FINANCIAL POST

FP survey
Industrials

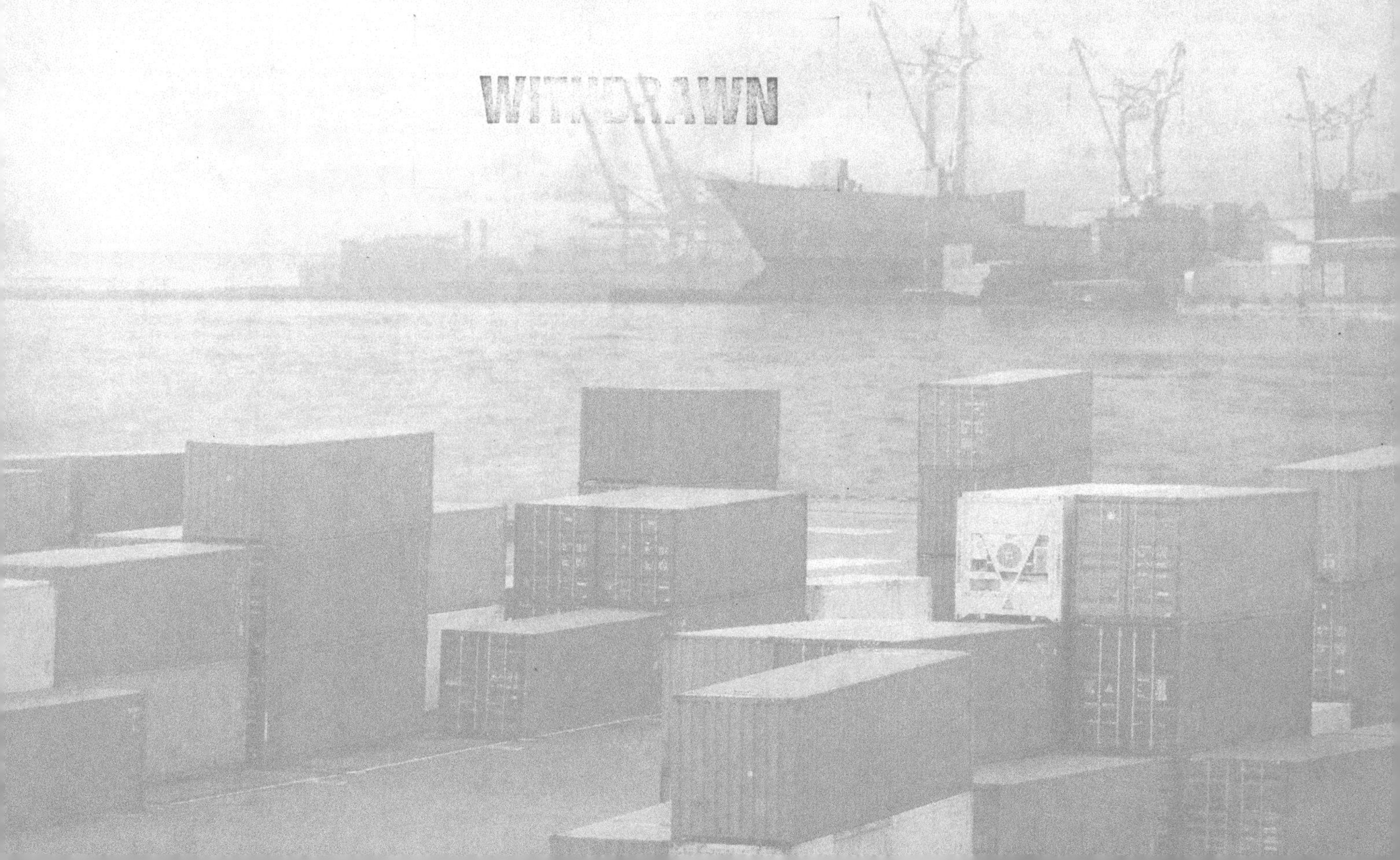

Additional Publications

For more detailed information or to place an order, see the back of the book.

CANADIAN ALMANAC & DIRECTORY 2024
Répetoire et almanach canadien

2,300 pages, 8 ½ x 11, Hardcover
177th edition, December 2023
ISBN 978-1-63700-702-0
ISSN 0068-8193
A combination of textual material, charts, colour photographs and directory listings, the *Canadian Almanac & Directory* provides the most comprehensive picture of Canada, from physical attributes to economic and business summaries to leisure and recreation.

CANADIAN WHO'S WHO 2024

1,200 pages, 8 3/8 x 10 7/8, Hardcover
December 2023
ISBN 978-1-63700-704-4
ISSN 0068-9963
Published for over 100 years, this authoritative annual publication offers access to the top 10,000 notable Canadians in all walks of life, including details such as date and place of birth, education, family details, career information, memberships, creative works, honours, languages, and awards, together with full addresses. Included are outstanding Canadians from business, academia, politics, sports, the arts and sciences, and more, selected because of the positions they hold in Canadian society, or because of the contributions they have made to Canada.

CANADIAN PARLIAMENTARY GUIDE 2023
Guide parlementaire canadien

1,326 pages, 6 x 9, Hardcover
157th edition, March 2023
ISBN 978-1-63700-682-5
ISSN 0315-6168
Published annually since before Confederation, this indispensable guide to government in Canada provides information on federal and provincial governments, with biographical sketches of government members, descriptions of government institutions, and historical text and charts. With significant bilingual sections, the Guide covers elections from Confederation to the present, including the most recent provincial elections.

FINANCIAL POST DIRECTORY OF DIRECTORS 2024
Répertoire des administrateurs

1,600 pages, 5 7/8 x 9, Hardcover
77th edition, September 2023
ISBN 978-1-63700-700-6
ISSN 0071-5042
Published biennially and annually since 1931, this comprehensive resource offers readers access to approximately 16,800 executive contacts from Canada's top 1,400 corporations. The directory provides a definitive list of directorships and offices held by noteworthy Canadian business people, as well as details on prominent Canadian companies (both public and private), including company name, contact information and the names of executive officers and directors. Includes all-new front matter and three indexes.

ASSOCIATIONS CANADA 2023
Associations du Canada

2,136 pages, 8 ½ x 11, Softcover
44th edition, March 2023
ISBN 978-1-64265-915-3
ISSN 1186-9798
Over 20,000 entries profile Canadian and international organizations active in Canada. Over 2,000 subject classifications index activities, professions and interests served by associations. Includes listings of NGOs, institutes, coalitions, social agencies, federations, foundations, trade unions, fraternal orders, and political parties. Fully indexed by subject, acronym, budget, conference, executive name, geographic location, mailing list availability, and registered charitable organization.

FINANCIAL SERVICES CANADA 2023-2024
Services financiers au Canada

1,516 pages, 8 1/2 x 11, Softcover
25th edition, May 2023
ISBN 978-1-63700-692-4
ISSN 1484-2408
This directory of Canadian financial institutions and organizations includes banks and depository institutions, non-depository institutions, investment management firms, financial planners, insurance companies, accountants, major law firms, associations, and financial technology companies. Fully indexed.

LIBRARIES CANADA 2023-2024
Bibliothèques Canada

900 pages, 8 ½ x 11, Softcover
37th edition, July 2023
ISBN 978-1-67300-690-0
ISSN 1920-2849
Libraries Canada offers comprehensive information on Canadian libraries, resource centres, business information centres, professional associations, regional library systems, archives, library schools, government libraries, and library technical programs.

CANADIAN ENVIRONMENTAL RESOURCE GUIDE 2022-2023
Guide des ressources environnementales canadiennes

1,063 pages, 8 1/2 x 11, Softcover
25th edition, July 2022
ISBN 978-1-63700-314-5
ISSN 1484-2408
Canada's most complete national listing of environmental organizations, product and service companies and governmental bodies, all indexed and categorized for quick and easy reference. Also included is the Environmental Update, with recent events, maps, rankings, statistics, and trade shows and conferences. The online version features even more content, including associations, special libraries, and federal/provincial government information.

CAREERS & EMPLOYMENT CANADA 2021
Carrières et emploi Canada 2021

970 pages, 8 ½ x 11, Softcover
1st edition, October 2020
ISBN 978-1-64265-713-5
Careers & Employment Canada is a new go-to resource for job-seekers across Canada, with detailed, current information on everything from industry associations to summer job opportunities. Divided into five helpful sections, plus three indexes, this guide contains 10,000 organizations and 20,000 industry contacts to aid in research and jump-start careers in a variety of fields.

HEALTH GUIDE CANADA 2020-2021
Guide canadien de la santé

1,098 pages, 8 ½ x 11, Softcover
4th edition, June 2020
ISBN: 978-1-64265-239-0
Health Guide Canada contains thousands of ways to deal with the many aspects of chronic or mental health disorders. It includes associations, government agencies, libraries and resource centres, educational facilities, hospitals and publications, as well as disease descriptions, relevant reports, and statistics.

CANNABIS CANADA
Cannabis au Canada

836 pages, 8 ½ x 11, Softcover
1st edition, April 2019
ISBN 978-1-64265-243-7
Cannabis Canada is a one-of-a-kind resource covering all aspects of this growing industry, including a history of cannabis, current reports, trade show listings, regulations, and a wealth of statistics. Company listings include a comprehensive industry buyer's guide, government resources, associations, venture capital and law firms, schools offering cannabis-related courses, and more.

FINANCIAL POST

FP survey Industrials 2023

97th Edition

GREY HOUSE PUBLISHING CANADA

Grey House Publishing Canada
PUBLISHER: Leslie Mackenzie
GENERAL MANAGER: Bryon Moore

Grey House Publishing
EDITORIAL DIRECTOR: Stuart Paterson
MARKETING DIRECTOR: Jessica Moody

Grey House Publishing Canada
3 - 1500 Upper Middle Road, P.O. Box 76017
Oakville, ON L6M 3H5
866-433-4739
FAX 416-644-1904
www.greyhouse.ca
e-mail: info@greyhouse.ca

Grey House Publishing Canada Inc. is a wholly owned subsidiary of Grey House Publishing Inc. USA.

Printed in Canada by Marquis Book Printing Inc.

97th edition published 2023
ISBN: 978-1-63700-694-8
ISSN: 1486-4266

Cataloguing in Publication Data is available from Libraries and Archives Canada.

Contents

Introduction

We are pleased to present **FPsurvey – Industrials 2023**, a guide to all industrial companies publicly traded and reporting in Canada.

Our listings cover companies involved in manufacturing, real estate development, forestry, investment holding, and financial management, as well as communications, transportation, banking, retailing, and other service industries. Also listed are those companies which provide service to these areas as well as investment trusts whose operating activities are in these areas. Since the 2008 edition, we stopped coverage of receivership companies in the main listings and moved these companies to the At Last Report list.

First established in 1927, **FPsurvey – Industrials** continues to address the very real needs of the private and corporate investor for a comprehensive securities manual. This is the 8th edition to be published by Grey House Publishing Canada.

We provide an overview of investment opportunities: companies' key assets and operations, their management and ownership, their financial position, and highlights of events affecting the companies over the past year. Together with its companion publication, **FPsurvey – Mines & Energy**, this book provides a wealth of information for both investment decisions and general interest purposes.

For a more comprehensive look at corporate Canada, we also provide ***The Year in Review.*** This section contains a tabular summary of rights offerings and name changes that have altered the corporate landscape over the previous 12 months. This material supplements the year end summary of the **FPdividends Annual Record & 10-Year Price Range.**

To assist with comparative analysis in and between industries we include the ***Top Ten by Industry*** section containing key financial ratios for the top companies in each of the Industry Groups under the Global Industry Classification Standard (GICS).

We are grateful to those corporate officials who provide updated information on their companies in time for our deadlines.

Special thanks to our team of dedicated analysts who spend many hours sifting through volumes of electronic files, financial reports, press releases and questionnaires to bring you this publication.

Additional Financial Post Data offerings include our **FP Advisor** web-based financial products designed to meet your personal and corporate information needs. Cross-referenced and updated daily, subscribe to FP Advisor which includes:

FP Corporate Surveys – News and in-depth research on all Canadian publicly traded companies

FP Corporate Analyzer – Fundamental data items on 1,002 Canadian companies, ready for you to retrieve, screen and analyze.

FP Corporate Reports – Historical, Investor and Industry Reports on Canada's top 327 publicly traded companies, with interactive charting capabilities.

FP Dividends – Distributions for all Canadian and foreign interlisted companies, trusts and mutual funds.

FP New Issues – A thorough up-to-date overview of Canadian IPOs and New Issues.

FP Predecessor & Defunct – A comprehensive collection of corporate changes which have occurred over the years since 1929.

FP Mergers & Acquistions - Information on mergers, acquisitions and divestitures involving Canadian companies.

FP Directory of Directors - Information on 30,693 directors and executives of Canadian companies.

Also available, our **FP Corporate Connection** electronic product puts corporate Canada at your fingertips with quick access to financial, operational and up-to-date contact information on 3,976 companies and 30,693 executive profiles. Screen data by geographic area, industry type, assets, revenues, number of employees and more. Create informed, accurate and targeted mailing lists with FP Corporate Connection.

Corporate Surveys information is also available electronically through partnerships with Lexis-Nexis.

The Editors,

August 28, 2023

Key Features

What information sections can a listing contain?

Each listing begins with **Full Legal Name.**

Introductory Paragraph: A summary of frequently used data items grouped together for ease of reference: listing information (exchange, base 3-character symbol for regular exchanges; if suspended, (S) will follow the exchange), CUSIP, address (head office, executive office, mailing), telephone number, toll-free telephone number, fax number, website and email, investor relations contact and telephone number, auditors, bankers, lawyers, transfer agents, top 800 FP 500 revenue ranking (if applicable), and number of employees and date.

Profile begins with the current jurisdiction of incorporation and year, followed by a brief summary of the company's business. Depending on how each specific company reports, this section may consist of several paragraphs covering the company as a whole, or may be divided by appropriate headings into various topics. For many industrial companies, operations are presented by division, product or geographical area. Information provided could include plant or store locations, capacity, production details, recent (or planned) expansions or downsizings. For resource companies (oil, gas, mining), operations include details of landholdings, exploration and development work done on and planned for various properties, along with tabular presentations of reserves and production statistics.

Recent Merger and Acquistions Activity lists transactions that took place over the past 18 months from date of extract. Only transactions with a value equal to or greater than $5,000,000 are displayed.

Predecessor Detail shows the most recent predecessor information on the company.

Directors, Trustees and Other Executive Officers provides a list of directors or trustees and officers of the company with their city, province/state and country. Executive directors are shown first, with their positions with the company, followed by the lead director, other directors, and other executive officers who are not directors. For many income trusts, directors or trustees and other executive officers of the underlying operating trust, management company or subsidiary are provided under the headings: Oper. Subsid./Mgt. Co. Trustees/Directors/Officers.

Capital Stock shows authorized and outstanding shares for each issue at a specified date (plus par value if applicable), followed by a brief summary of key provisions for each issue. As most common shares carry one vote per share, only exceptions are noted.

Major Shareholder shows holders of more than 10% of voting stock.

Price Range covers the lead share (major trading share), and shows ticker symbol, volume, high, low and close for five calendar years. Prices are blended prices from all Canadian exchanges on which the stock is listed. Note that some U.S. interlisted companies seldom trade in Canada, and their price range may be empty or represent very few trades. Price Range does not display where there is no trading or where there were only odd-lot trades.

Recent Close is at **date of extraction,** or the most recent trade within the preceding 12 months.

Capital Stock Changes are summarized for the previous two years, for most companies.

Dividends provides current and previous dividend rates (if within two years from date of publication) for each security. If a security does not pay on a set rate, up to four recent payments will be detailed. If a security is on a floating rate, the most recent four payments plus a summary of the totals for the previous two calendar years will be provided.

Long-Term Debt summarizes authorized and issued amounts outstanding at a specific date, along with key details of specific issues. For certain industries, debt, not long-term debt, is reported. Textual debt coverage for small and mid-capitalization companies has been discontinued since the 2011 edition.

Related Companies are categorized as follows: **Wholly Owned Subsidiaries, Subsidiaries** (in which a controlling interest is held, but are not wholly owned), and **Investments**, in which a non-controlling interest is held. Percentage ownership, location and corporate structures (i.e. subsidiaries of subsidiaries) are displayed.

Financial Statistics are provided in tabular form for companies with more than $100,000 in assets, subject to editorial discretion. Information is provided for two fiscal years. Preliminary, restated and pro forma figures are used if available, and are footnoted when used. (See also separate Guide to Financial Statistics Tables.) Interim results are presented in tabular form. Historical Summary provides Revenue, Net Income before discontinued operations, and Earnings per Share before discontinued operations (all on an originally reported basis). Capital Pool companies do not have financials presented. Per share figures are rounded to 2 decimal places; "0.00" indicates a value between nil and 0.005; "(0.00)" indicates a negative value between -0.005 and nil.

How are stock splits handled?

All per share data (earnings and price range) is adjusted for stock splits and consolidations, and a note is provided when this has been done. As a result, if a company was trading at $10 per share, and the stock subsequently split on a 2-new-for-1-old basis, that historical $10 price would be adjusted to $5, as you now have twice as many shares as you held before the split. Likewise, if the stock was consolidated on a 1-new-for-5-old basis, that historical $10 price would now be $50, as you now have only 1/5 the number of shares as you held before the consolidation. If you want to know the actual historical trading price, just do the arithmetic to un-adjust.

How many companies are covered in the Surveys?

Survey of Mines & Energy = 1,893 main listings plus 899 At Last Report (ALR)

Survey of Industrials = 1,903 main listings plus 763 At Last Report (ALR)

What were the cut-off dates for information in the Surveys?

Survey of Mines & Energy - August 27, 2023.

Survey of Industrials - August 27, 2023.

Recent Close - Date for recent close was August 25, 2023.

What are the sources for the Survey data?

We gather our information from corporate reports (annuals and interims, prospectuses, listing and filing statements), news releases, company websites, SEDAR, Ontario Securities Commission's filings, stock exchange bulletins, price feeds from stock exchanges, plus solicitations to the companies via data forms, telephone calls, faxes and email.

How do you ensure the data is accurate?

Our analysts update the database on a continuous basis from a variety of sources. Our computer system highlights all changes for a quality control check by experienced staff members. Data forms showing the listing data are mailed to each company annually for verification.

What are the unique features of our database?

- Quality control is system-driven. Balance checks are provided for financials, ensuring that entries add to both sub-totals and totals, with year-to-year checks on key figures.
- Financials are coded to pre-defined categories, which ensures consistency within the database from company to company, and also permits the calculation of ratios and % changes.
- Financial tables are provided in different flavours for different industry-reporting styles; in addition to the basic style, there are special financial templates for bank, trust, real estate, insurance and management (both regular and non-time format) presentations.

Guide to Financial Statistics Tables

DEFINITIONS:

The numbers presented in our Financial Statistics Tables use specific criteria, making the data consistent and comparable for all companies in our coverage. Most items such as net income, current assets and total assets are defined by generally accepted accounting principles. Other items are defined as follows:

Income Statement items:

Operating revenue — Pertains to sales generated from the primary business(es) of the company, net of royalties paid; in most cases it excludes interest and other investment income. Revenue components such as management fees, engineering fees, royalties received, service income, premium income and rental income are included. Royalty tax credits are not included. For banks and trust companies, operating revenue consists of interest income; fees and commissions are included in other income. For management and investment holding companies, the figure displayed as "Total revenue" may include investment and equity income, as well as realized and unrealized gains and losses on investments, and therefore in some cases may be a negative number.

Investment income — Includes interest and dividend income, and pre-tax equity income of the company in the net income of its unconsolidated subsidiaries and affiliates. Does not include gains or losses incurred upon disposition of investments.

Write-downs — Includes write-downs, write-offs and abandonments of resource properties (and associated capitalized exploration and development expenditures), asset impairment charges and write-downs and write-offs of investments, including provisions for such charged to net income.

Unusual items and Extraordinary items — Pertain to items explicitly identified as such on the company's income statement, subject to analyst's discretion.

Balance Sheet items:

Fixed assets, net — Pertains to all property, plant and equipment used in the generation of revenue, net of accumulated depreciation and depletion. Includes producing oil and gas properties and producing mineral properties.

Explor./devel. properties — Pertains to resource properties at the exploration or the development stage. Includes both the acquisition costs of the properties and capitalized exploration and development expenditures.

The number of common shares (or equivalent) are shown at the end of the fiscal period within the financial tables. If the company has more than one class of common shares, the total will be shown.

Cash Flow Statement items:

Cash from operating activities — Adds back non-cash charges to net income, including net changes in non-cash working capital balances related to operations.

Cash from financing activities — Represents the net change in cash received from or repaid to owners and creditors.

Cas from investing of activities — Represents the net change in cash from the acquisition or sale of income-generating assets.

Net cash position — Net cash as defined by the company at the end of the period covered in the Statement of Cash Flows.

PERCENTAGE CHANGES:

Year-over-year percentage changes for key financial items are not calculated if either item is less than zero, or if the periods utilize a different currency. if the percentage change is greater than 999% , n.m. is displayed.

RATIOS:

Formulae and rules for the calculation of our ratios are as follows. Note that ratios are not calculated if the numerator is from a period other than 11 to 13 months or 48 weeks to 56 weeks.

Return on Equity:

$$\frac{\text{Net Inc. before Disc. Opers. - Preferred Dividends - Net Inc. attrib. to Non-controlling Int.}}{\text{2-year average of Common Shareholders' Equity}} \times 100$$

Note: Not calculated if both numerator and denominator are less than zero.

Return on Assets:

$$\frac{\text{Net Income before Discontinued Operations + Finance Costs (1-Tax Rate)}}{\text{2-year average of Total Assets}} \times 100$$

$$\text{Tax Rate} = \frac{\text{Income Tax Expense}}{\text{Pre-tax Income}}$$

Net Profit Margin:

$$\frac{\text{Net Income before Discontinued Operations}}{\text{Operating Revenue}} \times 100$$

Note: Shown as n.a. if operating revenue is nil or not available.

Net Profit Margin for Banks and Trust companies:

$$\frac{\text{Net Income before Discontinued Operations}}{\text{Net Interest Income + Investment Income}} \times 100$$

Note: Shown as n.a. if operating revenue is nil or not available.

Top Ten by Industry

The following pages provide an industry study for the Top Ten companies in each of 25 Industry Groups of the Global Industry Classification Standard (GICS®). We have performed this screening on 1,002 companies covered in FP Corporate Surveys and in FP Corporate Analyzer. As part of our web-based FP Advisor, Corporate Analyzer allows the user to perform extracts based on a wide number of criteria to establish investment worthiness.

We hope you find this sample useful and will consider a subscription to FP Corporate Analyzer and to other Financial Post Data investment analysis products in FP Advisor.

Visit legacy-fpadvisor.financialpost.com for samples of FP Corporate Analyzer and other FP Advisor products.

NOTE: All data is for calendar 2022 year end results, or for fiscal years ended between July 2022 and June 2023. Net income in the following tables is defined as net income attributable to equityholders. The three key ratios: Net Profit Margin, Return on Equity and Return on Assets are based on the same calculations which appear in the financial table attached to the individual coverage for each company. All financial data is in Canadian dollars having been converted from foreign currencies for those companies whose statements are reported in such foreign currencies. Data for periods other than 11 to 13 months or 48 weeks to 56 weeks is annualized.

Automobiles & Components

Companies	Total Revenue $000s	Net income $000s	Total Assets $000s	Earns. per sh. $	Net Profit Margin %	Return on Equity %	Return on Assets %
Magna International Inc.	49,267,680	770,784	37,626,306	2.66	1.69	5.20	2.58
Linamar Corporation	7,917,911	426,194	8,576,391	6.67	5.38	9.06	5.76
Martinrea International Inc.	4,757,588	132,838	4,143,119	1.65	2.79	10.43	4.27
AirBoss of America Corp.	621,256	(41,523)	596,797	(1.54)	(6.68)	(14.76)	(6.19)

Banks

Companies	Total Revenue $000s	Net income $000s	Total Assets $000s	Earns. per sh. $	Net Profit Margin %	Return on Equity %	Return on Assets %
The Toronto-Dominion Bank	41,032,000	17,429,000	1,917,528,000	9.48	35.55	17.68	0.96
Royal Bank of Canada	40,771,000	15,794,000	1,917,219,000	11.08	32.27	16.13	0.87
The Bank of Nova Scotia	33,558,000	9,916,000	1,349,418,000	8.05	32.38	14.87	0.80
Bank of Montreal	26,897,000	13,537,000	1,139,199,000	20.04	40.16	22.80	1.27
Canadian Imperial Bank of Commerce	22,179,000	6,220,000	943,597,000	6.70	28.59	13.97	0.70
National Bank of Canada	9,545,000	3,384,000	403,740,000	9.72	35.05	18.84	0.89
EQB Inc.	1,616,231	270,181	51,144,957	7.63	34.54	12.49	0.62
Canadian Western Bank	1,561,905	336,896	41,440,143	3.39	31.30	10.15	0.86
Laurentian Bank of Canada	1,474,358	226,583	50,716,758	4.96	21.91	8.71	0.47
VersaBank	126,817	22,658	3,265,998	0.79	27.50	6.91	0.80

Capital Goods

Companies	Total Revenue $000s	Net income $000s	Total Assets $000s	Earns. per sh. $	Net Profit Margin %	Return on Equity %	Return on Assets %
Brookfield Business Partners L.P.	74,923,590	71,610	121,180,292	0.95	0.62	3.00	0.46
Brookfield Business Corporation	13,798,596	1,186,122	37,067,104	n.a.	10.15	n.m.	4.97
WSP Global Inc.	11,932,900	431,800	14,841,700	3.59	3.64	8.09	4.16
Finning International Inc.	9,279,000	503,000	7,269,000	3.25	5.40	21.11	8.64
Bombardier Inc.	9,000,726	(192,696)	16,686,696	(2.45)	(1.85)	n.m.	2.37
SNC-Lavalin Group Inc.	7,549,031	9,750	9,459,986	0.06	0.09	0.57	(0.38)
Russel Metals Inc.	5,070,600	371,900	2,506,900	5.91	7.33	26.49	16.23
Aecon Group Inc.	4,696,450	30,381	3,567,017	0.50	0.65	3.25	2.06
Toromont Industries Ltd.	4,230,736	454,198	4,182,125	5.52	10.74	21.23	12.21
CAE Inc.	4,203,300	222,700	10,436,500	0.70	5.52	5.23	3.81

Commercial & Professional Services

Companies	Total Revenue $000s	Net income $000s	Total Assets $000s	Earns. per sh. $	Net Profit Margin %	Return on Equity %	Return on Assets %
Waste Connections, Inc.	9,389,840	1,088,032	23,200,252	4.23	11.59	11.86	6.27
GFL Environmental Inc.	8,803,213	(405,964)	26,765,330	(0.95)	(2.71)	(4.52)	0.35
Thomson Reuters Corporation	8,628,354	1,742,076	29,396,694	3.59	20.99	10.89	6.34
Stantec Inc.	5,677,200	247,000	5,652,900	2.23	4.35	11.52	5.64
TELUS International (Cda) Inc.	3,213,336	238,266	4,814,824	0.90	7.41	10.48	5.93
Boyd Group Services Inc.	3,166,878	53,333	2,847,235	2.49	1.68	5.56	3.24
RB Global, Inc.	2,257,418	416,193	3,877,486	3.76	18.44	27.09	11.32
GDI Integrated Facility Services Inc.	2,172,000	36,000	1,220,000	1.57	1.66	8.67	3.12
Nuvei Corporation	1,098,007	73,865	4,772,402	0.52	7.35	2.85	2.24
Dexterra Group Inc.	971,517	3,433	611,401	0.05	0.38	1.16	2.46

Consumer Discretionary Distribution & Retail

Companies	Total Revenue $000s	Net income $000s	Total Assets $000s	Earns. per sh. $	Net Profit Margin %	Return on Equity %	Return on Assets %
Canadian Tire Corporation, Limited	17,810,600	1,044,100	22,102,300	17.70	6.64	19.44	6.25
AutoCanada Inc.	6,040,619	85,436	2,858,331	3.28	1.51	17.96	7.34
Dollarama Inc.	5,052,741	801,863	4,819,656	2.77	15.87	n.m.	19.99
ADENTRA Inc.	3,358,598	167,526	1,934,831	7.16	4.99	27.94	10.12
Doman Building Materials Group Ltd.	3,039,017	78,740	1,445,193	0.91	2.59	14.77	7.29
Leon's Furniture Limited	2,517,659	179,429	2,193,643	2.66	7.13	20.86	8.57
Aritzia Inc.	2,195,630	187,588	1,836,543	1.70	8.54	30.84	12.87
Taiga Building Products Ltd.	2,192,705	88,628	617,832	0.82	4.04	28.12	15.66
Indigo Books & Music Inc.	1,057,740	(49,566)	738,081	(1.78)	(4.69)	n.m.	(6.41)
Pet Valu Holdings Ltd.	951,697	100,766	740,176	1.43	10.59	n.m.	18.24

Consumer Durables & Apparel

Companies	Total Revenue $000s	Net income $000s	Total Assets $000s	Earns. per sh. $	Net Profit Margin %	Return on Equity %	Return on Assets %
BRP Inc.	10,033,400	863,900	6,464,600	10.88	8.63	n.m.	16.54
Gildan Activewear Inc.	4,219,108	705,085	4,658,050	3.83	16.71	28.49	17.54
Spin Master Corp.	2,630,431	340,213	2,427,045	3.31	12.93	22.77	14.81
Dorel Industries Inc.	2,044,497	177,024	1,435,847	5.44	(7.57)	(31.70)	(6.32)
Canada Goose Holdings Inc.	1,217,000	72,700	1,590,000	0.69	5.66	16.20	6.86
Unisync Corp.	96,307	(1,545)	104,364	(0.08)	(1.40)	(5.35)	0.55
Mene Inc.	26,912	(1,463)	31,714	(0.01)	(5.44)	(8.34)	(3.53)
iFabric Corp.	19,743	(455)	27,369	(0.02)	(2.29)	(2.02)	(1.25)
Vitreous Glass Inc.	9,623	2,172	5,494	0.35	22.57	51.61	40.83
Taiga Motors Corporation	3,212	(59,516)	94,315	(1.88)	n.m.	(63.05)	(49.14)

Consumer Services

Companies	Total Revenue $000s	Net income $000s	Total Assets $000s	Earns. per sh. $	Net Profit Margin %	Return on Equity %	Return on Assets %
Restaurant Brands International Inc.	8,469,510	1,312,416	30,798,084	4.27	22.78	42.57	8.99
Transat A.T. Inc.	1,642,038	(445,324)	2,271,131	(11.77)	(27.12)	n.m.	(16.36)
MTY Food Group Inc.	716,522	74,817	2,325,303	3.06	10.49	10.91	4.51
Park Lawn Corporation	424,595	32,713	2,002,575	0.96	7.70	4.57	2.13
Goodfood Market Corp.	268,586	(121,761)	129,848	(1.62)	(45.33)	n.m.	(63.23)
TWC Enterprises Limited	190,806	18,761	727,343	0.76	9.78	3.71	3.24
Bragg Gaming Group Inc.	116,086	(4,773)	150,945	(0.22)	(4.11)	(5.13)	(1.81)
Canlan Ice Sports Corp.	73,728	4,730	121,713	0.35	6.42	10.87	6.01
Global Education Communities Corp.	73,235	(15,336)	477,733	(0.22)	(76.15)	(38.99)	(8.81)
Gamehost Inc.	69,700	12,700	183,400	0.56	18.65	11.99	8.11

Consumer Staples Distribution & Retail

Companies	Total Revenue $000s	Net income $000s	Total Assets $000s	Earns. per sh. $	Net Profit Margin %	Return on Equity %	Return on Assets %
Alimentation Couche-Tard Inc.	95,497,554	4,107,806	39,448,814	4.08	4.30	24.73	11.57
George Weston Limited	57,048,000	1,816,000	48,958,000	12.29	4.92	29.23	7.43
Loblaw Companies Limited	56,504,000	1,921,000	38,147,000	5.82	3.53	17.02	6.77
Empire Company Limited	30,478,100	686,000	16,483,700	2.65	2.39	13.46	5.74
METRO Inc.	18,888,900	846,100	13,401,300	3.53	4.50	13.01	7.03
The North West Company Inc.	2,352,760	122,190	1,336,890	2.55	5.35	20.49	10.79
Neighbourly Pharmacy Inc.	749,149	(15,499)	1,102,001	(0.37)	(1.98)	(3.26)	0.37
Colabor Group Inc.	574,071	4,065	240,691	0.04	0.79	8.39	3.39
CareRx Corporation	381,727	(34,353)	264,535	(0.72)	(9.00)	(46.82)	(7.23)
DAVIDsTEA INC.	83,026	(14,868)	62,593	(0.56)	(17.91)	(35.82)	(20.03)

Energy

Companies	Total Revenue $000s	Net income $000s	Total Assets $000s	Earns. per sh. $	Net Profit Margin %	Return on Equity %	Return on Assets %
Cenovus Energy Inc.	66,897,000	6,450,000	55,869,000	3.29	9.64	25.59	12.83
Imperial Oil Limited	59,413,000	7,340,000	43,524,000	11.47	12.35	33.25	17.52
Suncor Energy Inc.	58,336,000	9,077,000	84,618,000	6.54	15.56	23.89	12.54
Enbridge Inc.	53,309,000	3,003,000	179,608,000	1.28	5.51	4.88	2.87
Canadian Natural Resources Limited	42,298,000	10,937,000	76,142,000	9.64	25.86	29.12	15.01
Parkland Corporation	35,462,000	310,000	14,288,000	1.94	0.98	12.38	4.81
Ovintiv Inc.	16,228,128	4,735,374	20,385,824	18.67	29.18	56.99	27.30
TC Energy Corporation	14,977,000	748,000	114,348,000	0.64	5.24	2.09	0.72
Pembina Pipeline Corporation	11,611,000	2,971,000	31,475,000	5.14	25.59	22.46	10.87
Gibson Energy Inc.	11,035,411	223,245	3,194,998	1.53	2.02	36.68	8.25

Equity Real Estate Investment Trusts (REITs)

Companies	Total Revenue $000s	Net income $000s	Total Assets $000s	Earns. per sh. $	Net Profit Margin %	Return on Equity %	Return on Assets %
Choice Properties Real Estate Investment Trust	1,264,594	744,253	16,819,527	n.a.	58.85	20.86	7.77
Canadian Apartment Properties Real Estate Investment Trust	1,007,268	13,637	17,741,888	n.a.	1.35	0.13	3.98
RioCan Real Estate Investment Trust	991,779	236,772	15,101,859	0.77	23.87	3.03	2.75
H&R Real Estate Investment Trust	834,640	844,823	11,412,603	n.a.	101.22	16.47	9.51
SmartCentres Real Estate Investment Trust	804,598	516,049	11,702,153	n.a.	79.04	10.32	6.82
First Capital Real Estate Investment Trust	693,096	(159,997)	9,581,938	n.a.	(23.05)	(3.60)	(0.03)
CT Real Estate Investment Trust	532,795	148,264	6,844,789	1.39	60.93	8.93	6.52
Allied Properties Real Estate Investment Trust	519,468	368,855	11,906,350	2.69	33.62	2.59	2.22
Boardwalk Real Estate Investment Trust	494,806	283,096	7,067,275	6.17	57.21	8.43	5.54
NorthWest Healthcare Properties Real Estate Investment Trust	464,052	64,295	8,514,000	n.a.	27.07	2.65	2.85

Financial Services

Companies	Total Revenue $000s	Net income $000s	Total Assets $000s	Earns. per sh. $	Net Profit Margin %	Return on Equity %	Return on Assets %
Brookfield Corporation	122,915,310	2,676,912	597,498,536	1.59	5.50	4.66	3.25
IGM Financial Inc.	3,357,249	867,244	18,873,176	3.64	25.99	13.72	5.26
CI Financial Corp.	2,334,307	299,757	9,708,358	1.59	12.93	18.74	4.35
Element Fleet Management Corp.	1,959,793	409,643	14,332,218	0.96	20.90	12.20	4.51
First National Financial Corporation	1,574,293	197,732	43,763,672	3.25	12.56	36.00	0.69
Canaccord Genuity Group Inc.	1,510,397	(90,104)	6,302,400	(1.16)	(3.62)	(11.10)	0.47
Partners Value Investments LP	1,481,660	1,460,121	7,623,333	21.93	98.55	19.54	16.79
TMX Group Limited	1,116,600	542,700	55,983,100	9.74	52.10	14.11	1.03
goeasy Ltd.	1,019,336	140,161	3,302,889	8.61	13.75	16.89	7.37
Home Capital Group Inc.	1,001,613	150,228	22,727,106	3.68	15.00	9.61	2.43

Food, Beverage & Tobacco

Companies	Total Revenue $000s	Net income $000s	Total Assets $000s	Earns. per sh. $	Net Profit Margin %	Return on Equity %	Return on Assets %
Saputo Inc.	17,843,000	622,000	14,425,000	1.49	3.49	9.12	5.00
Premium Brands Holdings Corporation	6,029,800	160,100	5,078,600	3.59	2.66	8.93	5.15
Maple Leaf Foods Inc.	4,739,063	(311,893)	4,439,436	(2.52)	(6.58)	(16.88)	(5.74)
Primo Water Corporation	2,884,060	38,539	4,965,118	0.23	1.34	2.27	1.94
Lassonde Industries Inc.	2,150,975	53,938	1,604,715	7.85	2.48	6.40	4.05
High Liner Foods Incorporated	1,392,768	71,258	1,358,720	2.11	5.12	15.51	7.64
SunOpta Inc.	1,216,930	(6,303)	1,158,824	(0.09)	(1.02)	(4.05)	0.36
Rogers Sugar Inc.	1,006,134	(16,568)	937,956	(0.16)	(1.65)	(5.43)	(1.82)
Andrew Peller Limited	382,140	(3,352)	566,748	(0.08)	(0.88)	(1.29)	1.68
Swiss Water Decaffeinated Coffee Inc.	176,935	2,387	219,039	0.26	1.35	4.32	3.37

Health Care Equipment & Services

Companies	Total Revenue $000s	Net income $000s	Total Assets $000s	Earns. per sh. $	Net Profit Margin %	Return on Equity %	Return on Assets %
Bausch + Lomb Corporation	4,905,936	7,812	15,088,976	0.03	0.40	0.07	0.41
dentalcorp Holdings Ltd.	1,250,300	(16,600)	3,375,200	(0.09)	(1.33)	(1.01)	(0.05)
Extendicare Inc.	1,221,577	69,554	781,579	0.78	(0.37)	(4.45)	2.02
Akumin Inc.	976,020	(204,103)	2,389,966	(2.28)	(20.22)	n.m.	(1.45)
Savaria Corporation	789,091	35,311	1,109,963	0.55	4.47	7.96	4.32
Sienna Senior Living Inc.	718,590	10,668	1,680,428	0.15	1.48	2.54	2.25
Chartwell Retirement Residences	707,992	49,531	3,510,342	n.a.	3.87	3.43	2.41
WELL Health Technologies Corp.	569,136	1,369	1,319,031	0.01	3.28	0.20	3.53
Medical Facilities Corporation	539,534	(5,735)	511,529	(0.20)	2.97	(4.13)	5.27
Quipt Home Medical Corp.	178,604	6,179	181,265	0.18	3.46	7.00	4.02

Household & Personal Products

Companies	Total Revenue $000s	Net income $000s	Total Assets $000s	Earns. per sh. $	Net Profit Margin %	Return on Equity %	Return on Assets %
Jamieson Wellness Inc.	547,369	52,808	1,107,263	1.29	9.65	13.65	7.06
MAV Beauty Brands Inc.	118,081	(202,902)	169,567	(5.52)	(171.83)	n.m.	(70.35)

Insurance

Companies	Total Revenue $000s	Net income $000s	Total Assets $000s	Earns. per sh. $	Net Profit Margin %	Return on Equity %	Return on Assets %
Power Corporation of Canada	48,695,000	1,965,000	733,650,000	2.85	7.28	8.24	0.59
Great-West Lifeco Inc.	44,662,000	3,349,000	701,455,000	3.46	7.91	13.47	0.59
Fairfax Financial Holdings Limited	36,521,100	1,493,654	124,737,385	60.70	4.59	7.25	1.82
Sun Life Financial Inc.	23,322,000	3,130,000	330,906,000	5.22	14.16	12.42	1.09
Intact Financial Corporation	21,289,000	2,424,000	64,959,000	13.46	11.37	16.54	3.91
Manulife Financial Corporation	17,147,000	7,294,000	848,941,000	3.68	41.88	13.87	0.94
iA Financial Corporation Inc.	8,595,000	842,000	87,425,000	7.68	9.31	12.30	0.97
Brookfield Reinsurance Ltd.	5,610,318	649,698	58,842,132	n.a.	11.63	32.07	2.18
Sagicor Financial Company Ltd.	3,307,408	150,466	14,576,989	1.05	6.68	10.42	1.85
Definity Financial Corporation	3,180,700	252,000	8,316,800	2.19	7.94	10.57	3.12

Materials

Companies	Total Revenue $000s	Net income $000s	Total Assets $000s	Earns. per sh. $	Net Profit Margin %	Return on Equity %	Return on Assets %
Nutrien Ltd.	48,189,624	9,973,320	73,909,444	18.51	20.77	30.97	15.55
Teck Resources Limited	16,821,000	3,317,000	52,359,000	6.30	24.20	16.87	8.41
Newmont Corporation	15,513,330	(558,558)	52,104,628	(0.70)	(3.35)	(2.22)	4.69
Barrick Gold Corporation	13,759,536	562,464	62,236,610	0.31	9.62	1.85	2.71
West Fraser Timber Co. Ltd.	12,630,702	2,571,450	13,503,442	27.42	20.36	25.86	19.58
First Quantum Minerals Ltd.	9,390,024	1,346,268	33,958,320	1.95	15.93	9.89	6.62
Agnico Eagle Mines Limited	7,474,993	872,664	31,811,970	1.99	11.67	6.03	4.28
Canfor Corporation	7,426,700	787,300	6,739,200	6.39	11.59	20.43	13.68
CCL Industries Inc.	6,382,200	622,700	8,664,400	3.50	9.76	15.54	8.38
Methanex Corporation	5,613,167	460,687	8,979,024	6.44	10.72	18.64	8.90

Media & Entertainment

Companies	Total Revenue $000s	Net income $000s	Total Assets $000s	Earns. per sh. $	Net Profit Margin %	Return on Equity %	Return on Assets %
Quebecor Inc.	4,531,900	599,700	10,625,300	2.55	13.17	45.90	7.80
COGECO Inc.	2,995,012	149,108	9,468,025	9.43	15.28	17.17	7.23
Cogeco Communications Inc.	2,900,654	423,299	9,278,509	9.16	15.64	16.39	7.32
Corus Entertainment Inc.	1,598,586	(245,058)	3,502,480	(1.19)	(14.53)	(26.94)	(2.79)
Cineplex Inc.	1,268,562	113	2,150,454	0.00	0.01	n.m.	0.50
TVA Group Inc.	594,409	(8,869)	676,070	(0.21)	(1.50)	(2.30)	(1.18)
Postmedia Network Canada Corp.	458,224	(74,712)	211,375	(0.78)	(16.30)	n.m.	(17.55)
Stingray Group Inc.	323,944	30,119	895,202	0.43	9.30	10.76	3.39
Boat Rocker Media Inc.	304,281	(7,506)	796,547	(0.13)	0.59	(3.22)	0.50
Yellow Pages Limited	268,278	73,432	207,298	3.10	27.37	80.73	30.02

Pharmaceuticals, Biotechnology & Life Sciences

Companies	Total Revenue $000s	Net income $000s	Total Assets $000s	Earns. per sh. $	Net Profit Margin %	Return on Equity %	Return on Assets %
Bausch Health Companies Inc.	10,577,448	(292,950)	34,778,844	(0.81)	(2.61)	n.m.	7.99
Tilray Brands, Inc.	837,838	(1,940,748)	5,857,872	(3.14)	(230.10)	(37.66)	(28.63)
Canopy Growth Corporation	402,904	(3,278,158)	2,439,098	(7.07)	(821.42)	(150.78)	(79.05)
TerrAscend Corp.	322,673	(429,540)	949,949	(1.76)	(120.81)	(112.08)	(46.65)
Knight Therapeutics Inc.	293,563	(29,892)	1,054,836	(0.26)	(10.18)	(3.58)	(2.48)
OrganiGram Holdings Inc.	145,809	(14,283)	577,107	(0.05)	(9.80)	(2.89)	(2.45)
Cronos Group Inc.	119,659	(219,692)	1,642,414	(0.59)	(183.60)	(13.60)	(12.92)
DRI Healthcare Trust	113,629	15,101	857,649	0.39	13.29	3.09	3.41
Theratechnologies Inc.	103,674	(61,172)	125,994	(0.65)	(59.00)	n.m.	(37.62)
Charlotte's Web Holdings, Inc.	96,529	(77,226)	254,067	(0.52)	(80.00)	(57.05)	(32.73)

Real Estate Management & Development

Companies	Total Revenue $000s	Net income $000s	Total Assets $000s	Earns. per sh. $	Net Profit Margin %	Return on Equity %	Return on Assets %
Colliers International Group Inc.	5,806,252	60,221	6,902,932	1.39	4.36	8.63	4.34
FirstService Corporation	4,877,077	157,638	3,756,692	3.57	3.87	14.18	5.49
Morguard Corporation	1,136,675	122,771	11,705,252	11.08	9.88	3.28	2.61
Tricon Residential Inc.	1,101,758	1,053,241	16,858,581	3.84	92.10	22.61	8.87
Altus Group Limited	735,451	(886)	1,263,886	(0.02)	(0.12)	(0.15)	(0.22)
Real Matters Inc.	433,723	(11,840)	187,832	(0.15)	(2.73)	(6.76)	(5.47)
DREAM Unlimited Corp.	343,768	164,445	3,956,494	3.86	47.84	11.05	5.58
StorageVault Canada Inc.	261,828	(41,242)	2,020,752	(0.11)	(15.75)	(19.21)	1.16
Invesque Inc.	253,498	(63,551)	1,485,798	(1.12)	(21.58)	(24.20)	0.07
Melcor Developments Ltd.	241,747	89,354	2,167,050	2.75	36.96	7.79	4.77

Semiconductors & Semiconductor Equipment

Companies	Total Revenue $000s	Net income $000s	Total Assets $000s	Earns. per sh. $	Net Profit Margin %	Return on Equity %	Return on Assets %
Spectra7 Microsystems Inc.	14,705	(9,167)	11,248	(0.27)	(62.34)	(340.64)	(54.47)

Software & Services

Companies	Total Revenue $000s	Net income $000s	Total Assets $000s	Earns. per sh. $	Net Profit Margin %	Return on Equity %	Return on Assets %
CGI Inc.	12,867,201	1,466,142	15,175,420	6.13	11.39	20.56	10.18
Constellation Software Inc.	8,621,844	666,624	10,672,228	31.48	8.32	36.93	9.30
Shopify Inc.	7,291,023	(4,505,464)	14,565,182	(3.55)	(61.79)	(35.73)	(28.69)
Open Text Corporation	6,009,873	201,508	22,626,101	0.75	3.36	3.74	3.01
Converge Technology Solutions Corp.	2,164,647	27,283	2,248,876	0.13	1.06	4.50	1.26
Ceridian HCM Holding Inc.	1,622,552	(95,567)	10,719,889	(0.62)	(5.89)	(3.38)	(0.97)
Topicus.com Inc.	1,255,853	72,511	1,872,272	0.90	9.56	n.m.	7.54
Softchoice Corporation	1,208,535	28,345	833,154	0.48	2.35	44.28	5.77
Lightspeed Commerce Inc.	966,459	(1,415,622)	3,610,794	(9.41)	(146.48)	(36.29)	(33.96)
BlackBerry Limited	861,984	(964,476)	2,285,119	(1.67)	(111.89)	(60.84)	(34.29)

Technology Hardware & Equipment

Companies	Total Revenue $000s	Net income $000s	Total Assets $000s	Earns. per sh. $	Net Profit Margin %	Return on Equity %	Return on Assets %
Celestica Inc.	9,439,500	189,441	7,620,312	1.54	2.01	9.27	3.66
Evertz Technologies Limited	454,578	64,032	436,652	0.84	14.20	27.02	15.69
Quarterhill Inc.	305,690	2,766	411,944	0.02	0.90	1.11	1.14
Haivision Systems Inc.	125,697	(6,192)	148,596	(0.21)	(4.93)	(6.91)	(3.75)
Baylin Technologies Inc.	120,860	(16,877)	74,384	(0.21)	(13.96)	n.m.	(20.16)
Firan Technology Group Corporation	89,624	698	83,746	0.03	0.86	1.42	0.94
Blackline Safety Corp.	72,931	(53,646)	108,049	(0.86)	(73.56)	(85.35)	(49.23)
Tantalus Systems Holding Inc.	51,563	(6,764)	50,585	(0.16)	(13.12)	(100.19)	(12.52)
Midwest Energy Emissions Corp.	28,149	(2,058)	12,646	(0.03)	(7.31)	n.m.	0.08
Nanalysis Scientific Corp.	24,821	(9,101)	69,902	(0.10)	(39.95)	(25.45)	(18.41)

Telecommunication Services

Companies	Total Revenue $000s	Net income $000s	Total Assets $000s	Earns. per sh. $	Net Profit Margin %	Return on Equity %	Return on Assets %
BCE Inc.	24,174,000	2,868,000	69,329,000	2.98	12.10	14.70	5.51
TELUS Corporation	18,292,000	1,615,000	54,046,000	1.16	9.39	10.19	4.31
Rogers Communications Inc.	15,396,000	1,680,000	55,655,000	3.33	10.91	16.29	5.65
Telesat Corporation	759,169	(23,396)	6,479,593	(1.90)	(10.55)	(5.22)	7.92
TeraGo Inc.	27,215	(11,571)	55,383	(0.61)	(42.52)	(33.13)	(12.76)

Transportation

Companies	Total Revenue $000s	Net income $000s	Total Assets $000s	Earns. per sh. $	Net Profit Margin %	Return on Equity %	Return on Assets %
Canadian National Railway Company	17,107,000	5,118,000	50,662,000	7.46	29.92	23.20	11.15
Air Canada	16,556,000	(1,700,000)	29,507,000	(4.75)	(10.27)	n.m.	(2.86)
TFI International Inc.	11,473,863	1,071,848	7,454,894	11.99	9.34	35.16	15.75
Canadian Pacific Kansas City Limited	8,814,000	3,517,000	73,495,000	3.78	39.90	9.67	4.96
Exchange Income Corporation	2,059,373	109,669	3,548,836	2.72	5.33	12.06	5.42
Mullen Group Ltd.	1,999,453	158,619	1,996,131	1.70	7.93	17.04	9.46
Chorus Aviation Inc.	1,595,804	48,890	4,055,909	0.13	3.25	2.78	3.47
Cargojet Inc.	979,900	190,600	1,986,300	11.04	19.45	25.28	12.64
Logistec Corporation	897,565	53,543	983,672	4.15	6.02	15.89	7.10
Algoma Central Corporation	677,942	119,966	1,365,697	3.17	17.70	17.56	10.68

Utilities

Companies	Total Revenue $000s	Net income $000s	Total Assets $000s	Earns. per sh. $	Net Profit Margin %	Return on Equity %	Return on Assets %
Brookfield Infrastructure Partners L.P.	18,783,954	443,982	98,800,026	0.18	9.53	5.98	3.67
AltaGas Ltd.	14,087,000	523,000	23,965,000	1.42	4.07	6.26	3.67
Fortis Inc.	11,043,000	1,394,000	64,252,000	2.78	13.71	7.18	4.00
Hydro One Limited	7,780,000	1,050,000	31,457,000	1.75	13.60	9.46	4.68
Emera Incorporated	7,588,000	1,008,000	39,742,000	3.56	13.30	10.11	2.73
Brookfield Renewable Partners L.P.	6,133,722	(158,844)	86,806,294	(0.78)	2.93	(3.38)	2.30
ATCO Ltd.	4,978,000	370,000	24,139,000	3.25	14.20	8.72	4.42
Brookfield Renewable Corporation	4,918,956	1,956,906	58,611,952	n.a.	48.97	31.51	4.34
Canadian Utilities Limited	4,048,000	632,000	21,974,000	2.07	15.79	10.74	4.41
Algonquin Power & Utilities Corp.	3,600,232	(276,010)	23,867,788	(0.43)	(11.14)	(4.12)	(0.44)

The Year in Review

Many changes have crossed the Canadian corporate landscape since our last annual survey publication. The details are located within the individual coverages found throughout this book and its sister publication, FP Survey – Mines & Energy 2023.

Our team of dedicated analysts follows these companies on a daily basis and compiles a collection of subscription products that provide the breadth and depth of corporate activity on a calendar year basis.

The following synopsis of activity covers the period from July 1, 2022, to August 27, 2023, and has been extracted from our FP Dividends service.

For additional information on this and other product offerings, visit legacy-fpadvisor.financialpost.com or email legacy-fpadvisor@postmedia.com

Corporate Name Changes

Original Name	New Name	Current Name	Effective Date
AEX Gold Inc.		Amaroq Minerals Ltd.	Jul 12/22
AMV Capital Corporation		Abasca Resources Inc.	Dec 29/22
ANC Capital Ventures Inc.		VIP Entertainment Technologies Inc.	Jul 6/22
ATS Automation Tooling Systems Inc.		ATS Corporation	Nov 21/22
Aben Resources Ltd.		Aben Minerals Ltd.	Feb 21/23
Abundant Solar Energy Inc.		SolarBank Corporation	Oct 7/22
Academy Metals Inc.		Bedford Metals Corp.	Oct 28/22
AcuityAds Holdings Inc.		illumin Holdings Inc.	Jun 14/23
AGFiQ Canadian Equity ETF		AGF Systematic Canadian Equity ETF	Jan 27/23
AGFiQ Emerging Markets Equity ETF		AGF Systematic Emerging Markets Equity ETF	Jan 27/23
AGFiQ International Equity ETF		AGF Systematic International Equity ETF	Jan 27/23
AGFiQ US Equity ETF		AGF Systematic US Equity ETF	Jan 27/23
AGFiQ US Market Neutral Anti-Beta CAD-Hedged ETF		AGF US Market Neutral Anti-Beta CAD-Hedged ETF	Jan 27/23
Agra Ventures Ltd.		Digicann Ventures Inc.	Aug 2/23
Aguila Copper Corp.		T2 Metals Corp.	Oct 20/22
Alchemist Mining Inc.		Lithos Energy Ltd.	Aug 15/23
Alianza Minerals Ltd.		Silver North Resources Ltd.	Aug 14/23
Alkaline Fuel Cell Power Corp.		Cleantech Power Corp.	May 4/23
Allied Copper Corp.		Volt Lithium Corp.	Apr 27/23
Alpha Metaverse Technologies Inc.		AlphaGen Intelligence Corp.	Jun 15/23
Altaley Mining Corporation		Luca Mining Corp.	Mar 21/23
Altan Rio Minerals Limited		Golden Horse Minerals Limited	Jul 21/23
American Manganese Inc.		RecycLiCo Battery Materials Inc.	Oct 3/22
Angel Gold Corp.		Eon Lithium Corp	Dec 19/22
Anglo Pacific Group plc		Ecora Resources plc	Oct 6/22
Antalis Ventures Corp.		Plantify Foods, Inc.	Jul 28/22
Aquarius AI Inc.		P2Earn Inc.	Mar 27/23
ArcPacific Resources Corp.		Avante Mining Corp.	May 15/23
Arctic Fox Minerals Corp.		Collective Metals Inc.	Mar 6/23
Arctic Fox Ventures Inc.		Arctic Fox Lithium Corp.	Mar 24/23
Aris Gold Corporation		Aris Mining Holdings Corp.	Sep 28/22
Arrow Canadian Advantage Alternative Class		Arrow Long/Short Alternative Class	Jun 20/23
Avante Logixx Inc.		Avante Corp.	Jun 1/23
Avanti Energy Inc.		Avanti Helium Corp.	Aug 22/22
BGP Acquisition Corp.		CRAFT 1861 Global Holdings Inc.	Mar 1/23
BMGB Capital Corp.		NAVCO Pharmaceuticals Inc.	Apr 13/23
Baden Resources Inc.		NorthStar Gaming Holdings Inc.	Mar 2/23
Bald Eagle Gold Corp.		Hercules Silver Corp.	Aug 18/22
Bastion Square Partners Inc.		Aluula Composites Inc.	Apr 14/23
Benchmark Metals Inc.		Thesis Gold Inc.	Aug 23/23
Benz Capital Corp.		Avaron Mining Corp.	Jul 25/23
Beyond Minerals Inc.		Beyond Lithium Inc.	May 15/23
Billy Goat Brands Ltd.		GOAT Industries Ltd.	Sep 12/22
Black Mountain Gold USA Corp.		Millennial Potash Corp.	Jan 25/23
Black Tusk Resources Inc.		Q Battery Metals Corp.	Mar 1/23
Brascan Gold Inc.		Brascan Resources Inc.	Apr 3/23
Braveheart Resources Inc.		Canadian Critical Minerals Inc.	Jan 19/23
Brookfield Asset Management Inc.		Brookfield Corporation	Dec 9/22
Brookfield Asset Management Reinsurance Partners Ltd.		Brookfield Reinsurance Ltd.	Dec 9/22
Burin Gold Corp.		Infinico Metals Corp.	Aug 23/23
CI Auspice Broad Commodity ETF		CI Auspice Broad Commodity Fund	May 5/23
CI Bio-Revolution ETF		CI Bio-Revolution Index ETF	Apr 21/23
CI Digital Security ETF		CI Digital Security Index ETF	Apr 21/23
CI Galaxy Blockchain ETF		CI Galaxy Blockchain Index ETF	Apr 21/23
CI Galaxy Metaverse ETF		CI Galaxy Metaverse Index ETF	Apr 21/23
CIBT Education Group Inc.		Global Education Communities Corp.	Apr 17/23
Canada House Cannabis Group Inc.		MTL Cannabis Corp.	Jul 28/23
Canada House Wellness Group Inc.	Canada House Cannabis Group Inc.	MTL Cannabis Corp.	Aug 23/22
Canadian Pacific Railway Limited		Canadian Pacific Kansas City Limited	Apr 14/23
Candente Copper Corp.		Alta Copper Corp.	May 19/23
Capitan Mining Inc.		Capitan Silver Corp.	Mar 23/23

Original Name	New Name	Current Name	Effective Date
Carl Data Solutions Inc.		infinitii ai inc.	Oct 7/22
Cartier Iron Corporation		Cartier Silver Corporation	Nov 15/22
Cashbox Ventures Ltd.		Volta Metals Ltd.	May 31/23
Chemesis International Inc.		Refined Metals Corp.	Nov 22/22
Cirrus Gold Corp.		American Copper Development Corporation	Jul 22/22
Clarity Gold Corp.		Clarity Metals Corp.	Dec 15/22
Clear Sky Lithium Corp.		POWR Lithium Corp.	Jan 30/23
ClearStream Energy Services Inc.		FLINT Corp.	Dec 1/22
Cloud Nine Web3 Technologies Inc.		Anonymous Intelligence Company Inc.	May 12/23
Column Capital Corp.		Largo Physical Vanadium Corp.	Sep 15/22
Copper Ridge Exploration Inc.		Norris Lithium Inc.	Jan 16/23
Cover Technologies Inc.		PlasCred Circular Innovations Inc.	Aug 3/23
Cross Border Capital I Inc.		SuperBuzz Inc.	Jul 7/22
Cub Energy Inc.		Carcetti Capital Corp.	Dec 30/22
CurrencyWorks Inc.		MetaWorks Platforms, Inc.	Aug 24/22
Cypress Development Corp.		Century Lithium Corp.	Jan 30/23
DLV Resources Ltd.		West Red Lake Gold Mines Ltd.	Dec 29/22
Decarbonization Plus Acquisition Corporation IV		Hammerhead Energy Inc.	Feb 23/23
Diamond Fields Resources Inc.		DFR Gold Inc.	Jan 30/23
DigiMax Global Inc.		Spetz Inc.	Dec 9/22
Dominion Water Reserves Corp.		Prime Drink Group Corp.	Nov 23/22
Dragonfly Capital Corp.		Black Swan Graphene Inc.	Aug 2/22
Dynamic Active Retirement Income+ ETF		Dynamic Active Retirement Income ETF	Nov 4/22
E3 Metals Corp.		E3 Lithium Ltd.	Jul 7/22
EEE Exploration Corp.		Spod Lithium Corp.	Sep 21/22
ESG Capital 1 Inc.		Full Circle Lithium Corp.	Apr 19/23
ESG Global Impact Capital Inc.		AI Artificial Intelligence Ventures Inc.	Jun 29/23
EV Ventures Inc.		Atco Mining Inc.	Sep 19/22
EVP CPC Inc.		EVP Capital Inc.	Apr 25/23
EYEFI Group Technologies Inc.		Sparc AI Inc.	Aug 9/23
Eagle I Capital Corporation		Weekapaug Lithium Limited	Feb 6/23
El Nino Ventures Inc.		MetalQuest Mining Inc.	Dec 30/22
Elemental Royalties Corp.		Elemental Altus Royalties Corp.	Sep 26/22
Engine Gaming and Media, Inc.		GameSquare Holdings, Inc.	Apr 11/23
Erin Ventures Inc.		Boron One Holdings Inc.	Feb 3/23
Essex Minerals Inc.		Optegra Ventures Inc.	Aug 25/23
Facedrive Inc.		Steer Technologies Inc.	Oct 4/22
Field Trip Health Ltd.		Reunion Neuroscience Inc.	Aug 11/22
Filo Mining Corp.		Filo Corp.	Jun 23/23
First Energy Metals Limited		FE Battery Metals Corp.	Nov 1/22
Fission 3.0 Corp.		F3 Uranium Corp.	Jan 31/23
Flexwork Properties Ltd.		Blockchain Venture Capital Inc.	Aug 3/22
Franklin Bissett Core Plus Bond Active ETF		Franklin Bissett Core Plus Bond Fund	Jul 10/23
Franklin Bissett Corporate Bond Active ETF		Franklin Bissett Corporate Bond Fund	Jul 10/23
Franklin Bissett Short Duration Bond Active ETF		Franklin Bissett Short Duration Bond Fund	Jul 10/23
Franklin Bissett Ultra Short Bond Active ETF		Franklin Bissett Ultra Short Bond ETF	Aug 8/23
Franklin Brandywine Global Sustainable Income Optimiser Active ETF		Franklin Brandywine Global Sustainable Income Optimiser Fund	Jul 10/23
Franklin ClearBridge Sustainable Global Infrastructure Income Active ETF		Franklin ClearBridge Sustainable Global Infrastructure Income Fund	Jul 10/23
Franklin ClearBridge Sustainable International Growth Active ETF		Franklin ClearBridge Sustainable International Growth Fund	Jul 10/23
Franklin Global Aggregate Bond Active ETF (CAD-Hedged)		Franklin Global Core Bond Fund	Aug 8/23
Franklin Global Growth Active ETF		Franklin Global Growth Fund	Jul 10/23
Franklin Innovation Active ETF		Franklin Innovation Fund	Jul 10/23
Franklin Western Asset Core Plus Bond Active ETF		Franklin Western Asset Core Plus Bond Fund	Jul 10/23
Freedom Battery Metals Inc.		Reflex Advanced Materials Corp.	Oct 14/22
Fuse Cobalt Inc.		Fuse Battery Metals Inc.	Feb 2/23
Future Fuel Corporation		American Future Fuel Corporation	Jul 8/22
GCM Mining Corp.		Aris Mining Corporation	Sep 28/22
Galane Gold Ltd.		Golconda Gold Ltd.	Oct 21/22
Gallagher Security Corp.		Genesis AI Corp.	Jul 11/23
Galway Gold Inc.		Montauk Metals Inc.	Jul 21/23
Gambier Gold Corp.		EGR Exploration Ltd.	Oct 17/22
Gamelancer Gaming Corp.		Gamelancer Media Corp.	Sep 27/22
Givex Information Technology Group Limited		Givex Corp.	Nov 10/22
Global Cannabis Applications Corp.		Global Compliance Applications Corp.	Jul 14/22
Global Care Capital Inc.		Polaris Northstar Capital Corp.	Mar 29/23
Gold Lion Resources Inc.		Lithium Lion Metals Inc.	Jul 31/23
Gold State Resources Inc.		International Metals Mining Corp.	Oct 31/22
Gold Tree Resources Ltd.		Live Energy Minerals Corp.	Mar 1/23
Golden Dawn Minerals Inc.		CanXGold Mining Corp.	Sep 22/22
Golden Sun Mining Corp.		Pan American Energy Corp.	Jul 14/22
Goldplay Mining Inc.		Europacific Metals Inc.	Jan 6/23
GoldSpot Discoveries Corp.		EarthLabs Inc.	Sep 2/22
Gravitas II Capital Corp.		Parvis Invest Inc.	Mar 3/23
Gravitas III Capital Corp.		Monaghan Capital Fund Ltd.	Jul 12/23
Gravitas Financial Inc.		New Frontier Ventures Inc.	Oct 4/22
The Green Organic Dutchman Holdings Ltd.		BZAM Ltd.	Feb 23/23
Greenfield Acquisition Corp.		Inspire Semiconductor Holdings Inc.	Sep 20/22
The Gummy Project Inc.		Vice Health and Wellness Inc.	Jun 19/23

Original Name	New Name	Current Name	Effective Date
HIVE Blockchain Technologies Ltd.		HIVE Digital Technologies Ltd.	Jul 12/23
HPQ-Silicon Resources Inc.		HPQ Silicon Inc.	Jul 4/22
Hansa Resources Limited		Tribeca Resources Corporation	Nov 2/22
Hanwei Energy Services Corp.		Peak Discovery Capital Ltd.	Apr 20/23
Harborside Inc.		StateHouse Holdings Inc	Jul 25/22
Hardwoods Distribution Inc.		ADENTRA Inc.	Dec 2/22
Harvest One Cannabis Inc.		Delivra Health Brands Inc.	Sep 8/22
Hawkmoon Resources Corp.		Earthwise Minerals Corp.	Apr 21/23
HeliosX Lithium & Technologies Corp.		D2 Lithium Corp.	Jun 21/23
High Fusion Inc.		Vertical Peak Holdings Inc.	May 8/23
Highbury Projects Inc.	IFS Global Software Inc.	Interfield Global Software Inc.	Feb 15/23
Hill Street Beverage Company Inc.		Hill Incorporated	May 30/23
Hilo Mining Ltd.		European Energy Metals Corp.	Apr 25/23
Holy Cow Foods Inc.		NextGen Food Robotics Corp.	Jan 24/23
Hopefield Ventures Inc.		CyberCatch Holdings, Inc.	Apr 12/23
Horizons Balanced TRI ETF Portfolio		Horizons Balanced Asset Allocation ETF	Aug 25/23
Horizons Conservative TRI ETF Portfolio		Horizons Conservative Asset Allocation ETF	Aug 25/23
Horizons Growth TRI ETF Portfolio		Horizons All-Equity Asset Allocation ETF	Aug 25/23
Hylands International Holdings Inc.		Ocham's Razor Capital Limited	Dec 5/22
I-Minerals Inc.		Highcliff Metals Corp.	Apr 11/23
IFS Global Software Inc.		Interfield Global Software Inc.	May 1/23
ITOK Capital Corp.		Blue Sky Global Energy Corp.	Jul 18/23
Icanic Brands Company Inc.		Leef Brands Inc.	Dec 7/22
Idaho Champion Gold Mines Canada Inc.		Champion Electric Metals Inc.	May 29/23
Idle Lifestyle Inc.		Generative AI Solutions Corp.	Feb 4/23
Îledor Exploration Corporation		LSL Pharma Group Inc.	Feb 17/23
Invictus Financial Inc.		Mapath Capital Corp.	Dec 22/22
Jasper Mining Corporation		Tuktu Resources Ltd.	Oct 19/22
Jazz Resources Inc.		JZR Gold Inc.	Oct 19/22
Jerico Explorations Inc.		Cumberland Resources Nickel Corp.	Dec 16/22
Jessy Ventures Corp.		Generation Gold Corp.	Dec 13/22
Jourdan Resources Inc.		Consolidated Lithium Metals Inc.	Jun 28/23
Justify Capital Corp.		Everyday People Financial Corp.	Aug 31/22
K.B. Recycling Industries Ltd.		Oceansix Future Paths Ltd.	Mar 29/23
King's Bay Resources Corp.		Lion Rock Resources Inc.	Jul 8/22
Kona Bay Technologies Inc.		Yerbaé Brands Corp.	Feb 9/23
LFNT Capital Corp.		LFNT Resources Corp.	Feb 10/23
LQwD FinTech Corp.		LQWD Technologies Corp.	Jul 28/23
Labrador Technologies Inc.		Labrador Resources Inc.	Feb 3/23
Labrador Uranium Inc.		Latitude Uranium Inc.	Jun 29/23
Leviathan Natural Products Inc.		1CM Inc.	Sep 6/22
Liberty One Lithium Corp.		Three Sixty Solar Ltd.	Aug 4/22
Lingo Media Corporation		Everybody Loves Languages Corp.	Oct 17/22
Lithoquest Resources Inc.		Storm Exploration Inc.	Nov 9/22
Loon Energy Corporation		Optimind Pharma Corp.	Jul 27/22
Love Pharma Inc.		Jolt Health Inc.	May 26/23
Luff Enterprises Ltd.		Herbal Dispatch Inc.	Jan 20/23
MLK Gold Ltd.		Triple One Metals Inc.	Apr 13/23
Madi Minerals Ltd.		Pegmatite One Lithium and Gold Corp.	Jan 27/23
Magen Ventures I Inc.		Grey Wolf Animal Health Corp.	Nov 11/22
Merida Minerals Holdings Inc.		Hispania Resources Inc.	Dec 14/22
Metallum Resources Inc.		Waroona Energy Inc.	May 11/23
Meteorite Capital Inc.		Kobo Resources Inc.	Mar 29/23
Miata II Capital Corp.		Miata Metals Corp.	Mar 7/23
Millrock Resources Inc.		Alaska Energy Metals Corporation	Mar 22/23
Minerva Intelligence Inc.		Aisix Solutions Inc.	Aug 17/23
Mineworx Technologies Ltd.		Regenx Tech Corp.	Oct 31/22
Miza II Resources Inc.		Great Eagle Gold Corp.	Jul 4/23
Mountain Boy Minerals Ltd.		MTB Metals Corp.	Mar 30/23
Myriad Metals Corp.		Myriad Uranium Corp.	Dec 12/22
Navion Capital Inc.		NOA Lithium Brines Inc.	Mar 1/23
NeonMind Biosciences Inc.		Lancaster Resources Inc.	Jun 7/23
Nevada Silver Corporation		Electric Metals (USA) Limited	May 16/23
Nevada Sunrise Gold Corporation		Nevada Sunrise Metals Corporation	Sep 23/22
New Tech Minerals Corp.		American Potash Corp.	Aug 31/22
Nickel Rock Resources Inc.		Grid Battery Metals Inc.	Apr 5/23
Ninepoint Bitcoin ETF		Ninepoint Web3 Innovators Fund	May 31/23
North American Nickel Inc.		Premium Nickel Resources Ltd.	Jul 29/22
Northview Fund		Northview Residential REIT	Aug 21/23
Nurosene Health Inc.		NetraMark Holdings Inc.	Feb 1/23
10000259749 Ontario Inc.		Arway Corporation	Aug 3/22
1000268474 Ontario Ltd.		NiCAN Limited	Jul 26/22
1111 Exploration Corp.		Teako Minerals Corp.	Feb 17/23
1287390 B.C. Ltd.	1000268474 Ontario Ltd.	NiCAN Limited	Jul 13/22
1319275 B.C. Ltd.		Critical Infrastructure Technologies Ltd.	Feb 13/23
1319738 B.C. Ltd.		DevvStream Holdings Inc.	Nov 4/22
Orefinders Resources Inc.		Orecap Invest Corp.	May 18/23
Ortho Regenerative Technologies Inc.		ChitogenX Inc.	Sep 12/22
Oz Lithium Corporation		Critical Reagent Processing Corp.	Aug 17/23
Pacific Paradym Energy Inc.		Olivier Ventures Inc.	Mar 3/23
Pancontinental Resources Corporation		Carolina Rush Corporation	Mar 2/23
Pascal Biosciences Inc.		Nevis Brands Inc.	Jun 12/23

Original Name	New Name	Current Name	Effective Date
Patriot One Technologies Inc.		Xtract One Technologies Inc.	Nov 28/22
Perihelion Capital Ltd.		Hydreight Technologies Inc.	Nov 25/22
PetroCorp Group Inc.		First Lithium Minerals Corp.	Jul 27/22
Phoenix Canada Oil Company Limited		ZYUS Life Sciences Corporation	Jun 9/23
Pima Zinc Corp.		Cybeats Technologies Corp.	Nov 9/22
Pinedale Energy Limited		MCF Energy Ltd.	Dec 23/22
Pinehurst Capital II Inc.		Halcones Precious Metals Corp.	Sep 15/22
Plant&Co. Brands Ltd.		Happy Belly Food Group Inc.	Sep 1/22
Plymouth Rock Technologies Inc.		Aether Global Innovations Corp.	Jul 31/23
Polaris Infrastructure Inc.		Polaris Renewable Energy Inc.	Jul 5/22
Predictmedix Inc.		Predictmedix AI Inc.	Jul 13/23
Prime Meridian Resources Corp.		Sonoran Desert Copper Corporation	Mar 21/23
Probe Metals Inc.		Probe Gold Inc.	Jan 9/23
Prodigy Ventures Inc.		genifi inc.	Jul 1/23
Prosperity Exploration Corp.		First American Uranium Inc.	Sep 16/22
Purpose Global Climate Opportunities Fund		Purpose Energy Transition Fund	Apr 14/23
Purpose Healthcare Innovation Yield ETF		Purpose Healthcare Innovation Yield Fund	Oct 17/22
Purpose High Interest Savings ETF		Purpose High Interest Savings Fund	Jan 16/23
Quebec Silica Resources Corp.		Quebec Innovative Materials Corp.	Jan 12/23
Queensland Gold Hills Corp.		Q2 Metals Corp.	Jan 9/23
RSI International Systems Inc.		ARCpoint Inc.	Oct 20/22
Razore Rock Resources Inc.		American Critical Elements Inc.	Sep 23/22
Ready Set Gold Corp.		Newpath Resources Inc.	Dec 8/22
Rebel Capital 2.0 Corp.		Arya Resources Ltd.	Dec 20/22
Ritchie Bros. Auctioneers Incorporated		RB Global, Inc.	May 23/23
Roadman Investments Corp.		Right Season Investments Corp.	Jan 3/23
RooGold Inc.		Metalite Resources Inc.	Mar 27/23
Royal Coal Corp.		EV Minerals Corporation	Dec 13/22
Royalty North Partners Ltd.		Horizon Copper Corp.	Aug 31/22
Rritual Superfoods Inc.		Aretto Wellness Inc.	Nov 25/22
Rugby Mining Limited		Rugby Resources Ltd.	Aug 29/22
Rush Uranium Corp.		Rush Rare Metals Corp.	Mar 16/23
SPARQ Corp.		SPARQ Systems Inc.	Jan 1/23
St. Anthony Gold Corp.		Spark Energy Minerals Inc.	Dec 23/22
Samoth Oilfield Inc.		Lycos Energy Inc.	Dec 12/22
Sassy Resources Corporation		Sassy Gold Corp.	Jul 20/22
Satori Resources Inc.		Canadian Gold Corp.	May 5/23
Scout Minerals Corp.		Eureka Lithium Corp.	Jun 1/23
ScreenPro Security Inc.		Justera Health Ltd.	May 17/23
Sebastiani Ventures Corp.		EvokAI Creative Labs Inc.	Apr 11/23
Secova Metals Corp.		ESGold Corp.	Jul 14/22
ShinyBud Corp.		Shiny Health & Wellness Corp.	Aug 15/22
Silk Road Energy Inc.		Record Resources Inc.	Mar 21/23
Silver Eagle Mines Inc.		Nevada Organic Phosphate Inc.	May 3/23
Silver Phoenix Resources Inc.		Atlas Global Brands Inc.	Dec 30/22
Silverton Metals Corp.		Lodestar Battery Metals Corp.	Nov 7/22
Softrock Minerals Ltd.		Criterium Energy Ltd.	Sep 26/22
SolidusGold Inc.		Valhalla Metals Inc.	Sep 16/22
Solitario Zinc Corp.		Solitario Resources Corp.	Jul 18/23
Sonora Gold & Silver Corp.		BTQ Technologies Corp.	Feb 17/23
St Charles Resources Inc.		BULGOLD Inc.	May 5/23
Stallion Gold Corp.		Stallion Discoveries Corp.	Jan 19/23
Stone Gold Inc.		Copper Road Resources Inc.	Sep 8/22
Straightup Resources Inc.		Battery X Metals Inc.	Jul 6/23
Strathmore Plus Energy Corp.		Strathmore Plus Uranium Corp.	Sep 26/22
TPCO Holding Corp.		Gold Flora Corporation	Jul 7/23
Thesis Gold Inc.		Thesis Gold (Holdings) Inc.	Aug 17/23
3iQ CoinShares Bitcoin ETF		3iQ Bitcoin ETF	Apr 11/23
3iQ CoinShares Ether ETF		3iQ Ether ETF	Apr 11/23
Titus Energy Corp.		Free Battery Metal Limited	Jun 8/23
TraceSafe Inc.		ShiftCarbon Inc.	Dec 20/22
Trillium Gold Mines Inc.		Renegade Gold Inc.	Jul 17/23
U3O8 Corp.		Green Shift Commodities Ltd.	Oct 18/22
United Hunter Oil & Gas Corp.		Bocana Resources Corp.	Dec 29/22
Uravan Minerals Inc.		Nuclear Fuels Inc.	Jul 7/23
VAR Resources Corp.		Grounded Lithium Corp.	Aug 25/22
VPN Technologies Inc.		Energy Plug Technologies Corp.	Jun 1/23
Valorem Resources Inc.		Avanti Gold Corp.	Apr 21/23
Valour Inc.		DeFi Technologies Inc.	Jul 10/23
Vejii Holdings Ltd.		Veji Holdings Ltd.	Aug 26/22
Verde Agritech Plc		Verde Agritech Ltd.	Jul 29/22
Verses Technologies Inc.		Verses AI Inc.	Mar 31/23
Victory Resources Corporation		Victory Battery Metals Corp.	Dec 19/22
Visionary Gold Corp.		Visionary Metals Corp.	Jul 10/23
Warrior Gold Inc.		Kirkland Lake Discoveries Corp.	May 10/23
WeCommerce Holdings Ltd.		Tiny Ltd.	Apr 17/23
West Red Lake Gold Mines Inc.		West Red Lake Gold Mines (Ontario) Ltd.	Feb 20/23
Westbridge Energy Corporation		Westbridge Renewable Energy Corp.	Sep 29/22
Western Troy Capital Resources Inc.		Li3 Lithium Corp.	Aug 2/22
White Metal Resources Corp.		Thunder Gold Corp.	Jul 14/22
Whitehorse Gold Corp.		Tincorp Metals Inc.	Feb 22/23
World Class Extractions Inc.		Stock Trend Capital Inc.	Feb 27/23

Original Name	New Name	Current Name	Effective Date
X-Terra Resources Inc.		Comet Lithium Corporation	Jun 1/23
X1 Esports and Entertainment Ltd.		X1 Entertainment Group Inc.	Oct 19/22
XPhyto Therapeutics Corp.		BioNxt Solutions Inc.	Nov 14/22
Xebec Adsorption Inc.		FormerXBC Inc.	Mar 9/23
Xtierra Inc.		Royalties Inc.	Feb 27/23
Yellow Stem Tech Inc.		Sweet Poison Spirits Inc.	Jun 1/23
Zoglo's Incredible Food Corp.		Zoglo's Food Corp.	Feb 28/23

Corporate Actions

Company Name	Split or Consolidation	Effective Date
AEterna Zentaris Inc.	1-for-25 cons.	Jul 21/22
ARCpoint Inc.	1-for-2.49308 cons.	Oct 27/22
Abaxx Technologies Inc.	1-for-3 cons.	May 23/23
Aben Minerals Ltd.	1-for-10 cons.	Feb 22/23
Acasti Pharma Inc.	1-for-6 cons.	Jul 10/23
African Energy Metals Inc.	1-for-4 cons.	Apr 10/23
Alaska Energy Metals Corporation	1-for-10 cons.	Mar 22/23
Algernon Pharmaceuticals Inc.	4-for-1 split	Mar 3/23
The Alkaline Water Company Inc.	1-for-15 cons.	Apr 5/23
Alset Capital Inc.	1-for-2 cons.	Aug 17/23
Alta Copper Corp.	1-for-4 cons.	May 19/23
Angold Resources Ltd.	1-for-10 cons.	Jun 7/23
Aptose Biosciences Inc.	1-for-15 cons.	Jun 6/23
Archer Exploration Corp.	1-for-3 cons.	Nov 29/22
Aretto Wellness Inc.	1-for-20 cons.	Nov 25/22
Atlas Global Brands Inc.	1-for-5 cons.	Jan 13/23
Atmofizer Technologies Inc.	1-for-20 cons.	Jan 12/23
Avante Mining Corp.	1-for-10 cons.	Dec 15/22
Avanti Gold Corp.	1-for-35 cons.	Jul 22/22
Azarga Metals Corp.	1-for-10 cons.	Jun 27/23
BTQ Technologies Corp.	1-for-10 cons.	Feb 17/23
BULGOLD Inc.	1-for-3 cons.	May 5/23
BZAM Ltd.	1-for-10 cons.	Nov 8/22
Basin Uranium Corp.	1-for-4 cons.	Jun 26/23
Bathurst Metals Corp.	1-for-2.5 cons.	Oct 31/22
Battery X Metals Inc.	1-for-3 cons.	Jul 6/23
BetaPro Bitcoin ETF	1-for-4 cons.	Aug 2/22
BetaPro Bitcoin ETF	1-for-4 cons.	Aug 2/22
BetaPro Crude Oil Inverse Leveraged Daily Bear ETF	1-for-4 cons.	Aug 2/22
BetaPro Equal Weight Canadian REIT -2x Daily Bear ETF	2-for-1 split	Nov 7/22
BetaPro Marijuana Companies Inverse ETF	2-for-1 split	Nov 7/22
BetaPro Marijuana Companies 2x Daily Bull ETF	1-for-2 cons.	Nov 7/22
BetaPro Marijuana Companies 2x Daily Bull ETF	1-for-2 cons.	Aug 2/22
BetaPro Marijuana Companies 2x Daily Bull ETF	1-for-15 cons.	Aug 8/23
BetaPro NASDAQ-100 -2x Daily Bear ETF	1-for-4 cons.	Feb 21/23
BetaPro NASDAQ-100 -2x Daily Bear ETF	1-for-4 cons.	Feb 21/23
BetaPro Natural Gas Inverse Leveraged Daily Bear ETF	1-for-10 cons.	Sep 6/22
BetaPro Natural Gas Leveraged Daily Bull ETF	1-for-15 cons.	Feb 21/23
BetaPro S&P 500 -2x Daily Bear ETF	1-for-4 cons.	Feb 21/23
BetaPro S&P 500 VIX Short-Term Futures ETF	1-for-6 cons.	Feb 21/23
BetaPro S&P/TSX Capped Energy -2x Daily Bear ETF	1-for-4 cons.	Aug 2/22
BetaPro S&P/TSX Capped Energy 2x Daily Bull ETF	2-for-1 split	Nov 7/22
BetaPro S&P/TSX Capped Financials -2x Daily Bear ETF	1-for-2 cons.	Nov 7/22
BetaPro S&P/TSX 60 Daily Inverse ETF	1-for-4 cons.	Feb 21/23
BetaPro Silver 2x Daily Bull ETF	1-for-2 cons.	Nov 7/22
Bettermoo(d) Food Corporation	1-for-10 cons.	Mar 13/23
Beyond Medical Technologies Inc.	1-for-10 cons.	Dec 30/22
Blanton Resources Corp.	1-for-2 cons.	Jul 21/23
Blender Bites Limited	1-for-10 cons.	Jul 13/22
Blockchain Venture Capital Inc.	1-for-21.2535 cons.	Aug 12/22
Blue Moon Metals Inc.	1-for-10 cons.	Mar 7/23
Blue Thunder Mining Inc.	1-for-4.7 cons.	Jan 20/23
BlueRush Inc.	1-for-5 cons.	Dec 19/22
Bocana Resources Corp.	1-for-1.6877 cons.	Jan 5/23
Bolt Metals Corp.	1-for-10 cons.	Mar 6/23
Boundary Gold and Copper Mining Ltd.	1-for-20 cons.	Apr 20/23
Bright Minds Biosciences Inc.	1-for-5 cons.	Jul 14/23
Brompton Oil Split Corp.	1-for-1.15625 cons.	Apr 11/23
Butte Energy Inc.	1-for-5 cons.	Mar 9/23
CLS Holdings USA, Inc.	1-for-4 cons.	Sep 21/22
CULT Food Science Corp.	1-for-4 cons.	Aug 23/23

Company Name	Split or Consolidation	Effective Date
Canacol Energy Ltd.	1-for-5 cons.	Jan 20/23
Canadian Nexus Team Ventures Corp.	1-for-7 cons.	Jun 22/23
Cannara Biotech Inc.	1-for-10 cons.	Feb 13/23
Carcetti Capital Corp.	1-for-300 cons.	Jan 4/23
Carlin Gold Corporation	1-for-10 cons.	Jun 8/23
Carlyle Commodities Corp.	1-for-10 cons.	Sep 6/22
Carolina Rush Corporation	1-for-10 cons.	Mar 2/23
Cartier Silver Corporation	1-for-5 cons.	Nov 18/22
Centaurus Energy Inc.	1-for-500 cons.	Dec 23/22
Central Iron Ore Limited	1-for-3 cons.	Jul 18/22
Centurion Minerals Ltd.	1-for-2 cons.	Jul 6/22
CleanGo Innovations Inc.	1-for-5 cons.	Jan 13/23
Clearmind Medicine Inc.	1-for-30 cons.	Sep 30/22
Collective Metals Inc.	1-for-10 cons.	Mar 13/23
Comet Lithium Corporation	1-for-7 cons.	Feb 8/23
Crest Resources Inc.	1-for-3 cons.	Mar 23/23
Criterium Energy Ltd.	1-for-5 cons.	Jun 7/23
CyberCatch Holdings, Inc.	1-for-3.87 cons.	Apr 24/23
Cypher Metaverse Inc.	1-for-10 cons.	Dec 20/22
Decade Resources Ltd.	1-for-5 cons.	Jul 12/22
DeepMarkit Corp.	1-for-40 cons.	Jun 22/23
Denarius Metals Corp.	1-for-10 cons.	Nov 21/22
Digicann Ventures Inc.	1-for-25 cons.	Aug 8/23
Direct Communication Solutions, Inc.	1-for-7 cons.	Feb 10/23
Discovery Harbour Resources Corp.	1-for-10 cons.	Jun 6/23
Dream Impact Trust	1-for-4 cons.	Jun 20/23
EGF Theramed Health Corp.	1-for-20 cons.	Jul 11/22
EGR Exploration Ltd.	1-for-3 cons.	Oct 17/22
Earthwise Minerals Corp.	1-for-10 cons.	Dec 22/22
Eat & Beyond Global Holdings Inc.	1-for-7 cons.	Mar 9/23
Edgemont Gold Corp.	1-for-2 cons.	Mar 2/23
Edison Lithium Corp.	1-for-8 cons.	Aug 1/23
Electrovaya Inc.	1-for-5 cons.	Jun 16/23
Empower Clinics Inc.	1-for-5 cons.	Jun 21/23
enCore Energy Corp.	1-for-3 cons.	Sep 14/22
Engineer Gold Mines Ltd.	1-for-4 cons.	May 31/23
EvokAI Creative Labs Inc.	1-for-2.66285 cons.	Apr 14/23
FE Battery Metals Corp.	1-for-3.8 cons.	Nov 1/22
Fabled Copper Corp.	1-for-10 cons.	Apr 13/23
Fabled Silver Gold Corp.	1-for-5 cons.	Jan 26/23
First Lithium Minerals Corp.	1-for-81.9672 cons.	Jul 27/22
First Responder Technologies Inc.	1-for-25 cons.	Dec 20/22
Flow Metals Corp.	1-for-10 cons.	Jul 21/22
Foremost Lithium Resource & Technology Ltd.	1-for-50 cons.	Jul 4/23
Full Circle Lithium Corp.	1-for-1.17 cons.	May 1/23
G2 Energy Corp.	1-for-5 cons.	Jun 9/23
G6 Materials Corp.	1-for-10 cons.	Jul 12/23
GOAT Industries Ltd.	1-for-100 cons.	Jul 19/23
Gaia Grow Corp.	1-for-25 cons.	Aug 9/22
Galway Metals Inc.	1-for-3 cons.	Jan 27/23
GameSquare Holdings, Inc.	1-for-4 cons.	Apr 11/23
Generative AI Solutions Corp.	1-for-30 cons.	Feb 13/23
Global Health Clinics Ltd.	1-for-20 cons.	Jul 11/22
Golconda Gold Ltd.	1-for-5 cons.	Oct 21/22
Golden Goliath Resources Ltd.	1-for-7 cons.	Jun 5/23
Golden Independence Mining Corp.	1-for-15 cons.	Nov 1/22
Golden Minerals Company	1-for-25 cons.	Jun 9/23
Goldgroup Mining Inc.	1-for-10 cons.	Sep 27/22
GoldHaven Resources Corp.	1-for-6 cons.	Jun 28/23
GoldMoney Inc.	1-for-5 cons.	Jun 23/23
Goodbody Health Inc.	1-for-10 cons.	Aug 22/22
Gran Tierra Energy Inc.	1-for-10 cons.	May 8/23
Graph Blockchain Inc.	1-for-10 cons.	Nov 16/22
Great Eagle Gold Corp.	2.5-for-1 split	Jul 6/23
Great Panther Mining Limited	1-for-10 cons.	Jul 25/22
Grey Wolf Animal Health Corp.	1-for-16.6667 cons.	Nov 23/22
HAVN Life Sciences Inc.	1-for-30 cons.	Aug 3/22

Company Name	Split or Consolidation	Effective Date
HEXO Corp.	1-for-14 cons.	Dec 19/22
Halcones Precious Metals Corp.	0.471698-for-1 cons.	Sep 22/22
Halo Collective Inc.	1-for-5 cons.	Oct 28/22
Hawkeye Gold & Diamond Inc.	1-for-10 cons.	Apr 18/23
The Hempshire Group, Inc.	1-for-4 cons.	Aug 11/22
Highcliff Metals Corp.	1-for-10 cons.	Apr 11/23
Hill Incorporated	1-for-75 cons.	May 30/23
Hillcrest Energy Technologies Ltd.	1-for-6 cons.	Jun 8/23
Honey Badger Silver Inc.	1-for-5.7 cons.	Jan 20/23
Horizons Canadian Large Cap Equity Covered Call ETF	1-for-2 cons.	Nov 7/22
Horizons Equal Weight Canadian Bank Covered Call ETF	1-for-2 cons.	Nov 7/22
Horizons Gold Yield ETF	1-for-2 cons.	Nov 7/22
Horizons Marijuana Life Sciences ETF	1-for-2 cons.	Nov 7/22
Horizons Marijuana Life Sciences ETF	1-for-2 cons.	Nov 7/22
Horizons Marijuana Life Sciences ETF	1-for-2 cons.	Aug 2/22
Horizons Marijuana Life Sciences ETF	1-for-2 cons.	Aug 2/22
Horizons NASDAQ-100 Covered Call ETF	1-for-2 cons.	Nov 7/22
Horizons Psychedelic Stock Index ETF	1-for-4 cons.	Aug 2/22
Horizons US Marijuana Index ETF	1-for-4 cons.	Aug 2/22
Horizons US Marijuana Index ETF	1-for-4 cons.	Aug 2/22
Hunter Technology Corp.	1-for-2 cons.	Nov 8/22
Huntsman Exploration Inc.	1-for-10 cons.	Mar 10/23
Hydreight Technologies Inc.	1-for-6.46805 cons.	Nov 25/22
IM Cannabis Corp.	1-for-10 cons.	Nov 17/22
IMV Inc.	1-for-10 cons.	Dec 13/22
ISM Resources Corp.	1-for-2 cons.	Feb 1/23
iMining Technologies Inc.	1-for-3 cons.	Aug 12/22
Infinity Stone Ventures Corp.	1-for-2 cons.	Jul 13/23
Integra Resources Corp.	1-for-2.5 cons.	May 26/23
Interfield Global Software Inc.	1-for-2.86 cons.	Feb 16/23
Interfield Global Software Inc.	3.44-for-1 split	Feb 15/23
International Metals Mining Corp.	1-for-10 cons.	Oct 31/22
Jinhua Capital Corporation	1-for-2 cons.	Aug 11/23
Jolt Health Inc.	1-for-10 cons.	Mar 2/23
KWESST Micro Systems Inc.	1-for-70 cons.	Oct 28/22
Kiaro Holdings Corp.	1-for-10 cons.	Sep 29/22
King Global Ventures Inc.	1-for-10 cons.	Jan 27/23
King Global Ventures Inc.	1-for-5 cons.	Jul 28/23
Kingman Minerals Ltd.	1-for-10 cons.	Oct 20/22
Kingsmen Resources Ltd.	1-for-2 cons.	Mar 28/23
Kirkland Lake Discoveries Corp.	1-for-4 cons.	May 10/23
Kobo Resources Inc.	1-for-5 cons.	Mar 31/23
Komo Plant Based Foods Inc.	1-for-10 cons.	Jan 30/23
LQWD Technologies Corp.	1-for-10 cons.	Nov 14/22
LSL Pharma Group Inc.	1-for-25 cons.	Mar 1/23
Lancaster Resources Inc.	1-for-30 cons.	Jan 24/23
Largo Physical Vanadium Corp.	1-for-7.547 cons.	Sep 15/22
Lincoln Gold Mining Inc.	1-for-10 cons.	Mar 8/23
Lion Rock Resources Inc.	1-for-2.5 cons.	Mar 6/23
Luca Mining Corp.	1-for-8 cons.	Dec 20/22
Lupaka Gold Corp.	1-for-10 cons.	Aug 15/22
Lycos Energy Inc.	1-for-8 cons.	Dec 15/22
M3 Metals Corp.	1-for-10 cons.	Sep 16/22
MTL Cannabis Corp.	1-for-30 cons.	Aug 23/22
MacDonald Mines Exploration Ltd.	1-for-10 cons.	Dec 7/22
Mako Mining Corp.	1-for-10 cons.	Mar 8/23
Margaret Lake Diamonds Inc.	1-for-10 cons.	Jun 16/23
Masivo Silver Corp.	1-for-5 cons.	Sep 6/22
McEwen Mining Inc.	1-for-10 cons.	Jul 28/22
Medivolve Inc.	1-for-15 cons.	Dec 8/22
MegaWatt Lithium and Battery Metals Corp.	1-for-10 cons.	May 9/23
Metallica Metals Corp.	1-for-5 cons.	Apr 13/23
MetalQuest Mining Inc.	1-for-2.5 cons.	Dec 30/22
Mexican Gold Mining Corp.	1-for-10 cons.	Mar 15/23
Mind Medicine (MindMed) Inc.	1-for-15 cons.	Aug 29/22
Mogo Inc.	1-for-3 cons.	Aug 14/23
Montego Resources Inc.	1-for-10 cons.	Dec 23/22
Musk Metals Corp.	1-for-4 cons.	Jun 9/23
Naturally Splendid Enterprises Ltd.	1-for-15 cons.	Sep 22/22
Nevada Exploration Inc.	1-for-25 cons.	Feb 15/23
Nevis Brands Inc.	1-for-5 cons.	Jun 12/23
New Frontier Ventures Inc.	1-for-25 cons.	Oct 4/22
New Leaf Ventures Inc.	1-for-5 cons.	Sep 12/22
New Wave Holdings Corp.	1-for-3 cons.	May 30/23
Newpath Resources Inc.	1-for-5 cons.	Aug 15/22
NewRange Gold Corp.	1-for-6 cons.	Jun 4/23
NexLiving Communities Inc.	1-for-20 cons.	Aug 3/23
Nexus Gold Corp.	1-for-10 cons.	May 18/23
Niocorp Developments Ltd.	1-for-10 cons.	Mar 21/23

Company Name	Split or Consolidation	Effective Date
Nortec Minerals Corp.	1-for-5 cons.	Dec 23/22
Northern Shield Resources Inc.	1-for-5 cons.	Sep 9/22
NorthStar Gaming Holdings Inc.	1-for-3.33333 cons.	Mar 2/23
Northview Residential REIT	1-for-1.75 cons.	Aug 23/23
Nuclear Fuels Inc.	0.8-for-1 cons.	Jul 10/23
O2Gold Inc.	1-for-10 cons.	Sep 13/22
Ocham's Razor Capital Limited	1-for-65 cons.	Dec 5/22
Olivier Ventures Inc.	1-for-3 cons.	Mar 3/23
Opawica Explorations Inc.	1-for-10 cons.	Mar 8/23
Optegra Ventures Inc.	1-for-10 cons.	Aug 25/23
Optimind Pharma Corp.	1-for-1.71308 cons.	Jul 27/22
OrganiGram Holdings Inc.	1-for-4 cons.	Jul 7/23
PR Technology Inc.	1-for-9 cons.	Aug 10/22
P2Earn Inc.	1-for-4 cons.	Mar 27/23
Parvis Invest Inc.	1-for-2.49 cons.	Mar 10/23
Peak Discovery Capital Ltd.	1-for-10 cons.	Oct 21/22
PeakBirch Commerce Inc.	1-for-10 cons.	Apr 14/23
Pegasus Resources Inc.	1-for-10 cons.	Apr 26/23
Permex Petroleum Corporation	1-for-60 cons.	Nov 2/22
PlantFuel Life Inc.	1-for-10 cons.	Jun 7/23
PlantX Life Inc.	1-for-10 cons.	Mar 30/23
PlantX Life Inc.	1-for-20 cons.	Sep 26/22
PlasCred Circular Innovations Inc.	1-for-2 cons.	Aug 8/23
Polaris Northstar Capital Corp.	1-for-20 cons.	Mar 29/23
PowerTap Hydrogen Capital Corp.	1-for-20 cons.	Jun 15/23
Premium Nickel Resources Ltd.	1-for-5 cons.	Aug 18/22
Pushfor Tech Inc.	1-for-2 cons.	Jan 12/23
Q Battery Metals Corp.	1-for-10 cons.	Nov 4/22
Quadro Resources Ltd.	1-for-3 cons.	Nov 22/22
RDARS Inc.	1-for-20 cons.	Jun 6/23
RT Minerals Corp.	1-for-10 cons.	Mar 17/23
Recharge Resources Ltd.	1-for-2 cons.	Aug 18/23
RediShred Capital Corp.	1-for-5 cons.	Aug 23/22
Regenx Tech Corp.	1-for-2 cons.	Sep 20/22
Renegade Gold Inc.	1-for-10 cons.	Jul 17/23
Reunion Neuroscience Inc.	1-for-5 cons.	Aug 17/22
Ridgestone Mining Inc.	1-for-20 cons.	Jan 9/23
Rover Metals Corp.	1-for-6 cons.	Oct 31/22
SBD Capital Corp.	1-for-12 cons.	Dec 23/22
SKRR Exploration Inc.	1-for-5 cons.	Jul 10/23
Sabre Gold Mines Corp.	1-for-10 cons.	Nov 9/22
Shoal Point Energy Ltd.	1-for-2 cons.	Apr 3/23
Signature Resources Ltd.	1-for-5 cons.	Dec 6/22
Silver North Resources Ltd.	1-for-5 cons.	Aug 14/23
Sixty North Gold Mining Ltd.	1-for-10 cons.	Oct 18/22
Sky Gold Corp.	1-for-3 cons.	Jan 23/23
Spark Energy Minerals Inc.	1-for-10 cons.	Aug 3/23
Spectra Products Inc.	1-for-5 cons.	Oct 31/22
Storm Exploration Inc.	1-for-4 cons.	Jan 19/23
Strategic Resources Inc.	1-for-6 cons.	Apr 12/23
Sweet Earth Holdings Corporation	1-for-8 cons.	Apr 24/23
Sweet Poison Spirits Inc.	1-for-2 cons.	May 1/23
TMX Group Limited	5-for-1 split	Jun 14/23
Temas Resources Corp.	1-for-9 cons.	Jun 26/23
Terrace Energy Corp.	1-for-10 cons.	Jul 25/22
Theratechnologies Inc.	1-for-4 cons.	Jul 31/23
Thesis Gold Inc.	1-for-2.6 cons.	Aug 25/23
Thomson Reuters Corporation	0.963957-for-1 cons.	Jun 23/23
Three Sixty Solar Ltd.	1-for-2 cons.	Jul 26/22
Thunderstruck Resources Ltd.	1-for-5 cons.	Apr 24/23
Treatment.com International Inc.	1-for-10 cons.	Jul 14/23
Tribeca Resources Corporation	1-for-5 cons.	Nov 2/22
Triumph Gold Corp.	1-for-10 cons.	Dec 23/22
Troy Minerals Inc.	2.5-for-1 split	Oct 12/22
VIP Entertainment Technologies Inc.	1-for-5 cons.	Mar 1/23
Valhalla Metals Inc.	1-for-5 cons.	Sep 28/22
Vegano Foods Inc.	1-for-10 cons.	Oct 25/22
Vice Health and Wellness Inc.	1-for-10 cons.	Nov 4/22
Victory Battery Metals Corp.	1-for-3 cons.	Dec 28/22
Vinergy Capital Inc.	1-for-5 cons.	May 19/23
Vizsla Copper Corp.	1-for-3.5 cons.	Dec 15/22
Volta Metals Ltd.	1-for-10 cons.	May 31/23
Walker River Resources Corp.	1-for-6 cons.	Jul 25/22
West Red Lake Gold Mines Ltd.	1-for-5 cons.	Jul 15/22
Western Energy Services Corp.	1-for-120 cons.	Aug 4/22
Westport Fuel Systems Inc.	1-for-10 cons.	Jun 6/23
Xebra Brands Ltd.	1-for-5 cons.	Feb 28/23
Xigem Technologies Corporation	1-for-10 cons.	Jul 21/22
Yerbaé Brands Corp.	1-for-5.8 cons.	Feb 10/23
Zincore Metals Inc.	1-for-2 cons.	May 11/23

Rights Offerings

Company	Basis	Price	Record Date	Ex. Rights	Expiry
Buffalo Coal Corp.	1 rt. for 1 com. sh., 1 rt. to buy 1 com. sh.	$0.01	Nov. 18/22	Nov. 17/22	Dec. 22/22
Builders Capital Mortgage Corp.	1 rt. for 1 cl. A sh., 3 rts. to buy 1 cl. A sh.	$9.30	Oct. 28/22	Oct. 27/22	Nov. 25/22
Canagold Resources Ltd.	1 rt. for 1 com. sh., 2 rts. to buy 1 com. sh.	$0.18	Nov. 10/22	Nov. 9/22	Dec. 9/22
Century Global Commodities Corporation	1 rt. for 1 ord. sh., 5 rts. to buy 1 ord. sh.	$0.02	June 9/23	June 8/23	July 7/23
Denarius Metals Corp.	1 rt. for 1 com. sh., 1 rt. to buy 1 Denarius Metals unit consisting of 1 com. sh. and 1 sh. pur. wt.	$0.40	Jan. 24/23	Jan. 23/23	Feb. 24/23
Eastern Platinum Limited	1 rt. for 1 com. sh., 1 rt. to buy 1 com. sh.	$0.11	Apr. 6/23	Apr. 5/23	May 5/23
Kore Mining Ltd.	0.75 rts. for 1 com. sh., 1 rt. to buy 1 com. sh.	$0.01	Oct. 20/22	Oct. 19/22	Nov. 15/22
MAS Gold Corp.	1 rt. for 1 com. sh., 1 rt. to buy 1 com. sh.	$0.01	June 30/23	June 29/23	Sept. 5/23
MCAN Mortgage Corporation	1 rt. for 1 com. sh., 13 rts. to buy 1 com. sh.	$14.00	Nov. 24/22	Nov. 23/22	Dec. 20/22
Mineworx Technologies Ltd.	1 rt. for 1 com. sh., 1 rt. to buy 1 com. sh.	$0.02	July 18/22	July 15/22	Sept. 12/22
NXT Energy Solutions Inc.	1 rt. for 1 com. sh., 2.95 rts. to buy 1 com. sh.	$0.18	Nov. 7/22	Nov. 4/22	Nov. 30/22
Planet Ventures Inc.	1 rt. for 1 com. sh., 1 rt. to buy 1 com. sh.	$0.02	Feb. 24/23	Feb. 23/23	Mar. 23/23
Plantify Foods, Inc.	1 rt. for 1 com. sh., 1 rt. to buy 1 com. sh.	$0.01	Aug. 22/23	Aug. 21/23	Sept. 15/23
PolyMet Mining Corp.	1 rt. for 1 com. sh., 1 rt. to buy 0.910688 com. shs.	US$2.11	Mar. 10/23	Mar. 9/23	Apr. 4/23
Razor Energy Corp.	1 rt. for 1 com. sh., 1 rt. to buy 0.494555 Razor Energy unit consisting of 1 com. sh. and 1 sh. pur. wt.	$0.80	May 16/23	May 15/23	June 7/23

Foreign Currency Dividends

The following companies have at least one class of stock on which dividends are paid in currency other than Canadian funds.

AIP Realty Trust US$
Agnico Eagle Mines Limited US$
Alamos Gold Inc. US$
Algoma Steel Group Inc. US$
Algonquin Power & Utilities Corp. US$
Alpine Summit Energy Partners, Inc. US$
AltaGas Ltd. US$
Alvopetro Energy Ltd. US$
American Hotel Income Properties REIT LP US$
Aura Minerals Inc. US$
Austral Gold Limited A$
BMO Covered Call Canadian Banks ETF US$
BMO High Yield US Corporate Bond Index ETF US$
BMO Laddered Preferred Share Index ETF US$
BMO Long-Term US Treasury Bond Index ETF US$
BMO Low Volatility US Equity ETF US$
BMO MSCI USA High Quality Index ETF US$
BMO Mid-Term US IG Corporate Bond Index ETF US$
BMO Mid-Term US Treasury Bond Index ETF US$
BMO Monthly Income ETF US$
BMO Nasdaq 100 Equity Index ETF US$
BMO Premium Yield ETF US$
BMO S&P US Mid Cap Index ETF US$
BMO S&P US Small Cap Index ETF US$
BMO S&P 500 Index ETF US$
BMO Short-Term US TIPS Index ETF US$
BMO Short-Term US Treasury Bond Index ETF US$
BMO US Aggregate Bond Index ETF US$
BMO US Dividend ETF US$
BMO US High Dividend Covered Call ETF US$
BMO US Preferred Shares Index ETF US$
BMO US Put Write ETF US$
BMO US TIPS Index ETF US$
BMO Ultra Short-Term US Bond ETF US$
BSR Real Estate Investment Trust US$
B2Gold Corp. US$
Barrick Gold Corporation US$
Brompton Flaherty & Crumrine Enhanced Investment Grade Preferred ETF US$
Brompton Flaherty & Crumrine Investment Grade Preferred ETF US$
Brompton Global Healthcare Income & Growth ETF US$
Brompton North American Financials Dividend ETF US$
Brompton Tech Leaders Income ETF US$
Brookfield Asset Management Ltd. US$
Brookfield Business Partners L.P. US$
Brookfield Corporation US$
Brookfield Infrastructure Corporation US$
Brookfield Infrastructure Partners L.P. US$
Brookfield Reinsurance Ltd. US$
Brookfield Renewable Corporation US$
Brookfield Renewable Partners L.P. US$
CI Alternative Diversified Opportunities Fund US$
CI Alternative Investment Grade Credit Fund US$
CI DoubleLine Core Plus Fixed Income US$ Fund US$
CI DoubleLine Income US$ Fund US$
CI DoubleLine Total Return Bond US$ Fund US$
CI Emerging Markets Alpha ETF US$
CI Energy Giants Covered Call ETF US$
CI Enhanced Government Bond ETF US$
CI Enhanced Short Duration Bond Fund US$
CI Global High Yield Credit Private Pool US$
CI Global Investment Grade ETF US$
CI Gold+ Giants Covered Call ETF US$
CI Health Care Giants Covered Call ETF US$
CI Investment Grade Bond ETF US$
CI Marret Alternative Absolute Return Bond Fund US$
CI Marret Alternative Enhanced Yield Fund US$
CI Tech Giants Covered Call ETF US$
CI U.S. Money Market ETF US$
Caribbean Utilities Company, Ltd. US$
Centamin plc US$
China Gold International Resources Corp. Ltd. US$
Colliers International Group Inc. US$
Constellation Software Inc. US$
DRI Healthcare Trust US$
Desjardins Alt Long/Short Equity Market Neutral ETF US$
Desjardins Alt Long/Short Global Equity Markets ETF US$
Dorel Industries Inc. US$
Dream Residential Real Estate Investment Trust US$
Dundee Precious Metals Inc. US$
Emerge EMPWR Sustainable Dividend Equity ETF US$
Emerge EMPWR Sustainable Emerging Markets Equity ETF US$
Emerge EMPWR Sustainable Global Core Equity ETF US$
Emerge EMPWR Sustainable Select Growth Equity ETF US$
Emerge EMPWR Unified Sustainable Equity ETF US$
Enbridge Inc. US$
Endeavour Mining plc US$
Enerplus Corporation US$
European Residential Real Estate Investment Trust □
Evolve Automobile Innovation Index Fund US$
Evolve Cyber Security Index Fund US$
Evolve European Banks Enhanced Yield ETF US$
Evolve FANGMA Index ETF US$
Evolve Future Leadership Fund US$
Evolve Global Healthcare Enhanced Yield Fund US$
Evolve Innovation Index Fund US$
Evolve S&P 500® Enhanced Yield Fund US$
Evolve US Banks Enhanced Yield Fund US$
Fairfax Financial Holdings Limited US$
Fidelity Global Core Plus Bond ETF US$
Fidelity Global Investment Grade Bond ETF US$
Fidelity International High Quality Index ETF US$
Fidelity U.S. Dividend for Rising Rates Index ETF US$
Fidelity U.S. High Dividend Index ETF US$
Fidelity U.S. High Quality Index ETF US$
Fidelity U.S. Low Volatility Index ETF US$
Fidelity U.S. Momentum Index ETF US$
Fidelity U.S. Value Index ETF US$
Firm Capital Apartment Real Estate Investment Trust US$
First Majestic Silver Corp. US$
FirstService Corporation US$
Flagship Communities Real Estate Investment Trust US$
Franco-Nevada Corporation US$
GFL Environmental Inc. US$
Gildan Activewear Inc. US$
Guardian Ultra-Short U.S. T-Bill Fund US$
Hamilton Enhanced U.S. Covered Call ETF US$

Hamilton U.S. Mid/Small-Cap Financials ETF US$
Harvest Brand Leaders Plus Income ETF US$
Harvest Energy Leaders Plus Income ETF US$
Harvest Healthcare Leaders Income ETF US$
Harvest Tech Achievers Growth & Income ETF US$
Harvest US Bank Leaders Income ETF US$
Horizons Active Ultra-Short Term US Investment Grade Bond ETF US$
Horizons Big Data & Hardware Index ETF US$
Horizons Global Semiconductor Index ETF US$
Horizons Marijuana Life Sciences ETF US$
Horizons Robotics and Automation Index ETF US$
Horizons US Large Cap Equity Covered Call ETF US$
Horizons 0-3 Month U.S. T-Bill ETF US$
Invesco FTSE RAFI U.S. Index ETF II US$
Invesco FTSE RAFI Global Small-Mid ETF US$
Invesco S&P 500 Equal Weight Index ETF US$
Invesco S&P 500 Low Volatility Index ETF US$
iShares Core MSCI All Country World ex Canada Index ETF US$
iShares Core MSCI EAFE IMI Index ETF US$
iShares Core MSCI Emerging Markets IMI Index ETF US$
iShares Core MSCI Global Quality Dividend Index ETF US$
iShares Core MSCI US Quality Dividend Index ETF US$
iShares Core S&P 500 Index ETF US$
iShares Core S&P U.S. Total Market Index ETF US$
iShares MSCI Min Vol USA Index ETF US$
iShares MSCI Multifactor USA Index ETF US$
iShares 1-5 Year U.S. IG Corporate Bond Index ETF US$
iShares S&P U.S. Mid-Cap Index ETF US$
iShares 20+ Year U.S. Treasury Bond Index ETF US$
iShares U.S. Aggregate Bond Index ETF US$
iShares U.S. IG Corporate Bond Index ETF US$
iShares 0-5 Year TIPS Bond Index ETF US$
Kinross Gold Corporation US$
Lundin Gold Inc. US$
Mackenzie Global Sustainable Dividend Index ETF US$
Mackenzie US Large Cap Equity Index ETF US$
Magna International Inc. US$
Manulife Smart U.S. Defensive Equity ETF US$
Manulife Smart U.S. Dividend ETF US$
Methanex Corporation US$
Mineros S.A. US$
Molson Coors Canada Inc. US$
Newcrest Mining Limited US$
Newmont Corporation US$
Nova Net Lease REIT US$
Nutrien Ltd. US$
OceanaGold Corporation US$
Open Text Corporation US$
Ovintiv Inc. US$
PIMCO Monthly Income Fund US$
Pan American Silver Corp. US$
Partners Value Investments LP US$
PetroTal Corp. US$
Polaris Renewable Energy Inc. US$
Primo Water Corporation US$
Purpose Bitcoin Yield ETF US$
Purpose Credit Opportunities Fund US$
Purpose Ether Yield ETF US$
Purpose Global Flexible Credit Fund US$
Purpose Premium Yield Fund US$
Purpose US Cash Fund US$
Purpose USD Cash Management Fund US$
RB Global, Inc. US$
RBC Quant EAFE Dividend Leaders ETF US$
RBC Quant EAFE Equity Leaders ETF US$
RBC Quant Emerging Markets Dividend Leaders ETF US$
RBC Quant Emerging Markets Equity Leaders ETF US$
RBC Quant European Dividend Leaders ETF US$
RBC Quant U.S. Dividend Leaders ETF US$
RBC Quant U.S. Equity Leaders ETF US$
RBC Short Term U.S. Corporate Bond ETF US$
RBC U.S. Banks Yield Index ETF US$
RBC U.S. Discount Bond ETF US$
RBC U.S. Dividend Covered Call ETF US$
Restaurant Brands International Inc. US$
Restaurant Brands International Limited Partnership US$
SSR Mining Inc. US$
Sagicor Financial Company Ltd. US$
Sailfish Royalty Corp. US$
Sierra Metals Inc. US$
Silvercorp Metals Inc. US$
Slate Grocery REIT US$
Sprott Inc. US$
Starlight U.S. Multi-Family (No. 2) Core Plus Fund US$
Starlight U.S. Residential Fund US$
TD Active Global Enhanced Dividend ETF US$
TD Active U.S, Enhanced Dividend ETF US$
TD Global Healthcare Leaders Index ETF US$
TD Global Technology Leaders Index ETF US$
TD Select U.S. Short Term Corporate Bond Ladder ETF US$
TD U.S. Index ETF US$
TFI International Inc. US$
Thomson Reuters Corporation US$
Tricon Residential Inc. US$
Triple Flag Precious Metals Corp. US$
US High Interest Savings Account Fund US$
US Premium Cash Management Fund US$
Vox Royalty Corp. US$
Waste Connections, Inc. US$
West Fraser Timber Co. Ltd. US$
Wheaton Precious Metals Corp. US$

Dividend Reinvestment Plans

The following companies are among those offering dividend reinvestment plans on at least one class of their capital stock.

A&W Revenue Royalties Income Fund
AGF Management Limited
ARC Resources Ltd.
abrdn Asia-Pacific Income Fund VCC
Agnico Eagle Mines Limited
Algonquin Power & Utilities Corp.
AltaGas Ltd.
Altius Minerals Corporation
Altus Group Limited
Andrew Peller Limited
Atrium Mortgage Investment Corporation
Australian REIT Income Fund
BCE Inc.
BMO Dow Jones Industrial Average Hedged to CAD Index ETF
BMO Emerging Markets Bond Hedged to CAD Index ETF
BMO Equal Weight Banks Index ETF
BMO Equal Weight Global Base Metals Hedged to CAD Index ETF
BMO Equal Weight Oil & Gas Index ETF
BMO Equal Weight REITs Index ETF
BMO Equal Weight US Banks Hedged to CAD Index ETF
BMO Equal Weight US Health Care Hedged to CAD Index ETF
BMO Equal Weight Utilities Index ETF
BMO Global Infrastructure Index ETF
BMO High Yield US Corporate Bond Hedged to CAD Index ETF
BMO Junior Gold Index ETF
BMO Long Corporate Bond Index ETF
BMO Long Federal Bond Index ETF
BMO MSCI EAFE Headged to CAD Index ETF
BMO MSCI Emerging Markets Index ETF
BMO MSCI India ESG Leaders Index ETF
BMO Mid Corporate Bond Index ETF
BMO Mid Federal Bond Index ETF
BMO MSCI China ESG Leaders Index ETF
BMO Nasdaq 100 Equity Hedged To CAD Index ETF
BMO Real Return Bond Index ETF
BMO S&P 500 Hedged to CAD Index ETF
BMO S&P/TSX Capped Composite Index ETF
BMO Short Corporate Bond Index ETF
BMO Short Federal Bond Index ETF
BMO Short Provincial Bond Index ETF
BMO Ultra Short-Term Bond ETF
BMO Ultra Short-Term US Bond ETF
BTB Real Estate Investment Trust
Bank of Montreal
The Bank of Nova Scotia
Barrick Gold Corporation
Baytex Energy Corp.
Bloom Select Income Fund
Blue Ribbon Income Fund
Bombardier Inc.
Brompton Flaherty & Crumrine Investment Grade Preferred ETF
Brompton Lifeco Split Corp.
Brompton Oil Split Corp.
Brompton Split Banc Corp.
Brookfield Corporation
Brookfield Global Infrastructure Securities Income Fund
Brookfield Infrastructure Partners L.P.
Brookfield Renewable Partners L.P.
Builders Capital Mortgage Corp.
CI Canadian Convertible Bond ETF

CI Canadian REIT ETF
CI Global Financial Sector ETF
CI Global Minimum Downside Volatility Index ETF
CI Gold+ Giants Covered Call ETF
CI Morningstar Canada Momentum Index ETF
CI Morningstar International Momentum Index ETF
CI Morningstar International Value Index ETF
CI Morningstar National Bank Quebec Index ETF
CI Morningstar US Value Index ETF
CI Tech Giants Covered Call ETF
CT Real Estate Investment Trust
Canadian Apartment Properties Real Estate Investment Trust
Canadian General Investments, Limited
Canadian High Income Equity Fund
Canadian Imperial Bank of Commerce
Canadian Natural Resources Limited
Canadian Tire Corporation, Limited
Canadian Utilities Limited
Canadian Western Bank
Canoe EIT Income Fund
Capital Power Corporation
Cardinal Energy Ltd.
Caribbean Utilities Company, Ltd.
Cenovus Energy Inc.
Chartwell Retirement Residences
Chemtrade Logistics Income Fund
Citadel Income Fund
Corus Entertainment Inc.
Crombie Real Estate Investment Trust
Decisive Dividend Corporation
Diversified Royalty Corp.
Dividend Growth Split Corp.
Dream Impact Trust
Dream Industrial Real Estate Investment Trust
Dream Office Real Estate Investment Trust
E Split Corp.
EQB Inc.
Element Fleet Management Corp.
Emera Incorporated
Energy Income Fund
Exchange Income Corporation
Extendicare Inc.
Fiera Capital Corporation
Firm Capital Apartment Real Estate Investment Trust
Firm Capital Mortgage Investment Corporation
Firm Capital Property Trust
First Capital Real Estate Investment Trust
First National Financial Corporation
First Quantum Minerals Ltd.
Fortis Inc.
Franco-Nevada Corporation
Freehold Royalties Ltd.
Gibson Energy Inc.
Global Dividend Growth Split Corp.
goeasy Ltd.
Hamilton Australian Bank Equal-Weight Index ETF
Hamilton Global Financials ETF
Harvest Brand Leaders Plus Income ETF
Harvest Energy Leaders Plus Income ETF
Harvest Global REIT Leaders Income ETF
Harvest Healthcare Leaders Income ETF
Harvest Tech Achievers Growth & Income ETF
Horizons Active Cdn Bond ETF
Horizons Active Cdn Dividend ETF
Horizons Active Cdn Municipal Bond ETF
Horizons Active Corporate Bond ETF
Horizons Active Floating Rate Senior Loan ETF
Horizons Active Global Dividend ETF
Horizons Active Global Fixed Income ETF
Horizons Active High Yield Bond ETF
Horizons Active Hybrid Bond and Preferred Share ETF
Horizons Active Preferred Share ETF
Horizons Active Ultra-Short Term Investment Grade Bond ETF
Horizons Active Ultra-Short Term US Investment Grade Bond ETF
Horizons Canadian Large Cap Equity Covered Call ETF
Horizons Canadian Oil and Gas Equity Covered Call ETF
Horizons Equal Weight Canadian Bank Covered Call ETF
Horizons Gold Producer Equity Covered Call ETF
Horizons NASDAQ-100 Covered Call ETF
Horizons Pipelines & Energy Services Index ETF
Horizons Seasonal Rotation ETF
Horizons US Large Cap Equity Covered Call ETF
Hydro One Limited
iA Financial Corporation Inc.
Imperial Oil Limited
Inovalis Real Estate Investment Trust
International Clean Power Dividend Fund
InterRent Real Estate Investment Trust
Invesco ESG Canadian Core Plus Bond ETF
iShares CNX Nifty India Index ETF
iShares Canadian Financial Monthly Income ETF
iShares Canadian Fundamental Index ETF
iShares Canadian Growth Index ETF
iShares Canadian HYBrid Corporate Bond Index ETF
iShares Canadian Real Return Bond Index ETF
iShares Canadian Select Dividend Index ETF
iShares Canadian Value Index ETF
iShares China Index ETF
iShares Convertible Bond Index ETF
iShares Core Balanced ETF Portfolio
iShares Core Canadian Corporate Bond Index ETF
iShares Core Canadian Government Bond Index ETF
iShares Core Canadian Long Term Bond Index ETF
iShares Core Canadian Short Term Bond Index ETF
iShares Core Canadian Short Term Corporate Bond Index ETF
iShares Core Canadian Universe Bond Index ETF
iShares Core Growth ETF Portfolio
iShares Core S&P 500 Index ETF (CAD-Hedged)
iShares Core S&P 500 Index ETF
iShares Core S&P/TSX Capped Composite Index ETF
iShares Diversified Monthly Income ETF
iShares Emerging Markets Fundamental Index ETF
iShares Equal Weight Banc & Lifeco ETF
iShares Floating Rate Note Index ETF
iShares Global Infrastructure Index ETF
iShares Global Monthly Dividend Index ETF (CAD hedged)
iShares Global Real Estate Index ETF
iShares High Quality Canadian Bond Index ETF
iShares International Fundamental Index ETF
iShares J.P. Morgan USD Emerging Markets Bond Index ETF (CAD-Hedged)
iShares Jantzi Social Index ETF
iShares Japan Fundamental Index ETF (CAD-Hedged)
iShares MSCI EAFE Index ETF (CAD-Hedged)
iShares MSCI Emerging Markets Index ETF
iShares MSCI World Index ETF
iShares MSCI Min Vol Canada Index ETF
iShares MSCI Min Vol EAFE Index ETF
iShares MSCI Min Vol Emerging Markets Index ETF
iShares MSCI Min Vol Global Index ETF
iShares MSCI Min Vol USA Index ETF
iShares MSCI Multifactor Canada Index ETF
iShares MSCI Multifactor EAFE Index ETF
iShares MSCI Multifactor EAFE Index ETF (CAD-Hedged)
iShares MSCI Multifactor USA Index ETF
iShares MSCI Multifactor USA Index ETF (CAD-Hedged)
iShares NASDAQ 100 Index ETF (CAD-Hedged)
iShares 1-5 Year Laddered Corporate Bond Index ETF
iShares 1-5 Year Laddered Government Bond Index ETF
iShares 1-10 Year Laddered Corporate Bond Index ETF
iShares 1-10 Year Laddered Government Bond Index ETF
iShares Premium Money Market ETF
iShares S&P/TSX Composite High Dividend Index ETF
iShares S&P/TSX Capped Energy Index ETF
iShares S&P Global Healthcare Index ETF (CAD-Hedged)
iShares S&P Global Water Index ETF
iShares S&P/TSX Capped REIT Index ETF
iShares S&P/TSX Canadian Dividend Aristocrats Index ETF
iShares S&P/TSX Capped Consumer Staples Index ETF
iShares S&P/TSX Capped Financials Index ETF
iShares S&P/TSX Capped Information Technology Index ETF
iShares S&P/TSX Capped Materials Index ETF
iShares S&P/TSX Capped Utilities Index ETF
iShares S&P/TSX CDN Preferred Share Index ETF
iShares S&P/TSX Completion Index ETF
iShares S&P/TSX Global Base Metals Index ETF
iShares S&P/TSX Global Gold Index ETF
iShares S&P/TSX North American Preferred Stock Index ETF (CAD-Hedged)
iShares S&P/TSX 60 Index ETF
iShares S&P/TSX SmallCap Index ETF
iShares S&P US Dividend Growers Index ETF (CAD-Hedged)
iShares U.S. High Dividend Equity Index ETF (CAD-Hedged)
iShares U.S. High Yield Bond Index ETF (CAD-Hedged)
iShares U.S. IG Corporate Bond Index ETF (CAD-Hedged)
iShares U.S. Small Cap Index ETF (CAD-Hedged)
iShares US Fundamental Index ETF
KP Tissue Inc.
Killam Apartment Real Estate Investment Trust
Laurentian Bank of Canada
Life & Banc Split Corp.
Loblaw Companies Limited
MCAN Mortgage Corporation
MINT Income Fund

Mackenzie Core Plus Canadian Fixed Income ETF
Mackenzie Core Plus Global Fixed Income ETF
Mackenzie Global High Yield Fixed Income ETF
Mackenzie Global Women's Leadership ETF
Mackenzie Unconstrained Bond ETF
Magna International Inc.
Manulife Financial Corporation
Middlefield Global Real Asset Fund
Middlefield Healthcare Dividend ETF
Middlefield Real Estate Dividend ETF
Middlefield U.S. Equity Dividend ETF
Morguard Corporation
Morguard North American Residential Real Estate Investment Trust
Morguard Real Estate Investment Trust
National Bank of Canada
Nexus Industrial REIT
Northland Power Inc.
NorthWest Healthcare Properties Real Estate Investment Trust
Nutrien Ltd.
Onex Corporation
Osisko Gold Royalties Ltd.
Ovintiv Inc.
PHX Energy Services Corp.
PIMCO Global Income Opportunities Fund
PIMCO Multi-Sector Income Fund
PIMCO Tactical Income Fund
PIMCO Tactical Income Opportunities Fund
PRO Real Estate Investment Trust
Park Lawn Corporation
Parkland Corporation
Peyto Exploration & Development Corp.
Picton Mahoney Tactical Income Fund
Pine Trail Real Estate Investment Trust
Plaza Retail REIT
Precious Metals and Mining Trust
Purpose Premium Yield Fund
Queen's Road Capital Investment Ltd.
Real Estate Split Corp.
Rogers Communications Inc.
Royal Bank of Canada
Saputo Inc.
Sienna Senior Living Inc.
Slate Grocery REIT
Slate Office Real Estate Investment Trust
SmartCentres Real Estate Investment Trust
Source Rock Royalties Ltd.
Starlight Global Infrastructure Fund
Starlight Global Real Estate Fund
StorageVault Canada Inc.
Sun Life Financial Inc.
Superior Plus Corp.
Sustainable Innovation & Health Dividend Fund
Symphony Floating Rate Senior Loan Fund
TC Energy Corporation
TELUS Corporation
TWC Enterprises Limited
Thomson Reuters Corporation
Tier One Capital Limited Partnership
Timbercreek Financial Corp.
The Toronto-Dominion Bank
TransAlta Corporation
Tricon Residential Inc.
True North Commercial Real Estate Investment Trust
Urbanfund Corp.
Vanguard Canadian Aggregate Bond Index ETF
Vanguard Canadian Short-Term Bond Index ETF
Vanguard Canadian Short-Term Corporate Bond Index ETF
Vanguard FTSE Canada All Cap Index ETF
Vanguard FTSE Canada Index ETF
Vanguard FTSE Canadian Capped REIT Index ETF
Vanguard FTSE Canadian High Dividend Yield Index ETF
Vanguard FTSE Developed All Cap ex North America Index ETF (Cad Hedged)
Vanguard FTSE Developed All Cap ex North America Index ETF
Vanguard FTSE Developed All Cap Ex U.S. Index ETF (CAD-hedged)
Vanguard FTSE Emerging Markets All Cap Index ETF
Vanguard FTSE Global All Cap ex Canada Index ETF
Vanguard Global Minimum Volatility ETF
Vanguard Global Momentum Factor ETF
Vanguard Global Value Factor ETF
Vanguard S&P 500 Index ETF
Vanguard S&P 500 Index ETF (CAD-hedged)
Vanguard U.S. Dividend Appreciation Index
Vanguard U.S. Total Market Index ETF (CAD-hedged)
Vermilion Energy Inc.
George Weston Limited
Wheaton Precious Metals Corp.

Dividend Changes

The following sections list companies that have reported dividend changes on a class of their capital stock during the previous and current calendar years. Dividend increases or decreases reported by companies that have not established a set dividend rate are excluded. The section includes companies paying a initial dividend after a split, consolidation, capital reorganization or merger, companies declaring a dividend on a stock that has not paid a dividend in over two years as well as companies paying any dividends that are unusual in nature. Details of the dividend can be found under the company listings in this edition.

Dividend Omitted

Brompton Oil Split Corp.
CI Auspice Broad Commodity Fund
CI Galaxy Blockchain Index ETF
CI Morningstar US Momentum Index ETF
CI WisdomTree Europe Hedged Equity Index ETF
Dividend 15 Split Corp.
Dividend Growth Split Corp.
Dynamic Active International Dividend ETF
First Trust AlphaDEX U.S. Health Care Sector Index ETF
First Trust Cloud Computing ETF
First Trust Nasdaq Cybersecurity ETF
First Trust Tactical Bond Index ETF
Franklin Brandywine Global Sustainable Income Optimiser Fund
Franklin ClearBridge Sustainable Global Infrastructure Income Fund
Franklin ClearBridge Sustainable International Growth Fund
Franklin Global Dividend Quality Index ETF
Franklin Global Growth Fund
Franklin Innovation Fund
Franklin U.S. Investment Grade Corporate Bond Active ETF (CAD-Hedged)
HLS Therapeutics Inc.
IA Clarington Loomis Global Allocation Fund
IA Clarington Loomis Global Multisector Bond Fund
i3 Energy plc
iShares S&P/TSX Capped Information Technology Index ETF
iShares 0-5 Year TIPS Bond Index ETF
iShares 0-5 Year TIPS Bond Index ETF (CAD-Hedged)
Jaguar Mining Inc.
Mackenzie US High Yield Bond Index ETF (CAD-Hedged)
NBI Liquid Alternatives ETF
NFI Group Inc.
North American Financial 15 Split Corp.
Prime Dividend Corp.
Quarterhill Inc.
Ravensource Fund
S Split Corp.
Summit Industrial Income REIT
TDb Split Corp.
Titan Mining Corporation
Velan Inc.

Dividend Deferred

RealCap Holdings Limited

Dividend Increase

A&W Revenue Royalties Income Fund
ADENTRA Inc.
AGF Management Limited
ARC Resources Ltd.
ATCO Ltd.
Alaris Equity Partners Income Trust

Algoma Central Corporation
Alimentation Couche-Tard Inc.
Allied Properties Real Estate Investment Trust
Alpine Summit Energy Partners, Inc.
AltaGas Ltd.
Altius Minerals Corporation
Alvopetro Energy Ltd.
Andlauer Healthcare Group Inc.
BCE Inc.
BMO Clean Energy Index ETF
BMO MSCI Fintech Innovation Index ETF
BMO MSCI Tech & Industrial Innovation Index ETF
BMO Nasdaq 100 Equity Index ETF
BRP Inc.
Badger Infrastructure Solutions Ltd.
Bank of Montreal
The Bank of Nova Scotia
Birchcliff Energy Ltd.
Bird Construction Inc.
Boardwalk Real Estate Investment Trust
Boyd Group Services Inc.
Brompton Oil Split Corp.
Brompton Split Banc Corp.
Brookfield Infrastructure Corporation
Brookfield Infrastructure Partners L.P.
Brookfield Renewable Corporation
Brookfield Renewable Partners L.P.
CCL Industries Inc.
CI Financial Corp.
CIBC Emerging Markets Equity Index ETF
CIBC Global Growth ETF
CIBC International Equity ETF
COGECO Inc.
CT Real Estate Investment Trust
Canadian Banc Corp.
Canadian Imperial Bank of Commerce
Canadian Life Companies Split Corp.
Canadian National Railway Company
Canadian Natural Resources Limited
Canadian Net Real Estate Investment Trust
Canadian Tire Corporation, Limited
Canadian Utilities Limited
Canadian Western Bank
Capital Power Corporation
Caribbean Utilities Company, Ltd.
Cenovus Energy Inc.
Chesswood Group Limited
Choice Properties Real Estate Investment Trust
Citigroup Inc.
Cogeco Communications Inc.
Crescent Point Energy Corp.
DREAM Unlimited Corp.
Decisive Dividend Corporation
Definity Financial Corporation
Diversified Royalty Corp.
Dollarama Inc.
Dynacor Group Inc.
Dynamic Active International ETF
E-L Financial Corporation Limited
EQB Inc.
Element Fleet Management Corp.
Emera Incorporated
Empire Company Limited
Enbridge Inc.
Enerplus Corporation
Enghouse Systems Limited
Evertz Technologies Limited
Exchange Income Corporation
Fidelity Canadian Momentum Index ETF
Fidelity U.S. Momentum Index ETF
Financial 15 Split Corp.
Finning International Inc.
First Capital Real Estate Investment Trust
First National Financial Corporation
FirstService Corporation
Flagship Communities Real Estate Investment Trust
Fortis Inc.
Franco-Nevada Corporation
Freehold Royalties Ltd.
GFL Environmental Inc.
Gear Energy Ltd.
Geodrill Limited
Gibson Energy Inc.
Global Water Resources, Inc.
goeasy Ltd.
Granite Real Estate Investment Trust
Great-West Lifeco Inc.
Guardian Capital Group Limited
Hammond Power Solutions Inc.
High Liner Foods Incorporated
Horizons Global Semiconductor Index ETF
Horizons Global Uranium Index ETF
Hydro One Limited
iA Financial Corporation Inc.
Imperial Oil Limited
Intact Financial Corporation
InterRent Real Estate Investment Trust
Jamieson Wellness Inc.
Keyera Corp.
Labrador Iron Ore Royalty Corporation
Laurentian Bank of Canada
Linamar Corporation
Loblaw Companies Limited
Logistec Corporation
Lorne Park Capital Partners Inc.
MCAN Mortgage Corporation
METRO Inc.
Magna International Inc.
Manulife Financial Corporation
Maple Leaf Foods Inc.
Marwest Apartment Real Estate Investment Trust
Melcor Developments Ltd.
Methanex Corporation
Mineros S.A.
Minto Apartment Real Estate Investment Trust
Morguard North American Residential Real Estate Investment Trust
NBI Active International Equity ETF
NBI Global Private Equity ETF
NBI Sustainable Global Equity ETF
NCM Core Global
National Bank of Canada
North American Construction Group Ltd.
North American Financial 15 Split Corp.
The North West Company Inc.
Northview Residential REIT
Nutrien Ltd.
Olympia Financial Group Inc.
Open Text Corporation
Osisko Gold Royalties Ltd.
Ovintiv Inc.
PHX Energy Services Corp.
PIMCO Multi-Sector Income Fund
Parex Resources Inc.
Parkland Corporation
Pason Systems Inc.
Pembina Pipeline Corporation
Perseus Mining Limited
Pet Valu Holdings Ltd.
Peyto Exploration & Development Corp.
Pine Cliff Energy Ltd.
Pizza Pizza Royalty Corp.
Power Corporation of Canada
PrairieSky Royalty Ltd.
Premium Brands Holdings Corporation
Primaris Real Estate Investment Trust
Primo Water Corporation
Propel Holdings Inc.
RB Global, Inc.
Restaurant Brands International Inc.
Richelieu Hardware Ltd.
RioCan Real Estate Investment Trust
Royal Bank of Canada
Russel Metals Inc.
Saputo Inc.
Savaria Corporation
Secure Energy Services Inc.
Sleep Country Canada Holdings Inc.
Softchoice Corporation
Source Rock Royalties Ltd.
Stantec Inc.
Starbucks Corporation
Stella-Jones Inc.
StorageVault Canada Inc.
Sun Life Financial Inc.
Suncor Energy Inc.
Symphony Floating Rate Senior Loan Fund
TC Energy Corporation
TECSYS Inc.
TELUS Corporation
TFI International Inc.
TMX Group Limited
TWC Enterprises Limited

Tamarack Valley Energy Ltd.
TerraVest Industries Inc.
Thomson Reuters Corporation
Topaz Energy Corp.
Toromont Industries Ltd.
The Toronto-Dominion Bank
Tourmaline Oil Corp.
TransAlta Corporation
Triple Flag Precious Metals Corp.
United Corporations Limited
Urbana Corporation
Vox Royalty Corp.
Wajax Corporation
Waste Connections, Inc.
George Weston Limited
Westshore Terminals Investment Corporation
Whitecap Resources Inc.
Yellow Pages Limited

Dividend Decrease

AGF US Market Neutral Anti-Beta CAD-Hedged ETF
AIP Realty Trust
abrdn Asia-Pacific Income Fund VCC
Algonquin Power & Utilities Corp.
Automotive Properties Real Estate Investment Trust
Barrick Gold Corporation
Brookfield Corporation
Brookfield Reinsurance Ltd.
Brookfield Renewable Partners L.P.
Canadian Banc Corp.
Centamin plc
Corby Spirit and Wine Limited
Corus Entertainment Inc.
Definity Financial Corporation
Dream Impact Trust
Faircourt Split Trust
Fidelity International Momentum Index ETF
Fidelity U.S. Momentum Currency Neutral Index ETF
First Majestic Silver Corp.
Gear Energy Ltd.
Horizons Emerging Markets Leaders ETF
Inovalis Real Estate Investment Trust
Labrador Iron Ore Royalty Corporation
Lassonde Industries Inc.
Lundin Gold Inc.
Mackenzie Master Limited Partnership
Magellan Aerospace Corporation
Newmont Corporation
Northview Residential REIT
Pan American Silver Corp.
Perseus Mining Limited
Picton Mahoney Tactical Income Fund
Pine Trail Real Estate Investment Trust
Savaria Corporation
Slate Office Real Estate Investment Trust
Starbucks Corporation
Sylogist Ltd.
Thomson Reuters Corporation
True North Commercial Real Estate Investment Trust

Initial Dividend

AbbVie Inc.
Alphabet (GOOGL) Yield Shares Purpose ETF
Amazon (AMZN) Yield Shares Purpose ETF
Apple (AAPL) Yield Shares Purpose ETF
BMO ARK Genomic Revolution Fund
BMO ARK Innovation Fund
BMO Covered Call Energy ETF
BMO Covered Call Health Care ETF
BMO Growth ETF
BMO US Aggregate Bond Index ETF
Berkshire Hathaway (BRK) Yield Shares Purpose ETF
BioSyent Inc.
Brompton Enhanced Multi-Asset Income ETF
Brompton Split Corp. Preferred Share ETF
Brookfield Asset Management Ltd.
Brookfield Corporation
CI Auspice Broad Commodity Fund
CI Balanced Growth Asset Allocation ETF
CI Balanced Income Asset Allocation ETF
CI Bio-Revolution Index ETF
CI Conservative Asset Allocation ETF
CI Digital Security Index ETF
CI Galaxy Metaverse Index ETF
CI Galaxy Multi-Crypto ETF
CI Global Bond Currency Neutral Fund
CI Global Green Bond Fund
CI Global Investment Grade ETF
CI Global Minimum Downside Volatility Index ETF
CI Global Sustainable Infrastructure Fund
CI Money Market ETF
CI U.S. Minimum Downside Volatility Index ETF
CI U.S. Money Market ETF
CI U.S. TrendLeaders Index ETF
CI Utilities Giants Covered Call ETF
CIBC Canadian Short-Term Bond Index ETF
CIBC International Equity Index ETF (CAD-Hedged)
CIBC Sustainable Global Equity Fund
CIBC U.S. Equity Index ETF (CAD-Hedged)
CVS Health Corporation
Carcetti Capital Corp.
Chevron Corporation
Citigroup Inc.
The Coca-Cola Company
Converge Technology Solutions Corp.
Desjardins Alt Long/Short Equity Market Neutral ETF
Desjardins Alt Long/Short Global Equity Markets ETF
Dynamic Active Discount Bond ETF
Dynamic Active Enhanced Yield Covered Options ETF
Emerge EMPWR Sustainable Dividend Equity ETF
Emerge EMPWR Sustainable Emerging Markets Equity ETF
Emerge EMPWR Sustainable Global Core Equity ETF
Emerge EMPWR Unified Sustainable Equity ETF
Enbridge Inc.
Evermore Retirement 2025 ETF
Evermore Retirement 2030 ETF
Evermore Retirement 2035 ETF
Evermore Retirement 2040 ETF
Evermore Retirement 2045 ETF
Evermore Retirement 2050 ETF
Evermore Retirement 2055 ETF
Evermore Retirement 2060 ETF
Evolve S&P 500® Enhanced Yield Fund
Evolve S&P/TSX 60 Enhanced Yield Fund
Evolve Slate Global Real Estate Enhanced Yield Fund
Exxon Mobil Corporation
Fidelity All-in-One Conservative ETF Fund
Fidelity All-in-One Equity ETF
Franklin Bissett Ultra Short Bond ETF
Franklin Global Growth Fund
Guardian i3 US Quality Growth ETF
Guardian Ultra-Short Canadian T-Bill Fund
GuardPath Managed Decumulation 2042 Fund
Hamilton Canadian Bank Equal-Weight Index ETF
Hamilton Enhanced Utilities ETF
Harvest Brand Leaders Enhanced Income ETF
Harvest Canadian Equity Enhanced Income Leaders ETF
Harvest Diversified Equity Income ETF
Harvest ESG Equity Income Index ETF
Harvest Equal Weight Global Utilities Enhanced Income ETF
Harvest Healthcare Leaders Enhanced Income ETF
Harvest Tech Achievers Enhanced Income ETF
Harvest Travel & Leisure Income ETF
Headwater Exploration Inc.
Horizons Canadian Utility Services High Dividend Index ETF
Horizons Copper Producers Index ETF
Horizons Enhanced Canadian Large Cap Equity Covered Call ETF
Horizons Enhanced Equal Weight Banks Index ETF
Horizons Enhanced Equal Weight Canadian Banks Covered Call ETF
Horizons Enhanced S&P/TSX 60 Index ETF
Horizons Enhanced US Large Cap Equity Covered Call ETF
Horizons Equal Weight Banks Index ETF
Horizons Global Lithium Producers Index ETF
Horizons Global Vaccines and Infectious Diseases Index ETF
Horizons North American Infrastructure Development Index ETF
InPlay Oil Corp.
Intel Corporation
iShares Core Canadian 15+ Year Federal Bond Index ETF
iShares Cybersecurity and Tech Index ETF
iShares MSCI Emerging Markets ex China Index ETF
iShares 20+ Year U.S. Treasury Bond Index ETF

iShares 20+ Year U.S. Treasury Bond Index ETF (CAD Hedged)
Lundin Gold Inc.
Mackenzie Emerging Markets Equity Index ETF
Manulife Smart International Defensive Equity ETF
Manulife Smart International Dividend ETF
Manulife Smart U.S. Dividend ETF
Mulvihill Premium Yield Fund
Mulvihill U.S. Health Care Enhanced Yield ETF
NIKE, Inc.
Ninepoint Target Income Fund
Pembina Pipeline Corporation
Picton Mahoney Fortified Core Bond Fund
Pine Trail Real Estate Investment Trust
Pipestone Energy Corp.
Purpose Cash Management Fund
Purpose Credit Opportunities Fund
Purpose USD Cash Management Fund
RBC Canadian Dividend Covered Call ETF
RBC Canadian Equity Income Fund
RBC Emerging Markets Dividend Fund
RBC Target 2024 Government Bond ETF
RBC Target 2025 Government Bond ETF
RBC Target 2026 Government Bond ETF
RBC Target 2027 Government Bond ETF
RBC Target 2028 Corporate Bond Index ETF
RBC Target 2028 Government Bond ETF
RBC Target 2029 Government Bond ETF
RBC U.S. Discount Bond (CAD Hedged) ETF
RBC U.S. Discount Bond ETF
RBC U.S. Dividend Covered Call ETF
Scotia Emerging Markets Equity Index Tracker ETF
SmartBe U.S. Quantitative Momentum Index ETF
Spin Master Corp.
Sun Residential Real Estate Investment Trust
TD Active U.S. Enhanced Dividend CAD Hedged ETF
TD Canadian Bank Dividend Index ETF
Tempus Capital Inc.
Tesla (TSLA) Yield Shares Purpose ETF
Tethys Petroleum Limited
TransAlta Corporation
US High Interest Savings Account Fund
United Parcel Service, Inc.
UnitedHealth Group Incorporated
Verizon Communications Inc.
Vox Royalty Corp.

Special Dividend

Advent-AWI Holdings Inc.
Algoma Central Corporation
Artis Real Estate Investment Trust
BMO ARK Genomic Revolution Fund
BMO ARK Innovation Fund
BMO All-Equity ETF
BMO Balanced ETF
BMO Canadian Dividend ETF
BMO Equal Weight Banks Index ETF
BMO Equal Weight Industrials Index ETF
BMO Equal Weight REITs Index ETF
BMO Equal Weight US Banks Index ETF
BMO Equal Weight US Banks Hedged to CAD Index ETF
BMO Equal Weight Utilities Index ETF
BMO Europe High Dividend Covered Call Hedged to CAD ETF
BMO Global Communications Index ETF
BMO Global Consumer Discretionary Hedged to CAD Index ETF
BMO Global Infrastructure Index ETF
BMO Growth ETF
BMO International Dividend Hedged to CAD ETF
BMO Japan Index ETF
BMO Low Volatility Canadian Equity ETF
BMO Low Volatility US Equity ETF
BMO MSCI EAFE Headged to CAD Index ETF
BMO MSCI Emerging Markets Index ETF
BMO MSCI Europe High Quality Hedged to CAD Index ETF
BMO MSCI USA High Quality Index ETF
BMO Monthly Income ETF
BMO MSCI Canada ESG Leaders Index ETF
BMO MSCI USA Value Index ETF
BMO Nasdaq 100 Equity Hedged To CAD Index ETF
BMO Nasdaq 100 Equity Index ETF
BMO Real Return Bond Index ETF
BMO S&P US Mid Cap Index ETF
BMO S&P/TSX Capped Composite Index ETF
BMO SIA Focused Canadian Equity Fund
BMO SIA Focused North American Equity Fund
BMO Short Corporate Bond Index ETF
BMO Short Federal Bond Index ETF
BMO Short Provincial Bond Index ETF
BMO Short-Term US TIPS Index ETF
BMO Sustainable Global Multi-Sector Bond Fund
BMO Ultra Short-Term Bond ETF
BMO Ultra Short-Term US Bond ETF
Barrick Gold Corporation
Big Banc Split Corp.
Birchcliff Energy Ltd.
Boston Pizza Royalties Income Fund
Brookfield Corporation
Brookfield Reinsurance Ltd.
CI Alternative Investment Grade Credit Fund
CI Auspice Broad Commodity Fund
CI Bio-Revolution Index ETF
CI Digital Security Index ETF
CI DoubleLine Core Plus Fixed Income US$ Fund
CI DoubleLine Income US$ Fund
CI DoubleLine Total Return Bond US$ Fund
CI Emerging Markets Alpha ETF
CI Energy Giants Covered Call ETF
CI Enhanced Government Bond ETF
CI Enhanced Short Duration Bond Fund
CI First Asset MSCI World ESG Impact ETF
CI Floating Rate Income Fund
CI Galaxy Blockchain Index ETF
CI Galaxy Metaverse Index ETF
CI Galaxy Multi-Crypto ETF
CI Global Asset Allocation Private Pool
CI Global Bond Currency Neutral Fund
CI Global Green Bond Fund
CI Global Healthcare Leaders Index ETF
CI Global High Yield Credit Private Pool
CI Global Investment Grade ETF
CI Global Minimum Downside Volatility Index ETF
CI Global Sustainable Infrastructure Fund
CI High Interest Savings ETF
CI Morningstar Canada Momentum Index ETF
CI Morningstar Canada Value Index ETF
CI Morningstar International Momentum Index ETF
CI Morningstar International Value Index ETF
CI Morningstar National Bank Quebec Index ETF
CI MSCI Europe Low Risk Weighted ETF
CI MSCI International Low Risk Weighted ETF
CI MSCI World Low Risk Weighted ETF
CI 1-5 Year Laddered Government Strip Bond Index ETF
CI ONE Global Equity ETF
CI Preferred Share ETF
CI U.S. Treasury Inflation-Linked Bond Index ETF (CAD Hedged)
CI U.S. 500 Index ETF
CI U.S. 1000 Index ETF
CI U.S. TrendLeaders Index ETF
CI WisdomTree U.S. MidCap Dividend Index ETF
CI WisdomTree U.S. Quality Dividend Growth Variably Hedged Index ETF
CI Yield Enhanced Canada Short-Term Aggregate Bond Index ETF
Caldwell U.S. Dividend Advantage Fund
Canadian Apartment Properties Real Estate Investment Trust
Canadian Natural Resources Limited
Canso Credit Income Fund
Carcetti Capital Corp.
Cenovus Energy Inc.
China Gold International Resources Corp. Ltd.
Clairvest Group Inc.
Crescent Point Energy Corp.
DREAM Unlimited Corp.
DRI Healthcare Trust
Desjardins Canadian Preferred Share Index ETF
Desjardins RI Global Multifactor - Fossil Fuel Free ETF
Desjardins RI Canada - Low CO2 Index ETF
Desjardins RI Canada Multifactor - Low CO2 ETF
Desjardins RI USA - Low CO2 Index ETF
Dream Office Real Estate Investment Trust
Dynamic Active Canadian Dividend ETF
Dynamic Active Enhanced Yield Covered Options ETF
Dynamic Active Global Infrastructure ETF
Dynamic Active U.S. Mid-Cap ETF
Emerge EMPWR Sustainable Dividend Equity ETF
Emerge EMPWR Sustainable Emerging Markets Equity ETF
Emerge EMPWR Sustainable Global Core Equity ETF
Evolve Active Global Fixed Income Fund

Evolve Cryptocurrencies ETF
Evolve Cyber Security Index Fund
Evolve Innovation Index Fund
Fidelity All-in-One Balanced ETF
Fidelity All-in-One Conservative ETF Fund
Fidelity All-in-One Equity ETF
Fidelity All-in-One Growth ETF
Fidelity Canadian Low Volatility Index ETF
Fidelity Canadian Value Index ETF
Fidelity U.S. Dividend for Rising Rates Curency Neutral Index ETF
Fidelity U.S. Dividend for Rising Rates Index ETF
Fidelity U.S. High Dividend Currency Neutral Index ETF
Fidelity U.S. High Dividend Index ETF
Fidelity U.S. High Quality Index ETF
Fidelity U.S. Low Volatility Index ETF
Fidelity U.S. Value Index ETF
Firm Capital Mortgage Investment Corporation
First Trust Cboe Vest U.S. Equity Buffer ETF - February
First Trust Cboe Vest U.S. Equity Buffer ETF - May
First Trust JFL Global Equity ETF
First Trust Nasdaq Cybersecurity ETF
Franklin FTSE Canada All Cap Index ETF
Franklin FTSE Europe ex U.K. Index ETF
Franklin FTSE U.S. Index ETF
Franklin Global Dividend Quality Index ETF
Franklin Risk Managed Canadian Equity Active ETF
Franklin U.S. Large Cap Multifactor Index ETF
Genesis Land Development Corp.
Guardian Canadian Sector Controlled Equity Fund
Guardian i3 Global Quality Growth ETF
Guardian i3 Global REIT ETF
Guardian i3 US Quality Growth ETF
HTC Purenergy Inc.
Hamilton Australian Bank Equal-Weight Index ETF
Hamilton Canadian Bank Mean Reversion Index ETF
Hamilton Global Financials ETF
Hamilton U.S. Mid/Small-Cap Financials ETF
Hampton Financial Corporation
High Interest Savings Account ETF
Horizons Active Cdn Dividend ETF
Horizons All-Equity Asset Allocation ETF
Horizons Balanced Asset Allocation ETF
Horizons Global Uranium Index ETF
Horizons Pipelines & Energy Services Index ETF
Horizons Robotics and Automation Index ETF
Horizons Seasonal Rotation ETF
Inventronics Limited
Invesco FTSE RAFI Canadian Small-Mid Index ETF
Invesco FTSE RAFI US Index ETF
Invesco Canadian Dividend Index ETF
Invesco FTSE RAFI Canadian Index ETF
Invesco FTSE RAFI Global Small-Mid ETF
Invesco Low Volatility Portfolio ETF
Invesco NASDAQ 100 Index ETF
Invesco S&P/TSX Composite ESG Index ETF
Invesco S&P 500 High Dividend Low Volatility Index ETF
Invesco S&P International Developed ESG Index ETF
Invesco S&P/TSX Composite ESG Tilt Index ETF
Invesco S&P/TSX Composite Low Volatility Index ETF
Invesco S&P/TSX REIT Income Index ETF
Invesco S&P/TSX 60 ESG Tilt Index ETF
iShares CNX Nifty India Index ETF
iShares Canadian Fundamental Index ETF
iShares Canadian Growth Index ETF
iShares Canadian Real Return Bond Index ETF
iShares Canadian Select Dividend Index ETF
iShares Canadian Value Index ETF
iShares Core Balanced ETF Portfolio
iShares Core Equity ETF Portfolio
iShares Core Growth ETF Portfolio
iShares Core MSCI All Country World ex Canada Index ETF
iShares Core MSCI Canadian Quality Dividend Index ETF
iShares Core MSCI EAFE IMI Index ETF
iShares Core MSCI EAFE IMI Index ETF (CAD-Hedged)
iShares Core MSCI Global Quality Dividend Index ETF
iShares Core MSCI US Quality Dividend Index ETF
iShares Core S&P 500 Index ETF
iShares Core S&P/TSX Capped Composite Index ETF
iShares Core S&P U.S. Total Market Index ETF
iShares Cybersecurity and Tech Index ETF
iShares Emerging Markets Fundamental Index ETF
iShares Equal Weight Banc & Lifeco ETF
iShares ESG Advanced MSCI Canada Index ETF
iShares ESG Aware MSCI Canada Index ETF
iShares ESG MSCI EAFE Leaders Index ETF
iShares Exponential Technologies Index ETF
iShares Global Agriculture Index ETF
iShares Global Infrastructure Index ETF
iShares International Fundamental Index ETF
iShares Japan Fundamental Index ETF (CAD-Hedged)
iShares MSCI EAFE Index ETF (CAD-Hedged)
iShares MSCI Europe IMI Index ETF (CAD-Hedged)
iShares MSCI World Index ETF
iShares MSCI Min Vol Canada Index ETF
iShares MSCI Min Vol Global Index ETF
iShares MSCI Min Vol Global Index ETF (CAD-Hedged)
iShares MSCI Multifactor USA Index ETF
iShares NASDAQ 100 Index ETF (CAD-Hedged)
iShares Premium Money Market ETF
iShares S&P/TSX Composite High Dividend Index ETF
iShares S&P U.S. Mid-Cap Index ETF
iShares S&P/TSX Capped Energy Index ETF
iShares S&P Global Consumer Discretionary Index ETF (CAD-Hedged)
iShares S&P/TSX Capped REIT Index ETF
iShares S&P/TSX Canadian Dividend Aristocrats Index ETF
iShares S&P/TSX Capped Consumer Staples Index ETF
iShares S&P/TSX Capped Financials Index ETF
iShares S&P/TSX Capped Utilities Index ETF
iShares S&P/TSX Completion Index ETF
iShares S&P/TSX Global Base Metals Index ETF
iShares S&P/TSX SmallCap Index ETF
iShares S&P US Dividend Growers Index ETF (CAD-Hedged)
iShares US Fundamental Index ETF
JFT Strategies Fund
Jade Power Trust
Mackenzie Balanced Allocation ETF
Mackenzie Canadian Aggregate Bond Index ETF
Mackenzie Canadian All Corporate Bond Index ETF
Mackenzie Canadian Equity Index ETF
Mackenzie Canadian Short-Term Bond Index ETF
Mackenzie Conservative Allocation ETF
Mackenzie Core Plus Canadian Fixed Income ETF
Mackenzie Core Plus Global Fixed Income ETF
Mackenzie Developed ex-North America Aggregate Bond ETF (CAD Hedged)
Mackenzie Developed Markets Real Estate Index ETF
Mackenzie Emerging Markets Bond Index ETF (CAD-Hedged)
Mackenzie Emerging Markets Local Currency Bond Index ETF
Mackenzie Floating Rate Income ETF
Mackenzie Global High Yield Fixed Income ETF
Mackenzie Global Infrastructure Index ETF
Mackenzie Global Sustainable Dividend Index ETF
Mackenzie Global Women's Leadership ETF
Mackenzie Growth Allocation ETF
Mackenzie International Equity Index ETF (CAD-Hedged)
Mackenzie International Equity Index ETF
Mackenzie Ivy Global Equity ETF
Mackenzie Maximum Diversification All World Developed Index ETF
Mackenzie Maximum Diversification Canada Index ETF
Mackenzie Maximum Diversification Emerging Markets Index ETF
Mackenzie Portfolio Completion ETF
Mackenzie US High Yield Bond Index ETF (CAD-Hedged)
Mackenzie US TIPS Index ETF (CAD-Hedged)
Mackenzie Unconstrained Bond ETF
Mackenzie U.S. Aggregate Bond Index ETF (CAD-Hedged)
Manulife Multifactor Canadian Large Cap Index ETF
Manulife Multifactor Canadian SMID Cap Index ETF
Manulife Multifactor U.S. Large Cap Index ETF
Manulife Smart Dividend ETF
Mackenzie Maximum Diversification All World Developed ex North America Index ETF
Metalla Royalty & Streaming Ltd.
Morien Resources Corp.
NBI Active Canadian Preferred Shares ETF
NBI Active U.S. Equity ETF
NBI Canadian Family Business ETF
NBI Global Private Equity ETF
NBI Liquid Alternatives ETF
NBI Sustainable Canadian Bond ETF
NBI Unconstrained Fixed Income ETF
Newcrest Mining Limited
Ninepoint Energy Fund
Ninepoint Energy Income Fund
Noranda Income Fund
Paramount Resources Ltd.
Picton Mahoney Fortified Alpha Alternative Fund
Pulse Seismic Inc.
Purpose Crypto Opportunities ETF
Purpose Energy Transition Fund
RB Global, Inc.
RBC Canadian Bank Yield Index ETF
RBC Quant Canadian Dividend Leaders ETF
RBC Quant Canadian Equity Leaders ETF
RBC Quant EAFE Dividend Leaders (CAD Hedge) ETF

RBC Quant EAFE Equity Leaders (CAD Hedged) ETF
RBC Quant EAFE Equity Leaders ETF
RBC Quant Emerging Markets Equity Leaders ETF
RBC Quant U.S. Dividend Leaders ETF
RBC Quant U.S. Equity Leaders (CAD Hedged) ETF
RBC Quant U.S. Equity Leaders ETF
RBC Vision Women's Leadership MSCI Canada Index ETF
Reko International Group Inc.
Ridgewood Canadian Investment Grade Bond Fund
SIR Royalty Income Fund
Scotia Emerging Markets Equity Index Tracker ETF
SmartBe Canadian Quantitative Momentum Index ETF
SmartBe Canadian Quantitative Value Index ETF
SmartBe U.S. Quantitative Momentum Index ETF
SmartBe U.S. Quantitative Value Index ETF
Spartan Delta Corp.
Standard Mercantile Acquisition Corp.
Stelco Holdings Inc.
Teck Resources Limited
Tethys Petroleum Limited
Titan Mining Corporation
Tourmaline Oil Corp.
Tree Island Steel Ltd.
Trilogy International Partners Inc.
US High Interest Savings Account Fund
Vanguard All-Equity ETF Portfolio
Vanguard Balanced ETF Portfolio
Vanguard Conservative ETF Portfolio
Vanguard FTSE Canada All Cap Index ETF
Vanguard FTSE Canadian Capped REIT Index ETF
Vanguard FTSE Canadian High Dividend Yield Index ETF
Vanguard FTSE Developed All Cap ex North America Index ETF (Cad Hedged)
Vanguard FTSE Developed All Cap Ex U.S. Index ETF
Vanguard FTSE Developed All Cap Ex U.S. Index ETF (CAD-hedged)
Vanguard FTSE Emerging Markets All Cap Index ETF
Vanguard FTSE Global All Cap ex Canada Index ETF
Vanguard Global Value Factor ETF
Vanguard Growth ETF Portfolio
Vanguard S&P 500 Index ETF
Vanguard U.S. Total Market Index ETF
Vitreous Glass Inc.
Wealthsimple Developed Markets ex North America Socially Responsible Index ETF
Wealthsimple North America Socially Responsible Index ETF
Wealthsimple Shariah World Equity Index ETF

Special Tax

Mackenzie Master Limited Partnership

Capital Gains

Artis Real Estate Investment Trust
BIP Investment Corporation
BMO ARK Genomic Revolution Fund
BMO ARK Innovation Fund
BMO All-Equity ETF
BMO Balanced ETF
BMO Canadian Dividend ETF
BMO Equal Weight Banks Index ETF
BMO Equal Weight Industrials Index ETF
BMO Equal Weight REITs Index ETF
BMO Equal Weight US Banks Index ETF
BMO Equal Weight US Banks Hedged to CAD Index ETF
BMO Equal Weight Utilities Index ETF
BMO Europe High Dividend Covered Call Hedged to CAD ETF
BMO Global Communications Index ETF
BMO Global Consumer Discretionary Hedged to CAD Index ETF
BMO Global Infrastructure Index ETF
BMO Growth ETF
BMO International Dividend Hedged to CAD ETF
BMO Japan Index ETF
BMO Low Volatility Canadian Equity ETF
BMO Low Volatility US Equity ETF
BMO MSCI EAFE Headged to CAD Index ETF
BMO MSCI Emerging Markets Index ETF
BMO MSCI Europe High Quality Hedged to CAD Index ETF
BMO MSCI USA High Quality Index ETF
BMO Monthly Income ETF
BMO MSCI Canada ESG Leaders Index ETF
BMO MSCI USA Value Index ETF
BMO Nasdaq 100 Equity Hedged To CAD Index ETF
BMO Nasdaq 100 Equity Index ETF
BMO Real Return Bond Index ETF
BMO S&P US Mid Cap Index ETF
BMO S&P/TSX Capped Composite Index ETF
BMO SIA Focused Canadian Equity Fund
BMO SIA Focused North American Equity Fund
BMO Short Corporate Bond Index ETF
BMO Short Federal Bond Index ETF
BMO Short Provincial Bond Index ETF
BMO Short-Term US TIPS Index ETF
BMO Sustainable Global Multi-Sector Bond Fund
BMO Ultra Short-Term Bond ETF
BMO Ultra Short-Term US Bond ETF
Big Banc Split Corp.
CI Alternative Investment Grade Credit Fund
CI Auspice Broad Commodity Fund
CI Bio-Revolution Index ETF
CI DoubleLine Core Plus Fixed Income US$ Fund
CI DoubleLine Income US$ Fund
CI DoubleLine Total Return Bond US$ Fund
CI Emerging Markets Alpha ETF
CI Energy Giants Covered Call ETF
CI Enhanced Government Bond ETF
CI Enhanced Short Duration Bond Fund
CI First Asset MSCI World ESG Impact ETF
CI Floating Rate Income Fund
CI Galaxy Blockchain Index ETF
CI Galaxy Metaverse Index ETF
CI Galaxy Multi-Crypto ETF
CI Global Asset Allocation Private Pool
CI Global Bond Currency Neutral Fund
CI Global Green Bond Fund
CI Global Healthcare Leaders Index ETF
CI Global High Yield Credit Private Pool
CI Global Investment Grade ETF
CI Global Minimum Downside Volatility Index ETF
CI High Interest Savings ETF
CI Morningstar Canada Momentum Index ETF
CI Morningstar International Momentum Index ETF
CI Morningstar International Value Index ETF
CI Morningstar National Bank Quebec Index ETF
CI MSCI Europe Low Risk Weighted ETF
CI MSCI International Low Risk Weighted ETF
CI MSCI World Low Risk Weighted ETF
CI 1-5 Year Laddered Government Strip Bond Index ETF
CI ONE Global Equity ETF
CI Preferred Share ETF
CI U.S. Treasury Inflation-Linked Bond Index ETF (CAD Hedged)
CI U.S. 500 Index ETF
CI U.S. 1000 Index ETF
CI U.S. TrendLeaders Index ETF
CI WisdomTree U.S. MidCap Dividend Index ETF
CI WisdomTree U.S. Quality Dividend Growth Variably Hedged Index ETF
CI Yield Enhanced Canada Short-Term Aggregate Bond Index ETF
Canadian Apartment Properties Real Estate Investment Trust
Canso Credit Income Fund
DRI Healthcare Trust
Desjardins Canadian Preferred Share Index ETF
Desjardins RI Global Multifactor - Fossil Fuel Free ETF
Desjardins RI Canada - Low CO2 Index ETF
Desjardins RI Canada Multifactor - Low CO2 ETF
Desjardins RI USA - Low CO2 Index ETF
Dream Office Real Estate Investment Trust
Dynamic Active Canadian Dividend ETF
Dynamic Active Enhanced Yield Covered Options ETF
Dynamic Active Global Infrastructure ETF
Dynamic Active U.S. Mid-Cap ETF
Emerge EMPWR Sustainable Dividend Equity ETF
Emerge EMPWR Sustainable Emerging Markets Equity ETF
Emerge EMPWR Sustainable Global Core Equity ETF
Evolve Cyber Security Index Fund
Fidelity All-in-One Balanced ETF
Fidelity All-in-One Conservative ETF Fund
Fidelity All-in-One Equity ETF
Fidelity All-in-One Growth ETF
Fidelity Canadian Low Volatility Index ETF
Fidelity Canadian Value Index ETF
Fidelity U.S. Dividend for Rising Rates Curency Neutral Index ETF
Fidelity U.S. Dividend for Rising Rates Index ETF
Fidelity U.S. High Dividend Currency Neutral Index ETF
Fidelity U.S. High Dividend Index ETF
Fidelity U.S. High Quality Index ETF

Fidelity U.S. Low Volatility Index ETF
Fidelity U.S. Value Index ETF
First Trust Cboe Vest U.S. Equity Buffer ETF - February
First Trust Cboe Vest U.S. Equity Buffer ETF - May
First Trust JFL Global Equity ETF
First Trust Nasdaq Cybersecurity ETF
Franklin FTSE Canada All Cap Index ETF
Franklin FTSE Europe ex U.K. Index ETF
Franklin FTSE U.S. Index ETF
Franklin Global Dividend Quality Index ETF
Franklin Risk Managed Canadian Equity Active ETF
Franklin U.S. Large Cap Multifactor Index ETF
Guardian Canadian Sector Controlled Equity Fund
Guardian i3 Global Quality Growth ETF
Guardian i3 Global REIT ETF
Guardian i3 US Quality Growth ETF
Hamilton Australian Bank Equal-Weight Index ETF
Hamilton Global Financials ETF
Hamilton U.S. Mid/Small-Cap Financials ETF
Horizons Active Cdn Dividend ETF
Horizons All-Equity Asset Allocation ETF
Horizons Balanced Asset Allocation ETF
Horizons Global Uranium Index ETF
Horizons Pipelines & Energy Services Index ETF
Horizons Robotics and Automation Index ETF
Horizons Seasonal Rotation ETF
Invesco FTSE RAFI Canadian Small-Mid Index ETF
Invesco FTSE RAFI US Index ETF
Invesco Canadian Dividend Index ETF
Invesco FTSE RAFI Canadian Index ETF
Invesco FTSE RAFI Global Small-Mid ETF
Invesco Low Volatility Portfolio ETF
Invesco NASDAQ 100 Index ETF
Invesco S&P/TSX Composite ESG Index ETF
Invesco S&P 500 High Dividend Low Volatility Index ETF
Invesco S&P International Developed ESG Index ETF
Invesco S&P/TSX Composite ESG Tilt Index ETF
Invesco S&P/TSX Composite Low Volatility Index ETF
Invesco S&P/TSX REIT Income Index ETF
Invesco S&P/TSX 60 ESG Tilt Index ETF
iShares CNX Nifty India Index ETF
iShares Canadian Fundamental Index ETF
iShares Canadian Growth Index ETF
iShares Canadian Real Return Bond Index ETF
iShares Canadian Select Dividend Index ETF
iShares Canadian Value Index ETF
iShares Core Balanced ETF Portfolio
iShares Core Equity ETF Portfolio
iShares Core Growth ETF Portfolio
iShares Core MSCI All Country World ex Canada Index ETF
iShares Core MSCI Canadian Quality Dividend Index ETF
iShares Core MSCI EAFE IMI Index ETF
iShares Core MSCI EAFE IMI Index ETF (CAD-Hedged)
iShares Core MSCI Global Quality Dividend Index ETF
iShares Core MSCI US Quality Dividend Index ETF
iShares Core S&P 500 Index ETF
iShares Core S&P/TSX Capped Composite Index ETF
iShares Core S&P U.S. Total Market Index ETF
iShares Cybersecurity and Tech Index ETF
iShares Emerging Markets Fundamental Index ETF
iShares Equal Weight Banc & Lifeco ETF
iShares ESG Advanced MSCI Canada Index ETF
iShares ESG Aware MSCI Canada Index ETF
iShares ESG MSCI EAFE Leaders Index ETF
iShares Exponential Technologies Index ETF
iShares Global Agriculture Index ETF
iShares Global Infrastructure Index ETF
iShares International Fundamental Index ETF
iShares Japan Fundamental Index ETF (CAD-Hedged)
iShares MSCI EAFE Index ETF (CAD-Hedged)
iShares MSCI Europe IMI Index ETF (CAD-Hedged)
iShares MSCI World Index ETF
iShares MSCI Min Vol Canada Index ETF
iShares MSCI Min Vol Global Index ETF
iShares MSCI Min Vol Global Index ETF (CAD-Hedged)
iShares MSCI Multifactor USA Index ETF
iShares NASDAQ 100 Index ETF (CAD-Hedged)
iShares Premium Money Market ETF
iShares S&P/TSX Composite High Dividend Index ETF
iShares S&P U.S. Mid-Cap Index ETF
iShares S&P/TSX Capped Energy Index ETF
iShares S&P Global Consumer Discretionary Index ETF (CAD-Hedged)
iShares S&P/TSX Capped REIT Index ETF
iShares S&P/TSX Canadian Dividend Aristocrats Index ETF
iShares S&P/TSX Capped Consumer Staples Index ETF
iShares S&P/TSX Capped Financials Index ETF
iShares S&P/TSX Capped Utilities Index ETF
iShares S&P/TSX Completion Index ETF
iShares S&P/TSX Global Base Metals Index ETF
iShares S&P/TSX SmallCap Index ETF
iShares S&P US Dividend Growers Index ETF (CAD-Hedged)
iShares US Fundamental Index ETF
JFT Strategies Fund
Mackenzie Balanced Allocation ETF
Mackenzie Canadian Aggregate Bond Index ETF
Mackenzie Canadian All Corporate Bond Index ETF
Mackenzie Canadian Equity Index ETF
Mackenzie Canadian Short-Term Bond Index ETF
Mackenzie Conservative Allocation ETF
Mackenzie Core Plus Canadian Fixed Income ETF
Mackenzie Core Plus Global Fixed Income ETF
Mackenzie Developed ex-North America Aggregate Bond ETF (CAD Hedged)
Mackenzie Developed Markets Real Estate Index ETF
Mackenzie Emerging Markets Bond Index ETF (CAD-Hedged)
Mackenzie Emerging Markets Local Currency Bond Index ETF
Mackenzie Floating Rate Income ETF
Mackenzie Global High Yield Fixed Income ETF
Mackenzie Global Infrastructure Index ETF
Mackenzie Global Sustainable Dividend Index ETF
Mackenzie Global Women's Leadership ETF
Mackenzie Growth Allocation ETF
Mackenzie International Equity Index ETF (CAD-Hedged)
Mackenzie International Equity Index ETF
Mackenzie Ivy Global Equity ETF
Mackenzie Maximum Diversification All World Developed Index ETF
Mackenzie Maximum Diversification Canada Index ETF
Mackenzie Maximum Diversification Emerging Markets Index ETF
Mackenzie Portfolio Completion ETF
Mackenzie US High Yield Bond Index ETF (CAD-Hedged)
Mackenzie US TIPS Index ETF (CAD-Hedged)
Mackenzie Unconstrained Bond ETF
Mackenzie U.S. Aggregate Bond Index ETF (CAD-Hedged)
Manulife Multifactor Canadian Large Cap Index ETF
Manulife Multifactor Canadian SMID Cap Index ETF
Manulife Multifactor U.S. Large Cap Index ETF
Manulife Smart Dividend ETF
Mackenzie Maximum Diversification All World Developed ex North America Index ETF
NBI Active Canadian Preferred Shares ETF
NBI Active U.S. Equity ETF
NBI Canadian Family Business ETF
NBI Global Private Equity ETF
NBI Liquid Alternatives ETF
NBI Sustainable Canadian Bond ETF
NBI Unconstrained Fixed Income ETF
Ninepoint Energy Fund
Ninepoint Energy Income Fund
RBC Canadian Bank Yield Index ETF
RBC Quant Canadian Dividend Leaders ETF
RBC Quant Canadian Equity Leaders ETF
RBC Quant EAFE Dividend Leaders (CAD Hedge) ETF
RBC Quant EAFE Equity Leaders (CAD Hedged) ETF
RBC Quant U.S. Dividend Leaders ETF
RBC Quant U.S. Equity Leaders ETF
RBC Vision Women's Leadership MSCI Canada Index ETF
Scotia Emerging Markets Equity Index Tracker ETF
SmartBe Canadian Quantitative Momentum Index ETF
SmartBe Canadian Quantitative Value Index ETF
SmartBe U.S. Quantitative Momentum Index ETF
SmartBe U.S. Quantitative Value Index ETF
US High Interest Savings Account Fund
Vanguard All-Equity ETF Portfolio
Vanguard Balanced ETF Portfolio
Vanguard Conservative ETF Portfolio
Vanguard FTSE Canada All Cap Index ETF
Vanguard FTSE Canadian Capped REIT Index ETF
Vanguard FTSE Canadian High Dividend Yield Index ETF
Vanguard FTSE Developed All Cap ex North America Index ETF (Cad Hedged)
Vanguard FTSE Developed All Cap Ex U.S. Index ETF
Vanguard FTSE Developed All Cap Ex U.S. Index ETF (CAD-hedged)
Vanguard FTSE Emerging Markets All Cap Index ETF
Vanguard FTSE Global All Cap ex Canada Index ETF
Vanguard Global Value Factor ETF
Vanguard Growth ETF Portfolio
Vanguard S&P 500 Index ETF
Vanguard U.S. Total Market Index ETF
Wealthsimple Developed Markets ex North America Socially Responsible Index ETF
Wealthsimple North America Socially Responsible Index ETF
Wealthsimple Shariah World Equity Index ETF

Return of Capital

Atlas Salt Inc.
Brookfield Reinsurance Ltd.
CI Alternative Investment Grade Credit Fund
CI Digital Security Index ETF
CI Emerging Markets Alpha ETF
CI Global Green Bond Fund
CI Global Investment Grade ETF
CI Global Sustainable Infrastructure Fund
CI Morningstar Canada Momentum Index ETF
Evolve Active Global Fixed Income Fund
Evolve Cryptocurrencies ETF
Evolve Innovation Index Fund
genifi inc.
Standard Mercantile Acquisition Corp.
Trilogy International Partners Inc.
ValOre Metals Corp.

Extra Dividend

Atrium Mortgage Investment Corporation
BMO Money Market Fund
Economic Investment Trust Limited
H&R Real Estate Investment Trust
Richards Packaging Income Fund

Abbreviations

A.C.T. – Australian Capital Territory
A.I. – Auditores Independentes
A.P.A. – Authorized Public Accountant
Aberdeen. – Aberdeenshire
ABR – Alternate Base Rate
acctg. – accounting
accum. – accumulated
acq(s). – acquisition(s)
acting CEO – acting chief executive officer
acting CFO – acting chief financial officer
acting chr. – acting chair
acting pres. – acting president
admin. – administration
ADR – American Depository Receipt
adv. board mbr. – advisory board member
advtg. – advertising
agri. – agriculture; agricultural
Ala. – Alabama
Alta. – Alberta
amalg. – amalgamation
AMEX – American Stock Exchange
Apr. – April
Argyll. – Argyllshire
Ariz. – Arizona
Ark. – Arkansas
ASC – Alberta Securities Commission
ASE – Alberta Stock Exchange
Assn. – Association
assoc. – associate
assoc. gen. counsel – associate general counsel
asst. – assistant
asst. sec. – assistant secretary
asst. treas. – assistant treasurer
asst. v-p, fin. – assistant vice-president, finance
Aug. – August
avg. – average
Ayr. – Ayrshire
B.C. – British Columbia
Banff. – Banffshire
bbl – barrel
bcf – billion cubic feet
BCSC – British Columbia Securities Commission
bdu – bone dry unit
Beds. – Bedfordshire
Berks. – Berkshire
Berwick. – Berwickshire
bldg. – building(s)
BOE – barrels of oil equivalent
BOPD – barrels oil produced per day
Brecon. – Breconshire
Bucks. – Buckinghamshire
bus. – business
Bute. – Buteshire
C.A. – Chartered Accountant
C.G.A. – Certified General Accountant
C.P.A. – Certified Public Accountant
Caernarvon. – Caernarvonshire
Calif. – California
Cambs. – Cambridgeshire
CAO – chief administrative officer
Cardigan. – Cardiganshire
Carmarthen. – Carmarthenshire
CBCA – Canada Business Corporation Act
Cdn. – Canadian
CDNX – Canadian Venture Exchange
CDOR – Canadian Dollar Offer Rate
CEO – chief executive officer
CFO – chief financial officer
chief acctg. officer – chief accounting officer
chief AML officer – chief anti-money laundering officer
chief bus. devel. officer – chief business development officer
chief bus. officer – chief business officer
chief comml. officer – chief commercial officer
chief commun. officer – chief communication officer
chief corp. devel. officer – chief corporate development officer
chief corp. officer – chief corporate officer
chief cust. officer – chief customer officer
chief devel. officer – chief development officer
chief distrib. officer – chief distribution officer
chief finl. & admin. officer – chief financial & administrative officer
chief HR officer – chief human resources officer
chief info. security officer – chief information security officer
chief invest. officer – chief investment officer
chief IT officer – chief information & technology officer
chief legal & admin. officer – chief legal & administration officer
chief legal & compliance office – chief legal & compliance officer
chief mdsg. officer – chief merchandising officer
chief mktg. officer – chief marketing officer
chief opers. officer – chief operations officer
chief sales & mktg. officer – chief sales & marketing officer
chief tech. officer – chief technology officer
chief. exec. – chief executive
chr. – chair
chr., emeritus – chair, emeritus
CICA – Canadian Institute of Chartered Accountants
CIO – chief information officer
Cl.A – Class A
Clack. – Clackmannanshire
CMO – chief medical officer
CNQ – Canadian Trading & Quotation System
CNSX – Canadian National Stock Exchange
co-CEO – co-chief executive officer
co-CFO – co-chief financial officer
co-chr. – co-chair
co-pres. – co-president
Colo. – Colorado
com. – common
Comm. – Commission
comml. – Commercial
commun. – communications
compt. – comptroller
Conn. – Connecticut
cons. – consulting
consol. – consolidated
const. – construction
contr. – controller
conv. – convertible
COO – chief operating officer
corp. – corporate
corp. counsel – corporate counsel
corp. sec. – corporate secretary
CRTC – Canadian Radio-Television Commission
CSE – Canadian Securities Exchange
CTO – Cease Trade Order
ctrl. – control
cty. – county
cum. – cumulative
Cumbs. – Cumberland
cust. – customer
D.C. – District of Columbia
dba – doing business as
deb(s). – debenture(s)
Dec. – December
def. – deferred
Del. – Delaware
Denbigh. – Denbighshire
depr. – depreciation
dept. – department
deputy CEO – deputy chief executive officer
deputy chr. – deputy chair
Derbys. – Derbyshire
Derry – Co. Londonderry
devel. – development
dir. – board of directors
dir. – director
dir., fin. – director, finance
dir., fin. & admin. – director, finance & administration
dist. – district
distrib(s). – distribution(s)
div. – division
divd(s). – dividend(s)
DPSP – Deferred Profit Sharing Plan
Dumfries. – Dumfriesshire
Dunbarton. – Dunbartonshire
EBITDA – Earns. bef. int., taxes, deprec. & amort.
eng. – engineering
envir. – environment
envirl. – environmental
EONIA – Euro OverNight Index Average
equip. – equipment
equiv. – equivalent
etc. – et cetera
EURIBOR – European Inter-Bank Offered Rate
eval. – evaluation
exch. – exchangeable
exec. – executive
exec. chr. – executive chair
exec. co-chr. – executive co-chair
exec. dir. – executive director
exec. v-chr. – executive vice-chair
exec. v-p – executive vice-president
exec. v-p, bus. devel. – executive vice-president, business development
exec. v-p, corp. devel. – executive vice-president, corporate development
exec. v-p, explor. – executive vice-president, exploration
exec. v-p, fin. – executive vice-president, finance
exec. v-p, HR – executive vice-president, human resources
exec. v-p, IT – executive vice-president, information technology
exec. v-p, mktg. – executive vice-president, marketing
exec. v-p, opers. – executive vice-president, operations
exec. v-p, sales – executive vice-president, sales

exec. v-p, sales & mktg. — executive vice-president, sales & marketing
exec. v-p, tech. — executive vice-president, technology
explor. — exploration
fbm — foot board measure
FDA — Food and Drug Administration
Feb. — February
fin. — finance
finl. — financial
Fla. — Florida
Flint. — Flintshire
fltg. — floating
ft. — feet
g/t — grams per tonne
Ga. — Georgia
GAAP — Generally Accepted Accounting Principles
gen. — general
gen. counsel — general counsel
gen. mgr. — general manager
geol. — geology
GJ — gigajoules
Gloucs. — Gloucestershire
govt. — government
GP — General Partnership
grp. — group
grp. head — group head
grp. pres. — group president
grp. v-p — group vice-president
GW — gigawatt(s)
GWh — gigawatt hour(s)
Hants. — Hampshire
Hereford. — Herefordshire
Herts. — Hertfordshire
honry. — honorary
HR — human resources
hr. — hour
hrs. — hours
Hunts. — Huntingdonshire
Ill. — Illinois
Ind. — Indiana
ind. — industrial
info. — information
insce. — insurance
instr. — instrument
int. — interest
interim CEO — interim chief executive officer
interim CFO — interim chief financial officer
interim chr. — interim chair
interim pres. — interim president
intl. — international
Inverness. — Inverness-shire
invest(s). — investment(s)
IR — investor relations
IT — Information Technology
Jan. — January
JIBAR — Johannesburg Inter-Bank Agreed Rate
jr. — junior
JV — Joint Venture
Kan. — Kansas
kgU — kilogram uranium
Kincard. — Kincardineshire
Kinross. — Kinrossshire
Kirkcud. — Kirkcudbrightshire
km — kilometre(s)
km^2 — square kilometre(s)
kV — kilovolt(s)
kVA — kilovolt-ampere
KW — kilowatt(s)
KWh — kilowatt hour(s)
Ky. — Kentucky
l-t — long-term
La. — Louisiana
Lanark. — Lanarkshire
Lancs. — Lancashire
lb. — pound(s)
lead dir. — lead director
Leics. — Leicestershire
LIBID — London Inter-Bank Bid Rate
LIBOR — London Inter-Bank Offered Rate
LIF — Life Income Fund
LIMEAN — London Inter-Bank Mean Rate
Lincs. — Lincolnshire
LISBOR — Lisbon Inter-Bank Offered Rate
LLP — Limited Liability Partnership
LP — Limited Partnership
m — metre(s)
M&A — mergers & acquisitions
m^2 — square metre(s)
m^3 — cubic metre(s)
maint. — maintenance
man. — managing
Man. — Manitoba
man. dir. — managing director
man. partner — managing partner
Mar. — March
Mass. — Massachusetts
mbbl — thousand barrels
mbr. — member
mcf — thousand cubic feet
Md. — Maryland
mdse. — merchandise
mdsg. — merchandising
ME — Montreal Exchange
Me. — Maine
mech. — mechanical
Merioneth. — Merionethshire
mfbm — thousand board feet
mfg. — manufacturing
mfr. — manufacture
mgr. — manager
mgt. — management
Mich. — Michigan
Middx. — Middlesex
min. — mining
Minn. — Minnesota
MIS — management information systems
Miss. — Mississippi
mktg. — marketing
mmcf — million cubic feet
mmfbm — million board feet
mmsf — million square feet
Mo. — Missouri
Monmouth. — Monmouthshire
Mont. — Montana
Montgomery. — Montgomeryshire
Moray. — Morayshire
msf — thousand square feet
mtge(s). — mortgage(s)
MW — megawatt(s)
MWac — megawatt(s), alternating current
MWh — megawatt hour(s)
N.B. — New Brunswick
N.C. — North Carolina
N.D. — North Dakota
N.H. — New Hampshire
N.J. — New Jersey
N.L. — Newfoundland & Labrador
N.M. — New Mexico
n.p.v. — no par value
N.S. — Nova Scotia
N.S.W. — New South Wales
N.T. — Northern Territory
N.W.T. — Northwest Territories
N.Y. — New York
Nairn. — Nairnshire
NASDAQ — National Association of Securities Dealers Automated Quotation (U.S.)
natl. — national
natl. v-p — national vice-president
NEB — National Energy Board
Neb. — Nebraska
Nev. — Nevada
Nfld. — Newfoundland
NGL — natural gas liquids
Northants. — Northamptonshire
Northumbs. — Northumberland
Notts. — Nottinghamshire
Nov. — November
NSR — Net Smelter Royalty
NYSE — New York Stock Exchange
o/s — outstanding
obligs. — obligations
Oct. — October
OEM — original equipment manufacturer
Okla. — Oklahoma
Ont. — Ontario
oper. — operating
oper. partner — operating partner
opers. — operations
opt — ounces per ton
ord. — ordinary
Ore. — Oregon
org. — organizational
orig. — originally
OSB — oriented strand board
OSC — Ontario Securities Commission
OTC BB — Over-the-counter Bulletin Board
Oxon. — Oxfordshire
oz. — ounce(s)
p.a. — per annum
P.E.I. — Prince Edward Island
P.R. — Puerto Rico
Pa. — Pennsylvania
pay. — payable
Peeble. — Peeblesshire
Pembroke. — Pembrokeshire
Perth. — Perthshire
pfce. — preference
PIP — Petroleum Incentive Payment
PJ — petajoules
ppm — parts per million
PR — public relations
pref. — preferred
pres. — president
pres. — president of division/subsidiary
proc. — process
prod. — production
prof. — professional
prop. — property
purch. — purchasing
Qld. — Queensland
Que. — Quebec
R&D — research & development
R.I. — Rhode Island
Radnor. — Radnorshire
redeem. — redeemable

regl. – regional
regl. head – regional head
regl. v-p – regional vice-president
rel. – relations (except PR)
Renfrew. – Renfrewshire
rep. – representative
retract. – retractable
rev. – revenue
revolv. – revolving
RIF – Retirement Income Fund
Roxburgh. – Roxburghshire
RRSP – Registered Retirement Savings Plan
rt. – right
S&P – Standard & Poor's
s-t – short-term
s.a. – semiannually
S.A. – South Australia
S.C. – South Carolina
S.D. – South Dakota
s.f. – sinking fund
Sask. – Saskatchewan
SEC – Securities and Exchange Commission (U.S.)
sec. – secretary
sec.-treas. – secretary-treasurer
secs. – securities
Selkirk. – Selkirkshire
Sept. – September
Ser.A – Series A
sh. – share
Shrops. – Shropshire
SOFR – Secured Overnight Financing Rate
Somt. – Somerset
sq. – square
sr. – senior
sr. counsel – senior counsel
sr. dir. – senior director
sr. exec. v-p – senior executive vice-president
sr. man. dir – senior managing director
sr. man. partner – senior managing partner
sr. mgr. – senior manager
sr. v-p – senior vice-president
sr. v-p, bus. devel. – senior vice-president, business development
sr. v-p, corp. devel. – senior vice-president, corporate development
sr. v-p, explor. – senior vice-president, exploration
sr. v-p, fin. – senior vice-president, finance
sr. v-p, fin. & admin. – senior vice-president, finance & administration
sr. v-p, HR – senior vice-president, human resources
sr. v-p, IT – senior vice-president, information technology
sr. v-p, mktg. – senior vice-president, marketing
sr. v-p, opers. – senior vice-president, operations
sr. v-p, sales – senior vice-president, sales
sr. v-p, sales & mktg. – senior vice-president, sales & marketing
sr. v-p, tech. – senior vice-president, technology
srvc(s). – service(s)
Staffs. – Staffordshire
Stirling. – Stirlingshire
subord. – subordinate
subsid. – subsidiary
supt. – superintendent
supvr. – supervisor
sys. – system(s)
Tas. – Tasmania
tax. – taxation
tcf – trillion cubic feet
tech. – technology
telecom. – telecommunication(s)
Tenn. – Tennessee
Tex. – Texas
TJ – terajoule(s)
tpd – tons per day
tr. – trust
trans. – transportation
treas. – treasurer
TSE, TSX – Toronto Stock Exchange
TSX-VEN – TSX Venture Exchange
TWh – terawatt hour(s)
twp. – township
U.A.E. – United Arab Emirates
U.K. – United Kingdom
U.S. – United States (of America)
v-chr. – vice-chair
v-p – vice-president
v-p, bus. devel. – vice-president, business development
v-p, corp. devel. – vice-president, corporate development
v-p, explor. – vice-president, exploration
v-p, fin. – vice-president, finance
v-p, fin. & admin. – vice-president, finance & administration
v-p, HR – vice-president, human resources
v-p, IR – vice-president, investor relations
v-p, IT – vice-president, information technology
v-p, mktg. – vice-president, marketing
v-p, opers. – vice-president, operations
v-p, sales – vice-president, sales
v-p, sales & mktg. – vice-president, sales & marketing
v-p, tech. – vice-president, technology
Va. – Virginia
Vic. – Victoria
VSE – Vancouver Stock Exchange
Vt. – Vermont
vtg. – voting
W.A. – Western Australia
W.Va. – West Virginia
w/d – write-down(s)
w/o – write-off(s)
Warks. – Warwickshire
Wash. – Washington
Westmlnd. – Westmorland
Wigtown. – Wigtownshire
Wilts. – Wiltshire
Wisc. – Wisconsin
Worcs. – Worcestershire
WSE – Winnipeg Stock Exchange
wt. – warrant
Wyo. – Wyoming
Yorks. – Yorkshire

Dividend Abbreviations

◆ – special
** – Reinvestment Option
† – extra
A – annually
a – other income
accr. – accrued
Adj. – adjustable
auc. – auction
b – base cost adjustment
c – interest income
cap – capital
cl – class
cum. – cumulative
cv – convertible
e – estimate
ea – each
eff. – effective
est – established
exch. – exchangeable
f – final dividend
Fltg. – floating
foll. – following
g – capital gain
i – initial payment
instlmt rcpt – instalment receipt
ltd ptnrshp – limited partnership
M – monthly
M.V. – multiple voting
N.V. – non-voting
pa – per annum
pd – paid
pfd/pref – preferred
Prev – previous
pt – participating
Q – quarterly
r – return of capital
Ra – rate
red. – redeemable
ret. – retractable
rt. – right
S – semiannually
S.V. – subordinate voting
stk – stock
t – special tax status
Tr unit – trust unit
Var. – variable
vt – special voting rights
wt. – warrant

Currency Abbreviations

€ – Euro (EUR)
¢ – cent(s)
£ – British Pound (GBP)
A$ – Australian Dollar (AUD)
B$ – Bahamian Dollar (BSD)
Baht – Thai Baht (THB)
Bds$ – Barbadian Dollar (BBD)
BFr – Belgian Franc (BEF)*
BZ$ – Belize Dollar (BZD)
Cdn$ – Canadian Dollar (CAD)
CI$ – Cayman Islands Dollar (KYD)
CKr – Czech Koruna (CZK)
Cn¥ – Chinese Yuan (CNY)
COL$ – Colombian Peso (COP)
DGu – Dutch Guilder (NLG)*
Dhs. – U.A.E. Dirham (AED)
DKr – Danish Kroner (DKK)
DM – Deutschemark (DEM)*
FFr – French Franc (FRF)*
FJ$ – Fiji Dollar (FJD)
Ft – Hungarian Forint (HUF)
GDr – Greek Drachma (GRD)*
GH¢ – Ghanaian Cedi (GHS)
HK$ – Hong Kong Dollar (HKD)
IKr – Icelandic Króna (ISK)
IR£ – Irish Punt (IEP)*
JA$ – Jamaican Dollar (JMD)
Jp¥ – Japanese Yen (JPY)
L – Italian Lira (ITL)*
N$ – Namibian Dollar (NAD)
NKr – Norwegian Krone (NOK)

NT$ — New Taiwan Dollar (TWD)
NZ$ — New Zealand Dollars (NZD)
PEs — Portuguese Escudo (PTE)*
Pts — Spanish Peseta (ESP)*
R — South African Rand (ZAR)
R$ — Brazilian Real (BRL)
RD$ — Dominican Rep. Peso (DOP)
Rs — Indian Rupee (INR)
SFr — Swiss Franc (CHF)
SKr — Swedish Krona (SEK)
TT$ — Trinidad & Tobago Dollar (TTD)
US$ — United States Dollar (USD)
Won — Korean Won (KRW)
zl — Polish Zloty (PLN)

* Replaced with euros since 2002

Miscellaneous Abbreviations

™ — Trademark
© — Copyright
® — Registered
SM — Special Mark

International Corporate Abbreviations

(Pty) Ltd. — Proprietary Limited (South Africa, Namibia, Botswana)
(Pvt.) Ltd. — Private Limited (Sri Lanka)
a.d. — akcionarsko društvo (Bosnia & Herzegovina, Croatia, Serbia - joint stock company)
A.E. — Anonimos Eteria (Greece - public limited company)
A.O. — Anonim Ortaklari/Ortakligi (Turkey)
a.s. — akciová spolecnost (Czech Republic, Slovakia - public limited company)
A.S. — Aktsiaselts (Estonia); Anonim Sirketi (Turkey - joint stock company)
A.V.V. — Aruba Vrijgestelde Vennootschap (Aruba)
A/S — Aktieselskap (Denmark - public limited company)
AARPI — Association d'Avocats à Responsabilité Professionnelle Individuelle (France - association)
Ab — Aktiebolag (Finland - private company)
AB — Aktiebolag (Sweden - private stock company)
AB (publ) — Publikt Aktiebolag (Sweden - public limited company)
AD — Aktsionerno drujestvo (Bulgaria - public limited company)
AG — Aktiengesellschaft (Austria, Germany, Switzerland - public limited company)
AG mvK — Aktiengesellschaft mit veränderlichem Kapital (Liechtenstein - variable capital investment company)
AL — Andelslag (Norway - cooperative; formerly A.L. and A/L)
AO — Aktsionernoye Obshchestvo (Russia - joint stock company); precedes name of company
ApS — Anpartsselskab (Denmark - limited liability company)
AS — Aksjeselskap (Norway - private stock company)
ASA — Allmennaksjeselskap (Norway - public limited company)
Ay — Avoinyhtio (Finland - general partnership)
B.M. — Be'eravon Mugbal (Israel - limited liability company
B.S.C. — Bahrain Shareholding Company (Bahrain)
B.V. — Besloten Vennootschap (Belgium, Netherlands, Netherlands Antilles - limited liability company)
B.V.B.A. — Besloten Vennootschap met Beperkte Aansprakelijkheid (Belgium - private limited company)
BH — Bosnia & Herzegovina
Bpk — Beperk (South Africa - limited liability company)
C. de R.L. — Compania de Responsabilidad Limitada (Spain)
C.A. — Compania Anonima (Ecuador, Venezuela)
C.I.C. — Community Interest Company (U.K. - limited company)
C.V. — Commanditaire Vennootschap (Netherlands - limited partnership)
C.V.B.A. — Coöperatieve Vennootschap met Beperkte Aansprakelijkheid (Belgium - limited liability cooperative)
CJSC — Closed Joint Stock Company (Russia; English equivalent of ZAO); precedes name of company
Co. Ltd. — Company Limited (South Korea)
CRL — Cooperativa de Responsabilidade Limitida (Portugal - limited liability cooperative)
d.d. — dionicko društvo (Bosnia & Herzegovina, Croatia, Serbia - joint stock company); delniška družba (Slovenia - public limited company)
d.o.o. — društvo sa ogranicenom odgovornošcu (Bosnia & Herzegovina, Croatia, Serbia - private limited liability company); družba z omejeno odgovornostjo (Slovenia - limited liability company)
d.o.o.e.l. — društvo sa ogranicenom odgovornošcu od edno lice (Bosnia & Herzegovina, Croatia, Macedonia, Serbia - private limited liability company with single member)
DAC — Designated Activity Company (Ireland - private limited company)
DMCC — Dubai Multi Commodities Centre
E.P.E. — Eteria Periorismenis Euthinis (Greece - limited liability company)
EAD — Ednolichno Aktsionerno Drujestvo (Bulgaria - joint stock company)
ehf. — Einkahlutafelag (Iceland - private limited liability company)
EmbH — Experten mit beschränkter Haftung (Germany)
EOOD — Ednolichno Drujestvo s Ogranichena Otgovornost (Bulgaria - limited liability company)
Est. — Establishment (Abu Dhabi, U.A.E.)
EURL — Entreprise unipersonnelle à responsabilité limitée (Algeria, France - sole proprietorship with limited liability)
FZCO — Free Zone Company Middle East
FZE — Free Zone Establishment (Qatar, U.A.E.)
GK — Godo Kaisha (Japan - limited liability company)
GmbH — Gesellschaft mit beschränkter Haftung (Austria, Bahamas, Germany, Switzerland - limited liability company)
GmbH & Co. KG — Gesellschaft mit beschränkter Haftung & Company Kommanditgesellschaft (Germany - limited partnership)
HB — Handelsbolag (Sweden - general partnership)
hf. — Hlutafelag (Iceland - limited liability company)
I/S — Interessentselskab (Denmark - general partnership); Interesentselskap (Norway - general partnership)
JSC — Joint Stock Company (Russia; English equivalent of AO); precedes name of company

Jusik Hoesa – (Korea - stock company)
k.d. – komanditno društvo (Bosnia & Herzegovina, Croatia & Serbia - limited partnership)
K.S.C.P. – Kuwaiti Shareholding Company (Kuwait - public company)
K/S – Kommanditselskap (Denmark - limited partnership)
KB – Kommanditbolag (Sweden - limited partnership)
KD – Komanditno Drugestvo (Bulgaria - limited partnership)
Kft. – Korlátolt felelosségu társaság (Hungary - limited liability company)
KG – Kommanditgesellschaft (Austria, Germany & Switzerland - limited partnership)
KgaA – Kommanditgesellschaft auf Aktien (Germany - limited partnership)
KK – Kabushiki Kaishi (Japan - stock company)
Lda. – Sociedade por Quotas Limitada (Portugal)
LDC – Limited Duration Company (Bahamas)
LLC or LC – Limited Liability Company (U.S.)
LLLP – Limited Liability Limited Partnership (U.S.)
LLP – Limited Liability Partnership (U.S.)
Ltd. Sti. – Limited Sirketi (Turkey - limited company)
Ltda. – Sociedade por Quotax de Responsabiliadade Limitada (Brazil)
mbH – mit beschränkter Haftung (Germany - with limited liability)
N.A. – National Association (U.S. - national bank)
N.P.L. – No Personal Liability (Canada)
N.V. – Naamloze Vennootschap (Belgium, Netherlands, Netherlands Antilles - public/private stock company)
NL – No Liability (Australia - restricted to mining companies)
Nyrt. – Nyilvánosan muködo részvénytársaság (Hungary - public limited company)
o.d. – ortacko društvo (Bosnia & Herzegovina, Croatia, Serbia - general partnership)
OAO – Otkrytoye aktsionernoye obshchestvo (Russia - open joint stock company); precedes name of company
OJSC – Open Joint Stock Company (Russia; English equivalent of OAO); precedes or after name of company
OOD – Drujestvo s ogranichena otgovornost (Bulgaria - limited company)
OOO – Obshchestvo s ogranichennoy otvetstvennostyu (Russia - limited liability company); precedes name of company
OÜ – Osaühing (Estonia - private limited company)
Oy – Osakeyhtiö (Finland - stock company)
Oyj – Julkinen Osakeyhtiö (Finland - public limited company)
P.C. or PC – Professional Corporation (U.S.)
P.S.C. – Professional Service Corporation
P/F – Partafelag (Faroe Islands - public company)
P/S – Partnerselskaber (Denmark - limited liability partnership)
PBC – Public Benefit Company (U.S.)
PJSC – Public Joint Stock Company (Middle East)
plc – private limited company (U.K.)
PLLC – Professional Limited Liability Company (U.S.)
PT – Perseroan Terbatas (Indonesia - limited company); precedes name of company
PT Tbk. – Perseroan Terbatas, Terbuka (Indonesia - public limited company)
Pte. Ltd. – Private Limited (Singapore)
Pty Ltd. – Proprietary Limited (Australia - small to medium-sized companies)
Pvt. Ltd. – Private Limited (India, Pakistan)
RAS – Riiklik Aktsiaselts (Estonia - state-owned joint stock company)
Rt. – Részvénytársaság (Hungary - public/private stock company)
S. Com. por A. – Sociedad Commanditaria por Acciones (Spain - incorporated partnership)
S. de R.L. – Sociedad de Responsabilidad Limitada (Mexico - limited partnership)
S. de R.L. de C.V. – Sociedad de Responsabilidad Limitada de Capital Variable (Mexico - limited liability company)
S.A. – Sociedade Anónima (Portugal); Société Anonyme (Bahamas, Belgium, Côte d'Ivoire, France, Greece, Luxembourg, Morocco, Switzerland); Sociedad Anónima (Argentina, Chile, Colombia, Mexico, Peru, Spain); Spólka Akcyjna (Poland); Societate pe Actiuni (Romania)
S.A. de C.V. – Sociedad Anónima de Capital Variable (Mexico - corporation)
S.A. E.S.P. – Sociedad Anónima Empresa de Servicios Públicos (Argentina, Chile, Colombia, Peru, Spain)
S.A.A. – Sociedad Anónima Abierta (Peru - open company)
S.A.B. – Sociedad Agente de Bolsa (Peru - private company)
S.A.B. de C.V. – Sociedad Anónima Bursátil de Capital Variable (Mexico - public limited company)
S.A.C. – Sociedad Anónima Cerrada (Peru - closed company)
S.A.E. – Sharikat al-Mossahamah (Egypt - public limited company)
S.A.L. – Société Anonyme Libanaise (France)
S.A.M. – Société Anonyme Monegasque (Monaco - general business company)
S.A.P.I. de C.V. – Sociedad Anónima Promotora de Inversiones de Capital Variable (Mexico)
S.A.R.L. – Société à Responsabilité Limitée (France, Luxembourg, Switzerland); Sociedad Anonima de Responsibilidade Limitada (Portugal)
S.A.R.L.U. – Société à Responsabilité Limitée Uni-personnelle (France - limited liability joint limited company)
S.a.s. – Società in accomandita semplice (Italy - limited partnership)
S.A.S. – Société par Actions Simplifiée (France - simplified joint-stock company); Sociedad por Acciones Simplificada (Colombia - simplified share company)
S.A.S.U. – Société par Actions Simplifiée Unipersonnelle (France)
S.A.U. – Sociedad Anónima Unipersonal (Argentina, Spain - single shareholder company)
S.C. – Sociedad en Commandita (Mexico, Spain - general partnership); Share Company (Eritrea, Ethiopia)

S.C.A. — Société en Commandite par Actions (France - share-based limited partnership); Sociedad en Comandita por Acciones (Colombia - share-based limited partnership)
S.C.C. — Sociedad Civil y Comercial (Ecuador)
S.C.I. — Société Civile Immobilière (France - property company)
S.C.M. — Sociedad Contractual Minera (Chile)
S.C.R.L. — Société Coopérative à Responsabilité Limitée (France - limited liability cooperative)
S.C.S. — Société en Commandite par Simple (France - limited partnership)
S.E. — Societas Europaea (EU - public company)
S.E.C. — Société en Commandite (France - limited partnership)
S.E.C.S. — Société en Commandite par Simple (Luxembourg - limited partnership)
S.E.N.C.R.L. — Société en Nom Collectif à Responsabilité Limitée (France - limited liability general partnership)
S.L. — Sociedad Limitada (Latin America, Portugal, Spain - limited company)
S.L.P. — Sociedad Limitada Profesional (Spain - professional limited liability company)
S.L.U. — Sociedad Limitada Unipersonal (Spain)
S.M.R.L. — Sociedad Minera de Responsabilidad Limitada (Peru); precedes or follows name of company
S.n.c. — Società in nome collettivo (Italy - general partnership)
S.N.C./S.E.N.C. — Société en Nom Collectif (France - general partnership)
S.p.A. — Sociedad por Acciones (Chile - limited partnership with shares); Società per Azioni (Italy - stock company)
S.P.R.L. — Société Privée à Responsabilité Limitée (Belgium, France - private limited company)
S.R.L. — Sociedad de Responsabilidad Limitada (Argentina, Bolivia, Peru, Spain - limited liability company); Societate cu Raspundere Limitata (Romania - limited liability company)
S.r.l. — Sociedad de responsabilidad limitada (Chile, Mexico); Società a Responsabilità Limitata (Italy - limited liability company)
s.r.o. — spolecnost s rucením omezeným (Czech Republic, Slovakia - limited liability company)
S.U.A.R.L. — Société Unipersonnelle à Responsabilité Limitée (Senegal - one-man limited liability company)
S.U.R.L. — Société Unipersonnelle à Responsabilité Limitée (France - one-man limited liability company)
S/A — Sociedade por Ações (Brazil)
SCA — Société en Commandite par Actions (Belgium - limited partnership); Societe in Còmandita pe Actiuni (Romania - limited partnership)
Sdn. Bhd. — Sendirian Berhad (Malaysia - limited liability company)
SE — Societas Europaea (EU - public company)
SEZC — Special Economic Zone Company (Cayman Islands)
sf. — sameignarfélag (Iceland - general partnership)
Sh.a. — Shoqëri Aksionare (Albania - public limited company)
Sh.p.k. — Shoqëri me Përgjegjësi të Kufizuar (Albania - limited company)
SIA — Sabiedriba ar ierobežotu atbildibu (Latvia - limited liability company)
SK — Spólka komandytowa (Poland - limited partnership)
slhf. — samlagshlutafélag (Iceland - limited parternship)
Sp.zo.o — Spólka z ograniczona odpowiedzialnoscia (Poland - private limited company)
SRL — Society with Restricted Liability (Barbados)
U.A. — Uitgesloten Aansprakelijkheid (Netherlands - cooperative with excluded liability)
UAB — Uždaroji Akcine Bendrove (Ukraine - private limited company)
UG — Unternehmergesellschaft (Germany - private limited company)
ULC — Unlimited Liability Company
UÜ — Usaldusühing (Estonia - limited partnership)
V.O.F./S.N.C. — Vennootschap Onder Firma / Société en Nom Collectif (Belgium/France - general partnership)
W.L.L. — With Limited Liability (Bahrain, Kuwait, Qatar, Saudi Arabia)
XK — Joint Stock Company (Mongolia)
XXK — Limited Liability Company (Mongolia)
ZAO — Zakrytoe aktionernoye obshchestvo (Russia - closed joint stock company); precedes name of company
Zrt. — Zártköruen muködo részvénytársaság (Hungary - closely held company)

A

A.1 A-Labs Capital II Corp.

Symbol - ALAB.P **Exchange** - TSX-VEN **CUSIP** - 00167A
Head Office - 1000-595 Howe St, Vancouver, BC, V6C 2T5
Email - doron@a-labs.ventures
Investor Relations - Doron Cohen 972-545-224-017
Auditors - RSM Canada LLP C.A., Toronto, Ont.
Lawyers - DuMoulin Black LLP, Vancouver, B.C.
Transfer Agents - Odyssey Trust Company, Calgary, Alta.
Profile - (B.C. 2018) Capital Pool Company.

Recent Merger and Acquisition Activity

Status: terminated **Revised:** Mar. 22, 2023
UPDATE: The transaction was terminated. PREVIOUS: A-Labs Capital II Corp. entered into a letter of intent for the Qualifying Transaction reverse takeover acquisition of Givatayim, Israel-based Orcanos Ltd., which provides an integrated software solution for application lifecycle management and quality management systems, that includes regulatory compliance, with a specialized focus on the medical device industry, for issuance of 86,443,500 common shares. Mar. 31, 2022 - A definitive agreement was entered into. A-Labs would acquire Orcanos for issuance of 72,628,395 post-consolidated common shares (following a 1-for-1.200604 share consolidation) at a deemed price of Cdn$0.32 per share. A-Labs would change its name to Orcanos Holdings Inc. Closing was expected on May 30, 2022, and conditional on the completion of one or more private placements of subscription receipts by Orcanos and/or a special purpose entity established by the directors of Orcanos for a minimum of Cdn$5,120,000 and a maximum of Cdn$8,050,000. June 1, 2022 - Deadline for completion was extended to June 30, 2022. July 4, 2022 - Deadline for completion was extended to Sept. 30, 2022. Sept. 30, 2022 - Deadline for completion was extended to Dec. 29, 2022. Dec. 22, 2022 - The minimum offering amount was lowered to Cdn$3,350,000. Deadline for completion was extended to Jan. 31, 2023.

Directors - Doron Cohen, CEO, Kfar Saba, Israel; Noah Hershcoviz, CFO & corp. sec., Tel Aviv, Israel; Konstantin Lichtenwald, Vancouver, B.C.; Michael Mire, Montréal, Qué.; W. Bruce Rowlands, Toronto, Ont.

Capital Stock

	Authorized (shs.)	Outstanding (shs.)[1]
Common	unlimited	5,762,900

[1] At May 26, 2023

Major Shareholder - Doron Cohen held 34.7% interest and Enrico (Rick) Paolone held 12.15% interest at Apr. 1, 2022.

Price Range - ALAB.P/TSX-VEN

Year	Volume	High	Low	Close
2020............	7,000	$0.12	$0.12	$0.12
2019............	106,250	$0.20	$0.07	$0.07

Capital Stock Changes - There were no changes to capital stock during 2022.

A.2 A-Labs Capital IV Corp.

Symbol - ALCC.P **Exchange** - TSX-VEN **CUSIP** - 00166L
Head Office - 2800 Park Place, 666 Burrard St, Vancouver, BC, V6C 2Z7 **Telephone** - (604) 687-9444
Email - chay.benhamou@gmail.com
Investor Relations - Shay Benhamou (604) 687-9444
Auditors - RSM Canada LLP C.A., Toronto, Ont.
Lawyers - DLA Piper (Canada) LLP
Transfer Agents - TSX Trust Company, Toronto, Ont.
Profile - (B.C. 2018) Capital Pool Company.

Recent Merger and Acquisition Activity

Status: pending **Announced:** Mar. 15, 2022
A-Labs Capital IV Corp. entered into a letter of intent for the Qualifying Transaction acquisition of private Israel-based Nanomedic Technologies Ltd., a biomedical technology company developing and commercializing EHF (Electrospun Healing Fibre) Technology™ and Spincare System which are both used for advanced wound management. The transaction valued Nanomedic at US$60,000,000, prior to giving effect to Nanomedic's planned US$15,000,000 private placement concurrent with (or prior to) the completion of the transaction.

Directors - Shay Benhamou, CEO, Ashdod, Israel; Yosef (Yossi) Shemesh, CFO & corp. sec., Caesarea, Israel; Hillar Lilles, Calgary, Alta.; Robert Wilson, Toronto, Ont.

Capital Stock

	Authorized (shs.)	Outstanding (shs.)[1]
Common	unlimited	4,000,000

[1] At Feb. 28, 2023

Major Shareholder - Shay Benhamou held 27.5% interest and Yosef (Yossi) Shemesh held 12.5% interest at Aug. 20, 2021.

Price Range - ALCC.P/TSX-VEN

Year	Volume	High	Low	Close
2022............	5,000	$0.07	$0.07	$0.07
2021............	3,000	$0.12	$0.12	$0.12
2020............	12,000	$0.16	$0.10	$0.12

Capital Stock Changes - There were no changes to capital stock during fiscal 2021 or fiscal 2022.

A.3 A-Labs Capital V Corp.

Symbol - ALBA.P **Exchange** - TSX-VEN **CUSIP** - 00166V
Head Office - 1110-5255 Yonge St, Toronto, ON, M2N 6P4
Email - rita@alabs.co
Investor Relations - Rita Alter (972) 545-4914
Auditors - RSM Canada LLP C.A., Toronto, Ont.
Transfer Agents - TSX Trust Company, Toronto, Ont.
Profile - (Can. 2018) Capital Pool Company.
Directors - Rita Alter, CEO & corp. sec., Israel; Yosef (Yossi) Shemesh, CFO, Caesarea, Israel; Hillar Lilles, Calgary, Alta.; Wayne Miller, Montréal, Qué.; Jason A. Saltzman, Toronto, Ont.

Capital Stock

	Authorized (shs.)	Outstanding (shs.)[1]
Common	unlimited	6,651,281

[1] At June 21, 2022

Major Shareholder - Rita Alter held 23.63% interest at June 29, 2022.

Price Range - ALBA.P/TSX-VEN

Year	Volume	High	Low	Close
2022............	146,000	$0.14	$0.02	$0.02
2021............	20,000	$0.11	$0.11	$0.11

Recent Close: $0.03

A.4 A2ZCryptocap Inc.

Symbol - AZC.P **Exchange** - TSX-VEN **CUSIP** - 00249B
Head Office - 800-333 7 Ave SW, Calgary, AB, T2P 1Z1 **Telephone** - (403) 262-2803
Email - cgulka@workingcapitalcorp.com
Investor Relations - Christopher Gulka (403) 262-2803
Auditors - Crowe MacKay LLP C.A.
Transfer Agents - Odyssey Trust Company, Calgary, Alta.
Profile - (Alta. 2021) Capital Pool Company.
Directors - Christopher Gulka, pres., CEO, CFO & corp. sec., Alta.; V. E. Dale Burstall, Calgary, Alta.; David Turk, Thornhill, Ont.

Capital Stock

	Authorized (shs.)	Outstanding (shs.)[1]
Common	unlimited	6,040,000

[1] At June 23, 2022

Major Shareholder - V. E. Dale Burstall held 11.26% interest, Christopher Gulka held 11.26% interest and David Turk held 11.26% interest at June 23, 2022.

Price Range - AZC.P/TSX-VEN

Year	Volume	High	Low	Close
2022............	1,347,501	$0.30	$0.12	$0.18

Recent Close: $0.19
Capital Stock Changes - On June 23, 2022, an initial public offering of 4,000,000 common shares was completed at 10¢ per share.

A.5 A2Z Smart Technologies Corp.

Symbol - AZ **Exchange** - TSX-VEN **CUSIP** - 00249W
Head Office - 1600-609 Granville St, Vancouver, BC, V7Y 1C3 **Toll-free** - (866) 824-8938
Website - www.a2zas.com
Email - gadi@a2zas.com
Investor Relations - Gadi P. Levin (866) 824-8938
Auditors - BDO Ziv Haft C.P.A., Tel Aviv, Israel
Transfer Agents - Computershare Trust Company of Canada Inc., Vancouver, B.C.
Employees - 119 at Dec. 31, 2022
Profile - (B.C. 2018) Develops and commercializes retail automation solutions, in particular for large grocery stores and supermarkets, through its Cust2Mate system. Also manufactures precision metal parts; provides maintenance services utilizing the application of advanced engineering capabilities and produces unmanned remote-controlled vehicles and energy power packs for Israeli military/security market; and develops automotive products for the military and civilian automotive industry.

Through 76.77%-owned **Cust2Mate Ltd.**, offers Cust2Mate system which incorporates a smart cart enabling shoppers to checkout automatically without having to unload and reload purchases. Cust2Mate provides unique features for shoppers and retailers such as product information and location, an on-cart scale to weigh items and automatically calculate costs, bar-code scanner and on-board payment system to bypass checkout lines. In addition, the Cust2Mate platform includes big data smart algorithms and computer vision capabilities, allowing for customer specific targeted advertising. Cust2Mate also offers a product that prevents theft when using traditional shopping carts and another product that increases efficiency when picking goods to meet online orders. The platform is being marketed throughout the world, with pilots in North and South America and in the Middle East, and a roll out of product in Israel.

Also developing automotive products including Fuel Tank Inertia Capsule (FTIC) System, a capsule that can be placed in a fuel tank to prevent gas tank explosions; and a vehicle cover device that will protect automobiles from the elements while the vehicle is not in use.

Historically, the company's revenue has primarily been generated from the maintenance services that are provided to the Israeli military/security market. Services include maintenance of technological systems and electrical and electronic equipment, maintenance of refrigeration systems and maintenance of power supplies. Produces products for the Israeli military/security market including unmanned remote-controlled vehicles of various sizes and capabilities designed for intricate bomb disposal, counter terrorism, and firefighting, as well as energy storage power packs, all of which are fully commercialized for military use. Further development of military products has been suspended.

Predecessor Detail - Name changed from A2Z Technologies Canada Corp., July 27, 2020.
Directors - Joseph Ben-Tsur, pres. & CEO, Yavne, Israel; Yonatan de Jongh, Rishon LeZion, Israel; Gadi Graus, Israel; Niv Raz Haim, Israel; Alan Rootenberg, Toronto, Ont.
Other Exec. Officers - Gadi P. Levin, CFO; Amnon Peleg, chief tech. officer; Sam Cole, corp. sec.

Capital Stock

	Authorized (shs.)	Outstanding (shs.)[1]
Preferred	unlimited	nil
Common	unlimited	36,642,158

[1] At July 4, 2023

Major Shareholder - Joseph Ben-Tsur held 31.26% interest at Mar. 27, 2023.

Price Range - AZ/TSX-VEN

Year	Volume	High	Low	Close
2022............	504,888	$14.00	$1.25	$1.90
2021............	4,223,988	$15.00	$2.19	$13.72
2020............	2,575,572	$3.12	$0.81	$2.85
2019............	18,596	$1.95	$0.63	$1.83
2018............	114,285	$0.63	$0.63	$0.63

Consolidation: 1-for-3 cons. in Aug. 2021; 1-for-1.4 cons. in Dec. 2019
Recent Close: $3.09
Capital Stock Changes - In June 2023, private placement of 3,818,275 units (1 common share & ½ warrant) at US$1.80 (CdnS$2.41) per unit was completed, with warrants exercisable at US$2.20 (Cdn$2.93) per share for two years.

In February 2022, 273,774 common shares were issued pursuant to the acquisition of Isramat Ltd. In November 2022, private placement of 2,978,337 units (1 common share & ½ warrant) at US$1.35 per unit was completed. Also during 2022, common shares were issued as follows: 630,161 on exercise of warrants, 545,000 under restricted share unit plan and 116,667 on exercise of options and 74,985 to a trustee.

Wholly Owned Subsidiaries

A2Z Advanced Solutions Ltd., Israel.
- 100% int. in **A2Z Military Solutions Ltd.**, Israel.
- 76.77% int. in **Cust2Mate Ltd.**, Israel.

Isramat Ltd., Israel.

Subsidiaries

80% int. in **AAI Advanced Automotive Innovations, Inc.**, Ont.
Note: The preceding list includes only the major related companies in which interests are held.

Financial Statistics

Periods ended:	12m Dec. 31/22[A]		12m Dec. 31/21[A]
	US$000s	%Chg	US$000s
Operating revenue	**9,351**	**+248**	**2,685**
Cost of sales	5,033		933
Salaries & benefits	7,240		2,633
Research & devel. expense	3,594		2,712
General & admin expense	4,414		4,406
Stock-based compensation	4,868		842
Operating expense	**25,120**	**+118**	**11,526**
Operating income	**(15,769)**	**n.a.**	**(8,841)**
Deprec., depl. & amort.	551		321
Finance costs, gross	1,391		91
Write-downs/write-offs	(382)		nil
Pre-tax income	**(18,347)**	**n.a.**	**(40,148)**
Income taxes	nil		142
Net income	**(18,347)**	**n.a.**	**(40,290)**
Net inc. for equity hldrs	**(16,557)**	**n.a.**	**(39,163)**
Net inc. for non-cont. int.	**(1,790)**	**n.a.**	**(1,127)**
Cash & equivalent	2,616		8,470
Inventories	375		1,147
Accounts receivable	1,373		857
Current assets	6,942		10,968
Fixed assets, net	2,357		1,072
Intangibles, net	3,395		2,091
Total assets	**142,694**	**+910**	**14,131**
Accts. pay. & accr. liabs	3,180		2,088
Current liabilities	6,237		2,372
Long-term debt, gross	1,744		641
Long-term debt, net	341		483
Long-term lease liabilities	605		151

Shareholders' equity	5,286		11,514
Non-controlling interest	(2,397)		(607)
Cash from oper. activs	**(9,431)**	**n.a.**	**(9,378)**
Cash from fin. activs	6,096		12,355
Cash from invest. activs	(1,559)		(280)
Net cash position	**2,616**	**-69**	**8,470**
Capital expenditures	(727)		(412)
Pension fund surplus	33		167
	US$		US$
Earnings per share*	(0.60)		(1.70)
Cash flow per share*	(0.34)		(0.40)
	shs		shs
No. of shs. o/s*	30,945,322		26,326,488
Avg. no. of shs. o/s*	27,681,778		23,340,621
	%		%
Net profit margin	(196.20)		n.m.
Return on equity	(197.11)		n.m.
Return on assets	(21.62)		(349.81)
No. of employees (FTEs)	119		19

* Common
[A] Reported in accordance with IFRS

Latest Results

Periods ended:	3m Mar. 31/23[A]		3m Mar. 31/22[A]
	US$000s	%Chg	US$000s
Operating revenue	4,608	+219	1,446
Net income	(3,843)	n.a.	(2,732)
Net inc. for equity hldrs.	(3,573)	n.a.	(2,347)
Net inc. for non-cont. int.	(270)		(385)
	US$		US$
Earnings per share*	(0.11)		(0.09)

* Common
[A] Reported in accordance with IFRS

Historical Summary
(as originally stated)

Fiscal Year	Oper. Rev.	Net Inc. Bef. Disc.	EPS*
	US$000s	US$000s	US$
2022[A]	9,351	(18,347)	(0.60)
2021[A]	2,685	(40,290)	(1.70)
2020[A]	1,068	(5,953)	(0.36)
2019[A1]	1,306	(2,808)	(0.21)
2018[A2]	1,327	41	0.00

* Common
[A] Reported in accordance with IFRS
[1] Results reflect the Dec. 12, 2019, Qualifying Transaction reverse takeover acquisition of an initial 99.46% interest in A2Z Advanced Solutions Ltd.
[2] Results pertain to A2Z Advanced Solutions Ltd.
Note: Adjusted throughout for 1-for-3 cons. in Aug. 2021; 1-for-1.4 cons. in Dec. 2019

A.6 AADirection Capital Corp.

Symbol - AAD.P **Exchange** - TSX-VEN **CUSIP** - 00253Y
Head Office - 2110 28 St, West Vancouver, BC, V7V 4M3 **Telephone** - (604) 925-0551
Email - maryxm@shaw.ca
Investor Relations - Xiao Qin Ma (604) 779-0016
Auditors - Mao & Ying LLP C.A., Vancouver, B.C.
Transfer Agents - Odyssey Trust Company, Vancouver, B.C.
Profile - (B.C. 2020) Capital Pool Company.
In February 2023, the company agreed to acquire **Centenario Gold Corp.**, which holds option to acquire Eden gold prospect in Mexico, for issuance of 23,138,818 common shares for deemed consideration of $2,257,000. The transaction would constitute the company's Qualifying Transaction and would be completed by way of a three-corned amalgamation. On closing, the company plans to change its name to **Centenario Gold Corp.**
Directors - Xiao Qin (Mary) Ma, CEO & CFO, B.C.; Michael H. Woods, corp. sec., West Vancouver, B.C.; Jackie Cheung, Vancouver, B.C.; Joanne F. Q. Yan, Vancouver, B.C.

Capital Stock

	Authorized (shs.)	Outstanding (shs.)[1]
Common	unlimited	6,000,000

[1] At June 2, 2022
Major Shareholder - Jackie Cheung held 14.17% interest and Joanne F. Q. Yan held 14.17% interest at Apr. 27, 2022.

Price Range - AAD.P/TSX-VEN

Year	Volume	High	Low	Close
2022	57,000	$0.14	$0.13	$0.13
2021	50,000	$0.15	$0.14	$0.14

Recent Close: $0.13
Capital Stock Changes - In February 2023, bought deal public offering of 11,666,667 subscription receipts at $0.15 per receipt was announced, each entitling the holder to receive 1 unit (1 common share & ½ warrant), without payment of additional consideration or further action, upon closing of the proposed Qualifying Transaction acquisition of Centenario Gold Corp.

A.7 AAJ Capital 3 Corp.

Symbol - AAAJ.P **Exchange** - TSX-VEN **CUSIP** - 00036L
Head Office - Royal Centre, 2050-1055 Georgia St W, PO Box 11121, Vancouver, BC, V6E 3P3 **Telephone** - (604) 684-2181
Email - praveen@varshneycapital.com
Investor Relations - Praveen K. Varshney (604) 684-2181
Auditors - Dale Matheson Carr-Hilton LaBonte LLP C.A., Vancouver, B.C.
Lawyers - McMillan LLP, Vancouver, B.C.
Transfer Agents - Olympia Trust Company, Vancouver, B.C.
Profile - (B.C. 2021) Capital Pool Company.
In November 2022, the company entered into a letter of intent for the Qualifying Transaction reverse takeover acquisition of **Iron Bull Mining Inc.** on a share-for-share basis (following a 1-for-4 share consolidation). Iron Bull has mineral interests in Spain and Namibia. In connection, the company would change its name to a name acceptable to Iron Bull and applicable regulatory authorities. Upon closing of the transaction, **Regenx Tech Corp.** (formerly **Mineworx Technologies Ltd.**), which holds 20,000,000 Iron Bull shares, would transfer 17,358,929 shares of the resulting issuer to its shareholders by way of a return of capital.
Directors - Praveen K. Varshney, CEO, CFO & corp. sec., Vancouver, B.C.; Peeyush K. Varshney, Vancouver, B.C.; Tina Wu, Vancouver, B.C.; Besar Xhelili, Ont.

Capital Stock

	Authorized (shs.)	Outstanding (shs.)[1]
Common	unlimited	6,450,000

[1] At Nov. 25, 2022
Major Shareholder - Praveen K. Varshney held 17.05% interest at Aug. 11, 2022.

Price Range - AAAJ.P/TSX-VEN

Year	Volume	High	Low	Close
2022	23,000	$0.15	$0.14	$0.14

Recent Close: $0.14
Capital Stock Changes - On June 14, 2022, an initial public offering of 2,500,000 common shares was completed at 10¢ per share.

A.8 A&W Revenue Royalties Income Fund

Symbol - AW.UN **Exchange** - TSX **CUSIP** - 000255
Head Office - 300-171 Esplanade W, North Vancouver, BC, V7M 3K9 **Telephone** - (604) 988-2141 **Fax** - (604) 988-5531
Website - www.awincomefund.ca
Email - investorrelations@aw.ca
Investor Relations - Kelly A. Blankstein (604) 988-2141
Auditors - PricewaterhouseCoopers LLP C.A., Vancouver, B.C.
Transfer Agents - Computershare Trust Company of Canada Inc., Vancouver, B.C.
Administrators - A&W Trade Marks Inc., North Vancouver, B.C.
Profile - (B.C. 2001) Through indirect subsidiary **A&W Trade Marks Limited Partnership**, holds the A&W trademarks and licenses these trademarks to **A&W Food Services of Canada Inc.** for use in operating and franchising A&W restaurants in Canada.
Indirect subsidiary **A&W Trade Marks Limited Partnership** has granted **A&W Food Services of Canada Inc.** a licence to use the A&W trademarks in Canada expiring on Dec. 30, 2100, in consideration for a royalty, payable by A&W Food Services to the partnership, equal to 3% of the franchise revenue from A&W restaurants across Canada included in the royalty pool.
A&W Food Services and its franchisees operate freestanding restaurants with drive-through facilities, restaurants in shopping centres, urban restaurants or gas/convenience store restaurants on shared sites in Canada. The A&W product line includes The Burger Family® hamburgers, Chubby Chicken® chicken products, A&W Root Beer®, A&W Brew Bar® frozen and espresso beverages, russet thick-cut fries, sweet potato fries, fresh hand-cut onion rings, soft drinks, coffee and breakfast items.
At Jan. 5, 2023, there were 1,037 A&W restaurants in the royalty pool.
On Jan. 5, 2023, 29 restaurants were added and 7 restaurants were removed from the royalty pool.
Trustees - Kevin Mahoney, chr., Vancouver, B.C.; Andrew W. Dunn, Toronto, Ont.; Fern Glowinsky, Toronto, Ont.
Oper. Subsid./Mgt. Co. Officers - Susan D. Senecal, pres. & CEO; Kelly A. Blankstein, CFO; Catherine Anderson, sec.

Capital Stock

	Authorized (shs.)	Outstanding (shs.)[1]
Trust Unit	unlimited	14,585,673
Limited Voting Unit	n.a.	1,507,020
Exchangeable Sec.	n.a.	3,800,721[2]

[1] At Dec. 31, 2022
[2] Securities of A&W Trade Marks Inc.
Trust Unit - Represents an equal undivided interest in the assets of the fund. Redeemable at any time at amounts related to market prices, subject to a maximum of $50,000 in cash redemptions in any one month. Redemption in excess of these amounts, assuming no waiving of the limitation by the trustees of the fund, shall be paid by way of distribution in specie of a pro rata number of securities of A&W Trade Marks Inc. held by the fund. One vote per trust unit.
Limited Voting Unit - Entitled to one vote for each limited voting unit that would be received on conversion of exchangeable securities, provided that such holders are not entitled to more than 40% of the votes cast upon a resolution for the appointment or removal of a trustee or any votes upon a resolution to amend the declaration of trust by which the fund is governed. Held by A&W Food Services of Canada Inc.
Exchangeable Security - Common shares of A&W Trade Marks Inc. Indirectly exchangeable for trust units of the fund on 1-for-2 basis. Held by A&W Food Services of Canada Inc.
Major Shareholder - A&W Food Services of Canada Inc. held 28.1% interest at Mar. 24, 2023.

Price Range - AW.UN/TSX

Year	Volume	High	Low	Close
2022	3,399,407	$43.50	$32.50	$35.61
2021	3,792,408	$41.39	$30.65	$39.80
2020	9,207,861	$39.65	$16.75	$34.06
2019	6,438,992	$47.65	$33.50	$38.58
2018	3,636,742	$37.74	$28.36	$34.13

Recent Close: $33.01
Capital Stock Changes - There were no changes to capital stock during 2022.

Dividends

AW.UN unit Ra $1.92 pa M est. Nov. 30, 2022**[1]
Prev. Rate: $1.86 est. Nov. 30, 2021
Prev. Rate: $1.80 est. Aug. 31, 2021
Prev. Rate: $1.62 est. July 30, 2021
$0.05◆ Dec. 31/21
Paid in 2023: $1.28 2022: $1.87 2021: $1.635 + $0.05◆
[1] Monthly divd normally payable in Apr/20 has been omitted.
** Reinvestment Option ◆ Special

Subsidiaries

83.6% int. in **A&W Trade Marks Inc.**
- 99.9% int. in **A&W Trade Marks Limited Partnership**

Financial Statistics

Periods ended:	12m Dec. 31/22[A]		12m Dec. 31/21[A]
	$000s	%Chg	$000s
Operating revenue	**52,181**	**+11**	**47,081**
General & admin expense	983		817
Operating expense	**983**	**+20**	**817**
Operating income	**51,198**	**+11**	**46,264**
Finance costs, net	3,163		2,558
Pre-tax income	**53,922**	**+17**	**45,955**
Income taxes	12,533		8,101
Net income	**41,389**	**+9**	**37,854**
Net inc. for equity hldrs.	**33,801**	**+12**	**30,051**
Net inc. for non-cont. int.	**7,588**	**-3**	**7,803**
Cash & equivalent	17,109		10,064
Accounts receivable	3,792		3,332
Current assets	21,748		15,943
Intangibles, net	385,429		360,871
Total assets	**411,658**	**+9**	**377,374**
Accts. pay. & accr. liabs	583		631
Current liabilities	9,348		4,108
Long-term debt, gross	59,870		59,803
Long-term debt, net	59,870		59,803
Shareholders' equity	220,984		217,357
Non-controlling interest	105,260		80,240
Cash from oper. activs	**44,264**	**+30**	**34,113**
Cash from fin. activs	(37,219)		(32,597)
Net cash position	**17,109**	**+70**	**10,064**
	$		$
Earnings per share*	2.10		1.94
Cash flow per share*	2.75		2.20
Cash divd. per share*	1.88		1.69
Extra divd. - cash*	nil		0.05
Total divd. per share*	**1.88**		**1.74**
	shs		shs
No. of shs. o/s*	16,092,693		16,092,693
Avg. no. of shs. o/s*	16,092,693		15,509,290
	%		%
Net profit margin	79.32		80.40
Return on equity	15.42		16.30
Return on assets	10.49		10.37

* Trust unit
[A] Reported in accordance with IFRS

Historical Summary
(as originally stated)

Fiscal Year	Oper. Rev.	Net Inc. Bef. Disc.	EPS*
	$000s	$000s	$
2022[A]	52,181	41,389	2.10
2021[A]	47,081	37,854	1.94
2020[A]	40,422	28,374	1.53
2019[A]	44,470	32,558	1.86
2018[A]	40,890	31,575	1.87

* Trust unit
[A] Reported in accordance with IFRS

A.9 ABC Technologies Holdings Inc.

Symbol - ABCT **Exchange** - TSX **CUSIP** - 00076T
Head Office - 2 Norelco Dr, Toronto, ON, M9L 2X6 **Telephone** - (416) 246-1782
Website - abctechnologies.com
Email - investors@abctech.com
Investor Relations - Nathan Barton (416) 246-1782

Auditors - KPMG LLP C.A., Vaughan, Ont.
Lawyers - Blake, Cassels & Graydon LLP
Transfer Agents - Computershare Trust Company of Canada Inc., Toronto, Ont.
FP500 Revenue Ranking - 300
Employees - 8,689 at June 30, 2022
Profile - (B.C. 2018; orig. Ont., 2016) Manufactures and supplies custom, highly engineered, technical plastics and lightweighting innovations to the North American light vehicle industry.

Service offering includes manufacturing, design, engineering, material compounding, machine tooling and equipment building, with more than 25 original equipment manufacturer (OEM) customers served worldwide. Product groups consist of heating, ventilation and air conditioning (HVAC) systems, including IP, battery cooling, console, defroster, floor and overhead ducts; interior systems, including interior garnish, interior trim, load floor and cargo systems, and centre consoles; exterior systems, including bumper, spoilers and winglets, running boards, bed extender, wheel flares, RamBox and rocker panel; fluid management, including coolant reservoir, washer system and power steering reservoir; passenger car air induction systems, including air induction, high temperature turbo duct and air filter; and flexible and other, including prop shaft, constant velocity joint and rack and pinion boots.

Manufacturing capabilities include continuous extrusion/soft-hard-soft, co-injection, hybrid/compression moulding, wrapping, complex assembly, injection moulding, blow moulding, 2-shot moulding/over-moulding, infrared (IR) welding, 3D flashless blow moulding and painting.

Operations are also conducted through the following 50%-owned joint venture companies: **ABC INOAC Exterior Systems Inc.**, a spoiler and body molding manufacturer with class A painting capabilities and facilities in both Canada and Mexico; **ABC INOAC Exterior Systems, LLC**, a spoiler and body molding manufacturer in the U.S. with class A painting capabilities; **Ningbo ABC INOAC Huaxiang Automotive Parts Co., Ltd.**, a manufacturer of HVAC systems, fluid management systems and flexible products in the People's Republic of China (PRC); **ABCOR Filters Inc.**, an automotive air filter manufacturer in Canada used exclusively in the company's in-house air induction systems.

The company's 246,000-sq.-ft. headquarters facility is located in Toronto, Ont., which includes its primary engineering and testing technical centre and manufacturing space. Operations consist of 28 manufacturing facilities principally located throughout North America, as well as in Spain, Poland, Germany, Brazil, PRC and Japan. Also has eight wholly owned regional technical customer and/or design centres, and two regional technical customer and/or design centres operated by the joint ventures, as well as multiple warehouse facilities worldwide.

In October 2022, the company announced plans to shut down its plant in Poland.

Recent Merger and Acquisition Activity

Status: completed **Revised:** Mar. 1, 2023
UPDATE: The transaction was completed. PREVIOUS: ABC Technologies Holdings Inc. agreed to acquire private Windsor, Ont.-based Windsor Mold, Inc. (dba WMG Technologies), a manufacturer of tools for injection molded interior and exterior automotive parts, for US$165,000,000.

Status: completed **Announced:** Feb. 2, 2023
ABC Technologies Holdings Inc. exercised its option to purchase the remaining 10.1% interest in Karl Etzel GmbH for €6,000,000.

Status: completed **Revised:** Feb. 1, 2023
UPDATE: The transaction was completed. PREVIOUS: ABC Technologies Holdings Inc. agreed to sell its 50% interest in ABC INOAC Exterior Systems, LLC. to INOAC Corporation for US$10,000,000.

Status: completed **Revised:** Feb. 1, 2023
UPDATE: The transaction was completed. PREVIOUS: ABC Technologies Holdings Inc. agreed to sell its 50% interest in ABC INOAC Exterior Systems, Inc. to INOAC Canada limited for US$13,000,000.

Status: terminated **Revised:** Jan. 12, 2023
UPDATE: The transaction was terminated. PREVIOUS: ABC Technologies Holdings Inc. agreed to acquire a washer systems product line from Continental Automotive GmbH, a manufacturer of parts for the automotive industry, for €20,500,000. The transaction is expected to close in the second quarter of 2023.

Status: pending **Revised:** Aug. 31, 2022
UPDATE: Part of the transaction was closed for €37,200,000, the remaining transaction is expected to be completed by the second quarter of fiscal 2023. PREVIOUS: ABC Technologies Holdings Inc. agreed to the sale and leaseback of all its real estate properties located in Mühlacker, Germany, obtained through the acquisition of Karl Etzel, for €51,800,000.

Status: completed **Revised:** Mar. 4, 2022
UPDATE: The transaction was completed. PREVIOUS: ABC Technologies Holdings Inc. agreed to acquire an 89.9% interest in Germany-based Karl Etzel GmbH, which manufactures and supplies injection molding plastic products, including plastic components for the automotive industry, for US$95,000,000.

Status: completed **Revised:** Mar. 1, 2022
UPDATE: The transaction was completed. PREVIOUS: ABC Technologies Holdings Inc. agreed to acquire North Canton, Ohio-based dlhBOWLES, Inc., which designs, develops and manufactures automotive fluid management and systems components, for US$255,000,000. dlhBOWLES' products include camera and sensor cleaning systems, windshield washer systems, sunroof drains, powertrain and chassis solutions.

Directors - Barry L. Engle, chr., Utah; Terry Campbell, pres. & CEO, Ont.; Mel Carlisle, Calif.; Patrick C. George, Calif.; Burt Jordan, Mich.; Michael Reiss, N.Y.; Brooke Sorensen, Conn.; James R. (Jim) Voss, Mo.; Jonathan Williams, New York, N.Y.

Other Exec. Officers - Scott Roggenbauer, CFO; Mark Decker, chief HR officer; John Loehr, chief transformation officer; Ryan Conacher, exec. v-p, general counsel & corp. sec.; Mike Fritts, exec. v-p, opers.; Leonard Roelant, exec. v-p, customer experience; Philip Grella, v-p, product and process engineering; François Bérubé, treas.

Capital Stock

	Authorized (shs.)	Outstanding (shs.)[1]
Common	unlimited	115,664,147

[1] At Feb. 11, 2023

Major Shareholder - AP IX Alpha Holdings (Lux) S.A.R.L. held 65.1% interest and Oaktree Capital Management, L.P. held 28.3% interest at Nov. 4, 2022.

Price Range - ABCT/TSX

Year	Volume	High	Low	Close
2022............	1,503,110	$7.37	$3.57	$5.44
2021............	4,718,639	$10.38	$5.75	$7.25

Recent Close: $6.00

Capital Stock Changes - In January 2022, private placement of 5,253,642 common shares was completed at US$4.60 per share. In February 2022, 57,790,064 common shares were issued at Cdn$5.83 per share pursuant to a rights offering. Also during fiscal 2022, 14,030 common shares were issued under a restricted share unit plan.

Dividends

ABCT com Ra $0.15 pa Q est. June 30, 2021
Listed Feb 22/21.
$0.015833i.......... June 30/21
i Initial Payment

Wholly Owned Subsidiaries

ABC Group Intermediate Holdings Inc., Ont.
- 100% int. in **ABC Technologies Inc.**, Toronto, Ont.
  - 100% int. in **ABC Group Japan Inc.**, Japan.
  - 100% int. in **ABC Group Limited**, Ont.
    - 100% int. in **ABC Group Holdings Inc.**, Del.
      - 100% int. in **ABC Automotive Systems Inc.**, Del.
      - 100% int. in **ABC Group Sales & Engineering Inc.**, Del.
      - 100% int. in **ABC Technologies dlhB Holdings Inc.**, Del.
        - 100% int. in **dlhBOWLES, Inc.**, North Canton, Ohio.
          - 99% int. in **dlhBOWLES de Mexico, S. de R.L. de C.V.**, Mexico.
          - 99% int. in **dlhBOWLES Mexico Services, S. de. R.L. de C.V.**, Mexico.
          - 100% int. in **dlhBOWLES Mexsub, LLC**, Mexico.
            - 1% int. in **dlhBOWLES de Mexico, S. de R.L. de C.V.**, Mexico.
            - 1% int. in **dlhBOWLES Mexico Services, S. de. R.L. de C.V.**, Mexico.
    - 100% int. in **ABC Technologies Inc.**, Tenn.
    - 100% int. in **Salga, Inc.**, Ind.
    - 100% int. in **Salga Plastics Inc.**, Tenn.
    - 100% int. in **Undercar Products Group Inc.**, Del.
- 100% int. in **ABC Plastic Moulding Group GmbH**, Germany.
  - 100% int. in **ABC Automobil-Formteile GmbH**, Germany.
  - 100% int. in **Karl Etzel GmbH**, Germany.
  - 100% int. in **Plasticos ABC Spain S.A.**, Spain.
  - 89% int. in **SAM-GmbH**, Germany.
- 100% int. in **ABC Technologies do Brasil Ltda.**, Brazil.
- 100% int. in **ABCHK Global Ventures Limited**, Hong Kong, People's Republic of China.
  - 50% int. in **ABC Auto Parts (Shanghai) Co., Ltd.**, People's Republic of China.
  - 100% int. in **Ningbo ABC INOAC Huaxiang Automotive Parts Co., Ltd.**, People's Republic of China.
  - 100% int. in **Shanghai ABC INOAC Huaxiang Automotive Parts Co., Ltd.**, People's Republic of China.
  - 100% int. in **Shenyang ABC INOAC Huaxiang Automotive Parts Co., Ltd.**, People's Republic of China.
- 50% int. in **ABCOR Filters Inc.**, Ont.
- 100% int. in **Grupo ABC de México, S.A. de C.V.**, Mexico.

Financial Statistics

Periods ended:	12m June 30/22[A]		12m June 30/21[A]
	US$000s	%Chg	US$000s
Operating revenue........................	**971,878**	**0**	**970,850**
Cost of sales..................................	823,596		753,949
Salaries & benefits.........................	49,365		50,372
General & admin expense...............	51,113		55,796
Stock-based compensation............	2,576		1,925
Operating expense........................	**926,650**	**+7**	**862,042**
Operating income.........................	**45,228**	**-58**	**108,808**
Deprec., depl. & amort.....................	93,526		78,615
Finance costs, gross.......................	31,582		46,336
Investment income..........................	498		5,669
Pre-tax income...........................	**(86,988)**	**n.a.**	**(11,248)**
Income taxes...................................	(22,448)		413
Net income...................................	**(64,540)**	**n.a.**	**(11,661)**
Cash & equivalent...........................	79,751		14,912
Inventories......................................	154,661		82,170
Accounts receivable........................	113,456		73,662
Current assets.................................	399,935		208,207
Long-term investments...................	45,556		47,412
Fixed assets, net.............................	371,294		334,775
Right-of-use assets.........................	165,679		153,628
Intangibles, net...............................	265,975		92,290
Total assets..................................	**1,278,272**	**+49**	**855,629**
Accts. pay. & accr. liabs..................	245,693		190,062
Current liabilities.............................	289,118		216,476
Long-term debt, gross.....................	400,000		280,000
Long-term debt, net.........................	400,000		280,000
Long-term lease liabilities...............	175,940		156,400
Shareholders' equity........................	375,760		165,204
Cash from oper. activs..................	**26,805**	**-77**	**115,337**
Cash from fin. activs.......................	363,406		(129,602)
Cash from invest. activs..................	(378,649)		(45,331)
Net cash position.........................	**25,400**	**+70**	**14,912**
Capital expenditures........................	(44,118)		(36,178)
Capital disposals.............................	nil		171
	US$		US$
Earnings per share*.........................	(0.85)		(0.22)
Cash flow per share*.......................	0.35		2.20
Cash divd. per share*......................	$0.15		$0.02
	shs		shs
No. of shs. o/s*...............................	115,580,128		52,522,392
Avg. no. of shs. o/s*........................	76,356,040		52,522,392
	%		%
Net profit margin..............................	(6.64)		(1.20)
Return on equity...............................	(23.86)		(7.52)
Return on assets..............................	(3.85)		4.21
Foreign sales percent.......................	73		74
No. of employees (FTEs)..................	8,689		5,820

* Common
[A] Reported in accordance with IFRS

Latest Results

Periods ended:	6m Dec. 31/22[A]		6m Dec. 31/21[A]
	US$000s	%Chg	US$000s
Operating revenue...........................	639,865	+74	366,854
Net income.......................................	(46,188)	n.a.	(44,612)
	US$		US$
Earnings per share*.........................	(0.40)		(0.85)

* Common
[A] Reported in accordance with IFRS

Historical Summary
(as originally stated)

Fiscal Year	Oper. Rev.	Net Inc. Bef. Disc.	EPS*
	US$000s	US$000s	US$
2022[A]...................	971,878	(64,540)	(0.85)
2021[A]...................	970,850	(11,661)	(0.22)
2020[A1].................	822,887	(26,120)	(0.50)
2019[A1].................	1,057,608	65,156	1.24
2018[A1].................	1,028,336	61,528	1.17

* Common
[A] Reported in accordance with IFRS
[1] As shown in the prospectus dated Feb. 12, 2021. Shares and per share figures adjusted to reflect 525.22392-for-1 split effective immediately prior to the initial public offering by way of secondary offering completed on Feb. 22, 2021.

A.10 AD4 Capital Corp.

Symbol - ADJ.P **Exchange** - TSX-VEN **CUSIP** - 00687F
Head Office - 423 10 St E, North Vancouver, BC, V6L 2E5 **Telephone** - (604) 619-0225
Email - ad4capital@shaw.ca
Investor Relations - Alfredo De Lucrezia (604) 619-0225
Auditors - Davidson & Company LLP C.A., Vancouver, B.C.
Lawyers - Lotz & Company, Vancouver, B.C.
Transfer Agents - Odyssey Trust Company, Vancouver, B.C.

Profile - (B.C. 2021) Capital Pool Company.

Recent Merger and Acquisition Activity

Status: pending **Announced:** Apr. 13, 2023
AD4 Capital Corp. entered into a letter of intent for the Qualifying Transaction reverse takeover acquisition of Nevada-based EEL Energy Limited, which develops, manufactures and markets the kCell energy storage technology and its applications, for issuance of 18,000,000 post-consolidated common shares at a deemed price of US$0.33 per share (following a 1-for-3 share consolidation). One kCell is a 48-volt direct current system than can store 1.38 kW of power. Four kCells (5.5 kW) are combined to create an EEL Power Stack.

Status: pending **Announced:** Apr. 13, 2023
AD4 Capital Corp. agreed to acquire private Whitehorse, Yukon-based 42256 Yukon Inc., which provides engineering, construction and project management services to clients across Canada, for $5,250,000, consisting of $1,250,000 cash and issuance of 10,000,000 post-consolidated common shares valued at $4,000,000 (following a 1-for-3 share consolidation). The transaction would be completed concurrent with the completion of AD4's proposed Qualifying Transaction reverse takeover acquisition of Nevada-based EEL Energy Limited.

Directors - Alfredo De Lucrezia, pres. & CEO, North Vancouver, B.C.; Maurizio Grande, v-p, Vancouver, B.C.; Jeffrey A. Bacha, Vancouver, B.C.; Gordon R. Kettleson, Tsawwassen, B.C.; John L. Pallot, New Westminster, B.C.

Other Exec. Officers - Gary R. McDonald, CFO; Benito J. (Ben) Colangelo, corp. sec.

Capital Stock

	Authorized (shs.)	Outstanding (shs.)[1]
Common	unlimited	15,500,001

[1] At Apr. 14, 2023

Major Shareholder - Alfredo De Lucrezia held 25.81% interest at June 29, 2022.

Price Range - ADJ.P/TSX-VEN

Year	Volume	High	Low	Close
2022	197,505	$0.15	$0.06	$0.06

Recent Close: $0.10

Capital Stock Changes - On June 29, 2022, an initial public offering of 5,000,000 common shares was completed at 10¢ per share.

A.11 ADENTRA Inc.

Symbol - ADEN **Exchange** - TSX **CUSIP** - 00686A
Head Office - Building B, 340-20161 86 Ave, Langley, BC, V2Y 1N2
Telephone - (604) 881-1988 **Fax** - (604) 881-1995
Website - adentragroup.com
Email - ian.tharp@loderockadvisors.com
Investor Relations - Ian Tharp (416) 567-2563
Auditors - KPMG LLP C.A., Vancouver, B.C.
Bankers - Bank of America Canada
Lawyers - Osler, Hoskin & Harcourt LLP, Vancouver, B.C.
Transfer Agents - Computershare Trust Company of Canada Inc., Vancouver, B.C.
FP500 Revenue Ranking - 162
Employees - 3,080 at Dec. 31, 2022

Profile - (Can. 2011; orig. B.C., 2004) Distributes speciality architectural building products to customers that supply products to the repair and remodel, residential construction, and commercial and diversified markets in North America.

Operates 87 distribution facilities (as at Mar. 10, 2023) across the U.S. and Canada that are organized into five flagship brands consisting of: Hardwoods Specialty Products Canada (8) and Hardwoods Specialty Products US (24); Rugby Architectural Building Products (33); Paxton Hardwoods (4); Novo Building Products (13); and Mid-Am Building Supply (5). Product portfolio includes architectural panels, trim, moulding and millwork, stair parts and railings, interior and exterior doors, windows, kitchen cabinets, decorative surfaces, decorative and functional hardware, plywood, hardwood lumber and boards, veneers, fasteners and adhesives, roofing, decking and siding.

Provides supply solutions to more than 75,000 customers and clients using four channels to market: industrial, consisting primarily of small and mid-sized manufacturers of residential, commercial and institutional cabinets, furniture, retail fixtures, mouldings and millwork, and specialty markets such as custom motor coaches and yacht interiors; ProDealers, consisting of small to large traditional retail lumberyards that supply building materials to contractors and custom and production home builders and renovators; home centres, consisting of big box building material retailers that sell directly to consumers and contractors; and architects and designers, with the needs of 24,000 North American architects and designer clients supported through the company's DesignOneSource specification team.

On Feb. 13, 2023, the company acquired all the assets and certain liabilities of Lubbock, Tex.-based **Rojo Distributors, Inc.**, a wholesale distributor of laminate, solid surface and quartz surfacing products and adhesives serving the West Texas market, for US$1,300,000.

Predecessor Detail - Name changed from Hardwoods Distribution Inc., Dec. 2, 2022.

Directors - Graham M. Wilson, chr., North Vancouver, B.C.; Robert J. (Rob) Brown, pres. & CEO, B.C.; Peter M. Bull, B.C.; Charlotte F. Burke, Toronto, Ont.; George R. Judd, Ga.; Michelle A. Lewis, Tex.; Jim C. Macaulay, Mich.; Qi Tang, Toronto, Ont.; Robert L. (Rob) Taylor, Tex.

Exec. Officers - Lance R. Blanco, sr. v-p, corp. devel.; David (Dave) Hughes, sr. v-p, acqs.; Dan B. Figgins, v-p, imports; Faiz H. Karmally, v-p, CFO & corp. sec.; Renee V. Murdoch, v-p, HR; Jason R. West, v-p, Canada; Drew H. Dickinson, pres., U.S. industrials; Jeffrey W. (Jeff) Leys, pres., ProDealer & Home Center

Capital Stock

	Authorized (shs.)	Outstanding (shs.)[1]
Common	unlimited	22,343,886

[1] At May 11, 2023

Normal Course Issuer Bid - The company plans to make normal course purchases of up to 1,735,401 common shares representing 10% of the public float. The bid commenced on Jan. 3, 2023, and expires on Dec. 31, 2023.

Major Shareholder - Peter M. Bull held 18.9% interest at Mar. 21, 2023.

Price Range - ADEN/TSX

Year	Volume	High	Low	Close
2022	18,765,167	$49.58	$22.66	$28.34
2021	15,152,478	$49.34	$24.35	$44.80
2020	13,394,580	$29.00	$7.40	$25.32
2019	10,390,417	$16.75	$10.75	$16.30
2018	8,948,590	$21.41	$10.04	$10.99

Recent Close: $33.10

Capital Stock Changes - During 2022, 240,482 common shares were issued under long-term incentive plan and 1,245,028 common shares were repurchased under a Normal Course Issuer Bid.

Dividends

ADEN com Ra $0.52 pa Q est. Jan. 27, 2023
Prev. Rate: $0.48 est. Jan. 28, 2022
Prev. Rate: $0.40 est. Jan. 29, 2021
Prev. Rate: $0.34 est. Jan. 31, 2020

Wholly Owned Subsidiaries

HDI Insurance Ltd., Barbados.
Hardwoods Specialty Products GP II Inc., B.C.
Hardwoods Specialty Products GP Inc., Canada.
- 1% int. in **Hardwoods Specialty Products LP**, Man.

Subsidiaries

99% int. in **Hardwoods Specialty Products LP**, Man.
- 1% int. in **Hardwoods Specialty Products (Washington) Corp.**, Wash.

99% int. in **Hardwoods Specialty Products (Washington) Corp.**, Wash.
- 1% int. in **Hardwoods Finance Company Inc.**, Del.
- 100% int. in **Hardwoods Specialty Products ULC**, B.C.
  - 1% int. in **Hardwoods USLP II LP**, Del.
- 100% int. in **Hardwoods Specialty Products US GP, Inc.**, Del.
  - 1% int. in **Hardwoods Specialty Products US LP, Inc.**, Del.
- 20% int. in **Hardwoods Specialty Products US LP, Inc.**, Del.
  - 100% int. in **Hardwoods Holdco 3 LLC**, Del.
  - 100% int. in **Mid-Am Holdings, LLC**, Del.
  - 100% int. in **Novo Building Products Holdings, LLC**, Mich.
    - 100% int. in **Novo Building Products, LLC**, Del.
      - 100% int. in **Novo Distribution, LLC**, Mich.
      - 100% int. in **Novo Manufacturing, LLC**, Del.
  - 100% int. in **Paxton Hardwoods LLC**, Del.
  - 100% int. in **Rugby Holdings LLC**, N.H.

99% int. in **Hardwoods USLP II LP**, Del.
- 100% int. in **Hardwoods Holdco 1 ULC**, B.C.
  - 100% int. in **Hardwoods US LLC**, Del.
- 100% int. in **Hardwoods Holdco 2 ULC**, B.C.
  - 100% int. in **Hardwoods Finance LLC**, Del.

Financial Statistics

Periods ended:	12m Dec. 31/22^A		12m Dec. 31/21^A
	US$000s	%Chg	US$000s
Operating revenue	**2,579,568**	**+60**	**1,616,199**
Cost of goods sold	1,988,597		1,216,495
Salaries & benefits	241,205		159,304
General & admin expense	83,780		49,953
Stock-based compensation	3,899		5,537
Operating expense	**2,317,481**	**+62**	**1,431,289**
Operating income	**262,087**	**+42**	**184,910**
Deprec., depl. & amort.	65,455		36,579
Finance costs, net	33,862		10,680
Pre-tax income	**162,770**	**+18**	**137,651**
Income taxes	34,102		34,506
Net income	**128,668**	**+25**	**103,145**
Cash & equivalent	65,068		7,762
Inventories	485,758		463,572
Accounts receivable	188,122		164,945
Current assets	759,206		668,692
Fixed assets, net	36,116		27,844
Right-of-use assets	158,861		140,770
Intangibles, net	462,250		265,651
Total assets	**1,428,974**	**+28**	**1,114,924**
Bank indebtedness	5,890		7,677
Accts. pay. & accr. liabs	129,197		113,696
Current liabilities	433,428		292,449
Long-term debt, gross	610,400		407,514
Long-term debt, net	346,032		273,573
Long-term lease liabilities	135,877		124,053
Shareholders' equity	506,972		414,032
Cash from oper. activs	**210,685**	**n.a.**	**(65,418)**
Cash from fin. activs	128,608		378,850
Cash from invest. activs	(279,470)		(306,627)
Net cash position	**65,068**	**+738**	**7,762**
Capital expenditures	(7,859)		(4,463)
Capital disposals	771		559
	US$		US$
Earnings per share*	5.50		4.81
Cash flow per share*	9.01		(3.05)
Cash divd. per share*	$0.48		$0.40
	shs		shs
No. of shs. o/s*	22,694,088		23,698,634
Avg. no. of shs. o/s*	23,394,072		21,436,451
	%		%
Net profit margin	4.99		6.38
Return on equity	27.94		31.15
Return on assets	10.12		12.94
Foreign sales percent	92		89
No. of employees (FTEs)	3,080		2,734

* Common
A Reported in accordance with IFRS

Latest Results

Periods ended:	3m Mar. 31/23^A		3m Mar. 31/22^A
	US$000s	%Chg	US$000s
Operating revenue	579,857	-10	644,883
Net income	9,597	-78	43,487
	US$		US$
Earnings per share*	0.43		1.83

* Common
A Reported in accordance with IFRS

Historical Summary
(as originally stated)

Fiscal Year	Oper. Rev.	Net Inc. Bef. Disc.	EPS*
	US$000s	US$000s	US$
2022^A	2,579,568	128,668	5.50
2021^A	1,616,199	103,145	4.81
	$000s	$000s	$
2020^A	1,245,312	37,602	1.78
2019^A	1,171,921	29,581	1.38
2018^A	1,134,267	32,159	1.50

* Common
A Reported in accordance with IFRS

A.12 ADF Group Inc.

Symbol - DRX **Exchange** - TSX **CUSIP** - 00089N
Head Office - 300 rue Henry-Bessemer, Terrebonne, QC, J6Y 1T3
Telephone - (450) 965-1911 **Toll-free** - (800) 263-7560 **Fax** - (450) 965-8558
Website - www.adfgroup.com
Email - jeanfrancois.boursier@adfgroup.com
Investor Relations - Jean-François Boursier (800) 263-7560
Auditors - PricewaterhouseCoopers LLP C.A., Montréal, Qué.
Bankers - National Bank of Canada, Montréal, Qué.
Lawyers - Fasken Martineau DuMoulin LLP, Montréal, Qué.
Transfer Agents - Computershare Trust Company of Canada Inc., Montréal, Qué.
FP500 Revenue Ranking - 603

Employees - 638 at Jan. 31, 2023

Profile - (Can. 1979) Provides connections design and engineering, fabrication, including industrial coating, and installation services for complex steel structures, heavy built-ups, and miscellaneous and architectural metalwork to the non-residential construction industry in the U.S. and Canada.

Services are provided to the non-residential construction industry including general contractors, project owners, engineering firms and project architects, structural steel erectors and other structural steel fabricators of commercial, institutional, industrial and public segments.

Facilities include a 630,000-sq.-ft. steel fabrication complex, including a 42,000-sq.-ft. paint shop, in Terrebonne, Que., with an annual fabrication capacity of 100,000 tons of steel; a 100,000-sq.-ft. steel fabrication plant, with an annual fabrication capacity of 25,000 tons of steel, and an adjacent 48,000-sq.-ft. paint shop in Great Falls, Mont.; and a 13,200-sq.-ft. sales office and equipment warehouse in Pompano Beach, Fla.

At Jan. 31, 2023, the company's order backlog was $376,500,000 compared with $373,100,000 at Jan. 31, 2022.

Directors - Jean Paschini, chr. & CEO, Rosemère, Qué.; Pierre Paschini, pres. & COO, Boisbriand, Qué.; Marise Paschini, exec. v-p, treas. & corp. sec., Saint-Léonard, Qué.; Jean Rochette†, Longueuil, Qué.; Myriam Blouin, Qué.; Danilo D'Aronco, Qué.; Richard Martel, Qué.; Guy Pelletier, Montréal, Qué.

Other Exec. Officers - Jean-François Boursier, CFO

† Lead director

Capital Stock

	Authorized (shs.)	Outstanding (shs.)[1]
Preferred	unlimited	nil
Multiple Voting	unlimited	14,343,107
Subordinate Voting	unlimited	18,297,099

[1] At Apr. 14, 2023

Multiple Voting - Convertible at any time, at the holder's option, into one subordinate voting share. Ten votes per share.

Subordinate Voting - Non-convertible. One vote per share.

Major Shareholder - Jean Paschini held 29.67% interest, Pierre Paschini held 29.67% interest and Marise Paschini held 29.66% interest at Apr. 14, 2023.

Price Range - DRX/TSX

Year	Volume	High	Low	Close
2022............	2,647,210	$2.29	$1.36	$2.10
2021............	8,254,228	$2.38	$1.30	$1.61
2020............	4,477,356	$1.65	$0.55	$1.49
2019............	4,058,957	$1.75	$0.97	$1.30
2018............	981,958	$2.28	$0.94	$1.03

Recent Close: $4.15

Capital Stock Changes - During fiscal 2023, 5,000 subordinate voting shares were issued on exercise of options.

Dividends

DRX com S.V. Ra $0.02 pa S est. May 16, 2011

Wholly Owned Subsidiaries

ADF Group USA Inc., Del.
- 100% int. in **ADF Industrial Coating Inc.**, Great Falls, Mont.
- 100% int. in **ADF International Inc.**, Fort Lauderdale, Fla.
  - 100% int. in **ADF Structural Steel Inc.**, Calif.
- 100% int. in **ADF Steel Corp.**, Plattsburgh, N.Y.

Financial Statistics

Periods ended:	12m Jan. 31/23[A]		12m Jan. 31/22[A]
	$000s	%Chg	$000s
Operating revenue........................	**250,890**	**-11**	**280,740**
Cost of goods sold..........................	211,194		252,316
General & admin expense...............	13,577		10,665
Operating expense........................	**224,771**	**-15**	**262,981**
Operating income........................	**26,119**	**+47**	**17,759**
Deprec., depl. & amort....................	5,323		5,054
Finance costs, gross........................	1,999		1,174
Pre-tax income............................	**16,854**	**+52**	**11,059**
Income taxes..................................	1,919		1,496
Net income...................................	**14,935**	**+56**	**9,563**
Cash & equivalent...........................	7,193		7,130
Inventories......................................	10,679		9,690
Accounts receivable........................	75,793		26,391
Current assets................................	154,380		91,102
Fixed assets, net.............................	90,378		83,629
Right-of-use assets.........................	21,848		21,587
Intangibles, net...............................	3,640		3,357
Total assets..................................	**271,617**	**+35**	**201,050**
Accts. pay. & accr. liabs..................	39,985		34,421
Current liabilities............................	88,781		52,389
Long-term debt, gross.....................	47,185		32,059
Long-term debt, net.........................	44,927		28,702
Long-term lease liabilities................	3,528		3,772
Shareholders' equity........................	124,985		108,450
Cash from oper. activs..................	**2,612**	**-2**	**2,669**
Cash from fin. activs........................	14,157		9,202
Cash from invest. activs...................	(12,081)		(21,989)
Net cash position..........................	**7,193**	**+1**	**7,130**
Capital expenditures........................	(11,463)		(21,477)
	$		$
Earnings per share*.........................	0.46		0.29
Cash flow per share*.......................	0.08		0.08
Cash divd. per share*......................	0.02		0.02
	shs		shs
No. of shs. o/s*...............................	32,640,206		32,635,206
Avg. no. of shs. o/s*........................	32,640,206		32,635,206
	%		%
Net profit margin............................	5.95		3.41
Return on equity..............................	12.80		9.19
Return on assets..............................	7.07		5.41
Foreign sales percent......................	85		86
No. of employees (FTEs).................	638		579

* M.V. & S.V.

[A] Reported in accordance with IFRS

Historical Summary
(as originally stated)

Fiscal Year	Oper. Rev.	Net Inc. Bef. Disc.	EPS*
	$000s	$000s	$
2023[A]...................	250,890	14,935	0.46
2022[A]...................	280,740	9,563	0.29
2021[A]...................	172,593	6,867	0.21
2020[A]...................	179,710	(2,132)	(0.07)
2019[A]...................	135,073	(374)	(0.01)

* M.V. & S.V.

[A] Reported in accordance with IFRS

A.13 AEterna Zentaris Inc.

Symbol - AEZS **Exchange** - TSX **CUSIP** - 007975

Head Office - 315 Sigma Dr, Suite 302D, Charleston, SC, United States, 29486 **Telephone** - (843) 900-3223

Website - www.zentaris.com

Email - aezs@jtcir.com

Investor Relations - Jenene Thomas (833) 475-8247

Auditors - Deloitte LLP C.A.

Lawyers - Ropes & Gray LLP; Norton Rose Fulbright Canada LLP, Montréal, Qué.

Transfer Agents - Computershare Trust Company of Canada Inc., Montréal, Qué.

Employees - 21 at Dec. 31, 2022

Profile - (Can. 1990) Develops and commercializes pharmaceutical and diagnostic products for various medical conditions.

Lead product, Macrilen™ (macimorelin), is an orally available peptidomimetic ghrelin receptor agonist which stimulates the secretion of growth hormone from the pituitary gland into the circulatory system by binding to the ghrelin receptor (GHSR-1a), and which has potential uses in both endocrinology and oncology indications. It has been approved by the U.S. FDA and European Medicines Agency as a diagnostic test for adult growth hormone deficiency (AGHD). Macrilen is commercialized in the U.S. and Canada as well as in the U.K., Europe and the Republic of Korea under the Ghryvelin™ brand . The company is also leveraging the Phase 3 clinical success and compelling safety profile of macimorelin for the diagnosis of childhood-onset growth hormone deficiency (CGHD) and is pursuing business development opportunities for the commercialization of macimorelin in Asia and other countries.

Development pipeline includes macimorelin therapeutic for the treatment of Lou Gehrig's disease or amyotrophic lateral sclerosis (ALS); autoimmunity modifying therapeutics for the treatment of neuromyelitis optica spectrum disorder (NMOSD) and Parkinson's disease (PD); and delayed clearance parathyroid hormone (DC-PTH) fusion polypeptides for the therapeutic treatment of chronic hypoparathyroidism.

In March 2023, **Atnahs Pharma U.K. Limited** (Pharmanovia) acquired from the company's existing partner **Consilient Health, Ltd.** the exclusive rights and licence for commercialization of macimorelin in Europe and the United Kingdom under the Ghryvelin™ brand for an undisclosed amount.

In January 2023, the company decided to discontiue the development of an oral prophylactic bacterial vaccines against each of SARS-CoV-2 (COVID-19) and chlamydia trachomatis.

In August 2022, **Novo Nordisk A/S** exercised its right to terminate the development and commercialization licence agreement signed by the company and Novo Nordisk for Macrilen™ (macimorelin) in the U.S. and Canada. As a result, the companyregained full U.S. and Canadian rights to the product.

Predecessor Detail - Name changed from AEterna Laboratories Inc., June 3, 2004; basis 1 com. for 1 subord. vtg. sh.

Directors - Carolyn Egbert, chr., Houston, Tex.; Dr. Klaus Paulini, pres., CEO & man. dir., AEterna Zentaris GmbH, Hessen, Germany; Peter G. Edwards, Ohio; Gilles R. Gagnon, Sherbrooke, Qué.; Dennis Turpin, Qué.

Other Exec. Officers - Dr. Nicola Ammer, sr. v-p, clinical devel. & CMO; Dr. Matthias Gerlach, sr. v-p, mfg. & supply chain; Dr. Eckhard G. Guenther, sr. v-p, bus. devel. & alliance mgt.; Giuliano La Fratta, sr. v-p & CFO; Dr. Michael Teifel, sr. v-p, non-clinical devel. & chief scientific officer; Güenther Grau, v-p, fin.

Capital Stock

	Authorized (shs.)	Outstanding (shs.)[1]
First Preferred	unlimited	nil
Second Preferred	unlimited	nil
Common	unlimited	4,855,876

[1] At May 9, 2023

Major Shareholder - Widely held at May 9, 2023.

Price Range - AEZS/TSX

Year	Volume	High	Low	Close
2022............	580,209	$13.50	$4.00	$4.30
2021............	2,434,144	$115.75	$11.25	$11.38
2020............	478,110	$50.00	$9.25	$13.50
2019............	196,708	$185.75	$25.25	$29.75
2018............	189,310	$128.50	$37.50	$101.50

Consolidation: 1-for-25 cons. in July 2022

Recent Close: $3.65

Capital Stock Changes - On July 21, 2022, common shares were consolidated on a 1-for-25 basis.

Wholly Owned Subsidiaries

AEterna Zentaris GmbH, Frankfurt am Main, Germany.
- 100% int. in **Zentaris IVF GmbH**, Frankfurt am Main, Germany.

AEterna Zentaris, Inc., Charleston, S.C.

Financial Statistics

Periods ended:	12m Dec. 31/22[A]		12m Dec. 31/21[A]
	US$000s	%Chg	US$000s
Operating revenue	**5,640**	**+7**	**5,260**
Cost of sales	157		90
Research & devel. expense	12,506		6,574
General & admin expense	8,095		7,122
Operating expense	**20,758**	**+51**	**13,786**
Operating income	**(15,118)**	**n.a.**	**(8,526)**
Deprec., depl. & amort.	135		145
Finance costs, net	(876)		(194)
Write-downs/write-offs	(8,350)		nil
Pre-tax income	**(22,727)**	**n.a.**	**(8,477)**
Income taxes	nil		(109)
Net income	**(22,727)**	**n.a.**	**(8,368)**
Cash & equivalent	50,611		65,300
Inventories	229		73
Accounts receivable	732		1,314
Current assets	55,488		70,820
Fixed assets, net	40		42
Right-of-use assets	176		150
Intangibles, net	nil		8,755
Total assets	**56,026**	**-30**	**80,102**
Accts. pay. & accr. liabs	3,828		2,672
Current liabilities	7,044		7,766
Long-term lease liabilities	65		31
Shareholders' equity	35,776		52,986
Cash from oper. activs	**(13,680)**	**n.a.**	**(8,581)**
Cash from fin. activs	(118)		51,037
Cash from invest. activs	(12)		(658)
Net cash position	**50,611**	**-22**	**65,300**
Capital expenditures	(11)		(30)
Capital disposals	nil		1
	US$		US$
Earnings per share*	(4.68)		(1.75)
Cash flow per share*	(2.82)		(1.87)
	shs		shs
No. of shs. o/s*	4,855,876		4,855,880
Avg. no. of shs. o/s*	4,855,876		4,596,980
	%		%
Net profit margin	(402.96)		(159.09)
Return on equity	(51.21)		(25.28)
Return on assets	(33.39)		(14.26)
Foreign sales percent	100		100
No. of employees (FTEs)	21		17

* Common
[A] Reported in accordance with IFRS

Latest Results

Periods ended:	3m Mar. 31/23[A]		3m Mar. 31/22[A]
	US$000s	%Chg	US$000s
Operating revenue	2,128	+40	1,517
Net income	(4,255)	n.a.	(2,640)
	US$		US$
Earnings per share*	(0.88)		(0.50)

* Common
[A] Reported in accordance with IFRS

Historical Summary
(as originally stated)

Fiscal Year	Oper. Rev. US$000s	Net Inc. Bef. Disc. US$000s	EPS* US$
2022[A]	5,640	(22,727)	(4.68)
2021[A]	5,260	(8,368)	(1.75)
2020[A]	3,652	(5,118)	(3.00)
2019[A]	532	(6,042)	(8.75)
2018[A]	26,881	4,187	6.25

* Common
[A] Reported in accordance with IFRS
Note: Adjusted throughout for 1-for-25 cons. in July 2022

A.14 AF2 Capital Corp.

Symbol - AF.P **Exchange** - TSX-VEN **CUSIP** - 001094
Head Office - Five Bentall Centre, 2300-550 Burrard St, Vancouver, BC, V6C 2B5
Email - jheld@aloefinance.com
Investor Relations - Jonathan Held (416) 907-5644
Auditors - SRCO Professional Corporation C.A., Richmond Hill, Ont.
Lawyers - Gowling WLG (Canada) LLP
Transfer Agents - Odyssey Trust Company, Vancouver, B.C.
Profile - (B.C. 2020) Capital Pool Company.
Directors - Michael B. Galloro, CEO, Toronto, Ont.; John Muffolini, Toronto, Ont.; Peter Simeon, Oakville, Ont.
Other Exec. Officers - Jonathan Held, CFO & corp. sec.

Capital Stock

	Authorized (shs.)	Outstanding (shs.)[1]
Preferred	unlimited	nil
Common	unlimited	5,000,000

[1] At Jan. 27, 2023

Major Shareholder - Michael B. Galloro held 26% interest at Mar. 15, 2021.

Price Range - AF.P/TSX-VEN

Year	Volume	High	Low	Close
2022	68,000	$0.18	$0.08	$0.09
2021	104,950	$0.20	$0.10	$0.15

Recent Close: $0.09
Capital Stock Changes - There were no changes to capital stock during fiscal 2022.

A.15 AGF Management Limited*

Symbol - AGF.B **Exchange** - TSX **CUSIP** - 001092
Head Office - CIBC Square, Tower One, 3900-81 Bay St, Toronto, ON, M5J 0G1 **Telephone** - (416) 367-1900 **Toll-free** - (888) 243-4668
Website - www.agf.com
Email - investorrelations@agf.com
Investor Relations - Courtney Learmont (888) 243-4668
Auditors - PricewaterhouseCoopers LLP C.A., Toronto, Ont.
Transfer Agents - Computershare Trust Company of Canada Inc.
FP500 Revenue Ranking - 482
Employees - 634 at Nov. 30, 2022
Profile - (Ont. 1960) Provides investment management for mutual funds, factor-based exchange traded funds (ETF), institutions and corporations, private wealth clients and access to private markets. Has investment operations and client servicing teams in North America and Europe.

Investment Capabilities

Fundamental includes equity and fixed income strategies covering a spectrum of objectives from wealth accumulation and risk management to income-generating solutions. The company has capabilities in global and North American equity and fixed income, as well as in the areas of sustainable and alternative investing.

Quantitative delivers custom solutions designed to provide better risk-adjusted returns by utilizing a multi-factor process. The company has developed a proprietary research and database platform which allows to define customized factors and build risk models and portfolio optimizations tailored to achieve investment objectives of each strategy.

Private Wealth provides customized investment services for high net worth individuals, endowments and foundations in key markets across Canada. The platform includes wholly owned **Cypress Capital Management Limited**, **Doherty & Associates Ltd.** and **Highstreet Asset Management Inc.**

Private Capital includes joint ventures with **Stream Asset Financial Management LP** and **AGF SAF Private Credit Management LP**, and fee-earning arrangements with **Instar Group Inc.** and **First Ascent Ventures**. Private Capital is a diversified private markets business that caters to the needs of retail brokers, family offices and institutions. Private Capital generates multiple streams for the company including management fee-related earnings, carried interest, other fee arrangements and invested capital.

Assets Under Management

Year ended Nov. 30	2022	2021
	$000,000s	$000,000s
Mutual funds[1]	23,898	24,006
Institutional, sub-advisory & ETF	8,514	9,082
Private client	7,275	7,366
Private alternatives	2,132[2]	2,181[3]
	41,819	42,635

[1] Includes retail, pooled funds and institutional client AUM invested in customized series offered within mutual funds.
[2] Includes $2.08 billion of fee-earning assets.
[3] Includes $2.11 billion of fee-earning assets.

Other Operations

The company offers fund administration services to its mutual funds, and through wholly owned **AGF Investments LLC**, has the capability to deliver a comprehensive trading infrastructure for ETFs and 40-Act vehicles in the United States. In addition, through its joint venture, **AGFWave Asset Management Inc.**, the company provides asset management services and products in The People's Republic of China and South Korea.

Predecessor Detail - Name changed from A.G.F. Management Limited, Dec. 2, 1994.
Directors - Col. (honry.) Blake C. Goldring, exec. chr., Toronto, Ont.; Kevin McCreadie, CEO & chief invest. officer, Toronto, Ont.; Judy G. Goldring, pres. & head, global distrib., Toronto, Ont.; G. Wayne Squibb†, Toronto, Ont.; Dr. Jane M. Buchan, Newport Beach, Calif.; Kathleen M. Camilli, New York, N.Y.; Ian L. T. Clarke, Pickering, Ont.; Charles Guay, Outremont, Qué.; Cybele Negris, B.C.
Other Exec. Officers - Chris Jackson, COO; Ken Tsang, CFO; Jenny Quinn, chief acctg. officer; Ashley (Ash) Lawrence, sr. v-p & head, alternatives; W. Robert Farquharson, v-chr., emeritus
† Lead director

Capital Stock

	Authorized (shs.)	Outstanding (shs.)[1]
Class A Vtg.	unlimited	57,600
Class B Non-vtg.	unlimited	65,125,966

[1] At May 31, 2023

Class A Voting - Rank junior to the class B shares. Privately held. One vote per share.
Class B Non-Voting - Rank senior to the class A shares. Dividends may be paid either in cash or in the form of additional class B shares at the shareholder's option. Non-voting.
Options - At Nov. 30, 2022, options were outstanding to purchase 4,701,833 class B non-voting shares at a weighted average exercise price of $5.90 per share with a weighted average remaining life of 2.9 years.
Normal Course Issuer Bid - The company plans to make normal course purchases of up to 4,397,923 class B non-voting shares representing 10% of the public float. The bid commenced on Feb. 8, 2023, and expires on Feb. 7, 2024.
Major Shareholder - Col. (honry.) Blake C. Goldring held 80% interest and W. Robert Farquharson held 20% interest at Nov. 30, 2022.

Price Range - AGF.B/TSX

Year	Volume	High	Low	Close
2022	30,334,983	$8.52	$5.63	$7.07
2021	35,023,001	$8.50	$5.95	$8.35
2020	56,392,201	$7.26	$2.50	$6.08
2019	31,285,099	$6.50	$4.51	$6.44
2018	27,801,385	$8.27	$4.27	$4.82

Recent Close: $7.56
Capital Stock Changes - In November 2022, 3,488,646 class B non-voting shares were repurchased under a Substantial Issuer Bid. Also during fiscal 2022, class B non-voting shares were issued as follows: 612,243 on exercise of options, 357,750 under employee benefit trust and 65,477 under dividend reinvestment plan. In addition, 2,795,892 class B non-voting shares were repurchased under a Normal Course Issuer Bid and 300,000 class B non-voting shares were repurchased for the employee benefit trust.

Dividends

AGF.B cl B cum. part. N.V. Ra $0.44 pa Q est. Apr. 21, 2023**
Prev. Rate: $0.40 est. Apr. 20, 2022
Prev. Rate: $0.36 est. July 20, 2021
Prev. Rate: $0.32 est. Apr. 17, 2015
** Reinvestment Option

Long-Term Debt - At Nov. 30, 2022, outstanding long-term debt totaled $21,587,000 (none current) and consisted entirely of borrowings under an unsecured revolving credit facility due on Nov. 6, 2025.

Wholly Owned Subsidiaries

AGF International Advisors Company Ltd., Ireland.
AGF Investments America Inc., Ont.
AGF Quantitative Advisors, Inc., Del.
- 99.9% int. in **AGF Investments LLC**, Del.

AGF Quantitative Advisors #2, Inc., Del.
- 0.1% int. in **AGF Investments LLC**, Del.

1801882 Alberta Ltd., Alta.
- 100% int. in **1936874 Ontario Ltd.**, Ont.

20/20 Financial Corporation, Oakville, Ont.
- 100% int. in **AGF Investments Inc.**, Toronto, Ont.
  - 100% int. in **Cypress Capital Management Limited**, Vancouver, B.C.
    - 100% int. in **Cypress Capital Management US Limited**, Vancouver, B.C.
  - 100% int. in **Doherty & Associates Ltd.**, Ottawa, Ont.
  - 100% int. in **Highstreet Asset Management Inc.**, London, Ont.

2593269 Ontario Inc., Ont.

Investments

50% int. in **AGFWave Asset Management Inc.**, Ont.
15% int. in **Priviti Capital Corporation**, Alta.

Financial Statistics

Periods ended:	12m Nov. 30/22^A		12m Nov. 30/21^oA
	$000s	%Chg	$000s
Total revenue	**469,004**	**+2**	**461,679**
Salaries & benefits	126,277		132,160
General & admin. expense	60,883		54,164
Stock-based compensation	7,703		9,638
Other operating expense	172,537		200,633
Operating expense	**367,400**	**-7**	**396,595**
Operating income	**101,604**	**+56**	**65,084**
Deprec. & amort.	11,652		10,490
Finance costs, gross	2,693		2,796
Pre-tax income	**87,259**	**+68**	**51,798**
Income taxes	20,612		12,501
Net income	**66,647**	**+70**	**39,297**
Cash & equivalent	79,301		109,558
Current assets	122,468		153,016
Long-term investments	200,721		161,504
Fixed assets, net	29,227		19,009
Right-of-use assets	70,178		76,065
Intangibles	941,063		941,147
Total assets	**1,368,989**	**+1**	**1,359,365**
Accts. pay. & accr. liabs	74,481		82,247
Current liabilities	75,717		86,817
Long-term debt, gross	21,587		nil
Long-term debt, net	21,587		nil
Long-term lease liabilities	80,279		80,710
Shareholders' equity	1,030,546		1,031,123
Cash from oper. activs	**64,600**	**+35**	**47,803**
Cash from fin. activs	(52,130)		(30,727)
Cash from invest. activs	(40,334)		(24,601)
Net cash position	**58,620**	**-32**	**86,484**
Capital expenditures, net	(16,339)		(13,273)
	$		$
Earnings per share*	0.97		0.56
Cash flow per share*	0.94		0.68
Cash divd. per share*	0.39		0.34
	shs		shs
No. of shs. o/s*	64,465,414		70,014,484
Avg. no. of shs. o/s*	68,430,165		70,009,123
	%		%
Net profit margin	14.21		8.51
Return on equity	6.47		3.84
Return on assets	5.04		3.06
No. of employees (FTEs)	634		631

* Class A & B
^o Restated
^A Reported in accordance with IFRS

Latest Results

Periods ended:	6m May 31/23^A		6m May 31/22^A
	$000s	%Chg	$000s
Total revenue	243,687	+1	242,361
Net income	47,856	+109	22,952
	$		$
Earnings per share*	0.73		0.33

* Class A & B
^A Reported in accordance with IFRS

Historical Summary
(as originally stated)

Fiscal Year	Total Rev.	Net Inc. Bef. Disc.	EPS*
	$000s	$000s	$
2022^A	469,004	66,647	0.97
2021^A	461,679	39,297	0.56
2020^A	543,919	173,908	2.25
2019^A	436,687	47,858	0.61
2018^A	450,203	72,993	0.94

* Class A & B
^A Reported in accordance with IFRS

A.16 AI Artificial Intelligence Ventures Inc.

Symbol - AIVC **Exchange** - TSX-VEN **CUSIP** - 00135V
Head Office - 1000-409 Granville St, Vancouver, BC, V6C 1T2 **Telephone** - (604) 689-5002
Email - chris@cherryconsulting.ca
Investor Relations - Christopher P. Cherry (604) 908-3095
Auditors - De Visser Gray LLP C.A., Vancouver, B.C.
Lawyers - Norton Rose Fulbright Canada LLP, Calgary, Alta.
Transfer Agents - TSX Trust Company, Toronto, Ont.
Profile - (B.C. 2017; orig. Can., 2010) Invests in businesses and projects which promote positive environmental and social impacts.

Holdings include equity and debt investments in various companies; wholly owned **Soilgenic Nutrients Inc.**, which is focused on developing sustainable and organic fertilizers; and 22.96% interest (**Encanto Potash Corp.** 77.04%) in Muskowekwan First Nation potash project in Saskatchewan, carried at nominal value.

In December 2022, the company acquired 14,000,000 common shares at 2¢ per share of **Glenmac Capital Inc.** for debt settlement of $280,000. The common shares represented 91.4% of the issued and outstanding shares of Glenmac.

Predecessor Detail - Name changed from ESG Global Impact Capital Inc., June 29, 2023.

Directors - David A. Berg, interim CEO, La Quinta, Calif.; Christopher P. (Chris) Cherry, CFO, Vancouver, B.C.; Eugene A. Hodgson, Vancouver, B.C.; Nicholas F. (Nick) Watters, Victoria, B.C.

Other Exec. Officers - Todd Violette, chief invest. officer; Jeff Ivan, CEO, Soilgenic Nutrients Inc.

Capital Stock

	Authorized (shs.)	Outstanding (shs.)[1]	Par
Series B Preferred	5,000,000	730,000[2]	$10
Common	unlimited	32,025,453	n.p.v.

[1] At June 29, 2023
[2] All held by Encanto Potash Corp.

Series B Preferred - Entitled to dividends. Convertible, at the company's option, into 10 common shares based upon either of the following options: redeem $1.00 every 180 days or a maximum of $2.00 within a 12-month period. One vote per share.

Common - One vote per share.

Major Shareholder - Widely held at July 13, 2020.

Price Range - AIVC/TSX-VEN

Year	Volume	High	Low	Close
2022	4,965,637	$0.16	$0.02	$0.04
2021	3,627,710	$0.44	$0.12	$0.13
2020	12,386,487	$0.33	$0.03	$0.20
2019	5,756,957	$0.83	$0.03	$0.03
2018	14,493,907	$3.81	$0.29	$0.39

Consolidation: 1-for-3 cons. in Apr. 2020
Recent Close: $0.23
Capital Stock Changes - During fiscal 2022, 2,307,692 common shares were issued for debt settlement.

Wholly Owned Subsidiaries

Soilgenic Nutrients Inc., B.C.

Financial Statistics

Periods ended:	12m Aug. 31/22^A		12m Aug. 31/21^oA
	$000s	%Chg	$000s
Realized invest. gain (loss)	278		2,325
Unrealized invest. gain (loss)	(5,433)		2,961
Total revenue	**(5,139)**	**n.a.**	**5,314**
General & admin. expense	302		891
Operating expense	**302**	**-66**	**891**
Operating income	**(5,441)**	**n.a.**	**4,423**
Finance costs, gross	8		18
Write-downs/write-offs	(57)		(6,388)
Pre-tax income	**(5,505)**	**n.a.**	**(1,299)**
Net income	**(5,505)**	**n.a.**	**(1,299)**
Cash & equivalent	4,316		9,478
Current assets	5,101		10,552
Total assets	**5,101**	**-52**	**10,552**
Bank indebtedness	nil		72
Accts. pay. & accr. liabs	426		470
Current liabilities	834		862
Long-term debt, gross	260		371
Long-term debt, net	nil		100
Preferred share equity	6,388		6,388
Shareholders' equity	4,266		9,590
Cash from oper. activs	**(87)**	**n.a.**	**(62)**
Cash from fin. activs	(72)		72
Cash from invest. activs	292		(887)
Net cash position	**188**	**+236**	**56**
	$		$
Earnings per share*	(0.18)		(0.04)
Cash flow per share*	(0.00)		(0.00)
	shs		shs
No. of shs. o/s*	31,825,453		29,517,761
Avg. no. of shs. o/s*	30,549,641		29,490,638
	%		%
Net profit margin	n.m.		(24.44)
Return on equity	n.m.		(33.76)
Return on assets	(70.24)		(11.72)

* Common
^o Restated
^A Reported in accordance with IFRS

Latest Results

Periods ended:	3m Nov. 30/22^A		3m Nov. 30/21^A
	$000s	%Chg	$000s
Total revenue	1,017	n.a.	(887)
Net income	967	n.a.	(930)
	$		$
Earnings per share*	0.03		(0.03)

* Common
^A Reported in accordance with IFRS

Historical Summary
(as originally stated)

Fiscal Year	Total Rev.	Net Inc. Bef. Disc.	EPS*
	$000s	$000s	$
2022^A	(5,139)	(5,505)	(0.18)
2021^A	5,314	(1,299)	(0.04)
2020^A	32	1,797	0.08
2019^A	26	(3,812)	(0.17)
2018^A	69	(10,109)	(0.52)

* Common
^A Reported in accordance with IFRS

Note: Adjusted throughout for 1-for-3 cons. in Apr. 2020

A.17 AI/ML Innovations Inc.

Symbol - AIML **Exchange** - CSE **CUSIP** - 00143Y
Head Office - 203-645 Fort St, Victoria, BC, V8W 1G2 **Telephone** - (778) 405-0882 **Toll-free** - (833) 751-0882
Website - aiml-innovations.com
Email - info@aiml-innovations.com
Investor Relations - Tim Daniels (778) 405-0882
Auditors - Baker Tilly WM LLP C.A., Vancouver, B.C.
Bankers - Royal Bank of Canada
Lawyers - Dentons Canada LLP, Vancouver, B.C.
Transfer Agents - Endeavor Trust Corporation, Vancouver, B.C.
Profile - (B.C. 2009; orig. B.C., 1983) Invests in the digital health and well being companies that leverage artificial intelligence (AI), machine learning (ML), cloud computing and digital platforms to drive transformative healthcare management solutions and precision support delivery.

Health Gauge Inc. (70% owned; formerly **Salu Design Group Inc.**) has developed Phoenix smart watch, a wearable solution which provides health monitoring (blood pressure, heart rate, sleep, activity and stress). Also provides digital health solutions utilizing accelerometers, ECG (electrocardiogram), PPG (photoplethysmorgram; used to measure blood volume changes in tissue) and other forms of physiological sensors to measure heart rate, heart rate variability, pulse oximetry, pulse wave velocity, pulse transit time, blood pressure and activity. The intellectual property also includes proprietary methods and intellectual property relating to behavioural tagging for the purposes of psychometric analysis. Also developing Alakin, a digital therapy and remote patient monitoring platform which allows hospitals and clinics to undertake "no code" value-based care programs with their patients.

Along with the digital health monitoring devices and AI-based software, a cloud computing platform is combined to help caregivers, patients and healthcare professionals access and utilize relevant health data.

AI Rx Inc. (70% owned; 30% **Tech2Health S.A.S.**) holds exclusive North American commercial usage rights to Tech2Health's complete portfolio of digital mental wellness and health-tech products and platform services, patents, technologies, brands and trademarks. The company also holds 9.44% interest in Tech2Health, a digital mental health provider.

In September 2021, the company agreed to acquire up to a 22.22% interest in Paris, France-based **Tech2Heal S.A.S.** for €2,000,000 cash and formed a joint venture, **AI Rx Inc.**, owned 70% by the company and 30% by Tech2Health. AI Rx was granted 100% of the North American rights to the exclusive commercial use of all products, brands and trademarks owned by Tech2Health for issuance of 1,500,000 common shares by the company at a deemed price of Cdn$0.80 per share. Tech2Health has developed Qookka Live, which provides mental and emotional health preventive and support services to corporations and health insurers from within one cohesive app. As at December 2022, the company has paid €1,000,000 for a 9.44% interest in Tech2Heal.

In November 2022, the company agreed to acquire the remaining 30% interest in **Health Gauge Inc.**, a private technology company operating in the digital health care space, in exchange for 1,800,000 incentive warrant Bs, with each warrant exchangeable for no further consideration into one common shares of the company upon completion of certain revenue performance conditions. Upon completion, the company would own 100% interest in Health Gauge.

Predecessor Detail - Name changed from Aiml Resources Inc., Nov. 6, 2020.

Directors - Tim Daniels, exec. chr., Florence, Italy; Randy Duguay, pres. & CEO, Edmonton, Alta.; Bruce Matichuk, chief technical officer, Edmonton, Alta.; Nicholas F. (Nick) Watters, Victoria, B.C.

Other Exec. Officers - David A. (Dave) Cross, CFO

Capital Stock

	Authorized (shs.)	Outstanding (shs.)[1]
Common	unlimited	36,692,770

[1] At Dec. 29, 2022

Major Shareholder - Widely held at June 20, 2022.

Price Range - AIML/CSE

Year	Volume	High	Low	Close
2022	9,186,393	$0.30	$0.03	$0.08
2021	29,280,903	$1.59	$0.21	$0.26
2020	1,233,711	$0.31	$0.10	$0.29
2019	275,381	$0.35	$0.10	$0.15
2018	243,175	$0.55	$0.25	$0.25

Consolidation: 1-for-10 cons. in Feb. 2020
Recent Close: $0.11
Capital Stock Changes - During fiscal 2022, common shares were issued as follows: 4,000,000 by private placement, 1,186,800 on

exercise of warrants, 350,000 on exercise of options and 311,799 for services.

Subsidiaries

70% int. in **AI Rx Inc.**, United States.
70% int. in **Health Gauge Inc.**, Edmonton, Alta. Formerly Salu Design Group Inc.

Investments

Carolina Rush Corporation, Toronto, Ont. (see Survey of Mines)
9.44% int. in **Tech2Health S.A.S.**, Paris, France.
• 30% int. in **AI Rx Inc.**, United States.

Financial Statistics

Periods ended:	12m Apr. 30/22[A]		12m Apr. 30/21[oA]
	$000s	%Chg	$000s
Operating revenue	**65**	**n.a.**	**nil**
Salaries & benefits	565		158
Research & devel. expense	392		94
General & admin expense	2,080		698
Stock-based compensation	338		482
Operating expense	**3,375**	**+136**	**1,431**
Operating income	**(3,310)**	**n.a.**	**(1,431)**
Deprec., depl. & amort.	42		nil
Finance costs, gross	66		41
Investment income	(26)		nil
Write-downs/write-offs	nil		(1,417)
Pre-tax income	**(3,550)**	**n.a.**	**(2,827)**
Net income	**(3,550)**	**n.a.**	**(2,827)**
Net inc. for equity hldrs	**(3,173)**	**n.a.**	**(2,726)**
Net inc. for non-cont. int.	**(377)**	**n.a.**	**(101)**
Cash & equivalent	525		3,485
Inventories	5		2
Accounts receivable	25		35
Current assets	895		3,594
Long-term investments	1,060		nil
Right-of-use assets	84		n.a.
Total assets	**2,040**	**-43**	**3,594**
Bank indebtedness	12		163
Accts. pay. & accr. liabs	483		409
Current liabilities	1,460		1,465
Long-term debt, gross	157		157
Long-term debt, net	40		40
Long-term lease liabilities	51		n.a.
Shareholders' equity	1,084		2,307
Non-controlling interest	(595)		(218)
Cash from oper. activs	**(3,024)**	**n.a.**	**(931)**
Cash from fin. activs	1,275		4,172
Cash from invest. activs	(1,143)		(11)
Net cash position	**475**	**-86**	**3,367**
Capital expenditures	nil		(28)
	$		$
Earnings per share*	(0.11)		(0.17)
Cash flow per share*	(0.10)		(0.06)
	shs		shs
No. of shs. o/s*	34,930,270		29,081,671
Avg. no. of shs. o/s*	30,586,669		16,662,352
	%		%
Net profit margin	n.m.		n.a.
Return on equity	(187.14)		n.m.
Return on assets	(123.68)		(142.36)

* Common
[o] Restated
[A] Reported in accordance with IFRS

Latest Results

Periods ended:	6m Oct. 31/22[A]		6m Oct. 31/21[A]
	$000s	%Chg	$000s
Operating revenue	172	n.a.	nil
Net income	(890)	n.a.	(2,240)
Net inc. for equity hldrs	(845)	n.a.	(2,044)
Net inc. for non-cont. int	(45)		(195)
	$		$
Earnings per share*	(0.03)		(0.07)

* Common
[A] Reported in accordance with IFRS

Historical Summary
(as originally stated)

Fiscal Year	Oper. Rev.	Net Inc. Bef. Disc.	EPS*
	$000s	$000s	$
2022[A]	65	(3,550)	(0.11)
2021[A]	nil	(2,827)	(0.17)
2020[A]	nil	(216)	(0.02)
2019[A]	nil	(167)	(0.02)
2018[A]	nil	(124)	(0.01)

* Common
[A] Reported in accordance with IFRS
Note: Adjusted throughout for 1-for-10 cons. in Feb. 2020

A.18 AIM5 Ventures Inc.

Symbol - AIME.P **Exchange** - TSX-VEN **CUSIP** - 00901M
Head Office - 400-77 King St W, Toronto, ON, M5K 0A1 **Telephone** - (647) 987-5083
Email - zach@libertyvp.co
Investor Relations - Zachary Goldenberg (647) 987-5083
Auditors - MNP LLP C.A., Toronto, Ont.
Transfer Agents - TSX Trust Company, Toronto, Ont.
Profile - (Ont. 2020) Capital Pool Company.

Recent Merger and Acquisition Activity

Status: terminated **Revised:** Jan. 3, 2023
UPDATE: The transaction was terminated. PREVIOUS: AIM5 Ventures Inc. entered into a letter of intent for the Qualifying Transaction reverse takeover acquisition of private Grand Bend, Ont.-based ChargerQuest Inc., which owns and operates electric vehicle (EV) charging infrastructure hosted at real estate properties, businesses, municipalities and high-traffic hubs. Terms of the transaction were to be subsequently disclosed.

Directors - Zachary Goldenberg, CEO & corp. sec., Toronto, Ont.; Aaron Salz, CFO, Toronto, Ont.; Alan Friedman, Toronto, Ont.; Marc Sontrop, Toronto, Ont.; Aaron Unger, Toronto, Ont.

Capital Stock

	Authorized (shs.)	Outstanding (shs.)[1]
Common	unlimited	6,550,000

[1] At Oct. 31, 2022

Major Shareholder - Widely held at Nov. 24, 2020.

Price Range - AIME.P/TSX-VEN

Year	Volume	High	Low	Close
2022	5,000	$0.16	$0.16	$0.16
2021	294,100	$0.24	$0.14	$0.14
2020	19,000	$0.20	$0.20	$0.20

Recent Close: $0.07

Capital Stock Changes - There were no changes to capital stock during fiscal 2022.

A.19 AIM6 Ventures Inc.

Symbol - AIMF.P **Exchange** - TSX-VEN **CUSIP** - 00147P
Head Office - 400-77 King St W, Toronto, ON, M5K 0A1 **Telephone** - (647) 987-5083
Email - zach@libertyvp.co
Investor Relations - Zachary Goldenberg (647) 987-5083
Auditors - MNP LLP C.A., Toronto, Ont.
Lawyers - Dentons Canada LLP, Toronto, Ont.
Transfer Agents - TSX Trust Company, Toronto, Ont.
Profile - (Ont. 2021) Capital Pool Company.

On Apr. 17, 2023, the company entered into a letter of intent for the Qualifying Transaction reverse takeover acquisition of **Copper Bullet Mines Inc.**, which holds Copper Springs prospect in Arizona.

Directors - Zachary Goldenberg, CEO & corp. sec., Toronto, Ont.; Aaron Salz, CFO, Toronto, Ont.; Alan Friedman, Toronto, Ont.; Marc Sontrop, Toronto, Ont.; Aaron Unger, Toronto, Ont.

Capital Stock

	Authorized (shs.)	Outstanding (shs.)[1]
Common	unlimited	8,900,000

[1] At Mar. 31, 2022

Major Shareholder - Widely held at Apr. 30, 2021.

Price Range - AIMF.P/TSX-VEN

Year	Volume	High	Low	Close
2022	337,100	$0.20	$0.07	$0.07
2021	61,000	$0.18	$0.12	$0.13

Recent Close: $0.08

A.20 AIP Realty Trust

Symbol - AIP.U **Exchange** - TSX-VEN **CUSIP** - 00149W
Head Office - HSBC Building, 2200-885 Georgia St W, Vancouver, BC, V6C 3E8 **Telephone** - (778) 918-8262
Website - www.aiprealtytrust.com
Email - greg.vorwaller@aiprealtytrust.com
Investor Relations - Gregory S. Vorwaller (778) 918-8262
Auditors - MNP LLP C.A., Calgary, Alta.
Transfer Agents - TSX Trust Company, Calgary, Alta.
Profile - (Alta. 2017) Acquires light industrial flex facilities focused on the trades and services sectors.

The trust owns a 22,400-sq.-ft. light industrial flex multi-tenant property (Eagle Court) in Lewisville, Tex., a suburb within the Dallas-Fort Worth (DFW) Metroplex. At April 2022, the trust has an agreement to acquire five more facilities under development in the DFW Metroplex totaling 376,000 sq. from **AllTrades Industrial Properties, Inc.**, a Dallas, Tex.-based developer and manager of light industrial flex properties. Also has an exclusive agreement to acquire all completed and leased AllTrades facilities being developed across North America and will provide mezzanine financing to AllTrades to acquire new locations and develop and construct facilities.

AllTrades' space are designed to meet the needs of trades and services business. Producing offerings include WorkSpace Shops, WorkSpace Studios and WorkSpace Parking.

Recent Merger and Acquisition Activity

Status: completed **Revised:** Apr. 14, 2022
UPDATE: The transaction was completed. PREVIOUS: Value Capital Trust entered into a letter of intent for the reverse takeover acquisition of private Toronto, Ont.-based AIP Yield Fund, LP (AIPYF), which finances the construction of, acquires and manages light industrial flex multi-tenant properties being developed across North America, on a unit-for-unit basis, which would have an implied value of US$3.75 per AIPYF unit (following a proposed 1-for-30 class A consolidation by Value). AIPYF holds the exclusive rights to purchase all completed AllTrades Industrial Properties, Inc. properties being developed across North America, including six facilities under development in the Dallas Fort Worth, Tex., submarkets with a projected completion value of US$86,000,000. In addition, as part of the transaction, Value would acquire all of the assets of AIP Eagle Court, LLC (AIPEC) for US$5,200,000, consisting of U$1,900,000 cash and assumption of AIPEC's permanent mortgage of US$3,300,000. Feb. 18, 2021 - As part of the transaction, AIPYF would amalgamate with a wholly owned subsidiary of Value to form a newly amalgamated company as the general partner of AIPYF, resulting in Value being the sole limited partner of AIPYF and a subsidiary of Value would be the general partner of AIPYF. Upon completion, Value would change its name to AIP Yield Fund Trust. In conjunction with, and prior to completion of the transaction, AIPYF planned to complete a private placement of up to US$20,000,000 of units. Oct. 1, 2021 - The letter of intent was extended to Sept. 30, 2021. Private placement was amended to US$5,000,000 and up to US$8,500,000 art US$2.00 per unit. Dec. 17, 2021 - A fourth extension to Jan. 31, 2022, was agreed to. Private placement of 2,752,500 subscription receipts at US$2.00 per receipt was completed. Feb. 4, 2022 - The parties entered into a definitive agreement. Prior to completion, AIPGP ULC would be appointed by AIPYF as its general partner and AIPGP would resign as general partner of AIPYF, and (ii) holders of class A units of AIPYF, including those issued upon the conversion of the subscription receipts and class B units of AIPYF would receive one post-consolidated unit of Value for each AIPYF unit held. Immediately thereafter, it is expected that AIPGP ULC and a subsidiary would then amalgamate. Upon completion of the amalgamation, the newly amalgamated entity would be the general partner of AIPYF and Value would be the limited partner of AIPYF. Following the amalgamation, the amalgamated entity and AIPYF would be wound up into Value and the assets of AIPYF (including AIP Realty, the sole beneficial owner of AIPEC, which holds the Eagle Court property, would be transferred to Value.

Predecessor Detail - Name changed from Value Capital Trust, Apr. 21, 2022, pursuant to the Qualifying Transaction reverse takeover acquisition of AIP Yield Fund, LP.; basis 1 new for 20 old shs.

Trustees - Leslie Wulf, exec. chr. & chief capital officer, Richardson, Tex.; Gregory S. (Greg) Vorwaller, pres. & CEO, Vancouver, B.C.; Bruce Hall, CFO, Tex.; Samantha Adams, Vancouver, B.C.; Kobi Dorenbush, Ont.; Brian Shibley, Tex.; Nathan Smith, Grand Cayman, Cayman Islands

Capital Stock

	Authorized (shs.)	Outstanding (shs.)[1]
Preferred Unit	unlimited	nil
Trust Unit	unlimited	3,421,985

[1] At May 25, 2023

Major Shareholder - Alpha Carta Ltd. held 35.84% interest at Apr. 21, 2022.

Price Range - AIP.U/TSX-VEN

Year	Volume	High	Low	Close
2022	351,930	US$2.59	US$1.11	US$1.25
2019	15,950	US$1.70	US$0.80	US$0.80
2018	48,290	US$3.60	US$1.60	US$1.70

Consolidation: 1-for-20 cons. in Apr. 2022
Recent Close: US$0.66

Capital Stock Changes - In April 2022, trust units were consolidated on a 1-for-20 basis and 2,837,861 post-consolidated trust units were issued pursuant to the Qualifying Transaction reverse takeover acquisition of AIP Yield Fund, LP.

Dividends

AIP.U cl A unit Ra US$0.08 pa Q est. Apr. 17, 2023
Listed Apr 21/22.
Prev. Rate: US$0.16 est. July 15, 2022
US$0.04**i** July 15/22
i Initial Payment

Wholly Owned Subsidiaries

AIP Eagle Court, LLC, Tex.
AIP Realty, LLC, Nev.
AIP Realty Management LLC, Nev.
AIP Realty USA, Inc., Nev.

A.21 AKITA Drilling Ltd.*

Symbol - AKT.A **Exchange** - TSX **CUSIP** - 009905
Head Office - 1000-333 7 Ave SW, Calgary, AB, T2P 2Z1 **Telephone** - (403) 292-7979 **Fax** - (403) 292-7990
Website - www.akita-drilling.com
Email - darcy.reynolds@akita-drilling.com
Investor Relations - Darcy Reynolds (403) 292-7530
Auditors - PricewaterhouseCoopers LLP C.A., Calgary, Alta.
Bankers - ATB Financial, Calgary, Alta.
Lawyers - Bennett Jones LLP, Calgary, Alta.
Transfer Agents - Odyssey Trust Company, Calgary, Alta.
FP500 Revenue Ranking - 652
Employees - 1,067 at Dec. 31, 2022
Profile - (Alta. 1992) Provides contract drilling services to the oil and gas industry in Canada and the U.S. In addition to conventional drilling, specializes in purpose-built drilling rigs, including self-moving pad rigs, and is active in directional, horizontal and underbalanced drilling.

The company is hired by independent oil and gas companies, major international oil and gas companies and their affiliates, and mining companies, as an independent contractor to drill oil and gas wells, potash exploration and development wells, and geothermal wells and wells to be developed into storage caverns for gas. At Dec. 31, 2022, the company had 36 drilling rigs (14 were wholly owned), of which 20 were in western Canada, which consists of 13 electric drilling rigs and seven mechanical drilling rigs; and 16 in the U.S., which consists of 14 electric drilling rigs and two diesel electric rigs. During 2022, the company provided drilling services to 27 different customers in Canada and 27 different customers in the U.S.

The company has its head office in Calgary, Alta., and operation facilities in Nisku, Alta., Evans, Colo., and Midland, Tex.

Operating Statistics:

	2022	2021
Operating days		
Canada	2,518	1,594
United States	4,088	2,871
Revenue per oper. day		
Canada	$30,753	$25,515
United States	$31,996	$24,878
Utilization rate		
Canada	34%	22%
United States	70%	49%

During the first quarter of 2023, the company sold certain components, including the centre section of one of its idle rigs in the U.S., for $2,027,000.

Periods ended:	12m Dec. 31/22	12m Dec. 31/21
No. of drill rigs	36	36
Drill rig operating days	6,606	4,465
Drill rig rev. per oper. day $	62,749	50,393
Drill rig util. rate, %	50	34

Directors - Linda A. Southern-Heathcott, exec. chr., Calgary, Alta.; Nancy C. Southern, deputy chr., Calgary, Alta.; Loraine M. Charlton, Calgary, Alta.; Douglas A. (Doug) Dafoe, Calgary, Alta.; Harish K. Mohan, Calgary, Alta.; Robert J. (Rob) Peabody, Calgary, Alta.; Henry G. (Harry) Wilmot, Calgary, Alta.; Charles W. Wilson, Boulder, Colo.

Other Exec. Officers - Colin A. Dease, pres. & CEO; Darcy Reynolds, v-p, fin. & CFO

Capital Stock

	Authorized (shs.)	Outstanding (shs.)[1]
First Preferred	unlimited	nil
Second Preferred	unlimited	nil
Class A Non-Vtg.	unlimited	37,996,407
Class B Common	unlimited	1,653,784

[1] At Aug. 1, 2023

Class A Non-Voting - Entitled to dividends.

Class B Common - Entitled to dividends. Convertible into class A non-voting shares at the shareholders' option on a share-for-share basis. One vote per share.

Options - At Dec. 31, 2022, options were outstanding to purchase 1,422,500 class A non-voting shares at a weighted average exercise price of $1.94 per share with a weighted average remaining contractual life of 6.6 years.

Major Shareholder - Nancy Southern, Linda Southern-Heathcott & Margaret E. Southern Spousal Trust held 86% interest at Mar. 20, 2023.

Price Range - AKT.A/TSX

Year	Volume	High	Low	Close
2022	20,529,992	$2.96	$0.89	$1.73
2021	7,237,398	$1.54	$0.50	$0.94
2020	21,337,476	$1.22	$0.25	$0.48
2019	8,875,312	$4.42	$0.75	$1.19
2018	2,192,743	$8.38	$3.41	$4.07

Recent Close: $1.77

Capital Stock Changes - During 2022, 42,000 class A non-voting shares were issued on exercise of options.

Long-Term Debt - At Dec. 31, 2022, outstanding long-term debt totaled $93,514,000 (none current) and consisted entirely of borrowings under a $110,000,000 operating loan facility, bearing interest at prime plus 2.25% to 3.5% and due September 2024.

Wholly Owned Subsidiaries

AKITA Equipment Corp., United States.
- 100% int. in **AKITA Drilling U.S.A. Corp.**, Tex.

Xtreme Drilling Corp., Houston, Tex. Inactive.

Investments

50% int. in **Akita Equtak Drilling Ltd.**
50% int. in **Akita Mistiyapew Aski Drilling Ltd.**
50% int. in **Akita Wood Buffalo Drilling Ltd.**

Financial Statistics

Periods ended:	12m Dec. 31/22[A]		12m Dec. 31/21[A]
	$000s	%Chg	$000s
Operating revenue	**200,996**	**+83**	**110,088**
Cost of goods sold	151,884		89,835
General & admin expense	13,864		11,706
Stock-based compensation	677		507
Operating expense	**166,425**	**+63**	**102,048**
Operating income	**34,571**	**+330**	**8,040**
Deprec., depl. & amort.	30,263		28,838
Finance income	41		5
Finance costs, gross	6,777		3,553
Investment income	5,954		1,981
Pre-tax income	**3,539**	**n.a.**	**(21,782)**
Income taxes	(749)		(792)
Net income	**4,288**	**n.a.**	**(20,990)**
Cash & equivalent	13,311		1,773
Accounts receivable	46,868		27,228
Current assets	61,778		30,223
Long-term investments	2,887		2,376
Fixed assets, net	200,550		211,469
Right-of-use assets	1,515		1,829
Total assets	**268,281**	**+8**	**247,574**
Accts. pay. & accr. liabs	12,238		6,987
Current liabilities	30,657		23,721
Long-term debt, gross	93,514		86,156
Long-term debt, net	93,514		84,439
Long-term lease liabilities	803		1,341
Shareholders' equity	137,851		131,485
Cash from oper. activs	**18,198**	**n.a.**	**(3,461)**
Cash from fin. activs	5,970		10,197
Cash from invest. activs	(13,598)		(11,805)
Net cash position	**13,311**	**+651**	**1,773**
Capital expenditures	(17,982)		(16,416)
Capital disposals	133		272
Unfunded pension liability	4,279		5,463
	$		$
Earnings per share*	0.11		(0.53)
Cash flow per share*	0.46		(0.09)
	shs		shs
No. of shs. o/s*	39,650,191		39,608,191
Avg. no. of shs. o/s*	39,622,805		39,608,191
	%		%
Net profit margin	2.13		(19.07)
Return on equity	3.18		(14.79)
Return on assets	4.85		(7.04)
Foreign sales percent	72		74
No. of employees (FTEs)	1,067		1,060

* Class A & B
[A] Reported in accordance with IFRS

Latest Results

Periods ended:	6m June 30/23[A]		6m June 30/22[A]
	$000s	%Chg	$000s
Operating revenue	123,349	+40	87,946
Net income	15,699	n.a.	(7,185)
	$		$
Earnings per share*	0.40		(0.18)

* Class A & B
[A] Reported in accordance with IFRS

Historical Summary
(as originally stated)

Fiscal Year	Oper. Rev.	Net Inc. Bef. Disc.	EPS*
	$000s	$000s	$
2022[A]	200,996	4,288	0.11
2021[A]	110,088	(20,990)	(0.53)
2020[A]	119,664	(93,274)	(2.35)
2019[A]	175,890	(19,875)	(0.50)
2018[A]	118,361	(15,939)	(0.65)

* Class A & B
[A] Reported in accordance with IFRS

A.22 ALDD Ventures Corp.

Symbol - ALDD.P **Exchange** - TSX-VEN **CUSIP** - 00160Y

Head Office - 600-905 Pender St W, Vancouver, BC, V6C 1L6 **Telephone** - (604) 721-9191

Email - simon@athenacpa.ca

Investor Relations - Tak Tsan Tso (604) 721-9191

Auditors - Mao & Ying LLP C.A., Vancouver, B.C.

Lawyers - Segev LLP, Vancouver, B.C.

Transfer Agents - Odyssey Trust Company, Vancouver, B.C.

Profile - (B.C. 2022) Capital Pool Company.

Common listed on TSX-VEN, May 5, 2023.

Directors - Chun Sing Cheung, CEO, Vancouver, B.C.; Tak Tsan (Simon) Tso, CFO & corp. sec., Vancouver, B.C.; Robert L. (Rob) Birmingham, North Vancouver, B.C.; Yee Sing (Simon) Cheng, Calgary, Alta.

Capital Stock

	Authorized (shs.)	Outstanding (shs.)[1]
Common	unlimited	7,600,000

[1] At May 5, 2023

Major Shareholder - Chun Sing Cheung held 22.37% interest and Tak Tsan (Simon) Tso held 22.37% interest at May 5, 2023.

Recent Close: $0.08

Capital Stock Changes - On May 5, 2023, an initial public offering of 4,000,000 common shares was completed at 10¢ per share.

A.23 AMG Acquisition Corp.

Symbol - AMG.P **Exchange** - TSX-VEN **CUSIP** - 031160

Head Office - 230-997 Seymour St, Office 9, Vancouver, BC, V6B 3M1 **Telephone** - (778) 833-1984

Email - kl@lpc-cpa.com

Investor Relations - Konstantin Lichtenwald (604) 609-6189

Auditors - SHIM & Associates LLP C.A., Vancouver, B.C.

Lawyers - Oziel Law, Toronto, Ont.

Transfer Agents - Odyssey Trust Company, Vancouver, B.C.

Profile - (B.C. 2021) Capital Pool Company.

Directors - Steven Pearce, CEO, Singapore, Singapore; Konstantin Lichtenwald, CFO & corp. sec., Vancouver, B.C.; Clarke Barlow, W.A., Australia; Michael Edwards, W.A., Australia

Capital Stock

	Authorized (shs.)	Outstanding (shs.)[1]
Common	unlimited	7,800,120

[1] At May 31, 2022

Major Shareholder - Steven Pearce held 12.39% interest at May 31, 2022.

Price Range - AMG.P/TSX-VEN

Year	Volume	High	Low	Close
2022	186,696	$0.20	$0.08	$0.10

Recent Close: $0.07

Capital Stock Changes - On May 31, 2022, an initial public offering of 2,550,000 common shares was completed at 10¢ per share.

A.24 AMPD Ventures Inc.

Symbol - AMPD **Exchange** - CSE **CUSIP** - 00175D

Head Office - 210-577 Great Northern Way, Vancouver, BC, V5T 1E1 **Telephone** - (604) 332-3329

Website - www.ampd.tech

Email - john.ross@ampd.tech

Investor Relations - John C. Ross (647) 291-4234

Auditors - Dale Matheson Carr-Hilton LaBonte LLP C.A., Vancouver, B.C.

Lawyers - Fasken Martineau DuMoulin LLP, Vancouver, B.C.

Transfer Agents - Olympia Trust Company, Vancouver, B.C.

Profile - (B.C. 2018) Supplies high-performance computing solutions to companies that have adopted artificial intelligence, machine learning, big data collection, analysis and visualization alongside reality technologies, as well as provides a range of offsite and hybrid solutions, connecting customers via Metro Area Network to data centres, including its own.

Solutions are provided to the video games industry, including eSports; the animation and visual effects industry; and mainstream companies utilizing mixed reality technologies for data visualization and analysis.

Solutions include AMPD Virtual Studio, AMPD Virtual Workstation, AMPD Render, AMPD Storage, AMPD Metal server, AMPD Cloud Plus, AMPD Flexible Edge, AMPD Virtual Production Services, AMPD Machine Learning PLatform, AMPD CDN, AMPD Game Hosting and AMPD Studio. Also sells **IO Industries Inc.**'s digital camera and video solutions.

The company has an operating data centre in Vancouver, B.C. Also developing an adjacent data centre and has plans to build a third data centre on the North Shore Campus of Capilano University in Vancouver.

Predecessor Detail - Name changed from E-Gaming Ventures Corp., July 25, 2019, pursuant to the reverse takeover acquisition of AMPD Holdings Corp.

Directors - Anthony Brown, chr. & interim CEO, White Rock, B.C.; Donald (Don) Bustin, chief tech. officer, Saint John, N.B.

Other Exec. Officers - John C. Ross, CFO & corp. sec.; Paul Mari, v-p, opers.; Ian P. Wilms, v-p, bus. devel. & govt. affairs

Capital Stock

	Authorized (shs.)	Outstanding (shs.)[1]
Common	unlimited	120,333,339

[1] At Apr. 27, 2023

Major Shareholder - Widely held at Oct. 14, 2022.

Price Range - AMPD/CSE

Year	Volume	High	Low	Close
2022	41,731,106	$0.45	$0.10	$0.11
2021	54,368,242	$0.52	$0.17	$0.43
2020	16,832,562	$0.39	$0.08	$0.22
2019	13,812,076	$0.70	$0.21	$0.24

Recent Close: $0.01

Capital Stock Changes - In August and September 2022, private placement of 13,053,571 units (1 common share & 1 warrant) at 14¢ per unit was completed, with warrants exercisable at 20¢ per share for 18 months.

In June 2021, private placement of 120,000 units (1 common share & 1 warrant) at 25¢ per unit was completed, with warrants exercisable at 40¢ per share for two years. In addition, 1,760,001 common shares were issued pursuant to the acquisition of Cloud-A Computing Inc. In November 2021, private placement of 22,639,663 units (1 common share & 1 warrant) at 30¢ per unit was completed, with warrants exercisable at 50¢ per share for two years. In December 2021, 3,598,195 common shares were issued pursuant to the acquisition of Departure Lounge Inc.

Wholly Owned Subsidiaries

AMPD Technologies (Canada) Inc., Vancouver, B.C.
AMPD Technologies (Europe) Limited, Dublin, Ireland.
AMPD Technologies (US) Inc., Wash.
Cloud-A Computing Inc., Canada.
Departure Lounge Inc., Vancouver, B.C.

Financial Statistics

Periods ended:	12m May 31/21[A]		12m May 31/20[A1]
	$000s	%Chg	$000s
Operating revenue	**1,550**	**+32**	**1,174**
Cost of sales	573		701
Salaries & benefits	1,445		1,191
General & admin expense	972		4,424
Stock-based compensation	946		2,790
Operating expense	**3,936**	**-57**	**9,107**
Operating income	**(2,386)**	**n.a.**	**(7,933)**
Deprec., depl. & amort.	645		345
Finance income	17		nil
Finance costs, gross	116		134
Pre-tax income	**(3,279)**	**n.a.**	**(8,237)**
Net income	**(3,279)**	**n.a.**	**(8,237)**
Cash & equivalent	1,608		939
Inventories	16		nil
Accounts receivable	268		336
Current assets	2,020		1,303
Fixed assets, net	904		1,468
Total assets	**2,939**	**+6**	**2,771**
Accts. pay. & accr. liabs.	352		394
Current liabilities	1,053		1,306
Long-term debt, gross	470		673
Long-term debt, net	nil		133
Long-term lease liabilities	89		325
Equity portion of conv. debs.	28		28
Shareholders' equity	1,746		1,007
Cash from oper. activs	**(1,596)**	**n.a.**	**(1,481)**
Cash from fin. activs	2,352		572
Cash from invest. activs	(80)		1,736
Net cash position	**1,608**	**+71**	**939**
Capital expenditures	(80)		(555)
	$		$
Earnings per share*	(0.07)		(0.26)
Cash flow per share*	(0.03)		(0.05)
	shs		shs
No. of shs. o/s*	59,214,506		41,266,340
Avg. no. of shs. o/s*	47,366,119		31,854,245
	%		%
Net profit margin	(211.55)		(701.62)
Return on equity	(238.21)		n.m.
Return on assets	(110.79)		(556.33)
Foreign sales percent	nil		4

* Common
[A] Reported in accordance with IFRS
[1] Results prior to Oct. 11, 2019, pertain to and reflect the reverse takeover acquisition of AMPD Holdings Corp.

Latest Results

Periods ended:	3m Aug. 31/21[A]		3m Aug. 31/20[A]
	$000s	%Chg	$000s
Operating revenue	333	-23	432
Net income	(1,091)	n.a.	(627)
	$		$
Earnings per share*	(0.02)		(0.01)

* Common
[A] Reported in accordance with IFRS

Historical Summary
(as originally stated)

Fiscal Year	Oper. Rev.	Net Inc. Bef. Disc.	EPS*
	$000s	$000s	$
2021[A]	1,550	(3,279)	(0.07)
2020[A]	1,174	(8,237)	(0.26)
2019[A]	1,343	(605)	(0.04)
2018[A]	994	(466)	(0.05)

* Common
[A] Reported in accordance with IFRS

A.25 ARCpoint Inc.

Symbol - ARC **Exchange** - TSX-VEN **CUSIP** - 03966D
Head Office - 101 North Main St, Suite 301, Greenville, SC, United States, 29601 **Toll-free** - (864) 271-3210
Website - arcpointlabs.com
Email - jconstantine@arcpointcorporate.com
Investor Relations - John Constantine (864) 271-3210
Auditors - Davidson & Company LLP C.A., Vancouver, B.C.
Transfer Agents - Computershare Trust Company of Canada Inc., Vancouver, B.C.
Employees - 43 at June 30, 2022
Profile - (Can. 2022; orig. B.C., 1998) Provides drug testing, alcohol screening, DNA and clinical lab testing, corporate wellness programs, and employment and background screening.

At June 30, 2022, the company operated 122 physical lab locations, of which 121 were franchisee-owned and one was corporate-owned. An additional 12 locations were expected to be opened in the second half of 2022.

Recent Merger and Acquisition Activity

Status: completed **Revised:** Oct. 20, 2022
UPDATE: The transaction was completed. A total of 12,525,744 class A subordinate voting shares at Cdn$0.45 per share and 123,894 class B proportionate voting shares at Cdn$225 per share were issued. ARCpoint Inc.'s class A subordinate voting shares commenced trading on the TSX Venture Exchange effective Oct. 27, 2022. PREVIOUS: RSI International Systems Inc. entered into a letter of intent for the reverse takeover acquisition of Greenville, S.C.-based ARCpoint Group LLC, which provides drug testing, alcohol screening, DNA and clinical lab testing, corporate wellness programs, and employment and background screening. Terms of the share consideration would be subsequently disclosed. Apr. 27, 2022 - A definitive agreement was entered into. The basis of share consideration was one-for-one. Upon completion, RSI would consolidate its common shares on a 1-for-3.1579031 basis and redesignate them as class A subordinate voting shares, continue its incorporation into Canada from British Columbia, change its name to ARCpoint Inc. and create a new class of class B proportionate voting shares. In addition, RSI's wholly owned 1000151427 Ontario Inc. and ARCpoint Group's wholly owned ARCpoint Finance Corp. would amalgamate. June 28, 2022 - The basis of share consolidation was amended to 1-for-2.4930814.

Predecessor Detail - Name changed from RSI International Systems Inc., Oct. 20, 2022, pursuant to the reverse takeover acquisition of Greenville, S.C.-based ARCpoint Group LLC; basis 1 new for 2.49308 old shs.

Directors - John Constantine, pres. & CEO, S.C.; Zelong (Roger) He, Vancouver, B.C.; Adam Ho, Alta.; David Keys, Nev.; Felix Mirando, S.C.

Other Exec. Officers - Dano Jukanovich, COO; Jason Tong, CFO & corp. sec.

Capital Stock

	Authorized (shs.)	Outstanding (shs.)[1]
Cl.A Subordinate Vtg.	unlimited	27,300,744
Cl.B Proportionate Vtg.	unlimited	123,894

[1] At Dec. 31, 2022

Class A Subordinate Voting - Each convertible, at the holder's option, into class B proportionate voting shares on a 1-for-500 basis. One vote per share.

Class B Proportionate Voting - Each convertible, at the holder's option, into 500 class A subordinate voting shares. 500 votes per share.

Major Shareholder - Felix Mirando held 33.27% interest and John Constantine held 29.74% interest at Oct. 27, 2022.

Price Range - ARC/TSX-VEN

Year	Volume	High	Low	Close
2022	399,836	$0.50	$0.17	$0.20
2021	1,712,903	$0.32	$0.20	$0.22
2020	272,389	$0.42	$0.20	$0.25
2019	579,852	$0.30	$0.19	$0.24
2018	397,523	$0.49	$0.01	$0.10

Consolidation: 1-for-2.49308 cons. in Oct. 2022
Recent Close: $0.19

Capital Stock Changes - On Oct. 20, 2022, common shares were consolidated on a 1-for-2.4930814 basis and redesignated as class A subordinate voting shares (effective on the TSX Venture Exchange on Oct. 27, 2022), a new class of class B proportionate voting shares was created, and 12,525,744 class A subordinate voting shares and 123,894 class B proportionate voting shares were issued pursuant to the reverse takeover acquisition of ARCpoint Group LLC.

Wholly Owned Subsidiaries

ARCpoint Group LLC, Greenville, S.C.
- 100% int. in **AFG Services LLC**, S.C.
- 100% int. in **ARCpoint Corporate Labs LLC**, S.C.
- 100% int. in **ARCpoint Franchise Group LLC**, S.C.
- 100% int. in **ARCpoint Holdings LLC**, S.C.
- 60% int. in **Achieve Behavioral Health Greenville LLC**, S.C.
- 100% int. in **Total Reporting, LLC**, Del.

1000151427 Ontario Inc., Ont.

Financial Statistics

Periods ended:	12m Dec. 31/21[A1]		12m Dec. 31/20[A]
	$000s	%Chg	$000s
General & admin expense	138		173
Stock-based compensation	nil		28
Operating expense	**138**	**-31**	**201**
Operating income	**(138)**	**n.a.**	**(201)**
Finance income	33		80
Finance costs, gross	2		5
Write-downs/write-offs	nil		(18)
Pre-tax income	**(107)**	**n.a.**	**(160)**
Net income	**(107)**	**n.a.**	**(160)**
Cash & equivalent	5,010		5,039
Accounts receivable	6		56
Current assets	5,030		5,309
Total assets	**5,030**	**-5**	**5,309**
Accts. pay. & accr. liabs.	60		57
Current liabilities	60		232
Shareholders' equity	4,970		5,078
Cash from oper. activs	**(80)**	**n.a.**	**(235)**
Cash from fin. activs	nil		(34)
Cash from invest. activs	77		28
Net cash position	**27**	**-10**	**30**
	$		$
Earnings per share*	(0.01)		(0.01)
Cash flow per share*	(0.01)		(0.02)
	shs		shs
No. of shs. o/s*	14,775,000		14,775,000
Avg. no. of shs. o/s*	14,775,000		14,775,000
	%		%
Net profit margin	n.a.		n.a.
Return on equity	(2.13)		(3.11)
Return on assets	(2.03)		(2.79)

* Cl.A Subord. Vtg.
[A] Reported in accordance with IFRS
[1] Results for 2021 and prior years pertain to RSI International Systems Inc.

Latest Results

Periods ended:	6m June 30/22[A]		6m June 30/21[A]
	$000s	%Chg	$000s
Net income	(94)	n.a.	(38)
	$		$
Earnings per share*	(0.01)		(0.00)

* Cl.A Subord. Vtg.
[A] Reported in accordance with IFRS

Historical Summary
(as originally stated)

Fiscal Year	Oper. Rev.	Net Inc. Bef. Disc.	EPS*
	$000s	$000s	$
2021[A]	nil	(107)	(0.01)
2020[A]	nil	(160)	(0.01)
2019[A]	447	4,535	0.30
2018[A]	4,913	(60)	(0.00)
2017[A]	4,910	(541)	(0.02)

* Cl.A Subord. Vtg.
[A] Reported in accordance with IFRS
Note: Adjusted throughout for 1-for-2.4930814 cons. in Oct. 2022

A.26 AREV Life Sciences Global Corp.

Symbol - AREV **Exchange** - CSE (S) **CUSIP** - 04019J
Head Office - 18-91 Golden Dr, Coquitlam, BC, V3K 6R2 **Telephone** - (778) 896-6536
Website - arevlifesciences.com
Email - mike@arevbrands.com
Investor Relations - Michael C. Withrow (778) 929-6536
Auditors - BF Borgers CPA PC C.P.A., Lakewood, Colo.
Lawyers - Fang & Associates, Vancouver, B.C.
Transfer Agents - Odyssey Trust Company, Vancouver, B.C.
Profile - (B.C. 2016; orig. Alta., 1986) Produces and sells functional ingredients produced via proprietary extraction systems targeted for the natural health, medical, functional food, nutraceutical and sport nutrition markets.

The company offers Ready-to-Use Therapeutic Food (RUTF) product for severe acute malnutrition (SAM) and an enteral formula targeting the long-term effects of COVID-19, which include products under development SUS-TAINN™ (Superior Utility Supplementation Therapeutic Agent for Indicated Nutritional Needs), a true ready to use therapeutic food; and RES-TORE™, which provides a proprietary blend of high quality proteins, antioxidants, minerals and proven anabolic agents, combined with pre and probiotics.

The company owns a unique extraction technology that has the capability to flash freeze active ingredients, oils and oleoresins for use as ingredients in food, nutraceuticals, cosmetics and other consumer products. The equipment and system allows for oils to be extracted from plants and feedstocks without the use of destructive high-temperature, pressure or aggressive solvents. The company extract ingredients from sea cucumber, sea buckthorn, hops, moringa, ginseng, fungi and cannabis.

Consumer end products include natural health products, including cannabidiol (CBD)-infused products such as Canna-Mulsion and NaturVax, an anti-viral supplement; NaturRelax, a natural sleep aid; NaturRelief, an anti-inflator and pain relief product; a line of Tetrahydrocannabinol products; white label cannabis products; a line of cannabis/CBD skincare products; and medicinal oils and edibles. Products are sold under the company's proprietary brands: Wright & Well and BARE or would be produced by third parties on a white label basis. The Company would also license its formulations to third parties for similar consumer markets.

In addition, the company is developing its technology platform Medicine Merchant™, which would support cannabis marketplace and similar retail supply chains and serve commercial products and telemedicine.

Common suspended from CSE, July 20, 2023.

Predecessor Detail - Name changed from AREV NanoTech Brands Inc., Aug. 11, 2021.

Directors - Michael C. (Mike) Withrow, chr. & CEO, B.C.; Denby Greenslade, interim CFO & corp. sec., Vancouver, B.C.; Allan Echino, B.C.; Brian V. Elliott, Meath, Ireland; Kevin J. Phelps, N.Y.

Other Exec. Officers - Donald (Don) Shaxon, v-p, mktg.

Capital Stock

	Authorized (shs.)	Outstanding (shs.)[1]
Preferred	20,000,000	nil
Redeem. Preferred	20,000,000	nil
Common	unlimited	31,537,363

[1] At Nov. 23, 2022

Major Shareholder - Michael C. (Mike) Withrow held 43.2% interest at Nov. 21, 2022.

Price Range - PA.H/TSX-VEN (D)

Year	Volume	High	Low	Close
2022	1,849,101	$0.39	$0.07	$0.07
2021	11,478,748	$0.47	$0.10	$0.31
2020	8,202,247	$0.33	$0.05	$0.31
2019	3,570,270	$2.52	$0.18	$0.21
2018	2,896,271	$3.84	$1.20	$1.50

Consolidation: 1-for-6 cons. in Mar. 2020

Recent Close: $0.09

Wholly Owned Subsidiaries

AREV Life Sciences Inc., Del.

Bare Topicals Ltd., B.C.

Deutsche Medizinal Cannabis UG, Germany. Inactive.

Phytomedicine Inc., Qué.

Wright & Well Essentials Inc.

Subsidiaries

51% int. in **AREV (Cambodia) Brands Co., Ltd.**, Cambodia.

Financial Statistics

Periods ended:	12m Dec. 31/21[A]		12m Dec. 31/20[A]
	$000s	%Chg	$000s
Operating revenue	**255**	**+34**	**191**
Research & devel. expense	148		128
General & admin expense	1,171		461
Stock-based compensation	455		106
Operating expense	**1,775**	**+155**	**695**
Operating income	**(1,520)**	**n.a.**	**(504)**
Deprec., depl. & amort.	146		149
Finance costs, gross	46		59
Write-downs/write-offs	(5)		(280)
Pre-tax income	**(990)**	**n.a.**	**(1,049)**
Net income	**(990)**	**n.a.**	**(1,049)**
Cash & equivalent	158		298
Inventories	20		5
Accounts receivable	129		26
Current assets	338		858
Fixed assets, net	237		324
Right-of-use assets	47		95
Total assets	**623**	**-51**	**1,277**
Bank indebtedness	nil		163
Accts. pay. & accr. liabs	586		549
Current liabilities	716		1,866
Long-term debt, gross	23		473
Long-term lease liabilities	nil		52
Equity portion of conv. debs	5		50
Shareholders' equity	(94)		(641)
Cash from oper. activs	**(1,470)**	**n.a.**	**(24)**
Cash from fin. activs	1,282		728
Cash from invest. activs	48		(436)
Net cash position	**158**	**-47**	**298**
Capital expenditures	(12)		(308)
	$		$
Earnings per share*	(0.05)		(0.07)
Cash flow per share*	(0.08)		(0.00)
	shs		shs
No. of shs. o/s*	26,892,140		20,207,807
Avg. no. of shs. o/s*	19,586,366		15,361,496
	%		%
Net profit margin	(388.24)		(549.21)
Return on equity	n.m.		n.m.
Return on assets	(99.37)		(91.84)

* Common

[A] Reported in accordance with IFRS

Latest Results

Periods ended:	9m Sept. 30/22[A]		9m Sept. 30/21[A]
	$000s	%Chg	$000s
Operating revenue	42	-63	113
Net income	(1,524)	n.a.	(1,492)
	$		$
Earnings per share*	(0.05)		(0.06)

* Common

[A] Reported in accordance with IFRS

Historical Summary
(as originally stated)

Fiscal Year	Oper. Rev.	Net Inc. Bef. Disc.	EPS*
	$000s	$000s	$
2021[A]	255	(990)	(0.05)
2020[A]	191	(1,049)	(0.07)
2019[A]	195	(3,193)	(0.36)
2018[A]	nil	(8,427)	(1.32)
2017[A]	nil	(1,020)	(0.42)

* Common

[A] Reported in accordance with IFRS

Note: Adjusted throughout for 1-for-6 cons. in Mar. 2020

A.27 ARHT Media Inc.

Symbol - ART **Exchange** - TSX-VEN **CUSIP** - 040328

Head Office - Unit 2, 195 Bentworth Ave, Toronto, ON, M6A 1P9 **Telephone** - (416) 782-8042 **Toll-free** - (800) 490-9210 **Fax** - (416) 861-8165

Website - www.arhtmedia.com

Email - hayyad@arhtmedia.com

Investor Relations - Hanna Ayyad (416) 782-8042

Auditors - McGovern Hurley LLP C.A., Toronto, Ont.

Transfer Agents - TSX Trust Company, Toronto, Ont.

Profile - (Ont. 1987) Develops, produces and distributes technology which captures, transmits and displays holograms for in-person, hybrid and online events.

The ARHT Engine™ is the technology that powers the company's hologram platform. The technology consists of the patented transmission software installed on premium purpose-built hardware that enables the transmission and delivery of real-time and pre-recorded holograms to in-person audiences.

Products include ARHT Capsule, a portable full-body and touchscreen LCD hologram with 2D and 3D depth-sensing cameras for live or pre-recorded presentations; ARHT Virtual Global Stage™, an one-in-all system that allows multiple presenters from different places to jointly present and interact with one another on the same stage with no latency as if they were physically next to each other; ARHT Screens, which are high resolution holographic displays available in different sizes used for immersive presentations; and ARHT Capture Studio, a complete solution for recording and transmitting live and pre-recorded presentations.

Also provides various related services including content creation and production, consultation on hologram creation, execution and management, technical training and support on the company's technology and software, customer support and hologram project management.

Predecessor Detail - Name changed from Vast Exploration Inc., Oct. 14, 2014, following reverse takeover acquisition of Delebrity Inc.

Directors - William C. (Con) Steers, chr., Toronto, Ont.; Jonathan M. Pollack, v-chr., Toronto, Ont.; Larry O'Reilly, pres. & CEO, Ont.; Deborah Beatty, Ont.; Richard G. Carl, Toronto, Ont.; Timothy W. (Tim) Casgrain, Toronto, Ont.; David C. Wetherald, Oakville, Ont.

Other Exec. Officers - Hanna Ayyad, CFO; Palash Ghosh, chief tech. officer; Chris Appleton, sr. v-p, opers.; Terry Davis, sr. v-p; Andrew Dorcas, sr. v-p, sales & strategy; B. J. Hjelholt, v-p, prod. & tech.; John Morning, v-p, military & defense; Jennifer Pelletier, v-p, projects; Roger Pollock, v-p, global entertainment; Gorona Seelay, v-p, global retail; Ellen Van de Woestij, v-p, strategic devel. global; Jeane Weber, v-p, global education

Capital Stock

	Authorized (shs.)	Outstanding (shs.)[1]
Common	unlimited	192,309,642

[1] At May 30, 2023

Major Shareholder - Widely held at Apr. 17, 2023.

Price Range - ART/TSX-VEN

Year	Volume	High	Low	Close
2022	33,493,252	$0.29	$0.14	$0.17
2021	90,293,374	$0.43	$0.16	$0.23
2020	127,538,730	$1.00	$0.06	$0.30
2019	12,089,237	$0.18	$0.08	$0.12
2018	22,241,072	$1.60	$0.07	$0.10

Recent Close: $0.13

Capital Stock Changes - In February 2022, private placement of 36,363,636 units (1 common share & ½ warrant) at $0.275 per unit was completed. Also during 2022, common shares were issued as follows: 7,411,538 on exercise of warrants, 1,191,667 on exercise of options and 407,166 for financing fees.

Wholly Owned Subsidiaries

ARHT Media Singapore Pte. Ltd., Singapore.

ARHT Media (USA) Inc., Calif.

ARHT Media (UK) Limited, United Kingdom.

Be There Networks Inc., Calif.

Investments

49% int. in **ARHT Asia Limited**, Hong Kong, People's Republic of China.

Financial Statistics

Periods ended:	12m Dec. 31/22[A]		12m Dec. 31/21[A]
	$000s	%Chg	$000s
Operating revenue	**7,511**	**+58**	**4,758**
Cost of sales	3,928		2,413
Salaries & benefits	5,628		3,569
Research & devel. expense	1,066		785
General & admin expense	2,851		1,870
Stock-based compensation	925		650
Operating expense	**14,398**	**+55**	**9,286**
Operating income	**(6,887)**	**n.a.**	**(4,528)**
Deprec., depl. & amort.	710		323
Finance costs, gross	n.a.		184
Finance costs, net	(11)		n.a.
Pre-tax income	**(7,576)**	**n.a.**	**(5,356)**
Net income	**(7,576)**	**n.a.**	**(5,356)**
Cash & equivalent	4,225		3,076
Inventories	1,570		633
Accounts receivable	2,478		1,529
Current assets	8,835		5,753
Fixed assets, net	2,489		930
Total assets	**11,324**	**+69**	**6,683**
Accts. pay. & accr. liabs	2,826		2,142
Current liabilities	3,469		2,803
Long-term debt, gross	nil		40
Long-term debt, net	nil		40
Long-term lease liabilities	17		152
Shareholders' equity	7,837		3,688
Cash from oper. activs	**(7,113)**	**n.a.**	**(4,364)**
Cash from fin. activs	10,531		7,649
Cash from invest. activs	(2,269)		(696)
Net cash position	**4,225**	**+37**	**3,076**
Capital expenditures	(2,269)		(696)
	$		$
Earnings per share*	(0.04)		(0.04)
Cash flow per share*	(0.04)		(0.03)
	shs		shs
No. of shs. o/s*	192,309,642		146,935,635
Avg. no. of shs. o/s*	181,479,187		125,932,001
	%		%
Net profit margin	(100.87)		(112.57)
Return on equity	(131.47)		n.m.
Return on assets	(84.15)		(114.97)
Foreign sales percent	84		78

* Common
[A] Reported in accordance with IFRS

Latest Results

Periods ended:	3m Mar. 31/23[A]		3m Mar. 31/22[A]
	$000s	%Chg	$000s
Operating revenue	1,280	-8	1,398
Net income	(2,808)	n.a.	(1,332)
	$		$
Earnings per share*	(0.02)		(0.01)

* Common
[A] Reported in accordance with IFRS

Historical Summary
(as originally stated)

Fiscal Year	Oper. Rev.	Net Inc. Bef. Disc.	EPS*
	$000s	$000s	$
2022[A]	7,511	(7,576)	(0.04)
2021[A]	4,758	(5,356)	(0.04)
2020[A]	2,215	(3,690)	(0.04)
2019[A]	3,281	(3,768)	(0.06)
2018[A1]	1,603	(5,838)	(0.19)

* Common
[A] Reported in accordance with IFRS
[1] 11 months ended Dec. 31, 2018.

A.28 ASEP Medical Holdings Inc.

Symbol - ASEP **Exchange** - CSE **CUSIP** - 04368A
Head Office - 420-730 View St, Victoria, BC, V8W 3Y7 **Telephone** - (778) 600-0509
Website - asepmedical.com
Email - chris@asepmedical.com
Investor Relations - Chris Dallin (604) 362-3654
Auditors - Manning Elliott LLP C.A., Vancouver, B.C.
Transfer Agents - Odyssey Trust Company, Vancouver, B.C.
Profile - (B.C. 2021) Develops and commercializes diagnostic and therapeutic solutions for the treatment of antibiotic-resistant infections as well as a peptide medical device coating technology.

Subsidiary **Sepset Biosciences Inc.** is developing and commercializing Sepset[ER (TM)], a blood-based gene expression assay that can detect an accurate diagnosis of severe incidences of sepsis in 60-90 minutes.

Subsidiary **ABT Innovations Inc.** is commercializing a proprietary peptide technology for the treatment of bacterial biofilm infections such as medical device infections, chronic infections, lung, bladder, wound, dental, skin, ear-nose and throat, sinusitis and orthopaedic. Other applications of the technology include anti-inflammatory activity; as non-steroidal anti-inflammatories like indomethacin; anti-infective immune-modulation that by itself can treat infection diseases (bacterial, viral and fungal); and activities as adjuvants for vaccines.

Subsidiary **SafeCoat Medical Inc.** is developing and commercializing a peptide medical device coating technology.

In December 2022, the company acquired a 50.1% interest in **SafeCoat Medical Inc.** by assisting in the negotiations with the University of British Columbia and SafeCoat for the grant of a licence for the development and commercialization of a peptide medical device coating technology. The company has the option to acquire the remaining 49.9% interest in SafeCoat for issuance of 6,000,000 common shares at a deemed price of 20¢ per share.

On Nov. 10, 2022, common shares were listed on the Frankfurt Stock Exchange under the symbol FSX: JJ8.

Predecessor Detail - Name changed from Trenchant Life Sciences Investment Corp., Nov. 9, 2021, pursuant to the reverse takeover acquisition of ASEP Medical Inc. and concurrent amalgamation of ASEP with wholly owned 1295277 B.C. Ltd.

Directors - Dr. Robert E. W. Hancock, chr. & CEO, Vancouver, B.C.; Timothy W. (Tim) Murphy, COO, Vancouver, B.C.; Dr. Richard Heinzl, Ont.; Derrold Norgaard, Victoria, B.C.

Other Exec. Officers - Jacqueline M. Tucker, CFO; Dr. Evan Haney, chief scientific officer; Dr. Fadia J. Saad, chief bus. devel. officer

Capital Stock

	Authorized (shs.)	Outstanding (shs.)[1]
Preferred	unlimited	nil
Common	unlimited	62,130,344

[1] At May 24, 2023

Major Shareholder - Widely held at May 24, 2023.

Price Range - ASEP/CSE

Year	Volume	High	Low	Close
2022	8,190,930	$0.78	$0.14	$0.64
2021	332,790	$1.03	$0.44	$0.50

Recent Close: $0.21

Wholly Owned Subsidiaries

ASEP Medical Inc., Victoria, B.C.
- 50.1% int. in **ABT Innovations Inc.**, Vancouver, B.C.
- 50.1% int. in **Sepset Biosciences Inc.**, Vancouver, B.C.

Subsidiaries

50.1% int. in **SafeCoat Medical Inc.**

Financial Statistics

Periods ended:	49w Dec. 31/21[A1]
	$000s
Salaries & benefits	82
Research & devel. expense	74
General & admin expense	689
Stock-based compensation	956
Operating expense	**1,800**
Operating income	**(1,800)**
Deprec., depl. & amort.	177
Finance costs, gross	102
Pre-tax income	**(2,344)**
Net income	**(2,344)**
Net inc. for equity hldrs	**(2,200)**
Net inc. for non-cont. int	**(143)**
Cash & equivalent	5,290
Current assets	5,754
Fixed assets, net	64
Intangibles, net	24,898
Total assets	**30,716**
Accts. pay. & accr. liabs	125
Current liabilities	144
Shareholders' equity	18,259
Non-controlling interest	12,313
Cash from oper. activs	**(1,191)**
Cash from fin. activs	6,335
Cash from invest. activs	146
Net cash position	**5,290**
Capital expenditures	(65)
	$
Earnings per share*	(0.10)
Cash flow per share*	(0.06)
	shs
No. of shs. o/s*	56,130,344
Avg. no. of shs. o/s*	21,357,895
	%
Net profit margin	n.a.
Return on equity	n.m.
Return on assets	n.a.

* Common
[A] Reported in accordance with IFRS
[1] Results reflect the Nov. 9, 2022, reverse takeover acquisition of ASEP Medical Inc.

Latest Results

Periods ended:	9m Sept. 30/22[A]		36w Sept. 30/21[A]
	$000s	%Chg	$000s
Net income	(4,215)	n.a.	(461)
Net inc. for equity hldrs	(3,307)	n.a.	(461)
Net inc. for non-cont. int	(908)		nil
	$		$
Earnings per share*	(0.08)		n.a.

* Common
[A] Reported in accordance with IFRS

A.29 ATCO Ltd.*

Symbol - ACO.X **Exchange** - TSX **CUSIP** - 046789
Head Office - West Building, 400-5302 Forand St SW, Calgary, AB, T3E 8B4 **Telephone** - (403) 292-7500 **Toll-free** - (800) 511-3447 **Fax** - (403) 292-7532
Website - www.atco.com
Email - colin.jackson@atco.com
Investor Relations - Colin R. Jackson (403) 808-2636
Auditors - PricewaterhouseCoopers LLP C.A., Calgary, Alta.
Lawyers - Bennett Jones LLP, Calgary, Alta.
Transfer Agents - TSX Trust Company, Calgary, Alta.
FP500 Revenue Ranking - 114
Employees - 7,580 at Dec. 31, 2022
Profile - (Alta. 1962) Provides services and business solutions in Canada, the U.S., Latin America, Australia and eastern and southern Europe through subsidiaries engaged in structures and logistics (workforce and residential housing, modular facilities, construction, site support services, workforce lodging services, facility operations and maintenance, defence operations services, and disaster and emergency management services); utilities (electricity and natural gas transmission and distribution, and international operations); energy infrastructure (energy storage, energy generation, industrial water solutions, and clean fuels); retail energy (electricity and natural gas retail sales, and whole-home solutions); transportation (ports and transportation logistics); and commercial real estate.

Structures & Logistics

Wholly owned **ATCO Structures & Logistics Ltd.** operates through two businesses: ATCO Structures, which provides workforce housing, space rentals, permanent modular construction and residential housing; and ATCO Frontec, which provides workforce lodging and site support services, facility operations and maintenance services, defence operations services, and disaster and emergency management services. Workforce housing division manufactures, sells and leases modular workforce housing, including short-term and permanent modular construction, pre-fabricated and relocatable modular buildings. Space rentals division sells and leases relocatable modular units used for commercial offices, lunchrooms, storage facilities, lavatories, medical facilities, locker rooms and other temporary structures. Permanent modular construction solutions include the design, manufacture and assembly of permanent modular buildings for classrooms, community centres, hotels, independent apartment complexes, and health and correctional facilities among others. Residential housing division manufactures and sells pre-fabricated, modular residential homes. ATCO Structures & Logistics has offices and/or operations in Canada, the U.S., Mexico, Chile, Hungary, Bosnia and Herzegovina, Kosovo and Australia, with manufacturing facilities located in Calgary and Lethbridge, Alta.; Diboll, Tex.; Perth, W.A.; Brisbane, Qld.; Guadalajara, Mexico; and Santiago, Chile.

Canadian Utilities Limited

Through 52.9%-owned Canadian Utilities Limited, operates utilities (electricity and natural gas), energy infrastructure, and retail energy businesses.

Utilities - Operations include regulated electricity and natural gas distribution and transmission in Canada and international electricity and natural gas services in Puerto Rico and Australia. In Canada, operations are conducted through **CU Inc.** and its subsidiaries, which distribute and transmit electricity and natural gas primarily in Alberta, Yukon, the Northwest Territories and the Lloydminster area of Saskatchewan. International operations consist of **LUMA Energy, LLC** (50% owned), which provides services to transform, modernize and operate Puerto Rico's 30,000-km electricity transmission and distribution system under an agreement with the Government of Puerto Rico; and **ATCO Gas Australia Pty Ltd.**, which provides regulated natural gas distribution services in Perth and neighbouring regions in Western Australia, and also distributes liquefied petroleum gas (LPG) in Albany.

Energy Infrastructure - Operations include non-regulated electricity generation from hydroelectric, natural gas and solar facilities in Alberta, Ontario, Mexico, Australia and Chile; non-regulated electricity transmission in Alberta; non-regulated natural gas storage and transmission, natural gas liquids (NGL) storage and industrial water services in Alberta and a regulated natural gas distribution system in the Northwest Territories; and a clean fuels business. Non-regulated electricity assets include 75% interest in the 32-MW Oldman River hydroelectric plant in Pincher Creek, Alta.; the 202-MW Forty Mile phase 1 wind farm in Bow Island, Alta.; 75% interest in the 40-MW Adelaide wind farm in Strathroy, Ont.; the 35-MW Electricidad del Golfo hydroelectric plant in Veracruz state, Mexico; 79% interest in an 11-MW gas-fired distributed generation facility in San Luis Potosí, Mexico; 50% interest in the 180-MW Osborne gas-fired combined-cycle facility near Adelaide, S.A.; the 86-MW Karratha gas-fired open-cycle plant in the Pilbara region of Western Australia; a 1-MW solar facility in Perth, W.A.;

95% interest in the 3-MW El Resplandor solar facility in Cabrero, Chile; and the Scotford, Muskeg River, Grand Rapids and Air Products transmission lines and substations in Alberta. **ATCO Energy Solutions Ltd.** builds, owns and operates non-regulated industrial water, natural gas storage, NGL storage and natural gas related infrastructure in Alberta. ATCO Energy Solutions assets include a natural gas storage facility in Carbon, Alta.; the Alberta Hub underground natural gas storage facility near Edson, Alta.; 60% interest in an NGL storage facility (ATCO Heartland Energy Centre) near Fort Saskatchewan, Alta.; the Muskeg River gas pipeline near Fort McMurray, Alta.; and an industrial water business in Alberta's Industrial Heartland region which provides integrated water services including pipeline transportation, storage, water treatment, recycling and disposal. ATCO Energy Solutions also owns a 33.3% interest in the regulated Ikhil gas plant in the Northwest Territories. In addition, ATCO Energy Solutions includes a clean fuels business, which develops and operates large-scale hydrogen and renewable natural gas (RNG) production projects.

Retail Energy - ATCO Energy Ltd. sells electricity and natural gas to residential customers in Alberta under the ATCOenergy name; offers lifestyle home products, home maintenance services and professional advice to home and business owners in Alberta under the Rümi name; and, through Blue Flame Kitchen, provides recipes and how-to guides, school programs, cooking classes and events online and at locations in Edmonton and Calgary, Alta., and Jandakot, W.A., as well as offers wholesale pre-packaged fresh and frozen foods to convenience stores, gas stations and grocers in Alberta.

Transportation

Through 40%-owned **Neltume Ports S.A.**, operates and develops multipurpose, bulk cargo and container terminals in Chile, Uruguay, Argentina, Brazil and the U.S. Operations include 17 port facilities and six port operation services businesses which handle various cargo products including copper, forestry products, consumer goods and agricultural products.

Other

Wholly owned **ATCO Land and Development Ltd.** holds 11 commercial real estate investments for sale, lease or development primarily in Alberta. Properties include 380,000 sq. ft. of office space, 20,000 sq. ft. of industrial space and 315 acres of land. Wholly owned **ASHCOR Technologies Ltd.** processes and markets live ash and ash reclaimed from landfills for the North American market.

Operating Statistics

Year ended Dec. 31	2022	2021
Structure & Logistics		
Workforce housing fleet	2,652	2,879
Housing fleet utilization, %	75	71
Space rental fleet	22,433	19,684
Space rental utilization, %	79	82
CU Inc. (Gas)		
Distribution mains, km	41,500	41,000
Natural gas distributed, PJ	276.5	270.4
Customers	1,271,541	1,254,731
ATCO Gas Australia		
Distribution pipelines, km	14,000	14,000
Natural gas distributed, PJ	27.7	28.3
Customers	791,557	780,891

Periods ended:	12m Dec. 31/22	12m Dec. 31/21
Generating capacity, MW	248	248
Transmission lines, km	11,000	11,000
Distribution lines, km	60,000	60,000
Electric. dist., million KWh	12,489	12,491
Electric. customers	262,578	261,370
Nat gas dist pipelines, km	55,500	55,000
Nat gas transmn pipelines, km	9,100	9,200
Nat. gas distrib., pj	304	299
Nat. gas customers	2,063,098	2,035,622

Recent Merger and Acquisition Activity

Status: completed **Announced:** Dec. 7, 2022

ATCO Ltd. acquired private Lethbridge, Alta.-based Triple M Housing Ltd., which manufactures modular homes and permanent modular structures in western Canada from a 230,000-sq.-ft. manufacturing facility, for $44,000,000. Triple M would operate as a specialized housing division for ATCO Structures within Canada.

Predecessor Detail - Name changed from ATCO Industries Ltd., Sept. 13, 1978.

Directors - Nancy C. Southern, chr. & CEO, Calgary, Alta.; Linda A. Southern-Heathcott, v-chr., Calgary, Alta.; Dr. Robert J. (Rob) Routs†, Brunnen, Switzerland; Robert T. (Bob) Booth, Calgary, Alta.; The Hon. Jason T. Kenney, Calgary, Alta.; Norman M. Steinberg, Côte Saint-Luc, Qué.; Dr. Roger J. Urwin, London, Middx., United Kingdom; Susan R. Werth, Calgary, Alta.

Other Exec. Officers - Marshall F. Wilmot, chief digital officer & pres., ATCO Energy Ltd.; M. George Constantinescu, exec. v-p & chief transformation officer; Katherine-Jane (Katie) Patrick, exec. v-p & chief finl. & invest. officer; Rebecca A. (Becky) Penrice, exec. v-p, corp. srvcs.; Sarah J. Shortreed, exec. v-p & chief tech. officer; Kyle M. Brunner, sr. v-p, gen. counsel & corp. sec.; P. Derek Cook, sr. v-p & contr.; Lisa Cooke, sr. v-p & chief mktg. officer; G. Dale Friesen, sr. v-p, corp. affairs & chief govt. affairs officer; Colin R. Jackson, sr. v-p, fin., treasury & sustainability; Adam M. Beattie, pres., ATCO Structures & Logistics Ltd.; Jim Landon, pres., Frontec

† Lead director

Capital Stock

	Authorized (shs.)	Outstanding (shs.)[1]
Preferred	20,000,000	nil
Junior Preferred	8,000,000	nil
Class I	300,000,000	100,933,882
Class II	50,000,000	12,424,996

[1] At July 25, 2023

Class I & II - Rank equally in all respects, except that the class I shares are non-voting and class II shares are voting. Class II voting shares are convertible into class I non-voting shares on a share-for-share basis. In the event an offer to purchase class II voting shares is made to all holders of class II voting shares, and is accepted and taken up by holders of a majority of such shares pursuant to the offer, then, provided an offer is not made to holders of class I non-voting shares on the same terms and conditions, the class I non-voting shares shall be entitled to the same voting rights as the class II voting shares.

Options - At Dec. 31, 2022, options were outstanding to purchase 1,882,600 class I non-voting shares at prices ranging from $38.40 to $51.97 per share with a weighted average remaining contractual life of 5.8 years.

Normal Course Issuer Bid - The company plans to make normal course purchases of up to 1,014,881 class I shares representing 1% of the total outstanding. The bid commenced on Mar. 13, 2023, and expires on Mar. 12, 2024.

Major Shareholder - Nancy Southern, Linda Southern-Heathcott & Margaret E. Southern Spousal Trust held 92.4% interest at Mar. 9, 2023.

Price Range - ACO.X/TSX

Year	Volume	High	Low	Close
2022	61,473,563	$48.46	$39.80	$42.38
2021	71,151,180	$46.19	$35.70	$42.70
2020	72,091,561	$54.97	$27.72	$36.49
2019	46,116,445	$51.29	$37.74	$49.77
2018	41,295,538	$45.04	$34.95	$38.61

Recent Close: $37.64

Capital Stock Changes - During 2022, class I non-voting shares were issued as follows: 652,695 on conversion of a like number of class II voting shares and 15,200 on exercise of options; 486,400 class I non-voting shares were repurchased under a Normal Course Issuer Bid and 10,383 (net) class I non-voting shares were purchased and held in trust.

Dividends

ACO.X cl I N.V. Ra $1.9024 pa Q est. Mar. 31, 2023
Prev. Rate: $1.8468 est. Mar. 31, 2022
Prev. Rate: $1.7932 est. Mar. 31, 2021
Prev. Rate: $1.7408 est. Mar. 31, 2020
ACO.Y cl II Ra $1.9024 pa Q est. Mar. 31, 2023
Prev. Rate: $1.8468 est. Mar. 31, 2022
Prev. Rate: $1.7932 est. Mar. 31, 2021
Prev. Rate: $1.7408 est. Mar. 31, 2020

Long-Term Debt - Outstanding at Dec. 31, 2022:

Revolv. credit facility[1]	$84,000,000
Subord. notes due Nov. 2078[2]	200,000,000
CU Inc. debs.	8,525,000,000
CU Inc. other debt due June 2024	7,000,000
ATCO Power Australia[3]	42,000,000
ATCO Structures & Logistics[4]	149,000,000
ATCO Gas Australia[5]	656,000,000
Canadian Utilities Limited debs.[6]	250,000,000
Electricidad del Golfo[7]	23,000,000
ATCO Energy Sol. & ATCO Power[8]	88,000,000
ATCO Investments Ltd. mtge.[9]	88,000,000
ATCO Sabinco[10]	27,000,000
Less: Def. fin. charges	52,000,000
	10,087,000,000
Less: Current portion	109,000,000
	9,978,000,000

[1] Bears interest at bankers' acceptance rate and due November 2025.

[2] Bears interest at 5.5% to Oct. 31, 2028; at a rate reset on February 1, May 1, August 1 and November 1 of each year equal to the three-month bankers' acceptance rate plus 2.92% from Nov. 1, 2028, to Nov. 1, 2048; and thereafter at a rate reset on February 1, May 1, August 1 and November 1 of each year equal to the three-month bankers' acceptance rate plus 3.67% until Nov. 1, 2078.

[3] A$45,000,000. Credit facility payable in Australian dollars, bearing interest at bank bill swap benchmark rates and due June 2025. Secured by a pledge of project assets and contracts.

[4] Credit facilities bearing interest at bankers' acceptance, LIBOR and bank bill swap benchmark rates and due from August 2024 to July 2025. Secured by a general assignment of ATCO Structures & Logistics' present and future property, assets, undertakings and equity interests in certain of its restricted subsidiaries and joint ventures.

[5] A$712,000,000, consisting of A$350,000,000 and A$362,000,000 credit facilities due August 2024 and August 2026, respectively. Both payable in Australian dollars and bearing interest at bank bill swap benchmark rates.

[6] Bears interest at 4.851% and due June 2052.

[7] 335,000,000 Mexican pesos. Credit facility payable in Mexican pesos, bearing interest at Mexican interbank rates and due November 2025.

[8] Credit facility bearing interest at CDOR or prime rates and due December 2025. Secured by ATCO Energy Solutions and ATCO Power's present and future properties, assets and equity interests in certain subsidiaries and joint ventures.

[9] Bears interest at bankers' acceptance rate and due March 2028. Secured by certain of the company's real estate holdings.

[10] 17 billion Chilean pesos. Credit facility payable in Chilean pesos, bearing interest at LIBOR rates and due August 2024.

Wholly Owned Subsidiaries

ASHCOR Technologies Ltd., Calgary, Alta.
ATCO Frontec Ltd., N.W.T.
ATCO Land and Development Ltd., Calgary, Alta.
ATCO Structures & Logistics Ltd., Alta.
- 70% int. in **ATCO Espaciomovil S.A.P.I. de C.V.**, Zapopan, Jal., Mexico.

Inversiones ATCO Chile Limitada, Chile.
- 40% int. in **Neltume Ports S.A.**, Santiago, Chile.

Subsidiaries

52.9% int. in **Canadian Utilities Limited**, Calgary, Alta. Holds 37.9% of class A non-voting shares and 96.7% of class B common shares. (see separate coverage)

Note: The preceding list includes only the major related companies in which interests are held.

Financial Statistics

Periods ended:	12m Dec. 31/22[A]		12m Dec. 31/21[A]
	$000s	%Chg	$000s
Operating revenue	**4,978,000**	**+16**	**4,289,000**
Salaries & benefits	599,000		573,000
Other operating expense	2,452,000		2,034,000
Operating expense	**3,051,000**	**+17**	**2,607,000**
Operating income	**1,927,000**	**+15**	**1,682,000**
Deprec., depl. & amort.	717,000		717,000
Finance income	45,000		14,000
Finance costs, gross	436,000		437,000
Investment income	95,000		75,000
Pre-tax income	**921,000**	**+49**	**617,000**
Income taxes	214,000		148,000
Net income	**707,000**	**+51**	**469,000**
Net inc. for equity hldrs	**370,000**	**+50**	**246,000**
Net inc. for non-cont. int.	**337,000**	**+51**	**223,000**
Cash & equivalent	1,033,000		1,091,000
Inventories	80,000		61,000
Accounts receivable	956,000		844,000
Current assets	2,361,000		2,221,000
Long-term investments	737,000		673,000
Fixed assets, net	19,504,000		18,791,000
Right-of-use assets	109,000		87,000
Intangibles, net	959,000		825,000
Total assets	**24,139,000**	**+5**	**23,004,000**
Bank indebtedness	nil		209,000[1]
Accts. pay. & accr. liabs	1,161,000		852,000
Current liabilities	1,526,000		1,586,000
Long-term debt, gross	10,087,000		9,852,000
Long-term debt, net	9,978,000		9,502,000
Long-term lease liabilities	99,000		76,000
Shareholders' equity	4,376,000		4,111,000
Non-controlling interest	3,968,000		3,838,000
Cash from oper. activs	**2,396,000**	**+29**	**1,864,000**
Cash from fin. activs	(953,000)		(486,000)
Cash from invest. activs	(1,496,000)		(1,383,000)
Net cash position	**1,033,000**	**-5**	**1,088,000**
Capital expenditures	(1,435,000)		(1,200,000)
Capital disposals	5,000		30,000
Unfunded pension liability	107,000		72,000
	$		$
Earnings per share*	3.25		2.16
Cash flow per share*	21.03		16.33
Cash divd. per share*	1.85		1.79
	shs		shs
No. of shs. o/s*	113,658,557		114,140,140
Avg. no. of shs. o/s*	113,957,680		114,171,978
	%		%
Net profit margin	14.20		10.93
Return on equity	8.72		6.03
Return on assets	4.42		3.54
Foreign sales percent	16		14
No. of employees (FTEs)	7,580		6,358

* Class I & II

[A] Reported in accordance with IFRS

[1] Includes $206,000,000 of commercial paper and $3,000,000 of bank indebtedness.

Latest Results

Periods ended:	6m June 30/23[A]		6m June 30/22[A]
	$000s	%Chg	$000s
Operating revenue	2,462,000	0	2,472,000
Net income	459,000	+10	416,000
Net inc. for equity hldrs	246,000	+13	218,000
Net inc. for non-cont. int	213,000		198,000
	$		$
Earnings per share*	2.17		1.91

* Class I & II

[A] Reported in accordance with IFRS

Historical Summary
(as originally stated)

Fiscal Year	Oper. Rev.	Net Inc. Bef. Disc.	EPS*
	$000s	$000s	$
2022[A]	4,978,000	707,000	3.25
2021[A]	4,289,000	469,000	2.16
2020[A]	3,944,000	497,000	2.21
2019[A]	4,706,000	1,007,000	4.49
2018[A]	4,888,000	671,000	2.87

* Class I & II

[A] Reported in accordance with IFRS

A.30 ATI AirTest Technologies Inc.

Symbol - AAT **Exchange** - TSX-VEN **CUSIP** - 00208E
Head Office - 9-1520 Cliveden Ave, Delta, BC, V3M 6J8 **Telephone** - (604) 517-3888 **Toll-free** - (888) 855-8880 **Fax** - (604) 517-3900
Website - www.airtest.com
Email - ted.konyi@airtest.com
Investor Relations - Theodore H. Konyi (888) 855-8880
Auditors - Dale Matheson Carr-Hilton LaBonte LLP C.A., Vancouver, B.C.
Bankers - Canadian Imperial Bank of Commerce, Vancouver, B.C.
Lawyers - Watson Goepel LLP, Vancouver, B.C.
Transfer Agents - Computershare Trust Company of Canada Inc., Vancouver, B.C.

Profile - (B.C. 1996) Develops, manufactures and distributes air testing equipment and related services that ensure the comfort, security, health and energy efficiency of commercial and institutional buildings in Canada and the U.S., measuring humidity, air velocity, temperature, carbon dioxide, refrigerants and a wide variety of industrial gases which may be present.

The company's sensors and controllers measure and control building functions which contribute in reducing energy use and optimizing the operational efficiency and safety of buildings. Products are offered to building contractors, building owners, property management companies, energy management companies and large equipment and controls manufacturers. Also provide data on levels of indoor air quality required by schools, retail stores and offices.

Product portfolio includes proprietary IAQEye™, a wireless carbon dioxide sensor and more than 300 sensor products that can be configured to work with any monitoring or building control system which includes ventilation control in buildings, humidity and moisture control, parking garage ventilation control, air velocity measurement, refrigerant gas leak detection and health and safety.

Directors - George B. Graham, chr., Burnaby, B.C.; Theodore H. (Ted) Konyi, CEO, Vancouver, B.C.; Robert B. Mebruer, St. Louis, Mo.

Other Exec. Officers - Lorne Stewart, pres.; D. Murray Graham, CFO & corp. sec.; Mike Schell, chief tech. officer

Capital Stock

	Authorized (shs.)	Outstanding (shs.)[1]
Common	unlimited	222,672,582

[1] At Aug. 15, 2023

Major Shareholder - Widely held at Nov. 10, 2022.

Price Range - AAT/TSX-VEN

Year	Volume	High	Low	Close
2022	20,701,755	$0.08	$0.01	$0.01
2021	33,009,872	$0.18	$0.06	$0.07
2020	19,793,843	$0.12	$0.01	$0.08
2019	2,444,102	$0.04	$0.01	$0.01
2018	9,001,447	$0.11	$0.01	$0.03

Recent Close: $0.02

Capital Stock Changes - In January and February 2023, private placement of 80,100,000 units (1 common share & 1 warrant) at 1¢ per unit was completed, with warrants exercisable at 5¢ per share for two years.

In April 2022, private placement of 33,540,000 units (1 common share & 1 warrant) at 5¢ per unit was completed.

Wholly Owned Subsidiaries

Airtest Technologies Corp., United States. Inactive.
Airwave Environmental Technologies Inc., Alta. Inactive.
Clairtec Inc., United States. Inactive.

Financial Statistics

Periods ended:	12m Dec. 31/22[A]		12m Dec. 31/21[A]
	$000s	%Chg	$000s
Operating revenue	**2,391**	**+12**	**2,130**
Cost of goods sold	1,497		1,281
Salaries & benefits	899		1,060
Research & devel. expense	61		117
General & admin expense	675		807
Stock-based compensation	nil		718
Operating expense	**3,132**	**-21**	**3,983**
Operating income	**(741)**	**n.a.**	**(1,853)**
Deprec., depl. & amort	34		35
Finance costs, gross	424		456
Write-downs/write-offs	(19)		(15)
Pre-tax income	**(416)**	**n.a.**	**(1,304)**
Net income	**(416)**	**n.a.**	**(1,304)**
Cash & equivalent	16		nil
Inventories	986		544
Accounts receivable	419		181
Current assets	1,550		959
Fixed assets, net	5		8
Right-of-use assets	113		145
Total assets	**1,669**	**+50**	**1,112**
Accts. pay. & accr. liabs	2,103		1,981
Current liabilities	5,016		5,613
Long-term debt, gross	1,305		1,500
Long-term debt, net	986		1,196
Long-term lease liabilities	98		131
Shareholders' equity	(4,431)		(5,828)
Cash from oper. activs	**(1,169)**	**n.a.**	**(1,515)**
Cash from fin. activs	1,194		1,431
Net cash position	**16**	**n.a.**	**(9)**
	$		$
Earnings per share*	(0.00)		(0.01)
Cash flow per share*	(0.01)		(0.02)
	shs		shs
No. of shs. o/s*	142,572,582		109,032,582
Avg. no. of shs. o/s*	120,855,507		96,596,439
	%		%
Net profit margin	(17.40)		(61.22)
Return on equity	n.m.		n.m.
Return on assets	0.58		(98.20)
Foreign sales percent	69		71

* Common

[A] Reported in accordance with IFRS

Latest Results

Periods ended:	3m Mar. 31/23[A]		3m Mar. 31/22[A]
	$000s	%Chg	$000s
Operating revenue	513	-30	729
Net income	(394)	n.a.	(225)
	$		$
Earnings per share*	(0.00)		(0.00)

* Common

[A] Reported in accordance with IFRS

Historical Summary
(as originally stated)

Fiscal Year	Oper. Rev.	Net Inc. Bef. Disc.	EPS*
	$000s	$000s	$
2022[A]	2,391	(416)	(0.00)
2021[A]	2,130	(1,304)	(0.01)
2020[A]	2,660	(2,879)	(0.05)
2019[A]	3,481	(278)	(0.02)
2018[A]	2,703	(1,274)	(0.03)

* Common

[A] Reported in accordance with IFRS

A.31 ATS Corporation*

Symbol - ATS **Exchange** - TSX **CUSIP** - 00217Y
Head Office - Building 2, 730 Fountain St N, Cambridge, ON, N3H 4R7 **Telephone** - (519) 653-6500 **Fax** - (519) 650-6545
Website - www.atsautomation.com
Email - dgalison@atsautomation.com
Investor Relations - David Galison (519) 653-4483 ext. 87185
Auditors - Ernst & Young LLP C.A., Toronto, Ont.
Bankers - The Bank of Nova Scotia
Transfer Agents - Computershare Trust Company of Canada Inc., Toronto, Ont.
FP500 Revenue Ranking - 207
Employees - 6,500 at May 17, 2023

Profile - (Ont. 1992 amalg.) Designs, builds, installs and services automated manufacturing and assembly systems for customers in the life sciences, food and beverage, transportation, consumer products and energy markets.

The company designs, manufactures, assembles and services automation systems on behalf of multinational companies throughout the world. It offers specialized equipment for specific applications or markets, as well as a number of automation and integration services including engineering design, prototyping, process verification, specification writing, software and manufacturing process controls development, equipment design and build, standard automation products/platforms, third party equipment qualification, procurement and integration, automation system installation, product line commissioning, validation and documentation. Has more than 60 manufacturing facilities and more than 80 sales and engineering offices in North America, Europe, Southeast Asia and the People's Republic of China.

During fiscal 2023, order bookings totaled $3.256 billion compared with $2.456 billion in the year earlier and order backlog was $2.153 billion at Mar. 31, 2023, compared with $1.438 billion at Mar. 31, 2022.

In July 2023, the company acquired Kildare, Ireland-based **Odyssey Validation Consultants Limited**, which provides digitalization solutions for the life science industry. Terms were not disclosed.

In May 2023, common shares were listed on the New York Stock Exchange under the symbol ATS.

During fiscal 2022, the company completed a reorganization plan which included the closure of two underperforming **CFT S.p.A.** facilities and the consolidation of an **SP Industries Inc.** facility, along with other cost reductions. Restructuring costs of $5,949,000 were recorded during fiscal 2022.

Common listed on NYSE, May 25, 2023.

Recent Merger and Acquisition Activity

Status: completed **Announced:** June 30, 2023
ATS Corporation acquired private Belgium-based Yazzoom B.V. for $5,283,000 cash. Yazzoom provides artificial intelligence and machine-learning-based production process software solutions with a focus on advanced data analytics.

Status: completed **Announced:** Mar. 28, 2023
ATS Corporation acquired Cedar City, Utah-based Triad Unlimited LLC for Cdn$12,387,000 cash plus contingent consideration of Cdn$7,953,000 upon achievement of certain performance targets within two years of the acquisition date. Triad provides engineering consulting services specializing on asset management by utilizing data analytics through cloud-based tools, a robust learning management system and database development.

Status: completed **Revised:** Mar. 3, 2023
UPDATE: The transaction was completed. PREVIOUS: ATS Automation Tooling Systems Inc. agreed to acquire Bangkok, Thailand-based ZI-Argus Ltd., an independent automation systems integrator in the ASEAN region and Australia, from Zuellig Industrial for US$18,015,000.

Status: completed **Revised:** Dec. 22, 2022
UPDATE: The transaction was completed. PREVIOUS: ATS Corporation agreed to acquire Leuven, Belgium-based IPCOS Group N.V. for Cdn$21,469,000 cash. IPCOS provides process optimization and digitalization solutions, serving a wide range of international process and allied industries. IPCOS had six locations across the U.S., Europe and India.

Predecessor Detail - Name changed from ATS Automation Tooling Systems Inc.

Directors - David L. McAusland, chr., Baie-d'Urfé, Qué.; Andrew P. Hider, CEO, N.C.; Dave W. Cummings, Vancouver, B.C.; Joanne S. Ferstman, Toronto, Ont.; Kirsten Lange, Ulm, Germany; Michael E. Martino, New Canaan, Conn.; Sharon C. Pel, Toronto, Ont.; Philip B. Whitehead, Basingstoke, Hants., United Kingdom

Other Exec. Officers - Ryan McLeod, CFO; Jeff Adamson, CIO; Angella V. Alexander, chief HR officer; Fiona Cleland Nielsen, sr. v-p, strategy & corp. devel.; Simon Roberts, sr. v-p, global after sales srvc.; Steve Emery, v-p, global procurement; Stewart McCuaig, v-p, gen. counsel & corp. sec.; Cameron Moyer, v-p, ATS bus. model; Christian Debus, pres., process automation solutions; Udo Panenka, pres., ind. automation; Jeremy Patten, pres., products & food tech.; Dr. Heinrich Sielemann, pres. & man. dir., IWK Verpackungstechnik GmbH

Capital Stock

	Authorized (shs.)	Outstanding (shs.)[1]
Common	unlimited	98,881,550

[1] At Aug. 8, 2023

Options - At Mar. 31, 2023, options were outstanding to purchase 785,429 common shares at prices ranging from $10.46 to $45.75 per share with a weighted average remaining contractual life of 4.67 years.

Normal Course Issuer Bid - The company plans to make normal course purchases of up to 7,335,032 common shares representing 10% of the public float. The bid commenced on Dec. 15, 2022, and expires on Dec. 14, 2023.

Major Shareholder - Mason Capital Management, LLC held 18.05% interest at June 16, 2023.

Price Range - ATS/TSX

Year	Volume	High	Low	Close
2022	54,272,006	$53.65	$30.60	$42.09
2021	54,000,029	$52.62	$21.67	$50.24
2020	74,527,418	$23.55	$14.27	$22.35
2019	48,767,636	$22.38	$14.04	$21.43
2018	61,377,825	$24.67	$13.28	$14.39

Recent Close: $58.38

Capital Stock Changes - In May 2023, public offering of 6,900,000 common shares was completed at US$41 per share, including additional 900,000 common shares on exercise of over-allotment option.

During fiscal 2023, 291,659 common shares were issued on exercise of options, 619,695 common shares were repurchased under a Normal Course Issuer Bid and 337,496 common shares were purchased and held in trust.

During fiscal 2022, 190,621 common shares were issued on exercise of options.

Long-Term Debt - Outstanding at Mar. 31, 2023:

Sr. sec. credit facility[1]	$691,906,000
4.125% sr. notes due Dec. 2028	472,990,000
Other credit facilities[2]	202,000
Less: Issuance costs	9,312,000
	1,155,786,000
Less: Current portion	65,000
	1,155,721,000

[1] Consists of amounts drawn on a $750,000,000 senior secured credit facility due Nov. 4, 2026, and a $300,000,000 non-amortized secured term credit facility due Nov. 4, 2024, bearing interest at prime rate or U.S. dollar base rate in Canada plus 0.45% to 2%, or bankers' acceptances, term SOFR rate, EURIBOR rate or Daily Simple SONIA rate plus 1.45% to 3%.

[2] Bear interest at rates ranging from 0.7% to 6.9%.

Wholly Owned Subsidiaries

ATS Automation Global Services USA, Inc., Del.
ATS Automation Holdings Italy S.r.l., Italy.
ATS Automation LLC, Del.
ATS Automation Malaysia Sdn. Bhd., Malaysia.
ATS Automation Solutions Limited, United Kingdom.
ATS Automation Tooling Systems GmbH, Munich, Germany.
- 100% int. in **IWK Verpackungstechnik GmbH**, Germany.
  - 100% int. in **IWK (Thailand) Ltd.**, Thailand.
- 100% int. in **Process Automation Solutions GmbH**, Germany.
  - 100% int. in **Advanced Applications GmbH**, Germany.
  - 100% int. in **Process Automation Solutions N.V.**, Belgium.
  - 100% int. in **Process Automation Solutions s.r.o.**, Prague, Czech Republic.

ATS Automation USA Holdings 6, Inc., Ohio
ATS Automation USA PA Holdings Inc., Del.
ATS Delaware 5 LLC, Del.
ATS Delaware 1 LP, Del.
ATS Food Technologies Inc., Del.
ATS Industrial Automation GmbH & Co. KG, Germany.
ATS Industrial Automation Inc., Ont.
ATS Industrial Automation s.r.o., Slovakia.
ATS Process Automation Solutions Corp., Ont.
ATS Test Inc., Ont.
Automation Tooling Systems Enterprises England Limited, United Kingdom.
- 100% int. in **MARCO Limited**, Kent, United Kingdom.

Automation Tooling Systems Enterprises GmbH, Germany.
Automation Tooling Systems Enterprises, Inc., Del.
- 100% int. in **ATS Assembly and Test, Inc.**, Mich.
- 100% int. in **ATS Ohio, Inc.**, Columbus, Ohio.
- 100% int. in **IWK Packaging Systems, Inc.**, Del.

Bel-art Products, N.J.
BioDot, Inc., Irvine, Calif.
BioDot Limited, United Kingdom.
BioDot Trading Shanghai, Co. Ltd., People's Republic of China.
CFT (Beijing) Technology Co., Ltd., People's Republic of China.
CFT Packaging USA Inc., Del.
Co.mac S.r.l., Italy.
Comecer, Inc., Del.
Comecer Medical System Pvt. Ltd., India.
Comecer Netherlands B.V., Netherlands.
Comecer S.p.A., Italy.
Control and Information Management Ltd., Dublin, Ireland.
DF S.r.l., Italy.
Genevac Limited, United Kingdom.
HSG Engineering S.r.l., Pistoia, Italy.
IPCOS B.V., Netherlands.
IPCOS DOF B.V., Netherlands.
IPCOS Engineering Solutions Pvt. Ltd., India.
IPCOS Group N.V., Leuven, Belgium.
IPCOS Inc., Del.
IPCOS N.V., Belgium.
IPCOS POE Engineering Solutions Pvt. Ltd., India.
IPCOS UK Ltd., United Kingdom.
IWK India Pvt. Ltd., India.
Industrial Automation Partners B.V., Netherlands.
Inimco B.V., Belgium.
Irta Dosificacio I Technologia S.L., Spain.
Kimberly Audrey Ltd., United Kingdom.
NCC Automated Systems, Inc., Pa.
Olimon Hungary Kft., Hungary.
PA Process Automation Solutions (Shanghai) Co. Ltd., Republic of China.
PA Solutions, Inc., Mich.
PT PAS Argus, Indonesia.
Process Automation Solutions B.V., Belgium.
Process Automation Solutions, Inc., Conn.
Process Automation Solutions Limited, Ireland.
Process Automation Solutions Pte. Ltd., Singapore.
ROLEC Prozess- und Brautechnik GmbH, Germany.
Raytec Service USA LLC, Calif.
Raytec Vision S.p.A., Italy.
SP Industries, Inc., Warminster, Pa.
Siapi S.r.l., Italy.
Techn'Agro SAS, France.
Triad Unlimited LLC, Cedar City, Utah.
2269187 Ontario Inc., Ont.
ZI-Argus Ltd., Bangkok, Thailand.
Zi-Argus Australia Pty Ltd., Australia.

Subsidiaries

97.69% int. in **CFT S.p.A.**, Parma, Italy.

Note: The preceding list includes only the major related companies in which interests are held.

Financial Statistics

Periods ended:	12m Mar. 31/23[A]		12m Mar. 31/22[A]
	$000s	%Chg	$000s
Operating revenue	**2,577,384**	**+18**	**2,182,717**
Cost of sales	1,808,146		1,534,156
General & admin expense	363,181		307,818
Stock-based compensation	30,592		32,762
Operating expense	**2,201,919**	**+17**	**1,874,736**
Operating income	**375,465**	**+22**	**307,981**
Deprec., depl. & amort.	125,489		115,421
Finance income	1,961		508
Finance costs, gross	64,679		32,708
Pre-tax income	**159,771**	**+3**	**154,411**
Income taxes	32,070		33,019
Net income	**127,701**	**+5**	**121,392**
Net inc. for equity hldrs	**127,433**	**+4**	**122,101**
Net inc. for non-cont. int	**268**	**n.a.**	**(709)**
Cash & equivalent	159,867		135,282
Inventories	256,866		207,873
Accounts receivable	399,741		348,631
Current assets	1,451,974		1,146,462
Fixed assets, net	263,119		222,123
Right-of-use assets	94,212		81,289
Intangibles, net	1,711,472		1,592,970
Total assets	**3,543,793**	**+15**	**3,069,397**
Bank indebtedness	5,824		1,766
Accts. pay. & accr. liabs	614,139		457,783
Current liabilities	1,043,571		845,009
Long-term debt, gross	1,155,786		1,016,711
Long-term debt, net	1,155,721		1,016,668
Long-term lease liabilities	73,255		62,856
Shareholders' equity	1,126,848		981,596
Non-controlling interest	3,735		4,087
Cash from oper. activs	**127,800**	**-41**	**216,163**
Cash from fin. activs	4,882		531,535
Cash from invest. activs	(109,022)		(797,467)
Net cash position	**159,867**	**+18**	**135,282**
Capital expenditures	(56,104)		(36,309)
Capital disposals	1,460		817
	$		$
Earnings per share*	1.39		1.32
Cash flow per share*	1.39		2.34
	shs		shs
No. of shs. o/s*	91,602,192		92,267,724
Avg. no. of shs. o/s*	91,835,740		92,206,291
	%		%
Net profit margin	4.95		5.56
Return on equity	12.09		13.01
Return on assets	5.43		5.59
Foreign sales percent	96		94
No. of employees (FTEs)	6,500		6,000

* Common
[A] Reported in accordance with IFRS

Latest Results

Periods ended:	3m July 2/23[A]		3m July 3/22[A]
	$000s	%Chg	$000s
Operating revenue	753,649	+23	610,591
Net income	47,724	+21	39,393
Net inc. for equity hldrs	47,563	+21	39,204
Net inc. for non-cont. int	161		189
	$		$
Earnings per share*	0.50		0.43

* Common
[A] Reported in accordance with IFRS

Historical Summary
(as originally stated)

Fiscal Year	Oper. Rev. $000s	Net Inc. Bef. Disc. $000s	EPS* $
2023[A]	2,577,384	127,701	1.39
2022[A]	2,182,717	121,392	1.32
2021[A]	1,430,052	64,103	0.70
2020[A]	1,429,734	52,951	0.57
2019[A]	1,253,616	70,762	0.76

* Common
[A] Reported in accordance with IFRS

A.32 ATW Tech Inc.

Symbol - ATW **Exchange** - TSX-VEN **CUSIP** - 002107
Head Office - 19 place d'Epernay, Lorraine, QC, J6Z 4K9 **Toll-free** - (844) 298-5932
Website - www.atwtech.com
Email - mguay@atwtech.com
Investor Relations - Michel Guay (844) 298-5932 ext. 301
Auditors - Guimond Lavallée Inc. C.A., Brossard, Qué.
Lawyers - Dentons Canada LLP, Montréal, Qué.
Transfer Agents - Computershare Trust Company of Canada Inc.
Profile - (Can. 2007) Owns technology platforms including VoxTel, Option.vote and Semeon.

VoxTel specializes in telephone billing and alternative payment solutions for fixed and mobile lines. Option.vote provides a large scale, customizable and secure multi-method voting system designed to reduce voting costs and to improve participation rates for unions, political parties, professional associations and others. Semeon is a highly accurate and flexible text analysis platform for customer reviews.

In June 2022, the company entered into a letter of intent to acquire a technology company offering data analytics tools and expert consulting services for $2,600,000 consisting of $1,600,000 cash minus the debt and (ii) issuance of $1,000,000 of common shares. The company would not disclose the name of the target company until a definitive agreement has been reached for commercial and confidentiality reasons.

Recent Merger and Acquisition Activity

Status: pending **Announced:** June 21, 2022
ATW Tech Inc. entered into a letter of intent to acquire a technology company that develops, markets and deploys public safety software for $8,500,000, consisting of a combination of (i) $4,750,000 cash, minus the debt, and a balance of the purchase price payable on the achievement of certain objectives and (ii) issuance of $2,250,000 of ATW common shares. ATW would not disclose the name of the target company until a definitive agreement has been reached for commercial and confidentiality reasons.

Predecessor Detail - Name changed from AtmanCo Inc., June 12, 2018.

Directors - Christian Trudeau, chr., Montréal, Qué.; Michel Guay, pres., CEO & acting CFO, Lorraine, Qué.; Carlos Bedran, France; Louis Lessard, Montréal, Qué.

Other Exec. Officers - Raymond Cyr, v-p, R&D & strategic mktg. & corp. sec.

Capital Stock

	Authorized (shs.)	Outstanding (shs.)[1]
Common	unlimited	243,512,412

[1] At Aug. 10, 2023

Major Shareholder - Widely held at Aug. 10, 2023.

Price Range - ATW/TSX-VEN

Year	Volume	High	Low	Close
2022	27,191,490	$0.09	$0.02	$0.03
2021	149,846,526	$0.23	$0.04	$0.06
2020	24,526,879	$0.08	$0.01	$0.04
2019	15,817,451	$0.07	$0.01	$0.01
2018	24,786,936	$0.22	$0.06	$0.06

Recent Close: $0.02

Capital Stock Changes - In June 2023, private placement of 14,500,000 units (1 common share & 1 warrant) at 5¢ per unit was announced, with warrants exercisable at 7¢ per share for three years.

During 2022, 10,700,000 common shares were issued by private placement.

Wholly Owned Subsidiaries

RNIS Telecommunications Inc., Canada.
Semeon Analytics Inc., Montréal, Qué.

Financial Statistics

Periods ended:	12m Dec. 31/22^A		12m Dec. 31/21^oA
	$000s	%Chg	$000s
Operating revenue	**1,711**	**-20**	**2,142**
Cost of sales	1,700		1,899
General & admin expense	1,606		1,466
Stock-based compensation	87		219
Operating expense	**3,393**	**-5**	**3,584**
Operating income	**(1,682)**	**n.a.**	**(1,442)**
Deprec., depl. & amort.	417		700
Finance costs, gross	206		83
Write-downs/write-offs	(41)		(2,865)
Pre-tax income	**(2,133)**	**n.a.**	**(5,017)**
Income taxes	nil		(141)
Net income	**(2,133)**	**n.a.**	**(4,876)**
Cash & equivalent	22		240
Accounts receivable	140		272
Current assets	323		660
Fixed assets, net	4		11
Right-of-use assets	nil		3
Intangibles, net	1,042		1,217
Total assets	**1,369**	**-28**	**1,891**
Bank indebtedness	1,165		250
Accts. pay. & accr. liabs	1,387		1,234
Current liabilities	2,648		1,530
Long-term debt, gross	97		152
Long-term debt, net	nil		109
Long-term lease liabilities	nil		1
Shareholders' equity	(1,280)		252
Cash from oper. activs	**(1,344)**	**n.a.**	**(1,203)**
Cash from fin. activs	1,382		1,412
Cash from invest. activs	(252)		(402)
Net cash position	**22**	**-91**	**240**
	$		$
Earnings per share*	(0.01)		(0.02)
Cash flow per share*	(0.01)		(0.01)
	shs		shs
No. of shs. o/s*	224,612,412		213,812,412
Avg. no. of shs. o/s*	214,164,193		201,261,501
	%		%
Net profit margin	(124.66)		(227.64)
Return on equity	n.m.		(269.02)
Return on assets	(118.22)		(129.24)
Foreign sales percent	11		18

* Common
o Restated
A Reported in accordance with IFRS

Latest Results

Periods ended:	3m Mar. 31/23^A		3m Mar. 31/22^A
	$000s	%Chg	$000s
Operating revenue	250	-57	577
Net income	(310)	n.a.	(630)
	$		$
Earnings per share*	(0.00)		(0.00)

* Common
A Reported in accordance with IFRS

Historical Summary
(as originally stated)

Fiscal Year	Oper. Rev.	Net Inc. Bef. Disc.	EPS*
	$000s	$000s	$
2022^A	1,711	(2,133)	(0.01)
2021^A	2,142	(4,876)	(0.02)
2020^A	2,372	(1,456)	(0.01)
2019^A	5,713	(3,611)	(0.04)
2018^A	11,985	(890)	(0.01)

* Common
A Reported in accordance with IFRS

A.33 AZN Capital Corp.

Symbol - AZN.H **Exchange** - TSX-VEN (S) **CUSIP** - 00249G
Head Office - 3123-595 Burrard St, Vancouver, BC, V7X 1J1 **Telephone** - (604) 609-6110 **Toll-free** - (877) 557-1053
Email - lle@fiorecorporation.com
Investor Relations - Lindsay Le Ho (604) 609-6118
Auditors - Davidson & Company LLP C.A., Vancouver, B.C.
Lawyers - Fang & Associates, Vancouver, B.C.
Transfer Agents - Computershare Trust Company of Canada Inc., Vancouver, B.C.
Profile - (B.C. 1980) Seeking new business opportunities.

Previously held contracts to operate shared mobility systems at 25 colleges and 45 municipalities in the U.S., under the OjO and Gotcha brands.

Common suspended from TSX-VEN, May 10, 2021.

Predecessor Detail - Name changed from Last Mile Holdings Ltd., Feb. 10, 2021.

Directors - Maxwell (Max) Smith, CEO & acting CFO, Venice, Calif.; Brian T. O'Neill†, Port Coquitlam, B.C.; Doug Deluca, Malibu, Calif.
Other Exec. Officers - Matt Tolan, sr. v-p, partnerships & corp. devel.
† Lead director

Capital Stock

	Authorized (shs.)	Outstanding (shs.)[1]
Preferred Multiple Vtg.	unlimited	nil
Limited Voting	unlimited	217,387,553

[1] At Aug. 22, 2023

Preferred - Issuable in series. **Preferred Multiple Voting** - Convertible into limited voting shares on a 1-for-1 basis in certain circumstances. Automatically converted into limited voting shares in certain circumstances. 1,000 votes per share.
Limited Voting - One vote per share.
New Common A & New Common A-1 Units - Membership units of wholly owned OjO Electric, LLC. Convertible into limited voting shares on a 1-for-1 basis in certain circumstances. Automatically redeemable for limited voting shares on a 1-for-1 basis in October 2026.
Class B Units - Membership units of wholly owned OjO Electric, LLC. Non-voting. Convertible into up to 7,069,707 new common A units. Automatically cancelled in October 2026.
Major Shareholder - Widely held at Apr. 21, 2021.

Price Range - AZN.H/TSX-VEN (S)

Year	Volume	High	Low	Close
2021	241,244,531	$0.13	$0.01	$0.03
2020	122,371,788	$0.29	$0.01	$0.01
2019	4,418,809	$0.97	$0.05	$0.50
2018	116,814	$0.16	$0.09	$0.09

Wholly Owned Subsidiaries

Gotcha Bike LLC, United States.
Gotcha Mobility LLC, United States.
Gotcha Ride LLC, United States.
OjO Electric Inc., Calif.

Subsidiaries

58% int. in **OjO Electric, LLC**, Oxnard, Calif.
- 100% int. in **OjO Electric US Holdings Corp.**, Nev.

A.34 Aardvark 2 Capital Corp.

Symbol - ACCB.P **Exchange** - TSX-VEN **CUSIP** - 00259B
Head Office - 400-77 King St W, Toronto, ON, M5K 0A1 **Telephone** - (647) 987-5083
Email - zach@libertyvp.co
Investor Relations - Zachary Goldenberg (647) 987-5083
Auditors - MNP LLP C.A., Toronto, Ont.
Transfer Agents - TSX Trust Company, Toronto, Ont.
Profile - (Ont. 2021) Capital Pool Company.
Directors - Zachary Goldenberg, CEO, CFO & corp. sec., Toronto, Ont.; Dennis Beker, Ont.; Raymond D. Harari, Panama City, Panama; Marc Sontrop, Toronto, Ont.

Capital Stock

	Authorized (shs.)	Outstanding (shs.)[1]
Common	unlimited	7,200,000

[1] At May 25, 2022

Major Shareholder - Zachary Goldenberg held 13.89% interest and Marc Sontrop held 13.89% interest at May 25, 2022.

Price Range - ACCB.P/TSX-VEN

Year	Volume	High	Low	Close
2022	13,563	$0.22	$0.12	$0.12

Recent Close: $0.09
Capital Stock Changes - On May 25, 2022, an initial public offering of 2,500,000 common shares was completed at 10¢ per share.

A.35 Abaxx Technologies Inc.

Symbol - ABXX **Exchange** - NEO **CUSIP** - 00258V
Head Office - 902-18 King St E, Toronto, ON, M5C 1C4 **Telephone** - (416) 777-6772 **Fax** - (416) 352-5693
Website - www.investors.abaxx.tech
Email - ir@abaxx.tech
Investor Relations - Steve Fray (416) 786-4381
Auditors - KPMG LLP C.A., Toronto, Ont.
Transfer Agents - Computershare Trust Company of Canada Inc., Toronto, Ont.
Employees - 42 at Mar. 31, 2022
Profile - (Alta. 2003) Develops and commercializing software infrastructure and tools for commodity exchanges and digital marketplace.

Has developed a suite of software applications which include trading and clearing software, verified-credential management, authentication, digital identity and access management, end-to-end encrypted financial messaging and video chat, financial data storage, electronic document, smart contract signing, digital-contract custody and other financial management applications. These applications enhance data privacy and security, accelerate transaction velocity and improve risk management strategies.

Also developing the operation of ACX (Abaxx Exchange and Clearing), a 91%-owned commodity futures exchange and clearinghouse based in Singapore, awaiting final regulatory approvals from the Monetary Authority of Singapore (MAS) to commence operations. ACX utilizes the company's software technologies. ACX has foundational products in liquefied natural gas (LNG) benchmark contracts and also developing a new derivative market product suite for previous metals, battery metals and emerging ESG (Environmental, Social and Corporate Governance) certified-commodity markets.

Also owns Taconite project, straddling Newfoundland and Labrador and Quebec, which consists of 80% interest in LabMag iron deposit, 64 km^2, 220 km north of Labrador City, N.L., and 100% interest in KéMag iron project, 83 km^2, 50 km north of Schefferville, Que. Proven and probable reserves were 3.932 billion tonnes grading 29.7% iron at LabMag at March 2014; and 815,000,000 tonnes grading 31.4% iron at KéMag at June 2016.

Predecessor Detail - Name changed from New Millennium Iron Corp., Dec. 14, 2020, pursuant to the reverse takeover acquisition of (old) Abaxx Technologies Inc. and concurrent amalgamation of (old) Abaxx with wholly owned 12404206 Canada Inc. (and continued as Abaxx Technologies Holdco Inc.).
Directors - Joshua D. (Josh) Crumb, chr., pres. & CEO, Huntsville, Ont.; Margot Naudie†, Toronto, Ont.; Catherine A. Flax, N.Y.; Cyrus Hiramanek, N.Y.; W. Scott Leckie, Toronto, Ont.; Thomas (Thom) McMahon, Singapore, Singapore
Other Exec. Officers - Steve Fray, CFO; Tafadzwa (Taf) Mganba, head, corp. devel.; Jeff Lipton, gen. counsel; Dan McElduff, pres., Abaxx Singapore Pte. Ltd.
† Lead director

Capital Stock

	Authorized (shs.)	Outstanding (shs.)[1]
Preferred	unlimited	nil
Common	unlimited	24,437,763

[1] At May 23, 2023

Major Shareholder - Joshua D. (Josh) Crumb held 15.72% interest at Mar. 31, 2023.

Price Range - ABXX/NEO

Year	Volume	High	Low	Close
2022	1,059,933	$10.50	$2.58	$7.50
2021	1,677,233	$13.44	$8.70	$10.80
2020	3,324,283	$14.22	$1.26	$12.15
2019	912,298	$3.96	$1.80	$1.80
2018	667,681	$4.68	$1.44	$2.70

Consolidation: 1-for-3 cons. in May 2023; 1-for-12 cons. in Dec. 2020
Recent Close: $8.03
Capital Stock Changes - On May 23, 2023, common shares were consolidated on a 1-for-3 basis.

During 2022, common shares were issued as follows; 1,997,328 on exercise of options and 21,233 under restricted share unit plan.

Wholly Owned Subsidiaries

Abaxx Technologies Holdco Inc., Toronto, Ont.
- 100% int. in **Abaxx Technologies Corp.**, Barbados.
  - 91% int. in **Abaxx Singapore Pte. Ltd.**, Singapore.
    - 100% int. in **Abaxx Clearing Pte. Ltd.**, Singapore.
    - 100% int. in **Abaxx Exchange Pte. Ltd.**, Singapore.

Labmag Services Inc., Canada.

Subsidiaries

80% int. in **LabMag GP Inc.**, Alta.
80% int. in **LabMag Limited Partnership**, Alta.

Investments

AirCarbon Pte. Ltd., Singapore.
15.7% int. in **Base Carbon Inc.**, Toronto, Ont. (see separate coverage)
Pasig & Hudson Private, Limited, Singapore.

Financial Statistics

Periods ended:	12m Dec. 31/22[A]		12m Dec. 31/21[A]
	$000s	%Chg	$000s
Salaries & benefits	3,428		2,111
Research & devel. expense	8,345		4,850
General & admin expense	4,856		4,645
Stock-based compensation	3,305		2,583
Operating expense	**19,934**	**+40**	**14,188**
Operating income	**(19,934)**	**n.a.**	**(14,188)**
Finance income	nil		425
Investment income	(2,174)		(382)
Pre-tax income	**(18,286)**	**n.a.**	**(12,905)**
Net income	**(18,286)**	**n.a.**	**(12,905)**
Net inc. for equity hldrs	**(17,026)**	**n.a.**	**(11,929)**
Net inc. for non-cont. int	**(1,260)**	**n.a.**	**(976)**
Cash & equivalent	9,606		21,873
Accounts receivable	439		350
Current assets	11,868		23,842
Long-term investments	2,135		5,451
Total assets	**14,003**	**-52**	**29,294**
Accts. pay. & accr. liabs	3,201		1,353
Current liabilities	3,201		1,353
Shareholders' equity	14,759		30,637
Non-controlling interest	(3,957)		(2,697)
Cash from oper. activs	**(15,301)**	**n.a.**	**(10,960)**
Cash from fin. activs	1,273		23,768
Cash from invest. activs	(1,835)		(3,011)
Net cash position	**4,581**	**-76**	**19,357**
	$		$
Earnings per share*	(0.69)		(0.51)
Cash flow per share*	(0.62)		(0.48)
	shs		shs
No. of shs. o/s*	24,411,695		23,738,841
Avg. no. of shs. o/s*	24,509,752		22,848,550
	%		%
Net profit margin	n.a.		n.a.
Return on equity	(75.01)		n.m.
Return on assets	(84.47)		n.a.

* Common
[A] Reported in accordance with IFRS

Latest Results

Periods ended:	3m Mar. 31/23[A]		3m Mar. 31/22[A]
	$000s	%Chg	$000s
Net income	(6,567)	n.a.	(686)
Net inc. for equity hldrs	(6,122)	n.a.	(542)
Net inc. for non-cont. int	(445)		(143)
	$		$
Earnings per share*	(0.24)		(0.03)

* Common
[A] Reported in accordance with IFRS

Historical Summary
(as originally stated)

Fiscal Year	Oper. Rev. $000s	Net Inc. Bef. Disc. $000s	EPS* $
2022[A]	nil	(18,286)	(0.69)
2021[A]	nil	(12,905)	(0.51)
2020[A1]	nil	(10,551)	(0.72)
2019[A2]	nil	(5,360)	(1.08)
2018[A]	nil	300	0.06

* Common
[A] Reported in accordance with IFRS
[1] Results reflect the Dec. 14, 2020, reverse takeover acquisition of (old) Abaxx Technologies Inc.
[2] Results for 2019 and prior years pertain to New Millenium Iron Corp.
Note: Adjusted throughout for 1-for-3 cons. in May 2023; 1-for-12 cons. in Dec. 2020

A.36 AbCellera Biologics Inc.

Symbol - ABCL **Exchange** - NASDAQ **CUSIP** - 00288U
Head Office - 2215 Yukon St, Vancouver, BC, V5Y 0A1 **Telephone** - (604) 559-9005
Website - www.abcellera.com
Email - tryn.stimart@abcellera.com
Investor Relations - Tryn T. Stimart (604) 559-9005
Auditors - KPMG LLP C.A., Vancouver, B.C.
Transfer Agents - Philadelphia Stock Transfer, Inc., Ardmore, Pa.
FP500 Revenue Ranking - 424
Employees - 495 at Dec. 31, 2022
Profile - (B.C. 2012) Searches, decodes and analyzes natural immune systems using its full-stack, artificial intelligence (AI)-powered drug discovery platform to find antibodies that its partners can develop into drugs to prevent and treat disease. Partners with pharmaceutical and biotechnology companies as well as non-profit and government organizations which select a target and define the antibody properties needed for drug development.

The company's platform is an operating system designed to support many antibody modalities; unlock new targets; integrates expert teams, technology and facilities with the data science and automation needed to propel antibody-based medicines increasing the speed and precision to clinical development for its partners; and increase the potential clinical and commercial success for its partners. Partnership agreements include near-term payments for technology access, research and intellectual property rights; downstream payments in the form of clinical and commercial milestones; and royalties on net sales of any approved therapeutics.

At Mar. 31, 2023, the company had 177 discovery programs that were either completed, in progress or under contract with 41 partners.

Directors - Dr. Carl L. G. Hansen, co-founder, pres. & CEO; Dr. Véronique Lecault, co-founder & COO; Dr. Michael R. Hayden†, Vancouver, B.C.; Dr. Andrew W. Lo; John S. Montalbano, Vancouver, B.C.; Peter Thiel, San Francisco, Calif.

Other Exec. Officers - Andrew Booth, CFO; Neil Aubuchon, chief comml. officer; Tryn T. Stimart, chief legal officer, chief compliance officer & corp. sec.; Adam Clarke, sr. v-p, complex membrane protein tech.; Murray McCutcheon, sr. v-p, partnering; Tiffany Chiu, v-p, comms.; Anne M. Stevens, v-p, bus. devel.
† Lead director

Capital Stock

	Authorized (shs.)	Outstanding (shs.)[1]
Common	unlimited	288,728,094

[1] At May 1, 2023

Major Shareholder - Dr. Carl L. G. Hansen held 20.59% interest at Apr. 1, 2023.

Price Range - ABCL/NASDAQ

Year	Volume	High	Low	Close
2022	167,883,955	US$14.97	US$5.42	US$10.13
2021	109,275,047	US$55.22	US$12.20	US$14.30
2020	8,104,563	US$71.91	US$37.75	US$40.24

Capital Stock Changes - During 2022, 3,594,491 common shares were issued on vesting of restricted share units.

Wholly Owned Subsidiaries

AbCellera Australia Pty Ltd., Australia.
AbCellera Biologics UK Ltd., United Kingdom.
AbCellera Boston, Inc., N.Y.
AbCellera Properties Columbia Inc., B.C.
AbCellera Properties Evans Inc., Canada.
AbCellera Properties Inc., B.C.
AbCellera US, Inc., Del.
Biologiques AbCellera Quebec, Inc., Qué.
Lineage Biosciences, Inc., Palo Alto, Calif.
Trianni, Inc., San Francisco, Calif.
Note: The preceding list includes only the major related companies in which interests are held.

Financial Statistics

Periods ended:	12m Dec. 31/22[A]		12m Dec. 31/21[0A]
	US$000s	%Chg	US$000s
Operating revenue	**485,424**	**+29**	**375,203**
Research & devel. expense	107,879		62,062
General & admin expense	66,755		48,761
Other operating expense	66,436		45,516
Operating expense	**241,070**	**+54**	**156,339**
Operating income	**244,354**	**+12**	**218,864**
Deprec., depl. & amort	27,843		14,451
Finance income	16,079		3,330
Finance costs, gross	4,045		6,080
Pre-tax income	**239,099**	**+9**	**219,149**
Income taxes	80,580		65,685
Net income	**158,519**	**+3**	**153,464**
Cash & equivalent	886,485		722,977
Inventories	1,532		1,672
Accounts receivable	38,593		160,576
Current assets	1,025,491		929,800
Long-term investments	72,522		50,313
Fixed assets, net	217,255		111,616
Intangibles, net	179,308		196,198
Total assets	**1,540,907**	**+17**	**1,318,569**
Accts. pay. & accr. liabs	14,828		14,924
Current liabilities	118,320		120,676
Long-term lease liabilities	76,675		36,413
Shareholders' equity	1,233,277		1,025,733
Cash from oper. activs	**277,360**	**+13**	**244,584**
Cash from fin. activs	(1,628)		(3,886)
Cash from invest. activs	(352,625)		(332,247)
Net cash position	**414,650**	**-17**	**501,142**
Capital expenditures	(70,660)		(58,452)
	US$		US$
Earnings per share*	0.56		0.56
Cash flow per share*	0.97		0.89
	shs		shs
No. of shs. o/s*	286,851,595		283,257,104
Avg. no. of shs. o/s*	285,056,606		275,763,745
	%		%
Net profit margin	32.66		40.90
Return on equity	14.03		16.53
Return on assets	11.27		13.57
No. of employees (FTEs)	495		386

* Common
[0] Restated
[A] Reported in accordance with U.S. GAAP

Latest Results

Periods ended:	3m Mar. 31/23[A]		3m Mar. 31/22[A]
	US$000s	%Chg	US$000s
Operating revenue	21,192	-93	316,581
Net income	(40,110)	n.a.	168,573
	US$		US$
Earnings per share*	(0.14)		0.59

* Common
[A] Reported in accordance with U.S. GAAP

Historical Summary
(as originally stated)

Fiscal Year	Oper. Rev. US$000s	Net Inc. Bef. Disc. US$000s	EPS* US$
2022[A]	485,424	158,519	0.56
2021[A]	375,203	153,464	0.56
2020[A]	233,155	118,918	0.53
2019[A]	11,612	(2,211)	(0.01)
2018[A]	8,831	309	0.00

* Common
[A] Reported in accordance with U.S. GAAP

A.37 Aberdeen International Inc.

Symbol - AAB **Exchange** - TSX **CUSIP** - 003069
Head Office - 198 Davenport Rd, Toronto, ON, M5R 1J2 **Telephone** - (416) 861-5875 **Fax** - (416) 861-8165
Website - aberdeen.green
Email - martin.schuermann@aberdeen.green
Investor Relations - Martin Schuermann (416) 861-5882
Auditors - McGovern Hurley LLP C.A., Toronto, Ont.
Lawyers - Cassels Brock & Blackwell LLP, Toronto, Ont.
Transfer Agents - TSX Trust Company, Toronto, Ont.
Profile - (Ont. 2006; orig. B.C., 1987) Conducts investment and merchant banking activities globally, focusing on small capitalization companies in the metals and mining sector and renewal energy sectors.

Primary investment objective is to realize exceptional earnings by investing in pre-initial public offering and/or early stage public resource and green energy companies with undeveloped or undervalued high quality resources and assets; obtain in-depth knowledge of the investee company and a working relationship with existing and/or proposed management; and seek multiple exit strategies for optimal realization of value of structured transactions. Transactions generally take the form of equity or debt, usually with equity rights attached.

At Apr. 30, 2023, the investment portfolio consisted of 13 publicly traded investments and 14 privately held investments with a total fair value of $25,438,580.

Primary investment is an indirect 16.9% interest in **African Thunder Platinum Limited**, which holds the 678-hectare Smokey Hills platinum-palladium mine located 300 km north of Johannesburg, South Africa. The mine was placed on care and maintenance in April 2016.

Recent Merger and Acquisition Activity

Status: completed **Announced:** Jan. 9, 2023

Aberdeen International Inc. sold its remaining 41.67% interest in Progressus Clean Technologies Inc. to AmmPower Corp. issuance of 41,254,125 AmmPower common shares at a deemed value of 30¢ per share. On closing, Aberdeen held a 27.35% interest in AmmPower.

Predecessor Detail - Name changed from International Catalyst Ventures Inc., Nov. 23, 2001; basis 1 new for 3 old shs.

Directors - Martin Schuermann, exec. chr. & CEO, Germany; Dr. Bernard R. (Bernie) Wilson†, Toronto, Ont.; Gregory Biniowsky, Vancouver, B.C.; Gen. (ret.) Lewis W. (Lew) MacKenzie, Ottawa, Ont.

Other Exec. Officers - Ryan Ptolemy, CFO & corp. sec.; Kenny Choi, legal counsel

† Lead director

Capital Stock

	Authorized (shs.)	Outstanding (shs.)[1]
Common	unlimited	144,877,282

[1] At June 14, 2023

Major Shareholder - Stan Bharti held 13.2% interest at June 10, 2023.

Price Range - AAB/TSX

Year	Volume	High	Low	Close
2022	18,719,432	$0.17	$0.04	$0.04
2021	87,693,541	$0.48	$0.12	$0.14
2020	63,804,888	$0.15	$0.02	$0.15
2019	23,989,342	$0.07	$0.03	$0.04
2018	19,310,809	$0.21	$0.05	$0.06

Recent Close: $0.03

Capital Stock Changes - During fiscal 2023, common shares were issued as follows: 7,750,000 on exercise of warrants and 75,000 under deferred share unit plan.

Wholly Owned Subsidiaries

Aberdeen (Barbados) Inc., Barbados.

Investments

16.9% int. in **African Thunder Platinum Limited**, Mauritius.

Note: The preceding list includes only the major related companies in which interests are held.

Financial Statistics

Periods ended:	12m Jan. 31/23[A]		12m Jan. 31/22[A]
	$000s	%Chg	$000s
Realized invest. gain (loss)	4,153		5,104
Unrealized invest. gain (loss)	(13,496)		3,722
Total revenue	**(8,715)**	**n.a.**	**9,094**
Salaries & benefits	2,934		4,363
General & admin. expense	1,039		1,410
Operating expense	**3,974**	**-31**	**5,772**
Operating income	**(12,689)**	**n.a.**	**3,322**
Finance costs, gross	62		59
Write-downs/write-offs	(349)		(2,368)
Pre-tax income	**(13,097)**	**n.a.**	**901**
Net income	**(13,097)**	**n.a.**	**901**
Cash & equivalent	39		2,049
Accounts receivable	105		216
Investments	29,602		39,399
Total assets	**30,415**	**-29**	**43,096**
Bank indebtedness	40		668
Accts. pay. & accr. liabs	1,592		1,663
Shareholders' equity	28,782		40,765
Cash from oper. activs	**(2,610)**	**n.a.**	**690**
Cash from fin. activs	543		1,347
Net cash position	**39**	**-98**	**2,049**
	$		$
Earnings per share*	(0.09)		0.02
Cash flow per share*	(0.02)		0.01
	shs		shs
No. of shs. o/s*	144,877,282		137,052,282
Avg. no. of shs. o/s*	141,560,433		136,367,350
	%		%
Net profit margin	n.m.		9.91
Return on equity	(37.66)		2.46
Return on assets	(35.46)		2.48

* Common

[A] Reported in accordance with IFRS

Latest Results

Periods ended:	3m Apr. 30/23[A]		3m Apr. 30/22[A]
	$000s	%Chg	$000s
Total revenue	(3,871)	n.a.	284
Net income	(4,541)	n.a.	(1,219)
	$		$
Earnings per share*	(0.03)		(0.01)

* Common

[A] Reported in accordance with IFRS

Historical Summary
(as originally stated)

Fiscal Year	Total Rev. $000s	Net Inc. Bef. Disc. $000s	EPS* $
2023[A]	(8,715)	(13,097)	(0.09)
2022[A]	9,094	901	0.02
2021[A]	5,689	2,918	0.03
2020[A]	3,775	1,869	0.02
2019[A]	(24,292)	(25,954)	(0.27)

* Common

[A] Reported in accordance with IFRS

A.38 abrdn Asia-Pacific Income Fund VCC

Symbol - FAP **Exchange** - TSX **CUSIP** - Y0040X

Head Office - c/o abrdn Inc., 1735 Market St, 32nd Flr, Philadelphia, PA, United States, 19103 **Telephone** - (215) 405-5700 **Toll-free** - (800) 992-6341 **Fax** - (866) 354-4005

Website - www.abrdn.com/en-ca/canada

Email - investor.relations@abrdn.com

Investor Relations - Investor Relations (800) 992-6341

Auditors - KPMG LLP C.A., Toronto, Ont.

Lawyers - Stikeman Elliott LLP, Toronto, Ont.

Transfer Agents - Computershare Trust Company of Canada Inc., Toronto, Ont.

Investment Managers - abrdn Asia Limited, Singapore, Singapore

Investment Advisors - Aberdeen Asset Managers Limited, London, Middx. United Kingdom

Administrators - State Street Bank and Trust Company, Singapore, Singapore; abrdn Canada Limited, Toronto, Ont.

Profile - (Singapore 1986) Invests in a fully managed portfolio consisting primarily of Asian and Oceanian debt securities.

Top 10 country allocation at Oct. 31, 2022 (as a percentage of net asset value):

Country	Percentage
Indonesia	32.7%
India	29.4%
Australia	9.1%
China	5.7%
Mexico	4.8%
United Kingdom	4.8%
Thailand	4.3%
Philippines	3.9%
Uruguay	3.4%
United Arab Emirates	3.2%
Bahrain	3.1%

Predecessor Detail - Name changed from Aberdeen Asia-Pacific Income Investment Company Limited, Dec. 17, 2021.

Directors - William J. Braithwaite, chr., Toronto, Ont.; Radhika Ajmera, London, Middx., United Kingdom; P. Gerald Malone, London, Middx., United Kingdom; Henny Muliany, Singapore; Warren C. Smith, Beaconsfield, Qué.; Hugh Young, Singapore

Other Exec. Officers - Christian Pittard, man. dir.; Andrea Melia, CFO & treas.; Joseph Andolina, chief compliance officer; Kenneth Akintewe, v-p; Mark Baker, v-p; Chris Demetriou, v-p; Alan Goodson, v-p; Beverley (Bev) Hendry, v-p; Megan Kennedy, v-p & joint sec.; Adam McCabe, v-p; James O'Connor, v-p; Lucia Sitar, v-p; Sharon Ferrari, asst. treas.

Capital Stock

	Authorized (shs.)	Outstanding (shs.)[1]
Preferred	50,000,000	nil
Redeemable	100,000,000	45,670,155

[1] At Dec. 31, 2022

Redeemable - Redeemable annually on March 31 for a price equal to equal to the average net asset value per share less any expenses and charges incurred by the company to fund such redemption payment.

Major Shareholder - Widely held at Jan. 17, 2022.

Price Range - FAP/TSX

Year	Volume	High	Low	Close
2022	10,174,090	$3.18	$2.27	$2.55
2021	14,852,178	$3.36	$2.85	$3.06
2020	12,348,531	$3.67	$2.51	$3.27
2019	13,650,816	$4.05	$3.31	$3.56
2018	12,533,416	$4.64	$3.19	$3.64

Recent Close: $2.58

Capital Stock Changes - In November 2021, the fund's ordinary shares were reclassified to redeemable shares. During fiscal 2022, 5,074,461 redeemable shares were repurchased under a Normal Course Issuer Bid.

Dividends

FAP ord Ra $0.21 pa M est. Feb. 28, 2023**[1]

Prev. Rate: $0.27 est. May 31, 2019

[1] Distributions are interest income.

** Reinvestment Option

Financial Statistics

Periods ended:	12m Oct. 31/22[A]		12m Oct. 31/21[A]
	$000s	%Chg	$000s
Realized invest. gain (loss)	(10,495)		(8,991)
Unrealized invest. gain (loss)	(23,998)		(8,666)
Total revenue	**(19,935)**	**n.a.**	**(1,508)**
General & admin. expense	2,887		3,971
Operating expense	**2,887**	**-27**	**3,971**
Operating income	**(22,822)**	**n.a.**	**(5,479)**
Finance costs, gross	2,077		1,255
Pre-tax income	**(24,821)**	**n.a.**	**(6,735)**
Income taxes	268		440
Net income	**(25,089)**	**n.a.**	**(7,175)**
Cash & equivalent	1,350		14,147
Accounts receivable	3,893		4,456
Investments	182,749		239,106
Total assets	**188,553**	**-28**	**261,944**
Accts. pay. & accr. liabs	680		883
Debt	56,743		74,123
Shareholders' equity	nil		184,344
Cash from oper. activs	**39,730**	**+237**	**11,781**
Cash from fin. activs	(52,847)		(4,152)
Net cash position	**1,350**	**-90**	**14,147**
	$		$
Earnings per share*	(0.53)		(0.14)
Cash flow per share*	0.83		0.23
Net asset value per share*	2.84		3.63
Cash divd. per share*	0.27		0.27
	shs		shs
No. of shs. o/s*	45,670,155		50,744,616
Avg. no. of shs. o/s*	47,755,550		50,744,616
	%		%
Net profit margin	n.m.		n.m.
Return on equity	n.m.		(3.68)
Return on assets	(10.21)		(2.14)

* Redeemable

[A] Reported in accordance with IFRS

Note: Net income reflects increase/decrease in net assets from operations.

Historical Summary
(as originally stated)

Fiscal Year	Total Rev. $000s	Net Inc. Bef. Disc. $000s	EPS* $
2022[A]	(19,935)	(25,089)	(0.53)
2021[A]	(1,508)	(7,175)	(0.14)
2020[A]	(5,614)	(11,701)	(0.23)
2019[A]	40,836	32,311	0.63
2018[A]	(19,806)	(28,712)	(0.56)

* Redeemable

[A] Reported in accordance with IFRS

A.39 Acadian Timber Corp.

Symbol - ADN **Exchange** - TSX **CUSIP** - 004272

Head Office - 365 Canada Rd, Edmundston, NB, E3V 1W2 **Telephone** - (506) 737-2345

Website - acadiantimber.com

Email - ir@acadiantimber.com

Investor Relations - Susan Wood (506) 737-2345

Auditors - PricewaterhouseCoopers LLP C.A., Halifax, N.S.

Lawyers - Lawson Lundell LLP, Vancouver, B.C.

Transfer Agents - TSX Trust Company

FP500 Revenue Ranking - 786

Employees - 52 at Dec. 31, 2022

Profile - (Can. 2010 amalg.) Supplies primary forest products from freehold timberlands in New Brunswick and north-central Maine, and provides harvesting and management services related to Crown-licensed timberlands in New Brunswick.

Owns and manages timberlands covering 761,000 acres primarily in Madawaska and Victoria ctys., N.B., and 300,000 acres in northern Penobscot and Piscataquis ctys., Me., with annual sustainable harvest volume of 1,000,000 m^3. Crown lands under management consist of 1,326,000 acres in New Brunswick.

Products include softwood and hardwood sawlogs, pulpwood and biomass by-products, which are sold to approximately 90 regional customers in eastern Canada and the northeastern United States.

Harvest

Year ended Dec. 31	2022 m^3	2021 m^3
N.B. Timberlands:		
Softwood	373,900	340,300
Hardwood	236,400	310,100
Biomass	85,100	110,900
Maine Timberlands:		
Softwood	151,000	221,700
Hardwood	59,900	83,200
Biomass	8,800	1,400

Directors - Malcolm Cockwell, chr., Haliburton, Ont.; Adam Sheparski, pres. & CEO, Saint-Jacques, N.B.; Karen Oldfield†, Halifax, N.S.; Heather M. Fitzpatrick, Toronto, Ont.; Erika N. Reilly, Vancouver, B.C.; Bruce K. Robertson, Toronto, Ont.

Other Exec. Officers - Susan Wood, CFO; Kevin Topolniski, chief forester

† Lead director

Capital Stock

	Authorized (shs.)	Outstanding (shs.)[1]
Common	unlimited	16,958,881

[1] At Mar. 24, 2023

Normal Course Issuer Bid - The company plans to make normal course purchases of up to 847,944 common shares representing 5% of the total outstanding. The bid commenced on Feb. 14, 2023, and expires on Feb. 13, 2024.

Major Shareholder - Macer Forest Holdings Inc. held 45.85% interest at Mar. 24, 2023.

Price Range - ADN/TSX

Year	Volume	High	Low	Close
2022	1,954,211	$19.83	$14.52	$14.97
2021	3,481,472	$21.57	$15.67	$19.18
2020	3,244,906	$18.62	$11.11	$16.10
2019	2,810,384	$17.97	$14.75	$16.64
2018	2,357,828	$20.24	$14.25	$15.13

Recent Close: $17.48

Capital Stock Changes - During 2022, 198,508 common shares were issued under the dividend reinvestment plan.

Dividends

ADN com Ra $1.16 pa Q est. Apr. 15, 2019

Wholly Owned Subsidiaries

Acadian Timber GP Inc., Ont.

Acadian Timber Limited Partnership, Man.

- 100% int. in **AT Limited Partnership**, Man.
- 100% int. in **AT Timberlands (N.S.) ULC**, N.S.
  - 100% int. in **Acadian Timber (U.S.), Inc.**, Del.
    - 100% int. in **Acadian US Timber GP Inc.**, Del.
      - 1% int. in **Katahdin Forest Management LLC**, Del.
    - 99% int. in **Katahdin Forest Management LLC**, Del.

Financial Statistics

Periods ended:	12m Dec. 31/22[A]		12m Dec. 31/21[A]
	$000s	%Chg	$000s
Operating revenue	**90,473**	**-5**	**95,729**
Cost of sales	62,894		64,933
General & admin expense	8,066		7,622
Other operating expense	1,375		1,156
Operating expense	**72,335**	**-2**	**73,711**
Operating income	**18,138**	**-18**	**22,018**
Deprec., depl. & amort.	273		261
Finance costs, net	3,098		2,978
Pre-tax income	**49,134**	**+86**	**26,453**
Income taxes	13,627		7,769
Net income	**35,507**	**+90**	**18,684**
Cash & equivalent	6,230		7,316
Inventories	1,850		1,450
Accounts receivable	8,265		8,386
Current assets	16,345		17,256
Fixed assets, net	87,986		99,183
Intangibles, net	6,140		6,140
Total assets	**547,836**	**+6**	**516,642**
Accts. pay. & accr. liabs.	11,206		8,800
Current liabilities	16,123		13,639
Long-term debt, gross	107,937		100,888
Long-term debt, net	107,937		100,888
Shareholders' equity	303,723		291,485
Cash from oper. activs	**15,235**	**-6**	**16,229**
Cash from fin. activs	(16,002)		(19,357)
Cash from invest. activs	(319)		186
Net cash position	**6,230**	**-15**	**7,316**
Capital expenditures	(378)		(333)
Capital disposals	59		519
	$		$
Earnings per share*	2.11		1.12
Cash flow per share*	0.91		0.97
Cash divd. per share*	1.16		1.16
	shs		shs
No. of shs. o/s*	16,885,424		16,686,916
Avg. no. of shs. o/s*	16,791,973		16,686,916
	%		%
Net profit margin	39.25		19.52
Return on equity	11.93		6.39
Return on assets	6.67		3.63
Foreign sales percent	28		33
No. of employees (FTEs)	52		58

* Common

[A] Reported in accordance with IFRS

Historical Summary
(as originally stated)

Fiscal Year	Oper. Rev. $000s	Net Inc. Bef. Disc. $000s	EPS* $
2022[A]	90,473	35,507	2.11
2021[A]	95,729	18,684	1.12
2020[A]	91,031	22,080	1.32
2019[A]	100,048	17,325	1.04
2018[A]	99,848	26,264	1.57

* Common

[A] Reported in accordance with IFRS

A.40 Acasti Pharma Inc.

Symbol - ACST **Exchange** - NASDAQ **CUSIP** - 00430K

Head Office - 102-3009 boul de la Concorde E, Laval, QC, H7E 2B5 **Telephone** - (450) 686-4555 **Toll-free** - (888) 664-9166 **Fax** - (450) 686-2505

Website - www.acasti.com/en

Email - info@acasti.com

Investor Relations - Prashant Kohli (450) 686-4555

Auditors - KPMG LLP C.A., Montréal, Qué.

Lawyers - Norton Rose Fulbright Canada LLP, Montréal, Qué.

Transfer Agents - Computershare Trust Company of Canada Inc., Montréal, Qué.

Profile - (Que. 2002) Develops formulations and drug delivery technologies to address rare and orphan diseases with unmet medical needs.

The company applies its proprietary formulation and drug delivery technologies to existing marketed drugs to achieve improvements over the current standard of care or provide treatment for diseases with no currently approved therapy. The lead drug candidate, GTX-104, an intravenous infusion targeting Subarachnoid Hemorrhage (SAH), a rare and life-threatening medical emergency in which bleeding occurs over the surface of the brain in the subarachnoid space between the brain and skull. Other drug candidates include: GTX-102, an oral mucosal spray targeting Ataxia-telangiectasia (A-T), a progressive, neurodegenerative genetic disease that primarily impacts children causing severe disability, for which no treatment presently exists; and GTX-101, a topical spray, targeting Postherpetic Neuralgia (PHN), a persistent and often debilitating neuropathic pain caused by nerve damage from the varicella zoster virus (shingles). Each candidate has received Orphan Drug designation from the U.S. FDA.

At June 23, 2023, the company had more than 40 granted and pending patents in various global jurisdictions, including six U.S. issued patents and four filed U.S. patent applications.

Class A delisted from TSX-VEN, Mar. 28, 2023.

Directors - Michael L. Derby, Conn.; Vimal Kavuru, United States; Donald Olds, Montréal, Qué.

Other Exec. Officers - Prashant Kohli, CEO & chief comml. officer; Brian D. Ford, CFO; Dr. R. Loch Macdonald, CMO; Carrie D'Andrea, v-p, clinical opers.; Dr. Amresh Kumar, v-p, program mgt.; Janelle (Jan) D'Alvise, corp. sec.

Capital Stock

	Authorized (shs.)	Outstanding (shs.)[1]
Class A	unlimited	7,435,472
Class B	unlimited	nil
Class C	unlimited	nil
Class D	unlimited	nil
Class E	unlimited	nil

[1] At July 10, 2023

Major Shareholder - Widely held at Aug. 24, 2022.

Price Range - ACST/TSX-VEN (D)

Year	Volume	High	Low	Close
2022	235,553	$12.06	$2.82	$4.50
2021	1,624,665	$74.40	$7.98	$9.72
2020	1,239,730	$158.88	$10.56	$20.16
2019	599,131	$194.40	$49.44	$153.60
2018	637,777	$109.92	$27.36	$54.72

Consolidation: 1-for-6 cons. in July 2023; 1-for-8 cons. in Aug. 2021

Capital Stock Changes - On July 10, 2023, class A shares were consolidated on a 1-for-6 basis.

During fiscal 2023, 324,648 class A shares were issued under an at-the-market offering.

On Aug. 31, 2021, class A shares were consolidated on a 1-for-8 basis. Also during fiscal 2022, 18,241,233 post-consolidated class A shares were issued pursuant to the acquisition of Grace Therapeutics, Inc.

Wholly Owned Subsidiaries

Acasti Innovation AG, Switzerland.

Acasti Pharma U.S., Inc., Del.

Financial Statistics

Periods ended:	12m Mar. 31/23[A]		12m Mar. 31/22[◻A]
	US$000s	%Chg	US$000s
Research & devel. expense	9,972		5,559
General & admin expense	6,340		8,444
Stock-based compensation	1,811		1,337
Operating expense	**18,123**	**+18**	**15,340**
Operating income	**(18,123)**	**n.a.**	**(15,340)**
Deprec., depl. & amort.	124		nil
Finance costs, net	(184)		(5,122)
Write-downs/write-offs	(33,908)		(249)
Pre-tax income	**(51,971)**	**n.a.**	**(10,467)**
Income taxes	(9,542)		(648)
Net income	**(42,429)**	**n.a.**	**(9,819)**
Cash & equivalent	27,890		43,661
Accounts receivable	802		548
Current assets	29,290		45,281
Fixed assets, net	104		250
Right-of-use assets	463		315
Intangibles, net	49,266		82,774
Total assets	**79,123**	**-38**	**128,620**
Accts. pay. & accr. liabs.	3,336		3,156
Current liabilities	3,411		3,260
Long-term lease liabilities	410		191
Shareholders' equity	67,955		108,270
Cash from oper. activs	**(15,913)**	**n.a.**	**(17,234)**
Cash from fin. activs	304		nil
Cash from invest. activs	13,153		(3,522)
Net cash position	**27,875**	**-8**	**30,339**
Capital expenditures	(17)		nil
	US$		US$
Earnings per share*	(5.70)		(1.62)
Cash flow per share*	(2.14)		(2.81)
	shs		shs
No. of shs. o/s*	7,435,472		7,381,364
Avg. no. of shs. o/s*	7,435,472		6,140,294
	%		%
Net profit margin	n.a.		n.a.
Return on equity	(48.15)		(11.98)
Return on assets	(40.85)		(10.28)

* Class A

◻ Restated

[A] Reported in accordance with U.S. GAAP

Historical Summary
(as originally stated)

Fiscal Year	Oper. Rev.	Net Inc. Bef. Disc.	EPS*
	US$000s	US$000s	US$
2023^A	nil	(42,429)	(5.70)
2022^A	nil	(9,819)	(1.62)
2021^A	196	(19,678)	(8.16)
2020^A	nil	(25,513)	(14.40)
	$000s	$000s	$
2019^B	nil	(51,566)	(45.60)

* Class A
^A Reported in accordance with U.S. GAAP
^B Reported in accordance with IFRS

Note: Adjusted throughout for 1-for-6 cons. in July 2023; 1-for-8 cons. in Aug. 2021

A.41 Acceleware Ltd.

Symbol - AXE **Exchange** - TSX-VEN **CUSIP** - 00433V
Head Office - 435 10 Ave SE, Calgary, AB, T2G 0W3 **Telephone** - (403) 249-9099 **Fax** - (403) 249-9881
Website - www.acceleware.com
Email - geoff.clark@acceleware.com
Investor Relations - Geoffrey Clark (403) 249-9099
Auditors - MNP LLP C.A., Calgary, Alta.
Lawyers - Lindsey MacCarthy LLP, Calgary, Alta.
Transfer Agents - Computershare Trust Company of Canada Inc., Calgary, Alta.
Employees - 15 at Mar. 31, 2023
Profile - (Alta. 2011, amalg.) Developing radio frequency (RF) heating technologies that enable the electrification of industrial heat and develops and markets special purpose computational software for the oil and gas and other markets.

Operates through two business segments: Radio Frequency Heating (RF Heating); and High-Performance Computing Scientific Software.

The **RF Heating** business segment is focused on providing decarbonized industrial heating through the company's proprietary industrial heating technology, Clean Tech Inverter (CTI). CTI converts electricity from various clean power sources into RF energy to provide decarbonized heat directly to the material being heated. Initial application of CTI is in the extraction of heavy oil and bitumen through the company's RF XL technology. RF XL, a patented production technology for heavy oil and oil sands, is being developed as an environmentally friendly alternative to steam assisted gravity drainage (SAGD) methods. RF XL acts as an underground, inside out microwave that heats the water already in the formation to produce steam, mobilizing the bitumen and allowing it to flow to the producing well. The technology can be redeployed to different sites and eliminates the use of external water, solvents, water treatment facilities and trailing ponds. A commercial pilot test of RF XL is being conducted at a site in Marwayne, Alta. The pilot project commenced in March 2022 and achieved first oil production in April 2022. In addition to heavy oil and bitumen production, additional applications of CTI include turquoise hydrogen production, commercial building heat, and bulk solids and crop drying.

The **High-Performance Computing Scientific Software** business segment sells proprietary computing software, primarily seismic imaging and electromagnetic (EM) simulation software. Seismic imaging software products are offered primarily to the oil and gas exploration industry and include AxRTM, which provides the core numerical functionality of reverse time migration (RTM) as a library that can be integrated into an existing seismic processing framework; AxWave, a finite-difference application used for the simulation of seismic wave propagation through the subsurface simulation of 2D and 3D seismic energy in an acoustic medium; and AxFWI, a modular full waveform inversion (FWI) application which provides the highest level of subsurface velocity model accuracy. For the EM simulation software market, provides AxFDTD™, an accelerated finite difference time domain (FDTD) solution, which is sold primarily to independent software vendors that have integrated the company's solution into their software packages.

Predecessor Detail - Succeeded Acceleware Corp., Apr. 26, 2011, pursuant to a plan of arrangement whereby all assets and liabilities, with the exception of certain tax assets, were transferred to the new company.

Directors - Bohdan S. (Don) Romaniuk, chr., Calgary, Alta.; Geoffrey (Geoff) Clark, pres. & CEO, Calgary, Alta.; Dr. Michal Okoniewski, chief scientific officer, Calgary, Alta.; Caralyn Bennett, Calgary, Alta.; Jim Boucher, Fort McKay, Alta.; Dr. Peter Neweduk, Victoria, B.C.

Other Exec. Officers - Michael (Mike) Tourigny, COO; Tracy Grierson, CFO

Capital Stock

	Authorized (shs.)	Outstanding (shs.)[1]
First Preferred	unlimited	nil
Second Preferred	unlimited	nil
Common	unlimited	116,277,007

[1] At May 23, 2023

Major Shareholder - Widely held at Apr. 18, 2023.

Price Range - AXE/TSX-VEN

Year	Volume	High	Low	Close
2022	7,601,389	$0.80	$0.19	$0.35
2021	14,304,010	$0.77	$0.20	$0.69
2020	6,701,713	$0.24	$0.05	$0.24
2019	4,754,782	$0.22	$0.07	$0.09
2018	14,705,069	$0.39	$0.12	$0.15

Recent Close: $0.20

Capital Stock Changes - In November 2022, private placement of 6,666,667 units (1 common share & 1 warrant) at 27¢ per unit was completed. Also during 2022, 310,000 common shares were issued on exercise of options.

Financial Statistics

Periods ended:	12m Dec. 31/22^A		12m Dec. 31/21^A
	$000s	%Chg	$000s
Operating revenue	**328**	**-56**	**753**
Cost of sales	19		42
Salaries & benefits	2,097		1,513
Research & devel. expense	2,153		2,093
General & admin expense	926		881
Stock-based compensation	277		219
Operating expense	**5,472**	**+15**	**4,748**
Operating income	**(5,144)**	**n.a.**	**(3,995)**
Deprec., depl. & amort.	71		52
Finance costs, gross	342		9
Pre-tax income	**(5,142)**	**n.a.**	**(4,080)**
Net income	**(5,142)**	**n.a.**	**(4,080)**
Cash & equivalent	1,146		1,948
Accounts receivable	1,035		2,961
Current assets	2,445		5,197
Fixed assets, net	4		44
Right-of-use assets	80		111
Total assets	**2,529**	**-53**	**5,352**
Accts. pay. & accr. liabs	2,308		5,251
Current liabilities	3,080		6,109
Long-term debt, gross	1,257		nil
Long-term debt, net	1,257		nil
Long-term lease liabilities	61		94
Shareholders' equity	(7,159)		(4,123)
Cash from oper. activs	**(4,582)**	**n.a.**	**(305)**
Cash from fin. activs	3,781		343
Cash from invest. activs	nil		(33)
Net cash position	**1,146**	**-41**	**1,948**
Capital expenditures	nil		(33)
	$		$
Earnings per share*	(0.05)		(0.04)
Cash flow per share*	(0.04)		(0.00)
	shs		shs
No. of shs. o/s*	115,072,007		108,095,340
Avg. no. of shs. o/s*	109,281,222		106,632,852
	%		%
Net profit margin	n.m.		(541.83)
Return on equity	n.m.		n.m.
Return on assets	(121.81)		(88.43)
Foreign sales percent	64		80
No. of employees (FTEs)	18		19

* Common
^A Reported in accordance with IFRS

Latest Results

Periods ended:	3m Mar. 31/23^A		3m Mar. 31/22^A
	$000s	%Chg	$000s
Operating revenue	104	+27	82
Net income	(256)	n.a.	(1,905)
	$		$
Earnings per share*	(0.00)		(0.02)

* Common
^A Reported in accordance with IFRS

Historical Summary
(as originally stated)

Fiscal Year	Oper. Rev.	Net Inc. Bef. Disc.	EPS*
	$000s	$000s	$
2022^A	328	(5,142)	(0.05)
2021^A	753	(4,080)	(0.04)
2020^A	899	(2,100)	(0.02)
2019^A	1,454	(1,559)	(0.01)
2018^A	4,317	(99)	(0.00)

* Common
^A Reported in accordance with IFRS

A.42 Accord Financial Corp.*

Symbol - ACD **Exchange** - TSX **CUSIP** - 00435L
Head Office - 602-40 Eglinton Ave E, Toronto, ON, M4P 3A2 **Telephone** - (416) 961-0007 **Toll-free** - (800) 967-0015 **Fax** - (416) 961-9443
Website - www.accordfinancial.com
Email - ieddy@accordfinancial.com
Investor Relations - Irene Eddy (800) 967-0015
Auditors - KPMG LLP C.A., Toronto, Ont.
Bankers - M&T Bank Corporation; Bank of Montreal; HSBC Bank Canada; Canadian Imperial Bank of Commerce, Toronto, Ont.; The Toronto-Dominion Bank, Toronto, Ont.; The Bank of Nova Scotia, Montréal, Qué.
Lawyers - Stikeman Elliott LLP, Toronto, Ont.
Transfer Agents - Computershare Trust Company of Canada Inc., Toronto, Ont.
Employees - 98 at Dec. 31, 2022
Profile - (Ont. 1992) Provides asset-based financial services to small and medium-sized companies in Canada and the U.S., including receivables financing, factoring, inventory financing, lease and equipment financing, working capital financing, film and media financing, credit protection and receivables management, as well as supply chain financing for importers.

The company's business primarily involves: (i) asset-based lending, which entails financing or purchasing accounts receivable on a recourse basis, as well as financing other tangible assets, such as inventory and equipment; (ii) lease and equipment financing and working capital financing to small businesses; (iii) film and media production financing; and (iv) credit protection and receivables management, which principally involves providing credit guarantees and collection services, generally without financing.

Accord Financial Inc. (AFI Canada) - Provides asset-based lending services, consisting of receivables financing, including recourse factoring (which consists primarily of the purchase of accounts receivable), as well as inventory, equipment and real estate financing to a wide range of small and medium-sized companies based in Canada. Also provides purchase order and supply chain financing. Client companies include financial services, leasing, manufacturing, retail, transportation, food processing, printing, packaging, apparel, electronics, telecommunication and industrial products enterprises.

Accord Financial Canada Corp. (dba Accord Small Business Finance) - Finances equipment in the form of lease financing and equipment loans, and provides unsecured working capital financing for small and medium-sized businesses primarily in western Canada, serving industries ranging from forestry and energy, to construction and manufacturing. Also offers AccordExpress, a program designed for small businesses that provides up to $250,000 of working capital and up to $1,000,000 when backed by receivables or equipment collateral, all with flexible terms.

Accord Financial, Inc. (AFI U.S.) - Engages in asset-based lending, which primarily consists of the financing of accounts receivable including recourse factoring, as well as inventory and equipment financing. Its operations are similar to those of AFI Canada. AFI U.S.' clients are located throughout the U.S. and are engaged in industries such as financial services, manufacturing, retailing, temporary staffing, automotive financing, professional services, pharmaceutical supply, advertising, food services and industrial products.

BondIt Media Capital (60% owned) - Engages in providing financing to films and television projects. Offers flexible financing options for media projects, business and producers. Also offers financing for minimum guarantees, gap loans, bridge loans, sales receivables, union deposits and film tax credit loans.

Accord CapX LLC (dba Accord Equipment Finance) - Provides equipment financing to small and medium-sized businesses by creating flexible solutions that support their client's needs for growth or liquidity. Accord Equipment Finance is an alternate debt provider focusing on equipment loans and leases. Clients include multiple industries such as manufacturing, transportation and retail trade throughout the U.S. and Canada.

Accord Financial Ltd. (AFL) - Provides credit protection (credit guarantees) and receivables management services, as well as supply chain financing, mostly to international factoring companies through its Factors Chain International affiliation. Operates out of leased premises in Toronto, Ont.

Predecessor Detail - Name changed from Delta Star Resources Inc., Mar. 31, 1992, pursuant to reverse takeover acquisition of Accord Business Credit Inc.; basis 1 new for 5 old shs.

Directors - David Beutel, chr., Toronto, Ont.; Simon J. Hitzig, pres., CEO, corp. sec. & pres., Accord Financial Ltd., Toronto, Ont.; Burt Feinberg, New York, N.Y.; Jean K. Holley, Alpharetta, Ga.; Gary J. Prager, Wake Forest, N.C.; David Spivak, Vancouver, B.C.; Stephen D. Warden, Oakville, Ont.

Other Exec. Officers - Barrett Carlson, sr. v-p, corp. devel. & pres., Accord CapX LLC; Irene Eddy, sr. v-p & CFO; Todd Eubanks, sr. v-p, underwriting & portfolio risk; Cathy Osborne, sr. v-p, HR; Jean (Jim) Bates, pres., Canada receivables mgt.; Matthew Helderman, pres., BondIt Media Capital; Jim Hogan, pres., Accord Financial, Inc. & pres., Accord equipment fin.; James Jang, pres., Accord small bus. fin.; Jason Rosenfeld, pres., Accord Financial Inc.

Capital Stock

	Authorized (shs.)	Outstanding (shs.)[1]
First Preferred	unlimited	nil
Common	unlimited	8,558,913

[1] At Aug. 13, 2023

Major Shareholder - Oakwest Corporation Limited held 24.78% interest, Simon J. Hitzig held 23.37% interest and 3502236 Canada Inc. held 12.24% interest at Apr. 25, 2023.

Price Range - ACD/TSX

Year	Volume	High	Low	Close
2022	468,950	$9.50	$7.50	$7.70
2021	748,579	$9.20	$6.23	$8.40
2020	713,647	$10.15	$3.51	$6.70
2019	479,002	$10.42	$8.37	$10.07
2018	311,284	$10.45	$8.22	$9.09

Recent Close: $5.99

Capital Stock Changes - There were no changes to capital stock during 2021 or 2022.

Dividends

ACD com Ra $0.30 pa Q est. Mar. 1, 2022
Prev. Rate: $0.20 est. June 1, 2020

Long-Term Debt - Outstanding at Dec. 31, 2022:

7% conv. debs. due Dec. 2023[1]	$24,863,761
Demand & term notes[2]	18,605,161
	43,469,022

[1] Convertible into common shares at $13.50 per share. An equity component of $1,005,105 was classified as part of shareholders' equity.
[2] Bearing interest at prime or at rates varying between 7% and 11%, respectively, due on various dates to July 2025.

Note - In August 2023, amendments to the company's 7% convertible debentures were approved, including an increase in the interest rate to 10% effective as of Jan. 2, 2024; extending the maturity date to Jan. 31, 2026, from Dec. 31, 2023; removing the company's right to repay the principal amount in common shares on the new maturity date or any redemption date; and removing the conversion right of the debentureholders.

Wholly Owned Subsidiaries

Accord Financial Canada Corp., Alta.
Accord Financial Inc., Montréal, Qué. Formerly Montcap Financial Corporation.
Accord Financial, Inc., Del.
- 100% int. in **Accord CapX LLC**, Chicago, Ill.
- 60% int. in **BondIt Media Capital**, Santa Monica, Calif.

Accord Financial Ltd., Ont. Formerly Accord Business Credit Inc.
Note: The preceding list includes only the major related companies in which interests are held.

Financial Statistics

Periods ended:	12m Dec. 31/22[A]		12m Dec. 31/21[A]
	$000s	%Chg	$000s
Total revenue	**67,491**	**+6**	**63,480**
General & admin. expense	29,599		31,456
Operating expense	**29,599**	**-6**	**31,456**
Operating income	**37,892**	**+18**	**32,024**
Deprec. & amort.	834		836
Provision for loan losses	8,293		(614)
Finance costs, gross	24,087		15,887
Write-downs/write-offs	(2,031)		(873)
Pre-tax income	**2,646**	**-82**	**14,949**
Income taxes	1,001		1,727
Net income	**1,645**	**-88**	**13,222**
Net inc. for equity hldrs	**1,427**	**-88**	**11,887**
Net inc. for non-cont. int.	**218**	**-84**	**1,335**
Cash & equivalent	11,630		13,839
Investments	444,458		472,899
Fixed assets, net	1,746		1,273
Intangibles, net	15,276		16,253
Total assets	**491,761**	**-5**	**520,109**
Bank indebtedness	323,094		356,819
Accts. pay. & accr. liabs	11,224		11,863
Debt	43,469		40,145
Lease liabilities	1,496		979
Equity portion of conv. debs	1,005		1,005
Shareholders' equity	100,972		99,967
Non-controlling interest	5,640		3,992
Cash from oper. activs	**31,507**	**n.a.**	**(101,647)**
Cash from fin. activs	(37,271)		120,375
Cash from invest. activs	(175)		(83)
Net cash position	**18,255**	**-24**	**24,148**
Capital expenditures	(175)		(83)
	$		$
Earnings per share*	0.17		1.39
Cash flow per share*	3.68		(11.88)
Cash divd. per share*	0.30		0.20
	shs		shs
No. of shs. o/s*	8,558,913		8,558,913
Avg. no. of shs. o/s*	8,558,913		8,558,913
	%		%
Net profit margin	2.44		20.83
Return on equity	1.42		12.52
Return on assets	3.28		6.03
Foreign sales percent	43		49
No. of employees (FTEs)	98		90

* Common
[A] Reported in accordance with IFRS

Latest Results

Periods ended:	6m June 30/23[A]		6m June 30/22[A]
	$000s	%Chg	$000s
Total revenue	36,377	+11	32,668
Net income	1,517	-56	3,416
Net inc. for equity hldrs	1,756	-46	3,260
Net inc. for non-cont. int.	(239)		156
	$		$
Earnings per share*	0.21		0.38

* Common
[A] Reported in accordance with IFRS

Historical Summary
(as originally stated)

Fiscal Year	Total Rev.	Net Inc. Bef. Disc.	EPS*
	$000s	$000s	$
2022[A]	67,491	1,645	0.17
2021[A]	63,480	13,222	1.39
2020[A]	48,501	608	0.05
2019[A]	56,175	5,341	0.76
2018[A]	46,927	11,227	1.24

* Common
[A] Reported in accordance with IFRS

A.43 Ackroo Inc.

Symbol - AKR **Exchange** - TSX-VEN **CUSIP** - 00461T
Head Office - Unit A3-1, 1250 Service Rd S, Hamilton, ON, L8E 5R9 **Telephone** - (613) 599-2396 **Toll-free** - (888) 405-0066 **Fax** - (613) 280-1551
Website - www.ackroo.com
Email - slevely@ackroo.com
Investor Relations - Steve Levely (613) 599-2396 ext. 730
Auditors - MNP LLP C.A.
Lawyers - Cassels Brock & Blackwell LLP, Vancouver, B.C.
Transfer Agents - Computershare Trust Company of Canada Inc., Vancouver, B.C.
Profile - (Can. 2000; orig. Alta., 1998 amalg.) Provides cloud-based gift card and loyalty technology platform to automotive, petroleum, retail and hospitality businesses of all sizes across North America.

The company's products include AckrooMKTG, a self-serve, data driven, cloud-based marketing platform which helps merchants in-store and online process and manage loyalty, gift card and promotional transactions at the point of sale; AckrooPAY, which provides merchants with payment processing options through some of the payment technology and service providers; and AckrooPOS, a hybrid management and point-of-sale solutions which helps manage and optimize the general operations of automotive dealers (Interactive DMS platform).

Also offers marketing services including email and direct mail marketing as well as design; and payment services including credit and debit card processing.

In April 2023, the company sold all customer contracts and related intellectual property of **3916715 Canada Inc.** (dba GGGolf), a golf course management solution, to Quebec-based investment group for a total consideration of $1,600,000 including $1,200,000 cash and eight monthly payments of $50,000. The acquiror would operate under the name **GGGolf Technologies Inc.**

In January 2023, the company acquired all customer contracts and related intellectual property (IP) of U.S.-based **Simpliconnect Inc.** for a total consideration of US$2,000,000 including issuance of 5,625,000 common shares at a deemed price of Cdn$0.12 per share, US$750,000 cash and six monthly cash payments of US$125,000 commencing on July 1, 2023. Simpliconnect is a Software-as-a-Service provider which focuses on driving client engagement for small to medium sized convenience store and petroleum chains.

Predecessor Detail - Name changed from Rare Earth Industries Ltd., Oct. 1, 2012, following reverse takeover acquisition of MoneyBar Rewards Inc.; basis 1 new for 2.5 old shs.
Directors - Steve Levely, CEO & acting CFO, Ont.; Philippe Bergeron-Belanger, Qué.; Jon Clare, Ont.; Sam Cole, B.C.; Bradley (Brad) French, Ont.; Jeremy Jagt, Ont.
Other Exec. Officers - Kevin Kennedy, v-p, product; Cheryl Lewis, v-p, opers.; Tyler Moss, v-p, fin. & admin.

Capital Stock

	Authorized (shs.)	Outstanding (shs.)[1]
Preferred	unlimited	nil
Common	unlimited	121,373,633

[1] At Mar. 31, 2023

Normal Course Issuer Bid - The company plans to make normal course purchases of up to 6,068,681 common shares representing 5% of the total outstanding. The bid commenced on June 16, 2023, and expires on June 15, 2024.
Major Shareholder - Rivemont MicroCap Fund held 14.83% interest, M3 Rebel Corporation held 14.46% interest and 2700715 Ontario Inc. held 10.57% interest at Sept. 1, 2022.

Price Range - AKR/TSX-VEN

Year	Volume	High	Low	Close
2022	16,885,218	$0.15	$0.05	$0.05
2021	17,556,038	$0.38	$0.11	$0.13
2020	14,333,803	$0.20	$0.08	$0.20
2019	14,317,698	$0.20	$0.10	$0.19
2018	25,399,997	$0.17	$0.07	$0.10

Recent Close: $0.09
Capital Stock Changes - In December 2022, 5,625,000 common shares were issued on acquisition of certain assets of Simpliconnect Inc.

Wholly Owned Subsidiaries

Ackroo Canada Inc., Ottawa, Ont.
Ackroo Corporation
3916715 Canada Inc., Longueuil, Qué.

Financial Statistics

Periods ended:	12m Dec. 31/22[A]		12m Dec. 31/21[A]
	$000s	%Chg	$000s
Operating revenue	**6,264**	**+5**	**5,978**
Cost of sales	579		707
Research & devel. expense	1,154		1,170
General & admin expense	3,191		3,692
Stock-based compensation	230		506
Operating expense	**5,154**	**-15**	**6,075**
Operating income	**1,110**	**n.a.**	**(97)**
Deprec., depl. & amort.	1,659		2,055
Finance costs, gross	386		512
Pre-tax income	**(2,037)**	**n.a.**	**(2,663)**
Net income	**(2,037)**	**n.a.**	**(2,663)**
Cash & equivalent	11		772
Inventories	8		21
Accounts receivable	461		470
Current assets	1,812		1,328
Fixed assets, net	84		110
Right-of-use assets	1,376		1,619
Intangibles, net	4,118		5,488
Total assets	**7,702**	**-14**	**8,953**
Bank indebtedness	515		nil
Accts. pay. & accr. liabs	553		598
Current liabilities	2,089		1,007
Long-term debt, gross	2,976		3,414
Long-term debt, net	2,745		3,336
Long-term lease liabilities	1,341		1,502
Shareholders' equity	1,527		3,080
Cash from oper. activs	**463**	**n.m.**	**29**
Cash from fin. activs	62		(223)
Cash from invest. activs	(1,286)		(967)
Net cash position	**11**	**-99**	**772**
Capital expenditures	(12)		(42)
Capital disposals	25		nil
	$		$
Earnings per share*	(0.02)		(0.02)
Cash flow per share*	0.00		0.00
	shs		shs
No. of shs. o/s*	121,373,633		115,748,633
Avg. no. of shs. o/s*	115,794,866		111,777,657
	%		%
Net profit margin	(32.52)		(44.55)
Return on equity	(88.43)		(77.21)
Return on assets	(19.83)		(21.37)

* Common
[A] Reported in accordance with IFRS

Latest Results

Periods ended:	3m Mar. 31/23[A]		3m Mar. 31/22[A]
	$000s	%Chg	$000s
Operating revenue	1,825	+17	1,556
Net income	502	n.a.	(476)
	$		$
Earnings per share*	0.00		(0.00)

* Common
[A] Reported in accordance with IFRS

Historical Summary
(as originally stated)

Fiscal Year	Oper. Rev.	Net Inc. Bef. Disc.	EPS*
	$000s	$000s	$
2022[A]	6,264	(2,037)	(0.02)
2021[A]	5,978	(2,663)	(0.02)
2020[A]	6,048	(1,303)	(0.02)
2019[A]	5,233	(1,179)	(0.01)
2018[A]	4,435	(1,067)	(0.01)

* Common
[A] Reported in accordance with IFRS

A.44 Acreage Holdings, Inc.

Symbol - ACRG.A.U **Exchange** - CSE **CUSIP** - 00489Y
Head Office - 450 Lexington Ave, Suite 3308, New York, NY, United States, 10163 **Telephone** - (646) 600-9181
Website - www.acreageholdings.com
Email - investors@acreageholdings.com
Investor Relations - Dennis Curran (646) 600-9181
Auditors - Marcum LLP C.P.A., New York, N.Y.
Transfer Agents - Odyssey Trust Company, Vancouver, B.C.
FP500 Revenue Ranking - 558
Employees - 1,016 at Feb. 28, 2023
Profile - (B.C. 2018; orig. Ont., 1989) Owns, manages and operates cannabis cultivation, processing, manufacturing and dispensary operations in U.S. states where medical or recreational use of cannabis is legal.

The company holds licences or is a party to management or consulting services agreements to operate in the cultivation, processing and manufacturing, wholesale, and retail sales of legal cannabis in the U.S. Operations include cultivating and processing cannabis plants;

manufacturing branded consumer products; wholesale distribution of cannabis flower and manufactured products, and retailing dosable cannabis products to consumers.

Products include pre-rolls and concentrated extracts for use in gel caps, edibles, beverages, and vape cartridges. Product brands include The Botanist, Prime Wellness Superflux and Innocent, as well as licensed brands such as **Canopy Growth Corporation**'s Tweed.

At June 30, 2022, the company owned and operated 27 dispensaries located in Oregon (4), New York (4), New Jersey (3), Connecticut (3), Massachusetts (2), Illinois (2), Ohio (5) and Maine (4). It also owned and operated nine cultivation and processing facilities located in Massachusetts (2), California, Illinois, Maine, New Jersey, New York, Ohio and Pennsylvania; indoor and greenhouse cultivation space totaled 104,094 sq. ft.

Also owns **Universal Hemp, LLC**, which is focused on thee distribution, marketing and sale of CBD products throughout the U.S.

On July 5, 2022, the company sold its four Oregon retail dispensaries branded as Cannabliss & Co. to **Chalice Brands Ltd.** for US$6,200,000, consisting of US$350,000 cash and issuance of a US$5,850,000 promissory note.

On May 3, 2022, the company completed the sale of a 30,000-sq.-ft. indoor cultivation facility in Medford, Ore., and a dispensary in Portland, Ore., to **Grown Rogue International Inc.** for US$3,000,000 payable in tranches. Grown Rogue had assumed operations of the cultivation facility under a management services agreement in February 2021 following announcement of the sale.

Recent Merger and Acquisition Activity

Status: pending **Revised:** Oct. 25, 2022

UPDATE: Canopy announced the formation of a new U.S. domiciled entity Canopy USA, LLC which would complete the transaction with Acreage. Canopy USA would acquire all of the issued and outstanding class D subordinate voting shares of Acreage for consideration of 0.45 Canopy common share in exchange for each class D share. Concurrently, Canopy irrevocably waived its option to acquire the class D shares pursuant to the plan of arrangement implemented on Sept. 23, 2020, pursuant to the arrangement agreement between Canopy and Acreage dated Apr. 18, 2019. Canopy has agreed to exercise its option under the existing arrangement to acquire Acreage's outstanding class E subordinate voting shares, representing 70% of the total shares of Acreage, at a fixed exchange ratio of 0.3048 Canopy common share for each class E share. Upon completion of the acquisition of the Acreage class D and class E shares, Canopy USA would own all the shares. Under the existing arrangement, Canopy was not obligated to acquire the class D shares but rather had an option to acquire those shares at a minimum price of US$6.41 per class D share. The acquisition of the class D shares was expected to close in the second half of 2023, and the acquisition of the class E shares to immediately follow. PREVIOUS: Canopy Growth Corp. entered into an agreement with Acreage Holdings, Inc. that grants Canopy the rights to acquire 100% of Acreage once cannabis becomes federally legal in the United States. Under the agreement, Acreage shareholders would receive an upfront payment of US$300,000,000 or US$2.55 per subordinate voting share. The upfront cash payment would be made to holders of Acreage subordinate voting shares, class B proportionate voting shares and class C multiple voting shares as well as holders of units of High Street Capital Partners, LLC and shares of Acreage Holdings WC, Inc. Upon the exercise of the right, Acreage subordinate voting shares, including those outstanding on conversion of multiple voting shares and other convertible securities, would receive 0.5818 Canopy Growth common shares for each Acreage subordinate voting share held. Upon exercise of the right, the total consideration payable is valued at US$3.4 billion. The companies would also execute a licensing agreement granting Acreage access to Canopy's brands such as Tweed and Tokyo Smoke and other intellectual property. The transaction would require the approval of shareholders of both Canopy Growth and Acreage at special meetings expected to take place in June 2019. The agreement includes termination fee of US$150,000,000 payable by Acreage in the event that the transaction is terminated in certain circumstances. June 19, 2019 - Canopy and Acreage shareholders approved the transaction. The initial payment was expected to be made to Acreage shareholders on June 27, 2019. June 21, 2019 - Acreage received an approval for the transaction from the Supreme Court of British Columbia. June 27, 2019 - The option was completed. Acreage shareholders received approximately US$2.63 per subordinate voting share, being their pro rata portion of US$300,000,000. The payment was to be distributed on or before July 3, 2019. June 25, 2020 - The terms of the agreement were amended including an upfront payment of US$37,500,000, creation of two new classes of shares in the capital of Acreage, with each existing Acreage subordinate voting shares being converted into 0.7 of new S.V. shares; and new floating shares that are not tied to fixed exchange ratio. In addition, Canopy has agreed to loan up to US$100,000,000 to Acreage in the form of a secured debenture. Sept. 23, 2020 - Acreage created the following new classes of shares: class E subordinate voting, class D subordinate voting and class F multiple voting. Each outstanding Acreage class A subordinate voting share was exchanged for 0.7 class E shares and 0.3 class D shares; each outstanding Acreage class B proportionate voting share was exchanged for 28 class E shares and 12 class D shares; and each outstanding Acreage class C multiple voting share was exchanged for 0.3 class D shares and 0.7 class F shares. Under an amended agreement, Canopy would only be required to acquire all outstanding class E shares upon a federal legalization event on the basis of 0.3048 Canopy common shares for each Acreage class E share held. Immediately prior to the acquisition, all Acreage class F shares would be automatically convertible into class E shares on a one-for-one basis. The class D shares would then act as an option for Canopy, should Canopy desire to acquire a 100% interest in Acreage, with the acquisition price of the class D shares to be based on the 30-day weighted average price of the shares, subject to a floor price of US$6.41 per share.

Predecessor Detail - Name changed from Applied Inventions Management Corp., Nov. 14, 2018, following reverse takeover acquisition of High Street Capital Partners, LLC (dba Acreage Holdings).

Directors - Dennis Curran, chr. & CEO; Carl Nesbitt, CFO; Corey Sheahan, exec. v-p, gen. counsel & corp. sec.

Other Exec. Officers - Dr. Corey Burchman, CMO; Katrina Yolen, chief mktg. officer; Bryan Murray, exec. v-p, govt. rel.; Laurence Wolfe, sr. v-p, mfg. & distrib.; Gretchen McCarthy, v-p, retail opers.

Capital Stock

	Authorized (shs.)	Outstanding (shs.)[1]
Cl.E Subord. Vtg.	unlimited	79,255,991
Cl.D Subord. Vtg.	unlimited	34,192,028
Cl.F Multiple Vtg.	117,600	117,600

[1] At Apr. 14, 2023

Class E Subordinate Voting - Entitled to dividends. Canopy Growth Corporation is required to acquire all outstanding class E shares upon the federal legalization of cannabis in the United States on the basis of 0.3048 Canopy common shares for one Acreage class E share. One vote per share.

Class D Subordinate Voting - Entitled to dividends. Canopy Growth Corporation holds an option to acquire all outstanding class D shares upon the federal legalization of cannabis in the United States at the 30-day volume weighted average price of the shares, subject to a floor price of US$6.41 per share. One vote per share.

Class F Multiple Voting - Entitled to dividends. Automatically convertible into class E subordinate voting shares on a one-for-one basis immediately prior to the acquisition of all outstanding class E subordinate voting shares by Canopy Growth Corporation. 4,300 votes per share.

Major Shareholder - Kevin P. Murphy held 82.4% interest at Apr. 14, 2023.

Price Range - ACRG.A.U/CSE

Year	Volume	High	Low	Close
2022	6,126,896	US$2.01	US$0.45	US$0.50
2021	14,548,938	US$8.99	US$1.49	US$1.65
2020	4,023,091	US$4.51	US$2.00	US$3.15

ACRG.U/CSE (D)

Year	Volume	High	Low	Close
2020	25,261,175	US$7.08	US$1.49	US$2.77
2019	38,724,282	US$28.30	US$3.88	US$5.92
2018	6,378,238	US$26.90	US$11.99	US$19.00

Recent Close: US$0.14

Wholly Owned Subsidiaries

Acreage Holdings America, Inc., Nev.

- 82.76% int. in **High Street Capital Partners, LLC**, New York, N.Y.
  - 100% int. in **Acreage-CCF, Inc.**, N.J.
  - 100% int. in **Acreage CCF New Jersey, LLC**, N.J.
  - 100% int. in **Acreage California Holding Company, LLC**, Calif.
  - 100% int. in **Acreage Chicago 1, LLC**, Ill.
  - 100% int. in **Acreage Connecticut, LLC**, Conn.
  - 100% int. in **Acreage Desert Hot Springs, LLC**, Del.
  - 100% int. in **Acreage Finance Delaware, LLC**, Del.
  - 100% int. in **Acreage Hoboken, LLC**, N.J.
  - 100% int. in **Acreage Holdings of NJ, LLC**, N.J.
  - 100% int. in **Acreage IP California, LLC**, Calif.
  - 100% int. in **Acreage IP Connecticut, LLC**, Conn.
  - 100% int. in **Acreage IP Holdings, LLC**, Nev.
  - 100% int. in **Acreage IP Massachusetts, LLC**, Mass.
  - 100% int. in **Acreage IP Michigan, LLC**, Mich.
  - 100% int. in **Acreage IP Nevada, LLC**, Nev.
  - 100% int. in **Acreage IP New Jersey, LLC**, N.J.
  - 100% int. in **Acreage IP New York, LLC**, N.Y.
  - 100% int. in **Acreage IP Ohio, LLC**, Ohio
  - 100% int. in **Acreage IP Oregon, LLC**, Ore.
  - 100% int. in **Acreage IP Pennsylvania, LLC**, Pa.
  - 100% int. in **Acreage Illinois 5, LLC**, Ill.
  - 100% int. in **Acreage Illinois 4, LLC**, Ill.
  - 100% int. in **Acreage Illinois Holding Company, LLC**, Ill.
  - 100% int. in **Acreage Illinois 1, LLC**, Ill.
  - 100% int. in **Acreage Illinois 6, LLC**, Ill.
  - 100% int. in **Acreage Illinois 3, LLC**, Ill.
  - 0.1% int. in **Acreage Illinois 2, LLC**, Ill.
  - 100% int. in **Acreage Iowa, LLC**, Iowa
  - 100% int. in **Acreage Massachusetts, LLC**, Mass.
  - 100% int. in **Acreage Michigan 5, LLC**, Mich.
  - 100% int. in **Acreage Michigan 4, LLC**, Mich.
  - 100% int. in **Acreage Michigan Holding Company, LLC**, Del.
  - 100% int. in **Acreage Michigan, LLC**, Mich.
  - 100% int. in **Acreage Michigan 1, LLC**, Mich.
  - 100% int. in **Acreage Michigan Operating, LLC**, Mich.
  - 100% int. in **Acreage Michigan 7, LLC**, Mich.
  - 100% int. in **Acreage Michigan 6, LLC**, Mich.
  - 100% int. in **Acreage Michigan 3, LLC**, Mich.
  - 100% int. in **Acreage Michigan 2, LLC**, Mich.
  - 100% int. in **Acreage New York, LLC**, N.Y.
  - 100% int. in **Acreage OZ RE, LLC**, Del.
  - 100% int. in **Acreage PA Management, LLC**, Pa.
  - 100% int. in **Acreage Pasadena, LLC**, Calif.
  - 100% int. in **Acreage Properties, LLC**, Del.
  - 100% int. in **Acreage RE State Holdings, LLC**, Del.
  - 100% int. in **Acreage Real Estate Holdco, LLC**, Del.
  - 100% int. in **Acreage Real Estate, LLC**, Del.
  - 100% int. in **Acreage Transportation, LLC**, Pa.
  - 100% int. in **Acreage Virginia, LLC**, Va.
  - 100% int. in **Armstrong Merger Sub, Inc.**, Calif.
  - 100% int. in **Balaton Foods, LLC**, Mich.
  - 100% int. in **Blue Tire Holdings, LLC**, Mich.
  - 100% int. in **The Botanist, Inc.**, Mass.
  - 100% int. in **Braeburn, LLC**, Calif.
  - 100% int. in **CWG Botanicals, Inc.**, Calif.
  - 100% int. in **Challenger Merger Sub, LLC**, Nev.
  - 100% int. in **D&B Wellness, LLC**, Conn. dba Compassionate Care Center of Connecticut
  - 100% int. in **East 11th, Inc.**, Ore.
  - 100% int. in **The Firestation 23, Inc.**, Ore.
  - 100% int. in **Form Factory Holdings, LLC**, Portland, Ore.
  - 100% int. in **Gesundheit Foods, LLC**, Ore.
  - 100% int. in **Gravenstein Foods, LLC**
  - 100% int. in **Greenleaf Apothecaries, LLC**, Ohio
  - 100% int. in **Greenleaf Gardens, LLC**, Ohio
  - 100% int. in **Greenleaf Therapeutics, LLC**, Ohio
  - 100% int. in **Gruner Apfel-CA, LLC**, Ore.
  - 100% int. in **Gruner Apfel LLC**, Ore.
  - 100% int. in **HSC Solutions, LLC**, Ill.
  - 100% int. in **HSCP CN Holdings II ULC**, Alta.
  - 100% int. in **HSCP CN Holdings ULC**, Alta.
  - 100% int. in **HSCP Holding Corporation**, Del.
  - 100% int. in **HSCP Oregon, LLC**, Ore.
  - 100% int. in **HSCP Service Company Holdings, Inc.**, Del.
  - 100% int. in **HSCP Service Company, LLC**, Del.
  - 100% int. in **HSPC Holding Corporation**, Del.
  - 100% int. in **HSRC Norcal, LLC**, Calif.
  - 100% int. in **Health Circle, Inc.**, Mass.
  - 100% int. in **High Street Capital Partners Management, LLC**, Del.
  - 100% int. in **Impire State Holdings LLC**, N.Y.
  - 100% int. in **In Grown Farms, LLC**, Ill.
  - 100% int. in **In Grown Farms 2, LLC**, Ill.
  - 100% int. in **Iowa Relief, LLC**, Iowa
  - 100% int. in **Joy Sellers Enterprises, LLC**, Ill.
  - 100% int. in **Kanna, Inc.**, Calif.
  - 100% int. in **Karma Merger Sub Inc.**, Calif.
  - 100% int. in **Kind Care, LLC**, Conn.
  - 100% int. in **MA RMD SVCS, LLC**, Mass.
  - 100% int. in **Made by Science LLC**, Calif.
  - 100% int. in **Maine HSCP, Inc**, Me.
  - 100% int. in **NCC, LLC**, Ill.
  - 100% int. in **NCC Real Estate, LLC**, Ill.
  - 100% int. in **NPG, LLC**, Me.
  - 100% int. in **NPG Portland, LLC**, Me.
  - 100% int. in **NY Medicinal Research & Caring, LLC**, N.Y.
  - 100% int. in **NYCANNA, LLC**, N.Y.
  - 100% int. in **Northeast Patients Group**, Me.
  - 100% int. in **Prime Alternative Treatment Center Consulting, LLC**, N.H.
  - 100% int. in **Prime Consulting Group, LLC**, Mass.
  - 100% int. in **Prime Wellness of Connecticut, LLC**, Conn.
  - 100% int. in **Prime Wellness of Pennsylvania, LLC**, Pa.
  - 100% int. in **Ryan Shirley Enterprises LLC**, Ill.
  - 100% int. in **South Shore Bio Pharma, LLC**, Mass.
  - 100% int. in **Tatich 3, LLC**, Ill.
  - 100% int. in **Thames Valley Apothecary, LLC**, Conn.
  - 100% int. in **22nd and Burn, Inc.**, Ore.
  - 100% int. in **Universal Hemp II, LLC**, Del.
  - 100% int. in **Universal Hemp, LLC**, Del.
  - 100% int. in **The Wellness & Pain Management Connection, LLC**, Me.
  - 100% int. in **Wonka Merger Sub, Inc.**, Del.

Subsidiaries

71.33% int. in **Acreage Holdings WC, Inc.**, Nev.

Financial Statistics

Periods ended:	12m Dec. 31/22[A]		12m Dec. 31/21[A]
	US$000s	%Chg	US$000s
Operating revenue	**237,138**	**+26**	**188,859**
Cost of goods sold	129,611		89,831
Salaries & benefits	55,905		45,769
General & admin expense	41,452		33,669
Stock-based compensation	10,138		19,946
Operating expense	**237,106**	**+25**	**189,215**
Operating income	**32**	**n.a.**	**(356)**
Deprec., depl. & amort.	13,661		14,262
Finance income	1,860		1,275
Finance costs, gross	24,036		19,964
Write-downs/write-offs	(129,799)[1]		(32,081)[2]
Pre-tax income	**(158,673)**	**n.a.**	**(55,352)**
Income taxes	10,022		17,805
Net income	**(168,695)**	**n.a.**	**(73,157)**
Net inc. for equity hldrs	**(139,876)**	**n.a.**	**(63,010)**
Net inc. for non-cont. int	**(28,819)**	**n.a.**	**(10,147)**
Cash & equivalent	24,067		43,180
Inventories	49,446		41,804
Accounts receivable	10,512		8,202
Current assets	118,193		112,979
Long-term investments	34,046		62,789
Fixed assets, net	133,405		126,797
Right-of-use assets	22,443		24,598
Intangibles, net	48,885		163,005
Total assets	**360,573**	**-27**	**491,551**
Accts. pay. & accr. liabs	29,566		23,861
Current liabilities	72,333		66,793
Long-term debt, gross	215,080		170,734
Long-term debt, net	213,496		169,151
Long-term lease liabilities	21,692		24,255
Shareholders' equity	61,384		197,267
Non-controlling interest	(21,205)		7,003
Cash from oper. activs	**(50,095)**	**n.a.**	**(40,530)**
Cash from fin. activs	39,270		(12,977)
Cash from invest. activs	(9,609)		43,369
Net cash position	**24,067**	**-46**	**44,501**
Capital expenditures	(18,482)		(33,049)
Capital disposals	nil		5
	US$		US$
Earnings per share*	(1.28)		(0.60)
Cash flow per share*	(0.46)		(0.39)
	shs		shs
No. of shs. o/s*	112,437,000		106,903,000
Avg. no. of shs. o/s*	109,690,000		105,087,000
	%		%
Net profit margin	(71.14)		(38.74)
Return on equity	(108.16)		(28.75)
Return on assets	(33.60)		(8.88)
Foreign sales percent	100		100

* Class D, E & F

[A] Reported in accordance with U.S. GAAP

[1] Includes impairment of US$100,866,000 on intangible assets and US$16,590,000 on goodwill.

[2] Includes impairment losses of US$32,828,000 on certain intangible assets and capital assets.

Historical Summary
(as originally stated)

Fiscal Year	Oper. Rev. US$000s	Net Inc. Bef. Disc. US$000s	EPS* US$
2022[A]	237,138	(168,695)	(1.28)
2021[A]	188,859	(73,157)	(0.60)
2020[A]	114,545	(360,118)	(2.87)
2019[A]	74,109	(195,162)	(1.74)
2018[B1]	21,124	(219,685)	(3.08)

* Class D, E & F

[A] Reported in accordance with U.S. GAAP

[B] Reported in accordance with IFRS

[1] Results reflect the Nov. 14, 2018, reverse takeover acquisition of High Street Capital Partners, LLC (dba Acreage Holdings).

A.45 Adagio Capital Inc.

Symbol - ADC.P **Exchange** - TSX-VEN **CUSIP** - 00535E
Head Office - 1510-789 Pender St W, Vancouver, BC, V6C 1H2
Telephone - (604) 728-7715
Email - dhallaazim@gmail.com
Investor Relations - Azim Dhalla (604) 728-7715
Auditors - Dale Matheson Carr-Hilton LaBonte LLP C.A., Vancouver, B.C.
Transfer Agents - Endeavor Trust Corporation, Vancouver, B.C.
Profile - (B.C. 2021) Capital Pool Company.
Common listed on TSX-VEN, Dec. 21, 2022.
Directors - Azim Dhalla, pres., CEO, CFO & corp. sec., Vancouver, B.C.; Nizar Y. Bharmal, Burnaby, B.C.; Christopher P. (Chris) Cherry, Vancouver, B.C.; James W. (Jim) Mustard, Vancouver, B.C.

Capital Stock

	Authorized (shs.)	Outstanding (shs.)[1]
Common	unlimited	5,000,000

[1] At Dec. 21, 2022

Major Shareholder - Azim Dhalla held 34% interest and James W. (Jim) Mustard held 16% interest at Dec. 21, 2022.
Recent Close: $0.14
Capital Stock Changes - On Dec. 21, 2022, an initial public offering of 2,000,000 common shares was completed at 10¢ per share.

A.46 Adamant Holdings Inc.

Symbol - ADMT **Exchange** - CSE (S) **CUSIP** - 00547K
Head Office - 1200-750 Pender St W, Vancouver, BC, V6C 2T8
Telephone - (778) 218-9638 **Fax** - (778) 218-9623
Website - adamantglobal.com
Email - apagani@adamantglobal.com
Investor Relations - Andrea Pagani (778) 218-9638
Auditors - GreenGrowth C.P.A., Los Angeles, Calif.
Lawyers - MacDonald Tuskey Corporate & Securities Lawyers, Vancouver, B.C.
Transfer Agents - Odyssey Trust Company
Profile - (B.C. 2012) Operates as a global telecom carrier in regions including Asia, Canada, Europe and the U.S.

The company is a licensed global telecom carrier within the international Voice over Internet Protocol (VoIP) wholesale business focusing on wholesale international long distance traffic termination. The company provides subscribers of global and local partner telecom companies with reasonable pricing on high-quality on-network international calls, while still providing customers with free texting, international airtime top-up capabilities, and other social media features available with most over-the-top applications around the world.

Has developed Upco Mobile Messenger, a mobile-based data application similar to SKYPE and WhatsApp and available on Apple iOS and Android. The app enables fully secure communications with other users including phone calls, sending messages, sharing pictures and locations and international balance transfer. Users can call non-Upco users at attractive rates or flexible calling plans using Upco-Out. In addition, the company has developed UpcoPay, an e-wallet payment solution which allows users to send and receive money anonymously without the use of any credit or debit card.

On Aug. 26, 2022, the company agreed to acquire 51% interest in **Domooptik d.o.o.**, a licensed public electronic communication networks operator in Saravejo, Bosnia and specializing in IT consulting, and set up and maintenance of fibre optic networks. Terms were not disclosed.

On Aug. 19, 2022, the company agreed to acquire 51% interest in **Europronet**, a licensed carrier operator and internet service provider in Saravejo, Bosnia. Terms were not disclosed.

Common suspended from CSE, May 9, 2023.

Predecessor Detail - Name changed from Upco International Inc., May 3, 2022.
Directors - Andrea Pagani, chr., pres. & CEO, Milan, Italy; Estanislao Peña; Juan Ramos Taboada, Buenos Aires, Argentina
Other Exec. Officers - Osvaldo Navarro, CFO; Trent Collett, exec. v-p, corp. devel. & IR

Capital Stock

	Authorized (shs.)	Outstanding (shs.)[1]
Common	unlimited	136,405,489

[1] At Sept. 30, 2022

Major Shareholder - Aduna Holding GmbH held 16.53% interest at Mar. 23, 2022.

Price Range - ADMT/CSE (S)

Year	Volume	High	Low	Close
2022	6,485,041	$0.07	$0.02	$0.02
2021	128,416,309	$0.46	$0.05	$0.05
2020	39,561,506	$0.12	$0.03	$0.07
2019	12,499,434	$0.18	$0.03	$0.07
2018	11,842,879	$0.45	$0.08	$0.15

Recent Close: $0.02

Wholly Owned Subsidiaries

Brilliance Global LLC, Del.
Oktacom Inc., N.Y.

Financial Statistics

Periods ended:	12m Dec. 31/21[A]		12m Dec. 31/20[oA]
	US$000s	%Chg	US$000s
Operating revenue	**496**	**n.a.**	**nil**
Cost of sales	459		nil
General & admin expense	814		1,314
Operating expense	**814**	**-38**	**1,314**
Operating income	**(318)**	**n.a.**	**(1,314)**
Deprec., depl. & amort.	1		70
Finance income	1		1
Finance costs, gross	49		33
Write-downs/write-offs	(24)		(188)
Pre-tax income	**(717)**	**n.a.**	**(1,501)**
Net income	**(717)**	**n.a.**	**(1,501)**
Cash & equivalent	1,394		5
Accounts receivable	42		38
Current assets	1,456		45
Fixed assets, net	9		nil
Total assets	**1,465**	**n.m.**	**45**
Bank indebtedness	nil		6
Accts. pay. & accr. liabs	169		406
Current liabilities	169		412
Long-term debt, gross	204		173
Long-term debt, net	204		173
Equity portion of conv. debs	120		120
Shareholders' equity	943		(684)
Cash from oper. activs	**(647)**	**n.a.**	**(144)**
Cash from fin. activs	2,109		160
Cash from invest. activs	(10)		nil
Net cash position	**1,394**	**n.m.**	**5**
Capital expenditures	(10)		nil
	US$		US$
Earnings per share*	(0.01)		(0.02)
Cash flow per share*	(0.01)		(0.00)
	shs		shs
No. of shs. o/s*	131,668,739		114,590,095
Avg. no. of shs. o/s*	107,133,151		90,349,181
	%		%
Net profit margin	(144.56)		n.a.
Return on equity	n.m.		n.m.
Return on assets	(88.48)		(477.40)

* Common

[o] Restated

[A] Reported in accordance with IFRS

Latest Results

Periods ended:	9m Sept. 30/22[A]		9m Sept. 30/21[A]
	US$000s	%Chg	US$000s
Operating revenue	1,166	+489	198
Net income	(668)	n.a.	(892)
	US$		US$
Earnings per share*	(0.00)		(0.01)

* Common

[A] Reported in accordance with IFRS

Historical Summary
(as originally stated)

Fiscal Year	Oper. Rev. US$000s	Net Inc. Bef. Disc. US$000s	EPS* US$
2021[A]	496	(717)	(0.01)
2020[A]	nil	(1,501)	(0.02)
2019[A]	304	(1,967)	(0.03)
2018[A]	2,515	(2,527)	(0.04)
2017[A1]	6,688	(1,212)	(0.05)

* Common

[A] Reported in accordance with IFRS

[1] Results reflect the Oct. 24, 2017, reverse takeover acquisition of Upco Systems Inc.

A.47 Adaptogenics Health Corp.

Symbol - ADPT **Exchange** - CSE **CUSIP** - 00654R
Head Office - 1100-1111 Melville St, Vancouver, BC, V6E 3V6
Telephone - (604) 782-4264
Website - adaptogenicshealth.com/home-page/
Email - info@adaptogenicshealth.com
Investor Relations - Hani Zabaneh (604) 782-4264
Auditors - Crowe MacKay LLP C.A., Vancouver, B.C.
Transfer Agents - Odyssey Trust Company, Vancouver, B.C.
Profile - (B.C. 2021) Formulates and distributes functional mushroom products and nutritional supplement alternatives.

Products are formulated combining functional mushrooms and adaptogenic herbs which are aimed to support holistic health.

Plans to launch five premium functional mushroom liquid tonics consisting of Reishi, Chaga, Turkey Tail, Lions Mane and Cordyceps. Products would be sold directly to customers primarily through the company's website, as well as wholesaling to retailers throughout Canada with a target on natural health food, supplement and grocery stores that currently sell mushroom products.

Common listed on CSE, Jan. 9, 2023.

Directors - Daryl Ware-Lane, CEO, Vancouver, B.C.; Hani Zabaneh, COO, North Vancouver, B.C.; Dave Heel, v-p, sales, Vancouver, B.C.; Martin Bajic, Burnaby, B.C.; Dr. Pavandeep Mehat, Victoria, B.C.

Other Exec. Officers - Ming Jang, CFO & corp. sec.

Capital Stock

	Authorized (shs.)	Outstanding (shs.)[1]
Common	unlimited	16,397,701

[1] At Jan. 9, 2023

Major Shareholder - Widely held at Jan. 9, 2023.

Recent Close: $0.05

Capital Stock Changes - On Apr. 1, 2021, 1 common share was issued upon incorporation. In July 2021, private placement of 5,000,000 common shares was completed at 2¢ per share. In January 2022, private placement of 11,397,700 common shares was completed at 5¢ per share.

Financial Statistics

Periods ended:	12m Mar. 31/22[A]
	$000s
General & admin expense	141
Operating expense	**141**
Operating income	**(141)**
Pre-tax income	**(141)**
Net income	**(141)**
Cash & equivalent	534
Accounts receivable	4
Current assets	577
Total assets	**577**
Accts. pay. & accr. liabs	38
Current liabilities	48
Shareholders' equity	529
Cash from oper. activs	**(136)**
Cash from fin. activs	670
Net cash position	**534**
	$
Earnings per share*	(0.03)
Cash flow per share*	(0.02)
	shs
No. of shs. o/s*	16,397,701
Avg. no. of shs. o/s*	5,622,007
	%
Net profit margin	n.a.
Return on equity	n.m.
Return on assets	n.a.

* Common

[A] Reported in accordance with IFRS

A.48 Adastra Holdings Ltd.

Symbol - XTRX **Exchange** - CSE **CUSIP** - 00654D

Head Office - 5451 275 St, Langley, BC, V4W 3X8 **Telephone** - (778) 715-5011 **Fax** - (844) 874-9893

Website - www.adastraholdings.ca

Email - michael@adastraholdings.ca

Investor Relations - Michael Forbes (778) 715-5011

Auditors - Davidson & Company LLP C.A., Vancouver, B.C.

Transfer Agents - National Securities Administrators Ltd., Vancouver, B.C.

Profile - (B.C. 1987) Manufactures and supplies ethnobotanical and cannabis science products designed for the adult-use and medical markets as well as for therapeutic applications.

The company has been granted a licence to produce and sell cannabis extracts, edibles and topicals under the Cannabis Act as well as a licence by Health Canada to conduct analytical testing for the cannabis industry at its facility in Langley, B.C. The 13,035-sq.-ft. facility, which commenced operations on Apr. 23, 2020, operates supercritical carbon dioxide primary extraction line for crude cannabis/hemp oil production, wiped film short path distillation line for production of high grade cannabis distillate, formulation and filling line for tincture bottles and vaporizer products, and packaging for finished packaged goods. Extracts are incorporated into edibles, beverages, topicals, tinctures, vape cartridges and other products that serve the Canadian medical and adult-use cannabis markets. Products are available at more than 1,400 adult-use retailers across Canada.

The company also operates a multidisciplinary centre in Victoria, B.C., for medical cannabis and psychedelic therapies, where a team of nurses, pharmacists, physicians, specialists and educators help create remedies that address the needs of patients. In addition, the company has been granted a license to procure and process controlled substances, including synthesis, propagation, cultivation and harvesting of psychedelic mushrooms for psilocybin extraction, research and manufacture controlled substances such as psilocybin and psilocin and business-to-business sale of controlled substances, including by export.

In March 2022, the company entered into a private label manufacturing agreement with **Zyre Brands Corp.**, whereby the company would manufacture custom-formulated cured resin vape products to sell under the Zyre brand in the Canadian adult-use market.

Predecessor Detail - Name changed from Phyto Extractions Inc., Sept. 1, 2021.

Directors - Michael Forbes, pres., CEO & corp. sec., B.C.; Paul Morgan, B.C.; J. Smoke Wallin, Calif.

Other Exec. Officers - Lachlan McLeod, CFO

Capital Stock

	Authorized (shs.)	Outstanding (shs.)[1]
Common	unlimited	55,970,547

[1] At Nov. 28, 2022

Major Shareholder - Widely held at May 13, 2022.

Price Range - XTRX/CSE

Year	Volume	High	Low	Close
2022	1,035,729	$1.03	$0.11	$0.25
2021	2,223,987	$1.60	$0.64	$0.89
2020	4,127,591	$2.97	$0.72	$1.38
2018	188,459	$1.80	$0.75	$1.80

Consolidation: 1-for-3 cons. in Apr. 2021; 1-for-5 cons. in Dec. 2019

Recent Close: $0.32

Capital Stock Changes - In April 2022, 10,000,000 common shares were returned to treasury and cancelled.

Wholly Owned Subsidiaries

Adastra Labs Holdings (2019) Ltd., Langley, B.C.
- 100% int. in **Adastra Brands Inc.**, B.C.
- 100% int. in **Adastra Labs Inc.**, B.C.
  - 100% int. in **1225140 B.C. Ltd.**, B.C.
- 100% int. in **Chemia Analytics Inc.**, Fla.
- 100% int. in **1178562 B.C. Ltd.**, B.C.

1204581 B.C. Ltd., B.C.

Financial Statistics

Periods ended:	12m Dec. 31/21[A]		12m Dec. 31/20[oA]
	$000s	%Chg	$000s
Operating revenue	**5,629**	**+125**	**2,499**
Cost of sales	3,685		1,714
Salaries & benefits	1,129		526
Research & devel. expense	89		182
General & admin expense	1,820		1,754
Stock-based compensation	891		5,333
Operating expense	**7,614**	**-20**	**9,509**
Operating income	**(1,985)**	**n.a.**	**(7,010)**
Deprec., depl. & amort.	273		93
Finance income	nil		8
Finance costs, gross	277		457
Write-downs/write-offs	(134)		(63)
Pre-tax income	**(2,765)**	**n.a.**	**(7,616)**
Income taxes	(15)		nil
Net income	**(2,750)**	**n.a.**	**(7,616)**
Cash & equivalent	745		1,145
Inventories	1,828		1,421
Accounts receivable	1,498		973
Current assets	4,221		3,696
Fixed assets, net	9,775		10,037
Intangibles, net	14,650		nil
Total assets	**28,755**	**+109**	**13,734**
Bank indebtedness	3,502		2,443
Accts. pay. & accr. liabs	1,829		1,148
Current liabilities	5,341		3,591
Shareholders' equity	22,373		10,086
Cash from oper. activs	**(1,054)**	**n.a.**	**(2,808)**
Cash from fin. activs	916		3,395
Cash from invest. activs	(263)		(1,819)
Net cash position	**745**	**-35**	**1,145**
Capital expenditures	(581)		(1,827)
	$		$
Earnings per share*	(0.05)		(0.19)
Cash flow per share*	(0.02)		(0.07)
	shs		shs
No. of shs. o/s*	65,970,547		43,334,100
Avg. no. of shs. o/s*	50,225,704		39,695,235
	%		%
Net profit margin	(48.85)		(304.76)
Return on equity	(16.94)		(100.40)
Return on assets	(11.65)		(57.08)

* Common

[o] Restated

[A] Reported in accordance with IFRS

Latest Results

Periods ended:	9m Sept. 30/22[A]		9m Sept. 30/21[A]
	$000s	%Chg	$000s
Operating revenue	9,142	+151	3,639
Net income	(1,602)	n.a.	(1,081)
	$		$
Earnings per share*	(0.03)		(0.02)

* Common

[A] Reported in accordance with IFRS

Historical Summary
(as originally stated)

Fiscal Year	Oper. Rev.	Net Inc. Bef. Disc.	EPS*
	$000s	$000s	$
2021[A]	5,629	(2,750)	(0.05)
2020[A]	2,499	(7,616)	(0.19)
2019[A1,2]	nil	(2,658)	(0.09)
2018[A3]	nil	(424)	(0.30)
2017[A]	nil	(529)	(0.30)

* Common

[A] Reported in accordance with IFRS

[1] 8 months ended Dec. 31, 2019.

[2] Results reflect the Dec. 19, 2019, reverse takeover acquisition of Adastra Labs Holdings Ltd.

[3] Results for 2018 and prior years pertain to Arrowstar Resources Ltd.

Note: Adjusted throughout for 1-for-3 cons. in Apr. 2021; 1-for-5 cons. in Dec. 2019

A.49 Adcore Inc.

Symbol - ADCO **Exchange** - TSX **CUSIP** - 00654B

Head Office - 105 Allenby St, Tel Aviv, Israel, 6513444 **Overseas Tel** - 972-3-566-3444

Website - www.adcore.com

Email - martijn@adcore.com

Investor Relations - Martin van den Bemd (647) 497-5337

Auditors - BDO Ziv Haft C.P.A., Tel Aviv, Israel

Lawyers - Gowling WLG (Canada) LLP, Toronto, Ont.

Transfer Agents - Computershare Trust Company of Canada Inc., Toronto, Ont.

Employees - 62 at Dec. 31, 2022

Profile - (Can. 2017) Provides automated solutions for day-to-day search engine marketing tasks that are designed for advertising agencies, in-house marketing professionals and freelancers.

The company's ADCORE technology utilizes smart algorithms and machine learning, a branch of artificial intelligence (AI) involving systems that learn from data.

Products are targeted at three market segments: Search, Social Media and Shopping. Product offerings include Feeditor, a shopping campaign automation solution for advertisers; Views, a search engine marketing solution, designed to help marketing professionals and ad agencies streamline, optimize and scale their operations, and altogether provide better service to their clients; Semdoc, a powerful account auditing solution for advertisers to formulate 52 key insights and metrics at the account and campaign level; Alerter, a digital asset monitoring tool including websites, data feeds, ad accounts and other online assets, providing status overview including email alerts and in-app notifications whenever action is required; Effortless Marketing, a holistic marketing solution for Shopify store owners from feed creation and submission to smart campaign creation and performance tracking; Couponer, which offers coupons for Google Ads and Microsoft Ads; and Amphy, a platform which provides a live online learning marketplace where learners can choose classes across various categories.

The company earns a commission on each dollar spent on ads managed through its platform at different rates for direct and indirect customers. Direct customers are business-to-business online advertisers and indirect customers are advertising agencies.

The company is headquartered in Tel Aviv, Israel, and has satellite offices in Melbourne, Australia; Toronto, Ont.; and Hong Kong and Shanghai, People's Republic of China. The data collected by the company is hosted in Canada and Israel on cloud-based hosting services.

Predecessor Detail - Name changed from County Capital One Ltd., May 27, 2019, Qualifying Transaction reverse takeover acquisition of Podium Advertising Technologies Ltd.; basis 1 new for 4.5738 old shs.

Directors - Omri Brill, chr., pres. & CEO, Tel Aviv, Israel; Roy Nevo, COO, Tel Aviv, Israel; Nancy H. Goertzen, Vancouver, B.C.; Ronnie (Ronen) Jaegermann, Tel Aviv, Israel; Sokhie S. Puar, Vancouver, B.C.

Other Exec. Officers - Yatir Sadot, CFO; Yossi Elchanan, chief mktg. officer; Vadim Malkin, chief tech. officer; Martijn van den Bemd, chief partnerships officer; Zehavit Dan, gen. counsel & corp. sec.

Capital Stock

	Authorized (shs.)	Outstanding (shs.)[1]
Common	unlimited	60,489,043

[1] At May 23, 2023

Normal Course Issuer Bid - The company plans to make normal course purchases of up to 3,024,452 common shares representing 5% of the total outstanding. The bid commenced on May 19, 2023, and expires on May 18, 2024.

Major Shareholder - Omri Brill held 68.08% interest at May 23, 2023.

Price Range - ADCO/TSX

Year	Volume	High	Low	Close
2022	7,401,682	$0.72	$0.17	$0.30
2021	18,912,117	$3.34	$0.59	$0.70
2020	12,375,697	$0.99	$0.32	$0.98
2019	1,770,369	$0.63	$0.38	$0.45

Recent Close: $0.21

Capital Stock Changes - During 2022, 387,654 common shares were issued on vesting of restricted share units, 1,254,000 common shares were repurchased under a Normal Course Issuer Bid and 2,171,400 common shares were cancelled.

Wholly Owned Subsidiaries

Adcore Australia Pty Ltd., Australia.
Adcore East Limited, Hong Kong, People's Republic of China.
• 100% int. in **Adcore China**, Shanghai, People's Republic of China.
Adcore US Inc., Del.
Amphy EdTech Ltd., Tel Aviv, Israel.
Amphy Inc., Del.
Podium Advertising Technologies Ltd., Tel Aviv, Israel.

Financial Statistics

Periods ended:	12m Dec. 31/22[A]		12m Dec. 31/21[A]
	US$000s	%Chg	US$000s
Operating revenue	**19,693**	**-30**	**27,966**
Cost of sales	10,214		18,231
Salaries & benefits	4,833		4,263
Research & devel. expense	244		251
General & admin expense	3,671		2,996
Stock-based compensation	381		716
Operating expense	**19,343**	**-27**	**26,457**
Operating income	**350**	**-77**	**1,509**
Deprec., depl. & amort.	786		684
Finance income	234		702
Finance costs, gross	1,993		1,487
Pre-tax income	**(2,195)**	**n.a.**	**40**
Income taxes	40		317
Net income	**(2,235)**	**n.a.**	**(277)**
Cash & equivalent	6,525		11,057
Accounts receivable	4,947		3,530
Current assets	...		14,587
Fixed assets, net	437		691
Intangibles, net	2,634		1,977
Total assets	**14,543**	**-16**	**17,284**
Accts. pay. & accr. liabs	4,453		4,172
Current liabilities	4,641		4,393
Long-term lease liabilities	nil		213
Shareholders' equity	9,734		12,195
Cash from oper. activs	**(2,547)**	**n.a.**	**(1,436)**
Cash from fin. activs	(853)		4,666
Cash from invest. activs	(1,207)		(931)
Net cash position	**6,525**	**-41**	**11,057**
Capital expenditures	(1,233)		(974)
	US$		US$
Earnings per share*	(0.04)		(0.01)
Cash flow per share*	(0.04)		(0.02)
	shs		shs
No. of shs. o/s*	60,443,699		63,481,445
Avg. no. of shs. o/s*	62,413,498		61,074,196
	%		%
Net profit margin	(11.35)		(0.99)
Return on equity	(20.38)		(2.90)
Return on assets	(1.29)		(70.45)
No. of employees (FTEs)	62		55

* Common
[A] Reported in accordance with IFRS

Latest Results

Periods ended:	3m Mar. 31/23[A]		3m Mar. 31/22[A]
	US$000s	%Chg	US$000s
Operating revenue	5,044	+36	3,706
Net income	(450)	n.a.	(662)
	US$		US$
Earnings per share*	(0.01)		(0.01)

* Common
[A] Reported in accordance with IFRS

Historical Summary
(as originally stated)

Fiscal Year	Oper. Rev. US$000s	Net Inc. Bef. Disc. US$000s	EPS* US$
2022[A]	19,693	(2,235)	(0.04)
2021[A]	27,966	(277)	(0.01)
2020[A]	16,997	648	0.01
2019[A1]	11,301	1,318	0.03
2018[A2]	8,570	1,680	n.a.

* Common
[A] Reported in accordance with IFRS
[1] Results reflect the May 27, 2019, reverse takeover acquisition of Podium Advertising Technologies Ltd.
[2] Results for 2018 and prior years pertain to Podium Advertising Technologies Ltd.
Note: Adjusted throughout for 1-for-4.5738 cons. in May 2019

A.50 AdRabbit Limited

Symbol - RABI **Exchange** - TSX-VEN **CUSIP** - Q01383
Head Office - 8 Pinchas Sapir, Ness Ziona, Israel
Website - ad-rabbit.com
Email - noah@alabs.co
Investor Relations - Noah Hershcoviz (604) 283-6110
Auditors - BDO Audit (WA) Pty Ltd. C.A., Subiaco, W.A. Australia
Transfer Agents - Computershare Trust Company of Canada Inc., Vancouver, B.C.; Automic Registry Services, Perth, W.A. Australia
Profile - (Australia 2018) Develops a suite of online and mobile-based products to support small-to-medium sized businesses (SMBs).

Has paused further development and rollout of AdRabbit, an artificial intelligence (AI)-based advertising and marketing platform for SMB's that enables them to run automated large-scale advertising and marketing campaigns online and on social media. The platform leverages the company's JARVIS backend technology, which is integrated with Facebook, Instagram, Google and TikTok, to ensure each campaign yields maximum customer reach, call to action and user conversation results. A beta version of the AdRabbit app was launched in 2021, which was subsequently removed from the app market in the third quarter of 2022 due to market conditions.

The company maintains its legacy product AppsVillage platform, a Software-as-a-Service (SaaS) solution which allows SMBs to automate the creation and management of apps and digital marketing campaigns for their businesses.

In June 2022, the company's ordinary shares were delisted from the Australian Stock Exchange.

Recent Merger and Acquisition Activity

Status: terminated **Revised:** Feb. 27, 2023
UPDATE: The transaction was terminated. PREVIOUS: AdRabbit Limited entered into an agreement for the reverse takeover acquisition of Nesher, Israel-based Sanolla Ltd., which manufactures, sells and distributes AI-based infrasound auscultation clinical device technologies. It is expected that the parties will complete one or more financing(s) for aggregate proceeds between US$10,000,000 to US$15,000,000. Sanolla's first product is VoqX, a smartstethoscope. Dec. 9, 2022 - The agreement expired but the companies are continuing to negotiate the parameters of the proposed transaction

Predecessor Detail - Name changed from AppsVillage Australia Limited, Jan. 31, 2022.
Directors - Noah Hershcoviz, chr. & interim CEO, Tel Aviv, Israel; Moshe Cohen, v-p, bus. devel., Ramat HaSharon, Israel; Daniel-Paul Corsello, Australia; Frederic W. R. (Fred) Leigh, Toronto, Ont.
Other Exec. Officers - Gidi Krupnik, CFO

Capital Stock

	Authorized (shs.)	Outstanding (shs.)[1]
Preference	unlimited	nil
Ordinary	unlimited	190,048,497

[1] At June 30, 2023

Major Shareholder - 12.64 Fund Limited Partnership held 11.28% interest at Feb. 7, 2022.

Price Range - RABI/TSX-VEN

Year	Volume	High	Low	Close
2022	53,048,367	$0.30	$0.01	$0.02

Recent Close: $0.01
Capital Stock Changes - In February 2022, 78,262,709 units (1 ordinary share & 1 warrant) were issued at Cdn$0.05 per unit on conversion of loans, with warrants exercisable at Cdn$0.05 per share for five years.

Wholly Owned Subsidiaries

AppsVillage Ltd., Israel.

Financial Statistics

Periods ended:	12m Dec. 31/21[A]		12m Dec. 31/20[oA]
	US$000s	%Chg	US$000s
Operating revenue	**407**	**-59**	**993**
Cost of sales	36		106
Research & devel. expense	1,122		790
General & admin expense	1,837		3,167
Stock-based compensation	216		249
Operating expense	**3,211**	**-26**	**4,312**
Operating income	**(2,804)**	**n.a.**	**(3,319)**
Deprec., depl. & amort.	33		29
Finance income	nil		9
Finance costs, gross	62		26
Pre-tax income	**(2,899)**	**n.a.**	**(3,365)**
Net income	**(2,899)**	**n.a.**	**(3,365)**
Cash & equivalent	117		818
Accounts receivable	171		117
Current assets	332		979
Fixed assets, net	8		14
Right-of-use assets	22		47
Total assets	**362**	**-65**	**1,040**
Bank indebtedness	1,060		nil
Accts. pay. & accr. liabs	905		522
Current liabilities	2,220		857
Long-term lease liabilities	nil		20
Shareholders' equity	(1,858)		163
Cash from oper. activs	**(2,423)**	**n.a.**	**(3,377)**
Cash from fin. activs	1,732		1,551
Cash from invest. activs	(1)		(9)
Net cash position	**117**	**-86**	**818**
Capital expenditures	(1)		(9)
	US$		US$
Earnings per share*	(0.03)		(0.04)
Cash flow per share*	(0.02)		(0.04)
	shs		shs
No. of shs. o/s*	107,538,748		99,182,445
Avg. no. of shs. o/s*	105,470,217		85,695,992
	%		%
Net profit margin	(712.29)		(338.87)
Return on equity	n.m.		(368.77)
Return on assets	(404.71)		(172.16)
No. of employees (FTEs)	n.a.		10

* Ordinary
[o] Restated
[A] Reported in accordance with IFRS

Latest Results

Periods ended:	9m Sept. 30/22[A]		9m Sept. 30/21[A]
	US$000s	%Chg	US$000s
Operating revenue	147	-60	363
Net income	(1,764)	n.a.	(2,099)
	US$		US$
Earnings per share*	(0.01)		(0.02)

* Ordinary
[A] Reported in accordance with IFRS

Historical Summary
(as originally stated)

Fiscal Year	Oper. Rev. US$000s	Net Inc. Bef. Disc. US$000s	EPS* US$
2021[A]	407	(2,899)	(0.03)
2020[A]	993	(3,365)	(0.07)
2019[A]	611	(5,017)	(0.14)

* Ordinary
[A] Reported in accordance with IFRS

A.51 Aduro Clean Technologies Inc.

Symbol - ACT **Exchange** - CSE **CUSIP** - 007408
Head Office - 104-1086 Modeland Rd, Sarnia, ON, N7S 6L2
Telephone - (647) 680-3515
Website - www.adurocleantech.com
Email - ovicus@adurocleantech.com
Investor Relations - Ofer Vicus (647) 680-3515
Auditors - De Visser Gray LLP C.A., Vancouver, B.C.
Transfer Agents - Computershare Trust Company of Canada Inc., Vancouver, B.C.
Profile - (B.C. 2018) Developed and commercialized the water-based Hydrochemolytic™ technology (HCT) to transform waste plastics and low-grade renewable oils into renewable fuels and specialty chemicals.

Applications are in three markets: Hydrochemolytic™ Plastics Upcycling (HPU), which transforms plastics, foam and rubber from used tires into transforming plastics into useful feedstocks for production of new plastics and foams, paints and coatings, and detergents; Hydrochemolytic™ Bitumen Upgrading (HBU), which transforms heavy crude oil and bitumen into light synthetic crude using feedstock such as Municipal Solid Waste or biomass; and Hydrochemolytic™ Renewables Upgrading (HRU), which transforms renewable oils into renewable motor fuels, bio-jet fuel and specialty chemicals at relatively low temperatures without requirement of molecular hydrogen from external sources. As at Aug, 31, 2022, the company owns seven patents, six granted and one pending.

Potential customers include: refineries, airlines, shipping industry, global and local energy companies, remote communities, national and international waste collection companies, municipalities and governments for HPU; Canadian provincial heavy oil producers, international heavy oil producers and refineries for HBU; and ethanol producers, seed crushing plants, biodiesel plants, farmers, and poultry and beef producers for HRU.

The company is developing partnerships by means of demonstration projects. Deliverables include reports that detail the technology; performance; key parameters and operational variables; economic, operational and environmental considerations including green house gases footprint; and life cycle analysis.

Predecessor Detail - Name changed from Dimension Five Technologies Inc., Apr. 23, 2021, pursuant to the reverse takeover acquisition of Aduro Energy Inc.; basis 1 new for 3 old shs.

Directors - William Marcus Trygstad, co-founder & chief tech. officer, Tex.; Ofer Vicus, co-founder, chr. & CEO, Ont.; Peter Kampian, Cambridge, Ont.; Chris Parr, B.C.; James E. (Jim) Scott, Colo.

Other Exec. Officers - Gene Cammack, COO; Mena Beshay, CFO; Abe Dyck, v-p, strategy & bus. devel.; Dr. Anil Jhawar, v-p, tech. & process devel.

Capital Stock

	Authorized (shs.)	Outstanding (shs.)[1]
Preferred	unlimited	nil
Common	unlimited	55,965,667

[1] At Oct. 31, 2022

Major Shareholder - Ofer Vicus held 28.51% interest at Oct. 20, 2021.

Price Range - ACT/CSE

Year	Volume	High	Low	Close
2022	15,117,632	$1.04	$0.48	$0.91
2021	20,625,095	$1.30	$0.59	$0.77
2019	960,986	$0.21	$0.09	$0.21

Consolidation: 1-for-3 cons. in Apr. 2021

Recent Close: $0.92

Capital Stock Changes - In July 2022, private placement of 2,599,579 units (1 common share & ½ warrant) at 72¢ per unit was completed, with warrants exercisable at $1.00 per share for two years. In December 2022, 1,757,025 common shares were issued on exercise of warrants. In April 2023, private placement of 4,222,056 units (1 common share & ½ warrant) at 93¢ per unit was completed, with warrants exercisable at $1.30 per share for two years.

During fiscal 2022, common shares were issued as follows: 15,033,729 on exercise of warrants and 3,360,952 by private placement.

Wholly Owned Subsidiaries

Aduro Clean Technologies Europe B.V., Geleen, Netherlands.
Aduro Energy Inc., Kitchener, Ont.

Financial Statistics

Periods ended:	12m May 31/22[A]		6m May 31/21[□A]
	$000s	%Chg	$000s
Operating revenue	**nil**	**n.a.**	**38**
Salaries & benefits	102		11
Research & devel. expense	1,038		200
General & admin expense	1,775		1,674
Stock-based compensation	1,790		987
Operating expense	**4,705**	**n.a.**	**2,872**
Operating income	**(4,705)**	**n.a.**	**(2,834)**
Deprec., depl. & amort.	61		29
Finance costs, gross	47		35
Pre-tax income	**(5,081)**	**n.a.**	**(2,877)**
Net income	**(5,081)**	**n.a.**	**(2,877)**
Cash & equivalent	2,111		2,860
Accounts receivable	158		77
Current assets	2,582		2,937
Fixed assets, net	450		56
Right-of-use assets	184		15
Intangibles, net	5		21
Total assets	**3,221**	**+6**	**3,029**
Accts. pay. & accr. liabs	565		447
Current liabilities	662		584
Long-term debt, gross	58		656
Long-term debt, net	27		626
Long-term lease liabilities	137		nil
Shareholders' equity	2,395		1,819
Cash from oper. activs	**(3,299)**	**n.a.**	**(702)**
Cash from fin. activs	2,961		3,585
Cash from invest. activs	(411)		(11)
Net cash position	**2,111**	**-26**	**2,860**
Capital expenditures	(411)		(11)
	$		$
Earnings per share*	(0.13)		(0.16)
Cash flow per share*	(0.08)		(0.04)
	shs		shs
No. of shs. o/s*	52,303,039		33,908,358
Avg. no. of shs. o/s*	40,318,441		17,860,687
	%		%
Net profit margin	n.a.		...
Return on equity	(241.15)		...
Return on assets	(161.09)		...

* Common
[□] Restated
[A] Reported in accordance with IFRS

Latest Results

Periods ended:	3m Aug. 31/22[A]		3m Aug. 31/21[A]
	$000s	%Chg	$000s
Net income	(1,234)	n.a.	(1,253)
	$		$
Earnings per share*	(0.02)		(0.07)

* Common
[A] Reported in accordance with IFRS

Historical Summary
(as originally stated)

Fiscal Year	Oper. Rev. $000s	Net Inc. Bef. Disc. $000s	EPS* $
2022[A]	nil	(5,081)	(0.13)
2021[A]	38	(3,209)	(0.24)
2020[A1]	42	(428)	(0.32)
2020[A2]	80	(511)	(0.06)
2019[A]	110	(245)	(0.03)

* Common
[A] Reported in accordance with IFRS
[1] Results reflect the Apr. 23, 2021, reverse takeover acquisition of Aduro Energy Inc.
[2] Results for fiscal 2020 and prior fiscal years pertain to Dimension Five Technologies Inc.
Note: Adjusted throughout for 1-for-3 cons. in Apr. 2021

A.52 Advanced Proteome Therapeutics Corporation

Symbol - APC.H **Exchange** - TSX-VEN **CUSIP** - 007628
Head Office - 104-8337 Eastlake Dr, Burnaby, BC, V5A 4W2 **Telephone** - (604) 690-3797
Website - www.advancedproteome.com
Email - paul@conation.ca
Investor Relations - Paul Woodward (604) 690-3797
Auditors - Crowe MacKay LLP C.A., Vancouver, B.C.
Transfer Agents - Endeavor Trust Corporation, Vancouver, B.C.
Profile - (B.C. 2005) Seeking new business opportunities.

On Mar. 15, 2023, the company transferred its assets and liabilities to wholly owned **Linceis Capital Corp.** in exchange for 41,127,080 common shares with a deemed value of $2,521,236, which were distributed to shareholders of the company on a pro rata basis. The assets transferred consisted of 198,005,400 common shares of Boston, Mass.-based **Advanced Proteome Therapeutics Inc.** (APTI), representing a 76.02% interest; and 1,145,189 common shares of Burnaby, B.C.-based **Aether Catalyst Solutions, Inc.**, representing a 2.3% interest. APTI develops and commercializes a technology platform that is intended for the chemical modification of protein therapeutics in the areas of therapeutics and diagnostics, protein drugs and personalized medicine.

The company retained certain assets for working capital purposes and is seeking new business opportunities. Linceis is seeking to list its common shares on the Canadian Securities Exchange.

Predecessor Detail - Succeeded ThrillTime Entertainment International, Inc., Oct. 25, 2006, pursuant to plan of arrangement whereby newly incorporated wholly owned subsidiary Advanced Proteome Therapeutics Corporation acquired 56% interest in Advanced Proteome Therapeutics, Inc. and completed a share exchange to become parent of ThrillTime.

Directors - Paul Woodward, pres. & CEO, B.C.; Cory Brandolini, B.C.; W. Benjamin (Ben) Catalano, Burnaby, B.C.; Martin J. C. Woodward, B.C.

Other Exec. Officers - Kenneth C. (Ken) Phillippe, CFO

Capital Stock

	Authorized (shs.)	Outstanding (shs.)[1]
Common	unlimited	40,127,080

[1] At Mar. 28, 2023

Major Shareholder - Widely held at Dec. 27, 2022.

Price Range - APC.H/TSX-VEN

Year	Volume	High	Low	Close
2022	6,702,504	$0.25	$0.03	$0.04
2021	7,702,970	$0.51	$0.12	$0.18
2020	5,171,613	$0.19	$0.04	$0.15
2019	2,744,757	$0.65	$0.05	$0.06
2018	12,315,009	$1.55	$0.35	$0.35

Consolidation: 1-for-10 cons. in May 2019

Recent Close: $0.01

Capital Stock Changes - During fiscal 2022, common shares were issued as follows: 1,826,443 on exercise of warrants and 100,000 on exercise of options.

Dividends

APC.H com N.S.R.
stk.[1] Mar. 15/23
Paid in 2023: stk. 2022: n.a. 2021: n.a.

[1] Stk. divd. of 1 Linceis Capital Corp com. sh. for ea. 1 sh. held.

Subsidiaries

91.67% int. in **1090573 B.C. Ltd.**, B.C.

Financial Statistics

Periods ended:	12m July 31/22[A]		12m July 31/21[□A]
	US$000s	%Chg	US$000s
Salaries & benefits	512		261
Research & devel. expense	260		128
General & admin expense	442		150
Stock-based compensation	nil		132
Operating expense	**1,214**	**+81**	**671**
Operating income	**(1,214)**	**n.a.**	**(671)**
Deprec., depl. & amort.	5		3
Finance income	2		1
Finance costs, gross	29		27
Pre-tax income	**597**	**n.a.**	**(1,920)**
Net income	**597**	**n.a.**	**(1,920)**
Net inc. for equity hldrs	**760**	**n.a.**	**(1,835)**
Net inc. for non-cont. int	**(162)**	**n.a.**	**(86)**
Cash & equivalent	544		822
Current assets	621		891
Fixed assets, net	16		6
Total assets	**636**	**-29**	**898**
Accts. pay. & accr. liabs	665		580
Current liabilities	1,245		999
Long-term debt, gross	227		172
Long-term debt, net	227		172
Shareholders' equity	1,068		(302)
Non-controlling interest	(1,919)		(1,757)
Cash from oper. activs	**(694)**	**n.a.**	**(545)**
Cash from fin. activs	429		1,415
Cash from invest. activs	(14)		(50)
Net cash position	**544**	**-34**	**822**
Capital expenditures	(14)		(2)
	US$		US$
Earnings per share*	0.01		(0.06)
Cash flow per share*	(0.02)		(0.02)
	shs		shs
No. of shs. o/s*	39,677,080		37,750,637
Avg. no. of shs. o/s*	39,088,324		31,706,444
	%		%
Net profit margin	n.a.		n.a.
Return on equity	n.m.		n.m.
Return on assets	81.62		(412.42)

* Common
[□] Restated
[A] Reported in accordance with IFRS

Latest Results

Periods ended:	3m Oct. 31/22[A]		3m Oct. 31/21[A]
	US$000s	%Chg	US$000s
Net income	(259)	n.a.	640
Net inc. for equity hldrs	(210)	n.a.	676
Net inc. for non-cont. int	(49)		(36)
	US$		US$
Earnings per share*	(0.01)		0.02

* Common
[A] Reported in accordance with IFRS

Historical Summary
(as originally stated)

Fiscal Year	Oper. Rev. US$000s	Net Inc. Bef. Disc. US$000s	EPS* US$
2022[A]	nil	597	0.01
2021[A]	nil	(1,920)	(0.06)
2020[A]	nil	(541)	(0.02)
2019[A]	nil	(461)	(0.02)
2018[A]	nil	(893)	(0.10)

* Common
[A] Reported in accordance with IFRS
Note: Adjusted throughout for 1-for-10 cons. in May 2019

A.53 Advantex Marketing International Inc.

Symbol - ADX **Exchange** - CSE **CUSIP** - 00756J
Head Office - 1600-100 King St W, Toronto, ON, M5X 1G5 **Telephone** - (905) 470-9558 **Toll-free** - (800) 663-1114 **Fax** - (905) 946-2984
Website - www.advantex.com
Email - mukesh.sabharwal@advantex.com
Investor Relations - Mukesh Sabharwal (416) 560-5173
Auditors - BDO Canada LLP C.A., Markham, Ont.
Lawyers - Norton Rose Fulbright Canada LLP, Toronto, Ont.
Transfer Agents - TSX Trust Company, Toronto, Ont.
Profile - (Ont. 1994 amalg.) Operates a merchant cash advance program for independent merchants and resells Aeroplan points to merchants under an agreement with **Air Canada**.

The company's merchants operate across Canada and include restaurants, independent inns, resorts and hotels, spas, retailers of men's and ladies' fashion, footwear and accessories, florists and garden centres, health and beauty centres, gift stores and home décor.

Operations are organized into two segments: Merchant Cash Advance; and Aeroplan Loyalty Program.

The **Merchant Cash Advance** (MCA) segment provides cash advance to a portfolio of about 125 merchants. It is the core business of the company. In the MCA program, the company provides merchants' with working capital through pre-purchase, at a discount, of merchants' future receivables and the company earns its revenue, per contract terms, as it collects against the pre-purchased receivables.

The **Aeroplan Loyalty Program** segment consists of an agreement with **Air Canada** to operate as a re-seller of **Aeroplan Inc.**'s (wholly owned by Air Canada) Aeroplan travel loyalty program. Under the Aeroplan program the company operates as a re-seller for Aeroplan and is dependent upon ongoing consumer interest in accumulating frequent flyer miles for the purpose of obtaining reward air travel on Air Canada. The company sells Aeroplan points to small and mid-sized retailers and service providers. Revenue is recognized, at the agreed price per Aeroplan point, when the participating merchant issues Aeroplan points to an Aeroplan member completing a qualifying transaction at the merchant.

Predecessor Detail - Name changed from Meacon Bay Resources Inc., Sept. 16, 1991.

Directors - Kelly E. Ambrose, pres., CEO & corp. sec., Ont.; Marc B. Lavine, Paris, France; David Moscovitz, Toronto, Ont.

Other Exec. Officers - Mukesh Sabharwal, v-p & CFO

Capital Stock

	Authorized (shs.)	Outstanding (shs.)[1]
Class A Preference	500,000	461,887
Class B Preference	unlimited	nil
Class C Preference	125,000	nil
Common	unlimited	253,392,507

[1] At Nov. 29, 2022

Class A Preference - Entitled to 8% non-cumulative dividends. Redeemable and non-participating. Non-voting.

Common - One vote per share.

Major Shareholder - Randall Abramson, Generation IACP Inc. & Generation PMCA Corp. held 59.75% interest, Herbert J. Abramson held 19.28% interest and Kelly E. Ambrose held 10.03% interest at Sept. 30, 2022.

Price Range - ADX/CSE

Year	Volume	High	Low	Close
2022	7,331,219	$0.06	$0.01	$0.01
2019	54,892	$0.15	$0.15	$0.15
2018	7,068,219	$1.80	$0.15	$0.15

Consolidation: 1-for-30 cons. in May 2022
Recent Close: $0.01

Capital Stock Changes - In September 2021 and March 2022, 224,167,268 post-consolidated common shares were issued as bonus shares and compensation. On May 29, 2022, common shares were consolidated on a 1-for-30 basis.

Wholly Owned Subsidiaries

Advantex Dining Corporation, Ont.
Advantex GP Inc., Canada.
- 7% int. in **Advantex Systems Limited Partnership**

Advantex Marketing Corporation, Ont.
- 100% int. in **Advantex Marketing International Inc.**, Del.

Advantex Marketing International (Maryland) Inc.
Advantex Smartadvance Inc.

Subsidiaries

93% int. in **Advantex Systems Limited Partnership**
- 100% int. in **1600011 Ontario Limited**, Ont.

Financial Statistics

Periods ended:	12m June 30/22[A]		12m June 30/21[A]
	$000s	%Chg	$000s
Operating revenue	**1,740**	**+41**	**1,230**
Cost of sales	742		369
Salaries & benefits	n.a.		969
General & admin expense	1,286		317
Operating expense	**2,392**	**+45**	**1,654**
Operating income	**(652)**	**n.a.**	**(425)**
Deprec., depl. & amort	nil		45
Finance costs, gross	2,055		1,569
Write-downs/write-offs	nil		(53)
Pre-tax income	**(2,708)**	**n.a.**	**(2,092)**
Net income	**(2,708)**	**n.a.**	**(2,092)**
Cash & equivalent	93		83
Accounts receivable	83		93
Current assets	3,530		1,946
Total assets	**3,530**	**+81**	**1,946**
Bank indebtedness	4,080		2,447
Accts. pay. & accr. liabs	2,826		2,731
Current liabilities	6,918		5,251
Long-term debt, gross	6,954		4,695
Long-term debt, net	6,954		4,695
Long-term lease liabilities	nil		13
Preferred share equity	4		4
Shareholders' equity	(10,342)		(8,012)
Cash from oper. activs	**(2,608)**	**n.a.**	**1,824**
Cash from fin. activs	2,619		(1,908)
Net cash position	**93**	**+12**	**83**
	$		$
Earnings per share*	(0.01)		(0.07)
Cash flow per share*	(0.01)		0.06
	shs		shs
No. of shs. o/s*	253,392,507		29,298,280
Avg. no. of shs. o/s*	199,545,395		29,298,280
	%		%
Net profit margin	(155.63)		(170.08)
Return on equity	n.m.		n.m.
Return on assets	(23.85)		(16.57)

* Common
[A] Reported in accordance with IFRS

Latest Results

Periods ended:	3m Sept. 30/22[A]		3m Sept. 30/21[A]
	$000s	%Chg	$000s
Operating revenue	585	+57	373
Net income	(531)	n.a.	(556)
	$		$
Earnings per share*	(0.00)		(0.01)

* Common
[A] Reported in accordance with IFRS

Historical Summary
(as originally stated)

Fiscal Year	Oper. Rev. $000s	Net Inc. Bef. Disc. $000s	EPS* $
2022[A]	1,740	(2,708)	(0.01)
2021[A]	1,230	(2,092)	(0.07)
2020[A]	2,610	(2,927)	(0.10)
2019[A]	6,101	(912)	(0.04)
2018[A]	7,587	1,224	0.08

* Common
[A] Reported in accordance with IFRS
Note: Adjusted throughout for 1-for-30 cons. in May 2022

A.54 Advent-AWI Holdings Inc.

Symbol - AWI **Exchange** - TSX-VEN **CUSIP** - 007642
Head Office - 719-550 Broadway W, Vancouver, BC, V5Z 0E9 **Telephone** - (604) 279-8868 **Fax** - (604) 279-0880
Email - adventwireless@advent-awi.com
Investor Relations - Alice Man Yee Chiu (604) 428-0028
Auditors - MNP LLP C.A., Vancouver, B.C.
Bankers - The Toronto-Dominion Bank, Richmond, B.C.
Lawyers - K MacInnes Law Group, Vancouver, B.C.
Transfer Agents - Computershare Trust Company of Canada Inc.
Profile - (B.C. 1984) Retails cellular and wireless products, services and accessories, and operates a consumer lending business. Also distributes and sells certain health products and services.

Wholly owned **Am-Call Wireless Inc.** is an authorized dealer of **Rogers Communications Inc.** and **Fido Solutions Inc.** and carries the full line of Rogers and Fido products and services, including wireless voice and data, high-speed Internet, digital cable television, home phone, Smart Home Monitoring and Rogers Platinum MasterCard. At Mar. 31, 2022, the company operated two Rogers and two Fido stores in the Greater Toronto Area.

Subsidiary **Adwell Financial Services Inc.** operates a consumer lending business in Vancouver, B.C.

Wholly owned **Advent TeleMedicare Ltd.** holds licence from **DynoSense Corp.** to sell and distribute certain DynoSense health products and services in Hong Kong and Macau, People's Republic of China. Products and services under the licence include handheld health scanners which are wirelessly connected with cloud-based artificial intelligence via user-friendly and channel-customized software and mobile applications. The devices monitor certain vital signs and health conditions of the user and send the information via the cloud to the user's medical care professionals.

In June 2022, the company entered into an agreement with **Wealth Blooming Holdings Ltd.** to sell 54.05% interest in wholly owned **Advent Telemedicare Limited** (ATL). Pursuant to the agreement, the company would receive 2,000 preference shares and 12,000 ordinary shares of ATL in payment of an outstanding loan of HK$15,000,000 owed by ATL to the company. Concurrently, the company would sell 1,950 ordinary shares to Wealth Blooming for HK$1,950,000 and Wealth Blooming would acquire 4,550 ordinary shares from ATL for HK$4,550,000 on or before July 30, 2022. In addition, Wealth Blooming would acquire additional 6,500 ordinary shares from ATL for HK$6,500,000 on or before Dec. 31, 2022. Upon completion of all these transactions, the company's interest would decrease from 100% to 45.95%.

Predecessor Detail - Name changed from Advent Wireless Inc., Mar. 23, 2017.

Directors - Alice Man Yee Chiu, pres. & CEO, West Vancouver, B.C.; Gen Wong, COO, Richmond, B.C.; Edgar Pang, CFO & corp. sec., Markham, Ont.; Kei Fat (Anthony) Chan, Coquitlam, B.C.; Bill Hui, Vancouver, B.C.; Ken Vong, Markham, Ont.; Sin-Kuen Yau, Hong Kong, Hong Kong, People's Republic of China

Capital Stock

	Authorized (shs.)	Outstanding (shs.)[1]
Common	100,000,000	11,935,513

[1] At May 30, 2022

Major Shareholder - Alice Man Yee Chiu held 26.95% interest at May 25, 2022.

Price Range - AWI/TSX-VEN

Year	Volume	High	Low	Close
2022	169,154	$1.09	$0.66	$0.66
2021	244,595	$1.25	$0.90	$1.00
2020	298,085	$1.15	$0.91	$0.97
2019	302,804	$1.19	$0.85	$1.00
2018	858,361	$1.29	$0.87	$0.90

Recent Close: $0.80

Dividends

AWI com N.S.R.
$0.05◆ Aug. 10/23 $0.05◆ Aug. 5/22
$0.05◆ June 24/21
Paid in 2023: $0.05◆ 2022: $0.05◆ 2021: $0.05◆
◆ Special

Wholly Owned Subsidiaries

Advent Marketing Inc.
Advent TeleMedicare Ltd., Hong Kong, People's Republic of China.
Am-Call Wireless Inc.
1013929 B.C. Ltd.

Subsidiaries

70% int. in **Adwell Financial Services Inc.**, Canada.
- 100% int. in **Adwell Mortgage Solutions Inc.**

Financial Statistics

Periods ended:	12m Dec. 31/21^A		12m Dec. 31/20^A
	$000s	%Chg	$000s
Operating revenue	**5,588**	**+35**	**4,137**
Cost of sales	3,160		2,012
Salaries & benefits	1,567		1,506
General & admin expense	1,383		1,043
Operating expense	**6,111**	**+34**	**4,561**
Operating income	**(523)**	**n.a.**	**(424)**
Deprec., depl. & amort.	336		305
Finance income	75		154
Finance costs, gross	75		68
Pre-tax income	**(762)**	**n.a.**	**928**
Income taxes	(71)		68
Net income	**(691)**	**n.a.**	**860**
Net inc. for equity hldrs	**(719)**	**n.a.**	**828**
Net inc. for non-cont. int.	**28**	**-12**	**32**
Cash & equivalent	13,239		14,061
Inventories	541		140
Accounts receivable	1,009		848
Current assets	16,367		17,003
Long-term investments	230		230
Fixed assets, net	1,467		1,519
Right-of-use assets	315		418
Intangibles, net	324		450
Total assets	**19,210**	**-5**	**20,207**
Accts. pay. & accr. liabs	2,346		2,050
Current liabilities	2,555		2,262
Long-term debt, gross	190		180
Long-term debt, net	190		180
Long-term lease liabilities	154		258
Shareholders' equity	16,264		17,487
Non-controlling interest	48		20
Cash from oper. activs	**(87)**	**n.a.**	**(326)**
Cash from fin. activs	(780)		(1,970)
Cash from invest. activs	51		2,710
Net cash position	**9,205**	**-8**	**10,031**
Capital expenditures	(18)		(32)
Capital disposals	nil		2,084
	$		$
Earnings per share*	(0.06)		0.07
Cash flow per share*	(0.01)		(0.03)
Extra divd. - cash*	0.05		0.15
	shs		shs
No. of shs. o/s*	11,935,513		11,935,513
Avg. no. of shs. o/s*	11,935,513		11,935,513
	%		%
Net profit margin	(12.37)		20.79
Return on equity	(4.26)		4.61
Return on assets	(3.16)		4.47

* Common
^A Reported in accordance with IFRS

Latest Results

Periods ended:	3m Mar. 31/22^A		3m Mar. 31/21^A
	$000s	%Chg	$000s
Operating revenue	895	-10	994
Net income	(366)	n.a.	(131)
Net inc. for equity hldrs	(376)	n.a.	(146)
Net inc. for non-cont. int.	10		15
	$		$
Earnings per share*	(0.03)		(0.01)

* Common
^A Reported in accordance with IFRS

Historical Summary
(as originally stated)

Fiscal Year	Oper. Rev. $000s	Net Inc. Bef. Disc. $000s	EPS* $
2021^A	5,588	(691)	(0.06)
2020^A	4,137	860	0.07
2019^A	6,321	847	0.07
2018^A	9,159	2,259	0.19
2017^A	12,942	1,388	0.12

* Common
^A Reported in accordance with IFRS

A.55 Adya Inc.

Symbol - ADYA **Exchange** - TSX-VEN **CUSIP** - 00783P
Head Office - North Tower, 100-675 Cochrane Dr, Markham, ON, L3R 0B8 **Telephone** - (416) 494-5893 **Toll-free** - (866) 814-3627 **Fax** - (416) 494-3788
Website - www.telehop.com
Email - sbishay@iristel.com
Investor Relations - Samer Bishay (888) 846-7654
Auditors - Clearhouse LLP C.A., Mississauga, Ont.
Transfer Agents - TSX Trust Company, Toronto, Ont.

Profile - (Ont. 1993) Provides full-service long-distance, Internet, business services and re-sale wireless services to residential and business customers across Canada and the U.S.

The company is a licensed Class "A" telecom carrier and offers wholesale services; provides equal access long distance services; markets a Hosted PBX (private branch exchange) service under its Telehop business services brand; provides global cellular phone communication services, SIM cards, roaming devices and Wi-Fi roaming solutions; offers prepaid long distance calling cards; offers Internet (DSL & cable), along with HomePhone/Internet/IPTV bundle packages; and resells a Voice over Internet Protocol (VoIP) service branded BroadTalk™. The company's core network resides in Toronto, Ont., with virtual points-of-presence in major cities, provinces and states across Canada and the U.S.

Dial-around services appear on the customers' regular, monthly telephone bills at the company's discounted rates. The company has billing and collection agreements with all the major Local Exchange Carriers across Canada.

Predecessor Detail - Name changed from Telehop Communications Inc., Feb. 10, 2017.

Directors - Samer Bishay, pres. & CEO, Ont.; Maged Bishara, Qué.; Stephen (Steve) Gregory, Qué.; Magdi Wanis, Ont.

Other Exec. Officers - Kyle Appleby, CFO

Capital Stock

	Authorized (shs.)	Outstanding (shs.)[1]
Common	unlimited	23,613,540

[1] At Aug. 18, 2022

Major Shareholder - Samer Bishay held 90% interest at June 30, 2022.

Price Range - ADYA/TSX-VEN

Year	Volume	High	Low	Close
2022	202,156	$0.18	$0.07	$0.08
2021	268,601	$0.30	$0.09	$0.10
2020	229,179	$0.15	$0.07	$0.07
2019	390,756	$0.50	$0.07	$0.09
2018	63,969	$1.00	$0.20	$0.20

Consolidation: 1-for-20 cons. in Aug. 2019
Recent Close: $0.04

Wholly Owned Subsidiaries

ALO Telecom Inc.
Communications Interlink Inc.
Elite Communications Inc.
Ellora Telecom Philippines Inc.
The Friend Network Inc.
The Friend Network Services Inc.
G3 Telecom USA Inc.
International Telehop Network Systems Inc., Toronto, Ont.
iRoam Mobile Solutions Ltd.
179766 Ontario Inc.
Telehop Agencies Inc.
Telehop Carrier Services Inc.
Telehop Global Israel Inc., Israel.
Telehop Management Inc.
Telehop Rebillers Limited
Ten-Ten-Six-Twenty Ltd.
Worldhop.Com Inc.

Financial Statistics

Periods ended:	12m Dec. 31/21^A		12m Dec. 31/20^A
	$000s	%Chg	$000s
Operating revenue	**4,911**	**-14**	**5,730**
Cost of sales	2,603		3,321
Research & devel. expense	306		328
General & admin expense	2,467		2,478
Operating expense	**5,376**	**-12**	**6,127**
Operating income	**(465)**	**n.a.**	**(397)**
Deprec., depl. & amort.	331		295
Finance costs, net	118		99
Pre-tax income	**(745)**	**n.a.**	**(782)**
Income taxes	nil		1
Net income	**(745)**	**n.a.**	**(784)**
Cash & equivalent	96		93
Inventories	34		36
Accounts receivable	267		347
Current assets	884		968
Fixed assets, net	119		210
Right-of-use assets	379		608
Intangibles, net	1		8
Total assets	**1,383**	**-23**	**1,794**
Accts. pay. & accr. liabs	1,060		772
Current liabilities	2,419		2,264
Long-term debt, gross	879		801
Long-term debt, net	701		301
Long-term lease liabilities	218		439
Shareholders' equity	(1,955)		(1,210)
Cash from oper. activs	**(70)**	**n.a.**	**(227)**
Cash from fin. activs	77		251
Cash from invest. activs	(4)		(19)
Net cash position	**96**	**+3**	**93**
Capital expenditures	(4)		(19)
	$		$
Earnings per share*	(0.03)		(0.03)
Cash flow per share*	(0.00)		(0.01)
	shs		shs
No. of shs. o/s*	23,613,540		23,613,540
Avg. no. of shs. o/s*	23,613,540		23,613,540
	%		%
Net profit margin	(15.17)		(13.68)
Return on equity	n.m.		n.m.
Return on assets	(46.90)		(42.85)
Foreign sales percent	17		21

* Common
^A Reported in accordance with IFRS

Latest Results

Periods ended:	6m June 30/22^A		6m June 30/21^A
	$000s	%Chg	$000s
Operating revenue	2,187	-11	2,461
Net income	(517)	n.a.	(360)
	$		$
Earnings per share*	(0.01)		(0.02)

* Common
^A Reported in accordance with IFRS

Historical Summary
(as originally stated)

Fiscal Year	Oper. Rev. $000s	Net Inc. Bef. Disc. $000s	EPS* $
2021^A	4,911	(745)	(0.03)
2020^A	5,730	(784)	(0.03)
2019^A	7,018	(193)	(0.04)
2018^A	8,508	(61)	(0.02)
2017^A	10,993	(438)	(0.18)

* Common
^A Reported in accordance with IFRS
Note: Adjusted throughout for 1-for-20 cons. in Aug. 2019

A.56 Aecon Group Inc.*

Symbol - ARE **Exchange** - TSX **CUSIP** - 00762V
Head Office - 105-20 Carlson Crt, Toronto, ON, M9W 7K6 **Telephone** - (416) 297-2600 **Toll-free** - (877) 232-2677 **Fax** - (416) 293-0271
Website - www.aecon.com
Email - aborgatti@aecon.com
Investor Relations - Adam Borgatti (877) 232-2677
Auditors - PricewaterhouseCoopers LLP C.A., Toronto, Ont.
Bankers - Canadian Imperial Bank of Commerce, Toronto, Ont.; The Toronto-Dominion Bank, Toronto, Ont.
Lawyers - Osler, Hoskin & Harcourt LLP, Toronto, Ont.
Transfer Agents - Computershare Trust Company of Canada Inc., Toronto, Ont.
FP500 Revenue Ranking - 119
Employees - 10,532 at Dec. 31, 2022
Profile - (Can. 1957) Provides design, procurement, materials supply, fabrication, construction, project management, financing and facilities operations services to both the public and private sector clients throughout Canada and, on a select basis, internationally.

Operations are carried out through two segments: Construction and Concessions.

Construction - This segment undertakes all aspects of construction of both public and private infrastructure primarily in Canada, and on a selected basis, internationally through five operating areas: Heavy Civil, Utilities, Industrial, Nuclear Power and Urban Transportation Systems.

Concessions - This segment includes the development, financing, design, construction and operation of infrastructure projects by way of public-private partnership contract structures, as well as by integrating the services of all project participants. Focuses primarily on the development of domestic and international public-private partnership (P3) projects, private finance solutions, developing effective strategic partnership, operations and maintenance, and leading/actively participating in development teams.

For the year ended Dec. 31, 2022, the company was involved in the design and/or construction of 22 major projects.

In May 2023, a joint venture of the company, **SNC-Lavalin** and **United Engineers & Constructors**, of which the company is lead partner, was awarded a $1.3 billion Fuel Channel and Feeder Replacement (FCFR) contract by **Bruce Power Inc.** for Units 4, 5, 7 and 8 at the Bruce Nuclear Generating Station in Tiverton, Ont. The company's share of the contract is $1 billion.

Recent Merger and Acquisition Activity

Status: completed **Revised:** May 1, 2023
UPDATE: The transaction was completed. PREVIOUS: Aecon Group Inc. agreed to sell its Aecon Transportation East roadbuilding services, aggregates and other materials supply businesses to Green Infrastructure Partners Inc. (GIP) for $235,000,000. Upon completion, Aecon and GIP would enter into a strategic cooperation agreement for certain major projects and pursuits in Ontario that leverage both Aecon's heavy civil construction services and GIP's roadbuilding capabilities. The transaction was expected to be completed in the first half of 2023.

Status: pending **Announced:** Mar. 15, 2023
Aecon Group Inc. agreed to sell a 49.9% interest in the L.F. Wade International Airport (Bermuda International Airport) concessionaire, Bermuda Skyport Corporation Limited, to Connor, Clark & Lunn Infrastructure for US$$128,500,000. Aecon would retain the management contract for the airport and remain the controlling shareholder of Skyport, owning a 50.1% interest. Connor, Clark and & Lunn Infrastructure is an affiliate of Connor, Clark & Lunn Financial Group Ltd. Skyport is responsible for the airport's operations, maintenance and commercial functions, as well as coordinating the overall delivery of the Bermuda International Airport Redevelopment Project over a 30-year concession term that commenced in 2017. The transaction was expected to close in the second quarter of 2023.

Predecessor Detail - Name changed from Armbro Enterprises Inc., June 28, 2001.

Directors - John M. Beck, chr., Toronto, Ont.; Jean-Louis Servranckx, pres. & CEO, Toronto, Ont.; Anthony P. (Tony) Franceschini†, Edmonton, Alta.; James D. (J.D.) Hole, Edmonton, Alta.; Stuart A. Lee, Edmonton, Alta.; Eric S. Rosenfeld, Harrison, N.Y.; Monica E. Sloan, Calgary, Alta.; Deborah S. (Debbie) Stein, Calgary, Alta.; Scott W. Thon, Calgary, Alta.; Susan Wolburgh Jenah, Toronto, Ont.

Other Exec. Officers - Thomas Clochard, exec. v-p, civil & nuclear; Eric MacDonald, exec. v-p, utilities; Steven N. (Steve) Nackan, exec. v-p & pres., Aecon Concessions grp.; Mark H. Scherer, exec. v-p & chief safety officer; David Smales, exec. v-p & CFO; Adam Borgatti, sr. v-p, corp. devel. & IR; Blair Brandon, sr. v-p, major projects, Civil West; Michael Derksen, sr. v-p & exec. lead, Civil West; Marty Harris, sr. v-p & exec. lead, Civil East; Mathew Kattapuram, sr. v-p, strategic bus. devel.; Eitan Ladizinsky, sr. v-p, concessions; Alistair MacCallum, sr. v-p, fin.; Dereck Oikawa, sr. v-p, U.S. opers., utilities; Manuel Rivaya, sr. v-p, urban trans. solutions; John Singleton, sr. v-p, ind.; Gordana Terkalas, sr. v-p, HR

† Lead director

Capital Stock

	Authorized (shs.)	Outstanding (shs.)[1]
Common	unlimited	61,695,316

[1] At July 26, 2023

Major Shareholder - Widely held at Apr. 10, 2023.

Price Range - ARE/TSX

Year	Volume	High	Low	Close
2022	85,109,070	$18.15	$8.29	$9.11
2021	63,751,444	$22.28	$15.95	$16.88
2020	79,103,733	$18.24	$10.94	$16.36
2019	80,029,366	$21.83	$16.62	$17.52
2018	89,163,125	$20.06	$14.27	$17.61

Recent Close: $11.02

Capital Stock Changes - During 2022, 713,036 common shares were issued as equity settled shares.

Dividends

ARE com Ra $0.74 pa Q est. Apr. 4, 2022
Prev. Rate: $0.70 est. Apr. 5, 2021
Prev. Rate: $0.64 est. Apr. 2, 2020

Long-Term Debt - Outstanding at Dec. 31, 2022:

5% conv. debs. due 2023[1]	$178,878,000
5.9% proj. financing due 2042	375,654,000
Equipment loans & other[2]	59,243,000
Lease liabs.	170,959,000
	784,734,000
Less: Current portion	235,442,000
	549,292,000

[1] Convertible into common shares at $22.95 per share. An equity component of $12,707,000 was classified as part of shareholders' equity.

[2] Bear interest at fixed and floating rates averaging 3.08%.

Wholly Owned Subsidiaries

Aecon Construction and Materials Limited, Brampton, Ont.
Aecon Construction Group Inc., Toronto, Ont.
Aecon Industrial Management Corp., Alta.
Aecon Infrastructure Management Inc., Alta.
Aecon Transportation West Ltd., Medicine Hat, Alta.
Bermuda Skyport Corporation Limited, Bermuda.
Groupe Aecon Québec Ltée, Qué.
Pacific Electrical Installations Ltd., Abbotsford, B.C.
Voltage Power Ltd., Winnipeg, Man.

Note: The preceding list includes only the major related companies in which interests are held.

Financial Statistics

Periods ended:	12m Dec. 31/22[A]		12m Dec. 31/21[A]
	$000s	%Chg	$000s
Operating revenue	**4,696,450**	**+18**	**3,977,322**
Cost of sales	4,340,493		3,610,505
General & admin expense	196,439		182,281
Operating expense	**4,536,932**	**+20**	**3,792,786**
Operating income	**159,518**	**-14**	**184,536**
Deprec., depl. & amort.	94,153		88,368
Finance income	2,899		610
Finance costs, gross	57,065		45,630
Investment income	17,703		15,101
Pre-tax income	**42,988**	**-42**	**73,788**
Income taxes	12,607		24,106
Net income	**30,381**	**-39**	**49,682**
Cash & equivalent	378,012		532,681
Inventories	37,620		25,195
Accounts receivable	1,023,578		824,803
Current assets	2,323,254		2,145,716
Long-term investments	107,871		69,294
Fixed assets, net	395,101		379,506
Intangibles, net	662,353		646,949
Total assets	**3,567,017**	**+9**	**3,286,817**
Bank indebtedness	120,979		23,305
Accts. pay. & accr. liabs	1,064,048		920,653
Current liabilities	1,834,463		1,469,519
Long-term debt, gross	784,734		753,373
Long-term debt, net	549,292		694,805
Equity portion of conv. debs.	12,707		12,707
Shareholders' equity	953,995		913,566
Cash from oper. activs	**(112,861)**	**n.a.**	**(31,410)**
Cash from fin. activs	(11,864)		(52,282)
Cash from invest. activs	(35,897)		(39,629)
Net cash position	**377,212**	**-29**	**532,681**
Capital expenditures	(32,708)		(35,379)
Capital disposals	12,544		10,343
Unfunded pension liability	857		n.a.
Pension fund surplus	n.a.		1,138
	$		$
Earnings per share*	0.50		0.82
Cash flow per share*	(1.85)		(0.52)
Cash divd. per share*	0.74		0.70
	shs		shs
No. of shs. o/s*	61,535,925		60,822,889
Avg. no. of shs. o/s*	60,977,009		60,345,615
	%		%
Net profit margin	0.65		1.25
Return on equity	3.25		5.56
Return on assets	2.06		2.45
Foreign sales percent	4		3
No. of employees (FTEs)	10,532		5,900

* Common
[A] Reported in accordance with IFRS

Latest Results

Periods ended:	6m June 30/23[A]		6m June 30/22[A]
	$000s	%Chg	$000s
Operating revenue	2,274,073	+8	2,109,152
Net income	18,770	n.a.	(23,794)
	$		$
Earnings per share*	0.30		(0.39)

* Common
[A] Reported in accordance with IFRS

Historical Summary
(as originally stated)

Fiscal Year	Oper. Rev.	Net Inc. Bef. Disc.	EPS*
	$000s	$000s	$
2022[A]	4,696,450	30,381	0.50
2021[A]	3,977,322	49,682	0.82
2020[A]	3,643,618	88,030	1.47
2019[A]	3,460,418	72,853	1.20
2018[A]	3,266,291	59,014	0.99

* Common
[A] Reported in accordance with IFRS

A.57 Aegis Brands Inc.

Symbol - AEG **Exchange** - TSX **CUSIP** - 00775H
Head Office - 200B-2040 Yonge St, Toronto, ON, M4S 1Z9 **Telephone** - (437) 747-4334 **Toll-free** - (855) 222-0875
Website - www.aegisbrands.ca
Email - mlee@aegisbrands.ca
Investor Relations - Melinda M. Lee (437) 747-4334
Auditors - Baker Tilly WM LLP C.A., Vancouver, B.C.
Transfer Agents - Computershare Trust Company of Canada Inc., Toronto, Ont.
Employees - 230 at Dec. 25, 2022

Profile - (Ont. 2011, amalg.) Owns and operates coffee houses, including a flagship roastery, under the Bridgehead® trade name, as well as casual dining bar and grill restaurants under the St. Louis Bar and Grill® trademark, across Canada.

Bridgehead® coffee houses serve premium coffee, baked goods and fresh foods made daily using local and seasonal ingredients. Bridgehead products are also available for purchase through their website, through Amazon, as well as at various grocery retailers throughout Ontario. At May 4, 2023, the cafe network consisted of 21 Bridgehead coffee houses.

St. Louis Bar and Grill® restaurants' menu includes wings, ribs, poutines, tacos, quesadillas, burgers and salads, and has 75 locations across Canada. St. Louis' products are also available for purchase at grocery retailers in Canada and through their application and Amazon.

Recent Merger and Acquisition Activity

Status: completed **Revised:** Nov. 17, 2022
UPDATE: The transaction was completed. PREVIOUS: Aegis Brands Inc. agreed to acquire substantially all of the assets and intellectual property of St. Louis Bar & Grill brand and trademark for $50,000,000 cash. St. Louis Bar & Grill is a Toronto, Ont.-based franchised casual dining bar and grill company with 72 locations across Canada. St. Louis Bar & Grill restaurants serve signature wings, ribs and garlic dill sauce.

Predecessor Detail - Name changed from The Second Cup Ltd., Sept. 24, 2020.

Directors - Michael D. Bregman, chr., Toronto, Ont.; Steven J. (Steve) Pelton, pres. & CEO, Oakville, Ont.; Stephen S. Kelley, Waterloo, Qué.; Alton McEwen, Carmel, Calif.; Aaron Serruya, Toronto, Ont.; Michael Serruya, Toronto, Ont.

Other Exec. Officers - Melinda M. Lee, CFO; Tara Ramsay, v-p, people; Dru Tailor, v-p, fin.; Kate Burnett, pres., Bridgehead (2000) Inc.

Capital Stock

	Authorized (shs.)	Outstanding (shs.)[1]
Common	unlimited	85,287,167

[1] At May 4, 2023

Major Shareholder - Ewing Morris & Co. Investment Partners Ltd. held 10.88% interest at Mar. 31, 2023.

Price Range - AEG/TSX

Year	Volume	High	Low	Close
2022	1,236,330	$0.85	$0.30	$0.62
2021	2,214,159	$1.60	$0.70	$0.71
2020	3,540,603	$1.76	$0.70	$0.92
2019	2,283,735	$2.29	$1.30	$1.68
2018	13,305,938	$4.05	$1.69	$1.85

Recent Close: $0.31

Capital Stock Changes - In January 2023, 51,639,175 common shares were issued on conversion of debentures.

In September 2022, 10,417,765 common shares were issued without further consideration on exchange of subscription receipts sold previously by private placement at $0.324 each.

Wholly Owned Subsidiaries

Bridgehead (2000) Inc., Ottawa, Ont.
SLF IP Operations Inc.
SLF Operations GP Inc.
SLF Operations Limited Partnership
2707048 Ontario Corporation, Canada. Inactive.

Investments

17.99% int. in **Kiaro Holdings Corp.**, Vancouver, B.C. (see separate coverage)

Financial Statistics

Periods ended:	52w Dec. 25/22^A		52w Dec. 26/21^A
	$000s	%Chg	$000s
Operating revenue	**15,159**	**+39**	**10,876**
Cost of sales	4,530		4,070
Salaries & benefits	8,351		4,852
General & admin expense	4,307		3,446
Operating expense	**17,188**	**+39**	**12,368**
Operating income	**(2,029)**	**n.a.**	**(1,492)**
Deprec., depl. & amort.	1,724		1,845
Finance income	209		12
Finance costs, gross	1,448		505
Write-downs/write-offs	(331)		(2,184)
Pre-tax income	**(10,708)**	**n.a.**	**(5,266)**
Income taxes	(1,460)		(404)
Net inc. bef. disc. opers	**(9,248)**	**n.a.**	**(4,862)**
Income from disc. opers	nil		(3,052)
Net income	**(9,248)**	**n.a.**	**(7,914)**
Cash & equivalent	6,508		1,765
Inventories	919		670
Accounts receivable	808		255
Current assets	10,092		2,993
Long-term investments	66		4,995
Fixed assets, net	2,080		2,714
Right-of-use assets	3,062		3,968
Intangibles, net	54,984		5,263
Total assets	**73,880**	**+264**	**20,320**
Accts. pay. & accr. liabs	5,621		3,316
Current liabilities	10,869		4,979
Long-term debt, gross	29,874		nil
Long-term debt, net	28,795		nil
Long-term lease liabilities	7,717		5,545
Shareholders' equity	7,045		7,903
Cash from oper. activs	**(734)**	**n.a.**	**(3,976)**
Cash from fin. activs	55,346		(3,449)
Cash from invest. activs	(49,869)		8,241
Net cash position	**6,508**	**+269**	**1,765**
Capital expenditures	(65)		(81)
Capital disposals	196		nil
	$		$
Earns. per sh. bef disc opers*	(0.38)		(0.21)
Earnings per share*	(0.38)		(0.34)
Cash flow per share*	(0.03)		(0.17)
	shs		shs
No. of shs. o/s*	33,647,992		23,230,227
Avg. no. of shs. o/s*	24,346,416		23,066,671
	%		%
Net profit margin	(61.01)		(44.70)
Return on equity	(123.74)		(42.17)
Return on assets	(16.98)		(7.15)
No. of employees (FTEs)	230		230

* Common
^A Reported in accordance with IFRS

Latest Results

Periods ended:	13w Mar. 26/23^A		3m Mar. 27/22^A
	$000s	%Chg	$000s
Operating revenue	7,053	+177	2,542
Net income	(973)	n.a.	(1,656)
	$		$
Earnings per share*	(0.02)		(0.07)

* Common
^A Reported in accordance with IFRS

Historical Summary
(as originally stated)

Fiscal Year	Oper. Rev.	Net Inc. Bef. Disc.	EPS*
	$000s	$000s	$
2022^A	15,159	(9,248)	(0.38)
2021^A	10,876	(4,862)	(0.21)
2020^A	11,201	(7,730)	(0.34)
2019^A	27,037	(4,674)	(0.23)
2018^A	25,714	1,151	0.06

* Common
^A Reported in accordance with IFRS

A.58 Aequus Pharmaceuticals Inc.

Symbol - AQS **Exchange** - TSX-VEN **CUSIP** - 007636
Head Office - 2820-200 Granville St, Vancouver, BC, V6C 1S4
Telephone - (604) 336-7906 **Fax** - (604) 563-5033
Website - www.aequuspharma.ca
Email - afehr@aequuspharma.ca
Investor Relations - Ann Fehr (604) 336-7906
Auditors - Smythe LLP C.A.
Lawyers - Blake, Cassels & Graydon LLP, Vancouver, B.C.
Transfer Agents - Computershare Trust Company of Canada Inc., Toronto, Ont.
Employees - 12 at Dec. 31, 2022

Profile - (B.C. 2013) Develops and commercializes enhanced delivery systems and differentiated products for specialized therapeutic areas including ophthalmology and transplant.

Commercial products include Evolve® line of preservative free dry eye products, including Evolve® Daily Intensive and Evolve® Intensive Gel; Zimed-PF, a preservative-free prostaglandin analog which reduces elevated intraocular pressure (IOP) in patients with open-angled glaucoma or ocular hypertension and is expected to begin commercial sales in August 2023; and 10 products of **Scope Ophthalmics Ltd.**'s portfolio of over-the-counter ophthalmology products including the OPTASE® range of preservative free dry eye products.

Products under development include REV-0100, which reduces the levels of lipofuscin to alter the course of Stargardt disease progression; and AQS1303, for the treatment of nausea and vomiting during pregnancy. The company has de-prioritized the development of AQS1303 and currently await development partners.

In April 2023, the company terminated its agreement with U.S.-based **Supernus Pharmaceuticals, Inc.** for the commercial rights to Topiramate XR and Oxcarbazepine XR , which are once-daily, extended-release anti-epileptic drugs and related costs of $478,940 were written off in December 2019 due to the company's limited ability to pay the future milestone payments in the short term.

In November 2022, the company announced that it ended its promotional service agreement with **Sandoz Canada Inc.** on Tacrolimus IR, an immunosuppressive therapy used for the treatment and prevention of acute rejection following organ transplantation, and PTVistitan™, a treatment for the reduction of elevated intraocular pressure in patients with open angle glaucoma or ocular hypertension. Sandoz Canada develops, manufactures and distributes generic pharmaceutical products across various therapeutic areas in Canada.

Directors - Douglas G. (Doug) Janzen, chr., pres. & CEO, Vancouver, B.C.; Christopher (Chris) Clark, Vancouver, B.C.; Marc Lustig, Vancouver, B.C.; Anne M. Stevens, B.C.

Other Exec. Officers - Ann Fehr, CFO & corp. sec.; Grant Larsen, chief comml. officer; Dr. Donald A. (Don) McAfee, chief scientific officer

Capital Stock

	Authorized (shs.)	Outstanding (shs.)[1]
Class A Preferred	unlimited	nil
Common	unlimited	132,634,431

[1] At May 30, 2023

Major Shareholder - Widely held at June 22, 2022.

Price Range - AQS/TSX-VEN

Year	Volume	High	Low	Close
2022	15,477,192	$0.12	$0.02	$0.04
2021	66,644,905	$0.29	$0.10	$0.12
2020	28,693,911	$0.16	$0.07	$0.12
2019	28,331,302	$0.25	$0.12	$0.13
2018	42,086,767	$0.45	$0.13	$0.16

Recent Close: $0.04

Capital Stock Changes - There were no changes to capital stock during 2022.

Wholly Owned Subsidiaries

Aequus Pharma (Canada) Ltd., Canada.

Financial Statistics

Periods ended:	12m Dec. 31/22^A		12m Dec. 31/21^oA
	$000s	%Chg	$000s
Operating revenue	**1,380**	**-49**	**2,715**
Cost of goods sold	104		43
Salaries & benefits	2,157		2,139
Research & devel. expense	169		297
General & admin expense	1,278		1,260
Stock-based compensation	41		216
Operating expense	**3,749**	**-5**	**3,955**
Operating income	**(2,369)**	**n.a.**	**(1,240)**
Deprec., depl. & amort.	130		128
Finance income	25		13
Finance costs, gross	181		455
Pre-tax income	**(3,210)**	**n.a.**	**(1,810)**
Net income	**(3,210)**	**n.a.**	**(1,810)**
Cash & equivalent	295		2,436
Inventories	94		140
Accounts receivable	310		941
Current assets	903		3,593
Fixed assets, net	6		13
Right-of-use assets	783		230
Total assets	**1,691**	**-61**	**4,348**
Accts. pay. & accr. liabs	289		379
Current liabilities	2,378		2,457
Long-term debt, gross	nil		1,927
Long-term lease liabilities	694		76
Shareholders' equity	(1,380)		1,789
Cash from oper. activs	**(1,953)**	**n.a.**	**(1,172)**
Cash from fin. activs	(189)		2,398
Cash from invest. activs	nil		(508)
Net cash position	**250**	**-90**	**2,392**
Capital expenditures	nil		(4)
	$		$
Earnings per share*	(0.02)		(0.01)
Cash flow per share*	(0.01)		(0.01)
	shs		shs
No. of shs. o/s*	132,634,431		132,634,431
Avg. no. of shs. o/s*	132,634,431		128,849,859
	%		%
Net profit margin	(232.61)		(66.67)
Return on equity	n.m.		(153.20)
Return on assets	(100.31)		(36.22)
No. of employees (FTEs)	12		14

* Common
^o Restated
^A Reported in accordance with IFRS

Latest Results

Periods ended:	3m Mar. 31/23^A		3m Mar. 31/22^A
	$000s	%Chg	$000s
Operating revenue	92	-70	302
Net income	(744)	n.a.	(917)
	$		$
Earnings per share*	(0.01)		(0.01)

* Common
^A Reported in accordance with IFRS

Historical Summary
(as originally stated)

Fiscal Year	Oper. Rev.	Net Inc. Bef. Disc.	EPS*
	$000s	$000s	$
2022^A	1,380	(3,210)	(0.02)
2021^A	2,715	(1,810)	(0.01)
2020^A	2,593	(1,045)	(0.01)
2019^A	1,633	(3,106)	(0.04)
2018^A	1,410	(2,804)	(0.04)

* Common
^A Reported in accordance with IFRS

A.59 Aether Catalyst Solutions, Inc.

Symbol - ATHR **Exchange** - CSE **CUSIP** - 00810C
Head Office - Unit 104, 8337 Eastlake Dr, Burnaby, BC, V5A 4W2
Telephone - (604) 608-2886
Website - www.aethercatalyst.com
Email - paul@aethercatalyst.com
Investor Relations - Paul Woodward (604) 690-3797
Auditors - Crowe MacKay LLP C.A., Vancouver, B.C.
Transfer Agents - National Securities Administrators Ltd., Vancouver, B.C.

Profile - (B.C. 2011) Commercializing a patent pending catalyst technology, initially for use in gasoline engine automotive emissions abatement.

The company has developed a low-cost, high-performance three-way catalyst to replace the costly precious metal based catalysts used in today's automotive catalytic converters. Its technology does not contain any platinum, palladium, or rhodium and could be processed using simple wash-coating methods that are scalable to high volume and low costs. Other possible applications for the technology include diesel, stationary power and volatile organic compounds. The company expects to license its technology for royalty payments.

In September 2022, the company relinquished its 80.41% equity interest in **Cap Clean Energy Corp.**, which is exploring opportunities in the clean air industry for further applications of the company's technology or the acquisition and deployment of complementary technologies.

Directors - Paul Woodward, pres. & CEO, B.C.; Derek Lew, CFO & corp. sec., Vancouver, B.C.; Dr. Neil Branda, B.C.; Jason W. Moreau, Vancouver, B.C.

Other Exec. Officers - Taylor Procyk, COO; Greg James, v-p, research; Glenn Kerr, v-p, IR

Capital Stock

	Authorized (shs.)	Outstanding (shs.)[1]
Common	unlimited	53,657,794

[1] At May 18, 2023

Major Shareholder - Conation Capital Corp. held 34.29% interest at May 18, 2023.

Price Range - ATHR/CSE

Year	Volume	High	Low	Close
2022	14,818,695	$0.33	$0.05	$0.07
2021	8,219,694	$0.55	$0.09	$0.27
2020	689,474	$0.40	$0.09	$0.10
2019	343,025	$0.40	$0.06	$0.20

Recent Close: $0.04

Capital Stock Changes - During 2022, common shares were issued as follows: 120,000 for debt settlement and 100,000 on exercise of options.

Financial Statistics

Periods ended:	12m Dec. 31/22[A]		12m Dec. 31/21[A]
	$000s	%Chg	$000s
Salaries & benefits	241		186
General & admin expense	306		238
Stock-based compensation	25		103
Operating expense	**572**	**+9**	**527**
Operating income	**(572)**	**n.a.**	**(527)**
Deprec., depl. & amort.	57		71
Finance costs, gross	11		17
Pre-tax income	**(587)**	**n.a.**	**(469)**
Net income	**(587)**	**n.a.**	**(469)**
Cash & equivalent	64		589
Accounts receivable	48		31
Current assets	127		643
Fixed assets, net	55		47
Right-of-use assets	39		72
Total assets	**221**	**-71**	**762**
Accts. pay. & accr. liabs	65		76
Current liabilities	148		113
Long-term debt, gross	40		40
Long-term debt, net	nil		40
Long-term lease liabilities	8		51
Shareholders' equity	65		559
Cash from oper. activs	**(475)**	**n.a.**	**(427)**
Cash from fin. activs	(64)		971
Cash from invest. activs	15		nil
Net cash position	**64**	**-89**	**589**
Capital expenditures	(32)		nil
	$		$
Earnings per share*	(0.01)		(0.01)
Cash flow per share*	(0.01)		(0.01)
	shs		shs
No. of shs. o/s*	49,657,794		49,437,794
Avg. no. of shs. o/s*	49,489,027		46,220,930
	%		%
Net profit margin	n.a.		n.a.
Return on equity	(188.14)		n.m.
Return on assets	(117.19)		(85.77)

* Common

[A] Reported in accordance with IFRS

Latest Results

Periods ended:	3m Mar. 31/23[A]		3m Mar. 31/22[A]
	$000s	%Chg	$000s
Net income	(132)	n.a.	(214)
	$		$
Earnings per share*	(0.00)		(0.00)

* Common

[A] Reported in accordance with IFRS

Historical Summary

(as originally stated)

Fiscal Year	Oper. Rev. $000s	Net Inc. Bef. Disc. $000s	EPS* $
2022[A]	nil	(587)	(0.01)
2021[A]	nil	(469)	(0.01)
2020[A]	nil	(427)	(0.01)
2019[A]	nil	(543)	(0.01)
2018[A]	nil	(309)	(0.01)

* Common

[A] Reported in accordance with IFRS

A.60 Aether Global Innovations Corp.

Symbol - AETH **Exchange** - CSE **CUSIP** - 00810E

Head Office - 700-1199 Hastings St W, Vancouver, BC, V6E 3T5 **Telephone** - (604) 729-2500 **Toll-free** - (888) 509-1353

Website - aethergic.com

Email - phil@aethergic.com

Investor Relations - Philip Lancaster (888) 509-1353

Auditors - Reliant CPA PC C.P.A.

Transfer Agents - Computershare Trust Company of Canada Inc., Vancouver, B.C.

Profile - (B.C. 2011) Developing certain systems and technologies primarily related to remotely detecting concealed mass casualty threat items and designs and manufactures Unmanned Aircraft Systems (UAS) for multiple applications such emergency services, search and rescue, surveillance, reconnaissance, inspection, mapping/surveying and non-destructive testing.

Technologies include MiRIAD (Millimetre-wave Remote Imaging from Airborne Drone), a compact sensor package that is mounted on an UAS which captures radar images of subjects within a wide, elevated field of view, detecting concealed threats on a person and structural weaknesses in valuable infrastructure assets; SS1 Shoe Scanner system, a floor-mounted 3D imaging system for inspecting footwear using millimetre-wave imaging techniques; CODA 1 (Cognitive Object Detection Apparatus), a ultra-compact modular radar device for stand-off threat detection; and Wi-Ti system (Wireless Threat Indication), a passive radar used in Wi-Fi enabled zones in buildings and places to detect threat items concealed on people over a wide coverage area.

The company has developed a fleet of seven multirotor (X-Lite, X1, X1-H and XMR) and fixed-wing (XV, XV-H and XV-L) UAS.

Generates revenue from the sale of engineering design services and radar components to U.S. government agencies and prime contractors.

Common reinstated on CSE, Jan. 17, 2023.

Common suspended from CSE, Nov. 7, 2022.

Predecessor Detail - Name changed from Plymouth Rock Technologies Inc., July 31, 2023.

Directors - Douglas Smith, chr., Washington, D.C.; Philip (Phil) Lancaster, pres. & CEO, Kelowna, B.C.; Dr. Khalid Al-Ali, Qatar; Zahara (Zara) Kanji, Vancouver, B.C.; Alan Treddenick, Cobourg, Ont.

Other Exec. Officers - Karen M. Parrin, CFO & corp. sec.

Capital Stock

	Authorized (shs.)	Outstanding (shs.)[1]
Common	unlimited	92,997,461

[1] At May 30, 2023

Major Shareholder - Widely held at Aug. 30, 2021.

Price Range - AETH/CSE

Year	Volume	High	Low	Close
2022	8,834,158	$0.32	$0.06	$0.06
2021	61,224,532	$1.82	$0.22	$0.22
2020	23,303,096	$0.67	$0.11	$0.23
2019	7,992,184	$0.74	$0.35	$0.49
2018	3,442,565	$0.93	$0.50	$0.61

Recent Close: $0.05

Capital Stock Changes - In March 2023, private placement of 33,680,000 units (1 common share & 1 warrant) at 5¢ per unit was completed, with warrants exercisable at 10¢ per share for three years. In April 2023, private placement of up to 16,666,667 units (1 common share & 1 warrant) at 6¢ per unit was arranged, with warrants exercisable at 10¢ per share for five years.

Wholly Owned Subsidiaries

Plymouth Rock Technologies Inc., Dover, Del.

Plymouth Rock Technologies UK Limited, United Kingdom.

Tetra Drones Limited, United Kingdom.

Financial Statistics

Periods ended:	12m Nov. 30/21[A]		12m Nov. 30/20[oA]
	$000s	%Chg	$000s
Operating revenue	**184**	**+159**	**71**
Cost of sales	103		31
Salaries & benefits	818		292
Research & devel. expense	985		386
General & admin expense	1,908		1,845
Stock-based compensation	1,144		479
Operating expense	**4,958**	**+63**	**3,033**
Operating income	**(4,774)**	**n.a.**	**(2,962)**
Deprec., depl. & amort.	144		41
Finance costs, gross	15		21
Pre-tax income	**(4,975)**	**n.a.**	**(2,924)**
Net income	**(4,975)**	**n.a.**	**(2,924)**
Cash & equivalent	375		25
Accounts receivable	12		3
Current assets	633		80
Fixed assets, net	294		67
Right-of-use assets	73		115
Intangibles, net	550		nil
Total assets	**1,549**	**+493**	**261**
Accts. pay. & accr. liabs	608		242
Current liabilities	707		323
Long-term debt, gross	29		nil
Long-term debt, net	23		nil
Long-term lease liabilities	47		91
Shareholders' equity	773		(152)
Cash from oper. activs	**(3,441)**	**n.a.**	**(2,115)**
Cash from fin. activs	4,326		1,587
Cash from invest. activs	(573)		(61)
Net cash position	**375**	**n.m.**	**25**
Capital expenditures	(204)		(58)
	$		$
Earnings per share*	(0.09)		(0.08)
Cash flow per share*	(0.06)		(0.06)
	shs		shs
No. of shs. o/s*	59,239,336		42,762,264
Avg. no. of shs. o/s*	53,075,143		37,525,451
	%		%
Net profit margin	n.m.		n.m.
Return on equity	n.m.		n.m.
Return on assets	(548.07)		(580.02)

* Common

[o] Restated

[A] Reported in accordance with IFRS

Latest Results

Periods ended:	6m May 31/22[A]		6m May 31/21[A]
	$000s	%Chg	$000s
Operating revenue	497	n.m.	23
Net income	(1,228)	n.a.	(2,374)
	$		$
Earnings per share*	(0.02)		(0.05)

* Common

[A] Reported in accordance with IFRS

Historical Summary

(as originally stated)

Fiscal Year	Oper. Rev. $000s	Net Inc. Bef. Disc. $000s	EPS* $
2021[A]	184	(4,975)	(0.09)
2020[A]	71	(2,924)	(0.08)
2019[A]	28	(4,367)	(0.14)
2018[A]	nil	(987)	(0.04)
2017[A]	nil	(116)	(0.01)

* Common

[A] Reported in accordance with IFRS

A.61 Affinor Growers Inc.

Symbol - AFI **Exchange** - CSE (S) **CUSIP** - 00830Q

Head Office - 400-595 Howe St, Vancouver, BC, V6C 2T5 **Telephone** - (604) 356-0411

Website - www.affinorgrowers.com

Email - nick@affinorgrowers.com

Investor Relations - Nicolas Brusatore (604) 356-0411

Auditors - Zeifmans LLP C.A., Toronto, Ont.

Lawyers - McCullough O'Connor Irwin LLP, Vancouver, B.C.

Transfer Agents - Computershare Trust Company of Canada Inc., Montréal, Qué.

Profile - (Can. 1996) Develops and commercializes various agriculture technologies and vertical farming technology for both indoor controlled environment and outdoor greenhouse agriculture industry.

The company's patented vertical farming technologies use the least possible resources such as land, water and energy to produce high quality, sustainable crops including leafy greens, flowering fruits and floral products. The company generates revenue through one-time licensing fees, royalties on production and margin on the sale of the company's patented technology.

Common suspended from CSE, Dec. 20, 2022.

Predecessor Detail - Name changed from Affinor Resources Inc., May 29, 2014.

Directors - Ben Hogervorst, chr.; Nicolas (Nick) Brusatore, pres., CEO & interim CFO, Port Coquitlam, B.C.; Dr. Alan R. Boyco, Port Moody, B.C.; Rick Easthom, B.C.

Other Exec. Officers - Ron Fraser, COO

Capital Stock

	Authorized (shs.)	Outstanding (shs.)[1]
Common	unlimited	24,439,915

[1] At May 30, 2023

Major Shareholder - Widely held at Jan. 28, 2021.

Price Range - AFI.H/TSX-VEN (D)

Year	Volume	High	Low	Close
2022	9,321,337	$0.60	$0.04	$0.04
2021	20,106,192	$0.90	$0.25	$0.35
2020	6,919,307	$0.70	$0.10	$0.30
2019	3,990,344	$0.70	$0.15	$0.30
2018	22,076,338	$2.75	$0.25	$0.40

Consolidation: 1-for-10 cons. in June 2022

Recent Close: $0.04

Capital Stock Changes - On June 20, 2022, common shares were consolidated on a 1-for-10 basis.

In January 2022, private placement of 10,430,005 units (1 common share & 1 warrant) at $0.035 per unit was completed, with warrants exercisable at $0.05 per share for two years.

Wholly Owned Subsidiaries

Affinor Analytics LLC Inactive.

Financial Statistics

Periods ended:	12m May 31/21[A]		12m May 31/20[oA]
	$000s	%Chg	$000s
Operating revenue	**nil**	**n.a.**	**54**
Cost of goods sold	nil		41
Salaries & benefits	126		156
Research & devel. expense	nil		35
General & admin expense	758		313
Other operating expense	8		19
Operating expense	**892**	**+58**	**563**
Operating income	**(892)**	**n.a.**	**(509)**
Deprec., depl. & amort.	81		80
Finance costs, gross	88		104
Write-downs/write-offs	(45)		(37)
Pre-tax income	**(1,024)**	**n.a.**	**(694)**
Income taxes	(2)		nil
Net income	**(1,022)**	**n.a.**	**(694)**
Cash & equivalent	434		15
Accounts receivable	33		20
Current assets	554		61
Fixed assets, net	304		64
Intangibles, net	903		922
Total assets	**1,773**	**+69**	**1,047**
Accts. pay. & accr. liabs	659		205
Current liabilities	684		779
Long-term debt, gross	nil		530
Long-term debt, net	nil		530
Shareholders' equity	1,089		267
Cash from oper. activs	**(606)**	**n.a.**	**(525)**
Cash from fin. activs	1,311		500
Cash from invest. activs	(286)		(24)
Net cash position	**434**	**n.m.**	**15**
Capital expenditures	(233)		(24)
	$		$
Earnings per share*	(0.10)		(0.05)
Cash flow per share*	(0.03)		(0.03)
	shs		shs
No. of shs. o/s*	21,103,362		15,290,811
Avg. no. of shs. o/s*	17,863,191		15,290,811
	%		%
Net profit margin	n.a.		n.m.
Return on equity	(150.74)		(113.03)
Return on assets	(66.25)		(52.87)

* Common
[o] Restated
[A] Reported in accordance with IFRS

Latest Results

Periods ended:	3m Aug. 31/21[A]		3m Aug. 31/20[A]
	$000s	%Chg	$000s
Net income	(137)	n.a.	(120)
	$		$
Earnings per share*	(0.01)		(0.01)

* Common
[A] Reported in accordance with IFRS

Historical Summary
(as originally stated)

Fiscal Year	Oper. Rev.	Net Inc. Bef. Disc.	EPS*
	$000s	$000s	$
2021[A]	nil	(1,022)	(0.10)
2020[A]	54	(694)	(0.04)
2019[A]	3	(2,404)	(0.20)
2018[A]	nil	(4,699)	(0.40)
2017[A]	nil	(1,717)	(0.10)

* Common
[A] Reported in accordance with IFRS

Note: Adjusted throughout for 1-for-10 cons. in June 2022

A.62 Ag Growth International Inc.*

Symbol - AFN **Exchange** - TSX **CUSIP** - 001181

Head Office - 198 Commerce Dr, Winnipeg, MB, R3P 0Z6 **Telephone** - (204) 489-1855 **Fax** - (204) 488-6929

Website - www.aggrowth.com

Email - investor-relations@aggrowth.com

Investor Relations - Andrew Jacklin (204) 489-1855

Auditors - Ernst & Young LLP C.A., Winnipeg, Man.

Lawyers - Burnet, Duckworth & Palmer LLP, Calgary, Alta.

Transfer Agents - Computershare Trust Company of Canada Inc., Toronto, Ont.

FP500 Revenue Ranking - 276

Employees - 4,987 at Dec. 31, 2022

Profile - (Can. 2001 amalg.) Provides equipment and services for agriculture bulk commodities including storage, transport and processing for grain, fertilizer, feed, seed and food. Products are manufactured in Canada, the United States, the United Kingdom, Brazil, Italy, France and India, and distributed globally.

Operations are organized into two business segments: Farm and Commercial.

The **Farm** business includes the sale of grain and fertilizer handling equipment, aeration products and storage bins primarily to farmers in North America where on-farm storage practices are conducive to the sale of portable handling equipment and storage bins for grain and fertilizer. Portable grain handling equipment include augers, grain vacuums and belt conveyors, used to move grain, oilseeds and lentils into and out of storage on the farm; stationary grain handling equipment forms part of a grain storage system that includes larger diameter grain storage bins and grain dryers; and storage and conditioning equipment include permanent storage such as corrugated storage bins, smoothwall storage bins and conditioning equipment used in aeration, heating and drying, including furnaces, heaters and fans. Also includes the manufacture and sale of portable and stationary liquid fuel containment tanks, used both in farm and industrial settings and are sold primarily through a dealer network; and offers an automated level monitoring system for tanks, complete with alerts and mobile access. In addition, offers grain storage monitoring which avoids physical bin-entry and provides remote visibility to grain conditions including automated alerts, remote control of aeration equipment and automated in-bin conditioning capabilities; and machine monitoring hardware and software which supports verification of field activities.

The **Commercial** business includes the sale of larger diameter storage bins, high capacity stationary grain handling equipment, fertilizer storage and handling systems, feed handling and storage equipment, aeration products, hazard monitoring systems, automated blending systems, control systems and food processing solutions which include design engineering, project management services and equipment supply. Also manufactures portable and stationary liquid fuel containment tank and rice milling and processing equipment such as cleaners, boilers, par-boilers, dryers, specialized colour sorters, graders and bagging equipment. Customers include large multi-national agri-businesses, grain handlers, regional cooperatives, contractors, food and animal feed manufacturers, and fertilizer blenders and distributors. Commercial equipment is used at port facilities for both the import and export of grains, inland grain terminals, corporate farms, fertilizer distribution sites, ethanol production, oilseed crushing, commercial feed mills, rice mills, and flour mills.

Production, warehousing and distribution facilities with an aggregate area of 2,929,007 sq. ft. are located in Exeter, Newton, Toronto, Vaughan and Woodstock, Ont.; Winnipeg, Rosenort and Oak Bluff, Man.; Saskatoon and Swift Current, Sask.; Nobleford, Olds and Rycroft, Alta.; Wynne, Ark.; Horace, N.D.; Sioux Falls and Watertown, S.D.; Decatur, Marshall and Monmouth, Ill.; Boone and Cedar Rapids, Iowa; Georgetown and Charlottetown, P.E.I.; Albion, Falls City, Grand Island and North Omaha, Neb.; Clay Center and Lenexa, Kan.; Joplin, Mo.; Assis, Brazil; NEste, Fiesso and Ozzano, Italy; Chauche and Naizin, France; and Bangalore, India. In addition, the company has inventory stocking points at strategic locations throughout its market areas to ensure ready supply across its distribution networks.

Predecessor Detail - Name changed from Benachee Resources Inc., June 3, 2009.

Directors - Janet P. Giesselman, chr., Fla.; Paul Householder, pres. & CEO, Ariz.; Rohit Bhardwaj, Ont.; Anne De Greef-Safft, S.C.; Michael J. (Mike) Frank, London, Middx., United Kingdom; William A. (Bill) Lambert, Toronto, Ont.; William S. (Bill) Maslechko, Calgary, Alta.; Malcolm F. (Mac) Moore, Naples, Fla.; Claudia Roessler, Wash.; David A. White, Asheville, N.C.

Other Exec. Officers - James D. (Jim) Rudyk, CFO; Paul Brisebois, sr. v-p, Canada farm; Neal Dilawri, sr. v-p, ERP solutions; Ryan Kipp, sr. v-p, legal, gen. counsel & corp. sec.; Gurcan Kocdag, sr. v-p, mfg. & supply; Marie McKeegan, sr. v-p, HR; Scott McKernan, sr. v-p, USA; Nicolle Parker, sr. v-p, fin. & info. sys.; David Postill, sr. v-p, mktg. & cust. experience; Noam Silberstein, sr. v-p, global feed; Rajan Aggarwal, v-p, India & CEO, AGI MILLTEC; Harsha Bhojraj, v-p, mfg.; Cristiano Carpin, v-p, EMEA; Mike Hand, v-p, North America comml.; Brian Harder, v-p, global foods; Shannon Hinrichs, v-p, sales execution; Rustom Mistry, v-p, South East Asia; Henry Palomino, v-p, global supply chain; Justin Paterson, v-p, global eng.; Francisco Prado, v-p, Brazil opers.; Subroto Pyne, v-p, global product mgt.

Capital Stock

	Authorized (shs.)	Outstanding (shs.)[1]
First Preferred	unlimited	nil
Second Preferred	unlimited	nil
Class A Preferred	unlimited	nil
Common	unlimited	19,003,873

[1] At Aug. 10, 2023

Major Shareholder - Widely held at Mar. 24, 2023.

Price Range - AFN/TSX

Year	Volume	High	Low	Close
2022	15,826,817	$45.94	$28.80	$43.35
2021	19,251,508	$48.47	$25.85	$31.68
2020	25,412,611	$48.07	$15.00	$29.81
2019	16,686,418	$63.11	$37.84	$46.44
2018	10,493,636	$64.72	$43.76	$46.80

Recent Close: $58.00

Capital Stock Changes - During 2022, 107,388 common shares were issued as dividends on share award incentive plan.

Dividends

AFN com Ra $0.60 pa Q est. July 15, 2020[1]

Prev. Rate: $2.40 est. Dec. 30, 2010

[1] Dividends paid monthly prior to July/20. Dividend reinvestment plan suspended eff. April 30, 2018.

Long-Term Debt - Outstanding at Dec. 31, 2022:

Revolv. credit facility due 2025[1]	$443,420,000
Debs. due to 2026[2]	252,750,000
Conv. debs. due to 2027[3]	183,481,000
Equipment financing	1,788,000
Less: Def. financing costs	4,270,000
	877,169,000
Less: Current portion	479,000
	876,690,000

[1] Consists of borrowings under a Canadian revolver and a U.S. revolver facility, bearing interest at bankers' acceptance or SOFR plus 1.2% to 2.75% and prime plus 0.2% to 1.75%.

[2] Net of accretion and financing fees. Consist of 5.4% debentures due June 30, 2024; 5.25% debentures due Dec. 31, 2024; and 5.25% debentures due Dec. 31, 2026.

[3] Net of accretion and financing fees. Consist 5% debentures due June 30, 2027, and convertible into common shares at $45.14 per share; and 5.2% debentures due Dec. 31, 2027, and convertible into common shares at $70.5 per share. An equity component totaling $22,851,000 was classified as part of shareholders' equity.

Wholly Owned Subsidiaries

AG Growth International Australia Pty Ltd., Australia.
AGI Agricultural Equipment (Nigeria) Limited, Nigeria.
AGI Agricultural Equipment Proprietary Limited, South Africa.
AGI EMEA S.R.L., Italy.
AGI Suretrack Ltd., Ont.
Ag Growth Holdings Corp.
- 100% int. in **AGI Brasil Indústria e Comércio S.A.**, Brazil.
- 100% int. in **Westfield Distributing (North Dakota) Inc.**
  - 100% int. in **AGI Suretrack LLC**, Archie, Mo.
  - 100% int. in **Airlanco Inc.**, Neb.
  - 100% int. in **CMC Industrial Electronics USA, Inc.**, Wash.
  - 100% int. in **Danmare, Inc.**, Del.
  - 100% int. in **Global Industries, Inc.**, Grand Island, Neb.
  - 100% int. in **Hansen Manufacturing Corp.**, Sioux Falls, S.D.
  - 100% int. in **Junge Control Inc.**, Cedar Rapids, Iowa.
  - 100% int. in **Mitchell Mill Systems USA, Inc.**, Mo.
  - 100% int. in **Tramco Inc.**, Wichita, Kan.
    - 100% int. in **Tramco Europe Limited**, United Kingdom.
  - 100% int. in **Union Iron, Inc.**, Decatur, Ill.
  - 100% int. in **Yargus Manufacturing, Inc.**, Ill.

Ag Growth International (Thailand) Ltd., Thailand.
CMC Industrial Electronics Ltd., Burnaby, B.C.
Danmare Group Inc., Ont.
Eastern Fabricators Inc., P.E.I.
Euro-Tramco B.V., Netherlands.
- 100% int. in **AGI Netherlands B.V.**, Netherlands.
- 99.99% int. in **Milltec Machinery Limited**, Bangalore, India.

Farmobile, Inc., Leawood, Kan.
Improtech Ltd., North York, Ont.
Sabe S.A.S., France.

Financial Statistics

Periods ended:	12m Dec. 31/22[A]		12m Dec. 31/21[A]
	$000s	%Chg	$000s
Operating revenue	**1,458,082**	**+22**	**1,198,523**
Cost of goods sold	792,965		677,525
Salaries & benefits	331,160		288,460
General & admin expense	152,100		107,363
Stock-based compensation	15,620		8,551
Operating expense	**1,300,450**	**+19**	**1,088,803**
Operating income	**157,632**	**+44**	**109,720**
Deprec., depl. & amort.	75,429		62,049
Finance income	327		377
Finance costs, gross	70,008		46,591
Investment income	nil		(1,077)
Write-downs/write-offs	(75,846)[1]		(5,074)
Pre-tax income	**(45,313)**	**n.a.**	**9,383**
Income taxes	5,270		(1,175)
Net income	**(50,583)**	**n.a.**	**10,558**
Cash & equivalent	59,644		61,307
Inventories	279,318		243,250
Accounts receivable	220,861		206,271
Current assets	642,846		572,819
Fixed assets, net	336,385		349,310
Right-of-use assets	31,360		19,211
Intangibles, net	568,862		611,652
Total assets	**1,646,051**	**+3**	**1,593,654**
Accts. pay. & accr. liabs	236,111		195,646
Current liabilities	412,217		464,647
Long-term debt, gross	877,169		876,636
Long-term debt, net	876,690		779,501
Long-term lease liabilities	33,482		17,263
Equity portion of conv. debs	22,851		12,905
Shareholders' equity	265,670		268,751
Cash from oper. activs	**102,170**	**+161**	**39,115**
Cash from fin. activs	(18,065)		35,054
Cash from invest. activs	(85,768)		(75,318)
Net cash position	**59,644**	**-3**	**61,307**
Capital expenditures	(33,283)		(28,676)
Capital disposals	1,587		511
Pension fund surplus	3,000		1,536
	$		$
Earnings per share*	(2.68)		0.56
Cash flow per share*	5.41		2.08
Cash divd. per share*	0.60		0.60
	shs		shs
No. of shs. o/s*	18,900,958		18,793,570
Avg. no. of shs. o/s*	18,870,453		18,778,726
	%		%
Net profit margin	(3.47)		0.88
Return on equity	(18.93)		3.97
Return on assets	1.70		4.10
Foreign sales percent	77		78
No. of employees (FTEs)	4,987		4,258

* Common

[A] Reported in accordance with IFRS

[1] Includes impairment of property, plant and equipment, right-of-use assets and intangible assets of the Digital business segment.

Latest Results

Periods ended:	6m June 30/23[A]		6m June 30/22[A]
	$000s	%Chg	$000s
Operating revenue	737,285	+8	681,974
Net income	32,452	+216	10,256
	$		$
Earnings per share*	1.71		0.54

* Common

[A] Reported in accordance with IFRS

Historical Summary
(as originally stated)

Fiscal Year	Oper. Rev. $000s	Net Inc. Bef. Disc. $000s	EPS* $
2022[A]	1,458,082	(50,583)	(2.68)
2021[A]	1,198,523	10,558	0.56
2020[A]	994,030	(61,648)	(3.30)
2019[A]	995,787	14,633	0.79
2018[A]	931,664	26,618	1.58

* Common

[A] Reported in accordance with IFRS

A.63 AgriFORCE Growing Systems Ltd.

Symbol - AGRI **Exchange** - NASDAQ **CUSIP** - 753992
Head Office - 300-2233 Columbia St, Vancouver, BC, V5Y 0M6 **Telephone** - (604) 757-0952 **Toll-free** - (866) 226-3514
Website - agriforcegs.com
Email - rwong@agriforcegs.com
Investor Relations - Richard S. Wong (604) 757-0952
Auditors - Marcum LLP C.P.A., Costa Mesa, Calif.
Transfer Agents - VStock Transfer. LLC, Woodmere, N.Y.
Employees - 15 at July 27, 2022
Profile - (B.C. 2017) Develops and acquires intellectual property (IP) and technology to improve farming including a controlled-environment agriculture (CEA) facility design, as well as provides agricultural technology (AgTech) consulting services. Also develops and commercializes plant-based ingredients and products that deliver healthier and more nutritious solutions.

Operations are carried out into two divisions: AgriFORCE Solutions; and AgriFORCE Brands.

AgriFORCE Solutions - The company has developed specific, data-driven cultivation strategies that start at tissue culture or micropropagation to allow crops to reach their full genetic potential. The company's expertise is delivered through a range of services and IP including its proprietary facility design and hydroponics-based automated grow system, FORCEGH+, that is to be leased to agricultural producers; and AgTech consulting services that are applied by customers across various sectors and at every phase of cultivation.

AgriFORCE Brands - This division is focused on the development and commercialization of plant-based ingredients and consumer products that deliver healthier and more nutritious solutions. The company owns intellectual property for a technology to naturally process and convert grains, pulses and root vegetables that results in low-starch, low-sugar, high-protein, fibre-rich baking flour products, and nutrition liquid.

Recent Merger and Acquisition Activity

Status: pending **Revised:** Sept. 26, 2022
UPDATE: The agreement was amended to reduce the consideration to US$17,660,000, plus an earn-out consideration of up to US$5,990,000 over two years based on achievement of certain performance milestones. In addition, the companies agreed to extend further the closing date of the transaction to before 2022 ends. PREVIOUS: AgriFORCE Growing Systems Ltd. entered into a letter of intent for the acquisition of a European agriculture/horticulture and AgTech consulting firm for US$29,000,000 in cash and common shares. Feb. 15, 2022 - A definitive agreement was entered into. The target company was identified as Netherlands-based Delphy Groep B.V. , which optimizes production of plant-based foods and flowers, with clients including agriculture companies, governments, universities and leading AgTech suppliers. May 12, 2022 - The companies mutually agreed to extend the closing date until the end of July 2022.

Status: pending **Announced:** Sept. 22, 2022
AgriFORCE Growing Systems Ltd. agreed to acquire 34 acres of land in Coachella, Calif., which would serve as the first Coachella Campus for AgriFORCE's controlled environment agriculture facilities for issuance of US$2,800,000 of common shares and US$1,500,000 cash. In connection, AgriFORCE agreed to develop the property with Stronghold Power Systems Inc. (SPSI) and Stronghold Engineering Inc. (SEI), with SEI bearing most of the infrastructure cost. The campus would include cultivation facilities, featuring advanced facility design, automated integrated growing systems and advanced environmental control systems.

Status: completed **Revised:** May 18, 2022
UPDATE: The transaction was completed, effective Sept. 10, 2021. PREVIOUS: AgriFORCE Growing Systems Ltd. agreed to acquire a food production and processing intellectual property (IP) from Boise, Idaho-based Manna Nutritional Group LLC for up to US$14,475,000 consisting of issuance of US$13,000,000 common shares and US$1,475,000 cash. The IP encompasses patent-pending technologies to naturally process and convert grain, pulses and root vegetables, resulting in low-starch, low-sugar, high-protein, high-fibre baking flour products, as well as a wide range of breakfast cereals, juices, natural sweeteners and baking enhancers.

Status: pending **Announced:** Mar. 10, 2022
AgriFORCE Growing Systems Ltd. entered into a letter to acquire private Sleidinge, Belgium-based Deroose Plants N.V., one of the largest tissue culture propagation companies in the world, for US$69,000,000. Deroose Plants produces and supplies young plant material for floriculture and production of plantation crops, fruits and vegetables, as well as offers Propagation-as-a-Service to young plant breeders and propagators. Deroose Plants is a subsidiary of SIAT S.A., which is a subsidiary of the Vandebeeck family's holding company, Fimave N.V.

Predecessor Detail - Name changed from Canivate Growing Systems Ltd., Nov. 22, 2019.

Directors - Ingo W. Mueller, chr. & CEO; Amy E. Griffith; Richard Levychin; W. John Meekison, Scottsdale, Ariz.; David Welch

Other Exec. Officers - Richard S. Wong, CFO; Dr. Laila Benkrima, chief scientist; Gideon De Jager, chief strategy & bus. devel. officer; Mauro Pennella, chief mktg. officer & pres., AgriFORCE Brands div.; John Dol, v-p, opers.; Dawn Longshaw, v-p, HR; André Beaulieu, gen. counsel; Troy T. McClellan, pres., AgriFORCE Solutions div.

Capital Stock

	Authorized (shs.)	Outstanding (shs.)[1]
Series A Preferred	unlimited	nil
Common	unlimited	15,555,118

[1] At Aug. 15, 2022

Series A Preferred - Entitled to cumulative dividends at 12% per annum. Convertible into common shares on a one-for-one basis. One vote per share. All outstanding Series A Preferred shares were converted to common shares on July 12, 2021.

Common - One vote per share.

Major Shareholder - Widely held at Oct. 19, 2022.

Price Range - AGRI/NASDAQ

Year	Volume	High	Low	Close
2022	75,734,230	US$6.09	US$0.95	US$1.13
2021	50,869,652	US$8.45	US$1.79	US$2.08

Wholly Owned Subsidiaries

AGI IP Co., Nev.
AgriFORCE Investments Inc., Del.
DayBreak Ag Systems Ltd., B.C.
West Pender Holdings, Inc., Del.
West Pender Management Co., Nev.

Financial Statistics

Periods ended:	12m Dec. 31/21[A]		12m Dec. 31/20[A1]
	US$000s	%Chg	US$000s
Salaries & benefits	1,766		1,072
Research & devel. expense	474		124
General & admin expense	3,880		1,569
Stock-based compensation	796		571
Operating expense	**6,917**	**+107**	**3,336**
Operating income	**(6,917)**	**n.a.**	**(3,336)**
Deprec., depl. & amort.	12		9
Finance costs, gross	484		nil
Pre-tax income	**(6,643)**	**n.a.**	**(3,222)**
Net income	**(6,643)**	**n.a.**	**(3,222)**
Cash & equivalent	7,775		653
Accounts receivable	32		9
Current assets	8,117		875
Fixed assets, net	2,121		2,100
Total assets	**11,765**	**+250**	**3,366**
Accts. pay. & accr. liabs	1,532		1,931
Current liabilities	1,532		1,931
Long-term debt, gross	47		31
Long-term debt, net	47		31
Preferred share equity	nil		6,718
Shareholders' equity	8,000		1,403
Cash from oper. activs	**(5,137)**	**n.a.**	**(1,852)**
Cash from fin. activs	13,405		605
Cash from invest. activs	(1,007)		(172)
Net cash position	**7,775**	**n.m.**	**653**
Capital expenditures	(26)		(2)
	US$		US$
Earnings per share*	(0.66)		(0.53)
Cash flow per share*	(0.46)		(0.23)
	shs		shs
No. of shs. o/s*	15,176,698		8,441,617
Avg. no. of shs. o/s*	11,164,311		7,907,233
	%		%
Net profit margin	n.a.		n.a.
Return on equity	(549.65)		n.m.
Return on assets	(81.41)		(83.30)

* Common

[A] Reported in accordance with U.S. GAAP

[1] Shares and per share figures adjusted to reflect 1-for-4.75 consolidation effective Nov. 29, 2020.

Latest Results

Periods ended:	6m June 30/22[A]		6m June 30/21[A]
	US$000s	%Chg	US$000s
Net income	(6,724)	n.a.	(2,092)
	US$		US$
Earnings per share*	(0.43)		(0.30)

* Common

[A] Reported in accordance with U.S. GAAP

Historical Summary
(as originally stated)

Fiscal Year	Oper. Rev. US$000s	Net Inc. Bef. Disc. US$000s	EPS* US$
2021[A]	nil	(6,643)	(0.66)
2020[A1]	nil	(3,222)	(0.53)
2019[A1]	nil	(5,119)	(0.67)

* Common

[A] Reported in accordance with U.S. GAAP

[1] Shares and per share figures adjusted to reflect 1-for-4.75 consolidation effective Nov. 29, 2020.

A.64 Agrinam Acquisition Corporation

Symbol - AGRI.U **Exchange** - TSX **CUSIP** - 00857H
Head Office - 801 Brickell Ave, 8th Floor, Miami, FL, United States, 33131
Website - agrinamspac.com
Email - agustin.tristan@agrinamspac.com
Investor Relations - Agustin Tristan 52-55-6698-9326
Auditors - MNP LLP C.A., Toronto, Ont.
Lawyers - Dorsey & Whitney LLP; Borden Ladner Gervais LLP, Toronto, Ont.
Transfer Agents - TSX Trust Company, Toronto, Ont.
Profile - (B.C. 2021) A Special Purpose Acquisition Corporation formed for the purpose of effecting an acquisition of one or more businesses or assets by way of a merger, share exchange, asset acquisition, share purchase, reorganization or any other similar business combination involving the company.

The company has 15 months from June 15, 2022, or up to 21 months if the company exercises its two successive three-month extension options, to complete a Qualifying Acquisition, and may be extended to up to 36 months if the company has exercised its applicable extension options and the requisite amounts have been deposited into the escrow account. The company plans to execute a Qualifying Acquisition with one or more companies that operate across the agricultural industries in North America, either in the primary sector (with a focus on superfoods and specialty products produced in high-tech greenhouses) or the value-added sector (with a focus on food tech as well as wine and spirits produced in new regions that have a nice differentiator relative to the competition). However, the company's search for a Qualifying Acquisition is not limited to a particular industry or geographic region.

Directors - Nicholas Thadaney, chr., Toronto, Ont.; Agustin Tristan, CEO, Mexico City, D.F., Mexico; Guillermo E. Cruz, COO, Mexico City, D.F., Mexico; Donald Olds, Montréal, Qué.; Jennifer Reynolds, Toronto, Ont.; Lara Zink, Toronto, Ont.

Other Exec. Officers - Jeronimo Peralta, CFO; Gustavo Castellanos, chief sustainability officer & corp. sec.; Luis A. Ibarra, chief invest. officer

Capital Stock

	Authorized (shs.)	Outstanding (shs.)[1]
Cl.A Restricted Vtg.	unlimited	13,800,001
Class B	unlimited	3,450,000

[1] At Aug. 11, 2023

Class A Restricted Voting - Automatically convertible into common shares upon closing of Qualifying Acquisition on a 1-for-1 basis. Not permitted to redeem more than 15% of class A restricted voting shares outstanding. Automatically redeemable if no Qualifying Acquisition is completed. One vote per share on all matters requiring shareholder approval including a proposed Qualifying Acquisition but not on the election and/or removal of directors and auditors.

Class B - Non-redeemable. Automatically convertible into proportionate voting shares upon closing of Qualifying Acquisition on the basis of 1 proportionate voting share for 100 class B shares. One vote per share.

Common - Not issuable prior to closing of Qualifying Acquisition. Would be convertible, at the holder's option, into proportionate voting shares on the basis of 1 proportionate voting share for 100 common shares. One vote per share.

Proportionate Voting - Not issuable prior to closing of Qualifying Acquisition. Would be convertible, at the holder's option, into common shares on the basis of 100 common shares for 1 proportionate share. 100 votes per share.

Major Shareholder - Agrinam Investments, LLC held 19.36% interest at Aug. 15, 2023.

Price Range - AGRI.U/TSX

Year	Volume	High	Low	Close
2022............	232,020	US$9.85	US$9.14	US$9.82

AGRI.V/TSX (D)

Year	Volume	High	Low	Close
2022............	587,300	US$10.06	US$9.90	US$9.96

Recent Close: US$10.47

Capital Stock Changes - On June 15, 2022, an initial public offering of 13,800,000 units (1 class A restricted voting share & 1 warrant) at US$10 per unit was completed, including 1,800,000 units on exercise of over-allotment option. Also during fiscal 2023, 3,450,000 class B shares were issued to founders.

A.65 Aimia Inc.*

Symbol - AIM **Exchange** - TSX **CUSIP** - 00900Q
Head Office - 600-176 Yonge St, Toronto, ON, M5C 2L7 **Telephone** - (416) 359-3999
Website - www.aimia.com
Email - albert.matousek@aimia.com
Investor Relations - Albert Matousek (416) 359-3999
Auditors - PricewaterhouseCoopers LLP C.A., Montréal, Qué.
Lawyers - Borden Ladner Gervais LLP
Transfer Agents - TSX Trust Company
FP500 Revenue Ranking - 479
Employees - 18 at Dec. 31, 2022
Profile - (Can. 2008) Holds investments in public and private companies.

The company operates an investment advisory business through wholly owned **Mittleman Investment Management, LLC**, an SEC-registered investment adviser that provides portfolio management to institutional investors and high-net-worth individuals. At Dec. 31, 2022, assets under management were US$93,900,000.

Holdings include wholly owned **Tufropes Pvt. Ltd.**, a global leader in the manufacturing of high-performance synthetic fiber ropes and netting solutions for global aquaculture, maritime, and other various industrial customers; 94% interest in **Giovanni Bozzetto S.p.A.**, an environmental, social, and governance (ESG)-focused providers of specialty sustainable chemicals; 48.9% interest in **Kognitiv Corporation**, a business-to-business (B2B) global Software-as-a-Service company which inspires customer loyalty through data-driven personalization; 11.9% interest in **Trade X Group of Companies Inc.**, a global B2B cross-border automotive trading platform; 10.85% interest in **Ever Harmonic Global Limited**, owner of **Clear Media Limited**, a bus shelter advertising firm in China; and minority stakes in various public company securities and limited partnerships.

On Apr. 14, 2023, wholly owned **Mittleman Investment Management, LLC**'s operations was wound down.

During 2022, the company sold all 10,355,900 common shares of **Capital A Bhd.** (formerly **AirAsia Group Bhd.**) it held for total proceeds of $2,100,000.

Recent Merger and Acquisition Activity

Status: completed **Revised:** May 9, 2023
UPDATE: The transaction was completed, with Aimia invested $206,300,000 for an equity interest of 94% and Bozzetto's management reinvested $13,300,000 which represents 6% minority interest in Bonzzetto. PREVIOUS: Aimia Inc. agreed to acquire Giovanni Bozzetto S.p.A. (Bozzetto Group) from Chequers Capital and other minority shareholders for $328,000,000. Filago, Italy-based Bozzetto is a manufacturer of over 2,000 proprietary specialty sustainable chemicals to service its core textile, water solutions, and dispersion end markets. Paladin Private Equity, LLC will act as Aimia's partner on the transaction and would be granted an option to acquire up to a 19.9% minority equity position of Bozzetto within one year of closing. The transaction was expected to close before the end of the second quarter of 2023.

Status: completed **Revised:** Mar. 17, 2023
UPDATE: The transaction was completed. PREVIOUS: Aimia Inc. agreed to acquire India-based Tufropes Pvt. Ltd., which manufactures synthetic fibre ropes and netting solutions for the aquaculture and maritime sectors, as well as diversified industrial end makers, for $249,600,000. Tufropes was capable of producing 70,000 tonnes of rope and netting solutions per year.

Status: completed **Revised:** July 18, 2022
UPDATE: The transaction was completed. PREVIOUS: Aimia Inc. agreed to sell its 48.9% interest in PLM Premier, S.A.P.I. de C.V., owner and operator of Mexican coalition loyalty program Club Premier, to Grupo Aeromexico, S.A.B. de C.V. (Aeromexico) for US$386,000,000 in net cash proceeds on closing plus an earnout of up US$19,000,000 on a net basis. The transaction would be consummated pursuant to the joint chapter 11 plan of reorganization of Grupo Aeromexico and its affiliates that are also debtors in the debtors' chapter 11 bankruptcy cases pending in the United States Bankruptcy Court for the Southern District of New York. June 30, 2022 - A definitive agreement was entered into and Mexican antitrust approval was received. Net cash proceeds were expected to be Cdn$531,000,00, subject to certain adjustments to be made post-closing plus an earnout of Cdn$27,000,000.

Predecessor Detail - Name changed from Groupe Aeroplan Inc., May 4, 2012.

Directors - Karen Basian, interim chr., Ont.; Philip C. Mittleman, CEO, Ponte Vedra Beach, Fla.; Michael Lehmann, pres., Rye, N.Y.; Kristen M. Dickey, N.Y.; Linda S. Habgood, N.J.; Thomas (Tom) Little, Ont.; Jon E. Mattson, Hobe Sound, Fla.; Jordan G. Teramo, New York, N.Y.

Other Exec. Officers - Steven (Steve) Leonard, CFO; Eric Blondeau, chief legal officer & corp. sec.

Capital Stock

	Authorized (shs.)	Outstanding (shs.)[1]
Preferred	unlimited	nil
Series 1		5,083,140
Series 2		nil
Series 3		4,355,263
Common	unlimited	84,164,614

[1] At Mar. 31, 2023

Preferred - Issuable in series. Non-voting.

Series 1 - Entitled to fixed cumulative preferential annual dividends of $1.2005 per share payable quarterly to Mar. 31, 2025, and thereafter at a rate reset every five years equal to the five-year Government of Canada bond yield plus 3.75%. Redeemable on Mar. 31, 2025, and on March 31 every five years thereafter at $25 per share plus declared and unpaid dividends. Convertible at the holder's option, on Mar. 31, 2025, and on March 31 every five years thereafter, into floating rate preferred series 2 shares on a share-for-share basis, subject to certain conditions. The preferred series 2 shares would pay a quarterly dividend equal to the 90-day Canadian Treasury bill rate plus 3.75%.

Series 3 - Entitled to fixed cumulative preferential annual dividends of $1.5025 payable quarterly to Mar. 31, 2024, and thereafter at a rate reset every five years equal to the five-year Government of Canada bond yield plus 4.2%. Redeemable on Mar. 31, 2024, and on March 31 every five years thereafter at $25 per share plus declared and unpaid dividends. Convertible at the holder's option, on Mar. 31, 2024, and on March 31 every five years thereafter, into floating rate preferred series 4 shares on a share-for-share basis, subject to certain conditions. The preferred series 4 shares would pay a quarterly dividend equal to the 90-day Canadian Treasury bill rate plus 4.2%.

Common - One vote per share.

Options - At Dec. 31, 2022, options were outstanding to purchase 75,142 common shares at a weighted average exercise price of $3.25 per share expiring to 2026.

Major Shareholder - Mithaq Capital SPC held 19.99% interest at Mar. 6, 2023.

Price Range - AIM/TSX

Year	Volume	High	Low	Close
2022............	43,615,646	$6.43	$3.29	$3.69
2021............	22,097,303	$5.58	$3.91	$4.95
2020............	58,985,679	$4.25	$1.60	$4.13
2019............	129,341,603	$4.30	$2.99	$3.60
2018............	201,218,148	$4.60	$1.49	$3.69

Recent Close: $3.24

Capital Stock Changes - During 2022, 8,323,598 common shares were repurchased under a Normal Course Issuer Bid.

Dividends

AIM.PR.A pfd ser 1 cum. red. exch. Adj. Ra $1.2005 pa Q est. June 30, 2020
AIM.PR.C pfd ser 3 cum. red. exch. Adj. Ra $1.5025 pa Q est. June 28, 2019

Long-Term Debt - At Dec. 31, 2022, the company had no long-term debt.

Wholly Owned Subsidiaries

Mittleman Brothers, LLC, New York, N.Y.
- 100% int. in **Mittleman Investment Management, LLC**, Melville, N.Y.

Tufropes Pvt. Ltd., India.

Subsidiaries

94% int. in **Giovanni Bozzetto S.p.A.**, Italy.

Investments

10.85% int. in **Ever Harmonic Global Limited**, Cayman Islands.
- 100% int. in **Clear Media Limited**, Hong Kong, Hong Kong, People's Republic of China.

48.9% int. in **Kognitiv Corporation**, Toronto, Ont.
11.9% int. in **Trade X Group of Companies Inc.**, Ont.

Financial Statistics

Periods ended:	12m Dec. 31/22[A]		12m Dec. 31/21[A]
	$000s	%Chg	$000s
Realized invest. gain (loss)...............	(2,200)		17,200
Unrealized invest. gain (loss)............	(37,300)		(5,300)
Total revenue..............................	**476,500**	**n.m.**	**12,600**
Salaries & benefits.........................	10,400		9,100
Stock-based compensation............	(2,400)		7,300
Other operating expense.................	12,600		7,900
Operating expense........................	**20,600**	**-15**	**24,300**
Operating income.........................	**455,900**	**n.a.**	**(11,700)**
Deprec. & amort..............................	100		700
Finance costs, net...........................	3,000		(300)
Write-downs/write-offs....................	(11,400)		nil
Pre-tax income..............................	**445,300**	**n.a.**	**(12,100)**
Income taxes....................................	5,200		5,000
Net inc. bef. disc. opers.................	**440,100**	**n.a.**	**(17,100)**
Income from disc. opers..................	nil		700
Net income....................................	**440,100**	**n.a.**	**(16,400)**
Cash & equivalent...........................	558,200		112,300
Accounts receivable........................	700		900
Current assets..................................	563,300		117,400
Long-term investments...................	189,100		267,200
Intangibles.......................................	1,100		12,100
Total assets...................................	**804,000**	**+87**	**431,000**
Accts. pay. & accr. liabs..................	7,300		4,700
Current liabilities.............................	9,500		10,100
Preferred share equity.....................	231,100		231,100
Shareholders' equity........................	776,900		404,000
Cash from oper. activs..................	**(17,700)**	**n.a.**	**21,400**
Cash from fin. activs........................	(49,100)		(12,600)
Cash from invest. activs..................	526,000		(118,900)
Net cash position..........................	**505,300**	**n.m.**	**34,800**
	$		$
Earns. per sh. bef disc opers*..........	4.88		(0.33)
Earnings per share*.........................	4.88		(0.32)
Cash flow per share*.......................	(0.20)		0.24
	shs		shs
No. of shs. o/s*................................	84,164,614		92,488,212
Avg. no. of shs. o/s*........................	87,682,533		90,922,527
	%		%
Net profit margin.............................	92.36		(135.71)
Return on equity...............................	118.96		(15.92)
Return on assets..............................	71.27		(3.91)
Foreign sales percent......................	100		100
No. of employees (FTEs)..................	18		18

* Common
[A] Reported in accordance with IFRS

Latest Results

Periods ended:	3m Mar. 31/23[A]		3m Mar. 31/22[A]
	$000s	%Chg	$000s
Total revenue..................................	14,100	n.a.	(14,300)
Net income......................................	(20,500)	n.a.	(18,900)
	$		$
Earnings per share*.........................	(0.29)		(0.24)

* Common
[A] Reported in accordance with IFRS

Historical Summary
(as originally stated)

Fiscal Year	Total Rev. $000s	Net Inc. Bef. Disc. $000s	EPS* $
2022A	476,500	440,100	4.88
2021A	12,600	(17,100)	(0.33)
2020A	14,300	(15,100)	(0.30)
2019A	134,000	42,900	0.37
2018A	167,100	(161,600)	(1.18)

* Common
A Reported in accordance with IFRS

A.66 Aion Therapeutic Inc.

Symbol - AION **Exchange** - CSE **CUSIP** - 00905T
Head Office - 703-45 Sheppard Ave E, Toronto, ON, M2N 5W9 **Telephone** - (416) 450-3270
Email - info@aiontherapeutic.com
Investor Relations - J. Graham Simmonds (416) 843-2881
Auditors - Kreston GTA LLP C.A., Markham, Ont.
Bankers - Alterna Savings and Credit Union Limited, Ottawa, Ont.
Transfer Agents - Capital Transfer Agency Inc., Toronto, Ont.
Profile - (B.C. 2011) Researches and develops therapeutic pharmaceuticals, nutraceuticals, and cosmeceuticals products utilizing combine healing compounds from medical cannabis and medicinal mushrooms.

The company is researching the healing potential of plant-based and fungal-based medicines, remedies and treatments for conditions such as psychiatric disorders, viral infections, bladder diseases and obesity using data mining and artificial intelligence (AI) techniques.

Has opened the Aion International Center for Psychedelic Psychiatry in Jamaica, which would specialize in the use of psilocybin for the treatment of addiction (tobacco, alcohol and other drug misuse), depression and anxiety associated with life-threatening illnesses, and treatment-resistant depression. In addition, the centre would be studying the effectiveness of psilocybin as a new therapy for opioid addiction, Alzheimer's disease, post-traumatic stress disorder (PTSD) and anorexia nervosa.

In June 2022, the company sold four patent applications and all associated data with the treatment of cancer and inflammation to **Apollon Formularies plc** for issuance of 4,348,679 common shares at a deemed price of £0.066 per share. In addition, the company would receive indefinite royalty fee of 4% of the global net revenue generated by the intellectual property. The patent applications consist of compositions and methods for treatment of cancers; compositions and methods for treatment of inflammation; methods for treatment of human cancers using mushroom compositions; and methods for treatment of human cancers using cannabis compositions.

Predecessor Detail - Name changed from Osoyoos Cannabis Inc., Aug. 28, 2020.

Directors - J. Graham Simmonds, exec. v-chr. & CEO, Toronto, Ont.; Paul J. Crath†, Toronto, Ont.; Dr. Anthony Hall, Fort Lauderdale, Fla.; Larry Horwitz, Lake Forest, Calif.; Sara L. Irwin, Toronto, Ont.

Other Exec. Officers - Rakesh Malhotra, CFO; Patricia L. (Pat) Purdy, corp. sec.

† Lead director

Capital Stock

	Authorized (shs.)	Outstanding (shs.)[1]
Preferred	unlimited	nil
Common	unlimited	147,299,269

[1] At Apr. 3, 2023

Major Shareholder - Plant-Based Investment Corp. held 16.96% interest at June 11, 2021.

Price Range - AION/CSE

Year	Volume	High	Low	Close
2022	40,534,716	$0.04	$0.01	$0.01
2021	94,235,545	$0.19	$0.02	$0.03
2020	33,202,198	$0.17	$0.01	$0.12
2019	36,046,420	$0.35	$0.05	$0.07

Recent Close: $0.02

Capital Stock Changes - In June 2021, private placement of 16,994,475 units (1 common share & ½ warrant) at $0.0875 per unit was completed.

Wholly Owned Subsidiaries

1160516 B.C. Ltd., Oliver, B.C.
- 100% int. in **Bare Root Production Osoyoos Inc.**, B.C.

1196691 B.C. Ltd., B.C.
- 100% int. in **Al Pharmaceuticals Jamaica Limited**, Jamaica.

Oservco Management Corp.

Financial Statistics

Periods ended:	12m Apr. 30/22A		12m Apr. 30/21A
	$000s	%Chg	$000s
Research & devel. expense	953		nil
General & admin expense	1,801		2,200
Stock-based compensation	nil		452
Operating expense	**2,754**	**+4**	**2,652**
Operating income	**(2,754)**	**n.a.**	**(2,652)**
Deprec., depl. & amort.	65		128
Finance costs, gross	76		186
Write-downs/write-offs	(1,000)		(5,157)
Pre-tax income	**(3,818)**	**n.a.**	**(8,265)**
Net income	**(3,818)**	**n.a.**	**(8,265)**
Cash & equivalent	nil		240
Current assets	150		475
Fixed assets, net	nil		500
Right-of-use assets	nil		64
Total assets	**150**	**-91**	**1,604**
Bank indebtedness	744		nil
Accts. pay. & accr. liabs	1,813		626
Current liabilities	2,557		1,206
Long-term debt, gross	nil		500
Equity portion of conv. debs	nil		110
Shareholders' equity	(2,407)		397
Cash from oper. activs	**(1,347)**	**n.a.**	**(2,133)**
Cash from fin. activs	1,197		3,002
Cash from invest. activs	nil		(1,380)
Net cash position	**nil**	**n.a.**	**240**
	$		$
Earnings per share*	(0.03)		(0.09)
Cash flow per share*	(0.01)		(0.02)
	shs		shs
No. of shs. o/s*	141,799,269		124,804,794
Avg. no. of shs. o/s*	139,890,301		93,897,086
	%		%
Net profit margin	n.a.		n.a.
Return on equity	n.m.		(653.10)
Return on assets	(426.68)		(327.09)

* Common
A Reported in accordance with IFRS

Latest Results

Periods ended:	3m July 31/22A		3m July 31/21A
	$000s	%Chg	$000s
Net income	808	n.a.	(747)
	$		$
Earnings per share*	0.01		(0.01)

* Common
A Reported in accordance with IFRS

Historical Summary
(as originally stated)

Fiscal Year	Oper. Rev. $000s	Net Inc. Bef. Disc. $000s	EPS* $
2022A	nil	(3,818)	(0.03)
2021A	nil	(8,265)	(0.09)
2020A	nil	(673)	(0.02)
2019A1	nil	(4,934)	(0.18)
2018A2,3	nil	(2,131)	(0.24)

* Common
A Reported in accordance with IFRS
[1] Results reflect the Oct. 31, 2018, reverse takeover acquisition of (new) Osoyoos Cannabis Inc.
[2] 38 weeks ended Apr. 30, 2018.
[3] Results pertain to (old) Osoyoos Cannabis Inc.

A.67 Air Canada*

Symbol - AC **Exchange** - TSX **CUSIP** - 008911
Head Office - Air Canada Centre, 7373 boul Côte-Vertu O, Saint-Laurent, QC, H4S 1Z3 **Telephone** - (514) 422-6644 **Toll-free** - (888) 247-2262 **Fax** - (514) 422-0296
Website - www.aircanada.com
Email - valerie.durand@aircanada.ca
Investor Relations - Valerie Durand (514) 422-7849
Auditors - PricewaterhouseCoopers LLP C.A., Montréal, Qué.
Lawyers - Stikeman Elliott LLP, Montréal, Qué.
Transfer Agents - TSX Trust Company, Montréal, Qué.
FP500 Revenue Ranking - 37
Employees - 30,478 at Dec. 31, 2022
Profile - (Can. 1988, via The Air Canada Public Participation Act; orig. Can., 1937, via Special Act of Parliament) Provides scheduled and charter air transportation for passengers and cargo to destinations in the Americas, Europe, Asia, Africa, Australia, the Middle East and the Caribbean. Also owns and operates Aeroplan travel loyalty program and provides tour operator services, leisure vacation packages and ground handling services to third parties.

At Dec. 31, 2022, the company's operating fleet totaled 192 aircraft (excluding chartered freighter, **Jazz Aviation LP**'s, aircraft covered under capacity purchase agreements), consisting of 110 Boeing and Airbus narrow-body aircraft, and 82 Boeing and Airbus wide-body aircraft. Wholly owned **Air Canada rouge LP**, dba Air Canada Rouge®, provides lower-cost leisure travel services with a fleet of 39 Airbus narrow-body aircraft. During 2022, the company, together with Jazz Airlines, operated an average of 945 scheduled flights each day and carried 37,000,000 passengers to 185 direct destinations on six continents. Through its membership in the Star Alliance® network, the company offers customers access to a vast global network, as well as reciprocal participation in frequent flyer programs and use of airport lounges and other airport facilities. The Star Alliance® network includes 26 member airlines.

Revenue is also generated from Air Canada Cargo which provides air cargo services on passenger flights and on all-cargo flights on domestic and U.S. transborder routes as well as on international routes (including on dedicated freighter aircraft) between Canada and major markets in Europe, Asia, South America and Australia; and wholly owned **Touram Limited Partnership**, dba Air Canada Vacations®, which provides tour and travel services.

Operating Statistics

Year ended Dec. 31	2022	2021
Passenger:		
Rev. pass. miles (RPM)[1]	66,495	21,045
Avail. seat miles (ASM)[1]	82,558	33,384
Pass. load factor (%)	80.5	63
Yield per RPM	21.4¢	21.4¢
Revenue per ASM	17.2¢	13.5¢
Operations:		
Average stage length[2]	1,755	1,582
Fuel price per litre	130.1¢	74.7¢
Fuel litres[1]	4,057	2,108

[1] Millions.
[2] Miles.

The Aeroplan program offers its more than 7,000,000 active members the ability to accumulate Aeroplan Miles throughout its partner network through purchases of products and services. Partnerships include brands in financial services, including credit and charge cards; travel; and retail and others including car rental, hotels and travel. Once members have accumulated a sufficient number of Aeroplan Miles, they can redeem them for flight rewards with the company and 45 partner airlines, as well as for a wide range of non-air rewards. The company also offers the Air Canada Altitude program to eligible Aeroplan members. Rewards include a range of premium travel privileges and benefits corresponding to their travel activity, such as priority check-in, complimentary checked baggage and upgrades to business class.

In October 2022, the company converted its options to acquire an additional 15 Airbus A220-300 aircraft, bringing the total number it would acquire to 60. Previously, the company elected to proceed with the acquisition of an additional 10 Airbus A220 aircraft, in addition to the two A220 aircraft that were added in 2021.

In September 2022, the company announced an agreement to purchase 30 ES-30 electric-hybrid regional aircraft from Göteborg, Sweden-based **Heart Aerospace AB** as well as the acquisition of a US$5,000,000 equity interest in the electric aircraft manufacturer. The ES-30s are expected to enter service in 2028 and have an all-electric, zero-emission range of 200 km.

In March, 2022, the company agreed to acquire 26 extra-long range (XLR) versions of the Airbus A321neo aircraft. Deliveries would begin in the first quarter of 2024 with the final aircraft to arrive in the first quarter of 2027. Fifteen of the aircraft would be leased from **Air Lease Corporation**, five would be leased from **AerCap Holdings N.V.** and six are being acquired under a purchase agreement with **Airbus S.A.S.**, which would include purchase rights to acquire an additional 14 of the aircraft between 2027 and 2030.

Directors - Vagn Sørensen, chr., London, Middx., United Kingdom; Michael S. Rousseau, pres. & CEO, Saint-Lambert, Qué.; Amee Chande, West Vancouver, B.C.; Christie J. B. (Chris) Clark, Toronto, Ont.; The Hon. Gary A. Doer, Winnipeg, Man.; Rob Fyfe, Auckland, New Zealand; Michael M. Green, East Hampton, N.Y.; Jean Marc Huot, Montréal, Qué.; Claudette McGowan, Aurora, Ont.; Madeleine M. Paquin, Montréal, Qué.; Kathleen P. (Katie) Taylor, Toronto, Ont.; Annette M. Verschuren, Toronto, Ont.; Michael M. (Mike) Wilson, Bragg Creek, Alta.

Other Exec. Officers - Marc B. Barbeau, exec. v-p & chief legal officer; John Di Bert, exec. v-p & CFO; Mark Galardo, exec. v-p, network planning & rev. mgt.; Craig Landry, exec. v-p & COO; Arielle Meloul-Wechsler, exec. v-p, chief HR officer & public affairs; Mark Nasr, exec. v-p, mktg. & digital & pres., Aeroplan Inc.; Kevin O'Connor, sr. v-p, global airports & opers. control; Capt. Murray Storm, sr. v-p, flight opers.; Carolyn M. Hadrovic, v-p & corp. sec.

Capital Stock

	Authorized (shs.)	Outstanding (shs.)[1]
Class A Variable Vtg.	unlimited	75,874,233
Class B Voting	unlimited	282,582,573

[1] At June 30, 2023

Class A Variable Voting - Held only by non-Canadians and entitled to one vote per share, with the following exceptions: (i) the number of variable voting shares outstanding, as a percentage of the total number of shares outstanding, exceeds 49%, or (ii) the total number of votes cast by or on behalf of holders of the variable voting shares at any meeting exceeds 49% of the total number of votes that may be cast at said meeting. If either of the above noted thresholds would otherwise be surpassed at any time, the vote attached to each variable voting share will decrease proportionately such that: (i) the number of variable voting shares as a class do not carry more than 49% of the aggregate votes attached to all issued and outstanding voting shares and (ii) the total number of votes cast by or on behalf of holders of variable voting shares at any meeting do not exceed 49% of the total number of votes that may be cast at said meeting. In addition, the votes attached to variable voting shares are subject to an automatic reduction in the event that any single non-Canadian or the aggregate of non-Canadian air carriers hold more than 25% of the votes. Convertible into one voting share automatically if the variable voting share becomes held, beneficially owned or controlled, directly or indirectly, by a Canadian, or if the provisions under the Canada Transportation Act relating to foreign ownership restrictions are repealed and not replaced with other similar provisions.

Class B Voting - Held only by Canadians. Convertible into one variable voting share only if the foreign ownership restrictions of the Canada Transportation Act are repealed and not replaced with similar restrictions. One vote per share.

Options - At Dec. 31, 2022, options were outstanding to purchase 5,304,745 class A variable and class B voting shares at a weighted average exercise price of $26.39 per share and expiring on various dates to 2031.

Major Shareholder - Widely held at Mar. 21, 2023.

Price Range - AC/TSX

Year	Volume	High	Low	Close
2022	722,570,967	$25.98	$15.57	$19.39
2021	875,547,715	$31.00	$19.31	$21.13
2020	1,369,872,181	$52.71	$9.26	$22.77
2019	288,280,461	$51.07	$24.75	$48.51
2018	312,570,715	$29.39	$20.33	$25.96

Recent Close: $22.32

Capital Stock Changes - During 2022, class A variable or class B voting shares were issued as follows: 350,535 on exercise of options and 169,866 on settlement of restricted share units.

Long-Term Debt - Outstanding at Dec. 31, 2022:

Aircraft financing[1]	$5,350,000,000
3.88% sr. notes due 2026[2]	1,626,000,000
4.63% sr. notes due 2029[3]	2,000,000,000
4% convertible notes due 2025[4]	313,000,000
Credit facility[5]	4,156,000,000
Lease liabilities	3,038,000,000
Less: Debt issuance costs	177,000,000
	16,306,000,000
Less: Current portion	1,263,000,000
	15,043,000,000

[1] Secured primarily by specific aircraft; bears interest at weighted average rates between 1.84% and 6.61% and due to 2033.

[2] US$1.2 billion.

[3] US$2 billion.

[4] Convertible into class A variable and/or class B voting shares at US$15.35 per share.

[5] Consists of Cdn$1.404 billion 1.21% unsecured credit facility due 2028 and US$2.3 billion 4.25% senior secured credit facility due 2028.

Wholly Owned Subsidiaries

Aeroplan Inc., Montréal, Qué.
Air Canada rouge General Partner Inc., Canada.
Air Canada rouge LP, Canada.
Touram General Partner Inc., Canada.
Touram Limited Partnership, Qué.

Investments

Heart Aerospace AB, Göteborg, Sweden.

Note: The preceding list includes only the major related companies in which interests are held.

Financial Statistics

Periods ended:	12m Dec. 31/22[A]		12m Dec. 31/21[¤A]
	$000s	%Chg	$000s
Operating revenue	**16,556,000**	**+159**	**6,400,000**
Salaries & benefits	3,260,000		2,143,000
Other operating expense	11,839,000		5,595,000
Operating expense	**15,099,000**	**+95**	**7,738,000**
Operating income	**1,457,000**	**n.a.**	**(1,338,000)**
Deprec., depl. & amort.	1,640,000		1,616,000
Finance income	168,000		72,000
Finance costs, gross	753,000		924,000
Write-downs/write-offs	(4,000)		(38,000)
Pre-tax income	**(1,524,000)**	**n.a.**	**(3,981,000)**
Income taxes	176,000		(379,000)
Net income	**(1,700,000)**	**n.a.**	**(3,602,000)**
Cash & equivalent	7,988,000		8,969,000
Inventories	318,000		224,000
Accounts receivable	1,037,000		691,000
Current assets	9,665,000		10,053,000
Long-term investments	887,000		653,000
Fixed assets, net	11,950,000		11,740,000
Intangibles, net	4,327,000		4,353,000
Total assets	**29,507,000**	**-4**	**30,614,000**
Accts. pay. & accr. liabs.	2,691,000		2,603,000
Current liabilities	9,353,000		6,924,000
Long-term debt, gross	16,306,000		16,523,000
Long-term debt, net	15,043,000		15,511,000
Shareholders' equity	(1,555,000)		9,000
Cash from oper. activs.	**2,368,000**	**n.a.**	**(1,502,000)**
Cash from fin. activs.	(1,612,000)		4,011,000
Cash from invest. activs.	(2,498,000)		(1,869,000)
Net cash position	**2,693,000**	**-39**	**4,415,000**
Capital expenditures	(1,572,000)		(1,073,000)
Capital disposals	36,000		30,000
Pension fund surplus	4,451,000		4,615,000
	$		$
Earnings per share*	(4.75)		(10.25)
Cash flow per share*	6.61		(4.28)
	shs		shs
No. of shs. o/s*	358,362,258		357,841,857
Avg. no. of shs. o/s*	358,000,000		351,000,000
	%		%
Net profit margin	(10.27)		(56.28)
Return on equity	n.m.		(417.87)
Return on assets	(2.86)		(9.29)
No. of employees (FTEs)	30,478		19,769

* Cl. A & B
¤ Restated
[A] Reported in accordance with IFRS

Latest Results

Periods ended:	6m June 30/23[A]		6m June 30/22[A]
	$000s	%Chg	$000s
Operating revenue	10,314,000	+57	6,554,000
Net income	842,000	n.a.	(1,360,000)
	$		$
Earnings per share*	2.35		(3.80)

* Cl. A & B
[A] Reported in accordance with IFRS

Historical Summary
(as originally stated)

Fiscal Year	Oper. Rev. $000s	Net Inc. Bef. Disc. $000s	EPS* $
2022[A]	16,556,000	(1,700,000)	(4.75)
2021[A]	6,400,000	(3,602,000)	(10.25)
2020[A]	5,833,000	(4,647,000)	(16.47)
2019[A]	19,131,000	1,476,000	5.51
2018[A]	18,065,000	167,000	0.61

* Cl. A & B
[A] Reported in accordance with IFRS

A.68 AirBoss of America Corp.*

Symbol - BOS **Exchange** - TSX **CUSIP** - 00927V
Head Office - 16441 Yonge St, Newmarket, ON, L3X 2G8 **Telephone** - (905) 751-1188 **Fax** - (905) 751-1101
Website - airboss.com
Email - cfigel@airboss.com
Investor Relations - Chris Figel (905) 751-1188
Auditors - KPMG LLP C.A., Toronto, Ont.
Lawyers - Davies Ward Phillips & Vineberg LLP, Toronto, Ont.
Transfer Agents - Computershare Trust Company of Canada Inc., Toronto, Ont.
FP500 Revenue Ranking - 427
Employees - 1,295 at Dec. 31, 2022

Profile - (Ont. 1989 amalg.) Designs, develops, manufactures and sells custom survivability solutions, compounded rubber and anti-vibration components for various applications and industries worldwide.

Operations are organized into three segments: AirBoss Defense Group; Rubber Solutions; and Engineered Products.

The **AirBoss Defense Group** develops, manufactures and sells chemical, biological, radioactive, nuclear and explosives (CBRN-E) protective equipment and related products for military, first response and healthcare applications. Products include hand, foot, respiratory protective wear (gloves, over-boots, extreme cold weather footwear, gas masks and filters), respiratory systems such as powered air purifying respirators (PAPRs) and shelters and infectious disease isolation systems (ISOPODs). Also supplies route clearance vehicles, countermine capability and survivability products to U.S. and foreign military forces. CBRN-E boots, gloves and gas mask face plates and related rubber compounds are manufactured at its 260,000-sq.-ft. facility in Acton-Vale, Que., and the engineered products facility in Auburn Hills; gas mask filters, PAPRs, decontamination shelters, ISOPODs, and thermal targeting materials are manufactured, assembled, inspected and packaged at its 105,000-sq.-ft. facility in Jessup, Md.; and route clearance vehicles and survivability products are manufactured at a 14,000-sq.-ft. facility in Charleston, S.C. Also, through wholly owned **BlackBox Biometrics, Inc.**, develops Blast Gauge® System of lightweight wearable blast overpressure sensors that monitor, record and analyze blast and impact events to help identify individuals such as warfighters, first responders and athletes with blast exposures that could put them at risk of brain injury. The Blast Gauge® System is manufactured at its 2,500-sq.-ft. facility in Rochester, N.Y.

The **Rubber Solutions** segment includes the development and manufacturing of over 2,000 different natural and synthetic custom rubber compounds, calendered and extruded material and moulded products for the mining, transportation, industrial rubber products, military, automotive, conveyor belting, and oil and gas industries, primarily in North America. Rubber compounds are manufactured at a 950,000-sq.-ft. facility in Kitchener, Ont.; a 150,000-sq.-ft. facility in Scotland Neck, N.C.; a 40,000-sq.-ft. facility in The Rock Hill, S.C.; and a 24,000-sq.-ft. facility in Chicago, Ill., providing a combined custom rubber compound capacity of 600,000,000 turn lbs. annually (inclusive of the rubber compounding operations in Acton-Vale, Que.).

The **Engineered Products** segment designs, engineers, manufactures and sells injection moulded metal bonded anti-vibration and noise-suppression products, including hydro mounts, exhaust hangers, engine mounts, boots, dampers, sway bar bushings and spring insulators, to the North American automotive industry and adjacent sectors. The company leases two facilities totaling 275,000-sq.-ft. in Auburn Hills, Mich.

In July 2023, the company's AirBoss Defense Group (ADG) was awarded contracts with a combined value of US$22,300,000. The contracts include supplying ADG AirBoss molded gloves to the Defense Logistics Agency and the Bandolier multipurpose line charge system to a partner nation for use by its military.

Predecessor Detail - Name changed from IATCO Industries Inc., May 4, 1994.

Directors - P. Grenville (Gren) Schoch, chr. & co-CEO, Aurora, Ont.; Stephen M. Ryan†, Washington, D.C.; Anita Antenucci, Washington, D.C.; David Camilleri, Waterloo, Ont.; Mary Matthews, Toronto, Ont.; Robert L. McLeish, Port Carling, Ont.; Alan J. D. Watson, Sydney, N.S.W., Australia

Other Exec. Officers - Chris Bitsakakis, pres. & co-CEO; Frank Ientile, CFO & treas.; Chris Figel, exec. v-p, gen. counsel & corp. sec.; Patrick Callahan, CEO, AirBoss defense grp.

† Lead director

Capital Stock

	Authorized (shs.)	Outstanding (shs.)[1]
Common	unlimited	27,130,556

[1] At Aug. 9, 2023

Options - At Dec. 31, 2022, options were outstanding to purchase 1,670,409 common shares at a weighted average exercise price of Cdn$12.23 per share with a weighted average contract life of 0.22 to 4.21 years.

Normal Course Issuer Bid - The company plans to make normal course purchases of up to 500,000 common shares representing 1.9% of the public float. The bid commenced on Dec. 6, 2022, and expires on Dec. 5, 2023.

Major Shareholder - P. Grenville (Gren) Schoch held 17.9% interest and J. Gordon Flatt held 14.5% interest at Mar. 14, 2023.

Price Range - BOS/TSX

Year	Volume	High	Low	Close
2022	35,539,680	$47.00	$5.62	$7.44
2021	38,613,893	$46.61	$15.22	$46.22
2020	27,983,041	$26.67	$4.59	$15.76
2019	3,784,835	$10.40	$7.07	$8.77
2018	3,997,336	$16.06	$7.82	$8.58

Recent Close: $4.63

Capital Stock Changes - During 2022, common shares were issued as follows: 79,079 on exercise of options and 19,781 for services.

Dividends

BOS com Ra $0.40 pa Q est. July 15, 2021[1]
Prev. Rate: $0.28 est. Apr. 17, 2017

[1] Divds. paid semiannually prior to April 2010.

Long-Term Debt - At Dec. 31, 2022, outstanding long-term debt totaled US$143,642,000 (US$2,286,000 current and net of US$1,413,000 deferred financing costs) and consisted of US$130,048,000 of term debt bearing interest at LIBOR plus 1.45% to 2.50% due September 2026 and US$15,007,000 of lease liabilities.

Wholly Owned Subsidiaries

AirBoss Defense Group, Inc., Del.
- 100% int. in **AirBoss Defense Group, LLC**, Del.
- 100% int. in **Critical Solutions International, LLC**, Tex.
  - 100% int. in **BlackBox Biometrics, Inc.**, Rochester, N.Y.

AirBoss Defense Group Ltd., Qué.
AirBoss Holdings Inc., Del.
- 100% int. in **AirBoss Rubber Compounding (NC) Inc.**, Scotland Neck, N.C.
  - 100% int. in **Ace Elastomer, LLC**, Rock Hill, S.C.
    - 100% int. in **Ace Midwest, LLC**, S.C.
  - 100% int. in **AirBoss Flexible Products, LLC**, Auburn Hills, Mich.

SunBoss Chemicals Corp., Ont.

Financial Statistics

Periods ended:	12m Dec. 31/22[A]		12m Dec. 31/21[A]
	US$000s	%Chg	US$000s
Operating revenue	**477,155**	**-19**	**586,858**
Cost of sales	441,111		438,118
Research & devel. expense	3,324		3,631
General & admin expense	36,552		44,499
Other operating expense	8,223		20,729
Operating expense	**489,210**	**-4**	**506,977**
Operating income	**(12,055)**	**n.a.**	**79,881**
Deprec., depl. & amort.	21,905		20,882
Finance costs, gross	5,738		4,178
Pre-tax income	**(40,412)**	**n.a.**	**54,532**
Income taxes	(8,520)		7,829
Net income	**(31,892)**	**n.a.**	**46,703**
Cash & equivalent	18,552		7,131
Inventories	92,833		122,147
Accounts receivable	94,628		82,440
Current assets	223,789		227,886
Fixed assets, net	89,292		93,148
Intangibles, net	113,237		121,075
Total assets	**440,766**	**-1**	**443,264**
Accts. pay. & accr. liabs.	85,239		103,026
Current liabilities	90,242		108,222
Long-term debt, gross	143,642		80,563
Long-term debt, net	141,356		78,207
Shareholders' equity	196,997		235,148
Cash from oper. activs.	**(30,775)**	**n.a.**	**2,023**
Cash from fin. activs.	52,202		(17,526)
Cash from invest. activs.	(10,189)		(64,559)
Net cash position	**18,552**	**+160**	**7,131**
Capital expenditures	(8,800)		(16,912)
Capital disposals	3		9
	US$		US$
Earnings per share*	(1.18)		1.73
Cash flow per share*	(1.14)		0.08
Cash divd. per share*	$0.40		$0.37
	shs		shs
No. of shs. o/s*	27,092,041		26,993,181
Avg. no. of shs. o/s*	27,071,000		26,970,000
	%		%
Net profit margin	(6.68)		7.96
Return on equity	(14.76)		21.74
Return on assets	(6.19)		12.41
Foreign sales percent	85		92
No. of employees (FTEs)	1,295		1,361

* Common
[A] Reported in accordance with IFRS

Latest Results

Periods ended:	6m June 30/23[A]		6m June 30/22[A]
	US$000s	%Chg	US$000s
Operating revenue	231,134	-9	255,020
Net income	(1,158)	n.a.	12,068
	US$		US$
Earnings per share*	(0.04)		0.45

* Common
[A] Reported in accordance with IFRS

Historical Summary
(as originally stated)

Fiscal Year	Oper. Rev. US$000s	Net Inc. Bef. Disc. US$000s	EPS* US$
2022[A]	477,155	(31,892)	(1.18)
2021[A]	586,858	46,703	1.73
2020[A]	501,572	56,262	1.40
2019[A]	328,126	10,219	0.44
2018[A]	316,603	8,536	0.37

* Common
[A] Reported in accordance with IFRS

A.69 AirIQ Inc.

Symbol - IQ **Exchange** - TSX-VEN **CUSIP** - 009120
Head Office - 207-1099 Kingston Rd, Pickering, ON, L1V 1B5 **Telephone** - (905) 831-6444 **Toll-free** - (888) 606-6444 **Fax** - (905) 581-3121
Website - www.airiq.com
Email - mrobb@airiq.com
Investor Relations - Michael J. Robb (888) 606-6444
Auditors - McGovern Hurley LLP C.A., Toronto, Ont.
Lawyers - Blake, Cassels & Graydon LLP, Toronto, Ont.
Transfer Agents - Computershare Trust Company of Canada Inc., Vancouver, B.C.
Profile - (Can. 2003; orig. B.C., 1991) Offers wireless asset management and location services that allow fleet operators and commercial businesses to effectively and efficiently monitor assets in near real time.

The company offers an intuitive web-based platform that provides fleet operators and vehicle owners with a suite of asset management solutions to reduce cost, improve efficiency and monitor, manage and protect their assets. Services are available online or via a mobile app, and include instant vehicle locating, boundary notification, automated inventory reports, maintenance reminders, security alerts and vehicle disabling and unauthorized movement alerts.

Also offers an application program interface which allows integration of the customers' custom specific software with the company's infrastructure. Other products offered are IQ-CAM™, a full integrated dual facing camera for Global Positioning System (GPS) tracking and real-time video for vehicle fleets and drivers; a battery powered device, which is ruggedized and weatherproof, that provides 'smart' movement-based tracking for theft recovery and for use in monitoring of assets such as containers, trailers, large tools, generators, porta potties and livestock; and electronic logging devices (ELD), which read movements of the user's vehicle and changes its setting when crossing the border and analyzes the user's driving behaviour to reduce any possibility of accidents and fuel wastage.

Predecessor Detail - Name changed from eDispatch.com Wireless Data Inc., July 31, 2002.

Directors - Vernon Lobo, chr., Toronto, Ont.; Michael J. (Mike) Robb, pres. & CEO, Brantford, Ont.; Gabriel Bouchard-Phillips, Westmount, Qué.; Geoffrey A. Rotstein, Toronto, Ont.

Other Exec. Officers - Bora (Kate) Kwak, CFO

Capital Stock

	Authorized (shs.)	Outstanding (shs.)[1]
Common	unlimited	29,367,574

[1] At July 12, 2023

Normal Course Issuer Bid - The company plans to make normal course purchases of up to 1,468,379 common shares representing 5% of the total outstanding. The bid commenced on June 27, 2023, and expires on June 26, 2024.

Major Shareholder - Mosaic Capital Partners, L.P. held 20.12% interest at Aug. 16, 2022.

Price Range - IQ/TSX-VEN

Year	Volume	High	Low	Close
2022	2,714,324	$0.35	$0.25	$0.27
2021	7,813,438	$0.44	$0.26	$0.29
2020	9,244,408	$0.50	$0.15	$0.35
2019	2,502,201	$0.28	$0.13	$0.25
2018	3,183,315	$0.20	$0.14	$0.15

Recent Close: $0.38

Capital Stock Changes - During fiscal 2023, 360,500 common shares were repurchased under a Normal Course Issuer Bid.

During fiscal 2022, 150,000 common shares were issued on exercise of options and 507,000 common shares were repurchased under a Normal Course Issuer Bid.

Wholly Owned Subsidiaries

AirIQ, LLC, Del.
AirIQ U.S. Holdings, Inc., Del.
- 100% int. in **AirIQ U.S., Inc.**, Irvine, Calif.

Financial Statistics

Periods ended:	12m Mar. 31/23[A]		12m Mar. 31/22[A]
	$000s	%Chg	$000s
Operating revenue	**5,049**	**+16**	**4,370**
Cost of sales	2,013		1,691
Research & devel. expense	114		118
General & admin expense	1,771		1,652
Stock-based compensation	81		4
Operating expense	**3,979**	**+15**	**3,465**
Operating income	**1,070**	**+18**	**905**
Deprec., depl. & amort.	347		306
Finance income	36		2
Finance costs, gross	3		4
Write-downs/write-offs	(34)		(8)
Pre-tax income	**863**	**+52**	**567**
Income taxes	(2,830)		nil
Net income	**3,693**	**+551**	**567**
Cash & equivalent	2,176		1,900
Inventories	639		515
Accounts receivable	567		433
Current assets	3,515		2,930
Fixed assets, net	1,688		1,581
Right-of-use assets	nil		46
Intangibles, net	286		nil
Total assets	**8,437**	**+85**	**4,557**
Accts. pay. & accr. liabs.	767		736
Current liabilities	1,353		1,284
Long-term lease liabilities	nil		28
Shareholders' equity	6,960		3,167
Cash from oper. activs.	**1,072**	**-11**	**1,211**
Cash from fin. activs.	(123)		(180)
Cash from invest. activs.	(673)		(960)
Net cash position	**2,176**	**+15**	**1,900**
Capital expenditures	(673)		(960)
	$		$
Earnings per share*	0.13		0.02
Cash flow per share*	0.04		0.04
	shs		shs
No. of shs. o/s*	29,367,574		29,728,074
Avg. no. of shs. o/s*	29,504,709		30,200,778
	%		%
Net profit margin	73.14		12.97
Return on equity	72.93		19.26
Return on assets	57.04		13.49
Foreign sales percent	52		68

* Common
[A] Reported in accordance with IFRS

Historical Summary
(as originally stated)

Fiscal Year	Oper. Rev. $000s	Net Inc. Bef. Disc. $000s	EPS* $
2023[A]	5,049	3,693	0.13
2022[A]	4,370	567	0.02
2021[A]	3,708	449	0.02
2020[A]	5,040	713	0.02
2019[A]	3,682	231	0.01

* Common
[A] Reported in accordance with IFRS

A.70 Aisix Solutions Inc.

Symbol - AISX **Exchange** - TSX-VEN **CUSIP** - 00956C
Head Office - 810-1166 Alberni St, Vancouver, BC, V6E 3Z3 **Telephone** - (604) 620-1051
Website - www.aisix.ca
Email - slam@aisix.ca
Investor Relations - Sharon Lam (604) 620-1051
Auditors - Baker Tilly WM LLP C.A., Vancouver, B.C.
Transfer Agents - TSX Trust Company, Vancouver, B.C.
Profile - (B.C. 2017) Develops and markets artificial intelligence (AI) software products for climate risk identification and mitigation.

The company's flagship product, climate85, is a data and analytic platform providing access to physical climate risk information at every location in Canada, including extreme temperature, humidex, precipitation and wind gust speed. climate85 consists of floods, heatwaves and wildfire risk scores. In addition, it offers tools and functionalities designed for banks and institutions, real estate investments trusts, insurers and underwriters, physical infrastructure owners, engineers, scientists and governments.

In December 2022, the company sold its geology division including the DRIVER software platform, which automates and accelerates 3D modelling of drilling numeric datasets, to U.S.-based **Bentley Systems, Incorporated** for $1,000,000.

Predecessor Detail - Name changed from Minerva Intelligence Inc., Aug. 17, 2023.

Directors - Dr. David Poole, co-founder & chief software architect, Vancouver, B.C.; Mihalis (Mike) Belantis, CEO, Calgary, Alta.; Scott C. Davis, Vancouver, B.C.; Marvin Pestcoe, N.Y.

Other Exec. Officers - Jake McGregor, pres.; Sharon Lam, COO; Charles E. (Chuck) Jenkins, CFO & corp. sec.; Chris Ahern, chief tech. officer; Grant R. Jay, v-p, sales & partnerships

Capital Stock

	Authorized (shs.)	Outstanding (shs.)[1]
Common	unlimited	96,958,037

[1] At Aug. 17, 2023

Major Shareholder - Widely held at Nov. 15, 2022.

Price Range - AISX/TSX-VEN

Year	Volume	High	Low	Close
2022............	15,303,783	$0.21	$0.02	$0.03
2021............	10,767,861	$0.40	$0.13	$0.18
2020............	4,803,904	$0.24	$0.05	$0.19
2019............	1,551,737	$0.50	$0.08	$0.13
2018............	369,362	$0.40	$0.24	$0.25

Consolidation: 1-for-2 cons. in June 2019

Recent Close: $0.12

Capital Stock Changes - In July 2023, private placement of 20,000,000 common shares was completed at 5¢ per share.

There were no changes to capital stock during 2022.

Wholly Owned Subsidiaries

Minerva Intelligence (Canada) Ltd., Vancouver, B.C.
Minerva Intelligence GmbH, Germany.
Minerva Intelligence (U.S.), Inc., Del. Inactive.

Financial Statistics

Periods ended:	12m Dec. 31/22[A]		12m Dec. 31/21[oA]
	$000s	%Chg	$000s
Operating revenue........................	**105**	**-61**	**269**
Cost of sales....................................	70		235
Salaries & benefits..........................	1,049		1,041
Research & devel. expense.............	nil		19
General & admin expense................	916		745
Stock-based compensation.............	40		163
Operating expense........................	**2,075**	**-6**	**2,203**
Operating income.........................	**(1,970)**	**n.a.**	**(1,934)**
Deprec., depl. & amort.....................	148		194
Finance income................................	nil		2
Finance costs, gross........................	11		2
Pre-tax income.............................	**(2,052)**	**n.a.**	**(2,141)**
Net inc. bef. disc. opers................	**(2,052)**	**n.a.**	**(2,141)**
Income from disc. opers.................	(428)		(698)
Net income....................................	**(2,480)**	**n.a.**	**(2,839)**
Cash & equivalent...........................	1,140		3,177
Accounts receivable........................	7		120
Current assets.................................	1,228		3,537
Fixed assets, net.............................	54		38
Right-of-use assets.........................	237		5
Intangibles, net...............................	nil		157
Total assets..................................	**1,520**	**-59**	**3,736**
Accts. pay. & accr. liabs..................	271		203
Current liabilities............................	334		270
Long-term lease liabilities...............	141		nil
Shareholders' equity.......................	1,045		3,466
Cash from oper. activs..................	**(2,940)**	**n.a.**	**(2,701)**
Cash from fin. activs.......................	953		4,528
Cash from invest. activs..................	(51)		(10)
Net cash position..........................	**1,140**	**-64**	**3,177**
Capital expenditures.......................	(51)		(10)
	$		$
Earnings per share*.........................	(0.03)		(0.04)
Cash flow per share*.......................	(0.04)		(0.05)
	shs		shs
No. of shs. o/s*...............................	76,958,037		76,958,037
Avg. no. of shs. o/s*........................	76,958,037		55,042,198
	%		%
Net profit margin.............................	n.m.		(795.91)
Return on equity..............................	(90.98)		(86.19)
Return on assets..............................	(77.66)		(76.37)

* Common
[o] Restated
[A] Reported in accordance with IFRS

Latest Results

Periods ended:	3m Mar. 31/23[A]		3m Mar. 31/22[A]
	$000s	%Chg	$000s
Operating revenue..........................	53	-57	123
Net income......................................	(434)	n.a.	(944)
	$		$
Earnings per share*.........................	(0.01)		(0.01)

* Common
[A] Reported in accordance with IFRS

Historical Summary
(as originally stated)

Fiscal Year	Oper. Rev.	Net Inc. Bef. Disc.	EPS*
	$000s	$000s	$
2022[A]...................	105	(2,052)	(0.03)
2021[A]...................	1,049	(2,839)	(0.05)
2020[A]...................	341	(2,774)	(0.06)
2019[A1].................	185	(4,090)	(0.10)
2018[A]...................	28	(1,127)	n.a.

* Common
[A] Reported in accordance with IFRS
[1] Results prior to May 28, 2019, pertain to and reflect the Qualifying Transaction reverse takeover acquisition of (old) Minerva Intelligence Inc.

Note: Adjusted throughout for 1-for-2 cons. in June 2019

A.71 Akanda Corp.

Symbol - AKAN **Exchange** - NASDAQ **CUSIP** - 00971M
Head Office - 1a, 1b Learoyd Rd, New Romney, KEN, United Kingdom, TN28 8XU **Overseas Tel** - 44-203-488-9514
Website - www.akandacorp.com
Email - ir@akandacorp.com
Investor Relations - Matt Chesler 44-203-488-9514
Auditors - BF Borgers CPA PC C.P.A., Lakewood, Colo.
Transfer Agents - Continental Stock Transfer & Trust Company, New York, N.Y.

Profile - (Ont. 2021) Has medical cannabis cultivation, manufacturing and distribution operations in Lesotho, imports and sells medical cannabis-based products to the domestic market in the United Kingdom and has cannabis cultivation, manufacturing and distributions operations in Portugal.

In Lesotho, wholly owned **Bophelo Bioscience and Wellness (Pty) Ltd.** holds licence to cultivate, manufacture, import and export medical cannabis products. Bophelo has a 200-hectare cultivation site located in Mafeteng.

In the United Kingdom, wholly owned **Canmart Limited** holds licence to import, export, wholesale, distribute and manufacture medical cannabis products. Canmart operates a 25,000-sq.-ft. warehouse located southeast of England.

In Portugal, wholly owned **RPK Biopharma Unipessoal Lda.**, has a 21,500-sq.-ft. indoor cultivation, processing and research and development facility in Sintra; and a 7,000,000-sq.-ft. outdoor cultivation site in Aljustrel.

In July 2022, the company placed indirect wholly owned **Bophelo Bioscience and Wellness (Pty) Ltd.** into liquidation.

Recent Merger and Acquisition Activity

Status: completed **Revised:** May 2, 2022
UPDATE: The transaction was completed. PREVIOUS: The Flowr Corporation agreed to sell Holigen Limited to Cannahealth Limited, wholly owned by Akanda Corp., for Cdn$35,000,000 consisting of Cdn$3,750,000 in cash, 1,900,000 Akanda common shares valued at US$10.30 per share, assumption of US$4,300,000 (€4,000,000) of indebtedness and at least Cdn$834,000 of interim funding to Holigen. Akanda has also agreed to subscribe for 14,285,714 Flowr common shares at a price per share of Cdn$0.07 per share. Holigen, through RPK Biopharma Unipessoal, Lda., owns and operates a 21,500-sq.-ft. indoor cultivation, processing and research and development facility in Sintra, Portugal; and a 7,000,000-sq.-ft. outdoor cultivation site in Aljustrel, Portugal.

Directors - Tejinder Virk, CEO; Jatinder (Jay) Dhaliwal, Vancouver, B.C.; Katharyn M. (Katie) Field, Los Angeles, Calif.; Mohsen Rahimi, B.C.; Harvinder Singh

Other Exec. Officers - Dr. Aslihan Akkar-Schenkl, pres.; Thomas (Tom) Flow, COO; Shailesh Bhushan, CFO

Capital Stock

	Authorized (shs.)	Outstanding (shs.)[1]
Common	unlimited	3,403,737

[1] At Mar. 9, 2023

Major Shareholder - Halo Collective Inc. held 43.8% interest at Mar. 17, 2022.

Price Range - AKAN/NASDAQ

Year	Volume	High	Low	Close
2022............	2,505,705	US$310.00	US$1.25	US$1.49

Consolidation: 1-for-10 cons. in Mar. 2023

Capital Stock Changes - On Mar. 9, 2023, common shares were consolidated on a 1-for-10 basis.

On Mar. 17, 2022, an initial public offering of 4,000,000 common shares was completed at US$4.00 per share.

In November 2021, 13,129,212 common shares were issued pursuant to acquisition of Cannahealth Limited from Halo Collective Inc.

Wholly Owned Subsidiaries

Cannahealth Limited, Malta.
- 100% int. in **Bophelo Holdings Limited**, United Kingdom.
  - 100% int. in **Bophelo Bioscience and Wellness (Pty) Ltd.**, Mafeteng, Lesotho.
- 100% int. in **Canmart Limited**, United Kingdom.
- 100% int. in **Holigen Limited**, Malta.
  - 100% int. in **GreyCan Pty Ltd.**, Australia.
  - 100% int. in **RPK Biopharma Unipessoal Lda**, Portugal.

A.72 Akumin Inc.

Symbol - AKU **Exchange** - TSX **CUSIP** - 01021X
Head Office - 8300 W Sunrise Blvd, Plantation, FL, United States, 33322 **Telephone** - (954) 320-6910
Website - www.akumin.com
Email - jeffrey.white@akumin.com
Investor Relations - R. Jeffrey White (866) 640-5222
Auditors - Ernst & Young LLP C.P.A., Miami, Fla.
Transfer Agents - Continental Stock Transfer & Trust Company, New York, N.Y.; TSX Trust Company, Toronto, Ont.
FP500 Revenue Ranking - 350
Employees - 3,631 at Mar. 13, 2023

Profile - (Del. 2022; orig. Ont., 2015 amalg.) Owns and operates radiology diagnostic imaging clinics and oncology radiation therapy sites across the U.S. Also provides end-to-end outsourced radiology and oncology services to U.S. hospitals, physician groups and other healthcare providers.

The company owns and/or operates fixed-site and mobile diagnostic imaging centres and radiation therapy sites in 48 U.S. states. Diagnostic imaging centres provide magnetic resonance imaging (MRI), computerized tomography (CT), positron emission tomography (PET), ultrasound, X-ray, mammography, nuclear medicine and other diagnostic or interventional radiology procedures; and radiation therapy facilities provide cancer treatment procedures primarily through linear accelerator therapies, such as intensity modulated radiation therapy (IMRT) and stereotactic body radiotherapy (SBRT), and guided robotic stereotactic radiosurgery. At Mar. 31, 2023, the company's fixed-site locations consisted of 180 diagnostic imaging centres and 30 radiation therapy sites.

The company provides outsourced medical services in the areas of radiology and oncology to about 1,100 hospitals and health systems in the U.S. Services include operations management, staffing, sales and marketing, scheduling, billing and full management of cancer care programs.

On Sep. 30, 2022, the company continued into Delaware from Ontario.

Predecessor Detail - Name changed from Elite Imaging Inc., Mar. 22, 2017.

Directors - Stanley G. (Stan) Dunford, chr., emeritus, Woodbridge, Ont.; Riadh Zine, chr. & CEO, Toronto, Ont.; Murray Lee†, Calgary, Alta.; Thomas (Tom) Davies, Toronto, Ont.; Haichen (Delphino) Huang, London, Middx., United Kingdom; L. Ross Sinclair, Toronto, Ont.; Paul S. Viviano, Huntington Beach, Calif.; John Wagner, Cambridge, Ont.; James Webb, Tex.; James Wyper, New York, N.Y.

Other Exec. Officers - Krishna Kumar, pres. & COO; David Kretschmer, interim CFO; Laurie Miller, chief HR officer; Paul Nelis, CIO; Tracy Weise, chief strategy & mktg. officer; Rohit Navani, exec. v-p & chief transformation officer; Douglas McCracken, pres., oncology; Gina M. Bonica, asst. sec.

† Lead director

Capital Stock

	Authorized (shs.)	Outstanding (shs.)[1]	Par
Preferred	50,000,000	nil	US$0.01
Common	300,000,000	90,998,491	US$0.01

[1] At June 30, 2023

Major Shareholder - Thaihot Investment Company US Limited held 15.72% interest and SCW Capital Management, LP held 12.6% interest at Apr. 17, 2023.

Price Range - AKU/TSX

Year	Volume	High	Low	Close
2022............	5,799,269	$3.05	$0.58	$0.96
2021............	8,204,691	$4.98	$1.90	$2.22
2020............	7,928,823	$5.16	$1.75	$3.81
2019............	1,960,925	$5.88	$3.30	$4.86
2018............	125,775	$7.05	$3.98	$3.99

AKU.U/TSX (D)

Year	Volume	High	Low	Close
2018............	27,573,535	US$4.94	US$2.70	US$3.40

Recent Close: $0.24

Capital Stock Changes - During 2022, common shares were issued as follows: 634,516 on vesting of restricted share units and 150,000 on exercise of options.

Wholly Owned Subsidiaries

Akumin Holdings Corp., Del.
- 100% int. in **Akumin Corp.**, Del.
  - 100% int. in **Akumin FL, LLC**, Fla.
  - 100% int. in **Akumin Florida Holdings, LLC**, Fla.
  - 100% int. in **Akumin Health Illinois, LLC**, Ill.
  - 100% int. in **Akumin Imaging Texas, LLC**, Tex.
  - 100% int. in **MSA Management, LLC**, Del.
  - 100% int. in **Medical Diagnostics, LLC**, Del.
  - 100% int. in **Medical Outsourcing Services, LLC**, Del.
  - 100% int. in **SyncMed, LLC**, Tex.
  - 100% int. in **Thaihot Investment Company US Limited**, Irvine, Calif.
    - 100% int. in **Alliance HealthCare Services, Inc.**, Irvine, Calif.
    - 100% int. in **Alliance Oncology, LLC**, Del.

Note: The preceding list includes only the major related companies in which interests are held.

Financial Statistics

Periods ended:	12m Dec. 31/22[A]		12m Dec. 31/21[oA]
	US$000s	%Chg	US$000s
Operating revenue	**749,631**	**+78**	**421,079**
Cost of sales	282,765		167,674
Salaries & benefits	279,906		160,840
General & admin expense	45,706		27,853
Stock-based compensation	3,242		2,792
Operating expense	**611,619**	**+70**	**359,159**
Operating income	**138,012**	**+123**	**61,920**
Deprec., depl. & amort.	98,205		44,895
Finance costs, gross	118,012		62,575
Investment income	972		291
Write-downs/write-offs	(47,202)[1]		nil
Pre-tax income	**(143,177)**	**n.a.**	**(65,205)**
Income taxes	8,410		(30,391)
Net income	**(151,587)**	**n.a.**	**(34,814)**
Net inc. for equity hldrs	**(156,761)**	**n.a.**	**(43,291)**
Net inc. for non-cont. int	**5,174**	**-39**	**8,477**
Cash & equivalent	59,424		48,419
Accounts receivable	114,166		121,525
Current assets	191,945		185,165
Fixed assets, net	221,214		259,122
Right-of-use assets	166,823		194,565
Intangibles, net	1,161,205		1,254,499
Total assets	**1,765,115**	**-8**	**1,918,826**
Accts. pay. & accr. liabs	123,534		122,139
Current liabilities	168,518		164,182
Long-term debt, gross	1,274,613		1,206,088
Long-term debt, net	1,254,652		1,192,074
Long-term lease liabilities	179,980		205,848
Shareholders' equity	(48,200)		105,189
Non-controlling interest	189,491		215,959
Cash from oper. activs	**65,367**	**+283**	**17,050**
Cash from fin. activs	(15,659)		766,144
Cash from invest. activs	(38,703)		(779,171)
Net cash position	**59,424**	**+23**	**48,419**
Capital expenditures	(44,762)		(17,867)
	US$		US$
Earnings per share*	(1.75)		(0.56)
Cash flow per share*	0.73		0.22
	shs		shs
No. of shs. o/s*	89,811,513		89,026,997
Avg. no. of shs. o/s*	89,459,812		76,836,032
	%		%
Net profit margin	(20.22)		(8.27)
Return on equity	n.m.		(46.54)
Return on assets	(1.45)		(0.11)
Foreign sales percent	100		100

* Common
[o] Restated
[A] Reported in accordance with U.S. GAAP
[1] Includes a US$46,500,000 goodwill impairment charge related to Oncology reporting unit.

Latest Results

Periods ended:	3m Mar. 31/23[A]		3m Mar. 31/22[A]
	US$000s	%Chg	US$000s
Operating revenue	187,592	+1	186,263
Net income	(29,190)	n.a.	(26,432)
Net inc. for equity hldrs	(35,148)	n.a.	(30,811)
Net inc. for non-cont. int	5,958		4,379
	US$		US$
Earnings per share*	(0.39)		(0.35)

* Common
[A] Reported in accordance with U.S. GAAP

Historical Summary
(as originally stated)

Fiscal Year	Oper. Rev. US$000s	Net Inc. Bef. Disc. US$000s	EPS* US$
2022[A]	749,631	(151,587)	(1.75)
2021[A]	421,079	(34,814)	(0.56)
2020[A]	245,626	(34,156)	(0.52)
2019[B]	247,436	8,651	0.10
2018[B]	154,782	7,574	0.09

* Common
[A] Reported in accordance with U.S. GAAP
[B] Reported in accordance with IFRS

A.73 Alaris Equity Partners Income Trust*

Symbol - AD.UN **Exchange** - TSX **CUSIP** - C01097
Head Office - 250-333 24 Ave SW, Calgary, AB, T2S 3E6 **Telephone** - (403) 228-0873 **Fax** - (403) 228-0906
Website - www.alarisequitypartners.com
Email - mervin@alarisequity.com
Investor Relations - Michael Ervin (403) 260-1457
Auditors - KPMG LLP C.A., Calgary, Alta.
Lawyers - Burnet, Duckworth & Palmer LLP, Calgary, Alta.
Transfer Agents - Computershare Trust Company of Canada Inc., Calgary, Alta.
FP500 Revenue Ranking - 657
Employees - 17 at Dec. 31, 2022

Profile - (Alta. 2020) Provides alternative financing primarily to private companies in North America in return for royalties or distributions.

The trust enables private, closely-held businesses to raise equity capital without losing control of their business and without the need to face a forced exit several years down the road. Cash financing is provided to private companies at an agreed upon valuation in exchange for a pre-determined distribution or royalty. The distribution is received monthly or quarterly by the trust but is determined a year in advance and is adjusted annually based on the percentage change in a mutually agreed upon performance metric based upon a "top-line" financial performance measure such as gross revenues, gross profit, same-store sales, same-clinic sales or same customer net sales.

Private company partners (annual royalties or distributions), consist of **3E, LLC** (US$5,987,000), a utility service provider that installs, inspects, maintains and replaces critical infrastructure for investor-owned utility companies throughout southeastern and midwestern U.S.; **Accscient, LLC** (US$9,693,000), a provider of IT consulting, staffing and outsourcing services, and specializes in digital infrastructure management, enterprise resource planning, business intelligence and database administration; **Amur Financial Group Inc.** (Cdn$6,869,000), an independent originator, manager and servicer of home equity loans in Canada; **Body Contour Centers, LLC** (dba Sono Bello, US$13,825,000), a provider of private plastic surgery in the U.S. with over 70 locations across the country; **Brown & Settle Investments, LLC** (US$8,447,000), a full-service large-parcel site development contractor based in northern Virginia; **Carey Electric Contracting, LLC** (US$1,773,000), an electrical contracting services company; **DNT Construction, LLC** (US$11,678,000), a provider of turnkey civil construction services to residential, commercial and municipal end markets; **Edgewater Technical Associates, LLC** (US$4,262,000), a provider of assistance to organizations performing nuclear and hazardous operations; **Fleet Advantage, LLC** (US$2,968,000), a provider of flexible truck leasing, finance structure and management, turn-key administration, truck lifecycle performance monitoring, data analytics and remarketing to large corporations; **GWM Holdings, Inc.** (US$8,401,000), a provider of data-driven digital marketing solutions for advertising globally; **Heritage Restoration, Holdings, LLC** (US$2,945,000), a specialty contractor providing masonry and masonry-related services to the commercial building industry; **LMS Reinforcing Steel Group** (Cdn$5,474,000), a fabricator and installer of rebar and provider of post tensioning, trucking and crane services primarily in western Canada; **PF Growth Partners, LLC** (US$12,952,000), a franchisee of over 70 Planet Fitness® fitness clubs in Maryland, Washington, D.C., Tennessee, Florida, Washington State and California; **SCR Mining and Tunnelling LP** (Cdn$4,200,000), a provider of surface and underground mining, construction, electrical and mechanical services in northern Ontario; **Sagamore Plumbing and Heating, LLC** (US$3,000,000), a provider of commercial plumbing, heating, ventilation and air conditioning (HVAC), and facilities maintenance services to clients across all industries in New England; **Stride Consulting LLC** (US$589,000), an Agile software development consultancy firm; **Unify Consulting LLC** (US$1,655,000), a management consulting firm that provides companies with local, customized consulting solutions; **Vehicle Leasing Holdings, LLC** (dba D&M Leasing, US$9,080,000), an independent direct-to-consumer provider of vehicle sourcing and leasing services in the U.S.; and **Federal Management Partners, LLC** (US$4,270,000), a professional services firm that provides evidence-based workforce and organizational management services to transform the public sector.

In April 2023, the trust invested US$36,500,000 in **Federal Management Partners, LLC**, consisting of US$30,500,000 in preferred equity and US$6,000,000 for a minority common equity ownership interest. The preferred equity would entitle the trust to an annualized distribution of US$4,300,000. Commencing on Jan. 1, 2024, the distribution would be adjusted annually based on the percentage change in gross revenue subject to a collar of 7%. Arlington, Va.-based Federal Management Partners is a professional services firm that provides evidence-based workforce and organizational management services to transform the public sector.

On Feb. 14, 2023, the trust completed a strategic transaction involving **Body Contour Centers LLC** (dba Sono Bello) and Brookfield Special Investments, a fund managed by **Brookfield Corporation**, through its Special Investments program. The transaction includes the trust exchanging US$145,000,000 of its existing preferred units in Sono Bello for newly issued convertible preferred units in Sono Bello, Brookfield investing US$400,000,000 in exchange for newly created convertible preferred units in Sono Bello and the trust receiving cash proceeds of US$20,300,000 for the redemption of its remaining existing preferred units. The convertible preferred units are entitled to receive a preferred distribution of 8.5% per annum, payable quarterly resulting in an annual distribution entitlement for the trust of US$12,400,000 and participate in as-converted value of Sono Bello. The trust would also receive: (i) an over allocation of profits relative to the other convertible preferred units not held by the trust if certain return-based performance thresholds are met; and (ii) an annual transaction fee of US$1,500,000 in connection with the transaction.

In December 2022, the trust made a US$2,100,000 follow-on investment in **PF Growth Partners, LLC**, consisting of US$1,700,000 in preferred equity and US$400,000 in common equity.

On Nov. 8, 2022, the trust invested US$24,000,000 in **Sagamore Plumbing and Heating, LLC**, consisting of US$20,000,000 in preferred equity and US$4,000,000 for a minority common equity ownership interest. The preferred equity would entitle the trust to an annualized distribution of US$3,000,000. Commencing on Jan. 1, 2024, the distribution would be adjusted annually based on the percentage change in gross revenue subject to a collar of 6%. Hingham, Mass.-based Sagamore offers a complete range of commercial plumbing, heating, ventilation and air conditioning (HVAC), and facilities maintenance services to clients across all industries in New England.

On Oct. 1, 2022, **Falcon Master Holdings LLC** (dba FNC Title Services), a full-service title and settlement company, redeemed all its preferred and common units held by the trust totaling US$40,000,000. The trust received gross proceeds of US$58,300,000, consisting of US$48,600,000 for the preferred equity (including US$5,200,000 for distributions owed up to January 2024) and US$9,700,000 for the common equity.

On Aug. 8, 2022, the trust made a US$26,000,000 follow-on investment in **Accscient, LLC**, consisting of US$16,000,000 in preferred equity and US$10,000,000 in common equity which entitle the trust to an additional annualized distribution of US$2,100,000.

In May 2022, the trust made a US$3,500,000 follow-on investment in **Heritage Restoration, Holdings, LLC**, consisting of US$2,500,000 in preferred equity at an initial yield of 15% as well as US$1,000,000 in common equity.

In April 2022, **Kimco Holdings, LLC**, a provider of route-based commercial janitorial services throughout the U.S., was acquired by a third party which resulted in total redemption proceeds of US$68,200,000 to the trust.

In March 2022, the trust made a US$65,000,000 follow-on investment in **Body Contour Centers LLC** (dba Sono Bello) in exchange for preferred equity with an initial annualized distribution of US$8,500,000.

Predecessor Detail - Succeeded Alaris Royalty Corp., Sept. 4, 2020, pursuant to plan of arrangement whereby Alaris Equity Partners Income Trust was formed to facilitate the conversion of the corporation into an income trust.

Trustees - Peter F. Grosskopf, chr., Toronto, Ont.; Stephen W. (Steve) King, pres. & CEO, Calgary, Alta.; Robert G. (Bob) Bertram, Aurora, Ont.; Sophia J. Langlois, Calgary, Alta.; Kim Lynch Proctor, Calgary, Alta.; E. Mitchell (Mitch) Shier, Calgary, Alta.

Other Exec. Officers - Amanda Frazer, CFO; Gregg Delcourt, chief invest. officer; Michael (Mike) Ervin, chief legal officer & corp. sec.; Curtis Krawetz, sr. v-p, invests.; Dan MacEahern, sr. v-p, invests.; Brandon Fagerheim, v-p, bus. devel.; Elizabeth (Liz) McCarthy, v-p, legal; Matthew McIntyre, v-p, invests.; Shawn Ostrow, v-p, bus. devel.; Jordan Primeau, v-p, legal; Deanne Erker, contr.

Capital Stock

	Authorized (shs.)	Outstanding (shs.)[1]
Trust Units	unlimited	45,498,191

[1] At Aug. 2, 2023

Normal Course Issuer Bid - The company plans to make normal course purchases of up to 1,000,000 trust units representing 2% of the total outstanding. The bid commenced on May 25, 2023, and expires on May 24, 2024.

Major Shareholder - Widely held at Mar. 28, 2023.

Price Range - AD.UN/TSX

Year	Volume	High	Low	Close
2022	22,845,735	$20.77	$14.61	$16.04
2021	42,116,644	$20.45	$14.48	$18.79
2020	79,805,327	$23.34	$5.83	$15.11

AD/TSX (D)

Year	Volume	High	Low	Close
2020	65,649,571	$23.34	$5.83	$12.27
2019	40,539,784	$22.50	$16.57	$21.93
2018	41,069,408	$20.94	$15.30	$16.99

Recent Close: $14.83

Capital Stock Changes - During 2022, 131,299 trust units were issued upon vesting of restricted trust units.

Dividends

AD.UN tr unit Ra $1.36 pa Q est. Jan. 16, 2023[1]
Prev. Rate: $1.32 est. Oct. 15, 2021
Prev. Rate: $1.24 est. Oct. 15, 2020
[1] Alaris Royalty Corp. com prior to Sept. 4, 2020.

Long-Term Debt - Outstanding at Dec. 31, 2022:

Revolv. credit facilities[1]	$216,077,000
5.5% conv. debs. due 2024[2]	93,446,000
6.25% sr. unsec. debs. due 2027	62,613,000
	372,136,000
Less: Current portion	nil
	372,136,000

[1] Borrowings under a $450,000,000 secured revolving credit facility, bearing interest at 5.3% and due September 2026.
[2] Convertible into trust units at $24.25 per unit.

Wholly Owned Subsidiaries

Alaris Equity Partners Inc., Canada.
- 100% int. in **Alaris Equity Partners USA Inc.**, Del.
  - 100% int. in **Salaris USA Royalty Inc.**, Del.
- 100% int. in **Alaris IGF Corp.**, Alta.
- 100% int. in **Alaris Management Holding Corp.**, Canada.
  - 100% int. in **Alaris Management US Holding Corp.**, United States.
    - 50% int. in **Alaris Splitter LLC**, Del.
- 100% int. in **Alaris Strategic Opportunities Inc.**, Canada.

Note: The preceding list includes only the major related companies in which interests are held.

Financial Statistics

Periods ended:	12m Dec. 31/22[A]		12m Dec. 31/21[A]
	$000s	%Chg	$000s
Realized invest. gain (loss)	37,941		9,921
Unrealized invest. gain (loss)	(29,906)		53,275
Total revenue	**198,081**	**-8**	**214,890**
General & admin. expense	22,032		13,273
Stock-based compensation	2,762		5,362
Other operating expense	4,640		4,246
Operating expense	**29,434**	**+29**	**22,881**
Operating income	**168,647**	**-12**	**192,009**
Deprec. & amort.	216		211
Finance costs, gross	28,185		24,988
Pre-tax income	**154,956**	**-7**	**166,045**
Income taxes	24,280		21,801
Net income	**130,676**	**-9**	**144,244**
Cash & equivalent	60,193		18,447
Accounts receivable	2,689		3,181
Current assets	88,064		64,245
Long-term investments	1,248,159		1,185,327
Fixed assets, net	485		658
Total assets	**1,370,103**	**+7**	**1,275,209**
Accts. pay. & accr. liabs	11,517		8,214
Current liabilities	30,388		24,353
Long-term debt, gross	372,136		416,161
Long-term debt, net	372,136		416,161
Shareholders' equity	898,255		788,859
Cash from oper. activs	**152,416**	**+46**	**104,158**
Cash from fin. activs	(125,158)		128,465
Cash from invest. activs	14,850		(228,991)
Net cash position	**60,193**	**+226**	**18,447**
	$		$
Earnings per share*	2.89		3.28
Cash flow per share*	3.37		2.37
Cash divd. per share*	1.33		1.28
	shs		shs
No. of shs. o/s*	45,280,685		45,149,386
Avg. no. of shs. o/s*	45,249,000		43,994,000
	%		%
Net profit margin	65.97		67.12
Return on equity	15.49		20.70
Return on assets	11.68		14.87
No. of employees (FTEs)	17		16

* Trust Unit
[A] Reported in accordance with IFRS

Latest Results

Periods ended:	6m June 30/23[A]		6m June 30/22[A]
	$000s	%Chg	$000s
Total revenue	84,350	-20	105,621
Net income	33,940	-49	66,031
	$		$
Earnings per share*	0.75		1.46

* Trust Unit
[A] Reported in accordance with IFRS

Historical Summary
(as originally stated)

Fiscal Year	Total Rev. $000s	Net Inc. Bef. Disc. $000s	EPS* $
2022[A]	198,081	130,676	2.89
2021[A]	214,890	144,244	3.28
2020[A]	68,082	20,291	0.56
2019[A1]	69,493	36,258	0.99
2018[A]	119,687	60,796	1.67

* Trust Unit
[A] Reported in accordance with IFRS
[1] Results for 2019 and prior years pertain to Alaris Royalty Corp.

A.74 Alaska Hydro Corporation

Symbol - AKH.H **Exchange** - TSX-VEN **CUSIP** - 01170T
Head Office - 2633 Carnation St, North Vancouver, BC, V7H 1H6 **Telephone** - (604) 929-3961 **Fax** - (866) 571-1068
Website - www.alaskahydro.com
Email - grandiso@telus.net
Investor Relations - Clifford A. Grandison (604) 929-3961
Auditors - De Visser Gray LLP C.A., Vancouver, B.C.
Bankers - Canadian Imperial Bank of Commerce, Vancouver, B.C.
Lawyers - MLT Aikins LLP, Vancouver, B.C.
Transfer Agents - Computershare Trust Company of Canada Inc., Vancouver, B.C.
Profile - (B.C. 2006) Develops renewable energy projects with a focus on hydroelectric power generation.

The company is developing the More Creek project which consists of a three-turbine generator facility with capacity of 75 MW and a hydroelectric storage dam on More Creek in northwestern British Columbia which was expected to produce 346 GWh of electricity annually. The project includes a diversion dam on Forrest Kerr Creek that would redirect water from the Forrest Kerr Creek to More Creek which would increase the energy produced by the More Creek hydroelectric generators to 448 GWh annually.

Predecessor Detail - Name changed from Project Finance Corp., Sept. 3, 2010, pursuant to Qualifying Transaction reverse takeover acquisition of Cascade Creek, LLC.

Directors - Matthew Bell, co-chr., Kake, Alaska; Clifford A. (Cliff) Grandison, co-chr., pres., CEO & corp. sec., North Vancouver, B.C.; Michael E. Hoole, Sechelt, B.C.; Russel Ker, Vancouver, B.C.; Gregory J. (Greg) Sunell, West Vancouver, B.C.

Other Exec. Officers - Robert W. (Bob) Anderson, CFO

Capital Stock

	Authorized (shs.)	Outstanding (shs.)[1]
Preferred	unlimited	nil
Common	100,000,000	38,369,750[2]

[1] At Aug. 29, 2022
[2] Net of 5,868,603 treasury shares.

Major Shareholder - Clifford A. (Cliff) Grandison held 14.2% interest at Oct. 18, 2021.

Price Range - AKH.H/TSX-VEN

Year	Volume	High	Low	Close
2022	3,228,382	$0.05	$0.01	$0.03
2021	4,719,691	$0.11	$0.03	$0.04
2020	7,285,135	$0.11	$0.02	$0.06
2019	3,322,147	$0.07	$0.01	$0.02
2018	2,882,826	$0.09	$0.03	$0.04

Recent Close: $0.02

Financial Statistics

Periods ended:	12m Dec. 31/21[A]		12m Dec. 31/20[A]
	$000s	%Chg	$000s
General & admin expense	61		59
Operating expense	**61**	**+3**	**59**
Operating income	**(61)**	**n.a.**	**(59)**
Finance costs, gross	10		nil
Pre-tax income	**19**	**n.a.**	**(59)**
Net income	**19**	**n.a.**	**(59)**
Cash & equivalent	25		4
Accounts receivable	4		2
Current assets	30		8
Total assets	**41**	**+116**	**19**
Accts. pay. & accr. liabs	92		84
Current liabilities	133		116
Long-term debt, gross	85		100
Long-term debt, net	85		100
Shareholders' equity	(178)		(197)
Cash from oper. activs	**21**	**n.a.**	**(45)**
Cash from fin. activs	nil		45
Net cash position	**25**	**+525**	**4**
	$		$
Earnings per share*	0.00		(0.00)
Cash flow per share*	0.00		(0.00)
	shs		shs
No. of shs. o/s*	38,369,750		38,369,750
Avg. no. of shs. o/s*	38,369,750		38,369,750
	%		%
Net profit margin	n.a.		n.a.
Return on equity	n.m.		n.m.
Return on assets	96.67		(318.92)

* Common
[A] Reported in accordance with IFRS

Latest Results

Periods ended:	6m June 30/22[A]		6m June 30/21[A]
	$000s	%Chg	$000s
Net income	(90)	n.a.	33
	$		$
Earnings per share*	(0.00)		0.00

* Common
[A] Reported in accordance with IFRS

Historical Summary
(as originally stated)

Fiscal Year	Oper. Rev. $000s	Net Inc. Bef. Disc. $000s	EPS* $
2021[A]	nil	19	0.00
2020[A]	nil	(59)	(0.00)
2019[A]	nil	(145)	(0.00)
2018[A]	nil	(70)	(0.00)
2017[A]	nil	(146)	(0.00)

* Common
[A] Reported in accordance with IFRS

A.75 Albatros Acquisition Corporation Inc.

Symbol - ALBT.P **Exchange** - TSX-VEN **CUSIP** - 01260K
Head Office - 2500-1100 boul René-Levesque O, Montréal, QC, H3B 5C9 **Telephone** - (514) 581-1473
Email - jpronovost@capepartners.ca
Investor Relations - Jean-Robert Pronovost (514) 581-1473
Auditors - Raymond Chabot Grant Thornton LLP C.A., Montréal, Qué.
Transfer Agents - TSX Trust Company, Montréal, Qué.
Profile - (Can. 2021) Capital Pool Company.

Directors - Jean-Robert Pronovost, CEO, Mont-Tremblant, Qué.; Joseph Cianci, CFO, Laval, Qué.; Éric Chouinard, Rosemère, Qué.; Louis E. Doyle, Kirkland, Qué.; Martin Legault, Blainville, Qué.

Other Exec. Officers - Gilles Seguin, corp. sec.

Capital Stock

	Authorized (shs.)	Outstanding (shs.)[1]
Common	unlimited	5,057,170

[1] At Feb. 14, 2023

Major Shareholder - Éric Chouinard held 10.55% interest at Feb. 14, 2023.

Price Range - ALBT.P/TSX-VEN

Year	Volume	High	Low	Close
2022	116,487	$0.20	$0.10	$0.20

Recent Close: $0.20

Capital Stock Changes - On July 5, 2022, an initial public offering of 1,340,000 common shares was completed at 15¢ per share.

A.76 Albert Labs International Corp.

Symbol - ABRT **Exchange** - CSE **CUSIP** - 012784
Head Office - 201-6996 Merritt Ave, Burnaby, BC, V5J 4R6 **Telephone** - (778) 819-0740
Website - albertlabs.com
Email - chandjagpal@albertlabs.com
Investor Relations - Navchand Jagpal (778) 819-0740
Auditors - Sam S. Mah Inc. C.A., Burnaby, B.C.
Lawyers - Kaminsky & Company, Surrey, B.C.
Transfer Agents - Computershare Trust Company of Canada Inc., Vancouver, B.C.
Profile - (B.C. 2009) Developing and commercializing psychedelic-based treatments with a focus on cancer-related distress.

The company is using Real World Evidence (RWE) studies to demonstrate psychedelic-assisted psychotherapy. Its first drug target, KRN-101, is a potential solution for cancer-related anxiety.

Common reinstated on CSE, July 7, 2023.

Common suspended from CSE, May 9, 2023.

Recent Merger and Acquisition Activity

Status: completed **Revised:** Mar. 10, 2022

UPDATE: The transaction was completed. PREVIOUS: ME Resources Corp. (MEC) entered into a letter of intent for the reverse takeover acquisition of private Burnaby, B.C.-based Albert Labs Inc. for issuance of 37,000,000 post-consolidated MEC common shares (following a 1-for-10 share consolidation). Albert Labs conducts clinical research and development focused on psychedelic-assisted therapies. Prior to completion, Albert Labs would complete a $4,000,000 equity financing. On closing, MEC would change its name to Albert Labs Inc. Mar. 5, 2021 - The companies entered into a definitive agreement, whereby MEC would issue 38,663,700 post-consolidated MEC common shares, excluding the shares to be issued from Albert Labs' equity financing, to Albert Labs shareholders.

Predecessor Detail - Name changed from ME Resource Corp., Mar. 10, 2022, pursuant to the reverse takeover acquisition of private Burnaby, B.C.-based Albert Labs Inc.; basis 1 new for 10 old shs.

Directors - Dr. Michael E. D. Raymont, chr. & CEO, Calgary, Alta.; Navchand (Chand) Jagpal, CFO, Surrey, B.C.; Ravinder (Robert) Kang, Vancouver, B.C.; Katie Shelton-Innes; Mike Thompson

Other Exec. Officers - Santoke S. Naal, COO; Dr. Malcolm Barratt-Johnson, CMO; Ali Gulamhusein, chief devel. officer; Toby Sorabjee, chief commun. officer; Barney Neal, v-p, opers.

Capital Stock

	Authorized (shs.)	Outstanding (shs.)[1]
Prefered	unlimited	nil
Common	unlimited	68,163,267

[1] At Aug. 29, 2022

Price Range - ABRT/CSE

Year	Volume	High	Low	Close
2022	3,570,796	$0.40	$0.03	$0.04
2018	3,500	$0.75	$0.55	$0.55

Consolidation: 1-for-10 cons. in Mar. 2022

Recent Close: $0.03

Capital Stock Changes - In March 2022, common shares were consolidated on a 1-for-10 basis, 38,663,700 post-consolidated common shares were issued pursuant to the reverse takeover acquisition of Albert Labs Inc., and 18,947,500 post-consolidated common shares were issued pursuant to debt settlement and private placement at $0.25 per share.

Wholly Owned Subsidiaries

Albert Labs Inc., Burnaby, B.C.

Financial Statistics

Periods ended:	12m Dec. 31/21[A1]		12m Dec. 31/20[A]
	$000s	%Chg	$000s
General & admin expense	280		280
Operating expense	**280**	**0**	**280**
Operating income	**(280)**	**n.a.**	**(280)**
Finance costs, gross	2		4
Pre-tax income	**(282)**	**n.a.**	**(284)**
Net income	**(282)**	**n.a.**	**(284)**
Bank indebtedness	nil		57
Accts. pay. & accr. liabs	482		382
Current liabilities	2,092		1,810
Shareholders' equity	(2,092)		(1,810)
Cash from oper. activs	**57**	**n.a.**	**(18)**
Cash from fin. activs	(57)		18
	$		$
Earnings per share*	(0.04)		(0.05)
Cash flow per share*	0.01		(0.00)
	shs		shs
No. of shs. o/s*	6,367,194		6,367,194
Avg. no. of shs. o/s*	6,367,194		6,367,194
	%		%
Net profit margin	n.a.		n.a.
Return on equity	n.m.		n.m.
Return on assets	n.m.		n.m.

* Common

[A] Reported in accordance with IFRS

[1] Results for 2021 and prior periods pertain to ME Resources Corp.

Historical Summary
(as originally stated)

Fiscal Year	Oper. Rev.	Net Inc. Bef. Disc.	EPS*
	$000s	$000s	$
2021[A]	nil	(282)	(0.04)
2020[A]	nil	(284)	(0.04)
2019[A]	nil	(135)	(0.02)
2018[A]	90	(280)	(0.04)
2017[A]	87	(426)	(0.10)

* Common

[A] Reported in accordance with IFRS

Note: Adjusted throughout for 1-for-10 cons. in Mar. 2022

A.77 Aleafia Health Inc.

Symbol - AH **Exchange** - TSX (S) **CUSIP** - 01444Q
Head Office - 85 Basaltic Rd, Concord, ON, L4K 1G4 **Telephone** - (416) 860-5665 **Toll-free** - (844) 258-0583 **Fax** - (416) 860-5626
Website - www.aleafiahealth.com
Email - ir@aleafiahealth.com
Investor Relations - Matthew Sale (833) 879-2533
Auditors - Accell Audit & Compliance C.P.A., Tampa, Fla.
Transfer Agents - Odyssey Trust Company
Employees - 225 at June 29, 2022
Profile - (Ont. 2018; orig. B.C., 2007) Cultivates, produces, distributes and sells cannabis products in Canada and international markets. Also operates a virtual network of medical cannabis clinics in Canada.

Cannabis Production and Distribution - Owns and operates three production facilities, consisting of a 35,000-sq.-ft. indoor cultivation, extraction, manufacturing and packaging facility in Paris, Ont.; a facility in Port Perry, Ont., with a 7,000-sq.-ft. indoor cultivation facility, an 86-acre outdoor cultivation site and 35,000 sq. ft. of drying and storage buildings; and a non-operating facility in Grimsby (Niagara), Ont., with 140,000 sq. ft. of greenhouse cultivation area and 20,000 sq. ft. of drying and storage space. Also operates a distribution centre in Concord, Ont. The company produces a portfolio of cannabis products, including dried flower, pre-rolls, vape cartridges, oils, capsules, sublingual strips, edibles and bath and body products. Medical cannabis products are sold under the Emblem brand, and adult-use products are sold under the Sunday Market parent brand, including Divvy, Bogart's Kitchen, Nith & Grand, Noon & Night and Kin Slips. In Canada, products are sold and distributed through its Emblem e-commerce marketplace, along with its home delivery service for medical patients in the Grater Toronto Area and surrounding communities; through business-to-business transactions with other licensed producers; and supply agreements with provincial distributors and retailers in Ontario, British Columbia, Alberta, Saskatchewan and Manitoba. Internationally, the company exports products for the medical cannabis markets in various regions, including Germany and Australia.

Medical Clinics - Owns and operates virtual medical cannabis clinics under the Canabo Medical Clinics name. Clinics are staffed by physicians and nurse practitioners which provide medical cannabis evaluations and consultation for patients.

On July 25, 2023, the company obtained creditor protection under the Companies' Creditors Arrangement Act to pursue restructuring and sale process. **Red White & Bloom Brands Inc.** agreed to provide debtor-in-possession financing of $6,600,000 to the company.

In November 2022, the company announced the wind down and cessation of operations at its 160,000-sq.-ft. greenhouse facility in Grimsby, Ont. The initiative impacted 41 employees.

The company changed its year end to March 31 from December 31, effective Mar. 31, 2022.

Common suspended from TSX, July 26, 2023.

Recent Merger and Acquisition Activity

Status: terminated **Revised:** July 14, 2023
UPDATE: The transaction was terminated. PREVIOUS: Red White & Bloom Brands Inc. (RWB) agreed to acquire Aleafia Health Inc. on the basis of 0.35 RWB common share for each Aleafia common share held. As part of the agreement, the loan agreement between Aleafia and NE SPC II LP was assigned by NE SPC II LP to RWB.

Predecessor Detail - Name changed from Canabo Medical Inc., Mar. 26, 2018.

Directors - Mark J. Sandler, chr., Ont.; Luciano (Lu) Galasso, Toronto, Ont.; David Pasieka, Oakville, Ont.; Jon P. Pereira, Toronto, Ont.; Carlo Sistilli, Ont.; Ian Troop, Georgetown, Ont.

Other Exec. Officers - Patricia (Tricia) Symmes-Rizakos, CEO; Matthew (Matt) Sale, CFO; Dr. Michael Verbora, CMO; Dave Shepherd, sr. v-p, HR

Capital Stock

	Authorized (shs.)	Outstanding (shs.)[1]
Common	unlimited	403,038,591

[1] At Nov. 9, 2022

Major Shareholder - Widely held at Aug. 19, 2022.

Price Range - AH/TSX (S)

Year	Volume	High	Low	Close
2022	74,059,188	$0.16	$0.04	$0.07
2021	199,607,303	$1.28	$0.10	$0.14
2020	150,789,508	$0.85	$0.31	$0.47
2019	292,050,857	$2.93	$0.54	$0.60
2018	300,836,368	$4.70	$0.47	$1.43

Recent Close: $0.02

Capital Stock Changes - In June 2022, private placement of 68,151,515 units (1 common share & ½ warrant) at $0.0825 per unit was completed, with warrants exercisable at $0.1025 per share for four years.

In March 2021, bought deal public offering of 27,390,000 units (1 common share & ½ warrant) at 83¢ per unit was completed, including 3,390,000 units on exercise of over-allotment option. Also during the 15-month period ended Mar. 31, 2022, common shares were issued as follows: 1,050,890 on exercise of warrants, 781,250 on exercise of options, 387,500 under an at-the-market program, 155,316 under restricted share unit plan and 89,709 under deferred share unit plan.

Wholly Owned Subsidiaries

Aleafia Brands Inc., Ont.
Aleafia Retail Inc., Ont.
- 9.4% int. in **One Plant (Retail) Corp.**, Ont.

Canabo Medical Corporation, Vancouver, B.C.
- 100% int. in **Aleafia Inc.**, Vaughan, Ont.
  - 100% int. in **Aleafia Farms Inc.**, Durham, Ont.

Emblem Corp., Toronto, Ont.
- 100% int. in **Emblem Cannabis Corp.**, Canada.
  - 100% int. in **Emblem Realty Ltd.**, Ont.
  - 100% int. in **GrowWise Health Limited**, Canada.

2672533 Ontario Inc., Ont.
2676063 Ontario Inc., Ont.

Investments

10% int. in **CannaPacific Pty Ltd.**, Australia.
Wellbeing Digital Sciences Inc., Vancouver, B.C.

Financial Statistics

Periods ended:	15m Mar. 31/22[A]		12m Dec. 31/20[oA]
	$000s	%Chg	$000s
Operating revenue	**43,122**	**n.a.**	**36,275**
Cost of sales	52,107		49,107
General & admin expense	39,153		28,186
Stock-based compensation	2,899		2,690
Operating expense	**94,159**	**n.a.**	**79,983**
Operating income	**(51,037)**	**n.a.**	**(43,708)**
Deprec., depl. & amort	12,427		10,166
Finance costs, net	10,787		11,636
Write-downs/write-offs	(95,075)[1]		(201,484)[2]
Pre-tax income	**(172,721)**	**n.a.**	**(258,045)**
Income taxes	(2,854)		(2,540)
Net income	**(169,867)**	**n.a.**	**(255,505)**
Cash & equivalent	2,546		29,968
Inventories	21,664		27,242
Accounts receivable	11,085		9,311
Current assets	40,462		74,656
Long-term investments	2,391		6,620
Fixed assets, net	40,448		78,469
Right-of-use assets	1,844		2,782
Intangibles, net	nil		66,029
Total assets	**85,145**	**n.a.**	**229,016**
Accts. pay. & accr. liabs	27,626		20,239
Current liabilities	76,622		45,041
Long-term debt, gross	53,549		56,802
Long-term debt, net	5,075		32,441
Long-term lease liabilities	1,833		2,726
Shareholders' equity	1,615		145,954
Cash from oper. activs	**(36,218)**	**n.a.**	**(7,629)**
Cash from fin. activs	11,917		13,116
Cash from invest. activs	(4,659)		(16,205)
Net cash position	**1,569**	**n.a.**	**30,529**
Capital expenditures	(4,659)		(17,777)
	$		$
Earnings per share*	(0.52)		(0.88)
Cash flow per share*	(0.11)		(0.03)
	shs		shs
No. of shs. o/s*	331,124,351		301,269,686
Avg. no. of shs. o/s*	327,012,541		291,589,929
	%		%
Net profit margin	...		(704.36)
Return on equity	...		(96.33)
Return on assets	...		(73.91)

* Common

[o] Restated

[A] Reported in accordance with IFRS

[1] Includes fixed assets write-down of $28,800,000, intangible assets write-down of $53,093,000 and goodwill write-down of $11,314,000.

[2] Includes goodwill write-down of $177,476,000 and intangible assets write-down of $22,116,000.

Latest Results

Periods ended:	6m Sept. 30/22[A]		6m Sept. 30/21[oA]
	$000s	%Chg	$000s
Operating revenue	22,664	+10	20,693
Net income	2,577	n.a.	(75,103)
	$		$
Earnings per share*	0.01		(0.23)

* Common

[o] Restated

[A] Reported in accordance with IFRS

Historical Summary
(as originally stated)

Fiscal Year	Oper. Rev.	Net Inc. Bef. Disc.	EPS*
	$000s	$000s	$
2022[A1]	43,122	(169,867)	(0.52)
2020[A]	44,542	(247,238)	(0.85)
2019[A]	16,351	(39,607)	(0.18)
2018[A2]	3,330	(18,533)	(0.16)

* Common

[A] Reported in accordance with IFRS

[1] 15 months ended Mar. 31, 2022.

[2] Results reflect the Mar. 26, 2018, reverse takeover acquisition of Aleafia Inc.

A.78 Algernon Pharmaceuticals Inc.

Symbol - AGN **Exchange** - CSE **CUSIP** - 01559R
Head Office - 400-601 Broadway W, Vancouver, BC, V5Z 4C2 **Telephone** - (604) 646-1553
Website - www.algernonpharmaceuticals.com
Email - chris@algernonpharmaceuticals.com
Investor Relations - Christopher J. Moreau (604) 398-4175 ext. 701
Auditors - Smythe LLP C.A., Vancouver, B.C.
Lawyers - McMillan LLP, Vancouver, B.C.

Transfer Agents - TSX Trust Company, Vancouver, B.C.
Employees - 1 at Dec. 16, 2022
Profile - (B.C. 2015) Developing repurposed therapeutic drugs for certain diseases including non-alcoholic steatohepatitis, chronic kidney disease, inflammatory bowel disease, idiopathic pulmonary fibrosis, chronic cough, acute lung injury and stroke.

Wholly owned **Nash Pharmaceuticals Inc.** develops data which supports the advancement of up to seven drug candidates into phase II trials in the areas of non-alcoholic steatohepatitis, chronic kidney disease, inflammatory bowel disease, idiopathic pulmonary fibrosis and chronic cough. Nash's drug candidates include NP-120 (Ifenprodil), the company's lead product, for multiple indications including treatment of idiopathic pulmonary fibrosis and for treatment of chronic cough; and NP-251 (Repirinast) for care treatment for chronic kidney disease. In addition, the company plans to conduct a 180 patient, 90-day phase 2b clinical study of Ifenprodil for chronic cough in the third quarter of 2023.

Wholly owned **Algernon NeuroScience Inc.** (AGN Neuro) researches and develops AP-188 DMT (N, N-Dimethyltryptamine) for the treatment of stroke. AGN Neuro focuses on the phase I DMT study which covers the investigation of prolonged intravenous infusion of DMT.

In December 2022, the company transferred all assets of the DMT research program to newly formed wholly owned **Algernon NeuroScience Inc.** (AGN Neuro) for 20,000,000 AGN Neuro common shares.

Predecessor Detail - Name changed from Breathtec Biomedical, Inc., Feb. 19, 2019.

Directors - Harry J. F. Bloomfield, chr., Montréal, Qué.; Christopher J. Moreau, CEO, Winnipeg, Man.; Dr. Raj Attariwala, lead engineer, Vancouver, B.C.; Howard Gutman, Washington, D.C.; Dr. Mark Williams, Winnipeg, Man.

Other Exec. Officers - James Kinley, CFO; Dr. Ahmad Khalil, CMO; Dr. Christopher Bryan, v-p, research & opers.

Capital Stock

	Authorized (shs.)	Outstanding (shs.)[1]
Preferred	unlimited	nil
Common	unlimited	9,653,724

[1] At Mar. 3, 2023

Major Shareholder - AlphaNorth Asset Management Inc. held 13.05% interest at Aug. 23, 2022.

Price Range - AGN/CSE

Year	Volume	High	Low	Close
2022	5,037,352	$2.98	$0.54	$0.54
2021	4,727,988	$10.25	$0.81	$1.03
2020	12,071,412	$14.50	$1.38	$5.50
2019	1,668,510	$13.75	$1.00	$1.38
2018	1,106,827	$26.00	$2.50	$3.00

Split: 4-for-1 split in Mar. 2023; 1-for-100 cons. in Nov. 2021
Recent Close: $0.18

Capital Stock Changes - On Mar. 3, 2023, common shares were split on a 3-for-1 basis.

On Nov. 24, 2021, common shares were consolidated on a 1-for-100 basis. In July and August 2022, private placement of 683,017 post-consolidated units (1 common share & 1 warrant) at $3.75 per unit was completed.

Wholly Owned Subsidiaries

Algernon NeuroScience Inc., B.C.
Nash Pharmaceuticals Inc., Vancouver, B.C.
- 100% int. in **Algernon Research Pty Ltd.**, Australia.

Financial Statistics

Periods ended:	12m Aug. 31/22^A		12m Aug. 31/21^A
	$000s	%Chg	$000s
Salaries & benefits	1,066		657
Research & devel. expense	2,330		4,797
General & admin expense	2,130		1,770
Stock-based compensation	531		827
Operating expense	**6,057**	**-25**	**8,051**
Operating income	**(6,057)**	**n.a.**	**(8,051)**
Finance income	2		12
Pre-tax income	**(6,054)**	**n.a.**	**(7,734)**
Net income	**(6,054)**	**n.a.**	**(7,734)**
Cash & equivalent	1,409		2,411
Accounts receivable	666		2,295
Current assets	2,827		4,909
Intangibles, net	5,256		5,171
Total assets	**8,141**	**-20**	**10,138**
Current liabilities	2,516		1,022
Shareholders' equity	5,625		9,115
Cash from oper. activs	**(2,913)**	**n.a.**	**(7,823)**
Cash from fin. activs	2,055		4,245
Cash from invest. activs	(145)		(124)
Net cash position	**1,409**	**-42**	**2,411**
	$		$
Earnings per share*	(0.87)		(1.24)
Cash flow per share*	(0.42)		(1.26)
	shs		shs
No. of shs. o/s*	9,431,540		6,698,752
Avg. no. of shs. o/s*	6,952,608		6,230,448
	%		%
Net profit margin	n.a.		n.a.
Return on equity	(82.14)		(72.51)
Return on assets	(66.24)		(67.36)
No. of employees (FTEs)	1		1

* Common
^A Reported in accordance with IFRS

Latest Results

Periods ended:	3m Nov. 30/22^A		3m Nov. 30/21^A
	$000s	%Chg	$000s
Net income	(1,880)	n.a.	(1,201)
	$		$
Earnings per share*	(0.20)		(0.18)

* Common
^A Reported in accordance with IFRS

Historical Summary
(as originally stated)

Fiscal Year	Oper. Rev.	Net Inc. Bef. Disc.	EPS*
	$000s	$000s	$
2022^A	nil	(6,054)	(0.87)
2021^A	nil	(7,734)	(1.24)
2020^A	nil	(8,538)	(2.50)
2019^A	nil	(1,896)	(1.00)
2018^A	nil	(938)	(1.00)

* Common
^A Reported in accordance with IFRS

Note: Adjusted throughout for 4-for-1 split in Mar. 2023; 1-for-100 cons. in Nov. 2021; 1-for-2 cons. in Oct. 2018

A.79 Algoma Central Corporation*

Symbol - ALC **Exchange** - TSX **CUSIP** - 015644
Head Office - 600-63 Church St, St. Catharines, ON, L2R 3C4
Telephone - (905) 687-7888 **Fax** - (905) 687-7840
Website - www.algonet.com
Email - peter.winkley@algonet.com
Investor Relations - Peter D. Winkley (905) 687-7897
Auditors - Deloitte LLP C.A., Toronto, Ont.
Bankers - Canadian Imperial Bank of Commerce
Lawyers - Borden Ladner Gervais LLP
Transfer Agents - TSX Trust Company, Toronto, Ont.
FP500 Revenue Ranking - 410
Employees - 1,600 at Dec. 31, 2022
Profile - (Can. 1899, via Special Act of Parliament) Operates a fleet of dry and liquid-bulk carriers, including self-unloading dry-bulk carriers, gearless dry-bulk carriers and product tankers, throughout the Great Lakes-St. Lawrence Waterway, with interests in a fleet of self-unloaders, cement carriers and deep sea bulkers. Also owns and operates a ship repair and steel fabrication facility in Ontario.

Operations are organized into four segments: Domestic Dry-Bulk; Product Tankers; Ocean Self-Unloaders; and Global Short Sea Shipping.

The **Domestic Dry-Bulk** marine transportation segment consists of 11 self-unloading and eight gearless bulk carriers, including one owned by a third party, and Algoma Ship Repair, a division that provides ship repair and steel fabricating services. The vessels are designed to carry a variety of dry-bulk products including iron ore, grain, coal and coke, salt and aggregates, and operate throughout the Great Lakes-St. Lawrence Waterway, from the Gulf of St. Lawrence through all five Great Lakes.

The **Product Tankers** segment provides safe and reliable transportation of liquid petroleum products and serves domestic oil refiners, leading wholesale distributors and large consumers of petroleum products. The domestic fleet of six product tankers, which operate within the Great Lakes, the St. Lawrence Seaway and Atlantic Canada regions, is owned and operated through wholly owned **Algoma Tankers Limited**. Also owns and manages three vessels operating under international flag. This segment includes 50% interests in **FureBear AB,** an international venture currently constructing eight tanker vessels for European operations.

The **Ocean Self-Unloaders** segment consists of **Marbulk Canada Inc.**, which is jointly owned with **CSL Group Inc.**; and wholly owned **Algoma Shipping Ltd.** Marbulk owns an ocean self-unloader and another self-unloader that is jointly owned with Bernhard Schulte. Algoma Shipping owns eight ocean self-unloading vessels. The Algoma self-unloaders are part of 18 ocean self-unloaders that form the CSL International commercial pool.

The **Global Short Sea Shipping** segment consists of 50% interest in **NovaAlgoma Cement Carriers Limited**, which operates a fleet of 26 cement carriers; 50% interest in **NovaAlgoma Short-Sea Holding Ltd.**, which operates a fleet of 17 short sea mini bulkers; and 50% interest in **NovaAlgoma Bulk Holdings Ltd.**, which participates in the trade of purchasing and selling handy-sized vessels.

During the first quarter of 2023, the company sold product tanker Algoma Hansa for $4,640,000.

During 2022, the company sold one cement carrier and two mini-bulkers for an undisclosed amount.

In December 2022, the company acquired two 2007-built product tankers. Terms were not disclosed. The vessels would be re-named as Algoberta and Algotitan.

In August 2022, the company entered into a joint venture agreement with Sweden-based **Furetank AB**, whereby the company and Furetank would construct four dual-fuel ice class 1A 17,999 DWT climate fiendly product tankers. The company and Furetank would own 50% interest each on the joint venture which is to be named as FureBear.

In July 2022, the company acquired the Birgit Knutsen as a potential future replacement vessel for its domestic tanker fleet. Terms were not disclosed. The vessel operated under a bare boat charter in international markets throughout 2022.

Recent Merger and Acquisition Activity

Status: completed **Announced:** June 30, 2023
Algoma Central Corporation acquired a self-unloading dry-bulk carrier for $85,663,000. The vessel was expected to join the fleet in 2027.

Status: completed **Announced:** June 19, 2023
Algoma Central Corporation acquired two 37,000-deadweight tonnage (DWT) ice class product tankers from South Korea-based Hyundai Mipo Dockyard Co., Ltd. for $127,000,000. The vessels would be entered on a long-term time charter under the Canadian flag in partnership with Irving Oil Limited and was expected to join the fleet in the first quarter of 2025. Hyundai Mipo manufactures mid-sized vessels, including petrochemical carriers, container ships and asphalt carriers. Irving Oil is engaged in petroleum refining and production of allied petroleum products.

Status: completed **Announced:** Mar. 31, 2023
Algoma Central Corporation sold product tanker Algonorth to subsidiary FureBear AB for $14,485,000. The vessel would be re-named as Fure Skagen.

Status: completed **Announced:** June 30, 2022
Algoma Central Corporation sold Station Mall, a 555,000-sq.-ft. enclosed shopping centre in Sault Ste. Marie, Ont., for $30,000,000.

Predecessor Detail - Name changed from Algoma Central Railway, Oct. 24, 1990.

Directors - Duncan N. R. Jackman, chr., Toronto, Ont.; Gregg A. Ruhl, pres. & CEO, Buffalo, N.Y.; Mats H. Berglund, Gothenburg, Sweden; Richard B. Carty, Toronto, Ont.; Jens Gronning, Copenhagen, Denmark; E. M. Blake Hutcheson, Toronto, Ont.; Dr. Trinity O. Jackman, Toronto, Ont.; Mark R. McQueen, Toronto, Ont.; Clive P. Rowe, Delray Beach, Fla.; Eric Stevenson, Toronto, Ont.

Other Exec. Officers - J. Wesley Newton, exec. v-p, strategy & bus. devel. & corp. sec.; Barton R. (Bart) Reynolds, exec. v-p, opers. & technical; Peter D. Winkley, exec. v-p & CFO; Steve Wright, sr. v-p, technical; Mario Battista, v-p, fin. & process innovation; Charlie Bungard, v-p, opers.; Jeffrey M. DeRosario, v-p, comml.; Fredrik Hanson, v-p, fin. & admin.; Christopher A. L. Lazarz, v-p, corp. fin.; Cathy Smith, v-p, HR

Capital Stock

	Authorized (shs.)	Outstanding (shs.)[1]
Preferred	unlimited	nil
Common	unlimited	38,432,882

[1] At June 30, 2023

Normal Course Issuer Bid - The company plans to make normal course purchases of up to 1,926,915 common shares representing 5% of the total outstanding. The bid commenced on Mar. 21, 2023, and expires on Mar. 20, 2024.

Major Shareholder - Amogla Holdings Limited held 30% interest and E-L Financial Corporation Limited held 27.3% interest at Mar. 10, 2023.

Price Range - ALC/TSX

Year	Volume	High	Low	Close
2022	1,977,509	$18.90	$14.81	$18.22
2021	2,307,713	$18.93	$13.26	$17.03
2020	2,183,549	$16.17	$7.01	$13.92
2019	1,722,350	$14.23	$12.27	$13.04
2018	1,222,934	$16.00	$11.61	$12.68

Recent Close: $15.19

Capital Stock Changes - During 2022, 227,454 common shares were issued on conversion of debentures and 26,525 common shares were repurchased under a Normal Course Issuer Bid.

Dividends

ALC com Ra $0.72 pa Q est. Mar. 1, 2023
Prev. Rate: $0.68 est. Mar. 1, 2021
Prev. Rate: $0.52 est. Sept. 1, 2020
$1.35◆................ Jan. 18/23 $2.65◆............ Jan. 12/21
Paid in 2023: $0.54 + $1.35◆ 2022: $0.68 2021: $0.68 + $2.65◆
◆ Special

Long-Term Debt - Outstanding at Dec. 31, 2022:

4.73% mtge. pay. due 2023	$5,197,000
5.25% conv. unsec. debs. due 2024[1]	78,068,000
Sr. secured notes:	
3.37% due 2027[2]	27,088,000
3.60% due 2030[3]	56,885,000
3.70% due 2032[4]	47,404,000
3.80% due 2035[5]	67,720,000
4.01% due 2035	128,000,000
Less: Unamort. financing exp.	8,008,000
	402,354,000
Less: Current portion	5,197,000
	397,157,000

[1] Convertible into common shares at $15.95 per share. Repayable in common shares on maturity at the company's option. An equity component of $2,270,000 was included as part of shareholders' equity.
[2] US$20,000,000.
[3] US$42,000,000.
[4] US$35,000,000.
[5] US$50,000,000.

Principal debt repayments were reported as follows:

2023	$5,197,000
2024	78,068,000
2027	27,088,000
Thereafter	300,009,000

Note - In January 2023, the conversion rate of the 5.25% convertible debentures was decreased to $14.59 per share from $15.95 per share.

Wholly Owned Subsidiaries

Algoma International Shipholdings Ltd., Bermuda.
Algoma Shipping Ltd., Hamilton, Bermuda.
Algoma Tankers Limited, St. Catharines, Ont.

Investments

50% int. in **FureBear AB**, Sweden.
50% int. in **NovaAlgoma Bulk Holdings Ltd.**, Bermuda.
50% int. in **NovaAlgoma Cement Carriers Limited**, Bermuda.
• 50% int. in **JT Cement AS**, Bergen, Norway.
50% int. in **NovaAlgoma Short-Sea Holding Limited**, Bermuda.

Financial Statistics

Periods ended:	12m Dec. 31/22[A]		12m Dec. 31/21[A]
	$000s	%Chg	$000s
Operating revenue	**677,942**	**+13**	**598,873**
Cost of goods sold	490,044		402,967
General & admin expense	34,567		32,551
Operating expense	**524,611**	**+20**	**435,518**
Operating income	**153,331**	**-6**	**163,355**
Deprec., depl. & amort.	65,429		67,852
Finance income	1,736		81
Finance costs, gross	20,450		20,733
Write-downs/write-offs	14,759		(5,864)
Pre-tax income	**101,388**	**+34**	**75,577**
Income taxes	16,917		11,812
After-tax income (expense)	35,495		18,405
Net income	**119,966**	**+46**	**82,170**
Cash & equivalent	141,968		108,942
Inventories	19,126		12,455
Accounts receivable	52,957		41,761
Current assets	250,330		190,574
Long-term investments	208,992		155,140
Fixed assets, net	850,538		818,922
Right-of-use assets	506		640
Intangibles, net	7,910		7,910
Total assets	**1,365,697**	**+14**	**1,200,083**
Accts. pay. & accr. liabs.	84,548		78,045
Current liabilities	150,828		84,511
Long-term debt, gross	402,354		391,682
Long-term debt, net	397,157		391,532
Long-term lease liabilities	321		403
Equity portion of conv. debs.	2,270		2,309
Shareholders' equity	726,024		640,283
Cash from oper. activs.	**133,130**	**-18**	**162,381**
Cash from fin. activs.	(42,368)		(141,016)
Cash from invest. activs.	(65,872)		(16,225)
Net cash position	**141,968**	**+30**	**108,942**
Capital expenditures	(69,054)		(31,882)
Capital disposals	11,543		8,530
Unfunded pension liability	n.a.		7,756
Pension fund surplus	8,255		n.a.
	$		$
Earnings per share*	3.17		2.17
Cash flow per share*	3.52		4.30
Cash divd. per share*	0.68		0.68
	shs		shs
No. of shs. o/s*	38,001,872		37,800,943
Avg. no. of shs. o/s*	37,818,215		37,800,943
	%		%
Net profit margin	17.70		13.72
Return on equity	17.56		13.68
Return on assets	10.68		8.23
Foreign sales percent	22		27
No. of employees (FTEs)	1,600		1,600

* Common
[A] Reported in accordance with IFRS

Latest Results

Periods ended:	6m June 30/23[A]		6m June 30/22[A]
	$000s	%Chg	$000s
Operating revenue	314,010	+17	268,566
Net income	13,504	-51	27,474
	$		$
Earnings per share*	0.35		0.73

* Common
[A] Reported in accordance with IFRS

Historical Summary
(as originally stated)

Fiscal Year	Oper. Rev.	Net Inc. Bef. Disc.	EPS*
	$000s	$000s	$
2022[A]	677,942	119,966	3.17
2021[A]	598,873	82,170	2.17
2020[A]	545,660	45,850	1.21
2019[A]	567,908	24,159	0.63
2018[A]	508,201	50,943	1.32

* Common
[A] Reported in accordance with IFRS

A.80 Algoma Steel Group Inc.

Symbol - ASTL **Exchange** - TSX **CUSIP** - 015658
Head Office - 105 West St, Sault Ste. Marie, ON, P6A 7B4 **Telephone** - (705) 945-2351 **Fax** - (705) 945-2203
Website - www.algoma.com
Email - john.naccarato@algoma.com
Investor Relations - John Naccarato (705) 945-2351
Auditors - Deloitte LLP C.A., Toronto, Ont.
Lawyers - Lawson Lundell LLP, Vancouver, B.C.
Transfer Agents - Continental Stock Transfer & Trust Company, New York, N.Y.; TSX Trust Company, Toronto, Ont.

FP500 Revenue Ranking - 144
Employees - 2,847 at Mar. 31, 2023
Profile - (B.C. 2021) Manufactures and sells hot and cold rolled steel products including coiled sheet and plate, with direct applications in the automotive, construction, energy, defence and manufacturing sectors.

Facilities include the Direct Strip Production Complex (DSPC), a hot strip mill; two blast furnaces, Blast Furnace No. 6 (idled) and 7 (operating);three coke batteries; and two 260,000-ton basic oxygen furnaces; the ladle metallurgy furnace No. 2 (LMF2) facility (which started up in 2021); a twin strand conventional slab caster; and a combination mill consisting of a 106-inch-wide hot strip mill and a 166-inch wide plate rolling mill. All facilities are located in Sault Ste. Marie, Ont. Production capacity is estimated at 2,800,000 tons per year.

Coil sheet steel products (representing 91% of total steel shipment volumes in fiscal 2023) include a wide variety of widths, gauges and grades, and are available unprocessed and with value-added temper processing for hot rolled coil, annealed and full hard cold-rolled coil, hot-rolled pickled and oiled products, floor plate and cut-to-length products. Primary end-users of the sheet products include service centers, and the automotive, manufacturing, construction and tubular industries.

Plate steel products (representing 9% of volumes) consist of various carbon-manganese, high-strength and low-alloy grades, and are sold in the as-rolled condition as well as subsequent value-added heat-treated conditions. The primary end-user of the plate products is the fabrication industry, which uses the plate products in the manufacturing or construction of railcars, buildings, bridges, off-highway equipment, storage tanks, ships, military applications, large diameter pipelines and power generation equipment.

Significant projects include a proposed $700,000,000 electric arc furnace (EAF) steelmaking facility, which is to be built adjacent to the current steel shop ($267,100,000 had been spent to Mar. 31, 2023, towards building and preparing the EAF transformation), which would increase annual steelmaking capacity by 900,000 tons following which production would transition away from the current blast furnace steelmaking; and a $120,000,000 plate mill modernization, which would allow for improved product quality with respect to surface and flatness, increase high strength capability with availability of new grades, ensure reliability of plate production with direct ship capability and increase capacity through debottlenecking and automation.

Predecessor Detail - Name changed from 1295908 B.C. Ltd., July 2, 2021.

Directors - Andrew S. (Andy) Harshaw, chr., Grimsby, Ont.; Michael D. Garcia, CEO, Sault Ste. Marie, Ont.; Mary Anne Bueschkens, Oakville, Ont.; James C. Gouin, Belle River, Ont.; Ave G. Lethbridge, Toronto, Ont.; Michael A. (Mike) McQuade, Grimsby, Ont.; Sanjay Nakra, Toronto, Ont.; Eric S. Rosenfeld, Harrison, N.Y.; Gale Rubenstein, Toronto, Ont.; Andrew E. Schultz, New Canaan, Conn.; David D. Sgro, Princeton, N.J.

Other Exec. Officers - Rajat Marwah, CFO; Danielle Baker, chief HR officer; Mike Panzeri, sr. v-p, prod.; Rory Brandow, v-p, sales; Loris Molino, v-p, maint. & oper. srvcs.; John Naccarato, v-p, strategy & chief legal officer; Mark Nogalo, v-p, strategic transformation

Capital Stock

	Authorized (shs.)	Outstanding (shs.)[1]
Common	unlimited	103,603,263

[1] At Aug. 8, 2023

Normal Course Issuer Bid - The company plans to make normal course purchases of up to 5,178,394 common shares representing 5% of the total outstanding. The bid commenced on Mar. 6, 2023, and expires on Mar. 5, 2024.

Major Shareholder - Widely held at Aug. 8, 2023.

Price Range - ASTL/TSX

Year	Volume	High	Low	Close
2022	45,462,337	$15.69	$7.70	$8.55
2021	3,208,573	$17.27	$11.31	$13.58

Recent Close: $9.74

Capital Stock Changes - In July 2022, 41,025,641 common shares were repurchased under a Substantial Issuer Bid. Also during fiscal 2023, 3,364,262 common shares were repurchased under a Normal Course Issuer Bid.

On Oct. 18, 2021, common shares were consolidated on a 0.71767775-for-1 basis and on Oct. 19, 2021, 30,306,320 post-consolidated common shares were issued pursuant to the acquisition of Legato Merger Corp. and private placement of 10,000,000 post-consolidated common shares was completed at US$10 per share. On Feb. 9, 2022, 35,883,692 post-consolidated common shares were issued in connection with earnout rights granted to non-management shareholders that existed prior to the Legato transaction.

Dividends

ASTL com Ra US$0.20 pa Q est. Mar. 31, 2022
Listed Oct 20/21.
US$0.05**i**.............. Mar. 31/22
i Initial Payment

Wholly Owned Subsidiaries

Algoma Steel Holdings Inc., B.C.
• 100% int. in **Algoma Steel Intermediate Holdings Inc.**, B.C.
  • 100% int. in **Algoma Steel Inc.**, Sault Ste. Marie, Ont.
    • 100% int. in **Algoma Docks GP Inc.**, B.C.
    • 100% int. in **Algoma Docks Limited Partnership**, B.C.

Financial Statistics

Periods ended:	12m Mar. 31/23[A]		12m Mar. 31/22[A]
	$000s	%Chg	$000s
Operating revenue	**2,778,500**	**-27**	**3,806,000**
Cost of sales	2,293,400		2,205,300
Salaries & benefits	43,200		54,200
General & admin expense	56,100		48,800
Operating expense	**2,392,700**	**+4**	**2,308,300**
Operating income	**385,800**	**-74**	**1,497,700**
Deprec., depl. & amort.	95,300		87,000
Finance income	13,300		500
Finance costs, gross	35,800		60,200
Pre-tax income	**376,100**	**-67**	**1,156,600**
Income taxes	77,600		298,900
Net income	**298,500**	**-65**	**857,700**
Cash & equivalent	247,400		915,300
Inventories	722,700		480,000
Accounts receivable	291,200		402,300
Current assets	1,366,300		1,916,500
Fixed assets, net	1,081,300		773,700
Intangibles, net	900		1,100
Total assets	**2,455,600**	**-9**	**2,693,600**
Bank indebtedness	1,900		100
Accts. pay. & accr. liabs.	204,600		261,900
Current liabilities	343,400		537,500
Long-term debt, gross	120,400		95,200
Long-term debt, net	110,400		85,200
Shareholders' equity	1,462,200		1,582,600
Cash from oper. activs.	**177,300**	**-86**	**1,263,400**
Cash from fin. activs.	(569,600)		(198,700)
Cash from invest. activs.	(333,500)		(165,700)
Net cash position	**247,400**	**-73**	**915,300**
Capital expenditures	(333,500)		(166,200)
Unfunded pension liability	184,000		118,100
	$		$
Earnings per share*	2.43		8.53
Cash flow per share*	1.45		12.56
Cash divd. per share*	0.20		0.05
	shs		shs
No. of shs. o/s*	103,567,884		147,957,787
Avg. no. of shs. o/s*	122,700,000		100,600,000
	%		%
Net profit margin	10.74		22.54
Return on equity	19.61		97.67
Return on assets	12.70		42.49
Foreign sales percent	63		66
No. of employees (FTEs)	2,847		2,734

* Common

[A] Reported in accordance with IFRS

Historical Summary

(as originally stated)

Fiscal Year	Oper. Rev.	Net Inc. Bef. Disc.	EPS*
	$000s	$000s	$
2023[A]	2,778,500	298,500	2.43
2022[A]	3,806,000	857,700	8.53
2021[A1]	1,794,900	(76,100)	(1.06)
2020[A]	1,956,900	(175,900)	(2.46)

* Common

[A] Reported in accordance with IFRS

[1] Results prior to Mar. 29, 2021, pertain to Algoma Steel Holdings Inc. Adjusted for 0.71767775-for-1 share consolidation on Oct. 18, 2021.

A.81 Algonquin Power & Utilities Corp.*

Symbol - AQN **Exchange** - TSX **CUSIP** - 015857

Head Office - 354 Davis Rd, Oakville, ON, L6J 2X1 **Telephone** - (905) 465-4500 **Toll-free** - (800) 387-0825 **Fax** - (905) 465-4514

Website - algonquinpower.com

Email - investorrelations@apucorp.com

Investor Relations - Brian Chin (905) 465-4500

Auditors - Ernst & Young LLP C.A., Toronto, Ont.

Lawyers - Blake, Cassels & Graydon LLP, Toronto, Ont.

Transfer Agents - American Stock Transfer & Trust Company, LLC, New York, N.Y.; TSX Trust Company, Toronto, Ont.

FP500 Revenue Ranking - 150

Employees - 3,951 at Dec. 31, 2022

Profile - (Can. 1988) Provides utility services related to electricity, natural gas, water and wastewater in the U.S., Canada, Bermuda and Chile. Also generates and sells electrical energy through a diverse portfolio of clean, renewable power generation and thermal power generation facilities across North America.

Operations are organized into two business units: Regulated Services Group and Renewable Energy Group.

Regulated Services Group

The group owns and operates a portfolio of electric distribution systems, water distribution and wastewater collection systems, natural gas distribution systems, and electric and natural gas transmission facilities, collectively providing distribution services to 1,256,000 customer connections. The group serves 308,000 electric customer connections in California, New Hampshire, Missouri, Kansas, Oklahoma, Arkansas and Bermuda; 375,000 natural gas customer connections in New Hampshire, Illinois, Iowa, Missouri, Georgia, New York, Massachusetts and New Brunswick; and 573,000 water distribution and wastewater collection utility systems customer connections in Arkansas, Arizona, California, Illinois, Missouri, Texas, New York and Chile. The group also owns and manages generating assets with a gross capacity of approximately 2.0 GW and has investments in a further 0.3 GW of net generation capacity.

Renewable Energy Group

The group generates and sells non-regulated renewable and thermal electricity through its portfolio of wind, hydroelectric, solar, renewable natural gas and thermal facilities, with a combined gross generating capacity of approximately 2.7 GW. About 82% of the electrical output from these facilities is sold pursuant to long term contractual arrangements. The group also has investments in generating assets with net generating capacity of 1.4 GW, which includes 51% interest in Stella, Cranell, West Raymond and East Raymond wind facilities in Texas and 42% interest in **Atlantica Sustainable Infrastructure plc** (formerly **Atlantica Yield plc**), which acquires, owns and manages an international portfolio of contracted renewable energy, power generation, electric transmission and water assets.

Year ended Dec. 31	2022	2021
	MWh sold	MWh sold
Renewable Energy:		
Quebec region	440,700	337,400
Ontario region	350,200	304,200
Manitoba region	435,000	422,500
Saskatchewan region	658,700	198,400
Western region	52,100	49,900
Maritime region	149,100	124,200
Pennsylvania region	105,500	134,800
Illinois region	1,720,500	1,367,700
Texas region	2,110,900	1,999,700
Minnesota region	869,300	720,300
California region	67,200	66,000
Michigan region	554,900	515,900
Maryland region	214,700	208,400
Virginia region	167,700	127,500
New York region	5,400	200
	7,901,900	6,577,100
Thermal Energy:		
Connecticut region	127,500	128,800
California region	149,100	145,400

In March 2023, the company achieved full commercial operations at its 112 MW Deerfield II wind facility in Huron cty., Mich.

On Apr. 14, 2022, the company's 175-MW Blue Hill wind facility in Saskatchewan, achieved full commercial operations.

Recent Merger and Acquisition Activity

Status: terminated **Revised:** Apr. 17, 2023

UPDATE: The transaction was terminated. PREVIOUS: Algonquin Power & Utilities Corp. (AQN) agreed to acquire Kentucky Power Company and AEP Kentucky Transmission Company, Inc. (Kentucky TransCo) from American Electric Power Company, Inc. for a total purchase price of US$2.846 billion, including assumption of US$1.221 billion of debt. Kentucky Power is a state rate-regulated electricity generation, distribution and transmission utility operating within the Commonwealth of Kentucky, serving 228,000 active customer connections and operations include a 1,075-MW natural gas fired power plant and a 50% interest in a coal-fueled plant. Kentucky TransCo is an electricity transmission business operating in the Kentucky portion of the transmission infrastructure that is part of the Pennsylvania – New Jersey – Maryland regional transmission organization (PJM). AQN plans to finance the acquisition with a US$2.725 billion syndicated acquisition financing commitment from CIBC and Scotiabank and a Cdn$800,000,000 offering of common shares. Sept. 29, 2022 - The purchase price was revised to US$2.646 billion, including assumption of US$1.221 billion of debt. Dec. 15, 2022 - Federal Energy Regulatory Commission (FERC) issued an order denying, without prejudice, authorization for the proposed transaction. Feb. 14, 2023 - A new application was filed with FERC for the approval of the transaction.

Status: completed **Revised:** Dec. 29, 2022

UPDATE: The transaction was completed for US$277,500,000 cash for the U.S. facilities and Cdn$108,610,000 cash for the Blue Hill facility. PREVIOUS: Algonquin Power & Utilities Corp. (AQN) agreed to sell ownership interests in a portfolio of operating wind projects in the U.S. and Canada to InfraRed Capital Partners Limited, an international infrastructure manager which is 80%-owned by Sun Life Financial Inc. The sale includes 49% interest in three wind facilities (Odell facility in Minnesota, Deerfield facility in Michigan and Sugar Creek facility in Illinois), totaling 551 MW, and 80% interest in the 175-MW Blue Hill wind facility in Saskatchewan. Total consideration was US$277,500,000 for the U.S. facilities and Cdn$107,300,000 for the Blue Hill facility. AQN would continue to oversee day-to-day operations and provide management services to the facilities. The transaction was expected to close by the end 2022.

Status: completed **Announced:** Aug. 5, 2022

Algonquin Power & Utilities Corp. acquired Sandhill Advanced Biofuels, LLC, a developer of renewable natural gas (RNG) anaerobic digestion projects located on dairy farms, with a portfolio of four projects in Wisconsin. Terms were not disclosed. Two of the projects recently achieved full commercial operations, while the other two projects are in late-stage development. Once fully constructed, the portfolio was expected to produce RNG at a rate of 500,000,000 BTUs per day. The projects represent Algonquin's first investment in the non-regulated RNG space

Predecessor Detail - Name changed from Hydrogenics Corporation, Oct. 27, 2009, pursuant to a plan of arrangement with Algonquin Power Income Fund to convert the fund into a corp., resulting in the fund becoming a wholly owned subsidiary; basis 1 Algonquin Power sh. for 1 Algonquin Power trust unit. All Hydrogenics assets and liabilities were transferred (except tax assets) to newly formed publicly listed Hydrogenics Corporation. Hydrogenics shldrs. exchanged shs. on a 1-for-1 basis for shs. of new Hydrogenics.

Directors - Kenneth (Ken) Moore, chr., Toronto, Ont.; Dr. Christopher G. (Chris) Huskilson, interim CEO, Wellington, N.S.; Amee Chande, West Vancouver, B.C.; Daniel S. (Dan) Goldberg, Ottawa, Ont.; D. Randy Laney, Farmington, Ark.; Masheed H. Saidi, Dana Point, Calif.; Dilek L. Samil, Las Vegas, Nev.; Melissa Stapleton Barnes, Carmel, Ind.

Other Exec. Officers - Anthony (Johnny) Johnston, COO; Darren G. Myers, CFO; Jeffery T. (Jeff) Norman, chief devel. officer; Kirsten Olsen, chief HR officer; Mary Ellen Paravalos, chief compliance & risk officer; Jennifer S. Tindale, chief legal officer & corp. sec.; Helen Bremner, exec. v-p, strategy & corp. planning; Colin Penny, exec. v-p, IT & digital transformation

Capital Stock

	Authorized (shs.)	Outstanding (shs.)[1]
Preferred	unlimited	nil
Series A		4,800,000
Series C		100
Series D		4,000,000
Common	unlimited	688,664,543[2]

[1] At Mar. 31, 2023

[2] At May 9, 2023.

Preferred Series A - Entitled to fixed cumulative annual dividends of Cdn$1.2905 payable quarterly to Dec. 30, 2023, and thereafter at a rate reset every five years equal to the five-year Government of Canada bond yield plus 2.94%. Redeemable on Dec. 31, 2023, and on December 31 every five years thereafter at Cdn$25 per share plus declared and unpaid dividends. Convertible on Dec. 31, 2023, and on December 31 every five years thereafter, into non-cumulative floating rate preferred series B shares on a share-for-share basis, subject to certain conditions. The series B shares would pay a quarterly dividend equal to the 90-day Canadian Treasury bill rate plus 2.94%. Non-voting.

Preferred Series D - Entitled to fixed cumulative annual dividends of Cdn$1.2728 payable quarterly to Mar. 31, 2024, and thereafter at a rate reset every five years equal to the five-year Government of Canada bond yield plus 3.28%. Redeemable on Mar. 31, 2024, and on March 31 every five years thereafter at Cdn$25 per share plus declared and unpaid dividends. Convertible on Mar. 31, 2024, and on March 31 every five years thereafter, into non-cumulative floating rate preferred series E shares on a share-for-share basis, subject to certain conditions. The series E shares would pay a quarterly dividend equal to the 90-day Canadian Treasury bill rate plus 3.28%. Non-voting.

Preferred Series C - Entitled to cumulative cash dividend payable quarterly until the date of redemption based on a prescribed payment schedule indexed in proportion to the increase in Consumer Price Index over the term of the shares. Mandatorily redeemable in 2031 for Cdn$53,400 per share. Convertible into common shares at any time after May 20, 2031, and before June 19, 2031, at Cdn$53,400 per share. Of the 100 shares outstanding, 36 are controlled by executives of the company. Non-voting. Classified as long-term liability.

Common - One vote per share.

Options - At Dec. 31, 2022, options were outstanding to purchase 2,626,780 common shares at a weighted average exercise price of Cdn$16.02 per share with a weighted average remaining contractual term of 5.63 years.

Major Shareholder - Widely held at Apr. 27, 2023.

Price Range - AQN/TSX

Year	Volume	High	Low	Close
2022	745,910,455	$20.19	$8.70	$8.82
2021	569,045,634	$22.67	$17.16	$18.27
2020	577,326,743	$22.39	$13.84	$20.95
2019	352,823,615	$19.34	$13.38	$18.37
2018	281,872,333	$14.68	$12.18	$13.73

Recent Close: $10.07

Capital Stock Changes - During 2022, common shares were issued as follows: 7,676,666 under dividend reinvestment plan, 2,861,709 under an at-the-market offering, 1,115,398 on exercise of share-based awards and 754 on conversion of debentures.

Dividends

AQN com Ra US$0.434 pa Q est. Apr. 14, 2023**

Prev. Rate: US$0.7232 est. July 15, 2022

Prev. Rate: US$0.6824 est. July 15, 2021

Prev. Rate: US$0.6204 est. July 15, 2020

AQN.PR.A pfd ser A cum. red. exch. Adj. Ra $1.2905 pa Q est. Apr. 1, 2019

AQN.PR.D pfd ser D cum. red. exch. Adj. Ra $1.4775 pa Q est. July 2, 2019

** Reinvestment Option

Long-Term Debt - Outstanding at Dec. 31, 2022:

Bank credit facilities due to 2031	US$773,643,000
Cmml. paper due 2023	407,000,000
Revolv. credit facilities due to 2027	351,786,000
Conv. debs	245,000
Cdn$ Notes:	
10.21% sr. notes due 2027[1]	15,024,000
3.68% sr. notes due to 2050[2]	882,899,000
US$ Notes & Bonds:	
1.18% sr. notes due 2026	1,142,814,000
6.34% sr. notes due to 2035	154,271,000
4.71% sr. bonds due to 2044	554,822,000
3.39% sr. notes due to 2047	1,496,101,000
Fixed-to-fixed rate jr. sub. notes:	
5.25% due 2082[3]	291,238,000
5.56% due 2078 to 2082	1,365,213,000
Chilean Unidad de Fomento borrowing:	
4.05% sr. bonds due to 2040[4]	77,206,000
	7,512,262,000
Less: Current portion	424,519,000
	7,087,743,000

[1] Cdn$20,349,000.
[2] Cdn$1,200,000.
[3] Cdn$400,000,000.
[4] CLF 1,637,000.

Minimum long-term debt repayment, excluding capital leases and convertible debentures, were reported as follows:

2023	US$1,128,660,000
2024	359,371,000
2025	45,262,000
2026	1,265,711,000
2027	719,144,000
Thereafter	4,019,166,000

Note - In March 2023, the senior unsecured revolving credit facility was amended whereby the borrowing capacity was increased from US$500,000,000 to US$1 billion with a new maturity date of Mar. 31, 2028.

Wholly Owned Subsidiaries

Algonquin Power Co., Oakville, Ont. Formerly Algonquin Power Income Fund.
- 100% int. in **Altavista Solar, LLC**, Va.
- 51% int. in **Deerfield Wind Energy, LLC**, Del.
- 100% int. in **GSG6, LLC**, Ill.
- 100% int. in **Maverick Creek Wind, LLC**, Del.
- 100% int. in **Minonk Wind, LLC**, Del.
- 51% int. in **Odell Wind Farm, LLC**, Minn.
- 100% int. in **St. Leon Wind Energy LP**, Man.
- 100% int. in **Senate Wind, LLC**, Del.
- 51% int. in **Sugar Creek Wind One LLC**, Del.

Bermuda Electric Light Company Limited, Bermuda.

Liberty (AY Holdings) B.V., Netherlands.
- 42% int. in **Atlantica Sustainable Infrastructure plc**, Middx., United Kingdom.

Liberty Utilities (Canada) Corp.
- 100% int. in **Liberty Utilities Co.**
  - 100% int. in **The Empire District Electric Company**, Mo.
    - 100% int. in **Kings Point Wind, LLC**, Del.
    - 100% int. in **Neosho Ridge Wind, LLC**, Del.
    - 100% int. in **North Fork Ridge Wind, LLC**, Del.
  - 100% int. in **The Empire District Gas Company**, Kan.
  - 100% int. in **Liberty Utilities (St. Lawrence Gas) Corp.**, Massena, N.Y.
  - 100% int. in **Liberty Utilities (CalPeco Electric) LLC**, Calif.
  - 100% int. in **Liberty Utilities (EnergyNorth Natural Gas) Corp.**, N.H.
  - 100% int. in **Liberty Utilities (Granite State Electric) Corp.**, N.H.
  - 100% int. in **Liberty Utilities (Litchfield Park Water & Sewer) Corp.**, Ariz.
  - 100% int. in **Liberty Utilities (Midstates Natural Gas) Corp.**, Mo.
  - 100% int. in **Liberty Utilities (New England Natural Gas Company) Corp.**, Mass.
  - 100% int. in **Liberty Utilities (New York Water) Corp.**, Merrick, N.Y.
  - 100% int. in **Liberty Utilities (Peach State Natural Gas) Corp.**, Ga.

Liberty Utilities (Canada) LP, Oakville, Ont.
- 100% int. in **Liberty Utilities (Gas New Brunswick) LP**, N.B.

Subsidiaries

64% int. in **Empresa de Servicios Sanitarios de Los Lagos S.A.**, Chile.

Note: The preceding list includes only the major related companies in which interests are held.

Financial Statistics

Periods ended:	12m Dec. 31/22[A]		12m Dec. 31/21[oA]
	US$000s	%Chg	US$000s
Operating revenue	**2,765,155**	**+22**	**2,274,142**
General & admin expense	80,232		66,726
Other operating expense	1,717,985		1,416,043
Operating expense	**1,798,217**	**+21**	**1,482,769**
Operating income	**966,938**	**+22**	**791,373**
Deprec., depl. & amort.	455,520		402,963
Finance income	24,102		20,776
Finance costs, gross	278,574		209,554
Investment income	85,727		75,186
Write-downs/write-offs	(235,478)		n.a.
Pre-tax income	**(369,668)**	**n.a.**	**142,232**
Income taxes	(61,513)		(43,425)
Net income	**(308,155)**	**n.a.**	**185,657**
Net inc. for equity hldrs	**(211,989)**	**n.a.**	**264,859**
Net inc. for non-cont. int.	**(96,166)**	**n.a.**	**(79,202)**
Cash & equivalent	57,623		125,157
Inventories	224,921		177,761
Accounts receivable	528,057		403,426
Current assets	1,094,481		938,743
Long-term investments	1,806,532		2,344,282
Fixed assets, net	11,944,885		11,042,446
Intangibles, net	1,417,262		1,306,360
Total assets	**17,627,613**	**+5**	**16,797,503**
Accts. pay. & accr. liabs	741,872		614,024
Current liabilities	1,534,460		1,364,712
Long-term debt, gross	7,512,262		6,211,375
Long-term debt, net	7,087,743		5,854,978
Long-term lease liabilities	21,834		22,512
Preferred share equity	184,299		184,299
Shareholders' equity	5,219,647		5,858,997
Non-controlling interest	1,616,792		1,523,082
Cash from oper. activs	**619,096**	**+293**	**157,466**
Cash from fin. activs	1,110,236		1,673,716
Cash from invest. activs	(1,788,409)		(1,798,109)
Net cash position	**101,185**	**-37**	**161,389**
Capital expenditures	(1,089,024)		(1,345,045)
Capital disposals	nil		6,023
Unfunded pension liability	58,880		116,754
	US$		US$
Earnings per share*	(0.33)		0.41
Cash flow per share*	0.91		0.25
Cash divd. per share*	0.71		0.67
	shs		shs
No. of shs. o/s*	683,614,803		683,614,803
Avg. no. of shs. o/s*	677,862,207		622,347,677
	%		%
Net profit margin	(11.14)		8.16
Return on equity	(4.12)		4.79
Return on assets	(0.44)		3.06
Foreign sales percent	93		93
No. of employees (FTEs)	3,951		3,445

* Common
[o] Restated
[A] Reported in accordance with U.S. GAAP

Latest Results

Periods ended:	3m Mar. 31/23[A]		3m Mar. 31/22[oA]
	US$000s	%Chg	US$000s
Operating revenue	778,627	+6	733,237
Net income	249,610	+375	52,598
Net inc. for equity hldrs	270,139	+197	90,965
Net inc. for non-cont. int	(20,529)		(38,367)
	US$		US$
Earnings per share*	0.39		0.13

* Common
[o] Restated
[A] Reported in accordance with U.S. GAAP

Historical Summary
(as originally stated)

Fiscal Year	Oper. Rev.	Net Inc. Bef. Disc.	EPS*
	US$000s	US$000s	US$
2022[A]	2,765,155	(308,155)	(0.33)
2021[A]	2,285,479	185,657	0.41
2020[A]	1,677,058	727,828	1.38
2019[A]	1,624,921	484,950	1.05
2018[A]	1,647,387	79,089	0.38

* Common
[A] Reported in accordance with U.S. GAAP

A.82 Alimentation Couche-Tard Inc.*

Symbol - ATD **Exchange** - TSX **CUSIP** - 01626P
Head Office - 4204 boul Industriel, Laval, QC, H7L 0E3 **Telephone** - (450) 662-6632 **Toll-free** - (800) 361-2612 **Fax** - (450) 662-6633
Website - corpo.couche-tard.com/en/
Email - investor.relations@couche-tard.com
Investor Relations - Jean Philippe Lachance (450) 662-6632 ext. 4619
Auditors - PricewaterhouseCoopers LLP C.A., Montréal, Qué.
Transfer Agents - TSX Trust Company, Montréal, Qué.
FP500 Revenue Ranking - 2
Employees - 128,000 at Apr. 30, 2023
Profile - (Que. 1988 amalg.) Operates and licenses a network of convenience stores and service stations across Canada, the United States, Europe, Hong Kong and 14 other countries and territories.

Convenience stores and service stations throughout North America, Scandinavia (Norway, Sweden and Denmark), Ireland, the Baltics (Estonia, Latvia and Lithuania), Poland and Hong Kong primarily operate under the Circle K® brand, with the exception of stores in Quebec and the northern tier region of the U.S. that operate under the brands Couche-Tard® and Holiday®, respectively, and automated fuel stations in Europe that operate under the Ingo® brand. Other North American store banners include Mac's®, Kangaroo®, Kangaroo Express®, On the Run®, Dairy Mart® and Corner Store®. Affiliate programs in North America operate under the Provi-Soir®, 7-jours®, Becker's®, Daisy Mart® and Winks® banners. North American stores range between 800 and 6,500 sq. ft., European stores range between 500 and 5,000 sq. ft., and stores in Hong Kong range from 200 to 2,000 sq. ft.

Offers traditional convenience store items such as tobacco products and alternative tobacco products, grocery items, candy and snacks, beverages, beer, wine and fresh food offerings, including quick service restaurants. In addition, services such as car wash, automatic teller machines (ATMs), sales of lottery tickets, calling cards, gift cards, postage stamps and bus tickets, money orders and electric vehicle charging are provided in numerous retail sites.

Also sells road transportation fuel at its store locations, which include full-service and automated stations. In Europe, bulk sales of fuel are also provided to industrial and commercial customers such as hospitals, car rental fleets, road construction crews, bus services, factories and independent resellers and retailers. During fiscal 2023, road transportation fuel sales represented about 74% of the company's total revenue. The company also sells stationary energy, home heating oil and aviation fuel products in Europe. Fuel terminals are operated in Alabama, Minnesota, Arizona, Florida, Illinois, North Carolina, Norway, Denmark, Sweden, Latvia, Lithuania and Ireland.

At Apr. 30, 2023, the company had 12,432 stores, which consisted of 9,983 company-owned and operated stores, 344 stores which are company owned but dealer operated, 820 stores which are dealer owned and operated, and 1,285 affiliated stores. The total store network consisted of 9,331 convenience stores across North America, including 8,326 stores with road transportation fuel dispensing; 2,711 service stations located in Europe, including 973 automated fuel stations; and 390 convenience stores in Hong Kong.

Store Network at Apr. 30, 2023:

Location	Stores
Eastern Canada	1,223
Central Canada	745
Western Canada	293
U.S. Heartland	369
U.S. Midwest	438
U.S. Great Lakes	467
Northern Tier	559
U.S. Coastal Carolinas	443
U.S. Southeast	531
U.S. South Atlantic	372
Florida	667
U.S. Gulf Coast	680
U.S. Rocky Mountains	413
Texas	670
U.S. Grand Canyon	662
U.S. West Coast	799
Denmark	435
Estonia	78
Ireland	407
Latvia	86
Lithuania	95
Norway	468
Poland	397
Sweden	745
Hong Kong	390

In addition, 2,036 Circle K® stores were operated under licence agreements in Cambodia (23), Egypt (123), Guam (13), Guatemala (1), Honduras (46), Indonesia (485), Jamaica (4), Macau (33), Mexico (871), New Zealand (4), Saudi Arabia (4), South Africa (4), United Arab Emirates (1) and Vietnam (424).

During fiscal 2023, the company sold 47 sites in the U.S. to various buyers for total consideration of US$56,000,000.

In May 2022, the company began the rollout of electric vehicle (EV) fast chargers in the U.S., starting at a new prototype Circle K store in Rock Hill, S.C. The company plans to bring EV charging units to 200 Circle K and Couche-Tard stores across North America over the next two years.

On May 20, 2022, the company invested US$30,100,000 in a joint venture with Houston, Tex.-based **Musket Corporation**, which then acquired four road transportation fuel terminals in Florida, Illinois and North Carolina.

On Mar. 7, 2022, the company announced the suspension of operations in Russia in light of the Russian war against Ukraine. Subsequently, the company lost control of and deconsolidated its wholly owned Russian subsidiaries effective Apr. 8, 2022. The company had 38 stores located in St. Petersburg, Murmansk and Pskov.

Recent Merger and Acquisition Activity

Status: pending **Revised:** June 22, 2023
UPDATE: TotalEnergies accepted Couche-Tard's firm offer which would lead to entering into definitive agreements. PREVIOUS: Alimentation Couche-Tard Inc. announced a firm offer to acquire certain European retail assets from TotalEnergies SE for a total cash consideration of €3.1 billion, to be financed using cash on hand, existing credit facilities, U.S. commercial paper program and a new term loan. The acquisition consists of 100% of TotalEnergies retail assets in Germany and the Netherlands and 60% interest in the Belgium and Luxembourg entities. At the end of 2022, TotalEnergies had 1,195 sites in Germany, 566 sites in Belgium, 387 sites in the Netherlands and 45 sites in Luxembourg, majority of which were company-owned (68%) with the balance being dealer-owned (32%). The transaction remains subject to an information and consultation process involving employee representative bodies and the approval of relevant authorities. Closing of the transaction was expected before the end of 2023, if the firm offer was accepted by TotalEnergies.

Status: pending **Announced:** Apr. 27, 2023
Alimentation Couche-Tard Inc. agreed to acquire 112 gas station and convenience store sites in the U.S. from MAPCO Express Inc., a wholly owned subsidiary of Santiago, Chile-based Empresas Copec S.A. Terms of the transaction were not disclosed. The sites were primarily located in Tennessee and Alabama, with additional locations in Kentucky and Georgia. The acquisition would also include surplus property and a logistics fleet. The transaction was contingent on a separate transaction in which MAPCO and its other locations would be acquired by Lawrenceville, Ga.-based Majors Management LLC.

Status: completed **Announced:** Apr. 21, 2023
Alimentation Couche-Tard Inc. acquired 10 company-owned and company-operated convenience retail and fuel sites operating under the Dion's Quik Chik brand in Florida. Terms were not disclosed.

Status: completed **Revised:** Apr. 17, 2023
UPDATE: The transaction was completed for US$285,700,000, which was financed using cash on hand and existing credit facilities. PREVIOUS: Alimentation Couche-Tard Inc. agreed to acquire 45 company-owned and company-operated convenience retail and fuel sites operating under the Big Red Stores brand in Arkansas. Terms were not disclosed.

Status: completed **Announced:** Mar. 1, 2023
Alimentation Couche-Tard Inc. sold 52 convenience retail and fuel sites, operating under the Esso, Wilsons Gas Stops, Go! Stores and Coast Gas brands (Wilsons), in New Brunswick, Newfoundland and Labrador, Nova Scotia and Prince Edward Island to Harnois Énergies for Cdn$77,600,000. The sites included 47 locations (34 company-owned and operated, one company-owned and dealer-operated and 12 dealer-owned and operated) acquired by Couche-Tard on Aug. 30, 2022, as part of the acquisition of the entities that operate the Wilsons convenience store and fuel network in Atlantic Canada. The divestiture of the sites was part of Couche-Tard's agreement with the Canadian Competition Bureau in relation to the Wilsons acquisition.

Status: completed **Revised:** Feb. 8, 2023
UPDATE: The transaction was completed for US$395,900,000, including debt repayment and financed using existing credit facilities and cash on hand. PREVIOUS: Alimentation Couche-Tard Inc. agreed to acquire Scottsdale, Ariz.-based True Blue Car Wash, LLC, which operates 65 car washes in Arizona, Texas, Illinois and Indiana under the Clean Freak and Rainstorm banners, for an undisclosed amount. The transaction was expected to be completed in the first half of 2023, subject to regulatory approvals and closing conditions.

Status: completed **Revised:** Aug. 30, 2022
UPDATE: The transaction was completed. The consideration was Cdn$346,800,000, including debt repayment. PREVIOUS: Alimentation Couche-Tard Inc. agreed to acquire Cape D'Or Holdings Limited, Barrington Terminals Limited and other related holding entities, which operate an independent convenience store and fuel network under the Esso, Wilsons Gas Stops and Go! Store brands in Atlantic Canada (collectively Wilsons). Terms of the transaction were not disclosed. The Wilsons network included 79 corporate-owned and operated convenience retail and fuel locations, 139 dealer locations (of which two were corporately owned), and a marine fuel terminal in Halifax, N.S. Couche-Tard plans to acquire the Wilsons network with some assets to be purchased by a third-party acquisition partner to be determined following a review of the proposed transaction by the Canadian Competition Bureau. The transaction was expected to close in the first half of the 2022 calendar year.

Predecessor Detail - Name changed from Actidev Inc., Dec. 15, 1994.

Directors - Alain Bouchard, co-founder & exec. chr., Montréal, Qué.; Jacques D'Amours, co-founder, Saint-Bruno-de-Montarville, Qué.; Richard Fortin, co-founder, Boucherville, Qué.; Réal Plourde, co-founder, Westmount, Qué.; Brian P. Hannasch, pres. & CEO, Columbus, Ind.; Louis O. Vachon†, Montréal, Qué.; Jean Bernier, Westmount, Qué.; Karinne Bouchard, Montréal, Qué.; Eric Boyko, Montréal, Qué.; Janice L. Fields, Naples, Fla.; Eric Fortin, Longueuil, Qué.; Mélanie Kau, Westmount, Qué.; Marie-Josée Lamothe, Montréal, Qué.; Monique F. Leroux, Montréal, Qué.; Daniel Rabinowicz, Saint-Lambert, Qué.; Louis Têtu, Québec, Qué.

Other Exec. Officers - Filipe da Silva, exec. v-p & CFO; Ed Dzadovsky, exec. v-p & chief tech. officer; Hans-Olav Hoidahl, exec. v-p, opers., Europe; Kevin A. Lewis, exec. v-p & chief growth officer; Timothy A. (Alex) Miller, exec. v-p & COO; Ina Strand, exec. v-p & chief people officer; Niall Anderton, sr. v-p, opers., Europe; Brian Bednarz, sr. v-p, opers.; Aaron Brooks, sr. v-p, real estate; Kathleen K. Cunnington, sr. v-p, global shared srvcs.; Jorn Madsen, sr. v-p, opers.; Suzanne Poirier, sr. v-p, opers.; Sophie Provencher, sr. v-p, global mdsg.; Louise Warner, sr. v-p, global fuels; Valéry Zamuner, sr. v-p, gen. counsel & corp. sec.; Mette Uglebjerg, interim sr. v-p, opers.

† Lead director

Capital Stock

	Authorized (shs.)	Outstanding (shs.)[1]
First Preferred	unlimited	nil
Second Preferred	unlimited	nil
Common	unlimited	976,908,984

[1] At July 10, 2023

Options - At Apr. 30, 2023, options were outstanding to purchase 3,417,700 common shares at prices ranging from Cdn$14 to Cdn$57 per share with a weighted average remaining contractual life of up to 6.77 years.

Normal Course Issuer Bid - The company plans to make normal course purchases of up to 49,066,629 common shares representing 5% of the total outstanding. The bid commenced on May 1, 2023, and expires on Apr. 30, 2024.

Major Shareholder - Alain Bouchard held 12.61% interest at July 10, 2023.

Price Range - ATD.B/TSX (D)

Year	Volume	High	Low	Close
2021	482,719,647	$52.42	$36.03	$49.67
2020	448,596,641	$47.49	$30.40	$43.38
2019	421,057,416	$44.57	$32.63	$41.21
2018	463,905,472	$35.13	$26.04	$33.96

Split: 2-for-1 split in Sept. 2019

ATD/TSX

Year	Volume	High	Low	Close
2022	412,815,489	$63.54	$45.23	$59.50
2021	31,218,441	$53.97	$36.90	$53.00
2020	2,701,710	$47.57	$30.57	$43.50
2019	1,371,518	$44.59	$32.75	$41.38
2018	1,477,538	$35.40	$26.28	$33.98

Split: 2-for-1 split in Sept. 2019

Recent Close: $71.29

Capital Stock Changes - On July 31, 2023, the company arranged to repurchase 10,820,837 common shares held by Alimentation Couche-Tard Inc., for a purchase price of Cdn$64.69 per share.

Effective Sept. 1, 2022, a new class of common shares was created, all class A multiple voting shares were converted into common shares on a 1-for-1 basis and class A multiple voting and class B subordinate voting shares were removed from authorized share capital. During fiscal 2023, 400,000 common shares were issued on exercise of options and 52,000,000 common shares were repurchased under a Normal Course Issuer Bid.

Prior to Dec. 8, 2021, 4,800,000 class B subordinate voting shares were issued on conversion of a like number of class A multiple voting shares, 100,000 class B subordinate voting shares were issued on exercise of options and 17,700,000 class B subordinate voting shares were repurchased under a Normal Course Issuer Bid. On Dec. 8, 2021, all 813,000,000 remaining class B subordinate voting shares were automatically converted into class A multiple voting shares on a 1-for-1 basis as a result of all four company co-founders reaching the age of 65. Also during fiscal 2022, 29,100,000 class A multiple voting shares were repurchased under a Normal Course Issuer Bid.

Dividends

ATD com M.V. Ra $0.56 pa Q est. Dec. 15, 2022
Prev. Rate: $0.44 est. Dec. 16, 2021
Prev. Rate: $0.35 est. Dec. 17, 2020
cl B S.V. Ra $0.44 pa Q est. Dec. 16, 2021
Delisted Dec 8/21.
Prev. Rate: $0.35 est. Dec. 17, 2020

Long-Term Debt - Outstanding at Apr. 30, 2023:

Cdn$ sr. notes[1]	US$1,025,200,000
3.85% NKr sr. notes due Feb. 2026[2]	62,700,000
1.88% Euro sr. notes due May 2026[3]	821,900,000
US$ sr. notes[4]	3,969,500,000
Other debts	9,700,000
	5,889,000,000
Less: Current portion	700,000
	5,888,300,000

[1] Consist of Cdn$700,000,000 principal amount of 3.06% senior notes due July 2024 and Cdn$700,000,000 principal amount of 3.6% senior notes due June 2025.

[2] NKr675,000,000.

[3] €750,000,000.

[4] Consist of US$1 billion principal amount of 3.55% senior notes due July 2027, US$750,000,000 principal amount of 2.95% senior notes due January 2030, US$650,000,000 principal amount of 3.44% senior notes due May 2041, US$500,000,000 principal amount of 4.5% senior notes due July 2047, US$750,000,000 principal amount of 3.8% senior notes due January 2050 and US$350,000,000 principal amount of 3.63% senior notes due May 2051.

Wholly Owned Subsidiaries

Couche-Tard Inc., Canada.
- 100% int. in **Mac's Convenience Stores Inc.**, Toronto, Ont.
  - 100% int. in **Big Diamond, LLC**, Tex.
  - 100% int. in **Circle K Danmark A/S**, Denmark.
  - 100% int. in **Circle K Ireland Fuel Trading Limited**, Ireland.
  - 100% int. in **Circle K Norge AS**, Norway.
  - 100% int. in **Circle K Polska Sp.zo.o**, Poland.
  - 100% int. in **Circle K Stores Inc.**, Tex.
  - 100% int. in **Circle K Sverige AB**, Sweden.
  - 100% int. in **Holiday Stationstores, LLC**, Bloomington, Minn.
  - 100% int. in **Mac's Convenience Stores LLC**, Del.
- 50% int. in **RDK Ventures LLC**, Chicago, Ill.

Investments

35.7% int. in **Fire & Flower Holdings Corp.**, Toronto, Ont.

Note: The preceding list includes only the major related companies in which interests are held.

Financial Statistics

Periods ended:	53w Apr. 30/23[A]		52w Apr. 24/22[A]
	US$000s	%Chg	US$000s
Operating revenue	**71,856,700**	**+14**	**62,809,900**
Cost of sales	59,804,600		51,805,100
General & admin expense	6,333,500		5,860,900
Stock-based compensation	28,300		23,600
Operating expense	**66,166,400**	**+15**	**57,689,600**
Operating income	**5,690,300**	**+11**	**5,120,300**
Deprec., depl. & amort.	1,502,000		1,455,800
Finance income	78,200		24,100
Finance costs, gross	384,900		305,100
Investment income	3,800		20,100
Write-downs/write-offs	(23,900)[1]		(89,900)[2]
Pre-tax income	**3,929,100**	**+15**	**3,417,600**
Income taxes	838,200		734,300
Net income	**3,090,900**	**+15**	**2,683,300**
Cash & equivalent	834,200		2,143,900
Inventories	2,176,000		2,403,000
Accounts receivable	2,298,500		2,497,500
Current assets	5,669,600		7,328,300
Long-term investments	303,000		418,900
Fixed assets, net	11,873,000		11,286,200
Right-of-use assets	3,385,100		3,302,200
Intangibles, net	7,383,700		6,781,600
Total assets	**29,049,200**	**-2**	**29,591,600**
Accts. pay. & accr. liabs	4,497,900		5,256,100
Current liabilities	5,165,000		6,017,400
Long-term debt, gross	5,889,000		5,965,000
Long-term debt, net	5,888,300		5,963,600
Long-term lease liabilities	3,138,800		3,049,500
Shareholders' equity	12,564,500		12,437,600
Cash from oper. activs	**4,344,600**	**+10**	**3,944,900**
Cash from fin. activs	(3,349,700)		(2,951,100)
Cash from invest. activs	(2,275,600)		(1,799,400)
Net cash position	**834,200**	**-61**	**2,143,900**
Capital expenditures	(1,803,800)		(1,664,500)
Capital disposals	262,100		403,300
Unfunded pension liability	10,500		17,300
	US$		US$
Earnings per share*	3.07		2.53
Cash flow per share*	4.31		3.71
Cash divd. per share*	$0.50		$0.40
	shs		shs
No. of shs. o/s*	981,332,584		1,032,935,943
Avg. no. of shs. o/s*	1,007,700,000		1,062,000,000
	%		%
Net profit margin	4.30		4.27
Return on equity	24.73		21.80
Return on assets	11.57		10.08
Foreign sales percent	88		87
No. of employees (FTEs)	128,000		122,000

* Common

[A] Reported in accordance with IFRS

[1] Pertains to impairment loss on investment in Fire & Flower Holdings Corp.

[2] Includes US$56,200,000 loss from the deconsolidation and impairment of Russian subsidiaries and US$33,700,000 impairment loss on investment in Fire & Flower Holdings Corp.

Historical Summary
(as originally stated)

Fiscal Year	Oper. Rev.	Net Inc. Bef. Disc.	EPS*
	US$000s	US$000s	US$
2023[A1]	71,856,700	3,090,900	3.07
2022[A]	62,809,900	2,683,300	2.53
2021[A]	45,760,100	2,705,500	2.45
2020[A]	54,132,400	2,357,600	2.10
2019[A]	59,117,600	1,821,300	1.62

* Common

[A] Reported in accordance with IFRS

[1] 53 weeks ended Apr. 30, 2023.

Note: Adjusted throughout for 2-for-1 split in Sept. 2019

A.83 Alithya Group inc.

Symbol - ALYA **Exchange** - TSX **CUSIP** - 01643B
Head Office - 400-1100 boul Robert-Bourassa, Montréal, QC, H3B 3A5 **Telephone** - (514) 285-5552
Website - www.alithya.com
Email - benjamin.cerantola@alithya.com
Investor Relations - Benjamin Cerantola (514) 285-5552 ext. 6480
Auditors - KPMG LLP C.A., Montréal, Qué.
Lawyers - Osler, Hoskin & Harcourt LLP, Montréal, Qué.

Transfer Agents - TSX Trust Company, Montréal, Qué.
FP500 Revenue Ranking - 496
Employees - 3,600 at Mar. 31, 2023
Profile - (Que. 2018) Provides consulting services including strategy and digital transformation in the areas of information technology to clients in the financial services, insurance, healthcare, government, renewable energy, manufacturing, telecommunications, transportation and logistics, and professional services sectors in Canada, the U.S. and internationally.
Operations are grouped into four segments: Business Strategy; Application Solutions Services; Enterprise Solutions; and Data and Analytics.
Business Strategy - Helps clients in decision-making processes regarding strategic planning, change management, systems evolution, operational processes, employee experience and transformative change enablement. Services include strategic consulting, digital transformation, organizational performance and enterprise architecture.
Application Solutions Services - Helps clients in migrating from legacy systems, developing new technological solutions and selecting hosting strategies, whether cloud, on- premise or hybrid hosting. Services include streamlining app development and operations, legacy systems modernization, control and software engineering, cloud infrastructure, quality assurance and automated testing.
Enterprise Solutions - Helps clients deploy company-wide systems for finance, human capital, operations and marketing functions. Services include enterprise resource planning, corporate performance management, customer relationship management and human capital management.
Data and Analytics - Helps clients gain business insight and improve decision-making by leveraging specialized IT systems and software. Services include business intelligence, data management, artificial intelligence and machine learning, as well as Internet of Things.
Has also established partnerships with companies including Microsoft, Oracle and Amazon Web Services.
During fiscal 2022, wholly owned **Pro2p Services Conseils Inc.** and **Alithya Askida Solutions Inc.** were dissolved.

Recent Merger and Acquisition Activity

Status: completed **Revised:** July 1, 2022
UPDATE: The transaction was completed. PREVIOUS: Alithya Group inc. agreed to acquire Indianapolis, Ind.-based Datum Consulting Group, LLC, which owns 14 cloud-based Software-as-a-Service proprietary products offering information capture, content management and application, and rules modernization for insurance companies, for $30,300,000 cash, issuance of 1,867,262 class A subordinate voting shares with a total value of $10,200,000 and contingent consideration of up to $16,400,000.
Directors - Ghyslain Rivard, founder, Qué.; Pierre Turcotte, chr., Qué.; Paul Raymond, pres. & CEO, Qué.; Robert Comeau†, Montréal, Qué.; Dana Ades-Landy, Montréal, Qué.; André P. Brosseau, Montréal, Qué.; Mélissa Gilbert, Québec, Qué.; Lucie Martel, Montréal, Qué.; James B. Renacci, Ohio; C. Lee Thomas, Ohio
Other Exec. Officers - Bernard Dockrill, COO; Claude Thibault, CFO; Giulia Cirillo, chief human capital officer; Nathalie Forcier, chief legal officer & corp. sec.; Robert Lamarre, CIO; Amar Bukkasagaram, sr. v-p, data solutions; Mike Feldman, sr. v-p, Oracle practice; Nigel Fonseca, sr. v-p, Ont. & western Canada; Barry O'Donnell, sr. v-p, digital adoption practice; Dany Paradis, sr. v-p, Quebec; John Scandar, sr. v-p, Microsoft practice; Russell Smith, pres., Alithya U.S.A., Inc.
† Lead director

Capital Stock

	Authorized (shs.)	Outstanding (shs.)[1]
Preferred	unlimited	nil
Cl.A Subord. Vtg.	unlimited	88,445,257
Cl.B Multiple Vtg.	unlimited	7,324,248

[1] At Aug. 8, 2023
Preferred - Issuable in series.
Class A Subordinate Voting - One vote per share.
Class B Multiple Voting - Convertible at any time, at the holder's option, into one class A subordinate voting share. Ten votes per share.
Normal Course Issuer Bid - The company plans to make normal course purchases of up to 2,491,128 class A subordinate voting shares representing 2.9% of the total outstanding. The bid commenced on Sept. 20, 2022, and expires on Sept. 19, 2023.
Major Shareholder - Ghyslain Rivard held 29.61% interest and Pierre Turcotte held 10.46% interest at July 17, 2023.

Price Range - ALYA/TSX

Year	Volume	High	Low	Close
2022	9,274,284	$3.95	$1.95	$2.03
2021	18,546,974	$6.91	$2.53	$3.24
2020	6,469,495	$4.23	$1.50	$2.70
2019	14,408,302	$4.80	$2.73	$3.62
2018	948,387	$7.94	$3.20	$3.20

Recent Close: $2.31
Capital Stock Changes - In July 2022, 1,867,262 class A subordinate voting shares were issued pursuant to the acquisition of Datum Consulting Group, LLC and its international affiliates. Also during fiscal 2023, class A subordinate voting shares were issued as follows: 738,382 as share-based compensation and 83,449 pursuant to the acquisition of Trafic 3W inc.; 371,525 class A subordinate voting shares were repurchased under a Normal Course Issuer Bid. In addition, 152,632 class B multiple voting shares were issued on exercise of options.
In April 2021, 25,182,676 class A subordinate voting shares were issued pursuant to the acquisition of R3D Consulting Inc. In February 2022, private placement of 8,143,322 class A subordinate voting shares was completed at $3.07 per share. Also during fiscal 2022, class A subordinate voting shares were issued as follows: 834,324 as share-based compensation, 302,632 in exchange for a like number of class B multiple voting shares, 63,874 in settlement of deferred share units and 2,750 on exercise of options; 349,400 class A subordinate voting shares were repurchased under a Normal Course Issuer Bid. In addition, 152,632 class B multiple voting shares were issued on exercise of options.

Wholly Owned Subsidiaries

Alithya Canada inc., Qué.
- 100% int. in **Alithya Consulting Inc.**, Qué.
- 100% int. in **Alithya Digital Technology Corporation**
- 100% int. in **Alithya Financial Solutions, Inc.**, Del.
- 100% int. in **Alithya France S.A.S.**

Alithya Numérique Maroc SARLAU, Morocco.
Alithya USA, Inc., Wakefield, Mass.
- 100% int. in **Alithya Fullscope Solutions, Inc.**
- 100% int. in **Alithya Ranzal LLC**
- 100% int. in **Vitalyst, LLC**, Bala Cynwyd, Pa.

DCG Team UK Limited, United Kingdom.
Datum Consulting Group Australia Pty Limited, Australia.
Datum Consulting Group, LLC, Indianapolis, Ind.
Datum Cybertech India Pvt Ltd., India.
Note: The preceding list includes only the major related companies in which interests are held.

Financial Statistics

Periods ended:	12m Mar. 31/23[A]		12m Mar. 31/22[oA]
	$000s	%Chg	$000s
Operating revenue	**522,701**	**+19**	**437,885**
Cost of sales	370,927		321,732
General & admin expense	119,782		95,522
Stock-based compensation	6,740		3,316
Operating expense	**497,449**	**+18**	**420,570**
Operating income	**25,252**	**+46**	**17,315**
Deprec., depl. & amort.	34,033		19,720
Finance income	349		80
Finance costs, gross	9,684		4,659
Pre-tax income	**(36,354)**	**n.a.**	**(18,575)**
Income taxes	(6,257)		(3,027)
Net income	**(30,097)**	**n.a.**	**(15,548)**
Cash & equivalent	22,583		17,655
Accounts receivable	92,453		100,867
Current assets	156,080		153,725
Fixed assets, net	8,724		10,412
Right-of-use assets	9,353		15,146
Intangibles, net	270,728		248,015
Total assets	**464,101**	**+4**	**447,721**
Accts. pay. & accr. liabs	91,263		89,660
Current liabilities	130,219		132,895
Long-term debt, gross	127,190		106,676
Long-term debt, net	114,382		87,360
Long-term lease liabilities	14,643		17,753
Shareholders' equity	187,068		199,751
Cash from oper. activs	**28,882**	**n.m.**	**1,850**
Cash from fin. activs	(11,326)		27,917
Cash from invest. activs	(13,728)		(18,938)
Net cash position	**22,583**	**+28**	**17,655**
Capital expenditures	(1,736)		(1,719)
	$		$
Earnings per share*	(0.32)		(0.18)
Cash flow per share*	0.30		0.02
	shs		shs
No. of shs. o/s*	95,195,816		92,725,616
Avg. no. of shs. o/s*	94,178,549		85,297,843
	%		%
Net profit margin	(5.76)		(3.55)
Return on equity	(15.56)		(10.10)
Return on assets	(4.84)		(3.37)
Foreign sales percent	40		35
No. of employees (FTEs)	3,600		3,700

* Cl.A subord. vtg.
[o] Restated
[A] Reported in accordance with IFRS

Latest Results

Periods ended:	3m June 30/23[A]		3m June 30/22[A]
	$000s	%Chg	$000s
Operating revenue	131,595	+4	126,764
Net income	(7,245)	n.a.	(4,164)
	$		$
Earnings per share*	(0.08)		(0.04)

* Cl.A subord. vtg.
[A] Reported in accordance with IFRS

Historical Summary
(as originally stated)

Fiscal Year	Oper. Rev. $000s	Net Inc. Bef. Disc. $000s	EPS* $
2023[A]	522,701	(30,097)	(0.32)
2022[A]	437,885	(15,548)	(0.18)
2021[A]	287,643	(17,338)	(0.30)
2020[A]	279,007	(39,667)	(0.70)
2019[A]	209,478	(12,475)	(0.34)

* Cl.A subord. vtg.
[A] Reported in accordance with IFRS

A.84 Allied Properties Real Estate Investment Trust*

Symbol - AP.UN **Exchange** - TSX **CUSIP** - 019456
Head Office - 1700-134 Peter St, Toronto, ON, M5V 2H2 **Telephone** - (416) 977-9002 **Fax** - (416) 306-8704
Website - www.alliedreit.com
Email - cwilliams@alliedreit.com
Investor Relations - Cecilia C. Williams (416) 977-9002
Auditors - Deloitte LLP C.A., Toronto, Ont.
Lawyers - Aird & Berlis LLP, Toronto, Ont.
Transfer Agents - TSX Trust Company, Toronto, Ont.
FP500 Revenue Ranking - 460
Employees - 386 at Dec. 31, 2022
Profile - (Ont. 2002) Owns, operates and develops a portfolio of urban office and retail properties in the downtown areas of Toronto, Kitchener and Ottawa, Ont.; Montreal, Que.; Edmonton and Calgary, Alta.; and Vancouver, B.C.
At June 30, 2023, the trust had 217 investment properties, consisting of 199 rental properties, three of which are partially under development; 13 development properties; and five properties held for sale (sold on Aug. 16, 2023).
The trust's rental portfolio at June 30, 2023:

Properties	Office[1]	Retail[1]
Toronto (117[2])	4,503,355	622,106
Kitchener (5)	536,493	25,810
Ottawa (2)	224,048	7,222
Montreal (31)	5,978,204	229,992
Calgary (31)	1,158,203	215,843
Vancouver (13)	824,860	153,104
	13,225,163	1,254,077

[1] Gross leasable area (sq. ft.).
[2] Includes 13 ancillary residential properties and 10 ancillary parking facilities with 840 spaces.
The 13 development properties and three rental properties partially under development had an estimated gross leasable area on completion of 2,860,053 sq. ft. and are located in Toronto (6), Kitchener (1), Montreal (5), Edmonton (1) and Vancouver (3).
The five properties held for sale were located in Montreal (1) and Toronto (4), including three urban data centres.
On June 12, 2023, the trust completed its conversion from a closed-end trust to an open-end trust.
In July 2022, the trust acquired 121 John Street, consisting of 2,444 sq. ft. of office space and 798 sq. ft. of retail space, in Toronto, Ont., for $4,350,000.

Recent Merger and Acquisition Activity

Status: completed **Revised:** Aug. 16, 2023
UPDATE: The transaction was completed. PREVIOUS: Allied Properties Real Estate Investment Trust agreed to sell its Toronto data centre portfolio to Tokyo, Japan-based KDDI Corporation for $1.35 billion. The portfolio included freehold interests in 151 Front St. West and 905 King St. West, and a leasehold interest in 250 Front St. West. The transaction was expected to be completed by the end of the third quarter of 2023, and was subject to Competition Act approval and customary closing conditions.
Status: completed **Revised:** Oct. 31, 2022
UPDATE: The transaction was completed. PREVIOUS: Allied Properties Real Estate Investment Trust agreed to acquire 700 Rue Saint-Hubert in Montreal, Que., from Jesta Group for $121,400,000. The property is an office building being developed by Jesta Group, consisting of 145,743 sq. ft. of gross leasable area and 145 underground parking spaces. The transaction was expected to close upon completion of the development of the building in the second half of 2022, subject to various closing conditions.
Status: completed **Announced:** Aug. 16, 2022
Allied Properties Real Estate Investment Trust sold a 44,671-sq.-ft. office property in Toronto, Ont. (100 Lombard Street) for $26,000,000.
Status: completed **Announced:** June 30, 2022
Allied Properties Real Estate Investment Trust sold a 33,731-sq.-ft. office property in Toronto, Ont. (662 King Street West) for $38,954,000.
Status: completed **Announced:** June 30, 2022
Allied Properties Real Estate Investment Trust sold a 6,934-sq.-ft. retail property in Toronto, Ont. (668 King Street West) for $9,991,000.
Status: completed **Announced:** Apr. 8, 2022
Allied Properties Real Estate Investment Trust acquired a 5,935-sq.-ft. retail property in Toronto, Ont. (540 King Street West) for $25,000,000.
Status: completed **Revised:** Mar. 31, 2022
UPDATE: The transaction was completed. PREVIOUS: Choice Properties Real Estate Investment Trust agreed to sell six urban office properties to Allied Properties Real Estate Investment Trust for $733,810,000, consisting of the issuance of $550,660,000 (11,809,145) of class B limited partnership units of a subsidiary limited partnership at $46.63 per unit and a $200,000,000 promissory note. The properties were

located at 110 Yonge Street (50% interest), 525 University Avenue and 175 Bloor Street East (50% interest) in Toronto, Ont.; 1508 West Broadway and 1185 West Georgia Street in Vancouver, B.C.; and 1010 Sherbrooke Street West in Montreal, Que.

Trustees - Michael R. Emory, founder & exec. chr., Toronto, Ont.; Cecilia C. Williams, pres. & CEO, Toronto, Ont.; Jennifer A. Tory‡, Toronto, Ont.; Matthew Andrade, Calgary, Alta.; Kay Brekken, Whistler, B.C.; Thomas G. (Tom) Burns, Toronto, Ont.; Hazel Claxton, Toronto, Ont.; Lois Cormack, Bradford, Ont.; Antonia (Toni) Rossi, Toronto, Ont.; Stephen L. Sender, Thornhill, Ont.

Other Exec. Officers - Douglas (Doug) Riches, exec. v-p, special opers.; Jean-François Burdet, sr. v-p, Montreal & Ottawa; David Doull, sr. v-p, people & brand; Tim Low, sr. v-p, leasing; J. P. Mackay, sr. v-p, natl. opers.; Nanthini Mahalingam, sr. v-p & CFO; Anne E. Miatello, sr. v-p, gen. counsel & corp. sec.; Travis Vokey, sr. v-p, tech. & innovation; Scott Brasil, v-p & assoc. gen. counsel; Jo Flatt, v-p, corp. planning & sustainability; Hersha Leung, v-p, technical srvcs. & const.; John Lindsay, v-p, devel.; Ana Lopes, v-p, lease documentation; Assmae Loudyi, v-p, portfolio opers., Montreal & Ottawa; Gord Oughton, v-p, leasing, central & western Canada; Christopher Thorne, v-p, leasing, Montreal & Ottawa; Leslie Chen, contr.

‡ Lead trustee

Capital Stock

	Authorized (shs.)	Outstanding (shs.)[1]
Trust Unit	unlimited	127,955,983
Special Voting Unit	unlimited	11,809,145
Class B LP Unit	unlimited	11,809,145[2]

[1] At July 26, 2023

[2] Held by Choice Properties Real Estate Investment Trust.

Trust Unit - One vote per unit.

Special Voting Unit - Issued to holders of class B limited partnership units of subsidiary Allied Properties Exchangeable Limited Partnership. Each special voting unit entitles the holder to a number of votes at unitholder meetings equal to the number of trust units into which the class B limited partnership units are exchangeable.

Class B Limited Partnership Unit - Entitled to distributions equal to those provided to trust units. Exchangeable into trust units on a 1-for-1 basis at any time by the holder. Classified as non-controlling interest.

Options - At Dec. 31, 2022, options were outstanding to purchase 1,717,043 trust units at a weighted average exercise price of $41.98 per unit with a weighted average remaining contractual life of 6.13 years.

Normal Course Issuer Bid - The company plans to make normal course purchases of up to 12,582,628 trust units representing 10% of the public float. The bid commenced on Feb. 24, 2023, and expires on Feb. 23, 2024.

Major Shareholder - Widely held at Mar. 21, 2023.

Price Range - AP.UN/TSX

Year	Volume	High	Low	Close
2022	70,091,479	$48.89	$24.77	$25.60
2021	62,775,419	$46.55	$35.40	$43.95
2020	96,503,326	$60.14	$31.49	$37.83
2019	53,864,773	$54.98	$43.06	$52.07
2018	41,035,141	$46.07	$38.71	$44.32

Recent Close: $20.80

Capital Stock Changes - During 2022, trust units were issued as follows: 211,800 under an at-the-market program and 6,332 on exercise of options.

Dividends

AP.UN unit Ra $1.80 pa M est. Feb. 15, 2023
Prev. Rate: $1.75 est. Feb. 15, 2022
Prev. Rate: $1.70 est. Feb. 16, 2021
Prev. Rate: $1.65 est. Feb. 18, 2020

Long-Term Debt - Outstanding at Dec. 31, 2022:

Construction loans[1]	$223,725,000
Revolv. credit facility[2]	440,000,000
Promissory note[3]	195,673,000
Term loans[4]	649,026,000
Debs.[5]	2,589,939,000
Mtges. payable[6]	112,822,000
	4,211,185,000
Less: Current portion	346,929,000
	3,864,256,000

[1] Consist of a $50,472,000 loan, bearing interest at prime or bankers' acceptance plus 1.2% with a standby fee of 0.2% and a letter of credit fee of 1% and due June 2023; a $85,485,000 loan, bearing interest at prime plus 0.35% or bankers' acceptance plus 1.35% with a standby fee of 0.25% and a letter of credit fee of 1% and due August 2023; a $71,762,000 loan, bearing interest at prime plus 0.45% or bankers' acceptance plus 1.45% with a standby fee of 0.25% and a letter of credit fee of 1% and due December 2024; and a $16,006,000 loan, bearing interest at prime plus 0.35% or bankers' acceptance plus 1.35% with a standby fee of 0.27% and a letter of credit fee of 1% and due December 2025.

[2] Borrowings from a $600,000,000 revolving credit facility, bearing interest at prime plus 0.2% or bankers' acceptance plus 1.2% with a standby fee of 0.24% and due January 2025.

[3] Bears interest of 1% for 2022 and 2% for 2023.

[4] $250,000,000 principal amount of 3.496% term loan due January 2024; and $400,000,000 principal amount of 4.865% term loan due October 2025.

[5] $200,000,000 principal amount of 3.636% series C debentures due April 2025; $300,000,000 principal amount of 3.394% series D debentures due August 2029; $300,000,000 principal amount of 3.113% series E debentures due April 2027; $400,000,000 principal amount of 3.117% series F debentures due February 2030; $300,000,000 principal amount of 3.131% series G debentures due May 2028; $600,000,000 principal amount of 1.726% series H debentures due February 2026; and $500,000,000 principal amount of 3.095% series I debentures due February 2032.

[6] Bear interest at a weighted average contractual rate of 3.37% at Dec. 31, 2022.

Minimum mortgage repayments were reported as follows:

2023	$15,299,000
2024	49,197,000
2025	6,423,000
2026	21,834,000
2027	487,000
Thereafter	19,750,000

Wholly Owned Subsidiaries

Allied Properties Exchangeable GP Inc., Canada.

Allied Properties Exchangeable Limited Partnership, Canada.
Represents class A limited partnership units.

Allied Properties Management GP Limited, Ont.

Allied Properties Management Trust, Ont.

- 100% int. in **Allied Properties Management Limited Partnership**, Canada.

Financial Statistics

Periods ended:	12m Dec. 31/22[A]		12m Dec. 31/21[oA]
	$000s	%Chg	$000s
Total revenue	**519,468**	**+10**	**472,799**
Rental operating expense	224,260		204,792
General & admin. expense	23,195		26,407
Operating expense	**247,455**	**+7**	**231,199**
Operating income	**272,013**	**+13**	**241,600**
Investment income	(3,161)		(451)
Deprec. & amort.	1,325		1,167
Finance income	32,080		28,023
Finance costs, gross	72,802		114,196
Write-downs/write-offs	(15,729)		nil
Pre-tax income	**174,669**	**-47**	**331,381**
Net inc bef disc ops, eqhldrs	168,161		331,381
Net inc bef disc ops, NCI	6,508		nil
Net inc. bef. disc. opers	**174,669**	**-47**	**331,381**
Disc. opers., equity hldrs	200,694		111,770
Income from disc. opers	200,694		111,770
Net income	**375,363**	**-15**	**443,151**
Net inc. for equity hldrs	**368,855**	**-17**	**443,151**
Net inc. for non-cont. int	**6,508**	**n.a.**	**nil**
Cash & equivalent	20,990		22,548
Accounts receivable	48,793		31,875
Current assets	1,812,744		310,175
Long-term investments	7,089		124,790
Fixed assets	25,145		29,352
Income-producing props	8,139,565		8,288,275
Properties under devel	1,529,440		1,238,830
Residential inventory	187,272		170,980
Property interests, net	9,880,097		9,726,270
Total assets	**11,906,350**	**+15**	**10,384,691**
Accts. pay. & accr. liabs	268,956		203,861
Current liabilities	824,967		339,596
Long-term debt, gross	4,211,185		3,453,284
Long-term debt, net	3,864,256		3,417,138
Long-term lease liabilities	50,851		157,550
Shareholders' equity	6,581,166		6,425,772
Non-controlling interest	541,672		nil
Cash from oper. activs	**321,193**	**+33**	**241,114**
Cash from fin. activs	331,598		476,844
Cash from invest. activs	(654,349)		(740,922)
Net cash position	**20,990**	**-7**	**22,548**
Capital expenditures	(398,174)		(428,248)
Increase in property	(190,753)		(288,887)
Decrease in property	89,691		71,592
	$		$
Earns. per sh. bef disc opers*	1.23		2.60
Earnings per share*	2.69		3.48
Cash flow per share*	2.35		1.89
Funds from opers. per sh.*	2.44		1.99
Adj. funds from opers. per sh.*	2.17		2.09
Cash divd. per share*	1.75		1.70
Total divd. per share*	**1.75**		**1.70**
	shs		shs
No. of shs. o/s*	127,955,983		127,737,851
Avg. no. of shs. o/s*	136,880,675		127,305,384
	%		%
Net profit margin	33.62		70.09
Return on equity	2.59		5.26
Return on assets	2.22		4.50
No. of employees (FTEs)	386		355

* Trust unit
[o] Restated
[A] Reported in accordance with IFRS

Latest Results

Periods ended:	6m June 30/23[A]		6m June 30/22[oA]
	$000s	%Chg	$000s
Total revenue	274,627	+9	251,721
Net inc. bef. disc. opers	(20,621)	n.a.	154,390
Income from disc. opers	133,203		132,838
Net income	112,582	-61	287,228
Net inc. for equity hldrs	107,585	-62	285,059
Net inc. for non-cont. int	4,997		2,169
	$		$
Earns. per sh. bef. disc. opers.*	(0.18)		1.14
Earnings per share*	0.77		2.14

* Trust unit
[o] Restated
[A] Reported in accordance with IFRS

Historical Summary
(as originally stated)

Fiscal Year	Total Rev. $000s	Net Inc. Bef. Disc. $000s	EPS* $
2022[A]	519,468	174,669	1.23
2021[A]	568,886	443,151	3.48
2020[A]	560,505	500,729	4.02
2019[A]	541,450	629,223	5.60
2018[A]	436,396	540,276	5.53

* Trust unit
[A] Reported in accordance with IFRS

A.85 Alpha Cognition Inc.

Symbol - ACOG **Exchange** - CSE **CUSIP** - 02074J

Head Office - 301-1228 Hamilton St, Vancouver, BC, V6B 6L2 **Telephone** - (604) 837-7990

Website - alphacognition.com

Email - mmcfadden@alphacognition.com

Investor Relations - Michael McFadden (604) 564-9244

Auditors - Manning Elliott LLP C.A., Vancouver, B.C.

Transfer Agents - Computershare Trust Company of Canada Inc., Vancouver, B.C.

Employees - 6 at Nov. 14, 2022

Profile - (B.C. 2017) Developing treatments for neurodegenerative diseases such as Alzheimer's Disease, cognitive impairment with traumatic brain injury and Amyotrophic Lateral Sclerosis (ALS).

Lead product under development is ALPHA-1062, a patented new chemical entity being developed as a new acetylcholine esterase inhibitor for the treatment of Alzheimer's disease, with minimal gastrointestinal side effects and novel routes of administration. ALPHA-1062 is also being developed in combination with memantine to treat moderate to severe Alzheimer's dementia and in a nasal spray formulation to treat traumatic brain injury. ALPHA-1062 has demonstrated safety and improved tolerability in human clinical trials.

Other products under development include ALPHA-0602, a gene therapy program delivering progranulin, a neurotrophic protein, and is under preclinical development for the treatment of ALS and has received Orphan Drug Designation from the U.S. FDA; and ALPHA-0702 and ALPHA-0802, a granulin epithelin motifs (GEMs) derived from full length progranulin, which have therapeutic potential across multiple neurodegenerative diseases.

Has offices in Vancouver, B.C., and Texas, and pre-clinical laboratory facilities in Charlottetown, P.E.I.

In May 2023, the company proposed to out-license ALPHA-1062IN (Intranasal) for treating cognitive impairment with mild traumatic brain injury (mtbi) to a new entity (TBI Company). **Spartan Securities LLC** has agreed to act as agent, on a best efforts basis, for financing TBI Company in exchange for an initial 37.5% interest in TBI Company on completion of a minimum US$1,000,000 financing. Resulting ownership of TBI Company would be as follows: 37.5% for Spartan, 47.5% for the company and 15% for key management of TBI Company. The out-licensing plan would permit the company to remain focused on advancing ALPHA-1062 for use in the treatment of symptoms of Alzheimer's disease.

Common delisted from TSX-VEN, May 1, 2023.

Common listed on CSE, May 1, 2023.

Predecessor Detail - Name changed from Crystal Bridge Enterprises Inc., Mar. 31, 2021, pursuant to Qualifying Transaction reverse takeover acquisition of Alpha Cognition Inc. (renmaed Alpha Cognition Canada Inc.); basis 1 new for 7.14 old shs.

Directors - Len Mertz, chr., Tex.; Michael McFadden, CEO, Tex.; Kenneth A. (Ken) Cawkell, corp. sec., New Westminster, B.C.; Rajeev (Rob) Bakshi, White Rock, B.C.; John Havens, Tex.; Phillip Mertz, Va.

Other Exec. Officers - Don Kalkofen, CFO; Lauren D'Angelo, chief comml. officer; Dr. Denis Kay, chief scientific officer

Capital Stock

	Authorized (shs.)	Outstanding (shs.)[1]
Preferred	unlimited	7,916,380
Restricted Vtg.	unlimited	7,000,000
Common	unlimited	87,950,664

[1] At June 26, 2023

Preferred - Convertible into common shares on a one-for-one basis at holder's option and automatically under certain conditions. One vote per share.

Restricted Voting - Issued to U.S. residents. Convertible into common shares on a one-for-one basis at holder's option, subject to conditions. One vote per share except for election or removal of directors.
Common - One vote per share.
Major Shareholder - Len Mertz held 11.05% interest at May 15, 2023.

Price Range - ACOG/TSX-VEN (D)

Year	Volume	High	Low	Close
2022	4,275,879	$1.19	$0.24	$0.30
2021	4,922,948	$2.49	$0.75	$1.08
2020	12,745	$0.79	$0.71	$0.71
2019	77,402	$1.43	$0.43	$0.75
2018	14,810	$1.29	$0.79	$1.07

Consolidation: 1-for-7.14 cons. in Mar. 2021
Recent Close: $0.35
Capital Stock Changes - In February and March 2023, private placement of 23,747,648 units (1 common share & 1 warrant) at Cdn$0.255 per unit was completed, with warrants exercisable at Cdn$0.39 per share for five years. In May 2023, private placement of 29,545,455 common shares at US$0.22 per unit was announced, with warrants exercisable at US$0.31 per share for three years.
During 2022, 416,519 common shares were issued on exercise of options.

Wholly Owned Subsidiaries

Alpha Cognition Canada Inc., Vancouver, B.C.
- 100% int. in **Alpha Cognition USA Inc.**, Tex.

Financial Statistics

Periods ended:	12m Dec. 31/22[A]		12m Dec. 31/21[A1]
	US$000s	%Chg	US$000s
Research & devel. expense	8,817		7,973
General & admin expense	3,407		2,526
Stock-based compensation	1,151		980
Operating expense	**13,375**	**+17**	**11,479**
Operating income	**(13,375)**	**n.a.**	**(11,479)**
Deprec., depl. & amort.	91		90
Finance income	2		2
Finance costs, gross	173		529
Pre-tax income	**(12,115)**	**n.a.**	**(19,545)**
Net income	**(12,115)**	**n.a.**	**(19,545)**
Cash & equivalent	2,084		11,302
Current assets	2,333		12,171
Fixed assets, net	4		13
Intangibles, net	614		697
Total assets	**2,951**	**-77**	**12,880**
Accts. pay. & accr. liabs	2,845		727
Current liabilities	4,057		1,803
Long-term debt, gross	1,211		1,076
Shareholders' equity	(1,320)		9,030
Cash from oper. activs	**(9,242)**	**n.a.**	**(9,879)**
Cash from fin. activs	25		14,878
Cash from invest. activs	(5)		459
Net cash position	**2,084**	**-82**	**11,302**
Capital expenditures	(5)		(14)
	US$		US$
Earnings per share*	(0.18)		(0.37)
Cash flow per share*	(0.14)		(0.19)
	shs		shs
No. of shs. o/s*	61,023,450		60,606,931
Avg. no. of shs. o/s*	67,972,194		53,333,061
	%		%
Net profit margin	n.a.		n.a.
Return on equity	n.m.		(432.12)
Return on assets	(150.87)		(179.18)

* Common
[A] Reported in accordance with IFRS
[1] Results reflect the Mar. 22, 2021, Qualifying Transaction reverse takeover acquisition of (old) Alpha Cognition Inc.

Latest Results

Periods ended:	3m Mar. 31/23[A]		3m Mar. 31/22[A]
	US$000s	%Chg	US$000s
Net income	(1,861)	n.a.	(2,913)
	US$		US$
Earnings per share*	(0.02)		(0.04)

* Common
[A] Reported in accordance with IFRS

Historical Summary
(as originally stated)

Fiscal Year	Oper. Rev. US$000s	Net Inc. Bef. Disc. US$000s	EPS* US$
2022[A]	nil	(12,115)	(0.18)
2021[A]	nil	(19,545)	(0.37)
2020[A1]	nil	(5,784)	n.a.
2019[A]	nil	(6,607)	n.a.
2018[A]	nil	(3,030)	n.a.

* Common
[A] Reported in accordance with IFRS
[1] Results for 2020 and prior years pertains to (old) Alpha Cognition Inc.
Note: Adjusted throughout for 1-for-7.14 cons. in Mar. 2021

A.86 AlphaGen Intelligence Corp.

Symbol - AIC **Exchange** - CSE **CUSIP** - 02080J
Head Office - 1930-1177 Hastings St W, Vancouver, BC, V6E 4T5 **Telephone** - (604) 359-1256
Website - alphametaverse.com
Email - ir@alphametaverse.com
Investor Relations - Investor Relations (604) 398-3379
Auditors - De Visser Gray LLP C.A., Vancouver, B.C.
Transfer Agents - Odyssey Trust Company, Vancouver, B.C.
Profile - (B.C. 2019) Focuses on the development of artificial intelligence (AI) for gaming, entertainment and the metaverse.
The company holds a portfolio of assets in gaming, generative AI, technology and content production services: Shape Immersive, a full-service metaverse studio building the future of web3 gaming and virtual retail experiences for Fortune 500 companies and beyond through 3D, non-fungible tokens (NFT), XR and game production; MANA, a Software-as-a-Service solution that offers a fully customizable white label tournament engine that supports Web3 assets such as cryptocurrencies and "Play 2 Earn" games; and GamerzArena, an eSports platform available online and mobile app which hosts daily, weekly and monthly contests and tournaments where gamers can compete for cash and prizes, with the ability to live-stream their gameplay.

Recent Merger and Acquisition Activity

Status: completed **Revised:** May 5, 2022
UPDATE: The transaction was completed. PREVIOUS: Alpha Metaverse Technologies Inc. entered into a letter of intent to acquire private Vancouver, B.C.-based Shape Immersive Entertainment Inc. for $1,000,000 cash and issuance of 14,840,000 class A common shares. Shape designs and develops metaverse experiences, including 3D non-fungible tokens (NFTs), holograms, augmented and virtual reality, and play-to-earn games, for clients in various industries. Apr. 13, 2022 - A definitive agreement was entered into.
Predecessor Detail - Name changed from Alpha Metaverse Technologies Inc., June 15, 2023.
Directors - Jonathan Anastas, chr., Calif.; Brian Wilneff, CEO, B.C.; Eli Dusenbury, CFO, Vancouver, B.C.; Mike Aujla, Vancouver, B.C.; Harwinder Parmar, Vancouver, B.C.
Other Exec. Officers - Adam Morrison, pres.

Capital Stock

	Authorized (shs.)	Outstanding (shs.)[1]
Cl.A Common	unlimited	90,823,380
Cl.B Common	unlimited	nil

[1] At May 30, 2023
Class A Common - One vote per share.
Class B Common - Non-voting.
Major Shareholder - Widely held at Mar. 30, 2022.

Price Range - AIC/CSE

Year	Volume	High	Low	Close
2022	21,671,002	$0.46	$0.04	$0.06
2021	28,760,255	$0.99	$0.20	$0.25

Recent Close: $0.12
Capital Stock Changes - In March 2022, private placement of 11,020,500 units (1 class A common share & 1 warrant) at 25¢ per unit was completed. On May 5, 2022, 14,840,000 class A common shares were issued pursuant to the acquisition of Shape Immersive Entertainment Inc. Also during fiscal 2022, class A common shares were issued as follows: 3,214,239 for debt settlement and 1,442,143 under restricted share unit plan.

Wholly Owned Subsidiaries

Esports Enterprises, Inc., Del.
- 100% int. in **GamerzArena, LLC**, Del.

Shape Immersive Entertainment Inc., Vancouver, B.C.

Financial Statistics

Periods ended:	12m June 30/22[A]		12m June 30/21[A1]
	$000s	%Chg	$000s
Operating revenue	**210**	**n.m.**	**17**
Cost of goods sold	108		nil
General & admin expense	4,146		2,897
Stock-based compensation	1,886		1,911
Other operating expense	119		35
Operating expense	**6,259**	**+29**	**4,843**
Operating income	**(6,049)**	**n.a.**	**(4,826)**
Deprec., depl. & amort.	716		474
Write-downs/write-offs	(1,806)		(18)
Pre-tax income	**(8,833)**	**n.a.**	**(5,340)**
Net income	**(8,833)**	**n.a.**	**(5,340)**
Cash & equivalent	1,208		1,717
Accounts receivable	73		nil
Current assets	1,459		3,319
Fixed assets, net	nil		2
Intangibles, net	2,425		2,210
Total assets	**3,884**	**-30**	**5,531**
Accts. pay. & accr. liabs	724		941
Current liabilities	1,224		941
Long-term debt, gross	60		nil
Long-term debt, net	60		nil
Shareholders' equity	2,601		4,590
Cash from oper. activs	**(2,116)**	**n.a.**	**(3,920)**
Cash from fin. activs	2,450		5,820
Cash from invest. activs	(843)		(192)
Net cash position	**1,208**	**-30**	**1,717**
	$		$
Earnings per share*	(0.13)		(0.11)
Cash flow per share*	(0.03)		(0.08)
	shs		shs
No. of shs. o/s*	90,823,380		60,306,498
Avg. no. of shs. o/s*	67,781,626		49,239,705
	%		%
Net profit margin	n.m.		n.m.
Return on equity	(245.67)		(213.69)
Return on assets	(187.64)		(158.11)

* Cl.A Common
[A] Reported in accordance with IFRS
[1] Shares and per share figures adjusted to reflect 2-for-1 share split in August 2020.

Latest Results

Periods ended:	3m Sept. 30/22[A]		3m Sept. 30/21[A]
	$000s	%Chg	$000s
Operating revenue	109	n.m.	4
Net income	(338)	n.a.	(2,216)
	$		$
Earnings per share*	(0.00)		(0.04)

* Cl.A Common
[A] Reported in accordance with IFRS

Historical Summary
(as originally stated)

Fiscal Year	Oper. Rev. $000s	Net Inc. Bef. Disc. $000s	EPS* $
2022[A]	210	(8,833)	(0.13)
2021[A1]	17	(5,340)	(0.11)
2020[A1]	nil	(2,323)	(0.07)
2019[A1,2]	nil	(258)	(0.04)

* Cl.A Common
[A] Reported in accordance with IFRS
[1] Shares and per share figures adjusted to reflect 2-for-1 share split in August 2020.
[2] 4 months ended June 30, 2019.

A.87 Alphinat inc.

Symbol - NPA **Exchange** - TSX-VEN **CUSIP** - 02081Y
Head Office - 680-2000 rue Peel, Montréal, QC, H3A 2W5 **Telephone** - (514) 398-9799 **Toll-free** - (877) 773-9799 **Fax** - (514) 398-9353
Website - www.alphinat.com
Email - info@alphinat.com
Investor Relations - Curtis Page (514) 398-9799 ext. 225
Auditors - Raymond Chabot Grant Thornton LLP C.A., Montréal, Qué.
Transfer Agents - Computershare Trust Company of Canada Inc., Montréal, Qué.
Profile - (Can. 2004) Offers SmartGuide®, an enterprise application development tool that enables organizations to easily build, deploy and manage web and mobile applications that smartly guide users through complex processes.
SmartGuide® is a drag-and-drop development platform complete with features that many other solutions require developers to code, making applications easier to build, test and maintain. The platform also provides easy support for accessibility standards with translation capacity supporting multiple languages and can automatically generate customizable documentation of the application being built. The product

is marketed to the public, healthcare, banking, insurance, telecommunications and other sectors.

Focuses on five main areas of solution development: SmartGuide® Grants and Contributions solution, which offers financial program creations for applications, adjudications and payments for federal, state and municipal clients creating calls for grants; SmartGuide® Portal Edition for Dynamics 3651, which optimizes the way that clients create and deploy online services on top of Microsoft Dynamics 365 CRM solutions; SmartGuide® GreenHouse Gas Registry, which is a green fintech solution allowing governments and industry to work together in reducing the harmful effects of greenhouse gases; SmartGuide® Claims, which offers unparalleled productivity to federal, state and municipal clients for financial claims applications, adjudication and settlements for financial compensation and class action settlements with customizable citizen-facing services and internal applications; and SmartGuide® CIVIC Portal, CIVIC Portal for Permits and Licensing and SmartGuide® Municipal Cloud, which are Municipal Cloud and on-premises solutions front ending partner solutions and other digital services for improved user experience for both the client cities and their citizens.

Directors - Michel Lemoine, chr., emeritus, Montréal, Qué.; Eric David, chr., Toronto, Ont.; Curtis Page, pres. & CEO, Ottawa, Ont.; Edwin (Ed) Shepherdson, Ottawa, Ont.; Benoit Ste-Marie, Montréal, Qué.; Sridhar (Sri) Subramanian, Markham, Ont.

Other Exec. Officers - Marc Chartrand, CFO; Denis Michaud, v-p & chief solution & security officer

Capital Stock

	Authorized (shs.)	Outstanding (shs.)[1]
Common	unlimited	63,148,956

[1] At Jan. 20, 2023

Major Shareholder - Andrée Lecoq held 11.96% interest at Jan. 20, 2023.

Price Range - NPA/TSX-VEN

Year	Volume	High	Low	Close
2022	2,520,070	$0.10	$0.05	$0.06
2021	6,891,478	$0.12	$0.06	$0.07
2020	3,538,250	$0.08	$0.04	$0.06
2019	1,801,518	$0.06	$0.04	$0.04
2018	4,487,307	$0.12	$0.04	$0.04

Recent Close: $0.05

Capital Stock Changes - There were no changes to capital stock from fiscal 2020 to fiscal 2022, inclusive.

Financial Statistics

Periods ended:	12m Aug. 31/22[A]		12m Aug. 31/21[A]
	$000s	%Chg	$000s
Operating revenue	**1,651**	**+6**	**1,558**
Cost of sales	290		333
Salaries & benefits	1,126		935
Stock-based compensation	14		75
Operating expense	**1,430**	**+6**	**1,343**
Operating income	**221**	**+3**	**215**
Deprec., depl. & amort.	75		77
Finance costs, gross	72		66
Pre-tax income	**113**	**+23**	**92**
Net income	**113**	**+23**	**92**
Cash & equivalent	7		nil
Accounts receivable	460		392
Current assets	500		453
Fixed assets, net	6		3
Right-of-use assets	124		199
Intangibles, net	1		4
Total assets	**631**	**-4**	**658**
Bank indebtedness	nil		22
Accts. pay. & accr. liabs	952		986
Current liabilities	1,306		1,388
Long-term debt, gross	48		162
Long-term debt, net	48		42
Long-term lease liabilities	70		147
Shareholders' equity	(792)		(919)
Cash from oper. activs	**254**	**+647**	**34**
Cash from fin. activs	(223)		(118)
Cash from invest. activs	(5)		(1)
Net cash position	**7**	**n.a.**	**(19)**
Capital expenditures	(5)		(1)
	$		$
Earnings per share*	0.00		0.00
Cash flow per share*	0.00		0.00
	shs		shs
No. of shs. o/s*	63,148,956		63,148,956
Avg. no. of shs. o/s*	63,148,956		63,148,956
	%		%
Net profit margin	6.84		5.91
Return on equity	n.m.		n.m.
Return on assets	28.70		26.07
Foreign sales percent	12		16

* Common

[A] Reported in accordance with IFRS

Latest Results

Periods ended:	3m Nov. 30/22[A]		3m Nov. 30/21[A]
	$000s	%Chg	$000s
Operating revenue	366	-9	403
Net income	10	-92	122
	$		$
Earnings per share*	0.00		0.00

* Common

[A] Reported in accordance with IFRS

Historical Summary
(as originally stated)

Fiscal Year	Oper. Rev. $000s	Net Inc. Bef. Disc. $000s	EPS* $
2022[A]	1,651	113	0.00
2021[A]	1,558	92	0.00
2020[A]	1,372	128	0.00
2019[A]	1,299	1	0.00
2018[A]	1,117	(347)	(0.01)

* Common

[A] Reported in accordance with IFRS

A.88 Alset Capital Inc.

Symbol - KSUM.H **Exchange** - TSX-VEN **CUSIP** - 02115L

Head Office - 488-1090 Georgia St W, Vancouver, BC, V6E 3V7 **Telephone** - (250) 307-2900 **Toll-free** - (844) 927-6278

Email - morganrgood@gmail.com

Investor Relations - Morgan Good (604) 715-4751

Auditors - Davidson & Company LLP C.A., Vancouver, B.C.

Transfer Agents - Endeavor Trust Corporation, Vancouver, B.C.

Profile - (B.C. 2009; orig. Nev., 1999) Seeking new business opportunities.

Formerly provided sports software for youth and amateur adult league teams.

Predecessor Detail - Name changed from ProSmart Enterprises Inc., Feb. 16, 2021; basis 1 new for 10 old shs.

Directors - Morgan Good, CEO, B.C.; Leighton Bocking, Vancouver, B.C.; Jeremy Hanson, B.C.; Zelong (Roger) He, Vancouver, B.C.; Vikas Ranjan, Toronto, Ont.

Other Exec. Officers - Anu Thomas, CFO; Greg Bobolo, exec. v-p, sports content & media

Capital Stock

	Authorized (shs.)	Outstanding (shs.)[1]
Preferred	unlimited	nil
Common	unlimited	13,155,925

[1] At Aug. 17, 2023

Major Shareholder - Widely held at Nov. 5, 2021.

Price Range - KSUM.H/TSX-VEN

Year	Volume	High	Low	Close
2022	210,827	$0.21	$0.04	$0.06
2021	817,998	$1.20	$0.16	$0.21
2020	66,641	$1.40	$0.20	$1.20
2018	606,564	$20.00	$0.70	$0.80

Consolidation: 1-for-2 cons. in Aug. 2023; 1-for-10 cons. in Feb. 2021

Recent Close: $0.04

Capital Stock Changes - On Aug. 17, 2023, common shares were consolidated on a 1-for-2 basis.

In October 2021, 14,444,444 units (1 common share & 1 warrant) were issued at 9¢ per unit for debt settlement and private placement of 8,333,366 units (1 common share & 1 warrant) at 9¢ per unit was completed, with warrants exercisable at 12¢ per share for one year.

Financial Statistics

Periods ended:	12m Sept. 30/21[A]		12m Sept. 30/20[A]
	$000s	%Chg	$000s
Salaries & benefits	nil		296
Research & devel. expense	nil		27
General & admin expense	239		285
Stock-based compensation	nil		2
Other operating expense	nil		17
Operating expense	**239**	**-62**	**625**
Operating income	**(239)**	**n.a.**	**(625)**
Pre-tax income	**460**	**n.a.**	**(530)**
Net income	**460**	**n.a.**	**(530)**
Cash & equivalent	1		1
Accounts receivable	14		11
Current assets	14		12
Total assets	**14**	**+17**	**12**
Bank indebtedness	1,498		1,446
Accts. pay. & accr. liabs	613		459
Current liabilities	2,112		2,598
Long-term debt, gross	nil		693
Shareholders' equity	(2,097)		(2,587)
Cash from oper. activs	**(9)**	**n.a.**	**(12)**
Cash from fin. activs	13		17
Net cash position	**1**	**0**	**1**
	$		$
Earnings per share*	0.28		(0.40)
Cash flow per share*	(0.01)		(0.01)
	shs		shs
No. of shs. o/s*	1,767,021		1,605,405
Avg. no. of shs. o/s*	1,665,623		1,605,405
	%		%
Net profit margin	n.a.		n.a.
Return on equity	n.m.		n.m.
Return on assets	n.m.		n.m.

* Common

[A] Reported in accordance with IFRS

Historical Summary
(as originally stated)

Fiscal Year	Oper. Rev. $000s	Net Inc. Bef. Disc. $000s	EPS* $
2021[A]	nil	460	0.28
2020[A]	nil	(530)	(0.40)
2019[A]	214	(931)	(0.60)
2018[A]	248	(13,519)	(10.00)
2017[A]	nil	(2,284)	(4.00)

* Common

[A] Reported in accordance with IFRS

Note: Adjusted throughout for 1-for-2 cons. in Aug. 2023; 1-for-10 cons. in Feb. 2021; 1-for-4 cons. in Mar. 2018

A.89 AltaGas Ltd.*

Symbol - ALA **Exchange** - TSX **CUSIP** - 021361

Head Office - 1700-355 4 Ave SW, Calgary, AB, T2P 0J1 **Telephone** - (403) 691-7575 **Toll-free** - (888) 890-2715 **Fax** - (403) 691-7576

Website - www.altagas.ca

Email - jon.morrison@altagas.ca

Investor Relations - Jon Morrison (877) 691-7199

Auditors - Ernst & Young LLP C.A., Calgary, Alta.

Lawyers - Stikeman Elliott LLP, Calgary, Alta.

Transfer Agents - Computershare Trust Company of Canada Inc., Calgary, Alta.

FP500 Revenue Ranking - 43

Employees - 3,045 at Dec. 31, 2022

Profile - (Can. 2010, amalg.) Extracts, gathers, processes and sells natural gas as well as owns and operates rate-regulated natural gas distribution and storage utilities in Canada and the U.S. Also holds interest in natural gas-fired power generation asset in California.

Operations are carried out through three divisions: Midstream, which includes global export terminals, gathering and extraction as well as fractionation and liquid handling of natural gas and natural gas liquids; Utilities, which consists of rate-regulated natural gas distribution and storage utilities that provides safe and affordable energy to residential and commercial customers; and Corporate, which consists of generation and sale of capacity, electricity, ancillary services and related products primarily in California.

Midstream

The Midstream division consists of global export terminals; natural gas gathering & extraction; fractionation and liquids handling; and terminals & storage.

Global export terminal assets include 70% interest in Ridley Island Propane Export Terminal in British Columbia, with export volumes of 92,000 bbl per day and 600,000 bbl of storage capacity; and wholly owned midstream company **Petrogas Energy Corp.**, owner of the Ferndale storage terminal in Washington State, with export volumes of 75,000 bbl per day and 800,000 bbl of storage capacity.

Natural gas gathering & extraction facilities include the Townsend complex in Fort St. John, B.C., which includes a 550-mmcf-per-day gas processing facility and natural gas liquid (NGL) treatment, storage and services infrastructure; the 150-mmcf-per-day Gordondale facility in Bonanza, Alta.; the 120-mmcf-per-day Blair Creek facility in Fort St.

John, B.C.; the Harmattan gas processing complex in Sundre, Alta., with 490-mmcf-per-day sour gas treating, co-stream processing and NGL extraction capacity; the 250-mmcf-per-day Joffre Ethane Extraction Plant in Joffre, Alberta; the 390-mmcf-per-day Edmonton Ethane Extraction Plant in Edmonton, Alta.; 11% interest in the 135-mmcf-per-day Pembina Empress Extraction Plant in Empress, Alta.; and 28.33% interest in the 213-mmcf-per-day processing and extraction assets in the Younger facility in Taylor, B.C.

Fractionation and liquids handling consists of NGL pipelines, treating, storage, truck and rail terminal infrastructure. Assets include the North Pine facility near Fort St. John, B.C., with capacity of 20,000-bbl-per-day fractionation of propane plus NGL mix; the Harmattan gas processing complex in Sundre, Alta., with 35,000-bbl-per-day NGL fractionation capacity, 450-bbl-per-day oil fractionation capacity and 200-tonne-per-day industrial grade carbon dioxide facility; and 50% interest in the 9,750-bbl-per-day fractionation and terminalling assets in the Younger facility in Taylor, B.C.

Terminals and storage business consists of crude oil and NGL assets which provide storage, blending, rail and truck logistical support and waterborne LPG export capabilities. Assets include Griffith terminal in Griffith, Ind., with 12,000-bbl-per-day LPG operational capacity and 700,000-bbl storage capacity; Fort Saskatchewan terminal located in Fort Saskatchewan, Alta., with 25,000-bbl-per-day NGL operational capacity and 180,000-bbl storage capacity; 50% interest in Sarnia facility in Sarnia, Ont., with 2,100,000-bbl crude oil and refined product storage capacity supported by 10,000-bbl-per-day rail loading capacity; 40% interest in Strathcona storage located in Fort Saskatchewan, Alta., with 3,215,500-bbl storage capacity; 50% interest in Sarnia NGL storage facility, with a 6.4 bcf storage capacity connected to the Dawn Hub in eastern Canada; five blending terminals located throughout Alberta and southern Saskatchewan, with an average capacity of 25,700 bbl per day; and owned and leased storage assets across North America to support marketing and distribution and terminal activities, with locations in Yakh, B.C., propane truck terminal, Scranton propane terminal, Guernsey and Edmonton leased crude tanks and various other strategic leased NGL storage at key hubs.

Trucking and wellsite fluids includes three primary trucking entities, which provide transportation related services within the Western Canadian Sedimentary Basin and the United States Pacific northwest by hauling frac fluid, produced water, crude oil and NGLs between producers, terminals, customers and end users; and through wholly owned Petrogas produces and distributes hydrocarbon fluids for fracturing and drilling of oil and gas wells to improve productivity and to resolve oilfield production for downstream producers in two facilities in Sundre and Slave Lake, Alta., with 1,500,000 bbl of processing capacity and 150,000 bbl of storage capacity.

This division also holds a rail logistics network consisting of 4,600 rail cars that the company manages to support liquid petroleum gas and NGL handling; 10% interest in Mountain Valley pipeline (under construction) in Virginia, which has a 2-bcf-per-day NGL transportation capacity from Wetzel cty., W.Va., to Pittsylvania cty., Va.; and 5% equity interest in the Mountain Valley Pipeline Southgate expansion, which would receive gas from Pittsylvania cty., Va., to Rockingham and Alamance ctys., N.C.

Utilities

The Utility division consists of assets that store and deliver natural gas to end users in the U.S., through indirect 100% interests in **Washington Gas Light Company (WGLC)**, which serves 1,200,000 customers in Virginia, Maryland and metropolitan Washington, D.C., area; **SEMCO Energy, Inc.**, which delivers essential energy to 325,000 customers in southern Michigan and Michigan's upper peninsula; and **Hampshire Gas Company**, which provides regulated natural gas storage in West Virginia. Also includes wholly owned **WGL Energy Services Inc.**, which sells natural gas and electricity directly to residential, commercial, and industrial customers in Maryland, Virginia, Delaware, Pennsylvania, Ohio and the District of Columbia.

Corporate

The division includes the 507-MW gas-fired Blythe Energy Center in California; 1 MW of distributed generation in different regions in the United States; and general corporate investment and trading activities.

Operating Statistics

Year ended Dec. 31	2022	2021
Midstream		
Inlet gas processed, mmcf/day[1]	1,268	1,498
NGLs & ethane, bbl/day[2]	56,669	64,319
Export volumes, bbl/day[3]	101,654	89,331
Fractionated volumes, bbl/day	33,602	30,715
Utilities		
End-use deliveries, bcf	164.6	155.9
Transportation deliveries, bcf	126.9	124.5
Service sites	1,704,000	1,689,000

[1] Average for the period.
[2] Total extraction volumes.
[3] Includes propane and butane exported at Ferndale.

Recent Merger and Acquisition Activity

Status: completed **Revised:** Mar. 1, 2023
UPDATE: The transaction was completed. PREVIOUS: AltaGas Ltd. agreed to sell its Alaskan utilities business to TriSummit Utilities Inc., which was owned by Public Sector Pension Investment Board and Alberta Teachers' Retirement Fund Board, for $1.025 billion. The sale included ENSTAR Natural Gas Company, a gas distribution business in Alaska with about 150,000 customers; Alaska Pipeline Co., which operated transmission and distribution pipelines for ENSTAR; 65% indirect interest in Cook Inlet Natural Gas Storage Alaska, LLC, a regulated natural gas storage utility; and other ancillary operations. The transaction was subject to customary closing conditions including regulatory approvals, and was expected to be completed by the first quarter of 2023. Dec. 22, 2022 - The transaction received approval from the Regulatory Commission of Alaska, the last remaining material regulatory closing condition to be satisfied in connection with the sale.

Status: completed **Announced:** July 5, 2022
AltaGas Ltd. acquired Idemitsu Canada Corporation's, a wholly owned subsidiary of Idemitsu Kosan Co., Ltd., 25.97% equity interest in Calgary, Alta.-based Petrogas Energy Corp. for total cash consideration of $285,000,000. As a result, AltaGas owned 100% of Petrogas.

Status: completed **Revised:** May 27, 2022
UPDATE: The transaction was completed for $1,000,000. PREVIOUS: AltaGas Ltd. agreed to sell the 70-MW Brush II gas-fired generation power plant in Colorado for an undisclosed amount. The transaction was expected to close in the second quarter of 2022.

Status: completed **Announced:** Apr. 12, 2022
Tourmaline Oil Corp. acquired the remaining 50% non-operated interest in two Aitken area gas plants in northeastern British Columbia from AltaGas Ltd. for $235,300,000. The plants have a combined processing capacity of 290 mmcf per day.

Predecessor Detail - Succeeded AltaGas Income Trust, July 1, 2010, pursuant to plan of arrangement whereby AltaGas Ltd. was formed to facilitate the conversion of the trust into a corporation and the trust was subsequently dissolved.

Directors - David W. Cornhill, founder, Calgary, Alta.; Pentti O. Karkkainen, chr., West Vancouver, B.C.; Vern D. Yu, pres. & CEO, Calgary, Alta.; Prof. Victoria A. Calvert, Calgary, Alta.; Randall L. (Randy) Crawford, Naples, Fla.; Jon-Al Duplantier, Houston, Tex.; Robert B. (Bob) Hodgins, Calgary, Alta.; Cynthia Johnston, Victoria, B.C.; Phillip R. (Phil) Knoll, Calgary, Alta.; Linda G. Sullivan, Va.; Nancy G. Tower, Calgary, Alta.

Other Exec. Officers - Shaheen Amirali, exec. v-p & chief external affairs & sustainability officer; Corine R. K. Bushfield, exec. v-p & CAO; Fredrick K. Dalena, exec. v-p, comml. strategy & bus. devel.; Bradley B. (Brad) Grant, exec. v-p, chief legal officer & corp. sec.; D. James Harbilas, exec. v-p & CFO; Donald M. (Blue) Jenkins, exec. v-p, pres., utilities & pres., Washington Gas Light Company; Randy W. Toone, exec. v-p & pres., midstream

Capital Stock

	Authorized (shs.)	Outstanding (shs.)[1]
Preferred	unlimited	
Series A		6,746,679
Series B		1,253,321
Series E		8,000,000
Series G		6,885,823
Series H		1,114,177
Common	unlimited	281,721,708

[1] At July 21, 2023

Preferred - Issuable in series and non-voting.

Series A - Entitled to cumulative preferential annual dividends of $0.765 per share payable quarterly to Sept. 30, 2025, and thereafter at a rate reset every five years equal to the five-year Government of Canada bond yield plus 2.66%. Redeemable on Sept. 30, 2025, and on September 30 every five years thereafter at $25 per share plus accrued and unpaid dividends. Convertible at the holder's option, on Sept. 30, 2025, and on September 30 every five years thereafter, into floating rate preferred series B shares on a share-for-share basis, subject to certain conditions.

Series B - Entitled to cumulative preferential dividends payable quarterly equal to the 90-day Canadian Treasury bill rate plus 2.66%. Redeemable on Sept. 30, 2025, and on September 30 every five years thereafter at $25 per share plus accrued and unpaid dividends or at $25.50 per share on any other non-conversion date. Convertible at the holder's option, on Sept. 30, 2025, and on September 30 every five years thereafter, into preferred series A shares on a share-for-share basis, subject to certain conditions.

Series E - Entitled to cumulative preferential annual dividends of $1.3483 per share to Dec. 31, 2023, and thereafter at a rate reset every five years equal to the five-year Government of Canada bond yield plus 3.17%. Redeemable on Dec. 31, 2023, and on December 31 every five years thereafter, for $25 per share plus accrued and unpaid dividends. Convertible on Dec. 31, 2023, and on December 31 every five years thereafter, into floating rate preferred series F shares on a share-for-share basis, subject to certain conditions. The series F shares would pay a quarterly dividend equal to the 90-day Canadian Treasury bill rate plus 3.17%.

Series G - Entitled to cumulative preferential annual dividends of $1.0605 per share to Sept. 30, 2024, and thereafter at a rate reset every five years equal to the five-year Government of Canada bond yield plus 3.06%. Redeemable on Sept. 30, 2024, and on September 30 every five years thereafter, for $25 per share plus accrued and unpaid dividends. Convertible on Sept. 30, 2024, and on September 30 every five year thereafter, into floating rate preferred series H shares on a share-for-share basis, subject to certain conditions.

Series H - Entitled to cumulative preferential dividends payable quarterly equal to the 90-day Canadian Treasury bill rate plus 3.06%. Redeemable on Sept. 30, 2024, and on September 30 every five years thereafter at $25 per share plus accrued and unpaid dividends or at $25.50 per share on any other non-conversion date. Convertible at the holder's option, on Sept. 30, 2024, and on September 30 every five years thereafter, into preferred series G shares on a share-for-share basis, subject to certain conditions.

Common - One vote per share.

Options - At Dec. 31, 2022, options were outstanding to purchase 6,958,139 common shares at prices ranging from $14.52 to $37.86 per share with a weighted average remaining contractual life of 2.72 years.

Preferred Series K (old) - Were entitled to cumulative preferential annual dividends of $1.25 per share to Mar. 31, 2022. Redeemed on Mar. 31, 2022, at $25 per share.

Preferred Series C (old) - Were entitled to cumulative preferential annual dividends of US$1.3225 per share payable quarterly to Sept. 30, 2022. Redeemed on Sept. 30, 2022, at $25 per share.

Major Shareholder - Widely held at Mar. 8, 2023.

Price Range - ALA/TSX

Year	Volume	High	Low	Close
2022	218,715,775	$31.16	$22.05	$23.38
2021	184,012,707	$27.45	$18.51	$27.31
2020	290,358,859	$22.74	$8.71	$18.72
2019	220,649,673	$20.87	$13.25	$19.78
2018	310,326,899	$29.34	$11.87	$13.90

Recent Close: $25.99

Capital Stock Changes - On Mar. 31, 2022, all 12,000,000 preferred shares series K were redeemed at $25 per share. On Sept. 30, 2022, all 8,000,000 preferred shares series C were redeemed at $25 per share. Also during 2022, 1,262,795 common shares were issued on exercise of options.

Dividends

ALA com Ra $1.12 pa Q est. Mar. 31, 2023**[1]
Prev. Rate: $1.06 est. Mar. 31, 2022
Prev. Rate: $0.96 est. Jan. 15, 2019
ALA.PR.A pfd ser A cum. red. exch. Adj. Ra $0.765 pa Q est. Dec. 31, 2020
ALA.PR.E pfd ser E cum. red. exch. Adj. Ra $1.34825 pa Q est. Mar. 29, 2019
ALA.PR.G pfd ser G cum. red. exch. Adj. Ra $1.0605 pa Q est. Dec. 31, 2019
ALA.PR.B pfd ser B cum. red. exch. Fltg. Ra pa Q
$0.45515 Sept. 29/23 $0.45026 June 30/23
$0.41875 Mar. 31/23 $0.3767 Dec. 30/22
Paid in 2023: $1.32416 2022: $1.00733 2021: $0.69436

ALA.PR.H pfd ser H cum. red. exch. Fltg. Ra pa Q
$0.48035 Sept. 29/23 $0.47519 June 30/23
$0.443404 Mar. 31/23 $0.4019 Dec. 30/22
Paid in 2023: $1.398944 2022: $1.107322 2021: $0.794372

pfd ser C cum. red. exch. Adj. Ra US$1.3225 pa Q est. Dec. 29, 2017[2]
US$0.330625**f** Sept. 29/22
pfd ser K cum. red. exch. Adj. Ra $1.25 pa Q est. June 30, 2017[3]
$0.3125**f** Mar. 31/22
[1] Divds. paid monthly prior to March 2022.
[2] Redeemed Sept. 30, 2022 at US$25 per sh.
[3] Redeemed March 31, 2022 at $25 per sh.
** Reinvestment Option **f** Final Payment

Long-Term Debt - Outstanding at Dec. 31, 2022:

Commercial paper due 2024	$386,000,000
Term loan due 2024	450,000,000
Revolv. credit facility due 2026[1]	188,000,000
Revolv. credit facility due 2027[2]	860,000,000
Medium-term notes due to 2047[3]	3,750,000,000
SEMCO debt due to 2050[4]	610,000,000
WGL & Wash. Gas notes due to 2052[5]	2,724,000,000
5.25% subord. series 1 notes due 2082	300,000,000
7.35% subord. series 2 notes due 2082	250,000,000
Finance lease obligs.	22,000,000
Fair value adj. on WGL acq.	79,000,000
Debt issuance costs	(47,000,000)
	9,572,000,000
Less: Current portion	334,000,000
	9,238,000,000

[1] US$150,000,000.
[2] $2 billion.
[3] Bears interest at rates ranging from 1.23% to 45.16%.
[4] Bears interest at rates ranging from 2.45% to 3.15%.
[5] Bears interest at rates ranging from 2.98% to 7.5%.

Note - In May 2023, private placement of $400,000,000 of 4.638% senior unsecured medium term notes due 2026 was completed.

Wholly Owned Subsidiaries

AltaGas Holdings (5) Inc., Canada.
- 0.01% int. in **AltaGas Pacific Partnership**, Alta.

AltaGas Holdings (4) Inc., Canada.
- 100% int. in **AltaGas LPG General Partner Inc.**, Canada.
  - 0.01% int. in **AltaGas LPG Limited Partnership**, B.C.
- 70% int. in **Ridley Island LPG Export GP Inc.**, Canada.
  - 0.01% int. in **Ridley Island LPG Export Limited Partnership**, B.C.

AltaGas Holdings Inc.
- 0.01% int. in **AltaGas Extraction and Transmission Limited Partnership**, Alta.
- 0.01% int. in **AltaGas Northwest Processing Limited Partnership**
- 0.17% int. in **AltaGas Pipeline Partnership**, Alta.

- 0.02% int. in **AltaGas Processing Partnership**, Alta.
- 100% int. in **Taylor Processing Inc.**
  - 0.1% int. in **Harmattan Gas Processing Limited Partnership**, Alta.

AltaGas Services (U.S.) Inc.
- 100% int. in **AltaGas Power Holdings (U.S.) Inc.**, United States.
- 100% int. in **AltaGas Utility Holdings (U.S.) Inc.**
  - 100% int. in **SEMCO Holding Corporation**, Del.
    - 100% int. in **SEMCO Energy, Inc.**, Port Huron, Mich.
  - 100% int. in **Wrangler 1 LLC**, Del.
    - 100% int. in **WGL Holdings, Inc.**, Washington, D.C.
      - 100% int. in **Hampshire Gas Company**, W.Va.
      - 100% int. in **Washington Gas Resources Corporation**, Washington, D.C.
        - 100% int. in **WGL Energy Services, Inc.**, Vienna, Va.
      - 100% int. in **Wrangler SPE LLC**, Del.
        - 100% int. in **Washington Gas Light Company**, Washington, D.C.

Subsidiaries

99.99% int. in **AltaGas Pacific Partnership**, Alta.
- 99.99% int. in **AltaGas LPG Limited Partnership**, B.C.
  - 69.99% int. in **Ridley Island LPG Export Limited Partnership**, B.C.
- 100% int. in **Petrogas Energy Corp.**, Calgary, Alta.
  - 99.99% int. in **Petrogas Holdings Partnership**, Alta.
    - 100% int. in **Petrogas, Inc.**, Del.

99.83% int. in **AltaGas Pipeline Partnership**, Alta.

99.98% int. in **AltaGas Processing Partnership**, Alta.
- 99.99% int. in **AltaGas Extraction and Transmission Limited Partnership**, Alta.
  - 99.9% int. in **Harmattan Gas Processing Limited Partnership**, Alta.
- 99.99% int. in **AltaGas Northwest Processing Limited Partnership**

Note: The preceding list includes only the major related companies in which interests are held.

Financial Statistics

Periods ended:	12m Dec. 31/22[A]		12m Dec. 31/21[A]
	$000s	%Chg	$000s
Operating revenue	**14,087,000**	**+33**	**10,573,000**
Cost of sales	11,138,000		7,708,000
General & admin expense	1,568,000		1,476,000
Operating expense	**12,706,000**	**+38**	**9,184,000**
Operating income	**1,381,000**	**-1**	**1,389,000**
Deprec., depl. & amort.	439,000		422,000
Finance income	17,000		11,000
Finance costs, gross	330,000		275,000
Investment income	13,000		(261,000)
Pre-tax income	**716,000**	**+61**	**446,000**
Income taxes	143,000		106,000
Net income	**573,000**	**+69**	**340,000**
Net inc. for equity hldrs	**523,000**	**+85**	**283,000**
Net inc. for non-cont. int.	**50,000**	**-12**	**57,000**
Cash & equivalent	53,000		63,000
Inventories	1,060,000		782,000
Accounts receivable	2,091,000		1,427,000
Current assets	4,638,000		2,624,000
Long-term investments	654,000		623,000
Fixed assets, net	11,686,000		11,323,000
Right-of-use assets	281,000		311,000
Intangibles, net	5,370,000		5,324,000
Total assets	**23,965,000**	**+11**	**21,593,000**
Bank indebtedness	293,000		169,000
Accts. pay. & accr. liabs	1,902,000		1,544,000
Current liabilities	3,407,000		2,657,000
Long-term debt, gross	9,572,000		8,195,000
Long-term debt, net	9,238,000		7,684,000
Long-term lease liabilities	215,000		253,000
Preferred share equity	586,000		1,076,000
Shareholders' equity	7,456,000		6,949,000
Non-controlling interest	162,000		652,000
Cash from oper. activs	**539,000**	**-27**	**738,000**
Cash from fin. activs	435,000		(245,000)
Cash from invest. activs	(997,000)		(483,000)
Net cash position	**64,000**	**-24**	**84,000**
Capital expenditures	(945,000)		(805,000)
Capital disposals	245,000		346,000
Unfunded pension liability	9,000		46,000
	$		$
Earnings per share*	1.42		0.82
Cash flow per share*	1.92		2.64
Cash divd. per share*	1.06		1.00
	shs		shs
No. of shs. o/s*	281,531,833		280,269,038
Avg. no. of shs. o/s*	281,000,000		279,900,000
	%		%
Net profit margin	4.07		3.22
Return on equity	6.26		3.89
Return on assets	3.67		2.55
Foreign sales percent	37		40
No. of employees (FTEs)	3,045		2,926

* Common

[A] Reported in accordance with U.S. GAAP

Latest Results

Periods ended:	6m June 30/23[A]		6m June 30/22[A]
	$000s	%Chg	$000s
Operating revenue	6,679,000	-6	7,133,000
Net income	600,000	+29	466,000
Net inc. for equity hldrs	591,000	+39	426,000
Net inc. for non-cont. int.	9,000		40,000
	$		$
Earnings per share*	2.05		1.40

* Common

[A] Reported in accordance with U.S. GAAP

Historical Summary
(as originally stated)

Fiscal Year	Oper. Rev.	Net Inc. Bef. Disc.	EPS*
	$000s	$000s	$
2022[A]	14,087,000	573,000	1.42
2021[A]	10,573,000	340,000	0.82
2020[A]	5,587,000	572,000	1.74
2019[A]	5,495,000	840,300	2.78
2018[A]	4,256,700	(453,700)	(2.25)

* Common

[A] Reported in accordance with U.S. GAAP

A.90 Altina Capital Corp.

Symbol - ALTN.P **Exchange** - TSX-VEN **CUSIP** - 02157A
Head Office - 2500-700 Georgia St W, Vancouver, BC, V7Y 1B3 **Telephone** - (604) 319-9000
Email - altinacapitalcorp@gmail.com
Investor Relations - Mirza Rahimani (604) 319-9000
Auditors - Davidson & Company LLP C.A., Vancouver, B.C.
Lawyers - Farris LLP, Vancouver, B.C.
Transfer Agents - Computershare Trust Company of Canada Inc., Vancouver, B.C.
Profile - (B.C. 2019) Capital Pool Company.

Recent Merger and Acquisition Activity

Status: terminated **Revised:** Mar. 31, 2023

UPDATE: The transaction was terminated. PREVIOUS: Altina Capital Corporation entered into a letter of intent for the Qualifying Transaction reverse takeover acquisition of private Vancouver, B.C.-based Omega Gold Corp. on a one-for-one basis. Omega Gold would complete a financing of between $1,500,000 and $3,000,000 concurrent to closing. Omega Gold has a pending transfer of a 51% interest in Peru-based Formacion Yura Exploracion S.A.C., which holds Rio Bravo gold claims near Arequipa, Peru and is in the process of arranging five staged options to acquire an additional 48.69% interest in Formacion Yura over up to a five-year period. On closing, Altina Capital would change its name to Omega Gold Corp. June 1, 2021 - A definitive agreement was entered into.

Directors - Mirza Rahimani, CEO, CFO & corp. sec., North Vancouver, B.C.; Gordon K. (Gord) Neal, Vancouver, B.C.; Terrance K. (Terry) Salman, Vancouver, B.C.; Theofilos (Theo) Sanidas, North Vancouver, B.C.

Capital Stock

	Authorized (shs.)	Outstanding (shs.)[1]
Common	unlimited	8,000,000

[1] At Nov. 29, 2022

Major Shareholder - Terrance K. (Terry) Salman held 11.25% interest at Aug. 11, 2021.

Price Range - ALTN.P/TSX-VEN

Year	Volume	High	Low	Close
2020	545,075	$0.40	$0.25	$0.32

Recent Close: $0.07

A.91 Altius Renewable Royalties Corp.

Symbol - ARR **Exchange** - TSX **CUSIP** - 02156G
Head Office - 200-38 Duffy Pl, St. John's, NL, A1B 4M5 **Toll-free** - (877) 576-2209
Website - arr.energy
Email - ben@arr.energy
Investor Relations - Ben Lewis (877) 576-2209
Auditors - Deloitte LLP C.A., St. John's, N.L.
Transfer Agents - TSX Trust Company, Toronto, Ont.
Profile - (Alta. 2018) Owns and manages a portfolio of diversified renewable power royalties and royalty-like interests.

Holds interests in a portfolio of 10 operational wind, solar and hydroelectric energy projects in Texas, Kansas, California and Vermont, totaling 2,068 MW; 23 construction and development stage wind and solar energy projects in Texas, Illinois, Pennsylvania, Virginia, Wyoming, Nebraska, Colorado and Indiana, totaling 5,961 MW; and royalty entitlements to 9,200 MW of renewable projects to be developed in North America. All royalties are held through **Great Bay Renewables, LLC** and **Great Bay Renewables II, LLC**, 50/50 joint ventures with certain funds managed by affiliates of **Apollo Global Management, Inc.**

Operational royalties include variable royalties on the 150-MW Old Settler and the 50-MW Cotton Plains wind projects in Floyd cty., Tex.; 1.5% gross revenue royalty (GRR) on the 175-MW Appaloosa wind project in Upton cty., Tex.; fixed dollar amount per MWh royalty produced from a distinct 658 MW of a larger 1,000-MW undisclosed wind project in Hansford cty., Tex.; 2.5% GRR on the 500-MW Young Wind wind project in Young cty., Tex.; variable royalties on the 250-MW Prospero 2 solar project in Andrews cty., and 15-MW Phantom solar project in Bell cty., both in Texas; 2.5% GRR on the 195-MW Jayhawk wind project in Crawford and Bourbon ctys., Kan.; variable royalty on the 70-MW Titan solar project in Imperial cty., Calif.; and 10% GRR on the Clyde River project, consisting of 5-MW hydroelectric and 150-KW solar projects in Orleans cty., Vt.

Construction and development royalties include 2.5% GRR on the 300-MW El Sauz wind project in Willacy cty., Tex.; phased GRR of 2% on the first 150 MW, 2.5% on the next 50 MW and 3% on anything above 200 MW on the 360-MW Canyon wind project, 3% GRRs on the 300-MW Easter, 300-MW Cone/Crosby III and 150-MW Water Valley wind projects, 1.5% GRRs on the 350-MW Cadillac Solar - Deville and 400-MW Cadillac Solar - El Dorado solar projects, and escalating fixed payments on the 180-MW Flatland solar project, all in Texas; 3% GRRs on the 255-MW Vermillion Grove, 400-MW Panther Grove I and 150-MW Shannon wind projects and 1.5% GRR on the 150-MW Vermilion solar project, all in Illinois; 1.5% GRR on the 175-MW Lawrence solar project in Pennsylvania; 1.5% GRR on the 150-MW Gloucester solar project in Virginia; 3% GRR on the 250-MW Wyoming I wind project in Wyoming; 3% GRR on the 150-MW Sugar Loaf wind project in Nebraska; 3% GRRs on the 200-MW Blackford and 180-MW Hoosier Line wind projects and 1.5% GRRs on the 150-MW Blackford and 400-MW Honey Creek solar projects, all in Indiana; and 1.5% GRRs on three solar projects, totaling 1,011 MW, in western U.S.

On June 21, 2023, affiliate **Great Bay Renewables, LLC** (GBR) entered into a US$45,000,000 royalty investment with **Hexagon Energy, LLC**, a Charlottesville, Va.-based renewable energy developer, to gain future royalties related to Hexagon's portfolio of 43 solar, solar plus battery storage and standalone battery storage development projects, totaling 5.3 GWac, located across 12 U.S. states and four regional transmission organizations as well as any additional projects added in the future. The royalty investment would be provided in tranches over the next three years as Hexagon achieves certain project advancement milestones, with an initial investment on closing of US$15,000,000. GBR would receive a 2.5% gross revenue royalty (GRR) on each solar and solar plus storage project and a 1% GRR on each standalone storage project until a minimum total return threshold is achieved.

On Jan. 6, 2023, affiliate **Great Bay Renewables, LLC** (GBR) sold the assets of wholly owned **NEO Geothermal, LLC**, which consisted of geothermal well fields in Portsmouth, N.H., for US$435,000.

On Dec. 20, 2022, affiliate **Great Bay Renewables II, LLC** (GBR II) acquired an existing royalty agreement on a portion of an operating 1,000-MW wind project in Hansford cty., Tex., from **Apex Clean Energy Holdings, LLC** for US$18,000,000. GBR II would receive a fixed dollar amount per MWh produced from a distinct 658 MW of the project.

On Dec. 1, 2022, affiliate **Great Bay Renewables II, LLC** entered into a US$46,000,000 royalty investment with **Longroad Energy Holdings, LLC**, a U.S.-based developer, owner and operator of renewable energy projects, to support Longroad's acquisition of 98.03 MWdc (70MWac) Titan solar project in Imperial cty., Calif. The royalty investment was structured using royalty rates that vary over time and would remain in place for the life of the project, including any extensions or enhancements.

On July 29, 2022, affiliate **Great Bay Renewables, LLC** (GBR) entered into a US$40,000,000 royalty investment with **Hodson Energy, LLC**, a New York-based renewable energy developer, to gain future royalties related to Hodson's entire portfolio of solar plus battery storage development projects, totaling 1.8 GWac, located primarily in the Mid-Atlantic region of the U.S. and any additional projects added in the future. The royalty investment would be provided in tranches over the next three years as Hodson achieves certain project advancement milestones, with an initial investment on closing of US$14,000,000. GBR would receive a 3% gross revenue royalty on each project developed and vended by Hodson until a minimum total return threshold is achieved.

On May 4, 2022, affiliate **Great Bay Renewables, LLC** (GBR) announced an investment totaling US$32,500,000 into **Bluestar Energy Capital LLC**, a new global renewables development platform. GBR would invest US$25,000,000 of the total commitment into **Nova Clean Energy, LLC**, the North American renewables development subsidiary of Bluestar, in exchange for royalties on 1.5 GW of renewable energy projects commercialized by Nova as well as a minority equity interest in Nova.

Directors - Earl A. Ludlow, chr., Paradise, N.L.; David J. Bronicheski, Oakville, Ont.; Karen E. Clarke-Whistler, Toronto, Ont.; Anna El-Erian, B.C.; André Gaumond, Lac-Beauport, Qué.

Other Exec. Officers - Brian F. Dalton, pres. & CEO; Ben Lewis, CFO

Capital Stock

	Authorized (shs.)	Outstanding (shs.)[1]
Common	unlimited	30,787,607

[1] At Aug. 1, 2023

Major Shareholder - Altius Minerals Corporation held 58% interest at June 30, 2023.

Price Range - ARR/TSX

Year	Volume	High	Low	Close
2022	14,513,737	$14.73	$6.70	$8.85
2021	6,637,165	$11.93	$7.80	$10.99

Recent Close: $8.98

Capital Stock Changes - In December 2022, bought deal public offering of 4,268,800 common shares was completed at Cdn$9.00 per share, including 368,800 common shares on exercise of over-allotment option.

Wholly Owned Subsidiaries

Altius GBR Holdings, Inc., Canada.
- 50% int. in **Great Bay Renewables Holdings II, LLC**, United States.
  - 100% int. in **Great Bay Renewables II, LLC**, Portsmouth, N.H.
- 50% int. in **Great Bay Renewables Holdings, LLC**, United States.
  - 100% int. in **GBR MemberCo., LLC**, United States.
    - 0.01% int. in **Great Bay Renewables, LLC**, Portsmouth, N.H.
- 99.99% int. in **Great Bay Renewables, LLC**, Portsmouth, N.H.

Financial Statistics

Periods ended:	12m Dec. 31/22[A]		12m Dec. 31/21[A]
	US$000s	%Chg	US$000s
Operating revenue	**781**	**+852**	**82**
Salaries & benefits	n.a.		278
General & admin expense	1,972		1,566
Stock-based compensation	320		290
Operating expense	**2,292**	**+7**	**2,134**
Operating income	**(1,511)**	**n.a.**	**(2,052)**
Investment income	521		(1,534)
Pre-tax income	**(690)**	**n.a.**	**(2,879)**
Income taxes	90		537
Net income	**(780)**	**n.a.**	**(3,416)**
Cash & equivalent	50,092		49,304
Accounts receivable	191		122
Current assets	50,518		49,426
Long-term investments	151,095		116,140
Total assets	**201,613**	**+22**	**165,565**
Accts. pay. & accr. liabs	566		511
Current liabilities	566		2,363
Shareholders' equity	195,048		159,056
Cash from oper. activs	**(1,172)**	**n.a.**	**(1,366)**
Cash from fin. activs	26,598		78,531
Cash from invest. activs	(24,637)		(27,881)
Net cash position	**50,092**	**+2**	**49,304**
	US$		US$
Earnings per share*	(0.03)		(0.14)
Cash flow per share*	(0.04)		(0.06)
	shs		shs
No. of shs. o/s*	30,782,689		26,513,889
Avg. no. of shs. o/s*	26,775,809		24,780,083
	%		%
Net profit margin	(99.87)		n.m.
Return on equity	(0.44)		(2.98)
Return on assets	(0.42)		(2.88)

* Common
[A] Reported in accordance with IFRS

Latest Results

Periods ended:	6m June 30/23[A]		6m June 30/22[A]
	US$000s	%Chg	US$000s
Operating revenue	1,171	+569	175
Net income	(202)	n.a.	(711)
	US$		US$
Earnings per share*	(0.01)		(0.03)

* Common
[A] Reported in accordance with IFRS

Historical Summary
(as originally stated)

Fiscal Year	Oper. Rev.	Net Inc. Bef. Disc.	EPS*
	US$000s	US$000s	US$
2022[A]	781	(780)	(0.03)
2021[A]	82	(3,416)	(0.14)
2020[A]	184	(1,975)	(0.15)
2019[A]	239	(1,511)	(0.49)

* Common
[A] Reported in accordance with IFRS

A.92 Altus Group Limited*

Symbol - AIF **Exchange** - TSX **CUSIP** - 02215R
Head Office - 500-33 Yonge St, Toronto, ON, M5E 1G4 **Telephone** - (416) 641-9500 **Toll-free** - (877) 953-9948 **Fax** - (416) 641-9501
Website - www.altusgroup.com
Email - camilla.bartosiewicz@altusgroup.com
Investor Relations - Camilla Bartosiewicz (416) 641-9773
Auditors - Ernst & Young LLP C.A., Toronto, Ont.
Bankers - HSBC Bank Canada; Bank of Montreal
Lawyers - Stikeman Elliott LLP, Toronto, Ont.
Transfer Agents - TSX Trust Company, Montréal, Qué.
FP500 Revenue Ranking - 394
Employees - 2,458 at Dec. 31, 2022
Profile - (Ont. 2011, amalg.) Provides software, data analytics and advisory services to the global commercial real estate (CRE) industry.

Operations are conducted through three segments: Analytics; Property Tax; and Appraisals and Development Advisory.

Analytics segment includes a portfolio of software, data analytics and advisory solutions used primarily to support and facilitate CRE asset valuations for performance, development and investment management. The segment helps clients gain data-based transparency and digitize their CRE asset and fund management valuation processes to make better decisions, maximize valuations, reduce risk and enhance the value of their CRE investments. Clients range from small-to-medium sized businesses to large global firms, as well as equity and debt investors, service providers, owner operators and developers. Solutions include software tools consisting of ARGUS Enterprise, a comprehensive software solution for CRE valuation and portfolio management; ARGUS Developer and ARGUS EstateMaster, a software for development feasibility analysis; ARGUS Voyanta, a cloud-based data management solution; ARGUS Taliance, cloud-based fund solution; ARGUS Acquire, a deal management solution for CRE acquisitions; ARGUS API, an application programming interface; and Finance Active, which provides software-as-a-service debt and financial risk management solution. Also offers data solutions, which include Altus Data Studio, which provides comprehensive real estate information on the Canadian residential, office, industrial and investment markets, and Reonomy, which provides an Artificial Intelligence (AI) and machine learning-powered commercial real estate data and analytics platform for real estate industry professionals; analytics, which include ARGUS Value Insight, which allows institutional real estate investors to perform quarterly performance reviews, benchmarking and attribution analysis of their portfolios, and Stratodem Analytics, which offers data-science-as-a-service through cloud-based platform that integrates vast amounts of granular local demographic and economic datasets to generate predictive models and analytical tools to better understand the factors influencing the market and build more accurate models and forecasts; and advisory, which includes wholly owned **One11 Advisors, LLC**'s strategic advisory and managed services for real estate organizations' front-to-back-office strategies, processes and technology. The segment operates in Canada, the U.S., Europe and Asia Pacific.

Property Tax segment includes expert services and technology for tax management. Core service offered is conducting property tax assessment reviews for commercial properties of clients. Based on the results of these reviews, the company selectively pursue appeals with government agencies to minimize the tax liability of clients. Primary technology used is itamlink property tax management software, a comprehensive tax management solution used by many organizations to optimize property tax processes. Services are offered in Canada, the U.S. and the U.K. primarily to landlords, CRE owners and tenants.

Appraisals and Development Advisory segment includes valuation appraisals of real estate portfolios, valuation of properties for transactional purposes, due diligence, and litigation and economic consulting. The segment also provides services in the areas of construction feasibility studies, budgeting, cost and loan monitoring and project management. Services are primarily offered in Canada and Australia, and clients include institutional CRE investors, developers, lenders and government agencies for infrastructure-related projects.

The company also holds 49% interest (**WSP Global Inc.** 51%) in **GeoVerra Inc.**, a Canadian geomatics business with offices across western Canada and Ontario. Provides land surveying, forestry and geospatial solutions to clients in diverse industries.

In May 2022, the company acquired the remaining 30% interest in subsidiary **Verifino GmbH & Co. KG** for $2,802,000 cash. As a result, the company now holds 100% interest in Verifino.

Recent Merger and Acquisition Activity

Status: completed **Announced:** May 1, 2022
Altus Group Limited acquired Toronto, Ont.-based Rethink Solutions Inc., which developed the itamlink property tax management software, a comprehensive tax management solution used by many organizations across the U.S. and Canada to optimize property tax processes, for $28,000,000 cash and issuance of $9,000,000 common shares.

Predecessor Detail - Succeeded Altus Group Income Fund, Jan. 1, 2011, pursuant to plan of arrangement whereby Altus Group Limited was formed to facilitate the conversion of the fund into a corporation and the fund was subsequently dissolved.

Directors - Raymond C. (Ray) Mikulich, chr., New York, N.Y.; Wai-Fong Au, Surrey, United Kingdom; Angela L. Brown, Lake Mary, Fla.; Colin Dyer, Washington, D.C.; Anthony (Tony) Gaffney, Toronto, Ont.; Michael (Mike) Gordon, Mass.; Anthony Long, Tex.; Diane B. MacDiarmid, Toronto, Ont.; Carolyn M. Schuetz, Toronto, Ont.; Janet P. Woodruff, West Vancouver, B.C.

Other Exec. Officers - James (Jim) Hannon, CEO; Pawan Chhabra, CFO; Camilla Bartosiewicz, chief commun. officer; Steve Bezner, chief devel. officer; Jorge Blanco, chief comml. officer & pres., Altus Analytics bus. unit; Kim Carter, chief people officer; Ernest Clark, chief mktg. officer; Terrie-Lynn Devonish, chief legal officer & corp. sec.; David Ross, CIO; Terry Bishop, pres., property tax, Canada; Michael Commons, pres., cost & product mgt.; Colin B. Johnston, pres., research, valuation & advisory, Canada; Alex Probyn, pres., property tax

Capital Stock

	Authorized (shs.)	Outstanding (shs.)[1]
Preferred	unlimited	nil
Common	unlimited	45,308,183

[1] At May 2, 2023

Options - At Dec. 31, 2022, options were outstanding to purchase 2,330,062 common shares at a weighted average exercise price of $45.42 per share with weighted average remaining contractual life 3.25 years.

Normal Course Issuer Bid - The company plans to make normal course purchases of up to 1,364,718 common shares representing 3% of the total outstanding. The bid commenced on Feb. 8, 2023, and expires on Feb. 7, 2024.

Major Shareholder - Mackenzie Financial Corporation held 14.4% interest at Mar. 20, 2023.

Price Range - AIF/TSX

Year	Volume	High	Low	Close
2022	23,309,499	$71.40	$41.27	$54.04
2021	22,147,774	$72.33	$47.57	$70.97
2020	32,326,018	$61.11	$33.41	$49.14
2019	21,101,801	$40.29	$21.67	$37.96
2018	21,424,556	$37.55	$21.74	$23.67

Recent Close: $51.02

Capital Stock Changes - In May 2022, 181,892 common shares were issued on acquisition of Rethink Solutions Inc. During 2022, common shares were issued as follows: 310,991 as share-based compensation, 262,945 on exercise of options, 136,945 treasury shares (net) were released (issued) under share-based compensation plans and 46,638 under dividend reinvestment plan; 188,838 common shares were repurchased under a Normal Course Issuer Bid.

Dividends

AIF com Ra $0.60 pa Q est. July 15, 2011**
** Reinvestment Option

Long-Term Debt - At Dec. 31, 2022, outstanding long-term debt totaled $317,828,000 (none current and net of $1,756,000 of deferred financing fees) and consisted entirely of borrowings under $550,000,000 of bank credit facilities with weighted average effective interest rate of 3.66% and maturing on Mar. 24, 2027.

Wholly Owned Subsidiaries

Altus Group II LLC
Altus Group (ACT) Pty Limited
Altus Group Asia Pacific Limited, Ont.
- 100% int. in **Altus Group Australia Pty Limited**, Australia.
  - 100% int. in **Altus Group Consulting Pty Limited**, Australia.
  - 100% int. in **Altus Group Cost Management Pty Limited**, Australia.
  - 100% int. in **EstateMaster Group Holdings Pty Limited**, Sydney, N.S.W., Australia.
    - 100% int. in **Estate Master FZ LLC**
    - 100% int. in **Estate Master Pty Limited**, Australia.
    - 100% int. in **Estate Master UK Limited**, United Kingdom.

Altus Group Bay Partnership Pty Limited
Altus Group Construction Professionals (Thailand) Company Limited, Thailand.
Altus Group Consulting (Thailand) Company Limited, Thailand.
Altus Group Data Solutions Inc., Canada.
Altus Group (Hong Kong) Limited, People's Republic of China.
Altus Group (India) Private Limited, India.
Altus Group Management Holdings (Thailand) Company Limited, Thailand.
Altus Group Queensland Pty Limited
Altus Group S.à.r.l., Luxembourg.
Altus Group Services (Thailand) Company Limited, Thailand.
Altus Group Tax Consulting Paralegal Professional Corporation, Ont.
Altus Group (UK) Limited, United Kingdom.
Altus Group (UK2) Limited, United Kingdom.
Altus Group U.S. Inc., Del.
- 100% int. in **Argus Software, Inc.**, Del.
  - 100% int. in **One11 Advisors, LLC**, Chicago, Ill.
  - 100% int. in **Scryer, Inc.**, Del.

Altus Group (Vietnam) Limited, Vietnam.
Altus UK LLP, United Kingdom.
Argus Software (Asia) Pte. Ltd.
Argus Software (Canada), Inc., Canada.
Argus Software (Oceanic) Pty Ltd.
Argus Software (UK) Limited, United Kingdom.
- 100% int. in **Altus Group (France) Holdings SAS**, France.
- 100% int. in **Finance Active S.A.S.**, Paris, France.
- 100% int. in **Taliance Group S.A.S.**, Paris, France.
  - 100% int. in **Taliance, Inc.**
  - 100% int. in **Taliance Limited**
  - 100% int. in **Taliance Solutions Canada Inc.**, Canada.

CVS (Commercial Valuers & Surveyors) Limited, United Kingdom.
Circle Software Acquisition Limited
Circle Software International Limited, United Kingdom.
Finance Active GmbH, Germany.
Finance Active SPRL
Finance Active S.à.r.l, Luxembourg.
Finance Active S.A.R.L., Luxembourg.
Finance Active S.r.l., Italy.
Finance Active UK Limited, United Kingdom.
Lambournes Holdings Limited
- 100% int. in **Lambournes Trading Services Limited**

R2G Limited, Herts., United Kingdom.
Rethink Solutions Inc., Toronto, Ont.
2262070 Ontario Limited, Ont.
Verifino GmbH & Co. KG, Germany.
Verifino Verwaltungs GmbH, Germany.
Voyanta Limited, United Kingdom.

Subsidiaries

85% int. in **Altus Egypt LLC**, Egypt.

Investments

49% int. in **Altus Group Property Tax Legal Services Inc.**
49% int. in **GeoVerra Inc.**, Edmonton, Alta. 50% voting interest
Note: The preceding list includes only the major related companies in which interests are held.

Financial Statistics

Periods ended:	12m Dec. 31/22[A]		12m Dec. 31/21[A]
	$000s	%Chg	$000s
Operating revenue	**735,451**	**+18**	**625,387**
Salaries & benefits	434,569		377,517
Stock-based compensation	29,380		23,938
Other operating expense	159,925		130,766
Operating expense	**623,874**	**+17**	**532,221**
Operating income	**111,577**	**+20**	**93,166**
Deprec., depl. & amort.	59,525		46,582
Finance income	505		246
Finance costs, gross	7,702		6,595
Investment income	3,013		1,187
Pre-tax income	**3,880**	**-89**	**34,200**
Income taxes	4,769		8,627
Net income	**(889)**	**n.a.**	**25,573**
Net inc. for equity hldrs	**(886)**	**n.a.**	**25,688**
Net inc. for non-cont. int.	**(3)**	**n.a.**	**(115)**
Cash & equivalent	55,267		51,271
Accounts receivable	169,433		151,355
Current assets	319,878		283,734
Long-term investments	38,822		37,302
Fixed assets, net	21,582		21,624
Right-of-use assets	38,873		59,992
Intangibles, net	790,388		753,980
Total assets	**1,263,886**	**+5**	**1,199,200**
Accts. pay. & accr. liabs	7,348		10,625
Current liabilities	239,860		209,931
Long-term debt, gross	317,828		286,924
Long-term debt, net	317,828		286,924
Long-term lease liabilities	45,459		57,225
Shareholders' equity	599,870		589,478
Non-controlling interest	nil		(115)
Cash from oper. activs	**77,085**	**+37**	**56,308**
Cash from fin. activs	(18,665)		300,430
Cash from invest. activs	(54,057)		(373,315)
Net cash position	**55,267**	**+8**	**51,271**
Capital expenditures	(5,433)		(5,965)
	$		$
Earnings per share*	(0.02)		0.62
Cash flow per share*	1.73		1.35
Cash divd. per share*	0.60		0.60
	shs		shs
No. of shs. o/s*	44,869,676		44,119,103
Avg. no. of shs. o/s*	44,635,448		41,684,077
	%		%
Net profit margin	(0.12)		4.09
Return on equity	(0.15)		5.28
Return on assets	(0.22)		3.15
Foreign sales percent	73		70
No. of employees (FTEs)	2,458		2,600

* Common
[A] Reported in accordance with IFRS

Latest Results

Periods ended:	3m Mar. 31/23[A]		3m Mar. 31/22[A]
	$000s	%Chg	$000s
Operating revenue	190,824	+14	167,584
Net income	(2,413)	n.a.	(11,456)
Net inc. for equity hldrs	(2,413)	n.a.	(11,518)
Net inc. for non-cont. int.	nil		62
	$		$
Earnings per share*	(0.05)		(0.26)

* Common
[A] Reported in accordance with IFRS

Historical Summary
(as originally stated)

Fiscal Year	Oper. Rev.	Net Inc. Bef. Disc.	EPS*
	$000s	$000s	$
2022[A]	735,451	(889)	(0.02)
2021[A]	625,387	25,573	0.62
2020[A]	561,156	27,009	0.67
2019[A]	567,415	18,194	0.46
2018[A]	510,429	(18,439)	(0.48)

* Common
[A] Reported in accordance with IFRS

A.93 Aluula Composites Inc.

Symbol - AUUA **Exchange** - TSX-VEN **CUSIP** - 022317
Head Office - 2233 Theatre Lane, Victoria, BC, V8R 6T1 **Toll-free** - (888) 724-2470
Website - aluula.com
Email - peter.dorrius@aluula.com
Investor Relations - Peter Dorrius (888) 724-2470
Auditors - Kingston Ross Pasnak LLP C.A., Edmonton, Alta.
Transfer Agents - Odyssey Trust Company, Vancouver, B.C.

Profile - (B.C. 2021) Manufactures composite textiles for a variety of applications in the wind sports, outdoor gear and equipment, sailing and aerospace markets.

The company leverages a patented fusion process to fuse high tech fibres and technical films together without the use of heavy glues. In particular, the company bonds materials at the molecular level which results in extremely light, strong and durable composites that are also recyclable at the end of life. Its composite textiles are more tear resistant, stretch resistant and are easier to be fabricated into different products. Products are ALUULA Durltye™, ALUULA Gold™ and ALUULA Graflyte™.

Wholly owned **Ocean Rodeo Sports Inc.** specializes in the design and production of wind sports equipment, such as kites and boards as well as a range of accessories and apparel for wind sports enthusiasts. Ocean Rodeo uses composite materials in the production of its products to ensure high performance and durability. Ocean Rodeo purchases finished products containing these composite materials from its manufacturer and sells them within the wind sport sector.

Recent Merger and Acquisition Activity

Status: completed **Revised:** Apr. 18, 2023
UPDATE: The transaction was completed. PREVIOUS: Bastion Square Partners Inc. (BSP) agreed to the Qualifying Transaction reverse takeover acquisition of Victoria, B.C.-based Aluula Composites Inc., a manufacturer of composite fabrics, by way of three-cornered amalgamation pursuant to which a wholly owned subsidiary of BSP would amalgamate with Aluula. BSP would issue such number of BSP common shares to Aluula shareholders as will equal a share value commensurate with a valuation that is a multiple of Aluula and its Ocean Rodeo subsidiary's trailing 12-month revenues for the period ending Oct. 31, 2022. On closing, BSP plans to change its name to Aluula Composites Inc.

Predecessor Detail - Name changed from Bastion Square Partners Inc., Apr. 14, 2023, pursuant to the Qualifying Transaction reverse takeover acquisition of (old) Aluula Composites Inc.

Directors - Richard Myerscough, CEO, B.C.; Briony Bayer, B.C.; Peter G. Berrang, Victoria, B.C.; Dr. Hannes Blum, B.C.; Peter B. Gustavson, B.C.; Jeremy South, West Vancouver, B.C.

Other Exec. Officers - John Zimmerman, pres. & chief opers. officer; Peter Dorrius, CFO & corp. sec.

Capital Stock

	Authorized (shs.)	Outstanding (shs.)[1]
Common	unlimited	225,009,365

[1] At Apr. 20, 2023

Major Shareholder - Richard Myerscough held 33.29% interest, Peter G. Berrang held 21.42% interest and Laurie Clarke held 10.21% interest at Apr. 20, 2023.

Price Range - AUUA/TSX-VEN

Year	Volume	High	Low	Close
2022	1,490,102	$0.20	$0.10	$0.10
2021	864,329	$0.40	$0.13	$0.20

Recent Close: $0.15

Capital Stock Changes - In July 2023, private placement of 24,489,953 units (1 common share & 1 warrant) at 15¢ per unit was completed, with warrants exercisable at 25¢ per share for two years.

In April 2023, 225,009,365 common shares were issued pursuant to the Qualifying Transaction reverse takeover acquisition of (old) Aluula Composites Inc., including 18,223,330 common shares issued on exchange of subscription receipts sold previously by private placement at 12¢ each and 6,776,670 common shares issued on exchange of common shares of a subsidiary sold previously by private placement at 12¢ per share.

On Oct. 12, 2021, Bastion Square Partners Inc. completed an initial public offering of 15,000,000 common shares was completed at 10¢ per share.

Wholly Owned Subsidiaries

Aluula Composites Inc., Victoria, B.C.
- 100% int. in **Ocean Rodeo Sports Inc.**, B.C.

Financial Statistics

Periods ended:	12m Oct. 31/22[A1]		12m Oct. 31/21[A]
	$000s	%Chg	$000s
Operating revenue	**2,784**	**+37**	**2,033**
Cost of sales	2,136		982
Salaries & benefits	952		768
Research & devel. expense	172		122
General & admin expense	503		265
Stock-based compensation	20		32
Operating expense	**3,783**	**+74**	**2,169**
Operating income	**(999)**	**n.a.**	**(136)**
Deprec., depl. & amort.	95		45
Finance costs, gross	134		29
Pre-tax income	**(583)**	**n.a.**	**10**
Income taxes	(101)		(501)
Net income	**(482)**	**n.a.**	**511**
Cash & equivalent	295		3
Accounts receivable	1,294		583
Current assets	5,156		1,640
Long-term investments	45		1
Fixed assets, net	1,206		839
Intangibles, net	8,242		13
Total assets	**14,679**	**+481**	**2,528**
Bank indebtedness	2,745		106
Accts. pay. & accr. liabs	894		199
Current liabilities	5,593		709
Long-term debt, gross	1,259		38
Long-term debt, net	967		38
Long-term lease liabilities	745		903
Shareholders' equity	14,679		2,528
Cash from oper. activs	**(945)**	**n.a.**	**(334)**
Cash from fin. activs	(581)		107
Cash from invest. activs	(819)		(101)
Net cash position	**(2,449)**	**n.a.**	**(104)**
Capital expenditures	(215)		(96)
	$		$
Earnings per share*	n.a.		n.a.
	shs		shs
No. of shs. o/s	n.a.		n.a.
	%		%
Net profit margin	(17.31)		25.14
Return on equity	(5.60)		n.m.
Return on assets	(4.31)		n.a.

[A] Reported in accordance with IFRS
[1] Results for fiscal 2022 and prior periods pertain to (old) Aluula Composites Inc.

A.94 Ambari Brands Inc.

Symbol - AMB **Exchange** - CSE **CUSIP** - 02316X
Head Office - 600-905 Pender St W, Vancouver, BC, V6C 1L6 **Telephone** - (604) 229-9772
Website - ambaribeauty.com
Email - ngrewal@ambaribrands.com
Investor Relations - Nisha Grewal (604) 229-9772
Auditors - Crowe MacKay LLP C.A., Vancouver, B.C.
Transfer Agents - Odyssey Trust Company, Vancouver, B.C.

Profile - (B.C. 2019) Produces, retails and distributes luxury skin care products infused with active ingredients, smart adaptogens and cannabidiol (CBD) in the United States, Europe and India. Also developing an artificial intelligence (AI)-powered beauty software and application for beauty product recommendations.

The company's products are based on its customized Modern Blend, which combines high levels of active ingredients, smart adaptogens such as reishi, shiitake and maitake mushrooms and broad spectrum CBD. Its three core products are the Gold Profection22® Mask, the PM Active12® Serum, AM Active10® Essence and the Complex4 Hydrator® Cream. All are vegan, cruelty-free, and formulated without silicones, parabens, fragrance or phthalates. Production and co-packing is carried out in collaboration with a Utah-based product development and manufacturing company.

Sales are made directly through the company's e-commerce platform www.ambaribeauty.com as well as through select luxury retailers online including Bergdorf Goodman, Neiman Marcus, Saks Fifth Avenue and El Corte Ingles and some brick-and-mortar locations.

Under development is Scarlett, an AI-powered beauty software and application for personalized beauty experiences. The application's AI-powered colour matching feature analyzes skin tones and undertones, providing recommendations for foundation, blush, lipstick, and eyeshadow shades. Scarlett also features a virtual makeup try-on function.

Directors - Nisha Grewal, CEO & corp. sec., Vancouver, B.C.; Gurcharn S. (Charn) Deol, interim CFO, Richmond, B.C.; Meissam Hagh Panah, Saint-Jean-sur-Richelieu, Qué.

Capital Stock

	Authorized (shs.)	Outstanding (shs.)[1]
Common	unlimited	52,095,195

[1] At May 23, 2023

Major Shareholder - Nisha Grewal held 20.12% interest at July 25, 2022.

Price Range - AMB/CSE

Year	Volume	High	Low	Close
2022	3,708,952	$0.50	$0.20	$0.25

Recent Close: $0.56

Capital Stock Changes - On July 25, 2022, 11,093,154 units (1 common share & ½ warrant) were issued without further consideration on exchange of special warrants sold in September and November 2021 at $0.50 each. Also during 2022, 1,471,180 common shares were cancelled.

Wholly Owned Subsidiaries

Ambari Beauty USA, Inc., Nev.

Financial Statistics

Periods ended:	12m Dec. 31/22[A]		12m Dec. 31/21[A]
	$000s	%Chg	$000s
Operating revenue	**204**	**+40**	**146**
Cost of sales	160		64
Salaries & benefits	33		nil
Research & devel. expense	5		26
General & admin expense	1,281		3,721
Operating expense	**1,479**	**-61**	**3,811**
Operating income	**(1,275)**	**n.a.**	**(3,665)**
Finance income	16		17
Finance costs, gross	23		13
Pre-tax income	**(1,317)**	**n.a.**	**(3,662)**
Net income	**(1,317)**	**n.a.**	**(3,662)**
Cash & equivalent	247		1,688
Inventories	724		652
Accounts receivable	23		21
Current assets	1,081		2,829
Total assets	**1,081**	**-62**	**2,829**
Accts. pay. & accr. liabs	234		174
Current liabilities	234		174
Shareholders' equity	846		2,655
Cash from oper. activs	**(1,338)**	**n.a.**	**(3,935)**
Cash from fin. activs	(150)		4,102
Cash from invest. activs	nil		(388)
Net cash position	**247**	**-85**	**1,688**
	$		$
Earnings per share*	(0.03)		(0.08)
Cash flow per share*	(0.03)		(0.08)
	shs		shs
No. of shs. o/s*	50,095,195		40,473,221
Avg. no. of shs. o/s*	44,893,717		46,966,372
	%		%
Net profit margin	(645.59)		n.m.
Return on equity	(75.24)		(149.78)
Return on assets	(66.19)		(141.71)

* Common
[A] Reported in accordance with IFRS

Latest Results

Periods ended:	3m Mar. 31/23[A]		3m Mar. 31/22[A]
	$000s	%Chg	$000s
Operating revenue	55	-37	87
Net income	(174)	n.a.	(386)
	$		$
Earnings per share*	(0.00)		(0.01)

* Common
[A] Reported in accordance with IFRS

Historical Summary
(as originally stated)

Fiscal Year	Oper. Rev.	Net Inc. Bef. Disc.	EPS*
	$000s	$000s	$
2022[A]	204	(1,317)	(0.03)
2021[A]	146	(3,662)	(0.08)
2020[A]	nil	(433)	(0.01)

* Common
[A] Reported in accordance with IFRS

A.95 Amcomri Entertainment Inc.

Symbol - AMEN **Exchange** - NEO **CUSIP** - 02341J
Head Office - 1800-510 Georgia St W, Vancouver, BC, V6B 0M3
Telephone - (604) 638-4890
Website - amcomrientertainmentinc.com
Email - larry.howard@amcomri.com
Investor Relations - Laurence Howard (416) 879-9425
Auditors - MNP LLP C.A., Toronto, Ont.
Transfer Agents - Odyssey Trust Company, Vancouver, B.C.
Profile - (B.C. 2015) Produces, sells and distributes independent films, feature documentaries, scripted and non-scripted television series on a global basis.

Operates through four wholly owned subsidiaries: **101 Films Limited**, **101 Films International Limited**, **Abacus Media Rights Limited**, and **Hollywood Classics International Limited** (HCI).

101 Films is an all-rights media distribution company owning and controlling the rights to over 1,750 movie titles in the U.K., and Irish markets.

101 Films International is an international sales agency that acquires distribution rights for movie titles on a global basis often enabling pre-production sales of rights to territories around the world through a series of long-established partnerships including major media platforms such as Netflix,Amazon, Apple, and Sky as well as studios including Universal, Paramount, Entertainment One and leading independent international distributors.

Abacus acquires and distributes the rights to television programmes and series worldwide including popular service providers such as Sky, Netflix, Amazon, Apple and BBC.

HCI sells physical copies of titles in global markets, as opposed to only licensing titles to which it has the rights.

Predecessor Detail - Name changed from Appreciated Media Holdings Inc., Jan. 7, 2022, pursuant to the reverse takeover acquisition of Trinity Pictures Distribution Limited.; basis 1 new for 25 old shs.

Directors - Paul McGowan, chr., Monaco; Robert Price, CEO, Somt., United Kingdom; Laurence (Larry) Howard, CFO & corp. sec., Wicklow, Ireland; Michael Walker, v-p, productions, Stoney Creek, Ont.; Martin A. (Andy) Lyon, United Kingdom; Michèle Maheux, Toronto, Ont.; Michelle Sangster; Alexander (Alex) Stojanovic, Toronto, Ont.

Capital Stock

	Authorized (shs.)	Outstanding (shs.)[1]
Common	unlimited	73,606,424

[1] At Mar. 31, 2023

Major Shareholder - Paul McGowan held 39.98% interest and Laurence (Larry) Howard held 13.26% interest at Jan. 13, 2022.

Price Range - AMEN/NEO

Year	Volume	High	Low	Close
2022	91,500	$1.14	$0.30	$0.36
2020	513,298	$4.63	$1.13	$1.25
2019	661,683	$15.00	$2.50	$3.25
2018	193,840	$18.00	$8.00	$14.50

Consolidation: 1-for-25 cons. in Jan. 2022
Recent Close: $0.13

Capital Stock Changes - In October 2021, private placement of 32,708,000 common shares was completed at 5¢ per share. In January 2022, common shares were consolidated on a 1-for-25 basis and 66,666,667 post-consolidated common shares were issued pursuant to the reverse takeover acquisition of Trinity Pictures Distribution Limited.

Wholly Owned Subsidiaries

Agatha Media Corp., Canada. Inactive.
Impossible Dream Entertainment Inc., Canada. Inactive.
Trinity Pictures Distribution Limited, United Kingdom.
- 100% int. in **Abacus Media Rights Limited**, United Kingdom.
- 49.9% int. in **Appreciated Media Global Limited**, British Virgin Islands.
- 100% int. in **101 Films International Limited**, United Kingdom.
- 100% int. in **101 Films Limited**, United Kingdom.
  - 100% int. in **Devil Lies Beneath Limited**, United Kingdom. Inactive.
  - 100% int. in **Elwood Plains Limited**, United Kingdom. Inactive.
  - 100% int. in **Hollywood Classics International Limited**, United Kingdom.
- 100% int. in **Silentpoint Limited**, Ireland.

Subsidiaries

50.1% int. in **Appreciated Media Global Limited**, British Virgin Islands.

A.96 Amego Capital Corp.

Symbol - MEGO.P **Exchange** - TSX-VEN **CUSIP** - 02343T
Head Office - 2050-1055 Georgia St W, Vancouver, BC, V6E 3P3
Telephone - (559) 318-5582
Email - kirkexner@yahoo.com
Investor Relations - Kirk Exner (559) 318-5592
Auditors - Dale Matheson Carr-Hilton LaBonte LLP C.A., Vancouver, B.C.
Transfer Agents - Olympia Trust Company, Vancouver, B.C.
Profile - (B.C. 2021) Capital Pool Company.
Directors - Kirk Exner, pres., CEO & corp. sec., Langley, B.C.; Andreas (Andy) Edelmeier, CFO, Vancouver, B.C.; Fraser Atkinson, Vancouver, B.C.; Nicole Marchand, Toronto, Ont.

Capital Stock

	Authorized (shs.)	Outstanding (shs.)[1]
Common	unlimited	3,675,000

[1] At Apr. 8, 2022

Major Shareholder - Kirk Exner held 14.97% interest and Andreas (Andy) Edelmeier held 10.2% interest at Apr. 8, 2022.

Price Range - MEGO.P/TSX-VEN

Year	Volume	High	Low	Close
2022	143,500	$0.26	$0.21	$0.22

Recent Close: $0.20

Capital Stock Changes - On Apr. 8, 2022, an initial public offering of 1,500,000 common shares was completed at 20¢ per share.

A.97 American Aires Inc.

Symbol - WIFI **Exchange** - CSE **CUSIP** - 02377G
Head Office - 100-400 Applewood Cres, Vaughan, ON, L4K 0C3
Telephone - (647) 404-4416
Website - www.airestech.com
Email - dimitry@airestech.com
Investor Relations - Dimitry Serov (905) 482-4667
Auditors - AGT Partners LLP C.A., Woodbridge, Ont.
Lawyers - Irwin Lowy LLP, Toronto, Ont.
Transfer Agents - Computershare Trust Company of Canada Inc., Toronto, Ont.
Profile - (Ont. 2012) Manufactures, distributes and sells devices intended to protect persons from the harmful effects of electromagnetic emissions.

Offers electromagnetic radiation (EMR) protection devices intended to protect users from the harmful effects of electromagnetic emissions emitted by data transmitting electronic devices such as cell phones, cordless phones, bluetooth earpieces, bluetooth headsets, computers, laptops, monitors, smart TVs, smart meters, Wi-Fi routers and other similar products. The company's devices, which are designed to be stuck or attached to a key ring, are sold under the Lifetune™ brand through e-commerce and distribution platforms.

Common reinstated on CSE, Mar. 13, 2023.

Directors - Drew Green, chr., Vancouver, B.C.; Josh Bruni, CEO, Tex.; Dimitry Serov, pres. & chief product officer, Richmond Hill, Ont.; Ruslan Elensky, Vaughan, Ont.; Andrew Michrowski, Ont.

Other Exec. Officers - Christoffer Guajala, COO; Vitali Savitski, CFO; Jo-Anne Archibald, corp. sec.

Capital Stock

	Authorized (shs.)	Outstanding (shs.)[1]
Common	unlimited	158,756,453

[1] At Dec. 31, 2022

Major Shareholder - Dimitry Serov held 28.98% interest at May 6, 2021.

Price Range - WIFI/CSE

Year	Volume	High	Low	Close
2022	15,068,635	$0.11	$0.04	$0.04
2021	85,701,637	$0.41	$0.05	$0.06
2020	64,996,239	$0.75	$0.14	$0.20
2019	7,445,532	$0.52	$0.27	$0.51

Recent Close: $0.02

Wholly Owned Subsidiaries

American Aires USA Inc., United States.

Financial Statistics

Periods ended:	12m Dec. 31/21[A]		12m Dec. 31/20[A]
	$000s	%Chg	$000s
Operating revenue	**2,553**	**+10**	**2,314**
Cost of sales	1,568		1,612
Salaries & benefits	454		520
Research & devel. expense	nil		215
General & admin expense	5,154		4,259
Stock-based compensation	1,143		3,015
Operating expense	**8,318**	**-14**	**9,622**
Operating income	**(5,765)**	**n.a.**	**(7,308)**
Deprec., depl. & amort	130		171
Finance income	nil		9
Finance costs, gross	94		8
Pre-tax income	**(6,087)**	**n.a.**	**(7,588)**
Net income	**(6,087)**	**n.a.**	**(7,588)**
Cash & equivalent	276		502
Inventories	409		264
Accounts receivable	1		1
Current assets	1,743		1,483
Fixed assets, net	12		1
Intangibles, net	513		641
Total assets	**2,267**	**+7**	**2,124**
Bank indebtedness	763		40
Accts. pay. & accr. liabs	649		628
Current liabilities	1,419		736
Shareholders' equity	848		1,388
Cash from oper. activs	**(3,032)**	**n.a.**	**(3,991)**
Cash from fin. activs	2,818		1,280
Cash from invest. activs	(13)		14
Net cash position	**276**	**-45**	**502**
Capital expenditures	(13)		nil
Capital disposals	nil		14
	$		$
Earnings per share*	(0.04)		(0.07)
Cash flow per share*	(0.02)		(0.04)
	shs		shs
No. of shs. o/s*	151,365,225		118,870,000
Avg. no. of shs. o/s*	141,585,537		111,940,355
	%		%
Net profit margin	(238.43)		(327.92)
Return on equity	(544.45)		(250.10)
Return on assets	(272.97)		(207.98)
Foreign sales percent	84		81

* Common
[A] Reported in accordance with IFRS

Latest Results

Periods ended:	9m Sept. 30/22[A]		9m Sept. 30/21[A]
	$000s	%Chg	$000s
Operating revenue	3,369	+110	1,606
Net income	(3,755)	n.a.	(4,666)
	$		$
Earnings per share*	(0.02)		(0.03)

* Common
[A] Reported in accordance with IFRS

Historical Summary
(as originally stated)

Fiscal Year	Oper. Rev.	Net Inc. Bef. Disc.	EPS*
	$000s	$000s	$
2021[A]	2,553	(6,087)	(0.04)
2020[A]	2,314	(7,588)	(0.07)
2019[A]	693	(3,400)	(0.04)
2018[A1]	532	(1,681)	(0.02)
2017[A1]	353	(918)	(0.02)

* Common
[A] Reported in accordance with IFRS
[1] As shown in the prospectus dated Oct. 2, 2019.

A.98 American Biofuels Inc.

Symbol - ABS.H **Exchange** - TSX-VEN (S) **CUSIP** - 02461V
Head Office - 303-595 Howe St, PO Box 4, Vancouver, BC, V6C 2T5 **Telephone** - (604) 718-2800 **Toll-free** - (888) 945-5056 **Fax** - (604) 718-2808
Email - teresa@simcoservices.ca
Investor Relations - Teresa M. Cherry (604) 718-2800
Auditors - Dale Matheson Carr-Hilton LaBonte LLP C.A., Vancouver, B.C.
Lawyers - DuMoulin Black LLP, Vancouver, B.C.
Transfer Agents - Computershare Trust Company of Canada Inc., Toronto, Ont.
Profile - (B.C. 1980) Pursuing acquisition of a manufacturer of industrial hemp products.
Common suspended from TSX-VEN, Sept. 2, 2022.

Recent Merger and Acquisition Activity

Status: pending **Revised:** Aug. 26, 2022
UPDATE: American Biofuels was advised that there have been restructuring activities within the members of Paragon. The parties have been in continuous communications regarding recovery of the advanced funds and/or restructuring of the agreement. PREVIOUS: American Biofuels Inc. agreed to the reverse takeover acquisition of Colorado-based Paragon Processing, LLC, which manufactures and distributes industrial hemp products. Pursuant to the agreement, American Biofuels would create a new class of proportionate voting shares and reclassify the current common shares as subordinate voting shares in order to retain its foreign private issuer status. American Biofuels would then issue the proportionate voting shares in exchange for all the membership interests of Paragon. The new proportionate voting shares are entitled to 100 votes per share, and are convertible to subordinate voting shares on the basis of one proportionate voting share for 100 subordinate voting share. Apr. 30, 2020 - The agreement has lapsed. Neither party has extended or terminated and the agreement is pending further negotiation.

Predecessor Detail - Name changed from TransAmerican Energy Inc., Sept. 12, 2018; basis 1 new for 10 old shs.
Directors - Keturah M. Nathe, interim pres. & interim CEO, Pitt Meadows, B.C.; Richard (Rick) Barnett, Port Moody, B.C.; Christopher P. (Chris) Cherry, Vancouver, B.C.; Ronald E. (Ron) Hughes, Point Roberts, Wash.; Stephen Watts, S.A., Australia; Jurgen A. Wolf, Vancouver, B.C.
Other Exec. Officers - Teresa M. Cherry, CFO & corp. sec.

Capital Stock

	Authorized (shs.)	Outstanding (shs.)[1]
Common	unlimited	9,866,224

[1] At Dec. 28, 2022

Major Shareholder - Widely held at Aug. 8, 2019.

Price Range - ABS.H/TSX-VEN (S)

Year	Volume	High	Low	Close
2019	2,383,378	$3.20	$0.85	$1.99
2018	2,874,216	$1.90	$0.10	$1.00

Capital Stock Changes - There were no changes to capital stock from fiscal 2020 to fiscal 2022, inclusive.

Wholly Owned Subsidiaries

1205742 B.C. Ltd., Canada.

Financial Statistics

Periods ended:	12m Apr. 30/22[A]		12m Apr. 30/21[□A]
	$000s	%Chg	$000s
General & admin expense	112		105
Operating expense	**112**	**+7**	**105**
Operating income	**(112)**	**n.a.**	**(105)**
Finance income	132		nil
Finance costs, gross	185		1
Write-downs/write-offs	(132)		(2,098)
Pre-tax income	**(296)**	**n.a.**	**(2,406)**
Net income	**(296)**	**n.a.**	**(2,406)**
Accounts receivable	7		4
Current assets	8		6
Total assets	**8**	**+33**	**6**
Bank indebtedness	2,486		2,300
Accts. pay. & accr. liabs	410		299
Current liabilities	2,896		2,599
Shareholders' equity	(2,914)		(2,618)
Cash from oper. activs	**(2)**	**n.a.**	**(32)**
Cash from fin. activs	nil		32
	$		$
Earnings per share*	(0.03)		(0.24)
Cash flow per share*	(0.00)		(0.00)
	shs		shs
No. of shs. o/s*	9,866,224		9,866,224
Avg. no. of shs. o/s*	9,866,224		9,866,224
	%		%
Net profit margin	n.a.		n.a.
Return on equity	n.m.		n.m.
Return on assets	n.m.		n.m.

* Common
□ Restated
[A] Reported in accordance with IFRS

Latest Results

Periods ended:	6m Oct. 31/22[A]		6m Oct. 31/21[A]
	$000s	%Chg	$000s
Net income	(170)	n.a.	(144)
	$		$
Earnings per share*	(0.02)		(0.02)

* Common
[A] Reported in accordance with IFRS

Historical Summary
(as originally stated)

Fiscal Year	Oper. Rev.	Net Inc. Bef. Disc.	EPS*
	$000s	$000s	$
2022[A]	nil	(296)	(0.03)
2021[A]	nil	(2,406)	(0.24)
2020[A]	nil	(426)	(0.04)
2019[A]	nil	(327)	(0.04)
2018[A]	nil	170	0.10

* Common
[A] Reported in accordance with IFRS
Note: Adjusted throughout for 1-for-10 cons. in Sept. 2018

A.99 American Hotel Income Properties REIT LP

Symbol - HOT.UN **Exchange** - TSX **CUSIP** - 026695
Head Office - 800-925 Georgia St W, Vancouver, BC, V6C 3L2 **Telephone** - (604) 630-3134 **Fax** - (604) 629-0790
Website - www.ahipreit.com
Email - tbeatty@ahipreit.com
Investor Relations - D. Travis Beatty (604) 630-3134
Auditors - KPMG LLP C.A., Vancouver, B.C.
Lawyers - Farris LLP, Vancouver, B.C.
Transfer Agents - Computershare Trust Company of Canada Inc., Vancouver, B.C.
FP500 Revenue Ranking - 529
Employees - 13 at Dec. 31, 2022
Profile - (Ont. 2012) Owns and acquires premium branded hotels in the United States.

The limited partnership indirectly owned, at Mar. 31, 2023, 71 premium branded hotels in 22 U.S. states, totaling 8,024 rooms, which cater primarily to corporate, extended stay and leisure travelers. Premium branded hotels are select-service hotel properties that have franchise agreements with international hotel brands, such as **Marriott International Inc.**, **Hilton Worldwide**, **InterContinental Hotels Group**, and **Choice Hotels International Inc.**

Properties are managed by **One Lodging Holding LLC**, wholly owned by **Aimbridge Hospitality, L.P.**

Recent Merger and Acquisition Activity

Status: pending **Announced:** Mar. 31, 2023
American Hotel Income Properties REIT LP agreed to sell the 107-room Springhill Suites hotel in Pinehurst, N.C., for US$11,700,000. The transaction was expected to be completed in June 2023.

Status: completed **Revised:** Dec. 31, 2022
UPDATE: The transaction was completed. PREVIOUS: American Hotel Income Properties REIT LP agreed to sell four premium branded hotels in Oklahoma, for US$26,250,000. The transaction consists of 147-room Holiday Inn, 103-room Staybridge Suites and 109-room Holiday Inn, all in Oklahoma City and an 81-room Hampton Inn in Woodward.

Status: completed **Revised:** Oct. 31, 2022
UPDATE: The transaction was completed. PREVIOUS: American Hotel Income Properties REIT LP agreed to sell the 116-room Hampton Inn hotel in Cranberry Township, Pa., for US$5,317,000.

Status: completed **Revised:** June 30, 2022
UPDATE: The transaction was completed. PREVIOUS: American Hotel Income Properties REIT LP agreed to sell the 132-room Hampton Inn hotel in Pittsburgh, Pa., for US$5,675,000.

Oper. Subsid./Mgt. Co. Directors - W. Michael Murphy, chr., Atlanta, Ga.; Charles W. (Chuck) van der Lee, v-chr., Vancouver, B.C.; Matthew Cervino, New York, N.Y.; Stephen J. (Steve) Evans, North Vancouver, B.C.; Richard Frank, Dallas, Tex.; Mahmood Khimji, Irving, Tex.; Tamara L. Lawson, Toronto, Ont.; Robert F. (John) O'Neill, West Vancouver, B.C.; Josef Vejvoda, Oakville, Ont.
Oper. Subsid./Mgt. Co. Officers - Jonathan Korol, CEO; Bruce Pittet, COO; D. Travis Beatty, CFO & corp. sec.; Stephanie Li, v-p, fin.

Capital Stock

	Authorized (shs.)	Outstanding (shs.)[1]
Preferred		
Series C	50,000	50,000[2]
L.P. Unit	unlimited	78,826,076[3]

[1] At Mar. 7, 2023
[2] Shares of wholly owned owned American Hotel Income Properties REIT Inc.
[3] At Apr. 25, 2023.

Series C Preferred - Issued by wholly owned American Hotel Income Properties REIT Inc. (AHIP REIT) to HCI-BGO Victoria JV LP. Entitled to a quarterly dividend of 8% per annum for the first three years, and, to the extent still outstanding, increases to 9% per annum for the fourth and fifth year, with further escalations after the fifth year of the issuance. The company has the option to pay the dividends through cash or issuance of additional series C preferred shares. Redeemable by AHIP REIT subject to (i) on or after the second year prior to the third year of issuance equal to the sum of (a) US$1,000 per share plus 0.5% of U.S. treasury bills rate, and (b) 1.5% of US$1,000 liquidation price; (ii) on or after the third year of issuance for US$1,000 per share plus all accrued and unpaid dividends; and (iii) the redemption of preferred C shares paid as dividends at a rate of US$1,000 per share plus all accrued and unpaid dividends. In case of liquidation, entitled to receive US$1,000 per share. Classified as non-controlling interest. Non voting.
Common - One vote per share.
Major Shareholder - Widely held at Apr. 25, 2023.

Price Range - HOT.UN/TSX

Year	Volume	High	Low	Close
2022	26,919,848	$4.53	$2.34	$2.79
2021	32,746,583	$4.84	$3.07	$3.77
2020	68,383,407	$7.49	$1.12	$3.12
2019	37,449,700	$7.59	$6.21	$7.04
2018	38,147,607	$9.47	$5.80	$6.34

Recent Close: $2.22
Capital Stock Changes - During 2022, 72,915 limited partnership units were issued under securities-based compensation plan.

Dividends

HOT.UN unit Ra US$0.18 pa M est. Feb. 15, 2023
HOT.U unit Ra US$0.18 pa M est. Feb. 15, 2023

Wholly Owned Subsidiaries

American Hotel Income Properties REIT (GP) Inc., Vancouver, B.C.
American Hotel Income Properties REIT Inc., Wichita, Kan.
- 100% int. in **AHIP Enterprises LLC**, Del.
  - 100% int. in **AHIP Enterprises II LLC**, Del.
- 100% int. in **AHIP Management Ltd.**, Vancouver, B.C.
- 100% int. in **AHIP Properties LLC**, Del.
  - 100% int. in **AHIP Properties II LLC**, Del.

Financial Statistics

Periods ended:	12m Dec. 31/22[A]		12m Dec. 31/21[□A]
	US$000s	%Chg	US$000s
Total revenue	**281,367**	**+17**	**241,307**
Rental operating expense	192,213		152,390
General & admin. expense	17,861		18,114
Operating expense	**210,074**	**+23**	**170,504**
Operating income	**71,293**	**+1**	**70,803**
Deprec. & amort.	37,952		43,087
Finance income	110		113
Finance costs, gross	31,615		40,452
Write-downs/write-offs	(44,081)		(12,403)
Pre-tax income	**(35,607)**	**n.a.**	**(10,729)**
Income taxes	(494)		1,119
Net inc. bef. disc. opers	**(35,113)**	**n.a.**	**(11,848)**
Income from disc. opers	(469)		(18)
Net income	**(35,582)**	**n.a.**	**(11,866)**
Net inc. for equity hldrs	**(39,637)**	**n.a.**	**(15,610)**
Net inc. for non-cont. int	**4,055**	**+8**	**3,744**
Cash & equivalent	12,945		14,700
Accounts receivable	9,214		9,082
Current assets	66,771		69,226
Fixed assets	918,063		1,027,765
Properties under devel.	35,266		17,232
Property interests, net	953,329		1,044,997
Intangibles, net	4,837		5,692
Total assets	**1,052,795**	**-9**	**1,152,388**
Accts. pay. & accr. liabs	35,534		27,728
Current liabilities	62,882		103,445
Long-term debt, gross	687,541		738,245
Long-term debt, net	663,578		668,852
Shareholders' equity	278,536		331,034
Non-controlling interest	43,570		43,570
Cash from oper. activs	**44,910**	**+150**	**17,954**
Cash from fin. activs	(61,961)		(4,340)
Cash from invest. activs	15,296		(18,632)
Net cash position	**12,945**	**-12**	**14,700**
Capital expenditures	(28,250)		(6,209)
Decrease in property	47,542		nil
	US$		US$
Earns. per sh. bef disc opers*	(0.45)		(0.15)
Earnings per share*	(0.46)		(0.15)
Cash flow per share*	0.57		0.23
Funds from opers. per sh.*	0.48		0.53
Adj. funds from opers. per sh.*	0.35		0.47
Cash divd. per share*	0.17		nil
Total divd. per share*	**0.17**		**nil**
	shs		shs
No. of shs. o/s*	78,795,444		78,722,529
Avg. no. of shs. o/s*	78,754,918		78,589,920
	%		%
Net profit margin	(12.48)		(4.91)
Return on equity	(12.85)		(4.64)
Return on assets	(0.36)		2.80
Foreign sales percent	100		100
No. of employees (FTEs)	13		13

* L.P. unit
□ Restated
[A] Reported in accordance with IFRS

Latest Results

Periods ended:	3m Mar. 31/23[A]		3m Mar. 31/22[A]
	US$000s	%Chg	US$000s
Total revenue	65,458	+6	61,776
Net income	(1,600)	n.a.	(3,875)
Net inc. for equity hldrs	(2,600)	n.a.	(4,875)
Net inc. for non-cont. int	1,000		1,000
	US$		US$
Earnings per share*	(0.02)		(0.05)

* L.P. unit
[A] Reported in accordance with IFRS

Historical Summary
(as originally stated)

Fiscal Year	Total Rev.	Net Inc. Bef. Disc.	EPS*
	US$000s	US$000s	US$
2022[A]	281,367	(35,113)	(0.45)
2021[A]	241,307	(11,848)	(0.15)
2020[A]	174,855	(65,766)	(0.84)
2019[A]	269,545	2,181	0.03
2018[A]	338,561	8,353	0.11

* L.P. unit
[A] Reported in accordance with IFRS

A.100 AmmPower Corp.

Symbol - AMMP **Exchange** - CSE **CUSIP** - 03169D
Head Office - 5 Hazelton Ave, Toronto, ON, M5R 2E1
Website - www.ammpower.com
Email - invest@ammpower.com
Investor Relations - Dr. Gary Benninger (248) 662-5565
Auditors - Crowe MacKay LLP C.A., Vancouver, B.C.
Lawyers - Cassels Brock & Blackwell LLP
Transfer Agents - Odyssey Trust Company, Vancouver, B.C.
Profile - (B.C. 2019) Has mineral interest in Quebec. Also developing technology to produce a carbon-free energy source.

In Quebec, holds Whabouchi South lithium prospect, 1,280 hectares, James Bay.

Also developing scientific solutions, methodologies and technologies for the production of green ammonia, a potential carbon-free energy source.

In July 2023, the company sold lithium claims covering 1,283 hectares in Quebec to **Consolidated Lithium Metals Inc.** for $60,000 and a 1% NSR royalty on the properties.

During fiscal 2022, option to acquire Klotz Lake (formerly Titan) gold prospect in Ontario was terminated and related costs written off.

Recent Merger and Acquisition Activity

Status: completed **Announced:** Jan. 9, 2023
Aberdeen International Inc. sold its remaining 41.67% interest in Progressus Clean Technologies Inc. to AmmPower Corp. issuance of 41,254,125 AmmPower common shares at a deemed value of 30¢ per share. On closing, Aberdeen held a 27.35% interest in AmmPower.

Predecessor Detail - Name changed from Soldera Mining Corp., Apr. 23, 2021.

Directors - Dr. Gary Benninger, exec. chr. & CEO, Mich.; Dr. Luisa Moreno, v-p, tech. & govt. rel., Ont.; Alia Comai, Mich.

Other Exec. Officers - René Bharti, pres.; Ryan Ptolemy, CFO; Dr. Zhenyu Zhang, chief technologist; Geoffrey (Geoff) Balderson, corp. sec.

Capital Stock

	Authorized (shs.)	Outstanding (shs.)[1]
Common	unlimited	99,437,970

[1] At Sept. 28, 2022

Major Shareholder - Aberdeen International Inc. held 27.35% interest at Jan. 9, 2023.

Price Range - AMMP/CSE

Year	Volume	High	Low	Close
2022	22,274,887	$0.66	$0.20	$0.30
2021	97,218,537	$2.15	$0.38	$0.38
2020	1,680,817	$0.50	$0.30	$0.46

Recent Close: $0.15

Capital Stock Changes - In September 2022, private placement of 4,769,739 units (1 common share & 1 warrant) at 23¢ per unit was completed, with warrants exercisable at 31¢ per share for two years.

In June 2021, private placement of 5,877,384 units (1 common share & ½ warrant) at 72¢ per unit was completed. In February 2022, private placement of 7,142,858 units (1 common share & 1 warrant) at 42¢ per unit was completed. Also during fiscal 2022, common shares were issued as follows: 7,295,832 on exercise of warrants, 5,937,153 on vesting of restricted share units and 215,547 for debt settlement.

Wholly Owned Subsidiaries

AmmPower America LLC, Mich.
AmTek Inc., Canada.

Subsidiaries

50.05% int. in **Progressus Clean Technologies Inc.**, Canada.

Financial Statistics

Periods ended:	12m May 31/22[A]		12m May 31/21[A]
	$000s	%Chg	$000s
Salaries & benefits	1,409		31
Exploration expense	54		212
General & admin expense	9,129		11,814
Stock-based compensation	9,800		2,795
Operating expense	**20,392**	**+37**	**14,852**
Operating income	**(20,392)**	**n.a.**	**(14,852)**
Deprec., depl. & amort.	257		nil
Pre-tax income	**(20,519)**	**n.a.**	**(16,432)**
Net income	**(20,519)**	**n.a.**	**(16,432)**
Cash & equivalent	627		1,895
Accounts receivable	42		72
Current assets	1,699		2,730
Fixed assets, net	583		nil
Right-of-use assets	1,451		nil
Explor./devel. properties	9		49
Total assets	**3,741**	**+35**	**2,779**
Accts. pay. & accr. liabs	755		112
Current liabilities	967		118
Long-term lease liabilities	1,363		nil
Shareholders' equity	1,410		2,661
Cash from oper. activs	**(9,709)**	**n.a.**	**(3,127)**
Cash from fin. activs	9,086		4,692
Cash from invest. activs	(620)		(200)
Net cash position	**627**	**-67**	**1,895**
Capital expenditures	(620)		(200)
	$		$
Earnings per share*	(0.24)		(0.42)
Cash flow per share*	(0.12)		(0.08)
	shs		shs
No. of shs. o/s*	94,437,064		67,968,290
Avg. no. of shs. o/s*	84,157,081		39,549,517
	%		%
Net profit margin	n.a.		n.a.
Return on equity	(1,008.06)		(1,019.99)
Return on assets	(629.42)		(980.14)

* Common
[A] Reported in accordance with IFRS

Historical Summary
(as originally stated)

Fiscal Year	Oper. Rev.	Net Inc. Bef. Disc.	EPS*
	$000s	$000s	$
2022[A]	nil	(20,519)	(0.24)
2021[A]	nil	(16,432)	(0.42)
2020[A1]	nil	(76)	(0.00)

* Common
[A] Reported in accordance with IFRS
[1] 25 weeks ended May 31, 2020.
Note: Adjusted throughout for 2-for-1 split in Oct. 2020

A.101 Anacott Acquisition Corporation

Symbol - AAC.P **Exchange** - TSX-VEN **CUSIP** - 032472
Head Office - 3000-360 Main St, Winnipeg, MB, R3C 4G1 **Telephone** - (204) 724-0613
Email - romanikm@mymts.net
Investor Relations - Michael Romanik (204) 726-0151
Auditors - Scarrow & Donald LLP C.A., Winnipeg, Man.
Lawyers - MLT Aikins LLP
Transfer Agents - Computershare Trust Company of Canada Inc., Vancouver, B.C.
Profile - (Can. 2020) Capital Pool Company.

In April 2022, the company's proposed Qualifying Transaction reverse takeover acquisition of **Botanical Holdings plc**, announced in October 2021, was terminated. Botancial Holdings invests in the medical cannabis sector.

Recent Merger and Acquisition Activity

Status: pending **Announced:** Mar. 2, 2023
Anacott Acquisition Corporation entered into a letter of intent for the Qualifying Transaction reverse takeover acquisition of Ramp Metals Inc., which as nickel-copper interests in Saskatchewan. Terms were to be entered into.

Directors - Michael Romanik, CEO, CFO & corp. sec., Brandon, Man.; Joseph J. (Jeff) Smulders, Richmond, B.C.; Glen Wallace, North Saanich, B.C.

Capital Stock

	Authorized (shs.)	Outstanding (shs.)[1]
Common	unlimited	4,400,896

[1] At July 22, 2022

Major Shareholder - Michael Romanik held 31.8% interest at May 25, 2022.

Price Range - AAC.P/TSX-VEN

Year	Volume	High	Low	Close
2022	48,001	$0.17	$0.10	$0.13
2021	265,865	$0.32	$0.15	$0.16

Recent Close: $0.10

A.102 Anaergia Inc.

Symbol - ANRG **Exchange** - TSX **CUSIP** - 03253E
Head Office - 4210 South Service Rd, Burlington, ON, L7L 4X5 **Telephone** - (905) 407-0647
Website - www.anaergia.com
Email - ir@anaergia.com
Investor Relations - Hani El-Kaissi (905) 766-3333
Auditors - Deloitte LLP C.A., Toronto, Ont.
Transfer Agents - TSX Trust Company, Toronto, Ont.
FP500 Revenue Ranking - 694
Employees - 400 at Dec. 31, 2022
Profile - (B.C. 2018; orig. Can., 2010) Develops technologies and services used to design, build, own, operate and finance projects that process organic waste, primarily solid waste, wastewater and agricultural waste, into renewable natural gas (RNG), clean water and natural fertilizer.

Has a portfolio of end-to-end solutions that integrates solid waste processing as well as wastewater treatment with organics recovery, high-efficiency anaerobic digestion, RNG production, and recovery of fertilizer and water from organic residuals.

Operates in three segments: **Capital Sales**, which consists of technology packaged solutions, equipment and services to third party customers, primarily municipalities, private entities and project developers, and includes engineering services, product sales, engineering procurement and construction contracts; **Services**, which offers third-party operation and maintenance and field service contracts, which are typically for periods of five to 10 years, with customers that typically include municipalities and project developers; and **Build, Own and Operate (BOO)**, where the company builds, owns and operates its own greenfield or brownfield facilities. Its flagship BOO asset is the Rialto bioenergy facility (51% owned) in Rialto, Calif., which is the largest organic waste diversion and energy recovery facility in North America.

Solutions are provided through nine offices in Burlington, Ont., Carlsbad, Calif., Cambridgeshire, U.K., Treviglio, Italy, Oldenzaal, Netherlands, Lippetal, Germany, Singapore, Cape Town, South Africa, and Aabenraa, Denmark; and two manufacturing plants in Grüntegernbach, Germany, and Ovada, Italy.

At Dec. 31, 2022, the company had a backlog of $5 billion consisting primarily of BOO and a development pipeline that included over 50 potential BOO opportunities.

Recent Merger and Acquisition Activity

Status: completed **Announced:** Feb. 22, 2023
Anaergia Inc. agreed to sell Envo Biogas plant, an anaerobic digestion facility, in Tonder, Denmark to Copenhagen Infrastructure Partners' (CIP) Advanced Bioenergy Fund I for €56,000,000.

Directors - Dr. Andrew Benedek, founder & chr., Calif.; The Hon. Frank J. McKenna†, Cap-Pelé, N.B.; Peter Gross, Minn.; Dr. Diana Mourato Benedek, Calif.; D. Fridrik (Rik) Parkhill, Ont.; Stan Simmons, Calif.; Alan Viterbi, Calif.

Other Exec. Officers - Brett Hodson, CEO; Dr. Yaniv Scherson, COO; Andrew Spence, CFO; Hani El-Kaissi, chief devel. officer; Juan Josse, chief engineer; Kunal Shah, chief growth officer; Ashwani Kumar, v-p, global opers.; Rober Murray, v-p, global project execution; Sasha Rollings-Scattergood, v-p, tech.; Thor Erickson, gen. counsel
† Lead director

Capital Stock

	Authorized (shs.)	Outstanding (shs.)[1]
Subord. Vtg.	unlimited	32,685,716
Multiple Vtg.	unlimited	32,222,369

[1] At June 23, 2023

Subordinate Voting - One vote per share.
Multiple Voting - All held by the company's founder, chairman and chief executive officer, Dr. Andrew Benedek. Convertible into subordinate voting shares on a 1-for-1 basis at the option of holder and automatically in certain circumstances. Four votes per share.
Major Shareholder - Dr. Andrew Benedek held 80% interest at June 23, 2023.

Price Range - ANRG/TSX

Year	Volume	High	Low	Close
2022	28,345,100	$20.10	$3.67	$4.34
2021	12,372,362	$26.77	$13.03	$20.20

Recent Close: $0.32
Capital Stock Changes - In April 2022, bought deal public offering of 4,800,000 subordinate voting shares was completed at $12.50 per share. Also during 2022, 883,158 subordinate voting shares were issued on exercise of options.

Wholly Owned Subsidiaries

Anaergia A/S, Aabenraa, Denmark.
- 100% int. in **EBT Holdco ApS**, Denmark.
  - 100% int. in **Envo Biogas Tonder A/S**, Tonder, Denmark.

Anaergia Bioenergy Facilitites, LLC, United States.
Anaergia B.V., Netherlands.
- 100% int. in **Anaergia Orex Manufacturing S.r.l.**, Italy.

Anaergia DB Inc., Canada.
Anaergia Future Fuel, LLC, United States.
Anaergia GmbH, Germany.
- 100% int. in **Anaergia Africa (Pty) Ltd.**, South Africa.

Anaergia ITA B.V., Netherlands.
Anaergia Infrastructure S.r.l., Italy.
Anaergia Ltd., United Kingdom.
Anaergia Nutrients Holdco, LLC, United States.
- 100% int. in **Anaergia Nutrients, LLC**, United States.

Anaergia Services LLC, United States.
- 100% int. in **Biogas Power Systems Mojave LLC**, United States.
- 100% int. in **Camden Bioenergy LLC**, United States.
- 100% int. in **Charlotte Bioenergy Facility HoldCo, LLLC**, United States.
  - 100% int. in **Charlotte Bioenergy Facility, LLLC**, United States.
- 100% int. in **Escondido Bioenergy Facility LLC**, United States.
- 100% int. in **Rhode Island Bioenergy Facility HoldCo, LLC**, United States.
  - 100% int. in **Rhode Island Bioenergy Facility, LLC**, United States.
- 51% int. in **Rialto Bioenergy Facility, LLC**, United States.
- 100% int. in **SoCal Biomethane Holdco LLC**, United States.
  - 100% int. in **SoCal Biomethane LLC**, United States.

Anaergia Singapore Pte. Ltd., Singapore.
Anaergia South Africa Services (Pty) Ltd., South Africa.
Anaergia S.r.l., Italy.
- 70% int. in **Bioener S.p.A.**, Italy.
  - 80% int. in **Bionet S.r.l**, Italy.
- 55% int. in **WTE Holdings S.r.l.**, Italy.

Anaergia Systems A/S, Denmark.
Anaergia Technologies GmbH, Germany.
- 92% int. in **UTS Biogastechnik GmbH**, Germany.

Anaergia Technologies, LLC, Del.
Db Technologies B.V., Netherlands.
Kent County Bioenergy Facility Holdco, LLC, United States.
- 100% int. in **Kent County Bioenergy Facility, LLC**, United States.

SoCal Organics Recycling Facility Holdco, LLC, United States.
- 100% int. in **SoCal Organics Recycling Facility, LLC**, United States.

UTS BioEnergy, LLC, United States.
Victor Valley Bioenergy Facility Holdco, LLC, United States.
- 100% int. in **Victor Valley Bioenergy Facility, LLC**, United States.

Investments

47% int. in **Fibracast Ltd.**, Ont.

Financial Statistics

Periods ended:	12m Dec. 31/22[A]		12m Dec. 31/21[oA]
	$000s	%Chg	$000s
Operating revenue	**162,853**	**+25**	**129,873**
Cost of sales	134,256		105,019
Research & devel. expense	2,465		(1,029)
General & admin expense	55,024		37,222
Operating expense	**191,745**	**+36**	**141,212**
Operating income	**(28,892)**	**n.a.**	**(11,339)**
Deprec., depl. & amort.	3,541		3,354
Finance costs, net	1,211		(917)
Investment income	(5,860)		(3,316)
Write-downs/write-offs	(4,304)		(1,349)
Pre-tax income	**(60,189)**	**n.a.**	**(12,591)**
Income taxes	14,523		1,516
Net income	**(74,712)**	**n.a.**	**(14,107)**
Net inc. for equity hldrs	**(64,282)**	**n.a.**	**(17,214)**
Net inc. for non-cont. int	**(10,430)**	**n.a.**	**3,107**
Cash & equivalent	110,135		79,317
Inventories	10,068		5,509
Accounts receivable	39,410		34,788
Current assets	205,270		226,362
Long-term investments	21,771		29,148
Fixed assets, net	488,860		327,510
Right-of-use assets	15,803		14,194
Intangibles, net	19,428		5,157
Total assets	**935,105**	**+35**	**693,386**
Bank indebtedness	5,451		5,113
Accts. pay. & accr. liabs	119,755		69,259
Current liabilities	171,743		109,186
Long-term debt, gross	356,202		201,378
Long-term debt, net	344,385		196,115
Long-term lease liabilities	14,836		13,975
Preferred share equity	47,678		23,679
Shareholders' equity	208,837		203,526
Non-controlling interest	133,303		119,870
Cash from oper. activs	**(30,558)**	**n.a.**	**(59,598)**
Cash from fin. activs	198,135		239,550
Cash from invest. activs	(192,504)		(138,602)
Net cash position	**55,378**	**-30**	**79,317**
Capital expenditures	(110,037)		(71,123)
	$		$
Earnings per share*	(0.83)		(0.53)
Cash flow per share*	(0.49)		(1.58)
	shs		shs
No. of shs. o/s*	64,434,522		58,750,869
Avg. no. of shs. o/s*	62,783,467		37,648,305
	%		%
Net profit margin	(45.88)		(10.86)
Return on equity	(37.72)		(30.93)
Return on assets	(9.18)		(2.46)
No. of employees (FTEs)	400		345

* S.V. & M.V.
[o] Restated
[A] Reported in accordance with IFRS

Latest Results

Periods ended:	3m Mar. 31/23[A]		3m Mar. 31/22[A]
	$000s	%Chg	$000s
Operating revenue	36,611	+3	35,616
Net income	(11,277)	n.a.	(16,390)
Net inc. for equity hldrs	(10,203)	n.a.	(12,282)
Net inc. for non-cont. int	(1,074)		(4,108)
	$		$
Earnings per share*	(0.14)		(0.15)

* S.V. & M.V.
[A] Reported in accordance with IFRS

Historical Summary
(as originally stated)

Fiscal Year	Oper. Rev.	Net Inc. Bef. Disc.	EPS*
	$000s	$000s	$
2022[A]	162,853	(74,712)	(0.83)
2021[A]	127,048	(15,565)	(0.53)
2020[A]	128,042	(16,821)	(4.11)
2019[A]	89,677	8,659	0.59

* S.V. & M.V.
[A] Reported in accordance with IFRS

A.103 AnalytixInsight Inc.

Symbol - ALY **Exchange** - TSX-VEN **CUSIP** - 03268Y
Head Office - 235-100 2 Toronto St, Toronto, ON, M5C 2B5 **Toll-free** - (866) 824-8938
Website - www.analytixinsight.com
Email - prakash.hariharan@analytixinsight.com
Investor Relations - Prakash Hariharan (416) 561-9461
Auditors - McGovern Hurley LLP C.A., Toronto, Ont.
Transfer Agents - TSX Trust Company, Toronto, Ont.
Profile - (Ont. 2014; orig. Man., 1999) Provides financial research and content for investors, information providers, finance portals and media; and system integration services for the workforce management industry. Also focuses on mobile opportunities especially in the business-to-business (B2B) and B2B-to-consumer spaces.

The company's flagship product, CapitalCube, provides financial research and content for investors, information providers, finance portals and media through its online portal www.capitalcube.com and through its institutional partner Connect platform. CapitalCube also includes on-demand daily updated fundamental research, portfolio evaluation and screening tools on the relative value of 50,000 global publicly traded companies and on more than 4,000 exchange-traded funds on North American Stock Exchanges.

Through wholly owned **Euclides Technologies, Inc.**, offers workforce optimization software solutions including IFS Field Service Management™, IFS Planning and Scheduling Optimization™ and ClickSoftware.

Affiliate **Marketwall S.R.L.** develops fintech solutions for financial institutions and provides mobile access to financial data and data analytics. Key products include InvestoPro, a European online digital trading platform which allows retail investors to trade stocks, bonds and derivatives, as well as delivers financial analysis, news, research, educational formats and other exclusive content aided by artificial intelligence; InvestoPro EVO, an online stock trading and fin-tech enabled services on multi-device trading platforms, including mobile, wearables and smart-TV, combined with research and financial education; InvestoPro GO, a simplified version of the online digital trading platform catered to **Samsung Electronics Italia S.p.A.**'s consumers; Investo, a stock trading application designed for retail users and available under license for deployment by banks and brokers; Gemina, a trading platform for banks and brokers available as white label business to business product offering; and Morningstar Global Market, an enterprise research and market data platform for institutional users of financial data and related investment products.

Predecessor Detail - Name changed from OMT Inc., July 11, 2013, following acquisition of AnalytixInsight Inc.; basis 1 new for 3 old shs.
Directors - Prakash Hariharan, chr. & CEO, Mississauga, Ont.; Chaith Kondragunta, man. dir., New York, N.Y.; Scott Gardner, Panama; Vincent Kadar, Ont.; Jith Veeravalli, Calif.
Other Exec. Officers - Natalie Hirsch, COO; Paul S. Bozoki, CFO; Scott Urquhart, v-p, corp. devel.; Aaron Atin, corp. sec.

Capital Stock

	Authorized (shs.)	Outstanding (shs.)[1]
Preferred	unlimited	nil
Common	unlimited	97,216,741

[1] At July 31, 2023

Major Shareholder - Widely held at July 31, 2023.

Price Range - ALY/TSX-VEN

Year	Volume	High	Low	Close
2022	19,166,977	$0.83	$0.29	$0.35
2021	52,513,365	$1.25	$0.55	$0.80
2020	27,000,796	$0.84	$0.21	$0.73
2019	22,738,884	$0.58	$0.29	$0.54
2018	47,520,996	$0.87	$0.27	$0.29

Recent Close: $0.16
Capital Stock Changes - During 2022, common shares were issued as follows: 765,000 under restricted share unit plan and 150,000 on exercise of options.

Wholly Owned Subsidiaries

Euclides Technologies, Inc., New York, N.Y.

Investments

49% int. in **Marketwall S.R.L.**, Milan, Italy.
- 100% int. in **InvestoPro Sim S.p.A.**, Milan, Italy.

Financial Statistics

Periods ended:	12m Dec. 31/22[A]		12m Dec. 31/21[A]
	$000s	%Chg	$000s
Operating revenue	**1,672**	**-44**	**3,001**
Cost of sales	1,647		2,243
Salaries & benefits	1,732		1,759
General & admin expense	1,562		1,250
Stock-based compensation	387		799
Operating expense	**5,328**	**-12**	**6,051**
Operating income	**(3,656)**	**n.a.**	**(3,049)**
Deprec., depl. & amort.	85		223
Finance costs, gross	4		10
Investment income	(152)		(132)
Write-downs/write-offs	(308)		(676)
Pre-tax income	**(4,170)**	**n.a.**	**(4,082)**
Net income	**(4,170)**	**n.a.**	**(4,082)**
Cash & equivalent	2,519		6,075
Accounts receivable	510		316
Current assets	3,160		6,531
Long-term investments	4,182		4,334
Fixed assets, net	42		72
Total assets	**7,384**	**-32**	**10,936**
Accts. pay. & accr. liabs	628		395
Current liabilities	679		537
Long-term lease liabilities	14		5
Shareholders' equity	6,691		10,394
Cash from oper. activs	**(3,505)**	**n.a.**	**(2,072)**
Cash from fin. activs	(56)		8,618
Cash from invest. activs	nil		(2,112)
Net cash position	**2,519**	**-59**	**6,075**
	$		$
Earnings per share*	(0.04)		(0.05)
Cash flow per share*	(0.04)		(0.02)
	shs		shs
No. of shs. o/s*	97,216,741		96,301,741
Avg. no. of shs. o/s*	96,557,563		89,310,894
	%		%
Net profit margin	(249.40)		(136.02)
Return on equity	(48.81)		(53.20)
Return on assets	(45.48)		(49.30)

* Common
[A] Reported in accordance with IFRS

Latest Results

Periods ended:	3m Mar. 31/23[A]		3m Mar. 31/22[A]
	$000s	%Chg	$000s
Operating revenue	178	-61	455
Net income	(215)	n.a.	(986)
	$		$
Earnings per share*	(0.00)		(0.01)

* Common
[A] Reported in accordance with IFRS

Historical Summary
(as originally stated)

Fiscal Year	Oper. Rev.	Net Inc. Bef. Disc.	EPS*
	$000s	$000s	$
2022[A]	1,672	(4,170)	(0.04)
2021[A]	3,001	(4,082)	(0.05)
2020[A]	3,179	(1,980)	(0.03)
2019[A]	3,673	(1,670)	(0.02)
2018[A]	4,838	(2,302)	(0.03)

* Common
[A] Reported in accordance with IFRS

A.104 Andean Precious Metals Corp.

Symbol - APM **Exchange** - TSX-VEN **CUSIP** - 03349X
Head Office - Ignacio L. Vallarta, No. 811 Sur Col. El Mirador Centro, Monterrey, NL, Mexico, 64070 **Telephone** - (437) 371-2820
Website - www.andeanpm.com
Email - tmoran@andeanpm.com
Investor Relations - Patricia Moran (416) 564-4290
Auditors - KPMG LLP C.A., Toronto, Ont.
Lawyers - McMillan LLP, Toronto, Ont.
Transfer Agents - Computershare Trust Company of Canada Inc., Vancouver, B.C.
FP500 Revenue Ranking - 723
Profile - (B.C. 2018) Owns and operates San Bartolomé open-pit silver mine and has other mineral interests in Bolivia.

Holds San Bartolomé open-pit silver mine, 1,800 hectares, near Potosí, where commercial production commenced in June 2008. As at Dec. 31, 2022, measured and indicated resource at Tatasi-Portugalete deposit was 82,000 tonnes grading 304 g/t silver, measured and indicated resource at Pallacos deposit was 2,237,000 tonnes grading 83 g/t silver and indicated resource at FDF Oxides was 10,148,000 tonnes grading 50 g/t silver.

Also holds Jiwaki II prospect; and Rio Blanco gold prospect, 3,745 hectares, 117 km south of San Bartolomé mine.

Periods ended:	12m Dec. 31/22	12m Dec. 31/21
Gold prod., oz	2,560	6,075
Gold sales, oz	2,341	5,888
Avg real. gold price, US$/oz	1,814	1,767
Silver prod., oz	4,788,000	5,358,000
Silver sales, oz	4,769,000	5,366,000
Avg real. silver price, US$/oz	21.76	24.94

Note: Reflects operations of San Bartolomé silver mine owned and operated by indirect wholly owned Empresa Minera Manquiri, S.A., which was indirectly acquired through the company's Qualifying Transaction reverse takeover acquisition of 1254688 B.C. Ltd. effective Mar. 18, 2021.

Predecessor Detail - Name changed from Buckhaven Capital Corp., Mar. 18, 2021, pursuant to the Qualifying Transaction reverse takeover acquisition of 1254688 B.C. Ltd. and concurrent amalgamation of 1254688 B.C. with wholly owned 1271860 B.C. Ltd.; basis 1 new for 1.5 old shs.

Directors - Alberto Morales, exec. chr. & CEO, Santo Domingo, Dominican Republic; Grant Angwin†, Utah; Yohann Bouchard, Oakville, Ont.; Felipe C. Canales, N.L., Mexico; Peter V. Gundy, Toronto, Ont.; Ramiro G. Villarreal, N.L., Mexico

Other Exec. Officers - Juan Carlos Sandoval, CFO; Segun Odunuga, exec. v-p, fin.; Sarai Cardoso, v-p, special projects; Federico Gil, v-p, legal & admin.; Patricia (Trish) Moran, v-p, IR; Melissa Terui, corp. sec.; Humberto Rada Gómez, pres., Manquiri

† Lead director

Capital Stock

	Authorized (shs.)	Outstanding (shs.)[1]
Common	unlimited	158,032,756

[1] At Mar. 17, 2023

Normal Course Issuer Bid - The company plans to make normal course purchases of up to 7,895,706 common shares representing 5% of the total outstanding. The bid commenced on Oct. 4, 2022, and expires on Oct. 3, 2023.

Major Shareholder - Alberto Morales held 50.3% interest and Eric S. Sprott held 13.5% interest at July 29, 2022.

Price Range - APM/TSX-VEN

Year	Volume	High	Low	Close
2022	33,645,560	$2.30	$0.65	$1.11
2021	26,546,964	$2.03	$0.92	$1.75
2020	35,333	$0.36	$0.19	$0.36
2019	119,333	$0.46	$0.27	$0.27

Consolidation: 1-for-1.5 cons. in Mar. 2021
Recent Close: $0.64

Capital Stock Changes - During 2022, 881,250 common shares were issued on vesting of restricted share units and 322,000 common shares were repurchased under a Normal Course Issuer Bid.

Wholly Owned Subsidiaries

1295229 B.C. Limited, B.C.
- 100% int. in **Ag-Mining Investments AB**, Sweden.
- 100% int. in **Empresa Minera Manquiri, S.A.**, Bolivia.
- 100% int. in **Minera Pukaraju S.A.**, Bolivia.

Financial Statistics

Periods ended:	12m Dec. 31/22[A]		12m Dec. 31/21[A]
	US$000s	%Chg	US$000s
Operating revenue	**108,049**	**-25**	**144,207**
Cost of sales	91,133		95,013
Salaries & benefits	8,597		6,831
Exploration expense	3,615		3,894
General & admin expense	4,156		5,877
Stock-based compensation	2,156		2,017
Operating expense	**109,657**	**-3**	**113,632**
Operating income	**(1,608)**	**n.a.**	**30,575**
Deprec., depl. & amort.	7,212		10,388
Finance income	828		120
Finance costs, gross	1,279		1,292
Pre-tax income	**(10,074)**	**n.a.**	**19,981**
Income taxes	17		15,713
Net income	**(10,091)**	**n.a.**	**4,268**
Cash & equivalent	86,067		91,453
Inventories	11,720		8,733
Current assets	109,300		105,144
Fixed assets, net	16,565		20,695
Total assets	**133,857**	**-5**	**140,293**
Accts. pay. & accr. liabs	13,113		11,879
Current liabilities	19,025		19,434
Shareholders' equity	94,427		102,558
Cash from oper. activs	**(2,740)**	**n.a.**	**33,615**
Cash from fin. activs	724		19,401
Cash from invest. activs	(3,724)		(3,911)
Net cash position	**80,729**	**-8**	**87,276**
Capital expenditures	(2,204)		(3,383)
	US$		US$
Earnings per share*	(0.06)		0.03
Cash flow per share*	(0.02)		0.22
	shs		shs
No. of shs. o/s*	157,473,506		157,473,506
Avg. no. of shs. o/s*	157,911,600		149,641,719
	%		%
Net profit margin	(9.34)		2.96
Return on equity	(10.25)		4.83
Return on assets	(6.43)		3.55

* Common
[A] Reported in accordance with IFRS

Historical Summary
(as originally stated)

Fiscal Year	Oper. Rev.	Net Inc. Bef. Disc.	EPS*
	US$000s	US$000s	US$
2022[A]	108,049	(10,091)	(0.06)
2021[A]	144,207	4,268	0.03
2020[A1]	130,672	45,959	n.a.
2019[A1]	88,655	(12,801)	n.a.
2018[A1]	64,284	40,556	n.a.

* Common
[A] Reported in accordance with IFRS
[1] Results pertain to Ag-Mining Investments AB.
Note: Adjusted throughout for 1-for-1.5 cons. in Mar. 2021

A.105 Andlauer Healthcare Group Inc.

Symbol - AND **Exchange** - TSX **CUSIP** - 034223
Head Office - 100 Vaughan Valley Rd, Vaughan, ON, L4H 3C5 **Telephone** - (416) 744-4900
Website - www.andlauerhealthcare.com
Email - pbromley@andlauer.ca
Investor Relations - Peter Bromley (416) 744-4916
Auditors - KPMG LLP C.A., Toronto, Ont.
Lawyers - Goodmans LLP, Toronto, Ont.
Transfer Agents - TSX Trust Company, Toronto, Ont.
FP500 Revenue Ranking - 419
Employees - 2,230 at Dec. 31, 2022
Profile - (Ont. 2019) Provides customized third-party logistics (3PL) and specialized transportation services for the healthcare sector in Canada and the United States.

Services are offered to healthcare manufacturers, wholesalers, distributors and 3PL providers through a platform of high quality, technology-enabled supply chain solutions for a range of products, including pharmaceuticals, vaccines, biologics, blood products narcotics, precursors, active pharmaceutical ingredients, over-the-counter, natural health, animal health, consumer health, cosmetics, health and beauty aids, and medical devices.

Principal product lines are customized logistics and distribution, and packaging solutions (representing the healthcare logistics segment); ground transportation, air freight forwarding, and dedicated delivery and last mile services (representing the specialized transportation segment).

The company's ATS Healthcare brand nation-wide distribution network operates through a fleet of 611 customized, qualified, calibrated and temperature monitored vehicles consisting of 45 vans, 150 three-ton trucks, 45 five-ton trucks, 301 trailers and 70 tractors. Operations are conducted from 37 facilities across Canada, consisting of nine distribution centres and 22 branches as well as operating from six third-party owned cross-docks. In addition, the company has 190 trucks and 260 trailers under the Skelton brand operating across Canada and the United States; and has 95 trucks and 170 trailers under the Boyle Transportation brand operating across 48 contiguous United States.

Recent Merger and Acquisition Activity

Status: completed **Revised:** Mar. 1, 2022

UPDATE: The transaction was completed. The share consideration was satisfied through the issuance of 154,639 Andlauer subordinate voting shares. PREVIOUS: Andlauer Healthcare Group Inc. agreed to acquire private Boucherville, Que.-based Logistics Support Unit (LSU) Inc. for $30,000,000, consisting of $22,500,000 cash, to be financed through a combination of cash on hand and by drawing on credit facilities, and issuance of $7,500,000 of Andlauer subordinate voting shares. LSU provides third-party logistics offering specialty pharmacy, warehousing, distribution and order management services throughout Canada to national and international companies as well as government clients in the pharmaceutical, medical and biotechnology sectors. LSU also was the exclusive distributor of immunizing agents for the Quebec public health system.

Directors - Peter Jelley, chr., East York, Ont.; Michael N. Andlauer, CEO, Oakville, Ont.; The Hon. Ronalee H. (Rona) Ambrose†, Calgary, Alta.; Cameron Joyce, Cambridge, Ont.; Joseph Schlett, Waterdown, Ont.; Evelyn Sutherland, East York, Ont.; Thomas G. Wellner, Toronto, Ont.

Other Exec. Officers - Peter Bromley, CFO & corp. sec.; Graham Cromb, chief strategy officer; Stephen Barr, pres., trans.; Dean Berg, pres., logistics; C. Robert (Bob) Brogan, pres., specialty solutions

† Lead director

Capital Stock

	Authorized (shs.)	Outstanding (shs.)[1]
Preferred	unlimited	nil
Subordinate Voting	unlimited	20,074,253
Multiple Voting	unlimited	21,840,000[2]

[1] At Mar. 2, 2023.

[2] All held by Michael N. Andlauer.

Subordinate Voting - One vote per share.

Multiple Voting - Convertible, at the holder's option, into subordinate voting shares on a one-for-one basis. Four votes per share.

Normal Course Issuer Bid - The company plans to make normal course purchases of up to 1,856,857 subordinate voting shares representing 10% of the public float. The bid commenced on Mar. 29, 2023, and expires on Mar. 28, 2024.

Major Shareholder - Michael N. Andlauer held 81.32% interest at Mar. 2, 2023.

Price Range - AND/TSX

Year	Volume	High	Low	Close
2022	6,579,640	$55.97	$37.57	$47.35
2021	7,522,949	$55.84	$31.81	$54.03
2020	7,102,732	$50.00	$19.00	$40.94
2019	2,199,335	$20.25	$18.00	$20.05

Recent Close: $40.93

Capital Stock Changes - On Mar. 1, 2022, 154,639 subordinate voting shares were issued pursuant to the acquisition of Logistics Support Unit (LSU) Inc. Also during 2022, 90,000 subordinate voting shares were issued on exercise of options.

Dividends

AND sub vtg Ra $0.32 pa Q est. Apr. 17, 2023
Prev. Rate: $0.28 est. Oct. 17, 2022
Prev. Rate: $0.24 est. Apr. 15, 2022
Prev. Rate: $0.20 est. July 15, 2020

Wholly Owned Subsidiaries

Associated Logistics Solutions Inc., Ont.
- 100% int. in **Accuristix Inc.**, Canada.
  - 100% int. in **Accuristix**, Ont.
    - 100% int. in **Accuristix Healthcare Logistics Inc.**, Ont.
    - 100% int. in **Nova Pack Ltd.**, Ont.
- 100% int. in **Concord Supply Chain Solutions Inc.**, Del. Inactive.
- 100% int. in **Logistics Support Unit (LSU) Inc.**, Boucherville, Qué.
- 100% int. in **13811361 Canada Inc.**, Canada.
- 100% int. in **2040637 Ontario Limited**, Ont.
  - 100% int. in **Accuristix**, Ont.

Credo Systems Canada Inc., Ont.

Skelton Canada Inc., Ont.
- 52% int. in **Andlauer Healthcare Group (USA), Inc.**, Del.
  - 100% int. in **Skelton Truck Lines, Inc.**, Del.
  - 48% int. in **Skelton USA Inc.**, Ohio
  - 100% int. in **T.F. Boyle Transportation, Inc.**, Billerica, Mass.
- 100% int. in **Skelton USA Inc.**, Ohio

2186940 Ontario Inc., Ont.
- 100% int. in **ATS Andlauer Transportation Services GP Inc.**, Canada.
  - 100% int. in **ATS Andlauer Transportation Services Limited Partnership**, Man.
    - 100% int. in **MEDDS Canada - A Medical Delivery Services Corporation**, Canada.
      - 25% int. in **MEDDS Winnipeg - A Medical Delivery Services Corporation**, Man.
    - 75% int. in **MEDDS Winnipeg - A Medical Delivery Services Corporation**, Man.
    - 100% int. in **McAllister Courier Inc.**, Chatham, Ont.
    - 100% int. in **TDS Logistics Inc.**, London, Ont.
- 100% int. in **2721275 Ontario Limited**, Ont.
  - 100% int. in **ATS Andlauer Transportation Services Limited Partnership**, Man.

Note: The preceding list includes only the major related companies in which interests are held.

Financial Statistics

Periods ended:	12m Dec. 31/22[A]		12m Dec. 31/21[A]
	$000s	%Chg	$000s
Operating revenue	**648,423**	**+47**	**440,115**
Cost of sales	425,124		286,645
General & admin expense	47,201		35,190
Stock-based compensation	1,301		1,861
Operating expense	**473,626**	**+46**	**323,696**
Operating income	**174,797**	**+50**	**116,419**
Deprec., depl. & amort.	64,452		42,716
Finance income	599		198
Finance costs, gross	6,858		6,219
Pre-tax income	**103,758**	**-4**	**108,440**
Income taxes	27,483		18,486
Net income	**76,275**	**-15**	**89,954**
Cash & equivalent	65,855		24,990
Inventories	3,326		2,331
Accounts receivable	98,423		90,093
Current assets	172,076		122,178
Fixed assets, net	175,880		178,112
Intangibles, net	357,698		335,200
Total assets	**712,460**	**+11**	**644,169**
Accts. pay. & accr. liabs	42,918		39,404
Current liabilities	85,778		90,529
Long-term debt, gross	49,557		60,288
Long-term debt, net	49,557		49,288
Long-term lease liabilities	87,182		100,517
Shareholders' equity	440,992		352,119
Cash from oper. activs	**137,128**	**+63**	**84,091**
Cash from fin. activs	(51,587)		93,889
Cash from invest. activs	(45,557)		(183,382)
Net cash position	**65,855**	**+164**	**24,990**
Capital expenditures	(25,748)		(8,026)
Capital disposals	1,721		258
	$		$
Earnings per share*	1.82		2.30
Cash flow per share*	3.28		2.15
Cash divd. per share*	0.26		0.20
	shs		shs
No. of shs. o/s*	41,914,000		41,669,000
Avg. no. of shs. o/s*	41,813,000		39,036,000
	%		%
Net profit margin	11.76		20.44
Return on equity	19.23		40.30
Return on assets	11.99		21.21
Foreign sales percent	20		4
No. of employees (FTEs)	2,230		1,800

* Subord. Vtg.

[A] Reported in accordance with IFRS

Historical Summary
(as originally stated)

Fiscal Year	Oper. Rev.	Net Inc. Bef. Disc.	EPS*
	$000s	$000s	$
2022[A]	648,423	76,275	1.82
2021[A]	440,115	89,954	2.30
2020[A]	314,340	37,714	1.00
2019[A]	289,988	30,345	0.79
2018[A1]	277,010	28,185	n.a.

* Subord. Vtg.

[A] Reported in accordance with IFRS

[1] Represents the collective results of Associated Logistics Solutions Inc., Credo Canada Systems Inc. and 2186940 Ontario Inc. (which were acquired concurrent with the completion of the Dec. 11, 2019, initial public offering). As shown in the prospectus dated Dec. 4, 2019.

A.106 Andrew Peller Limited*

Symbol - ADW.A **Exchange** - TSX **CUSIP** - 03444Q

Head Office - 697 South Service Rd, Grimsby, ON, L3M 4E8 **Telephone** - (905) 643-4131 **Toll-free** - (800) 564-6253 **Fax** - (905) 643-4944

Website - www.andrewpeller.com

Email - paul.dubkowski@andrewpeller.com

Investor Relations - Paul Dubkowski (800) 564-6253

Auditors - PricewaterhouseCoopers LLP C.A., Oakville, Ont.

Bankers - Rabobank Canada, Toronto, Ont.; National Bank of Canada; Bank of Montreal; The Toronto-Dominion Bank; Royal Bank of Canada

Lawyers - Osler, Hoskin & Harcourt LLP, Toronto, Ont.

Transfer Agents - Computershare Trust Company of Canada Inc., Toronto, Ont.

FP500 Revenue Ranking - 524

Employees - 1,629 at Mar. 31, 2023

Profile - (Can. 1965) Produces, bottles, imports and markets wines and craft beverage alcohol products, and produces wine kits and related accessories for the personal winemaking market mainly in Canada.

Operates wineries in British Columbia, Ontario and Nova Scotia, and markets wines produced from grapes grown in the Niagara Peninsula in Ontario, the Okanagan Valley and Similkameen Valley in British Columbia, and other countries around the world.

Premium and ultra-premium brands include Peller Estates, Trius, Thirty Bench, Wayne Gretzky, Sandhill, Red Rooster, Black Hills Estate Winery, Tinhorn Creek Vineyards, Gray Monk Estate Winery, Raven Conspiracy and Conviction. Popularly priced varietal brands include Peller Family Vineyards, Copper Moon, XOXO and Black Cellar. Value-priced wine blends include Hochtaler, Domaine D'Or, Schloss Laderheim, Royal and Sommet. Craft beverage alcohol products include No Boats on Sunday ciders and seltzers, and various spirits and cream whisky products under the Wayne Gretzky No. 99 brand. Products are sold primarily through government liquor distribution systems and the company's chain of 101 independent retail locations in Ontario under The Wine Shop, Wine Country Vintners and Wine Country Merchants store banners. The company also imports and markets bottled premium wines from around the world through Andrew Peller Import Agency in Vancouver, B.C., and wholly owned **The Small Winemakers Collection Inc.** in Toronto, Ont.

Through wholly owned **Global Vintners Inc.**, the company manufactures and markets premium and ultra-premium winemaking products through more than 200 Winexpert, Vineco and Wine Kitz authorized retailers and more than 400 independent retailers across Canada plus distributors in the U.S., the U.K., New Zealand, Australia and China.

Predecessor Detail - Name changed from Andrés Wines Ltd., Sept. 20, 2006; basis 3 new for 1 old sh.

Directors - John E. Peller, exec. chr., pres. & CEO, Burlington, Ont.; Dr. A. Angus Peller, v-chr., Toronto, Ont.; Perry J. Miele†, Burlington, Ont.; Shauneen E. Bruder, Toronto, Ont.; David Mongeau, Monte Carlo, Monaco; François Vimard, Ont.

Other Exec. Officers - Patrick R. O'Brien, chief comml. officer; Paul Dubkowski, exec. v-p, IT & CFO; Craig D. McDonald, exec. v-p, opers.; Sara E. Presutto, exec. v-p, people & culture; José Salgado, exec. v-p, corp. planning & devel., VQA & DTC & legal counsel; Stefan Barker, v-p, integrated supply chain; Gregory J. (Greg) Berti, v-p, industry rel. & bus. devel.; Mark Torrance, v-p, estate wine grp. opers.

† Lead director

Capital Stock

	Authorized (shs.)	Outstanding (shs.)[1]
Preference	unlimited	
Series A	33,315	nil
Class A Non-vtg.	unlimited	35,084,089
Class B Vtg.	unlimited	8,144,183

[1] At June 30, 2023

Class A Non-Voting - Entitled to dividends amounting to 115% of any dividend paid or declared on class B voting shares. In event of liquidation, etc., equal in all respects to class B voting shares. Non-voting.

Class B Voting - Convertible into class A non-voting shares on a share-for-share basis. One vote per share.

Options - At Mar. 31, 2023, options were outstanding to purchase 1,641,335 class A non-voting shares at exercise prices ranging from $5.01 to $20 per share with a weighted average remaining contractual life of 90 months.

Normal Course Issuer Bid - The company plans to make normal course purchases of up to 1,000,000 class A non-voting shares representing 2.9% of the total outstanding. The bid commenced on Sept. 16, 2022, and expires on Sept. 15, 2023.

Major Shareholder - Peller family held 61.3% interest and John E. Peller held 11.7% interest at July 31, 2023.

Price Range - ADW.A/TSX

Year	Volume	High	Low	Close
2022	7,515,269	$8.28	$4.60	$4.99
2021	11,466,702	$11.60	$7.67	$8.16
2020	7,251,351	$12.09	$6.00	$10.48
2019	5,610,000	$15.45	$11.53	$11.81
2018	9,121,591	$19.04	$11.64	$13.69

Recent Close: $4.37

Capital Stock Changes - During fiscal 2023, class A shares were issued as follows: 58,851 on exercise of performance, restricted and deferred share units and 3,794 as dividends.

During fiscal 2022, class A shares were issued as follows: 49,056 on exercise of performance and deferred share units and 1,916 as dividends; 598,600 class A shares were repurchased under a Normal Course Issuer Bid.

Dividends

ADW.B cl B Ra $0.214 pa Q est. July 9, 2021**[1]
Prev. Rate: $0.1964 est. Apr. 9, 2021
Prev. Rate: $0.1872 est. July 5, 2019
ADW.A cl A N.V. Ra $0.246 pa Q est. July 9, 2021**[1]
Prev. Rate: $0.2256 est. Apr. 9, 2021
Prev. Rate: $0.2152 est. July 5, 2019

[1] Dividend reinvestment plan implemented eff. Sept. 9, 2016.

** Reinvestment Option

Long-Term Debt - At Mar. 31, 2023, outstanding long-term debt totaled $208,089,000 (none current and net of $40,000 of financing costs) and consisted entirely of borrowings under a $350,000,000 revolving credit facility due Dec. 8, 2024.

Note - In June 2023, the company replaced its existing revolving credit facility with a $275,000,000 asset-backed lending credit facility maturing on June 13, 2027.

Wholly Owned Subsidiaries

Canrim Packaging Ltd., Vancouver, B.C.

Global Vintners Inc., Ont.
- 100% int. in **Wine Kitz Franchise Inc.**, Ont.

Riverbend Inn & Winery Inc., Ont.

Sandhill Vineyards Ltd., Vancouver, B.C.

The Small Winemakers Collection Inc., Toronto, Ont.

Financial Statistics

Periods ended:	12m Mar. 31/23[A]		12m Mar. 31/22[A]
	$000s	%Chg	$000s
Operating revenue	**382,140**	**+2**	**373,944**
Cost of goods sold	240,248		234,952
General & admin expense	103,880		99,804
Operating expense	**344,128**	**+3**	**334,756**
Operating income	**38,012**	**-3**	**39,188**
Deprec., depl. & amort.	22,520		21,353
Finance costs, gross	16,185		7,068
Pre-tax income	**(4,240)**	**n.a.**	**17,075**
Income taxes	(888)		4,607
Net income	**(3,352)**	**n.a.**	**12,468**
Cash & equivalent	nil		1,297
Inventories	209,154		197,042
Accounts receivable	25,297		27,376
Current assets	246,168		236,213
Fixed assets, net	210,265		209,015
Right-of-use assets	13,612		15,215
Intangibles, net	96,703		97,628
Total assets	**566,748**	**+2**	**558,071**
Bank indebtedness	4,942		nil
Accts. pay. & accr. liabs	46,178		45,961
Current liabilities	59,850		54,381
Long-term debt, gross	208,089		192,065
Long-term debt, net	208,089		192,065
Long-term lease liabilities	10,205		12,193
Shareholders' equity	253,638		265,401
Cash from oper. activs	**13,754**	**-12**	**15,592**
Cash from fin. activs	5,283		(2,924)
Cash from invest. activs	(20,334)		(14,108)
Net cash position	**nil**	**n.a.**	**1,297**
Capital expenditures	(17,301)		(13,612)
Capital disposals	nil		8,793
Pension fund surplus	879		669
	$		$
Earnings per share*	(0.08)		0.29
Earnings per share**	(0.07)		0.26
Cash flow per share***	0.32		0.36
Cash divd. per share*	0.25		0.25
Cash divd. per share**	0.21		0.21
	shs		shs
No. of shs. o/s***	43,184,839		43,122,194
Avg. no. of shs. o/s***	43,163,640		43,345,152
	%		%
Net profit margin	(0.88)		3.33
Return on equity	(1.29)		4.70
Return on assets	1.68		3.20
Foreign sales percent	3		4
No. of employees (FTEs)	1,629		1,622

* Class A
** Class B
*** Class A & Class B
[A] Reported in accordance with IFRS

Latest Results

Periods ended:	3m June 30/23[A]		3m June 30/22[A]
	$000s	%Chg	$000s
Operating revenue	100,481	+3	97,699
Net income	(931)	n.a.	2,863
	$		$
Earnings per share*	(0.02)		0.07
Earnings per share**	(0.02)		0.06

* Class A
** Class B
[A] Reported in accordance with IFRS

Historical Summary
(as originally stated)

Fiscal Year	Oper. Rev.	Net Inc. Bef. Disc.	EPS*
	$000s	$000s	$
2023[A]	382,140	(3,352)	(0.08)
2022[A]	373,944	12,468	0.29
2021[A]	393,036	27,786	0.65
2020[A]	382,306	23,494	0.55
2019[A]	381,796	21,958	0.51

* Class A
[A] Reported in accordance with IFRS

A.107 Aneesh Capital Corp.

Symbol - EESH.P **Exchange** - TSX-VEN **CUSIP** - 034582
Head Office - 2050-1055 Georgia St W, Vancouver, BC, V6E 3P3 **Telephone** - (604) 684-2181
Email - peeyush@varshneycapital.com
Investor Relations - Peeyush K. Varshney (604) 684-2181
Auditors - Dale Matheson Carr-Hilton LaBonte LLP C.A., Vancouver, B.C.
Transfer Agents - Olympia Trust Company, Vancouver, B.C.
Profile - (B.C. 2017) Capital Pool Company.
Directors - Peeyush K. Varshney, CEO & CFO, Vancouver, B.C.; Capt. Mervyn J. Pinto, Surrey, B.C.; Besar Xhelili, Ont.
Other Exec. Officers - Debbie Lew, corp. sec.

Capital Stock

	Authorized (shs.)	Outstanding (shs.)[1]
Common	unlimited	6,250,001

[1] At June 28, 2022

Major Shareholder - Peeyush K. Varshney held 28.79% interest at Mar. 17, 2022.

Price Range - EESH.P/TSX-VEN

Year	Volume	High	Low	Close
2022	56,500	$0.17	$0.10	$0.10
2021	30,000	$0.21	$0.20	$0.20

Recent Close: $0.08

A.108 Ankh II Capital Inc.

Symbol - AUNK.P **Exchange** - TSX-VEN **CUSIP** - 03539U
Head Office - 2000-250 Howe St, Vancouver, BC, V6C 3R8 **Telephone** - (604) 690-2680
Email - roger@friendshipfoods.net
Investor Relations - Roger E. Milad (604) 690-2680
Auditors - Baker Tilly WM LLP C.A., Vancouver, B.C.
Lawyers - Dentons Canada LLP, Vancouver, B.C.
Transfer Agents - TSX Trust Company, Vancouver, B.C.
Profile - (Can. 2022) Capital Pool Company.
Common listed on TSX-VEN, May 12, 2023.
Directors - Roger E. Milad, CEO & CFO, Vancouver, B.C.; Gary Musil, New Westminster, B.C.; D. Richard (Rick) Skeith, Calgary, Alta.

Capital Stock

	Authorized (shs.)	Outstanding (shs.)[1]
Common	unlimited	6,041,801

[1] At May 12, 2023

Major Shareholder - Roger E. Milad held 16.55% interest at May 12, 2023.
Capital Stock Changes - On May 12, 2023, an initial public offering of 4,041,800 common shares was completed at 10¢ per share.

A.109 Ankh Capital Inc.

Symbol - ANKH.P **Exchange** - TSX-VEN **CUSIP** - 03539R
Head Office - 2000-250 Howe St, Vancouver, BC, V6C 3R8 **Telephone** - (604) 690-2680
Email - roger@friendshipfoods.net
Investor Relations - Roger E. Milad (604) 690-2680
Auditors - Baker Tilly HMA LLP C.A., Winnipeg, Man.
Lawyers - Dentons Canada LLP
Transfer Agents - Odyssey Trust Company, Vancouver, B.C.
Profile - (B.C. 2020) Capital Pool Company.

Recent Merger and Acquisition Activity

Status: pending **Announced:** Mar. 1, 2023
Ankh Capital Inc. entered into a non-binding letter of intent for the Qualifying Transaction reverse takeover acquisition of Quetzal Copper Limited, which has mineral interests in British Columbia and Mexico. The transaction was expected to be completed by way of a three-cornered amalgamation, share purchase, share exchange or alternate transaction. Ankh would consolidate its common shares on a 1-for-2 basis and each Quetzal common share would be exchanged for Ankh post-consolidated common shares at a ratio to be determined based on a valuation of Quetzal determined in connection with a private placement to be completed by Quetzal. A private placement of common shares for minimum gross proceeds of $3,000,000 would be completed by Quetzal.
Status: terminated **Revised:** Nov. 8, 2022
UPDATE: The transaction has lapsed. PREVIOUS: Ankh Capital Inc. entered into a non-binding letter of intent for the Qualifying Transaction reverse takeover acquisition of Calgary, Alta.-based Home Run Oil & Gas Inc., which explores for and develops oil and gas in the Ante Creek area of Alberta, for issuance of one post-consolidated common share (following a 1-for-4 share consolidation) per Home Run common share at a ratio to be determined at a later date.
Directors - Roger E. Milad, CEO & CFO, Vancouver, B.C.; T. Barry Coughlan, Vancouver, B.C.; D. Richard (Rick) Skeith, Calgary, Alta.

Capital Stock

	Authorized (shs.)	Outstanding (shs.)[1]
Common	unlimited	15,620,000

[1] At Oct. 24, 2022

Major Shareholder - Widely held at Oct. 15, 2021.

Price Range - ANKH.P/TSX-VEN

Year	Volume	High	Low	Close
2022	222,500	$0.10	$0.09	$0.09
2021	10,000	$0.10	$0.10	$0.10

Capital Stock Changes - On Oct. 15, 2021, an initial public offering of 10,000,000 common shares was completed at 10¢ per share.

A.110 Anonymous Intelligence Company Inc.

Symbol - ANON **Exchange** - CSE **CUSIP** - 03634K
Head Office - 610-700 Pender St W, Vancouver, BC, V6C 1G8 **Telephone** - (778) 240-7724 **Fax** - (604) 699-9768
Website - cloud9web3.com
Email - info@c9eg.com
Investor Relations - Nilda Rivera (604) 669-9788
Auditors - WDM Chartered Accountants C.A., Vancouver, B.C.
Lawyers - DuMoulin Black LLP, Vancouver, B.C.
Transfer Agents - Odyssey Trust Company, Vancouver, B.C.
Profile - (B.C. 2015) Develops and offers peer-to-peer or decentralized infrastructure products.
Owns the Limitless Virtual Private Network (VPN), a proprietary software product that is offered to users which relates to the usage of network infrastructure to perform distributed computational processing and to provide the user secure and encrypted connection to the Internet.
The company does not mine nor intends to mine cryptocurrencies, but intends to monetize the Limitless VPN using **NICEHASH Ltd.**, which operates as a hash rate broker and marketplace, by allowing third parties to use the hash rate of the Limitless VPN's userbase to mine cryptocurrencies.
Also offers the Haller.ai and Turminal.ai artificial intelligence (AI)-powered software-as-a-service (SaaS) platforms.
On July 14, 2023, the company acquired **Haller.ai Technologies Inc.**, which offers artificial intelligence (AI)-powered sofware-as-a-service (SaaS) platform, for issuance of 20,000,000 common shares at a deemed price of 10¢ per share.
On May 12, 2023, the company changed its business from an educational technology company to a technology company focused on developing and offering peer-to-peer or decentralized infrastructure products.
Predecessor Detail - Name changed from Cloud Nine Web3 Technologies Inc., May 12, 2023, pursuant to change of business from an educational technology company to a technology company focused on developing and offering peer-to-peer or decentralized infrastructure products.
Directors - John M. Bean, West Vancouver, B.C.; Tyler Koverko; Kant Trivedi, Nobleton, Ont.; Anthony Zelen, Coldstream, B.C.
Other Exec. Officers - Lucas Stemshorn-Russell, pres. & CEO; Nilda Rivera, CFO & corp. sec.; Justin Jacobson, v-p, opers.

Capital Stock

	Authorized (shs.)	Outstanding (shs.)[1]
Common	unlimited	82,180,753

[1] At May 18, 2023

Major Shareholder - Widely held at May 18, 2023.

Price Range - ANON/CSE

Year	Volume	High	Low	Close
2022	22,805,887	$0.55	$0.04	$0.06
2021	80,311,730	$2.60	$0.06	$0.30
2020	4,603,382	$0.15	$0.06	$0.06
2019	2,582,736	$0.32	$0.05	$0.07
2018	1,073,291	$0.45	$0.10	$0.13

Consolidation: 1-for-5 cons. in Mar. 2019
Recent Close: $0.07
Capital Stock Changes - In April 2023, private placement of 13,215,600 units (1 common share & 1 warrant) at 5¢ per unit was completed, with warrants exercisable at 6¢ per share for five years. On July 14, 2023, 20,000,000 common shares were issued pursuant to the acquisition of Haller.ai Technologies Inc.
During fiscal 2022, common shares were issued as follows: 4,000,000 on conversion of debentures, 1,277,000 on exercise of warrants and 250,000 for vested restricted share units.

Wholly Owned Subsidiaries

BHR Capital Corp., B.C. Inactive.
- 100% int. in **English Canada World Organization Inc.**, N.S. Inactive.

Haller.ai Technologies Inc.

Investments

16% int. in **Next Decentrum Technologies Inc.**

Financial Statistics

Periods ended:	12m Sept. 30/22^A		12m Sept. 30/21^A
	$000s	%Chg	$000s
Salaries & benefits	381		199
General & admin expense	765		3,732
Stock-based compensation	1,402		136
Operating expense	**2,547**	**-37**	**4,067**
Operating income	**(2,547)**	**n.a.**	**(4,067)**
Deprec., depl. & amort.	583		68
Finance income	1		nil
Finance costs, gross	23		113
Write-downs/write-offs	(1,088)		nil
Pre-tax income	**(3,550)**	**n.a.**	**(3,981)**
Net income	**(3,550)**	**n.a.**	**(3,981)**
Cash & equivalent	1,105		2,509
Current assets	1,326		2,901
Long-term investments	903		145
Fixed assets, net	2		3
Intangibles, net	3,800		5,295
Total assets	**6,892**	**-18**	**8,449**
Accts. pay. & accr. liabs	212		377
Current liabilities	370		706
Long-term debt, gross	158		381
Long-term debt, net	nil		52
Shareholders' equity	6,522		7,691
Cash from oper. activs	**(1,088)**	**n.a.**	**(4,229)**
Cash from fin. activs	89		7,597
Cash from invest. activs	(405)		(861)
Net cash position	**1,105**	**-56**	**2,509**
Capital expenditures	nil		(4)
	$		$
Earnings per share*	(0.05)		(0.11)
Cash flow per share*	(0.02)		(0.11)
	shs		shs
No. of shs. o/s*	68,122,653		62,595,653
Avg. no. of shs. o/s*	66,166,880		37,715,705
	%		%
Net profit margin	n.a.		n.a.
Return on equity	(49.95)		n.m.
Return on assets	(45.98)		(90.94)

* Common
^A Reported in accordance with IFRS

Latest Results

Periods ended:	3m Dec. 31/22^A		3m Dec. 31/21^A
	$000s	%Chg	$000s
Net income	(429)	n.a.	666
	$		$
Earnings per share*	(0.01)		0.01

* Common
^A Reported in accordance with IFRS

Historical Summary
(as originally stated)

Fiscal Year	Oper. Rev. $000s	Net Inc. Bef. Disc. $000s	EPS* $
2022^A	nil	(3,550)	(0.05)
2021^A	nil	(3,981)	(0.11)
2020^A	10	(510)	(0.03)
2019^A	nil	(610)	(0.05)
2018^A	14	(96)	(0.05)

* Common
^A Reported in accordance with IFRS
Note: Adjusted throughout for 1-for-5 cons. in Mar. 2019

A.111 Anquiro Ventures Ltd.

Symbol - AQR.P **Exchange** - TSX-VEN (S) **CUSIP** - 03633L
Head Office - 303-595 Howe St, Vancouver, BC, V6C 2T5 **Telephone** - (604) 718-2800 **Fax** - (604) 718-2808
Email - teresa@simcoservices.ca
Investor Relations - Teresa M. Cherry (604) 718-2800
Auditors - Dale Matheson Carr-Hilton LaBonte LLP C.A., Vancouver, B.C.
Lawyers - DuMoulin Black LLP, Vancouver, B.C.
Transfer Agents - Computershare Trust Company of Canada Inc., Vancouver, B.C.
Profile - (B.C. 2012) Capital Pool Company.
Common suspended from TSX-VEN, Feb. 28, 2020.

Recent Merger and Acquisition Activity

Status: pending **Announced:** Feb. 21, 2023
Anquiro Ventures Ltd. entered into a letter of intent for the Qualifying Transaction reverse takeover acquisition of private Vancouver, B.C.-based Black Pine Resources Corp., which holds an option to acquire the Sugarloaf copper project in southwestern New Mexico, on a share-for-share basis at a deemed issuance price of 20¢ per Anquiro share. Upon completion, Black Pine would amalgamate with a wholly owned subsidiary of Anquiro.

Directors - Keturah M. Nathe, pres. & CEO, Pitt Meadows, B.C.; Richard (Rick) Barnett, Port Moody, B.C.; Christopher P. (Chris) Cherry, Vancouver, B.C.; Joe DeVries, Delta, B.C.; Huitt Tracey, Vancouver, B.C.
Other Exec. Officers - Teresa M. Cherry, CFO & corp. sec.

Capital Stock

	Authorized (shs.)	Outstanding (shs.)[1]
Common	unlimited	4,500,001

[1] At Sept. 9, 2022
Major Shareholder - Widely held at June 3, 2021.

Price Range - AQR.P/TSX-VEN (S)

Year	Volume	High	Low	Close
2020	40,000	$0.09	$0.04	$0.04
2019	166,500	$0.18	$0.11	$0.14
2018	289,500	$0.30	$0.11	$0.12

Capital Stock Changes - There were no changes to capital stock from fiscal 2019 to fiscal 2022, inclusive.

A.112 Antera Ventures II Corp.

Symbol - AVII.P **Exchange** - TSX-VEN **CUSIP** - 03675K
Head Office - Royal Centre, 1500-1055 Georgia St W, PO Box 11117, Vancouver, BC, V6E 4N7
Email - raj.dewan@mcmillan.ca
Investor Relations - Rajeev Dewan (416) 865-7878
Auditors - MNP LLP C.A., Vancouver, B.C.
Transfer Agents - Odyssey Trust Company, Vancouver, B.C.
Profile - (B.C. 2021) Capital Pool Company.
Directors - Arinder S. Mahal, CEO, Toronto, Ont.; Dushan Batrovic, CFO, Georgetown, Ont.; Rajeev (Raj) Dewan, corp. sec., Richmond Hill, Ont.; Thomas B. (Tom) Astle, Aurora, Ont.; Pardeep S. Sangha, Vancouver, B.C.

Capital Stock

	Authorized (shs.)	Outstanding (shs.)[1]
Common	unlimited	15,000,000

[1] At May 20, 2022
Major Shareholder - Arinder S. Mahal held 21.33% interest at Aug. 4, 2021.

Price Range - AVII.P/TSX-VEN

Year	Volume	High	Low	Close
2022	309,500	$0.11	$0.06	$0.06
2021	59,000	$0.11	$0.10	$0.10

Recent Close: $0.03

A.113 Antibe Therapeutics Inc.

Symbol - ATE **Exchange** - TSX **CUSIP** - 037025
Head Office - 15 Prince Arthur Ave, Toronto, ON, M5R 1B2 **Telephone** - (416) 922-3460
Website - www.antibethera.com
Email - christina@antibethera.com
Investor Relations - Christina Cameron (416) 577-1443
Auditors - Ernst & Young LLP C.A., Toronto, Ont.
Bankers - The Bank of Nova Scotia, Toronto, Ont.
Lawyers - WeirFoulds LLP, Toronto, Ont.
Transfer Agents - Computershare Trust Company of Canada Inc., Toronto, Ont.
Employees - 11 at Mar. 31, 2023
Profile - (Ont. 2009) Originates, develops and out-licenses patent-protected new pharmaceuticals for pain and inflammation.

The company's lead drug, Otenaproxesul (formerly ATB-346; Phase I clinical study), is a novel non-steroidal anti-inflammatory drug (NSAID) that releases hydrogen sulfide combines with naproxen, a widely used NSAID, for the treatment of acute pain associated with, amongst other, post-operative pain. The company has completed clinical pharmacokinetic (PK) and pharmacodynamic (PD) study in healthy volunteers to confirm the optimal dosing regimens for the Phase II bunionectomy trial in the fourth quarter of 2023. Phase II clinical study for bunionectomy trial of otenaproxesul is anticipated to commence in the first quarter of 2024 and would deliver top-line data in the second quarter of 2024. The company also plans to rapidly expand to the full range of acute pain indications such as migraine, dysmenorrhea, traumatic injury, dental pain and gout.

Other pain and inflammation drug candidates in the pipeline include ATB-352 (under pre-clinical studies), a hydrogen sulfide-releasing derivative of ketoprofen targeting specialized pain indication; and a new inflammatory bowel disease (IBD) candidate using the architecuture of ATB-429, a hydrogen sulfide-releasing derivative of low-dose aspirin targeting gastrointestinal safety commonly prescribed to patients with ulcerative colitis and Crohn's disease.

In November 2022, the company sold wholly owned **Citagenix Inc.**, which holds a portfolio of bone grafts, dental membranes and other products that support specialized surgical procedures in the dental and orthopedic market places, to **HANSAmed Limited** for $3,500,000 cash plus an additional $3,000,000 upon achieving certain milestones.

Directors - Dr. John Wallace, founder & v-chr., Toronto, Ont.; Robert E. Hoffman, chr., San Diego, Calif.; Walter (Walt) Macnee, v-chr., Toronto, Ont.; Daniel (Dan) Legault, pres., CEO & corp. sec., Toronto, Ont.; Dr. Roderick Flower, Bath, Somt., United Kingdom; Amal Khouri, Montréal, Qué.; Jennifer McNealey, Mill Valley, Calif.; Yung Wu, Toronto, Ont.
Other Exec. Officers - Scott Curtis, COO; Alain Wilson, CFO; Dr. Joseph Stauffer, CMO; Dr. David Vaughan, chief devel. officer; Christina Cameron, v-p, IR; Ella Korets-Smith, v-p, bus. devel.; Philip Stern, v-p, commun.

Capital Stock

	Authorized (shs.)	Outstanding (shs.)[1]
Common	unlimited	52,637,091

[1] At July 28, 2023
Major Shareholder - Widely held at July 28, 2023.

Price Range - ATE/TSX

Year	Volume	High	Low	Close
2022	7,409,081	$0.83	$0.41	$0.47
2021	51,920,133	$7.52	$0.64	$0.66
2020	32,784,219	$8.90	$3.05	$3.93
2019	16,665,039	$5.40	$2.35	$4.50
2018	25,795,894	$7.90	$1.50	$3.10

Consolidation: 1-for-10 cons. in Dec. 2020
Recent Close: $0.50
Capital Stock Changes - During fiscal 2023, 517,816 common shares were issued on vesting of restricted share units.

On June 3, 2021, 5,873,092 common shares were issued pursuant to the acquisition of Antibe Holdings Inc. Also during fiscal 2022, common shares were issued as follows: 460,939 on vesting of restricted share units and 42,640 on exercise of warrants.

Financial Statistics

Periods ended:	12m Mar. 31/23^A		12m Mar. 31/22^A
	$000s	%Chg	$000s
Salaries & benefits	3,763		4,198
Research & devel. expense	9,403		11,959
General & admin expense	4,572		3,851
Stock-based compensation	2,808		5,521
Operating expense	**20,546**	**-20**	**25,529**
Operating income	**(20,546)**	**n.a.**	**(25,529)**
Finance costs, net	(1,255)		(279)
Pre-tax income	**(19,291)**	**n.a.**	**(25,250)**
Net inc. bef. disc. opers	**(19,291)**	**n.a.**	**(25,250)**
Income from disc. opers	(184)		190
Net income	**(19,475)**	**n.a.**	**(25,060)**
Cash & equivalent	38,892		54,807
Accounts receivable	1,615		1,121
Current assets	41,546		61,364
Intangibles, net	26,352		26,352
Total assets	**70,561**	**-21**	**89,158**
Accts. pay. & accr. liabs	2,764		2,816
Current liabilities	2,764		4,694
Shareholders' equity	40,166		56,833
Cash from oper. activs	**(16,305)**	**n.a.**	**(16,920)**
Cash from fin. activs	80		(26)
Cash from invest. activs	(11,827)		(20,220)
Net cash position	**6,755**	**-81**	**34,807**
Capital expenditures	(9)		(245)
Capital disposals	319		nil
	$		$
Earnings per share*	(0.37)		(0.50)
Cash flow per share*	(0.31)		(0.33)
	shs		shs
No. of shs. o/s*	52,617,092		52,099,276
Avg. no. of shs. o/s*	52,286,301		50,774,440
	%		%
Net profit margin	n.a.		n.a.
Return on equity	(39.78)		(47.15)
Return on assets	(24.16)		(29.55)
No. of employees (FTEs)	11		37

* Common
^A Reported in accordance with IFRS

Historical Summary
(as originally stated)

Fiscal Year	Oper. Rev. $000s	Net Inc. Bef. Disc. $000s	EPS* $
2023^A	nil	(19,291)	(0.37)
2022^A	nil	(25,250)	(0.50)
2021^A	9,713	(24,734)	(0.70)
2020^A	9,987	(19,342)	(0.70)
2019^A	9,539	(12,816)	(0.60)

* Common
^A Reported in accordance with IFRS
Note: Adjusted throughout for 1-for-10 cons. in Dec. 2020

A.114 ApartmentLove Inc.

Symbol - APLV **Exchange** - CSE **CUSIP** - 03750A
Head Office - 1600-421 7 St SW, Calgary, AB, T2P 4K9
Website - apartmentlove.com
Email - tdavidson@apartmentlove.com
Investor Relations - Trevor Davidson (647) 272-9702
Auditors - RSM Alberta LLP C.A., Calgary, Alta.
Lawyers - Dentons Canada LLP; Gowling WLG (Canada) LLP
Transfer Agents - Odyssey Trust Company, Calgary, Alta.
Employees - 9 at Nov. 15, 2022
Profile - (Can. 2015) Operates multiple Internet listing services that promote residential homes, apartments, and vacation properties on behalf of property managers, apartment building owners and operators, and private landlords and hosts in the United States, Canada, Mexico, the Caribbean and elsewhere around the world.

Operates apartmentlove.com, a website for searching and viewing residential properties for rent in the United States, Canada and elsewhere around the world, and ownerdirect.com, a website for short-terms vacation rentals. Visitors to the websites can view the listings for free and may contact landlords, property managers, owners, and hosts, free of charge to make vacation travel arrangements, schedule a property viewing, or ask other relevant questions to help make informed rental decisions. The company also offers listing contracts to landlords to provide an unlimited number of listings each month over a defined service period for a monthly recurring rate. Landlords for residential listings include property management companies, apartment building owners and operators, industry associations and private landlords.

At Nov. 29, 2022, apartmentlove.com had 309,438 active listings compared with 257,201 properties listed for rent on May 18, 2022, and ownerdirect.com had 8,919 active listings in more than 30 countries.

On Nov. 16, 2022, the company's common shares commenced trading on the OTCQB Venture Market under the ticker symbol APMLF.

In November 2022, the company agreed to acquire an Internet listing services company in Ontario for $940,000.

In July 2022, the company acquired ownerdirect.com, a short-term vacation rental website with operations in Canada, the U.S., Mexico and the Caribbean, for $375,000 cash.

Recent Merger and Acquisition Activity

Status: pending **Announced:** June 26, 2023

ApartmentLove Inc. signed a letter of intent to acquire a private Canadian financial technology company that operates a "pay your rent online" software platform that has 50,000 monthly recurring users. Terms of the transaction were not disclosed. The acquisition would include 150 property managers that process more than $750,000,000 in annual transaction volume.

Predecessor Detail - Name changed from Culada Asset Management, Inc., June 19, 2018.

Directors - Trevor Davidson, pres., CEO & corp. sec., Kelowna, B.C.; George Davidson, CFO, Calgary, Alta.; Monique Hutchins, Toronto, Ont.; Ian Korman, Toronto, Ont.; Scott MacMillan, Toronto, Ont.; Mackenzie Regent, Calgary, Alta.; Frank Y. Sur, Calgary, Alta.

Other Exec. Officers - Kenneth (Ken) Lang, chief tech. officer

Capital Stock

	Authorized (shs.)	Outstanding (shs.)[1]
Preferred	unlimited	nil
Common	unlimited	51,213,340

[1] At May 1, 2023

Major Shareholder - Trevor Davidson held 16% interest at Apr. 14, 2022.

Price Range - APLV/CSE

Year	Volume	High	Low	Close
2022............	6,391,169	$0.38	$0.08	$0.11
2021............	4,719,072	$0.50	$0.17	$0.22

Recent Close: $0.18

Capital Stock Changes - In May, June and September 2022, private placement of 9,356,664 units (1 common shares & ½ warrant) at 15¢ per unit was completed, with warrants exercisable at 25¢ per share for two years.

Financial Statistics

Periods ended:	12m Dec. 31/21[A]		12m Dec. 31/20[oA]
	$000s	%Chg	$000s
Operating revenue	**6**	**-60**	**15**
Cost of sales	1		5
Salaries & benefits	117		228
General & admin expense	526		142
Stock-based compensation	236		102
Operating expense	**880**	**+84**	**477**
Operating income	**(874)**	**n.a.**	**(462)**
Deprec., depl. & amort.	100		75
Finance costs, gross	45		6
Write-downs/write-offs	nil		(16)
Pre-tax income	**(831)**	**n.a.**	**(523)**
Net income	**(831)**	**n.a.**	**(523)**
Cash & equivalent	553		47
Accounts receivable	24		6
Current assets	613		58
Fixed assets, net	2		1
Intangibles, net	267		90
Total assets	**881**	**+491**	**149**
Accts. pay. & accr. liabs	418		256
Current liabilities	418		256
Long-term debt, net	452		49
Long-term lease liabilities	452		49
Equity portion of conv. debs	56		4
Shareholders' equity	12		(157)
Cash from oper. activs	**(176)**	**n.a.**	**(177)**
Cash from fin. activs	959		254
Cash from invest. activs	(278)		(73)
Net cash position	**553**	**n.m.**	**47**
Capital expenditures	(2)		nil
	$		$
Earnings per share*	(0.02)		(0.02)
Cash flow per share*	(0.00)		(0.01)
	shs		shs
No. of shs. o/s*	38,575,350		34,194,990
Avg. no. of shs. o/s*	36,498,917		33,289,529
	%		%
Net profit margin	n.m.		n.m.
Return on equity	n.m.		n.m.
Return on assets	(152.62)		(305.01)

* Common

[o] Restated

[A] Reported in accordance with IFRS

Latest Results

Periods ended:	9m Sept. 30/22[A]		9m Sept. 30/21[A]
	$000s	%Chg	$000s
Operating revenue	186	n.m.	3
Net income	(1,034)	n.a.	(241)
	$		$
Earnings per share*	(0.02)		(0.01)

* Common

[A] Reported in accordance with IFRS

Historical Summary
(as originally stated)

Fiscal Year	Oper. Rev.	Net Inc. Bef. Disc.	EPS*
	$000s	$000s	$
2021[A]	6	(831)	(0.02)
2020[A]	15	(523)	(0.02)
2019[A]	53	(597)	(0.02)

* Common

[A] Reported in accordance with IFRS

A.115 Apolo IV Acquisition Corp.

Symbol - AIV.P **Exchange** - TSX-VEN **CUSIP** - 03769K
Head Office - 2100-40 King St W, Toronto, ON, M5H 3C2 **Telephone** - (416) 806-5216
Email - rr@rr1.co
Investor Relations - Ryan Roebuck (416) 806-5216
Auditors - MNP LLP C.A., Toronto, Ont.
Transfer Agents - TSX Trust Company, Toronto, Ont.
Profile - (Ont. 2021) Capital Pool Company.
Directors - Ryan Roebuck, CEO & CFO, Toronto, Ont.; Michael Galego, Toronto, Ont.; Michael Young, Nashville, Tenn.
Other Exec. Officers - Stephen Arbib, corp. sec.

Capital Stock

	Authorized (shs.)	Outstanding (shs.)[1]
Common	unlimited	20,000,000

[1] At Mar. 31, 2022

Major Shareholder - Stephen Arbib held 16.5% interest at Apr. 1, 2021.

Price Range - AIV.P/TSX-VEN

Year	Volume	High	Low	Close
2022............	203,000	$0.14	$0.04	$0.05
2021............	266,425	$0.35	$0.11	$0.20

Recent Close: $0.08

A.116 Appili Therapeutics Inc.

Symbol - APLI **Exchange** - TSX **CUSIP** - 03783R
Head Office - 21-1344 Summer St, Halifax, NS, B3H 0A8 **Telephone** - (902) 442-4655 **Fax** - (902) 442-4651
Website - www.appilitherapeutics.com
Email - info@appilitherapeutics.com
Investor Relations - Jenna McNeil (902) 442-4655
Auditors - PricewaterhouseCoopers LLP C.A., Halifax, N.S.
Transfer Agents - Computershare Trust Company of Canada Inc., Montréal, Qué.

Profile - (Can. 2018; orig. N.S., 2015) Acquires, discovers, develops and commercializes novel infectious disease therapeutics and vaccines.

The company's anti-infective portfolio includes ATI-1701, a biodefense vaccine candidate for Francisella tularensis, a Category A pathogen which has the capability to be aerosolized and causes tularemia; ATI-1801, a topical paromomycin product to treat cutaneous leishmaniasis, a disfiguring infection of the skin; and ATI-1501, a taste-masked oral liquid formulation of the antibiotic metronidazole, which is being developed with **Saptalis Pharmaceuticals LLC**.

In November 2022, the company announced the funding from the U.S. Defense Threat Reduction Agency in partnership with the U.S. Air Force Academy of at least US$14,000,000 for the development of ATI-1701, a biodefense vaccine candidate for Francisella tularensis.

On Nov. 10, 2022, the company announced plans to discontinue development of ATI-2307, an antifungal product candidate and ATI-1503, an antibiotic targeting multi-drug resistant Gram-negative bacteria.

Directors - Dr. Armand Balboni, chr., Va.; Dr. Don Cilla, pres. & CEO, Md.; Dr. Theresa Matkovits†, N.J.; Brian M. Bloom, Toronto, Ont.; Dr. Juergen Froehlich, Mass.; Rochelle Stenzler, Toronto, Ont.

Other Exec. Officers - Kenneth G. Howling, acting CFO; Dr. Yoav Golan, CMO; Dr. Gary Nabors, chief devel. officer

† Lead director

Capital Stock

	Authorized (shs.)	Outstanding (shs.)[1]
Preferred	unlimited	nil
Non-vtg. Common	unlimited	nil
Class A Common	unlimited	121,266,120

[1] At Nov. 10, 2022

Major Shareholder - Bloom Burton & Co. Inc. held 11.84% interest at Aug. 12, 2022.

Price Range - APLI/TSX

Year	Volume	High	Low	Close
2022............	43,305,383	$0.18	$0.04	$0.05
2021............	47,816,329	$1.43	$0.09	$0.12
2020............	32,834,057	$1.89	$0.50	$1.22
2019............	1,754,077	$1.09	$0.32	$0.75

Recent Close: $0.05

Capital Stock Changes - In May 2022, public offering of 50,000,000 units (1 class A common share & ½ warrant) was completed at $0.09 per unit, with warrants exercisable at $0.15 per share for five years.

In October 2021, public offering of 8,434,000 units (1 class A common share & ½ warrant) was completed at $0.83 per unit.

Wholly Owned Subsidiaries

Appili Therapeutics (USA) Inc., United States.

Financial Statistics

Periods ended:	12m Mar. 31/22^A		12m Mar. 31/21^A
	$000s	%Chg	$000s
Operating revenue	**1,391**	**n.a.**	**nil**
Research & devel. expense	19,674		8,925
General & admin expense	5,317		5,440
Operating expense	**24,991**	**+74**	**14,365**
Operating income	**(23,600)**	**n.a.**	**(14,365)**
Deprec., depl. & amort.	13		15
Finance income	34		117
Finance costs, gross	1,555		70
Pre-tax income	**(25,118)**	**n.a.**	**(14,325)**
Net income	**(25,118)**	**n.a.**	**(14,325)**
Cash & equivalent	6,665		16,125
Accounts receivable	467		1,035
Current assets	8,239		18,262
Fixed assets, net	42		55
Total assets	**8,282**	**-55**	**18,317**
Accts. pay. & accr. liabs	6,446		4,531
Current liabilities	6,669		4,617
Long-term debt, gross	4,977		1,033
Long-term debt, net	4,883		947
Shareholders' equity	(3,271)		12,753
Cash from oper. activs	**(19,081)**	**n.a.**	**(11,451)**
Cash from fin. activs	9,564		17,018
Cash from invest. activs	5,062		(4,993)
Net cash position	**6,665**	**-40**	**11,063**
Capital expenditures	nil		(8)
	$		$
Earnings per share*	(0.38)		(0.24)
Cash flow per share*	(0.29)		(0.19)
	shs		shs
No. of shs. o/s*	71,266,120		62,777,469
Avg. no. of shs. o/s*	66,731,000		59,178,590
	%		%
Net profit margin	n.m.		n.a.
Return on equity	n.m.		(132.65)
Return on assets	(177.17)		(96.67)

* Cl.A. Common
[A] Reported in accordance with IFRS

Latest Results

Periods ended:	6m Sept. 30/22^A		6m Sept. 30/21^A
	$000s	%Chg	$000s
Net income	(3,963)	n.a.	(18,546)
	$		$
Earnings per share*	(0.04)		(0.30)

* Cl.A. Common
[A] Reported in accordance with IFRS

Historical Summary
(as originally stated)

Fiscal Year	Oper. Rev.	Net Inc. Bef. Disc.	EPS*
	$000s	$000s	$
2022^A	1,391	(25,118)	(0.38)
2021^A	nil	(14,325)	(0.24)
2020^A	199	(5,416)	(0.16)
2019^A1	nil	(4,331)	(0.14)
2018^A	nil	(3,976)	(0.16)

* Cl.A. Common
[A] Reported in accordance with IFRS
[1] Results adjusted to reflect May 3, 2019, 3.86-for-1 split of class A common shares.

A.117 Appulse Corporation

Symbol - APL **Exchange** - TSX-VEN **CUSIP** - 03833A
Head Office - 3504 64 Ave SE, Calgary, AB, T2C 1P4 **Telephone** - (403) 236-2883 **Toll-free** - (877) 336-2883 **Fax** - (403) 279-3342
Website - www.appulsecorp.net
Email - dbaird@centrifuges.net
Investor Relations - Douglas A. Baird (877) 336-2883
Auditors - MNP LLP C.A., Calgary, Alta.
Bankers - ATB Financial, Calgary, Alta.
Lawyers - Morris McManus Professional Corporation, Calgary, Alta.
Transfer Agents - Computershare Trust Company of Canada Inc., Calgary, Alta.
Profile - (Alta. 2001) Sells, rents, services and refurbishes centrifuge equipment to industries throughout North America and internationally. Also provides oilfield and refinery waste services.

Sells new and refurbished centrifuge machines and parts, and provides rentals of centrifuge equipment. Also provides maintenance services and consulting and design advice to a wide variety of industries with a focus on food and beverage processors and environmental applications; and value added services including a balancing service for large equipment including centrifuge bowls. Wholly owned **Centrifuges Unlimited Inc.** manufactures parts for centrifuge machines and provides specialized machining services for equipment repairs. In addition, provides oilfield and refinery waste services such as recovery of pipeline quality oil, and separates water and solids to international oil companies through wholly owned **Rolyn Oilfield Services Inc.**

Directors - Franklin T. (Frank) Bailey, chr., Calgary, Alta.; Douglas A. (Doug) Baird, pres. & CEO, Calgary, Alta.; Dennis R. Schmidt, CFO & corp. sec., Calgary, Alta.; Robert D. Richards, pres., Centrifuges Unlimited Inc., Calgary, Alta.; Michael Forgo, Alta.; James A. (Jim) Maldaner, Calgary, Alta.

Capital Stock

	Authorized (shs.)	Outstanding (shs.)[1]
Preferred	unlimited	nil
Common	unlimited	14,484,304

[1] At July 25, 2023

Major Shareholder - Robert D. Richards held 28.44% interest and Evelyn A. Richards held 14.15% interest at July 25, 2023.

Price Range - APL/TSX-VEN

Year	Volume	High	Low	Close
2022	455,394	$0.38	$0.24	$0.24
2021	1,967,135	$0.46	$0.29	$0.32
2020	1,646,146	$0.48	$0.10	$0.46
2019	372,700	$0.29	$0.16	$0.17
2018	166,035	$0.28	$0.14	$0.17

Recent Close: $0.31
Capital Stock Changes - During 2022, 295,000 common shares were issued on exercise of options.

Wholly Owned Subsidiaries

Centrifuges Unlimited Inc.
- 100% int. in **Rolyn Oilfield Services Inc.**, United States.
- 100% int. in **Rolyn Oilfield Services (U.S.) Inc.**, United States. Inactive.

Financial Statistics

Periods ended:	12m Dec. 31/22^A		12m Dec. 31/21^A
	$000s	%Chg	$000s
Operating revenue	**10,452**	**+13**	**9,233**
Cost of sales	6,387		5,063
Salaries & benefits	2,577		2,478
General & admin expense	405		363
Stock-based compensation	80		nil
Operating expense	**9,449**	**+20**	**7,905**
Operating income	**1,003**	**-24**	**1,328**
Deprec., depl. & amort.	511		509
Finance costs, gross	111		102
Pre-tax income	**334**	**-55**	**742**
Income taxes	97		nil
Net income	**238**	**-68**	**742**
Cash & equivalent	339		374
Inventories	6,913		6,874
Accounts receivable	1,706		1,376
Current assets	9,022		8,684
Fixed assets, net	887		899
Right-of-use assets	477		772
Total assets	**10,386**	**0**	**10,355**
Bank indebtedness	1,241		891
Accts. pay. & accr. liabs	1,809		1,532
Current liabilities	3,508		3,542
Long-term lease liabilities	228		565
Shareholders' equity	6,607		6,248
Cash from oper. activs	**119**	**-87**	**916**
Cash from fin. activs	49		(594)
Cash from invest. activs	(203)		(233)
Net cash position	**339**	**-9**	**374**
Capital expenditures	(221)		(233)
Capital disposals	18		nil
	$		$
Earnings per share*	0.02		0.05
Cash flow per share*	0.01		0.07
	shs		shs
No. of shs. o/s*	14,242,304		13,947,304
Avg. no. of shs. o/s*	14,239,879		13,962,896
	%		%
Net profit margin	2.28		8.04
Return on equity	3.70		12.63
Return on assets	3.05		8.29
Foreign sales percent	21		18

* Common
[A] Reported in accordance with IFRS

Latest Results

Periods ended:	3m Mar. 31/23^A		3m Mar. 31/22^A
	$000s	%Chg	$000s
Operating revenue	2,388	+15	2,079
Net income	58	+123	26
	$		$
Earnings per share*	0.00		0.00

* Common
[A] Reported in accordance with IFRS

Historical Summary
(as originally stated)

Fiscal Year	Oper. Rev.	Net Inc. Bef. Disc.	EPS*
	$000s	$000s	$
2022^A	10,452	238	0.02
2021^A	9,233	742	0.05
2020^A	10,461	1,096	0.08
2019^A	11,095	859	0.06
2018^A	9,749	168	0.01

* Common
[A] Reported in accordance with IFRS

A.118 Aptose Biosciences Inc.

Symbol - APS **Exchange** - TSX **CUSIP** - 03835T
Head Office - 1105-251 Consumers Rd, Toronto, ON, M2J 4R3 **Telephone** - (647) 479-9828
Website - www.aptose.com
Email - spietropaolo@aptose.com
Investor Relations - Susan Pietropaolo (647) 479-9828
Auditors - KPMG LLP C.A., Toronto, Ont.
Lawyers - McCarthy Tétrault LLP, Toronto, Ont.
Transfer Agents - Computershare Trust Company of Canada Inc., Toronto, Ont.
Employees - 35 at Dec. 31, 2022
Profile - (Can. 2006) Researches and develops pharmaceutical products and technologies for the treatment of cancer.

The company's two leading clinical stage investigational products under development are Tuspetinib (HM43239), an oral, myeloid kinome inhibitor in an international Phase 1/2 trial in patients with relapsed or refractory acute myeloid leukemia (AML); and Luxeptinib (CG-806), an oral, dual lymphoid and myeloid kinome inhibitor in a Phase 1a/b trial in patients with relapsed or refractory B-cell malignancies who have failed or are intolerant to standard therapies, and in a separate Phase 1a/b trial in patients with relapsed or refractory AML or high risk myelodysplastic syndrome (MDS). The U.S. FDA has granted Fast Track designation for HM43239 for the treatment of relapsed or refractory AML.

In addition, the company together with **Ohm Inc.** is also developing APL-581, a dual bromodomain and extra-terminal domain motif protein and kinase inhibitor program.

Predecessor Detail - Name changed from Lorus Therapeutics Inc., Aug. 28, 2014.
Directors - Dr. William G. Rice, chr., pres., CEO & chief acctg. officer, Del Mar, Calif.; Dr. Denis R. Burger†, Ore.; Carol G. Ashe, Pa.; Dr. Erich M. Platzer, Basel, Switzerland; Dr. Bernd R. Seizinger, N.J.; Dr. Mark D. Vincent, Ont.; Warren Whitehead, Toronto, Ont.
Other Exec. Officers - Phillippe Ledru, chief comml. officer; Dr. Rafael Bejar, sr. v-p & CMO; Fletcher Payne, sr. v-p & CFO; Janet Clennett, v-p, fin.; Roger Davies, v-p, opers.; Brooks Ensign, v-p & contr.; Dr. Yuying Jin, v-p, biometrics; Dr. Robert B. Killion Jr., v-p, chemistry, mfg. & controls; Victor Montalgo Lugo, v-p, clinical opers.; Dr. George P. Melko, v-p, regulatory affairs
† Lead director

Capital Stock

	Authorized (shs.)	Outstanding (shs.)[1]
Common	unlimited	6,200,352

[1] At June 6, 2023

Major Shareholder - Widely held at Apr. 3, 2023.

Price Range - APS/TSX

Year	Volume	High	Low	Close
2022	435,072	$29.25	$9.00	$11.70
2021	897,509	$135.00	$20.85	$25.95
2020	1,149,541	$189.30	$75.00	$83.85
2019	512,851	$118.35	$31.20	$110.25
2018	733,349	$89.55	$35.10	$39.00

Consolidation: 1-for-15 cons. in June 2023
Recent Close: $5.60
Capital Stock Changes - On June 6, 2023, common shares were consolidated on a 1-for-15 basis.

During 2022, common shares were issued as follows: 128,000 under at-the-market equity facility, 14,000 on exercise of options and 11,000 under employee stock purchase plan.

Wholly Owned Subsidiaries

Aptose Biosciences USA Inc., Del.

Subsidiaries

80% int. in **NuChem Pharmaceuticals Inc.**, Toronto, Ont. Inactive since 2012.

Financial Statistics

Periods ended:	12m Dec. 31/22[A]		12m Dec. 31/21[A]
	US$000s	%Chg	US$000s
Salaries & benefits	7,181		7,593
Research & devel. expense	18,650		34,590
General & admin expense	11,444		10,164
Stock-based compensation	5,207		12,950
Operating expense	**42,482**	**-35**	**65,297**
Operating income	**(42,482)**	**n.a.**	**(65,297)**
Deprec., depl. & amort.	120		150
Finance income	788		94
Pre-tax income	**(41,823)**	**n.a.**	**(65,354)**
Net income	**(41,823)**	**n.a.**	**(65,354)**
Cash & equivalent	46,959		79,128
Current assets	49,519		81,737
Fixed assets, net	211		323
Right-of-use assets	1,297		465
Total assets	**51,027**	**-38**	**82,525**
Accts. pay. & accr. liabs	11,983		7,715
Current liabilities	12,284		8,174
Long-term lease liabilities	1,002		115
Shareholders' equity	37,741		74,236
Cash from oper. activs	**(32,322)**	**n.a.**	**(43,304)**
Cash from fin. activs	116		226
Cash from invest. activs	30,066		(35,208)
Net cash position	**36,970**	**-5**	**39,114**
Capital expenditures	(24)		(212)
	US$		US$
Earnings per share*	(6.75)		(10.95)
Cash flow per share*	(5.25)		(7.29)
	shs		shs
No. of shs. o/s*	6,157,818		6,147,668
Avg. no. of shs. o/s*	6,151,133		5,939,067
	%		%
Net profit margin	n.a.		n.a.
Return on equity	(74.70)		(67.67)
Return on assets	(62.63)		(62.60)
No. of employees (FTEs)	35		41

* Common
[A] Reported in accordance with U.S. GAAP

Latest Results

Periods ended:	3m Mar. 31/23[A]		3m Mar. 31/22[A]
	US$000s	%Chg	US$000s
Net income	(13,676)	n.a.	(11,481)
	US$		US$
Earnings per share*	(2.25)		(1.80)

* Common
[A] Reported in accordance with U.S. GAAP

Historical Summary
(as originally stated)

Fiscal Year	Oper. Rev.	Net Inc. Bef. Disc.	EPS*
	US$000s	US$000s	US$
2022[A]	nil	(41,823)	(6.75)
2021[A]	nil	(65,354)	(10.95)
2020[A]	nil	(55,238)	(10.05)
2019[A]	nil	(26,277)	(7.80)
2018[A]	nil	(28,868)	(12.90)

* Common
[A] Reported in accordance with U.S. GAAP
Note: Adjusted throughout for 1-for-15 cons. in June 2023

A.119 Aquarius Surgical Technologies Inc.

Symbol - ASTI **Exchange** - CSE **CUSIP** - 03842P
Head Office - 89 Scollard St, Toronto, ON, M5R 1G4 **Telephone** - (647) 308-0685 **Toll-free** - (877) 740-2784
Website - aquariussurgical.com
Email - lornemac@eastlink.ca
Investor Relations - Lorne S. MacFarlane (902) 496-7594
Auditors - Grant Thornton LLP C.A., Mississauga, Ont.
Bankers - Royal Bank of Canada, Richmond Hill, Ont.
Lawyers - Christopher H. Freeman, King City, Ont.
Transfer Agents - TSX Trust Company, Toronto, Ont.
Profile - (Ont. 1986) Develops and markets minimally invasive medical laser systems and consumables for multiple medical disciplines including urology, gynecology, ophthalmology, thoracic, ENT, cardiovascular and neurosurgery.

Solutions consist of multiple laser systems, consumables, clinical education, service, support and maintenance.

Current product portfolio consists of the Pathfinder, a high performance, compact and portable surgical diode laser, used for procedures such as benign prostatic hyperplasia (BPH) surgery, strictures and tumours; HYPHO (holmium), a portable laser for lithotripsy, including treatment of upper ureter and kidney stones; and Uni-core fibre, an optical fibre used for the delivery of medical laser during medical procedures.

Products are sold through distribution agreements covering all countries in North America, and its target market segments include end users, hospitals, private practices (solo practitioners, group practices and surgical centres) and mobilizers (service providers providing all-inclusive service to hospitals in the form of a rental agreement).

Predecessor Detail - Name changed from Aquarius Coatings Inc., Feb. 24, 2017, pursuant to acquisition of Surgical Lasers Inc.; basis 1 new for 20 old shs.

Directors - David J. Hennigar, chr., Bedford, N.S.; Charlotte M. Janssen, Toronto, Ont.; Dr. Rajiv Singal, Toronto, Ont.; Dr. Stanley Swierzewski III, Holyoke, Mass.

Other Exec. Officers - Michael Machika, interim CEO; Lorne S. MacFarlane, CFO; Christopher H. Freeman, corp. sec.

Capital Stock

	Authorized (shs.)	Outstanding (shs.)[1]
Common	unlimited	27,599,172
Special	unlimited	nil

[1] At Mar. 7, 2023

Common - One vote per share.
Series A Special - Redeemed during fiscal 2021 at $0.0001 per share.
Major Shareholder - David J. Hennigar held 39.95% interest and Gordon S. Willox held 19.92% interest at Jan. 5, 2022.

Price Range - ASTI/CSE

Year	Volume	High	Low	Close
2022	1,045,394	$0.09	$0.02	$0.02
2021	2,053,023	$0.65	$0.01	$0.09
2020	916,071	$0.45	$0.12	$0.20
2019	553,996	$0.51	$0.20	$0.35
2018	610,040	$0.65	$0.25	$0.35

Recent Close: $0.01
Capital Stock Changes - During fiscal 2022, 600,000 common shares were issued for services.

Wholly Owned Subsidiaries

Scotiachemco Holdings Limited, N.S.
Scotiachemco Inc., N.S.
Surgical Lasers Inc., Newmarket, Ont.
- 100% int. in **Surgical Lasers Inc.**, Del.

Investments

Woodland Biofuels Inc., Toronto, Ont.

Financial Statistics

Periods ended:	12m Mar. 31/22[A]		12m Mar. 31/21[oA]
	$000s	%Chg	$000s
Operating revenue	**328**	**-44**	**583**
Cost of sales	197		367
General & admin expense	767		854
Stock-based compensation	nil		20
Operating expense	**964**	**-22**	**1,241**
Operating income	**(636)**	**n.a.**	**(658)**
Deprec., depl. & amort.	51		136
Finance income	14		35
Finance costs, gross	213		371
Pre-tax income	**(859)**	**n.a.**	**(1,810)**
Net income	**(859)**	**n.a.**	**(1,810)**
Cash & equivalent	158		146
Inventories	45		21
Accounts receivable	87		204
Current assets	609		642
Long-term investments	281		nil
Fixed assets, net	6		305
Total assets	**895**	**-5**	**946**
Bank indebtedness	156		150
Accts. pay. & accr. liabs	868		415
Current liabilities	1,647		946
Long-term debt, gross	663		660
Long-term debt, net	663		229
Shareholders' equity	(3,215)		(2,395)
Cash from oper. activs	**(109)**	**n.a.**	**(451)**
Cash from fin. activs	126		591
Cash from invest. activs	(5)		(100)
Net cash position	**158**	**+8**	**146**
Capital expenditures	(5)		(100)
	$		$
Earnings per share*	(0.04)		(0.08)
Cash flow per share*	(0.00)		(0.02)
	shs		shs
No. of shs. o/s*	23,679,172		23,079,172
Avg. no. of shs. o/s*	23,089,035		22,935,165
	%		%
Net profit margin	(261.89)		(310.46)
Return on equity	n.m.		n.m.
Return on assets	(70.18)		(110.48)
Foreign sales percent	100		100

* Common
[o] Restated
[A] Reported in accordance with IFRS

Latest Results

Periods ended:	3m June 30/22[A]		3m June 30/21[A]
	$000s	%Chg	$000s
Operating revenue	104	+108	50
Net income	(194)	n.a.	(243)
	$		$
Earnings per share*	(0.01)		(0.01)

* Common
[A] Reported in accordance with IFRS

Historical Summary
(as originally stated)

Fiscal Year	Oper. Rev.	Net Inc. Bef. Disc.	EPS*
	$000s	$000s	$
2022[A]	328	(859)	(0.04)
2021[A]	583	(1,810)	(0.08)
2020[A]	959	(1,611)	(0.08)
2019[A]	393	(1,587)	(0.08)
2018[A]	975	(6,252)	(0.35)

* Common
[A] Reported in accordance with IFRS

A.120 Arbutus Biopharma Corporation

Symbol - ABUS **Exchange** - NASDAQ **CUSIP** - 03879J
Head Office - 701 Veterans Cir, Warminster, PA, United States, 18974
Telephone - (267) 469-0914 **Fax** - (267) 282-0411
Website - www.arbutusbio.com
Email - lcaperelli@arbutusbio.com
Investor Relations - Lisa Caperelli (267) 332-8869
Auditors - Ernst & Young LLP C.A.
Lawyers - Dorsey & Whitney LLP, Seattle, Wash.; Farris LLP, Vancouver, B.C.
Transfer Agents - TSX Trust Company, Vancouver, B.C.
Employees - 96 at Dec. 31, 2022
Profile - (B.C. 2005) Developing drug candidates for people suffering from chronic hepatitis B infection (HBV).

The pipeline is focused on finding a cure for chronic HBV infection, and developing a combination of products that intervene at different points in the viral life cycle. It consists of multiple drug candidates, with complementary mechanisms of action, which are expected to be used in combination to effect patient benefit.

Lead compound AB-729, is a proprietary subcutaneously-delivered RNA interference (RNAi) therapeutic product candidate that suppresses hepatitis B surface antigen (HBsAg) expression, which is a key prerequisite to enable reawakening of a patient's immune system to respond to HBV. AB-729 is under one Phase Ia/Ib study that inhibits viral replication and reduces all HBV antigens, including HBsAg; and two Phase IIa proof-of-concept clinical trials in combination with other agents with potentially complementary mechanisms of action.

The HBV portfolio also includes AB-101, an oral PD-L1 inhibitor which mediates activation and reinvigoration of HBV-specific T-cells; and AB-161, an oral RNA destabilizer to treat chronic HBV.

Has a drug discovery and development program for treating coronaviruses including COVID-19. Lead coronavirus drug candidate, AB-343, inhibits the SARS-CoV-2 Mpro, a validated target for the treatment of COVID-19 and potential future coronavirus outbreaks. The company also intend to nominate a nsp12 clinical candidate and initiate IND-enabling studies in the second half of 2023. An nsp12 viral polymerase could potentially be combined with AB-343 to achieve better patient treatment outcomes and for use in prophylactic settings.

The company has entered into a separate clinical collaboration agreement with **Vaccitech Plc** to evaluate the company's AB-729 as the cornerstone agent in combination with Vaccitech's T-cell stimulating therapeutic vaccine for the treatment of patients with chronic HBV infection. Also has a collaboration agreement with **X-Chem, Inc.** and **Proteros Biostructures GmbH** for the research and license agreement on the discovery of novel inhibitors targeting the SARS-CoV-2 nsp5 main protease to accelerate the development of pan-coronavirus agents to treat COVID-19 and potential future coronavirus outbreaks.

Also receiving royalties from Onpattro® (Patisiran/ALN-TTR02), an FDA-approved RNAi therapeutic targeting transthyretin (TTR) for the treatment of TTR-mediated amyloidosis (ATTR) in patients with FAP.

Predecessor Detail - Name changed from Tekmira Pharmaceuticals Corporation, Aug. 3, 2015.

Directors - Dr. Frank Torti, chr., United States; William H. Collier, pres. & CEO, Wayne, Pa.; Daniel Burgess, Rancho Santa Fe, Calif.; Richard C. Henriques Jr., United States; Dr. Keith Manchester, N.Y.; James Meyers, San Francisco, Calif.; Dr. Melissa V. Rewolinski

Other Exec. Officers - Michael J. McElhaugh, COO; David C. Hastings, CFO; Christopher Naftzger, chief compliance officer & gen. counsel; Dr. Karen Sims, CMO; Dr. Michael J. Sofia, chief scientific officer; Shannon Briscoe, v-p, HR; Lisa Caperelli, v-p, IR

Capital Stock

	Authorized (shs.)	Outstanding (shs.)[1]
Preferred	unlimited	nil
Series A	1,164,000	nil
Common	unlimited	166,133,563

[1] At May 2, 2023

Major Shareholder - Roivant Sciences Ltd. held 23.5% interest at Mar. 27, 2023.

Price Range - ABUS/NASDAQ

Year	Volume	High	Low	Close
2022	92,796,325	US$4.01	US$1.86	US$2.33
2021	194,980,195	US$6.50	US$2.43	US$3.89
2020	186,769,685	US$9.00	US$0.88	US$3.55
2019	24,598,552	US$4.75	US$0.82	US$2.78
2018	22,560,420	US$12.50	US$3.21	US$3.83

Capital Stock Changes - During 2022, common shares were issued as follows: 8,645,426 under an open-market-sale agreement, 3,579,952 pursuant to the acquisition of interest in Anchor Life Limited, 171,224 under employee stock purchase plan and 71,025 on exercise of stock options.

Wholly Owned Subsidiaries

Arbutus Biopharma, Inc., Warminster, Pa.
- 100% int. in **Enantigen Therapeutics, Inc.**, Warminster, Pa.

Investments

16% int. in **Genevant Sciences Ltd.**

Financial Statistics

Periods ended:	12m Dec. 31/22[A]		12m Dec. 31/21[A]
	US$000s	%Chg	US$000s
Operating revenue	**39,019**	**+255**	**10,988**
Research & devel. expense	80,069		60,972
General & admin expense	13,564		13,489
Stock-based compensation	7,182		6,424
Operating expense	**100,815**	**+25**	**80,885**
Operating income	**(61,796)**	**n.a.**	**(69,897)**
Deprec., depl. & amort.	1,427		1,753
Finance income	2,192		127
Finance costs, gross	1,726		2,857
Pre-tax income	**(65,012)**	**n.a.**	**(76,247)**
Income taxes	4,444		nil
Net income	**(69,456)**	**n.a.**	**(76,247)**
Cash & equivalent	146,913		155,317
Accounts receivable	1,352		899
Current assets	151,139		160,661
Fixed assets, net	5,070		5,983
Right-of-use assets	1,744		2,092
Total assets	**195,419**	**-4**	**204,485**
Accts. pay. & accr. liabs	16,028		10,812
Current liabilities	32,857		11,221
Long-term lease liabilities	1,815		2,231
Shareholders' equity	136,852		169,439
Cash from oper. activs	**(35,356)**	**n.a.**	**(67,532)**
Cash from fin. activs	31,814		137,236
Cash from invest. activs	(74,942)		(12,678)
Net cash position	**30,776**	**-72**	**109,282**
Capital expenditures	(512)		(809)
	US$		US$
Earnings per share*	(0.46)		(0.83)
Cash flow per share*	(0.23)		(0.64)
	shs		shs
No. of shs. o/s*	157,455,363		144,987,736
Avg. no. of shs. o/s*	150,939,337		106,242,452
	%		%
Net profit margin	(178.01)		(693.91)
Return on equity	(45.35)		(144.90)
Return on assets	(33.81)		(42.97)
No. of employees (FTEs)	96		85

* Common
[A] Reported in accordance with U.S. GAAP

Latest Results

Periods ended:	3m Mar. 31/23[A]		3m Mar. 31/22[A]
	US$000s	%Chg	US$000s
Operating revenue	6,687	-47	12,581
Net income	(16,339)	n.a.	(15,765)
	US$		US$
Earnings per share*	(0.10)		(0.11)

* Common
[A] Reported in accordance with U.S. GAAP

Historical Summary
(as originally stated)

Fiscal Year	Oper. Rev. US$000s	Net Inc. Bef. Disc. US$000s	EPS* US$
2022[A]	39,019	(69,456)	(0.46)
2021[A]	10,988	(76,247)	(0.83)
2020[A]	6,914	(63,745)	(1.00)
2019[A]	6,011	(153,723)	(2.89)
2018[A]	5,945	(57,060)	(1.21)

* Common
[A] Reported in accordance with U.S. GAAP

A.121 Arch Biopartners Inc.

Symbol - ARCH **Exchange** - TSX-VEN **CUSIP** - 03938C
Head Office - 545 King St W, Toronto, ON, M5V 1M1
Website - www.archbiopartners.com
Email - rm@archbiopartners.com
Investor Relations - Richard Muruve (647) 428-7031
Auditors - Baker Tilly HMA LLP C.A., Winnipeg, Man.
Transfer Agents - TSX Trust Company, Toronto, Ont.

Profile - (Can. 2003; orig. Ont., 1983) Develops and manages a portfolio of early stage biotechnology projects in the discovery stage and advances them to the later stages of development and commercialization.

The company is focused on the clinical development of its lead drug candidate Metablok™ (LSALT peptide) which has the potential to treat or prevent dipeptidase-1 (DPEP-1) mediated organ inflammation in the lungs, liver or kidneys which often results in organ damage or failure, including in the case of sepsis and COVID-19. Other technology platforms under going research and development include: AB569, a new drug candidate for the treatment or prevention of antibiotic resistant bacterial infections, primarily as a topical treatment for wounds; Borg: Peptide-Solid Surface Interface, a binding of proprietary peptides to solid metal and plastic surfaces to inhibit biofilm formation and reduce corrosion; and MetaMx™, proprietary synthetic molecules that target brain tumour initiation cells and invasive glioma cells. The company either owns the intellectual property emanating from its research programs or it has exclusive licences.

Predecessor Detail - Name changed from Foccini International Inc., May 3, 2010, pursuant to reverse takeover acquisition of Arch Biotech Inc.

Directors - Richard Muruve, pres. & CEO, Toronto, Ont.; Andrew Bishop, acting CFO, Toronto, Ont.; Claude Allary, Paris, France; Dr. Richard Rossman, Hamilton, Ont.

Other Exec. Officers - Daniel Muruve, chief scientific officer

Capital Stock

	Authorized (shs.)	Outstanding (shs.)[1]
Preferred	unlimited	nil
Common	unlimited	62,598,815

[1] At May 30, 2023

Major Shareholder - Richard Muruve held 14.56% interest at Feb. 13, 2023.

Price Range - ARCH/TSX-VEN

Year	Volume	High	Low	Close
2022	3,337,136	$4.25	$2.65	$2.81
2021	10,033,486	$5.30	$1.12	$3.45
2020	8,965,262	$1.70	$0.74	$1.49
2019	2,786,889	$1.38	$0.85	$0.97
2018	6,627,582	$1.84	$0.44	$1.31

Recent Close: $1.59

Capital Stock Changes - During fiscal 2022, common shares were issued as follows: 250,000 on exercise of options and 117,990 for settlement of interest.

Wholly Owned Subsidiaries

Arch Bio Ireland Ltd., Ireland.
Arch Bio Ohio Inc. Inactive.
Arch Biophysics Ltd., Alta.
Arch Biotech Inc., Ont.
Arch Cancer Therapeutics Ltd., Alta.
Arch Clinical Pty Ltd., Australia.

Financial Statistics

Periods ended:	12m Sept. 30/22[A]		12m Sept. 30/21[A]
	$000s	%Chg	$000s
Salaries & benefits	195		193
Research & devel. expense	1,272		3,778
General & admin expense	553		698
Stock-based compensation	25		110
Operating expense	**2,045**	**-57**	**4,779**
Operating income	**(2,045)**	**n.a.**	**(4,779)**
Finance costs, gross	309		273
Pre-tax income	**(1,408)**	**n.a.**	**(1,170)**
Net income	**(1,408)**	**n.a.**	**(1,170)**
Cash & equivalent	506		448
Accounts receivable	87		2,201
Current assets	622		2,668
Total assets	**621**	**-77**	**2,668**
Bank indebtedness	nil		1,802
Accts. pay. & accr. liabs	489		962
Current liabilities	2,779		3,189
Long-term debt, gross	4,152		3,100
Long-term debt, net	2,052		3,100
Shareholders' equity	(4,471)		(3,882)
Cash from oper. activs	**479**	**n.a.**	**(2,981)**
Cash from fin. activs	(421)		2,775
Net cash position	**506**	**+13**	**448**
	$		$
Earnings per share*	(0.02)		(0.02)
Cash flow per share*	0.01		(0.05)
	shs		shs
No. of shs. o/s*	62,330,292		61,962,302
Avg. no. of shs. o/s*	62,158,611		61,323,206
	%		%
Net profit margin	n.a.		n.a.
Return on equity	n.m.		n.m.
Return on assets	(66.83)		(52.63)

* Common
[A] Reported in accordance with IFRS

Latest Results

Periods ended:	6m Mar. 31/23[A]		6m Mar. 31/22[A]
	$000s	%Chg	$000s
Net income	(3,120)	n.a.	(662)
	$		$
Earnings per share*	(0.05)		(0.01)

* Common
[A] Reported in accordance with IFRS

Historical Summary
(as originally stated)

Fiscal Year	Oper. Rev. $000s	Net Inc. Bef. Disc. $000s	EPS* $
2022[A]	nil	(1,408)	(0.02)
2021[A]	nil	(1,170)	(0.02)
2020[A]	nil	(4,629)	(0.08)
2019[A]	nil	(2,358)	(0.04)
2018[A]	nil	(3,198)	(0.06)

* Common
[A] Reported in accordance with IFRS

A.122 Arctic Fox Lithium Corp.

Symbol - AFX **Exchange** - CSE **CUSIP** - 03967C
Head Office - 905-1030 Georgia St W, Vancouver, BC, V6E 2Y3
Telephone - (604) 689-2646 **Fax** - (604) 689-1289
Website - www.arcticfoxlithium.com
Email - hchew@pacificparagon.com
Investor Relations - Harry Chew (604) 899-6500
Auditors - Saturna Group Chartered Accountants LLP C.A., Vancouver, B.C.
Transfer Agents - Odyssey Trust Company, Vancouver, B.C.

Profile - (B.C. 2013) Has mineral interest in British Columbia, and developed a gaming application.

In British Columbia, holds option from **Pacific Ridge Exploration Ltd.** to earn 60% interest in Spius copper-molybdenum prospect, 2,206 hectares, 10 km east-northeast of Boston Bar.

In addition, the company has developed a gaming application entitled "After: The Lawless", a multiplayer online role-playing game that has been designed to be easily scaled to be played on Apple devices. The company plans to divest this application to focus on the mineral exploration of its Spius prospect.

In February 2023, the company entered into a letter of intent to acquire Pontax North lithium prospect in James Bay region of Quebec for issuance of up to 6,000,000 common shares and $50,000 in cash.

In January 2023, the company entered into a letter of intent to acquire Kana lithium prospect in the James Bay region of Quebec for issuance of 12,000,000 common shares and Cdn$150,000 cash in instalments.

Recent Merger and Acquisition Activity

Status: terminated **Revised:** Mar. 9, 2022

UPDATE: The transaction was terminated. PREVIOUS: Arctic Fox Ventures Inc. entered into a letter of agreement to acquire private Las Vegas, Nev.-based Global A Brands, Inc. (GAB) for issuance of 115,000,000 AFX common shares at Cdn$0.40 per share. GAB acquires and develops early-stage businesses in the luxury goods and lifestyle markets including companies engaged in liquor, cosmetics, distribution and gaming. The transaction would constitute a change of business.

Predecessor Detail - Name changed from Arctic Fox Ventures Inc., Mar. 24, 2023.

Directors - Harry Chew, pres. & CEO, Vancouver, B.C.; Sonny Chew, CFO & corp. sec., Vancouver, B.C.; Dr. Gerald G. (Gerry) Carlson, West Vancouver, B.C.; Dr. Terrance G. Owen, Abbotsford, B.C.; Eddy Sui, Richmond, B.C.

Capital Stock

	Authorized (shs.)	Outstanding (shs.)[1]
Common	100,000,000	45,893,416

[1] At Mar. 24, 2023

Major Shareholder - Harry Chew held 20.4% interest at Jan. 11, 2022.

Price Range - AFX/CSE

Year	Volume	High	Low	Close
2022	306,995	$0.20	$0.06	$0.06
2021	100,000	$0.16	$0.14	$0.14

Recent Close: $0.12

Capital Stock Changes - During fiscal 2022, 805,000 common shares were issued by private placement.

Financial Statistics

Periods ended:	12m June 30/22[A]		12m June 30/21[A]
	$000s	%Chg	$000s
General & admin expense	127		128
Other operating expense	19		25
Operating expense	**146**	**-5**	**153**
Operating income	**(146)**	**n.a.**	**(153)**
Pre-tax income	**(146)**	**n.a.**	**(150)**
Net income	**(146)**	**n.a.**	**(150)**
Cash & equivalent	11		132
Current assets	26		141
Explor./devel. properties	163		163
Total assets	**202**	**-36**	**316**
Bank indebtedness	9		59
Current liabilities	9		59
Shareholders' equity	192		258
Cash from oper. activs	**(202)**	**n.a.**	**(118)**
Cash from fin. activs	81		128
Cash from invest. activs	nil		(105)
Net cash position	**11**	**-92**	**132**
Capital expenditures	nil		(93)
	$		$
Earnings per share*	(0.01)		(0.00)
Cash flow per share*	(0.01)		(0.00)
	shs		shs
No. of shs. o/s*	27,273,416		26,468,416
Avg. no. of shs. o/s*	26,547,813		30,382,277
	%		%
Net profit margin	n.a.		n.a.
Return on equity	(64.89)		(61.48)
Return on assets	(56.37)		(54.74)

* Common

[A] Reported in accordance with IFRS

Latest Results

Periods ended:	3m Sept. 30/22[A]		3m Sept. 30/21[A]
	$000s	%Chg	$000s
Net income	(27)	n.a.	(32)
	$		$
Earnings per share*	(0.00)		(0.00)

* Common

[A] Reported in accordance with IFRS

Historical Summary
(as originally stated)

Fiscal Year	Oper. Rev.	Net Inc. Bef. Disc.	EPS*
	$000s	$000s	$
2022[A]	nil	(146)	(0.01)
2021[A]	nil	(150)	(0.00)
2020[A]	nil	(98)	(0.00)
2019[A]	nil	(769)	(0.06)

* Common

[A] Reported in accordance with IFRS

A.123 Aretto Wellness Inc.

Symbol - ARTO **Exchange** - CSE **CUSIP** - 03990C

Head Office - 151 Hastings St W, Vancouver, BC, V6B 1H4 **Telephone** - (604) 394-2082

Website - rritual.com

Email - investors@arettowellness.com

Investor Relations - Nathan Nowak (778) 724-1301

Auditors - Davidson & Company LLP C.A., Vancouver, B.C.

Lawyers - Clark Wilson LLP, Vancouver, B.C.

Transfer Agents - Odyssey Trust Company, Vancouver, B.C.

Profile - (B.C. 2019) Develops, markets, sells and distributes plant-based products featuring functional mushrooms and adaptogen ingredients for health and wellness.

Product line consists of elixir powders and frozen, ready-to-serve smoothie mixes which are sold direct to consumer through e-commerce channels and wholesale to brick and mortar retailers throughout North America.

Predecessor Detail - Name changed from Rritual Superfoods Inc., Nov. 25, 2022; basis 1 new for 20 old shs.

Directors - David Lubotta, chr., Toronto, Ont.; Nathan Nowak, CEO; Warren Spence, acting CFO, Port Coquitlam, B.C.

Other Exec. Officers - Douglas (Doug) Campbell, v-p, sales

Capital Stock

	Authorized (shs.)	Outstanding (shs.)[1]
Common	unlimited	5,532,862

[1] At Nov. 25, 2022

Major Shareholder - Widely held at Nov. 26, 2021.

Price Range - ARTO/CSE

Year	Volume	High	Low	Close
2022	8,868,860	$3.50	$0.05	$0.06
2021	3,613,666	$23.40	$1.70	$1.90

Consolidation: 1-for-20 cons. in Nov. 2022

Recent Close: $0.04

Capital Stock Changes - On Nov. 25, 2022, common shares were consolidated on a 1-for-20 basis.

In September 2021, bought deal public offering of 8,000,000 units (1 common share & ½ warrant) at 50¢ per unit was completed. In February 2022, 33,000,000 common shares were issued pursuant to the acquisition of JustGo Juice Nutrition Ltd. Also during fiscal 2022, common shares were issued as follows: 1,830,000 on exercise of options, 420,000 on vesting of restricted share units and 75,000 on exercise of warrants.

Wholly Owned Subsidiaries

JustGo Juice Nutrition Ltd., Vancouver, B.C.
- 100% int. in **JustGo Plant Nutrition Ltd.**, Vancouver, B.C.

Rritual USA Inc., Nev.

Financial Statistics

Periods ended:	12m June 30/22[A]		12m June 30/21[A]
	$000s	%Chg	$000s
Operating revenue	**94**	**-52**	**197**
Cost of goods sold	463		250
General & admin expense	4,551		5,375
Stock-based compensation	651		683
Operating expense	**5,665**	**-10**	**6,308**
Operating income	**(5,571)**	**n.a.**	**(6,111)**
Deprec., depl. & amort.	nil		30
Write-downs/write-offs	(6,513)		nil
Pre-tax income	**(12,083)**	**n.a.**	**(6,142)**
Net income	**(12,083)**	**n.a.**	**(6,142)**
Cash & equivalent	4		672
Inventories	nil		1,091
Accounts receivable	nil		175
Current assets	37		3,480
Total assets	**37**	**-99**	**3,480**
Accts. pay. & accr. liabs	1,622		498
Current liabilities	1,622		498
Shareholders' equity	(1,585)		2,982
Cash from oper. activs	**(4,887)**	**n.a.**	**(6,986)**
Cash from fin. activs	4,161		7,296
Cash from invest. activs	72		nil
Net cash position	**4**	**-99**	**672**
	$		$
Earnings per share*	(3.00)		(3.00)
Cash flow per share*	(1.18)		(3.31)
	shs		shs
No. of shs. o/s*	5,277,617		3,111,367
Avg. no. of shs. o/s*	4,135,930		2,111,867
	%		%
Net profit margin	n.m.		n.m.
Return on equity	n.m.		(380.31)
Return on assets	(687.12)		(323.18)
Foreign sales percent	100		100

* Common

[A] Reported in accordance with IFRS

Latest Results

Periods ended:	3m Sept. 30/22[A]		3m Sept. 30/21[A]
	$000s	%Chg	$000s
Operating revenue	nil	n.a.	51
Net income	(392)	n.a.	(1,813)
	$		$
Earnings per share*	(0.07)		(0.60)

* Common

[A] Reported in accordance with IFRS

Historical Summary
(as originally stated)

Fiscal Year	Oper. Rev.	Net Inc. Bef. Disc.	EPS*
	$000s	$000s	$
2022[A]	94	(12,083)	(3.00)
2021[A]	197	(6,142)	(3.00)
2020[A]	nil	(161)	(6.60)

* Common

[A] Reported in accordance with IFRS

Note: Adjusted throughout for 1-for-20 cons. in Nov. 2022

A.124 Argo Living Soils Corp.

Symbol - ARGO **Exchange** - CSE **CUSIP** - 04018T

Head Office - 820-1130 Pender St W, Vancouver, BC, V6E 4A4 **Telephone** - (250) 539-0837

Website - argolivingsoils.com

Email - peter.hoyle@shaw.ca

Investor Relations - Peter J. Hoyle (604) 787-2811

Auditors - Dale Matheson Carr-Hilton LaBonte LLP C.A., Vancouver, B.C.

Transfer Agents - Odyssey Trust Company, Vancouver, B.C.

Profile - (B.C. 2018) Produces and develops organic products including soil amendments, living soils, bio-fertilizers, vermicompost, and compost tea kits formulated specifically for high value crops.

Products developed include Living Soil, which is a proprietary vermicast (worm castings) formulated soil for the vegetative and flowering stages of plant growth; Vermicasts, which are derived from a proprietary feed-input that can be used as a microbial and fungal inoculant, usually called a soil additive and/or a soil amendment; Aerobic compost tea kits; which are used to manage soil regeneration and microbiology; mixed dry soil amendments, which are used for improving soil texture, structure, fertility and porosity; and blends of essential oils, which are used to controls pests such as spider mites, thrips, fungus gnats and root aphids.

The company produces Vermicasts at its farm and production facilities located on farmland in Galiano Island, B.C. The Galiano Island farm site includes two vermicast barns, a mixing plant and an office building, and would also be the site of a research facility, greenhouse for producing cultivars and facilities for developing and producing natural fertilizers and pesticides. The company sells Vermicasts on its website.

Directors - Peter J. Hoyle, interim CEO, CFO & corp. sec., Ont.; Ken Bowman, chief agri. oper. officer, B.C.; Hector Diakow, B.C.; Robert Intile, B.C.

Capital Stock

	Authorized (shs.)	Outstanding (shs.)[1]
Common	unlimited	21,376,301

[1] At Apr. 28, 2023

Major Shareholder - Widely held at Apr. 20, 2022.

Price Range - ARGO/CSE

Year	Volume	High	Low	Close
2022	2,365,604	$0.35	$0.07	$0.09
2021	2,642,309	$0.35	$0.17	$0.32

Recent Close: $0.12

Financial Statistics

Periods ended:	12m Nov. 30/21[A]		12m Nov. 30/20[A]
	$000s	%Chg	$000s
Research & devel. expense	nil		23
General & admin expense	416		64
Stock-based compensation	4		nil
Operating expense	**420**	**+383**	**87**
Operating income	**(420)**	**n.a.**	**(87)**
Deprec., depl. & amort.	16		2
Pre-tax income	**(433)**	**n.a.**	**(89)**
Net income	**(433)**	**n.a.**	**(89)**
Cash & equivalent	326		198
Current assets	336		199
Fixed assets, net	80		13
Right-of-use assets	20		21
Total assets	**437**	**+87**	**234**
Accts. pay. & accr. liabs	13		10
Current liabilities	49		32
Long-term lease liabilities	5		5
Shareholders' equity	383		196
Cash from oper. activs	**(429)**	**n.a.**	**(58)**
Cash from fin. activs	629		262
Cash from invest. activs	(72)		(14)
Net cash position	**326**	**+65**	**198**
	$		$
Earnings per share*	(0.03)		(0.02)
	shs		shs
No. of shs. o/s*	18,193,300		10,070,000
Avg. no. of shs. o/s*	12,787,511		4,178,137
	%		%
Net profit margin	n.a.		n.a.
Return on equity	(149.57)		(89.00)
Return on assets	(129.06)		(73.25)

* Common

[A] Reported in accordance with IFRS

Latest Results

Periods ended:	3m Feb. 28/22[A]		3m Feb. 28/21[A]
	$000s	%Chg	$000s
Net income	(93)	n.a.	(78)
	$		$
Earnings per share*	(0.01)		(0.01)

* Common
[A] Reported in accordance with IFRS

Historical Summary
(as originally stated)

Fiscal Year	Oper. Rev. $000s	Net Inc. Bef. Disc. $000s	EPS* $
2021[A]	nil	(433)	(0.03)
2020[A]	nil	(89)	(0.02)
2019[A]	nil	(2)	(0.00)

* Common
[A] Reported in accordance with IFRS

A.125 Argo Opportunity Corp.

Symbol - AROC.P **Exchange** - TSX-VEN **CUSIP** - 04019W
Head Office - PO Box 3566 Stn Terminal, Vancouver, BC, V6B 3Y6 **Telephone** - (604) 722-5225
Email - mike@pacwest.ca
Investor Relations - Michele N. Marrandino (604) 722-5225
Auditors - Dale Matheson Carr-Hilton LaBonte LLP C.A., Vancouver, B.C.
Lawyers - Aluvion Professional Corporation, Toronto, Ont.
Transfer Agents - Odyssey Trust Company, Vancouver, B.C.
Profile - (Can. 2021) Capital Pool Company.
Common listed on TSX-VEN, May 18, 2023.
Directors - Michele N. (Mike) Marrandino, pres., CEO, CFO & corp. sec., Vancouver, B.C.; Mark Fekete, Montréal, Qué.; David Franklin, Thornhill, Ont.; John Gibson, Toronto, Ont.

Capital Stock

	Authorized (shs.)	Outstanding (shs.)[1]
Common	unlimited	6,221,700

[1] At May 18, 2023

Major Shareholder - John Gibson held 19.29% interest at May 18, 2023.
Capital Stock Changes - On May 18, 2023, an initial public offering of 3,221,700 common shares was completed at 10¢ per share.

A.126 Aritzia Inc.*

Symbol - ATZ **Exchange** - TSX **CUSIP** - 04045U
Head Office - 118-611 Alexander St, Vancouver, BC, V6A 1E1 **Telephone** - (604) 251-3132
Website - investors.aritzia.com/investor-relations/default.aspx
Email - breed@aritzia.com
Investor Relations - Beth Reed (646) 603-9844
Auditors - PricewaterhouseCoopers LLP C.A., Vancouver, B.C.
Lawyers - Stikeman Elliott LLP, Vancouver, B.C.
Transfer Agents - TSX Trust Company, Vancouver, B.C.
FP500 Revenue Ranking - 205
Employees - 8,300 at Feb. 26, 2023
Profile - (B.C. 2008) Designs and retails premium women's apparel and accessories under the Aritzia brand as well as premium athletic wear for men and women under the Reigning Champ brand primarily in North America through its own stores, online channels and third party retailers.

The company's women's products include t-shirts, blouses, sweaters, jackets, coats, pants, shorts, skirts, dresses, denim, intimates, swimwear and accessories for each season. Brands include Wilfred, Babaton, TNA, Wilfred Free, Denim Forum, The Group by Babaton, Ten by Babaton, Sunday Best, Talula, Super World™, TnAction™ and Auxiliary. The majority of stores are operated under the Aritzia banner, with selectively operated TNA, Wilfred, Super World™ and Babaton exclusive brand stores.

The company contracts and maintains direct relationships with a diversified base of independent suppliers and manufacturers located primarily in Asia and Europe for its exclusive brands.

At May 2, 2023, the company operated 68 stores in Canada in Alberta (10), British Columbia (17), Manitoba, Nova Scotia, Ontario (31), Québec (7) and Saskatchewan, and 46 stores in the U.S., in California (10), Colorado, Florida (2), Georgia, Hawaii, Illinois (4), Massachusetts, Michigan, Minnesota, New Jersey (3), Nevada, New York (8), Ohio, Oregon, Pennsylvania, Tennessee, Texas (4), Virginia, Washington (2) and Washington D.C., averaging about 8,000 sq. ft., with flagship stores up to 20,000 sq. ft., and all in prime locations. The company's products are sold exclusively through its stores and aritzia.com.

Distribution centres include a 223,000-sq.-ft. facility located in New Westminster, B.C.; a 150,000-sq.-ft facility in Mississauga, Ont.; and a 240,000-sq.-ft. facility in Columbus, Ohio.

In addition, wholly owned **CYC Design Corporation** designs and manufactures men's and women's athletic wear under the Reigning Champ brand. Products are sold worldwide through Reigning Champ stores, online channels and third party retailers. Operated stores are located in British Columbia (2) and Ontario (2).

On Nov. 30, 2022, a secondary offering of 1,500,000 subordinate voting shares of the company by certain entities controlled by Brian Hill, the company's founder and executive chairman, was completed at $51.60 per share. The company did not receive any proceeds from the offering. On closing, Brian Hill's voting interest decreased to 69.5% from 71.2%.

Recent Merger and Acquisition Activity

Status: completed **Announced:** May 26, 2023
Aritzia Inc. acquired the remaining 25% equity interest in CYC Design Corporation for issuance of 419,047 subordinate voting shares valued at $15,400,000. In addition, Aritzia may issue to the CYC selling shareholders, by Mar. 31, 2026, additional subordinate voting shares with an estimated value of up to $9,400,000 based on certain operational performance metrics of the Reigning Champ brand.

Directors - Brian Hill, founder & exec. chr., B.C.; Jennifer Wong, CEO & corp. sec., B.C.; John E. Currie†, North Vancouver, B.C.; Aldo Bensadoun, Qué.; Daniel Habashi, Ont.; David Labistour, North Vancouver, B.C.; John S. Montalbano, Vancouver, B.C.; Marni Payne, Mass.; Glen T. Senk, Palm Beach, Fla.; Marcia M. Smith, Vancouver, B.C.
Other Exec. Officers - Todd Ingledew, CFO; Karen Kwan, chief people & culture officer; Dave MacIver, CIO; Pippa Morgan, exec. v-p, retail
† Lead director

Capital Stock

	Authorized (shs.)	Outstanding (shs.)[1]
Preferred	unlimited	nil
Multiple Voting	unlimited	20,437,349
Subordinate Voting	unlimited	90,297,811

[1] At July 10, 2023

Multiple Voting - Convertible into subordinate voting shares on a 1-for-1 basis at any time at the option of the holder and automatically under certain circumstances. Ten votes per share.
Subordinate Voting - One vote per share.
Normal Course Issuer Bid - The company plans to make normal course purchases of up to 3,860,745 subordinate voting shares representing 5% of the public float. The bid commenced on Jan. 20, 2023, and expires on Jan. 19, 2024.
Major Shareholder - Brian Hill held 69.4% interest at May 11, 2023.

Price Range - ATZ/TSX

Year	Volume	High	Low	Close
2022	87,334,308	$60.64	$31.67	$47.35
2021	74,117,118	$53.46	$24.39	$52.35
2020	77,747,066	$26.37	$9.20	$25.79
2019	71,338,509	$19.59	$15.08	$19.05
2018	55,259,048	$19.79	$11.59	$16.40

Recent Close: $24.65
Capital Stock Changes - During fiscal 2023, subordinate voting shares were issued as follows: 1,500,000 on conversion of a like number of multiple voting shares and 943,772 on exercise of options; 1,619,580 subordinate voting shares were repurchased under a Normal Course Issuer Bid.
Long-Term Debt - At Feb. 26, 2023, the company had no long-term debt.

Wholly Owned Subsidiaries

Aritzia GP Inc., B.C.
- 0.01% int. in **Aritzia LP**, Ont.

CYC Design Corporation, Vancouver, B.C.

Subsidiaries

99.99% int. in **Aritzia LP**, Ont.
- 100% int. in **Aritzia US Holdings Inc.**, B.C.
  - 100% int. in **United States of Aritzia Inc.**, Del.

Financial Statistics

Periods ended:	52w Feb. 26/23[A]		52w Feb. 27/22[A]
	$000s	%Chg	$000s
Operating revenue	**2,195,630**	**+47**	**1,494,630**
Cost of goods sold	1,162,199		740,219
General & admin expense	588,006		379,634
Stock-based compensation	24,369		26,131
Operating expense	**1,774,574**	**+55**	**1,145,984**
Operating income	**421,056**	**+21**	**348,646**
Deprec., depl. & amort.	133,902		112,627
Finance income	2,841		1,600
Finance costs, gross	31,263		25,202
Pre-tax income	**263,807**	**+20**	**219,600**
Income taxes	76,219		62,683
Net income	**187,588**	**+20**	**156,917**
Cash & equivalent	86,510		265,245
Inventories	467,634		208,125
Accounts receivable	18,184		8,147
Current assets	611,848		521,536
Fixed assets, net	308,608		223,190
Right-of-use assets	614,061		362,887
Intangibles, net	285,228		286,244
Total assets	**1,836,543**	**+29**	**1,424,586**
Accts. pay. & accr. liabs.	221,712		179,344
Current liabilities	417,300		387,325
Long-term lease liabilities	654,690		417,067
Shareholders' equity	685,787		530,811
Cash from oper. activs.	**74,913**	**-78**	**338,353**
Cash from fin. activs.	(122,537)		(124,093)
Cash from invest. activs.	(131,213)		(99,576)
Net cash position	**86,510**	**-67**	**265,245**
Capital expenditures	(122,767)		(65,427)
	$		$
Earnings per share*	1.70		1.42
Cash flow per share*	0.68		3.06
	shs		shs
No. of shs. o/s*	110,442,610		111,118,418
Avg. no. of shs. o/s*	110,259,000		110,401,000
	%		%
Net profit margin	8.54		10.50
Return on equity	30.84		35.22
Return on assets	12.87		13.64
Foreign sales percent	51		45
No. of employees (FTEs)	8,300		6,569

* M.V. & S.V.
[A] Reported in accordance with IFRS

Latest Results

Periods ended:	13w May 28/23[A]		13w May 29/22[A]
	$000s	%Chg	$000s
Operating revenue	462,665	+13	407,910
Net income	17,470	-47	33,261
	$		$
Earnings per share*	0.16		0.30

* M.V. & S.V.
[A] Reported in accordance with IFRS

Historical Summary
(as originally stated)

Fiscal Year	Oper. Rev. $000s	Net Inc. Bef. Disc. $000s	EPS* $
2023[A]	2,195,630	187,588	1.70
2022[A]	1,494,630	156,917	1.42
2021[A]	857,323	19,227	0.18
2020[A]	980,589	90,594	0.84
2019[A1]	874,296	78,728	0.70

* M.V. & S.V.
[A] Reported in accordance with IFRS
[1] 53 weeks ended Mar. 3, 2019.

A.127 Arkadia Capital Corp.

Symbol - AKC.H **Exchange** - TSX-VEN (S) **CUSIP** - 040724
Head Office - 1400-350 7 Ave SW, Calgary, AB, T2P 3N9 **Telephone** - (403) 299-9600 **Fax** - (403) 299-9601
Email - arock@nerlandlindsey.com
Investor Relations - Adam Rock (403) 299-9600
Auditors - MNP LLP C.A., Calgary, Alta.
Bankers - Royal Bank of Canada
Lawyers - Lindsey MacCarthy LLP
Transfer Agents - Olympia Trust Company, Calgary, Alta.
Profile - (Alta. 2011) Capital Pool Company.
Common suspended from TSX-VEN, Aug. 7, 2018.

Recent Merger and Acquisition Activity

Status: pending **Revised:** Aug. 16, 2022
UPDATE: A definitive agreement was entered into. PREVIOUS: Arkadia Capital Corp. entered into a letter of intent for the Qualifying Transaction reveres takeover acquisition of private British Columbia-based Moduurn Mobility Inc., which has developed a commission-free, white label digital

ordering and delivery service that connects restaurant brands and corporate cafeterias to the on-demand world, on a share-for-share basis (following a 1-for-40 share consolidation). Upon completion, Moduurn would amalgamate with Arkadia's wholly owned 1324976 B.C. Ltd., and Arkadia would change its name to Moduurn Mobility Limited. In conjunction with the transaction, Moduurn proposed to complete a private placement of up to 5,000,000 common shares at $1.00 per share.

Directors - Adam Rock, CEO & corp. sec., Alta.

Other Exec. Officers - Kalvie Legat, CFO

Capital Stock

	Authorized (shs.)	Outstanding (shs.)[1]
Preferred	unlimited	nil
Common	unlimited	6,523,343

[1] At Aug. 22, 2023

Major Shareholder - Widely held at Jan. 11, 2014.

A.128 Armada Data Corporation

Symbol - ARD **Exchange** - TSX-VEN **CUSIP** - 042084

Head Office - 215-5080 Timberlea Blvd, Mississauga, ON, L4W 4M2 **Telephone** - (905) 624-4913 **Toll-free** - (866) 453-6995 **Fax** - (905) 624-3259

Website - www.armadadata.com

Email - ematthews@armadadatacorp.ca

Investor Relations - Elizabeth Matthews (866) 453-6995

Auditors - Philip Gigan C.A., Toronto, Ont.

Bankers - HSBC Bank Canada, Mississauga, Ont.

Lawyers - Harris + Harris LLP, Mississauga, Ont.

Transfer Agents - Computershare Trust Company of Canada Inc., Toronto, Ont.

Profile - (B.C. 1999) Provides real-time automobile pricing, comparative and related data to institutional and retail customers on a fee-for-service basis through company-operated automotive related websites and offers information technology and marketing services to its clients.

Operations consist of three segments: Insurance Services; CarCostCanada; and Information Technology (IT) Services.

The Insurance Services division sells total-loss replacement vehicle pricing reports to Canadian insurance companies. The CarCostCanada division sells new car pricing data to consumers through the www.CarCostCanada.com website; resells new car pricing data to qualified third party vendors; sells online advertising for third parties; sells new vehicle leads to automobile dealers; and offers consulting and other vehicle-related marketing services. The IT services division offers website and email hosting, dedicated servers, technical and network support services, and resells software and hardware solutions from Microsoft, Barracuda, Dropbox and Webroot.

Predecessor Detail - Name changed from CCC Internet Solutions Inc., Jan. 26, 2004.

Directors - R. James Matthews, pres., CEO & corp. sec., Mississauga, Ont.; Eli Oszlak, v-p & chief tech. officer, Mississauga, Ont.; Gregory Harris, Toronto, Ont.; Glen Hrabovsky, Ont.; Fred Marotta, Ont.

Other Exec. Officers - Elizabeth Matthews, CFO & contr.

Capital Stock

	Authorized (shs.)	Outstanding (shs.)[1]
Common	unlimited	17,670,265

[1] At Sept. 28, 2022

Major Shareholder - R. James Matthews held 20.1% interest, Daniela Timoteo held 19.7% interest and Eli Oszlak held 10.7% interest at Oct. 13, 2021.

Price Range - ARD/TSX-VEN

Year	Volume	High	Low	Close
2022	2,300,665	$0.11	$0.04	$0.05
2021	5,699,786	$0.20	$0.08	$0.10
2020	4,380,521	$0.16	$0.05	$0.16
2019	2,622,935	$0.10	$0.04	$0.06
2018	2,169,989	$0.18	$0.07	$0.11

Recent Close: $0.04

Capital Stock Changes - There were no changes to capital stock from fiscal 2014 to fiscal 2022, inclusive.

Dividends

ARD com N.S.R.
$0.01 May 31/21
Paid in 2023: n.a. 2022: n.a. 2021: $0.01

Wholly Owned Subsidiaries

CCC Internet Solutions Inc., Ont.

Subsidiaries

90% int. in **The Big & Easy Bottle Brewing Company Inc.** Inactive.
- 100% int. in **Mister Beer Inc.** Inactive.
- 100% int. in **Mister Beer U Brew Inc.** Inactive.

Financial Statistics

Periods ended:	12m May 31/22[A]		12m May 31/21[A]
	$000s	%Chg	$000s
Operating revenue	**2,526**	**-20**	**3,150**
Salaries & benefits	1,509		1,592
General & admin expense	1,124		1,423
Operating expense	**2,633**	**-13**	**3,015**
Operating income	**(107)**	**n.a.**	**135**
Deprec., depl. & amort.	96		82
Finance costs, gross	26		30
Write-downs/write-offs	(180)		nil
Pre-tax income	**(408)**	**n.a.**	**22**
Income taxes	(73)		6
Net income	**(335)**	**n.a.**	**16**
Cash & equivalent	160		432
Accounts receivable	364		460
Current assets	644		1,037
Fixed assets, net	19		22
Right-of-use assets	168		173
Intangibles, net	24		234
Total assets	**855**	**-42**	**1,466**
Accts. pay. & accr. liabs	225		366
Current liabilities	277		507
Long-term lease liabilities	126		133
Shareholders' equity	602		936
Non-controlling interest	(150)		(150)
Cash from oper. activs	**(209)**	**n.a.**	**302**
Cash from fin. activs	(129)		(308)
Cash from invest. activs	67		86
Net cash position	**160**	**-63**	**432**
Capital expenditures	(14)		(2)
	$		$
Earnings per share*	(0.02)		0.00
Cash flow per share*	(0.01)		0.02
Cash divd. per share*	nil		0.01
	shs		shs
No. of shs. o/s*	17,670,265		17,670,265
Avg. no. of shs. o/s*	17,670,265		17,670,265
	%		%
Net profit margin	(13.26)		0.51
Return on equity	(43.56)		1.57
Return on assets	(27.03)		2.49

* Common
[A] Reported in accordance with IFRS

Historical Summary (as originally stated)

Fiscal Year	Oper. Rev. $000s	Net Inc. Bef. Disc. $000s	EPS* $
2022[A]	2,526	(335)	(0.02)
2021[A]	3,150	16	0.00
2020[A]	3,281	50	0.00
2019[A]	2,885	(37)	(0.00)
2018[A]	2,952	272	0.02

* Common
[A] Reported in accordance with IFRS

A.129 Armada Mercantile Ltd.

Symbol - ARM **Exchange** - CSE **CUSIP** - 041904

Head Office - 100-1616 3 Ave W, Vancouver, BC, V6J 1K2 **Telephone** - (604) 687-7300

Website - www.armadamercantile.com

Email - cole@armadamercantile.com

Investor Relations - Patrick D. Cole (916) 746-0029

Auditors - Sam S. Mah Inc. C.A., Vancouver, B.C.

Transfer Agents - Computershare Trust Company of Canada Inc., Vancouver, B.C.

Profile - (B.C. 1987) Provides merchant banking services primarily through wholly owned **Armada Group USA, Inc.**

The company provides specialized merchant banking, broker-dealer, venture lending and corporate finance services internationally, as well as advising clients on corporate strategy, structure, mergers and acquisitions, and raising capital. Armada USA provides broker-dealer products and services through its relationship with **Redrock Trading Partners, LLC**. International corporate finance services, which are offered through **Oxygen Funding, Inc.** (30% owned), include account receivables factoring, supply chain, equipment leasing, merchant cash advance, and purchase order and other types of specialized finance. Through **Empire Factors LLC**, offers commercial finance services including account receivables factoring, supply chain and revenue lines of credit primarily to companies in New York and New Jersey. In addition, subsidiary **RichGrandDad Financial Ltd.** (51% owned) offers real estate and merchant lending services through its affiliate companies including Empire Factors, **Hard Money Mobile LLC**, **Lend on Land**, **Quantak**, **Century Capital Partners, LLC** and **Solid Oak Investments, Inc.**; and holds a 33% interest in **SNM Brothers LLC** (dba Ace Foods), which imports and distributes London Dairy ice cream in more than 35 countries around the world.

Predecessor Detail - Name changed from Armada Gold and Minerals Ltd., Mar. 4, 1992.

Directors - Patrick D. Cole, pres., Roseville, Calif.; Michelle Cole, CFO & corp. sec., Roseville, Calif.; Mark Varley, chief tech. officer, Richmond, B.C.

Other Exec. Officers - Victor Cohen, CEO

Capital Stock

	Authorized (shs.)	Outstanding (shs.)[1]
Preferred	100,000,000	nil
Series A		526,315
Series B		nil
Series C		nil
Common	200,000,000	19,104,409

[1] At June 28, 2023

Preferred - Issuable in series. Non-voting.

Series A - Convertible into common shares on a 1-for-1 basis, if the market trading price of the common shares of Vocalscape Networks, Inc. of Nevada is trading at less than US$1.00 per share as of the first anniversary date of the issuance of the series A preferred shares. Redeemable at US$0.285 per share.

Common - One vote per share.

Major Shareholder - Patrick D. Cole held 27% interest at July 13, 2021.

Price Range - ARM/CSE

Year	Volume	High	Low	Close
2022	267,707	$0.41	$0.18	$0.35
2021	741,428	$0.38	$0.13	$0.25
2020	164,620	$0.48	$0.07	$0.18
2019	651,950	$0.54	$0.03	$0.03
2018	216,851	$0.76	$0.20	$0.40

Recent Close: $0.47

Capital Stock Changes - There were no changes to capital stock during fiscal 2023.

Wholly Owned Subsidiaries

Armada Group USA, Inc., Del.
- 100% int. in **Armada Finance, LLC**, United States.
- **Empire Factors, LLC**, United States.
- 30% int. in **Oxygen Funding Inc.**, Calif.
- 51% int. in **RichGrandDad Financial Ltd.**, B.C.
- **Zero Nox, Inc.**

Financial Statistics

Periods ended:	12m Feb. 28/23[A]		12m Feb. 28/22[oA]
	$000s	%Chg	$000s
Operating revenue	**51**	**n.m.**	**3**
General & admin expense	179		238
Operating expense	**179**	**-25**	**238**
Operating income	**(128)**	**n.a.**	**(235)**
Finance income	403		312
Finance costs, gross	1		1
Pre-tax income	**268**	**+267**	**73**
Income taxes	25		19
Net income	**243**	**+350**	**54**
Net inc. for equity hldrs	**242**	**+394**	**49**
Net inc. for non-cont. int	**1**	**-80**	**5**
Cash & equivalent	5,815		5,630
Accounts receivable	6		6
Current assets	5,922		5,637
Long-term investments	460		nil
Total assets	**6,381**	**+13**	**5,637**
Bank indebtedness	7		7
Accts. pay. & accr. liabs	489		84
Current liabilities	529		120
Preferred share equity	171		171
Shareholders' equity	5,853		5,516
Cash from oper. activs	**428**	**+851**	**45**
Cash from fin. activs	(108)		(25)
Cash from invest. activs	(367)		nil
Net cash position	**400**	**+97**	**203**
	$		$
Earnings per share*	0.01		0.00
Cash flow per share*	0.02		0.00
	shs		shs
No. of shs. o/s*	19,104,409		19,104,409
Avg. no. of shs. o/s*	19,025,418		19,025,418
	%		%
Net profit margin	476.47		n.m.
Return on equity	4.39		0.96
Return on assets	4.06		0.98

* Common
[o] Restated
[A] Reported in accordance with IFRS

Historical Summary
(as originally stated)

Fiscal Year	Oper. Rev. $000s	Net Inc. Bef. Disc. $000s	EPS* $
2023[A]	51	243	0.01
2022[A]	3	48	0.00
2021[A]	9	5,530	0.31
2020[A]	3	(268)	(0.01)
2019[A]	17	(19)	(0.00)

* Common
[A] Reported in accordance with IFRS

A.130 Artis Real Estate Investment Trust*

Symbol - AX.UN **Exchange** - TSX **CUSIP** - 04315L
Head Office - 600-220 Portage Ave, Winnipeg, MB, R3C 0A5 **Telephone** - (204) 947-1250 **Toll-free** - (800) 941-4751 **Fax** - (204) 947-0453
Website - www.artisreit.com
Email - hnikkel@artisreit.com
Investor Relations - Heather Nikkel (800) 941-4751
Auditors - Deloitte LLP C.A., Winnipeg, Man.
Bankers - The Bank of Nova Scotia, Winnipeg, Man.
Lawyers - Norton Rose Fulbright LLP
Transfer Agents - Odyssey Trust Company
FP500 Revenue Ranking - 525
Employees - 172 at Dec. 31, 2022
Profile - (Man. 2004) Owns, manages, leases and develops a portfolio of office, retail and industrial properties in Canada and the U.S.

At June 30, 2023, the trust owned 120 income-producing properties totaling 13,686,000 sq. ft. of leasable area in Alberta, British Columbia, Manitoba, Ontario, Saskatchewan, Arizona, Colorado, Minnesota, Texas and Wisconsin.

Property portfolio at June 30, 2023:

Type	Props.	Sq. Ft.[1]
Canada:		
Office	13	1,888,000
Retail	28	1,803,000
Industrial	37	2,570,000
	78	6,261,000
U.S.:		
Office	27	4,362,000
Industrial	15	3,063,000
	42	7,425,000
Total:	120	13,686,000

[1] Owned share of leasable area.

At June 30, 2023, the trust had an industrial property under development in Minnesota totaling 99,000 sq. ft. and an office property under redevelopment in Colorado totaling 257,000 sq. ft.

On Aug. 2, 2023, the trust initiated a strategic review process to consider and evaluate strategic alternatives that may be available to the trust to unlock and maximize value for unitholders.

In June 2023, the trust sold a parcel of office development land in Madison, Wisc., for an undisclosed amount.

In September 2022, the trust acquired the remaining 5% interest in Park 8Ninety II, a 543,210-sq.-ft. industrial property in Greater Houston, Tex., for US$2,508,283.

On June 22, 2022, trust announced the acquisition of an additional 1,045,271 REIT units, series A of **Dream Office Real Estate Investment Trust** (Dream Office REIT) at an average price of $21.76 per share. As a result, the trust's interest in Dream Office REIT increased to 7,486,187 units from 6,,440,916 units, representing a 14.32% ownership interest.

Recent Merger and Acquisition Activity

Status: completed **Revised:** June 27, 2023
UPDATE: The transaction was completed. PREVIOUS: Artis Real Estate Investment Trust agreed to sell six industrial properties totaling 700,000 sq. ft. of leasable area in the Twin Cities area of Minnesota for US$74,800,000. The transaction was expected to close in March 2023.

Status: completed **Announced:** June 16, 2023
Artis Real Estate Investment Trust sold Eagle Creek, a 122,900-sq.-ft. warehouse and distribution complex with office space in Savage, Minn. Terms were not disclosed.

Status: completed **Revised:** June 16, 2023
UPDATE: The transaction was completed. PREVIOUS: Artis Real Estate Investment Trust entered into unconditional agreement to sell St. Vital Square, a six-building retail centre totaling 116,500 sq. ft. of leasable area in Winnipeg, Man., for $42,100,000.

Status: pending **Announced:** June 8, 2023
Artis Real Estate Investment Trust entered into unconditional agreement to sell seven industrial properties and one parcel of land in the United States for a purchase price of US$88,700,000.

Status: completed **Revised:** June 7, 2023
UPDATE: The transaction was completed. PREVIOUS: Artis Real Estate Investment Trust agreed to sell Clearwater Creek Distribution Center, a 402,500-sq.-ft. industrial property in Lino Lakes, Minn., for US$28,900,000. The transaction was expected to close in June 2023.

Status: completed **Revised:** May 30, 2023
UPDATE: Namao South was sold. PREVIOUS: Artis Real Estate Investment Trust agreed to sell three retail properties in Alberta, 44,600-sq.-ft. Gateway Power Centre in Grande Prairie, 50,000-sq.-ft. Visions Building in Calgary and 108,000-sq.-ft. Namao South in Edmonton. Total consideration was $71,550,000. The transaction was expected to close in May 2023. May 15, 2023 - Gateway Power Centre was sold. May 29, 2023 - Visions Building was sold.

Status: completed **Announced:** Apr. 19, 2023
Artis Real Estate Investment Trust sold Liberton Square, a 20,700-sq.-ft. shopping centre in St. Albert, Alta., for $8,000,000.

Status: completed **Announced:** Mar. 14, 2023
Artis Real Estate Investment Trust sold North 48 Commercial Centre, a 64,147-sq.-ft. office property in Saskatoon, Sask., for $14,600,000.

Status: completed **Revised:** Nov. 15, 2022
UPDATE: The transaction was completed. PREVIOUS: Artis Real Estate Investment Trust agreed to sell Hartford Corporate Plaza, a 123,210-sq.-ft. office property in New Hartford, N.Y., for US$13,700,000. The transaction was expected to close on Nov. 15, 2022.

Status: completed **Announced:** Nov. 4, 2022
Artis Real Estate Investment Trust sold 17 industrial properties totaling 2,500,000 sq. ft. of leasable area in the Twin Cities area of Minnesota for US$248,900,000.

Status: completed **Announced:** Sept. 19, 2022
Artis Real Estate Investment Trust sold New Brighton Office Center, a 116,011-sq.-ft. office property in the Twin Cities area of Minnesota, for $24,163,000.

Status: completed **Announced:** June 30, 2022
Artis Real Estate Investment Trust sold Rocky Mountain Business Center, a 137,868-sq.-ft. industrial property in Aurora, Colo. Terms were not disclosed.

Status: completed **Announced:** June 24, 2022
Artis Real Estate Investment Trust sold Meadowvale Office, a 99,828-sq.-ft. class A office building in Mississauga, Ont. Terms were not disclosed.

Status: completed **Revised:** Mar. 10, 2022
UPDATE: The transaction was completed. PREVIOUS: Artis Real Estate Investment Trust agreed to sell 2150-2180 Dunwin Drive, a 75,900-sq.-ft. industrial property in the Greater Toronto Area of Ontario, for $29,200,000. The transaction was expected to close in March 2022.

Status: completed **Revised:** Mar. 1, 2022
UPDATE: The transaction was completed. PREVIOUS: Iris Acquisition II LP, an entity created by a consortium led by Canderel Real Estate Property Inc. and including Artis Real Estate Investment Trust, partnerships managed by the Sandpiper Group Holdings Inc., and FrontFour Capital Group LLC, agreed to acquire Cominar Real Estate Investment Trust for $11.75 per unit in cash. The equity value is $2.2 billion and the enterprise value is $5.7 billion. Artis has committed a total of up to $214,000,000 to the transaction, which includes participation in multiple aspects of the consortium's overall capital structure, including $100,000,000 of junior preferred units that carry a distribution rate of 18% per annum and up to $114,000,000 in common equity units. Koch Real Estate Investments, LLC is also providing preferred equity for the transaction. The consortium plans to retain portions of Cominar's retail portfolio, as well as components of Cominar's office portfolio, and has agreed to sell Cominar's industrial portfolio to Blackstone and certain Cominar retail and office properties to Group Mach Acquisition Inc. for $1.5 billion. A termination fee of $55,000,000 would be payable by Cominar to the consortium in certain circumstances and reverse termination fee of $110,000,000 would be payable by the consortium to Cominar in the event the consortium fails to pay the consideration. The transaction was to close in the first quarter of 2022. Dec. 23, 2021 - The Superior Court of Québec issued a final order approving the transaction

Status: completed **Revised:** Mar. 1, 2022
UPDATE: The transaction was completed. PREVIOUS: Groupe Mach Inc. agreed to acquire certain retail and office properties of Cominar Real Estate Investment Trust from Iris Acquisition II LP, an entity created by a consortium led by Canderel Real Estate Property Inc., and including FrontFour Capital Group LLC, Artis Real Estate Investment Trust and partnerships managed by the Sandpiper Group, for $1.5 billion. The consortium has an agreement to acquire Cominar for an enterprise value of $5.7 billion.

Status: completed **Revised:** Mar. 1, 2022
UPDATE: The transaction was completed. PREVIOUS: Blackstone Real Estate, an affiliate of The Blackstone Inc., agreed to acquire the industrial property portfolio of Cominar Real Estate Investment Trust from Iris Acquisition II LP, an entity created by a consortium led by Canderel Real Estate Property Inc., and including FrontFour Capital Group LLC, Artis Real Estate Investment Trust and partnerships managed by the Sandpiper Group. Terms were not disclosed. The consortium has an agreement to acquire Cominar for an enterprise value of $5.7 billion. Feb. 21, 2021 - Investment Canada approval was received.

Predecessor Detail - Name changed from Westfield Real Estate Investment Trust, Feb. 15, 2007.

Trustees - Ben Rodney‡, chr., Toronto, Ont.; Samir A. Manji, pres. & CEO, West Vancouver, B.C.; Heather-Anne Irwin, Ont.; Michael H. (Mike) Shaikh, Calgary, Alta.; Aida Tammer, Toronto, Ont.; Elisabeth S. (Lis) Wigmore, Toronto, Ont.; Lauren Zucker, Westport, Conn.

Other Exec. Officers - Kim Riley, COO; Jaclyn Koenig, CFO; David L. (Dave) Johnson, exec. v-p, asset mgt., central region; Philip Martens, exec. v-p, U.S. region; Kara Watson, exec. v-p, gen. counsel & corp. sec.; Marie Dunn, sr. v-p, asset mgt., U.S. region; Brad Goerzen, sr. v-p, leasing, central region; Amy Melchior, sr. v-p, asset mgt., Minn.; Gregory D. Moore, sr. v-p, real estate, Canada; Heather Nikkel, sr. v-p, IR & sustainability; Ron Wieler, sr. v-p, const. & devel.; Leon Wilkosz, sr. v-p, asset mgt., Wisc.; Lyndsay Jones, v-p, prop. mgt., central region; Lena Laluk, v-p, finl. reporting; Toni Lazaruk, v-p, treasury; Jayelle Morris, v-p, HR; Lec Mroczek, v-p, leasing, western region; Danielle Robert, v-p, acctg.; Eric Sawatzky, v-p, IT

‡ Lead trustee

Capital Stock

	Authorized (shs.)	Outstanding (shs.)[1]
Preferred Unit	unlimited	
Series A		nil
Series E		3,284,210
Series I		4,732,940
Special Voting Unit	unlimited	nil
Class B LP Unit	unlimited	nil
Trust Unit	unlimited	109,145,591

[1] At Aug. 2, 2023

Preferred Unit - Issuable in series. Fully and unconditionally guaranteed by the trust. Non-voting.

Series E - Entitled to cumulative preferential annual distributions of $1.368 per unit payable quarterly to Sept. 30, 2023, and thereafter at a rate reset every five years equal to the five-year Government of Canada bond yield plus 3.3%. Redeemable by the trust on Sept. 30, 2023, and on September 30 every five years thereafter, at $25 per unit plus declared and unpaid distributions. Convertible at the holder's option, on Sept. 30, 2023, and on September 30 every five years thereafter, into floating rate preferred series F units on a unit-for-unit basis, subject to certain conditions. The series F units would pay a quarterly distribution equal to the 90-day Canadian Treasury bill rate plus 3.3%.

Series I - Entitled to cumulative preferential annual distributions of $1.7482 per unit payable quarterly to Apr. 30, 2028, and thereafter at a rate reset every five years equal to the greater of: (i) five-year Government of Canada bond yield plus 3.93%; and (ii) 6%. Redeemable by the trust on Apr. 30, 2028, and on April 30 every five years thereafter at $25 per unit plus declared and unpaid distributions. Convertible at the holder's option, on Apr. 30, 2028, and on April 30 every five years thereafter, into floating rate preferred series J units on a unit-for-unit basis, subject to certain conditions. The series J units would pay a quarterly distribution equal to the 90-day Canadian Treasury bill rate plus 3.93%.

Trust Unit - One vote per trust unit.

Special Voting Unit - Issued to holders of class B limited partnership units of wholly owned AX L.P. Each special voting unit entitles the holder to a number of votes at unitholder meetings equal to the number of trust units into which the class B limited partnership units are exchangeable.

Class B Limited Partnership Unit - Partnership units of wholly owned AX L.P. entitled to distributions equal to those paid to trust units. Exchangeable into trust units on a 1-for-1 basis at any time at the holder's option.

Preferred Series A (old) - Were entitled to cumulative preferential annual distributions of $1.4155 payable quarterly. Redeemed on Sept. 30, 2022, at $25 per unit plus declared and unpaid distributions.

Normal Course Issuer Bid - The company plans to make normal course purchases of up to 7,860,942 trust units representing 10% of the public float. The bid commenced on Dec. 19, 2022, and expires on Dec. 18, 2023.

The company plans to make normal course purchases of up to 361,001 preferred series E units representing 10% of the public float. The bid commenced on Dec. 19, 2022, and expires on Dec. 18, 2023.

The company plans to make normal course purchases of up to 480,534 preferred series I units representing 10% of the public float. The bid commenced on Dec. 19, 2022, and expires on Dec. 18, 2023.

Major Shareholder - Sandpiper Group Holdings Inc. held 16.9% interest and Steven Joyce held 16% interest at May 1, 2023.

Price Range - AX.UN/TSX

Year	Volume	High	Low	Close
2022	87,945,228	$13.76	$8.77	$9.01
2021	102,145,501	$12.12	$10.31	$11.94
2020	101,243,905	$13.67	$5.41	$10.66
2019	82,738,172	$12.83	$9.13	$11.90
2018	82,568,352	$14.42	$8.75	$9.24

Recent Close: $6.93

Capital Stock Changes - On Sept. 30, 2022, all 3,248,300 preferred series A units were redeemed at $25 per unit plus declared and unpaid distributions. Also during 2022, 20,974 trust units were issued on redemption of restricted units and 8,156,276 trust units were repurchased under a Normal Course Issuer Bid. In addition, 94,400 preferred series E units and 68,800 preferred series I units were repurchased under a Normal Course Issuer Bid.

Dividends

AX.UN tr unit Ra $0.60 pa M est. Apr. 15, 2021[1]
Prev. Rate: $0.5562 est. Jan. 15, 2021

stk.[2]◆**g**	Dec. 31/22	$0.08◆	Dec. 31/22
stk.[3]◆**g**	Dec. 31/21	$0.32◆	Dec. 31/21

Paid in 2023: $0.45 2022: $0.55 + $0.08◆ + stk.◆**g** 2021: $0.58905 + $0.32◆ + stk.◆**g**

AX.PR.E pfd ser E cum. red. exch. Adj. Ra $1.368 pa Q est. Dec. 31, 2018
AX.PR.I pfd ser I cum. red. exch. Adj. Ra $1.74825 pa Q est. July 31, 2023
pfd ser A cum. red. exch. Adj. Ra $1.4155 pa Q est. Dec. 29, 2017[4]

[1] Distribution reinvestment plan suspended eff. Jan. 13/17.
[2] Distribution will be automatically reinvested and the units will be consolidated immediately after distribution. Equiv to $0.08.
[3] Distribution will be automatically reinvested and the units will be consolidated immediately after distribution. Equiv to $2.07
[4] Redeemed Sept. 30, 2022 at $25 per sh. plus accr. divds. of $0.353875.
◆ Special **g** Capital Gain

Long-Term Debt - Outstanding at Dec. 31, 2022:

Mtge. & loans pay.[1]	$864,698,000
Revolv. credit facilities[2]	601,934,000
Non-revolv. credit facilities[3]	300,000,000
3.824% sr. ser.D debs. due 2023	249,723,000
5.6% sr. ser.E debs. due 2025	199,368,000
Less: Financing costs	775,000
	2,214,948,000
Less: Current portion	1,252,276,000
	962,672,000

[1] Bearing interest at a weighted average nominal rate of 4.46% at Dec. 31, 2022. Maturity dates range from Jan. 13, 2023, to June 1, 2031.

[2] Consists of $226,588,000 and $375,346,000 revolving credit facilities, due in April 2023 and December 2024, respectively. Both facilities bear interest at banker's acceptance rate plus 1.7% or prime plus 0.7%, or LIBOR plus 1.7% or U.S. base rate plus 0.7%.

[3] Consists of $50,000,000 and $150,000,000 non-revolving credit facilities due in February 2023 and July 2023, respectively, both bearing interest at banker's acceptance rate plus 1.7% or prime plus 0.7%; and $100,000,000 non-revolving credit facility due in February 2023, which bears interest at banker's acceptance rate plus 1.6% or prime plus 0.6%.

Note - In January 2023, the trust extended the maturity of its $50,000,000 non-revolving credit facility to April 2023 from February 2023 and $100,000,000 non-revolving credit facility to February 2024 from February 2023. In February 2023, the trust extended the maturity of its $150,000,000 non-revolving credit facility to July 2024 from July 2023 and $280,000,000 revolving credit facility to April 2025 from April 2023.

Wholly Owned Subsidiaries

Artis General Partner Ltd., Winnipeg, Man.
- 100% int. in **AX LP**, Winnipeg, Man.
  - 75% int. in **AR GL LP**, Canada.
  - 75% int. in **AR GL General Partner Ltd.**
  - 100% int. in **AX QC Ltd.**, Man.
  - 100% int. in **Artis US Holdings II, LLC**, United States.
    - 100% int. in **Artis US Holdings II GP, Inc.**, United States.
      - 100% int. in **Artis US Holdings II LP**, United States.
  - 100% int. in **Artis US Holdings III, LLC**, United States.
    - 100% int. in **Artis US Holdings III GP, Inc.**, United States.
      - 100% int. in **Artis US Holdings III LP**, United States.
  - 100% int. in **Artis US Holdings IV, LLC**, United States.
    - 100% int. in **Artis US Holdings IV GP, Inc.**, United States.
      - 100% int. in **Artis US Holdings IV LP**, United States.
  - 100% int. in **Artis US Holdings, Inc.**, United States.
    - 100% int. in **AX US Management, Inc.**, United States.
  - 50% int. in **Ice II L.P.**, Ont.
  - 51% int. in **Ice GP Inc.**, Ont.
  - 50% int. in **Ice L.P.**, Ont.

Artis Property Management General Partner Ltd., Canada.
- 100% int. in **AX Property Management LP**, Canada.

Investments

14.77% int. in **Dream Office Real Estate Investment Trust**, Toronto, Ont. (see separate coverage)

Note: The preceding list includes only the major related companies in which interests are held.

Financial Statistics

Periods ended:	12m Dec. 31/22[A]		12m Dec. 31/21[◻A]
	$000s	%Chg	$000s
Total revenue	**372,512**	**-11**	**419,499**
Cost of real estate sales	nil		16,038
General & admin. expense	8,297		11,165
Property taxes	60,082		64,857
Other operating expense	102,450		100,819
Operating expense	**170,829**	**-11**	**192,879**
Operating income	**201,683**	**-11**	**226,620**
Investment income	85,369		17,693
Deprec. & amort.	1,254		1,362
Finance income	18,944		1,885
Finance costs, gross	89,437		69,648
Pre-tax income	**9,061**	**-98**	**390,464**
Income taxes	14,355		1,289
Net income	**(5,294)**	**n.a.**	**389,175**
Cash & equivalent	29,168		221,474
Accounts receivable	17,307		14,674
Current assets	406,108		340,074
Long-term investments	794,704		292,712
Fixed assets	13,788		13,668
Income-producing props.	3,156,206		3,741,544
Properties under devel.	191,552		195,161
Property interests, net	3,353,101		3,943,116
Total assets	**4,553,913**	**0**	**4,576,024**
Accts. pay. & accr. liabs.	56,655		74,145
Current liabilities	1,350,691		954,548
Long-term debt, gross	2,214,948		1,965,638
Long-term debt, net	962,672		1,164,118
Preferred share equity	205,806		288,221
Shareholders' equity	2,229,159		2,455,353
Cash from oper. activs.	**140,744**	**-29**	**199,499**
Cash from fin. activs.	(46,571)		(622,974)
Cash from invest. activs.	(288,989)		610,260
Net cash position	**29,168**	**-87**	**221,474**
Capital expenditures	(21)		(5)
Increase in property	(141,861)		(132,645)
Decrease in property	340,735		791,725
	$		$
Earnings per share*	(0.18)		2.87
Cash flow per share*	1.19		1.54
Funds from opers. per sh.*	1.40		1.35
Adj. funds from opers. per sh.*	0.95		0.96
Cash divd. per share*	0.60		0.59
Extra divd. - cash*	0.08		0.32
Stk. divd. - cash equiv.*	0.08		2.07
Total divd. per share*	**0.76**		**2.98**
	shs		shs
No. of shs. o/s*	115,409,234		123,544,536
Avg. no. of shs. o/s*	117,932,876		129,553,433
	%		%
Net profit margin	(1.42)		92.77
Return on equity	(1.01)		17.67
Return on assets	(1.26)		9.72
Foreign sales percent	59		51
No. of employees (FTEs)	172		188

* Trust unit
◻ Restated
[A] Reported in accordance with IFRS

Latest Results

Periods ended:	6m June 30/23[A]		6m June 30/22[A]
	$000s	%Chg	$000s
Total revenue	174,533	-5	184,296
Net income	(107,715)	n.a.	217,457
	$		$
Earnings per share*	(1.00)		1.74

* Trust unit
[A] Reported in accordance with IFRS

Historical Summary
(as originally stated)

Fiscal Year	Total Rev. $000s	Net Inc. Bef. Disc. $000s	EPS* $
2022[A]	372,512	(5,294)	(0.18)
2021[A]	419,499	389,175	2.87
2020[A]	458,917	21,543	0.03
2019[A]	521,660	122,737	0.72
2018[A]	512,870	158,636	0.89

* Trust unit
[A] Reported in accordance with IFRS

A.131 Arway Corporation

Symbol - ARWY **Exchange** - CSE **CUSIP** - 04336A
Head Office - 501-121 Richmond St W, Toronto, ON, M5K 2K1
Telephone - (631) 655-6733
Website - www.arway.ai
Email - evan@nextechar.com
Investor Relations - Evan Gappelberg (631) 655-6733
Auditors - Saturna Group Chartered Accountants LLP C.A., Vancouver, B.C.
Transfer Agents - Computershare Trust Company of Canada Inc., Vancouver, B.C.

Profile - (Ont. 2022) Developing the ARway mobile application, a no-code spatial computing platform, with an augmented reality indoor wayfinding solution for large, multi-purpose venues activated with visual marker tracking.

Users can access a venue map to navigate to any Point of Interest (POI) with step-by-step directions and interact with augmented reality experiences and content. ARway only requires end-users to scan a QR code with their smartphone to activate.

The company was incorporated on July 15, 2022, as a wholly owned subsidiary of **NexTech AR Solutions Corp.** to facilitate the transfer of NexTech's ARway mobile application, an augmented reality spatial computing platform, and associated assets to the company. The transfer was completed in October 2022 and NexTech spun out the company, with NexTech receiving 15,599,900 common shares of the company and NexTech shareholders receiving 4,000,000 common shares, which were distributed on a pro rata basis. Immediately following completion of the spin-out, NexTech transferred 3,000,000 of the common shares to certain service providers; as a result, NexTech held 13,000,000 common shares of the company (inclusive of 100 shares previously held), representing a 48.82% interest.

Common listed on CSE, Oct. 26, 2022.

Predecessor Detail - Name changed from 10000259749 Ontario Inc., Aug. 3, 2022.

Directors - Evan Gappelberg, CEO, Fla.; Belinda Tyldesley, corp. sec., B.C.; Jeff Dawley, Ont.; Anthony Pizzonia, Toronto, Ont.

Other Exec. Officers - Andrew Chan, CFO

Capital Stock

	Authorized (shs.)	Outstanding (shs.)[1]
Common	unlimited	26,629,554

[1] At Oct. 26, 2022

Major Shareholder - NexTech AR Solutions Corp. held 48.82% interest and Evan Gappelberg held 10.86% interest at Oct. 26, 2022.

Price Range - ARWY/CSE

Year	Volume	High	Low	Close
2022	638,268	$2.95	$0.67	$1.51

Recent Close: $0.60

Capital Stock Changes - In October 2022, 19,999,900 common shares were issued pursuant to the transfer of the ARway mobile application and associated assets from NexTech AR Solutions Corp. to the company and 6,629,554 units (1 common share & 1 warrant) were issued without further consideration on exchange of subscription receipts sold previously by private placement at 25¢ each, with warrants exercisable at 50¢ per share for three years.

Wholly Owned Subsidiaries

1373221 B.C. Ltd., B.C.

Financial Statistics

Periods ended:	12m July 31/22[A1]		12m July 31/21[A1]
	$000s	%Chg	$000s
Operating revenue	**6**	**-33**	**9**
Salaries & benefits	551		34
Research & devel. expense	nil		188
General & admin expense	15		31
Operating expense	**566**	**+124**	**253**
Operating income	**(560)**	**n.a.**	**(244)**
Deprec., depl. & amort.	nil		14
Pre-tax income	**(560)**	**n.a.**	**(258)**
Net income	**(560)**	**n.a.**	**(258)**
Cash & equivalent	nil		4
Current assets	nil		4
Total assets	**nil**	**n.a.**	**4**
Accts. pay. & accr. liabs.	nil		5
Current liabilities	nil		5
Long-term debt, gross	nil		87
Long-term debt, net	nil		87
Shareholders' equity	nil		(88)
Cash from oper. activs.	**(565)**	**n.a.**	**(243)**
Cash from fin. activs.	558		121
Net cash position	**nil**	**n.a.**	**4**
	$		$
Earnings per share*	n.a.		n.a.
	shs		shs
No. of shs. o/s	n.a.		n.a.
	%		%
Net profit margin	n.m.		n.m.
Return on equity	n.m.		n.m.
Return on assets	n.m.		(355.86)

[A] Reported in accordance with IFRS
[1] Results were prepared on a carve-out basis reflecting the ARway business transferred from NexTech AR Solutions Corp.

Historical Summary
(as originally stated)

Fiscal Year	Oper. Rev.	Net Inc. Bef. Disc.	EPS*
	$000s	$000s	$
2022[A1]	6	(560)	n.a.
2021[A1]	9	(258)	n.a.
2020[A1]	26	(65)	n.a.

* Common
[A] Reported in accordance with IFRS
[1] Results were prepared on a carve-out basis reflecting the ARway business transferred from NexTech AR Solutions Corp.

A.132 Ascend Wellness Holdings, Inc.

Symbol - AAWH.U **Exchange** - CSE **CUSIP** - 04351N
Head Office - 1411 Broadway, 16th Flr, New York, NY, United States, 10018 **Telephone** - (646) 661-7600 **Fax** - (781) 703-7777
Website - awholdings.com
Email - ir@awholdings.com
Investor Relations - Rebecca Conti Koar (646) 661-7600
Auditors - Macias Gini & O'Connell LLP C.P.A., San Francisco, Calif.
Transfer Agents - Odyssey Trust Company, Calgary, Alta.
Employees - 1,800 at Aug. 10, 2022
Profile - (Del. 2018) Owns, manages and operates cannabis cultivation facilities and dispensaries in Illinois, Massachusetts, Michigan, New Jersey, Ohio and Pennsylvania.

At August 2022, the company had five cultivation and manufacturing facilities with 213,000 sq. ft. of operational canopy and total capacity of 107,000 lbs. per year; and 22 open and operating retail locations under the Ascend banner. Facilities include a 113,000-sq.-ft. indoor and greenhouse facility in Barry, Ill.; a 54,000-sq.-ft. indoor facility in Athol, Mass.; a 28,000-sq.-ft. indoor facility in Lansing, Mich.; a 16,000-sq.-ft. indoor facility in Franklin, N.J.; and a 2,000-sq.-ft. indoor facility in Monroe, Ohio. Products are produced and sold under the in-house brands Simply Herb, Ozone and Ozone Reserve as well as under partner brands, including Lowell Smokes, Flower by Edie Parker and 1906.

In August 2022, the company agreed to acquire two non-operating dispensaries in Illinois, under two separate agreements, for US$5,500,000 and US$5,600,000 each.

On Aug. 12, 2022, the company signed an option to acquire **Ohio Patient Access LLC**, owner of three provisionally licensed dispensaries under development in Cincinnati, Piqua and Sandusky, Ohio. Total consideration for the acquisition was US$22,300,000.

In June 2022, the company sold and leased back two of its properties in Pennsylvania for US$3,825,000.

On Apr. 19, 2022, the company acquired the remaining 99% interest in **Story of PA CR, LLC** for US$53,127,000, consisting of US$10,170,000 cash and issuance of 12,900,000 class A common shares. Story intends to open a 100,000-sq.-ft. cultivation and processing facility and up to six dispensaries in Pennsylvania.

Recent Merger and Acquisition Activity

Status: terminated **Revised:** Aug. 15, 2022
UPDATE: The transaction was terminated. PREVIOUS: Ascend Wellness Holdings, Inc. (AWH) agreed to invest US$73,000,000 in MedMen NY, Inc. (MMNY), which operates a cultivation and manufacturing facility in Utica, N.Y., and has four operational medical cannabis dispensaries in the state. MMNY is owned by MedMen Enterprises Inc. Under terms of the agreement, MMNY would assume US$73,000,000 of MedMen's secured debt, AWH would invest US$35,000,000 in cash in MMNY and a subsidiary of AWH would issue a senior secured promissory note in favour of MMNY's senior secured lender in the principal amount of US$28,000,000. Following its investment, AWH would hold a controlling interest in MMNY equal to approximately 86.7% of the equity in MMNY. Jan. 3, 2022 - MedMen announced the termination of the agreement. Jan. 13, 2022 - AWH filed a lawsuit with the Supreme Court of the State of New York, New York County - Commercial Division, claiming the agreement was improperly terminated and seeking specific performance of agreement. May 11, 2022 - AWH agreed to purchase 100% interest in MedMen's New York state operations for US$88,000,000, consisting of US$15,000,000 cash and assumption of US$73,000,000 of debt. The agreement resolves the litigation between MedMen and AWH concerning the transaction.

Predecessor Detail - Name changed from Ascend Wellness Holdings, LLC, Apr. 22, 2021.

Directors - Abner Kurtin, co-founder & exec. chr., Miami Beach, Fla.; Francis (Frank) Perullo, co-founder, Lexington, Mass.; John Hartmann, CEO, Ill.; Sam Brill†, N.Y.; Joseph (Joe) Hinrichs; Emily Paxhia, San Francisco, Calif.; Scott Swid, Sag Harbor, N.Y.

Other Exec. Officers - David Gacom, COO; Daniel (Dan) Neville, CFO; Robin Debiase, chief people officer; Christopher (Chris) Melillo, chief revenue officer; Brian Miesieski, chief brand officer; Rebecca Conti Koar, sr. v-p, IR; Danielle Drummond, v-p, social equity; Douglas (Doug) Fischer, gen. counsel
† Lead director

Capital Stock

	Authorized (shs.)	Outstanding (shs.)[1]	Par
Preferred	10,000,000	nil	US$0.001
Class A Common	750,000,000	188,163,575	US$0.001
Class B Common	100,000	65,000	US$0.001

[1] At Aug. 10, 2022

Class A Common - One vote per share.
Class B Common - All controlled by Abner Kurtin and Frank Perullo. Convertible into class A common shares on a 1-for-1 basis. Automatically convert into class A common shares under certain conditions. 1,000 votes per share.

Major Shareholder - Abner Kurtin held 39.6% interest at Mar. 15, 2022.

Price Range - AAWH.U/CSE

Year	Volume	High	Low	Close
2022	11,506,141	US$6.40	US$1.00	US$1.15
2021	3,723,127	US$11.71	US$5.15	US$6.61

Recent Close: US$0.49

Capital Stock Changes - In April 2022, 12,900,000 class A common shares were issued pursuant to the acquisition of the remaining 99% interest in Story of PA CR, LLC.

Wholly Owned Subsidiaries

AGP Investments, LLC, United States.
AWH Management Group LLC, Ill.
AWH New York, LLC, N.Y.
AWH NJ Holdco, LLC, N.J.
- 100% int. in **Ascend New Jersey, LLC**, N.J.
  - 100% int. in **AW Franklin LLC**, N.J.
  - 100% int. in **NJ Management Group LLC**, N.J.

AWH Pennsylvania, LLC, Pa.
- 100% int. in **Story of PA CR, LLC**, Pa.

AWHM, LLC, Mich.
Ascend Athol RE LLC, Mass.
Ascend Friend Street RE LLC, Mass.
Ascend GI Borrower, LLC, N.J.
Ascend Illinois II, LLC, Ill.
- 100% int. in **AWH Fairview, LLC**, Ill.
- 100% int. in **AWH Springfield Opco, LLC**, Ill.

Ascend Illinois Holdings, LLC, Ill.
- 100% int. in **Chicago Alternative Health Center Holdings, LLC**, Ill.
- 100% int. in **Chicago Alternative Health Center, LLC**, Ill.
- 100% int. in **Moca, LLC**, Ill.

Ascend Illnois, LLC, Ill.
- 100% int. in **AWH Fairview Opco, LLC**, Ill.
- 100% int. in **Healthcentral, LLC**, Ill.
- 100% int. in **Revolution Cannabis-Barry, LLC**, Ill.
- 100% int. in **Springfield Partners II, LLC**, Ill.

Ascend Mass Holdco, LLC, Mass.
Ascend Mass, Inc., Mass.
- 100% int. in **Ascend Mass, LLC**, Mass.

Ascend Ohio, LLC, Ohio
- 100% int. in **BCCO, LLC**, Ohio
- 100% int. in **Hemma Operations, LLC**, Ohio
  - 100% int. in **Hemma, LLC**, Ohio
- 100% int. in **Marichron Pharma, LLC**, Ohio
- 100% int. in **Marichron Properties, LLC**, Ohio
- 100% int. in **Ohio Cannabis Clinic, LLC**, Ohio
- 100% int. in **Ohio Management Group LLC**, Ohio

Ascend Virginia, LLC, Va.
Blue Jay Botanicals Holdings, LLC, Mass.
Blue Jay RE, LLC, Mass.
Massgrow, Inc., Mass.
- 100% int. in **Mass Management Group LLC**, Mass.
- 100% int. in **Massgrow, LLC**, Mass.

Met Real Estate, LLC, Mass.
Southcoast Apothecary, LLC, Mass.

Subsidiaries

99.9% int. in **FPAW Michigan 2, Inc.**, Mich.
- 100% int. in **FPAW Michigan, LLC**, Mich.
  - 100% int. in **MSP Management Group LLC**, Mich.

Financial Statistics

Periods ended:	12m Dec. 31/21[A]		12m Dec. 31/20[oA]
	US$000s	%Chg	US$000s
Operating revenue	**332,381**	**+131**	**143,732**
Cost of goods sold	186,797		79,122
Salaries & benefits	55,773		15,986
General & admin expense	50,251		28,881
Operating expense	**292,821**	**+136**	**123,989**
Operating income	**39,560**	**+100**	**19,743**
Deprec., depl. & amort.	19,648		11,610
Finance costs, gross	63,989		12,993
Pre-tax income	**(80,937)**	**n.a.**	**(5,139)**
Income taxes	41,720		18,702
Net income	**(122,657)**	**n.a.**	**(23,841)**
Net inc. for equity hldrs	**(122,657)**	**n.a.**	**(25,439)**
Net inc. for non-cont. int.	**nil**	**n.a.**	**1,598**
Cash & equivalent	155,481		56,547
Inventories	65,588		28,997
Accounts receivable	7,612		6,227
Current assets	258,012		134,178
Fixed assets, net	239,656		120,540
Right-of-use assets	103,958		84,642
Intangibles, net	102,238		73,259
Total assets	**723,436**	**+69**	**427,748**
Accts. pay. & accr. liabs.	45,454		31,224
Current liabilities	117,395		115,285
Long-term debt, gross	258,786		211,607
Long-term debt, net	230,846		152,277
Long-term lease liabilities	197,295		156,400
Shareholders' equity	176,477		3,786
Cash from oper. activs.	**(41,738)**	**n.a.**	**(6,004)**
Cash from fin. activs.	252,355		82,168
Cash from invest. activs.	(113,233)		(30,872)
Net cash position	**155,481**	**+168**	**58,097**
Capital expenditures	(88,428)		(26,419)
Capital disposals	930		26,750
	US$		US$
Earnings per share*	(0.82)		(0.27)
Cash flow per share*	(0.28)		n.a.
	shs		shs
No. of shs. o/s*	171,586,000		n.a.
Avg. no. of shs. o/s*	149,434,000		n.a.
	%		%
Net profit margin	(36.90)		(16.59)
Return on equity	(136.09)		(135.39)
Return on assets	(4.46)		11.68
No. of employees (FTEs)	1,500		900

* Cl.A Common
[o] Restated
[A] Reported in accordance with U.S. GAAP

Latest Results

Periods ended:	6m June 30/22[A]		6m June 30/21[A]
	US$000s	%Chg	US$000s
Operating revenue	182,589	+22	149,504
Net income	(48,987)	n.a.	(93,120)
	US$		US$
Earnings per share*	(0.27)		(0.73)

* Cl.A Common
[A] Reported in accordance with U.S. GAAP

Historical Summary
(as originally stated)

Fiscal Year	Oper. Rev.	Net Inc. Bef. Disc.	EPS*
	US$000s	US$000s	US$
2021[A]	332,381	(122,657)	(0.82)
2020[A]	143,732	(23,841)	(0.27)
2019[A]	12,032	(33,242)	(0.37)

* Cl.A Common
[A] Reported in accordance with U.S. GAAP

A.133 Asia Green Biotechnology Corp.

Symbol - ASIA **Exchange** - CSE **CUSIP** - 04522C
Head Office - 1150-707 7 Ave SW, Calgary, AB, T2P 3H6 **Telephone** - (403) 612-5655 **Fax** - (403) 264-5455
Website - www.asiagreenbiotechnology.com
Investor Relations - David E. T. Pinkman (403) 863-6034
Auditors - Paul J. Rozek Professional Corporation C.A., Calgary, Alta.
Lawyers - Heighington Law Firm, Calgary, Alta.
Transfer Agents - TSX Trust Company, Calgary, Alta.
Profile - (Alta. 2017) Researches and develops organic hybridization technology and certain products derived from that technology through exclusive rights for use in the hemp industry in Asia.

The company has secured exclusive rights to use the proprietary organic hybridization technology developed by **InPlanta Biotechnology Inc.** for planting, growth and harvesting of new and valuable hemp strains and related crops in commercial quantities which is intended to be applied to hemp industry in Asia with an initial focus in Cambodia, Thailand and South Korea, with future activities to be directed at Japan,

People's Republic of China, India, Malaysia and Singapore. Hybridization is a specialized breeding process which allows isolation of plants with unique traits to be used for cross-pollination with other strains, potentially creating a new variety with a unique and desirable trait combination. Also holds a licence to deploy **Swysh Inc.**'s proprietary technology for creation of topical treatments for a variety of external and internal conditions and ailments including various anti-viral and preventative health-care applications; and exclusive licence to clinically develop and commercialize **Pathway Rx Inc.**'s cannabis sativa varieties for prevention and treatment of COVID-19 and other infectious diseases. The company plans to commercialize the technology from Swysh and Pathway in the greater region of Asia.

Predecessor Detail - Name changed from Asia Cannabis Corp., Apr. 16, 2020.

Directors - David E. T. Pinkman, interim pres. & interim CEO, Calgary, Alta.; Vincent E. (Vince) Ghazar, CFO, Calgary, Alta.; Igor Kovalchuk, Lethbridge, Alta.; Alisdair Leeson

Capital Stock

	Authorized (shs.)	Outstanding (shs.)[1]
Preferred	unlimited	nil
Common	unlimited	36,247,100

[1] At May 30, 2023

Major Shareholder - Johannes J. (Joe) Kingma held 38.14% interest and Igor Kovalchuk held 12.28% interest at Sept. 15, 2021.

Price Range - ASIA/CSE

Year	Volume	High	Low	Close
2022	780,525	$0.09	$0.01	$0.02
2021	1,775,823	$0.26	$0.03	$0.04
2020	4,900,166	$0.30	$0.04	$0.10
2019	5,387,768	$0.79	$0.04	$0.05

Recent Close: $0.01

Financial Statistics

Periods ended:	12m Dec. 31/21[A]		12m Dec. 31/20[A]
	$000s	%Chg	$000s
Research & devel. expense	159		116
General & admin expense	330		437
Stock-based compensation	35		nil
Operating expense	**523**	**-5**	**553**
Operating income	**(523)**	**n.a.**	**(553)**
Finance costs, gross	1		nil
Pre-tax income	**(525)**	**n.a.**	**(553)**
Net income	**(525)**	**n.a.**	**(553)**
Cash & equivalent	67		381
Current assets	116		441
Total assets	**116**	**-74**	**441**
Accts. pay. & accr. liabs	43		28
Current liabilities	43		28
Long-term debt, gross	150		nil
Long-term debt, net	150		nil
Shareholders' equity	(77)		413
Cash from oper. activs	**(464)**	**n.a.**	**(641)**
Cash from fin. activs	150		nil
Net cash position	**67**	**-82**	**381**
	$		$
Earnings per share*	(0.02)		(0.02)
Cash flow per share*	(0.01)		(0.02)
	shs		shs
No. of shs. o/s*	36,247,100		36,247,100
Avg. no. of shs. o/s*	32,608,992		28,116,667
	%		%
Net profit margin	n.a.		n.a.
Return on equity	n.m.		(80.20)
Return on assets	(188.15)		(73.93)

* Common

[A] Reported in accordance with IFRS

Latest Results

Periods ended:	9m Sept. 30/22[A]		9m Sept. 30/21[A]
	$000s	%Chg	$000s
Net income	(132)	n.a.	(386)
	$		$
Earnings per share*	(0.00)		(0.01)

* Common

[A] Reported in accordance with IFRS

Historical Summary
(as originally stated)

Fiscal Year	Oper. Rev. $000s	Net Inc. Bef. Disc. $000s	EPS* $
2021[A]	nil	(525)	(0.02)
2020[A]	nil	(553)	(0.02)
2019[A]	nil	(767)	(0.03)
2018[A]	nil	(922)	(0.06)
2018[A1,2]	nil	(725)	(0.03)

* Common

[A] Reported in accordance with IFRS

[1] 32 weeks ended July 31, 2018.

[2] As shown in the prospectus dated Oct. 29, 2018.

A.134 Asian Television Network International Limited

Symbol - SAT **Exchange** - TSX-VEN **CUSIP** - 044919

Head Office - 330 Cochrane Dr, Markham, ON, L3R 8E4 **Telephone** - (905) 948-8199 **Fax** - (905) 948-8108

Website - www.asiantelevision.com

Email - saurab@asiantelevision.com

Investor Relations - Saurab Mehta (905) 948-8199

Auditors - AGT Partners LLP C.A., Woodbridge, Ont.

Transfer Agents - Computershare Trust Company of Canada Inc., Toronto, Ont.

Profile - (Ont. 1993) Owns and operates specialty television channels primarily aimed at the South Asian community in Canada and the U.S.

The company's 50 specialty digital television channels include the flagship ATN-HD general interest service, several Bollywood movie channels with several hundred movies a month, and a variety of channels that include sports, news, music, lifestyle, spiritual and several regional language channels. The company also broadcasts world class Cricket through ATN Cricket Plus & CBN, airs a 24-hour South Asian channel and operates a South Asian radio service on Satellite Radio across Canada and the U.S. The broadcast centre is located in Markham, Ont.

Directors - Dr. Shan Chandrasekar, chr., pres. & CEO, Gormley, Ont.; Jaya Chandrasekar, v-p, programming, Gormley, Ont.; Prakash Naidoo, v-p, sales, corp. sec. & gen. mgr., Aurora, Ont.; John E. (Ted) Boyle, Mississauga, Ont.; Bruce G. Buckley, Toronto, Ont.

Other Exec. Officers - Saurab Mehta, CFO

Capital Stock

	Authorized (shs.)	Outstanding (shs.)[1]
Preference	unlimited	
Class A		nil
Class B		nil
Common	unlimited	24,402,914

[1] At Sept. 30, 2022

Major Shareholder - Dr. Shan Chandrasekar held 72.4% interest at May 25, 2022.

Price Range - SAT/TSX-VEN

Year	Volume	High	Low	Close
2022	532,653	$0.30	$0.12	$0.25
2021	418,004	$0.55	$0.12	$0.30
2020	636,818	$0.15	$0.08	$0.13
2019	1,525,175	$0.15	$0.09	$0.13
2018	2,838,749	$0.54	$0.13	$0.14

Recent Close: $0.14

Wholly Owned Subsidiaries

Asian Television Network Inc.
Commonwealth Broadcasting Limited
JCTV Productions Limited
South Asian Television Canada Limited
South Asian Television Network LTD.

Financial Statistics

Periods ended:	12m Dec. 31/21[A]		12m Dec. 31/20[A]
	$000s	%Chg	$000s
Operating revenue	**9,487**	**-5**	**10,037**
Salaries & benefits	1,584		1,421
General & admin expense	7,027		7,058
Operating expense	**8,611**	**+2**	**8,479**
Operating income	**877**	**-44**	**1,558**
Deprec., depl. & amort.	1,159		1,583
Finance income	17		38
Finance costs, gross	56		66
Pre-tax income	**(324)**	**n.a.**	**(56)**
Income taxes	(157)		478
Net income	**(167)**	**n.a.**	**(535)**
Cash & equivalent	55		69
Accounts receivable	1,947		2,221
Current assets	2,637		2,839
Long-term investments	2,000		2,200
Fixed assets, net	732		1,153
Right-of-use assets	2,820		510
Intangibles, net	5		96
Total assets	**8,289**	**+21**	**6,842**
Bank indebtedness	200		60
Accts. pay. & accr. liabs	2,698		3,283
Current liabilities	3,418		3,853
Long-term lease liabilities	2,420		214
Shareholders' equity	2,451		2,618
Cash from oper. activs	**439**	**+86**	**236**
Cash from fin. activs	(370)		(483)
Cash from invest. activs	(83)		212
Net cash position	**55**	**-20**	**69**
Capital expenditures	(18)		(6)
	$		$
Earnings per share*	(0.01)		(0.02)
Cash flow per share*	0.02		0.01
	shs		shs
No. of shs. o/s*	24,402,914		24,402,914
Avg. no. of shs. o/s*	24,402,914		24,402,914
	%		%
Net profit margin	(1.76)		(5.33)
Return on equity	(6.59)		(18.54)
Return on assets	(1.83)		1.24

* Common

[A] Reported in accordance with IFRS

Latest Results

Periods ended:	3m Mar. 31/22[A]		3m Mar. 31/21[A]
	$000s	%Chg	$000s
Operating revenue	2,037	-12	2,328
Net income	(292)	n.a.	(337)
	$		$
Earnings per share*	(0.01)		(0.01)

* Common

[A] Reported in accordance with IFRS

Historical Summary
(as originally stated)

Fiscal Year	Oper. Rev. $000s	Net Inc. Bef. Disc. $000s	EPS* $
2021[A]	9,487	(167)	(0.01)
2020[A]	10,037	(535)	(0.02)
2019[A]	11,920	(2,329)	(0.10)
2018[A]	14,766	(1,502)	(0.06)
2017[A]	20,042	(164)	(0.01)

* Common

[A] Reported in accordance with IFRS

A.135 Aster Acquisition Corp.

Symbol - ATR.P **Exchange** - TSX-VEN **CUSIP** - 045938

Head Office - 478-6647 Fraser St, Vancouver, BC, V5X 0K3 **Telephone** - (604) 909-4880

Email - aster-ir@outlook.com

Investor Relations - Vincent Wong (604) 909-4880

Auditors - Baker Tilly HMA LLP C.A., Winnipeg, Man.

Transfer Agents - Endeavor Trust Corporation, Vancouver, B.C.

Profile - (B.C. 2021) Capital Pool Company.

Directors - Vincent Wong, chr., CEO & corp. sec., Vancouver, B.C.; Robert (Rob) Goehring, Coquitlam, B.C.; Frank P. Harley, Vancouver, B.C.; Warren Jung, Vancouver, B.C.; Ryan Maarschalk, Kelowna, B.C.; Dr. Jeffrey R. (Jeff) Wilson, Vancouver, B.C.

Other Exec. Officers - Xiao-Dong Song, CFO

Capital Stock

	Authorized (shs.)	Outstanding (shs.)[1]
Common	unlimited	6,700,000

[1] At June 22, 2022

Major Shareholder - Vincent Wong held 17.91% interest and Warren Jung held 11.94% interest at June 22, 2022.

Price Range - ATR.P/TSX-VEN

Year	Volume	High	Low	Close
2022............	53,000	$0.15	$0.10	$0.10

Recent Close: $0.08

Capital Stock Changes - On June 22, 2022, an initial public offering of 5,000,000 common shares was completed at 10¢ per share.

A.136 Astron Connect Inc.

Symbol - AST **Exchange** - TSX-VEN **CUSIP** - 04640L
Head Office - 500-666 Burrard St, Vancouver, BC, V6C 3P6 **Telephone** - (604) 620-2092
Website - www.astronconnect.com
Email - irisd@astronconnect.com
Investor Relations - Hong Duan (778) 373-8586
Auditors - Smythe LLP C.A., Vancouver, B.C.
Transfer Agents - TSX Trust Company, Vancouver, B.C.

Profile - (B.C. 2017) Operates Sachiel Connect, an online information service platform that helps Canadian-based food and beverage producers export their products primarily to the People's Republic of China (PRC). Also exports bottled spring water from British Columbia to the PRC and other emerging markets.

Sachiel Connect is an online information services platform for Canadian food and beverage producers and agricultural sector to promote and market their products to international buyers in the PRC and emerging markets, as well as in Canada. The company places each supplier's product offerings onto the portal and passes on the appropriate marketing information to its strategic partnerships with order aggregators that assist the company in adding buyers/members to the platform. Also handles logictics, distribution, marketing, sales and legal documentation in importing Canadian food and beverages, skin care, supplements and agricultural products to the PRC.

Also exports and supplies Canadian bottled spring water under the Sachiel Water and Manna Water brands primarily in the PRC.

Predecessor Detail - Name changed from Exalt Capital Corp., Aug. 23, 2018, pursuant to Qualifying Transaction reverse takeover acquisition of Sachiel Connect Inc.

Directors - S. Randall (Randy) Smallbone, chr. & interim CEO, Burlington, Ont.; Hong (Iris) Duan, interim CFO, West Vancouver, B.C.; Wei Kang, v-p, fin., Vancouver, B.C.; Herrick Lau, Vancouver, B.C.

Other Exec. Officers - Jack Austin, chief consultant

Capital Stock

	Authorized (shs.)	Outstanding (shs.)[1]
Common	unlimited	16,937,901

[1] At May 26, 2023

Major Shareholder - Bei Nie held 19.36% interest at July 29, 2022.

Price Range - AST/TSX-VEN

Year	Volume	High	Low	Close
2022............	990,911	$0.17	$0.05	$0.11
2021............	403,781	$1.36	$0.09	$0.17
2020............	124,939	$0.40	$0.20	$0.24
2019............	122,179	$1.76	$0.40	$0.48
2018............	43,195	$2.48	$1.52	$2.00

Consolidation: 1-for-8 cons. in June 2021
Recent Close: $0.03

Capital Stock Changes - In April 2022, private placement of 5,000,000 units (1 common share & 1 warrant) at 10¢ per unit was completed. Also during fiscal 2022, 1,500,000 common shares were issued for loan.

Wholly Owned Subsidiaries

Manna Resources Inc., B.C.
Sachiel Holdings Ltd., B.C.
Sachiel Water Inc., B.C.

Financial Statistics

Periods ended:	12m Sept. 30/22[A]		12m Sept. 30/21[A]
	$000s	%Chg	$000s
Operating revenue	**176**	**+319**	**42**
Cost of sales	129		71
Salaries & benefits	184		170
General & admin expense	284		348
Stock-based compensation	nil		14
Operating expense	**597**	**-1**	**603**
Operating income	**(421)**	**n.a.**	**(561)**
Deprec., depl. & amort.	51		220
Write-downs/write-offs	(486)		(333)
Pre-tax income	**(937)**	**n.a.**	**(1,134)**
Net income	**(937)**	**n.a.**	**(1,134)**
Cash & equivalent	505		952
Inventories	66		66
Accounts receivable	17		11
Current assets	660		1,134
Fixed assets, net	nil		7
Right-of-use assets	nil		44
Intangibles, net	10		10
Total assets	**670**	**-44**	**1,195**
Accts. pay. & accr. liabs	143		157
Current liabilities	180		418
Shareholders' equity	430		717
Cash from oper. activs	**(569)**	**n.a.**	**(482)**
Cash from fin. activs	451		(163)
Cash from invest. activs	(330)		nil
Net cash position	**505**	**-47**	**952**
	$		$
Earnings per share*	(0.07)		(0.11)
Cash flow per share*	(0.04)		(0.05)
	shs		shs
No. of shs. o/s*	16,937,901		10,437,901
Avg. no. of shs. o/s*	13,111,874		10,437,901
	%		%
Net profit margin	(532.39)		n.m.
Return on equity	(163.38)		(88.80)
Return on assets	(100.48)		(60.85)

* Common
[A] Reported in accordance with IFRS

Latest Results

Periods ended:	6m Mar. 31/23[A]		6m Mar. 31/22[A]
	$000s	%Chg	$000s
Operating revenue	nil	n.a.	32
Net income	(212)	n.a.	(252)
	$		$
Earnings per share*	(0.01)		(0.02)

* Common
[A] Reported in accordance with IFRS

Historical Summary
(as originally stated)

Fiscal Year	Oper. Rev. $000s	Net Inc. Bef. Disc. $000s	EPS* $
2022[A]	176	(937)	(0.07)
2021[A]	42	(1,134)	(0.11)
2020[A]	401	(1,299)	(0.16)
2019[A]	1,276	(1,756)	(0.24)
2018[A]	849	(2,707)	(0.64)

* Common
[A] Reported in accordance with IFRS
Note: Adjusted throughout for 1-for-8 cons. in June 2021

A.137 Athabasca Minerals Inc.

Symbol - AMI **Exchange** - TSX-VEN **CUSIP** - 046826
Head Office - Canada Place, 620-407 2 St SW, Calgary, AB, T2P 2Y3
Telephone - (587) 392-5862 **Fax** - (780) 430-9865
Website - www.athabascaminerals.com
Email - cheryl.grue@athabascaminerals.com
Investor Relations - Cheryl Grue (403) 200-5093
Auditors - Grant Thornton LLP C.A., Edmonton, Alta.
Transfer Agents - TSX Trust Company, Calgary, Alta.
Employees - 32 at Apr. 28, 2022

Profile - (Alta. 2006 amalg.) Manages, acquires, develops and explores for aggregates and industrial minerals in Alberta and British Columbia. Also operates RockChain™ digital platform.

The company operates through three segments: AMI Aggregates; AMI Silica; and AMI RockChain.

AMI Aggregates - This segment includes the production and sale of aggregates from the Coffey Lake gravel pit, 335 hectares, 90 km north of Fort McMurray, Alta., managed by the company on behalf of Alberta Ministry of Environment and Parks until 2034. Operations on Coffey Lake commenced in March 2020. The company also operates the True North Staging hub for crushing and stockpiling of aggregates from Coffey Lake. Also holds Firebag sand deposit, 32 hectares, which commenced production in February 2022; 65-hectare House River pit, 11 km east of Highway 63 on the House River, which commenced operation in fiscal 2012; 32-hectare Kearl pit, which commenced production in June 2021; and 32-hectare Hargwen pit, 17 km east of Hinton, which commenced production in June 2022.

Also in Alberta, holds project sunder development including the 81-hectare Logan pit, 160 km south of Fort McMurray; the 32-hectare Pelican Hill pit, 70 km southeast of Wabasca; the 30-hectare Emerson pit, 27 km southeast of Hinton; and Richardson granite-dolomite project, 3,904 hectares, 130 km north of Fort McMurray, with inferred resource of 683,140,000 tonnes of crush rock aggregate (dolomite and granite) at October 2019. The company also has stockpile and distribution hubs in Conklin, Sunday Creek and KM248 (near Anzac, Alta.).

AMI Silica - This segment includes the mineral properties in Alberta including Prosvita (formerly Duvernay) frac sand project, 356 hectares, consisting of White Rabbit property, with measured resource of 18,800,000 tonnes fine-to-coarse grain sands on White Rabbit at May 2021; and Whitetail property, 336 hectares, 45 km northeast of Athabasca, with measured and indicated resource of 11,900,000 tonnes fine-to-coarse grain sands at June 2021. In British Columbia, holds Montney In-Basin frac sand project, 150,000 hectares, near Dawson Creek and Fort St John. Also holds 50% interest in **AMI Silica LLC**, which holds an operational sand mine and processing plant capable of up to 2,000,000 tons production per annum in Wisconsin.

AMI RockChain - This segment includes RockChain™, a digital platform with optimized supply-transport solutions for more than $763,000,000 in construction materials bids with a growing network of suppliers, transportation and equipment companies across western Canada, and an algorithm module that determines the best supply transport combination to help improve utilization for aggregate producers and trucking companies, with price and service benefits to customers. In addition, wholly owned **TerraShift Engineering Ltd.** offers TerraMaps™ software that support resource exploration and development, environmental and regulatory planning, resource management, compliance reporting and reclamation for a growing customer base across western Canada and Ontario.

In March 2022, **AMI Silica LLC**, owned 50/50 by the company and **JMAC Resources Limited**, completed the acquisition of an operational sand mine and facilities in Wisconsin for US$1,000,000 and the assumption of US$6,400,000 of reclamation liabilities. The assets acquired include 1,100 acres of real-estate, a processing plant capable of up to 2,000,000 tons production per annum, fixed storage, two rail transloads, mobile equipment and active supply chain contracts. JMAC is controlled by Jon McCreay, a major shareholder of the company.

Common reinstated on TSX-VEN, June 16, 2023.
Common suspended from TSX-VEN, May 10, 2023.

Predecessor Detail - Formed from Hali Capital Corporation in Alberta, Dec. 31, 2006, on Qualifying Transaction amalgamation with Athabasca Minerals Inc., constituting a reverse takeover by Athabasca; basis 1 com. sh. for 1 Athabasca cl. A com. sh. and 1 com. sh. for 2.5 Hali shs.

Directors - Don Paulencu, chr., Sherwood Park, Alta.; Jon McCreary, Wenatchee, Wash.; Dale G. Nolan, Lacombe, Alta.

Other Exec. Officers - Dana Archibald, CEO, COO & pres., AMI RockChain Inc.; J. David Churchill, CFO; Ryan Lissel, v-p, projects & opers.

Capital Stock

	Authorized (shs.)	Outstanding (shs.)[1]
Preferred	unlimited	nil
Common	unlimited	77,628,388

[1] At May 25, 2022

Major Shareholder - Jon McCreary held 19.7% interest at May 2, 2022.

Price Range - AMI/TSX-VEN

Year	Volume	High	Low	Close
2022............	15,458,306	$0.70	$0.18	$0.21
2021............	16,798,962	$0.40	$0.14	$0.36
2020............	13,038,718	$0.38	$0.08	$0.13
2019............	28,744,520	$0.79	$0.22	$0.27
2018............	13,584,116	$0.35	$0.12	$0.25

Recent Close: $0.09

Wholly Owned Subsidiaries

AMI Aggregates Inc.
AMI Rockchain Inc.
• 100% int. in **TerraShift Engineering Ltd.**, Edmonton, Alta.
AMI Silica Inc.
2132561 Alberta Ltd., Alta.
2140534 Alberta Ltd., Alta.

Investments

50% int. in **AMI Silica LLC**, Wis.
49% int. in **Metis North Sand & Gravel GP Ltd.**

Financial Statistics

Periods ended:	12m Dec. 31/21[A]		12m Dec. 31/20[A]
	$000s	%Chg	$000s
Operating revenue	**11,792**	**+506**	**1,945**
Cost of sales	10,298		1,898
General & admin expense	2,934		2,765
Stock-based compensation	248		337
Operating expense	**13,480**	**+101**	**6,700**
Operating income	**(1,688)**	**n.a.**	**(4,755)**
Deprec., depl. & amort.	389		447
Finance income	13		22
Finance costs, gross	44		87
Investment income	nil		(109)
Write-downs/write-offs	nil		(106)
Pre-tax income	**(2,176)**	**n.a.**	**(3,500)**
Income taxes	11		31
Net income	**(2,187)**	**n.a.**	**(3,531)**
Cash & equivalent	2,517		1,954
Inventories	847		847
Accounts receivable	1,292		491
Current assets	4,783		3,413
Long-term investments	nil		3,524
Fixed assets, net	540		739
Right-of-use assets	87		251
Intangibles, net	36		85
Explor./devel. properties	12,127		6,251
Total assets	**20,937**	**+13**	**18,543**
Accts. pay. & accr. liabs.	1,765		1,004
Current liabilities	2,792		2,495
Long-term debt, gross	1,055		1,427
Long-term debt, net	300		140
Long-term lease liabilities	5		79
Shareholders' equity	15,151		13,185
Cash from oper. activs.	**(1,210)**	**n.a.**	**(2,039)**
Cash from fin. activs.	1,253		2,709
Cash from invest. activs.	521		(711)
Net cash position	**2,517**	**+29**	**1,954**
Capital expenditures	(606)		(1,565)
Capital disposals	50		8
	$		$
Earnings per share*	(0.03)		(0.07)
Cash flow per share*	(0.02)		(0.04)
	shs		shs
No. of shs. o/s*	76,964,088		59,110,153
Avg. no. of shs. o/s*	67,947,084		49,657,351
	%		%
Net profit margin	(18.55)		(181.54)
Return on equity	(15.44)		(25.72)
Return on assets	(10.86)		(18.71)

* Common

[A] Reported in accordance with IFRS

Latest Results

Periods ended:	3m Mar. 31/22[A]		3m Mar. 31/21[A]
	$000s	%Chg	$000s
Operating revenue	6,984	+537	1,097
Net income	22,580	n.a.	(602)
	$		$
Earnings per share*	0.29		(0.01)

* Common

[A] Reported in accordance with IFRS

Historical Summary
(as originally stated)

Fiscal Year	Oper. Rev.	Net Inc. Bef. Disc.	EPS*
	$000s	$000s	$
2021[A]	11,792	(2,187)	(0.03)
2020[A]	1,945	(3,531)	(0.07)
2019[A]	2,597	(2,721)	(0.06)
2018[A]	5,132	(2,510)	(0.07)
2017[A]	7,476	(2,687)	(0.08)

* Common

[A] Reported in accordance with IFRS

A.138 Atlas Engineered Products Ltd.

Symbol - AEP **Exchange** - TSX-VEN **CUSIP** - 049304
Head Office - 2005 Boxwood Rd, Nanaimo, BC, V9S 5X9 **Telephone** - (250) 754-1400 **Toll-free** - (877) 250-2211 **Fax** - (250) 754-1403
Website - www.atlasengineeredproducts.com
Email - mmacrae@atlasep.ca
Investor Relations - Melissa MacRae (250) 739-0908
Auditors - PricewaterhouseCoopers LLP C.A., Vancouver, B.C.
Transfer Agents - Computershare Trust Company of Canada Inc., Vancouver, B.C.

Profile - (B.C. 1984) Designs, manufactures and distributes engineered roof trusses, floor trusses, wall panels and wood products to the residential and commercial builders across Canada.

Products include roof trusses, floor joists, floor trusses, floor panels, wall panels, I-joists, open joists, engineered beams, rim boards, knee wall and patio doors. Also offers services such as design, engineering and permitting services, and project management and site assembly services.

Operations include manufacturing and distribution facilities in British Columbia, Manitoba and Ontario.

Recent Merger and Acquisition Activity

Status: completed **Announced:** Aug. 23, 2023
Atlas Engineered Products Ltd. acquired private New Brunswick-based Léon Chouinard et Fils Co. Ltd. (LCF), which manufactures roof trusses, floor systems and wall panels, and supplies engineered wood products, for $26,000,000 plus $2,884,737 in net closing adjustments for LCF's cash, income taxes receivable and payable, and working capital excluding inventory as at June 30, 2023. The purchase price included the land and buildings on which LCF's facilities were located and had been appraised at $2,792,000. The consideration was satisfied by $26,884,737 cash, financed using a combination of Atlas's existing cash and a term loan and mortgage, and issuance of 1,739,129 Atlas class A common shares at a deemed price of $1.14 per share. During 2022, LCF generated $25,700,000 in revenues.

Status: completed **Revised:** Mar. 1, 2022
UPDATE: The transaction was completed for $5,800,000 cash. Also acquired the land and buildings on which Hi-Tec Industries' facilities located for the appraised value of $3,250,000 cash. PREVIOUS: Atlas Engineered Products Ltd. entered into a letter of intent to acquire a B.C.-based Hi-Tec Industries Ltd., a truss manufacturing company (target), for $5,800,000. Atlas also intends to acquire the land and buildings on which the target's facilities are located for $2,700,000 cash, subject to completion of an independent appraisal.

Predecessor Detail - Name changed from Archer Petroleum Corp., Nov. 9, 2017, pursuant to the reverse takeover acquisition of (old) Atlas Engineered Products Ltd.

Directors - Don Hubbard, chr., Nanaimo, B.C.; Mohammad Hadi Abassi, pres. & CEO, Nanaimo, B.C.; Paul Andreola, Vancouver, B.C.; Greg Smith, Vancouver, B.C.; Kevin Smith, North Vancouver, B.C.

Other Exec. Officers - Gurmit Dhaliwal, COO; Melissa MacRae, CFO

Capital Stock

	Authorized (shs.)	Outstanding (shs.)[1]
Class B Preferred	unlimited	nil
Class A Common	unlimited	57,881,215

[1] At May 25, 2023

Normal Course Issuer Bid - The company plans to make normal course purchases of up to 4,732,015 common shares representing 10% of the public float. The bid commenced on Dec. 1, 2022, and expires on Dec. 1, 2023.

Major Shareholder - Widely held at Sept. 20, 2022.

Price Range - AEP/TSX-VEN

Year	Volume	High	Low	Close
2022	19,674,432	$0.79	$0.42	$0.75
2021	24,313,305	$0.68	$0.26	$0.60
2020	15,742,090	$0.48	$0.19	$0.41
2019	13,016,836	$0.60	$0.29	$0.40
2018	10,572,876	$0.72	$0.34	$0.36

Recent Close: $1.21

Capital Stock Changes - On Aug. 23, 2023, 1,739,129 common shares were issued pursuant to the acquisition of Léon Chouinard et Fils Co. Ltd.

During 2022, class A common shares were issued as follows: 2,102,819 on exercise of warrants and 880,000 on exercise of options; 2,886,286 class A common shares were repurchased under a Normal Course Issuer Bid.

Wholly Owned Subsidiaries

Atlas Building Systems Ltd., Nanaimo, B.C.
Clinton Building Components Ltd., Ont.
Hi-Tec Industries Ltd., B.C.
Léon Chouinard et Fils Co. Ltd., N.B.
Novum Building Components Ltd., Abbotsford, B.C.
Pacer Building Components Inc., Ilderton, Ont.
Satellite Building Components Ltd., Merrickville, Ont.
South Central Building Systems Ltd., Canada.

Financial Statistics

Periods ended:	12m Dec. 31/22[A]		12m Dec. 31/21[A]
	$000s	%Chg	$000s
Operating revenue	**61,900**	**+13**	**54,998**
Cost of sales	29,212		27,906
Salaries & benefits	14,652		12,692
General & admin expense	2,287		1,736
Stock-based compensation	254		91
Operating expense	**46,405**	**+9**	**42,426**
Operating income	**15,495**	**+23**	**12,572**
Deprec., depl. & amort.	2,942		2,639
Finance income	234		32
Finance costs, gross	674		424
Write-downs/write-offs	(23)		(52)
Pre-tax income	**12,008**	**+29**	**9,305**
Income taxes	3,178		2,351
Net income	**8,830**	**+27**	**6,954**
Cash & equivalent	16,119		8,947
Inventories	4,592		3,370
Accounts receivable	5,825		6,731
Current assets	26,898		19,308
Fixed assets, net	11,885		8,468
Intangibles, net	11,302		7,716
Total assets	**50,491**	**+41**	**35,781**
Accts. pay. & accr. liabs.	2,836		3,049
Current liabilities	6,862		6,781
Long-term debt, gross	13,484		6,971
Long-term debt, net	11,665		6,019
Long-term lease liabilities	843		1,430
Shareholders' equity	28,873		19,813
Cash from oper. activs.	**11,296**	**+18**	**9,579**
Cash from fin. activs.	5,463		(1,239)
Cash from invest. activs.	(9,588)		(1,209)
Net cash position	**16,119**	**+80**	**8,947**
Capital expenditures	(3,648)		(1,323)
Capital disposals	nil		85
	$		$
Earnings per share*	0.15		0.12
Cash flow per share*	0.19		0.17
	shs		shs
No. of shs. o/s*	57,847,263		57,750,730
Avg. no. of shs. o/s*	58,702,361		57,728,196
	%		%
Net profit margin	14.26		12.64
Return on equity	36.27		42.48
Return on assets	21.62		23.13

* Cl.A com.

[A] Reported in accordance with IFRS

Latest Results

Periods ended:	3m Mar. 31/23[A]		3m Mar. 31/22[A]
	$000s	%Chg	$000s
Operating revenue	9,629	-23	12,434
Net income	543	-65	1,563
	$		$
Earnings per share*	0.01		0.03

* Cl.A com.

[A] Reported in accordance with IFRS

Historical Summary
(as originally stated)

Fiscal Year	Oper. Rev.	Net Inc. Bef. Disc.	EPS*
	$000s	$000s	$
2022[A]	61,900	8,830	0.15
2021[A]	54,998	6,954	0.12
2020[A]	35,734	229	0.00
2019[A]	34,764	(755)	(0.02)
2018[A1]	13,353	(1,250)	(0.04)

* Cl.A com.

[A] Reported in accordance with IFRS

[1] 7 months ended Dec. 31, 2018.

A.139 Atlas Global Brands Inc.

Symbol - ATL **Exchange** - CSE (S) **CUSIP** - 04933Q
Head Office - Unit 104, 566 Riverview Dr, Chatham, ON, N7M 0N2 **Telephone** - (416) 453-4790 **Toll-free** - (855) 510-4769
Website - atlasglobalbrands.com
Email - bernie@atlasglobalbrands.com
Investor Relations - Bernard Yeung (416) 453-4790
Auditors - BDO Canada LLP C.A., Vancouver, B.C.
Bankers - Bank of Montreal
Lawyers - Cassels Brock & Blackwell LLP, Vancouver, B.C.
Transfer Agents - Computershare Trust Company of Canada Inc., Vancouver, B.C.

Profile - (B.C. 2003) Cultivates, manufactures and distributes cannabis and cannabis products in Canada and Israel.

Wholly owned **Atlas Biotechnologies Inc.** is a licensed Canadian cultivator and processor, with a focus on health and wellness and adult-use products. Both medical and adult-use products are distributed across Canada, with bulk dried flower also distributed through various supply agreements to Germany, Spain and Australia. Produces and sells smokeless tetrahydrocannabinol (THC) and cannabidiol (CBD) products such as transdermal patches, creams, tinctures and chewing gums under the Atlas Thrive brand, and inhalable adult-use focused products such as flower, pre-rolls, vapes, concentrates and seeds under the Natural History brand. Operates a 38,000-sq.-ft. indoor cannabis facility west of Edmonton, Alta., in Lac Ste. Anne cty.

Subsidiary **AgMedica Bioscience Inc.** (99% owned) is a licensed Canadian cultivator and processor, as well as EU-GMP (European Union Good Manufacturing Practices) certified for production of cannabis dried flower and oil, and exports medically formatted cannabis products to medically legalized global markets. Produces and sells medical and adult-use cannabis, cannabis-derived extracts and derivative cannabis products in Canada, and also distributes cannabis flower and extracts internationally to Australia, Israel, Denmark and the U.K. Medical cannabis products are sold under the AgMedica brand and adult-use products under the Vertical and Five Founders brands. Operates a 114,000-sq.-ft. EU-GMP indoor facility in Chatham, Ont.

Wholly owned **Cambrosia Ltd.** develops products derived from cannabis extracts, and imports, distributes and retails medical cannabis throughout Israel.

Subsidiaries **Tlalim Pappo Ltd.**, **Pharmacy Baron Ltd.** and **R.J. Regavim Ventures Ltd.** (all 51% owned) operate cannabis pharmacies in Israel.

In February 2023, the company changed its fiscal year end to March 31 from December 31, effective Feb. 28, 2023.

Common suspended from CSE, Aug. 9, 2023.

Recent Merger and Acquisition Activity

Status: completed **Revised:** Dec. 30, 2022

UPDATE: The transaction was completed. PREVIOUS: Silver Phoenix Resources Inc. (SPR) agreed to the reverse takeover acquisition of Atlas Biotechnologies Inc., AgMedica Bioscience Inc. and Cambrosia Ltd. for issuance of common shares with a deemed value of $189,000,000. Edmonton, Alta.-based Atlas was a licensed producer of cannabis products; Chatham, Ont.-based AgMedica was a vertically integrated licensed producer of cannabis supplying the Canadian and Australian medical cannabis markets; and Israel-based Cambrosia Ltd. was an international holding company, active, through its subsidiaries, across key stages of the cannabis value chain: development of products derived from cannabis extracts, and import, distribution and retailing of medical cannabis. July 14, 2022 - A definitive agreement was entered into. Under the agreement, SPR's wholly owned 2432998 Alberta Ltd. and 14060407 Canada Inc. would amalgamate with Atlas and AgMedica, respectively; and SPR would acquire Cambrosia on a share-for-share basis. Atlas, AgMedica and Cambrosia shareholders would receive 38,550,838, 38,550,870 and 70,519,693 SPR post-consolidated common shares, respectively (following a 1-for-5 share consolidation). Upon completion, SPR would change its name to Atlas Global Brands Inc.

Predecessor Detail - Name changed from Silver Phoenix Resources Inc., Dec. 30, 2022, pursuant to the reverse takeover acquisition of Atlas Biotechnologies Inc., AgMedica Bioscience Inc. and Cambrosia Ltd. and concurrent amalgamation of Atlas Biotechnologies and AgMedica with wholly owned 2432998 Alberta Ltd. and 14060407 Canada Inc., respectively; basis 1 new for 5 old shs.

Directors - Cale Alacer; Dr. Trevor Henry, Ont.; Elan MacDonald, Alta.; Peter Van Mol, Blenheim, Ont.

Other Exec. Officers - Bernard (Bernie) Yeung, CEO; Jason Cervi, CFO; Natalie Douglas, corp. sec.

Capital Stock

	Authorized (shs.)	Outstanding (shs.)[1]
Common	unlimited	151,066,781

[1] At Jan. 13, 2023

Major Shareholder - S.H.R. Group Management (KSN) Ltd. held 18.46% interest and Dr. Tamir Gedo held 18.46% interest at Jan. 13, 2023.

Price Range - ATL/CSE (S)

Year	Volume	High	Low	Close
2022	28,526	$2.00	$1.18	$1.53
2021	74,486	$4.50	$1.15	$1.40
2020	40,592	$6.13	$2.50	$3.00
2019	5,497	$5.00	$3.00	$3.00
2018	3,923	$7.98	$0.73	$3.26

Consolidation: 1-for-5 cons. in Jan. 2023; 1-for-5 cons. in June 2021; 1-for-1.45 cons. in Feb. 2019

Recent Close: $0.15

Capital Stock Changes - On Dec. 30, 2022, common shares were consolidated on a 1-for-5 basis (effective on the Canadian Securities Exchange on Jan 13, 2023) and 38,550,838, 38,550,870 and 70,519,693 post-consolidated common shares were issued pursuant to the reverse takeover acquisition of Atlas Biotechnologies Inc., AgMedica Bioscience Inc. and Cambrosia Ltd., respectively.

Wholly Owned Subsidiaries

Atlas Biotechnologies Inc., Edmonton, Alta.
- 100% int. in **Atlas Growers Denmark A/S**, Denmark.
- 100% int. in **Atlas Growers Ltd.**, Alta.

Cambrosia Ltd., Rishon LeZion, Israel.
- 51% int. in **Pharmacy Baron Ltd.**, Israel.
- 51% int. in **R.J. Regavim Ventures Ltd.**, Israel.
- 51% int. in **Tlalim Papo Ltd.**, Israel.

Subsidiaries

99% int. in **AgMedica Bioscience Inc.**, Chatham, Ont.
- 100% int. in **5047346 Ontario Inc.**, Ont.
- 100% int. in **Tavivat Naturals Inc.**, Canada.
  - 100% int. in **8050678 Canada Inc.**, Canada.
  - 100% int. in **Unique Beverages (USA) Inc.**, United States.
- 80% int. in **Wellworth Health Corp.**, Canada.

Financial Statistics

Periods ended:	12m Dec. 31/21[A1]		12m Dec. 31/20[A]
	$000s	%Chg	$000s
General & admin expense	195		172
Operating expense	**195**	**+13**	**172**
Operating income	**(195)**	**n.a.**	**(172)**
Finance costs, gross	4		15
Pre-tax income	**(199)**	**n.a.**	**(186)**
Net income	**(199)**	**n.a.**	**(186)**
Cash & equivalent	3		1
Accounts receivable	9		15
Current assets	13		16
Total assets	**13**	**-19**	**16**
Bank indebtedness	97		27
Current liabilities	73		209
Shareholders' equity	(157)		(221)
Cash from oper. activs	**(130)**	**n.a.**	**(35)**
Cash from fin. activs	132		27
Net cash position	**3**	**+200**	**1**
	$		$
Earnings per share*	(0.10)		(0.12)
Cash flow per share*	(0.08)		(0.02)
	shs		shs
No. of shs. o/s*	1,682,313		1,542,314
Avg. no. of shs. o/s*	1,671,573		1,542,314
	%		%
Net profit margin	n.a.		n.a.
Return on equity	n.m.		n.m.
Return on assets	n.m.		(777.27)

* Common

[A] Reported in accordance with IFRS

[1] Results for 2021 and prior years pertain to Silver Phoenix Resources Inc.

Historical Summary
(as originally stated)

Fiscal Year	Oper. Rev. $000s	Net Inc. Bef. Disc. $000s	EPS* $
2021[A]	nil	(199)	(0.10)
2020[A]	nil	(186)	(0.12)
2019[A]	nil	(123)	(0.09)
2018[A]	nil	(1,223)	(2.17)
2017[A]	nil	(204)	(0.38)

* Common

[A] Reported in accordance with IFRS

Note: Adjusted throughout for 1-for-5 cons. in Jan. 2023; 1-for-5 cons. in June 2021; 1-for-1.45 cons. in Feb. 2019

A.140 Atlas One Capital Corporation

Symbol - ACAP.P **Exchange** - TSX-VEN **CUSIP** - 04941B

Head Office - 300-20 Holly St, Toronto, ON, M4S 3B1 **Telephone** - (416) 865-0123

Email - drosenkrantz@patica.ca

Investor Relations - David A. Rosenkrantz (416) 865-0123

Auditors - MNP LLP C.A., Toronto, Ont.

Transfer Agents - Odyssey Trust Company, Toronto, Ont.

Profile - (Ont. 2022) Capital Pool Company.

Recent Merger and Acquisition Activity

Status: terminated **Revised:** June 5, 2023

UPDATE: The transaction was terminated. PREVIOUS: Atlas One Capital Corporation entered into a letter of intent for the Qualifying Transaction reverse takeover acquisition of Zodiac Gold Inc., which holds Mount Coffee gold prospect in Liberia. Terms were to be negotiated. A concurrent financing for proceeds of at least $3,000,000 would be completed by Zodiac Gold.

Directors - David A. Rosenkrantz, pres., CEO & CFO, Etobicoke, Ont.; Ilana Prussky, treas. & corp. sec., Toronto, Ont.; Tracy A. Graf, Sylvan Lake, Alta.; Maurice (Maish) Kagan, Toronto, Ont.

Capital Stock

	Authorized (shs.)	Outstanding (shs.)[1]
Common	unlimited	5,320,000

[1] At June 9, 2022

Major Shareholder - Ilana Prussky held 18.8% interest and David A. Rosenkrantz held 18.8% interest at June 9, 2022.

Price Range - ACAP.P/TSX-VEN

Year	Volume	High	Low	Close
2022	53,001	$0.10	$0.08	$0.10

Recent Close: $0.10

Capital Stock Changes - On June 9, 2022, an initial public offering of 2,660,000 common shares was completed at 10¢ per share.

A.141 Atmofizer Technologies Inc.

Symbol - ATMO **Exchange** - CSE **CUSIP** - 04952E

Head Office - Five Bentall Centre, 2300-550 Burrard St, Vancouver, BC, V6C 2B5

Website - www.atmofizer.com

Email - brian@atmofizer.com

Investor Relations - Brian Meadows (305) 902-1858

Auditors - Davidson & Company LLP C.A., Vancouver, B.C.

Transfer Agents - Odyssey Trust Company, Calgary, Alta.

Profile - (B.C. 2021; orig. Can., 1930) Develops, manufactures and distributes proprietary and patented products, such as commercial air decontaminators and anti-virus coating and decals, under the Atmofizer brand.

The products are based on a patented technology for ultrafine particle agglomeration and neutralization, which address the wide range of dangerous nano-scale particles, viruses and bacteria that are too small to be effectively managed by conventional HEPA filters and ultraviolet lights.

Owned and licensed product lines include wearable, portable and mobile use for personal air treatment, as well as larger systems to handle higher air volumes for commercial, industrial, institutional and residential applications.

Predecessor Detail - Name changed from Consolidated HCI Holdings Corporation, Nov. 15, 2021, pursuant to the reverse takeover acquisition of Vaxxinator USA LLC (dba Vaxxinator Enterprises Inc.).; basis 1 new for 24.691 old shs.

Directors - Olivier Centner, CEO, Toronto, Ont.; Michael B. Galloro, Toronto, Ont.; Joshua Helman, Tampa, Fla.; Nareda Mills, London, Ont.; Peter Simeon, Oakville, Ont.

Other Exec. Officers - Whit Pepper, pres. & chief comml. officer; Brian Meadows, CFO & corp. sec.

Capital Stock

	Authorized (shs.)	Outstanding (shs.)[1]
Common	unlimited	6,687,390

[1] At Jan. 12, 2023

Major Shareholder - Widely held at Oct. 21, 2022.

Price Range - ATMO/CSE

Year	Volume	High	Low	Close
2022	6,892,173	$54.80	$0.20	$0.20
2021	334,470	$150.00	$44.40	$52.60
2020	132	$93.83	$29.63	$93.83
2019	84	$59.26	$49.38	$49.38
2018	175	$148.15	$56.79	$61.73

Consolidation: 1-for-20 cons. in Jan. 2023; 1-for-24.691 cons. in Nov. 2021

Recent Close: $0.08

Capital Stock Changes - On Jan. 12, 2023, common shares were consolidated on a 1-for-20 basis.

Wholly Owned Subsidiaries

Atmofizer Canada Inc., B.C.
- 100% int. in **Atmofizer USA, LLC**, Miami Beach, Fla. dba Vaxxinator Enterprises Inc.
  - 60% int. in **Vaxxinator Lease Co., LLC**, Nev.

Financial Statistics

Periods ended:	12m Dec. 31/21[A1]		12m Dec. 31/20[A2]
	US$000s	%Chg	US$000s
Operating revenue	**497**	**n.a.**	**nil**
Cost of goods sold	414		nil
Salaries & benefits	340		nil
Research & devel. expense	943		162
General & admin expense	7,136		993
Stock-based compensation	4,280		nil
Operating expense	**13,113**	**n.m.**	**1,155**
Operating income	**(12,616)**	**n.a.**	**(1,155)**
Deprec., depl. & amort.	841		nil
Finance income	3		nil
Finance costs, gross	2		nil
Write-downs/write-offs	(1,240)		nil
Pre-tax income	**(21,424)**	**n.a.**	**(1,168)**
Net income	**(21,424)**	**n.a.**	**(1,168)**
Net inc. for equity hldrs	**(21,431)**	**n.a.**	**(1,168)**
Net inc. for non-cont. int	**7**	**n.a.**	**nil**
Cash & equivalent	1,910		1,415
Inventories	668		47
Accounts receivable	488		20
Current assets	5,921		2,381
Fixed assets, net	24		nil
Intangibles, net	9,044		nil
Total assets	**16,489**	**+593**	**2,381**
Accts. pay. & accr. liabs	1,483		153
Current liabilities	1,777		153
Long-term debt, gross	294		nil
Shareholders' equity	14,705		2,228
Non-controlling interest	7		nil
Cash from oper. activs	**(6,727)**	**n.a.**	**(1,254)**
Cash from fin. activs	13,486		2,669
Cash from invest. activs	(6,264)		nil
Net cash position	**1,910**	**+35**	**1,415**
Capital expenditures	(30)		nil
	US$		US$
Earnings per share*	(6.58)		(2.91)
Cash flow per share*	(2.07)		(3.11)
	shs		shs
No. of shs. o/s*	3,696,514		n.a.
Avg. no. of shs. o/s*	3,253,453		401,693
	%		%
Net profit margin	n.m.		n.a.
Return on equity	(253.13)		n.m.
Return on assets	(227.05)		(93.71)

* Class B

[A] Reported in accordance with IFRS

[1] Results reflect the Nov. 12, 2021, reverse takeover acquisition of Vaxxinator USA LLC (dba Vaxxinator Enterprises Inc.).

[2] Results pertain to Vaxxinator USA LLC (dba Vaxxinator Enterprises Inc.).

Latest Results

Periods ended:	9m Sept. 30/22[A]		9m Sept. 30/21[oA]
	US$000s	%Chg	US$000s
Operating revenue	210	+173	77
Net income	(16,010)	n.a.	(5,859)
	US$		US$
Earnings per share*	(3.20)		(1.88)

* Class B

[o] Restated

[A] Reported in accordance with IFRS

Historical Summary
(as originally stated)

Fiscal Year	Oper. Rev.	Net Inc. Bef. Disc.	EPS*
	US$000s	US$000s	US$
2021[A]	497	(21,424)	(6.58)
2020[A]	nil	(1,168)	(2.91)
	$000s	$000s	$
2020[A1]	nil	(279)	(6.91)
2019[A]	nil	(326)	(7.90)
2018[A]	nil	(328)	(7.90)

* Class B

[A] Reported in accordance with IFRS

[1] Results for fiscal 2020 and prior fiscal years pertain to Consolidated HCI Holdings Corporation.

Note: Adjusted throughout for 1-for-20 cons. in Jan. 2023; 1-for-24.691 cons. in Nov. 2021

A.142 Atoro Capital Corp.

Symbol - TTO.H **Exchange** - TSX-VEN **CUSIP** - 04962D
Head Office - 610-700 Pender St W, Vancouver, BC, V6C 1G8 **Telephone** - (778) 628-1202
Email - plee@kowestcapital.com
Investor Relations - Peter Lee (778) 628-1202
Auditors - Dale Matheson Carr-Hilton LaBonte LLP C.A., Vancouver, B.C.
Transfer Agents - Computershare Trust Company of Canada Inc., Toronto, Ont.
Profile - (B.C. 2011) Capital Pool Company.

Recent Merger and Acquisition Activity

Status: terminated **Revised:** July 7, 2022
UPDATE: The transaction was terminated. PREVIOUS: Atoro Capital Corp. entered into a letter of intent for the Qualifying Transaction reverse takeover acquisition of private Lyte Investments Inc. for issuance of 20,000,000 post-consolidated common shares (following a 1-for-1.85 share consolidation). An additional 1,666,667 post-consolidated common shares would be issued to Lyte as consideration for its proposed acquisition of a certain licence and technology. In addition, Atoro would issue up to 8,666,667 post-consolidated common shares to Lyte shareholders to be released against achieving certain pre-defined performance milestones, and assume commitments to issue up to 4,000,000 post-consolidated common shares and warrants for certain services, and 9,746,667 post-consolidated common shares upon conversion of outstanding convertible notes of Lyte. Lyte offers an integrated telehealth platform which provides individuals, employees and customers access to medical doctors and nurses in real time through their mobile devices or personal computers.

Directors - Clive Brookes, pres. & CEO, White Rock, B.C.; Peter Lee, CFO & corp. sec., Vancouver, B.C.; John Hewlett, Surrey, B.C.

Capital Stock

	Authorized (shs.)	Outstanding (shs.)[1]
Common	unlimited	10,171,340

[1] At Apr. 19, 2023

Major Shareholder - Widely held at Sept. 26, 2022.

Price Range - TTO.H/TSX-VEN

Year	Volume	High	Low	Close
2022	68,767	$0.10	$0.02	$0.02
2021	70,400	$0.18	$0.11	$0.18
2020	435,722	$0.15	$0.04	$0.12
2019	52,575	$0.08	$0.05	$0.06
2018	534,223	$0.12	$0.07	$0.07

Recent Close: $0.04

Capital Stock Changes - There were no changes to capital stock during fiscal 2022.

A.143 Atrium Mortgage Investment Corporation

Symbol - AI **Exchange** - TSX **CUSIP** - 04964G
Head Office - 900-20 Adelaide St E, Toronto, ON, M5C 2T6 **Telephone** - (416) 867-1053 **Fax** - (416) 867-1303
Website - www.atriummic.com
Email - rob.goodall@cmcapitalcorp.com
Investor Relations - Robert G. Goodall (416) 867-1053
Auditors - Crowe Soberman LLP C.A., Toronto, Ont.
Lawyers - Fogler, Rubinoff LLP, Toronto, Ont.
Transfer Agents - Computershare Trust Company of Canada Inc., Toronto, Ont.; TSX Trust Company, Toronto, Ont.
Managers - Canadian Mortgage Capital Corporation, Toronto, Ont.
Profile - (Ont. 2001) Provides residential and commercial mortgages in major urban centres in Canada.

The company focuses on single family residential mortgages; multi-family residential, investment properties and commercial mortgages; developer and builder loans; mezzanine and subordinated debt financing; and discounted or distresses mortgage debt. The weighted average loan-to-value ratio of the mortgage portfolio, as a whole, at the time of underwriting each loan will not exceed 75%. A typical loan in the portfolio has an interest rate of 6.99% to 6.99% per annum, a one or two-year term and monthly interest-only mortgage payments. Mortgage loan amounts are generally $300,000 to a maximum of $30,000,000. For loan amounts in excess of $30,000,000, the company co-lends with one or more private lenders or financial institutions.

At Dec. 31, 2022, the number of residential and commercial mortgages totaled 260 valued at $866,262,000 with an average loan-to-value ratio of 59.4% and average term to maturity of 10.9 months.

Directors - Mark L. Silver, chr., Toronto, Ont.; Robert G. (Rob) Goodall, pres. & CEO, Toronto, Ont.; Peter P. Cohos, Calgary, Alta.; Robert H. DeGasperis, Toronto, Ont.; Andrew Grant, Vancouver, B.C.; Maurice (Maish) Kagan, Toronto, Ont.; Nancy H. O. Lockhart, Toronto, Ont.; Jennifer Scoffield, Mississauga, Ont.

Other Exec. Officers - Marianne Dobslaw, man. dir., B.C.; Phil Fiuza, man. dir., single family mtges., Ont.; Bram Rothman, man. dir., Ont.; Sunny Sarai, man. dir., single family mtges., B.C.; Richard Munroe, COO; John Ahmad, CFO & corp. sec.; Adam McDonald, v-p, fin. & admin.

Capital Stock

	Authorized (shs.)	Outstanding (shs.)[1]
Common	unlimited	43,649,883

[1] At June 9, 2023

Normal Course Issuer Bid - The company plans to make normal course purchases of up to 4,176,336 common shares representing 10% of the public float. The bid commenced on June 24, 2023, and expires on June 23, 2024.

Major Shareholder - Widely held at Mar. 24, 2023.

Price Range - AI/TSX

Year	Volume	High	Low	Close
2022	10,558,580	$14.55	$10.15	$10.73
2021	8,468,385	$15.49	$12.32	$14.05
2020	14,914,415	$14.87	$6.72	$12.65
2019	8,848,088	$14.81	$12.55	$14.50
2018	9,367,584	$14.49	$11.20	$12.59

Recent Close: $11.23

Capital Stock Changes - During 2022, common shares were issued as follows: 470,927 under dividend reinvestment plan, 41,614 under deferred share incentive plan and 16,440 under employee share purchase plan.

Dividends

AI com Ra $0.90 pa M est. Feb. 12, 2018**
$0.23† Feb. 28/23 $0.07† Feb. 28/22
$0.02◆ Feb. 26/21
Paid in 2023: $0.675 + $0.23† 2022: $0.90 + $0.07† 2021: $0.90 + $0.02◆

** Reinvestment Option † Extra ◆ Special

Financial Statistics

Periods ended:	12m Dec. 31/22[A]		12m Dec. 31/21[A]
	$000s	%Chg	$000s
Total revenue	**78,371**	**+22**	**64,235**
General & admin. expense	9,448		8,281
Stock-based compensation	336		310
Operating expense	**9,784**	**+14**	**8,591**
Operating income	**68,587**	**+23**	**55,644**
Provision for loan losses	1,914		1,289
Finance costs, gross	19,719		12,530
Write-downs/write-offs	(1,832)		nil
Pre-tax income	**46,332**	**+11**	**41,793**
Net income	**46,332**	**+11**	**41,793**
Investments	880,564		768,232
Total assets	**874,780**	**+13**	**775,487**
Accts. pay. & accr. liabs	7,041		3,574
Debt	378,958		295,540
Equity portion of conv. debs	3,786		2,222
Shareholders' equity	475,564		470,167
Cash from oper. activs	**58,070**	**-14**	**67,885**
Cash from fin. activs	29,741		(34,864)
Cash from invest. activs	(87,811)		(33,021)
	$		$
Earnings per share*	1.08		0.98
Cash flow per share*	1.35		1.59
Cash divd. per share*	0.90		0.90
Extra divd. - cash*	0.23		0.07
Total divd. per share*	**1.13**		**0.97**
	shs		shs
No. of shs. o/s*	43,335,995		42,807,014
Avg. no. of shs. o/s*	43,057,886		42,596,713
	%		%
Net profit margin	59.12		65.06
Return on equity	9.80		8.96
Return on assets	8.00		7.10

* Common

[A] Reported in accordance with IFRS

Historical Summary
(as originally stated)

Fiscal Year	Total Rev.	Net Inc. Bef. Disc.	EPS*
	$000s	$000s	$
2022[A]	78,371	46,332	1.08
2021[A]	64,235	41,793	0.98
2020[A]	65,019	39,188	0.93
2019[A]	66,171	38,568	0.97
2018[A]	58,316	33,769	0.95

* Common

[A] Reported in accordance with IFRS

A.144 Audrey Capital Corporation

Symbol - AUD.P **Exchange** - TSX-VEN **CUSIP** - 050813
Head Office - 905-1111 Hastings St W, Vancouver, BC, V6E 2J3 **Telephone** - (604) 638-2545 **Fax** - (604) 638-2546
Email - martensen@slater.group
Investor Relations - Melissa Martensen (604) 638-2545
Auditors - Davidson & Company LLP C.A., Vancouver, B.C.
Lawyers - Farris LLP, Vancouver, B.C.
Transfer Agents - Olympia Transfer Services Inc., Calgary, Alta.
Profile - (B.C. 2021) Capital Pool Company.
Directors - Ian P. Slater, pres., CEO & CFO, Vancouver, B.C.; Paul Beattie, Montréal, Qué.; Peter Roth, Vancouver, B.C.; Jay Sujir, Vancouver, B.C.
Other Exec. Officers - Melissa Martensen, corp. sec.

Capital Stock

	Authorized (shs.)	Outstanding (shs.)[1]
Preferred	unlimited	nil
Common	unlimited	20,000,000

[1] At May 5, 2022

Major Shareholder - Paul Beattie held 20% interest, Jackie Cheung held 20% interest and Ian P. Slater held 20% interest at May 5, 2022.

Price Range - AUD.P/TSX-VEN

Year	Volume	High	Low	Close
2022............	241,502	$0.30	$0.10	$0.19

Recent Close: $0.08

Capital Stock Changes - In January 2022, private placement of 1,500,000 common shares was completed at 10¢ per share.

A.145 Auka Capital Corp.

Symbol - AUK.P **Exchange** - TSX-VEN **CUSIP** - 002235
Head Office - 1600-421 7 Ave SW, Calgary, AB, T2P 4K9 **Telephone** - (780) 237-9270
Email - rcole@tytataholdings.com
Investor Relations - Robert Cole (780) 237-9270
Auditors - EBT Chartered Accountants LLP C.A., Medicine Hat, Alta.
Lawyers - Gowling WLG (Canada) LLP, Calgary, Alta.
Transfer Agents - Odyssey Trust Company, Calgary, Alta.
Profile - (Alta. 2021) Capital Pool Company.
Common listed on TSX-VEN, Dec. 12, 2022.
Directors - Robert Cole, pres. & CEO, Edmonton, Alta.; Michael Kaiser, CFO, Edmonton, Alta.; Frank Y. Sur, corp. sec., Calgary, Alta.; Jay Baraniecki, Edmonton, Alta.; Ralf Kaiser, Sherwood Park, Alta.; Jeff Lloyd, Edmonton, Alta.; Dave Muddle, Edmonton, Alta.

Capital Stock

	Authorized (shs.)	Outstanding (shs.)[1]
Preferred	unlimited	nil
Common	unlimited	12,500,000

[1] At Dec. 13, 2022

Major Shareholder - Widely held at Dec. 13, 2022.

Price Range - AUK.P/TSX-VEN

Year	Volume	High	Low	Close
2022............	20,000	$0.11	$0.11	$0.11

Recent Close: $0.10

Capital Stock Changes - On Dec. 13, 2022, an initial public offering of 7,500,000 common shares was completed at 10¢ per share.

A.146 Aurinia Pharmaceuticals Inc.

Symbol - AUPH **Exchange** - NASDAQ **CUSIP** - 05156V
Head Office - 140-14315 118 Ave, Edmonton, AB, T5L 4S6 **Telephone** - (250) 744-2487 **Fax** - (250) 744-2498
Website - www.auriniapharma.com
Email - dsheel@auriniapharma.com
Investor Relations - DeDe Sheel (250) 744-2487
Auditors - PricewaterhouseCoopers LLP C.A., Edmonton, Alta.
Lawyers - Borden Ladner Gervais LLP, Vancouver, B.C.
Transfer Agents - Computershare Trust Company, N.A., Golden, Colo.; Computershare Trust Company of Canada Inc., Toronto, Ont.
Employees - 316 at Dec. 31, 2022
Profile - (Alta. 2009) Develops and commercializes LUPKYNIS® (voclosporin) primarily for the treatment of adult patients with active lupus nephritis (LN).

Owns and distributes LUPKYNIS™ (voclosporin), an oral medication for the treatment of lupus nephritis, an inflammation of the kidneys that can lead to end-stage renal disease, in the United States. Voclosporin, the active ingredient in LUPKYNIS™, is a calcineurin inhibitor (CNI), structurally similar to cyclosporine A, but chemically modified on the amino acid-1 residue to offer relevant clinical benefits as compared to the older off-patent CNIs. Customers include specialty pharmacies and distributors which resell the company's products to health care providers and patients.

Has received U.S. FDA approval for LUPKYNIS™ for adult patients with active lupus nephritis (LN), making it the first FDA-approved oral therapy for LN; and Swiss Agency for Therapeutic Products (Swissmedic) regulatory approval in Switzerland for LUPKYNIS™ in combination with a background immunosuppressive therapy to treat adults with active class III, IV and V (including mixed classes III/V and IV/V) LN, a serious complication of systemic lupus erythematosus. The company has marketing authorizations for LUPKYNIS™ from European Commission (EC) with **Otsuka Pharmaceutical Co., Ltd.**, its collaboration partner for the development and commercializatioin of LUPKYNIS™ for the treatment of adult patients with active LN, which is valid in all European (EU) member states as well as in Iceland, Liechtenstein, Norway and Northern Ireland; and Medicines and Healthcare Products Regulatory Agency (MHRA) authorization of voclosporin licensed in Great Britain for the treatment of active LN in adult patients.

The company is also developing AUR200, a recombinant Fc fusion protein designed to specifically block B-cell activating factor (BAFF) and A Proliferation-Inducing Ligand (APRIL) to treat autoimmune and nephrology conditions; and holds global license to develop and commercialize AUR300, a novel peptide therapeutic that modulates M2 macrophages (a type of white blood cells) via the macrophage mannose receptor CD206 to treat autoimmune and fibrotic diseases. AUR200 and AUR300 is currently under pre-clinical study with submission of Investigational New Drug Application (IND) to FDA expected in 2023 for AUR200 and in 2024 for AUR300.

The company has three facilities located in Victoria, B.C.; Edmonton, Alta.; and Rockville, Md.

Predecessor Detail - Name changed from Isotechnika Pharma Inc., Oct. 23, 2013, following acquisition of (old) Aurinia Pharmaceuticals Inc.; basis 1 new for 50 old shs.

Directors - Dr. Daniel G. Billen, chr., Mississauga, Ont.; Peter Greenleaf, pres. & CEO, Potomac, Md.; Jeffrey A. Bailey; Dr. Brinda Balakrishna, San Francisco, Calif.; Dr. David R. W. Jayne, Cambridge, Cambs., United Kingdom; Jill D. Leversage, Vancouver, B.C.; R. Hector MacKay-Dunn, Vancouver, B.C.; Dr. Karen Smith

Other Exec. Officers - Joseph (Joe) Miller, CFO; Scott Habig, chief comml. officer; Michael R. Martin, chief bus. officer; Matthew (Max) Donley, exec. v-p, internal opers. & strategy; Volker Knappertz, exec. v-p, R&D; Stephen P. Robertson, exec. v-p, chief compliance officer, gen. counsel & corp. sec.; Dr. Glenn Schulman, sr. v-p, corp. commun. & IR; Tim Hermes, v-p, market access; Fran Lynch, v-p, sales; DeDe Sheel, v-p, IR

Capital Stock

	Authorized (shs.)	Outstanding (shs.)[1]
Common	unlimited	143,034,009

[1] At May 3, 2023

Major Shareholder - Widely held at Apr. 12, 2023.

Price Range - AUPH/NASDAQ

Year	Volume	High	Low	Close
2022............	180,160,503	US$23.42	US$4.07	US$4.32
2021............	225,913,662	US$33.95	US$9.74	US$22.87

AUP/TSX (D)

Year	Volume	High	Low	Close
2021............	33,564,768	$26.00	$11.77	$16.76
2020............	42,895,451	$28.39	$14.38	$17.56
2019............	20,816,088	$28.59	$4.70	$26.29
2018............	10,024,658	$9.87	$5.70	$9.28

Capital Stock Changes - During 2022, common shares were issued as follows: 383,000 on vesting of restricted share units and 285,000 under employee stock purchase plan and 77,000 on exercise of options.

Wholly Owned Subsidiaries

Aurinia Pharma Limited, United Kingdom.
Aurinia Pharma U.S., Inc., Del.

Financial Statistics

Periods ended:	12m Dec. 31/22[A]		12m Dec. 31/21[A]
	US$000s	%Chg	US$000s
Operating revenue........................	**134,030**	**+194**	**45,605**
Cost of sales....................................	5,664		1,091
Salaries & benefits..........................	96,163		89,999
Research & devel. expense...............	27,683		35,689
General & admin expense.................	83,098		65,352
Stock-based compensation...............	31,709		30,874
Operating expense........................	**244,317**	**+10**	**223,005**
Operating income.........................	**(110,287)**	**n.a.**	**(177,400)**
Deprec., depl. & amort.....................	2,706		2,761
Finance income................................	5,118		529
Pre-tax income..............................	**(106,352)**	**n.a.**	**(180,206)**
Income taxes...................................	1,828		760
Net income.....................................	**(108,180)**	**n.a.**	**(180,966)**
Cash & equivalent............................	389,390		466,078
Inventories......................................	24,752		19,326
Accounts receivable.........................	13,483		15,414
Current assets.................................	442,539		513,324
Fixed assets, net..............................	3,650		4,418
Right-of-use assets..........................	4,907		5,383
Intangibles, net................................	6,425		8,404
Total assets...................................	**470,860**	**-13**	**543,367**
Accts. pay. & accr. liabs....................	39,990		34,947
Current liabilities..............................	46,107		40,646
Long-term lease liabilities................	7,152		7,680
Shareholders' equity.........................	405,435		479,091
Cash from oper. activs...................	**(79,529)**	**n.a.**	**(157,692)**
Cash from fin. activs.........................	2,433		221,112
Cash from invest. activs....................	(60,632)		(103,870)
Net cash position...........................	**94,172**	**-59**	**231,900**
Capital expenditures.........................	(292)		(297)
	US$		US$
Earnings per share*.........................	(0.76)		(1.40)
Cash flow per share*........................	(0.56)		(1.22)
	shs		shs
No. of shs. o/s*...............................	142,268,000		141,600,000
Avg. no. of shs. o/s*.........................	141,915,000		129,369,000
	%		%
Net profit margin..............................	(80.71)		(396.81)
Return on equity...............................	(24.46)		(40.81)
Return on assets...............................	(21.33)		(35.94)
Foreign sales percent........................	100		100
No. of employees (FTEs)..................	316		300

* Common
[A] Reported in accordance with U.S. GAAP

Latest Results

Periods ended:	3m Mar. 31/23[A]		3m Mar. 31/22[A]
	US$000s	%Chg	US$000s
Operating revenue...........................	34,409	+59	21,625
Net income......................................	(26,206)	n.a.	(37,630)
	US$		US$
Earnings per share*.........................	(0.18)		(0.27)

* Common
[A] Reported in accordance with U.S. GAAP

Historical Summary
(as originally stated)

Fiscal Year	Oper. Rev.	Net Inc. Bef. Disc.	EPS*
	US$000s	US$000s	US$
2022[A]..................	134,030	(108,180)	(0.76)
2021[A]..................	45,605	(180,966)	(1.40)
2020[A]..................	50,118	(102,680)	(0.87)
2019[B]..................	318	(123,846)	(1.33)
2018[B]..................	463	(64,120)	(0.76)

* Common
[A] Reported in accordance with U.S. GAAP
[B] Reported in accordance with IFRS

A.147 Aurora Cannabis Inc.*

Symbol - ACB **Exchange** - TSX **CUSIP** - 05156X
Head Office - 3498 63 Ave, Leduc, AB, T9E 0G8 **Toll-free** - (844) 928-7672
Website - www.auroramj.com
Email - media@auroramj.com
Investor Relations - Kevin Niland (855) 279-4652
Auditors - KPMG LLP C.A., Vancouver, B.C.
Bankers - Bank of Montreal, Vancouver, B.C.
Lawyers - Paul, Weiss, Rifkind, Wharton & Garrison LLP, New York, N.Y.; Stikeman Elliott LLP, Vancouver, B.C.
Transfer Agents - Computershare Trust Company, N.A., Canton, Mass.; Computershare Trust Company of Canada Inc., Vancouver, B.C.
FP500 Revenue Ranking - 635
Employees - 1,130 at Mar. 31, 2023
Profile - (B.C. 2006) Produces, distributes and sells medical and recreational cannabis and cannabis-derivative products in Canada and other international jurisdictions. Also owns 50.1% interest in **Bevo Agtech Inc.**, a supplier of propagated vegetables and ornamental plants in North America.

In Canada, primary cannabis cultivation and manufacturing facilities are located in Bradford, Ont. (Aurora River, 210,000 sq. ft.), Markham, Ont. (Aurora Ridge, 55,000 sq. ft.), Townsend, Ont. (Thrive, 14,000 sq. ft. indoor and 6 acres outdoor) and Pemberton, B.C. (WMMC, 62,000 sq. ft.). These facilities produce across all major product categories: flower, pre-rolls, oils, concentrates, capsules, vapes and edibles. The company also operates a 22,500-sq.-ft. research facility (Aurora Coast) in Comox, B.C., which is dedicated to cannabis breeding as well as supports the company's genetics licensing business unit, Occo. Occo provides the company's catalogue of cannabis genetics for licensing to other producers. Other operations include wholly owned **CanvasRx Inc.**, a medical cannabis patient counselling and outreach service provider, serving patients across Canada virtually and through owned and third-party clinic locations.

International activities are conducted primarily in Europe, Australia, Israel and Uruguay through a combination of strategic investments, domestic production and supply agreements. Operations include wholly owned **Aurora Deutschland GmbH**, a wholesale importer, exporter and distributor of medical cannabis in the European Union, with a 29,400-sq.-ft. production facility in Leuna, Germany; 10% interest in **Indica Industries Pty Ltd.** (dba MedReleaf Australia), which cultivates, manufactures, imports, exports and distributes medical cannabis primarily in Australia; an extraction facility near the Montevideo airport in Uruguay; and wholly owned **Reliva, LLC**, which produces, distributes and sells hemp-derived CBD products under the Reliva and KG7 brands that are sold in retail stores and online in the U.S.

Medical cannabis products are sold under the brands Aurora, CanniMed, MedReleaf, WMMC, Pedanios, Bidiol and CraftPlant, and recreational brands include Whistler Cannabis Co., San Rafael '71, Aurora Drift, Daily Special, Being and Greybeard Cannabis.

Subsidiary **Bevo Agtech Inc.** (50.1% owned) produces and supplies greenhouse and outdoor field crop seedlings and floral plants for greenhouses, nurseries, field farms and wholesalers in North America.

On June 13, 2023, the company decided to exit its interest in Netherlands-based **Growery B.V.** in order to focus on other international growth priorities. The company held a 40% interest in Growery, which was one of the licence holders entitled to participate in the Netherlands' proposed adult-use cannabis pilot program, the Controlled Cannabis Supply Chain Experiment.

In May 2023, the company decided to close its 100,000-sq.-ft. Aurora Nordic greenhouse facility in Odense, Denmark.

In April 2023, wholly owned **Thrive Cannabis Inc.** wound up **2755757 Ontario Inc.** (dba Venn Cannabis), a 50/50 joint venture with **Canary RX Inc.**, wholly owned by **Target Group Inc.** Venn Cannabis was formed to operate and manage Canary's 44,000-sq.-ft. indoor cultivation facility in Simcoe, Ont.

The company changed its fiscal year end to March 31 from June 30, effective Mar. 31, 2023.

In May 2022, the company announced the closure of the Aurora Sky greenhouse and processing facility in Edmonton, Alta.; the Aurora Valley outdoor farm in Westwold, B.C., used for cultivation research; its testing, research and genetics division, wholly owned **Anandia Laboratories Inc.**, which has facilities in Vancouver (2), B.C., and Toronto, Ont.; and the Whistler Alpha Lake production facility in Alpha Lake, B.C. Aurora Valley, Anandia and Whistler Alpha Lake were closed in the fourth quarter of 2022 and Aurora Sky ceased production in September 2022.

Recent Merger and Acquisition Activity

Status: completed **Announced:** July 24, 2023
Aurora Cannabis Inc. sold its Medicine Hat, Alta.-facility (Aurora Sun Facility) to Bevo Farms Ltd., a wholly owned subsidiary of Bevo Agtech Inc., for up to $15,000,000 payable over time based on Bevo Farms successfully achieving certain financial milestones at the Aurora Sun Facility. Aurora has a controlling interest in Bevo Agtech Inc.

Status: completed **Announced:** Jan. 4, 2023
Aurora Cannabis Inc. sold its former 300,000-sq.-ft. Aurora Polaris manufacturing and distribution facility in Edmonton, Alta., for $15,000,000.

Status: completed **Revised:** Sept. 30, 2022
UPDATE: The transaction was completed. PREVIOUS: Aurora Cannabis Inc. agreed to sell its 800,000-sq.-ft. Aurora Sky greenhouse and processing facility in Edmonton, Alta., to Bevo Agtech Inc., the owner of Bevo Farms Ltd., for contingent consideration of up to $25,000,000 payable over time based on Bevo successfully achieving certain financial milestones at the Aurora Sky facility. Bevo plans to repurpose the facility for non-cannabis agriculture.

Status: completed **Announced:** Sept. 20, 2022
Aurora Cannabis Inc. acquired CannaHealth Therapeutics Inc., which has assets in the Canadian medical aggregator space, for $21,900,000.

Status: terminated **Revised:** Sept. 19, 2022
UPDATE: The transaction was terminated. PREVIOUS: Aurora Cannabis Inc. agreed to sell its Aurora Sun greenhouse and processing facility in Medicine Hat, Alta., for $46,800,000, consisting of $20,000,000 cash on closing and a $26,800,000 vendor take back promissory note payable within five years of closing the transaction. The half-completed Aurora Sun facility, which was originally designed to measure 1,600,000 sq. ft., has been vacant since construction was halted in late 2020.

Status: completed **Announced:** Aug. 25, 2022
Aurora Cannabis Inc. acquired a 50.1% interest in Bevo Agtech Inc., the sole parent of Bevo Farms Ltd., one of the largest suppliers of propagated vegetables and ornamental plants in North America, for $45,000,000 in cash on closing. Concurrently with closing of the transaction, Bevo agreed to acquire Aurora's Aurora Sky facility in Edmonton, Alta. Bevo, which operates 63 acres of greenhouse in British Columbia, generated revenues of $39,000,000 for the 12 months-ended June 30, 2022. Up to an additional $12,000,000 shall be payable by a subsidiary of Aurora to the Bevo selling shareholder over the three years following closing, conditional on Bevo successfully achieving certain financial milestones at its Site One facility in Langley, B.C.

Status: completed **Revised:** Aug. 15, 2022
UPDATE: The transaction was completed. PREVIOUS: Aurora Cannabis Inc. agreed to sell its Aurora Valley outdoor farm in Westwold, B.C., for $5,900,000. Aurora Valley was used for cultivation research to develop new technology, genetics and intellectual property until its closure in late fiscal 2022.

Status: completed **Revised:** May 5, 2022
UPDATE: The transaction was completed. Aurora issued 2,467,421 common shares to satisfy the share consideration. PREVIOUS: Aurora Cannabis Inc. agreed to acquire TerraFarma Inc. (parent company of Thrive Cannabis) for total consideration of $38,000,000 payable in cash and Aurora common shares. The transaction also included earnout consideration of up to $10,000,000 for satisfying certain near-term revenue targets and up to $20,000,000 for satisfying certain long-term revenue targets within two years of the closing of the transaction, each payable in cash, Aurora shares or a combination of both. Simcoe, Ont.-based Thrive is a licensed producer of super-premium cannabis concentrates and craft dried flower, whose brands include Greybeard Cannabis Co. and Being Cannabis. The transaction was expected to close during Aurora's fiscal fourth quarter ending June 30, 2022.

Status: completed **Revised:** Mar. 15, 2022
UPDATE: The transaction was completed. PREVIOUS: Aurora Cannabis Inc. agreed to sell its shuttered semi-complete Nordic Sky greenhouse facility in Odense, Denmark, for $7,500,000. Construction of Nordic Sky was suspended in November 2019; the facility was originally designed to measure 1,000,000 sq. ft.

Predecessor Detail - Name changed from Prescient Mining Corp., Oct. 2, 2014, pursuant to reverse takeover acquisition of Aurora Marijuana Inc.

Directors - Ronald F. (Ron) Funk, chr., Ont.; Miguel Martin, CEO, Va.; Norma Beauchamp, Toronto, Ont.; Theresa S. Firestone, Toronto, Ont.; Chitwant S. Kohli, Ont.; Michael Singer, Montréal, Qué.; Adam K. Szweras, Toronto, Ont.

Other Exec. Officers - W. Glen Ibbott, CFO; David (Dave) Aird, exec. v-p, IT; Nathalie Clark, exec. v-p, gen. counsel & corp. sec.; André Jérôme, exec. v-p, global bus. devel.; Alex Miller, exec. v-p, opers. & supply chain; Lori Schick, exec. v-p, HR

Capital Stock

	Authorized (shs.)	Outstanding (shs.)[1]	Par
Class A	unlimited	nil	$1.00
Class B	unlimited	nil	$5.00
Common	unlimited	354,205,652	n.p.v.

[1] At June 19, 2023

Options - At Mar. 31, 2023, options were outstanding to purchase 6,721,503 common shares at prices ranging from $1.67 to $163.56 per share expiring on various dates to Sept. 30, 2027.

Warrants - At Mar. 31, 2023, warrants were outstanding to purchase 89,124,788 common shares at prices ranging from $4.38 to $116.09 per share expiring on various dates to Nov. 30, 2025.

Major Shareholder - Widely held at June 19, 2023.

Price Range - ACB/TSX

Year	Volume	High	Low	Close
2022	584,934,902	$7.61	$1.11	$1.25
2021	591,524,078	$24.10	$6.82	$6.85
2020	730,125,395	$36.24	$4.93	$10.60
2019	200,700,272	$164.04	$29.40	$33.48
2018	388,688,832	$194.88	$63.48	$81.36

Consolidation: 1-for-12 cons. in May 2020
Recent Close: $0.61

Capital Stock Changes - During the nine-month period ended Mar. 31, 2023, common shares were issued as follows: 44,551,253 under an at-the-market program, 2,614,995 for earn-out payment and 330,824 on exercise of restricted, deferred and performance share units.

In May 2022, 2,467,421 common shares were issued pursuant to the acquisition of TerraFarma Inc. In June 2022, bought deal public offering of 70,408,750 units (1 common share & 1 warrant) at US$2.45 per unit was completed, including 9,183,750 units on exercise of over-allotment option. Also during fiscal 2022, common shares were issued as follows: 26,161,388 under an at-the-market program, 375,193 on exercise of restricted, deferred and performance share units, 193,554 for earn-out payment and 97,009 for services.

Long-Term Debt - At Mar. 31, 2023, outstanding long-term debt totaled $178,305,000 ($142,142,000 current) and consisted of $132,571,000 of 5.5% convertible senior notes due Feb. 28, 2024, convertible into common shares at US$86.72 per share, and $45,734,000 in borrowings under term loan credit facilities, bearing interest at prime plus a margin.

Wholly Owned Subsidiaries

ACB Captive Insurance Company Inc., Canada.
Aurora Cannabis Enterprises Inc., Alta.
Aurora Deutschland GmbH, Germany.
Aurora Nordic Cannabis A/S, Odense, Denmark.
CannaHealth Therapeutics Inc., Canada.
CanvasRx Inc., Markham, Ont.
Reliva, LLC, Natick, Mass.
TerraFarma Inc., Simcoe, Ont.
• 100% int. in **Thrive Cannabis Inc.**, Canada.
Whistler Medical Marijuana Corporation, Whistler, B.C.

Subsidiaries

50.1% int. in **Bevo Agtech Inc.**, B.C.
• 100% int. in **Bevo Farms Ltd.**, Milner, B.C.

Investments

19.19% int. in **Choom Holdings Inc.**, Vancouver, B.C. (see separate coverage)
10% int. in **Indica Industries Pty Ltd.**, Australia. dba MedReleaf Australia.
Radient Technologies Inc., Edmonton, Alta. (see separate coverage)

Financial Statistics

Periods ended:	9m Mar. 31/23[A]		12m June 30/22[oA]
	$000s	%Chg	$000s
Operating revenue	**174,968**	**n.a.**	**221,339**
Cost of sales	174,193		200,114
Research & devel. expense	4,921		10,389
General & admin expense	122,639		175,237
Stock-based compensation	10,764		13,757
Operating expense	**312,517**	**n.a.**	**399,497**
Operating income	**(137,549)**	**n.a.**	**(178,158)**
Deprec., depl. & amort.	14,916		48,602
Finance income	14,252		4,507
Finance costs, gross	29,596		71,813
Investment income	33		(293)
Write-downs/write-offs	(45,982)		(1,463,796)[1]
Pre-tax income	**(221,532)**	**n.a.**	**(1,720,120)**
Income taxes	(15,237)		(2,141)
Net inc bef disc ops, eqhldrs	(198,997)		(1,717,624)
Net inc bef disc ops, NCI	(7,298)		(355)
Net income	**(206,295)**	**n.a.**	**(1,717,979)**
Net inc. for equity hldrs	**(198,997)**	**n.a.**	**(1,717,624)**
Net inc. for non-cont. int	**(7,298)**	**n.a.**	**(355)**
Cash & equivalent	234,942		439,138
Inventories	106,132		116,098
Accounts receivable	41,308		46,995
Current assets	479,927		745,121
Long-term investments	nil		1,207
Fixed assets, net	322,969		233,465
Intangibles, net	78,395		70,696
Total assets	**926,322**	**n.a.**	**1,084,356**
Accts. pay. & accr. liabs	75,825		69,874
Current liabilities	242,305		130,857
Long-term debt, gross	178,305		226,504
Long-term debt, net	36,163		199,650
Long-term lease liabilities	43,804		36,837
Shareholders' equity	486,076		661,843
Non-controlling interest	31,061		511
Cash from oper. activs	**(115,821)**	**n.a.**	**(110,267)**
Cash from fin. activs	(71,406)		147,779
Cash from invest. activs	(27,291)		(36,171)
Net cash position	**234,942**	**n.a.**	**437,807**
Capital expenditures	(12,132)		(32,213)
Capital disposals	20,253		19,648
	$		$
Earnings per share*	(0.62)		(7.99)
Cash flow per share*	(0.36)		(0.51)
	shs		shs
No. of shs. o/s*	345,269,310		297,772,238
Avg. no. of shs. o/s*	322,735,165		214,912,605
	%		%
Net profit margin	...		(776.18)
Return on equity	...		(127.25)
Return on assets	...		(89.25)
Foreign sales percent	14		28
No. of employees (FTEs)	1,130		1,338

* Common
[o] Restated
[A] Reported in accordance with IFRS
[1] Includes $914,275,000 full impairment of goodwill, $284,927,000 impairment of intangible assets and $259,115,000 impairment of property, plant and equipment.

Historical Summary
(as originally stated)

Fiscal Year	Oper. Rev.	Net Inc. Bef. Disc.	EPS*
	$000s	$000s	$
2023[A1]	174,968	(206,295)	(0.62)
2022[A]	221,339	(1,717,979)	(7.99)
2021[A]	245,252	(693,477)	(4.09)
2020[A]	278,906	(3,300,493)	(33.84)
2019[A]	247,939	(297,924)	(3.48)

* Common
[A] Reported in accordance with IFRS
[1] 9 months ended Mar. 31, 2023.
Note: Adjusted throughout for 1-for-12 cons. in May 2020

A.148 Aurora Solar Technologies Inc.

Symbol - ACU **Exchange** - TSX-VEN (S) **CUSIP** - 05207J
Head Office - 100-788 Harbourside Dr, North Vancouver, BC, V7P 3R7 **Telephone** - (778) 241-5000 **Fax** - (604) 688-2205
Website - www.aurorasolartech.com
Email - corpcomm@aurorasolartech.com
Investor Relations - Jake Bouma (604) 317-3936
Auditors - BDO Canada LLP C.A., Vancouver, B.C.
Transfer Agents - Computershare Trust Company of Canada Inc., Toronto, Ont.
Profile - (B.C. 2006) Develops, manufactures and markets material inspection and inline quality control systems for solar polysilicon, wafer, cell and module manufacturing industries.

Products include DM™ and TCM™ Instruments, a series of systems that use safe infrared light to measure key properties of crystalline silicon photovoltaic (PV) wafers; Visualize™ software, which uses the real-time data provided by DM and TCM product to show the relationship between the per-wafer measurements and the changing spatial variations in chemical layer properties induced by variations in the behaviour of manufacturing equipment used to create these layers; Insight™, a data science package that analyses the large volume of data available from the sequence of finished solar cells in a production line and reveals the links between unwanted variations in their efficiency and the causes in production; and BT Imaging, which offers offline and inline photoluminescence inspection equipment for PV materials including silicon, perovskite and thin film materials for use at different processing stages including ingots, as-cut wafers, cells and solar modules. Services provided include system configuration and performance planning, system engineering, operations training courses and optimization services.

Also developing Insight™ Essentials, which is the first of a planned series of Insight™ versions that is focused on plant-wide yield (and quality control) visualization and reporting.

Common suspended from TSX-VEN, Aug. 15, 2023.

Recent Merger and Acquisition Activity

Status: completed **Revised:** Aug. 26, 2022

UPDATE: The transaction was completed. PREVIOUS: Aurora Solar Technologies Inc. agreed to acquire private Australia-based BT Imaging PTY Ltd. for $13,799,180 consisting of issuance of 62,969,351 common shares and $1,205,310 cash. BT imaging designs and develops photoluminescence imaging tools for PV material inspection and quality control during production and for laboratory use during product development.

Predecessor Detail - Name changed from ACT Aurora Control Technologies Corp., May 28, 2015.

Directors - Kevin Dodds, CEO, Vancouver, B.C.; Dr. Roger G. Buckeridge, N.S.W., Australia; Gordon Deans, West Vancouver, B.C.; R. David Toyoda, Vancouver, B.C.

Other Exec. Officers - Tricia Pederson, CFO; Steve McDonald, v-p, bus. devel.; Wei Deng, gen. mgr., Asia Pacific; Shirley Kancs, corp. sec.

Capital Stock

	Authorized (shs.)	Outstanding (shs.)[1]
Common	unlimited	222,194,076

[1] At Aug. 26, 2022

Major Shareholder - Widely held at Apr. 14, 2022.

Price Range - ACU/TSX-VEN (S)

Year	Volume	High	Low	Close
2022	33,637,620	$0.17	$0.05	$0.05
2021	161,040,123	$0.85	$0.13	$0.15
2020	96,436,838	$0.39	$0.06	$0.37
2019	43,387,625	$0.12	$0.03	$0.08
2018	19,961,412	$0.30	$0.06	$0.06

Recent Close: $0.03

Capital Stock Changes - In August 2022, 62,969,351 common shares were issued pursuant to the acquisition of BT Imaging PTY Ltd. and a concurrent private placement of 11,650,000 units (1 common share & 1 warrant) at 10¢ per unit was completed, with warrants exercisable at 20¢ per share for one year.

In May 2021, private placement of 14,200,000 units (1 common share & ½ warrant) at 25¢ per unit was completed. Also during fiscal 2022, 1,050,000 common shares were issued on exercise of options.

Wholly Owned Subsidiaries

Aurora Solar Technologies (Canada) Inc.

BT Imaging Pty Ltd., Australia.

Financial Statistics

Periods ended:	12m Mar. 31/22[A]		12m Mar. 31/21[A]
	$000s	%Chg	$000s
Operating revenue	**nil**	**n.a.**	**1,866**
Cost of sales	nil		1,395
Salaries & benefits	1,637		1,206
Research & devel. expense	1,137		566
General & admin expense	1,232		927
Stock-based compensation	494		384
Operating expense	**4,500**	**0**	**4,478**
Operating income	**(4,500)**	**n.a.**	**(2,612)**
Deprec., depl. & amort.	148		105
Finance costs, gross	11		14
Write-downs/write-offs	nil		(49)
Pre-tax income	**(4,247)**	**n.a.**	**(3,520)**
Net income	**(4,247)**	**n.a.**	**(3,520)**
Cash & equivalent	2,017		2,772
Inventories	324		334
Accounts receivable	118		20
Current assets	2,494		3,184
Fixed assets, net	193		70
Right-of-use assets	241		312
Intangibles, net	202		197
Total assets	**3,189**	**-16**	**3,816**
Accts. pay. & accr. liabs.	395		589
Current liabilities	477		673
Long-term debt, gross	60		60
Long-term debt, net	60		60
Long-term lease liabilities	177		232
Shareholders' equity	2,476		2,851
Cash from oper. activs.	**(3,848)**	**n.a.**	**(2,070)**
Cash from fin. activs.	3,284		3,084
Cash from invest. activs.	(191)		(63)
Net cash position	**2,017**	**-27**	**2,772**
	$		$
Earnings per share*	(0.03)		(0.03)
Cash flow per share*	(0.03)		(0.02)
	shs		shs
No. of shs. o/s*	144,974,725		129,724,725
Avg. no. of shs. o/s*	142,725,547		113,667,348
	%		%
Net profit margin	n.a.		(188.64)
Return on equity	(159.45)		(124.58)
Return on assets	(120.94)		(95.18)

* Common

[A] Reported in accordance with IFRS

Latest Results

Periods ended:	3m June 30/22[A]		3m June 30/21[A]
	$000s	%Chg	$000s
Net income	(1,003)	n.a.	(1,103)
	$		$
Earnings per share*	(0.01)		(0.01)

* Common

[A] Reported in accordance with IFRS

Historical Summary
(as originally stated)

Fiscal Year	Oper. Rev.	Net Inc. Bef. Disc.	EPS*
	$000s	$000s	$
2022[A]	nil	(4,247)	(0.03)
2021[A]	1,866	(3,520)	(0.03)
2020[A]	3,298	(504)	(0.01)
2019[A]	438	(2,258)	(0.03)
2018[A]	2,508	(738)	(0.01)

* Common

[A] Reported in accordance with IFRS

A.149 Aurora Spine Corporation

Symbol - ASG **Exchange** - TSX-VEN **CUSIP** - 05206X

Head Office - 300-20 Holly St, Toronto, ON, M4S 3B1

Website - www.aurora-spine.com

Email - dmeyer@auroraspine.us

Investor Relations - David M. Meyer (760) 424-2004

Auditors - MNP LLP C.A., Waterloo, Ont.

Transfer Agents - TSX Trust Company, Toronto, Ont.

Profile - (Ont. 2013) Develops and distributes minimally invasive, regenerative spinal implant technologies, with a focus on spinal implant and pain care markets.

The company's primary product lines are interlaminar fusion devices (ZIP), which provide an alternative to pedicle screws and rods to fix and ultimately allow two or more vertebrae to fuse together by using two interlocking titanium side plates with a hollow titanium core chamber to host bone or biologic grafting material for stabilization and load sharing in patients with degenerative disc disease; DEXA Technology™ interbody cages, which consist of series of implants manufactured with varying densities to match a patient's bone density score; and invasive sacroiliac (SI) joint fusion, which consists of series of patented titanium implants and instruments used to implant them to solve musculoskeletal disorders of the spine and sacropelvic. ZIP lumbar (lower spine) fusion devices include ZIP®, ZIP ULTRA®, ZIP LP™ and ZIP-51™. Some of the ZIP products have been used mid-spine (thoracic). DEXA implants include DEXA-C™ cervical interbody cages for anterior cervical discectomy with fusion (ACDF) procedures, DEXA-L™ standalone anterior lumbar interbody fusion device (ALIF) and Apollo™ anterior cervical plate system. SI joint fusion products include SiLO™ posterior SI fusion system, which is made of human cortical bone and used in stabilizing and fusing the iliac bone (pelvis) to the spine (sacrum); SiLO-TFX™, a titanium/non-bone version of SiLO™; and SOLO™ standalone ALIF cage system, a 3D printed standalone fusion device which is used as an integrated plate and spacer system that helps to preserve the natural spine shape while providing support and stability. Other product includes titanium-coated PEEK (polyether ether ketone) interbody cages, which are used to fill the space between vertebrae after removal of damaged disc to provide spacing and stability between the vertebrae while allowing bone to grow through it during the fusion process. Product under development stage includes ZIPFlex™, a posterior interlaminar implant for motion preservation.

In addition, the company offers third party products, including cervical and lumbar plates and screws.

Directors - David A. Rosenkrantz, chr., Etobicoke, Ont.; Trent J. Northcutt, pres. & CEO, Calif.; Tracy A. Graf, Sylvan Lake, Alta.; J. Daryl MacLellan, Toronto, Ont.; Michael Seid, San Diego, Calif.; James Snow, Calif.

Other Exec. Officers - Chad Clouse, CFO; Laszlo Garamszegi, v-p, eng. & chief tech. officer; David M. (Dave) Meyer, v-p, chief legal officer & corp. sec.

Capital Stock

	Authorized (shs.)	Outstanding (shs.)[1]
Preferred	unlimited	nil
Common	unlimited	64,325,083
Restricted Vtg. Com.	unlimited	5,071,427

[1] At May 26, 2023

Common - One vote per share.

Restricted Voting Common - Carries the same voting right as the common shares, except does not carry the right to vote in respect of the election of directors of the company.

Major Shareholder - David A. Rosenkrantz held 14.93% interest at May 26, 2023.

Price Range - ASG/TSX-VEN

Year	Volume	High	Low	Close
2022	6,068,560	$0.59	$0.22	$0.46
2021	7,671,902	$1.04	$0.26	$0.35
2020	3,402,264	$0.49	$0.13	$0.40
2019	3,740,522	$0.45	$0.20	$0.28
2018	10,049,826	$0.45	$0.09	$0.38

Recent Close: $0.25

Capital Stock Changes - During 2022, 325,000 common shares were issued on exercise of warrants.

Wholly Owned Subsidiaries

Aurora Spine Europe Limited, United Kingdom. Inactive.

Aurora Spine, Inc., Nev.

Financial Statistics

Periods ended:	12m Dec. 31/22[A]		12m Dec. 31/21[A]
	US$000s	%Chg	US$000s
Operating revenue	**14,877**	**+41**	**10,545**
Cost of goods sold	7,068		5,711
Salaries & benefits	2,973		2,229
Research & devel. expense	1,160		941
General & admin expense	4,010		3,423
Stock-based compensation	142		141
Operating expense	**15,353**	**+23**	**12,445**
Operating income	**(476)**	**n.a.**	**(1,900)**
Deprec., depl. & amort.	869		649
Finance costs, gross	164		159
Write-downs/write-offs	(62)		nil
Pre-tax income	**(1,501)**	**n.a.**	**(2,359)**
Net income	**(1,501)**	**n.a.**	**(2,359)**
Cash & equivalent	423		3,173
Inventories	3,054		1,890
Accounts receivable	3,666		2,668
Current assets	7,331		8,405
Fixed assets, net	1,911		1,304
Intangibles, net	881		854
Total assets	**10,123**	**-4**	**10,564**
Accts. pay. & accr. liabs	2,833		2,449
Current liabilities	3,030		2,627
Long-term debt, gross	2,418		2,286
Long-term debt, net	2,418		2,274
Long-term lease liabilities	356		94
Shareholders' equity	4,317		5,569
Cash from oper. activs	**(1,558)**	**n.a.**	**(2,129)**
Cash from fin. activs	(318)		4,312
Cash from invest. activs	(873)		(721)
Net cash position	**423**	**-87**	**3,173**
Capital expenditures	(771)		(721)
	US$		US$
Earnings per share*	(0.02)		(0.04)
Cash flow per share*	(0.02)		(0.04)
	shs		shs
No. of shs. o/s*	67,055,510		66,730,510
Avg. no. of shs. o/s*	66,797,291		58,706,898
	%		%
Net profit margin	(10.09)		(22.37)
Return on equity	(30.37)		(53.31)
Return on assets	(12.93)		(24.83)

* Common
[A] Reported in accordance with IFRS

Latest Results

Periods ended:	3m Mar. 31/23[A]		3m Mar. 31/22[A]
	US$000s	%Chg	US$000s
Operating revenue	2,958	-17	3,552
Net income	(663)	n.a.	(387)
	US$		US$
Earnings per share*	(0.01)		(0.01)

* Common
[A] Reported in accordance with IFRS

Historical Summary
(as originally stated)

Fiscal Year	Oper. Rev.	Net Inc. Bef. Disc.	EPS*
	US$000s	US$000s	US$
2022[A]	14,877	(1,501)	(0.02)
2021[A]	10,545	(2,359)	(0.04)
2020[A]	8,646	(232)	(0.00)
2019[A]	11,153	(1,254)	(0.03)
2018[A]	8,682	(68)	(0.00)

* Common
[A] Reported in accordance with IFRS

A.150 Aurum Lake Mining Corporation

Symbol - ARL.P **Exchange** - TSX-VEN **CUSIP** - 05209U
Head Office - Brookfield Place, 4400-181 Bay St, Toronto, ON, M5J 2T3 **Telephone** - (647) 530-1117
Email - patrick.sapphire@principlecp.com
Investor Relations - Patrick Sapphire (647) 530-1117
Auditors - MNP LLP C.A., Vancouver, B.C.
Transfer Agents - Odyssey Trust Company, Vancouver, B.C.
Profile - (B.C. 2021) Capital Pool Company.
Directors - Patrick Sapphire, CEO & CFO, Toronto, Ont.; G. Wesley (Wes) Roberts, Toronto, Ont.; Weizhe Zhong
Other Exec. Officers - Rajeev (Raj) Dewan, corp. sec.

Capital Stock

	Authorized (shs.)	Outstanding (shs.)[1]
Common	unlimited	16,500,000

[1] At May 28, 2023

Major Shareholder - Patrick Sapphire held 24.2% interest, Dr. Jingbin Wang held 18.8% interest and Khione Gateway Inc. held 12.1% interest at July 19, 2022.

Price Range - ARL.P/TSX-VEN

Year	Volume	High	Low	Close
2022	126,200	$0.11	$0.10	$0.11

Recent Close: $0.11
Capital Stock Changes - On July 19, 2022, an initial public offering of 3,500,000 common shares was completed at 10¢ per share.

A.151 Auston Capital Corp.

Symbol - ASTN.P **Exchange** - TSX-VEN **CUSIP** - 052504
Head Office - 608-409 Granville St, Vancouver, BC, V6C 1T2 **Telephone** - (604) 642-0115 **Fax** - (604) 642-0116
Email - stevesmith15@shaw.ca
Investor Relations - Stephen Smith (604) 642-0115
Auditors - De Visser Gray LLP C.A., Vancouver, B.C.
Lawyers - S. Paul Simpson Law Corporation, Vancouver, B.C.
Transfer Agents - Computershare Trust Company of Canada Inc., Vancouver, B.C.
Profile - (B.C. 2017) Capital Pool Company.

Recent Merger and Acquisition Activity

Status: pending **Announced:** Sept. 1, 2022
Auston Capital Corp. entered into a letter of intent for the Qualifying Transaction reverse takeover acquisition of Eastport Ventures Inc., which has mineral interests in Botswana. Terms were not disclosed.
Status: terminated **Revised:** July 22, 2022
UPDATE: The transaction was terminated. PREVIOUS: Auston Capital Corp. entered into a letter of intent for the Qualifying Transaction (QT) reverse takeover acquisition of private Toronto, Ont.-based Southern Sky Resources Corp. on a share-for-share basis, which would result in the issuance of 20,500,000 post-consolidated Auston common shares (following a 1-for-2.25 share consolidation). Concurrent with closing, Southern Sky would complete a $2,000,000 financing structured as either a common share offering, a subscription receipt offering, or such other security offering as determined by Southern Sky based on discussions with investors. Southern Sky has mineral interests in Guyana and Colombia. Oct. 5, 2021 - A definitive agreement was entered into whereby the QT reverse takeover acquisition of Southern Sky would be completed by way of a three-cornered amalgamation of Southern Sky and a wholly owned subsidiary of Auston. Auston would issue 21,427,500 post-consolidated common shares to Southern Sky shareholders. In addition, Southern Sky would complete a private placement of 8,000,000 subscription receipts at 40¢ per receipt, with each receipt exchangeable for 1 post-consolidated Auston common share without further consideration on closing of the transaction. Apr. 4, 2022 - Conditional TSX Venture Exchange approval was received.
Directors - Mark Fekete, pres., CEO, CFO & corp. sec., Montréal, Qué.; Iqbal J. (Ick) Boga, Vancouver, B.C.; Zachery (Zak) Dingsdale, Cobourg, Ont.; Kenneth (Ken) MacLeod, West Vancouver, B.C.; Stephen (Steve) Smith, White Rock, B.C.; James Taylor, Surrey, B.C.

Capital Stock

	Authorized (shs.)	Outstanding (shs.)[1]
Common	unlimited	6,200,000

[1] At Dec. 10, 2021

Major Shareholder - Kenneth (Ken) MacLeod held 17.74% interest at Mar. 23, 2021.

Price Range - ASTN.P/TSX-VEN

Year	Volume	High	Low	Close
2022	17,060	$0.15	$0.04	$0.04
2021	141,000	$0.08	$0.05	$0.08
2020	25,000	$0.06	$0.06	$0.06
2019	212,803	$0.16	$0.06	$0.06

A.152 Australian REIT Income Fund

Symbol - HRR.UN **Exchange** - TSX **CUSIP** - 05257X
Head Office - c/o Harvest Portfolios Group Inc., 209-710 Dorval Dr, Oakville, ON, L6K 3V7 **Telephone** - (416) 649-4541 **Toll-free** - (866) 998-8298 **Fax** - (416) 649-4542
Website - www.harvestportfolios.com
Email - mkovacs@harvestportfolios.com
Investor Relations - Michael Kovacs (416) 494-4541
Auditors - PricewaterhouseCoopers LLP C.A., Toronto, Ont.
Lawyers - Borden Ladner Gervais LLP, Toronto, Ont.
Transfer Agents - TSX Trust Company, Toronto, Ont.
Trustees - Harvest Portfolios Group Inc., Oakville, Ont.
Investment Managers - Harvest Portfolios Group Inc., Oakville, Ont.
Managers - Harvest Portfolios Group Inc., Oakville, Ont.
Profile - (Ont. 2013) Invests in an actively managed portfolio consisting primarily of equity securities listed on the Australian Stock Exchange issued by Australian real estate investment trusts and, to a lesser extent, issuers engaged in the real estate industry in Australia.
The fund focuses on real estate issuers providing an attractive current cash yield and/or capital appreciation opportunities in various sectors, including industrial, residential, office, retail and other real estate sectors. The fund may from time to time invest in debt securities and from time to time the value of the portfolio is intended to be 100% hedged back to the Canadian dollar or 100% unhedged. The fund may borrow against the assets of the fund to a maximum of 40% of total assets for purposes of acquiring assets for the portfolio.
The manager receives a management fee at an annual rate equal to 1.3% of the net asset value per unit calculated and payable monthly in arrears.
Top 10 holdings at June 30, 2023 (as a percentage of net asset value):

Holdings	Percentage
Goodman Group	22%
Stockland Corporation Limited	14.3%
Mirvac Group	12.9%
HomeCo Daily Needs REIT	12.8%
The GPT Group	12.7%
Charter Hall Group	11.3%
Vicinity Centres	10.8%
Scentre Group	10%
Charter Hall Retail REIT	9.8%
DEXUS Property Group	8.5%

The fund does not have a fixed termination date but may be terminated by the manager upon the approval of the unitholders.
Oper. Subsid./Mgt. Co. Directors - Michael Kovacs, chr., pres., CEO & corp. sec., Oakville, Ont.; Mary Medeiros, COO, Oakville, Ont.; Dr. Nick Bontis, Ancaster, Ont.; Townsend Haines, Toronto, Ont.
Oper. Subsid./Mgt. Co. Officers - Daniel Lazzer, CFO; David K. Balsdon, chief compliance officer; Paul MacDonald, chief invest. officer & portfolio mgr.

Capital Stock

	Authorized (shs.)	Outstanding (shs.)[1]
Class A Unit	unlimited	655,948
Class F Unit	unlimited	8,100

[1] At Dec. 31, 2022

Class A Unit - Entitled to monthly cash distributions equal to $0.055 per unit (5.5% per annum based on an issue price of $12 per unit). Retractable on the second last business day in September of each year at a price equal to the net asset value (NAV) per class A unit less any costs associated with the retraction. Retractable on the last business day in any other month at a price equal to the lesser of: (i) 95% of the weighted average trading price on the TSX for the 20 trading days immediately preceding the retraction date, and (ii) the closing price per unit. One vote per unit.
Class F Unit - Issued to fee-based and/or institutional accounts. Entitled to same distributions and retraction privileges as class A unitholders, provided that the retraction price is equal to the product of: (i) the class A monthly retraction price, and (ii) a fraction, the numerator of which is the most recently calculated NAV per class F unit and the denominator of which is the most recently calculated NAV per class A unit. Convertible monthly into class A units based on the NAV per class F unit divided by the NAV per class A unit. One vote per unit.
Major Shareholder - Widely held at Mar. 1, 2023.

Price Range - HRR.UN/TSX

Year	Volume	High	Low	Close
2022	78,809	$12.90	$7.52	$8.65
2021	101,789	$12.74	$9.11	$12.74
2020	152,244	$13.35	$5.00	$10.49
2019	566,810	$12.95	$9.70	$12.80
2018	326,096	$11.59	$9.42	$9.73

Recent Close: $8.00
Capital Stock Changes - During 2022, 814 class A units were issued under distribution reinvestment plan and 3,133 class A units and 4,495 class F units were retracted.

Dividends

HRR.UN cl A unit Ra $0.66 pa M est. May 15, 2013**
** Reinvestment Option

Financial Statistics

Periods ended:	12m Dec. 31/22^A		12m Dec. 31/21^A
	$000s	%Chg	$000s
Realized invest. gain (loss)	(97)		332
Unrealized invest. gain (loss)	(2,244)		1,659
Total revenue	**(1,903)**	**n.a.**	**2,442**
General & admin. expense	288		364
Operating expense	**288**	**-21**	**364**
Operating income	**(2,191)**	**n.a.**	**2,078**
Finance costs, gross	96		48
Pre-tax income	**(2,287)**	**n.a.**	**2,030**
Net income	**(2,287)**	**n.a.**	**2,030**
Cash & equivalent	63		19
Accounts receivable	130		115
Investments	8,683		11,372
Total assets	**8,875**	**-24**	**11,712**
Debt	2,694		2,699
Shareholders' equity	6,145		8,940
Cash from oper. activs	**559**	**-43**	**989**
Cash from fin. activs	(514)		(1,093)
Net cash position	**63**	**+232**	**19**
	$		$
Earnings per share*	(3.38)		2.85
Earnings per share**	(5.13)		3.53
Cash flow per share***	0.84		1.39
Net asset value per share*	9.22		13.27
Cash divd. per share*	0.66		0.66
	shs		shs
No. of shs. o/s***	664,048		670,862
Avg. no. of shs. o/s***	668,464		709,890
	%		%
Net profit margin	n.m.		83.13
Return on equity	(30.32)		23.97
Return on assets	(21.29)		18.28

* Cl.A unit
** Cl.F unit
*** Cl.A unit & Cl.F unit
^A Reported in accordance with IFRS

Note: Net income reflects increase/decrease in net assets from operations.

Historical Summary
(as originally stated)

Fiscal Year	Total Rev. $000s	Net Inc. Bef. Disc. $000s	EPS* $
2022^A	(1,903)	(2,287)	(3.38)
2021^A	2,442	2,030	2.85
2020^A	(526)	(952)	(1.18)
2019^A	4,329	3,656	3.17
2018^A	610	(131)	(0.08)

* Cl.A unit
^A Reported in accordance with IFRS

A.153 Australis Capital Inc.

Symbol - AUSA **Exchange** - CSE (S) **CUSIP** - 05259R
Head Office - 376 E. Warm Springs Rd, Suite 190, Las Vegas, NV, United States, 89119 **Telephone** - (702) 817-2214 **Toll-free** - (800) 898-0648
Website - ausa-corp.com
Email - marc.lakmaaker@ausa-corp.com
Investor Relations - Marc Lakmaaker (800) 898-0648
Auditors - BF Borgers CPA PC C.P.A., Lakewood, Colo.
Transfer Agents - Odyssey Trust Company
Profile - (Alta. 2015) Owns cannabis brands and operations in the U.S. Also provides design and engineering services for the cannabis and horticultural sectors worldwide; and offers a dispensary technology platform in North America.

Owns medical and recreational cannabis brands, Tsunami, Provisions, GT Flowers and Mr. Natural, which are marketed in the U.S. The company enters into supply arrangement and partnerships with cannabis producers for the production of products under its brands.

Subsidiary **2750176 Ontario Inc.** (51% owned; dba ALPS) is an engineering consulting firm which specializes in the cannabis and traditional horticultural sectors, including fruits, vegetables, mushrooms and ornamentals. ALPS serves customers around the world, providing standardized, custom turn-key facility designs and a suite of services, including facility design (greenhouses, indoor, hoop house and outdoor facilities), crop consulting, project management, commissioning, operational support and maintenance. ALPS also offers APIS, a computerized compliance and maintenance management system.

In addition, offers Cocoon Platform, a platform-as-a-service solution for cannabis dispensaries in North America which supports order fulfillment, cash management, bankcard acceptance, data analytics, customer loyalty, marketing, privacy and compliance. The platform includes CocoonPod, self-service kiosks deployed in dispensaries which facilitate contactless transactions through its capabilities to accept and manage cash transactions and analyze customer identification; and CocoonRewards, a mobile loyalty application which is under development. The Cocoon Platform integrates with existing Enterprise Resource Planning (ERP) systems.

Common suspended from CSE, Oct. 19, 2022.

Directors - Hanoz Kapadia, chr., Ont.; Terrence (Terry) Booth, CEO, Edmonton, Alta.; Dr. Duke Fu, COO, Nev.; Dr. Jason R. B. Dyck, chief science officer, Sherwood Park, Alta.; John Esteireiro, Ont.; Jillian (Jill) Swainson, Alta.
Other Exec. Officers - Robert Wilson, CFO; Leah S. Bailey, chief bus. devel. officer; Marc Lakmaaker, sr. v-p, commun. & capital markets; Thomas Larssen, pres., ALPS, Inc.

Capital Stock

	Authorized (shs.)	Outstanding (shs.)[1]
Preferred	unlimited	nil
Common	unlimited	349,885,023

[1] At June 14, 2023

Major Shareholder - Terrence (Terry) Booth held 12.5% interest and Thomas Larssen held 11.1% interest at Nov. 2, 2021.

Price Range - AUSA/CSE (S)

Year	Volume	High	Low	Close
2022	63,970,740	$0.17	$0.02	$0.03
2021	132,114,735	$0.78	$0.13	$0.18
2020	71,349,117	$0.39	$0.10	$0.17
2019	129,270,764	$1.46	$0.32	$0.45
2018	87,052,456	$16.00	$0.61	$0.73

Recent Close: $0.03

Capital Stock Changes - In June 2022, private placement of 17,369,317 common shares was completed at $0.095 per share.

In December 2021, private placement 18,428,584 units (1 common share & 1 warrant) at 17¢ per unit was completed, with warrants exercisable at 35¢ per share for two years.

Wholly Owned Subsidiaries

Australis CA LLC, Calif.
Australis Capital (Nevada) Inc., Nev.
Australis Holdings LLP, Bellingham, Wash.
Australis Perennial, LLC, Nev.
Australis Prosper, LLC, Nev.
Australis Terrain, LLC, Nev.
Cocoon Technology, LLC, Nev.
GT Acquisition LLC, Nev.
GT Intellectual Property LLP, Nev.
Rthm Technologies Inc., Toronto, Ont.

Subsidiaries

51% int. in **2750176 Ontario Inc.**, Ont.
- 100% int. in **ALPS B.V.**, Netherlands.
- 100% int. in **ALPS Empco Inc.**, Ont.
- 100% int. in **ALPS (Ontario) Inc.**, Ont.
- 100% int. in **APIS Inc.**, Ont.
- 100% int. in **Larssen GC Ltd.**, Ont.
- 100% int. in **Larssen Ltd.**, Burlington, Ont.

Investments

Body and Mind Inc., Vancouver, B.C. (see separate coverage)
Quality Green Inc., Hamilton, Ont.

Financial Statistics

Periods ended:	12m Mar. 31/21^A		12m Mar. 31/20^A
	$000s	%Chg	$000s
Operating revenue	**717**	**+224**	**221**
Cost of goods sold	746		nil
Salaries & benefits	5,899		4,817
Research & devel. expense	120		nil
General & admin expense	5,828		3,861
Stock-based compensation	1,390		5,339
Operating expense	**13,983**	**0**	**14,017**
Operating income	**(13,266)**	**n.a.**	**(13,796)**
Deprec., depl. & amort.	769		601
Finance income	107		937
Finance costs, gross	125		197
Investment income	(1,162)		(1,126)
Write-downs/write-offs	(7,685)		(1,549)
Pre-tax income	**(25,537)**	**n.a.**	**(23,342)**
Income taxes	(78)		nil
Net income	**(25,459)**	**n.a.**	**(23,342)**
Net inc. for equity hldrs	**(25,261)**	**n.a.**	**(23,342)**
Net inc. for non-cont. int.	**(198)**	**n.a.**	**nil**
Cash & equivalent	3,531		7,647
Inventories	473		nil
Accounts receivable	1,697		381
Current assets	23,842		23,716
Long-term investments	1,130		11,797
Fixed assets, net	298		4,931
Right-of-use assets	1,097		745
Intangibles, net	29,285		15,365
Total assets	**82,455**	**+29**	**63,700**
Accts. pay. & accr. liabs	5,916		2,585
Current liabilities	7,422		3,875
Long-term debt, gross	747		nil
Long-term debt, net	747		nil
Long-term lease liabilities	686		610
Shareholders' equity	61,301		57,766
Non-controlling interest	5,394		nil
Cash from oper. activs	**(9,466)**	**n.a.**	**(8,323)**
Cash from fin. activs	(305)		2,272
Cash from invest. activs	(2,915)		(2,102)
Net cash position	**3,531**	**-78**	**16,333**
Capital expenditures	(1,478)		(705)
Capital disposals	19		nil
	$		$
Earnings per share*	(0.14)		(0.14)
Cash flow per share*	(0.05)		(0.05)
	shs		shs
No. of shs. o/s*	226,044,436		169,943,997
Avg. no. of shs. o/s*	177,116,372		162,361,059
	%		%
Net profit margin	n.m.		n.m.
Return on equity	(42.43)		(39.42)
Return on assets	(34.67)		(35.95)

* Common
^A Reported in accordance with IFRS

Latest Results

Periods ended:	9m Dec. 31/21^A		9m Dec. 31/20^A
	$000s	%Chg	$000s
Operating revenue	6,371	n.m.	258
Net income	(18,691)	n.a.	(28,550)
Net inc. for equity hldrs	(18,366)	n.a.	(28,550)
Net inc. for non-cont. int.	(325)		nil
	$		$
Earnings per share*	(0.08)		(0.17)

* Common
^A Reported in accordance with IFRS

Historical Summary
(as originally stated)

Fiscal Year	Oper. Rev. $000s	Net Inc. Bef. Disc. $000s	EPS* $
2021^A	717	(25,459)	(0.14)
2020^A	221	(23,342)	(0.14)
2019^A	130	(4,171)	(0.04)
2018^A1	nil	(43)	n.a.
2017^A1	nil	(51)	n.a.

* Common
^A Reported in accordance with IFRS
[1] As shown in the prospectus dated Aug. 14, 2018.

A.154 AutoCanada Inc.*

Symbol - ACQ **Exchange** - TSX **CUSIP** - 05277B
Head Office - 200-15511 123 Ave NW, Edmonton, AB, T5V 0C3 **Telephone** - (780) 732-3135 **Toll-free** - (866) 938-0561 **Fax** - (780) 447-0651
Website - www.autocan.ca
Email - alalani@autocan.ca

Investor Relations - Azim Lalani (866) 938-0561
Auditors - PricewaterhouseCoopers LLP C.A., Edmonton, Alta.
Bankers - HSBC Bank Canada
Lawyers - Borden Ladner Gervais LLP
Transfer Agents - Computershare Trust Company of Canada Inc.
FP500 Revenue Ranking - 101
Employees - 6,000 at Dec. 31, 2022
Profile - (Can. 2009) Operates 83 franchised automotive dealerships in eight Canadian provinces and Illinois.

The company sells Chrysler, Dodge, Jeep, Ram, Fiat, Alfa Romeo, Chevrolet, GMC, Buick, Cadillac, Ford, Hyundai, Kia, Nissan, Infiniti, Volkswagen, Audi, Subaru, Mazda, Mercedes-Benz, BMW, MINI, Porsche, Volvo, Toyota, Lincoln, Acura and Honda branded vehicles. The dealerships offer new and used vehicles, vehicle leasing, vehicle parts, vehicle maintenance and collision repair services, extended service contracts, vehicle protection products, after-market products and auction services. Also arranges financing and insurance for vehicles purchased by its customers through third party finance and insurance sources in exchange for a fee from lenders.

During 2022, dealerships sold 101,719 vehicles and processed 989,006 service and collision repair orders in its 1,367 service bays.

Geographic breakdown of automobile dealerships and collision centres at Dec. 31, 2022:

Location	Dealerships/collision centres[1]
British Columbia	10
Alberta	20
Saskatchewan	5
Manitoba	6
Ontario	27
Quebec	6
New Brunswick	1
Nova Scotia	1
Illinois	10

[1] Includes dealerships that operate under the company's Used Digital Retail division. The company's interest in the dealerships are held by **AutoCanada UD LP**, in which a wholly owned subsidiary of the company is a general partner.

Canadian operations include 11 RightRide used vehicle locations in British Columbia (1), Alberta (3), Saskatchewan (1), Manitoba (1), Ontario (4) and New Brunswick (1) and 25 collision centres, including 10 stand-alone centres.

In November 2022, the company acquired the remaining 5% interest in **156023 Canada Inc.** (dba Planète Mazda) for $433,000.

Recent Merger and Acquisition Activity

Status: completed **Announced:** May 1, 2023
AutoCanada Inc. acquired London Auto Collision Limited, which operates a collision centre in London, Ont. Terms of the transaction were not disclosed. The collision centre generate more than $5,000,000 in annual revenue.

Status: completed **Announced:** Apr. 18, 2023
AutoCanada Inc. acquired Premier Chevrolet Cadillac Buick GMC, a new and used vehicle Chevrolet Cadillac Buick dealership and collision centre in Windsor, Ont. Terms of the transaction were not disclosed. The dealership, including the collision centre, generate more than $70,000,000 in annual revenue.

Status: completed **Announced:** Feb. 23, 2023
AutoCanada Inc. acquired private Calgary, Alta.-based 5121175 Manitoba Ltd. (dba DCCHail), which provides paintless dent repair services throughout Canada. Terms were not disclosed. DCCHail generates in excess of $15,000,000 in annual revenue.

Status: completed **Announced:** Dec. 1, 2022
AutoCanada Inc. acquired Sterling Honda automobile dealership in Hamilton, Ont. Terms of the transaction were not disclosed; the consideration would be funded from a drawdown of AutoCanada's credit facility. The dealership generates more than $65,000,000 in annual revenue.

Status: completed **Announced:** Nov. 4, 2022
AutoCanada Inc. acquired Excellence Auto Collision Limited, which operates two luxury collision centres in Scarborough and Toronto, Ont., Excellence Auto Collision Silver Star and Excellence Auto Collision Midwest. Terms were not disclosed. The two collision centres generate in excess of $10,000,000 in annual revenue.

Status: completed **Announced:** Oct. 27, 2022
AutoCanada Inc. acquired private KAVIA Auto Body, Inc. for an undisclosed amount. KAVIA provides auto-body repair services, including collision repair, automotive refinishing, frame straightening, automotive glass replacement and auto detailing for imported and domestic vehicles in Saskatchewan. KAVIA generates in excess of $5,500,000 in annual revenue.

Status: completed **Announced:** Sept. 28, 2022
AutoCanada Inc. acquired Northern Auto Auctions of Canada Inc. (North Toronto Auction, [NTA]), a fee-based used vehicle auction business, serving dealers and consumers alike, located in Innisfil, Ont. Terms were not disclosed. NTA generates in excess of $4,500,000 in annual revenue and would operate within AutoCanada's Used Digital Retail division.

Status: completed **Announced:** Sept. 22, 2022
AutoCanada Inc. acquired Auto Gallery of Winnipeg Inc., an independent used vehicle dealership in Winnipeg, Man. Terms were not disclosed. The acquired dealership generates more than $15,000,000 in annual revenue.

Status: completed **Announced:** Aug. 12, 2022
AutoCanada Inc. acquired Velocity Auto Body Inc., a Tesla certified, I-CAR Gold Class collision centre in Markham, Ont. Terms of the transaction were not disclosed. Velocity operates a 12,000-sq.-ft. facility with more than 25 production bays.

Status: completed **Announced:** Aug. 2, 2022
AutoCanada Inc. acquired Kelleher Ford, a new and used Ford dealership and collision centre in Brandon, Man., for an undisclosed amount. The transaction would be funded from a drawdown of AutoCanada's credit facility. Kelleher Ford had been operating for more than 25 years with facilities of more than 35,000 sq. ft. on seven acres. The acquired dealership, including the collision centre, generated more than $50,000,000 in annual revenue.

Status: completed **Announced:** June 30, 2022
AutoCanada Inc. acquired Burwell Auto Body Limited, which operates a luxury-brand focused collision centre in London, Ont. Terms of the transaction were not disclosed. Burwell Auto Body, which operates out of a 20,000-sq.-ft. facility, was a certified BMW, Audi, Tesla, Volvo, Porsche and Subaru collision centre.

Status: completed **Announced:** May 2, 2022
AutoCanada Inc. acquired two dealerships in Ontario, Porsche of London and Audi Windsor. Terms were not disclosed. The acquired dealerships generate in excess of $80,000,000 in annual revenue.

Directors - Paul W. Antony, exec. chr., London, Ont.; Stephen Green†, N.Y.; Dennis S. DesRosiers, Toronto, Ont.; Rhonda English, Ont.; Barry L. James, Edmonton, Alta.; Joseph L. (Lee) Matheson, Toronto, Ont.; Elias Olmeta, San Diego, Calif.

Other Exec. Officers - Azim Lalani, CFO; Peter Hong, chief strategy officer & gen. counsel; Brian Feldman, sr. v-p, opers. & disruptive technologies; Lee Wittick, sr. v-p, opers. & OEM rel.; Casey Charleson, v-p, fin.; Arthur Crawford, v-p, collision centres; Derrick Edmunds, v-p, domestic platform; Darnelle Funk, v-p, software devel.; Andrew Gowan, v-p, used vehicle strategy & acq.; Patrycja Kujawa, v-p, info. mgt.; Jennifer Lennox, v-p, people & culture; Jonathan Parker, v-p, special fin.; David Pestrak, v-p, acq. opers.; Mikel Pestrak, v-p, fin. & insce.; Robert Smoczynski, v-p, imports OEM platform; Jeffrey (Jeff) Thorpe, pres., Cdn. opers.

† Lead director

Capital Stock

	Authorized (shs.)	Outstanding (shs.)[1]
Preferred	unlimited	nil
Common	unlimited	23,551,137

[1] At May 3, 2023

Options - At Dec. 31, 2022, options were outstanding to purchase 1,996,544 common shares at an average exercise price of $13.47 per share with a weighted average remaining contractual life of 5.19 years.

Normal Course Issuer Bid - The company plans to make normal course purchases of up to 1,350,048 common shares representing 10% of the public float. The bid commenced on Dec. 28, 2022, and expires on Dec. 27, 2023.

Major Shareholder - EdgePoint Investment Group Inc. held 27% interest and BloombergSen Inc. held 12.05% interest at Mar. 20, 2023.

Price Range - ACQ/TSX

Year	Volume	High	Low	Close
2022	26,012,230	$43.03	$20.76	$23.31
2021	41,256,247	$59.26	$22.62	$42.70
2020	45,936,939	$30.65	$4.60	$23.61
2019	28,429,434	$14.32	$7.33	$12.39
2018	50,786,164	$23.86	$8.36	$11.35

Recent Close: $24.88

Capital Stock Changes - During 2022, common shares were issued as follows: 800,000 on exercise of options and 194,639 for settlement of treasury shares; 3,011,558 common shares were repurchased under a Substantial Issuer Bid and 1,730,321 common shares were repurchased under a Normal Course Issuer Bid.

Long-Term Debt - Outstanding at Dec. 31, 2022:

Credit facility due 2025[1]	$180,000,000
Non-recourse mtges.[2]	31,979,000
5.75% sr. notes due 2029	350,000,000
Other long-term debt	136,000
Less: Unamortized def. fin. costs	6,987,000
	555,128,000
Less: Current portion	777,000
	554,351,000

[1] Bearing interest at prime rate or U.S. base rate plus 0.75% or at the banker's acceptance rate or LIBOR plus 1.75% for the $275,000,000 revolving facility; bearing interest at CDOR plus 1.75% for the $15,000,000 wholesale leasing facilities; bear interest rates of CDOR plus 1% for the $1.06 billion wholesale floorplan facilities except for the facility for floorplan of used export vehicles which bears interest rates of CDOR plus 1.25%.

[2] Consist of a mortgage bearing interest at prime rate plus 1.5% due 2025; and two mortgages bearing interest at 7.07% due 2027.

Note - In February 2023, the credit facility was amended whereby the maturity date was extended to Apr. 14, 2026. In addition, the revolving facility was increased from $275,000,000 to $375,000,000 and the wholesale floorplan facility was increased from $1.06 billion to $1.22 billion.

Wholly Owned Subsidiaries

AutoCanada Holdings Inc., Canada.

Note: The preceding list includes only the major related companies in which interests are held.

Financial Statistics

Periods ended:	12m Dec. 31/22[A]		12m Dec. 31/21[A]
	$000s	%Chg	$000s
Operating revenue	**6,040,619**	**+30**	**4,653,415**
Cost of sales	4,997,746		3,819,232
Salaries & benefits	514,714		385,576
General & admin expense	238,496		179,772
Stock-based compensation	5,801		3,569
Operating expense	**5,756,757**	**+31**	**4,388,149**
Operating income	**283,862**	**+7**	**265,266**
Deprec., depl. & amort.	52,007		43,692
Finance income	4,144		810
Finance costs, gross	131,478		35,189
Write-downs/write-offs	8,691		39,846
Pre-tax income	**123,884**	**-44**	**221,220**
Income taxes	32,824		54,021
Net income	**91,060**	**-46**	**167,199**
Net inc. for equity hldrs	**85,436**	**-48**	**164,207**
Net inc. for non-cont. int.	**5,624**	**+88**	**2,992**
Cash & equivalent	108,301		102,480
Inventories	979,540		737,299
Accounts receivable	217,790		132,913
Current assets	1,315,773		982,264
Fixed assets, net	345,592		248,109
Right-of-use assets	396,369		370,998
Intangibles, net	737,345		599,210
Total assets	**2,858,331**	**+27**	**2,258,673**
Bank indebtedness	992,254		708,561
Accts. pay. & accr. liabs.	229,696		189,731
Current liabilities	1,297,279		953,437
Long-term debt, gross	555,128		285,908
Long-term debt, net	554,351		285,908
Long-term lease liabilities	457,111		427,215
Shareholders' equity	457,899		493,411
Non-controlling interest	28,898		25,998
Cash from oper. activs.	**147,974**	**+31**	**112,942**
Cash from fin. activs.	82,837		97,003
Cash from invest. activs.	(228,024)		(215,374)
Net cash position	**108,301**	**+6**	**102,480**
Capital expenditures	(52,667)		(34,576)
Capital disposals	123		2,399
	$		$
Earnings per share*	3.28		5.98
Cash flow per share*	5.68		4.11
	shs		shs
No. of shs. o/s*	23,502,470		27,249,710
Avg. no. of shs. o/s*	26,050,206		27,474,106
	%		%
Net profit margin	1.51		3.59
Return on equity	17.96		39.32
Return on assets	7.34		9.32
Foreign sales percent	15		15
No. of employees (FTEs)	6,000		5,400

* Common
[A] Reported in accordance with IFRS

Latest Results

Periods ended:	6m June 30/23[A]		6m June 30/22[A]
	$000s	%Chg	$000s
Operating revenue	3,295,588	+9	3,028,464
Net income	53,612	+24	43,380
Net inc. for equity hldrs	50,369	+25	40,165
Net inc. for non-cont. int.	3,243		3,215
	$		$
Earnings per share*	2.14		1.50

* Common
[A] Reported in accordance with IFRS

Historical Summary
(as originally stated)

Fiscal Year	Oper. Rev.	Net Inc. Bef. Disc.	EPS*
	$000s	$000s	$
2022[A]	6,040,619	91,060	3.28
2021[A]	4,653,415	167,199	5.98
2020[A]	3,329,494	(6,623)	(0.27)
2019[A]	3,476,111	(27,073)	(1.03)
2018[A]	3,150,781	(77,428)	(2.85)

* Common
[A] Reported in accordance with IFRS

A.155 Automotive Finco Corp.

Symbol - AFCC.H **Exchange** - TSX-VEN **CUSIP** - 05329N
Head Office - 3000-222 Bay St, Toronto, ON, M5K 1E7 **Telephone** - (647) 351-2886 **Fax** - (647) 351-2880
Website - www.autofincocorp.com
Email - kbillan@autofincocorp.com
Investor Relations - Kuldeep Billan (647) 351-8870
Auditors - Raymond Chabot Grant Thornton LLP C.A., Val-d'Or, Qué.
Lawyers - Norton Rose Fulbright Canada LLP, Toronto, Ont.

Transfer Agents - Computershare Trust Company of Canada Inc., Montréal, Qué.

Profile - (Can. 1986) Provides debt financing and makes other investments, including some with royalty-like features, in connection with the financing of automotive dealerships, automotive dealer groups and/or other related businesses and assets globally, with an initial focus in Canada. Also has a mineral interest in Quebec.

The company makes its investments as the sole limited partner of subsidiary **Automotive Finance Limited Partnership**, which has entered into an alliance agreement with **AA Finance Co LP** (AAFC), a member of a privately held group involved in the acquisition, ownership and operation of automotive dealerships. AAFC would provide the partnership with a right of first offer (ROFO) on certain debt financing opportunities undertaken by affiliates of AAFC for acquisitions and/or recapitalizations of automobile retailers and/or auto dealership groups.

Also holds 32% interest in Duncan Lake iron prospect, James Bay area, Que., carried at nominal value. The company considers the interest to be immaterial.

Predecessor Detail - Name changed from Augyva Mining Resources Inc., Mar. 8, 2017, pursuant to change of business from mineral exploration to automotive dealership financing; basis 1 new for 15 old shs.

Directors - Farhad Abasov, chr., Dubai, United Arab Emirates; Kuldeep Billan, CEO, Toronto, Ont.; Curtis Johansson, Vancouver, B.C.

Oper. Subsid./Mgt. Co. Officers - Shannon C. Penney, CFO; André Lacroix, corp. sec.

Capital Stock

	Authorized (shs.)	Outstanding (shs.)[1]
Common	unlimited	19,819,377

[1] At May 30, 2023

Major Shareholder - Kuldeep Billan held 21.86% interest and Eastwood Capital Corp. held 19.58% interest at May 23, 2023.

Price Range - AFCC.H/TSX-VEN

Year	Volume	High	Low	Close
2022	1,866,390	$2.05	$1.38	$1.54
2021	3,461,126	$2.25	$1.49	$2.04
2020	2,458,254	$1.74	$0.50	$1.53
2019	6,511,582	$1.90	$1.25	$1.74
2018	2,735,151	$2.34	$1.31	$1.31

Recent Close: $0.62

Capital Stock Changes - There were no changes to capital stock during 2022.

Dividends

AFCC.H com Ra $0.2052 pa M est. July 31, 2017

Wholly Owned Subsidiaries

Automotive Finance Limited Partnership, Ont.

Financial Statistics

Periods ended:	12m Dec. 31/22[A]		12m Dec. 31/21[A]
	$000s	%Chg	$000s
Operating revenue	**304**	**n.a.**	**nil**
General & admin expense	921		1,129
Stock-based compensation	(15)		15
Operating expense	**906**	**-21**	**1,145**
Operating income	**(602)**	**n.a.**	**(1,145)**
Pre-tax income	**(602)**	**n.a.**	**(1,145)**
Net income	**(602)**	**n.a.**	**(1,145)**
Cash & equivalent	1,770		27,807
Accounts receivable	304		nil
Current assets	23,131		27,823
Total assets	**23,131**	**-17**	**27,823**
Accts. pay. & accr. liabs	397		420
Current liabilities	397		420
Shareholders' equity	22,734		27,403
Cash from oper. activs	**(970)**	**n.a.**	**(473)**
Cash from fin. activs	(4,067)		(9,689)
Cash from invest. activs	(21,000)		nil
Net cash position	**1,770**	**-94**	**27,807**
	$		$
Earnings per share*	(0.03)		(0.06)
Cash flow per share*	(0.05)		(0.02)
Cash divd. per share*	0.21		0.21
	shs		shs
No. of shs. o/s*	19,819,377		19,819,377
Avg. no. of shs. o/s*	19,819,377		20,588,894
	%		%
Net profit margin	(198.03)		n.a.
Return on equity	(2.40)		(3.49)
Return on assets	(2.36)		(3.44)

* Common

[A] Reported in accordance with IFRS

Latest Results

Periods ended:	3m Mar. 31/23[A]		3m Mar. 31/22[A]
	$000s	%Chg	$000s
Operating revenue	625	n.a.	nil
Net income	387	n.a.	(243)
	$		$
Earnings per share*	0.02		(0.01)

* Common

[A] Reported in accordance with IFRS

Historical Summary
(as originally stated)

Fiscal Year	Oper. Rev.	Net Inc. Bef. Disc.	EPS*
	$000s	$000s	$
2022[A]	304	(602)	(0.03)
2021[A]	nil	(1,145)	(0.06)
2020[A]	nil	(903)	(0.04)
2019[A]	4,683	(62)	(0.01)
2018[A]	8,015	3,488	0.15

* Common

[A] Reported in accordance with IFRS

A.156 Automotive Properties Real Estate Investment Trust

Symbol - APR.UN **Exchange** - TSX **CUSIP** - 05329M

Head Office - 300-133 King St E, Toronto, ON, M5C 1G6 **Telephone** - (647) 789-2440

Website - www.automotivepropertiesreit.ca

Email - akalra@automotivereit.ca

Investor Relations - Andrew A. Kalra (647) 789-2436

Auditors - BDO Canada LLP C.A., Toronto, Ont.

Lawyers - Torys LLP, Toronto, Ont.

Transfer Agents - Computershare Trust Company of Canada Inc., Toronto, Ont.

FP500 Revenue Ranking - 791

Profile - (Ont. 2015) Owns and acquires primarily income-producing automotive dealership properties across Canada.

At Mar. 16, 2023, the trust's portfolio consisted of 76 properties, totaling 2,821,724 sq. ft. of gross leasable area (GLA), within the major metropolitan centres of six provinces in Canada.

Property portfolio at Mar. 16, 2023:

Location	Props.	GLA (Sq. Ft.)
British Columbia	8	199,244
Alberta	13	467,508
Saskatchewan	9	203,560
Manitoba	2	96,135
Ontario	27	1,058,889
Quebec	17	796,388
	76	2,821,724

Of the 76 properties, 37 are exclusively occupied by the Dilawri Group of Companies for use as automotive dealerships or, in one case, an automotive repair facility, one is jointly occupied by the Dilawri Group and third parties for use as automotive dealerships or complementary uses, including restaurants, and the remaining 38 are exclusively occupied by other dealership groups for use as automotive dealerships or for automotive dealership ancillary services, such as a vehicle service compound facility or a repair facility. Dilawri Group is the largest automotive dealership group in Canada and represents 32 automotive brands.

Recent Merger and Acquisition Activity

Status: completed **Announced:** June 2, 2023
Automotive Properties Real Estate Investment Trust (50%) and StorageVault Canada Inc. (50%) jointly acquired a 50,415-sq.-ft. automotive dealership property located at 9425 Taschereau Boulevard in Brossard, Que., for $16,100,000 (each having funded 50% of the acquisition price). StorageVault owned a self-storage property adjacent to the dealership.

Status: completed **Revised:** Jan. 4, 2023
UPDATE: The transaction was completed. PREVIOUS: Automotive Properties Real Estate Investment Trust agreed to acquire six automotive dealership properties in Laval (3), Sorel-Tracy (2) and St. Eustache (1), Que., totaling 187,421 sq. ft. of gross leasable area, for $98,500,000, which would be funded through the increase to one of the REIT's credit facilities, draws on revolving credit facilities and cash on hand.

Status: completed **Revised:** Nov. 30, 2022
UPDATE: The transaction was completed. PREVIOUS: Automotive Properties Real Estate Investment Trust agreed to sell the Kingston Toyota and Lexus of Kingston automotive dealership properties in Kingston, Ont., totaling 41,356 sq. ft. of gross leasable area, for $18,000,000.

Trustees - Kapil (Kap) Dilawri, chr., Toronto, Ont.; Milton Lamb, pres. & CEO, Ont.; John R. Morrison‡, Toronto, Ont.; Patricia Kay, Boston, Mass.; Stuart Lazier, Ont.; James Matthews, Ont.; Julie Morin, Ottawa, Ont.

Other Exec. Officers - Andrew A. Kalra, CFO & corp. sec.

‡ Lead trustee

Capital Stock

	Authorized (shs.)	Outstanding (shs.)[1]
Trust Unit	unlimited	39,727,346
Special Voting Unit	unlimited	9,327,487
Class B LP Unit		9,327,487[2 3]

[1] At Apr. 13, 2023

[2] Classified as debt.

[3] Securities of Automotive Properties Limited Partnership.

Trust Unit - One vote per unit.

Special Voting Unit - Issued to holders of class B limited partnership units of subsidiary Automotive Properties Limited Partnership. Each special voting unit entitles the holder to a number of votes at unitholder meetings equal to the number of trust units into which the class B limited partnership units are exchangeable.

Class B Limited Partnership Unit - Entitled to distributions equal to those provided to trust units. Directly exchangeable into trust units on a 1-for-1 basis at any time by holder. All held by the Dilawri Group of Companies. Classified as debt.

Major Shareholder - Dilawri Group of Companies held 32.1% interest and TWC Enterprises Limited held 19.3% interest at Apr. 13, 2023.

Price Range - APR.UN/TSX

Year	Volume	High	Low	Close
2022	12,543,848	$15.09	$11.14	$12.97
2021	11,696,112	$14.97	$10.56	$14.95
2020	25,690,450	$12.89	$5.30	$10.71
2019	20,058,516	$12.77	$8.79	$12.15
2018	8,704,563	$11.47	$8.45	$8.97

Recent Close: $10.95

Capital Stock Changes - During 2022, trust units were issued as follows: 605,766 on exchange of a like number of class B limited partnership units and 41,426 on vesting of deferred units and income deferred units

Dividends

APR.UN unit Ra $0.80 pa M est. Jan. 16, 2023
Prev. Rate: $0.804 est. Aug. 16, 2021
Prev. Rate: $0.80 est. Sept. 15, 2015

Wholly Owned Subsidiaries

Automotive Properties REIT GP Inc., Ont.

Subsidiaries

71.2% int. in **Automotive Properties Limited Partnership**, Toronto, Ont.

Financial Statistics

Periods ended:	12m Dec. 31/22[A]		12m Dec. 31/21[A]
	$000s	%Chg	$000s
Total revenue	**82,861**	**+6**	**78,218**
Rental operating expense	12,286		11,414
General & admin. expense	4,865		4,490
Operating expense	**17,151**	**+8**	**15,904**
Operating income	**65,710**	**+5**	**62,314**
Deprec. & amort.	696		183
Finance costs, gross	25,578		23,568
Write-downs/write-offs	nil		277
Pre-tax income	**83,365**	**-2**	**85,418**
Net income	**83,365**	**-2**	**85,418**
Cash & equivalent	396		474
Fixed assets	3,275		5,886
Income-producing props	1,068,033		1,019,321
Property interests, net	1,071,308		1,025,207
Right-of-use assets	191		90
Total assets	**1,093,818**	**+4**	**1,051,650**
Accts. pay. & accr. liabs	4,134		3,152
Long-term debt, gross	552,053		562,485
Long-term lease liabilities	3,820		6,602
Shareholders' equity	520,944		460,371
Cash from oper. activs	**64,547**	**+4**	**62,212**
Cash from fin. activs	(39,885)		(37,178)
Cash from invest. activs	(24,740)		(24,868)
Net cash position	**396**	**-16**	**474**
Increase in property	(42,692)		(423)
Decrease in property	17,952		nil
	$		$
Earnings per share*	n.a.		n.a.
Cash flow per share*	1.62		1.59
Funds from opers. per sh.*	0.95		0.95
Adj. funds from opers. per sh.*	0.91		0.90
Cash divd. per share*	0.80		0.80
Total divd. per share*	**0.80**		**0.80**
	shs		shs
No. of shs. o/s*	39,727,346		39,080,154
	%		%
Net profit margin	100.61		109.21
Return on equity	16.99		20.06
Return on assets	10.16		10.96

* Trust unit

[A] Reported in accordance with IFRS

Historical Summary
(as originally stated)

Fiscal Year	Total Rev.	Net Inc. Bef. Disc.	EPS*
	$000s	$000s	$
2022A	82,861	83,365	n.a.
2021A	78,218	85,418	n.a.
2020A	75,124	26,965	n.a.
2019A	67,580	(4,499)	n.a.
2018A	48,254	39,150	n.a.

* Trust unit
A Reported in accordance with IFRS

A.157 Auxly Cannabis Group Inc.

Symbol - XLY **Exchange** - TSX **CUSIP** - 05335P
Head Office - Unit 002, 777 Richmond St W, Toronto, ON, M6J 0C2 **Telephone** - (647) 812-0121 **Toll-free** - (833) 695-2414 **Fax** - (647) 812-0120
Website - www.auxly.com
Email - jcannon@auxly.com
Investor Relations - Julie Cannon (833) 695-2414
Auditors - Ernst & Young LLP C.A., Toronto, Ont.
Lawyers - McCarthy Tétrault LLP, Toronto, Ont.
Transfer Agents - Computershare Trust Company of Canada Inc., Vancouver, B.C.
FP500 Revenue Ranking - 779
Employees - 420 at Dec. 31, 2022
Profile - (Ont. 2021; orig. B.C., 1987) Cultivates, manufactures and distributes cannabis products in Canada.

Products are sold under the brands Kolab Project, Foray, Dosecann, Back Forty and Parcel and distributed across Canada, except Quebec, through provincial agencies, medical cannabis sales channels and licensed cannabis retailers. Cultivation, research and development (R&D), and manufacturing operations include a 52,000-sq.-ft. facility in Charlottetown, P.E.I., with R&D, product formulation, testing and manufacturing activities; and a 1,100,000-sq.-ft. greenhouse and processing facility in Leamington, Ont., 876,000 sq. ft. of which is operational and used for cultivation, processing and manufacturing.

On May 30, 2023, the company transitioned the operations of its facility in Carleton Place, Ont., to its facility in Leamington, Ont. Wholly owned **Auxly Ottawa Inc.** owned and operated the 10,000-sq.-ft. facility in Carleton Place, which ceased cultivation in 2020 and shifted focus to the manufacturing, processing and distribution of dried flower and pre-roll cannabis products. The company intends to sell Auxly Ottawa's facility.

In February 2022, the company closed its 27,700-sq.-ft. indoor cultivation facility in Kentville, N.S., which was owned and operated by wholly owned **Auxly Annapolis Inc.**, and its outdoor cultivation project in Hortonville, N.S., which consisted of over 158 acres of land owned by wholly owned **Auxly Annapolis OG Inc.** The company never commenced outdoor cultivation activities at the Auxly Annapolis OG facility, and the facility was used for additional storage and processing capacity.

In July and August 2022, the Auxly Annapolis and Auxly Annapolis OG facilities were sold to private purchasers for $6,000,000 and $4,150,000, respectively.

Recent Merger and Acquisition Activity

Status: completed **Announced:** July 5, 2022
Auxly Cannabis Group Inc. sold its 27,700-sq.-ft. indoor cultivation facility in Kentville, N.S., which was owned and operated by wholly owned Auxly Annapolis Inc., for $6,000,000. The facility ceased operations in February 2022.

Predecessor Detail - Name changed from Cannabis Wheaton Income Corp., June 8, 2018.
Directors - Hugo M. Alves, co-founder & CEO, Toronto, Ont.; Genevieve Young, chr., Ottawa, Ont.; Vikram Bawa, Mississauga, Ont.; Troy J. Grant, Bedford, N.S.; Conrad Tate, Bristol, Gloucs., United Kingdom
Other Exec. Officers - Michael (Mike) Lickver, pres.; Travis Wong, interim CFO; Ian Rapsey, chief creative officer; Vladimir Klacar, sr. v-p, regulatory affairs & planning; Andrew B. MacMillan, sr. v-p, comml.; Carla Nawrocki, sr. v-p, corp. devel. & strategy; Ronald (Ron) Fichter, gen. counsel & corp. sec.

Capital Stock

	Authorized (shs.)	Outstanding (shs.)[1]
Common	unlimited	1,002,014,308

[1] At Aug. 11, 2023

Major Shareholder - Widely held at May 19, 2023.

Price Range - XLY/TSX

Year	Volume	High	Low	Close
2022	299,216,922	$0.20	$0.02	$0.02
2021	379,951,451	$0.51	$0.18	$0.19
2020	350,712,844	$0.76	$0.12	$0.26
2019	268,505,689	$1.08	$0.52	$0.54
2018	848,384,826	$2.97	$0.60	$0.91

Recent Close: $0.02
Capital Stock Changes - In February 2023, private placement of 96,000,000 units (1 common share & 1 warrant) at $0.035 per unit was completed, with warrants exercisable at $0.045 per share for five years.

During 2022, common shares were issued as follows: 57,928,500 under an at-the-market offering and 4,347,826 as convertible debenture amendment fee.

Wholly Owned Subsidiaries

Auxly Annapolis Inc., Kentville, N.S. Formerly Robinson's Cannabis Incorporated.
Auxly Annapolis OG Inc., N.S. Formerly Robinson's Outdoor Grow Incorporated.
Auxly Charlottetown Inc., Stoney Creek, Ont. Formerly Dosecann LD Inc.
Auxly Leamington Inc., Leamington, Ont. Formerly Sunens Farms Inc.
Auxly Ottawa Inc., Carleton Place, Ont. Formerly Kolab Project Inc.

Subsidiaries

80% int. in **Inverell S.A.**, Montevideo, Uruguay.

Investments

Herbal Dispatch Inc., Vancouver, B.C. (see separate coverage)
MediPharm Labs Corp., Barrie, Ont. (see separate coverage)
Wellbeing Digital Sciences Inc., Vancouver, B.C.
Note: The preceding list includes only the major related companies in which interests are held.

Financial Statistics

Periods ended:	12m Dec. 31/22A		12m Dec. 31/21oA
	$000s	%Chg	$000s
Operating revenue	**94,472**	**+13**	**83,829**
Cost of sales	77,960		64,539
Salaries & benefits	18,665		17,828
General & admin expense	27,984		26,460
Stock-based compensation	4,023		1,433
Operating expense	**128,632**	**+17**	**110,260**
Operating income	**(34,160)**	**n.a.**	**(26,431)**
Deprec., depl. & amort.	14,816		12,507
Finance income	337		1,597
Finance costs, gross	21,578		17,668
Investment income	nil		(4,661)
Write-downs/write-offs	(67,180)[1]		(11,426)
Pre-tax income	**(136,555)**	**n.a.**	**(50,240)**
Income taxes	(6,262)		(4,330)
Net inc. bef. disc. opers	**(130,293)**	**n.a.**	**(45,910)**
Income from disc. opers	nil		12,156
Net income	**(130,293)**	**n.a.**	**(33,754)**
Net inc. for equity hldrs	**(130,293)**	**n.a.**	**(33,739)**
Net inc. for non-cont. int	**nil**	**n.a.**	**(15)**
Cash & equivalent	14,779		14,894
Inventories	46,953		52,378
Accounts receivable	17,533		31,209
Current assets	89,903		118,543
Long-term investments	1,090		3,897
Fixed assets, net	195,274		226,476
Intangibles, net	45,466		98,493
Total assets	**331,820**	**-26**	**450,422**
Accts. pay. & accr. liabs	33,046		30,569
Current liabilities	92,685		52,854
Long-term debt, gross	174,475		168,809
Long-term debt, net	119,801		151,362
Long-term lease liabilities	14,866		17,252
Equity portion of conv. debs	34,306		35,170
Shareholders' equity	90,406		212,520
Non-controlling interest	(4,719)		(4,407)
Cash from oper. activs	**(2,481)**	**n.a.**	**(49,758)**
Cash from fin. activs	1,184		26,529
Cash from invest. activs	1,179		17,326
Net cash position	**14,636**	**-1**	**14,754**
Capital expenditures	(9,192)		(378)
Capital disposals	10,300		nil
	$		$
Earns. per sh. bef disc opers*	(0.15)		(0.06)
Earnings per share*	(0.15)		(0.04)
Cash flow per share*	(0.00)		(0.06)
	shs		shs
No. of shs. o/s*	906,014,308		843,737,982
Avg. no. of shs. o/s*	889,871,187		783,379,798
	%		%
Net profit margin	(137.92)		(54.77)
Return on equity	(86.02)		(22.47)
Return on assets	(28.05)		(7.18)
No. of employees (FTEs)	420		558

* Common
o Restated
A Reported in accordance with IFRS
1 Includes impairment of $19,059,000 on property, plant and equipment and $23,413,000 on intangible assets, as well as $25,398,000 full impairment of goodwill.

Latest Results

Periods ended:	6m June 30/23A		6m June 30/22A
	$000s	%Chg	$000s
Operating revenue	45,958	-8	49,961
Net income	(23,112)	n.a.	(54,135)
	$		$
Earnings per share*	(0.02)		(0.06)

* Common
A Reported in accordance with IFRS

Historical Summary
(as originally stated)

Fiscal Year	Oper. Rev.	Net Inc. Bef. Disc.	EPS*
	$000s	$000s	$
2022A	94,472	(130,293)	(0.15)
2021A	83,829	(45,910)	(0.06)
2020A	50,796	(87,431)	(0.14)
2019A	8,352	(108,618)	(0.17)
2018A	747	(67,209)	(0.14)

* Common
A Reported in accordance with IFRS

A.158 Avant Brands Inc.

Symbol - AVNT **Exchange** - TSX **CUSIP** - 05353D
Head Office - 335-1632 Dickson Ave, Kelowna, BC, V1Y 7T2 **Telephone** - (778) 760-8338 **Toll-free** - (800) 351-6358
Website - avantbrands.ca
Email - miguel@avantbrands.ca
Investor Relations - Miguel Martinez (778) 760-8338
Auditors - Ernst & Young LLP C.A., Vancouver, B.C.
Transfer Agents - Computershare Trust Company of Canada Inc., Vancouver, B.C.
Employees - 220 at Feb. 27, 2023
Profile - (B.C. 2017; orig. Can., 2012) Produces and distributes cannabis products across Canada.

Owns and operates indoor cultivation and processing facilities consisting of a 14,000-sq.-ft. facility in Edmonton, Alta; a 15,000-sq.-ft. facility in Tiverton (Kincardine), Ont.; a 10,000-sq.-ft. facility in Chase, B.C.; a 60,000-sq.-ft. facility in Vernon, B.C. and a 80,000-sq.-ft. facility in Kelowna, B.C.

Also has a 20,000-sq.-ft. facility (GreenTec) under construction in Kelowna, B.C., which was intended to serve as the company's flagship cultivation facility. The company has resumed the build-out of facility in preparation for future demand after its construction had been previously suspended.

Products are marketed and sold under the BLK MKT™, Tenzo™, Cognoscente™ and Treehugger™ recreational cannabis brands, which are distributed through supply agreements in British Columbia, Ontario, Saskatchewan, Manitoba, Quebec, Alberta, New Brunswick, Yukon, Newfoundland and Labrador, and Prince Edward Island; Pristine™, which provides a variety of quality cannabis seeds; and the GreenTec™ medical cannabis brand, which is distributed across Canada through the company's online medical cannabis platform and through other licensed producers.

In March 2023, the company, through wholly owned **GreenTec Holdings Ltd.**, acquired the remaining 50% interest in **Avant Brands K1 Inc.** for $4,560,000 consisting of $1,450,000 12% promissory note due Aug. 13, 2023, and the issuance of 18,137,780 common shares.

Recent Merger and Acquisition Activity

Status: completed **Revised:** Feb. 3, 2023
UPDATE: The transaction was completed for $5,115,000 satisfied by $3,850,000 in cash, issuance of 7,402,186 common shares valued at $1,265,000 plus the amount of the closing DIP loan and the assumed liabilities. DIP debt was $2,500,000 at Jan. 31, 2023. PREVIOUS: The Flowr Corporation agreed to sell its 91.5% interest in The Flowr Group (Okanagan) Inc. (Flowr Okanagan) to Avant Brands K1 Inc., a 50%-owned subsidiary of Avant Brands Inc. for total consideration of $5,115,000 plus the amount of the closing debtor-in-possession (DIP) loan and the assumed liabilities. Flowr Okanagan has an 85,000-sq.-ft. indoor cultivation and production facility in Kelowna, B.C.

Status: completed **Revised:** Feb. 3, 2023
UPDATE: The transaction was completed. Consideration included the issuance of 22,249,734 common shares. PREVIOUS: Avant Brands Inc. agreed to acquire the remaining 50% interest in private 3PL Ventures Inc., which produces and distributes cannabis products from a 60,000-sq.-ft. facility in Vernon, B.C., for $15,000,000, consisting of $1,500,000 cash, issuance of a $9,500,000 convertible promissory note and issuance of $4,000,000 of common shares. The transaction was expected to be completed on or around Feb. 1, 2023.

Predecessor Detail - Name changed from GTEC Holdings Ltd., July 9, 2021.
Directors - Jürgen Schreiber, chr., Toronto, Ont.; Norton Singhavon, CEO, Kelowna, B.C.; Michael (Mike) Blady, Kelowna, B.C.; Sylvia Lee, Kelowna, B.C.; Duane Lo, Kelowna, B.C.; Derek Sanders, Kelowna, B.C.
Other Exec. Officers - David Lynn, COO; Miguel Martinez, CFO

Capital Stock

	Authorized (shs.)	Outstanding (shs.)[1]
Preference	unlimited	nil
Common	unlimited	257,580,816

[1] At July 17, 2023

Major Shareholder - Widely held at Apr. 11, 2023.

Price Range - AVNT/TSX

Year	Volume	High	Low	Close
2022	16,989,094	$0.38	$0.16	$0.17
2021	164,002,470	$1.10	$0.11	$0.35
2020	42,007,267	$0.22	$0.08	$0.11
2019	58,628,457	$0.81	$0.17	$0.21
2018	53,302,214	$1.40	$0.45	$0.49

Recent Close: $0.19

Capital Stock Changes - During fiscal 2022, common shares were issued as follows: 3,099,324 for services, 2,403,530 as share-based compensation and 1,000,000 for contingent consideration.

Wholly Owned Subsidiaries

GreenTec Holdings Ltd., Kelowna, B.C.
- 100% int. in **Alberta Craft Cannabis Inc.**, Edmonton, Alta.
- 100% int. in **Avant Brands K1 Inc.**, Ont.
  - 100% int. in **The Flowr Group (Okanagan) Inc.**, Ont.
- 100% int. in **GreenTec Bio-Pharmaceuticals Corp.**, B.C.
- 100% int. in **GreenTec Retail Ventures Inc.**, Canada.
  - 100% int. in **1203648 B.C. Ltd.**, B.C.
- 100% int. in **Grey Bruce Farms Incorporated**, Canada.
- 100% int. in **Spectre Labs Inc.**, Kelowna, B.C.
- 100% int. in **3PL Ventures Inc.**, B.C.
- 100% int. in **Tumbleweed Farms Corp.**, B.C.

Note: The preceding list includes only the major related companies in which interests are held.

Financial Statistics

Periods ended:	12m Nov. 30/22^A		12m Nov. 30/21^A
	$000s	%Chg	$000s
Operating revenue	**20,149**	**+112**	**9,499**
Cost of sales	16,235		7,600
Salaries & benefits	2,573		2,292
General & admin expense	4,410		3,614
Stock-based compensation	3,597		473
Operating expense	**26,815**	**+92**	**13,979**
Operating income	**(6,666)**	**n.a.**	**(4,480)**
Deprec., depl. & amort.	1,876		915
Finance costs, gross	37		1,148
Investment income	1,233		(270)
Write-downs/write-offs	nil		(5,916)
Pre-tax income	**(6,254)**	**n.a.**	**(12,330)**
Income taxes	364		(1,199)
Net inc. bef. disc. opers	**(6,618)**	**n.a.**	**(11,131)**
Income from disc. opers	nil		(103)
Net income	**(6,618)**	**n.a.**	**(11,234)**
Net inc. for equity hldrs	**(7,542)**	**n.a.**	**(11,234)**
Net inc. for non-cont. int.	**924**	**n.a.**	**nil**
Cash & equivalent	6,780		14,489
Inventories	10,461		6,171
Accounts receivable	4,409		2,348
Current assets	27,487		26,166
Long-term investments	1,000		3,951
Fixed assets, net	28,651		17,069
Intangibles, net	9,893		3,384
Total assets	**67,031**	**+33**	**50,570**
Accts. pay. & accr. liabs	2,683		2,073
Current liabilities	3,294		2,395
Long-term lease liabilities	2,400		301
Shareholders' equity	43,919		47,874
Non-controlling interest	4,324		nil
Cash from oper. activs	**(3,461)**	**n.a.**	**(5,623)**
Cash from fin. activs	(993)		20,960
Cash from invest. activs	(3,095)		(1,649)
Net cash position	**6,764**	**-53**	**14,313**
Capital expenditures	(1,443)		(594)
Capital disposals	91		500
	$		$
Earnings per share*	(0.04)		(0.06)
Cash flow per share*	(0.02)		(0.03)
	shs		shs
No. of shs. o/s*	206,094,740		199,591,886
Avg. no. of shs. o/s*	201,221,147		182,070,266
	%		%
Net profit margin	(32.85)		(117.18)
Return on equity	(16.43)		(29.18)
Return on assets	(11.19)		(22.10)
No. of employees (FTEs)	150		125

* Common
^A Reported in accordance with IFRS

Latest Results

Periods ended:	6m May 31/23^A		6m May 31/22^A
	$000s	%Chg	$000s
Operating revenue	15,015	+82	8,271
Net income	(398)	n.a.	(4,339)
Net inc. for equity hldrs	(433)	n.a.	(4,339)
Net inc. for non-cont. int	35		nil
	$		$
Earnings per share*	(0.00)		(0.02)

* Common
^A Reported in accordance with IFRS

Historical Summary
(as originally stated)

Fiscal Year	Oper. Rev.	Net Inc. Bef. Disc.	EPS*
	$000s	$000s	$
2022^A	20,149	(6,618)	(0.04)
2021^A	9,499	(11,131)	(0.06)
2020^A	7,907	(9,744)	(0.08)
2019^A	2,361	(9,574)	(0.09)
2018^A1	58	(10,537)	(0.14)

* Common
^A Reported in accordance with IFRS
[1] Results reflect the June 12, 2018, Qualifying Transaction reverse takeover acquisition of GreenTec Holdings Ltd.

A.159 Avante Corp.

Symbol - XX **Exchange -** TSX-VEN **CUSIP -** 05352F
Head Office - 1959 Leslie St, Toronto, ON, M3B 2M3 **Telephone -** (416) 923-6984 **Fax -** (416) 923-5198
Website - www.avantecorp.ca
Email - manny@avantecorp.ca
Investor Relations - Emmanuel Mounouchos (416) 923-6984
Auditors - RSM Canada LLP C.A., Toronto, Ont.
Transfer Agents - TSX Trust Company, Toronto, Ont.
Employees - 118 at Mar. 31, 2023

Profile - (Ont. 2006) Provides technology-enabled security systems and services to residential and condominium customers within the Toronto and Muskoka regions of Ontario.

Wholly owned **Avante Security Inc.** offers the following products and services: **Protective Services**, which includes physical protection services such as guarding, patrol and rapid response, intelligent perimeter protection, international security travel advisory and secure transport services; **Electronic Security**, which consists of a suite of home security services including system design, access control, video and systems installation; and **Monitoring and Managed Services**, which includes monitoring services through physical on-site inspections or via closed circuit television (CCTV) and web cameras and also includes alarm and video monitoring, analytics, verification and electronic building management utilizing the company's Avante Control Centre hub, for monitoring, dispatch and response via its 24-hour emergency call centre.

In December 2022, wholly owned **Avante Security Inc.** acquired the business and assets of Bracebridge, Ont.-based **C&B Alarms Ltd.** for $575,000. C&B provides security services in the Muskoka region that complements the company's operations in the region.

Recent Merger and Acquisition Activity

Status: completed **Revised:** June 1, 2022
UPDATE: The transaction was completed. PREVIOUS: SSC Security Services Corp. agreed to acquire Toronto, Ont.-based Logixx Security Inc., a provider of security protection (including security guards and patrols) for enterprise and commercial clients across Canada, from Avante Logixx Inc. for $23,950,000. The transaction was entered into as an alternative to SSC's proposed acquisition of Avante, which was concurrently terminated.

Status: terminated **Revised:** Mar. 30, 2022
UPDATE: The transaction was terminated. PREVIOUS: SSC Security Services Corp. agreed to acquire Avante Logixx Inc. for 52¢ cash and 0.4155 SSC common shares for each Avante share held, which implied a total consideration of $1.75 per Avante share. The transaction was valued at $46,500,000, including the assumption of $9,400,000 of Avante debt. Avante provides and develops technology-enabled security systems and services for residential and commercial clients. Avante's operating subsidiaries are Avante Security Inc., and Logixx Security Inc.

Predecessor Detail - Name changed from Avante Logixx Inc., June 1, 2023.

Directors - Emmanuel (Manny) Mounouchos, chr. & CEO, Toronto, Ont.; Daniel N. Argiros, Toronto, Ont.; Bruce Bronfman, Toronto, Ont.; Wade Burton, Ont.; Robert Klopot, Toronto, Ont.

Other Exec. Officers - Raj Kapoor, CFO

Capital Stock

	Authorized (shs.)	Outstanding (shs.)[1]
Common	unlimited	26,489,438

[1] At Aug. 1, 2023

Major Shareholder - Fairfax Financial Holdings Limited held 20% interest and Emmanuel (Manny) Mounouchos held 10.35% interest at Aug. 19, 2022.

Price Range - XX/TSX-VEN

Year	Volume	High	Low	Close
2022	10,566,965	$1.60	$0.65	$0.76
2021	8,127,532	$2.25	$1.25	$1.49
2020	6,259,318	$1.73	$0.66	$1.44
2019	5,698,323	$2.10	$1.01	$1.49
2018	8,466,980	$2.50	$1.40	$1.95

Recent Close: $0.88

Capital Stock Changes - There were no changes to capital stock during fiscal 2023.

During fiscal 2022, 5,297,434 common shares were issued on conversion of debentures.

Wholly Owned Subsidiaries

Avante Security Inc., Toronto, Ont.

Financial Statistics

Periods ended:	12m Mar. 31/23^A		12m Mar. 31/22^A
	$000s	%Chg	$000s
Operating revenue	**19,960**	**+10**	**18,156**
Cost of sales	11,838		10,308
Salaries & benefits	3,608		4,990
General & admin expense	3,246		2,887
Stock-based compensation	654		131
Operating expense	**19,345**	**+6**	**18,316**
Operating income	**615**	**n.a.**	**(160)**
Deprec., depl. & amort.	1,099		1,224
Finance costs, gross	548		747
Pre-tax income	**(3,262)**	**n.a.**	**(5,876)**
Income taxes	594		61
Net inc. bef. disc. opers	**(3,856)**	**n.a.**	**(5,937)**
Income from disc. opers	3,888		1,545
Net income	**32**	**n.a.**	**(4,392)**
Cash & equivalent	10,114		354
Inventories	929		936
Accounts receivable	5,601		3,520
Current assets	17,320		5,625
Fixed assets, net	2,443		1,738
Intangibles, net	4,832		4,650
Total assets	**25,583**	**-40**	**42,943**
Accts. pay. & accr. liabs	4,197		6,163
Current liabilities	7,406		9,365
Long-term debt, gross	500		8,865
Long-term debt, net	nil		8,422
Long-term lease liabilities	1,064		335
Shareholders' equity	16,781		16,052
Cash from oper. activs	**(3,758)**	**n.a.**	**1,825**
Cash from fin. activs	(9,504)		(178)
Cash from invest. activs	23,022		(801)
Net cash position	**10,114**	**n.m.**	**354**
Capital expenditures	(380)		(61)
Capital disposals	309		44
	$		$
Earns. per sh. bef disc opers*	(0.15)		(0.27)
Earnings per share*	0.00		(0.27)
Cash flow per share*	(0.14)		0.08
	shs		shs
No. of shs. o/s*	26,489,438		26,489,438
Avg. no. of shs. o/s*	26,489,438		21,830,599
	%		%
Net profit margin	(19.32)		(32.70)
Return on equity	(23.49)		(42.89)
Return on assets	(9.36)		(11.91)
No. of employees (FTEs)	118		1,828

* Common
^A Reported in accordance with IFRS

Historical Summary
(as originally stated)

Fiscal Year	Oper. Rev.	Net Inc. Bef. Disc.	EPS*
	$000s	$000s	$
2023^A	19,960	(3,856)	(0.15)
2022^A	18,156	(5,937)	(0.27)
2021^A	91,716	(3,172)	(0.15)
2020^A	55,741	(2,717)	(0.13)
2019^A	32,081	(2,119)	(0.11)

* Common
^A Reported in accordance with IFRS

A.160 Avicanna Inc.

Symbol - AVCN **Exchange -** TSX **CUSIP -** 05368K
Head Office - 1502-480 University Ave, Toronto, ON, M5G 1V2 **Telephone -** (647) 243-5283
Website - www.avicanna.com
Email - ir@avicanna.com
Investor Relations - Aras Azadian (647) 243-5283
Auditors - Kingston Ross Pasnak LLP C.A., Edmonton, Alta.
Lawyers - DLA Piper (Canada) LLP
Transfer Agents - Odyssey Trust Company, Vancouver, B.C.
Employees - 80 at Mar. 31, 2023

Profile - (Ont. 2016) Develops, manufactures and commercializes plant-derived cannabinoid-based products for medical and pharmaceutical markets.

Products are divided into four market segments: medical cannabis and wellness products, such as oil drops, sublingual sprays, topicals, capsules, tablets and water-soluble infusers, available in Canada, Colombia and the Caribbean under the RHO Phyto™ brand; CBD consumer and derma-cosmetic products, consisting of topical skincare product lines under the Pura H&W™ and Pura Earth™ brands or private label brands in Canada, the U.S., Colombia, Ecuador, the European Union, Germany, Switzerland, and Austria; pharmaceutical preparations and products, consisting of cannabinoid-based drug candidates which are under various stages of development, registration and commercialization in the areas of neurology, depression, sleep, dermatology, and pain, including the first pharmaceutical preparation (Trunerox™) which is in drug registration stage in several Latin American countries for the treatment of refractory epilepsy; and cannabinoid active pharmaceutical ingredients, which are marketed under the Aureus™ brand, offering cannabinoid active pharmaceutical ingredients including cannabidiol (CBD), cannabigerol (CBG) and tetrahydrocannabinol (THC) in addition to standardized seeds through its organic, economical, and industrial-scale subsidiary based in Colombia. The company has also licensed the Viola and re+PLAY cannabis brands for commercialization in Canada.

In addition, the company owns and operates MyMedi.ca medical cannabis care platform, which features diverse and scientifically curated products from leading Canadian licensed producers in addition to pharmacist-led patient support programs and educational resources to facilitate the incorporation of medical cannabis into health care regimens. MyMedi.ca is also providing specialty services to distinct patient groups such as veterans and collaborating with public and private providers for adjudication and reimbursement.

Research and development activities for the company's products are conducted in the Johnson & Johnson Innovation Centre (JLABS @ Toronto) as well as in collaboration with Canadian academic and medical institutions. Activities include the conception, development, pre-clinical analysis and clinical studies of pharmaceutical, medical cannabis and consumer products. Pharmaceutical programs include cannabinoid-based products for addiction and withdrawal from alcohol and nicotine, neuropathic and chronic pain, seizures and sudden death in epilepsy, inflammation, anxiety and depression, epidermolysis bullosa, oseteoarthritis and multiple sclerosis.

Subsidiary **Santa Marta Golden Hemp S.A.S.** (SMGH; 60% owned) is licensed to cultivate, extract and process cannabis from facilities in Santa Marta, Colombia, producing and manufacturing products for the company's operations in Colombia and produces the Aureus™ products for distribution worldwide. SMGH's facilities include 150,000-sq.-ft. shadehouse space, 156,000-sq.-ft. outdoor space and 14,000-sq.-ft. customized greenhouse space.

On May 29, 2023, the company agreed to acquire specific assets of the Medical Cannabis by Shoppers business from **Shoppers Drug Mart Corporation**, wholly owned by **Loblaw Companies Limited**, for $2,600,000 and pay Shoppers an earnout based on net revenues for a period of two years. The final closing was scheduled for July 31, 2023.

In July 2022, the company formed a partnership with **Ei.Ventures, Inc.** to develop and commercialize functional fungi-based products under the brand Psilly.

In June 2022, the company sold its 63% interest in Colombia-based **Sativa Nativa S.A.S.**, which cultivates, extracts and processes cannabis from facilities in Santa Marta, for $675,000. Sativa's facilities include 50,000-sq.-ft. shadehouse space, 50,000-sq.-ft. outdoor space and 20,000-sq.-ft. customized greenhouse space.

During the second quarter of 2022, the company divested its non-core medical cannabis program in Colombia. The program was launched in December 2020 through a compound pharmacy model (Formulaciones Magistrales) in which the company provided its cannabinoid formulations to patients and the medical community.

Directors - Aras Azadian, co-founder & CEO, Ont.; Dr. Chandrakant J. (Chandra) Panchal, chr., Pierrefonds, Qué.; Giancarlo D. Char, Miami, Fla.; Eileen McCormack, Ont.; John McVicar, Ont.

Other Exec. Officers - Phillip Cardella, CFO; Dr. Frantz Le Devedec, exec. v-p, R&D; Ivana Maric, exec. v-p, mktg.; Arash Moghani, exec. v-p, opers. & tech.; Dr. Karolina Urban, exec. v-p, scientific & medical affairs; Ingrid Diaz, v-p, assoc. gen. counsel & corp. compliance officer; Brennan Kerr, v-p, commercialization; Samantha Watt, v-p, Cdn. opers.

Capital Stock

	Authorized (shs.)	Outstanding (shs.)[1]
Preferred	unlimited	nil
Common	unlimited	83,198,475

[1] At May 15, 2023

Major Shareholder - Sheldon Inwentash held 11.88% interest at Apr. 10, 2023.

Price Range - AVCN/TSX

Year	Volume	High	Low	Close
2022	13,568,861	$0.80	$0.16	$0.41
2021	9,411,635	$1.65	$0.62	$0.78
2020	12,664,042	$3.00	$0.66	$1.31
2019	10,601,430	$7.40	$1.23	$2.54

Recent Close: $0.38

Capital Stock Changes - In March 2023, private placement of 3,096,230 units (1 common share & ½ warrant) at 40¢ per unit was completed, with warrants exercisable at 50¢ per share for three years.

From March to December 2022, private placement of 26,215,870 units (1 common share & ½ warrant) at 35¢ per unit was completed. Also during 2022, 2,852,648 common shares were issued on vesting of restricted share units.

Wholly Owned Subsidiaries

Avicanna LATAM S.A.S., Colombia.
Avicanna (UK) Limited, United Kingdom.
Avicanna USA Inc., Del.
2516167 Ontario Inc., Ont. dba My Cannabis.

Subsidiaries

60% int. in **Santa Marta Golden Hemp S.A.S.**, Colombia.
60% int. in **Sigma Magdalena Canada Inc.**, Ont.
- 100% int. in **Sigma Analytical Magdalena S.A.S.**, Colombia.

Financial Statistics

Periods ended:	12m Dec. 31/22^A		12m Dec. 31/21^A
	$000s	%Chg	$000s
Operating revenue	**4,048**	**+24**	**3,269**
Cost of sales	527		437
Salaries & benefits	4,179		4,893
Research & devel. expense	277		304
General & admin expense	4,764		6,672
Stock-based compensation	1,043		1,313
Operating expense	**10,790**	**-21**	**13,619**
Operating income	**(6,742)**	**n.a.**	**(10,350)**
Deprec., depl. & amort.	887		894
Finance costs, gross	1,672		738
Write-downs/write-offs	(1,118)		(4,161)
Pre-tax income	**(14,735)**	**n.a.**	**(16,761)**
Income taxes	nil		14
Net income	**(14,735)**	**n.a.**	**(16,775)**
Net inc. for equity hldrs	**(13,421)**	**n.a.**	**(15,371)**
Net inc. for non-cont. int	**(1,314)**	**n.a.**	**(1,403)**
Cash & equivalent	1,194		31
Inventories	3,110		3,002
Accounts receivable	2,149		2,336
Current assets	7,064		7,354
Long-term investments	nil		180
Fixed assets, net	10,017		14,322
Right-of-use assets	370		147
Intangibles, net	168		299
Total assets	**17,619**	**-21**	**22,302**
Accts. pay. & accr. liabs	4,753		7,289
Current liabilities	11,405		12,196
Long-term debt, gross	2,838		1,506
Long-term debt, net	180		416
Shareholders' equity	(384)		1,146
Non-controlling interest	3,842		5,762
Cash from oper. activs	**(7,435)**	**n.a.**	**(11,663)**
Cash from fin. activs	9,901		10,060
Cash from invest. activs	810		761
Net cash position	**1,194**	**n.m.**	**31**
Capital expenditures	(51)		(769)
Capital disposals	28		300
	$		$
Earnings per share*	(0.23)		(0.37)
Cash flow per share*	(0.13)		(0.28)
	shs		shs
No. of shs. o/s*	74,952,800		45,884,282
Avg. no. of shs. o/s*	59,167,116		41,285,084
	%		%
Net profit margin	(364.01)		(513.15)
Return on equity	n.m.		(429.27)
Return on assets	(65.44)		(61.14)

* Common
^A Reported in accordance with IFRS

Latest Results

Periods ended:	3m Mar. 31/23^A		3m Mar. 31/22^A
	$000s	%Chg	$000s
Operating revenue	1,170	+13	1,038
Net income	(2,508)	n.a.	(939)
Net inc. for equity hldrs	(2,934)	n.a.	(1,366)
Net inc. for non-cont. int	426		427
	$		$
Earnings per share*	(0.04)		(0.03)

* Common
^A Reported in accordance with IFRS

Historical Summary
(as originally stated)

Fiscal Year	Oper. Rev.	Net Inc. Bef. Disc.	EPS*
	$000s	$000s	$
2022^A	4,048	(14,735)	(0.23)
2021^A	3,269	(16,775)	(0.37)
2020^A	1,570	(32,862)	(1.07)
2019^A	168	(22,213)	(1.05)
2018^A	118	(7,289)	(0.52)

* Common
^A Reported in accordance with IFRS

A.161 Avivagen Inc.

Symbol - VIV **Exchange** - TSX-VEN **CUSIP** - 05382F
Head Office - 100 Sussex Dr, Ottawa, ON, K1A 0R6 **Telephone** - (613) 949-8164 **Toll-free** - (855) 210-2355 **Fax** - (613) 993-0796
Website - www.avivagen.com
Email - d.basek@avivagen.com
Investor Relations - Drew Basek (416) 540-0733
Auditors - McGovern Hurley LLP C.A., Toronto, Ont.
Lawyers - LaBarge Weinstein LLP, Ottawa, Ont.
Transfer Agents - Computershare Trust Company of Canada Inc., Toronto, Ont.

Profile - (Can. 2005 amalg.) Develops and commercializes products to replace antibiotics in livestock feeds to optimize the health and growth of the animals, as well as products intended to improve or maintain quality of life in companion animals and human health.

The company's proprietary product, OxC-beta™ (fully-oxidized beta-carotene) Livestock, is a non-antibiotic means of maintaining optimal health and growth in livestock animals such as poultry, swine, farmed fish and dairy cattle, which reduces the development of antibiotic resistant pathogens that are widely thought to occur in food animal production and can threaten human health. OxC-beta™ Livestock is currently approved for sale in New Zealand, the Philippines, Malaysia, China, Mexico, Australia, the U.S., Taiwan, Brazil, Vietnam and Thailand. Other products include a soft chew natural supplement for both cats and dogs under the Vivamune™ Health Chews and the Dr. Tobias All-in-One Dog Chews brands.

In addition, has launched Dr. Tobias Beta Blend, human dietary supplements based on the beta-carotene. The product line consists of bottles of capsules and were developed as a direct-to-consumer human health product available online.

The company is headquartered and has laboratories in Ottawa, Ont. Inventories are produced in Taipei, Taiwan and Vermont, U.S.

Predecessor Detail - Name changed from Chemaphor Inc., May 25, 2012.

Directors - Jeffrey Kraws, chr., N.Y.; David Hankinson, v-chr., Paradise, N.S.; G. F. Kym Anthony, CEO, Toronto, Ont.; Dr. Graham Burton, chief scientific officer, Ottawa, Ont.; Paul Mesburis†, B.C.

Other Exec. Officers - Dr. James (Jamie) Nickerson, pres.; Ira Levy, interim CFO

† Lead director

Capital Stock

	Authorized (shs.)	Outstanding (shs.)[1]
Common	unlimited	77,694,700

[1] At June 6, 2023

Major Shareholder - Widely held at Mar. 3, 2023.

Price Range - VIV/TSX-VEN

Year	Volume	High	Low	Close
2022	13,887,718	$0.32	$0.06	$0.08
2021	18,675,465	$0.78	$0.28	$0.30
2020	14,378,116	$0.77	$0.39	$0.65
2019	9,792,265	$0.99	$0.37	$0.58
2018	5,385,479	$1.10	$0.33	$0.40

Recent Close: $0.02

Capital Stock Changes - In April and July 2022, private placement of 11,026,180 units (1 common share & 1 warrant) at 20¢ per unit was completed,. Also during fiscal 2022, common shares were issued as follow: 5,678,000 to debenture holders, 3,025,000 by private placement and 498,680 in settlement of maintenance fees.

Investments

50% int. in **Centre Beach, Inc.**

Financial Statistics

Periods ended:	12m Oct. 31/22^A		12m Oct. 31/21^A
	$000s	%Chg	$000s
Operating revenue	**939**	**-28**	**1,296**
Cost of goods sold	539		762
Salaries & benefits	1,745		1,612
General & admin expense	3,364		2,750
Stock-based compensation	152		327
Operating expense	**5,800**	**+6**	**5,451**
Operating income	**(4,861)**	**n.a.**	**(4,155)**
Deprec., depl. & amort.	87		125
Finance income	1		5
Finance costs, gross	1,769		1,585
Pre-tax income	**(6,066)**	**n.a.**	**(6,394)**
Net income	**(6,066)**	**n.a.**	**(6,394)**
Cash & equivalent	290		1,408
Inventories	314		1,232
Accounts receivable	573		439
Current assets	1,271		3,216
Fixed assets, net	94		262
Total assets	**1,365**	**-61**	**3,478**
Accts. pay. & accr. liabs	1,200		560
Current liabilities	2,098		6,014
Long-term debt, gross	6,061		6,713
Long-term debt, net	5,251		1,397
Long-term lease liabilities	nil		20
Shareholders' equity	(5,984)		(3,953)
Cash from oper. activs	**(3,117)**	**n.a.**	**(4,599)**
Cash from fin. activs	1,999		5,347
Cash from invest. activs	nil		(9)
Net cash position	**290**	**-79**	**1,408**
Capital expenditures	nil		(9)
	$		$
Earnings per share*	(0.09)		(0.12)
Cash flow per share*	(0.05)		(0.09)
	shs		shs
No. of shs. o/s*	77,187,355		56,959,495
Avg. no. of shs. o/s*	66,027,861		52,444,157
	%		%
Net profit margin	(646.01)		(493.36)
Return on equity	n.m.		n.m.
Return on assets	(177.45)		(170.11)
Foreign sales percent	100		100
No. of employees (FTEs)	n.a.		13

* Common
^A Reported in accordance with IFRS

Latest Results

Periods ended:	6m Apr. 30/23^A		6m Apr. 30/22^A
	$000s	%Chg	$000s
Operating revenue	144	-60	360
Net income	(2,399)	n.a.	(2,857)
	$		$
Earnings per share*	(0.03)		(0.05)

* Common
^A Reported in accordance with IFRS

Historical Summary
(as originally stated)

Fiscal Year	Oper. Rev. $000s	Net Inc. Bef. Disc. $000s	EPS* $
2022^A	939	(6,066)	(0.09)
2021^A	1,296	(6,394)	(0.12)
2020^A	1,178	(4,751)	(0.12)
2019^A	977	(4,836)	(0.14)
2018^A	1,073	(4,834)	(0.15)

* Common
^A Reported in accordance with IFRS

A.162 Avricore Health Inc.

Symbol - AVCR **Exchange** - TSX-VEN **CUSIP** - 054521
Head Office - 1120-789 Pender St W, Vancouver, BC, V6C 1H2 **Telephone** - (604) 773-8943
Website - www.avricorehealth.com
Email - info@avricorehealth.com
Investor Relations - Hector D. Bremner (604) 773-8943
Auditors - Manning Elliott LLP C.A., Vancouver, B.C.
Lawyers - Max Pinsky Personal Law Corporation, Vancouver, B.C.
Transfer Agents - Computershare Trust Company of Canada Inc., Vancouver, B.C.
Profile - (B.C. 2000) Provides a turnkey point-of-care testing system, HealthTab™, to pharmacies that screens patients for health markers and tests for infections like streptococcus (strep) or COVID-19.

HealthTab™ combines point-of-care technologies with a secure, cloud-based platform for tackling pressing global health issues. With just a few drops of blood from a finger prick, the system generates lab-accurate results on the spot and data is reported in real time. The test menu includes up to 23 key biomarkers for screening and managing chronic diseases, such as diabetes and heart disease. Test menu includes hemoglobin A1C (HbA1c), lipid profile and estimated glomerular filtration rate (eGFR) tests, as well as its recently added capabilities for bacterial and viral tests, such as strep and COVID-19 tests.

The company has a master services agreement with Shoppers Drug Mart® to deploy HealthTab™ in 532 pharmacies across Canada. At Dec. 31, 2022, 416 participating Shoppers Drug Mart® pharmacies Ontario (378), British Columbia (23), Nova Scotia (6), Alberta (5) and New Brunswick (4) had received their HealthTab™ systems and are offering screening tests to patients. Has also placed HealthTab™ in the first pharmacist-led primary healthcare clinic located in Lethbridge, Alta., and in a Real Canadian Superstore®. Future applications for HealthTab™ include seniors living facilities and electronic health record service providers.

Has an agreement with **Abbott Laboratories** to distribute and integrate Afinion 2™ and associated tests for diabetes and heart disease screening in Canadian community pharmacies, including HbA1c testing, a critical marker for the screening and management of diabetes, to its HealthTab™ platform. The agreement also includes Abbott's ID NOW™ molecular testing device for SARS-CoV-2 as well as respiratory syncytial virus, influenza A & B and strep, and the handheld blood chemistry analyzer, point-of-care i-STAT Alinity and its associated tests for creatinine.

Predecessor Detail - Name changed from Vanc Pharmaceuticals Inc., Nov. 5, 2018.

Directors - David M. Hall, chr., Vancouver, B.C.; Hector D. Bremner, CEO, Vancouver, B.C.; Rodger Seccombe, chief tech. officer, Vancouver, B.C.; Alan Arnstein, Alta.; Christine J. Hrudka, Saskatoon, Sask.; Dr. Robert Sindelar, Vancouver, B.C.; Thomas W. Teahen, Ont.

Other Exec. Officers - Kiriaki (Kiki) Smith, CFO & corp. sec.

Capital Stock

	Authorized (shs.)	Outstanding (shs.)[1]
Common	unlimited	99,644,664

[1] At May 30, 2023

Major Shareholder - Widely held at May 15, 2023.

Price Range - AVCR/TSX-VEN

Year	Volume	High	Low	Close
2022	19,453,172	$0.41	$0.08	$0.32
2021	117,874,875	$0.69	$0.09	$0.16
2020	154,336,025	$0.18	$0.01	$0.10
2019	19,293,172	$0.15	$0.02	$0.03
2018	33,670,023	$0.75	$0.08	$0.10

Recent Close: $0.17

Capital Stock Changes - During 2022, common shares were issued as follows: 909,400 on exercise of warrants and 800,000 on exercise of options.

Wholly Owned Subsidiaries

HealthTab, Inc., Vancouver, B.C.

Financial Statistics

Periods ended:	12m Dec. 31/22^A		12m Dec. 31/21^A
	$000s	%Chg	$000s
Operating revenue	**1,768**	**n.m.**	**123**
Cost of goods sold	1,312		92
General & admin expense	937		1,256
Stock-based compensation	332		496
Operating expense	**2,581**	**+40**	**1,844**
Operating income	**(813)**	**n.a.**	**(1,721)**
Deprec., depl. & amort.	1		18
Finance income	8		1
Finance costs, gross	5		45
Write-downs/write-offs	(9)		nil
Pre-tax income	**(818)**	**n.a.**	**(1,708)**
Net income	**(818)**	**n.a.**	**(1,708)**
Cash & equivalent	621		2,013
Accounts receivable	770		92
Current assets	1,431		2,159
Fixed assets, net	1,108		91
Intangibles, net	30		32
Total assets	**2,569**	**+13**	**2,281**
Accts. pay. & accr. liabs	313		44
Current liabilities	605		84
Long-term debt, gross	40		40
Long-term debt, net	40		40
Shareholders' equity	1,964		2,197
Cash from oper. activs	**(438)**	**n.a.**	**(1,234)**
Cash from fin. activs	254		3,085
Cash from invest. activs	(1,209)		(140)
Net cash position	**621**	**-69**	**2,013**
Capital expenditures	(1,193)		(105)
	$		$
Earnings per share*	(0.01)		(0.02)
Cash flow per share*	(0.00)		(0.01)
	shs		shs
No. of shs. o/s*	99,244,664		97,535,264
Avg. no. of shs. o/s*	97,859,216		92,610,766
	%		%
Net profit margin	(46.27)		n.m.
Return on equity	(39.32)		n.m.
Return on assets	(33.53)		(122.23)

* Common
^A Reported in accordance with IFRS

Latest Results

Periods ended:	3m Mar. 31/23^A		3m Mar. 31/22^A
	$000s	%Chg	$000s
Operating revenue	629	n.m.	43
Net income	(192)	n.a.	(186)
	$		$
Earnings per share*	(0.00)		(0.00)

* Common
^A Reported in accordance with IFRS

Historical Summary
(as originally stated)

Fiscal Year	Oper. Rev. $000s	Net Inc. Bef. Disc. $000s	EPS* $
2022^A	1,768	(818)	(0.01)
2021^A	123	(1,708)	(0.02)
2020^A	33	(1,174)	(0.02)
2019^A	33	(1,916)	(0.04)
2018^A	828	(4,137)	(0.12)

* Common
^A Reported in accordance with IFRS

A.163 Awakn Life Sciences Corp.

Symbol - AWKN **Exchange** - NEO **CUSIP** - 05455W
Head Office - 301-217 Queen St W, Toronto, ON, M5V 0R2 **Telephone** - (416) 270-9566
Website - awaknlifesciences.com
Email - jonathanh@awaknlifesciences.com
Investor Relations - Jonathan Held (416) 361-2517
Auditors - MNP LLP C.A., Burlington, Ont.
Transfer Agents - Endeavor Trust Corporation, Vancouver, B.C.
Profile - (B.C. 2018) Researches, develops and delivers psychedelic medicines and therapies focused on treating substance and behavioural addictions.

Therapy and drug development pipeline includes Ketamine-assisted psychotherapy and 3,4-Methylenedioxymethamphetamine (MDMA)-assisted psychotherapy for alcohol use disorder (AUD) and Ketamine-assisted psychotherapy for behavioural addictions. Also undertaking pre-clinical drug discovery to generate new molecules with even better properties than those presented by Ketamine and MDMA, to treat both substance and behavioural addictions. Ketamine-assisted psychotherapy for AUD is being used to treat clients in the company's clinics and Ketamine-assisted psychotherapy for behavioural addictions is targeted to be introduced into the company's clinics in 2023.

Psychedelic-assisted psychotherapies are delivered in clinics in Bristol and London, U.K., and in Oslo, Norway. A larger clinic in Oslo is being constructed and is targeted to open in May 2023, by which time the current location in Oslo will close. Another clinic in Trondheim, Norway is under renovation and is targeted to operate in March 2023.

Also licenses the proprietary Ketamine-assisted psychotherapy for AUD to other addiction treatment centres in territories where the company does not operate.

Predecessor Detail - Name changed from 1169082 B.C. Ltd., June 15, 2021, pursuant to the reverse takeover acquisition of Awakn Life Sciences Inc. and concurrent amalgamation of (old) Awakn with wholly owned 2835517 Ontario Ltd.

Directors - George Scorsis, chr., Toronto, Ont.; Anthony Tennyson, pres. & CEO, Dublin, Ireland; Paul Carter, Wilts., United Kingdom; Stephen Page, London, Middx., United Kingdom; Prof. John Papastergiou, Ont.

Other Exec. Officers - James Collins, COO; Dr. Arun Dhandayudham, CMO; Jonathan Held, chief bus. officer & interim CFO; Shaun McNulty, chief scientific officer; Prof. David J. Nutt, chief research officer; Gordo Whittaker, chief mktg. officer

Capital Stock

	Authorized (shs.)	Outstanding (shs.)[1]
Common	unlimited	32,476,187

[1] At Dec. 11, 2022

Major Shareholder - Widely held at June 23, 2021.

Price Range - AWKN/NEO

Year	Volume	High	Low	Close
2022	401,400	$3.36	$0.26	$0.34
2021	312,100	$3.33	$1.51	$2.68

Recent Close: $0.28

Capital Stock Changes - In March 2022, private placement of 2,031,250 units (1 common share & ½ warrant) at $1.60 per unit was completed, with warrants exercisable at $2.20 per share for two years. From September and November 2022, private placement of 5,557,630 units (1 common share & ½ warrant) at 55¢ per unit was completed, with warrants exercisable at 68¢ per share for two years.

Wholly Owned Subsidiaries

Awakn Clinics Oslo AS, Norway.
Awakn Life Sciences Inc., Toronto, Ont.
- 51% int. in **Awakn Bristol Limited**, United Kingdom.
- 100% int. in **Awakn LS Europe Holdings Limited**, Ireland.
  - 100% int. in **Awakn LS Partnerships Limited**, Ireland.
- 100% int. in **Awakn Life Sciences UK Ltd.**, United Kingdom.
  - 100% int. in **Awakn London Limited**, United Kingdom.
  - 100% int. in **Awakn Manchester Ltd.**, United Kingdom.

1233705 B.C. Ltd., B.C.

Financial Statistics

Periods ended:	12m Jan. 31/22[A]		40w Jan. 31/21[A1]
	$000s	%Chg	$000s
Operating revenue	**236**	**n.a.**	**nil**
Research & devel. expense	3,309		nil
General & admin expense	5,449		577
Stock-based compensation	1,090		40
Operating expense	**9,849**	**n.a.**	**617**
Operating income	**(9,613)**	**n.a.**	**(617)**
Deprec., depl. & amort.	181		13
Finance costs, gross	205		10
Pre-tax income	**(16,472)**	**n.a.**	**(1,106)**
Net income	**(16,472)**	**n.a.**	**(1,106)**
Net inc. for equity hldrs	**(15,946)**	**n.a.**	**(945)**
Net inc. for non-cont. int	**(526)**	**n.a.**	**(161)**
Cash & equivalent	1,623		366
Accounts receivable	29		nil
Current assets	2,112		477
Fixed assets, net	1,865		204
Right-of-use assets	1,748		144
Intangibles, net	979		nil
Total assets	**6,876**	**+733**	**825**
Accts. pay. & accr. liabs	1,287		228
Current liabilities	1,856		242
Long-term lease liabilities	1,453		118
Shareholders' equity	3,411		328
Non-controlling interest	(388)		137
Cash from oper. activs	**(8,586)**	**n.a.**	**(473)**
Cash from fin. activs	11,502		1,058
Cash from invest. activs	(1,685)		(216)
Net cash position	**1,623**	**+343**	**366**
Capital expenditures	(1,702)		(201)
	$		$
Earnings per share*	(0.73)		(0.09)
Cash flow per share*	(0.39)		(0.04)
	shs		shs
No. of shs. o/s*	24,887,307		n.a.
Avg. no. of shs. o/s*	21,962,237		12,628,816
	%		%
Net profit margin	n.m.		...
Return on equity	(852.96)		...
Return on assets	(422.46)		...

* Common

[A] Reported in accordance with IFRS

[1] Results pertain to Awakn Life Sciences Inc.

Latest Results

Periods ended:	6m July 31/22[A]		6m July 31/21[A]
	$000s	%Chg	$000s
Operating revenue	593	n.a.	nil
Net income	(5,189)	n.a.	(9,186)
Net inc. for equity hldrs	(5,016)	n.a.	(8,960)
Net inc. for non-cont. int	(173)		(226)
	$		$
Earnings per share*	(0.19)		(0.47)

* Common

[A] Reported in accordance with IFRS

A.164 Axcap Ventures Inc.

Symbol - AXCP **Exchange** - CSE **CUSIP** - 05455X

Head Office - 488-1090 Georgia St W, Vancouver, BC, V6E 3V7 **Telephone** - (604) 687-7130

Email - shannon@commoditypartners.ca

Investor Relations - Shannon Anderson (604) 687-7130

Auditors - Manning Elliott LLP C.A., Vancouver, B.C.

Transfer Agents - Odyssey Trust Company, Vancouver, B.C.

Profile - (B.C. 2018; orig. Ont., 1987) Invests in securities of private and public companies, with a focus on the mineral exploration, technology, software development and biotechnology industries.

In April 2022, the company completed a change of business from an industrial issuer to an investment company, with a focus on investing in both private and public companies in the mineral exploration, technology, software development and biotechnology industries. In conjunction, the company changed its name to **Axcap Ventures Inc.** The company previously developed software to better facilitate the purchase and sale of Bitcoin for end users.

Predecessor Detail - Name changed from Netcoins Holdings Inc., Apr. 20, 2022, following change of business from an industrial issuer to an investment company.

Directors - Kenneth (Ken) Cotiamco, interim CEO, Vancouver, B.C.; Robert Dubeau, pres., B.C.; Desmond M. (Des) Balakrishnan, Vancouver, B.C.; Carson Seabolt, B.C.; Mario Vetro, Vancouver, B.C.

Other Exec. Officers - Jonathan Yan, CFO

Capital Stock

	Authorized (shs.)	Outstanding (shs.)[1]
Common	unlimited	21,811,241

[1] At May 1, 2023

Major Shareholder - Carson Seabolt held 26.57% interest, Mario Vetro held 25.87% interest and Forestxholdings Ltd. held 14.59% interest at May 17, 2022.

Price Range - AXCP/CSE

Year	Volume	High	Low	Close
2022	747,097	$0.17	$0.06	$0.10
2020	2,199,347	$0.25	$0.06	$0.12
2019	4,898,122	$3.75	$0.11	$0.14
2018	15,140,793	$16.25	$1.75	$2.75

Consolidation: 1-for-25 cons. in Nov. 2019

Recent Close: $0.04

Capital Stock Changes - In February and March 2022, private placement of 16,836,486 units (1 common share & 1 warrant) at 11¢ per unit was completed, with warrants exercisable at $0.115 per share for five years.

Financial Statistics

Periods ended:	12m Dec. 31/21[A]		12m Dec. 31/20[A]
	$000s	%Chg	$000s
General & admin expense	894		984
Operating expense	**894**	**-9**	**984**
Operating income	**(894)**	**n.a.**	**(984)**
Deprec., depl. & amort.	nil		1
Finance income	55		15
Write-downs/write-offs	nil		(393)
Pre-tax income	**(751)**	**n.a.**	**650**
Net income	**(751)**	**n.a.**	**650**
Cash & equivalent	829		165
Current assets	834		165
Long-term investments	825		2,927
Total assets	**2,172**	**-30**	**3,092**
Accts. pay. & accr. liabs	452		621
Current liabilities	452		621
Shareholders' equity	1,720		2,471
Cash from oper. activs	**(722)**	**n.a.**	**(871)**
Cash from invest. activs	1,387		(899)
Net cash position	**829**	**+402**	**165**
	$		$
Earnings per share*	(0.15)		0.13
Cash flow per share*	(0.15)		(0.18)
	shs		shs
No. of shs. o/s*	4,856,589		4,856,589
Avg. no. of shs. o/s*	4,856,589		4,856,589
	%		%
Net profit margin	n.a.		n.a.
Return on equity	(35.84)		30.29
Return on assets	(28.53)		24.26

* Common

[A] Reported in accordance with IFRS

Historical Summary
(as originally stated)

Fiscal Year	Oper. Rev.	Net Inc. Bef. Disc.	EPS*
	$000s	$000s	$
2021[A]	nil	(751)	(0.15)
2020[A]	nil	650	0.13
2019[A]	43,379	(1,008)	(0.26)
2018[A1]	58,357	(22,148)	(5.75)
2018[A2]	nil	(1,985)	(2.50)

* Common

[A] Reported in accordance with IFRS

[1] Results reflect the Mar. 9, 2018, reverse takeover acquisition of Netcoins Inc.

[2] Results for 2018 and prior years pertain to GAR Limited (old).

Note: Adjusted throughout for 1-for-25 cons. in Nov. 2019

A.165 Axe2 Acquisitions Inc.

Symbol - AXET.P **Exchange** - TSX-VEN **CUSIP** - 05460C

Head Office - 2900-25 King St W, Toronto, ON, M5L 1G3 **Telephone** - (416) 848-1008

Email - ddattels@newgenfunds.com

Investor Relations - David Dattels (416) 848-1008

Auditors - Goodman & Associates LLP C.A., Toronto, Ont.

Lawyers - Fasken Martineau DuMoulin LLP, Calgary, Alta.

Transfer Agents - Odyssey Trust Company, Vancouver, B.C.

Profile - (B.C. 2020) Capital Pool Company.

Common listed on TSX-VEN, Nov. 23, 2022.

Directors - Chris Rowan, CFO, Toronto, Ont.; Norm Chang, Toronto, Ont.; William Lamb, West Vancouver, B.C.; Krisztian Tóth, Toronto, Ont.

Other Exec. Officers - David Dattels, interim CEO & corp. sec.

Capital Stock

	Authorized (shs.)	Outstanding (shs.)[1]
Class A Preferred	unlimited	nil
Common	unlimited	6,886,468

[1] At May 30, 2023

Major Shareholder - Widely held at Nov. 23, 2022.

Price Range - AXET.P/TSX-VEN

Year	Volume	High	Low	Close
2022	165,000	$0.10	$0.10	$0.10

Recent Close: $0.08

Capital Stock Changes - On Nov. 23, 2022, an initial public offering of 4,286,468 common shares was completed at 10¢ per share.

A.166 Axiom Capital Advisors Inc.

Symbol - ACA **Exchange** - CSE **CUSIP** - 05465N

Head Office - 210-2020 4 St SW, Calgary, AB, T2S 1W3 **Telephone** - (604) 940-8826 **Fax** - (888) 739-9875

Website - www.axiomadvisors.ca

Email - evan@axiomadvisors.ca

Investor Relations - L. Evan Baergen (604) 940-8826

Auditors - Kenway Mack Slusarchuk Stewart LLP C.A., Calgary, Alta.

Transfer Agents - Alliance Trust Company, Calgary, Alta.

Profile - (Alta. 2020) Forms and sells minority ownership interests of subsidiaries it forms to small businesses, allowing the subsidiary to receive investment capital from registered accounts such as registered retirement savings plan (RRSP), registered education savings plan, retirement income fund (RIF) and tax free savings accounts (TFSA).

The company receives an upfront fee as well as a percentage of the funds raised by the subsidiary and an annual renewal fee. Also offers to manage the administration portion of the capital raised by the subsidiary under a separate administration agreement. The company may also receive additional compensation from the subsidiaries, such as dividends.

Directors - Dwight Martin, chr. & CEO, B.C.; L. Evan Baergen, CFO & corp. sec., Delta, B.C.; Douglas T. (Doug) McCartney, Calgary, Alta.; Paul H. Shelley, Calgary, Alta.

Capital Stock

	Authorized (shs.)	Outstanding (shs.)[1]
Class A Preferred	unlimited	nil
Class B Preferred	unlimited	nil
Class C Preferred	unlimited	nil
Class A Common	unlimited	6,472,100

[1] At Sept. 30, 2022

Major Shareholder - L. Evan Baergen held 38.6% interest and Dwight Martin held 38.6% interest at Apr. 5, 2022.

Recent Close: $0.11

Capital Stock Changes - There were no changes to capital stock during fiscal 2021 or fiscal 2022.

Financial Statistics

Periods ended:	12m June 30/22[A]		12m June 30/21[A]
	$000s	%Chg	$000s
Operating revenue	**104**	**+160**	**40**
General & admin expense	57		67
Operating expense	**57**	**-15**	**67**
Operating income	**47**	**n.a.**	**(27)**
Deprec., depl. & amort.	nil		42
Write-downs/write-offs	nil		(86)
Pre-tax income	**47**	**n.a.**	**(154)**
Net income	**47**	**n.a.**	**(154)**
Cash & equivalent	6		2
Accounts receivable	18		nil
Current assets	23		6
Total assets	**24**	**+300**	**6**
Bank indebtedness	15		44
Accts. pay. & accr. liabs	6		6
Current liabilities	21		50
Shareholders' equity	3		(44)
Cash from oper. activs	**33**	**n.a.**	**(89)**
Cash from fin. activs	(29)		44
Net cash position	**6**	**+200**	**2**
	$		$
Earnings per share*	0.01		(0.02)
Cash flow per share*	0.01		(0.01)
	shs		shs
No. of shs. o/s*	6,472,100		6,472,100
Avg. no. of shs. o/s*	6,472,100		6,472,100
	%		%
Net profit margin	45.19		(385.00)
Return on equity	n.m.		n.m.
Return on assets	313.33		(191.30)

* Cl.A Common

[A] Reported in accordance with IFRS

Latest Results

Periods ended:	3m Sept. 30/22[A]		3m Sept. 30/21[A]
	$000s	%Chg	$000s
Operating revenue	16	n.a.	nil
Net income	(4)	n.a.	(13)
	$		$
Earnings per share*	(0.00)		(0.00)

* Cl.A Common

[A] Reported in accordance with IFRS

Historical Summary
(as originally stated)

Fiscal Year	Oper. Rev. $000s	Net Inc. Bef. Disc. $000s	EPS* $
2022^A	104	47	0.01
2021^A	40	(154)	(0.02)
2020^A	25	(79)	n.a.

* Cl.A Common
^A Reported in accordance with IFRS

A.167 Axion Ventures Inc.

Symbol - AXV **Exchange** - TSX-VEN (S) **CUSIP** - 05465L
Head Office - 1000-595 Burrard St, Vancouver, BC, V7X 1S8 **Telephone** - (604) 219-2140
Website - www.axionventures.com
Email - grant.kim@axionventures.com
Investor Relations - Grant Kim (604) 219-2140
Auditors - Davidson & Company LLP C.A., Vancouver, B.C.
Lawyers - Boughton Law Corporation, Vancouver, B.C.; Clark Wilson LLP, Vancouver, B.C.
Transfer Agents - Computershare Trust Company of Canada Inc., Vancouver, B.C.
Profile - (B.C. 2011) Invests primarily in companies in the online video gaming and other information technology (IT) sectors.
Holds direct and indirect interests in **Axion Games Limited** (AG), an online video game development and publishing company with primary operations in Shanghai, People's Republic of China. AG focuses on cross platform development and publication of online video games, as well as licensing its proprietary titles to third party publishers globally.
Holds 49% indirect interest in **True Axion Interactive Ltd.** (TAI), a video game academy and development studio with primary operations in Bangkok, Thailand. TAI develops mobile focused games with design and infrastructure extendable to multiple platforms.
Holds 15% interest in **Red Anchor Trading Corp.**, a British Virgin Islands-based company which operates the HotNow mobile application, a marketing automation platform for retailers to offer various promotions.
Holds 60% indirect interest in **Longroot Limited**, which operates a digital assets business in Thailand and is currently in the process of obtaining its local business licence.
Common suspended from TSX-VEN, Aug. 5, 2020.
Predecessor Detail - Name changed from Capstream Ventures Inc., Mar. 10, 2017.
Directors - Yasuyo Yamazaki, exec. chr., Tokyo, Japan; Grant Kim, interim CEO, Vancouver, B.C.; Kunio Hamada, Tokyo, Japan; Mana Prapakamol, Bangkok, Thailand; Stephen R. (Steve) Willey, Bellevue, Wash.
Other Exec. Officers - Peemtat Utsahajit, COO & interim CFO; Matthew (Matt) Sroka, v-p, corp. devel.

Capital Stock

	Authorized (shs.)	Outstanding (shs.)[1]
Preferred	unlimited	nil
Common	unlimited	255,893,504

[1] At Nov. 24, 2022
Major Shareholder - Grant Kim held 10.92% interest at Mar. 8, 2021.

Price Range - AXV/TSX-VEN (S)

Year	Volume	High	Low	Close
2020	2,214,381	$0.35	$0.10	$0.20
2019	9,890,334	$1.25	$0.28	$0.31
2018	6,736,542	$1.25	$0.79	$0.90

Wholly Owned Subsidiaries
Axia Corporation Ltd., Hong Kong, People's Republic of China.
Axia Corporation (Thailand) Co., Ltd., Thailand.
Axia Technologies Pte Ltd., Singapore.
Axion Entertainment Holdings Ltd., British Virgin Islands.
Axion Entertainment International Holdings Limited, British Virgin Islands.
Axion Interactive (Hong Kong) Ltd., Hong Kong, People's Republic of China.
- 100% int. in **Axion Interactive Entertainment (Chengdu) Co., Ltd.**, People's Republic of China.
- 100% int. in **Axion Interactive Entertainment (Shanghai) Co., Ltd.**, People's Republic of China.

Axion Interactive Inc., British Virgin Islands.
- 49% int. in **True Axion Games Ltd.**, Thailand.

Subsidiaries
54.22% int. in **Axion Games Limited**, Cayman Islands.
- 100% int. in **Mega Marble International Limited**, British Virgin Islands.
  - 100% int. in **Digital Arts Academy International Group Limited**, British Virgin Islands.
    - 70% int. in **Taozhi Digital Technology (Shanghai) Co., Ltd.**, Shanghai, People's Republic of China.
  - 100% int. in **Ying Pei Digital Technology (Shanghai) Co., Ltd.**, Shanghai, People's Republic of China.
    - 100% int. in **Shanghai Ying Pei Digital Technology Co., Ltd.**, Shanghai, People's Republic of China.
    - 100% int. in **Shanghai Ying Pei Software Co., Ltd.**, People's Republic of China.
    - 100% int. in **Shanghai Zhenyou Network Technology Limited**, People's Republic of China.
  - 100% int. in **Ying Pei Digital Technology (Suzhou) Co., Ltd.**, Suzhou, Jiangsu, People's Republic of China.
- 100% int. in **Mocool Limited**, Hong Kong, People's Republic of China.

99% int. in **Axion Ventures (BKK) Co., Ltd.**, Thailand.
60% int. in **Longroot Limited**, Cayman Islands.
- 100% int. in **Axion Intelligence Ltd.**, British Virgin Islands.
- 100% int. in **Longroot (Thailand) Ltd.**, Thailand.

60% int. in **True Axion Interactive Ltd.**, Thailand.

Investments
15% int. in **Red Anchor Trading Corp.**, Bangkok, Thailand.
50% int. in **Trajectory Games Ltd.**, Russia.
- 100% int. in **Trajectory Games Ru Ltd.**, Russia.

Note: The preceding list includes only the major related companies in which interests are held.

A.168 Axis Auto Finance Inc.

Symbol - AXIS **Exchange** - TSX **CUSIP** - 05465J
Head Office - 200-165 Galaxy Blvd, Toronto, ON, M9W 0C8 **Toll-free** - (855) 964-5626 **Fax** - (866) 765-8164
Website - www.axisautofinance.com
Email - ir@axisautofinance.com
Investor Relations - Richard Lloyd (855) 964-5626
Auditors - Ernst & Young LLP C.A., Toronto, Ont.
Transfer Agents - TSX Trust Company, Toronto, Ont.
Employees - 150 at Sept. 28, 2022
Profile - (Can. 2008) Provides alternative used vehicle financing to individuals that do not qualify for traditional bank financing as well as commercial equipment leasing and financing solutions.
Operations are organized into two segments:
Automotive Lending - Originates and services loans and leases granted primarily to non-prime consumers to finance the purchase of motor vehicles. Non-prime consumers are borrowers who may have had previous financial difficulties or may not yet have sufficient credit history. Loans are originated through a network of over 2,500 independent and franchised used vehicles dealers across Canada, as well as through the company's DriveAxis.ca platform, a direct-to-consumer e-commerce solution for buying and financing used vehicles. Through DriveAxis.ca, customers can choose their next used vehicle, customize financing terms and get the car delivered to their home, while the dealer gets paid the full retail price for the vehicles.
Equipment Financing - Wholly owned **Pivotal Capital Corp.** originates and services leases for commercial customers to finance the purchase of industrial and manufacturing machinery, commercial heavy vehicles and other business equipment.
At Sept. 30, 2022, the lending portfolio consisted of automotive leases and loans with an aggregate receivables balance of $145,625,977 and equipment finance leases and loans with an aggregate receivables balance of $31,247,007. In addition, the company managed $98,868,521 of automotive finance receivables originated and serviced on behalf of **Westlake Financial Services Inc.**
Predecessor Detail - Name changed from Verdant Financial Partners I Inc., July 25, 2016, following Qualifying Transaction reverse takeover acquisition of 8095981 Canada Inc. (operated as Axis Auto Finance); basis 1 new for 6 old shs.
Directors - Paul J. Stoyan, chr., Toronto, Ont.; Todd Hudson, CEO, Toronto, Ont.; Ilja Troitschanski, pres., Toronto, Ont.; Ian Anderson, Los Angeles, Calif.; Lesley Gallinger, Toronto, Ont.; Wes Neichenbauer, Toronto, Ont.; James (Jim) Nikopoulos, Toronto, Ont.; Bruce Smith, Toronto, Ont.
Other Exec. Officers - Steven Koster, man. dir.; Richard Lloyd, CFO

Capital Stock

	Authorized (shs.)	Outstanding (shs.)[1]
Preferred	unlimited	nil
Common	unlimited	122,109,949

[1] At Nov. 18, 2022
Normal Course Issuer Bid - The company plans to make normal course purchases of up to 6,105,497 common shares representing 5% of the total outstanding. The bid commenced on Nov. 26, 2022, and expires on Nov. 25, 2023.
Major Shareholder - Westlake Services, LLC held 24.57% interest and Ilja Troitschanski held 11.4% interest at Oct. 31, 2022.

Price Range - AXIS/TSX

Year	Volume	High	Low	Close
2022	8,345,505	$0.73	$0.42	$0.48
2021	10,960,201	$0.57	$0.25	$0.54
2020	12,070,906	$0.51	$0.14	$0.32
2019	9,534,829	$0.52	$0.21	$0.22
2018	11,337,440	$0.81	$0.39	$0.43

Recent Close: $0.16
Capital Stock Changes - In November 2021, private placement of 30,000,000 common shares was completed at 50¢ per share. Also during fiscal 2022, common shares were issued as follows: 1,115,957 on vesting of restricted share units and 234,666 on exercise of warrants; 5,694,000 common shares were repurchased under a Normal Course Issuer Bid.

Wholly Owned Subsidiaries
Axis Auto Finance Lending Corp., Canada.
Axis Auto Finance Services Corp., Canada.
- 100% int. in **Pivotal Capital Corp.**, Canada.

Cars on Credit Financial Inc., Newmarket, Ont.
Trend Financial Corp., Toronto, Ont.
- 100% int. in **TAuto Ontario Inc.**, Ont.
- 100% int. in **Trend Dealer Services GP Inc.**, Ont.
  - 0.1% int. in **Trend Dealers Services LP**, Ont.
- 99.9% int. in **Trend Dealers Services LP**, Ont.

Financial Statistics

Periods ended:	12m June 30/22^A		12m June 30/21^A
	$000s	%Chg	$000s
Total revenue	**40,163**	**+5**	**38,369**
General & admin. expense	16,362		13,248
Stock-based compensation	403		505
Other operating expense	94		150
Operating expense	**16,859**	**+21**	**13,902**
Operating income	**23,304**	**-5**	**24,467**
Deprec. & amort.	1,557		1,494
Provision for loan losses	11,569		10,326
Finance costs, gross	7,887		9,185
Pre-tax income	**1,985**	**-39**	**3,253**
Income taxes	500		932
Net income	**1,485**	**-36**	**2,321**
Cash & equivalent	1,477		3,448
Inventories	2,002		2,144
Accounts receivable	2,354		1,257
Investments	...		117,084
Fixed assets, net	1,625		1,453
Right-of-use assets	902		610
Intangibles, net	18,635		18,642
Total assets	**186,997**	**+20**	**155,842**
Accts. pay. & accr. liabs	6,094		7,272
Debt	130,569		111,838
Lease liabilities	917		645
Equity portion of conv. debs	3,211		3,211
Shareholders' equity	49,416		36,086
Cash from oper. activs	**(29,946)**	**n.a.**	**(1,308)**
Cash from fin. activs	28,641		(3,252)
Cash from invest. activs	(1,266)		(1,684)
Net cash position	**4,076**	**-39**	**6,647**
Capital expenditures	(994)		(476)
	$		$
Earnings per share*	0.01		0.02
Cash flow per share*	(0.26)		(0.01)
	shs		shs
No. of shs. o/s*	122,927,046		97,270,423
Avg. no. of shs. o/s*	116,124,032		97,034,085
	%		%
Net profit margin	3.70		6.05
Return on equity	3.47		6.70
Return on assets	4.31		5.73

* Common
^A Reported in accordance with IFRS

Latest Results

Periods ended:	3m Sept. 30/22^A		3m Sept. 30/21^A
	$000s	%Chg	$000s
Total revenue	10,197	+3	9,948
Net income	(908)	n.a.	651
	$		$
Earnings per share*	(0.01)		0.01

* Common
^A Reported in accordance with IFRS

Historical Summary
(as originally stated)

Fiscal Year	Total Rev. $000s	Net Inc. Bef. Disc. $000s	EPS* $
2022^A	40,163	1,485	0.01
2021^A	38,369	2,321	0.02
2020^A	37,202	(675)	(0.01)
2019^A	31,922	(3,864)	(0.04)
2018^A	15,798	(3,702)	(0.06)

* Common
^A Reported in accordance with IFRS

A.169 Ayr Wellness Inc.

Symbol - AYR.A **Exchange** - NEO **CUSIP** - 05475P
Head Office - 2601 South Bayshore Dr, Suite 900, Miami, FL, United States, 33133
Website - www.ayrwellness.com
Email - ir@ayrwellness.com
Investor Relations - Jon DeCourcey (786) 885-0397
Auditors - Marcum LLP C.P.A., New York, N.Y.
Transfer Agents - Odyssey Trust Company, Toronto, Ont.
FP500 Revenue Ranking - 430

Employees - 2,800 at Dec. 31, 2022

Profile - (B.C. 2019; orig. Ont., 2017) Cultivates, manufactures, distributes and retails cannabis products in the United States.

The company had 86 retail dispensaries (at August 2023) in Florida (62), Massachusetts (4), Nevada (6), New Jersey (3), Pennsylvania (9) and Illinois (2). Dispensaries primarily operate under brand names including AYR Cannabis Dispensary and The Dispensary.

Cultivation and production facilities total 1,300,000 sq. ft. across 16 facilities located in Florida, Massachusetts, Nevada, New Jersey, Ohio, Pennsylvania and Illinois, which produce consumer-packaged goods brands including Kynd, Origyn Extracts, Levia, STiX Preroll Co., Secret Orchard, Lost in Translation, Haze, Road Tripper, Wicked, CannaPunch and Entourage.

On July 13, 2023, the company entered into an option agreement to acquire **Twice the Wellness, LLC**, which intends to open a medical marijuana dispensary in Woodmere, Ohio.

In April 2023, the company acquired **Tahoe Hydroponics Company, LLC**, a cannabis cultivator and producer with cultivation and manufacturing facilities in Carson City and Sparks, Nev., totaling 33,000 sq. ft., for US$1,500,000 cash and issuance of 232,795 exchangeable shares valued at US$115,000. The second part of the acquisition involves **NV Green, Inc.**, a producer of concentrates, which has not yet closed. The company would issue an additional 58,196 exchangeable shares on closing of NV Green.

In March 2023, the company sold wholly owned **Blue Camo, LLC** (dba Oasis), which consisted of the company's Arizona assets, to **AZ Goat, LLC**, a group consisting primarily of former owners of Blue Camo, for US$20,000,000 cash and assumption of US$15,000,000 in lease obligations. The sale included three Oasis-branded dispensaries in the greater Phoenix area, a 10,000-sq.-ft. cultivation and processing facility in Chandler and an 80,000-sq.-ft. cultivation facility in Phoenix, as well as 60% interest in **Willcox OC, LLC**, a joint venture developing an outdoor cultivation facility.

On Feb. 9, 2023, the company entered into option agreements to acquire two entities each provisionally licensed to operate a medical marijuana dispensary in Riverside and Clermont cty., both in Ohio, from **Daily Releaf, LLC** and **Heaven Wellness, LLC**, respectively.

In January 2023, the company terminated its agreement to acquire **Gentle Ventures, LLC** and certain of its affiliates (dba Dispensary 33), owner and operator of two dispensaries in Chicago, Ill., for US$55,000,000, consisting of US$12,000,00 cash, US$40,000,000 in stock and US$3,000,000 in seller notes.

In May 2022, the company acquired **Herbal Remedies Dispensaries, LLC**, an operator of two dispensaries in Quincy, Ill., for US$19,000,000, consisting of US$3,000,000 cash, issuance of 353,000 exchangeable shares valued at US$1,900,000 and a US$14,200,000 promissory note.

Predecessor Detail - Name changed from Ayr Strategies Inc., Feb. 12, 2021.

Directors - Jonathan (Jon) Sandelman, exec. chr. & corp. sec., Miami, Fla.; Joyce Johnson-Miller†, Chicago, Ill.; Glenn Isaacson, New York, N.Y.; Louis F. Karger, Needham, Mass.; Charles Miles, New York, N.Y.; Michael Warren

Other Exec. Officers - David Goubert, pres. & CEO; Brad Asher, CFO; Robert (Jamie) Mendola, chief bus. devel. officer, natl. head, wholesale & purch. & gen. mgr., western region; Anya Varga, chief people officer

† Lead director

Capital Stock

	Authorized (shs.)	Outstanding (shs.)[1]
Subordinate Vtg.	unlimited	10,066,000
Restricted Vtg.	unlimited	6,370,000
Limited Vtg.	unlimited	47,282,000
Multiple Vtg.	unlimited	3,696,486
Exchangeable	unlimited	9,710,707[2]

[1] At June 30, 2023

[2] Securities of wholly owned CSAC Acquisition Inc.

Subordinate Voting - May be held, beneficially owned or controlled only by non-U.S. persons; if, at any given time, the shares are held, beneficially owned or controlled by a U.S. person, they will automatically convert into restricted voting shares on a one-for-one basis. One vote per share. Are traded along with restricted voting and limited voting shares under a single designation.

Restricted Voting - May be held, beneficially owned or controlled only by U.S. persons; if, at any given time, the shares are held, beneficially owned or controlled by non-U.S. persons, they will automatically convert into subordinate voting shares on a one-for-one basis. If, at any given time, the total number of restricted voting shares represents a number equal to or in excess of the foreign portfolio investors (FPI) threshold (less than 50% of the company's outstanding voting securities held by residents of the U.S.), then the minimum number of restricted voting shares required to stay within the FPI threshold would be automatically converted into limited voting shares on a one-for-one basis. In connection with a formal bid whereby a bidder would own or control more than 50% of the total voting power of the company for the election of directors, the bidder may elect that the restricted voting shares it so acquires not be automatically converted into limited voting shares. If, at any given time, the total number of restricted voting shares represents a number below the FPI threshold, then a number of limited voting shares would be automatically converted into restricted voting shares on a one-for-one basis, to the maximum extent possible such that the restricted voting shares then represent a number of shares that is one share less than the FPI threshold. One vote per share.

Limited Voting - May be held, beneficially owned or controlled only by U.S. persons; if, at any given time, the shares are held, beneficially owned or controlled by non-U.S. persons, they will automatically convert into subordinate voting shares on a one-for-one basis. One vote per share on all matters except the election of directors.

Multiple Voting - Entitled to dividends. Convertible at any time into subordinate voting shares on a one-for-one basis. Automatically convertible into subordinate voting shares on a one-for-one basis on May 24, 2024 (representing five years following closing of the Qualifying Acquisition). 25 votes per share.

Exchangeable - Exchangeable for subordinate voting shares on a one-for-one basis and are the economic equivalent of subordinate voting shares. Non-voting.

Major Shareholder - Jonathan (Jon) Sandelman held 59.8% interest at May 16, 2023.

Price Range - AYR.A/NEO

Year	Volume	High	Low	Close
2022	36,674,159	$23.28	$1.61	$1.64
2021	30,474,083	$47.44	$15.76	$19.14
2020	11,570,583	$31.48	$5.01	$30.25
2019	2,891,076	$26.79	$10.00	$12.25
2018	130,100	$19.93	$10.00	$12.57

Recent Close: $1.08

Capital Stock Changes - During 2022, subordinate, restricted or limited voting shares were issued as follows: 2,109,000 on vesting of restricted share units, 2,006,000 on conversion of a like number of exchangeable shares, 1,029,000 as earn-out consideration, 76,000 for services and 33,000 on exercise of options; 5,000 subordinate voting shares were repurchased under a Normal Course Issuer Bid and 676,000 subordinate, restricted or limited voting shares were cancelled. In addition, 353,000 and 329,000 exchangeable shares were issued pursuant to the acquisitions of Herbal Remedies Dispensaries, LLC and Cultivauna, LLC, respectively.

Wholly Owned Subsidiaries

Ayr Wellness Holdings LLC, Nev.

- 100% int. in **CSAC Holdings Inc.**, Nev.
  - 100% int. in **CSAC Acquisition Inc.**, Nev.
    - 100% int. in **Ayr NJ, LLC**, Nev.
    - 100% int. in **Ayr Ohio LLC**, Ohio
      - 100% int. in **Greenlight Holdings, LLC**, Ohio
      - 100% int. in **Greenlight Management, LLC**, Ohio
    - 100% int. in **CSAC Acquisition AZ Corp.**, Ariz.
    - 100% int. in **CSAC Acquisition FL Corp.**, Fla.
      - 100% int. in **DFMMJ Investments, LLC**, Fla.
      - 100% int. in **242 Cannabis, LLC**, Fla.
    - 100% int. in **CSAC Acquisition IL Corp.**, Ill.
      - 100% int. in **Herbal Remedies Dispensaries, LLC**, Ill.
    - 100% int. in **CSAC Acquisition MA Corp.**, Mass.
      - 100% int. in **Cultivauna, LLC**, Mass.
      - 100% int. in **Eskar Holdings, LLC**, Mass.
      - 100% int. in **Sira Naturals, Inc.**, Cambridge, Mass.
    - 100% int. in **CSAC Acquisition NJ Corp.**, N.J.
      - 100% int. in **GSD NJ LLC**, N.J.
    - 100% int. in **CSAC Acquisition NV Corp.**, Nev.
      - 100% int. in **CannaPunch of Nevada LLC**, Henderson, Nev.
      - 100% int. in **Kynd-Strainz, LLC**, Nev.
      - 100% int. in **Lemon Aide, LLC**, Nev.
      - 100% int. in **LivFree Wellness LLC**, Las Vegas, Nev.
        - 100% int. in **BP Solutions LLC**, Nev.
      - 100% int. in **Tahoe Hydroponics Company, LLC**, Carson City, Nev.
      - 100% int. in **Tahoe-Reno Botanicals, LLC**, Nev.
      - 100% int. in **Tahoe-Reno Extractions, LLC**, Nev.
    - 100% int. in **CSAC Acquisition PA Corp.**, Pa.
      - 100% int. in **CannTech PA, LLC**, Pa.
      - 100% int. in **DocHouse, LLC**, Pa.
      - 100% int. in **PA Natural Medicine, LLC**, Pa.
    - 100% int. in **CSAC Ohio, LLC**, Ohio
    - 100% int. in **DWC Investments, LLC**, Nev.
    - 100% int. in **Klymb Project Management, Inc.**, Nev.

Financial Statistics

Periods ended:	12m Dec. 31/22[A]		12m Dec. 31/21[A]
	US$000s	%Chg	US$000s
Operating revenue	**465,618**	**+30**	**357,608**
Cost of goods sold	239,190		201,335
General & admin expense	175,270		117,290
Stock-based compensation	46,822		27,155
Operating expense	**461,282**	**+33**	**345,780**
Operating income	**4,336**	**-63**	**11,828**
Deprec., depl. & amort.	92,839		58,834
Finance income	275		204
Finance costs, gross	30,575		16,550
Investment income	nil		(32)
Write-downs/write-offs	(148,531)[1]		nil
Pre-tax income	**(210,109)**	**n.a.**	**12,309**
Income taxes	45,376		29,261
Net income	**(255,485)**	**n.a.**	**(16,952)**
Net inc. for equity hldrs	**(245,466)**	**n.a.**	**(16,952)**
Net inc. for non-cont. int	**(10,019)**	**n.a.**	**nil**
Cash & equivalent	80,640		154,342
Inventories	115,053		93,363
Accounts receivable	8,949		7,413
Current assets	213,527		266,067
Fixed assets, net	326,918		275,222
Right-of-use assets	182,130		106,247
Intangibles, net	1,032,835		1,208,825
Total assets	**1,763,880**	**-5**	**1,859,912**
Accts. pay. & accr. liabs	54,771		59,707
Current liabilities	228,994		152,336
Long-term debt, gross	480,206		379,265
Long-term debt, net	439,683		371,154
Long-term lease liabilities	159,408		97,173
Shareholders' equity	833,324		1,020,063
Non-controlling interest	2,000		nil
Cash from oper. activs	**(34,165)**	**n.a.**	**(27,781)**
Cash from fin. activs	26,960		274,514
Cash from invest. activs	(66,497)		(219,629)
Net cash position	**80,640**	**-48**	**154,342**
Capital expenditures	(77,424)		(100,003)
Capital disposals	31,433		nil
	US$		US$
Earnings per share*	(3.58)		(0.30)
Cash flow per share*	(0.50)		(0.48)
	shs		shs
No. of shs. o/s*	70,650,317		67,401,946
Avg. no. of shs. o/s*	68,635,000		57,329,350
	%		%
Net profit margin	(54.87)		(4.74)
Return on equity	(26.49)		(2.90)
Return on assets	(12.05)		(3.21)
Foreign sales percent	100		100
No. of employees (FTEs)	2,800		2,300

* S.V., M.V. & Exch.

[A] Reported in accordance with U.S. GAAP

[1] Pertains to goodwill impairment.

Latest Results

Periods ended:	6m June 30/23[A]		6m June 30/22[□A]
	US$000s	%Chg	US$000s
Operating revenue	234,402	+18	198,417
Net inc. bef. disc. opers	(43,586)	n.a.	(44,683)
Income from disc. opers	(184,686)		(4,759)
Net income	(228,272)	n.a.	(49,442)
Net inc. for equity hldrs	(224,536)	n.a.	(45,934)
Net inc. for non-cont. int	(3,736)		(3,508)
	US$		US$
Earns. per sh. bef. disc. opers.*	(0.56)		(0.60)
Earnings per share*	(3.15)		(0.67)

* S.V., M.V. & Exch.

□ Restated

[A] Reported in accordance with U.S. GAAP

Historical Summary

(as originally stated)

Fiscal Year	Oper. Rev.	Net Inc. Bef. Disc.	EPS*
	US$000s	US$000s	US$
2022[A]	465,618	(255,485)	(3.58)
2021[A]	357,608	(16,952)	(0.30)
2020[B]	155,114	(176,333)	(6.32)
2019[B]	75,196	(164,180)	(9.43)
	$000s	$000s	$
2018[B]	nil	(58,923)	(15.94)

* S.V., M.V. & Exch.

[A] Reported in accordance with U.S. GAAP

[B] Reported in accordance with IFRS

A.170 Ayurcann Holdings Corp.

Symbol - AYUR **Exchange** - CSE **CUSIP** - 05476A
Head Office - Unit 6, 1080 Brock Rd, Pickering, ON, L1W 3H3 **Telephone** - (905) 492-3322
Website - ayurcann.com
Email - igal@ayurcann.com
Investor Relations - Igal Sudman (905) 492-3322
Auditors - Clearhouse LLP C.A., Mississauga, Ont.
Transfer Agents - Odyssey Trust Company
Profile - (Ont. 2012 amalg.) Provides post-harvest outsourcing solutions, including extraction, product formulation and manufacturing, for licensed cannabis producers and cannabis brands.

Operations are conducted out of a 10,300-sq.-ft. facility in Pickering, Ont., with processing capacity of up to 300,000 kg of biomass per year and manufacturing capacity for up to 3,000,000 product units per year for vapes, tinctures, topicals, flowers and edibles. End-to-end outsourcing services provided include extraction, refinement, bulk oil sales, product research and development, formulation, packaging, fulfillment and distribution for the Canadian adult use and medical cannabis markets. Also produces products under proprietary brands including Fuego, Xplor, Joints and Hustle and Shake.

In addition, operates Ayurcann Marketplace, an online cannabis marketplace for medical cannabis consumers in Canada.

Recent Merger and Acquisition Activity

Status: completed **Revised:** Sept. 7, 2022
UPDATE: The transaction was completed. 32,352,941 common shares were issued to Tetra to satisfy the transaction. As a result, Tetra's voting interest increased to 23.06% from 2.64%. PREVIOUS: Ayurcann Holdings Corp. entered a share purchase agreement with Tetra Oils Inc. to acquire Joints and Hustle & Shake Inc. for $5,500,000 common shares at a deemed price of 17¢ per share. Joints and Hustle offers cannabis products including oils, vapes, flowers, tinctures and hash.

Predecessor Detail - Name changed from Canada Coal Inc., Mar. 25, 2021, pursuant to the reverse takeover acquisition of Ayurcann Inc. and concurrent amalgamation of Ayurcann with wholly owned 12487772 Canada Inc.; basis 1 new for 2 old shs.

Directors - Igal Sudman, chr., CEO & corp. sec., Maple, Ont.; Roman Buzaker, pres., CFO & COO, Toronto, Ont.; Alison Gordon, Toronto, Ont.; David Hackett, Toronto, Ont.; Maor Shayit, Vaughan, Ont.

Capital Stock

	Authorized (shs.)	Outstanding (shs.)[1]
Common	unlimited	155,556,863

[1] At Nov. 29, 2022

Major Shareholder - Tetra Oils Inc. held 22.87% interest, Igal Sudman held 17.28% interest, Roman Buzaker held 17.1% interest and Weed Me Inc. held 10.18% interest at Nov. 21, 2022.

Price Range - AYUR/CSE

Year	Volume	High	Low	Close
2022	14,121,257	$0.18	$0.03	$0.03
2021	14,673,064	$0.75	$0.13	$0.17
2020	3,361,415	$0.14	$0.02	$0.12
2019	7,250,625	$0.14	$0.02	$0.05
2018	1,998,779	$0.23	$0.05	$0.05

Consolidation: 1-for-2 cons. in Mar. 2021
Recent Close: $0.02

Capital Stock Changes - In October 2021, private placement of 7,710,354 units (1 common share & 1 warrant) at 18¢ per unit was completed and 5,159,958 common shares were issued for completion of the production and manufacturing facility in Pickering, Ont. Also during fiscal 2022, 5,071,372 common shares were issued on vesting of restricted share units; 1,682,000 common shares were repurchased under Normal Course Issuer Bid.

Wholly Owned Subsidiaries

Ayurcann Inc., Thornhill, Ont.
Joints and Hustle & Shake Inc., Ont.

Financial Statistics

Periods ended:	12m June 30/22[A]	%Chg	12m June 30/21[A1]
	$000s	%Chg	$000s
Operating revenue	**11,082**	**+45**	**7,634**
Cost of goods sold	7,165		2,805
Salaries & benefits	998		754
General & admin expense	2,405		1,569
Stock-based compensation	2,105		134
Operating expense	**12,673**	**+141**	**5,262**
Operating income	**(1,591)**	**n.a.**	**2,372**
Deprec., depl. & amort.	321		212
Finance costs, gross	91		315
Write-downs/write-offs	(38)		nil
Pre-tax income	**(3,423)**	**n.a.**	**57**
Income taxes	(335)		335
Net income	**(3,088)**	**n.a.**	**(278)**
Cash & equivalent	1,355		725
Inventories	2,948		2,317
Accounts receivable	1,400		2,059
Current assets	6,095		5,431
Fixed assets, net	939		884
Right-of-use assets	249		362
Total assets	**7,283**	**+9**	**6,677**
Accts. pay. & accr. liabs	1,994		1,084
Current liabilities	2,168		1,572
Long-term debt, gross	40		40
Long-term debt, net	40		40
Long-term lease liabilities	181		316
Shareholders' equity	4,894		4,749
Cash from oper. activs	**(50)**	**n.a.**	**(199)**
Cash from fin. activs	943		538
Cash from invest. activs	(263)		363
Net cash position	**1,355**	**+87**	**725**
Capital expenditures	(263)		(509)
	$		$
Earnings per share*	(0.03)		(0.00)
Cash flow per share*	(0.00)		(0.00)
	shs		shs
No. of shs. o/s*	120,857,317		104,597,633
Avg. no. of shs. o/s*	118,511,846		84,994,390
	%		%
Net profit margin	(27.87)		(3.64)
Return on equity	n.m.		(9.49)
Return on assets	n.a.		(46.49)

* Common
[A] Reported in accordance with IFRS
[1] Results reflect the Mar. 26, 2021, reverse takeover acquisition of Ayurcann Inc.

Latest Results

Periods ended:	3m Sept. 30/22[A]	%Chg	3m Sept. 30/21[A]
	$000s	%Chg	$000s
Operating revenue	3,358	+80	1,866
Net income	(935)	n.a.	125
	$		$
Earnings per share*	(0.01)		0.00

* Common
[A] Reported in accordance with IFRS

Historical Summary
(as originally stated)

Fiscal Year	Oper. Rev.	Net Inc. Bef. Disc.	EPS*
	$000s	$000s	$
2022[A]	11,082	(3,088)	(0.03)
2021[A]	7,634	(278)	(0.00)
2020[A1]	nil	(237)	(0.02)
2019[A]	nil	(223)	(0.02)
2018[A]	nil	(273)	(0.02)

* Common
[A] Reported in accordance with IFRS
[1] Results for fiscal 2020 and prior fiscal years pertain to Canada Coal Inc.
Note: Adjusted throughout for 1-for-2 cons. in Mar. 2021

B

B.1 BBTV Holdings Inc.

Symbol - BBTV **Exchange** - TSX **CUSIP** - 05551N
Head Office - 1205 Melville St, Vancouver, BC, V6E 0A6 **Telephone** - (604) 900-5202
Website - www.bbtv.com
Email - nglaister@bbtv.com
Investor Relations - Nancy Glaister (604) 900-5202
Auditors - PricewaterhouseCoopers LLP C.A., Vancouver, B.C.
Lawyers - Torys LLP; Clark Wilson LLP, Vancouver, B.C.
Transfer Agents - Computershare Trust Company of Canada Inc., Vancouver, B.C.
FP500 Revenue Ranking - 512
Employees - 241 at Dec. 31, 2022
Profile - (B.C. 2019) Provides VISO®, a proprietary suite of managed services and Software-as-a-Service (SaaS) products to help content creators from content management to content protection and collaborations.

Has two main solutions:

Base Solutions - Solutions that help creators get their content discovered, collaborate with one another and gain insights from their performance, as well as help them monitor content for brand safety. Base Solutions also offers audience development and educational services, which provides resources for creators to stay informed and updated to the latest trends; and partner experience services, which provides assistance to creators in reporting and payments.

Plus Solutions - Solutions that help creators expand their growth and monetization opportunities through direct advertising sales to brands and advertising agencies; content management, which includes monetizing, tracking and removing copies of creator's content, and management of official video channels; and development and publishing of mobile gaming applications in partnership with creators.

The company activates content owners to Base Solutions before migrating their content to Plus Solutions. Exclusive digital content rights are generally acquired by way of licence from content owners, which the company then enhances their content.

Recent Merger and Acquisition Activity

Status: completed **Announced:** Oct. 26, 2022
BBTV Holdings Inc. acquired the assets of Detroit, Mich.-based Outloud Media for up to $5,000,000 subject to a five-year performance-based earn-out mechanism. Outloud Media is a creator economy business which distributes and monetizes digital content on various social media platforms.

Directors - Shahrzad Rafati, chr. & CEO, Vancouver, B.C.; Hamed Shahbazi†, Vancouver, B.C.; John M. Kim, Toronto, Ont.; Dr. Marcel Reichart, Lisbon, Portugal; Michele Romanow, Christ Church, Barbados; Catherine Warren, Vancouver, B.C.
Other Exec. Officers - Khamphiou (KB) Brinkley, CFO; Lewis Ball, chief strategy officer; Martin Cass, chief mktg. officer; Blake Corbet, chief corp. devel. officer; Doug Johnson, chief of ad sales & branded entertainment; Erich Lochner, sr. v-p, creator partnerships; Nancy Glaister, gen. counsel
† Lead director

Capital Stock

	Authorized (shs.)	Outstanding (shs.)[1]
Preferred	unlimited	nil
Multiple Voting	unlimited	6,408,505
Subordinate Voting	unlimited	15,239,042

[1] At May 12, 2023

Subordinate Voting - Non-convertible. One vote per share.
Multiple Voting - Convertible at any time, at the holder's option, into subordinate voting shares on a one-for-one basis. 10 votes per share.
Major Shareholder - Shahrzad Rafati held 81.55% interest at May 10, 2023.

Price Range - BBTV/TSX

Year	Volume	High	Low	Close
2022	13,243,215	$3.53	$0.43	$0.53
2021	16,946,293	$15.29	$2.95	$3.03
2020	6,400,685	$16.00	$9.85	$14.19

Recent Close: $0.31
Capital Stock Changes - During 2022, 771,197 common shares were issued under restricted and performance share unit plan.

Wholly Owned Subsidiaries

BroadbandTV Corp., Vancouver, B.C.
- 100% int. in **BroadbanTV (USA) Inc.**, Wash.
- 100% int. in **1189065 B.C. Ltd.**, B.C.
  - 0.01% int. in **YoBoHo New Media Private Limited**, India.
- 99.99% int. in **YoBoHo New Media Private Limited**, India.
  - 100% int. in **YoBoHo New Media Inc.**, Del.

Financial Statistics

Periods ended:	12m Dec. 31/22[A]		12m Dec. 31/21[A]
	$000s	%Chg	$000s
Operating revenue	**402,335**	**-16**	**476,622**
Cost of sales	365,615		437,261
Research & devel. expense	5,237		4,614
General & admin expense	45,875		43,985
Stock-based compensation	3,532		1,183
Operating expense	**420,259**	**-14**	**487,043**
Operating income	**(17,924)**	**n.a.**	**(10,421)**
Deprec., depl. & amort.	35,302		34,857
Finance costs, gross	8,952		6,849
Write-downs/write-offs	(156,705)[1]		nil
Pre-tax income	**(210,545)**	**n.a.**	**(49,770)**
Income taxes	(13,269)		(16,930)
Net income	**(197,276)**	**n.a.**	**(32,840)**
Cash & equivalent	19,549		30,899
Accounts receivable	16,163		30,026
Current assets	43,687		67,350
Fixed assets, net	1,577		2,246
Intangibles, net	152,069		337,272
Total assets	**197,934**	**-51**	**407,369**
Accts. pay. & accr. liabs	76,195		88,137
Current liabilities	88,563		88,809
Long-term debt, gross	58,484		51,056
Long-term debt, net	46,764		51,056
Long-term lease liabilities	729		1,394
Shareholders' equity	49,923		243,594
Cash from oper. activs	**(16,707)**	**n.a.**	**3,254**
Cash from fin. activs	10,242		14,127
Cash from invest. activs	(4,703)		(2,075)
Net cash position	**19,549**	**-37**	**30,899**
Capital expenditures	(267)		(197)
Capital disposals	6		nil
	$		$
Earnings per share*	(9.26)		(1.59)
Cash flow per share*	(0.78)		0.16
	shs		shs
No. of shs. o/s*	21,484,238		20,713,041
Avg. no. of shs. o/s*	21,299,900		20,619,973
	%		%
Net profit margin	(49.03)		(6.89)
Return on equity	(134.42)		(12.94)
Return on assets	(62.41)		(6.62)
No. of employees (FTEs)	241		284

* S.V. & M.V.
[A] Reported in accordance with IFRS
[1] Pertains to impairment of goodwill.

Historical Summary
(as originally stated)

Fiscal Year	Oper. Rev. $000s	Net Inc. Bef. Disc. $000s	EPS* $
2022[A]	402,335	(197,276)	(9.26)
2021[A]	476,622	(32,840)	(1.59)
2020[A]	109,685	(7,359)	(2.05)
2019[A1]	372,389	(8,158)	(0.62)
2018[A1]	334,893	(7,842)	(0.63)

* S.V. & M.V.
[A] Reported in accordance with IFRS
[1] Results pertain to BroadbandTV Corp.

B.2 The BC Bud Corporation

Symbol - BCBC **Exchange** - CSE **CUSIP** - 05553A
Head Office - 1500-409 Granville St, Vancouver, BC, V6C 1T2 **Telephone** - (778) 656-0377
Website - thebcbc.com
Email - daniel@thebcbc.com
Investor Relations - Daniel Southan-Dwyer (778) 619-2122
Auditors - BF Borgers CPA PC C.P.A., Lakewood, Colo.
Transfer Agents - Computershare Trust Company of Canada Inc., Vancouver, B.C.
Profile - (B.C. 2000; orig. Alta., 1987) Manufactures premium cannabis products in Canada through partnerships with licensed producers.

The company's business model is focused initially around strategic manufacturing and distribution agreements and joint venture agreements with established licensed producers. Partnerships include cannabis dried flower supply agreement with **Dunesberry Farms Ltd.**; manufacturing agreement of CannaBeans™, a chocolate covered coffee bean with cannabis with **Black Rose Organics Cannabis Inc.**; production of chemical-free concentrates including vaporizer cartridges under Solventless Solutions™ brand with **Habitat Craft Cannabis Ltd.**; development of Buds™, a cannabis infused beverage, with **2682130 Ontario Limited** (dba Peak Processing Solutions); and packaging solutions for cannabis flower, pre-rolls and concentrates with **Tricanna Industries Inc.**

Predecessor Detail - Name changed from Entheos Capital Corporation, pursuant to the reverse takeover acquisition of The BC Bud Corporation (renamed BC Bud Holdings Corp.).
Directors - Brayden R. Sutton, chr. & CEO, Chilliwack, B.C.; Thomas Joshua (Josh) Taylor, pres., B.C.; Justin Chorbajian, Langley, B.C.; Dayna Lange, B.C.; Brian Taylor, B.C.
Other Exec. Officers - Tak Tsan (Simon) Tso, CFO; Daniel Southan-Dwyer, v-p, corp. devel. & creative dir.

Capital Stock

	Authorized (shs.)	Outstanding (shs.)[1]
Preferred	unlimited	nil
Common	unlimited	46,220,565

[1] At Nov. 30, 2022

Major Shareholder - Brayden R. Sutton held 31.06% interest, Thomas Joshua (Josh) Taylor held 24% interest and Marc Lustig held 14.27% interest at Sept. 12, 2022.

Price Range - BCBC/CSE

Year	Volume	High	Low	Close
2022	4,759,788	$0.19	$0.04	$0.06
2021	2,874,896	$0.46	$0.15	$0.15
2020	1,034,513	$0.50	$0.10	$0.28
2019	534,167	$0.90	$0.40	$0.80
2018	844,078	$1.80	$0.20	$0.60

Consolidation: 1-for-10 cons. in Apr. 2020
Recent Close: $0.08

Wholly Owned Subsidiaries

BC Bud Holdings Corp., Vancouver, B.C.

Financial Statistics

Periods ended:	12m Feb. 28/22[A1]		12m Feb. 28/21[A2]
	$000s	%Chg	$000s
Operating revenue	**nil**	**n.a.**	**1**
Research & devel. expense	21		nil
General & admin expense	359		55
Stock-based compensation	417		nil
Operating expense	**797**	**n.m.**	**55**
Operating income	**(797)**	**n.a.**	**(54)**
Deprec., depl. & amort.	18		nil
Finance costs, gross	7		1
Pre-tax income	**(2,858)**	**n.a.**	**(56)**
Net income	**(2,858)**	**n.a.**	**(56)**
Cash & equivalent	1,403		340
Inventories	7		6
Current assets	1,887		351
Fixed assets, net	59		69
Intangibles, net	2		1
Total assets	**1,949**	**+363**	**421**
Accts. pay. & accr. liabs	84		26
Current liabilities	177		26
Long-term debt, gross	93		86
Long-term debt, net	nil		86
Shareholders' equity	1,772		308
Cash from oper. activs	**(876)**	**n.a.**	**(41)**
Cash from fin. activs	nil		450
Cash from invest. activs	1,938		(69)
Net cash position	**1,403**	**+313**	**340**
Capital expenditures	nil		(69)
	$		$
Earnings per share*	(0.10)		(0.01)
Cash flow per share*	(0.03)		(0.01)
	shs		shs
No. of shs. o/s*	44,843,482		n.a.
Avg. no. of shs. o/s*	29,524,989		4,294,521
	%		%
Net profit margin	n.a.		n.m.
Return on equity	(274.81)		(9.77)
Return on assets	(240.59)		(8.41)

* Common
[A] Reported in accordance with IFRS
[1] Results reflect the Sept. 29, 2021, reverse takeover acquisition of The BC Bud Co.
[2] Results pertain to BC Bud Holdings Corp. (formerly (old) The BC Bud Corporation).

Latest Results

Periods ended:	6m Aug. 31/22[A]		6m Aug. 31/21[oA]
	$000s	%Chg	$000s
Operating revenue	620	n.a.	nil
Net income	(720)	n.a.	(92)
	$		$
Earnings per share*	(0.02)		(0.01)

* Common
[o] Restated
[A] Reported in accordance with IFRS

Historical Summary
(as originally stated)

Fiscal Year	Oper. Rev. $000s	Net Inc. Bef. Disc. $000s	EPS* $
2022[A]	nil	(2,858)	(0.10)
2021[A]	1	(56)	(0.01)
2020[A1]	1	(143)	(0.01)
2019[A]	6	(292)	(0.07)
2018[A]	(3)	(508)	(0.10)

* Common
[A] Reported in accordance with IFRS
[1] Results for 2020 and prior periods pertain to Entheos Capital Corporation
Note: Adjusted throughout for 1-for-10 cons. in Apr. 2020

B.3 BC Craft Supply Co. Ltd.

Symbol - CRFT **Exchange** - CSE (S) **CUSIP** - 07335D
Head Office - 810-789 Pender St W, Vancouver, BC, V6C 1H2 **Telephone** - (604) 687-2038 **Fax** - (604) 687-3141
Website - bccraftsupplyco.ca
Email - info@bccraftsupplyco.com
Investor Relations - Brett Walker (604) 396-1776
Auditors - Abu-Farah Professional Corporation C.A., Mississauga, Ont.
Transfer Agents - National Securities Administrators Ltd., Vancouver, B.C.
Profile - (B.C. 2012) Develops and curates cannabis and psychedelic brands and assets.

Operations consist of:

CRFT, which curates and aggregates craft cannabis brands, providing access for small-batch growers in Canada. Brand portfolio covers various product categories and includes Grizzlers (pre-rolls), Earth Dragon Organics (CBD-infused skincare and bath products) and Roll Model (pre-rolls).

Wholly owned **Medcann Health Products Ltd.** is a licensed cannabis cultivator and processor with a 10,000-sq.-ft. facility being reconstructed in Chemainus, B.C.

Wholly owned **Somo Industries Inc.** (dba Feelwell Brands) owns Clix, a cannabis brand in California consisting of herbal blended pre-rolls and micro-dosed tablets, and General Principle, an athletic wellness brand featuring functional, sports-oriented cannabis products.

Wholly owned **Ava Pathways Inc.** researches and develops psychoactive therapies using psilocybin and compounds derived from mushrooms to treat common and debilitating medical conditions, such as depression, anxiety, PTSD and substance use disorder.

Wholly owned **Olympic View Botanicals Ltd.** is building an indoor micro cannabis cultivation facility in Sooke, B.C. Olympic has submitted an application to Health Canada for a micro cultivation licence.

Common suspended from CSE, Feb. 4, 2022.

Predecessor Detail - Name changed from Pasha Brands Ltd., May 19, 2020.

Directors - Brett Walker, interim CEO; Anthony Laud, CFO; Ilona Kiss

Capital Stock

	Authorized (shs.)	Outstanding (shs.)[1]
Common	unlimited	2,276,454

[1] At Dec. 23, 2021

Major Shareholder - Widely held at July 23, 2021.

Price Range - BCP/TSX-VEN (D)

Year	Volume	High	Low	Close
2022	160,259	$0.79	$0.13	$0.50
2021	2,344,263	$17.50	$0.50	$0.70
2020	494,156	$40.00	$4.00	$10.00
2019	51,560	$1,260.00	$96.00	$102.00
2018	64	$1,032.00	$432.00	$552.00

Consolidation: 1-for-100 cons. in Dec. 2021; 1-for-12 cons. in Mar. 2020; 1-for-2 cons. in June 2019

Capital Stock Changes - On Dec. 23, 2021, common shares were consolidated on a 1-for-100 basis.

Wholly Owned Subsidiaries

Pasha Brands Holdings Ltd., Nanaimo, B.C.
- 100% int. in **Ava Pathways Inc.**, Vancouver, B.C.
- 100% int. in **Medcann Health Products Ltd.**, B.C.
- 100% int. in **Olympic View Botanicals Ltd.**, B.C.
- 100% int. in **1198937 B.C. Ltd.**, B.C.
- 100% int. in **Royal Green Acres Manufacturing Ltd.**, B.C.
  - 100% int. in **1178558 B.C. Ltd.**, B.C.

Somo Industries Inc., Calif. dba Feelwell Brands.

B.4 BCE Inc.*

Symbol - BCE **Exchange** - TSX **CUSIP** - 05534B
Head Office - Bldg A, 8e étage, 1 carref Alexander-Graham-Bell, Verdun, QC, H3E 3B3 **Toll-free** - (888) 932-6666 **Fax** - (514) 786-3970
Website - www.bce.ca
Email - thane.fotopoulos@bell.ca
Investor Relations - Thane Fotopoulos (800) 339-6353
Auditors - Deloitte LLP C.A., Montréal, Qué.
Transfer Agents - American Stock Transfer & Trust Company, LLC, New York, N.Y.; TSX Trust Company, Montréal, Qué.
FP500 Revenue Ranking - 22
Employees - 44,610 at Dec. 31, 2022
Profile - (Can. 1970) Operates wireless and wireline networks across Canada, providing mobile, Internet, television and other communication services to residential, business and wholesale customers. Also operates a media business with assets in television, radio, digital and out-of-home advertising.

Bell Communication and Technology Services (Bell CTS)

Provides integrated digital wireless voice and data communication products and services to residential and business customers across Canada under the Bell, Virgin Plus and Lucky Mobile brands. Wireless network includes LTE coverage of more than 99% of the population, with LTE-A covering 96%, and 5G coverage of 82% of Canada's population, with 5G+ covering 38%, at Dec. 31, 2022. Products and services include postpaid and prepaid data and voice plans; consumer electronic products; international roaming services in more than 230 outbound destinations worldwide (209 of them supporting LTE and 63 supporting 5G); mobile business solutions; and Internet of Things (IoT) solutions, including asset and fleet management, smart buildings, smart cities and smart supply chain. Products and services are distributed in more than 8,000 retail points, including more than 1,000 Bell, Virgin Plus, Lucky Mobile and The Source locations, and other third party dealer and retail locations, as well as through call centres, sales representatives, certified resellers and online channels.

Provides data, including Internet, Internet protocol television (IPTV), cloud-based services and business solutions, voice and other communication services and products to residential, small and medium-sized business and large enterprise customers, primarily in Ontario, Quebec, the Atlantic provinces and Manitoba, and satellite TV service and connectivity to customers across Canada. Broadband fibre network consists of fibre-to-the-premise (FTTP) and fibre-to-the-node (FTTN) locations, covering 10,000,000 homes and businesses in Ontario, Quebec, the Atlantic provinces and Manitoba. Wireline network also includes wireless-to-the-premise (WTTP), a 5G-capable fixed wireless service delivered over the company's LTE network to provide broadband Internet to residents in smaller and underserved communities, and digital subscriber line (DSL) technology in areas where fibre and WTTP connections are not available. Residential customers are offered with high-speed Internet marketed as Fibe Internet and Virgin Plus Internet; television services, including IPTV (namely Fibe TV, the Fibe TV application and Virgin Plus TV) and satellite TV under the Bell TV brand; home phone, including local and long distance telephone services; and smart home services, which include home security, monitoring and automation services. Products and services offered to business customers include Internet and network solutions, including Internet access, software-defined solutions, private networks, global networks, managed and professional services; communications solutions, including IP telephony, local and long distance, audio, video and web conferencing and webcasting, and contact centre solutions such as cloud-based, hybrid and on-premise services; cloud solutions, including cloud professional and managed services, cloud computing, public multi-access edge computing (MEC), cloud connect, and cloud backup and disaster recovery; and network and cloud security, and managed services and professional services. Operations also include the wholesale business, which buys and sells local telephone, long distance, data and other services from or to resellers and other carriers; wireline operations in the Northern Territories under the NorthwesTel brand; and competitive local exchange carrier (CLEC) services in Alberta and British Columbia.

Bell Media

Owns and operates 35 conventional TV stations, including CTV and Noovo; 27 specialty TV channels, including TSN and RDS; four pay TV services and four direct-to-consumer (DTC) streaming services, including Crave, TSN and RDS; 109 licensed radio stations in 58 markets across Canada; digital media, including websites, applications and platforms associated with the company's news, sports, entertainment and lifestyle properties; and Astral, an out-of-home advertising business with a network of more than 45,000 advertising faces in key urban markets across Canada. Also holds broadcast rights for sports properties, HBO, HBO Max, STARZ and iHeartRadio. Other assets include 50% equity interest in **Dome Productions Partnership**, a provider of sports and other event production and broadcast facilities; partnership in Just For Laughs, a live comedy event and TV producer; minority interest in Grandé Studios, a provider of TV and film production facilities, equipment rentals and technical services in Montreal; and operations of **Octane Racing Group Inc.**, promoter of the Formula 1 Canadian Grand Prix.

In addition, the company holds 37.5% interest (**Rogers Communications Inc.** 37.5%, **Kilmer Van Nostrand Co. Limited** 25%) in **Maple Leaf Sports & Entertainment Ltd.**, owner of Scotiabank Arena in Toronto, the NHL's Toronto Maple Leafs, the NBA's Toronto Raptors, the MLS' Toronto FC, the CFL's Toronto Argonauts, the AHL's Toronto Marlies and associated real estate holdings; 50% interest in **GLENTEL Inc.** (50% Rogers), a retailer of mobile products and services; and 18.4% interest in entities that operate the Montreal Canadiens Hockey Club, evenko (a promoter and producer of cultural and sports events), the Bell Centre in Montreal and Place Bell in Laval.

Periods ended:	12m Dec. 31/22	12m Dec. 31/21
Retail network access services	2,190,771[1]	2,298,605[1]
Wireless subscribers	12,400,904[2]	11,708,979[2]
Retail internet subscribers	4,258,570	3,861,653
TV subscribers[3]	2,751,498	2,735,010

[1] Consists of residential network access services lines.
[2] Consists of mobile phone subscribers and mobile connected device subscribers, such as tablets, wearables and Internet of Things (IoT) units.
[3] Includes satellite and IPTV.

Recent Merger and Acquisition Activity

Status: completed **Revised:** June 1, 2023
UPDATE: The transaction was completed for cash consideration of $157,000,000, of which $12,000,000 is payable within two years, and an estimated $6,000,000 of additional cash consideration contingent on the achievement of certain performance objectives. PREVIOUS: Bell Canada, wholly owned by BCE Inc., agreed to acquire Montreal, Que.-based FX Innovation Inc., a provider of cloud-focused managed and professional services and workflow automation services for business clients. Terms were not disclosed. Upon closing, FX Innovation will continue to operate independently. The transaction was expected to close in the second or third quarter of 2023.

Status: completed **Revised:** May 3, 2023
UPDATE: The transaction was completed for net cash proceeds of $211,000,000. PREVIOUS: BCE Inc. agreed to sell its 63% interest in certain production studios and production studios under construction, which were included within its Bell Media segment, for estimated cash proceeds of $220,000,000. The transaction was expected to close in the first half of 2023 upon substantial completion of the production studios.

Status: completed **Announced:** Jan. 1, 2023
BCE Inc. repurchased BCE Master Trust Fund's 9.5% interest in Maple Leaf Sports & Entertainment Ltd. (MLSE), which owns and operates sports teams including the Toronto Maple Leafs, the Toronto Raptors, the Toronto Argonauts and Toronto FC, as well as the Scotiabank Arena, for $149,000,000. As a result, BCE's indirect interest in MLSE increased to 37.5% from 28%.

Status: completed **Revised:** Dec. 1, 2022
UPDATE: The transaction was completed for $303,000,000. Bell added 128,065 Internet subscribers, 2,315 IPTV subscribers and 64,498 retail network access customers (NAS) customers. PREVIOUS: Bell Canada, wholly owned by BCE Inc., agreed to acquire independent communications provider Distributel Communications Limited. Terms were not disclosed. Distributel, which offers high-speed Internet, TV, mobile and home phone services in Ontario, Quebec, Alberta and British Columbia, as well as business solutions across Canada, would continue to operate independently.

Status: completed **Revised:** Mar. 1, 2022
UPDATE: The transaction was completed. PREVIOUS: BCE Inc. agreed to sell wholly owned 6362222 Canada Inc. (dba Createch) to Paris, France-based innovation and technology consulting firm Talan SAS for $55,000,000. Createch carries on a consulting business specializing in designing and implementing technology services and solutions for North American clients in the industrial, distribution, retail, financial, service and public sectors.

Predecessor Detail - Name changed from Bell Canada Enterprises Inc., Jan. 1, 1988.

Directors - Gordon M. Nixon, chr., Toronto, Ont.; Mirko Bibic, pres. & CEO, Toronto, Ont.; David F. Denison, Toronto, Ont.; Robert P. (Rob) Dexter, Halifax, N.S.; Katherine M. Lee, Toronto, Ont.; Monique F. Leroux, Montréal, Qué.; Sheila A. Murray, Toronto, Ont.; Louis P. (Lou) Pagnutti, Toronto, Ont.; Calin Rovinescu, Toronto, Ont.; Karen H. Sheriff, Picton, Ont.; Robert C. Simmonds, Toronto, Ont.; Jennifer A. Tory, Toronto, Ont.; Louis O. Vachon, Montréal, Qué.; Cornell C. V. Wright, Toronto, Ont.

Other Exec. Officers - Wade Oosterman, v-chr. & pres., Bell Media; Glen LeBlanc, exec. v-p, CFO & v-chr., Atlantic Canada; Robert Malcolmson, exec. v-p & chief legal & regulatory officer; Nikki Moffat, exec. v-p, corp. srvcs. & chief HR officer; Curtis Millen, sr. v-p, corp. strategy & treas.

Capital Stock

	Authorized (shs.)	Outstanding (shs.)[1]
First Preferred	unlimited	
Series Q	8,000,000	nil
Series R	8,000,000	7,992,000
Series S	8,000,000	2,125,067
Series T	8,000,000	5,820,633
Series Y	10,000,000	7,009,252
Series Z	10,000,000	2,973,348
Series AA	20,000,000	12,254,761
Series AB	20,000,000	7,664,939
Series AC	20,000,000	6,716,274
Series AD	20,000,000	13,148,226
Series AE	24,000,000	6,460,913
Series AF	24,000,000	9,472,387
Series AG	22,000,000	8,921,530
Series AH	22,000,000	4,987,870
Series AI	22,000,000	9,477,640
Series AJ	22,000,000	4,454,760
Series AK	25,000,000	23,119,512
Series AL	25,000,000	1,797,188
Series AM	30,000,000	10,422,778
Series AN	30,000,000	1,052,822
Series AQ	30,000,000	9,108,800
Second Preferred	unlimited	nil
Common	unlimited	912,289,567
Class B	unlimited	nil

[1] At June 30, 2023

First Preferred - Total authorized amount of first preferred shares is unlimited. Issuable in one or more series at the discretion of directors. All series rank pari passu with each other and in priority to the second preferred and common shares with respect to payment of dividends and distribution of assets in the event of liquidation, dissolution, etc. Non-voting.

Series R - Entitled to cumulative preferential annual dividends of $0.7545 per share payable quarterly to Dec. 1, 2025, and thereafter at a rate reset every five years to a fixed rate not less than 80% of the Government of Canada yield. Redeemable on Dec. 1, 2025, and on December 1 every five years thereafter at $25 per share. Convertible at the holder's option, on Dec. 1, 2025, and on December 1 every five years thereafter, into floating rate first preferred series Q shares on a share-for-share basis, subject to certain conditions. The series Q shares would pay a monthly dividend at a rate between 50% and 100% of the prime rate adjusted upwards or downwards on a monthly basis whenever the calculated trading price of the shares is $24.875 or less or $25.125 or more, respectively.

Series S - Entitled to cumulative preferential floating rate dividends payable monthly at a rate between 50% and 100% of the prime rate adjusted upwards or downwards on a monthly basis whenever the calculated trading price of the shares is $24.875 or less or $25.125 or more, respectively. Redeemable at $25.50 per share at any time. Convertible at the holder's option, on Nov. 1, 2026, and on November 1 every five years thereafter, into first preferred series T shares on a share-for-share basis, subject to certain conditions.

Series T - Entitled to cumulative preferential annual dividends of $1.2475 per share payable quarterly to Nov. 1, 2026, and thereafter at a rate reset every five years to a fixed rate not less than 80% of the Government of Canada yield. Redeemable on Nov. 1, 2026, and on November 1 every five years thereafter at $25 per share. Convertible at the holder's option, on Nov. 1, 2026, and on November 1 every five years thereafter, into floating rate first preferred series S shares on a share-for-share basis, subject to certain conditions.

Series Y - Entitled to cumulative preferential floating rate dividends payable monthly at a rate between 50% and 100% of the prime rate adjusted upwards or downwards on a monthly basis whenever the calculated trading price of the shares is $24.875 or less or $25.125 or more, respectively. Redeemable at $25.50 per share at any time. Convertible at the holder's option, on Dec. 1, 2027, and on December 1 every five years thereafter, into first preferred series Z shares on a share-for-share basis, subject to certain conditions.

Series Z - Entitled to cumulative preferential annual dividends of $1.3365 per share payable quarterly to Dec. 1, 2027, and thereafter at a rate reset every five years to a fixed rate not less than 80% of the Government of Canada yield. Redeemable on Dec. 1, 2027, and on December 1 every five years thereafter at $25 per share. Convertible at the holder's option, on Dec. 1, 2027, and on December 1 every five years thereafter, into floating rate first preferred series Y shares on a share-for-share basis, subject to certain conditions.

Series AA - Entitled to cumulative preferential annual dividends of $1.235 per share payable quarterly to Sept. 1, 2027, and thereafter at a rate reset every five years to a fixed rate not less than 80% of the Government of Canada yield. Redeemable on Sept. 1, 2027, and on September 1 every five years thereafter at $25 per share. Convertible at the holder's option, on Sept. 1, 2027, and on September 1 every five years thereafter, into floating rate first preferred series AB shares on a share-for-share basis, subject to certain conditions.

Series AB - Entitled to cumulative preferential floating rate dividends payable monthly at a rate between 50% and 100% of the prime rate adjusted upwards or downwards on a monthly basis whenever the calculated trading price of the shares is $24.875 or less or $25.125 or more, respectively. Redeemable at $25.50 per share at any time. Convertible at the holder's option, on Sept. 1, 2027, and on September 1 every five years thereafter, into first preferred series AA shares on a share-for-share basis, subject to certain conditions.

Series AC - Entitled to cumulative preferential annual dividends of $1.27 per share payable quarterly to Mar. 1, 2028, and thereafter at a rate reset every five years to a fixed rate not less than 80% of the Government of Canada yield. Redeemable on Mar. 1, 2028, and on March 1 every five years thereafter at $25 per share. Convertible at the holder's option, on Mar. 1, 2028, and on March 1 every five years thereafter, into floating rate first preferred series AD shares on a share-for-share basis, subject to certain conditions.

Series AD - Entitled to cumulative preferential floating rate dividends payable monthly at a rate between 50% and 100% of the prime rate adjusted upwards or downwards on a monthly basis whenever the calculated trading price of the shares is $24.875 or less or $25.125 or more, respectively. Redeemable at $25.50 per share at any time. Convertible at the holder's option, on Mar. 1, 2028, and on March 1 every five years thereafter, into first preferred series AC shares on a share-for-share basis, subject to certain conditions.

Series AE - Entitled to cumulative preferential floating rate dividends payable monthly at a rate between 50% and 100% of the prime rate adjusted upwards or downwards on a monthly basis whenever the calculated trading price of the shares is $24.875 or less or $25.125 or more, respectively. Redeemable at $25.50 per share at any time. Convertible at the holder's option, on Feb. 1, 2025, and on February 1 every five years thereafter, into first preferred series AF shares on a share-for-share basis, subject to certain conditions.

Series AF - Entitled to cumulative preferential annual dividends of $0.9663 per share payable quarterly to Feb. 1, 2025, and thereafter at a rate reset every five years to a fixed rate not less than 80% of the Government of Canada yield. Redeemable on Feb. 1, 2025, and on February 1 every five years thereafter at $25 per share. Convertible at the holder's option, on Feb. 1, 2025, and on February 1 every five years thereafter, into floating rate first preferred series AE shares on a share-for-share basis, subject to certain conditions.

Series AG - Entitled to cumulative preferential annual dividends of $0.8425 per share payable quarterly to May 1, 2026, and thereafter at a rate reset every five years to a fixed rate not less than 80% of the Government of Canada yield. Redeemable on May 1, 2026, and on May 1 every five years thereafter at $25 per share. Convertible at the holder's option, on May 1, 2026, and on May 1 every five years thereafter, into floating rate first preferred series AH shares on a share-for-share basis, subject to certain conditions.

Series AH - Entitled to cumulative preferential floating rate dividends payable monthly at a rate between 50% and 100% of the prime rate adjusted upwards or downwards on a monthly basis whenever the calculated trading price of the shares is $24.875 or less or $25.125 or more, respectively. Redeemable at $25.50 per share at any time. Convertible at the holder's option, on May 1, 2026, and on May 1 every five years thereafter, into first preferred series AG shares on a share-for-share basis, subject to certain conditions.

Series AI - Entitled to cumulative preferential annual dividends of $0.8475 per share payable quarterly to Aug. 1, 2026, and thereafter at a rate reset every five years to a fixed rate not less than 80% of the Government of Canada Yield. Redeemable on Aug. 1, 2026, and on August 1 every five years thereafter at $25 per share. Convertible at the holder's option, on Aug. 1, 2026, and on August 1 every five years thereafter, into floating rate first preferred series AJ shares on a share-for-share basis, subject to certain conditions.

Series AJ - Entitled to cumulative preferential floating rate dividends payable monthly at a rate between 50% and 100% of the prime rate adjusted upwards or downwards on a monthly basis whenever the calculated trading price of the shares is $24.875 or less or $25.125 or more, respectively. Redeemable at $25.50 per share at any time. Convertible at the holder's option, on Aug. 1, 2026, and on August 1 every five years thereafter, into first preferred series AI shares on a share-for-share basis, subject to certain conditions.

Series AK - Entitled to cumulative preferential annual dividends of $0.8265 per share payable quarterly to Dec. 31, 2026, and thereafter at a rate reset every five years equal to the five-year Government of Canada yield plus 1.88%. Redeemable on Dec. 31, 2026, and on December 31 every five years thereafter at $25 per share. Convertible at the holder's option, on Dec. 31, 2026, and on December 31 every five years thereafter, into floating rate first preferred series AL shares on a share-for-share basis, subject to certain conditions.

Series AL - Entitled to cumulative preferential annual dividends payable quarterly equal to the 90-day Canadian Treasury bill rate plus 1.88%. Redeemable on Dec. 31, 2026, and on December 31 every five years thereafter at $25 per share, or at $25.50 per share in the case of redemptions on any other date. Convertible at the holder's option, on Dec. 31, 2026, and on December 31 every five years thereafter, into first preferred series AK shares on a share-for-share basis, subject to certain conditions.

Series AM - Entitled to cumulative preferential annual dividends of $0.7348 per share payable quarterly to Mar. 31, 2026, and thereafter at a rate reset rate every five years equal to the five-year Government of Canada yield plus 2.09%. Redeemable on Mar. 31, 2026, and on March 31 every five years thereafter at $25 per share. Convertible at the holder's option, on Mar. 31, 2026, and on March 31 every five years thereafter, into floating rate first preferred series AN shares on a share-for-share basis, subject to certain conditions.

Series AN - Entitled to cumulative preferential annual dividends payable quarterly equal to the 90-day Canadian Treasury bill rate plus 2.09%. Redeemable on Mar. 31, 2026, and on March 31 every five years thereafter at $25 per share, or at $25.50 per share in the case of redemptions on any other date. Convertible at the holder's option, on Mar. 31, 2026, and on March 31 every five years thereafter, into first preferred series AM shares on a share-for-share basis, subject to certain conditions.

Series AQ - Entitled to cumulative preferential annual dividends of $1.203 per share payable quarterly to Sept. 30, 2023, and thereafter at a rate reset every five years equal to the five-year Government of Canada yield plus 2.64%. Redeemable on Sept. 30, 2023, and on September 30 every five years thereafter at $25 per share. Convertible at the holder's option, on Sept. 30, 2023, and on September 30 every five years thereafter, into floating rate first preferred series AR shares on a share-for-share basis, subject to certain conditions. The series AR shares would pay a quarterly dividend equal to the 90-day Canadian Treasury bill rate plus 2.64%.

Second Preferred - Total authorized amount of second preferred shares is unlimited. The second preferred shares rank after the first preferred but before the common shares with respect to payment of dividends and distribution of assets.

Common - One vote per share.

Options - At Dec. 31, 2022, options were outstanding to purchase 7,802,108 common shares at prices ranging from $50 to more than $60 per share with a weighted average remaining life of five years.

First Preferred Series AO (old) - Were entitled to cumulative preferential annual dividends of $1.065 per share payable quarterly to Mar. 31, 2022. Redeemed on Mar. 31, 2022, at $25 per share.

Normal Course Issuer Bid - The company plans to make normal course purchases of up to 212,826 first preferred series S shares representing 10% of the public float. The bid commenced on Nov. 9, 2022, and expires on Nov. 8, 2023.

The company plans to make normal course purchases of up to 807,929 first preferred series Y shares representing 10% of the public float. The bid commenced on Nov. 9, 2022, and expires on Nov. 8, 2023.

The company plans to make normal course purchases of up to 799,890 first preferred series R shares representing 10% of the public float. The bid commenced on Nov. 9, 2022, and expires on Nov. 8, 2023.

The company plans to make normal course purchases of up to 1,230,766 first preferred series AA shares representing 10% of the public float. The bid commenced on Nov. 9, 2022, and expires on Nov. 8, 2023.

The company plans to make normal course purchases of up to 191,850 first preferred series Z shares representing 10% of the public float. The bid commenced on Nov. 9, 2022, and expires on Nov. 8, 2023.

The company plans to make normal course purchases of up to 1,002,799 first preferred series AC shares representing 10% of the public float. The bid commenced on Nov. 9, 2022, and expires on Nov. 8, 2023.

The company plans to make normal course purchases of up to 587,013 first preferred series T shares representing 10% of the public float. The bid commenced on Nov. 9, 2022, and expires on Nov. 8, 2023.

The company plans to make normal course purchases of up to 651,291 first preferred series AE shares representing 10% of the public float. The bid commenced on Nov. 9, 2022, and expires on Nov. 8, 2023.

The company plans to make normal course purchases of up to 948,148 first preferred series AF shares representing 10% of the public float. The bid commenced on Nov. 9, 2022, and expires on Nov. 8, 2023.

The company plans to make normal course purchases of up to 897,953 first preferred series AG shares representing 10% of the public float. The bid commenced on Nov. 9, 2022, and expires on Nov. 8, 2023.

The company plans to make normal course purchases of up to 501,757 first preferred series AH shares representing 10% of the public float. The bid commenced on Nov. 9, 2022, and expires on Nov. 8, 2023.

The company plans to make normal course purchases of up to 953,504 first preferred series AI shares representing 10% of the public float. The bid commenced on Nov. 9, 2022, and expires on Nov. 8, 2023.

The company plans to make normal course purchases of up to 768,873 first preferred series AB shares representing 10% of the public float. The bid commenced on Nov. 9, 2022, and expires on Nov. 8, 2023.

The company plans to make normal course purchases of up to 996,320 first preferred series AD shares representing 10% of the public float. The bid commenced on Nov. 9, 2022, and expires on Nov. 8, 2023.

The company plans to make normal course purchases of up to 2,319,031 first preferred series AK shares representing 10% of the public float. The bid commenced on Nov. 9, 2022, and expires on Nov. 8, 2023.

The company plans to make normal course purchases of up to 446,496 first preferred series AJ shares representing 10% of the public float. The bid commenced on Nov. 9, 2022, and expires on Nov. 8, 2023.

The company plans to make normal course purchases of up to 1,043,997 first preferred series AM shares representing 10% of the public float. The bid commenced on Nov. 9, 2022, and expires on Nov. 8, 2023.

The company plans to make normal course purchases of up to 920,000 first preferred series AQ shares representing 10% of the public float. The bid commenced on Nov. 9, 2022, and expires on Nov. 8, 2023.

The company plans to make normal course purchases of up to 105,472 first preferred series AN shares representing 10% of the public float. The bid commenced on Nov. 9, 2022, and expires on Nov. 8, 2023.

The company plans to make normal course purchases of up to 179,938 first preferred series AL shares representing 10% of the public float. The bid commenced on Nov. 9, 2022, and expires on Nov. 8, 2023.

Major Shareholder - Widely held at Mar. 2, 2023.

Price Range - BCE/TSX

Year	Volume	High	Low	Close
2022	781,152,513	$74.09	$55.66	$59.49
2021	876,448,631	$67.08	$54.18	$65.81
2020	706,764,192	$65.28	$46.03	$54.43
2019	446,029,139	$65.45	$53.05	$60.16
2018	411,436,670	$60.49	$50.72	$53.93

Recent Close: $56.32

Capital Stock Changes - On Mar. 1, 2023, 3,635,351 first preferred series AC shares were converted into a like number of first preferred series AD shares and 351,634 first preferred series AD shares were converted into a like number of first preferred series AC shares.

On Mar. 31, 2022, all 4,600,000 first preferred series AO shares were redeemed at $25 per share. On Sept. 1, 2022, 1,067,517 first preferred series AA shares were converted into a like number of first preferred series AB shares and 1,977,982 first preferred series AB shares were converted into a like number of first preferred series AA shares. On Dec. 1, 2022, 1,196,313 first preferred series Y shares were converted into a like number of first preferred series Z shares and 137,274 first preferred series Z shares were converted into a like number of first preferred series Y shares. Also during 2022, common shares were issued as follows: 2,952,992 under employee stock option plan and 11,003 under deferred share plan. In addition, 6,900 first preferred series R shares, 3,200 first preferred series S shares, 49,500 first preferred series T shares, 11,000 first preferred series Y shares, 4,200 first preferred series Z shares, 52,900 first preferred series AA shares, 23,800 first preferred series AB shares, 20,200 first preferred series AC shares, 12,100 first preferred series AD shares, 52,000 first preferred series AE shares, 9,100 first preferred series AF shares, 58,000 first preferred series AG shares, 29,700 first preferred series AH shares, 57,400 first preferred series AI shares, 10,200 first preferred series AJ shares, 70,800 first preferred series AK shares, 2,200 first preferred series AL shares, 17,200 first preferred series AM shares, 1,900 first preferred series AN shares and 91,200 first preferred series AQ shares were repurchased under a Normal Course Issuer Bid.

Dividends

BCE com Ra $3.87 pa Q est. Apr. 17, 2023†† **
Prev. Rate: $3.68 est. Apr. 15, 2022
Prev. Rate: $3.50 est. Apr. 15, 2021
Prev. Rate: $3.33 est. Apr. 15, 2020

BCE.PR.S pfd 1st ser S cum. red. exch. Fltg. Ra pa M**[1]

$0.15	Sept. 12/23	$0.14798	Aug. 12/23
$0.14358	July 12/23	$0.13958	June 12/23

Paid in 2023: $1.26728 2022: $0.95079 2021: $0.61248

BCE.PR.Y pfd 1st ser Y cum. red. exch. Fltg. Ra pa M**[1]

$0.15	Sept. 12/23	$0.14798	Aug. 12/23
$0.14358	July 12/23	$0.13958	June 12/23

Paid in 2023: $1.26728 2022: $0.95079 2021: $0.61248

BCE.PR.R pfd 1st ser R cum. red. exch. Adj. Ra $0.7545 pa Q est. Mar. 1, 2021**[1]

BCE.PR.A pfd 1st ser AA cum. red. exch. Adj. Ra $1.235 pa Q est. Dec. 1, 2022

BCE.PR.Z pfd 1st ser Z cum. red. exch. Adj. Ra $1.3365 pa Q est. Mar. 1, 2023**[1]

BCE.PR.C pfd 1st ser AC cum. red. exch. Adj. Ra $1.27 pa Q est. June 1, 2023

BCE.PR.T pfd 1st ser T cum. red. exch. Adj. Ra $1.2475 pa Q est. Feb. 1, 2022**[1]

BCE.PR.E pfd 1st ser AE cum. red. exch. Fltg. Ra pa M**

$0.15	Sept. 12/23	$0.14798	Aug. 12/23
$0.14358	July 12/23	$0.13958	June 12/23

Paid in 2023: $1.26728 2022: $0.95079 2021: $0.61248

BCE.PR.F pfd 1st ser AF cum. red. exch. Adj. Ra $0.96625 pa Q est. May 1, 2020

BCE.PR.G pfd 1st ser AG cum. red. exch. Adj. Ra $0.8425 pa Q est. Aug. 3, 2021

BCE.PR.H pfd 1st ser AH cum. red. exch. Fltg. Ra pa M

$0.15	Sept. 12/23	$0.14798	Aug. 12/23
$0.14358	July 12/23	$0.13958	June 12/23

Paid in 2023: $1.26728 2022: $0.95079 2021: $0.61248

BCE.PR.I pfd 1st ser AI cum. red. exch. Adj. Ra $0.8475 pa Q est. Nov. 1, 2021

BCE.PR.B pfd 1st ser AB cum. red. exch. Fltg. Ra pa M

$0.15	Sept. 12/23	$0.14798	Aug. 12/23
$0.14358	July 12/23	$0.13958	June 12/23

Paid in 2023: $1.26628 2022: $0.94627 2021: $0.61248

BCE.PR.D pfd 1st ser AD cum. red. exch. Fltg. Ra pa M

$0.15	Sept. 12/23	$0.14798	Aug. 12/23
$0.14358	July 12/23	$0.13958	June 12/23

Paid in 2023: $1.26728 2022: $0.95079 2021: $0.61248

BCE.PR.K pfd 1st ser AK cum. red. exch. Adj. Ra $0.8265 pa Q est. Mar. 31, 2022

BCE.PR.J pfd 1st ser AJ cum. red. exch. Fltg. Ra pa M

$0.15	Sept. 12/23	$0.14798	Aug. 12/23
$0.14358	July 12/23	$0.13958	June 12/23

Paid in 2023: $1.26728 2022: $0.95079 2021: $0.61248

BCE.PR.M pfd 1st ser AM cum. red. exch. Adj. Ra $0.73475 pa Q est. June 30, 2021

BCE.PR.Q pfd 1st ser AQ cum. red. exch. Adj. Ra $1.203 pa Q est. Dec. 31, 2018

BCE.PR.N pfd 1st ser AN cum. red. exch. Fltg. Ra pa Q

$0.41923	Sept. 30/23	$0.41474	June 30/23
$0.38361	Mar. 31/23	$0.34078	Jan. 4/23

Paid in 2023: $1.55836 2022: $0.53016 2021: $0.55186

BCE.PR.L pfd 1st ser AL cum. red. exch. Fltg. Ra pa Q

$0.406	Sept. 30/23	$0.40165	June 30/23
$0.37066	Mar. 31/23	$0.32755	Jan. 4/23

Paid in 2023: $1.50586 2022: $0.49089 2021: $0.49935

pfd 1st ser AO cum. red. exch. Adj. Ra $1.065 pa Q est. June 30, 2017[2]
$0.26625f Mar. 31/22

[1] Shareholders who are also holders of com. shs. are eligible to participate in the dividend reinvestment plan.
[2] Redeemed March 31, 2022 at $25 per sh.
†† Currency Option ** Reinvestment Option f Final Payment

Long-Term Debt - Outstanding at Dec. 31, 2022:

Debt securities[1]:	
2011 trust indenture[2]	$225,000,000
1996 trust indenture[3]	275,000,000
1997 trust indenture[4]	16,747,000,000
2016 U.S. trust indenture[5]	6,525,000,000
1976 trust indenture[6]	975,000,000
Lease liabs.	4,402,000,000
Other	449,000,000
Less: Net unamort. discount	34,000,000
Less: Unamort. debt costs	101,000,000
	29,463,000,000
Less: Current portion	1,680,000,000
	27,783,000,000

[1] Amounts pertain to wholly owned Bell Canada.
[2] Weighted average interest rate of 4% at Dec. 31, 2022, and due 2024.
[3] Weighted average interest rate of 8.21% at Dec. 31, 2022, and due to 2031.
[4] Weighted average interest rate of 3.82% at Dec. 31, 2022, and due to 2051.
[5] Weighted average interest rate of 3.32% at Dec. 31, 2022, and due to 2052.
[6] Weighted average interest rate of 9.38% at Dec. 31, 2022, and due to 2054.

Note - In February 2023, Bell Canada completed a public offering of $1.05 billion principal amount of 4.55% series M-58 MTN debentures due Feb. 9, 2030, and $450,000,000 principal amount of 5.15% series M-59 MTN debentures due Feb. 9, 2053. In May 2023, Bell Canada completed a public offering of US$850,000,000 principal amount of 5.1% series US-8 MTN notes due May 11, 2033.

Wholly Owned Subsidiaries

Bell MTS Inc., Winnipeg, Man.
- 5.9% int. in **Bell Canada**, Montréal, Qué.

FX Innovation Inc., Montréal, Qué.

Subsidiaries

94.1% int. in **Bell Canada**, Montréal, Qué.
- 100% int. in **Bell Aliant Inc.**, Halifax, N.S.
- 100% int. in **Bell Media Inc.**, Toronto, Ont.
  - 100% int. in **Dome Productions Inc.**, Toronto, Ont.
    - 50% int. in **Dome Productions Partnership**, Toronto, Ont.
- 100% int. in **Bell Mobility Holdings Inc.**, Dorval, Qué.
  - 100% int. in **Bell Mobility Inc.**, Montréal, Qué.
- 100% int. in **Distributel Communications Limited**, Toronto, Ont.
- 100% int. in **NorthernTel, Limited Partnership**, New Liskeard, Ont.
- 100% int. in **Northwestel Inc.**, Yellowknife, N.W.T.
- 100% int. in **The Source (Bell) Electronics Inc.**, Barrie, Ont.
- 100% int. in **Télébec, Limited Partnership**, Qué.

Investments

37.5% int. in **Maple Leaf Sports & Entertainment Ltd.**, Toronto, Ont.
50% int. in **9275711 Canada Inc.**, Canada.
- 100% int. in **GLENTEL Inc.**, Burnaby, B.C.

Financial Statistics

Periods ended:	12m Dec. 31/22[A]		12m Dec. 31/21[□A]
	$000s	%Chg	$000s
Operating revenue	**24,174,000**	**+3**	**23,449,000**
Cost of sales	7,641,000		7,284,000
Salaries & benefits	4,168,000		4,181,000
Other operating expense	1,917,000		1,825,000
Operating expense	**13,975,000**	**+3**	**13,556,000**
Operating income	**10,199,000**	**+3**	**9,893,000**
Deprec., depl. & amort.	4,723,000		4,609,000
Finance costs, gross	1,095,000		1,102,000
Investment income	(61,000)		(95,000)
Write-downs/write-offs	(279,000)		(197,000)
Pre-tax income	**3,893,000**	**-1**	**3,936,000**
Income taxes	967,000		1,044,000
Net inc bef disc ops, eqhldrs	2,868,000		2,840,000
Net inc bef disc ops, NCI	58,000		52,000
Net income	**2,926,000**	**+1**	**2,892,000**
Net inc. for equity hldrs	**2,868,000**	**+1**	**2,840,000**
Net inc. for non-cont. int.	**58,000**	**+12**	**52,000**
Cash & equivalent	149,000		289,000
Inventories	656,000		482,000
Accounts receivable	4,090,000		3,828,000
Current assets	6,487,000		6,198,000
Long-term investments	1,007,000		1,036,000
Fixed assets, net	29,256,000		28,235,000
Intangibles, net	27,089,000		26,142,000
Total assets	**69,329,000**	**+4**	**66,764,000**
Bank indebtedness	2,457,000		1,635,000
Accts. pay. & accr. liabs.	4,317,000		3,584,000
Current liabilities	11,469,000		9,113,000
Long-term debt, gross	29,463,000		28,038,000
Long-term debt, net	27,783,000		27,048,000
Preferred share equity	3,870,000		4,003,000
Shareholders' equity	22,178,000		22,635,000
Non-controlling interest	337,000		306,000
Cash from oper. activs	**8,365,000**	**+4**	**8,008,000**
Cash from fin. activs	(2,988,000)		(925,000)
Cash from invest. activs	(5,517,000)		(7,018,000)
Net cash position	**149,000**	**-48**	**289,000**
Capital expenditures, net	(5,133,000)		(4,852,000)
Pension fund surplus	4,060,000		3,496,000
	$		$
Earnings per share*	2.98		2.99
Cash flow per share*	9.18		8.84
Cash divd. per share*	3.68		3.50
	shs		shs
No. of shs. o/s*	911,982,866		909,018,871
Avg. no. of shs. o/s*	911,500,000		906,300,000
	%		%
Net profit margin	12.10		12.33
Return on equity	14.70		15.21
Return on assets	5.51		5.81
No. of employees (FTEs)	44,610		49,781

* Common
□ Restated
[A] Reported in accordance with IFRS

Latest Results

Periods ended:	6m June 30/23[A]		6m June 30/22[A]
	$000s	%Chg	$000s
Operating revenue	12,120,000	+3	11,711,000
Net income	1,185,000	-25	1,588,000
Net inc. for equity hldrs	1,146,000	-26	1,542,000
Net inc. for non-cont. int.	39,000		46,000
	$		$
Earnings per share*	1.16		1.62

* Common
[A] Reported in accordance with IFRS

Historical Summary
(as originally stated)

Fiscal Year	Oper. Rev.	Net Inc. Bef. Disc.	EPS*
	$000s	$000s	$
2022[A]	24,174,000	2,926,000	2.98
2021[A]	23,449,000	2,892,000	2.99
2020[A]	22,883,000	2,473,000	2.51
2019[A]	23,964,000	3,253,000	3.37
2018[A]	23,468,000	2,973,000	3.10

* Common
[A] Reported in accordance with IFRS

B.5 BEACN Wizardry & Magic Inc.

Symbol - BECN **Exchange** - TSX-VEN **CUSIP** - 07355C
Head Office - 410-325 Howe St, Vancouver, BC, V6C 1Z7 **Telephone** - (604) 687-3520 **Fax** - (888) 889-4874
Website - www.ir.beacn.com
Email - investment@beacn.com

Investor Relations - Craig Fraser (604) 687-3520
Auditors - De Visser Gray LLP C.A., Vancouver, B.C.
Lawyers - DuMoulin Black LLP, Vancouver, B.C.
Transfer Agents - Computershare Trust Company of Canada Inc., Vancouver, B.C.
Profile - (B.C. 2020) Manufactures and sells microphones and audio controllers under the BEACN brand targeted for online content creators and gamers.
The company's products include BEACN Mic, an advanced USB-C microphone; BEACN Mix, an intuitive audio controller; and BEACN Mix Create, an audio mixer for content creators. The company has four warehouse facilities in Canada, the U.S. (2) and the U.K.
Predecessor Detail - Name changed from Germinate Capital Ltd., Nov. 2, 2021, pursuant to the Qualifying Transaction reverse takeover acquisition of Beacon Hill Innovations Ltd.
Directors - Sarah Weber, chr., Port Coquitlam, B.C.; Daniel Davies, pres., interim CFO & chief tech. officer, B.C.; Kevin Alexander, B.C.; Scott Christopher, B.C.
Other Exec. Officers - Craig Fraser, CEO

Capital Stock

	Authorized (shs.)	Outstanding (shs.)[1]
Common	unlimited	48,496,836

[1] At May 30, 2023

Major Shareholder - James (Jim) Elliott held 18.37% interest, Kenneth B. (Ken) Hallat held 13.07% interest and David Howard held 12.38% interest at May 30, 2023.

Price Range - BECN/TSX-VEN

Year	Volume	High	Low	Close
2022	931,812	$0.48	$0.20	$0.27
2021	466,927	$0.48	$0.16	$0.40

Recent Close: $0.19

Capital Stock Changes - In November 2022, private placement of 5,600,000 units (1 common share & 1 warrant) at 25¢ per unit was completed. Also during 2022, 112,500 common shares were issued on exercise of options.

Wholly Owned Subsidiaries

Beacon Hill Innovations Ltd., Victoria, B.C.

Financial Statistics

Periods ended:	12m Dec. 31/22[A]		12m Dec. 31/21[oA]
	$000s	%Chg	$000s
Operating revenue	**4,325**	**n.a.**	**nil**
Cost of goods sold	2,689		nil
Salaries & benefits	1,129		813
General & admin expense	976		636
Stock-based compensation	123		198
Operating expense	**4,917**	**+199**	**1,647**
Operating income	**(592)**	**n.a.**	**(1,647)**
Deprec., depl. & amort.	135		45
Finance costs, gross	51		22
Pre-tax income	**(723)**	**n.a.**	**(2,957)**
Income taxes	(272)		(243)
Net income	**(451)**	**n.a.**	**(2,714)**
Cash & equivalent	1,287		2,040
Inventories	1,555		537
Accounts receivable	222		42
Current assets	4,144		3,042
Fixed assets, net	252		322
Right-of-use assets	61		nil
Total assets	**4,457**	**+32**	**3,364**
Accts. pay. & accr. liabs	365		270
Current liabilities	689		270
Long-term debt, gross	418		494
Long-term debt, net	175		494
Long-term lease liabilities	38		nil
Shareholders' equity	3,555		2,560
Cash from oper. activs	**(1,840)**	**n.a.**	**(1,950)**
Cash from fin. activs	1,138		3,734
Cash from invest. activs	(50)		(79)
Net cash position	**1,287**	**-37**	**2,040**
Capital expenditures	(50)		(271)
	$		$
Earnings per share*	(0.01)		(0.09)
Cash flow per share*	(0.04)		(0.06)
	shs		shs
No. of shs. o/s*	48,496,836		42,784,336
Avg. no. of shs. o/s*	43,356,391		31,834,302
	%		%
Net profit margin	(10.43)		n.a.
Return on equity	(14.75)		(199.71)
Return on assets	(10.72)		(140.82)

* Common
[o] Restated
[A] Reported in accordance with IFRS

Latest Results

Periods ended:	3m Mar. 31/23[A]		3m Mar. 31/22[A]
	$000s	%Chg	$000s
Operating revenue	600	-64	1,649
Net income	(530)	n.a.	251
	$		$
Earnings per share*	(0.01)		0.01

* Common
[A] Reported in accordance with IFRS

Historical Summary
(as originally stated)

Fiscal Year	Oper. Rev.	Net Inc. Bef. Disc.	EPS*
	$000s	$000s	$
2022[A]	4,325	(451)	(0.01)
2021[A1]	nil	(2,714)	(0.09)
2020[A2]	nil	(779)	(0.06)

* Common
[A] Reported in accordance with IFRS
[1] Results for 2021and prior periods pertain to Beacon Hill Innovations Ltd.
[2] 46 weeks ended Dec. 31, 2020.

B.6 B.E.S.T. Venture Opportunities Fund Inc.

Symbol - BVOF.A **Exchange** - CSE **CUSIP** - 054971
Head Office - 503-56 The Esplanade, Toronto, ON, M5E 1A7 **Telephone** - (416) 203-7331 **Fax** - (416) 203-6630
Website - bestfunds.ca
Email - tlunan@bestfunds.ca
Investor Relations - Thomas W. R. Lunan (416) 203-7331 ext. 230
Auditors - BDO Canada LLP C.A., Toronto, Ont.
Transfer Agents - Convexus Managed Services Inc., Thornhill, Ont.
Investment Managers - B.E.S.T. Investment Counsel Limited, Toronto, Ont.
Portfolio Advisors - B.E.S.T. Investment Counsel Limited, Toronto, Ont.
Profile - (Can. 1993) Labour-sponsored investment fund.
The fund makes investments in eligible Canadian businesses.
Top 10 holdings at Feb. 28, 2022 (as a percentage of net asset value):

Holdings	Percentage
Ruby Corp.	39.9%
Province of Ontario[1]	31.6%
Royal Bank of Canada[2]	13.8%
Spectra Products Inc.	5.6%
EQ Inc.	3.1%
Northern Graphite Corporation	2.1%
Cash	1.5%
Redline Communications Group Inc.	0.6%
Medcan Health Management Inc.	0.5%
SQI Diagnostics Inc.	0.5%

[1] 8.1% Sept. 8, 2023.
[2] Banker's acceptance.

Class A ser I listed on CSE, Nov. 25, 2022.
Class A ser II listed on CSE, Nov. 25, 2022.
Predecessor Detail - Name changed from Dynamic Venture Opportunities Fund Ltd., Oct. 22, 2018.
Directors - Geoffrey R. (Geoff) Bedford, chr., Burlington, Ont.; John-David Alkema, Hamilton, Ont.; Brent W. Bere, Waterdown, Ont.; Harold F. Jones, Oro-Medonte, Ont.
Other Exec. Officers - John M. A. Richardson, CEO; Thomas W. R. (Tom) Lunan, CFO; Mark D. Donatelli, corp. sec.

Capital Stock

	Authorized (shs.)	Outstanding (shs.)[1]
Class A	unlimited	
Series I		250,381
Series II		770,704
Class B	1,000	4
Class C	unlimited	nil

[1] At Nov. 25, 2022

Class A - Issuable in series.
Series I & II - Entitled to receive dividends, provided that no dividend will be declared or paid unless the same dividend per share is declared or paid to holders of class C shares. Not redeemable by class A shareholders until at least Dec. 31, 2024. One vote per share.
Class B - Not entitled to receive dividends. Redeemable by the fund at a redemption price equal to the issue price of the shares. Held by the Christian Labour Association of Canada (2), UNITE HERE Canada (1) and the United Brotherhood of Carpenters and Joiners of America (1), who are entitled to elect a majority of the fund's directors. One vote per share.
Class C - Issuable in series. Entitled to receive dividends, provided that no dividend will be declared or paid unless the same dividend per share is declared or paid to holders of class A shares. One vote per share. The fund does not intend to issue any class C shares.
Major Shareholder - Widely held at Nov. 25, 2022.

Price Range - BVOF.A/CSE

Year	Volume	High	Low	Close
2022	300	$5.00	$5.00	$5.00

BVOF.B/CSE

Year	Volume	High	Low	Close
2022	3,239	$5.00	$3.00	$3.00

Recent Close: $2.11

Financial Statistics

Periods ended:	12m Aug. 31/21[A]		12m Aug. 31/21[A]
	$000s	%Chg	$000s
Realized invest. gain (loss)	(3)		(3)
Unrealized invest. gain (loss)	(434)		(434)
Total revenue	**1,057**	**n.a.**	**1,057**
General & admin. expense	786		786
Operating expense	**786**	**n.a.**	**786**
Operating income	**271**	**n.a.**	**271**
Finance costs, gross	14		14
Pre-tax income	**257**	**n.a.**	**257**
Net income	**257**	**n.a.**	**257**
Cash & equivalent	127		127
Current assets	13,610		13,610
Total assets	**13,610**	**n.a.**	**13,610**
Accts. pay. & accr. liabs	141		141
Current liabilities	163		163
Cash from oper. activs	**2,992**	**n.a.**	**2,992**
Cash from fin. activs	(3,389)		(3,389)
Net cash position	**127**	**n.a.**	**127**
	$		$
Earnings per share*	0.39		0.39
Cash flow per share*	2.50		2.50
Net asset value per share*	25.67		25.67
	shs		shs
No. of shs. o/s*	1,070,555		1,070,555
Avg. no. of shs. o/s*	1,195,496		1,195,496
	%		%
Net profit margin	24.31		24.31
Return on equity	n.m.		n.m.
Return on assets	1.79		1.79

* Cl.A Series I & II
[A] Reported in accordance with IFRS

Latest Results

Periods ended:	6m Feb. 28/22[A]
	$000s
Total revenue	534
Net income	201
	$
Earnings per share*	0.38

* Cl.A Series I & II
[A] Reported in accordance with IFRS

B.7 BIGG Digital Assets Inc.

Symbol - BIGG **Exchange** - CSE **CUSIP** - 089804
Head Office - 1220-1130 Pender St W, Vancouver, BC, V6E 4A4 **Telephone** - (778) 819-4675 **Toll-free** - (844) 282-2140
Website - www.biggdigitalassets.com
Email - mark@biggdigitalassets.com
Investor Relations - Mark Binns (844) 515-2646
Auditors - KPMG LLP C.A., Vancouver, B.C.
Transfer Agents - Computershare Trust Company of Canada Inc., Vancouver, B.C.
Employees - 60 at June 28, 2023
Profile - (B.C. 2014) Owns, operates and invests in cryptocurrency businesses that support and enhance a compliant and regulated ecosystem.
The company operates two businesses: Netcoins; and Blockchain Intelligence Group (BIG).
Netcoins is a digital currency sales brokerage that enables clients in the Canada and the U.S., to buy, sell, stack and stake cryptocurrency. The Netcoins platform is available via a mobile app and on the web. Also offers Netcoins Pay in Canada, a physical and virtual prepaid Mastercard that enables users to earn Bitcoin rewards.
BIG offers QLUE™ (Qualitative Law Enforcement Unified Edge), a blockchain-agnostic search and analytics platform which allows law enforcement, regulatory technology (regtech), regulators and government agencies to forensically and visually trace, track and monitor cryptocurrency transactions to aid in the fight against terrorist financing, money laundering, human trafficking, drug trafficking, weapons trafficking and other illicit activities; BitRank Verified®, a risk-scoring platform that provides real-time monitoring and scoring of cryptocurrency transactions and wallets enabling regtech, banks, ATMs, exchanges and retailers to meet traditional regulatory/compliance requirements; and Address Watch, an automated cryptocurrency alert service which enables investigators and compliance teams to track activity tied to supported cryptocurrency addresses and groups of addresses. Also provides Certified Cryptocurrency Investigator (CCI) program, a training program on how to track, trace and investigate

cryptocurrency transactions and/or crimes; and cryptocurrency forensic investigation services to financial institutions and law enforcement through a network of certified investigators. These products are sold via subscriptions.

In addition, holds investments in businesses that support and enhance a compliant and regulated ecosystem for cryptocurrency.Primary investments include **TerraZero Technologies Inc.**, which acquires, designs, builds and operates virtual assets and solutions to monetize the Metaverse space, as well as owns digital real estate and provides offices and services to those interested in the Metaverse.

In November 2022, sold its 15% interest in **Luxxfolio Holdings Inc.** for an undisclosed amount. The company acquired the interest in June 2022 consisting of 12,500,000 units (1 common share & 1 warrant) at 16¢ per unit. Luxxfolio is a digital infrastructure provider for bitcoin mining and data hosting operations.

Recent Merger and Acquisition Activity

Status: terminated **Revised:** June 6, 2023

UPDATE: The transaction was terminated. PREVIOUS: Whatcom Capital II Corp. entered into a letter of intent for the Qualifying Transaction reverse takeover acquisition of Terrazero Technologies Inc., a Metaverse company. A total of 52,947,539 post-consolidated common shares (following a 1-for-3.5 share consolidation) were expected to be issued at a deemed price of $0.70 per share to Terrazero shareholders. Terrazero was expected to complete a private placement financing for gross proceeds of up to $2,000,000. Terrazero has a studio division, which creates immersive Metaverse activations for global brands and companies, a technology division, which creates solutions to bridge the real world with the virtual world, and a data analytics division, which aggregates data from across the Metaverse to help guide Terrazero's and its clients' decision making. BIGG Digital Assets Inc. holds a 29% interest in Terrazero. Feb. 1, 2023 - The companies entered into a definitive agreement whereby Terrazero would amalgamated with a wholly owned subsidiary of Whatcom to continue as TZ technologies Corp. Whatcom would change its name to TerraZero Technologies Inc.

Predecessor Detail - Name changed from BIG Blockchain Intelligence Group Inc., Oct. 4, 2019.

Directors - Mark Binns, CEO, North Vancouver, B.C.; Lance Morginn, pres. & pres., Blockchain Technology Group Inc., Vancouver, B.C.; D. Kim Evans, CFO, North Vancouver, B.C.; Robert L. (Rob) Birmingham, North Vancouver, B.C.; Mark Healy, Paris, Ont.; Kalle Radage, B.C.

Other Exec. Officers - Fraser Matthews, pres., Netcoins Inc.

Capital Stock

	Authorized (shs.)	Outstanding (shs.)[1]
Preferred	unlimited	nil
Common	unlimited	255,310,401

[1] At June 28, 2023

Major Shareholder - Widely held at Nov. 10, 2022.

Price Range - BIGG/CSE

Year	Volume	High	Low	Close
2022............	185,781,219	$1.53	$0.22	$0.23
2021............	492,349,542	$5.05	$0.37	$1.04
2020............	142,975,357	$0.58	$0.03	$0.51
2019............	88,214,545	$0.14	$0.04	$0.04
2018............	153,352,932	$1.95	$0.07	$0.10

Recent Close: $0.29

Capital Stock Changes - During 2022, common shares were issued as follows: 5,708,675 on exercise of warrants and 3,223,232 on exercise of options.

Wholly Owned Subsidiaries

BIG Blockchain Intelligence Group Inc., Tex.
BitRank Verification Services Inc., B.C.
Blockchain Technology Group Inc., Vancouver, B.C.
- 100% int. in **2140 Software Solutions Inc.**, B.C.

CFC Digital Inc., B.C.
Dark Fibre Systems Inc., B.C.
1208810 B.C. Ltd., B.C.
- 100% int. in **NTC Holdings Corp.**, Canada.
- 100% int. in **Netcoins Inc.**, Vancouver, B.C.
- 100% int. in **Netcoins USA Inc.**, Wyo.

QLUE Forensic Systems Inc., B.C.

Investments

LQWD Technologies Corp., Vancouver, B.C. (see separate coverage)
30.33% int. in **Terrazero Technologies Inc.**, Vancouver, B.C.
ZenLedger, Inc., Bellevue, Wash.

Financial Statistics

Periods ended:	12m Dec. 31/22[A]		12m Dec. 31/21[A]
	$000s	%Chg	$000s
Operating revenue........................	**7,473**	**-47**	**14,115**
Cost of sales..................................	365		230
Salaries & benefits..........................	7,588		5,466
Research & devel. expense.............	912		730
General & admin expense................	14,850		11,007
Stock-based compensation............	1,766		6,283
Operating expense........................	**25,481**	**+7**	**23,716**
Operating income.........................	**(18,008)**	**n.a.**	**(9,601)**
Deprec., depl. & amort....................	382		544
Finance income..............................	195		106
Finance costs, gross.......................	5		5
Investment income.........................	(2,178)		nil
Write-downs/write-offs....................	(68)		(5)
Pre-tax income............................	**(44,153)**	**n.a.**	**(6,891)**
Income taxes..................................	nil		153
Net income...................................	**(44,153)**	**n.a.**	**(7,044)**
Cash & equivalent...........................	5,678		31,846
Inventories......................................	39,592		92,364
Accounts receivable.......................	2,206		2,963
Current assets................................	53,884		135,061
Long-term investments..................	10,639		17,622
Fixed assets, net............................	545		258
Right-of-use assets........................	24		55
Intangibles, net..............................	1,194		1,402
Total assets..................................	**67,403**	**-56**	**154,397**
Accts. pay. & accr. liabs..................	3,403		2,132
Current liabilities...........................	44,275		85,414
Long-term lease liabilities...............	7		36
Shareholders' equity.......................	23,120		68,947
Cash from oper. activs..................	**(18,413)**	**n.a.**	**(22,617)**
Cash from fin. activs........................	1,162		52,304
Cash from invest. activs..................	(8,929)		(10,611)
Net cash position.........................	**5,678**	**-82**	**31,846**
Capital expenditures.......................	(431)		(261)
Capital disposals............................	nil		5
	$		$
Earnings per share*.........................	(0.18)		(0.03)
Cash flow per share*.......................	(0.07)		(0.10)
	shs		shs
No. of shs. o/s*...............................	253,785,401		244,853,494
Avg. no. of shs. o/s*........................	248,367,113		229,561,348
	%		%
Net profit margin............................	(590.83)		(49.90)
Return on equity.............................	(95.91)		(16.83)
Return on assets............................	(39.81)		(7.65)
Foreign sales percent.....................	26		9

* Common
[A] Reported in accordance with IFRS

Latest Results

Periods ended:	3m Mar. 31/23[A]		3m Mar. 31/22[A]
	$000s	%Chg	$000s
Operating revenue..........................	1,525	-39	2,510
Net income.....................................	(751)	n.a.	(5,534)
	$		$
Earnings per share*.........................	(0.00)		(0.02)

* Common
[A] Reported in accordance with IFRS

Historical Summary
(as originally stated)

Fiscal Year	Oper. Rev.	Net Inc. Bef. Disc.	EPS*
	$000s	$000s	$
2022[A]...................	7,473	(44,153)	(0.18)
2021[A]...................	14,115	(7,044)	(0.03)
2020[A]...................	2,515	(2,949)	(0.02)
2019[A]...................	566	(8,302)	(0.07)
2018[A]...................	84	(9,625)	(0.09)

* Common
[A] Reported in accordance with IFRS

B.8 BIOSENTA Inc.

Symbol - ZRO **Exchange** - CSE **CUSIP** - 09072N
Head Office - 704-18 Wynford Dr, Toronto, ON, M3C 3S2 **Telephone** - (416) 410-2019 **Toll-free** - (855) 410-2019 **Fax** - (416) 410-6703
Website - www.biosenta.com
Email - am@biosenta.com
Investor Relations - Amarvir Gill (416) 410-2019
Auditors - MS Partners LLP C.A., Toronto, Ont.
Transfer Agents - Heritage Trust Company, Toronto, Ont.

Profile - (Ont. 1986) Develops and manufactures chemical compounds for household and industrial applications using advanced encapsulated nanotechnology.

Developing two business units within the anti-microbial industry: Industrial and Consumer.

Through the Industrial division, plans to manufacture and distribute Tri-filler™, an anti-microbial filler that performs filing and bulking functions like calcium carbonate; and prohibits mould infestation. The company had commissioned its production plant in Party Sound, Ont., to produce the filler product and the plant was producing a test product. However, commercial operations have not commenced due to shortage of funds.

Through the Consumer division, has developed True™, a disinfectant that eliminates moulds, mildew, viruses, bacteria fungi and prevents regrowth. It is the second generation of the Zeromold™ anti-microbial retail product line and has received regulatory approvals for distribution in Canada and the United States.

In October 2022, the company entered into a memorandum of understanding with **Voran Group Ventures Ltd.** to commercialize Tri-Filler™ antimicrobial products worldwide. Voran is a Sherwood, Alta.-based company that develops, commercializes and distributes advanced antimicrobial solutions.

Predecessor Detail - Name changed from RXT 110 Inc., May 31, 2012.

Directors - Edwin (Ed) Korhonen, chr., Ont.; Amarvir (Am) Gill, pres., CEO & acting CFO, Alta.; David Butler, Ont.; Nicholas Iacono, New Canaan, Conn.; Dene L. Rogers, San Francisco, Calif.

Capital Stock

	Authorized (shs.)	Outstanding (shs.)[1]
Class C Preferred	unlimited	nil
Class A	unlimited	23,006,591
Class B	unlimited	nil

[1] At Mar. 31, 2023

Major Shareholder - CDS & Co. held 45.31% interest, 1698791 Ontario Ltd. held 17.88% interest and Amarvir (Am) Gill held 13.63% interest at July 6, 2022.

Price Range - ZRO/CSE

Year	Volume	High	Low	Close
2022............	611,378	$0.63	$0.07	$0.53
2021............	1,743,194	$2.50	$0.19	$0.26
2020............	1,693,157	$2.43	$0.04	$1.50
2019............	12,200	$0.11	$0.07	$0.07
2018............	564,114	$0.75	$0.01	$0.04

Recent Close: $0.45

Capital Stock Changes - During fiscal 2022, 3,625,315 class A shares were issued for debt settlement.

Wholly Owned Subsidiaries

Biosenta U.S.A. Inc., United States.

Financial Statistics

Periods ended:	12m Sept. 30/22[A]		12m Sept. 30/21[A]
	$000s	%Chg	$000s
Operating revenue........................	**1**	**-99**	**168**
Cost of sales..................................	nil		69
Salaries & benefits..........................	627		778
Research & devel. expense.............	103		81
General & admin expense................	366		368
Stock-based compensation............	113		892
Operating expense........................	**1,209**	**-45**	**2,188**
Operating income.........................	**(1,208)**	**n.a.**	**(2,020)**
Finance costs, gross.......................	223		10
Write-downs/write-offs....................	(31)		(8)
Pre-tax income............................	**(1,458)**	**n.a.**	**(2,042)**
Net income...................................	**(1,458)**	**n.a.**	**(2,042)**
Cash & equivalent...........................	27		112
Inventories......................................	45		77
Current assets................................	256		264
Total assets..................................	**256**	**-3**	**264**
Bank indebtedness..........................	35		92
Accts. pay. & accr. liabs..................	1,300		1,396
Current liabilities...........................	3,121		2,797
Shareholders' equity.......................	(2,925)		(2,594)
Cash from oper. activs..................	**(504)**	**n.a.**	**(672)**
Cash from fin. activs........................	420		740
Net cash position.........................	**27**	**-76**	**112**
	$		$
Earnings per share*.........................	(0.07)		(0.11)
Cash flow per share*.......................	(0.02)		(0.04)
	shs		shs
No. of shs. o/s*...............................	23,006,591		19,381,276
Avg. no. of shs. o/s*........................	21,303,490		17,796,546
	%		%
Net profit margin............................	n.m.		n.m.
Return on equity.............................	n.m.		n.m.
Return on assets............................	(475.00)		n.m.

* Class A
[A] Reported in accordance with IFRS

Historical Summary
(as originally stated)

Fiscal Year	Oper. Rev. $000s	Net Inc. Bef. Disc. $000s	EPS* $
2022A	1	(1,458)	(0.07)
2021A	168	(2,042)	(0.11)
2020A	2	(762)	(0.05)
2019A	nil	(530)	(0.04)
2018A	1	(1,190)	(0.09)

* Class A
A Reported in accordance with IFRS

B.9 BIP Investment Corporation

CUSIP - 09075W
Head Office - Royal Centre, 1500-1055 Georgia St W, PO Box 11117, Vancouver, BC, V6E 4N7
Website - www.brookfield.com/infrastructure
Email - bip.enquiries@brookfield.com
Investor Relations - Rene Lubianski (416) 956-5129
Auditors - Deloitte LLP C.A., Toronto, Ont.
Transfer Agents - Computershare Trust Company of Canada Inc.
Profile - (B.C. 2018) Operates primarily for the purpose of issuing preferred shares and serves as an investment holding company for **Brookfield Infrastructure Partners L.P.** (BIP LP).

The company's investments consist of indirect interests in **Enercare Inc.**, BIP LP's North American residential energy infrastructure operation (acquired in 2018), which provides water heaters, furnaces, air conditioners and other HVAC rental products, protection plans, sub-metering and related services; **NorthRiver Midstream Inc.**, BIP LP's western Canadian natural gas gathering and processing business (acquired from **Enbridge Inc.** in 2018 and 2019); and **Inter Pipeline Ltd.**, BIP LP's Canadian diversified midstream business (acquired in 2021).

The company does not prepare separate financial statements due to an exemption from the continuous disclosure requirements under the Securities Act. One of the conditions of the exemption is that the company is required to file with the Canadian securities commissions all documents filed by parent entity BIP LP.

Directors - Samuel J. B. (Sam) Pollock, CEO, Toronto, Ont.; David Krant, CFO; Jeffrey M. (Jeff) Blidner, Toronto, Ont.; Anne Schaumburg, N.J.

Capital Stock

	Authorized (shs.)	Outstanding (shs.)[1]
Senior Preferred	unlimited	
Series 1		4,000,000
Jr. Preferred	unlimited	16,731,501
Common	unlimited	10,001,020

[1] At Jan. 10, 2023

Note: Jr. preferred and common shares all held by Brookfield Infrastructure Holdings (Canada) Inc., a wholly subsidiary of Brookfield Infrastructure Partners L.P.

Senior Preferred - Issuable in series. Fully and unconditionally guaranteed by Brookfield Infrastructure Partners L.P. Non-voting.

Series 1 - Entitled to fixed cumulative preferential annual dividends of $1.4625 per share payable quarterly to Mar. 31, 2024, and thereafter at a rate reset every five years equal to the greater of the five-year Government of Canada bond yield plus 3.96%; and 5.85%. Retractable in each month for a price equal to the lesser of: (i) 95% of the volume weighted average price on the TSX for three business days; and (ii) $23.75. Redeemable on Mar. 31, 2024, and on March 31 every five years thereafter at $25 per share plus declared and unpaid dividends. Convertible at the holder's option on Mar. 31, 2024, and on March 31 every five years thereafter, into floating rate senior preferred series 2 shares on a share-for-share basis, subject to certain conditions.

Major Shareholder - Brookfield Infrastructure Partners L.P. held 100% interest at Jan. 10, 2023.

Dividends

BIK.PR.A pfd ser 1 cum. red. exch. Adj. Ra $1.4625 pa Q est. Mar. 29, 2019
$0.365625**g** Sept. 29/23 $0.365625**g** Mar. 31/23
$0.365625**g** Dec. 30/22 $0.365625**g** Sept. 29/22
Paid in 2023: $0.365625 + $0.73125**g** 2022: $0.73125 + $0.73125**g** 2021: $1.462125

g Capital Gain

Investments

Enercare Inc., Markham, Ont.
Inter Pipeline Ltd., Calgary, Alta.
NorthRiver Midstream Inc., Calgary, Alta.

B.10 BMTC Group Inc.*

Symbol - GBT **Exchange** - TSX **CUSIP** - 05561N
Head Office - 8500 place Marien, Montréal-Est, QC, H1B 5W8 **Telephone** - (514) 648-5757 **Toll-free** - (877) 881-4050 **Fax** - (514) 881-4056
Website - www.bmtc.ca
Email - m.desgroseillers@bmtc.ca
Investor Relations - Michèle Des Groseillers (514) 648-5757
Auditors - PricewaterhouseCoopers LLP C.A., Montréal, Qué.
Bankers - Desjardins Bank, N.A.; National Bank of Canada
Lawyers - Davies Ward Phillips & Vineberg LLP, Montréal, Qué.; Fasken Martineau DuMoulin LLP, Montréal, Qué.; Norton Rose Fulbright LLP
Transfer Agents - Computershare Trust Company of Canada Inc., Montréal, Qué.
FP500 Revenue Ranking - 399
Employees - 954 at Jan. 31, 2023
Profile - (Que. 1982) Operates stores in Quebec selling furniture, household appliances and electronic products.

The company's sales and distribution network includes eight Brault & Martineau stores, nine Ameublements Tanguay stores, 11 EconoMax stores and two liquidation centres located in the areas of LaSalle, Gatineau, Brossard, Sherbrooke, Kirkland, Ste-Rose, St-Hubert, Montreal, Ste-Thérèse, Laval, St-Eustache, Joliette, Granby, Drummondville, Lévis, Beauport, Trois-Rivières, Rimouski, Chicoutimi, Rivière-du-Loup, St-Georges-de-Beauce, Ste-Foy and Quebec City. The network also includes three distribution and administrative centres in Montreal and Quebec City.

The majority of these stores are used solely as showrooms and points of sale with delivery being made principally from distribution centres. All deliveries of Brault & Martineau and EconoMax divisions of the company are carried out by subcontractors on an ad-hoc basis, while its Ameublements Tanguay division delivers the goods it sells by its corporate-owned fleet of delivery trucks and also uses outsourcing, as well as uses subcontractors on an ad-hoc basis.

On Dec. 1, 2022, wholly owned **Ameublements Tanguay Inc.** was amalgamated into the company.

Recent Merger and Acquisition Activity

Status: completed **Announced:** Feb. 1, 2023
BMTC Group Inc. completed the sale and leaseback of its distribution centre in Montreal, Que., for $66,500,000.

Predecessor Detail - Name changed from Cantrex Group Inc., Nov. 2, 1989.

Directors - Yves Des Groseillers, chr., Qué.; Marie-Berthe Des Groseillers, pres. & CEO, Qué.; André Bérard†, Montréal, Qué.; Lucien Bouchard, Montréal, Qué.; Gabriel Castiglio, Montréal, Qué.; Charles Des Groseillers, Qué.; Tony Fionda, Qué.; Anne-Marie Leclair, Montréal, Qué.

Other Exec. Officers - Jacques Tanguay, COO; Sylvie Bélanger, CFO; Michèle Des Groseillers, corp. sec.; Charles Tanguay, pres., Brault & Martineau, EconoMax & Ameublements Tanguay div.
† Lead director

Capital Stock

	Authorized (shs.)	Outstanding (shs.)[1]
First Preferred	unlimited	nil
Second Preferred	unlimited	nil
Common	unlimited	32,974,250

[1] At Apr. 30, 2023

Normal Course Issuer Bid - The company plans to make normal course purchases of up to 1,650,085 common shares representing 5% of the total outstanding. The bid commenced on Apr. 15, 2023, and expires on Apr. 14, 2024.

Major Shareholder - Yves Des Groseillers held 64.77% interest and Fidelity Management & Research Company held 19.11% interest at Apr. 27, 2023.

Price Range - GBT/TSX

Year	Volume	High	Low	Close
2022	783,443	$16.00	$11.15	$13.39
2021	999,208	$16.28	$10.50	$15.69
2020	795,230	$13.02	$5.69	$12.40
2019	830,421	$15.68	$9.89	$10.39
2018	1,230,036	$18.74	$12.58	$12.99

Recent Close: $15.25

Capital Stock Changes - During fiscal 2023, 382 600 common shares were repurchased under a Normal Course Issuer Bid.

Dividends

GBT com Ra $0.36 pa S est. Jan. 5, 2022
Prev. Rate: $0.32 est. July 2, 2021
Prev. Rate: $0.30 est. Jan. 5, 2021

Long-Term Debt - At Jan. 31, 2023, the company had no long-term debt.

Wholly Owned Subsidiaries

Le Corbusier-Concorde inc., Laval, Qué.
- 100% int. in **Le Corbusier-Concorde S.E.C.**, Laval, Qué.

Financial Statistics

Periods ended:	12m Jan. 31/23A		12m Jan. 31/22A
	$000s	%Chg	$000s
Operating revenue	**717,972**	**-12**	**819,445**
Cost of sales	424,442		483,736
General & admin expense	239,408		240,905
Operating expense	**663,850**	**-8**	**724,641**
Operating income	**54,122**	**-43**	**94,804**
Deprec., depl. & amort.	10,005		11,468
Finance income	2,001		626
Finance costs, gross	412		550
Investment income	4,812		3,370
Pre-tax income	**54,039**	**-50**	**107,858**
Income taxes	13,201		25,927
Net income	**40,838**	**-50**	**81,931**
Cash & equivalent	3,050		18,983
Inventories	113,627		113,818
Accounts receivable	8,760		5,334
Current assets	133,826		139,158
Long-term investments	227,614		218,343
Fixed assets, net	142,158		148,915
Total assets	**581,964**	**+6**	**549,926**
Bank indebtedness	11,034		nil
Accts. pay. & accr. liabs.	97,932		130,843
Current liabilities	112,260		139,527
Long-term lease liabilities	5,432		8,726
Shareholders' equity	440,899		387,866
Cash from oper. activs	**(1,935)**	**n.a.**	**62,226**
Cash from fin. activs	(21,785)		(22,510)
Cash from invest. activs	(3,247)		(17,539)
Net cash position	**(7,984)**	**n.a.**	**18,983**
Capital expenditures	(3,755)		(2,245)
Capital disposals	135		172
Pension fund surplus	76,617		41,761
	$		$
Earnings per share*	1.23		2.43
Cash flow per share*	(0.06)		1.85
Cash divd. per share*	0.36		0.34
	shs		shs
No. of shs. o/s*	33,040,400		33,423,000
Avg. no. of shs. o/s*	33,255,566		33,723,642
	%		%
Net profit margin	5.69		10.00
Return on equity	9.86		24.88
Return on assets	7.27		16.47
No. of employees (FTEs)	954		1,251

* Common
A Reported in accordance with IFRS

Latest Results

Periods ended:	3m Apr. 30/23A		3m Apr. 30/22A
	$000s	%Chg	$000s
Operating revenue	135,102	-23	175,659
Net income	38,017	n.m.	807
	$		$
Earnings per share*	1.15		0.02

* Common
A Reported in accordance with IFRS

Historical Summary
(as originally stated)

Fiscal Year	Oper. Rev. $000s	Net Inc. Bef. Disc. $000s	EPS* $
2023A	717,972	40,838	1.23
2022A	819,445	81,931	2.43
2021A	649,056	54,842	1.61
2020A	720,169	36,034	1.05
2019A	740,017	45,165	1.29

* Common
A Reported in accordance with IFRS

B.11 BQE Water Inc.

Symbol - BQE **Exchange** - TSX-VEN **CUSIP** - 055640
Head Office - 250-900 Howe St, Vancouver, BC, V6Z 2M4 **Telephone** - (604) 685-1243 **Toll-free** - (800) 537-3073 **Fax** - (604) 685-7778
Website - www.bqewater.com
Email - hwong@bqewater.com
Investor Relations - Heman Wong (604) 685-1243
Auditors - MNP LLP C.A., Vancouver, B.C.
Bankers - HSBC Bank Canada, Vancouver, B.C.
Lawyers - McCarthy Tétrault LLP, Vancouver, B.C.
Transfer Agents - Computershare Trust Company of Canada Inc., Vancouver, B.C.
Profile - (B.C. 1999) Designs, operates and maintains water treatment plants that remove, recover and recycle dissolved metals, sulphate, selenium, cyanide, ammonia and other nitrogen species from contaminated water using patented BioSulphide®, ChemSulphide®™, Met-IX™, Sulf-IX™, Sulf-IXC™, Selen-IX™ and SART processes. Also provides water management related services.

Operational services consist of the operation of water treatment plants, which generate revenues from the sale of recovered metals, as well as from water treatment and operations support fees. The company operates three water treatment plants located at Dexing and Yinshan mines in Jiangxi province, PRC, operated by 50%-owned **JCC-BioteQ Environmental Technologies Co. Ltd.**; a water treatment plant in Shandong province, PRC, operated by 20%-owned **Shandong MWT BioteQ Environmental Technologies Co. Ltd.**; four water treatment plants at **Glencore plc**'s Raglan mine in northern Quebec; a water treatment plant in **Minto Metals Corp.**'s Minto mine in Yukon; two water treatment plants at two metallurgical facilities in eastern China that are owned by **Shandong Zhongkuang Group Co., Ltd.** and **Zhaojin Mining Industry Co., Ltd.**; a water treatment plant utilizing Selen-IX™ process to remove selenium from ash pond water in Virginia owned by **WesTech Engineering Inc.**; and a water treatment plant utilizing a combination of nanofiltration and selenium electro-reduction process for simultaneous removal of selenium and sulphate from mine water for the base metal project in Arizona.

Technical services consist of water management consulting and technical innovation services including feasibility and assessment studies, toxicity investigations, process engineering design, treatment plant commissioning, plant optimization, laboratory treatability assessments and field pilot demonstrations.

Predecessor Detail - Name changed from BioteQ Environmental Technologies Inc., Mar. 1, 2017.

Directors - Peter Gleeson, exec. chr., Seattle, Wash.; Dr. David Kratochvil, pres. & CEO, Vancouver, B.C.; Sara C. Elford, Shawnigan Lake, B.C.; Dr. Christopher A. (Chris) Fleming, Lakefield, Ont.; Robert D. (Rob) Henderson, Vancouver, B.C.

Other Exec. Officers - Heman Wong, CFO & corp. sec.; Brent Baker, v-p, eng.; Jonathan (Jon) Reynolds, v-p, projects; Songlin Ye, v-p, Asia; Oscar Lopez, gen. mgr., Latin America

Capital Stock

	Authorized (shs.)	Outstanding (shs.)[1]
Common	unlimited	1,252,528

[1] At May 30, 2023

Normal Course Issuer Bid - The company plans to make normal course purchases of up to 62,556 common shares representing 5% of the total outstanding. The bid commenced on Dec. 12, 2022, and expires on Dec. 11, 2023.

Major Shareholder - Dr. Richard Hubbard held 19.21% interest, Hall Tingley held 16.97% interest and Robert Stein held 10.32% interest at May 15, 2023.

Price Range - BQE/TSX-VEN

Year	Volume	High	Low	Close
2022	40,667	$32.50	$24.00	$29.50
2021	57,799	$34.00	$18.02	$26.50
2020	121,350	$20.00	$7.41	$19.10
2019	96,798	$9.00	$5.00	$8.55
2018	70,709	$12.50	$4.50	$5.50

Consolidation: 1-for-100 cons. in Mar. 2019

Recent Close: $25.00

Capital Stock Changes - During 2022, 11,960 common shares were issued on exercise of options.

Wholly Owned Subsidiaries

BQE Water (Hangzhou) Co. Ltd., Hangzhou, Zhejiang, People's Republic of China.

BQE Water Delaware, Inc., Del.

Biomet Mining Corporation, Richmond, B.C.

BioteQ Water (Chile) S.p.A., Santiago, Chile.

BioteQ Water Mexico S.A. de C.V., Hermosillo, Son., Mexico.

Investments

49% int. in **BQE Water Nuvumiut Development Inc.**, Canada.

50% int. in **JCC-BioteQ Environmental Technologies Co. Ltd.**, People's Republic of China.

20% int. in **Shangdong MWT BioteQ Environmental Technologies Co. Ltd.**, People's Republic of China.

Financial Statistics

Periods ended:	12m Dec. 31/22[A]		12m Dec. 31/21[A]
	$000s	%Chg	$000s
Operating revenue	**12,158**	**+62**	**7,511**
Salaries & benefits	7,369		4,696
General & admin expense	3,655		2,236
Stock-based compensation	671		303
Other operating expense	316		214
Operating expense	**12,011**	**+61**	**7,448**
Operating income	**147**	**+133**	**63**
Deprec., depl. & amort.	264		168
Finance income	53		6
Finance costs, gross	27		29
Investment income	1,487		2,803
Write-downs/write-offs	(8)		95
Pre-tax income	**1,471**	**-47**	**2,760**
Income taxes	309		130
Net income	**1,162**	**-56**	**2,629**
Cash & equivalent	6,234		3,944
Accounts receivable	3,207		2,009
Current assets	9,959		6,269
Long-term investments	5,301		6,855
Fixed assets, net	395		255
Intangibles, net	315		399
Total assets	**15,988**	**+16**	**13,803**
Accts. pay. & accr. liabs	1,241		1,042
Current liabilities	2,794		1,712
Long-term debt, gross	268		351
Long-term debt, net	186		268
Long-term lease liabilities	86		86
Shareholders' equity	12,638		11,313
Cash from oper. activs	**(364)**	**n.a.**	**(250)**
Cash from fin. activs	(195)		(14)
Cash from invest. activs	2,768		988
Net cash position	**6,234**	**+58**	**3,944**
Capital expenditures	(81)		(45)
	$		$
Earnings per share*	0.93		2.13
Cash flow per share*	(0.29)		(0.20)
	shs		shs
No. of shs. o/s*	1,256,928		1,244,968
Avg. no. of shs. o/s*	1,248,890		1,231,673
	%		%
Net profit margin	9.56		35.00
Return on equity	9.70		27.10
Return on assets	7.94		21.90
Foreign sales percent	65		56

* Common

[A] Reported in accordance with IFRS

Latest Results

Periods ended:	3m Mar. 31/23[A]		3m Mar. 31/22[A]
	$000s	%Chg	$000s
Operating revenue	2,691	+9	2,467
Net income	(340)	n.a.	190
	$		$
Earnings per share*	(0.27)		0.15

* Common

[A] Reported in accordance with IFRS

Historical Summary
(as originally stated)

Fiscal Year	Oper. Rev.	Net Inc. Bef. Disc.	EPS*
	$000s	$000s	$
2022[A]	12,158	1,162	0.93
2021[A]	7,511	2,629	2.13
2020[A]	7,696	1,167	0.96
2019[A]	5,640	241	0.20
2018[A]	4,270	150	0.16

* Common

[A] Reported in accordance with IFRS

Note: Adjusted throughout for 1-for-100 cons. in Mar. 2019

B.12 BRP Inc.*

Symbol - DOO **Exchange** - TSX **CUSIP** - 05577W

Head Office - 726 rue Saint-Joseph, Valcourt, QC, J0E 2L0 **Telephone** - (450) 532-2211 **Toll-free** - (888) 272-9222 **Fax** - (450) 532-6494

Website - www.brp.com

Email - philippe.deschenes@brp.com

Investor Relations - Philippe Deschênes (450) 532-6462

Auditors - Deloitte LLP C.A., Montréal, Qué.

Transfer Agents - Computershare Trust Company of Canada Inc., Montréal, Qué.

FP500 Revenue Ranking - 61

Employees - 23,000 at Jan. 31, 2023

Profile - (Can. 2003) Designs, develops, manufactures, distributes and markets powersports vehicles and marine products.

Powersports Vehicles - Portfolio of brands and products consists of Can-Am® all-terrain vehicles (ATVs), side-by-side vehicles (SSVs), and Spyder and Ryker three-wheeled vehicles (3WVs); Ski-Doo® and Lynx® snowmobiles; Sea-Doo® personal watercraft and pontoons; and Rotax® engines for karts and recreational aircraft.

Marine Products - Portfolio of brands and products consists of Alumacraft® fishing; Manitou® pontoon boats; Rotax® engines for jet boats; and aluminum boats and trailers under the brands Quintrex®, Stacer® and Yellowfin®.

Products are sold in more than 130 countries primarily directly through a network of 2,600 dealers in 21 countries as well as through 150 distributors serving 350 dealers. Products are manufactured at 13 facilities in Australia, Austria, Canada, Finland, Mexico (4) and the U.S. (5).

In January 2023, the company launched a design and innovation centre in Palm Bay, Fla., to conduct advanced concepts studies for all on-water products and introduce innovations to the marine industry.

In January 2023, the company announced the construction of an additional boat manufacturing facility in Chihuahua City, Mexico to increase its production capacity of marine products including Manitou® pontoons and Alumacraft® boats. The facility was expected to be operational in 2025 at a cost of $220,000,000.

In December 2022, the company launched a design studio in south of France to conduct advanced concept studies in renewable mobility.

In October 2022, the company announced the construction of an electric vehicle (EV) manufacturing facility in Querétaro, Mexico to produce Can-Am® electric two-wheel motorcycles. The facility was expected to be operational in 2024.

On Mar. 25, 2022, the company announced its plans to launch a new all-electric two-wheel motorcycle lineup under the Can-Am brand. The first models of the complete lineup are expected to be available in mid-2024.

Recent Merger and Acquisition Activity

Status: completed **Revised:** Oct. 3, 2022

UPDATE: The transaction was completed. PREVIOUS: BRP Inc. agreed to acquire substantially all the assets related to the Shawinigan, Que.-based powersports business of Kongsberg Inc., a developer and manufacturer of electronic and mechatronic products and long-standing BRP supplier, from Kongsberg Automotive ASA. Terms were not disclosed. The plant produces a variety products of including displays, keypads, sensors, actuators and electronic power steering, wire harnesses and dashboard assemblies. The transaction was expected to be completed by the end of fiscal 2023.

Status: completed **Announced:** Aug. 5, 2022

BRP Inc. acquired an 80% interest in Denkendorf, Germany-based Pinion GmbH, which designs, manufactures and sells mechanical gearboxes for traditional and electric bicycles, for €62,000,000 in cash.

Status: completed **Revised:** July 27, 2022

UPDATE: The transaction was completed. PREVIOUS: BRP Inc. agreed to acquire Kottingbrunn, Austria-based Great Wall Motor Austria GmbH, a research and development center which specializes in e-drive systems and transmissions for electric vehicles, from Great Wall Motor Co. Ltd. Terms were not disclosed.

Directors - José Boisjoli, chr., pres. & CEO, Qué.; Barbara J. Samardzich†, Mich.; Élaine Beaudoin, Montréal, Qué.; Pierre Beaudoin, Knowlton, Qué.; Joshua (Josh) Bekenstein, Wayland, Mass.; Charles Bombardier, Montréal, Qué.; Ernesto M. Hernández, Méx., Mexico; Katherine (Kathy) Kountze, Mass.; Estelle Métayer, Westmount, Qué.; Nicholas G. (Laki) Nomicos, Mass.; Edward (Ted) Philip, Fla.; Michael Ross, Qué.

Other Exec. Officers - Laurent Beaudoin, chr., emeritus; Sébastien Martel, CFO; Stéphane Bilodeau, CIO; Anne-Marie LaBerge, chief mktg. officer; Martin Langelier, chief legal officer; Denys Lapointe, chief design officer; Thomas Uhr, chief tech. officer; Bernard Guy, exec. v-p, global product strategy; Anne Le Breton, exec. v-p, people & culture; Josée Perreault, exec. v-p, omnichannel; Minh Thanh Tran, exec. v-p, corp. strategy & low voltage & human assisted grp.; Karim Donnez, pres., marine grp.; Sandy Scullion, pres., powersports grp.

† Lead director

Capital Stock

	Authorized (shs.)	Outstanding (shs.)[1]
Preferred	unlimited	nil
Multiple Vtg.	unlimited	42,384,200
Subordinate Vtg.	unlimited	35,697,171

[1] At May 30, 2023

Multiple Voting - Convertible at any time into subordinate voting shares on a 1-for-1 basis. Six votes per share.

Subordinate Voting - One vote per share.

Options - At Jan. 31, 2023, options were outstanding to purchase 3,546,663 subordinate voting shares at a weighted average exercise price of $58.60 per share with weighted average remaining life of 7.2 years.

Normal Course Issuer Bid - The company plans to make normal course purchases of up to 3,519,398 subordinate voting shares representing 10% of the public float. The bid commenced on Dec. 5, 2022, and expires on Dec. 4, 2023.

Major Shareholder - Bombardier-Beaudoin family held 45% interest, Bain Capital, LLC held 32.6% interest and Caisse de dépôt et placement du Québec held 10.1% interest at Apr. 19, 2023.

Price Range - DOO/TSX

Year	Volume	High	Low	Close
2022	53,358,818	$113.84	$73.74	$103.23
2021	62,009,850	$129.98	$80.72	$110.80
2020	103,282,081	$87.75	$18.56	$84.09
2019	75,527,669	$67.00	$33.90	$59.16
2018	63,325,073	$74.67	$32.36	$35.34

Recent Close: $104.43

Capital Stock Changes - During fiscal 2023, 570,779 subordinate voting shares were issued on exchange of a like number of multiple voting shares, 299,102 subordinate voting shares were issued on exercise of options, 2,427,184 subordinate voting shares were repurchased under a Substantial Issuer bid and 463,950 subordinate voting shares were repurchased under a Normal Course Issuer Bid.

Dividends

DOO com S.V. Ra $0.72 pa Q est. Apr. 17, 2023[1]
Prev. Rate: $0.64 est. Apr. 18, 2022
Prev. Rate: $0.52 est. Jan. 14, 2022
[1] Quarterly divd normally payable in Apr/20 has been omitted.

Long-Term Debt - Outstanding at Jan. 31, 2023:

Term facility due 2027[1]	Cdn$1,969,500,000
Term facility due 2029[2]	665,100,000
Austrian term loans[3]	178,800,000
Less: Unamort. cost	23,200,000
	2,790,200,000
Less: Current portion	59,400,000
	2,730,800,000

[1] US$1.477 billion. Bears interest at LIBOR plus 2%, U.S. base rate plus 1% or U.S. prime rate plus 1.00%.
[2] US$498,800,000. Bears interest at SOFR plus 3.5%.
[3] €128,600,000. Bears interest at rates ranging between 0.87% and 3.41% and maturing between March 2023 and December 2030.

Wholly Owned Subsidiaries

Bombardier Recreational Products Inc., Valcourt, Qué.
- 100% int. in **BRP Sweden AB**, Sweden.
  - 100% int. in **BRP European Distribution S.A.**, Switzerland.
  - 100% int. in **BRP Finland Oy**, Finland.
  - 100% int. in **BRP Holdings (Austria) GmbH**, Austria.
    - 100% int. in **BRP-Rotax GmbH & Co. KG**, Austria.
      - 100% int. in **Great Wall Motor Austria GmbH**, Austria.
- 100% int. in **BRP US Inc.**, Del.

Telwater Pty Ltd., Australia.

Subsidiaries

80% int. in **BRP Commerce & Trade Co. Ltd.**, People's Republic of China.
80% int. in **Pinion GmbH**, Germany.
75% int. in **Regionales Innovations Centrum GmbH**, Austria.
Note: The preceding list includes only the major related companies in which interests are held.

Financial Statistics

Periods ended:	12m Jan. 31/23[A]		12m Jan. 31/22[A]
	$000s	%Chg	$000s
Operating revenue	**10,033,400**	**+31**	**7,647,900**
Cost of sales	7,223,600		5,242,100
Research & devel. expense	367,700		289,800
General & admin expense	774,900		664,900
Operating expense	**8,366,200**	**+35**	**6,196,800**
Operating income	**1,667,200**	**+15**	**1,451,100**
Deprec., depl. & amort.	310,400		273,600
Finance income	6,000		3,800
Finance costs, gross	114,800		128,900
Pre-tax income	**1,165,900**	**+8**	**1,076,700**
Income taxes	300,500		282,100
Net income	**865,400**	**+9**	**794,600**
Net inc. for equity hldrs	**863,900**	**+9**	**793,900**
Net inc. for non-cont. int.	**1,500**	**+114**	**700**
Cash & equivalent	202,300		265,800
Inventories	2,290,100		1,691,300
Accounts receivable	655,000		465,700
Current assets	3,380,600		2,668,100
Fixed assets, net	1,810,400		1,441,900
Right-of-use assets	180,300		132,700
Intangibles, net	741,300		494,900
Total assets	**6,464,600**	**+28**	**5,030,900**
Bank indebtedness	29,000		nil
Accts. pay. & accr. liabs	1,548,200		1,622,900
Current liabilities	2,483,300		2,619,400
Long-term debt, gross	2,790,200		2,040,500
Long-term debt, net	2,730,800		1,937,400
Long-term lease liabilities	152,200		117,500
Shareholders' equity	534,900		(135,600)
Non-controlling interest	5,200		2,800
Cash from oper. activs	**649,500**	**-16**	**770,000**
Cash from fin. activs	190,300		(1,142,700)
Cash from invest. activs	(853,400)		(687,700)
Net cash position	**202,300**	**-24**	**265,800**
Capital expenditures	(601,000)		(628,900)
Capital disposals	nil		400
Unfunded pension liability	158,000		220,200
	$		$
Earnings per share*	10.88		9.57
Cash flow per share*	8.18		9.28
Cash divd. per share*	0.64		0.52
	shs		shs
No. of shs. o/s*	78,906,708		81,498,740
Avg. no. of shs. o/s*	79,382,008		82,973,284
	%		%
Net profit margin	8.63		10.39
Return on equity	n.m.		n.m.
Return on assets	16.54		17.94
Foreign sales percent	84		83
No. of employees (FTEs)	23,000		20,000

* M.V. & S.V.
[A] Reported in accordance with IFRS

Latest Results

Periods ended:	3m Apr. 30/23[A]		3m Apr. 30/22[A]
	$000s	%Chg	$000s
Operating revenue	2,429,400	+34	1,809,300
Net income	154,500	+28	121,000
Net inc. for equity hldrs	154,200	+28	120,900
Net inc. for non-cont. int.	300		100
	$		$
Earnings per share*	1.96		1.49

* M.V. & S.V.
[A] Reported in accordance with IFRS

Historical Summary
(as originally stated)

Fiscal Year	Oper. Rev. $000s	Net Inc. Bef. Disc. $000s	EPS* $
2023[A]	10,033,400	865,400	10.88
2022[A]	7,647,900	794,600	9.57
2021[A]	5,952,900	362,900	4.15
2020[A]	6,052,700	370,600	4.00
2019[A]	5,243,800	227,300	2.31

* M.V. & S.V.
[A] Reported in accordance with IFRS

B.13 BSR Real Estate Investment Trust

Symbol - HOM.UN **Exchange** - TSX **CUSIP** - 05585D
Head Office - 3400-333 Bay St, Toronto, ON, M5H 2S7
Website - www.bsrreit.com
Email - bsrinvestorrelations@bsrtrust.com
Investor Relations - Susan Rosenbaum Koehn (501) 371-6335
Auditors - KPMG LLP C.A., Toronto, Ont.
Transfer Agents - TSX Trust Company, Toronto, Ont.
FP500 Revenue Ranking - 650

Employees - 250 at Dec. 31, 2022

Profile - (Ont. 2018) Acquires, owns and operates garden-style, multi-family residential properties primarily in the sunbelt region of the United States.

Garden-style, multi-family communities are generally characterized as a cluster of low-rise buildings, usually two to four stories with an average of 200 to 400 total apartment units.

The trust's portfolio is located in five suburban primary and secondary markets in three bordering states within the sunbelt region of the U.S. At Dec. 31, 2022, the trust's portfolio consisted of 31 garden-style, multi-family apartment properties, totaling 8,666 apartment units.

State	Props.	Units
Texas	24	7,397
Arkansas	3	304
Oklahoma	4	965
	31	8,666

Trustees - Neil J. Labatte, chr., Toronto, Ont.; John S. Bailey, exec. v-chr., Little Rock, Ark.; Daniel M. Oberste, pres. & CEO, Little Rock, Ark.; William A. Halter, Little Rock, Ark.; Bryan H. Held, Etobicoke, Ont.; W. Daniel Hughes Jr., Montgomery, Ala.; S. Jane Marshall, Toronto, Ont.; Teresa Neto, Etobicoke, Ont.; Graham D. Senst, Toronto, Ont.; Elizabeth A. Wademan, Toronto, Ont.

Oper. Subsid./Mgt. Co. Officers - Susan Rosenbaum Koehn, COO; Brandon R. Barger, CFO & corp. sec.; Scott A. Ray, CAO; Davi Miesner, sr. v-p, opers.; Mike Cirillo, v-p, asset mgt.; Steven Etchison, v-p, acctg.; Genevieve Garcia, v-p, Texas; Randy Jackson, v-p, invests.; Nick Stefanov, v-p, IT; Debby Pratt, contr.

Capital Stock

	Authorized (shs.)	Outstanding (shs.)[1]
Trust Unit	unlimited	36,369,787
Class B Unit	unlimited	20,521,710

[1] At Mar. 8, 2023

Trust Unit - One vote per unit.

Class B Unit - Issued by wholly owned BSR Trust, LLC. Economically equivalent to trust units and entitled to receive distributions on the same per unit basis as holders of trust units. Redeemable for cash or trust units on a 1-for-1 basis. Non-voting. Classified as liabilities.

Normal Course Issuer Bid - The company plans to make normal course purchases of up to 3,322,107 trust units representing 10% of the public float. The bid commenced on Oct. 6, 2022, and expires on Oct. 5, 2023.

Major Shareholder - Widely held at Mar. 8, 2023.

Price Range - HOM.UN/TSX

Year	Volume	High	Low	Close
2022	7,613,470	$28.08	$17.31	$17.76
2021	5,292,591	$23.00	$13.19	$22.98
2020	5,339,207	$17.74	$10.97	$14.46
2019	3,074,481	$17.34	$12.53	$15.19

HOM.U/TSX

Year	Volume	High	Low	Close
2019	9,079,816	US$12.75	US$7.77	US$11.65
2018	6,622,042	US$9.70	US$7.12	US$8.00

Recent Close: $16.44

Capital Stock Changes - In April 2022, bought deal public offering of 5,888,000 trust units was completed at US$19.55 per unit, including 768,000 units on exercise of over-allotment option. Also during 2022, trust units were issued as follows: 147,970 on exchange of a like number of class B units, 104,071 under unit-based compensation plan and 45,137 on conversion of debentures; 1,079,507 trust units were repurchased under a Normal Course Issuer Bid.

Dividends

HOM.U unit Ra US$0.52 pa M est. July 17, 2023
Prev. Rate: US$0.52 est. Nov. 15, 2022
Prev. Rate: US$0.52 est. May 16, 2022
Prev. Rate: US$0.50 est. Aug. 15, 2018
HOM.UN unit Ra US$0.52 pa M est. May 16, 2022
Prev. Rate: US$0.50 est. July 15, 2019

Wholly Owned Subsidiaries

BSR REIT Holdings, Inc., United States.
- 100% int. in **BSR Trust, LLC**, Little Rock, Ark.
  - 100% int. in **BSR Management, LLC**, Ark.
- 100% int. in **Peace of Mind Insurance Company, Inc.**, Ark.

Financial Statistics

Periods ended:	12m Dec. 31/22[A]		12m Dec. 31/21[A]
	US$000s	%Chg	US$000s
Total revenue	**158,518**	**+33**	**119,582**
Rental operating expense	28,278		21,660
Salaries & benefits	17,526		14,727
General & admin. expense	9,394		8,373
Property taxes	21,198		17,501
Operating expense	**76,396**	**+23**	**62,261**
Operating income	**82,122**	**+43**	**57,321**
Deprec. & amort.	133		130
Finance income	216		216
Finance costs, gross	39,663		44,292
Pre-tax income	**227,230**	**-20**	**283,214**
Net income	**227,230**	**-20**	**283,214**
Cash & equivalent	7,196		6,838
Accounts receivable	3,227		4,240
Current assets	31,436		21,147
Income-producing props.	2,021,095		1,918,167
Property interests, net	2,021,095		1,918,167
Right-of-use assets	300		33
Total assets	**2,063,275**	**+6**	**1,948,095**
Accts. pay. & accr. liabs.	50,434		34,588
Current liabilities	52,213		37,677
Long-term debt, gross	1,036,785		1,244,591
Long-term debt, net	1,035,006		1,242,877
Long-term lease liabilities	307		34
Shareholders' equity	975,749		666,569
Cash from oper. activs.	**89,506**	**+53**	**58,404**
Cash from fin. activs.	(62,629)		377,290
Cash from invest. activs.	(26,519)		(434,120)
Net cash position	**7,196**	**+5**	**6,838**
Increase in property	(30,724)		(657,055)
Decrease in property	nil		215,253
	US$		US$
Earnings per share*	n.a.		n.a.
Cash flow per share*	2.47		1.87
Funds from opers. per sh.*	0.86		0.60
Adj. funds from opers. per sh.*	0.80		0.59
Cash divd. per share*	0.52		0.50
Total divd. per share*	**0.52**		**0.50**
	shs		shs
No. of shs. o/s*	36,309,281		31,203,610
	%		%
Net profit margin	143.35		236.84
Return on equity	27.67		57.49
Return on assets	13.31		21.39
Foreign sales percent	100		100
No. of employees (FTEs)	250		250

* Trust Unit

[A] Reported in accordance with IFRS

Historical Summary
(as originally stated)

Fiscal Year	Total Rev.	Net Inc. Bef. Disc.	EPS*
	US$000s	US$000s	US$
2022[A]	158,518	227,230	n.a.
2021[A]	119,582	283,214	n.a.
2020[A]	113,286	27,577	n.a.
2019[A]	111,664	(53,207)	n.a.
2018[A1]	64,073	143,952	n.a.

* Trust Unit

[A] Reported in accordance with IFRS

[1] 51 weeks ended Dec. 31, 2018.

B.14 BTB Real Estate Investment Trust

Symbol - BTB.UN **Exchange** - TSX **CUSIP** - 11777P
Head Office - 300-1411 rue Crescent, Montréal, QC, H3G 2B3 **Telephone** - (514) 286-0188 **Fax** - (514) 286-0011
Website - www.btbreit.com
Email - psoulie@btbreit.com
Investor Relations - Philippine Soulié (514) 286-0188 ext. 236
Auditors - KPMG LLP C.A., Montréal, Qué.
Bankers - Laurentian Bank of Canada, Montréal, Qué.
Lawyers - De Grandpré Chait LLP, Montréal, Qué.
Transfer Agents - Computershare Trust Company of Canada Inc., Montréal, Qué.
FP500 Revenue Ranking - 743
Employees - 81 at Dec. 31, 2022
Profile - (Qué. 2006) Owns and acquires income-producing mid-market office, commercial and industrial properties in Quebec, Ontario, Alberta and Saskatchewan.

The trust focuses on office, commercial and industrial properties in primary and secondary markets east of Ottawa, Ont. The property portfolio at Mar. 31, 2023, consisted of 74 office, retail and industrial properties in eastern Canada totaling 6,033,436 sq. ft. of gross leasable area.

Property portfolio at Mar. 31, 2023:

Type	Props.	Leasable Area[1]
Office	35	2,819,123
Industrial	28	1,822,138
Retail	11	1,392,175
	74	6,033,436

[1] Sq. ft.

On Dec. 8, 2022, the trust sold a 24,925-sq.-ft. office property in Sainte-Thérèse, Que., for $4,580,000.

On Sept. 19, 2022, the trust sold a 10,773-sq.-ft. retail and office property in Montreal, Que., for $4,400,000.

On June 16, 2022, the trust sold an industrial property in Magog, Que., for $1,800,000.

Recent Merger and Acquisition Activity

Status: completed **Announced:** May 3, 2023
BTB Real Estate Investment Trust acquired a 83,292-sq.-ft. industrial property in Edmonton, Alta., for $7,350,000, consisting of issuance of 550,000 class B limited partnership units of wholly owned BTB Real Estate Limited Partnership at a deemed price of $4.50 per unit and the balance to be funded via a mortgage.

Status: completed **Announced:** Feb. 2, 2023
BTB Real Estate Investment Trust acquired The Lion Electric Company's newly constructed battery manufacturing building located near Mirabel airport in Mirabel, Que., for a purchase price of Cdn$28,000,000, excluding fees and adjustments. The 176,819-sq.-ft. battery factory for motorized electric transport, such as trucks and buses, was leased back by Lion Electric. The transaction excluded the innovation centre building, which remained the property of Lion Electric.

Status: completed **Announced:** Dec. 14, 2022
BTB Real Estate Investment Trust sold a 25,322-sq.-ft. office property in Montreal, Que., for $5,900,000.

Status: completed **Announced:** Sept. 8, 2022
BTB Real Estate Investment Trust acquired a 72,088-sq.-ft. industrial property in Edmonton, Alta., for $15,750,000. The property was fully leased to the Redco Equipment sales group, which was involved in the wellhead completion tools sector in the Canadian market of fossil energies.

Status: completed **Announced:** June 29, 2022
BTB Real Estate Investment Trust acquired a 51,747-sq.-ft. industrial property in Edmonton, Alta., for $12,950,000.

Status: completed **Announced:** June 17, 2022
BTB Real Estate Investment Trust acquired a 67,162-sq.-ft. class A industrial property in Vaudreuil-Dorion, Que., for $15,000,000. The property was fully leased to Amylior, which designs, develops and manufactures high-end motorized wheelchairs, seating and positioning systems and accessories.

Status: completed **Announced:** Apr. 5, 2022
BTB Real Estate Investment Trust acquired a 46,400-sq.-ft. industrial property at 110 Algoma Road Ottawa, Ont., for $12,500,000.

Trustees - Michel Léonard, founder, pres. & CEO, Westmount, Qué.; Jocelyn Proteau, chr., Montréal, Qué.; Jean-Pierre Janson, v-chr., Outremont, Qué.; Armand Des Rosiers, Saint-Lambert, Qué.; Lucie Ducharme, Montréal, Qué.; Sylvie Lachance, Ont.; Christine Marchildon, Pointe-Claire, Qué.; Luc Martin, Laval, Qué.; Fernand Perreault, Longueuil, Qué.

Other Exec. Officers - Mathieu Bolté, exec. v-p & chief operating & finl. officer

Capital Stock

	Authorized (shs.)	Outstanding (shs.)[1]
Trust Unit	unlimited	85,842,255
Class B LP Unit	unlimited	747,265[2 3]
Special Voting Unit	unlimited	747,265

[1] At May 8, 2023

[2] Classified as debt.

[3] Securities of wholly owned BTB Real Estate Limited Partnership.

Trust Unit - One vote per unit.

Class B Limited Partnership Unit - Exchangeable into trust units on a one-for-one basis. Entitled to receive the same distributions as declared on trust units. Classified a debt under IFRS. Non-voting.

Special Voting Unit - No economic entitlement in the trust or in the distribution or assets of the trust. Only issued in connection with or in relation to securities exchangeable into units, including class B LP units. Non-transferable separately from exchangeable securities to which they are attached and will automatically be transferred upon the transfer of any such exchangeable securities. One vote per unit.

Normal Course Issuer Bid - The company plans to make normal course purchases of up to 5,838,023 trust units representing 7% of the public float. The bid commenced on Nov. 10, 2022, and expires on Nov. 9, 2023.

Major Shareholder - Widely held at May 8, 2023.

Price Range - BTB.UN/TSX

Year	Volume	High	Low	Close
2022	41,509,434	$4.42	$3.07	$3.65
2021	41,442,439	$4.38	$3.45	$4.08
2020	60,294,293	$5.50	$2.29	$3.53
2019	25,632,248	$5.20	$4.27	$5.17
2018	27,055,506	$4.94	$4.03	$4.35

Recent Close: $3.31

Capital Stock Changes - In March 2022, bought deal public offering of 9,584,100 trust units was completed at $4.05 per unit, including 1,250,100 trust units on exercise of over-allotment option. Also during 2022, trust units were issued as follows: 872,983 under dividend reinvestment plan, 511,804 on conversion of debentures, 130,506 under restricted unit compensation plan and 11,915 under employee unit purchase plan.

Dividends

BTB.UN tr unit Ra $0.30 pa M est. June 15, 2020**[1]
Prev. Rate: $0.42 est. Sept. 15, 2014

[1] Distribution reinvestment plan implemented eff. Sept. 30, 2011.

** Reinvestment Option

Wholly Owned Subsidiaries

BTB Acquisition and Operating Trust, Qué. formerly TB Subsidiary Trust
- 100% int. in **BTB Real Estate General Partner Inc.**, Canada.
- 100% int. in **BTB Real Estate Limited Partnership**, Qué.
  - 8.18% int. in **Société immobilière Cagim, L.P.**, Qué.
- 100% int. in **BTB Real Estate Management Inc.**
- 100% int. in **Cagim Real Estate Corporation**, Québec, Qué.
  - 100% int. in **Complexe Lebourgneuf Phase II Inc.**, Qué.
  - 0.1% int. in **Lombard, LP**, Canada.
  - 0.1% int. in **Place d'affaires Lebourgneuf Phase II GP**
  - 0.1% int. in **Société immobilière Cagim, L.P.**, Qué.
- 100% int. in **Immeuble BTB Crescent Sainte-Catherine Inc**, Canada.
  - 0.1% int. in **Immeuble BTB Crescent Sainte-Catherine S.E.N.C**, Qué.
- 99.9% int. in **Immeuble BTB Crescent Sainte-Catherine S.E.N.C**, Qué.
- 99.9% int. in **Lombard, LP**, Canada.
- 99.9% int. in **Place d'affaires Lebourgneuf Phase II GP**
  - 27.13% int. in **Société immobilière Cagim, L.P.**, Qué.
- 64.69% int. in **Société immobilière Cagim, L.P.**, Qué.

Financial Statistics

Periods ended:	12m Dec. 31/22[A]		12m Dec. 31/21[A]
	$000s	%Chg	$000s
Total revenue	**119,495**	**+19**	**100,343**
Rental operating expense	48,943		43,920
General & admin. expense	7,437		6,842
Operating expense	**56,380**	**+11**	**50,762**
Operating income	**63,115**	**+27**	**49,581**
Deprec. & amort.	122		87
Finance income	624		739
Finance costs, gross	16,166		28,127
Pre-tax income	**38,154**	**-8**	**41,568**
Net income	**38,154**	**-8**	**41,568**
Cash & equivalent	2,404		7,191
Accounts receivable	4,816		5,528
Fixed assets	1,436		1,438
Income-producing props.	1,164,881		1,110,971
Property interests, net	1,165,203		1,111,417
Total assets	**1,179,340**	**+4**	**1,129,901**
Accts. pay. & accr. liabs.	20,058		21,731
Long-term debt, gross	689,218		684,914
Long-term lease liabilities	4,203		4,219
Shareholders' equity	462,072		404,425
Cash from oper. activs.	**66,240**	**+17**	**56,538**
Cash from fin. activs.	(5,319)		13,321
Cash from invest. activs.	(65,708)		(71,730)
Net cash position	**2,404**	**-67**	**7,191**
Capital expenditures	n.a.		(199)
Increase in property	(96,497)		(73,240)
Decrease in property	30,787		1,709
	$		$
Earnings per share*	0.46		0.58
Cash flow per share*	0.79		0.79
Funds from opers. per sh.*	0.44		0.42
Adj. funds from opers. per sh.*	0.39		0.38
Cash divd. per share*	0.30		0.30
Total divd. per share*	**0.30**		**0.30**
	shs		shs
No. of shs. o/s*	85,238,279		74,126,971
Avg. no. of shs. o/s*	83,438,658		71,547,334
	%		%
Net profit margin	31.93		41.43
Return on equity	8.81		11.14
Return on assets	4.70		6.78
No. of employees (FTEs)	81		79

* Trust unit

[A] Reported in accordance with IFRS

Latest Results

Periods ended:	3m Mar. 31/23[A]		3m Mar. 31/22[A]
	$000s	%Chg	$000s
Total revenue	32,911	+13	29,068
Net income	8,802	+36	6,449
	$		$
Earnings per share*	0.10		0.08

* Trust unit

[A] Reported in accordance with IFRS

Historical Summary
(as originally stated)

Fiscal Year	Total Rev. $000s	Net Inc. Bef. Disc. $000s	EPS* $
2022[A]	119,495	38,154	0.46
2021[A]	100,343	41,568	0.58
2020[A]	92,969	2,919	0.05
2019[A]	93,602	51,881	0.88
2018[A]	87,423	41,337	0.79

* Trust unit
[A] Reported in accordance with IFRS

B.15 BTQ Technologies Corp.

Symbol - BTQ **Exchange** - NEO **CUSIP** - 055869
Head Office - 2500-700 Georgia St W, Vancouver, BC, V7Y 1B3 **Telephone** - (778) 373-5499 **Fax** - (604) 357-3086
Website - www.btq.com
Email - bill@btq.com
Investor Relations - Bill Mitoulas (778) 373-5499
Auditors - BDO Canada LLP C.A., Vancouver, B.C.
Lawyers - Farris LLP, Vancouver, B.C.
Transfer Agents - Computershare Trust Company of Canada Inc., Vancouver, B.C.
Profile - (B.C. 1983) Develops software and hardware for post-quantum security, eco-friendly blockchain mining and a blockchain network secured with post-quantum cryptography.

The company is building a portfolio of intellectual property (IP) to safeguard the crypto asset class with energy efficient quantum processes. The IP covers a wide range of applications including blockchain, defence, financial services, insurance and Internet of Things (IoT) devices.

Has an office in Taipei, Taiwan, which would focus on research and development related to post-quantum cryptography, eco-friendly proof of work mining and formal verification within smart contracts platforms.

Common delisted from TSX-VEN, Feb. 10, 2023.
Common listed on NEO, Feb. 10, 2023.

Recent Merger and Acquisition Activity

Status: completed **Revised:** Feb. 17, 2023
UPDATE: The transaction was completed. PREVIOUS: Sonora Gold & Silver Corp. entered into a letter of intent to acquire private Liechtenstein-based BTQ AG for issuance of 56,000,000 post-consolidated common shares (following a 1-for-1.71 share consolidation). In addition, BTQ was building a portfolio of intellecual property to safeguard the Bitcoin network with energy efficient quantum processes and currently holds several patent applications for generating quantum algorithms. Upon completion, Sonora would change its name to BTQ Technology Corp. Dec. 31, 2021 - A definitive agreement was entered into whereby Sonora would acquire BTQ for issuance of 92,000,000 post-consolidated common shares at a deemed price of 40¢ per share (following a 1-for-6 share consolidation). May 5, 2022 - The consolidation ratio to be effected was amended to 1-for-10.

Predecessor Detail - Name changed from Sonora Gold & Silver Corp., Feb. 17, 2023, pursuant to the reverse takeover acquisition of BTQ AG; basis 1 new for 10 old shs.

Directors - Olivier F. Roussy Newton, CEO, Zug, Switzerland; Nicolas Roussy Newton, COO, Taipei, Republic of China; Kevin Mulhern, Toronto, Ont.; Michael D. Resendes, Toronto, Ont.; Johan Wattenstrom, Zug, Switzerland

Other Exec. Officers - Lonny Wong, CFO; Chen-Mou Cheng, chief cryptographer; Ming-Yang Chih, chief strategy officer; Po-Chun Kuo, chief tech. officer; Peter Lavelle, chief legal officer & corp. sec.

Capital Stock

	Authorized (shs.)	Outstanding (shs.)[1]
Common	unlimited	121,248,879

[1] At May 15, 2023

Major Shareholder - Olivier F. Roussy Newton held 34.38% interest at Feb. 21, 2023.

Price Range - SOC/TSX-VEN (D)

Year	Volume	High	Low	Close
2021	462,588	$0.95	$0.40	$0.90
2020	950,687	$1.00	$0.15	$0.50
2019	339,430	$0.70	$0.25	$0.40
2018	1,124,112	$1.95	$0.50	$0.55

Consolidation: 1-for-10 cons. in Feb. 2023
Recent Close: $0.61

Capital Stock Changes - In February 2023, common shares were consolidated on a 1-for-10 basis, 92,000,000 post-consolidated common shares were issued pursuant to the reverse takeover acquisition of BTQ AG, 18,001,250 post-consolidated common shares were issued without further consideration on exchange of subscription receipts sold previously by private placement at 40¢ each and 2,500,000 post-consolidated common shares were issued for finders' fees.

There were no changes to capital stock during fiscal 2023.

Wholly Owned Subsidiaries

BTQ AG, Liechtenstein.

Financial Statistics

Periods ended:	12m Jan. 31/23[A1]		12m Jan. 31/22[A]
	$000s	%Chg	$000s
General & admin expense	644		208
Operating expense	**644**	**+210**	**208**
Operating income	**(644)**	**n.a.**	**(208)**
Write-downs/write-offs	(512)		nil
Pre-tax income	**(1,156)**	**n.a.**	**(208)**
Net income	**(1,156)**	**n.a.**	**(208)**
Cash & equivalent	7,240		263
Accounts receivable	25		7
Current assets	7,265		270
Explor./devel. properties	nil		512
Total assets	**7,268**	**+826**	**785**
Accts. pay. & accr. liabs	469		30
Current liabilities	469		30
Shareholders' equity	6,799		755
Cash from oper. activs	**(223)**	**n.a.**	**(159)**
Cash from fin. activs	7,201		48
Net cash position	**7,240**	**n.m.**	**263**
	$		$
Earnings per share*	(0.13)		(0.02)
Cash flow per share*	(0.03)		(0.02)
	shs		shs
No. of shs. o/s*	8,747,629		8,747,617
Avg. no. of shs. o/s*	8,747,629		8,631,261
	%		%
Net profit margin	n.a.		n.a.
Return on equity	(30.61)		(25.37)
Return on assets	(28.71)		(24.84)

* Common
[A] Reported in accordance with IFRS
[1] Results for fiscal 2022 and prior fiscal years pertain to Sonora Gold & Silver Corp.

Latest Results

Periods ended:	3m Mar. 31/23[A]		3m Apr. 30/22[A]
	$000s	%Chg	$000s
Net income	(6,933)	n.a.	(78)
	$		$
Earnings per share*	(0.07)		(0.10)

* Common
[A] Reported in accordance with IFRS

Historical Summary
(as originally stated)

Fiscal Year	Oper. Rev. $000s	Net Inc. Bef. Disc. $000s	EPS* $
2023[A]	nil	(1,156)	(0.13)
2022[A]	nil	(208)	(0.02)
2021[A]	nil	(216)	(0.03)
2020[A]	nil	(138)	(0.02)
2019[A]	nil	(147)	(0.02)

* Common
[A] Reported in accordance with IFRS
Note: Adjusted throughout for 1-for-10 cons. in Feb. 2023

B.16 BYND Cannasoft Enterprises Inc.

Symbol - BYND **Exchange** - CSE **CUSIP** - 05608P
Head Office - 2264 11 Ave E, Vancouver, BC, V5N 1Z6 **Telephone** - (604) 833-6820
Website - cannasoft-crm.com
Email - gkabazo@gmail.com
Investor Relations - Gabriel Kabazo (604) 833-6820
Auditors - Reliant CPA PC C.P.A., Lakewood, Colo.
Transfer Agents - Computershare Trust Company of Canada Inc., Vancouver, B.C.
Employees - 8 at Dec. 31, 2022
Profile - (B.C. 2021 amalg.; orig. B.C., 2019) Develops customer relationship management (CRM) software for small and medium-sized businesses and for the medical cannabis industry. Also plans to build a cannabis farm and indoor growing facility in Israel and developing the EZ-G device for female health issues.

Wholly owned **BYND - Beyond Solutions Ltd.** is developing Benefit CRM cloud-based software which enables small and medium-sized businesses in Israel to optimize their day-to-day activities such as sales management, personnel management, marketing, call centre activities and assets management. A next-generation, cloud-based version of the Benefit CRM is also being developed to allow customization of the software and to include an online marketplace that can identify clients and resellers who might be able to supply the buyer's needs. A cannabis CRM platform for the medical cannabis sector was also developed to enable the growers, manufacturers, laboratories, distributors, pharmacies and end users to establish a 'shop front' where each will be able to provide desired information about its operations to other users of the platform.

Subsidiary **B.Y.B.Y. Investments and Promotions Ltd.** (Cannasoft) plans to build a 3.7-acre cannabis farm and 2,400-m^2 indoor cannabis growing facility on five acres of land in Moshav Kochav Michael, Israel, which is leased by the Brzezinski family to Cannasoft. The construction of the facility is subject to approval of the transfer of a growing licence from Dalia Brzezinski to Cannasoft. Also has a licence to engage in medical cannabis without direct contact with the substance from the Ministry of Health of Israel. This licence would allow Cannasoft to trade medical cannabis products through an agreement with a licensed cannabis grower in Israel. Cannasoft is also working to build a private label of medical cannabis inflorescences for pharmacies in Israel.

Wholly owned **Zigi Carmel Initiatives & Investments Ltd.** develops patent-pending products including the EZ-G device, a therapeutic device that, combined with proprietary software, regulates the flow of low-concentration cannabidiol (CBD) oils into the soft tissues of the female reproductive system, which can relieve female health issues such as candida, dryness and scars; a condom with a double pocket to contain lubricant that can be diluted with natural oils such as CBD; female and male treatment devices for external use that utilize artificial intelligence to control operational parameters based on the user's physiological parameters collected from sensors.

Recent Merger and Acquisition Activity

Status: completed **Revised:** Sept. 22, 2022
UPDATE: The transaction was completed. PREVIOUS: BYND Cannasoft Enterprises Inc. agreed to acquire Israel-based Zigi Carmel Initiatives & Investments Ltd., which holds the EZ-G device, for issuance of 7,920,000 common shares at a deemed price of $4.735 per share. The EZ-G device was a patent pending therapeutic device that, combined with proprietary software, regulates the flow of low-concentration cannabidiol (CBD) oils into the soft tissues of the female reproductive system, which can relieve female health issues such as candida, dryness and scars.

Predecessor Detail - Formed from Lincoln Acquisitions Corp. in British Columbia, Mar. 29, 2021, pursuant to the amalgamation with Israel-based 1232986 B.C. Ltd., and concurrently completed the reverse takeover acquisition of Israel-based BYND - Beyond Solutions Ltd.

Directors - Yftah Ben Yaackov, CEO, Ashkelon, Israel; Marcel (Moti) Maram, pres., Israel; Gabriel (Gabi) Kabazo, CFO, Vancouver, B.C.; Avner Tal, v-p, sales & mktg. & chief tech. officer, Kiryat Ata, Israel; Niv Shirazi, Israel; Dr. Stefánia Szabó, Toronto, Ont.; Harold M. Wolkin, Toronto, Ont.; Carmel Zigdon, Givatayim, Israel

Capital Stock

	Authorized (shs.)	Outstanding (shs.)[1]
Common	unlimited	37,899,386

[1] At May 15, 2023

Major Shareholder - Yftah Ben Yaackov held 21.6% interest, Carmel Zigdon held 20.9% interest, Marcel (Moti) Maram held 10.8% interest and Avner Tal held 10.8% interest at Apr. 21, 2023.

Price Range - BYND/CSE

Year	Volume	High	Low	Close
2022	520,902	$20.68	$2.98	$4.91
2021	339,809	$5.05	$0.83	$5.00

Recent Close: $1.40

Capital Stock Changes - On Sept. 22, 2022, 7,920,000 common shares were issued pursuant to the acquisition of Zigi Carmel Initiatives & Investments Ltd. Also during 2022, common shares were issued as follows: 290,000 on exercise of options, 183,378 by private placement and 13,454 on vesting of restricted share units.

Wholly Owned Subsidiaries

BYND - Beyond Solutions Ltd., Israel.
- 76% int. in **B.Y.B.Y. Investments and Promotions Ltd.**, Israel.

Zigi Carmel Initiatives & Investments Ltd., Israel.

Financial Statistics

Periods ended:	12m Dec. 31/22^A		12m Dec. 31/21^A1
	$000s	%Chg	$000s
Operating revenue	**1,123**	**-8**	**1,217**
Cost of sales	504		590
General & admin expense	2,176		632
Stock-based compensation	154		551
Operating expense	**2,834**	**+60**	**1,773**
Operating income	**(1,711)**	**n.a.**	**(556)**
Deprec., depl. & amort.	33		56
Finance costs, net	14		14
Pre-tax income	**(1,658)**	**n.a.**	**(4,843)**
Income taxes	6		35
Net income	**(1,665)**	**n.a.**	**(4,879)**
Cash & equivalent	2,393		3,025
Accounts receivable	228		197
Current assets	3,446		5,747
Fixed assets, net	1,317		443
Intangibles, net	45,140		1,300
Total assets	**49,903**	**+566**	**7,491**
Accts. pay. & accr. liabs.	191		181
Current liabilities	458		260
Long-term debt, gross	136		193
Long-term debt, net	88		143
Shareholders' equity	49,271		7,000
Cash from oper. activs	**(2,067)**	**n.a.**	**(345)**
Cash from fin. activs	849		6,048
Cash from invest. activs	(2,008)		(843)
Net cash position	**2,393**	**-21**	**3,025**
Capital expenditures	(939)		(393)
Capital disposals	2		nil
	$		$
Earnings per share*	(0.05)		(0.22)
Cash flow per share*	(0.06)		(0.02)
	shs		shs
No. of shs. o/s*	37,885,932		29,479,100
Avg. no. of shs. o/s*	31,865,960		22,332,694
	%		%
Net profit margin	(148.26)		(400.90)
Return on equity	(5.92)		n.m.
Return on assets	(5.80)		(116.14)
No. of employees (FTEs)	8		8

* Common
^A Reported in accordance with IFRS
[1] Results reflect the Mar. 29, 2021, reverse takeover acquisition of BYND - Beyond Solutions Ltd.

Latest Results

Periods ended:	3m Mar. 31/23^A		3m Mar. 31/22^A
	$000s	%Chg	$000s
Operating revenue	421	-7	455
Net income	(740)	n.a.	(165)
	$		$
Earnings per share*	(0.02)		(0.01)

* Common
^A Reported in accordance with IFRS

Historical Summary
(as originally stated)

Fiscal Year	Oper. Rev.	Net Inc. Bef. Disc.	EPS*
	$000s	$000s	$
2022^A	1,123	(1,665)	(0.05)
2021^A	1,217	(4,879)	(0.22)
2020^A1	1,555	161	n.a.
2019^A1	1,610	(291)	n.a.
2018^A1	1,543	32	n.a.

* Common
^A Reported in accordance with IFRS
[1] Results pertain to BYND - Beyond Solutions Ltd.

B.17 BYT Holdings Ltd.

Symbol - BYT **Exchange** - CSE (S) **CUSIP** - 056067
Head Office - 1570-505 Burrad St, PO Box, Vancouver, BC, V6E 3P3
Website - bytholdings.com
Email - raj.dewan@mcmillan.ca
Investor Relations - Rajeev Dewan (416) 865-7878
Auditors - HML PLT C.A., Kuala Lumpur, Malaysia
Transfer Agents - Computershare Trust Company of Canada Inc., Vancouver, B.C.
Profile - (B.C. 2019) Provides engineering, procurement and construction management (EPCM) solutions to the electronics, food and beverage, oil and gas, semiconductor and waste management sectors.

EPCM solutions provided range from consultancy and design services, to the construction of projects involving high technology production facilities, primarily in Singapore and mainland People's Republic of China (PRC). Engineering services include the design and/or construction of new facilities in new and existing buildings, the refurbishment and upgrading of existing facilities, and corrective or routine maintenance services, which are primarily provided to customers in the semiconductor industry. EPCM and in-house semiconductor engineering services consist of the installation of cleanrooms and controlled environments, design and implementation of heat ventilation and air conditioning systems, and mechanical and electrical systems. EPCM solutions also includes provision of waste management services which convert waste into organic compost, primarily operating in Shanghai, PRC.

Common suspended from CSE, Dec. 6, 2021.

Predecessor Detail - Name changed from SLE Synergy Ltd., Jan. 27, 2021.

Directors - Cunkou (Sunny) Li, exec. chr. & CEO, Singapore; Ricky Ng, Singapore; Patrick Sapphire, Toronto, Ont.; Tee Ween Tan, Singapore; Zhang Yiwen, Singapore

Other Exec. Officers - Hong Beng (Ben) Lim, COO; Jun Wah Lai, CFO; San San (Michelle) Neo, chief corp. officer; Rajeev (Raj) Dewan, corp. sec.

Capital Stock

	Authorized (shs.)	Outstanding (shs.)[1]
Common	unlimited	104,107,638

[1] At Dec. 7, 2022

Major Shareholder - Chor Gee (Vincent) Lim held 23.96% interest, Yuan Yuan held 23.25% interest and Cunkou (Sunny) Li held 23.04% interest at July 6, 2021.

Price Range - BYT/CSE (S)

Year	Volume	High	Low	Close
2021	2,161,035	$0.50	$0.03	$0.05
2020	438,556	$0.40	$0.09	$0.09

Wholly Owned Subsidiaries

Springleaf Engineering Pte. Ltd., Singapore.
- 100% int. in **BYT Singapore Pte. Ltd.**, Singapore.
  - 100% int. in **BYT Malaysia Sdn. Bhd.**, Malaysia.
- 100% int. in **Shanghai Xin Da Process Engineering Co., Ltd.**, Shanghai, Shanghai, People's Republic of China.
- 60% int. in **Springleaf-Biomax (Shanghai) Pte. Ltd.**, Shanghai, Shanghai, People's Republic of China.

B.18 BZAM Ltd.

Symbol - BZAM **Exchange** - CSE **CUSIP** - 12464X
Head Office - 402-5520 Explorer Rd, Mississauga, ON, L4W 5L1
Telephone - (905) 304-4201 **Toll-free** - (844) 473-3663
Website - bzam.com
Email - lstewart@bzam.com
Investor Relations - Lisa Stewart (604) 341-8177 ext. 269
Auditors - KPMG LLP C.A., Vaughan, Ont.
Transfer Agents - Odyssey Trust Company, Calgary, Alta.
Employees - 580 at Dec. 18, 2022
Profile - (Can. 2016) Produces, distributes and sells medical and recreational cannabis and cannabis-related products in Canada.

Cultivation, extraction, manufacturing and packaging operations include a 166,000-sq.-ft. hybrid greenhouse and processing facility in Ancaster (Hamilton), Ont.; a 26,000-sq.-ft. manufacturing facility in Puslinch, Ont.; and facilities in Lower Mainland, West Kootenay and Vancouver Island, B.C., and Edmonton, Alta., including three indoor cultivation facilities, with total potential of 160,000 sq. ft., a 40,000-sq.-ft. processing facility and 100-acre of outdoor grow. Also has access to 15,000 sq. ft. of cultivation and processing space in Vaudreil, Que. These facilities produce medical and recreational cannabis products, including flower, pre-rolls, vapes, oils and edibles, which are sold through authorized retailers or distributors and licensed entities. Brands include BZAM, The Green Organic Dutchman, -ness, Highly Dutch Organic, Ripple by TGOD, Table Top, Cruuzy, Wyld, GRx and partner brands FRESH, Dunn Cannabis, Superflower and Snackbar.

The company also operates retail cannabis stores in Winnipeg, Man., and Regina, Sask., as well as pursuing distribution of cannabis-derived medical products in Germany.

In December 2022, the company terminated its cannabis manufacturing agreement with **Cannara Biotech Inc.** at its Valleyfield, Que., facility.

In September 2022, the company sold its wholly owned hemp business based in Poland, **HemPoland Sp.zo.o**, a manufacturer and marketer of premium hemp-derived cannabidiol (CBD) products in Europe, to **Ramm Pharma Corp.** for $1,350,000 in cash and $5,460,000 in debt forgiveness.

In May 2022, the company sold and leased back the leasehold improvements at its facility in Puslinch, Ont., for $3,000,000, consisting of $1,900,000 cash and settlement of $1,100,000 of debt.

Recent Merger and Acquisition Activity

Status: completed **Revised:** Nov. 3, 2022
UPDATE: The transaction was completed for issuance of 650,313,607 common shares at a deemed price of $0.0596 per share. PREVIOUS: The Green Organic Dutchman Holdings Ltd. (TGOD) agreed to acquire private Vancouver, B.C.-based BZAM Holdings Inc., which cultivates and produces cannabis and cannabis products, for issuance of common shares in two tranches which would result in BZAM's sole shareholder holding 49.5% of TGOD's issued and outstanding post-consolidated common shares upon completion of the transaction (following a 1-for-10 share consolidation). In addition, BZAM's sole shareholder was entitled to earn up to $33,000,000 in TGOD common shares upon the achievement of certain milestones. BZAM sells vapes, infused pre-rolls and high quality flower under the BZAM™, -ness™, Table Top™, Dunn Cannabis and FRESH brands, with products sold in British Columbia and Alberta. BZAM has operating facilities in the Lower Mainland, West Kootenay and Vancouver Island, B.C., and Edmonton, Alta., as well as retail cannabis stores in Winnipeg, Man., and Regina, Sask.

Predecessor Detail - Name changed from The Green Organic Dutchman Holdings Ltd., Feb. 23, 2023.

Directors - Bassam Alghanim, chr., Kuwait; Sean Bovingdon, CFO, Oakville, Ont.; Wendy Kaufman, Toronto, Ont.; Keith Merker, London, Ont.; Chris Schnarr, Mississauga, Ont.; Sherry Tross, Va.

Other Exec. Officers - Matt Milich, CEO; Michel Gagné, COO; Jordan Winnett, chief comml. officer; Nadine Jean-Francois, v-p, supply chain; Rosanna Mastropietro, corp. sec.

Capital Stock

	Authorized (shs.)	Outstanding (shs.)[1]
Common	unlimited	163,637,836

[1] At Jan. 4, 2023

Major Shareholder - BZAM International Ltd. held 46% interest at Dec. 22, 2022.

Price Range - BZAM/CSE

Year	Volume	High	Low	Close
2022	12,250,363	$1.45	$0.29	$0.33
2021	54,098,324	$6.50	$0.90	$0.95
2020	58,676,264	$8.40	$2.10	$2.35
2019	79,326,888	$58.10	$6.20	$7.50
2018	46,219,564	$102.40	$21.90	$24.60

Consolidation: 1-for-10 cons. in Nov. 2022
Recent Close: $0.16

Capital Stock Changes - In January 2023, 6,500,000 common shares were issued for settlement of $2,600,000 of debt.

On Nov. 3, 2022, 65,031,361 post-consolidated common shares were issued pursuant to the acquisition of BZAM Holdings Inc. and 491,421 post-consolidated common shares were issued as finders' fees. On Nov. 8, 2022, common shares were consolidated on a 1-for-10 basis. In December 2022, public offering of 12,707,500 units (1 post-consolidated common share & 1 warrant) at 40¢ per unit was completed, with warrants exercisable at 50¢ per share for five years.

Wholly Owned Subsidiaries

BZAM Holdings Inc., Vancouver, B.C.
- 100% int. in **BZAM Management Ltd.**, B.C.
- 100% int. in **10050999 Manitoba Ltd.**, Man.

Galaxie Brands Corporation, Puslinch, Ont.
The Green Organic Dutchman Ltd., Ancaster, Ont.
Medican Organic Inc., Valleyfield, Qué.
TGOD Europe B.V., Netherlands.

Financial Statistics

Periods ended:	12m Dec. 31/21[A]		12m Dec. 31/20[□A]
	$000s	%Chg	$000s
Operating revenue	**30,241**	**+137**	**12,744**
Cost of sales	18,508		11,375
Research & devel. expense	528		942
General & admin expense	24,401		30,957
Stock-based compensation	3,381		4,873
Operating expense	**46,818**	**-3**	**48,147**
Operating income	**(16,577)**	**n.a.**	**(35,403)**
Deprec., depl. & amort.	12,164		5,561
Finance income	89		243
Finance costs, gross	10,395		5,011
Investment income	nil		(148)
Write-downs/write-offs	16,693[1]		(123,684)[2]
Pre-tax income	**(39,980)**	**n.a.**	**(171,778)**
Income taxes	(436)		nil
Net inc. bef. disc. opers	**(39,544)**	**n.a.**	**(171,778)**
Income from disc. opers	(2,753)		(11,353)
Net income	**(42,297)**	**n.a.**	**(183,131)**
Net inc. for equity hldrs	**(42,138)**	**n.a.**	**(182,541)**
Net inc. for non-cont. int	**(159)**	**n.a.**	**(590)**
Cash & equivalent	4,089		11,212
Inventories	20,942		17,135
Accounts receivable	9,180		10,183
Current assets	55,107		44,380
Long-term investments	nil		1,272
Fixed assets, net	117,980		147,263
Intangibles, net	19,524		8,933
Total assets	**194,346**	**-8**	**211,575**
Bank indebtedness	5,492		nil
Accts. pay. & accr. liabs	18,259		24,453
Current liabilities	29,391		66,377
Long-term debt, gross	20,225		40,755
Long-term debt, net	18,204		nil
Long-term lease liabilities	6,517		4,551
Shareholders' equity	137,674		140,949
Non-controlling interest	(863)		(1,145)
Cash from oper. activs	**(18,038)**	**n.a.**	**(35,958)**
Cash from fin. activs	(13,443)		60,470
Cash from invest. activs	25,796		(42,176)
Net cash position	**4,089**	**-64**	**11,212**
Capital expenditures	(9,121)		(50,259)
Capital disposals	27,210		1,415
	$		$
Earns. per sh. bef disc opers*	(0.72)		(4.65)
Earnings per share*	(0.76)		(4.94)
Cash flow per share*	(0.33)		(0.97)
	shs		shs
No. of shs. o/s*	74,966,065		48,667,576
Avg. no. of shs. o/s*	55,210,913		36,969,878
	%		%
Net profit margin	(130.76)		n.m.
Return on equity	(28.27)		(83.69)
Return on assets	(14.42)		(60.23)

* Common
□ Restated
[A] Reported in accordance with IFRS
[1] Includes $46,475,000 impairment of fixed assets in Valleyfield, Que., and $68,286,000 impairment reversal of fixed assets and intangibles in Ancaster (Hamilton), Ont.
[2] Includes $120,602,000 fixed asset impairment related to operations at Valleyfield, Que., and Ancaster (Hamilton), Ont.

Note: Cost of sales is net of changes in fair value of biological assets and inventory sold.

Latest Results

Periods ended:	9m Sept. 30/22[A]		9m Sept. 30/21[A]
	$000s	%Chg	$000s
Operating revenue	32,124	+55	20,775
Net inc. bef. disc. opers	(26,696)	n.a.	(33,266)
Income from disc. opers	(432)		(1,295)
Net income	(27,128)	n.a.	(34,561)
Net inc. for equity hldrs	(27,128)	n.a.	(34,451)
Net inc. for non-cont. int	nil		(110)
	$		$
Earns. per sh. bef. disc. opers.*	(0.36)		(0.64)
Earnings per share*	(0.36)		(0.66)

* Common
[A] Reported in accordance with IFRS

Historical Summary
(as originally stated)

Fiscal Year	Oper. Rev. $000s	Net Inc. Bef. Disc. $000s	EPS* $
2021[A]	30,241	(39,544)	(0.72)
2020[A]	21,495	(183,131)	(4.94)
2019[A]	10,957	(195,750)	(7.08)
2018[A]	1,879	(45,203)	(2.05)
2017[A]	nil	(13,459)	(1.20)

* Common
[A] Reported in accordance with IFRS

Note: Adjusted throughout for 1-for-10 cons. in Nov. 2022

B.19 Backstageplay Inc.

Symbol - BP **Exchange** - TSX-VEN **CUSIP** - 056362
Head Office - 350-409 Granville St, Vancouver, BC, V6C 1T2 **Telephone** - (604) 241-8400
Website - www.backstageplay.com
Email - sean@backstageplay.com
Investor Relations - Sean P. Hodgins (778) 318-1514
Auditors - MNP LLP C.A., Toronto, Ont.
Lawyers - Fasken Martineau DuMoulin LLP, Toronto, Ont.
Transfer Agents - TSX Trust Company, Toronto, Ont.

Profile - (B.C. 2014; orig. Ont., 2004 amalg.) Operates an online platform focused on social gaming and retention using software and back office systems which manage players and their gaming activity.

The company provides game developers with access to its iGaming platform, which serves up games and other content, as well as function as software and back office systems which manage players and their gaming activity. The platform features chat management, hosting tools, foul words management, game management and reporting suite, among others, allowing game publishers to focus on game development rather than platform development. Also provides a technology infrastructure allowing businesses or their entertainment professionals to generate subscription, top up and advertising revenue while artists or other social media engaged celebrities generate fan loyalty.

On Feb. 19, 2022, the company entered into product co-development and revenue share agreements with **Cash Live Entertainment Inc.**, the operator of a live poker mobile gaming app, Cash Live. Each party would contribute specified game and software source code to develop two new live format games. The terms of the agreements are for one year and amount to US$125,000 for each game. In addition, the company would receive up to US$250,000 of Cash Live Entertainment shares for the company's contribution of game source code and specified managed services. The net revenues after direct costs from the two new games would be split 25% to the company and 75% to Cash Live Entertainment. During 2023, Cash Live advised the company that it had suspended development efforts until it could either obtain funding to support additional development efforts or make other arrangements.

Predecessor Detail - Name changed from Oramericas Corp., Feb. 9, 2016.

Directors - Simon Collins, chr., London, Middx., United Kingdom; Scott F. White, CEO, Campbellville, Ont.; Sean P. Hodgins, CFO & corp. sec., Richmond, B.C.; Robert (Bob) Williams, CIO, Sliema, Malta; Andrew Branscombe, Oakville, Ont.

Capital Stock

	Authorized (shs.)	Outstanding (shs.)[1]
Common	unlimited	20,687,833

[1] At May 30, 2023

Major Shareholder - Scott F. White held 29.5% interest at Nov. 2, 2022.

Price Range - BP/TSX-VEN

Year	Volume	High	Low	Close
2022	696,642	$0.33	$0.05	$0.10
2021	2,282,013	$0.45	$0.08	$0.30
2020	1,114,740	$0.30	$0.06	$0.20
2019	2,373,295	$0.30	$0.03	$0.16
2018	2,068,804	$0.92	$0.10	$0.10

Consolidation: 1-for-2 cons. in Feb. 2020
Recent Close: $0.10

Capital Stock Changes - There were no changes to capital stock during 2022.

Wholly Owned Subsidiaries

Backstageplay (Delaware) Inc., Del.
Parlay Malta (Holding) Limited, Malta.
- 100% int. in **Parlay Malta Limited**, Malta.

Financial Statistics

Periods ended:	12m Dec. 31/22[A]		12m Dec. 31/21[A]
	$000s	%Chg	$000s
Research & devel. expense	14		1
General & admin expense	378		101
Stock-based compensation	nil		92
Operating expense	**379**	**+95**	**194**
Operating income	**(379)**	**n.a.**	**(194)**
Finance costs, gross	1		1
Pre-tax income	**(393)**	**n.a.**	**(195)**
Net income	**(393)**	**n.a.**	**(195)**
Cash & equivalent	81		301
Current assets	84		477
Total assets	**84**	**-82**	**477**
Accts. pay. & accr. liabs	323		323
Current liabilities	323		323
Shareholders' equity	(240)		154
Cash from oper. activs	**(390)**	**n.a.**	**(86)**
Cash from fin. activs	(170)		319
Net cash position	**81**	**-73**	**301**
	$		$
Earnings per share*	(0.02)		(0.01)
Cash flow per share*	(0.02)		(0.00)
	shs		shs
No. of shs. o/s*	20,687,833		20,687,833
Avg. no. of shs. o/s*	20,687,833		18,496,053
	%		%
Net profit margin	n.a.		n.a.
Return on equity	n.m.		n.m.
Return on assets	(139.75)		(68.67)

* Common
[A] Reported in accordance with IFRS

Latest Results

Periods ended:	3m Mar. 31/23[A]		3m Mar. 31/22[A]
	$000s	%Chg	$000s
Net income	(20)	n.a.	(22)
	$		$
Earnings per share*	(0.00)		(0.00)

* Common
[A] Reported in accordance with IFRS

Historical Summary
(as originally stated)

Fiscal Year	Oper. Rev. $000s	Net Inc. Bef. Disc. $000s	EPS* $
2022[A]	nil	(393)	(0.02)
2021[A]	nil	(195)	(0.01)
2020[A]	nil	(274)	(0.02)
2019[A]	nil	(72)	(0.01)
2018[A]	2	(1,192)	(0.09)

* Common
[A] Reported in accordance with IFRS

Note: Adjusted throughout for 1-for-2 cons. in Feb. 2020

B.20 BacTech Environmental Corporation

Symbol - BAC **Exchange** - CSE **CUSIP** - 070490
Head Office - 409-37 King St E, Toronto, ON, M5C 1E9 **Telephone** - (416) 813-0303
Website - www.bactechgreen.com
Email - borr@bactechgreen.com
Investor Relations - M. Ross Orr (416) 813-0303 ext. 222
Auditors - McGovern Hurley LLP C.A., Toronto, Ont.
Bankers - Canadian Imperial Bank of Commerce, Toronto, Ont.
Transfer Agents - Trans Canada Transfer Inc., Toronto, Ont.

Profile - (Can. 2010) Holds exclusive licence for patented BACOX bioleaching technology for reclamation of historic mine tailings and mining waste materials.

The company's proprietary bioleaching technology utilizes bacteria to extract precious and base metals from difficult-to-treat ores, concentrates and tailings. The production of sulphur dioxide emissions, which is the primary source of acid rain, and arsenic trioxide is eliminated by replacing smelting and/or roasting with a bioleach process. Metals extracted include gold, silver, cobalt, nickel, copper, uranium and zinc.

Developing a 18,250-tonne-per-annum bioleaching plant for a gold recovery/arsenic stabilization project in Ponce Enriquez, Equador, and holds an adjacent 100-acre property that would be used for the operations in Tenguel. An updated bankable feasibility study released in February 2022 for the bioleaching plant in Equador contemplated annual production of 30,900 oz. gold over a 20-year mine life. Initial capital costs were estimated at US$17,000,000. Other projects include the development of a bioleach plant for extracting battery metals from tailings in the Sudbury Basin in Ontario. The company is also investigating project opportunities in the Trujillo area of Peru and a gold and silver mine tailings in Medellín, Colombia.

In September 2022, common shares were listed on OTCQB Venture Market under the symbol BCCEF.

In September 2022, the company acquired a 100-acre land package for its proposed processing plant in Tenguel, Ecuador for an undisclosed amount.

In May 2022, the company entered into an investment protection agreement (IPA) with the Government of Ecuador for the gold recovery/arsenic stabilization project in Tenguel, Ecuador. The IPA terms explicitly cover both the company's prior and forthcoming investment commitments in Ecuador of up to US$95,500,000 in plant construction and gold production activity through 2024. Under the IPA, the Ecuadorian State has granted the company the applicable protections and guarantees in accordance with the Organic Code of Production, Trade and Investments and Organic Law for Productive Promotion, Investment Attraction, Employment Generation, and Fiscal Stability.

Directors - The Hon. Timothy (Tim) Lewin, chr., United Kingdom; M. Ross Orr, pres. & CEO, Toronto, Ont.; W. Walter Cimowsky, Delray Beach, Fla.; Jay L. Naster, Toronto, Ont.; James A. (Jay) Richardson, Toronto, Ont.; Donald A. (Don) Whalen, Unionville, Ont.

Other Exec. Officers - David Tingey, COO; Louis R. (Lou) Nagy, CFO & corp. sec.; Dr. Paul C. Miller, v-p, tech. & eng.

Capital Stock

	Authorized (shs.)	Outstanding (shs.)[1]
Common	unlimited	183,460,334

[1] At Mar. 31, 2023

Major Shareholder - Option Three Advisory Services Limited held 11.3% interest at Aug. 13, 2021.

Price Range - BAC/CSE

Year	Volume	High	Low	Close
2022	40,876,540	$0.16	$0.06	$0.07
2021	274,826,234	$0.24	$0.02	$0.15
2020	17,519,824	$0.04	$0.01	$0.02
2019	19,932,537	$0.04	$0.01	$0.02
2018	44,176,423	$0.07	$0.02	$0.03

Recent Close: $0.07

Capital Stock Changes - In March and June 2023, private placement of 11,050,000 units (1 common share & 1 warrant) at 8¢ per unit was completed, with warrants exercisable at 12¢ per share for two years.

From February to May 2022, private placement of 10,550,000 units (1 common share & 1 warrant) at 20¢ per unit was completed. Also during 2022, common shares were issued as follows: 5,053,260 on exercise of warrants and 851,515 by private placement.

Wholly Owned Subsidiaries

BacTechVerde S.A.S., Ecuador.

Subsidiaries

98% int. in **Empresa Minera Ambiental Bactech S.A.**, Bolivia.

Financial Statistics

Periods ended:	12m Dec. 31/22[A]		12m Dec. 31/21[A]
	$000s	%Chg	$000s
Salaries & benefits	619		179
Research & devel. expense	954		208
General & admin expense	1,227		539
Stock-based compensation	400		398
Operating expense	**3,200**	**+142**	**1,324**
Operating income	**(3,200)**	**n.a.**	**(1,324)**
Finance costs, gross	174		235
Pre-tax income	**(3,371)**	**n.a.**	**(1,596)**
Net income	**(3,371)**	**n.a.**	**(1,596)**
Cash & equivalent	10		64
Current assets	157		235
Fixed assets, net	981		nil
Total assets	**1,138**	**+384**	**235**
Bank indebtedness	221		221
Accts. pay. & accr. liabs	1,713		1,150
Current liabilities	2,907		1,471
Long-term debt, gross	972		100
Equity portion of conv. debs	136		nil
Shareholders' equity	(1,950)		(1,417)
Cash from oper. activs	**(2,226)**	**n.a.**	**(1,191)**
Cash from fin. activs	3,153		1,236
Cash from invest. activs	(981)		nil
Net cash position	**10**	**-84**	**64**
Capital expenditures	(981)		nil
	$		$
Earnings per share*	(0.02)		(0.01)
Cash flow per share*	(0.01)		(0.01)
	shs		shs
No. of shs. o/s*	174,210,334		157,755,559
Avg. no. of shs. o/s*	168,769,069		139,135,066
	%		%
Net profit margin	n.a.		n.a.
Return on equity	n.m.		n.m.
Return on assets	(465.70)		n.m.

* Common

[A] Reported in accordance with IFRS

Historical Summary
(as originally stated)

Fiscal Year	Oper. Rev.	Net Inc. Bef. Disc.	EPS*
	$000s	$000s	$
2022[A]	nil	(3,371)	(0.02)
2021[A]	nil	(1,596)	(0.01)
2020[A]	nil	861	0.01
2019[A]	nil	(1,085)	(0.01)
2018[A]	nil	(1,274)	(0.02)

* Common

[A] Reported in accordance with IFRS

B.21 Badger Capital Corp.

Symbol - YVR.P **Exchange** - TSX-VEN **CUSIP** - 05652M

Head Office - 1090-510 Burrard St, Vancouver, BC, V6C 3B9 **Telephone** - (604) 569-2209

Email - neil@cem.ca

Investor Relations - Neil Currie (604) 569-2209

Auditors - MNP LLP C.A., Vancouver, B.C.

Transfer Agents - Computershare Trust Company of Canada Inc., Vancouver, B.C.

Profile - (B.C. 2020) Capital Pool Company.

Directors - Neil Currie, pres., CEO, CFO & corp. sec., Vancouver, B.C.; James A. (Jim) Currie, Vancouver, B.C.; Benjamin Curry, Vancouver, B.C.; John A. Hansen, Vancouver, B.C.

Capital Stock

	Authorized (shs.)	Outstanding (shs.)[1]
Common	unlimited	8,600,100

[1] At Aug. 31, 2022

Major Shareholder - Neil Currie held 11.63% interest and John A. Hansen held 11.63% interest at June 14, 2021.

Price Range - YVR.P/TSX-VEN

Year	Volume	High	Low	Close
2022	513,501	$0.15	$0.06	$0.15
2021	282,500	$0.20	$0.12	$0.12

Recent Close: $0.06

Capital Stock Changes - In February 2023, private placement of up to 2,400,000 common shares at 5¢ per share was announced.

B.22 Badger Infrastructure Solutions Ltd.*

Symbol - BDGI **Exchange** - TSX **CUSIP** - 056533

Head Office - ATCO Centre II, 400-919 11 Ave SW, Calgary, AB, T2R 1P3 **Telephone** - (403) 264-8500 **Toll-free** - (800) 465-4273 **Fax** - (403) 228-9773

Website - www.badgerinc.com

Email - pbhatia@badgerinc.com

Investor Relations - Pramod Bhatia (800) 465-4273

Auditors - Deloitte LLP C.A., Calgary, Alta.

Bankers - The Toronto-Dominion Bank, Calgary, Alta.

Transfer Agents - Computershare Trust Company of Canada Inc., Calgary, Alta.

FP500 Revenue Ranking - 392

Employees - 2,254 at Dec. 31, 2022

Profile - (Alta. 2010) Provides non-destructive excavating services to the utility, industrial, construction, transportation and other industries throughout Canada and the United States.

Designs and manufactures the Badger Hydrovac System, a truck-mounted hydrovac excavation unit that is used primarily for safe excavation around critical infrastructure and in congested underground conditions. The Badger Hydrovac uses a pressurized stream of water to liquefy the soil cover which is then removed with a powerful vacuum system and deposited into a storage tank. In addition, the company offers Badger Airvac™ which is also used for safe excavation but utilizes compressed air instead of water to loosen the cover soil before vacuuming and depositing excavation materials into a storage tank. Hydrovac and airvac units are manufactured at the company's 62,000-sq.-ft. office and manufacturing facility in Red Deer, Alta.

Provides services in various regions throughout Canada and the U.S. either directly to customers through its Badger Corporate division or through operating partners and franchisees. At Dec. 31, 2022, Badger Corporate operated a total of 1,182 excavation units, of which 197 were operated in five Canadian provinces and 985 in 43 U.S. states; and 174 excavation units in four Canadian provinces and 31 excavation units in three U.S. states were operated by operating partners and franchisees.

Other services include sewer cleaning and inspection, locating services, trenching, shielding, disposition of excavated materials, supply of water, supplies, and coordinating or arranging for various services required by the customer from third party providers which may include items such as backfilling or other material purchases.

Predecessor Detail - Name changed from Badger Daylighting Ltd., May 5, 2021.

Directors - Glen D. Roane, chr., Calgary, Alta.; Robert (Rob) Blackadar, pres. & CEO, Ga.; David J. Bronicheski, Oakville, Ont.; Stephanie Cuskley, N.J.; William (Bill) Derwin, Denver, Colo.; G. Keith Graham, Chatham, Ont.; Stephen J. Jones, Pa.; Mary B. Jordan, Vancouver, B.C.; William J. (Bill) Lingard, Calgary, Alta.; Patricia (Tribby) Warfield, Fla.

Other Exec. Officers - Robert P. (Rob) Dawson, CFO; Julie Lee, chief HR officer; Elizabeth (Liz) Peterson, sr. v-p, opers.; Pradeep Atluri, v-p, info. strategy & tech.; Pramod Bhatia, v-p, fin.; Francisco Brondo, v-p, mfg.; Trevor Carson, v-p, IR & corp. devel.; Christopher (Chris) Gunn, v-p, field sales

Capital Stock

	Authorized (shs.)	Outstanding (shs.)[1]
Common	unlimited	34,473,438

[1] At Aug. 3, 2023

Major Shareholder - The Turtle Creek Group held 18.01% interest and EdgePoint Investment Group Inc. held 10.97% interest at Mar. 23, 2023.

Price Range - BDGI/TSX

Year	Volume	High	Low	Close
2022	13,557,636	$33.21	$22.54	$26.66
2021	24,448,988	$46.58	$28.89	$31.79
2020	35,564,585	$41.82	$18.00	$38.03
2019	44,508,840	$49.57	$30.12	$35.14
2018	37,652,648	$34.35	$22.37	$32.25

Recent Close: $34.30

Capital Stock Changes - There were no changes to capital stock during 2022.

Dividends

BDGI com Ra $0.69 pa Q est. Apr. 14, 2023[1]

Prev. Rate: $0.66 est. Apr. 15, 2022

Prev. Rate: $0.63 est. Apr. 15, 2021

Prev. Rate: $0.60 est. Apr. 15, 2020

[1] Divds. paid monthly prior to April 2022.

Long-Term Debt - At Dec. 31 2022, outstanding long-term debt totaled US$138,882,000 (none current and net of US$1,156,000 unamortized issuance cost) and consisted entirely of borrowings under a Cdn$400,000,000 credit facility bearing interest at prime rate plus margin, or banker's acceptance rate or SOFR plus margin, and matures on Aug. 31, 2027.

Wholly Owned Subsidiaries

Badger Daylighting (Fort McMurray) Inc., Alta.
Badger Edmonton Ltd., Alta.
Badger Leasing (Canada) Ltd., Canada.
Badger Manufacturing (Canada) Ltd., Canada.
Badger Manufacturing (USA) LLC, United States.
Badger Transportation LLC, United States.
Badger US Holdings (Canada) Ltd., Canada.

- 100% int. in **Badger Finance Hungary Kft.**, Hungary.
- 100% int. in **Badger Infrastructure Solutions USA Inc**, United States.
  - 100% int. in **Badger Daylighting Corp.**, Nev.
    - 100% int. in **Badger Leasing (USA) LLC**, United States.

Fieldtek Ltd., Lloydminster, Alta.

- 1% int. in **Badger Daylighting Limited Partnership**, Alta.

Subsidiaries

99% int. in **Badger Daylighting Limited Partnership**, Alta.

Financial Statistics

Periods ended:	12m Dec. 31/22^A		12m Dec. 31/21^oA
	US$000s	%Chg	US$000s
Operating revenue	**570,812**	**+26**	**453,910**
Cost of sales	431,662		358,857
General & admin expense	39,194		37,120
Stock-based compensation	5,507		2,453
Operating expense	**476,363**	**+20**	**398,430**
Operating income	**94,449**	**+70**	**55,480**
Deprec., depl. & amort.	59,584		57,125
Finance costs, gross	8,066		4,406
Pre-tax income	**22,883**	**n.a.**	**(11,272)**
Income taxes	4,593		(2,535)
Net income	**18,290**	**n.a.**	**(8,737)**
Cash & equivalent	5,398		4,137
Inventories	25,213		10,700
Accounts receivable	141,495		113,807
Current assets	181,656		145,035
Fixed assets, net	298,636		289,388
Right-of-use assets	29,679		18,960
Intangibles, net	23,029		24,931
Total assets	**533,000**	**+11**	**478,314**
Accts. pay. & accr. liabs	68,831		50,651
Current liabilities	104,333		102,215
Long-term debt, gross	138,882		120,620
Long-term debt, net	138,882		95,620
Long-term lease liabilities	18,356		9,541
Shareholders' equity	222,847		221,815
Cash from oper. activs	**68,329**	**+25**	**54,610**
Cash from fin. activs	(7,180)		(20,243)
Cash from invest. activs	(59,946)		(43,635)
Net cash position	**5,398**	**+30**	**4,137**
Capital expenditures	(65,545)		(42,794)
Capital disposals	2,858		1,899
	US$		US$
Earnings per share*	0.53		(0.25)
Cash flow per share*	1.98		1.58
Cash divd. per share*	$0.66		$0.63
	shs		shs
No. of shs. o/s*	34,473,438		34,473,438
Avg. no. of shs. o/s*	34,473,438		34,600,681
	%		%
Net profit margin	3.20		(1.92)
Return on equity	8.17		(3.59)
Return on assets	4.85		(1.09)
Foreign sales percent	82		81
No. of employees (FTEs)	2,254		2,119

* Common
^o Restated
^A Reported in accordance with IFRS

Latest Results

Periods ended:	6m June 30/23^A		6m June 30/22^A
	US$000s	%Chg	US$000s
Operating revenue	315,102	+22	258,305
Net income	13,777	n.a.	(460)
	US$		US$
Earnings per share*	0.40		(0.01)

* Common
^A Reported in accordance with IFRS

Historical Summary
(as originally stated)

Fiscal Year	Oper. Rev.	Net Inc. Bef. Disc.	EPS*
	US$000s	US$000s	US$
2022^A	570,812	18,290	0.53
	$000s	$000s	$
2021^A	568,752	(11,249)	(0.33)
2020^A	558,627	24,749	0.71
2019^A	654,282	59,732	1.67
2018^A	615,442	67,817	1.83

* Common
^A Reported in accordance with IFRS

B.23 Ballard Power Systems Inc.*

Symbol - BLDP **Exchange** - TSX **CUSIP** - 058586
Head Office - 9000 Glenlyon Pky, Burnaby, BC, V5J 5J8 **Telephone** - (604) 454-0900 **Fax** - (604) 412-4700
Website - www.ballard.com
Email - investors@ballard.com
Investor Relations - Kate Charlton (604) 453-3939
Auditors - KPMG LLP C.A., Vancouver, B.C.
Lawyers - Seed Intellectual Property Law Group PLLC, Seattle, Wash.; Dorsey & Whitney LLP, Seattle, Wash.; Stikeman Elliott LLP, Vancouver, B.C.
Transfer Agents - Computershare Trust Company of Canada Inc., Vancouver, B.C.
FP500 Revenue Ranking - 760
Employees - 1,296 at Dec. 31, 2022
Profile - (Can. 2008) Designs, develops, manufactures, sells and services zero-emission proton exchange membrane (PEM) fuel cell products for a variety of applications, including heavy-duty motive, material handling, stationary power generation and delivery of technology solutions.

Offers fuel cell products and services for public transit systems, including buses, light rail, marine vessels and for commercial trucks, as well as material handling for industrial vehicles such as forklifts, automated guided vehicles and ground support equipment; stationary power generation for telecommunications equipment and other critical infrastructure; and powertrain integration solutions.

Products include FCgen®-LCS membrane electrode assemblies (MEA) and FCveloCity®-9SSL MEA fuel cell stacks for buses, commercial vehicles, light rail, and material handling applications; FCgen®-HPS, FCgen®-LCS, FCveloCity®-9SSL and FCgen®-1020ACS stacks for passenger car, buses, commercial vehicles, light rail, material handling and backup power applications; FCveloCity®, FCmove™, FCmove™-HD+ and FCwave™ modules for buses, commercial vehicles, light rail, marine and stationary applications; FCrail™ for passenger rail applications; A-drive energy system and powertrain products for buses, trucks and light rail; FCgen®-1020 ACS and FCgen®-H2PM fuel cell and system products for backup power applications; ClearGen® for distributed generation systems; and FCgen®-200 for power generation.

Also helps customers solve difficult technical and business challenges in their PEM fuel cell programs or address new business opportunities by offering customized, bundled technology solutions, including specialized PEM fuel cell engineering services, access to the company's intellectual property portfolio and know-how, as well as the supply of technology components.

Research, development and manufacturing facilities are located in Burnaby, B.C.; and Hobro, Denmark.

During the second quarter of 2023, the company assigned its option held to purchase additional series A preferred shares of **Wisdom Group Holdings Ltd.** (Wisdom Motor) for consideration of US$1,000,000. As a result, the company's interest in Wisdom Motor decreased from 7.17% to 6.7%.

During the second quarter of 2023, the company agreed to sell its 10% interest in **Guangdong Synergy Ballard Hydrogen Power Co., Ltd.** (Synergy Ballard JVco) to **Synergy Group** for a nominal consideration. The transaction was expected to close in the first half of 2023.

In March 2023, the company made a US$1,000,000 cash contribution in **Quantron AG** to exercise its option to purchase an additional 793 shares. As part of the option, the company made an additional contribution of €3,000,000 in April 2023, resulting in a non-controlling interest of 3% in Quantron.

On Sept. 30, 2022, the company announced it would establish its new China headquarters, membrane electrode assembly (MEA) manufacturing facility and research and development centre at a site strategically located at the Jiading Hydrogen Port. It would invest US$130,000,000 over the next three years, which would enable annual production capacity at the new MEA production facility of 13,000,000 MEAs, which would supply 20,000 engines. The facility would also include space to assemble 600 engines annually to support the production and sale of the company's engines in the rail, marine, off-road and stationary markets in China, as well as for certain export markets.

In June 2022, the company acquired a 7.169% interest in **Wisdom Group Holdings Ltd.** through the purchase of 898 series A preferred shares of Wisdom for US$10,000,000.

Recent Merger and Acquisition Activity

Status: completed **Announced:** Sept. 19, 2022
Ballard Power Systems Inc. acquired a minority interest in Quantron AG, which is developing truck fuel cell vehicle platforms. Terms were not disclosed. In addition, Ballard would be the exclusive fuel cell supplier to Quantron for these platforms.

Directors - James N. (Jim) Roche, chr., Ottawa, Ont.; R. Randall (Randy) MacEwen, pres. & CEO, Vancouver, B.C.; Kathleen (Kathy) Bayless, Calif.; Douglas P. Hayhurst, North Vancouver, B.C.; Kui (Kevin) Jiang, Shandong, People's Republic of China; Hubertus M. Mühlhäuser, Switzerland; Marty T. Neese, Menlo Park, Calif.; Shaojun (Sherman) Sun, Shandong, People's Republic of China; Janet P. Woodruff, West Vancouver, B.C.

Other Exec. Officers - Mark Biznek, sr. v-p & COO; Dr. Kevin Colbow, sr. v-p & chief tech. officer; Paul Dobson, sr. v-p & CFO; Dr. Mircea Gradu, sr. v-p & chief eng. officer; David Mucciacciaro, sr. v-p & chief comml. officer; Sarbjot (Jyoti) Sidhu, sr. v-p & chief people & culture officer; Kerry B. Hillier, gen. counsel & corp. sec.; Jesper Themsen, pres. & CEO, Ballard Power Systems Europe A/S

Capital Stock

	Authorized (shs.)	Outstanding (shs.)[1]
Preferred	unlimited	nil
Common	unlimited	298,702,372

[1] At Aug. 8, 2023

Options - At Dec. 31, 2022, options were outstanding to purchase 4,807,620 common shares at a weighted average exercise price of US$9 per share with a weighted average remaining contractual life of 4.3 years.

Major Shareholder - Weichai Power Co., Ltd. held 15.4% interest at Apr. 10, 2023.

Price Range - BLDP/TSX

Year	Volume	High	Low	Close
2022	315,016,946	$16.14	$6.02	$6.48
2021	345,856,563	$53.90	$15.03	$15.89
2020	302,575,445	$30.60	$9.55	$29.78
2019	72,722,927	$9.65	$3.34	$9.28
2018	64,473,875	$5.95	$3.05	$3.28

Recent Close: $5.59

Capital Stock Changes - During 2022, common shares were issued as follows: 304,635 on exercise of options, 217,832 on redemption of restricted share units, 112,451 pursuant to the acquisition of Ballard Motive Solutions Ltd. (formerly Arcola Energy Limited) and 58,990 on redemption of deferred share units.

Long-Term Debt - At Dec. 31, 2022, the company had no long-term debt.

Wholly Owned Subsidiaries

Ballard Hong Kong Limited, Hong Kong, People's Republic of China.
- 100% int. in **Ballard Power Systems (China) Co., Ltd.**, People's Republic of China.
- 10% int. in **Guangdong Synergy Ballard Hydrogen Power Co., Ltd.**, Guangdong, People's Republic of China.
- 100% int. in **Guangzhou Ballard Power Systems Co., Ltd.**, People's Republic of China.
- 49% int. in **Weichai Ballard Hy-Energy Technologies Co., Ltd.**, People's Republic of China.

Ballard Motive Solutions Ltd., London, Middx., United Kingdom.
Ballard Power Corporation, Del.
- 100% int. in **Ballard Fuel Cell Systems Inc.**, Ore.
- 100% int. in **Ballard Unmanned Systems Inc.**, Southborough, Mass.

Ballard Power Systems Europe A/S, Denmark.
- 100% int. in **Ballard Norge AS**, Norway.

Ballard Services Inc., B.C.

Investments

34% int. in **BDF I.P. Holdings Ltd.**, Vancouver, B.C.
9.8% int. in **Forsee Power S.A.S.**, France.
3% int. in **Quantron AG**, Augsburg, Germany.
6.7% int. in **Wisdom Group Holdings Ltd.**, Cayman Islands.

Financial Statistics

Periods ended:	12m Dec. 31/22^A		12m Dec. 31/21^A
	US$000s	%Chg	US$000s
Operating revenue	**83,786**	**-20**	**104,505**
Research & devel. expense	84,048		52,539
General & admin expense	35,581		31,762
Stock-based compensation	9,408		9,669
Other operating expense	92,044		86,561
Operating expense	**221,081**	**+22**	**180,531**
Operating income	**(137,295)**	**n.a.**	**(76,026)**
Deprec., depl. & amort.	13,357		9,752
Finance costs, net	3,381		10,107
Investment income	(11,617)		(16,140)
Write-downs/write-offs	(13,097)		(317)
Pre-tax income	**(177,030)**	**n.a.**	**(114,613)**
Income taxes	(3,536)		(216)
Net inc. bef. disc. opers	**(173,494)**	**n.a.**	**(114,397)**
Income from disc. opers	nil		164
Net income	**(173,494)**	**n.a.**	**(114,233)**
Cash & equivalent	915,741		1,126,899
Inventories	58,050		51,518
Accounts receivable	35,915		26,009
Current assets	1,028,507		1,229,186
Long-term investments	66,357		70,292
Fixed assets, net	82,361		56,061
Intangibles, net	69,482		85,056
Total assets	**1,247,077**	**-13**	**1,440,943**
Accts. pay. & accr. liabs	40,333		39,555
Current liabilities	73,168		83,159
Long-term lease liabilities	11,836		13,882
Shareholders' equity	1,158,911		1,328,217
Cash from oper. activs	**(132,171)**	**n.a.**	**(80,476)**
Cash from fin. activs	(2,406)		526,908
Cash from invest. activs	(75,557)		(85,630)
Net cash position	**913,730**	**-19**	**1,123,895**
Capital expenditures	(33,932)		(13,158)
Unfunded pension liability	348		1,814
	US$		US$
Earnings per share*	(0.58)		(0.39)
Cash flow per share*	(0.44)		(0.27)
	shs		shs
No. of shs. o/s*	298,394,203		297,700,295
Avg. no. of shs. o/s*	298,093,270		295,293,438
	%		%
Net profit margin	(207.07)		(109.47)
Return on equity	(13.95)		(10.26)
Return on assets	(12.91)		(9.47)
Foreign sales percent	95		97
No. of employees (FTEs)	1,296		1,367

* Common
^A Reported in accordance with IFRS

Latest Results

Periods ended:	6m June 30/23[A]		6m June 30/22[A]
	US$000s	%Chg	US$000s
Operating revenue	28,653	-32	41,979
Net income	(64,014)	n.a.	(96,186)
	US$		US$
Earnings per share*	(0.21)		(0.32)

* Common
[A] Reported in accordance with IFRS

Historical Summary
(as originally stated)

Fiscal Year	Oper. Rev.	Net Inc. Bef. Disc.	EPS*
	US$000s	US$000s	US$
2022[A]	83,786	(173,494)	(0.58)
2021[A]	104,505	(114,397)	(0.39)
2020[A]	103,877	(49,469)	(0.20)
2019[A]	106,327	(39,050)	(0.17)
2018[A]	96,586	(27,323)	(0.15)

* Common
[A] Reported in accordance with IFRS

B.24 Baltic I Acquisition Corp.

Symbol - BLTC.P **Exchange** - TSX-VEN **CUSIP** - 058826
Head Office - 2500-700 Georgia St W, Vancouver, BC, V7Y 1B3 **Telephone** - (604) 363-7742
Email - baltic1acquisition@gmail.com
Investor Relations - Harry Pokrandt (604) 363-7742
Auditors - Davidson & Company LLP C.A., Vancouver, B.C.
Lawyers - Farris LLP, Vancouver, B.C.
Transfer Agents - Computershare Trust Company of Canada Inc., Vancouver, B.C.
Profile - (B.C. 2018) Capital Pool Company.
Directors - Harry Pokrandt, CEO, North Vancouver, B.C.; Jessica Van Den Akker, CFO, Vancouver, B.C.; Jay Sujir, corp. sec., Vancouver, B.C.; Luke Alexander, Vancouver, B.C.; Karlene Collier, Vancouver, B.C.; Thezpaul (Taje) Dhatt, B.C.

Capital Stock

	Authorized (shs.)	Outstanding (shs.)[1]
Preferred	unlimited	nil
Common	unlimited	10,074,350

[1] At Apr. 28, 2022

Major Shareholder - Harry Pokrandt held 62% interest at Mar. 24, 2021.

Price Range - BLTC.P/TSX-VEN

Year	Volume	High	Low	Close
2022	263,500	$0.16	$0.11	$0.11
2021	138,000	$0.23	$0.12	$0.12
2020	166,500	$0.25	$0.11	$0.20

Recent Close: $0.07

B.25 Bank of Montreal*

Symbol - BMO **Exchange** - TSX **CUSIP** - 063671
Head Office - 129 rue Saint-Jacques, Montréal, QC, H2Y 1L6 **Telephone** - (514) 877-1285 **Toll-free** - (877) 255-5266 **Exec. Office** - 1 First Canadian Place, 100 King St W, PO Box 1, Toronto, ON, M5X 1A1 **Telephone** - (416) 867-5000 **Toll-free** - (800) 555-3000
Website - www.bmo.com
Email - bill2.anderson@bmo.com
Investor Relations - Bill Anderson (416) 867-7834
Auditors - KPMG LLP C.A., Toronto, Ont.
Transfer Agents - Computershare Trust Company, N.A., Golden, Colo.; Computershare Investor Services plc, London, Middx. United Kingdom; Computershare Trust Company of Canada Inc., Toronto, Ont.
FP500 Revenue Ranking - 14
Employees - 46,722 at Oct. 31, 2022
Profile - (Can. 1871, via Bank Act; orig. Can., 1822) A Schedule I Canadian chartered bank providing personal and commercial banking, wealth management, global markets and investment banking products and services. The bank has more than 12,000,000 customers through more than 1,400 bank branches and operates in Canada, the U.S., and select markets globally through its offices in a number of jurisdictions around the world.

Personal & Commercial Banking (P&C) - This group consists of the bank's two retail and commercial banking operating segments: Canadian P&C and U.S. P&C.

Canadian P&C provides products and services to 8,000,000 customers throughout Canada, including chequing and savings accounts, credit cards, mortgages, personal loans, small business lending, cash management and everyday financial and investment advice to retail customers. Also offers multiple financing options, treasury and payment solutions, and risk management products. The bank delivers services through its network of almost 900 BMO Bank of Montreal branches, contact centres, digital banking platforms and more than 3,200 automated teller machines (ATMs).

U.S. P&C provides deposits, home lending, consumer credit, small business lending, credit cards, as well as financing options and treasury and payment solutions, and risk management products to over 3,800,000 personal and commercial clients in 32 U.S. states under the BMO Harris and Bank of the West brands. Products and services are provided through more than 1,000 branches, contact centres, digital banking platforms and access to more than 42,000 ATMs.

BMO Wealth Management - This group provides asset, wealth management and insurance products and services worldwide, serving individuals, families, business owners and institutions through its BMO Private Wealth, BMO InvestorLine, BMO Wealth Management U.S., BMO Global Asset Management and BMO Insurance business lines. BMO Private wealth provides investing, banking and wealth advisory services, as well as investment management, business succession planning, trust and estate services, and philanthropy to high net worth and ultra-high net worth clients. BMO InvestorLine is an online brokerage which offers three options: self-directed service, adviceDirect™, and SmartFolio™. BMO Wealth Management U.S. offers financial solutions to mass affluent, high net worth and ultra-high net worth individuals, families and businesses. BMO Global Asset Management provides investment management services to institutional, retail and high net worth investors, offering client-focused solutions and strategies to help clients meet their investment objectives. BMO Insurance provides life insurance, critical illness insurance, annuity products, segregated funds, group creditor insurance and travel insurance to bank customers in Canada.

BMO Capital Markets - Through 32 locations around the world, including 18 in North America, provides investment and corporate banking and global market products and services to corporate, institutional and government clients.

Investment and corporate banking business includes capital-raising services loan origination and syndication, balance sheet management solutions and treasury management services. The bank provides strategic advice on mergers and acquisitions, restructurings and recapitalizations, trade finance and risk mitigation services to support international business activities. The bank also provides banking and other operating services tailored to North American and international financial institutions.

Global markets business includes sales, trading and research activities. The bank offers integrated debt, foreign exchange, interest rate, credit, equity, securitization and commodities solutions to institutional, corporate and retail clients. In addition, provides new product development, origination, risk management, advisory services, funding and liquidity management to its clients.

Corporate Services - This group, consisting of Corporate Units and Technology and Operations (T&O), provides services to the bank's three operating groups. Corporate Units provide strategic planning, risk management, treasury, finance, legal and regulatory compliance, sustainability, human resources, communications, marketing, real estate and procurement. T&O develops, monitors, manages and maintains governance over information technology including data and analytics, as well as provides cyber security and operations services.

In December 2022, the bank acquired Calgary-based **Radicle Group Inc.**, which provides sustainability advisory services and solutions as well as technology-driven emissions measurement and management. Terms were not disclosed. The acquisition was not considered material to the bank.

In November 2022, pursuant to a lawsuit filed in the U.S. Bankruptcy Court for the District of Minnesota against wholly owned **BMO Harris Bank N.A.**, the jury awarded damages of US$564,000,000 against BMO Harris. The lawsuit is in relation to a ponzi scheme carried out by Thomas J. Petters and certain affiliated individuals and entities that operated a deposit account at a predecessor bank, **M&I Marshall and Ilsley Bank**. The bank intends to file an appeal to the U.S. Court of Appeals for the Eighth Circuit to contest the jury verdict and award.

Recent Merger and Acquisition Activity

Status: completed **Revised:** June 1, 2023
UPDATE: The transaction was completed. The consideration paid by BMO was US$160,000,000. PREVIOUS: Bank of Montreal (BMO) agreed to acquire LoyaltyOne, Co.'s AIR MILES Reward Program business. Terms of the transaction were not disclosed. BMO was a founding partner of the AIR MILES program. LoyaltyOne, a Canadian subsidiary of Loyalty Ventures Inc., has filed for protection under the Companies' Creditors Arrangement Act (CCAA) and was seeking approval under CCAA for a sale and investment solicitation process to solicit any other interest in the AIR MILES business. BMO's acquisition or a proposed acquisition by any other bidder would be subject to Court approval.

Status: completed **Revised:** Feb. 1, 2023
UPDATE: The transaction was completed. PREVIOUS: Bank of Montreal (BMO) agreed to acquire Bank of the West, Inc. from BNP Paribas for US$16.3 billion, or US$13.4 billion net of estimated US$2.9 billion of excess capital (at closing) at Bank of the West. BMO would finance a portion of the consideration with net proceeds from a proposed Cdn$2.7 billion bought deal public offering. Bank of the West represents all of BNP Paribas' retail & commercial banking activities in the United States. The acquisition would add nearly 1,800,000 customers to BMO and 514 branches and commercial and wealth offices in key U.S. growth markets. BMO expects to incur pre-tax merger and integration costs of Cdn$1.7 billion and achieve pre-tax cost savings of Cdn$860,000,000. Upon closing, BMO plans to merge Bank of the West into BMO Harris Bank N.A. The transaction was expected to close in the first quarter of calendar 2023, subject to customary closing conditions, including regulatory approvals. Jan. 17, 2023 - BMO announced it had received all regulatory approvals required to complete its acquisition of Bank of the West from BNP Paribas

Predecessor Detail - Name changed from The President, Directors and Company of the Bank of Montreal, June 1, 1831.

Directors - George A. Cope, chr., Orleans, Ont.; W. Darryl White, pres. & CEO, Toronto, Ont.; Janice M. (Jan) Babiak, Nashville, Tenn.; Sophie Brochu, Bromont, Qué.; Craig W. Broderick, Greenwich, Conn.; Stephen J. Dent, Toronto, Ont.; Christine A. Edwards, Lake Forest, Ill.; Dr. Martin S. Eichenbaum, Glencoe, Ill.; David E. Harquail, Toronto, Ont.; Linda S. Huber, New York, N.Y.; Eric R. La Flèche, Mount Royal, Qué.; Lorraine Mitchelmore, Calgary, Alta.; Madhu Ranganathan, Saratoga, Calif.

Other Exec. Officers - Amb. David Jacobson, v-chr.; The Hon. Brian V. Tobin, v-chr.; Douglas J. Porter, man. dir. & chief economist; Tayfun Tuzun, CFO; Piyush Agrawal, chief risk officer; Cameron Fowler, chief strategy & opers. officer; Mona Malone, chief HR officer & head, people & culture; Herbert (Herb) Mazariegos, chief AML officer; Gail S. Palac, chief auditor; Steven L. (Steve) Tennyson, chief tech. & opers. officer; Nadim Hirji, grp. head, BMO Commercial Banking; Erminia (Ernie) Johannson, grp. head, North American personal & bus. banking; Deland Kamanga, grp. head, BMO Wealth Management; Paul Noble, sr. v-p, chief legal officer, enterprise legal & corp. sec.; Sharon Haward-Laird, gen. counsel; Grégoire Baillargeon, pres. & v-chr., Que.; Daniel (Dan) Barclay, CEO & grp. head, BMO Capital Markets; Darrel Hackett, CEO, BMO Financial Corp. & pres. & CEO, BMO Harris Bank N.A; Albert Yu, CEO, Asia

Capital Stock

	Authorized (shs.)	Outstanding (shs.)[1]
Class A Preferred	unlimited	nil
Class B Preferred	unlimited	
Series 27		20,000,000
Series 29		16,000,000
Series 31		12,000,000
Series 33		8,000,000
Series 44		16,000,000
Series 46		14,000,000
Series 50		500,000
Series 52		650,000
Limited Recourse Capital Notes	n.a.	
LRCN, Series 1		1,250,000
LRCN, Series 2		750,000
LRCN, Series 3		1,000,000
Common	unlimited	713,025,530

[1] At Apr. 30, 2023

Class A Preferred - Issuable in series. The class A preferred shares as a class rank on a parity with the class B preferred shares as a class. The class A preferred shares of each series will rank on a parity with the class A preferred shares of every other series and are entitled to preference over the common shares with respect to payment of dividends and distribution of assets. Non-voting.

Class B Preferred - Issuable in series. The class B preferred shares rank on a parity with the class A preferred shares. The class B preferred shares may be issued for a consideration expressed and payable in Canadian dollars or in a currency other than Canadian dollars and all amounts to be paid to the holders thereof may be paid in Canadian dollars or any other currency. Non-voting.

Series 27 - Entitled to non-cumulative preferential annual dividends of $0.963 payable quarterly to May 25, 2024, and thereafter at a rate reset every five years equal to the five-year Government of Canada bond yield plus 2.33%. Redeemable on May 25, 2024, and on May 25 every five years thereafter at $25 per share. Convertible at the holder's option, on May 25, 2024, and on May 25 every five years thereafter, into floating rate class B preferred series 28 shares on a share-for-share basis, subject to certain conditions. The series 28 shares would pay a quarterly dividend equal to the 90-day Canadian Treasury bill rate plus 2.33%. Convertible into common shares upon occurrence of certain trigger events related to financial viability. The contingent conversion formula is 1.0 multiplied by $25 plus declared and unpaid dividends divided by the greater of (i) a floor price of $5.00; and (ii) current market price of the common shares.

Series 29 - Entitled to non-cumulative preferential annual dividends of $0.906 payable quarterly to Aug. 25, 2024, and thereafter at a rate reset every five years equal to the five-year Government of Canada bond yield plus 2.24%. Redeemable on Aug. 25, 2024, and on August 25 every five years thereafter at $25 per share. Convertible at the holder's option, on Aug. 25, 2024, and on August 25 every five years thereafter, into floating rate class B preferred series 30 shares on a share-for-share basis, subject to certain conditions. The series 30 shares would pay a quarterly dividend equal to the 90-day Canadian Treasury bill rate plus 2.24%. Convertible into common shares upon occurrence of certain trigger events related to financial viability. The contingent conversion formula is 1.0 multiplied by $25 plus declared and unpaid dividends divided by the greater of (i) a floor price of $5.00; and (ii) current market price of the common shares.

Series 31 - Entitled to non-cumulative preferential annual dividends of $0.9628 payable quarterly to Nov. 25, 2024, and thereafter at a rate reset every five years equal to the five-year Government of Canada bond yield plus 2.22%. Redeemable on Nov. 25, 2024, and on November 25 every five years thereafter at $25 per share. Convertible at the holder's option, on Nov. 25, 2024, and on November 25 every five years thereafter, into floating rate class B preferred series 32 shares on a share-for-share basis, subject to certain conditions. The series 32 shares would pay a quarterly dividend equal to the 90-day Canadian Treasury bill rate plus 2.22%. Convertible into common shares upon occurrence of certain trigger events related to financial viability. The contingent conversion formula is 1.0 multiplied by $25 plus declared and unpaid dividends divided by the greater of (i) a floor price of $5.00; and (ii) current market price of the common shares.

Series 33 - Entitled to non-cumulative preferential annual dividends of $0.7635 payable quarterly to Aug. 25, 2025, and thereafter at a rate reset every five years equal to the five-year Government of Canada bond yield plus 2.71%. Redeemable on Aug. 25, 2025, and on August 25 every five years thereafter at $25 per share. Convertible at the holder's option, on Aug. 25, 2025, and on August 25 every five years thereafter, into floating rate class B preferred series 34 shares on a share-for-share basis, subject to certain conditions. The series 34 shares would pay a quarterly dividend equal to the 90-day Canadian Treasury bill rate plus 2.71%. Convertible into common shares upon occurrence of certain trigger events related to financial viability. The contingent conversion formula is 1.0 multiplied by $25 plus declared and unpaid dividends divided by the greater of (i) a floor price of $5.00; and (ii) current market price of the common shares.

Series 44 - Entitled to non-cumulative preferential annual dividends of $1.2125 payable quarterly to Nov. 25, 2023, and thereafter at a rate reset every five years equal to the five-year Government of Canada bond yield plus 2.68%. Redeemable on Nov. 25, 2023, and on November 25 every five years thereafter at $25 per share. Convertible at the holder's option, on Nov. 25, 2023, and on November 25 every five years thereafter, into floating rate class B preferred series 45 shares on a share-for-share basis, subject to certain conditions. The series 45 shares would pay a quarterly dividend equal to the 90-day Canadian Treasury bill rate plus 2.68%. Convertible into common shares upon occurrence of certain trigger events related to financial viability. The contingent conversion formula is 1.0 multiplied by $25 plus declared and unpaid dividends divided by the greater of (i) a floor price of $5.00; and (ii) current market price of the common shares.

Series 46 - Entitled to non-cumulative preferential annual dividends of $1.275 payable quarterly to May 25, 2024, and thereafter at a rate reset every five years equal to the five-year Government of Canada bond yield plus 3.51%. Redeemable on May 25, 2024, and on May 25 every five years thereafter at $25 per share. Convertible at the holder's option, on May 25, 2024, and on May 25 every five years thereafter, into floating rate class B preferred series 47 shares on a share-for-share basis, subject to certain conditions. The series 47 shares would pay a quarterly dividend equal to the 90-day Canadian Treasury bill rate plus 3.51%. Convertible into common shares upon occurrence of certain trigger events related to financial viability. The contingent conversion formula is 1.0 multiplied by $25 plus declared and unpaid dividends divided by the greater of (i) a floor price of $5.00; and (ii) current market price of the common shares.

Series 50 - Entitled to non-cumulative preferential annual dividends of $73.73 payable semi-annually to Nov. 26, 2027, and thereafter at a rate reset every five years equal to the five-year Government of Canada bond yield plus 4.25%. Redeemable on Nov. 26, 2027, and on November 26 every five years thereafter at $1,000 per share. Convertible at the holder's option into a new series of additional Tier 1 capital preferred shares of the bank on a share-for-share basis. Convertible into common shares upon occurrence of certain trigger events related to financial viability. The contingent conversion formula is 1.0 multiplied by $1,000 plus declared and unpaid dividends divided by the greater of (i) a floor price of $5.00; and (ii) current market price of the common shares.

Series 52 - Entitled to non-cumulative preferential annual dividends of $70.57 payable semi-annually to May 26, 2028, and thereafter at a rate reset every five years equal to the five-year Government of Canada bond yield plus 4.25%. Redeemable on May 26, 2028, and on May 26 every five years thereafter at $1,000 per share. Convertible at the holder's option into a new series of additional Tier 1 capital preferred shares of the bank on a share-for-share basis. Convertible into common shares upon occurrence of certain trigger events related to financial viability. The contingent conversion formula is 1.0 multiplied by $1,000 plus declared and unpaid dividends divided by the greater of (i) a floor price of $5.00; and (ii) current market price of the common shares.

Limited Recourse Capital Notes (LRCNs) - Notes with recourse limited to assets held in a consolidated trust managed by a third party trustee. **Series 1** - Bear interest at 4.3% per annum until Nov. 26, 2025, and thereafter at an annual rate reset every five years equal to the five-year Government of Canada bond yield plus 3.938% until maturity on Nov. 26, 2080. Trust assets consist of non-cumulative five-year reset class B preferred series 48 shares. **Series 2** - Bear interest at 5.625% per annum until May. 26, 2027, and thereafter at an annual rate reset every five years equal to the five-year Government of Canada bond yield plus 4.03% until maturity May 26, 2082. Trust assets consist of non-cumulative five-year reset class B preferred series 49 shares. **Series 3** - Bear interest at 7.325% per annum until Nov. 26, 2027, and thereafter at an annual rate reset every five years equal to the five-year Government of Canada bond yield plus 4.1% until maturity on Nov. 26, 2082. Trust assets consist of non-cumulative five-year reset class B preferred series 51 shares.

Common - One vote per share.

Reserved - At Oct. 31, 2022, 25,669,677 common shares were reserved for issuance under the shareholder dividend reinvestment and share purchase plan and 5,976,870 common shares for the potential exercise of stock options. These options were outstanding at a weighted average exercise price of $98.12 per share with a weighted average remaining contractual life of 0.9 to 7.6 years.

Class B Preferred Series 38 (old) - Were entitled to non-cumulative preferential annual dividends of $1.2125 payable quarterly. Redeemed on Feb. 25, 2022, at $25 per share.

Class B Preferred Series 40 (old) - Were entitled to non-cumulative preferential annual dividends of $1.125 payable quarterly. Redeemed on May 25, 2022, at $25 per share.

Class B Preferred Series 42 (old) - Were entitled to non-cumulative preferential annual dividends of $1.10 payable quarterly. Redeemed on Aug. 25, 2022, at $25 per share.

Major Shareholder - Widely held at May 24, 2023.

Price Range - BMO/TSX

Year	Volume	High	Low	Close
2022	585,120,568	$154.47	$113.73	$122.66
2021	575,882,997	$141.37	$94.90	$136.19
2020	777,363,612	$104.75	$55.76	$96.78
2019	416,516,802	$106.51	$87.91	$100.64
2018	360,679,469	$109.00	$86.25	$89.19

Recent Close: $112.16

Capital Stock Changes - In December 2022, public offering of 13,575,750 common shares, including 1,770,750 shares on exercise of over-allotment option, and concurrent private placement of 8,431,700 common shares at $118.60 per share to Caisse de dépôt et placement du Québec, OMERS, Alberta Investment Management Corporation, Healthcare of Ontario Pension Plan, Public Sector Pension Investment Board and Canada Pension Plan Investment Board were completed all at $118.60 per share. Net proceeds would be used to align the bank's capital position with increased regulatory requirements and for general corporate purposes. An additional 6,323,777 common shares were issued by issued BNP Paribas S.A. at $118.60 per share upon closing of the acquisition of Bank of the West, Inc. On Dec. 1, 2022, 1,162,711 common shares were issued on acquisition of Radicle Group Inc. On Jan. 31, 2023, offering of 650,000 class B preferred series 52 shares was completed at $25 per share.

On Feb. 25, 2022, all 24,000,000 class B preferred series 38 shares were redeemed at $25 per share. In March 2022, bought deal public offering of 20,843,750 common shares was completed at $149 per share, including 2,718,750 common shares on exercise of over-allotment option. Also in March 2022, 750,000 class B preferred series 49 shares were issued in conjunction with issuance of $750,000,000 of limited recourse capital notes, series 2 priced at $1,000 per note. On May 25, 2022, all 20,000,000 class B preferred series 40 shares were redeemed at $25 per share. On July 27, 2022, offering of 500,000 class B preferred series 50 shares was completed at $1,000 per share. On Aug. 25, 2022, all 16,000,000 class B preferred series 42 shares were redeemed at $25 per share. In September 2022, 1,000,000 class B preferred series 51 shares were issued in conjunction with issuance of $1,000,000,000 of limited recourse capital notes, series 3 priced at $1,000 per note. Also during fiscal 2022, common shares were issued as follows: 7,531,233 under dividend reinvestment and share purchase plan and 733,591 on exercise of options; 138,168 common shares were returned to treasury.

Dividends

BMO com Ra $5.88 pa Q est. Aug. 28, 2023**
Prev. Rate: $5.72 est. Feb. 28, 2023
Prev. Rate: $5.56 est. Aug. 26, 2022
Prev. Rate: $5.32 est. Feb. 28, 2022
Prev. Rate: $4.24 est. Feb. 26, 2020
BMO.PR.S pfd B ser 27 red. exch. Adj. Ra $0.963 pa Q est. Aug. 26, 2019**
BMO.PR.T pfd B ser 29 red. exch. Adj. Ra $0.906 pa Q est. Nov. 25, 2019**
BMO.PR.W pfd B ser 31 red. exch. Adj. Ra $0.96275 pa Q est. Feb. 25, 2020**
BMO.PR.Y pfd B ser 33 red. exch. Adj. Ra $0.7635 pa Q est. Nov. 25, 2020**
BMO.PR.E pfd B ser 44 red. exch. Adj. Ra $1.2125 pa Q est. Feb. 25, 2019**
BMO.PR.F pfd B ser 46 red. exch. Adj. Ra $1.275 pa Q est. Aug. 26, 2019
pfd B ser 25 red. exch. Adj. Ra $0.45125 pa Q est. Nov. 25, 2016**[1]
$0.112813f........... Aug. 25/21
pfd B ser 26 red. exch. Fltg. Ra pa Q**[1]
$0.078704f........... Aug. 25/21 $0.073516........ May 25/21
$0.078011........... Feb. 25/21
Paid in 2023: n.a. 2022: n.a. 2021: $0.230231**f**
pfd B ser 38 red. exch. Adj. Ra $1.2125 pa Q est. Feb. 27, 2017**[2]
pfd B ser 40 red. exch. Adj. Ra $1.125 pa Q est. Aug. 25, 2017**[3]
$0.28125f............ May 25/22
pfd B ser 42 red. exch. Adj. Ra $1.10 pa Q est. Nov. 27, 2017**[4]
$0.275f................ Aug. 25/22

[1] Redeemed Aug. 25, 2021 at $25 per sh.
[2] Redeemed Feb. 25, 2022 at $25 per sh.
[3] Redeemed May 25, 2022 at $25 per sh.
[4] Redeemed Aug. 25, 2022 at $25 per sh.
** Reinvestment Option **f** Final Payment

Long-Term Debt - All bank debentures and notes are direct unsecured and subordinated to deposits and other liabilities.

Outstanding at Oct. 31, 2022:	
Ser.20 debs. due to 2040[1]	$146,000,000
Subord. notes:	
4.338% due 2028[2]	1,135,000,000
3.803% due 2032[3]	1,497,000,000
3.088% due 2037[4]	1,393,000,000
Medium-term notes:	
2.88% ser.J due 2029	998,000,000
2.08% ser.J due 2030	1,248,000,000
1.93% ser.K due 2031	984,000,000
6.53% ser.L due 2032	749,000,000
	8,150,000,000

[1] Bearing interest at 8.25% and due December 2025 to 2040.
[2] US$850,000,000.
[3] US$1.25 billion.
[4] US$1.25 billion.

Wholly Owned Subsidiaries

BMO Capital Markets Limited, London, Middx., United Kingdom. Book value of common and preferred shares owned by the bank at Oct. 31, 2022, totaled $289,000,000.

BMO Financial Corp., Chicago, Ill. Formerly Harris Financial Corp. Book value of common and preferred shares owned by the bank at Oct. 31, 2022, totaled $32,490,000,000.

- 100% int. in **BMO Asset Management Corp.**, Chicago, Ill.
- 100% int. in **BMO Capital Markets Corp.**, N.Y.
- 100% int. in **BMO Harris Bank N.A.**, Chicago, Ill.
  - 100% int. in **BMO Harris Investment Company, LLC**, Las Vegas, Nev.

BMO Japan Securities Ltd., Tokyo, Japan. Book value of common and preferred shares owned by the bank at Oct. 31, 2022, totaled $6,000,000.

BMO Life Insurance Company, Toronto, Ont. Book value of common and preferred shares owned by the bank at Oct. 31, 2022, totaled $1,610,000,000.

- 100% int. in **BMO Life Holdings (Canada), ULC**, Halifax, N.S.
  - 100% int. in **BMO Life Assurance Company**, Toronto, Ont.

BMO Trust Company, Toronto, Ont. Book value of common and preferred shares owned by the bank at Oct. 31, 2022, totaled $597,000,000.

Bank of Montreal (China) Co. Ltd., Beijing, Beijing, People's Republic of China. Book value of common and preferred shares owned by the bank at Oct. 31, 2022, totaled $463,000,000.

Bank of Montreal Europe plc, Dublin, Ireland. Formerly Bank of Montreal Ireland plc. Book value of common and preferred shares owned by the bank at Oct. 31, 2022, totaled $1,130,000,000.

Bank of Montreal Holding Inc., Toronto, Ont. Book value of common and preferred shares owned by the bank at Oct. 31, 2022, totaled $36,913,000,000.

- 100% int. in **BMO Investments Inc.**, Toronto, Ont.
- 100% int. in **BMO Investments Limited**, Hamilton, Bermuda.
  - 100% int. in **BMO Reinsurance Limited**, St. Michael, Barbados.
- 100% int. in **BMO InvestorLine Inc.**, Toronto, Ont.
- 100% int. in **BMO Nesbitt Burns Inc.**, Toronto, Ont.
- 100% int. in **Bank of Montreal Mortgage Corporation**, Toronto, Ont.
  - 100% int. in **BMO Mortgage Corp.**, Vancouver, B.C.

Bank of the West, Inc., San Francisco, Calif.

- 51% int. in **CLAAS Financial Services, LLC**, San Francisco, Calif.

Note: The preceding list includes only the major related companies in which interests are held.

Financial Statistics

Periods ended:	12m Oct. 31/22[A]		12m Oct. 31/21[A]
	$000s	%Chg	$000s
Interest income	**26,897,000**	**+35**	**19,887,000**
Interest expense	11,012,000		5,577,000
Net interest income	**15,885,000**	**+11**	**14,310,000**
Provision for loan losses	313,000		20,000
Other income	17,825,000		12,876,000
Salaries & pension benefits	8,795,000		8,322,000
Non-interest expense	15,511,000		16,908,000
Pre-tax income	**17,886,000**	**+74**	**10,258,000**
Income taxes	4,349,000		2,504,000
Net income	**13,537,000**	**+75**	**7,754,000**
Cash & equivalent	93,200,000		101,564,000
Securities	273,262,000		232,849,000
Net non-performing loans	1,447,000		1,671,000
Total loans	664,533,000		565,644,000
Fixed assets, net	4,841,000		4,454,000
Total assets	**1,139,199,000**	**+15**	**988,175,000**
Deposits	769,478,000		685,631,000
Other liabilities	290,533,000		238,128,000
Subordinated debt	8,150,000		6,893,000
Preferred share equity	6,308,000		5,558,000
Shareholders' equity	71,038,000		57,523,000
Cash from oper. activs	**4,957,000**	**-89**	**44,049,000**
Cash from fin. activs	15,980,000		(5,122,000)
Cash from invest. activs	(29,471,000)		(299,000)
Pension fund surplus	1,179,000		809,000
	$		$
Earnings per share*	20.04		11.60
Cash flow per share*	7.47		68.06
Cash divd. per share*	5.44		4.24
	shs		shs
No. of shs. o/s*	677,106,878		648,136,472
Avg. no. of shs. o/s*	663,990,000		647,163,000
	%		%
Basel III Common Equity Tier 1	16.70		13.70
Basel III Tier 1	18.40		15.40
Basel III Total	20.70		17.60
Net profit margin	40.16		28.52
Return on equity	22.80		14.73
Return on assets	1.27		0.80
Foreign sales percent	53		41
No. of employees (FTEs)	46,722		43,863

* Common
[A] Reported in accordance with IFRS

Latest Results

Periods ended:	6m Apr. 30/23[A]		6m Apr. 30/22[A]
	$000s	%Chg	$000s
Net interest income	8,835,000	+12	7,921,000
Net income	1,306,000	-83	7,689,000
Net inc. for equity hldrs	1,303,000	-83	7,689,000
Net inc. for non-cont. int	3,000		nil
	$		$
Earnings per share*	1.62		11.61

* Common
[A] Reported in accordance with IFRS

Historical Summary
(as originally stated)

Fiscal Year	Int. Inc.	Net Inc. Bef. Disc.	EPS*
	$000s	$000s	$
2022[A]	26,897,000	13,537,000	20.04
2021[A]	19,887,000	7,754,000	11.60
2020[A]	23,315,000	5,097,000	7.56
2019[A]	26,152,000	5,758,000	8.68
2018[A]	19,451,000	5,450,000	8.19

* Common
[A] Reported in accordance with IFRS

B.26 The Bank of Nova Scotia*

Symbol - BNS **Exchange** - TSX **CUSIP** - 064149
Head Office - Bank of Nova Scotia Building, 1709 Hollis St, Halifax, NS, B3J 3B7 **Telephone** - (902) 420-3567 **Toll-free** - (800) 265-6978 **Fax** - (902) 422-8332 **Exec. Office** - 40 Temperance St, Toronto, ON, M5H 0B4 **Telephone** - (416) 866-6161 **Fax** - (416) 866-3750
Website - www.scotiabank.com
Email - john.mccartney@scotiabank.com
Investor Relations - John McCartney (416) 863-7579
Auditors - KPMG LLP C.A., Toronto, Ont.
Transfer Agents - Computershare Trust Company, N.A., Louisville, Ky.; Computershare Trust Company of Canada Inc., Toronto, Ont.
FP500 Revenue Ranking - 13
Employees - 90,979 at Oct. 31, 2022
Profile - (Can. 1871, via Bank Act; orig. N.S., 1832) A Schedule I Canadian chartered bank providing a full range of personal and commercial banking, wealth management and private banking, corporate and investment banking, and capital markets products and services primarily in Canada, the U.S. and the Pacific Alliance countries.
Canadian Banking - Provides banking products and services to over 10,000,000 personal and business customers across Canada through a network of more than 940 branches and 3,725 automated banking machines (ABMs), as well as online, mobile and telephone banking and specialized sales teams. Operations consist of Retail Banking and Business Banking units. Retail Banking provides financial advice and solutions and day-to-day banking products, including debit cards, chequing accounts, credit cards, investments, mortgages, personal loans and insurance products, as well as retail automotive financing solutions to retail customers. Also includes the operations of digital bank **Tangerine Bank** which serves over 2,000,000 customers. Business Banking delivers advisory services and a full product suite, including lending, deposit, cash management and trade finance solutions, to small, medium and large businesses.
International Banking - Provides retail, corporate and commercial banking products and services to over 11,000,000 customers in select countries outside of Canada, with a network of more than 1,200 branches and 4,800 automated teller machines (ATMs). Operations are focused on Latin America, including the Pacific Alliance countries of Mexico, Peru, Chile and Colombia, and supported by markets in Central America and the Caribbean.
Global Wealth Management - Provides wealth management advice, products and services to retail and institutional customers across 13 countries. Solutions include online and full-service brokerage, trust and estate services, wealth planning, investment management, private banking, mutual funds, exchange traded funds and institutional asset management.
Global Banking & Markets (GBM) - Provides wholesale banking and capital markets products and services to corporate, government and institutional investor clients across 21 countries. GBM is a full-service wholesale bank and investment dealer in Canada and Mexico, and offers a range of products and services in the U.S., Latin America (excluding Mexico), Europe and the Asia-Pacific region. GBM provides corporate lending; transaction banking, including trade finance and cash management; investment banking, including corporate finance and mergers and acquisitions; fixed income and equity underwriting, sales, trading and research; prime brokerage and securities lending; foreign exchange sales and trading; commodity derivatives; precious and base metals sales, trading, financing and physical services; and collateral management.
In October 2022, the bank sold its 26.8% interest in **Banco del Caribe, C.A.** and 23.4% interest in **Inversiones Americana del Caribe (IAC), B.V.**, both operating in Venezuela, as well as its interest in Thailand-based **Thanachart Insurance Public Company Limited** and **Thanachart Securities Public Company Limited**. The financial and capital impacts of the transactions were not significant.
Also during the fourth quarter of fiscal 2022, the bank wound down its operations in India and Malaysia in relation to its realignment of the business in the Asia-Pacific region.

Recent Merger and Acquisition Activity

Status: terminated **Revised:** June 9, 2022
UPDATE: The transaction was terminated. PREVIOUS: The Bank of Nova Scotia agreed to sell its banking operations in Guyana to First Citizens Bank Limited. The transaction is subject to regulatory approvals and customary closing conditions. Terms were not disclosed.
Status: completed **Announced:** June 7, 2022
Empire Company Limited announced the acquisition of an ownership interest in Scene+ loyalty rewards program, making it a co-owner with Cineplex Inc. and The Bank of Nova Scotia. Terms were not disclosed. Scene+ rollout in Empire banners would begin with stores in Atlantic Canada in August 2022, and then continue across the country, culminating in early 2023. Scene+ has over 10,000,000 members and offers an assortment of opportunities to earn and redeem points across a broad spectrum of partners. AIR MILES collectors would continue to earn and redeem in Empire store until the Scene+ program is available in that region.
Status: completed **Revised:** Apr. 29, 2022
UPDATE: The transaction was completed. PREVIOUS: The Bank of Nova Scotia (BNS) agreed to acquire Grupo Said's remaining 16.76% interest in Scotiabank Chile, S.A. for Cdn$1.3 billion (US$1 billion), consisting of Cdn$650,000,000 cash and issuance of 7,000,000 common shares valued at Cdn$650,000,000. The acquisition would result in BNS owning 99.79% of its Chilean unit, with the transaction expected to add Cdn$35,000,000 per quarter to BNS' profits. Grupo Said was a company controlled by Chile's Said family.
Directors - Aaron W. Regent, chr., Toronto, Ont.; L. Scott Thomson, pres. & CEO, West Vancouver, B.C.; Nora A. Aufreiter, Toronto, Ont.; Guillermo E. Babatz, Mexico City, D.F., Mexico; Scott B. Bonham, Atherton, Calif.; Daniel H. (Don) Callahan, Fairfield, Conn.; W. Dave Dowrich, Brooklyn, N.Y.; Lynn K. Patterson, Toronto, Ont.; Michael D. Penner, London, Middx., United Kingdom; Una M. Power, Vancouver, B.C.; Calin Rovinescu, Toronto, Ont.; Benita M. Warmbold, Toronto, Ont.
Other Exec. Officers - Philip (Phil) Thomas, chief risk officer; Francisco A. Aristeguieta, grp. head, intl. banking; Glen B. Gowland, grp. head, global wealth mgt.; Barbara F. (Barb) Mason, grp. head & chief HR officer; Dan Rees, grp. head, Cdn. banking; Rajagopal (Raj) Viswanathan, grp. head & CFO; Dr. Michael Zerbs, grp. head, tech. & opers.; Ian Arellano, exec. v-p & gen. counsel; Anique Asher, exec. v-p, fin. & strategy; Stephen Bagnarol, exec. v-p, Cdn. bus. banking; Paul Baroni, exec. v-p & chief auditor; Alex Besharat, exec. v-p, Cdn. wealth mgt.; Tracy Bryan, exec. v-p, global opers.; Stuart Davis, exec. v-p, finl. crimes risk mgt. & grp. chief AML officer; John W. Doig, exec. v-p, retail sales; Nicole Frew, exec. v-p & chief compliance officer; Loretta Marcoccia, exec. v-p & COO, global banking & markets; Diego Masola, exec. v-p & country head, Chile; Adrián Otero, exec. v-p & country head, Mexico; Gillian Riley, exec. v-p, Tangerine; Shawn Rose, exec. v-p & chief tech. officer; Francisco Sardón, exec. v-p & country head, Peru; Anya M. Schnoor, exec. v-p, Caribbean, Central America & Uruguay; Kevin J. Teslyk, exec. v-p & COO, Cdn. banking; Maria Theofilaktidis, exec. v-p, fin.; Martin Weeks, exec. v-p & treas.; Terri-Lee Weeks, exec. v-p, retail cust.; Julie A. Walsh, sr. v-p, chief corp. governance officer & corp. sec.; James A. Neate, pres. & grp. head, corp. & invest. banking; Jake P. Lawrence, CEO & grp. head, global banking & markets

Capital Stock

	Authorized (shs.)	Outstanding (shs.)[1]
Preferred	unlimited	
Series 40		12,000,000
Common	unlimited	1,198,175,000

[1] At May 12, 2023

Preferred - Issuable in series. Each preferred series ranks pari passu with other existing preferred series. Non-voting.
Series 40 - Entitled to non-cumulative preferential annual dividends of $1.2125 payable quarterly to Jan. 26, 2024, and thereafter at a rate reset every five years equal to the five-year Government of Canada bond yield plus 2.43%. Redeemable on Jan. 27, 2024, and on January 27 every five years thereafter at $25 per share. Convertible at the holder's option on Jan. 27, 2024, and on January 27 every five years thereafter, into floating rate preferred series 41 shares on a share-for-share basis, subject to certain conditions. The series 41 shares would pay a quarterly dividend equal to the 90-day Canadian Treasury bill rate plus 2.43%. Convertible upon occurrence of certain trigger events related to financial viability into common shares equal to 1.0 multiplied by $25 plus declared and unpaid dividends divided by the greater of: (i) $5.00; and (ii) current market price of the common shares.
Common - One vote per share.
Options - At Oct. 31, 2022, options were outstanding to purchase 9,907,000 common shares at prices ranging from $55.63 to $85.46 per share with a weighted average remaining contractual life of 5.85 years.
Preferred Series 38 (old) - Were entitled to non-cumulative preferential annual dividends of $1.2125 payable quarterly to Jan. 26, 2022. Redeemed on Jan. 27, 2022, at $25 per share.
Major Shareholder - Widely held at May 24, 2023.

Price Range - BNS/TSX

Year	Volume	High	Low	Close
2022	1,138,985,647	$95.00	$63.19	$66.34
2021	1,005,126,499	$91.77	$67.43	$89.55
2020	1,162,910,110	$74.92	$46.38	$68.80
2019	635,723,369	$76.75	$67.17	$73.35
2018	569,893,133	$83.22	$66.36	$68.05

Recent Close: $62.12
Capital Stock Changes - On Jan. 27, 2022, all 20,000,000 preferred series 38 shares were redeemed at $25 per share. In April 2022, 7,000,000 common shares were issued pursuant to the acquisition of an additional 16.76% interest in Scotiabank Chile, S.A. Also during fiscal 2022, 1,951,372 common shares were issued under stock option plans and 32,913,800 common shares were repurchased under a Normal Course Issuer Bid.

Dividends

BNS com Ra $4.24 pa Q est. July 27, 2023**
Prev. Rate: $4.12 est. July 27, 2022
Prev. Rate: $4.00 est. Jan. 27, 2022
Prev. Rate: $3.60 est. Oct. 29, 2019
BNS.PR.I pfd ser 40 red. exch. Adj. Ra $1.2125 pa Q est. Jan. 29, 2019**
pfd ser 32 red. exch. Adj. Ra $0.51575 pa Q est. Apr. 27, 2016**[1]
$0.009891**f**........... Feb. 2/21
pfd ser 34 red. exch. Adj. Ra $1.375 pa Q est. Apr. 27, 2016**[2]
$0.34375**f**............ Apr. 26/21
pfd ser 33 red. exch. Fltg. Ra pa Q**[3]
$0.006976**f**........... Feb. 2/21 $0.093638........ Jan. 27/21
Paid in 2023: n.a. 2022: n.a. 2021: $0.100614**f**
pfd ser 36 red. exch. Adj. Ra $1.375 pa Q est. July 27, 2016**[4]
$0.34375**f**............ July 26/21
pfd ser 38 red. exch. Adj. Ra $1.2125 pa Q est. Jan. 27, 2017**[5]
$0.303125**f**........... Jan. 27/22
[1] Redeemed Feb. 2, 2021 at $25 per sh. plus accr. divds. of $0.009891.
[2] Redeemed April 26, 2021 at $25 per sh.
[3] Redeemed Feb. 2, 2021 at $25 per sh. plus accr. divds. of $0.006976.
[4] Redeemed July 26, 2021 at $25 per sh.
[5] Redeemed Jan. 27, 2022 at $25 per sh.
** Reinvestment Option **f** Final Payment

Long-Term Debt - Outstanding at Oct. 31, 2022:

Fixed rate subord. debs.:	
8.9% due June 2025	$253,000,000
4.5% due December 2025[1]	1,690,000,000
3.89% due January 2029[2]	1,770,000,000
2.836% due July 2029[3]	1,459,000,000
3.934% due May 2032[4]	1,575,000,000
4.588% due May 2037[1,5]	1,644,000,000
Fltg. rate subord. debs. due 2085[6]	78,000,000
	8,469,000,000

[1] US$1.25 billion.
[2] After Jan. 18, 2024, bears interest at an annual rate equal to the 90-day bankers' acceptance rate plus 1.58%.
[3] After July 3, 2024, bears interest at an annual rate equal to the 90-day bankers' acceptance rate plus 1.18%.
[4] After May 3, 2027, bears interest at a quarterly rate equal to the prevailing 90-day bankers' acceptance rate plus 1.52%.
[5] Bears interest at 4.588% to May 3, 2032, and thereafter at the prevailing five-year U.S. treasury rate plus 2.05%.
[6] US$57,000,000. Bears interest at the offered rate for six-month U.S. dollar LIBOR plus 0.125%.

Wholly Owned Subsidiaries

BNS International (Bahamas) Limited, Nassau, Bahamas. Carrying value of shares owned by the bank at Oct. 31, 2022, totaled $17,180,000,000.
- 100% int. in **BNS Asia Limited**, Singapore.
- 100% int. in **The Bank of Nova Scotia Trust Company (Bahamas) Limited**, Nassau, Bahamas.
- 100% int. in **Grupo BNS de Costa Rica, S.A.**, San Jose, Costa Rica.
- 100% int. in **Scotiabank & Trust (Cayman) Ltd.**, Grand Cayman, Cayman Islands.
- 100% int. in **Scotiabank (Bahamas) Limited**, Nassau, Bahamas.
- 100% int. in **Scotiabank (Ireland) Designated Activity Company**, Dublin, Ireland.

BNS Investments Inc., Toronto, Ont. Carrying value of shares owned by the bank at Oct. 31, 2022, totaled $15,750,000,000.
- 100% int. in **Montréal Trust Company of Canada**, Toronto, Ont.
- 100% int. in **Scotia Holdings (US) Inc.**, New York, N.Y.
  - 100% int. in **Scotia Capital (USA) Inc.**, New York, N.Y.

The Bank of Nova Scotia Trust Company, Toronto, Ont. Carrying value of shares owned by the bank at Oct. 31, 2022, totaled $214,000,000.
Jarislowsky, Fraser Limited, Montréal, Qué. Carrying value of shares owned by the bank at Oct. 31, 2022, totaled $988,000,000.
MD Financial Management Inc., Ottawa, Ont. Carrying value of shares owned by the bank at Oct. 31, 2022, totaled $2,781,000,000.
National Trust Company, Toronto, Ont. Carrying value of shares owned by the bank at Oct. 31, 2022, totaled $374,000,000.
Nova Scotia Inversiones Limitada, Santiago, Chile. Carrying value of shares owned by the bank at Oct. 31, 2022, totaled $6,114,000,000.
- 99.79% int. in **Scotiabank Chile, S.A.**, Santiago, Chile.

1832 Asset Management L.P., Toronto, Ont. Carrying value of shares owned by the bank at Oct. 31, 2022, totaled $3,785,000,000.
RoyNat Inc., Toronto, Ont. Carrying value of shares owned by the bank at Oct. 31, 2022, totaled $594,000,000.
Scotia Capital Inc., Toronto, Ont. Carrying value of shares owned by the bank at Oct. 31, 2022, totaled $3,215,000,000.
Scotia Dealer Advantage Inc., Burnaby, B.C. Carrying value of shares owned by the bank at Oct. 31, 2022, totaled $867,000,000.

Scotia Mortgage Corporation, Toronto, Ont. Carrying value of shares owned by the bank at Oct. 31, 2022, totaled $810,000,000.
Scotia Peru Holdings S.A., Lima, Peru. Carrying value of shares owned by the bank at Oct. 31, 2022, totaled $4,961,000,000.
- 100% int. in **Profuturo AFP S.A.**, Lima, Peru.
- 99.31% int. in **Scotiabank Peru S.A.A.**, Lima, Peru.

Scotia Securities Inc., Toronto, Ont. Carrying value of shares owned by the bank at Oct. 31, 2022, totaled $63,000,000.
Scotiabank (Barbados) Limited, Bridgetown, Barbados. Carrying value of shares owned by the bank at Oct. 31, 2022, totaled $273,000,000.
Scotiabank Brasil S.A. Banco Multiplo, São Paulo, Brazil. Carrying value of shares owned by the bank at Oct. 31, 2022, totaled $788,000,000.
Scotiabank Caribbean Holdings Ltd., Bridgetown, Barbados. Carrying value of shares owned by the bank at Oct. 31, 2022, totaled $1,550,000,000.
- 100% int. in **Integra Properties Ltd., S.A.**, Panama City, Panama.
- 71.8% int. in **Scotia Group Jamaica Limited**, Kingston, Jamaica.
  - 100% int. in **The Bank of Nova Scotia Jamaica Limited**, Kingston, Jamaica.
- 50.9% int. in **Scotiabank Trinidad and Tobago Limited**, Port of Spain, Trinidad and Tobago.

Scotiabank Europe plc, London, Middx., United Kingdom. Carrying value of shares owned by the bank at Oct. 31, 2022, totaled $2,478,000,000.
Scotiabank Uruguay S.A., Montevideo, Uruguay. Carrying value of shares owned by the bank at Oct. 31, 2022, totaled $478,000,000.
Tangerine Bank, Toronto, Ont. Carrying value of shares owned by the bank at Oct. 31, 2022, totaled $3,827,000,000.

Subsidiaries

51% int. in **Scotiabank Colpatria S.A.**, Bogota, Colombia. Carrying value of shares owned by the bank at Oct. 31, 2022, totaled $842,000,000.
97.4% int. in **Grupo Financiero Scotiabank Inverlat, S.A. de C.V.**, Mexico City, D.F., Mexico. Carrying value of shares owned by the bank at Oct. 31, 2022, totaled $5,960,000,000.
99.8% int. in **Scotiabank Republica Dominicana, S.A. - Banco Múltiple**, Santo Domingo, Dominican Republic. Carrying value of shares owned by the bank at Oct. 31, 2022, totaled $906,000,000.

Investments

18.11% int. in **Bank of Xi'an Co. Ltd.**, Shaanxi, People's Republic of China. Carrying value of shares owned by the bank at Oct. 31, 2022, totaled $1,007,000,000.
20% int. in **CTFS Holdings Limited**, Toronto, Ont. Carrying value of shares owned by the bank at Oct. 31, 2022, totaled $579,000,000.
48.1% int. in **Maduro & Curiel's Bank N.V.**, Curacao. Carrying value of shares owned by the bank at Oct. 31, 2022, totaled $438,000,000.
Note: The preceding list includes only the major related companies in which interests are held.

Financial Statistics

Periods ended:	12m Oct. 31/22[A]		12m Oct. 31/21[A]
	$000s	%Chg	$000s
Interest income	**33,558,000**	**+34**	**24,986,000**
Interest expense	15,443,000		8,025,000
Net interest income	**18,115,000**	**+7**	**16,961,000**
Provision for loan losses	1,382,000		1,808,000
Other income	13,301,000		14,291,000
Salaries & pension benefits	8,836,000		8,541,000
Non-interest expense	17,102,000		16,618,000
Pre-tax income	**12,932,000**	**+1**	**12,826,000**
Income taxes	2,758,000		2,871,000
Net income	**10,174,000**	**+2**	**9,955,000**
Net inc. for equity hldrs	**9,916,000**	**+3**	**9,624,000**
Net inc. for non-cont. int	**258,000**	**-22**	**331,000**
Cash & equivalent	66,438,000		87,078,000
Securities	223,162,000		221,511,000
Net non-performing loans	3,151,000		2,801,000
Total loans	920,300,000		764,725,000
Fixed assets, net	5,700,000		5,621,000
Total assets	**1,349,418,000**	**+14**	**1,184,844,000**
Deposits	916,181,000		797,259,000
Other liabilities	350,019,000		308,359,000
Subordinated debt	8,469,000		6,334,000
Preferred share equity	8,075,000		6,052,000
Shareholders' equity	73,225,000		70,802,000
Non-controlling interest	1,524,000		2,090,000
Cash from oper. activs	**16,943,000**	**n.a.**	**(12,807,000)**
Cash from fin. activs	(4,579,000)		(2,777,000)
Cash from invest. activs	(11,293,000)		14,697,000
Unfunded pension liability	n.a.		120,000
Pension fund surplus	679,000		n.a.
	$		$
Earnings per share*	8.05		7.74
Cash flow per share*	14.13		(10.55)
Cash divd. per share*	4.06		3.60
	shs		shs
No. of shs. o/s*	1,191,375,095		1,215,337,523
Avg. no. of shs. o/s*	1,199,000,000		1,214,000,000
	%		%
Basel III Common Equity Tier 1	11.50		12.30
Basel III Tier 1	13.20		13.90
Basel III Total	15.30		15.90
Net profit margin	32.38		31.85
Return on equity	14.87		14.72
Return on assets	0.80		0.86
Foreign sales percent	43		41
No. of employees (FTEs)	90,979		89,488

* Common
[A] Reported in accordance with IFRS

Latest Results

Periods ended:	6m Apr. 30/23[A]		6m Apr. 30/22[A]
	$000s	%Chg	$000s
Net interest income	9,035,000	+2	8,817,000
Net income	3,931,000	-28	5,487,000
Net inc. for equity hldrs	3,865,000	-27	5,321,000
Net inc. for non-cont. int	66,000		166,000
	$		$
Earnings per share*	3.07		4.32

* Common
[A] Reported in accordance with IFRS

Historical Summary
(as originally stated)

Fiscal Year	Int. Inc. $000s	Net Inc. Bef. Disc. $000s	EPS* $
2022[A]	33,558,000	10,174,000	8.05
2021[A]	24,986,000	9,955,000	7.74
2020[A]	29,712,000	6,853,000	5.43
2019[A]	32,784,000	8,798,000	6.72
2018[A]	28,067,000	8,724,000	6.90

* Common
[A] Reported in accordance with IFRS

B.27 Banxa Holdings Inc.

Symbol - BNXA **Exchange** - TSX-VEN **CUSIP** - 06683R
Head Office - Level 2, 2-6 Gwynne St, Melbourne, VIC, Australia, 3121
Overseas Tel - 61-4-1119-6979
Website - www.banxa.com
Email - dom@banxa.com
Investor Relations - Domenico Carosa 61-4-1554-9103
Auditors - PKF Antares Professional Corporation C.A., Calgary, Alta.
Transfer Agents - TSX Trust Company, Vancouver, B.C.
Profile - (B.C. 2020; orig. Can., 2018) Has developed and operates payment infrastructures and compliance systems to facilitate fiat to cryptocurrency conversions primarily for business-to-business (B2B) clients.

The company has a payment gateway infrastructure that includes online payments across multiple currencies and payment types. Through global and local payment options, the company offers payment and compliance rails to major cryptocurrency businesses. Global exchanges and wallets can utilize the company's B2B platform to offer their users a fast and reliant fiat to cryptocurrency conversion service (and vice versa) within the company's partner's platforms. The service allows the company's platform to focus on their cryptocurrency business without touching payments and fiat currency. Bitcoin and Ethereum are the primary cryptocurrencies transacted with the company.

The company earns revenue from the sale of crypto-currencies (fiat off-ramp services); commission fees; and spread (fiat on-ramp services).

In March 2023, the company sold bitcoin.ca, a domain name which offers bitcoin products and services in Canada, for US$250,000.

In September 2022, the company sold domain names and website assets including coinloft.com.au, buyabitcoin.com.au and bitcoin.com.au to **Independent Reserve Pty Ltd** for A$2,250,000 cash and issuance of A$750,000 common shares. The domains are formerly a part of company's business-to-commerce portfolio which offers bitcoin services and purchases in Australia and New Zealand.

Common reinstated on TSX-VEN, July 10, 2023.

Common suspended from TSX-VEN, Nov. 4, 2022.

Predecessor Detail - Name changed from A-Labs Capital I Corp., Dec. 23, 2020, pursuant to Qualifying Transaction reverse takeover acquisition of BTC Corporation Holdings Pty Ltd.; basis 1 new for 4.66667 old shs.

Directors - Domenico (Dom) Carosa, chr., Australia; Matthew Cain, Melbourne, Vic., Australia; Doron Cohen, Kfar Saba, Israel; Joshua (Jim) Landau, Melbourne, Vic., Australia

Other Exec. Officers - Holger Arians, CEO; Sean Moynihan, COO & CFO; Tom Chalmers, chief product officer; Iain Clark, chief tech. officer; Gregor Cooney, chief mktg. officer; Josh D'Ambrosio, chief comml. officer; Richard Mico, gen. counsel

Capital Stock

	Authorized (shs.)	Outstanding (shs.)[1]
Common	unlimited	45,563,056

[1] At Mar. 31, 2023

Major Shareholder - Domenico (Dom) Carosa held 13.73% interest at Feb. 16, 2022.

Price Range - BNXA/TSX-VEN

Year	Volume	High	Low	Close
2022	10,827,206	$3.16	$0.62	$1.08
2021	52,553,091	$8.30	$0.90	$3.02
2020	8,571	$0.16	$0.16	$0.16
2019	5,357	$0.70	$0.14	$0.14
2018	9,107	$1.14	$0.47	$1.14

Consolidation: 1-for-4.66667 cons. in Jan. 2021

Recent Close: $0.65

Capital Stock Changes - During fiscal 2022, common shares were issued as follows: 492,941 on conversion of debt, 164,706 on exercise of warrants, 91,375 on exercise of options and 70,000 for services.

Wholly Owned Subsidiaries

BNXA USA Holding Inc., United States.
- 100% int. in **BNXA Brazil Ltda.**, Brazil.
- 100% int. in **BNXA Teknoloji Anonim Sirketi**, Türkiye.
- 100% int. in **BNXA UK Vasp Limited**, United Kingdom.
- 100% int. in **BNXA USA MTL Inc.**, United States.
- 100% int. in **BNXA USA NV Inc.**, United States.
- 100% int. in **BNXA USA Operating Inc.**, United States.

BTC Corporation Holdings Pty Ltd., Vic., Australia.
- 100% int. in **BC Cloud Mining Pty Ltd.**, Australia.
- 100% int. in **BNXA UK Holding Limited**, United Kingdom.
  - 50% int. in **Banxa.com Pty Ltd.**, Australia.
- 100% int. in **BTC Sing SPV Pte. Ltd.**, Singapore.
- 50% int. in **Banxa.com Pty Ltd.**, Australia.
- 100% int. in **EU Internet Ventures B.V.**, Netherlands.
- 100% int. in **Global Internet Ventures Pty Ltd.**, Australia.
- 100% int. in **Internet SG Ventures Pte Ltd.**, Singapore.
- 100% int. in **LT Internet Ventures UAB**, Lithuania.
- 100% int. in **Rhino Loft Pty Ltd.**, Australia.
- 100% int. in **Richmond Internet Ventures Corporation**, Canada.

Financial Statistics

Periods ended:	12m June 30/22[A]		12m June 30/21[◊A]
	A$000s	%Chg	A$000s
Operating revenue	**71,596**	**+56**	**45,971**
Cost of sales	50,758		29,120
Salaries & benefits	18,048		7,266
General & admin expense	12,542		5,019
Stock-based compensation	2,925		2,081
Other operating expense	562		449
Operating expense	**84,835**	**+93**	**43,935**
Operating income	**(13,239)**	**n.a.**	**2,036**
Deprec., depl. & amort.	455		39
Finance costs, gross	488		879
Pre-tax income	**(17,042)**	**n.a.**	**(5,688)**
Income taxes	229		140
Net income	**(17,271)**	**n.a.**	**(5,828)**
Cash & equivalent	9,364		18,616
Inventories	884		45
Accounts receivable	2,767		5,502
Current assets	13,479		24,456
Fixed assets, net	495		35
Right-of-use assets	763		nil
Intangibles, net	152		152
Total assets	**15,395**	**-38**	**24,896**
Accts. pay. & accr. liabs.	5,720		3,816
Current liabilities	7,062		5,933
Long-term debt, gross	nil		445
Long-term lease liabilities	822		nil
Shareholders' equity	7,447		18,934
Cash from oper. activs.	**(8,033)**	**n.a.**	**(1,108)**
Cash from fin. activs.	(578)		16,833
Cash from invest. activs.	(198)		(40)
Net cash position	**9,364**	**-50**	**18,616**
Capital expenditures	(198)		(69)
	A$		A$
Earnings per share*	(0.38)		(0.15)
Cash flow per share*	(0.18)		(0.03)
	shs		shs
No. of shs. o/s*	45,563,056		44,744,034
Avg. no. of shs. o/s*	45,389,074		38,258,594
	%		%
Net profit margin	(24.12)		(12.68)
Return on equity	(130.94)		(57.82)
Return on assets	(83.28)		(34.04)

* Common
[◊] Restated
[A] Reported in accordance with IFRS

Latest Results

Periods ended:	9m Mar. 31/23[A]		9m Mar. 31/22[A]
	A$000s	%Chg	A$000s
Operating revenue	57,768	+2	56,528
Net income	(2,341)	n.a.	(8,426)
	A$		A$
Earnings per share*	(0.05)		(0.19)

* Common
[A] Reported in accordance with IFRS

Historical Summary
(as originally stated)

Fiscal Year	Oper. Rev.	Net Inc. Bef. Disc.	EPS*
	A$000s	A$000s	A$
2022[A]	71,596	(17,271)	(0.38)
2021[A1]	45,971	(5,828)	(0.15)
2020[A2]	6,787	(4,135)	n.a.
2019[A]	7,988	(2,067)	n.a.

* Common
[A] Reported in accordance with IFRS
[1] Results reflect the Dec. 23, 2020, reverse takeover acquisition of BTC Corporation Holdings Pty Ltd.
[2] Results for fiscal 2020 and prior periods pertain to BTC Corporation Holdings Pty Ltd.
Note: Adjusted throughout for 1-for-4.66667 cons. in Jan. 2021

B.28 Base Carbon Inc.

Symbol - BCBN **Exchange** - NEO **CUSIP** - 06975E
Head Office - 902-18 King St E, Toronto, ON, M5C 1C4 **Telephone** - (647) 264-5305
Website - www.basecarbon.com
Email - ryan@basecarbon.com
Investor Relations - Ryan Hornby (647) 264-5305
Auditors - KPMG LLP C.A., Toronto, Ont.
Transfer Agents - Marrelli Trust Company Limited, Vancouver, B.C.
Employees - 10 at Mar. 1, 2022
Profile - (Ont. 2022; orig. B.C., 2021) Sources, finances and develops carbon offset projects and trading carbon credits.

Pipeline of potential carbon reduction projects include energy efficiency (cook stoves/water purifiers), forestry (afforestation/reforestation) and nascent (biochar, mangroves, seagrass, regenerative agriculture) projects, with a focus on those that have higher quality nature-based solutions such as reforestation, soil carbon and other projects attributed with permanent removal such as carbon capture, usage and storage technologies. The pipeline of projects could collectively account for an estimated reduction of more than 1 billion tonnes of carbon credits.

Predecessor Detail - Name changed from 1287411 B.C. Ltd., Feb. 22, 2022, pursuant to the reverse takeover acquisition of Base Carbon Corp. and concurrent amalgamation of Base Carbon with wholly owned 1000095223 Ontario Inc.

Directors - Michael Costa, chr. & CEO, Toronto, Ont.; Andrew Fedak, chief strategy officer, Menlo Park, Calif.; Catherine A. Flax†, N.Y.; Margot Naudie, Toronto, Ont.; Bruce Tozer, Wilts., United Kingdom

Other Exec. Officers - Wesley (Wes) Fulford, pres.; Philip Hardwick, COO; Kwesi Marshall, CFO; Ryan Hornby, chief legal officer & corp. sec.
† Lead director

Capital Stock

	Authorized (shs.)	Outstanding (shs.)[1]
Preference	unlimited	nil
Common	unlimited	121,108,302

[1] At June 9, 2023

Normal Course Issuer Bid - The company plans to make normal course purchases of up to 7,974,471 common shares representing 6.6% of the total outstanding. The bid commenced on June 21, 2023, and expires on June 20, 2024.

Major Shareholder - Abaxx Technologies Inc. held 15.7% interest at Mar. 31, 2023.

Price Range - BCBN/NEO

Year	Volume	High	Low	Close
2022	2,014,000	$0.95	$0.42	$0.45

Recent Close: $0.50

Capital Stock Changes - On Feb. 23, 2022, 124,579,300 common shares were issued pursuant to the reverse takeover acquisition of Base Carbon Corp.

Wholly Owned Subsidiaries

Base Carbon Corp., Ont.
- 78% int. in **Base Carbon Capital Partners Corp.**, Barbados.
- 49.9% int. in **Hardwick Climate Business Limited**, United Kingdom.
  - 22% int. in **Base Carbon Capital Partners Corp.**, Barbados.

B.29 Battery Mineral Resources Corp.

Symbol - BMR **Exchange** - TSX-VEN **CUSIP** - 07133G
Head Office - 1900-1040 Georgia St W, Vancouver, BC, V6E 4H3 **Telephone** - (604) 229-3830
Website - www.bmrcorp.com
Email - mkostuik@bmrcorp.com
Investor Relations - Martin Kostuik (604) 229-3830
Auditors - Grant Thornton LLP C.A., Toronto, Ont.
Transfer Agents - Odyssey Trust Company, Vancouver, B.C.
Profile - (B.C. 2007) Has mineral interests in Chile, Ontario, Quebec, Idaho, Nevada and South Korea. Also supplies pipeline equipment in western Canada and the U.S

In Chile, holds lease on formerly producing Punitaqui Mining Complex, 118 km^2, 35 km south of Ovalle, with indicated resource of 6,172,000 tonnes grading 1.14% copper and 2.47 g/t silver at August 2022. Mining operation was placed on care and maintenance in 2020, with the potential commencement of restart mining activities in the third or fourth quarter of 2023.

In Ontario, holds McAra cobalt prospect, 252 km^2; Gowganda cobalt project; Shining Tree cobalt prospect, 26 km^2; Elk Lake cobalt prospect, 209 km^2, 55 km northwest of Temiskaming Shores, which includes Silverstrike cobalt prospect, Maps-Johnson cobalt prospect and 60% interest in Sunvest cobalt prospect; Wilder cobalt prospect, 220 km^2, which includes Kell claims and Thompson claims; White Reserve cobalt prospect, 130 km^2; and Cobra. At March 2020, measured and indicated resource at McAra was 34,000 tonnes grading 1.47% cobalt and 10.28 g/t silver.

In Quebec, holds formerly producing Fabre cobalt property, 18 km^2, 30 km southeast of Cobalt.

In Idaho, holds Bonanza cobalt prospect, 32 km^2, Idaho cobalt belt; and East Fork prospect.

In Nevada, Amargosa lithium prospect, 5 km^2, 130 km west of Las Vegas.

In South Korea, holds formerly producing Geuman graphite property; and formerly producing Taehwa graphite property, 79 km east-northeast of Seoul.

Wholly owned **ESI Energy Services Inc.** (dba Ozzie's) rents and sells backfill separation machines (padding machines) to mainline pipeline and utility contractors, renewables and utility construction contractors as well as oilfield pipeline and construction contractors. Ozzie's has operations in Leduc, Alta., and Phoenix, Ariz.

In November 2022, the company sold an industrial real estate property in Leduc, Alta. for an undisclosed amount.

In March 2023, option to earn 60% interest in Gowganda Big Four and Gowganda East cobalt-silver claims in Ontario was terminated and $2,043,406 related costs were written off.

Recent Merger and Acquisition Activity

Status: completed **Revised:** June 13, 2022
PREVIOUS: The transaction was completed. UPDATE: Battery Mineral Resources Corp. entered into an agreement to sell and leaseback its industrial property and building at 7102 West Sherman Street in Phoenix, Ariz., for US$6,900,000.

Predecessor Detail - Name changed from Fusion Gold Ltd., Feb. 12, 2021, pursuant to the Qualifying Transaction reverse takeover acquisition of (old) Battery Mineral Resources Corp. and concurrent amalgamation of (old) Battery Mineral with wholly owned 1234525 B.C. Ltd.; basis 1 new for 2 old shs.

Directors - Lazaros (Laz) Nikeas, exec. chr., New Canaan, Conn.; Martin Kostuik, CEO, Nashville, Tenn.; Julia B. Aspillaga, Maldonado, Uruguay; Dr. Stephen Dunmead, Ga.; John Kiernan, Vancouver, B.C.; Joseph (Joe) Tuso, N.Y.; Derek C. White, West Vancouver, B.C.

Other Exec. Officers - Max Satel, CFO; Peter J. Doyle, v-p, explor.; Dr. Henry J. Sandri, v-p, bus. devel.; Jacob Willoughby, v-p, corp. devel. & strategy; Sheryl Dhillon, corp. sec.

Capital Stock

	Authorized (shs.)	Outstanding (shs.)[1]
Common	unlimited	172,309,777

[1] At May 29, 2023

Major Shareholder - Weston Energy, LLC held 53.14% interest at Apr. 21, 2023.

Price Range - BMR/TSX-VEN

Year	Volume	High	Low	Close
2022	14,261,099	$0.48	$0.15	$0.15
2021	4,524,215	$0.90	$0.33	$0.42
2019	66,750	$0.60	$0.21	$0.33
2018	91,615	$0.60	$0.27	$0.28

Consolidation: 1-for-2 cons. in Feb. 2021
Recent Close: $0.15

Capital Stock Changes - During 2022, 833,333 common shares were issued under the restricted share unit plan.

Wholly Owned Subsidiaries

BMR Holdings Limited, Vancouver, B.C.
- 100% int. in **ESI Energy Services Inc.**, Calgary, Alta.
- 100% int. in **North American Cobalt Inc.**, United States.

Battery Mineral Resources (Nevada), Inc., United States.
Battery Mineral Resources Korea, South Korea.
ESI Energy Services (Australia) Pty Ltd., Australia.
Minera BMR S.p.A., Chile.
North American Cobalt Inc., Toronto, Ont.
Opirus Minerals Group Pty Ltd., Australia.
Ozzies, Inc., United States.

Financial Statistics

Periods ended:	12m Dec. 31/22[A]		12m Dec. 31/21[A1]
	$000s	%Chg	$000s
Operating revenue	**12,671**	**+9**	**11,614**
Cost of sales	1,254		512
General & admin expense	11,890		12,202
Stock-based compensation	3,758		2,458
Operating expense	**16,902**	**+11**	**15,173**
Operating income	**(4,231)**	**n.a.**	**(3,559)**
Deprec., depl. & amort.	3,015		3,615
Finance income	n.a.		127
Finance costs, gross	2,448		267
Write-downs/write-offs	(841)		(2,402)[2]
Pre-tax income	**(2,189)**	**n.a.**	**(12,198)**
Income taxes	1,307		1,554
Net inc bef disc ops, eqhldrs	(3,496)		(13,329)
Net inc bef disc ops, NCI	nil		(424)
Net income	**(3,496)**	**n.a.**	**(13,752)**
Net inc. for equity hldrs	**(3,496)**	**n.a.**	**(13,329)**
Net inc. for non-cont. int	**nil**	**n.a.**	**(424)**
Cash & equivalent	4,254		2,630
Accounts receivable	3,178		3,746
Current assets	7,660		8,896
Fixed assets, net	53,089		40,564
Intangibles, net	160		182
Explor./devel. properties	46,655		31,505
Total assets	**107,563**	**+33**	**81,147**
Bank indebtedness	2,073		nil
Accts. pay. & accr. liabs	3,121		3,767
Current liabilities	14,291		12,092
Long-term debt, gross	13,089		4,715
Long-term debt, net	12,461		4,187
Long-term lease liabilities	1,351		nil
Shareholders' equity	64,489		59,789
Cash from oper. activs	**(112)**	**n.a.**	**1,997**
Cash from fin. activs	6,604		11,913
Cash from invest. activs	(4,943)		(25,494)
Net cash position	**4,254**	**+62**	**2,630**
Capital expenditures	(16,267)		(24,497)
Capital disposals	14,417		nil
	$		$
Earnings per share*	(0.02)		(0.09)
Cash flow per share*	(0.00)		0.01
	shs		shs
No. of shs. o/s*	171,705,612		170,872,279
Avg. no. of shs. o/s*	171,500,133		158,099,142
	%		%
Net profit margin	(27.59)		(118.41)
Return on equity	(5.63)		(23.08)
Return on assets	0.44		(17.82)
Foreign sales percent	79		81

* Common

[A] Reported in accordance with IFRS

[1] Results reflect the Feb. 12, 2021, reverese takeover acquisition of (old) Battery Mineral Resources Corp.

[2] Includes a $2,23,808 impairment on certain claims in Gowganda cobalt project.

Latest Results

Periods ended:	3m Mar. 31/23[A]		3m Mar. 31/22[oA]
	$000s	%Chg	$000s
Operating revenue	2,725	+9	2,489
Net income	(2,383)	n.a.	(1,783)
	$		$
Earnings per share*	(0.01)		(0.01)

* Common

[o] Restated

[A] Reported in accordance with IFRS

Historical Summary
(as originally stated)

Fiscal Year	Oper. Rev.	Net Inc. Bef. Disc.	EPS*
	$000s	$000s	$
2022[A]	12,671	(3,496)	(0.02)
2021[A]	11,614	(13,752)	n.a.
2020[A1]	nil	(3,872)	n.a.
2019[A]	nil	(252)	n.a.

* Common

[A] Reported in accordance with IFRS

[1] Results for 2020 and prior year pertain to (old) Battery Mineral Resources Corp.

Note: Adjusted throughout for 1-for-2 cons. in Feb. 2021

B.30 Bausch + Lomb Corporation

Symbol - BLCO **Exchange** - TSX **CUSIP** - 071705
Head Office - 520 Applewood Cres, Vaughan, ON, L4K 4B4 **Telephone** - (905) 695-7700 **Toll-free** - (800) 686-7720
Website - www.bausch.com
Email - ir@bauschhealth.com
Investor Relations - Mark Maico (877) 281-6642
Auditors - PricewaterhouseCoopers LLP C.P.A., Florham Park, N.J.
Transfer Agents - TSX Trust Company, Toronto, Ont.
FP500 Subsidiary Revenue Ranking - 16
Employees - 12,900 at Dec. 31, 2022

Profile - (Can. 2020) Develops, manufactures and markets branded and branded generic pharmaceuticals, over-the-counter (OTC) products and medical devices in the area of eye health.

Operations consist of three segments: Vision Care; Ophthalmic Pharmaceuticals; and Surgical.

Vision care products include contact lens, eye vitamin and mineral supplements, multipurpose solutions, OTC eye drops, cleaning and conditioning solutions for rigid gas permeable (RGP) lenses, re-wetting drops and saline solutions. Key brands include Bausch + Lomb INFUSE®, Bausch + Lomb ULTRA®, Biotrue® ONEday, AQUALOX™, PureVision® and SofLens® (contact lens); PreserVision® AREDS 2 and Ocuvite® (eye vitamin and nutritional supplement); Biotrue®, Bausch + Lomb Renu® and Boston® (contact lens solution); Artelac® (eye moisturizer eye drop); and LUMIFY® (ocular redness reliever eye drop).

Ophthalmic pharmaceuticals products include proprietary and generic pharmaceutical products for post-operative treatments and treatments for a number of eye conditions such as glaucoma, eye inflammation, ocular hypertension, dry eyes and retinal diseases. Key brands include XIPERE® (macular edema associated with uveitis); Vyzulta® (intraocular pressure related with open angle glaucoma or ocular hypertension); Lotemax® (post-ocular surgery inflammation and pain); Besivance® (bacterial conjunctivitis); Visudyne® (predominantly classic subfoveal choroidal neovascularization); Minims® portfolio which includes ocular anaesthetics, corticosteroids, mydriatics, cycloplegics, artificial tears, irrigating solutions and diagnostic stain products; Prolensa® (post-cataract surgery inflammation and pain); Lotemax® (post-ocular surgery inflammation and pain); Alrex® (seasonal allergic conjunctivitis); and Zylet® (steroid-responsive inflammatory ocular conditions).

Surgical products include medical device equipment, consumables and instrumental tools, and technologies. Key brands include Stellaris Elite® (vision enhancement system for vitreoretinal surgery and cataract procedures); Synergetics® (vitreoretinal surgery instruments); VICTUS® (femtosecond laser for cataract and corneal refractive surgery); Teneo™ (excimer laser system for corneal refractive surgery); Akreos®, enVista®, Crystalens® and Trulign® (ophthalmic surgical intraocular lenses); and Storz® (ophthalmic instruments).

On Dec. 12, 2022, the company acquired private Red Bud, Ill.-based **Total Titanium, Inc.**, an ophthalmic microsurgical instrument and machined parts manufacturing company. Terms were not disclosed.

On Nov. 21, 2022, the company acquired private Portland, Ore.-based **Paragon BioTeck, Inc.**, an eye-care focused drug development company primarily focused on the early detection of ocular diseases. Terms were not disclosed.

Recent Merger and Acquisition Activity

Status: pending **Announced:** June 30, 2023
Bausch + Lomb Corporation agreed to acquire XIIDRA® (lifitegrast ophthalmic solution) 5%, a prescription eye drop solution indicated for the treatment of the signs and symptoms of dry eye disease, as well as libvatrep and AcuStream from Novartis AG for up to US$2.5 billion, including an upfront payment of US$1.75 billion in cash with potential milestone obligations up to US$750,000,000 based on sales thresholds and pipeline commercialization. The transaction is expected to close by the end of 2023

Status: completed **Announced:** Jan. 17, 2023
Bausch + Lomb Corporation acquired Irvine, Calif.-based AcuFocus, Inc. for an upfront purchase price of US$35,000,000, of which US$31,000,000 was paid and the remaining purchase price was to be paid within 18 months following the transaction, less any amounts that are the subject of any indemnification claims. AcuFocus develops and manufactures small aperture intraocular products for cataract patients. Products include IC-8® Apthera™ intraocular lens (IOL), a wavefront-filtering intraocular lens for unilateral implantation in certain patients who have been diagnosed with bilateral operable cataracts.

Status: completed **Revised:** May 10, 2022
UPDATE: The offering was completed. PREVIOUS: Bausch Health Companies Inc. priced a secondary initial public offering (IPO) of 35,000,000 common shares of Bausch + Lomb Corporation at US$18 per share. Underwriters were granted an option to purchase up to an additional 5,250,000 common shares from Bausch Health. Bausch + Lomb would not receive any of the proceeds from the IPO. The common shares of Bausch + Lomb commenced trading on the NYSE and on an "if, as and when issued basis" on the TSX on May 6, 2022. On closing, Bausch Health, would hold 90% of the common shares of Bausch + Lomb (88.5% if over-allotment option is exercised in full).

Directors - Brenton L. (Brent) Saunders, chr. & CEO, Fla.; Thomas W. Ross Sr.†, N.C.; Nathalie Bernier, Montréal, Qué.; Richard U. (Dick) DeSchutter, Calif.; Gary Hu, Fla.; Brett Icahn, Fla.; Sarah B. Kavanagh, Toronto, Ont.; John A. Paulson, N.Y.; Russel C. Robertson, Toronto, Ont.; Dr. Andrew C. von Eschenbach, Tex.

Other Exec. Officers - T. J. Crawford, chief commun. officer; Jonathan Kellerman, chief compliance officer; Manisha Narasimhan, chief corp. devel. & digital officer; Robert D. (Bob) Bailey, exec. v-p & chief legal officer; Sam Eldessouky, exec. v-p & CFO; Asli Gevgilili, exec. v-p & chief HR officer; Dr. Yehia Hashad, exec. v-p, R&D & CMO; Al Waterhouse, exec. v-p & chief supply chain & opers. officer; Louis Yu, exec. v-p & chief quality officer; Joseph F. (Joe) Gordon, pres., global consumer, surgical & vision care; Andrew Stewart, pres., ophthalmic pharmaceuticals

† Lead director

Capital Stock

	Authorized (shs.)	Outstanding (shs.)[1]
Common	unlimited	350,258,115

[1] At Apr. 28, 2023

Major Shareholder - Bausch Health Companies Inc. held 89% interest at Aug. 3, 2023.

Price Range - BLCO/TSX

Year	Volume	High	Low	Close
2022	1,063,437	$25.75	$15.95	$21.04

Recent Close: $24.61

Capital Stock Changes - During 2022, 749 common shares were issued for cash.

Wholly Owned Subsidiaries

AcuFocus Australia Pty. Ltd., Australia.
AcuFocus Holdings, Inc., Del.
AcuFocus, Inc., Irvine, Calif.
Alden Optical Laboratories, Inc., N.Y.
Audrey Enterprise, LLC, Del.
BAUSCH HEALTH LLC, Belarus.
BL Indústria Ótica Ltda., Brazil.
BLEP Holding GmbH, Germany.
B.L.J. Company, Ltd., Japan.
Bausch & Lomb Americas Inc., Del.
Bausch & Lomb Argentina S.R.L., Argentina.
Bausch & Lomb Australia Holdings Pty Limited, Australia.
Bausch & Lomb (Australia) Pty Limited, Australia.
Bausch & Lomb France S.A.S., France.
Bausch & Lomb Gesellschaft m.b.H., Austria.
Bausch & Lomb GmbH, Germany.
Bausch & Lomb (Hong Kong) Limited, Hong Kong, People's Republic of China.
Bausch & Lomb IOM S.p.A., Italy.
Bausch & Lomb Incorporated, Rochester, N.Y.
Bausch & Lomb India Private Limited, India.
Bausch + Lomb Ireland Limited, Ireland.
Bausch & Lomb Korea Co. Ltd., South Korea.
Bausch & Lomb (Malaysia) Sdn. Bhd., Malaysia.
Bausch & Lomb México Holdings S.A. de C.V., Mexico.
Bausch & Lomb (New Zealand) Limited, New Zealand.
Bausch & Lomb Nordic AB, Sweden.
Bausch & Lomb Pharma S.A., Belgium.
Bausch & Lomb Philippines Inc., Philippines.
Bausch & Lomb Poland sp. z.o.o., Poland.
Bausch & Lomb S.A., Spain.
Bausch & Lomb Saglik ve Optik Urunleri Tic. A.S., Türkiye.
Bausch & Lomb (Shanghai) Trading Co., Ltd., People's Republic of China.
Bausch & Lomb (Singapore) Private Limited, Singapore.
Bausch & Lomb (South Africa) (Pty) Ltd., South Africa.
Bausch & Lomb South Asia, Inc., Del.
Bausch & Lomb Swiss AG, Switzerland.
Bausch & Lomb Taiwan Limited, Republic of China.
Bausch & Lomb (Thailand) Limited, Thailand.
Bausch & Lomb U.K. Limited, United Kingdom.
Bausch Foundation, LLC, Del.
Bausch Health Hellas Single-Member Pharmaceuticals S.A., Greece.
Bausch Health Korea Co., Limited, South Korea.
Bausch Health Limited Liability Company, Russia.
"Bausch Health" LLC, Ukraine.
Bausch Health LLP, Kazakhstan.
Bausch Health Perú S.R.L., Peru.
Bausch Health Romania S.R.L., Romania.
Bausch Health Trading DWC-LLC, United Arab Emirates.
Bausch+Lomb Dutch Holdings B.V., Netherlands.
Bausch+Lomb Netherlands B.V., Netherlands.
Beijing Bausch & Lomb Eyecare Co., Ltd., People's Republic of China.
Bescon Co., Ltd., South Korea.
Dr. Gerhard Mann chem.-pharm. Fabrik GmbH, Germany.
Dr. Robert Winzer Pharma GmbH, Germany.
Eye Essentials LLC, Del.
Grundstücksverwaltungsgesellschaft Dr. Gerhard Mann chem.-pharm. Fabrik GmbH, Germany.
Laboratoire Chauvin S.A.S., France.
Natur Produkt Europe B.V., Netherlands.
PT Bausch Lomb Indonesia, Indonesia.
Paragon BioTeck, Inc., Nev.
PharmaSwiss drustvo s ogranicenom odgovornoscu za trgovinu i usluge, Croatia.
Shandong Bausch & Lomb Freda New Packing Materials Co., Ltd., People's Republic of China.
Shandong Bausch & Lomb Freda Pharmaceutical Co., Ltd., People's Republic of China.
Sino Concept Technology Limited, Hong Kong, People's Republic of China.
Soflens (Pty) Ltd., South Africa.
Sterimedix Limited, United Kingdom.
Synergetics IP, Inc., Del.
Synergetics, Inc., Mo.
Technolas Perfect Vision GmbH, Germany.
Total Titanium, Inc., Ill.
Unilens Corp. USA, Largo, Fla.
Unilens Vision Sciences, Inc., Wilmington, Del.
Valeant Med Sp.zo.o, Poland.
Visioncare Devices, Inc., Calif.
Waicon Vision S.A., Argentina.

Financial Statistics

Periods ended:	12m Dec. 31/22^A		12m Dec. 31/21^A1
	US$000s	%Chg	US$000s
Operating revenue	**3,768,000**	**0**	**3,765,000**
Cost of goods sold	1,511,000		1,458,000
Cost of sales	8,000		9,000
Research & devel. expense	307,000		271,000
General & admin expense	1,343,000		1,266,000
Operating expense	**3,169,000**	**+5**	**3,004,000**
Operating income	**599,000**	**-21**	**761,000**
Deprec., depl. & amort.	379,000		415,000
Finance income	6,000		nil
Finance costs, gross	146,000		nil
Pre-tax income	**73,000**	**-77**	**318,000**
Income taxes	58,000		125,000
Net income	**15,000**	**-92**	**193,000**
Net inc. for equity hldrs	**6,000**	**-97**	**182,000**
Net inc. for non-cont. int.	**9,000**	**-18**	**11,000**
Cash & equivalent	380,000		177,000
Inventories	628,000		572,000
Accounts receivable	724,000		721,000
Current assets	2,137,000		1,635,000
Fixed assets, net	1,300,000		1,225,000
Intangibles, net	6,565,000		6,850,000
Total assets	**11,144,000**	**+3**	**10,823,000**
Accts. pay. & accr. liabs.	370,000		239,000
Current liabilities	1,296,000		1,099,000
Long-term debt, gross	2,436,000		nil
Long-term debt, net	2,411,000		nil
Shareholders' equity	7,033,000		9,329,000
Non-controlling interest	68,000		73,000
Cash from oper. activs.	**345,000**	**-60**	**873,000**
Cash from fin. activs.	81,000		(712,000)
Cash from invest. activs.	(215,000)		(214,000)
Net cash position	**380,000**	**+115**	**177,000**
Capital expenditures	(175,000)		(193,000)
Unfunded pension liability	20,000		43,000
	US$		US$
Earnings per share*	0.02		n.a.
Cash flow per share*	0.99		n.a.
	shs		shs
No. of shs. o/s*	350,000,749		n.a.
Avg. no. of shs. o/s*	350,000,000		n.a.
	%		%
Net profit margin	0.40		5.13
Return on equity	0.07		1.89
Return on assets	0.41		1.75
Foreign sales percent	97		97
No. of employees (FTEs)	12,900		n.a.

* Common

^A Reported in accordance with U.S. GAAP

[1] Represent the results of Bausch + Lomb (a Business of Bausch Health Companies Inc.)

Latest Results

Periods ended:	3m Mar. 31/23^A		3m Mar. 31/22^A
	US$000s	%Chg	US$000s
Operating revenue	931,000	+5	889,000
Net income	(88,000)	n.a.	23,000
Net inc. for equity hldrs.	(90,000)	n.a.	20,000
Net inc. for non-cont. int.	2,000		3,000
	US$		US$
Earnings per share*	(0.26)		n.a.

* Common

^A Reported in accordance with U.S. GAAP

Historical Summary
(as originally stated)

Fiscal Year	Oper. Rev.	Net Inc. Bef. Disc.	EPS*
	US$000s	US$000s	US$
2022^A	3,768,000	15,000	0.02
2021^A	3,765,000	193,000	n.a.
2020^A	3,412,000	(17,000)	n.a.

* Common

^A Reported in accordance with U.S. GAAP

B.31 Bausch Health Companies Inc.*

Symbol - BHC **Exchange** - TSX **CUSIP** - 071734
Head Office - 2150 boul St Elzéar O, Laval, QC, H7L 4A8 **Telephone** - (514) 744-6792 **Toll-free** - (800) 361-1448 **Fax** - (514) 744-6272
Exec. Office - 400 Somerset Corporate Blvd, Bridgewater, NJ, United States, 08807 **Telephone** - (908) 927-1400 **Toll-free** - (866) 246-8245
Website - www.bauschhealth.com
Email - ir@bauschhealth.com
Investor Relations - Mark Maico (877) 281-6642
Auditors - PricewaterhouseCoopers LLP C.P.A., Florham Park, N.J.
Bankers - The Bank of Nova Scotia
Lawyers - Sullivan & Cromwell LLP; Proskauer Rose LLP, New York, N.Y.; Davies Ward Phillips & Vineberg LLP, Toronto, Ont.
Transfer Agents - TSX Trust Company, Montréal, Qué.
FP500 Revenue Ranking - 57
Employees - 19,900 at Dec. 31, 2022
Profile - (B.C. 2013; orig. Ont., 1994 amalg.) Develops, manufactures and markets branded, generic and branded generic pharmaceuticals, over-the-counter (OTC) products and medical aesthetic devices primarily in the areas of gastroenterology and dermatology. Also owns 89% interest in **Bausch + Lomb Corporation**, which develops, manufactures and markets branded and branded generic pharmaceuticals, OTC products and medical devices in the area of eye health.

Products are organized into five segments: Bausch + Lomb; Salix; International; Diversified Products; and Solta Medical. The product portfolio consists of 1,100 products, which are sold directly or indirectly to pharmacies, hospitals, physicians, drug store chains and wholesalers in 100 countries.

Bausch + Lomb

This segment consists of the global Bausch + Lomb eye health business conducted through subsidiary Bausch + Lomb Corporation, which includes vision care, surgical and ophthalmic pharmaceuticals products.

Principal products of Bausch + Lomb includes PreserVision® AREDS 2 and Ocuvite® (eye vitamin and nutritional supplement); Biotrue® and Bausch + Lomb Renu® (contact lens solution); LUMIFY® (ocular redness reliever eye drop); Bausch + Lomb INFUSE®, Bausch + Lomb ULTRA® and Biotrue® ONEday (contact lens); Stellaris Elite® (vision enhancement system for vitreoretinal surgery and cataract procedures); Synergetics® (vitreoretinal surgery instruments); VICTUS® (femtosecond laser for cataract and corneal refractive surgery); and Lotemax® SM (gel drop for postoperative inflammation and pain treatment).

Salix

This segment consists of sales in the U.S. of gastrointestinal products including Xifaxan® (irritable bowel syndrome with diarrhoea, hepatic encephalopathy and travelers' diarrhoea), Relistor® (opioid-induced constipation), Trulance® (chronic idiopathic constipation and irritable bowel syndrome with constipation) and Glumetza® (type 2 diabetes).

International

This segment consists of sales of branded and branded generic pharmaceutical products and OTC products (other than sales of Bausch + Lomb products and Solta aesthetic medical devices) in Canada, Europe, Asia, Latin America, Africa and the Middle East. Principal products are Bisocard® (hypertension, angina pectoris or heart failure), Thrombo ASS® (thrombotic complications), Contrave®/Mysimba® (obesity), Jublia® (toenail fungus), Espaven® (a line of gastrointestinal treatments) and Bedoyecta® (multivitamin) and Arazlo® Lotion (acne).

Diversified Products

This segment consists of sales in the U.S. of: (i) pharmaceutical products in the areas of neurology and certain other therapeutic classes; (ii) generic products; (iii) Ortho Dermatologics (dermatological) products; and (iv) dentistry products.

Principal products are Wellbutrin XL® and Aplenzin® (anti-depressants), Cuprimine® (Wilson's disease, cystinuria and severe arthritis), Mysoline® (anticonvulsant), Ativan® (anxiety disorders), Xenazine® (chorea associated with Huntington's disease), Syprine® (Wilson's disease) and Librax® (emotional and somatic factors in gastrointestinal disorders, peptic ulcers, irritable bowel syndrome and acute enterocolitis) under neurology and other pharmaceuticals product portfolio; Diastat® rectal gel (epilepsy), Uceris® (ulcerative colitis) and Elidel® (atopic dermatitis) under the generic product portfolio; Targretin® (skin problems from cutaneous T-cell lymphoma), Bryhali®, Siliq® and Duobrii® (moderate-to-severe psoriasis), Jublia® (toenail fungus) and an acne portfolio including Solodyn®, Retin-A®, Clindagel®, Altreno®, Arazlo® and Onexton® Gel under the dermatological unit; and Arestin® (dental antibiotic), NeutraSal® (dryness of the mouth and oral mucosa) and OSSIX® (a line of cross-linked collagen regenerative products for guided bone and tissue regeneration procedures) for the dentistry segment.

Solta Medical

This segment consists of global sales of Solta aesthetic medical devices such as Thermage®, Fraxel®, Clear + Brilliant® and VASERlipo® that are collectively tailored to address and improve a broad range of skin and body treatment needs including skin tightening, resurfacing and rejuvenation.

On June 16, 2022, the company announced it has suspended plans for an initial public offering (IPO) of its Solta Medical business, which develops, manufactures and sells aesthetic medical devices.

On Aug. 6, 2020, the company announced its intention to spin off its Bausch + Lomb eye health business into an independent publicly traded company. In connection, wholly owned **Bausch + Lomb Corporation** was formed to represent the company's global eye health business. Bausch + Lomb began trading on the New York Stock Exchange and the Toronto Stock Exchange on May 6, 2022, and completed an initial public offering (IPO) on May 10, 2022. The full separation of Bausch + Lomb was expected to be completed after the expiry of customary lockups related to the IPO and achievement of targeted debt leverage ratios, subject to the receipt of applicable shareholder and other necessary approvals and market conditions.

Recent Merger and Acquisition Activity

Status: completed **Revised:** May 10, 2022
UPDATE: The offering was completed. PREVIOUS: Bausch Health Companies Inc. priced a secondary initial public offering (IPO) of 35,000,000 common shares of Bausch + Lomb Corporation at US$18 per share. Underwriters were granted an option to purchase up to an additional 5,250,000 common shares from Bausch Health. Bausch + Lomb would not receive any of the proceeds from the IPO. The common shares of Bausch + Lomb commenced trading on the NYSE and on an "if, as and when issued basis" on the TSX on May 6, 2022. On closing, Bausch Health, would hold 90% of the common shares of Bausch + Lomb (88.5% if over-allotment option is exercised in full).

Predecessor Detail - Name changed from Valeant Pharmaceuticals International, Inc., July 13, 2018.

Directors - John A. Paulson, chr., N.Y.; Thomas J. (Tom) Appio, CEO, N.J.; Brett Icahn, Fla.; Sarah B. Kavanagh, Toronto, Ont.; Steven D. Miller, Fla.; Dr. Richard C. Mulligan, Mass.; Robert N. Power, Pa.; Russel C. Robertson, Toronto, Ont.; Thomas W. Ross Sr., N.C.; Dr. Amy B. Wechsler, N.Y.

Other Exec. Officers - Dr. Tage Ramakrishna, CMO & pres., R&D; Seana Carson, exec. v-p & gen. counsel; Thomas G. (Tom) Vadaketh, exec. v-p & CFO; John Barresi, sr. v-p, chief acctg. officer & contr.; Mirza Dautbegovic, sr. v-p & COO; Kathleen Fitzpatrick, sr. v-p & chief HR officer; Jeff Hartness, sr. v-p, market access, comml. opers., neurology, generics & govt. affairs; Cees Heiman, sr. v-p, Europe & Canada; Dr. Graham Jackson, sr. v-p & chief quality officer; Donald Pearl, sr. v-p, ortho dermatologics; Fernando Zarate, v-p, Latin America

Capital Stock

	Authorized (shs.)	Outstanding (shs.)[1]
Common	unlimited	364,334,264

[1] At July 28, 2023

Options - At Dec. 31, 2022, options were outstanding to purchase 10,800,000 common shares at a weighted average exercise price of US$26.83 per share with a weighted average remaining contractual life of 6 years.

Major Shareholder - Widely held at Mar. 17, 2023.

Price Range - BHC/TSX

Year	Volume	High	Low	Close
2022	280,322,948	$35.68	$5.10	$8.50
2021	128,295,198	$43.97	$26.51	$34.94
2020	185,799,548	$39.70	$16.30	$26.41
2019	189,755,630	$42.15	$24.89	$38.87
2018	303,149,556	$36.52	$18.62	$25.25

Recent Close: $11.23

Capital Stock Changes - During 2022, 2,493,098 common shares were issued under share-based compensation plans.

Long-Term Debt - Outstanding at Dec. 31, 2022:

Revolv. credit facility due Feb. 2027[1]	US$470,000,000
Term loan facility due Feb. 2027[2]	2,392,000,000
Senior notes:	
5.5% due Nov. 2025	1,672,000,000
9% due Dec. 2025	951,000,000
9.25% due Apr. 2026	737,000,000
8.5% due Jan. 2027	644,000,000
6.125% due Feb. 2027	987,000,000
5.75% due Aug. 2027	496,000,000
7% due Jan. 2028	170,000,000
5% due Jan. 2028	429,000,000
4.875% due June 2028	1,583,000,000
11% due Sept. 2028	2,826,000,000
6.25% due Feb. 2029	813,000,000
5% due Feb. 2029	448,000,000
7.25% due May 2029	334,000,000
5.25% due Jan. 2030	771,000,000
14% due Oct. 2030	711,000,000
5.25% due Feb. 2031	458,000,000
Other debt	12,000,000
Bausch + Lomb Corp. cr. facility	2,439,000,000
1375209 B.C. Ltd.	
9% notes due Jan. 2028	1,423,000,000
	20,766,000,000
Less: Current portion	432,000,000
	20,334,000,000

[1] Bears interest at either: (i) term SOFR rate for the interest period relevant to such borrowing; or (ii) a base rate determined by reference to the highest of: (a) the prime rate (as defined in the 2022 Amended Credit Agreement), (b) federal funds effective rate plus 0.5% and (c) term SOFR rate for a period of one month plus 1% (or if such rate shall not be ascertainable, 1.5%) (provided, however that the term SOFR rate with respect to the facility shall at no time be less than 0.5% per annum). In each case, plus an applicable margin.

[2] Borrowings can be made in U.S. dollars, Canadian dollars or Euros. For U.S. dollar borrowings, bears interest at either: (i) term SOFR rate (subject to a floor of 0.00% per annum); or (ii) a U.S. dollar base rate. For Canadian dollar borrowings, bears interest at either: (i) CDOR; or (ii) a Canadian dollar prime rate. For Euro borrowings, bears interest at EURIBOR for the interest period relevant to such borrowing (subject to a floor of 0.00% per annum). In each case, plus an applicable margin. Term SOFR rate loans are subject to a credit spread adjustment ranging from 0.10%-0.25%.

Minimum long-term debt repayments were reported as follows:

2023	US$150,000,000
2024	150,000,000
2025	2,789,000,000
2026	891,000,000
2027	6,938,000,000
Thereafter	8,192,000,000

Wholly Owned Subsidiaries

Amoun Pharmaceutical Romania SRL, Romania.
Bausch & Lomb Americas Inc., Del.
Bausch & Lomb Mexico, S.A. de C.V., Mexico.
Bausch & Lomb Saglik ve Optik Urunleri Tic. A.S., Türkiye.
Bausch Health Americas, Inc., Del.
Bausch Health Australia Pty Ltd., Australia.
Bausch Health, Canada Inc., Canada.

Bausch Health France S.A.S., France.
Bausch Health HoldCo Limited, Ireland.
Bausch Health Ireland Limited, Ireland.
Bausch Health Magyarország Korlátolt Felelősségû Társaság, Hungary.
Bausch Health Poland sp.zo.o, Poland.
Bausch Health Slovakia s.r.o., Slovakia.
Bausch Health US, LLC, Del.
Bausch Health Ukraine Limited Liability Company, Ukraine.
Bausch Pharma Kazakhstan LLP, Kazakhstan.
Bausch RUMO Holdings Limited Liability, Russia.
Bausch+Lomb OPS B.V., Netherlands.
Cambridge Pharmaceutical S.A.S., Colombia.
Emo-Farm Sp.zo.o, Poland.
Farmatech S.A., Colombia.
Humax Pharmaceutical S.A., Colombia.
ICN Egypt LLC, Egypt.
ICN Polfa Rzeszow S.A., Poland.
Laboratorios Fedal, S.A., Mexico.
Laboratorios Grossman, S.A., Mexico.
Medicis Pharmaceutical Corporation, Del.
Medpharma Pharmaceutical & Chemical Industries LLC, Sharjah, United Arab Emirates.
Nysco de Mexico, S.A. de C.V., Mexico.
Oceana Therapeutics Limited, Ireland.
Oceanside Pharmaceuticals, Inc., Del.
12279967 Canada Ltd., Canada.
12283778 Canada Ltd., Canada.
1261229 B.C. Ltd., B.C.
1375209 B.C. Ltd., B.C.
OraPharma, Inc., Horsham, Pa.
PharmaSwiss BH drustvo za trgovinu na veliko d.o.o., Bosnia and Herzegovina.
PharmaSwiss Ceska republika s.r.o., Czech Republic.
PharmaSwiss d.o.o., Beograd, Serbia.
PharmaSwiss d.o.o., Slovenia.
PharmaSwiss EOOD, Bulgaria.
PharmaSwiss S.A., Zug, Switzerland.
PharmaSwiss, UAB, Lithuania.
PreCision Dermatology, Inc., Cumberland, R.I.
Przedsiebiorstwo Farmaceutyczne Jelfa S.A., Poland.
Salix Pharmaceuticals, Inc., Calif.
Salix Pharmaceuticals, Ltd., Raleigh, N.C.
Santarus, Inc., Del.
Solta Malaysia Sdn. Bhd., Malaysia.
Solta Medical Australia Pty Limited, Australia.
Solta Medical Corporation, Canada.
Solta Medical Distribution, LLC, Del.
Solta Medical Dutch Holdings B.V., Netherlands.
Solta Medical France, France.
Solta Medical Germany GmbH, Germany.
Solta Medical Hong Kong Limited, Hong Kong, People's Republic of China.
Solta Medical Iberia S.L., Spain.
Solta Medical, Inc, Hayward, Calif.
Solta Medical Ireland Limited, Ireland.
Solta Medical Italy S.R.L., Italy.
Solta Medical Korea Limited, South Korea.
Solta Medical Philippines Inc., Philippines.
Solta Medical Poland sp. z.o.o., Poland.
Solta Medical Singapore Private Limited, Singapore.
Solta Medical (Thailand) Limited, Thailand.
Solta Medical UK Limited, United Kingdom.
Solta (Shanghai) Health Management Co., Ltd., People's Republic of China.
Solta Taiwan Limited, Republic of China.
Tecnofarma, S.A. de C.V., Mexico.
UAB PharmaSwiss, Lithuania.
V-BAC Holding Corp., Canada.
VRX Holdco LLC, Del.
Valeant Canada GP Limited, Canada.
Valeant Canada Limited, Canada.
Valeant Canada S.E.C., Canada.
Valeant Farmacéutica Panamá, S.A., Panama.
Valeant Finance Luxembourg S.A.R.L., Luxembourg.
Valeant Holdings Ireland Unlimited Company, Ireland.
Valeant Servicios y Administración, S. de R.L. de C.V., Mexico.
Wirra Holdings Pty Ltd., Australia.

Subsidiaries

89% int. in **Bausch + Lomb Corporation**, Vaughan, Ont. (see separate coverage)

Financial Statistics

Periods ended:	12m Dec. 31/22[A]		12m Dec. 31/21[A]
	US$000s	%Chg	US$000s
Operating revenue	**8,124,000**	**-4**	**8,434,000**
Cost of goods sold	2,336,000		2,361,000
Cost of sales	28,000		33,000
Research & devel. expense	529,000		465,000
General & admin expense	2,446,000		2,447,000
Operating expense	**5,339,000**	**+1**	**5,306,000**
Operating income	**2,785,000**	**-11**	**3,128,000**
Deprec., depl. & amort.	1,394,000		1,552,000
Finance income	14,000		7,000
Finance costs, gross	1,464,000		1,426,000
Write-downs/write-offs	(839,000)[1]		(703,000)[2]
Pre-tax income	**(129,000)**	**n.a.**	**(1,024,000)**
Income taxes	83,000		(87,000)
Net income	**(212,000)**	**n.a.**	**(937,000)**
Net inc. for equity hldrs	**(225,000)**	**n.a.**	**(948,000)**
Net inc. for non-cont. int.	**13,000**	**+18**	**11,000**
Cash & equivalent	591,000		2,119,000
Inventories	1,090,000		993,000
Accounts receivable	1,790,000		1,775,000
Current assets	4,247,000		5,607,000
Fixed assets, net	1,600,000		1,598,000
Right-of-use assets	221,000		247,000
Intangibles, net	17,347,000		19,405,000
Total assets	**25,686,000**	**-12**	**29,202,000**
Accts. pay. & accr. liabs	521,000		407,000
Current liabilities	3,941,000		5,198,000
Long-term debt, gross	20,766,000		22,654,000
Long-term debt, net	20,334,000		22,654,000
Long-term lease liabilities	184,000		214,000
Shareholders' equity	(692,000)		(106,000)
Non-controlling interest	952,000		72,000
Cash from oper. activs	**(728,000)**	**n.a.**	**1,426,000**
Cash from fin. activs	(474,000)		(1,513,000)
Cash from invest. activs	(303,000)		409,000
Net cash position	**591,000**	**-72**	**2,119,000**
Capital expenditures	(218,000)		(269,000)
Unfunded pension liability	30,000		53,000
Pension fund surplus	n.a.		4,000
	US$		US$
Earnings per share*	(0.62)		(2.64)
Cash flow per share*	(2.01)		3.97
	shs		shs
No. of shs. o/s*	361,898,846		359,405,748
Avg. no. of shs. o/s*	362,000,000		358,900,000
	%		%
Net profit margin	(2.61)		(11.11)
Return on equity	n.m.		n.m.
Return on assets	7.99		1.22
Foreign sales percent	96		96
No. of employees (FTEs)	19,900		19,100

* Common
[A] Reported in accordance with U.S. GAAP
[1] Includes US$824,000,000 goodwill impairment of Diversified Products reporting unit.
[2] Includes US$469,000,000 goodwill impairment of Ortho Dermatologics reporting unit.

Latest Results

Periods ended:	6m June 30/23[A]		6m June 30/22[A]
	US$000s	%Chg	US$000s
Operating revenue	4,068,000	+5	3,885,000
Net income	(182,000)	n.a.	(205,000)
Net inc. for equity hldrs	(175,000)	n.a.	(214,000)
Net inc. for non-cont. int.	(7,000)		9,000
	US$		US$
Earnings per share*	(0.48)		(0.59)

* Common
[A] Reported in accordance with U.S. GAAP

Historical Summary
(as originally stated)

Fiscal Year	Oper. Rev.	Net Inc. Bef. Disc.	EPS*
	US$000s	US$000s	US$
2022[A]	8,124,000	(212,000)	(0.62)
2021[A]	8,434,000	(937,000)	(2.64)
2020[A]	8,027,000	(559,000)	(1.58)
2019[A]	8,601,000	(1,783,000)	(5.08)
2018[A]	8,380,000	(4,144,000)	(11.81)

* Common
[A] Reported in accordance with U.S. GAAP

B.32 Baylin Technologies Inc.

Symbol - BYL **Exchange** - TSX **CUSIP** - 072819
Head Office - 503-4711 Yonge St, Toronto, ON, M2N 6K8 **Telephone** - (416) 805-9127
Website - www.baylintech.com
Email - kelly.myles@baylintech.com
Investor Relations - Kelly Myles (416) 805-9127
Auditors - RSM Canada LLP C.A., Toronto, Ont.
Lawyers - Miller Thomson LLP, Toronto, Ont.
Transfer Agents - Computershare Trust Company of Canada Inc., Toronto, Ont.
FP500 Revenue Ranking - 740
Employees - 684 at Dec. 31, 2022

Profile - (Ont. 2013) Designs, manufactures and sells passive and active radio frequency (RF) and satellite communications products and services under the Advantech Wireless brand and mobile, networking and wireless infrastructure devices under the Galtronics brand.

The company operates through two segments: Galtronics; and Satellite Communications (SATCOM).

Galtronics - This segment includes wholly owned **Galtronics USA, Inc.**, which designs and manufactures wireless antenna solutions for its customers. Antennas and products are custom engineered to meet the specifications for customers' mobile, embedded and wireless infrastructure needs, including products such as distributed antenna systems (DAS), base station antennas (BSA), small cells and 5G massive MMU (multiple-input, multiple output unit) antenna modules. The segment has three interrelated antenna product lines including Asia Pacific, where the company works with original equipment manufacturer (OEM) customers to design and produce antennas from the company's plant in Vietnam for mobile phones, smartphones and tablets; Embedded Antenna, where the company works with OEM customers to design and produce antennas from the company's plant in China for home networking devices, including Wi-Fi routers, set-top boxes, 5G products and land mobile radio products; and Wireless Infrastructure, where the company works with network carrier customers and other businesses to design and produce small cell system antennas, DAS and BSA from the company's plant in China that support wireless coverage and mobile data capacity requirements.

SATCOM - This segment includes wholly owned **Advantech Wireless Technologies Inc.**, which designs and manufactures customizable radio frequency and terrestrial microwave products for highly specialized wireless communications markets; and supplies RF and microwave solid state power amplifiers, pulsed amplifiers for radar applications, transmitter and transceiver products as well as RF passive components and systems. Products are designed for broadcast, maritime and cruise ships, government and military, homeland security, direct-to-home satellite, oil and gas and wireless communications.

In February 2023, wholly owned **Galtronics Vietnam Dai Dong Co., Ltd.** (GTD) had completed the transfer of the lease of its MMU (multiple-input multiple-output unit) facility in Vietnam to third party, with the assumption of GTD's obligations under the lease. The facility was intended to be an MMU antenna contract manufacturing facility, but never became operational, in part due to the COVID-19 pandemic. The original term of the lease ran until May 29, 2029. The rental and related costs associated with the lease over its remaining term were expected to total approximately $2,700,000.

Directors - Jeffrey C. Royer, chr., Toronto, Ont.; Harold M. Wolkin, v-chr., Toronto, Ont.; Barry J. Reiter†, Toronto, Ont.; Janice Davis, Detroit, Mich.; Bejoy Pankajakshan, Tex.; David J. Saska, Mich.; Donald E. (Don) Simmonds, Uxbridge, Ont.

Other Exec. Officers - Leighton Carroll, pres. & CEO; Dan Nohdomi, sr. v-p & CFO; Mark Waddell, sr. v-p, Galtronics global mfg.; Clifford (Cliff) Gary, v-p, fin.; Neil Smith, v-p, operational fin.; Phil Mohtadi, gen. counsel; Dr. Minya Gavrilovic, pres. & chief tech. officer, Galtronics U.S.A.; John Restivo, pres., Advantech Wireless Technologies

† Lead director

Capital Stock

	Authorized (shs.)	Outstanding (shs.)[1]
Preferred	unlimited	nil
Common	unlimited	80,340,954

[1] At Mar. 30, 2023

Major Shareholder - Jeffrey C. Royer held 58% interest at Mar. 30, 2023.

Price Range - BYL/TSX

Year	Volume	High	Low	Close
2022	10,208,603	$1.00	$0.19	$0.38
2021	28,239,682	$2.14	$0.70	$0.90
2020	15,113,054	$2.50	$0.47	$0.93
2019	15,734,273	$4.50	$1.56	$2.06
2018	7,302,397	$4.29	$2.90	$3.81

Recent Close: $0.30

Capital Stock Changes - During 2022, 209,961 common shares were issued as share-based compensation.

Wholly Owned Subsidiaries

Advantech Wireless Technologies Inc., Kirkland, Qué.
- 100% int. in **Advantech Wireless Technologies (USA) Inc.**, Del.
- 99.7% int. in **Baylin Technologies Do Brasil Produtos De Telecomunicacoes Ltda.**, Brazil.

Galtronics Electronics (Wuxi) Co., Ltd., People's Republic of China.
Galtronics Korea Ltd., South Korea.
Galtronics USA, Inc., Del.
- 100% int. in **Galtronics Corporation Ltd.**, Del.

Galtronics Vietnam Co., Limited

Investments

0.3% int. in **Baylin Technologies Do Brasil Produtos De Telecomunicacoes Ltda.**, Brazil.
19% int. in **Galonics Canada Ltd.**, Ont.

Financial Statistics

Periods ended:	12m Dec. 31/22[A]		12m Dec. 31/21[A]
	$000s	%Chg	$000s
Operating revenue	**120,860**	**+18**	**102,494**
Cost of sales	67,698		68,624
Salaries & benefits	29,739		29,103
Research & devel. expense	12,918		13,358
General & admin expense	12,412		9,331
Operating expense	**122,767**	**+2**	**120,416**
Operating income	**(1,907)**	**n.a.**	**(17,922)**
Deprec., depl. & amort.	10,467		10,982
Finance costs, net	4,252		4,098
Investment income	(56)		70
Write-downs/write-offs	(72)		(25,954)
Pre-tax income	**(16,494)**	**n.a.**	**(60,749)**
Income taxes	383		6,671
Net income	**(16,877)**	**n.a.**	**(67,420)**
Cash & equivalent	7,379		19,674
Inventories	18,370		15,831
Accounts receivable	20,294		20,232
Current assets	50,453		61,086
Long-term investments	133		189
Fixed assets, net	10,344		12,491
Right-of-use assets	9,114		9,771
Intangibles, net	4,261		9,282
Total assets	**74,384**	**-20**	**93,033**
Bank indebtedness	12,688		10,787
Accts. pay. & accr. liabs.	29,963		28,573
Current liabilities	65,505		61,852
Long-term debt, gross	20,836		25,931
Long-term debt, net	nil		4,853
Long-term lease liabilities	9,611		10,651
Shareholders' equity	(3,260)		11,781
Cash from oper. activs.	**(4,981)**	**n.a.**	**(6,877)**
Cash from fin. activs.	(6,595)		16,857
Cash from invest. activs.	(1,739)		(1,412)
Net cash position	**7,379**	**-62**	**19,674**
Capital expenditures	(1,759)		(1,412)
Capital disposals	20		nil
	$		$
Earnings per share*	(0.21)		(1.09)
Cash flow per share*	(0.06)		(0.11)
	shs		shs
No. of shs. o/s*	80,304,975		80,095,014
Avg. no. of shs. o/s*	80,165,063		61,844,708
	%		%
Net profit margin	(13.96)		(65.78)
Return on equity	n.m.		(222.35)
Return on assets	(20.16)		(59.53)
Foreign sales percent	96		98
No. of employees (FTEs)	684		676

* Common
[A] Reported in accordance with IFRS

Historical Summary
(as originally stated)

Fiscal Year	Oper. Rev. $000s	Net Inc. Bef. Disc. $000s	EPS* $
2022[A]	120,860	(16,877)	(0.21)
2021[A]	102,494	(67,420)	(1.09)
2020[A]	119,739	(16,924)	(0.42)
2019[A]	153,323	(19,614)	(0.49)
2018[A]	136,214	(5,444)	(0.13)

* Common
[A] Reported in accordance with IFRS

B.33 Baymount Incorporated

Symbol - BYM.H **Exchange** - TSX-VEN **CUSIP** - 07287U
Head Office - 1901-130 Adelaide St W, Toronto, ON, M5H 3P5 **Telephone** - (416) 843-2881 **Fax** - (416) 947-9804
Email - jgrahamsimmonds@gmail.com
Investor Relations - J. Graham Simmonds (416) 843-2881
Auditors - RSM Canada LLP C.A., Toronto, Ont.
Transfer Agents - Capital Transfer Agency Inc., Toronto, Ont.
Profile - (Ont. 2004) Seeking opportunities in the gaming, technology, consumer products and other regulated industries.
Predecessor Detail - Name changed from Academy Capital Corp., Jan. 18, 2006.
Directors - J. Graham Simmonds, chr., pres., CEO & corp. sec., Toronto, Ont.; Gordon Ashworth, Toronto, Ont.; Helmut Biemann, Irvine, Calif.; Pierre G. Gagnon, Oakville, Ont.; Gerald (Gerry) Goldberg, Toronto, Ont.
Other Exec. Officers - Cameron Wickham, CFO

Capital Stock

	Authorized (shs.)	Outstanding (shs.)[1]
Common	unlimited	32,193,286

[1] At Aug. 19, 2022

Major Shareholder - Widely held at Apr. 29, 2019.

Price Range - BYM.H/TSX-VEN

Year	Volume	High	Low	Close
2022	3,054,786	$0.02	$0.01	$0.01
2021	2,422,053	$0.04	$0.02	$0.02
2020	4,284,552	$0.05	$0.01	$0.03
2019	3,435,348	$0.05	$0.01	$0.01
2018	15,322,294	$0.05	$0.01	$0.02

Recent Close: $0.01

Wholly Owned Subsidiaries

Baymount Corporation, Toronto, Ont.
Baymount Development Corp.
Baymount Financial Corp.
Odds On Media Inc.
1794254 Ontario Inc.

Investments

45% int. in **AltPresence Inc.**
Gilla Inc., Nev.

Financial Statistics

Periods ended:	12m Dec. 31/21[A]		12m Dec. 31/20[A]
	$000s	%Chg	$000s
Salaries & benefits	193		193
General & admin expense	88		112
Operating expense	**281**	**-8**	**305**
Operating income	**(281)**	**n.a.**	**(305)**
Finance costs, gross	7		nil
Pre-tax income	**(287)**	**n.a.**	**(310)**
Net income	**(287)**	**n.a.**	**(310)**
Cash & equivalent	17		1
Current assets	17		1
Total assets	**17**	**n.m.**	**1**
Bank indebtedness	62		nil
Accts. pay. & accr. liabs.	2,729		2,487
Current liabilities	2,791		2,487
Shareholders' equity	(2,773)		(2,486)
Cash from oper. activs.	**(38)**	**n.a.**	**nil**
Cash from fin. activs.	55		nil
Net cash position	**17**	**n.m.**	**1**
	$		$
Earnings per share*	(0.01)		(0.01)
Cash flow per share*	(0.00)		nil
	shs		shs
No. of shs. o/s*	32,193,286		32,193,286
Avg. no. of shs. o/s*	32,193,286		32,193,286
	%		%
Net profit margin	n.a.		n.a.
Return on equity	n.m.		n.m.
Return on assets	n.m.		n.m.

* Common
[A] Reported in accordance with IFRS

Historical Summary
(as originally stated)

Fiscal Year	Oper. Rev. $000s	Net Inc. Bef. Disc. $000s	EPS* $
2021[A]	nil	(287)	(0.01)
2020[A]	nil	(310)	(0.01)
2019[A]	nil	(261)	(0.01)
2018[A]	nil	(350)	(0.01)
2017[A]	nil	(196)	(0.01)

* Common
[A] Reported in accordance with IFRS

B.34 The Becker Milk Company Limited*

Symbol - BEK.B **Exchange** - TSX **CUSIP** - 075653
Head Office - 200-82 Richmond St E, Toronto, ON, M5C 1P1 **Telephone** - (416) 606-2984
Investor Relations - Brian Rattenbury (416) 606-2984
Auditors - Grant Thornton LLP C.A., Mississauga, Ont.
Transfer Agents - TSX Trust Company, Toronto, Ont.
Employees - 4 at Apr. 30, 2023
Profile - (Ont. 1988 amalg.) Owns and manages 39 retail commercial properties in southern Ontario.

Most of the properties are single-store sites with a few multi-store plazas, including one residential unit above a retail store. At Apr. 30, 2023, the company had leased to third parties 51 retail units, of which 36 were leased to **Circle K Stores Inc.** (a successor to **Mac's Convenience Stores Inc.**), a subsidiary of **Alimentation Couche-Tard Inc.**, and the remaining 15 stores and one residential unit were leased to other tenants. At Apr. 30, 2023, 83% of the company's income is generated from Circle K in the form of rent. The length of the terms of the leases with Circle K varies from one to six years.

Most of the operational commitments of the company are performed by outside contractors. These mainly consist of upgrading the company's store properties and industrial buildings to conform to structural and environmental standards. In addition, the company is bearing the cost of one parcel of unoccupied land at Apr. 30, 2023.

During fiscal 2023, the company sold four properties for total proceeds of $1,171,923.

Directors - Dr. Geoffrey W. J. Pottow, chr., pres. & CEO, Toronto, Ont.; Robert Bazos, v-chr., Senneville, Qué.; George A. Duguay, Toronto, Ont.; George S. Panos, Toronto, Ont.; Donald Stewart, Ont.
Other Exec. Officers - Brian Rattenbury, CFO

Capital Stock

	Authorized (shs.)	Outstanding (shs.)[1]
Class A Preference	8,000	nil
Class B Special	2,459,250	1,267,610
Common	640,750	540,750

[1] At July 17, 2023

Class A Preference - Entitled to fixed cumulative preferential cash dividends of $6.00 per share per annum, payable annually. Ranks senior to class B special and common shares and entitled to $100 per share in the event of liquidation, dissolution, winding-up or other distribution of assets. Redeemable in whole or in part at any time on 30 days' notice at $100 plus accrued and unpaid dividends. Non-voting unless dividends in arrears for an aggregate two years, then entitled to one vote per share.

Class B Special - Participating and entitled to non-cumulative dividends when set and declared by the board of directors, and to share equally share for share with common stock in any further distribution. In the event of liquidation, dissolution, winding-up or other distribution of assets, entitled to share equally, share for share, with common stock in any distribution of assets. Non-voting except on changes in terms and conditions attached to class B shares, then entitled to one vote per share.

Common - One vote per share.

Major Shareholder - Euclid Securities Limited held 100% interest at July 17, 2023.

Price Range - BEK.B/TSX

Year	Volume	High	Low	Close
2022	126,233	$14.91	$12.31	$12.70
2021	156,917	$14.85	$12.00	$14.00
2020	89,182	$14.29	$10.46	$12.01
2019	185,541	$16.11	$12.10	$14.25
2018	116,407	$16.42	$12.20	$12.71

Recent Close: $12.95

Capital Stock Changes - There were no changes to capital stock from fiscal 2008 to fiscal 2023, inclusive.

Dividends

BEK.B cl B spl N.V. Ra $0.80 pa S est. Apr. 8, 2013

Long-Term Debt - At Apr. 30, 2023, the company had no long-term debt.

Investments

Alimentation Couche-Tard Inc., Laval, Qué. (see separate coverage)

Financial Statistics

Periods ended:	12m Apr. 30/23[A]		12m Apr. 30/22[A]
	$000s	%Chg	$000s
Operating revenue	**2,860**	**+7**	**2,670**
Cost of sales	418		508
General & admin expense	1,298		1,373
Other operating expense	41		103
Operating expense	**1,757**	**-11**	**1,984**
Operating income	**1,103**	**+61**	**686**
Pre-tax income	**(602)**	**n.a.**	**6,675**
Income taxes	176		1,009
Net income	**(778)**	**n.a.**	**5,666**
Cash & equivalent	4,847		4,448
Accounts receivable	699		1,375
Current assets	6,507		7,882
Long-term investments	2,204		1,864
Fixed assets, net	31,540		33,190
Total assets	**40,325**	**-6**	**43,021**
Accts. pay. & accr. liabs.	359		999
Current liabilities	359		999
Shareholders' equity	34,869		36,799
Cash from oper. activs.	**904**	**+441**	**167**
Cash from fin. activs.	(1,447)		(1,447)
Cash from invest. activs.	297		834
Net cash position	**135**	**-65**	**381**
Capital expenditures	(240)		(34)
Capital disposals	1,172		190
	$		$
Earnings per share*	(0.43)		3.13
Cash flow per share*	0.50		0.09
Cash divd. per share*	0.80		0.80
	shs		shs
No. of shs. o/s*	1,808,360		1,808,360
Avg. no. of shs. o/s*	1,808,360		1,808,360
	%		%
Net profit margin	(27.20)		212.21
Return on equity	(2.17)		16.44
Return on assets	(1.87)		14.07
No. of employees (FTEs)	4		4

* Cl.B & com.
[A] Reported in accordance with IFRS

Historical Summary
(as originally stated)

Fiscal Year	Oper. Rev.	Net Inc. Bef. Disc.	EPS*
	$000s	$000s	$
2023^A	2,860	(778)	(0.43)
2022^A	2,670	5,666	3.13
2021^A	3,097	3,536	1.96
2020^A	3,174	834	0.46
2019^A	3,144	1,310	0.72

* Cl.B & com.
^A Reported in accordance with IFRS

B.35 Bee Vectoring Technologies International Inc.

Symbol - BEE **Exchange** - CSE **CUSIP** - 076588
Head Office - 7-4160 Sladeview Cres, Mississauga, ON, L5L 0A1 **Telephone** - (647) 660-5119
Website - www.beevt.com
Email - investor@beevt.com
Investor Relations - Ashish Malik (647) 660-5119
Auditors - Davidson & Company LLP C.A., Vancouver, B.C.
Lawyers - CP LLP, Toronto, Ont.
Transfer Agents - Endeavor Trust Corporation, Vancouver, B.C.
Profile - (B.C. 2011) Owns, develops and commercializes a patented and/or patent-pending bee vectoring technology designed to utilize bees as natural delivery mechanisms for a variety of powdered mixtures comprised of organic compounds or currently used products that inhibit or eliminate common crop diseases, while at the same time fertilizing the same crops without the use of water.

The company has patents granted and/or pending for the following technologies: BVT-CR7, an organic strain of a natural occurring endophytic fungus that controls targeted crop diseases and increases crop yield; Vectorite™, a recipe of ingredients that allows bees to carry BVT-CR7 and other beneficial fungi or bacteria in their outbound flights to the crops; an integrated dispenser and removable and sealable tray system for bumble bee hives in which the Vectorite™ containing BVT-CR7 or other third party microbial products is placed through which the bees pass and pick up the Vectorite™; and a computer-controlled dispenser system for use with honeybee hives which can dispense in a controlled manner a determinate amount of the Vectorite™ containing BVT-CR7 or other third-party microbial products for delivery to crops using honey bees. The company is also developing new applications and new revenue stream opportunities for its proprietary beneficial microbe Clonostachys rosea Strain BVT CR-7 such as foliar spray applications and applications on seeds.

The company targets two main diseases: Botrytis, a grey fuzz that grows over time on strawberries, blueberries and raspberries and causes blossom blight and berry rot; and Sclerotinia, a soil borne pathogen causing white mould diseases which can seriously damage and in some cases quickly and completely destroy numerous kinds of crops including canola, sunflowers, tomatoes, blueberries and strawberries.

At Jan. 31, 2023, the company had more than 65 patents granted worldwide and more than 35 pending, including the new honey bee system. Patents cover North America, South America, Europe, Asia and Australia. Operations include a 7,000-sq.-ft. production and research facility in Mississauga, Ont.

Predecessor Detail - Name changed from Unique Resources Corp., June 30, 2015, following reverse takeover acquisition of Bee Vectoring Technology Inc.; basis 1 new for 2.4 old shs.

Directors - Michael Collinson, chr., Caledon, Ont.; Ashish Malik, pres. & CEO, Calif.; James (Jim) Molyneux, corp. sec., Etobicoke, Ont.

Other Exec. Officers - Kyle Appleby, CFO

Capital Stock

	Authorized (shs.)	Outstanding (shs.)[1]
Common	unlimited	133,501,369

[1] At Jan. 30, 2023

Major Shareholder - Widely held at Jan. 12, 2023.

Price Range - BEE/CSE

Year	Volume	High	Low	Close
2022	19,425,651	$0.45	$0.11	$0.12
2021	28,222,975	$0.48	$0.23	$0.29
2020	38,791,321	$0.68	$0.24	$0.39
2019	30,432,063	$0.54	$0.14	$0.46
2018	13,963,882	$0.34	$0.13	$0.15

Recent Close: $0.08

Capital Stock Changes - During fiscal 2022, common shares were issued follows: 12,732,941 by private placement, 2,120,241 for debt settlement, 845,000 on vesting of restricted share units, 431,770 for interest and 200,000 on exercise of options.

Wholly Owned Subsidiaries

Bee Vectoring Technology Inc., Caledon, Ont.
Bee Vectoring Technology U.S.A. Corp., United States.

Financial Statistics

Periods ended:	12m Sept. 30/22^A		12m Sept. 30/21^A
	$000s	%Chg	$000s
Operating revenue	**497**	**+25**	**399**
Cost of sales	250		233
Salaries & benefits	855		740
Research & devel. expense	915		576
General & admin expense	2,245		2,466
Stock-based compensation	543		357
Operating expense	**4,809**	**+10**	**4,372**
Operating income	**(4,313)**	**n.a.**	**(3,973)**
Deprec., depl. & amort.	240		196
Finance income	nil		21
Finance costs, gross	31		nil
Write-downs/write-offs	(39)		(1)
Pre-tax income	**(4,932)**	**n.a.**	**(4,123)**
Net income	**(4,932)**	**n.a.**	**(4,123)**
Cash & equivalent	210		2,711
Accounts receivable	227		107
Current assets	3,269		2,925
Fixed assets, net	313		327
Right-of-use assets	422		82
Intangibles, net	1,919		1,918
Total assets	**5,922**	**+13**	**5,253**
Accts. pay. & accr. liabs.	1,189		486
Current liabilities	1,254		565
Long-term debt, gross	550		150
Long-term debt, net	550		150
Long-term lease liabilities	357		7
Shareholders' equity	3,761		4,531
Cash from oper. activs	**(2,895)**	**n.a.**	**(2,850)**
Cash from fin. activs	580		5,620
Cash from invest. activs	(179)		(352)
Net cash position	**210**	**-92**	**2,711**
Capital expenditures	(100)		(191)
Capital disposals	46		nil
	$		$
Earnings per share*	(0.04)		(0.04)
Cash flow per share*	(0.02)		(0.03)
	shs		shs
No. of shs. o/s*	132,829,563		116,499,611
Avg. no. of shs. o/s*	120,206,835		114,143,762
	%		%
Net profit margin	(992.35)		n.m.
Return on equity	(118.96)		(136.73)
Return on assets	(87.71)		(106.77)
Foreign sales percent	100		100

* Common
^A Reported in accordance with IFRS

Historical Summary
(as originally stated)

Fiscal Year	Oper. Rev.	Net Inc. Bef. Disc.	EPS*
	$000s	$000s	$
2022^A	497	(4,932)	(0.04)
2021^A	399	(4,123)	(0.04)
2020^A	289	(6,715)	(0.08)
2019^A	58	(2,898)	(0.04)
2018^A	nil	(2,993)	(0.04)

* Common
^A Reported in accordance with IFRS

B.36 Belgravia Hartford Capital Inc.

Symbol - BLGV **Exchange** - CSE **CUSIP** - 07785T
Head Office - 1410-120 Adelaide St W, Toronto, ON, M5H 1T1 **Telephone** - (416) 779-3268
Website - www.belgraviahartford.com
Email - mazodi@blgv.ca
Investor Relations - Mehdi Azodi (416) 779-3268
Auditors - Davidson & Company LLP C.A., Vancouver, B.C.
Lawyers - Cassels Brock & Blackwell LLP, Toronto, Ont.
Transfer Agents - Computershare Trust Company of Canada Inc., Vancouver, B.C.
Profile - (B.C. 2019; orig. Can., 2002) Owns and manages a portfolio of investments on private and public companies and investment funds focusing on technology, blockchain, healthcare and mineral resources, and provides management services.

Operates through three divisions: Incubation; Investments; and Royalty & Management Services.

The **Incubation** division provides capital to support the development of early stage companies in the biotechnology/healthcare, technology, resources and medical sectors.

The **Investments** division invests in various private and public companies. At June 30, 2022, the company's investment portfolio included shares of nine public and private companies with a fair value of $5,138,528.

The **Royalty & Management Services** division provides corporate governance, restructuring and related administrative services, and earns royalties from water and other resources.

In March 2022, the company sold 8,000,000 common shares of **Imperial Mining Group Ltd.** at 14¢ per share. As a result, the company's interest in Imperial decreased from 10.17% to 5.27% (representing 8,600,000 common shares).

Predecessor Detail - Name changed from Belgravia Capital International Inc., Dec. 20, 2019.

Directors - John Stubbs, chr., Winchester, Hants., United Kingdom; Mehdi Azodi, pres. & CEO, Toronto, Ont.; Deena Siblock, COO & corp. sec., Toronto, Ont.; Ernest Angelo Jr., Midland, Tex.; The Hon. Pierre S. Pettigrew, Toronto, Ont.

Other Exec. Officers - Paul L. Kania, CFO; Hang Tran, contr.

Capital Stock

	Authorized (shs.)	Outstanding (shs.)[1]
Common	unlimited	46,233,333

[1] At Jan. 12, 2023

Major Shareholder - Mehdi Azodi held 17.95% interest at July 15, 2022.

Price Range - BLGV/CSE

Year	Volume	High	Low	Close
2022	6,716,672	$0.16	$0.03	$0.03
2021	13,725,024	$0.40	$0.15	$0.15
2020	18,709,844	$0.45	$0.05	$0.25
2019	14,106,706	$0.40	$0.05	$0.10
2018	53,290,504	$3.60	$0.15	$0.20

Consolidation: 1-for-10 cons. in Mar. 2021
Recent Close: $0.02

Wholly Owned Subsidiaries

Belgravia Hartford Estates Corp., United States. Formerly Trigon Exploration Utah Inc.
- 9.29% int. in **East Peak BK34 LLC**, Colo.

Belgravia Hartford Gold Assets Corp., Canada. Formerly Intercontinental Potash Corp.

Financial Statistics

Periods ended:	12m Dec. 31/21^A		12m Dec. 31/20^{oA}
	$000s	%Chg	$000s
Realized invest. gain (loss)	511		1,300
Unrealized invest. gain (loss)	1,498		8,366
Total revenue	**1,751**	**-82**	**9,816**
Salaries & benefits	3,337		1,332
General & admin. expense	2,500		1,256
Stock-based compensation	nil		926
Operating expense	**5,838**	**+66**	**3,514**
Operating income	**(4,087)**	**n.a.**	**6,302**
Deprec. & amort.	2		1
Write-downs/write-offs	nil		(97)
Pre-tax income	**(4,094)**	**n.a.**	**6,203**
Net income	**(4,094)**	**n.a.**	**6,203**
Cash & equivalent	185		109
Accounts receivable	nil		73
Current assets	12,711		15,525
Long-term investments	74		4
Fixed assets, net	4		4
Total assets	**12,790**	**-18**	**15,533**
Accts. pay. & accr. liabs.	280		185
Current liabilities	280		185
Shareholders' equity	12,510		15,348
Cash from oper. activs	**426**	**n.a.**	**(542)**
Cash from fin. activs	(348)		nil
Cash from invest. activs	(2)		(3)
Net cash position	**185**	**+70**	**109**
Capital expenditures	(2)		(3)
	$		$
Earnings per share*	(0.09)		0.15
Cash flow per share*	0.01		(0.06)
	shs		shs
No. of shs. o/s*	47,224,724		40,179,252
Avg. no. of shs. o/s*	45,262,353		40,179,252
	%		%
Net profit margin	(233.81)		63.19
Return on equity	(29.39)		52.64
Return on assets	(28.91)		51.58

* Common
^o Restated
^A Reported in accordance with IFRS

Latest Results

Periods ended:	6m June 30/22^A		6m June 30/21^{oA}
	$000s	%Chg	$000s
Total revenue	(5,516)	n.a.	3,096
Net income	(7,314)	n.a.	(903)
Net inc. for equity hldrs	(7,314)	n.a.	(901)
Net inc. for non-cont. int	nil		(2)
	$		$
Earnings per share*	(0.16)		(0.09)

* Common
^o Restated
^A Reported in accordance with IFRS

Historical Summary
(as originally stated)

Fiscal Year	Total Rev.	Net Inc. Bef. Disc.	EPS*
	$000s	$000s	$
2021^A	1,751	(4,094)	(0.09)
2020^A	144	6,203	0.15
2019^A	233	(239)	(0.01)
2018^A	815	(7,034)	(0.20)
2017^A	nil	(8,407)	(0.40)

* Common
^A Reported in accordance with IFRS
Note: Adjusted throughout for 1-for-10 cons. in Mar. 2021

B.37 Beretta Ventures Ltd.

Symbol - BRTA.H **Exchange** - TSX-VEN **CUSIP** - 08374J
Head Office - 1600-609 Granville St, Vancouver, BC, V7Y 1C3 **Telephone** - (778) 331-8505 **Fax** - (778) 508-9923
Email - sackerman@emprisecapital.com
Investor Relations - Scott Ackerman (778) 331-8505
Auditors - Davidson & Company LLP C.A., Vancouver, B.C.
Bankers - Bank of Montreal
Lawyers - Cassels Brock & Blackwell LLP, Vancouver, B.C.
Transfer Agents - Computershare Trust Company of Canada Inc., Vancouver, B.C.
Profile - (B.C. 2011) Capital Pool Company.
Predecessor Detail - Name changed from Folkstone Capital Corp., Jan. 18, 2021; basis 1 new for 3 old shs.
Directors - Scott Ackerman, CEO, CFO & corp. sec., Surrey, B.C.; Rick Cox, B.C.; Michael Lucas, Alta.

Capital Stock

	Authorized (shs.)	Outstanding (shs.)[1]
Common	unlimited	9,622,249

[1] At Oct. 28, 2022

Major Shareholder - 685733 B.C. Ltd. held 19.9% interest, 8185735 Canada Corp. held 19.9% interest, The Emprise Special Opportunities Fund (2017) Limited Partnership held 19.9% interest and Scott Ackerman held 12.2% interest at Aug. 6, 2021.

Price Range - BRTA.H/TSX-VEN

Year	Volume	High	Low	Close
2022	146,359	$0.22	$0.10	$0.11
2021	229,400	$0.25	$0.11	$0.25

Consolidation: 1-for-3 cons. in Jan. 2021
Recent Close: $0.12

B.38 Berkley Renewables Inc.

Symbol - BKS **Exchange** - CSE (S) **CUSIP** - 084494
Head Office - 900-570 Granville St, Vancouver, BC, V6C 3P1 **Telephone** - (604) 682-3701
Email - pam@saulnierconsulting.com
Investor Relations - Pamela A. Saulnier (778) 231-0996
Auditors - Mao & Ying LLP C.A., Vancouver, B.C.
Lawyers - Bacchus Law Corporation, Vancouver, B.C.; Borden Ladner Gervais LLP, Vancouver, B.C.
Transfer Agents - Computershare Trust Company of Canada Inc.
Profile - (B.C. 1986 amalg.) Provides consulting services relating to photovoltaic power generation and has gas interests in Alberta.
Through its Solar Management division, provides consulting services relating to the financing, strategy and operations management to companies in photovoltaic power generation.
Also has interests in producing natural gas wells in Alberta.
Common suspended from CSE, May 7, 2019.
Predecessor Detail - Name changed from Berkley Resources Inc., Apr. 16, 2012; basis 1 new for 10 old shs.
Directors - Matthew J. (Matt) Wayrynen, exec. chr., pres. & CEO, West Vancouver, B.C.; Tyrone M. Docherty, Delta, B.C.; Lindsay E. Gorrill, Coeur d'Alene, Idaho
Other Exec. Officers - Pamela A. (Pam) Saulnier, CFO

Capital Stock

	Authorized (shs.)	Outstanding (shs.)[1]
Common	unlimited	15,811,451

[1] At Mar. 31, 2023

Major Shareholder - Widely held at Mar. 31, 2023.

Price Range - BKS/TSX-VEN (D)

Year	Volume	High	Low	Close
2019	87,630	$0.04	$0.04	$0.04
2018	1,392,601	$0.11	$0.02	$0.04

Capital Stock Changes - In January 2022, private placement of 5,400,000 units (1 common share & 1 warrant) at 5¢ per unit was completed, with warrants exercisable at 5¢ per share for three years and 10¢ per share in the following two years.

Subsidiaries

53% int. in **Blue Star Global Inc.**, Nev.
95% int. in **Solar Flow-Through 2012-I General Partner Ltd.**, Canada.
95% int. in **Solar Flow-Through 2012-I Management Ltd.**, Canada.
95% int. in **Solar Flow-Through 2013-I General Partner Ltd.**, Canada.
95% int. in **Solar Flow-Through 2013-I Management Ltd.**, Canada.
95% int. in **Solar Flow-Through 2014-I General Partner Ltd.**, Canada.
95% int. in **Solar Flow-Through 2014-I Management Ltd.**, Canada.
95% int. in **Solar Flow-Through 2015-I General Partner Ltd.**, Canada.
95% int. in **Solar Flow-Through 2015-I Management Ltd.**, Canada.
95% int. in **Solar Flow-Through 2016-I General Partner Ltd.**, Canada.
95% int. in **Solar Flow-Through 2016-I Management Ltd.**, Canada.
83.38% int. in **Solar Flow-Through 2017-I General Partner Ltd.**, Canada.
83.38% int. in **Solar Flow-Through 2017-I Management Ltd.**, Canada.
83.38% int. in **Solar Flow-Through 2017-A General Partner Ltd.**, Canada.
83.38% int. in **Solar Flow-Through 2017-A Management Ltd.**, Canada.
83.38% int. in **Solar Flow-Through 2018-I General Partner Ltd.**, Canada.
83.38% int. in **Solar Flow-Through 2018-I Management Ltd.**, Canada.
83.38% int. in **Solar Flow-Through 2018-A General Partner Ltd.**, Canada.
83.38% int. in **Solar Flow-Through 2018-A Management Ltd.**, Canada.

Investments

RepliCel Life Sciences Inc., Vancouver, B.C. (see separate coverage)

B.39 Better Plant Sciences Inc.

Symbol - PLNT.X **Exchange** - CSE **CUSIP** - 087737
Head Office - 1-2770 Fraser St, Vancouver, BC, V5T 3V7 **Telephone** - (604) 632-1700 **Toll-free** - (833) 515-2677
Website - www.betterplantsciences.com
Email - cole@betterplantsciences.com
Investor Relations - Cole Drezdoff
Auditors - Mao & Ying LLP C.A., Vancouver, B.C.
Lawyers - DuMoulin Black LLP, Vancouver, B.C.
Transfer Agents - Endeavor Trust Corporation, Vancouver, B.C.
Profile - (B.C. 2014) Pursuing new business opportunities.
In May 2022, the company discontinued the sales NeonMind-branded mushroom coffees in the United States. Canadian sales and distribution were discontinued in October 2021.
In April 2022, the company sold wholly owned **Jusu Wellness Inc.** to an unrelated party for a nominal amount. Jusu Wellness produces and sells a line of plant-based products, including skin care, body and home cleaning products.
On Apr. 12, 2022, wholly owned **Urban Juve Provisions Inc.** and **Jusu Bars Corp.** amalgamated to form **Metaversive Holdings Inc.**

Recent Merger and Acquisition Activity

Status: terminated **Revised:** Jan. 30, 2023
UPDATE: The transaction was terminated. PREVIOUS: Better Plant Sciences Inc. entered into a letter of intent for the reverse takeover acquisition of West Vancouver, B.C.-based Metaversive Networks Inc. on a share-for-share basis by way of an amalgamation of Metaversive and a wholly owned subsidiary of Better Plant. Metaversive is developing products and services within the Metaverse. On closing, the largest shareholder of the resulting issuer would be Ztudium Inc., a company owned by Dinis Guarda. Ztudium is a global maker of industry 4IR Fourth Industrial Revolution technologies and research. Apr. 14, 2022 - Metaversive changed its name to FreedomX Metaversive Networks Inc. Apr. 26, 2022 - A definitive agreement was entered into. Better Plant would consolidate its common shares on a 1-for-2 basis and change its name to FreedomX Metaversive Inc. Each of Better Plant and Metaversive intends to complete an equity financing for maximum proceeds of $6,000,000 and $1,152,299, respectively, at a price not less than 35¢ per share.
Predecessor Detail - Name changed from The Yield Growth Corp., Aug. 18, 2020.
Directors - Cole Drezdoff, pres. & CEO, B.C.; Spiros Margaris, Switzerland; Bruce W. Mullen, B.C.
Other Exec. Officers - Yucai (Rick) Huang, CFO

Capital Stock

	Authorized (shs.)	Outstanding (shs.)[1]
Common	unlimited	19,917,970

[1] At Aug. 2, 2022

Major Shareholder - Bruce W. Mullen held 10.3% interest at Apr. 13, 2021.

Price Range - PLNT.X/CSE

Year	Volume	High	Low	Close
2022	892,089	$0.30	$0.13	$0.19
2021	13,052,438	$1.80	$0.25	$0.25
2020	17,116,980	$3.10	$0.60	$1.60
2019	16,370,330	$9.40	$1.85	$1.90
2018	1,274,044	$3.75	$1.65	$2.35

Consolidation: 1-for-10 cons. in Jan. 2022
Recent Close: $0.04

Wholly Owned Subsidiaries

Metaversive Holdings Inc., Vancouver, B.C.
1233392 B.C. Ltd., B.C.

Investments

Komo Plant Based Foods Inc., Vancouver, B.C. (see separate coverage)
10.5% int. in **Lancaster Lithium Inc.**, Vancouver, B.C.

Financial Statistics

Periods ended:	12m Nov. 30/21^A		12m Nov. 30/20^oA
	$000s	%Chg	$000s
Operating revenue	**1,658**	**+49**	**1,115**
Cost of sales	846		267
Salaries & benefits	989		1,694
Research & devel. expense	188		366
General & admin expense	2,578		4,342
Stock-based compensation	1,011		1,427
Operating expense	**5,612**	**-31**	**8,096**
Operating income	**(3,954)**	**n.a.**	**(6,981)**
Deprec., depl. & amort.	308		177
Finance costs, gross	125		59
Investment income	(2,099)		(357)
Write-downs/write-offs	(2,566)		(1,309)
Pre-tax income	**(5,046)**	**n.a.**	**(9,682)**
Net inc. bef. disc. opers	**(5,046)**	**n.a.**	**(9,682)**
Income from disc. opers	(46)		(230)
Net income	**(5,092)**	**n.a.**	**(9,912)**
Net inc. for equity hldrs	**(4,893)**	**n.a.**	**(9,111)**
Net inc. for non-cont. int.	**(199)**	**n.a.**	**(801)**
Cash & equivalent	576		197
Inventories	208		1,170
Accounts receivable	113		382
Current assets	1,058		1,903
Long-term investments	1,853		425
Fixed assets, net	107		194
Right-of-use assets	253		213
Intangibles, net	nil		1,924
Total assets	**3,355**	**-28**	**4,658**
Accts. pay. & accr. liabs	785		832
Current liabilities	982		1,114
Long-term debt, gross	729		80
Long-term debt, net	729		80
Long-term lease liabilities	184		184
Equity portion of conv. debs	34		nil
Shareholders' equity	1,452		3,828
Non-controlling interest	nil		(548)
Cash from oper. activs	**(1,943)**	**n.a.**	**(6,370)**
Cash from fin. activs	1,599		6,767
Cash from invest. activs	206		(362)
Net cash position	**25**	**-86**	**181**
Capital expenditures	(10)		(122)
	$		$
Earns. per sh. bef disc opers*	(0.26)		(0.72)
Earnings per share*	(0.26)		(0.74)
Cash flow per share*	(0.10)		(0.47)
	shs		shs
No. of shs. o/s*	19,917,970		17,847,325
Avg. no. of shs. o/s*	19,213,775		13,463,800
	%		%
Net profit margin	(304.34)		(868.34)
Return on equity	(183.60)		(355.17)
Return on assets	(122.83)		(237.96)

* Common
^o Restated
^A Reported in accordance with IFRS

Latest Results

Periods ended:	6m May 31/22^A		6m May 31/21^oA
	$000s	%Chg	$000s
Operating revenue	309	-22	396
Net inc. bef. disc. opers	(1,374)	n.a.	330
Income from disc. opers	(375)		(513)
Net income	(1,748)	n.a.	(184)
Net inc. for equity hldrs	(1,748)	n.a.	15
Net inc. for non-cont. int.	nil		(199)
	$		$
Earns. per sh. bef. disc. opers.*	(0.07)		0.02
Earnings per share*	(0.09)		0.00

* Common
^o Restated
^A Reported in accordance with IFRS

Historical Summary
(as originally stated)

Fiscal Year	Oper. Rev.	Net Inc. Bef. Disc.	EPS*
	$000s	$000s	$
2021^A	1,658	(5,046)	(0.26)
2020^A	1,135	(9,912)	(0.70)
2019^A	4,019	(16,021)	(1.80)
2018^A	3,055	(9,708)	(1.30)
2017^A1	nil	(1,230)	(0.60)

* Common
^A Reported in accordance with IFRS
[1] As shown in the prospectus dated Nov. 19, 2018. Figures adjusted to reflect 2-for-1 share split effective June 4, 2018.
Note: Adjusted throughout for 1-for-10 cons. in Jan. 2022

B.40 BetterLife Pharma Inc.

Symbol - BETR **Exchange** - CSE **CUSIP** - 08772P
Head Office - 300-1275 6 Ave W, Vancouver, BC, V6H 1A6 **Telephone** - (604) 221-0595
Website - abetterlifepharma.com
Email - david.melles@blifepharma.com
Investor Relations - David Melles (778) 887-1928
Auditors - MNP LLP C.A., Vancouver, B.C.
Lawyers - Alexander Holburn Beaudin & Lang LLP, Vancouver, B.C.
Transfer Agents - National Securities Administrators Ltd., Vancouver, B.C.

Profile - (B.C. 2002) Developing and commercializing non-hallucinogenic psychedelic compounds for the treatment of neuropsychiatric and neurological disorders.

The company is also refining and developing drug candidates from a broad set of complementary interferon-based technologies which have the potential to engage the immune system to fight viral infectionsis.

Lead products under development and preclinical stage include BETR-001, a nonhallucinogenic second-generation lysergic acid diethylamide (LSD) derivative molecule that mimics the projected therapeutic potential of LSD in the treatment of disorders such as depression, posttraumatic stress disorder (PTSD) and migraines; BETR-002, a novel formulation of a derivative of dihydrohonokiol, a known antianxiety compound, with potential to treat benzodiazepine dependency, anxiety and spasticity; and MM-003, a patent pending proprietary Interferon a2b (IFNa2b) inhalation formulation to treat viral infections such as SARS-CoV-2 (COVID-19).

Other products include MM-001, a topical IFNa2b product for the treatment of human papiloma virus (HPV) infection that can cause cervical cancer; and AP-002, an oral gallium-based novel small molecule which finished drug product is an enteric protected tablet for oral administration for potential treatment of cancer.

Predecessor Detail - Name changed from Pivot Pharmaceuticals Inc., Dec. 6, 2019.

Directors - Dr. Ahmad Doroudian, founder & CEO, Vancouver, B.C.; Robert J. Metcalfe, Toronto, Ont.; R. Anthony Pullen, Ont.; Dr. Wolfgang Renz, Germany

Other Exec. Officers - Dr. Hooshmand Sheshbaradaran, COO; Moira Ong, CFO & corp. sec.

Capital Stock

	Authorized (shs.)	Outstanding (shs.)[1]
Preferred	unlimited	nil
Common	unlimited	85,401,241

[1] At Aug. 31, 2022

Major Shareholder - Widely held at May 31, 2022.

Price Range - BETR/CSE

Year	Volume	High	Low	Close
2022	17,339,534	$0.31	$0.08	$0.16
2021	46,877,364	$2.27	$0.19	$0.22
2020	10,074,729	$3.00	$0.40	$2.01
2019	3,280,257	$5.20	$1.15	$1.55
2018	5,339,818	$27.90	$2.50	$2.90

Consolidation: 1-for-10 cons. in June 2020
Recent Close: $0.08

Wholly Owned Subsidiaries

BetterLife Pharma US Inc., Seattle, Wash.
Blife Therapeutics Inc., Vancouver, B.C.
MedMelior Inc., Vancouver, B.C.
- 100% int. in **Altum Pharma (Australia) Pty Ltd.**, Melbourne, Vic., Australia.
- 100% int. in **Altum Pharmaceuticals (HK) Limited**, Hong Kong, Hong Kong, People's Republic of China.

Financial Statistics

Periods ended:	12m Jan. 31/22[A]		12m Jan. 31/21[A]
	$000s	%Chg	$000s
Salaries & benefits	1,742		1,720
Research & devel. expense	5,421		285
General & admin expense	1,557		5,035
Stock-based compensation	1,231		827
Operating expense	**9,951**	**+26**	**7,867**
Operating income	**(9,951)**	**n.a.**	**(7,867)**
Deprec., depl. & amort.	18		88
Finance costs, gross	58		40
Write-downs/write-offs	192		(11,312)
Pre-tax income	**(11,993)**	**n.a.**	**(36,351)**
Income taxes	167		nil
Net income	**(12,159)**	**n.a.**	**(36,351)**
Cash & equivalent	174		155
Accounts receivable	325		520
Current assets	1,143		1,330
Fixed assets, net	18		37
Total assets	**1,161**	**-13**	**1,336**
Accts. pay. & accr. liabs	3,341		4,503
Current liabilities	4,143		5,847
Long-term debt, gross	312		500
Long-term debt, net	35		nil
Shareholders' equity	(3,881)		(4,612)
Cash from oper. activs	**(11,203)**	**n.a.**	**(7,165)**
Cash from fin. activs	11,234		4,090
Cash from invest. activs	nil		(72)
Net cash position	**174**	**+12**	**155**
Capital expenditures	nil		(10)
	$		$
Earnings per share*	(0.16)		(1.34)
Cash flow per share*	(0.15)		(0.27)
	shs		shs
No. of shs. o/s*	85,241,238		51,445,842
Avg. no. of shs. o/s*	75,469,531		27,027,028
	%		%
Net profit margin	n.a.		n.a.
Return on equity	n.m.		n.m.
Return on assets	(969.18)		(757.50)
No. of employees (FTEs)	4		3

* Common
[A] Reported in accordance with IFRS

Latest Results

Periods ended:	3m Apr. 30/22[A]		3m Apr. 30/21[A]
	$000s	%Chg	$000s
Net income	(2,989)	n.a.	(2,444)
	$		$
Earnings per share*	(0.04)		(0.04)

* Common
[A] Reported in accordance with IFRS

Historical Summary
(as originally stated)

Fiscal Year	Oper. Rev.	Net Inc. Bef. Disc.	EPS*
	$000s	$000s	$
2022[A]	nil	(12,159)	(0.16)
2021[A]	nil	(36,351)	(1.34)
2020[A]	nil	(19,589)	(1.30)
2019[B]	nil	(9,146)	(1.00)
	US$000s	US$000s	US$
2018[B]	nil	(121)	(0.01)

* Common
[A] Reported in accordance with IFRS
[B] Reported in accordance with U.S. GAAP
Note: Adjusted throughout for 1-for-10 cons. in June 2020

B.41 Bettermoo(d) Food Corporation

Symbol - MOOO **Exchange** - CSE **CUSIP** - 08772W
Head Office - 800-1199 Hastings St W, Vancouver, BC, V6E 3T5 **Telephone** - (236) 521-8783 **Toll-free** - (855) 715-1865
Website - www.bettermoo.com
Email - gb@winchesteradvisory.com
Investor Relations - Geoffrey Balderson (855) 715-1865
Auditors - Dale Matheson Carr-Hilton LaBonte LLP C.A., Vancouver, B.C.
Transfer Agents - TSX Trust Company, Toronto, Ont.

Profile - (B.C. 2019; orig. Ont., 1936) Develops, produces and sells dairy-free beverages and cheese alternatives under the Moodrink, Moofrais and Moobert brands. Also produces and sells cannabidiol (CBD)-infused products including tea sachets, creams, gummies and oils under the Happy Tea brand.

Moodrink is a proprietary blend of oat milk and herbs. The original flavour of Moodrink is expected to launch in the third quarter of 2023, followed by additional flavours such as vanilla, matcha and chai. Plans are also in place to launch more plant-based dairy alternative products including butter, yogurt, cheese, ice cream, sour cream and créme fraîche.

Moofrais and Moobert are vegan nut-based cheese alternative products that are manufactured and sold in Austria, with more than ten varieties of camembert and cream cheese alternatives, as well as a smoky parmesan cheese alternative available.

In addition, produces and sells Happy Tea products which are infused with hemp extracts, adaptogens or CBD. These products, available both in brick-and-mortar stores and online, are divided into four categories: tea sachets, CBD creams, CBD gummies, and CBD oil. A CBD-infused water is also under development.

In August 2022, the company changed its fiscal year end to July 31 from December 31.

In June 2022, the company acquired 80% interest in private Austrian-based **Bella's Organic GmbH** for issuance of 362,500 common shares valued at $500,000 and $137,500 cash. Bella's Organic develops, manufactures and markets vegan and organic artisan cheese products.

Predecessor Detail - Name changed from Happy Gut Brands Limited, May 19, 2022.

Directors - Steve Pear, chr., Tex.; Nima Bahrami, CEO, Vancouver, B.C.; Geoffrey (Geoff) Balderson, CFO & corp. sec., Vancouver, B.C.; Patrick C. T. (Pat) Morris, Vancouver, B.C.; Joel Shacker, Vancouver, B.C.

Capital Stock

	Authorized (shs.)	Outstanding (shs.)[1]
Common	unlimited	7,483,236

[1] At Mar. 13, 2023

Major Shareholder - Joel Shacker held 11.84% interest at Oct. 18, 2022.

Price Range - MOOO/CSE

Year	Volume	High	Low	Close
2022	1,205,890	$16.70	$3.30	$4.00
2021	1,625,472	$19.90	$3.20	$15.00
2020	27,671	$7.00	$2.80	$5.50

Consolidation: 1-for-10 cons. in Mar. 2023; 1-for-10 cons. in May 2020; 1-for-10 cons. in Aug. 2019
Recent Close: $2.80

Capital Stock Changes - In February 2023, private placement of 863,256 post-consolidated units (1 common share & 1 warrant) at $3.30 per unit was completed, with warrants exercisable at $4.10 per share for two years. On Mar. 13, 2023, common shares were consolidated on a 1-for-10 basis. In June 2023, private placement of 238,185 units (1 post-consolidated common share & ½ warrant) at $2.33 per unit was completed, with warrants exercisable at $3.50 per share for three years.

During the seven-month period ended July 31, 2022, common shares were issued as follows: 9,000,000 on exercise of warrants, 369,750 pursuant to the acquisition of Bella's Organic GmbH and 1,000 on exercise of options

Wholly Owned Subsidiaries

Bettermoo(d) Holdings Corp., B.C.
Happy Tea Supplements LLC, Fla.

Subsidiaries

80% int. in **Bettermoo(d) GmbH**, Austria.

Financial Statistics

Periods ended:	7m July 31/22[A]		12m Dec. 31/21[□A]
	$000s	%Chg	$000s
Operating revenue	**5**	**n.a.**	**14**
Cost of sales	3		11
Salaries & benefits	105		164
Research & devel. expense	508		32
General & admin expense	1,592		2,068
Stock-based compensation	1,104		1,810
Operating expense	**3,312**	**n.a.**	**4,085**
Operating income	**(3,307)**	**n.a.**	**(4,071)**
Write-downs/write-offs	(1,159)		(281)
Pre-tax income	**(4,478)**	**n.a.**	**(28,842)**
Income taxes	(30)		nil
Net income	**(4,449)**	**n.a.**	**(28,842)**
Cash & equivalent	299		2,052
Inventories	2		nil
Accounts receivable	115		65
Current assets	439		2,122
Fixed assets, net	59		nil
Intangibles, net	221		522
Total assets	**719**	**n.a.**	**3,143**
Accts. pay. & accr. liabs	463		488
Current liabilities	534		553
Long-term debt, gross	71		66
Shareholders' equity	51		2,589
Non-controlling interest	110		nil
Cash from oper. activs	**(2,056)**	**n.a.**	**(2,272)**
Cash from fin. activs	456		3,745
Cash from invest. activs	(132)		267
Net cash position	**299**	**n.a.**	**2,052**
	$		$
Earnings per share*	(0.70)		(6.50)
Cash flow per share*	(0.33)		(0.52)
	shs		shs
No. of shs. o/s*	6,462,817		5,525,742
Avg. no. of shs. o/s*	6,232,409		4,413,804
	%		%
Net profit margin	...		n.m.
Return on equity	...		(1,981.59)
Return on assets	...		n.m.

* Common
□ Restated
A Reported in accordance with IFRS

Latest Results

Periods ended:	3m Oct. 31/22[A]		3m Sept. 30/21[□A]
	$000s	%Chg	$000s
Operating revenue	10	+400	2
Net income	(511)	n.a.	(3,179)
Net inc. for equity hldrs	(485)	n.a.	(3,179)
Net inc. for non-cont. int	(26)		nil
	$		$
Earnings per share*	(0.10)		(0.70)

* Common
□ Restated
A Reported in accordance with IFRS

Historical Summary
(as originally stated)

Fiscal Year	Oper. Rev.	Net Inc. Bef. Disc.	EPS*
	$000s	$000s	$
2022[A1]	5	(4,449)	(0.70)
2021[A]	14	(28,842)	(6.50)
2020[A2]	9	(1,331)	(0.40)
2019[A3]	nil	81	1.00
2018[A]	nil	(66)	(1.00)

* Common
A Reported in accordance with IFRS
1 7 months ended July 31, 2022.
2 4 months ended Dec. 31, 2020.
3 Results for 2019 and prior periods pertain to Viking Gold Exploration Inc.

Note: Adjusted throughout for 1-for-10 cons. in Mar. 2023; 1-for-10 cons. in May 2020; 1-for-10 cons. in Aug. 2019

B.42 BevCanna Enterprises Inc.

Symbol - BEV **Exchange** - CSE (S) **CUSIP** - 08783B
Head Office - 300-1008 Homer St, Vancouver, BC, V6B 2X1 **Telephone** - (604) 569-1414
Website - www.bevcanna.com
Email - bryce@bevcanna.com
Investor Relations - Bryce Allen (778) 766-3744
Auditors - GreenGrowth C.P.A., Los Angeles, Calif.
Transfer Agents - Olympia Trust Company

Profile - (B.C. 2017) Develops and manufactures traditional and cannabinoid-infused beverages and supplements. Also operates an e-commerce platform for health and wellness products.

Owns and operates a 40,000-sq.-ft. beverage manufacturing facility in Bridesville, B.C., with a bottling capacity of up to 210,000,000 bottles annually. The facility consists of a 10,000-sq.-ft. plant for cannabinoid-infused beverages and a 30,000-sq.-ft. plant for conventional beverages. The site also includes a naturally alkaline spring water aquifer and 315 acres of agricultural land. Products manufactured include the company's TRACE brand, a line of alkaline and plant-based mineral water, mineral concentrates and shots, Keef, a licensed brand of cannabis-infused soda, as well as white label/private label brands of conventional and cannabinoid-based beverage and wellness products.

Also owns Pure Therapy, an e-commerce platform selling various nutraceutical and hemp-based CBD health products in the U.S. and Western Europe.

Common suspended from CSE, Aug. 4, 2022.

Predecessor Detail - Name changed from Nutrivida Biotech Investments Inc., Sept. 14, 2018.

Directors - Marcello Leone, chr. & CEO, Vancouver, B.C.; N. John Campbell, CFO, chief strategy officer & corp. sec., Vancouver, B.C.; Howard A. Blank, Vancouver, B.C.; Martino Ciambrelli, Vancouver, B.C.; William L. (Bill) Macdonald, West Vancouver, B.C.; Douglas L. Mason, West Vancouver, B.C.

Other Exec. Officers - Bruce Dawson-Scully, pres.; Raffael Kapusty, v-p, sales & insights; Bill Niarchos, v-p, sales & sales opers.

Capital Stock

	Authorized (shs.)	Outstanding (shs.)[1]
Common	unlimited	179,756,069

1 At Nov. 29, 2021

Major Shareholder - Widely held at Oct. 20, 2021.

Price Range - BEV/CSE (S)

Year	Volume	High	Low	Close
2022	17,122,315	$0.23	$0.05	$0.06
2021	92,570,419	$1.47	$0.20	$0.20
2020	107,052,611	$1.07	$0.18	$0.98
2019	21,728,432	$1.00	$0.26	$0.36

Capital Stock Changes - In January 2023, 54,926,021 common shares were issued pursuant to acquisition of Embark Health Inc.

Wholly Owned Subsidiaries

BevCanna Operating Corp., B.C.
Carmanah Craft Corp., B.C.
Embark Health Inc., Toronto, Ont.
Exceler Holdings Ltd., B.C.
Naturally Pure Therapy Products Corp., B.C.
Naturo Group Enterprises Inc., B.C.
- 87% int. in **Naturo Springs Inc.**, Canada.

B.43 BeWhere Holdings, Inc.

Symbol - BEW **Exchange** - TSX-VEN **CUSIP** - 08825T
Head Office - 2475 Skymark Ave, Unit 4, Mississauga, ON, L4W 4Y6
Toll-free - (844) 229-4373 **Fax** - (416) 533-7890
Website - www.bewhere.com
Email - info@bewhere.com
Investor Relations - Owen Moore (844) 229-4373
Auditors - Dale Matheson Carr-Hilton LaBonte LLP C.A., Vancouver, B.C.
Transfer Agents - Capital Transfer Agency Inc., Toronto, Ont.

Profile - (B.C. 2015; orig. Ont., 1994) Designs and sells beacons, and develops mobile applications, middleware and cloud-based solutions, which provide businesses with real-time information on equipment, tools and inventory in transit and at facilities.

Manufactures cellular-based products (M-IoT) with sensors that works on either Long Term Evolution for Machine (LTE-M) or Narrowband IoT (NB-IoT) cellular-based networks, both which qualify as low power area networks. The company also designs and contract manufactures Bluetooth® Low Energy Beacons and has built a suite of asset tracking applications for mobile devices and websites. Its solutions are designed to monitor location, temperature, air pressure, humidity, light and motion/impact. Also offers fixed Bluetooth/Wi-Fi gateways for use in warehouses, loading docks, construction trailers, gatehouses, equipment lock-ups and work sites. Products are offered to the emergency service, construction, utility and transportation industries.

Predecessor Detail - Name changed from Greenock Resources Inc., Feb. 3, 2016, following reverse takeover acquisition of BeWhere Inc.

Directors - Owen Moore, CEO, Mississauga, Ont.; Chris Panczuk, COO, Brampton, Ont.; Paul Christie, Toronto, Ont.; Joanne De Laurentiis, Toronto, Ont.; Nauby Jacob, Ont.

Other Exec. Officers - Rajiv Khanna, CFO & sec.-treas.; Brian Boychuk, sr. v-p, sales & mktg.; Margaux Berry, v-p, strategy & growth; Carmen Morra, v-p, opers.

Capital Stock

	Authorized (shs.)	Outstanding (shs.)[1]
Preference	unlimited	nil
Common	unlimited	87,901,988

1 At May 9, 2023

Normal Course Issuer Bid - The company plans to make normal course purchases of up to 4,391,349 common shares representing 5% of the total outstanding. The bid commenced on June 7, 2023, and expires on June 6, 2024.

Major Shareholder - Owen Moore held 10.2% interest and Chris Panczuk held 10.02% interest at May 9, 2023.

Price Range - BEW/TSX-VEN

Year	Volume	High	Low	Close
2022	9,466,131	$0.28	$0.20	$0.23
2021	23,586,838	$0.38	$0.19	$0.27
2020	31,013,197	$0.28	$0.08	$0.28
2019	28,171,979	$0.34	$0.14	$0.24
2018	46,734,050	$0.59	$0.16	$0.24

Recent Close: $0.19

Capital Stock Changes - During 2022, 50,000 common shares were issued on exercise of warrants and 363,000 were repurchased under a Normal Course Issuer Bid.

Wholly Owned Subsidiaries

BeWhere Inc., Mississauga, Ont.
BeWhere, Inc., Del.

Financial Statistics

Periods ended:	12m Dec. 31/22[A]		12m Dec. 31/21[A]
	$000s	%Chg	$000s
Operating revenue	**10,025**	**+17**	**8,541**
Cost of sales	6,254		5,975
Salaries & benefits	1,387		998
Research & devel. expense	512		nil
General & admin expense	1,026		777
Stock-based compensation	37		51
Operating expense	**9,216**	**+18**	**7,801**
Operating income	**809**	**+9**	**740**
Deprec., depl. & amort	409		342
Finance income	27		8
Finance costs, gross	51		3
Pre-tax income	**526**	**+26**	**417**
Income taxes	(1,559)		nil
Net income	**2,085**	**+400**	**417**
Cash & equivalent	3,227		2,559
Inventories	855		859
Accounts receivable	1,996		1,228
Current assets	6,165		4,897
Fixed assets, net	503		23
Intangibles, net	485		737
Total assets	**8,712**	**+54**	**5,657**
Accts. pay. & accr. liabs	1,232		912
Current liabilities	1,448		1,006
Long-term debt, gross	228		35
Long-term debt, net	228		35
Long-term lease liabilities	416		nil
Shareholders' equity	6,650		4,584
Cash from oper. activs	**640**	**-7**	**690**
Cash from fin. activs	62		96
Cash from invest. activs	(34)		(694)
Net cash position	**3,227**	**+26**	**2,559**
Capital expenditures	(34)		(26)
	$		$
Earnings per share*	0.02		0.00
Cash flow per share*	0.01		0.01
	shs		shs
No. of shs. o/s*	87,983,488		88,296,488
Avg. no. of shs. o/s*	88,203,057		88,076,587
	%		%
Net profit margin	20.80		4.88
Return on equity	37.12		9.67
Return on assets	31.83		7.44

* Common
A Reported in accordance with IFRS

Latest Results

Periods ended:	3m Mar. 31/23[A]		3m Mar. 31/22[A]
	$000s	%Chg	$000s
Operating revenue	2,675	+13	2,367
Net income	103	+544	16
	$		$
Earnings per share*	0.00		0.00

* Common
A Reported in accordance with IFRS

Historical Summary
(as originally stated)

Fiscal Year	Oper. Rev.	Net Inc. Bef. Disc.	EPS*
	$000s	$000s	$
2022[A]	10,025	2,085	0.02
2021[A]	8,541	417	0.00
2020[A]	7,037	(1,972)	(0.02)
2019[A]	6,097	(1,230)	(0.01)
2018[A]	3,609	(1,408)	(0.02)

* Common
A Reported in accordance with IFRS

B.44 Beyond Medical Technologies Inc.

Symbol - DOCT **Exchange** - CSE **CUSIP** - 088641
Head Office - 715-6388 3 Rd, Richmond, BC, V6Y 0L4 **Telephone** - (604) 805-4602

Email - kal@bullruncapital.ca
Investor Relations - Kulwant Malhi (604) 805-4602
Auditors - BF Borgers CPA PC C.P.A., Lakewood, Colo.
Bankers - Bank of Montreal, Vancouver, B.C.
Lawyers - McMillan LLP, Vancouver, B.C.
Transfer Agents - Computershare Trust Company of Canada Inc., Vancouver, B.C.
Profile - (B.C. 2006) Seeking new business opportunities.

Has manufacturing facility located in Delta, B.C., where the company previously operated its waste digester business in the food and pharmaceutical industries as well as its personal protective equipment manufacturing business.

In March 2022, the company announced its intention to operate its Micron Technologies' facility at reduced capacity or potentially terminating its mask manufacturing business and to seek new business opportunities.

Predecessor Detail - Name changed from Micron Waste Technologies Inc., Jan. 12, 2021.

Directors - Kulwant (Kal) Malhi, chr. & CEO, Vancouver, B.C.; Harveer Sidhu, pres., B.C.; Michael C. Kelly, Langley, B.C.; Dr. Hyder A. Khoja, B.C.

Other Exec. Officers - Zahara (Zara) Kanji, CFO; Ziba Hajizadeh, v-p, eng.; Karen Lauriston, v-p

Capital Stock

	Authorized (shs.)	Outstanding (shs.)[1]
Common	unlimited	7,913,975

[1] At Feb. 17, 2023

Major Shareholder - Widely held at Feb. 17, 2023.

Price Range - DOCT/CSE

Year	Volume	High	Low	Close
2022	1,805,484	$0.95	$0.05	$0.06
2021	3,692,539	$2.50	$0.25	$0.40
2020	2,455,016	$2.40	$0.40	$1.15
2019	1,328,041	$10.80	$0.90	$1.00
2018	3,745,393	$16.00	$5.00	$5.70

Consolidation: 1-for-10 cons. in Dec. 2022; 1-for-2 cons. in May 2020

Recent Close: $0.07

Capital Stock Changes - On Dec. 30, 2022, common shares were consolidated on a 1-for-10 basis.

Wholly Owned Subsidiaries

Micron Technologies Holding Inc., Canada.
Micron Technologies Inc., B.C.

Financial Statistics

Periods ended:	12m Dec. 31/21[A]		12m Dec. 31/20[A]
	$000s	%Chg	$000s
Operating revenue	**943**	**+351**	**209**
Cost of sales	1,194		184
Salaries & benefits	90		588
Research & devel. expense	21		29
General & admin expense	1,420		1,334
Stock-based compensation	200		7
Operating expense	**2,835**	**+32**	**2,141**
Operating income	**(1,891)**	**n.a.**	**(1,932)**
Deprec., depl. & amort.	214		142
Finance income	nil		7
Finance costs, gross	14		25
Pre-tax income	**(2,913)**	**n.a.**	**(6,521)**
Net income	**(2,913)**	**n.a.**	**(6,521)**
Cash & equivalent	1,431		624
Inventories	322		369
Accounts receivable	28		97
Current assets	1,808		1,195
Fixed assets, net	114		444
Right-of-use assets	nil		144
Intangibles, net	nil		25
Total assets	**1,953**	**+6**	**1,844**
Accts. pay. & accr. liabs	175		197
Current liabilities	413		274
Long-term lease liabilities	nil		88
Shareholders' equity	1,540		1,482
Cash from oper. activs	**(1,399)**	**n.a.**	**(1,834)**
Cash from fin. activs	2,674		(66)
Cash from invest. activs	(468)		(260)
Net cash position	**1,431**	**+129**	**624**
Capital expenditures	(68)		(234)
Capital disposals	nil		5
	$		$
Earnings per share*	(0.40)		(1.40)
Cash flow per share*	(0.19)		(0.39)
	shs		shs
No. of shs. o/s*	7,913,975		5,601,184
Avg. no. of shs. o/s*	7,538,754		4,744,627
	%		%
Net profit margin	(308.91)		n.m.
Return on equity	(192.79)		(259.85)
Return on assets	(152.70)		(228.45)

* Common
[A] Reported in accordance with IFRS

Latest Results

Periods ended:	3m Mar. 31/22[A]		3m Mar. 31/21[A]
	$000s	%Chg	$000s
Operating revenue	126	-52	263
Net income	(461)	n.a.	(807)
	$		$
Earnings per share*	(0.10)		0.10

* Common
[A] Reported in accordance with IFRS

Historical Summary
(as originally stated)

Fiscal Year	Oper. Rev.	Net Inc. Bef. Disc.	EPS*
	$000s	$000s	$
2021[A]	943	(2,913)	(0.40)
2020[A]	209	(6,521)	(1.40)
2019[A]	nil	(5,366)	(1.40)
2018[A]	nil	(3,208)	(0.80)
2017[A1]	nil	(8,590)	(6.60)

* Common
[A] Reported in accordance with IFRS
[1] Results reflect the Oct. 19, 2017, reverse takeover of (old) Micron Waste Technologies Inc.

Note: Adjusted throughout for 1-for-10 cons. in Dec. 2022; 1-for-2 cons. in May 2020

B.45 Beyond Oil Ltd.

Symbol - BOIL **Exchange** - CSE **CUSIP** - 088669
Head Office - 1208 Rosewood Cres, North Vancouver, BC, V7P 1H4
Telephone - (778) 809-0250
Website - www.beyondoil.co
Email - denise@vancouvercorporate.ca
Investor Relations - Denise Pilla (778) 809-0250
Auditors - BDO Ziv Haft C.P.A., Tel Aviv, Israel
Transfer Agents - Endeavor Trust Corporation, Vancouver, B.C.
Profile - (B.C. 2012) Has developed and manufactures an innovative proprietary and patented formulation which eliminates the free fatty acids from cooking oil while preserving the oil's quality and nutritional values.

Initial product is a filtering and processing aid marketed under the name FryDay™, which is a filter powder that uses natural ingredients that is added to frying oil to extend its life. The product is marketed to food-service and industrial frying businesses.

The filtering process includes mixing the powder into the hot oil to absorb and prevent the formation of harmful components such as total particulate matter, free fatty acids, trans fats, acrylamide, polycyclic aromatic hydrocarbons and other impurities. The oil would then be passed through a microfiltration paper.

FryDay™ is produced and packaged at Jezreel Valley, Israel, which will then be shipped to distributors and customers in Israel, Turkey, Canada and the U.S.

Recent Merger and Acquisition Activity

Status: completed **Revised:** May 12, 2022
UPDATE: The transaction was completed. Beyond Oil Ltd. issued a total of 24,410,505 common shares. The common shares of Beyond Oil Ltd. commenced trading on the CSE effective May 25, 2022. PREVIOUS: FTC Cards Inc. entered into a letter of intent to acquire Israel-based (old) Beyond Oil Ltd., a developer and manufacturer of an innovative proprietary and patented formulation which eliminates the free fatty acids from cooking oil while preserving the oil's quality and nutritional values. Terms of the transaction were not disclosed. Upon completion, FTC would become a public company whose common shares would be listed on a Canadian stock exchange. Sept. 26, 2021 - A definitive agreement was entered into whereby FTC would acquire Beyond Oil via a reverse takeover. Beyond Oil shareholders would be issued such number of FTC common shares that equalled 50% plus one share of the total number of issued and outstanding resulting issuer shares after giving effect to the transaction. Upon completion, FTC would change its name to Beyond Oil Ltd. and apply to list its common shares on the Canadian Securities Exchange (CSE). May 4, 2022 - FTC changed its name to Beyond Oil Ltd.

Predecessor Detail - Name changed from FTC Cards Inc., May 4, 2022, pursuant to the reverse takeover acquisition of Beyond Oil Inc.

Directors - Dan Itzhaki, chr., Beit Horon, Israel; Jonathan Or, interim CEO & chief mktg. officer, Tel Aviv, Israel; Michael Pinhas Or, pres., Israel; Robert Kiesman, v-p, Richmond, B.C.; Dr. Gad Penini, Netanya, Israel; Hanadi Said, Haifa, Israel; Erez Winner, Beit Horon, Israel

Other Exec. Officers - Shany Touboul, CFO; Michal Werner, chief tech. officer; Denise Pilla, corp. sec.

Capital Stock

	Authorized (shs.)	Outstanding (shs.)[1]
Common	unlimited	52,091,849

[1] At Mar. 31, 2023

Major Shareholder - Jonathan Or held 12.32% interest at Mar. 24, 2023.

Price Range - BOIL/CSE

Year	Volume	High	Low	Close
2022	3,673,956	$2.25	$0.40	$0.71

Recent Close: $0.67

Capital Stock Changes - In March 2023, private placement of 1,600,000 units (1 common share & ½ warrant) at Cdn$0.75 per unit was completed, with warrants exercisable at Cdn$1.00 per share for one year.

On May 12, 2022, 24,410,505 common shares were issued pursuant to the reverse takeover acquisition of (old) Beyond Oil Ltd. In addition, 4,666,667 units (1 common share & 0.57 warrants) were issued without further consideration on exchange of special warrants sold from February to April 2022 at $0.75 each. Also during 2022, common shares were issued as follows: 1,708,735 as finders' fees and 92,000 on exercise of warrants.

Wholly Owned Subsidiaries

Beyond Oil Ltd., Israel.

Financial Statistics

Periods ended:	12m Dec. 31/22[A1]		12m Dec. 31/21[A2]
	US$000s	%Chg	US$000s
Operating revenue	**nil**	**n.a.**	**(43)**
Salaries & benefits	612		461
Research & devel. expense	685		317
General & admin expense	906		606
Stock-based compensation	344		384
Other operating expense	5		nil
Operating expense	**2,551**	**+44**	**1,768**
Operating income	**(2,551)**	**n.a.**	**(1,811)**
Deprec., depl. & amort.	306		294
Finance costs, gross	474		367
Pre-tax income	**(13,612)**	**n.a.**	**(2,463)**
Net income	**(13,612)**	**n.a.**	**(2,463)**
Cash & equivalent	876		388
Accounts receivable	113		62
Current assets	995		473
Fixed assets, net	155		151
Right-of-use assets	178		78
Intangibles, net	3,463		4,163
Total assets	**4,791**	**-2**	**4,866**
Bank indebtedness	nil		791
Accts. pay. & accr. liabs	573		312
Current liabilities	1,012		1,490
Long-term debt, gross	nil		735
Long-term debt, net	nil		735
Long-term lease liabilities	179		94
Shareholders' equity	3,261		2,547
Cash from oper. activs	**(2,373)**	**n.a.**	**(828)**
Cash from fin. activs	2,561		758
Cash from invest. activs	325		(41)
Net cash position	**876**	**+126**	**388**
Capital expenditures	(57)		(21)
	US$		US$
Earnings per share*	(0.34)		(0.91)
Cash flow per share*	(0.06)		(0.31)
	shs		shs
No. of shs. o/s*	48,913,006		n.a.
Avg. no. of shs. o/s*	40,041,032		2,699,094
	%		%
Net profit margin	n.a.		n.m.
Return on equity	(468.73)		(80.42)
Return on assets	(272.09)		(42.16)

* Common
[A] Reported in accordance with IFRS
[1] Results reflect the May 12, 2022, reverse takeover acquisition of (old) Beyond Oil Ltd.
[2] Results pertain to (old) Beyond Oil Ltd.

Latest Results

Periods ended:	3m Mar. 31/23[A]		3m Mar. 31/22[A]
	US$000s	%Chg	US$000s
Operating revenue	10	n.a.	nil
Net income	(451)	n.a.	(601)
	US$		US$
Earnings per share*	(0.01)		(0.22)

* Common
[A] Reported in accordance with IFRS

Historical Summary
(as originally stated)

Fiscal Year	Oper. Rev.	Net Inc. Bef. Disc.	EPS*
	US$000s	US$000s	US$
2022[A]	nil	(13,612)	(0.34)
2021[A1]	(43)	(2,463)	(0.91)
2020[A1]	nil	(3,285)	(1.27)
2019[A1]	59	(1,171)	(0.48)

* Common
[A] Reported in accordance with IFRS
[1] Results pertain to (old) Beyond Oil Ltd.

B.46 Bhang Inc.

Symbol - BHNG **Exchange** - CSE (S) **CUSIP** - 08862K
Head Office - 6815 Biscayne Blvd, Suite 103, Miami, FL, United States, 33138
Website - www.bhangnation.com

Email - invest@bhangcorporation.com
Investor Relations - J. Graham Simmonds (786) 953-4281
Auditors - DNTW Toronto LLP C.A., Toronto, Ont.
Transfer Agents - Capital Transfer Agency Inc., Toronto, Ont.
Profile - (Ont. 1997 amalg.) Produces and distributes cannabis and hemp-derived and terpene products in seven U.S. states and across Canada, with a focus on tetrahydrocannabinol (THC) chocolates and other edibles. Also operates its own e-commerce platform.

The company has three types of branded products: cannabis-derived products containing THC and CBD; hemp-derived CBD products; and terpene products. Products include chocolates, pre-rolls, vapes, gums, beverages and gummies.

CBD products are all manufactured by co-packers and are sold by licensees or by the company directly in states where they are permitted to be sold. THC products are manufactured by licensees and sold by such licensees where they are permitted to sell such products, primarily in Canada and California, Florida, Nevada, New Mexico, Michigan, Illinois and Massachusetts. The company licenses only its brand and recipes to these licensees and also facilitates their purchases of Bhang-branded packaging and moulds to assist them with production and distribution. Terpene-flavoured products are cannabis-inspired and do not contain any marijuana or hemp.

Also operates a CBD e-commerce store as well as online merchandise of products including hats, hoodies, mugs and other Bhang™ branded products.

In May 2022, the company sold 2,060,000 common shares of **Plant-Based Investment Corp.** it held for Cdn$412,000, decreasing its ownership interest to 3.96% from 11.45%.

Sub vtg suspended from CSE, May 8, 2023.

Predecessor Detail - Name changed from Pele Mountain Resources Inc., May 24, 2019, pursuant to reverse takeover acquistion of Bhang Corporation; basis 1 new for 10 old shs.

Directors - J. Graham Simmonds, exec. chr. & interim CEO, Toronto, Ont.; Stephen M. Gledhill, CFO, Aurora, Ont.; Sara L. Irwin, Toronto, Ont.; Daniel Nauth, Toronto, Ont.; Paul Pellegrini, Toronto, Ont.

Other Exec. Officers - Samantha (Sam) Ford Collins, chief mktg. officer; DJ Muggs, chief brand strategist; Wes Eder, v-p, rev.; Heather Vigil, v-p, sales

Capital Stock

	Authorized (shs.)	Outstanding (shs.)[1]
Subord. Vtg.	unlimited	234,751,747
Multiple Vtg.		7,516

[1] At Nov. 29, 2022

Subordinate Voting - One vote per share.

Multiple Voting - Convertible into subordinate voting shares on 1,000-for-1 basis, subject to restrictions. 1,000 votes per share.

Major Shareholder - Plant-Based Investment Corp. held 30.58% interest, Scott J. Van Rixel held 21.17% interest and Richard Sellers held 11.53% interest at Sept. 28, 2020.

Price Range - GEM/TSX-VEN (D)

Year	Volume	High	Low	Close
2022	15,599,608	$0.09	$0.02	$0.02
2021	43,106,903	$0.24	$0.05	$0.09
2020	20,436,880	$0.19	$0.05	$0.06
2019	7,520,213	$1.23	$0.08	$0.15
2018	292,076	$0.75	$0.30	$0.40

Consolidation: 1-for-10 cons. in May 2019
Recent Close: $0.02
Capital Stock Changes - On August 19, 2022, 17,382,609 subordinate voting shares were issued on the conversion of multiple voting shares on a 1000-for-1 basis.

Wholly Owned Subsidiaries

Bhang Canada Corp., Canada.
Bhang Corporation, Miami, Fla.
- 100% int. in **CB Brands, LLC**
- 100% int. in **CB Productions, LLC**, United States.
- 100% int. in **Euro Brand IP Holdings, LLC**
- 100% int. in **Founding Fathers' Hemp Company**

2838301 Ontario Inc., Ont.

Investments

Plant-Based Investment Corp., Toronto, Ont.

Financial Statistics

Periods ended:	12m Dec. 31/21[A]		12m Dec. 31/20[A]
	US$000s	%Chg	US$000s
Operating revenue	**1,266**	**-22**	**1,627**
Cost of sales	413		708
Salaries & benefits	1,023		961
General & admin expense	2,217		1,941
Stock-based compensation	586		761
Operating expense	**4,239**	**-3**	**4,371**
Operating income	**(2,973)**	**n.a.**	**(2,744)**
Deprec., depl. & amort.	45		90
Finance costs, gross	31		84
Write-downs/write-offs	(15)		(368)
Pre-tax income	**(3,298)**	**n.a.**	**(4,422)**
Net inc. bef. disc. opers	**(3,298)**	**n.a.**	**(4,422)**
Income from disc. opers	nil		3
Net income	**(3,298)**	**n.a.**	**(4,418)**
Cash & equivalent	1,100		70
Inventories	185		205
Accounts receivable	190		246
Current assets	1,640		745
Long-term investments	nil		990
Fixed assets, net	79		153
Total assets	**1,719**	**-9**	**1,887**
Accts. pay. & accr. liabs	978		1,176
Current liabilities	1,342		2,523
Long-term debt, gross	nil		8
Long-term debt, net	nil		2
Shareholders' equity	(258)		(1,388)
Cash from oper. activs	**(2,121)**	**n.a.**	**(2,199)**
Cash from fin. activs	2,533		1,600
Cash from invest. activs	(3)		339
Net cash position	**491**	**+601**	**70**
Capital expenditures	(38)		(88)
Capital disposals	35		100
	US$		US$
Earnings per share*	(0.02)		(0.03)
Cash flow per share*	(0.01)		(0.02)
	shs		shs
No. of shs. o/s*	204,967,115		104,837,537
Avg. no. of shs. o/s*	192,723,258		139,419,484
	%		%
Net profit margin	(260.51)		(271.79)
Return on equity	n.m.		n.m.
Return on assets	(181.20)		n.a.

* Subord. Vtg.
[A] Reported in accordance with IFRS

Latest Results

Periods ended:	9m Sept. 30/22[A]		9m Sept. 30/21[A]
	US$000s	%Chg	US$000s
Operating revenue	1,013	+15	882
Net income	(2,743)	n.a.	(1,374)
	US$		US$
Earnings per share*	(0.01)		(0.01)

* Subord. Vtg.
[A] Reported in accordance with IFRS

Historical Summary
(as originally stated)

Fiscal Year	Oper. Rev.	Net Inc. Bef. Disc.	EPS*
	US$000s	US$000s	US$
2021[A]	1,266	(3,298)	(0.02)
2020[A]	1,627	(4,422)	(0.03)
2019[A1]	4,778	(15,079)	(0.15)
	$000s	$000s	$
2018[A2]	nil	110	0.03
2017[A]	nil	(138)	(0.07)

* Subord. Vtg.
[A] Reported in accordance with IFRS
[1] Results reflect the July 9, 2019, reverse takeover acquisition of Bhang Corporation.
[2] Results for fiscal 2018 and prior periods pertain to Pele Mountain Resources Inc.
Note: Adjusted throughout for 1-for-10 cons. in May 2019

B.47 Big Banc Split Corp.

Symbol - BNK **Exchange** - TSX **CUSIP** - 088893
Head Office - c/o Purpose Investments Inc., 3100-130 Adelaide St W, PO Box 109, Toronto, ON, M5H 3P5 **Telephone** - (416) 583-3850
Toll-free - (877) 789-1517 **Fax** - (416) 583-3851
Website - www.purposeinvest.com
Email - vladt@purposeinvest.com
Investor Relations - Vladimir Tasevski (416) 583-3860
Auditors - Ernst & Young LLP C.A., Toronto, Ont.
Lawyers - Blake, Cassels & Graydon LLP, Toronto, Ont.
Transfer Agents - TSX Trust Company, Toronto, Ont.
Managers - Purpose Investments Inc., Toronto, Ont.

Profile - (Ont. 2020) Holds an equally weighted portfolio of common shares of **Bank of Montreal, Canadian Imperial Bank of Commerce, National Bank of Canada, Royal Bank of Canada, The Bank of Nova Scotia** and **The Toronto-Dominion Bank**.

In order to generate additional returns and enhance the portfolio's income, the manager may write covered call options and cash covered put options in respect of some or all of the shares held in the portfolio. The fund is rebalanced on a quarterly basis.

The company has a scheduled termination date of Nov. 30, 2023, subject to extension for successive terms of up to three years.

The manager is entitled to a management fee at an annual rate of 0.75% of net asset value, calculated and payable monthly in arrears.

Portfolio at June 16, 2023 (as a percentage of the portfolio):

Holdings	Percentage
Canadian Imperial Bank of Commerce	15.32%
The Bank of Nova Scotia	14.92%
Royal Bank of Canada	14.81%
Bank of Montreal	14.69%
National Bank of Canada	14.44%
The Toronto-Dominion Bank	14.36%

Directors - Som Seif, chr., pres. & CEO, Toronto, Ont.; Randall C. Barnes, Las Vegas, Nev.; Jean M. Fraser, Toronto, Ont.; Douglas G. Hall, Halifax, N.S.

Other Exec. Officers - Jeffrey J. (Jeff) Bouganim, CFO; Vladimir Tasevski, v-p; Alessia Crescenzi, sr. counsel & chief compliance officer

Capital Stock

	Authorized (shs.)	Outstanding (shs.)[1]
Preferred	unlimited	1,391,104[2]
Class A	unlimited	1,391,104
Class J	unlimited	100[2 3]

[1] At Dec. 31, 2022
[2] Classified as debt.
[3] All shares are held by Big Banc Split Trust.

Preferred - Entitled to fixed cumulative preferential monthly distributions of 5¢ per share. Retractable in November of each year at a price per unit equal to the net asset value (NAV) per unit (one class A share and one preferred share), less any costs associated with the retraction. Retractable in any other month at a price per share equal to 95% of the lesser of: (i) the NAV per unit less the cost to the company to purchase a class A share for cancellation; and (ii) $10. All outstanding preferred shares will be redeemed on Nov. 30, 2023, at a price per share equal to the lesser of: (i) $10 plus any accrued and unpaid distributions; and (ii) the NAV per preferred share. Rank in priority to class A shares and class J shares with respect to payment of distributions and repayment of capital on the dissolution, liquidation or winding up of the company. Non-voting.

Class A - Entitled to monthly non-cumulative cash distributions targeted to be $0.067 per share. No distributions will be paid if the distributions payable on the preferred shares are in arrears or in respect of a cash distribution, after payment of the distribution, the NAV per unit would be less than $15. Retractable in November of each year along with an equal number of preferred shares at a price per share equal to the NAV per unit, less any costs associated with the retraction, including commissions. Retractable in any other month at a price per share equal to 95% of the difference between: (i) the NAV per unit on the retraction date; and (ii) the cost to the company to purchase a preferred share for cancellation. All outstanding class A shares will be redeemed on Nov. 30, 2023, at a price per share equal to the greater of: (i) the NAV per unit minus $10 and any accrued and unpaid distributions on a preferred share; and (ii) nil. Rank subsequent to preferred shares with respect to payment of distributions and repayment of capital on the dissolution, liquidation or winding up of the company. Non-voting.

Class J - Not entitled to dividends. Redeemable and retractable at $1.00 per share. Rank subsequent to preferred and prior to class A shares with respect to the payment of dividends and the repayment of capital on the dissolution, liquidation or winding up of the company. One vote per share.

Major Shareholder - Big Banc Split Trust held 100% interest at Dec. 31, 2022.

Price Range - BNK/TSX

Year	Volume	High	Low	Close
2022	1,156,080	$19.08	$10.67	$11.78
2021	755,361	$17.30	$10.67	$17.23
2020	944,986	$11.19	$8.43	$10.85

Recent Close: $10.20
Capital Stock Changes - During 2022, 169,100 class A shares and 169,100 preferred shares were retracted.

Dividends

BNK cl A Ra $0.7944 pa M est. Nov. 13, 2020
Prev. Rate: $2.5836 est. Oct. 15, 2020
$1.915◆**g**............ Feb. 1/23 stk.[1]◆**g**........... Jan. 31/22
Paid in 2023: $0.5958 + $1.915◆**g** 2022: $0.7944 + stk.◆**g** 2021: $0.7944
BNK.PR.A pfd cum. Ra $0.60 pa M
[1] Distribution will be automatically reinvested and the units will be consolidated immediately after distribution. Equiv to $1.2410.
◆ Special **g** Capital Gain

Financial Statistics

Periods ended:	12m Dec. 31/22^A		12m Dec. 31/21^A
	$000s	%Chg	$000s
Realized invest. gain (loss)	5,275		6,749
Unrealized invest. gain (loss)	(10,473)		5,235
Total revenue	**(3,641)**	**n.a.**	**13,730**
General & admin. expense	459		461
Operating expense	**459**	**0**	**461**
Operating income	**(4,100)**	**n.a.**	**13,269**
Finance costs, gross	3		nil
Pre-tax income	**(4,103)**	**n.a.**	**13,269**
Net income	**(4,103)**	**n.a.**	**13,269**
Cash & equivalent	nil		242
Accounts receivable	134		227
Investments	32,110		43,966
Total assets	**32,272**	**-28**	**44,903**
Bank indebtedness	201		nil
Accts. pay. & accr. liabs	117		559
Debt	13,936		15,627
Shareholders' equity	17,856		28,506
Cash from oper. activs	**5,195**	**+162**	**1,980**
Cash from fin. activs	(5,638)		(5,770)
Net cash position	**(201)**	**n.a.**	**242**
	$		$
Earnings per share*	(3.26)		6.85
Cash flow per share*	3.36		1.11
Net asset value per share*	12.84		18.27
Cash divd. per share*	0.79		0.79
Extra stk. divd. - cash equiv.*	1.24		nil
Total divd. per share*	**2.04**		**0.79**
	shs		shs
No. of shs. o/s*	1,391,104		1,560,304
Avg. no. of shs. o/s*	1,545,379		1,781,711
	%		%
Net profit margin	n.m.		96.64
Return on equity	(21.71)		48.26
Return on assets	(10.63)		31.09

* Class A

^A Reported in accordance with IFRS

Note: Net income reflects increase/decrease in net assets resulting from operations.

Historical Summary
(as originally stated)

Fiscal Year	Total Rev.	Net Inc. Bef. Disc.	EPS*
	$000s	$000s	$
2022^A	(3,641)	(4,103)	(3.26)
2021^A	13,730	13,269	6.85
2020^A1	7,617	5,310	2.62

* Class A

^A Reported in accordance with IFRS

[1] 6 months ended Dec. 31, 2020.

B.48 Big Pharma Split Corp.

Symbol - PRM **Exchange** - TSX **CUSIP** - 08934P
Head Office - 204-610 Chartwell Rd, Oakville, ON, L6J 4A5 **Telephone** - (416) 649-4541 **Toll-free** - (866) 998-8298 **Fax** - (416) 649-4542
Website - www.harvestportfolios.com
Email - mkovacs@harvestportfolios.com
Investor Relations - Michael Kovacs (416) 649-4541
Auditors - PricewaterhouseCoopers LLP C.A., Oakville, Ont.
Lawyers - Blake, Cassels & Graydon LLP
Transfer Agents - TSX Trust Company, Toronto, Ont.
Managers - Harvest Portfolios Group Inc., Oakville, Ont.
Profile - (Ont. 2017) Invests in an initially equally weighted portfolio consisting of equity securities of 10 dividend-paying healthcare and pharmaceutical companies listed on a North American stock exchange as selected by the portfolio manager.

The portfolio is rebalanced at least semi-annually, to reflect the impact of a merger or acquisition affecting one or more of the healthcare or pharmaceutical companies and to adjust for changes in the market values of investments. To generate additional income, the company may write call options each month in respect of equity securities held in the portfolio. The company will terminate on Dec. 31, 2027, unless extended.

The manager is entitled to a management fee at an annual rate of 0.75% of net asset value, calculated and payable monthly in arrears.

Top 10 holdings at May 31, 2023 (as a percentage of total assets):

Holdings	Percentage
AstraZeneca plc	10.9%
Sanofi S.A.	10.4%
Merck & Co., Inc.	10.3%
Johnson & Johnson	10.0%
Zoetis Inc.	9.8%
Bristol-Myers Squibb Company	9.5%
Amgen Inc.	9.3%
Eli Lilly and Company	9.2%
Pfizer Inc.	9.2%
AbbVie Inc.	8.9%

In November 2022, an extension of the company an additional five years, to Dec. 31, 2027, was approved.

Directors - Michael Kovacs, pres., CEO & corp. sec., Oakville, Ont.; Mary Medeiros, COO, Oakville, Ont.; Dr. Nick Bontis, Ancaster, Ont.; Townsend Haines, Toronto, Ont.

Other Exec. Officers - Daniel Lazzer, CFO; David K. Balsdon, chief compliance officer; Paul MacDonald, chief invest. officer & portfolio mgr.

Capital Stock

	Authorized (shs.)	Outstanding (shs.)[1]
Preferred	unlimited	985,438[2]
Class A	unlimited	1,280,832
Class J	unlimited	100[2]

[1] At Dec. 31, 2022

[2] Classified as debt.

Preferred - Entitled to fixed cumulative preferential quarterly distributions of $0.125 per share (to yield 5% per annum on the original $10 issue price). Retractable in June of each year at the NAV per unit, less any costs associated with the retraction. Retractable in any other month at a price per share equal to 96% of the lesser of: (i) the net asset value (NAV) per unit (one class A share and one preferred share) less the cost to the company to purchase a class A share for cancellation; and (ii) $10. All outstanding preferred shares will be redeemed on Dec. 31, 2027, at a price per share equal to the lesser of: (i) $10 plus any accrued and unpaid distributions; and (ii) the NAV per preferred share. Rank in priority to class A shares and class J shares with respect to payment of distributions and repayment of capital on the dissolution, liquidation or winding-up of the company. Non-voting.

Class A - Entitled to non-cumulative monthly cash distributions of $0.1031 per share (to yield 8.25% per annum on the original $15 issue price). No distributions will be paid if the distributions payable on the preferred shares are in arrears or after payment of the distribution, the NAV per unit would be less than $15. Retractable in June of each year concurrently with a preferred share at a price equal to the lesser of NAV per unit less any costs associated with the retraction. Retractable in any other month at a price per share equal to 96% of the difference between: (i) the NAV per unit; and (ii) the cost to the company to purchase a preferred share for cancellation. All outstanding class A shares will be redeemed on Dec. 31, 2027, at a price per share equal to the greater of: (i) the NAV per unit minus $10 and minus any accrued and unpaid dividends on the preferred share; and (ii) nil. Rank subsequent to preferred shares but in priority to class J shares with respect to payment of distributions and the repayment of capital on the dissolution, liquidation or winding-up of the company. Non-voting.

Class J - Not entitled to receive dividends. Redeemable and retractable at $1.00 per share. Rank subsequent to preferred shares and class A shares with respect to distributions on dissolution, liquidation or winding-up of company. One vote per share.

Major Shareholder - Harvest Big Pharma Split Trust held 100% interest at Dec. 31, 2022.

Price Range - PRM/TSX

Year	Volume	High	Low	Close
2022	764,606	$16.77	$12.50	$14.58
2021	829,490	$15.49	$12.55	$14.67
2020	350,067	$14.75	$8.12	$13.40
2019	553,006	$14.53	$11.39	$14.05
2018	761,895	$14.75	$11.60	$12.38

Recent Close: $15.00

Capital Stock Changes - During 2022, 47,700 preferred shares and 27,700 class A shares were issued under an at-the-market equity program, and 548,527 preferred shares and 233,133 class A shares were retracted.

Dividends

PRM cl A Ra $1.2372 pa M est. Jan. 12, 2018
$0.716◆**g**............ Feb. 24/21
Paid in 2023: $0.9279 2022: $1.2372 2021: $1.2372 + $0.716◆**g**

PRM.PR.A pfd cum. ret. Ra $0.50 pa Q
◆ Special **g** Capital Gain

Financial Statistics

Periods ended:	12m Dec. 31/22^A		12m Dec. 31/21^A
	$000s	%Chg	$000s
Realized invest. gain (loss)	3,027		(2)
Unrealized invest. gain (loss)	(94)		4,745
Total revenue	**4,028**	**-28**	**5,621**
General & admin. expense	882		768
Operating expense	**882**	**+15**	**768**
Operating income	**3,146**	**-35**	**4,853**
Finance costs, gross	756		687
Pre-tax income	**2,389**	**-43**	**4,210**
Net income	**2,389**	**-43**	**4,210**
Cash & equivalent	819		1,430
Accounts receivable	85		103
Investments	23,728		35,318
Total assets	**39,096**	**+3**	**37,814**
Debt	9,854		14,863
Shareholders' equity	19,731		22,404
Cash from oper. activs	**1,128**	**n.a.**	**(9,000)**
Cash from fin. activs	(1,737)		10,194
Net cash position	**819**	**-43**	**1,430**
	$		$
Earnings per share*	1.58		3.27
Cash flow per share*	0.75		(6.98)
Net asset value per share*	15.40		15.07
Cash divd. per share*	1.24		1.24
Extra divd. - cash*	nil		0.72
Capital gains divd.*	nil		0.72
Total divd. per share*	**1.24**		**2.67**
	shs		shs
No. of shs. o/s*	1,280,832		1,486,265
Avg. no. of shs. o/s*	1,509,259		1,289,340
	%		%
Net profit margin	59.31		74.90
Return on equity	11.34		23.66
Return on assets	8.18		16.12

* Class A

^A Reported in accordance with IFRS

Note: Net income reflects increase/decrease in net assets from operations.

Historical Summary
(as originally stated)

Fiscal Year	Total Rev.	Net Inc. Bef. Disc.	EPS*
	$000s	$000s	$
2022^A	4,028	2,389	1.58
2021^A	5,621	4,210	3.27
2020^A	789	(217)	(0.22)
2019^A	3,779	2,580	2.16
2018^A	3,507	2,105	1.56

* Class A

^A Reported in accordance with IFRS

B.49 Big Rock Brewery Inc.

Symbol - BR **Exchange** - TSX **CUSIP** - 08947P
Head Office - 5555 76 Ave SE, Calgary, AB, T2C 4L8 **Telephone** - (403) 720-3239 **Toll-free** - (800) 242-3107 **Fax** - (403) 720-3641
Website - bigrockbeer.com/investors/investors-corporate
Email - investors@bigrockbeer.com
Investor Relations - Stephen J. Giblin (800) 242-3107
Auditors - MNP LLP C.A.
Lawyers - Bennett Jones LLP
Transfer Agents - Odyssey Trust Company, Calgary, Alta.
Employees - 78 at Dec. 30, 2022
Profile - (Alta. 2010) Produces, markets and distributes craft beers, ciders and other alcoholic beverages in Canada.

Has two reportable business segments: wholesale, which manufactures and distributes beer, cider and other alcoholic beverages to provincial liquor boards, grocery chains and on-premise customers, which is subsequently sold to end consumers; and retail, which sells beverages, food and merchandise to end consumers through premises owned and/or operated by the company.

Offers a selection of beer, ciders and ready-to-drink beverages under brands including Big Rock, Tree Brewing, Rock Creek Cider, Dukes Cider, AGD, Shaftbury, Bow Valley, White Peaks and Cottage Spring.

Brewing operations are located in Calgary, Alta., Vancouver, B.C., and Toronto, Ont., with the facility in Calgary serving as the primary brewing, packaging and warehousing facility. Distribution facilities are located in Calgary and Edmonton, Alta., with sales staff residents in Alberta, British Columbia, Saskatchewan, Manitoba and Ontario. The company also has a restaurant brewery in Calgary and in Toronto.

In March 2023, the company initiated a process to evaluate potential strategic alternatives with a view to enhancing shareholder value (strategic review). The strategic review would review the company's operations and investigate alternate courses of actions including, but not limited to, further cost reductions, restructuring, refinancing, a potential sale of all or part of the company's assets, a business combination with another party or other strategic initiatives.

Predecessor Detail - Succeeded Big Rock Brewery Income Trust, Jan. 7, 2011, pursuant to plan of arrangement whereby Big Rock

Brewery Inc. was formed to facilitate the conversion of the trust into a corporation and the trust was subsequently dissolved.

Directors - Stephen J. (Steve) Giblin, chr., interim pres. & interim CEO, Vancouver, B.C.; Kathleen McNally-Leitch, v-chr., Calgary, Alta.; Alanna McDonald, Harrison, N.Y.; P. Donnell Noone, Greensboro, N.C.

Other Exec. Officers - Michael Holditch, interim CFO; Sam Galick, v-p, opers.; Brad Goddard, dir., bus. devel. & govt. rel.

Capital Stock

	Authorized (shs.)	Outstanding (shs.)[1]
Preferred	unlimited	nil
Common	unlimited	6,978,000

[1] At May 15, 2023

Major Shareholder - VN Capital Management, LLC held 28.6% interest, The estate of Edward E. McNally held 14.3% interest and JC Clark Ltd. held 12.3% interest at Apr. 18, 2023.

Price Range - BR/TSX

Year	Volume	High	Low	Close
2022	365,242	$6.40	$1.25	$1.95
2021	709,815	$7.25	$4.51	$6.10
2020	462,714	$5.50	$2.70	$4.75
2019	695,143	$7.25	$4.50	$4.97
2018	936,677	$7.51	$4.67	$6.37

Recent Close: $1.60

Capital Stock Changes - During fiscal 2022, 32,000 common shares were released from treasury.

Wholly Owned Subsidiaries

Big Rock Brewery Operations Corp., Calgary, Alta.
- 0.01% int. in **Big Rock Brewery Limited Partnership**, Calgary, Alta.

Subsidiaries

99.99% int. in **Big Rock Brewery Limited Partnership**, Calgary, Alta.

Financial Statistics

Periods ended:	12m Dec. 30/22[A]		12m Dec. 30/21[A]
	$000s	%Chg	$000s
Operating revenue	**47,098**	**+2**	**45,982**
Cost of sales	26,620		21,639
Salaries & benefits	13,159		12,597
General & admin expense	9,753		9,620
Stock-based compensation	600		802
Operating expense	**50,132**	**+12**	**44,658**
Operating income	**(3,034)**	**n.a.**	**1,324**
Deprec., depl. & amort.	3,885		3,335
Finance costs, gross	982		1,373
Pre-tax income	**(9,068)**	**n.a.**	**(4,076)**
Income taxes	(1,967)		(819)
Net income	**(7,101)**	**n.a.**	**(3,257)**
Cash & equivalent	612		228
Inventories	5,769		6,719
Accounts receivable	2,549		2,167
Current assets	9,924		9,577
Fixed assets, net	36,427		39,226
Right-of-use assets	3,085		3,428
Intangibles, net	2,190		2,591
Total assets	**51,626**	**-6**	**54,822**
Accts. pay. & accr. liabs	8,100		5,753
Current liabilities	15,102		9,817
Long-term debt, gross	13,750		10,214
Long-term debt, net	8,045		7,529
Long-term lease liabilities	3,099		3,628
Shareholders' equity	25,202		31,703
Cash from oper. activs	**(1,335)**	**n.a.**	**962**
Cash from fin. activs	2,685		4,264
Cash from invest. activs	(966)		(5,250)
Net cash position	**612**	**+168**	**228**
Capital expenditures	(1,062)		(7,536)
Capital disposals	318		2,554
	$		$
Earnings per share*	(1.02)		(0.47)
Cash flow per share*	(0.19)		0.14
	shs		shs
No. of shs. o/s*	6,978,000		6,946,000
Avg. no. of shs. o/s*	6,978,000		6,925,000
	%		%
Net profit margin	(15.08)		(7.08)
Return on equity	(24.96)		(9.79)
Return on assets	(11.90)		(4.05)
No. of employees (FTEs)	78		129

* Common
[A] Reported in accordance with IFRS

Latest Results

Periods ended:	3m Mar. 30/23[A]		3m Mar. 31/22[A]
	$000s	%Chg	$000s
Operating revenue	10,451	+19	8,787
Net income	(255)	n.a.	(1,271)
	$		$
Earnings per share*	(0.04)		(0.18)

* Common
[A] Reported in accordance with IFRS

Historical Summary
(as originally stated)

Fiscal Year	Oper. Rev. $000s	Net Inc. Bef. Disc. $000s	EPS* $
2022[A]	47,098	(7,101)	(1.02)
2021[A]	45,982	(3,257)	(0.47)
2020[A]	43,984	(666)	(0.10)
2019[A]	42,653	(2,922)	(0.42)
2018[A]	48,748	360	0.05

* Common
[A] Reported in accordance with IFRS

B.50 Big Tree Carbon Inc.

Symbol - BIGT **Exchange** - TSX-VEN **CUSIP** - 08969W
Head Office - 3600-22 Adelaide St W, Toronto, ON, M5H 4E3 **Telephone** - (416) 844-9969 **Fax** - (416) 865-6636
Website - aurcrest.ca
Email - christopherangeconeb@gmail.com
Investor Relations - Christopher C. J. Angeconeb (416) 844-9969
Auditors - Wasserman Ramsay C.A., Markham, Ont.
Bankers - Royal Bank of Canada, Toronto, Ont.
Lawyers - Gardiner Roberts LLP, Toronto, Ont.
Transfer Agents - TSX Trust Company, Toronto, Ont.

Profile - (Ont. 1982) Developing natural resources carbon sequestration projects and has mineral interests in Ontario.

Developing forestry-based carbon sequestration projects as well as local renewable energy infrastructure and innovative renewable energy technologies, both in partnership with First Nations and indigenous groups, for long-term greenhouses gas emissions reduction benefits which could be monetized through carbon credit trading. Forest carbon projects under development include Lac Seul, 22,063 hectares; and Agoke projects, 974,000 hectares, all in Ontario.

Holds Richardson Lake gold prospect, 3,295 hectares, 100 km northeast of Red Lake, including Richardson, Richardson South and Richardson North gold prospects; nearby Ranger Lake gold prospect, 4,790 hectares, including Ranger East prospect; 35% interest (**Evolution Mining Limited** 65%) in Bridget Lake gold prospect, 144 hectares, 25 km west of Red Lake; and McFaulds Lake prospect, 450 hectares, Lower James Bay region, carried at nil value.

During 2022, Trout Lake South gold prospect (formerly Dancing Man) was abandoned and related costs written off.

Predecessor Detail - Name changed from AurCrest Gold Inc., Apr. 22, 2022.

Directors - Christopher C. J. (Chris) Angeconeb, pres. & CEO, Sioux Lookout, Ont.; William R. (Bill) Johnstone, corp. counsel & corp. sec., Toronto, Ont.; Stan Beardy, Thunder Bay, Ont.; Ian A. Brodie-Brown, Toronto, Ont.; Alex Carpenter, Scarborough, Ont.

Other Exec. Officers - J. Errol Farr, CFO

Capital Stock

	Authorized (shs.)	Outstanding (shs.)[1]
Preference	unlimited	nil
Common	unlimited	113,319,856

[1] At Aug. 13, 2023

Major Shareholder - Widely held at Feb. 28, 2022.

Price Range - BIGT/TSX-VEN

Year	Volume	High	Low	Close
2022	11,680,567	$0.32	$0.06	$0.07
2021	34,270,063	$0.39	$0.07	$0.31
2020	17,618,613	$0.09	$0.02	$0.08
2019	7,814,928	$0.05	$0.02	$0.04
2018	10,129,778	$0.04	$0.01	$0.02

Recent Close: $0.06

Capital Stock Changes - During 2022, common shares were issued as follows: 3,413,333 on exercise of warrants and 250,000 on exercise of options.

Wholly Owned Subsidiaries

Big Tree Carbon Corp., Canada.

Subsidiaries

97% int. in **Wiigwaasaatig Energy Inc.**

Investments

NewRange Gold Corp., Vancouver, B.C. (see Survey of Mines)
Pegasus Resources Inc., Vancouver, B.C. (see Survey of Mines)

Financial Statistics

Periods ended:	12m Dec. 31/22[A]		12m Dec. 31/21[◻A]
	$000s	%Chg	$000s
Exploration expense	179		1,199
General & admin expense	372		510
Stock-based compensation	nil		446
Operating expense	**551**	**-74**	**2,155**
Operating income	**(551)**	**n.a.**	**(2,155)**
Finance income	63		nil
Write-downs/write-offs	(34)		nil
Pre-tax income	**647**	**-70**	**2,124**
Net income	**647**	**-70**	**2,124**
Cash & equivalent	60		472
Accounts receivable	7		28
Current assets	68		520
Explor./devel. properties	71		105
Total assets	**847**	**-15**	**997**
Accts. pay. & accr. liabs	328		189
Current liabilities	1,148		881
Shareholders' equity	(302)		116
Cash from oper. activs	**(243)**	**n.a.**	**(1,891)**
Cash from fin. activs	251		1,900
Cash from invest. activs	(273)		(410)
Net cash position	**1**	**-100**	**266**
Capital expenditures	nil		(38)
	$		$
Earnings per share*	0.01		0.02
Cash flow per share*	(0.00)		(0.02)
	shs		shs
No. of shs. o/s*	113,319,856		109,656,523
Avg. no. of shs. o/s*	112,209,409		102,133,625
	%		%
Net profit margin	n.a.		n.a.
Return on equity	n.m.		n.m.
Return on assets	70.17		219.08

* Common
◻ Restated
[A] Reported in accordance with IFRS

Latest Results

Periods ended:	3m Mar. 31/23[A]		3m Mar. 31/22[A]
	$000s	%Chg	$000s
Net income	54	+54	35
	$		$
Earnings per share*	0.00		0.00

* Common
[A] Reported in accordance with IFRS

Historical Summary
(as originally stated)

Fiscal Year	Oper. Rev. $000s	Net Inc. Bef. Disc. $000s	EPS* $
2022[A]	nil	647	0.01
2021[A]	nil	2,124	0.02
2020[A]	nil	(407)	(0.01)
2019[A]	nil	(199)	(0.00)
2018[A]	nil	(274)	(0.00)

* Common
[A] Reported in accordance with IFRS

B.51 Bigstack Opportunities I Inc.

Symbol - STAK.P **Exchange** - TSX-VEN **CUSIP** - 09000L
Head Office - 902-18 King St W, Toronto, ON, M5C 1C4 **Telephone** - (905) 330-7948
Email - eszustak@jbrlimited.com
Investor Relations - Eric E. V. Szustak (905) 330-7948
Auditors - Clearhouse LLP C.A., Mississauga, Ont.
Transfer Agents - Marrelli Trust Company Limited, Vancouver, B.C.
Profile - (Ont. 2020) Capital Pool Company.
Directors - Eric E. V. Szustak, pres., CEO, CFO & corp. sec., Oakville, Ont.; Magaly Bianchini, Toronto, Ont.; Dennis H. Peterson, Toronto, Ont.

Capital Stock

	Authorized (shs.)	Outstanding (shs.)[1]
Common	unlimited	9,260,001

[1] At Mar. 31, 2023

Major Shareholder - Widely held at Oct. 31, 2021.

Price Range - STAK.P/TSX-VEN

Year	Volume	High	Low	Close
2022	51,000	$0.11	$0.06	$0.10

Recent Close: $0.09

Capital Stock Changes - There were no changes to capital stock during 2022.

B.52 Binovi Technologies Corp.

Symbol - VISN.H **Exchange** - TSX-VEN (S) **CUSIP** - 09076N
Head Office - 574 Chartwell Rd, Oakville, ON, L6J 4A8 **Telephone** - (416) 943-6271 **Toll-free** - (855) 416-7158
Website - www.binovi.com
Email - invest@binovi.com
Investor Relations - Jatinder Dhaliwal (647) 289-6640
Auditors - Saturna Group Chartered Accountants LLP C.A., Vancouver, B.C.
Lawyers - Armstrong Simpson, Vancouver, B.C.
Transfer Agents - Computershare Trust Company of Canada Inc., Vancouver, B.C.
Profile - (B.C. 2011) Develops and commercializes visual and neuro-cognitive processing products and manufactures hardware and software for diagnosing and remediating visual perception disorders in Canada and the U.S.

The Binovi™ platform is a system which integrates software, hardware, data, expert knowledge and insights to help patients, kindergarten to grade 12 (K-12) students and athletes improve vision and vision-related skills. The system includes Binovi™ Touch, a tool which is designed to help visual performance by improving reaction times, improving hand-eye coordination and visual perception, and increasing visual memory; Binovi™ Pro, which allows doctors/trainers to manage their patient/athlete's vision training regimens; Binovi™ Coach, which provides users with automatic updates on their training regimen; Binovi™ Academy, an ePub-based learning and teaching tool which includes testing and therapy protocols and pre-set activities for Binovi™ Pro, as well as custom test configurations for Binovi™ Touch; Binovi™ Balance, which is designed to incorporate balance and gross motor skills to fine-motor and hand-eye coordination exercises; and Binovi™ kit, which contains materials for vision therapy that can be paired with Binovi™ Coach and Binovi™ Pro for multimedia instructions and properly complete home therapies. Beta product which is expected to be available in the third quarter of 2021 include Binovi™ Connect, an application supported by specialized expert knowledge, data insights and supporting hardware to deliver customized one-on-one cognitive training and learning protocols ideal for K-12 students, vision care specialists and sports performance testing and training.

The company also manufactures VIMA Rev strobe lenses which incorporates stroboscopic lenses used to improve sensory and sensory motor skills. Also developing Binovi™ Agile, which is a bundle of Binovi™ Touch, Binovi™ Pro, Binovi™ Balance and Binovi Vima strobe lenses aligned with data and expert knowledge within sports vision therapy.

Wholly owned **VTA Software Corp.** offers vision screening and vision therapy software platform developed and marketed under the VERA™ brand.

Wholly owned **Samurai Motion Tracking Corp.** offers computer aided vision therapy which contains 12 therapy procedures for developing saccadic eye movements, span of recognition, and visual sequential memory skills that are essential for fast and accurate reading.

Common suspended from TSX-VEN, July 6, 2022.

Predecessor Detail - Name changed from Eyecarrot Innovations Corp., June 30, 2020.

Directors - Jatinder (Jay) Dhaliwal, CEO & interim CFO, Vancouver, B.C.; Usama (Sam) Chaudhry, Vancouver, B.C.; David M. (Dave) Jenkins, Langley, B.C.; Mohsen Rahimi, B.C.

Other Exec. Officers - Dr. Sam Mithani, chief tech. officer; Dr. Leonard Press, chief scientific officer; Dr. Patrick Quaid, chief scientific officer, Binocular Vision

Capital Stock

	Authorized (shs.)	Outstanding (shs.)[1]
Common	unlimited	26,613,490

[1] At Sept. 19, 2022

Major Shareholder - Widely held at Sept. 19, 2022.

Price Range - VISN.H/TSX-VEN (S)

Year	Volume	High	Low	Close
2022	2,216,013	$0.16	$0.08	$0.09
2021	17,553,581	$2.00	$0.12	$0.12
2020	15,727,298	$6.90	$1.15	$1.55
2019	1,191,629	$20.00	$1.05	$3.60
2018	193,444	$33.00	$11.00	$14.00

Consolidation: 1-for-10 cons. in Oct. 2021; 1-for-10 cons. in Aug. 2019

Capital Stock Changes - On Oct. 21, 2021, common shares were consolidated on a 1-for-10 basis. In December 2021, private placement of 10,033,334 post-consolidated common shares was completed at 15¢ per share.

Wholly Owned Subsidiaries

Call Connect Me Inc., Canada.
1252796 B.C. Ltd., Canada.
Samurai Motion Tracking Corp.
2270377 Alberta Ltd., Canada.
VTA Software Corp., Canada.
Wayne Engineering Inc., United States.

Financial Statistics

Periods ended:	12m Feb. 28/21[A]		12m Feb. 29/20[A]
	$000s	%Chg	$000s
Operating revenue	**646**	**-6**	**687**
Cost of sales	205		102
Salaries & benefits	254		456
Research & devel. expense	467		484
General & admin expense	5,980		5,313
Stock-based compensation	1,138		741
Other operating expense	nil		(45)
Operating expense	**8,045**	**+14**	**7,052**
Operating income	**(7,399)**	**n.a.**	**(6,365)**
Deprec., depl. & amort.	773		185
Finance costs, gross	53		41
Pre-tax income	**(9,028)**	**n.a.**	**(7,689)**
Net income	**(9,028)**	**n.a.**	**(7,689)**
Cash & equivalent	117		231
Inventories	267		269
Accounts receivable	286		296
Current assets	2,096		1,942
Fixed assets, net	17		22
Right-of-use assets	35		95
Intangibles, net	10,030		842
Total assets	**12,296**	**+254**	**3,471**
Bank indebtedness	nil		8
Accts. pay. & accr. liabs	2,165		1,894
Current liabilities	2,292		2,044
Long-term debt, gross	34		nil
Long-term debt, net	34		nil
Long-term lease liabilities	nil		40
Shareholders' equity	9,877		1,387
Cash from oper. activs	**(6,067)**	**n.a.**	**(6,525)**
Cash from fin. activs	5,952		4,617
Cash from invest. activs	nil		(17)
Net cash position	**117**	**-49**	**231**
Capital expenditures	nil		(17)
	$		$
Earnings per share*	(1.00)		(4.20)
Cash flow per share*	(0.72)		(3.59)
	shs		shs
No. of shs. o/s*	12,856,677		4,167,025
Avg. no. of shs. o/s*	8,403,769		1,817,135
	%		%
Net profit margin	n.m.		n.m.
Return on equity	(160.30)		(302.54)
Return on assets	(113.85)		(182.73)
Foreign sales percent	86		84

* Common
[A] Reported in accordance with IFRS

Latest Results

Periods ended:	6m Aug. 31/21[A]		6m Aug. 31/20[A]
	$000s	%Chg	$000s
Operating revenue	202	-25	269
Net income	(3,017)	n.a.	(3,202)
	$		$
Earnings per share*	(1.90)		(0.54)

* Common
[A] Reported in accordance with IFRS

Historical Summary
(as originally stated)

Fiscal Year	Oper. Rev.	Net Inc. Bef. Disc.	EPS*
	$000s	$000s	$
2021[A]	646	(9,028)	(1.00)
2020[A]	687	(7,689)	(4.20)
2019[A]	667	(4,773)	(4.80)
2018[A]	99	(2,713)	(4.00)
2017[A]	97	(4,336)	(8.00)

* Common
[A] Reported in accordance with IFRS

Note: Adjusted throughout for 1-for-10 cons. in Oct. 2021; 1-for-10 cons. in Aug. 2019

B.53 biOasis Technologies Inc.

Symbol - BTI **Exchange** - TSX-VEN **CUSIP** - 09064N
Head Office - 157 Church St, 19 Flr, New Haven, CT, United States, 06510 **Telephone** - (203) 533-7082
Website - www.bioasis.us
Email - deborah@bioasis.us
Investor Relations - Deborah Rathjen (203) 533-7082
Auditors - Manning Elliott LLP C.A., Vancouver, B.C.
Lawyers - Bereskin & Parr LLP; Cooley LLP; Thomas, Rondeau LLP, Vancouver, B.C.
Transfer Agents - Computershare Trust Company of Canada Inc., Vancouver, B.C.
Profile - (B.C. 2006) Researches, develops and commercializes technologies and products intended for the treatment of central nervous system diseases and disorders.

The company is developing a proprietary carrier for the transport of therapeutic agents across the blood brain barrier (BBB), through its xB³™ platform. The BBB protects the brain by preventing almost all foreign substances from entering. The company collaborates with pharmaceutical companies to research if xB³ platform can be used to deliver their therapeutic compounds to the brain.

Also developing epidermal growth factor (EGF) platform for treating rare and orphan neurodegenerative and neuroinflammatory disorders. EGF is a protein that stimulates cell growth and diffentiation, notably for myelin producing cells. EGF is anticipated to stimulate myeline regeneration and protect nerve cells in addition to inducing nerve cell growth and differentiation.

Programs under development include xB³-001, which targets HER2-positive breast cancer brain metastases; xB³-002, which targets glioblastoma; xB³-004, which targets neuropathic pain and neuroinflammation; xB³-007, which targets neurodegenerative diseases including Gaucher's, Parkinson's and Lewy body dementia; xB³-008, for the treatment of Hunter Syndrome; xB³-009, which targets Frontotemporal Lobe dementia, neuronal ceoird lipofusinosis and amyotrophic lateral sclerosis; and EGF1-48, which stimulates myelination and downregulating neuroinflammation, thus offering neuroprotective properties that support development in Guillain-Barre Syndrome, Chronic Inflammatory Demyelinating Polyneuropathy and other clinical manifestations related to onset and/or progression of multiple sclerosis, including optic neuritis and relapses of the disease.

Has over 150 U.S. and foreign patents related to its technologies for delivering therapeutic agents across the BBB which include the xB³ peptide vectors, pharmaceutical compositions and methods of use.

In June 2022, the company acquired all rights, title and interest in the intellectual property of Norway-based **Cresence AS** related to the epidermal growth factor (EGM) platform, which would be used for the treatment of Guillain-Barre Syndrome and Chronic Inflammatory Demyelinating Polyneuropathy, among other indications, for issuance of 6,500,000 common shares and up to an additional of 6,000,0000 common shares upon achieving certain milestones.

In May 2022, the company entered into a research collaboration and licensing agreement with Seoul, South Korea-based **Neuramedy Co. Ltd.** whereby Neuramedy obtained worldwide rights to research, develop and commercialize an xB³™ version of its antibody, Tomaralimab, directed at the Toll-like receptor 2, for an upfront payment and may receive an additional of US$72,000,000 milestone payments and a royalty on net sales.

Recent Merger and Acquisition Activity

Status: terminated **Revised:** Jan. 23, 2023
UPDATE: Midatech shareholders did not approve the transaction and the agreement was terminated. PREVIOUS: Midatech Pharma plc agreed to acquire BiOasis Technologies Inc. on the basis of 0.9556 Midatech ordinary shares (or 0.0382 American depositary shares, (ADSs)) for each BiOasis common share held. The transaction is subject to a number of conditions, including Midatech completing a financing and Midatech shareholder approval.

Predecessor Detail - Name changed from W.R. Partners Ltd., Mar. 27, 2008, following Qualifying Transaction acquisition of biOasis Technologies Inc.

Directors - Dr. Deborah A. Rathjen, exec. chr., pres. & CEO, S.A., Australia; David M. Wurzer†, Conn.; John E. Curran, Conn.; John Hemeon, Kingsville, Ont.; Dr. Mario Saltarelli, Boston, Mass.

Other Exec. Officers - David P. (Dave) Jenkins, CFO; May Orfali, CMO; Mei Mei Tian, v-p & head, external research
† Lead director

Capital Stock

	Authorized (shs.)	Outstanding (shs.)[1]
Common	unlimited	79,414,015

[1] At Jan. 5, 2023

Major Shareholder - Widely held at Jan. 5, 2023.

Price Range - BTI/TSX-VEN

Year	Volume	High	Low	Close
2022	7,164,372	$0.31	$0.04	$0.05
2021	12,905,636	$0.70	$0.23	$0.27
2020	8,841,752	$0.46	$0.15	$0.35
2019	5,622,073	$0.63	$0.18	$0.25
2018	11,826,754	$0.97	$0.26	$0.48

Recent Close: $0.01

Capital Stock Changes - In June 2022, 6,500,000 common shares were issued on acquisition of intangible assets.

Wholly Owned Subsidiaries

biOasis Advanced Technologies Inc., B.C.
Bioasis Biosciences Corp., United States.
Bioasis Royalty Fund, LLC, United States.

Financial Statistics

Periods ended:	12m Feb. 28/22^A		12m Feb. 28/21^oA
	$000s	%Chg	$000s
Operating revenue	**38**	**-99**	**4,078**
Salaries & benefits	1,378		1,611
Research & devel. expense	920		1,004
General & admin expense	841		743
Stock-based compensation	441		279
Operating expense	**3,580**	**-2**	**3,637**
Operating income	**(3,542)**	**n.a.**	**441**
Deprec., depl. & amort.	55		60
Pre-tax income	**(2,960)**	**n.a.**	**698**
Net income	**(2,960)**	**n.a.**	**698**
Cash & equivalent	1,731		2,737
Accounts receivable	98		30
Current assets	2,107		3,059
Fixed assets, net	nil		5
Intangibles, net	159		213
Total assets	**2,266**	**-31**	**3,276**
Accts. pay. & accr. liabs	1,489		1,843
Current liabilities	2,989		1,899
Long-term debt, gross	1,902		nil
Long-term debt, net	402		nil
Shareholders' equity	1,917		407
Cash from oper. activs	**(3,636)**	**n.a.**	**1,771**
Cash from fin. activs	2,636		312
Cash from invest. activs	nil		7
Net cash position	**1,731**	**-37**	**2,737**
Capital disposals	nil		7
	$		$
Earnings per share*	(0.04)		0.01
Cash flow per share*	(0.05)		0.03
	shs		shs
No. of shs. o/s*	72,914,015		72,914,015
Avg. no. of shs. o/s*	72,167,220		68,115,456
	%		%
Net profit margin	n.m.		17.12
Return on equity	(254.73)		n.m.
Return on assets	(106.82)		33.10

* Common
^o Restated
^A Reported in accordance with IFRS

Latest Results

Periods ended:	6m Aug. 31/22^A		6m Aug. 31/21^A
	$000s	%Chg	$000s
Operating revenue	120	n.a.	nil
Net income	(1,323)	n.a.	(1,121)
	$		$
Earnings per share*	(0.02)		(0.02)

* Common
^A Reported in accordance with IFRS

Historical Summary
(as originally stated)

Fiscal Year	Oper. Rev. $000s	Net Inc. Bef. Disc. $000s	EPS* $
2022^A	38	(2,960)	(0.04)
2021^A	4,078	698	0.01
2020^A	606	(4,056)	(0.07)
2019^A	1,422	(3,473)	(0.06)
2018^A	590	(5,308)	(0.10)

* Common
^A Reported in accordance with IFRS

B.54 Biocure Technology Inc.

Symbol - CURE **Exchange** - CSE **CUSIP** - 09075T
Head Office - 300-1055 Hastings St W, Vancouver, BC, V6E 2E9 **Telephone** - (604) 609-7146 **Fax** - (604) 685-5120
Website - www.biocuretech.com
Email - info@biocuretech.com
Investor Relations - Konstantin Lichtenwald (604) 609-7146
Auditors - Dale Matheson Carr-Hilton LaBonte LLP C.A., Vancouver, B.C.
Lawyers - Armstrong Simpson, Vancouver, B.C.
Transfer Agents - Computershare Trust Company of Canada Inc., Vancouver, B.C.

Profile - (B.C. 2007) Developing biosimilar pharmaceutical products for the treatment of multiple sclerosis, neutropenia, macular edema and macular degeneration. Also developing Chimeric Antigen Receptor T-Cell (CAR-T) therapy for the treatment of chronic lymphocytic leukemia and lung and ovarian cancer, as well as a foot and mouth disease vaccine, and hair growth production and skin regeneration products.

Biopharmaceutical products under pre-clinical development include Interferon beta-1b for treatment of relapsing forms of multiple sclerosis; Ranibizumab for treatment of macular degeneration and macular edema; and PEG-Filgrastim for treatment of neutropenia.

Also developing CAR-T, a cell-based therapy that uses the patient's immune system to treat cancer. T cells are isolated and then transformed with specific CAR that recognize the cancer. The transformed T cells are infused back into the patient to effect the treatment. The company has selected to develop ROR1 CAR-T for the treatment of chronic lymphocytic leukemia and lung and ovarian cancer.

Other products include a foot and mouth disease vaccine using recombined protein; and hair growth agent and skin regeneration products which uses stem-cell culture technology to identify growth factors, which are then applied to cosmetic products.

In June 2023, the company sold its 1,773,879 common shares and 57,954 preferred shares in **Biocurepharm Corporation** to Dr. Sang Mok Lee. As consideration Dr. Lee would transfer to the company an aggregate of 27,317,506 common shares of the company held by him for cancellation and return to treasury.

Predecessor Detail - Name changed from Gravis Energy Corp., Nov. 24, 2017, following reverse takeover acquisition of BiocurePharm Corporation; basis 1 new for 6.03348 old shs.

Directors - Dr. Sang Mok Lee, CEO, Daejeon, South Korea; Konstantin Lichtenwald, CFO, Vancouver, B.C.; Sang Goo (Collin) Kim, corp. sec., Vancouver, B.C.; Berkan Unal, Berlin, Germany

Other Exec. Officers - Dr. Björn Cocholovius, pres.

Capital Stock

	Authorized (shs.)	Outstanding (shs.)[1]
Common	unlimited	81,603,652

[1] At June 1, 2023

Major Shareholder - Widely held at June 1, 2023.

Price Range - CURE/CSE

Year	Volume	High	Low	Close
2022	1,231,515	$0.12	$0.01	$0.01
2021	1,986,051	$0.33	$0.12	$0.13
2020	1,309,136	$0.54	$0.09	$0.28
2019	2,496,016	$0.81	$0.18	$0.22
2018	12,735,469	$1.89	$0.24	$0.48

Recent Close: $0.04

Capital Stock Changes - During 2022, 2,300,000 common shares were issued for debt settlement.

Subsidiaries

92.11% int. in **BiocurePharm Corporation**, South Korea.

Investments

10% int. in **Korea Waterbury Uranium Corporation**
9.95% int. in **Korea Waterbury Uranium Limited Partnership**, B.C.

Financial Statistics

Periods ended:	12m Dec. 31/22^A		12m Dec. 31/21^oA
	$000s	%Chg	$000s
Salaries & benefits	8		32
General & admin expense	688		606
Stock-based compensation	nil		1,165
Operating expense	**696**	**-61**	**1,803**
Operating income	**(696)**	**n.a.**	**(1,803)**
Finance costs, gross	5		67
Pre-tax income	**(403)**	**n.a.**	**(1,869)**
Net inc. bef. disc. opers	**(403)**	**n.a.**	**(1,869)**
Income from disc. opers	(1,112)		722
Net income	**(1,515)**	**n.a.**	**(1,148)**
Net inc. for equity hldrs	**(1,450)**	**n.a.**	**(1,128)**
Net inc. for non-cont. int	**(65)**	**n.a.**	**(20)**
Cash & equivalent	38		159
Inventories	nil		4
Accounts receivable	22		13
Current assets	118		2,134
Long-term investments	1,966		1,966
Fixed assets, net	nil		5
Right-of-use assets	nil		3
Intangibles, net	nil		1
Total assets	**2,084**	**-50**	**4,153**
Bank indebtedness	81		1,197
Accts. pay. & accr. liabs	713		939
Current liabilities	4,411		3,752
Long-term debt, gross	nil		1,254
Long-term debt, net	nil		1,254
Shareholders' equity	(1,978)		(533)
Non-controlling interest	(349)		(320)
Cash from oper. activs	**(818)**	**n.a.**	**(1,083)**
Cash from fin. activs	631		1,169
Cash from invest. activs	75		27
Net cash position	**38**	**-76**	**159**
	$		$
Earnings per share*	(0.00)		(0.02)
Cash flow per share*	(0.01)		(0.01)
	shs		shs
No. of shs. o/s*	108,921,158		106,621,158
Avg. no. of shs. o/s*	106,917,322		103,038,873
	%		%
Net profit margin	n.a.		n.a.
Return on equity	n.m.		n.m.
Return on assets	(12.76)		(41.41)

* Common
^o Restated
^A Reported in accordance with IFRS

Latest Results

Periods ended:	3m Mar. 31/23^A		3m Mar. 31/22^A
	$000s	%Chg	$000s
Net income	(328)	n.a.	(327)
Net inc. for equity hldrs	(313)	n.a.	(308)
Net inc. for non-cont. int	(15)		(19)
	$		$
Earnings per share*	(0.00)		(0.00)

* Common
^A Reported in accordance with IFRS

Historical Summary
(as originally stated)

Fiscal Year	Oper. Rev. $000s	Net Inc. Bef. Disc. $000s	EPS* $
2022^A	nil	(403)	(0.00)
2021^A	nil	(1,148)	(0.01)
2020^A	nil	(3,078)	(0.03)
2019^A	nil	(4,791)	(0.05)
2018^A	nil	(6,586)	(0.07)

* Common
^A Reported in accordance with IFRS

B.55 BioHarvest Sciences Inc.

Symbol - BHSC **Exchange** - CSE **CUSIP** - 09076J
Head Office - 1140-625 Howe St, Vancouver, BC, V6C 2T6 **Telephone** - (604) 689-5722 **Fax** - (604) 685-9182
Website - www.bioharvest.com
Email - dave@bioharvest.com
Investor Relations - David K. Ryan (604) 622-1186
Auditors - BDO Ziv Haft C.P.A., Tel Aviv, Israel
Transfer Agents - National Securities Administrators Ltd., Vancouver, B.C.

Profile - (B.C. 2013) Owns Bio-Plant CELLicitation™, a proprietary and patented platform technology for growing plant cells in liquid bioreactors in order to produce the active plant ingredients without the need to grow the whole plant.

The technology allows the production of the desired plant metabolites in their natural state to ensure the highest bio-availability and efficacy without the undesired elements, such as pesticides, chemicals and residues. The original plant is used only once to collect the plant cells with the active ingredients that are subsequently perpetually reproduced with the same quality and consistency.

The company operates within two segments: Nutraceuticals and Pharmaceuticals.

Nutraceuticals

The company engages in research and development of unique science-based therapeutic solutions for the nutraceutical industry. Its first polyphenol/antioxidant nutraceutical superfruits product is VINIA®, a functional food and dietary supplement powder from red grape cells containing the whole matrix of polyphenols with a high concentration of piceid resveratrol. VINIA® has been approved and available for sale in Israel and the U.S. through e-commerce and business-to-business channels.

Pharmaceuticals

The company focuses on the development of plant cell-based Active Pharmaceutical Ingredients (APIs) that can assist in the treatment of specific medical indications including the ability of its red grape cell active ingredient to treat and improve eye, cardio-vascular, mental and skin health. In addition, the company has been growing trichomes, the natural micro-factories producing cannabinoids, terpenes and other phytochemicals in the cannabis plant, sourced from multiple plant strains. Commercialization of cannabis biomass, consisting of cannabis cells which include trichomes, was put on hold in 2022.

During the second quarter of 2022, wholly owned **Dolarin Ltd.** was amalgamated into wholly owned **BioHarvest Ltd.**

Predecessor Detail - Name changed from Canna-V-Cell Sciences Inc., Mar. 31, 2020, pursuant to the reverse takeover acquisition of Israel-based BioHarvest Ltd. and concurrent amalgamation of BioHarvest with wholly owned BioFarming Ltd.

Directors - Dr. Zaki Rakib, chr. & pres., San Jose, Calif.; David K. (Dave) Ryan, v-p, IR & corp. sec., Langley, B.C.; John A. (Jake) Fiddick, Burnaby, B.C.; Vivien Rakib, Tel Aviv, Israel; David Tsur, Israel

Other Exec. Officers - Ilan Sobel, CEO; Dr. Ilana Belzer, COO; Alan Rootenberg, CFO; Dr. Brian S. Cornblatt, CMO; Dr. Yochi Hagay, chief tech. officer; Malkit Azachi, v-p, R&D; Michal Sapir, v-p, regulation affairs

Capital Stock

	Authorized (shs.)	Outstanding (shs.)[1]
Preferred	unlimited	nil
Common	unlimited	472,723,419

[1] At May 30, 2023

Major Shareholder - Vivien Rakib held 22.02% interest and GreenSoil Investments Management Ltd. held 10.37% interest at June 12, 2023.

Price Range - BHSC/CSE

Year	Volume	High	Low	Close
2022	28,341,076	$0.54	$0.23	$0.29
2021	56,460,600	$0.71	$0.22	$0.46
2020	29,205,840	$0.35	$0.10	$0.23
2019	14,972,173	$0.34	$0.11	$0.15
2018	1,789,739	$0.40	$0.11	$0.19

Recent Close: $0.17

Capital Stock Changes - During 2022, 164,000 common shares were issued on exercise of warrants.

Wholly Owned Subsidiaries

BioHarvest Ltd., Israel.
• 100% int. in **BioHarvest Inc.**, Del.
Superfood Nutraceuticals Inc., Del.

Financial Statistics

Periods ended:	12m Dec. 31/22[A]		12m Dec. 31/21[A]
	US$000s	%Chg	US$000s
Operating revenue	**5,498**	**+162**	**2,102**
Cost of sales	4,279		1,432
Research & devel. expense	2,186		4,062
General & admin expense	9,352		4,759
Operating expense	**15,817**	**+54**	**10,253**
Operating income	**(10,319)**	**n.a.**	**(8,151)**
Deprec., depl. & amort.	293		340
Finance costs, net	624		1,336
Pre-tax income	**(11,236)**	**n.a.**	**(9,827)**
Net income	**(11,236)**	**n.a.**	**(9,827)**
Cash & equivalent	1,736		4,117
Inventories	1,378		928
Accounts receivable	1,208		620
Current assets	4,322		5,665
Fixed assets, net	4,908		4,364
Total assets	**9,393**	**-8**	**10,208**
Accts. pay. & accr. liabs.	2,237		1,901
Current liabilities	11,519		2,923
Long-term debt, gross	8,549		nil
Long-term debt, net	8,549		nil
Long-term lease liabilities	1,670		2,273
Shareholders' equity	(5,929)		2,855
Cash from oper. activs.	**(9,241)**	**n.a.**	**(6,794)**
Cash from fin. activs.	8,138		10,772
Cash from invest. activs.	(1,256)		(1,640)
Net cash position	**1,736**	**-58**	**4,117**
Capital expenditures	(1,256)		(1,640)
	US$		US$
Earnings per share*	(0.02)		(0.02)
Cash flow per share*	(0.02)		(0.02)
	shs		shs
No. of shs. o/s*	460,716,275		453,630,137
Avg. no. of shs. o/s*	456,877,572		435,669,422
	%		%
Net profit margin	(204.37)		(467.51)
Return on equity	n.m.		n.m.
Return on assets	(114.65)		n.a.
Foreign sales percent	100		100

* Common
[A] Reported in accordance with IFRS

Latest Results

Periods ended:	3m Mar. 31/23[A]		3m Mar. 31/22[A]
	US$000s	%Chg	US$000s
Operating revenue	2,163	+209	699
Net income	(752)	n.a.	(2,130)
	US$		US$
Earnings per share*	(0.00)		(0.00)

* Common
[A] Reported in accordance with IFRS

Historical Summary
(as originally stated)

Fiscal Year	Oper. Rev.	Net Inc. Bef. Disc.	EPS*
	US$000s	US$000s	US$
2022[A]	5,498	(11,236)	(0.02)
2021[A]	2,102	(9,827)	(0.02)
2020[A1]	396	(6,584)	(0.02)
2019[A2]	nil	(5,135)	(0.09)
	$000s	$000s	$
2018[A3]	nil	(210)	(0.01)

* Common
[A] Reported in accordance with IFRS
[1] Results reflect the Mar. 31, 2020, reverse takeover acquisition of BioHarvest Ltd.
[2] Results reflect the Sept. 27, 2018, reverse takeover acquisition of Dolarin Ltd.
[3] Results for fiscal 2018 and prior fiscal years pertain to Midnight Star Ventures Corp.

B.56 BioMark Diagnostics Inc.

Symbol - BUX **Exchange** - CSE **CUSIP** - 09073K
Head Office - 130-3851 Shell Rd, Richmond, BC, V6X 2W2 **Telephone** - (604) 370-0779
Website - www.biomarkdiagnostics.com
Email - rahmed@biomarkdiagnostics.com
Investor Relations - Rashid A. M. Bux (604) 836-6950
Auditors - MNP LLP C.A., Vancouver, B.C.
Transfer Agents - Computershare Trust Company of Canada Inc.
Employees - 6 at Aug. 3, 2023
Profile - (B.C. 2014) Developing a cancer diagnostics technology platform based on metabolomics and machine learning.

The company is focused on bringing its blood-based cancer diagnostic tests and detection solution to commercialization standards starting with its early lung cancer assay. Also plans to expand into other hard to detect and treat cancers such as brain, ovarian, breast, pancreatic, head and neck.

The intellectual property (IP) portfolio of the company includes more than eight distinct families of patents offering worldwide protection on early lung cancer detection and spermidine/spermine N1-acetyltransferase (SSAT1) use for response to treatment in lung and brain cancers.

The company's legacy novel Acetylated Biomarker Assay Red Alert technology, a metabolomic screening technology, is used to determine the amount of cancer in the body. The technology works by screening for the acetylated form of an approved drug (amantadine) which is given to patients prior to measurement in body fluids using liquid chromatography-mass spectrometry. The amantadine acetylation is performed by an enzyme, spermidine/spermine N-acetyltransferase (SSAT). Analysis of SSAT mRNA levels in tissue samples allows determination of cancer type. In addition, this technology can help assess response to treatment and determine potential early relapse.

Affiliate **Bio-Stream Diagnostics Inc.** is developing a low-cost pathogen detection platform based on OCET platform and was conducting several clinical proof of concept studies on several pathogens and biomarkers for point of care applications.

Directors - Rashid A. M. Bux, pres. & CEO, B.C.; Kai-Ming (Brian) Cheng, chief technical officer, Pa.; Dr. Bramhanand (Bram) Ramjiawan, Man.

Other Exec. Officers - Guoyu (Gina) Huang, interim CFO; Jean-François (Jeff) Haince, chief scientific officer & gen. mgr.

Capital Stock

	Authorized (shs.)	Outstanding (shs.)[1]
Common	unlimited	83,286,229

[1] At July 28, 2023

Major Shareholder - Biomark Technologies Inc. held 49.23% interest at Nov. 4, 2022.

Price Range - BUX/CSE

Year	Volume	High	Low	Close
2022	4,679,730	$0.31	$0.15	$0.22
2021	22,166,982	$0.63	$0.14	$0.27
2020	8,368,294	$0.29	$0.07	$0.15
2019	9,264,034	$0.30	$0.03	$0.23
2018	5,335,070	$0.11	$0.04	$0.05

Recent Close: $0.24

Capital Stock Changes - In May 2022, private placement of 5,062,000 units (1 common share & 1 warrant) at 25¢ per unit was completed. Also during fiscal 2023, 250,000 common shares were issued on exercise of options.

During fiscal 2022, 1,190,000 common shares were issued on exercise of warrants.

Wholly Owned Subsidiaries

BioMark Cancer Diagnostics USA Inc., Del.
Biomark Cancer Systems Inc.
BioMark Diagnostic Solutions Inc., Qué.

Investments

20.53% int. in **Bio-Stream Diagnostics Inc.**, Alta.

Financial Statistics

Periods ended:	12m Mar. 31/23[A]		12m Mar. 31/22[□A]
	$000s	%Chg	$000s
Operating revenue	**153**	**+248**	**44**
Research & devel. expense	546		498
General & admin expense	824		864
Stock-based compensation	330		nil
Operating expense	**1,700**	**+25**	**1,362**
Operating income	**(1,547)**	**n.a.**	**(1,318)**
Deprec., depl. & amort.	386		180
Finance costs, gross	110		50
Pre-tax income	**(1,842)**	**n.a.**	**(1,454)**
Net income	**(1,842)**	**n.a.**	**(1,454)**
Cash & equivalent	72		383
Accounts receivable	34		82
Current assets	126		499
Long-term investments	3		3
Fixed assets, net	45		53
Right-of-use assets	543		916
Total assets	**732**	**-50**	**1,472**
Bank indebtedness	229		144
Accts. pay. & accr. liabs.	220		128
Current liabilities	1,664		1,501
Long-term debt, gross	nil		96
Long-term debt, net	nil		96
Long-term lease liabilities	217		510
Shareholders' equity	(1,150)		(636)
Cash from oper. activs.	**(914)**	**n.a.**	**(1,204)**
Cash from fin. activs.	609		768
Cash from invest. activs.	(5)		(59)
Net cash position	**72**	**-81**	**383**
Capital expenditures	(5)		(59)
	$		$
Earnings per share*	(0.02)		(0.02)
Cash flow per share*	(0.01)		(0.02)
	shs		shs
No. of shs. o/s*	83,286,229		77,974,229
Avg. no. of shs. o/s*	82,777,884		77,928,585
	%		%
Net profit margin	n.m.		n.m.
Return on equity	n.m.		n.m.
Return on assets	(157.17)		(115.79)

* Common
□ Restated
[A] Reported in accordance with IFRS

Historical Summary
(as originally stated)

Fiscal Year	Oper. Rev.	Net Inc. Bef. Disc.	EPS*
	$000s	$000s	$
2023[A]	153	(1,842)	(0.02)
2022[A]	44	(1,454)	(0.02)
2021[A]	nil	(1,094)	(0.02)
2020[A]	263	(1,215)	(0.02)
2019[A]	nil	(546)	(0.01)

* Common
[A] Reported in accordance with IFRS

B.57 Biome Grow Inc.

Symbol - BIO **Exchange** - CSE **CUSIP** - 09075M
Head Office - 1401-480 University Ave, Toronto, ON, M5G 1V2 **Telephone** - (416) 875-8395 **Toll-free** - (833) 333-2588 **Fax** - (416) 805-7895
Website - www.biomegrow.com
Email - kmalik@biomegrow.com
Investor Relations - Khurram Malik (833) 333-2588
Auditors - Manning Elliott LLP C.A., Vancouver, B.C.
Transfer Agents - Computershare Trust Company of Canada Inc., Vancouver, B.C.
Profile - (Can. 2014) Seeking new business opportunities.

Prior to July 2020, owned licensed Canadian cannabis producer **Highland Grow Inc.**

On May 21, 2021, the company exchanged all its 88,904,428 remaining exchangeable shares held of **MYM Nutraceuticals Inc.** for a like number of common shares. As a result, the company held a total of 122,768,413 MYM common shares, representing a 33.3% interest. Subsequently in July 2021, MYM was acquired by **IM Cannabis Corp.** (IMC) and all MYM common shares held by the company were converted into 2,700,905 common shares of IMC.

Predecessor Detail - Name changed from Orca Touchscreen Technologies Ltd., Oct. 3, 2018, following reverse takeover acquisition of Cultivator Catalyst Corp. (CCC) and concurrent amalgamation of CCC with wholly owned 1151856 B.C. Ltd.; basis 1 new for 50 old shs.

Directors - Khurram Malik, CEO & interim CFO, Toronto, Ont.; J. Mark Lievonen, Stouffville, Ont.; Steven Poirier, Toronto, Ont.

Other Exec. Officers - Laird Choi, v-p, corp. srvcs.; David Callahan, pres., The Back Home Medical Cannabis Corporation; Frank MacMaster, pres., Highland Grow Inc.

Capital Stock

	Authorized (shs.)	Outstanding (shs.)[1]
Class B Preferred	unlimited	nil
Common	unlimited	112,417,435
Special Class C	unlimited	1

[1] At Aug. 29, 2022

Class B Preferred - Issuable in series. Non-voting.

Common - One vote per share.

Special Class C - Not entitled to dividends. Convertible into common shares, under certain circumstances. Non-voting.

Major Shareholder - Sasha Jacob held 44.3% interest at June 24, 2021.

Price Range - BIO/CSE

Year	Volume	High	Low	Close
2022	2,765,472	$0.04	$0.01	$0.01
2021	9,565,530	$0.18	$0.03	$0.04
2020	13,058,144	$0.19	$0.03	$0.05
2019	11,975,139	$0.80	$0.14	$0.16
2018	6,910,938	$2.10	$0.47	$0.69

Recent Close: $0.01

Wholly Owned Subsidiaries

Cultivator Catalyst Corp., Toronto, Ont.
- 100% int. in **Great Lakes Cannabis Company Inc.**, Ont.
- 100% int. in **Red Sands Craft Cannabis Co.**, P.E.I. Inactive.
- 100% int. in **Weed Virtual Retail Inc.**, Ont. Inactive.

Investments

IM Cannabis Corp., Tel Aviv, Israel. (see separate coverage)

Financial Statistics

Periods ended:	12m Dec. 31/21[A]		12m Dec. 31/20[A]
	$000s	%Chg	$000s
Salaries & benefits	106		1,393
General & admin expense	902		2,427
Stock-based compensation	52		28
Operating expense	**1,061**	**-72**	**3,849**
Operating income	**(1,061)**	**n.a.**	**(3,849)**
Finance costs, gross	454		1,840
Write-downs/write-offs	(3)		(381)
Pre-tax income	**(140)**	**n.a.**	**(1,717)**
Net inc. bef. disc. opers	**(140)**	**n.a.**	**(1,717)**
Income from disc. opers	nil		1,478
Net income	**(140)**	**n.a.**	**(239)**
Cash & equivalent	10,831		11,251
Accounts receivable	86		38
Current assets	11,007		12,068
Long-term investments	nil		512
Total assets	**11,074**	**-12**	**12,581**
Accts. pay. & accr. liabs	1,139		2,359
Current liabilities	4,645		3,609
Long-term debt, gross	3,506		3,706
Long-term debt, net	nil		2,456
Shareholders' equity	6,429		6,516
Cash from oper. activs	**(1,840)**	**n.a.**	**(1,009)**
Cash from fin. activs	(310)		(2,294)
Cash from invest. activs	2,163		1,808
Net cash position	**583**	**+2**	**569**
	$		$
Earns. per sh. bef disc opers*	(0.00)		(0.02)
Earnings per share*	(0.00)		(0.00)
Cash flow per share*	(0.02)		(0.01)
	shs		shs
No. of shs. o/s*	112,417,435		112,417,435
Avg. no. of shs. o/s*	112,417,435		111,891,383
	%		%
Net profit margin	n.a.		n.a.
Return on equity	(2.16)		(25.56)
Return on assets	2.65		0.94

* Common

[A] Reported in accordance with IFRS

Latest Results

Periods ended:	6m June 30/22[A]		6m June 30/21[A]
	$000s	%Chg	$000s
Net income	(8,562)	n.a.	4,762
	$		$
Earnings per share*	(0.08)		0.04

* Common

[A] Reported in accordance with IFRS

Historical Summary
(as originally stated)

Fiscal Year	Oper. Rev.	Net Inc. Bef. Disc.	EPS*
	$000s	$000s	$
2021[A]	nil	(140)	(0.00)
2020[A]	nil	(1,717)	(0.02)
2019[A]	4,679	(9,481)	(0.09)
2018[A1]	nil	(8,862)	(0.09)
2017[A2]	nil	186	0.17

* Common

[A] Reported in accordance with IFRS

[1] Results reflect the Oct. 3, 2018 reverse takeover acquisition of Cultivator Catalyst Corp.

[2] Results for 2017 and prior years pertain to Orca Touchscreen Technologies Ltd.

Note: Adjusted throughout for 1-for-50 cons. in Oct. 2018

B.58 Biomind Labs Inc.

Symbol - BMND **Exchange** - NEO **CUSIP** - 090702

Head Office - Pando Science and Technology Park, Camino Aparico Saravia s/n Pando, Canelones, Uruguay, 91000 **Overseas Tel** - 598-9-225-1500

Website - biomindlabs.com

Email - alejandro.antalich@biomindlabs.com

Investor Relations - Alejandro Antalich 598-9-770-2500

Auditors - MNP LLP C.A., Toronto, Ont.

Transfer Agents - Odyssey Trust Company, Calgary, Alta.

Employees - 5 at Dec. 31, 2022

Profile - (Ont. 2021; orig. Alta., 2005) Researching and developing psychedelic-derived regulated medicines for psychiatric and neurological conditions.

Develops novel pharmaceutical formulations and drug delivery systems based on psychedelic molecules (N, N-dimenthyltryptamine (DMT) and 5-MeO-DMT) and phenethylamine (mescaline).

Priority drug development programs include: BMND01, which is under Phase II clinical trial for treatment-resistant depression with inhaled administration; BMND02, for Fibromyalgia; BMND03, for addictive disorders; BMND07, for major depressive disorder; BMND05, for chronic pain; BMND08, which is under Phase II clinical trial for the treatment of depression and anxiety in patients with Alzheimer's-type cognitive impairment; BMND09, for Parkinson's disease; and BMND06, based on the psychedelic molecule mescaline, for inflammatory disorders. Also developing new chemical entity, Triptax™, which could be used as an active pharmaceutical ingredient or as a chemical precursor of the company's novel formulations to treat depression.

Predecessor Detail - Name changed from Crosswinds Holdings Inc., July 14, 2021, pursuant to the reverse takeover acquisition of Biomind Research Corp. and concurrent amalgamation of Biomind with wholly owned Crosswinds Mergersub Inc.; basis 1 new for 32.5 old shs.

Directors - Ravi Sood, chr., Toronto, Ont.; Alejandro Antalich, CEO, Montevideo, Uruguay; Oscar A. León, CFO, Montevideo, Uruguay; Fraser A. Buchan, Toronto, Ont.; Dr. Ben Illigens, Berlin, Germany

Other Exec. Officers - Paola Diaz Dellavalle, chief scientific officer; Juan Presa, chief legal officer

Capital Stock

	Authorized (shs.)	Outstanding (shs.)[1]
Common	unlimited	74,761,853

[1] At May 15, 2023

Major Shareholder - Union Group Ventures Limited held 39.79% interest at May 15, 2023.

Price Range - BMND/NEO

Year	Volume	High	Low	Close
2022	73,000	$1.45	$0.16	$0.89
2021	22,500	$1.88	$1.12	$1.39
2019	1,689	$4.39	$3.58	$3.90
2018	1,072,636	$7.80	$2.54	$4.39

Consolidation: 1-for-32.5 cons. in July 2021

Recent Close: $0.33

Capital Stock Changes - In June 2023, a share consolidation of up to 1-for-10 was approved by shareholders.

There were no changes to capital stock during 2022.

Wholly Owned Subsidiaries

Biomind Labs UK Limited, United Kingdom.

Biomind Research Corp., Canelones, Uruguay.
- 100% int. in **Liverdome Development Inc.**, British Virgin Islands.
  - 100% int. in **Biomind Labs Pesquisas Científicas Ltda.**, Brazil.
- 100% int. in **Mindcore Labs Limited**, British Virgin Islands.

Financial Statistics

Periods ended:	12m Dec. 31/22[A]		12m Dec. 31/21[A1]
	US$000s	%Chg	US$000s
Research & devel. expense	574		571
General & admin expense	1,763		2,284
Stock-based compensation	554		1,381
Operating expense	**2,891**	**-32**	**4,236**
Operating income	**(2,891)**	**n.a.**	**(4,236)**
Deprec., depl. & amort	44		28
Finance costs, gross	1		4
Pre-tax income	**(2,986)**	**n.a.**	**(4,332)**
Net income	**(2,986)**	**n.a.**	**(4,332)**
Cash & equivalent	26		2,274
Current assets	45		2,440
Fixed assets, net	36		45
Right-of-use assets	8		44
Total assets	**89**	**-96**	**2,528**
Accts. pay. & accr. liabs	329		290
Current liabilities	337		325
Long-term lease liabilities	nil		10
Shareholders' equity	(248)		2,193
Cash from oper. activs	**(2,150)**	**n.a.**	**(2,123)**
Cash from fin. activs	(39)		4,471
Cash from invest. activs	nil		(44)
Net cash position	**26**	**-99**	**2,274**
	US$		US$
Earnings per share*	(0.04)		(0.06)
Cash flow per share*	(0.03)		(0.03)
	shs		shs
No. of shs. o/s*	74,761,853		74,761,853
Avg. no. of shs. o/s*	74,761,853		72,060,404
	%		%
Net profit margin	n.a.		n.a.
Return on equity	n.m.		(386.13)
Return on assets	(228.12)		(327.19)
No. of employees (FTEs)	5		9

* Common

[A] Reported in accordance with IFRS

[1] Results reflect the July 23, 2021, reverse takeover acquisition of Biomind Research Corp.

Latest Results

Periods ended:	3m Mar. 31/23[A]		3m Mar. 31/22[A]
	US$000s	%Chg	US$000s
Net income	(434)	n.a.	(768)
	US$		US$
Earnings per share*	(0.01)		(0.01)

* Common

[A] Reported in accordance with IFRS

Historical Summary
(as originally stated)

Fiscal Year	Oper. Rev.	Net Inc. Bef. Disc.	EPS*
	US$000s	US$000s	US$
2022[A]	nil	(2,986)	(0.04)
2021[A]	nil	(4,332)	(0.06)
	$000s	$000s	$
2020[A1]	3	(242)	(0.97)
2019[A]	(82)	(471)	(1.63)
2018[A]	1,224	(1,550)	(5.53)

* Common

[A] Reported in accordance with IFRS

[1] Results for 2020 and prior years pertain to Crosswinds Holdings Inc.

Note: Adjusted throughout for 1-for-32.5 cons. in July 2021

B.59 BioNeutra Global Corporation

Symbol - BGA **Exchange** - TSX-VEN **CUSIP** - 09073L

Head Office - 1101-1030 Georgia St W, Vancouver, BC, V6E 2Y3 **Telephone** - (604) 210-5669

Website - www.bioneutra.ca

Email - jianhua.zhu@bioneutra.ca

Investor Relations - Dr. Jianhua Zhu (780) 466-1481 ext. 132

Auditors - Kenway Mack Slusarchuk Stewart LLP C.A., Calgary, Alta.

Bankers - The Toronto-Dominion Bank, Edmonton, Alta.

Transfer Agents - Computershare Trust Company of Canada Inc., Calgary, Alta.

Profile - (Alta. 1996) Researches, develops, produces and commercializes ingredients, specifically isomalto-oligosaccharides (IMO), for nutraceutical, functional and mainstream foods and beverages.

Lead product is VitaFiber™ IMO, an advanced functional and health food and beverage ingredient scientifically made from natural agricultural cereal crop products including tapioca, field pea or corn, which are naturally sweet and lower in calories than sugar, and a natural source of dietary fibre used in various consumer packaged products including ice cream and frozen dairy, sports drinks, gummies, nutrition and energy bars, jams and jellies, pet foods, confectionary and baked goods. The sugar alternative is sold to small and medium enterprises and food manufacturers in Canada, the U.S., Europe, Australia and southeast Asia as well as worldwide through direct-to-consumer retail channels such as Amazon.com and Shopify.com.

Has health approvals in place from the U.S. FDA, Canada Health, and the European Food Safety Authority (EFSA) for the use of VitaFiber in a wide variety of consumer products.

Predecessor Detail - Name changed from INTERCAP eCommerce Inc., Oct. 29, 2014, following the reverse takeover acquistion of BioNeutra North America Inc. (deemed acquiror) and BioNeutra International Limited; basis 1 new for 10 old shs.

Directors - Dr. Jianhua Zhu, pres. & CEO, Edmonton, Alta.; C. H. William (Bill) Cheung, Edmonton, Alta.; Dr. Stephen C. (Steve) Jakeway, Edmonton, Alta.; Robin G. Le Fevre, Edmonton, Alta.; Michael Z. C. Li, Vancouver, B.C.; Ken Lin, Vancouver, B.C.; Michael Tse, Hong Kong, Hong Kong, People's Republic of China

Other Exec. Officers - Ross Montagano, COO; Yiyuan Jiang, CFO

Capital Stock

	Authorized (shs.)	Outstanding (shs.)[1]
Preferred	unlimited	nil
Common	unlimited	46,448,787

[1] At May 19, 2023

Major Shareholder - Dr. Jianhua Zhu held 22.33% interest and Frederick Lee held 13.4% interest at May 19, 2023.

Price Range - BGA/TSX-VEN

Year	Volume	High	Low	Close
2022	667,383	$0.17	$0.02	$0.02
2021	1,223,164	$0.36	$0.11	$0.17
2020	876,698	$0.48	$0.12	$0.19
2019	1,004,967	$0.68	$0.21	$0.30
2018	1,536,318	$0.75	$0.27	$0.57

Recent Close: $0.03

Capital Stock Changes - There were no changes to capital stock from 2020 to 2022, inclusive.

Wholly Owned Subsidiaries

BioNeutra Hong Kong Ltd., Hong Kong, People's Republic of China.
BioNeutra International Limited, British Virgin Islands.
BioNeutra North America Inc., Edmonton, Alta.
VitaCanada Inc., Canada.

Financial Statistics

Periods ended:	12m Dec. 31/22^A		12m Dec. 31/21^oA
	$000s	%Chg	$000s
Operating revenue	**13,391**	**-13**	**15,401**
Cost of sales	11,042		12,510
Salaries & benefits	2,047		1,715
Research & devel. expense	(16)		12
General & admin expense	2,584		2,722
Stock-based compensation	nil		483
Operating expense	**15,657**	**-10**	**17,441**
Operating income	**(2,266)**	**n.a.**	**(2,040)**
Deprec., depl. & amort.	201		315
Finance income	nil		3
Finance costs, gross	450		391
Pre-tax income	**(2,921)**	**n.a.**	**(2,830)**
Net income	**(2,921)**	**n.a.**	**(2,830)**
Cash & equivalent	723		839
Inventories	7,180		8,022
Accounts receivable	1,097		1,726
Current assets	9,715		10,933
Fixed assets, net	9,642		9,751
Intangibles, net	425		401
Total assets	**19,782**	**-6**	**21,085**
Accts. pay. & accr. liabs	15,430		14,123
Current liabilities	16,910		15,780
Long-term debt, gross	5,870		6,422
Long-term debt, net	5,566		5,867
Shareholders' equity	(3,756)		(1,034)
Cash from oper. activs	**838**	**n.a.**	**(113)**
Cash from fin. activs	(309)		(298)
Cash from invest. activs	(197)		(277)
Net cash position	**723**	**-14**	**839**
Capital expenditures	(119)		(277)
	$		$
Earnings per share*	(0.06)		(0.06)
Cash flow per share*	0.02		(0.00)
	shs		shs
No. of shs. o/s*	46,448,787		46,448,787
Avg. no. of shs. o/s*	46,448,787		46,448,787
	%		%
Net profit margin	(21.81)		(18.38)
Return on equity	n.m.		n.m.
Return on assets	(12.09)		(10.90)
Foreign sales percent	86		85

* Common
o Restated
A Reported in accordance with IFRS

Latest Results

Periods ended:	3m Mar. 31/23^A		3m Mar. 31/22^A
	$000s	%Chg	$000s
Operating revenue	2,993	-24	3,926
Net income	(925)	n.a.	116
	$		$
Earnings per share*	(0.02)		0.00

* Common
A Reported in accordance with IFRS

Historical Summary
(as originally stated)

Fiscal Year	Oper. Rev. $000s	Net Inc. Bef. Disc. $000s	EPS* $
2022^A	13,391	(2,921)	(0.06)
2021^A	15,401	(2,830)	(0.06)
2020^A	24,116	(3,707)	(0.08)
2019^A	37,701	(12,443)	(0.27)
2018^A	37,717	3,103	0.07

* Common
A Reported in accordance with IFRS

B.60 BioNxt Solutions Inc.

Symbol - BNXT **Exchange** - CSE **CUSIP** - 090974
Head Office - 270-1820 Fir St, Vancouver, BC, V6J 3B1 **Telephone** - (780) 818-6422
Website - bionxt.com
Email - info@bionxt.com
Investor Relations - Hugh A. D. Rogers (780) 818-6422
Auditors - Davidson & Company LLP C.A., Vancouver, B.C.
Transfer Agents - Computershare Trust Company of Canada Inc., Vancouver, B.C.

Profile - (B.C. 2017) Developing and commercializing next-generation pharmaceutical and diagnostic solutions, including infectious disease and oral health diagnostic and screening tests, drug delivery formulations and pharmaceutical production, including psychedelic compounds and cannabinoids.

Diagnostic and Screening Tests - Wholly owned **3a-Dignostics GmbH** is developing and commercializing a portfolio of pathogen and oral health diagnostic and biosensor screening tests for the detection of bacterial and viral infectious diseases, including influenza A, group A streptococcus, stomatitis, periimplantitis and periodontitis. Commercial products include Covid-ID Lab, a rapid point-of-care RT-PCR test for the detection of SARS-CoV-2 (COVID-19); and an oral dissolvable biosensor test for oral inflammation. Additional tests for other pandemic threats are in planning and development, specifically for H1N1 (swine flu) and H5N1 (avian flu).

Drug Delivery - Wholly owned **Vektor Pharma TF GmbH** is developing a thin film drug formulation business, with a focus on generic and hybrid-generic drug products based on approved active pharmaceutical ingredients (API). Vektor designs, tests and manufactures thin film drug delivery systems, including transdermal patches and sub-lingual (oral) strips. Drug delivery programs include a transdermal patch for the delivery of Rotigotine, a non-ergoline dopamine agonist approved for the treatment of Parkinson's disease and restless legs syndrome in Europe and the U.S.; an oral dissolvable film (ODF) for the delivery of cannabidiol (CBD) for treatment-resistant Epilepsy; ODF delivery of tetrahydrocannabinol (THC) for anorexia and nausea; and ODF delivery of a combination of CBD and THC for Multiple Sclerosis-associated spasticity. Vektor plans to construct a 32,000-sq.-ft. commercial drug manufacturing facility at its own property in Biberach, Germany.

Psychedelics - Focused on the development of psychedelic medicine to treat mental health-related medical conditions, such as depression, anxiety, addiction and trauma-related stress disorder, through wholly owned **XPhyto Laboratories Inc.** in Canada and Vektor in Germany. The company is developing industrial-scale production of pharmaceutical-grade psychedelic compounds, including psilocybin and mescaline, through advanced biosynthesis process.

Predecessor Detail - Name changed from XPhyto Therapeutics Corp., Nov. 14, 2022.

Directors - Hugh A. D. Rogers, pres. & CEO, Vancouver, B.C.; Peter Damouni, London, Middx., United Kingdom; Dr. Raimar Löbenberg, Edmonton, Alta.; Wolfgang Probst, Germany; Per S. Thoresen, Oslo, Norway

Other Exec. Officers - P. Joseph Meagher, CFO

Capital Stock

	Authorized (shs.)	Outstanding (shs.)[1]
Common	unlimited	98,386,873

[1] At May 29, 2023

Major Shareholder - Widely held at Sept. 6, 2022.

Price Range - BNXT/CSE

Year	Volume	High	Low	Close
2022	7,750,892	$1.70	$0.36	$0.59
2021	16,921,735	$3.45	$1.03	$1.08
2020	24,050,560	$3.55	$0.99	$1.88
2019	7,681,451	$1.42	$0.73	$0.96

Recent Close: $0.45

Capital Stock Changes - In March 2023, private placement of 4,050,000 units (1 common share & ½ warrant) at 50¢ per unit was completed, with warrants exercisable at 80¢ per share for two years.

In March and April 2022, private placement of 2,300,000 common shares was completed at $1.00 per share. In August and September 2022, private placement of 10,000,000 units (1 common share & ½ warrant) at 36¢ per unit was completed. Also during 2022, common shares were issued as follows: 714,000 on exercise of options, 442,839 for debt settlement, 200,000 were released from treasury and 100,000 on conversion of debentures.

Wholly Owned Subsidiaries

Bunker Pflanzenextrakte GmbH, Germany.
- 100% int. in **XP Diagnostics GmbH**, Germany.

SCUR-Alpha 1108 GmbH, Germany.
- 100% int. in **Vektor Pharma TF GmbH**, Germany.
  - 100% int. in **Vektor Vermogens und Grundbesitz GmbH**, Germany.

3a-Diagnostics GmbH, Germany.
XPhyto Laboratories Inc., Alta.

Financial Statistics

Periods ended:	12m Dec. 31/22^A		12m Dec. 31/21^A
	$000s	%Chg	$000s
Operating revenue	**297**	**+4**	**286**
Cost of sales	102		87
Salaries & benefits	833		859
Research & devel. expense	2,111		3,343
General & admin expense	2,981		8,228
Stock-based compensation	114		3,275
Operating expense	**6,141**	**-61**	**15,792**
Operating income	**(5,843)**	**n.a.**	**(15,506)**
Deprec., depl. & amort.	216		823
Finance costs, gross	1,143		732
Write-downs/write-offs	(6,512)		(3,677)
Pre-tax income	**(12,870)**	**n.a.**	**(20,748)**
Income taxes	(494)		(111)
Net income	**(12,376)**	**n.a.**	**(20,637)**
Cash & equivalent	136		1,352
Inventories	nil		736
Accounts receivable	459		546
Current assets	691		2,704
Fixed assets, net	891		1,058
Right-of-use assets	31		71
Intangibles, net	nil		5,894
Total assets	**1,613**	**-83**	**9,727**
Accts. pay. & accr. liabs	1,370		2,320
Current liabilities	2,017		5,450
Long-term debt, gross	4,336		4,638
Long-term debt, net	3,724		1,661
Long-term lease liabilities	nil		665
Equity portion of conv. debs	615		367
Shareholders' equity	(4,128)		1,669
Cash from oper. activs	**(6,230)**	**n.a.**	**(12,155)**
Cash from fin. activs	5,023		16,230
Cash from invest. activs	(4)		(5,308)
Net cash position	**136**	**-90**	**1,352**
Capital expenditures	(4)		(452)
	$		$
Earnings per share*	(0.15)		(0.29)
Cash flow per share*	(0.07)		(0.17)
	shs		shs
No. of shs. o/s*	91,209,873		77,453,034
Avg. no. of shs. o/s*	83,773,816		70,234,876
	%		%
Net profit margin	n.m.		n.m.
Return on equity	n.m.		(727.30)
Return on assets	(198.89)		(221.08)
Foreign sales percent	100		100

* Common
A Reported in accordance with IFRS

Latest Results

Periods ended:	3m Mar. 31/23^A		3m Mar. 31/22^A
	$000s	%Chg	$000s
Operating revenue	169	+40	121
Net income	(1,496)	n.a.	(1,760)
	$		$
Earnings per share*	(0.06)		(0.02)

* Common
A Reported in accordance with IFRS

Historical Summary
(as originally stated)

Fiscal Year	Oper. Rev. $000s	Net Inc. Bef. Disc. $000s	EPS* $
2022^A	297	(12,376)	(0.15)
2021^A	286	(20,637)	(0.29)
2020^A	346	(16,890)	(0.30)
2019^A	208	(7,669)	(0.17)
2018^A	nil	(861)	(0.04)

* Common
A Reported in accordance with IFRS

B.61 Biorem Inc.

Symbol - BRM **Exchange** - TSX-VEN **CUSIP** - 09068G
Head Office - 7496 Wellington Road 34, RR 3, Puslinch, ON, N0B 2J0 **Telephone** - (519) 767-9100 **Toll-free** - (800) 353-2087 **Fax** - (519) 767-1824
Website - www.biorem.biz
Email - dnewman@biorem.biz
Investor Relations - Douglas Newman (519) 767-9100 ext. 287
Auditors - MNP LLP C.A.
Transfer Agents - TSX Trust Company, Toronto, Ont.
Profile - (Ont. 2003) Designs, manufactures and distributes high-efficiency air emissions control systems used to eliminate odours, volatile organic compounds (VOCs) and hazardous air pollutants (HAPs), and offers Biogas Conditioning technologies specializing in biological treatment of hydrogen sulfide (H_2S).

Product offerings include Biofilters, which are biologically based biofilter technologies for the elimination of odours, H_2S, VOCs and HAPs, with the capacity to treat air flows from as little as 50 cubic feet per hour (cfh) to greater than 500,000 cfh; Biotrickling Filters, which are designed for the removal of high level H_2S and other water soluble odorous compounds; Multi-Stage Systems, which are a combination of biotrickling filters, biofilter technologies and activated carbon system for treatment of complex odours associated with various municipal wastewater treatment processes; Biogas Solutions, which are biogas conditioning systems designed to protect equipment from the damaging effects caused by H_2S, siloxanes and VOCs; Biogas Sweetening System, designed for the removal of hydrogen sulfide from landfill gas and other methane gas mixtures; Dry Scrubber Adsorption Systems, removes using medias such as activated carbon and impregnated activated alumina allow the lowest outlet concentrations for dense urban applications.; Organics and Anaerobic Digestion, a biological odour control system for composting facilities; and Biofiltration Media, which are permanent filter media products (Biosorbens®, Biopak™, Bioroll™ & Bioblok™ and XLD™) for the treatment of a wide array of air emissions.

The company is headquartered in Guelph, Ont., with offices in Victor, N.Y., and Beijing, People's Republic of China. The company has more than 1,800 installed systems worldwide.

Predecessor Detail - Name changed from Ontario Capital Opportunities Inc., Jan. 17, 2005, following Qualifying Transaction reverse takeover acquisition of Biorem Technologies Inc.; basis 1 new for 4 old shs.

Directors - Derek S. Webb, pres. & CEO, Waterloo, Ont.; Alex Gill, Toronto, Ont.; William B. (Bill) White, Palm Coast, Fla.
Other Exec. Officers - Douglas (Doug) Newman, CFO & corp. sec.

Capital Stock

	Authorized (shs.)	Outstanding (shs.)[1]
Common	unlimited	15,697,437

[1] At May 10, 2023

Major Shareholder - Widely held at May 10, 2023.

Price Range - BRM/TSX-VEN

Year	Volume	High	Low	Close
2022	1,289,848	$0.99	$0.66	$0.88
2021	5,112,110	$0.96	$0.43	$0.90
2020	3,575,648	$0.60	$0.26	$0.54
2019	2,820,672	$0.44	$0.32	$0.40
2018	2,881,622	$0.47	$0.32	$0.38

Recent Close: $1.04

Capital Stock Changes - During 2022, 20,000 common shares were issued under a stock-based compensation plan.

Wholly Owned Subsidiaries

Biorem (Beijing) Environmental Technologies Company Limited, People's Republic of China.
Biorem Environmental Inc., Victor, N.Y.
Biorem Environmental (US) Ltd., United States.
Biorem (Hong Kong) Limited, People's Republic of China.
Biorem Technologies Inc., Guelph, Ont.
Biorem Wuhu Environmental Technology Ltd.
Tianjin Biqing Environmental Technology Co., Ltd., People's Republic of China.

Financial Statistics

Periods ended:	12m Dec. 31/22[A]		12m Dec. 31/21[A]
	$000s	%Chg	$000s
Operating revenue	**28,863**	**+18**	**24,478**
Cost of goods sold	19,814		17,971
Research & devel. expense	97		14
General & admin expense	5,722		3,840
Operating expense	**25,633**	**+17**	**21,826**
Operating income	**3,230**	**+22**	**2,652**
Deprec., depl. & amort	351		344
Finance costs, gross	257		36
Pre-tax income	**2,383**	**+17**	**2,034**
Income taxes	770		737
Net income	**1,613**	**+24**	**1,297**
Cash & equivalent	3,775		4,471
Inventories	888		902
Accounts receivable	8,357		6,507
Current assets	17,775		16,165
Fixed assets, net	1,016		1,145
Total assets	**20,730**	**+8**	**19,166**
Accts. pay. & accr. liabs	7,374		7,579
Current liabilities	12,922		13,231
Long-term debt, gross	4,276		5,010
Long-term debt, net	2,975		3,501
Long-term lease liabilities	312		470
Shareholders' equity	4,521		1,964
Cash from oper. activs	**1,445**	**-62**	**3,782**
Cash from fin. activs	(952)		(7,556)
Cash from invest. activs	(203)		(76)
Net cash position	**3,775**	**-16**	**4,471**
Capital expenditures	(203)		(76)
	$		$
Earnings per share*	0.10		0.04
Cash flow per share*	0.09		0.11
	shs		shs
No. of shs. o/s*	15,497,437		15,477,437
Avg. no. of shs. o/s*	15,484,937		35,922,293
	%		%
Net profit margin	5.59		5.30
Return on equity	49.75		16.75
Return on assets	8.96		6.42
Foreign sales percent	73		52

* Common
[A] Reported in accordance with IFRS

Latest Results

Periods ended:	3m Mar. 31/23[A]		3m Mar. 31/22[A]
	$000s	%Chg	$000s
Operating revenue	3,169	-28	4,381
Net income	(557)	n.a.	(101)
	$		$
Earnings per share*	(0.04)		(0.01)

* Common
[A] Reported in accordance with IFRS

Historical Summary
(as originally stated)

Fiscal Year	Oper. Rev. $000s	Net Inc. Bef. Disc. $000s	EPS* $
2022[A]	28,863	1,613	0.10
2021[A]	24,478	1,297	0.04
2020[A]	24,375	2,089	0.05
2019[A]	20,649	(1,302)	(0.03)
2018[A]	24,333	4,666	0.12

* Common
[A] Reported in accordance with IFRS

B.62 BioSyent Inc.

Symbol - RX **Exchange** - TSX-VEN **CUSIP** - 090690
Head Office - 402-2476 Argentia Rd, Mississauga, ON, L5N 6M1 **Telephone** - (905) 206-0013 **Toll-free** - (888) 439-0013 **Fax** - (905) 206-1413
Website - www.biosyent.com
Email - rmarch@biosyent.com
Investor Relations - Robert March (905) 206-0013
Auditors - MNP LLP C.A., Toronto, Ont.
Bankers - Canadian Imperial Bank of Commerce, Toronto, Ont.; Royal Bank of Canada, Toronto, Ont.
Lawyers - Caravel Law Professional Corporation, Toronto, Ont.; Wildeboer Dellelce LLP, Toronto, Ont.
Transfer Agents - Computershare Trust Company of Canada Inc., Toronto, Ont.
Profile - (Can. 1999; orig. B.C., 1947) Sources, acquires or in-licenses and further develops pharmaceutical and other healthcare products for sale in Canada and certain international markets. Also markets biologically and health friendly non-chemical insecticides.

Manufactures and/or markets FeraMAX® Pd Therapeutic 150, FeraMAX® Pd Maintenance 45 and FeraMAX® Pd Powder 15, capsules and water soluble oral iron supplements, all used for the prevention and treatment of iron deficiency.

Also holds licensing and distribution agreements for Combogesic®, a combination of acetaminophen and ibuprofen for pain relief and has been approved in Canada; for Cathejell® Jelly, a product indicated for surface anaesthesia and lubrication for various procedures including cystoscopies, catheterizations and other endourethral operations, endoscopies, proctoscopies, rectoscopies and tracheal intubations; for RepaGyn®, a vaginal suppository which helps relieve dryness and promote healing of vaginal mucosa, and for Proktis-M®, a rectal suppository which helps healing of the anus and rectum; and for Tibella®, a hormone replacement therapy consisting of tibolone for the short-term treatment of vasomotor symptoms due to estrogen deficiency in postmenopausal women, more than one year after menopause.

The company's legacy business includes the manufacturing and marketing of Protect-It®, a non-chemical food-safe grain insecticide which is registered for use in Canada and the U.S.

Predecessor Detail - Name changed from Hedley Technologies Inc., June 13, 2006.

Directors - René C. Goehrum, chr., pres. & CEO, Toronto, Ont.; Peter D. Lockhard†, Toronto, Ont.; Larry Andrews, Ont.; Joseph Arcuri, Ont.; Sara C. Elford, Shawnigan Lake, B.C.; Stephen Wilton, Unionville, Ont.
Other Exec. Officers - Robert March, v-p, fin. & CFO; Joost van der Mark, v-p, corp. devel.; Kevin Wilson, v-p, community health bus.
† Lead director

Capital Stock

	Authorized (shs.)	Outstanding (shs.)[1]
Preferred	25,000,000	nil
Common	100,000,000	12,091,919

[1] At May 25, 2023

Normal Course Issuer Bid - The company plans to make normal course purchases of up to 690,000 common shares representing 5.7% of the total outstanding. The bid commenced on Dec. 19, 2022, and expires on Dec. 18, 2023.

Major Shareholder - René C. Goehrum held 18.25% interest and FAX Capital Corp. held 17.75% interest at Apr. 13, 2023.

Price Range - RX/TSX-VEN

Year	Volume	High	Low	Close
2022	1,172,216	$10.00	$6.24	$7.00
2021	1,596,445	$9.59	$6.76	$8.26
2020	3,374,917	$8.49	$3.13	$7.91
2019	1,714,401	$8.88	$5.51	$6.10
2018	2,416,284	$10.26	$6.93	$8.06

Recent Close: $7.80

Capital Stock Changes - During 2022, 5,903 common shares were issued on exercise of options and 424,700 common shares were repurchased under a Normal Course Issuer Bid. In addition, 39,800 common shares were held in treasury.

Dividends

RX com Ra $0.16 pa Q est. Dec. 15, 2022
$0.04**i** Dec. 15/22
i Initial Payment

Wholly Owned Subsidiaries

BioSyent Pharma Inc., Mississauga, Ont.
BioSyent Pharma International Inc., Barbados.
Hedley Technologies Ltd., B.C.
Hedley Technologies (USA) Inc., Wash.

Financial Statistics

Periods ended:	12m Dec. 31/22[A]		12m Dec. 31/21[A]
	$000s	%Chg	$000s
Operating revenue	**27,925**	**-2**	**28,618**
Cost of goods sold	5,067		5,980
Salaries & benefits	6,877		5,904
Research & devel. expense	121		161
General & admin expense	7,868		7,412
Stock-based compensation	536		404
Other operating expense	97		116
Operating expense	**20,566**	**+3**	**19,977**
Operating income	**7,359**	**-15**	**8,641**
Deprec., depl. & amort.	451		457
Finance income	526		155
Finance costs, gross	77		85
Pre-tax income	**7,431**	**-11**	**8,378**
Income taxes	1,972		2,097
Net income	**5,458**	**-13**	**6,282**
Cash & equivalent	28,696		28,212
Inventories	4,535		2,204
Accounts receivable	3,498		2,787
Current assets	37,143		34,079
Fixed assets, net	1,673		1,932
Intangibles, net	1,201		874
Total assets	**40,485**	**+9**	**37,167**
Accts. pay. & accr. liabs.	5,063		3,563
Current liabilities	5,719		4,137
Long-term lease liabilities	1,221		1,395
Shareholders' equity	33,363		31,555
Cash from oper. activs.	**4,949**	**+6**	**4,675**
Cash from fin. activs.	(4,371)		(2,076)
Cash from invest. activs.	(10,790)		(4,837)
Net cash position	**7,865**	**-56**	**18,035**
Capital expenditures, net	(47)		(85)
	$		$
Earnings per share*	0.44		0.50
Cash flow per share*	0.40		0.37
Cash divd. per share*	0.04		nil
	shs		shs
No. of shs. o/s*	12,097,861		12,556,458
Avg. no. of shs. o/s*	12,303,121		12,689,163
	%		%
Net profit margin	19.55		21.95
Return on equity	16.82		21.53
Return on assets	14.20		17.94
Foreign sales percent	3		6

* Common

[A] Reported in accordance with IFRS

Latest Results

Periods ended:	3m Mar. 31/23[A]		3m Mar. 31/22[A]
	$000s	%Chg	$000s
Operating revenue	6,483	-8	7,037
Net income	1,175	-26	1,588
	$		$
Earnings per share*	0.10		0.13

* Common

[A] Reported in accordance with IFRS

Historical Summary
(as originally stated)

Fiscal Year	Oper. Rev.	Net Inc. Bef. Disc.	EPS*
	$000s	$000s	$
2022[A]	27,925	5,458	0.44
2021[A]	28,618	6,282	0.50
2020[A]	22,332	3,795	0.29
2019[A]	21,424	4,369	0.31
2018[A]	21,527	5,705	0.39

* Common

[A] Reported in accordance with IFRS

B.63 BioVaxys Technology Corp.

Symbol - BIOV **Exchange** - CSE **CUSIP** - 09076M
Head Office - 503-905 Pender St W, Vancouver, BC, V6C 1L6 **Telephone** - (604) 722-9842
Website - biovaxys.com
Email - jpassin@biovaxys.com
Investor Relations - James C. Passin (646) 452-7054
Auditors - Dale Matheson Carr-Hilton LaBonte LLP C.A., Vancouver, B.C.
Transfer Agents - Odyssey Trust Company, Vancouver, B.C.
Profile - (B.C. 2018) Developing immunotherapeutic vaccines for life-threatening various cancers and viral infections as well as an immunodiagnostic test for COVID-19. Also distributes products for the treatment of cervical lesions.

The company has haptenized protein vaccines under clinical development for ovarian cancer (BVX-0918), for colorectal cancer (BVX-0922), for SARS-CoV-2 [COVID-19] (BVX-0320), and for the strain of coronavirus that causes severe acute respiratory syndrome (SARS1) (BVX-1021). In addition, the company has a diagnostic platform called CoviDTH®, which is a disposable diagnostic tool to identify a T-cell immune response to the presence of Covid-19. Also holds licences to market Papilocare®, a vaginal gel product which prevents and treats Human Papillomavirus (HPV) cervical lesions and Oral Immunocaps®, an over-the-counter nutritional supplement which supports immune function and vaginal microbiota to help re-epithelialization of cervical lesions. The company plans to begin stocking and distributing Oral Immunocaps® in early 2023.

The company plans to commercialize its products in the United States and seek commercial partners via licensing agreements for the European Union, Asia/Pacific and Latin American markets.

In March 2023, the company acquired Vancouver-based **TAETSoftware Corp.**, a clinical studies management company which develops and commercializes the Trial Adverse Events Tracker (TAET) technology platform, for issuance of 24,500,000 common shares and an additional 2,500,000 common shares payable upon the successful testing of the beta version of the application. TAET is a software application which would enable clinical study subjects to record and submit clinical Adverse Drug Events (ADE) reports to study sponsors in real time.

Predecessor Detail - Name changed from Lions Bay Mining Corp., Sept. 30, 2020, pursuant to reverse takeover acquisition of BioVaxys LLC.

Directors - James C. Passin, CEO, interim CFO & interim corp. sec., Ill.; Anthony J. Dutton, Vancouver, B.C.; Craig Loverock, Toronto, Ont.

Other Exec. Officers - Kenneth Kovan, pres. & COO; Dr. David Berd, CMO

Capital Stock

	Authorized (shs.)	Outstanding (shs.)[1]
Common	unlimited	148,014,057

[1] At May 2, 2023

Major Shareholder - Widely held at May 2, 2023.

Price Range - BIOV/CSE

Year	Volume	High	Low	Close
2022	30,646,683	$0.27	$0.09	$0.12
2021	96,766,326	$0.78	$0.14	$0.21
2020	35,591,288	$0.60	$0.04	$0.19
2019	5,526,676	$0.10	$0.02	$0.04
2018	127,410	$0.08	$0.05	$0.06

Split: 2-for-1 split in Apr. 2020
Recent Close: $0.02

Capital Stock Changes - In November 2022, private placement of 4,050,000 units (1 common share & 1 warrant) at 10¢ per unit and 940,000 units (1 common share & 1 warrant) at $0.125 per unit was completed, both with warrants exercisable at 20¢ per share for two years. In March 2023, private placement of 5,360,00 common shares was completed at $0.125 per share.

In February 2022, private placement of 5,323,333 units (1 common share & 1 warrant) at 15¢ per unit was completed. In August and September 2022, private placement of 3,350,000 units (1 common share & 1 warrant) at 10¢ per unit was completed. Also during fiscal 2022, common shares were issued as follows: 7,178,544 for debt settlement and 773,797 for services.

Wholly Owned Subsidiaries

BioVaxys Inc., New York, N.Y.

Financial Statistics

Periods ended:	12m Oct. 31/22[A]		12m Oct. 31/21[A]
	$000s	%Chg	$000s
Research & devel. expense	963		726
General & admin expense	2,619		4,579
Stock-based compensation	500		1,137
Operating expense	**4,082**	**-37**	**6,442**
Operating income	**(4,082)**	**n.a.**	**(6,442)**
Finance income	16		8
Finance costs, gross	248		nil
Write-downs/write-offs	(7,397)[1]		nil
Pre-tax income	**(11,727)**	**n.a.**	**(6,458)**
Net income	**(11,727)**	**n.a.**	**(6,458)**
Cash & equivalent	142		593
Current assets	715		874
Intangibles, net	nil		7,397
Total assets	**866**	**-90**	**8,504**
Accts. pay. & accr. liabs.	1,434		255
Current liabilities	1,639		327
Shareholders' equity	(774)		8,177
Cash from oper. activs.	**(1,575)**	**n.a.**	**(5,294)**
Cash from fin. activs.	1,108		3,439
Net cash position	**142**	**-76**	**593**
	$		$
Earnings per share*	(0.12)		(0.08)
Cash flow per share*	(0.02)		(0.06)
	shs		shs
No. of shs. o/s*	108,812,635		92,186,961
Avg. no. of shs. o/s*	98,179,801		82,930,053
	%		%
Net profit margin	n.a.		n.a.
Return on equity	n.m.		(72.82)
Return on assets	(245.02)		(68.11)

* Common

[A] Reported in accordance with IFRS

[1] Includes impairment losses of $5,513,993 for the Hapten-based cancer vaccines development and $1,882,828 for the COVID diagnostic and vaccine development.

Latest Results

Periods ended:	3m Jan. 31/23[A]		3m Jan. 31/22[A]
	$000s	%Chg	$000s
Net income	(956)	n.a.	(1,211)
	$		$
Earnings per share*	(0.01)		(0.01)

* Common

[A] Reported in accordance with IFRS

Historical Summary
(as originally stated)

Fiscal Year	Oper. Rev.	Net Inc. Bef. Disc.	EPS*
	$000s	$000s	$
2022[A]	nil	(11,727)	(0.12)
2021[A]	nil	(6,458)	(0.08)
2020[A1]	nil	(1,103)	(0.04)
2019[A2]	nil	(230)	(0.01)
2018[A3]	nil	(161)	(0.03)

* Common

[A] Reported in accordance with IFRS

[1] Results reflect the Oct. 6, 2020, reverse takeover acquisition of New York, N.Y.-based BioVaxys LLC.

[2] Results for fiscal 2019 and prior periods pertain to Lions Bay Mining Corp.

[3] 28 weeks ended Oct. 31, 2018.

Note: Adjusted throughout for 2-for-1 split in Apr. 2020

B.64 Birchtree Investments Ltd.

Symbol - BRCH **Exchange** - CSE **CUSIP** - 09077K
Head Office - 2900-550 Burrard St, Vancouver, BC, V6C 0A3
Email - svitaliy@gmail.com
Investor Relations - Vitali Savitski (416) 300-0625
Auditors - Stern & Lovrics LLP C.A., Toronto, Ont.
Transfer Agents - Marrelli Trust Company Limited, Vancouver, B.C.
Profile - (B.C. 2021) Invests in the securities of early stage private and public companies.

Plans to invest in early or strategic financing rounds of a target company to take advantage of favourable valuations and larger exit multiples.

At Jan. 31, 2023, held investments in four public companies, **ThreeD Capital Inc.**, **EHave Inc.**, **Xebra Brands Ltd.**, and **American Aires Inc.**, and three private companies, **Bluecorp Capital Corp.**, **Firstpayment Inc.**, and **Somerset Energy Partners Corp.**

Common listed on CSE, Mar. 1, 2023.

Predecessor Detail - Name changed from Birchtree Investments Inc., July 14, 2021.

Directors - Vitali Savitski, CEO; James S. (Jim) Greig, Vancouver, B.C.; Andrew Lindzon, Toronto, Ont.; Ivan Riabov

Other Exec. Officers - Carmelo (Carm) Marrelli, CFO

Capital Stock

	Authorized (shs.)	Outstanding (shs.)[1]
Common	unlimited	77,515,500

[1] At Mar. 1, 2023

Major Shareholder - ThreeD Capital Inc. held 12.9% interest and Anthony Heller held 12.9% interest at Mar. 1, 2023.

Recent Close: $0.01

Capital Stock Changes - During fiscal 2022, 20,810,000 common shares were issued on conversion of special warrants.

Financial Statistics

Periods ended:	12m Aug. 31/22[A]		30w Aug. 31/21[A]
	$000s	%Chg	$000s
Realized invest. gain (loss)	858		17
Unrealized invest. gain (loss)	(20)		(652)
Total revenue	**874**	**n.a.**	**(634)**
General & admin. expense	185		53
Operating expense	**185**	**n.a.**	**53**
Operating income	**689**	**n.a.**	**(687)**
Finance costs, gross	180		nil
Pre-tax income	**867**	**n.a.**	**(3,455)**
Net income	**867**	**n.a.**	**(3,455)**
Cash & equivalent	289		409
Current assets	825		435
Long-term investments	2,148		1,612
Total assets	**2,972**	**+45**	**2,048**
Accts. pay. & accr. liabs	110		52
Current liabilities	110		52
Shareholders' equity	2,863		1,996
Cash from oper. activs	**(102)**	**n.a.**	**(14)**
Cash from fin. activs	nil		914
Cash from invest. activs	(17)		(491)
Net cash position	**289**	**-29**	**409**
	$		$
Earnings per share*	0.01		(0.12)
Cash flow per share*	(0.00)		(0.00)
	shs		shs
No. of shs. o/s*	77,515,500		56,705,500
Avg. no. of shs. o/s*	73,353,500		28,505,655
	%		%
Net profit margin	99.20		...
Return on equity	35.69		...
Return on assets	41.71		...

* Common

[A] Reported in accordance with IFRS

B.65 Bird Construction Inc.*

Symbol - BDT **Exchange** - TSX **CUSIP** - 09076P

Head Office - 400-5700 Explorer Dr, Mississauga, ON, L4W 0C6 **Telephone** - (905) 602-4122 **Fax** - (905) 602-1516

Website - www.bird.ca

Email - investor.relations@bird.ca

Investor Relations - Terrance L. McKibbon (905) 602-4122

Auditors - KPMG LLP C.A., Winnipeg, Man.

Bankers - Bank of Montreal, Toronto, Ont.

Transfer Agents - Computershare Trust Company of Canada Inc., Calgary, Alta.

FP500 Revenue Ranking - 192

Employees - 1,648 at Dec. 31, 2022

Profile - (Ont. 2010) Provides construction services across Canada to industrial, commercial, and institutional markets, including industrial maintenance, repair and operations services, shutdowns and turnarounds, civil infrastructure and steel modular construction, mine support services, utility contracting, fabrication and specialty trades.

The company focuses primarily on projects in the industrial, infrastructure, institutional and commercial sectors of the general contracting industry.

Industrial work includes provision of general contracting for industrial buildings including manufacturing, processing, distribution and warehouse facilities. Also provides maintenance services such as insulation, metal siding and cladding, ductwork, asbestos abatement, mechanical and electrical and instrumentation abilities including high voltage testing and commissioning, as well as power line construction, structural, mechanical, and piping, including off-site metal and modular fabrication for clients primarily operating in the oil and gas, liquified natural gas (LNG), mining, water and wastewater, renewables and nuclear sectors.

Infrastructure sector offers civil construction including site preparation and earthworks, underground piping, foundations and other concrete services. Also provides mine support services and hydroelectric construction; and key civil infrastructure sub-sectors, including road, bridge, rail, and underground utilities installation.

Institutional projects include construction and renovation of hospitals, post-secondary educational facilities, K-12 schools, recreation facilities, prisons, courthouses, government buildings, long term care and senior housing, as well as environmental facilities that include water and wastewater treatment centres, composting facilities, and biosolids treatment and management facilities.

Commercial projects include the construction and renovation of shopping malls, big box stores, office buildings, hotels, and selected mixed use mid- to high-rise condominiums and apartments.

The company is headquartered in Mississauga, Ont., and has offices across Canada.

At Dec. 31, 2022, the company had a backlog of contracts totaling $2.64 billion compared with $3.0 billion at Dec. 31, 2021.

In July 2023, the company was awarded contracts for a combined value of $350,000,000. The contracts include a design-build contract to complete a pre-construction and design phase for the campus centre redevelopment project of Southern Alberta Institute of Technology, as well as construction management contracts for the Victor Phillip Dahdaleh Hall project at St. Francis Xavier University, the Dykeland Lodge long-term care facility replacement and the Glen Haven Manor long-term care facility replacement in Nova Scotia.

In July 2023, the company was awarded multiple contracts valued at $180,000,000. The contracts include civil and concrete scopes to support processing infrastructure development at the Blackwater mine project in central British Columbia for **Sedgman Canada Limited**, rehabilitation work on hydroelectric power-related structures in northeastern Ontario and final site earthworks, grading and asphalt paving at an existing project site in northwestern British Columbia.

Recent Merger and Acquisition Activity

Status: completed **Announced:** Feb. 1, 2023

Bird Construction Inc. acquired Ontario-based Trinity Communication Services Ltd. for $6,800,000, consisting of cash, issuance of common shares and a holdback liability. Trinity is telecommunications and utility infrastructure contractor that provides services including underground, aerial, commercial inside plant and multi-dwelling unit installations.

Predecessor Detail - Succeeded Bird Construction Income Fund, Jan. 1, 2011, pursuant to plan of arrangement whereby Bird Construction Inc. was formed to facilitate the conversion of the fund into a corporation and the fund was subsequently wound up.

Directors - Paul R. Raboud, chr., Toronto, Ont.; Terrance L. (Teri) McKibbon, pres. & CEO, Canmore, Alta.; Luc J. Messier†, Houston, Tex.; Dr. J. Richard Bird, Calgary, Alta.; Karyn A. Brooks, Calgary, Alta.; Bonnie D. DuPont, Calgary, Alta.; Steven L. (Steve) Edwards, Kansas City, Mo.; J. Kim Fennell, Los Gatos, Calif.; Jennifer F. Koury, Calgary, Alta.; Gary Merasty, Saskatoon, Sask.; Arni C. Thorsteinson, Winnipeg, Man.

Other Exec. Officers - Gilles G. Royer, COO; Wayne R. Gingrich, CFO & treas.; Rick Begg, CIO; Brian C. Henry, chief people officer; J. Paul Bergman, exec. v-p, bldgs. east; Charles J. Caza, exec. v-p, chief legal officer & corp. sec.; David Keep, exec. v-p, MRO & comml. sys.; Peter Lineen, exec. v-p, health, safety & envir.; Rob Otway, exec. v-p, bldgs. west; Tannis Proulx, exec. v-p, ind. const.; Arthur Krehut, sr. v-p, operational srvcs.; Paul Pastirik, sr. v-p, strategic devel.; Denis Bigioni, pres., Dagmar Construction Inc.

† Lead director

Capital Stock

	Authorized (shs.)	Outstanding (shs.)[1]
Preferred	unlimited	nil
Common	unlimited	53,774,639

[1] At Aug. 9, 2023

Major Shareholder - Canso Investment Counsel Ltd. held 17.97% interest at Mar. 16, 2023.

Price Range - BDT/TSX

Year	Volume	High	Low	Close
2022	22,609,383	$9.90	$5.74	$8.12
2021	35,445,582	$10.78	$7.79	$9.82
2020	14,938,280	$8.18	$3.96	$8.00
2019	13,625,821	$8.20	$4.88	$7.15
2018	20,805,211	$10.15	$5.11	$6.11

Recent Close: $10.86

Capital Stock Changes - There were no changes to capital stock during 2022.

Dividends

BDT com Ra $0.4296 pa M est. Apr. 20, 2023

Prev. Rate: $0.39 est. Feb. 17, 2017

Long-Term Debt - Outstanding at Dec. 31, 2022:

Revolv. credit facility[1]	$22,725,000
Non-revolv. term loan facility[1]	47,500,000
Fixed rate term loans[2]	4,866,000
	75,091,000
Less: Current portion	7,084,000
	68,007,000

[1] Bears interest at prime plus a spread and due December 2025.

[2] Bear interest at rates ranging from 2.04% to 4.70% and due on various dates through 2027.

Wholly Owned Subsidiaries

BFL Fabricators Ltd.
Bird Capital OMP Project Co. Inc.
Bird Civil et mines Ltée
Bird Construction Company Limited, Toronto, Ont.
- 99.5% int. in **Bird Capital Limited Partnership**, Ont.
  - 100% int. in **Bird Capital MDC Project Co. Inc.**, Ont.
  - 100% int. in **Bird Casey House GP Inc.**, Ont.
    - 0.5% int. in **Bird Casey House Limited Partnership**, Ont.
  - 99.5% int. in **Bird Casey House Limited Partnership**, Ont.
- 100% int. in **Bird Capital Limited**, Ont.
  - 0.05% int. in **Bird Capital Limited Partnership**, Ont.
- 99.5% int. in **Bird Construction Company**, Ont.
- 100% int. in **Bird Construction GP Limited**, Ont.
  - 0.5% int. in **Bird Construction Group Limited Partnership**, Alta.
- 99.5% int. in **Bird Construction Group Limited Partnership**, Alta.
- 100% int. in **Bird Heavy Civil Limited**, N.L. formerly H.J. O'Connell Limited.
- 100% int. in **Bird Management Ltd.**, Ont.
  - 0.5% int. in **Bird Construction Company**, Ont.
  - 100% int. in **Bird Design-Build Construction Inc.**, Ont.
  - 100% int. in **Bird Design-Build Limited**, Alta.
  - 100% int. in **Bird Industrial Group Limited**

Bird Construction Group Ltd., Canada.
Bird Construction Group, Ont.
Bird Construction Industrial Services Ltd., Canada.
Bird General Contractors Ltd., Canada.
Canadian Consulting Group Limited
Dagmar Construction Inc., Ont.
411007 Alberta Ltd., Canada.
Innovative Trenching Solutions Field Services Ltd.
Innovative Trenching Solutions Ltd.
Innovative Trenching USA Inc., Del.
NCGL Construction Ltd.
NCGL Industrial Ltd.
Nason Contracting Group Ltd., St. Albert, Alta.
Stuart Olson Inc., Calgary, Alta.
- 100% int. in **The Churchill Corporation**, Alta.
  - 100% int. in **Canem Holdings Ltd.**, B.C.
    - 100% int. in **Canem Systems Ltd.**, B.C.
    - 100% int. in **McCaine Electric Ltd.**, Winnipeg, Man.
- 100% int. in **Stuart Olson Asset Corp.**, Canada.
- 100% int. in **Stuart Olson Buildings Ltd.**, Alta.
  - 100% int. in **Stuart Olson Construction Ltd.**, Calgary, Alta.
- 100% int. in **Stuart Olson Industrial Constructors Inc.**, B.C.
- 100% int. in **Stuart Olson Industrial Inc.**, Alta.
  - 100% int. in **ARC Line Construction Ltd.**, Alta.
  - 100% int. in **Fuller Austin Inc.**, Edmonton, Alta.
  - 100% int. in **Laird Electric Inc.**, Edmonton, Alta.
  - 100% int. in **Northern Industrial Insulation Contractors Inc.**, Edmonton, Alta.
  - 100% int. in **Sigma Power Services Inc.**, Edmonton, Alta.
  - 100% int. in **Stuart Olson Industrial Projects Inc.**, Alta.
    - 100% int. in **Stuart Olson Northern Ventures Inc.**, Alta.
  - 100% int. in **Stuart Olson Industrial Services Ltd.**, Alta.
  - 100% int. in **Stuart Olson Water Inc.**, Calgary, Alta.
  - 100% int. in **Studon Industrial Inc.**, Red Deer, Alta.
  - 100% int. in **Tartan Canada Corporation**, Calgary, Alta.

TCC Holdings Inc., Canada.
Trinity Communication Services Ltd., Brampton, Ont.

Note: The preceding list includes only the major related companies in which interests are held.

Financial Statistics

Periods ended:	12m Dec. 31/22[A]		12m Dec. 31/21[A]
	$000s	%Chg	$000s
Operating revenue	**2,377,549**	**+7**	**2,220,026**
Cost of sales	2,146,013		2,005,062
General & admin expense	125,721		120,756
Operating expense	**2,271,734**	**+7**	**2,125,818**
Operating income	**105,815**	**+12**	**94,208**
Deprec., depl. & amort.	36,439		34,537
Finance income	10,341		1,322
Finance costs, gross	9,818		7,550
Investment income	(2,714)		4,187
Pre-tax income	**67,185**	**+17**	**57,630**
Income taxes	17,322		14,847
Net income	**49,863**	**+17**	**42,783**
Cash & equivalent	174,607		190,191
Accounts receivable	708,161		597,814
Current assets	970,301		873,070
Long-term investments	9,786		13,471
Fixed assets, net	55,471		55,004
Right-of-use assets	66,136		67,497
Intangibles, net	90,482		86,218
Total assets	**1,229,279**	**+8**	**1,137,148**
Accts. pay. & accr. liabs	573,224		514,330
Current liabilities	785,669		721,260
Long-term debt, gross	75,091		78,681
Long-term debt, net	68,007		71,211
Long-term lease liabilities	55,469		59,576
Shareholders' equity	272,988		243,488
Cash from oper. activs	**43,399**	**+21**	**35,826**
Cash from fin. activs	(44,278)		(34,246)
Cash from invest. activs	(14,812)		(23,305)
Net cash position	**174,607**	**-8**	**190,191**
Capital expenditures	(16,817)		(8,550)
Capital disposals	6,444		3,614
Unfunded pension liability	n.a.		232
Pension fund surplus	368		n.a.
	$		$
Earnings per share*	0.93		0.80
Cash flow per share*	0.81		0.67
Cash divd. per share*	0.39		0.39
	shs		shs
No. of shs. o/s*	53,695,293		53,695,293
Avg. no. of shs. o/s*	53,695,293		53,258,316
	%		%
Net profit margin	2.10		1.93
Return on equity	19.31		18.76
Return on assets	4.83		4.40
No. of employees (FTEs)	1,648		1,588

* Common
[A] Reported in accordance with IFRS

Latest Results

Periods ended:	6m June 30/23[A]		6m June 30/22[A]
	$000s	%Chg	$000s
Operating revenue	1,222,874	+16	1,052,209
Net income	18,863	-8	20,465
	$		$
Earnings per share*	0.35		0.38

* Common
[A] Reported in accordance with IFRS

Historical Summary
(as originally stated)

Fiscal Year	Oper. Rev.	Net Inc. Bef. Disc.	EPS*
	$000s	$000s	$
2022[A]	2,377,549	49,863	0.93
2021[A]	2,220,026	42,783	0.80
2020[A]	1,504,432	36,103	0.80
2019[A]	1,376,408	9,484	0.22
2018[A]	1,381,784	(1,013)	(0.02)

* Common
[A] Reported in accordance with IFRS

B.66 Bird River Resources Inc.

Symbol - BDR **Exchange** - CSE **CUSIP** - 090823
Head Office - 5204 Roblin Blvd, Winnipeg, MB, R3R 0H1 **Telephone** - (204) 589-2848 **Toll-free** - (877) 587-0777 **Fax** - (204) 586-6238
Website - www.birdriverresources.com
Email - jonbirdriver@gmail.com
Investor Relations - Jon D. Bridgman (877) 587-0777
Auditors - MNP LLP C.A., Vancouver, B.C.
Lawyers - Garfinkle Biderman LLP, Toronto, Ont.
Transfer Agents - Capital Transfer Agency Inc., Toronto, Ont.
Profile - (Man. 1958) Pursuing acquisition of two hydroelectric power plants in Quebec.

Periods ended:	12m July 31/21	12m July 31/20
Oil reserves, net, mbbl	n.a.	411
NGL reserves, net, mbbl	n.a.	45
Gas reserves, net, mmcf	n.a.	1,628
BOE reserves, net, mbbl	n.a.	727

Predecessor Detail - Name changed from Bird River Mines Inc., Feb. 7, 2011.
Directors - Jon D. Bridgman, CEO, Toronto, Ont.; Edward L. (Ed) Thompson, sec.-treas., Winnipeg, Man.; Donal V. Carroll, Etobicoke, Ont.; Warren Hawkins, Toronto, Ont.
Other Exec. Officers - Vincent E. (Vince) Ghazar, CFO

Capital Stock

	Authorized (shs.)	Outstanding (shs.)[1]
Common	unlimited	16,666,757

[1] At Dec. 29, 2021

Major Shareholder - Widely held at Nov. 21, 2021.

Price Range - BDR/CSE

Year	Volume	High	Low	Close
2022	4,616,817	$0.22	$0.06	$0.09
2021	9,249,215	$0.26	$0.09	$0.12
2020	4,742,786	$0.24	$0.04	$0.09
2019	2,289,786	$0.54	$0.06	$0.12
2018	4,030,875	$5.16	$0.36	$0.42

Consolidation: 1-for-12 cons. in Nov. 2020
Recent Close: $0.05
Capital Stock Changes - In September 2021, private placement of 14,000,000 common shares at 25¢ per share was proposed.

Financial Statistics

Periods ended:	12m July 31/21[A]		12m July 31/20[A]
	$000s	%Chg	$000s
Operating revenue	**nil**	**n.a.**	**7**
Cost of sales	nil		8
General & admin expense	245		211
Stock-based compensation	214		nil
Operating expense	**459**	**+110**	**219**
Operating income	**(459)**	**n.a.**	**(212)**
Pre-tax income	**(459)**	**n.a.**	**(212)**
Net inc. bef. disc. opers	**(459)**	**n.a.**	**(212)**
Income from disc. opers	157		(8,533)
Net income	**(302)**	**n.a.**	**(8,745)**
Cash & equivalent	552		113
Accounts receivable	33		11
Current assets	590		4,160
Total assets	**590**	**-86**	**4,160**
Accts. pay. & accr. liabs	99		167
Current liabilities	99		4,203
Shareholders' equity	491		(58)
Cash from oper. activs	**(185)**	**n.a.**	**58**
Cash from fin. activs	621		40
Cash from invest. activs	4		(189)
Net cash position	**553**	**+389**	**113**
Capital expenditures	nil		(279)
	$		$
Earns. per sh. bef disc opers*	(0.04)		(0.02)
Earnings per share*	(0.02)		(0.90)
Cash flow per share*	(0.02)		(0.01)
	shs		shs
No. of shs. o/s*	16,666,861		9,666,861
Avg. no. of shs. o/s*	12,177,055		9,666,861
	%		%
Net profit margin	n.a.		n.m.
Return on equity	n.m.		n.m.
Return on assets	(19.33)		(2.97)

* Common
[A] Reported in accordance with IFRS

Latest Results

Periods ended:	3m Oct. 31/21[A]		3m Oct. 31/20[A]
	$000s	%Chg	$000s
Operating revenue	nil	n.a.	2
Net inc. bef. disc. opers	(79)	n.a.	(13)
Income from disc. opers	nil		137
Net income	(79)	n.a.	124
	$		$
Earns. per sh. bef. disc. opers.*	(0.00)		(0.02)
Earnings per share*	(0.00)		0.15

* Common
[A] Reported in accordance with IFRS

Historical Summary
(as originally stated)

Fiscal Year	Oper. Rev.	Net Inc. Bef. Disc.	EPS*
	$000s	$000s	$
2021[A]	nil	(459)	(0.04)
2020[A]	7	(212)	(0.02)
2019[A]	1,129	(693)	(0.12)
2018[A]	35	(2,007)	(0.36)
2017[A]	95	(184)	(0.24)

* Common
[A] Reported in accordance with IFRS
Note: Adjusted throughout for 1-for-12 cons. in Nov. 2020

B.67 Birks Group Inc.

Symbol - BGI **Exchange** - NYSE MKT **CUSIP** - 09088U
Head Office - 200-2020 boul Robert Bourassa, Montréal, QC, H3A 2A5 **Telephone** - (514) 397-2501 **Fax** - (514) 397-2537
Website - www.maisonbirks.com
Email - kfontana@birksgroup.com
Investor Relations - Katia Fontana (514) 397-2592
Auditors - KPMG LLP C.A., Montréal, Qué.
Lawyers - Holland & Knight LLP, Fort Lauderdale, Fla.
Transfer Agents - Computershare Trust Company, N.A., Canton, Mass.
FP500 Revenue Ranking - 676
Employees - 296 at Mar. 26, 2022
Profile - (Can. 1879) Designs, manufactures and retails fine jewelry, timepieces, sterling silver and gifts in Canada.
Products include designer jewelry, rings, wedding bands, earrings, bracelets, necklaces, charms, baby jewelry, timepieces and giftware. The company also offers repair and custom design services.
At June 23, 2022, the company operated 24 luxury jewelry stores under the Maison Birks brand across Canada; one retail store in Calgary, Alta., under the Brinkhaus brand; and two retail stores in Vancouver, B.C., under the Graff and Patek Philippe brands. Products are also offered through select SAKS Fifth Avenue stores in Canada and the U.S., Mappin & Webb and Goldsmiths locations in the United Kingdom and Mayors stores in the U.S., as well as certain jewelry retailers across North America and the European Union. Manufacturing and warehousing facilities are located in Montreal, Que. Products are also sold on e-commerce platforms, as well as through wholesale and gold exchange. During fiscal 2022, 35% (fiscal 2021 - 31%) of jewelry products acquired for sale was internally designed, sourced or manufactured.
During fiscal 2022, the company closed three Maison Birks stores in Oshawa, Ont., Saskatoon, Sask., and Victoria, B.C.
Predecessor Detail - Name changed from Birks & Mayors Inc., Oct. 1, 2013.
Directors - Niccolò Rossi di Montelera, exec. chr., Florence, Italy; Jean-Christophe Bédos, pres. & CEO, Montréal, Qué.; Davide Barberis Canonico, United Kingdom; Shirley A. Dawe, Toronto, Ont.; Frank Di Tomaso, Montréal, Qué.; Emilio B. Imbriglio, Montréal, Qué.; Deborah Shannon-Trudeau, Montréal, Qué.; Joseph F. X. Zahra, Malta
Other Exec. Officers - Maryame El Bouwab, v-p, mdsg., planning & supply chain; Katia Fontana, v-p & CFO; Miranda Melfi, v-p, HR, chief legal officer & corp. sec.

Capital Stock

	Authorized (shs.)	Outstanding (shs.)[1]
Series A Preferred	unlimited	nil
Class A Common	unlimited	10,967,417
Class B Common	unlimited	7,717,970
Non-voting Common	unlimited	nil

[1] At July 29, 2022

Class A Common - One vote per share.
Class B Common - Ten votes per share.
Major Shareholder - Grande Rousse Trust held 89.65% interest at July 29, 2022.

Price Range - BGI/NYSE MKT

Year	Volume	High	Low	Close
2022	1,313,452	US$8.09	US$4.33	US$7.93
2021	14,016,833	US$8.63	US$0.82	US$4.85
2020	9,339,942	US$1.97	US$0.34	US$0.86
2019	276,748	US$1.25	US$0.82	US$0.90
2018	1,656,088	US$2.76	US$0.77	US$0.95

Capital Stock Changes - During fiscal 2022, class A common shares were issued as follows: 138,147 on exercise of options and 46,323 on exercise of warrants.

Wholly Owned Subsidiaries

Birks Investments Inc., Canada.
Birks Jewellers Limited, Hong Kong, Hong Kong, People's Republic of China.
Cash, Gold & Silver Inc., Canada.
Cash, Gold & Silver USA, Inc., United States.
RMBG Retail Vancouver ULC, B.C.

Financial Statistics

Periods ended:	52w Mar. 26/22[A]		52w Mar. 27/21[A]
	$000s	%Chg	$000s
Operating revenue	**181,342**	**+27**	**143,068**
Cost of sales	105,122		86,718
General & admin expense	65,942		53,713
Operating expense	**171,064**	**+22**	**140,431**
Operating income	**10,278**	**+290**	**2,637**
Deprec., depl. & amort.	5,809		5,458
Finance costs, gross	3,182		3,017
Pre-tax income	**1,287**	**n.a.**	**(5,838)**
Net income	**1,287**	**n.a.**	**(5,838)**
Cash & equivalent	2,013		1,807
Inventories	78,907		97,789
Accounts receivable	8,037		7,307
Current assets	90,779		108,947
Fixed assets, net	22,781		24,496
Right-of-use assets	58,071		57,670
Intangibles, net	6,031		4,894
Total assets	**183,261**	**-9**	**201,680**
Bank indebtedness	43,157		53,387
Accts. pay. & accr. liabs	36,631		49,184
Current liabilities	88,880		111,829
Long-term debt, gross	23,500		26,022
Long-term debt, net	21,371		23,062
Long-term lease liabilities	66,757		66,713
Shareholders' equity	5,864		(1,422)
Cash from oper. activs	**18,648**	**n.a.**	**(1,723)**
Cash from fin. activs	(12,631)		5,957
Cash from invest. activs	(5,811)		(2,992)
Net cash position	**2,013**	**+11**	**1,807**
Capital expenditures	(4,612)		(2,976)
	$		$
Earnings per share*	0.07		(0.32)
Cash flow per share*	1.02		(0.10)
	shs		shs
No. of shs. o/s*	18,515,913		18,328,943
Avg. no. of shs. o/s*	18,346,000		18,005,000
	%		%
Net profit margin	0.71		(4.08)
Return on equity	n.m.		n.m.
Return on assets	2.32		(1.37)
No. of employees (FTEs)	296		319

* Cl.A & B com.

[A] Reported in accordance with U.S. GAAP

Historical Summary
(as originally stated)

Fiscal Year	Oper. Rev.	Net Inc. Bef. Disc.	EPS*
	$000s	$000s	$
2022[A]	181,342	1,287	0.07
2021[A]	143,068	(5,838)	(0.32)
2020[A]	169,420	(12,227)	(0.68)
2019[A]	151,049	(18,305)	(1.02)
	US$000s	US$000s	US$
2018[A1]	114,378	(16,778)	(0.93)

* Cl.A & B com.

[A] Reported in accordance with U.S. GAAP

[1] 53 weeks ended Mar. 31, 2018.

B.68 The Bitcoin Fund

Symbol - QBTC **Exchange** - TSX **CUSIP** - 09175G
Head Office - 2700-161 Bay St, Toronto, ON, M5J 2S1 **Telephone** - (416) 639-2130 **Fax** - (416) 848-4202
Website - www.3iq.ca
Email - fred.pye@3iq.ca
Investor Relations - Frederick T. Pye (514) 775-0010
Auditors - Raymond Chabot Grant Thornton LLP C.A., Montréal, Qué.
Transfer Agents - Computershare Trust Company of Canada Inc., Toronto, Ont.
Trustees - 3iQ Corp., Toronto, Ont.
Managers - 3iQ Corp., Toronto, Ont.
Profile - (Ont. 2020) Invests in Bitcoin.

The fund invests in Bitcoin purchased from reputable bitcoin trading platforms (commonly referred to as Bitcoin exchanges) and over-the-counter counterparties. Bitcoin trading platforms are spot markets on which Bitcoin can be exchanged for U.S. dollars. Bitcoin trading platforms are not regulated as securities exchanges or commodity futures exchanges under the securities or commodity futures laws of Canada, the United States or other global jurisdictions.

The value of Bitcoin held by the fund is based on the MVIS CryptoCompare Bitcoin Benchmark Rate Index maintained by **MV Index Solutions GmbH** (MVIS). Prior to May 2, 2022, the fund's Bitcoin was valued based on MVIS CryptoCompare Institutional Bitcoin Index also maintained by MVIS.

The manager is entitled to a management fee at an annual rate of 1.95% of net asset value, calculated daily and payable monthly, plus taxes. The fund does not have a fixed termination date but may be terminated at the discretion of the manager without unitholder approval.

Directors - Frederick T. (Fred) Pye, chr. & CEO, Pointe-Claire, Qué.; John Loeprich, CFO, Moffat, Ont.; Anthony Cox, exec. v-p, Toronto, Ont.

Oper. Subsid./Mgt. Co. Officers - Pascal St-Jean, pres.; Diana Escobar Bold, chief compliance officer

Capital Stock

	Authorized (shs.)	Outstanding (shs.)[1]
Class A Unit	unlimited	7,883,051
Class F Unit	unlimited	nil

[1] At Mar. 31, 2023

Class A & F Units - Denominated in U.S. dollars. The fund does not intend to pay distributions. Class F units are designed for fee-based investors and/or institutional accounts. Retractable in June of each year at a price equal to the net asset value (NAV) per unit on the first business day following June 15, less any costs and expenses associated with the retraction. Payment of proceeds of annual redemption will be made in U.S. dollars or, at the request of a unitholder who is redeeming at least 20,000 units, in bitcoin. In connection with annual redemption, unitholders may elect to convert their units on a NAV basis into units of 3iQ CoinShares Bitcoin ETF. Class A units are retractable monthly at a price per unit equal to the lesser of: (a) 95% of the closing market price; and (b) the NAV per class A unit on the applicable monthly retraction date less, in each case, any costs and expenses associated with the retraction. In any event, the class A retraction price will not be an amount that is more than the NAV per class A unit. Class F units are retractable monthly at a price per unit equal to the class A retraction price multiplied by a fraction, the numerator of which shall be the NAV per class F unit and the denominator of which shall be the NAV per class A unit. Class F units issued are reclassified immediately as class A units on a 1-for-1 basis. Class F units may be issued in the future that may not be reclassified immediately as class A units and as such, there may be outstanding class F units in the future. One vote per unit.

Normal Course Issuer Bid - The company plans to make normal course purchases of up to 680,633 class A units representing 10% of the public float. The bid commenced on Mar. 1, 2023, and expires on Feb. 29, 2024.

Major Shareholder - Widely held at Dec. 31, 2022.

Price Range - QBTC/TSX

Year	Volume	High	Low	Close
2022	8,053,091	$65.00	$19.01	$20.84
2021	31,752,865	$89.50	$38.10	$61.02
2020	7,774,651	$51.80	$21.96	$48.39

QBTC.U/TSX

Year	Volume	High	Low	Close
2020	18,256,975	US$40.75	US$10.01	US$37.68

Recent Close: $34.81

Capital Stock Changes - During 2022, 3,591,213 class A units were converted into units of 3iQ CoinShares Bitcoin ETF, 120,800 class A units were repurchased under a Normal Course Issuer Bid and 35,512 class A units were retracted.

Financial Statistics

Periods ended:	12m Dec. 31/22[A]		12m Dec. 31/21[A]
	US$000s	%Chg	US$000s
Realized invest. gain (loss)	53,217		202,684
Unrealized invest. gain (loss)	(363,670)		69,707
Total revenue	**(310,414)**	**n.a.**	**272,393**
General & admin. expense	8,158		20,783
Operating expense	**8,158**	**-61**	**20,783**
Operating income	**(318,572)**	**n.a.**	**251,610**
Finance costs, gross	nil		194
Pre-tax income	**(318,572)**	**n.a.**	**251,416**
Net income	**(318,572)**	**n.a.**	**251,416**
Cash & equivalent	48		145
Investments	139,650		587,918
Total assets	**139,698**	**-76**	**588,063**
Accts. pay. & accr. liabs	344		1,472
Shareholders' equity	139,354		586,591
Cash from oper. activs	**4,928**	**n.a.**	**(174,335)**
Cash from fin. activs	(5,023)		172,136
Net cash position	**48**	**-67**	**145**
	US$		US$
Earnings per share*	(33.83)		16.36
Cash flow per share*	0.52		(11.34)
Net asset value per share*	17.68		50.44
	shs		shs
No. of shs. o/s*	7,883,051		11,630,577
Avg. no. of shs. o/s*	9,416,790		15,371,675
	%		%
Net profit margin	n.m.		92.30
Return on equity	(87.77)		45.11
Return on assets	(87.55)		44.65

* Cl.A Unit

[A] Reported in accordance with IFRS

Historical Summary
(as originally stated)

Fiscal Year	Total Rev.	Net Inc. Bef. Disc.	EPS*
	US$000s	US$000s	US$
2022[A]	(310,414)	(318,572)	(33.83)
2021[A]	272,393	251,416	16.36
2020[A1]	270,022	267,167	36.23

* Cl.A Unit

[A] Reported in accordance with IFRS

[1] 38 weeks ended Dec. 31, 2020.

B.69 Bitcoin Well Inc.

Symbol - BTCW **Exchange** - TSX-VEN **CUSIP** - 09173W
Head Office - 10142 82 Ave NW, Edmonton, AB, T6E 1Z4 **Toll-free** - (888) 711-3866
Website - bitcoinwell.com
Email - heather.barnhouse@dentons.com
Investor Relations - Heather Barnhouse (888) 711-3866
Auditors - Kingston Ross Pasnak LLP C.A., Edmonton, Alta.
Transfer Agents - Odyssey Trust Company, Calgary, Alta.
Profile - (Alta. 2017) Operates bitcoin ATMs across Canada and provides in-person and online services to buy, sell and use bitcoin.

At Mar. 31, 2023, the company had 266 ATMs in operation, including 93 machines operating in partner locations. The company also facilitates bitcoin transactions through Bitcoin Well Infinite, which offers in-person cryptocurrency services in Edmonton and Calgary, Alta., as well as through its non-custodial online bitcoin platform at bitcoinwell.com/app.

In March 2023, the company entered into an agreement with an undisclosed partner to offer its non-custodial bitcoin services to customers in the U.S., planned for launch in the second quarter of 2023.

During the first quarter of 2022, wholly owned **Paradime Ltd.** (dba AlphaVend) ceased operations of its bitcoin ATMs in the U.K. following revocation of its licence. AlphaVend had 26 machines across England, Scotland and Wales.

Predecessor Detail - Name changed from Red River Capital Corp., June 11, 2021, pursuant to the Qualifying Transaction reverse takeover acquisition of 1739001 Alberta Ltd. (dba Bitcoin Well) and concurrent amalgamation of Bitcoin Well with wholly owned 2283971 Alberta Ltd. (and continued as Bitcoin Well Holdings Inc.).

Directors - Adam O'Brien, pres. & CEO, Sherwood Park, Alta.; David Bradley, chief revenue officer, Calgary, Alta.; Mitchell W. Demeter, Grand Cayman, Cayman Islands; Terry Rhode, Sherwood Park, Alta.; Allen D. Stephen, Sherwood Park, Alta.

Other Exec. Officers - Luke Thibodeau, CFO; Heather Barnhouse, corp. sec.

Capital Stock

	Authorized (shs.)	Outstanding (shs.)[1]
Preferred	unlimited	nil
Common	unlimited	174,382,887

[1] At May 1, 2023

Major Shareholder - Adam O'Brien held 46.83% interest and Richard Gauthier held 14.66% interest at May 1, 2023.

Price Range - BTCW/TSX-VEN

Year	Volume	High	Low	Close
2022	17,607,056	$0.20	$0.04	$0.04
2021	15,464,301	$0.60	$0.17	$0.18
2020	11,000	$0.04	$0.03	$0.04
2019	330,100	$0.13	$0.02	$0.12
2018	111,500	$0.20	$0.10	$0.10

Recent Close: $0.04

Capital Stock Changes - During 2022, common shares were issued as follows: 478,244 for services and 373,830 on exercise of options.

Wholly Owned Subsidiaries

Bitcoin Well Holdings Inc., Edmonton, Alta.
- 100% int. in **Enterprises Equibytes Inc.**, Montréal, Qué.
- 100% int. in **Ghostlab Inc.**, Edmonton, Alta.
- 100% int. in **1196302 B.C. Ltd.**, B.C.
- 100% int. in **Paradime Ltd.**, United Kingdom.

Financial Statistics

Periods ended:	12m Dec. 31/22[A]		12m Dec. 31/21[A1]
	$000s	%Chg	$000s
Operating revenue	**66,731**	**-33**	**99,613**
Cost of sales	62,307		94,440
Salaries & benefits	3,801		4,079
General & admin expense	3,899		5,721
Stock-based compensation	314		530
Operating expense	**70,321**	**-33**	**104,770**
Operating income	**(3,590)**	**n.a.**	**(5,157)**
Deprec., depl. & amort.	2,149		1,365
Finance costs, gross	1,741		549
Write-downs/write-offs	(3,164)		(1,306)
Pre-tax income	**(5,213)**	**n.a.**	**(14,131)**
Income taxes	778		(528)
Net income	**(5,992)**	**n.a.**	**(13,603)**
Cash & equivalent	3,947		4,800
Inventories	711		376
Accounts receivable	102		364
Current assets	11,080		14,813
Long-term investments	350		929
Fixed assets, net	1,391		2,229
Right-of-use assets	33		135
Intangibles, net	1,170		5,042
Total assets	**14,024**	**-40**	**23,561**
Bank indebtedness	13,716		15,651
Accts. pay. & accr. liabs	681		1,245
Current liabilities	14,540		17,225
Long-term debt, gross	100		100
Long-term debt, net	100		100
Long-term lease liabilities	nil		29
Shareholders' equity	5,832		5,990
Cash from oper. activs	**(9,076)**	**n.a.**	**(2,431)**
Cash from fin. activs	8,944		6,298
Cash from invest. activs	(721)		(3,122)
Net cash position	**3,967**	**-17**	**4,800**
Capital expenditures	(147)		(1,591)
	$		$
Earnings per share*	(0.03)		(0.09)
Cash flow per share*	(0.05)		(0.02)
	shs		shs
No. of shs. o/s*	174,382,887		173,530,813
Avg. no. of shs. o/s*	174,203,993		146,811,422
	%		%
Net profit margin	(8.98)		(13.66)
Return on equity	(101.37)		n.m.
Return on assets	(21.24)		(73.28)

* Common
[A] Reported in accordance with IFRS
[1] Results reflect the June 11, 2021, Qualifying Transaction reverse takeover acquisition of 1739001 Alberta Ltd. (dba Bitcoin Well).

Latest Results

Periods ended:	3m Mar. 31/23[A]		3m Mar. 31/22[A]
	$000s	%Chg	$000s
Operating revenue	12,417	-8	13,529
Net income	(3,523)	n.a.	(2,061)
	$		$
Earnings per share*	(0.02)		(0.01)

* Common
[A] Reported in accordance with IFRS

Historical Summary
(as originally stated)

Fiscal Year	Oper. Rev.	Net Inc. Bef. Disc.	EPS*
	$000s	$000s	$
2022[A]	66,731	(5,992)	(0.03)
2021[A]	99,613	(13,603)	(0.09)
2020[A1]	51,971	(2,743)	(0.23)
2019[A1]	14,539	117	n.a.

* Common
[A] Reported in accordance with IFRS
[1] Results pertain to 1739001 Alberta Ltd. (dba Bitcoin Well).

B.70 Bitfarms Ltd.

Symbol - BITF **Exchange** - TSX **CUSIP** - 09173B
Head Office - 902-18 King St E, Toronto, ON, M5C 1C4 **Telephone** - (416) 804-8535
Website - www.bitfarms.com
Email - gmorphy@bitfarms.com
Investor Relations - L. Geoffrey Morphy (647) 259-1790
Auditors - PricewaterhouseCoopers LLP C.A., Oakville, Ont.
Transfer Agents - TSX Trust Company, Toronto, Ont.
FP500 Revenue Ranking - 673
Employees - 150 at Dec. 31, 2022
Profile - (Can. 2018) Owns and operates server farms in Quebec, Washington State, Paraguay and Argentina that mine for cryptocurrencies.

Operations are carried out through two segments: Backbone; and Volta.

Wholly owned **Backbone Hosting Solutions Inc.** operates ten server farms, which mine Bitcoin, located in Quebec (7), Washington, Paraguay and Argentina, consisting of computers or miners, designed for validating transactions primarily on cryptocurrency network blockchains. Also exchanges cryptocurrencies mined into U.S. dollars regularly through reputable and established cryptocurrency trading platforms.

Operating power at May 14, 2023:

Country	MW
Canada	148
United States	20
Paraguay	10
Argentina	18
	196

Wholly owned **9159-9290 Quebec Inc.** (dba Volta) assists the company in building and maintaining its server farms and provides electrician services to both commercial and residential customers in Quebec.

In April 2023, the company entered into agreements to acquire 22 MW of hydro power capacity and to lease a site in Baie-Comeau, Que., for a total consideration of US$1,800,000.

In December 2022, the company sold its Sherbrooke, Que.-based De la Pointe power facility to **Société de transport de Sherbrooke**, for US$3,600,000.

In September 2022, the company commenced production at its 50-MW mining facility in Rio Cuarto, Argentina.

In March 2022, the company acquired Garlock power facility in Sherbrooke, Que., for Cdn$2,250,000 and 25,000 common share purchase warrants, with an exercise price of Cdn$4.43. An 18-MW electrical infrastructure would be developed at the site intended to replace de la Pointe power facility scheduled to be retired in February 2023.

Directors - Nicolas Bonta, founder & chr., Buenos Aires, Argentina; L. Geoffrey (Geoff) Morphy, pres. & CEO, Toronto, Ont.; Brian M. Howlett†, Mississauga, Ont.; Andres Finkielsztain, Buenos Aires, Argentina; Emiliano J. Grodzki, Buenos Aires, Argentina; Edith M. (Edie) Hofmeister, Berkeley, Calif.

Other Exec. Officers - Jeffrey Lucas, CFO; Ben Gagnon, chief min. officer; Benoit Gobeil, sr. v-p, opers. & infrastructure; Marc-André Ammann, v-p, fin. & acctg.; Philippe Fortier, v-p, corp. devel.; Jeffrey (Jung Feng) Gao, v-p, risk mgt.; Paul Magrath, v-p, tax; Patricia Osorio, v-p, corp. affairs; Andrea K. Souza, v-p, HR; Stephanie Wargo, v-p, mktg. & commun.

† Lead director

Capital Stock

	Authorized (shs.)	Outstanding (shs.)[1]
Class A Preferred	unlimited	nil
Common	unlimited	244,726,000

[1] At May 14, 2023

Major Shareholder - Widely held at Apr. 4, 2023.

Price Range - BITF/TSX

Year	Volume	High	Low	Close
2022	225,195,921	$6.83	$0.52	$0.56
2021	465,715,341	$11.60	$2.26	$6.38
2020	76,966,822	$3.66	$0.28	$2.50
2019	22,344,850	$4.20	$0.48	$0.50

Recent Close: $1.71

Capital Stock Changes - During 2022, common shares were issued as follows: 29,324,000 under an at-the-market offering and 70,000 on exercise of options.

Wholly Owned Subsidiaries

Bitfarms Ltd., Tel Aviv, Israel.
- 100% int. in **AU Acquisition VI, LLC**, Nev.
- 34.7% int. in **Backbone Hosting Solutions Inc.**, Brossard, Qué.
  - 90% int. in **Backbone Hosting Solutions Paraguay S.A.**, Paraguay.
  - 100% int. in **Backbone Hosting Solutions S.A.U.**, Argentina.
  - 100% int. in **Backbone Hosting Solutions (U.S.A.) Inc.**, Del.
  - 100% int. in **9159-9290 Quebec Inc.**, Qué.
- 10% int. in **Backbone Hosting Solutions Paraguay S.A.**, Paraguay.
- 100% int. in **Pembroke & Timberland, LLC**, Me.
- 100% int. in **2872246 Ontario Inc.**, Ont.
  - 100% int. in **Backbone Mining Solutions LLC**, Del.

Subsidiaries

65.3% int. in **Backbone Hosting Solutions Inc.**, Brossard, Qué.

Financial Statistics

Periods ended:	12m Dec. 31/22[A]		12m Dec. 31/21[□A]
	US$000s	%Chg	US$000s
Operating revenue	**142,428**	**-16**	**169,491**
Cost of sales	59,490		33,895
Salaries & benefits	30,040		30,334
General & admin expense	21,466		12,904
Operating expense	**110,996**	**+44**	**77,133**
Operating income	**31,432**	**-66**	**92,358**
Deprec., depl. & amort.	72,420		24,476
Finance income	51,649		6,149
Finance costs, gross	24,089		27,152
Write-downs/write-offs	(93,113)[1]		60
Pre-tax income	**(256,462)**	**n.a.**	**42,637**
Income taxes	(17,412)		20,507
Net income	**(239,050)**	**n.a.**	**22,130**
Cash & equivalent	30,887		125,595
Inventories	588		548
Accounts receivable	701		1,038
Current assets	69,088		287,127
Fixed assets, net	219,428		136,850
Right-of-use assets	16,364		9,397
Intangibles, net	33		18,636
Total assets	**343,098**	**-37**	**542,587**
Accts. pay. & accr. liabs	20,541		14,480
Current liabilities	67,244		101,178
Long-term debt, gross	47,147		11,167
Long-term debt, net	4,093		910
Long-term lease liabilities	14,215		9,227
Shareholders' equity	255,567		422,582
Cash from oper. activs	**36,250**	**n.a.**	**(43,319)**
Cash from fin. activs	24,010		371,986
Cash from invest. activs	(155,011)		(208,998)
Net cash position	**30,887**	**-75**	**125,595**
Capital expenditures	(153,138)		(108,161)
Capital disposals	10,500		1,109
	US$		US$
Earnings per share*	(1.15)		0.14
Cash flow per share*	0.17		(0.27)
	shs		shs
No. of shs. o/s*	224,200,000		194,806,000
Avg. no. of shs. o/s*	207,776,000		157,652,000
	%		%
Net profit margin	(167.84)		13.06
Return on equity	(70.50)		10.10
Return on assets	(48.91)		12.19
No. of employees (FTEs)	150		n.a.

* Common
[□] Restated
[A] Reported in accordance with IFRS
[1] Includes US$84,081,000 impairment related to Argentina cryptocurrency mining operations.

Latest Results

Periods ended:	3m Mar. 31/23[A]		3m Mar. 31/22[A]
	US$000s	%Chg	US$000s
Operating revenue	30,050	-25	40,329
Net income	(2,479)	n.a.	4,519
	US$		US$
Earnings per share*	(0.01)		0.02

* Common
[A] Reported in accordance with IFRS

Historical Summary
(as originally stated)

Fiscal Year	Oper. Rev.	Net Inc. Bef. Disc.	EPS*
	US$000s	US$000s	US$
2022[A]	142,428	(239,050)	(1.15)
2021[A]	169,491	22,130	0.14
2020[A]	34,703	(16,289)	(0.19)
2019[A]	32,421	2,107	0.04
2018[A1]	33,805	(18,236)	n.a.

* Common
[A] Reported in accordance with IFRS
[1] Results pertain to Bitfarms Ltd. (Israel).

B.71 BitRush Corp.

Symbol - BRH **Exchange** - CSE (S) **CUSIP** - 09173X
Head Office - 2905-77 King St W, Toronto, ON, M5K 1H1 **Telephone** - (416) 847-1831 **Fax** - (416) 603-8436
Website - www.bitrush.com
Email - karsten.arend@bitrush.com
Investor Relations - Karsten Arend (647) 660-8703
Auditors - Manning Elliott LLP C.A., Vancouver, B.C.
Transfer Agents - Capital Transfer Agency Inc., Toronto, Ont.
Profile - (Ont. 1999 amalg.) Seeking new business opportunities.

Previously developed cryptographic payment, cryptographic gaming and advertising technologies. The company operated AdBit, an online advertising platform which used Bitcoin (BTC) as a payment method.

Common suspended from CSE, Dec. 5, 2016.

Predecessor Detail - Name changed from The Streetwear Corporation, Aug. 25, 2015, following reverse takeover acquisition of MezzaCap GmbH.

Directors - Karsten Arend, pres. & CEO, Toronto, Ont.; Harold Morgan; Hansjoerg Wagner, Singapore

Other Exec. Officers - Keith Li, CFO & corp. sec.

Capital Stock

	Authorized (shs.)	Outstanding (shs.)[1]
Common	unlimited	99,848,607

[1] At May 17, 2022

Major Shareholder - HSRC Investments Ltd. held 38.5% interest at July 8, 2021.

Financial Statistics

Periods ended:	12m Dec. 31/21[A]		12m Dec. 31/20[A]
	$000s	%Chg	$000s
General & admin expense	459		220
Operating expense	**459**	**+109**	**220**
Operating income	**(459)**	**n.a.**	**(220)**
Finance costs, gross	5		nil
Pre-tax income	**(242)**	**n.a.**	**(58)**
Net income	**(242)**	**n.a.**	**(58)**
Cash & equivalent	99		20
Accounts receivable	49		28
Current assets	153		50
Intangibles, net	nil		160
Total assets	**153**	**-27**	**210**
Accts. pay. & accr. liabs	132		267
Current liabilities	132		338
Long-term debt, gross	60		60
Long-term debt, net	60		60
Shareholders' equity	(39)		(188)
Cash from oper. activs	**(261)**	**n.a.**	**(179)**
Cash from fin. activs	300		71
Cash from invest. activs	40		(50)
Net cash position	**99**	**+395**	**20**
	$		$
Earnings per share*	(0.00)		(0.00)
Cash flow per share*	(0.00)		(0.00)
	shs		shs
No. of shs. o/s*	99,848,607		89,809,234
Avg. no. of shs. o/s*	92,984,750		89,809,234
	%		%
Net profit margin	n.a.		n.a.
Return on equity	n.m.		n.m.
Return on assets	(130.58)		(27.88)

* Common

[A] Reported in accordance with IFRS

Latest Results

Periods ended:	3m Mar. 31/22[A]		3m Mar. 31/21[A]
	$000s	%Chg	$000s
Net income	(77)	n.a.	(52)
	$		$
Earnings per share*	(0.00)		(0.00)

* Common

[A] Reported in accordance with IFRS

Historical Summary
(as originally stated)

Fiscal Year	Oper. Rev.	Net Inc. Bef. Disc.	EPS*
	$000s	$000s	$
2021[A]	nil	(242)	(0.00)
2020[A]	nil	(58)	(0.00)
2019[A]	nil	(264)	(0.00)
2018[A]	nil	10	0.00
2017[A]	nil	(1,005)	(0.01)

* Common

[A] Reported in accordance with IFRS

B.72 Black Diamond Group Limited*

Symbol - BDI **Exchange** - TSX **CUSIP** - 09202D

Head Office - 1000-440 2 Ave SW, Calgary, AB, T2P 5E9 **Telephone** - (403) 206-4747 **Toll-free** - (888) 569-4880 **Fax** - (403) 264-9281

Website - www.blackdiamondgroup.com

Email - jzhang@blackdiamondgroup.com

Investor Relations - Jason Zhang (403) 206-4739

Auditors - Ernst & Young LLP C.A., Calgary, Alta.

Lawyers - Torys LLP, Calgary, Alta.

Transfer Agents - Odyssey Trust Company

FP500 Revenue Ranking - 549

Employees - 427 at Dec. 31, 2022

Profile - (Alta. 2009) Rents and sells modular space solutions and workforce accommodation solutions to customers in various industries in Canada, the U.S. and Australia.

Operates two complementary business units: Modular Space Solutions and Workforce Solutions.

Modular Space Solutions - This business unit provides modular buildings for temporary office, storage and training space primarily on construction sites and at industrial and commercial facilities in British Columbia, Alberta, Saskatchewan, Ontario, Quebec, New Brunswick, California, Texas, Pennsylvania, North Carolina, Maine, Massachusetts and Georgia. Structures provided include office units, lavatories, storage units, office complexes, classroom facilities, banking facilities, health care facilities, high security modular buildings, custom manufactured modular facilities and blast resistant structures. Customers include general contractors, construction trades, real estate developers, manufacturers, commercial businesses, education providers, financial institutions, resource companies and government agencies. At Dec. 31, 2022, the rental fleet consisted of 11,173 units of which 6,922 were located in Canada and 4,251 in the U.S.

Workforce Solutions - This unit consists of large format workforce accommodations, and small format workforce accommodation and industrial services in North America; workforce solution in Australia; and LodgeLink, which offers travel management logistics. During 2022, workforce solutions' rental fleet capacity consisted of 5,038 units in Canada, 449 units in the U.S. and 1,207 units in Australia.

The large format workforce accommodations provides workforce accommodations and associated services to oil and gas exploration and development companies, mineral and metals mining and processing companies, large catering and food services providers, engineering and construction companies, drillers, general contractors, pipeline constructors, disaster recovery organizations and municipal and provincial governments throughout Canada and certain regions of the U.S. Facilities include relocatable dormitories, kitchen/diner complexes, recreation facilities and supporting utility assets. Also offers both new and used units for sale, provides delivery, installation, project management and ancillary products, turnkey lodging services, remote facility management and supply chain management service.

The small format workforce accommodation and industrial services provides rental of industrial equipment such as tanks, environmental containment systems, fluids management and transfer equipment, light towers, matting, power generation and industrial heaters; and staff quarters and rapid deployment accommodation camps provide living amenities to work crews and support staff along with full installation and maintenance services from operations in Fort St. John, B.C.; Grande Prairie, Alta.; Midland and Fort Worth, Tex.

The workforce solution in Australia rents and sells remote workforce accommodations across the continent and modular workspace solutions, classrooms for the education sector and provides associated services in or near the major centres of Sydney, Brisbane and Perth. Customer base in Australia includes natural resource companies, building and construction companies, commercial and general industrial companies, public and private education and government.

Wholly owned **LodgeLink Inc.** operates a digital marketplace for business-to-business crew accommodation, travel and logistics services in North America. LodgeLink aggregates available hotels and lodges in an online platform and allows customers to book and manage all aspects of crew travel and accommodations. At Dec. 31, 2022, LodgeLink had a capacity of 996,865 rooms across 10,248 listed properties and over 753 corporate customers. During 2022, the marketplace handled 356,328 room nights sold.

In January 2023, the company announced an expansion into Atlantic Canada with plans to open a BOXX Modular branch and a Black Diamond Camps business development office in Moncton, N.B.

Recent Merger and Acquisition Activity

Status: completed **Announced:** Oct. 31, 2022

Black Diamond Group Limited acquired Flordale, Ont.-based C.L. Martin & Co. Limited for $54,500,000, including the assumption of debt. C.L. Martin provides a turnkey lease and delivery package of modular buildings for use as classrooms and storage rooms for school boards, private schools, businesses or individuals. The acquisition includes 1,851 units primarily focused on the education and government sector and $33,000,000 of contracted revenue.

Status: completed **Announced:** May 2, 2022

Black Diamond Group Limited acquired all of the operating assets of Cambrian Trailer Rentals Ltd., consisting of a fleet of 150 rental units and associated rental agreements in southern Alberta. Terms were not disclosed.

Directors - Trevor Haynes, chr., pres. & CEO, Calgary, Alta.; Robert Wagemakers†, Calgary, Alta.; Brian R. Hedges, Toronto, Ont.; Robert J. (Bob) Herdman, Calgary, Alta.; Barbara J. Kelley, Colo.; Edward H. Kernaghan, Toronto, Ont.; Leilani Latimer, San Francisco, Calif.; Steven Stein, Calgary, Alta.

Other Exec. Officers - Toby LaBrie, exec. v-p & CFO; Patrick Melanson, exec. v-p, shared srvcs. & CIO; Edward J. (Ted) Redmond, exec. v-p & COO, modular space solutions; Michael L. (Mike) Ridley, exec. v-p & COO, workforce solutions

† Lead director

Capital Stock

	Authorized (shs.)	Outstanding (shs.)[1]
Preferred	unlimited	nil
Common	unlimited	60,220,000[2]

[1] At Aug. 3, 2023

[2] Net of 798,000 shares held in trust.

Options - At Dec. 31, 2022, options were outstanding to purchase 3,299,000 common shares at a weighted average exercise price of $2.75 per share with average remaining contractual life of 2.44 years.

Normal Course Issuer Bid - The company plans to make normal course purchases of up to 4,395,507 common shares representing 10% of the public float. The bid commenced on Mar. 14, 2023, and expires on Mar. 13, 2024.

Major Shareholder - Edward H. Kernaghan held 14.2% interest at Mar. 20, 2023.

Price Range - BDI/TSX

Year	Volume	High	Low	Close
2022	12,893,268	$5.23	$3.10	$4.83
2021	11,148,581	$5.65	$2.47	$4.43
2020	9,037,836	$2.75	$0.90	$2.72
2019	11,066,956	$2.75	$1.51	$2.15
2018	25,243,280	$3.96	$1.65	$2.09

Recent Close: $6.03

Capital Stock Changes - During 2022, common shares were issued as follows: 1,325,000 on exercise of options and 934,000 pursuant to vesting of share awards; 583,000 common shares were cancelled and 552,000 common shares were repurchased under a Normal Course Issuer Bid.

Dividends

BDI com N.S.R.

$0.02	Oct. 15/23	$0.02	July 15/23
$0.02	Apr. 15/23	$0.02	Jan. 15/23

Paid in 2023: $0.08 2022: $0.0575 2021: $0.0125◆

◆ Special

Long-Term Debt - Outstanding at Dec. 31, 2022:

Revolv. credit facility due Oct. 2026[1]	$225,292,000
Bank term loans due to Dec. 2026[2]	2,503,000
Less: Debt issuance costs	882,000
	226,913,000
Less: Current portion	nil
	226,913,000

[1] Bears interest at prime rate plus 0.25% to 0.75%, or bankers' acceptance rate plus 1.5% to 2%.

[2] Bear interest at 3.05% to 3.79%.

Wholly Owned Subsidiaries

Black Diamond Capital Ltd., Alta.

Black Diamond GPI Inc., Alta.

- 49% int. in **3340698 Nova Scotia Limited**, N.S.

Black Diamond Group Inc., Alta.

- 0.5% int. in **Black Diamond Dene Limited Partnership**, B.C.
- 0.01% int. in **Black Diamond Nehiyawak Limited Partnership**, Alta.
- 0.1% int. in **Black Diamond West Moberly Limited Partnership**, B.C.
- 1.1% int. in **Whitecap Black Diamond Limited Partnership**, Sask.

Black Diamond Group International Ltd., Barbados.

- 100% int. in **Black Diamond Australia Holdings Pty Ltd.**, Australia.
  - 100% int. in **A.C.N. 161717531 Pty Ltd.**, Australia.
  - 100% int. in **Black Diamond Group Company Pty Ltd.**, Australia.
    - 100% int. in **Black Diamond Modular Buildings Pty Ltd.**, Australia.
      - 100% int. in **Australian Portable Buildings Pty Ltd.**, Australia.

Black Diamond Limited Partnership, Calgary, Alta.

- 49.5% int. in **Black Diamond Dene Limited Partnership**, B.C.
- 49.99% int. in **Black Diamond Nehiyawak Limited Partnership**, Alta.
- 49.9% int. in **Black Diamond West Moberly Limited Partnership**, B.C.
- 99.99% int. in **Britco BOXX Limited Partnership**, Alta.
- 49% int. in **Nova Scotia Mi'kmaq Black Diamond Limited Partnership**, N.S.
- 100% int. in **1373901 Alberta Ltd.**, Alta.
  - 100% int. in **BOXX Modular Holdings Inc.**, Del.
    - 100% int. in **BDG Finance LLC**, Del.
    - 100% int. in **BOXX Modular, Inc.**, Del.
    - 100% int. in **Black Diamond Capital U.S.A. Inc.**, Del.
    - 100% int. in **Black Diamond Energy Services Inc.**, Del.
    - 100% int. in **Black Diamond Finance U.S.A. Inc.**, Del.
    - 100% int. in **Black Diamond Real Estate Inc.**, Del.
    - 100% int. in **MPA Systems, LLC**, Tex.
  - 100% int. in **1563539 Alberta ULC**, Alta.
    - 100% int. in **BDG Holdings Inc.**, Sask.
- 49% int. in **3340675 Nova Scotia Limited**, N.S.
- 48.99% int. in **Whitecap Black Diamond Limited Partnership**, Sask.

Britco BOXX GP Ltd., Alta.

- 0.01% int. in **Britco BOXX Limited Partnership**, Alta.

C.L. Martin & Co. Limited, Ont.

LodgeLink Inc., Canada.

- 100% int. in **LodgeLink Inc.**, Del.

1743170 Alberta Ltd., Alta.

Investments

50% int. in **BDK Lodges Inc.**, B.C.

Financial Statistics

Periods ended:	12m Dec. 31/22[A]		12m Dec. 31/21[A]
	$000s	%Chg	$000s
Operating revenue	**324,544**	**-4**	**339,550**
Salaries & benefits	57,097		50,518
General & admin expense	15,361		11,861
Stock-based compensation	4,876		3,408
Other operating expense	168,104		213,124
Operating expense	**245,438**	**-12**	**278,911**
Operating income	**79,106**	**+30**	**60,639**
Deprec., depl. & amort	35,177		35,170
Finance costs, net	8,851		6,036
Write-downs/write-offs	6,329		nil
Pre-tax income	**40,239**	**+101**	**20,027**
Income taxes	11,911		(1,754)
Net income	**28,328**	**+30**	**21,781**
Net inc. for equity hldrs	**26,384**	**+30**	**20,359**
Net inc. for non-cont. int	**1,944**	**+37**	**1,422**
Cash & equivalent	8,308		4,558
Accounts receivable	72,229		58,228
Current assets	99,351		75,967
Fixed assets, net	491,436		404,479
Right-of-use assets	16,839		18,778
Intangibles, net	32,727		20,850
Total assets	**649,442**	**+22**	**530,341**
Accts. pay. & accr. liabs	38,254		40,114
Current liabilities	69,180		66,251
Long-term debt, gross	226,913		155,639
Long-term debt, net	226,913		155,639
Long-term lease liabilities	15,421		17,765
Shareholders' equity	268,531		234,455
Non-controlling interest	4,012		12,344
Cash from oper. activs	**70,789**	**0**	**71,137**
Cash from fin. activs	34,514		(36,558)
Cash from invest. activs	(101,937)		(33,631)
Net cash position	**8,308**	**+82**	**4,558**
Capital expenditures	(51,053)		(36,284)
Capital disposals	nil		2,277
	$		$
Earnings per share*	0.45		0.35
Cash flow per share*	1.20		1.23
Cash divd. per share*	0.07		0.01
Extra divd. - cash*	nil		0.01
Total divd. per share*	**0.07**		**0.03**
	shs		shs
No. of shs. o/s*	59,282,000		58,158,000
Avg. no. of shs. o/s*	59,189,000		57,621,000
	%		%
Net profit margin	8.73		6.41
Return on equity	10.49		9.11
Return on assets	4.80		4.18
Foreign sales percent	56		55
No. of employees (FTEs)	427		376

* Common
[A] Reported in accordance with IFRS

Latest Results

Periods ended:	6m June 30/23[A]		6m June 30/22[A]
	$000s	%Chg	$000s
Operating revenue	172,609	+24	139,639
Net income	9,554	+6	8,981
Net inc. for equity hldrs	8,985	+12	7,997
Net inc. for non-cont. int	569		984
	$		$
Earnings per share*	0.15		0.14

* Common
[A] Reported in accordance with IFRS

Historical Summary
(as originally stated)

Fiscal Year	Oper. Rev.	Net Inc. Bef. Disc.	EPS*
	$000s	$000s	$
2022[A]	324,544	28,328	0.45
2021[A]	339,550	21,781	0.35
2020[A]	179,857	(2,387)	(0.06)
2019[A]	185,936	(7,042)	(0.14)
2018[A]	165,931	(11,621)	(0.21)

* Common
[A] Reported in accordance with IFRS

B.73 Black Swan Graphene Inc.

Symbol - SWAN **Exchange** - TSX-VEN **CUSIP** - 09226M
Head Office - 1410-120 Adelaide St W, Toronto, ON, M5H 1T1
Telephone - (416) 844-7365
Website - blackswangraphene.com
Email - phardy@blackswangraphene.com
Investor Relations - Paul Hardy (416) 844-7365
Auditors - McGovern Hurley LLP C.A., Toronto, Ont.
Transfer Agents - Endeavor Trust Corporation, Vancouver, B.C.
Profile - (B.C. 2010) Developing graphene products aimed at several industrial sectors including concrete, polymers and lithium-ion batteries.

Has a patented graphene processing technology that allows for the production of high performance graphene at a cost sufficiently low to engender rapid commercial penetration in industrial applications requiring large volumes of graphene.

Has access to a pilot and small-scale production plant in Consett, U.K., for research and development. The pilot plant has the capacity to produce approximately 20 to 40 tonnes of graphene nanoplatelets (GNP) in dispersion using the patented and proven homogenization process.

The company plans to conduct a preliminary economic assessment and a feasibility study to plan the construction of a large-scale facility in Quebec. Aims to produce, manufacture and distribute atomically thin two-dimensional (2D) materials, including GNP and focus on its commercialization with an initial focus on the polymer, concrete and rubber industries.

Recent Merger and Acquisition Activity

Status: completed **Revised:** Aug. 2, 2022
UPDATE: The transaction was completed. PREVIOUS: Dragonfly Capital Corp. enter into a letter of intent for the Qualifying Transaction reverse takeover acquisition of private Toronto, Ont.-based Black Swan Graphite Inc., a graphene processing technology company that recently acquired strategic assets related to the patented Graphene Technology from Thomas Swan & Co. Limited. Terms and structure of the transaction were to be negotiated. Black Swan planned to complete a concurrent financing for gross proceeds of $5,000,000. Principal Black Swan shareholders were Mason Graphite Inc. (56.03% interest), Thomas Swan & Co. and Fahad Al-Tamimi, chair and second largest shareholder of Mason Graphite. Jan. 17, 2022 - A definitive agreement was entered into. Dragonfly would acquire Black Swan for issuance of 210,229,434 common shares at a deemed price of 15¢ per share. Mar. 14, 2022 - Dragonfly completed a private placement of 46,669,665 subscription receipts at 15¢ per receipt for gross proceeds of $7,000,500. Apr. 21, 2022 - The closing date was extended to June 17, 2022, and the exchange ratio was modified whereby Black Swan shareholders would receive 15.2 Dragonfly common shares for each share held, which would result in the issuance of 210,230,349 Dragonfly common shares. July 22, 2022 - Conditional TSX Venture Exchange approval was received.

Predecessor Detail - Name changed from Dragonfly Capital Corp., Aug. 2, 2022, pursuant to the Qualifying Transaction reverse takeover acquisition of (old) Black Swan Graphite Inc.

Directors - Harry Swan, chr., United Kingdom; Simon Marcotte, pres. & CEO, Oakville, Ont.; Michael Edwards, COO, Hereford., United Kingdom; Peter Damouni, London, Middx., United Kingdom; Dr. David S. Deak, Los Gatos, Calif.; Bradley (Brad) Humphrey, Toronto, Ont.; Roy McDowall, Chambly, Qué.

Other Exec. Officers - Gregory F. (Greg) Duras, CFO & corp. sec.; Paul Hardy, v-p, corp. devel.; Dr. Chris Herron, v-p, research & product devel.

Capital Stock

	Authorized (shs.)	Outstanding (shs.)[1]
Common	unlimited	283,938,008

[1] At Sept. 28, 2022

Major Shareholder - Mason Graphite Inc. held 41.49% interest and Harry Swan held 15.56% interest at Sept. 28, 2022.

Price Range - SWAN/TSX-VEN

Year	Volume	High	Low	Close
2022	12,459,988	$0.28	$0.07	$0.08
2021	202,050	$0.26	$0.13	$0.14
2020	86,500	$0.14	$0.13	$0.13
2019	30,000	$0.18	$0.18	$0.18
2018	352,000	$0.25	$0.10	$0.17

Recent Close: $0.12

Capital Stock Changes - In August 2022, 210,230,343 common shares were issued pursuant to the Qualifying Transaction reverse takeover acquisition of (old) Black Swan Graphite Inc., and 46,669,665 common shares were issued without further consideration on exchange of subscription receipts sold previously by private placement at 15¢ each. In addition, 10,727,000 common shares were issued as a finder's fee.

There were no changes to capital stock of Dragonfly Capital Corp. from fiscal 2019 to fiscal 2022, inclusive.

Financial Statistics

Periods ended:	12m Dec. 31/21[A1]
	$000s
General & admin expense	516
Stock-based compensation	1,014
Other operating expense	95
Operating expense	**1,625**
Operating income	**(1,625)**
Deprec., depl. & amort	315
Pre-tax income	**(1,941)**
Net income	**(1,941)**
Cash & equivalent	4,900
Accounts receivable	39
Current assets	4,959
Intangibles, net	9,144
Total assets	**14,103**
Accts. pay. & accr. liabs	100
Current liabilities	100
Shareholders' equity	14,003
Cash from oper. activs	**(571)**
Cash from fin. activs	10,686
Cash from invest. activs	(5,216)
Net cash position	**4,900**
	$
Earnings per share*	(0.43)
Cash flow per share*	(0.13)
	shs
No. of shs. o/s*	13,830,944
Avg. no. of shs. o/s*	4,528,998
	%
Net profit margin	n.a.
Return on equity	n.m.
Return on assets	n.a.

* Common
[A] Reported in accordance with IFRS
[1] Results for 2021 pertain to (old) Black Swan Graphene Inc.

B.74 BlackBerry Limited*

Symbol - BB **Exchange** - TSX **CUSIP** - 09228F
Head Office - 2200 University Ave E, Waterloo, ON, N2K 0A7
Telephone - (519) 888-7465 **Toll-free** - (877) 255-2377 **Fax** - (519) 888-7884
Website - www.ca.blackberry.com
Email - investor_relations@blackberry.com
Investor Relations - Steve Rai (519) 888-7465 ext. 75950
Auditors - PricewaterhouseCoopers LLP C.A., Toronto, Ont.
Transfer Agents - Computershare Trust Company, Inc., Denver, Colo.; Computershare Trust Company of Canada Inc., Toronto, Ont.
FP500 Revenue Ranking - 368
Employees - 3,181 at Feb. 28, 2023
Profile - (Ont. 1984) Provides intelligent security software and services to enterprises and governments around the world. The company secures more than 500,000,000 endpoints, including more than 235,000,000 vehicles, and leverages artificial intelligence (AI) and machine learning to deliver innovative solutions in the areas of cybersecurity, safety and data privacy solutions, and is a leader in the areas of endpoint security and management, encryption, and embedded systems.

Products and services are organized into three groups: Cybersecurity, Internet of Things (IoT), and Licensing and Other.

Cybersecurity - The company's core offering is the BlackBerry Spark software platform, which integrates a unified endpoint security (UES) layer with BlackBerry unified endpoint management (UEM) to enable secure endpoint communications in a zero trust environment. BlackBerry UES is a set of complementary cybersecurity products offering endpoint protection platform (EPP), endpoint detection and response (EDR), mobile threat defence (MTD), zero-trust network access (ZTNA) and user and entity behaviour analytics (UEBA) capabilities. The BlackBerry Spark platform is informed by the company's AI and machine learning capabilities, continuous innovations, professional cybersecurity services and threat research, industry partnerships and academic collaborations. BlackBerry Spark solutions are available through the BlackBerry® Cyber suite and the BlackBerry Spark® UEM suite, which are also marketed together as the BlackBerry Spark® suite, which offers a broad range of tailored cybersecurity and endpoint management options.

The BlackBerry Spark UES suite offers Cylance® AI and machine learning-based cybersecurity solutions, including: CylancePROTECT®, an EPP and available MTD solution that uses an automated, prevention-first approach to protect against the execution of malicious code on an endpoint; CylanceOPTICS®, an EDR solution that provides both visibility into and prevention of malicious activity on an endpoint; CylanceGUARD®, a managed detection and response solution that provides 24/7 threat hunting and monitoring; CylanceGATEWAY™, an AI-empowered ZTNA solution; CylancePERSONA™, a UEBA solution that provides continuous authentication by validating user identity in real time; and CylancePROTECT Mobile™, a MTD cybersecurity solution that uses the power of AI to block malware infections, prevent URL phishing attacks, and check application integrity.

The BlackBerry Spark® UEM suite includes BlackBerry UEM, a central software component of the Company's secure communications platform offering a single pane of glass, or unified console view, for managing and securing devices, applications, identity, content and endpoints across all leading operating systems; BlackBerry® Dynamics™, a development platform and secure container for mobile applications, including the company's own enterprise applications such as BlackBerry® Work and BlackBerry® Connect for secure collaboration; and BlackBerry® Workspaces, a secure enterprise-grade file sharing solution for secure file storage, synchronization and sharing.

In addition, the company offers BlackBerry® AtHoc and BlackBerry® Alert, which are secure critical event management solutions that enable people, devices and organizations to exchange critical information in real time during business continuity and life safety operations; SecuSUITE®, a secure voice and text messaging solution with advanced encryption, and anti-eavesdropping and continuous authentication capabilities; and BBM Enterprise, an enterprise-grade secure instant messaging solution for messaging, voice and video.

IoT - This business consists of BlackBerry Technology Solutions (BTS) and BlackBerry IVY™. The principal component of BTS is BlackBerry QNX®, which provides real-time operating systems, hypervisors, middleware, development tools and professional services for connected embedded systems in the automotive, medical, industrial automation and other markets. Solutions include Neutrino® operating system and the BlackBerry QNX® CAR platform, a secure automotive over-the-air software update management services that allows original equipment manufacturers (OEM's) to manage the life cycle of the software and security in their vehicles; BlackBerry Certicom®, which leverages patented elliptic curve cryptography to provide device security, anti-counterfeiting and product authentication solutions; and BlackBerry Radar asset tracking solution. The BlackBerry IVY™ is an intelligent vehicle data platform leveraging BlackBerry QNX's automotive capabilities which allow automakers to safely access a vehicle's sensor data, normalize it, and apply machine learning to generate and share predictive insights and inferences.

Licensing and Other - The Licensing business is responsible for the management and monetization of the company's global patent portfolio. At Feb. 28, 2023, the company owned 37,500 worldwide patents and applications. The company's Other business generates revenue from service access fees charged to subscribers using its legacy BlackBerry 7 and prior BlackBerry operating systems.

The company is headquartered in Waterloo, Ont., with additional facilities in the U.S., Asia-Pacific, Europe, Africa and the Middle East.

On May 1, 2023, the company announced it plans to initiate a review of its portfolio of businesses. These alternatives include, but are not limited to, the possible separation of one or more of the company's businesses.

In September 2022, the U.S. District Court for the Southern District of New York granted final approval for the settlement in relation to the lawsuits alleging that the company and certain of its former officers made materially false and misleading statements regarding the company's financial condition and business prospects and that certain of the company's financial statements contain material misstatements. The company paid $165,000,000 cash to settle the claims.

In March 2022, the company ceased all business activities in Russia.

Recent Merger and Acquisition Activity

Status: completed **Revised:** May 11, 2023

UPDATE: The transaction was completed. PREVIOUS: BlackBerry Limited agreed to sell substantially all of its non-core patents and patent applications to Maliki Innovations Limited, a newly formed subsidiary of Dublin, Ireland-based Key Patent Innovations Limited, for US$200,000,000, of which US$170,000,000 would be paid on closing and an additional US$30,000,000 would be paid no later than the third anniversary of closing. BlackBerry would also be entitled to receive annual cash royalties from the profits generated from the BlackBerry patents, which would initially be capped at US$700,000,000, subject to an annual cap increase of an amount equal to 4% of the remaining portion of the US$700,000,000 that has not been paid to BlackBerry as of the date of the increase. The transaction would include the sale of 32,000 patents and applications relating primarily to mobile devices, messaging and wireless networking, but would exclude patents and applications that are necessary to support BlackBerry's current core business operations, as well as excludes 120 monetizable non-core patent families relating to mobile devices (representing 2,000 patents and applications which were primarily standards essential), as well as all existing revenue generating agreements. BlackBerry would receive a licence back to the patents being sold, and the transaction would not impact customers' use of any of BlackBerry's products, solutions or services. The transaction was conditional upon conditions including satisfaction of all regulatory conditions under the Hart–Scott–Rodino Antitrust Improvements Act in the U.S. and the Investment Canada Act.

Status: terminated **Revised:** Mar. 21, 2023

UPDATE: The transaction was terminated as Catapult was unable to secure financing to complete the transaction. PREVIOUS: BlackBerry Limited agreed to sell substantially all of its non-core patent assets to Catapult IP Innovations Inc., a special purpose vehicle formed to acquire the patent assets, for US$600,000,000, consisting of US$450,000,000 cash and a US$150,000,000 promissory note. BlackBerry would receive a licence back to the patents being sold, which relate primarily to mobile devices, messaging and wireless networking. The transaction was conditional upon conditions including satisfaction of all regulatory conditions under the Hart–Scott–Rodino Antitrust Improvements Act in the U.S. and the Investment Canada Act.

Predecessor Detail - Name changed from Research In Motion Limited, July 9, 2013.

Directors - John S. Chen, exec. chr. & CEO, Calif.; V. Prem Watsa†, Toronto, Ont.; Michael A. Daniels, Colo.; Timothy Dattels, Calif.; Lisa S. Disbrow, Va.; Richard J. (Dick) Lynch, New Hope, Pa.; Dr. Laurie Smaldone Alsup, N.J.; The Hon. Wayne G. Wouters, Vancouver, B.C.

Other Exec. Officers - Steve Rai, CFO; Marjorie Dickman, chief govt. affairs & public policy officer; Charles Eagan, chief tech. officer; Jesse Harold, CIO; Phil Kurtz, chief legal officer & corp. sec.; Nita White-Ivy, chief HR officer; Mark Wilson, chief mktg. officer; Sai Yuen (Billy) Ho, exec. v-p, product eng., BlackBerry Spark; Vito Giallorenzo, sr. v-p, corp. devel. & COO, BlackBerry tech. solutions; Arvind Raman, sr. v-p & chief info. security officer; Neelam Sandhu, sr. v-p, sustainability & chief elite cust. success officer; John Wall, sr. v-p & co-head, BlackBerry tech. solutions, products, eng. & opers.; Mattias Eriksson, pres. & gen. mgr., BlackBerry IoT bus. unit; John J. Giamatteo, pres., Cybersecurity

† Lead director

Capital Stock

	Authorized (shs.)	Outstanding (shs.)[1]
Preferred	unlimited	nil
Class A Common	unlimited	nil
Common	unlimited	583,239,813

[1] At June 26, 2023

Options - At Feb. 28, 2023, options were outstanding to purchase 489,000 common shares at a weighted average exercise price of US$4.63 per share with an average remaining contractual life of 4.74 years.

Major Shareholder - Widely held at May 5, 2023.

Price Range - BB/TSX

Year	Volume	High	Low	Close
2022	524,005,666	$12.05	$4.31	$4.41
2021	1,205,543,109	$36.00	$8.34	$11.82
2020	648,390,714	$12.54	$3.94	$8.44
2019	387,841,088	$13.74	$6.48	$8.35
2018	494,415,797	$18.14	$8.94	$9.71

Recent Close: $7.08

Capital Stock Changes - During fiscal 2023, common shares were issued as follows: 4,872,000 on vesting of restricted share units, 960,000 under the employee share purchase plan and 97,000 on exercise of options.

Long-Term Debt - At Feb. 28, 2023, outstanding long-term debt totaled US$367,000,000 (all current) and consisted entirely of 1.75% unsecured convertible debentures due November 2023; convertible into common shares at US$6.00 per share.

Wholly Owned Subsidiaries

BlackBerry Corporation, Del.
BlackBerry UK Limited, United Kingdom.
Cylance Inc., Irvine, Calif.
Secusmart GmbH, Germany.

Note: The preceding list includes only the major related companies in which interests are held.

Financial Statistics

Periods ended:	12m Feb. 28/23[A]		12m Feb. 28/22[A]
	US$000s	%Chg	US$000s
Operating revenue	**656,000**	**-9**	**718,000**
Cost of sales	203,000		215,000
Research & devel. expense	207,000		219,000
General & admin expense	340,000		297,000
Stock-based compensation	34,000		36,000
Operating expense	**784,000**	**+2**	**767,000**
Operating income	**(128,000)**	**n.a.**	**(49,000)**
Deprec., depl. & amort.	96,000		165,000
Finance income	11,000		27,000
Finance costs, gross	6,000		6,000
Write-downs/write-offs	(480,000)[1]		nil
Pre-tax income	**(720,000)**	**n.a.**	**19,000**
Income taxes	14,000		7,000
Net income	**(734,000)**	**n.a.**	**12,000**
Cash & equivalent	426,000		712,000
Accounts receivable	132,000		163,000
Current assets	743,000		1,043,000
Long-term investments	34,000		30,000
Fixed assets, net	25,000		41,000
Right-of-use assets	44,000		50,000
Intangibles, net	798,000		1,366,000
Total assets	**1,679,000**	**-35**	**2,567,000**
Accts. pay. & accr. liabs	143,000		151,000
Current liabilities	729,000		397,000
Long-term debt, gross	367,000		507,000
Long-term debt, net	nil		507,000
Long-term lease liabilities	52,000		66,000
Shareholders' equity	857,000		1,556,000
Cash from oper. activs	**(263,000)**	**n.a.**	**(28,000)**
Cash from fin. activs	6,000		10,000
Cash from invest. activs	176,000		207,000
Net cash position	**322,000**	**-21**	**406,000**
Capital expenditures	(7,000)		(8,000)
Capital disposals	17,000		nil
	US$		US$
Earnings per share*	(1.27)		0.02
Cash flow per share*	(0.45)		(0.05)
	shs		shs
No. of shs. o/s*	582,157,203		576,227,898
Avg. no. of shs. o/s*	578,654,000		570,607,000
	%		%
Net profit margin	(111.89)		1.67
Return on equity	(60.84)		0.78
Return on assets	(34.29)		0.59
No. of employees (FTEs)	3,181		3,325

* Common

[A] Reported in accordance with U.S. GAAP

[1] Includes a US$245,000,000 goodwill impairment charge related to BlackBerry Spark reporting unit and a US$231,000,000 impairment charge related to long-lived assets in UES asset group.

Latest Results

Periods ended:	3m May 31/23[A]		3m May 31/22[A]
	US$000s	%Chg	US$000s
Operating revenue	373,000	+122	168,000
Net income	(11,000)	n.a.	(181,000)
	US$		US$
Earnings per share*	(0.02)		(0.31)

* Common

[A] Reported in accordance with U.S. GAAP

Historical Summary
(as originally stated)

Fiscal Year	Oper. Rev. US$000s	Net Inc. Bef. Disc. US$000s	EPS* US$
2023[A]	656,000	(734,000)	(1.27)
2022[A]	718,000	12,000	0.02
2021[A]	893,000	(1,104,000)	(1.97)
2020[A]	1,040,000	(152,000)	(0.27)
2019[A]	904,000	93,000	0.17

* Common

[A] Reported in accordance with U.S. GAAP

B.75 Blackhawk Growth Corp.

Symbol - BLR **Exchange** - CSE **CUSIP** - 09237D
Head Office - Bankers Hall West, 3810-888 3 St SW, Calgary, AB, T2P 5C5 **Telephone** - (403) 531-1710 **Fax** - (403) 265-6535
Website - www.blackhawkgrowth.com
Email - info@blackhawkgrowth.com
Investor Relations - Trevor P. Wong-Chor (403) 991-7737
Auditors - SHIM & Associates LLP C.A., Vancouver, B.C.
Bankers - ATB Financial, Calgary, Alta.
Lawyers - DLA Piper (Canada) LLP, Calgary, Alta.
Transfer Agents - Odyssey Trust Company, Calgary, Alta.

Profile - (B.C. 2020; orig. Alta., 1986) Invests in equity and debt instruments of companies across a variety of sectors with a focus on the health, cannabis and cannabidiol (CBD) sectors in Canada and the U.S.

At Dec. 31, 2022, total fair value of the company's equity investments totaled $27,954,218.

The investments include wholly owned **Blum Distributors Ltd.**, an established mycology supplier with its own leased production facility in British Columbia; wholly owned **TERP Wholesale, LLC**, a fully licensed distribution centre in California that packages and manufactures tetrahydrocannabinol (THC) products; wholly owned **Stable Foods Co.** (formerly **NuWave Foods Inc.**), a fully licensed commercial kitchen and baked goods manufacturer in Edmonton, Alta., specializing in preservative free shelf stable baked goods; wholly owned **SAC Pharma Partners Inc.**, a licensed cannabis producer located in Sacramento, Calif.; **Gaia Grow Corp.**, an operator of cannabis extraction facility in Calgary, Alta.; wholly owned **Noble Line Inc.**, an online seller of CBD-based hemp products in the U.S.; wholly owned **Trip Pharma Inc.**, a psychedelic development and wellness company; **Fantasy Aces Daily Fantasy Sports Corp.**, a provider of fantasy sports, games, social media and advertising in the U.S.; and wholly owned **Spaced Food Inc.**, a distributor of edible cannabis products.

On May 29, 2023, the company agreed to acquire Australia-based **Hardenbrook Group Pty Ltd.**, an investment company leading a portfolio of four companies to go public, for issuance of 70,000,000 common shares at a deemed price of 5¢ per share.

On May 1, 2023, a plan of arrangement was completed whereby Australia-based wholly owned **MindBio Therapeutics Pty Ltd.** and **Digital Mind Technology Pty Ltd.** was transferred to wholly owned **1286409 B.C. Ltd.**, and 1286409 B.C. was spun out to shareholders on a one-for-one basis. Upon completion of the arrangement, 1286409 B.C. was renamed **MindBio Therapeutics Corp.**, and shares of MindBio would commence trading on the Canadian Securities Exchange on or about May 5, 2023. MindBio Therapeutics Corp. would focus on the psychedelics and mental health technologies business.

In April 2022, the company acquired British Columbia-based **Blum Distributors Ltd.**, an established mycology supplier with its own leased production facility, for issuance of 9,650,000 common shares at $0.415 per share.

On Mar. 2, 2022, the company acquired the remaining 49% interest in **Stable Foods Co.** (formerly **NuWave Foods Inc.**) for issuance of 3,200,000 common shares at a deemed price of $0.425 per share.

Predecessor Detail - Name changed from Blackhawk Resource Corp., Mar. 11, 2020.

Directors - Anoosh Manzoori, chr., Melbourne, Vic., Australia; Justin A. Hanka, CEO, Vic., Australia; John Dinan, CFO, Melbourne, Vic., Australia; Anthony Habberfield

Other Exec. Officers - Trevor P. Wong-Chor, corp. sec.

Capital Stock

	Authorized (shs.)	Outstanding (shs.)[1]
Preferred	unlimited	nil
Common	unlimited	77,995,593

[1] At May 30, 2023

Major Shareholder - Widely held at Nov. 17, 2022.

Price Range - BLR/CSE

Year	Volume	High	Low	Close
2022............	16,957,655	$0.58	$0.07	$0.15
2021............	27,383,288	$1.04	$0.32	$0.52
2020............	23,549,531	$2.00	$0.24	$0.33
2019............	1,186,462	$2.50	$0.38	$0.50
2018............	362,322	$4.00	$1.00	$1.25

Consolidation: 1-for-25 cons. in Nov. 2020

Recent Close: $0.02

Capital Stock Changes - In December 2021, 3,623,188 and 8,661,290 common shares were issued pursuant to the acquisitions of TERP Wholesale, LLC and Digital Mind Technology Pty Ltd., respectively. On Mar. 2, 2022, 3,200,000 common shares were issued pursuant to the acquisition of the remaining 49% interest in Stable Foods Co. Also during fiscal 2022, common shares were issued as follows; 22,095,180 on acquisition of MindBio Therapeutics Pty Ltd., 9,650,000 on acquisition of Blum Distributors Ltd., 2,340,476 under restricted share unit plan, 1,100,000 on exercise of options, 1,000,000 on exercise of warrants, 870,000 as finder's fees, 115,384 on conversion of debt and 87,500 for debt settlement.

Wholly Owned Subsidiaries

Blum Distributors Ltd., B.C.
Digital Mind Technology Pty Ltd., Australia.
MindBio Therapeutics Pty Ltd., Australia.
Noble Line Inc., United States.
SAC Pharma Partners Inc., B.C.
• 100% int. in **SAC Pharma Partners USA, Inc.**, Sacramento, Calif.
Spaced Food Inc., Canada.
Stable Foods Co., Edmonton, Alta. Formerly NuWave Foods Inc.
TERP Wholesale, LLC, Calif.
Trip Pharma Inc., Edmonton, Alta.

Investments

Fantasy Aces Daily Fantasy Sports Corp., Aliso Viejo, Calif.
Gaia Grow Corp., Vancouver, B.C. (see separate coverage)
MindBio Therapeutics Corp., Melbourne, Vic., Australia. (see separate coverage)

Financial Statistics

Periods ended:	12m June 30/22[A]		12m June 30/21[rA]
	$000s	%Chg	$000s
Realized invest. gain (loss)..............	nil		21
Unrealized invest. gain (loss)...........	(4,089)		775
Total revenue...............................	**(4,045)**	**n.a.**	**833**
General & admin. expense..............	1,540		2,583
Stock-based compensation............	4,050		757
Operating expense.......................	**5,590**	**+67**	**3,340**
Operating income.........................	**(9,635)**	**n.a.**	**(2,507)**
Finance costs, gross.......................	373		nil
Write-downs/write-offs....................	(263)		nil
Pre-tax income............................	**(10,272)**	**n.a.**	**(2,520)**
Net income...................................	**(10,272)**	**n.a.**	**(2,520)**
Cash & equivalent...........................	437		420
Accounts receivable........................	562		175
Current assets................................	29,425		7,655
Total assets..................................	**29,425**	**+284**	**7,655**
Accts. pay. & accr. liabs................	91		60
Current liabilities............................	91		60
Long-term debt, gross.....................	1,688		nil
Shareholders' equity.......................	27,646		7,594
Cash from oper. activs..................	**(3,527)**	**n.a.**	**(2,834)**
Cash from fin. activs.......................	3,545		2,635
Net cash position..........................	**437**	**+4**	**420**
	$		$
Earnings per share*.........................	(0.18)		(0.14)
Cash flow per share*........................	(0.06)		(0.16)
	shs		shs
No. of shs. o/s*...............................	77,995,593		25,252,575
Avg. no. of shs. o/s*.......................	56,367,711		17,493,276
	%		%
Net profit margin.............................	n.m.		(302.52)
Return on equity..............................	n.m.		n.m.
Return on assets..............................	n.a.		n.a.

* Common
[r] Restated
[A] Reported in accordance with IFRS

Latest Results

Periods ended:	3m Sept. 30/22[A]		3m Sept. 30/21[A]
	$000s	%Chg	$000s
Total revenue..................................	(163)	n.a.	(633)
Net income......................................	(938)	n.a.	(2,475)
	$		$
Earnings per share*.........................	(0.01)		(0.10)

* Common
[A] Reported in accordance with IFRS

Historical Summary
(as originally stated)

Fiscal Year	Total Rev.	Net Inc. Bef. Disc.	EPS*
	$000s	$000s	$
2022[A]...................	(4,045)	(10,272)	(0.18)
2021[A]...................	833	(2,520)	(0.14)
2020[A]...................	(154)	(1,865)	(0.25)
2019[A]...................	(2,159)	(2,427)	(1.25)
2018[A]...................	(67)	(710)	(0.50)

* Common
[A] Reported in accordance with IFRS

Note: Adjusted throughout for 1-for-25 cons. in Nov. 2020

B.76 Blackline Safety Corp.

Symbol - BLN **Exchange** - TSX **CUSIP** - 092382
Head Office - Unit 100, 803 24 Ave SE, Calgary, AB, T2G 1P5
Telephone - (403) 451-0327 **Toll-free** - (877) 869-7212 **Fax** - (403) 451-9981
Website - www.blacklinesafety.com
Email - investors@blacklinesafety.com
Investor Relations - Matt Glover (403) 451-0327
Auditors - PricewaterhouseCoopers LLP C.A., Calgary, Alta.
Lawyers - DLA Piper (Canada) LLP, Calgary, Alta.
Transfer Agents - Odyssey Trust Company
Employees - 477 at Oct. 31, 2022

Profile - (Alta. 2006) Develops, manufactures and markets portable, rugged and compact safety employee monitoring products for industrial and professional applications.

Products and services include G6 single-gas cloud-connected gas monitor; G7c safety wearable for indoor and outdoor locations covered by 4G wireless; G7x safety wearable for remote locations in North America, South America, Australia and New Zealand that are not covered by 4G wireless; G7 EXO area gas monitor; Field replaceable cartridges in G7c, G7x and G7 EXO connected devices capable to accommodate a wide variety of configurations proprietary to the company; G7 Bridge, a portable satellite base station for remote locations which communicates with G7x; G7 Dock and G6 Dock, an accessory product used to calibrate G6, G7c and G7x devices; Loner Mobile, a safety monitoring application for mainstream smartphones; Blackline Location Beacon, an indoor/outdoor location technology that provides precise positioning where GPS signals are weak or unavailable; Blackline monitoring, a 24/7/365 live monitoring service offered by the company or approved partner; Blackline Live, a cloud-hosted, live safety monitoring portal for safety alert management; Blackline Analytics, a data analytics package built into Blackline Live; and Blackline Vision, a data science consulting and software services. Products are available through a number of distributor and dealer channels throughout Canada, the U.S., Europe, Australia, New Zealand and other international locations.

On Mar. 31, 2022, the company acquired private Kitchener, Ont.-based **Swift Labs Inc.**, an Internet of Things (IoT) design and engineering consulting firm, for fair value consideration of $4,541,000, consisting of $3,200,000 cash, net of note payable acquired, and issuance of 270,776 common shares at a fair value of $5.74 per share.

Predecessor Detail - Name changed from BlackLine GPS Corp., July 7, 2015.

Directors - Cody Z. Slater, chr. & CEO, Calgary, Alta.; Michael F. Hayduk, corp. sec., Calgary, Alta.; Dr. Cheemin Bo-Linn†, San Francisco, Calif.; Jason W. Cohenour, Blaine, Wash.; Brad Gilewich, Edmonton, Alta.; Robert J. (Bob) Herdman, Calgary, Alta.; Barbara Holzapfel, Wash.

Other Exec. Officers - Sean Stinson, pres. & chief growth officer; Kevin Meyers, COO; Shane Grennan, CFO; Brendon Cook, CIO; Christine Gillies, chief product & mktg. officer; Meaghan Whitney, chief people officer

† Lead director

Capital Stock

	Authorized (shs.)	Outstanding (shs.)[1]
Preferred	unlimited	nil
Common	unlimited	72,139,344

[1] At Feb. 7, 2023

Major Shareholder - DAK Capital Inc. held 25.4% interest at Feb. 7, 2023.

Price Range - BLN/TSX

Year	Volume	High	Low	Close
2022............	7,728,858	$6.96	$1.53	$1.81
2021............	5,782,818	$9.50	$5.78	$6.18
2020............	4,268,043	$7.55	$3.53	$7.55
2019............	4,241,119	$6.74	$4.99	$6.20
2018............	3,222,501	$6.80	$4.26	$4.82

Recent Close: $3.45

Capital Stock Changes - On Mar. 31, 2022, 270,776 common shares were issued pursuant to the acquisition of Swift Labs Inc. In August 2022, bought deal offering of 5,405,885 common shares and concurrent private placement of 5,909,091 common shares was completed all at $2.20 per share. Also during fiscal 2022, common shares were issued as follows: 173,097 as stock-based compensation and 82,518 on exercise of options.

Wholly Owned Subsidiaries

Blackline Safety Australia Pty Ltd., Australia.
Blackline Safety Europe Limited, Colchester, Essex, United Kingdom.
Blackline Safety Europe S.A.S., France.
Blackline Safety U.S.A. Corp., United States.
Swift Labs Inc., Kitchener, Ont.
Wearable Technologies Limited, United Kingdom.

Financial Statistics

Periods ended:	12m Oct. 31/22[A]		12m Oct. 31/21[A]
	$000s	%Chg	$000s
Operating revenue	**72,931**	**+34**	**54,312**
Cost of sales	36,824		24,675
Research & devel. expense	23,556		15,750
General & admin expense	57,915		41,130
Operating expense	**118,295**	**+45**	**81,555**
Operating income	**(45,364)**	**n.a.**	**(27,243)**
Deprec., depl. & amort	6,616		5,055
Finance income	409		279
Finance costs, gross	142		106
Pre-tax income	**(53,252)**	**n.a.**	**(33,116)**
Income taxes	394		188
Net income	**(53,646)**	**n.a.**	**(33,305)**
Cash & equivalent	22,640		34,433
Inventories	18,712		12,710
Accounts receivable	22,881		20,257
Current assets	75,969		90,652
Fixed assets, net	12,807		9,866
Right-of-use assets	2,513		2,234
Intangibles, net	7,078		2,417
Total assets	**108,049**	**-1**	**109,303**
Accts. pay. & accr. liabs	19,155		16,139
Current liabilities	35,662		28,702
Long-term debt, gross	8,575		nil
Long-term debt, net	8,575		nil
Long-term lease liabilities	1,793		1,589
Shareholders' equity	52,362		73,339
Cash from oper. activs	**(50,560)**	**n.a.**	**(28,970)**
Cash from fin. activs	32,233		38,722
Cash from invest. activs	249		(3,045)
Net cash position	**22,640**	**-34**	**34,433**
Capital expenditures	(8,663)		(5,464)
	$		$
Earnings per share*	(0.86)		(0.67)
Cash flow per share*	(0.81)		(0.59)
	shs		shs
No. of shs. o/s*	72,063,093		60,221,726
Avg. no. of shs. o/s*	62,584,204		49,418,060
	%		%
Net profit margin	(73.56)		(61.32)
Return on equity	(85.35)		(47.69)
Return on assets	(49.23)		(33.55)
Foreign sales percent	73		76
No. of employees (FTEs)	477		481

* Common
[A] Reported in accordance with IFRS

Historical Summary
(as originally stated)

Fiscal Year	Oper. Rev. $000s	Net Inc. Bef. Disc. $000s	EPS* $
2022[A]	72,931	(53,646)	(0.86)
2021[A]	54,312	(33,305)	(0.67)
2020[A]	38,377	(8,021)	(0.16)
2019[A]	33,271	(9,924)	(0.21)
2018[A]	17,772	(9,002)	(0.23)

* Common
[A] Reported in accordance with IFRS

B.77 Blender Bites Limited

Symbol - BITE **Exchange** - CSE **CUSIP** - 09353K
Head Office - 800-1199 Hastings St W, Vancouver, BC, V6E 3T5 **Toll-free** - (888) 997-2055
Website - blenderbites.com
Email - investors@blenderbites.com
Investor Relations - Investor Relations (888) 997-2055
Auditors - Crowe MacKay LLP C.A., Vancouver, B.C.
Transfer Agents - Endeavor Trust Corporation, Vancouver, B.C.
Profile - (B.C. 2016 amalg.) Manufactures, develops and distributes natural and organic frozen smoothie pucks under the Blender Bites brand in Canada and the U.S.

Blender Bites pucks are made fresh from fruits and other functional ingredients such as greens and plant-based vitamins, minerals and fibre. These can be added to any liquid of choice, together with additional ingredients such as water, protein powders, nut butters and milk, to create smoothies as well as bowls and desserts. Products are available in more than 900 retail stores and online in Canada and the U.S. In addition, the company plans to launch products incorporating plant-based proteins and functional greens focused on immune support, cognition, skin health, stress reduction and gut health.

Predecessor Detail - Name changed from Balsam Technologies Corp., Sept. 21, 2021, following reverse takeover acquisition of Blender Bites Incorporated.

Directors - Chelsie Hodge, CEO, Vancouver, B.C.; Nima Bahrami, Vancouver, B.C.; Christopher (Chris) Mackay, Vancouver, B.C.; Patrick C. T. (Pat) Morris, Vancouver, B.C.; Grant Smith, Markham, Ont.

Other Exec. Officers - Steve Pear, COO; Geoffrey (Geoff) Balderson, CFO; Nicole Lacson, corp. sec.

Capital Stock

	Authorized (shs.)	Outstanding (shs.)[1]
Common	unlimited	5,702,558

[1] At June 27, 2023

Major Shareholder - Chelsie Hodge held 15.74% interest at Sept. 27, 2022.

Price Range - BITE/CSE

Year	Volume	High	Low	Close
2022	1,466,692	$11.60	$1.26	$1.65
2021	1,404,214	$27.12	$1.56	$11.84
2020	193,240	$16.00	$0.80	$1.48
2019	835	$12.00	$9.20	$11.20
2018	41,352	$44.00	$6.80	$11.60

Consolidation: 1-for-10 cons. in July 2022; 1.25-for-1 split in Jan. 2022; 1-for-10 cons. in Apr. 2020

Recent Close: $3.20

Capital Stock Changes - In March 2023, private placement of 649,350 units (1 common share & 1 warrant) at $3.08 per unit was completed, with warrants exercisable at $5.50 per share for five years. In June 2023, private placement of 443,072 units (1 common share & ½ warrant) at $3.50 per unit was completed, with warrants exercisable at $4.55 per share for three years.

On Jan. 18, 2022, common shares were split on a 1.25-for-1 basis. On July 13, 2022, common shares were consolidated on a 1-for-10 basis. Also during fiscal 2022, post-split/consolidated common shares were issued as follows: 298,846 on exercise of warrants, 95,000 for services and 20,989 for debt settlement.

Wholly Owned Subsidiaries

Blender Bites (Holdings) Limited, Vancouver, B.C.

Financial Statistics

Periods ended:	12m Oct. 31/22[A]		12m Oct. 31/21[A1]
	$000s	%Chg	$000s
Operating revenue	**3,845**	**+308**	**942**
Cost of goods sold	3,435		810
Salaries & benefits	395		43
Research & devel. expense	175		84
General & admin expense	4,040		1,045
Stock-based compensation	422		nil
Operating expense	**8,467**	**+327**	**1,981**
Operating income	**(4,622)**	**n.a.**	**(1,039)**
Deprec., depl. & amort	9		8
Finance costs, gross	2		45
Pre-tax income	**(4,633)**	**n.a.**	**(15,953)**
Net income	**(4,633)**	**n.a.**	**(15,953)**
Cash & equivalent	221		2,588
Inventories	385		nil
Accounts receivable	643		455
Current assets	1,291		4,358
Fixed assets, net	426		84
Intangibles, net	36		21
Total assets	**1,753**	**-61**	**4,463**
Bank indebtedness	35		33
Accts. pay. & accr. liabs	742		742
Current liabilities	777		775
Shareholders' equity	977		3,688
Cash from oper. activs	**(2,703)**	**n.a.**	**(2,604)**
Cash from fin. activs	741		4,184
Cash from invest. activs	(405)		801
Net cash position	**221**	**-91**	**2,588**
Capital expenditures	(386)		(77)
	$		$
Earnings per share*	(1.17)		(9.46)
Cash flow per share*	(0.68)		(1.24)
	shs		shs
No. of shs. o/s*	4,091,672		3,676,839
Avg. no. of shs. o/s*	3,958,493		1,686,953
	%		%
Net profit margin	(120.49)		n.m.
Return on equity	n.m.		n.m.
Return on assets	n.a.		(677.80)

* Common
[A] Reported in accordance with IFRS
[1] Results reflect the Sept. 20, 2021, reverse takeover acquisition of Blender Bites (Holdings) Limited (formerly Blender Bites Incorporated).

Latest Results

Periods ended:	6m Apr. 30/23[A]		6m Apr. 30/22[A]
	$000s	%Chg	$000s
Operating revenue	657	-67	1,975
Net income	(2,664)	n.a.	(2,304)
	$		$
Earnings per share*	(0.61)		(0.60)

* Common
[A] Reported in accordance with IFRS

Historical Summary
(as originally stated)

Fiscal Year	Oper. Rev. $000s	Net Inc. Bef. Disc. $000s	EPS* $
2022[A]	3,845	(4,633)	(1.17)
2021[A]	942	(15,953)	(9.46)
2020[A1]	441	(119)	n.a.
2020[A2]	nil	(285)	(1.12)
2019[A]	nil	(888)	(4.00)

* Common
[A] Reported in accordance with IFRS
[1] Results pertain to Blender Bites (Holdings) Limited (formerly Blender Bites Incorporated).
[2] Results for fiscal 2020 and prior fiscal years pertain to Balsam Technologies Corp.

Note: Adjusted throughout for 1-for-10 cons. in July 2022; 1.25-for-1 split in Jan. 2022; 1-for-10 cons. in Apr. 2020

B.78 Blockchain Venture Capital Inc.

Symbol - BVCI **Exchange** - CSE **CUSIP** - 09370B
Head Office - 1800-130 King St W, Toronto, ON, M5X 1E3 **Telephone** - (416) 420-4250
Website - www.bvcadt.com
Email - steven@bvcadt.com
Investor Relations - Steven Olsthoorn (416) 420-4250
Auditors - NVS Chartered Accountants Professional Corporation C.A., Markham, Ont.
Transfer Agents - TSX Trust Company, Toronto, Ont.
Employees - 5 at Aug. 8, 2022
Profile - (Ont. 2022 amalg.) Developing a proprietary blockchain platform and ledger technology (BVC Chain), a digital asset wallet (BvcPay) and a native digital currency (CADT).

BVC Chain can be customized and implemented by organizations wishing to deploy blockchain platform-based products and services. BVC Chain also serves as the platform and infrastructure for BvcPay and CADT. BvcPay is a cloud-based mobile application which functions as a Digital Currency wallet and which can facilitate point of sale and online transactions over the BVC Chain using Bitcoin, Etherum, CADT and Canadian dollars. CADT is the company's native digital currency of the BVC Chain and is intend to be a Stablecoin.

Whyth Trust, a subsidiary of **Whyth Financial** and a Schedule I Canadian financial institution, acts a custodian to hold the Canadian funds represented by CADT.

Recent Merger and Acquisition Activity

Status: completed **Revised:** Aug. 4, 2022

UPDATE: The transaction was completed. Flexwork and (old) BVCI amalgamated to form Blockchain Venture Capital Inc. PREVIOUS: Reliant Gold Corp. (Flexwork) agreed to the reverse takeover acquisition of private Toronto, Ont.-based Blockchain Venture Capital Inc. (BVCI) on a share-for-share basis (following an up to 1-for-21.5 share consolidation). BVCI developed BvcPay, a mobile application which functions as a decentralized digital currency wallet, a blockchain explorer and an over-the-counter trading and decentralized digital currency exchange platform; CADT, a stablecoin issued by BVCI; and BVC Chain, a proprietary blockchain which supports the issuance of CADT and the BvcPay functions. Prior to closing, BVCI would complete a private placement of $1,500,000 to $2,000,000 of common shares at $1.50 per share. Reliant's 2018 name change to Flexwork Properties Ltd. never received Canadian Securities Exchange approval. Upon closing, Reliant Gold would change its name to Blockchain Venture Capital Inc.

Predecessor Detail - Formed from Flexwork Properties Ltd. in Ontario, Aug. 3, 2022, pursuant to amalgamation with (old) Blockchain Venture Capital Inc. (deemed acquiror); basis 1 new for 21.2535 old shs.

Directors - Richard Zhou, pres. & CEO, Richmond Hill, Ont.; Steven Olsthoorn, CFO & corp. sec., Richmond Hill, Ont.; Monika Cywinska, Etobicoke, Ont.; Yongbiao (Winfield) Ding, Toronto, Ont.; Justin Poy, Richmond Hill, Ont.

Capital Stock

	Authorized (shs.)	Outstanding (shs.)[1]
Preference	unlimited	nil
Common	unlimited	25,699,179

[1] At Aug. 12, 2022

Major Shareholder - Richard Zhou held 58.28% interest at Aug. 12, 2022.

Price Range - BVCI/CSE

Year	Volume	High	Low	Close
2022	1,603,484	$5.50	$0.50	$1.10
2018	100,966	$0.85	$0.43	$0.43

Consolidation: 1-for-21.2535 cons. in Aug. 2022

Recent Close: $0.46

Capital Stock Changes - Pursuant to amalgamation completed on Aug. 3, 2022, 24,414,219 common shares were issued to shareholders of (old) Blockchain Venture Capital Inc. (1-for-1 basis) and 1,284,960 common shares were issued to shareholders of Flexwork Properties Ltd. (1-for-21.25353 basis).

Financial Statistics

Periods ended:	12m Dec. 31/21[A1]		12m Dec. 31/20[A]
	$000s	%Chg	$000s
Salaries & benefits	7		7
General & admin expense	26		25
Operating expense	**33**	**+3**	**32**
Operating income	**(33)**	**n.a.**	**(32)**
Pre-tax income	**17**	**n.a.**	**(32)**
Net income	**17**	**n.a.**	**(32)**
Cash & equivalent	27		1
Current assets	28		1
Total assets	**28**	**n.m.**	**1**
Accts. pay. & accr. liabs	101		91
Current liabilities	101		91
Shareholders' equity	(73)		(90)
Cash from oper. activs	**27**	**n.a.**	**nil**
Net cash position	**27**	**n.m.**	**1**
	$		$
Earnings per share*	0.01		(0.03)
Cash flow per share*	0.02		nil
	shs		shs
No. of shs. o/s*	1,188,455		1,188,455
Avg. no. of shs. o/s*	1,188,455		1,101,756
	%		%
Net profit margin	n.a.		n.a.
Return on equity	n.m.		n.m.
Return on assets	117.24		n.m.

* Common

[A] Reported in accordance with IFRS

[1] Results for 2021 and prior periods pertain to Flexwork Properties Ltd.

Historical Summary
(as originally stated)

Fiscal Year	Oper. Rev. $000s	Net Inc. Bef. Disc. $000s	EPS* $
2021[A]	nil	17	0.01
2020[A]	nil	(32)	(0.03)
2019[A]	nil	(27)	(0.03)
2018[A]	nil	(180)	(0.21)
2017[A]	nil	(117)	(0.21)

* Common

[A] Reported in accordance with IFRS

Note: Adjusted throughout for 1-for-21.25353 cons. in Aug. 2022

B.79 BlockchainK2 Corp.

Symbol - BITK **Exchange** - TSX-VEN **CUSIP** - 09369M
Head Office - 400-837 Hastings St W, Vancouver, BC, V6C 3N6
Telephone - (604) 630-8746 **Toll-free** - (888) 241-5996
Website - blockchaink2.com
Email - yliang@jacksoncompany.ca
Investor Relations - Yuying Liang (604) 630-8746
Auditors - Dale Matheson Carr-Hilton LaBonte LLP C.A., Vancouver, B.C.
Transfer Agents - Computershare Trust Company of Canada Inc., Toronto, Ont.

Profile - (Alta. 2013; orig. B.C., 1983) Invests in blockchain technology solutions for capital markets and other sectors.

The investment portfolio includes wholly owned **Amplify Games Inc.**, which is developing a blockchain-enabled technology platform for the distribution and promotion of digital games; wholly owned **iRecover Inc.**, which is developing a blockchain-based application to support individuals recovering from addiction; **Sobe Organics, Inc.** (51% owned), which distributes CBD infused health and beauty products under the Lux Beauty Club brand throughout the U.S.; investment in **Envexergy Inc.** (dba RealBlocks), which has a platform that provides tokenized secondary trading of limited partnership interest for private equity, private credit and real estate; and a profit sharing partnership with **500 N 4th LLC** (dba Standard Power), which provides colocation facilities in the U.S. for advanced data processing operations, including cryptocurrency mining.

Predecessor Detail - Name changed from Africa Hydrocarbons Inc., May 25, 2018.

Directors - Douglas L. Wu, chr., New York, N.Y.; Sergei Stetsenko, CEO, Dubai, United Arab Emirates; Robert Jarva; Dr. Steven Sangha, Richmond, B.C.; Balazs Veszpremi

Other Exec. Officers - Yuying Liang, CFO & corp. sec.; Tony Caputo, pres. & CEO, Amplify Games Inc.

Capital Stock

	Authorized (shs.)	Outstanding (shs.)[1]
Preferred	unlimited	nil
Common	unlimited	16,780,962

[1] At Feb. 28, 2023

Major Shareholder - Widely held at Sept. 30, 2020.

Price Range - BITK/TSX-VEN

Year	Volume	High	Low	Close
2022	5,144,232	$0.30	$0.07	$0.11
2021	25,516,280	$2.30	$0.20	$0.27
2020	4,784,122	$0.89	$0.05	$0.78
2019	2,987,910	$0.39	$0.12	$0.13
2018	2,451,610	$1.25	$0.18	$0.37

Recent Close: $0.12

Capital Stock Changes - There were no changes to capital stock during fiscal 2022.

Wholly Owned Subsidiaries

Africa Hydrocarbons (Bahamas) Ltd., Bahamas.
Africa Hydrocarbons Tunisia Ltd., Tunisia.
Amplify Games Inc., United States.
iRecover Inc., United States.
Watutatu Inc., Ont.

Subsidiaries

51% int. in **Sobe Organics, Inc.**, Aventura, Fla.

Investments

Envexergy Inc., N.Y. dba RealBlocks

Financial Statistics

Periods ended:	12m Sept. 30/22[A]		12m Sept. 30/21[A]
	$000s	%Chg	$000s
Operating revenue	**73**	**-37**	**115**
Cost of sales	40		77
Salaries & benefits	225		194
General & admin expense	1,056		967
Stock-based compensation	nil		985
Operating expense	**1,321**	**-41**	**2,223**
Operating income	**(1,248)**	**n.a.**	**(2,108)**
Finance income	nil		25
Finance costs, gross	43		17
Write-downs/write-offs	nil		(215)
Pre-tax income	**(1,154)**	**n.a.**	**(2,221)**
Net income	**(1,154)**	**n.a.**	**(2,221)**
Net inc. for equity hldrs	**(1,081)**	**n.a.**	**(2,206)**
Net inc. for non-cont. int	**(73)**	**n.a.**	**(15)**
Cash & equivalent	45		574
Inventories	14		8
Accounts receivable	2		12
Current assets	69		607
Long-term investments	1,284		1,223
Total assets	**1,354**	**-28**	**1,871**
Bank indebtedness	424		20
Accts. pay. & accr. liabs	465		277
Current liabilities	889		296
Long-term debt, gross	80		66
Long-term debt, net	80		66
Shareholders' equity	413		1,463
Non-controlling interest	(28)		47
Cash from oper. activs	**(1,001)**	**n.a.**	**(748)**
Cash from fin. activs	419		104
Cash from invest. activs	54		(186)
Net cash position	**45**	**-92**	**574**
	$		$
Earnings per share*	(0.06)		(0.13)
Cash flow per share*	(0.06)		(0.05)
	shs		shs
No. of shs. o/s*	16,780,962		16,780,962
Avg. no. of shs. o/s*	16,780,962		16,401,917
	%		%
Net profit margin	n.m.		n.m.
Return on equity	(115.25)		(108.00)
Return on assets	(68.90)		(94.47)
Foreign sales percent	100		100

* Common

[A] Reported in accordance with IFRS

Historical Summary
(as originally stated)

Fiscal Year	Oper. Rev. $000s	Net Inc. Bef. Disc. $000s	EPS* $
2022[A]	73	(1,154)	(0.06)
2021[A]	115	(2,221)	(0.13)
2020[A]	36	(321)	(0.02)
2019[A]	nil	(685)	(0.04)
2018[A]	nil	(2,573)	(0.19)

* Common

[A] Reported in accordance with IFRS

B.80 Blockmate Ventures Inc.

Symbol - MATE **Exchange** - TSX-VEN **CUSIP** - 09370U
Head Office - 505 Kootenay St, Nelson, BC, V1L 1K9
Website - www.blockmate.com
Email - david@blockmate.com
Investor Relations - David Wong 44-20-7448-3081
Auditors - Kingston Ross Pasnak LLP C.A., Edmonton, Alta.
Bankers - Royal Bank of Canada, Toronto, Ont.
Lawyers - McMillan LLP, Vancouver, B.C.
Transfer Agents - TSX Trust Company, Toronto, Ont.

Profile - (B.C. 2010) Operates Midpoint, a peer-to-peer foreign exchange matching platform that matches buyers and sellers of foreign currency and transfers the funds to their desired location through an intermediary third party payment provider. Also builds consumer-focused blockchain-based products and owns premium domain names Blockchain.eu, Blockchain.com.au and Hivello.com

The Midpoint platform allows any registered and authorized individual or company to conduct foreign exchange transactions for a transparent fee at the Interbank midpoint or mid-market rate through the company's website. The platform currently supports 24 major currencies with over 244 payout countries available. Target clients include small and medium-sized enterprises which engage in frequent foreign exchange transactions, leisure and tourism, accountancy practices and independent financial advisory, and software and technologies; and individuals which are ex-patriot white-collar workers, foreign homeowners and migrant workers.

Also offers Virtual International Bank Account Numbers (Virtual IBAN) in the U.K., which was launched in November 2020, wherein the company's clients could open a number of business and personal Virtual IBANs and have the payments that are made to them rerouted to the same master account. This mimics the effect of having multiple bank accounts without the banking fee expenses and the hassle to maintain them. The company has also commenced bet testing of a new mobile app developed to provide peer-to-peer foreign exchange services.

Through wholly owned **Blockchain World Ltd.**, operates Blockchain.eu (for Europe) and Blockchain.com.au (for Australia), which are easy-to-use platforms where users can buy and sell cryptocurrencies from exchanges around the world; and Hivello, a specialist in deployment of blockchain Internet of Things (IoT) infrastructure which offers a blockchain IoT platform where individuals and property owners can earn passive income by hosting a Hivello hotspot at their premise, similar to homeowner renting out their room on Airbnb.

In July 2022, wholly owned **Hivello Operations B.V.** entered into a partnership with **DLTx ASA** to expand the Hivello network of Internet of Things (IoT) hotspots. Through the partnership, Hivello would secure access to DLTx's suppliers, financiers and management expertise. DLTx would receive a 40% interest in Hivello and the company would retain the remaining 60% which are both subject to dilution from new capital on a pro rata basis.

In March 2022, the company acquired **Blockchain World Ltd.**, which offers blockchain-based products and owns premium domain names Blockchain.eu (Europe) and Blockchain.com.au (Australia) and would be launching new offerings in early 2022, for issuance of 10,000,000 common shares and additional common shares issuable on certain milestones being met.

Predecessor Detail - Name changed from Midpoint Holdings Ltd., May 16, 2022.

Directors - David Wong, chr., London, Middx., United Kingdom; Justin Rosenberg, CEO, Toronto, Ont.; Domenico (Dom) Carosa, Australia; Corbin Comishin, Nelson, B.C.; Dr. Georg Hochwimmer, Munich, Germany

Other Exec. Officers - Konstantin Lichtenwald, CFO & corp. sec.; Michael (Mike) Hampson, pres., Midpoint & Transfer Ltd.

Capital Stock

	Authorized (shs.)	Outstanding (shs.)[1]
Common	unlimited	79,794,997

[1] At Nov. 28, 2022

Major Shareholder - Domenico (Dom) Carosa held 14.1% interest at Nov. 17, 2022.

Price Range - MATE/TSX-VEN

Year	Volume	High	Low	Close
2022	6,047,740	$0.25	$0.02	$0.02
2021	12,463,239	$0.44	$0.12	$0.25
2020	11,260,979	$0.34	$0.08	$0.15
2019	5,397,696	$0.60	$0.08	$0.10
2018	3,710,789	$1.28	$0.16	$0.16

Consolidation: 1-for-4 cons. in Jan. 2020

Recent Close: $0.04

Capital Stock Changes - In November 2022 and January 2023, private placement of 18,065,337 units (1 common share & 1 warrant) at 5¢ per unit was completed, with warrants exercisable at $0.075 per share for three years.

In March 2022, 10,000,000 common shares were issued pursuant to acquisition of Blockchain World Ltd.

Wholly Owned Subsidiaries

Blockchain World Ltd.
- 60% int. in **Hivello Operations B.V.**, Amsterdam, Netherlands.

Midpoint & Transfer Ltd., United Kingdom.
Midpoint Hong Kong Ltd., Hong Kong, People's Republic of China.

Financial Statistics

Periods ended:	12m June 30/22[A]		12m June 30/21[□A]
	$000s	%Chg	$000s
Operating revenue	**436**	**+12**	**388**
Cost of sales	232		180
Salaries & benefits	740		296
General & admin expense	1,444		753
Operating expense	**2,416**	**+97**	**1,229**
Operating income	**(1,980)**	**n.a.**	**(841)**
Deprec., depl. & amort.	109		26
Finance income	4		nil
Write-downs/write-offs	(342)		nil
Pre-tax income	**(4,639)**	**n.a.**	**(787)**
Net income	**(4,639)**	**n.a.**	**(787)**
Cash & equivalent	740		2,984
Accounts receivable	12		27
Current assets	771		3,031
Fixed assets, net	23		9
Intangibles, net	nil		28
Total assets	**794**	**-74**	**3,067**
Accts. pay. & accr. liabs	379		156
Current liabilities	385		156
Shareholders' equity	409		2,911
Cash from oper. activs	**(1,693)**	**n.a.**	**(715)**
Cash from fin. activs	(34)		(124)
Cash from invest. activs	(437)		(52)
Net cash position	**740**	**-75**	**2,984**
Capital expenditures	(359)		(11)
	$		$
Earnings per share*	(0.08)		(0.02)
Cash flow per share*	(0.03)		(0.02)
	shs		shs
No. of shs. o/s*	63,501,660		53,501,660
Avg. no. of shs. o/s*	56,834,993		44,675,632
	%		%
Net profit margin	n.m.		(202.84)
Return on equity	(279.46)		(45.73)
Return on assets	(240.30)		(40.56)

* Common
□ Restated
[A] Reported in accordance with IFRS

Latest Results

Periods ended:	3m Sept. 30/22[A]		3m Sept. 30/21[A]
	$000s	%Chg	$000s
Operating revenue	80	-26	108
Net income	(519)	n.a.	(268)
	$		$
Earnings per share*	(0.01)		(0.00)

* Common
[A] Reported in accordance with IFRS

Historical Summary
(as originally stated)

Fiscal Year	Oper. Rev.	Net Inc. Bef. Disc.	EPS*
	$000s	$000s	$
2022[A]	436	(4,639)	(0.08)
2021[A]	388	(787)	(0.02)
2020[A]	428	(1,158)	(0.04)
2019[A]	399	(567)	(0.02)
2018[A]	482	(706)	(0.03)

* Common
[A] Reported in accordance with IFRS
Note: Adjusted throughout for 1-for-4 cons. in Jan. 2020

B.81 Blockmint Technologies Inc.

Symbol - BKMT **Exchange** - TSX-VEN **CUSIP** - 09370A
Head Office - 220 NW 8 Ave, Portland, OR, United States, 97209 **Telephone** - (971) 713-5550
Website - www.blockmint.ai
Email - info@blockmint.ai
Investor Relations - Nelson Ijih (503) 961-4022
Auditors - Baker Tilly WM LLP C.A., Vancouver, B.C.
Bankers - Bank of Montreal
Transfer Agents - Computershare Trust Company of Canada Inc., Toronto, Ont.
Profile - (B.C. 1980) Operates a cryptocurrency mining operation in Washington, and develops distributed systems and networks that enable a more decentralized deployment of blockchain-based applications such as cryptocurrency mining.
The company commenced mining bitcoin in December 2021. As of Mar. 31, 2022, the company, through its S19 Antminers bitcoin mining equipment, have mined approximately 2.07 bitcoin with an equivalent value of US$85,309.
The company has developed Minter, a secure and private web browser that allows users to use their spare computing power to mine cryptocurrencies to earn either: (i) carbon credits to offset their carbon footprint; or (ii) fractional ownership in a non-fungible token (NFT) from the company's NFT portfolio. The current version of Minter is for use on desktops and laptops with a Windows operating system. Additional integrated features include a virtual private network (VPN) and an ad-blocker. The product is available for download at the website getminter.com.
The company was also developing MintAccess, a software product that allows website owners/hosts to earn cryptocurrency from users when they visit the owner's site by utilizing the site visitor's computing power from their connected device to mine cryptocurrency. Website owners could monetize the content on their site without having a site visitor pay a fee or view paid/sponsored advertisements. Development was suspended in 2019 due to the depressed price of cryptocurrencies.
Predecessor Detail - Name changed from SMC Ventures Inc., Feb. 19, 2019, pursuant to reverse takeover acquisition of (old) Blockmint Technologies Inc. (renamed Blockmint (Canada) Technologies Inc.); basis 1 new for 2 old shs.
Directors - Nelson Ijih, CEO & chief tech. officer, Ore.; Jeffrey B. (Jeff) Lightfoot, Richmond, B.C.; David M. (Dave) Patterson, West Vancouver, B.C.; Colin Watt, Vancouver, B.C.
Other Exec. Officers - Victor J. (Vic) Hugo, CFO; Erin L. Walmesley, corp. sec.

Capital Stock

	Authorized (shs.)	Outstanding (shs.)[1]
Common	unlimited	48,242,605

[1] At Aug. 9, 2022
Major Shareholder - Widely held at Aug. 9, 2022.

Price Range - BKMT/TSX-VEN

Year	Volume	High	Low	Close
2022	2,798,688	$0.12	$0.02	$0.02
2021	21,094,742	$0.78	$0.09	$0.11
2020	1,788,623	$0.45	$0.06	$0.44
2019	2,564,331	$0.31	$0.05	$0.09
2018	89,463	$1.00	$0.36	$0.54

Consolidation: 1-for-2 cons. in Feb. 2019
Recent Close: $0.05

Wholly Owned Subsidiaries

Blockmint (Canada) Technologies Inc., Vancouver, B.C.
- 100% int. in **Blockmint (USA) Technologies Inc.**, Del.

Financial Statistics

Periods ended:	12m Dec. 31/21[A]		12m Dec. 31/20[A]
	US$000s	%Chg	US$000s
Operating revenue	**34**	**n.a.**	**nil**
Cost of sales	4		nil
Salaries & benefits	20		18
General & admin expense	763		383
Stock-based compensation	355		nil
Operating expense	**1,142**	**+185**	**401**
Operating income	**(1,108)**	**n.a.**	**(401)**
Deprec., depl. & amort.	29		nil
Finance costs, gross	2		nil
Write-downs/write-offs	nil		(18)
Pre-tax income	**(1,126)**	**n.a.**	**(426)**
Net income	**(1,126)**	**n.a.**	**(426)**
Cash & equivalent	2,032		2,601
Accounts receivable	9		3
Current assets	2,085		2,605
Fixed assets, net	515		nil
Right-of-use assets	160		nil
Total assets	**2,760**	**+6**	**2,605**
Accts. pay. & accr. liabs	51		62
Current liabilities	160		62
Shareholders' equity	2,549		2,544
Cash from oper. activs	**(800)**	**n.a.**	**(363)**
Cash from fin. activs	769		nil
Cash from invest. activs	(538)		nil
Net cash position	**2,032**	**-22**	**2,601**
Capital expenditures	(537)		nil
	US$		US$
Earnings per share*	(0.02)		(0.01)
Cash flow per share*	(0.02)		(0.01)
	shs		shs
No. of shs. o/s*	48,242,605		44,269,068
Avg. no. of shs. o/s*	47,948,642		44,269,068
	%		%
Net profit margin	n.m.		n.m.
Return on equity	(44.22)		(15.47)
Return on assets	(41.90)		(15.24)

* Common
[A] Reported in accordance with IFRS

Latest Results

Periods ended:	3m Mar. 31/22[A]		3m Mar. 31/21[A]
	US$000s	%Chg	US$000s
Operating revenue	85	n.a.	nil
Net income	(90)	n.a.	(549)
	US$		US$
Earnings per share*	(0.00)		(0.01)

* Common
[A] Reported in accordance with IFRS

Historical Summary
(as originally stated)

Fiscal Year	Oper. Rev.	Net Inc. Bef. Disc.	EPS*
	US$000s	US$000s	US$
2021[A]	34	(1,126)	(0.02)
2020[A]	nil	(426)	(0.01)
2019[A1]	nil	(4,149)	(0.10)
	$000s	$000s	$
2018[A2]	nil	(94)	(0.01)
2017[A]	nil	(44)	(0.02)

* Common
[A] Reported in accordance with IFRS
[1] Results reflect the Feb. 2, 2019, reverse takeover acquisition of (old) Blockmint Technologies Inc.
[2] Results for 2018 and prior periods pertain to SMC Ventures Inc.
Note: Adjusted throughout for 1-for-2 cons. in Feb. 2019

B.82 Bloom Select Income Fund

Symbol - BLB.UN **Exchange** - TSX **CUSIP** - 093734
Head Office - c/o Bloom Investment Counsel, Inc., 1710-150 York St, Toronto, ON, M5H 3S5 **Telephone** - (416) 861-9941 **Toll-free** - (855) 256-6618 **Fax** - (416) 861-9943
Website - www.bloomfunds.ca
Email - ir@bloomfunds.ca
Investor Relations - Fiona E. Mitra (855) 256-6618
Auditors - PricewaterhouseCoopers LLP C.A., Toronto, Ont.
Lawyers - Blake, Cassels & Graydon LLP, Toronto, Ont.
Transfer Agents - TSX Trust Company, Toronto, Ont.
Trustees - Bloom Investment Counsel, Inc., Toronto, Ont.
Managers - Bloom Investment Counsel, Inc., Toronto, Ont.
Portfolio Managers - Bloom Investment Counsel, Inc., Toronto, Ont.
Administrators - CIBC Mellon Global Securities Services Company, Toronto, Ont.
Profile - (Ont. 2012) Invests in an actively managed portfolio of Canadian dividend paying equity securities, income trusts and real estate investment trusts that exhibit low volatility.
The fund's investment portfolio consists of securities that have a Beta of less than one at the time of investment. Beta is a measure of volatility of a security in comparison to the market as a whole. It reflects the tendency of a security's returns to respond to changes in the market. A Beta of one indicates that the security's price has historically moved with the market, a Beta of less than one means that the security has historically been less volatile than the market, and a Beta of greater than one indicates that the security's price has historically been more volatile than the market.
The fund does not have a fixed termination date but may be terminated upon the approval of the unitholders. The fund may also employ leverage of up to 20% of the net asset value.
Portfolio allocation at Dec. 31, 2022 (as a percentage of total investment portfolio):

Sector	Percentage
Financials	16.3%
Real estate	12.3%
Energy infrastructure	12%
Cash and cash equivalents	10.2%
Telecommunication services	9.5%
Consumer discretionary	8.5%
Utilities	7.7%
Consumer staples	7.4%
Materials	6.5%
Industrials	6.3%
Oil & gas distribution	3.3%

Oper. Subsid./Mgt. Co. Directors - M. Paul Bloom, chr., pres., chief compliance officer, portfolio mgr. & corp. sec., Toronto, Ont.; Adina Bloom Somer, v-p & portfolio mgr., Toronto, Ont.; Beverly Lyons, Jerusalem, Israel
Oper. Subsid./Mgt. Co. Officers - Fiona E. Mitra, CFO; Kevin G. Willis, v-p

Capital Stock

	Authorized (shs.)	Outstanding (shs.)[1]
Fund Unit	unlimited	1,257,840

[1] At Dec. 31, 2022
Fund Unit - Entitled to a monthly cash distribution of $0.04167 per unit (5% per annum based on an issue price of $10 per unit). Retractable on the second last business day in October of each year at a price equal to the net asset value per unit less any costs incurred to fund the retraction. One vote per fund unit.

Price Range - BLB.UN/TSX

Year	Volume	High	Low	Close
2022............	240,416	$9.60	$7.68	$8.08
2021............	262,071	$10.11	$8.73	$9.18
2020............	572,895	$10.25	$5.83	$8.67
2019............	591,959	$9.96	$8.35	$9.51
2018............	572,302	$10.66	$8.33	$8.39

Recent Close: $7.66

Capital Stock Changes - During 2022, 7,144 fund units were issued under the dividend reinvestment plan and 88,300 fund units were retracted.

Dividends

BLB.UN unit Ra $0.50 pa M est. June 15, 2012**
** Reinvestment Option

Financial Statistics

Periods ended:	12m Dec. 31/22[A]		12m Dec. 31/21[A]
	$000s	%Chg	$000s
Realized invest. gain (loss)..............	386		341
Unrealized invest. gain (loss)...........	(1,532)		1,082
Total revenue...............................	**(709)**	**n.a.**	**1,880**
General & admin. expense..............	390		367
Operating expense.......................	**390**	**+6**	**367**
Operating income.........................	**(1,099)**	**n.a.**	**1,513**
Pre-tax income.............................	**(1,099)**	**n.a.**	**1,513**
Net income...................................	**(1,099)**	**n.a.**	**1,513**
Cash & equivalent...........................	1,078		978
Accounts receivable........................	49		50
Investments....................................	9,516		12,023
Total assets..................................	**10,651**	**-18**	**13,065**
Accts. pay. & accr. liabs..................	74		72
Shareholders' equity........................	10,525		12,937
Cash from oper. activs..................	**1,417**	**+177**	**511**
Cash from fin. activs........................	(1,317)		(890)
Net cash position..........................	**1,078**	**+10**	**978**
	$		$
Earnings per share*........................	(0.83)		1.11
Cash flow per share*.......................	1.07		0.38
Net asset value per share*..............	8.37		9.66
Cash divd. per share*......................	0.50		0.50
	shs		shs
No. of shs. o/s*...............................	1,257,840		1,338,996
Avg. no. of shs. o/s*........................	1,326,749		1,358,758
	%		%
Net profit margin.............................	n.m.		80.48
Return on equity..............................	(9.37)		11.98
Return on assets.............................	(9.27)		11.86

* Fund Unit
[A] Reported in accordance with IFRS

Note: Net income reflects increase/decrease in net assets from operations.

Historical Summary
(as originally stated)

Fiscal Year	Total Rev.	Net Inc. Bef. Disc.	EPS*
	$000s	$000s	$
2022[A]...................	(709)	(1,099)	(0.83)
2021[A]...................	1,880	1,513	1.11
2020[A]...................	(470)	(846)	(0.55)
2019[A]...................	3,571	3,150	1.88
2018[A]...................	(2,663)	(3,118)	(1.61)

* Fund Unit
[A] Reported in accordance with IFRS

B.83 Blue Ribbon Income Fund

Symbol - RBN.UN **Exchange -** TSX **CUSIP -** 095819
Head Office - c/o Brompton Group Limited, Bay Wellington Tower, Brookfield Place, 2930-181 Bay St, PO Box 793, Toronto, ON, M5J 2T3 **Telephone -** (416) 642-9061 **Toll-free -** (866) 642-6001 **Fax -** (416) 642-6001
Website - www.bromptongroup.com
Email - wong@bromptongroup.com
Investor Relations - Ann P. Wong (866) 642-6001
Auditors - PricewaterhouseCoopers LLP C.A., Toronto, Ont.
Lawyers - Stikeman Elliott LLP, Toronto, Ont.
Transfer Agents - Computershare Trust Company of Canada Inc., Toronto, Ont.
Trustees - Computershare Trust Company of Canada Inc., Toronto, Ont.
Investment Managers - Bloom Investment Counsel, Inc., Toronto, Ont.
Managers - Brompton Funds Limited, Toronto, Ont.
Portfolio Managers - Brompton Funds Limited, Toronto, Ont.
Administrators - Blue Ribbon Fund Management Ltd., Toronto, Ont.
Profile - (Ont. 1997) Invests primarily in Canadian income trusts, royalty trusts, real estate investment trusts, common and preferred shares, and debt instruments.

Brompton Funds Limited is the sub-administrator of the fund. The fund may also employ leverage of up to 25% of its total assets. The fund does not have a fixed termination date but may be terminated by the manager upon the approval of the unitholders.

Top 10 holdings at Mar. 31, 2023 (as a percentage of net asset value):

Holdings	Percentage
Cash and short-term investments............	15.4%
Ag Growth International Inc.......................	6.3%
Premium Brands Holdings Corp................	6.2%
Parkland Corporation................................	5.8%
Canadian Tire Corporation Limited...........	4.6%
Chemtrade Logistics Income Fund...........	4.6%
Park Lawn Corporation.............................	4.2%
Enbridge Inc..	4.1%
Transcontinental Inc., class A..................	4.1%
Manulife Financial Corporation..................	4.1%

Predecessor Detail - Name changed from Citadel Diversified Investment Trust, Nov. 24, 2009, pursuant to reorganization with Blue Ribbon Fund Management Ltd. as manager.
Oper. Subsid./Mgt. Co. Directors - M. Paul Bloom, chr. & exec. v-p, Toronto, Ont.; Mark A. Caranci, pres., Toronto, Ont.; Adina Bloom Somer, Toronto, Ont.
Oper. Subsid./Mgt. Co. Officers - Ann P. Wong, CFO; Kathryn A. H. Banner, sr. v-p & corp. sec.

Capital Stock

	Authorized (shs.)	Outstanding (shs.)[1]
Trust Unit	unlimited	9,564,164

[1] At July 14, 2023

Trust Unit - Entitled to receive monthly distributions of 4¢ per unit. Retractable in November of each year at a price equal to the net asset value per unit, less any costs to fund the retraction. One vote per trust unit.

Price Range - RBN.UN/TSX

Year	Volume	High	Low	Close
2022............	1,280,705	$9.23	$6.97	$7.36
2021............	2,013,143	$8.80	$7.48	$8.68
2020............	3,169,828	$8.89	$4.18	$7.48
2019............	3,255,609	$8.53	$7.31	$8.30
2018............	4,379,795	$9.94	$7.12	$7.39

Recent Close: $7.32

Capital Stock Changes - During 2022, 686,813 trust units were retracted and 2,724 trust units were issued under a distribution reinvestment plan.

Dividends

RBN.UN tr unit Ra $0.48 pa M est. May 14, 2020**
Prev. Rate: $0.60 est. May 13, 2016
** Reinvestment Option

Financial Statistics

Periods ended:	12m Dec. 31/22[A]		12m Dec. 31/21[A]
	$000s	%Chg	$000s
Realized invest. gain (loss)..............	2,051		4,273
Unrealized invest. gain (loss)...........	(10,252)		10,100
Total revenue...............................	**(4,992)**	**n.a.**	**17,653**
General & admin. expense..............	900		1,405
Operating expense.......................	**900**	**-36**	**1,405**
Operating income.........................	**(5,892)**	**n.a.**	**16,248**
Finance costs, gross.......................	nil		9
Pre-tax income.............................	**(6,069)**	**n.a.**	**16,238**
Net income...................................	**(6,069)**	**n.a.**	**16,238**
Cash & equivalent...........................	1,232		1,118
Accounts receivable........................	322		298
Investments....................................	71,788		88,451
Total assets..................................	**73,390**	**-18**	**89,866**
Accts. pay. & accr. liabs..................	67		218
Shareholders' equity........................	72,940		89,238
Cash from oper. activs..................	**10,371**	**-23**	**13,512**
Cash from fin. activs........................	(10,256)		(13,570)
Net cash position..........................	**1,232**	**+10**	**1,118**
	$		$
Earnings per share*........................	(0.60)		1.47
Cash flow per share*.......................	1.02		1.22
Net asset value per share*..............	7.63		8.71
Cash divd. per share*......................	0.48		0.48
	shs		shs
No. of shs. o/s*...............................	9,564,164		10,248,253
Avg. no. of shs. o/s*........................	10,183,942		11,073,607
	%		%
Net profit margin.............................	n.m.		91.98
Return on equity..............................	(7.48)		18.48
Return on assets.............................	(7.43)		18.35

* Trust unit
[A] Reported in accordance with IFRS

Note: Net income reflects increase/decrease in net assets from operations.

Historical Summary
(as originally stated)

Fiscal Year	Total Rev.	Net Inc. Bef. Disc.	EPS*
	$000s	$000s	$
2022[A]...................	(4,992)	(6,069)	(0.60)
2021[A]...................	17,653	16,238	1.47
2020[A]...................	(5,459)	(6,828)	(0.54)
2019[A]...................	25,521	23,358	1.66
2018[A]...................	(22,306)	(24,900)	(1.52)

* Trust unit
[A] Reported in accordance with IFRS

B.84 Blueberries Medical Corp.

Symbol - BBM **Exchange -** CSE **CUSIP -** 09609Y
Head Office - 2200-885 Georgia St W, Vancouver, BC, V6C 3E8
Website - www.blueberriesmed.com
Email - grodriguez@blueberriesmed.com
Investor Relations - Guillermo P. Rodriguez (416) 562-3220
Auditors - MNP LLP C.A., Toronto, Ont.
Transfer Agents - Computershare Trust Company of Canada Inc., Vancouver, B.C.
Profile - (B.C. 2013 amalg.) Holds licences to cultivate, produce, domestically distribute and internationally export cannabidiol (CBD) and tetrahydrocannabinol (THC)-based medical cannabis and cannabis-derived products from its primary operations in central Colombia.

Operation include 30,000-sq.-ft. processing and extraction facility in Tocancipa; 442,000-sq.-ft. nursery, propagation and production center in Guatavita; and 1,614,585-sq.-ft. of outdoor cultivation facility in Cogua.

The company owns 142 exclusive Colombian cannabis strains with high contents of CBD and THC.

Also holds 75% interest in **SATIN S.A.S.**, a joint venture with **Cannabis Avatara, S.E.** (Cannava) whereby the company would build a cultivation facility and processing centre of excellence on Cannava's 74-acre agricultural property in Jujuy Province, Argentina.

Revenues are earned through sale of cuttings to local licensed producers, extraction/processing services for third party producers, sale of raw materials including oil and standardized formulas as well as finished products, sale of CBD cosmetics and sale and production of medical and finished formulations.

Predecessor Detail - Name changed from CDN MSolar Corp., Feb. 5, 2019, following reverse takeover acquisition of Blueberries Cannabis Corp. and concurrent amalgamation of Blueberries Cannabis with wholly owned 2663895 Ontario Inc. (and continued as Blueberries Research Corp.).
Directors - Facundo Garretón, chr. & interim CEO, Maldonado, Uruguay; Joaquín Barbera; Sebastian Hochbaum, Buenos Aires, Argentina; Catherine Lathwell, Toronto, Ont.; Patricio Villalba, Bogota, Colombia
Other Exec. Officers - Guillermo P. Rodriguez, CFO; José María Forero, pres., Latin American opers.

Capital Stock

	Authorized (shs.)	Outstanding (shs.)[1]
Common	unlimited	163,810,263

[1] At Aug. 25, 2022

Major Shareholder - Facundo Garretón held 19.56% interest at Aug. 25, 2022.

Price Range - BBM/CSE

Year	Volume	High	Low	Close
2022............	15,702,698	$0.07	$0.02	$0.02
2021............	40,723,372	$0.25	$0.06	$0.07
2020............	45,025,825	$0.18	$0.04	$0.10
2019............	79,641,740	$0.88	$0.09	$0.12

Recent Close: $0.03

Wholly Owned Subsidiaries

BBV Labs Inc., Panama.
• 75% int. in **SATIN S.A.S.**, Argentina.
Blueberries Research Corp., Toronto, Ont.
• 100% int. in **Blueberries S.A.S.**, Colombia.
Centro De Dessarollo e Investigacion, Colombia.

Financial Statistics

Periods ended:	12m Dec. 31/21[A]		12m Dec. 31/20[A]
	$000s	%Chg	$000s
Operating revenue	**139**	**+111**	**66**
Cost of sales	384		4
Salaries & benefits	444		857
General & admin expense	475		1,261
Stock-based compensation	(340)		806
Other operating expense	91		549
Operating expense	**1,055**	**-70**	**3,477**
Operating income	**(916)**	**n.a.**	**(3,411)**
Deprec., depl. & amort.	828		714
Finance costs, gross	311		192
Write-downs/write-offs	(3,389)		nil
Pre-tax income	**(5,147)**	**n.a.**	**(4,940)**
Net income	**(5,147)**	**n.a.**	**(4,940)**
Cash & equivalent	1,343		307
Accounts receivable	202		204
Current assets	1,564		523
Fixed assets, net	1,602		2,737
Right-of-use assets	nil		609
Intangibles, net	nil		841
Total assets	**3,594**	**-51**	**7,270**
Accts. pay. & accr. liabs.	312		999
Current liabilities	1,936		2,097
Long-term debt, gross	1,107		837
Long-term debt, net	nil		837
Long-term lease liabilities	223		446
Shareholders' equity	1,435		3,890
Cash from oper. activs.	**(1,680)**	**n.a.**	**(2,390)**
Cash from fin. activs.	2,766		784
Cash from invest. activs.	(49)		(611)
Net cash position	**1,343**	**+337**	**307**
Capital expenditures	(10)		(832)
	$		$
Earnings per share*	(0.04)		(0.04)
Cash flow per share*	(0.01)		(0.02)
	shs		shs
No. of shs. o/s*	163,810,263		126,701,831
Avg. no. of shs. o/s*	148,504,538		123,931,339
	%		%
Net profit margin	n.m.		n.m.
Return on equity	(193.31)		n.m.
Return on assets	(89.03)		n.a.

* Common
[A] Reported in accordance with IFRS

Latest Results

Periods ended:	6m June 30/22[A]		6m June 30/21[A]
	$000s	%Chg	$000s
Operating revenue	74	+95	38
Net income	(1,168)	n.a.	(859)
	$		$
Earnings per share*	(0.01)		(0.01)

* Common
[A] Reported in accordance with IFRS

Historical Summary
(as originally stated)

Fiscal Year	Oper. Rev.	Net Inc. Bef. Disc.	EPS*
	$000s	$000s	$
2021[A]	139	(5,147)	(0.04)
2020[A]	66	(4,940)	(0.04)
2019[A1]	nil	(10,788)	(0.10)
2018[A2]	nil	(15)	(0.01)
2017[A]	nil	(416)	(0.20)

* Common
[A] Reported in accordance with IFRS
[1] Results reflect the Feb. 5, 2019, reverse takeover acquisition of Blueberries Cannabis Corp.
[2] Results for fiscal 2018 and prior fiscal years pertain to CDN MSolar Corp.
Note: Adjusted throughout for 1-for-10 cons. in July 2018

B.85 BlueRush Inc.

Symbol - BTV **Exchange** - TSX-VEN **CUSIP** - 09629N
Head Office - 200-5700 Yonge St, Toronto, ON, M2M 4K2 **Telephone** - (416) 203-0618 **Toll-free** - (844) 455-2583 **Fax** - (416) 848-0021
Website - www.bluerush.com
Email - steve.taylor@bluerush.com
Investor Relations - Stephen Taylor (416) 457-9391
Auditors - MNP LLP C.A., Toronto, Ont.
Lawyers - DLA Piper (Canada) LLP, Toronto, Ont.
Transfer Agents - TSX Trust Company, Toronto, Ont.
Profile - (Ont. 2004) Provides a Software-as-a-Service (SaaS)-based marketing and sales platform that enables organizations to achieve greater engagement with its customers primarily aimed for customer communication management (CCM) providers, and the financial services, insurance, and telecommunications and utilities industries.

Through wholly owned **BlueRush Digital Media Corp.**, develops and markets IndiVideo™, an interactive personalized video platform which enables the clients to capture knowledge and data from their customers' video interactions, creating new and compelling data-driven customer insights. IndiVideo has a self-serve functionality that allows users to improve pre-existing videos by adding personalization, interactive calls to action (CTAs), data tracking and closed-captions and audio transcripts for full accessibility compliance. The self-serve platform integrates with Adobe After-Effects to make the technology accessible to clients. The company also has partnership agreements for the reselling of IndiVideo solution.

The company also offers a full suite of customizable and licensable financial tools and calculators, which simplify financial products and create educational experiences that empower the client's customers to make a confident decision; and provides professional services, including digital strategies to personalize customer experience, mobile-first web development, and video marketing services that covers everything from video script development, audio and video production to post-production.

Predecessor Detail - Name changed from BlueRush Media Group Corp., Apr. 30, 2018.

Directors - Laurence (Larry) Lubin, chr. & pres., Thornhill, Ont.; Stephen (Steve) Taylor, CEO, Ont.; John Eckert, Toronto, Ont.; Chris Rasmussen, Ont.; Paul G. Smith, Toronto, Ont.; Mark Soane

Other Exec. Officers - Sandra Clarke, CFO; Savitri Ponnambalam, chief cust. officer; Len Smofsky, exec. v-p & chief experience officer; Jeffrey Liberman, v-p, sales & mktg.; Richard Pineault, v-p, technical architecture; Robbie Grossman, corp. sec.

Capital Stock

	Authorized (shs.)	Outstanding (shs.)[1]
Common	unlimited	34,110,217

[1] At Dec. 20, 2022

Major Shareholder - Round 13 Capital Founders Fund, L.P. held 29% interest at Sept. 6, 2022.

Price Range - BTV/TSX-VEN

Year	Volume	High	Low	Close
2022	2,387,360	$0.58	$0.08	$0.15
2021	2,507,944	$1.20	$0.35	$0.58
2020	883,537	$0.60	$0.18	$0.60
2019	1,861,136	$0.60	$0.28	$0.33
2018	898,553	$1.00	$0.38	$0.53

Consolidation: 1-for-5 cons. in Dec. 2022
Recent Close: $0.05

Capital Stock Changes - On Dec. 19, 2022, common shares were consolidated on a 1-for-5 basis.

In April 2022, private placement of 8,434,375 units (1 common share & ½ warrant) at $0.064 per unit was completed. Also during fiscal 2022, 10,000 common share were issued on exercise of options.

Wholly Owned Subsidiaries

BlueRush Digital Media Corp., Toronto, Ont.

Financial Statistics

Periods ended:	12m July 31/22[A]		12m July 31/21[oA]
	$000s	%Chg	$000s
Operating revenue	**4,769**	**+30**	**3,675**
Cost of sales	1,235		1,447
Research & devel. expense	1,295		1,402
General & admin expense	4,818		4,054
Stock-based compensation	501		292
Operating expense	**7,849**	**+9**	**7,195**
Operating income	**(3,080)**	**n.a.**	**(3,520)**
Deprec., depl. & amort.	201		256
Finance costs, gross	158		894
Write-downs/write-offs	(84)		(6)
Pre-tax income	**(3,522)**	**n.a.**	**(4,158)**
Income taxes	(2)		(30)
Net income	**(3,520)**	**n.a.**	**(4,129)**
Cash & equivalent	1,265		2,158
Inventories	nil		8
Accounts receivable	939		730
Current assets	2,920		3,427
Fixed assets, net	67		82
Right-of-use assets	33		124
Intangibles, net	nil		17
Total assets	**3,021**	**-18**	**3,676**
Accts. pay. & accr. liabs.	1,895		1,684
Current liabilities	3,248		3,046
Long-term debt, gross	785		998
Long-term debt, net	770		740
Shareholders' equity	(2,617)		(112)
Cash from oper. activs.	**(2,615)**	**n.a.**	**(3,236)**
Cash from fin. activs.	1,776		4,079
Cash from invest. activs.	(53)		(46)
Net cash position	**1,248**	**-42**	**2,141**
Capital expenditures	(15)		(46)
	$		$
Earnings per share*	(0.10)		(0.15)
Cash flow per share*	(0.08)		(0.14)
	shs		shs
No. of shs. o/s*	34,100,217		32,411,342
Avg. no. of shs. o/s*	32,833,561		23,997,209
	%		%
Net profit margin	(73.81)		(112.35)
Return on equity	n.m.		n.m.
Return on assets	(100.41)		(103.98)
Foreign sales percent	63		61

* Common
[o] Restated
[A] Reported in accordance with IFRS

Latest Results

Periods ended:	3m Oct. 31/22[A]		3m Oct. 31/21[A]
	$000s	%Chg	$000s
Operating revenue	1,219	+10	1,110
Net income	(837)	n.a.	(985)
	$		$
Earnings per share*	(0.03)		(0.03)

* Common
[A] Reported in accordance with IFRS

Historical Summary
(as originally stated)

Fiscal Year	Oper. Rev.	Net Inc. Bef. Disc.	EPS*
	$000s	$000s	$
2022[A]	4,769	(3,520)	(0.10)
2021[A]	3,675	(4,129)	(0.15)
2020[A]	3,783	(3,350)	(0.20)
2019[A]	3,605	(3,841)	(0.25)
2018[A]	3,022	(3,350)	(0.30)

* Common
[A] Reported in accordance with IFRS
Note: Adjusted throughout for 1-for-5 cons. in Dec. 2022

B.86 Bluesky Digital Assets Corp.

Symbol - BTC **Exchange** - CSE **CUSIP** - 09629B
Head Office - First Canadian Place, 5700-100 King St W, Toronto, ON, M5X 1C9 **Telephone** - (416) 363-3833
Website - www.blueskydigitalassets.com
Email - frank.kordy@blueskydigitalassets.com
Investor Relations - Frank Kordy (647) 466-4037
Auditors - Raymond Chabot Grant Thornton LLP C.A., Montréal, Qué.
Lawyers - Garfinkle Biderman LLP, Toronto, Ont.
Transfer Agents - TSX Trust Company, Toronto, Ont.
Profile - (Ont. 2006) Carries out cryptocurrency mining operations. Also develops value-added technology services for the digital currency market.

The company mines digital currencies, Bitcoin and Ether, at a mining facility in Quebec. Also developing value-added technology services for the digital currency market, such as proprietary technology solutions.

Research and development and software product initiatives are conducted through Bluesky Intel (BSI) or Bluesky Intelligence, which covers areas including decentralized finance (DeFi), stablecoin, Artificial Intelligence (AI) and all blockchain-related opportunities. BSI would serve as a platform for businesses to adopt blockchain technology.

In March 2022, the company acquired application-specific integrated circuits (ASIC) and graphics processing unit (GPU) mining rigs from **Monbanc Corporation** for the issuance of 6,060,606 common shares at a deemed price of $0.165.

Predecessor Detail - Name changed from Gunpowder Capital Corp., Dec. 2, 2019.

Directors - Ben Gelfand, CEO, Oakville, Ont.; Frank Kordy, corp. sec., Brampton, Ont.; Alan J. Grant, Toronto, Ont.; Daniel W. K. Rafuse

Other Exec. Officers - Anthony R. Pearlman, COO; Victor J. (Vic) Hugo, CFO

Capital Stock

	Authorized (shs.)	Outstanding (shs.)[1]
Preferred	6,591,157	
Class A		493,020
Class B		1,250
Common	unlimited	115,376,796

[1] At May 30, 2023

Class A and Class B Preferred - Entitled to an annual dividend of 8%. Non-voting.

Common - One vote per share.

Major Shareholder - Widely held at May 18, 2022.

Price Range - BTC/CSE

Year	Volume	High	Low	Close
2022	63,928,136	$0.28	$0.02	$0.03
2021	82,154,003	$1.90	$0.27	$0.27
2020	50,407,763	$0.79	$0.06	$0.49
2019	1,675,813	$0.84	$0.06	$0.12
2018	581,103	$1.20	$0.48	$0.48

Consolidation: 1-for-12 cons. in May 2020

Recent Close: $0.04

Capital Stock Changes - In March 2023, 17,557,884 common shares were issued for debt settlement. In May 2023, private placement of 14,750,000 units (1 common share & 1 warrant) at $0.045 per unit was completed, with warrants exercisable at $0.065 per share for two years.

In January 2022, private placement of 9,235,000 units (1 common share & 1 warrant) at 25¢ was completed. Also during 2022, common shares were issued as follows: 6,666,666 for debt settlement and 1,400,000 by private placement.

Wholly Owned Subsidiaries

Bluesky Digital Assets Inc., Canada.

GP Realty Inc., Canada.

- 100% int. in **Bluesky Defi Inc.**, Canada.
- 100% int. in **Bluesky Intelligence Inc.**, Canada.

GP Self Storage Inc., Canada.

MethodeVerte Inc., Canada.

Investments

Astro Aerospace Ltd., Tex.

Cheetah Canyon Resources Corp., North Vancouver, B.C.

EastWest Bioscience Inc., Penticton, B.C. (see separate coverage)

Hemp Inc., Las Vegas, Nev.

Target Group Inc., Ont.

Worksport Ltd., Ont.

Financial Statistics

Periods ended:	12m Dec. 31/22[A]		12m Dec. 31/21[A]
	$000s	%Chg	$000s
Operating revenue	**1,415**	**-62**	**3,726**
Cost of sales	2,386		1,561
General & admin expense	1,842		1,998
Stock-based compensation	479		4,949
Operating expense	**4,707**	**-45**	**8,508**
Operating income	**(3,292)**	**n.a.**	**(4,782)**
Deprec., depl. & amort.	1,819		1,401
Finance costs, gross	19		7
Investment income	(104)		(35)
Write-downs/write-offs	(3,984)[1]		nil
Pre-tax income	**(7,361)**	**n.a.**	**(6,365)**
Income taxes	36		(65)
Net inc. bef. disc. opers	**(7,398)**	**n.a.**	**(6,300)**
Income from disc. opers	nil		(6)
Net income	**(7,398)**	**n.a.**	**(6,306)**
Cash & equivalent	282		3,412
Accounts receivable	8		127
Current assets	524		3,788
Fixed assets, net	1,280		4,708
Right-of-use assets	161		224
Total assets	**1,966**	**-77**	**8,720**
Accts. pay. & accr. liabs	981		999
Current liabilities	1,106		1,036
Long-term debt, gross	95		70
Long-term debt, net	35		70
Long-term lease liabilities	106		190
Preferred share equity	2,055		2,055
Shareholders' equity	557		4,883
Cash from oper. activs	**(439)**	**n.a.**	**(1,941)**
Cash from fin. activs	2,176		7,062
Cash from invest. activs	(2,313)		(5,450)
Net cash position	**232**	**-73**	**854**
Capital expenditures	(2,448)		(5,891)
Capital disposals	nil		119
	$		$
Earnings per share*	(0.11)		(0.16)
Cash flow per share*	(0.01)		(0.05)
	shs		shs
No. of shs. o/s*	67,258,480		49,956,814
Avg. no. of shs. o/s*	65,890,727		38,772,639
	%		%
Net profit margin	(522.83)		(169.08)
Return on equity	n.m.		(961.10)
Return on assets	(138.10)		(117.21)

* Common

[A] Reported in accordance with IFRS

[1] Pertains to the impairment of data miners of $4,118,887 and the reversal of impairment for a financial instrument totaling $135,037.

Latest Results

Periods ended:	3m Mar. 31/23[A]		3m Mar. 31/22[A]
	$000s	%Chg	$000s
Operating revenue	nil	n.a.	581
Net income	(997)	n.a.	(586)
	$		$
Earnings per share*	(0.01)		(0.01)

* Common

[A] Reported in accordance with IFRS

Historical Summary
(as originally stated)

Fiscal Year	Oper. Rev. $000s	Net Inc. Bef. Disc. $000s	EPS* $
2022[A]	1,415	(7,398)	(0.11)
2021[A]	3,726	(6,300)	(0.16)
2020[A]	695	(1,505)	(0.08)
2019[A]	337	(4,834)	(0.51)
2018[A]	749	(2,808)	(1.10)

* Common

[A] Reported in accordance with IFRS

Note: Adjusted throughout for 1-for-12 cons. in May 2020

B.87 BluMetric Environmental Inc.

Symbol - BLM **Exchange** - TSX-VEN **CUSIP** - 096427

Head Office - 1682 Woodward Dr, Ottawa, ON, K2C 3R8 **Telephone** - (613) 839-3053 **Toll-free** - (877) 487-8436 **Fax** - (877) 487-8436

Website - www.blumetric.ca

Email - vkaraiskos@blumetric.ca

Investor Relations - Vivian Karaiskos (877) 487-8436

Auditors - MNP LLP C.A., Ottawa, Ont.

Bankers - Bank of Montreal

Transfer Agents - Computershare Trust Company of Canada Inc., Toronto, Ont.

Employees - 177 at Sept. 30, 2022

Profile - (Can. 1985) Provides professional environmental consulting services and water and wastewater solutions to clients in the mining, military, government, commercial and industrial sectors in Canada and the U.S.

The company focuses on environmental earth sciences and engineering, contaminated site remediation, water resource management, industrial hygiene, occupational health and safety, and water and wastewater design-build and pre-engineered solutions. Professional services offered include environmental permitting and compliance, environmental reporting, environmental site assessments, geomatics and data management, industrial hygiene, management systems, occupational health and safety and ergonomics, physical hydrogeology and clean water, property assessments and environmental due diligence, waste management and waterpower and hydraulic structures.

Predecessor Detail - Name changed from Seprotech Systems Incorporated, Nov. 6, 2012, pursuant to reverse takeover acquisition of WESA Group Inc.; basis 1 new for 10 old shs.

Directors - Ian Mor Macdonald, chr., Toronto, Ont.; Scott A. MacFabe, CEO, Ottawa, Ont.; Ian Murray Macdonald, Kitchener, Ont.; Wanda Richardson, Cambridge, Ont.; Dr. David L. Rudolph, Ont.

Other Exec. Officers - Vivian Karaiskos, CFO & corp. sec.; Andy Benson, v-p & dir., opers.; Wayne Ingham, v-p & dir., strategic bus. devel.

Capital Stock

	Authorized (shs.)	Outstanding (shs.)[1]
Special	unlimited	nil
Common	unlimited	29,435,695

[1] At Feb. 28, 2023

Major Shareholder - Roger M. Woeller held 12.8% interest at Feb. 15, 2023.

Price Range - BLM/TSX-VEN

Year	Volume	High	Low	Close
2022	3,857,680	$0.80	$0.30	$0.38
2021	6,755,459	$0.92	$0.18	$0.74
2020	2,629,842	$0.23	$0.07	$0.19
2019	1,158,584	$0.25	$0.12	$0.13
2018	1,445,790	$0.31	$0.13	$0.16

Recent Close: $0.34

Capital Stock Changes - During fiscal 2022, 540,000 common shares were issued on exercise of options.

Financial Statistics

Periods ended:	12m Sept. 30/22[A]		12m Sept. 30/21[A]
	$000s	%Chg	$000s
Operating revenue	**34,318**	**-3**	**35,479**
Cost of sales	13,311		13,353
Salaries & benefits	15,652		14,471
General & admin expense	3,112		2,413
Operating expense	**32,075**	**+6**	**30,237**
Operating income	**2,243**	**-57**	**5,242**
Deprec., depl. & amort.	516		604
Finance costs, gross	99		312
Write-downs/write-offs	nil		(91)
Pre-tax income	**1,628**	**-62**	**4,327**
Income taxes	305		601
Net income	**1,323**	**-64**	**3,726**
Cash & equivalent	4,911		4,727
Accounts receivable	7,565		4,717
Current assets	17,923		15,681
Fixed assets, net	169		183
Right-of-use assets	775		609
Intangibles, net	73		51
Total assets	**19,670**	**+13**	**17,420**
Accts. pay. & accr. liabs	5,905		3,935
Current liabilities	7,010		5,968
Long-term debt, gross	1,321		1,934
Long-term debt, net	823		1,321
Long-term lease liabilities	468		269
Shareholders' equity	11,369		9,862
Cash from oper. activs	**1,197**	**-67**	**3,654**
Cash from fin. activs	(930)		(1,205)
Cash from invest. activs	(83)		(192)
Net cash position	**4,911**	**+4**	**4,727**
Capital expenditures	(46)		(144)
	$		$
Earnings per share*	0.05		0.13
Cash flow per share*	0.04		0.13
	shs		shs
No. of shs. o/s*	29,435,695		28,895,695
Avg. no. of shs. o/s*	29,365,996		28,773,174
	%		%
Net profit margin	3.86		10.50
Return on equity	12.46		46.76
Return on assets	7.57		24.26
No. of employees (FTEs)	177		160

* Common

[A] Reported in accordance with IFRS

Latest Results

Periods ended:	3m Dec. 31/22^A		3m Dec. 31/21^A
	$000s	%Chg	$000s
Operating revenue	10,478	+34	7,816
Net income	456	-17	552
	$		$
Earnings per share*	0.02		0.02

* Common
^A Reported in accordance with IFRS

Historical Summary
(as originally stated)

Fiscal Year	Oper. Rev.	Net Inc. Bef. Disc.	EPS*
	$000s	$000s	$
2022^A	34,318	1,323	0.05
2021^A	35,479	3,726	0.13
2020^A	28,621	471	0.02
2019^A	28,252	351	0.01
2018^A	32,247	2,659	0.09

* Common
^A Reported in accordance with IFRS

B.88 BnSellit Technology Inc.

Symbol - BNSL **Exchange** - CSE **CUSIP** - 09662H
Head Office - 3000-421 7 Ave SW, Calgary, AB, T2P 4K9 **Telephone** - (403) 700-6466
Website - bnsellit.com
Email - tc@bnsellit.com
Investor Relations - Antonio Comparelli (403) 630-2779
Auditors - Kenway Mack Slusarchuk Stewart LLP C.A., Calgary, Alta.
Transfer Agents - Alliance Trust Company, Calgary, Alta.
Profile - (Alta. 2021) Develops BnSellit™ and BnBuylt™ mobile applications (app) and BnSellit™ host portal that allow short-term rental (STR) property owners and hotels to sell or rent out items such as bicycles, golf clubs, toiletries, snacks and art pieces, as well as offer high-speed Internet access to their guests.

The mobile app and host portal are accessed by the guests through QR codes placed in the room. The platform includes real time payment processing integrations, inventory control, guest management and support, host management and support, performance reporting and real time guest-to-host chat/phone communications. The platform also allows guests to buy tickets to local experiences such as attractions, tours, events, day trips and adventures, with the host earning a percentage of all experience sales. In addition, a full enterprise hotel platform is offered which includes automated housekeeping, maintenance and service requests, hotel managed concierge services, essential information access, hotel amenity details, express room checkout, guest to staff communication and self-serve point of sale.

Multi-unit hotel operators are also offered a variety of licensing options for the platform including white label, private branding or hybrid combinations.

Directors - John Napier, chr., New Zealand; Antonio (Tony) Comparelli, pres. & CEO, Ont.; L. Evan Baergen, Delta, B.C.; Colin Keddy, Oman; Douglas T. (Doug) McCartney, Calgary, Alta.
Other Exec. Officers - Christopher (Chris) Carmichael, CFO

Capital Stock

	Authorized (shs.)	Outstanding (shs.)[1]
Class A Common	unlimited	46,813,565
Class B Common	unlimited	nil

[1] At Aug. 25, 2022

Major Shareholder - John Napier held 43.3% interest, Bolloré S.E. held 13.2% interest and Antonio (Tony) Comparelli held 10.3% interest at May 11, 2022.

Price Range - BNSL/CSE

Year	Volume	High	Low	Close
2022	2,747,129	$0.55	$0.07	$0.20
2021	350,056	$1.40	$0.20	$0.36

Recent Close: $0.20

Wholly Owned Subsidiaries

BnSellit Technology (US) Incorporated, Del.

Financial Statistics

Periods ended:	11m Dec. 31/21^A
	$000s
Operating revenue	**1**
Cost of sales	1
Salaries & benefits	192
General & admin expense	666
Operating expense	**859**
Operating income	**(858)**
Deprec., depl. & amort.	9
Finance costs, gross	1
Pre-tax income	**(869)**
Net income	**(869)**
Cash & equivalent	478
Accounts receivable	59
Current assets	545
Fixed assets, net	3
Right-of-use assets	186
Intangibles, net	1,313
Total assets	**2,076**
Accts. pay. & accr. liabs	123
Current liabilities	223
Long-term lease liabilities	87
Shareholders' equity	1,766
Cash from oper. activs	**(831)**
Cash from fin. activs	1,458
Cash from invest. activs	(150)
Net cash position	**478**
Capital expenditures	(4)
	$
Earnings per share*	(0.02)
Cash flow per share*	(0.02)
	shs
No. of shs. o/s*	45,804,039
Avg. no. of shs. o/s*	39,629,195
	%
Net profit margin	n.m.
Return on equity	n.m.
Return on assets	n.a.

* Common
^A Reported in accordance with IFRS

Latest Results

Periods ended:	6m June 30/22^A
	$000s
Operating revenue	3
Net income	(734)
	$
Earnings per share*	(0.02)

* Common
^A Reported in accordance with IFRS

B.89 Boardwalk Real Estate Investment Trust*

Symbol - BEI.UN **Exchange** - TSX **CUSIP** - 096631
Head Office - First West Place, 200-1501 1 St SW, Calgary, AB, T2R 0W1 **Telephone** - (403) 531-9255 **Fax** - (403) 531-9565
Website - www.bwalk.com
Email - investor@bwalk.com
Investor Relations - J. Eric Bowers (403) 531-9255
Auditors - Deloitte LLP C.A., Calgary, Alta.
Bankers - The Toronto-Dominion Bank, Calgary, Alta.
Lawyers - First West Law LLP, Calgary, Alta.; Gowling WLG (Canada) LLP, Calgary, Alta.
Transfer Agents - Computershare Trust Company of Canada Inc., Calgary, Alta.
FP500 Revenue Ranking - 470
Employees - 1,558 at Dec. 31, 2022
Profile - (Alta. 2004) Acquires, develops, owns, operates and manages a portfolio of multi-family residential rental properties in Alberta, Saskatchewan, Ontario, Quebec and British Columbia.

The trust's residential properties are located in Edmonton, Calgary, Red Deer, Grande Prairie, Fort McMurray, Banff, Canmore and Spruce Grove, Alta.; Saskatoon and Regina, Sask.; Brampton, London, Kitchener, Cambridge and Waterloo, Ont.; Montreal and Quebec City, Que.; and Victoria, B.C. At Dec. 31, 2022, the trust's property portfolio consisted of direct and indirect interests in 33,810 rental units totaling 29,309755 net rentable sq. ft.. The average occupancy rate in 2022 was of 96.81%.

Geographic distribution of the trust's properties at Dec. 31, 2022:

Location	Units	Sq. Ft.
Alberta	21,084	18,080,443
Saskatchewan	3,505	3,065,330
Ontario	3,107	2,672,534
Quebec	6,000	5,395,692
British Columbia	114	95,756
	33,810	29,309,755

Recent Merger and Acquisition Activity

Status: completed **Announced:** Apr. 25, 2023
Boardwalk Real Estate Investment Trust acquired The Vue, a 124-unit apartment community in Langford, B.C., for $60,000,000.

Status: completed **Announced:** Aug. 8, 2022
Boardwalk Real Estate Investment Trust acquired The Level, a 158-unit apartment community in Calgary, Alta., for $41,900,000, including the assumption of a $29,200,000 mortgage.

Status: completed **Revised:** June 1, 2022
UPDATE: The transaction was completed. PREVIOUS: Boardwalk Real Estate Investment Trust agreed to acquire three parcels of land in Victoria, B.C., which is planned for the development of new rental units, for $12,000,000. The transaction was expected to close on June 1, 2022.

Status: completed **Announced:** Mar. 30, 2022
Boardwalk Real Estate Investment Trust acquired two properties in Canmore, Alta., and Brampton, Ont., for a combined purchase price of $117,500,000, financed with cash on hand and mortgage financing. The properties are Peak Estates in Canmore, consisting of three A-class, four-storey buildings totaling 148 units, and Ardglen Place in Brampton, which consists of 152 townhouse units.

Trustees - Sam Kolias, chr. & CEO, Calgary, Alta.; Brian G. Robinson‡, Calgary, Alta.; Mandy Abramsohn, Toronto, Ont.; Andrea Goertz, Alta.; Gary M. Goodman, Toronto, Ont.; Samantha A. Kolias-Gunn, Calgary, Alta.; Scott Morrison, Toronto, Ont.
Oper. Subsid./Mgt. Co. Officers - James Ha, pres.; Lisa Smandych, CFO; Leonora Davids, sr. v-p, opers.; Van Kolias, sr. v-p, quality control; Boyd Belisle, v-p, community & culture; J. Eric Bowers, v-p, fin. & IR; Razvan Costin, v-p, opers., northern Alta.; Bhavnesh Jairam, v-p, tech. & CIO; Haroon Khan, v-p, opers., B.C., southern Alta. & Sask.; Jeffrey (Jeff) Klaus, v-p, asset mgt. & devel.; Helen Mix, v-p, people
‡ Lead trustee

Capital Stock

	Authorized (shs.)	Outstanding (shs.)[1]
Trust Unit	unlimited	45,724,155
Special Voting Unit	unlimited	4,475,000
Class B Unit	unlimited	4,475,000[2 3]

[1] At Mar. 31, 2023
[2] Classified as debt.
[3] Securities of Boardwalk REIT Limited Partnership.

Trust Unit - The trust will endeavour to make monthly cash distributions. Redeemable at any time at price per unit equal to the lesser of: (i) 90% of the market price of the units on the TSX during the 21-day trading period prior to the redemption date; and (ii) 100% of the closing price. One vote per trust unit.

Special Voting Unit - Provide voting rights to holders of class B units of Boardwalk REIT Limited Partnership. Holders are not entitled to receive distributions or any amount upon liquidation, dissolution or winding-up of the trust. Each special voting unit entitles the holder to a number of votes at unitholder meetings equal to the number of trust units into which the class B units are exchangeable. The number of special voting units outstanding will be equal to the number of class B units outstanding.

Class B Unit - The class B units were issued to certain former shareholders of BPCL Holdings Inc. pursuant to the Plan of Arrangement completed on May 3, 2004. The class B units are non-transferable, except under certain circumstances, but are exchangeable, on a one-for-one basis, into trust units. Entitled to receive distributions on the same basis as trust units.

Normal Course Issuer Bid - The company plans to make normal course purchases of up to 3,693,000 trust units representing 10% of the public float. The bid commenced on Nov. 22, 2022, and expires on Nov. 21, 2023.

Major Shareholder - Sam and Van Kolias held 26.2% interest at Mar. 17, 2023.

Price Range - BEI.UN/TSX

Year	Volume	High	Low	Close
2022	31,634,243	$61.77	$41.12	$49.43
2021	32,452,449	$57.10	$33.06	$54.83
2020	51,712,620	$51.84	$15.80	$33.74
2019	30,850,469	$49.14	$36.47	$45.93
2018	32,597,539	$52.43	$36.83	$37.81

Recent Close: $66.69

Capital Stock Changes - During 2022, 25,810 trust units were issued for vested deferred units and 440,000 trust units were repurchased under a Normal Course Issuer Bid.

Dividends

BEI.UN unit Ra $1.17 pa M est. Apr. 17, 2023[1]
Prev. Rate: $1.08 est. Apr. 15, 2022
Prev. Rate: $1.0008 est. Feb. 15, 2018
stk.[2]◆g................ Dec. 31/21
Paid in 2023: $1.1475 2022: $1.0602 2021: $1.0008 + stk.◆g

[1] Distribution reinvestment plan terminated eff. Feb. 15/08.
[2] Distribution will be automatically reinvested and the units will be consolidated immediately after distribution. Equiv to $0.325.
◆ Special **g** Capital Gain

Long-Term Debt - Outstanding at Dec. 31, 2022:

Mtges. payable[1]	$3,214,554,000
Class B units[2]	221,199,000
	3,435,753,000
Less: Current portion	504,953,000
	2,930,800,000

[1] Bear interest at a weighted average interest rate of 2.72%.
[2] Issued to certain former shareholders of BPCL Holdings Inc.

Minimum mortgage repayments were reported as follows:

2023	$504,953,000
2024	468,332,000
2025	559,501,000
2026	551,118,000
2027	599,359,000
Thereafter	652,763,000

Wholly Owned Subsidiaries

Boardwalk Real Estate Management Ltd.
Top Hat Operating Trust, B.C.
- 100% int. in **Boardwalk REIT Limited Partnership**, B.C.
  - 100% int. in **Boardwalk GP Holding Trust**
    - 99.99% int. in **Boardwalk General Partnership**
      - 50% int. in **BRIO Holdings Ltd.**
      - 100% int. in **Boardwalk REIT Properties Holdings Ltd.**
      - 100% int. in **Carlisle Ave Development B.C. Ltd.**, B.C.
      - 100% int. in **Helmcken RD Development B.C. Ltd.**, B.C.
      - 100% int. in **Island Highway Development (B.C.) Ltd.**, B.C.
      - 50% int. in **Redwalk Brampton Inc.**
        - 0.01% int. in **Redwalk Brampton Limited Partnership**
      - 49.99% int. in **Redwalk Brampton Limited Partnership**
      - 100% int. in **Watkiss Eagle Creek Property Ltd.**, B.C.
- 100% int. in **Boardwalk Quebec Trust**, Qué.
  - 99.99% int. in **Boardwalk St-Laurent LP**, Saint-Laurent, Qué.
- 100% int. in **Boardwalk REIT Properties Holdings (Alberta) Ltd.**
- 100% int. in **Boardwalk REIT Quebec Inc.**
- 100% int. in **Metropolitan Structures (MSI) Inc.**
- 100% int. in **9108-4749 Quebec Inc.**
  - 100% int. in **9165-5795 Quebec Inc.**, Qué.
    - 0.01% int. in **Boardwalk St-Laurent LP**, Saint-Laurent, Qué.
- 100% int. in **Nun's Island Trust 1**
- 100% int. in **Nun's Island Trust 2**
- 100% int. in **6222285 Canada Inc.**
  - 100% int. in **Boardwalk GP Operating Trust**
    - 0.01% int. in **Boardwalk General Partnership**

Financial Statistics

Periods ended:	12m Dec. 31/22^A		12m Dec. 31/21^A
	$000s	%Chg	$000s
Total revenue	**494,806**	**+5**	**470,531**
Rental operating expense	155,099		146,596
General & admin. expense	33,859		33,282
Stock-based compensation	2,556		2,392
Property taxes	51,047		49,595
Operating expense	**242,561**	**+5**	**231,865**
Operating income	**252,245**	**+6**	**238,666**
Investment income	(247)		nil
Deprec. & amort.	7,782		7,809
Finance income	935		331
Finance costs, gross	97,021		90,080
Pre-tax income	**283,174**	**-37**	**446,157**
Income taxes	78		(110)
Net income	**283,096**	**-37**	**446,267**
Cash & equivalent	52,816		64,300
Inventories	7,765		8,015
Accounts receivable	4,641		6,155
Current assets	90,145		93,470
Long-term investments	44,174		43,137
Fixed assets	129,879		120,622
Income-producing props	6,900,745		6,492,969
Property interests, net	6,932,097		6,522,846
Total assets	**7,067,275**	**+6**	**6,660,653**
Accts. pay. & accr. liabs	59,974		59,773
Current liabilities	584,942		606,127
Long-term debt, gross	3,435,753		3,244,988
Long-term debt, net	2,930,800		2,716,378
Long-term lease liabilities	76,602		76,182
Shareholders' equity	3,466,998		3,253,178
Cash from oper. activs	**160,904**	**-1**	**161,860**
Cash from fin. activs	24,670		(12,643)
Cash from invest. activs	(197,058)		(137,877)
Net cash position	**52,816**	**-18**	**64,300**
Capital expenditures	(5,467)		(5,511)
Increase in property	(193,791)		(172,319)
Decrease in property	nil		43,309
	$		$
Earnings per share*	6.17		9.59
Cash flow per share*	3.51		3.48
Funds from opers. per sh.*	3.13		2.94
Adj. funds from opers. per sh.*	2.51		2.31
Cash divd. per share*	1.07		1.00
Extra stk. divd. - cash equiv.*	nil		0.33
Total divd. per share*	**1.07**		**1.33**
	shs		shs
No. of shs. o/s*	45,722,922		46,137,112
Avg. no. of shs. o/s*	45,856,070		46,532,264
	%		%
Net profit margin	57.21		94.84
Return on equity	8.43		14.56
Return on assets	5.54		8.40
No. of employees (FTEs)	1,558		1,560

* Trust Unit
^A Reported in accordance with IFRS

Latest Results

Periods ended:	3m Mar. 31/23^A		3m Mar. 31/22^A
	$000s	%Chg	$000s
Total revenue	130,531	+10	118,277
Net income	221,389	+219	69,428
	$		$
Earnings per share*	4.84		1.51

* Trust Unit
^A Reported in accordance with IFRS

Historical Summary
(as originally stated)

Fiscal Year	Total Rev.	Net Inc. Bef. Disc.	EPS*
	$000s	$000s	$
2022^A	494,806	283,096	6.17
2021^A	470,531	446,267	9.59
2020^A	465,572	(197,279)	(4.24)
2019^A	455,313	34,781	0.75
2018^A	434,616	193,200	4.17

* Trust Unit
^A Reported in accordance with IFRS

B.90 Boardwalktech Software Corp.

Symbol - BWLK **Exchange** - TSX-VEN **CUSIP** - 096639
Head Office - 10050 N Wolfe Rd, Suite SW1-276, Cupertino, CA, United States, 95014 **Telephone** - (650) 618-6200
Website - www.boardwalktech.com
Email - charlie.glavin@boardwalktech.com
Investor Relations - Charles Glavin (650) 618-6118
Auditors - MNP LLP C.A., Calgary, Alta.
Lawyers - Owens, Wright LLP, Toronto, Ont.
Transfer Agents - Odyssey Trust Company, Vancouver, B.C.
Employees - 50 at Aug. 17, 2022
Profile - (B.C. 2018; orig. Alta., 1996) Designs and licenses a patented and cloud-based digital ledger for collaborative, multi-party enterprise planning applications.

The company's Boardwalk Enterprise Digital Ledger platform is a cloud-based platform service that runs mission-critical applications worldwide. It manages a vast amount of structured and unstructured data, allowing multiple parties to effectively work on the same data simultaneously while preserving the fidelity and provenance of the data. The technology could be used to build and maintain applications with multiple internal or external users working in Excel, a web form, or a mobile environment as the user interface.

Clients use the company's technology for supply chain management, retail, information technology, financial planning and analysis, payroll management, performance management, project and portfolio management, deal price management, trade and procurement spend management and tax management.

Operations are located in the United States and India, which provide enterprise software-as-a-service (SaaS) to global customers.

Predecessor Detail - Name changed from Wood Composite Technologies Inc., June 4, 2018, following reverse takeover acquisition of Boardwalktech, Inc.; basis 1 new for 410 old shs.

Directors - Andrew T. Duncan, chr., pres. & CEO, Menlo Park, Calif.; Charles (Charlie) Glavin, CFO & corp. sec., Lafayette, Calif.; Ravi (Ganesh) Krishnan, chief tech. officer, Cupertino, Calif.; Steve Bennet, Palo Alto, Calif.

Other Exec. Officers - Dharmesh Dadbhawala, chief product officer; Glenn Cordingley, sr. v-p, bus. devel.; James B. Kuppe, sr. v-p, sales & mktg.; Sarang Kulkarni, v-p, eng.

Capital Stock

	Authorized (shs.)	Outstanding (shs.)[1]
Common	unlimited	4,810,099
Non-vtg. Com.	unlimited	1,399,146

[1] At June 27, 2023

Common - One vote per share.
Non-voting Common - Entitled to the same rights as the common shares, including dividend rights. Convertible into common shares on a one-for-one basis.
Major Shareholder - SQN Venture Income Fund held 16.9% interest at Apr. 20, 2022.

Price Range - BWLK/TSX-VEN

Year	Volume	High	Low	Close
2022	9,787,147	$0.94	$0.28	$0.82
2021	12,932,899	$1.44	$0.61	$0.70
2020	2,922,676	$0.84	$0.33	$0.61
2019	2,265,856	$0.70	$0.34	$0.35
2018	795,194	$5.25	$0.55	$0.71

Recent Close: $0.51
Capital Stock Changes - During fiscal 2023, common shares were issued as follows: 4,296,533 on vesting of restricted share units and 1,245,656 on exercise of warrants.

During fiscal 2022, 541,795 common shares were issued on exercise of warrants.

Wholly Owned Subsidiaries

Boardwalktech, Inc., Cupertino, Calif.
- 98% int. in **BoardwalkTech Solutions Private Limited**, India.

Financial Statistics

Periods ended:	12m Mar. 31/23^A		12m Mar. 31/22^A
	US$000s	%Chg	US$000s
Operating revenue	**6,475**	**+48**	**4,375**
Cost of sales	608		587
Salaries & benefits	5,266		4,738
General & admin expense	2,213		979
Stock-based compensation	1,566		1,265
Operating expense	**9,653**	**+28**	**7,568**
Operating income	**(3,178)**	**n.a.**	**(3,194)**
Deprec., depl. & amort.	345		337
Pre-tax income	**(3,564)**	**n.a.**	**(3,549)**
Income taxes	20		15
Net income	**(3,584)**	**n.a.**	**(3,564)**
Cash & equivalent	2,187		869
Accounts receivable	1,331		2,515
Current assets	3,669		3,537
Fixed assets, net	14		17
Right-of-use assets	100		432
Total assets	**3,783**	**-5**	**3,986**
Accts. pay. & accr. liabs	1,229		412
Current liabilities	4,746		3,432
Long-term lease liabilities	nil		128
Shareholders' equity	(962)		426
Cash from oper. activs	**1,121**	**n.a.**	**(2,297)**
Cash from fin. activs	215		88
Cash from invest. activs	(15)		(22)
Net cash position	**2,187**	**+152**	**869**
Capital expenditures	(15)		(22)
	US$		US$
Earnings per share*	(0.08)		(0.08)
Cash flow per share*	0.02		(0.05)
	shs		shs
No. of shs. o/s*	48,100,998		42,558,809
Avg. no. of shs. o/s*	45,434,261		42,637,114
	%		%
Net profit margin	(55.35)		(81.46)
Return on equity	n.m.		(245.45)
Return on assets	(92.26)		(84.23)

* Com. & N.V. Com.
^A Reported in accordance with IFRS

Historical Summary
(as originally stated)

Fiscal Year	Oper. Rev.	Net Inc. Bef. Disc.	EPS*
	US$000s	US$000s	US$
2023^A	6,475	(3,584)	(0.08)
2022^A	4,375	(3,564)	(0.08)
2021^A	4,343	(3,610)	(0.15)
2020^A	4,636	(5,819)	(0.45)
	$000s	$000s	$
2019^A1	4,917	(20,859)	(2.11)

* Com. & N.V. Com.
^A Reported in accordance with IFRS
[1] Results reflect the June 6, 2018 reverse takeover acquisition of Boardwalktech, Inc.

B.91 Boat Rocker Media Inc.

Symbol - BRMI **Exchange** - TSX **CUSIP** - 09664U
Head Office - 310 King St E, Toronto, ON, M5A 1K6 **Telephone** - (416) 591-0065 **Fax** - (416) 591-0075
Website - www.boatrocker.com
Email - sam@boatrocker.com
Investor Relations - Samantha Traub (416) 591-5725
Auditors - PricewaterhouseCoopers LLP C.A., Toronto, Ont.
Transfer Agents - TSX Trust Company, Toronto, Ont.
Employees - 950 at Dec. 31, 2022
Profile - (Ont. 2003) Creates, produces and distributes television programs for all platforms and provides talent management services to celebrities and performers.

Operations are carried out through three business segments: Television; Kids and Family; and Representation.

The **Television** segment includes live action scripted and unscripted video content production and owned IP (intellectual property) distribution, but excluding kids and family content.

The **Kids and Family** segment includes kids and family live-action scripted and unscripted content and all animated content, as well as owned IP distribution, franchise management and brand management.

The **Representation** segment includes brand and management services provided to talent and IP representation services to third-party IP owners.

Brands include Boat Rocker Studios, Scripted, Proper Productions, Insight Productions, Matador Content, Jam Filled Entertainment and Untitled Entertainment.

Directors - David Fortier, co-founder & exec. co-chr., Toronto, Ont.; Ivan Schneeberg, co-founder & exec. co-chr., Toronto, Ont.; John Young, CEO, Toronto, Ont.; Sangeeta Desai†, Founex, Switzerland; Katherine Cunningham, Toronto, Ont.; Ellis Jacob, Toronto, Ont.; Quinn McLean, Toronto, Ont.

Other Exec. Officers - Michel Pratte, pres.; Judy Adam, CFO; Samantha (Sam) Traub, chief corp. officer & gen. counsel; Cindy Brown, exec. v-p, HR; Kyle MacDougall, pres., Jam Filled Entertainment Inc.; Jay Peterson, pres., Boat Rocker Studios, unscripted; Jon Rutherford, pres., Boat Rocker Studios, kids & family & rights

† Lead director

Capital Stock

	Authorized (shs.)	Outstanding (shs.)[1]
Multiple Vtg.	unlimited	23,553,050
Subordinate Vtg.	unlimited	32,774,434

[1] At Apr. 25, 2023

Multiple Voting - Convertible into subordinate voting shares on a one-for-one basis. Entitled to up to 10 votes per share. The number of votes to which a holder of multiple voting shares is entitled to will be determined by whether such holder is a Canadian person (10 votes) or non-Canadian person (a variable number of votes, not less than one and not exceeding 10). All held by Fairfax Financial Holdings Limited, David Fortier, Ivan Schneeberg and John Young.

Subordinate Voting - One vote per share.

Normal Course Issuer Bid - The company plans to make normal course purchases of up to 1,000,000 subordinate voting shares representing 3% of the total outstanding. The bid commenced on Sept. 1, 2022, and expires on Aug. 31, 2023.

Major Shareholder - Fairfax Financial Holdings Limited held 56.1% interest and David Fortier & Ivan Schneeberg collectively held 32.4% interest at Apr. 28, 2023.

Price Range - BRMI/TSX

Year	Volume	High	Low	Close
2022	1,095,277	$7.04	$2.05	$2.58
2021	1,831,676	$9.19	$6.12	$6.90

Recent Close: $1.81

Capital Stock Changes - During 2022, 99,722 subordinate voting shares were issued on vesting of restricted share units and 12,562 subordinate voting shares were repurchased under the Normal Course Issuer Bid.

Wholly Owned Subsidiaries

Boat Rocker Media (U.S.) Inc., Del.
- 100% int. in **Boat Rocker Media (U.S.) LLC**, Del.
  - 100% int. in **Boat Rocker Studios, Scripted, LLC**, Los Angeles, Calif.
    - 100% int. in **Platform One Media Productions LLC**, Del.
      - 100% int. in **Ceteri Production, LLC**, Del.
      - 100% int. in **Fidelis Productions, LLC**, Del.
      - 100% int. in **Rubigo LLC**, Del.
      - 100% int. in **Salvos, LLC**, Del.
  - 51% int. in **Untitled Entertainment LLC**, Los Angeles, Calif.
- 100% int. in **Matador Content, LLC**, New York, N.Y.

Boat Rocker Rights (HK) Ltd., Hong Kong, People's Republic of China.
Boat Rocker Rights Inc., Ont.
Boat Rocker Rights (U.K.) Ltd., United Kingdom.
Boat Rocker Rights (US) Inc., Toronto, Ont.
Boat Rocker Sports Inc., Ont.
Boat Rocker Ventures Inc., Ont.
Proper Productions Inc., Ont.
Temple Street Development Corporation, Ont.
TritonHQ Inc., Ont.

Subsidiaries

70% int. in **Insight Productions Ltd.**, Toronto, Ont.

Note: The preceding list includes only the major related companies in which interests are held.

Financial Statistics

Periods ended:	12m Dec. 31/22[A]		12m Dec. 31/21[A]
	$000s	%Chg	$000s
Operating revenue	**304,281**	**-48**	**580,369**
Cost of sales	94,416		148,907
Salaries & benefits	70,384		66,544
General & admin expense	21,112		19,550
Stock-based compensation	1,089		4,594
Operating expense	**187,001**	**-22**	**239,595**
Operating income	**117,280**	**-66**	**340,774**
Deprec., depl. & amort.	107,179		347,247
Finance income	542		380
Finance costs, gross	6,768		5,122
Investment income	529		(26)
Pre-tax income	**7,252**	**n.a.**	**(5,928)**
Income taxes	5,456		6,153
Net income	**1,796**	**n.a.**	**(12,081)**
Net inc. for equity hldrs	**(7,506)**	**n.a.**	**(20,656)**
Net inc. for non-cont. int.	**9,302**	**+8**	**8,575**
Cash & equivalent	85,794		96,950
Accounts receivable	107,277		109,608
Current assets	270,585		271,204
Long-term investments	1,424		895
Fixed assets, net	7,337		9,056
Right-of-use assets	17,753		21,103
Intangibles, net	128,943		132,873
Total assets	**796,547**	**+32**	**603,539**
Accts. pay. & accr. liabs.	73,944		80,714
Current liabilities	450,966		255,813
Long-term lease liabilities	15,480		18,600
Shareholders' equity	231,752		235,069
Non-controlling interest	29,900		28,710
Cash from oper. activs.	**(74,131)**	**n.a.**	**(16,875)**
Cash from fin. activs.	68,081		47,794
Cash from invest. activs.	(1,890)		(5,667)
Net cash position	**85,794**	**-12**	**96,950**
Capital expenditures	(1,183)		(2,705)
	$		$
Earnings per share*	(0.13)		(0.41)
Cash flow per share*	(1.32)		(0.34)
	shs		shs
No. of shs. o/s*	56,255,575		56,168,415
Avg. no. of shs. o/s*	56,227,941		50,111,674
	%		%
Net profit margin	0.59		(2.08)
Return on equity	(3.22)		(15.51)
Return on assets	0.50		(0.26)
Foreign sales percent	74		91
No. of employees (FTEs)	950		850

* S.V. & M.V.

[A] Reported in accordance with IFRS

Historical Summary
(as originally stated)

Fiscal Year	Oper. Rev.	Net Inc. Bef. Disc.	EPS*
	$000s	$000s	$
2022[A]	304,281	1,796	(0.13)
2021[A]	580,369	(12,081)	(0.41)
2020[A]	226,803	(43,990)	(3.09)
2019[A]	244,165	(19,483)	(1.60)
2018[A]	164,845	9,757	0.62

* S.V. & M.V.

[A] Reported in accordance with IFRS

B.92 Body and Mind Inc.

Symbol - BAMM **Exchange** - CSE **CUSIP** - 09689V
Head Office - 750-1095 Pender St W, Vancouver, BC, V6E 2M6
Telephone - (604) 376-3567 **Toll-free** - (800) 361-6312
Website - www.bodyandmind.com
Email - dongshim@shimaccounting.com
Investor Relations - Dong H. Shim (604) 376-3567
Auditors - Sadler, Gibb & Associates, LLC C.P.A.
Lawyers - McMillan LLP, Vancouver, B.C.
Transfer Agents - New Horizon Transfer Inc., Vancouver, B.C.

Profile - (Nev. 2010) Has cannabis cultivation, processing, distribution and retail operations in Nevada, California, Ohio, Arkansas and Michigan.

Owns and operates an 18,000-sq.-ft. cultivation facility and a 7,500-sq.-ft. production facility in Las Vegas, Nev.; three dispensaries in San Diego, Long Beach and Seaside, Calif.; a 4,000-sq.-ft. production facility and dispensary in Elyria, Ohio; a 6,500-sq.-ft. cultivation facility and dispensary in West Memphis, Ark; and 5,000 sq. ft. of processing; and a dispensary in Muskegon, Mich. Also developing a manufacturing facility in California; cultivation and production facilities in Manistee, Mich., with 50,000 sq. ft. of cultivation; and dispensary in New Jersey.

Products produced include cannabis flower, pre-rolls, oils, concentrates, vape pens, cartridges and edibles which are marketed under the Body and Mind brand as well as licensed third-party brands such as Her Highness and Gpen.

In December 2022, the company acquired **CarftedPlants NJ, Inc.**, which owns a retail location with local cannabis-use approval in New Jersey, for US$170,000 cash and issuance of 16,666,667 common shares at a deemed price of Cdn$0.08 per share.

In December 2022, the company acquired the remaining 20% of **Canopy Monterey Bay, LLC.**, which owns a retail dispensary in Seaside, Calif., for issuance of 16,301,694 common shares. The company previously acquired 80% interest in Canopy for US$1,250,000 cash, issuance of US$1,250,000 of common shares and a US$2,300,000 10% secured promissory note due 2027.

In March 2022, wholly owned **NMG Cathedral, LLC** was dissolved.

Predecessor Detail - Name changed from Deploy Technologies Inc., Dec. 7, 2017; basis 1 new for 3 old shs.

Directors - Michael Mills, pres. & CEO; Stephen (Trip) Hoffman, COO; Alexis Podesta; Brent Reuter, Vancouver, B.C.; Joshua N. (Josh) Rosen, Scottsdale, Ariz.

Other Exec. Officers - Dong H. (Don) Shim, CFO; Darren Tindale, corp. sec.

Capital Stock

	Authorized (shs.)	Outstanding (shs.)[1]	Par
Common	900,000,000	146,636,974	US$0.0001

[1] At Feb. 3, 2023

Major Shareholder - Widely held at Feb. 3, 2023.

Price Range - BAMM/CSE

Year	Volume	High	Low	Close
2022	29,317,275	$0.40	$0.07	$0.09
2021	33,631,042	$1.14	$0.30	$0.39
2020	24,807,582	$0.72	$0.22	$0.49
2019	78,977,100	$3.71	$0.51	$0.55
2018	39,218,703	$2.09	$0.33	$0.54

Recent Close: $0.08

Capital Stock Changes - In December 2022, 16,301,694 common shares were issued pursuant to the acquisition of the remaining 20% of Canopy Monterey Bay, LLC.

In December 2021, 2,728,156 common shares were issued pursuant to the acquisition of an 80% interest in Canopy Monterey Bay, LLC. Also during fiscal 2022, 1,862,679 common shares were issued for operating leases.

Wholly Owned Subsidiaries

DEP Nevada Inc., Nev.
- 100% int. in **BaM Body and Mind Dispensary NJ Inc.**, N.J. formerly CraftedPlants NJ Corp.
- 100% int. in **Canopy Monterey Bay, LLC**, Calif.
- 100% int. in **NMG CA C1, LLC**, Calif.
- 100% int. in **NMG CA P1, LLC**, Calif.
- 100% int. in **NMG MI C1 Inc.**, Mich.
- 100% int. in **NMG MI 1, Inc.**, Mich.
- 100% int. in **NMG MI P1 Inc.**, Mich.
- 100% int. in **NMG OH P1, LLC**, Ohio
- 100% int. in **NMG OH1, LLC**, Ohio
- 100% int. in **Nevada Medical Group LLC**, Nev.
  - 100% int. in **NMG Long Beach, LLC**, Calif.
  - 100% int. in **NMG Ohio, LLC**, Ohio
  - 60% int. in **NMG San Diego, LLC**, Calif.

Financial Statistics

Periods ended:	12m July 31/22[A]		12m July 31/21[oA]
	US$000s	%Chg	US$000s
Operating revenue	**31,638**	**+18**	**26,901**
Cost of sales	19,702		13,110
Salaries & benefits	3,908		3,400
General & admin expense	7,773		5,138
Stock-based compensation	435		976
Operating expense	**31,818**	**+41**	**22,624**
Operating income	**(180)**	**n.a.**	**4,277**
Deprec., depl. & amort.	1,486		1,197
Finance income	72		164
Finance costs, gross	1,372		53
Investment income	nil		13
Write-downs/write-offs	(20,517)		(593)
Pre-tax income	**(25,635)**	**n.a.**	**190**
Income taxes	2,593		2,167
Net income	**(28,228)**	**n.a.**	**(1,976)**
Net inc. for equity hldrs	**(28,677)**	**n.a.**	**(2,261)**
Net inc. for non-cont. int	**448**	**+58**	**284**
Cash & equivalent	1,854		7,374
Inventories	3,880		2,936
Accounts receivable	476		1,545
Current assets	7,998		14,307
Fixed assets, net	5,641		4,894
Right-of-use assets	4,163		2,539
Intangibles, net	11,861		25,024
Total assets	**31,026**	**-36**	**48,126**
Accts. pay. & accr. liabs	2,815		1,792
Current liabilities	6,617		6,454
Long-term debt, gross	7,406		4,816
Long-term debt, net	7,394		4,799
Long-term lease liabilities	5,515		2,324
Shareholders' equity	9,630		34,324
Non-controlling interest	475		27
Cash from oper. activs	**(3,444)**	**n.a.**	**295**
Cash from fin. activs	(27)		6,166
Cash from invest. activs	(2,145)		(832)
Net cash position	**1,854**	**-75**	**7,374**
Capital expenditures	(828)		(402)
	US$		US$
Earnings per share*	(0.25)		(0.02)
Cash flow per share*	(0.03)		0.00
	shs		shs
No. of shs. o/s*	113,668,613		109,077,778
Avg. no. of shs. o/s*	112,209,254		108,463,019
	%		%
Net profit margin	(89.22)		(7.35)
Return on equity	(130.48)		(6.66)
Return on assets	(67.51)		(5.82)
Foreign sales percent	100		100

* Common
[o] Restated
[A] Reported in accordance with U.S. GAAP

Latest Results

Periods ended:	3m Oct. 31/22[A]		3m Oct. 31/21[A]
	US$000s	%Chg	US$000s
Operating revenue	7,832	+3	7,571
Net income	(2,953)	n.a.	(677)
Net inc. for equity hldrs	(3,055)	n.a.	(789)
Net inc. for non-cont. int	102		112
	US$		US$
Earnings per share*	(0.03)		(0.01)

* Common
[A] Reported in accordance with U.S. GAAP

Historical Summary
(as originally stated)

Fiscal Year	Oper. Rev. US$000s	Net Inc. Bef. Disc. US$000s	EPS* US$
2022[A]	31,638	(28,228)	(0.25)
2021[A]	25,700	(1,976)	(0.02)
2020[A]	5,287	(4,598)	(0.04)
2019[A]	4,612	(3,753)	(0.05)
2018[A1]	2,413	(1,781)	(0.05)

* Common
[A] Reported in accordance with U.S. GAAP
[1] Results reflect the Nov. 14, 2017, reverse takeover acquisition of Nevada Medical Group LLC.

B.93 Bold Capital Enterprises Ltd.

Symbol - BOLD.P **Exchange** - TSX-VEN **CUSIP** - 09753B
Head Office - 3500-800 rue du Square Victoria, Montréal, QC, H4Z 1E9 **Telephone** - (514) 332-1656
Email - peter.rona@sympatico.ca
Investor Relations - Peter Rona (514) 332-1656
Auditors - Mallette LLP C.A., Québec, Qué.
Lawyers - Fasken Martineau DuMoulin LLP, Montréal, Qué.
Transfer Agents - TSX Trust Company, Toronto, Ont.
Profile - (Can. 2018) Capital Pool Company.

Recent Merger and Acquisition Activity

Status: terminated **Revised:** Mar. 31, 2023
UPDATE: The transaction was terminated. PREVIOUS: Bold Capital Enterprises Ltd. entered into a letter of intent for the Qualifying Transaction reverse takeover acquisition of SinuSafe Medical Ltd., which develops, manufactures, and sells minimal invasive medical devices for otolaryngologists (ENT physicians) to facilitate earlier surgical interventions for Sinusitis patients. A total of 134,000,000 common shares were expected to be issued to SinuSafe shareholders at a deemed price of 20¢ per share. In addition, up to an additional 84,000,000 common shares of the resulting issuer may be issued to the shareholders of SinuSafe upon the resulting issuer achieving four performance milestones. Bold plans to complete a concurrent private placement of units (1 common share & 1 warrant) for gross proceeds of a minimum of $6,500,000 and a maximum of $9,000,000.

Directors - Peter Rona, pres., CEO & corp. sec., Montréal, Qué.; Nabil Ishak, CFO, Pierrefonds, Qué.; Edward Ierfino, Saint-Bruno, Qué.; John Paradias, Laval, Qué.

Capital Stock

	Authorized (shs.)	Outstanding (shs.)[1]
Common	unlimited	47,264,500

[1] At May 30, 2023

Major Shareholder - John Paradias held 11.9% interest at May 26, 2021.

Price Range - BOLD.P/TSX-VEN

Year	Volume	High	Low	Close
2022	287,000	$0.24	$0.16	$0.16
2021	377,100	$0.21	$0.06	$0.20
2020	158,000	$0.12	$0.06	$0.06
2019	692,000	$0.25	$0.09	$0.12

Capital Stock Changes - There were no changes to capital stock during 2022.

B.94 Bombardier Inc.*

Symbol - BBD.B **Exchange** - TSX **CUSIP** - 097751
Head Office - 400 ch de la Côte-Vertu O, Dorval, QC, H4S 1Y9
Telephone - (514) 861-9481 **Fax** - (514) 861-2746
Website - www.bombardier.com
Email - francis.richer.de.la.fleche@bombardier.com
Investor Relations - Francis Richer de la Flèche (514) 240-9679
Auditors - Ernst & Young LLP C.A., Montréal, Qué.
Transfer Agents - Computershare Trust Company of Canada Inc., Montréal, Qué.
FP500 Revenue Ranking - 67
Employees - 15,900 at Dec. 31, 2022
Profile - (Can. 1902, via letters patent) Designs, manufactures and services business aircraft.

The company designs, manufactures and provides aftermarket support for Challenger (consists of the Challenger 350, Challenger 3500 and Challenger 650) and Global (consists of the Global 5000, Global 5500, Global 6000, Global 6500 and Global 7500, as well as the Global 8000, which was expected to enter into service in 2025) families of business jets. Also provides pre-owned aircraft, through its Certified Pre-owned Aircraft program.

Through Bombardier Defence, its specialized aircraft division, supports the needs of government and other special mission providers around the world by adapting its jets to cover a broad range of mission types including surveillance and reconnaissance, medical evacuations and dignitary transport. Services range from turnkey packages consisting the complete design, building, testing and certification activities, through to specialist engineering support and technical oversight of customer specific projects.

Through Customer Services group, the company offers maintenance, parts and smart services, and 24/7 customer support. Maintenance services include refurbishment and modification of business aircraft, and component repair and overhaul services. Smart parts and smart services include the offering of manufacturer approved parts, as well as repairs to customer-owned parts, and a portfolio of cost-per-flight-hour parts and maintenance plans available for Learjet, Challenger and Global aircraft. 24/7 customer support includes 24-hour customer response centres, enhanced online services tools, customer services engineering, mobile response team, structural repair, technical publications and Entry-Into-Service support.

Has a fleet of 5,000 aircraft in-service with a variety of multinational corporations, charter and fractional ownership providers, governments and private individuals.

Has production and engineering sites in Montreal, Que., Toronto, Ont., Wichita, Kan., Red Oak, Tex., and Querétaro, Mexico, as well as international service and support network across the globe.

Business Aircraft Deliveries

Year ended Dec. 31	2022	2021
Learjet[1]	3	10
Challenger	50	44
Global	70	66
	123	120

[1] The company delivered its last Learjet aircraft in the first quarter of 2022, but continues to provide aftermarket support for the Learjet family of aircraft.

In July 2023, the company acquired the Latécoère's electrical wiring interconnection system business in Querétaro, Mexico, for an undisclosed amount. The business manufactures electrical harnesses.

During 2022, new service centres were opened in Singapore, Melbourne, Australia and Miami-Dade cty., Fla., and broke ground on a new service centre in Abu Dhabi, U.A.E., which was targeted to open in 2025.

On Sept. 20, 2022, the Challenger 3500 business jet, which represents a major update to the Challenger 350 platform, entered into service.

On Apr. 19, 2022, the company announced the designation of its Wichita, Kan., site as its new U.S. headquarters. This site would also be home to the newly renamed Bombardier Defence division, reflecting the company's strategic expansion of its existing Specialized Aircraft division.

Also in April 2022, the company announced additional firm orders for modified versions of its Global 6000 aircraft, as part of a potential US$465,000,000 order from the United States Air Force in support of the Battlefield Airborne Communications Node program.

Predecessor Detail - Name changed from Bombardier-MLW Ltd., June 23, 1978.

Directors - Pierre Beaudoin, chr., Knowlton, Qué.; Éric Martel, pres. & CEO, Mont-Royal, Qué.; Douglas R. (Doug) Oberhelman†, Ill.; Joanne Bissonnette, Montréal, Qué.; Charles Bombardier, Montréal, Qué.; Rose Damen, Netherlands; Diane Fontaine, Montréal, Qué.; Ji-Xun Foo, Shanghai, Shanghai, People's Republic of China; Diane Giard, Shefford, Qué.; Anthony R. Graham, Toronto, Ont.; Melinda M. Rogers-Hixon, Toronto, Ont.; Eric Sprunk, Seattle, Wash.; Antony N. Tyler, Hong Kong, People's Republic of China

Other Exec. Officers - Barton W. (Bart) Demosky, exec. v-p & CFO; Éric Filion, exec. v-p, programs & supply chain; Jean-Christophe Gallagher, exec. v-p, aircraft sales & Bombardier defense; David Murray, exec. v-p, mfg., IT & Bombardier operational excellence sys.; Paul Sislian, exec. v-p, Bombardier aftermarket srvcs. & strategy; Daniel (Dan) Brennan, sr. v-p, people & sustainability; Peter Likoray, sr. v-p, sales, new aircraft; François Ouellette, sr. v-p, legal srvcs. & contracts; Annie Torkia Lagacé, sr. v-p, gen. counsel & corp. sec.; Ève Laurier, v-p, commun., public affairs & mktg.; Martin LeBlanc, v-p & chief ethics & compliance officer
† Lead director

Capital Stock

	Authorized (shs.)	Outstanding (shs.)[1]
Preferred	unlimited	
Series 2	12,000,000	2,684,527
Series 3	12,000,000	9,315,473
Series 4	9,400,000	9,400,000
Cl.A Mult. Vtg.	143,680,000	12,349,370
Cl.B Subord. Vtg.	143,680,000	83,198,483

[1] At Aug. 1, 2023

Preferred - Non-voting and issuable in series.

Series 2 Preferred - Entitled to cumulative preferential cash dividends at a floating rate set between 50% to 100% of the Canadian prime rate, adjusted upwards or downwards on a monthly basis to a monthly maximum of 4% if the trading price of the series 2 preferred shares is less than Cdn$24.90 per share or more than Cdn$25.10 per share. Redeemable at Cdn$25.50 per share. Convertible on a 1-for-1 basis on Aug. 1, 2027, and on August 1 of every fifth year thereafter into series 3 preferred shares.

Series 3 Preferred - Entitled to cumulative preferential cash dividends of 4.588% (Cdn$1.147) per share per annum for the period from Aug. 1, 2022, to July 31, 2027. For each succeeding five-year period, the applicable fixed annual dividend rate shall not be less than 80% of the Government of Canada bond yield. Redeemable at Cdn$25 per share on Aug. 1, 2027, and on August 1 of every fifth year thereafter. Convertible on a 1-for-1 basis on Aug. 1, 2027, and on August 1 of every fifth year thereafter into series 2 preferred shares.

Series 4 Preferred - Entitled to cumulative preferential cash dividends of 6.25% (Cdn$1.5625) per share per annum. Redeemable at Cdn$25 per share. Convertible into class B subordinate voting shares on the basis of dividing the then applicable redemption price together with all accrued and unpaid dividends by the greater of Cdn$2.00 and 95% of the weighted average trading price of the class B shares for a period of 20 consecutive trading days.

Class A Multiple Voting - Convertible, at option of holder, at any time into class B subordinate voting shares on a share-for-share basis. Ten votes per share.

Class B Subordinate Voting - In the event of liquidation, dissolution or winding-up, class B shares rank on a parity with class A shares except that class B shareholders are entitled to vote separately as a class. Convertible into class A shares on a share-for-share basis in the event that an offer to all or substantially all holders of class A shares to acquire such shares is accepted by the present controlling shareholder of the company; or if the controlling shareholder ceases to hold more than 50% of the outstanding class A shares. One vote per share.

Options - At Dec. 31, 2022, options were outstanding to purchase 3,683,172 class B subordinate voting shares at a weighted average exercise price of Cdn$56.52 per share with a weighted average remaining life of up to 3 years.

Normal Course Issuer Bid - The company plans to make normal course purchases of up to 600,000 class B subordinate voting shares representing 0.7% of the total outstanding. The bid commenced on May 23, 2023, and expires on May 22, 2024.

Major Shareholder - Bombardier family held 48.13% interest at Mar. 6, 2023.

Price Range - BBD.B/TSX

Year	Volume	High	Low	Close
2022	93,826,440	$55.50	$18.30	$52.27
2021	76,365,688	$56.88	$11.58	$42.00
2020	118,781,376	$49.25	$6.50	$12.00
2019	79,980,736	$75.75	$38.25	$48.25
2018	97,350,032	$139.50	$39.63	$50.75

Consolidation: 1-for-25 cons. in June 2022

Recent Close: $52.84

Capital Stock Changes - On June 13, 2022, class A multiple voting shares and class B subordinate voting shares were consolidated on a 1-for-25 basis. In August 2022, 3,127,209 series 2 preferred shares were converted into a like number of series 3 preferred shares. Also during 2022, 288,363 post-consolidated class B subordinate voting shares were issued for cash and 149,592 post-consolidated class B subordinate voting share were repurchased under a Normal Course Issuer Bid. In addition, 1,578,085 post-consolidated class B subordinate voting shares were purchased and held in trust under the performance and restricted share unit plans and 23,669 post-consolidated class B subordinate voting shares were distributed and held in trust under the performance and restricted share unit plans.

Dividends

BBD.PR.B pfd ser 2 cum. red. exch. Fltg. Ra pa M

$0.15**e**	Sept. 15/23	$0.148	Aug. 15/23
$0.1436	July 15/23	$0.1396	June 15/23

Paid in 2023: $1.2674**e** 2022: $0.9507 2021: $0.612

BBD.PR.C pfd ser 4 cum. red. cv exch. Ra $1.5625 pa Q**

BBD.PR.D pfd ser 3 cum. red. exch. Adj. Ra $1.147 pa Q est. Oct. 31, 2022**

** Reinvestment Option **e** Estimate

Long-Term Debt - Outstanding at Dec. 31, 2022:

7.5% sr. notes due Dec. 2024	US$395,000,000
7.5% sr. notes due Mar. 2025	1,136,000,000
7.13% sr. notes due June 2026	1,191,000,000
7.88% sr. notes due Apr. 2027	1,880,000,000
6% sr. notes due Feb. 2028	743,000,000
7.45% sr. notes due May 2034	507,000,000
7.35% debs. due Dec. 2026[1]	110,000,000
Other loans[2]	18,000,000
	5,980,000,000
Less: Current portion	nil
	5,980,000,000

[1] Cdn$150,000,000.

[2] Bearing interest at a weighted average rate of 7.95% and due in April 2026.

Note - In January 2023, offering of US$750,000,000 7.5% senior notes due Feb. 1, 2029, was completed. Net proceeds were used to redeem all outstanding 7.5% senior notes due 2024 and to finance the cash tender offer to purchase US$500,000,000 of its 7.5% senior notes due 2025.

Wholly Owned Subsidiaries

Learjet Inc., Wichita, Kan.

Note: The preceding list includes only the major related companies in which interests are held.

Financial Statistics

Periods ended:	12m Dec. 31/22^A		12m Dec. 31/21^A
	US$000s	%Chg	US$000s
Operating revenue	**6,913,000**	**+14**	**6,085,000**
Cost of sales	5,241,000		4,744,000
Research & devel. expense	360,000		338,000
General & admin expense	395,000		355,000
Operating expense	**5,996,000**	**+10**	**5,437,000**
Operating income	**917,000**	**+42**	**648,000**
Deprec., depl. & amort.	415,000		417,000
Finance income	33,000		324,000
Finance costs, gross	817,000		936,000
Write-downs/write-offs	(3,000)		nil
Pre-tax income	**(246,000)**	**n.a.**	**(371,000)**
Income taxes	(118,000)		(122,000)
Net inc bef disc ops, eqhldrs	(128,000)		(249,000)
Net inc. bef. disc. opers	**(128,000)**	**n.a.**	**(249,000)**
Disc. opers., equity hldrs	(20,000)		5,290,000
Disc. opers., NCI	nil		29,000
Income from disc. opers	(20,000)		5,319,000
Net income	**(148,000)**	**n.a.**	**5,070,000**
Net inc. for equity hldrs	**(148,000)**	**n.a.**	**5,041,000**
Net inc. for non-cont. int	**nil**	**n.a.**	**29,000**
Cash & equivalent	1,291,000		1,675,000
Inventories	3,322,000		3,242,000
Accounts receivable	252,000		269,000
Current assets	5,585,000		5,481,000
Fixed assets, net	1,214,000		837,000
Intangibles, net	3,873,000		4,129,000
Total assets	**12,324,000**	**-3**	**12,764,000**
Accts. pay. & accr. liabs	1,286,000		1,164,000
Current liabilities	5,437,000		4,768,000
Long-term debt, gross	5,980,000		7,047,000
Long-term debt, net	5,980,000		7,047,000
Long-term lease liabilities	448,000		269,000
Preferred share equity	347,000		347,000
Shareholders' equity	(2,762,000)		(3,089,000)
Cash from oper. activs	**1,072,000**	**n.a.**	**(289,000)**
Cash from fin. activs	(1,132,000)		(2,965,000)
Cash from invest. activs	(325,000)		2,500,000
Net cash position	**1,291,000**	**-23**	**1,675,000**
Capital expenditures	(355,000)		(237,000)
Capital disposals	18,000		5,000
Unfunded pension liability	277,000		747,000
	US$		US$
Earns. per sh. bef disc opers*	(1.67)		(3.00)
Earnings per share*	(1.88)		52.00
Cash flow per share*	11.34		(2.92)
	shs		shs
No. of shs. o/s*	94,095,684		95,511,329
Avg. no. of shs. o/s*	94,496,000		96,333,640
	%		%
Net profit margin	(1.85)		(4.09)
Return on equity	n.m.		n.m.
Return on assets	2.37		2.12
Foreign sales percent	95		92
No. of employees (FTEs)	15,900		13,800

* Class A & B

^A Reported in accordance with IFRS

Latest Results

Periods ended:	6m June 30/23^A		6m June 30/22^A
	US$000s	%Chg	US$000s
Operating revenue	3,128,000	+12	2,803,000
Net inc. bef. disc. opers	312,000	n.a.	(396,000)
Income from disc. opers	(45,000)		(20,000)
Net income	267,000	n.a.	(416,000)
	US$		US$
Earns. per sh. bef. disc. opers.*	3.13		(4.31)
Earnings per share*	2.65		(4.52)

* Class A & B

^A Reported in accordance with IFRS

Historical Summary
(as originally stated)

Fiscal Year	Oper. Rev. US$000s	Net Inc. Bef. Disc. US$000s	EPS* US$
2022^A	6,913,000	(128,000)	(1.67)
2021^A	6,085,000	(249,000)	(3.00)
2020^A	6,487,000	(170,000)	(2.00)
2019^A	15,757,000	(1,607,000)	(19.00)
2018^A	16,236,000	318,000	2.50

* Class A & B

^A Reported in accordance with IFRS

Note: Adjusted throughout for 1-for-25 cons. in June 2022

B.95 Bonanza Mining Corporation

Symbol - BNZ **Exchange** - TSX-VEN **CUSIP** - 09790B

Head Office - 423 10 St E, North Vancouver, BC, V7L 2E5 **Telephone** - (604) 619-0225 **Fax** - (604) 980-6264

Email - bonanzamining@shaw.ca

Investor Relations - Alfredo De Lucrezia (604) 619-0225

Auditors - Davidson & Company LLP C.A., Vancouver, B.C.

Lawyers - Tupper Jonsson & Yeadon, Vancouver, B.C.

Transfer Agents - Computershare Trust Company of Canada Inc., Vancouver, B.C.

Profile - (B.C. 2016) Has mineral interests in British Columbia.

Holds MC polymetallic prospect, 903 hectares, 14 km northeast of Stewart; option to acquire Shag zinc-lead-silver prospect, 4,052 hectares, 24 km northeast of Canal Flats, requiring exploration expenditures of $1,000,000 over four years to Dec. 31, 2025; and option to acquire Frog polymetallic prospect, 9,429 hectares, Liard Mining dist., requiring exploration expenditures of $1,000,000 over four years to Dec. 31, 2025.

Predecessor Detail - Name changed from Califfi Capital Corp., Aug. 5, 2021.

Directors - Alfredo De Lucrezia, pres. & CEO, North Vancouver, B.C.; Christopher W. Graf, v-p, explor., Wardner, B.C.; Andrew S. (Drew) Burgess, Calgary, Alta.; Charles J. (Charlie) Greig, Penticton, B.C.; Dayton R. Marks, Ont.; John L. Pallot, New Westminster, B.C.

Other Exec. Officers - Daniel (Dan) Martino, CFO; Glenn R. Yeadon, corp. sec.

Capital Stock

	Authorized (shs.)	Outstanding (shs.)[1]
Common	unlimited	50,142,202

[1] At July 20, 2023

Major Shareholder - Alfredo De Lucrezia held 11.38% interest at Oct. 3, 2022.

Price Range - BNZ/TSX-VEN

Year	Volume	High	Low	Close
2022	1,275,726	$0.18	$0.05	$0.06
2021	2,406,120	$0.21	$0.11	$0.12
2019	36,000	$0.17	$0.15	$0.15
2018	522,175	$0.30	$0.15	$0.17

Recent Close: $0.05

Capital Stock Changes - During fiscal 2023, common shares were issued as follows: 3,636,000 by private placement, 200,000 on acquisition of mineral properties and 48,000 as finders' fees.

Financial Statistics

Periods ended:	12m Feb. 28/23^A		12m Feb. 28/22^A1
	$000s	%Chg	$000s
Salaries & benefits	108		118
General & admin expense	178		219
Stock-based compensation	21		343
Operating expense	**307**	**-55**	**679**
Operating income	**(307)**	**n.a.**	**(679)**
Finance income	6		nil
Pre-tax income	**(113)**	**n.a.**	**(2,347)**
Net income	**(113)**	**n.a.**	**(2,347)**
Cash & equivalent	248		1,317
Accounts receivable	5		28
Current assets	266		1,363
Explor./devel. properties	2,210		1,022
Total assets	**2,517**	**+3**	**2,451**
Accts. pay. & accr. liabs	42		25
Current liabilities	130		234
Shareholders' equity	2,387		2,217
Cash from oper. activs	**(270)**	**n.a.**	**(543)**
Cash from fin. activs	326		1,610
Cash from invest. activs	(1,125)		104
Net cash position	**248**	**-81**	**1,317**
Capital expenditures	(1,153)		(452)
	$		$
Earnings per share*	(0.00)		(0.05)
Cash flow per share*	(0.01)		(0.01)
	shs		shs
No. of shs. o/s*	49,942,202		46,058,202
Avg. no. of shs. o/s*	47,442,903		44,131,797
	%		%
Net profit margin	n.a.		n.a.
Return on equity	(4.91)		(170.13)
Return on assets	(4.55)		(154.87)

* Common

^A Reported in accordance with IFRS

[1] Results prior to Mar. 23, 2021, pertain to and reflect the Qualifying Transaction acquisition of (old) Bonanza Mining Corporation.

Historical Summary
(as originally stated)

Fiscal Year	Oper. Rev. $000s	Net Inc. Bef. Disc. $000s	EPS* $
2023[A]	nil	(113)	(0.00)
2022[A]	nil	(2,347)	(0.05)
2021[A1]	nil	(33)	n.a.

* Common
[A] Reported in accordance with IFRS
[1] 14 months ended Feb. 28, 2021.

B.96 Boosh Plant-Based Brands Inc.

Symbol - VEGI **Exchange** - CSE **CUSIP** - 099403
Head Office - 205-18428 53 Ave, Surrey, BC, V3S 7A4 **Telephone** - (604) 300-5069
Website - www.booshfood.com
Email - connie@booshfood.com
Investor Relations - Connie Marples (778) 840-1700
Auditors - Smythe LLP C.A.
Transfer Agents - Olympia Trust Company, Vancouver, B.C.
Profile - (B.C. 2020) Produces, distributes and sells plant-based snacks, entrees and appetizers to retailers, consumers and to food service industry in Canada and the United States.

Plant-based products include frozen entrees such as veggie, bolognese bowl, coconut curry cauli and shepherd's pie; refrigerated (cooler) entrees such as sloppy joe, gravy and chili; and shelf stable mac and cheese entrees all under the boosh brand. Also offers vegan cheese under the Pulse Kitchen brand; végé pâté and seed-based spreadable dips under the Salt Spring Harvest brand; and bean-based chips under the Beanfields brand. Products are distributed to retailers and to the food service industry including restaurants and pubs. Products are also sold online and delivered to consumers through Shopveji.com and booshfood.com.

Directors - Connie Marples, pres. & interim CEO, Surrey, B.C.; Lance Marples, acting CFO, Surrey, B.C.; David Coburn, Ariz.; Jennifer Eged, Vancouver, B.C.

Other Exec. Officers - TJ Walsh, v-p, sales, North America; Frank Kordy, corp. sec.; Nobu Mano, contr.

Capital Stock

	Authorized (shs.)	Outstanding (shs.)[1]
Common	unlimited	33,784,499

[1] At Oct. 6, 2022

Major Shareholder - Connie Marples held 10.67% interest and Lance Marples held 10.67% interest at Jan. 19, 2022.

Price Range - VEGI/CSE

Year	Volume	High	Low	Close
2022	11,391,248	$1.05	$0.03	$0.03
2021	11,446,823	$1.73	$0.80	$0.80

Recent Close: $0.02

Capital Stock Changes - On May 26, 2021, an initial public offering of 5,750,000 units (1 common share & 1 warrant) at 50¢ per unit was completed. In February 2022, 8,000,000 common shares were issued on acquisition of Beanfields, Inc. Also during fiscal 2022, common shares were issued as follows: 3,308,522 by private placement, 2,078,882 on exercise of warrants, 1,304,000 as finders' fees, 297,504 for services, 100,000 on conversion of debt, 50,000 on acquisition of Pulse Kitchen Specialty Foods Ltd., 28,409 on acquisition of assets of Saltspring Harvest Ltd.'s business and 5,000 on acquisition of certain recipes and formulas for shelf stable vegan cheese sauce.

Wholly Owned Subsidiaries

Beautiful Beanfields, Inc.
Boosh Food Inc., B.C.
Pulse Kitchen Specialty Foods Ltd.

Financial Statistics

Periods ended:	12m Mar. 31/22[A]	%Chg	12m Mar. 31/21[A]
	$000s	%Chg	$000s
Operating revenue	**684**	**+533**	**108**
Cost of sales	831		113
Salaries & benefits	673		11
Research & devel. expense	63		11
General & admin expense	4,863		498
Stock-based compensation	755		182
Operating expense	**7,185**	**+783**	**814**
Operating income	**(6,501)**	**n.a.**	**(706)**
Deprec., depl. & amort.	198		20
Finance costs, net	6		11
Pre-tax income	**(7,977)**	**n.a.**	**(946)**
Net income	**(7,977)**	**n.a.**	**(946)**
Cash & equivalent	217		98
Inventories	516		98
Accounts receivable	1,236		51
Current assets	2,413		285
Fixed assets, net	88		23
Right-of-use assets	42		101
Intangibles, net	8,604		52
Total assets	**11,149**	**n.m.**	**462**
Accts. pay. & accr. liabs	2,629		337
Current liabilities	3,164		627
Long-term debt, gross	nil		148
Long-term lease liabilities	2		14
Shareholders' equity	7,983		(178)
Cash from oper. activs	**(6,438)**	**n.a.**	**(436)**
Cash from fin. activs	6,722		157
Cash from invest. activs	(299)		375
Net cash position	**217**	**+121**	**98**
Capital expenditures	(67)		(24)
	$		$
Earnings per share*	(0.47)		(0.14)
Cash flow per share*	(0.37)		(0.06)
	shs		shs
No. of shs. o/s*	29,937,817		9,015,500
Avg. no. of shs. o/s*	17,277,381		6,805,520
	%		%
Net profit margin	n.m.		(875.93)
Return on equity	n.m.		n.m.
Return on assets	(137.40)		(359.70)

* Common
[A] Reported in accordance with IFRS

Latest Results

Periods ended:	3m June 30/22[A]	%Chg	3m June 30/21[A]
	$000s	%Chg	$000s
Operating revenue	1,449	n.m.	33
Net income	(1,111)	n.a.	(995)
	$		$
Earnings per share*	(0.04)		(0.09)

* Common
[A] Reported in accordance with IFRS

Historical Summary
(as originally stated)

Fiscal Year	Oper. Rev. $000s	Net Inc. Bef. Disc. $000s	EPS* $
2022[A]	684	(7,977)	(0.47)
2021[A]	108	(946)	(0.14)
2020[A1]	128	(150)	(0.02)
2019[A]	26	(135)	(0.03)

* Common
[A] Reported in accordance with IFRS
[1] Results for fiscal 2020 and prior periods pertain to Boosh Food Inc.

B.97 Boralex Inc.*

Symbol - BLX **Exchange** - TSX **CUSIP** - 09950M
Head Office - 36 rue Lajeunesse, Kingsey Falls, QC, J0A 1B0 **Telephone** - (819) 363-6363 **Fax** - (819) 363-6399 **Exec. Office** - 2400-900 boul de Maisonneuve O, Montréal, QC, H3A 0A8 **Telephone** - (514) 284-9890 **Fax** - (514) 284-9895
Website - www.boralex.com
Email - stephane.milot@boralex.com
Investor Relations - Stéphane Milot (514) 213-1045
Auditors - PricewaterhouseCoopers LLP C.A., Montréal, Qué.
Lawyers - Stikeman Elliott LLP, Montréal, Qué.
Transfer Agents - Computershare Trust Company of Canada Inc., Montréal, Qué.
FP500 Revenue Ranking - 374
Employees - 626 at Dec. 31, 2022
Profile - (Can. 1982) Develops, builds and operates renewable power stations in Canada, France, the U.S. and the U.K., including wind, hydroelectric and solar power, with installed capacity of 3,017 MW.

The company is active in three sectors: wind power; hydroelectric power; and solar power.

Wind Power - Holds interests in 96 wind power stations in France (68), Canada (23) and the United States (5) with a total installed capacity of 2,584 MW. Projects under various stages of development include 1,125 and 1,242 MW of wind power stations in Canada and the U.S., as well as in France and elsewhere.

Hydroelectric Power - Owns 16 run-of-river hydroelectric power stations in New York (7), Quebec (6), British Columbia (2) and Ontario (1) with a total installed capacity of 181 MW. These stations are operated and managed from a control centre in Kingsey Falls, Que.

Solar Power - Operates 12 solar power stations in California (5), Alabama (1), Indiana (1) and France (5) with a total installed capacity of 255 MW. Projects under various stages of development include 1,100 MW of solar power stations in Canada and the U.S., as well as 616 MW of solar power stations in France and elsewhere.

Power production (proportionate consolidation), in MWh:

Year ended Dec. 31	2022	2021
Wind power	4,972,000	4,798,000
Hydroelectric power	752,000	789,000
Thermal power[1]	40,000	145,000
Solar power	536,000	483,000
	1,991,000	6,215,000

[1] Sold on Apr. 1, 2022.

In May 2023, the company commissioned its second energy storage unit, with a storage capacity of more than 3.3 MWh, at the site of the Plouguin wind farm in France.

In December 2022, the 12-MW Grange du Causse solar farm, 13-MW Mont de Bezard 2 wind farm and 65-MW Moulins du Lohan wind farm, all in France, were commissioned.

In May and June 2022, three wind farms in France totaling 53 MW of operating capacity were commissioned. The projects include the 25-MW Bois des Fontaines and the repowering of Evits et Josaphat and Remise de Reclainville to increase capacity.

In June 2022, five company solar farms totaling 540 MW of electric generation and 77 MW of storage were selected under a Request for Proposals in New York State. Once constructed, the solar farms would generate more than 1 TWh of solar electricity annually, enough to power more than 141,200 homes annually. The selected photovoltaic solar electricity generation projects would be located across upstate New York.

On Apr. 19, 2022, the company, **Énergir Inc.**, and **Hydro-Québec** announced a partnership to develop three wind projects of 400 MW each on the Seigneurie de Beaupré territory in Quebec. The companies would participate equally in the projects through affiliated companies. The energy generated would be purchased by Hydro-Québec under three power purchase agreements and included in the volume of energy available to supply its various markets. The total investments for the three projects could reach $3 billion.

Recent Merger and Acquisition Activity

Status: completed **Announced:** Dec. 29, 2022
Boralex Inc. acquired a 50% interest in five operating wind farms in Texas (3) and New Mexico (2) with a total installed capacity of 894 MW from EDF Renewables North America for a purchase price of US$249,800,000 (Cdn$339,700,000). EDF Renewables' interest represents 447 MW of installed capacity. EDF Renewables is a subsidiary of Électricité de France S.A. (EDF Group).

Status: completed **Announced:** July 4, 2022
Boralex Inc. acquired WW Holdco Ltd.'s (Infinergy) interests in the United Kingdom for £24,000,000 (Cdn$37,000,000). The transaction included 100% of Infinergy Ltd., which has a portfolio of 338 MW of wind and solar power and energy storage projects under development, including 232 MW owned by the joint venture with Boralex and 106 MW owned directly by Infinergy.

Status: completed **Revised:** Apr. 29, 2022
UPDATE: The transaction was completed. PREVIOUS: Boralex Inc. agreed to sell a 30% interest in its portfolio of operating assets and development pipeline in France to Energy Infrastructure Partners AG for €532,000,000 (Cdn$766,000,000) cash. The assets include operating facilities consisting of 67 wind power and four solar power stations, totaling 1,081 MW, as well as 1,500 MW of projects under construction or development. Boralex would retain a 70% interest and remain as manager of the portfolio. The transaction was expected to close in the first half of 2022.

Status: completed **Announced:** Apr. 27, 2022
Boralex Inc. sold its 10-MW La Bouleste wind power station in France for $7,000,000.

Status: completed **Revised:** Apr. 1, 2022
UPDATE: The transaction was completed for $9,000,000. PREVIOUS: Boralex Inc. agreed to sell its 35-MW wood-residue thermal power station in Senneterre, Que., to Resolute Forest Products Inc. for an undisclosed amount.

Predecessor Detail - Name changed from Boralex Energy Corporation, May 28, 1984.

Directors - Alain Rhéaume, chr., Lac-Delage, Qué.; Patrick Decostre, pres. & CEO, Montréal, Qué.; André Courville, Montréal, Qué.; Lise Croteau, Mont-Tremblant, Qué.; Ghyslain Deschamps, Qué.; Marie-Claude Dumas, Qué.; Marie Giguère, Montréal, Qué.; Ines Kolmsee, Germany; Patrick Lemaire, Kingsey Falls, Qué.; Dr. Zin Smati, Houston, Tex.; Dany St-Pierre, Chicago, Ill.

Other Exec. Officers - Marie-Josée Arsenault, exec. v-p & chief people & culture officer; Hugues Girardin, exec. v-p & gen. mgr., North America; Bruno Guilmette, exec. v-p & CFO; Pascal Hurtubise, exec. v-p & chief legal officer; Nicolas Wolff, exec. v-p & gen. mgr., Europe; Julie Cusson, sr. v-p, enterprise risk mgt. & corp. social responsibility; Isabelle Fontaine, sr. v-p, corp. public affairs & commun.; Pascal Laprise-Demers, sr. v-p, corp. strategy & bus. performance; Nicolas

Mabboux, sr. v-p, IT & digital transformation; Mihaela Stefanov, sr. v-p, enterprise risk mgt.; Eric Cantin, v-p, fin.; Linda Filion, corp. sec.

Capital Stock

	Authorized (shs.)	Outstanding (shs.)[1]
Preferred	unlimited	nil
Class A	unlimited	102,766,104

[1] At Mar. 31, 2023

Options - At Dec. 31, 2022, options were outstanding to purchase 220,860 class A shares at prices ranging from $13.87 to $37.16 per share expiring to 2032.

Major Shareholder - Caisse de dépôt et placement du Québec held 12.5% interest at Mar. 2, 2023.

Price Range - BLX/TSX

Year	Volume	High	Low	Close
2022	83,309,118	$51.55	$30.04	$40.02
2021	114,033,548	$56.70	$32.94	$34.68
2020	99,087,444	$47.82	$17.91	$47.24
2019	57,847,861	$25.36	$16.67	$24.46
2018	51,582,557	$25.03	$15.96	$16.84

Recent Close: $33.54

Capital Stock Changes - During 2022, 144,148 class A shares were issued on exercise of options.

Dividends

BLX cl A Ra $0.66 pa Q est. Dec. 17, 2018

Long-Term Debt - Outstanding at Dec. 31, 2022:

Credit facilities[1]	$185,000,000
5.64% subord. loan due 2028	300,000,000
2.95% term loan due 2028	198,000,000
Term loans due to 2044[2]	1,170,000,000
Term loans due to 2056[3]	1,487,000,000
Other	6,000,000
Less: Financing costs	69,000,000
	3,277,000,000
Less: Current portion	404,000,000
	2,873,000,000

[1] Consists of $146,000,000 construction facility due 2024, bearing interest at 1.86%; and 39,000,000 revolving credit facility due 2027, bearing interest at 1.9%.

[2] Bearing interest at rates from 1% to 4.05%.

[3] Bearing interest at rates from 2.91% to 7.05%.

Wholly Owned Subsidiaries

Boralex Ontario Energy Holdings LP, Canada.
Boralex Ontario Energy Holdings 2 LP, Canada.
Boralex Power Limited Partnership, Qué.
Borlax US Solar CIA LLC, United States.
Des Moulins Wind Power LP, Canada.
Éoliennes Témiscouata II L.P., Canada.
NR Capital GP, Canada.
Le Plateau Wind Power LP, Man.

Subsidiaries

70% int. in **Boralex Europe S.A.**, Luxembourg. Formerly Boralex Luxembourg S.A.
- 100% int. in **Boralex Energie France S.A.S.**, France.
- 100% int. in **Boralex Énergie Verte S.A.S.**, France.
- 100% int. in **Boralex Production S.A.S.**, France.
- 100% int. in **Boralex Sainte Christine S.A.S.**, France.

Investments

50% int. in **FWRN LP**, Canada.

Note: The preceding list includes only the major related companies in which interests are held.

Financial Statistics

Periods ended:	12m Dec. 31/22[A]		12m Dec. 31/21[A]
	$000s	%Chg	$000s
Operating revenue	**818,000**	**+22**	**671,000**
Research & devel. expense	33,000		24,000
General & admin expense	55,000		37,000
Other operating expense	258,000		153,000
Operating expense	**346,000**	**+62**	**214,000**
Operating income	**472,000**	**+3**	**457,000**
Deprec., depl. & amort	295,000		297,000
Finance costs, gross	130,000		144,000
Investment income	37,000		9,000
Write-downs/write-offs	(85,000)		(4,000)
Pre-tax income	**18,000**	**-59**	**44,000**
Income taxes	10,000		18,000
Net income	**8,000**	**-69**	**26,000**
Net inc. for equity hldrs	**30,000**	**+76**	**17,000**
Net inc. for non-cont. int	**(22,000)**	**n.a.**	**9,000**
Cash & equivalent	361,000		256,000
Accounts receivable	234,000		148,000
Current assets	638,000		460,000
Long-term investments	536,000		107,000
Fixed assets, net	3,335,000		3,227,000
Right-of-use assets	340,000		407,000
Intangibles, net	1,292,000		1,365,000
Total assets	**6,539,000**	**+14**	**5,751,000**
Bank indebtedness	12,000		nil
Accts. pay. & accr. liabs	377,000		145,000
Current liabilities	821,000		395,000
Long-term debt, gross	3,277,000		3,603,000
Long-term debt, net	2,873,000		3,383,000
Long-term lease liabilities	300,000		290,000
Shareholders' equity	1,681,000		1,001,000
Non-controlling interest	345,000		210,000
Cash from oper. activs	**513,000**	**+49**	**345,000**
Cash from fin. activs	261,000		75,000
Cash from invest. activs	(684,000)		(433,000)
Net cash position	**349,000**	**+36**	**256,000**
Capital expenditures	(135,000)		(106,000)
	$		$
Earnings per share*	0.30		0.16
Cash flow per share*	4.99		3.36
Cash divd. per share*	0.66		0.66
	shs		shs
No. of shs. o/s*	102,762,850		102,618,702
Avg. no. of shs. o/s*	102,726,063		102,618,657
	%		%
Net profit margin	0.98		3.87
Return on equity	2.24		1.71
Return on assets	1.07		2.01
Foreign sales percent	60		54
No. of employees (FTEs)	626		562

* Class A
[A] Reported in accordance with IFRS

Latest Results

Periods ended:	3m Mar. 31/23[A]		3m Mar. 31/22[A]
	$000s	%Chg	$000s
Operating revenue	298,000	+31	227,000
Net income	55,000	-4	57,000
Net inc. for equity hldrs	43,000	-14	50,000
Net inc. for non-cont. int	12,000		7,000
	$		$
Earnings per share*	0.41		0.49

* Class A
[A] Reported in accordance with IFRS

Historical Summary
(as originally stated)

Fiscal Year	Oper. Rev.	Net Inc. Bef. Disc.	EPS*
	$000s	$000s	$
2022[A]	818,000	8,000	0.30
2021[A]	671,000	26,000	0.16
2020[A]	619,000	61,000	0.55
2019[A]	564,000	(43,000)	(0.43)
2018[A]	471,000	(44,000)	(0.45)

* Class A
[A] Reported in accordance with IFRS

B.98 Boston Pizza Royalties Income Fund

Symbol - BPF.UN **Exchange** - TSX **CUSIP** - 101084
Head Office - 201-13571 Commerce Pky, Richmond, BC, V6V 2R2
Telephone - (604) 270-1108 **Fax** - (604) 270-4168
Website - www.bpincomefund.com
Email - investorrelations@bostonpizza.com
Investor Relations - Michael E. Harbinson (604) 270-1108
Auditors - KPMG LLP C.A., Vancouver, B.C.
Lawyers - Borden Ladner Gervais LLP, Vancouver, B.C.
Transfer Agents - Computershare Trust Company of Canada Inc., Vancouver, B.C.

Profile - (B.C. 2002) Owns the Canadian trademarks used by **Boston Pizza International Inc.** in the operation of Boston Pizza restaurants in Canada. At Jan. 1, 2023, the royalty pool included 377 restaurants.

Subsidiary **Boston Pizza Royalties Limited Partnership** has granted **Boston Pizza International Inc.** (BPI) an exclusive 99-year licence to use the Boston Pizza rights in Canada in consideration for a royalty, payable by BPI to the partnership, equal to 4.0% of the franchise revenue from Boston Pizza restaurants in Canada included in the royalty pool. In addition, through **Boston Pizza Canada Limited Partnership**, the fund receives 1.5% of franchise revenue from BPI less the pro rata portion payable to BPI.

Boston Pizza restaurants in operation at Dec. 31, 2022:

Location	Restaurants[1]
Alberta	108
British Columbia	54
Manitoba	21
New Brunswick	5
Newfoundland & Labrador	4
Northwest Territories & Yukon	2
Nova Scotia	12
Ontario	113
Prince Edward Island	1
Quebec	32
Saskatchewan	25
	377

[1] All included in the royalty pool.

Effective Jan. 1, 2023, six restaurants were removed from the royalty pool.

Trustees - Marc Guay, chr., Oakville, Ont.; Paulina Hiebert, Edmonton, Alta.; Shelley C. Williams, Langley, B.C.

Oper. Subsid./Mgt. Co. Officers - Jordan Holm, pres.; Michael E. Harbinson, CFO

Capital Stock

	Authorized (shs.)	Outstanding (shs.)[1]
Fund Unit	unlimited	21,521,463[2]
Special Voting Unit	unlimited	359,193,322[3]
Class B General Partnership Unit	unlimited	2,872,800[4]
Class 2 General Partnership Unit	unlimited	59,184,161[5]

[1] At Feb. 8, 2023

[2] At June 15, 2023.

[3] All held by Boston Pizza International Inc.

[4] Securities of Boston Pizza Royalties Limited Partnership.

[5] Securities of Boston Pizza Canada Limited Partnership.

Fund Unit - Entitled to monthly cash distributions. Redeemable at a price per unit equal to the lesser of (i) 90% of the weighted average price per unit during the 20-trading day period immediately following the date on which the units were surrendered for redemption and (ii) an amount equal to (a) the closing price of the units on the redemption date; (b) the average of the highest and lowest prices of the units on the redemption date; or (c) the average of the last bid and ask prices if there was no trading on the redemption date. One vote per fund unit.

Special Voting Unit - Issued to holders of Boston Pizza Royalties Limited Partnership class B units and Boston Pizza Canada Limited Partnership class 2 units, class 3 units, class 4 units and class 5 units. Each class B units and class 2 units entitles the holder to a vote at the unitholder meetings of the fund equal to the number of fund units into which the class B units and class 2 units are exchangeable.

Class B General Partnership Unit - Entitled to receive a proportionate distribution based on the incremental royalty paid by Boston Pizza International Inc. to Boston Pizza Royalties Limited Partnership from new Boston Pizza restaurants. Exchangeable into fund units on the basis of class B exchange multiplier applicable at the date of such exchange. The multiplier, adjusted on January 1 each year, is based on a defined calculation which is based in part on the net franchise revenue from restaurants opened. Class B general partnership units are all held by Boston Pizza International Inc. Classified as financial liability.

Class 2 General Partnership Unit - Entitled to receive a proportionate distribution based on the incremental franchise revenue paid by Boston Pizza International Inc. to Boston Pizza Canada Limited Partnership from new Boston Pizza restaurants. Exchangeable into fund units on the basis of class 2 exchange multiplier applicable at the date of such exchange. The multiplier, adjusted on January 1 each year, is based on a defined calculation which is based in part on the net franchise revenue from restaurants opened. Class 2 general partnership units are all held by Boston Pizza International Inc.

Normal Course Issuer Bid - The company plans to make normal course purchases of up to 400,000 fund units representing 1.9% of the total outstanding. The bid commenced on June 20, 2023, and expires on June 19, 2024.

Major Shareholder - Boston Pizza International Inc. held 13.2% interest at Feb. 8, 2023.

Price Range - BPF.UN/TSX

Year	Volume	High	Low	Close
2022	12,312,750	$17.66	$14.02	$15.08
2021	13,680,382	$16.19	$10.06	$15.45
2020	23,073,018	$14.83	$5.34	$10.83
2019	12,929,188	$18.17	$13.13	$13.46
2018	7,965,648	$22.06	$13.82	$15.11

Recent Close: $16.25

Capital Stock Changes - There were no changes to capital stock during 2021 or 2022.

Dividends

BPF.UN unit Var. Ra pa M

$0.107	Aug. 31/23	$0.107	July 31/23
$0.107	June 30/23	$0.107	May 31/23

Paid in 2023: $0.841 2022: $1.097 + $0.085◆ 2021: $0.84 + $0.20◆

◆ Special

Wholly Owned Subsidiaries

Boston Pizza Holdings GP Inc., B.C.

Boston Pizza Holdings Trust, Vancouver, B.C.

- 100% int. in **Boston Pizza Holdings Limited Partnership**, B.C.
  - 100% int. in **Boston Pizza Canada Limited Partnership**, B.C.
  - 100% int. in **Boston Pizza Royalties Limited Partnership**, B.C.

Subsidiaries

80% int. in **Boston Pizza GP Inc.**, Vancouver, B.C.

Financial Statistics

Periods ended:	12m Dec. 31/22[A]		12m Dec. 31/21[A]
	$000s	%Chg	$000s
Operating revenue	**45,473**	**+29**	**35,154**
General & admin expense	1,390		1,299
Operating expense	**1,390**	**+7**	**1,299**
Operating income	**44,083**	**+30**	**33,855**
Finance income	107		94
Finance costs, gross	7,304		6,385
Pre-tax income	**39,657**	**-10**	**43,844**
Income taxes	9,074		6,437
Net income	**30,583**	**-18**	**37,407**
Cash & equivalent	5,213		5,162
Accounts receivable	4,372		3,422
Current assets	11,298		8,904
Long-term investments	115,587		117,606
Intangibles, net	284,188		284,188
Total assets	**413,701**	**+1**	**411,313**
Accts. pay. & accr. liabs	544		586
Current liabilities	3,076		91,027
Long-term debt, gross	86,440		87,963
Long-term debt, net	86,440		nil
Shareholders' equity	280,578		275,799
Cash from oper. activs	**34,355**	**+13**	**30,475**
Cash from fin. activs	(34,304)		(33,013)
Net cash position	**5,213**	**+1**	**5,162**
	$		$
Earnings per share*	1.42		1.74
Cash flow per share*	1.60		1.42
Cash divd. per share*	1.11		0.86
Extra divd. - cash*	0.09		nil
Total divd. per share*	**1.20**		**0.86**
	shs		shs
No. of shs. o/s*	21,521,463		21,521,463
Avg. no. of shs. o/s*	21,521,463		21,521,463
	%		%
Net profit margin	67.26		106.41
Return on equity	10.99		14.04
Return on assets	8.78		10.69

* Fund unit

[A] Reported in accordance with IFRS

Latest Results

Periods ended:	3m Mar. 31/23[A]		3m Mar. 31/22[A]
	$000s	%Chg	$000s
Operating revenue	11,917	+25	9,507
Net income	6,669	-48	12,899
	$		$
Earnings per share*	0.31		0.60

* Fund unit

[A] Reported in accordance with IFRS

Historical Summary
(as originally stated)

Fiscal Year	Oper. Rev.	Net Inc. Bef. Disc.	EPS*
	$000s	$000s	$
2022[A]	45,473	30,583	1.42
2021[A]	35,154	37,407	1.74
2020[A]	32,642	9,570	0.44
2019[A]	45,395	22,503	1.03
2018[A]	45,611	8,669	0.40

* Fund unit

[A] Reported in accordance with IFRS

B.99 Bow Lake Capital Corp.

Symbol - BLCC.P **Exchange** - TSX-VEN **CUSIP** - 10215F

Head Office - Roslyn Building, 300-400 5 Ave SW, Calgary, AB, T2P 0L6 **Telephone** - (403) 999-7808

Email - arthur_h_kwan@hotmail.com

Investor Relations - Arthur H. Kwan (403) 999-7808

Auditors - Kenway Mack Slusarchuk Stewart LLP C.A., Calgary, Alta.

Lawyers - Borden Ladner Gervais LLP, Calgary, Alta.

Transfer Agents - Alliance Trust Company, Calgary, Alta.

Profile - (B.C. 2021) Capital Pool Company.

Directors - Arthur H. Kwan, CEO, Calgary, Alta.; Murray R. Hinz, CFO, Calgary, Alta.; Michael J. Saliken, corp. sec., Calgary, Alta.; Michael J. Lang, Calgary, Alta.; Jeremy T. Ross, Vancouver, B.C.

Capital Stock

	Authorized (shs.)	Outstanding (shs.)[1]
Preferred	unlimited	nil
Common	unlimited	7,800,000

[1] At May 10, 2023

Major Shareholder - Widely held at Mar. 24, 2022.

Price Range - BLCC.P/TSX-VEN

Year	Volume	High	Low	Close
2022	40,000	$0.15	$0.01	$0.01

Recent Close: $0.01

Capital Stock Changes - On Mar. 24, 2022, an initial public offering of 5,000,000 common shares was completed at 10¢ per share.

B.100 Boyd Group Services Inc.*

Symbol - BYD **Exchange** - TSX **CUSIP** - 103310

Head Office - Unit C1, 1745 Ellice Ave, Winnipeg, MB, R3H 1A6 **Telephone** - (204) 895-1244 **Fax** - (204) 895-1283

Website - www.boydgroup.com

Email - jeff.murray@boydgroup.com

Investor Relations - Jeff Murray (204) 895-1244 ext. 33841

Auditors - Deloitte LLP C.A., Winnipeg, Man.

Bankers - The Toronto-Dominion Bank, Toronto, Ont.

Lawyers - Thompson Dorfman Sweatman LLP, Winnipeg, Man.

Transfer Agents - Computershare Trust Company of Canada Inc., Toronto, Ont.

FP500 Revenue Ranking - 164

Employees - 12,391 at Dec. 31, 2022

Profile - (Can. 2019) Owns and operates non-franchised automotive collision and glass repair centres in Canada and the U.S. Also operates a retail auto glass business and a third party administrator that offers glass, emergency roadside, and first notice of loss services.

Wholly owned **The Boyd Group Inc.** (Boyd) operates 128 locations under the trade names Boyd Autobody & Glass and Assured Automotive in Ontario (82), Alberta (16), Manitoba (12), British Columbia (14) and Saskatchewan (4), and 761 locations under the trade name Gerber Collision & Glass in 32 U.S. states. Collision repair services are provided to insurance companies and individual vehicle owners.

Boyd is also a major retail auto glass operator in the United States under the trade names Gerber Collision & Glass, Glass America, Auto Glass Services, Auto Glass Authority and Autoglassonly.com. In addition, operates Gerber National Claims Services, which offers glass, emergency roadside and first notice of loss services.

During the six-month period ended June 30, 2023, the company acquired a two location glass business in Minnesota and a single location glass business in Texas for an undisclosed amount. In addition, the company added 48 collision repair locations, including 35 through acquisition and 13 start-up locations.

During 2022, 40 new collision locations were added.

Subsequent to the third quarter of 2022, the company acquired a single location glass business in Wisconsin for an undisclosed amount.

During the nine-months ended Sept. 30, 2022, the company acquired a single location glass business in Minnesota and a four location glass business in Florida for an undisclosed amount. In addition, the company added 28 locations, including 17 through acquisition, six start-up locations and five intake centres.

Recent Merger and Acquisition Activity

Status: completed **Announced:** Sept. 30, 2022

Boyd Group Services Inc. sold and leased back 35 properties for total consideration of US$53,404,000. Of the 35 properties, 24 relate to operating locations and 11 relate to start-up locations under development.

Predecessor Detail - Succeeded Boyd Group Income Fund, Jan. 2, 2020, pursuant to plan of arrangement whereby Boyd Group Services Inc. was formed to facilitate the conversion of the income fund into a corporation.

Directors - David G. (Dave) Brown, chr., Winnipeg, Man.; Timothy J. (Tim) O'Day, pres. & CEO, Chicago, Ill.; W. Brock Bulbuck, Winnipeg, Man.; Robert B. (Bob) Espey, Calgary, Alta.; Christine Feuell, Mich.; Robert G. Gross, Las Vegas, Nev.; John Hartmann, Ill.; Violet A. M. (Vi) Konkle, Ont.; Dr. William Onuwa, Ont.; Sally A. Savoia, Orlando, Fla.

Other Exec. Officers - Jeff Murray, exec. v-p & CFO; Jason Hope, v-p, corp. devel. & strategic projects; Peter Toni, asst. sec. & corp. counsel

Capital Stock

	Authorized (shs.)	Outstanding (shs.)[1]
Common	unlimited	21,472,194

[1] At June 30, 2023

Major Shareholder - Fidelity Management & Research Company held 10.49% interest and Mackenzie Financial Corporation held 10.18% interest at Mar. 24, 2023.

Price Range - BYD/TSX

Year	Volume	High	Low	Close
2022	14,162,983	$222.74	$117.48	$209.16
2021	10,687,937	$267.00	$183.00	$199.62
2020	17,993,341	$231.52	$125.01	$219.56

BYD.UN/TSX (D)

Year	Volume	High	Low	Close
2019	11,099,652	$209.13	$106.75	$202.00
2018	11,270,536	$133.00	$97.99	$112.95

Recent Close: $239.98

Capital Stock Changes - There were no changes to capital stock during 2021 or 2022.

Dividends

BYD com Ra $0.588 pa Q est. Jan. 27, 2023[1]

Prev. Rate: $0.576 est. Jan. 17, 2022

Prev. Rate: $0.564 est. Jan. 27, 2021

[1] Boyd Group Income Fund unit prior to Jan. 2, 2020. Divds. paid monthly prior to Mar/20.

Long-Term Debt - Outstanding at Dec. 31, 2022:

Revolv. credit facility[1]	US$192,343,000
Term loan[2]	124,759,000
Vendor notes[3]	43,069,000
	360,171,000
Less: Current portion	15,365,000
	344,806,000

[1] Bears interest rates between prime, banker's acceptance, U.S. prime or LIBOR and due March 2025.

[2] Bears interest at 3.455% and due March 2027.

[3] Bear interest at rates ranging from 3% to 8% and due on various dates through January 2028.

Wholly Owned Subsidiaries

The Boyd Group Inc., Winnipeg, Man.

- 100% int. in **Assured Automotive (2017) Inc.**
- 100% int. in **The Boyd Group (U.S.) Inc.**, Del.
  - 100% int. in **AMPB Acquisition Corp.**, Nev.
  - 100% int. in **Collex Collision Experts Inc.**, Mich.
  - 100% int. in **Collision Revision, Inc.**, Ill.
  - 100% int. in **Collision Service Repair Center, Inc.**, Wash.
  - 100% int. in **Gerber Collision & Glass (Kansas) Inc.**, Kan.
  - 100% int. in **Gerber Collision (California), Inc.**, Calif.
  - 100% int. in **Gerber Collision (Colorado) Inc.**, Colo.
  - 100% int. in **Gerber Collision (Idaho), Inc.**, Coeur d'Alene, Idaho.
  - 100% int. in **Gerber Collision (Louisiana), Inc.**
    - 100% int. in **Champ's Holding Company, LLC**, La.
  - 100% int. in **Gerber Collision (Midwest), Inc.**, United States.
  - 100% int. in **Gerber Collision (NY), Inc.**
    - 100% int. in **Carubba Collision Corp.**, N.Y.
  - 100% int. in **Gerber Collision (Northeast), Inc.**, N.C.
  - 100% int. in **Gerber Collision (Oregon), Inc.**
  - 100% int. in **Gerber Collision (Tennessee), Inc.**
  - 100% int. in **Gerber Collision (Texas), Inc.**
  - 100% int. in **Gerber Collision (Utah), Inc.**
  - 100% int. in **Gerber Collision (Wisconsin), Inc.**
  - 100% int. in **Gerber Glass Holdings Inc.**, Del.
    - 100% int. in **Gerber Glass, LLC**
      - 100% int. in **Glass America LLC**
        - 100% int. in **Auto Glass Only, LLC**
          - 100% int. in **Glass America Alabama LLC**
          - 100% int. in **Glass America Illinois LLC**
          - 100% int. in **Glass America Kentucky LLC**
          - 100% int. in **Glass America Maryland LLC**
          - 100% int. in **Glass America Massachusetts LLC**
          - 100% int. in **Glass America Michigan LLC**
          - 100% int. in **Glass America Midwest Lindenhurst LLC**
          - 100% int. in **Glass America Midwest North Canton LLC**
          - 100% int. in **Glass America Missouri LLC**
          - 100% int. in **Glass America New York LLC**
          - 100% int. in **Glass America Ohio LLC**
          - 100% int. in **Glass America Texas LLC**
          - 100% int. in **Glass America Vermont LLC**
          - 100% int. in **Glass America Virginia LLC**
        - 100% int. in **Gerber Glass (District 5), LLC**
          - 100% int. in **S&L Auto Glass, LLC**
        - 100% int. in **Gerber Glass (District 4), LLC**
        - 100% int. in **Gerber Glass (District 7), LLC**
        - 100% int. in **Gerber Glass (District 6), LLC**
        - 100% int. in **Gerber Glass (District 3), LLC**
        - 100% int. in **Gerber Glass (District 2), LLC**
        - 100% int. in **Gerber National Claim Services, LLC**
        - 100% int. in **Glass America (California), LLC**, Calif.
        - 100% int. in **Glass America Midwest LLC**
        - 100% int. in **Glass America Southeast LLC**
        - 100% int. in **Hansen Auto Glass, LLC**
- 100% int. in **The Gerber Group Inc.**, Skokie, Ill.
  - 100% int. in **Cars Collision Center, LLC**, Colo.
  - 100% int. in **True2Form Collision Repair Centers, Inc.**, United States.
    - 100% int. in **True2Form Collision Repair Centers, LLC**
- 100% int. in **Gerber Payroll Services Inc.**, Del.
- 100% int. in **Gerber Real Estate Inc.**
- 100% int. in **Hansen Collision, Inc.**
  - 100% int. in **Hansen Leasing, Inc.**
- 100% int. in **Kingswood Collision, Inc.**, Ariz.

- 100% int. in **Master Collision Repair, Inc.**, Tampa, Fla.
- 100% int. in **Mobile Auto Solutions (2021), Inc.**, Del.
- 100% int. in **Service Collision Center (Georgia) Inc.**
- 100% int. in **Service Collision Center (Oklahoma) Inc.**
  - 100% int. in **Collision Works Holdings II, LLC**, Okla.
  - 100% int. in **Collision Works of Kansas, LLC**, Okla.
  - 100% int. in **Collision Works of Oklahoma, LLC**, Okla.
  - 100% int. in **Collision Works Real Estate Holdings, LLC**, Okla.
    - 100% int. in **Collision Works of Tulsa, LLC**, Okla.
  - 100% int. in **Hail Works, LLC**, Okla.

Financial Statistics

Periods ended:	12m Dec. 31/22[A]		12m Dec. 31/21[A]
	US$000s	%Chg	US$000s
Operating revenue	**2,432,318**	**+30**	**1,872,670**
Cost of sales	1,344,998		1,033,410
Other operating expense	813,820		619,716
Operating expense	**2,158,818**	**+31**	**1,653,126**
Operating income	**273,500**	**+25**	**219,544**
Deprec., depl. & amort.	175,619		153,694
Finance costs, gross	37,308		27,653
Pre-tax income	**58,727**	**+82**	**32,214**
Income taxes	17,765		8,674
Net income	**40,962**	**+74**	**23,540**
Cash & equivalent	15,068		27,714
Inventories	78,784		66,784
Accounts receivable	139,266		103,024
Current assets	275,304		234,652
Fixed assets, net	314,564		332,189
Right-of-use assets	568,437		502,036
Intangibles, net	934,645		950,718
Total assets	**2,102,832**	**+4**	**2,027,127**
Accts. pay. & accr. liabs	307,729		258,423
Current liabilities	424,294		367,673
Long-term debt, gross	360,171		442,073
Long-term debt, net	344,806		428,186
Long-term lease liabilities	519,056		450,423
Shareholders' equity	746,597		726,434
Cash from oper. activs	**264,247**	**+34**	**196,714**
Cash from fin. activs	(228,369)		124,368
Cash from invest. activs	(47,925)		(354,097)
Net cash position	**15,068**	**-46**	**27,714**
Capital expenditures	(33,370)		(31,479)
Capital disposals	2,745		1,145
	US$		US$
Earnings per share*	1.91		1.10
Cash flow per share*	12.31		9.16
Cash divd. per share*	$0.58		$0.57
	shs		shs
No. of shs. o/s*	21,472,194		21,472,194
Avg. no. of shs. o/s*	21,472,194		21,472,194
	%		%
Net profit margin	1.68		1.26
Return on equity	5.56		3.23
Return on assets	3.24		2.40
Foreign sales percent	92		92
No. of employees (FTEs)	12,391		10,145

* Common
[A] Reported in accordance with IFRS

Latest Results

Periods ended:	6m June 30/23[A]		6m June 30/22[A]
	US$000s	%Chg	US$000s
Operating revenue	1,468,176	+26	1,169,561
Net income	47,092	+216	14,906
	US$		US$
Earnings per share*	2.19		0.69

* Common
[A] Reported in accordance with IFRS

Historical Summary
(as originally stated)

Fiscal Year	Oper. Rev.	Net Inc. Bef. Disc.	EPS*
	US$000s	US$000s	US$
2022[A]	2,432,318	40,962	1.91
2021[A]	1,872,670	23,540	1.10
	$000s	$000s	$
2020[A]	2,089,115	57,734	2.75
2019[A]	2,283,325	64,147	3.23
2018[A]	1,864,613	77,639	3.94

* Common
[A] Reported in accordance with IFRS

B.101 Brachium2 Capital Corp.

Symbol - BRCB.P **Exchange** - TSX-VEN **CUSIP** - 10378A
Head Office - 1800-510 Georgia St W, Vancouver, BC, V6B 0M3 **Telephone** - (604) 838-0110 **Fax** - (604) 646-2510
Email - bpike@btlgcapital.com
Investor Relations - Bryant Pike (778) 609-8660
Auditors - Baker Tilly WM LLP C.A., Vancouver, B.C.
Transfer Agents - Odyssey Trust Company, Vancouver, B.C.
Profile - (B.C. 2021) Capital Pool Company.
Directors - Bryant Pike, CEO & CFO, Richmond, B.C.; Kris Miks, B.C.; Larry Nevsky, Toronto, Ont.
Other Exec. Officers - Benjamin Iscoe, corp. sec.

Capital Stock

	Authorized (shs.)	Outstanding (shs.)[1]
Common	unlimited	9,316,597

[1] At May 31, 2023

Major Shareholder - Widely held at June 8, 2021.

Price Range - BRCB.P/TSX-VEN

Year	Volume	High	Low	Close
2022	68,000	$0.12	$0.05	$0.05
2021	280,000	$0.20	$0.10	$0.10

Recent Close: $0.15
Capital Stock Changes - There were no changes to capital stock during fiscal 2023.

B.102 Bragg Gaming Group Inc.

Symbol - BRAG **Exchange** - TSX **CUSIP** - 104833
Head Office - 1955-130 King St W, Toronto, ON, M5X 1E3 **Telephone** - (647) 490-6889
Website - www.bragg.games
Email - info@bragg.games
Investor Relations - Yaniv Spielberg (647) 800-2282
Auditors - MNP LLP C.A., Toronto, Ont.
Lawyers - Bennett Jones LLP, Toronto, Ont.
Transfer Agents - Computershare Trust Company of Canada Inc., Toronto, Ont.
FP500 Revenue Ranking - 749
Employees - 432 at Mar. 31, 2023
Profile - (Can. 2004) Offers a suite of turnkey business-to-business (B2B) gaming solutions, including content, technology and services, to online and land-based gaming operators worldwide.
Content - Consists of a portfolio of casino games developed by the company's in-house studios, Wild Streak Gaming, Spin Games, Atomic Slot Lab, Indigo Magic and Oryx Gaming, as well as exclusive gaming content from third party studios. Also offers a wide range of over 6,500 aggregated casino gaming titles from third party suppliers.
Technology - Develops and deploys technology platforms including Bragg PAM, an omnichannel player account management platform which features a comprehensive set of tools required for gaming operations, including player overview and segmentation, player profiling, loyalty programs, customer relationship management (CRM) and promotions, bonuses and rewards, payments management, fraud and risk management, compliance, analytics, reporting and content management system (CMS); Bragg Hub, a content delivery platform where clients can access the company's portfolio of proprietary, exclusive and aggregated gaming content; Bragg RGS (remote gaming server), which provides toolset for game development that enable clients to deliver gaming content that can be played on any device and web browser; and Fuze, a player engagement platform which offers tools such as tournaments with real-time leaderboards, quests, recommendation engine, free rounds, mystery jackpots, achievements, bounties and a campaign management system.
Services - Provides managed marketing and operational services, such as customer support, know-your-customer (KYC) process, compliance, payment, risk and fraud management.

In October 2022, the company entered into a licensing agreement with **Sega Sammy Creation Inc.**, a unit of Japan-based **SEGA SAMMY Group**, for the exclusive rights to distribute select titles from Sega's content portfolio to online gaming operators in the U.S., the U.K. and other global markets.

In September 2022, the company entered into an iGaming content development partnership with Bally's Interactive, the digital arm of **Bally's Corporation**, whereby Bally's Interactive's online brands such as Virgin Casino, JackpotJoy and Vera&John would launch content from the company's proprietary slots studios, including Atomic Slot Lab and Indigo Magic, as well as from a range of exclusive proprietary and third-party titles from the company's existing and future portfolio. In addition, the company would distribute titles on an exclusive basis via its Remote Game Server from a select number of Bally's Interactive's third-partner partner studios.

In March 2022, the company was awarded a gaming licence to supply its content, technology and services in the Bahamas. In addition, the company was granted a licence by the Alcohol and Gaming Commission of Ontario to supply its solutions to local iGaming and sports betting operators in the province starting Apr. 4, 2022.

Recent Merger and Acquisition Activity

Status: completed **Revised:** June 1, 2022
UPDATE: The transaction was completed. PREVIOUS: Bragg Gaming Group Inc. agreed to acquire Reno, Nev.-based Spin Games LLC, which designs and develops gaming content and interactive technologies for regulated business-to-business (B2B) social and real money gaming markets, for US$30,000,000, consisting of US$10,000,000 cash and issuance of US$20,000,000 of common shares, of which US$5,000,000 of common shares would be issued on closing and the balance over three years. The transaction was expected to be completed in late 2021, following final approval from state gaming regulators and satisfaction of other customary closing conditions.
Predecessor Detail - Name changed from Breaking Data Corp., Dec. 27, 2018.
Directors - Matevz Mazij, v-chr., Croatia; Yaniv Sherman, CEO, Chicago, Ill.; Ron Baryoseph, Toronto, Ont.; Mark Clayton, Las Vegas, Nev.; Holly Gagnon, Mass.; Don Robertson, Hawkestone, Ont.; Kent Young, Reno, Nev.
Other Exec. Officers - Lara Falzon, pres. & COO; Ronen Kannor, CFO; Peter Lavric, chief tech. officer; Chris Looney, chief comml. officer; Giles Potter, chief mktg. officer; Yaniv Spielberg, chief strategy officer & corp. sec.

Capital Stock

	Authorized (shs.)	Outstanding (shs.)[1]
Common	unlimited	21,764,009

[1] At May 19, 2023

Major Shareholder - Matevz Mazij held 22.3% interest at May 19, 2023.

Price Range - BRAG/TSX

Year	Volume	High	Low	Close
2022	15,135,633	$10.10	$3.92	$5.25
2021	38,246,925	$31.80	$6.30	$6.42
2020	11,656,117	$18.60	$1.50	$14.30
2019	4,662,233	$13.90	$1.80	$2.45
2018	2,379,285	$31.00	$4.15	$8.10

Consolidation: 1-for-10 cons. in May 2021
Recent Close: $7.28
Capital Stock Changes - In June 2022, 285,135 common shares were issued pursuant to the acquisition of Spin Games LLC. Also during 2022, common shares were issued as follows: 761,754 as deferred consideration, 97,045 on exercise of deferred share units and 8,000 on exercise of options.

Wholly Owned Subsidiaries

Bragg Gaming Group - Group Services Ltd., United Kingdom.
Bragg Gaming Group - Parent Services Ltd., United Kingdom.
Bragg Oryx Holdings Inc., Toronto, Ont.
- 100% int. in **Oryx Gaming International LLC**, Las Vegas, Nev.
  - 100% int. in **Oryx Gaming Limited**, Malta.
  - 100% int. in **Oryx Marketing Poslovne Storitve d.o.o.**, Slovenia.
  - 100% int. in **Oryx Podpora d.o.o.**, Slovenia.
  - 100% int. in **Oryx Razvojne-Storitve d.o.o.**, Slovenia.
  - 100% int. in **Oryx Sales Distribution Limited**, Cyprus.

Bragg U.S., Inc., Del.
- 100% int. in **Spin Games LLC**, Reno, Nev.
- 100% int. in **Wild Streak LLC**, Las Vegas, Nev.

Poynt Inc., Canada.

Financial Statistics

Periods ended:	12m Dec. 31/22[A]		12m Dec. 31/21[◻A]
	€000s	%Chg	€000s
Operating revenue	**84,734**	**+45**	**58,319**
Cost of sales	39,652		29,998
Salaries & benefits	19,367		14,821
General & admin expense	14,521		9,789
Stock-based compensation	3,773		4,667
Operating expense	**77,313**	**+30**	**59,275**
Operating income	**7,421**	**n.a.**	**(956)**
Deprec., depl. & amort.	8,454		4,797
Finance income	13		61
Finance costs, gross	985		245
Write-downs/write-offs	(649)		(602)
Pre-tax income	**(1,926)**	**n.a.**	**(6,686)**
Income taxes	1,558		826
Net income	**(3,484)**	**n.a.**	**(7,512)**
Cash & equivalent	11,287		16,006
Accounts receivable	16,628		8,454
Current assets	29,738		26,958
Fixed assets, net	660		252
Right-of-use assets	576		579
Intangibles, net	73,367		55,573
Total assets	**104,388**	**+25**	**83,390**
Accts. pay. & accr. liabs	19,549		14,357
Current liabilities	24,307		15,317
Long-term debt, gross	6,757		nil
Long-term debt, net	6,648		nil
Long-term lease liabilities	344		451
Shareholders' equity	69,534		66,195
Cash from oper. activs	**5,753**	**n.m.**	**115**
Cash from fin. activs	7,010		12,408
Cash from invest. activs	(16,873)		(23,883)
Net cash position	**11,287**	**-29**	**16,006**
Capital expenditures	(544)		(123)
	€		€
Earnings per share*	(0.16)		(0.39)
Cash flow per share*	0.27		0.01
	shs		shs
No. of shs. o/s*	21,107,968		19,956,034
Avg. no. of shs. o/s*	21,400,000		19,500,000
	%		%
Net profit margin	(4.11)		(12.88)
Return on equity	(5.13)		(14.16)
Return on assets	(1.81)		(9.31)
No. of employees (FTEs)	428		286

* Common
◻ Restated
[A] Reported in accordance with IFRS

Latest Results

Periods ended:	3m Mar. 31/23[A]		3m Mar. 31/22[A]
	€000s	%Chg	€000s
Operating revenue	22,859	+18	19,360
Net income	(476)	n.a.	(720)
	€		€
Earnings per share*	(0.02)		(0.04)

* Common
[A] Reported in accordance with IFRS

Historical Summary
(as originally stated)

Fiscal Year	Oper. Rev.	Net Inc. Bef. Disc.	EPS*
	€000s	€000s	€
2022[A]	84,734	(3,484)	(0.16)
2021[A]	58,319	(7,512)	(0.39)
2020[A]	46,421	(14,476)	(1.70)
2019[A]	26,592	(10,376)	(1.40)
	$000s	$000s	$
2018[A1]	8,810	(21,514)	(7.30)

* Common
[A] Reported in accordance with IFRS
[1] 9 months ended Dec. 31, 2018.
Note: Adjusted throughout for 1-for-10 cons. in May 2021

B.103 Braille Energy Systems Inc.

Symbol - BES **Exchange** - TSX-VEN **CUSIP** - 10489B
Head Office - 945 Princess St, Box 117, Kingston, ON, K7L 0E9 **Telephone** - (613) 241-4040 **Toll-free** - (800) 764-4708 **Fax** - (613) 900-4619
Website - brailleenergy.com
Email - jmazvihwa@mincomcapital.com
Investor Relations - Judith T. Mazvihwa-MacLean (613) 581-4040
Auditors - MNP LLP C.A., Ottawa, Ont.
Transfer Agents - Computershare Trust Company of Canada Inc., Montréal, Qué.
Profile - (Can. 2011) Holds 89.95% interest in **Braille Battery Inc.**, which manufactures, markets and sells lightweight high-powered battery systems for the professional motor sports industry and transportation market.
Braille Battery's products include lithium and Absorbent Glass Mat (AGM) batteries which consists of prefabricated components delivered by third party suppliers and in-house fabricated components and are assembled at its own facilities in Sarasota, Fla. and Kingston, Ont. Also distributes a full multi-level line of batteries and accessories pre-assembled by a network of suppliers in North America and Europe; and offers custom designed battery application solutions. Products are sold through distributors, online, to individuals and to companies in the automotive racing industry.
Braille Battery plans to create energy applications for the transportation electrification and energy storage sectors, with a focus on fast charging, long life battery materials and products from materials derived from graphite and graphene, and is working on portable battery solutions in partnership with a clean water technology company.
On Aug. 11, 2022, the company sold the 2,592-hectare Romer polymetallic prospect in Quebec to **Stria Lithium Inc.** for $125,000 cash and issuance of 7,500,000 common shares at a deemed price of 5¢ per share.
Predecessor Detail - Name changed from Mincom Capital Inc., June 21, 2018, pursuant to the reverse takeover acquisition of an 89.95% interest in Braille Holdings Inc.
Directors - Jeffrey (Jeff) York, chr., Ottawa, Ont.; Lindsay Weatherdon, pres. & CEO, Burlington, Ont.; Marc R. Roy, Ont.
Other Exec. Officers - Judith T. Mazvihwa-MacLean, CFO & corp. sec.; Ivan Gissing, chief tech. officer & gen. mgr.

Capital Stock

	Authorized (shs.)	Outstanding (shs.)[1]
Common	unlimited	91,675,037

[1] At May 29, 2023
Major Shareholder - Widely held at Feb. 28, 2023.

Price Range - BES/TSX-VEN

Year	Volume	High	Low	Close
2022	18,856,504	$0.23	$0.07	$0.07
2021	242,553,638	$1.82	$0.09	$0.21
2020	111,966,609	$0.55	$0.01	$0.10
2019	5,022,610	$0.04	$0.01	$0.02
2018	2,808,003	$0.13	$0.02	$0.04

Recent Close: $0.04
Capital Stock Changes - In April 2023, private placement of 10,735,290 units (1 common share & ½ warrant) at $0.085 per unit was completed, with warrants exercisable at 12¢ per share for two years.

Subsidiaries

89.95% int. in **Braille Holdings Inc.**, Sarasota, Fla.
- 100% int. in **Braille Battery Inc.**, Sarasota, Fla.

Investments

Stria Lithium Inc., Kingston, Ont. (see separate coverage)

Financial Statistics

Periods ended:	12m Sept. 30/21[A]		12m Sept. 30/20[A]
	$000s	%Chg	$000s
Operating revenue	**3,467**	**+18**	**2,929**
Cost of goods sold	1,884		1,699
Salaries & benefits	464		379
General & admin expense	1,286		934
Stock-based compensation	398		16
Other operating expense	nil		20
Operating expense	**4,032**	**+32**	**3,047**
Operating income	**(565)**	**n.a.**	**(118)**
Deprec., depl. & amort.	98		93
Finance costs, gross	107		93
Write-downs/write-offs	nil		(12)
Pre-tax income	**(771)**	**n.a.**	**(364)**
Income taxes	(37)		60
Net income	**(734)**	**n.a.**	**(424)**
Net inc. for equity hldrs	**(791)**	**n.a.**	**(464)**
Net inc. for non-cont. int	**56**	**+40**	**40**
Cash & equivalent	4,207		125
Inventories	578		279
Accounts receivable	176		150
Current assets	5,256		661
Fixed assets, net	122		104
Right-of-use assets	667		149
Total assets	**6,045**	**+562**	**913**
Bank indebtedness	nil		30
Accts. pay. & accr. liabs	371		483
Current liabilities	1,048		2,189
Long-term debt, gross	36		200
Long-term debt, net	36		24
Long-term lease liabilities	541		60
Shareholders' equity	4,432		(1,364)
Non-controlling interest	(36)		(95)
Cash from oper. activs	**(1,109)**	**n.a.**	**108**
Cash from fin. activs	5,237		47
Cash from invest. activs	(41)		(26)
Net cash position	**4,207**	**n.m.**	**125**
Capital expenditures	(41)		(26)
	$		$
Earnings per share*	(0.01)		(0.01)
Cash flow per share*	(0.02)		0.00
	shs		shs
No. of shs. o/s*	80,939,748		47,762,257
Avg. no. of shs. o/s*	65,721,221		47,106,778
	%		%
Net profit margin	(21.17)		(14.48)
Return on equity	n.m.		n.m.
Return on assets	(18.17)		(40.34)

* Common
[A] Reported in accordance with IFRS

Historical Summary
(as originally stated)

Fiscal Year	Oper. Rev.	Net Inc. Bef. Disc.	EPS*
	$000s	$000s	$
2021[A]	3,467	(734)	(0.01)
2020[A]	2,929	(424)	(0.01)
2019[A]	2,501	(2,896)	(0.06)
2018[A]	691	(2,529)	(0.10)
2017[A]	nil	(326)	(0.02)

* Common
[A] Reported in accordance with IFRS

B.104 Braxia Scientific Corp.

Symbol - BRAX **Exchange** - CSE **CUSIP** - 105736
Head Office - 1903-700 Bay St, Toronto, ON, M5G 1Z6 **Telephone** - (416) 762-2138
Website - braxiascientific.com
Email - info@braxiascientific.com
Investor Relations - Stephen R. Brooks (416) 762-2138
Auditors - Dale Matheson Carr-Hilton LaBonte LLP C.A., Vancouver, B.C.
Transfer Agents - National Securities Administrators Ltd., Vancouver, B.C.
Profile - (B.C. 2019) Owns and operates multidisciplinary clinics and a telemedicine platform providing treatment for mental health disorders. Also researches and develops novel psychedelic treatments and delivery systems.
Clinics operate under the Braxia Health name and specialize in providing rapid-onset treatments, such as intravenous ketamine infusion therapy, intranasal esketamine therapy and sublingual/oral ketamine therapy, for several treatment-resistant conditions such as major depressive disorder and bipolar disorder. Operations consist of five clinics in Mississauga, Toronto and Ottawa, Ont., and Montreal, Que.
Owns and operates KetaMD application, a telemedicine platform for safe, affordable and life-changing at-home ketamine treatments for people suffering from mental health disorders such as depression, bipolar disorder, anxiety and post-traumatic stress disorder.
Research and development activities focus on ketamine and derivatives and other psychedelics to develop novel drug formulations. Programs include ketamine trial for bipolar depression; ketamine trial to rapidly reduce suicidality; multiple-dose psilocybin trial for treatment-resistant depression; and development of topical ketamine formulation and intranasal ketamine product.
Also offers training programs to psychiatrists, physicians and other healthcare professionals, through Braxia Institute, relating to clinical practice of psychedelic treatment therapies.

Recent Merger and Acquisition Activity

Status: completed **Announced:** Aug. 3, 2022
Braxia Scientific Corp. acquired Florida-based KetaMD, Inc., which owns and operates KetaMD application, a telemedicine platform for safe, affordable and life-changing at-home ketamine treatments for people suffering from depression and related mental health conditions, for issuance of 42,144,629 Braxia common shares and $2,940,000 convertible debentures totaling $6,262,902.
Predecessor Detail - Name changed from Champignon Brands Inc., Apr. 29, 2021, pursuant to the reverse takeover acquisition of Altmed Capital Corp.
Directors - Dr. Roger McIntyre, chr. & CEO, Toronto, Ont.; Olga Cwiek, Port Hope, Ont.; Jerry Habuda, Toronto, Ont.; Leann Taylor, Delray Beach, Fla.
Other Exec. Officers - Stephen R. Brooks, CFO; Dr. Yena Lee, chief research officer; Dr. Joshua Rosenblat, chief medical & scientific officer; Jason Wolkove, CIO; Daniel Herrera, v-p, R&D & growth; Kevin Kratiuk, v-p, opers., Braxia Health; Peter Rizakos, gen. counsel

Capital Stock

	Authorized (shs.)	Outstanding (shs.)[1]
Common	unlimited	240,723,143

[1] At Nov. 29, 2022
Major Shareholder - Widely held at Sept. 16, 2022.

Price Range - BRAX/CSE

Year	Volume	High	Low	Close
2022	78,076,793	$0.13	$0.03	$0.03
2021	65,139,991	$0.82	$0.08	$0.08
2020	184,767,599	$2.40	$0.18	$0.89

Recent Close: $0.02
Capital Stock Changes - On Aug. 3, 2022, 42,144,629 common shares were issued pursuant to the acquisition of KetaMD, Inc.
In January 2022, private placement of 30,000,000 units (1 common share & 1 warrant) at 10¢ per unit was completed. Also during fiscal 2022, common shares were issued as follows: 468,302 on exercise of warrants. 250,000 for services, 200,000 for debt settlement and 150,000 on exercise of options; 9,780,000 common shares were returned to treasury.

Wholly Owned Subsidiaries

Altmed Capital Corp., Canada.
- 100% int. in **Canadian Rapid Treatment Center of Excellence Inc.**, Mississauga, Ont.
  - 50% int. in **Canadian Rapid Treatment Centre of Excellence (Quebec) Inc.**, Montréal, Qué.

Artisan Growers Ltd., Kelowna, B.C.
KetaMD, Inc., United States.
Novo Formulations Ltd., Canada.
Tassili Life Sciences Corp., Canada.

Financial Statistics

Periods ended:	12m Mar. 31/22[A]		12m Mar. 31/21[A1]
	$000s	%Chg	$000s
Operating revenue	**1,487**	**+48**	**1,008**
Cost of sales	1,240		863
Salaries & benefits	1,083		142
Research & devel. expense	193		1,979
General & admin expense	3,661		5,669
Stock-based compensation	2,423		2,875
Operating expense	**8,600**	**-25**	**11,527**
Operating income	**(7,113)**	**n.a.**	**(10,519)**
Deprec., depl. & amort.	23		20
Finance costs, gross	5		3
Write-downs/write-offs	(5,300)[2]		(129)
Pre-tax income	**(12,179)**	**n.a.**	**(88,828)**
Income taxes	(45)		nil
Net income	**(12,134)**	**n.a.**	**(88,828)**
Cash & equivalent	8,678		11,101
Accounts receivable	225		113
Current assets	9,663		11,396
Long-term investments	35		nil
Fixed assets, net	168		50
Intangibles, net	1,768		7,044
Total assets	**11,634**	**-37**	**18,490**
Bank indebtedness	50		50
Accts. pay. & accr. liabs	2,188		2,185
Current liabilities	2,538		2,552
Long-term debt, gross	53		49
Long-term debt, net	53		49
Long-term lease liabilities	81		nil
Shareholders' equity	8,963		15,890
Cash from oper. activs	**(4,518)**	**n.a.**	**(5,056)**
Cash from fin. activs	2,704		14,412
Cash from invest. activs	(609)		(1,306)
Net cash position	**8,678**	**-22**	**11,101**
Capital expenditures	(25)		(22)
	$		$
Earnings per share*	(0.07)		(0.56)
Cash flow per share*	(0.03)		(0.03)
	shs		shs
No. of shs. o/s*	198,578,514		177,290,212
Avg. no. of shs. o/s*	175,243,678		157,639,936
	%		%
Net profit margin	(816.01)		n.m.
Return on equity	n.m.		(941.22)
Return on assets	n.a.		(824.21)

* Common

[A] Reported in accordance with IFRS

[1] Results reflect the Apr. 30, 2020, reverse takeover acquisition of Altmed Capital Corp.

[2] Includes impairment of goodwill amounting to $5,275,374.

Latest Results

Periods ended:	6m Sept. 30/22[A]		6m Sept. 30/21[A]
	$000s	%Chg	$000s
Operating revenue	873	+10	793
Net income	(3,133)	n.a.	(2,802)
	$		$
Earnings per share*	(0.02)		(0.02)

* Common

[A] Reported in accordance with IFRS

Historical Summary
(as originally stated)

Fiscal Year	Oper. Rev. $000s	Net Inc. Bef. Disc. $000s	EPS* $
2022[A]	1,487	(12,134)	(0.07)
2021[A]	1,008	(88,828)	(0.56)
2020[A1,2]	nil	(1,925)	n.a.
2019[A3,4]	nil	(173)	(0.02)

* Common

[A] Reported in accordance with IFRS

[1] 29 weeks ended Mar. 31, 2020.

[2] Results pertain to Altmed Capital Corp.

[3] 27 weeks ended Sept. 30, 2019.

[4] Results pertain to Champignon Brands Inc.

B.105 Bri-Chem Corp.

Symbol - BRY **Exchange** - TSX **CUSIP** - 10778T
Head Office - 27075 Acheson Rd, Acheson, AB, T7X 6B1 **Telephone** - (780) 962-9490 **Fax** - (780) 962-9875
Website - www.brichem.com
Email - tpagnucco@brichem.com
Investor Relations - Tony Pagnucco (780) 571-8587
Auditors - Kingston Ross Pasnak LLP C.A., Edmonton, Alta.
Bankers - Canadian Imperial Bank of Commerce, Edmonton, Alta.
Lawyers - Dentons Canada LLP, Edmonton, Alta.
Transfer Agents - Computershare Trust Company of Canada Inc., Calgary, Alta.
FP500 Revenue Ranking - 767
Employees - 65 at Dec. 31, 2022
Profile - (Alta. 2007 amalg.) Distributes, blends, packages and manufactures primarily drilling fluids and chemicals to the oil and gas industry in Canada and the United States.

Provides more than 100 products in a wide variety of weights and clays, lost circulation materials, chemicals and oil mud products to mud engineering companies who sell directly to drilling firms engaged by oil and gas companies. Products include drilling fluids and completion, cementing, acidizing, stimulation and production of chemical fluids. Products are distributed from 12 stock points or warehouses across Alberta, Saskatchewan and British Columbia, and from 14 stock points in the U.S. Owned blending, packaging and warehouse facilities are located in Camrose, Acheson and Calgary, Alta.; Estevan, Sask.; Clinton and Chickasha, Okla.; Midland, Tex.; and Bakersfield, Calif., with capacity to blend, package and distribute specialty fluids for customer specific products.

In December 2022, the company acquired a 7,500-sq.-ft. warehouse facility in Midland, Tex., for an undisclosed amount.

Predecessor Detail - Formed from mBase Commerce Inc. in Alberta, Jan. 1, 2007, on amalgamation with Gwelan Supply Ltd., constituting a reverse takeover by Gwelan; basis 1 new for 1 Gwelan sh. and 0.2 new for 1 mBase sh.

Directors - Donald P. (Don) Caron, chr., pres. & CEO, Edmonton, Alta.; Brian Campbell, Edmonton, Alta.; Eric Sauze, Edmonton, Alta.; Albert Sharp, Parkland County, Alta.

Other Exec. Officers - Tony Pagnucco, CFO

Capital Stock

	Authorized (shs.)	Outstanding (shs.)[1]
Preferred	unlimited	nil
Common	unlimited	26,432,981

[1] At May 11, 2023

Major Shareholder - Widely held at May 11, 2023.

Price Range - BRY/TSX

Year	Volume	High	Low	Close
2022	11,438,130	$0.95	$0.16	$0.66
2021	5,425,190	$0.27	$0.08	$0.16
2020	8,538,717	$0.15	$0.04	$0.08
2019	6,352,896	$0.30	$0.06	$0.10
2018	7,916,182	$0.74	$0.12	$0.17

Recent Close: $0.42

Capital Stock Changes - During 2022, 2,500,000 common shares were issued on exercise of warrants.

Wholly Owned Subsidiaries

Bri-Chem Supply Ltd., Leduc, Alta.
Bri-Corp USA Inc., Thornton, Colo.
- 100% int. in **Bri-Chem Logistics, LLC**, Okla.
- 100% int. in **Bri-Chem Supply Corp. LLC**, Thornton, Colo.
- 100% int. in **Sun Coast Materials, LLC**, Bakersfield, Calif.

Sodium Solutions Inc., Acheson, Alta.
Solution Blend Service Ltd., Calgary, Alta.

Financial Statistics

Periods ended:	12m Dec. 31/22[A]		12m Dec. 31/21[A]
	$000s	%Chg	$000s
Operating revenue	**104,513**	**+73**	**60,405**
Cost of sales	83,424		48,161
Salaries & benefits	7,025		4,363
General & admin expense	4,607		3,435
Operating expense	**95,056**	**+70**	**55,959**
Operating income	**9,457**	**+113**	**4,446**
Deprec., depl. & amort.	1,089		940
Finance costs, gross	2,556		1,700
Write-downs/write-offs	(544)		(659)
Pre-tax income	**4,620**	**+259**	**1,287**
Income taxes	(4,023)		(29)
Net inc bef disc ops, eqhldrs	8,643		1,317
Net income	**8,643**	**+556**	**1,317**
Inventories	31,864		16,776
Accounts receivable	30,919		19,342
Current assets	63,407		36,793
Fixed assets, net	8,971		6,266
Right-of-use assets	1,632		624
Total assets	**78,500**	**+79**	**43,796**
Bank indebtedness	30,739		16,410
Accts. pay. & accr. liabs	16,428		8,193
Current liabilities	47,972		31,643
Long-term debt, gross	7,124		6,764
Long-term debt, net	6,918		nil
Long-term lease liabilities	1,204		437
Shareholders' equity	22,406		11,716
Cash from oper. activs	**(8,565)**	**n.a.**	**(9,220)**
Cash from fin. activs	10,667		9,179
Cash from invest. activs	(2,102)		40
Capital expenditures	(2,109)		(44)
Capital disposals	7		84
	$		$
Earnings per share*	0.33		0.06
Cash flow per share*	(0.32)		(0.39)
	shs		shs
No. of shs. o/s*	26,432,981		23,932,981
Avg. no. of shs. o/s*	26,432,981		23,932,981
	%		%
Net profit margin	8.27		2.18
Return on equity	50.66		11.83
Return on assets	21.95		8.72
Foreign sales percent	74		70
No. of employees (FTEs)	65		57

* Common

[A] Reported in accordance with IFRS

Historical Summary
(as originally stated)

Fiscal Year	Oper. Rev. $000s	Net Inc. Bef. Disc. $000s	EPS* $
2022[A]	104,513	8,643	0.33
2021[A]	60,405	1,317	0.06
2020[A]	45,156	(5,148)	(0.22)
2019[A]	91,726	(3,656)	(0.15)
2018[A]	121,436	(9,355)	(0.39)

* Common

[A] Reported in accordance with IFRS

B.106 BriaCell Therapeutics Corp.

Symbol - BCT **Exchange** - TSX **CUSIP** - 10778Y
Head Office - Bellevue Centre, 300-235 15 St W, West Vancouver, BC, V7T 2X1 **Telephone** - (604) 921-1810 **Toll-free** - (888) 485-6340 **Fax** - (604) 921-1898
Website - www.briacell.com
Email - glevin@briacell.com
Investor Relations - Gadi P. Levin (888) 485-6340
Auditors - MNP LLP C.A., Toronto, Ont.
Transfer Agents - Computershare Trust Company of Canada Inc., Toronto, Ont.
Employees - 11 at Oct. 27, 2022
Profile - (B.C. 2006) Develops immunotherapy treatments for advanced breast and other cancers.

Developing Bria-IMT™, a genetically engineered whole-cell vaccine derived from a human breast tumour cell line. This targeted vaccine is believed to boost the immune system by releasing granulocyte/macrophage colony-stimulating factor which activates both T-cells that destroy tumour cells directly or indirectly by inducing antibody-generating immune response and B-cells that generate anti-tumour antibodies of the immune system. The vaccine is under going clinical trials in select cases of breast cancer including a combination with immune checkpoint inhibitors such as the Incyte drugs INCMGA00012, an anti-PD-1 antibody similar to pembrolizumab (KEYTRUDA®); and epacadostat, an orally bioavailable smallmolecule inhibitor of indoleamine 2,3-dioxygenase 1 (IDO1).

Also under development is BriaDX™, a diagnostic test to determine which patients are most likely to respond to Bria-IMT™; Bria-OTS™, an off-the-shelf personalized immunotherapy in development for advanced breast cancer; novel, selective protein kinase C delta inhibitors, which represents a unique, highly-targeted approach to treat cancer and to boost the immune system; Bria-Pros™, an off-the-shelf personalized immunotherapy for prostate cancer; Bria-Mel™, an off-the-shelf personalized immunotherapy for melanoma; Bria-Lung™, an off-the-shelf personalized immunotherapy for lung cancer; and Bria-TILs-RX™, an off-the-shelf personalized immunotherapy for prostate, epithelial and glandular cancer. In addition, the company has exclusive license to develop and commercialize Soluble CD80 as a biologic agent for the treatment of cancer.

On Mar. 30, 2023, the company announced plans to spin-out certain pre-clinical assets, specifically Bria-TILsRx™, and protein kinase C delta (PKC) inhibitors for multiple indications including cancer, into a newly created entity. Shareholders of the company would receive one common share of the new entity for each common share of the company held. The company would retain a 66.67% ownership interest in the new entity.

Predecessor Detail - Name changed from Ansell Capital Corp., Nov. 25, 2014, following the reverse takeover acquisition of (old) BriaCell Therapeutics Corp.; basis 1 new for 3.25 old shs.

Directors - Jamieson Bondarenko, chr., Toronto, Ont.; Dr. William V. Williams, pres. & CEO, Pa.; Vaughn C. Embro-Pantalony, Toronto, Ont.; Dr. Jane Gross, Park City, Utah; Marc Lustig, Vancouver, B.C.; Martin Schmieg, Delray Beach, Fla.; Dr. Rebecca Taub, Villanova, Pa.

Other Exec. Officers - Gadi P. Levin, CFO & corp. sec.; Dr. Giuseppe Del Priore, CMO; Dr. Miguel A. Lopez-Lago, chief scientific officer; Farrah Dean, v-p, corp. devel.

Capital Stock

	Authorized (shs.)	Outstanding (shs.)[1]
Common	unlimited	15,518,018

[1] At Dec. 12, 2022

Major Shareholder - Marc Lustig held 10.7% interest at Dec. 12, 2022.

Price Range - BCT/TSX

Year	Volume	High	Low	Close
2022	1,987,233	$15.05	$5.32	$5.90
2021	3,121,737	$15.75	$3.50	$10.45
2020	187,608	$27.00	$4.40	$5.98
2019	243,038	$45.00	$10.50	$12.00
2018	232,876	$54.00	$21.00	$24.00

Consolidation: 1-for-300 cons. in Jan. 2020

Recent Close: $10.20

Capital Stock Changes - During fiscal 2022, 1,280,107 common shares were issued on exercise of warrants and 1,031,672 common shares were repurchased under a Normal Course Issuer Bid.

Wholly Owned Subsidiaries

BriaCell Therapeutics Corp., Los Angeles, Calif.
- 100% int. in **Sapientia Pharmaceuticals, Inc.**, Pa.

Financial Statistics

Periods ended:	12m July 31/22[A]		12m July 31/21[□A]
	US$000s	%Chg	US$000s
Research & devel. expense	7,586		1,301
General & admin expense	4,613		3,652
Stock-based compensation	3,075		1,968
Operating expense	**15,274**	**+121**	**6,921**
Operating income	**(15,274)**	**n.a.**	**(6,921)**
Deprec., depl. & amort.	15		15
Finance costs, net	11,550		6,840
Pre-tax income	**(26,839)**	**n.a.**	**(13,816)**
Net income	**(26,839)**	**n.a.**	**(13,816)**
Cash & equivalent	41,042		57,269
Accounts receivable	24		13
Current assets	42,347		57,798
Intangibles, net	230		246
Total assets	**42,577**	**-27**	**58,044**
Accts. pay. & accr. liabs.	941		557
Current liabilities	941		557
Shareholders' equity	10,329		27,672
Cash from oper. activs.	**(12,484)**	**n.a.**	**(7,750)**
Cash from fin. activs.	(3,743)		64,998
Net cash position	**41,042**	**-28**	**57,269**
	US$		US$
Earnings per share*	(1.73)		(3.06)
Cash flow per share*	(0.81)		(1.71)
	shs		shs
No. of shs. o/s*	15,518,018		15,269,583
Avg. no. of shs. o/s*	15,494,091		4,519,579
	%		%
Net profit margin	n.a.		n.a.
Return on equity	(79.42)		n.m.
Return on assets	(53.35)		(48.25)
No. of employees (FTEs)	8		5

* Common
[□] Restated
[A] Reported in accordance with IFRS

Latest Results

Periods ended:	3m Oct. 31/22[A]		3m Oct. 31/21[A]
	US$000s	%Chg	US$000s
Net income	(1,107)	n.a.	(27,533)
	US$		US$
Earnings per share*	(0.07)		(1.81)

* Common
[A] Reported in accordance with IFRS

Historical Summary
(as originally stated)

Fiscal Year	Oper. Rev.	Net Inc. Bef. Disc.	EPS*
	US$000s	US$000s	US$
2022[A]	nil	(26,839)	(1.73)
2021[A]	nil	(428)	(0.09)
	$000s	$000s	$
2020[A]	nil	(4,944)	(6.99)
2019[A]	nil	(5,790)	(9.00)
2018[A]	nil	(5,413)	(12.00)

* Common
[A] Reported in accordance with IFRS

Note: Adjusted throughout for 1-for-300 cons. in Jan. 2020

B.107 Bridgemarq Real Estate Services Inc.

Symbol - BRE **Exchange** - TSX **CUSIP** - 10808B
Head Office - 200-39 Wynford Dr, Toronto, ON, M3C 3K5 **Telephone** - (416) 510-5800 **Fax** - (416) 510-5856
Website - www.bridgemarq.com
Email - info@bridgemarq.com
Investor Relations - Anne-Elise Cugliari Allegritti (416) 510-5783
Auditors - Deloitte LLP C.A., Toronto, Ont.
Lawyers - Goodmans LLP, Toronto, Ont.
Transfer Agents - TSX Trust Company, Toronto, Ont.
Managers - Bridgemarq Real Estate Services Manager Limited, Toronto, Ont.

Profile - (Ont. 2010) Through subsidiary **Residential Income Fund L.P.**, provides services to a national network of real estate brokers and Realtors® in Canada under the Royal LePage, Via Capitale and Johnston & Daniel brand names.

Residential Income Fund L.P. (75% owned; RIFLP) receives fixed and variable franchise fees and other revenues from the services it provides to real estate professionals in facilitating the purchase and sale of real estate, including proprietary technological, marketing, promotional, communications and support systems. **Brookfield BBP (Canada) Holdings L.P.** holds the remaining 25% interest in RIFLP.

At Mar. 31, 2023, the franchise network consisted of 286 franchises with 20,619 Realtors® operating from 726 locations across Canada.

The company is managed by **Bridgemarq Real Estate Services Manager Limited** (formerly **Brookfield Real Estate Services Manager Limited**), a wholly owned subsidiary of **Brookfield Asset Management Inc.**

Predecessor Detail - Name changed from Brookfield Real Estate Services Inc., May 27, 2019.

Directors - Spencer Enright, chr., Oakville, Ont.; Colum P. Bastable, Toronto, Ont.; Lorraine D. Bell, New York, N.Y.; Jitanjli Datt, Toronto, Ont.; Joseph S. (Joe) Freedman, Toronto, Ont.; Gail Kilgour, Toronto, Ont.

Other Exec. Officers - Philip (Phil) Soper, pres. & CEO; Glen McMillan, CFO

Capital Stock

	Authorized (shs.)	Outstanding (shs.)[1]
Preferred	unlimited	nil
Restricted Voting	unlimited	9,483,850
Special Voting	1	1
Class A LP Unit	unlimited	9,983,000
Class B LP Unit	unlimited	3,327,667[2]

[1] At May 9, 2023
[2] Classified as debt.

Note: LP units are securities of subsidiary Residential Income Fund L.P.

Restricted Voting - One vote per share except that restricted voting shareholders do not vote for the directors who are appointed by the holder of the special voting share. Carry 74% of the aggregate votes attached to all issued and outstanding voting shares.

Special Voting - Held by Brookfield BBP (Canada) Holdings L.P. (BBP) and not transferable other than to affiliates of BBP. Entitled to appoint two-fifths of the directors of the company so long as BBP and/or its affiliates hold at least 10% of the restricted voting shares outstanding (calculated on the basis that all class B limited partnership units have been exchanged for restricted voting shares). Entitles the holder to a number of votes at shareholder meetings equal to the number of restricted voting shares into which the class B limited partnership units are exchangeable. Carry 26% of the aggregate votes attached to all issued and outstanding voting shares. Redeemable by the holder at 1¢ per share.

Class A Limited Partnership Unit - Represents the 75% interest in Residential Income Fund L.P. (RIFLP) held by the company.

Class B Limited Partnership Unit - Represents the 25% interest in RIFLP held by BBP. Exchangeable for restricted voting shares on a 1-for-1 basis. Equal in all other respects to class A limited partnership units.

Major Shareholder - Brookfield Corporation held 28.4% interest at Mar. 27, 2023.

Price Range - BRE/TSX

Year	Volume	High	Low	Close
2022	2,967,351	$17.13	$12.40	$12.84
2021	2,631,088	$18.00	$14.33	$16.31
2020	4,213,380	$15.85	$6.31	$14.80
2019	4,024,039	$17.48	$12.87	$14.72
2018	3,285,888	$20.15	$12.36	$14.57

Recent Close: $14.70

Capital Stock Changes - There were no changes to capital stock from 2011 to 2022, inclusive.

Dividends

BRE com Ra $1.35 pa M est. Sept. 30, 2017

Subsidiaries

75% int. in **Residential Income Fund General Partner Limited**, Ont.
75% int. in **Residential Income Fund L.P.**, Ont.
- 100% int. in **9120 Real Estate Network, L.P.**, Qué.

Financial Statistics

Periods ended:	12m Dec. 31/22[A]		12m Dec. 31/21[A]
	$000s	%Chg	$000s
Operating revenue	**49,871**	**-1**	**50,202**
Cost of sales	1,207		1,035
General & admin expense	20,992		20,804
Operating expense	**22,199**	**+2**	**21,839**
Operating income	**27,672**	**-2**	**28,363**
Deprec., depl. & amort.	7,168		7,631
Finance income	13,750		nil
Finance costs, gross	8,776		11,904
Write-downs/write-offs	154		nil
Pre-tax income	**25,324**	**+187**	**8,828**
Income taxes	4,355		4,066
Net income	**20,969**	**+340**	**4,762**
Cash & equivalent	6,419		6,217
Accounts receivable	3,502		3,425
Current assets	11,888		10,134
Intangibles, net	54,942		62,238
Total assets	**72,629**	**-8**	**78,596**
Accts. pay. & accr. liabs.	1,138		1,107
Current liabilities	70,250		3,231
Long-term debt, gross	109,686		122,693
Long-term debt, net	42,727		122,693
Shareholders' equity	(48,314)		(56,480)
Cash from oper. activs.	**15,103**	**0**	**15,139**
Cash from fin. activs.	(14,303)		(17,803)
Cash from invest. activs.	(598)		275
Net cash position	**6,419**	**+3**	**6,217**
	$		$
Earnings per share*	2.21		0.50
Cash flow per share*	1.59		1.60
Cash divd. per share*	1.35		1.35
	shs		shs
No. of shs. o/s*	9,483,850		9,483,850
Avg. no. of shs. o/s*	9,483,850		9,483,850
	%		%
Net profit margin	42.05		9.49
Return on equity	n.m.		n.m.
Return on assets	37.34		13.35

* Restricted Vtg.
[A] Reported in accordance with IFRS

Latest Results

Periods ended:	3m Mar. 31/23[A]		3m Mar. 31/22[A]
	$000s	%Chg	$000s
Operating revenue	11,991	-11	13,426
Net income	(4,705)	n.a.	4,719
	$		$
Earnings per share*	(0.50)		0.50

* Restricted Vtg.
[A] Reported in accordance with IFRS

Historical Summary
(as originally stated)

Fiscal Year	Oper. Rev.	Net Inc. Bef. Disc.	EPS*
	$000s	$000s	$
2022[A]	49,871	20,969	2.21
2021[A]	50,202	4,762	0.50
2020[A]	40,339	767	0.08
2019[A]	44,349	3,076	0.32
2018[A]	42,027	17,391	1.83

* Restricted Vtg.
[A] Reported in accordance with IFRS

B.108 Bright Minds Biosciences Inc.

Symbol - DRUG **Exchange** - CSE **CUSIP** - 10919W
Head Office - 1500-1055 Georgia St W, Vancouver, BC, V6E 4N7
Website - brightmindsbio.com

Email - ian@brightmindsbio.com
Investor Relations - Ian McDonald (647) 407-2515
Auditors - De Visser Gray LLP C.A., Vancouver, B.C.
Transfer Agents - Computershare Trust Company of Canada Inc., Vancouver, B.C.
Profile - (B.C. 2019) Developing serotonergic (5-HT) therapeutics to improve the lives of patients with severe and life-altering diseases, with a focus on new chemical entities for a variety of pain indications, seizures and neuropsychiatric disorders.

Pre-clinical stage drug pipeline consists of 5-HT_{2C}, which targets Dravet syndrome, epilepsy, opioid use disorder, binge eating disorder and Alzheimer's; 5-HT_{2A}, which targets depression and post-traumatic stress disorder (PTSD); and 5-HT_{2A} + 5-HT_{2C}, which targets undisclosed chronic pain disorder.

In September 2022, wholly owned **Psilocybinlabs Ltd.** was dissolved.

Directors - Ian McDonald, pres. & CEO, Toronto, Ont.; Dr. Jan Pedersen, chief science officer, Soborg, Denmark; Nils C. Bottler, Berlin, Germany; Jeremy Fryzuk, London, Middx., United Kingdom; Dr. Emer Lahey, Pa.; Dr. David Weiner, United States

Other Exec. Officers - Ryan E. Cheung, CFO; Dr. Mark A. Smith, CMO; Jianmin Duan, v-p, pharmacology; Thomas Grizzle, v-p, toxicology; Dr. Tom Lategan, v-p, regulatory affairs; Dr. Gideon Shapiro, v-p, discovery

Capital Stock

	Authorized (shs.)	Outstanding (shs.)[1]
Common	unlimited	3,772,071

[1] At July 14, 2023

Major Shareholder - Dr. Alan Kozikowski held 10.71% interest at Dec. 28, 2022.

Price Range - DRUG/CSE

Year	Volume	High	Low	Close
2022	1,171,659	$30.35	$4.50	$5.10
2021	504,017	$55.00	$20.05	$20.40

Consolidation: 1-for-5 cons. in July 2023
Recent Close: $3.60

Capital Stock Changes - In December 2022, private placement of 194,800 units (1 post-consolidated common share & 1 warrant) at $6.25 per unit was completed, with warrants exercisable at $6.75 per share for two years. On July 14, 2023, common shares were consolidated on a 1-for-5 basis.

During fiscal 2022, common shares were issued as follows: 2,874,998 on exercise of warrants, 2,858,000 by private placement and 25,000 for services.

Wholly Owned Subsidiaries

Bright Minds Bioscience Pty. Ltd., Australia.
Bright Minds Biosciences LLC, Del.

Financial Statistics

Periods ended:	12m Sept. 30/22[A]		12m Sept. 30/21[A]
	$000s	%Chg	$000s
Research & devel. expense	11,409		5,605
General & admin expense	2,543		2,290
Stock-based compensation	772		709
Other operating expense	243		182
Operating expense	**14,967**	**+70**	**8,786**
Operating income	**(14,967)**	**n.a.**	**(8,786)**
Deprec., depl. & amort.	6		nil
Finance costs, gross	2		nil
Write-downs/write-offs	(2)		nil
Pre-tax income	**(14,965)**	**n.a.**	**(8,651)**
Net income	**(14,965)**	**n.a.**	**(8,651)**
Cash & equivalent	11,628		19,760
Accounts receivable	115		110
Current assets	11,948		20,038
Right-of-use assets	139		nil
Intangibles, net	nil		2
Total assets	**12,087**	**-40**	**20,040**
Accts. pay. & accr. liabs	1,405		639
Current liabilities	1,472		639
Long-term lease liabilities	72		nil
Shareholders' equity	10,543		19,402
Cash from oper. activs	**(13,587)**	**n.a.**	**(7,319)**
Cash from fin. activs	5,196		26,056
Net cash position	**11,628**	**-41**	**19,760**
	$		$
Earnings per share*	(6.05)		(4.80)
Cash flow per share*	(5.50)		(4.08)
	shs		shs
No. of shs. o/s*	3,518,472		2,366,872
Avg. no. of shs. o/s*	2,470,383		1,794,805
	%		%
Net profit margin	n.a.		n.a.
Return on equity	(99.95)		(85.95)
Return on assets	(93.15)		(82.71)

* Common
[A] Reported in accordance with IFRS

Historical Summary
(as originally stated)

Fiscal Year	Oper. Rev.	Net Inc. Bef. Disc.	EPS*
	$000s	$000s	$
2022[A]	nil	(14,965)	(6.05)
2021[A]	nil	(8,651)	(4.80)
2020[A1]	nil	(480)	(0.65)
2019[A1,2]	nil	(79)	(0.20)

* Common
[A] Reported in accordance with IFRS
[1] Shares and per share figures adjusted to reflect 1-for-2.5 share consolidation effective Nov. 10, 2020.
[2] 4 months ended Sept. 30, 2019.
Note: Adjusted throughout for 1-for-5 cons. in July 2023

B.109 Britannia Life Sciences Inc.

Symbol - BLAB **Exchange** - CSE **CUSIP** - 11042D
Head Office - 2400-120 Adelaide St W, Toronto, ON, M5H 1T1
Telephone - (416) 433-9259
Website - britannia.life
Email - peter@britannia.life
Investor Relations - Peter J. Shippen (416) 930-7711
Auditors - Zeifmans LLP C.A., Toronto, Ont.
Lawyers - MLT Aikins LLP, Winnipeg, Man.
Transfer Agents - Odyssey Trust Company, Toronto, Ont.
Profile - (Can. 2000) Provides product testing, safety assessment and compliance services to the cosmetic, consumer packaged goods and nutraceutical industries in the United Kingdom and globally. Also develops and sells hemp-based cannabis consumer products for wellness for both women and men and adult sexual health.

Through subsidiary **Advanced Development & Safety Laboratories Limited** (ADSL) operates a formulation and laboratory testing facility in Devon, United Kingdom. Is licensed to test and approve cannabidiol (CBD) products in the U.K. ADSL's primary products and services include cosmetic product safety reports, global compliance & registration, microbiological & laboratory testing, consumer & clinical evaluation and CBD novel foods agreements. Also holds 50% interest in **Britannia Mining Solutions Inc.**, which operates and develops mining assay labs.

The RISE Life Sciences portfolio includes nanotized, hemp-based CBD wellness, sleep, sport recovery, intimacy, muscle recovery and PMS targeted oral sprays with non-GMO, lactose free all-natural ingredients, marketed under Life Bloom Organics™ brand; and a suite of CBD-based oral spray which combines nanotized hemp extracts with traditional herbs, adaptogens and essential oils designed to enhance intimate experiences for women and men, marketed under the Karezza™ brand. Also offers hemp-based CBD wellness, sleep, intimacy, muscle recovery and PMS targeted products delivered through quick-dissolve oral tables; and hemp-based CBD topical products, which includes muscle recovery lotion and muscle recovery balm, all marketed under the Life Bloom Organics™ brand. Products are sold through its website.

In March 2022, common shares were listed on the Frankfurt Stock Exchange under the symbol L020.

Predecessor Detail - Name changed from RISE Life Science Corp., Nov. 10, 2021, pursuant to the reverse takeover acquisition of London, U.K.-based Britannia Bud Canada Holdings Inc. (dba Britannia Life Sciences); basis 1 new for 10 old shs.

Directors - Peter J. Shippen, CEO, Toronto, Ont.; Scott Lawrence Secord, Toronto, Ont.; Greg Taylor, Ont.

Other Exec. Officers - Boris Novansky, pres.; Sarah Zilik, CFO & corp. sec.; Mark Bowes-Cavanagh, chief technical officer

Capital Stock

	Authorized (shs.)	Outstanding (shs.)[1]
Class A Common	unlimited	nil
Common	unlimited	162,254,339

[1] At Nov. 10, 2022

Major Shareholder - Peter J. Shippen held 22.8% interest and Mark Bowes-Cavanagh held 11.5% interest at Nov. 10, 2022.

Price Range - BLAB/CSE

Year	Volume	High	Low	Close
2022	25,832,275	$0.25	$0.05	$0.07
2021	9,039,552	$0.32	$0.16	$0.19
2020	601,917	$0.20	$0.05	$0.20
2019	1,498,216	$2.90	$0.05	$0.05
2018	1,909,815	$7.40	$0.45	$1.80

Consolidation: 1-for-10 cons. in Nov. 2021
Recent Close: $0.08

Capital Stock Changes - In May 2021, private placement of 10,301,940 post-consolidated units (1 common share & 1 warrant) at US$0.007 per unit was completed. In June 2021, 8,243,339 post-consolidated common shares were issued on conversion of notes and 3,389,834 post-consolidated common shares were issued for debt settlement. In October 2021, 2,335,680 post-consolidated common shares were issued on conversion of notes. In November 2021, common shares were consolidated on a 1-for-10 basis and pursuant to the reverse takeover acquisition of Britannia Bud Canada Holdings Inc. (BBCH) post-consolidated common shares were issued as follows: 77,626,332 to BBCH shareholders, 50,956,082 on conversion of BBCH debentures and 3,000,000 to an officer. Also during fiscal 2022, 20,000 post-consolidated common shares were issued on exercise of warrants.

Wholly Owned Subsidiaries

Britannia Bud Canada Holdings Inc., London, Middx., United Kingdom.
- 70% int. in **Advanced Development & Safety Laboratories Limited**, United Kingdom.
- 100% int. in **Britannia Bud Company Limited**, London, Middx., United Kingdom.

Jamaica-BLU Ltd., Canada.
RISE Life Science (Colorado) LLC, Colo.
- 100% int. in **Brandmax Inc.**, Malibu, Calif. dba Cultivate Kind.
- 100% int. in **Life Bloom Organics, LLC**, Malibu, Calif.

RISE Research Inc., Canada.
Scout Assessment Corp.

Investments

50% int. in **Britannia Mining Solutions Inc.**

Financial Statistics

Periods ended:	12m Mar. 31/22[A1]		12m Mar. 31/21[oA]
	$000s	%Chg	$000s
Operating revenue	**7,300**	**+412**	**1,425**
Cost of sales	2,038		253
Salaries & benefits	1,215		292
General & admin expense	1,136		561
Stock-based compensation	1,107		nil
Operating expense	**5,496**	**+397**	**1,106**
Operating income	**1,804**	**+466**	**319**
Deprec., depl. & amort.	190		35
Finance costs, gross	2,314		358
Pre-tax income	**(13,275)**	**n.a.**	**401**
Income taxes	712		258
Net income	**(13,986)**	**n.a.**	**143**
Net inc. for equity hldrs	**(15,458)**	**n.a.**	**(157)**
Net inc. for non-cont. int	**1,472**	**+391**	**300**
Cash & equivalent	1,631		828
Accounts receivable	1,792		1,686
Current assets	3,485		2,514
Fixed assets, net	546		703
Intangibles, net	17,059		18,234
Total assets	**21,090**	**-2**	**21,452**
Accts. pay. & accr. liabs	3,201		2,032
Current liabilities	8,322		10,189
Long-term debt, gross	122		2,363
Long-term debt, net	122		2,363
Shareholders' equity	1,352		(202)
Non-controlling interest	4,131		2,865
Cash from oper. activs	**2,799**	**n.a.**	**(587)**
Cash from fin. activs	(2,579)		6,202
Cash from invest. activs	654		(4,913)
Net cash position	**1,631**	**+97**	**828**
Capital expenditures	(87)		nil
Capital disposals	nil		43
	$		$
Earnings per share*	(0.14)		(0.02)
Cash flow per share*	0.03		(0.08)
	shs		shs
No. of shs. o/s*	161,904,339		n.a.
Avg. no. of shs. o/s*	109,501,513		7,762,633
	%		%
Net profit margin	(191.59)		10.04
Return on equity	n.m.		n.m.
Return on assets	(54.29)		2.49

* Common
[o] Restated
[A] Reported in accordance with IFRS
[1] Results reflect the Nov. 15, 2021, reverse takeover acquisition of Britannia Bud Canada Holdings Inc.

Latest Results

Periods ended:	6m Sept. 30/22[A]		6m Sept. 30/21[oA]
	$000s	%Chg	$000s
Operating revenue	3,104	-20	3,895
Net income	5,008	+669	651
Net inc. for equity hldrs	4,573	n.a.	(177)
Net inc. for non-cont. int	435		828
	$		$
Earnings per share*	0.03		(0.02)

* Common
[o] Restated
[A] Reported in accordance with IFRS

Historical Summary
(as originally stated)

Fiscal Year	Oper. Rev. $000s	Net Inc. Bef. Disc. $000s	EPS* $
2022[A1]	7,300	(13,986)	(0.14)
2020[A]	32	(3,204)	(0.50)
2019[A]	974	(7,127)	(1.20)
2018[A]	186	(11,856)	(2.40)

* Common
[A] Reported in accordance with IFRS
[1] Results reflect the Nov. 15, 2021, reverse takeover acquisition of Britannia Bud Canada Holdings Inc.
Note: Adjusted throughout for 1-for-10 cons. in Nov. 2021

B.110 British Columbia Hydro and Power Authority

CUSIP - 110601
Head Office - 333 Dunsmuir St, Vancouver, BC, V6B 5R3 **Telephone** - (604) 224-9376 **Toll-free** - (800) 224-9376
Website - www.bchydro.com
Email - connectwithus@bchydro.com
Investor Relations - Media Relations (800) 224-9376
Auditors - KPMG LLP C.A., Vancouver, B.C.
FP500 Revenue Ranking - 84
Employees - 5,863 at Mar. 31, 2022
Profile - (B.C. 1961) Generates, transmits and distributes electricity in British Columbia, serving 95% of the province's population.
Operates 30 hydroelectric plants and two thermal generating stations located throughout the Peace region in northeastern B.C. and Columbia region in southeastern B.C., as well as the Lower Mainland and Coast and on Vancouver Island. The hydroelectric system has 12,206 MW of installed generating capacity and a network of 80,241 km of transmission and distribution lines (at Mar. 31, 2022).

Periods ended:	12m Mar. 31/22	12m Mar. 31/21
Electric sales, GWh	84,719	83,780
Generating capacity, MW	12,206	12,204
Transmission lines, km	20,148	19,958
Distribution lines, km	60,093	59,907
Electric. customer accts	2,156,202	2,118,453

Directors - Lori Wanamaker, chr., B.C.; Lynette DuJohn, B.C.; Daryl A. Fields, B.C.; Amanda Hobson, Kamloops, B.C.; Irene Lanzinger, B.C.; Chief Clarence Louie, B.C.; Victoria J. McMillan, North Vancouver, B.C.; Nalaine Morin, B.C.; Vasee Navaratnam, Vancouver, B.C.; John Nunn, Sooke, B.C.; Catherine Roome, North Vancouver, B.C.
Other Exec. Officers - Chris O'Riley, pres. & CEO; Maureen Daschuk, exec. v-p, integrated planning; Al Leonard, exec. v-p, capital infrastructure project delivery; Charlotte Mitha, exec. v-p, opers.; Ken Duke, sr. v-p & gen. counsel; Kirsten Peck, sr. v-p, safety & chief compliance officer; Carolynn Ryan, sr. v-p, people & chief HR officer; Diana Stephenson, sr. v-p, cust. & corp. affairs
Major Shareholder - Province of British Columbia held 100% interest at Mar. 31, 2022.

Wholly Owned Subsidiaries
Powerex Corp., Vancouver, B.C.
Powertech Labs Inc., Surrey, B.C.
Note: The preceding list includes only the major related companies in which interests are held.

Financial Statistics

Periods ended:	12m Mar. 31/22[A]		12m Mar. 31/21[A]
	$000s	%Chg	$000s
Operating revenue	**7,591,000**	**+18**	**6,414,000**
Cost of sales	3,002,000		2,269,000
Salaries & benefits	736,000		711,000
Operating expense	**4,715,000**	**+21**	**3,889,000**
Operating income	**2,876,000**	**+14**	**2,525,000**
Deprec., depl. & amort.	1,079,000		1,009,000
Finance costs, gross	521,000		224,000
Pre-tax income	**668,000**	**-3**	**688,000**
Net income	**668,000**	**-3**	**688,000**
Cash & equivalent	99,000		37,000
Inventories	199,000		182,000
Accounts receivable	451,000		469,000
Current assets	1,571,000		1,291,000
Fixed assets, net	34,038,000		31,677,000
Right-of-use assets	1,248,000		1,317,000
Intangibles, net	705,000		688,000
Total assets	**42,734,000**	**+6**	**40,383,000**
Accts. pay. & accr. liabs	1,545,000		1,288,000
Current liabilities	5,380,000		5,246,000
Long-term debt, gross	25,951,000		24,980,000
Long-term debt, net	22,659,000		21,651,000
Long-term lease liabilities	1,327,000		1,352,000
Shareholders' equity	7,046,000		6,367,000
Cash from oper. activs	**2,415,000**	**+31**	**1,839,000**
Cash from fin. activs	774,000		996,000
Cash from invest. activs	(3,127,000)		(2,913,000)
Net cash position	**99,000**	**+168**	**37,000**
Capital expenditures	(3,127,000)		(2,913,000)
Unfunded pension liability	713,000		1,311,000
	$		$
Earnings per share*	n.a.		n.a.
	shs		shs
No. of shs. o/s	n.a.		n.a.
	%		%
Net profit margin	8.80		10.73
Return on equity	9.96		11.45
Return on assets	2.86		2.30
No. of employees (FTEs)	5,863		6,128

[A] Reported in accordance with IFRS

Historical Summary
(as originally stated)

Fiscal Year	Oper. Rev. $000s	Net Inc. Bef. Disc. $000s	EPS* $
2022[A]	7,591,000	668,000	n.a.
2021[A]	6,414,000	688,000	n.a.
2020[A]	6,269,000	705,000	n.a.
2019[A]	6,573,000	(428,000)	n.a.
2018[A]	6,237,000	684,000	n.a.

* Common
[A] Reported in accordance with IFRS

B.111 Brompton Lifeco Split Corp.

Symbol - LCS **Exchange** - TSX **CUSIP** - 112216
Head Office - c/o Brompton Group Limited, Bay Wellington Tower, Brookfield Place, 2930-181 Bay St, PO Box 793, Toronto, ON, M5J 2T3 **Telephone** - (416) 642-9061 **Toll-free** - (866) 642-6001 **Fax** - (416) 642-6001
Website - www.bromptongroup.com
Email - wong@bromptongroup.com
Investor Relations - Ann P. Wong (866) 642-6001
Auditors - PricewaterhouseCoopers LLP C.A., Toronto, Ont.
Transfer Agents - TSX Trust Company, Toronto, Ont.
Managers - Brompton Funds Limited, Toronto, Ont.
Portfolio Managers - Brompton Funds Limited, Toronto, Ont.
Profile - (Ont. 2007) Invests in a portfolio of the common shares of the four largest publicly traded Canadian life insurance companies.
The portfolio consists of common shares of **Great-West Lifeco Inc.**, **iA Financial Group Inc.**, **Manulife Financial Corporation** and **Sun Life Financial Inc.** The portfolio is rebalanced on an equally weighted basis, at least annually, to adjust for changes in the market values of investments, and to reflect the impact of a merger or acquisition affecting one or more of the life insurance companies.
To generate additional income, the company may write covered call or put options in respect of common shares held in the portfolio. The company will terminate on Apr. 29, 2024, unless extended.
The manager receives a management fee at an annual rate equal to 0.6% of the net asset value calculated and payable monthly in arrears.
On Aug. 10, 2023, the company announced an extension of the term of the class A and preferred shares an additional five years to Apr. 27, 2029.
Directors - Mark A. Caranci, pres. & CEO, Toronto, Ont.; Ann P. Wong, CFO & chief compliance officer, Toronto, Ont.; Christopher S. L. Hoffmann, Toronto, Ont.; Raymond R. Pether, Toronto, Ont.
Other Exec. Officers - Laura Lau, chief invest. officer; Kathryn A. H. Banner, sr. v-p & corp. sec.; Michael D. Clare, sr. v-p & sr. portfolio mgr.; Christopher Cullen, sr. v-p; Manith (Manny) Phanvongsa, sr. v-p; Michelle L. Tiraborelli, sr. v-p

Capital Stock

	Authorized (shs.)	Outstanding (shs.)[1]
Preferred	unlimited	9,017,415[2]
Class A	unlimited	9,017,415
Class J	unlimited	100[2]

[1] At Dec. 31, 2022
[2] Classified as debt.
Preferred - Entitled to receive fixed cumulative preferential quarterly dividends of $0.15625 per share (to yield 6.25% per annum on the original $10 issue price). Under a regular monthly retraction, a shareholder will receive, for each preferred share, an amount equal to 96% of the lesser of: (i) the net asset value (NAV) per unit (1 class A share and 1 preferred share) less the cost associated with the retraction of class A shares; and (ii) $10. Under a concurrent annual retraction on the April valuation date of each year, a shareholder will receive, for each unit, an amount equal to the NAV per unit less any costs related to liquidating the portfolio to pay such amount. All outstanding preferred shares will be redeemed on Apr. 29, 2029, at a price per share equal to the lesser of: (i) $10 plus any accrued and unpaid distributions; and (ii) the NAV per share. Rank in priority to the class A and class J shares with respect to the payment of dividends and the repayment of capital on the dissolution, liquidation or winding-up of the company. Non-voting.
Class A - Entitled to non-cumulative monthly cash distributions of $0.075 per share (to yield 6% per annum on the original $15 issue price). No distributions will be paid if the distributions payable on the preferred shares are in arrears or in respect of a cash distribution, after payment of the distribution, the NAV per unit (1 class A share and 1 preferred share) would be less than $15. In addition, no special distributions would be paid on the class A shares if, after payment of the distribution, the NAV per unit would be less than $25 unless the company has to make such distributions to fully recover refundable taxes. Under a regular monthly retraction, a shareholder will receive, for each class A share, the amount by which 96% of the NAV per unit exceeds the cost to the company of purchasing a preferred share in the market. Under a concurrent annual retraction on the April valuation date of each year, a shareholder will receive, for each unit, an amount equal to the NAV per unit less any costs related to liquidating the portfolio to pay such amount. All outstanding class A shares will be redeemed on Apr. 29, 2029, at a price equal to the greater of: (i) the NAV per unit minus $10 plus any accrued and unpaid distributions on a preferred share; and (ii) nil. Rank subsequent to the preferred shares but in priority to the class J shares with respect to the payment of dividends and the repayment of capital on the dissolution, liquidation or winding-up of the company. Non-voting.
Class J - Not entitled to receive dividends. Redeemable and retractable at a price of $1.00 per share. Rank subsequent to both the preferred shares and class A shares with respect to distributions on the dissolution, liquidation or winding-up of the company. One vote per share.
Major Shareholder - LCS Trust held 100% interest at Mar. 23, 2023.

Price Range - LCS/TSX

Year	Volume	High	Low	Close
2022	9,864,059	$7.19	$2.96	$4.43
2021	4,054,967	$7.19	$3.75	$6.88
2020	5,053,010	$6.87	$1.26	$3.75
2019	3,919,949	$6.25	$2.61	$6.23
2018	4,999,126	$7.89	$2.10	$2.74

Recent Close: $5.27
Capital Stock Changes - In January 2022, public offering of 2,382,400 preferred shares and 2,382,400 class A shares was completed at $10.05 and $6.95 per share, respectively. In March 2022, public offering of 1,788,100 preferred shares and 1,788,100 class A shares was completed at $10.05 and $6.70 per share, respectively. Also during 2022, 64,700 preferred shares and 64,700 class A shares were retracted.

Dividends

LCS cl A N.V. N.S.R. **[1]

$0.075	Sept. 15/23	$0.075	Aug. 15/23
$0.075	July 17/23	$0.075	June 14/23

Paid in 2023: $0.60 2022: $0.375 2021: $0.75
LCS.PR.A pfd cum. red. ret. Ra $0.625 pa Q
[1] No set frequency divd normally payable in Apr/20 has been omitted.
** Reinvestment Option

Financial Statistics

Periods ended:	12m Dec. 31/22[A]		12m Dec. 31/21[A]
	$000s	%Chg	$000s
Realized invest. gain (loss)	97		2,302
Unrealized invest. gain (loss)	(10,094)		13,736
Total revenue	**(3,894)**	**n.a.**	**19,315**
General & admin. expense	2,501		735
Operating expense	**2,501**	**+240**	**735**
Operating income	**(6,395)**	**n.a.**	**18,580**
Finance costs, gross	5,436		3,093
Pre-tax income	**(11,831)**	**n.a.**	**15,488**
Net income	**(11,831)**	**n.a.**	**15,488**
Cash & equivalent	1,282		1,049
Investments	133,093		79,418
Total assets	**134,580**	**+67**	**80,509**
Accts. pay. & accr. liabs	81		63
Debt	90,174		49,116
Shareholders' equity	43,318		30,447
Cash from oper. activs	**(64,883)**	**n.a.**	**11,178**
Cash from fin. activs	65,116		(11,106)
Net cash position	**1,282**	**+22**	**1,049**
	$		$
Earnings per share*	(1.38)		3.07
Cash flow per share*	(7.56)		2.22
Net asset value per share*	4.80		6.20
Cash divd. per share*	0.30		0.83
	shs		shs
No. of shs. o/s*	9,017,415		4,911,615
Avg. no. of shs. o/s*	8,578,677		5,046,174
	%		%
Net profit margin	n.m.		80.19
Return on equity	(32.08)		58.99
Return on assets	(5.95)		23.72

* Class A

[A] Reported in accordance with IFRS

Note: Net income reflects increase/decrease in net assets from operations.

Historical Summary
(as originally stated)

Fiscal Year	Total Rev. $000s	Net Inc. Bef. Disc. $000s	EPS* $
2022[A]	(3,894)	(11,831)	(1.38)
2021[A]	19,315	15,488	3.07
2020[A]	(13,085)	(17,181)	(3.04)
2019[A]	34,250	29,188	4.37
2018[A]	(20,358)	(26,165)	(3.71)

* Class A

[A] Reported in accordance with IFRS

B.112 Brompton Oil Split Corp.

Symbol - OSP **Exchange** - TSX **CUSIP** - 11222H
Head Office - c/o Brompton Group Limited, Bay Wellington Tower, Brookfield Place, 2930-181 Bay St, PO Box 793, Toronto, ON, M5J 2T3 **Telephone** - (416) 642-9061 **Toll-free** - (866) 642-6001 **Fax** - (416) 642-6001
Website - www.bromptongroup.com
Email - wong@bromptongroup.com
Investor Relations - Ann P. Wong (866) 642-6001
Auditors - PricewaterhouseCoopers LLP C.A., Toronto, Ont.
Transfer Agents - TSX Trust Company, Toronto, Ont.
Managers - Brompton Funds Limited, Toronto, Ont.
Portfolio Managers - Brompton Funds Limited, Toronto, Ont.
Profile - (Ont. 2014) Holds common shares of at least 15 large capitalization North American oil and gas issuers from the S&P/TSX Composite Index and S&P 500 Index.

The portfolio may be reconstituted and is rebalanced at least semi-annually at the manager's discretion. To be included in the portfolio, an issuer must be a constituent of the S&P 500 Index or the S&P/TSX Composite Index, have a market capitalization of at least $2 billion and pay a dividend at the time of investment, reconstitution or rebalancing. The portfolio is focused primarily on oil and gas issuers that have significant exposure to oil. The company may also invest up to 25% of the portfolio value, as measured at the time of investment, in equity securities of issuers that operate in energy subsectors including equipment, services, pipelines, transportation and infrastructure.

The manager receives a management fee at an annual rate equal to 0.70% of the net asset value calculated daily and payable monthly in arrears.

Top 10 holdings at Mar. 31, 2023 (as a percentage of net asset value):

Holding	Percentage
Pioneer Natural Resources Co.	5.9%
Tourmaline Oil Corp.	5.9%
Canadian Natural Resources Ltd.	5.9%
Imperial Oil Ltd.	5.8%
Occidental Petroleum Corp.	5.8%
Cenovus Energy Inc.	5.8%
Exxon Mobil Corp.	5.8%
Devon Energy Corp.	5.8%
Marathon Oil Corp.	5.8%
Diamondback Energy Inc.	5.8%

On Aug. 10, 2023, the company announced an extension of the term of the class A and preferred shares an additional one year to Mar. 28, 2025.

On Jan. 27, 2023, the company announced an extension of the term of the class A and preferred shares an additional one year to Mar. 28, 2024.

Directors - Mark A. Caranci, pres. & CEO, Toronto, Ont.; Ann P. Wong, CFO & chief compliance officer, Toronto, Ont.; Christopher S. L. Hoffmann, Toronto, Ont.; Raymond R. Pether, Toronto, Ont.

Other Exec. Officers - Laura Lau, chief invest. officer; Kathryn A. H. Banner, sr. v-p & corp. sec.; Michael D. Clare, sr. v-p & sr. portfolio mgr.; Christopher Cullen, sr. v-p; Manith (Manny) Phanvongsa, sr. v-p; Michelle L. Tiraborelli, sr. v-p

Capital Stock

	Authorized (shs.)	Outstanding (shs.)[1]
Preferred	unlimited	822,414[2]
Class A	unlimited	822,414
Class J	unlimited	100[2]

[1] At Apr. 11, 2023

[2] Classified as debt.

Preferred - Entitled to receive fixed cumulative preferential quarterly dividends of $0.20 per share (to yield 8% per annum on the original $10 issue price). Retractable in March of each year at a price per unit equal to the net asset value (NAV) per unit (one class A share and one preferred share), less any costs associated with the retraction. Retractable in any other month at a price per share equal to 96% of the lesser of: (i) the NAV per unit less the cost to the company to purchase a class A share for cancellation; and (ii) $10. All outstanding preferred shares will be redeemed on Mar. 28, 2025, at a price per share equal to the lesser of: (i) $10 plus any accrued and unpaid distributions; and (ii) the NAV per preferred share. Rank in priority to class A shares and class J shares with respect to payment of distributions and repayment of capital on the dissolution, liquidation or winding-up of company. Non-voting.

Class A - Entitled to monthly non-cumulative cash distributions of $0.10 per share (to yield 8% per annum on the original $15 issue price). No distributions will be paid if the distributions payable on the preferred shares are in arrears or in respect of a cash distribution, after payment of the distribution, the NAV per unit would be less than $15. In addition, no distributions in excess of 10¢ per month would be paid on the class A shares if, after payment of the distribution, the NAV per unit would be less than $23.50 unless the company has to make such distributions to fully recover refundable taxes. Under a regular monthly retraction, a shareholder will receive, for each class A share, the amount by which 96% of the NAV per unit exceeds the cost to the company of purchasing a preferred share in the market. Under a concurrent annual retraction on the March valuation date of each year, a shareholder will receive, for each unit, an amount equal to the NAV per unit less any costs associated with the retraction. All outstanding class A shares will be redeemed on Mar. 28, 2025, at a price equal to the greater of: (i) the NAV per unit minus $15 plus any accrued and unpaid distributions on a preferred share; and (ii) nil. Rank subsequent to the preferred shares but in priority to the class J shares with respect to the payment of dividends and the repayment of capital on the dissolution, liquidation or winding-up of the company. Non-voting.

Class J - Not entitled to dividends. Redeemable and retractable at $1.00 per share. Rank subsequent to both the preferred and class A shares with respect to the payment of dividends and the repayment of capital on the dissolution, liquidation or winding-up of the company. One vote per share.

Major Shareholder - Brompton Oil Split Trust held 100% interest at Mar. 23, 2023.

Price Range - OSP/TSX

Year	Volume	High	Low	Close
2022	1,384,283	$8.68	$2.29	$5.67
2021	601,751	$3.09	$0.58	$2.15
2020	1,072,759	$1.75	$0.39	$0.58
2019	1,635,376	$4.63	$1.10	$1.63
2018	3,100,536	$9.71	$1.16	$2.76

Consolidation: 1-for-1.15625 cons. in Apr. 2023
Recent Close: $3.85

Capital Stock Changes - On Mar. 30, 2023, 128,500 preferred shares were retracted. On Apr. 11, 2023, class A shares were consolidated on a 1-for-1.15 basis; the consolidation restored an equal number of outstanding preferred and class A shares following the Mar. 30, 2023 special retraction.

There were no changes to capital stock during 2021 or 2022.

Dividends

OSP cl A omitted **[1]
1-for-1 cons eff. Apr. 11, 2023
$0.10.................. Dec. 14/22
Paid in 2023: n.a. 2022: $0.10 2021: n.a.

OSP.PR.A pfd cum. ret. Ra $0.80 pa Q
Prev. Rate: $0.65

[1] Monthly divd normally payable in January/23 has been omitted.

** Reinvestment Option

Financial Statistics

Periods ended:	12m Dec. 31/22[A]		12m Dec. 31/21[A]
	$000s	%Chg	$000s
Realized invest. gain (loss)	585		418
Unrealized invest. gain (loss)	3,935		3,566
Total revenue	**5,109**	**+20**	**4,253**
General & admin. expense	272		202
Operating expense	**272**	**+35**	**202**
Operating income	**4,837**	**+19**	**4,051**
Finance costs, gross	619		618
Pre-tax income	**3,918**	**n.a.**	**nil**
Net income	**3,918**	**n.a.**	**nil**
Cash & equivalent	256		110
Accounts receivable	26		19
Investments	13,200		9,356
Total assets	**13,585**	**+43**	**9,485**
Accts. pay. & accr. liabs	56		57
Debt	9,509		9,261
Shareholders' equity	3,823		nil
Cash from oper. activs	**242**	**n.a.**	**(20)**
Cash from fin. activs	(95)		nil
Net cash position	**256**	**+133**	**110**
	$		$
Earnings per share*	4.76		nil
Cash flow per share*	0.29		(0.02)
Net asset value per share*	4.65		nil
Cash divd. per share*	0.12		nil
	shs		shs
No. of shs. o/s*	822,414		822,414
Avg. no. of shs. o/s*	822,414		822,414
	%		%
Net profit margin	76.69		n.a.
Return on equity	n.m.		n.m.
Return on assets	39.33		n.m.

* Class A

[A] Reported in accordance with IFRS

Note: Note: Net income reflects increase/decrease in net assets from operations.

Historical Summary
(as originally stated)

Fiscal Year	Total Rev. $000s	Net Inc. Bef. Disc. $000s	EPS* $
2022[A]	5,109	3,918	4.76
2021[A]	4,253	nil	nil
2020[A]	(18,497)	(2,562)	(0.92)
2019[A]	4,586	2,385	0.86
2018[A]	(13,704)	(16,015)	(5.77)

* Class A

[A] Reported in accordance with IFRS

Note: Adjusted throughout for 1-for-1.1562473 cons. in Apr. 2023

B.113 Brompton Split Banc Corp.

Symbol - SBC **Exchange** - TSX **CUSIP** - 11221E
Head Office - c/o Brompton Group Limited, Bay Wellington Tower, Brookfield Place, 2930-181 Bay St, PO Box 793, Toronto, ON, M5J 2T3 **Telephone** - (416) 642-9061 **Toll-free** - (866) 642-6001 **Fax** - (416) 642-6001
Website - www.bromptongroup.com
Email - wong@bromptongroup.com
Investor Relations - Ann P. Wong (866) 642-6001
Auditors - PricewaterhouseCoopers LLP C.A., Toronto, Ont.
Transfer Agents - TSX Trust Company, Toronto, Ont.
Managers - Brompton Funds Limited, Toronto, Ont.
Portfolio Managers - Brompton Funds Limited, Toronto, Ont.
Profile - (Ont. 2005) Invests in a portfolio of common shares of the six largest publicly traded Canadian banks and units of one North American Exchange Traded Fund (ETF).

The portfolio consists of common shares of **Bank of Montreal**, **Canadian Imperial Bank of Commerce**, **National Bank of Canada**, **Royal Bank of Canada**, **The Bank of Nova Scotia** and **The Toronto-Dominion Bank**, and units of **Brompton North American Financials Dividend ETF**. The portfolio is rebalanced to an equally weighted basis, at least annually, to adjust for changes in the market values of investments, and to reflect the impact of a merger, acquisition or other significant corporate action or event affecting portfolio constituents. Up to 10% of the portfolio may be invested in global financial companies.

To generate additional income, the company may write covered call or put options in respect of common shares held in the portfolio. The company will terminate on Nov. 29, 2027, unless extended.

The manager receives a management fee at an annual rate equal to 0.55% of the net asset value calculated and payable monthly in arrears.

In March 2022, the board of directors approved extention of the term of the company's preferred and class A shares an additional five years, to Nov. 29, 2027.

Directors - Mark A. Caranci, pres. & CEO, Toronto, Ont.; Ann P. Wong, CFO & chief compliance officer, Toronto, Ont.; Christopher S. L. Hoffmann, Toronto, Ont.; Raymond R. Pether, Toronto, Ont.

Other Exec. Officers - Laura Lau, chief invest. officer; Kathryn A. H. Banner, sr. v-p & corp. sec.; Michael D. Clare, sr. v-p & sr. portfolio mgr.; Christopher Cullen, sr. v-p; Manith (Manny) Phanvongsa, sr. v-p; Michelle L. Tiraborelli, sr. v-p

Capital Stock

	Authorized (shs.)	Outstanding (shs.)[1]
Preferred	unlimited	20,013,826[2]
Class A	unlimited	19,990,226
Class J	unlimited	100[2]

[1] At Apr. 27, 2023

[2] Classified as debt.

Preferred - Entitled to receive fixed cumulative preferential quarterly dividends of $0.125 per share (to yield 5% per annum on the original $10 issue price). Retractable in November of each year at a price per unit equal to the net asset value (NAV) per unit (one class A share and one preferred share), less any costs associated with the retraction. Retractable in any other month at a price per share equal to 96% of the lesser of: (i) the NAV per unit less the cost to the company to purchase a class A share for cancellation; and (ii) $10. All outstanding preferred shares will be redeemed on Nov. 29, 2027, at a price per share equal to the lesser of: (i) $10 plus any accrued and unpaid distributions; and (ii) the NAV per preferred share. Rank in priority to class A shares and class J shares with respect to payment of distributions and repayment of capital on the dissolution, liquidation or winding-up of company. Non-voting.

Class A - Entitled to monthly non-cumulative cash distributions of 10¢ per share (to yield 8% per annum on the original $15 issue price). No distributions will be paid if the distributions payable on the preferred shares are in arrears or in respect of a cash distribution, after payment of the distribution, the NAV per unit (1 class A share and 1 preferred share) would be less than $15. In addition, no distributions in excess of 10¢ per month would be paid on the class A shares if, after payment of the distribution, the NAV per unit would be less than $25 unless the company has to make such distributions to fully recover refundable taxes. Under a regular monthly retraction, a shareholder will receive, for each class A share, the amount by which 96% of the NAV per unit exceeds the cost to the company of purchasing a preferred share in the market. Under a concurrent annual retraction on the November valuation date of each year, a shareholder will receive, for each unit, an amount equal to the NAV per unit less any costs related to liquidating the portfolio to pay such amount. All outstanding class A shares will be redeemed on Nov. 29, 2027, at a price equal to the greater of: (i) the NAV per unit minus $10 plus any accrued and unpaid distributions on a preferred share; and (ii) nil. Rank subsequent to the preferred shares but in priority to the class J shares with respect to the payment of dividends and the repayment of capital on the dissolution, liquidation or winding-up of the company. Non-voting.

Class J - Not entitled to dividends. Redeemable and retractable at $1.00 per share. Rank subsequent to both the preferred and class A shares with respect to the payment of dividends and the repayment of capital on the dissolution, liquidation or winding-up of the company. One vote per share.

Major Shareholder - Brompton Split Banc Trust held 100% interest at Mar. 23, 2023.

Price Range - SBC/TSX

Year	Volume	High	Low	Close
2022	9,539,212	$14.74	$10.58	$11.48
2021	7,475,040	$13.35	$8.33	$13.07
2020	13,209,115	$10.80	$3.33	$8.48
2019	3,377,913	$10.96	$9.06	$10.43
2018	3,274,800	$12.18	$8.30	$9.21

Split: 1.25-for-1 split in Dec. 2021

Recent Close: $9.30

Capital Stock Changes - In April 2023, an offering of 1,444,390 class A shares and 1,467,890 preferred shares at $10.80 per class A share and $9.85 per preferred share, respectively, was completed.

In August 2022, an offering of 2,245,625 class A shares and 2,245,625 preferred shares at $12.20 per class A share and $10 per preferred share, respectively, was completed. On Nov. 24, 2022, an offering of 7,751,296 preferred shares at $9.55 per preferred share was completed. Also during 2022, 219,900 preferred shares and 491,500 class A shares were issued under an at-the-market equity program, and 7,584,001 preferred shares and 12,305 class A shares were retracted.

Dividends

SBC cl A Ra $1.20 pa M est. Jan. 17, 2022**
1-for-1 split eff. Dec. 16, 2021
Prev. Rate: $1.20 est. May 12, 2017
SBC.PR.A pfd cum. red. ret. Ra $0.625 pa Q
Prev. Rate: $0.50
** Reinvestment Option

Financial Statistics

Periods ended:	12m Dec. 31/22[A]		12m Dec. 31/21[A]
	$000s	%Chg	$000s
Realized invest. gain (loss)	6,218		5,486
Unrealized invest. gain (loss)	(59,734)		84,354
Total revenue	**(39,755)**	**n.a.**	**103,324**
General & admin. expense	2,293		2,117
Operating expense	**2,293**	**+8**	**2,117**
Operating income	**(42,048)**	**n.a.**	**101,207**
Finance costs, gross	8,841		6,855
Pre-tax income	**(54,059)**	**n.a.**	**93,811**
Net income	**(54,059)**	**n.a.**	**93,811**
Cash & equivalent	475		591
Accounts receivable	1,487		1,868
Investments	348,953		366,966
Total assets	**350,945**	**-5**	**369,573**
Accts. pay. & accr. liabs	69		109
Debt	181,130		158,210
Shareholders' equity	164,815		207,661
Cash from oper. activs	**(34,606)**	**n.a.**	**7,208**
Cash from fin. activs	34,490		(6,676)
Net cash position	**475**	**-20**	**591**
	$		$
Earnings per share*	(3.22)		5.59
Cash flow per share*	(2.06)		0.43
Net asset value per share*	8.89		13.13
Cash divd. per share*	1.20		0.98
	shs		shs
No. of shs. o/s*	18,545,836		15,821,016
Avg. no. of shs. o/s*	16,794,892		16,792,425
	%		%
Net profit margin	n.m.		90.79
Return on equity	(29.03)		53.38
Return on assets	(12.55)		30.89

* Class A
[A] Reported in accordance with IFRS

Note: Net income reflects increase/decrease in net assets from operations.

Historical Summary
(as originally stated)

Fiscal Year	Total Rev. $000s	Net Inc. Bef. Disc. $000s	EPS* $
2022[A]	(39,755)	(54,059)	(3.22)
2021[A]	103,324	93,811	5.59
2020[A]	11,153	2,149	0.14
2019[A]	28,994	22,572	1.92
2018[A]	(14,625)	(20,358)	(2.08)

* Class A
[A] Reported in accordance with IFRS

Note: Adjusted throughout for 1.25-for-1 split in Dec. 2021

B.114 Brookfield Asset Management Ltd.

Symbol - BAM **Exchange** - TSX **CUSIP** - 113004
Head Office - Brookfield Place, 100-181 Bay St, Toronto, ON, M5J 2T3 **Telephone** - (416) 369-2621
Website - bam.brookfield.com
Email - jason.fooks@brookfield.com
Investor Relations - Jason Fooks (866) 989-0311
Auditors - Deloitte LLP C.A., Toronto, Ont.
Transfer Agents - American Stock Transfer & Trust Company, LLC, New York, N.Y.; TSX Trust Company, Toronto, Ont.
Employees - 2,500 at Dec. 31, 2022

Profile - (B.C. 2022) Holds 25% interest in the global alternative asset management business of **Brookfield Corporation** (formerly **Brookfield Asset Management Inc.**).

Brookfield Asset Management ULC, owned 25% by the company and 75% by **Brookfield Corporation**, is the asset management business of Brookfield. At June 30, 2023, had US$850 billion in assets under management and US$440 billion in fee-bearing capital across renewable power and transition, infrastructure, private equity, real estate and credit. Offers investors a large portfolio of private funds that have global mandates and diversified strategies. Products are grouped into three categories: (i) long-term private funds, (ii) permanent capital vehicles and perpetual strategies and (iii) liquid strategies.

On Dec. 9, 2022, **Brookfield Corporation** (BN, formerly **Brookfield Asset Management Inc.**) completed its transaction for the public listing and distribution of a 25% interest in its asset management business, through the company by a plan of arrangement. The transaction resulted in the division of BN into two publicly traded companies, BN and the company, with the holders of BN's class A limited voting shares, class B limited voting shares and class A preferred series 8 and 9 shares becoming shareholders of the company on completion. Each holder of BN class A limited voting shares received 1 class A limited voting share of the company for every 4 BN class A limited voting shares held. Holders of BN class A preferred series 8 shares received 0.103 class A limited voting share of the company and a new BN class A preferred series 51 share for each series 8 share held and holders of BN class A preferred series 9 shares received 0.101 class A limited voting share of the company and a new BN class A preferred series 52 share for each series 9 share held.

Class A listed on TSX, Dec. 1, 2022.
Class A listed on NYSE, Dec. 1, 2022.

Recent Merger and Acquisition Activity

Status: pending **Announced:** June 9, 2023
Brookfield Asset Management Ltd. agreed to acquire Dubai, U.A.E.-based, London Stock Exchange-listed Network International Holdings plc, which provides digital payment solutions to merchants and financial institutions in the Middle East and Africa, for £4.00 cash per share. The transaction was valued at £2.2 billion (Cdn$3.7 billion). Brookfield planned to combine the business with Magnati Sole Proprietorship LLC, the former First Abu Dhabi Bank payments unit in which Brookfield holds a 60% interest in. Network's customers included more than 150,000 merchants and 200 financial institutions.

Directors - Dr. Mark J. Carney, chr. & head, transition investing, Ottawa, Ont.; J. Bruce Flatt, CEO, New York, N.Y.; Brian W. Kingston, man. partner & CEO, real estate, New York, N.Y.; Cyrus Madon, man. partner & CEO, private equity, Toronto, Ont.; Samuel J. B. (Sam) Pollock, man. partner & CEO, infrastructure, Toronto, Ont.; Marcel R. Coutu†, Calgary, Alta.; Olivia (Liv) Garfield, London, Middx., United Kingdom; Nili Gilbert, New York, N.Y.; Keith Johnson, Jackson, Wyo.; Allison Kirkby, Stockholm, Sweden; Diana Noble, London, Middx., United Kingdom; Satish Rai, Pickering, Ont.

Other Exec. Officers - Justin B. Beber, man. partner, CAO & gen. counsel; Bahir Manios, man. partner & CFO; Craig W. A. Noble, man. partner & CEO, alternative invest.; Connor D. Teskey, man. partner, pres. & CEO, renewable power & transition
† Lead director

Capital Stock

	Authorized (shs.)	Outstanding (shs.)[1]
Cl.A Preference	unlimited	nil
Cl.A Limited Voting	unlimited	412,563,905
Cl.B Limited Voting	21,280	21,280

[1] At July 26, 2023

Class A Limited Voting - Entitled to elect one half of the board of directors and as a class must approve the appointment of auditors. Rank on par with class B limited voting shares with respect to dividends and return of capital. Entitled to elect one-half of the board of directors. One vote per share.

Class B Limited Voting - Entitled to elect the other one half of the board of directors and as a class must approve the appointment of auditors. One vote per share.

Normal Course Issuer Bid - The company plans to make normal course purchases of up to 31,785,036 class A limited voting shares representing 10% of the public float. The bid commenced on Jan. 11, 2023, and expires on Jan. 10, 2024.

Major Shareholder - A partnership which includes current and former senior executives of the company collectively held 20.61% interest at Apr. 20, 2023.

Price Range - BAM/TSX

Year	Volume	High	Low	Close
2022	11,669,525	$50.14	$28.23	$38.77

Recent Close: $45.19

Capital Stock Changes - On Dec. 9, 2022, 409,477,357 class A limited voting shares were issued to shareholders of Brookfield Corporation and 2,725,500 class A limited voting shares were issued to shareholders to shareholders of Brookfield Resinsurance Ltd. (formerly Brookfield Asset Management Reinsurance Partners Ltd.), of which 16,048,129 class A limited voting shares were held in treasury, and 21,280 class B limited voting shares were issued to BAM Partnership.

Dividends

BAM cl A Ra US$1.28 pa Q est. Mar. 31, 2023
Listed Dec 1/22.
US$0.32i.............. Mar. 31/23
i Initial Payment

Investments

25% int. in **Brookfield Asset Management ULC**, Toronto, Ont.
- 100% int. in **Atlas Holdings II LLC**, Del.
- 100% int. in **BREP Holding LP**, Bermuda.
- 100% int. in **Brookfield Asset Management Private Institutional Capital Adviser US, LLC**, Del.
- 100% int. in **Brookfield Asset Management Private Institutional Capital Adviser (Canada), L.P.**, Man.
- 100% int. in **Brookfield Asset Management Private Institutional Capital Adviser (Private Equity), L.P.**, Man.
- 100% int. in **Brookfield Canada Renewable Manager LP**, Ont.
- 100% int. in **Brookfield Capital Partners LLC**, Del.
- 100% int. in **Brookfield Global Infrastructure Advisor Limited**, United Kingdom.
- 100% int. in **Brookfield Global Property Advisor Limited**, United Kingdom.
- 100% int. in **Brookfield Global Renewable Energy Advisor Limited**, United Kingdom.
- 100% int. in **Brookfield Infrastructure Group LLC**, Del.
- 100% int. in **Brookfield Infrastructure Group L.P.**, Ont.
- 100% int. in **Brookfield Property Group LLC**, Del.
- 100% int. in **Brookfield Public Securities Group Holdings LLC**, Del.
- 100% int. in **Brookfield Renewable Energy Group LLC**, Del.
- 100% int. in **Brookfield Strategic Real Estate Partners II GP of GP LLC**, Del.
- 100% int. in **Brookfield Strategic Real Estate Partners III GP of GP LLC**, Del.
- **Brookfield US Holdings Inc.**, Ont.
- 100% int. in **Brookfield US Inc.**, Del.
- 64% int. in **Oaktree AIF Investments LP**, Del.

- 64% int. in **Oaktree Capital II, LP**, Del.
- 64% int. in **Oaktree Capital Management (Cayman) LP**, Cayman Islands.
- 64% int. in **Oaktree Capital Management LP**, Del.

Financial Statistics

Periods ended:	5m Dec. 31/22[A]
	US$000s
Salaries & benefits	(37,000)
General & admin. expense	1,000
Other operating expense	38,000
Operating expense	**2,000**
Operating income	**(2,000)**
Pre-tax income	**19,000**
Net income	**19,000**
Cash & equivalent	1,000
Investments	2,378,000
Total assets	**3,161,000**
Bank indebtedness	3
Accts. pay. & accr. liabs	781,000
Shareholders' equity	2,377,000
Cash from oper. activs	**(2,000)**
Cash from fin. activs	3,000
Net cash position	**1,000**
	US$
Earnings per share*	0.05
Cash flow per share*	(0.00)
	shs
No. of shs. o/s*	396,154,728
Avg. no. of shs. o/s*	396,166,341
	%
No. of employees (FTEs)	2,500

* Class A
[A] Reported in accordance with U.S. GAAP

Latest Results

Periods ended:	6m June 30/23[A]
	US$000s
Net income	234,000
	US$
Earnings per share*	0.59

* Class A
[A] Reported in accordance with U.S. GAAP

B.115 Brookfield Business Corporation

Symbol - BBUC **Exchange** - TSX **CUSIP** - 11259V
Head Office - 250 Vesey St, 15th Flr, New York, NY, United States, 10281 **Telephone** - (212) 417-7000
Website - bbu.brookfield.com
Email - alan.fleming@brookfield.com
Investor Relations - Alan Fleming (416) 645-2736
Auditors - Deloitte LLP C.A., Toronto, Ont.
Transfer Agents - American Stock Transfer & Trust Company, LLC, New York, N.Y.; TSX Trust Company, Toronto, Ont.
FP500 Subsidiary Revenue Ranking - 7
Employees - 38,000 at Dec. 31, 2022
Profile - (B.C. 2021) Owns and operates services and industrial operations globally.

Operations include a construction services business with operations primarily in the U.K. and Australia; a North American automotive software provider; a healthcare services business in Australia; a global nuclear technology services provider; and a water and wastewater service provider in Brazil.

Wholly owned **Multiplex Global Limited** provides construction services including design, program and procurement, primarily on large-scale and complex landmark buildings and social infrastructure in Australia and the U.K.

Affiliate **CDK Global, Inc.** (29% economic interest, 100% voting interest) provides retail technology and software-as-a-service (SaaS) solutions that help dealers and auto manufacturers across North America run their businesses more efficiently.

Affiliate **Healthscope Pty Ltd.** (28% economic interest, 100% voting interest) operates 39 private hospitals in Australia.

Affiliate **Westinghouse Electric Company LLC** (27% economic interest, 100% voting interest) provides fuel, ongoing maintenance services, engineering solutions, instrumentation and control systems, manufactured components, and decontamination, decommissioning and remediation of power plant sites for the global nuclear power generation industry.

Affiliate **BRK Ambiental Participações S.A.** (26% economic interest, 70% voting interest) collects, treats and distributes water and wastewater to residential and governmental customers throughout Brazil.

The company is a controlled affiliate of **Brookfield Business Partners L.P.** which, through its 51.7%-owned subsidiary **Brookfield Business L.P.**, holds 25% economic interest and 75% voting interest in the company.

In February 2023, affiliate **Westinghouse Electric Company LLC** completed the sale of its wholly owned **BHI Energy, Inc.**'s power delivery business for US$270,000,000.

In May 2022, affiliate **Westinghouse Electric Company LLC** acquired Weymouth, Mass.-based **BHI Energy, Inc.**, a provider of specialty services and staffing solutions for industrial, oil and gas, power generation and power delivery businesses, for US$737,000,000.

In March 2022, affiliate **Westinghouse Electric Company LLC** acquired a Spanish engineering and outage services business for US$23,000,000.

Recent Merger and Acquisition Activity

Status: pending **Announced:** Oct. 11, 2022
Brookfield Business Corporation (BBPC) together with its institutional partners agreed to sell its nuclear technology services operation, Westinghouse Electric Company, to a consortium led by Cameco Corporation and Brookfield Renewable Partners L.P. (BEP LP) for a total enterprise value of US$7.875 billion. BBPC expects to receive US$1.8 billion for its 44% stake in Westinghouse, with the balance distributed to institutional partners. On closing, BEP LP and its institutional partners would own 51% interest in Westinghouse and Cameco would own 49%. Westinghouse's existing debt structure would remain in place, leaving an estimated US$4.5 billion equity cost to the consortium, subject to closing adjustments. This equity cost would be shared proportionately between BEP LP and its partners (US$2.3 billion) and Cameco (US$ $2.2 billion). BEP LP was expected to invest US$750,000,000 to acquire about 17% interest in Westinghouse. The transaction was expected to close in the second half of 2023.

Status: completed **Revised:** July 6, 2022
UPDATE: The transaction was completed through BBP LP subsidiary Brookfield Business Corporation, which acquired a 29% ownership interest. PREVIOUS: Brookfield Business Partners L.P. (BBP LP) together with institutional partners agreed to acquire Hoffman Estates, Ill.-based CDK Global, Inc. for US$54.87 per share for a deal value of US$8.3 billion. CDK Global provides technology services and software solutions that help automotive dealers and manufacturers in North America run their businesses more efficiently. The transaction would be funded with US$3.5 billion of equity, of which BBP LP intends to invest US$500,000,000, with the balance coming from institutional partners. BBP LP plans to fund its portion of the investment with a new US$500,000,000 commitment from Brookfield Asset Management Inc. to subscribe for 6% perpetual preferred equity securities of BBP LP. The transaction was expected to close in the third quarter of 2022.

Directors - Jeffrey M. (Jeff) Blidner, chr., Toronto, Ont.; John S. Lacey†, Thornhill, Ont.; David C. Court, Toronto, Ont.; Stephen J. Girsky, New York, N.Y.; Dr. David Hamill, Qld., Australia; Anne Ruth Herkes, Berlin, Germany; Donald Mackenzie, Bermuda; Michael J. Warren, Washington, D.C.; Patricia Zuccotti, Kirkland, Wash.

Other Exec. Officers - Cyrus Madon, CEO; Amanda Marshall, man. dir., tax; Jaspreet Dehl, CFO; A. J. Silber, sr. v-p; Denis A. Turcotte, man. partner

† Lead director

Capital Stock

	Authorized (shs.)	Outstanding (shs.)[1]
Cl.A Senior Preferred	unlimited	nil
Cl.B Junior Preferred	unlimited	nil
Cl.A Exch. Subord. Vtg.	unlimited	72,954,912[2]
Cl.B Multiple Vtg.	unlimited	1[2]
Cl.C Non.Vtg.	unlimited	25,934,120

[1] At Aug. 8, 2023
[2] Classified as debt.

Class A Senior and Class B Junior Preferred - Issuable in series. Non-voting.

Class A Exchangeable Subordinate Voting - Entitled to dividends. Exchangeable, at the holder's option, for one non-voting publicly traded limited partnership (LP) unit of Brookfield Business Partners L.P. (the partnership) for each exchangeable share held or its cash equivalent. The partnership, or any of its controlled subsidiaries, is entitled to convert each exchangeable share into class C non-voting shares on a one-for-one basis. One vote per share. Holders will vote together with the class B multiple voting shareholders and not as separate classes.

Class B Multiple Voting - Not entitled to dividends. Holders have the right to tender all or a portion of their class B shares for cash for each class B share equal to the NYSE closing price of one LP unit of the partnership on the date of the request for redemption. Transferable only to the partnership or persons controlled by the partnership. Entitled to a number of votes equal to three times the aggregate number of votes attached to the exchangeable shares. Will be voted together with the exchangeable shareholders and not as separate classes. All indirectly held by the partnership.

Class C Non-Voting - Entitled to dividends. Holders have the right to tender all or a portion of their class C shares for cash for each class C share equal to the NYSE closing price of one LP unit of the partnership on the date of the request for redemption. Transferable only to the partnership or persons controlled by the partnership. Non-voting. All indirectly held by the partnership.

Normal Course Issuer Bid - The company plans to make normal course purchases of up to 3,647,745 class A exchangeable subordinate voting shares representing 5% of the total outstanding. The bid commenced on Aug. 17, 2023, and expires on Aug. 16, 2024.

Major Shareholder - Brookfield Corporation, Brookfield Business Partners L.P. and Brookfield Business L.P. collectively held 91% interest at Apr. 25, 2023.

Price Range - BBUC/TSX

Year	Volume	High	Low	Close
2022	8,853,988	$44.26	$24.10	$25.44

Recent Close: $24.34

Capital Stock Changes - Pursuant to a special distribution completed on Mar. 15, 2022, 73,088,510 class A exchangeable subordinate voting shares were distributed (with Brookfield Business Partners L.P. (BBP LP) and Brookfield Asset Management Inc. receiving approximately 38,200,000 and 34,900,000 exchangeable shares, respectively) and all existing common shares were converted into 25,853,695 class C shares. All class A exchangeable subordinate voting shares received by BBP LP were subsequently distributed to BBP LP unitholders on the basis of one exchangeable share for each 2 limited partnership units of BBP LP held. Also during 2022, 80,425 class A exchangeable subordinate voting shares were converted into 80,425 class C shares and 52,500 class A exchangeable subordinate voting shares were exchanged for limited partnership units of BBP LP.

Dividends

BBUC cl A sub vtg Ra $0.25 pa Q est. June 30, 2022
Listed Mar 4/22.
$0.0625i............... June 30/22
i Initial Payment

Wholly Owned Subsidiaries

BBUC Holdings Inc., Ont.
- 100% int. in **BBUC Bermuda Holdco Limited**, Bermuda.
  - 26% int. in **BRK Ambiental Participações S.A.**, Brazil. Holds 70% voting interest.
  - 29% int. in **CDK Global, Inc.**, Hoffman Estates, Ill.
  - 100% int. in **Multiplex Global Limited**, United Kingdom.
- 28% int. in **Healthscope Pty Ltd.**, Melbourne, Vic., Australia. Holds 100% voting interest.
- 27% int. in **Westinghouse Electric Company LLC**, Cranberry, Pa. Holds 100% voting interest.

Financial Statistics

Periods ended:	12m Dec. 31/22[A]		12m Dec. 31/21[A]
	US$000s	%Chg	US$000s
Operating revenue	**10,598,000**	**+10**	**9,649,000**
Cost of sales	5,394,000		5,641,000
Salaries & benefits	3,180,000		2,557,000
General & admin expense	372,000		282,000
Operating expense	**8,946,000**	**+5**	**8,480,000**
Operating income	**1,652,000**	**+41**	**1,169,000**
Deprec., depl. & amort	892,000		603,000
Finance costs, net	(94,000)		401,000
Investment income	13,000		5,000
Write-downs/write-offs	(21,000)		nil
Pre-tax income	**671,000**	**+728**	**81,000**
Income taxes	(405,000)		(12,000)
Net income	**1,076,000**	**n.m.**	**93,000**
Net inc. for equity hldrs	**911,000**	**n.m.**	**36,000**
Net inc. for non-cont. int	**165,000**	**+189**	**57,000**
Cash & equivalent	736,000		894,000
Inventories	653,000		580,000
Accounts receivable	2,303,000		1,602,000
Current assets	4,880,000		3,866,000
Long-term investments	251,000		70,000
Fixed assets, net	3,765,000		4,036,000
Intangibles, net	16,209,000		6,442,000
Total assets	**27,376,000**	**+72**	**15,920,000**
Bank indebtedness	nil		1,860,000
Accts. pay. & accr. liabs	2,044,000		1,756,000
Current liabilities	5,985,000		5,629,000
Long-term debt, gross	12,913,000		5,246,000
Long-term debt, net	12,498,000		5,193,000
Long-term lease liabilities	423,000		401,000
Shareholders' equity	359,000		(516,000)
Non-controlling interest	3,712,000		1,652,000
Cash from oper. activs	**181,000**	**-71**	**618,000**
Cash from fin. activs	8,913,000		14,000
Cash from invest. activs	(9,230,000)		(478,000)
Net cash position	**736,000**	**-18**	**894,000**
Capital expenditures	(655,000)		(728,000)
Capital disposals	33,000		9,000
Unfunded pension liability	356,000		334,000
	US$		US$
Earnings per share*	n.a.		n.a.
Cash divd. per share*	$0.19		$n.a.
	shs		shs
No. of shs. o/s*	72,955,585		n.a.
	%		%
Net profit margin	10.15		0.96
Return on equity	n.m.		n.m.
Return on assets	4.97		0.57
No. of employees (FTEs)	38,000		35,000

* Cl.A Exch. Sub. Vtg.
[A] Reported in accordance with IFRS

Latest Results

Periods ended:	3m Mar. 31/23[A]		3m Mar. 31/22[A]
	US$000s	%Chg	US$000s
Operating revenue	2,921,000	+30	2,251,000
Net income	(185,000)	n.a.	(163,000)
Net inc. for equity hldrs	(140,000)	n.a.	(164,000)
Net inc. for non-cont. int	(45,000)		1,000
	US$		US$
Earnings per share*	n.a.		n.a.

[A] Reported in accordance with IFRS

Historical Summary
(as originally stated)

Fiscal Year	Oper. Rev.	Net Inc. Bef. Disc.	EPS*
	US$000s	US$000s	US$
2022[A]	10,598,000	1,076,000	n.a.
2021[A]	9,649,000	93,000	n.a.
2020[A1]	9,606,000	(127,000)	n.a.
2019[A1]	9,903,000	(134,000)	n.a.
2018[A1]	6,956,000	(119,000)	n.a.

* Cl.A Exch. Sub. Vtg.

[A] Reported in accordance with IFRS

[1] Results prepared on a carve-out basis of select services and industrial operations of Brookfield Business Partners L.P.

B.116 Brookfield Business Partners L.P.

Symbol - BBU.UN **Exchange** - TSX **CUSIP** - G16234
Head Office - 73 Front St, 5th Floor, Hamilton, Bermuda, HM 12 **Telephone** - (441) 294-3309
Website - www.bbu.brookfield.com
Email - alan.fleming@brookfield.com
Investor Relations - Alan Fleming (416) 645-2736
Auditors - Deloitte LLP C.A., Toronto, Ont.
Transfer Agents - American Stock Transfer & Trust Company, LLC, New York, N.Y.; TSX Trust Company, Toronto, Ont.
Employees - 102,000 at Dec. 31, 2022
Profile - (Bermuda 2016) Acquires, owns and operates businesses globally across the business services, infrastructure services and industrial sectors.

Business Services

This segment includes **Sagen MI Canada Inc.**, which underwrites mortgage insurance for residential properties across Canada; **La Trobe Financial Services Pty Ltd.**, a non-bank lender and asset manager in Australia; **Greenergy Fuels Holdings Limited**, which operates rail-fed fuel terminals and storage locations in Canada and the mid-western U.S. as well as 250 retail gas stations in Canada and Ireland; **Ontario Gaming GTA Limited Partnership**, which operates four entertainment facilities in the Greater Toronto Area; **Imagine Communications Group Limited**, which provides wireless broadband services in rural Ireland; **IndoStar Capital Finance Limited**, which provides non-bank financial services in India including vehicle and home financing for individuals and loans for small and medium-sized enterprises; **Magnati - Sole Proprietorship LLC**, which provides payment solutions and services for retail, hospitality, government and e-commerce businesses in the Middle East region; **Ouro Verde Locação e Seviços S.A.**, which provides heavy equipment and light vehicle leasing in Brazil; **Unidas Locadora S.A.**, which provides car rental services in Brazil; **Everise Holdings Pte. Ltd.**, which provides customer management solutions primarily for large global healthcare and technology clients; and **WatServ Holdings Ltd.**, which provides digital cloud services in Canada and the U.S.

In addition, through controlled publicly traded affiliate **Brookfield Business Corporation** (BBUC), has interests in a provider of retail technology and software-as-a-service (SaaS) solutions for the North American automotive industry; a healthcare services business in Australia; and a global construction business operating primarily in Australia and the U.K.

Infrastructure Services

This segment includes **Scientific Games, LLC**, which supplies products, services and technology to government-sponsored lottery programs globally; **Altera Infrastructure L.P.**, which provides marine transportation, facility storage, long-distance towing and offshore installation, maintenance and safety services to offshore oil producers globally; **Brand Industrial Holdings Inc.** (dba BrandSafway), which provides scaffolding and related services to global industrial and commercial markets; and **Modulaire Investments 2 S.à r.l.**, which provides modular building leasing services in Europe and Asia-Pacific.

Through BBUC, also has interest in a global nuclear technology services provider.

Industrial Operations

This segment includes **Clarios Global L.P.**, which manufactures automotive batteries; **GrafTech International Ltd.**, which manufactures graphite electrodes and petroleum needle coke; **Aldo Componentes Eletrônicos Ltda.**, which distributes solar power generators for the distributed generation market in Brazil; **DexKo Global Inc.**, which manufactures engineered components for providers of industrial trailers and other towable equipment worldwide; **Ember Resources Inc.**, a natural gas producer in western Canada; **CWC Energy Services Corp.**, a provider of well servicing and contract drilling services in western Canada; **Hammerstone Infrastructure Materials Ltd.**, operator of a limestone quarry in the Athabasca region of Alberta which supplies aggregates to large oil sands customers; **Schoeller Allibert Group B.V.**, which supplies reusable plastic packaging for various industries; and **Cardone Industries, Inc.**, which remanufactures automotive aftermarket parts for original equipment manufacturers (OEMs), warehouse distributors, fleets and retailers; and **CUPA Finance, S.L.**, which extracts and produces natural slate for roofing and cladding applications.

Through BBUC, also has interest in a water and wastewater service provider in Brazil.

The remaining 48.3% of managing general partnership units in **Brookfield Business L.P.** is held by **Brookfield Corporation** and its affiliates.

On Jan. 31, 2023, **Modulaire Investments 2 S.à r.l.**, the limited partnership's modular building leasing services operations, acquired **Mobile Mini UK Holdings Limited**, a provider of portable storage solutions in the U.K., for US$419,000,000.

On Oct. 5, 2022, **DexKo Global Inc.**, the limited partnership's (LP) engineered components manufacturer, together with institutional partners, acquired **TexTrail, Inc.**, a distributor of axles and trailer components, for US$922,000,000, inclusive of US$300,000,000 of equity funded by the LP and its institutional partners, of which the LP's share was US$100,000,000.

During the first quarter of 2022, the limited partnership (LP) together with institutional partners syndicated a portion of their investment and funded contingent consideration to the former shareholders of **Everise Holdings Pte. Ltd.**, a customer management solutions provider, which reduced the LP's economic interest to 29% from 36%.

The limited partnership (LP) created a new Canadian corporation, **Brookfield Business Corporation** (BBUC), on June 21, 2021, which would own and operate services and industrial operations globally of the LP. The services and operations included a construction services business with operations primarily in the U.K. and Australia; a healthcare services business in Australia; a global nuclear technology services provider; and a water and wastewater service provider in Brazil.

On Mar. 15, 2022, unitholders of the LP received 1 BBUC class A exchangeable subordinate voting share for each two LP units held in a form of a special distribution. The majority of the BBUC exchangeable shares were held by the unitholders of the LP after the effective split, with the LP also owning all the BBUC class B multiple voting and class C non-voting shares. The exchangeable and class B shareholders controlled 25% and 75%, respectively, of the aggregate voting rights of the shares of BBUC. **Brookfield Asset Management Inc.**, as a unitholder of the LP, held 64.7% of the BBUC exchangeable shares, which was equivalent to its effective ownership of the LP's units.

Recent Merger and Acquisition Activity

Status: completed **Announced:** Apr. 4, 2023
FirstService Corporation acquired private Toronto, Ont.-based Crossbridge Condominium Services Ltd., which provides residential management services to a portfolio of condominium companies across the Greater Toronto Area of Ontario. Terms of the transaction were not disclosed. Crossbridge had been an affiliate of Brookfield Business Partners L.P.

Status: completed **Revised:** Oct. 11, 2022
UPDATE: The transaction was completed. BBP LP acquired 7% ownership interest for US$400,000,000. PREVIOUS: Brookfield Business Partners L.P. (BBP LP) together with institutional partners agreed to acquire New York, N.Y.-based Nielsen Holdings plc for US$16 billion cash. Nielsen provides measurement, data and analytics across all channels and platforms for the global media industry. Together with institutional partners, BBP LP would invest US$2.65 billion by way of preferred equity, convertible into 45% of Nielsen's common equity. BBP LP's share of the preferred equity investment would be US$600,000,000. The transaction was expected to be completed in the second half of 2022.

Status: completed **Announced:** Oct. 1, 2022
Brookfield Business Partners L.P. (BBP LP) together with institutional partners acquired Unidas Locadora S.A., a full-service car rental business in Brazil, for US$726,000,000. BBP LP acquired 35% ownership interest for US$125,000,000.

Status: completed **Revised:** Aug. 8, 2022
UPDATE: The transaction was completed. BBP LP acquired 22% ownership interest for US$68,000,000. PREVIOUS: Brookfield Business Partners L.P. (BBP LP) together with institutional partners agreed to acquire a 60% interest in Abu Dhabi, U.A.E.-based Magnati - Sole Proprietorship LLC for US$400,000,000, with BBP LP funding US$65,000,000 for a 20% interest. Magnati offers payment solutions and services for all industries, including retail, hospitality, government and e-commerce businesses. The transaction was expected to be completed in the first half of 2022.

Status: completed **Revised:** July 6, 2022
UPDATE: The transaction was completed through BBP LP subsidiary Brookfield Business Corporation, which acquired a 29% ownership interest. PREVIOUS: Brookfield Business Partners L.P. (BBP LP) together with institutional partners agreed to acquire Hoffman Estates, Ill.-based CDK Global, Inc. for US$54.87 per share for a deal value of US$8.3 billion. CDK Global provides technology services and software solutions that help automotive dealers and manufacturers in North America run their businesses more efficiently. The transaction would be funded with US$3.5 billion of equity, of which BBP LP intends to invest US$500,000,000, with the balance coming from institutional partners. BBP LP plans to fund its portion of the investment with a new US$500,000,000 commitment from Brookfield Asset Management Inc. to subscribe for 6% perpetual preferred equity securities of BBP LP. The transaction was expected to close in the third quarter of 2022.

Status: completed **Revised:** May 31, 2022
UPDATE: The transaction was completed. BBP LP acquired 40% ownership interest. PREVIOUS: Brookfield Business Partners L.P. (BBP LP) together with institutional partners agreed to acquire Melbourne, Australia-based La Trobe Financial Services Pty Ltd., a non-bank lender and asset manager, for US$1.1 billion including a contingent payment tied to achievement of certain performance milestones. La Trobe has more than A$13 billion in assets under management and manages fixed income credit funds on behalf of more than 50,000 qualified retail investors, primarily in residential property-backed loans. La Trobe also plays a critical role in the Australian real estate credit market by financing loans to high-quality borrowers. BBP LP and its partners' initial investment would be funded with US$765,000,000 of equity, of which BBP LP would fund US$250,000,000. The Blackstone Inc. holds an 80% interest in La Trobe. Closing was expected in the second quarter of 2022.

Status: completed **Revised:** May 31, 2022
UPDATE: The transaction was completed for US$879,000,000. BBP LP acquired 23% ownership interest for US$100,000,000 and would account for CUPA as an equity investment. PREVIOUS: Brookfield Business Partners L.P. (BBP LP) together with institutional partners agreed to acquire Spain-based CUPA Finance, S.L. from The Carlyle Group Inc. for US$950,000,000. CUPA produces and distributes premium natural slates and stones for building and related applications. The transaction would be funded with US$390,000,000 of equity, of which BBP LP plans to fund US$100,000,000 for a 25% ownership interest, with the balance from institutional partners. Closing was expected in the second quarter of 2022.

Status: completed **Revised:** Apr. 4, 2022
UPDATE: The transaction was completed. Scientific Games, LLC was formed to hold the acquired business. BBP LP acquired a 35% ownership interest for US$860,000,000. PREVIOUS: Brookfield Business Partners L.P. (BBP LP) together with institutional partners agreed to acquire the business of Scientific Games Corporation for US$5.8 billion. BBP LP would fund 30% of the US$2.6 billion equity. The business supplies products, services and technology to government sponsored lottery programs and has long-term relationships with 130 lottery entities in more than 50 countries. The transaction was expected to be completed by the second quarter of 2022.

Oper. Subsid./Mgt. Co. Directors - Jeffrey M. (Jeff) Blidner, chr., Toronto, Ont.; John S. Lacey†, Thornhill, Ont.; Stephen J. Girsky, New York, N.Y.; Dr. David Hamill, Qld., Australia; Anne Ruth Herkes, Berlin, Germany; Donald Mackenzie, Bermuda; Patricia Zuccotti, Kirkland, Wash.

Other Exec. Officers - Cyrus Madon, CEO; Jaspreet Dehl, CFO
† Lead director

Capital Stock

	Authorized (shs.)	Outstanding (shs.)[1]
G.P. Unit	n.a.	4
L.P. Unit	unlimited	74,613,176[2]
Redeem/Exch. Ptnrshp. Unit	n.a.	69,705,497[3]
Special L.P. Unit	n.a.	4[4]
Preferred Share	n.a.	200,002[5]

[1] At Mar. 31, 2023

[2] At Aug. 8, 2023.

[3] Securities of subsidiary Brookfield Business L.P.

[4] Securities of subsidiary Brookfield Business L.P.

[5] Securities of subsidiaries.

General Partnership Unit - Entitles the managing general partner Brookfield Business Partners Limited to the right to govern the financial and operating policies of the partnership.

Limited Partnership Unit - Non-voting.

Redeemable/Exchangeable Partnership Unit - Issued by subsidiary Brookfield Business L.P. (BBP). Exchangeable for limited partnership units on a one-for-one basis and are the economic equivalent of limited partnership units. Redeemable at the option of the holder in whole or in part for cash equal to the market value of one of the limited partnership units multiplied by the number of units to be redeemed, subject to the right of the limited partnership to acquire such interests (in lieu of redemption) in exchange for limited partnership units. Non-voting. All held by Brookfield Corporation (BN) and its affiliates. Classified as part of non-controlling interest.

Special Limited Partnership Unit - Issued by subsidiary BBP. Entitled to incentive distributions calculated as: (i) 20% of the growth in the market value of the limited partnership units quarter-over-quarter (only after exceeding an incentive distribution threshold of US$31.53) multiplied by (ii) the number of limited partnership units outstanding at the end of each quarter. All held by BN and its affiliates. Classified as part of non-controlling interest.

Preferred Share - Issued by three of the limited partnership's subsidiaries. Entitled to cumulative annual dividends of 5% as and when declared by the board of the directors of the applicable entity. Redeemable at the option of the applicable entity at any time after 2036. All held by BN. Classified as part of non-controlling interest.

Normal Course Issuer Bid - The company plans to make normal course purchases of up to 3,730,658 limited partnership units representing 5% of the total outstanding. The bid commenced on Aug. 17, 2023, and expires on Aug. 16, 2024.

Major Shareholder - Brookfield Corporation held 100% interest at Dec. 31, 2022.

Price Range - BBU.UN/TSX

Year	Volume	High	Low	Close
2022	17,526,663	$61.24	$20.94	$22.89
2021	17,110,534	$65.35	$45.40	$58.05
2020	19,959,331	$62.09	$27.00	$48.29
2019	17,574,248	$55.95	$40.56	$53.73
2018	19,067,799	$59.66	$41.32	$41.58

Recent Close: $20.44

Capital Stock Changes - During 2022, 2,525,490 limited partnership units were repurchased under a Normal Course Issuer Bid and 52,500 limited partnership units were issued on conversion of class A exchangeable subordinate voting shares of Brookfield Business Corporation.

Dividends

BBU.UN ltd ptnrshp unit Ra US$0.25 pa Q est. June 30, 2017
stk.[1] ◆.................. Mar. 15/22
Paid in 2023: US$0.1875 2022: US$0.25 + stk.◆ 2021: US$0.25

[1] Stk. divd. of 0.5 Brookfield Business Corp cl. A sub vtg shs. for ea. 1 sh. held.
◆ Special

Subsidiaries

51.7% int. in **Brookfield Business L.P.**, Bermuda.
- 35% int. in **Aldo Componentes Eletrônicos Ltda.**, Maringá, Brazil. Holds 100% voting interest.
- 43% int. in **Altera Infrastructure L.P.**, Hamilton, Bermuda. Holds 99% voting interest.
- 17% int. in **Brand Industrial Services, Inc.**, Kennesaw, Ga. dba BrandSafway
- 100% int. in **Brookfield BBP Bermuda Holdings Limited**, Bermuda.
- 100% int. in **Brookfield BBP Canada Holdings Inc.**, Canada.
  - 25% int. in **Brookfield Business Corporation**, New York, N.Y. Holds 75% voting interest. (see separate coverage)
- 100% int. in **Brookfield BBP U.S. Holdings LLC**, United States.
- 23% int. in **CUPA Finance, S.L.**, Spain.
- 23.4% int. in **CWC Energy Services Corp.**, Calgary, Alta. (see separate coverage)
- 52% int. in **Cardone Industries, Inc.**, Philadelphia, Pa. Holds 98% voting interest.
- 28% int. in **Clarios Global L.P.**, Milwaukee, Wis. Holds 100% voting interest.
- 34% int. in **DexKo Global Inc.**, Novi, Mich. Holds 100% voting interest.
- 46% int. in **Ember Resources Inc.**, Calgary, Alta. Holds 100% voting interest.
- 28% int. in **Everise Holdings Pte. Ltd.**, Singapore, Singapore. Holds 84% voting interest.
- 8% int. in **GrafTech International Ltd.**, Ohio
- 18% int. in **Greenergy Fuels Holdings Ltd.**, London, Middx., United Kingdom. Holds 88% voting interest.
- 94% int. in **Hammerstone Infrastructure Materials Ltd.**, Canada. Holds 98% voting interest.
- 31% int. in **Imagine Communications Group Limited**, Dublin, Ireland. Holds 55% voting interest.
- 20% int. in **IndoStar Capital Finance Limited**, Mumbai, India. Holds 56% voring interest.
- 22% int. in **Magnati - Sole Proprietorship LLC**, Abu Dhabi, United Arab Emirates. 60% voting interest.
- 28% int. in **Modulaire Investments 2 S.à r.l.**, Luxembourg. Holds 100% voting interest.
- 7% int. in **Nielsen Holdings plc**, New York, N.Y.
- **Ontario Gaming GTA Limited Partnership**, Ont.
- 35% int. in **Ouro Verde Locação e Seviços S.A.**, Brazil. Holds 100% voting interest.
- 41% int. in **Sagen MI Canada Inc.**, Oakville, Ont. Holds 100% voting interest. (see separate coverage)
- 14% int. in **Schoeller Allibert Group B.V.**, Netherlands. Holds 52% voting interest.
- 36% int. in **Scientific Games, LLC**, Alpharetta, Ga. Hold 100% voting interest.
- 75% int. in **Sera Global Holding LP**, Canada.
- 40% int. in **La Trobe Financial Services Pty Ltd.**, Melbourne, Vic., Australia. 100% voting interest.
- 35% int. in **Unidas Locadora S.A.**, Brazil. 100% voting interest.
- 100% int. in **WatServ Holdings Ltd.**, Waterloo, Ont.

Financial Statistics

Periods ended:	12m Dec. 31/22[A]		12m Dec. 31/21[A]
	US$000s	%Chg	US$000s
Operating revenue	**57,545,000**	**+24**	**46,587,000**
Cost of sales	44,248,000		36,745,000
Salaries & benefits	5,594,000		4,123,000
General & admin expense	1,372,000		1,012,000
Operating expense	**51,250,000**	**+22**	**41,880,000**
Operating income	**6,295,000**	**+34**	**4,707,000**
Deprec., depl. & amort.	3,260,000		2,283,000
Finance costs, net	2,538,000		1,468,000
Investment income	165,000		13,000
Write-downs/write-offs	9,000		(440,000)
Pre-tax income	**77,000**	**-97**	**2,318,000**
Income taxes	(278,000)		165,000
Net income	**355,000**	**-84**	**2,153,000**
Net inc. for equity hldrs	**55,000**	**-79**	**258,000**
Net inc. for non-cont. int.	**300,000**	**-84**	**1,895,000**
Cash & equivalent	4,097,000		3,850,000
Inventories	5,186,000		4,512,000
Accounts receivable	6,401,000		4,945,000
Current assets	18,312,000		15,418,000
Long-term investments	4,747,000		5,081,000
Fixed assets, net	15,893,000		15,325,000
Intangibles, net	39,527,000		23,391,000
Total assets	**89,498,000**	**+39**	**64,219,000**
Bank indebtedness	636,000		727,000
Accts. pay. & accr. liabs	9,303,000		7,895,000
Current liabilities	16,954,000		13,912,000
Long-term debt, gross	46,693,000		29,076,000
Long-term debt, net	42,935,000		27,014,000
Long-term lease liabilities	1,274,000		1,293,000
Shareholders' equity	1,415,000		2,252,000
Non-controlling interest	17,050,000		10,748,000
Cash from oper. activs	**1,011,000**	**-40**	**1,693,000**
Cash from fin. activs	18,070,000		7,063,000
Cash from invest. activs	(18,721,000)		(8,926,000)
Net cash position	**2,870,000**	**+11**	**2,588,000**
Capital expenditures	(1,748,000)		(1,450,000)
Capital disposals	181,000		124,000
Unfunded pension liability	590,000		634,000
	US$		US$
Earnings per share*	0.73		3.28
Cash flow per share*	13.43		21.62
Cash divd. per share*	0.25		0.25
	shs		shs
No. of shs. o/s*	74,612,503		77,085,493
Avg. no. of shs. o/s*	75,300,000		78,300,000
	%		%
Net profit margin	0.62		4.62
Return on equity	3.00		12.34
Return on assets	0.46		3.62
No. of employees (FTEs)	102,000		90,000

* L.P. unit
[A] Reported in accordance with IFRS

Latest Results

Periods ended:	3m Mar. 31/23[A]		3m Mar. 31/22[oA]
	US$000s	%Chg	US$000s
Operating revenue	13,758,000	+2	13,472,000
Net income	203,000	n.a.	(10,000)
Net inc. for equity hldrs	25,000	+212	8,000
Net inc. for non-cont. int	178,000		(18,000)
	US$		US$
Earnings per share*	0.34		0.10

* L.P. unit
[o] Restated
[A] Reported in accordance with IFRS

Historical Summary
(as originally stated)

Fiscal Year	Oper. Rev.	Net Inc. Bef. Disc.	EPS*
	US$000s	US$000s	US$
2022[A]	57,545,000	355,000	0.73
2021[A]	46,587,000	2,153,000	3.28
2020[A]	37,635,000	580,000	(1.13)
2019[A]	43,032,000	434,000	0.62
2018[A]	37,168,000	1,203,000	1.11

* L.P. unit
[A] Reported in accordance with IFRS

B.117 Brookfield Corporation*

Symbol - BN **Exchange** - TSX **CUSIP** - 11271J
Head Office - Bay Wellington Tower, Brookfield Place, 100-181 Bay St, PO Box 762, Toronto, ON, M5J 2T3 **Telephone** - (416) 363-9491 **Fax** - (416) 365-9642
Website - bn.brookfield.com
Email - monica.thakur@brookfield.com
Investor Relations - Monica Thakur (866) 989-0311
Auditors - Deloitte LLP C.A., Toronto, Ont.
Transfer Agents - American Stock Transfer & Trust Company, LLC, New York, N.Y.; TSX Trust Company, Toronto, Ont.
FP500 Revenue Ranking - 1
Employees - 195,000 at Dec. 31, 2022

Profile - (Ont. 1997 amalg.) Global alternative asset management company which owns and operates assets with a focus on renewable power and transition, infrastructure, private equity, real estate and credit. At Dec. 31, 2022, assets under management totaled US$800 billion.

Asset Management - Operations, held through 75% owned **Brookfield Asset Management ULC** (**Brookfield Asset Management Ltd.** 25%), include managing long-term private funds, perpetual strategies and liquid strategies on behalf of clients and the company, as well as the asset management activities of subsidiary **Oaktree Capital Group, LLC**. At Dec. 31, 2022, the company managed US$418 billion in fee-bearing capital.

Renewable Power & Transition - Operations, held through publicly traded affiliate **Brookfield Renewable Partners L.P.**, include the ownership, operation and development of hydroelectric, wind, solar and energy transition power generating facilities. Asset portfolio includes 229 hydroelectric generating stations on 87 river systems in North America, Brazil and Colombia totaling 8,159 MW of generating capacity and an average annual generation of 37,843 GWh; 125 wind facilities in North America, Europe, Brazil and Asia totaling 6,935 MW of generating capacity and an average annual generation of 20,977 GWh; 149 solar facilities worldwide totaling 3,957 MW of generating capacity and an average annual generation of 8,476 GWh; 6,238 distributed generation facilities worldwide totaling 2,055 MW of generating capacity and an average annual generation of 2,439 GWh; pumped storage facilities in North America and Europe totaling 2,721 MW of generating capacity with 5,220 GWh of storage capacity; four biomass facilities in Brazil totaling 175 MW of generating capacity; and four cogeneration plants in North America, Europe and Colombia totaling 529 MW of generating capacity.

Infrastructure - Operations, held through publicly traded affiliate **Brookfield Infrastructure Partners L.P.**, include the ownership, operation and development of utilities (electricity and natural gas transmission and distribution, and water distribution), transport (port terminals, rail and toll roads), midstream (natural gas transmission, gathering and processing, and storage) and data infrastructure (telecommunications towers, fibre optic networks and data centres). Key infrastructure assets include 60,000 km of operating electricity transmission and distribution lines in Australia; 4,200 km of natural gas pipelines in Brazil, Mexico and India; 2,000 km of operating electricity transmission lines in Brazil, with an additional 900 km under development; 7,800,000 connections, predominantly electricity and natural gas, in the U.K. and Colombia; a residential energy infrastructure business which provides water heater, heating, ventilation and air conditioner (HVAC) rentals as well as home repair services in Canada, the U.S., Germany and the U.K.; a sub-metering business which has more than 540,000 long-term contracted sub-metering services within Canada and the U.S.; 1,700,000 installed smart meters in Australia and New Zealand; 11 terminals in the U.K. and Australia that facilitate global trade of goods, natural resources and commodities; a 30,000,000-tonne-per-annum liquefied natural gas export terminal in the U.S.; an 85,000,000-tonne-per-annum export facility in Australia; 22,000 km of rail track in North America and Europe; 5,500 km of rail track in Western Australia; 4,800 km of rail network in Brazil; 3,800 km of toll roads in Brazil, Peru and India; 15,000 km of natural gas transmission lines in the U.S.; 600 bcf of natural gas storage in the U.S. and Canada; 17 natural gas and natural gas liquids processing plants in Canada, with a capacity of 5.7 bcf per day; 10,600 km of pipelines, which include long-haul, conventional and natural gas gathering pipelines; 525,000-tonne-per-annum petrochemical facility for polypropylene production in Canada; 207,000 operational telecommunications towers in India, France, Germany, Austria, the U.K. and New Zealand; 46,600 km of fibre optic cable in France, Brazil and New Zealand; more than 70 distributed antenna systems in the U.K.; 881,000 fibre-to-the-premise connections in France and Australia; two semiconductor manufacturing foundries in the U.S.; and 50 data centres in five continents, with 230 MW of critical load capacity.

Private Equity - Operations, held through publicly traded subsidiary **Brookfield Business Partners L.P.**, include business services, infrastructure services and industrial operations. Business services include providing residential mortgage default insurance in Canada; providing cloud-based operations software to dealerships and original equipment manufacturers across automotive and related industries; operating private hospitals and providing essential social infrastructure in Australia; global construction services; financing of commercial vehicle and affordable housing in India; road fuels distribution and marketing in the U.K., Ireland, Canada and the U.S.; heavy equipment and light vehicle leasing in Brazil; providing payment processing platform for government, merchant and institutional clients in the U.A.E.; operating entertainment facilities in Canada; providing customer management solutions for managing customer interactions of large global healthcare and technology clients primarily based in the U.S.; wireless broadband services in rural Ireland; providing services to residential real estate brokers through franchise arrangements under a number of brands in Canada; residential condominium property management services in Canada; and providing third party audience measurement, data and analytics to the video and audio advertising industry. Infrastructure services include providing original equipment and technology to the global nuclear power generation industry; marine transportation, offshore oil production, facility storage, long-distance towing and offshore installation, maintenance and safety services to the offshore oil production industry; lottery services in more than 50 countries; modular building leasing in Europe and Asia Pacific; and scaffolding and related services to the global industrial and commercial markets. Industrial operations include manufacturing of automotive batteries; production of graphite electrodes; water and wastewater services in Brazil; manufacturing of engineered components for industrial trailers and other towable-equipment providers; distribution of solar power solutions in Brazil; providing returnable plastic packaging in Europe; natural gas exploration and production in Canada; contract drilling and well servicing in western Canada; remanufacturing of automotive aftermarket parts in the U.S.; manufacturing of graphite electrodes and petroleum needle coke; limestone quarrying in Alberta; and manufacturing of slate roofing tiles. Also operates a residential development business, which includes construction, sales and marketing of residential and commercial office units in Brazil.

Real Estate - Operations, held through wholly owned **Brookfield Property Partners L.P.** and **Brookfield Residential Properties ULC** (collectively Brookfield Property Group), include office properties, retail properties and limited partnership (LP) investments. The real estate portfolio includes interests in 132 office properties totaling 92,000,000 sq. ft. in leading commercial markets such as New York, N.Y., London, U.K., Toronto, Ont., Berlin, Germany, Dubai, U.A.E., Sydney, Australia, and Rio de Janeiro, Brazil; and 109 malls and urban retail properties totaling 110,000,000 sq. ft. primarily in the U.S. The LP investment portfolio includes real estate private funds managed by the company which holds assets in the multi-family, triple net lease, hospitality, office, retail, mixed-use, logistics, life science, senior living, manufactured housing and student housing sectors.

On Dec. 9, 2022, the company completed its transaction for the public listing and distribution of a 25% interest in its asset management business, through **Brookfield Asset Management Ltd.** (BAML) by a plan of arrangement. The transaction resulted in the division of the company into two publicly traded companies, the company (which was renamed **Brookfield Corporation**) and BAML, with the holders of the company's class A limited voting shares, class B limited voting shares and class A preferred series 8 and 9 shares becoming shareholders of BAML on completion. Each holder of class A limited voting shares of the company received 1 class A limited voting share of BAML for every 4 class A limited voting shares of the company held. Holders of class A preferred series 8 shares received 0.103 BAML class A limited voting share and a new Brookfield Corporation class A preferred series 51 share for each series 8 share held and holders of class A preferred series 9 shares received 0.101 BAML class A limited voting share and a new Brookfield Corporation class A preferred series 52 share for each series 9 share held. The class A shares of BAML commenced trading on NYSE and TSX on Dec. 12, 2022.

Recent Merger and Acquisition Activity

Status: completed **Revised:** Dec. 31, 2022
UPDATE: The transaction was completed. PREVIOUS: Brookfield Asset Management Inc. agreed to sell its U.K.-based student housing portfolio, known as Student Roost, to Singapore-based GIC Pte. Ltd. and U.S.-based Greystar Real Estate Partners, LLC for £3.3 billion (US$4.2 billion). Student Roost operated in more than 20 cities across the U.K., consisting of more than 23,000 beds, with plans to develop about 3,000 more.

Status: completed **Announced:** Mar. 14, 2022
Brookfield Asset Management Inc. (BAM) and Qatar Investment Authority (QIA) sold a 49% interest in One Manhattan West to Blackstone Real Estate. The deal values the office building at US$2.85 billion. One Manhattan West is a 67-storey, 2,100,000-sq.-ft. building that is part of Manhattan West, BAM and QIA's 8-acre, 8,000,000-sq.-ft. commercial complex on Manhattan's west side in New York.

Predecessor Detail - Name changed from Brookfield Asset Management Inc., Dec. 9, 2022.

Directors - The Hon. Frank J. McKenna, chr., Cap-Pelé, N.B.; Jeffrey M. (Jeff) Blidner, v-chr., Toronto, Ont.; Brian D. Lawson, v-chr., Toronto, Ont.; J. Bruce Flatt, man. partner & CEO, New York, N.Y.; M. Elyse Allan, Toronto, Ont.; Angela F. Braly, Indianapolis, Ind.; Jack L. Cockwell, Toronto, Ont.; Janice R. Fukakusa, Toronto, Ont.; V. Maureen Kempston Darkes, Lauderdale-by-the-Sea, Fla.; Howard S. Marks, New York, N.Y.; Rafael Miranda Robredo, Madrid, Spain; Lord Gus O'Donnell, London, Middx., United Kingdom; Hutham S. Olayan, New York, N.Y.; Diana L. Taylor, New York, N.Y.

Other Exec. Officers - Aleks Novakovic, head, global tax; Swati Mandava, legal counsel & corp. sec.; Nicholas H. (Nick) Goodman, man. partner, pres. & CFO; Brian W. Kingston, man. partner & CEO, real estate; Cyrus Madon, man. partner & CEO, private equity; Lori A. Pearson, man. partner & COO; Samuel J. B. (Sam) Pollock, man. partner & CEO, infrastructure; Sachin G. Shah, man. partner & CEO, insce. solutions; Connor D. Teskey, man. partner & CEO, renewable power & transition

Capital Stock

	Authorized (shs.)	Outstanding (shs.)[1]	Par
Cl.A Preferred	unlimited		
Series 2	10,220,175	10,220,175	$25
Series 4	3,983,910	3,983,910	$25
Series 6	111,633	nil	$25
Series 13	8,792,596	8,792,596	$25
Series 15	nil	nil	$25
Series 17	7,840,204	7,840,204	$25
Series 18	8,881,088	7,681,088	$25
Series 24	10,812,027	10,808,027	$25
Series 25	10,996,000	nil	$25
Series 26	9,770,928	9,770,928	$25
Series 27	10,000,000	nil	$25
Series 28	9,723,927	9,233,927	$25
Series 29	9,890,000	nil	$25
Series 30	9,787,090	9,787,090	$25
Series 31	10,000,000	nil	$25
Series 32	11,750,299	11,750,299	$25
Series 33	12,000,000	nil	$25
Series 34	9,876,735	9,876,735	$25
Series 35	10,000,000	nil	$25
Series 36	7,842,909	7,842,909	$25
Series 37	7,830,091	7,830,091	$25
Series 38	7,906,132	7,906,132	$25
Series 39	8,000,000	nil	$25
Series 40	11,841,025	11,841,025	$25
Series 41	12,000,000	nil	$25
Series 42	11,887,500	11,887,500	$25
Series 43	12,000,000	nil	$25
Series 44	9,831,929	9,831,929	$25
Series 45	10,000,000	nil	$25
Series 46	11,740,797	11,740,797	$25
Series 47	12,000,000	nil	$25
Series 48	11,885,972	11,885,972	$25
Series 49	12,000,000	nil	$25
Series 50	unlimited	nil	US$25
Series 51	4,500,000	3,320,486	$25
Series 52	4,500,000	1,177,580	$25
Cl.AA Preferred	unlimited	nil	$25
Cl.A Limited Voting	unlimited	1,638,066,244[2]	n.p.v.
Cl.B Limited Voting	85,120	85,120	n.p.v.

[1] At Aug. 11, 2023

[2] At Aug. 18, 2023.

Class A Preferred - Issuable from time to time in one or more series. Each series rank on a parity with every other series with respect to dividends and return of capital. Entitled to preference over the class AA preferred shares and any other shares ranking junior to the class A preferred shares. Non-voting unless provided by law and except if dividends thereon remain unpaid for two years.

Series 2 - Entitled to cumulative preferential dividends payable quarterly at a rate equal to 70% of the average prime rate. Redeemable at Cdn$25 per share plus accrued and unpaid dividends.

Series 4 - Entitled to cumulative preferential dividends payable quarterly at a rate equal to 70% of the average prime rate. Redeemable at Cdn$25 per share plus accrued and unpaid dividends.

Series 13 - Entitled to cumulative preferential dividends payable quarterly at a rate equal to 70% of the average prime rate. Redeemable at Cdn$25 per share plus accrued and unpaid dividends.

Series 17 - Entitled to cumulative preferential annual dividends of Cdn$1.1875 per share payable quarterly. Redeemable at Cdn$25 per share plus accrued and unpaid dividends. Convertible at any time into class A limited voting shares at a price equal to the greater of Cdn$2.00 and of 95% of the 20-day weighted average market price of class A limited voting shares at the time of conversion.

Series 18 - Entitled to cumulative preferential annual dividends of Cdn$1.1875 per share payable quarterly. Redeemable at Cdn$25 per share plus accrued and unpaid dividends. Convertible at any time into class A limited voting shares at a price equal to the greater of Cdn$2.00 and of 95% of the 20-day weighted average market price of class A limited voting shares at the time of conversion.

Series 24 - Entitled to cumulative preferential annual dividends of Cdn$0.80925 per share payable quarterly to June 30, 2026, and thereafter at a rate reset every five years equal to the five-year Government of Canada bond yield plus 2.3%. Redeemable on June 30, 2026, and on June 30 every five years thereafter at Cdn$25 per share plus declared and unpaid dividends. Convertible at the holder's option, on June 30, 2026, and on June 30 every five years thereafter, into floating rate class A preferred series 25 shares on a share-for-share basis, subject to certain conditions. The series 25 shares would pay a quarterly dividend equal to the 90-day Canadian Treasury bill rate plus 2.3%.

Series 26 - Entitled to cumulative preferential annual dividends of Cdn$0.9615 per share payable quarterly to Mar. 31, 2027, and thereafter at a rate reset every five years equal to the five-year Government of Canada bond yield plus 2.31%. Redeemable on Mar. 31, 2027, and on March 31 every five years thereafter at Cdn$25 per share plus declared and unpaid dividends. Convertible at the holder's option, on Mar. 31, 2027, and on March 31 every five years thereafter, into floating rate class A preferred series 27 shares on a share-for-share basis, subject to certain conditions. The series 27 shares would pay a quarterly dividend equal to the 90-day Canadian Treasury bill rate plus 2.31%.

Series 28 - Entitled to cumulative preferential annual dividends of Cdn$1.1515 per share payable quarterly to June 30, 2027, and thereafter at a rate reset every five years equal to the five-year Government of Canada bond yield plus 1.8%. Redeemable on June 30, 2027, and on June 30 every five years thereafter at Cdn$25 per share plus declared and unpaid dividends. Convertible at the holder's option, on June 30, 2027, and on June 30 every five years thereafter, into floating rate class A preferred series 29 shares on a share-for-share basis, subject to certain conditions. The series 29 shares would pay a quarterly dividend equal to the 90-day Canadian Treasury bill rate plus 1.8%.

Series 30 - Entitled to cumulative preferential annual dividends of Cdn$1.52225 per share payable quarterly to Dec. 31, 2027, and thereafter at a rate reset every five years equal to the five-year Government of Canada bond yield plus 2.96%. Redeemable on Dec. 31, 2027, and on December 31 every five years thereafter at Cdn$25 per share plus declared and unpaid dividends. Convertible at the holder's option, on Dec. 31, 2027, and on December 31 every five years thereafter, into floating rate class A preferred series 31 shares on a share-for-share basis, subject to certain conditions. The series 31 shares would pay a quarterly dividend equal to the 90-day Canadian Treasury bill rate plus 2.96%.

Series 32 - Entitled to cumulative preferential annual dividends of Cdn$1.2653 per share payable quarterly to Sept. 30, 2023, and thereafter at a rate reset every five years equal to the five-year Government of Canada bond yield plus 2.9%. Redeemable on Sept. 30, 2023, and on September 30 every five years thereafter at Cdn$25 per share plus declared and unpaid dividends. Convertible at the holder's option, on Sept. 30, 2023, and on September 30 every five years thereafter, into floating rate class A preferred series 33 shares on a share-for-share basis, subject to certain conditions. The series 33 shares would pay a quarterly dividend equal to the 90-day Canadian Treasury bill rate plus 2.9%.

Series 34 - Entitled to cumulative preferential annual dividends of Cdn$1.10925 per share payable quarterly to Mar. 31, 2024, and thereafter at a rate reset every five years equal to the five-year Government of Canada bond yield plus 2.63%. Redeemable on Mar. 31, 2024, and on March 31 every five years thereafter at Cdn$25 per share plus declared and unpaid dividends. Convertible at the holder's option, on Mar. 31, 2024, and on March 31 every five years thereafter, into floating rate class A preferred series 35 shares on a share-for-share basis, subject to certain conditions. The series 35 shares would pay a quarterly dividend equal to the 90-day Canadian Treasury bill rate plus 2.63%.

Series 36 - Entitled to cumulative preferential annual dividends of Cdn$1.2125 per share payable quarterly. Redeemable at Cdn$25 per share plus accrued and unpaid dividends.

Series 37 - Entitled to cumulative preferential annual dividends of Cdn$1.225 per share payable quarterly. Redeemable at Cdn$25 per share plus accrued and unpaid dividends.

Series 38 - Entitled to cumulative preferential annual dividends of Cdn$0.892 per share payable quarterly to Mar. 31, 2025, and thereafter at a rate reset every five years equal to the five-year Government of Canada bond yield plus 2.55%. Redeemable on Mar. 31, 2025, and on March 31 every five years thereafter at Cdn$25 per share plus declared and unpaid dividends. Convertible at the holder's option, on Mar. 31, 2025, and on March 31 every five years thereafter, into floating rate class A preferred series 39 shares on a share-for-share basis, subject to certain conditions. The series 39 shares would pay a quarterly dividend equal to the 90-day Canadian Treasury bill rate plus 2.55%.

Series 40 - Entitled to cumulative preferential annual dividends of Cdn$1.0073 per share payable quarterly to Sept. 30, 2024, and thereafter at a rate reset every five years equal to the five-year Government of Canada bond yield plus 2.86%. Redeemable on Sept. 30, 2024, and on September 30 every five years thereafter at Cdn$25 per share plus declared and unpaid dividends. Convertible at the holder's option, on Sept. 30, 2024, and on September 30 every five years thereafter, into floating rate class A preferred series 41 shares on a share-for-share basis, subject to certain conditions. The series 41 shares would pay a quarterly dividend equal to the 90-day Canadian Treasury bill rate plus 2.86%.

Series 42 - Entitled to cumulative preferential annual dividends of Cdn$0.8135 per share payable quarterly to June 30, 2025, and thereafter at a rate reset every five years equal to the five-year Government of Canada bond yield plus 2.84%. Redeemable on June 30, 2025, and on June 30 every five years thereafter at Cdn$25 per share plus declared and unpaid dividends. Convertible at the holder's option, on June 30, 2025, and on June 30 every five years thereafter, into floating rate class A preferred series 43 shares on a share-for-share basis, subject to certain conditions. The series 43 shares would pay a quarterly dividend equal to the 90-day Canadian Treasury bill rate plus 2.84%.

Series 44 - Entitled to cumulative preferential annual dividends of Cdn$1.25 per share payable quarterly to Dec. 31, 2025, and thereafter at a rate reset every five years equal to the greater of: (i) five-year Government of Canada bond yield plus 4.17%; and (ii) 5%. Redeemable on Dec. 31, 2025, and on December 31 every five years thereafter at Cdn$25 per share plus declared and unpaid dividends. Convertible at the holder's option, on Dec. 31, 2025, and on December 31 every five years thereafter, into floating rate class A preferred series 45 shares on a share-for-share basis, subject to certain conditions. The series 45 shares would pay a quarterly dividend equal to the 90-day Canadian Treasury bill rate plus 4.17%.

Series 46 - Entitled to cumulative preferential annual dividends of Cdn$1.3465 per share payable quarterly to Mar. 31, 2027, and thereafter at a rate reset every five years equal to the greater of: (i) five-year Government of Canada bond yield plus 3.85%; and (ii) 4.80%. Redeemable on Mar. 31, 2027, and on March 31 every five years thereafter at Cdn$25 per share plus declared and unpaid dividends. Convertible at the holder's option, on Mar. 31, 2027, and on March 31 every five years thereafter, into floating rate class A preferred series 47 shares on a share-for-share basis, subject to certain conditions. The series 47 shares would pay a quarterly dividend equal to the 90-day Canadian Treasury bill rate plus 3.85%.

Series 48 - Entitled to cumulative preferential annual dividends of Cdn$1.55725 per share payable quarterly to Jan. 1, 2028, and thereafter at a rate reset every five years equal to the greater of: (i) five-year Government of Canada bond yield plus 3.1%; and (ii) 4.75%. Redeemable on Dec. 31, 2027, and on December 31 every five years thereafter at Cdn$25 per share plus declared and unpaid dividends. Convertible at the holder's option, on Dec. 31, 2027, and on December 31 every five years thereafter, into floating rate class A preferred series 49 shares on a share-for-share basis, subject to certain conditions. The series 49 shares would pay a quarterly dividend equal to the 90-day Canadian Treasury bill rate plus 3.1%.

Series 51 - Entitled to cumulative preferential dividends payable monthly at a rate equal to between 50% and 100% of the prime rate. Redeemable at Cdn$22.44 per share plus accrued and unpaid dividends. Convertible at the holder's option, on Nov. 1, 2026, and on November 1 every five years thereafter, into class A preferred series 52 shares on a share-for-share basis, subject to certain conditions.

Series 52 - Entitled to fixed cumulative preferential annual dividends of Cdn$0.605 per share payable quarterly to Oct. 31, 2026, and thereafter at a rate reset every five years equal to a fixed rate not less than 80% of the Government of Canada bond yield. Redeemable on Nov. 1, 2026, and on November 1 every five years thereafter, at Cdn$22 per share plus accrued and unpaid dividends. Convertible at the holder's option, on Nov. 1, 2026, and on November 1 every five years thereafter, into class A preferred series 51 shares on a share-for-share basis, subject to certain conditions.

Class AA Preferred - Issuable from time to time in one or more series. Each series rank on a parity with every other series with respect to dividends and return of capital. Rank junior to class A preferred shares and are entitled to priority over all other classes of shares. Non-voting.

Class A Limited Voting - Entitled to elect one half of the board of directors and as a class must approve the appointment of auditors. Rank on par with class B limited voting shares with respect to dividends and return of capital. One vote per share.

Class B Limited Voting - Entitled to elect one half of the board of directors and as a class must approve the appointment of auditors. One vote per share.

Options - At Dec. 31, 2022, options were outstanding to purchase 44,093,000 New York Stock Exchange (NYSE) listed class A limited voting shares at a weighted average exercise price of US$25.16 per share with an average life of up to 8.2 years.

Class A Preferred Series 15 (old)- Were entitled to cumulative preferential dividends payable quarterly at a rate determined by negotiation, bid or auction, or at the bankers' acceptable rate plus 0.40%. Redeemed during the first quarter of 2023.

Class A Preferred Series 25 (old) - Were entitled to cumulative preferential annual dividends payable quarterly equal to the 90-day Canadian Treasury bill rate plus 2.3%. Converted into class A preferred series 24 shares on a share-for-share basis on June 30, 2021.

Normal Course Issuer Bid - The company plans to make normal course purchases of up to 142,042,619 class A limited voting shares representing 10% of the public float. The bid commenced on May 25, 2023, and expires on May 24, 2024.

The company plans to make normal course purchases of up to 1,022,018 class A preferred series 2 shares representing 10% of the public float. The bid commenced on Aug. 22, 2023, and expires on Aug. 21, 2024.

The company plans to make normal course purchases of up to 398,391 class A preferred series 4 shares representing 10% of the public float. The bid commenced on Aug. 22, 2023, and expires on Aug. 21, 2024.

The company plans to make normal course purchases of up to 879,260 class A preferred series 13 shares representing 10% of the public float. The bid commenced on Aug. 22, 2023, and expires on Aug. 21, 2024.

The company plans to make normal course purchases of up to 784,020 class A preferred series 17 shares representing 10% of the public float. The bid commenced on Aug. 22, 2023, and expires on Aug. 21, 2024.

The company plans to make normal course purchases of up to 768,109 class A preferred series 18 shares representing 10% of the public float. The bid commenced on Aug. 22, 2023, and expires on Aug. 21, 2024.

The company plans to make normal course purchases of up to 1,080,803 class A preferred series 24 shares representing 10% of the public float. The bid commenced on Aug. 22, 2023, and expires on Aug. 21, 2024.

The company plans to make normal course purchases of up to 977,093 class A preferred series 26 shares representing 10% of the public float. The bid commenced on Aug. 22, 2023, and expires on Aug. 21, 2024.

The company plans to make normal course purchases of up to 923,393 class A preferred series 28 shares representing 10% of the public float. The bid commenced on Aug. 22, 2023, and expires on Aug. 21, 2024.

The company plans to make normal course purchases of up to 978,709 class A preferred series 30 shares representing 10% of the public float. The bid commenced on Aug. 22, 2023, and expires on Aug. 21, 2024.

The company plans to make normal course purchases of up to 1,175,030 class A preferred series 32 shares representing 10% of the public float. The bid commenced on Aug. 22, 2023, and expires on Aug. 21, 2024.

The company plans to make normal course purchases of up to 987,674 class A preferred series 34 shares representing 10% of the public float. The bid commenced on Aug. 22, 2023, and expires on Aug. 21, 2024.

The company plans to make normal course purchases of up to 784,291 class A preferred series 36 shares representing 10% of the public float. The bid commenced on Aug. 22, 2023, and expires on Aug. 21, 2024.

The company plans to make normal course purchases of up to 783,009 class A preferred series 37 shares representing 10% of the public float. The bid commenced on Aug. 22, 2023, and expires on Aug. 21, 2024.

The company plans to make normal course purchases of up to 790,613 class A preferred series 38 shares representing 10% of the public float. The bid commenced on Aug. 22, 2023, and expires on Aug. 21, 2024.

The company plans to make normal course purchases of up to 1,184,103 class A preferred series 40 shares representing 10% of the public float. The bid commenced on Aug. 22, 2023, and expires on Aug. 21, 2024.

The company plans to make normal course purchases of up to 1,188,750 class A preferred series 42 shares representing 10% of the public float. The bid commenced on Aug. 22, 2023, and expires on Aug. 21, 2024.

The company plans to make normal course purchases of up to 983,193 class A preferred series 44 shares representing 10% of the public float. The bid commenced on Aug. 22, 2023, and expires on Aug. 21, 2024.

The company plans to make normal course purchases of up to 1,174,080 class A preferred series 46 shares representing 10% of the public float. The bid commenced on Aug. 22, 2023, and expires on Aug. 21, 2024.

The company plans to make normal course purchases of up to 1,188,597 class A preferred series 48 shares representing 10% of the public float. The bid commenced on Aug. 22, 2023, and expires on Aug. 21, 2024.

The company plans to make normal course purchases of up to 332,049 class A preferred series 51 shares representing 10% of the public float. The bid commenced on Aug. 22, 2023, and expires on Aug. 21, 2024.

The company plans to make normal course purchases of up to 117,758 class A preferred series 52 shares representing 10% of the public float. The bid commenced on Aug. 22, 2023, and expires on Aug. 21, 2024.

Major Shareholder - A partnership which includes current and former senior executives of the company collectively held 18.3% interest at Apr. 20, 2023.

Price Range - BN/TSX

Year	Volume	High	Low	Close
2022	438,600,146	$79.04	$41.78	$42.58
2021	415,291,842	$78.67	$48.34	$76.39
2020	582,975,362	$60.48	$31.35	$52.62
2019	398,599,840	$52.41	$33.73	$50.02
2018	377,837,824	$39.43	$31.14	$34.88

Recent Close: $44.17

Capital Stock Changes - During the first quarter of 2023, all outstanding 2,000,000 class A preferred series 15 shares were redeemed.

On Dec. 9, 2022, all outstanding 3,320,486 class A preferred series 8 shares were exchanged for a like number of class A preferred series 51 shares and all outstanding 1,177,580 class A preferred series 9 shares were exchanged for a like number of class A preferred series 52 shares. Also during 2022, class A limited voting shares were issued as follows: 19,138,775 under long-term share ownership plans, 1,406,586 on exercise of options and 1,245,226 under dividend reinvestment plan and others; 17,247,660 class A limited voting shares were repurchased. In addition, 1,188,000 class A preferred series 4 shares were issued and 237,510 class A preferred series 2 shares, 497,500 class A preferred series 13 shares and 185,661 class A preferred series 18 shares were redeemed.

Dividends

BN cl A Ra US$0.28 pa Q est. Mar. 31, 2023**
Prev. Rate: US$0.56 est. Mar. 31, 2022
Prev. Rate: US$0.52 est. Mar. 31, 2021
Prev. Rate: US$0.48 est. June 30, 2020
stk.[1]◆.................. Dec. 9/22 stk.[2]◆.............. June 28/21
Paid in 2023: US$0.21 2022: US$0.56 + stk.◆ 2021: US$0.52 + stk.◆

BN.PR.B pfd A ser 2 cum. red. Fltg. Ra pa Q
$0.293125............ June 30/23 $0.248813........ Mar. 31/23
$0.243688............ Dec. 30/22 $0.185063........ Sept. 29/22
Paid in 2023: $0.541938 2022: $0.665439 2021: $0.428752

BN.PR.C pfd A ser 4 cum. red. Fltg. Ra pa Q
$0.293125............ June 30/23 $0.284813........ Mar. 31/23
$0.243688............ Dec. 30/22 $0.185063........ Sept. 29/22
Paid in 2023: $0.577938 2022: $0.665439 2021: $0.428752

BN.PR.K pfd A ser 13 cum. red. Fltg. Ra pa Q
$0.293125............ June 30/23 $0.284813........ Mar. 31/23
$0.243688............ Dec. 30/22 $0.185063........ Sept. 29/22
Paid in 2023: $0.577938 2022: $0.665439 2021: $0.428752

BN.PR.M pfd A ser 17 cum. red. cv exch. Ra $1.1875 pa Q
BN.PR.N pfd A ser 18 cum. red. cv exch. Ra $1.1875 pa Q
BN.PR.R pfd A ser 24 cum. red. exch. Adj. Ra $0.80925 pa Q est. Sept. 29, 2021
BN.PR.T pfd A ser 26 cum. red. exch. Adj. Ra $0.9615 pa Q est. June 30, 2022
BN.PR.X pfd A ser 28 cum. red. exch. Adj. Ra $1.1515 pa Q est. Sept. 29, 2022
BN.PR.Z pfd A ser 30 cum. red. exch. Adj. Ra $1.52225 pa Q est. Mar. 31, 2023
BN.PF.A pfd A ser 32 cum. red. exch. Adj. Ra $1.26525 pa Q est. Dec. 31, 2018
BN.PF.B pfd A ser 34 cum. red. exch. Adj. Ra $1.10925 pa Q est. June 28, 2019
BN.PF.C pfd A ser 36 cum. red. Ra $1.2125 pa Q
BN.PF.D pfd A ser 37 cum. red. Ra $1.225 pa Q
BN.PF.E pfd A ser 38 cum. red. exch. Adj. Ra $0.892 pa Q est. June 30, 2020
BN.PF.F pfd A ser 40 cum. red. exch. Adj. Ra $1.00725 pa Q est. Dec. 31, 2019
BN.PF.G pfd A ser 42 cum. red. exch. Adj. Ra $0.8135 pa Q est. Sept. 30, 2020
BN.PF.H pfd A ser 44 cum. red. exch. Adj. Ra $1.25 pa Q est. Dec. 31, 2015
BN.PF.I pfd A ser 46 cum. red. exch. Adj. Ra $1.3465 pa Q est. June 30, 2022
BN.PF.J pfd A ser 48 cum. red. exch. Adj. Ra $1.55725 pa Q est. Mar. 31, 2023
BN.PF.K pfd A ser 51 cum. red. exch. Fltg. Ra pa M
Listed Dec 12/22.
$0.132.................. Sept. 12/23 $0.13023.......... Aug. 11/23
$0.12635.............. July 12/23 $0.12283.......... June 12/23
Paid in 2023: $1.11368**i** 2022: n.a. 2021: n.a.

BN.PF.L pfd A ser 52 cum. red. exch. Adj. Ra $0.605 pa Q est. Jan. 12, 2023
Listed Dec 12/22.
$0.151255**i**........... Jan. 12/23
pfd A ser 8 cum. red. exch. Fltg. Ra pa M
Delisted Dec 12/22.
$0.12396.............. Dec. 12/22 $0.11522.......... Nov. 10/22
$0.10977.............. Oct. 12/22 $0.09792.......... Sept. 12/22
Paid in 2023: n.a. 2022: $0.95064 2021: $0.61248

pfd A ser 9 cum. red. exch. Adj. Ra $0.6875 pa Q est. Feb. 1, 2017**
Delisted Dec 12/22.
pfd A ser 25 cum. red. exch. Fltg. Ra pa Q
Delisted Jul 2/21.
$0.147905............ June 30/21 $0.1485............ Mar. 31/21
Paid in 2023: n.a. 2022: n.a. 2021: $0.296405

[1] Stk. divd. of 0.25 Brookfield Asset Mgmt Ltd cl. A shs. for ea. 1 sh. held.
[2] Stk. divd. of 1 Brookfield Asset Management Reinsurance Partners Ltd. cl A exch sh. for ea. 145 shs. held.
** Reinvestment Option ◆ Special **i** Initial Payment

Long-Term Debt - Outstanding at Dec. 31, 2022:

Corporate borrowings[1]	US$11,390,000,000
Subsidiary preferred shares[2]	1,469,000,000
	12,859,000,000

[1] Net of deferred financing costs totaling US$77,000,000. Bear interest at a weighted average rate of 4.2% and due to 2080.

[2] Consist of Brookfield Property Split Corp. senior preferred shares, Rouse Properties, L.P. series A preferred shares, Brookfield India Real Estate Trust preferred units, preferred capital of Alstria Office Prime Portfolio GmbH & Co. KG, preferred capital of India Infrastructure Investment Trusts and BIP Investment Corporation series 1 senior preferred shares.

Note - In June 2023, public offering of US$550,000,000 principal amount of 6.087% senior notes due 2033 was completed. In July 2023, US$550,000,000 principal amount of senior notes due Apr. 1, 2024, were redeemed.

Wholly Owned Subsidiaries

Brookfield Property Partners L.P., Hamilton, Bermuda.
Brookfield Residential Properties ULC, Calgary, Alta.

Subsidiaries

75% int. in **Brookfield Asset Management ULC**, Toronto, Ont.
65% int. in **Brookfield Business Partners L.P.**, Hamilton, Bermuda. Holds 100% voting interest. (see separate coverage)
64% int. in **Oaktree Capital Group, LLC**, Los Angeles, Calif.

Investments

27% int. in **Brookfield Infrastructure Partners L.P.**, Hamilton, Bermuda. Holds 100% voting interest. (see separate coverage)
48% int. in **Brookfield Renewable Partners L.P.**, Hamilton, Bermuda. Holds 100% voting interest. (see separate coverage)

Note: The preceding list includes only the major related companies in which interests are held.

Financial Statistics

Periods ended:	12m Dec. 31/22^A		12m Dec. 31/21^A
	US$000s	%Chg	US$000s
Unrealized invest. gain (loss)	(977,000)		5,151,000
Total revenue	**94,405,000**	**+13**	**83,333,000**
Salaries & benefits	9,849,000		7,804,000
General & admin. expense	3,931,000		3,197,000
Other operating expense	57,170,000		46,678,000
Operating expense	**70,950,000**	**+23**	**57,679,000**
Operating income	**23,455,000**	**-9**	**25,654,000**
Deprec. & amort.	7,683,000		6,437,000
Finance costs, gross	10,702,000		7,604,000
Pre-tax income	**6,664,000**	**-55**	**14,712,000**
Income taxes	1,469,000		2,324,000
Net income	**5,195,000**	**-58**	**12,388,000**
Net inc. for equity hldrs	**2,056,000**	**-48**	**3,966,000**
Net inc. for non-cont. int.	**3,139,000**	**-63**	**8,422,000**
Cash & equivalent	41,295,000		29,240,000
Inventories	12,843,000		11,415,000
Accounts receivable	14,155,000		11,332,000
Investments	47,094,000		46,100,000
Fixed assets, net	124,268,000		115,489,000
Properties	115,100,000		100,865,000
Intangibles, net	67,073,000		50,836,000
Total assets	**441,284,000**	**+13**	**391,003,000**
Accts. pay. & accr. liabs	12,743,000		11,258,000
Debt	12,859,000		12,060,000
Lease liabilities	8,506,000		9,041,000
Preferred share equity	4,145,000		4,145,000
Shareholders' equity	43,753,000		46,355,000
Non-controlling interest	98,138,000		88,386,000
Cash from oper. activs	**8,751,000**	**+11**	**7,874,000**
Cash from fin. activs	32,460,000		16,261,000
Cash from invest. activs	(39,650,000)		(21,045,000)
Net cash position	**14,396,000**	**+13**	**12,694,000**
Capital expenditures	(7,236,000)		(6,881,000)
Capital disposals	595,000		723,000
	US$		US$
Earnings per share*	1.22		2.47
Cash flow per share*	5.58		5.12
Cash divd. per share*	0.56		0.52
	shs		shs
No. of shs. o/s*	1,573,371,868		1,568,828,941
Avg. no. of shs. o/s*	1,567,500,000		1,536,500,000
	%		%
Net profit margin	5.50		14.87
Return on equity	4.66		10.26
Return on assets	3.25		5.12
Foreign sales percent	88		90
No. of employees (FTEs)	195,000		177,300

* Class A & B
^A Reported in accordance with IFRS

Latest Results

Periods ended:	3m Mar. 31/23^A		3m Mar. 31/22^A
	US$000s	%Chg	US$000s
Total revenue	23,764,000	-3	24,505,000
Net income	424,000	-86	2,960,000
Net inc. for equity hldrs	120,000	-91	1,359,000
Net inc. for non-cont. int	304,000		1,601,000
	US$		US$
Earnings per share*	0.05		0.84

* Class A & B
^A Reported in accordance with IFRS

Historical Summary
(as originally stated)

Fiscal Year	Total Rev. US$000s	Net Inc. Bef. Disc. US$000s	EPS* US$
2022^A	94,405,000	5,195,000	1.22
2021^A	83,333,000	12,388,000	2.47
2020^A	61,250,000	707,000	(0.12)
2019^A	69,493,000	5,354,000	1.77
2018^A	59,653,000	7,488,000	2.31

* Class A & B
^A Reported in accordance with IFRS
Note: Adjusted throughout for 1.5-for-1 split in Apr. 2020

B.118 Brookfield Global Infrastructure Securities Income Fund

Symbol - BGI.UN **Exchange** - TSX **CUSIP** - 112720
Head Office - c/o Brookfield Corporation, Bay Wellington Tower, Brookfield Place, 100-181 Bay St, PO Box 762, Toronto, ON, M5J 2T3 **Telephone** - (416) 363-9491 **Fax** - (416) 365-9642
Website - www.brookfield.com
Email - monica.thakur@brookfield.com
Investor Relations - Monica Thakur (866) 989-0311
Auditors - Deloitte LLP C.A., Toronto, Ont.
Transfer Agents - Computershare Trust Company of Canada Inc., Toronto, Ont.
Trustees - Brookfield Investment Management (Canada) Inc., Toronto, Ont.
Investment Managers - Brookfield Public Securities Group LLC, New York, N.Y.
Managers - Brookfield Public Securities Group LLC, New York, N.Y.
Profile - (Ont. 2013) Invests primarily in equity securities of publicly traded global infrastructure companies.

The investment portfolio consists primarily of companies which own or operate infrastructure assets including physical structures, networks and systems for transportation, energy, water and sewage and communication. The fund does not have a fixed termination date but may be terminated by the manager upon the approval of the unitholders.

Top 10 holdings at Mar. 31, 2023 (as a percentage of net asset value):

Holdings	Percentage
Plains GP Holdings LP	8.0%
National Grid plc	7.2%
ONEOK, Inc.	7.0%
Energy Transfer LP	6.8%
Kinder Morgan, Inc.	6.7%
Entergy Corporation	5.9%
NiSource Inc.	5.7%
Crown Castle Inc.	5.6%
Ferrovial S.A.	5.2%
American Electric Power Co Inc.	4.5%

Oper. Subsid./Mgt. Co. Directors - Adam Sachs, chief compliance officer, Jersey City, N.J.; Liam O'Connor, dir., fin. & contr., Chicago, Ill.
Oper. Subsid./Mgt. Co. Officers - David Levi, CEO; Kevin English, COO; Brian Hurley, gen. counsel & corp. sec.; Brian Hourihan, global chief compliance officer

Capital Stock

	Authorized (shs.)	Outstanding (shs.)[1]
Trust Unit	unlimited	17,682,982

[1] At Mar. 28, 2023

Trust Unit - Entitled to quarterly cash distributions targeted to be 15¢ per unit (6% per annum based on an original issue price of $10 per unit). Retractable in September of each year at a price per unit equal to the net asset value (NAV) per unit, less any costs associated with the retraction. Retractable in any other month at a price per unit equal to the lesser of: (i) 95% of the weighted average price per unit on TSX for the 10 trading days immediately preceding the retraction date; and (ii) the closing price per unit. One vote per trust unit.
Major Shareholder - Widely held at Mar. 28, 2023.

Price Range - BGI.UN/TSX

Year	Volume	High	Low	Close
2022	4,705,761	$7.46	$4.84	$5.16
2021	4,887,260	$8.21	$5.71	$6.62
2020	8,372,355	$8.48	$3.49	$5.90
2019	7,587,386	$8.09	$5.51	$7.83
2018	10,713,952	$6.81	$5.44	$5.68

Recent Close: $4.27
Capital Stock Changes - During 2022, trust units were issued as follows: 962,200 under an at-the-market equity program and 89,270 under a dividend reinvestment plan; 16,211 trust units were retracted.

Dividends

BGI.UN unit Ra $0.60 pa Q est. Oct. 22, 2013**
** Reinvestment Option

Financial Statistics

Periods ended:	12m Dec. 31/22^A		12m Dec. 31/21^A
	$000s	%Chg	$000s
Realized invest. gain (loss)	(498)		5,817
Unrealized invest. gain (loss)	2,214		5,452
Total revenue	**6,282**	**-59**	**15,436**
General & admin. expense	1,255		1,309
Other operating expense	204		277
Operating expense	**1,459**	**-8**	**1,587**
Operating income	**4,823**	**-65**	**13,849**
Finance costs, gross	676		463
Pre-tax income	**4,148**	**-69**	**13,386**
Income taxes	531		582
Net income	**3,616**	**-72**	**12,803**
Cash & equivalent	4,421		2,165
Investments	100,336		101,269
Total assets	**105,125**	**+1**	**103,843**
Bank indebtedness	22,903		21,294
Accts. pay. & accr. liabs	331		448
Shareholders' equity	79,242		79,609
Cash from oper. activs	**4,415**	**-28**	**6,137**
Cash from fin. activs	(2,158)		(6,366)
Net cash position	**4,421**	**+104**	**2,165**
	$		$
Earnings per share*	0.21		0.79
Cash flow per share*	0.26		0.38
Net asset value per share*	4.49		4.79
Cash divd. per share*	0.60		0.60
	shs		shs
No. of shs. o/s*	17,655,293		16,620,034
Avg. no. of shs. o/s*	17,270,174		16,234,372
	%		%
Net profit margin	57.56		82.94
Return on equity	4.55		16.78
Return on assets	4.02		13.17

* Trust Unit
^A Reported in accordance with IFRS

Note: Net income reflects increase/decrease in net assets resulting from operations.

Historical Summary
(as originally stated)

Fiscal Year	Total Rev. $000s	Net Inc. Bef. Disc. $000s	EPS* $
2022^A	6,282	3,616	0.21
2021^A	15,436	12,803	0.79
2020^A	(24,562)	(27,676)	(1.72)
2019^A	34,127	29,665	1.73
2018^A	(780)	(5,700)	(0.29)

* Trust Unit
^A Reported in accordance with IFRS

B.119 Brookfield Infrastructure Corporation

Symbol - BIPC **Exchange** - TSX **CUSIP** - 11275Q
Head Office - 250 Vesey St, 15th Flr, New York, NY, United States, 10281-1023 **Telephone** - (212) 417-7000
Website - www.bip.brookfield.com
Email - stephen.fukuda@brookfield.com
Investor Relations - Stephen Fukuda (416) 956-5129
Auditors - Deloitte LLP C.A., Toronto, Ont.
Transfer Agents - Computershare Trust Company of Canada Inc., Toronto, Ont.
FP500 Subsidiary Revenue Ranking - 38
Employees - 2,300 at Dec. 31, 2022
Profile - (B.C. 2019) Owns and operates a regulated natural gas transmission business in Brazil; a regulated gas and electricity distribution business in the United Kingdom; and a regulated utility business in Australia.

In Brazil, holds 31% economic interest (92% voting interest) in **Nova Transportadora do Sudeste S.A.**, which operates more than 2,000 km of natural gas transportation pipelines in the states of Rio de Janeiro, Sao Paulo and Minas Gerais with a total capacity of 158 m^3 fully contracted under long-term "ship-or-pay" agreements.

In the U.K., holds 80% interest in **BUUK Infrastructure No 1 Limited**, an independent "last-mile", multi-utility connection provider with about 4,300,000 connections throughout England, Scotland and Wales. Customers consist primarily of large energy retailers who serve residential and commercial users.

In Australia, holds 8% interest in **AusNet Services Ltd.**, which operates 7,000 km of electricity transmission lines and 54,000 km of electricity distribution lines across Victoria, as well as a regulated gas distribution business.

The company is a controlled affiliate of **Brookfield Infrastructure Partners L.P.** which, through its 70.05%-owned subsidiary **Brookfield Infrastructure L.P.**, holds 1.9% economic interest and 75% voting interest in the company.

Recent Merger and Acquisition Activity

Status: pending **Announced:** Apr. 11, 2023
Brookfield Infrastructure Corporation (BIPC) and its institutional partners agreed to acquire Purchase, N.Y.-based Triton International Limited for US$85 per share, consisting of US$68.50 in cash and US$16.50 in BIPC

class A shares. The transaction values Triton's common equity at US$4.7 billion and reflects an enterprise value of US$13.3 billion. Triton is the world's largest lessor of intermodal freight containers, with a container fleet of more than 7,000,000 twenty-foot equivalent units. The transaction is expected to close in the fourth quarter of 2023.

Directors - Anne Schaumburg, chr., N.J.; Jeffrey M. (Jeff) Blidner, Toronto, Ont.; William J. Cox, Hamilton, Bermuda; Roslyn Kelly, London, Middx., United Kingdom; John Mullen, Sydney, N.S.W., Australia; Daniel Muñiz Quintanilla, Mexico City, D.F., Mexico; Suzanne P. Nimocks, Park City, Utah; Rajeev Vasudeva, London, Middx., United Kingdom

Other Exec. Officers - Samuel J. B. (Sam) Pollock, CEO; Michael Ryan, man. dir., gen. counsel & corp. sec.; Benjamin M. (Ben) Vaughan, COO; David Krant, CFO

Capital Stock

	Authorized (shs.)	Outstanding (shs.)[1]
Preferred	unlimited	nil
Cl.A Exchangeable S.V.	unlimited	110,614,288[2]
Class B Multiple Vtg.	unlimited	2[2]
Class C Non-vtg.	unlimited	2,103,677

[1] At Apr. 26, 2023

[2] Classified as debt.

Class A Exchangeable Subordinate Voting - Entitled to dividends equal to distributions on Brookfield Infrastructure Partners L.P. (BIP LP) limited partnership units. Exchangeable for limited partnership units of BIP LP on a 1-for-1 basis or its cash equivalent. One vote per share.

Class B Multiple Voting - Entitled to dividends. Entitled to number votes equal to: (i) the number that is three times the number of class A exchangeable shares then issued and outstanding divided by (ii) the number of class B shares then issued and outstanding. Redeemable for cash in an amount equal to the market price of a BIP LP limited partnership unit. All held by BIP LP and Brookfield Infrastructure L.P. (BILP).

Class C Non-voting - All held by BIP LP and BILP. Entitled to dividends as and when declared by board of directors. BIP LP is entitled to all of the residual value in the company after payment in full of the amount due to holders of class A exchangeable shares and class B shares and subject to the prior rights of holders of preferred shares. Redeemable for cash in an amount equal to the market price of a BIP LP limited partnership unit.

Normal Course Issuer Bid - The company plans to make normal course purchases of up to 9,737,380 class A exchangeable subordinate voting shares representing 10% of the public float. The bid commenced on Dec. 1, 2022, and expires on Nov. 30, 2023.

Major Shareholder - Brookfield Corporation, Brookfield Infrastructure Partners L.P. and Brookfield Infrastructure L.P. collectively held 78% interest at Apr. 26, 2023.

Price Range - BIPC/TSX

Year	Volume	High	Low	Close
2022............	36,051,514	$67.18	$51.57	$52.67
2021............	48,576,456	$67.05	$48.61	$57.55
2020............	37,470,976	$62.92	$32.23	$61.46

Split: 1.5-for-1 split in June 2022

Recent Close: $53.10

Capital Stock Changes - On June 13 2022, class A exchangeable subordinate voting shares were split on a 3-for-2 basis. Also during 2022, 427,643 post-split class A exchangeable subordinate voting shares were issued on exchange of class B exchangeable limited partnership units of Brookfield Infrastructure Corporation Exchange L.P. and 17,512 post-split class A exchangeable subordinate voting shares were exchanged for BIP LP limited partnership units.

Dividends

BIPC cl A exch Ra US$1.53 pa Q est. Mar. 31, 2023[1]
2-for-1 split eff. June 13, 2022
Prev. Rate: US$2.16 est. Mar. 31, 2022
Prev. Rate: US$2.04 est. Mar. 31, 2021
Prev. Rate: US$1.94 est. June 30, 2020

[1] Cdn. residents will receive the Cdn. dollar equivalent.

Wholly Owned Subsidiaries

BIPC Holdings Inc., Ont.

- 100% int. in **BIPC Bermuda Holdco Limited**, Bermuda.
  - 8% int. in **AusNet Services Ltd.**, Southbank, Vic., Australia.
  - 80% int. in **BUUK Infrastructure No 1 Limited**, United Kingdom.
  - 31% int. in **Nova Transportadora do Sudeste S.A.**, Rio de Janeiro, Brazil. Holds 92% voting interest.

Financial Statistics

Periods ended:	12m Dec. 31/22[A]		12m Dec. 31/21[A]
	US$000s	%Chg	US$000s
Operating revenue	**1,886,000**	**+15**	**1,643,000**
Cost of sales	272,000		246,000
Salaries & benefits	59,000		44,000
General & admin expense	69,000		49,000
Operating expense	**400,000**	**+18**	**339,000**
Operating income	**1,486,000**	**+14**	**1,304,000**
Deprec., depl. & amort.	211,000		236,000
Finance costs, net	(514,000)		741,000
Investment income	4,000		nil
Pre-tax income	**1,881,000**	**+335**	**432,000**
Income taxes	262,000		405,000
Net income	**1,619,000**	**n.m.**	**27,000**
Net inc. for equity hldrs	**1,094,000**	**n.a.**	**(368,000)**
Net inc. for non-cont. int.	**525,000**	**+33**	**395,000**
Cash & equivalent	445,000		469,000
Accounts receivable	441,000		402,000
Current assets	1,567,000		2,010,000
Long-term investments	428,000		nil
Fixed assets, net	4,718,000		4,803,000
Intangibles, net	3,365,000		3,176,000
Total assets	**10,178,000**	**+1**	**10,086,000**
Bank indebtedness	26,000		131,000
Accts. pay. & accr. liabs	606,000		452,000
Current liabilities	4,633,000		6,197,000
Long-term debt, gross	4,577,000		3,556,000
Long-term debt, net	4,249,000		3,556,000
Shareholders' equity	(1,119,000)		(2,127,000)
Non-controlling interest	758,000		703,000
Cash from oper. activs	**893,000**	**+6**	**839,000**
Cash from fin. activs	(4,000)		(868,000)
Cash from invest. activs	(1,047,000)		326,000
Net cash position	**445,000**	**-5**	**469,000**
Capital expenditures	(525,000)		(417,000)
Capital disposals	4,000		2,000
	US$		US$
Earnings per share*	n.a.		n.a.
Cash divd. per share*	1.44		1.36
	shs		shs
No. of shs. o/s*	110,567,671		110,156,270
	%		%
Net profit margin	85.84		1.64
Return on equity	n.m.		n.m.
Return on assets	15.98		0.28
Foreign sales percent	100		100
No. of employees (FTEs)	2,300		1,900

* Cl.A Exch.

[A] Reported in accordance with IFRS

Latest Results

Periods ended:	3m Mar. 31/23[A]		3m Mar. 31/22[A]
	US$000s	%Chg	US$000s
Operating revenue	497,000	+8	461,000
Net income	(195,000)	n.a.	(216,000)
Net inc. for equity hldrs	(301,000)	n.a.	(373,000)
Net inc. for non-cont. int.	106,000		157,000
	US$		US$
Earnings per share*	n.a.		n.a.

[A] Reported in accordance with IFRS

Historical Summary
(as originally stated)

Fiscal Year	Oper. Rev.	Net Inc. Bef. Disc.	EPS*
	US$000s	US$000s	US$
2022[A]	1,886,000	1,619,000	n.a.
2021[A]	1,643,000	27,000	n.a.
2020[A]	1,430,000	(232,000)	n.a.
2019[A1]	1,619,000	570,000	n.a.
2018[A]	1,561,000	581,000	n.a.

* Cl.A. Exch.

[A] Reported in accordance with IFRS

[1] Represent carve-out financial statements of utilities operations transferred from Brookfield Infrastructure Partners L.P.

Note: Adjusted throughout for 1.5-for-1 split in June 2022

B.120 Brookfield Infrastructure Partners L.P.

Symbol - BIP.UN **Exchange** - TSX **CUSIP** - G16252
Head Office - 73 Front St, 5th Floor, Hamilton, Bermuda, HM 12
Telephone - (441) 294-3309 **Fax** - (441) 296-4475
Website - www.bip.brookfield.com
Email - stephen.fukuda@brookfield.com
Investor Relations - Stephen Fukuda (416) 956-5129
Auditors - Deloitte LLP C.A., Toronto, Ont.
Transfer Agents - Computershare Trust Company, Inc., Canton, Mass.; Computershare Trust Company of Canada Inc., Toronto, Ont.

Profile - (Bermuda 2007) Acquires, owns and operates utilities, transport, midstream and data businesses in North and South America, Europe and the Asia Pacific region.

Utilities

This segment consists of 60,000 km of operational electricity transmission and distribution lines in Australia; 2,900 km of electricity transmission lines in Brazil, of which 2,000 km are operational; 4,200 km of natural gas pipelines in North America, South America and India; commercial and residential distribution businesses which have 7,900,000, connections, predominantly electricity and natural gas; a residential energy infrastructure business which provides water heater, heating, ventilation and air conditioner (HVAC) rentals, and other home services and policies to 10,500,000 customers in Canada, the U.S., Germany and the U.K.; a sub-metering business which has over 570,000 long-term contracted sub-metering services in Canada and the U.S.; and 1,800,000 installed smart meters in Australia and New Zealand.

Holdings include **Enercare Inc.**, **Vanti S.A. E.S.P.**, **Transmissora Sertaneja de Eletricidade S.A.**, **Pipeline Infrastructure Ltd.**, **BOXT Limited**, **Thermondo GmbH** and **HomeServe plc**. In addition, through controlled publicly traded affiliate **Brookfield Infrastructure Corporation**, holds controlling interests in **BUUK Infrastructure No 1 Limited** and **Nova Transportadora do Sudeste S.A.**, and an equity investment in **AusNet Services Ltd.**

Transport

This segment consists of 115 short line and regional freight railroads with over 22,000 km of track in North America and Europe; 5,500 km of railroad tracks and related infrastructure in Western Australia; 4,800 km of rail network in Brazil; 3,800 km of toll roads in Brazil, Peru and India; 11 port terminals in the U.K. and Australia; a 30,000,000-tonne-per-annum liquefied natural gas (LNG) export terminal in the U.S.; and an 85,000,000-tonne-per-annum export facility in Australia.

Holdings include **Genesee & Wyoming Inc.**, **Arc Infrastructure WA Pty Ltd.**, **BIF India Holdings Pte Ltd.**, **Simhapuri Expressway Limited**, **Rayalseema Expressway Private Limited**, **Rutas de Lima S.A.C.**, **Brookfield Port Acquisitions (UK) Limited** and **Linx Cargo Care Group Pty Ltd.**

Midstream

This segment consists of 15,000 km of natural gas transmission pipelines in the U.S.; 10,600 km of pipelines which include long-haul, conventional and natural gas gathering pipelines in Canada; 17 natural gas and natural gas liquids processing plants in western Canada with capacity of 5.7 bcf per day; 600 bcf of natural gas storage in the U.S. and Canada; and a petrochemical processing complex in Canada with capacity of 525,000 tonnes per year.

Holdings include **NorthRiver Midstream Inc.**, **Inter Pipeline Ltd.**, **Lodi Gas Storage LLC**, **Rockpoint Gas Storage Partners L.P.** and **Warwick Gas Storage L.P.**

Data

This segment consists of 209,000 operational telecommunication sites in India, France, Germany, Austria, the U.K. and New Zealand; 46,600 km of fibre optic cable in France, Brazil and New Zealand; more than 70 distributed antenna systems in the U.K.; 900,000 fibre-to-the-premise connections in France and Australia; two semiconductor manufacturing facilities under construction in the U.S.; and 50 data centres located in five continents with 1,400,000 sq. ft. of raised floors and 230 MW of critical load capacity.

Holdings include **Dawn Acquisitions LLC**, **Ruby Pooling Hold Trust**; **Summit Digitel Infrastructure Private Limited**; **Crest Digitel Private Limited** and **WIG Holdings I Limited**.

The remaining 29.95% of managing general partnership units in **Brookfield Infrastructure L.P.** is held by **Brookfield Corporation** and its affiliates.

On May 2, 2023, the limited partnership exercised its option to acquire an additional 15% interest in **Transmissora Sertaneja de Eletricidade S.A.**, a Brazilian electricity transmission operation, increasing its ownership to 31%. Consideration was not disclosed. As a result of governance rights obtained, the limited partnership will consolidate Sertaneja.

On Feb. 1, 2023, the limited partnership acquired an effective 6% interest in a German telecommunications business for about US$700,000,000.

On Nov. 22, 2022, the limited partnership (BIP LP) entered into a joint-venture agreement with **Intel Corporation** for the construction and operation of a semiconductor foundry. BIP LP was expected to fund about US$500,000,000 of equity capital toward the project for a 12% interest.

On Aug. 4, 2022, the limited partnership, through an equal joint venture with another infrastructure investor, acquired an effective 12% interest in **Uniti Group Ltd.**, which provides wholesale and retail telecommunications services to customers and businesses in Australia, for US$193,000,000.

In June 2022, the limited partnership, together with its institutional partners, agreed to sell its Indian toll road operations for net proceeds of about US$200,000,000. The sale was expected to close in the first quarter of 2023.

On June 13, 2022, the limited partnership sold an effective 19% interest in its North American container terminal operation for net proceeds of US$275,000,000.

On Apr. 1, 2022, the limited partnership acquired 13% interest in an Australian smart meter business for US$215,000,000.

On Mar. 10, 2022, the limited partnership acquired an effective 17% interest in an Indian telecommunications business for US$30,000,000.

Recent Merger and Acquisition Activity

Status: pending **Announced:** June 20, 2023

Brookfield Infrastructure Partners L.P. (BIP LP) together with its institutional partners and existing investor Ontario Teachers' Pension

Plan agreed to acquire Dallas, Tex.-based Compass Datacenters, LLC from RedBird Capital Partners and the Azrieli Group. Compass Datacenters designs and constructs custom data centres, as well as rents its own data centres, to cloud and Software-as-a-Service providers, enterprises, co-location and hosting companies. Terms were not disclosed. The transaction was expected to close by the end of 2023.

Status: pending **Announced:** Apr. 11, 2023
Brookfield Infrastructure Partners L.P. (BIP LP) together with its institutional partners agreed to acquire a controlling interest in Paris, France-based Data4 from a unit of AXA S.A. for about US$2.4 billion. Data4 designs, own and operates 31 data centres in France, Italy, Spain, Luxembourg, Poland and Germany; it has 100MW of in-place capacity with plans to add 400MW. The transaction is expected to close in the third quarter of 2023.

Status: completed **Revised:** Apr. 3, 2023
UPDATE: The transaction was completed. PREVIOUS: Enbridge Inc. agreed to acquire Tres Palacios Holdings LLC, which owns and operates a natural gas storage facility in Markham, Tex., from Crestwood Equity Partners LP, Brookfield Infrastructure Partners L.P. (BIP LP) and BIP LP's institutional partners for US$335,000,000. Crestwood owns 50.1% in Tres Palacios, and BIP LP and its partners own 49.9%. Tres Palacios consists of three natural gas storage salt caverns with a total working gas capacity of 35 bcf and an integrated 62-mile natural gas header pipeline system, with eleven inter- and intrastate natural gas pipeline connections, including Enbridge's Texas Eastern pipeline.

Status: completed **Announced:** Jan. 4, 2023
Brookfield Infrastructure Partners L.P. (BIP LP) and its institutional partners completed the acquisition of Walsall, U.K.-based HomeServe plc for US$6.1 billion. BIP LP paid US$1.5 billion for an effective 26% and 25% interest in HomeServe's North American and European businesses, respectively. HomeServe provides home emergency repairs and improvements in the U.K., the U.S., Canada, France, Belgium, Spain, Portugal and Japan.

Status: completed **Announced:** Nov. 30, 2022
Brookfield Infrastructure Partners L.P. (BIP LP) and its institutional partners completed the sale of five Brazilian electricity transmission concessions, held through Odoya Transmissora de Energia S.A., Esperanza Transmissora de Energia S.A., Jose Maria de Macedo de Eletricidade S.A, Giovanni Sanguinetti Transmissora de Energia S.A. and Veredas Transmissora de Eletricidade S.A. BIP LP received in net proceeds of US$250,000,000 for its 31% interest.

Status: completed **Revised:** Sept. 12, 2022
UPDATE: The transaction was completed. PREVIOUS: Enercare Inc., wholly owned by Brookfield Infrastructure Partners L.P. and its institutional partners, agreed to acquire private Montreal, Que.-based HydroSolution, L.P., which provides water heaters, heat pumps, electric vehicle charging stations and other equipment for the home, serving more than 275,000 customers throughout Quebec. Terms of the transaction were not disclosed.

Oper. Subsid./Mgt. Co. Directors - Anne Schaumburg, chr., N.J.; Jeffrey M. (Jeff) Blidner, Toronto, Ont.; William J. Cox, Hamilton, Bermuda; Roslyn Kelly, London, Middx., United Kingdom; Daniel Muñiz Quintanilla, Mexico City, D.F., Mexico; Suzanne P. Nimocks, Park City, Utah; Rajeev Vasudeva, London, Middx., United Kingdom

Oper. Subsid./Mgt. Co. Officers - Samuel J. B. (Sam) Pollock, CEO; Benjamin M. (Ben) Vaughan, COO; David Krant, CFO

Capital Stock

	Authorized (shs.)	Outstanding (shs.)[1]
Class A Pref. L.P. Unit	unlimited	
Series 1		4,989,265
Series 3		4,989,262
Series 9		7,986,595
Series 11		9,936,190
Series 13		8,000,000
Series 14		8,000,000
Limited Partnership Unit	unlimited	458,633,280[2]
Special G.P. Unit	n.a.	2,400,631[3 4]
Redeem. Partnership Unit	n.a.	193,587,223[3 5]
Managing G.P. Unit	n.a.	458,380,315[3 6]
Exchange L.P. Unit	n.a.	6,371,677[3 7]
BIPC Exchangeable L.P. Unit	n.a.	110,604,400[3 8]
Perpetual Subord. Notes	n.a.	12,000,000[3 9]

[1] At Dec. 31, 2022
[2] At Mar. 31, 2023.
[3] At Mar. 31, 2023.
[4] Securities of subsidiary Brookfield Infrastructure L.P.
[5] Securities of subsidiary Brookfield Infrastructure L.P.
[6] Securities of subsidiary Brookfield Infrastructure L.P.
[7] Securities of subsidiary Brookfield Infrastructure Partners Exchange L.P.
[8] Securities of subsidiary Brookfield Infrastructure Corporation Exchange L.P.
[9] Securities of subsidiary BIP Bermuda Holdings I Limited.

Class A Preferred Limited Partnership Unit, Series 1 - Entitled to cumulative preferential annual distributions of Cdn$0.9935 payable quarterly to June 30, 2025, and thereafter at a rate reset every five years equal to the five-year Government of Canada bond yield plus 3.56%. Redeemable on June 30, 2025, and on June 30 every five years thereafter at Cdn$25 per unit plus declared and unpaid distributions. Convertible at the holder's option on June 30, 2025, and on June 30 every five years thereafter, into floating rate class A preferred LP units, series 2, on a unit-for-unit basis, subject to certain conditions. The class A preferred LP units, series 2, would pay a quarterly distribution equal to the 90-day Canadian Treasury bill rate plus 3.56%.

Class A Preferred Limited Partnership Unit, Series 3 - Entitled to cumulative preferential annual distributions of Cdn$1.375 payable quarterly to Dec. 31, 2025, and thereafter at a rate reset every five years equal to the five-year Government of Canada bond yield plus 4.53%. Redeemable on Dec. 31, 2025, and on December 31 every five years thereafter at Cdn$25 per unit plus declared and unpaid distributions. Convertible at the holder's option on Dec. 31, 2025, and on December 31 every five years thereafter, into floating rate class A preferred LP units, series 4, on a unit-for-unit basis, subject to certain conditions. The class A preferred LP units, series 4, would pay a quarterly distribution equal to the 90-day Canadian Treasury bill rate plus 4.53%.

Class A Preferred Limited Partnership Unit, Series 9 - Entitled to cumulative preferential annual distributions of Cdn$1.6605 payable quarterly to Mar. 31, 2028, and thereafter at a rate reset every five years equal to greater of: (i) the five-year Government of Canada bond yield plus 3% and (ii) 5%. Redeemable on Mar. 31, 2028, and on March 31 every five years thereafter at Cdn$25 per unit plus declared and unpaid distributions. Convertible at the holder's option on Mar. 31, 2028, and on March 31 every five years thereafter, into floating rate class A preferred LP units, series 10, on a unit-for-unit basis, subject to certain conditions. The class A preferred LP units, series 10, would pay a quarterly distribution equal to the greater of: the 90-day Canadian Treasury bill rate plus 3%; and (ii) 5%.

Class A Preferred Limited Partnership Unit, Series 11 - Entitled to cumulative preferential annual distributions of Cdn$1.275 payable quarterly to Dec. 31, 2023, and thereafter at a rate reset every five years equal to greater of: (i) the five-year Government of Canada bond yield plus 2.92% and (ii) 5.1%. Redeemable on Dec. 31, 2023, and on December 31 every five years thereafter at Cdn$25 per unit plus declared and unpaid distributions. Convertible at the holder's option on Dec. 31, 2023, and on December 31 every five years thereafter, into floating rate class A preferred LP units, series 12, on a unit-for-unit basis, subject to certain conditions. The class A preferred LP units, series 12, would pay a quarterly distribution equal to the greater of: the 90-day Canadian Treasury bill rate plus 2.92%; and (ii) 5.1%.

Class A Preferred Limited Partnership Unit, Series 13 - Entitled to cumulative preferential annual distributions of US$1.28125 payable quarterly. Redeemable on or after Oct. 15, 2025, at US$25 per unit plus all accrued and unpaid distributions.

Class A Preferred Limited Partnership Unit, Series 14 - Entitled to cumulative preferential annual distributions of US$1.25 payable quarterly. Redeemable on or after Feb. 16, 2026, at US$25 per unit plus all accrued and unpaid distributions.

Limited Partnership Unit - One vote per unit.

Special General Partner Unit - Issued by subsidiary Brookfield Infrastructure L.P. (BILP). Participate in earnings and distributions on a per unit basis equivalent to the per unit participation of the managing general partner units. All held by Brookfield Asset Management Inc. (BAM) and its affiliates.

Redeemable Partnership Unit - Issued by subsidiary BILP. Exchangeable for limited partnership units on a one-for-one basis and are the economic equivalent of limited partnership units. Participate in earnings and distributions on a per unit basis equivalent to the per unit participation of the managing general partner units. Non-voting. All held by BAM and its affiliates. Classified as part of non-controlling interest.

Managing General Partner Unit - Issued by subsidiary BILP. Equal to the number of limited partnership units.

Exchange Limited Partnership Unit - Issued by subsidiary Brookfield Infrastructure Partners Exchange LP. Exchangeable for limited partnership units on a one-for-one basis and are the economic equivalent of limited partnership units. Classified as a separate component of non-controlling interests.

BIPC Exchangeable Limited Partnership Unit - Issued by subsidiary Brookfield Infrastructure Corporation Exchange LP. Exchangeable for Brookfield Infrastructure Corporation (BIPC) class A exchangeable subordinate voting shares (BIPC exchangeable shares) on a one-for-one basis and are the economic equivalent of limited partnership units. Classified as a separate component of non-controlling interests.

Perpetual Subordinated Notes - Issued by subsidiary BIP Bermuda Holdings I Limited. Have a fixed coupon rate of 5.125% per annum. Do not have a fixed maturity date and are not redeemable at the option of the holders. Redeemable at BIP Bermuda's option on or after Jan. 21, 2027. Classified as a separate component of non-controlling interests.

Normal Course Issuer Bid - The company plans to make normal course purchases of up to 22,914,157 limited partnership units representing 5% of the total outstanding. The bid commenced on Dec. 1, 2022, and expires on Nov. 30, 2023.

The company plans to make normal course purchases of up to 498,926 cl.A preferred LP units, series 1 representing 10% of the public float. The bid commenced on Dec. 1, 2022, and expires on Nov. 30, 2023.

The company plans to make normal course purchases of up to 498,586 cl.A preferred LP units, series 3 representing 10% of the public float. The bid commenced on Dec. 1, 2022, and expires on Nov. 30, 2023.

The company plans to make normal course purchases of up to 798,659 cl.A preferred LP units, series 9 representing 10% of the public float. The bid commenced on Dec. 1, 2022, and expires on Nov. 30, 2023.

The company plans to make normal course purchases of up to 993,619 cl.A preferred LP units, series 11 representing 10% of the public float. The bid commenced on Dec. 1, 2022, and expires on Nov. 30, 2023.

Major Shareholder - Brookfield Corporation held 100% interest at Dec. 31, 2022.

Price Range - BIP.UN/TSX

Year	Volume	High	Low	Close
2022	115,820,148	$57.08	$40.84	$41.94
2021	93,784,112	$51.76	$40.93	$51.33
2020	171,077,568	$49.77	$24.97	$41.99
2019	140,872,144	$46.89	$30.93	$43.24
2018	75,637,144	$37.73	$29.36	$31.43

Split: 1.5-for-1 split in June 2022
Recent Close: $43.25

Capital Stock Changes - On Jan. 21, 2022, public offering of 12,000,000 perpetual subordinated notes was completed at US$25 per note. On Mar. 31, 2022, all 11,979,750 class A preferred limited partnership units, series 7 were redeemed at Cdn$25 per unit. On June 13, 2022, limited partnership units and Brookfield Infrastructure Corporation (BIPC) exchangeable subordinate voting shares were split on a 3-for-2 basis. Also during 2022, post-split limited partnership units were issued as follows: 338,953 under a distribution reinvestment plan, 122,570 on conversion of Brookfield Infrastructure Partners Exchange LP limited partnership units and 17,512 on conversion of BIPC class A exchangeable subordinate voting shares.

Dividends

BIP.UN ltd ptnrshp unit Ra US$1.53 pa Q est. Mar. 31, 2023**
2-for-1 split eff. June 13, 2022
Prev. Rate: US$2.16 est. Mar. 31, 2022
Prev. Rate: US$2.04 est. Mar. 31, 2021
Prev. Rate: US$1.94 est. June 30, 2020
BIP.PR.A pfd A ser 1 cum. red. exch. Adj. Ra $0.9935 pa Q est. Sept. 30, 2020
BIP.PR.B pfd A ser 3 cum. red. exch. Adj. Ra $1.375 pa Q est. Mar. 31, 2016
BIP.PR.E pfd A ser 9 cum. red. exch. Adj. Ra $1.6605 pa Q est. June 30, 2023
BIP.PR.F pfd A ser 11 cum. red. exch. Adj. Ra $1.275 pa Q est. Dec. 31, 2018
pfd A ser 5 cum. red. exch. Adj. Ra $1.3375 pa Q est. Sept. 30, 2016[1]
pfd A ser 7 cum. red. exch. Adj. Ra $1.25 pa Q est. Mar. 31, 2017[2]
$0.3125**f**............... Mar. 31/22
[1] Redeemed Sept. 30, 2021 at $25 per sh.
[2] Redeemed March 31, 2022 at $25 per sh.
** Reinvestment Option **f** Final Payment

Subsidiaries

70.05% int. in **Brookfield Infrastructure L.P.**, Bermuda. Holds 100% voting interest.
- 100% int. in **Arc Infrastructure Holdings No. 1 Pty Ltd.**, Australia.
- 40% int. in **BIF India Holdings Pte. Ltd.**, Singapore. Holds 93% voting interest.
- 100% int. in **BIP Bermuda Holdings I Limited**, Bermuda.
- 15% int. in **BOXT Limited**, United Kingdom. Holds 60% voting interest.
- 100% int. in **Brookfield Infrastructure Holdings (Canada) Inc.**, Ont.
  - 100% int. in **BIP Investment Corporation**, Vancouver, B.C. (see separate coverage)
  - 1.9% int. in **Brookfield Infrastructure Corporation**, New York, N.Y. 75% voting interest. (see separate coverage)
- 100% int. in **Brookfield Infrastructure US Holdings I Corporation**, Del.
- 59% int. in **Brookfield Port Acquisitions (U.K.) Limited**, United Kingdom. Holds 100% voting interest.
- 17% int. in **Crest Digitel Private Limited**, India. Hold 62% voting interest.
- 29% int. in **Dawn Acquisitions LLC**, United States. Holds 100% voting interest.
- 26% int. in **Enercare Inc.**, Markham, Ont. Holds 100% voting interest.
- 9% int. in **Genesee & Wyoming Inc.**, Rochester, N.Y. Holds 72% voting interest.
- **HomeServe plc**, Walsall, Staffs., United Kingdom.
- 56% int. in **Inter Pipeline Ltd.**, Calgary, Alta. Holds 100% voting interest.
- 27% int. in **Linx Cargo Care Group Pty Ltd.**, Australia. Holds 67% voting interest.
- 40% int. in **Lodi Gas Storage, LLC**, Calif. Holds 100% voting interest.
- 29% int. in **NorthRiver Midstream Inc.**, Calgary, Alta. Holds 100% voting interest.
- 21% int. in **Pipeline Infrastructure Pvt. Ltd.**, India. Holds 75% voting interest.
- 29% int. in **Rayalseema Expressway Private Limited**, Hyderabad, India. Holds 95% voting interest.
- 40% int. in **Rockpoint Gas Storage Partners L.P.**, United States. Holds 100% voting interest.
- 29% int. in **Ruby Pooling Hold Trust**, Australia. Holds 100% voting interest.
- 17% int. in **Rutas de Lima S.A.C.**, Peru. Holds 57% voting interest.
- 29% int. in **Simhapuri Expressway Limited**, Hyderabad, India. Holds 95% voting interest.
- 17% int. in **Summit Digitel Infrastructure Pvt. Ltd.**, Ahmedabad, India. Holds 62% voting interest.
- 11% int. in **Thermondo GmbH**, Germany. Holds 51% voting interest.
- 31% int. in **Transmissora Sertaneja de Eletricidade S.A.**, Brazil.
- 21% int. in **Vanti S.A. E.S.P.**, Bogota, Colombia. Holds 75% voting interest.
- 24% int. in **WIG Holdings I Limited**, United Kingdom. Holds 98% voting interest.
- 25% int. in **Warwick Gas Storage L.P.**, Alta. Holds 100% voting interest.

Financial Statistics

Periods ended:	12m Dec. 31/22[A]		12m Dec. 31/21[□A]
	US$000s	%Chg	US$000s
Operating revenue	**14,427,000**	**+25**	**11,537,000**
Cost of sales	8,352,000		6,211,000
General & admin expense	433,000		406,000
Operating expense	**8,785,000**	**+33**	**6,617,000**
Operating income	**5,642,000**	**+15**	**4,920,000**
Deprec., depl. & amort.	2,158,000		2,036,000
Finance costs, gross	1,855,000		1,468,000
Investment income	12,000		88,000
Pre-tax income	**1,935,000**	**-42**	**3,333,000**
Income taxes	560,000		614,000
Net income	**1,375,000**	**-49**	**2,719,000**
Net inc. for equity hldrs	**341,000**	**-55**	**766,000**
Net inc. for non-cont. int	**1,034,000**	**-47**	**1,953,000**
Cash & equivalent	2,117,000		1,924,000
Inventories	531,000		400,000
Accounts receivable	2,276,000		1,847,000
Current assets	6,686,000		4,896,000
Long-term investments	6,194,000		5,548,000
Fixed assets, net	37,291,000		38,655,000
Intangibles, net	20,611,000		23,193,000
Total assets	**72,969,000**	**-1**	**73,961,000**
Accts. pay. & accr. liabs	3,267,000		2,980,000
Current liabilities	8,377,000		8,661,000
Long-term debt, gross	30,233,000		29,253,000
Long-term debt, net	27,202,000		26,121,000
Long-term lease liabilities	3,037,000		3,423,000
Preferred share equity	918,000		1,138,000
Shareholders' equity	5,317,000		6,871,000
Non-controlling interest	19,037,000		19,520,000
Cash from oper. activs	**3,131,000**	**+13**	**2,772,000**
Cash from fin. activs	56,000		(995,000)
Cash from invest. activs	(3,365,000)		(1,173,000)
Net cash position	**1,279,000**	**-9**	**1,406,000**
Capital expenditures	(2,775,000)		(2,067,000)
Capital disposals	41,000		85,000
Unfunded pension liability	25,000		192,000
	US$		US$
Earnings per share*	0.14		0.77
Cash flow per share*	6.83		6.23
Cash divd. per share*	1.44		1.36
	shs		shs
No. of shs. o/s*	458,380,315		457,898,247
Avg. no. of shs. o/s*	458,100,000		445,050,000
	%		%
Net profit margin	9.53		23.57
Return on equity	5.98		14.52
Return on assets	3.67		5.79
Foreign sales percent	69		79

* L.P. unit
[□] Restated
[A] Reported in accordance with IFRS

Latest Results

Periods ended:	3m Mar. 31/23[A]		3m Mar. 31/22[A]
	US$000s	%Chg	US$000s
Operating revenue	4,218,000	+24	3,411,000
Net income	143,000	-51	294,000
Net inc. for equity hldrs	40,000	-39	66,000
Net inc. for non-cont. int	103,000		228,000
	US$		US$
Earnings per share*	(0.07)		(0.01)

* L.P. unit
[A] Reported in accordance with IFRS

Historical Summary
(as originally stated)

Fiscal Year	Oper. Rev. US$000s	Net Inc. Bef. Disc. US$000s	EPS* US$
2022[A]	14,427,000	1,375,000	0.14
2021[A]	11,537,000	2,719,000	1.16
2020[A]	8,885,000	904,000	0.23
2019[A]	6,597,000	650,000	0.05
2018[A]	4,652,000	806,000	0.39

* L.P. unit
[A] Reported in accordance with IFRS
Note: Adjusted throughout for 1.5-for-1 split in June 2022

B.121 Brookfield Investments Corporation

CUSIP - 112741
Head Office - c/o Brookfield Corporation, Bay Wellington Tower, Brookfield Place, 100-181 Bay St, PO Box 762, Toronto, ON, M5J 2T3 **Telephone** - (416) 363-9491 **Fax** - (416) 363-2856
Website - www.brookfield.com
Email - angela.yulo@brookfield.com
Investor Relations - Anglea Yulo (866) 989-0311
Auditors - Deloitte LLP C.A., Toronto, Ont.
Transfer Agents - TSX Trust Company, Montréal, Qué.
Profile - (Ont. 2007 amalg.) Holds investments in the real estate and forest products sectors and owns a portfolio of preferred shares issued by **Brookfield Corporation**, which owns interests in renewable power and transition, infrastructure, private equity, real estate and credit businesses worldwide.
The company (since December 2015) does not issue separate financial statements due to an exemption from the continuous disclosure requirements on the basis that it relies on the continuous disclosure documents filed with Canadian securities commissions by parent company **Brookfield Corporation** (BN), which has provided a full and unconditional subordinated guarantee of the company's outstanding retractable class 1 senior preferred shares, series A (classified as debt), other than those held by BN or its affiliates.
Common delisted from CDN, Oct. 13, 2000.
Predecessor Detail - Name changed from Brascade Corporation, Nov. 27, 2007.
Directors - Edward C. (Ed) Kress, chr. & pres., Toronto, Ont.; Frank N. C. Lochan, Oakville, Ont.; Dr. George E. Myhal, Toronto, Ont.; Danesh K. Varma, Kingston upon Thames, Surrey, United Kingdom
Other Exec. Officers - Kathy Sarpash, sr. v-p, gen. counsel & corp. sec.; Patrick Taylor, sr. v-p & CFO; Geoffrey Gambrell, v-p & contr.

Capital Stock

	Authorized (shs.)	Outstanding (shs.)[1]
Class 1 Senior Preferred	unlimited	
Series A	25,000,000	5,711,935[2 3]
Class 1 Special Preferred	unlimited	
Series A	2,646,400	nil
Series B	100	nil
Series C	8,000,000	nil
Class 1 Junior Preferred	unlimited	
Series A	unlimited	17,999,719[2]
Series B		17,200,000
Common	unlimited	49,847,899

[1] At Sept. 30, 2015
[2] Classified as debt.
[3] At Dec. 31, 2022.

Class 1 Senior Preferred - Issuable in series. **Series A** - Entitled to cumulative fixed quarterly dividends of Cdn$1.175 per share to yield 4.7%. Non-voting. Retractable and redeemable at any time at Cdn$25 per share plus accrued and unpaid dividends.
Class 1 Junior Preferred - Issuable in series. **Series A** - Rank in priority to common shares with respect to payment of dividends in the event of dissolution, liquidation or winding-up of the company. Non-voting. Entitled to non-cumulative quarterly dividend rate of 4%. Retractable and redeemable at any time at US$31 per share plus accrued and unpaid dividends.
Common - One vote per share.
Major Shareholder - Brookfield Corporation held 100% interest at Dec. 31, 2022.

Dividends

BRN.PR.A pfd 1 ser A cum. red. Ra $1.175 pa Q

Investments

28.1% int. in **BPY II L.P.**, Hamilton, Bermuda.
- 26.6% int. in **Brookfield Property Partners L.P.**, Hamilton, Bermuda.

36.2% int. in **Brookfield Europe L.P.**
- 24.3% int. in **BPY I L.P.**, Hamilton, Bermuda.
  - 26% int. in **Brookfield Property Partners L.P.**, Hamilton, Bermuda.

Brookfield Residential Properties ULC, Calgary, Alta.
Norbord Inc., Toronto, Ont.

B.122 Brookfield Office Properties Inc.

CUSIP - 112900
Head Office - Bay Wellington Tower, Brookfield Place, 330-181 Bay St, PO Box 770, Toronto, ON, M5J 2T3 **Telephone** - (416) 369-2300 **Fax** - (416) 369-2301 **Exec. Office** - Brookfield Place New York, 250 Vesey St, 15th Flr, New York, NY, United States, 10281-1023 **Telephone** - (212) 417-7000 **Fax** - (212) 417-7214
Website - www.bpoinvestor.com
Email - rachel.nappi@brookfield.com
Investor Relations - Rachel Nappi (212) 417-7169
Auditors - Deloitte LLP C.A., Toronto, Ont.
Lawyers - Torys LLP, Toronto, Ont.
Transfer Agents - TSX Trust Company, Toronto, Ont.
Profile - (Can. 1978) Owns, manages and develops premier office properties, with signature properties located in New York, N.Y.; Washington, D.C.; Houston, Tex.; Los Angeles, Calif.; Toronto, Ont.; Calgary, Alta.; London, U.K.; Berlin, Germany; and Sydney and Perth, Australia.
The company (since August 2016) does not issue separate financial statements due to an exemption from the continuous disclosure requirements on the basis that it relies on the continuous disclosure documents filed with Canadian securities commissions by parent company **Brookfield Property Partners L.P.**, which has provided a full and unconditional subordinated guarantee of the company's class AAA preference shares and debt securities.
Common delisted from TSX, June 11, 2014.
Predecessor Detail - Name changed from Brookfield Properties Corporation, May 9, 2011.

Capital Stock

	Authorized (shs.)	Outstanding (shs.)[1]
Class AAA Preference	unlimited	
Series N	11,000,000	11,000,000
Series O	11,000,000	nil
Series P	12,000,000	12,000,000
Series Q	12,000,000	nil
Series R	10,000,000	10,000,000
Series S	10,000,000	nil
Series T	10,000,000	10,000,000
Series U	10,000,000	nil
Series V	1,805,489	1,805,489
Series W	3,816,527	3,816,527
Series Y	2,847,711	2,847,711
Series AA	12,000,000	12,000,000
Series CC	8,000,000	8,000,000
Series EE	11,000,000	11,000,000
Series GG	11,000,000	11,000,000
Series II	10,000,000	10,000,000
Common	unlimited	484,806,813[2]

[1] At June 30, 2023
[2] At June 30, 2016.

Class AAA Preference - Issuable in series. Non-voting.
Series N - Entitled to cumulative annual dividends of Cdn$1.002 per share payable quarterly to June 30, 2026, and thereafter at a rate reset every five years equal to the five-year Government of Canada bond yield plus 3.07%. Redeemable on June 30, 2026, and on June 30 every five years thereafter at Cdn$25 per share. Convertible at the holder's option, on June 30, 2026, and on June 30 every five years thereafter, into floating rate preferred series O shares on a share-for-share basis, subject to certain conditions. The series O would pay a quarterly dividend equal to the three-month Government of Canada Treasury Bill yield plus 3.07%.
Series P - Entitled to cumulative annual dividends of Cdn$1.134 per share payable quarterly to Mar. 31, 2027, and thereafter at a rate reset every five years equal to the five-year Government of Canada bond yield plus 3%. Redeemable on Mar. 31, 2027, and on March 31 every five years thereafter at Cdn$25 per share. Convertible at the holder's option, on Mar. 31, 2027, and on March 31 every five years thereafter, into floating rate preferred series Q shares on a share-for-share basis, subject to certain conditions. The series Q would pay a quarterly dividend equal to the three-month Government of Canada Treasury Bill yield plus 3%.
Series R - Entitled to cumulative annual dividends of Cdn$1.075 per share payable quarterly to Sept. 30, 2026, and thereafter at a rate reset every five years equal to the five-year Government of Canada bond yield plus 3.48%. Redeemable on Sept. 30, 2026, and on September 30 every five years thereafter at Cdn$25 per share. Convertible at the holder's option, on Sept. 30, 2026, and on September 30 every five years thereafter, into floating rate preferred series S shares on a share-for-share basis, subject to certain conditions. The series S would pay a quarterly dividend equal to the three-month Government of Canada Treasury Bill yield plus 3.48%.
Series T - Entitled to cumulative annual dividends of Cdn$1.34575 per share payable quarterly to Dec. 31, 2023, and thereafter at a rate reset every five years equal to the five-year Government of Canada bond yield plus 3.16%. Redeemable on Dec. 31, 2023, and on December 31 every five years thereafter at Cdn$25 per share. Convertible at the holder's option, on Dec. 31, 2023, and on December 31 every five years thereafter, into floating rate preferred series U shares on a share-for-share basis, subject to certain conditions. The series U would pay a quarterly dividend equal to the 90-day Canadian Treasury bill rate plus 3.16%.
Series V - Entitled to cumulative dividends at a rate equivalent to 70% of average bank prime rate. Redeemable at Cdn$25 per share plus accrued and unpaid dividends.
Series W - Entitled to cumulative dividends at a rate equivalent to 70% of average bank prime rate. Redeemable at Cdn$25 per share plus accrued and unpaid dividends.
Series Y - Terms are identical to those attached to series W preferred shares and the company may reclassify Series Y preferred shares as series W preferred shares without prior approval of series Y preferred shareholders.
Series AA - Entitled to cumulative annual dividends of Cdn$1.1775 per share payable quarterly to Dec. 31, 2024, and thereafter at a rate reset every five years equal to the five-year Government of Canada bond yield plus 3.15%. Redeemable on Dec. 31, 2024, and on December 31 every five years thereafter at Cdn$25 per share. Convertible at the holder's option, on Dec. 31, 2024, and on December 31 every five years thereafter, into floating rate preferred series BB shares on a share-for-share basis, subject to certain conditions. The series BB would pay a quarterly dividend equal to the 90-day Canadian Treasury bill rate plus 3.15%.
Series CC - Entitled to cumulative annual dividends of Cdn$1.50 per share payable quarterly to June 30, 2021, and thereafter at a rate reset every five years equal to greater of: (i) the five-year Government of Canada bond yield plus 5.18%; and (ii) 6%. Redeemable on June 30, 2021, and on June 30 every five years thereafter at Cdn$25 per share. Convertible at the holder's option, on June 30, 2021, and on June 30 every five years thereafter, into floating rate preferred series DD shares on a share-for-share basis, subject to certain conditions. The series DD would pay a quarterly dividend equal to the 90-day Canadian Treasury bill rate plus 5.18%.
Series EE - Entitled to cumulative annual dividends of Cdn$1.374 per share payable quarterly to Mar. 31, 2027, and thereafter at a rate reset every five years equal to greater of: (i) the five-year Government of

Canada bond yield plus 3.96%; and (ii) 5.1%. Redeemable on Mar. 31, 2027, and on March 31 every five years thereafter at Cdn$25 per share. Convertible at the holder's option, on Mar. 31, 2027, and on March 31 every five years thereafter, into floating rate preferred series FF shares on a share-for-share basis, subject to certain conditions. The series FF would pay a quarterly dividend equal to the 90-day Canadian Treasury bill rate plus 3.96%.

Series GG - Entitled to cumulative annual dividends of Cdn$1.6365 per share payable quarterly to June 30, 2027, and thereafter at a rate reset every five years equal to greater of: (i) the five-year Government of Canada bond yield plus 3.74%; and (ii) 4.85%. Redeemable on June 30, 2027, and on June 30 every five years thereafter at Cdn$25 per share. Convertible at the holder's option, on June 30, 2027, and on June 30 every five years thereafter, into floating rate preferred series HH shares on a share-for-share basis, subject to certain conditions. The series HH would pay a quarterly dividend equal to the 90-day Canadian Treasury bill rate plus 3.74%.

Series II - Entitled to cumulative annual dividends of Cdn$1.590 per share payable quarterly to Dec. 31, 2027, and thereafter at a rate reset every five years equal to greater of: (i) the five-year Government of Canada bond yield plus 3.23%; and (ii) 4.85%. Redeemable on Dec. 31, 2027, and on December 31 every five years thereafter at Cdn$25 per share. Convertible at the holder's option, on Dec. 31, 2027, and on December 31 every five years thereafter, into floating rate preferred series JJ shares on a share-for-share basis, subject to certain conditions. The series JJ would pay a quarterly dividend equal to the 90-day Canadian Treasury bill rate plus 3.23%.

Common - One vote per share.

Major Shareholder - Brookfield Property Partners L.P. held 100% interest at June 30, 2023.

Dividends

BPO.PR.N pfd AAA ser N cum. red. exch. Adj. Ra $1.0025 pa Q est. Sept. 30, 2021

BPO.PR.P pfd AAA ser P cum. red. exch. Adj. Ra $1.134 pa Q est. June 30, 2022

BPO.PR.R pfd AAA ser R cum. red. exch. Adj. Ra $1.075 pa Q est. Dec. 31, 2021

BPO.PR.T pfd AAA ser T cum. red. exch. Adj. Ra $1.34575 pa Q est. Mar. 29, 2019

BPO.PR.X pfd AAA ser V cum. red. Fltg. Ra pa Q

$0.293125...........	Aug. 14/23	$0.278582........	May 12/23
$0.23381.............	Feb. 14/23	$0.171731........	Nov. 14/22

Paid in 2023: $0.805517 2022: $0.386107 2021: $0.428752

BPO.PR.W pfd AAA ser W cum. red. Fltg. Ra pa Q

$0.295769...........	Aug. 14/23	$0.289965........	May 12/23
$0.259599...........	Feb. 14/23	$0.206814........	Nov. 14/22

Paid in 2023: $0.845333 2022: $0.568079 2021: $0.428752

BPO.PR.Y pfd AAA ser Y cum. red. Fltg. Ra pa Q

$0.295769...........	Aug. 14/23	$0.289965........	May 12/23
$0.259599...........	Feb. 14/23	$0.206814........	Nov. 14/22

Paid in 2023: $0.845333 2022: $0.568079 2021: $0.428752

BPO.PR.A pfd AAA ser AA cum. red. exch. Adj. Ra $1.17725 pa Q est. Mar. 31, 2020

BPO.PR.C pfd AAA ser CC cum. red. exch. Adj. Ra $1.53 pa Q est. Sept. 30, 2021

BPO.PR.E pfd AAA ser EE cum. red. exch. Adj. Ra $1.374 pa Q est. June 30, 2022

BPO.PR.G pfd AAA ser GG cum. red. exch. Adj. Ra $1.6365 pa Q est. Sept. 30, 2022

BPO.PR.I pfd AAA ser II cum. red. exch. Adj. Ra $1.58975 pa Q est. Mar. 31, 2023

pfd AAA ser S cum. red. exch. Fltg. Ra pa Q

Delisted Oct 1/21.

$0.22622............	Sept. 30/21	$0.221268........	June 30/21
$0.221303...........	Mar. 31/21		

Paid in 2023: n.a. 2022: n.a. 2021: $0.668791

B.123 Brookfield Property Preferred L.P.

CUSIP - G1624R

Head Office - 73 Front St, 5th Flr, Hamilton, Bermuda, HM 12 **Telephone** - (441) 294-3304 **Fax** - (441) 296-4475

Website - www.brookfield.com

Email - jane.sheere@brookfield.com

Investor Relations - Jane Sheere (441) 294-3304

Auditors - Deloitte LLP C.A.

Transfer Agents - TSX Trust Company

Profile - (Bermuda 2021) Wholly owned preferred share financing vehicle of **Brookfield Property Partners L.P.**, a subsidiary of **Brookfield Corporation**, which owns, operates and invests in commercial and other income producing property on a global basis.

The company does not prepare separate financial statements due to an exemption from the continuous disclosure requirements under the Securities Act. One of the conditions of the exemption is that the company is required to file with the Canadian securities commissions all documents filed by parent entity **Brookfield Property Partners L.P.**

Capital Stock

	Authorized (shs.)	Outstanding (shs.)[1]
Cl.A Preferred, Series 1	40,000,000	19,273,654

[1] At Mar. 31, 2023

Class A Cumulative Redeemable Preferred Units - 6.25% Series 1 - Entitled to cumulative annual dividends of US$1.5625 per unit payable quarterly. Redeemable at the limited partnership's option on or after July 26, 2026, at US$25 per unit, plus all accrued (whether or not declared) and unpaid dividends up to but excluding the date of payment or distribution. Non-convertible.

Major Shareholder - Brookfield Property Partners L.P. held 100% interest at Mar. 31, 2023.

Dividends

BPYP.PR.A cl A ser 1 unit red. Ra US$1.5625 pa Q

Listed Jul 27/21.

Prev. Rate: US$1.0936

US$0.2734i.......... Sept. 30/21

i Initial Payment

B.124 Brookfield Property Split Corp.

CUSIP - 112827

Head Office - c/o Brookfield Corporation, Bay Wellington Tower, Brookfield Place, 100-181 Bay St, PO Box 762, Toronto, ON, M5J 2T3 **Telephone** - (416) 363-9491 **Fax** - (416) 365-9642

Email - monica.thakur@brookfield.com

Investor Relations - Monica Thakur (866) 989-0311

Auditors - Deloitte LLP C.A., Toronto, Ont.

Transfer Agents - TSX Trust Company

Profile - (B.C. 2013) Wholly owned preferred share financing vehicle of **Brookfield Property Partners L.P.**, a subsidiary of **Brookfield Corporation**, which owns, operates and invests in commercial and other income producing property on a global basis.

The company does not prepare separate financial statements due to an exemption from the continuous disclosure requirements under the Securities Act. One of the conditions of the exemption is that the company is required to file with the Canadian securities commissions all documents filed by parent entity **Brookfield Property Partners L.P.**

Directors - Bryan K. Davis, Rye, N.Y.; P. Keith Hyde, Toronto, Ont.; Lance Liebman, New York, N.Y.; Robert L. Stelzl, Mont.

Capital Stock

	Authorized (shs.)	Outstanding (shs.)[1]
Class A Senior Preferred	unlimited	
Series 1		805,559
Series 2		543,506
Series 3		640,578
Series 4		525,893
Class A Junior Preferred		44,868,000
Class B Junior Preferred		22,434,000
Class C Junior Preferred		nil
Class D Junior Preferred		nil
Class A	unlimited	44,529,986
Class B	unlimited	44,086,898

[1] At Mar. 31, 2023

Class A Senior Preferred - Issuable in series. Rank senior to common shares and junior preferred shares as to payment of dividends and return of capital in the event of liquidation, etc. Non-voting. **Series 1** - Entitled to cumulative dividends at the rate of 5.25% per annum. Redeemable at US$25 per share. **Series 2** - Entitled to cumulative dividends at the rate of 5.75% per annum. Redeemable at Cdn$25 per share. **Series 3** - Entitled to cumulative dividends at the rate of 5% per annum. Redeemable at Cdn$25 per share. **Series 4** - Entitled to cumulative dividends at the rate of 5.2% per annum. Redeemable at Cdn$25 per share.

Class A & B Junior Preferred - Rank senior to common shares and junior to senior preferred shares as to payment of dividends and return of capital in the event of liquidation, etc. Non-voting. Entitled to fixed cumulative dividends of $1.50 per annum, payable on January 7 of each year. Redeemable and retractable at Cdn$25 per share at any time.

Common - One vote per share.

Major Shareholder - Brookfield Property Partners L.P. held 100% interest at Mar. 31, 2023.

Dividends

BPS.PR.U pfd A ser 1 cum. red. ret. Ra US$1.3125 pa Q

BPS.PR.A pfd A ser 2 cum. red. ret. Ra $1.4375 pa Q

BPS.PR.B pfd A ser 3 cum. red. ret. Ra $1.25 pa Q

BPS.PR.C pfd A ser 4 cum. red. ret. Ra $1.30 pa Q

B.125 Brookfield Reinsurance Ltd.

Symbol - BNRE **Exchange** - TSX **CUSIP** - G16250

Head Office - Ideation House, 94 Pitts Bay Rd, 1st Flr, Pembroke, Bermuda, HM08 **Telephone** - (441) 294-3316

Website - bnre.brookfield.com

Email - rachel.powell@brookfield.com

Investor Relations - Rachel Powell (416) 956-5141

Auditors - Deloitte LLP C.A., Toronto, Ont.

Lawyers - Torys LLP, Toronto, Ont.

Transfer Agents - TSX Trust Company, Toronto, Ont.

Employees - 3,500 at Dec. 31, 2022

Profile - (Bermuda 2020) Operates a financial services business providing reinsurance and other capital-based services to the insurance industry.

Operations are divided into three segments:

Direct Insurance - Wholly owned **American National Group, Inc.** (ANICO) operates in all 50 U.S. states, the District of Columbia and Puerto Rico, offering a broad line of products and services including life insurance, annuities, property and casualty insurance, health insurance, credit insurance and pension products for personal lines, agribusiness and certain commercial exposures. As of Dec. 31, 2022, ANICO and its subsidiaries had US$19.7 billion of future policy benefits and policyholder account balances.

Reinsurance - Wholly owned **North End Re (Cayman) SPC** (NER SPC) and **North End Re Ltd.** (NER Ltd.) reinsure annuity-based products, primarily fixed annuities, fixed index annuities and payout annuities, for direct insurers and other reinsurers operating in North America and western Europe. As of Dec. 31, 2022, NER SPC and NER Ltd. had US$5.9 billion and US$1.5 billion of future policy benefits, respectively.

Pension Risk Transfer (PRT) - This business involves the transfer by a corporate sponsor of the risks associated with the sponsorship and administration of a pension plan. The company's PRT business is conducted through wholly owned **Brookfield Annuity Company** (BAC), which provides PRT solutions for pension plan sponsors across Canada, and ANICO in the U.S. As of Dec. 31, 2022, BAC had US$3.0 billion of future policy benefits. ANICO launched its U.S. PRT business in the fourth quarter of 2022.

On Dec. 9, 2022, the company completed the special distribution of 2,725,500 class A limited voting shares of **Brookfield Asset Management Ltd.** (BAML) to the holders of its class A exchangeable limited voting shares and class B limited voting shares. Holders of the company's class A and class B shares of record on Dec. 2, 2022, received one BAML class A share for every 4 Brookfield Reinsurance class A shares or class B shares held, while retaining their shares of the company. **Brookfield Asset Management Inc.** (BAM, renamed **Brookfield Corporation**, BN) undertook a public listing and distribution of a 25% interest in its asset management business, BAML, by way of a plan of arrangement. The plan of arrangement resulted in the division of BAM into two publicly traded companies: BN and BAML.

On May 25, 2022, the company acquired Galveston, Tex.-based **American National Group, Inc.** (ANICO) for US$190 cash per share, in a transaction valued at US$5.1 billion. ANICO operates in all 50 states, offering a broad line of products and services including life insurance, annuities, health insurance, credit insurance, pension products, and property and casualty insurance for personal lines, agribusiness and certain commercial exposures.

Recent Merger and Acquisition Activity

Status: pending **Revised:** July 5, 2023

UPDATE: BNRE entered into a definitive agreement to acquire all of the shares of AEL its does not already own for US$55 per share consisting of US$38.85 in cash and 0.49707 Brookfield Asset Management Ltd. (BAM) class A limited voting shares (BAM shares) valued at US$16.15 per share. The acquisition would be facilitated by a merger of AEL with Arches Merger Sub, Inc., a wholly owned subsidiary of BNRE. BNRE plans to acquire from Brookfield Corporation (BN) the BAM shares required to satisfy the non-cash consideration offered to AEL shareholders. The transaction was expected to close in the first half of 2024. PREVIOUS: Brookfield Reinsurance Ltd. (BNRE) submitted a proposal to acquire all of the shares of West Des Moines, Iowa-based American Equity Investment Life Holding Company (AEL) it does not already own for US$55 per share in cash and stock. The offer values AEL at US$4.3 billion. BNRE holds an approximate 19% equity interest in AEL.

Status: pending **Announced:** Feb. 8, 2023

Brookfield Reinsurance Ltd. agreed to acquire Argo Group International Holding, Ltd. for US$30 per share in cash for a transaction value of $1.1 billion. NYSE-listed Argo Group is a U.S.-focused underwriter of specialty insurance products in the property and casualty market. The transaction was expected to close in the second half of 2023.

Predecessor Detail - Name changed from Brookfield Asset Management Reinsurance Partners Ltd., Dec. 9, 2022.

Directors - Sachin G. Shah, chr. & CEO, Toronto, Ont.; William J. Cox†, Hamilton, Bermuda; Barry Blattman, New York, N.Y.; Dr. Soonyoung Chang, Dubai, United Arab Emirates; Michelle Coleman Mayes, N.Y.; Gregory (Greg) Morrison, Hamilton, Bermuda; Lori A. Pearson, Toronto, Ont.; Lars Rodert, Stockholm, Sweden; Anne Schaumburg, N.J.; Jay Wintrob, Los Angeles, Calif.

Other Exec. Officers - Paul Forestell, COO & pres., CEO, Brookfield Annuity Company; Thomas Corbett, CFO; Lorenzo Lorilla, chief invest. officer; Lyndsay Hatlelid, gen. counsel; Anna Knapman-Scott, corp. sec.; Gregory McConnie, CEO, North End Re (Cayman) SPC & North End Re Ltd.

† Lead director

Capital Stock

	Authorized (shs.)	Outstanding (shs.)[1]	Par
Cl.A Junior Preferred	1,000,000,000		US$25
Series 1		100,460,280[2 3]	
Cl.B Junior Preferred	1,000,000,000	nil	$25
Cl.A Senior Preferred	100,000,000	nil	US$25
Cl.B Senior Preferred	100,000,000	nil	$25
Cl.A Exch. Limited Vtg.	1,000,000,000	10,450,952	US$39
Class B Limited Vtg.	500,000	24,000	US$39
Class C Non-Vtg.	1,000,000,000	41,314,891[4]	US$1.00

[1] At Mar. 31, 2023

[2] Classified as debt.

[3] All held by Brookfield Corporation

[4] All held by Brookfield Corporation

Class A Junior Preferred - Issuable in series.

Series 1 - Entitled to fixed cumulative 4.5% preferential cash dividend payable annually. Redeemable at the company's option at US$25 per share. Retractable by Brookfield Corporation (BN, formerly Brookfield Asset Management Inc.) at US$25 per share at any time on or after May 25, 2029. Non-voting.

Class B Junior Preferred - Issuable in series.

Class A & B Senior Preferred - Issuable in series.

Class A Exchangeable Limited Voting - Entitled to distributions, which would be received at the same time and in the same amount as the cash dividends paid on each BN class A limited voting share. Exchangeable at the holder's option for BN class A limited voting shares on a one-for-one basis. One vote per share.

Class B Limited Voting - Entitled to the same distributions as the class A exchangeable limited voting shares. May only be held by the BN Re class B partners, a company controlled by one or more of the partners or BN. BN does not have any intention to hold any class B shares. The BN Re class B partners will be entitled to elect one-half of the company's board of directors. One vote per share.

Class C Non-Voting - Entitled to distributions equal to the company's distributable earnings (as determined by the company's management) after payment of distributions on class A exchangeable limited voting shares, class B limited voting shares and any other shares ranking senior to the class C shares and after provision for expenses, anticipated cash needs and other similar adjustments. BN will be entitled, from time to time, to convert any class A exchangeable limited voting shares held by it or its subsidiaries into class C shares. May only be transferred within BN. Non-voting.

Major Shareholder - Widely held at May 24, 2022.

Price Range - BNRE/TSX

Year	Volume	High	Low	Close
2022	7,866,534	$81.49	$41.77	$42.33
2021	6,468,787	$99.00	$61.16	$79.44

Recent Close: $45.18

Capital Stock Changes - On May 25, 2022, 98,351,547 class A junior preferred shares, series 1 were issued for US$2.459 billion and 11,270,466 class C non-voting shares were issued for US$450,000,000 to Brookfield Asset Management Inc. (subsequently renamed Brookfield Corporation, BN). On Nov. 4, 2022, 675,000 class A exchangeable limited voting shares were converted by BN into 1,066,471 class C non-voting shares. On Dec. 1, 2022, 608,000 class A exchangeable limited voting shares were converted by BN into 1,066,471 class C non-voting shares. On Dec. 9, 2022, 2,108,733 class A junior preferred shares, series 1 were issued for $52,718,000 to BN.

Dividends

BNRE cl A exch Ra US$0.28 pa Q est. Mar. 31, 2023
Listed Jun 28/21.
Prev. Rate: US$0.56 est. Mar. 31, 2022
Prev. Rate: US$0.52 est. Dec. 31, 2021
Prev. Rate: $0.52 est. Sept. 29, 2021

US$0.07**r**............... Sept. 29/23 stk.[1]◆............... Dec. 9/22
US$0.14◆**r**............ Dec. 30/22 US$0.14◆**r**....... Sept. 29/22
Paid in 2023: US$0.14 + US$0.07**r** 2022: US$0.42 + US$0.14**r** + US$0.28◆**r** + stk.◆ 2021: $0.13**r** + US$0.13**r**

[1] Stk. divd. of 0.25 Pamorex Minerals Inc wts. for ea. 1 sh. held.

◆ Special **r** Return of Capital

Wholly Owned Subsidiaries

BAM Re Holdings Ltd., Bermuda.

- 100% int. in **Arches Merger Sub, Inc.**, Iowa
- 100% int. in **BAMR US Holdings (Bermuda) I Ltd.**, Bermuda.
  - 100% int. in **BAMR US Holdings LLC**, Del.
    - 100% int. in **American National Group, Inc.**, Galveston, Tex.
- 100% int. in **Brookfield Annuity Holdings Inc.**, Toronto, Ont.
  - 100% int. in **Brookfield Annuity Company**, Toronto, Ont.
- 100% int. in **North End Re (Cayman) SPC**, Cayman Islands.
  - 19% int. in **American Equity Investment Life Holding Company**, West Des Moines, Iowa.
- 100% int. in **North End Re Ltd.**, Bermuda.

Financial Statistics

Periods ended:	12m Dec. 31/22^A		12m Dec. 31/21^□A
	US$000s	%Chg	US$000s
Net premiums earned	3,011,000		1,016,000
Net investment income	1,074,000		25,000
Total revenue	**4,309,000**	**+314**	**1,041,000**
Policy benefits & claims	3,156,000		1,107,000
General & admin. expense	439,000		35,000
Other operating expense	78,000		11,000
Operating expense	**3,673,000**	**+219**	**1,153,000**
Operating income	**(2,520,000)**	**n.a.**	**(1,219,000)**
Finance costs, gross	104,000		1,000
Pre-tax income	**532,000**	**n.a.**	**(113,000)**
Income taxes	31,000		(1,000)
Net income	**501,000**	**n.a.**	**(112,000)**
Net inc. for equity hldrs	**499,000**	**n.a.**	**(112,000)**
Net inc. for non-cont. int	**2,000**	**n.a.**	**nil**
Cash & equivalent	2,145,000		393,000
Securities investments	17,569,000		2,778,000
Mortgages	5,888,000		390,000
Real estate	1,036,000		nil
Total investments	30,295,000		5,418,000
Total assets	**43,458,000**	**+275**	**11,577,000**
Claims provisions	1,786,000		nil
Debt	3,652,000		693,000
Policy liabilities & claims	28,152,000		7,007,000
Shareholders' equity	1,677,000		1,345,000
Non-controlling interest	8,000		nil
Cash from oper. activs	**644,000**	**-62**	**1,688,000**
Cash from fin. activs	5,994,000		2,640,000
Cash from invest. activs	(4,878,000)		(3,971,000)
Net cash position	**2,145,000**	**+446**	**393,000**
Pension fund surplus	98,000		n.a.
	US$		US$
Earnings per share*	n.a.		n.a.
Cash divd. per share*	0.84		0.26
Extra divd. - cash*	0.28		nil
Total divd. per share*	**1.12**		**0.26**
	shs		shs
No. of shs. o/s*	50,553,612		34,446,537
	%		%
Net profit margin	11.63		(10.76)
Return on equity	32.07		(15.69)
Return on assets	2.18		(1.71)
No. of employees (FTEs)	3,500		...

* Cl.A Exchang.
□ Restated
A Reported in accordance with U.S. GAAP

Latest Results

Periods ended:	3m Mar. 31/23^A		3m Mar. 31/22^□A
	US$000s	%Chg	US$000s
Total revenue	1,203,000	+333	278,000
Net income	(93,000)	n.a.	156,000
Net inc. for equity hldrs	(98,000)	n.a.	156,000
Net inc. for non-cont. int	5,000		nil
	US$		US$
Earnings per share*	n.a.		n.a.

□ Restated
A Reported in accordance with U.S. GAAP

Historical Summary
(as originally stated)

Fiscal Year	Total Rev. US$000s	Net Inc. Bef. Disc. US$000s	EPS* US$
2022^A	4,309,000	501,000	n.a.
2021^B	7,344,000	(44,000)	n.a.
2020^B	514,000	1,000	n.a.

* Cl.A Exchang.
A Reported in accordance with U.S. GAAP
B Reported in accordance with IFRS

B.126 Brookfield Renewable Corporation

Symbol - BEPC **Exchange** - TSX **CUSIP** - 11284V

Head Office - 250 Vesey St, 15th Flr, New York, NY, United States, 10281-1023 **Telephone** - (212) 417-7000 **Toll-free** - (833) 236-0278

Website - www.bep.brookfield.com/bepc

Email - alexander.jackson@brookfield.com

Investor Relations - Alex Jackson (416) 649-8196

Auditors - Ernst & Young LLP C.A., Toronto, Ont.

Transfer Agents - Computershare Trust Company of Canada Inc., Toronto, Ont.

FP500 Subsidiary Revenue Ranking - 15

Employees - 2,152 at Dec. 31, 2022

Profile - (B.C. 2019) Owns and operates hydroelectric, wind, solar, storage and ancillary power generation assets in Brazil, Colombia, Uruguay, Chile, the U.S., Canada, Spain, Portugal and the U.K.

At Dec. 31, 2022, the company held interests in 5,202 facilities with 25,377 MW of power generating capacity on a consolidated basis (12,857 MW attributable to the company on a proportionate basis) consisting of 196 hydroelectric facilities, 55 wind farms, 69 solar facilities and 4,882 energy transition facilities.

Hydroelectric - Holds interests in 196 hydroelectric generating stations on 68 river systems in the U.S. (136), Brazil (43) and Colombia (17) totaling 6,798 MW of power generating capacity and 6,246 GWh of storage capacity (proportionate basis).

Wind - Holds interests in 55 wind farms in the U.S., Spain, Portugal, Brazil, Uruguay and Canada totaling 2,595 MW of power generation capacity (proportionate basis).

Solar - Holds interests in 69 solar facilities in the U.S., Canada, Chile, Spain and the U.K. totaling 1,489 MW of power generating capacity (proportionate basis).

Energy Transition - Holds interests in 4,882 facilities totaling 1,975 MW of power generating capacity and 1,095 GWh of storage capacity (proportionate basis). Energy transition investments include investments in nuclear services, carbon capture and storage projects, renewable natural gas, recycling, offshore wind generation, hydrogen and ammonia production and investments focused on enhancing the energy efficiency of existing infrastructure.

The company is a controlled affiliate of **Brookfield Infrastructure Partners L.P.** which, through its 58.09%-owned subsidiary **Brookfield Infrastructure L.P.**, holds 46.7% economic interest and 75% voting interest in the company.

In March 2023, the company, together with institutional partners, acquired a 136-MW portfolio of wind assets in Brazil for US$95,000,000; the company acquired 22.5% economic interest.

Also in March 2023, the company's institutional partners sold 78% interest in a 378-MW operating hydroelectric portfolio in the U.S., of which 28% was sold to affiliates of **Brookfield Corporation**. The company retained its 22% interest and had ceased to consolidate this investment at Dec. 31, 2022.

During the first quarter of 2023, the company completed construction of a 1,200-MW solar facility in Brazil, a 226-MW wind facility in Brazil and a 57-MW wind facility in California.

During 2022, the company, together with its institutional partners, acquired a 248-MW development wind portfolio in Brazil (the company's economic interest is 25%) and an operating utility-scale solar asset in Colombia with total capacity of 40 MW (the company's economic interest is 22%). Terms were not disclosed.

In August 2022, the company, together with its institutional partners, formed a joint venture with **California Resources Corporation** to establish a carbon management business to develop carbon capture and storage in California. The company and its partners committed to invest up to US$500,000,000 to fund the development of identified projects in the state.

In June 2022, the company, together with its institutional partners, sold a 36-MW operating hydroelectric portfolio in Brazil for proceeds of US$90,000,000 (US$23,000,000 net to the company).

Periods ended:	12m Dec. 31/22	12m Dec. 31/21
Generating capacity, MW[1]	25,377	21,049
Electric gen., GWh[1]	63,036	56,629
Avg. electric price, $/MWh	88	82

[1] Consolidated basis

Recent Merger and Acquisition Activity

Status: pending **Announced:** June 12, 2023
Duke Energy Corporation agreed to sell its unregulated utility scale Commercial Renewables business to Brookfield Renewable Partners L.P., Brookfield Renewable Corporation and their institutional partners for US$1.05 billion (Brookfield Renewable's share is US$265,000,000), reflecting a enterprise value of US$2.8 billion. The business includes more than 3,400 MW (alternating current) of utility-scale solar, wind and battery storage across the U.S., net of joint venture partners ownership, in addition to operations and projects under development and construction.

Status: pending **Announced:** Mar. 27, 2023
A consortium consisting of Brookfield Renewable Partners L.P. and Brookfield Renewable Corporation, together with their institutional partners and global institutional investors Global Industrial Company and Temasek Holdings (Private) Limited, and MidOcean Energy, an LNG company formed and managed by EIG Management Company, LLC, has agreed to acquire Origin Energy Limited for A$8.91 per share, valuing Origin at an enterprise value of A$18.7 billion. Origin's board of directors unanimously recommended that its shareholders vote in favour of the transaction. Upon closing, Brookfield, its institutional partners and investors would own Origin's Energy Markets business, Australia's largest integrated power generator and energy retailer. MidOcean would separately own Origin's Integrated Gas segment including its upstream gas interests and the 27.5% stake in Australia Pacific LNG.

Directors - Jeffrey M. (Jeff) Blidner, chr., Toronto, Ont.; David McD. Mann†, Chester, N.S.; Scott Cutler, Utah; Sarah Deasley, London, Middx., United Kingdom; Eleazar de Carvalho Filho, São Paulo, Brazil; Nancy Dorn, Ga.; R. Randall (Randy) MacEwen, Vancouver, B.C.; Louis J. Maroun, Warwick, Bermuda; Stephen Westwell, London, Middx., United Kingdom; Patricia Zuccotti, Kirkland, Wash.

Other Exec. Officers - Connor D. Teskey, CEO; Wyatt Hartley, CFO; Jennifer Mazin, gen. counsel

† Lead director

Capital Stock

	Authorized (shs.)	Outstanding (shs.)[1]
Exch. Sr. Preferred	unlimited	nil
Cl.B Jr. Preferred	unlimited	nil
Cl.A Exchangeable S.V.	unlimited	172,227,909[2]
Class B Multiple Vtg.	unlimited	165[2]
Class C Non-vtg.	unlimited	189,600,000

[1] At May 9, 2023

[2] Classified as debt.

Class A Exchangeable Subordinate Voting - Entitled to dividends equal to distributions on Brookfield Renewable Partners L.P. (BEP) limited partnership units. Exchangeable for limited partnership units of BEP on a 1-for-1 basis or its cash equivalent. Convertible, at any time, into class C non-voting shares on a one-for-one basis. One vote per share.

Class B Multiple Voting - Entitled to dividends. Entitled to number votes equal to: (i) the number that is three times the number of class A exchangeable shares then issued and outstanding divided by (ii) the number of class B shares then issued and outstanding. Redeemable for cash in an amount equal to the market price of a limited partnership unit of BEP. All held by BEP and Brookfield Renewable Energy L.P. (BRELP) representing a 75% voting interest.

Class C Non-voting - All held by BEP and BRELP. Entitled to dividends as and when declared by board of directors. BEP is entitled to all of the residual value in the company after payment in full of the amount due to holders of class A exchangeable shares and class B shares and subject to the prior rights of holders of preferred shares. Redeemable for cash in an amount equal to the market price of a limited partnership unit of BEP.

Normal Course Issuer Bid - The company plans to make normal course purchases of up to 8,610,905 class A exchangeable subordinate voting shares representing 5% of the total outstanding. The bid commenced on Dec. 16, 2022, and expires on Dec. 15, 2023.

Major Shareholder - Brookfield Corporation, Brookfield Renewable Partners L.P. and Brookfield Renewable Energy L.P. collectively held 81.5% interest at May 9, 2023.

Price Range - BEPC/TSX

Year	Volume	High	Low	Close
2022	64,147,183	$55.55	$36.96	$37.27
2021	68,406,892	$80.30	$42.76	$46.55
2020	43,387,170	$78.90	$36.17	$74.26

Recent Close: $39.01

Capital Stock Changes - In June 2023, bought deal public offering of 7,430,000 class A exchangeable subordinate voting shares was completed at US$33.80 per share. Net proceeds would be used to fund current and future investment opportunities and for general corporate purposes.

During 2022, 27,064 class A exchangeable subordinate voting shares were issued on vesting of restricted stock units and 12,308 class A exchangeable subordinate voting shares were exchanged for a like number of Brookfield Renewable Partners L.P. limited partnership units.

Dividends

BEPC cl A exch sh S.V. Ra US$1.35 pa Q est. Mar. 31, 2023

Prev. Rate: US$1.28 est. Mar. 31, 2022

Prev. Rate: US$1.215 est. Mar. 31, 2021

Prev. Rate: US$1.736 est. Sept. 30, 2020

Wholly Owned Subsidiaries

BEP Subco Inc., Ont.
- 100% int. in **BEP Bermuda Holdings IV Limited**, Bermuda.
- 100% int. in **BRE Colombia Hydro Holdings L.P.**, Bermuda.
  - 100% int. in **BRE Colombia Co Invest I L.P.**, Bermuda.
  - 100% int. in **BRE Colombia Holdings Limited**, Bermuda.
    - 22% int. in **Isagen S.A. E.S.P.**, Colombia. Holds 99.7% voting interest.
  - **Brookfield Infrastructure Fund III**
    - **Isagen S.A. E.S.P.**, Colombia.
- 100% int. in **Brookfield Power US Holding America Co.**, Del.
- 100% int. in **TerraForm Power Parent, LLC**, N.Y.
  - **TerraForm Power, Inc.**, Bethesda, Md.

BP Brazil US Subco LLC, Del.

Financial Statistics

Periods ended:	12m Dec. 31/22[A]		12m Dec. 31/21[oA]
	US$000s	%Chg	US$000s
Operating revenue	**3,778,000**	**+12**	**3,367,000**
Salaries & benefits	224,000		206,000
Other operating expense	1,119,000		1,154,000
Operating expense	**1,343,000**	**-1**	**1,360,000**
Operating income	**2,435,000**	**+21**	**2,007,000**
Deprec., depl. & amort.	1,179,000		1,115,000
Finance costs, net	(768,000)		(367,000)
Investment income	6,000		2,000
Pre-tax income	**1,968,000**	**+94**	**1,017,000**
Income taxes	118,000		87,000
Net income	**1,850,000**	**+99**	**930,000**
Net inc. for equity hldrs	**1,503,000**	**+59**	**946,000**
Net inc. for non-cont. int	**347,000**	**n.a.**	**(16,000)**
Cash & equivalent	642,000		525,000
Inventories	18,000		20,000
Accounts receivable	581,000		579,000
Current assets	3,426,000		2,336,000
Long-term investments	743,000		455,000
Fixed assets, net	37,828,000		37,915,000
Intangibles, net	931,000		1,067,000
Total assets	**43,288,000**	**+3**	**41,986,000**
Accts. pay. & accr. liabs	412,000		313,000
Current liabilities	7,251,000		8,975,000
Long-term debt, gross	13,715,000		13,512,000
Long-term debt, net	12,416,000		12,060,000
Long-term lease liabilities	338,000		346,000
Shareholders' equity	5,873,000		3,667,000
Non-controlling interest	10,951,000		10,558,000
Cash from oper. activs	**1,284,000**	**+225**	**395,000**
Cash from fin. activs	(402,000)		678,000
Cash from invest. activs	(738,000)		(1,027,000)
Net cash position	**642,000**	**+22**	**525,000**
Capital expenditures	(847,000)		(1,354,000)
Capital disposals	92,000		376,000
	US$		US$
Earnings per share*	n.a.		n.a.
Cash divd. per share*	1.28		1.22
	shs		shs
No. of shs. o/s*	172,218,098		172,203,342
	%		%
Net profit margin	48.97		27.62
Return on equity	31.51		39.06
Return on assets	4.34		2.28
Foreign sales percent	100		100
No. of employees (FTEs)	2,152		2,080

* Cl.A Exch. S.V.

[o] Restated

[A] Reported in accordance with IFRS

Latest Results

Periods ended:	3m Mar. 31/23[A]		3m Mar. 31/22[A]
	US$000s	%Chg	US$000s
Operating revenue	1,066,000	+15	929,000
Net income	(920,000)	n.a.	(882,000)
Net inc. for equity hldrs	(1,065,000)	n.a.	(976,000)
Net inc. for non-cont. int	145,000		94,000
	US$		US$
Earnings per share*	n.a.		n.a.

[A] Reported in accordance with IFRS

Historical Summary
(as originally stated)

Fiscal Year	Oper. Rev. US$000s	Net Inc. Bef. Disc. US$000s	EPS* US$
2022[A]	3,778,000	1,850,000	n.a.
2021[A]	3,367,000	930,000	n.a.
2020[A]	3,087,000	(2,819,000)	n.a.
2019[A1]	2,236,000	425,000	n.a.
2018[A1]	2,164,000	362,000	n.a.

* Cl.A Exch. S.V.

[A] Reported in accordance with IFRS

[1] Results were prepared on a carve-out basis reflecting the U.S., Colombian and Brazilian operations transferred from Brookfield Renewable Partners L.P.

Note: Adjusted throughout for 1.5-for-1 split in Dec. 2020

B.127 Brookfield Renewable Partners L.P.

Symbol - BEP.UN **Exchange** - TSX **CUSIP** - G16258

Head Office - 73 Front Street, Fifth Floor, Hamilton, Bermuda, HM 12 **Telephone** - (441) 294-3304 **Toll-free** - (888) 327-2722 **Fax** - (441) 516-1988

Website - www.bep.brookfield.com

Email - alexander.jackson@brookfield.com

Investor Relations - Alex Jackson (647) 484-8525

Auditors - Ernst & Young LLP C.A., Toronto, Ont.

Transfer Agents - Computershare Trust Company of Canada Inc., Toronto, Ont.

Managers - BRP Energy Group L.P., Hamilton Parish, Bermuda

Employees - 3,400 at Dec. 31, 2022

Profile - (Bermuda 2011) Owns, operates and manages renewable power businesses with a focus on hydroelectric, wind, utility solar and distributed generation power generation as well as biomass power generation, cogeneration and storage businesses in North and South America, Europe and Asia.

At Dec. 31, 2022, the limited partnership held interests in 6,764 facilities with a total of 25,377 MW of power generating capacity and an average annual production of 69,735 GWh on a consolidated basis. Holdings consisted of 229 hydroelectric facilities, 125 wind farms, 149 utility-scale solar facilities, 6,238 distributed generation facilities and 23 storage & other facilities. Also holds interests in total development pipeline of 110,000 MW of renewable power and 8,000 thousand metric tons per annum (TMTPA) of carbon capture and storage projects.

Hydroelectric - Holds interests in 229 hydroelectric generating stations on 87 river systems in the U.S. (136), Canada (33), Colombia (17) and Brazil (43) totaling 8,159 MW of power generating capacity which can produce an average of 37,843 GWh of electricity per year and has 7,507 GWh of storage capacity.

Wind - Holds interests in 125 wind farms in the U.S., Canada, Brazil, Uruguay, the U.K., Poland, Spain, Portugal, India and China totaling 6,935 MW of power generating capacity which can produce an average of 20,977 GWh of electricity per year.

Solar - Holds interests in 149 utility-scale solar facilities in the U.S., Spain, Mexico, Chile, India and China totaling 3,957 MW of power generating capacity which can produce an average of 8,476 GWh of electricity per year.

Distributed Generation - Holds interests in 6,238 distributed generation facilities totaling 2,055 MW of power generating capacity with 2,439 GWh of electricity per year. The facilities include nine fuel cell facilities in North America totaling 10 MW of generating capacity, four biomass facilities in Brazil totaling 175 MW of power generating capacity; a 300-MW gas-fired cogeneration plant in Colombia; a 105-MW gas-fired cogeneration plant in North America; and two cogeneration plants in Europe totaling 124 MW of power generating capacity.

Storage & Other - Holds interests in 23 facilities totaling 4,271 MW of power generating capacity and 5,220 GWh of storage capacity, and includes pumped storage in North America (633 MW) and Europe (2,088 MW).

The remaining 42% of managing general partnership units in **Brookfield Business L.P.** is held by **Brookfield Corporation** and its affiliates. **Brookfield Corporation**'s subsidiary **Brookfield Renewable Partners Limited** is the limited partnership's general partner.

During 2022, the limited partnership (BEP LP), together with its institutional partners, acquired 32% interest in **Kishoa S.L.** (dba Powen) for US$56,000,000, with the BEP LP acquiring 6% economic interest for US$13,000,000. Powen is a distributed generation development platform in Spain and Mexico with 700 MW of operating and development assets.

In December 2022, the limited partnership (BEP LP), together with its institutional partners, acquired 10% interest (2% economic interest for BEP LP) in **California Bioenergy LLC**, a developer, operator and owner of renewable natural gas assets in the U.S., for US$150,000,000 (US$30,000,000 net to BEP LP). BEP LP and its partners also secured the option to invest up to US$350,000,000 (US$70,000,000 net to BEP LP) of follow-on equity capital for future projects.

In June 2022, the limited partnership (BEP LP), together with institutional partners, committed to invest US$500,000,000, of which US$122,000,000 was deployed for 20% common equity interest, in **Island Aggregator LP**, which owns and operates long-term contracted power and utility assets across the Americas with 1.2 GW of installed capacity and a 1.3-GW development pipeline.

During the second quarter of 2022, the limited partnership (BEP LP), together with its institutional partners, acquired additional shares in Warsaw, Poland-based **Polenergia S.A.** for US$122,000,000, with BEP LP paying US$10,000,000 for its share. Polenergia owns and operates wind and solar projects, as well as gas-fired and coke-oven-fired plants in Poland. Polenergia also operates electricity trading and distribution businesses. The acquisition increased BEP LP's voting interest to 32% and its economic interest to 8%.

In March 2022, the limited partnership (BEP LP), together with its institutional partners, agreed to invest $300,000,000 in **Entropy Inc.**, owned 90% by **Advantage Energy Ltd.**, to fund Entropy's near term projects including its Glacier Phase 1 and 2 carbon capture and storage (CCS) projects. BEP LP would invest in a hybrid security that implies a pre-money valuation of $300,000,000. The committed capital would be drawn down by Entropy to fund CCS projects that reach final investment decision as certain predetermined return thresholds are met. Advantage Energy would continue to control Entropy until substantially all of the BEP LP's committed capital was invested, at which time BEP LP would hold 50% voting interest in Entropy on an as-converted basis.

Periods ended:	12m Dec. 31/22	12m Dec. 31/21
Generating capacity, MW[1]	25,377	21,049
Electric gen., GWh[1]	63,036	56,629
Avg. electric price, $/MWh	88	82

[1] Consolidated basis.

Recent Merger and Acquisition Activity

Status: pending **Announced:** June 12, 2023

Duke Energy Corporation agreed to sell its unregulated utility scale Commercial Renewables business to Brookfield Renewable Partners L.P., Brookfield Renewable Corporation and their institutional partners for US$1.05 billion (Brookfield Renewable's share is US$265,000,000), reflecting a enterprise value of US$2.8 billion. The business includes more than 3,400 MW (alternating current) of utility-scale solar, wind and battery storage across the U.S., net of joint venture partners ownership, in addition to operations and projects under development and construction.

Status: pending **Announced:** Mar. 27, 2023
A consortium consisting of Brookfield Renewable Partners L.P. and Brookfield Renewable Corporation, together with their institutional partners and global institutional investors Global Industrial Company and Temasek Holdings (Private) Limited, and MidOcean Energy, an LNG company formed and managed by EIG Management Company, LLC, has agreed to acquire Origin Energy Limited for A$8.91 per share, valuing Origin at an enterprise value of A$18.7 billion. Origin's board of directors unanimously recommended that its shareholders vote in favour of the transaction. Upon closing, Brookfield, its institutional partners and investors would own Origin's Energy Markets business, Australia's largest integrated power generator and energy retailer. MidOcean would separately own Origin's Integrated Gas segment including its upstream gas interests and the 27.5% stake in Australia Pacific LNG.

Status: completed **Revised:** Dec. 16, 2022
UPDATE: The transaction was completed. PREVIOUS: Brookfield Renewable Partners L.P. (BEP LP), together with its institutional partners, agreed to acquire Scout Clean Energy LLC for US$1 billion with the potential to invest an additional US$350,000,000 to support the business' development activities (US$270,000,000 in total net to BEP LP). Scout's portfolio includes over 1,200 MW of operating wind assets, including 400 MW managed on behalf of third parties, and a pipeline of over 22,000 MW of wind, solar and storage projects across 24 U.S. states, including almost 2,500 MW of under construction and advanced-stage projects. Scout would continue to operate as independent business within the Brookfield Renewable U.S. platform.

Status: pending **Announced:** Oct. 11, 2022
Brookfield Business Corporation (BBPC) together with its institutional partners agreed to sell its nuclear technology services operation, Westinghouse Electric Company, to a consortium led by Cameco Corporation and Brookfield Renewable Partners L.P. (BEP LP) for a total enterprise value of US$7.875 billion. BBPC expects to receive US$1.8 billion for its 44% stake in Westinghouse, with the balance distributed to institutional partners. On closing, BEP LP and its institutional partners would own 51% interest in Westinghouse and Cameco would own 49%. Westinghouse's existing debt structure would remain in place, leaving an estimated US$4.5 billion equity cost to the consortium, subject to closing adjustments. This equity cost would be shared proportionately between BEP LP and its partners (US$2.3 billion) and Cameco (US$ $2.2 billion). BEP LP was expected to invest US$750,000,000 to acquire about 17% interest in Westinghouse. The transaction was expected to close in the second half of 2023.

Status: completed **Revised:** Sept. 29, 2022
Brookfield Renewable Partners L.P. (BEP LP), together with its institutional partners, acquired Standard Solar Inc. for US$540,000,000 with the potential to invest an additional US$160,000,000 (US$140,000,000 in total net to BEP LP). to support the business' growth initiatives. Standard Solar owns and operates solar projects and has 500 MW of operating and under construction contracted assets and a development pipeline of almost 2,000 MW. Standard Solar would continue to operate as independent business within the Brookfield Renewable U.S. platform.

Status: completed **Revised:** June 30, 2022
UPDATE: The transaction was completed for US$90,000,000, with BEP LP receiving US$23,000,000 for its 25% share. PREVIOUS: Brookfield Renewable Partners L.P. (BEP LP), together with its institutional partners, agreed to sell a 36-MW operating hydroelectric portfolio in Brazil for US$98,000,000.

Status: completed **Revised:** May 13, 2022
UPDATE: The transaction was completed for US$33,000,000, with BEP LP receiving US$10,000,000 for its share. PREVIOUS: Brookfield Renewable Partners L.P. (BEP LP), together with its institutional partners, agreed to sell a 19-MW solar portfolio in Malaysia for an undisclosed amount. The transaction was expected to close in the first half of 2021.

Status: terminated **Revised:** May 7, 2022
UPDATE: BEP LP and GROK Ventures announced their withdrawal to the proposed acquisition following AGL's rejection of the revised proposal. The transaction was terminated. PREVIOUS: Brookfield Renewable Partners L.P. (BEP LP), together with its institutional partners, and GROK Ventures, the private investing vehicle of Mike Cannon-Brookes, announced a proposal to acquire AGL Energy Limited, the largest integrated power generation and energy retailer in Australia, at A$7.50 per share, which values AGL at an equity value of A$5 billion. Feb. 21, 2022 - AGL rejected the proposal. May 6, 2022 - BEP LP and GROK Ventures raised their offer to acquire AGL at A$8.25 per share.

Status: completed **Revised:** Mar. 31, 2022
UPDATE: The transaction was completed. PREVIOUS: Brookfield Renewable Partners L.P. (BEP LP) and its institutional partners agreed to acquire a 47-MW solar development project in Italy for US$9,000,000, with BEP LP acquiring a 25% interest for US$2,000,000. The seller has also agreed to present BEP LP with renewable power development opportunities in Italy from its 500-MW development pipeline over the next three years. BEP LP is expected to hold 25% interest in future opportunities acquired from the seller's development pipeline.

Status: completed **Revised:** Mar. 31, 2022
UPDATE: The transaction was completed. PREVIOUS: Brookfield Renewable Partners L.P. (BEP LP) and its institutional partners agreed to acquire a 450-MW solar development project in India for US$66,000,000, with BEP LP investing US$17,000,000. The transaction was expected to close in early 2022.

Status: completed **Announced:** Mar. 17, 2022
Brookfield Renewable Partners L.P. (BEP LP) and its institutional partners acquired 83% interest in a 437 MW distributed generation portfolio of operating and development assets in Chile for US$31,000,000. BEP LP acquired 20% economic interest in the investment.

Predecessor Detail - Name changed from Brookfield Renewable Energy Partners L.P., May 4, 2016.

Oper. Subsid./Mgt. Co. Directors - Jeffrey M. (Jeff) Blidner, chr., Toronto, Ont.; David McD. Mann†, Chester, N.S.; Scott Cutler, Utah; Sarah Deasley, London, Middx., United Kingdom; Nancy Dorn, Ga.; Louis J. Maroun, Warwick, Bermuda; Stephen Westwell, London, Middx., United Kingdom; Patricia Zuccotti, Kirkland, Wash.

Oper. Subsid./Mgt. Co. Officers - Connor D. Teskey, CEO; Wyatt Hartley, sr. v-p, fin. & CFO; Jennifer Mazin, gen. counsel
† Lead director

Capital Stock

	Authorized (shs.)	Outstanding (shs.)[1]
Cl.A Preferred LP Unit		
Series 5		nil
Series 7		7,000,000
Series 11		nil
Series 13		10,000,000
Series 15		7,000,000
Series 17		8,000,000
Series 18		6,000,000
General Partnership Unit		3,977,260
Redeemable Partnership Unit		194,487,939[2]
Limited Partnership Unit	unlimited	275,432,611

[1] At Mar. 31, 2023
[2] Securities of Brookfield Renewable Energy L.P.

Class A Preferred Limited Partnership Unit - Issuable in series. Non-voting.

Series 7 - Entitled to cumulative preferential annual dividends of $1.375 payable quarterly to Jan. 31, 2026, and thereafter at a rate reset every five years equal to the five-year Government of Canada bond yield plus 4.7%. Redeemable on Jan. 31, 2026, and on January 31 every five years thereafter at Cdn$25 per share plus declared and unpaid distributions. Convertible at the holder's option, on Jan. 31, 2026, and on January 31 every five years thereafter, into floating rate class A preferred limited partnership units, series 8 on a share-for-share basis, subject to certain conditions. The series 8 units would pay a quarterly distribution equal to the 90-day Canadian Treasury bill rate plus 4.47%.

Series 13 - Entitled to cumulative preferential annual dividends of $1.5125 payable quarterly to Apr. 30, 2028, and thereafter at a rate reset every five years equal to the greater of: (i) the five-year Government of Canada bond yield plus 3%; and (ii) 5%. Redeemable on Apr. 30, 2028, and on April 30 every five years thereafter at Cdn$25 per share plus declared and unpaid distributions. Convertible at the holder's option, on Apr. 30, 2028, and on April 30 every five years thereafter, into floating rate class A preferred limited partnership units, series 14 on a share-for-share basis, subject to certain conditions. The series 14 units would pay a quarterly distribution equal to the 90-day Canadian Treasury bill rate plus 3%.

Series 15 - Entitled to cumulative preferential annual dividends of $1.4375 payable quarterly to Apr. 30, 2024, and thereafter at a rate reset every five years equal to the greater of: (i) the five-year Government of Canada bond yield plus 3.94%; and (ii) 5.75%. Redeemable on Apr. 30, 2024, and on April 30 every five years thereafter at Cdn$25 per share plus declared and unpaid distributions. Convertible at the holder's option, on Apr. 30, 2024, and on April 30 every five years thereafter, into floating rate class A preferred limited partnership units, series 16 on a share-for-share basis, subject to certain conditions. The series 16 units would pay a quarterly distribution equal to the 90-day Canadian Treasury bill rate plus 3.94%.

Series 17 - Entitled to a 5.25% cumulative preferential distribution, payable quarterly. Redeemable on or after Mar. 31, 2025, at US$25 per unit plus declared and unpaid distributions.

Series 18 - Entitled to a 5.5% cumulative preferential distribution, payable quarterly. Redeemable on or after Apr. 30, 2027, at Cdn$26 per unit and declining by Cdn$0.25 per share annually (on April 30) to Apr. 30, 2031, and at Cdn$25 per share thereafter.

General Partnership Unit - Indirectly held by Brookfield Asset Management Inc. Voting. Classified as non-controlling interest effective Dec. 31, 2012.

Redeemable Partnership Unit - Securities of subsidiary Brookfield Renewable Energy L.P. Exchangeable for cash or limited partnership units. Indirectly held by Brookfield Asset Management Inc. Participating and non-voting.

Limited Partnership Unit - Participating and non-voting.

Class A Preferred Limited Partnership Unit, Series 5 (old) - Were entitled to a 5.59% cumulative preferential annual distribution, payable quarterly. Redeemed at Cdn$25.25 per unit on Jan. 31, 2022.

Class A Preferred Limited Partnership Unit, Series 11 (old) - Were entitled to a 5% cumulative preferential distribution, payable quarterly, to Apr. 30, 2022. Redeemed at Cdn$25 per unit on Apr. 30, 2022.

Normal Course Issuer Bid - The company plans to make normal course purchases of up to 13,764,352 limited partnership units representing 5% of the total outstanding. The bid commenced on Dec. 16, 2022, and expires on Dec. 15, 2023.

The company plans to make normal course purchases of up to 700,000 class A preferred LP units, series 7 representing 10% of the public float. The bid commenced on Dec. 16, 2022, and expires on Dec. 15, 2023.

The company plans to make normal course purchases of up to 1,000,000 class A preferred LP units, series 13 representing 10% of the public float. The bid commenced on Dec. 16, 2022, and expires on Dec. 15, 2023.

The company plans to make normal course purchases of up to 700,000 class A preferred LP units, series 15 representing 10% of the public float. The bid commenced on Dec. 16, 2022, and expires on Dec. 15, 2023.

The company plans to make normal course purchases of up to 600,000 class A preferred LP units, series 18 representing 10% of the public float. The bid commenced on Dec. 16, 2022, and expires on Dec. 15, 2023.

Major Shareholder - Brookfield Corporation held 100% interest at Dec. 31, 2022.

Price Range - BEP.UN/TSX

Year	Volume	High	Low	Close
2022	67,763,398	$53.09	$32.58	$34.28
2021	61,420,131	$63.39	$41.88	$45.31
2020	109,565,801	$55.76	$29.16	$54.95
2019	68,024,360	$42.97	$23.61	$40.20
2018	47,834,984	$29.26	$22.21	$23.57

Split: 1.5-for-1 split in Dec. 2020
Recent Close: $35.77

Capital Stock Changes - In June 2023, bought deal public offering of 8,200,000 limited partnership units and concurrent private placement of 5,148,270 limited partnership units all at US$30.35 per unit were completed. Net proceeds would be used to fund current and future investment opportunities and for general corporate purposes.

On Jan. 31, 2022, all 2,885,496 class A preferred limited partnership units, series 5 were redeemed at Cdn$25.25 per unit. In April 2022, public offering of 6,000,000 class A preferred limited partnership units, series 18 was completed at CdnS$25 per unit and all 10,000,000 class A preferred limited partnership units, series 11 were redeemed at Cdn$25 per unit. Also during 2022, limited partnership units were issued as follows: 262,177 under distribution reinvestment plan and 12,308 on exchange of a like number of Brookfield Renewable Corporation exchangeable shares.

Dividends

BEP.UN unit Ra US$1.35 pa Q est. Mar. 31, 2023**
Prev. Rate: US$1.28 est. Mar. 31, 2022
Prev. Rate: US$1.215 est. Mar. 31, 2021
Prev. Rate: US$1.736 est. Sept. 30, 2020
BEP.PR.G pfd A ser 7 cum. red. exch. Adj. Ra $1.375 pa Q est. Feb. 1, 2016
BEP.PR.M pfd A ser 13 cum. red. exch. Adj. Ra $1.5125 pa Q est. July 31, 2023
BEP.PR.O pfd A ser 15 cum. red. exch. Adj. Ra $1.4375 pa Q est. Apr. 30, 2019
BEP.PR.R pfd A ser 18 cum. red. Ra $1.375 pa Q
Listed Apr 14/22.
Prev. Rate: $1.6272
$0.4068**i**............... Aug. 2/22
pfd A ser 5 cum. red. Ra $1.3976 pa Q[1]
$0.3494**f**............... Jan. 31/22
pfd A ser 9 cum. red. exch. Adj. Ra $1.4375 pa Q est. Aug. 2, 2016[2]
$0.359375**f**........... Aug. 3/21
pfd A ser 11 cum. red. exch. Adj. Ra $1.25 pa Q est. May 1, 2017
$0.3125**f**............... May 2/22
[1] Redeemed Jan. 31, 2022 at $25 per sh.
[2] Redeemed Aug. 4, 2021 at $25 per sh.
** Reinvestment Option **f** Final Payment **i** Initial Payment

Subsidiaries

58% int. in **Brookfield Renewable Energy L.P.**, Bermuda. The balance is held by Brookfield Corporation through Brookfield Renewable Power Inc.
- 100% int. in **BP Brazil US Subco LLC**, Del.
- 100% int. in **Brookfield BRP Canada Corp.**, Alta.
  - 47.6% int. in **Brookfield Renewable Corporation**, New York, N.Y. Holds 75% voting interest. (see separate coverage)
- 100% int. in **Brookfield BRP Europe Holdings (Bermuda) Limited**, Bermuda.
- 100% int. in **Brookfield Renewable Power Preferred Equity Inc.**, Toronto, Ont. (see separate coverage)
- 2% int. in **California Bioenergy LLC**, Visalia, Calif.
- 8% int. in **Entropy Inc.**, Calgary, Alta.
- 20% int. in **Island Aggregator L.P.**
- 6% int. in **Kishoa S.L.**, Madrid, Spain.
- 8% int. in **Polenergia S.A.**, Warsaw, Poland. Holds 32% voting interest.
- 12.5% int. in **X-Elio Energy S.L.**, Madrid, Spain. Holds 50% voting interest.

Note: The preceding list includes only the major related companies in which interests are held.

Financial Statistics

Periods ended:	12m Dec. 31/22[A]		12m Dec. 31/21[oA]
	US$000s	%Chg	US$000s
Operating revenue	**4,711,000**	**+15**	**4,096,000**
Cost of sales	1,434,000		1,365,000
General & admin expense	243,000		288,000
Operating expense	**1,677,000**	**+1**	**1,653,000**
Operating income	**3,034,000**	**+24**	**2,443,000**
Deprec., depl. & amort.	1,583,000		1,501,000
Finance income	68,000		59,000
Finance costs, gross	1,224,000		981,000
Investment income	96,000		22,000
Pre-tax income	**136,000**	**n.a.**	**(52,000)**
Income taxes	(2,000)		14,000
Net income	**138,000**	**n.a.**	**(66,000)**
Net inc. for equity hldrs	**(122,000)**	**n.a.**	**(136,000)**
Net inc. for non-cont. int	**260,000**	**+271**	**70,000**
Cash & equivalent	998,000		900,000
Inventories	42,000		31,000
Accounts receivable	672,000		629,000
Current assets	4,183,000		2,889,000
Long-term investments	1,392,000		1,107,000
Fixed assets, net	54,283,000		49,432,000
Intangibles, net	1,735,000		1,184,000
Total assets	**64,111,000**	**+15**	**55,867,000**
Accts. pay. & accr. liabs	716,000		520,000
Current liabilities	4,943,000		3,222,000
Long-term debt, gross	24,850,000		21,529,000
Long-term debt, net	22,574,000		19,711,000
Long-term lease liabilities	526,000		434,000
Shareholders' equity	4,856,000		4,973,000
Non-controlling interest	21,430,000		19,023,000
Cash from oper. activs	**1,711,000**	**+133**	**734,000**
Cash from fin. activs	3,489,000		2,143,000
Cash from invest. activs	(5,066,000)		(2,504,000)
Net cash position	**998,000**	**+11**	**900,000**
Capital expenditures	(2,190,000)		(1,967,000)
Capital disposals	140,000		827,000
	US$		US$
Earnings per share*	(0.60)		(0.69)
Cash flow per share*	6.22		2.67
Cash divd. per share*	1.28		1.22
	shs		shs
No. of shs. o/s*	275,358,750		275,084,265
Avg. no. of shs. o/s*	275,200,000		274,900,000
	%		%
Net profit margin	2.93		(1.61)
Return on equity	(3.38)		(3.88)
Return on assets	2.30		2.23
No. of employees (FTEs)	3,400		2,875

* L.P. & Red. unit
[o] Restated
[A] Reported in accordance with IFRS

Latest Results

Periods ended:	3m Mar. 31/23[A]		3m Mar. 31/22[A]
	US$000s	%Chg	US$000s
Operating revenue	1,331,000	+17	1,136,000
Net income	177,000	+436	33,000
Net inc. for equity hldrs	(16,000)	n.a.	(33,000)
Net inc. for non-cont. int	193,000		66,000
	US$		US$
Earnings per share*	(0.09)		(0.16)

* L.P. & Red. unit
[A] Reported in accordance with IFRS

Historical Summary
(as originally stated)

Fiscal Year	Oper. Rev. US$000s	Net Inc. Bef. Disc. US$000s	EPS* US$
2022[A]	4,711,000	138,000	(0.60)
2021[A]	4,096,000	(66,000)	(0.69)
2020[A]	3,810,000	(45,000)	(0.61)
2019[A]	2,980,000	273,000	(0.13)
2018[A]	2,982,000	403,000	0.09

* L.P. & Red. unit
[A] Reported in accordance with IFRS
Note: Adjusted throughout for 1.5-for-1 split in Dec. 2020

B.128 Brookfield Renewable Power Preferred Equity Inc.

CUSIP - 11283Q
Head Office - Bay Wellington Tower, Brookfield Place, 300-181 Bay St, PO Box 762, Toronto, ON, M5J 2T3 **Telephone** - (416) 359-1955 **Toll-free** - (888) 327-2722 **Fax** - (416) 363-2856
Website - www.brookfield.com
Email - alexander.jackson@brookfield.com
Investor Relations - Alex Jackson (416) 649-8196
Auditors - Ernst & Young LLP C.A., Toronto, Ont.
Transfer Agents - Computershare Trust Company of Canada Inc.
Managers - BRP Energy Group L.P., Hamilton Parish, Bermuda
Profile - (Can. 2010) Wholly owned preferred share financing vehicle of **Brookfield Renewable Partners L.P.**, which owns, operates and manages renewable power businesses with 25,377 MW of power generating capacity with assets in North and South America, Europe and Asia.

The company does not prepare separate financial statements due to an exemption from the continuous disclosure requirements under the Securities Act. One of the conditions of the exemption is that the company is required to file with the Canadian securities commissions all documents filed by parent entity **Brookfield Renewable Partners L.P.**

Capital Stock

	Authorized (shs.)	Outstanding (shs.)[1]
Class A Preference	unlimited	
Series 1		6,849,533
Series 2		3,110,531
Series 3		9,961,399
Series 5		4,114,504
Series 6		7,000,000
Class B Preference	unlimited	nil
Common	unlimited	1

[1] At Mar. 31, 2023

Class A Preference - Issuable in series. Fully and unconditionally guaranteed by Brookfield Renewable Energy Partners L.P. Non-voting.

Series 1 - Entitled to cumulative preferential annual dividends of $0.784252 per share payable quarterly to Apr. 30, 2025, and thereafter at a rate reset every five years equal to the five-year Government of Canada bond yield plus 2.62%. Redeemable on Apr. 30, 2025, and on April 30 every five years thereafter at $25 per share plus declared and unpaid dividends. Convertible at the holder's option on Apr. 30, 2025, and on April 30 every five years thereafter, into floating rate class A preference series 2 shares on a share-for-share basis, subject to certain conditions.

Series 2 - Entitled to cumulative preferential annual dividends payable quarterly equal to the 90-day Canadian Treasury bill rate plus 2.62%. Redeemable on Apr. 30, 2025, on April 30 every five years thereafter at $25 per share or at any non-conversion date at $25.50 per share. Convertible at the holder's option on Apr. 30, 2025, and on April 30 every five years thereafter, into preferred series 1 shares on a share-for-share basis, subject to certain conditions.

Series 3 - Entitled to cumulative preferential annual dividends of $1.08775 per share payable quarterly to July 31, 2024, and thereafter at a rate reset every five years equal to the five-year Government of Canada bond yield plus 2.94%. Redeemable on July 31, 2024, and on July 31 every five years thereafter at $25 per share plus declared and unpaid dividends. Convertible at the holder's option on July 31, 2024, and on July 31 every five years thereafter, into floating rate class A preference series 4 shares on a share-for-share basis, subject to certain conditions. The series 4 shares would pay a quarterly dividend equal to the 90-day Canadian Treasury bill rate plus 2.94%.

Series 5 - Entitled to cumulative preferential annual dividends of $1.25 per share, payable quarterly. Redeemable at Cdn$25 per share.

Series 6 - Entitled to cumulative preferential annual dividends of $1.25 per share, payable quarterly. Redeemable at Cdn$25.50 per share, and declining by Cdn$0.25 per share annually (on July 31) to July 31, 2022, and at Cdn$25 per share thereafter.

Common - One vote per share. Held by Brookfield Renewable Energy Partners L.P.

Normal Course Issuer Bid - The company plans to make normal course purchases of up to 684,953 class A preference series 1 shares representing 10% of the public float. The bid commenced on Dec. 16, 2022, and expires on Dec. 15, 2023.

The company plans to make normal course purchases of up to 996,139 class A preference series 3 shares representing 10% of the public float. The bid commenced on Dec. 16, 2022, and expires on Dec. 15, 2023.

The company plans to make normal course purchases of up to 411,450 class A preference series 5 shares representing 10% of the public float. The bid commenced on Dec. 16, 2022, and expires on Dec. 15, 2023.

The company plans to make normal course purchases of up to 700,000 class A preference series 6 shares representing 10% of the public float. The bid commenced on Dec. 16, 2022, and expires on Dec. 15, 2023.

The company plans to make normal course purchases of up to 311,053 class A preference series 2 shares representing 10% of the public float. The bid commenced on Dec. 16, 2022, and expires on Dec. 15, 2023.

Major Shareholder - Brookfield Renewable Partners L.P. held 100% interest at Mar. 31, 2023.

Capital Stock Changes - There were no changes to capital stock during 2021 or 2022.

Dividends

BRF.PR.A pfd A ser 1 cum. red. exch. Adj. Ra $0.78425 pa Q est. July 31, 2020
BRF.PR.C pfd A ser 3 cum. red. exch. Adj. Ra $1.08775 pa Q est. Oct. 31, 2019
BRF.PR.E pfd A ser 5 cum. red. Ra $1.25 pa Q
BRF.PR.F pfd A ser 6 cum. red. Ra $1.25 pa Q
BRF.PR.B pfd A ser 2 cum. red. exch. Fltg. Ra pa Q

$0.47588	Oct. 31/23	$0.442798	July 31/23
$0.422018	May 1/23	$0.395223	Jan. 31/23

Paid in 2023: $1.735919 2022: $0.85616 2021: $0.685578

B.129 Brüush Oral Care Inc.

Symbol - BRSH **Exchange** - NASDAQ **CUSIP** - 11750K
Head Office - Unit 210, 128 Hastings St W, Vancouver, BC, V6B 1G8 **Toll-free** - (844) 427-8774
Website - investors.bruush.com
Email - aneil@bruush.com
Investor Relations - Aneil Manhas (604) 808-5858
Auditors - Dale Matheson Carr-Hilton LaBonte LLP C.A., Vancouver, B.C.
Lawyers - Lucosky Brookman LLP, Woodbridge, Conn.; DuMoulin Black LLP, Vancouver, B.C.
Transfer Agents - Endeavor Trust Corporation, Vancouver, B.C.
Employees - 7 at July 29, 2022
Profile - (B.C. 2017) Manufactures and sells electric toothbrushes and toothbrush head refills directly to customers in the U.S. and Canada.

Other related oral products planned to be rolled out include toothpaste, mouthwash, dental floss and whitening pens, as well as an electronic toothbrush for kids.

Directors - Aneil Manhas, founder, chr. & CEO; Kia Besharat, Nassau, Bahamas; Dr. Robert Ward; Brett Yormark
Other Exec. Officers - Alan MacNevin, COO; Matthew (Matt) Kavanagh, CFO

Capital Stock

	Authorized (shs.)	Outstanding (shs.)[1]
Common	unlimited	511,368

[1] At Aug. 1, 2023

Major Shareholder - Aneil Manhas held 11.76% interest at Aug. 5, 2022.

Price Range - BRSH/NASDAQ

Year	Volume	High	Low	Close
2022	571,244	US$97.00	US$10.93	US$11.35

Consolidation: 1-for-25 cons. in Aug. 2023

Capital Stock Changes - On Aug. 1, 2023, common shares were consolidated on a 1-for-25 basis.

On Aug. 5, 2022, an initial public offering of 3,728,549 units (1 common share & 1 warrant) at US$4.16 per unit was completed, with warrants exercisable at US$4.16 per share.

Financial Statistics

Periods ended:	9m Oct. 31/21[A1]		12m Jan. 31/21[A1]
	US$000s	%Chg	US$000s
Operating revenue	**1,965**	**n.a.**	**901**
Cost of goods sold	978		291
Salaries & benefits	282		93
General & admin expense	4,717		3,910
Stock-based compensation	92		4,949
Operating expense	**6,069**	**n.a.**	**9,244**
Operating income	**(4,104)**	**n.a.**	**(8,343)**
Deprec., depl. & amort.	5		nil
Finance costs, gross	60		18
Pre-tax income	**(4,211)**	**n.a.**	**(8,890)**
Net income	**(4,211)**	**n.a.**	**(8,890)**
Cash & equivalent	15		693
Inventories	774		1,176
Accounts receivable	161		81
Current assets	1,031		2,068
Fixed assets, net	7		3
Intangibles, net	11		nil
Total assets	**1,050**	**n.a.**	**2,072**
Bank indebtedness	27		18
Accts. pay. & accr. liabs	3,366		309
Current liabilities	4,993		1,908
Shareholders' equity	(3,943)		163
Cash from oper. activs	**(671)**	**n.a.**	**(4,052)**
Cash from fin. activs	14		4,568
Cash from invest. activs	(21)		(3)
Net cash position	**15**	**n.a.**	**693**
Capital expenditures	(6)		(3)
	US$		US$
Earnings per share*	(26.75)		(89.50)
Cash flow per share*	(4.27)		(10.56)
	shs		shs
No. of shs. o/s*	157,246		157,154
Avg. no. of shs. o/s*	157,181		99,387
	%		%
Net profit margin	...		(986.68)
Return on equity	...		n.m.
Return on assets	...		n.a.
Foreign sales percent	63		57

* Common
[A] Reported in accordance with IFRS
[1] Shares and per share figures adjusted to reflect 1-for-3.86 consolidation effective July 2022.
Note: Adjusted throughout for 1-for-25 cons. in Aug. 2023

B.130 Buhler Industries Inc.*

Symbol - BUI **Exchange** - TSX **CUSIP** - 119918
Head Office - 1260 Clarence Ave, Winnipeg, MB, R3T 1T2 **Telephone** - (204) 661-8711 **Fax** - (204) 654-2503
Website - www.buhlerindustries.com
Email - wjanzen@buhler.com
Investor Relations - Willy H. Janzen (204) 654-5718
Auditors - Baker Tilly HMA LLP C.A., Winnipeg, Man.
Bankers - Canadian Imperial Bank of Commerce, Winnipeg, Man.
Lawyers - Thompson Dorfman Sweatman LLP, Winnipeg, Man.
Transfer Agents - Computershare Trust Company of Canada Inc., Calgary, Alta.
FP500 Revenue Ranking - 621
Employees - 813 at Dec. 31, 2022
Profile - (Can. 1994 amalg.) Designs, manufactures and distributes agricultural equipment in Canada and the United States.

The Versatile line of equipment consists of tractors, self-propelled sprayers, combines, precision seeding equipment and tillage. The Farm King division includes grain augers, mowers, bale carriers, snow blowers, compact implements, applicators and tillage as well as its Allied brand of commercial equipment. Also offers products under Ezee-On and Inland brands.

Owns four fully equipped manufacturing plants in Morden (1) and Winnipeg (3), Man., totaling more than 1,100,000 sq. ft. of manufacturing, assembly and distribution space. Products are sold throughout Canada and the United States by 1,200 active dealers, serviced by warehouses in Ontario, Manitoba, Indiana, Nebraska and Arkansas. The company also provides custom metal fabrication to the non-agricultural sector.

In May 2022, the company sold its land and former manufacturing facility in Willmar, Minn., for an undisclosed amount.

Recent Merger and Acquisition Activity

Status: completed **Announced:** Apr. 30, 2023
Buhler Industries Inc. sold its Vegreville, Alta. facility and completed the sale and leaseback of its Woodstock, Ont. property for total proceeds of $15,400,000 net of commission.

Directors - Grant Adolph, chr. & COO, Winnipeg, Man.; Yury Ryazanov, CEO, Russia; Adam Reid, v-p, sales & mktg., Man.; Ossama AbouZeid, Man.; Oleg Gorbunov, Russia; Allan L. V. Stewart, Man.; Dmitry Udras, Russia
Other Exec. Officers - Marat Nogerov, pres.; Willy H. Janzen, CFO; Maxim Loktionov, v-p

Capital Stock

	Authorized (shs.)	Outstanding (shs.)[1]
Class A Common	unlimited	25,000,000
Class B Common	unlimited	nil

[1] At June 30, 2023

Major Shareholder - Combine Factory Rostselmash Ltd. held 96.7% interest at June 30, 2023.

Price Range - BUI/TSX

Year	Volume	High	Low	Close
2022	97,322	$3.29	$1.51	$1.93
2021	172,238	$3.89	$2.60	$2.96
2020	65,329	$3.95	$2.20	$2.60
2019	222,671	$3.96	$2.60	$2.93
2018	121,545	$4.60	$3.53	$3.86

Recent Close: $2.52
Capital Stock Changes - There were no changes to capital stock during 2022.
Long-Term Debt - At Dec. 31, 2022, outstanding long-term debt totaled $11,244,000 (all current) and consisted of a $529,000 loan due to The City of Willmar, bearing interest at the annual rate of the implicit price deflator for Minnesota; and $10,715,000 drawn on a bank credit facility due October 2023.
Note - In January 2023, the loan due to The City of Willmar was repaid.

Wholly Owned Subsidiaries

Amarillo Service & Supply Inc., United States.
- 100% int. in **B.I.I. Fargo, Inc.**
- 100% int. in **Buhler Versatile USA Ltd.**
- 100% int. in **Implement Sales Company Inc.**
- 100% int. in **Isco Inc.**
  - 100% int. in **Ezee-On (USA) Ltd.**

Buhler Versatile Inc., Winnipeg, Man.
John Buhler Inc.
- 50% int. in **Bradley Steel Processors Inc.**, Man.
- 90% int. in **Buhler Manufacturing**
- 90% int. in **Buhler Trading Inc.**
- 100% int. in **70268 Manitoba Ltd.**

Progressive Manufacturing Ltd., Winnipeg, Man.
- 10% int. in **Buhler Manufacturing**
- 10% int. in **Buhler Trading Inc.**

Financial Statistics

Periods ended:	12m Dec. 31/22[A]		15m Dec. 31/21[A]
	$000s	%Chg	$000s
Operating revenue	**239,869**	**n.a.**	**317,178**
Cost of goods sold	203,440		281,339
Research & devel. expense	7,406		8,106
General & admin expense	22,569		26,774
Operating expense	**233,415**	**n.a.**	**316,219**
Operating income	**6,454**	**n.a.**	**959**
Deprec., depl. & amort.	2,420		2,760
Finance income	74		20
Finance costs, gross	5,946		7,429
Investment income	337		508
Pre-tax income	**(1,119)**	**n.a.**	**8,988**
Income taxes	(88)		77
Net income	**(1,031)**	**n.a.**	**8,911**
Inventories	175,312		166,404
Accounts receivable	23,366		22,366
Current assets	202,788		195,064
Long-term investments	6,869		6,594
Fixed assets, net	14,416		14,735
Total assets	**231,611**	**+3**	**224,949**
Bank indebtedness	27,943		22,074
Accts. pay. & accr. liabs	75,854		75,057
Current liabilities	116,056		110,166
Long-term debt, gross	11,244		13,250
Long-term debt, net	nil		393
Shareholders' equity	88,851		89,882
Cash from oper. activs	**(7,208)**	**n.a.**	**(26,769)**
Cash from fin. activs	(2,143)		5,024
Cash from invest. activs	4,179		6,475
Net cash position	**(27,943)**	**n.a.**	**(22,074)**
Capital expenditures	(3,131)		(4,961)
Capital disposals	7,310		11,436
	$		$
Earnings per share*	(0.04)		0.36
Cash flow per share*	(0.29)		(1.07)
	shs		shs
No. of shs. o/s*	25,000,000		25,000,000
Avg. no. of shs. o/s*	25,000,000		25,000,000
	%		%
Net profit margin	(0.43)		...
Return on equity	(1.15)		...
Return on assets	1.95		...
Foreign sales percent	62		61
No. of employees (FTEs)	813		760

* Common
[A] Reported in accordance with IFRS

Latest Results

Periods ended:	6m June 30/23[A]		6m June 30/22[A]
	$000s	%Chg	$000s
Operating revenue	123,582	+9	112,996
Net income	20,180	n.m.	1,448
	$		$
Earnings per share*	0.81		0.06

* Common
[A] Reported in accordance with IFRS

Historical Summary
(as originally stated)

Fiscal Year	Oper. Rev.	Net Inc. Bef. Disc.	EPS*
	$000s	$000s	$
2022[A]	239,869	(1,031)	(0.04)
2021[A1]	317,178	8,911	0.36
2020[A]	249,550	(25,809)	(1.03)
2019[A]	229,119	(29,489)	(1.18)
2018[A]	287,984	(49,532)	(1.98)

* Common
[A] Reported in accordance with IFRS
[1] 15 months ended Dec. 31, 2021.

B.131 BuildDirect.com Technologies Inc.

Symbol - BILD **Exchange** - TSX-VEN **CUSIP** - 12009C
Head Office - 90-200 Granville St, Vancouver, BC, V6C 1S4 **Telephone** - (604) 662-8100 **Toll-free** - (877) 631-2845
Website - www.builddirect.com
Email - ir@builddirect.com
Investor Relations - Matthew Alexander (778) 382-7748
Auditors - Grant Thornton LLP C.A., Vancouver, B.C.
Transfer Agents - Computershare Trust Company of Canada Inc., Vancouver, B.C.
FP500 Revenue Ranking - 741
Profile - (B.C. 2019) Operates an e-commerce marketplace (www.builddirect.com) for purchasing and selling home improvement and flooring materials.

The BuildDirect platform connects homeowners and home improvement professionals in North America with suppliers and sellers of quality building materials from around the world including flooring, tile, decking and more. The company is actively seeking to acquire independent flooring retailers that have extensive professional client networks in the U.S. and Canada.

Predecessor Detail - Name changed from VLCTY Capital Inc., Aug. 13, 2021, pursuant to the Qualifying Transaction reverse takeover acquisition of (old) BuildDirect.com Technologies Inc. and concurrent amalgamation of (old) BuildDirect with wholly owned 9923896 Canada Inc.; basis 1 new for 26.538 old shs.
Directors - Timothy (Tim) Howley, New Westminster, B.C.; Henry Lees-Buckley, Delta, B.C.; Eyal Ofir, Toronto, Ont.; Milan Roy, Vancouver, B.C.
Other Exec. Officers - Shawn Wilson, CEO; Matthew Alexander, interim CFO; David Montagliani, v-p, category mgt.

Capital Stock

	Authorized (shs.)	Outstanding (shs.)[1]
Common	unlimited	41,941,535

[1] At May 2, 2023

Major Shareholder - Anthony von Mandt held 37% interest, Charles Chang held 14% interest, Beedie Investments Limited held 13% interest and MDV IX, L.P. held 12% interest at May 9, 2023.

Price Range - BILD/TSX-VEN

Year	Volume	High	Low	Close
2022	1,198,507	$1.71	$0.27	$0.28
2021	530,632	$5.50	$1.39	$1.70
2020	3,881	$3.98	$3.32	$3.98

Consolidation: 1-for-26.538 cons. in Aug. 2021
Recent Close: $0.45
Capital Stock Changes - In January 2023, private placement of 1,121,622 common share was completed at Cdn$0.37 per share.

During 2022, common shares were issued as follows: 11,131,615 by private placement and 27,202 on exercise of options.

Wholly Owned Subsidiaries

BuildDirect (Asia) Inc.
BuildDirect Operations Limited, Vancouver, B.C.
- 100% int. in **BuildDirect Technologies India Pvt. Ltd.**, India.
- 100% int. in **BuildDirect Technology Holdings, Inc.**, United States.
  - 100% int. in **Charter Distributing Company**, United States. dba FloorSource Wholesale & Supply
  - 100% int. in **Superb Flooring & Design LLC**, Troy, Mich.
- 100% int. in **6702627 Canada Inc.**, Canada.

Financial Statistics

Periods ended:	12m Dec. 31/22[A]		12m Dec. 31/21[A1]
	US$000s	%Chg	US$000s
Operating revenue	**92,150**	**+2**	**90,668**
Cost of goods sold	60,182		58,833
Research & devel. expense	1,342		1,629
General & admin expense	22,597		26,999
Other operating expense	7,384		8,976
Operating expense	**91,505**	**-5**	**96,438**
Operating income	**645**	**n.a.**	**(5,770)**
Deprec., depl. & amort.	4,069		2,967
Finance income	62		96
Finance costs, gross	2,097		3,868
Write-downs/write-offs	(3,385)		nil
Pre-tax income	**(8,254)**	**n.a.**	**(9,957)**
Income taxes	(384)		371
Net income	**(7,870)**	**n.a.**	**(10,328)**
Cash & equivalent	4,426		1,835
Inventories	6,657		7,453
Accounts receivable	4,000		4,421
Current assets	16,952		16,112
Fixed assets, net	592		599
Right-of-use assets	3,566		4,306
Intangibles, net	10,686		16,931
Total assets	**33,991**	**-14**	**39,453**
Accts. pay. & accr. liabs	5,475		7,620
Current liabilities	15,345		19,437
Long-term debt, gross	12,366		8,236
Long-term debt, net	7,609		3,386
Long-term lease liabilities	2,860		3,930
Shareholders' equity	7,448		11,323
Cash from oper. activs	**(1,861)**	**n.a.**	**(6,791)**
Cash from fin. activs	4,124		12,408
Cash from invest. activs	197		(9,316)
Net cash position	**4,108**	**+139**	**1,717**
Capital expenditures	(47)		(110)
	US$		US$
Earnings per share*	(0.25)		(0.41)
Cash flow per share*	(0.06)		(0.27)
	shs		shs
No. of shs. o/s*	40,819,913		29,661,097
Avg. no. of shs. o/s*	31,762,336		25,003,793
	%		%
Net profit margin	(8.54)		(11.39)
Return on equity	(83.85)		n.m.
Return on assets	(15.99)		(18.53)
Foreign sales percent	100		100

* Common

[A] Reported in accordance with IFRS

[1] Results prior to Aug. 13, 2021, pertain to and reflect the Qualifying Transaction reverse takeover acquisition of (old) BuildDirect.com Technologies Inc.

Historical Summary
(as originally stated)

Fiscal Year	Oper. Rev. US$000s	Net Inc. Bef. Disc. US$000s	EPS* US$
2022[A]	92,150	(7,870)	(0.25)
2021[A]	90,668	(10,328)	(0.41)
2020[A]	52,110	(4,559)	(1.06)
2019[A]	40,536	(11,464)	(2.65)

* Common

[A] Reported in accordance with IFRS

Note: Adjusted throughout for 1-for-26.538 cons. in Aug. 2021

B.132 Builders Capital Mortgage Corp.

Symbol - BCF **Exchange** - TSX-VEN **CUSIP** - 12008G
Head Office - 260-1414 8 St SW, Calgary, AB, T2R 1J6 **Telephone** - (403) 685-9888 **Fax** - (403) 225-9470
Website - www.builderscapital.ca
Email - jstrangway@builderscapital.ca
Investor Relations - John Strangway (403) 685-9888
Auditors - MNP LLP C.A., Calgary, Alta.
Lawyers - Osler, Hoskin & Harcourt LLP, Calgary, Alta.
Transfer Agents - Computershare Trust Company of Canada Inc., Calgary, Alta.
Managers - Builders Capital Management Corp., Calgary, Alta.
Portfolio Advisors - Builders Capital Management Corp., Calgary, Alta.

Profile - (Alta. 2013) Provides short-term residential construction mortgages to home builders, with a focus on urban markets and their surrounding areas in western Canada and Nova Scotia.

The company holds a portfolio of 28 construction mortgages to builders of residential, wood frame construction projects in Calgary (10), Edmonton (1) and other locations (3) in Alberta, British Columbia (13) and Nova Scotia (1) with $35,654,413 in outstanding principal at Mar. 31, 2023. The mortgages have terms of one year or less and are all secured by real property with buildings at different stages of completion. **Builders CapitalManagement Corp.** is the company's manager.

Directors - Sandy L. Loutitt, chr., pres. & CEO, Calgary, Alta.; John Strangway, CFO & corp. sec., Abbotsford, B.C.; John A. Drummond, Calgary, Alta.; Victor P. Harwardt, Vancouver, B.C.; David E. T. Pinkman, Calgary, Alta.; Brent J. Walter, Calgary, Alta.

Capital Stock

	Authorized (shs.)	Outstanding (shs.)[1]
Class A Non-vtg.	unlimited	2,261,124
Class B Non-vtg.	unlimited	912,836
Voting	1,000	100

[1] At May 29, 2023

Class A Non-voting - Entitled to non-cumulative dividends of up to 8% per annum. Retractable in October of each year at a price equal to 95% of the net asset value (NAV) per share. Rank in priority to class B non-voting shares and voting shares with respect to the payment of dividends and the repayment of capital on the dissolution, liquidation or winding-up of the company. Non-voting.

Class B Non-voting - Entitled to non-cumulative dividends of up to 16% per annum. Retractable in October of each year at a price equal to: (i) 100% of the NAV per share if the shares are not listed for trading on the TSX or such other recognized stock exchange in Canada; or (ii) 95% of the NAV per share if the shares are listed for trading on the TSX or such other recognized stock exchange in Canada. Rank in priority to voting shares with respect to the payment of dividends and the repayment of capital on the dissolution, liquidation or winding-up of the company. Non-voting.

Voting - Entitled to dividends of up to 8% per annum. One vote per share.

Price Range - BCF/TSX-VEN

Year	Volume	High	Low	Close
2022	273,899	$11.04	$9.25	$9.32
2021	440,257	$10.55	$8.35	$10.10
2020	207,805	$10.05	$7.03	$8.56
2019	221,101	$10.05	$9.74	$9.81
2018	208,399	$10.24	$9.36	$10.00

Recent Close: $8.57

Capital Stock Changes - In November 2022, 247,501 class A non-voting shares were issued at $9.30 per share pursuant to a rights offering. Also during 2022, 5,578 class A non-voting shares were issued under the dividend reinvestment plan.

Dividends

BCF cl A N.V. Ra $0.80 pa Q est. Jan. 31, 2014**
** Reinvestment Option

Subsidiaries

99.99% int. in **Builders Capital Limited Partnership**

Financial Statistics

Periods ended:	12m Dec. 31/22[A]		12m Dec. 31/21[A]
	$000s	%Chg	$000s
Total revenue	**3,759**	**+23**	**3,061**
General & admin. expense	409		399
Operating expense	**409**	**+3**	**399**
Operating income	**3,350**	**+26**	**2,662**
Provision for loan losses	353		276
Finance costs, gross	288		57
Pre-tax income	**2,708**	**+16**	**2,330**
Net income	**2,708**	**+16**	**2,330**
Cash & equivalent	394		352
Accounts receivable	1		4
Investments	34,134		28,405
Total assets	**35,720**	**+17**	**30,518**
Bank indebtedness	5,718		3,019
Accts. pay. & accr. liabs	64		45
Shareholders' equity	29,270		26,888
Cash from oper. activs	**2,382**	**n.a.**	**(1,390)**
Cash from fin. activs	2,423		761
Net cash position	**394**	**+12**	**352**
	$		$
Earnings per share*	0.92		0.80
Cash flow per share*	0.81		(0.48)
Cash divd. per share*	0.80		0.80
	shs		shs
No. of shs. o/s*	3,163,308		2,910,229
Avg. no. of shs. o/s*	2,936,077		2,910,229
	%		%
Net profit margin	72.04		76.12
Return on equity	9.64		8.68
Return on assets	9.05		8.25

* Cl.A & Cl.B Non-vtg.

[A] Reported in accordance with IFRS

Latest Results

Periods ended:	3m Mar. 31/23[A]		3m Mar. 31/22[A]
	$000s	%Chg	$000s
Total revenue	1,085	+28	845
Net income	829	+25	665
	$		$
Earnings per share*	0.26		0.23

* Cl.A & Cl.B Non-vtg.

[A] Reported in accordance with IFRS

Historical Summary
(as originally stated)

Fiscal Year	Total Rev. $000s	Net Inc. Bef. Disc. $000s	EPS* $
2022[A]	3,759	2,708	0.92
2021[A]	3,061	2,330	0.80
2020[A]	3,231	2,125	0.72
2019[A]	2,922	1,446	0.50
2018[A]	3,429	1,925	0.70

* Cl.A & Cl.B Non-vtg.

[A] Reported in accordance with IFRS

B.133 Burcon NutraScience Corporation*

Symbol - BU **Exchange** - TSX **CUSIP** - 120831
Head Office - 1946 Broadway W, Vancouver, BC, V6J 1Z2 **Telephone** - (604) 733-0896 **Toll-free** - (888) 408-7960 **Fax** - (604) 733-8821
Website - www.burcon.ca
Email - plam@burcon.ca
Investor Relations - Paul Lam (888) 408-7960
Auditors - KPMG LLP C.A., Vancouver, B.C.
Lawyers - Stikeman Elliott LLP, Vancouver, B.C.
Transfer Agents - Computershare Trust Company of Canada Inc., Vancouver, B.C.
Employees - 24 at Mar. 31, 2023

Profile - (B.C. 2020; orig. Yuk., 1998) Owns a portfolio of composition, application and process patents covering plant-based proteins derived from pea, canola, soy, hemp, sunflower seed and other plant-based sources for the production of purified, nutritious, functional and nutraceutical plant proteins for the food and beverage industry worldwide. Also offers pilot plant processing and scale-up validation services.

Products include: Peazazz®, a pea protein isolate that is soluble, clean and neutral-tasting and suitable for dairy alternative food and beverages including plant-based milk, yogurt and ice cream; Peazac®, a pea protein isolate that has lower protein content, neutral flavour and moderate viscosity and is suitable for plant-based meat alternative products, ready-to-mix powders, ready-to-mix beverages, dairy alternatives and nutrition bars; Puratein®, a canola protein isolate, which consists mainly of globulin proteins used in meat alternatives such as burgers and sausages and nutrition bars; Supertein®, a highly soluble canola protein isolate, which consists of albumin proteins used in non-dairy frozen desserts, egg alternative, plant-based marshmallows, plant-based ready-to-mix beverages, whipped toppings and plant based bars; Nutratein®, a canola protein isolate, which consists of a mixture of globulin and albumin proteins used in meat and egg alternatives, and other plant-based functional foods; Nutratein-PS™, a blend of Peazazz® and Supertein® proteins that has a clean flavour with high solubility suitable for dairy-alternative beverages such as almond milk, or to formulate a stand-alone beverage with a nutritional value consistent with cow's milk; and Nutratein-TZ™, a combination of Peazac® and Supertein® proteins suited in the formulation of plant-based meat products such as veggie burgers or veggie sausages.The company is also seeking opportunities to commercialize its sunflower and soy protein intellectual property portfolio, as well as developing hemp and flax protein isolates.

In addition, the company provides pilot plant processing and scale-up validation services including consulting and contract as well as product and process development for plant proteins at its 10,333-sq.-ft. technical centre in Winnipeg, Man.

Also has 31.60% interest in **Merit Functional Foods Corporation**, which owns a 94,000-sq.-ft. pea and canola protein production facility in Manitoba. Merit's product portfolio includes three product family offerings: pea protein; non-genetically modified organism (GMO) canola protein; and MeritPro™, a unique lineup of nutritionally complete protein blends.

Patent portfolio consists of 267 issued worldwide, including 69 issued U.S. patents, and 125 additional patent applications, 19 of which are U.S. patent applications.

On May 8, 2023, the company announced that the bid submitted on Apr. 24, 2023, in cooperation with an industry plant protein company to acquire the assets of affiliate **Merit Functional Foods Corporation**, which was placed in receivership on Mar. 1, 2023, was not accepted. As a result, the company would continue to work with additional industry participants, who had interest in jointly acquiring the assets, to formulate an alternative bid.

In November 2022, joint venture **Merit Functional Foods Corporation** announced a partnership with **Konscious Foods Canada Inc.** and **Canadian Pacifico Seaweeds Ltd.** in a project co-invested by Protein Industries Canada, to develop a new line of more than 20 plant-based frozen seafood alternative products. The products would incorporate Merit's pea and canola proteins and Canadian Pacifico Seaweeds' seaweed ingredients. Konscious Foods would distribute the product line across North America to grocery stores and food service channels. A total of $15,3000,000 has been committed to the project, with Protein Industries Canada committing $5,500,000 and the partners committing the remaining $9,800,000.

On Sept. 12, 2022, common shares were delisted from the Nasdaq Capital Market in the U.S. under the symbol BRCN.

In April 2022, the company received a co-investment from Protein Industries Canada for the development of high-quality protein ingredients from sunflower seeds. The project would include the company and **Pristine Gourmet - Persall Fine Foods Co.** to further develop the company's novel process for the production of sunflower protein ingredients, with a total investment of $1,000,000.

Common delisted from NASDAQ, Sept. 12, 2022.

Predecessor Detail - Name changed from Burcon Capital Corp., Oct. 18, 1999.

Directors - Peter H. Kappel, chr., Vancouver, B.C.; Dr. D. Lorne J. Tyrrell†, Edmonton, Alta.; Alan Y. L. Chan, Hong Kong, Hong Kong, People's Republic of China; Debora S. Fang, London, Middx., United Kingdom; J. Douglas Gilpin, Edmonton, Alta.; Alfred Lau, B.C.; Jeanne McCaherty, Minn.; Aaron T. Ratner, Pa.

Other Exec. Officers - Kip Underwood, CEO; Jade Cheng, CFO & treas.; Dorothy K. T. Law, sr. v-p, legal & corp. sec.; Randy Willardsen, sr. v-p, process; Dr. Martin Schweizer, v-p, technical devel.

† Lead director

Capital Stock

	Authorized (shs.)	Outstanding (shs.)[1]
Common	unlimited	121,671,471

[1] At Aug. 2, 2023

Options - At Mar. 31, 2023, options were outstanding to purchase 7,161,803 common shares at a weighted average exercise price of $1.88 per share with a weighted average remaining contractual life of up to 5.65 years.

Major Shareholder - Alan Y. L. Chan held 21.08% interest at Aug. 2, 2023.

Price Range - BU/TSX

Year	Volume	High	Low	Close
2022	19,918,750	$1.61	$0.36	$0.39
2021	71,445,374	$5.92	$1.30	$1.49
2020	105,322,402	$3.67	$0.60	$3.44
2019	123,047,864	$1.98	$0.16	$0.97
2018	12,121,039	$0.77	$0.13	$0.17

Recent Close: $0.15

Capital Stock Changes - In May 2023, private placement of 12,880,829 units (1 common share & 1 warrant) at $0.265 per unit was completed, with warrants exercisable at 35¢ per share for three years.

There were no changes to capital stock during fiscal 2023.

During fiscal 2022, common shares were issued as follows: 191,615 on exercise of options and 105,750 on exercise of warrants.

Long-Term Debt - At Mar. 31, 2023, outstanding long-term debt totaled $5,112,381 (none current), representing the debt component of up to $10,000,000 secured loan bearing interest at 8% per annum, including $5,000,000 due July 1, 2024.

Wholly Owned Subsidiaries

Burcon NutraScience Holdings Corp., Canada.
- 31.6% int. in **Merit Functional Foods Corporation**, Canada.

Burcon NutraScience (MB) Corp., Winnipeg, Man.

Financial Statistics

Periods ended:	12m Mar. 31/23[A]		12m Mar. 31/22[□A]
	$000s	%Chg	$000s
Operating revenue	**364**	**+113**	**171**
Salaries & benefits	4,141		4,912
Research & devel. expense	1,035		(1,410)
General & admin expense	1,527		1,704
Other operating expense	946		2,049
Operating expense	**7,649**	**+5**	**7,255**
Operating income	**(7,285)**	**n.a.**	**(7,084)**
Deprec., depl. & amort	240		273
Finance income	425		434
Finance costs, gross	467		113
Investment income	(5,500)		(3,333)
Write-downs/write-offs	(12,346)[1]		nil
Pre-tax income	**(25,364)**	**n.a.**	**(10,258)**
Net income	**(25,364)**	**n.a.**	**(10,258)**
Cash & equivalent	1,457		7,001
Accounts receivable	332		200
Current assets	1,865		7,615
Long-term investments	nil		10,175
Fixed assets, net	984		859
Intangibles, net	1,255		1,255
Total assets	**9,899**	**-66**	**29,350**
Accts. pay. & accr. liabs	591		907
Current liabilities	625		1,044
Long-term debt, gross	5,112		nil
Long-term debt, net	5,112		nil
Long-term lease liabilities	24		59
Shareholders' equity	4,137		28,247
Cash from oper. activs	**(6,014)**	**n.a.**	**(5,914)**
Cash from fin. activs	4,896		174
Cash from invest. activs	(4,435)		(1,232)
Net cash position	**1,457**	**-79**	**7,001**
Capital expenditures	(360)		(52)
	$		$
Earnings per share*	(0.23)		(0.09)
Cash flow per share*	(0.06)		(0.05)
	shs		shs
No. of shs. o/s*	108,728,742		108,728,742
Avg. no. of shs. o/s*	108,728,742		108,588,454
	%		%
Net profit margin	n.m.		n.m.
Return on equity	(156.65)		(31.80)
Return on assets	(126.87)		(30.25)
No. of employees (FTEs)	24		26

* Common

□ Restated

[A] Reported in accordance with IFRS

[1] Includes $7,987,304 impairment of investment in affiliate Merit Functional Foods Corporation and $4,358,630 impairment of loans to Merit, due to Merit's assets being placed in receivership on Mar. 1, 2023.

Historical Summary
(as originally stated)

Fiscal Year	Oper. Rev.	Net Inc. Bef. Disc.	EPS*
	$000s	$000s	$
2023[A]	364	(25,364)	(0.23)
2022[A]	171	(10,258)	(0.09)
2021[A]	259	(617)	(0.01)
2020[A]	31	(4,633)	(0.06)
2019[A]	40	(4,777)	(0.11)

* Common

[A] Reported in accordance with IFRS

B.134 Butte Energy Inc.

Symbol - BEN.H **Exchange** - TSX-VEN **CUSIP** - 124102

Head Office - 3123-595 Burrard St, Vancouver, BC, V7X 1J1 **Telephone** - (604) 609-6130 **Fax** - (604) 609-6145

Email - krussell@fiorecorporation.com

Investor Relations - Kia Russell (604) 609-6130

Auditors - Davidson & Company LLP C.A., Vancouver, B.C.

Bankers - ATB Financial, Calgary, Alta.

Lawyers - Borden Ladner Gervais LLP, Calgary, Alta.

Transfer Agents - Computershare Trust Company of Canada Inc., Toronto, Ont.

Profile - (B.C. 2018; orig. Alta., 1992) Seeking new business opportunities.

Predecessor Detail - Name changed from Wavefire.com Inc., June 14, 2011.

Directors - Geir L. Liland, CEO, Richmond, B.C.; D. Jeffrey Harder, West Vancouver, B.C.; Travis Musgrave, B.C.

Other Exec. Officers - Kia Russell, CFO & corp. sec.

Capital Stock

	Authorized (shs.)	Outstanding (shs.)[1]
Class A Common	unlimited	65,662,841

[1] At May 15, 2023

Major Shareholder - Frank Giustra held 19.55% interest and Thomas (Tommy) Humphreys held 18.98% interest at Oct. 21, 2022.

Price Range - BEN.H/TSX-VEN

Year	Volume	High	Low	Close
2022	1,276,482	$0.88	$0.23	$0.30
2021	999,784	$1.30	$0.70	$0.90
2020	285,948	$1.50	$0.75	$1.20
2018	315,180	$0.50	$0.18	$0.48

Consolidation: 1-for-5 cons. in Mar. 2023

Recent Close: $0.17

Capital Stock Changes - On Mar. 9, 2023, class A common shares were consolidated on a 1-for-5 basis.

During 2022, 2,000,000 class A common shares were issued on exercise of options.

Financial Statistics

Periods ended:	12m Dec. 31/22[A]		12m Dec. 31/21[A]
	$000s	%Chg	$000s
General & admin expense	194		369
Stock-based compensation	238		nil
Operating expense	**432**	**+17**	**369**
Operating income	**(432)**	**n.a.**	**(369)**
Finance income	2		1
Write-downs/write-offs	32		7
Pre-tax income	**(398)**	**n.a.**	**(362)**
Net income	**(398)**	**n.a.**	**(362)**
Cash & equivalent	15		41
Accounts receivable	3		8
Current assets	117		150
Total assets	**117**	**-22**	**150**
Accts. pay. & accr. liabs	41		21
Current liabilities	83		95
Shareholders' equity	34		54
Cash from oper. activs	**(165)**	**n.a.**	**(406)**
Cash from fin. activs	140		200
Net cash position	**15**	**-63**	**41**
	$		$
Earnings per share*	(0.01)		(0.01)
Cash flow per share*	(0.00)		(0.01)
	shs		shs
No. of shs. o/s*	64,276,841		63,876,840
Avg. no. of shs. o/s*	63,959,032		63,739,478
	%		%
Net profit margin	n.a.		n.a.
Return on equity	(904.55)		(268.15)
Return on assets	(298.13)		(145.09)

* Cl.A com.

[A] Reported in accordance with IFRS

Latest Results

Periods ended:	3m Mar. 31/23[A]		3m Mar. 31/22[A]
	$000s	%Chg	$000s
Net income	(44)	n.a.	(42)
	$		$
Earnings per share*	(0.00)		(0.00)

* Cl.A com.

[A] Reported in accordance with IFRS

Historical Summary
(as originally stated)

Fiscal Year	Oper. Rev.	Net Inc. Bef. Disc.	EPS*
	$000s	$000s	$
2022[A]	nil	(398)	(0.01)
2021[A]	nil	(362)	(0.01)
2020[A]	nil	(935)	(0.02)
2019[A]	nil	(171)	(0.00)
2018[A]	nil	(190)	(0.00)

* Cl.A com.

[A] Reported in accordance with IFRS

Note: Adjusted throughout for 1-for-5 cons. in Mar. 2023

B.135 Buzz Capital Inc.

Symbol - BUZ.P **Exchange** - TSX-VEN **CUSIP** - 12429L

Head Office - 300-116 Albert St, Ottawa, ON, K1P 5G3 **Telephone** - (613) 366-3631

Email - gprekupec@dipchand.com

Investor Relations - Gregory M. Prekupec (416) 504-5805

Auditors - MNP LLP C.A., Toronto, Ont.

Lawyers - Sui & Company, Toronto, Ont.

Transfer Agents - TSX Trust Company, Toronto, Ont.

Profile - (Can. 2017) Capital Pool Company.

Common reinstated on TSX-VEN, Aug. 11, 2023.

Recent Merger and Acquisition Activity

Status: terminated **Revised:** Apr. 17, 2023

UPDATE: The transaction was terminated. PREVIOUS: Buzz Capital Inc. entered into a letter of intent for the Qualifying Transaction reverse takeover acquisition of private Toronto, Ont.-based Grata Technologies Inc., which develops a tenant engagement software platform and a smart lock system to enhance the living of multi-family residents, on a share-for-share basis (following a 1-for-29.94012 share consolidation). Prior to completion, Grata would complete a private placement at $6.14 per share for gross proceeds of a minimum of $10,000,000. Upon completion, Buzz would change its name to Grata Technologies Inc.

Directors - Gregory M. Prekupec, CEO & CFO, Ont.; Lorne Gertner, Toronto, Ont.; James W. Longshore, Nassau, Bahamas; W. Brett Wilson, Calgary, Alta.

Other Exec. Officers - Brian MacIntosh, corp. sec.

Capital Stock

	Authorized (shs.)	Outstanding (shs.)[1]
Common	unlimited	8,409,999

[1] At May 22, 2023

Major Shareholder - Widely held at Oct. 11, 2022.

Price Range - BUZ.P/TSX-VEN

Year	Volume	High	Low	Close
2019.............	1,015,570	$0.29	$0.11	$0.11
2018.............	1,577,745	$0.73	$0.18	$0.22

Recent Close: $0.08

Capital Stock Changes - There were no changes to capital stock from 2020 to 2022, inclusive.

B.136 Buzz Capital 2 Inc.

Symbol - BUZH.P **Exchange** - TSX-VEN **CUSIP** - 12430G
Head Office - 300-116 Albert St, Ottawa, ON, K1P 5G3 **Telephone** - (613) 239-0531
Email - patrick@terrahive.com
Investor Relations - Patrick M. Lalonde (613) 366-4242
Auditors - MNP LLP C.A., Toronto, Ont.
Lawyers - Sui & Company, Toronto, Ont.
Transfer Agents - TSX Trust Company, Toronto, Ont.
Profile - (Can. 2018) Capital Pool Company.

Recent Merger and Acquisition Activity

Status: terminated **Revised:** Nov. 10, 2022

UPDATE: The transaction was terminated. PREVIOUS: Buzz Capital 2 Inc. entered into a letter of intent for the Qualifying Transaction reverse takeover acquisition of private Sault Ste. Marie, Ont.-based Heliene Inc., which manufactures solar modules for the commercial and residential markets, on a share-for-share basis, which would result in the issuance of 79,381,265 Buzz 2 post-consolidated common shares (following a 1-for-5.8714 share consolidation). In conjunction, Heliene would complete a concurrent financing of $35,000,000 to $45,000,000 of subscription receipts at $1.00 per receipt; each subscription receipt would automatically be converted into 1 Buzz 2 unit (1 common share & 1 warrant) upon completion of the transaction, with warrants exercsiable at $1.25 per share for two years. Dec. 15, 2021 - The parties entered into a definitive agreement. Upon completion, Heliene would amalgamate with Buzz 2's wholly owned 1000047668 Ontario Inc., and Buzz 2's incorporation would be continued into Ontario from Canada. Apr. 18, 2022 - The parties extended the outside closing date of transaction to Oct. 31, 2022, and announced that the closing of the private placement of subscription receipts has been postponed.

Directors - Patrick M. Lalonde, pres., CEO & CFO, Ottawa, Ont.; Lorne Gertner, Toronto, Ont.; Charles (Chuck) Rifici, Ottawa, Ont.; W. Brett Wilson, Calgary, Alta.

Other Exec. Officers - Hugo M. Alves, corp. sec.

Capital Stock

	Authorized (shs.)	Outstanding (shs.)[1]
Common	unlimited	8,220,000

[1] At May 22, 2023

Major Shareholder - Widely held at Oct. 11, 2022.

Price Range - BUZH.P/TSX-VEN

Year	Volume	High	Low	Close
2021.............	9,000	$0.13	$0.13	$0.13
2020.............	176,500	$0.14	$0.06	$0.12
2019.............	365,400	$0.20	$0.10	$0.10
2018.............	123,650	$0.25	$0.12	$0.18

Recent Close: $0.05

Capital Stock Changes - There were no changes to capital stock from 2019 to 2022, inclusive.

C

C.1 C-COM Satellite Systems Inc.

Symbol - CMI **Exchange** - TSX-VEN **CUSIP** - 125009
Head Office - 2574 Sheffield Rd, Ottawa, ON, K1B 3V7 **Telephone** - (613) 745-4110 **Toll-free** - (877) 463-8886 **Fax** - (613) 745-7144
Website - www.c-comsat.com
Email - lklein@c-comsat.com
Investor Relations - Dr. Leslie Klein (877) 463-8886
Auditors - Welch LLP C.A., Ottawa, Ont.
Bankers - Bank of Montreal
Lawyers - LaBarge Weinstein LLP, Ottawa, Ont.
Transfer Agents - Computershare Trust Company of Canada Inc., Toronto, Ont.
Profile - (Can. 1997) Develops, manufactures and designs commercial grade, mobile auto-deploying satellite-based technology for the delivery of two-way high-speed Internet, Voice over Internet Protocol (VoIP) and video services into vehicles globally.

The company's proprietary fully motorized, auto-deploying iNetVu® mobile antennas deliver high-speed satellite-based Internet services to remote locations and transportable platforms which are sold to the oil and gas, military communications, disaster management, satellite news gathering, emergency communications, cellular backhaul, telemedicine, mobile education, government services, mobile banking, mobile office and other vertical markets. iNetVu® mobile products, which are available in Ka-band, Ku-band, C-band and X-band, include driveaways, flyaways, manpack versions as well as fixed motorized antennas complete with controllers and accessories.

Directors - Dr. Leslie Klein, pres. & CEO, Ottawa, Ont.; Eli Fathi, Ottawa, Ont.; Ronald A. (Ron) Leslie, Ottawa, Ont.; Dr. Arunas Slekys, Redondo Beach, Calif.
Other Exec. Officers - Art Slaughter, CFO; Bilal Awada, chief tech. officer; Shane McLean, corp. sec.

Capital Stock

	Authorized (shs.)	Outstanding (shs.)[1]
Common	unlimited	40,741,400

[1] At Apr. 18, 2023

Major Shareholder - Dr. Leslie Klein held 37.9% interest at Mar. 20, 2023.

Price Range - CMI/TSX-VEN

Year	Volume	High	Low	Close
2022	1,146,797	$2.42	$1.13	$1.34
2021	3,875,297	$4.48	$1.96	$2.42
2020	8,482,601	$3.39	$1.52	$2.69
2019	4,310,941	$1.98	$1.10	$1.68
2018	2,347,530	$1.30	$0.98	$1.18

Recent Close: $0.95
Capital Stock Changes - During fiscal 2022, 1,045,000 common shares were issued on exercise of options.

Dividends

CMI com Ra $0.05 pa Q est. Nov. 13, 2013

Financial Statistics

Periods ended:	12m Nov. 30/22[A]		12m Nov. 30/21[A]
	$000s	%Chg	$000s
Operating revenue	**11,645**	**+27**	**9,152**
Cost of sales	5,805		3,650
Research & devel. expense	909		743
General & admin expense	2,908		2,145
Stock-based compensation	588		625
Operating expense	**10,210**	**+43**	**7,162**
Operating income	**1,435**	**-28**	**1,990**
Deprec., depl. & amort.	26		33
Investment income	181		95
Pre-tax income	**1,867**	**-11**	**2,101**
Income taxes	728		678
Net income	**1,140**	**-20**	**1,423**
Cash & equivalent	18,851		17,074
Inventories	6,718		7,735
Accounts receivable	1,080		1,277
Current assets	26,794		26,281
Fixed assets, net	75		58
Intangibles, net	1		3
Total assets	**26,870**	**+2**	**26,342**
Accts. pay. & accr. liabs	1,123		1,410
Current liabilities	1,427		1,683
Shareholders' equity	25,218		24,529
Cash from oper. activs	**3,127**	**+25**	**2,506**
Cash from fin. activs	(1,038)		(334)
Cash from invest. activs	(570)		(121)
Net cash position	**10,131**	**+14**	**8,883**
Capital expenditures	(40)		(5)
	$		$
Earnings per share*	0.03		0.04
Cash flow per share*	0.08		0.06
Cash divd. per share*	0.05		0.05
	shs		shs
No. of shs. o/s*	41,786,400		40,741,400
Avg. no. of shs. o/s*	41,144,414		40,087,485
	%		%
Net profit margin	9.79		15.55
Return on equity	4.58		6.07
Return on assets	4.28		5.71
Foreign sales percent	99		99

* Common
[A] Reported in accordance with IFRS

Latest Results

Periods ended:	3m Feb. 28/23[A]		3m Feb. 28/22[A]
	$000s	%Chg	$000s
Operating revenue	684	-77	3,000
Net income	(176)	n.a.	594
	$		$
Earnings per share*	(0.00)		0.01

* Common
[A] Reported in accordance with IFRS

Historical Summary
(as originally stated)

Fiscal Year	Oper. Rev.	Net Inc. Bef. Disc.	EPS*
	$000s	$000s	$
2022[A]	11,645	1,140	0.03
2021[A]	9,152	1,423	0.04
2020[A]	6,456	(95)	(0.00)
2019[A]	13,978	2,843	0.08
2018[A]	13,527	2,300	0.06

* Common
[A] Reported in accordance with IFRS

C.2 C21 Investments Inc.

Symbol - CXXI **Exchange** - CSE **CUSIP** - 12675Q
Head Office - 170-601 Cordova St W, PO Box 107, Vancouver, BC, V6B 1G1 **Telephone** - (604) 336-8613 **Toll-free** - (833) 289-2994 **Fax** - (604) 718-2808
Website - www.cxxi.ca
Email - michael.kidd@cxxi.ca
Investor Relations - Michael Kidd (604) 908-3095
Auditors - Marcum LLP C.P.A., San Jose, Calif.
Transfer Agents - Continental Stock Transfer & Trust Company, New York, N.Y.; Computershare Trust Company of Canada Inc., Vancouver, B.C.
Employees - 110 at Jan. 31, 2023
Profile - (B.C. 1987) Cultivates, processes, distributes and sells cannabis and hemp-derived consumer products in Nevada.

Operates cultivation and processing operations include a 104,000-sq.-ft. indoor cultivation and processing facility in Sparks, Nev., with 37,000 sq. ft. used for cultivation and 1,200 sq. ft. dedicated for extraction. Products are sold through the company's two dispensaries in Sparks and Fernley, Nev., operating under the Silver State Relief name, as well as through wholesale channels. Products include flower, vaporizer pens, cured extracts, edibles and pre-rolls which are marketed under the brands Phantom Farms, Hood Oil and Silver State Relief. The company's remaining assets in Oregon, including facilities, licenses and equipments, are all held for sale.

In March 2023, the company terminated the lease-to-own arrangement for certain licences, land and equipment in southern Oregon. As part of the settlement agreement, the lessee paid $500,000 as consideration for two Oregon Liquor and Cannabis Commission recreational cannabis production licences. The company retained the land, building and equipment, which were being listed for sale.

In April 2022, the company agreed to sell certain assets including indoor production, wholesale and processing license as well as certain nominal equipment in Bend, Ore., for US$87,500.

In March 2022, the company terminated its management agreement with the third party whereby the third party commenced operating its 10,000-sq.-ft. extraction facility; adjacent 5,000-sq.-ft. wholesale distribution warehouse; dispensary (Pure Green) in Portland; and its 23,000-sq.-ft. indoor cultivation facility in Clackamas cty., Ore. The third party assumed all leasehold liabilities and costs at the facilities. The company ceased its processing and wholesale operations in Portland, Ore. at April 2020.

Common reinstated on CSE, June 16, 2023.
Common suspended from CSE, June 7, 2023.
Predecessor Detail - Name changed from Curlew Lake Resources Inc., Nov. 24, 2017.
Directors - D. Bruce Macdonald, chr., West Vancouver, B.C.; Michael Kidd, CFO & corp. sec., Richmond, B.C.; Todd Harrison, N.Y.; Leonard (Len) Werden, Vancouver, B.C.
Other Exec. Officers - Sonny Newman, pres. & CEO

Capital Stock

	Authorized (shs.)	Outstanding (shs.)[1]
Common	unlimited	120,047,814

[1] At June 29, 2023

Major Shareholder - Sonny Newman held 10.4% interest at May 31, 2023.

Price Range - CXXI/CSE

Year	Volume	High	Low	Close
2022	18,388,754	$0.81	$0.25	$0.26
2021	53,080,528	$2.59	$0.59	$0.64
2020	38,521,266	$1.95	$0.23	$1.77
2019	122,194,449	$2.52	$0.45	$0.74
2018	38,760,430	$3.00	$0.62	$0.78

Recent Close: $0.32
Capital Stock Changes - There were no changes to capital stock during fiscal 2023.

Wholly Owned Subsidiaries

320204 US Holdings Corp., Del.
- 100% int. in **Eco Firma Farms LLC**, Ore.
- 100% int. in **320204 Nevada Holdings Corp.**, Nev.
  - 100% int. in **Silver State Cultivation LLC**, Nev.
  - 100% int. in **Silver State Relief LLC**, Nev.
- 100% int. in **320204 Oregon Holdings Corp.**, Ore.
  - 100% int. in **Phantom Brands LLC**, Portland, Ore.
  - 100% int. in **Phantom Venture Group, LLC**, Portland, Ore.
    - 100% int. in **4964 BFH, LLC**, Ore.
    - 100% int. in **Phantom Distribution, LLC**, Ore.
    - 100% int. in **63353 Bend, LLC**, Ore.
    - 100% int. in **20727-4 Bend, LLC**, Ore.
- 100% int. in **320204 RE Holdings, LLC**, Ore.
- 100% int. in **Workforce Concepts 21, Inc.**, Ore.

Note: The preceding list includes only the major related companies in which interests are held.

Financial Statistics

Periods ended:	12m Jan. 31/23[A]		12m Jan. 31/22[o][A]
	US$000s	%Chg	US$000s
Operating revenue	**28,888**	**-12**	**32,983**
Cost of sales	15,487		14,173
Salaries & benefits	2,747		2,914
General & admin expense	5,124		4,494
Stock-based compensation	209		366
Operating expense	**23,568**	**+7**	**21,948**
Operating income	**5,320**	**-52**	**11,035**
Deprec., depl. & amort.	1,365		1,280
Finance costs, gross	457		1,308
Write-downs/write-offs	(21)		nil
Pre-tax income	**4,191**	**-76**	**17,132**
Income taxes	2,810		4,935
Net inc. bef. disc. opers	**1,382**	**-89**	**12,198**
Income from disc. opers	(1,088)		(2,243)
Net income	**293**	**-97**	**9,955**
Cash & equivalent	1,892		3,068
Inventories	4,174		4,054
Accounts receivable	412		210
Current assets	8,742		10,284
Fixed assets, net	4,685		4,870
Right-of-use assets	8,386		8,875
Intangibles, net	36,428		37,765
Total assets	**58,311**	**-6**	**61,844**
Accts. pay. & accr. liabs	2,921		2,509
Current liabilities	14,974		15,974
Long-term debt, gross	3,183		9,388
Long-term debt, net	3,183		2,027
Long-term lease liabilities	8,555		8,953
Shareholders' equity	34,315		33,729
Cash from oper. activs	**5,900**	**-14**	**6,836**
Cash from fin. activs	(6,684)		(7,845)
Cash from invest. activs	(391)		(1,394)
Net cash position	**1,892**	**-38**	**3,068**
Capital expenditures	(442)		(2,562)
	US$		US$
Earns. per sh. bef disc opers*	0.01		0.10
Earnings per share*	0.00		0.08
Cash flow per share*	0.05		0.06
	shs		shs
No. of shs. o/s*	120,047,814		120,047,814
Avg. no. of shs. o/s*	120,047,814		118,308,584
	%		%
Net profit margin	4.78		36.98
Return on equity	3.99		41.30
Return on assets	2.55		20.10
Foreign sales percent	100		100
No. of employees (FTEs)	110		142

* Common

[o] Restated

[A] Reported in accordance with U.S. GAAP

Latest Results

Periods ended:	3m Apr. 30/23[A]		3m Apr. 30/22[A]
	US$000s	%Chg	US$000s
Operating revenue	7,692	+3	7,472
Net inc. bef. disc. opers	(387)	n.a.	1,037
Income from disc. opers	(84)		(730)
Net income	(471)	n.a.	307
	US$		US$
Earns. per sh. bef. disc. opers.*	(0.00)		0.01
Earnings per share*	(0.00)		0.01

* Common

[A] Reported in accordance with U.S. GAAP

Historical Summary
(as originally stated)

Fiscal Year	Oper. Rev.	Net Inc. Bef. Disc.	EPS*
	US$000s	US$000s	US$
2023[A]	28,888	1,382	0.01
2022[A]	32,983	13,159	0.11
2021[B]	36,127	(6,106)	(0.06)
2020[B]	37,705	(32,556)	(0.42)
2019[B]	2,586	(23,601)	(0.77)

* Common

[A] Reported in accordance with U.S. GAAP

[B] Reported in accordance with IFRS

C.3 CAE Inc.*

Symbol - CAE **Exchange** - TSX **CUSIP** - 124765

Head Office - 8585 ch de la Côte-de-Liesse, Saint-Laurent, QC, H4T 1G6 **Telephone** - (514) 341-6780 **Toll-free** - (800) 564-6253 **Fax** - (514) 340-5530

Website - www.cae.com

Email - andrew.arnovitz@cae.com

Investor Relations - Andrew C. Arnovitz (866) 999-6223

Auditors - PricewaterhouseCoopers LLP C.A., Montréal, Qué.

Lawyers - Norton Rose Fulbright Canada LLP, Montréal, Qué.

Transfer Agents - Computershare Trust Company of Canada Inc., Montréal, Qué.

FP500 Revenue Ranking - 161

Employees - 13,000 at Mar. 31, 2023

Profile - (Can. 1947) Provides integrated training services and simulation and modelling technologies for the civil aviation, defence and security and healthcare industries worldwide. Trains civil and defence crew members and healthcare professionals annually through a network of 250 sites and training locations in more than 40 countries.

Operations are carried out through three segments: Civil Aviation Training Solutions; Defence and Security; and Healthcare.

Civil Aviation Training Solutions - Provides comprehensive training services and products for flight, cabin, maintenance and ground personnel in commercial, business and helicopter aviation; flight simulation training equipment including full-flight simulators; ab initio pilot training; crew sourcing services, and aircraft flight operations software products and services. Customers include major commercial airlines, regional airlines, business aircraft operators, civil helicopter operators, aircraft manufacturers, third-party training centres, flight training organizations, maintenance repair and overhaul organizations, and aircraft finance leasing companies. The training network includes 70 training centres and more than 324 full-flight simulators.

Defence and Security - Offers training, and mission and operational support products and services across multi-domain operations including air, land, maritime, space and cyber domains. Customers include defence forces, original equipment manufacturers, government agencies and public safety organizations. These customers are served through more than 145 locations across the United States, Canada, the United Kingdom, Germany, Middle East, India, Australia and New Zealand.

Healthcare - Offers integrated simulation-based education and training solutions to healthcare students and clinical professionals. These solutions include interventional and imaging simulations, curricula, mixed-reality and digital learning, audiovisual debriefing solutions, centre management platforms and patient simulators. Customers include hospital and university simulation centres, medical and nursing schools, paramedic organizations, defence forces, medical societies, public health agencies and original equipment manufacturers.

Manufacturing and assembly facilities are located in Montreal, Que.; Tampa and Sarasota, Fla.; Arlington, Tex.; and Stolberg, Germany.

In June 2023, the company was awarded a contract to provide critical flight training to U.S. Air Force (USAF) student pilots as part of the Helicopter Training Next program. The US$44,500,000 initial contract award supports the training of all initial USAF rotary-wing air, ground and simulation training. The program extends through 2033 with a maximum value of US$110,600,000 over the total contract term.

In May 2023, the company was awarded a 12-year US$455,000,000 contract from **General Dynamics Information Technology** to support Flight School Training Support Services at Fort Novosel, Ala. Under the terms of the contract, the company would build and deliver new full-flight simulators for the CH-47F and UH-60M platforms to meet the U.S. Army Aviation Center of Excellence's rotary-wing simulation services requirements. In addition to owning and operating the new training devices, the company would also implement CH-47F and UH-60M software configurations for reconfigurable collective training devices.

On Mar. 30, 2023, the company formed a joint venture with **AEGEAN**, Greece's largest airline, to establish AEGEAN CAE Flight Training Centre, an advanced flight training center in Athens, Greece. With a capacity for up to seven full-flight simulators, the training centre would be part of AEGEAN's new 85,000 m^2 technical base at Athens International Airport.

On Mar. 28, 2023, the company and **Chorus Aviation Inc.** launched **Cygnet Aviation Academy LP**, a pilot academy in Kingston, Ont. which offers integrated airline transport pilot license (ATPL) and airline-specific rating training programs and simulations for cadet pilots.

In January 2023, the company was awarded a contract by the United States Army to provide comprehensive initial and recurrent training for more than 600 U.S. Army and U.S. Air Force fixed-wing pilots annually. The firm-fixed-price award has an approximate total value of US$250,000,000 through 2032 distributed from an initial base period and seven single-year options. The company has provided Army Fixed-Wing training at its Dothan Training Center in Alabama since the initial contract award in 2016.

In August 2022, the company entered into a 15-year agreement with the **Qantas Group**, to develop and operate a new state-of-the-art pilot training centre in Sydney, Australia.

During fiscal 2022, subsidiary **Asian Aviation Centre of Excellence (Singapore) Pte Ltd.**, and wholly owned **CAE Beteiligungsgesellschaft mbH, CAE Machinery Ltd., CAE Railway Ltd., CAE Training Aircraft B.V., CAE Wood Products G.P.** and **Logitude OY** were dissolved.

Recent Merger and Acquisition Activity

Status: completed **Revised:** Mar. 1, 2022

UPDATE: The transaction was completed. PREVIOUS: CAE Inc. agreed to acquire Sabre Corporation's AirCentre airline operations portfolio for US$392,500,000. The transaction was expected to be completed in the first quarter of calendar 2022 and was subject to customary conditions and regulatory approvals. The acquisition includes the Sabre Airline Operations product portfolio which is a suite of flight and crew management and optimization solutions, related technology and intellectual property, as well as the transfer of workforce.

Predecessor Detail - Name changed from CAE Industries Ltd., Sept. 15, 1993.

Directors - Alan N. MacGibbon, chr., Toronto, Ont.; Marc Parent, pres. & CEO, Montréal, Qué.; Ayman Antoun, Oakville, Ont.; Margaret S. (Peg) Billson, Albuquerque, N.M.; Sophie Brochu, Bromont, Qué.; Elise Eberwein, Scottsdale, Ariz.; Marianne Harrison, Boston, Mass.; Mary Lou Maher, Toronto, Ont.; François Olivier, Montréal, Qué.; Gen. (ret.) David G. Perkins, Jackson, N.H.; Michael E. Roach, Montréal, Qué.; Patrick M. Shanahan, Seattle, Wash.; Andrew J. Stevens, Cheltenham, Gloucs., United Kingdom

Other Exec. Officers - Abha Dogra, chief tech. & product officer; Mark Hounsell, chief compliance officer, gen. counsel & corp. sec.; Bob Lockett, chief people officer; Daniel Gelston, grp. pres., defence & security & pres. & gen. mgr., CAE USA Inc.; Nick Leontidis, grp. pres., civil aviation; Sonya Branco, exec. v-p, fin. & CFO; Andrew C. Arnovitz, sr. v-p, IR & enterprise risk mgt.; Carter Copeland, sr. v-p, global strategy; Hélène V. Gagnon, sr. v-p, stakeholder engagement & chief sustainability officer; Pascal Grenier, sr. v-p, flight srvcs. & global opers.; Jeff Evans, pres., healthcare

Capital Stock

	Authorized (shs.)	Outstanding (shs.)[1]
Preferred	unlimited	nil
Common	unlimited	318,135,978

[1] At July 31, 2023

Options - At Mar. 31, 2023, options were outstanding to purchase 6,323,537 common shares at prices ranging from $16.15 to $38.01 per share with a weighted remaining contractual life of 3.44 years.

Major Shareholder - Widely held at June 15, 2023.

Price Range - CAE/TSX

Year	Volume	High	Low	Close
2022	174,838,382	$35.47	$20.90	$26.19
2021	176,135,618	$42.43	$27.72	$31.91
2020	235,617,601	$42.00	$14.26	$35.27
2019	128,569,366	$36.86	$24.64	$34.38
2018	131,886,776	$28.15	$21.12	$25.09

Recent Close: $31.79

Capital Stock Changes - During fiscal 2023, 882,167 common shares were issued on exercise of options.

On July 2, 2021, 22,400,000 common shares were issued without further consideration on exchange of subscription receipts sold previously by private placement at $31.25 each. Also during fiscal 2022, 1,268,660 common shares were issued on exercise of options.

Long-Term Debt - Outstanding at Mar. 31, 2023:

Revolv. credit facilities due 2027	$433,000,000
Term loans due 2023-2028	564,400,000
Sr. notes due 2024-2034[1]	1,300,700,000
R&D obligs. due 2023-2042[2]	496,100,000
Lease liabs	455,900,000
	3,250,100,000
Less: Current portion	214,600,000
	3,035,500,000

[1] Bearing interest rates ranging from 3.6% to 4.9%.

[2] Interest-bearing and non-interest-bearing obligations with the Governments of Canada and Quebec relative to R&D programs.

Note - In June 2023, private placement of $400,000,000 5.541% series 1 senior unsecured notes due on June 12, 2028, was completed.

Wholly Owned Subsidiaries

Advanced Medical Technologies, LLC, Wash.
Asian Aviation Centre of Excellence (Singapore) Pte Ltd., Singapore.
Aviation Personnel Support Services Limited, Ireland.
CAE Academia de Aviación España, S.L., Spain.
CAE Australia Pty Ltd., Australia.
CAE Aviation Services Pte. Ltd., Singapore.
CAE Aviation Training Australia Pty Ltd., Australia.
CAE Aviation Training B.V., Netherlands.
CAE Aviation Training Chile Limitada, Chile.
CAE Aviation Training International Ltd, Mauritius.
CAE Aviation Training Peru S.A., Peru.
CAE BC ULC, B.C.
CAE Bangkok Co., Limited, Bangkok, Thailand.
CAE Beyss Grundstücksgesellschaft GmbH, Germany.
CAE CFT B.V., Netherlands.
CAE CFT Holdings B.V., Netherlands.
CAE CFT Korea Ltd., South Korea.
CAE Center Amsterdam B.V., Netherlands.
CAE Center Brussels N.V., Belgium.
CAE Centre Copenhagen A/S, Denmark.
CAE Centre Hong Kong Limited, Hong Kong, People's Republic of China.
CAE Centre Oslo AS, Norway.
CAE Centre Stockholm AB, Sweden.
CAE Civil Aviation Training Solutions Inc., Fla.
CAE Colombia Flight Training S.A.S., Bogota, Colombia.
CAE Crew Solutions B.V., Netherlands.
CAE Crewing Services Limited, Ireland.
CAE Delaware Buyco Inc., Del.
CAE Digital Inc., Canada.
CAE Doss Aviation Inc., Tex.
CAE El Salvador Flight Training S.A. de C.V., El Salvador.
CAE Elektronik GmbH, Germany.
- 50% int. in **ARGE Rheinmetall Defence Electronics GmbH**, Germany.

CAE Engineering Kft., Hungary.
CAE Flight & Simulator Services Sdn. Bhd., Malaysia.
CAE Flight Services Austria GmbH, Austria.
CAE Flight Services New Zealand Limited, New Zealand.
CAE Flight Services Poland Sp z.o.o., Poland.
CAE Flight Services Sweden AB, Sweden.
CAE Flight Services USA, Inc., Del.
CAE Flight Services Uruguay S.A., Uruguay.

CAE Flight Solutions USA Inc., Del.
CAE Flight Training Center Mexico, S.A. de C.V., Mexico.
CAE Flight Training (India) Private Limited, Bangalore, India.
CAE France SAS, France.
CAE GAH Aviation Technology Services Co. Ltd., People's Republic of China.
CAE Global Academy Évora, S.A., Portugal.
CAE GmbH, Germany.
CAE Healthcare Canada Inc., Canada.
CAE Healthcare GmbH, Germany.
CAE Healthcare Inc., Del.
CAE Healthcare Kft., Hungary.
CAE Holdings B.V., Netherlands.
CAE Holdings Limited, United Kingdom.
CAE India Private Limited, Bangalore, India.
CAE Integrated Enterprise Solutions Australia Pty Ltd., Australia.
CAE International Holdings Limited, Saint-Laurent, Qué.
CAE Investments S.A.R.L., Luxembourg.
CAE Japan Flight Training Inc., Japan.
CAE Kuala Lumpur Sdn. Bhd., Malaysia.
CAE Luxembourg Acquisition, S.A.R.L., Luxembourg.
CAE Management Hungary Kft., Hungary.
CAE Military Aviation Training Inc., Canada.
CAE New Zealand Pty Limited, New Zealand.
CAE North East Training Inc., Del.
CAE Oslo - Aviation Academy AS, Oslo, Norway.
CAE Oxford Aviation Academy Amsterdam B.V., Netherlands.
CAE Oxford Aviation Academy Phoenix Inc., Ariz.
CAE Parc Aviation Jersey Limited, Jersey.
CAE STS Limited, United Kingdom.
CAE Screenplates S.A., France.
CAE Services GmbH, Germany.
CAE Services Italia, S.r.l., Italy.
CAE Servicios Globales de Instrucción de Vuelo (España) S.L., Spain.
CAE Shanghai Company, Limited, Shanghai, Shanghai, People's Republic of China.
CAE SimuFlite Inc., Dallas, Tex.
CAE Simulation Technologies Private Limited, India.
CAE Simulator Services Inc., Qué.
CAE Singapore (S.E.A.) Pte. Ltd., Singapore, Singapore.
CAE South America Flight Training do Brasil Ltda., Brazil.
CAE TSP Inc., Canada.
CAE Training & Services Brussels N.V., Belgium.
CAE Training & Services UK Ltd., United Kingdom.
CAE Training Norway AS, Norway.
CAE (UK) plc, United Kingdom.
CAE US Capital LLC, Del.
CAE US Capital Management LLC, Del.
CAE US Finance GP LLC, Del.
CAE US Finance LP, Del.
CAE (US) Inc., Del.
CAE US Management LLC, Del.
CAE USA Inc., Del.
CAE Verwaltungsgesellschaft mbH, Germany.
CAE Vietnam Limited Liability Company, Vietnam.
ETOPS (AS) UK Limited, United Kingdom.
ETOPS Aviation Services Malaysia Sdn. Bhd., Malaysia.
ETOPS SAS, France.
Flight Training Device (Mauritius) Limited, Mauritius.
Flightline Data Services, Inc., Ga.
GCAT Flight Academy Germany GmbH, Germany.
GCAT Flight Academy Malta Ltd., Malta.
International Flight School (Mauritius) Ltd., Mauritius.
Invertron Simulators plc, Sussex, United Kingdom.
iRIS Health Solutions Limited, United Kingdom.
Medicor Lab Inc., Qué.
Merlot Aero Inc., Del.
Merlot Aero International Limited, New Zealand.
Merlot Aero Ventures Limited, New Zealand.
9595058 Canada Inc., Canada.
Oxford Airline Training Center Inc., Ariz.
Oxford Aviation Academy Europe AB, Sweden.
Oxford Aviation Academy European Holdings AB, Sweden.
Oxford Aviation Academy Finance Ltd., Ireland.
Oxford Aviation Academy Ireland Holdings Ltd., Ireland.
Oxford Aviation Academy Norway Holdings AS, Norway.
Oxford Aviation Academy (Oxford) Limited, United Kingdom.
Parc Aviation Engineering Services Limited, Ireland.
Parc Aviation International Limited, Ireland.
Parc Aviation Japan Limited, Japan.
Parc Aviation Limited, Ireland.
Parc Aviation Services Limited, Isle of Man.
Parc Aviation Training Limited, Ireland.
Parc Aviation (UK) Limited, United Kingdom.
Parc Interim Limited, Ireland.
Parc Selection Limited, Isle of Man.
Parc U.S. Inc., Del.
Pegasus Uçus Egitim Merkezi A.S., Türkiye.
Pelesys Aviation Maintenance Training Inc., B.C.
Pelesys Learning Systems Inc., Vancouver, B.C.
Presagis Canada Inc., Saint-Laurent, Qué.
Presagis Europe (S.A.), France.
Presagis USA Inc., Calif.
RB Aero Development Services India Private Limited, India.
SIM-Industries Brasil Administração de Centros de Treinamento Ltda., Brazil.
Sim-Industries Production B.V., Netherlands.
Simubel N.V., Belgium.
Simulator Servicios Mexico, S.A. de C.V., Mexico.

Subsidiaries

76.5% int. in **CAE Aircrew Training Services plc**, United Kingdom.
60% int. in **CAE Brunei Multi Purpose Training Centre Sdn. Bhd.**, Brunei.
51% int. in **National Flying Training Institute Private Limited**, India.
80% int. in **SIV Ops Training, S.L.**, Spain.
80% int. in **Servicios de Instrucción de Vuelo, S.L.**, Spain.

Investments

50% int. in **Aviation Training Northeast Asia B.V.**, Netherlands.
50% int. in **CAE Aircraft Maintenance Pty Ltd.**, Australia.
50% int. in **CAE Arabia LLC**, Saudi Arabia.
50% int. in **CAE Austria**, Germany.
50% int. in **CAE Defence Solutions Middle East LLC**, Qatar.
50% int. in **CAE Flight and Simulator Services Korea Ltd.**, South Korea.
33.34% int. in **CAE Icelandair Flight Training ehf.**, Iceland.
50% int. in **CAE-LÍDER Training do Brasil Ltda.**, Brazil.
49% int. in **CAE Maritime Middle East LLC**, United Arab Emirates.
50% int. in **CAE Melbourne Flight Training Pty Ltd.**, Australia.
50% int. in **CAE Middle East Holdings Limited**, Dubai, United Arab Emirates.
49% int. in **CAE Middle East L.L.C.**, United Arab Emirates.
49% int. in **CAE Middle East Pilot Services LLC**, United Arab Emirates.
50% int. in **CAE Simulation Training Private Limited**, Greater Noida, India.
13.39% int. in **CVS Leasing Limited**, United Kingdom.
14.26% int. in **China Southern West Australia Flying College Pty Ltd.**, Australia.
49% int. in **Embraer CAE Training Services, LLC**, Del.
49% int. in **Emirates-CAE Flight Training LLC**, United Arab Emirates.
12% int. in **Eurofighter Simulation Systems GmbH**, Germany.
50% int. in **Flight Training Alliance GmbH**, Germany.
50% int. in **HATSOFF Helicopter Training Private Limited**, India.
25% int. in **HFTS Helicopter Flight Training Services GmbH**, Germany.
50% int. in **Helicopter Training Media International GmbH**, Germany.
50% int. in **JAL CAE Flight Training Co. Ltd.**, Japan.
49% int. in **KVDB Flight Training Services, Inc.**, Ariz.
50% int. in **Leonardo CAE Advanced Jet Training Sr.l.**, Italy.
50% int. in **Oxford Aviation Academy (Australia) Pty Ltd.**, Australia.
50% int. in **Oxford Aviation Academy Holdings Pty Ltd.**, Australia.
49% int. in **PTC Solutions JV, LLC**, Wis.
40% int. in **Philippine Academy for Aviation Training Inc.**, Philippines.
50% int. in **Rotorsim S.r.l.**, Italy.
50% int. in **Rotorsim USA LLC**, Del.
50% int. in **SIMCOM Holdings, Inc.**, Orlando, Fla.
34% int. in **Sabena Flight Academy - Africa**, South Africa.
50% int. in **SimCom Inc.**, Fla.
50% int. in **SimCom International Inc.**, Fla.
50% int. in **Singapore CAE Flight Training Pte. Ltd.**, Singapore.
50% int. in **SkyAlyne Canada Inc.**, Canada.
37% int. in **SkyWarrior Flight Training LLC**, Pensacola, Fla.
49% int. in **Xebec Government Services, LLC**, Del.

Financial Statistics

Periods ended:	12m Mar. 31/23^A		12m Mar. 31/22^¤A
	$000s	%Chg	$000s
Operating revenue	**4,203,300**	**+25**	**3,371,300**
Cost of sales	2,735,100		2,147,600
Research & devel. expense	114,100		89,700
General & admin expense	549,600		477,900
Operating expense	**3,398,800**	**+25**	**2,715,200**
Operating income	**804,500**	**+23**	**656,100**
Deprec., depl. & amort.	342,200		310,500
Finance income	13,400		12,800
Finance costs, gross	191,100		143,400
Investment income	53,200		48,500
Write-downs/write-offs	7,500		(37,100)
Pre-tax income	**296,300**	**+93**	**153,600**
Income taxes	64,400		3,600
Net income	**231,900**	**+55**	**150,000**
Net inc. for equity hldrs	**222,700**	**+57**	**141,700**
Net inc. for non-cont. int	**9,200**	**+11**	**8,300**
Cash & equivalent	217,600		346,100
Inventories	583,400		519,800
Accounts receivable	615,700		556,900
Current assets	2,235,000		2,148,600
Long-term investments	532,100		455,400
Fixed assets, net	2,387,100		2,129,300
Right-of-use assets	426,900		373,000
Intangibles, net	4,050,800		3,796,300
Total assets	**10,436,500**	**+9**	**9,578,800**
Accts. pay. & accr. liabs	1,020,700		950,900
Current liabilities	2,246,700		2,091,200
Long-term debt, gross	3,250,100		3,046,200
Long-term debt, net	3,035,500		2,804,400
Shareholders' equity	4,507,700		4,009,700
Non-controlling interest	81,200		76,900
Cash from oper. activs	**408,400**	**-2**	**418,200**
Cash from fin. activs	(152,600)		1,255,600
Cash from invest. activs	(400,700)		(2,237,100)
Net cash position	**217,600**	**-37**	**346,100**
Capital expenditures	(268,800)		(272,200)
Capital disposals	5,700		8,400
Unfunded pension liability	n.a.		14,800
Pension fund surplus	51,000		n.a.
	$		$
Earnings per share*	0.70		0.46
Cash flow per share*	1.29		1.34
	shs		shs
No. of shs. o/s*	317,906,290		317,024,123
Avg. no. of shs. o/s*	317,660,608		311,016,278
	%		%
Net profit margin	5.52		4.45
Return on equity	5.23		3.96
Return on assets	3.81		3.17
Foreign sales percent	91		89
No. of employees (FTEs)	13,000		13,000

* Common
¤ Restated
^A Reported in accordance with IFRS

Latest Results

Periods ended:	3m June 30/23^A		3m June 30/22^A
	$000s	%Chg	$000s
Operating revenue	1,054,400	+13	933,300
Net income	67,800	n.m.	3,700
Net inc. for equity hldrs	65,300	n.m.	1,700
Net inc. for non-cont. int	2,500		2,000
	$		$
Earnings per share*	0.21		0.01

* Common
^A Reported in accordance with IFRS

Historical Summary
(as originally stated)

Fiscal Year	Oper. Rev. $000s	Net Inc. Bef. Disc. $000s	EPS* $
2023^A	4,203,300	231,900	0.70
2022^A	3,371,300	150,000	0.46
2021^A	2,981,900	(47,500)	(0.17)
2020^A	3,623,200	318,900	1.17
2019^A	3,304,100	340,100	1.24

* Common
^A Reported in accordance with IFRS

C.4 CBD Global Sciences Inc.

Symbol - CBDN **Exchange** - CSE (S) **CUSIP** - 12482U
Head Office - 225 Union Blvd, Suite 350, Lakewood, CO, United States, 80228 **Telephone** - (720) 881-2541
Website - www.cbdglobalsciences.com
Email - sreeves@tinglemerrett.com

Investor Relations - Scott M. Reeves (888) 401-2239
Auditors - Dale Matheson Carr-Hilton LaBonte LLP C.A., Vancouver, B.C.
Transfer Agents - Capital Transfer Agency Inc., Toronto, Ont.
Profile - (Alta. 2018) Produces and distributes hemp-based cannabidiol (CBD) products in the U.S.

CBD products are marketed under the Aethics and CannaOil brands and include tinctures, capsules, topicals, hydration products and confectionary products. Products are sold across the U.S. through select distributors, brick and mortar retailers and online.

Also provides direct store delivery (DSD) distribution services for multiple vendors of CBD-infused products and non-CBD products throughout the Colorado and Wyoming territories that are servicing more than 6,000 convenience store and large box retailers through its distribution networks. In addition, has a manufacturing facility in Silver Cliff, Colo., that produces wholesale CBD products such as full-spectrum oil, distillate, isolate and THC-free oil, as well as provides white label, custom private label and co-packing services.

In April 2022, name change to **Global Sciences Inc.** and up to 1-for-25 share consolidation were proposed.

Common suspended from CSE, July 11, 2022.

Recent Merger and Acquisition Activity

Status: pending **Announced:** Sept. 9, 2022
CBD Global Sciences Inc. agreed to acquire a direct store distribution (DSD) business from Midvale, Utah-based NewAge, Inc. for US$4,500,000 cash. The DSD business distributes beverages, snacks and other products to grocers, big box retailers and convenience stores in Colorado. The acquisition includes certain specified tangible and intangible assets used in the operation and the assumption of certain specified liabilities. The transaction was expected to close in the fourth quarter of 2022.

Directors - Brad Wyatt, chr., pres. & CEO, Castle Pines, Colo.; Glenn Dooley, interim CFO & COO, Parker, Colo.; Scott M. Reeves, corp. sec., Calgary, Alta.; Jeff Hays, Parker, Colo.

Capital Stock

	Authorized (shs.)	Outstanding (shs.)[1]
Preferred	unlimited	
Series A	500,000	735,361
Common	unlimited	49,456,624

[1] At Oct. 12, 2022

Series A Preferred - Convertible into common shares on a 100-for-1 basis. 100 votes per share.
Common - One vote per share.
Major Shareholder - Widely held at Apr. 19, 2022.

Price Range - CBDN/CSE (S)

Year	Volume	High	Low	Close
2022	3,795,985	$0.30	$0.03	$0.05
2021	4,646,862	$0.65	$0.13	$0.21
2020	4,109,807	$0.42	$0.10	$0.27
2019	1,355,941	$0.75	$0.25	$0.42

Wholly Owned Subsidiaries

Bam Bam Productions LLC
Dog Unleashed CBD, LLC, Colo.
Energy Unleased LLC, Colo.
Global Sciences Holdings Inc.
Legacy Distribution Group LLC, Colo.
Resinosa LLC, Colo.

Financial Statistics

Periods ended:	12m Dec. 31/21[A]		12m Dec. 31/20[□A]
	US$000s	%Chg	US$000s
Operating revenue	**167**	**-42**	**289**
Cost of sales	126		225
Research & devel. expense	7		36
General & admin expense	2,479		1,965
Stock-based compensation	179		424
Operating expense	**2,791**	**+5**	**2,649**
Operating income	**(2,624)**	**n.a.**	**(2,360)**
Deprec., depl. & amort.	66		160
Finance income	1		1
Finance costs, gross	596		1,215
Write-downs/write-offs	(4,132)		(1,290)
Pre-tax income	**(5,201)**	**n.a.**	**(5,302)**
Net inc. bef. disc. opers	**(5,201)**	**n.a.**	**(5,302)**
Income from disc. opers	(52)		(3,626)
Net income	**(5,253)**	**n.a.**	**(8,928)**
Cash & equivalent	93		1
Inventories	189		nil
Accounts receivable	24		3
Current assets	320		308
Fixed assets, net	1,375		80
Intangibles, net	332		nil
Total assets	**2,092**	**+343**	**472**
Accts. pay. & accr. liabs	1,074		1,878
Current liabilities	2,056		3,548
Long-term debt, gross	1,899		4,310
Long-term debt, net	1,338		3,916
Long-term lease liabilities	384		72
Preferred share equity	9,766		2,079
Shareholders' equity	(1,696)		(8,275)
Cash from oper. activs	**(1,139)**	**n.a.**	**(1,340)**
Cash from fin. activs	1,011		1,263
Cash from invest. activs	221		55
Net cash position	**93**	**n.m.**	**1**
Capital expenditures	(3)		nil
Capital disposals	80		55
	US$		US$
Earns. per sh. bef disc opers*	(0.15)		(0.17)
Earnings per share*	(0.15)		(0.28)
Cash flow per share*	(0.03)		(0.04)
	shs		shs
No. of shs. o/s*	48,813,291		34,525,758
Avg. no. of shs. o/s*	35,684,841		31,501,446
	%		%
Net profit margin	n.m.		n.m.
Return on equity	n.m.		n.m.
Return on assets	(359.20)		(123.47)

* Common
□ Restated
[A] Reported in accordance with IFRS

Latest Results

Periods ended:	6m June 30/22[A]		6m June 30/21[□A]
	US$000s	%Chg	US$000s
Operating revenue	391	+598	56
Net inc. bef. disc. opers	(1,104)	n.a.	(1,849)
Income from disc. opers	nil		(52)
Net income	(1,104)	n.a.	(1,900)
	US$		US$
Earns. per sh. bef. disc. opers.*	(0.02)		(0.05)
Earnings per share*	(0.02)		(0.06)

* Common
□ Restated
[A] Reported in accordance with IFRS

Historical Summary
(as originally stated)

Fiscal Year	Oper. Rev. US$000s	Net Inc. Bef. Disc. US$000s	EPS* US$
2021[A]	167	(5,201)	(0.15)
2020[A]	305	(8,928)	(0.28)
2019[A]	2,317	(8,956)	(0.53)
2018[A1]	592	(2,653)	n.a.
2017[A]	338	(73)	n.a.

* Common
[A] Reported in accordance with IFRS
[1] Results pertain to Global NV Corp.

C.5 CCL Industries Inc.*

Symbol - CCL.B **Exchange** - TSX **CUSIP** - 124900
Head Office - 801-111 Gordon Baker Rd, Toronto, ON, M2H 3R1
Telephone - (416) 756-8500 **Fax** - (416) 756-8555
Website - www.cclind.com
Email - sfurtado@cclind.com
Investor Relations - Suzana Furtado (416) 756-8500
Auditors - KPMG LLP C.A., Toronto, Ont.
Lawyers - McMillan LLP, Toronto, Ont.
Transfer Agents - TSX Trust Company, Montréal, Qué.
FP500 Revenue Ranking - 96
Employees - 25,300 at Dec. 31, 2022
Profile - (Can. 1977; orig. Ont., 1957) Manufactures labels, consumer printable media products, technology-driven label solutions, polymer banknote substrates and specialty films for various markets including home and personal care, healthcare and specialty, premium food and beverage, automotive, electronics and consumer durables, security, and retail and apparel.

Operations are carried out through a decentralized organization of subsidiaries in North America, Europe, Latin America, Africa, Asia, Australia and the Middle East, through four operating segments: CCL division; Avery division; Checkpoint division; and Innovia division.

The **CCL division** produces pressure sensitive and extruded film materials for a range of decorative, instructional, functional and security applications for government institutions and global customers in the consumer packaging, healthcare, chemicals, consumer durables, electronic device and automotive markets. Also sells complementary products and services such as extruded and laminated plastic tubes, aluminum aerosols and specialty bottles, folded instructional leaflets, specialty folded cartons, precision decorated and die cut components, electronic displays, polymer bank note substrate and other complementary products and services to specific end-use markets. The division operates 149 facilities globally, with 37 in North America, 55 in Europe, 15 in Latin America, 42 in Asia and South Africa.

The **Avery division** supplies labels, specialty converted media and software solutions primarily in North America, Europe and Australia, with a small presence in Latin America. Products are split into five primary lines: printable media, which includes address labels, shipping labels, marketing and product identification labels, indexes and dividers, business cards and name badges supported by customized software solutions; organizational product, which includes binders, sheet protectors and writing instruments; direct to consumer digitally imaged media, which includes labels, business cards, name badges, event badges, key cards, wristbands, planners and journals, and family oriented identification labels supported by unique web-enabled e-commerce URLs; pressure sensitive tapes; and horticultural labels and tags. The division operates 23 manufacturing facilities globally.

The **Checkpoint division** manufactures and distributes technology-driven, loss-prevention, inventory management and labelling solutions, including radio-frequency (RF) and radio-frequency identification-based (RFID), to the retail and apparel industry. Products include merchandise availability solutions (MAS), which focus on electronic-article-surveillance systems and include hardware, software, labels and tags for loss prevention and inventory control systems including RFID solutions; apparel labelling solutions (ALS), which include apparel labels and tags, some of which are RFID capable; and Meto, which is a branded European-centric product line and includes hand-held pricing tools and labels and promotional in-store displays. The division operates 25 manufacturing facilities, ten distribution facilities, three product and software development centres and a sales office globally.

The **Innovia division** manufactures specialty high performance, multi-layer, surface engineered biaxially oriented polypropylene films for label, packaging and security applications. Products are sold to customers in the pressure sensitive label materials, flexible packaging and consumer packaged goods industries worldwide with a small percentage of the total volume consumed internally by the CCL division. The division operates eight manufacturing facilities, four sales offices and a research and development laboratory globally.

In April 2023, the company acquired the intellectual property of private Denmark-based **Alert Systems ApS** for $3,000,000. Alert provides patented protected anti-theft solutions which are sold alongside Checkpoint division's Merchandise Availability Solutions product lines.

In May 2022, the company announced its plan to build a new films manufacturing facility in Leipzig, Germany, which would produce highly engineered thin gauge label films. A total of $70,000,000 would be invested to construct the facility and commercial operations would commence in early 2025.

Recent Merger and Acquisition Activity

Status: completed **Announced:** July 6, 2023
CCL Industries Inc. acquired privately held Creaprint S.L., a specialist in mould label producer with a manufacturing facility in Alicante, Spain, for debt and cash-free purchase consideration of $38,100,000. The business would now trade as CCL Label, Spain and become a part of the Food & Beverage unit in Europe.

Status: completed **Announced:** Apr. 28, 2023
CCL Industries Inc. acquired Farmington, Conn-based Data Management, Incorporated (dba Threshold Visitor Management Systems), a privately owned supplier of visitor sign-in, tracking and identification badges using proprietary software, for $6,800,000.

Status: completed **Announced:** Apr. 3, 2023
CCL Industries Inc. acquired private Grand Rapids, Mich.-based eAgile Inc., a developer of hardware and software products for the healthcare industry supplied alongside RFID (radio frequency identification) inlays embedded into labels for $54,000,000 including $1,000,000 net cash assumed with $7,000,000 deferred for five years. eAgile would become an integral part of CCL's Healthcare and Specialty business while adding RFID know-how across CCL.

Status: completed **Announced:** May 31, 2022
CCL Industries Inc. acquired Netherlands-based Floramedia Group B.V., which designs and prints horticultural labels, for $53,100,000.

Status: completed **Revised:** Apr. 29, 2022
UPDATE: The transaction was completed. Final consideration was $149,900,000, including the assumption of $10,000,000 of debt. PREVIOUS: CCL Industries Inc. agreed to acquire Adelbras Indústria e

Comércio de Adesivos Ltda. and Amazon Tape Indústria e Comércio de Fitas Adesivas Ltda. (collectively Adelbras) in Sao Paolo, Brazil for $155,400,000. The transaction was expected to close in the second quarter of 2022. The Adelbras would be reported as part of Avery division. Adelbras produces adhesive tapes including masking, bonding and packaging sold through retails and distributors under the Adelbras brand name.

Predecessor Detail - Name changed from The Conn Chem Group Ltd., Nov. 28, 1979.

Directors - Donald G. Lang, exec. chr., Toronto, Ont.; Geoffrey T. Martin, pres. & CEO, Dover, Mass.; Kathleen L. Keller-Hobson†, Niagara-on-the-Lake, Ont.; Angella V. Alexander, Toronto, Ont.; Linda A. Cash, Atlanta, Ga.; Vincent J. (Vince) Galifi, Vaughan, Ont.; Erin M. Lang, Toronto, Ont.; Stuart W. Lang, Cambridge, Ont.; Dr. Douglas W. (Doug) Muzyka, Philadelphia, Pa.; Thomas C. (Tom) Peddie, Toronto, Ont.

Other Exec. Officers - James A. (Jim) Sellors, sr. v-p, Asia Pacific; Lalitha Vaidyanathan, sr. v-p, fin.-IT-HR; Sean P. Washchuk, sr. v-p & CFO; Kamal Kotecha, v-p, tax.; Mark A. McClendon, v-p & gen. counsel; Nick Vecchiarelli, v-p, corp. acctg.; Monika Vodermaier, v-p, corp. fin. Europe; Suzana Furtado, corp. sec.; Günther Birkner, pres., food & beverage, healthcare & specialty & pres., Innovia Films worldwide; Mark Cooper, pres., Avery & METO worldwide; Ben Lilienthal, pres., Checkpoint worldwide & grp. v-p, CCL Industries Mexico & Central America; Ben Rubino, pres., home & personal care worldwide

† Lead director

Capital Stock

	Authorized (shs.)	Outstanding (shs.)[1]
Class A Vtg.	unlimited	11,781,887
Class B Non-vtg.	unlimited	165,659,767

[1] At May 10, 2023

Class A Voting - Entitled to dividends at a rate set at 1¢ per share per annum less than the dividends declared on the class B non-voting shares. Convertible at any time into class B non-voting shares. One vote per share.

Class B Non-Voting - Entitled to receive, or have set aside for payment, dividends as declared by the Board of Directors from time to time. Non-voting unless consideration given for class A voting shares, under a takeover bid when voting control has been acquired, exceeds 115% of the market price of class B non-voting shares, when entitled to one vote per share. Ranks equally with class A voting shares in all other respects.

Options - At Dec. 31, 2022, options were outstanding to purchase 1,300,000 class B non-voting shares, exercisable at prices ranging from $55.73 to $66.87 per share (weighted average exercise price of $61.64 per share), with a weighted average remaining contractual life of 0.6 years. Of the total outstanding, 1,100,000 were exercisable at a weighted average exercise price of $62.71 per share.

Normal Course Issuer Bid - The company plans to make normal course purchases of up to 14,500,000 class B non-voting shares representing 9.9% of the public float. The bid commenced on May 25, 2023, and expires on May 24, 2024.

Major Shareholder - Donald G. Lang held 47.57% interest and Stuart W. Lang held 47.57% interest at Mar. 17, 2023.

Price Range - CCL.B/TSX

Year	Volume	High	Low	Close
2022	69,097,238	$69.38	$53.36	$57.84
2021	63,019,145	$75.19	$57.43	$67.83
2020	89,361,788	$61.53	$34.57	$57.79
2019	78,495,376	$68.49	$48.43	$55.32
2018	76,423,644	$67.74	$47.32	$50.06

Recent Close: $60.05

Capital Stock Changes - During 2022, class B non-voting shares were issued as follows: 100,000 on exercise of options and 100,000 on exercise of restricted units; 3,400,000 class B shares were repurchased under a Normal Course Issuer Bid.

Dividends

CCL.B cl B N.V. Ra $1.06 pa Q est. Mar. 31, 2023
Prev. Rate: $0.96 est. Mar. 31, 2022
Prev. Rate: $0.84 est. Mar. 31, 2021
Prev. Rate: $0.72 est. Mar. 31, 2020
CCL.A cl A Ra $1.05 pa Q est. Mar. 31, 2023
Prev. Rate: $0.95 est. Mar. 31, 2022
Prev. Rate: $0.83 est. Mar. 31, 2021
Prev. Rate: $0.71 est. Mar. 31, 2020

Long-Term Debt - Outstanding at Dec. 31, 2022:

Credit facilities[1]	$394,100,000
3.25% notes due 2026[2]	674,200,000
3.864% notes due 2028	298,900,000
3.05% notes due 2030[3]	806,400,000
Other loans[4]	8,600,000
	2,182,200,000
Less: Current portion	6,600,000
	2,175,600,000

[1] Borrowings under a US$1.2 billion revolving credit facility due on Feb. 28, 2025, bearing interest at the applicable benchmark interest rate plus an interest rate margin.

[2] US$500,000,000.

[3] US$600,000,000.

[4] Consist of term bank loans at various rates and repayment terms.

Wholly Owned Subsidiaries

CCL International Inc., Ont.
- 100% int. in **CCL Industries Corporation**, Del.
  - 100% int. in **Avery Products Corporation**, Del.
  - 100% int. in **CCL Label, Inc.**, Mich.
- 100% int. in **CCL Industries (U.K.) Limited**, United Kingdom.
  - 100% int. in **CCL Syrinx (U.K. Holding) Limited**, United Kingdom.
    - 100% int. in **CCL Syrinx (U.K.) Limited**, United Kingdom.
- 100% int. in **CCL Label A/S**, Denmark.
  - 100% int. in **Syrinx Holding Germany GmbH**, Germany.

Data Management, Incorporated, Farmington, Conn.
eAgile Inc., Grand Rapids, Mich.

Note: The preceding list includes only the major related companies in which interests are held.

Financial Statistics

Periods ended:	12m Dec. 31/22[A]		12m Dec. 31/21[A]
	$000s	%Chg	$000s
Operating revenue	**6,382,200**	**+11**	**5,732,800**
Cost of sales	4,301,700		3,798,300
General & admin expense	852,600		761,400
Operating expense	**5,154,300**	**+13**	**4,559,700**
Operating income	**1,227,900**	**+5**	**1,173,100**
Deprec., depl. & amort.	365,300		342,400
Finance income	12,900		7,700
Finance costs, gross	77,700		64,600
Investment income	19,900		11,200
Pre-tax income	**806,000**	**+3**	**780,600**
Income taxes	183,300		181,500
Net income	**622,700**	**+4**	**599,100**
Cash & equivalent	839,500		602,100
Inventories	785,100		677,300
Accounts receivable	1,100,500		1,083,800
Current assets	2,819,700		2,447,600
Long-term investments	79,500		68,400
Fixed assets, net	2,212,300		1,910,300
Right-of-use assets	180,200		145,500
Intangibles, net	3,211,800		2,966,200
Total assets	**8,664,400**	**+14**	**7,627,800**
Accts. pay. & accr. liabs.	1,394,400		1,321,500
Current liabilities	1,501,400		1,418,000
Long-term debt, gross	2,182,200		1,706,700
Long-term debt, net	2,175,600		1,691,400
Long-term lease liabilities	139,600		111,900
Shareholders' equity	4,265,200		3,747,000
Cash from oper. activs.	**992,800**	**+18**	**838,700**
Cash from fin. activs.	(72,600)		(370,000)
Cash from invest. activs.	(706,600)		(541,300)
Net cash position	**839,500**	**+39**	**602,100**
Capital expenditures	(447,200)		(323,800)
Capital disposals	27,800		16,900
Unfunded pension liability	257,900		313,900
	$		$
Earnings per share*	3.50		3.33
Earnings per share**	3.50		3.33
Cash flow per share***	5.58		4.67
Cash divd. per share*	0.96		0.84
Cash divd. per share**	0.95		0.83
	shs		shs
No. of shs. o/s***	177,000,000		180,200,000
Avg. no. of shs. o/s***	178,000,000		179,700,000
	%		%
Net profit margin	9.76		10.45
Return on equity	15.54		17.05
Return on assets	8.38		8.67
Foreign sales percent	98		98
No. of employees (FTEs)	25,300		25,100

* Class B
** Class A
*** Class B & Class A
[A] Reported in accordance with IFRS

Latest Results

Periods ended:	3m Mar. 31/23[A]		3m Mar. 31/22[A]
	$000s	%Chg	$000s
Operating revenue	1,652,100	+9	1,521,700
Net income	166,400	+11	150,200
	$		$
Earnings per share*	0.94		0.84

* Class B
[A] Reported in accordance with IFRS

Historical Summary
(as originally stated)

Fiscal Year	Oper. Rev.	Net Inc. Bef. Disc.	EPS*
	$000s	$000s	$
2022[A]	6,382,200	622,700	3.50
2021[A]	5,732,800	599,100	3.33
2020[A]	5,242,300	529,700	2.96
2019[A]	5,321,300	477,100	2.68
2018[A]	5,161,500	466,800	2.64

* Class B
[A] Reported in accordance with IFRS

C.6 CENTR Brands Corp.

Symbol - CNTR **Exchange** - CSE **CUSIP** - 15234A

Head Office - 100-2318 Oak St, Vancouver, BC, V6H 4J1 **Telephone** - (604) 773-1514

Website - www.findyourcentr.com

Email - info@findyourcentr.com

Investor Relations - Arjan J. Chima (778) 879-8613

Auditors - KPMG LLP C.A., Vancouver, B.C.

Transfer Agents - TSX Trust Company, Vancouver, B.C.

Employees - 18 at Sept. 22, 2022

Profile - (B.C. 2012 amalg.) Develops and markets beverages infused with hemp-derived extracts and derivatives.

The company's products include CENTR and CENTR Sugar Free, which are sparkling, low-calorie, cannabidiol (CBD) beverages, CENTR Instant, which is a single serve, ready-mix CBD drink powder and CENTR Enhanced, which is a zero calorie, non-CBD, nootropic and adaptogen-enriched sparkling water. The products are sold in 4,600 retail locations across 23 states in the U.S. through distribution agreements and its online store findyourcentr.com.

Predecessor Detail - Name changed from River Wild Exploration Inc., Apr. 1, 2019, pursuant to the reverse takeover acquisition of CBD Lifestyle Corp.

Directors - Robert W. C. Becher, chr., Caledon, Ont.; Arjan J. Chima, CEO & corp. sec., West Vancouver, B.C.; David T. Young, pres. & CFO, Naples, Fla.; Anton J. (Tony) Drescher, Vancouver, B.C.; Joseph P. Elmlinger, Greenwich, Conn.

Other Exec. Officers - Josh Rosinsky, v-p, sales

Capital Stock

	Authorized (shs.)	Outstanding (shs.)[1]
Common	unlimited	114,685,659

[1] At Apr. 25, 2023

Major Shareholder - Paul Meehan held 15.63% interest and David Lyall held 10.61% interest at Nov. 3, 2022.

Price Range - CNTR/CSE

Year	Volume	High	Low	Close
2022	6,769,802	$1.04	$0.26	$0.30
2021	10,927,964	$2.50	$0.60	$0.85
2020	5,844,796	$0.69	$0.30	$0.58
2019	5,395,519	$0.78	$0.38	$0.40
2018	1,809,615	$0.70	$0.02	$0.55

Recent Close: $0.20

Capital Stock Changes - From July to September 2021, private placement of 3,935,520 units (1 common share & 1 warrant) at Cdn$1.50 per unit was completed. In April and May 2022, private placement of 8,235,515 units (1 common share & 1 warrant) at Cdn$0.65 per unit was completed. Also during fiscal 2022, common shares were issued as follows: 5,550,000 on vesting of restricted share units, 603,347 on exercise of warrants and 202,305 for debt settlement; 120,000 common shares were held in treasury.

Wholly Owned Subsidiaries

CBD Lifestyle Corp., Vancouver, B.C.
CENTR Brands USA LLC, United States.

Financial Statistics

Periods ended:	12m May 31/22[A]		12m May 31/21[oA]
	US$000s	%Chg	US$000s
Operating revenue	**1,854**	**+143**	**763**
Cost of sales	1,320		606
Salaries & benefits	3,415		2,384
General & admin expense	1,946		1,733
Stock-based compensation	454		2,269
Operating expense	**7,135**	**+2**	**6,992**
Operating income	**(5,281)**	**n.a.**	**(6,229)**
Deprec., depl. & amort.	98		30
Pre-tax income	**485**	**n.a.**	**(14,257)**
Net income	**485**	**n.a.**	**(14,257)**
Cash & equivalent	3,856		832
Inventories	1,050		1,119
Accounts receivable	75		153
Current assets	5,421		2,359
Fixed assets, net	24		16
Right-of-use assets	443		4
Total assets	**5,888**	**+147**	**2,379**
Accts. pay. & accr. liabs	556		773
Current liabilities	773		1,401
Long-term debt, gross	32		33
Long-term debt, net	32		33
Long-term lease liabilities	349		nil
Shareholders' equity	4,095		(3,629)
Cash from oper. activs	**(5,571)**	**n.a.**	**(4,192)**
Cash from fin. activs	8,618		4,519
Cash from invest. activs	(24)		(9)
Net cash position	**3,856**	**+363**	**832**
Capital expenditures	(24)		(9)
	US$		US$
Earnings per share*	0.01		(0.22)
Cash flow per share*	(0.07)		(0.06)
	shs		shs
No. of shs. o/s*	95,492,731		77,086,044
Avg. no. of shs. o/s*	75,749,502		66,075,537
	%		%
Net profit margin	26.16		n.m.
Return on equity	n.m.		n.m.
Return on assets	11.73		(847.37)

* Common
[o] Restated
[A] Reported in accordance with IFRS

Latest Results

Periods ended:	3m Aug. 31/22[A]		3m Aug. 31/21[A]
	US$000s	%Chg	US$000s
Operating revenue	328	-64	920
Net income	(2,091)	n.a.	304
	US$		US$
Earnings per share*	(0.02)		0.00

* Common
[A] Reported in accordance with IFRS

Historical Summary
(as originally stated)

Fiscal Year	Oper. Rev.	Net Inc. Bef. Disc.	EPS*
	US$000s	US$000s	US$
2022[A]	1,854	485	0.01
2021[A]	763	(14,257)	(0.22)
2020[A]	463	(2,612)	(0.04)
	$000s	$000s	$
2019[A1,2]	nil	(3,127)	(0.09)
2018[A3]	nil	(100)	(0.00)

* Common
[A] Reported in accordance with IFRS
[1] 37 weeks ended May 31, 2019.
[2] Results reflect the Apr. 1, 2019, reverse takeover acquisition of CBD Lifestyle Corp.
[3] Results for fiscal 2018 and prior years pertain to (new) River Wild Exploration Inc.

C.7 CES Energy Solutions Corp.*

Symbol - CEU **Exchange** - TSX **CUSIP** - 15713J
Head Office - 1400-332 6 Ave SW, Calgary, AB, T2P 0B2 **Telephone** - (403) 269-2800 **Toll-free** - (888) 785-6695 **Fax** - (403) 266-5708
Website - www.cesenergysolutions.com
Email - anthony.aulicino@ceslp.ca
Investor Relations - Anthony M. Aulicino (403) 269-2800
Auditors - Deloitte LLP C.A., Calgary, Alta.
Bankers - The Bank of Nova Scotia, Calgary, Alta.
Lawyers - Crowe & Dunlevy, Oklahoma City, Okla.; Stikeman Elliott LLP, Calgary, Alta.
Transfer Agents - Computershare Trust Company of Canada Inc., Calgary, Alta.
FP500 Revenue Ranking - 227
Employees - 2,123 at Dec. 31, 2022

Profile - (Alta. 2020; orig. Can., 1986) Provides technically advanced consumable chemical solutions throughout the life-cycle of the oilfield, including total solutions at the drill-bit, at the point of completion and stimulation, at the wellhead and pump-jack, and finally through to the pipeline and midstream market.

Operates two core businesses: Drilling and Completion Fluids; and Production and Specialty Chemicals.

The **Drilling and Completion Fluids** business designs and implements drilling fluid systems and completion solutions for the North American oil and natural gas industry, operating in various basins in the U.S. and the Western Canadian Sedimentary Basin (WCSB), with an emphasis on servicing the ongoing major resource plays. The company operates under the AES Drilling Fluids brand in the U.S., and Canadian Energy Services brand in Canada. Proprietary drilling fluid systems consist of Seal-AX™, Polarbond™, ABS40™, Cotton Seal™, Enerdrill™, Bond Log Plus, PureStar™, Envirobond™, Liquidrill™, Invert/Ecovert™, Enerclear™, EnerLITE™, Micro Strength, Macro Strength, Brinex™, Glydex™, Liquislide™ Salt, Tarbreak™, Tarbreak #2, Bitencap™, Poly-Core™, Enerseal™, Enerseal HDD™, Enerhib C™, Enerscav C™ and ClearViewer™.

The **Production and Specialty Chemicals** business designs, develops and manufactures production and specialty chemicals, which provide solutions at the point of completion and stimulation, at the wellhead and pump-jack, and through to the pipeline and midstream market. The company operates under the trade names JACAM Catalysts and Proflow Solutions in the U.S., and through wholly owned **Sialco Materials Ltd.** and PureChem Services in the WCSB. Lab facilities are located in Sterling, Kan.; Midland, Gardendale and Sonora, Tex.; Delta, B.C.; Carlyle, Sask.; and Nisku, Calgary and Grande Prairie, Alta.

Other complementary businesses include **Clear Environmental Solutions**, which provides environmental consulting, water management services, and drilling fluids waste disposal services primarily to oil and gas producers active in the WCSB; **Superior Weighting**, based out of the Port of Corpus Christi, Tex., which custom grinds minerals including barite, which is the weighting agent utilized in most drilling fluids systems; and **CES Operations (SPC)**, which provides drilling fluids and production chemicals in Oman. In addition, the company sells production chemicals to a distributor in Nigeria.

Periods ended:	12m Dec. 31/22	12m Dec. 31/21
Drill rig operating days	71,665	49,809

Predecessor Detail - Name changed from Canadian Energy Services & Technology Corp., June 20, 2017.

Directors - Philip J. (Phil) Scherman, chr., Calgary, Alta.; Kenneth E. (Ken) Zinger, pres. & CEO, Calgary, Alta.; Spencer D. Armour III, Midland, Tex.; Stella Cosby, Calgary, Alta.; Ian Hardacre, Toronto, Ont.; John M. Hooks, Calgary, Alta.; Kyle D. Kitagawa, Calgary, Alta.; Edwin (Joseph) Wright, Midland, Tex.

Other Exec. Officers - Anthony M. (Tony) Aulicino, CFO; Matthew S. Bell, legal counsel & corp. sec.; Richard L. Baxter, pres., U.S. drilling fluids; Vernon J. (Vern) Disney, pres., U.S. prod. chemicals; Michael Hallat, pres., Sialco Materials Ltd.

Capital Stock

	Authorized (shs.)	Outstanding (shs.)[1]
Preferred	unlimited	nil
Common	unlimited	248,300,825

[1] At Aug. 10, 2023

Normal Course Issuer Bid - The company plans to make normal course purchases of up to 18,719,430 common shares representing 10% of the public float. The bid commenced on July 21, 2023, and expires on July 20, 2024.

Major Shareholder - EdgePoint Investment Group Inc. held 22.1% interest at May 11, 2023.

Price Range - CEU/TSX

Year	Volume	High	Low	Close
2022	198,442,895	$3.27	$2.01	$2.76
2021	120,130,655	$2.24	$1.28	$2.03
2020	132,640,096	$2.39	$0.53	$1.28
2019	154,356,843	$3.67	$1.68	$2.33
2018	178,845,426	$6.86	$2.89	$3.15

Recent Close: $3.60

Capital Stock Changes - During 2022, common shares were issued as follows: 2,747,074 as stock-based compensation and 69,212 as stock settled director fee; 2,131,500 common shares were repurchased under a Normal Course Issuer Bid.

Dividends

CEU com N.S.R. [1]

$0.025	July 14/23	$0.02	Apr. 14/23
$0.02	Jan. 13/23	$0.016	Oct. 14/22

Paid in 2023: $0.065 2022: $0.064 2021: $0.016

[1] Monthly divd normally payable in May/20 has been omitted.

Long-Term Debt - Outstanding at Dec. 31, 2022:

Senior facility due 2024[1]	$209,276,000
6.375% senior notes due 2024	287,954,000
Less: Unamort. debt issue costs	5,748,000
	491,482,000
Less: Current portion	nil
	491,482,000

[1] Consists of borrowings under a US$120,000,000 U.S. facility and a Cdn$270,000,000 Canadian facility, bearing interest at bank's prime rate or U.S. base rate plus an applicable pricing margin ranging from 0.25% to 1% or Canadian bankers' acceptance rate or SOFR plus an applicable pricing margin ranging from 1.25% to 2%.

Scheduled principal payments were reported as follows:

2023	nil
2024	$398,679,000
2025	nil
2026	nil
2027	nil
Thereafter	nil

Note - In April 2023, principal amount of the senior facility increased to Cdn$700,000,000, consisting of a of Cdn$450,000,000 revolving facility and a Cdn$250,000,000 Canadian term loan facility, with maturity date of Apr. 25, 2026.

Wholly Owned Subsidiaries

Canadian Energy Services Inc., Alta.
- 0.01% int. in **Canadian Energy Services L.P.**, Calgary, Alta.

Sialco Materials Ltd., Delta, B.C.

Subsidiaries

98.57% int. in **Canadian Energy Services L.P.**, Calgary, Alta.
- 100% int. in **CES Holdings Ltd.**, Alta.
  - 100% int. in **CES Operations Ltd.**, Calgary, Alta.
    - 100% int. in **AES Drilling Fluids Holdings, LLC**, Wilmington, Del.
      - 100% int. in **AES Drilling Fluids, LLC**, Denver, Colo.
      - 100% int. in **Jacam Chemical Company 2013, LLC**, United States.
        - 100% int. in **Catalyst Oilfield Services 2016, LLC**, Del.
          - 100% int. in **Jacam Catalyst, LLC**, United States.
            - 100% int. in **Proflow Solutions 2022, LLC**
          - 100% int. in **Jacam Logistics, LLC**, Del.
          - 100% int. in **Jacam Manufacturing 2013, LLC**, United States.
      - 100% int. in **Superior Weighting Products, LLC**, United States.
      - 100% int. in **Trenchless Fluid Systems, LLC**, Del.
    - 100% int. in **CES Operations (SPC)**, Oman.

Financial Statistics

Periods ended:	12m Dec. 31/22[A]		12m Dec. 31/21[A]
	$000s	%Chg	$000s
Operating revenue	**1,922,319**	**+61**	**1,196,420**
Cost of sales	1,250,544		726,108
Salaries & benefits	332,460		253,285
General & admin expense	82,293		61,256
Stock-based compensation	15,552		13,637
Operating expense	**1,680,849**	**+59**	**1,054,286**
Operating income	**241,470**	**+70**	**142,134**
Deprec., depl. & amort.	74,484		67,978
Finance costs, net	39,568		22,389
Pre-tax income	**126,754**	**+142**	**52,331**
Income taxes	31,536		2,447
Net income	**95,218**	**+91**	**49,884**
Inventories	428,144		273,501
Accounts receivable	479,360		308,836
Current assets	933,680		619,201
Long-term investments	5,403		17,006
Fixed assets, net	283,432		260,752
Right-of-use assets	62,199		46,482
Intangibles, net	85,243		83,678
Total assets	**1,411,003**	**+30**	**1,087,598**
Accts. pay. & accr. liabs	234,299		153,282
Current liabilities	267,344		175,762
Long-term debt, gross	491,482		395,184
Long-term debt, net	491,482		395,184
Long-term lease liabilities	36,414		25,706
Shareholders' equity	609,049		486,675
Cash from oper. activs	**(2,738)**	**n.a.**	**(74,405)**
Cash from fin. activs	49,529		68,914
Cash from invest. activs	(46,791)		(12,760)
Capital expenditures	(52,394)		(25,886)
Capital disposals	8,573		17,912
	$		$
Earnings per share*	0.37		0.20
Cash flow per share*	(0.01)		(0.29)
Cash divd. per share*	0.07		0.03
	shs		shs
No. of shs. o/s*	254,515,682		253,830,896
Avg. no. of shs. o/s*	255,223,348		255,269,304
	%		%
Net profit margin	4.95		4.17
Return on equity	17.38		10.59
Return on assets	7.62		5.13
Foreign sales percent	66		65
No. of employees (FTEs)	2,123		1,812

* Common
[A] Reported in accordance with IFRS

Latest Results

Periods ended:	6m June 30/23^A		6m June 30/22^A
	$000s	%Chg	$000s
Operating revenue	1,073,538	+29	834,931
Net income	66,903	+120	30,355
	$		$
Earnings per share*	0.26		0.12

* Common

^A Reported in accordance with IFRS

Historical Summary
(as originally stated)

Fiscal Year	Oper. Rev. $000s	Net Inc. Bef. Disc. $000s	EPS* $
2022^A	1,922,319	95,218	0.37
2021^A	1,196,420	49,884	0.20
2020^A	888,047	(222,903)	(0.85)
2019^A	1,277,257	30,106	0.11
2018^A	1,271,051	47,735	0.18

* Common

^A Reported in accordance with IFRS

C.8 CF Energy Corp.

Symbol - CFY **Exchange** - TSX-VEN **CUSIP** - 12529J
Head Office - 308-3100 Steeles Ave E, Markham, ON, L3R 8T3 **Telephone** - (647) 313-0066 **Fax** - (647) 313-0088
Website - www.cfenergy.com
Email - fred.wong@changfengenergy.cn
Investor Relations - Wong Wai Keung (647) 313-0066
Auditors - Deloitte Touche Tohmatsu C.P.A., Hong Kong, Hong Kong People's Republic of China
Lawyers - Miller Thomson LLP, Markham, Ont.
Transfer Agents - Computershare Trust Company of Canada Inc., Toronto, Ont.

Profile - (B.C. 2018; orig. Can., 2008 amalg.) Develops natural gas distribution networks and distributes natural gas in the People's Republic of China (PRC). Also builds and operates electric vehicle battery swap stations; and renewable and smart energy projects in Hainan and Sichuan provinces, PRC.

Operations are conducted through three segments: Gas Distribution Utility; Electric Vehicle (EV) Battery Swap Station; and Integrated Smart Energy.

Gas Distribution Utility provides gas pipeline installation and connection and distribution of natural gas to residential, commercial and industrial customers through its pipeline networks in Sanya City, Hainan province and Pingxiang City, Jiangxi province, PRC, and supplies natural gas to industrial customers including ceramic factories in Pingxiang City, Jiangxi province, PRC. Also operates two refuelling stations in Sanya and Changsha City for vehicles such as household cars, taxicabs, buses and trucks; and transports natural gas via the company's 2-km pipeline in Zhaoqing City, Guangdong province.

EV Battery Swap Station invests, builds and operates four EV battery stations to serve **BAIC Qingxiang Technology Co., Ltd**'s 200 swap-battery EVs for its network taxi hiring business operating in Sanya City, Hainan province, PRC, and its additional 200 EV network taxis for other cities in Hainan province, PRC. Also includes an additional EV battery station in Zhuhai City, Guangdong province, which commenced operation in March 2022.

Integrated Smart Energy includes the 70%-owned Haitang Bay project, which combines the use of multiple clean energy sources, including solar, hydro, electricity and natural gas to supply cooling, heating, as well as hot water to the hotels, shopping centers and households in the Haitang Bay area of Sanya City, Hainan province, PRC; and the 71.6%-owned Meishan project, which is a joint investment, construction and operation of an integrated district energy distribution project in the new economic development zone of Meishan City, Sichuan province, PRC.

Operating Statistics

Year ended Dec. 31	2021	2020
Residential:		
Cust. connected during year	20,273	35,059
Total customers connected	341,219	320,946
Gas sold, m³	16,882,321	16,197,400
Commercial:		
Cust. connected during year	148	87
Total customers connected	1,365	1,217
Gas sold, m³	34,537,403	29,909,513

Note - Gas sold by the CNG Refuelling Station in 2021 was 11,375,995 m³ compared with 12,720,078 m³ in 2020.

Predecessor Detail - Name changed from Changfeng Energy Inc., Apr. 12, 2019.

Directors - Si Yin (Ann) Lin, chr. & CEO, Toronto, Ont.; Hui Cai, Guangzhou, Guangdong, People's Republic of China; Yongbiao (Winfield) Ding, Toronto, Ont.; Wong Wai (Frederick) Keung; Dan Liu, Beijing, Beijing, People's Republic of China; Wencheng Zhang, Beijing, Beijing, People's Republic of China

Other Exec. Officers - Ling Cao, CFO; Ping Chen, v-p, project coordination

Capital Stock

	Authorized (shs.)	Outstanding (shs.)[1]
Common	unlimited	65,885,155

[1] At Dec. 31, 2022

Major Shareholder - The estate of Huajun Lin held 52.6% interest at Nov. 18, 2022.

Price Range - CFY/TSX-VEN

Year	Volume	High	Low	Close
2022	1,226,737	$0.54	$0.19	$0.32
2021	2,261,292	$0.72	$0.39	$0.52
2020	2,832,742	$0.66	$0.34	$0.54
2019	2,707,006	$1.10	$0.52	$0.67
2018	5,472,558	$1.18	$0.60	$0.95

Recent Close: $0.22

Wholly Owned Subsidiaries

CF Energy Group (Hainan) Co., Ltd., People's Republic of China.
CF Energy (Hong Kong) Limited, People's Republic of China.
Haikou Huapu New Energy Co., Ltd., People's Republic of China.
Hainan Hengtai Energy Co., Ltd., People's Republic of China.
Hainan Huapu Energy Co., Ltd., People's Republic of China.
Hainan Huapu Engineering Services Co., Ltd., People's Republic of China.
Hainan Huapu Green Energy Investment Co., Ltd., People's Republic of China.
Hainan Huapu Natural Gas Investment Co., Ltd., People's Republic of China.
Hainan Huapu Smart Energy Co., Ltd., People's Republic of China.
Sanya Changfeng Clean Energy Co., Ltd., People's Republic of China.
Sanya Changfeng International Natural Gas Trading Co., Ltd., People's Republic of China.
Sanya Changfeng New Energy Investment Co., Ltd., Hainan, People's Republic of China.
Sanya Changfeng Offshore Natural Gas Design Co. Ltd., Hainan, People's Republic of China.
Sanya Changfeng Offshore Natural Gas Distribution Co., Ltd., Hainan, People's Republic of China.
Sanya Changfeng Offshore Natural Gas Engineering Construction Co. Ltd., Hainan, People's Republic of China.
Sanya ChangfengWorld Entergy Forum Co., Ltd., People's Republic of China.
Yunnan Huapu New Energy Co., Ltd., People's Republic of China.
Zhuhai Changfeng Energy Import & Export Co. Ltd., People's Republic of China.
Zhuhai Huapu New Energy Co., Ltd., People's Republic of China.

Subsidiaries

70% int. in **EDF Changfeng (Sanya) Energy Co., Ltd.**, People's Republic of China.
60% int. in **Hebei Riheng Clean Energy Ltd.**, Hebei, People's Republic of China.
60% int. in **Hunan CNPC New Energy Investment Ltd.**, Hunan, People's Republic of China.
58% int. in **Hunan Changfeng - CNPC Energy Co. Ltd.**, Changsha, Hunan, People's Republic of China.
71.6% int. in **Meishan Hengtai Tianzhiyuan Energy Co., Ltd.**, People's Republic of China.
98% int. in **Zhaoqing Gaoyao Changheng Xinmingzhu Energy Co., Ltd.**, People's Republic of China.
61% int. in **Zhuhai Henghui Energy Co. Ltd.**, People's Republic of China.
- 100% int. in **Zhaoqing Gaoyao Hengtai Natural Gas Co., Ltd.**, People's Republic of China. Formerly Gaoyao Evergrowth Natural Gas Co., Ltd.

Financial Statistics

Periods ended:	12m Dec. 31/22^‡A		12m Dec. 31/21^A
	Cn¥000s	%Chg	Cn¥000s
Operating revenue	**334,239**	**-6**	**355,233**
Cost of sales	...		190,641
General & admin expense	...		87,564
Operating expense	**...**	**n.a.**	**278,205**
Operating income	**...**	**n.a.**	**77,028**
Deprec., depl. & amort.	...		30,560
Finance income	...		713
Finance costs, gross	18,024		10,092
Investment income	...		4,794
Write-downs/write-offs	...		(1,301)
Pre-tax income	**...**	**n.a.**	**37,351**
Income taxes	...		15,670
Net inc bef disc ops, eqhldrs	16,981		23,011
Net inc bef disc ops, NCI	(12,953)		(1,330)
Net inc. bef. disc. opers	**4,028**	**-81**	**21,681**
Disc. opers., equity hldrs	37		(1,330)
Disc. opers., NCI	25		(887)
Income from disc. opers	62		(2,217)
Net income	**4,090**	**-79**	**19,464**
Net inc. for equity hldrs	**17,018**	**-22**	**21,681**
Net inc. for non-cont. int	**(12,928)**	**n.a.**	**(2,217)**
Cash & equivalent	...		127,595
Inventories	...		3,988
Accounts receivable	...		96,923
Current assets	...		259,994
Long-term investments	...		51,268
Fixed assets, net	...		755,050
Right-of-use assets	...		77,637
Intangibles, net	...		13,683
Total assets	**1,245,108**	**+4**	**1,195,344**
Bank indebtedness	...		60,860
Accts. pay. & accr. liabs	...		133,744
Current liabilities	...		393,469
Long-term debt, gross	426,446		412,611
Long-term debt, net	380,530		351,257
Long-term lease liabilities	...		5,327
Shareholders' equity	385,949		367,788
Non-controlling interest	48,194		50,356
Cash from oper. activs	**39,237**	**-6**	**41,749**
Cash from fin. activs	...		173,756
Cash from invest. activs	...		(225,912)
Net cash position	**...**	**n.a.**	**128,062**
Capital expenditures	...		(200,957)
Capital disposals	...		1,006
	Cn¥		Cn¥
Earns. per sh. bef disc opers*	0.26		0.35
Earnings per share*	0.26		0.33
Cash flow per share*	0.60		0.63
	shs		shs
No. of shs. o/s*	65,885,155		65,885,155
Avg. no. of shs. o/s*	65,885,155		65,878,345
	%		%
Net profit margin	1.21		6.10
Return on equity	4.51		6.44
Return on assets	n.m.		2.52
Foreign sales percent	100		100

* Common

‡ Preliminary

^A Reported in accordance with IFRS

Historical Summary
(as originally stated)

Fiscal Year	Oper. Rev. Cn¥000s	Net Inc. Bef. Disc. Cn¥000s	EPS* Cn¥
2022^‡A	334,239	4,028	0.26
2021^A	355,233	21,681	0.35
2020^A	368,210	45,576	0.74
2019^A	438,021	47,158	0.72
2018^A	400,515	35,675	0.57

* Common

‡ Preliminary

^A Reported in accordance with IFRS

C.9 CGI Inc.*

Symbol - GIB.A **Exchange** - TSX **CUSIP** - 12532H
Head Office - 1500-1350 boul René-Lévesque O, Montréal, QC, H3G 1T4 **Telephone** - (514) 841-3200 **Fax** - (514) 841-3299
Website - www.cgi.com
Email - kevin.linder@cgi.com
Investor Relations - Kevin Linder (514) 841-3200
Auditors - PricewaterhouseCoopers LLP C.A., Montréal, Qué.
Transfer Agents - Computershare Trust Company of Canada Inc.
FP500 Revenue Ranking - 47
Employees - 90,000 at Sept. 30, 2022

Profile - (Que. 1981) Provides end-to-end information technology (IT) and business consulting services to clients worldwide.

The company delivers end-to-end services consisting of strategic IT and business consulting, systems integration, managed IT and business process outsourcing, and intellectual property (IP) solutions that cover the full spectrum of technology delivery from digital strategy and architecture to solution design, development, integration, implementation and operations.

The company's IP solutions include CGI Advantage, an enterprise resource planning (ERP) suite that is used by the public sector for financial management, vendor self-service, grants management, performance budgeting, collections, human resources management, case management and procurement; Momentum, an ERP solution used by more than 100 organizations across the three branches of the U.S. federal government, including intelligence and defence organizations; CGI Collections360, which is a collections system that combines various solutions consisting of default management software, hosting or application management, multi-channel and customer self service, compliance practice monitoring, gateway partner network, performance analytics, operations management systems implementation and consulting, and full business process operations; CGI CustomerAdvance, an end-to-end outsourcing solution which provides customer relationship management and business process services, such as global call centre support, fee processing, cash management and complex scheduling; and CGI Trade360, a fully integrated solution used in the global trade business of banks.

Target industries include financial services (including banking and insurance); government (including space), manufacturing; retail and distribution (including consumer services, transportation and logistics); communications and utilities (including energy and media); and health (including life sciences).

Operations are conducted through offices and delivery centres located in Canada, the U.S., Colombia, Europe, Morocco, India, Malaysia, the Philippines, The People's Republic of China and Australia.

At Sept. 30	2022	2021
	$million	$million
Contract backlog	24,055	23,059
New contract bookings	13,966	13,843

Recent Merger and Acquisition Activity

Status: completed **Revised:** July 29, 2022
UPDATE: The remaining shares were acquired. PREVIOUS: CGI Inc. agreed to acquire Paris, France-based Umanis S.A., which provides IT consulting services and data, digital and business solutions including data management and analysis, at €17.15 per share which values Umanis at €310,000,000. CGI would initially complete a block purchase for 70.6% interest in Umanis, followed by a mandatory tender offer to acquire the remaining shares of Umanis. The board of Umanis supported the transaction. May 31, 2022 - CGI completed the block purchase of 70.6% of Umanis' shares. July 13, 2022 - The tender offer was completed. CGI acquired 91.54% of Umanis, representing 91.42% of voting rights. July 18, 2022 - CGI launched a statutory squeeze out process to acquire all remaining outstanding shares of Umanis.

Status: completed **Revised:** May 30, 2022
UPDATE: The transaction was completed. PREVIOUS: CGI Inc. agreed to acquire Paris, France-based Harwell Management S.A.S., a management consulting firm specializing in the financial services industry, for $47,309,000. Harwell's offerings include strategy and organizational transformation, human resources transformation, digital and IT advisory, finance transformation, risk management, compliance and control, innovation and data strategy, and corporate social responsibility.

Predecessor Detail - Name changed from CGI Group Inc., Jan. 30, 2019.

Directors - Serge Godin, co-founder & exec. chr., Westmount, Qué.; André Imbeau, co-founder & advisor to the exec. chr., Beloeil, Qué.; Julie Godin, co-chr. & exec. v-p, strategic planning & corp. devel., Westmount, Qué.; George D. Schindler, pres. & CEO, Fairfax, Va.; George A. Cope†, Orleans, Ont.; Paule Doré, Outremont, Qué.; Gilles Labbé, Outremont, Qué.; Michael B. (Mike) Pedersen, Toronto, Ont.; Stephen S. Poloz, Orleans, Ont.; Mary G. Powell, Vt.; Alison C. Reed, London, Middx., United Kingdom; Michael E. Roach, Montréal, Qué.; Kathy N. Waller, Atlanta, Ga.; Joakim Westh, Stockholm, Sweden; Frank Witter, Braunschweig, Germany

Other Exec. Officers - Mark Boyajian, exec. v-p & chief bus. eng. officer; Benoit Dubé, exec. v-p, legal & economic affairs & corp. sec.; Bernard Labelle, exec. v-p & chief HR officer; Steve Perron, exec. v-p & CFO; Jean-Michel Baticle, pres. & COO, western, southern, northwest & central-east Europe, Finland, Poland, Baltics & Latin America; François Boulanger, pres. & COO, Canada, U.S. comml. & state govt., Asia-Pacific & global IP solutions; Caroline de Grandmaison, pres., France & Luxemberg; Dirk A. de Groot, pres., northwest & central-east Europe opers.; Laurent Gerin, pres., southern Europe & western & southern Europe delivery centres of excellence; David L. (Dave) Henderson, pres., global IP solutions; Timothy J. (Tim) Hurlebaus, pres., U.S. opers., comml. & state govt.; Leena-Mari Lähteenmaa, pres., Finland, Poland & Baltics opers.; Stephanie Mango, pres., CGI Federal Inc.; George J. Mattackal, pres., Asia Pacific global delivery centres of excellence; Tara McGeehan, pres., U.K. & Australia opers.; Torsten Strass, pres., Scandinavia & central Europe opers.; Guy Vigeant, pres., Canada opers.
† Lead director

Capital Stock

	Authorized (shs.)	Outstanding (shs.)[1]
First Preferred	unlimited	nil
Second Preferred	unlimited	nil
Class A Subordinate	unlimited	208,926,569
Class B	unlimited	26,445,706

[1] At July 21, 2023

First Preferred - Convertible into class A subordinate or class B shares under certain conditions. Rank prior to all other classes of shares with respect to dividends. One vote per share.

Second Preferred - Rank prior to class A subordinate and class B shares with respect to dividends. Non-voting.

Class A Subordinate - Participate equally with class B shares in dividends. Convertible into class B shares under certain conditions. One vote per share.

Class B - Participate equally with class A subordinate shares in dividends. Convertible into class A subordinate shares. Ten votes per share.

Options - At Sept. 30, 2022, options were outstanding to purchase 6,882,845 class A subordinate shares at prices ranging from $23.65 to $115.01 per share with a weighted average remaining contractual life of 4.54 years.

Normal Course Issuer Bid - The company plans to make normal course purchases of up to 18,769,394 class A subordinate shares representing 10% of the public float. The bid commenced on Feb. 6, 2023, and expires on Feb. 5, 2024.

Major Shareholder - Serge Godin held 53.72% interest at Dec. 5, 2022.

Price Range - GIB.A/TSX

Year	Volume	High	Low	Close
2022	95,431,214	$120.82	$95.45	$116.71
2021	105,791,431	$116.88	$93.88	$111.85
2020	172,561,236	$114.49	$67.23	$100.99
2019	125,686,786	$111.86	$80.27	$108.67
2018	138,355,025	$87.22	$66.06	$83.50

Recent Close: $138.07

Capital Stock Changes - During fiscal 2022, 941,059 class A subordinate shares were issued on exercise of options and 8,809,839 class A subordinate shares were repurchased under a Normal Course Issuer Bid.

Long-Term Debt - Outstanding at Sept. 30, 2022:

Term loan credit facilities[1]	$687,705,000
Sr. unsecured notes[2]	550,177,000
2.1% sr. unsecured notes due 2028[3]	595,900,000
Sr. unsecured notes[4]	11,361,974,000
Other	71,278,000
	3,267,034,000
Less: Current portion	93,447,000
	3,173,587,000

[1] US$500,000,000. Bearing interest at 30-day U.S. LIBOR, plus a variable margin expiring in December 2023.

[2] Consists of US$300,000,000 principal amount of senior U.S. unsecured notes due 2024; and US$150,000,000 principal amount of senior U.S. unsecured notes due from 2023 to 2024 . Bearing interest at weighted average rate of 3.98% at Sept. 30, 2022.

[3] Cdn$600,000,000.

[4] Consists of US$600,000,000 principal amount of senior U.S. unsecured notes due in September 2026; and US$400,000,000 principal amount of senior U.S. unsecured notes due in September 2031. Bearing interest at weighted average rate of 1.79% at Sept. 30, 2022.

Minimum long-term debt repayments were reported as follows:

Fiscal 2023	$93,447,000
Fiscal 2024-26	1,178,103,000
Fiscal 2027-29	863,125,000
Thereafter	1,132,359,000

Wholly Owned Subsidiaries

CGI Deutschland B.V. & Co. KG, Germany.
CGI Federal Inc., United States.
CGI France SAS, France.
CGI IT UK Limited, United Kingdom.
CGI Information Systems and Management Consultants Inc., Canada.
CGI Nederland B.V., Netherlands.
CGI Payroll Services Centre Inc., Canada.
CGI Suomi Oy, Finland.
CGI Sverige AB, Sweden.
CGI Technologies and Solutions Inc., United States.
Conseillers en gestion et informatique CGI inc., Qué.

Note: The preceding list includes only the major related companies in which interests are held.

Financial Statistics

Periods ended:	12m Sept. 30/22[A]		12m Sept. 30/21[oA]
	$000s	%Chg	$000s
Operating revenue	**12,867,201**	**+6**	**12,126,793**
Salaries & benefits	7,611,681		7,139,983
Stock-based compensation	186,726		177,130
Other operating expense	2,509,823		2,355,489
Operating expense	**10,308,230**	**+7**	**9,672,602**
Operating income	**2,558,971**	**+4**	**2,454,191**
Deprec., depl. & amort.	463,480		495,893
Finance income	3,194		3,111
Finance costs, gross	95,217		109,909
Write-downs/write-offs	(4,854)		(9,669)
Pre-tax income	**1,966,959**	**+7**	**1,837,992**
Income taxes	500,817		468,920
Net income	**1,466,142**	**+7**	**1,369,072**
Cash & equivalent	966,458		1,699,206
Inventories	1,191,844		1,045,058
Accounts receivable	1,363,545		1,231,452
Current assets	4,349,047		4,765,138
Long-term investments	16,826		19,354
Fixed assets, net	369,608		352,092
Right-of-use assets	535,121		586,207
Intangibles, net	9,359,027		8,877,056
Total assets	**15,175,420**	**+1**	**15,021,021**
Accts. pay. & accr. liabs	1,016,407		891,374
Current liabilities	3,649,331		3,803,472
Long-term debt, gross	3,267,034		3,401,656
Long-term debt, net	3,173,587		3,008,929
Long-term lease liabilities	551,257		609,121
Shareholders' equity	7,272,724		6,986,232
Cash from oper. activs	**1,864,998**	**-12**	**2,115,928**
Cash from fin. activs	(1,591,098)		(1,782,497)
Cash from invest. activs	(911,947)		(388,507)
Net cash position	**1,471,184**	**-13**	**1,699,206**
Capital expenditures	(156,136)		(121,806)
Capital disposals	3,790		nil
Unfunded pension liability	107,974		98,260
	$		$
Earnings per share*	6.13		5.50
Cash flow per share*	7.79		8.49
	shs		shs
No. of shs. o/s*	237,748,255		245,617,035
Avg. no. of shs. o/s*	239,262,004		249,119,219
	%		%
Net profit margin	11.39		11.29
Return on equity	20.56		19.21
Return on assets	10.18		9.49
Foreign sales percent	85		86
No. of employees (FTEs)	90,000		80,000

* Class A & B
[o] Restated
[A] Reported in accordance with IFRS

Latest Results

Periods ended:	9m June 30/23[A]		9m June 30/22[A]
	$000s	%Chg	$000s
Operating revenue	10,789,024	+12	9,619,980
Net income	1,216,773	+10	1,103,780
	$		$
Earnings per share*	5.18		4.59

* Class A & B
[A] Reported in accordance with IFRS

Historical Summary
(as originally stated)

Fiscal Year	Oper. Rev.	Net Inc. Bef. Disc.	EPS*
	$000s	$000s	$
2022[A]	12,867,201	1,466,142	6.13
2021[A]	12,126,793	1,369,072	5.50
2020[A]	12,164,115	1,117,862	4.27
2019[A]	12,111,236	1,263,207	4.63
2018[A]	11,506,825	1,141,402	4.02

* Class A & B
[A] Reported in accordance with IFRS

C.10 CI Financial Corp.*

Symbol - CIX **Exchange** - TSX **CUSIP** - 125491
Head Office - 200-15 York St, Toronto, ON, M5J 0A3 **Telephone** - (416) 364-1145 **Toll-free** - (800) 268-9374 **Fax** - (416) 364-6299
Website - www.cifinancial.com
Email - jweyeneth@ci.com
Investor Relations - Jason Weyeneth (800) 268-9374
Auditors - Ernst & Young LLP C.A., Toronto, Ont.
Lawyers - Blake, Cassels & Graydon LLP, Toronto, Ont.
Transfer Agents - Computershare Trust Company, N.A., Louisville, Ky.; Computershare Trust Company of Canada Inc., Toronto, Ont.
FP500 Revenue Ranking - 196

Employees - 2,300 at Dec. 31, 2022
Profile - (Ont. 2008) Manages, markets, distributes and administers mutual funds, segregated funds, exchange-traded funds, structured products and other fee-earning investment products for Canadian, Australian and New Zealand investors. Also provides financial planning, insurance, investment advice, wealth management, and estate and succession planning services in Canada and the U.S.

Operates in three reportable segments: Asset Management; Canada Wealth Management; and U.S. Wealth Management.

Asset Management - Operations include wholly owned **CI Investments Inc.**, operating as CI Global Asset Management (CI GAM), and subsidiaries **GSFM Pty Limited** and **Marret Asset Management Inc.** Revenues are derived principally from the fees earned on the management of investment funds and other fee-earning investment products, including mutual funds, segregated funds, pooled funds, alternative funds, closed-end and exchange-traded funds and discretionary accounts. At Dec. 31, 2022, CI GAM and Marret managed more than 260 core mutual/pooled funds and more than 130 exchange-traded funds, closed-end investment funds or limited partnerships which are offered across Canada primarily through investment dealers, mutual fund dealers and insurance advisors, as well as through the institutional investment marketplace. These funds are managed by in-house portfolio managers in addition to affiliated and outside investment advisory firms. GSFM serves retail and institutional investors in Australia and New Zealand. At Dec. 31, 2022, total assets under management were $117.8 billion.

Canada Wealth Management - Operations include wholly owned **Assante Wealth Management (Canada) Ltd.**, operating as CI Assante Wealth Management, which provides individuals and families with portfolio management, investment advisory services, distribution of securities, insurance products, banking products and wealth management services, including financial, tax, estate, succession and philanthropic planning, through affiliates and subsidiaries including **Assante Capital Management Ltd.** (a securities dealer), **Assante Financial Management Ltd.** (a mutual fund dealer) and **Assante Estate and Insurance Services Inc.** (insurance agents); wholly owned **CI Private Counsel LP**, operating as CI Private Wealth and Assante Private Client, which provides discretionary investment management and other services to high-net-worth and ultra-high-net-worth clients; subsidiary **Aligned Capital Partners Inc.**, an investment dealer and provider of investment management and wealth management services; wholly owned **Northwood Family Office Ltd.**, a multi-family office offering integrated planning, investment management, wealth administration and family engagement to ultra-high-net-worth individuals and families; wholly owned **WealthBar Financial Services Inc.**, which operates two online investment platforms, both under the CI Direct Investing name, offering investment portfolios and commission-free advice and for self-directed trading; and wholly owned **CI Investment Services Inc.**, a broker-dealer providing custodial and other services to portfolio managers and registered broker-dealers. At Dec. 31, 2022, total wealth management assets in Canada were $77.4 billion.

U.S. Wealth Management - Operations are conducted primarily through 80%-owned **CI US Holdings Inc.**, which holds interests in 27 registered investment advisor (RIA) firms operating under the CI Private Wealth brand. RIAs provide high-net-worth and ultra-high-net-worth clients with comprehensive wealth management services, including family office, trust, business succession planning, concierge, tax, estate and retirement planning, values-aligned investing and bill payment. The company also owns **Segall Bryant & Hamill, LLC**, an RIA which provides portfolio management services and products to institutional and individual clients; and holds minority interests in two alternative asset management firms, **Columbia Pacific Advisors, LLC** and **GLASfunds, LLC**. At Dec. 31, 2022, total wealth management assets in the U.S. were $180.6 billion.

In April 2023, subsidiary **CI Private Wealth, LLC** (CIPW) launched **CIPW Trust, LLC**, a South Dakota trust company offering corporate trustee services to CIPW's clients.

On Jan. 19, 2023, the company voluntarily delisted its common shares from the New York Stock Exchange.

In March 2022, affiliate **One Capital Management, LLC** acquired **FundX Investments Group LLC**, a San Francisco, Calif.-based fund manager.

Common delisted from NYSE, Jan. 20, 2023.

Recent Merger and Acquisition Activity

Status: completed **Announced:** Aug. 10, 2023
CI Financial Corp. acquired Montreal, Que.-based Coriel Capital Inc., a registered portfolio manager that provides outsourced chief investment officer services to high net worth families in Canada, with $1.3 billion in assets under management (AUM). Terms of the transaction were not disclosed.

Status: completed **Announced:** Aug. 10, 2023
CI Financial Corp. acquired San Antonio, Tex.-based Intercontinental Wealth Advisors, LLC, a registered investment advisor with US$1.7 billion in assets under management (AUM). Terms of the transaction were not disclosed.

Status: completed **Announced:** June 30, 2023
CI Financial Corp. acquired Garden City, N.Y.-based La Ferla Group, LLC, a registered investment advisor with US$275,600,000 in assets under management (AUM). Terms of the transaction were not disclosed.

Status: completed **Revised:** June 30, 2023
UPDATE: The transaction was completed. PREVIOUS:CI Financial Corp. agreed to sell its 45% interest in Boston, Mass.-based registered investment advisor firm Congress Wealth Management, LLC. Terms of the transaction were not disclosed.

Status: completed **Revised:** May 24, 2023
UPDATE: The transaction was completed. PREVIOUS: CI Financial Corp. agreed to sell a 20% minority interest in its U.S. wealth management business to a diversified group of institutional investors, including a wholly owned subsidiary of the Abu Dhabi Investment Authority (ADIA), Bain Capital, Flexpoint Ford, Ares Management funds, the State of Wisconsin, and others for US$1 billion (Cdn$1.34 billion). On closing, CI would hold an 80% interest in the business with the investors holding the remaining 20% in the form of convertible preferred equity.

Status: completed **Revised:** May 1, 2023
UPDATE: The transaction was completed. PREVIOUS: CI Financial Corp. agreed to acquire Houston, Tex.-based Avalon Advisors, LLC, a registered investment advisor with US$8.2 billion in assets under management (AUM). Terms of the transaction were not disclosed.

Status: completed **Announced:** Nov. 10, 2022
CI Financial Corp. acquired New York, N.Y.-based Kore Private Wealth, LLC, a registered investment advisory firm with US$5.1 billion in assets under management (AUM), serving ultra-high-net-worth individuals and families. Terms of the transaction were not disclosed. Kore was rebranded to CI Kore Private Wealth.

Status: completed **Announced:** Oct. 3, 2022
CI Financial Corp. acquired New York, N.Y.-based Inverness Counsel, LLC, a registered investment advisory firm with US$4.8 billion in assets under management (AUM), serving ultra-high-net-worth clients, families and trusts in the New York region. Terms of the transaction were not disclosed. Inverness was rebranded to CI Inverness Private Wealth.

Status: completed **Revised:** Oct. 3, 2022
UPDATE: The transaction was completed. PREVIOUS: CI Financial Corp. agreed to acquire certain assets of Boston, Mass.-based Eaton Vance WaterOak Advisors, LLC, formerly Eaton Vance Investment Counsel (EVIC). EVIC, a registered investment advisor and part of the asset management division of Morgan Stanley, acted as advisor for US$11.4 billion in assets on behalf of families, endowments, foundations and other institutions. Terms of the transaction were not disclosed. The transaction was expected to close in the fourth quarter of 2022, subject to regulatory approval and other customary closing conditions.

Status: completed **Revised:** Apr. 29, 2022
UPDATE: The transaction was completed. PREVIOUS: CI Financial Corp. agreed to acquire Corient Capital Partners, LLC, a Newport Beach, Calif.-based wealth management firm overseeing US$5 billion on behalf of ultra-high-net-worth individuals and families across the United States. Terms were not disclosed. The transaction was expected to close in the second quarter of 2022.

Status: completed **Revised:** Apr. 29, 2022
UPDATE: The transaction was completed. PREVIOUS: CI Financial Corp. agreed to acquire Houston, Tex.-based Galapagos Partners, L.P., a multi-family office and investment advisory firm providing comprehensive financial management services to a small number of wealthy families and private clients. Terms of the transaction were not disclosed.

Status: completed **Revised:** Apr. 1, 2022
UPDATE: The transaction was completed. PREVIOUS: CI Financial Corp. agreed to acquire Toronto, Ont.-based Northwood Family Office Ltd., a multi-family office managing and coordinating the integrated financial, investment and personal affairs of wealthy Canadian and global families with $10,000,000 to over $1 billion in family net worth. Northwood manages about $2.2 billion of investment assets and $9 billion of family net worth on behalf of clients. The acquisition was expected to increase CI's Canadian wealth management assets to about $81 billion and total assets globally to about $377 billion. Terms of the transaction were not disclosed. The transaction was expected to close in the second quarter of 2022, subject to regulatory approval and other customary closing conditions.

Directors - William T. (Bill) Holland, chr., Toronto, Ont.; Kurt MacAlpine, CEO, Miami, Fla.; David P. Miller†, Toronto, Ont.; William E. (Bill) Butt, Toronto, Ont.; Brigette Chang-Addorisio, Toronto, Ont.; Paul J. Perrow, Toronto, Ont.; Sarah M. Ward, Hobe Sound, Fla.

Other Exec. Officers - Darie P. Urbanky, pres., COO & head, asset mgt., CI Investments Inc.; Amarjit Anderson, chief risk officer & chief internal auditor; Manisha Burman, exec. v-p & chief HR officer; Edward D. (Ted) Kelterborn, exec. v-p & chief legal officer; Dr. Marc-André Lewis, exec. v-p & chief invest. officer; Amit Muni, exec. v-p & CFO; Julie Silcox, exec. v-p & chief mktg. officer; Sean Etherington, pres., Assante Wealth Management (Canada) Limited

† Lead director

Capital Stock

	Authorized (shs.)	Outstanding (shs.)[1]
Preference	unlimited	nil
Common	unlimited	167,640,863

[1] At June 30, 2023

Options - At Dec. 31, 2022, options were outstanding to purchase 506,000 common shares at prices ranging from $18.99 to $28.67 per share expiring on various dates to 2029.

Normal Course Issuer Bid - The company plans to make normal course purchases of up to 15,205,008 common shares representing 10% of the public float. The bid commenced on June 20, 2023, and expires on June 19, 2024.

Major Shareholder - Widely held at May 9, 2023.

Price Range - CIX/TSX

Year	Volume	High	Low	Close
2022	186,536,098	$27.70	$11.85	$13.51
2021	194,513,485	$30.88	$14.91	$26.44
2020	185,211,216	$25.81	$10.53	$15.78
2019	146,252,886	$22.24	$16.92	$21.71
2018	178,367,714	$30.23	$16.47	$17.28

Recent Close: $16.59

Capital Stock Changes - During 2022, common shares were issued as follows: 1,138,000 for share-based compensation and 74,000 pursuant to business acquisition; 14,116,000 common shares were repurchased under a Normal Course Issuer Bid.

Dividends

CIX com Ra $0.80 pa Q est. Jan. 15, 2024
Prev. Rate: $0.72 est. Oct. 15, 2018

Long-Term Debt - Outstanding at Dec. 31, 2022:

Prime rate loan due 2024	$320,000,000
3.215% debs. due 2024	300,636,000
3.759% debs. due 2025	448,684,000
7% debs. due 2025	398,050,000
3.904% debs. due 2027	249,178,000
3.2% debs. due 2030	1,293,467,000
4.1% debs. due 2051	1,206,199,000
	4,216,214,000
Less: Current portion	320,000,000
	3,896,214,000

Note - In May 2023, $234,775,000 of outstanding 3.215% debentures due 2024, $370,762,000 of outstanding 3.759% debentures due 2025 and $97,531,000 of outstanding 3.904% debentures due 2027 were repurchased under a tender offer.

Wholly Owned Subsidiaries

Assante Wealth Management (Canada) Ltd., Toronto, Ont.
- 100% int. in **Assante Capital Management Ltd.**, Canada.
- 100% int. in **Assante Estate and Insurance Services Inc.**, Ont.
- 100% int. in **Assante Financial Management Ltd.**, Ont.

CI Investment Services Inc., Toronto, Ont.
CI Investments Inc., Toronto, Ont.
CI Private Counsel LP, Man.
CI Private Wealth Canada Ltd., Canada.
- 100% int. in **Northwood Family Office Ltd.**, Toronto, Ont.

Coriel Capital Inc., Montréal, Qué.
Segall Bryant & Hamill, LLC, Chicago, Ill.
WealthBar Financial Services Inc., Vancouver, B.C.

Subsidiaries

80% int. in **CI US Holdings Inc.**, Del.
- 100% int. in **CIPW Holdings, LLC**, United States.
  - 100% int. in **CI Private Wealth, LLC**, Miami, Fla.
    - 100% int. in **Avalon Advisors, LLC**, Houston, Tex.
    - 100% int. in **Balasa Dinverno Foltz LLC**, Itasca, Ill.
    - 100% int. in **Barrett Asset Management, LLC**, New York, N.Y.
    - 100% int. in **Bowling Portfolio Management LLC**, Cincinnati, Ohio.
    - 100% int. in **Brightworth, LLC**, Atlanta, Ga.
    - 100% int. in **Budros, Ruhlin & Roe, Inc.**, Columbus, Ohio.
    - 100% int. in **CIPW Trust, LLC**, S.D.
    - 100% int. in **CPWM, LLC**, Seattle, Wash.
    - 49% int. in **The Cabana Group, LLC**, Ark.
    - 31% int. in **Columbia Pacific Advisors, LLC**, Seattle, Wash.
    - 100% int. in **Corient Capital Partners, LLC**, Newport Beach, Calif.
    - 100% int. in **Dowling & Yahnke, LLC**, San Diego, Calif.
    - 100% int. in **Doyle Wealth Management, LLC**, St. Petersburg, Fla.
    - 100% int. in **La Ferla Group, LLC**, Garden City, N.Y.
    - 30% int. in **GLAS Funds, LLC**, Cleveland, Ohio.
    - 100% int. in **Galapagos Partners, L.P.**, Houston, Tex.
    - 100% int. in **Gofen and Glossberg, LLC**, Chicago, Ill.
    - 100% int. in **Intercontinental Wealth Advisors, LLC**, San Antonio, Tex.
    - 100% int. in **Inverness Counsel, LLC**, New York, N.Y.
    - 100% int. in **Kore Private Wealth, LLC**, New York, N.Y.
    - 100% int. in **Matrix Capital Advisors, LLC**, Chicago, Ill.
    - 100% int. in **McCutchen Group LLC**, Seattle, Wash.
    - 100% int. in **One Capital Management, LLC**, Westlake Village, Calif.
    - 100% int. in **Portola Partners Group LLC**, Menlo Park, Calif.
    - 100% int. in **RGT Wealth Advisors, LLC**, Dallas, Tex.
    - 100% int. in **R.H. Bluestein & Company**, Birmingham, Mich.
    - 100% int. in **Radnor Financial Advisors, LLC**, Wayne, Pa.
    - 100% int. in **RegentAtlantic Capital, LLC**, Morristown, N.J.
    - 100% int. in **The Roosevelt Investment Group, LLC**, N.Y.
    - 100% int. in **Stavis & Cohen Private Wealth, LLC**, Houston, Tex.
    - 100% int. in **Surevest, LLC**, Phoenix, Ariz.

84% int. in **GSFM Pty Limited**, Sydney, N.S.W., Australia.
65% int. in **Marret Asset Management Inc.**, Toronto, Ont.

Investments

Aligned Capital Partners Inc., Burlington, Ont.

Note: The preceding list includes only the major related companies in which interests are held.

Financial Statistics

Periods ended:	12m Dec. 31/22[A]		12m Dec. 31/21[aA]
	$000s	%Chg	$000s
Total revenue	**2,334,307**	**+8**	**2,169,583**
Other operating expense	1,426,087		1,139,034
Operating expense	**1,426,087**	**+25**	**1,139,034**
Operating income	**908,220**	**-12**	**1,030,549**
Deprec. & amort.	153,247		94,105
Finance costs, gross	153,952		112,386
Pre-tax income	**476,204**	**-19**	**586,166**
Income taxes	174,375		173,792
Net income	**301,829**	**-27**	**412,374**
Net inc. for equity hldrs	**299,757**	**-27**	**409,328**
Net inc. for non-cont. int	**2,072**	**-32**	**3,046**
Cash & equivalent	194,068		362,551
Accounts receivable	298,778		272,962
Current assets	1,833,430		1,839,024
Long-term investments	310,035		306,968
Fixed assets, net	55,587		52,596
Right-of-use assets	139,422		142,606
Intangibles	7,227,700		6,185,237
Total assets	**9,708,358**	**+12**	**8,659,551**
Accts. pay. & accr. liabs	293,246		369,081
Current liabilities	3,288,055		2,698,401
Long-term debt, gross	4,216,214		3,776,038
Long-term debt, net	3,896,214		3,331,552
Long-term lease liabilities	149,360		153,540
Shareholders' equity	1,609,771		1,588,517
Non-controlling interest	13,891		27,123
Cash from oper. activs	**478,916**	**-28**	**665,960**
Cash from fin. activs	(47,542)		483,097
Cash from invest. activs	(508,533)		(1,401,876)
Net cash position	**153,620**	**-33**	**230,779**
Capital expenditures	(17,480)		(7,798)
	$		$
Earnings per share*	1.59		2.03
Cash flow per share*	2.53		3.30
Cash divd. per share*	0.72		0.72
	shs		shs
No. of shs. o/s*	184,517,832		197,422,270
Avg. no. of shs. o/s*	189,089,000		201,628,000
	%		%
Net profit margin	12.93		19.01
Return on equity	18.74		25.82
Return on assets	4.35		6.54
Foreign sales percent	27		15
No. of employees (FTEs)	2,300		2,416

* Common
[a] Restated
[A] Reported in accordance with IFRS

Latest Results

Periods ended:	6m June 30/23[A]		6m June 30/22[A]
	$000s	%Chg	$000s
Total revenue	1,413,908	+18	1,200,405
Net income	81,533	-72	295,775
Net inc. for equity hldrs	80,923	-73	294,357
Net inc. for non-cont. int	610		1,418
	$		$
Earnings per share*	0.45		1.52

* Common
[A] Reported in accordance with IFRS

Historical Summary
(as originally stated)

Fiscal Year	Total Rev. $000s	Net Inc. Bef. Disc. $000s	EPS* $
2022[A]	2,334,307	301,829	1.59
2021[A]	2,727,017	412,374	2.03
2020[A]	2,050,456	475,546	2.22
2019[A]	2,119,227	537,524	2.30
2018[A]	2,236,365	617,847	2.38

* Common
[A] Reported in accordance with IFRS

C.11 CLS Holdings USA, Inc.

Symbol - CLSH **Exchange** - CSE **CUSIP** - 12565J
Head Office - 1800 S. Industrial Rd, Suite 100, Las Vegas, NV, United States, 89102 **Toll-free** - (888) 260-7775
Website - www.clsholdingsinc.com
Email - investors@clsholdingsinc.com
Investor Relations - Andrew J. Glashow (888) 438-9132
Auditors - M&K CPAS, PLLC C.P.A., Houston, Tex.
Transfer Agents - Odyssey Trust Company, Calgary, Alta.; VStock Transfer. LLC, Woodmere, N.Y.
Employees - 108 at Aug. 11, 2022

Profile - (Nev. 2011) Produces, distributes and retails cannabis products in Nevada. Also has a patented proprietary method of extracting cannabinoids from cannabis plants and converting them into products.

Cultivation and manufacturing operations are conducted at a 10,000-sq.-ft. small-scale facility in North Las Vegas, Nev., which produces a line of cannabis concentrates and cannabis-infused products under the City Trees name. City Trees products are distributed through numerous dispensaries located across Nevada. Retail operations consist of a dispensary in Las Vegas, Nev., operating under the Oasis Cannabis name, which carries between 30 and 40 different strains of cannabis flowers and a variety of cannabis products such as vaporizers, concentrated oil, edibles, capsules, tinctures and beverages. The dispensary accounts for a majority of the company's revenue.

The company owns a proprietary method of extracting cannabinoids from cannabis plants and converting the resulting cannabinoid extracts into concentrates such as oils, waxes, edibles and shatter. Plans to generate revenue from the technology through licensing, fee-for-service and joint venture arrangements.

Directors - Andrew J. Glashow, pres. & CEO, R.I.; Ross Silver, Ore.; David Zelinger

Other Exec. Officers - Charlene Soco, exec. v-p, fin.

Capital Stock

	Authorized (shs.)	Outstanding (shs.)[1]	Par
Preferred	20,000,000	nil	US$0.001
Common	187,500,000	72,518,098	US$0.0001

[1] At Oct. 6, 2022

Major Shareholder - Navy Capital Green Management, LLC held 21.36% interest and Tribeca Investments Partners Pty Ltd. held 18.31% interest at Sept. 22, 2022.

Price Range - CLSH/CSE

Year	Volume	High	Low	Close
2022	1,751,590	$0.56	$0.05	$0.07
2021	982,670	$1.96	$0.22	$0.42
2020	705,982	$1.20	$0.26	$0.84
2019	932,349	$1.96	$0.84	$1.08

Consolidation: 1-for-4 cons. in Sept. 2022

CLSH.U/CSE (D)

Year	Volume	High	Low	Close
2019	4,632,748	US$0.75	US$0.25	US$0.30

Recent Close: $0.10

Capital Stock Changes - On Sept. 21, 2022, common shares were consolidated on a 1-for-4 basis.

During fiscal 2022, common shares were issued as follows: 936,666 on conversion of debt and 50,000 to officers.

Wholly Owned Subsidiaries

Alternative Solutions, LLC, Nev.
- 100% int. in **Serenity Wellness Center, LLC**, Nev. dba Oasis Cannabis
- 100% int. in **Serenity Wellness Growers, LLC**, Nev. dba City Trees Fresh Cannabis Cultivation, Wholesale
- 100% int. in **Serenity Wellness Products, LLC**, Nev. dba City Trees Fresh Cannabis Production, Wholesale

CLS Investments, Inc., Nev. Inactive.
CLS Labs Colorado, Inc., Colo. Inactive.
CLS Labs, Inc., Nev.
CLS Massachusetts, Inc., Mass.
CLS Nevada, Inc., Nev.
CLS Rhode Island, Inc., United States.
Cannabis Life Sciences Consulting, LLC, Fla.

Investments

50% int. in **Kealii Okamalu, LLC**, Nev.

Financial Statistics

Periods ended:	12m May 31/22[A]		12m May 31/21[A]
	US$000s	%Chg	US$000s
Operating revenue	**22,663**	**+17**	**19,292**
Cost of goods sold	11,124		9,645
General & admin expense	11,663		10,116
Operating expense	**22,787**	**+15**	**19,761**
Operating income	**(124)**	**n.a.**	**(469)**
Deprec., depl. & amort.	754		685
Finance costs, net	2,150		3,657
Investment income	(112)		nil
Write-downs/write-offs	nil		(2,499)
Pre-tax income	**(399)**	**n.a.**	**(13,400)**
Income taxes	2,041		2,490
Net income	**(2,440)**	**n.a.**	**(15,891)**
Net inc. for equity hldrs	**(2,343)**	**n.a.**	**(15,891)**
Net inc. for non-cont. int	**(97)**	**n.a.**	**nil**
Cash & equivalent	2,552		1,665
Inventories	3,418		1,228
Accounts receivable	618		685
Current assets	6,884		3,841
Long-term investments	470		nil
Fixed assets, net	4,342		3,476
Right-of-use assets	2,155		2,250
Intangibles, net	1,748		1,863
Total assets	**15,828**	**+36**	**11,597**
Accts. pay. & accr. liabs	2,318		1,609
Current liabilities	28,112		4,984
Long-term debt, gross	23,155		20,060
Long-term debt, net	2,694		19,730
Long-term lease liabilities	1,894		1,979
Shareholders' equity	(17,052)		(15,097)
Non-controlling interest	(97)		nil
Cash from oper. activs	**(3,158)**	**n.a.**	**(2,535)**
Cash from fin. activs	3,052		nil
Cash from invest. activs	992		1,275
Net cash position	**2,552**	**+53**	**1,665**
Capital expenditures	(1,105)		(269)
	US$		US$
Earnings per share*	(0.08)		(0.52)
Cash flow per share*	(0.10)		(0.08)
	shs		shs
No. of shs. o/s*	32,052,021		31,805,354
Avg. no. of shs. o/s*	32,032,244		31,666,210
	%		%
Net profit margin	(10.77)		(82.37)
Return on equity	n.m.		n.m.
Return on assets	(17.79)		(118.31)
Foreign sales percent	100		100

* Common
[A] Reported in accordance with U.S. GAAP

Latest Results

Periods ended:	3m Aug. 31/22[A]		3m Aug. 31/21[A]
	US$000s	%Chg	US$000s
Operating revenue	6,045	+10	5,501
Net income	(1,332)	n.a.	428
Net inc. for equity hldrs	(1,148)	n.a.	428
Net inc. for non-cont. int	(184)		nil
	US$		US$
Earnings per share*	(0.05)		0.01

* Common
[A] Reported in accordance with U.S. GAAP

Historical Summary
(as originally stated)

Fiscal Year	Oper. Rev. US$000s	Net Inc. Bef. Disc. US$000s	EPS* US$
2022[A]	22,663	(2,440)	(0.08)
2021[A]	19,292	(15,891)	(0.52)
2020[A]	11,918	(30,658)	(0.96)
2019[A]	8,459	(27,619)	(1.08)
2018[A1]	nil	(9,577)	(0.96)

* Common
[A] Reported in accordance with U.S. GAAP
[1] As shown in the prospectus dated Nov. 30, 2018.
Note: Adjusted throughout for 1-for-4 cons. in Sept. 2022

C.12 CNJ Capital Investments Inc.

Symbol - CNJ.P **Exchange** - TSX-VEN **CUSIP** - 12598T
Head Office - 700-401 Georgia St W, Vancouver, BC, V6B 5A1 **Telephone** - (778) 895-8888
Email - cnjcapitalinvestments@hotmail.com
Investor Relations - Shun Yui Lu (778) 895-8888
Auditors - MNP LLP C.A., Vancouver, B.C.
Lawyers - Richards Buell Sutton LLP, Vancouver, B.C.
Transfer Agents - TSX Trust Company, Vancouver, B.C.
Profile - (B.C. 2021) Capital Pool Company.

Common listed on TSX-VEN, June 21, 2023.

Directors - Christopher (Chris) Chung, pres. & CEO, Vancouver, B.C.; Shun Yui (Raymond) Lu, CFO & corp. sec., B.C.; Chi Wai D. (Jerry) Chan, B.C.; Michael B. (Mike) England, Port Coquitlam, B.C.; Ian M. Mallmann, Richmond, B.C.

Capital Stock

	Authorized (shs.)	Outstanding (shs.)[1]
Common	unlimited	6,200,000

[1] At June 21, 2023

Major Shareholder - Chi Wai D. (Jerry) Chan held 19.35% interest and Christopher (Chris) Chung held 19.35% interest at June 21, 2023.

Recent Close: $0.24

Capital Stock Changes - On June 21, 2023, an initial public offering of 3,000,000 common shares was completed at 10¢ per share.

C.13 COGECO Inc.*

Symbol - CGO **Exchange** - TSX **CUSIP** - 19238T
Head Office - 3301-1 Place Ville-Marie, Montréal, QC, H3B 3N2
Telephone - (514) 764-4600 **Fax** - (514) 874-0776
Website - corpo.cogeco.com/cgo/en
Email - andre-gilles.frigon@cogeco.com
Investor Relations - André-Gilles Frigon (514) 764-4795
Auditors - Deloitte LLP C.A., Montréal, Qué.
Lawyers - Stikeman Elliott LLP, Montréal, Qué.
Transfer Agents - Computershare Trust Company of Canada Inc., Montréal, Qué.
FP500 Revenue Ranking - 170
Employees - 4,700 at Aug. 31, 2022

Profile - (Que. 1957) Provides Internet, video and phone services to residential and business customers in Quebec, Ontario and 13 U.S. states through an 85% voting interest in **Cogeco Communications Inc.** Also operates 20 radio stations in Quebec and one station in Ontario, and a radio news agency.

Subsidiary **Cogeco Communications Inc.** provides Internet, video and phone services through its two-way broadband fibre networks in Canada and the U.S., primarily to residential customers, as well as to small and medium-sized businesses. Services are provided under the name Cogeco Connexion in Quebec and Ontario; and the name Breezeline (formerly Atlantic Broadband) in Pennsylvania, Florida, Maryland, Massachusetts, Delaware, South Carolina, Connecticut, Maine, New Hampshire, New York, Virginia, West Virginia and Ohio.

Wholly owned **Cogeco Media Inc.** owns and operates 20 radio stations across Quebec and one radio station in Ontario and also operates Cogeco Nouvelles, a news agency feeding more than 40 affiliated independent stations.

On Apr. 25, 2022, wholly owned **Cogeco Media Inc.** completed an agreement with **Arsenal Média** to acquire and sell radio stations in Quebec. Cogeco Media acquired from Arsenal Média a radio station in the Saguenay-Lac-Saint-Jean region known as CILM, and simultaneously sold to Arsenal Média two radio stations in the Abitibi-Témiscamingue region known as Capitale Rock and Wow. Terms were not disclosed.

Periods ended:	12m Aug. 31/22	12m Aug. 31/21
Video service customers	975,628	982,708
Internet service customers	1,480,554	1,436,201
Telephony service customers	551,139	553,164

Directors - Louis Audet, chr., Westmount, Qué.; Philippe Jetté, pres. & CEO, Montréal, Qué.; James C. Cherry†, Brockville, Ont.; Arun D. Bajaj, Westmount, Qué.; Mary-Ann Bell, Montréal, Qué.; Patricia Curadeau-Grou, Montréal, Qué.; Samih Elhage, Munich, Germany; Normand Legault, Lac-Brome, Qué.; Caroline Papadatos, Toronto, Ont.

Other Exec. Officers - Linda Gillespie, sr. v-p & chief HR officer; Christian Jolivet, sr. v-p, corp. affairs, chief legal officer & corp. sec.; Marie-Hélène Labrie, sr. v-p & chief public affairs, commun. & strategy officer; Dr. Zouheir Mansourati, sr. v-p & chief tech. officer; Patrice Ouimet, sr. v-p & CFO; Elizabeth Alves, v-p, enterprise strategy & sustainability; Paul Beaudry, v-p, regulatory affairs; France De Blois, v-p, fin.; Martin Grenier, v-p, procurement; Julie Latreille, v-p & treas.; François-Philippe Lessard, v-p, corp. devel.; Caroline Paquet, pres., Cogeco Media

† Lead director

Capital Stock

	Authorized (shs.)	Outstanding (shs.)[1]
Preferred	unlimited	nil
Multiple Voting	unlimited	1,602,217
Subordinate Voting	unlimited	14,009,952

[1] At June 30, 2023

Preferred - Issuable in series. Non-voting.

Multiple Voting - Convertible into subordinate voting shares on a one-for-one basis. Participates equally with subordinate voting shares. Twenty votes per share.

Subordinate Voting - One vote per share.

Normal Course Issuer Bid - The company plans to make normal course purchases of up to 325,000 subordinate voting shares representing 2.3% of the total outstanding. The bid commenced on Jan. 18, 2023, and expires on Jan. 17, 2024.

Major Shareholder - Gestion Audem Inc. held 69.2% interest and Rogers Communications Inc. held 12.9% interest at Nov. 14, 2022.

Price Range - CGO/TSX

Year	Volume	High	Low	Close
2022	3,923,192	$85.00	$52.06	$63.57
2021	3,946,008	$101.24	$75.50	$81.23
2020	8,447,471	$105.99	$70.95	$81.98
2019	4,187,160	$107.88	$57.49	$104.09
2018	3,992,889	$91.26	$54.93	$58.24

Recent Close: $47.92

Capital Stock Changes - During fiscal 2022, 222,902 subordinate voting shares were repurchased under a Normal Course Issuer Bid and 17,603 (net) subordinate voting shares held in trust were distributed.

Dividends

CGO com S.V. Ra $2.924 pa Q est. Nov. 24, 2022
Prev. Rate: $2.50 est. Dec. 9, 2021
Prev. Rate: $2.18 est. Nov. 24, 2020

Long-Term Debt - Outstanding at Aug. 31, 2022:

COGECO Inc.	
3.52% term facility due 2027[1]	$41,955,000
Lease liabilities	66,813,000
Subsidiaries:	
4.18% ser.4 sr. debs. due 2023	299,730,000
3.72% revolving facility due 2027[2]	106,199,000
4.52% sr. term facility tr.1 due 2025[3]	2,060,614,000
5.02% sr. term facility tr.2 due 2028[4]	1,155,801,000
4.14% ser.A sr. notes due 2024[5]	32,742,000
4.3% sr. notes due 2025[6]	281,450,000
4.29% ser.B sr. notes due 2026[7]	196,313,000
2.99% sr. notes due 2031	496,993,000
	4,738,610,000
Less: Current portion	340,468,000
	4,398,142,000

[1] US$32,000,000.
[2] US$81,000,000.
[3] US$1.593 billion.
[4] US$895,500,000.
[5] US$25,000,000.
[6] US$215,000,000.
[7] US$150,000,000.

Wholly Owned Subsidiaries

Cogeco Media Acquisition Inc., Canada.
- 100% int. in **Cogeco Media Inc.**, Qué.

Investments

35% int. in **Cogeco Communications Inc.**, Montréal, Qué. Represents 85% voting interest. (see separate coverage)

Note: The preceding list includes only the major related companies in which interests are held.

Financial Statistics

Periods ended:	12m Aug. 31/22[A]		12m Aug. 31/21[oA]
	$000s	%Chg	$000s
Operating revenue	**2,995,012**	**+15**	**2,603,845**
Salaries & benefits	516,427		472,440
Other operating expense	1,072,997		905,937
Operating expense	**1,589,424**	**+15**	**1,378,377**
Operating income	**1,405,588**	**+15**	**1,225,468**
Deprec., depl. & amort.	625,603		515,255
Finance costs, gross	189,914		128,212
Pre-tax income	**555,042**	**-3**	**573,257**
Income taxes	97,287		134,242
Net inc bef disc ops, eqhldrs	149,108		141,856
Net inc bef disc ops, NCI	308,647		297,159
Net income	**457,755**	**+4**	**439,015**
Net inc. for equity hldrs	**149,108**	**+5**	**141,856**
Net inc. for non-cont. int	**308,647**	**+4**	**297,159**
Cash & equivalent	379,001		551,968
Accounts receivable	123,617		97,624
Current assets	555,494		693,083
Fixed assets, net	3,061,177		2,391,467
Intangibles, net	5,667,300		4,330,228
Total assets	**9,468,025**	**+26**	**7,536,313**
Bank indebtedness	8,633		4,460
Accts. pay. & accr. liabs	396,480		287,915
Current liabilities	1,008,119		808,123
Long-term debt, gross	4,738,610		3,329,910
Long-term debt, net	4,398,142		3,067,940
Shareholders' equity	919,843		816,658
Non-controlling interest	2,349,670		2,074,679
Cash from oper. activs	**1,258,427**	**+22**	**1,029,767**
Cash from fin. activs	970,896		(73,408)
Cash from invest. activs	(2,409,442)		(802,708)
Net cash position	**379,001**	**-31**	**551,968**
Capital expenditures	(747,608)		(539,176)
Capital disposals	4,529		2,564
Unfunded pension liability	n.a.		516
Pension fund surplus	5,271		n.a.
	$		$
Earnings per share*	9.43		8.92
Cash flow per share*	79.55		64.78
Cash divd. per share*	2.50		2.18
	shs		shs
No. of shs. o/s*	15,696,088		15,901,387
Avg. no. of shs. o/s*	15,819,729		15,896,718
	%		%
Net profit margin	15.28		16.86
Return on equity	17.17		17.98
Return on assets	7.23		7.38
Foreign sales percent	49		43
No. of employees (FTEs)	4,700		3,844

* M.V. & S.V.
[o] Restated
[A] Reported in accordance with IFRS

Latest Results

Periods ended:	9m May 31/23[A]		9m May 31/22[A]
	$000s	%Chg	$000s
Operating revenue	2,314,484	+3	2,248,101
Net income	259,714	-25	346,376
Net inc. for equity hldrs	41,396	-63	112,675
Net inc. for non-cont. int	218,318		233,701
	$		$
Earnings per share*	2.65		7.11

* M.V. & S.V.
[A] Reported in accordance with IFRS

Historical Summary
(as originally stated)

Fiscal Year	Oper. Rev. $000s	Net Inc. Bef. Disc. $000s	EPS* $
2022[A]	2,995,012	457,755	9.43
2021[A]	2,603,845	439,015	8.92
2020[A]	2,479,474	401,833	8.05
2019[A]	2,444,062	368,165	7.38
2018[A]	2,538,175	371,713	7.65

* M.V. & S.V.
[A] Reported in accordance with IFRS

C.14 CO2 Gro Inc.

Symbol - GROW **Exchange** - TSX-VEN **CUSIP** - 12595N
Head Office - 5800-40 King St W, Box 1011, Toronto, ON, M5H 3S1
Telephone - (416) 315-7477
Website - www.co2gro.ca
Email - sam.kanes@co2gro.ca
Investor Relations - Samuel Kanes (416) 315-7477
Auditors - McGovern Hurley LLP C.A., Toronto, Ont.
Bankers - The Toronto-Dominion Bank

Lawyers - Miller Thomson LLP
Transfer Agents - Computershare Trust Company of Canada Inc., Toronto, Ont.
Profile - (Ont. 2010) Develops and markets CO_2 Delivery Solutions™ systems which infuse water with dissolved CO_2 that accelerates the growth and health of plants of indoor and protected plant growers.
The CO_2 Delivery Solutions™ create an aqueous CO_2 microfilm around the entire crop leaf which provides CO_2 enrichment as well as microdosing of other desired nutrients. It also boosts yield by up to 30% and provides protection to crops from pathogens such as powdery mildew. The technologies work best for indoor plant grow facilities that do not use CO_2 gassing and can work on farms for plants including cannabis, lettuce, kale, microgreens, peppers, flowers and medical tobacco.
Predecessor Detail - Name changed from BlueOcean NutraSciences Inc., Apr. 12, 2018.
Directors - Michael M. Boyd, chr., Toronto, Ont.; John H. Archibald, pres. & CEO, Grimsby, Ont.; Samuel Kanes, v-p, market research, Toronto, Ont.; Rose Marie Gage, Rockland, Ont.; Dr. Gord Surgeoner, Fergus, Ont.; Tom Wiltrout, Plainfield, Ind.
Other Exec. Officers - Stephen M. Gledhill, CFO & corp. sec.; Aaron Archibald, v-p, sales & strategic alliances

Capital Stock

	Authorized (shs.)	Outstanding (shs.)[1]
Common	unlimited	97,326,698

[1] At May 30, 2023

Major Shareholder - Ospraie AG Science, LLC held 20.5% interest at June 29, 2023.

Price Range - GROW/TSX-VEN

Year	Volume	High	Low	Close
2022	7,496,387	$0.26	$0.08	$0.10
2021	14,255,311	$0.47	$0.12	$0.20
2020	16,084,352	$0.25	$0.06	$0.15
2019	37,981,321	$0.70	$0.17	$0.24
2018	37,016,977	$0.35	$0.12	$0.23

Recent Close: $0.07
Capital Stock Changes - During 2022, common shares were issued as follows: 11,488,695 on exercise of warrants and 1,022,285 on exercise of options.

Wholly Owned Subsidiaries

Asta NutraSciences Inc., Ont. Inactive.
BlueOcean Algae Inc. Inactive.
BlueOcean Shrimp Products Inc, Ont. Inactive.
CO2 GRO (US) Inc., United States. Inactive.
Pure Polar Canada Inc. Inactive.
Pure Polar Labs Inc., Canada. Inactive.
70717 Newfoundland and Labrador Limited, N.L. Inactive.
Solutions4CO2 USA, Inc. Inactive.

Investments

50% int. in **2453969 Ontario Inc.** Inactive.

Financial Statistics

Periods ended:	12m Dec. 31/22[A]		12m Dec. 31/21[A]
	$000s	%Chg	$000s
Operating revenue	**285**	**+10**	**259**
Cost of sales	214		242
Salaries & benefits	569		401
Research & devel. expense	91		149
General & admin expense	679		559
Stock-based compensation	365		331
Operating expense	**1,919**	**+14**	**1,682**
Operating income	**(1,634)**	**n.a.**	**(1,423)**
Deprec., depl. & amort.	24		20
Finance income	14		1
Finance costs, gross	1		1
Write-downs/write-offs	(83)		(178)
Pre-tax income	**(1,765)**	**n.a.**	**(1,655)**
Net income	**(1,765)**	**n.a.**	**(1,655)**
Cash & equivalent	1,097		543
Accounts receivable	98		38
Current assets	1,255		675
Intangibles, net	97		165
Total assets	**1,424**	**+62**	**877**
Accts. pay. & accr. liabs.	207		264
Current liabilities	402		441
Shareholders' equity	921		436
Cash from oper. activs.	**(1,271)**	**n.a.**	**(1,192)**
Cash from fin. activs.	1,882		863
Cash from invest. activs.	(58)		(73)
Net cash position	**1,097**	**+102**	**543**
	$		$
Earnings per share*	(0.02)		(0.02)
Cash flow per share*	(0.01)		(0.01)
	shs		shs
No. of shs. o/s*	97,326,698		84,815,718
Avg. no. of shs. o/s*	96,027,511		83,680,191
	%		%
Net profit margin	(619.30)		(639.00)
Return on equity	(260.13)		(227.18)
Return on assets	(153.32)		(149.89)
Foreign sales percent	88		63

* Common
[A] Reported in accordance with IFRS

Latest Results

Periods ended:	3m Mar. 31/23[A]		3m Mar. 31/22[A]
	$000s	%Chg	$000s
Operating revenue	15	-53	32
Net income	(295)	n.a.	(393)
	$		$
Earnings per share*	(0.00)		(0.00)

* Common
[A] Reported in accordance with IFRS

Historical Summary
(as originally stated)

Fiscal Year	Oper. Rev.	Net Inc. Bef. Disc.	EPS*
	$000s	$000s	$
2022[A]	285	(1,765)	(0.02)
2021[A]	259	(1,655)	(0.02)
2020[A]	91	(994)	(0.01)
2019[A]	11	(1,474)	(0.02)
2018[A]	4	(1,297)	(0.03)

* Common
[A] Reported in accordance with IFRS

C.15 CRAFT 1861 Global Holdings Inc.

Symbol - HUMN **Exchange** - NEO **CUSIP** - 22414D
Head Office - 650-100 Sun Ave NE, Albuquerque, NM, United States, 87109 **Telephone** - (505) 228-8446
Website - craft1861global.com
Email - crystal.buckner@craft1861global.com
Investor Relations - Crystal Buckner (505) 228-8446
Auditors - GreenGrowth C.P.A., Los Angeles, Calif.
Lawyers - McMillan LLP, Vancouver, B.C.
Transfer Agents - Odyssey Trust Company, Vancouver, B.C.
Profile - (B.C. 2020) Produces hemp-derived cannabidiol (CBD) health and wellness products containing zero tetrahydrocannabinol (THC) and has cannabis cultivation, production and retail operations in New Mexico.
In New Mexico, operates an 87,210-sq.-ft. cultivation facility in Belen with 8,100 sq. ft. of mixed light covered canopy and 65,340 sq. ft. of outdoor canopy space with a capacity to produce 16,200 lbs. of cannabis fresh frozen flower and trim annually. Raw cannabis is grown from clones. Operations include finishing of dried/cured cannabis into finished flower, pre-rolls or other dried plant products, as well as the manufacturing of infused products such as edibles, concentrates and topicals. Has two adult-use cannabis retail outlets in Albuquerque under the 1861 Market banner.
CBD products consists of the Craft 1861 Restore line of balms, creams, serums and bath bombs. Sales are generated through the company's e-commerce site with business-to-business sales expected to commence in the first half of 2023.
The company enters into exclusive, multi-year strategic licensing rights partnerships with a number of the largest global athletic organizations in which they pay each strategic partner an annual fee in exchange as consideration of being its exclusive wellness partner. Plans to expands THC operations into other legal jurisdictions through the sale of its proprietary branded THC products.
Class A delisted from NEO, Mar. 2, 2023.
Sub vtg listed on NEO, Mar. 1, 2023.

Recent Merger and Acquisition Activity

Status: pending **Announced:** July 20, 2023
CRAFT 1861 Global Holdings Inc. enter into a letter of intent for a combination Nanocures International, Inc., which would constitute a reverse takeover transaction of CRAFT. Nanocures would acquire all of the issued and outstanding shares of CRAFT for US$474,040,780 cash and equity securities of the combined entity (New Nano), representing 25% of issued and outstanding shares of New Nano, with a total deemed value of approximately US$1,724,040,780. Upon closing, the total enterprise value of New Nano is required to be not less than US$5 billion. Following closing, New Nano would continue to operate the business of CRAFT and plans to rename itself Nanocures International, Inc.
Status: completed **Revised:** Feb. 28, 2023
UPDATE: The transaction was completed. BGP changed its name to CRAFT 1861 Global Holdings Inc. PREVIOUS: BGP Acquisition Corp. agreed to acquire Craft 1861 Global, Inc. for issuance of 430,000 proportionate voting shares valued at US$430,000,000 plus an earnout of an additional 100,000 proportionate voting shares. The transaction would constitute BGP's Qualifying Acquisition. In connection with the transaction, BGF's class A restricted voting shares not required to be redeemed would convert into subordinate voting shares on a one-for-one basis and class B shares would convert into proportionate voting Shares on a 1-for-100 basis. Craft 1861 produces non-psychoactive, hemp-derived CBD health and wellness products and is also a vertically integrated cannabis company with cultivation, production and dispensary operations in New Mexico. Following closing, BGP would continue to operate the business of Craft Global and plans to change its name CRAFT 1861 Global Holdings.
Predecessor Detail - Name changed from BGP Acquisition Corp., Mar. 1, 2023, pursuant to the Qualifying Acquisition of Craft 1861 Global, Inc.
Directors - Robert Aranda, chr. & CEO, Albuquerque, N.M.; Ruth Epstein, Mill Valley, Calif.; Shelly Lombard, N.J.; Dr. Harvey Schiller, N.Y.
Other Exec. Officers - Chris Fitzgerald, CFO; Crystal Buckner, CAO & corp. sec.; Jeffrey Frye, chief mktg. officer; Beverly Henson, CIO; Eric Lujan, chief bus. rev. & devel. officer; Ethan Weinstein, chief legal officer; Alex Robertson, assoc. gen. counsel

Capital Stock

	Authorized (shs.)	Outstanding (shs.)[1]
Proportionate Vtg.	unlimited	464,050
Subord. Vtg.	unlimited	93,406

[1] At Mar. 1, 2023

Subordinate Voting - One vote per share.
Proportionate Voting - Convertible, at the holder's option, into subordinate voting shares on the basis of 100 common shares for 1 proportionate share. 100 votes per share.
Major Shareholder - Robert Aranda held 60.36% interest and Brott LLC held 12.8% interest at Mar. 1, 2023.
Capital Stock Changes - In January 2023, 327,495 class A restricted voting shares were redeemed. On Feb. 28, 2023, all 93,406 remaining class A shares were converted into subordinate voting shares on a one-for-one basis and all 3,475,001 class B shares were converted into proportionate voting shares.
On Nov. 7, 2022, 11,148,381 class A restricted voting shares were redeemed.

Wholly Owned Subsidiaries

Craft 1861 Global, Inc., Albuquerque, N.M.
- 100% int. in **Craft 1861 Gold, LLC**, N.M.
- 100% int. in **Craft 1861, LLC**, N.M.
- 100% int. in **1861 Market, LLC**, N.M. Healthy Education Society.

Financial Statistics

Periods ended:	12m Dec. 31/21[A1]		12m Dec. 31/20[A1]
	US$000s	%Chg	US$000s
Operating revenue	**1,702**	**+78**	**954**
Cost of goods sold	(725)[2]		1,159
General & admin expense	11,443		9,330
Operating expense	**10,717**	**+2**	**10,489**
Operating income	**(9,015)**	**n.a.**	**(9,535)**
Finance income	855		813
Finance costs, gross	713		634
Pre-tax income	**(8,874)**	**n.a.**	**(9,356)**
Income taxes	539		(136)
Net income	**(9,413)**	**n.a.**	**(9,220)**
Cash & equivalent	886		29
Inventories	1,703		155
Accounts receivable	76		2
Current assets	3,234		356
Fixed assets, net	41		54
Right-of-use assets	258		183
Total assets	**3,533**	**+393**	**716**
Accts. pay. & accr. liabs	1,324		259
Current liabilities	31,911		22,668
Long-term debt, gross	103		nil
Long-term debt, net	80		nil
Long-term lease liabilities	309		189
Shareholders' equity	(29,129)		(22,142)
Cash from oper. activs	**(9,525)**	**n.a.**	**(9,190)**
Cash from fin. activs	10,628		9,437
Cash from invest. activs	(245)		(261)
Net cash position	**886**	**n.m.**	**29**
Capital expenditures	(245)		(261)
	US$		US$
Earnings per share*	n.a.		n.a.
	shs		shs
No. of shs. o/s	n.a.		n.a.
	%		%
Net profit margin	(553.06)		(966.46)
Return on equity	n.m.		n.m.
Return on assets	(407.47)		n.a.

[A] Reported in accordance with IFRS

[1] Results pertain to The Natively Group, a group of four cannabis companies (Healthy Education Society; Zia Plus, LLC; CRAFT 1861, LLC/Natively, LLC; CRAFT 1861 Gold, LLC).

[2] Net of unrealized gain on changes in fair value of biological assets of $1,481,417 and realized fair value on inventory sold of $22,306.

C.16 CT Real Estate Investment Trust

Symbol - CRT.UN **Exchange** - TSX **CUSIP** - 126462

Head Office - c/o Canadian Tire Corporation, Limited, 2180 Yonge St, PO Box 770 Stn K, Toronto, ON, M4P 2V8 **Telephone** - (416) 480-2029 **Toll-free** - (855) 770-7348 **Fax** - (416) 480-3216

Website - www.ctreit.com

Email - lesley.gibson@ctreit.com

Investor Relations - Lesley Gibson (855) 770-7348

Auditors - Deloitte LLP C.A., Toronto, Ont.

Transfer Agents - Computershare Trust Company of Canada Inc., Toronto, Ont.

FP500 Subsidiary Revenue Ranking - 92

Employees - 59 at Dec. 31, 2022

Profile - (Ont. 2013) Owns, manages and develops primarily net lease retail properties across Canada, leased 92% to parent company **Canadian Tire Corporation, Limited** (CTC). At Mar. 31, 2023, the trust held 365 retail properties, four industrial properties, a mixed-use commercial property and three development properties, totaling 30,040,543 sq. ft. of gross leasable area.

Parent company CTC licenses its associate dealers to operate more than 500 Canadian Tire retail stores across Canada and an additional 1,200 retail stores are operated under various other CTC banners including SportChek, Mark's, PartSource, Canadian Tire Gas+, Helly Hansen and Party City.

At Mar. 31, 2023, the trust's portfolio consisted of 261 Canadian Tire single tenant properties, 27 other single tenant properties, 69 multi-tenant properties anchored by a Canadian Tire store, eight multi-tenant properties not anchored by a Canadian Tire store, four industrial properties, one mixed-use property and three development properties. CTC represented 92% of the total gross leasable area (GLA).

Property portfolio mix at Mar. 31, 2023 (excluding properties under development):

Property type	GLA
Retail properties	
Canadian Tire stores	22,907,190
Third-party tenants	2,093,896
Other CTC banners[1]	632,869
	25,633,955
Industrial properties	4,205,749
Mixed-use property	200,839
Total	30,040,543

[1] Include Mark's, L'Équipeur, SportChek, Sports Experts and Canadian Tire Bank.

During 2022, the trust acquired a Canadian Tire store in Kingston, Ont., and development lands in Lloydminster, Alta., from **Canadian Tire Corporation, Limited**; land containing a Canadian Tire store from a third party in Kingston, Ont.; and development lands adjoining existing Canadian Tire stores and for the development of new Canadian Tire stores from third parties in Napanee, Ont., Sherbrooke, Que., Invermere, B.C., and Moose Jaw, Sask. Total investment cost was $210,291,000 for acquisitions of income-producing properties and intensification/development/redevelopment of existing properties.

Trustees - John O'Bryan, chr., Aurora, Ont.; Kevin Salsberg, pres. & CEO, Toronto, Ont.; Pauline Alimchandani, Toronto, Ont.; Heather Briant, Toronto, Ont.; Gregory C. (Greg) Craig, Toronto, Ont.; Anna Martini, Montréal, Qué.; Dean C. McCann, Toronto, Ont.; Kelly Smith, Toronto, Ont.

Other Exec. Officers - Lesley Gibson, CFO; Kimberley M. Graham, sr. v-p, gen. counsel & corp. sec.; Jodi M. Shpigel, sr. v-p, real estate; Clint Elenko, v-p, western Canada; David Goldstein, v-p, eastern Canada; Victor Iaccino, v-p, opers. & sustainable devel.; Glenn Wotton, v-p, const.

Capital Stock

	Authorized (shs.)	Outstanding (shs.)[1]
Preferred Unit	unlimited	nil
Trust Unit	unlimited	107,777,846
Special Voting Unit	unlimited	127,193,833
Class B LP Unit	unlimited	127,193,833
Class C LP Unit		[2]
Series 3		200,000
Series 4		200,000
Series 5		200,000
Series 6		200,000
Series 7		200,000
Series 8		200,000
Series 9		200,000
Series 16		16,550
Series 17		18,500
Series 18		4,900
Series 19		11,600

[1] At Mar. 31, 2023

[2] Classified as debt.

Note: Limited partnership units are securities of CT REIT Limited Partnership.

Trust Unit - One vote per unit.

Special Voting Unit - Issued to holders of class B limited partnership units of subsidiary CT REIT Limited Partnership and in limited circumstances to holders of class C limited partnership units of CT REIT. Each special voting unit entitles the holder to a number of votes at unitholder meetings equal to the number of trust units into which the class B limited partnership units are exchangeable.

Class B Limited Partnership Unit - Entitled to distributions equal to those provided to trust units. Directly exchangeable into trust units on a 1-for-1 basis at any time by holder. All held by Canadian Tire Corporation, Limited. Classified as non-controlling interest.

Class C Limited Partnership Unit - Issued at $1,000 per limited partnership unit. Entitled to cumulative preferential monthly distributions in priority to distributions to holders of class B limited partnership units. All held by Canadian Tire Corporation, Limited. Classified as debt. Non-voting. **Series 3** - The distribution rate during the initial fixed rate period expiring on May 31, 2025, is 2.37%. **Series 4** - The distribution rate during the initial fixed rate period expiring on May 31, 2024, is 4.5%. **Series 5** - The distribution rate during the initial fixed rate period expiring on May 31, 2028, is 4.5%. **Series 6** - The distribution rate during the initial fixed rate period expiring on May 31, 2031, is 5%. **Series 7** - The distribution rate during the initial fixed rate period expiring on May 31, 2034, is 5%. **Series 8** - The distribution rate during the initial fixed rate period expiring on May 31, 2035, is 5%. **Series 9** - The distribution rate during the initial fixed rate period expiring on May 31, 2038, is 5%. **Series 16** - The distribution rate during the initial fixed rate period expiring on May 31, 2025, is 2.37%. **Series 17** - The distribution rate during the initial fixed rate period expiring on May 31, 2025, is 2.37%. **Series 18** - The distribution rate during the initial fixed rate period expiring on May 31, 2025, is 2.37%. **Series 19** - The distribution rate during the initial fixed rate period expiring on May 31, 2025, is 2.37%.

Normal Course Issuer Bid - The company plans to make normal course purchases of up to 3,300,000 trust units representing 3.1% of the total outstanding. The bid commenced on Nov. 29, 2022, and expires on Nov. 28, 2023.

Major Shareholder - Canadian Tire Corporation, Limited held 68.6% interest at Mar. 31, 2023.

Price Range - CRT.UN/TSX

Year	Volume	High	Low	Close
2022	34,347,144	$18.46	$14.21	$15.59
2021	38,181,902	$18.42	$15.11	$17.32
2020	62,519,782	$17.22	$9.14	$15.67
2019	52,180,097	$16.30	$11.47	$16.14
2018	14,711,238	$14.68	$11.26	$11.53

Recent Close: $14.61

Capital Stock Changes - During 2022, 1,197,656 trust units were issued under distribution reinvestment plan.

Dividends

CRT.UN unit Ra $0.8982 pa M est. July 17, 2023**
Prev. Rate: $0.86784 est. July 15, 2022
Prev. Rate: $0.8393 est. July 15, 2021
Prev. Rate: $0.80316 est. Sept. 15, 2020
** Reinvestment Option

Wholly Owned Subsidiaries

CT REIT GP Corp., Ont.

Investments

45.9% int. in **CT REIT Limited Partnership**, Ont.

Financial Statistics

Periods ended:	12m Dec. 31/22[A]		12m Dec. 31/21[A]
	$000s	%Chg	$000s
Total revenue	**532,795**	**+4**	**514,537**
Rental operating expense	19,609		18,193
General & admin. expense	14,478		14,593
Property taxes	91,524		89,097
Operating expense	**125,611**	**+3**	**121,883**
Operating income	**407,184**	**+4**	**392,654**
Finance income	256		14
Finance costs, gross	110,672		105,720
Pre-tax income	**324,613**	**-29**	**456,859**
Net income	**324,613**	**-29**	**456,859**
Net inc. for equity hldrs	**148,264**	**-29**	**208,169**
Net inc. for non-cont. int	**176,349**	**-29**	**248,690**
Cash & equivalent	2,611		3,555
Accounts receivable	3,734		2,884
Current assets	9,926		9,444
Income-producing props	6,703,462		6,409,844
Properties under devel	129,538		79,156
Property interests, net	6,833,000		6,489,000
Total assets	**6,844,789**	**+5**	**6,500,102**
Bank indebtedness	99,884		79,300
Current liabilities	278,660		303,355
Long-term debt, gross	2,687,750		2,598,561
Long-term debt, net	2,631,583		2,438,394
Long-term lease liabilities	102,223		74,707
Shareholders' equity	1,698,250		1,622,365
Non-controlling interest	2,128,923		2,055,784
Cash from oper. activs	**399,273**	**-2**	**407,201**
Cash from fin. activs	(180,600)		(261,411)
Cash from invest. activs	(219,617)		(146,766)
Net cash position	**2,611**	**-27**	**3,555**
Capital expenditures	(197,953)		(94,722)
Increase in property	(21,664)		(73,229)
Decrease in property	nil		21,185
	$		$
Earnings per share*	1.39		1.97
Cash flow per share*	3.74		3.85
Funds from opers. per sh.*	1.27		1.24
Adj. funds from opers. per sh.*	1.15		1.11
Cash divd. per share*	0.86		0.82
Total divd. per share*	**0.86**		**0.82**
	shs		shs
No. of shs. o/s*	107,501,944		106,304,288
Avg. no. of shs. o/s*	106,893,856		105,714,887
	%		%
Net profit margin	60.93		88.79
Return on equity	8.93		13.41
Return on assets	6.52		8.88
No. of employees (FTEs)	59		58

* Trust Unit

[A] Reported in accordance with IFRS

Latest Results

Periods ended:	3m Mar. 31/23[A]		3m Mar. 31/22[A]
	$000s	%Chg	$000s
Total revenue	137,506	+4	131,950
Net income	70,511	-24	93,079
Net inc. for equity hldrs	32,319	-24	42,462
Net inc. for non-cont. int	38,192		50,617
	$		$
Earnings per share*	0.30		0.40

* Trust Unit

[A] Reported in accordance with IFRS

Historical Summary
(as originally stated)

Fiscal Year	Total Rev. $000s	Net Inc. Bef. Disc. $000s	EPS* $
2022[A]	532,795	324,613	1.39
2021[A]	514,537	456,859	1.97
2020[A]	502,348	183,305	0.80
2019[A]	489,013	307,193	1.38
2018[A]	472,483	300,906	1.40

* Trust Unit

[A] Reported in accordance with IFRS

C.17 CU Inc.

CUSIP - 126577

Head Office - c/o ATCO Ltd., West Building, 400-5302 Forand St SW, Calgary, AB, T3E 8B4 **Telephone** - (403) 292-7500 **Fax** - (403) 292-7532

Website - www.canadianutilities.com

Email - colin.jackson@atco.com
Investor Relations - Colin R. Jackson (403) 808-2636
Auditors - PricewaterhouseCoopers LLP C.A., Calgary, Alta.
Lawyers - Bennett Jones LLP, Calgary, Alta.
Transfer Agents - TSX Trust Company, Calgary, Alta.
FP500 Subsidiary Revenue Ranking - 30
Employees - 3,695 at Dec. 31, 2022

Profile - (Can. 1999) Distributes and transmits electricity and natural gas in western and northern Canada.

Wholly owned **ATCO Electric Ltd.** is engaged in the regulated business of transmitting and distributing electricity to about 263,000 customers in 240 communities and rural areas in northern and east-central Alberta; three communities in Saskatchewan; 19 communities in Yukon and one community in British Columbia (through wholly owned **ATCO Electric Yukon**); and nine communities in the Northwest Territories (through 50%-owned **Northland Utilities (NWT) Limited** and **Northland Utilities (Yellowknife) Limited**). Operations include 11,000 km of transmission lines, 60,000 km of distribution lines, and 20 diesel and two hydroelectric plants and 12 solar sites in Alberta, Yukon and the Northwest Territories. The company also delivers power to and operates 3,500 km of distribution lines owned by Rural Electrification Associations; and operates Alberta PowerLine (APL), a 500-km, 500-kV electricity transmission line running from Wabamun to Fort McMurray, Alta., on behalf of APL's owners under a 35-year contract.

Wholly owned **ATCO Gas and Pipelines Ltd.** conducts regulated natural gas distribution and transmission activities. Natural gas is distributed to about 1,300,000 customers throughout Alberta and in the Lloydminster area of Saskatchewan through 41,500 km of distribution mains, with principal markets in the communities of Edmonton, Calgary, Airdrie, Fort McMurray, Grande Prairie, Lethbridge, Lloydminster, Red Deer, Spruce Grove, St. Albert and Sherwood Park. Natural gas transmission operations consist of a natural gas transmission system in Alberta, with a peak delivery capacity of 4.85 bcf per day, consisting of 9,100 km of pipelines, 16 compressor sites, 3,700 receipt and delivery points, and a salt cavern storage peaking facility near Fort Saskatchewan, Alta. ATCO Gas and Pipelines receives natural gas on its pipeline system from various gas processing plants and from connections with other natural gas transmission systems, and transports the gas to end users within Alberta or to other pipeline systems for export out of the province.

Periods ended:	12m Dec. 31/22	12m Dec. 31/21
Generating capacity, MW	47	47
Transmission lines, km	11,000	11,000
Distribution lines, km	60,000	60,000
Electric. dist., million KWh	12,489	12,491
Electric. customers	262,578	261,370
Nat gas dist pipelines, km	41,500	41,000
Nat gas transmn pipelines, km	9,100	9,200
Nat. gas distrib., pj	277	270
Nat. gas customers	1,271,541	1,254,731

Directors - Nancy C. Southern, chr. & CEO, Calgary, Alta.; Linda A. Southern-Heathcott, v-chr., Calgary, Alta.; Robert T. (Bob) Booth, Calgary, Alta.; Loraine M. Charlton, Calgary, Alta.; Robert J. (Bob) Normand, Edmonton, Alta.

Other Exec. Officers - Rebecca A. (Becky) Penrice, exec. v-p, corp. srvcs.; Brian P. Shkrobot, exec. v-p & CFO; Kyle M. Brunner, sr. v-p, gen. counsel & corp. sec.; Colin R. Jackson, sr. v-p, fin., treasury & sustainability; Melanie L. Bayley, pres., ATCO Electric Ltd.; D. Jason Sharpe, pres., ATCO Gas and Pipelines Ltd.

Capital Stock

	Authorized (shs.)	Outstanding (shs.)[1]	Par
Preferred	unlimited		
4.6% Series 1		4,600,000	$25
2.292% Series 4		3,000,000	$25
Class A Non-vtg.	unlimited	3,570,322	n.p.v.
Class B Common	unlimited	2,188,262	n.p.v.

[1] At Apr. 25, 2023

Note: All class A non-voting and class B common shares are held by Canadian Utilities Limited, which is controlled by ATCO Ltd.

Preferred - Issuable in series and non-voting. **Series 1** - Entitled to fixed cumulative annual dividends of $1.15 per share payable quarterly. Redeemable at $25 per share plus accrued and unpaid dividends. **Series 4** - Entitled to fixed cumulative annual dividends of $0.5725 per share payable quarterly to June 1, 2026, and thereafter at a rate reset every five years equal to the five-year Government of Canada bond yield plus 1.36%. Redeemable on June 1, 2026, and on June 1 every five years thereafter at $25 per share plus accrued and unpaid dividends. Convertible at the holder's option on June 1, 2026, and on June 1 every five years thereafter, into floating rate preferred series 5 shares on a share-for-share basis, subject to certain conditions. The series 5 shares would pay a quarterly dividend equal to the 90-day Canadian Treasury bill rate plus 1.36%.

Class A Non-Voting - Non-voting. All held by Canadian Utilities Limited.

Class B Common - Convertible any time into class A non-voting shares on a 1-for-1 basis. One vote per share. All held by Canadian Utilities Limited.

Major Shareholder - Canadian Utilities Limited held 100% interest at Apr. 25, 2023.

Capital Stock Changes - There were no changes to capital stock during 2022.

Dividends

CIU.PR.A pfd ser 1 cum. red. Ra $1.15 pa Q
CIU.PR.C pfd ser 4 cum. red. exch. Adj. Ra $0.5725 pa Q est. Sept. 1, 2021

Wholly Owned Subsidiaries

ATCO Electric Ltd., Calgary, Alta.
- 100% int. in **ATCO Electric Yukon**, Yuk.
- 50% int. in **Northland Utilities Enterprises Ltd.**, N.W.T.
  - 100% int. in **Northland Utilities (NWT) Limited**, N.W.T.
  - 100% int. in **Northland Utilities (Yellowknife) Limited**, Calgary, Alta.

ATCO Gas and Pipelines Ltd., Alta.

Financial Statistics

Periods ended:	12m Dec. 31/22[A]		12m Dec. 31/21[A]
	$000s	%Chg	$000s
Operating revenue	**3,151,000**	**+12**	**2,823,000**
Salaries & benefits	223,000		221,000
Other operating expense	1,213,000		1,174,000
Operating expense	**1,436,000**	**+3**	**1,395,000**
Operating income	**1,715,000**	**+20**	**1,428,000**
Deprec., depl. & amort.	559,000		547,000
Finance income	5,000		1,000
Finance costs, gross	364,000		373,000
Pre-tax income	**797,000**	**+57**	**509,000**
Income taxes	193,000		122,000
Net income	**604,000**	**+56**	**387,000**
Cash & equivalent	7,000		121,000
Inventories	17,000		13,000
Accounts receivable	537,000		475,000
Current assets	576,000		688,000
Long-term investments	17,000		nil
Fixed assets, net	16,533,000		16,217,000
Right-of-use assets	15,000		11,000
Intangibles, net	755,000		674,000
Total assets	**17,950,000**	**+2**	**17,612,000**
Bank indebtedness	19,000		275,000
Accts. pay. & accr. liabs	645,000		489,000
Current liabilities	826,000		960,000
Long-term debt, gross	8,485,000		8,401,000
Long-term debt, net	8,385,000		8,276,000
Long-term lease liabilities	14,000		10,000
Preferred share equity	187,000		187,000
Shareholders' equity	5,029,000		4,894,000
Cash from oper. activs	**1,818,000**	**+23**	**1,480,000**
Cash from fin. activs	(991,000)		(323,000)
Cash from invest. activs	(891,000)		(1,083,000)
Net cash position	**(12,000)**	**n.a.**	**52,000**
Capital expenditures	(898,000)		(885,000)
	$		$
Earnings per share*	n.a.		n.a.
Cash divd. per share*	85.71		64.32
	shs		shs
No. of shs. o/s*	5,758,584		5,758,584
Avg. no. of shs. o/s*	5,758,584		5,758,584
	%		%
Net profit margin	19.17		13.71
Return on equity	12.50		8.05
Return on assets	4.95		3.88
No. of employees (FTEs)	3,695		3,242

* Class A & B
[A] Reported in accordance with IFRS

Latest Results

Periods ended:	3m Mar. 31/23[A]		3m Mar. 31/22[A]
	$000s	%Chg	$000s
Operating revenue	877,000	-4	917,000
Net income	209,000	-6	222,000
	$		$
Earnings per share*	n.a.		n.a.

[A] Reported in accordance with IFRS

Historical Summary
(as originally stated)

Fiscal Year	Oper. Rev. $000s	Net Inc. Bef. Disc. $000s	EPS* $
2022[A]	3,151,000	604,000	n.a.
2021[A]	2,823,000	387,000	n.a.
2020[A]	2,730,000	404,000	n.a.
2019[A]	2,787,000	746,000	n.a.
2018[A]	2,507,000	345,000	n.a.

* Class A & B
[A] Reported in accordance with IFRS

C.18 CULT Food Science Corp.

Symbol - CULT **Exchange** - CSE **CUSIP** - 230266
Head Office - 810-789 Pender St W, Vancouver, BC, V6C 1H2
Telephone - (604) 687-2038 **Toll-free** - (833) 439-2858
Website - www.cultfoodscience.com
Email - ir@cultfoodscience.com
Investor Relations - Nick Kuzyk (833) 439-2858
Auditors - SHIM & Associates LLP C.A., Vancouver, B.C.
Transfer Agents - Endeavor Trust Corporation, Vancouver, B.C.

Profile - (B.C. 1983) Invests in companies that operate in the cultivated meat and cultured dairy food technology sectors around the world, and operates the CULT Foods division.

Investments may include the acquisition of equity, debt or other securities of publicly traded or private companies or other entities, financing in exchange for pre-determined royalties or distributions and the acquisition of all or part of one or more businesses, portfolios or other assets.

Target investments may include companies involved in the following spaces: (i) cultivated meat, (ii) cultured dairy, (iii) food technology, (iv) cultured non-meat food products, (v) sponsored or collaborative cellular agricultural research and development opportunities, (vi) cellular agricultural intellectual property, (vii) cellular agricultural media and public relations companies.

At June 30, 2022, investments included Simple Agreement for Future Equity (SAFE) agreements with **Biftek Inc.**, **Cell AG Tech Inc.**, **MeliBio Inc.**, **Mogale Meat Co.**, **Novel Farms Inc.**, **De Novo Foods, Inc.**, **Fiction Foods Inc.**, **Jellatech**, **Ohayo Valley Inc.**, **Umami Meats Pte. Ltd.**, **Opalia Co.**, **California Cultured Inc.** and **Pearlita Foods**; equity investments in **Eat Just, Inc.**, **BSF Enterprise plc** and **Steakholder Foods Ltd.** (formerly **Meatech 3D Ltd.**); and equity and convertible notes investments in **Change Foods**. Total fair value of investments was $3,857,026.

The CULT Foods division develops and commercializes cell-based products in collaboration with its affiliate companies. The initial two new products launched are: Zero Coffee, a sparkling coffee beverage made with cell-based coffee; and Free Candy, a performance gummy made with cell-based collagen.

In January 2023, the company expanded its operations with the launch of a new products division, CULT Foods, which will develop and commercialize cell-based products in collaboration with its affiliate companies.

In September 2022, the company acquired **Food Revolution Media Inc.**, an online publisher of news, interviews and editorials focused on early-stage growth companies in the plant-based and cell-based foods sectors, for issuance of 15,000,000 common shares. An additional 15,000,000 common shares would be issued upon Food Revolution achieving certain quantitative milestones.

Predecessor Detail - Name changed from Triangle Industries Ltd., July 28, 2021.

Directors - Francis Rowe, CFO & corp. sec., Victoria, B.C.; Dorian Banks, Vancouver, B.C.; Kirill Kompaniyets, Toronto, Ont.

Other Exec. Officers - Lejjy Gafour, CEO; Joshua Errett, v-p, product devel.

Capital Stock

	Authorized (shs.)	Outstanding (shs.)[1]
Common	unlimited	50,583,136

[1] At Aug. 23, 2023

Major Shareholder - Marc Lustig held 13.6% interest at June 26, 2023.

Price Range - CULT/CSE

Year	Volume	High	Low	Close
2022	36,679,772	$2.60	$0.08	$0.12
2019	166,694	$6.00	$3.00	$3.00
2018	271,678	$8.60	$1.00	$5.30

Consolidation: 1-for-4 cons. in Aug. 2023; 2-for-1 split in Aug. 2021; 1-for-10 cons. in Dec. 2020

Recent Close: $0.16

Capital Stock Changes - On Aug. 23, 2023, common shares were consolidated on a 1-for-4 basis.

In September 2022, 15,000,000 common shares were issued pursuant to the acquisition of Food Revolution Media Inc.

Wholly Owned Subsidiaries

Food Revolution Media Inc.

Investments

BSF Enterprise plc, London, Middx., United Kingdom.
Change Foods, Palo Alto, Calif.
Eat Just, Inc., San Francisco, Calif.
Steakholder Foods Ltd., Rehovot, Israel.

Financial Statistics

Periods ended:	12m Dec. 31/21^A		12m Dec. 31/20^A
	$000s	%Chg	$000s
General & admin expense	919		96
Stock-based compensation	1,628		nil
Operating expense	**2,547**	**n.m.**	**96**
Operating income	**(2,547)**	**n.a.**	**(96)**
Deprec., depl. & amort.	4		6
Finance income	nil		6
Finance costs, gross	nil		1
Write-downs/write-offs	nil		(109)
Pre-tax income	**(2,552)**	**n.a.**	**(206)**
Net income	**(2,552)**	**n.a.**	**(206)**
Cash & equivalent	2,021		2
Current assets	2,936		2
Long-term investments	3,501		nil
Fixed assets, net	11		15
Total assets	**6,448**	**n.m.**	**17**
Accts. pay. & accr. liabs.	218		118
Current liabilities	218		140
Shareholders' equity	6,230		(123)
Cash from oper. activs.	**(1,636)**	**n.a.**	**(19)**
Cash from fin. activs.	7,156		20
Net cash position	**2,021**	**n.m.**	**2**
	$		$
Earnings per share*	(0.20)		(0.16)
Cash flow per share*	(0.12)		(0.01)
	shs		shs
No. of shs. o/s*	34,826,038		1,306,136
Avg. no. of shs. o/s*	13,853,907		1,306,136
	%		%
Net profit margin	n.a.		n.a.
Return on equity	n.m.		n.m.
Return on assets	(78.95)		(288.73)

* Common
^A Reported in accordance with IFRS

Latest Results

Periods ended:	3m Mar. 31/22^A		3m Mar. 31/21^A
	$000s	%Chg	$000s
Net income	(1,806)	n.a.	(26)
	$		$
Earnings per share*	(0.04)		(0.02)

* Common
^A Reported in accordance with IFRS

Historical Summary (as originally stated)

Fiscal Year	Oper. Rev.	Net Inc. Bef. Disc.	EPS*
	$000s	$000s	$
2021^A	nil	(2,552)	(0.20)
2020^A	nil	(206)	(0.16)
2019^A	nil	(238)	(0.20)
2018^A	nil	(1,003)	(1.00)
2017^A	nil	(29)	(0.11)

* Common
^A Reported in accordance with IFRS

Note: Adjusted throughout for 1-for-4 cons. in Aug. 2023; 2-for-1 split in Aug. 2021; 1-for-10 cons. in Dec. 2020; 1-for-2.5 cons. in Apr. 2018

C.19 CVR Medical Corp.

Symbol - CVM.H **Exchange** - TSX-VEN (S) **CUSIP** - 088895
Head Office - 409-221 Esplanade W, North Vancouver, BC, V7M 3J3 **Telephone** - (604) 669-0780 **Fax** - (604) 669-0774
Website - www.cvrmed.com
Email - paulblunden@cvrmed.com
Investor Relations - Dr. Paul Blunden (604) 669-0780
Auditors - Dale Matheson Carr-Hilton LaBonte LLP C.A., Vancouver, B.C.
Transfer Agents - TSX Trust Company, Vancouver, B.C.
Profile - (B.C. 1980) Commercializing a diagnostic device designed to detect and measure carotid arterial narrowing.

The Carotid Stenotic Scan (CSS) is a non-invasive device that listens to soundwaves produced by the flow of blood within the carotid arteries and analyzes the data to provide the clinician with a report detailing the level of narrowing present. **CVR Global, Inc.**, which originally developed the CSS, is responsible for managing all research and development, clinical pathway, governmental and regulatory filings including the submission with the U.S. FDA and maintaining the intellectual property portfolio under a commercialization agreement which has a 20-year term to 2038. CVR Global is entitled to a 7% royalty on all CSS devices sold paid quarterly, in arrears, with a 3% royalty on all consumables.

In April 2021, the company entered into an amended restructuring agreement with **CVR Global, Inc.**, whereby the company would acquire CVR Global's intellectual property necessary to commercialize Carotid Stenotic Scan (CSS) device and all of CVR Global's technology related to its proprietary sub-sonic, infrasonic and low frequency sound wave analysis for issuance of 20,000,000 units (1 common share & 1 warrant) and a royalty of 8% for manufacturer's suggested retail price of CSS products. The company would assume all operational control of the CSS device, and all duties, responsibilities, liabilities, and obligations related to the CSS, and should have the sole and exclusive obligation and responsibility to bring the CSS to market and to develop all improvements and innovations. The proposed acquisition requires shareholder and TSX Venture Exchange approval. At June 2022, the transaction was still pending.

Common suspended from TSX-VEN, May 9, 2022.

Predecessor Detail - Name changed from Big Bar Resources Corporation, Sept. 23, 2016, following purchase of patents relating to a diagnostic device.

Directors - Dr. Paul Blunden, pres. & CFO, Fla.; Dr. Phillip (Phil) Bendick, Mich.; Joseph Lynch; Trish Perzyk-Howell
Other Exec. Officers - Darren Day, CEO

Capital Stock

	Authorized (shs.)	Outstanding (shs.)[1]
Common	unlimited	107,233,206

[1] At Aug. 29, 2022

Major Shareholder - CVR Global Inc. held 28.1% interest at Feb. 28, 2022.

Price Range - CVM.H/TSX-VEN (S)

Year	Volume	High	Low	Close
2022	4,334,432	$0.05	$0.02	$0.02
2021	31,177,680	$0.15	$0.02	$0.04
2020	32,987,708	$0.09	$0.02	$0.03
2019	14,172,169	$0.37	$0.20	$0.20
2018	25,113,426	$0.50	$0.22	$0.25

Capital Stock Changes - In May 2022, private placement of 2,005,334 units (1 common share & 1 warrant) at Cdn$0.03 per unit was completed, with warrants exercisable at Cdn$0.05 per share for five years.

Wholly Owned Subsidiaries

CVRM, Inc., Del.

Financial Statistics

Periods ended:	12m Dec. 31/21^A		12m Dec. 31/20^A
	US$000s	%Chg	US$000s
Research & devel. expense	28		60
General & admin expense	599		318
Stock-based compensation	(43)		(248)
Operating expense	**584**	**+346**	**131**
Operating income	**(584)**	**n.a.**	**(131)**
Finance costs, net	75		76
Write-downs/write-offs	(1,173)		nil
Pre-tax income	**(1,818)**	**n.a.**	**(173)**
Net income	**(1,818)**	**n.a.**	**(173)**
Cash & equivalent	94		3
Current assets	98		66
Intangibles, net	nil		1,153
Total assets	**98**	**-92**	**1,219**
Accts. pay. & accr. liabs.	1,310		1,218
Current liabilities	4,280		3,564
Long-term debt, gross	528		364
Long-term debt, net	28		87
Shareholders' equity	(4,456)		(2,686)
Cash from oper. activs.	**(88)**	**n.a.**	**(180)**
Cash from fin. activs.	198		181
Net cash position	**94**	**n.m.**	**3**
	US$		US$
Earnings per share*	(0.02)		(0.00)
Cash flow per share*	(0.00)		(0.00)
	shs		shs
No. of shs. o/s*	105,227,872		101,377,872
Avg. no. of shs. o/s*	101,462,256		101,377,872
	%		%
Net profit margin	n.a.		n.a.
Return on equity	n.m.		n.m.
Return on assets	(276.08)		(14.24)

* Common
^A Reported in accordance with IFRS

Latest Results

Periods ended:	6m June 30/22^A		6m June 30/21^A
	US$000s	%Chg	US$000s
Net income	(325)	n.a.	(188)
	US$		US$
Earnings per share*	(0.00)		(0.00)

* Common
^A Reported in accordance with IFRS

Historical Summary (as originally stated)

Fiscal Year	Oper. Rev.	Net Inc. Bef. Disc.	EPS*
	US$000s	US$000s	US$
2021^A	nil	(1,818)	(0.02)
2020^A	nil	(173)	(0.00)
2019^A	nil	(5,137)	(0.05)
2018^A	nil	(7,442)	(0.10)
	$000s	$000s	$
2017^A	nil	(8,494)	(0.15)

* Common
^A Reported in accordance with IFRS

C.20 CWC Energy Services Corp.

Symbol - CWC **Exchange** - TSX-VEN **CUSIP** - 12671H
Head Office - 2910-605 5 Ave SW, Calgary, AB, T2P 3H5 **Telephone** - (403) 264-2177 **Toll-free** - (877) 341-3933 **Fax** - (403) 264-2842
Website - www.cwcenergyservices.com
Email - duncanau@cwcenergyservices.com
Investor Relations - Duncan T. Au (877) 341-3933
Auditors - Ernst & Young LLP C.A., Calgary, Alta.
Bankers - Canadian Western Bank, Edmonton, Alta.; HSBC Bank Canada, Toronto, Ont.; National Bank of Canada, Calgary, Alta.; ATB Financial, Calgary, Alta.
Lawyers - Burnet, Duckworth & Palmer LLP, Calgary, Alta.
Transfer Agents - Computershare Trust Company of Canada Inc., Calgary, Alta.
Employees - 665 at Dec. 31, 2022
Profile - (Alta. 2005 amalg.) Provides drilling and well services to oil and gas exploration and development companies in western Canada and the Unites States.

Operations are carried out through two segments: Contract Drilling, and Production Services.

The **Contract Drilling** segment operates under the name CWC Ironhand Drilling and consists of telescopic double and electric triple drilling rigs ideally suited for horizontal drilling in the Western Canadian Sedimentary Basin and select U.S. basins.

The **Production Services** segment operates under the name CWC Well Services and provides well services including completions, maintenance, workovers and well decommissioning through service rigs.

At Dec. 31, 2022, the company's fleet consisted of 143 service rigs, consisting of single (74), double (56) and slant (13) rigs; and 22 drilling rigs, consisting of telescopic double (9) and electric triple drilling rigs (13). Operations are conducted from facilities located in Nisku, Grande Prairie, Slave Lake, Sylvan Lake, Drayton Valley, Lloydminster, Provost and Brooks, Alta.; and Denver, Colo. and Casper, Wyo.

Periods ended:	12m Dec. 31/22	12m Dec. 31/21
No. of drill rigs	22	19
Drill rig operating days	3,288	1,252
No. of service rigs	143	144
Service rig operating hrs	110,241	105,570

Recent Merger and Acquisition Activity

Status: completed **Announced:** June 4, 2022
CWC Energy Services Corp. acquired three alternating current (AC) triple drilling rigs with operations in Montana, North Dakota, Wyoming, Utah, Colorado, New Mexico and Texas, as well as all related and ancillary equipment, for US$7,400,000 cash.

Predecessor Detail - Name changed from CWC Well Services Corp., May 15, 2014, following acquisition of Ironhand Drilling Inc.

Directors - James (Jim) Reid, chr., Calgary, Alta.; Duncan T. Au, pres. & CEO, Calgary, Alta.; Daryl G. Austin, Vegreville, Alta.; Gary L. Bentham, Calgary, Alta.; Jason Chehade, Calgary, Alta.; Nancy F. Foster, Calgary, Alta.; Wade J. McGowan, Calgary, Alta.

Other Exec. Officers - Stuart King, CFO; Robert (Bob) Apps, v-p, sales & mktg., drilling; Paul Donohue, v-p, opers., drilling; Michael (Mike) DuBois, v-p, sales & mktg., well srvcs.; Darwin L. McIntyre, v-p, opers., well srvcs.; James L. Kidd, corp. sec.

Capital Stock

	Authorized (shs.)	Outstanding (shs.)[1]
Preferred	unlimited	nil
Common	unlimited	518,806,894

[1] At Apr. 27, 2023

Normal Course Issuer Bid - The company plans to make normal course purchases of up to 25,620,671 common shares representing 5% of the total outstanding. The bid commenced on Nov. 16, 2022, and expires on Nov. 15, 2023.

Major Shareholder - BCP II AIV LP and Brookfield Business Partners Canada LP held 55.8% interest and Canada Pension Plan Investment Board held 16.5% interest at Apr. 10, 2023.

Price Range - CWC/TSX-VEN

Year	Volume	High	Low	Close
2022	34,508,981	$0.34	$0.15	$0.23
2021	29,974,983	$0.21	$0.11	$0.17
2020	15,173,919	$0.18	$0.05	$0.12
2019	11,930,953	$0.20	$0.07	$0.10
2018	24,394,071	$0.23	$0.10	$0.12

Recent Close: $0.19

Capital Stock Changes - During 2022, common shares were issued as follows: 4,615,000 on exercise of options and 4,607,636 under restricted share unit plan; 210,000 common shares were repurchased under a Normal Course Issuer Bid.

Financial Statistics

Periods ended:	12m Dec. 31/22[A]		12m Dec. 31/21[A]
	$000s	%Chg	$000s
Operating revenue	**205,332**	**+100**	**102,635**
Cost of sales	44,425		23,139
Salaries & benefits	105,785		58,321
General & admin expense	9,137		6,110
Stock-based compensation	1,049		782
Operating expense	**160,396**	**+82**	**88,352**
Operating income	**44,936**	**+215**	**14,283**
Deprec., depl. & amort.	12,162		10,563
Finance costs, gross	2,558		1,086
Write-downs/write-offs	23,207		(1,324)
Pre-tax income	**53,373**	**+889**	**5,396**
Income taxes	11,713		823
Net income	**41,660**	**+811**	**4,573**
Cash & equivalent	104		90
Accounts receivable	45,946		26,227
Current assets	49,925		27,911
Fixed assets, net	237,627		198,734
Total assets	**287,552**	**+27**	**226,645**
Accts. pay. & accr. liabs	13,983		8,945
Current liabilities	14,848		9,709
Long-term debt, gross	43,004		45,847
Long-term debt, net	42,139		45,083
Shareholders' equity	210,381		163,269
Cash from oper. activs	**29,802**	**+133**	**12,776**
Cash from fin. activs	(5,584)		13,413
Cash from invest. activs	(24,204)		(26,265)
Net cash position	**104**	**+16**	**90**
Capital expenditures	(25,358)		(28,836)
Capital disposals	1,154		2,571
	$		$
Earnings per share*	0.08		0.01
Cash flow per share*	0.06		0.03
	shs		shs
No. of shs. o/s*	518,084,727		509,072,091
Avg. no. of shs. o/s*	511,284,083		505,337,978
	%		%
Net profit margin	20.29		4.46
Return on equity	22.30		2.85
Return on assets	16.98		2.56
Foreign sales percent	31		7
No. of employees (FTEs)	665		516

* Common
[A] Reported in accordance with IFRS

Latest Results

Periods ended:	3m Mar. 31/23[A]		3m Mar. 31/22[A]
	$000s	%Chg	$000s
Operating revenue	57,538	+41	40,831
Net income	4,669	+36	3,439
	$		$
Earnings per share*	0.01		0.01

* Common
[A] Reported in accordance with IFRS

Historical Summary
(as originally stated)

Fiscal Year	Oper. Rev.	Net Inc. Bef. Disc.	EPS*
	$000s	$000s	$
2022[A]	205,332	41,660	0.08
2021[A]	102,635	4,573	0.01
2020[A]	67,893	(24,490)	(0.05)
2019[A]	108,446	(1,700)	(0.00)
2018[A]	144,762	(1,702)	(0.00)

* Common
[A] Reported in accordance with IFRS

C.21 The Caldwell Partners International Inc.*

Symbol - CWL **Exchange** - TSX **CUSIP** - 12913L
Head Office - TD South Tower, 2410-79 Wellington St W, PO Box 75, Toronto, ON, M5K 1E7 **Telephone** - (416) 920-7702 **Toll-free** - (888) 366-3827 **Fax** - (416) 920-8646
Website - www.caldwell.com
Email - cbeck@caldwell.com
Investor Relations - C. Christopher Beck (888) 366-3827
Auditors - KPMG LLP C.A., Vaughan, Ont.
Lawyers - Miller Thomson LLP, Toronto, Ont.
Transfer Agents - Computershare Trust Company of Canada Inc., Toronto, Ont.
FP500 Revenue Ranking - 699
Employees - 418 at Aug. 31, 2022
Profile - (Ont. 1979) Provides talent acquisition services at all levels, including candidate research and sourcing, full recruitment at the professional, executive and board levels, and a suite of talent strategy and assessment tools.

Operations are conducted through two segments: Caldwell and IQTalent Partners.

Caldwell

Provides executive search services in Canada, the U.S. and Europe, specializing in the recruitment of qualified individuals for board, CEO and senior leadership levels on behalf of its clients. Contracts with its clients, on an assignment basis, to provide consulting advice on the identification, evaluation, assessment and recommendation of qualified candidates for specific positions. Also concentrates its activities on providing executives on a variable basis for executive advisory positions. Other areas of specialization are the recruitment of candidates for corporate boards of directors, interim executives, onboarding, succession planning, compensation assessment and competitive analyses. In addition, provides talent assessment and strategy tools through Caldwell Analytics and The Predictive Index.

Clients include national, international and multinational businesses and public sector organizations. Industry specializations include the financial services, industrial, technology, media and telecommunications, life sciences, consumer and retail distribution, professional services, education and not-for-profit sectors.

Offices are located in Toronto, Ont.; Calgary, Alta.; Vancouver, B.C.; Stamford, Conn.; New York, N.Y.; Atlanta, Ga.; Nashville, Tenn.; Chicago, Ill.; Houston and Dallas, Tex.; Los Angeles and San Francisco, Calif.; Miami, Fla.; Philadelphia, Pa.; Charleston, S.C.; London, U.K.; and Zurich, Switzerland. Also has affiliation arrangements for mutual referral agreements with Australia-based **Johnson Advisory Pty Limited** (dba Johnson Partners) covering Australia and New Zealand; and Cayman Islands-based **Become Group Limited** covering Hong Kong, Beijing, Shanghai and Shenzhen, People's Republic of China, and Singapore.

IQTalent Partners

Provides on-demand talent acquisition augmentation as a managed service to clients, primarily in-house talent acquisition departments, with revenue generated per labour hour in the U.S. Services include research, candidate sourcing and full lifecycle recruitment services at the professional level. Operations are conducted in Nashville, Tenn.

On Mar. 1, 2023, the company spun off its software business, IQRecruit, from wholly owned **IQTalent Partners, Inc.** IQRecruit is a talent search and candidate management platform that combines the powers of artificial intelligence (AI), automation and expert research techniques to deliver high quality candidates to companies. The software was transferred into a newly formed entity, **IQRecruit, Inc.**, of which IQTalent held a 41.9% interest. David Windley invested US$250,000 into IQRecruit in exchange for 8.7% of the shares of IQRecruit, with a third party and IQRecruit's employees holding the remainder of the shares.

In March 2022, the company entered into an international affiliation agreement with Australian-based executive search firm, **Johnson Advisory Pty Ltd.** Under the agreement, Johnson became the company's exclusive external search partner for Australia and New Zealand, and the company became Johnson's exclusive external search partner for North America and the U.K. The agreement replaced the company's licensing agreement with Auckland, N.Z.-based **The Caldwell Partners International New Zealand Limited** (formerly **Simon Monks and Partners Limited**), which was acquired by Johnson. Caldwell New Zealand was the company's New Zealand licensee since Nov. 8, 2015.

Recent Merger and Acquisition Activity

Status: completed **Announced:** Oct. 1, 2022
The Caldwell Partners International Inc. acquired The Counsel Network Inc., a Canada-based executive search firm specializing in the Canadian legal market, for $2,406,000 cash.

Directors - Elias Vamvakas, chr., Toronto, Ont.; John N. Wallace, CEO, Toronto, Ont.; C. Christopher (Chris) Beck, pres. & CFO, Boston, Mass.; David Windley, pres., IQTalent Partners, Inc., Los Altos, Calif.; Terry Grayson-Caprio, S.C.; Darcy D. Morris, Toronto, Ont.; John Young, Toronto, Ont.; Rosemary Zigrossi, Toronto, Ont.

Other Exec. Officers - Michael R. J. Falagario, v-p, tech., bus. & legal opers.; Shreya Lathia, v-p, acctg. & reporting; Dianne Kelly, contr.; Pamela Cioffi, dir., talent & knowledge mgt.

Capital Stock

	Authorized (shs.)	Outstanding (shs.)[1]
Common	unlimited	25,880,693

[1] At May 31, 2023

Options - At Aug. 31, 2022, options were outstanding to purchase 400,000 common shares at a weighted average exercise price of 73¢ per share with a weighted average remaining contractual term of five years.

Major Shareholder - Ewing Morris & Co. Investment Partners Ltd. held 14.8% interest and C. Douglas Caldwell held 10.7% interest at Jan. 12, 2023.

Price Range - CWL/TSX

Year	Volume	High	Low	Close
2022	2,573,894	$2.99	$1.50	$1.55
2021	6,364,496	$2.96	$1.03	$2.00
2020	2,640,570	$1.38	$0.56	$1.12
2019	4,367,969	$1.50	$1.14	$1.24
2018	6,205,181	$1.66	$1.01	$1.30

Recent Close: $0.90

Capital Stock Changes - During fiscal 2022, 375,000 common shares were issued on exercise of options.

Long-Term Debt - At Aug. 31, 2022, the company had no long-term debt.

Wholly Owned Subsidiaries

The Caldwell Partners International Europe, Ltd., London, Middx., United Kingdom.
The Caldwell Partners International Ltd., Del.
- 100% int. in **IQTalent Partners, Inc.**, Nashville, Tenn.
  - 41.9% int. in **IQRecruit, Inc.**, Canada.

The Counsel Network Inc., Vancouver, B.C.

Financial Statistics

Periods ended:	12m Aug. 31/22[A]		12m Aug. 31/21[A]
	$000s	%Chg	$000s
Operating revenue	**156,165**	**+30**	**119,766**
Cost of sales	121,516		90,646
General & admin expense	18,881		18,344
Operating expense	**140,397**	**+29**	**108,990**
Operating income	**15,768**	**+46**	**10,776**
Deprec., depl. & amort.	2,567		2,394
Finance income	129		32
Finance costs, gross	419		491
Pre-tax income	**10,710**	**+98**	**5,417**
Income taxes	2,532		898
Net income	**8,178**	**+81**	**4,519**
Cash & equivalent	35,668		29,214
Accounts receivable	22,882		23,218
Current assets	69,083		58,981
Long-term investments	736		242
Fixed assets, net	2,035		1,970
Right-of-use assets	5,345		9,549
Intangibles, net	9,118		8,194
Total assets	**91,288**	**+5**	**87,133**
Bank indebtedness	nil		176
Accts. pay. & accr. liabs	47,887		41,492
Current liabilities	49,704		46,543
Long-term lease liabilities	4,414		8,560
Shareholders' equity	35,065		25,752
Cash from oper. activs	**7,101**	**-71**	**24,878**
Cash from fin. activs	499		(5,935)
Cash from invest. activs	(1,917)		(3,925)
Net cash position	**35,668**	**+22**	**29,214**
Capital expenditures	(466)		(251)
	$		$
Earnings per share*	0.32		0.19
Cash flow per share*	0.28		1.05
	shs		shs
No. of shs. o/s*	25,880,693		25,505,693
Avg. no. of shs. o/s*	25,707,748		23,800,655
	%		%
Net profit margin	5.24		3.77
Return on equity	26.89		21.26
Return on assets	9.53		7.70
Foreign sales percent	89		87
No. of employees (FTEs)	418		287

* Common
[A] Reported in accordance with IFRS

Latest Results

Periods ended:	9m May 31/23[A]		9m May 31/22[A]
	$000s	%Chg	$000s
Operating revenue	71,647	-40	120,246
Net income	(4,798)	n.a.	5,603
	$		$
Earnings per share*	(0.19)		0.22

* Common
[A] Reported in accordance with IFRS

Historical Summary
(as originally stated)

Fiscal Year	Oper. Rev.	Net Inc. Bef. Disc.	EPS*
	$000s	$000s	$
2022[A]	156,165	8,178	0.32
2021[A]	119,766	4,519	0.19
2020[A]	58,193	2,846	0.14
2019[A]	72,138	325	0.02
2018[A]	66,883	2,015	0.10

* Common
[A] Reported in accordance with IFRS

C.22 Calfrac Well Services Ltd.*

Symbol - CFW **Exchange** - TSX **CUSIP** - 129584
Head Office - 500-407 8 Ave SW, Calgary, AB, T2P 1E5 **Telephone** - (403) 266-6000 **Toll-free** - (866) 770-3722 **Fax** - (403) 266-7381
Website - www.calfrac.com
Email - molinek@calfrac.com
Investor Relations - Michael D. Olinek (403) 234-6673
Auditors - PricewaterhouseCoopers LLP C.A., Calgary, Alta.
Bankers - Canadian Western Bank; The Bank of Nova Scotia; Export Development Canada; Royal Bank of Canada, Calgary, Alta.; ATB Financial, Calgary, Alta.; HSBC Bank Canada, Calgary, Alta.
Lawyers - Bennett Jones LLP, Calgary, Alta.

Transfer Agents - Computershare Trust Company of Canada Inc., Calgary, Alta.
FP500 Revenue Ranking - 270
Employees - 2,270 at Dec. 31, 2022
Profile - (Can. 2020; orig. Alta., 2004 amalg.) Provides specialized oilfield services, including hydraulic fracturing, coiled tubing, cementing and other well stimulation services, in western Canada, the U.S. and Argentina.

Operations consist of three geographic business segments: Canada, United States and Argentina.

The **Canadian** segment provides fracturing and coiled tubing services to oil and gas exploration and production companies operating in Alberta and northeast British Columbia.

The **United States** segment provides fracturing services to oil and gas companies operating in the Williston Basin located in North Dakota as well as the Rockies region, which includes the Uinta Basin in Utah and the Powder Basin in Wyoming. Also provides fracturing services to natural gas-focused customers operating in the Appalachia basin in Pennsylvania, Ohio and West Virginia.

The **Argentina** segment provides pressure pumping services from operating bases in Argentina. Fracturing, cementing and coiled tubing services are provided to oil and natural gas companies operating in the Neuquén, Las Heras and Comodoro regions.

Hydraulic fracturing and well stimulation services are provided from operating districts located in Red Deer, Grande Prairie, Alta.; Grand Junction, Colo.; Williston, N.D.; Smithfield, Pa.; Artesia, N.M.; Gillette, Wyo.; Vernal, Utah; and Neuquén, Las Heras, Añelo and Comodoro Rivadavia, Argentina. The company's head office is located in Calgary, Alta., and its regional offices are located in Denver, Colo.; Houston, Tex.; and Buenos Aires, Argentina. At June 30, 2023, the company operated 1,238,000 hydraulic horsepower in its fracturing operations, and well servicing equipment including 13 coiled tubing units and 11 cementing units.

Operating Statistics

Year ended Dec. 31	2022	2021
Canada		
Fracturing jobs	13,503	11,769
Rev./fracturing job ($)	29,312	21,626
Coiled tubing jobs	1,453	1,339
Rev./coiled tubing job ($)	31,183	18,970
U.S.		
Fracturing jobs	15,054	13,833
Rev./fracturing job ($)	53,515	30,982
Argentina		
Fracturing jobs	1,973	1,800
Rev./fracturing job ($)	74,181	57,453
Coiled tubing jobs	1,296	1,063
Rev./coiled tubing job ($)	30,489	21,860
Cementing jobs	547	445
Rev./cementing job	76,193	59,558
Russia[1]		
Fracturing jobs	n.a.	1,847
Rev./fracturing job ($)	nil	61,313
Coiled tubing jobs	n.a.	240
Rev./coiled tubing job ($)	nil	37,091

[1] Discontinued in March 2022.

In March 2022, the company discontinued its operations in Russia, and committed to a plan to sell its Russian operations.

Predecessor Detail - Formed from Denison Energy Inc. in Alberta, Mar. 24, 2004, on reverse takeover acquisition of and amalgamation with Calfrac Well Services Ltd. Prior to the transaction, almost all of Denison's assets were transferred to 2 new cos.

Directors - Ronald P. Mathison, chr., Calgary, Alta.; Douglas R. (Doug) Ramsay, v-chr., Okotoks, Alta.; Patrick G. (Pat) Powell, CEO, Calgary, Alta.; George S. Armoyan, Halifax, N.S.; Holly A. Benson, Calgary, Alta.; Anuroop S, Duggal, Toronto, Ont.; Chetan Mehta, New York, N.Y.; Charles Pellerin, Victoriaville, Qué.

Other Exec. Officers - Michael D. (Mike) Olinek, CFO; Mark R. Ellingson, v-p, sales & mktg., U.S. div.; Jon Koop, v-p, HR; Brent W. Merchant, v-p, sales & mktg., Canada; Alif H. Noorani, v-p, fin.; Jeffrey I. Ellis, gen. counsel & corp. sec.; Gordon T. Milgate, pres., Cdn. opers.; Mark D. Rosen, pres., U.S. opers.

Capital Stock

	Authorized (shs.)	Outstanding (shs.)[1]
Common	unlimited	80,860,392

[1] At Aug. 8, 2023

Options - At Dec. 31, 2022, options were outstanding to purchase 3,587,769 common shares at an average exercise price of $4.90 per share with a weighted average remaining life of 3.86 years.

Warrants - At Dec. 31, 2022, warrants were outstanding exercisable for 5,219,150 common shares at $2.50 per share expiring on Dec. 18, 2023.

Major Shareholder - George & Simé Armoyan held 34.9% interest and Ronald P. Mathison held 11.6% interest at Mar. 22, 2023.

Price Range - CFW/TSX

Year	Volume	High	Low	Close
2022	22,561,362	$7.90	$4.08	$6.10
2021	18,566,576	$6.45	$2.75	$4.20
2020	3,887,337	$63.50	$3.65	$3.94
2019	1,442,259	$197.50	$39.00	$62.50
2018	2,979,968	$417.50	$101.50	$122.00

Consolidation: 1-for-50 cons. in Dec. 2020
Recent Close: $5.82
Capital Stock Changes - During 2022, common shares were issued as follows: 42,065,259 on conversion of notes, 531,706 on exercise of warrants and 435,567 on exercise of options.

Long-Term Debt - Outstanding at Dec. 31, 2022:

Revolv. term loan facility[1]	$170,000,000
10% notes due 2023	2,534,000
10.875% notes due 2026	162,528,000
Less: Unamort. issue costs	3,342,000
	331,720,000
Less: Current portion	2,534,000
	329,186,000

[1] Consists of $205,000,0000 revolving term loan facility and $45,000,000 operating facility due July 1, 2024. Bearing interest ranging from prime or U.S. base rate plus 1% to prime plus 3.5% for prime-based loans and U.S. base-rate loans and interest ranging from 2% to 4.5% above the respective base rates for SOFR-based loans and bankers' acceptance-based loans.

Principal repayments of long-term debt over the next five years are as follows:

2023	nil
2024	170,000,000
2025	nil
2026	162,528,000
2027	nil
Thereafter	nil

Wholly Owned Subsidiaries

CWS International LLC, Russia.
Calfrac (Canada) Inc., Alta.
• 0.28% int. in **Calfrac Holdings LP**, Del.
Calfrac Well Services (Argentina) S.A., Argentina.
Calfrac Well Services Corp., Colo.
12178711 Canada Inc., Canada.

Subsidiaries

99.72% int. in **Calfrac Holdings LP**, Del.

Note: The preceding list includes only the major related companies in which interests are held.

Financial Statistics

Periods ended:	12m Dec. 31/22[A]		12m Dec. 31/21[oA]
	$000s	%Chg	$000s
Operating revenue	**1,499,220**	**+70**	**880,249**
Cost of sales	1,222,587		788,156
General & admin expense	62,199		42,761
Operating expense	**1,284,786**	**+55**	**830,917**
Operating income	**214,434**	**+335**	**49,332**
Deprec., depl. & amort.	122,027		127,431
Finance costs, net	46,555		37,739
Write-downs/write-offs	(19,211)		(705)
Pre-tax income	**24,280**	**n.a.**	**(121,606)**
Income taxes	(11,023)		(26,875)
Net inc. bef. disc. opers	**35,303**	**n.a.**	**(94,731)**
Income from disc. opers	(23,626)		11,919
Net income	**11,677**	**n.a.**	**(82,812)**
Cash & equivalent	8,498		nil
Inventories	108,866		101,840
Accounts receivable	238,769		189,835
Current assets	414,370		307,533
Fixed assets, net	543,475		563,423
Right-of-use assets	22,908		22,005
Total assets	**995,753**	**+12**	**892,961**
Bank indebtedness	nil		1,351
Accts. pay. & accr. liabs	171,603		127,441
Current liabilities	203,702		136,796
Long-term debt, gross	331,720		388,479
Long-term debt, net	329,186		388,479
Long-term lease liabilities	13,443		12,560
Equity portion of conv. debs	212		4,764
Shareholders' equity	422,972		328,840
Cash from oper. activs	**107,532**	**n.a.**	**(15,337)**
Cash from fin. activs	(33,533)		45,852
Cash from invest. activs	(74,325)		(61,294)
Net cash position	**18,393**	**n.a.**	**(1,351)**
Capital expenditures	(79,810)		(63,434)
Capital disposals	5,485		2,140
	$		$
Earns. per sh. bef disc opers*	0.83		(2.52)
Earnings per share*	0.27		(2.21)
Cash flow per share*	2.52		(0.41)
	shs		shs
No. of shs. o/s*	80,733,504		37,700,972
Avg. no. of shs. o/s*	42,609,234		37,543,761
	%		%
Net profit margin	2.35		(10.76)
Return on equity	9.39		(25.64)
Return on assets	3.74		(10.49)
Foreign sales percent	70		68
No. of employees (FTEs)	2,270		2,684

* Common
[o] Restated
[A] Reported in accordance with IFRS

Latest Results

Periods ended:	6m June 30/23[A]		6m June 30/22[A]
	$000s	%Chg	$000s
Operating revenue	959,786	+57	613,035
Net inc. bef. disc. opers	86,844	n.a.	(24,806)
Income from disc. opers	4,754		(32,924)
Net income	91,598	n.a.	(57,730)
	$		$
Earns. per sh. bef. disc. opers.*	1.07		(0.65)
Earnings per share*	1.13		(1.51)

* Common
[A] Reported in accordance with IFRS

Historical Summary
(as originally stated)

Fiscal Year	Oper. Rev.	Net Inc. Bef. Disc.	EPS*
	$000s	$000s	$
2022[A]	1,499,220	35,303	0.83
2021[A]	1,002,395	(82,812)	(2.21)
2020[A]	705,436	(324,235)	(76.78)
2019[A]	1,620,955	(156,203)	(54.02)
2018[A]	2,256,426	(26,177)	(6.31)

* Common
[A] Reported in accordance with IFRS

Note: Adjusted throughout for 1-for-50 cons. in Dec. 2020

C.23 Calian Group Ltd.*

Symbol - CGY **Exchange** - TSX **CUSIP** - 12989J
Head Office - 400-770 Palladium Dr, Ottawa, ON, K2V 1C8 **Telephone** - (613) 599-8600 **Toll-free** - (877) 225-4264 **Fax** - (613) 592-3664
Website - www.calian.com
Email - ir@calian.com
Investor Relations - Patrick Houston (613) 599-8600
Auditors - KPMG LLP C.A., Ottawa, Ont.
Bankers - Royal Bank of Canada, Ottawa, Ont.
Lawyers - LaBarge Weinstein LLP, Ottawa, Ont.
Transfer Agents - TSX Trust Company, Toronto, Ont.
FP500 Revenue Ranking - 439
Employees - 4,500 at Sept. 30, 2022
Profile - (Can. 1982) Provides business services and products to both government and private industry clients in the areas of health, defence, security, aerospace, engineering, agricultural technology, satellite communications and information technology.

The company operates in four segments: Advanced Technologies, Health, Learning, and Information Technology (IT) and Cybersecurity Solutions.

Advanced Technologies - Provides internally developed products, engineering services and solutions for the space, communications, nuclear, agriculture, defence and government sectors. Services offered cover software development, product development, custom manufacturing, full life-cycle support, studies, requirements analysis, project management, multi-discipline engineered system solutions and training.

Health - Manages a network of more than 2,500 health care professionals delivering primary care, occupational health services and care coordination to public and private sector clients across Canada, the United States and Europe. Also provides management and strategy services to pharmaceutical companies conducting clinical trials and patient support programs. Clinics under the Primacy brand are located in Loblaw grocery stores across Canada including Real Canadian Superstore®, Zehrs®, Loblaws® and No Frills®.

Learning - Provides consulting services in emergency management, training and advanced training technologies to federal and provincial governments, municipalities, indigenous communities and the private sector primarily in Canada. Products and technologies offered, which complement its training services, includes VCCI (Virtual Command Control Interface); Calian MaestroEDE™, a tool used to design, develop and deliver high-fidelity, collective training exercises for military customers; and Calian ResponseReady™, an online platform and simulation tool that supports emergency management training exercise delivery and evaluation.

IT and Cybersecurity Solutions - Provides professional services and solutions for application-based infrastructure and cyber security. Services include IT & cyber staff augmentation, cyber consulting, solution provider and value added reselling (VAR), cyber incident management and managed security services provider (MSSP) services inclusive of managed IT services, network Operations-as-a-Service (NOCaaS) and security Operations-as-a-Service (SoCaaS).

Offices are located in Ottawa, Toronto, Kingston, Burlington and Smiths Falls, Ont.; Edmonton, Alta.; Oromocto, N.B.; Halifax, N.S.; Saskatoon and Regina, Sask.; Vaudreuil-Dorion, Que.; Germany; Norway; and the U.K. Also has R&D and manufacturing facilities in Saskatoon and Regina, Sask.; Ottawa, Ont.; Vaudreuil-Dorion, Que.; and Germany.

Recent Merger and Acquisition Activity

Status: pending **Announced:** Mar. 9, 2023
Calian Group Ltd. agreed to acquire the assets of Sonoma, Calif.-based Hawaii Pacific Teleport, L.P. (HPT) for Cdn$47,000,000 (US$35,000,000), with earnouts of up to an additional Cdn$15,000,000 (US$11,000,000) based on the achievement of certain level of EBITDA performance over the next two years. HPT provides satellite and fibre-based communications throughout the Asia Pacific region from its U.S.-based locations via its satellite teleports, datacentre, media management

centre and terrestrial networks. The transaction was expected to be completed by the third quarter of 2023, subject to regulatory approvals.
Status: completed **Revised:** Mar. 14, 2022
UPDATE: The transaction was completed. PREVIOUS: Calian Group Ltd. agreed to acquire the assets of Computex, Inc. (dba Computex Technology Solutions) from American Virtual Cloud Technologies, Inc. for $38,000,000 cash. Computex Technology Solutions is a Texas-based provider of IT and cyber solutions including data centre, enterprise networking, cloud services, managed IT solutions, cybersecurity and integration services. The transaction was expected to close in the second quarter of fiscal 2022.

Predecessor Detail - Name changed from Calian Technologies Ltd., Apr. 1, 2016.

Directors - George Weber, chr., Ottawa, Ont.; Kevin Ford, pres. & CEO, Ont.; Raymond G. (Ray) Basler, Saskatoon, Sask.; Lori M. O'Neill, Ottawa, Ont.; Young Park, Toronto, Ont.; Jo-Anne Poirier, Ottawa, Ont.; R. Ronald Richardson, Ont.; Valerie C. Sorbie, Toronto, Ont.

Other Exec. Officers - Patrick Houston, CFO & corp. sec.; Michele Bedford, chief comml. officer; Seann Hamer, chief tech. officer; Sue Ivay, chief HR officer; Michael (Mike) Muldner, CIO; Sacha Gera, pres., IT & cyber solutions; Gordon McDonald, pres., Calian health; Patrick Thera, pres., advanced tech.; Donald (Don) Whitty, pres., learning

Capital Stock

	Authorized (shs.)	Outstanding (shs.)[1]
Preferred	unlimited	nil
Common	unlimited	11,726,524

[1] At Mar. 31, 2023

Options - At Sept. 30, 2022, 220,800 options were outstanding to purchase common shares at a weighted average price of $52.55 per share with a weighted average remaining contractual life of 2.49 years.

Major Shareholder - Widely held at Dec. 19, 2022.

Price Range - CGY/TSX

Year	Volume	High	Low	Close
2022............	5,036,097	$72.11	$51.99	$66.79
2021............	4,134,835	$67.58	$53.35	$61.54
2020............	4,272,339	$71.91	$31.29	$66.16
2019............	1,307,120	$39.78	$28.70	$38.50
2018............	1,330,431	$33.99	$25.76	$29.40

Recent Close: $52.10

Capital Stock Changes - During fiscal 2022, common shares were issued as follows: 240,674 pursuant to acquisitions, 35,147 under the employee stock purchase plan, 24,759 on exercise of options and 20,983 under restricted share unit plan.

Dividends

CGY com Ra $1.12 pa Q est. Sept. 5, 2012

Long-Term Debt - At Sept. 30, 2022, the company had no long-term debt.

Wholly Owned Subsidiaries

Alio Health Services Inc., Ottawa, Ont.
Allphase Clinical Research Services Inc., Ottawa, Ont.
Calian International Ltd., Ottawa, Ont.
- 100% int. in **SatService, GmbH**, Germany.

Calian Ltd., Ottawa, Ont.
- 100% int. in **Dapasoft Inc.**, North York, Ont.
  - 100% int. in **iSecurity Inc.**, Ont.

IntraGrain Technologies Inc., Regina, Sask.
Tallysman Wireless Inc., Ottawa, Ont.

Note: The preceding list includes only the major related companies in which interests are held.

Financial Statistics

Periods ended:	12m Sept. 30/22[A]		12m Sept. 30/21[A]
	$000s	%Chg	$000s
Operating revenue........................	**582,172**	**+12**	**518,404**
Cost of sales....................................	412,946		391,667
Research & devel. expense.............	5,372		5,020
General & admin expense...............	95,995		67,853
Stock-based compensation............	1,927		1,935
Operating expense........................	**516,240**	**+11**	**466,475**
Operating income........................	**65,932**	**+27**	**51,929**
Deprec., depl. & amort....................	31,158		19,070
Finance costs, net...........................	746		810
Pre-tax income............................	**24,159**	**+36**	**17,707**
Income taxes..................................	10,555		6,552
Net income....................................	**13,604**	**+22**	**11,155**
Cash & equivalent...........................	42,646		78,611
Inventories......................................	58,508		61,924
Accounts receivable........................	171,453		111,138
Current assets.................................	296,510		262,174
Long-term investments...................	670		670
Fixed assets, net.............................	29,204		23,643
Right-of-use assets.........................	16,678		15,383
Intangibles, net...............................	203,046		154,622
Total assets..................................	**547,162**	**+19**	**457,969**
Bank indebtedness..........................	7,500		nil
Accts. pay. & accr. liabs..................	122,871		66,180
Current liabilities............................	211,658		121,180
Long-term lease liabilities...............	14,920		14,449
Shareholders' equity.......................	305,186		292,360
Cash from oper. activs..................	**43,141**	**-7**	**46,542**
Cash from fin. activs........................	(6,215)		64,440
Cash from invest. activs..................	(72,891)		(56,606)
Net cash position..........................	**42,646**	**-46**	**78,611**
Capital expenditures........................	(7,325)		(7,849)
	$		$
Earnings per share*.........................	1.19		1.08
Cash flow per share*.......................	3.80		4.39
Cash divd. per share*......................	1.12		1.12
	shs		shs
No. of shs. o/s*...............................	11,607,391		11,285,828
Avg. no. of shs. o/s*........................	11,343,615		10,599,693
	%		%
Net profit margin.............................	2.34		2.15
Return on equity..............................	4.55		4.53
Return on assets..............................	2.71		2.83
Foreign sales percent......................	29		22
No. of employees (FTEs).................	4,500		4,500

* Common
[A] Reported in accordance with IFRS

Latest Results

Periods ended:	6m Mar. 31/23[A]		6m Mar. 31/22[A]
	$000s	%Chg	$000s
Operating revenue..........................	316,086	+16	271,604
Net income......................................	9,093	+63	5,573
	$		$
Earnings per share*.........................	0.78		0.49

* Common
[A] Reported in accordance with IFRS

Historical Summary
(as originally stated)

Fiscal Year	Oper. Rev. $000s	Net Inc. Bef. Disc. $000s	EPS* $
2022[A]...................	582,172	13,604	1.19
2021[A]...................	518,404	11,155	1.08
2020[A]...................	432,320	20,360	2.25
2019[A]...................	343,044	19,992	2.55
2018[A]...................	304,958	16,077	2.08

* Common
[A] Reported in accordance with IFRS

C.24 California Nanotechnologies Corp.

Symbol - CNO **Exchange** - TSX-VEN **CUSIP** - 130492
Head Office - 17220 Edwards Rd, Cerritos, CA, United States, 90703
Telephone - (562) 991-5211 **Toll-free** - (800) 577-6664 **Fax** - (562) 926-6913
Website - www.calnanocorp.com
Email - e.eyerman@calnanocorp.com
Investor Relations - Eric Eyerman (562) 991-5211
Auditors - MNP LLP C.A., Calgary, Alta.
Transfer Agents - Computershare Trust Company of Canada Inc., Calgary, Alta.

Profile - (Alta. 2002) Provides nanotechnology solutions that allow metals and other materials to take on enhanced performance characteristics which can be tailored to customer's specific application.

The company's two core technologies are Spark Plasma Sintering (SPS), an advanced sintering and bonding technique for all varieties of materials including metallic alloys, high-temp ceramics and high entropy alloys; and Cryogenic Milling, a powder processing technique used for particle size reduction to nano scale, mechanical alloying and nano-grain refinement. Also offers other services including spark plasma sintering and hot pressing tooling fabrication and design; wire electrical discharge machining (EDM) and machining of metals and metallic alloys; tensile, compression and hardness testing; planetary ball milling; v-blending or tumble milling; and particle size analysis via laser diffraction.

Target markets are the microchip fabrication, aerospace, sports and recreation, defence, automotive, medical, and the oil and gas industries.

Predecessor Detail - Name changed from Veritek Technologies Inc., Feb. 1, 2007, following Qualifying Transaction reverse takeover acquisition of California Nanotechnologies, Inc.

Directors - Eric Eyerman, CEO & COO, Calif.; Roger Dent, acting CFO, Toronto, Ont.; Sébastien R. Goulet, Calif.; Enrique Lavernia, Calif.

Capital Stock

	Authorized (shs.)	Outstanding (shs.)[1]
Class A Common	unlimited	31,803,750

[1] At May 31, 2022

Major Shareholder - Omni-Lite Industries Canada Inc. held 18.88% interest and Dr. Patrick B. Berbon held 10.09% interest at Dec. 15, 2021.

Price Range - CNO/TSX-VEN

Year	Volume	High	Low	Close
2022............	6,062,275	$0.13	$0.06	$0.11
2021............	6,226,693	$0.20	$0.07	$0.09
2020............	4,081,276	$0.12	$0.02	$0.10
2019............	2,126,326	$0.13	$0.02	$0.04
2018............	6,395,731	$0.10	$0.04	$0.05

Recent Close: $0.18

Wholly Owned Subsidiaries

California Nanotechnologies, Inc., Cerritos, Calif.
- 100% int. in **White Roof Solutions, Inc.**, Culver City, Calif.

Financial Statistics

Periods ended:	12m Feb. 28/22[A]		12m Feb. 28/21[oA]
	US$000s	%Chg	US$000s
Operating revenue........................	**1,082**	**+36**	**795**
Cost of goods sold...........................	324		335
Salaries & benefits..........................	208		193
General & admin expense...............	200		222
Stock-based compensation............	10		12
Operating expense........................	**742**	**-3**	**762**
Operating income........................	**340**	**+930**	**33**
Deprec., depl. & amort....................	129		130
Finance costs, gross........................	75		59
Write-downs/write-offs....................	nil		(25)
Pre-tax income............................	**201**	**n.a.**	**(121)**
Net income....................................	**201**	**n.a.**	**(121)**
Cash & equivalent...........................	51		20
Accounts receivable........................	351		45
Current assets.................................	406		68
Fixed assets, net.............................	287		391
Right-of-use assets.........................	262		nil
Intangibles, net...............................	5		5
Total assets..................................	**959**	**+107**	**464**
Accts. pay. & accr. liabs..................	189		130
Current liabilities............................	1,783		1,649
Long-term debt, gross.....................	133		239
Long-term debt, net.........................	nil		123
Shareholders' equity.......................	(1,073)		(1,308)
Cash from oper. activs..................	**144**	**+71**	**84**
Cash from fin. activs........................	(105)		(106)
Cash from invest. activs..................	(8)		nil
Net cash position..........................	**51**	**+155**	**20**
Capital expenditures........................	(8)		nil
	US$		US$
Earnings per share*.........................	0.01		(0.00)
Cash flow per share*.......................	0.00		0.00
	shs		shs
No. of shs. o/s*...............................	31,803,750		31,430,296
Avg. no. of shs. o/s*........................	31,552,198		31,430,296
	%		%
Net profit margin.............................	18.58		(15.22)
Return on equity..............................	n.m.		n.m.
Return on assets..............................	38.79		(11.19)

* Cl.A com.
[o] Restated
[A] Reported in accordance with IFRS

Latest Results

Periods ended:	3m May 31/22[A]		3m May 31/21[A]
	US$000s	%Chg	US$000s
Operating revenue..........................	329	+60	206
Net income......................................	50	n.a.	(10)
	US$		US$
Earnings per share*.........................	0.00		(0.00)

* Cl.A com.
[A] Reported in accordance with IFRS

Historical Summary
(as originally stated)

Fiscal Year	Oper. Rev. US$000s	Net Inc. Bef. Disc. US$000s	EPS* US$
2022[A]	1,082	201	0.01
2021[A]	795	(121)	(0.00)
2020[A]	831	(56)	(0.00)
2019[A]	750	(59)	(0.00)
2018[A]	549	(47)	(0.00)

* Cl.A com.
[A] Reported in accordance with IFRS

C.25 Cameco Corporation*

Symbol - CCO **Exchange** - TSX **CUSIP** - 13321L
Head Office - 2121 11 St W, Saskatoon, SK, S7M 1J3 **Telephone** - (306) 956-6200 **Fax** - (306) 956-6201
Website - www.cameco.com
Email - rachelle_girard@cameco.com
Investor Relations - Rachelle Girard (306) 956-6403
Auditors - KPMG LLP C.A., Saskatoon, Sask.
Lawyers - Osler, Hoskin & Harcourt LLP
Transfer Agents - American Stock Transfer & Trust Company, LLC, New York, N.Y.; TSX Trust Company, Montréal, Qué.
FP500 Revenue Ranking - 233
Employees - 2,424 at Dec. 31, 2022
Profile - (Can. 1987) Produces, develops, evaluates and explores uranium in Canada (northern Saskatchewan), the United States (Nebraska and Wyoming), Kazakhstan and Western Australia. Refines and converts uranium in Ontario for sale as fuel for the generation of electricity in nuclear power reactors around the world.

Operations are carried out through two reportable segments: Uranium and Fuel Services.

The **Uranium** segment includes the exploration for, mining, milling, purchase and sale of uranium concentrate (U_3O_8). In Canada, uranium production is derived from the Cigar Lake underground mine (54.547% interest, **Orano S.A.** 40.453%, **TEPCO Resources Inc.** 5%); the McArthur River underground mine (69.805% interest, Orano 30.195%); and the Key Lake mill (83.33% interest, Orano 16.67%), all in Saskatchewan. In south Kazakhstan, production is from the Inkai in situ recovery project (40% ownership, Joint Stock Company National Atomic Company **Kazatomprom** 60%). Advanced projects include the Millennium underground project (69.9% interest, **UEX Corporation** 15.05%, **Denison Mines Corp.** 15.05%) in Saskatchewan; and the Kintyre and Yeelirrie open-pit projects, both in Western Australia. Also holds the Rabbit Lake mill in Saskatchewan, where production was suspended in 2016. Curtailed properties include the Crow Butte, Neb., and the Smith Ranch-Highland, Wyo., in situ recovery operations, where new wellfield development was stopped in April 2016 and production ceased in early 2018.

The **Fuel Services** segment consists of the refining and conversion of uranium concentrates, fabrication of finished fuel for heavy water reactors, and the purchase and sale of conversion services. Uranium is refined at a facility located west of Blind River, Ont., to produce high-purity uranium trioxide (UO_3), the feedstock for conversion plants. The Port Hope, Ont., facility converts UO_3 to uranium dioxide (UO_2), the fuel for CANDU heavy water reactors, and uranium hexafluoride (UF_6), the feedstock for enrichment processes required to produce fuel for light water reactors. Manufacturing of fuel bundles and reactor components for CANDU reactors are conducted from facilities in Port Hope and Cobourg, Ont.

Production

Year ended Dec. 31	2022	2021
Uranium concentrates[1]	10,400	6,100
Uranium fuel services[2]	13,000	12,100

[1] Thousands of lbs. of U_3O_8.
[2] Thousands of kg of uranium (as UO_2, UF_6, UO_3 and fuel fabrication).
Note - Figures represent the company's share.

Proven and Probable Reserves

	Tonnes 000s	Content[1] 000s	Cameco's share[1] 000s
2022	328,589	821,300	468,800
2021	347,686	828,200	464,300

[1] Lbs. of U_3O_8.

In November 2022, the company resumed operations at the McArthur River and Key Lake mill in northern Saskatchewan, where operations were suspended since January 2018.

Periods ended:	12m Dec. 31/22	12m Dec. 31/21
Uranium prod., lbs	10,400,000	6,100,000
Uranium sales, lbs	25,600,000	24,300,000
Avg real. uranium price, $/lb	57.85	43.34
Uranium reserves, lbs	468,800,000	464,300,000

Recent Merger and Acquisition Activity

Status: pending **Announced:** Oct. 11, 2022
Brookfield Business Corporation (BBPC) together with its institutional partners agreed to sell its nuclear technology services operation, Westinghouse Electric Company, to a consortium led by Cameco Corporation and Brookfield Renewable Partners L.P. (BEP LP) for a total enterprise value of US$7.875 billion. BBPC expects to receive US$1.8 billion for its 44% stake in Westinghouse, with the balance distributed to institutional partners. On closing, BEP LP and its institutional partners would own 51% interest in Westinghouse and Cameco would own 49%. Westinghouse's existing debt structure would remain in place, leaving an estimated US$4.5 billion equity cost to the consortium, subject to closing adjustments. This equity cost would be shared proportionately between BEP LP and its partners (US$2.3 billion) and Cameco (US$ $2.2 billion). BEP LP was expected to invest US$750,000,000 to acquire about 17% interest in Westinghouse. The transaction was expected to close in the second half of 2023.

Status: completed **Revised:** May 19, 2022
UPDATE: The transaction was completed. PREVIOUS: Cameco Corporation and Orano Canada Inc. agreed to acquire Idemitsu Canada Resources Ltd.'s 7.875% interest in the Cigar Lake underground uranium mine in northern Saskatchewan for $187,000,000 ($107,000,000 from Cameco and $80,000,000 from Orano). Upon closing, Cameco's ownership stake in the Cigar Lake would increase by 4.522% to 54.547%, while Orano's share would rise by 3.353% to 40.453%. TEPCO Resources Inc. retains the remaining 5% interest in the property. The transaction was expected to close in the second quarter of 2022.

Predecessor Detail - Name changed from Cameco - A Canadian Mining & Energy Corporation, Nov. 1, 1990.

Directors - Ian D. Bruce, chr., Calgary, Alta.; Timothy S. (Tim) Gitzel, pres. & CEO, Saskatoon, Sask.; Dr. Daniel Camus, Westmount, Qué.; Donald H. F. Deranger, Prince Albert, Sask.; Catherine A. Gignac, Mississauga, Ont.; James K. (Jim) Gowans, Surrey, B.C.; Dr. Kathryn J. (Kate) Jackson, Pittsburgh, Pa.; Donald B. (Don) Kayne, Delta, B.C.; Leontine van Leeuwen-Atkins, Calgary, Alta.

Other Exec. Officers - Dr. Grant E. Isaac, exec. v-p & CFO; Sean A. Quinn, sr. v-p, chief legal officer & corp. sec.; Brian A. Reilly, sr. v-p & COO; Heidi Shockey, sr. v-p & deputy CFO; Alice Wong, sr. v-p & chief corp. officer

Capital Stock

	Authorized (shs.)	Outstanding (shs.)[1]
First Preferred	unlimited	nil
Second Preferred	unlimited	nil
Common	unlimited	433,308,237
Class B	1	1

[1] At July 30, 2023

Common - One vote per share.

Class B - Entitles the Government of Saskatchewan to vote separately as a class in respect of any proposal to locate the company's head office outside of the province. The share has an assigned value of $1.00. One vote per share.

Options - At Dec. 31, 2022, options were outstanding to purchase 3,053,571 common shares at a weighted average exercise price of $15.75 per share with a weighted average remaining life of up to 3.2 years.

Major Shareholder - Widely held at Mar. 29, 2023.

Price Range - CCO/TSX

Year	Volume	High	Low	Close
2022	423,864,414	$41.05	$23.03	$30.69
2021	370,745,515	$35.47	$15.45	$27.58
2020	281,637,768	$18.38	$7.69	$17.05
2019	210,059,930	$17.12	$10.70	$11.54
2018	301,729,080	$16.70	$10.50	$15.48

Recent Close: $49.50

Capital Stock Changes - In October 2022, bought deal public offering of 34,057,250 common shares was completed at $21.95 per share, including 4,442,250 common shares on exercise of over-allotment option. Also during 2022, 401,955 common shares were issued on exercise of options.

Dividends

CCO com Ra $0.12 pa A est. Dec. 15, 2022[1]
Prev. Rate: $0.08 est. Dec. 14, 2018
[1] Dividends paid quarterly prior to December/18.

Long-Term Debt - Outstanding at Dec. 31, 2022:

Sr. unsecured debs.:	
Ser.G 4.19% due June 2024	$499,407,000
Ser.H 2.95% due Oct. 2027	398,238,000
Ser.F 5.09% due Nov. 2042	99,355,000
	997,000,000
Less: Current portion	nil
	997,000,000

Wholly Owned Subsidiaries

Cameco Australia Pty Ltd., Australia.
Cameco Europe Ltd., Switzerland.
Cameco Fuel Manufacturing Inc., Port Hope, Ont.
Cameco Inc., United States.
Cameco Marketing Inc., Saskatoon, Sask.
Crow Butte Resources, Inc., United States.
Power Resources, Inc., Denver, Colo.

Investments

49% int. in **GE-Hitachi Global Laser Enrichment LLC**, United States.
40% int. in **Inkai Limited Liability Partnership**, Kazakhstan.
Note: The preceding list includes only the major related companies in which interests are held.

Financial Statistics

Periods ended:	12m Dec. 31/22[A]		12m Dec. 31/21[A]
	$000s	%Chg	$000s
Operating revenue	**1,868,003**	**+27**	**1,474,984**
Cost of sales	1,457,336		1,282,635
Research & devel. expense	12,175		7,168
Exploration expense	10,578		8,016
General & admin expense	172,029		127,566
Operating expense	**1,652,118**	**+16**	**1,425,385**
Operating income	**215,885**	**+335**	**49,599**
Deprec., depl. & amort.	177,376		190,415
Finance income	37,499		6,804
Finance costs, gross	85,728		76,612
Investment income	93,988		68,283
Pre-tax income	**84,795**	**n.a.**	**(103,855)**
Income taxes	(4,469)		(1,201)
Net income	**89,264**	**n.a.**	**(102,654)**
Net inc. for equity hldrs	**89,382**	**n.a.**	**(102,577)**
Net inc. for non-cont. int	**(118)**	**n.a.**	**(77)**
Cash & equivalent	2,281,848		1,332,353
Inventories	664,698		409,521
Accounts receivable	183,944		276,139
Current assets	3,321,636		2,141,552
Long-term investments	210,972		233,240
Fixed assets, net	2,645,083		2,827,049
Right-of-use assets	9,452		4,156
Intangibles, net	47,117		51,247
Explor./devel. properties	818,955		745,394
Total assets	**8,632,793**	**+15**	**7,517,744**
Accts. pay. & accr. liabs	374,714		340,458
Current liabilities	560,841		413,743
Long-term debt, gross	997,000		996,250
Long-term debt, net	997,000		996,250
Long-term lease liabilities	9,287		4,872
Shareholders' equity	5,836,054		4,845,841
Non-controlling interest	11		127
Cash from oper. activs	**304,607**	**-34**	**458,288**
Cash from fin. activs	869,258		(46,772)
Cash from invest. activs	(1,290,822)		(80,298)
Net cash position	**1,143,674**	**-8**	**1,247,447**
Capital expenditures	(143,448)		(98,784)
Capital disposals	780		5,357
Unfunded pension liability	46,816		64,305
	$		$
Earnings per share*	0.22		(0.26)
Cash flow per share*	0.75		1.15
Cash divd. per share*	0.12		0.08
	shs		shs
No. of shs. o/s*	432,518,471		398,059,266
Avg. no. of shs. o/s*	405,494,353		397,630,947
	%		%
Net profit margin	4.78		(6.96)
Return on equity	1.67		(2.09)
Return on assets	2.22		(0.36)
Foreign sales percent	47		52
No. of employees (FTEs)	2,424		2,095

* Common
[A] Reported in accordance with IFRS

Latest Results

Periods ended:	6m June 30/23[A]		6m June 30/22[A]
	$000s	%Chg	$000s
Operating revenue	1,168,961	+22	955,615
Net income	132,657	+7	124,221
Net inc. for equity hldrs	132,662	+7	124,329
Net inc. for non-cont. int	(5)		(108)
	$		$
Earnings per share*	0.31		0.31

* Common
[A] Reported in accordance with IFRS

Historical Summary
(as originally stated)

Fiscal Year	Oper. Rev. $000s	Net Inc. Bef. Disc. $000s	EPS* $
2022[A]	1,868,003	89,264	0.22
2021[A]	1,474,984	(102,654)	(0.26)
2020[A]	1,800,073	(53,197)	(0.13)
2019[A]	1,862,925	73,941	0.19
2018[A]	2,091,661	166,235	0.42

* Common
[A] Reported in accordance with IFRS

C.26 Can-Gow Capital Inc.

Symbol - GOWC.P **Exchange** - TSX-VEN **CUSIP** - 13472T
Head Office - 1343-5328 Calgary Trail NW, Edmonton, AB, T9E 0V4 **Telephone** - (780) 439-8995
Email - doug@capitalwestventures.com
Investor Relations - Douglas Walker (780) 439-8995

Auditors - RSM Alberta LLP C.A., Edmonton, Alta.
Lawyers - Tupper Jonsson & Yeadon, Vancouver, B.C.
Transfer Agents - TSX Trust Company, Calgary, Alta.
Profile - (Alta. 2019) Capital Pool Company.
Common listed on TSX-VEN, Feb. 16, 2023.
Directors - Brendon McCutcheon, pres. & CEO, Edmonton, Alta.; Douglas Walker, CFO & corp. sec., Edmonton, Alta.; Dennis Bourgeault, Edmonton, Alta.; Peter Friesen, Edmonton, Alta.; Anwar Sleiman, Edmonton, Alta.

Capital Stock

	Authorized (shs.)	Outstanding (shs.)[1]
Preferred	unlimited	nil
Class A Common	unlimited	6,900,000
Class B Common	unlimited	nil
Class C Common	unlimited	nil

[1] At Feb. 16, 2023

Major Shareholder - Krystal Brewer held 23.19% interest, Brendon McCutcheon held 14.49% interest and Anwar Sleiman held 14.49% interest at Feb. 16, 2023.
Recent Close: $0.20
Capital Stock Changes - On Feb. 16, 2023, an initial public offering of 2,300,000 class A common shares was completed at 10¢ per share.

C.27 Canaccord Genuity G Ventures Corp.

Symbol - CGGV.UN **Exchange** - NEO **CUSIP** - 134818
Head Office - Brookfield Place, 3000-161 Bay St, Toronto, ON, M5J 2S1 **Telephone** - (416) 869-7368 **Toll-free** - (800) 382-9280
Email - jallen@cgf.com
Investor Relations - Jackie Allen (800) 382-9280
Auditors - MNP LLP C.A., Toronto, Ont.
Transfer Agents - Odyssey Trust Company, Toronto, Ont.
Profile - (Ont. 2021) A Special Purpose Acquisition Corporation formed for the purpose of effecting an acquisition of one or more businesses or assets by way of a merger, amalgamation, arrangement, share exchange, asset acquisition, share purchase, reorganization or any other similar business combination involving the company.
The company has 24 months from July 23, 2021, to complete a Qualifying Transaction or 27 months if it has executed a letter of intent, agreement in principle or definitive agreement for a Qualifying Transaction within 24 months from July 23, 2021. The company plans to focus primarily on acquiring companies with an enterprise value of between $30,000,000 and $150,000,000.
On July 24, 2023, the company's permitted timeline to complete a Qualifying Transaction has been automatically extended to Oct. 23, 2023.
Directors - Michael D. (Mike) Shuh, CEO, Toronto, Ont.; Roger Daher, Markham, Ont.; Kevin Kirby, Toronto, Ont.; Paul Pathak, Toronto, Ont.
Other Exec. Officers - Yu-Hyeon (Daniel) Chung, CFO; Jackie Allen, corp. sec.

Capital Stock

	Authorized (shs.)	Outstanding (shs.)[1]
Cl.A Restricted Vtg.	unlimited	5,000,000
Class B	unlimited	1,250,001

[1] At June 30, 2022

Class A Restricted Voting Share - Not redeemable in connection with completion of a Qualifying Transaction. On or following completion of a Qualifying Transaction, automatically convertible into common shares. Automatically redeemable if Qualifying Transaction not completed within permitted timeline for an amount payable in cash. One vote per share on all matters requiring shareholder approval including a proposed Qualifying Transaction but not on the election or removal of directors and auditors. Completion of the Qualifying Transaction will be subject to the approval of the holders of a majority of the class A shares.
Class B - Not redeemable in connection with a Qualifying Transaction or entitled to access the escrow account upon winding-up of company. On or following completion of a Qualifying Transaction, automatically convertible into common shares. All held by CG G-Corp Sponsor Inc. I, which is wholly owned by Canaccord Genuity Group Inc., and the company's founders Michael D. Shuh, Kevin Kirby, Paul Pathak and Roger Daher. Not entitled to vote at a meeting on a resolution requiring shareholder approval of the Qualifying Transaction.
Common - Not issuable prior to closing of the Qualifying Transaction. One vote per share.
Major Shareholder - Canaccord Genuity Group Inc. held 20% interest at June 30, 2022.

Price Range - CGGV.UN/NEO

Year	Volume	High	Low	Close
2022	29,900	$3.40	$2.70	$2.80
2021	76,500	$3.25	$2.70	$3.25

Recent Close: $2.81

C.28 Canaccord Genuity Group Inc.*

Symbol - CF **Exchange** - TSX **CUSIP** - 134801
Head Office - 2200-609 Granville St, PO Box 10337, Vancouver, BC, V7Y 1H2 **Telephone** - (604) 643-7300 **Toll-free** - (800) 663-1899
Website - canaccordgenuity.com
Email - cmarinoff@cgf.com
Investor Relations - Christina Marinoff (800) 382-9280
Auditors - Ernst & Young LLP C.A., Vancouver, B.C.
Transfer Agents - Computershare Trust Company of Canada Inc., Vancouver, B.C.
FP500 Revenue Ranking - 217
Employees - 2,829 at Mar. 31, 2023
Profile - (B.C. 1997) Provides independent, full-service financial services, with operations in two principal segments: capital markets and wealth management. Individual, institutional and corporate clients are offered comprehensive investment solutions, brokerage services and investment banking services.
Operations are carried out through two main segments: **Canaccord Genuity Capital Markets**; and **Canaccord Genuity Wealth Management**. Revenue is generated from commissions and fees associated with commission-based brokerage services and sale of fee-based products and services, investment banking, advisory fees, principal trading, interest and other. Commissions and fees revenue is principally generated from private client investment management trading activity and institutional sales and trading.
Canaccord Genuity Capital Markets - This group provides research, institutional equity sales and trading, investment banking, mergers and acquisitions and advisory services, international and principal trading, and fixed income trading to corporate, institutional and government clients through 20 offices in North America, the U.K. and Europe, Asia and Australia. Sectors covered are focused on technology, healthcare and life sciences, metals and mining, and consumer and retail, with additional exposure to diversified, transportation and industrials, energy, structured products and sustainability.
Canaccord Genuity Wealth Management - This group provides investment advice, brokerage services, managed accounts, portfolio management, fee-based accounts, wealth management services, insurance and estate planning, and financial planning to individual investors, private clients, institutions and intermediaries, and charities in Canada, the U.K. and Crown Dependencies, and Australia through 145 advisory teams and nine offices across Canada, 252 investment professionals and fund managers and 16 offices in the U.K., Guernsey, Jersey and Isle of Man, and 119 advisors and seven offices in Australia. At Mar. 31, 2023, assets under administration in Canada totaled $35.7 billion and assets under management (AUM) totaled $8.8 billion in Canada, AUM in the U.K. and Crown Dependencies totaled $55.1 billion, and AUM in Australia totaled $5.4 billion.
Outside the capital markets and wealth management segments, the company also operates a correspondent brokerage services division in Canada under the Pinnacle Correspondent Services banner. This division provides secure and confidential fully-integrated clearing and settlement, administrative, trading and research services to other brokerage firms.
In May 2023, the company sold wholly owned **Canaccord Genuity (Dubai) Ltd.**, which conducted capital markets operations in Dubai, for an undisclosed amount.
Subsequent to Mar. 31, 2023, wholly owned **Canaccord Genuity Management Company Limited** and 94.5%-owned subsidiaries, **Canaccord Genuity Financial Planning Limited**, **Punter Southall Wealth Limited** and **Adam & Company Investment Management Limited**, were wound up.
Concurrent with the company's acquisition of **Punter Southall Group Limited** on May 31, 2022, **HPS Investment Partners, LLC** acquired an additional £65,300,000 (Cdn$104,100,000) of convertible preferred shares of subsidiary **Canaccord Genuity Wealth Group Holdings (Jersey) Limited**.

Recent Merger and Acquisition Activity

Status: terminated **Revised:** June 14, 2023
UPDATE: The offer expired. The management group entered into a two-year standstill agreement which includes voting support commitments from certain members of the management group in favour of board-supported director nominees, reimbursement of certain reasonable expenses of the management group and continuation of an ad hoc independent committee, if required, for purposes of considering potential value enhancing alternative transactions. PREVIOUS: A management-led group of Canaccord Genuity Group Inc. proposed a going private transaction whereby it would acquire the remaining 78.7% interest in Canaccord Genuity for $11.25 cash per share. The transaction valued Canaccord Genuity at $1.127 billion. The employee group making the offer included president and CEO Daniel J. Daviau and chairman David J. Kassie, as well as all the members of Canaccord Genuity's global operating committee and additional senior and tenured employees from across its business. Canaccord Genuity's largest independent shareholder supported the transaction. Feb. 27, 2023 - 1373113 B.C. Ltd., on behalf of itself and the management-led group consisting of officers and employees of Canaccord, formally commenced the all-cash offer. The special committee of the board of directors of Canaccord does not support the offer and plans to recommend to the board that shareholders not tender to the offer, which expires on June 13, 2023. Mar. 22, 2023 - A new special committee was formed to evaluate the offer. June 5, 2023 - The board of directors of Canaccord Genuity has recommended that shareholders of the company reject the offer.
Status: completed **Revised:** May 29, 2023
UPDATE: The transaction was completed for $2,400,000 plus contingent consideration subject to achievement of certain performance targets. PREVIOUS: Canaccord Genuity Group Inc. agreed to acquire Mercer Global Investment Canada Limited's Canadian private wealth business. Terms were not disclosed. The acquisition would add $1.5 billion in client assets. Mercer Global Investment Canada is a business unit of Mercer, owned by Marsh & McLennan Companies, Inc.
Status: completed **Revised:** Aug. 17, 2022
UPDATE: The transaction was completed. Total consideration was £5,000,000 cash on closing, deferred consideration of £2,000,000 payable in cash or shares over three years following completion and contingent consideration of up to £17,000,000 payable over four years following completion, subject to achievement of performance targets related to revenue. PREVIOUS: Canaccord Genuity Group Inc. agreed to acquire the business of London, U.K.-based Results International Group LLP, an independent advisory firm focused in the technology and healthcare sectors which provides M&A and corporate finance services to entrepreneurs, corporates, private equity firms and investors. Results has executed more than 60 strategic advisory transactions in the past three years. Terms were not disclosed. The transaction was expected to close in the current fiscal quarter, subject to customary closing conditions.
Status: completed **Revised:** May 31, 2022
UPDATE: The transaction was completed. PREVIOUS: Canaccord Genuity Group Inc. agreed to acquire Punter Southall Wealth Limited (PSW), including the intermediary-facing brand Psigma, from Punter Southall Group Limited, a London, U.K.-based financial and professional services group, for £164,000,000 (Cdn$277,500,000) cash and issuance of ordinary shares in Canaccord's wealth management business in the U.K. and Crown Dependencies (CGWM UK) valued at £4,000,000. On closing, Canaccord would hold a 66.9% interest in CGWM UK. PSW offers financial planning, wealth management, investment management and retirement planning services to high net-worth individuals from offices in London, Guildford, Birmingham, Newcastle and Edinburgh, U.K. PSW has £5 billion (Cdn$8.5 billion) in client assets.
Predecessor Detail - Name changed from Canaccord Financial Inc., Oct. 1, 2013.
Directors - David J. Kassie, chr., Toronto, Ont.; Daniel J. (Dan) Daviau, pres. & CEO, Toronto, Ont.; Terrence A. (Terry) Lyons†, Vancouver, B.C.; Michael B. Auerbach, New York, N.Y.; Amy Freedman, Toronto, Ont.; Jo-Anne O'Connor, Toronto, Ont.; Rodney (Rod) Phillips, Toronto, Ont.
Other Exec. Officers - Marcus Freeman, man. dir. & CEO, Canaccord Genuity (Australia) Limited; Jennifer (Jen) Pardi, man. dir. & global head, equity capital markets; Fera Jeraj, chief tech. officer; Jason Melbourne, head, Cdn. capital markets & global head, Cdn. equities & distrib.; Mark Whaling, global head, secs.; Donald D. (Don) MacFayden, exec. v-p & CFO; Adrian Pelosi, exec. v-p, chief risk officer & treas.; Andrew F. (Andy) Viles, exec. v-p & chief legal officer; D'Arcy P. Doherty, gen. counsel & corp. sec.; Jeffrey G. Barlow, CEO, Canaccord Genuity LLC; David Esfandi, CEO, Canaccord Genuity Wealth Limited; Stuart R. Raftus, CEO, Canaccord Genuity Corp.; Nick Russell, CEO, Canaccord Genuity Limited
† Lead director

Capital Stock

	Authorized (shs.)	Outstanding (shs.)[1]
First Preferred	unlimited	nil
Series A		4,540,000
Series C		4,000,000
Common	unlimited	99,705,818

[1] At Aug. 7, 2023

First Preferred Series A - Entitled to fixed cumulative annual dividends of $1.007 per share payable quarterly to Sept. 30, 2026, and thereafter at a rate reset every five years equal to the five-year Government of Canada yield plus 3.21%. Redeemable on Sept. 30, 2026, and on September 30 every five years thereafter at $25 per share plus declared and unpaid dividends. Convertible at the holder's option on Sept. 30, 2026, and on September 30 every five years thereafter, into floating rate first preferred series B shares on a share-for-share basis, subject to certain conditions. The series B shares are entitled to cumulative preferential annual dividends payable quarterly equal to the 90-day Canadian Treasury bill rate plus 3.21%. Non-voting.
First Preferred Series C - Entitled to fixed cumulative annual dividends of $1.70925 per share payable quarterly to June 30, 2027, and thereafter at a rate reset every five years equal to the five-year Government of Canada yield plus 4.03%. Redeemable on June 30, 2027, and on June 30 every five years thereafter at $25 per share plus declared and unpaid dividends. Convertible at the holder's option on June 30, 2027, and on June 30 every five years thereafter, into floating rate first preferred series D shares on a share-for-share basis, subject to certain conditions. The series D shares are entitled to cumulative preferential annual dividends payable quarterly equal to the 90-day Canadian Treasury bill rate plus 4.03%. Non-voting.
Common - One vote per share.
Options - At Mar. 31, 2023, options were outstanding to purchase 5,222,335 common shares at a weighted average exercise price of $6.92 per share expiring to 2028.
Normal Course Issuer Bid - The company plans to make normal course purchases of up to 4,985,290 common shares representing 5% of the total outstanding. The bid commenced on Aug. 21, 2023, and expires on Aug. 20, 2024.
Major Shareholder - Widely held at June 12, 2023.

Price Range - CF/TSX

Year	Volume	High	Low	Close
2022	82,033,997	$16.05	$6.24	$8.39
2021	92,023,163	$16.62	$10.88	$15.08
2020	68,478,566	$11.44	$3.21	$11.16
2019	49,341,003	$6.88	$4.62	$4.84
2018	54,302,007	$7.49	$5.49	$5.77

Recent Close: $8.61
Capital Stock Changes - During fiscal 2023, common shares were issued as follows: 285,899 on exercise of options and 195,993 for deferred consideration; 585,300 common shares were repurchased under a Normal Course Issuer Bid.
In January 2022, 6,451,612 common shares were repurchased under a Substantial Issuer Bid. Also during fiscal 2022, common shares were issued as follows: 736,850 for deferred consideration and 609,046 on exercise of options; 3,387,816 common shares were repurchased under a Normal Course Issuer Bid.

Dividends

CF com Ra $0.34 pa Q est. Mar. 10, 2022[1]
Prev. Rate: $0.30 est. June 30, 2021
Prev. Rate: $0.26 est. Mar. 10, 2021
Prev. Rate: $0.22 est. Sept. 10, 2020

CF.PR.A pfd 1st ser A cum. red. exch. Adj. Ra $1.007 pa Q est. Dec. 31, 2021
CF.PR.C pfd 1st ser C cum. red. exch. Adj. Ra $1.70925 pa Q est. Sept. 30, 2022
[1] Quarterly divd normally payable in Mar/16 has been omitted.

Long-Term Debt - At Mar. 31, 2023, outstanding long-term debt totaled $314,622,000 ($20,842,000 current and net of $3,070,000 of unamortized financing fees) and consisted of $7,500,000 of subordinated debt, bearing interest at prime plus 4% and due on demand, and $307,122,000 of bank loan due September 2024.

Wholly Owned Subsidiaries

The Balloch Group Limited, British Virgin Islands.
CG G Sponsors Inc. I, Canada.
- 20% int. in **Canaccord Genuity G Ventures Corp.**, Toronto, Ont. (see separate coverage)

CG Investments Inc. III, Canada.
CG Investments Inc. IV, Canada.
CG Investments Inc. V, Canada.
CG Investments Inc. VI, Canada.
CG Investments Inc., Canada.
CG Sawaya, LLC, New York, N.Y.
Canaccord Adams (Delaware) Inc., Del.
Canaccord Adams Financial Group Inc., Del.
Canaccord Genuity Asia (Beijing) Limited, Beijing, People's Republic of China.
Canaccord Genuity Asia (Hong Kong) Limited, Hong Kong, People's Republic of China.
Canaccord Genuity Corp., Vancouver, B.C.
Canaccord Genuity Emerging Markets Ltd., Bahamas.
Canaccord Genuity Finance Corp., Canada.
Canaccord Genuity Group Finance Company Ltd., Canada.
Canaccord Genuity Hawkpoint Limited, London, Middx., United Kingdom.
Canaccord Genuity (Hong Kong) Limited, Hong Kong, People's Republic of China.
Canaccord Genuity Limited, United Kingdom.
- 100% int. in **Canaccord Asset Management Inc.**, Canada.

Canaccord Genuity LLC, Del.
Canaccord Genuity Petsky Prunier LLC, Del.
Canaccord Genuity S.A.S., France.
Canaccord Genuity Securities LLC, United States.
Canaccord Genuity (2021) GP ULC, Canada.
Canaccord Genuity (2021) Holdings ULC, Canada.
Canaccord Genuity (2021) Limited Partnership, Canada.
Canaccord Genuity (2021) LLC, United States.
Canaccord Genuity Wealth & Estate Planning Services Ltd., Canada.
Canaccord Genuity Wealth Group Holdings Ltd., Canada.
Canaccord Genuity Wealth Management (USA) Inc., Minn.
Collins Stewart Inc., United States.
FinLogiK Inc., Montréal, Qué.
- 75% int. in **FinLogiK Tunisie SARL**, Tunisia.

JitneyTrade Inc., Montréal, Qué.
Stockwave Equities Ltd., Vancouver, B.C.

Subsidiaries

65% int. in **Canaccord Financial Group (Australia) Pty Ltd.**, Australia.
- 100% int. in **Canaccord Genuity (Australia) Limited**, Australia.
- 100% int. in **Canaccord Genuity Financial Limited**, Perth, W.A., Australia.
  - 100% int. in **Patersons Asset Management Limited**, Australia.

94.5% int. in **Canaccord Genuity Wealth Group Holdings (Jersey) Limited**, Jersey.
- 100% int. in **Canaccord Genuity Wealth Group Limited**, United Kingdom.
- 100% int. in **Canaccord Genuity Wealth (International) Holdings Limited**, Guernsey.
  - 100% int. in **Canaccord Genuity Wealth (International) Limited**, Guernsey.
- 100% int. in **Canaccord Genuity Wealth Limited**, United Kingdom.
  - 100% int. in **CG Wealth Planning Limited**, London, Middx., United Kingdom.
  - 100% int. in **Canaccord Genuity Asset Management Limited**, United Kingdom.

Note: The preceding list includes only the major related companies in which interests are held.

Financial Statistics

Periods ended:	12m Mar. 31/23[A]		12m Mar. 31/22[A]
	$000s	%Chg	$000s
Total revenue	**1,510,397**	**-26**	**2,046,002**
Salaries & benefits	936,872		1,248,184
General & admin. expense	138,461		101,431
Other operating expense	203,551		196,771
Operating expense	**1,278,884**	**-17**	**1,546,386**
Operating income	**231,513**	**-54**	**499,616**
Deprec. & amort.	67,969		51,487
Finance costs, gross	54,539		23,598
Write-downs/write-offs	(102,571)[1]		nil
Pre-tax income	**(34,433)**	**n.a.**	**378,269**
Income taxes	20,309		107,704
Net income	**(54,742)**	**n.a.**	**270,565**
Net inc. for equity hldrs	**(90,104)**	**n.a.**	**246,314**
Net inc. for non-cont. int	**35,362**	**+46**	**24,251**
Cash & equivalent	1,723,510		2,839,490
Accounts receivable	3,355,203		3,438,655
Current assets	5,112,922		6,280,112
Long-term investments	18,101		22,928
Fixed assets, net	48,180		34,643
Right-of-use assets	103,729		117,066
Intangibles	928,735		697,272
Total assets	**6,302,400**	**-13**	**7,250,245**
Accts. pay. & accr. liabs	3,720,332		4,845,672
Current liabilities	4,363,351		5,485,756
Long-term debt, gross	314,622		159,541
Long-term debt, net	293,780		145,467
Long-term lease liabilities	92,526		101,620
Preferred share equity	205,641		205,641
Shareholders' equity	1,054,639		1,178,069
Non-controlling interest	343,998		238,700
Cash from oper. activs	**(584,416)**	**n.a.**	**263,253**
Cash from fin. activs	71,223		(142,859)
Cash from invest. activs	(288,111)		(201,995)
Net cash position	**1,008,432**	**-44**	**1,788,261**
Capital expenditures, net	(24,348)		(12,122)
	$		$
Earnings per share*	(1.16)		2.50
Cash flow per share*	(6.69)		2.77
Cash divd. per share*	0.34		0.31
	shs		shs
No. of shs. o/s*	99,594,391		99,697,799
Avg. no. of shs. o/s*	87,381,995		94,871,398
	%		%
Net profit margin	(3.62)		13.22
Return on equity	(11.10)		25.28
Return on assets	0.47		3.86
Foreign sales percent	70		66
No. of employees (FTEs)	2,829		2,587

* Common
[A] Reported in accordance with IFRS
[1] Consists of $101,729,000 goodwill impairment and $842,000 intangible asset impairment of the Canadian capital markets operation.

Latest Results

Periods ended:	3m June 30/23[A]		3m June 30/22[A]
	$000s	%Chg	$000s
Total revenue	343,324	+8	317,370
Net income	(268)	n.a.	(3,004)
Net inc. for equity hldrs	(10,536)	n.a.	(10,173)
Net inc. for non-cont. int	10,268		7,169
	$		$
Earnings per share*	(0.15)		(0.14)

* Common
[A] Reported in accordance with IFRS

Historical Summary
(as originally stated)

Fiscal Year	Total Rev.	Net Inc. Bef. Disc.	EPS*
	$000s	$000s	$
2023[A]	1,510,397	(54,742)	(1.16)
2022[A]	2,046,002	270,565	2.50
2021[A]	2,007,688	269,802	2.30
2020[A]	1,223,867	86,554	0.78
2019[A]	1,190,567	71,582	0.58

* Common
[A] Reported in accordance with IFRS

C.29 Canada Goose Holdings Inc.*

Symbol - GOOS **Exchange** - TSX **CUSIP** - 135086
Head Office - 250 Bowie Ave, Toronto, ON, M6E 4Y2 **Telephone** - (416) 780-9850
Website - www.canadagoose.com
Email - ir@canadagoose.com
Investor Relations - David M. Forrest (800) 865-0224
Auditors - Deloitte LLP C.A., Toronto, Ont.
Lawyers - Ropes & Gray LLP, San Francisco, Calif.; Stikeman Elliott LLP, Toronto, Ont.
Transfer Agents - Computershare Trust Company, N.A., Canton, Mass.; Computershare Trust Company of Canada Inc., Toronto, Ont.
FP500 Revenue Ranking - 324
Employees - 4,760 at Apr. 2, 2023

Profile - (B.C. 2013) Designs, manufactures, distributes and retails performance luxury apparel for men, women, youth, children and babies under the Canada Goose brand. Also designs and manufactures performance outdoor and industrial footwear under the Baffin brand.

The company's product offerings include various styles of parkas, lightweight down jackets, rainwear, windwear, apparel, fleece, footwear and accessories for fall, winter and spring seasons. The company continues to develop and introduce new products across styles, uses and climates including Canada Goose footwear and Baffin branded footwear.

Canada Goose products are sold in 62 countries through 57 national e-commerce sites and 51 directly operated permanent retail stores across North America, Europe and Asia Pacific; as well as through retailers and international distributors. Baffin products are predominantly sold through distributors and retailers in Canada and the United States.

The company operates eight Canada Goose manufacturing facilities in Toronto, Ont., Winnipeg, Man., and Greater Montreal, Que.; and one warehouse facility in Winnipeg. Baffin operates one manufacturing facility in Stoney Creek, Ont. The company also works with 12 subcontractors in Canada and 18 international manufacturing partners.

On Apr. 4, 2022, the company and **Sazaby League Ltd.** formed a 50/50 joint venture, **Canada Goose Japan K.K.** The company contributed $2,500,000 for its 50% share and controls the joint venture from the date of inception. Sazaby contributed cash, as well as certain assets and liabilities in exchange for its 50% share. The joint venture agreement replaces an exclusive national distributor arrangement between Sazaby League and the company. Canada Goose Japan would be the exclusive distributor of the company's products in Japan through a national e-commerce site, and retail and wholesale points of distribution across the country.

Directors - Dani Reiss, chr. & CEO, Toronto, Ont.; Maureen Chiquet†, N.Y.; John M. Davison†, Ont.; Michael D. Armstrong, Calif.; Joshua (Josh) Bekenstein, Wayland, Mass.; Jodi L. H. Butts, Ottawa, Ont.; Ryan Cotton, Mass.; Stephen K. Gunn, Toronto, Ont.; Ching Ying (Belinda) Wong, Hong Kong, People's Republic of China

Other Exec. Officers - Carrie Baker, pres.; John Moran, COO; Michael (Woody) Blackford, chief product officer; Penny Brook, chief mktg. & experience officer; Jessica (Jess) Johannson, chief HR officer; Ana Mihaljevic, head, global stores & pres., North America; Daniel Binder, exec. v-p, sales opers. & planning & chief transformation officer; Matt Blonder, exec. v-p & chief digital officer; Jonathan Sinclair, exec. v-p & CFO; Patrick Bourke, sr. v-p, strategy & corp. devel.; David M. Forrest, sr. v-p & gen. counsel; Paul Cadman, pres., Asia-Pacific; Juliette Streichenberger, pres., Canada Goose International AG & pres., EMEA; Paul Hubner, founder, pres. & CEO, Baffin Limited
† Lead director

Capital Stock

	Authorized (shs.)	Outstanding (shs.)[1]
Preferred	unlimited	nil
Multiple Vtg.	unlimited	51,004,076
Subord. Vtg.	unlimited	51,901,249

[1] At July 27, 2023

Preferred - Issuable in series. Non-voting.
Multiple Voting - Convertible into subordinate voting shares on a 1-for-1 basis. Ten votes per share.
Subordinate Voting - One vote per share.
Options - At Apr. 2, 2023, options were outstanding to purchase 4,055,199 subordinate voting shares at prices ranging from $0.02 to $83.53 per share with a weighted average remaining life of 1 to 9.2 years.
Normal Course Issuer Bid - The company plans to make normal course purchases of up to 5,421,685 subordinate voting shares representing 10% of the public float. The bid commenced on Nov. 22, 2022, and expires on Nov. 21, 2023.
Major Shareholder - Bain Capital, L.P. held 54.91% interest and Dani Reiss held 35.8% interest at June 20, 2023.

Price Range - GOOS/TSX

Year	Volume	High	Low	Close
2022	94,389,081	$48.14	$20.01	$24.08
2021	74,570,618	$67.33	$35.80	$46.88
2020	112,839,624	$51.13	$18.27	$37.84
2019	130,046,237	$79.89	$42.38	$47.01
2018	90,832,864	$95.58	$35.88	$59.68

Recent Close: $20.64

Capital Stock Changes - During fiscal 2023, subordinate voting shares were issued as follows: 87,034 for settlement of restricted share units and 60,248 on exercise of options; 1,152,802 subordinate voting shares were repurchased under a Normal Course Issuer Bid.

During fiscal 2022, subordinate voting shares were issued as follows: 342,148 on exercise of options and 49,968 for settlement of restricted share units; 5,636,763 subordinate voting shares were repurchased under a Normal Course Issuer Bid.

Long-Term Debt - At Apr. 2, 2023, outstanding long-term debt totaled $395,700,000 ($4,100,000 current and net of $600,000 unamortized deferred transaction costs) and consisted entirely of a US$300,000,000 term loan bearing interest at LIBOR plus 3.5% and due on Oct. 7, 2027.

Wholly Owned Subsidiaries

Canada Goose Inc., Toronto, Ont.
- 100% int. in **Baffin Limited**, Ont.
  - 100% int. in **Baffin Inc.**, Stoney Creek, Ont.
  - 100% int. in **Baffin US, Inc.**, Del.
- 100% int. in **Canada Goose EU B.V.**, Netherlands.
- 100% int. in **Canada Goose International Holdings Limited**, United Kingdom.
  - 100% int. in **Canada Goose Asia Holdings Limited**, Hong Kong, People's Republic of China.
    - 100% int. in **CG (Shanghai) Trading Co., Ltd.**, Shanghai, People's Republic of China.
    - 100% int. in **Canada Goose HK Limited**, Hong Kong, People's Republic of China.
  - 100% int. in **Canada Goose France Retail S.A.S.**, France.
  - 100% int. in **Canada Goose Germany Retail GmbH**, Frankfurt am Main, Germany.
  - 100% int. in **Canada Goose International AG**, Switzerland.
    - 50% int. in **Canada Goose Australia Pty Ltd.**, Australia.
    - 50% int. in **Canada Goose Japan, K.K.**, Japan.
  - 100% int. in **Canada Goose Italy Retail S.r.l.**, Italy.
  - 100% int. in **Canada Goose Services Limited**, United Kingdom.
  - 100% int. in **Canada Goose UK Retail Limited**, United Kingdom.
- 100% int. in **Canada Goose Netherlands Retail B.V.**, Netherlands.
- 100% int. in **Canada Goose US, Inc.**, United States.

Financial Statistics

Periods ended:	52w Apr. 2/23^A		53w Apr. 3/22^A
	$000s	%Chg	$000s
Operating revenue	**1,217,000**	**+11**	**1,098,400**
Cost of sales	392,100		350,100
General & admin expense	580,300		495,800
Operating expense	**972,400**	**+15**	**845,900**
Operating income	**244,600**	**-3**	**252,500**
Deprec., depl. & amort.	109,100		95,800
Finance income	900		400
Finance costs, gross	42,900		39,400
Pre-tax income	**93,500**	**-21**	**117,700**
Income taxes	24,600		23,100
Net income	**68,900**	**-27**	**94,600**
Net inc. for equity hldrs	**72,700**	**-23**	**94,600**
Net inc. for non-cont. int	**(3,800)**	**n.a.**	**nil**
Cash & equivalent	286,500		287,700
Inventories	472,600		393,300
Accounts receivable	50,900		42,700
Current assets	863,200		762,300
Fixed assets, net	156,000		114,200
Right-of-use assets	291,800		215,200
Intangibles, net	199,000		175,300
Total assets	**1,590,000**	**+19**	**1,340,600**
Bank indebtedness	23,500		nil
Accts. pay. & accr. liabs	192,300		165,800
Current liabilities	352,400		281,500
Long-term debt, gross	395,700		370,000
Long-term debt, net	391,600		366,200
Long-term lease liabilities	258,700		192,200
Shareholders' equity	469,500		427,900
Non-controlling interest	8,000		nil
Cash from oper. activs	**116,300**	**-23**	**151,600**
Cash from fin. activs	(80,700)		(298,200)
Cash from invest. activs	(45,300)		(37,200)
Net cash position	**286,500**	**0**	**287,700**
Capital expenditures	(45,200)		(34,500)
	$		$
Earnings per share*	0.69		0.87
Cash flow per share*	1.11		1.40
	shs		shs
No. of shs. o/s*	104,188,988		105,194,508
Avg. no. of shs. o/s*	105,058,643		108,296,802
	%		%
Net profit margin	5.66		8.61
Return on equity	16.20		18.40
Return on assets	6.86		8.87
Foreign sales percent	80		80
No. of employees (FTEs)	4,760		4,353

* M.V. & S.V.
^A Reported in accordance with IFRS

Latest Results

Periods ended:	13w July 2/23^A		13w July 3/22^A
	$000s	%Chg	$000s
Operating revenue	84,800	+21	69,900
Net income	(85,000)	n.a.	(63,600)
Net inc. for equity hldrs	(81,100)	n.a.	(62,400)
Net inc. for non-cont. int	(3,900)		(1,200)
	$		$
Earnings per share*	(0.78)		(0.59)

* M.V. & S.V.
^A Reported in accordance with IFRS

Historical Summary
(as originally stated)

Fiscal Year	Oper. Rev. $000s	Net Inc. Bef. Disc. $000s	EPS* $
2023^A	1,217,000	68,900	0.69
2022^A1	1,098,400	94,600	0.87
2021^A	903,700	70,200	0.64
2020^A	958,100	151,700	1.38
2019^A	830,500	143,600	1.31

* M.V. & S.V.
^A Reported in accordance with IFRS
[1] 53 weeks ended Apr. 3, 2022.

C.30 Canada Jetlines Operations Ltd.

Symbol - CJET **Exchange** - NEO **CUSIP** - 13527D
Head Office - 300-6299 Airport Rd, Mississauga, ON, L4V 1N3
Toll-free - (888) 221-0915
Website - www.jetlines.com
Email - percy.gyara@jetlines.ca
Investor Relations - Percy Gyara (604) 562-8690
Auditors - MNP LLP C.A., Toronto, Ont.
Transfer Agents - Computershare Trust Company of Canada Inc., Vancouver, B.C.

Profile - (Can. 2017 amalg.) Launching a Canadian ultra low-cost airline under the Canada Jetlines banner to provide tour operations with flights within Canada and to popular sun destinations in the U.S., Mexico and the Caribbean.

The airliner was created to provide travel services and vacation packages to leisure destinations within Canada and to the U.S., Mexico, Cuba, Jamaica, St. Lucia, Antigua, Bahamas and other Caribbean nations. A fleet of 15 Airbus A320 aircraft to be leased and introduced by 2025 is planned. The company intends to provide vacation packages through partnerships with airports, tourism bureaus, hotels, hospitality brands and attractions.

On Aug. 26, 2022, the company announced that its airline operations would begin on Sept. 22, 2022, with biweekly flights between Toronto (YYZ) and Calgary (YYC). The airline received its Air Operator Certificate from Transport Canada on Aug. 18, 2022, and domestic and international service licenses from the Canadian Transportation Agency on Aug. 22, 2022, giving it all government certification required to start operations. Domestic flights to Moncton, N.B. (YQM) and Winnipeg, Man. (YWG) were also planned.

On Apr. 7, 2022, the company announced that it has selected Toronto Pearson International Airport (YYZ) as its international travel hub for flights out of Canada.

Predecessor Detail - Formed from Canada Jetlines Ltd. in Canada, Feb. 28, 2017.

Directors - Brigitte Goersch, chr., Fla.; Eddy (Ed) Doyle, CEO, Toronto, Ont.; Regenold Christian, Ont.; Rossen Dimitrov, Doha, Qatar; Ryan Goepel, Fla.; Beth S. Horowitz, Toronto, Ont.; Shawn Klerer, Maple, Ont.; David Kruschell, Alta.; Ravinder Minhas, Alta.

Other Exec. Officers - Percy Gyara, CFO; Duncan Bureau, chief comml. officer; Capt. Vic Charlebois, v-p, flight opers.; Brad Warren, v-p, maint. & COO; Sheila Paine, corp. sec.

Capital Stock

	Authorized (shs.)	Outstanding (shs.)[1]
Common Voting	unlimited	35,670,326
Variable Voting	unlimited	26,589,561

[1] At June 30, 2022

Common Voting - May only be owned and controlled by Canadians. Automatically convertible into one variable voting share if such common voting share is or becomes beneficially owned or controlled, directly or indirectly, by a holder who is not Canadian. One vote per share.

Variable Voting - May only be owned and controlled by persons who are not Canadians. Automatically convertible into one common voting share if such variable voting share is or becomes beneficially owned or controlled, directly or indirectly, by a Canadian. One vote per share.

Major Shareholder - Global Crossing Airlines Group Inc. held 13.91% interest and Regenold Christian held 11.9% interest at May 5, 2022.

Price Range - CJET/NEO

Year	Volume	High	Low	Close
2022	2,242,000	$0.40	$0.21	$0.22
2021	272,500	$0.83	$0.38	$0.40

Recent Close: $0.14

Wholly Owned Subsidiaries

Canada Jetlines Vacations Ltd., Canada.

Financial Statistics

Periods ended:	12m Dec. 31/21^A		12m Dec. 31/20^A
	$000s	%Chg	$000s
Salaries & benefits	17		1
General & admin expense	1,634		62
Stock-based compensation	1,207		nil
Other operating expense	148		2
Operating expense	**3,006**	**n.m.**	**65**
Operating income	**(3,006)**	**n.a.**	**(65)**
Deprec., depl. & amort.	6		nil
Finance income	15		1
Pre-tax income	**(3,101)**	**n.a.**	**158**
Net income	**(3,101)**	**n.a.**	**158**
Cash & equivalent	3,580		3
Current assets	4,893		15
Fixed assets, net	130		nil
Right-of-use assets	214		nil
Total assets	**5,237**	**n.m.**	**15**
Accts. pay. & accr. liabs	759		351
Current liabilities	821		351
Long-term debt, gross	40		40
Long-term debt, net	40		40
Long-term lease liabilities	207		nil
Shareholders' equity	4,168		(377)
Cash from oper. activs	**(2,667)**	**n.a.**	**39**
Cash from fin. activs	6,270		(169)
Cash from invest. activs	(26)		29
Net cash position	**3,580**	**n.m.**	**3**
Capital expenditures	(26)		nil
Capital disposals	nil		29
	$		$
Earnings per share*	(0.07)		0.00
Cash flow per share*	(0.06)		0.00
	shs		shs
No. of shs. o/s*	50,463,474		33,403,145
Avg. no. of shs. o/s*	43,652,104		33,403,145
	%		%
Net profit margin	n.a.		n.a.
Return on equity	n.m.		n.m.
Return on assets	(118.09)		135.04

* Com. Vtg. & Var. Vtg
^A Reported in accordance with IFRS

Latest Results

Periods ended:	6m June 30/22^A		6m June 30/21^A
	$000s	%Chg	$000s
Net income	(5,562)	n.a.	(170)
	$		$
Earnings per share*	(0.10)		(0.01)

* Com. Vtg. & Var. Vtg
^A Reported in accordance with IFRS

Historical Summary
(as originally stated)

Fiscal Year	Oper. Rev. $000s	Net Inc. Bef. Disc. $000s	EPS* $
2021^A	nil	(3,101)	(0.07)
2020^A	nil	158	0.00
2019^A	nil	(6,554)	(0.20)

* Com. Vtg. & Var. Vtg
^A Reported in accordance with IFRS

C.31 CanadaBis Capital Inc.

Symbol - CANB **Exchange** - TSX-VEN **CUSIP** - 13530Q
Head Office - PO Box 850, Rocky Mountain House, AB, T4T 1A6
Toll-free - (888) 784-4621
Website - www.canadabis.com
Email - travis@stigmagrow.ca
Investor Relations - Travis McIntyre (888) 784-4621
Auditors - BDO Canada LLP C.A., Calgary, Alta.
Lawyers - Dentons Canada LLP
Transfer Agents - Computershare Trust Company of Canada Inc., Calgary, Alta.

Profile - (Alta. 2016) Produces and sells recreational cannabis and cannabis products in Canada.

Owns and operates a 66,000-sq.-ft. indoor cultivation and processing facility in Red Deer, Alta. Proprietary product brands include Dab Bods, Black NGL, White NGL, Chapter 1 and Stigma Grow. Products are sold and distributed through the company's cannabis retail store in Red Deer operating under the INDICAtive Collection name, and through wholesale transactions with provincial boards and other licensed establishments.

Also provides extraction and tolling services to other licensed producers; and holds 95% interest in a 13-acre undeveloped land on Vancouver Island, B.C., zoned for outdoor/greenhouse cannabis cultivation.

Directors - Travis McIntyre, pres. & CEO, Rocky Mountain House, Alta.; Shane Chana, interim CFO, Edmonton, Alta.; Barbara M. (Barb) O'Neill, corp. sec., Airdrie, Alta.; Nicole Bacsalmasi, Calgary, Alta.; Alex Michaud, Edmonton, Alta.

Capital Stock

	Authorized (shs.)	Outstanding (shs.)[1]
Preferred	unlimited	nil
Cl.A Common	unlimited	137,136,380
Cl.B Non-vtg. Common	unlimited	nil

[1] At Apr. 30, 2023

Major Shareholder - Kimberley (Kim) McIntyre held 25.1% interest, Travis McIntyre held 25.1% interest and 2011939 Alberta Ltd. held 16.1% interest at May 17, 2022.

Price Range - CANB/TSX-VEN

Year	Volume	High	Low	Close
2022	7,732,523	$0.12	$0.03	$0.08
2021	12,745,326	$0.25	$0.05	$0.06
2020	4,340,194	$0.23	$0.08	$0.10
2019	1,731,038	$0.68	$0.15	$0.16
2018	1,064,742	$0.49	$0.16	$0.36

Recent Close: $0.28

Capital Stock Changes - In December 2021, private placement of 1,153,846 units (1 class A common share & 1 warrant) at 13¢ per unit was completed.

Wholly Owned Subsidiaries

Full Spectrum Labs Ltd., Alta. dba Stigma Roots
Stigma Pharmaceuticals Inc., Red Deer, Alta.
• 100% int. in **1998643 Alberta Ltd.**, Alta. dba Stigma Grow
2103157 Alberta Ltd., Red Deer, Alta. dba INDICAtive Collection

Subsidiaries

95% int. in **Goldstream Cannabis Inc.**, B.C.

Financial Statistics

Periods ended:	12m July 31/22[A]		12m July 31/21[A]
	$000s	%Chg	$000s
Operating revenue	**11,669**	**+70**	**6,866**
Cost of sales	5,921		4,250
General & admin expense	4,174		4,021
Stock-based compensation	54		458
Operating expense	**10,150**	**+16**	**8,730**
Operating income	**1,519**	**n.a.**	**(1,864)**
Deprec., depl. & amort	481		422
Finance costs, gross	493		400
Pre-tax income	**608**	**n.a.**	**(2,681)**
Net income	**608**	**n.a.**	**(2,681)**
Net inc. for equity hldrs	**608**	**n.a.**	**(2,677)**
Net inc. for non-cont. int	**nil**	**n.a.**	**(4)**
Cash & equivalent	145		850
Inventories	2,935		1,222
Accounts receivable	2,139		673
Current assets	5,682		2,900
Fixed assets, net	9,506		10,090
Intangibles, net	nil		8
Total assets	**15,478**	**+17**	**13,284**
Accts. pay. & accr. liabs	3,538		1,334
Current liabilities	11,904		10,142
Long-term debt, gross	6,759		7,442
Long-term debt, net	474		455
Long-term lease liabilities	427		807
Shareholders' equity	2,540		1,728
Non-controlling interest	93		94
Cash from oper. activs	**(83)**	**n.a.**	**(1,807)**
Cash from fin. activs	(412)		2,366
Cash from invest. activs	(210)		123
Net cash position	**145**	**-83**	**850**
Capital expenditures	(210)		(152)
Capital disposals	nil		1
	$		$
Earnings per share*	0.00		(0.02)
Cash flow per share*	(0.00)		(0.01)
	shs		shs
No. of shs. o/s*	137,136,380		135,982,534
Avg. no. of shs. o/s*	136,747,550		135,220,903
	%		%
Net profit margin	5.21		(39.05)
Return on equity	28.49		(105.73)
Return on assets	7.66		(17.68)

* Cl.A Common
[A] Reported in accordance with IFRS

Latest Results

Periods ended:	3m Oct. 31/22[A]		3m Oct. 31/21[A]
	$000s	%Chg	$000s
Operating revenue	5,148	+179	1,845
Net income	700	n.a.	(271)
Net inc. for equity hldrs	700	n.a.	(270)
Net inc. for non-cont. int	nil		(1)
	$		$
Earnings per share*	0.01		(0.00)

* Cl.A Common
[A] Reported in accordance with IFRS

Historical Summary
(as originally stated)

Fiscal Year	Oper. Rev.	Net Inc. Bef. Disc.	EPS*
	$000s	$000s	$
2022[A]	11,669	608	0.00
2021[A]	6,866	(2,681)	(0.02)
2020[A]	4,429	(5,391)	(0.04)
2019[A]	nil	(9,003)	(0.09)
2018[A1]	nil	(346)	n.a.

* Cl.A Common
[A] Reported in accordance with IFRS
[1] Results pertain to 1926360 Alberta Ltd. (dba Stigma Pharmaceuticals).

C.32 Canadian Apartment Properties Real Estate Investment Trust*

Symbol - CAR.UN **Exchange** - TSX **CUSIP** - 134921
Head Office - 401-11 Church St, Toronto, ON, M5E 1W1 **Telephone** - (416) 861-9404
Website - www.capreit.ca
Email - ir@capreit.net
Investor Relations - Nicole Dolan (437) 219-1765
Auditors - Ernst & Young LLP C.A., Toronto, Ont.
Lawyers - Stikeman Elliott LLP, Toronto, Ont.
Transfer Agents - Computershare Trust Company of Canada Inc., Toronto, Ont.
FP500 Revenue Ranking - 338
Employees - 1,067 at Dec. 31, 2022

Profile - (Ont. 1997) Owns and operates a portfolio of multi-unit residential rental properties principally located in and near major urban centres across Canada and, through subsidiary **European Residential Real Estate Investment Trust** (ERES), in the Netherlands.

Properties consist of apartments, townhomes and manufactured home communities (MHCs). At Mar. 31, 2023, the trust owned or had co-ownership interests in 53,191 residential suites and 77 MHCs, consisting of 12,336 land lease sites, in Ontario, Quebec, British Columbia, Alberta, Nova Scotia, Saskatchewan, Prince Edward Island, New Brunswick and the Netherlands.

Geographic mix of residential suites at Mar. 31, 2023:

Location	Number
Greater Toronto Area	17,139
Ottawa	1,485
London/Kitchener/Waterloo	3,808
Greater Montreal Region	8,681
Quebec City	2,777
Greater Vancouver Region	3,743
Victoria & other B.C.	2,117
Edmonton	608
Calgary	1,775
Halifax	3,287
Regina	234
Charlottetown	637
The Netherlands[1]	6,900
	53,191

[1] Represents residential properties owned by ERES.

MHC land lease sites at Mar. 31, 2023:

Location	Number
Ontario	4,425
Quebec	429
British Columbia	496
Alberta	2,251
Nova Scotia	127
Saskatchewan	378
Prince Edward Island	791
New Brunswick	3,439
	12,336

In March 2023, the trust sold a 46-suite property in Wingham, Ont., for $250,000.

Recent Merger and Acquisition Activity

Status: completed **Announced:** June 8, 2023
Canadian Apartment Properties Real Estate Investment Trust sold a property consisting of 393 residential units and two commercial units in the Saint-Laurent neighbourhood of Montréal, Qué., for consideration of $68,900,000.

Status: completed **Announced:** June 8, 2023
Canadian Apartment Properties Real Estate Investment Trust sold a 60-suite residential portfolio in Charlottetown, P.E.I., for gross proceeds of $9,400,000, excluding disposition costs.

Status: completed **Announced:** June 8, 2023
Canadian Apartment Properties Real Estate Investment Trust sold a 162-suite residential property in Longueuil, a suburb of Montréal, Qué., for gross consideration of $25,000,000.

Status: completed **Announced:** May 11, 2023
Canadian Apartment Properties Real Estate Investment Trust sold a non-core portfolio totaling 180 residential suites and one commercial unit in Montréal, Que., for total consideration of $27,800,000.

Status: completed **Announced:** Apr. 12, 2023
Canadian Apartment Properties Real Estate Investment Trust acquire a newly constructed 89-suite residential building in Edmonton, Alta., for a purchase price of $27,200,000 which was funded by $6,800,000 in cash and assumption of $20,400,000 of mortgages.

Status: completed **Announced:** Mar. 6, 2023
Canadian Apartment Properties Real Estate Investment Trust (CAPREIT) sold a parking lot site located adjacent to an existing multi-residential building owned by CAPREIT in Montréal, Que., for $17,250,000 cash.

Status: completed **Announced:** Feb. 27, 2023
Canadian Apartment Properties Real Estate Investment Trust (CAPREIT) acquired a 143-suite residential property in Ottawa, Ont., for $61,000,000, which consists of $16,000,000 cash, assumption of a $42,000,000 mortgage and a $3,000,000 vendor take-back loan.

Status: completed **Announced:** Jan. 25, 2023
Canadian Apartment Properties Real Estate Investment Trust sold its 50% interest in three apartment properties in Ottawa, Ont., totaling 1,150 suites, for $136,250,000 cash.

Status: completed **Revised:** Aug. 24, 2022
UPDATE: The transaction was completed. PREVIOUS: Canadian Apartment Properties Real Estate Investment Trust agreed to sell a 253-unit apartment building in East York, Ont., for $90,100,000.

Status: completed **Announced:** July 26, 2022
Canadian Apartment Properties Real Estate Investment Trust (CAPREIT) acquired a newly built 65-unit residential property in Edmonton, Alta., for $22,500,000, which was funded by CAPREIT's acquisition and operating facility.

Status: completed **Announced:** July 19, 2022
Canadian Apartment Properties Real Estate Investment Trust (CAPREIT) acquired a newly built 235-unit residential property in Laval, Que., for $102,000,000, which was funded by CAPREIT's acquisition and operating facility.

Status: completed **Announced:** June 20, 2022
Canadian Apartment Properties Real Estate Investment Trust sold its 50% interest in two apartment properties in Ottawa, Ont., totaling 370 suites, for $35,125,000.

Status: completed **Announced:** June 15, 2022
Canadian Apartment Properties Real Estate Investment Trust sold two apartment properties in Scarborough, Ont., totaling 423 suites, for $165,000,000.

Status: completed **Announced:** May 4, 2022
Canadian Apartment Properties Real Estate Investment Trust (CAPREIT) acquired a portfolio of apartments and townhomes, consisting of 36 suites and 76 units, respectively, in Kanata, Ont., for $43,700,000, which was funded by CAPREIT's acquisition and operating facility and assumption of a $26,504,000 mortgage.

Status: completed **Announced:** Apr. 29, 2022
Canadian Apartment Properties Real Estate Investment Trust sold an 82-suite apartment property in Toronto, Ont., for $56,000,000.

Status: completed **Announced:** Mar. 31, 2022
Canadian Apartment Properties Real Estate Investment Trust (CAPREIT) acquired a 172-site manufactured home community in Red Deer, Alta., for $16,520,000, which was funded by CAPREIT's acquisition and operating facility.

Status: completed **Announced:** Mar. 7, 2022
Canadian Apartment Properties Real Estate Investment Trust acquired a six-property luxury portfolio of apartment buildings, namely Majestic, L'Onyx, Le Topaze, L'Opale, Le Jade and Le Quartz, in Montreal, Laval, Côte Saint-Luc and Saint-Hyacinthe, Que., for $281,000,000, which was funded by CAPREIT's acquisition and operating facility and the assumption of $55,500,000 in mortgages. The portfolio totals 516 residential suites including 44 bachelor, 236 one-bedroom, 211 two-bedroom and 25 three-bedroom apartments as well as three commercial units.

Trustees - Dr. Gina P. Cody, chr., Toronto, Ont.; Mark Kenney, pres. & CEO, Newmarket, Ont.; Lori-Ann Beausoleil, Toronto, Ont.; Harold Burke, Toronto, Ont.; Gervais Levasseur, Dollard-des-Ormeaux, Qué.; Kenneth E. (Ken) Silver, Toronto, Ont.; Dr. Jennifer Stoddart, Westmount, Qué.; Dr. Elaine Todres, Toronto, Ont.; René Tremblay, Montréal, Qué.

Other Exec. Officers - Stephen Co, CFO; Jodi Lieberman, chief people, culture & brand officer; Julian Schonfeldt, chief invest. officer; Archna Sharma, exec. v-p, risk & compliance; Andrew Wood, exec. v-p, tech.; Larry Geer, sr. v-p, tax & govt. rel.; Clayton Yeung, sr. v-p, finl. reporting & acctg.; Lou Canton, v-p, procurement; Fernanda Chackery, v-p, org. effectiveness; Jenny Chou, v-p, fin.; Karim Farouk, v-p, opers.; Judy Harkai, v-p, opers.; James Isenberg, v-p, HR; Adelia Machado, v-p, opers. partnership; Carmen Perez, v-p, opers.; Nick Savino, v-p, opers. srvcs.; Ravinder Singh, v-p, application devel.; Lily Thai, v-p, acqs.

Capital Stock

	Authorized (shs.)	Outstanding (shs.)[1]
Preferred Unit	25,840,600	nil
Trust Unit	unlimited	167,545,285
Special Voting Unit	unlimited	1,647,186
Class B LP Unit	n.a.	1,647,186[2]

[1] At Mar. 31, 2023
[2] Securities of CAPREIT Limited Partnership.

Trust Unit - One vote per trust unit.

Special Voting Unit - Issued to holders of class B limited partnership units of subsidiary CAPREIT Limited Partnership. Each special voting unit entitles the holder to a number of votes at unitholder meetings equal to the number of trust units into which the class B limited partnership units are exchangeable.

Class B Limited Partnership Unit - Entitled to distributions equal to those provided to trust units. Directly exchangeable into trust units on a 1-for-1 basis. Classified as current liabilities.

Normal Course Issuer Bid - The company plans to make normal course purchases of up to 16,901,348 trust units representing 10% of the public float. The bid commenced on Mar. 24, 2023, and expires on Mar. 23, 2024.

Major Shareholder - Widely held at Mar. 23, 2023.

Price Range - CAR.UN/TSX

Year	Volume	High	Low	Close
2022	114,163,343	$60.19	$39.08	$42.68
2021	86,560,094	$62.77	$48.45	$59.96
2020	139,527,535	$61.29	$36.40	$49.99
2019	95,941,378	$56.82	$43.03	$53.01
2018	81,933,922	$49.45	$34.43	$44.30

Recent Close: $47.90

Capital Stock Changes - During 2022, trust units were issued as follows: 865,001 under distribution reinvestment plan, 200,363 under restricted unit rights plan, 100,493 under deferred unit plan and 65,368 under employee unit purchase plan; 5,233,162 trust units were repurchased under a Normal Course Issuer Bid.

Dividends

CAR.UN unit Ra $1.45 pa M est. Sept. 15, 2021**
Prev. Rate: $1.38 est. Apr. 15, 2019
stk.[1]◆g................ Dec. 30/22
Paid in 2023: $1.0875 2022: $1.45 + stk.◆g 2021: $1.40333

[1] Distribution will be automatically reinvested and the units will be consolidated immediately after distribution. Equiv to $0.36.
** Reinvestment Option ◆ Special g Capital Gain

Long-Term Debt - At Dec. 31, 2022, outstanding long-term debt totaled $6,966,072,000 ($613,277,000 current) and consisted of $6,577,097,000 of mortgages payable bearing interest at a weighted average effective rate of 2.61% and mature between 2023 and 2036; and $388,975,000 drawn on credit facilities.

Minimum mortgage repayments were reported as follows:

2023	$599,243,000
2024	648,139,000
2025	921,048,000
2026	875,178,000
2027	935,513,000
Thereafter	2,771,836,000

Wholly Owned Subsidiaries

CAPREIT GP Inc., Ont.
CAPREIT Limited Partnership, Toronto, Ont. Class A limited partnership units.
- 100% int. in **ERESM European Residential Management B.V.**, Netherlands.
- **European Residential Real Estate Investment Trust**, Toronto, Ont. Holds 65% voting interest through ownership of 10,197,000 trust units of the REIT and 142,040,821 class B limited partnership units of ERES Limited Partnership. (see separate coverage)
- 18.68% int. in **Irish Residential Properties REIT plc**, Dublin, Ireland.

Financial Statistics

Periods ended:	12m Dec. 31/22^A		12m Dec. 31/21^A
	$000s	%Chg	$000s
Total revenue	**1,007,268**	**+8**	**933,137**
Rental operating expense	262,947		235,446
General & admin. expense	57,965		51,366
Stock-based compensation	(3,414)		15,111
Property taxes	93,912		87,698
Operating expense	**411,410**	**+6**	**389,621**
Operating income	**595,858**	**+10**	**543,516**
Investment income	647		18,455
Deprec. & amort.	7,462		8,250
Finance income	11,083		2,271
Finance costs, gross	182,869		160,463
Write-downs/write-offs	(14,278)		nil
Pre-tax income	**3,603**	**-100**	**1,473,976**
Income taxes	(10,034)		81,181
Net income	**13,637**	**-99**	**1,392,795**
Cash & equivalent	47,303		73,411
Accounts receivable	17,678		17,866
Current assets	249,588		137,182
Long-term investments	250,697		412,781
Fixed assets	52,495		47,430
Income-producing props	17,153,709		17,101,919
Property interests, net	17,166,373		17,115,743
Right-of-use assets	2,994		3,365
Intangibles, net	nil		15,133
Total assets	**17,741,888**	**0**	**17,712,973**
Accts. pay. & accr. liabs	137,908		141,499
Current liabilities	967,009		991,202
Long-term debt, gross	6,966,072		6,410,931
Long-term debt, net	6,352,795		5,767,471
Long-term lease liabilities	47,460		48,316
Shareholders' equity	10,003,695		10,399,886
Cash from oper. activs	**598,027**	**+8**	**551,433**
Cash from fin. activs	(132,324)		512,497
Cash from invest. activs	(502,974)		(1,107,986)
Net cash position	**47,303**	**-36**	**73,411**
Capital expenditures	(336,467)		(299,419)
Increase in property	(539,561)		(844,432)
Decrease in property	306,949		29,194
	$		$
Earnings per share*	n.a.		n.a.
Cash flow per share*	3.43		3.18
Funds from opers. per sh.*	2.29		2.26
Cash divd. per share*	1.45		1.41
Extra stk. divd. - cash equiv.*	0.36		nil
Total divd. per share*	**1.81**		**1.41**
	shs		shs
No. of shs. o/s*	169,404,469		173,406,406
Avg. no. of shs. o/s*	174,370,000		173,508,000
	%		%
Net profit margin	1.35		149.26
Return on equity	0.13		14.16
Return on assets	3.98		9.30
Foreign sales percent	12		12
No. of employees (FTEs)	1,067		1,076

* Trust unit
^A Reported in accordance with IFRS

Latest Results

Periods ended:	3m Mar. 31/23^A		3m Mar. 31/22^A
	$000s	%Chg	$000s
Total revenue	260,947	+6	246,628
Net income	(103,227)	n.a.	45,309
	$		$
Earnings per share*	n.a.		n.a.

^A Reported in accordance with IFRS

Historical Summary
(as originally stated)

Fiscal Year	Total Rev. $000s	Net Inc. Bef. Disc. $000s	EPS* $
2022^A	1,007,268	13,637	n.a.
2021^A	933,137	1,392,795	n.a.
2020^A	882,643	925,928	n.a.
2019^A	777,884	1,195,447	n.a.
2018^A	688,585	1,217,671	n.a.

* Trust unit
^A Reported in accordance with IFRS

C.33 Canadian Banc Corp.

Symbol - BK **Exchange** - TSX **CUSIP** - 13536V
Head Office - c/o Quadravest Capital Management Inc., 2510-200 Front St W, PO Box 51, Toronto, ON, M5V 3K2 **Telephone** - (416) 304-4440 **Toll-free** - (877) 478-2372
Website - www.quadravest.com
Email - info@quadravest.com
Investor Relations - Shari Payne (877) 478-2372

Auditors - PricewaterhouseCoopers LLP C.A., Toronto, Ont.
Lawyers - Blake, Cassels & Graydon LLP, Toronto, Ont.
Transfer Agents - Computershare Trust Company of Canada Inc., Toronto, Ont.
Investment Managers - Quadravest Capital Management Inc., Toronto, Ont.
Managers - Quadravest Capital Management Inc., Toronto, Ont.

Profile - (Ont. 2005) Invests in a portfolio of common shares primarily consisting of six Canadian financial services companies.

The portfolio may hold up to 20% of its net asset value in equity securities of other Canadian or foreign financial services corporations.

To supplement the dividends received on the investment portfolio and to reduce risk, the company may, from time to time, write covered call options in respect of all or part of the common shares in the portfolio.

The investment manager receives a management fee at an annual rate equal to 0.65% of the net asset value of the company calculated and payable monthly in arrears. In addition, the manager receives an administration fee at an annual rate equal to 0.2% of the net asset value of the company calculated and payable monthly in arrears, as well as service fee payable to dealers on the class A shares at a rate of 0.5% of the net asset value of class A shares per annum.

The company will terminate on Dec. 1, 2028, or earlier if the preferred shares or class A shares are delisted by the TSX or if the net asset value of the company declines to less than $5,000,000. At such time all outstanding preferred shares and class A shares will be redeemed. The termination date may be extended beyond Dec. 1, 2028, for a further five years and thereafter for additional successive periods of five years as determined by the board of directors.

Top 10 holdings at Feb. 28, 2023 (as a percentage of net assets):

Holdings	Percentage
Royal Bank of Canada	14.4%
The Toronto-Dominion Bank	11.7%
Bank of Montreal	11.6%
National Bank of Canada	11.4%
The Bank of Nova Scotia	8.8%
Canadian Imperial Bank of Commerce	8.8%
Bank of America Corporation	5.3%
Morgan Stanley	2.8%
JPMorgan Chase & Co.	2.5%
The Goldman Sachs Group, Inc.	1.9%

In March 2023, the maturity date of the company's preferred shares and class A shares was extended a further five years, to Dec. 1, 2028.

Predecessor Detail - Name changed from Canadian Banc Recovery Corp., Jan. 27, 2012.

Directors - S. Wayne Finch, chr., pres. & CEO, Caledon, Ont.; Laura L. Johnson, corp. sec., Oakville, Ont.; Peter F. Cruickshank, Oakville, Ont.; Michael W. Sharp, Toronto, Ont.; John D. Steep, Stratford, Ont.

Other Exec. Officers - Silvia Gomes, CFO

Capital Stock

	Authorized (shs.)	Outstanding (shs.)[1]
Preferred	unlimited	22,287,682[2]
Class B	1,000	1,000[2]
Class A	unlimited	22,082,182

[1] At May 15, 2023
[2] Classified as debt.

Preferred - Entitled to receive floating rate cumulative monthly cash dividends equal to the prime rate plus 1.5%, with a minimum annual rate of 5% and a maximum annual rate of 8%. Retractable in any month at a price equal to the lesser of (i) $10; and (ii) 96% of the net asset value (NAV) per unit (one class A share and one preferred share) less the cost of the purchase of a class A share in the market for cancellation. Under a concurrent annual retraction in July of each year, a shareholder will receive, for each unit, an amount equal to the NAV per unit, less any costs (to a maximum of 1% of the NAV per unit) to fund the retraction. All outstanding preferred shares will be redeemed on Dec. 1, 2028, at a price per share equal to $10. Rank in priority to class A and class B shares with respect to the payment of dividends and repayment of capital. Non-voting.

Class B - Not entitled to dividends. Retractable at $1.00 per share and are entitled to liquidation value of $1.00 per share. Rank subsequent to preferred shares and prior to the class A shares with respect to the repayment of capital on the dissolution, liquidation or winding-up of the company. One vote per share.

Class A - Entitled to receive monthly non-cumulative distributions targeted to be 15% per annum of the volume-weighted average market price of the class A shares for the last three trading days of the preceding month. In addition, a special year-end dividend will be payable on the last day of November in each year if such funds are available. No regular monthly distributions will be paid if any dividends on the preferred shares are in arrears or if the NAV per unit is equal to or less than $15 and no special year-end dividends will be paid if after such payment the NAV per unit would be less than $25. Retractable in any month at a price equal 96% of the NAV per unit less the cost of the purchase of a preferred share in the market for cancellation. Under a concurrent annual retraction in July of each year, shareholders will have the right to receive, for each unit, an amount equal to the NAV per unit less any costs (to a maximum of 1% of the NAV per unit) to fund the retraction. All outstanding class A shares will be redeemed on Dec. 1, 2028, at an amount representing all remaining assets of the company after redemption of the preferred and class B shares. Rank subordinate to preferred and class B shares with respect to payment of dividends and the repayment of capital. Non-voting.

Normal Course Issuer Bid - The company plans to make normal course purchases of up to 2,204,842 class A shares representing 10% of the public float. The bid commenced on May 29, 2023, and expires on May 28, 2024.

The company plans to make normal course purchases of up to 2,226,511 preferred shares representing 10% of the public float. The bid commenced on May 29, 2023, and expires on May 28, 2024.

Major Shareholder - Canadian Banc Corp. Holding Trust held 100% interest at Feb. 23, 2023.

Price Range - BK/TSX

Year	Volume	High	Low	Close
2022	12,939,143	$15.99	$12.13	$13.22
2021	4,524,258	$14.23	$8.73	$13.86
2020	6,413,101	$10.48	$4.98	$8.90
2019	3,083,774	$11.69	$9.35	$10.08
2018	4,253,019	$14.49	$8.40	$9.71

Recent Close: $12.88

Capital Stock Changes - In January 2023, public offering of 2,360,000 preferred shares at $10 per share and 1,560,000 class A shares at $13.75 per share was completed.

In February 2022, public offering of 1,544,000 preferred shares at $10 per share and 1,544,000 class A shares at $15.75 per share was completed. In June 2022, public offering of 1,167,000 preferred shares at $10 per share and 1,167,000 class A shares at $14.50 per share was completed. Also during fiscal 2022, 3,190,700 preferred shares and 3,302,100 class A shares were issued under an at-the-market equity program.

Dividends

BK cl A N.V. Ra $1.98 pa M est. Sept. 8, 2023[1]
Prev. Rate: $1.971 est. Aug. 10, 2023
Prev. Rate: $1.95756 est. July 10, 2023
Prev. Rate: $1.989 est. May 10, 2023
Prev. Rate: $2.064 est. Apr. 10, 2023
Prev. Rate: $2.04456 est. Mar. 10, 2023
Prev. Rate: $1.989 est. Feb. 10, 2023
Prev. Rate: $2.02056 est. Jan. 10, 2023
Prev. Rate: $1.95456 est. Dec. 9, 2022
Prev. Rate: $1.93056 est. Nov. 10, 2022
Prev. Rate: $1.98756 est. Sept. 9, 2022
Prev. Rate: $2.235 est. July 8, 2022
Prev. Rate: $2.16456 est. June 10, 2022
Prev. Rate: $2.23656 est. Apr. 8, 2022
Prev. Rate: $2.112 est. Feb. 10, 2022
Prev. Rate: $2.043 est. Jan. 10, 2022
Prev. Rate: $1.94256 est. Dec. 10, 2021
Prev. Rate: $1.215 est. Nov. 10, 2021
Prev. Rate: $1.24596 est. Oct. 8, 2021
Prev. Rate: $1.22004 est. Sept. 10, 2021
Prev. Rate: $1.23204 est. Aug. 10, 2021
Prev. Rate: $1.221 est. July 9, 2021
Prev. Rate: $1.13004 est. June 10, 2021
Prev. Rate: $1.10196 est. May 10, 2021

BK.PR.A pfd cum. ret. Fltg. Ra pa M

$0.06667	Sept. 8/23	$0.06667	Aug. 10/23
$0.06667	July 10/23	$0.06667	June 9/23

Paid in 2023: $0.59919 2022: $0.57461 2021: $0.50004

[1] Monthly divd normally payable in Apr/20 has been omitted.

Financial Statistics

Periods ended:	12m Nov. 30/22^A		12m Nov. 30/21^A
	$000s	%Chg	$000s
Realized invest. gain (loss)	2,083		2,976
Unrealized invest. gain (loss)	(5,745)		53,142
Total revenue	**6,838**	**-89**	**64,622**
General & admin. expense	2,957		2,813
Other operating expense	693		626
Operating expense	**3,650**	**+6**	**3,439**
Operating income	**3,188**	**-95**	**61,183**
Finance costs, gross	8,408		5,302
Pre-tax income	**(5,220)**	**n.a.**	**55,881**
Net income	**(5,220)**	**n.a.**	**55,881**
Cash & equivalent	60,391		5,273
Accounts receivable	80		10
Investments	291,726		233,242
Total assets	**353,118**	**+48**	**238,524**
Accts. pay. & accr. liabs	313		376
Debt	161,093		102,076
Shareholders' equity	184,350		133,821
Cash from oper. activs	**(52,793)**	**n.a.**	**26,787**
Cash from fin. activs	107,922		(27,315)
Net cash position	**60,391**	**n.m.**	**5,273**
	$		$
Earnings per share*	(0.39)		5.31
Cash flow per share*	(3.98)		2.54
Net asset value per share*	11.37		13.11
Cash divd. per share*	2.10		1.17
	shs		shs
No. of shs. o/s*	16,220,682		10,207,582
Avg. no. of shs. o/s*	13,271,924		10,531,870
	%		%
Net profit margin	(76.34)		86.47
Return on equity	(3.28)		48.57
Return on assets	1.08		27.51

* Class A
^A Reported in accordance with IFRS

Note: Net income reflects increase/decrease in net assets from operations.

Historical Summary
(as originally stated)

Fiscal Year	Total Rev.	Net Inc. Bef. Disc.	EPS*
	$000s	$000s	$
2022^A	6,838	(5,220)	(0.39)
2021^A	64,622	55,881	5.31
2020^A	(11,000)	(19,274)	(1.76)
2019^A	24,791	15,565	1.40
2018^A	(1,689)	(9,832)	(0.99)

* Class A
^A Reported in accordance with IFRS

C.34 Canadian General Investments, Limited*

Symbol - CGI **Exchange** - TSX **CUSIP** - 135825

Head Office - 10 Toronto St, Toronto, ON, M5C 2B7 **Telephone** - (416) 366-2931 **Toll-free** - (866) 443-6097 **Fax** - (416) 366-2729

Website - www.mmainvestments.com

Email - ffuernkranz@mmainvestments.com

Investor Relations - Frank C. Fuernkranz (866) 443-6097

Auditors - PricewaterhouseCoopers LLP C.A., Toronto, Ont.

Bankers - Bank of Montreal

Lawyers - Blake, Cassels & Graydon LLP, Toronto, Ont.

Transfer Agents - Computershare Investor Services plc, Bristol, Gloucs. United Kingdom; Computershare Trust Company of Canada Inc., Toronto, Ont.

Managers - Morgan Meighen & Associates Limited, Toronto, Ont.

Profile - (Ont. 1930) Closed-end investment fund focused on capital growth and income generation through a diversified portfolio of equity securities of Canadian companies. The portfolio has been managed by **Morgan Meighen & Associates Limited** since 1956.

Primarily invests in common shares of Canadian companies. Income is derived primarily from dividends on such shares and from interest on debentures, term deposits and cash balances.

The company qualifies as an investment corporation under the Income Tax Act (Canada) which entitles it to certain beneficial tax treatments. The company is subject to a reduced rate of tax on its investment income other than dividends received from taxable Canadian corporations and net taxable capital gains. Income taxes are paid by the company on realized gains on the sale of investments at an effective rate of about 20%. These taxes are recoverable by the company as long as it continues to qualify as an investment corporation. At Dec. 31, 2022, the company had refundable capital gains taxes of $8,373,000 (2021 - $8,594,000), which are refundable upon payment of capital gains dividends of $60,000,000 (2021 - $61,000,000). The company is also subject to a special tax of 38 1/3% on taxable dividends received from corporations resident in Canada. This special tax is refundable on payment of taxable dividends to shareholders at the rate of $0.3833 for each $1.00 of such dividends paid. The company had $620,000 refundable dividend tax on hand at Dec. 31, 2022 (2021 - $2,208,000).

Pursuant to a management agreement with **Morgan Meighen & Associates Limited**, a Toronto, Ont.-based investment management firm, the company is committed to pay monthly management fee for services received in connection with the management of the company's financial accounts and investment portfolio. Management fees are computed monthly at 1% per annum of the market value of the company's investments adjusted for cash, portfolio accounts receivable and portfolio accounts payable.

Top 10 holdings at July 31, 2023 (as a percentage of investment portfolio):

Holdings	Percentage
NIVDIA Corporation	6.8%
First Quantum Minerals Ltd.	5.1%
Canadian Pacific Kansas City Limited	4.5%
TFI International Inc.	4.3%
West Fraser Timber Co. Ltd.	4.1%
Franco-Nevada Corporation	4%
Apple Inc.	3.9%
WSP Global Inc.	3.1%
The Descartes Systems Group Inc.	3%
Mastercard Incorporated	2.9%

Predecessor Detail - Name changed from Second Canadian General Investments Limited, Aug. 17, 1931.

Directors - Vanessa L. Morgan, chr., Mississauga, Ont.; Jonathan A. Morgan, pres. & CEO, Toronto, Ont.; James F. Billett, Toronto, Ont.; Marcia Lewis Brown, Toronto, Ont.; A. Michelle Lally, Toronto, Ont.; Michael C. Walke, Toronto, Ont.

Other Exec. Officers - Frank C. Fuernkranz, CFO & corp. sec.; Christopher J. Esson, treas.; Laura M. Jess, asst. sec.

Capital Stock

	Authorized (shs.)	Outstanding (shs.)[1]
Class A Preference	unlimited	
Series 4		nil[2]
Common	unlimited	20,861,141

[1] At Feb. 28, 2023
[2] Classified as debt.

Major Shareholder - Jonathan A. Morgan and Vanessa L. Morgan jointly held 52.51% interest at Feb. 28, 2023.

Price Range - CGI/TSX

Year	Volume	High	Low	Close
2022	1,029,037	$44.70	$28.21	$32.60
2021	1,538,534	$45.60	$32.40	$44.05
2020	1,473,295	$34.86	$16.22	$34.81
2019	866,077	$26.73	$20.31	$26.21
2018	1,321,094	$26.44	$19.70	$20.51

Recent Close: $35.88

Capital Stock Changes - There were no changes to capital stock from 2017 to 2022, inclusive.

Dividends

CGI com Var. Ra pa Q**

$0.024	Sept. 15/23	$0.24	June 15/23
$0.24	Mar. 15/23	$0.23	Dec. 15/22

Paid in 2023: $0.504 2022: $0.92 2021: $0.66 + $0.22**g**

pfd A ser 4 3.75% cum. red. ret. Ra $0.9375 pa Q[1]

[1] Redeemed June 12, 2023 at $25 per sh. plus accr. divds. of $0.2286.
** Reinvestment Option **g** Capital Gain

Long-Term Debt - At Dec. 31, 2022, outstanding debt totaled $149,901,000 ($75,000,000 current and net of $99,000 deferred issuance costs) and consisted of $100,000,000 borrowings under a credit facility, bearing interest at the one-month CDOR plus 0.6% per annum, and $74,901,000 representing 3,000,000 class A preference series 4 shares.

Class A Preference Series 4 - Entitled to fixed annual cumulative preferential cash dividend in the amount of $0.9375 per share, payable quarterly. Redeemable at $25 per share. Retractable by holder on or after June 15, 2023, at $25 per share, together with accrued and unpaid dividends.

Note - On June 12, 2023, all $75,000,000 3.75% class A preference shares series 4 were redeemed for $75,685,800, including accrued and unpaid dividends.

Financial Statistics

Periods ended:	12m Dec. 31/22^A		12m Dec. 31/21^A
	$000s	%Chg	$000s
Realized invest. gain (loss)	(2,419)		82,689
Unrealized invest. gain (loss)	(254,131)		186,311
Total revenue	**(235,721)**	**n.a.**	**284,432**
Other operating expense	15,108		16,723
Operating expense	**15,108**	**-10**	**16,723**
Operating income	**(250,829)**	**n.a.**	**267,709**
Finance costs, gross	5,463		4,192
Pre-tax income	**(256,292)**	**n.a.**	**263,517**
Income taxes	(1,901)		8,726
Net income	**(254,391)**	**n.a.**	**254,791**
Cash & equivalent	3,598		16,599
Accounts receivable	2,168		2,547
Investments	1,150,182		1,445,969
Total assets	**1,157,849**	**-21**	**1,465,115**
Accts. pay. & accr. liabs	1,513		1,585
Debt	149,901		174,683
Shareholders' equity	1,006,312		1,279,896
Cash from oper. activs	**36,192**	**+14**	**31,626**
Cash from fin. activs	(49,193)		(21,959)
Net cash position	**3,598**	**-78**	**16,599**
	$		$
Earnings per share*	(12.19)		12.21
Cash flow per share*	1.73		1.52
Net asset value per share*	48.24		61.35
Cash divd. per share*	0.92		0.66
Capital gains divd.*	nil		0.22
Total divd. per share*	**0.92**		**0.88**
	shs		shs
No. of shs. o/s*	20,861,141		20,861,141
Avg. no. of shs. o/s*	20,861,141		20,861,141
	%		%
Net profit margin	n.m.		89.58
Return on equity	(22.25)		21.93
Return on assets	(18.98)		19.28

* Common
^A Reported in accordance with IFRS

Note: Net income reflects increase/decrease in net assets from operations.

Historical Summary
(as originally stated)

Fiscal Year	Total Rev.	Net Inc. Bef. Disc.	EPS*
	$000s	$000s	$
2022^A	(235,721)	(254,391)	(12.19)
2021^A	284,432	254,791	12.21
2020^A	307,826	289,436	13.87
2019^A	205,754	186,074	8.92
2018^A	(56,961)	(73,423)	(3.52)

* Common
^A Reported in accordance with IFRS

C.35 Canadian High Income Equity Fund

Symbol - CIQ.UN **Exchange** - TSX **CUSIP** - 136012
Head Office - c/o Brompton Group Limited, Bay Wellington Tower, Brookfield Place, 2930-181 Bay St, PO Box 793, Toronto, ON, M5J 2T3 **Telephone** - (416) 642-9061 **Toll-free** - (866) 642-6001 **Fax** - (416) 642-6001
Website - www.bromptongroup.com
Email - wong@bromptongroup.com
Investor Relations - Ann P. Wong (416) 642-6000
Auditors - PricewaterhouseCoopers LLP C.A., Toronto, Ont.
Bankers - Royal Bank of Canada, Toronto, Ont.
Transfer Agents - TSX Trust Company, Toronto, Ont.
Trustees - TSX Trust Company, Toronto, Ont.
Investment Managers - Bloom Investment Counsel, Inc., Toronto, Ont.
Managers - Brompton Funds Limited, Toronto, Ont.
Portfolio Managers - Brompton Funds Limited, Toronto, Ont.
Profile - (Ont. 2010) Invests primarily in Canadian income trusts, royalty trusts, real estate investment trusts, common and preferred shares, debt instruments and, to a lesser extent, non-dividend paying equities and foreign securities.

The fund does not have a fixed termination date but may be terminated upon the approval of the unitholders.

Top 10 holdings at Mar. 31, 2023 (as a percentage of net asset value):

Holdings	Percentage
Ag Growth International Inc.	6.4%
Premium Brands Holdings Corp.	6.0%
Parkland Corporation	5.4%
Chemtrade Logistics Income Fund	4.6%
Park Lawn Corporation	4.6%
Transcontinental Inc., class A	4.3%
Manulife Financial Corporation	4.3%
Sun Life Financial Inc.	4.2%
Canadian Tire Corporation Limited	4.1%
The Toronto-Dominion Bank	3.9%

Oper. Subsid./Mgt. Co. Directors - Mark A. Caranci, pres. & CEO, Toronto, Ont.; Ann P. Wong, CFO, Toronto, Ont.; Christopher S. L. Hoffmann, Toronto, Ont.; Raymond R. Pether, Toronto, Ont.
Oper. Subsid./Mgt. Co. Officers - Laura Lau, chief invest. officer; Kathryn A. H. Banner, sr. v-p & corp. sec.; Michael D. Clare, sr. v-p & sr. portfolio mgr.; Christopher Cullen, sr. v-p; Manith (Manny) Phanvongsa, sr. v-p; Michelle L. Tiraborelli, sr. v-p

Capital Stock

	Authorized (shs.)	Outstanding (shs.)[1]
Trust Unit	unlimited	1,209,185

[1] At July 14, 2023

Trust Unit - Entitled to monthly distributions of 4¢ per unit. Retractable in September of each year at a price equal to the net asset value per unit less any costs associated with the retraction. One vote per unit.

Price Range - CIQ.UN/TSX

Year	Volume	High	Low	Close
2022	296,299	$9.45	$6.25	$6.85
2021	502,010	$8.10	$7.03	$7.85
2020	538,271	$8.34	$4.24	$7.08
2019	512,905	$7.90	$6.98	$7.62
2018	593,280	$9.58	$6.77	$6.99

Recent Close: $6.72

Capital Stock Changes - During 2022, 140,040 trust units were retracted and 398 units were issued pursuant to a distribution reinvestment plan.

Dividends

CIQ.UN unit Ra $0.48 pa M est. May 14, 2020**
Prev. Rate: $0.60 est. May 13, 2016
** Reinvestment Option

Financial Statistics

Periods ended:	12m Dec. 31/22^A		12m Dec. 31/21^A
	$000s	%Chg	$000s
Realized invest. gain (loss)	413		1,184
Unrealized invest. gain (loss)	(1,259)		788
Total revenue	**(467)**	**n.a.**	**2,414**
General & admin. expense	259		299
Operating expense	**259**	**-13**	**299**
Operating income	**(726)**	**n.a.**	**2,115**
Pre-tax income	**(726)**	**n.a.**	**2,115**
Net income	**(726)**	**n.a.**	**2,115**
Cash & equivalent	235		116
Accounts receivable	34		34
Investments	8,279		10,702
Total assets	**8,548**	**-21**	**10,851**
Accts. pay. & accr. liabs	47		51
Shareholders' equity	8,453		10,746
Cash from oper. activs	**1,692**	**-49**	**3,290**
Cash from fin. activs	(1,573)		(3,422)
Net cash position	**235**	**+103**	**116**
	$		$
Earnings per share*	(0.55)		1.34
Cash flow per share*	1.29		2.08
Net asset value per share*	6.99		7.97
Cash divd. per share*	0.48		0.48
	shs		shs
No. of shs. o/s*	1,208,745		1,348,387
Avg. no. of shs. o/s*	1,311,005		1,579,858
	%		%
Net profit margin	n.m.		87.61
Return on equity	(7.56)		18.56
Return on assets	(7.48)		18.39

* Trust unit
^A Reported in accordance with IFRS

Historical Summary
(as originally stated)

Fiscal Year	Total Rev.	Net Inc. Bef. Disc.	EPS*
	$000s	$000s	$
2022^A	(467)	(726)	(0.55)
2021^A	2,414	2,115	1.34
2020^A	(323)	(616)	(0.34)
2019^A	3,173	2,766	1.36
2018^A	(3,755)	(4,279)	(1.72)

* Trust unit
^A Reported in accordance with IFRS

C.36 Canadian Imperial Bank of Commerce*

Symbol - CM **Exchange** - TSX **CUSIP** - 136069
Head Office - CIBC Square, 81 Bay St, Toronto, ON, M5J 0E7 **Telephone** - (416) 980-2211
Website - www.cibc.com
Email - geoffrey.weiss@cibc.com
Investor Relations - Geoffrey M. Weiss (416) 980-5093
Auditors - Ernst & Young LLP C.A., Toronto, Ont.
Lawyers - Mayer Brown LLP, Chicago, Ill.; Blake, Cassels & Graydon LLP, Toronto, Ont.
Transfer Agents - Computershare Trust Company, Inc., Canton, Mass.; TSX Trust Company, Toronto, Ont.
FP500 Revenue Ranking - 19
Employees - 50,427 at Oct. 31, 2022
Profile - (Can. 1961) A Schedule I Canadian chartered bank providing a full range of personal and business banking, commercial banking and wealth management and capital markets products and services to 13,000,000 personal banking, business, public sector and institutional clients in Canada, the U.S. and around the world.

Canadian Personal & Business Banking - Provides financial advice, services and solutions to personal and business clients across Canada through banking centres, mobile and online channels.

Canadian Commercial Banking & Wealth Management - Provides banking and wealth management services to middle-market companies, entrepreneurs, high-net-worth individuals and families across Canada, as well as asset management services to institutional investors.

U.S. Commercial Banking & Wealth Management - Provides commercial banking and private wealth services across the U.S., focusing on middle-market and mid-corporate companies, entrepreneurs, and high-net-worth individuals and families. This segment also provides personal and small business banking services in four U.S. Midwestern markets.

Capital Markets - Provides integrated global markets products and services, investment banking advisory and execution, corporate banking solutions and research to clients around the world.

Corporate & Other - Consists of technology, infrastructure and innovation, risk management, people, culture and brand, finance and enterprise strategy, as well as other support groups. This segment also includes subsidiary **FirstCaribbean International Bank Limited**, which has 47 branches, six international banking and private wealth management offices, 19 platinum offices, and seven mortgage and loans centres in 15 regional markets in the Caribbean, and strategic investments in the **CIBC Mellon** joint ventures with **The Bank of New York Mellon**, which provide trust and asset servicing in Canada.

On Feb. 17, 2023, the bank announced an agreement with the special purpose vehicle controlled by **Cerberus Capital Management L.P.** to fully settle the lawsuit filed by Cerberus against the bank including the most recent judgment of the New York Court. Under the settlement, the bank agreed to pay US$770,000,000 to Cerberus in full satisfaction of the judgment, and both parties have agreed to arrange for the immediate dismissal, with prejudice, of all claims, counterclaims and appeals relating to the litigation. The bank recorded a pre-tax provision of Cdn$1.169 billion in the first quarter of 2023, representing damages and pre-judgment interest totaling US$855,000,000 through Jan. 31, 2023.

During the third quarter of fiscal 2022, **FirstCaribbean International Bank Limited** (CIBC FirstCaribbean) received regulatory approval for the proposed sale of banking assets in St. Vincent and St. Kitts, with the sale expected to close by the third quarter of fiscal 2023. Previously, CIBC FirstCaribbean agreed to sell its banking assets in the Caribbean, specifically in St. Vincent, Grenada, Dominica, St. Kitts and Aruba. The sale of banking assets in Aruba was completed on Feb. 25, 2022. The proposed sale of banking assets in Dominica was terminated, with its operations ceasing on Jan. 31, 2023. Terms were not disclosed and the transactions are considered immaterial.

Recent Merger and Acquisition Activity

Status: completed **Revised:** Mar. 4, 2022
UPDATE: The acquisition of the credit card portfolio was completed for cash consideration of $3.1 billion, and CIBC became the exclusive issuer of Costco credit cards in Canada. PREVIOUS: Canadian Imperial Bank of Commerce (CIBC) agreed to acquire the Canadian Costco credit card portfolio, which had an outstanding balance of $3 billion. In connection, CIBC entered into a long-term agreement to become the exclusive issuer of Costco-branded Mastercard credit cards in Canada. Terms were not disclosed. Closing was expected in early 2022.

Directors - Katharine B. (Kate) Stevenson, chr., Toronto, Ont.; Victor G. Dodig, pres. & CEO, Toronto, Ont.; Ammar Al-Joundi, Toronto, Ont.; Charles J. G. Brindamour, Toronto, Ont.; Nanci E. Caldwell, Woodside, Calif.; Michelle L. Collins, Chicago, Ill.; Luc Desjardins, Toronto, Ont.; Kevin J. Kelly, Toronto, Ont.; Christine E. Larsen, Montclair, N.J.; Mary Lou Maher, Toronto, Ont.; William F. (Bill) Morneau Jr., Toronto, Ont.; Martine Turcotte, Verdun, Qué.; Barry L. Zubrow, West Palm Beach, Fla.

Other Exec. Officers - Michael G. (Mike) Capatides, v-chr., CIBC Bank USA; The Hon. Lisa Raitt, v-chr., global invest. banking; Shawn Beber, sr. exec. v-p, grp. head, U.S. region & pres. & CEO, CIBC Bank USA; Harry K. Culham, sr. exec. v-p & grp. head, capital markets & direct finl. srvcs.; Frank Guse, sr. exec. v-p & chief risk officer; Jon Hountalas, sr. exec. v-p & grp. head, Cdn. banking; Christina C. Kramer, sr. exec. v-p & grp. head, tech., infrastructure & innovation; Hratch Panossian, sr. exec. v-p & CFO; Sandy R. Sharman, sr. exec. v-p & grp. head, people, culture & brand; Kikelomo (Kike) Lawal, exec. v-p & chief legal officer; P. Michelle Caturay, sr. v-p, chief privacy officer, assoc. gen. counsel & corp. sec.

Capital Stock

	Authorized (shs.)	Outstanding (shs.)[1]
Class A Preferred	unlimited	
Series 39		16,000,000
Series 41		12,000,000
Series 43		12,000,000
Series 47		18,000,000
Series 49		13,000,000
Series 51		10,000,000
Series 56		600,000
Class B Preferred	unlimited	nil
Limited Recourse Capital Notes	n.a.	
Series 1		750,000
Series 2		750,000
Series 3		800,000
Common	unlimited	911,769,363

[1] At Apr. 30, 2023

Class A Preferred - Issuable in series. Entitled to non-cumulative dividends, payable quarterly. Total authorized amount is unlimited and issuable in series up to an aggregate consideration not exceeding $10 billion. The class A preferred shares shall rank in priority to the class B preferred shares and the common shares and each series of class A preferred shares shall rank pari passu with every other series with respect to the payment of dividends and the distribution of assets in the event of liquidation, dissolution, etc. Voting rights will be set by the directors for each series.

Series 39 - Entitled to non-cumulative annual dividends of $0.9283 per share payable quarterly to July 31, 2024, and thereafter at a rate reset every five years equal to the five-year Government of Canada bond yield plus 2.32%. Redeemable on July 31, 2024, and on July 31 every five years thereafter at $25 per share plus declared and unpaid dividends. Convertible at the holder's option, on July 31, 2024, and on July 31 every five years thereafter, into floating rate preferred series 40 shares on a share-for-share basis, subject to certain conditions. The series 40 shares would pay a quarterly dividend equal to the 90-day Canadian Treasury bill rate plus 2.32%. Convertible into common shares upon occurrence of certain trigger events related to financial viability. The contingent conversion formula is 1.0 multiplied by $25 plus declared and unpaid dividends divided by the greater of (i) a floor price of $5.00; and (ii) current market price of the common shares.

Series 41 - Entitled to non-cumulative annual dividends of $0.97725 per share payable quarterly to Jan. 31, 2025, and thereafter at a rate reset every five years equal to the five-year Government of Canada bond yield plus 2.24%. Redeemable on Jan. 31, 2025, and on January 31 every five years thereafter at $25 per share plus declared and unpaid dividends. Convertible at the holder's option, on Jan. 31, 2025, and on January 31 every five years thereafter, into floating rate preferred series 42 shares on a share-for-share basis, subject to certain conditions. The series 42 shares would pay a quarterly dividend equal to the 90-day Canadian Treasury bill rate plus 2.24%. Convertible into common shares upon occurrence of certain trigger events related to financial viability. The contingent conversion formula is 1.0 multiplied by $25 plus declared and unpaid dividends divided by the greater of (i) a floor price of $5.00; and (ii) current market price of the common shares.

Series 43 - Entitled to non-cumulative annual dividends of $0.78575 per share payable quarterly to July 31, 2025, and thereafter at a rate reset every five years equal to the five-year Government of Canada bond yield plus 2.79%. Redeemable on July 31, 2025, and on July 31 every five years thereafter at $25 per share plus declared and unpaid dividends. Convertible at the holder's option, on July 31, 2025, and on July 31 every five years thereafter, into floating rate preferred series 44 shares on a share-for-share basis, subject to certain conditions. The series 44 shares would pay a quarterly dividend equal to the 90-day Canadian Treasury bill rate plus 2.79%. Convertible into common shares upon occurrence of certain trigger events related to financial viability. The contingent conversion formula is 1.0 multiplied by $25 plus declared and unpaid dividends divided by the greater of (i) a floor price of $5.00; and (ii) current market price of the common shares.

Series 47 - Entitled to non-cumulative annual dividends of $1.4695 per share payable quarterly to Jan. 31, 2028, and thereafter at a rate reset every five years equal to the five-year Government of Canada bond yield plus 2.45%. Redeemable on Jan. 31, 2028, and on January 31 every five years thereafter at $25 per share plus declared and unpaid dividends. Convertible at the holder's option, on Jan. 31, 2028, and on January 31 every five years thereafter, into floating rate preferred series 48 shares on a share-for-share basis, subject to certain conditions. The series 48 shares would pay a quarterly dividend equal to the 90-day Canadian Treasury bill rate plus 2.45%. Convertible into common shares upon occurrence of certain trigger events related to financial viability. The contingent conversion formula is 1.0 multiplied by $25 plus declared and unpaid dividends divided by the greater of (i) a floor price of $5.00; and (ii) current market price of the common shares.

Series 49 - Entitled to non-cumulative annual dividends of $1.30 per share payable quarterly to Apr. 30, 2024, and thereafter at a rate reset every five years equal to the five-year Government of Canada bond yield plus 3.31%. Redeemable on Apr. 30, 2024, and on April 30 every five years thereafter at $25 per share plus declared and unpaid dividends. Convertible at the holder's option, on Apr. 30, 2024, and on April 30 every five years thereafter, into floating rate preferred series 50 shares on a share-for-share basis, subject to certain conditions. The series 50 shares would pay a quarterly dividend equal to the 90-day Canadian Treasury bill rate plus 3.31%. Convertible into common shares upon occurrence of certain trigger events related to financial viability. The contingent conversion formula is 1.0 multiplied by $25 plus declared and unpaid dividends divided by the greater of (i) a floor price of $5.00; and (ii) current market price of the common shares.

Series 51 - Entitled to non-cumulative annual dividends of $1.2875 per share payable quarterly to July 31, 2024, and thereafter at a rate reset every five years equal to the five-year Government of Canada bond yield plus 3.62%. Redeemable on July 31, 2024, and on July 31 every five years thereafter at $25 per share plus declared and unpaid dividends. Convertible at the holder's option, on July 31, 2024, and on July 31 every five years thereafter, into floating rate preferred series 52 shares on a share-for-share basis, subject to certain conditions. The series 52 shares would pay a quarterly dividend equal to the 90-day Canadian Treasury bill rate plus 3.62%. Convertible into common shares upon occurrence of certain trigger events related to financial viability. The contingent conversion formula is 1.0 multiplied by $25 plus declared and unpaid dividends divided by the greater of (i) a floor price of $5.00; and (ii) current market price of the common shares.

Series 56 - Entitled to non-cumulative annual dividends of $73.65 per share payable semi-annually to Oct. 28, 2027, and thereafter at a rate reset every five years equal to the five-year Government of Canada bond yield plus 4.2%. Redeemable from Sept. 28, 2027, to October 28, 2027 and from the September 28 to and including October 28 period five years thereafter at $1,000 per share plus declared and unpaid dividends.

Class B Preferred - Total authorized amount is unlimited, issuable in series up to an aggregate consideration not exceeding $10 billion. The class B preferred shares rank in priority to the common shares and junior to the class A preferred shares with respect to the payment of dividends and the distribution of assets. In addition to any shareholder approvals required by applicable law, holders of the class B preferred shares will be required to give assent to the creation of any new shares ranking prior to or on parity with the class B shares. However, for the issuance of any additional series of class B preferred shares or of any shares ranking prior to or on parity with the class B preferred shares, shareholder approval will only be required if dividends are in arrears on any outstanding series of class B preferred shares.

Limited Recourse Capital Notes (LRCNs) - Notes with recourse limited to assets held by a third party trustee in a consolidated trust.

LRCN Series 1 - Bear interest at 4.375% per annum until Oct. 28, 2025, and thereafter at an annual rate reset every five years equal to the five-year Government of Canada bond yield plus 4% until maturity on Oct. 28, 2080. Trust assets consist of non-cumulative five-year reset class A preferred series 53 shares.

LRCN Series 2 - Bear interest at 4% per annum until Jan. 28, 2027, and thereafter at an annual rate reset every five years equal to the five-year Government of Canada bond yield plus 3.102% until maturity on Jan. 28, 2082. Trust assets consist of non-cumulative five-year reset class A preferred series 54 shares.

LRCN Series 3 - Bear interest at 7.15% per annum until July 28, 2027, and thereafter at an annual rate reset every five years equal to the five-year Government of Canada bond yield plus 4% until maturity on July 28, 2082. Trust assets consist of non-cumulative five-year reset class A preferred series 55 shares.

Common - One vote per share.

Options - At Oct. 31, 2022, options were outstanding to purchase 11,438,024 common shares at prices ranging from $1 to $80 per share with a weighted average remaining contractual life of 6.52 years.

Class A Preferred Series 45 (old) - Were entitled to non-cumulative annual dividends of $1.10 per share payable quarterly to July 31, 2022. Redeemed on July 29, 2022, at $25 per share.

Major Shareholder - Widely held at May 25, 2023.

Price Range - CM/TSX

Year	Volume	High	Low	Close
2022	907,164,650	$83.75	$53.58	$54.77
2021	858,440,192	$76.44	$53.72	$73.73
2020	1,163,140,864	$56.22	$33.76	$54.36
2019	812,021,056	$57.98	$48.78	$54.03
2018	635,257,216	$62.61	$49.76	$50.84

Split: 2-for-1 split in May 2022

Recent Close: $53.98

Capital Stock Changes - On May 16, 2022, common shares were split on a 2-for-1 basis. On July 29, 2022, all 32,000,000 class A preferred series 45 shares were redeemed at $25 per share. In June 2022, 800,000 class A preferred series 55 shares were issued in conjunction with issuance of $800,000,000 of limited recourse capital notes, series 3 priced at $1,000 per note. On Sept. 16, 2022, 600,000 class A preferred series 56 shares were issued at $1,000 per share. Also during fiscal 2022, post-split common shares were issued as follows: 2,302,876 under employee share purchase plan, 2,272,831 under shareholder investment plan, 1,362,340 on exercise of options and 197,289 under share-based compensation plan. In addition, 1,800,000 post-split common shares were repurchased under a Normal Course Issuer Bid, 48,809 (net) post-split common shares were sold from treasury and 1,975,000 (net) class A preferred shares were purchased and returned to treasury.

Dividends

CM com Ra $3.48 pa Q est. July 28, 2023**
Prev. Rate: $3.40 est. Jan. 27, 2023
Prev. Rate: $3.32 est. July 28, 2022
2-for-1 split eff. May 16, 2022
Prev. Rate: $6.44 est. Jan. 28, 2022
Prev. Rate: $5.84 est. Apr. 28, 2020
CM.PR.O pfd A ser 39 red. exch. Adj. Ra $0.99525 pa Q est. Oct. 28, 2019
CM.PR.P pfd A ser 41 red. exch. Adj. Ra $0.97725 pa Q est. Apr. 28, 2020
CM.PR.Q pfd A ser 43 red. exch. Adj. Ra $0.78575 pa Q est. Oct. 28, 2020
CM.PR.S pfd A ser 47 red. exch. Adj. Ra $1.4695 pa Q est. Apr. 28, 2023
CM.PR.T pfd A ser 49 red. exch. Adj. Ra $1.30 pa Q est. Apr. 29, 2019
CM.PR.Y pfd A ser 51 red. exch. Adj. Ra $1.2875 pa Q est. Oct. 28, 2019
pfd A ser 45 red. exch. Adj. Ra $1.10 pa Q est. Oct. 27, 2017[1]
$0.275f................ July 28/22
[1] Redeemed July 29, 2022 at $25 per sh.
** Reinvestment Option f Final Payment

Long-Term Debt - All bank debentures are direct unsecured and subordinated to deposits and other liabilities.

Outstanding at Oct. 31, 2022:	
Fixed rate subord. debs.:	
5.75% due July 2024[1]	$36,000,000
3.45% due April 2028[2]	1,487,000,000
8.7% due May 2029	32,000,000
2.95% due June 2029[3]	1,426,000,000
2.01% due July 2030[4]	929,000,000
11.6% due Jan. 2031	174,000,000
1.96% due Apr. 2031[5]	916,000,000
10.8% due May 2031	129,000,000
4.2% due Apr. 2032[6]	963,000,000
8.7% due May 2032	34,000,000
8.7% due May 2033	34,000,000
8.7% due May 2035	36,000,000
Fltg. rate subord. debs.:	
Due July 2084[7]	52,000,000
Due August 2085[8]	13,000,000
Subord. debt held for trading purposes	31,000,000
	6,292,000,000

[1] TT$175,000,000 (denominated in Trinidad & Tobago dollars).
[2] After Apr. 4, 2023, bears interest at the three-month bankers' acceptance rate plus 1%.
[3] After June 19, 2024, bears interest at the three-month bankers' acceptance rate plus 1.18%.
[4] After July 21, 2025, bears interest at the three-month bankers' acceptance rate plus 1.28%.
[5] After Apr. 21, 2026, bears interest at the three-month bankers' acceptance rate plus 0.56%.
[6] After Apr. 7, 2027, bears interest at Daily Compounded Canadian Overnight Repo Rate Average (CORRA) plus 1.69%.
[7] US$38,000,000. Bears interest at the six-month US$ LIBOR plus 0.25%.
[8] US$10,000,000. Bears interest at the six-month US$ LIBOR plus 0.125%.

Note - In January 2023, public offering of $1 billion principal amount of 5.33% debentures due Jan. 20, 2033, was completed. The debentures bear a fixed rate of 5.33% until Jan. 20, 2028, and thereafter at the Daily Compounded Canadian Overnight Repo Rate Average (CORRA) plus 2.37%.

Wholly Owned Subsidiaries

CIBC Asset Management Inc., Toronto, Ont. Book value of voting shares owned by the bank at Oct. 31, 2022, totaled $444,000,000.

CIBC Australia Limited, Sydney, N.S.W., Australia. Book value of voting shares owned by the bank at Oct. 31, 2022, totaled $19,000,000.

CIBC BA Limited, Toronto, Ont.

CIBC Bancorp USA Inc., Chicago, Ill. Book value of voting shares owned by the bank at Oct. 31, 2022, totaled $10,595,000,000.

- 100% int. in **CIBC Bank USA**, Chicago, Ill.
- 100% int. in **CIBC Private Wealth Group, LLC**, Atlanta, Ga. Formerly Atlantic Trust Group, LLC.
  - 100% int. in **CIBC Delaware Trust Company**, Wilmington, Del. Formerly Atlantic Trust Company of Delaware.
  - 100% int. in **CIBC National Trust Company**, Atlanta, Ga. Formerly Atlantic Trust Company, N.A.
  - 100% int. in **CIBC Private Wealth Advisors, Inc.**, Chicago, Ill. Formerly AT Investment Advisers, Inc.
- 100% int. in **Canadian Imperial Holdings Inc.**, New York, N.Y.
  - 100% int. in **CIBC Inc.**, New York, N.Y.
    - 100% int. in **CIBC World Markets Corp.**, New York, N.Y.

CIBC Capital Markets (Europe) S.A., Luxembourg. Book value of voting shares owned by the bank at Oct. 31, 2022, totaled $550,000,000.

CIBC Holdings (Cayman) Limited, George Town, Cayman Islands. Book value of voting shares owned by the bank at Oct. 31, 2022, totaled $1,742,000,000.

- 100% int. in **CIBC Cayman Bank Limited**, George Town, Cayman Islands.

- 100% int. in **CIBC Cayman Capital Limited**, George Town, Cayman Islands.
- 100% int. in **CIBC Reinsurance Company Limited**, George Town, Cayman Islands.

CIBC Investments (Cayman) Limited, George Town, Cayman Islands. Book value of voting shares owned by the bank at Oct. 31, 2022, totaled $2,820,000,000.

- 91.7% int. in **FirstCaribbean International Bank Limited**, Warrens, Barbados.
  - 100% int. in **FirstCaribbean International Bank and Trust Company (Cayman) Limited**, George Town, Cayman Islands.
    - 100% int. in **CIBC Fund Administration Services (Asia) Limited**, Hong Kong, People's Republic of China.
  - 100% int. in **FirstCaribbean International Trust Company (Bahamas) Limited**, Nassau, Bahamas.
  - 95.2% int. in **FirstCaribbean International Bank (Bahamas) Limited**, Nassau, Bahamas.
    - 100% int. in **Sentry Insurance Brokers Ltd.**, Nassau, Bahamas.
  - 100% int. in **FirstCaribbean International Bank (Barbados) Limited**, Warrens, Barbados.
  - 100% int. in **FirstCaribbean International Bank (Cayman) Limited**, George Town, Cayman Islands.
    - 100% int. in **FirstCaribbean International Bank (Curacao) N.V.**, Curacao.
    - 100% int. in **FirstCaribbean International Finance Corporation (Netherlands Antilles) N.V.**, Curacao.
  - 100% int. in **FirstCaribbean International Bank (Jamaica) Limited**, Kingston, Jamaica.
  - 100% int. in **FirstCaribbean International Bank (Trinidad and Tobago) Limited**, Maraval, Trinidad and Tobago.
  - 100% int. in **FirstCaribbean International Wealth Management Bank (Barbados) Limited**, Warrens, Barbados.

CIBC Investor Services Inc., Toronto, Ont. Book value of voting shares owned by the bank at Oct. 31, 2022, totaled $25,000,000.

CIBC Life Insurance Company Limited, Toronto, Ont. Book value of voting shares owned by the bank at Oct. 31, 2022, totaled $23,000,000.

CIBC Mortgages Inc., Toronto, Ont. Book value of voting shares owned by the bank at Oct. 31, 2022, totaled $230,000,000.

CIBC Securities Inc., Toronto, Ont. Book value of voting shares owned by the bank at Oct. 31, 2022, totaled $2,000,000.

CIBC Trust Corporation, Toronto, Ont. Book value of voting shares owned by the bank at Oct. 31, 2022, totaled $306,000,000.

CIBC World Markets Inc., Toronto, Ont. Book value of voting shares owned by the bank at Oct. 31, 2022, totaled $306,000,000.

- 100% int. in **CIBC Wood Gundy Financial Services Inc.**, Toronto, Ont.
- 100% int. in **CIBC Wood Gundy Financial Services (Quebec) Inc.**, Montréal, Qué.

CIBC World Markets (Japan) Inc., Tokyo, Japan. Book value of voting shares owned by the bank at Oct. 31, 2022, totaled $48,000,000.

INTRIA Items Inc., Mississauga, Ont. Book value of voting shares owned by the bank at Oct. 31, 2022, totaled $100,000,000.

Investments

50% int. in **CIBC Mellon Global Securities Services Company**, Toronto, Ont.

50% int. in **CIBC Mellon Trust Company**, Toronto, Ont.

Note: The preceding list includes only the major related companies in which interests are held.

Financial Statistics

Periods ended:	12m Oct. 31/22^A		12m Oct. 31/21^A
	$000s	%Chg	$000s
Interest income	**22,179,000**	**+50**	**14,741,000**
Interest expense	9,538,000		3,282,000
Net interest income	**12,641,000**	**+10**	**11,459,000**
Provision for loan losses	1,057,000		158,000
Other income	9,192,000		8,556,000
Salaries & pension benefits	7,157,000		6,450,000
Non-interest expense	12,803,000		11,535,000
Pre-tax income	**7,973,000**	**-4**	**8,322,000**
Income taxes	1,730,000		1,876,000
Net income	**6,243,000**	**-3**	**6,446,000**
Net inc. for equity hldrs	**6,220,000**	**-3**	**6,429,000**
Net inc. for non-cont. int	**23,000**	**+35**	**17,000**
Cash & equivalent	63,861,000		56,997,000
Securities	175,879,000		161,401,000
Net non-performing loans	1,079,000		1,061,000
Total loans	586,296,000		519,493,000
Fixed assets, net	3,377,000		3,286,000
Total assets	**943,597,000**	**+13**	**837,683,000**
Deposits	697,572,000		621,158,000
Other liabilities	189,351,000		165,156,000
Subordinated debt	6,292,000		5,539,000
Preferred share equity	4,923,000		4,325,000
Shareholders' equity	50,181,000		45,648,000
Non-controlling interest	201,000		182,000
Cash from oper. activs	**22,715,000**	**n.a.**	**(3,332,000)**
Cash from fin. activs	(1,610,000)		(1,945,000)
Cash from invest. activs	(24,391,000)		(3,506,000)
Pension fund surplus	1,395,000		1,340,000
	$		$
Earnings per share*	6.70		6.99
Cash flow per share*	25.15		(3.71)
Cash divd. per share*	3.27		2.92
	shs		shs
No. of shs. o/s*	906,040,097		901,655,952
Avg. no. of shs. o/s*	903,312,000		897,906,000
	%		%
Basel III Common Equity Tier 1	11.70		12.40
Basel III Tier 1	13.30		14.10
Basel III Total	15.30		16.20
Net profit margin	28.59		32.21
Return on equity	13.97		15.90
Return on assets	0.70		0.80
Foreign sales percent	25		23
No. of employees (FTEs)	50,427		45,282

* Common

^A Reported in accordance with IFRS

Latest Results

Periods ended:	6m Apr. 30/23^A		6m Apr. 30/22^A
	$000s	%Chg	$000s
Net interest income	6,392,000	+3	6,220,000
Net income	2,120,000	-38	3,392,000
Net inc. for equity hldrs	2,100,000	-38	3,382,000
Net inc. for non-cont. int	20,000		10,000
	$		$
Earnings per share*	2.16		3.65

* Common

^A Reported in accordance with IFRS

Historical Summary
(as originally stated)

Fiscal Year	Int. Inc.	Net Inc. Bef. Disc.	EPS*
	$000s	$000s	$
2022^A	22,179,000	6,243,000	6.70
2021^A	14,741,000	6,446,000	6.99
2020^A	17,522,000	3,792,000	4.12
2019^A	20,697,000	5,121,000	5.61
2018^A	17,505,000	5,284,000	5.84

* Common

^A Reported in accordance with IFRS

Note: Adjusted throughout for 2-for-1 split in May 2022

C.37 Canadian Investment Grade Preferred Share Fund

Symbol - RIGP.UN **Exchange** - NEO **CUSIP** - 136188
Head Office - c/o Purpose Investments Inc., 3100-130 Adelaide St W, PO Box 109, Toronto, ON, M5H 3P5 **Telephone** - (416) 583-3850 **Toll-free** - (877) 789-1517 **Fax** - (416) 583-3851
Website - www.purposeinvest.com
Email - vladt@purposeinvest.com
Investor Relations - Vladimir Tasevski (416) 583-3860
Auditors - Ernst & Young LLP C.A., Toronto, Ont.
Lawyers - Fasken Martineau DuMoulin LLP, Toronto, Ont.
Transfer Agents - TSX Trust Company, Toronto, Ont.
Trustees - Purpose Investments Inc., Toronto, Ont.
Managers - Purpose Investments Inc., Toronto, Ont.

Profile - (Ont. 2016) Invests in an actively managed portfolio consisting primarily of preferred shares of Canadian issuers.

Not less than 80% of the total assets would be invested in Canadian preferred shares. The fund does not have a fixed termination date.

Top 10 holdings at July 13, 2023 (as a percentage of the portfolio):

Holding	Percentage
Royal Bank of Canada, Pref. Ser. Az	10.00%
ECN Capital Corp., Pref. Ser.C	9.76%
Toronto-Dominion Bank, Pref. Ser.A	7.14%
Brookfield Corp., Pref. Series	6.36%
Pembina Pipeline Corp., Pref. Series	4.60%
Brookfield Corp., Pref. Series	3.84%
Power Financial Corp., Pref. Series T	3.83%
Brookfield Corp., Pref. Series	3.69%
Brookfield Corp., Pref. Series	3.45%
Enbridge Inc, Cum Red Pref. Ser. F	3.22%

Predecessor Detail - Name changed from Canadian Investment Grade Preferred Share Fund (P2L), Sept. 24, 2018.

Oper. Subsid./Mgt. Co. Directors - Som Seif, chr., pres. & CEO, Toronto, Ont.; Jeffrey J. (Jeff) Bouganim, CFO, Oakville, Ont.; Vladimir Tasevski, v-p & COO, Toronto, Ont.

Oper. Subsid./Mgt. Co. Officers - Alessia Crescenzi, chief compliance officer

Capital Stock

	Authorized (shs.)	Outstanding (shs.)[1]
Class T	unlimited	611,443
Class A	unlimited	nil

[1] At Dec. 31, 2022

Class T - Entitled to monthly cash distributions of $0.1146 per unit to yield 5.5% per annum on the original $25 issue price. Retractable in January of each year for an amount equal to the net asset value per unit, less any costs associated with the retraction. Retractable in any other month for a price equal to the lesser of: (i) 95% of the weighted average price per unit on the NEO Exchange for the 10 trading days immediately preceding the retraction date; and (ii) the closing price per unit. One vote per unit.

Major Shareholder - Widely held at Mar. 1, 2023.

Price Range - RIGP.UN/TSX (D)

Year	Volume	High	Low	Close
2021	600	$27.56	$21.26	$27.00
2020	1,300	$20.66	$14.56	$19.75
2019	7,600	$20.85	$17.24	$19.81
2018	171,661	$29.85	$28.00	$29.00

Capital Stock Changes - During 2022, 29,476 class T units were retracted.

Dividends

cl T unit Ra $1.3752 pa M est. Jan. 16, 2017
Delisted Aug 28/23.

Financial Statistics

Periods ended:	12m Dec. 31/22^A		12m Dec. 31/21^A
	$000s	%Chg	$000s
Realized invest. gain (loss)	265		60
Unrealized invest. gain (loss)	(5,613)		4,948
Total revenue	**(4,402)**	**n.a.**	**6,033**
General & admin. expense	186		211
Other operating expense	(21)		5
Operating expense	**165**	**-24**	**216**
Operating income	**(4,567)**	**n.a.**	**5,817**
Finance costs, gross	95		42
Pre-tax income	**(4,662)**	**n.a.**	**5,775**
Net income	**(4,662)**	**n.a.**	**5,775**
Cash & equivalent	46		698
Accounts receivable	47		17
Investments	15,764		22,814
Total assets	**15,859**	**-33**	**23,530**
Accts. pay. & accr. liabs	202		281
Debt	3,899		5,216
Shareholders' equity	11,687		17,959
Cash from oper. activs	**2,279**	**-45**	**4,140**
Cash from fin. activs	(2,930)		(3,689)
Net cash position	**46**	**-93**	**698**
	$		$
Earnings per share*	(7.52)		8.54
Cash flow per share*	3.68		6.12
Net asset value per share*	19.11		28.02
Cash divd. per share*	0.80		0.92
	shs		shs
No. of shs. o/s*	611,443		640,919
Avg. no. of shs. o/s*	619,705		676,439
	%		%
Net profit margin	n.m.		95.72
Return on equity	(31.18)		32.74
Return on assets	(23.19)		25.85

* Class T

^A Reported in accordance with IFRS

Note: Net income reflects increase/decrease in net assets from operations.

Historical Summary
(as originally stated)

Fiscal Year	Total Rev.	Net Inc. Bef. Disc.	EPS*
	$000s	$000s	$
2022[A]	(4,402)	(4,662)	(7.52)
2021[A]	6,033	5,775	8.54
2020[A]	1,099	869	0.97
2019[A]	(576)	(1,280)	(0.14)
2018[A]	(5,830)	(7,225)	(4.28)

* Class T
[A] Reported in accordance with IFRS

C.38 Canadian Life Companies Split Corp.

Symbol - LFE **Exchange** - TSX **CUSIP** - 136290
Head Office - c/o Quadravest Capital Management Inc., 2510-200 Front St W, PO Box 51, Toronto, ON, M5V 3K2 **Telephone** - (416) 304-4440 **Toll-free** - (877) 478-2372
Website - www.quadravest.com
Email - info@quadravest.com
Investor Relations - Shari Payne (877) 478-2372
Auditors - PricewaterhouseCoopers LLP C.A., Toronto, Ont.
Lawyers - Blake, Cassels & Graydon LLP, Toronto, Ont.
Transfer Agents - Computershare Trust Company of Canada Inc., Toronto, Ont.
Investment Managers - Quadravest Capital Management Inc., Toronto, Ont.
Managers - Quadravest Capital Management Inc., Toronto, Ont.
Profile - (Ont. 2005) Invests in a portfolio of common shares primarily consisting of publicly traded Canadian insurance companies.

The portfolio includes **Manulife Financial Corporation, Sun Life Financial Inc., Great-West Lifeco Inc.** and **iA Financial Corporation Inc.** Shares held within the portfolio are expected to range between 10% and 30% in weight but may vary at any time. Up to 20% of the net asset value may be invested in equity securities of foreign life insurance companies or other Canadian or foreign financial services companies.

To supplement the dividends received on the investment portfolio and to reduce risk, the company will, from time to time, write covered call options in respect of all or part of the common shares in the portfolio.

The investment manager receives a management fee at an annual rate equal to 0.65% of the net asset value of the company calculated and payable monthly in arrears. In addition, the manager receives an administration fee at an annual rate equal to 0.1% of the net asset value of the company calculated and payable monthly in arrears, as well as service fee payable to dealers on the class A shares at a rate of 0.5% per annum.

The company will terminate on Dec. 1, 2024, or earlier at the discretion of the manager if the class A and 2012 preferred shares are delisted by the TSX or if the net asset value of the company declines to less than $5,000,000. At such time all outstanding class A and 2012 preferred shares will be redeemed. The termination date may be extended beyond Dec. 1, 2024, for a further six years and thereafter for additional successive periods of six years as determined by the board of directors.

Top 10 holdings at Feb. 28, 2023 (as a percentage of net assets):

Holdings	Percentage
Manulife Financial Corporation	28.4%
Sun Life Financial Inc.	23.3%
iA Financial Corporation Inc.	20.7%
Great-West Lifeco Inc.	11.0%
The Bank of Nova Scotia	3.9%
Prudential Financial Inc.	1.1%
Canadian Imperial Bank of Commerce	0.8%
The Toronto-Dominion Bank	0.8%
Aflac Incorporated	0.6%
Lincoln National Corp.	0.5%

Directors - S. Wayne Finch, chr., pres. & CEO, Caledon, Ont.; Laura L. Johnson, corp. sec., Oakville, Ont.; Peter F. Cruickshank, Oakville, Ont.; Michael W. Sharp, Toronto, Ont.; John D. Steep, Stratford, Ont.
Other Exec. Officers - Silvia Gomes, CFO

Capital Stock

	Authorized (shs.)	Outstanding (shs.)[1]
Class B	1,000	1,000[2]
2012 Preferred	unlimited	11,644,001[2]
Class A	unlimited	11,525,201

[1] At May 15, 2023
[2] Classified as debt.

Class B - Not entitled to receive dividends. Retractable at any time at $1.00 per share and have a liquidation entitlement of $1.00 per share. Rank prior to 2012 preferred shares and class A shares with respect to distributions on the dissolution, liquidation or winding-up of the company. One vote per share.

2012 Preferred - Entitled to receive monthly floating cumulative preferential dividend equal to the greater of (i) $0.05417 per share (to yield 6.5% per annum on the original $10 issue price) and (ii) the prevailing Canadian prime rate plus 2% annually based on the original $10 issue price, to a maximum of 8%. Under a monthly retraction, a shareholder will receive an amount equal to the lesser of (i) $10; and (ii) 98% of the net asset value (NAV) per unit (one class A share and one 2012 preferred share) less the cost to the company of purchasing a class A share for cancellation. Under a concurrent annual retraction in March of each year, a shareholder will receive, for each unit, an amount equal to the NAV per unit less any costs (to a maximum of 1% of the NAV per unit) to fund the retraction. All outstanding preferred shares will be redeemed on Dec. 1, 2024, at $10 per share. Rank in priority to class A and subordinate to class B shares with respect to the payment of dividends and the repayment of capital on the dissolution, liquidation or winding-up of the company. Non-voting.

Class A - Entitled to distributions at a dividend rate set by the board of directors at its discretion. In addition, a special year-end dividend will be payable on the last day of November in each year if such funds are available. No regular monthly distributions will be paid if any dividends on the 2012 preferred shares are in arrears or if the NAV per unit is equal to or less than $15 and no special year-end dividends will be paid if after such payment the NAV per unit would be less than $25. Retractable in any month at a price equal to the sum of (i) 98% of the NAV less the cost of the purchase of a 2012 preferred share in the market for cancellation; and (ii) all dividends owing on the class A share to but excluding the applicable retraction date. Under a concurrent annual retraction in March of each year, shareholders will have the right to receive, for each unit, an amount equal to the NAV per unit, less any costs (to a maximum of 1% of the NAV per unit) to fund the retraction. All outstanding class A shares will be redeemed upon termination of the company at an amount representing all remaining assets of the company after redemption of the preferred and class B shares. Rank subordinate to 2012 preferred and class B shares with respect to the payment of dividends and the repayment of capital on the dissolution, liquidation or winding-up of the company. Non-voting.

Normal Course Issuer Bid - The company plans to make normal course purchases of up to 1,085,432 class A shares representing 10% of the public float. The bid commenced on May 29, 2023, and expires on May 28, 2024.

The company plans to make normal course purchases of up to 1,156,200 2012 preferred shares representing 10% of the public float. The bid commenced on May 29, 2023, and expires on May 28, 2024.

Major Shareholder - Canadian Life Companies Split Corp. Holding Trust held 100% interest at Feb. 23, 2023.

Price Range - LFE/TSX

Year	Volume	High	Low	Close
2022	13,469,327	$5.57	$2.20	$2.66
2021	8,818,337	$4.64	$2.30	$4.09
2020	11,012,599	$4.82	$1.08	$2.44
2019	8,127,674	$4.46	$2.04	$4.09
2018	13,669,146	$6.68	$1.67	$2.12

Recent Close: $3.02

Capital Stock Changes - During fiscal 2022, 37,800 2012 preferred shares and 37,800 class A shares were issued under an at-the-market equity program.

Dividends

LFE cl A N.V. N.S.R. [1]
$0.10 Mar. 10/22 $0.10 Feb. 10/22
Paid in 2023: n.a. 2022: $0.20 2021: n.a.

LFE.PR.B 2012 pfd cum. ret. Ra $0.80 pa M
Prev. Rate: $0.795
Prev. Rate: $0.745
Prev. Rate: $0.67
Prev. Rate: $0.65

[1] No set frequency divd normally payable in Apr/20 has been omitted.

Financial Statistics

Periods ended:	12m Nov. 30/22[A]		12m Nov. 30/21[A]
	$000s	%Chg	$000s
Realized invest. gain (loss)	2,629		1,406
Unrealized invest. gain (loss)	(4,742)		20,640
Total revenue	**5,279**	**-82**	**28,932**
General & admin. expense	1,422		1,483
Other operating expense	429		495
Operating expense	**1,851**	**-6**	**1,978**
Operating income	**3,428**	**-87**	**26,954**
Finance costs, gross	8,571		8,282
Pre-tax income	**(5,143)**	**n.a.**	**18,672**
Net income	**(5,143)**	**n.a.**	**18,672**
Cash & equivalent	20,410		10,614
Accounts receivable	1,383		1,501
Investments	149,022		162,140
Total assets	**170,815**	**-2**	**174,851**
Accts. pay. & accr. liabs.	150		168
Debt	124,728		124,350
Shareholders' equity	42,070		49,603
Cash from oper. activs.	**20,022**	**-22**	**25,653**
Cash from fin. activs.	(10,430)		(21,384)
Net cash position	**20,410**	**+92**	**10,614**
	$		$
Earnings per share*	(0.41)		1.46
Cash flow per share*	1.61		2.01
Net asset value per share*	3.37		3.99
Cash divd. per share*	0.20		nil
	shs		shs
No. of shs. o/s*	12,472,701		12,434,901
Avg. no. of shs. o/s*	12,461,676		12,778,886
	%		%
Net profit margin	(97.42)		64.54
Return on equity	(11.22)		44.24
Return on assets	1.98		15.60

* Class A
[A] Reported in accordance with IFRS

Note: Net income reflects increase/decrease in net assets from operations.

Historical Summary
(as originally stated)

Fiscal Year	Total Rev.	Net Inc. Bef. Disc.	EPS*
	$000s	$000s	$
2022[A]	5,279	(5,143)	(0.41)
2021[A]	28,932	18,672	1.46
2020[A]	(19,958)	(30,686)	(2.27)
2019[A]	36,962	25,584	1.80
2018[A]	(16,524)	(28,039)	(1.80)

* Class A
[A] Reported in accordance with IFRS
Note: Adjusted throughout for 1.0497725-for-1 split in Dec. 2018

C.39 Canadian National Railway Company*

Symbol - CNR **Exchange** - TSX **CUSIP** - 136375
Head Office - 935 rue de la Gauchetière O, Montréal, QC, H3B 2M9 **Telephone** - (514) 399-5430 **Toll-free** - (888) 888-5909
Website - www.cn.ca
Email - investor.relations@cn.ca
Investor Relations - Stacy Alderson (514) 399-0052
Auditors - KPMG LLP C.A., Montréal, Qué.
Lawyers - Sullivan & Cromwell LLP, New York, N.Y.; Stikeman Elliott LLP, Montréal, Qué.
Transfer Agents - Computershare Trust Company, N.A., Louisville, Ky.; Computershare Trust Company of Canada Inc., Toronto, Ont.
FP500 Revenue Ranking - 34
Employees - 25,178 at June 30, 2023
Profile - (Can. 1919, via Special Act of Parliament) Operates a railroad network of 18,600 route miles of track which spans Canada and the United States, connecting Canada's Eastern and Western coasts with the U.S. South. Freight revenue is derived from the movement of a diversified and balanced portfolio of commodities: petroleum and chemicals, metals and minerals, forest products, coal, grain and fertilizers, intermodal and automotive. Other revenues are primarily derived from non-rail services that support the company's rail business.

The company's rail network reaches three coasts, from the Atlantic and Pacific oceans to the Gulf of Mexico, and serves the cities and ports of Vancouver and Prince Rupert, B.C.; Thunder Bay, Ont.; Montreal and Quebec, Que.; Halifax, N.S.; Saint John, N.B.; New Orleans, La.; and Mobile, Ala.; and the metropolitan areas of Toronto, Ont.; Edmonton,

Alta.; Winnipeg, Man.; Saskatoon, Sask.; Chicago, Ill.; Memphis, Tenn.; and Detroit, Mich., with connections to all points in North America.

Rail freight and related transportation activities are classified into seven commodity groups: **Petroleum and Chemicals**, including chemicals and plastics, refined petroleum products, natural gas liquids, crude oil and sulfur; **Metals and Minerals**, consisting primarily of materials related to oil and gas development such as frac sand, drilling pipe and large diameter pipe, steel, iron ore, non-ferrous base metals and ores, raw materials including scrap metal, industrial materials including aggregates, construction materials such as roofing and railway equipment, machinery and dimensional (large) loads; **Forest Products**, including various types of lumber, panels, paper, board and wrapping paper, wood pulp and other fibres such as logs, recycled paper, wood chips and wood pellets; **Coal**, consisting of thermal grades of bituminous coal, metallurgical coal and petroleum coke; **Grain and Fertilizers**, including wheat, oats, barley, flaxseed, rye, peas, lentils, corn, corn meal, ethanol, dried distillers grain, canola seed and canola products, soybeans and soybean products, sweeteners, animal fat, potash, ammonium nitrate, anhydrous ammonia, urea and other fertilizers; **Intermodal**, includes rail and trucking services and consists of the domestic segment, which transports consumer products and manufactured goods, serving retail, wholesale and logistics provider channels, in Canada, the U.S., Mexico and transborder, and the international intermodal, which handles import and export container traffic, serving the ports of Vancouver, Prince Rupert, Montreal, Halifax, New Orleans and Mobile; and **Automotive**, which moves both domestic finished vehicles and parts throughout North America, providing service to certain vehicle assembly plants in Ontario, Michigan and Mississippi, vehicle distribution facilities in Canada and the U.S., parts production facilities in Michigan and Ontario, as well as shippers of finished vehicle imports via the ports of Halifax and Vancouver and through interchange with other railroads.

Operating Statistics

Years ended Dec. 31	2022	2021
Route miles[1]	18,600	19,500
Carloads	5,697,000	5,701,000
Gross ton miles per employee	19,820,000	19,033,000
Revenue ton miles (RTM)[2]	235,788	233,138
Freight rev. per RTM	7.03¢	5.96¢
Freight rev. per carload	$2,908	$2,436

[1] Includes Canada and the U.S.
[2] 000,000s.

Carloads by Commodity Group

Years ended Dec. 31	2022	2021
Petroleum & chemicals	636,000	596,000
Metals & minerals	956,000	969,000
Forest products	330,000	339,000
Coal	503,000	379,000
Grain & fertilizers	614,000	628,000
Intermodal	2,450,000	2,611,000
Automotive	208,000	179,000
	5,697,000	5,701,000

Recent Merger and Acquisition Activity

Status: completed **Revised:** Apr. 3, 2023

UPDATE: The transaction was completed. PREVIOUS: ROK Resources Inc. agreed to sell certain non-core assets in Saskatchewan to Rife Resources Ltd., a wholly owned subsidiary of Canadian National Railway Company's CN Pension Trust Funds, for $47,250,000. The sale includes non-operated 2.11685% interest in Weyburn Unit.

Status: terminated **Revised:** June 7, 2022

UPDATE: The transaction was terminated. PREVIOUS: Canadian National Railway Company agreed to acquire the Massena rail line from CSX Corporation. Terms were not disclosed. The Massena rail line represents more than 220 miles of track between Valleyfield, Que., and Woodard, N.Y., and serves many cities in the province of Quebec, including Beauharnois and Huntingdon, and in the state of New York, including Massena, Norwood, Potsdam and Gouverneur. Apr. 6, 2020 - STB issued its decision conditionally approving the acquisition, which will become effective on May 21, 2020. June 6, 2020 - Canadian National Railway and CSX sought reconsideration to remove Surface Transportation Board's (STB) condition which requires a change to the line sale agreement for STB's review. Feb. 25, 2021 - STB denied the petitions for reconsideration. Apr. 23, 2021 - Canadian National Railway appealed STB's condition. The case is pending in the United States Court of Appeals for the Seventh Circuit. Briefing was suspended while the parties participate in the circuit mediation process.

Directors - Shauneen E. Bruder, chr., Toronto, Ont.; Tracy A. Robinson, pres. & CEO, Calgary, Alta.; Jo-ann de Pass Olsovsky, Tex.; David (Dave) Freeman, Tenn.; Denise Gray, Troy, Mich.; Justin M. Howell, Wash.; Susan C. Jones, Calgary, Alta.; Robert (Rob) Knight, Fla.; Michel Letellier, Saint-Lambert, Qué.; Margaret A. McKenzie, Calgary, Alta.; Al Monaco, Calgary, Alta.

Other Exec. Officers - Stephen Covey, chief security officer & chief of police; Edmond L. (Ed) Harris, exec. v-p & COO; Ghislain Houle, exec. v-p & CFO; Doug MacDonald, exec. v-p & chief mktg. officer; Dominique Malenfant, exec. v-p & chief IT officer; Olivier Chouc, sr. v-p & chief legal officer; Janet Drysdale, sr. v-p & chief stakeholder rel. officer; Dorothea Klein, sr. v-p & chief HR officer; Patrick Lortie, sr. v-p & chief strategy officer; Keith Reardon, sr. v-p, interline & network devel.; Derek Taylor, sr. v-p, trans.; Patrick Whitehead, sr. v-p, network opers.; Bernd Beyer, v-p & treas.; Mohit Bhat, v-p, cust. solutions & innovation; Dan Bresolin, v-p, intermodal; Cristina Circelli, v-p, gen. counsel & corp. sec.; Carrie-Ann Crozier, v-p, multimodal opers.; Sandra Ellis, v-p, bulk; Salvatore (Sam) Forgione, v-p & compt.; Mark Grubbs, v-p, mech.; Martin Guimond, v-p, trans., eastern region; Brent Laing, v-p, eng.; Mark Lerner, v-p, mktg. & chief of staff; Kelly Levis, v-p, ind. products; Jamie Lockwood, v-p, finl. planning; Helen Quirke, v-p, supply chain & bus. devel.; Robert (Buck) Rogers, v-p, petroleum & chemicals; James Thompson, v-p, trans., western region; Mike J. Jones, pres., TransX

Capital Stock

	Authorized (shs.)	Outstanding (shs.)[1]
Class A Preferred	unlimited	nil
Class B Preferred	unlimited	nil
Common	unlimited	655,600,000

[1] At July 25, 2023

Options - At Dec. 31, 2022, options were outstanding to purchase 3,300,000 common shares at prices ranging from $47.30 to $170.81 per share with a weighted average remaining life of 6.3 years.

Normal Course Issuer Bid - The company plans to make normal course purchases of up to 32,000,000 common shares representing 4.8% of the total outstanding. The bid commenced on Feb. 1, 2023, and expires on Jan. 31, 2024.

Major Shareholder - Widely held at Mar. 3, 2023.

Price Range - CNR/TSX

Year	Volume	High	Low	Close
2022	310,551,354	$175.39	$137.26	$160.84
2021	336,727,186	$168.66	$125.00	$155.38
2020	364,770,174	$149.11	$92.01	$139.94
2019	279,206,481	$127.96	$98.47	$117.47
2018	316,950,625	$118.62	$90.84	$101.11

Recent Close: $152.98

Capital Stock Changes - During 2022, 600,000 common shares were issued on exercise of options, 400,000 common shares were disbursed by share trusts, 30,200,000 common shares were repurchased under a Normal Course Issuer Bid and 700,000 common shares were purchased by share trusts.

Dividends

CNR com Ra $3.16 pa Q est. Mar. 31, 2023
Prev. Rate: $2.93 est. Mar. 31, 2022
Prev. Rate: $2.46 est. Mar. 31, 2021
Prev. Rate: $2.30 est. Mar. 31, 2020

Long-Term Debt - Outstanding at Dec. 31, 2022:

Notes & Debentures:	
Canadian National Series[1]:	
7.63% US$ debs. due 2023	Cdn$203,000,000
2.95% US$ notes due 2024	474,000,000
2.8% Cdn$ notes due 2025	350,000,000
2.75% US$ notes due 2026	678,000,000
6.9% US$ notes due 2028	644,000,000
3.2% Cdn$ notes due 2028	350,000,000
3% Cdn$ notes due 2029	350,000,000
7.38% US$ debs. due 2031	271,000,000
3.85% US$ notes due 2032	1,084,000,000
6.25% US$ notes due 2034	678,000,000
6.2% US$ notes due 2036	610,000,000
6.71% US$ PURS due 2036	339,000,000
6.38% US$ debs. due 2037	407,000,000
3.5% US$ notes due 2042	339,000,000
4.5% US$ notes due 2043	339,000,000
3.95% Cdn$ notes due 2045	400,000,000
3.2% US$ notes due 2046	881,000,000
3.6% Cdn$ notes due 2047	500,000,000
3.65% US$ notes due 2048	813,000,000
3.6% Cdn$ notes due 2048	450,000,000
4.45% US$ notes due 2049	881,000,000
3.6% Cdn$ notes due 2049	450,000,000
3.05% Cdn$ notes due 2050	450,000,000
2.45% US$ notes due 2050	813,000,000
4.4% US$ notes due 2052	949,000,000
4% Cdn$ notes due 2065	100,000,000
Illinois Central Series:	
7.7% US$ debs. due 2096	169,000,000
BC Rail Series:	
Subordinated notes due 2094[2]	842,000,000
Other:	
Commercial paper[3]	805,000,000
Equipment loans	779,000,000
Finance lease obligs	10,000,000
Less: Net unamort. disc. & debt costs	979,000,000
	15,429,000,000
Less: Current portion	1,057,000,000
	14,372,000,000

Note - All notes and debentures are unsecured.

[1] Fixed rate notes and debentures are redeemable, in whole or in part, at the company's option at any time, at the greater of par and a formula price based on interest rates at the time of redemption.

[2] Non-interest bearing. These notes are recorded as a discounted debt of Cdn$15,000,000, using an imputed interest rate of 5.75%. Discount of Cdn$827,000,000 is included in the net unamortized discount and debt issuance costs.

[3] Consists of US$594,000,000 (Cdn$805,000,000) and US$111,000,000 (Cdn$140,000,000) borrowings at a weighted average interest rate of 4.27% and 0.18%, respectively.

Long-term debt maturities, excluding finance lease liabilities, for the next five years and thereafter are as follows:

2023	Cdn$1,056,000,000
2024	509,000,000
2025	385,000,000
2026	713,000,000
2027	36,000,000
Thereafter	12,720,000,000

The aggregate amount of debt payable in U.S. currency at Dec. 31, 2022, was US$8,975,000,000 (Cdn$12,165,000,000).

Note - In May 2023, offering of Cdn$550,000,000 of 4.15% notes due 2030, Cdn$400,000,000 of 4.4% notes due 2033 and Cdn$800,000,000 of 4.7% notes due 2053 was completed. In addition, all US$150,000,000 (Cdn$203,000,000) principal amount of 7.63% notes due 2023, were repaid.

Wholly Owned Subsidiaries

North American Railways, Inc., Del.
- 100% int. in **Grand Trunk Corporation**, Del.
  - 100% int. in **Grand Trunk Western Railroad Company**, Mich.
- 100% int. in **Illinois Central Corporation**, Del.
  - 100% int. in **Illinois Central Railroad Company**, Ill.
- 100% int. in **Wisconsin Central Limited**, Del.

Note: The preceding list includes only the major related companies in which interests are held.

Financial Statistics

Periods ended:	12m Dec. 31/22[A]		12m Dec. 31/21[□A]
	$000s	%Chg	$000s
Operating revenue	**17,107,000**	**+18**	**14,477,000**
Salaries & benefits	2,935,000		2,879,000
Other operating expense	5,603,000		4,437,000
Operating expense	**8,538,000**	**+17**	**7,316,000**
Operating income	**8,569,000**	**+20**	**7,161,000**
Deprec., depl. & amort.	1,729,000		1,598,000
Finance income	498,000		407,000
Finance costs, gross	548,000		610,000
Investment income	(29,000)		20,000
Pre-tax income	**6,763,000**	**+7**	**6,342,000**
Income taxes	1,645,000		1,443,000
Net income	**5,118,000**	**+4**	**4,899,000**
Cash & equivalent	328,000		838,000
Inventories	692,000		589,000
Accounts receivable	1,371,000		1,074,000
Current assets	3,217,000		3,426,000
Long-term investments	94,000		119,000
Fixed assets, net	43,537,000		41,178,000
Right-of-use assets	470,000		445,000
Intangibles, net	207,000		209,000
Total assets	**50,662,000**	**+4**	**48,538,000**
Accts. pay. & accr. liabs	2,660,000		2,504,000
Current liabilities	3,842,000		3,120,000
Long-term debt, gross	15,429,000		12,485,000
Long-term debt, net	14,372,000		11,977,000
Long-term lease liabilities	341,000		322,000
Shareholders' equity	21,384,000		22,744,000
Cash from oper. activs	**6,667,000**	**-2**	**6,791,000**
Cash from fin. activs	(4,667,000)		(3,857,000)
Cash from invest. activs	(2,510,000)		(2,873,000)
Net cash position	**834,000**	**-38**	**1,341,000**
Capital expenditures	(2,750,000)		(2,891,000)
Capital disposals	273,000		nil
Pension fund surplus	2,680,000		2,603,000
	$		$
Earnings per share*	7.46		6.91
Cash flow per share*	9.71		9.59
Cash divd. per share*	2.93		2.46
	shs		shs
No. of shs. o/s*	671,000,000		700,900,000
Avg. no. of shs. o/s*	686,400,000		708,500,000
	%		%
Net profit margin	29.92		33.84
Return on equity	23.20		23.11
Return on assets	11.15		11.51
Foreign sales percent	32		31
No. of employees (FTEs)	23,971		22,604

* Common
□ Restated
[A] Reported in accordance with U.S. GAAP

Latest Results

Periods ended:	6m June 30/23[A]		6m June 30/22[A]
	$000s	%Chg	$000s
Operating revenue	8,370,000	+4	8,052,000
Net income	2,387,000	+6	2,243,000
	$		$
Earnings per share*	3.59		3.23

* Common
[A] Reported in accordance with U.S. GAAP

Historical Summary
(as originally stated)

Fiscal Year	Oper. Rev.	Net Inc. Bef. Disc.	EPS*
	$000s	$000s	$
2022^A	17,107,000	5,118,000	7.46
2021^A	14,477,000	4,892,000	6.90
2020^A	13,819,000	3,562,000	5.01
2019^A	14,917,000	4,216,000	5.85
2018^A	14,321,000	4,328,000	5.89

* Common
^A Reported in accordance with U.S. GAAP

C.40 Canadian Net Real Estate Investment Trust

Symbol - NET.UN **Exchange** - TSX-VEN **CUSIP** - 13639A
Head Office - 106 av Gun, Pointe-Claire, QC, H9R 3X3 **Telephone** - (450) 536-5328 **Fax** - (450) 446-1116
Website - www.cnetreit.com
Email - khenley@cnetreit.com
Investor Relations - Kevin Henley (450) 536-5328
Auditors - MNP LLP C.A., Montréal, Qué.
Lawyers - Davies Ward Phillips & Vineberg LLP
Transfer Agents - TSX Trust Company, Montréal, Qué.
Employees - 4 at Dec. 31, 2022
Profile - (Que. 2011; orig. Can., 2006) Owns 101 triple net and management-free commercial real estate properties in Quebec, Ontario, Nova Scotia and New Brunswick, that house quick services restaurants, gas/service stations, convenience stores, auto parts businesses and major retailers.

At Dec. 31, 2023, the trust's portfolio consisted of 101 commercial properties, including 32 co-owned properties, in Quebec (83), Ontario (9), Nova Scotia (8) and New Brunswick (1), totaling 1,460,210 sq. ft. of leasable area, of which 163,675 sq. ft. are co-owned.

On Apr. 3, 2023, the trust sold a 2,690-sq.-ft. commercial property located at 536 Algonquin Blvd. East in Timmins, Ont., for $1,300,000 cash.

On Jan. 18, 2023, the trust acquired a parcel of land in Lachine, Que., for $250,000.

On July 15, 2022, the trust acquired a 4,400-sq.-ft. auto service centre operated under the Midas banner in Fredericton, N.B., for $975,000.

On June 23, 2022, the trust, through 50%-owned **Fronsac Odacite Lachute LP**, acquired a parcel of land in Lachute, Que., for $1,800,000 cash.

Recent Merger and Acquisition Activity

Status: completed **Revised:** Aug. 3, 2022
UPDATE: The transaction was completed. PREVIOUS: Canadian Net Real Estate Investment Trust agreed to acquire a 53,151-sq.-ft. hardware store operated under the Rona banner in Châteauguay, Que., for $8,300,000.

Status: completed **Revised:** May 24, 2022
UPDATE: Canadian Net acquired three additional properties: a 29,698-sq.-ft. grocery store operated under the Metro banner in Chénéville, Que.; a 35,991-sq.-ft. grocery-anchored retail strip in St-André-Avellin, Que.; and a 3,500-sq.-ft. service station operated under the Couche-Tard banner in St-Jérôme, Que. Total consideration paid for the four properties was $18,800,000. PREVIOUS: Canadian Net Real Estate Investment Trust acquired a 30,500-sq.-ft. retail store operated under the Giant Tiger banner in Truro, N.S.

Status: completed **Announced:** Mar. 21, 2022
Canadian Net Real Estate Investment Trust acquired a 38,064-sq.-ft. and a 4,016-sq.-ft. retail properties in Saguenay, Que., for $8,800,000. The properties were leased to a grocery store operated under the IGA banner and to a National Bank of Canada branch.

Predecessor Detail - Name changed from Fronsac Real Estate Investment Trust, June 22, 2021.
Trustees - Michel C. Trudeau, chr., Montréal, Qué.; Guy P. Dancosse, Montréal, Qué.; Sandrine Debbanné, Qué.; Rita Ghorayeb, Qué.; Guy Laframboise, Montréal, Qué.; François-Olivier Laplante, Montréal, Qué.; Michael A. Zakuta, Montréal, Qué.
Other Exec. Officers - Kevin Henley, pres. & CEO; Charles B. (Ben) Gazith, CFO & treas.

Capital Stock

	Authorized (shs.)	Outstanding (shs.)[1]
Trust Unit	unlimited	20,528,502

[1] At July 19, 2023

Normal Course Issuer Bid - The company plans to make normal course purchases of up to 1,026,425 trust units representing 5% of the total outstanding. The bid commenced on Aug. 1, 2023, and expires on July 31, 2024.
Major Shareholder - Widely held at Apr. 6, 2023.

Price Range - NET.UN/TSX-VEN

Year	Volume	High	Low	Close
2022	2,234,878	$8.47	$6.01	$6.20
2021	2,643,472	$8.49	$6.49	$8.04
2020	2,451,681	$7.50	$4.45	$6.70
2019	477,527	$7.30	$5.10	$6.60
2018	443,614	$6.20	$4.50	$5.70

Consolidation: 1-for-10 cons. in Nov. 2020
Recent Close: $4.98
Capital Stock Changes - During 2022, trust units were issued as follows: 299,781 on exercise of warrants and 18,350 for services.

Dividends

NET.UN unit Ra $0.345 pa M est. Jan. 31, 2023
Prev. Rate: $0.34 est. Jan. 31, 2022
Prev. Rate: $0.30 est. Jan. 29, 2021
Prev. Rate: $0.02555 est. Jan. 31, 2020

Wholly Owned Subsidiaries

Fronsac Capital Inc.
- 100% int. in **Investissements Immobiliers Prodige Inc.**

Subsidiaries

75% int. in **Fronsac Odacite Trois-Pistoles LP**
82.5% int. in **Odacité Mercier LP**, Qué.
95% int. in **Odacité Ste-Sophie LP**, Qué.

Investments

50% int. in **Antigonish Beech Hill LP**
50% int. in **CDM-1 LP**, Qué.
50% int. in **FBO Mix Properties LP**, Qué.
40% int. in **FBO Simple LP**, Qué.
50% int. in **Fronsac Odacité Jules-Vernes LP**, Qué.
50% int. in **Fronsac Odacité Lachute LP**, Qué.
40% int. in **GMB Frondacité LP**, Qué.
50% int. in **Immeubles Frondacité LP**, Qué.
50% int. in **Nodasac Valleyfield LP**, Qué.
50% int. in **Somerled Pictou LP**, N.S.
50% int. in **Somerled Wilkinson LP**, Qué.

Financial Statistics

Periods ended:	12m Dec. 31/22^A		12m Dec. 31/21^A
	$000s	%Chg	$000s
Total revenue	**24,729**	**+30**	**18,954**
Rental operating expense	6,357		4,632
Salaries & benefits	521		434
General & admin. expense	370		350
Stock-based compensation	603		309
Operating expense	**7,851**	**+37**	**5,724**
Operating income	**16,878**	**+28**	**13,230**
Investment income	(901)		2,967
Finance income	320		244
Finance costs, gross	6,054		4,591
Write-downs/write-offs	nil		(28)
Pre-tax income	**(6,497)**	**n.a.**	**25,236**
Income taxes	(3)		145
Net income	**(6,494)**	**n.a.**	**25,090**
Cash & equivalent	205		607
Accounts receivable	1,992		1,173
Current assets	8,317		1,936
Long-term investments	15,671		18,843
Income-producing props	275,425		252,948
Property interests, net	275,425		252,948
Total assets	**303,060**	**+9**	**278,166**
Accts. pay. & accr. liabs	1,942		934
Current liabilities	38,923		17,230
Long-term debt, gross	160,878		144,707
Long-term debt, net	144,361		130,026
Shareholders' equity	118,688		129,814
Cash from oper. activs	**11,331**	**+22**	**9,263**
Cash from fin. activs	29,832		42,679
Cash from invest. activs	(41,565)		(55,794)
Net cash position	**205**	**-66**	**607**
Increase in property	(44,297)		(53,731)
	$		$
Earnings per share*	(0.32)		1.35
Cash flow per share*	0.55		0.50
Funds from opers. per sh.*	0.64		0.58
Adj. funds from opers. per sh.*	0.59		0.54
Cash divd. per share*	0.34		0.30
Total divd. per share*	**0.34**		**0.30**
	shs		shs
No. of shs. o/s*	20,592,733		20,274,602
Avg. no. of shs. o/s*	20,514,719		18,575,569
	%		%
Net profit margin	(26.26)		132.37
Return on equity	(5.23)		22.81
Return on assets	(0.15)		12.16
No. of employees (FTEs)	4		3

* Trust unit
^A Reported in accordance with IFRS

Latest Results

Periods ended:	3m Mar. 31/23^A		3m Mar. 31/22^A
	$000s	%Chg	$000s
Total revenue	6,416	+18	5,432
Net income	4,830	+226	1,481
	$		$
Earnings per share*	0.23		0.07

* Trust unit
^A Reported in accordance with IFRS

Historical Summary
(as originally stated)

Fiscal Year	Total Rev.	Net Inc. Bef. Disc.	EPS*
	$000s	$000s	$
2022^A	24,729	(6,494)	(0.32)
2021^A	18,954	25,090	1.35
2020^A	12,977	9,621	0.66
2019^A	9,388	4,081	0.37
2018^A	6,275	(1,889)	(0.21)

* Trust unit
^A Reported in accordance with IFRS
Note: Adjusted throughout for 1-for-10 cons. in Nov. 2020

C.41 Canadian Nexus Team Ventures Corp.

Symbol - TEAM **Exchange** - CSE **CUSIP** - 13640F
Head Office - 830-1100 Melville St, Vancouver, BC, V6B 6H5 **Telephone** - (604) 813-9995 **Fax** - (604) 662-7950
Email - info@canadiannexus.com
Investor Relations - Scott A. Young (604) 960-1878
Auditors - MNP LLP C.A., Vancouver, B.C.
Lawyers - Morton Law, LLP, Vancouver, B.C.
Transfer Agents - TSX Trust Company, Toronto, Ont.
Profile - (B.C. 1980) Invests in early to mid-stage companies primarily in food, health, wellness and technology industries. Also has mineral interests in Quebec.

Primary investments include **Gringo Restaurants Inc.** (100%-owned), which operates a full-service restaurant in Vancouver, B.C.; **AgriFORCE Growing Systems Ltd.** (formerly **Canivate Growing Systems Ltd.**), an agriculture technology company which has developed a way of growing high-value cannabis crop through facility design and growing system; **iComply Investor Services Inc.**, which offers intelligent compliance management solutions via its iComplyKYC and PREFACTO™ solutions that collects, maintains and analyzes KYC data for digital due diligence; and **OctoAI Technologies Corp.**, which offers artificial intelligence-based solutions for data extraction, servicing the real-estate and insurance markets.

Other investments include **MineHub Technologies Inc.**, **Adven Inc.**, **Magnum Gold Corp.**, **Deep Cove Productions Ltd.**, **Cleantek Industries Inc.**, **Aurista Exploration Corp.**, and **Polar Bear Universal Media Inc.** At Mar. 31, 2023, fair value of investments totaled $2,481,290.

In Quebec, holds option to acquire Urban Barry gold prospect, 1,126 hectares, requiring payment of $1,300,000 and exploration expenditures of $2,100,000 over three years to March 2024; and option to acquire nearby Abitibi prospect, 3,101 hectares, including Lac Herbert and Lac Lapointe deposits.

During the first quarter of 2023, the company sold 200,000 shares of **GameOn Entertainment Technologies Inc.** it held for proceeds of $8,890.

Predecessor Detail - Name changed from Brand X Lifestyle Corp., May 21, 2021.
Directors - Scott A. Young, CEO, Vancouver, B.C.; Jonathan G. E. Jackson, West Vancouver, B.C.; John W. Seaman, Thunder Bay, Ont.
Other Exec. Officers - Alexander B. (Alex) Helmel, CFO

Capital Stock

	Authorized (shs.)	Outstanding (shs.)[1]
Common	unlimited	8,976,697

[1] At June 22, 2023

Major Shareholder - Arni T. Johannson held 30% interest at Mar. 24, 2023.

Price Range - TEAM/CSE

Year	Volume	High	Low	Close
2022	660,599	$1.02	$0.18	$0.28
2021	1,426,677	$1.30	$0.28	$0.49
2020	2,557,533	$2.31	$0.42	$1.19
2019	726,220	$1.26	$0.35	$0.56
2018	1,662,405	$10.50	$0.21	$0.70

Consolidation: 1-for-7 cons. in June 2023; 1-for-2 cons. in Mar. 2020
Recent Close: $0.15
Capital Stock Changes - On June 22, 2023, common shares were consolidated on 1-for-7 basis.

During 2022, 6,407,000 common shares were issued by private placement and 50,000 common shares were repurchased under a Normal Course Issuer Bid.

Wholly Owned Subsidiaries

CNV Mining Holdings Corp., Canada.
- 100% int. in **Aurista Exploration Corp.**, Canada.

Canadian Copper & Gold Corp. Inactive.
Polar Bear Universal Media Corp.
Wooden Table Hospitality Corp., Canada.
- 100% int. in **Gringo Restaurants Inc.**, Canada.

Investments

Adven Inc.
AgriFORCE Growing Systems Ltd., Vancouver, B.C. (see separate coverage)
Cleantek Industries Inc., Calgary, Alta. (see separate coverage)
Deep Cove Productions Ltd.
Icomply Investor Services Inc., Vancouver, B.C.
MineHub Technologies Inc., Vancouver, B.C. (see separate coverage)
OctoAI Technologies Corp.

Financial Statistics

Periods ended:	12m Dec. 31/22[A]		12m Dec. 31/21[o][A]
	$000s	%Chg	$000s
Realized invest. gain (loss)	(2,259)		(4,075)
Total revenue	**(2,231)**	**n.a.**	**(3,949)**
General & admin. expense	676		725
Stock-based compensation	18		50
Operating expense	**694**	**-10**	**775**
Operating income	**(2,925)**	**n.a.**	**(4,724)**
Deprec. & amort.	71		14
Finance costs, gross	1		3
Write-downs/write-offs	(838)		nil
Pre-tax income	**(3,932)**	**n.a.**	**(4,741)**
Net income	**(3,932)**	**n.a.**	**(4,741)**
Cash & equivalent	2,688		5,606
Accounts receivable	30		2
Current assets	3,021		5,898
Right-of-use assets	nil		101
Total assets	**3,341**	**-52**	**6,932**
Bank indebtedness	9		nil
Accts. pay. & accr. liabs	158		48
Current liabilities	168		84
Long-term lease liabilities	nil		75
Shareholders' equity	3,173		6,773
Cash from oper. activs	**(474)**	**n.a.**	**(850)**
Cash from fin. activs	363		892
Cash from invest. activs	(64)		(197)
Net cash position	**27**	**-87**	**201**
Capital expenditures	(1)		(97)
	$		$
Earnings per share*	(0.49)		(0.63)
Cash flow per share*	(0.06)		(0.11)
	shs		shs
No. of shs. o/s*	8,976,697		8,068,554
Avg. no. of shs. o/s*	8,468,156		7,486,861
	%		%
Net profit margin	n.m.		n.m.
Return on equity	(79.07)		(61.08)
Return on assets	(76.53)		(60.08)

* Common
[o] Restated
[A] Reported in accordance with IFRS

Latest Results

Periods ended:	3m Mar. 31/23[A]		3m Mar. 31/22[A]
	$000s	%Chg	$000s
Total revenue	(278)	n.a.	433
Net income	(397)	n.a.	181
	$		$
Earnings per share*	(0.07)		0.02

* Common
[A] Reported in accordance with IFRS

Historical Summary
(as originally stated)

Fiscal Year	Total Rev. $000s	Net Inc. Bef. Disc. $000s	EPS* $
2022[A]	(2,231)	(3,932)	(0.49)
2021[A]	(3,949)	(4,741)	(0.63)
2020[A]	3,056	2,485	0.49
2019[A]	nil	1,181	0.34
2018[A]	nil	(3,242)	(0.98)

* Common
[A] Reported in accordance with IFRS

Note: Adjusted throughout for 1-for-7 cons. in June 2023; 1-for-2 cons. in Mar. 2020

C.42 Canadian Oil Recovery & Remediation Enterprises Ltd.

Symbol - CVR.H **Exchange** - TSX-VEN (S) **CUSIP** - 136424
Head Office - 1007-141 Adelaide St W, Toronto, ON, M5H 3L5 **Telephone** - (416) 368-4027 **Fax** - (416) 368-4469
Email - rkoroll@corre.com
Investor Relations - Randy Koroll (416) 662-9455
Auditors - Richter LLP C.A., Toronto, Ont.
Transfer Agents - Computershare Trust Company of Canada Inc.
Profile - (Can. 2007) Provides oil waste management solutions to the petroleum industry including the upstream petroleum sector (oil production and drilling companies) and downstream petroleum sector (oil refinery, transportation and distribution companies).

Services offered include remediating oil-contaminated soil; treating sludge, oil based muds and drilling waste; oil recovery; industrial waste management; oil storage tank cleaning; oil and gas engineering; and project management.

The company holds exclusive licences for two distinct Advanced Recovery Equipment Systems (ARES) technologies, the two soil washing plants known as ARES I and II technologies. The ARES I operating plant in Kuwait has a capacity of up to 20 tons per hour with a focus on cleaning heavy oil-contaminated soil, treating sludge and recovering oil. The ARES II operating facility in Canada is designed to clean oil-contaminated soil and recover oil at a rate up to 10 tons per hour. Also offers a specialized adaptation of the ARES technology, which is based on the use of hydrocarbon-degrading bacteria (bioremediation) to clean oil-contaminated soil when the hydrocarbon level in the soil is typically 2% or lower and site logistics do not permit the use of operating equipment.

The company also provides environmental solutions through strategic operating partnerships. Strategic operating partners include **TG Engineering Inc.**, providing engineering for liquids handling, power and cogeneration, oil and water separation and processing, gas compression processing and treating, and oil and gas engineering and project management; and Kuwait-based **CANAR Trading and Contracting Company**, providing exclusive logistical, mobilization, procurement and labour support.

Common suspended from TSX-VEN, May 7, 2021.

Predecessor Detail - Name changed from C Level II International Holding Inc., June 30, 2008, following Qualifying Transaction reverse takeover acquisition of Canadian Oil Recovery & Remediation Enterprises Inc.; basis 1 new for 3 old shs.

Directors - John Lorenzo, chr., pres. & CEO, Toronto, Ont.; Anton Ayoub, Toronto, Ont.; Sohail Khan, Jeddah, Saudi Arabia; Raymond J. Stapell, Buffalo, N.Y.

Other Exec. Officers - Randy Koroll, CFO

Capital Stock

	Authorized (shs.)	Outstanding (shs.)[1]
Common	unlimited	169,665,746

[1] At Aug. 22, 2023

Major Shareholder - Al-Najah Advanced Technology Co. Ltd. held 25.05% interest, TUNOQ Investment Ltd. held 12.91% interest and Estate of Hassan Dahlawi held 12.29% interest at Feb. 24, 2021.

Price Range - CVR.H/TSX-VEN (S)

Year	Volume	High	Low	Close
2018	14,373,506	$0.05	$0.01	$0.01

Wholly Owned Subsidiaries

B.D.E. Properties Inc., Toronto, Ont.
CORRE Inc., United Arab Emirates.
Mentra Life Sciences Inc., Toronto, Ont.

C.43 Canadian Pacific Kansas City Limited*

Symbol - CP **Exchange** - TSX **CUSIP** - 13646K
Head Office - 7550 Ogden Dale Rd SE, Calgary, AB, T2C 4X9 **Telephone** - (403) 319-7000 **Toll-free** - (888) 333-6370 **Fax** - (403) 319-6770
Website - www.cpkcr.com/en-ca
Email - investor@cpkcr.com
Investor Relations - Chris De Bruyn (403) 319-3591
Auditors - Ernst & Young LLP C.A., Calgary, Alta.
Lawyers - Bennett Jones LLP, Calgary, Alta.
Transfer Agents - Computershare Trust Company, N.A., Canton, Mass.; Computershare Trust Company of Canada Inc., Calgary, Alta.
FP500 Revenue Ranking - 69
Employees - 12,754 at Dec. 31, 2022
Profile - (Can. 2001) Owns and operates a 20,000-mile transnational freight railway network that connects Canada, the United States and Mexico. The rail network transports bulk commodities, merchandise freight and intermodal traffic.

The network consists of 5,200 miles located in western Canada, 2,500 miles in eastern Canada, 4,500 miles in the U.S. Midwest, 600 miles in the U.S. Northeast and 7,100 miles in the U.S. Midwest and Southeast regions and Mexico.

Markets served consist of: **Grain**, which is centred in the Canadian Prairies (Saskatchewan, Manitoba and Alberta) and Minnesota, North Dakota and Iowa, transporting whole grains and processed products for export and domestic consumption; **Coal**, which moves primarily Canadian metallurgical coal originating from southeastern British Columbia for export use and U.S. thermal coal from mines in the Powder River Basin in Montana and Wyoming to power-generating facilities in the U.S. Midwest; **Potash**, which moves mainly from Saskatchewan to offshore markets through the ports of Vancouver, Portland and Thunder Bay, and to markets in the U.S.; **Fertilizers and Sulphur**, which transports dry and wet fertilizers and sulphur primarily produced from Alberta; **Forest Products**, which include pulp, paper, lumber and panel products shipped from key producing areas in British COlumbia, Ontario, Alberta, Quebec, New Brunswick and the U.S. Southeast and Northeast to destinations throughout North America and to export markets; **Energy, Chemicals and Plastics**, which include energy products such as liquefied petroleum gas, fuel oil, asphalt and gasoline from western Canada, biofuels from the U.S. Midwest, crude primarily from western Canada, chemicals from Alberta, eastern Canada, the U.S. Midwest and Gulf of Mexico and plastics primarily from Alberta, transported to various North American destinations and overseas; **Metals, Minerals and Consumer Products**, include aggregates, steel, food and consumer products and non-ferrous metals shipped across North America; **Automotive**, which consists of Canadian-produced vehicles shipped to the U.S. from production facilities in Ontario, U.S.-produced vehicles shipped cross-border into Canada as well as within the U.S., Mexican-produced vehicles shipped to Canada and the U.S., import vehicles transported through the Port of Vancouver to eastern and western Canada, as well as pre-owned vehicles, machinery and automotive parts; and **Intermodal**, which consists of domestic intermodal freight of primarily manufactured consumer products moving within North America, and international intermodal freight moving to and from ports and North American inland markets.

Operating Statistics (Excludes Kansas City Southern)

Year ended Dec. 31	2022	2021
GTM of freight (millions)[1]	269,134	271,921
RTM of freight (millions)[2]	148,228	149,686
Train miles, 000s	28,899	29,397
Freight rev. per RTM (¢)[2]	5.82	5.22
Freight rev. per carload ($)	3,101	2,857

[1] GTM - Gross ton miles.
[2] RTM - Revenue ton miles.

Carloads by Market1

Year ended Dec. 31	2022	2021
Grain	382,100	426,200
Coal	269,800	291,500
Potash	160,000	150,900
Fertilizers & sulphur	61,800	64,400
Forest products	73,100	73,600
Energy, chemicals & plastics	297,400	320,100
Metals, mins. & consumer	248,300	236,700
Automotive	104,400	109,200
Intermodal	1,185,200	1,062,900
	2,782,100	2,735,500

[1] Excludes results of Kansas City Southern.

On Apr. 14, 2023, the transfer of the shares of **Kansas City Southern** (KCS) from a voting trust to an affiliate of the company was completed. The company changed its name to **Canadian Pacific Kansas City Limited**. On Mar. 15, 2023, the company's acquisition of KCS, completed on Dec. 14, 2021, received approval by the U.S. Surface Transportation Board (STB).

Recent Merger and Acquisition Activity

Status: pending **Announced:** June 28, 2023
Canadian Pacific Kansas City Limited (CPKC) and CSX Corporation each agreed to acquire or operate portions of Meridian & Bigbee Railroad, L.L.C. (MNBR), a Genesee & Wyoming Inc. (G&W)-owned railway in Mississippi and Alabama, to establish a new freight corridor for shippers that connects Mexico, Texas and the U.S. Southeast. Terrms were not disclosed. CPKC would acquire and operate the segment of the MNBR between Meridian and Myrtlewood, Ala., and CSX would operate the lines currently leased by MNBR east of Myrtlewood. As a result, CPKC and CSX would establish a direct CPKC-CSX interchange at or near Myrtlewood, Ala. In exchange, G&W would acquire certain Canadian properties owned by CPKC and other rights.

Predecessor Detail - Name changed from Canadian Pacific Railway Limited, Apr. 14, 2023.

Directors - Isabelle Courville, chr., Rosemère, Qué.; Keith E. Creel, pres. & CEO, Wellington, Fla.; The Hon. John R. Baird, Toronto, Ont.; Gillian H. (Jill) Denham, Toronto, Ont.; Antonio Garza, Mexico City, D.F., Mexico; David Garza-Santos, Monterrey, N.L., Mexico; Edward R. Hamberger, Delray Beach, Fla.; Janet H. Kennedy, Naples, Fla.; Henry Maier, Tenn.; Matthew H. Paull, Wilmette, Ill.; Jane L. Peverett, West Vancouver, B.C.; Andrea Robertson, Calgary, Alta.; Gordon T. Trafton II, Naperville, Ill.

Other Exec. Officers - John K. Brooks, exec. v-p & chief mktg. officer; James Clements, exec. v-p, strategic planning & tech.; Jeffrey J. Ellis, exec. v-p, chief legal officer & corp. sec.; John Orr, exec. v-p & chief transformation officer; Mark A. Redd, exec. v-p & COO; Nadeem S. Velani, exec. v-p & CFO; Coby Bullard, sr. v-p, sales & mktg., mdse., energy, chemicals & plastics & transloads; Mike Foran, sr. v-p, network & capacity mgt.; Justin Meyer, sr. v-p, eng. & mech.; Tracy L. Miller, sr. v-p, opers., southern & eastern region; Laird J. Pitz, sr. v-p & chief risk officer; Greg Squires, sr. v-p, opers., western region; Jonathan Wahba, sr. v-p, sales & mktg., intermodal, automotive & bulk; Maeghan Albiston, v-p & chief HR officer; Pam Arpin, v-p & CIO; Tom Bourgonje, v-p, eng.; Ian Gray, v-p, finl. planning & acctg.; Joan Hardy, v-p, sales & mktg., grain & fertilizer; Jason M. Ross, v-p, opers., southern region; Nicholas C. Walker, v-p, opers., western region; Oscar A. Del Cueto, pres. & gen. mgr., CPKC de Mexico

Capital Stock

	Authorized (shs.)	Outstanding (shs.)[1]
First Preferred	unlimited	nil
Second Preferred	unlimited	nil
Common	unlimited	931,460,732

[1] At July 26, 2023

Options - At Dec. 31, 2022, options were outstanding to purchase 7,353,133 common shares at exercise prices ranging from $23.84 to $111.52 per share with a weighted average contractual life of 3.3 years.

Major Shareholder - Widely held at Apr. 24, 2023.

Price Range - CP/TSX

Year	Volume	High	Low	Close
2022	356,436,929	$111.43	$86.12	$100.95
2021	392,619,580	$100.00	$82.12	$90.98
2020	446,384,000	$89.40	$50.40	$88.31
2019	379,207,360	$67.58	$47.00	$66.21
2018	437,128,928	$58.31	$42.50	$48.45

Split: 5-for-1 split in May 2021
Recent Close: $106.87

Capital Stock Changes - During 2022, 800,000 common shares were issued on exercise of options.

Dividends

CP com Ra $0.76 pa Q est. Oct. 26, 2020††
5-for-1 split eff. May 14, 2021
Prev. Rate: $3.32 est. July 29, 2019
†† Currency Option

Long-Term Debt - Outstanding at Dec. 31, 2022:

4.45% notes due 2023[1]	$474,000,000
1.589% notes due 2023	1,000,000,000
5.41% sr. secured notes due 2024[1]	76,000,000
6.91% equip. notes due 2024	40,000,000
1.35% notes due 2024[1]	2,030,000,000
2.9% notes due 2025[1]	948,000,000
3.7% notes due 2026[1]	338,000,000
1.75% notes due 2026[1]	1,353,000,000
2.54% notes due 2028	1,200,000,000
4% notes due 2028[1]	677,000,000
3.15% notes due 2029	399,000,000
2.05% notes due 2030[1]	676,000,000
7.125% debs. due 2031[1]	474,000,000
2.45% notes due 2031[1]	1,896,000,000
5.75% debs. due 2033[1]	333,000,000
4.8% notes due 2035[1]	405,000,000
5.95% notes due 2037[1]	603,000,000
6.45% notes due 2039	400,000,000
3% notes due 2041[1]	1,348,000,000
5.75% notes due 2042[1]	334,000,000
4.8% notes due 2045[1]	743,000,000
3.05% notes due 2050	298,000,000
3.1% notes due 2051[1]	2,422,000,000
6.125% notes due 2115[1]	1,219,000,000
4% debenture stock[1]	41,000,000
4% debenture stock[2]	6,000,000
Finance lease obligs	38,000,000
Less: Unamortized fees	120,000,000
	19,651,000,000
Less: Current portion	1,510,000,000
	18,141,000,000

[1] Payable in U.S. dollars.
[2] Payable in British pounds.

Debenture stock was created by an Act of Parliament in 1889 and constitutes a first charge upon and over the whole of the undertaking, railways, works, rolling stock, plant, property and effects of the company (with certain exceptions).

Minimum long-term debt repayments, excluding finance leases, were reported as follows:

2023	$1,504,000,000
2024	2,118,000,000
2025	948,000,000
2026	1,693,000,000
2027	nil
Thereafter	13,520,000,000

Wholly Owned Subsidiaries

CP (US) Holding Corporation, Del.
CPFL S.à.r.l., Luxembourg.
CPFS AG, Switzerland.
Canadian Pacific Railway Company, Toronto, Ont.
Cygnus Canadian Holding Company Limited, Canada.
- 100% int. in **Cygnus Holding Corporation**, Del.
  - 100% int. in **Kansas City Southern**, Kansas City, Mo.

6061338 Canada Inc., Canada.
Soo Line Corporation, Minn.
- 100% int. in **Soo Line Railroad Company**, Minn.

3939804 Canada Inc., Canada.

Note: The preceding list includes only the major related companies in which interests are held.

Financial Statistics

Periods ended:	12m Dec. 31/22[A]		12m Dec. 31/21[A]
	$000s	%Chg	$000s
Operating revenue	**8,814,000**	**+10**	**7,995,000**
Salaries & benefits	1,570,000		1,570,000
Other operating expense	3,062,000		2,408,000
Operating expense	**4,632,000**	**+16**	**3,978,000**
Operating income	**4,182,000**	**+4**	**4,017,000**
Deprec., depl. & amort	853,000		811,000
Finance income	n.a.		6,000
Finance costs, gross	n.a.		446,000
Finance costs, net	652,000		n.a.
Investment income	1,074,000		(141,000)
Pre-tax income	**4,145,000**	**+15**	**3,620,000**
Income taxes	628,000		768,000
Net income	**3,517,000**	**+23**	**2,852,000**
Cash & equivalent	451,000		82,000
Inventories	284,000		235,000
Accounts receivable	1,016,000		819,000
Current assets	1,889,000		1,352,000
Long-term investments	45,314,000		42,518,000
Fixed assets, net	22,385,000		21,200,000
Right-of-use assets	267,000		287,000
Intangibles, net	386,000		371,000
Total assets	**73,495,000**	**+8**	**68,177,000**
Accts. pay. & accr. liabs	1,244,000		1,164,000
Current liabilities	3,213,000		3,159,000
Long-term debt, gross	19,651,000		20,127,000
Long-term debt, net	18,141,000		18,577,000
Long-term lease liabilities	202,000		224,000
Shareholders' equity	38,886,000		33,829,000
Cash from oper. activs	**4,142,000**	**+12**	**3,688,000**
Cash from fin. activs	(2,297,000)		9,936,000
Cash from invest. activs	(1,496,000)		(13,730,000)
Net cash position	**451,000**	**+450**	**82,000**
Capital expenditures	(1,557,000)		(1,532,000)
Capital disposals	58,000		96,000
Unfunded pension liability	175,000		263,000
Pension fund surplus	3,101,000		2,317,000
	$		$
Earnings per share*	3.78		4.20
Cash flow per share*	4.45		5.43
Cash divd. per share*	0.76		0.76
	shs		shs
No. of shs. o/s*	930,500,000		929,700,000
Avg. no. of shs. o/s*	930,000,000		679,700,000
	%		%
Net profit margin	39.90		35.67
Return on equity	9.67		13.86
Return on assets	4.96		6.98
Foreign sales percent	27		25
No. of employees (FTEs)	12,754		11,834

* Common
[A] Reported in accordance with U.S. GAAP

Latest Results

Periods ended:	6m June 30/23[A]		6m June 30/22[A]
	$000s	%Chg	$000s
Operating revenue	5,440,000	+35	4,040,000
Net income	2,125,000	+57	1,355,000
Net inc. for equity hldrs	2,124,000	+57	1,355,000
Net inc. for non-cont. int	1,000		nil
	$		$
Earnings per share*	2.28		1.46

* Common
[A] Reported in accordance with U.S. GAAP

Historical Summary
(as originally stated)

Fiscal Year	Oper. Rev.	Net Inc. Bef. Disc.	EPS*
	$000s	$000s	$
2022[A]	8,814,000	3,517,000	3.78
2021[A]	7,995,000	2,852,000	4.20
2020[A]	7,710,000	2,444,000	3.61
2019[A]	7,792,000	2,440,000	3.52
2018[A]	7,316,000	1,951,000	2.73

* Common
[A] Reported in accordance with U.S. GAAP
Note: Adjusted throughout for 5-for-1 split in May 2021

C.44 Canadian Solar Inc.

Symbol - CSIQ **Exchange** - NASDAQ **CUSIP** - 136635
Head Office - 545 Speedvale Ave W, Guelph, ON, N1K 1E6 **Telephone** - (519) 837-1881 **Fax** - (519) 837-2550
Website - www.canadiansolar.com
Email - investor@canadiansolar.com
Investor Relations - Dr. Huifeng Chang (519) 837-1881
Auditors - Deloitte Touche Tohmatsu C.P.A., Shanghai, Shanghai People's Republic of China
Transfer Agents - Computershare Shareowner Services LLC, Jersey City, N.J.
FP500 Revenue Ranking - 62
Employees - 18,423 at Dec. 31, 2022
Profile - (Ont. 2022; orig. Ont., 2001) Designs, develops, manufactures and sells solar ingots, wafers, cells, modules, and other solar power and battery storage products primarily to distributors, system integrators, project developers, installers, engineering, procurement and construction (EPC) services companies worldwide including the U.S., Canada, Germany, Spain, the Netherlands, South Africa, the People's Republic of China (PRC), Japan, India, Thailand, Australia, Brazil and Mexico.

Operations are organized into two business segments: CSI Solar; and Global Energy.

CSI Solar

The CSI Solar segment involves the design, development, manufacturing and sale of solar power and battery storage products, including solar modules, solar system kits, battery storage solutions, and other materials, components and services including EPC.

Standard solar modules are arrays of interconnected solar cells in weatherproof encapsulation. The company produces standard solar modules, ranging from 3 W to over 665 W in power and using mono-crystalline or multi-crystalline cells in several different design patterns, including shingled cells.

EPC Services are turn-key solution for utility scale photovoltaic projects, including system design, procurement, installation, system testing and commissioning. EPC services are also provided in PRC to ground-mounted projects, as well as to large-scale distributed system projects of industrial and commercial customers.

Solar system kit is a ready-to-install package consisting of solar modules produced by the company and components, such as inverters, racking system and other accessories, supplied by third parties.

Battery storage solutions offer integrated battery, power conversion systems and energy management system, as well as comprehensive services and capabilities for project installations, including consulting and project EPC management.

Global Energy

Global Energy develops, sells and/or operates and maintains solar and battery storage projects primarily in the U.S., Brazil, Chile, the U.K., the European Union, Japan, PRC and Australia. Global Energy segment develops both stand-alone solar and stand-alone battery storage projects, as well as hybrid solar plus storage projects. The segment's monetization strategies vary between develop-to-sell, build-to-sell and build-to-own, depending on business strategies and market conditions. Global Energy also has a battery storage business which focuses on project development, including sourcing land, interconnection, structuring power purchase agreements and other permits and requirements for battery storage projects, as opposed to CSI Solar's battery storage business, which focuses on the system integration business that delivers turnkey battery storage technology solutions.

At Jan. 31, 2022, Global Energy's solar project development pipeline totaled 24.4 GWp, including 1.6 GWp under construction, 4.2 GWp of backlog and 18.6 GWp of earlier stage pipeline; its portfolio of solar power plants in operation totaled 445 MWp; and its battery storage project development backlog and pipeline totaled 27,142 MWp, including 2,681 MWp under construction, 841 MWp of backlog and 23,620 MWp of pipeline.

At Dec. 31, 2021, the company had 23.9 GW of total annual solar module manufacturing capacity of which about 19.7 GW was located in PRC, 4.2 GW South East Asia, and the rest in other regions; 13.9 GW of total annual solar cell manufacturing capacity of which about 4.2 GW was located in Southeast Asia and the rest in PRC; 11.5 GW of total annual wafer manufacturing capacity in PRC; and 5.4 GW of total annual ingot manufacturing capacity in PRC.

In July 2022, the company continued into Ontario from British Columbia.

Directors - Dr. Shawn (Xiaohua) Qu, chr., pres. & CEO, Suzhou, Jiangsu, People's Republic of China; Dr. Huifeng Chang, sr. v-p & CFO, Princeton, N.J.; Yan Zhuang, pres., CSI Solar Co., Ltd., Suzhou, Jiangsu, People's Republic of China; Leslie (Li Hsien) Chang, Hong Kong, Hong Kong, People's Republic of China; Dr. Harry E. Ruda, Toronto, Ont.; Lauren C. Templeton, Lookout Mountain, Tenn.; Arthur (Lap Tat) Wong, Beijing, Beijing, People's Republic of China; Luen Cheung (Andrew) Wong, Hong Kong, Hong Kong, People's Republic of China

Other Exec. Officers - Hanbing Zhang, chief sustainability officer; Dr. Guoqiang Xing, sr. v-p & chief tech. officer; Jianyi Zhang, sr. v-p, chief compliance officer & gen. counsel; Ismael Guerrero Arias, v-p & pres., Energy business

Capital Stock

	Authorized (shs.)	Outstanding (shs.)[1]
Common	unlimited	64,635,716[2]

[1] At Jan. 31, 2023
[2] Net of treasury shares.

Major Shareholder - Dr. Shawn (Xiaohua) Qu held 21.3% interest at Jan. 31, 2023.

Price Range - CSIQ/NASDAQ

Year	Volume	High	Low	Close
2022	92,532,727	US$47.69	US$22.15	US$30.90
2021	137,359,591	US$67.33	US$28.80	US$31.29
2020	114,087,811	US$56.40	US$12.00	US$51.24
2019	59,462,459	US$25.87	US$14.00	US$22.10
2018	54,352,463	US$17.97	US$11.38	US$14.34

Wholly Owned Subsidiaries

CSI Energy Project Technology (SuZhou) Co., Ltd., Argentina.

Canadian Solar Brasil I Fundo De Investimento Em Participacoes, Brazil.
Canadian Solar Construction (Australia) Pty Ltd., Australia.
Canadian Solar Energy Holding Singapore 1 Pte. Ltd., Singapore.
Canadian Solar Energy Singapore Pte. Ltd., Singapore.
Canadian Solar Investment Management Pty Ltd., Australia.
Canadian Solar Netherlands Cooperative U.A., Netherlands.
Canadian Solar New Energy Holding Company Limited, Hong Kong, People's Republic of China.
Canadian Solar O and M (Ontario) Inc., Ont.
Canadian Solar Project KK, Japan.
Canadian Solar Solutions Inc., Ont.
Canadian Solar UK Projects Ltd., United Kingdom.
FieldFare Argentina S.R.L., Australia.
Recurrent Energy, LLC, San Francisco, Calif.

Subsidiaries

79.59% int. in **CSI Solar Co., Ltd.**, Suzhou, Jiangsu, People's Republic of China.
- 100% int. in **CSI Cells Co., Ltd.**, Suzhou, Jiangsu, People's Republic of China.
- 100% int. in **CSI Electricity Sales (JiangSu) Co., Ltd.**, People's Republic of China.
- 90% int. in **CSI New Energy Development (Suzhou) Co., Ltd.**, People's Republic of China.
- 100% int. in **CSI New Energy Holding Co., Ltd.**, People's Republic of China.
- 100% int. in **CSI New Energy Technology (Zhejiang) Co., Ltd.**, People's Republic of China.
- 100% int. in **CSI Solar Manufacturing (Funing) Co., Ltd.**, People's Republic of China.
- **CSI Cells (Yancheng) Co., Ltd.**, People's Republic of China.
- 100% int. in **Canadian Solar Brazil Commerce, Import and Export of Solar Panels Ltd.**, Brazil.
- 100% int. in **Canadian Solar EMEA GmbH**, Germany.
- 100% int. in **Canadian Solar International Limited**, Hong Kong, Hong Kong, People's Republic of China.
- 100% int. in **Canadian Solar Japan KK**, Japan.
- 100% int. in **Canadian Solar Manufacturing (Changshu) Inc.**, Suzhou, Jiangsu, People's Republic of China.
  - **CSI Modules (DaFeng) Co., Ltd.**, People's Republic of China.
- 100% int. in **Canadian Solar Manufacturing (Luoyang) Inc.**, Henan, People's Republic of China.
- 100% int. in **Canadian Solar Manufacturing (Thailand) Co., Ltd.**, Thailand.
- 100% int. in **Canadian Solar Manufacturing Vietnam Co., Ltd.**, Vietnam.
- 100% int. in **Canadian Solar Photovoltaic Technology (Luoyang) Co., Ltd.**, People's Republic of China.
- 100% int. in **Canadian Solar SSES (UK) Ltd.**, United Kingdom.
- 100% int. in **Canadian Solar SSES (US) Ltd.**, United States.
- 100% int. in **Canadian Solar South East Asia Pte., Ltd.**, Singapore.
- 100% int. in **Canadian Solar Sunenergy (Baotou) Co., Ltd.**, People's Republic of China.
- 100% int. in **Canadian Solar Sunenergy (Jiaxing) Co. Ltd.**, People's Republic of China.
- 100% int. in **Canadian Solar (USA) Inc**, United States.
- 100% int. in **Changshu Tegu New Materials Technology Co., Ltd.**, People's Republic of China.
- 100% int. in **Changshu Tlian Co., Ltd.**, People's Republic of China.
- 100% int. in **Suzhou Sanysolar Materials Technology Co., Ltd.**, Suzhou, Jiangsu, People's Republic of China.

Note: The preceding list includes only the major related companies in which interests are held.

Financial Statistics

Periods ended:	12m Dec. 31/22‡A		12m Dec. 31/21A
	US$000s	%Chg	US$000s
Operating revenue	**7,468,610**	**+42**	**5,277,169**
Cost of sales	...		4,350,705
Research & devel. expense	...		58,407
General & admin expense	...		397,054
Operating expense	**...**	**n.a.**	**4,806,166**
Operating income	**...**	**n.a.**	**471,003**
Deprec., depl. & amort.	...		282,769
Finance income	...		11,051
Finance costs, gross	74,266		58,153
Investment income	...		18,634
Write-downs/write-offs	...		(44,921)
Pre-tax income	**...**	**n.a.**	**138,464**
Income taxes	...		35,844
After-tax income (expense)	...		7,256
Net income	**298,555**	**+172**	**109,876**
Net inc. for equity hldrs	**239,968**	**+152**	**95,248**
Net inc. for non-cont. int	**58,587**	**+301**	**14,628**
Cash & equivalent	...		869,831
Inventories	...		1,192,374
Accounts receivable	...		688,616
Current assets	5,644,657		4,771,827
Long-term investments	...		98,919
Fixed assets, net	...		1,510,140
Right-of-use assets	...		35,286
Intangibles, net	...		18,992
Total assets	**9,037,128**	**+22**	**7,388,342**
Bank indebtedness	...		1,973,513
Accts. pay. & accr. liabs	...		502,995
Current liabilities	5,258,768		4,038,148
Long-term debt, gross	1,372,904		927,195
Long-term debt, net	1,039,383		748,309
Long-term lease liabilities	...		23,215
Shareholders' equity	1,941,639		1,801,083
Non-controlling interest	365,055		325,355
Cash from oper. activs	**916,631**	**n.a.**	**(408,254)**
Cash from fin. activs	428,639		614,071
Cash from invest. activs	(630,488)		(429,570)
Net cash position	**1,969,503**	**+37**	**1,434,282**
Capital expenditures	...		(429,500)
Capital disposals	...		36,952
	US$		US$
Earnings per share*	3.73		1.55
Cash flow per share*	14.25		(6.63)
	shs		shs
No. of shs. o/s*	64,506,055		64,022,678
Avg. no. of shs. o/s*	64,324,558		61,614,391
	%		%
Net profit margin	4.00		2.08
Return on equity	12.82		5.65
Return on assets	n.m.		2.20
Foreign sales percent	99		99
No. of employees (FTEs)	18,423		13,535

* Common
‡ Preliminary
A Reported in accordance with U.S. GAAP

Historical Summary
(as originally stated)

Fiscal Year	Oper. Rev. US$000s	Net Inc. Bef. Disc. US$000s	EPS* US$
2022‡A	7,468,610	298,555	3.73
2021A	5,277,169	109,876	1.55
2020A	3,476,495	147,246	2.46
2019A	3,200,583	166,555	2.88
2018A	3,744,512	242,431	4.02

* Common
‡ Preliminary
A Reported in accordance with U.S. GAAP

C.45 Canadian Tire Corporation, Limited*

Symbol - CTC.A **Exchange** - TSX **CUSIP** - 136681
Head Office - 2180 Yonge St, PO Box 770 Stn K, Toronto, ON, M4P 2V8 **Telephone** - (416) 480-3000 **Toll-free** - (800) 387-8803 **Fax** - (416) 480-3500
Website - www.corp.canadiantire.ca
Email - karen.keyes@cantire.com
Investor Relations - Karen Keyes (647) 518-4461
Auditors - Deloitte LLP C.A., Toronto, Ont.
Transfer Agents - Computershare Trust Company of Canada Inc., Toronto, Ont.
FP500 Revenue Ranking - 31
Employees - 13,802 at Dec. 31, 2022
Profile - (Ont. 1927) Offers a range of retail goods and services, including general merchandise, apparel, sporting goods, petroleum, financial services including a bank, and real estate operations.

Operations are organized into three segments: Retail; Financial Services; and CT Real Estate Investment Trust (CT REIT).

Retail

This business is conducted primarily under the banners Canadian Tire, PartSource, Pro Hockey Life, Party City, Canadian Tire Gas+, the various banners of SportChek, Mark's and Helly Hansen.

Canadian Tire Retail - The retail selling space of Canadian Tire stores ranges from 3,200 sq. ft. to 136,000 sq. ft., totaling 22,700,000 sq. ft. across 504 stores throughout Canada. Product lines include more than 197,000 national and owned brand products in the automotive, fixing, living, playing and seasonal and gardening product divisions. Owned brands carried at stores include Canvas, For Living, Motomaster, Mastercraft, Noma and Paderno. Majority of the stores also provide various automotive services, such as oil changes, tire installations, brake and engine repairs and roadside assistance. The company also offers online shopping through www.canadiantire.ca. and its mobile application. Retail stores are operated by third-party associate dealers, who own the fixtures, equipment and inventory of the stores they operate. The company supports Canadian Tire associate dealers with category business management, marketing, product curation, distribution, administrative, financial and information technology services.

Operations also include PartSource, a chain of 80 specialty automotive parts stores which provide unique automotive parts and products and cater to serious "do-it-yourselfers" and professional installers. It also offers a broad selection of automotive parts and maintenance accessories to Canadian Tire stores and other retailers and commercial customers. The company also operates Pro Hockey Life, a specialty retailer selling high-end hockey products across 16 retail locations and online; and Party City, a provider of party supplies through 65 retail stores and online.

Petroleum - Operates under the Canadian Tire and Gas+ banners, with a network of 284 gas bars and associated convenience stores, of which 153 are located adjacent to Canadian Tire stores. Also operates 20 gas bars and associated convenience stores located at ONroute rest stops on major Ontario highways (Highway 401 and Highway 400). Select gas bars, ONroute locations and/or Canadian Tire stores include 124 electric vehicle (EV) charging stations. All of the petroleum sites are operated by independent operators.

SportChek - Retails an extensive range of sporting equipment and athletic, outdoor, leisure and recreational apparel, footwear and accessories across Canada. Retail network consists of 212 corporate stores operating under the SportChek (193) and Atmosphere (19) banners, and 163 franchise stores under the banners Sports Experts (96), Atmosphere (44), Hockey Experts (10) and Sports Rousseau/L'Entrepôt du Hockey (13). Also provides online shopping through websites including www.sportchek.ca, www.sportsexperts.ca and www.atmosphere.ca. There are also a number of third-party operated stores that have "buying member" status in SportChek's franchise program with access to products for their businesses which typically undertake their own merchandising, purchasing, advertising, transportation and general administration. Owned brands carried at SportChek banners include Diamondback, Forward With Design (FWD), Ripzone, Sherwood and Woods.

Mark's - Operates a chain of 348 corporate and 32 franchise stores across Canada under the banners Mark's and L'Equipeur (in Quebec), offering primarily casual and industrial apparel and footwear. Also offers online retailing through www.marks.com and www.lequipeur.com. Private labels include Denver Hayes, Dakota WorkPro and WindRiver. Mark's also conducts a business-to-business operation under the name Mark's Commercial which sells footwear, apparel and personal protective equipment, with a focus on employee safety and workwear needs.

Helly Hansen - Designs and manufactures professional grade outdoor apparel within core categories of sailing, skiing, mountain, urban, base-layer, workwear, lifestyle and adventure under the Helly Hansen and Musto brands. Products are sold through wholesale and retail channels across more than 40 countries worldwide, with core markets in Europe, Canada and the U.S.

Financial Services

Holds 80% interest (**The Bank of Nova Scotia** 20%) in **CTFS Holdings Limited** and its subsidiaries, including **Canadian Tire Bank** (CTB) and **CTFS Bermuda Ltd.** CTB markets and issues a range of Triangle-branded credit cards, including the Triangle Mastercard®, Triangle World Elite Mastercard®, Gas Advantage Mastercard® and Cash Advantage Mastercard®. CTB also offers in-store financing, insurance products, and retail and broker deposits including high-interest savings accounts, tax-free savings accounts and guaranteed investment certificates. CTFS Bermuda reinsures the creditor insurance that is marketed by CTB as well as a closed block of warranty business.

CT REIT

Subsidiary **CT Real Estate Investment Trust** (CT REIT) owns, develops and leases income-producing commercial properties located across Canada. At Dec. 31, 2022, CT REIT held a portfolio of 373 properties, totaling 30,100,000 sq. ft. of gross leasable area, consisting of 365 retail properties, four industrial properties, a mixed-use commercial property and three development properties.

On May 3, 2023, the company announced a new partnership with **Suncor Energy Inc.**'s Petro-Canada business. The partnership includes a partnership between the company's Triangle Rewards loyalty program, with more than 11,000,000 active members, and Suncor's Petro-Points loyalty program, with more than 3,000,000 active members; the rebranding of more than 200 Canadian Tire Gas+ retail fuel sites to Petro-Canada sites; and Suncor becoming the primary fuel provider to the company's retail fuel network over time, eventually supplying more than 1 billion litres of fuel to the company's retail fuel station network annually. Each company would retain full ownership and control of its respective loyalty program.

During the second quarter of fiscal 2022, the company exited its Helly Hansen operations in Russia which had 41 retail stores, an e-commerce site and more than 300 employees.

Directors - J. Michael Owens, chr., Toronto, Ont.; Gregory H. (Greg) Hicks, pres. & CEO, Markham, Ont.; Dr. Eric T. Anderson, Chicago, Ill.; Dr. Martha G. Billes, Calgary, Alta.; Owen G. Billes, St. Catharines, Ont.; Lyne Castonguay, Fort Lauderdale, Fla.; David C. Court, Toronto, Ont.; Cathryn E. (Cathy) Cranston, Toronto, Ont.; Steve Frazier, Mercer Island, Wash.; Norman Jaskolka, Montréal, Qué.; Sylvain Leroux, Montréal, Qué.; Donald A. Murray, Red Deer, Alta.; Nadir Patel, Ottawa, Ont.; Christine (Chris) Rupp, New Albany, Ohio; Sowmyanarayan Sampath, Short Hills, N.J.; Cynthia M. Trudell, Bonita Springs, Fla.

Other Exec. Officers - Paul Draffin, chief supply chain officer; Rex W. Lee, chief IT officer; Susan M. O'Brien, chief brand & cust. officer; James R. (Jim) Christie, exec. v-p, strategic advisor & gen. counsel; Gregory C. (Greg) Craig, exec. v-p & CFO; John E. Pershing, exec. v-p & chief HR officer; Stephen Brinkley, pres., SportChek; Peter J. (PJ) Czank, pres., Mark's Work Wearhouse Ltd.; Thomas J. (TJ) Flood, pres., Canadian Tire retail; Aayaz Pira, pres., Canadian Tire Financial Services

Capital Stock

	Authorized (shs.)	Outstanding (shs.)[1]
Class A Non-vtg.	100,000,000	53,306,998
Common	3,423,366	3,423,366

[1] At Apr. 1, 2023

Class A Non-Voting - Entitled to receive cumulative preferential dividends at the rate of 1¢ per share per annum. After payment of the cumulative preferential dividends of 1¢ per share per annum, entitled to further dividends declared and paid in each year in equal amounts per share on all class A non-voting shares and common shares without preference or distinction or priority of one share over another. Holders of class A non-voting shares are entitled to receive notice of and to attend all meetings of the shareholders. Holders, voting separately as a class, are entitled to elect the greater of three directors or one-fifth of the total number of directors. Should an offer to purchase common shares be made to all or substantially all of the holders of common shares (other than an offer to purchase both class A non-voting shares and common shares at the same price and on the same terms and conditions) and should a majority of the outstanding common shares be tendered and taken up pursuant to such offer, the class A non-voting shares shall be entitled to one vote per share. Non-voting.

Common - Entitled to further dividends declared and paid in each year in equal amounts per share on all class A non-voting shares and common shares after payment of non-cumulative dividend at the rate of 1¢ per share per annum. Convertible at any time into class A non-voting shares on a share-for-share basis. Common shares may not be created in excess of the shares currently authorized without the approval of the class A non-voting shareholders. One vote per share.

Options - At Dec. 31, 2022, options were outstanding to purchase 1,293,009 class A non-voting shares at prices ranging from $80.49 to $187.25 per share with a weighted average remaining contractual life of 4.22 years.

Normal Course Issuer Bid - The company plans to make normal course purchases of up to 5,100,000 class A non-voting shares representing 10% of the public float. The bid commenced on Mar. 2, 2023, and expires on Mar. 1, 2024.

Major Shareholder - Dr. Martha G. Billes held 40.9% interest, C.T.C. Dealer Holdings Limited held 20.6% interest, Owen G. Billes held 20.5% interest and Canadian Tire Corporation, Limited's Deferred Profit Sharing Plan held 12.2% interest at Mar. 16, 2023.

Price Range - CTC.A/TSX

Year	Volume	High	Low	Close
2022	58,201,231	$196.75	$139.24	$141.50
2021	50,632,669	$213.85	$159.44	$181.44
2020	100,684,265	$170.39	$67.15	$167.33
2019	60,810,638	$157.36	$131.31	$139.75
2018	54,777,652	$183.93	$137.10	$142.74

Recent Close: $152.63

Capital Stock Changes - During fiscal 2022, 121,009 class A non-voting shares were issued under the dividend reinvestment plan and 2,567,769 class A non-voting shares were repurchased under a Normal Course Issuer Bid.

Dividends

CTC com Ra $6.90 pa Q est. Mar. 1, 2023**
Prev. Rate: $6.50 est. Sept. 1, 2022
Prev. Rate: $5.20 est. Mar. 1, 2022
Prev. Rate: $4.70 est. Mar. 1, 2021
Prev. Rate: $4.55 est. Mar. 1, 2020
CTC.A cl A N.V. Ra $6.90 pa Q est. Mar. 1, 2023**
Prev. Rate: $6.50 est. Sept. 1, 2022
Prev. Rate: $5.20 est. Mar. 1, 2022
Prev. Rate: $4.70 est. Mar. 1, 2021
Prev. Rate: $4.55 est. Mar. 1, 2020
** Reinvestment Option

Long-Term Debt - Outstanding at Dec. 31, 2022:

Sr. notes[1]:	
Ser.2018-1, 3.138% due 2023	$545,600,000
Ser.2019-1, 2.28% due 2024	522,800,000
Ser.2020-1, 1.388% due 2025	447,600,000
Ser.2022-1, 4.958% due 2027	418,600,000
Subord. notes[1]:	
Ser.2018-1, 4.138% due 2023	38,000,000
Ser.2019-1, 3.43% due 2024	36,400,000
Ser.2020-1, 2.438% due 2025	31,200,000
Ser.2022-1, 6.108% due 2027	29,300,000
Debentures[2]:	
3.527% ser.B due 2025	199,600,000
3.289% ser.D due 2026	199,500,000
3.469% ser.E due 2027	174,500,000
3.865% ser.F due 2027	199,300,000
3.029% ser.H due 2029	248,700,000
2.371% ser.G due 2031	149,200,000
Medium-term notes:	
3.167% due 2023	399,800,000
6.5% due 2028	150,900,000
6.57% due 2034	201,700,000
5.61% due 2035	199,700,000
Mtges.	65,300,000
	4,257,700,000
Less: Current portion	1,040,200,000
	3,217,500,000

[1] Asset-backed debt issued by Glacier Credit Card Trust.
[2] Issued by CT Real Estate Investment Trust (CT REIT).

Minimum long-term debt repayment, excluding mortgages, were reported as follows:

2023	$984,000,000
2024	560,000,000
2025	680,000,000
2026	200,000,000
2027	825,100,000
Thereafter	950,000,000

Wholly Owned Subsidiaries

Canadian Tire Real Estate Limited, Ont.
- 68.6% int. in **CT Real Estate Investment Trust**, Toronto, Ont. (see separate coverage)

Canadian Tire Services Limited, Toronto, Ont. Formerly Canadian Tire Financial Services Limited.
- 80% int. in **CTFS Holdings Limited**, Toronto, Ont.
  - 100% int. in **CTFS Bermuda Ltd.**, Bermuda.
  - 100% int. in **Canadian Tire Bank**, Oakville, Ont.

FGL Sports Ltd., Calgary, Alta.
Helly Hansen Holding AS, Oslo, Norway.
Mark's Work Wearhouse Ltd., Calgary, Alta.

Note: The preceding list includes only the major related companies in which interests are held.

Financial Statistics

Periods ended:	52w Dec. 31/22[A]		52w Jan. 1/22[□A]
	$000s	%Chg	$000s
Operating revenue	**17,810,600**	**+9**	**16,292,100**
Cost of sales	11,688,200		10,439,200
Salaries & benefits	1,577,500		1,575,500
General & admin expense	1,925,000		1,675,000
Operating expense	**15,190,700**	**+11**	**13,689,700**
Operating income	**2,619,900**	**+1**	**2,602,400**
Deprec., depl. & amort.	743,500		701,500
Finance income	20,900		13,700
Finance costs, gross	251,900		236,200
Pre-tax income	**1,583,800**	**-7**	**1,701,900**
Income taxes	401,000		441,200
Net income	**1,182,800**	**-6**	**1,260,700**
Net inc. for equity hldrs	**1,044,100**	**-7**	**1,127,600**
Net inc. for non-cont. int	**138,700**	**+4**	**133,100**
Cash & equivalent	507,600		2,357,900
Inventories	3,216,100		2,480,600
Accounts receivable	7,373,400		6,479,500
Current assets	11,530,400		11,646,600
Long-term investments	894,000		1,010,900
Fixed assets, net	4,994,100		4,549,300
Right-of-use assets	1,932,000		1,786,100
Intangibles, net	2,341,600		2,372,200
Total assets	**22,102,300**	**+1**	**21,802,200**
Bank indebtedness	1,054,100		535,700
Accts. pay. & accr. liabs	2,804,400		2,601,400
Current liabilities	7,147,000		6,790,000
Long-term debt, gross	4,257,700		4,278,500
Long-term debt, net	3,217,500		3,558,700
Long-term lease liabilities	2,026,400		1,916,800
Shareholders' equity	5,618,500		5,123,800
Non-controlling interest	1,420,700		1,387,000
Cash from oper. activs	**566,000**	**-67**	**1,735,900**
Cash from fin. activs	(1,661,500)		(653,400)
Cash from invest. activs	(329,900)		(658,000)
Net cash position	**326,300**	**-81**	**1,751,700**
Capital expenditures	(712,000)		(630,600)
Capital disposals	5,200		61,700
	$		$
Earnings per share*	17.70		18.56
Cash flow per share*	9.60		28.58
Cash divd. per share*	5.85		4.70
	shs		shs
No. of shs. o/s*	57,700,364		60,147,124
Avg. no. of shs. o/s*	58,983,364		60,744,440
	%		%
Net profit margin	6.64		7.74
Return on equity	19.44		23.44
Return on assets	6.25		6.81
Foreign sales percent	4		4
No. of employees (FTEs)	13,802		13,435

* Cl.A N.V. & Common
□ Restated
[A] Reported in accordance with IFRS

Latest Results

Periods ended:	13w Apr. 1/23[A]		13w Apr. 2/22[A]
	$000s	%Chg	$000s
Operating revenue	3,707,200	-3	3,837,400
Net income	42,800	-80	217,600
Net inc. for equity hldrs	7,800	-96	182,100
Net inc. for non-cont. int	35,000		35,500
	$		$
Earnings per share*	0.14		3.05

* Cl.A N.V. & Common
[A] Reported in accordance with IFRS

Historical Summary
(as originally stated)

Fiscal Year	Oper. Rev. $000s	Net Inc. Bef. Disc. $000s	EPS* $
2022[A]	17,810,600	1,182,800	17.70
2021[A]	16,292,100	1,260,700	18.56
2020[A1]	14,871,000	862,600	12.35
2019[A]	14,534,400	894,800	12.60
2018[A]	14,058,700	783,000	10.67

* Cl.A N.V. & Common
[A] Reported in accordance with IFRS
[1] 53 weeks ended Jan. 2, 2021.

C.46 Canadian Utilities Limited*

Symbol - CU **Exchange** - TSX **CUSIP** - 136717
Head Office - West Building, 400-5302 Forand St SW, Calgary, AB, T3E 8B4 **Telephone** - (403) 292-7500 **Fax** - (403) 292-7532
Website - www.canadianutilities.com
Email - colin.jackson@atco.com

Investor Relations - Colin R. Jackson (403) 808-2636
Auditors - PricewaterhouseCoopers LLP C.A., Calgary, Alta.
Lawyers - Bennett Jones LLP, Calgary, Alta.
Transfer Agents - TSX Trust Company, Calgary, Alta.
FP500 Subsidiary Revenue Ranking - 21
Employees - 5,035 at Dec. 31, 2022
Profile - (Can. 1927) Provides services and business solutions in Canada, Australia, Mexico, Puerto Rico and Chile through subsidiaries engaged in utilities (electricity and natural gas transmission and distribution, and international operations); energy infrastructure (energy storage, energy generation, industrial water solutions, and clean fuels); and retail energy (electricity and natural gas retail sales, and whole-home solutions).

Utilities - Operations include regulated electricity and natural gas distribution and transmission in Canada and international electricity and natural gas services in Puerto Rico and Australia. Canadian regulated utilities are carried out by wholly owned **CU Inc.** and its subsidiaries. CU, through wholly owned **ATCO Electric Ltd.**, transmits and distributes electricity primarily in northern and east-central Alberta, Yukon, the Northwest Territories and the Lloydminster area of Saskatchewan. ATCO Electric owns and operates 11,000 km of transmission lines, 60,000 km of distribution lines, and 20 diesel and two hydroelectric plants and 12 solar sites with total capacity of 47 MW, as well as delivers power to and operates 3,500 km of distribution lines owned by Rural Electrification Associations. Also operates Alberta PowerLine (APL), a 500-km, 500-kV electricity transmission line running from Wabamun to Fort McMurray, Alta., on behalf of APL's owners. Natural gas distribution and transmission businesses are operated through CU's wholly owned **ATCO Gas and Pipelines Ltd.** Natural gas is distributed to municipal, residential, commercial and industrial customers in Alberta and the Lloydminster area of Saskatchewan, through 41,500 km of distribution mains. ATCO Gas and Pipelines owns and operates a natural gas transmission system in Alberta, with a peak delivery capacity of 4.85 bcf per day, consisting of 9,100 km of pipelines, 16 compressor sites, 3,700 receipt and delivery points, and a salt cavern storage peaking facility near Fort Saskatchewan, Alta. In Puerto Rico, **LUMA Energy, LLC** (50% owned; **Quanta Services, Inc.** 50%) provides services to transform, modernize and operate Puerto Rico's 30,000-km electricity transmission and distribution system under an agreement with the Government of Puerto Rico. Wholly owned **ATCO Gas Australia Pty Ltd.** provides regulated natural gas distribution services in Perth and neighbouring regions in Western Australia through 14,000 km of pipelines and related infrastructure, and also distributes liquefied petroleum gas (LPG) in Albany.

Energy Infrastructure - Operations include non-regulated electricity generation in western Canada, Mexico, Australia and Chile; non-regulated electricity transmission in Alberta; non-regulated natural gas storage and transmission, natural gas liquids (NGL) storage and industrial water services in Alberta and a regulated natural gas distribution system in the Northwest Territories; and a clean fuels business. Non-regulated electricity generation assets include 75% interest in the 32-MW Oldman River hydroelectric plant in Pincher Creek, Alta.; the 202-MW Forty Mile phase 1 wind farm in Bow Island, Alta.; 75% interest in the 40-MW Adelaide wind farm in Strathroy, Ont.; the 35-MW Electricidad del Golfo hydroelectric plant in Veracruz state, Mexico; 79% interest in an 11-MW gas-fired distributed generation facility in San Luis Potosí, Mexico; 50% interest in the 180-MW Osborne gas-fired combined-cycle facility near Adelaide, S.A.; the 86-MW Karratha gas-fired open-cycle plant in the Pilbara region of Western Australia; a 1-MW solar facility in Perth, W.A.; 95% interest in the 3-MW El Resplandor solar facility in Cabrero, Chile; and more than 1,500 MW of wind and solar development pipeline in Alberta and Ontario, including three solar projects totaling 103 MW (Deerfoot, Barlow and Empress) under construction in Alberta, and the proposed 325-MW Central West pumped storage hydro project in New South Wales. Non-regulated electricity transmission involves the operation of four transmission assets totaling 33 km in Alberta, including Scotford transmission line and substation, Muskeg River transmission line and substation, Grand Rapids substation and Air Products transmission line. Wholly owned **ATCO Energy Solutions Ltd.** builds, owns and operates non-regulated industrial water, natural gas storage, NGL storage and natural gas related infrastructure to serve the midstream and petrochemical sector of western Canada's energy industry. ATCO Energy Solutions assets include a natural gas storage facility in Carbon, Alta., with seasonal storage capacity of 68 petajoules; the Alberta Hub underground natural gas storage facility near Edson, Alta., with capacity of 49 petajoules; 60% interest in ATCO Heartland Energy Centre near Fort Saskatchewan, Alta., with NGL storage capacity of 544,000 m^3; the 116-km Muskeg River gas pipeline near Fort McMurray, Alta.; and an industrial water business in Alberta's Industrial Heartland region which provides integrated water services including pipeline transportation, storage, water treatment, recycling and disposal, with capacity of 85,200 m^3 per day. ATCO Energy Solutions also owns a 33.3% interest in the regulated Ikhil gas plant, a gas production, gathering and processing facility in the Northwest Territories. In addition, ATCO Energy Solutions includes a clean fuels business, which involves the development and operation of large-scale hydrogen and renewable natural gas (RNG) production projects. Clean fuel projects proposed or under development include the Two Hills RNG facility (in partnership with **Future Fuel Ltd.**) north of Vegreville, Alta., which would combine organic waste from nearby municipalities with agricultural byproducts to produce 230,000 gigajoules per year of RNG; a hydrogen production facility (in partnership with **Suncor Energy Inc.**) at the company's ATCO Heartland Energy Centre which would produce more than 300,000 tonnes per year of clean hydrogen; two hydrogen production and refueling facilities at **Canadian Pacific Kansas City Limited**'s rail yards in Calgary and Edmonton, Alta.; and the Atlas Carbon Sequestration Hub (in partnership with **Shell Canada Limited** and Suncor) east of Edmonton, which would capture 750,000 to 850,000 tonnes per year of carbon.

Retail Energy - Wholly owned **ATCO Energy Ltd.** sells electricity and natural gas to residential customers in Alberta under the ATCOenergy name; offers lifestyle home products online and provides home maintenance services and professional advice to home and business owners in Alberta under the Rümi name; and, through Blue Flame Kitchen, provides recipes and how-to guides, school programs, cooking classes and events online and at locations in Edmonton and Calgary, Alta., and Jandakot, W.A., as well as offers wholesale pre-packaged fresh and frozen foods to convenience stores, gas stations and grocers in Alberta.

Operating Statistics

Year ended Dec. 31	2022	2021
Canada:		
Reg. electric distribution[1]	12,489	12,491
Reg. nat. gas throughput[2]	276.5	270.4
Electric customers[3]	262,578	261,370
Gas customers[3]	1,271,541	1,254,731
Australia:		
Reg. nat. gas throughput[2]	27.7	28.3
Gas customers[3]	791,557	780,891

[1] GWh.
[2] Petajoules.
[3] Average monthly number of customers.

Recent Merger and Acquisition Activity

Status: completed **Revised:** Jan. 3, 2023
UPDATE: The transaction was completed. Canadian Utilities acquired Adelaide and Forty Mile wind farms as well as the 1,500-MW development pipeline for $713,000,000. Existing partners of Suncor on the Chin Chute and Magrath wind farms opted to acquire the additional interest in these facilities. Suncor received total proceeds of $730,000,000 for its entire wind and solar assets. PREVIOUS: Suncor Energy Inc. agreed to sell its wind and solar energy assets, consisting of 252 MW of operational wind facilities and more than 1,500 MW of wind and solar projects at various stages of development located in Alberta and Ontario, to Canadian Utilities Limited, a subsidiary of ATCO Ltd., for $730,000,000. The sale includes interest in the 30-MW Magrath (33.3%), 30-MW Chin Chute (33.3%) and 40-MW Adelaide (75%) wind farms, as well as the 202-MW Forty Mile wind farm which was expected to be operating by the end of 2022, and development stage renewable power assets. Suncor plans to focus on areas of energy expansion, hydrogen and renewable fuels.

Status: completed **Announced:** Mar. 31, 2022
Canadian Utilities Limited (CUL) sold a 36% interest in Northland Utilities Enterprises Ltd. (NUE), an electric utility operating in the Northwest Territories, to Denendeh Investments Incorporated (DII), representing 27 Dene First Nations across the Northwest Territories, for $8,000,000. As a result, CUL and DII each owned a 50% interest in NUE.

Directors - Nancy C. Southern, chr. & CEO, Calgary, Alta.; Linda A. Southern-Heathcott, v-chr., Calgary, Alta.; Dr. Roger J. Urwin†, London, Middx., United Kingdom; Dr. Matthias F. Bichsel, Lucerne, Switzerland; Loraine M. Charlton, Calgary, Alta.; Robert J. S. (Bob) Hanf, Calgary, Alta.; Kelly C. Koss-Brix, Calgary, Alta.; Robert J. (Bob) Normand, Edmonton, Alta.; Alexander J. (Alex) Pourbaix, Calgary, Alta.; Hector A. Rangel, Mexico City, D.F., Mexico; Laura A. Reed, Wynn Vale, S.A., Australia; Dr. Robert J. (Rob) Routs, Brunnen, Switzerland; The Hon. Wayne G. Wouters, Vancouver, B.C.

Other Exec. Officers - Robert J. (Bob) Myles, COO, ATCO EnPower; Wayne K. Stensby, COO, ATCO Energy Systems; Marshall F. Wilmot, chief digital officer & pres., ATCO Energy Ltd.; M. George Constantinescu, exec. v-p & chief transformation officer; Rebecca A. (Becky) Penrice, exec. v-p, corp. srvcs.; Brian P. Shkrobot, exec. v-p & CFO; Sarah J. Shortreed, exec. v-p & chief tech. officer; Kyle M. Brunner, sr. v-p, gen. counsel & corp. sec.; P. Derek Cook, sr. v-p & contr.; Lisa Cooke, sr. v-p & chief mktg. officer; Colin R. Jackson, sr. v-p, fin., treasury & sustainability; Melanie L. Bayley, pres., ATCO Electric Ltd.; D. Jason Sharpe, pres., ATCO Gas & Pipelines Ltd.
† Lead director

Capital Stock

	Authorized (shs.)	Outstanding (shs.)[1]	Par
Series Preferred	150,000	nil	n.p.v.
Series 2nd Preferred	unlimited		
5.196% Series Y		13,000,000	$25
4.9% Series AA		6,000,000	$25
4.9% Series BB		6,000,000	$25
4.5% Series CC		7,000,000	$25
4.5% Series DD		9,000,000	$25
5.25% Series EE		5,000,000	$25
4.5% Series FF		10,000,000	$25
4.75% Series HH		8,050,000	$25
Class A Non-Vtg.	unlimited	201,743,648	n.p.v.
Class B Common	unlimited	68,465,765	n.p.v.

[1] At July 25, 2023

Series Preferred - Issuable in series and rank prior to series second preferred, class A non-voting and class B common shares. Non-voting.
Series Second Preferred - Issuable in series and non-voting.
5.196% Series Y - Entitled to annual dividends of $1.299 per share payable quarterly to June 1, 2027, and thereafter at a rate reset every five years equal to the five-year Government of Canada bond yield plus 2.4%. Redeemable on June 1, 2027, and on June 1 every five years thereafter at $25 per share plus accrued and unpaid dividends. Convertible at the holder's option on June 1, 2027, and on June 1 every five years thereafter, into floating rate second preferred series Z shares on a share-for-share basis, subject to certain conditions. The series Z shares would pay a quarterly dividend equal to the 90-day Canadian Treasury bill rate plus 2.4%.
4.9% Series AA - Entitled to annual dividends of $1.225 per share payable quarterly. Redeemable at $25 per share plus accrued and unpaid dividends.
4.9% Series BB - Entitled to annual dividends of $1.225 per share payable quarterly. Redeemable at $25 per share plus accrued and unpaid dividends.
4.5% Series CC - Entitled to annual dividends of $1.125 per share payable quarterly. Redeemable at $25 per share plus accrued and unpaid dividends.
4.5% Series DD - Entitled to annual dividends of $1.125 per share payable quarterly. Redeemable at $25 per share plus accrued and unpaid dividends.
5.25% Series EE - Entitled to annual dividends of $1.3125 per share payable quarterly. Redeemable at $25.50 per share and declining by 25¢ per share annually to Sept. 1, 2024, and at $25 per share thereafter, plus accrued and unpaid dividends.
4.5% Series FF - Entitled to annual dividends of $1.125 per share payable quarterly to Dec. 1, 2025, and thereafter at a rate reset every five years equal to the five-year Government of Canada bond yield plus 3.69%. Redeemable on Dec. 1, 2025, and on December 1 every five years thereafter at $25 per share plus accrued and unpaid dividends. Convertible at the holder's option on Dec. 1, 2025, and on December 1 every five years thereafter, into floating rate second preferred series GG shares on a share-for-share basis, subject to certain conditions. The series GG shares would pay a quarterly dividend equal to the 90-day Canadian Treasury bill rate plus 3.69%.
4.75% Series HH - Entitled to annual dividends of $1.1875 per share payable quarterly. Redeemable at $26 per share on or after Mar. 1, 2027, and declining by 25¢ per share annually to Mar. 1, 2031, and at $25 per share thereafter, plus accrued and unpaid dividends.
Class A Non-Voting - Convertible into class B common shares on a share-for-share basis in the event of a takeover bid or if ATCO Ltd. ceases to own or control more than 10,000,000 of the outstanding class B shares. Entitled to dividends.
Class B Common - Convertible into class A non-voting shares on a share-for-share basis. Entitled to dividends. One vote per share.
Options - At Dec. 31, 2022, options were outstanding to purchase 1,998,600 class A non-voting shares at prices ranging from $29.97 to $41.54 per share with a weighted average remaining contractual life of 5.8 years.
Major Shareholder - ATCO Ltd. held 96.8% interest at Mar. 9, 2023.

Price Range - CU/TSX

Year	Volume	High	Low	Close
2022	179,145,716	$41.94	$33.24	$36.65
2021	142,875,789	$37.00	$29.96	$36.69
2020	141,989,376	$42.97	$25.25	$31.09
2019	76,144,431	$40.14	$30.91	$39.17
2018	67,732,748	$37.47	$29.12	$31.32

Recent Close: $32.19
Capital Stock Changes - During 2022, class A non-voting shares were issued as follows: 3,839,609 on conversion of a like number of class B common shares, 527,471 under the dividend reinvestment plan and 30,400 on exercise of options.

Dividends

CU.X cl B Ra $1.7944 pa Q est. Mar. 1, 2023**
Prev. Rate: $1.7768 est. Mar. 1, 2022
Prev. Rate: $1.7592 est. Mar. 1, 2021
Prev. Rate: $1.7416 est. Mar. 1, 2020
CU cl A N.V. Ra $1.7944 pa Q est. Mar. 1, 2023**
Prev. Rate: $1.7768 est. Mar. 1, 2022
Prev. Rate: $1.7592 est. Mar. 1, 2021
Prev. Rate: $1.7416 est. Mar. 1, 2020
CU.PR.C pfd 2nd ser Y cum. red. exch. Adj. Ra $1.30 pa Q est. Sept. 1, 2022
CU.PR.D pfd 2nd ser AA cum. red. Ra $1.225 pa Q
CU.PR.E pfd 2nd ser BB cum. red. Ra $1.225 pa Q
CU.PR.F pfd 2nd ser CC cum. red. Ra $1.125 pa Q
CU.PR.G pfd 2nd ser DD cum. red. Ra $1.125 pa Q
CU.PR.H pfd 2nd ser EE cum. red. Ra $1.3125 pa Q
CU.PR.I pfd 2nd ser FF cum. red. exch. Adj. Ra $1.125 pa Q est. Dec. 1, 2015
CU.PR.J pfd 2nd ser HH red. Ra $1.1875 pa Q
Listed Dec 9/21.
$0.26678i............ Mar. 1/22
** Reinvestment Option **i** Initial Payment

Long-Term Debt - Outstanding at Dec. 31, 2022:

4.851% debs. due June 2052	$250,000,000
CU Inc. debs.	8,525,000,000
CU Inc. other debt due June 2024	7,000,000
ATCO Power Australia[1]	42,000,000
ATCO Gas Australia[2]	656,000,000
Electricidad del Golfo[3]	23,000,000
ATCO Energy Sol. & ATCO Power[4]	88,000,000
Less: Def. fin. charges	51,000,000
	9,540,000,000
Less: Current portion	106,000,000
	9,434,000,000

[1] A$45,000,000. Credit facility payable in Australian dollars, bearing interest at bank bill swap benchmark rates and due June 2025. Secured by a pledge of project assets and contracts.
[2] A$712,000,000, consisting of A$350,000,000 and A$362,000,000 credit facilities due August 2024 and August 2026, respectively. Both

payable in Australian dollars and bearing interest at bank bill swap benchmark rates.

[3] 335,000,000 Mexican pesos. Credit facility payable in Mexican pesos, bearing interest at Mexican interbank rates and due November 2025.

[4] Credit facility bearing interest at CDOR or prime rates and due December 2025. Secured by ATCO Energy Solutions and ATCO Power's present and future properties, assets and equity interests in certain subsidiaries and joint ventures.

Credit Lines - At Dec. 31, 2022, the company had long-term committed credit lines of $2.718 billion, of which $744,000,000 was used and $1.974 billion was available; and $638,000,000 of uncommitted credit lines, of which $257,000,000 was used and $381,000,000 was available.

Wholly Owned Subsidiaries

ATCO Australia Pty Ltd., Australia.
ATCO Energy Ltd., Canada.
ATCO Energy Solutions Ltd., Calgary, Alta.
ATCO Gas Australia Pty Ltd., Australia.
ATCO Power (2010) Ltd., Canada.
CU Inc., Calgary, Alta. (see separate coverage)

Investments

50% int. in **LUMA Energy, LLC**, Puerto Rico.

Note: The preceding list includes only the major related companies in which interests are held.

Financial Statistics

Periods ended:	12m Dec. 31/22[A]		12m Dec. 31/21[A]
	$000s	%Chg	$000s
Operating revenue	**4,048,000**	**+15**	**3,515,000**
Salaries & benefits	374,000		362,000
Other operating expense	1,906,000		1,620,000
Operating expense	**2,280,000**	**+15**	**1,982,000**
Operating income	**1,768,000**	**+15**	**1,533,000**
Deprec., depl. & amort.	642,000		651,000
Finance income	36,000		11,000
Finance costs, gross	407,000		413,000
Investment income	76,000		58,000
Pre-tax income	**838,000**	**+56**	**538,000**
Income taxes	199,000		138,000
Net income	**639,000**	**+60**	**400,000**
Net inc. for equity hldrs	**632,000**	**+61**	**393,000**
Net inc. for non-cont. int.	**7,000**	**0**	**7,000**
Cash & equivalent	698,000		753,000
Inventories	24,000		21,000
Accounts receivable	873,000		759,000
Current assets	1,867,000		1,731,000
Long-term investments	237,000		204,000
Fixed assets, net	18,596,000		18,008,000
Right-of-use assets	50,000		51,000
Intangibles, net	819,000		726,000
Total assets	**21,974,000**	**+4**	**21,075,000**
Bank indebtedness	nil		209,000[1]
Accts. pay. & accr. liabs	989,000		739,000
Current liabilities	1,317,000		1,418,000
Long-term debt, gross	9,540,000		9,308,000
Long-term debt, net	9,434,000		8,977,000
Long-term lease liabilities	44,000		44,000
Preferred share equity	1,571,000		1,571,000
Shareholders' equity	6,879,000		6,635,000
Non-controlling interest	187,000		187,000
Cash from oper. activs	**2,140,000**	**+25**	**1,718,000**
Cash from fin. activs	(932,000)		(478,000)
Cash from invest. activs	(1,256,000)		(1,262,000)
Net cash position	**698,000**	**-7**	**750,000**
Capital expenditures	(1,224,000)		(1,078,000)
Capital disposals	1,000		30,000
Unfunded pension liability	96,000		59,000
	$		$
Earnings per share*	2.07		1.21
Cash flow per share*	7.95		6.37
Cash divd. per share*	1.78		1.76
	shs		shs
No. of shs. o/s*	269,469,984		268,911,219
Avg. no. of shs. o/s*	269,133,415		269,855,016
	%		%
Net profit margin	15.79		11.38
Return on equity	10.74		6.43
Return on assets	4.41		3.42
Foreign sales percent	6		7
No. of employees (FTEs)	5,035		4,796

* Class A & B

[A] Reported in accordance with IFRS

[1] Includes $206,000,000 of commercial paper and $3,000,000 of bank indebtedness.

Latest Results

Periods ended:	6m June 30/23[A]		6m June 30/22[A]
	$000s	%Chg	$000s
Operating revenue	2,010,000	-2	2,043,000
Net income	403,000	+5	382,000
Net inc. for equity hldrs	397,000	+5	378,000
Net inc. for non-cont. int.	6,000		4,000
	$		$
Earnings per share*	1.33		1.28

* Class A & B

[A] Reported in accordance with IFRS

Historical Summary
(as originally stated)

Fiscal Year	Oper. Rev.	Net Inc. Bef. Disc.	EPS*
	$000s	$000s	$
2022[A]	4,048,000	639,000	2.07
2021[A]	3,515,000	400,000	1.21
2020[A]	3,233,000	434,000	1.32
2019[A]	3,905,000	958,000	3.24
2018[A]	4,377,000	641,000	2.08

* Class A & B

[A] Reported in accordance with IFRS

C.47 Canadian Western Bank*

Symbol - CWB **Exchange** - TSX **CUSIP** - 13677F

Head Office - Canadian Western Bank Place, 3000-10303 Jasper Ave NW, Edmonton, AB, T5J 3X6 **Telephone** - (780) 423-8888 **Toll-free** - (800) 836-1886 **Fax** - (780) 423-8897

Website - www.cwb.com

Email - chris.williams@cwbank.com

Investor Relations - Chris Williams (800) 836-1886

Auditors - KPMG LLP C.A., Edmonton, Alta.

Transfer Agents - Computershare Trust Company of Canada Inc., Calgary, Alta.

FP500 Revenue Ranking - 243

Employees - 2,712 at Oct. 31, 2022

Profile - (Can. 1987 amalg.) A Schedule I Canadian chartered bank primarily operating through branches in Alberta, British Columbia, Saskatchewan, Manitoba Ontario and Quebec. Provides business and personal banking, specialized financing, wealth management and trust services offerings for business owners, organizations and individuals.

Full-service business and personal banking is offered through banking centre locations in Alberta, British Columbia, Saskatchewan, Manitoba, Ontario and Quebec; and personal banking through digital channels, including Motive Financial.

Specialized financing is delivered through under the banners CWB Optimum Mortgage, CWB Equipment Financing, CWB National Leasing, CWB Maxium Financial and CWB Franchise Finance.

Wealth management services are provided through CWB Wealth Management and its affiliate brands, including T.E. Wealth, Leon Frazer & Associates, CWB Wealth Partners and Canadian Western Financial.

Trust services are offered through CWB Trust Services, a division of wholly owned **Canadian Western Trust Company**.

During fiscal 2022, wholly owned **CWB McLean & Partners Wealth Management Ltd.** changed its name to **CWB Wealth Partners Ltd.**

Predecessor Detail - Formed from Bank of Alberta in Canada, Nov. 1, 1987, on amalgamation with Western & Pacific Bank of Canada.

Directors - Sarah A. Morgan-Silvester, chr., Vancouver, B.C.; Christopher H. (Chris) Fowler, pres. & CEO, Edmonton, Alta.; Andrew J. Bibby, Vancouver, B.C.; Dr. Marie Y. Delorme, Calgary, Alta.; Maria Filippelli, Toronto, Ont.; Linda M. O. Hohol, Calgary, Alta.; E. Gay Mitchell, Toronto, Ont.; Margaret J. (Peggy) Mulligan, Oakville, Ont.; Irfhan A. Rawji, Calgary, Alta.; Ian M. Reid, Edmonton, Alta.

Other Exec. Officers - R. Matthew (Matt) Rudd, CFO; Kelly S. Blackett, chief people & culture officer; Azfar Karimuddin, CIO; M. Carolina Parra, chief risk officer; Stephen H. E. Murphy, grp. head, comml., personal & wealth; Jeffrey I. L. (Jeff) Wright, grp. head, client solutions & specialty bus.; John Steeves, exec. v-p, banking; Trent A. Erickson, sr. v-p, credit risk mgt.; Kelly M. Martin, sr. v-p & chief internal auditor; Monique M. Petrin Nicholson, sr. v-p, gen. counsel & corp. sec.

Capital Stock

	Authorized (shs.)	Outstanding (shs.)[1]
First Preferred	unlimited	
Series 5		5,000,000
Series 7		nil
Series 9		5,000,000
Class A	33,964,324	nil
Limited Resource Capital Notes	n.a.	[2]
Series 1		175,000
Series 2		150,000
Common	unlimited	96,307,801

[1] At May 19, 2023

[2] Number of shares represent the number of notes issued.

First Preferred - Issuable in series provided that the aggregate consideration for all outstanding first preferred shares shall not exceed $1 billion. Non-voting.

Series 5 - Entitled to non-cumulative annual dividends of $1.07525 payable quarterly to Apr. 30, 2024, and thereafter at a rate reset every five years equal to the five-year Government of Canada bond yield plus 2.76%. Redeemable on Apr. 30, 2024, and on April 30 every five years thereafter at $25 per share plus declared and unpaid dividends. Convertible at the holder's option, on Apr. 30, 2024, and on April 30 every five years thereafter, into non-cumulative floating rate preferred series 6 shares on a share-for-share basis, subject to certain conditions. The series 6 shares would pay a quarterly dividend equal to the 90-day Canadian Treasury bill rate plus 2.76%. Convertible upon occurrence of certain trigger events related to financial viability into common shares equal to 1.0 multiplied by $25 plus declared and unpaid dividends divided by the greater of: (i) $5.00; and (ii) current market price of the common shares.

Series 9 - Entitled to non-cumulative annual dividends of $1.50 payable quarterly to Apr. 30, 2024, and thereafter at a rate reset every five years equal to the five-year Government of Canada bond yield plus 4.04%. Redeemable on Apr. 30, 2024, and on April 30 every five years thereafter at $25 per share plus declared and unpaid dividends. Convertible at the holder's option, on Apr. 30, 2024, and on April 30 every five years thereafter, into non-cumulative floating rate preferred series 10 shares on a share-for-share basis, subject to certain conditions. The series 10 shares would pay a quarterly dividend equal to the 90-day Canadian Treasury bill rate plus 4.04%. Convertible upon occurrence of certain trigger events related to financial viability into common shares equal to 1.0 multiplied by $25 plus declared and unpaid dividends divided by the greater of: (i) $5.00; and (ii) current market price of the common shares.

Limited Recourse Capital Notes (LRCNs) - Notes with recourse limited to assets held by an independent trustee in a consolidated limited recourse trust. **LRCN - Series 1** - Bear interest at 6% per annum until Apr. 30, 2026, exclusively and, thereafter, at an annual rate reset every five years equal to the five-year Government of Canada bond yield plus 5.621% until maturity on Apr. 30, 2081. Trust assets consist of non-cumulative five-year reset first preferred series 11 shares. **LRCN - Series 2** - Bear interest at 5% per annum until July 31, 2026, exclusively and, thereafter, at an annual rate reset every five years equal to the five-year Government of Canada bond yield plus 3.949% until maturity on July 31, 2081. Trust assets consist of non-cumulative five-year reset first preferred series 12 shares.

Common - One vote per share.

Options - At Oct. 31, 2022, options were outstanding to purchase 1,871,717 common shares at a weighted average exercise price of $31.63 per share with a weighted average remaining contractual life of 3.8 years.

Major Shareholder - Widely held at Mar. 2, 2023.

Price Range - CWB/TSX

Year	Volume	High	Low	Close
2022	98,333,815	$41.35	$21.21	$24.06
2021	59,837,593	$41.56	$28.12	$36.30
2020	86,225,404	$34.00	$15.70	$28.62
2019	56,630,722	$36.61	$25.62	$31.89
2018	68,041,440	$40.83	$24.33	$26.04

Recent Close: $25.33

Capital Stock Changes - During fiscal 2022, common shares were issued as follows: 4,725,271 under at-the-market offering, 164,251 under the dividend reinvestment plan and 46,255 on exercise of options.

Dividends

CWB com Ra $1.32 pa Q est. June 22, 2023**[1]
Prev. Rate: $1.28 est. Jan. 5, 2023
Prev. Rate: $1.24 est. June 23, 2022
Prev. Rate: $1.20 est. Jan. 6, 2022
Prev. Rate: $1.16 est. Mar. 26, 2020
CWB.PR.B pfd ser 5 red. exch. Adj. Ra $1.07525 pa Q est. July 31, 2019**
CWB.PR.D pfd ser 9 red. exch. Adj. Ra $1.50 pa Q est. Apr. 30, 2019
pfd ser 7 red. exch. Adj. Ra $1.5625 pa Q est. July 31, 2016[2]
$0.390625**f**.......... July 31/21

[1] Dividend reinvestment plan implemented eff. Aug./09.

[2] Redeemed Aug. 2, 2021 at $25 per sh.

** Reinvestment Option **f** Final Payment

Long-Term Debt - Outstanding at Oct. 31, 2022:

Subord. debs.:	
3.668% due June 2029[1]	$250,000,000
4.84% due June 2030[2]	125,000,000
Unamort. fin. costs	(1,198,000)
Securitization debt:	3,088,097,000
	3,461,899,000

[1] After June 11, 2024, bear interest at the three-month bankers' acceptance rate plus 1.99%.

[2] After June 29, 2025, bear interest at the three-month bankers' acceptance rate plus 4.1%.

Note - In December 2022, offering of $150,000,000 of 5.937% subordinated debentures due Dec. 22, 2032, was completed. The debentures bear interest at 5.937% until Dec. 22, 2027, and thereafter at the Daily Compounded Canadian Overnight Repo Rate Average (CORRA) plus 2.91%.

Wholly Owned Subsidiaries

CWB Maxium Financial Inc., Richmond Hill, Ont. Carrying value of voting shares owned by the bank totaled $30,812,000 at Oct. 31, 2022.

CWB National Leasing Inc., Winnipeg, Man. Carrying value of voting shares owned by the bank totaled $134,458,000 at Oct. 31, 2022.
CWB Wealth Management Ltd., Edmonton, Alta. Carrying value of voting shares owned by the bank totaled $118,660,000 at Oct. 31, 2022.
- 100% int. in **CWB Wealth Partners Ltd.**, Calgary, Alta.
- 100% int. in **Canadian Western Financial Ltd.**, Edmonton, Alta.

Canadian Western Trust Company, Edmonton, Alta. Carrying value of voting shares owned by the bank totaled $19,136,000 at Oct. 31, 2022.
Valiant Trust Company, Calgary, Alta. Carrying value of voting shares owned by the bank totaled $10,582,000 at Oct. 31, 2022.

Financial Statistics

Periods ended:	12m Oct. 31/22[A]		12m Oct. 31/21[oA]
	$000s	%Chg	$000s
Interest income	**1,561,905**	**+19**	**1,318,012**
Interest expense	621,929		425,649
Net interest income	**939,976**	**+5**	**892,363**
Provision for loan losses	45,997		27,055
Other income	136,311		123,670
Salaries & pension benefits	345,743		325,136
Non-interest expense	581,777		508,718
Pre-tax income	**448,513**	**-7**	**480,260**
Income taxes	111,617		123,007
Net inc bef disc ops, eqhldrs	336,896		356,963
Net inc bef disc ops, NCI	nil		290
Net income	**336,896**	**-6**	**357,253**
Net inc. for equity hldrs	**336,896**	**-6**	**356,963**
Net inc. for non-cont. int	**nil**	**n.a.**	**290**
Cash & equivalent	115,979		128,459
Securities	4,518,795		3,573,878
Net non-performing loans	119,982		163,027
Total loans	35,743,804		32,789,570
Fixed assets, net	153,026		130,698
Total assets	**41,440,143**	**+11**	**37,323,176**
Deposits	33,019,047		29,975,739
Other liabilities	1,226,221		798,487
Subordinated debt	3,461,899		3,015,065
Preferred share equity	575,000		575,000
Shareholders' equity	3,732,976		3,533,885
Cash from oper. activs	**1,192,067**	**+49**	**802,487**
Cash from fin. activs	(8,795)		(75,039)
Cash from invest. activs	(1,184,318)		(731,985)
	$		$
Earnings per share*	3.39		3.74
Cash flow per share*	13.04		9.16
Cash divd. per share*	1.22		1.16
	shs		shs
No. of shs. o/s*	94,326,112		89,390,335
Avg. no. of shs. o/s*	91,430,832		87,578,859
	%		%
Basel III Common Equity Tier 1	8.80		8.80
Basel III Tier 1	10.60		10.80
Basel III Total	12.10		12.40
Net profit margin	31.30		35.16
Return on equity	10.15		11.44
Return on assets	0.86		1.00
No. of employees (FTEs)	2,712		2,617

* Common
[o] Restated
[A] Reported in accordance with IFRS

Latest Results

Periods ended:	6m Apr. 30/23[A]		6m Apr. 30/22[A]
	$000s	%Chg	$000s
Net interest income	472,803	+3	459,181
Net income	177,604	+1	175,120
	$		$
Earnings per share*	1.72		1.80

* Common
[A] Reported in accordance with IFRS

Historical Summary
(as originally stated)

Fiscal Year	Int. Inc.	Net Inc. Bef. Disc.	EPS*
	$000s	$000s	$
2022[A]	1,561,905	336,896	3.39
2021[A]	1,318,012	357,253	3.74
2020[A]	1,368,914	271,550	2.86
2019[A]	1,418,700	287,846	3.05
2018[A]	1,225,295	264,647	2.81

* Common
[A] Reported in accordance with IFRS

C.48 CanaFarma Hemp Products Corp.

Symbol - CNFA **Exchange** - CSE (S) **CUSIP** - 13683D
Head Office - 2080-777 Hornby St, Vancouver, BC, V6Z 1S4 **Telephone** - (214) 704-7942 **Fax** - (972) 596-0017
Website - www.canafarmacorp.com
Email - vitaly@canafarmacorp.com
Investor Relations - Vitaly Fargesen (718) 757-4145
Auditors - Urish Popeck & Co., LLC C.P.A., Pittsburgh, Pa.
Transfer Agents - Reliable Stock Transfer Inc., Toronto, Ont.
Profile - (B.C. 2017) Sells hemp-based products to consumers through an online distribution platform.
Products include chewing gum, tinctures and creams which are sold in the U.S. under the proprietary brand YOOFORIC. Products are manufactured by third parties in Europe and the U.S.
Common suspended from CSE, Nov. 4, 2021.
Predecessor Detail - Name changed from KYC Technology Inc., Mar. 3, 2020, pursuant to the reverse takeover acquisition of private New York, N.Y.-based CanaFarma Corp.
Directors - Merdan Gurbanov, chr., Dubai, United Arab Emirates; Uri Mermelstein, N.Y.; Vitaliy Snagovskiy, Dubai, United Arab Emirates
Other Exec. Officers - Philip (Phil) Klauder, acting CFO; Edward J. Kirkham, chief grower; Vitaly Fargesen, sr. v-p, strategic planning; Igor Palatnik, sr. v-p, product acq.; Tyrone Ross Jr., v-p, commun.

Capital Stock

	Authorized (shs.)	Outstanding (shs.)[1]
Common	unlimited	213,211,781
Proportionate Vtg.	1,000,000	57,000

[1] At Dec. 5, 2022

Common - One vote per share.
Proportionate Voting - Entitled to dividends. Each convertible, at the holder's option, into 100 common shares. 100 votes per share.
Major Shareholder - Widely held at Nov. 3, 2020.

Price Range - CNFA/CSE (S)

Year	Volume	High	Low	Close
2021	15,708,326	$0.35	$0.05	$0.05
2020	11,182,661	$1.42	$0.10	$0.33

Wholly Owned Subsidiaries

CanaFarma Corp., New York, N.Y.
- 100% int. in **Simple Solutions by Hemp Inc.**, N.Y.

C.49 Canfor Corporation*

Symbol - CFP **Exchange** - TSX **CUSIP** - 137576
Head Office - 100-1700 75 Ave W, Vancouver, BC, V6P 6G2 **Telephone** - (604) 661-5241 **Fax** - (604) 661-5253
Website - www.canfor.com
Email - patrick.elliott@canfor.com
Investor Relations - Patrick A. J. Elliott (604) 661-5441
Auditors - KPMG LLP C.A., Vancouver, B.C.
Transfer Agents - TSX Trust Company, Vancouver, B.C.
FP500 Subsidiary Revenue Ranking - 10
Employees - 7,908 at Dec. 31, 2022
Profile - (B.C. 1966) Produces and markets softwood lumber, remanufactured lumber products, and specialized and customized wood products, with production facilities in British Columbia, Alberta, the U.S. and Sweden. Holds 54.8% interest in **Canfor Pulp Products Inc.** (CPPI), a producer of northern bleached softwood kraft (NBSK) pulp and specialty paper.
Operations include two segments: Lumber, and Pulp & Paper.
Lumber - Consists of woodlands, sawmilling and remanufacturing operations. At Dec. 31, 2022, the woodlands operations managed 10,287,662 m^3 of annual allowable cut in British Columbia and Alberta. Operates (at Dec. 31, 2022) nine sawmills in British Columbia, three in Alberta, four in South Carolina, three in Alabama, two in Georgia, one in North Carolina, one in Mississippi, one in Arkansas and 14 in Sweden, with a combined annual production capacity of 7,100 mmfbm lumber (including 100% capacity from 70%-owned **Vida AB**). Other operations include a whole-log chipping plant and two pellet plants in British Columbia; two laminating plants in Arkansas and Georgia; a finger joint plant in North Carolina; a specialty facility in Alberta; and a trucking division in South Carolina. The segment also includes the company's wood products sales and marketing division in Vancouver, B.C.; nine value-added facilities in Sweden, which include the manufactures of premium packaging, modular housing, industrial products and biofuel; and a 60% interest in **Houston Pellet Inc.**, which owns a 225,000-tonne wood pellet plant in Houston, B.C. The majority of lumber produced is construction and specialty grade dimension lumber and includes high-value engineered wood products, higher-grade machine stress rated lumber, strength-rated trusses, beams, and tongue-and-groove timber and premium specialty products. Products are sold throughout North America, Europe and Asia. Wood chips are produced at sawmills as a by-product and from converted pulpwood and are primarily sold to CPPI. Wood products sales offices are located in Canada, the U.S., Japan, Sweden, the U.K., Denmark, the Netherlands and Australia.
Pulp & Paper - Through subsidiary CPPI, owns and operates four pulp mills with an annual production capacity of over 1,100,000 tonnes of northern softwood market kraft pulp, majority of which is bleached to become NBSK, and 140,000 tonnes of kraft paper. The segment also includes CPPI's Taylor pulp mill near Taylor, B.C., with an annual production capacity of 230,000 tonnes of bleached chemi-thermo mechanical pulp. Pulp products are sold by CPPI's sales and marketing group to customers primarily in North America, Europe and Asia, and from offices in Vancouver, B.C.; Shanghai, People's Republic of China; Seoul, South Korea; and Tokyo, Japan.

Production

Year ended Dec. 31	2022	2021
Lumber (mfbm):		
Spruce-pine-fir	3,684,000	3,910,000
Southern yellow pine	1,618,000	1,641,000
Pulp & Paper:		
Pulp (tonnes)	718,000	1,018,000
Kraft paper (tonnes)	132,000	126,000

In April 2023, the company wound down and permanently closed its Chetwynd, B.C., sawmill and pellet plant and temporarily closed its Houston, B.C., sawmill for an extended period to facilitate a major redevelopment on the site. The closures removed 750 mmfbm of annual production capacity.
In July 2022, the company announced that it would invest $210,000,000 to build a new, state-of-the-art sawmill complex in southern Alabama, with an expected annual production of 250 mmfbm on a two-shift basis.
In April 2022, the company announced that it would invest $165,000,000 to upgrade and expand its sawmill and planer facility in Union cty., Ark. The improvements commenced in the third quarter of 2022 and were expected increase annual production by 115 mmfbm.

Recent Merger and Acquisition Activity

Status: completed **Revised:** Mar. 1, 2022
UPDATE: The transaction was completed. PREVIOUS: Canfor Corporation agreed to acquire the solid wood operations of Millar Western Forest Products Ltd. for $420,000,000, including $56,000,000 in working capital, and would be financed with cash and liquidity on hand. The assets consisted of two sawmill complexes in Whitecourt and Fox Creek and the Spruceland Millworks facility in Acheson, all in Alberta. The operations would add 630 mmfbm of production capacity. The transaction was expected to be completed in the first quarter of 2022 and was subject to customary closing conditions including regulatory approval.
Directors - The Hon. John R. Baird, chr., Toronto, Ont.; Donald B. (Don) Kayne, pres. & CEO, Delta, B.C.; Ryan Barrington-Foote, Vancouver, B.C.; Glen D. Clark, Vancouver, B.C.; Santhe Dahl, Växjö, Sweden; Dieter W. Jentsch, King City, Ont.; Conrad A. Pinette, Vancouver, B.C.; M. Dallas H. Ross, Vancouver, B.C.; Ross S. Smith, West Vancouver, B.C.; Frederick T. (Fred) Stimpson III, Mobile, Ala.; William W. Stinson, Vancouver, B.C.; Sandra J. Stuart, Vancouver, B.C.; Dianne L. Watts, Surrey, B.C.
Other Exec. Officers - Stephen Mackie, exec. v-p, North American opers.; David M. Calabrigo, sr. v-p, corp. devel., legal affairs & corp. sec.; Patrick A. J. (Pat) Elliott, sr. v-p, sustainability & CFO; Kevin Horsnell, sr. v-p, opers., Canada; Kevin Pankratz, sr. v-p, sales & mktg.; Katy Player, sr. v-p, people; David Trent, sr. v-p, global supply chain & digital; Susan L. Yurkovich, sr. v-p, global bus. devel.; Jim Bogle, v-p, tech. & digital; Bob Hayes, v-p, global supply chain; Andreas Kammenos, v-p, residual fibre & bus. analytics; Ross Lennox, v-p, woodlands, Canada; Bob Smith, v-p, North American sales; Katrina Wilson, v-p & contr.; Tony Sheffield, pres., Canfor Southern Pine; Måns Johansson, CEO, Vida grp.

Capital Stock

	Authorized (shs.)	Outstanding (shs.)[1]	Par
Preferred	10,000,000	nil	$25
Common	1,000,000,000	120,111,879	n.p.v.

[1] At July 27, 2023

Normal Course Issuer Bid - The company plans to make normal course purchases of up to 6,052,978 common shares representing 5% of the total outstanding. The bid commenced on Mar. 21, 2023, and expires on Mar. 20, 2024.
Major Shareholder - James A. (Jim) Pattison held 52.6% interest at Mar. 13, 2023.

Price Range - CFP/TSX

Year	Volume	High	Low	Close
2022	69,726,255	$33.89	$18.42	$21.31
2021	92,468,000	$35.53	$21.92	$32.06
2020	92,254,432	$23.93	$6.11	$22.98
2019	120,343,493	$18.92	$8.55	$12.14
2018	103,238,629	$34.04	$14.48	$16.53

Recent Close: $19.44
Capital Stock Changes - During 2022, 3,434,021 common shares were repurchased under a Normal Course Issuer Bid.
Long-Term Debt - Outstanding at Dec. 31, 2022:

1% to 2% project financing	$5,200,000
Fltg. rate sr. notes due Apr. 2023	100,000
Fltg. rate sr. notes due Nov. 2024	100,000
Fltg. rate sr. notes due Nov. 2025	50,000,000
4.4% sr. notes due 2025	135,400,000
Fltg. rate sr. notes due May 2028	400,000
Fltg. rate sr. notes due June 2031	67,700,000
	258,900,000
Less: Current portion	45,300,000
	213,600,000

Wholly Owned Subsidiaries

Canadian Forest Products Ltd., Vancouver, B.C.
- 54.8% int. in **Canfor Pulp Products Inc.**, Vancouver, B.C. (see separate coverage)
- 100% int. in **Canfor Southern Pine, Inc.**, Myrtle Beach, S.C.

Canfor Energy North Limited Partnership
Canfor Sweden AB, Sweden.
- 70% int. in **VIDA AB**, Sweden.

Elliott Sawmilling Co., Inc., S.C.

Subsidiaries

60% int. in **Houston Pellet Inc.**, Houston, B.C.

Financial Statistics

Periods ended:	12m Dec. 31/22A		12m Dec. 31/21A
	$000s	%Chg	$000s
Operating revenue	**7,426,700**	**-3**	**7,684,900**
General & admin expense	174,200		147,100
Other operating expense	5,634,700		4,974,700
Operating expense	**5,808,900**	**+13**	**5,121,800**
Operating income	**1,617,800**	**-37**	**2,563,100**
Deprec., depl. & amort.	397,200		376,800
Finance income	29,400		6,600
Finance costs, gross	28,400		30,700
Write-downs/write-offs	(138,600)		(293,500)
Pre-tax income	**1,108,500**	**-42**	**1,896,800**
Income taxes	247,400		438,000
Net income	**861,100**	**-41**	**1,458,800**
Net inc. for equity hldrs	**787,300**	**-41**	**1,341,600**
Net inc. for non-cont. int	**73,800**	**-37**	**117,200**
Cash & equivalent	1,268,700		1,354,800
Inventories	1,180,700		1,173,800
Accounts receivable	423,300		514,500
Current assets	3,064,900		3,163,400
Long-term investments	33,400		37,500
Fixed assets, net	2,576,900		2,125,900
Right-of-use assets	99,100		65,500
Intangibles, net	532,100		514,800
Total assets	**6,739,200**	**+9**	**6,173,900**
Bank indebtedness	27,800		18,700
Accts. pay. & accr. liabs	678,700		730,200
Current liabilities	883,600		1,081,600
Long-term debt, gross	258,900		246,000
Long-term debt, net	213,600		245,500
Long-term lease liabilities	79,500		49,200
Shareholders' equity	4,221,500		3,484,000
Non-controlling interest	541,300		525,100
Cash from oper. activs	**1,113,000**	**-42**	**1,914,900**
Cash from fin. activs	(179,400)		(504,100)
Cash from invest. activs	(1,046,600)		(468,400)
Net cash position	**1,268,700**	**-6**	**1,354,800**
Capital expenditures	(625,300)		(428,200)
Unfunded pension liability	74,500		92,300
	$		$
Earnings per share*	6.39		10.74
Cash flow per share*	9.03		15.33
	shs		shs
No. of shs. o/s*	121,059,579		124,493,600
Avg. no. of shs. o/s*	123,198,290		124,909,404
	%		%
Net profit margin	11.59		18.98
Return on equity	20.43		47.14
Return on assets	13.68		26.28
Foreign sales percent	89		91
No. of employees (FTEs)	7,908		7,391

* Common
A Reported in accordance with IFRS

Latest Results

Periods ended:	6m June 30/23A		6m June 30/22oA
	$000s	%Chg	$000s
Operating revenue	2,831,400	-35	4,387,000
Net income	(192,200)	n.a.	986,000
Net inc. for equity hldrs	(185,900)	n.a.	907,800
Net inc. for non-cont. int	(6,300)		78,200
	$		$
Earnings per share*	(1.54)		7.32

* Common
o Restated
A Reported in accordance with IFRS

Historical Summary
(as originally stated)

Fiscal Year	Oper. Rev. $000s	Net Inc. Bef. Disc. $000s	EPS* $
2022A	7,426,700	861,100	6.39
2021A	7,684,900	1,458,800	10.74
2020A	5,454,400	559,900	4.35
2019A	4,658,300	(269,700)	(2.10)
2018A	5,044,400	439,000	2.78

* Common
A Reported in accordance with IFRS

C.50 Canfor Pulp Products Inc.*

Symbol - CFX **Exchange** - TSX **CUSIP** - 137584
Head Office - c/o Canfor Corporation, 100-1700 75 Ave W, Vancouver, BC, V6P 6G2 **Telephone** - (604) 661-5241 **Fax** - (604) 661-5226
Website - www.canfor.com
Email - patrick.elliott@canfor.com
Investor Relations - Patrick A. J. Elliott (604) 661-5441
Auditors - KPMG LLP C.A., Vancouver, B.C.
Lawyers - Stikeman Elliott LLP, Vancouver, B.C.
Transfer Agents - TSX Trust Company, Vancouver, B.C.
FP500 Subsidiary Revenue Ranking - 65
Employees - 1,196 at Dec. 31, 2022

Profile - (B.C. 2010) Produces softwood kraft pulp and kraft paper in British Columbia for sale in North America, Europe and Asia.

The company has four pulp mills with an annual capacity to produce 1,100,000 tonnes of northern softwood market kraft pulp, majority of which is bleached to become northern bleached softwood kraft (NBSK) pulp, 230,000 tonnes of bleached chemi-thermo mechanical pulp (BCTMP), and 140,000 tonnes of bleached and unbleached kraft paper. Wood chips and hog fuel required by the mills are supplied by **Canfor Corporation** (the company's majority shareholder).

Operations

Northwood pulp mill - A two-line pulp mill with annual production capacity of 600,000 tonnes of NBSK pulp, which is used to make variety of products including printing and writing paper, premium tissue and specialty papers, and is primarily delivered to customers in North America and Asia.

Intercontinental pulp mill - A single-line pulp mill with annual production capacity of 320,000 tonnes of NBSK pulp, which is used to make substantially the same product as that from Northwoods, and is primarily delivered to customers in North America, Europe and Asia.

Prince George pulp and paper mill - An integrated two-line pulp and paper mill with an annual production capacity of 150,000 tonnes of kraft pulp, and kraft paper production capacity of 140,000 tonnes, which supplies products to pulp markets in North America, Europe and Asia, and its internal paper-making facilities, as well as supplies both bleached and unbleached kraft paper grades and specialty papers primarily to North American, Asian and European markets.

Taylor pulp mill - A BCTMP mill located in Taylor, B.C., with an annual production capacity of 230,000 tonnes of BCTMP, which supplies North America and Asia.

In April 2023, the company wound down and permanently closed the pulp line at its Prince George, B.C., pulp and paper mill, which resulted in a reduction of 280,000 tonnes of market kraft pulp annually. The specialty paper at the site would continue to operate.

Periods ended:	12m Dec. 31/22	12m Dec. 31/21
Market pulp prod., tonnes	717,983	1,018,309
Kraft paper prod., tonnes	131,824	125,784

Predecessor Detail - Succeeded Canfor Pulp Income Fund, Jan. 1, 2011, pursuant to plan of arrangement whereby Canfor Pulp Products Inc. was formed to facilitate the conversion of the fund into a corporation and the fund was subsequently dissolved.

Directors - The Hon. John R. Baird, chr., Toronto, Ont.; J. Craig Armstrong, Edmonton, Alta.; Dieter W. Jentsch, King City, Ont.; Donald B. (Don) Kayne, Delta, B.C.; Norman (Norm) Mayr, Port Moody, B.C.; Conrad A. Pinette, Vancouver, B.C.; William W. Stinson, Vancouver, B.C.; Sandra J. Stuart, Vancouver, B.C.

Other Exec. Officers - Kevin Edgson, pres. & CEO; David M. Calabrigo, sr. v-p, corp. devel., legal affairs & corp. sec.; Patrick A. J. (Pat) Elliott, sr. v-p, sustainability & CFO; Kevin Anderson, v-p, opers. & innovation; Brian Yuen, v-p, pulp & paper sales & mktg.

Capital Stock

	Authorized (shs.)	Outstanding (shs.)[1]
Common	unlimited	65,233,559

[1] At July 27, 2023

Major Shareholder - Canfor Corporation held 54.8% interest at July 27, 2023.

Price Range - CFX/TSX

Year	Volume	High	Low	Close
2022	6,971,205	$6.74	$3.90	$4.14
2021	19,469,500	$11.06	$5.90	$6.69
2020	17,690,172	$10.13	$4.01	$8.18
2019	21,248,260	$19.80	$7.36	$8.36
2018	23,082,011	$28.12	$12.95	$16.21

Recent Close: $1.87

Capital Stock Changes - There were no changes to capital stock from 2020 to 2022, inclusive.

Long-Term Debt - At Dec. 31, 2022, outstanding long-term debt totaled $50,000,000 (none current) and consisted entirely of a non-revolving term loan, bearing interest at Canadian prime rate, banker's acceptances, U.S. dollar base rate or U.S. dollar LIBOR rate, plus a margin and due November 2025.

Wholly Owned Subsidiaries

Canfor Pulp Ltd., Canada.

Financial Statistics

Periods ended:	12m Dec. 31/22A		12m Dec. 31/21A
	$000s	%Chg	$000s
Operating revenue	**1,085,600**	**-5**	**1,144,900**
Cost of goods sold	866,800		862,100
General & admin expense	29,000		28,300
Other operating expense	140,500		137,700
Operating expense	**1,036,300**	**+1**	**1,028,100**
Operating income	**49,300**	**-58**	**116,800**
Deprec., depl. & amort.	97,800		87,300
Finance income	nil		100
Finance costs, gross	7,300		5,100
Write-downs/write-offs	(49,600)		(95,000)
Pre-tax income	**(108,300)**	**n.a.**	**(61,000)**
Income taxes	(29,200)		(16,600)
Net income	**(79,100)**	**n.a.**	**(44,400)**
Cash & equivalent	14,700		73,300
Inventories	183,200		211,800
Accounts receivable	87,600		76,200
Current assets	314,400		372,100
Fixed assets, net	418,200		448,200
Right-of-use assets	1,800		2,100
Intangibles, net	13,200		16,600
Total assets	**756,000**	**-10**	**841,700**
Bank indebtedness	15,000		nil
Accts. pay. & accr. liabs	150,100		147,000
Current liabilities	166,000		150,900
Long-term debt, gross	50,000		50,000
Long-term debt, net	50,000		50,000
Long-term lease liabilities	1,900		2,100
Shareholders' equity	427,400		495,000
Cash from oper. activs	**45,300**	**-70**	**148,900**
Cash from fin. activs	8,300		(4,300)
Cash from invest. activs	(112,200)		(78,100)
Net cash position	**14,700**	**-80**	**73,300**
Capital expenditures	(112,600)		(78,700)
Unfunded pension liability	18,400		25,500
	$		$
Earnings per share*	(1.21)		(0.68)
Cash flow per share*	0.69		2.28
	shs		shs
No. of shs. o/s*	65,233,559		65,233,559
Avg. no. of shs. o/s*	65,233,559		65,233,559
	%		%
Net profit margin	(7.29)		(3.88)
Return on equity	(17.15)		(8.64)
Return on assets	(9.23)		(4.62)
Foreign sales percent	93		94
No. of employees (FTEs)	1,196		1,277

* Common
A Reported in accordance with IFRS

Latest Results

Periods ended:	6m June 30/23A		6m June 30/22oA
	$000s	%Chg	$000s
Operating revenue	492,800	-3	509,200
Net income	(47,200)	n.a.	(25,600)
	$		$
Earnings per share*	(0.72)		(0.39)

* Common
o Restated
A Reported in accordance with IFRS

Historical Summary
(as originally stated)

Fiscal Year	Oper. Rev. $000s	Net Inc. Bef. Disc. $000s	EPS* $
2022A	1,085,600	(79,100)	(1.21)
2021A	1,144,900	(44,400)	(0.68)
2020A	990,500	(22,400)	(0.34)
2019A	1,087,900	(30,500)	(0.47)
2018A	1,374,300	184,400	2.83

* Common
A Reported in accordance with IFRS

C.51 Canlan Ice Sports Corp.

Symbol - ICE **Exchange** - TSX **CUSIP** - 137639
Head Office - 6501 Sprott St, Burnaby, BC, V5B 3B8 **Telephone** - (604) 736-9152 **Fax** - (604) 736-9170
Website - www.canlansports.com
Email - iwu@canlansports.com
Investor Relations - Ivan C. Wu (604) 736-9152
Auditors - KPMG LLP C.A., Vancouver, B.C.
Lawyers - DLA Piper (Canada) LLP, Vancouver, B.C.
Transfer Agents - Computershare Trust Company of Canada Inc., Vancouver, B.C.
Employees - 950 at Dec. 31, 2022

Profile - (B.C. 2019 amalg.; orig. B.C., 2004 amalg.) Acquires, develops and operates recreational facilities in Canada and the United States.

Owns, leases or manages a network of 17 facilities, containing 49 full-sized ice sheets, five indoor turf fields, 20 multi-sport hard courts and outdoor beach volleyball courts in British Columbia, Saskatchewan, Manitoba, Ontario and Illinois. The company owns 12 of these facilities, operates one under a long-term lease arrangement, one under an operating agreement with a municipality, one under operating leases and manages two on behalf of third party owners.

Revenue is generated from ice and field rentals, internal programming, restaurant and concession operations, retail sports store operations, sponsorships and advertising, indoor and exterior space rentals, and management and consulting services.

Recent Merger and Acquisition Activity

Status: completed **Announced:** Feb. 28, 2023

Canlan Ice Sports Corp. exercised its option to acquire Canlan Sports Libertyville, a non-ice sports complex facility in Libertyville, Ill., for US$3,750,000. The sports complex contains two boarded soccer pitches, a fitness centre, rock climbing, nine sport courts, an outdoor baseball diamond and a concession.

Predecessor Detail - Name changed from Canlan Investment Corporation, Aug. 3, 1999.

Directors - Victor D'Souza, chr., Toronto, Ont.; Joey St-Aubin, pres. & CEO, Courtice, Ont.; Frank D. Barker, Vancouver, B.C.; Geoffrey J. Barker, Surrey, B.C.; Doug Brownridge, B.C.; Connie Carras, Ont.; Don Crowe, Redmond, Wash.; Chris McMullen, Toronto, Ont.

Other Exec. Officers - Ivan C. Wu, CFO; Michael F. Gellard, exec. v-p; Mark Faubert, sr. v-p, opers. & COO; Liana Guiry, v-p, sales, mktg. & cust. experience; Chad Mahabir, v-p, tech.; Rita Price, v-p, HR & chief privacy officer

Capital Stock

	Authorized (shs.)	Outstanding (shs.)[1]
Preferred	unlimited	nil
Common	500,000,000	13,337,448

[1] At May 17, 2023

Major Shareholder - Bartrac Investments Ltd. held 75.5% interest and the Article 6 Trust, created under the Jerry Zucker Revocable Trust held 17.2% interest at May 17, 2023.

Price Range - ICE/TSX

Year	Volume	High	Low	Close
2022	109,324	$4.35	$3.20	$3.90
2021	52,247	$4.81	$2.63	$3.40
2020	149,086	$5.58	$2.43	$3.65
2019	116,799	$5.34	$4.32	$5.10
2018	205,646	$5.94	$3.83	$4.73

Recent Close: $4.26

Capital Stock Changes - There were no changes to capital stock from 2010 to 2022, inclusive.

Dividends

ICE com N.S.R.

$0.03	Oct. 16/23	$0.03	July 17/23
$0.03	Apr. 14/23	$0.03	Jan. 16/23

Paid in 2023: $0.12 2022: n.a. 2021: n.a.

Wholly Owned Subsidiaries

Canlan Ice Sports (USA) Corp., Wash.
Canlan Ventures Ltd.
P.C. Development Inc., Ore.

Financial Statistics

Periods ended:	12m Dec. 31/22[A]		12m Dec. 31/21[A]
	$000s	%Chg	$000s
Total revenue	**73,728**	**+83**	**40,393**
Cost of real estate sales	26,685		16,331
Salaries & benefits	34,763		23,630
General & admin. expense	1,636		1,171
Operating expense	**63,084**	**+53**	**41,132**
Operating income	**10,644**	**n.a.**	**(739)**
Deprec. & amort.	8,379		7,801
Finance income	208		40
Finance costs, gross	2,636		2,625
Pre-tax income	**5,129**	**n.a.**	**(2,546)**
Income taxes	399		(1,454)
Net income	**4,730**	**n.a.**	**(1,092)**
Cash & equivalent	18,532		12,530
Inventories	607		490
Accounts receivable	2,184		2,298
Current assets	22,796		16,106
Fixed assets	205,261		202,637
Property interests, net	95,523		97,432
Total assets	**121,713**	**+4**	**116,612**
Accts. pay. & accr. liabs.	8,396		7,650
Current liabilities	31,034		25,896
Long-term debt, gross	39,812		43,796
Long-term debt, net	38,067		39,360
Long-term lease liabilities	4,816		9,970
Shareholders' equity	46,651		40,416
Cash from oper. activs.	**10,577**	**-13**	**12,136**
Cash from fin. activs.	(1,450)		(13,715)
Cash from invest. activs.	(3,397)		6,649
Net cash position	**18,532**	**+48**	**12,530**
Capital expenditures	(3,696)		(584)
Capital disposals	299		7,233
	$		$
Earnings per share*	0.35		(0.08)
Cash flow per share*	0.79		0.91
Cash divd. per share*	0.03		nil
	shs		shs
No. of shs. o/s*	13,337,448		13,337,448
Avg. no. of shs. o/s*	13,337,448		13,337,448
	%		%
Net profit margin	6.42		(2.70)
Return on equity	10.87		(2.66)
Return on assets	6.01		0.03
Foreign sales percent	16		19
No. of employees (FTEs)	950		800

* Common
[A] Reported in accordance with IFRS

Latest Results

Periods ended:	3m Mar. 31/23[A]		3m Mar. 31/22[A]
	$000s	%Chg	$000s
Total revenue	24,477	+29	18,948
Net income	3,445	+63	2,117
	$		$
Earnings per share*	0.26		0.16

* Common
[A] Reported in accordance with IFRS

Historical Summary
(as originally stated)

Fiscal Year	Total Rev.	Net Inc. Bef. Disc.	EPS*
	$000s	$000s	$
2022[A]	73,728	4,730	0.35
2021[A]	40,393	(1,092)	(0.08)
2020[A]	39,259	(6,363)	(0.48)
2019[A]	88,341	2,448	0.18
2018[A]	87,638	4,483	0.34

* Common
[A] Reported in accordance with IFRS

C.52 Cann-Is Capital Corp.

Symbol - NIS.P **Exchange** - TSX-VEN **CUSIP** - 13765T
Head Office - c/o 1 First Canadian Place, 1600-100 King St W, Toronto, ON, M5X 1G5 **Telephone** - (416) 862-4479
Email - jonathan@graffcapital.com
Investor Relations - Jonathan Graff (416) 862-3558
Auditors - MNP LLP C.A., Toronto, Ont.
Lawyers - Gowling WLG (Canada) LLP, Toronto, Ont.
Transfer Agents - TSX Trust Company, Toronto, Ont.
Profile - (Ont. 2017) Capital Pool Company.
Directors - James Lanthier, chr., Toronto, Ont.; Jonathan Graff, CEO, Toronto, Ont.; Joshua Hazenfratz, Ramat HaSharon, Israel; Geoffrey A. Rotstein, Toronto, Ont.
Other Exec. Officers - Ronnie (Ronen) Jaegermann, CFO

Capital Stock

	Authorized (shs.)	Outstanding (shs.)[1]
Preference	unlimited	nil
Common	unlimited	5,217,518

[1] At Aug. 24, 2022

Major Shareholder - Ronnie (Ronen) Jaegermann held 29.9% interest at Apr. 1, 2021.

Price Range - NIS.P/TSX-VEN

Year	Volume	High	Low	Close
2020	121,000	$0.15	$0.01	$0.15
2019	97,000	$0.13	$0.07	$0.08
2018	140,610	$0.24	$0.10	$0.10

C.53 Canna 8 Investment Trust

Symbol - RCR.P **Exchange** - TSX-VEN **CUSIP** - 13766K
Head Office - Wildeboer Dellelce Place, 800-365 Bay St, Toronto, ON, M5H 2V1 **Telephone** - (647) 218-2849
Email - gpillai@realcannareit.com
Investor Relations - Gopikannan Pillai (647) 218-2849
Auditors - RSM Canada LLP C.A., Toronto, Ont.
Lawyers - Wildeboer Dellelce LLP, Toronto, Ont.
Transfer Agents - TSX Trust Company, Toronto, Ont.
Profile - (Ont. 2018) Capital Pool Company.
Trustees - Dean Parmar, CEO, Edmonton, Alta.; Nebojsa Dobrijevic, CFO & corp. sec., Toronto, Ont.; Sundeep Cheema, Edmonton, Alta.; Gopikannan (Gopi) Pillai, Oakville, Ont.; Shant Poladian, Toronto, Ont.

Capital Stock

	Authorized (shs.)	Outstanding (shs.)[1]
Trust Unit	unlimited	12,120,000
Special Voting Unit	unlimited	nil

[1] At Aug. 22, 2022

Major Shareholder - Nebojsa Dobrijevic held 14.85% interest and Gopikannan (Gopi) Pillai held 14.85% interest at May 14, 2021.

Price Range - RCR.P/TSX-VEN

Year	Volume	High	Low	Close
2022	383,000	$0.03	$0.01	$0.01
2021	374,500	$0.07	$0.02	$0.02
2019	319,600	$0.15	$0.05	$0.06
2018	529,176	$0.39	$0.05	$0.15

Recent Close: $0.01

C.54 Cannabix Technologies Inc.

Symbol - BLO **Exchange** - CSE **CUSIP** - 13765L
Head Office - 501-3292 Production Way, Burnaby, BC, V5A 4R4 **Telephone** - (604) 551-7831 **Fax** - (604) 676-2767
Website - www.cannabixtechnologies.com
Email - info@cannabixtechnologies.com
Investor Relations - Ravinder S. Mlait (604) 551-7831
Auditors - Saturna Group Chartered Accountants LLP C.A., Vancouver, B.C.
Lawyers - Clark Wilson LLP, Vancouver, B.C.
Transfer Agents - TSX Trust Company, Vancouver, B.C.
Profile - (B.C. 2011) Developing the Cannabix marijuana breathalyzer for law enforcement and the workplace.

The company's marijuana breathalyzer device is being developed to provide rapid detection of tetrahydrocannabinol (THC) and can be used roadside to identify drivers intoxicated by the use of marijuana and test employees in the workplace where intoxication by THC can be hazardous. Cannabix devices are in advanced prototype and pre-clinical testing stages.

Holds a 20-year a licence agreement with the University of British Columbia (UBC) to develop a marijuana breath detection device based upon microfluid sensor technology developed at UBC. Also holds a licence agreement with University of Florida to develop a marijuana breath detection device based upon field asymmetric waveform ion mobility spectrometry (FAIMS) and mass spectrometry (MS).

In April 2022, the company announced that it has developed a Contactless Alcohol Breathalyzer (CAB) prototype for vehicle cabins and entered into a non-disclosure agreement with the Tier 1 global automobile parts manufacturer. The company filed a provisional patent application for its CAB technology, which is intended to measure breath samples in a contactless (no straw, no mouthpiece) method.

Predecessor Detail - Name changed from West Point Resources Inc., Aug. 12, 2014.

Directors - Ravinder S. (Rav) Mlait, CEO, Coquitlam, B.C.; Kulwant (Kal) Malhi, pres., Vancouver, B.C.; Bryan E. Loree, CFO & corp. sec., Burnaby, B.C.; Dr. Raj Attariwala, chief scientific officer, Vancouver, B.C.; Thomas W. Clarke, Calgary, Alta.

Other Exec. Officers - Dr. Moe Paknahad, v-p, tech. devel.

Capital Stock

	Authorized (shs.)	Outstanding (shs.)[1]
Preferred	unlimited	nil
Common	unlimited	114,144,104

[1] At Aug. 17, 2022

Major Shareholder - Widely held at June 3, 2022.

Price Range - BLO/CSE

Year	Volume	High	Low	Close
2022	10,741,105	$0.84	$0.26	$0.33
2021	40,380,970	$2.49	$0.50	$0.54
2020	36,438,040	$1.08	$0.31	$0.90
2019	34,792,139	$2.09	$0.35	$0.37
2018	172,922,661	$3.68	$1.02	$1.37

Recent Close: $0.27

Capital Stock Changes - During fiscal 2022, 1,765,000 common shares were issued on exercise of options.

Financial Statistics

Periods ended:	12m Apr. 30/22^A		12m Apr. 30/21^A
	$000s	%Chg	$000s
Research & devel. expense	1,261		1,104
General & admin expense	893		7,371
Stock-based compensation	1,214		810
Operating expense	**3,367**	**-64**	**9,285**
Operating income	**(3,367)**	**n.a.**	**(9,285)**
Deprec., depl. & amort.	29		26
Finance income	29		67
Pre-tax income	**(3,396)**	**n.a.**	**(9,243)**
Net income	**(3,396)**	**n.a.**	**(9,243)**
Cash & equivalent	8,454		10,095
Accounts receivable	46		14
Current assets	8,522		10,119
Fixed assets, net	192		216
Total assets	**8,760**	**-16**	**10,381**
Accts. pay. & accr. liabs	121		81
Current liabilities	121		81
Shareholders' equity	8,639		10,301
Cash from oper. activs	**(2,129)**	**n.a.**	**(1,710)**
Cash from fin. activs	493		3,490
Cash from invest. activs	(5)		(122)
Net cash position	**8,454**	**-16**	**10,095**
Capital expenditures	(5)		(76)
	$		$
Earnings per share*	(0.03)		(0.09)
Cash flow per share*	(0.02)		(0.02)
	shs		shs
No. of shs. o/s*	114,144,104		112,379,104
Avg. no. of shs. o/s*	114,057,227		107,137,394
	%		%
Net profit margin	n.a.		n.a.
Return on equity	(35.86)		(97.58)
Return on assets	(35.48)		(96.70)

* Common

^A Reported in accordance with IFRS

Historical Summary
(as originally stated)

Fiscal Year	Oper. Rev.	Net Inc. Bef. Disc.	EPS*
	$000s	$000s	$
2022^A	nil	(3,396)	(0.03)
2021^A	nil	(9,243)	(0.09)
2020^A	nil	(6,971)	(0.07)
2019^A	nil	(3,881)	(0.04)
2018^A	nil	(1,468)	(0.02)

* Common

^A Reported in accordance with IFRS

C.55 Cannara Biotech Inc.

Symbol - LOVE **Exchange** - TSX-VEN **CUSIP** - 13765U

Head Office - 200-333 boul Décarie, Saint-Laurent, QC, H4N 3M9 **Telephone** - (514) 543-4200

Website - www.cannara.ca

Email - nick@cannara.ca

Investor Relations - Nicholas Sosiak (514) 543-4200 ext. 254

Auditors - KPMG LLP C.A., Montréal, Qué.

Bankers - Canadian Imperial Bank of Commerce

Lawyers - Dentons Canada LLP, Montréal, Qué.

Transfer Agents - Computershare Trust Company of Canada Inc., Montréal, Qué.

Profile - (B.C. 2017) Cultivates, processes and sells cannabis and cannabis derivative products in Canada. Also leases out a portion of one of its cannabis facilities and operates an online e-commerce platform for hemp CBD (cannabidiol) products in the U.S.

In Quebec, owns a 625,000-sq.-ft. indoor cannabis cultivation and processing facility in Farnham, comprising of a 170,000 sq. ft. operational licensed cultivation area and a 455,000 sq. ft. leased house warehouse space; and a 1,034,000-sq.-ft. hybrid indoor/greenhouse cannabis cultivation and processing facility in Valleyfield, consisting of 24 independent growing zones totaling 600,000 sq. ft., a 225,000-sq.-ft. cannabis 2.0 processing centre and a 200,000-sq.-ft. rooftop greenhouse. The independent growing zones at the Valleyfield facility are being converted for indoor cultivation. Products are marketed under three flagship brands, Tribal, Nugz and Orchid CBD, which include dried flower, pre-roll, live resin full spectrum extract, live resin vape cartridges and hash products.

Operates www.shopCBD.com, an online e-commerce platform which offers a selection of hemp-based CBD products for U.S. consumers. Products include oils and tinctures, body and skin care products, edibles and drinks, capsules and pet-related products.

Predecessor Detail - Name changed from Dunbar Capital Corp., Dec. 31, 2018, pursuant to the Qualifying Transaction reverse takeover acquisition of (old) Cannara Biotech Inc. and concurrent amalgamation of (old) Cannara with wholly owned 11038427 Canada Inc.

Directors - Zohar Krivorot, chr., pres. & CEO, Montréal, Qué.; Donald Olds†, Montréal, Qué.; Mary Durocher, Ont.; Jack M. Kay, Toronto, Ont.; Derek Stern, Montréal, Qué.

Other Exec. Officers - Nicholas Sosiak, CFO; Avi Krivorot, chief tech. officer; Issam Ben Moussa, v-p, prod. & experimentation; Noémi Follain, v-p, fin.; France Landry, v-p, HR; Anthony Manouk, v-p, compliance & gen. mgr.; Brian Sherman, v-p, legal affairs & gen. counsel

† Lead director

Capital Stock

	Authorized (shs.)	Outstanding (shs.)[1]
Common	unlimited	87,748,132

[1] At Feb. 13, 2023

Normal Course Issuer Bid - The company plans to make normal course purchases of up to 15,000,000 common shares representing 1.7% of the total outstanding. The bid commenced on Dec. 3, 2022, and expires on Dec. 2, 2023.

Major Shareholder - Zohar Krivorot held 27.6% interest and Derek Stern held 19.01% interest at Dec. 12, 2022.

Price Range - LOVE/TSX-VEN

Year	Volume	High	Low	Close
2022	3,645,222	$1.50	$0.85	$0.95
2021	18,405,174	$1.85	$0.80	$1.35
2020	11,386,003	$1.75	$0.70	$0.80
2019	26,407,722	$3.45	$0.95	$1.25

Consolidation: 1-for-10 cons. in Feb. 2023

Recent Close: $1.05

Capital Stock Changes - On Feb. 13, 2023, common shares were consolidated on a 1-for-10 basis and 2,955,414 post-consolidated common shares were issued on conversion of $5,317,645 of debentures.

During fiscal 2022, 500,000 common shares were issued on exercise of options.

Wholly Owned Subsidiaries

Cannara Biotech (Québec) Inc., Canada.
Cannara Biotech (Ops) Inc., B.C.
Cannara Biotech (Valleyfield) Inc., Canada.
Global shopCBD.com Inc., Canada.
- 100% int. in **ShopCBD.com**, United States.

Financial Statistics

Periods ended:	12m Aug. 31/22^A		12m Aug. 31/21^A
	$000s	%Chg	$000s
Operating revenue	**35,483**	**+118**	**16,290**
Cost of sales	18,510		6,724
Salaries & benefits	2,969		2,056
Research & devel. expense	1,257		1,907
General & admin expense	6,708		4,924
Stock-based compensation	349		324
Operating expense	**29,793**	**+87**	**15,935**
Operating income	**5,689**	**n.m.**	**355**
Deprec., depl. & amort.	1,229		1,032
Finance income	679		53
Finance costs, gross	3,314		1,838
Pre-tax income	**2,305**	**n.a.**	**(1,528)**
Net income	**2,305**	**n.a.**	**(1,528)**
Cash & equivalent	12,115		8,159
Inventories	13,267		5,508
Accounts receivable	8,527		2,895
Current assets	40,989		19,247
Fixed assets, net	83,290		71,517
Right-of-use assets	114		233
Total assets	**125,617**	**+37**	**92,023**
Accts. pay. & accr. liabs	9,308		6,263
Current liabilities	11,861		6,834
Long-term debt, gross	48,155		20,454
Long-term debt, net	46,187		20,151
Long-term lease liabilities	17		217
Shareholders' equity	66,736		64,116
Cash from oper. activs	**(6,079)**	**n.a.**	**(2,093)**
Cash from fin. activs	25,464		33,252
Cash from invest. activs	(15,345)		(30,829)
Net cash position	**12,115**	**+48**	**8,159**
Capital expenditures	(15,096)		(30,606)
Capital disposals	63		217
	$		$
Earnings per share*	0.10		(0.02)
Cash flow per share*	(0.07)		(0.03)
	shs		shs
No. of shs. o/s*	87,698,132		87,648,132
Avg. no. of shs. o/s*	87,668,954		76,515,159
	%		%
Net profit margin	6.50		(9.38)
Return on equity	3.52		(2.98)
Return on assets	5.16		0.42

* Common

^A Reported in accordance with IFRS

Latest Results

Periods ended:	3m Nov. 30/22^A		3m Nov. 30/21^A
	$000s	%Chg	$000s
Operating revenue	10,241	+62	6,327
Net income	3	n.a.	(530)
	$		$
Earnings per share*	nil		(0.01)

* Common

^A Reported in accordance with IFRS

Historical Summary
(as originally stated)

Fiscal Year	Oper. Rev.	Net Inc. Bef. Disc.	EPS*
	$000s	$000s	$
2022^A	35,483	2,305	0.10
2021^A	16,290	(1,528)	(0.02)
2020^A	2,475	(13,094)	(0.20)
2019^A1	2,097	(12,972)	(0.20)
2018^A2,3	433	(2,113)	n.a.

* Common

^A Reported in accordance with IFRS

[1] Results reflect the Dec. 31, 2018, Qualifying Transaction reverse takeover acquisition of (old) Cannara Biotech Inc.

[2] 27 weeks ended Aug. 31, 2018.

[3] Results pertain to (old) Cannara Biotech Inc. As shown in the prospectus dated Dec. 14, 2018.

Note: Adjusted throughout for 1-for-10 cons. in Feb. 2023

C.56 Cannibble Foodtech Ltd.

Symbol - PLCN **Exchange** - CSE **CUSIP** - M2160A

Head Office - PO Box 4250, Rosh Haayin, Israel, 4856602 **Overseas Tel** - 972-54-430-9583

Website - cannibble.world

Email - yoav.b@cannibble.world

Investor Relations - Yoav Bar-Joseph 972-54-430-9583

Auditors - BDO Ziv Haft C.P.A., Tel Aviv, Israel

Transfer Agents - Odyssey Trust Company

Profile - (Israel 2018) Develops and manufactures powder food and drink mix products marketed under the brand name The Pelicann, that are subsequently infused with hemp seeds, hemp protein, cannabidiol (CBD) and tetrahydrocannabinol (THC).

The company has developed a proprietary process technology for the manufacture of "Black Box" product mixes, which are manufactured in Israel and then shipped to external markets to be subsequently infused with THC, CBD, or hemp by a local manufacturer operating under the company's directions. The company has developed over 100 product SKUs of which 32 have been manufactured as at Jan. 31, 2022, and has three product families, based on whether the products are infused with THC, CBD, or hemp. Pelicann product offerings include CannaShakes™, CannaShakes Sports™, CannaMix™, CannaSpices™ and CannaPop™. Has an online store at www.thepelicann.com and a store on Amazon.com (the Pelicann) where it sells its hemp-based products.

Directors - Yoav Bar-Joseph, co-founder, chr. & CEO, Rosh Haayin, Israel; Elad Barkan, co-founder & chief tech. officer, Israel; Sophie Mas, Vancouver, B.C.; Aaron Meckler, Toronto, Ont.

Other Exec. Officers - Ziv Turner, co-founder & v-p, bus. devel.; Uri Ben-Or, CFO

Capital Stock

	Authorized (shs.)	Outstanding (shs.)
Ordinary	1,000,000,000	21,721,399

Major Shareholder - Yoav Bar-Joseph held 18.8% interest, Elad Barkan held 18.8% interest, Ziv Turner held 12.6% interest, Jeffrey Low held 12.3% interest and Asaf Porat held 12.3% interest at Mar. 3, 2022.

Price Range - PLCN/CSE

Year	Volume	High	Low	Close
2022	956,450	$0.93	$0.20	$0.35

Recent Close: $0.35

Wholly Owned Subsidiaries

EAZY Tech Inc.

C.57 Canntab Therapeutics Limited

Symbol - PILL **Exchange** - CSE **CUSIP** - 137799

Head Office - 223 Riviera Dr, Markham, ON, L3R 5J6 **Telephone** - (289) 301-3812 **Toll-free** - (833) 301-3812 **Fax** - (833) 615-2855

Website - www.canntab.ca

Email - richard@canntab.ca

Investor Relations - Richard Goldstein (833) 301-3812

Auditors - Clearhouse LLP C.A., Mississauga, Ont.

Lawyers - Gardiner Roberts LLP, Toronto, Ont.

Transfer Agents - Capital Transfer Agency Inc., Toronto, Ont.

Profile - (Can. 2010) Manufactures and distributes hard pill cannabinoid formulations in multiple doses and timed-release combinations.

Has developed an in-house technology to deliver standardized medical cannabis extract from selective strains in a variety of extended/sustained release pharmaceutical dosages for therapeutic use. The Extended Release (XR) tablet product delivers standardized medical cannabis extract from selective strains in a solid, extended release pharmaceutical dosage. The XR was design to address the accuracy of dosing, onset times, duration of action, bioavailability, discreetness of consumption, ease of spoilage and the reduction of side effects. The company plans to manufacture and distribute the XR Tablet in legal medical cannabis jurisdictions including Canada, select states within the U.S., Australia and Germany.

Has patents and patent applications in Canada, the U.S. and internationally. The company holds a cannabis standard processing and sales for medical purposes license, and a cannabis research license from Health Canada under the Cannabis Act.

Hard pill manufacturing occurs at the company's facility in Markham, Ont.; and cannabis is cultivated at its farms located in Regina, Sask., and Caledon, Ont., which have total capacity of 560 acres.

Predecessor Detail - Name changed from Telferscot Resources Inc., Apr. 9, 2018, following reverse takeover acquisition of (old) Canntab Therapeutics Limited and concurrent amalgamation of (old) Canntab with wholly owned 2611780 Ontario Inc. to form Canntab Therapeutics Subsidiary Limited; basis 1 new for 200 old shs.

Directors - Richard Goldstein, co-founder, interim CEO, CFO & corp. sec., Toronto, Ont.; Barry M. Polisuk, chr., Vaughan, Ont.; Vitor M. Fonseca, Toronto, Ont.

Other Exec. Officers - Joshi Laxminarayan, chief scientific officer

Capital Stock

	Authorized (shs.)	Outstanding (shs.)[1]
Common	unlimited	38,909,159

[1] At Aug. 31, 2022

Major Shareholder - Richard Goldstein held 10.88% interest and Jeffrey W. (Jeff) Renwick held 10.83% interest at Dec. 5, 2020.

Price Range - PILL/CSE

Year	Volume	High	Low	Close
2022	8,279,152	$0.79	$0.01	$0.02
2021	8,366,407	$1.09	$0.57	$0.72
2020	6,246,760	$1.15	$0.27	$0.80
2019	6,396,508	$1.17	$0.40	$0.55
2018	21,326,128	$24.00	$0.50	$1.14

Recent Close: $0.01

Capital Stock Changes - During fiscal 2022, common shares were issued as follows: 1,970,722 on exercise of warrants, 960,000 on exercise of options and 40,000 for services.

Wholly Owned Subsidiaries

Canntab USA, Inc., Del.
420 Therapeutics Inc.

Financial Statistics

Periods ended:	12m May 31/22[A]		12m May 31/21[A]
	$000s	%Chg	$000s
Operating revenue	**293**	**n.a.**	**nil**
Cost of goods sold	224		nil
Salaries & benefits	1,058		786
Research & devel. expense	205		80
General & admin expense	1,319		1,286
Stock-based compensation	450		633
Operating expense	**3,256**	**+17**	**2,785**
Operating income	**(2,963)**	**n.a.**	**(2,785)**
Deprec., depl. & amort.	635		546
Finance costs, gross	567		189
Write-downs/write-offs	(1,408)		(263)
Pre-tax income	**(3,689)**	**n.a.**	**(4,420)**
Net income	**(3,689)**	**n.a.**	**(4,420)**
Cash & equivalent	691		1,491
Inventories	489		1,721
Accounts receivable	210		207
Current assets	1,465		3,515
Fixed assets, net	779		2,066
Right-of-use assets	305		491
Intangibles, net	304		289
Total assets	**2,852**	**-55**	**6,361**
Bank indebtedness	60		60
Accts. pay. & accr. liabs	968		1,421
Current liabilities	2,558		1,665
Long-term debt, gross	1,426		968
Long-term debt, net	126		968
Long-term lease liabilities	201		354
Shareholders' equity	(311)		2,269
Cash from oper. activs	**(2,846)**	**n.a.**	**(2,849)**
Cash from fin. activs	1,895		2,595
Cash from invest. activs	151		(345)
Net cash position	**691**	**-54**	**1,491**
Capital expenditures	(30)		(272)
	$		$
Earnings per share*	(0.10)		(0.13)
Cash flow per share*	(0.08)		(0.08)
	shs		shs
No. of shs. o/s*	38,909,159		35,938,467
Avg. no. of shs. o/s*	37,723,925		34,552,675
	%		%
Net profit margin	n.m.		n.a.
Return on equity	n.m.		(152.47)
Return on assets	(67.77)		(71.29)

* Common
[A] Reported in accordance with IFRS

Latest Results

Periods ended:	3m Aug. 31/22[A]		3m Aug. 31/21[A]
	$000s	%Chg	$000s
Operating revenue	39	+11	35
Net income	(468)	n.a.	(604)
	$		$
Earnings per share*	(0.01)		(0.02)

* Common
[A] Reported in accordance with IFRS

Historical Summary
(as originally stated)

Fiscal Year	Oper. Rev. $000s	Net Inc. Bef. Disc. $000s	EPS* $
2022[A]	293	(3,689)	(0.10)
2021[A]	nil	(4,420)	(0.13)
2020[A]	133	(2,607)	(0.01)
2019[A]	240	(2,459)	(0.10)
2018[A1]	27	(2,408)	(0.11)

* Common
[A] Reported in accordance with IFRS
[1] Results reflect the Apr. 12, 2018, reverse takeover acquisition of Canntab Therapeutics Limited.

C.58 Canoe EIT Income Fund

Symbol - EIT.UN **Exchange** - TSX **CUSIP** - 13780R
Head Office - 2750-421 7 Ave SW, Calgary, AB, T2P 4K9 **Telephone** - (403) 571-5550 **Toll-free** - (877) 434-2796 **Fax** - (403) 571-5554
Website - www.canoefinancial.com
Email - info@canoefinancial.com
Investor Relations - Renata Colic (877) 434-2796
Auditors - PricewaterhouseCoopers LLP C.A., Calgary, Alta.
Lawyers - Blake, Cassels & Graydon LLP
Transfer Agents - Alliance Trust Company, Calgary, Alta.
Trustees - Alliance Trust Company, Calgary, Alta.
Managers - Canoe Financial LP, Calgary, Alta.
Portfolio Managers - Canoe Financial LP, Calgary, Alta.

Profile - (Alta. 1997) Invests in a diversified portfolio of income producing investments including securities of publicly traded real estate investment trusts, qualified limited partnerships, corporations and similar issuers, corporate debt, convertible debentures and preferred shares.

The fund will terminate on Dec. 31, 2050, unless an alternative termination date is approved by unitholders.

Canoe Financial LP, the fund's manager, is paid monthly a management fee calculated daily equal to 1.5% per annum on the first $250,000,000 of the daily total asset value (TAV) of the fund plus 1% per annum in excess of $250,000,000. The TAV shall be the fund's net asset value (NAV) plus the amount representing any outstanding preferred units if they are deducted from the assets of the fund in calculating the fund's NAV.

Sector allocation at Dec. 31, 2022 (as a percentage of net asset value):

Sector	Percentage
Financials	24.7%
Energy	21.3%
Healthcare	20.7%
Materials	13.3%
Industrials	10.0%
Consumer discretionary	8.2%
Consumer staples	6.7%
Cash	4.5%
Communication services	3.8%
Real estate	1.1%
Corporate bonds	0.9%
Other net assets (liabs.)	(15.2%)

Predecessor Detail - Name changed from EnerVest Diversified Income Trust, Nov. 6, 2013.

Oper. Subsid./Mgt. Co. Directors - Darcy Hulston, pres. & CEO, Calgary, Alta.; David J. Rain, Calgary, Alta.

Oper. Subsid./Mgt. Co. Officers - Kim Jativa, COO; Renata Colic, CFO; Darren N. Cabral, sr. v-p; Darcy M. Lake, sr. v-p, chief compliance officer & gen. counsel; Steve Mantrop, sr. v-p & natl. sales dir.; Robert (Rob) Taylor, sr. v-p, chief invest. officer & portfolio mgr.

Capital Stock

	Authorized (shs.)	Outstanding (shs.)[1]
Preferred Unit	unlimited	
Series 1		5,635,000[2]
Series 2		3,220,000[2]
Trust Unit	unlimited	171,389,143[3]

[1] At Dec. 31, 2022
[2] Classified as debt.
[3] At July 31, 2023.

Preferred Unit - Issuable in series. Non-voting. Classified as financial liability under IFRS.

Series 1 - Entitled to fixed cumulative preferential annual cash distributions of $1.20 per unit payable quarterly. Redeemable at $25 per unit on or after Mar. 15, 2024, together with any accrued and unpaid distributions. Retractable on or after Mar. 15, 2024, at $25 per unit plus any accrued and unpaid distributions.

Series 2 - Entitled to fixed cumulative preferential annual cash distributions of $1.20 per unit payable quarterly. Redeemable at $25.50 per unit on or after Mar. 15, 2024, and at $25 per unit on or after Mar. 15, 2025, together, in each case, with any accrued and unpaid distributions. Retractable on or after Mar. 15, 2025, at $25 per unit plus any accrued and unpaid distributions.

Trust Unit - Entitled to monthly cash distributions derived from income and other distributions received on the portfolio, less expenses and taxes payable of the fund. Entitled on December 31 each year to distribution of (i) net realized capital gains of the fund for the year ended and (ii) any excess of income of the fund over distributions otherwise made during the year. Retractable on a date determined by the fund each year at a price equal to 95% of the average net asset value per unit based on the three trading days preceding the retraction date, less any costs associated with the retraction. One vote per unit.

Major Shareholder - Widely held at Feb. 24, 2023.

Price Range - EIT.UN/TSX

Year	Volume	High	Low	Close
2022	64,799,463	$14.89	$12.04	$13.38
2021	62,989,144	$13.33	$9.85	$13.25
2020	64,623,692	$10.86	$5.06	$9.84
2019	41,061,767	$11.56	$9.85	$10.41
2018	36,574,800	$12.16	$9.04	$10.33

Recent Close: $12.72

Capital Stock Changes - During 2022, 13,836,000 trust units were issued under an at-the-market equity program and 71,000 trust units were retracted.

Dividends

EIT.UN tr unit Ra $1.20 pa M est. Sept. 15, 2009**
$0.44◆ .... Jan. 13/22
Paid in 2023: $1.00 2022: $1.20 + $0.44◆ 2021: $1.20

EIT.PR.A pfd ser 1 cum. red. ret. Ra $1.20 pa Q
EIT.PR.B pfd ser 2 cum. red. ret. Ra $1.20 pa Q
** Reinvestment Option ◆ Special

Financial Statistics

Periods ended:	12m Dec. 31/22[A]		12m Dec. 31/21[A]
	$000s	%Chg	$000s
Realized invest. gain (loss)	150,530		243,602
Unrealized invest. gain (loss)	86,762		322,973
Total revenue	**301,386**	**-51**	**613,161**
General & admin. expense	33,230		25,789
Operating expense	**33,230**	**+29**	**25,789**
Operating income	**268,156**	**-54**	**587,372**
Finance costs, gross	12,785		11,512
Pre-tax income	**255,371**	**-56**	**575,860**
Net income	**255,371**	**-56**	**575,860**
Cash & equivalent	98,232		145,479
Accounts receivable	6,204		5,543
Investments	2,401,226		2,090,460
Total assets	**2,506,108**	**+12**	**2,241,647**
Accts. pay. & accr. liabs	3,004		2,608
Debt	317,480		309,818
Shareholders' equity	2,168,892		1,914,210
Cash from oper. activs	**(50,125)**	**n.a.**	**(12,090)**
Cash from fin. activs	8,681		115,415
Net cash position	**94,232**	**-35**	**145,479**
	$		$
Earnings per share*	1.67		4.35
Cash flow per share*	(0.33)		(0.09)
Net asset value per share*	13.68		13.22
Cash divd. per share*	1.20		1.20
Extra divd. - cash*	nil		0.44
Total divd. per share*	**1.20**		**1.64**
	shs		shs
No. of shs. o/s*	158,560,000		144,795,000
Avg. no. of shs. o/s*	152,543,000		132,445,000
	%		%
Net profit margin	84.73		93.92
Return on equity	12.51		36.68
Return on assets	11.30		30.98

* Trust unit
[A] Reported in accordance with IFRS

Note: Net income reflects increase/decrease in net assets from operations.

Historical Summary
(as originally stated)

Fiscal Year	Total Rev. $000s	Net Inc. Bef. Disc. $000s	EPS* $
2022[A]	301,386	255,371	1.67
2021[A]	613,161	575,860	4.35
2020[A]	96,619	59,566	0.50
2019[A]	205,200	167,648	1.47
2018[A]	(34,486)	(67,890)	(0.74)

* Trust unit
[A] Reported in accordance with IFRS

C.59 Canopy Growth Corporation*

Symbol - WEED **Exchange** - TSX **CUSIP** - 138035
Head Office - 1 Hershey Dr, Smiths Falls, ON, K7A 0A8 **Toll-free** - (855) 558-9333
Website - www.canopygrowth.com
Email - tyler.burns@canopygrowth.com
Investor Relations - Tyler Burns (855) 558-9333
Auditors - PKF O'Connor Davies, LLP C.P.A., New York, N.Y.
Transfer Agents - Odyssey Trust Company, Toronto, Ont.
FP500 Revenue Ranking - 458
Employees - 1,621 at Mar. 31, 2023
Profile - (Can. 2009) Produces, distributes and sells cannabis products for the recreational and medical markets across Canada and in other countries where cannabis and/or hemp operations are legally permissible including the U.S., Europe and Australia. Also manufactures and sells consumer packaged goods globally, including vaporizer devices, skincare and wellness products, and sports nutrition and hydration products.

In Canada, serves the recreational and medical cannabis markets through the production and sale of various cannabis products, including dried flower and pre-rolled joints, extracts and concentrates such as softgel capsules, beverages, gummies and vapes. Operations are primarily focused in two cultivation facilities located in Kincardine, Ont., and Kelowna, B.C., with a manufacturing site in Smiths Falls, Ont. Recreational brands include Tweed, 7ACRES, 7ACRES Craft Collective, DOJA, Deep Space, Vert, HiWay and Ace Valley which are sold to provincial and territorial agencies under a business-to-business wholesale model. Through Spectrum Therapeutics, the company's international medical brand, medical cannabis products are sold directly to consumers via an e-commerce shop.

Internationally, Spectrum Therapeutics imports and distributes medical cannabis in Europe, primarily Germany and Poland, and Australia. In addition, offers health and wellness hemp-derived cannabidiol (CBD) products under the Martha Stewart CDB brand.

Also operates wholly owned Tuttlingen, Germany-based **Storz & Bickel GmbH**, which designs, manufactures and sells medically approved vaporizers and other similar devices to 130 markets worldwide; wholly owned London, U.K.-based **This Works Products Limited**, which produces and sells beauty, skincare, wellness and sleep solution products, some of which have been blended with hemp-derived CBD, under the This Works brand globally; and subsidiary **BioSteel Sports Nutrition Inc.**, which produces and sells sports nutrition beverages, hydration mixes, proteins and other specialty nutrition products in North America.

On May 30, 2023, the company and **Indiva Limited** entered into a licence assignment and assumption agreement providing the company exclusive rights and interests to manufacture, distribute and sell Indiva's Wana™ branded sour gummies and soft chews in Canada. Indiva would also manufacture Wana™ for the company in Canada. As consideration for Indiva entering into the agreements, Indiva completed a private placement of common shares on June 16, 2023, with the company subscribing for 37,230,000 common shares for an aggregate purchase price of $2,155,617 at a price per share of $0.0579. Upon closing of the private placement, Canopy held control over 19.99% of the common shares of Indiva.

In June 2023, the company announced a partnership with Quebec-based cannabis cultivator **VASCO Cannabis Inc.** to produce and supply craft cannabis for distribution under the Vert Collab brand in Quebec. The company would also introduce Maitri, its second Quebec-focused flower brand.

In May 2023, the company modified the structure of its interest in U.S.-domiciled holding company **Canopy USA, LLC** to comply with NASDAQ listing requirements. Upon receiving shareholder approval for the creation of a new class of non-voting exchangeable shares in the capital of the company, Canopy USA was expected to exercise rights to acquire **Acreage Holdings, Inc.**; **Mountain High Products, LLC**, **Wana Wellness, LLC** and **The Cima Group, LLC** (collectively Wana); and **Lemurian, Inc.** (dba Jetty). Under the modified structure, the company would not be required to consolidate the financial results of Canopy USA with the company's financial statements. The agreed upon structural amendments to the company's interests in Canopy USA include reducing its economic interest in Canopy USA to no greater than 90%, adjustments to the composition and nomination rights of Canopy USA's board of managers, and modifications to the terms of the initial protection agreement.

During fiscal 2023, the company acquired an additional 11.8% interest in **BioSteel Sports Nutrition Inc.** for issuance of 8,692,128 common shares valued at $26,506,000, thereby increasing its interest to 90.4% from 78.6%.

On Feb. 9, 2023, the company announced a number of changes to its Canadian operations including exiting cannabis flower cultivation at its 1 Hershey Drive facility in Smith Falls, Ont.; ceasing the sourcing of cannabis flower from the leased Mirabel, Que., facility; consolidating cultivation at existing facilities in Kincardine, Ont., and Kelowna, B.C.; and moving to a third-party sourcing model for all cannabis beverages, edibles, vapes and extracts. Manufacturing of cannabis flower, pre-rolled joints, softgel and oils would be consolidated at the company's existing beverage production facility in Smiths Falls, and the company would migrate its existing genetics program to Quebec-based **EXKA Inc.** The 1 Hershey Drive facility would be closed and sold. In March 2023, the company acquired the remaining 45% interest in **Les Serres Vert Cannabis Inc.**, operator of the Mirabel facility, for an undisclosed amount and subsequently terminated its lease for the facility. The changes resulted in the reduction of 800 positions and pre-tax restructuring and other charges of $547,533,000 during fiscal 2023.

In January 2023, the company closed its Scarborough, Ont., research facility.

On Oct. 25, 2022, the company announced the formation of a new U.S.-domiciled holding company, named **Canopy USA, LLC**, to hold its U.S. cannabis investments, which would enable it to exercise its options to acquire **Acreage Holdings, Inc.**, **Mountain High Products, LLC**, **Wana Wellness, LLC** and **The Cima Group, LLC** (collectively Wana) and **Lemurian, Inc.** (dba Jetty). In addition, Canopy USA acquired 38,890,570 exchangeable shares of **TerrAscend Corp.** as well as an option to acquire 1,072,450 TerrAscend common shares and 22,474,130 TerrAscend warrants from the company. As a result, Canopy USA held 13.7% interest in TerrAscend, assuming conversion of its exchangeable shares and the exercise of its option but excluding the exercise of its warrants. The company only holds non-voting and non-participating shares of Canopy USA. Until such time as the company converts the non-voting shares into common shares of Canopy USA, the company would not have economic or voting interest in Canopy USA or any of its investments. Canopy USA, Wana, Jetty, TerrAscend and Acreage would continue to operate independently of the company.

The company also proposed to create a new class of non-voting and non-participating exchangeable shares, which are convertible into common shares. Major shareholder **Constellation Brands, Inc.** (CBI) has expressed its intention to convert all common shares of the company it holds into exchangeable shares. If Constellation elects to convert, certain other transactions between the company and CBI would occur, including: (i) CBI surrendering for cancellation for no consideration all warrants to purchase common shares of the company held by CBI; (ii) the termination of investor rights agreement, administrative services agreement, co-development agreement, and any and all other commercial arrangements between the company's affiliates, on the one hand, and CBI and its affiliates; (iii) CBI would no longer have the right to nominate persons to the company's board of directors, would no longer have any approval rights over certain transactions proposed to be undertaken by the company, and restrictive covenants previously agreed between the parties would terminate; and (iv) all of CBI's nominees serving on the board are expected to resign.

If CBI does not convert its common shares into exchangeable shares, Canopy USA would not be permitted to exercise the rights to acquire Acreage, Wana or Jetty and the agreement to acquire the class D subordinate voting shares of Acreage would be terminated. In such circumstances, the company would retain its option to acquire the class E subordinate voting shares of Acreage and Canopy USA would continue to hold an option to acquire Wana and Jetty as well as exchangeable shares and other securities in the capital of TerrAscend.

Recent Merger and Acquisition Activity

Status: pending **Announced:** Aug. 17, 2023
Canopy Growth Corporation agreed to sell its facility at 1 Hershey Drive in Smith Falls, Ont., to Mississauga, Ont.-based Hershey Canada Inc., wholly owned by The Hershey Company, for $53,000,000. The transaction would represent the sale of the facility back to Hershey, which used to be one of its chocolate factories.

Status: completed **Announced:** June 29, 2023
Canopy Growth Corporation sold its Modesto, Calif., industrial hemp manufacturing facility. Terms were not disclosed.

Status: completed **Revised:** Jan. 3, 2023
UPDATE: The transaction was completed. PREVIOUS: Canopy Growth Corporation agreed to sell its Canadian retail operations including stores operating under the Tweed and Tokyo Smoke retail banners. Terms of the transaction were not disclosed. OEG Retail Cannabis (OEGRC), an existing Canopy licensee partner that owns and operates Canopy's franchised Tokyo Smoke stores in Ontario, has agreed to acquire all of Canopy's 23 corporate Tokyo Smoke and Tweed stores across Manitoba, Saskatchewan and Newfoundland and Labrador, as well as all Tokyo Smoke-related intellectual property. The acquired Tweed stores would be rebranded. OEGRC is a division of privately held Katz Group Canada Ltd. Canopy has also agreed to sell its five corporate retail locations in Alberta to Calgary, Alta.-based cannabis retailer 420 Investments Ltd. These stores would be rebranded to FOUR20. In addition, the master licence agreement between Canopy and Alimentation Couche-Tard Inc. with respect to the use of the Tweed brand for brick-and-mortar retail stores operating in Ontario was also terminated. Canopy would continue to own and operate the Tweed brand.

Status: pending **Revised:** Oct. 25, 2022
UPDATE: Newly formed U.S. holding company Canopy USA, LLC would complete the acquisition of Jetty. Canopy Growth would not hold any direct interest in Jetty. PREVIOUS: Canopy Growth Corporation agreed to acquire private California-based Lemurian, Inc. (dba Jetty), which produces cannabis extracts including solventless vape, live resin vape, and other products. The transaction was structured as two separate option agreements whereby Canopy has a call option to acquire 100% of the equity interest in Jetty. Canopy would make an upfront payment of US$69,000,000 payable through combination of cash and issuance of common shares in exchange for a 75% interest in Jetty. Upon exercise of the rights to acquire up to 100% interest in Jetty, Canopy would make an additional payment to be satisfied through a combination of cash and issuance of common shares.

Status: pending **Revised:** Oct. 25, 2022
UPDATE: Newly formed U.S. holding company Canopy USA, LLC would complete the acquisition of Wana. Canopy Growth would not hold any direct interest in Wana. PREVIOUS: Canopy Growth Corporation agreed to acquire Mountain High Products, LLC, Wana Wellness, LLC and The Cima Group, LLC (collectively Wana), which manufacture and sell gummies in Colorado and licenses its intellectual property to partners, who manufacture, distribute and sell Wana-branded gummies across the U.S. The transaction was structured as three separate option agreements whereby Canopy has a call option to acquire 100% of the membership interests in each Wana entity. Canopy would make an upfront cash payment in the aggregate amount of US$297,500,000. Upon exercise of the right to acquire each Wana entity, Canopy would make a payment equal to 15% of the fair market value of such Wana entity at the time the option was exercised. As additional consideration, Canopy may make additional deferred payments in respect to each Wana entity as of the 2.5 and 5-year anniversary of the upfront payment, less certain deductions. The call option and deferred payments may be satisfied in cash, shares or a combination thereof at Canopy's sole discretion.

Status: pending **Revised:** Oct. 25, 2022
UPDATE: Canopy announced the formation of a new U.S. domiciled entity Canopy USA, LLC which would complete the transaction with Acreage. Canopy USA would acquire all of the issued and outstanding class D subordinate voting shares of Acreage for consideration of 0.45 Canopy common share in exchange for each class D share. Concurrently, Canopy irrevocably waived its option to acquire the class D shares pursuant to the plan of arrangement implemented on Sept. 23, 2020, pursuant to the arrangement agreement between Canopy and Acreage dated Apr. 18, 2019. Canopy has agreed to exercise its option under the existing arrangement to acquire Acreage's outstanding class E subordinate voting shares, representing 70% of the total shares of Acreage, at a fixed exchange ratio of 0.3048 Canopy common share for each class E share. Upon completion of the acquisition of the Acreage class D and class E shares, Canopy USA would own all the shares. Under the existing arrangement, Canopy was not obligated to acquire the class D shares but rather had an option to acquire those shares at a minimum price of US$6.41 per class D share. The acquisition of the class D shares was expected to close in the second half of 2023, and the acquisition of the class E shares to immediately follow. PREVIOUS: Canopy Growth Corp. entered into an agreement with Acreage Holdings, Inc. that grants Canopy the rights to acquire 100% of Acreage once cannabis becomes federally legal in the United States. Under the agreement, Acreage shareholders would receive an upfront payment of US$300,000,000 or US$2.55 per subordinate voting share. The upfront cash payment would be made to holders of Acreage subordinate voting shares, class B proportionate voting shares and class C multiple voting shares as well as holders of units of High Street Capital Partners, LLC and shares of Acreage Holdings WC, Inc. Upon the exercise of the right, Acreage subordinate voting shares, including those outstanding on conversion of multiple voting shares and other convertible securities, would receive 0.5818 Canopy Growth common shares for each Acreage subordinate voting share held. Upon exercise of the right, the total consideration payable is valued at US$3.4 billion. The companies would also execute a licensing agreement granting Acreage access to Canopy's brands such as Tweed and Tokyo Smoke and other intellectual property. The transaction would require the approval of shareholders of both Canopy Growth and Acreage at special meetings expected to take place in June 2019. The agreement includes termination fee of US$150,000,000 payable by Acreage in the event that the transaction is terminated in certain circumstances. June 19, 2019 - Canopy and Acreage shareholders approved the transaction. The initial payment was expected to be made to Acreage shareholders on June 27, 2019. June 21, 2019 - Acreage received an approval for the transaction from the Supreme Court of British Columbia. June 27, 2019 - The option was completed. Acreage shareholders received approximately US$2.63 per subordinate voting share, being their pro rata portion of US$300,000,000. The payment was to be distributed on or before July 3, 2019. June 25, 2020 - The terms of the agreement were amended including an upfront payment of US$37,500,000, creation of two new classes of shares in the capital of Acreage, with each existing Acreage subordinate voting shares being converted into 0.7 of new S.V. shares; and new floating shares that are not tied to fixed exchange ratio. In addition, Canopy has agreed to loan up to US$100,000,000 to Acreage in the form of a secured debenture. Sept. 23, 2020 - Acreage created the following new classes of shares: class E subordinate voting, class D subordinate voting and class F multiple voting. Each outstanding Acreage class A subordinate voting share was exchanged for 0.7 class E shares and 0.3 class D shares; each outstanding Acreage class B proportionate voting share was exchanged for 28 class E shares and 12 class D shares; and each outstanding Acreage class C multiple voting share was exchanged for 0.3 class D shares and 0.7 class F shares. Under an amended agreement, Canopy would only be required to acquire all outstanding class E shares upon a federal legalization event on the basis of 0.3048 Canopy common shares for each Acreage class E share held. Immediately prior to the acquisition, all Acreage class F shares would be automatically convertible into class E shares on a one-for-one basis. The class D shares would then act as an option for Canopy, should Canopy desire to acquire a 100% interest in Acreage, with the acquisition price of the class D shares to be based on the 30-day weighted average price of the shares, subject to a floor price of US$6.41 per share.

Predecessor Detail - Name changed from Tweed Marijuana Inc., Sept. 17, 2015.

Directors - Judy A. Schmeling, chr., Indian Rocks Beach, Fla.; David E. Klein, CEO, Rochester, N.Y.; Garth Hankinson, Rochester, N.Y.; Robert L. Hanson, San Francisco, Calif.; David A. Lazzarato, Toronto, Ont.; James A. Sabia Jr., Chicago, Ill.; Theresa (Terry) Yanofsky, Westmount, Qué.

Other Exec. Officers - Judy Hong, CFO; Jenny Brewer, chief HR officer; Chris Edwards, chief strategy officer; Brenna Eller, chief commun. officer; Dr. Christelle Gedeon, chief legal officer & corp. sec.; Tara Rozalowsky, chief growth officer; Thomas C. (Tom) Stewart, chief acctg. officer

Capital Stock

	Authorized (shs.)	Outstanding (shs.)[1]
Common	unlimited	717,196,302

[1] At Aug. 3, 2023

Options - At Mar. 31, 2023, options were outstanding to purchase 13,750,888 common shares at prices ranging from $0.06 to $67.64

per share with a weighted average remaining contractual life of three years.

Warrants - At Mar. 31, 2023, warrants were outstanding exercisable for 128,193,047 common shares at a weighted average exercise price of $58.04 per share.

Major Shareholder - Constellation Brands, Inc. held 23.9% interest at Aug. 3, 2023.

Price Range - WEED/TSX

Year	Volume	High	Low	Close
2022	738,414,471	$12.18	$2.79	$3.14
2021	379,714,488	$71.60	$11.03	$11.04
2020	531,308,444	$38.22	$12.96	$31.32
2019	607,421,408	$70.98	$18.23	$27.31
2018	1,418,138,616	$76.68	$20.85	$36.61

Recent Close: $0.54

Capital Stock Changes - In June and July 2023, 118,279,181 common shares were issued as part of settlement of debt totaling $205,500,000. In August 2023, a share consolidation at a ratio between 1-for-5 and 1-for-15 was proposed.

In June and July 2022, 76,804,412 common shares were issued for settlement of $262,620,000 of 4.25% convertible senior notes. Also during fiscal 2023, common shares were issued as follows: 14,142,066 on conversion of convertible debentures, 12,751,008 pursuant to the assignment of rights to Acreage Holdings, Inc.'s tax receivable agreement, 8,692,128 for acquisition of an additional 11.8% interest in BioSteel Sports Nutrition Inc., 8,426,539 pursuant to the option to acquire Lemurian, Inc. (dba Jetty), 1,464,934 under restricted and performance share unit plans, 222,421 for completion of certain milestones, 79,586 on exercise of options and 299,853 for others.

In June 2021, 9,013,400 common shares were issued pursuant to the acquisition of The Supreme Cannabis Company, Inc. Also during fiscal 2022, common shares were issued as follows: 1,295,285 for completion of certain milestones, 445,680 on exercise of options, 300,319 under restricted and performance share unit plans and 492,741 for others.

Long-Term Debt - Outstanding at Mar. 31, 2023:

4.25% sr. notes due July 2023	$337,380,000
8% conv. debs. due Sept. 2025[1]	31,503,000
Accretion debs. due Sept. 2025[2]	8,780,000
Credit facility due Mar. 2026[3]	840,058,000
5% conv. debs. due Feb. 2028[4]	93,228,000
Other debts	2,062,000
Accrued interest	3,148,000
Fair value adjustments	(9,278,000)
	1,306,881,000
Less: Current portion	556,890,000
	749,991,000

[1] Issued by wholly owned The Supreme Cannabis Company, Inc. Convertible into 40.907767 common shares plus 35¢ cash for each $1,000 principal amount.

[2] Issued by wholly owned The Supreme Cannabis Company, Inc. Bears interest which accretes at a rate of 11.06% based on the remaining principal amount of the Supreme convertible debentures.

[3] Bears interest at LIBOR plus 8.5% and is subject to a LIBOR floor of 1%.

[4] Convertible into common shares at a price equal to 92.5% of the volume-weighted average price of the common shares during the three consecutive trading days ending on the business day prior to the date of conversion.

Note - In April 2023, $100,000,000 principal amount of 4.25% senior notes due July 2023 were refinanced with a $100,000,000 4.25% promissory note due December 2024. In June 2023, $12,500,000 principal amount of 4.25% senior notes due July 2023 were exchanged for cash, including accrued and unpaid interest, and issuance of 24,342,740 common shares. In July 2023, $193,000,000 principal amount of 4.25% senior notes due July 2023 were redeemed for $101,000,000 cash, issuance of 93,936,441 common shares and issuance of $41,500,000 principal amount of debentures; convertible into common shares at 55¢ per share. In addition, the company decreased $100,000,000 of principal indebtedness under the credit facility for a cash payment of $93,000,000.

Wholly Owned Subsidiaries

Apollo Applied Research Inc., Canada.
BC Tweed Joint Venture Inc., B.C.
Batavia Bio Processing Limited, Batavia, Ill.
Beckley Canopy Therapeutics Limited, Oxford, Oxon., United Kingdom.
Canindica Capital Ltd., Bahamas.
Canopy Elevate I, LLC, Del.
Canopy Elevate II, LLC, Del.
Canopy Elevate III, LLC, Del.
Canopy Growth Australia Pty Ltd., Australia.
Canopy Growth Chile S.p.A., Chile.
Canopy Growth Corporation de Mexico S. de R.L. de C.V., Mexico.
Canopy Growth Corporation Insurance Limited, Bermuda.
Canopy Growth Czech s.r.o., Czech Republic. formerly Annabis Medical s.r.o.
Canopy Growth Germany GmbH, Germany.
Canopy Growth Hellas S.A., Greece.
Canopy Growth Holdings B.V., Netherlands.
Canopy Growth LATAM Holdings Corporation, Canada.
Canopy Growth Polska Sp.zo.o., Poland.
Canopy Growth UK Limited, United Kingdom.
Canopy Growth USA, LLC, United States.
Canopy Oak, LLC, Del.
Coldstream Real Estate Holdings I LLC, Del.
Coldstream Real Estate Holdings II LLC, Del.
Coldstream Real Estate Holdings III LLC, Del.
EB Transaction Corp., Del.
EB Transaction Sub I, LLC, Del.
Grow House JA Limited, Jamaica.
HIP Developments LLC, Del.
HIP NY Developments LLC, Del.
Lakessence North America LLC, Ill.
9388036 Canada Inc., Canada.
10007705 Manitoba Ltd., Man.
10663824 Canada Inc., Canada.
11065220 Canada Inc., Canada.
11239490 Canada Inc., Canada.
11318152 Canada Inc., Canada.
1208640 B.C. Ltd., B.C.
POS Bio-Sciences USA Inc., United States.
POS Management Corp., Canada.
POS Pilot Plant Corporation, Canada.
Les Serres Vert Cannabis Inc., Mirabel, Qué.
Spectrum Biomedical UK Limited, Milton Keynes, Bucks., United Kingdom.
Spectrum Labs Brasil S.A., Brazil.
Storz & Bickel America, Inc., United States.
Storz & Bickel GmbH, Germany.
The Supreme Cannabis Company, Inc., Toronto, Ont.
Supreme Cannabis Ltd., Canada.
TWP UK Holdings Ltd., United Kingdom.
- 100% int. in **TWP IP Ltd.**, United Kingdom.
- 100% int. in **TWP USA Inc.**, United States.
- 100% int. in **This Works Products Limited**, London, Middx., United Kingdom.

Tweed Inc., Smiths Falls, Ont.
Tweed Leasing Corp., Canada.
2344823 Ontario Inc., Ont.

Subsidiaries

90.4% int. in **BioSteel Sports Nutrition Inc.**, Toronto, Ont.
- 100% int. in **BioSteel Manufacturing LLC**, Del.
- 100% int. in **Biosteel Sports Nutrition USA LLC**, United States.

Investments

Canopy USA, LLC, United States.
19.99% int. in **Indiva Limited**, Ottawa, Ont. (see separate coverage)

Note: The preceding list includes only the major related companies in which interests are held.

Financial Statistics

Periods ended:	12m Mar. 31/23[A]		12m Mar. 31/22[oA]
	$000s	%Chg	$000s
Operating revenue	**402,904**	**-21**	**510,321**
Cost of goods sold	460,820		663,176
General & admin expense	417,932		408,619
Stock-based compensation	31,188		47,525
Operating expense	**909,940**	**-19**	**1,119,320**
Operating income	**(507,036)**	**n.a.**	**(608,999)**
Deprec., depl. & amort.	84,517		114,418
Finance income	24,282		6,601
Finance costs, gross	126,160		103,944
Investment income	nil		(100)
Write-downs/write-offs	(1,799,694)[1]		(66,813)
Pre-tax income	**(3,314,320)**	**n.a.**	**(339,515)**
Income taxes	(4,774)		(8,948)
Net income	**(3,309,546)**	**n.a.**	**(330,567)**
Net inc. for equity hldrs	**(3,278,158)**	**n.a.**	**(310,043)**
Net inc. for non-cont. int	**(31,388)**	**n.a.**	**(20,524)**
Cash & equivalent	794,367		1,383,872
Inventories	148,901		204,539
Accounts receivable	66,820		68,197
Current assets	1,077,254		1,727,612
Long-term investments	568,292		800,328
Fixed assets, net	499,466		942,780
Intangibles, net	274,282		2,119,198
Total assets	**2,439,098**	**-56**	**5,605,260**
Accts. pay. & accr. liabs	152,225		139,548
Current liabilities	803,842		213,190
Long-term debt, gross	1,306,881		1,500,991
Long-term debt, net	749,991		1,491,695
Long-term lease liabilities	80,625		101,125
Shareholders' equity	758,435		3,583,574
Non-controlling interest	1,587		36,841
Cash from oper. activs	**(557,546)**	**n.a.**	**(545,811)**
Cash from fin. activs	(19,694)		(45,533)
Cash from invest. activs	433,379		230,819
Net cash position	**677,007**	**-13**	**776,005**
Capital expenditures	(9,217)		(36,684)
Capital disposals	13,609		27,279
	$		$
Earnings per share*	(7.07)		(0.79)
Cash flow per share*	(1.20)		(1.39)
	shs		shs
No. of shs. o/s*	517,305,551		394,422,604
Avg. no. of shs. o/s*	463,724,414		391,324,285
	%		%
Net profit margin	(821.42)		(64.78)
Return on equity	(150.78)		(8.78)
Return on assets	(79.05)		(3.69)
Foreign sales percent	33		44
No. of employees (FTEs)	1,621		3,151

* Common

[o] Restated

[A] Reported in accordance with U.S. GAAP

[1] Includes goodwill impairment charges totaling $1,785,080,000 as follows: $1,725,368,000 for the Canadian cannabis operations; $57,401,000 for the BioSteel unit; and $2,311,000 for the This Works unit.

Historical Summary
(as originally stated)

Fiscal Year	Oper. Rev.	Net Inc. Bef. Disc.	EPS*
	$000s	$000s	$
2023[A]	402,904	(3,309,546)	(7.07)
2022[A]	520,325	(320,485)	(0.77)
2021[A]	546,649	(1,670,820)	(4.69)
2020[A]	398,772	(1,387,440)	(3.80)
2019[B]	226,341	(670,094)	(2.57)

* Common

[A] Reported in accordance with U.S. GAAP

[B] Reported in accordance with IFRS

C.60 Canso Credit Income Fund

Symbol - PBY.UN **Exchange** - TSX **CUSIP** - 138080

Head Office - 3037-3080 Yonge St, Toronto, ON, M4N 3N1 **Telephone** - (416) 640-4275 **Toll-free** - (877) 308-6979 **Fax** - (416) 855-6515

Website - www.lysanderfunds.com

Email - rusherjones@cansofunds.com

Investor Relations - Richard Usher-Jones (905) 881-8853

Auditors - Deloitte LLP C.A., Toronto, Ont.

Lawyers - Stikeman Elliott LLP, Toronto, Ont.

Transfer Agents - TSX Trust Company, Toronto, Ont.

Trustees - BNY Trust Company of Canada, Toronto, Ont.

Managers - Lysander Funds Limited, Richmond Hill, Ont.

Portfolio Managers - Canso Investment Counsel Ltd., Richmond Hill, Ont.

Profile - (Ont. 2010) Invests in diversified portfolio consisting of long and short positions primarily of corporate bonds and other income securities.

Lysander Funds Limited, the manager of the fund, receives a management fee equal to 0.75% per annum of the fund's net asset value (NAV), calculated daily and payable monthly in arrears plus applicable taxes, as well as a performance fee equal to 20% of the fund's outperformance of the FTSE TMX Canada All Corporate Bond Index, payable only if the NAV per unit exceeds the highest level previously reached for calculation of the performance fee and the NAV per unit exceeds the cumulative performance of the index during the same period.

The fund does not have a fixed termination date, but may be terminated based on the discretion of the fund's manager.

Oper. Subsid./Mgt. Co. Directors - Richard Usher-Jones, pres. & CEO, Toronto, Ont.; Timothy Hicks, chief invest. officer, Toronto, Ont.; John Carswell, Richmond Hill, Ont.; Heather Mason-Wood, Richmond Hill, Ont.; Raymond Oh, Richmond Hill, Ont.; Salvatore (Sam) Reda, Verdun, Qué.; Lee Wong, Markham, Ont.

Oper. Subsid./Mgt. Co. Officers - Paul Adair, COO; Raj Vijh, CFO; Ruth Liu, chief compliance officer, gen. counsel & corp. sec.; Jason Darling, v-p, natl. sales

Capital Stock

	Authorized (shs.)	Outstanding (shs.)[1]
Class A Unit	unlimited	10,123,880
Class F Unit	unlimited	303,844
Class N Unit	unlimited	nil

[1] At Dec. 31, 2022

Class A Unit - Entitled to monthly cash distributions of $0.04166 per unit (5% per annum based on an issue price of $10 per unit). Retractable monthly at a price per unit equal to the lesser of: (i) 94% of the weighted average price per unit on TSX during the preceding 10 trading days; (ii) the closing price per unit; and (iii) the net asset value (NAV) per unit at the monthly retraction date, less any costs associated with the retraction. Retractable in June each year at a price equal to the NAV per unit. One vote per unit.

Class F Unit - For fee-based or institutional accounts. Entitled to monthly cash distributions of $0.04166 per unit (5% per annum based on an issue price of $10 per unit). Convertible into class A units on a monthly basis, with each class F unit converted into a number of class A units equal to the class F NAV per unit divided by the class A NAV per unit. Retractable monthly at a price equal to the product of: (i) the monthly retraction amount of class A unit; and (ii) a fraction equal to the class F NAV per unit divided by the class A NAV per unit. Retractable in June each year at a price equal to the NAV per unit. One vote per unit.

Class N Unit - Automatically converted into class A units on the first business day following the end of the calendar year in which the class N units were issued, with each class N unit converted into a number of class A units equal to the class N NAV per unit divided by the class A NAV per unit. Retractable monthly at a price equal to the product of: (i) the monthly retraction amount of class A unit; and (ii) a fraction equal to the class N NAV per unit divided by the class A NAV per unit. One vote per unit.

Major Shareholder - Widely held at Mar. 29, 2023.

Price Range - PBY.UN/TSX

Year	Volume	High	Low	Close
2022	2,263,949	$15.71	$12.90	$13.66
2021	1,643,580	$15.68	$13.33	$15.15
2020	1,847,020	$13.99	$6.91	$13.41
2019	2,351,717	$11.50	$10.36	$10.90
2018	3,289,468	$12.33	$10.46	$11.16

Recent Close: $14.36

Capital Stock Changes - During 2022, 117,134 class F units were converted into 131,154 class A units and 32,300 class F units were retracted.

Dividends

PBY.UN cl A unit Ra $0.50 pa M est. Sept. 15, 2010
stk.[1] ◆g .... Dec. 30/22 $1.68989◆ .... Dec. 31/21
Paid in 2023: $0.49992 2022: $0.49992 + stk.◆g 2021: $0.49992 + $1.68989◆

[1] Distribution will be automatically reinvested and the units will be consolidated immediately after distribution. Equiv to $0.5578.
◆ Special **g** Capital Gain

Financial Statistics

Periods ended:	12m Dec. 31/22[A]		12m Dec. 31/21[A]
	$000s	%Chg	$000s
Realized invest. gain (loss)	15,890		19,663
Unrealized invest. gain (loss)	(20,753)		2,195
Total revenue	**2,054**	**-94**	**34,423**
General & admin. expense	1,562		10,554
Operating expense	**1,562**	**-85**	**10,554**
Operating income	**492**	**-98**	**23,869**
Finance costs, gross	1,380		1,649
Pre-tax income	**(888)**	**n.a.**	**22,220**
Net income	**(888)**	**n.a.**	**22,220**
Cash & equivalent	9,692		7,231
Accounts receivable	3,747		1,906
Investments	190,832		208,141
Total assets	**204,368**	**-6**	**217,355**
Accts. pay. & accr. liabs	97		8,879
Shareholders' equity	153,953		160,555
Cash from oper. activs	**8,109**	**-75**	**32,620**
Cash from fin. activs	(5,715)		(5,805)
Net cash position	**9,692**	**+34**	**7,231**
	$		$
Earnings per share*	(0.08)		2.09
Earnings per share**	(0.31)		2.68
Cash flow per share***	0.78		3.12
Net asset value per share*	14.71		15.29
Cash divd. per share*	0.50		0.50
Extra divd. - cash*	nil		1.69
Extra stk. divd. - cash equiv.*	0.56		nil
Total divd. per share*	**1.06**		**2.19**
	shs		shs
No. of shs. o/s***	10,427,724		10,446,004
	%		%
Net profit margin	(43.23)		64.55
Return on equity	(0.56)		14.59
Return on assets	0.23		10.20

* Cl.A Unit
** Cl.F Unit
*** Cl.A Unit & Cl.F Unit
[A] Reported in accordance with IFRS

Note: Net income reflects increase/decrease in net assets from operations.

Historical Summary
(as originally stated)

Fiscal Year	Total Rev. $000s	Net Inc. Bef. Disc. $000s	EPS* $
2022[A]	2,054	(888)	(0.08)
2021[A]	34,423	22,220	2.09
2020[A]	40,839	30,714	2.54
2019[A]	20,913	16,192	1.14
2018[A]	(1,987)	(6,390)	(0.44)

* Cl.A Unit
[A] Reported in accordance with IFRS

C.61 Canso Select Opportunities Corporation

Symbol - CSOC.A **Exchange** - TSX-VEN **CUSIP** - 13809N
Head Office - 550-100 York Blvd, Richmond Hill, ON, L4B 1J8 **Telephone** - (647) 956-6264
Website - www.selectopportunitiescorporation.com
Email - jmorin@selectopportunitiescorporation.com
Investor Relations - Joe Morin (647) 956-6264
Auditors - Deloitte LLP C.A., Toronto, Ont.
Lawyers - Borden Ladner Gervais LLP, Toronto, Ont.
Transfer Agents - TSX Trust Company, Toronto, Ont.

Profile - (Ont. 2018) Evaluates potential investments in debt, public and private equity, and other securities.

The company may invest in Canadian and foreign securities issued in both public and private markets; companies at all stages of development, including distressed, venture and start-up investments; and derivative securities, both for hedging and investment purposes.

At Mar. 31, 2023, the sole investment, which accounted for more than 10% of the company's portfolio market value, was **Lysander Funds Limited**, a retail fund management company.

On Jan. 13, 2023, the company acquired 70,000 class A common shares of Toronto, Ont.-based **Lysander Funds Limited**, a retail fund management company within the **Canso Investment Counsel** group, from **Canso Fund Management Ltd.** for issuance of 2,440,239 class B subordinate voting shares valued at $12,500,000. As a result, the company owns 9% interest in Lysander.

Directors - Heather Mason-Wood, chr., Richmond Hill, Ont.; Joe Morin, pres., CEO & chief invest. officer, Ont.; Shirley Sumsion, CFO, Ont.; Neda Bizzotto, v-p & corp. sec., Ont.; Brenda Burns, Richmond Hill, Ont.; John Carswell, Richmond Hill, Ont.; Margaret Dowdall-Logie; Tom Fernandes, Ont.; Steve Klubi, B.C.; Tony MacDougall, Ont.

Capital Stock

	Authorized (shs.)	Outstanding (shs.)[1]
Preference	unlimited	nil
Class A Multiple Vtg.	unlimited	1,611,460
Class B Subordinate Vtg.	unlimited	3,606,977

[1] At Apr. 3, 2023

Class A Multiple Voting - Entitled to dividends as declared by the board of directors from time to time. Convertible, at the holder's option at any time, into class B subordinate voting share on a share-for-share basis. 30 votes per share.

Class B Subordinate Voting - Entitled to dividends, which would only be declared concurrently with the declaration of a dividend on class A multiple voting shares, and would be 5¢ per share higher than the amount of dividend declared on the class A multiple voting shares. Subject to an offer made to acquire class A multiple voting shares, any holder may, at any time or from time-to-time during a conversion period (the period of time commencing on the eighth day after the offer date and terminating on the expiry date), convert any or all of the class B subordinate voting shares into class A multiple voting shares on a share-for-share basis, and tender the converted shares to the offer. One vote per share.

Major Shareholder - John Carswell held 45.1% interest at Apr. 3, 2023.

Price Range - CSOC.A/TSX-VEN

Year	Volume	High	Low	Close
2022	101,323	$2.50	$1.75	$2.05
2021	304,538	$2.91	$2.00	$2.26
2020	160,481	$3.24	$1.66	$2.56
2019	284,817	$3.69	$1.50	$1.72
2018	151,261	$6.00	$2.50	$2.69

CSOC.B/TSX-VEN

Year	Volume	High	Low	Close
2022	94,050	$2.72	$1.70	$2.20
2021	194,193	$2.67	$2.00	$2.50
2020	102,098	$2.65	$1.69	$2.55
2019	430,532	$3.20	$1.56	$1.75
2018	166,150	$5.00	$2.31	$2.35

Recent Close: $2.50

Capital Stock Changes - On Jan. 13, 2023, 2,440,239 class B subordinate voting shares were issued pursuant to the acquisition of 9% interest in Lysander Funds Limited.

During 2022, 10,000 class A multiple voting shares were converted into 10,000 class B subordinate voting shares.

Wholly Owned Subsidiaries

Canso Select Opportunities Fund, Richmond Hill, Ont.

Financial Statistics

Periods ended:	12m Dec. 31/22[A]		12m Dec. 31/22[A]
	$000s	%Chg	$000s
Realized invest. gain (loss)	446		446
Unrealized invest. gain (loss)	(1,289)		(1,289)
Total revenue	**(721)**	**n.a.**	**(721)**
General & admin. expense	237		237
Operating expense	**237**	**n.a.**	**237**
Operating income	**(958)**	**n.a.**	**(958)**
Finance costs, gross	1		1
Pre-tax income	**(959)**	**n.a.**	**(959)**
Income taxes	(155)		(155)
Net income	**(804)**	**n.a.**	**(804)**
Cash & equivalent	80		80
Investments	12,982		12,982
Total assets	**13,785**	**n.a.**	**13,785**
Accts. pay. & accr. liabs	179		179
Shareholders' equity	13,606		13,606
Cash from oper. activs	**10**	**n.a.**	**10**
Net cash position	**80**	**n.a.**	**80**
	$		$
Earnings per share*	(0.29)		(0.29)
Cash flow per share*	0.00		0.00
Net asset value per share*	4.90		4.90
	shs		shs
No. of shs. o/s*	2,778,198		2,778,198
	%		%
Net profit margin	n.m.		n.m.
Return on equity	(5.74)		(5.74)
Return on assets	(5.69)		(5.69)

* Cl.A Mult. Vtg.
[A] Reported in accordance with IFRS

Latest Results

Periods ended:	3m Mar. 31/23[A]
	$000s
Total revenue	(511)
Net income	(481)
	$
Earnings per share*	(0.09)

* Cl.A Mult. Vtg.
[A] Reported in accordance with IFRS

Historical Summary
(as originally stated)

Fiscal Year	Total Rev.	Net Inc. Bef. Disc.	EPS*
	$000s	$000s	$
2022[A]	(721)	(804)	(0.29)
2021[A]	2,941	2,377	0.86
2020[A]	(1,042)	(1,081)	(0.39)
2019[A]	(353)	(502)	(0.18)
2018[A1]	(1,986)	(1,817)	(0.65)

* Cl.A Mult. Vtg.
[A] Reported in accordance with IFRS
[1] 45 weeks ended Dec. 31, 2018.

C.62 Cansortium Inc.

Symbol - TIUM.U **Exchange** - CSE **CUSIP** - 13809L
Head Office - 82 NE 26 St, Suite 110, Miami, FL, United States, 33137 **Telephone** - (305) 902-2720
Website - getfluent.com
Email - todd.buchman@getfluent.com
Investor Relations - Todd Buchman (305) 441-9085
Auditors - Baker Tilly US, LLP C.P.A., Irvine, Calif.
Lawyers - Harris + Harris LLP, Mississauga, Ont.
Transfer Agents - Odyssey Trust Company, Calgary, Alta.
FP500 Revenue Ranking - 752
Profile - (Ont. 2018) Produces and retails medical cannabis in Florida and Texas, and retails medical cannabis in Pennsylvania.

Cultivation and processing operations include a 46,000-sq.-ft. indoor cultivation and production facility in Tampa, Fla.; a cultivation and production facility in Zolfo Springs, Fla., with 26,000 sq. ft. of indoor cultivation and production space and a 40,000-sq.-ft. greenhouse; and a cultivation facility in Schulenburg, Tex., with 1,300 sq. ft. in operation and the potential to expand to 400,000 sq. ft.

Retail operations include Fluent-branded medical cannabis dispensaries in Florida (27) and Pennsylvania (3) and home deliveries in Texas. Medical cannabis products are marketed under the Fluent name and include oral drops, capsules, topicals, syringes, dried flower, pre-rolls, cartridges and edibles. In Pennsylvania, the company's product offering consists of a variety of third-party branded medical cannabis products.

On June 30, 2022, the company terminated its agreement with **Green Standard, Inc.**, to acquire an 8.5-acre outdoor cultivation facility in Arlington twp., Mich., as well as cultivation, production and future retail dispensary licenses. As result, the company discontinued its operation in Michigan and wrote off related assets totaling US$7,884,000.

Also in June 2022, the company closed its 43,000-sq.-ft. greenhouse cultivation facility in Homestead, Fla., and wrote off related assets totaling US$688,000.

In May 2022, indirect wholly owned **Cansortium Beverage Company Inc.** was dissolved.

Directors - William (Bill) Smith, exec. chr., Gulf Breeze, Fla.; Robert Beasley, CEO, Pensacola, Fla.; Roger Daher, Markham, Ont.; Mark Eckenrode, Locust Grove, Ga.; John M. McKimm, Toronto, Ont.

Other Exec. Officers - Jeffrey Batliner, CFO; Todd Buchman, chief legal officer & corp. sec.; Samantha Hymes, exec. v-p; Liora Boudin, contr.

Capital Stock

	Authorized (shs.)	Outstanding (shs.)[1]
Common	unlimited	238,882,503
Proportionate Voting	unlimited	2,607,724

[1] At Dec. 31, 2022

Common - One vote per share.
Proportionate Voting - Convertible at any time, at the holder's option, into 10 common shares per proportionate voting share. Automatically convertible into common shares at the same ratio under certain circumstances. Ten votes per share.
Major Shareholder - William (Bill) Smith held 19.7% interest at May 26, 2022.

Price Range - TIUM.U/CSE

Year	Volume	High	Low	Close
2022	45,051,351	US$0.69	US$0.11	US$0.12
2021	63,668,777	US$1.30	US$0.50	US$0.66
2020	16,658,123	US$0.77	US$0.08	US$0.76
2019	22,484,677	US$2.20	US$0.34	US$0.44

Recent Close: US$0.07

Wholly Owned Subsidiaries

Cansortium International Inc., Ont.
- 10% int. in **Cansortium Brazil Ltda.**, Brazil.
- 100% int. in **Cansortium Canada Holdings Inc.**, Ont.
  - 90% int. in **Cansortium Brazil Ltda.**, Brazil.
  - 50% int. in **Cansortium Colombia S.A.S.**, Colombia.
- 100% int. in **Cansortium Holdings LLC**, Fla.
  - 100% int. in **Cansortium Florida, LLC**, Fla.
    - 100% int. in **Fluent Servicing, LLC**, Fla.
    - 100% int. in **Spirit Lake Road Nursery LLC**, Fla.
  - 100% int. in **Cansortium Michigan LLC**, Mich.
  - 100% int. in **Cansortium Pennsylvania, LLC**, Pa.
  - 100% int. in **Cansortium Puerto Rico LLC**, Puerto Rico.
  - 100% int. in **Cansortium Texas, LLC**, Tex.
  - 100% int. in **Cavern Capital Holdings LLC**, Wyo.
  - 100% int. in **Fluent Hemp LLC**, United States.
  - 100% int. in **Harvest Park Lot 9 Investors LLC**, Del.
  - 100% int. in **Harvest Park Lot 9 Investors No. 2 LLC**, Del.
- 100% int. in **16171 Slater Road Investors LLC**, Del.

Financial Statistics

Periods ended:	12m Dec. 31/22[‡A]		12m Dec. 31/21[A]
	US$000s	%Chg	US$000s
Operating revenue	**87,692**	**+34**	**65,437**
Cost of goods sold	...		29,650
General & admin expense	...		25,742
Stock-based compensation	...		4,304
Operating expense	**...**	**n.a.**	**59,696**
Operating income	**...**	**n.a.**	**5,741**
Deprec., depl. & amort.	...		6,384
Finance costs, net	16,087		15,760
Pre-tax income	**(26,770)**	**n.a.**	**(11,358)**
Income taxes	10,376		7,646
Net inc. bef. disc. opers	**(37,146)**	**n.a.**	**(19,004)**
Income from disc. opers	(277)		(35)
Net income	**(37,423)**	**n.a.**	**(19,039)**
Cash & equivalent	...		9,024
Inventories	...		8,981
Accounts receivable	...		26
Current assets	19,239		23,535
Fixed assets, net	...		34,160
Right-of-use assets	...		19,169
Intangibles, net	...		97,348
Total assets	**178,031**	**-2**	**182,457**
Accts. pay. & accr. liabs	...		14,364
Current liabilities	37,957		23,563
Long-term debt, gross	57,710		54,293
Long-term debt, net	56,969		53,674
Long-term lease liabilities	...		21,091
Equity portion of conv. debs	6,677		4,933
Shareholders' equity	27,560		62,566
Cash from oper. activs	**19,069**	**n.a.**	**(5,026)**
Cash from fin. activs	(13,048)		32,811
Cash from invest. activs	(6,774)		(22,111)
Net cash position	**8,359**	**-7**	**9,024**
Capital expenditures	...		(21,060)
	US$		US$
Earnings per share*	(0.15)		(0.08)
Cash flow per share*	0.08		(0.02)
	shs		shs
No. of shs. o/s*	264,959,743		251,976,742
Avg. no. of shs. o/s*	252,698,567		228,628,703
	%		%
Net profit margin	(42.36)		(29.04)
Return on equity	(82.43)		(42.05)
Return on assets	(20.61)		(11.28)
Foreign sales percent	100		100

* Common
‡ Preliminary
[A] Reported in accordance with IFRS

Note: Number of shares and average number of shares outstanding includes proportionate voting shares converted into common shares on a 10-for-1 basis.

Historical Summary
(as originally stated)

Fiscal Year	Oper. Rev.	Net Inc. Bef. Disc.	EPS*
	US$000s	US$000s	US$
2022[‡A]	87,692	(37,146)	(0.15)
2021[A]	65,437	(19,004)	(0.08)
2020[A]	52,388	(36,734)	(0.18)
2019[A]	28,511	(65,645)	(0.35)
2018[A]	8,061	(1,054)	(0.01)

* Common
‡ Preliminary
[A] Reported in accordance with IFRS

C.63 Canyon Creek Food Company Ltd.

Symbol - CYF **Exchange** - TSX-VEN **CUSIP** - 138908
Head Office - 8704 53 Ave, Edmonton, AB, T6E 5G2 **Telephone** - (780) 463-2991 **Toll-free** - (888) 217-1246 **Fax** - (780) 463-5511
Website - www.canyoncreekfood.com
Email - talty@canyoncreekfood.com
Investor Relations - Terence N. Alty (888) 217-1246
Auditors - PricewaterhouseCoopers LLP C.A., Edmonton, Alta.
Transfer Agents - Computershare Trust Company of Canada Inc., Calgary, Alta.
Profile - (Alta. 1995) Provides fresh soups and other prepared food products to both grocery retailers and various food service establishments including restaurants and institutions throughout Canada.

Products include fresh stews and chilies, refrigerated soups, sauces, gravies and side dishes. The company operates a food production facility in Edmonton, Alta.

Predecessor Detail - Name changed from Magna Power Corp., May 15, 1996.

Directors - Brian Halina, chr., Edmonton, Alta.; Terence N. (Terry) Alty, pres. & CEO, Calgary, Alta.; Belva Rode, CFO; David Harbinson, Edmonton, Alta.; Tim Holliday

Capital Stock

	Authorized (shs.)	Outstanding (shs.)[1]
Preferred	unlimited	nil
Common	unlimited	35,148,902

[1] At Jan. 30, 2023

Major Shareholder - Brian Halina held 55.75% interest at July 28, 2022.

Price Range - CYF/TSX-VEN

Year	Volume	High	Low	Close
2022	1,562,636	$0.12	$0.03	$0.04
2021	10,450,508	$0.32	$0.02	$0.08
2020	1,210,437	$0.03	$0.01	$0.03
2019	761,380	$0.05	$0.02	$0.02
2018	1,065,121	$0.10	$0.02	$0.03

Recent Close: $0.02

Capital Stock Changes - There were no changes to capital stock from fiscal 2007 to fiscal 2022, inclusive.

Wholly Owned Subsidiaries

Canyon Creek Soup Company Ltd. , Edmonton, Alta.

Financial Statistics

Periods ended:	12m May 31/22[A]		12m May 31/21[A]
	$000s	%Chg	$000s
Operating revenue	**9,555**	**+33**	**7,175**
Cost of sales	6,915		4,258
Salaries & benefits	2,368		1,308
Research & devel. expense	20		6
General & admin expense	564		389
Operating expense	**9,867**	**+66**	**5,961**
Operating income	**(312)**	**n.a.**	**1,214**
Deprec., depl. & amort.	587		477
Finance costs, gross	1,652		2,423
Write-downs/write-offs	(627)		nil
Pre-tax income	**(3,180)**	**n.a.**	**(1,686)**
Net income	**(3,180)**	**n.a.**	**(1,686)**
Cash & equivalent	1		200
Inventories	1,636		594
Accounts receivable	321		268
Current assets	2,083		1,148
Fixed assets, net	3,204		1,766
Right-of-use assets	3,529		2,535
Total assets	**7,816**	**+41**	**5,531**
Bank indebtedness	4,395		2,141
Accts. pay. & accr. liabs	4,116		2,065
Current liabilities	9,182		4,877
Long-term debt, gross	14,499		14,499
Long-term debt, net	14,154		14,154
Long-term lease liabilities	2,513		2,489
Shareholders' equity	(31,969)		(28,790)
Cash from oper. activs	**528**	**-49**	**1,026**
Cash from fin. activs	1,481		(318)
Cash from invest. activs	(2,209)		(508)
Net cash position	**1**	**-100**	**200**
Capital expenditures	(2,290)		(389)
	$		$
Earnings per share*	(0.09)		(0.05)
Cash flow per share*	0.02		0.03
	shs		shs
No. of shs. o/s*	35,148,902		35,148,902
Avg. no. of shs. o/s*	35,148,902		35,148,902
	%		%
Net profit margin	(33.28)		(23.50)
Return on equity	n.m.		n.m.
Return on assets	(22.90)		14.18
Foreign sales percent	12		15

* Common
[A] Reported in accordance with IFRS

Latest Results

Periods ended:	3m Aug. 31/22[A]		3m Aug. 31/21[A]
	$000s	%Chg	$000s
Operating revenue	1,912	+182	678
Net income	(829)	n.a.	(709)
	$		$
Earnings per share*	(0.02)		(0.02)

* Common
[A] Reported in accordance with IFRS

Historical Summary
(as originally stated)

Fiscal Year	Oper. Rev. $000s	Net Inc. Bef. Disc. $000s	EPS* $
2022[A]	9,555	(3,180)	(0.09)
2021[A]	7,175	(1,686)	(0.05)
2020[A]	10,357	(3,851)	(0.11)
2019[A]	7,479	(2,835)	(0.08)
2018[A]	7,200	(2,062)	(0.06)

* Common
[A] Reported in accordance with IFRS

C.64 Capital Power Corporation*

Symbol - CPX **Exchange** - TSX **CUSIP** - 14042M
Head Office - 1200-10423 101 St NW, Edmonton, AB, T5H 0E9 **Telephone** - (780) 392-5100 **Toll-free** - (866) 896-4636 **Fax** - (780) 392-5124
Website - www.capitalpower.com
Email - rmah@capitalpower.com
Investor Relations - Randy Mah (866) 896-4636
Auditors - KPMG LLP C.A., Edmonton, Alta.
Lawyers - Borden Ladner Gervais LLP, Calgary, Alta.
Transfer Agents - Computershare Trust Company of Canada Inc., Calgary, Alta.
FP500 Revenue Ranking - 179
Employees - 802 at Dec. 31, 2022
Profile - (Can. 2009) Develops, acquires, owns and operates power generation facilities across North America. Owns 7,500 MW of power generation capacity at 29 natural gas, wind, solid fuel and solar facilities.

Wholly owned **Capital Power L.P.** (CPLP) owns a portfolio of commercial plants that total 2,423 MW of owned and/or operated power generation capacity and generate electricity from coal, natural gas, wind and landfill gas, all located in Alberta. This portfolio consists of the 430-MW Genesee 1, the 450-MW Genesee 2 and the 516-MW Genesee 3 (100% owned) coal and natural gas co-fired generation plants near Warburg; the 480-MW Joffre (40% owned) gas-fired combined cycle cogeneration plant near Red Deer; the 243-MW Clover Bar Energy Centre (100% owned) natural gas-fired simple cycle plant and the 2-MW Clover Bar (100% owned) landfill gas-fired plant, both in Edmonton; the 150-MW Halkirk 1 (100% owned) wind farm in Halkirk; and the 881-MW Shepard Energy Centre (50% owned) natural gas-fired combined-cycle plant in Calgary.

Contracted plants owned by CPLP include the 353-MW Whitla wind facility, the 75-MW Clydesdale (formerly Enchant) solar project and the 41-MW Strathmore solar project, all in Alberta; the 40-MW Kingsbridge 1 wind facility near Goderich, Ont.; the 275-MW Island Generation natural gas-fired combined cycle plant at Campbell River, B.C.; the 142-MW Quality wind facility near Tumbler Ridge, B.C.; the 105-MW Port Dover and Nanticoke wind facilities in Norfolk and Haldimand ctys., Ont.; the 456-MW York Energy Centre (50% owned) natural gas-fired plant northwest of Newmarket, Ont.; the 875-MW Goreway natural gas-fired combined cycle facility in Brampton, Ont.; the 92-MW East Windsor natural gas-fired cogeneration plant adjacent to **Ford Motor Company of Canada, Limited**'s engine manufacturing site in Windsor, Ont.; and two 5-MW waste heat generation facilities in 150 Mile House and Savona, B.C. Output from these plants is sold primarily under long-term contracts with provincial government entities. Other contracted plants include the 885-MW Decatur Energy Centre natural gas-fired combined cycle plant in Decatur, Ala.; the 50-MW Macho Springs wind facility in Luna cty., N.M.; the 15-MW Beaufort solar facility in Chocowinity, N.C.; the 178-MW Bloom wind facility in Kansas; the 99-MW New Frontier wind facility in McHenry cty., N.D.; the 600-MW Arlington Valley natural gas-fired combined-cycle facility southwest of Phoenix, Ariz.; the 150-MW Cardinal Point wind facility in McDonough and Warren ctys., Ill.; the 101-MW Buckthorn wind facility south of Dallas, Tex.; and the 1,633-MW Midland Cogen (50% owned) natural gas-fired combine-cycle facility in Midland, Mich.

CPLP's facilities under construction or advanced development include the 151-MW Halkirk 2 wind farm; the repowering of Genesee 1 and 2 to transition both units into natural gas, which would add 538 MW when completed in 2024; and a battery storage, which would add 210 MW when completed in 2024, all located in Alberta. In addition, owns a portfolio of 20 solar development sites in the U.S., representing a total potential generation capacity of 1,298 MW and the option to co-locate 1,200 MWh of energy storage, which would be construction-ready by 2024 with commercial operation starting between 2025 and 2026.

On Dec. 13, 2022, the 75-MW Clydesdale (formerly Enchant) solar project in Alberta commenced commercial operations. The project was completed at a total cost of $124,000,000.

On Mar. 17, 2022, the 41-MW Strathmore solar project in Alberta commenced commercial operations. The project was completed at a total cost of US$58,000,000.

Recent Merger and Acquisition Activity

Status: completed **Revised:** Sept. 23, 2022
UPDATE: The transaction was completed. PREVIOUS: Capital Power Corporation and Manulife Investment Management (MIM), the global wealth and asset management segment of Manulife Financial Corporation, agreed to acquire MCV Holding Company LLC from OMERS Infrastructure Management Inc. and co-investors for a total of US$894,000,000, including the assumption of US$521,000,000 of project level debt. MCV, through wholly owned Midland Cogeneration Venture Limited Partnership, owns and operates a 1,633-MW natural gas combined-cycle cogeneration facility in Midland, Mich. Under a 50/50 joint venture, Capital Power and MIM would each contribute US$186,000,000 subject to working capital and other closing adjustments. Capital Power would finance the transaction using cash on hand and existing credit facilities. Capital Power would be responsible for operations and maintenance and asset management in exchange for an annual management fee. The transaction was expected to close in the third quarter of 2022, subject to regulatory approvals and other customary closing conditions.

Directors - Jill V. Gardiner, chr., Vancouver, B.C.; Avik Dey, pres. & CEO, Calgary, Alta.; Doyle N. Beneby Jr., West Palm Beach, Fla.; Gary A. Bosgoed, Alta.; Carolyn J. Graham, Edmonton, Alta.; Kelly Huntington, Indianapolis, Ind.; Barry V. Perry, St. John's, N.L.; Jane L. Peverett, West Vancouver, B.C.; Robert L. (Bob) Phillips, Anmore, B.C.; Keith Trent, Charlotte, N.C.

Other Exec. Officers - Bryan DeNeve, sr. v-p, opers.; Sandra A. Haskins, sr. v-p, fin. & CFO; Christopher (Chris) Kopecky, sr. v-p & chief legal, devel. & comml. officer; Steve Owens, sr. v-p, const. & eng.; Jacquelyn M. (Jacquie) Pylypiuk, sr. v-p, people, culture & tech.

Capital Stock

	Authorized (shs.)	Outstanding (shs.)[1]
Preference	unlimited	nil
Series 1		5,000,000
Series 3		6,000,000
Series 5		8,000,000
Series 7		nil
Series 9		nil
Series 11		6,000,000
Common	unlimited	116,950,000
Special Limited Vtg.	1	1[2]

[1] At July 27, 2023
[2] Held by EPCOR Utilities Inc.

Preference - Issuable in series. Each series of preference shares ranks on a parity with every other series of preference shares and in priority to the common shares in the event of the liquidation, dissolution or winding up, etc., of the company. Non-voting.

Series 1 - Entitled to cumulative preferential dividends of $0.6552 per share payable quarterly to Dec. 31, 2025, and thereafter at a rate reset every five years equal to the five-year Government of Canada yield plus 2.17%. Redeemable on Dec. 31, 2025, and on December 31 every five years thereafter at $25 per share plus declared and unpaid dividends. Convertible on Dec. 31, 2025, and on December 31 every five years thereafter, into floating rate preferred series 2 shares on a share-for-share basis, subject to certain conditions. The series 2 shares would pay a quarterly dividend equal to the 90-day Canadian Treasury bill rate plus 2.17%.

Series 3 - Entitled to cumulative preferential dividends of $1.3633 per share payable quarterly to Dec. 31, 2023, and thereafter at a rate reset every five years equal to the five-year Government of Canada yield plus 3.23%. Redeemable on Dec. 31, 2023, and on December 31 every five years thereafter at $25 per share plus declared and unpaid dividends. Convertible on Dec. 31, 2023, and on December 31 every five years thereafter, into floating rate preferred series 4 shares on a share-for-share basis, subject to certain conditions. The series 4 shares would pay a quarterly dividend equal to the 90-day Canadian Treasury bill rate plus 3.23%.

Series 5 - Entitled to cumulative preferential dividends of $1.6577 per share payable quarterly to June 30, 2028, and thereafter at a rate reset every five years equal to the five-year Government of Canada yield plus 3.15%. Redeemable on June 30, 2028, and on June 30 every five years thereafter at $25 per share plus declared and unpaid dividends. Convertible on June 30, 2028, and on June 30 every five years thereafter, into floating rate preferred series 6 shares on a share-for-share basis, subject to certain conditions. The series 6 shares would pay a quarterly dividend equal to the 90-day Canadian Treasury bill rate plus 3.15%.

Series 11 - Entitled to cumulative preferential dividends of $1.4375 per share payable quarterly to June 30, 2024, and thereafter at a rate reset every five years equal to the five-year Government of Canada yield plus 4.15%. Redeemable on June 30, 2024, and on June 30 every five years thereafter at $25 per share plus declared and unpaid dividends. Convertible on June 30, 2024, and on June 30 every five years thereafter, into floating rate preferred series 12 shares on a share-for-share basis, subject to certain conditions. The series 12 shares would pay a quarterly dividend equal to the 90-day Canadian Treasury bill rate plus 4.15%.

Common - One vote per share.

Special Limited Voting - Held by EPCOR Utilities Inc. Non-voting except with respect to its right to vote separately as a class in connection with any proposal to amend the articles of the company with respect to changing the head office location to a location other than Edmonton, Alta., and certain related matters.

Options - At Dec. 31, 2022, options were outstanding to purchase 1,710,709 common shares at a weighted average exercise price of $30.56 per share with a weighted average remaining contractual life of 3.72 years.

Preference Series 9 (old) - Were entitled to cumulative preferential dividends of $1.4375 per share payable quarterly to Sept. 30, 2022. Redeemed on Sept. 30, 2022, at $25 per share.

Normal Course Issuer Bid - The company plans to make normal course purchases of up to 5,800,000 common shares representing 5% of the public float. The bid commenced on Mar. 3, 2023, and expires on Mar. 2, 2024.

Major Shareholder - Widely held at Mar. 13, 2023.

Price Range - CPX/TSX

Year	Volume	High	Low	Close
2022	93,087,716	$51.90	$36.65	$46.33
2021	73,320,980	$45.05	$33.31	$39.46
2020	103,097,405	$38.88	$20.23	$34.98
2019	77,115,096	$35.09	$26.22	$34.39
2018	65,379,973	$29.79	$22.15	$26.59

Recent Close: $40.74

Capital Stock Changes - On Sept. 30, 2022, all 6,000,000 series 9 preference shares were redeemed at $25 per share. Also during 2022, 692,968 common shares were issued on exercise of options.

Dividends

CPX com Ra $2.46 pa Q est. Oct. 31, 2023
Prev. Rate: $2.32 est. Oct. 31, 2022
Prev. Rate: $2.19 est. Oct. 29, 2021
Prev. Rate: $2.05 est. Oct. 30, 2020
CPX.PR.A pfd ser 1 cum. red. exch. Adj. Ra $0.65525 pa Q est. Mar. 31, 2021
CPX.PR.C pfd ser 3 cum. red. exch. Adj. Ra $1.36325 pa Q est. Mar. 29, 2019
CPX.PR.E pfd ser 5 cum. red. exch. Adj. Ra $1.5775 pa Q est. Sept. 29, 2023
CPX.PR.K pfd ser 11 red. exch. Adj. Ra $1.4375 pa Q est. June 28, 2019
pfd ser 7 cum. red. exch. Adj. Ra $1.50 pa Q est. Dec. 30, 2016**[1]
$0.375**f** Dec. 31/21
pfd ser 9 cum. red. exch. Adj. Ra $1.4375 pa Q est. Sept. 29, 2017[2]
$0.359375**f** Sept. 30/22
[1] Redeemed Dec. 31, 2021 at $25 per sh.
[2] Redeemed Sept. 30, 2022 at $25 per sh.
** Reinvestment Option **f** Final Payment

Long-Term Debt - Outstanding at Dec. 31, 2022:

Tax-equity financing	$354,000,000
Revolv. credit facilities due 2027	340,000,000
4.28% sr. med.-term notes due 2024	450,000,000
5.61% sr. notes due 2026[1]	88,000,000
3.85% sr. notes due 2026	160,000,000
4.99% sr. med.-term notes due 2026	300,000,000
4.56% sr. notes due 2029	210,000,000
4.42% sr. med.-term notes due 2030	275,000,000
4.72% sr. notes due 2031	65,000,000
3.15% sr. med.-term notes due 2032	350,000,000
3.24% sr. notes due 2033[2]	203,000,000
4.96% sr. notes due 2034	50,000,000
7.95% sr. hybrid notes due 2082	350,000,000
Non-recourse financing:	
Fltng. rate Goreway bonds due 2027	426,000,000
6.28% East Windsor bonds due 2029	94,000,000
6.9% Macho Springs loans due 2031	43,000,000
Less: Deferred debt issue costs	32,000,000
	3,726,000,000
Less: Current portion	133,000,000
	3,593,000,000

[1] US$65,000,000.
[2] US$150,000,000.

Wholly Owned Subsidiaries

Capital Power L.P., Edmonton, Alta.
- 100% int. in **Arlington Valley, LLC**, Del.
- 100% int. in **CP Bloom Wind LLC**, Del.
- 100% int. in **CP Energy Marketing L.P.**, Alta.
- 100% int. in **CP Energy Marketing (US) Inc.**, Del.
- 100% int. in **Capital Power (Alberta) Limited Partnership**, Alta.
- 100% int. in **Capital Power (G3) Limited Partnership**, Alta.
- 100% int. in **Capital Power (Genesee) L.P.**, Alta.
- 100% int. in **Capital Power Investments LLC**, Del.
- 100% int. in **Capital Power (Whitla) L.P.**, Alta.
- 100% int. in **Cardinal Point LLC**, Del.
- 100% int. in **Decatur Energy Centre, LLC**, Del.
- 100% int. in **Goreway Station Partnership**, Ont.
- 100% int. in **Halkirk I Wind Project L.P.**, Alta.

Note: The preceding list includes only the major related companies in which interests are held.

Financial Statistics

Periods ended:	12m Dec. 31/22^A		12m Dec. 31/21^A
	$000s	%Chg	$000s
Operating revenue	**2,712,000**	**+54**	**1,757,000**
Cost of sales	1,578,000		667,000
Salaries & benefits	159,000		160,000
General & admin expense	297,000		265,000
Stock-based compensation	25,000		16,000
Operating expense	**2,059,000**	**+86**	**1,108,000**
Operating income	**653,000**	**+1**	**649,000**
Deprec., depl. & amort.	553,000		539,000
Finance costs, gross	156,000		174,000
Investment income	32,000		9,000
Write-downs/write-offs	nil		(58,000)
Pre-tax income	**141,000**	**-4**	**147,000**
Income taxes	13,000		60,000
Net income	**128,000**	**+47**	**87,000**
Net inc. for equity hldrs	**138,000**	**+41**	**98,000**
Net inc. for non-cont. int	**(10,000)**	**n.a.**	**(11,000)**
Cash & equivalent	307,000		387,000
Inventories	242,000		217,000
Accounts receivable	835,000		370,000
Current assets	1,686,000		1,186,000
Long-term investments	437,000		145,000
Fixed assets, net	6,360,000		6,203,000
Right-of-use assets	127,000		120,000
Intangibles, net	817,000		784,000
Total assets	**10,135,000**	**+12**	**9,073,000**
Accts. pay. & accr. liabs	1,176,000		529,000
Current liabilities	2,212,000		1,205,000
Long-term debt, gross	3,726,000		3,360,000
Long-term debt, net	3,593,000		3,234,000
Long-term lease liabilities	146,000		137,000
Preferred share equity	603,000		753,000
Shareholders' equity	2,454,000		2,841,000
Non-controlling interest	6,000		18,000
Cash from oper. activs	**935,000**	**+8**	**867,000**
Cash from fin. activs	(102,000)		(275,000)
Cash from invest. activs	(910,000)		(565,000)
Net cash position	**307,000**	**-21**	**387,000**
Capital expenditures	n.a.		(781,000)
Capital expenditures, net	(682,000)		n.a.
Unfunded pension liability	28,000		32,000
	$		$
Earnings per share*	0.85		0.39
Cash flow per share*	8.02		7.74
Cash divd. per share*	2.26		2.12
	shs		shs
No. of shs. o/s*	116,886,649		116,193,681
Avg. no. of shs. o/s*	116,537,927		112,054,541
	%		%
Net profit margin	4.72		4.95
Return on equity	5.03		2.18
Return on assets	2.81		2.11
Foreign sales percent	12		11
No. of employees (FTEs)	802		773

* Common
^A Reported in accordance with IFRS

Latest Results

Periods ended:	6m June 30/23^A		6m June 30/22^A
	$000s	%Chg	$000s
Operating revenue	2,037,000	+85	1,103,000
Net income	370,000	+89	196,000
Net inc. for equity hldrs	373,000	+85	202,000
Net inc. for non-cont. int	(3,000)		(6,000)
	$		$
Earnings per share*	3.06		1.56

* Common
^A Reported in accordance with IFRS

Historical Summary
(as originally stated)

Fiscal Year	Oper. Rev.	Net Inc. Bef. Disc.	EPS*
	$000s	$000s	$
2022^A	2,712,000	128,000	0.85
2021^A	1,757,000	87,000	0.39
2020^A	1,791,000	130,000	0.78
2019^A	1,713,000	119,000	0.73
2018^A	1,249,000	267,000	2.25

* Common
^A Reported in accordance with IFRS

C.65 Capitan Investment Ltd.

Symbol - CAI **Exchange** - TSX-VEN **CUSIP** - 14058L
Head Office - 610-700 4 Ave SW, Calgary, AB, T2P 3J4 **Telephone** - (403) 237-5411 **Fax** - (403) 232-1307
Email - fiona.w@gccapholdings.com
Investor Relations - Shu Wang (403) 232-1359
Auditors - MNP LLP C.A., Calgary, Alta.
Lawyers - Miles Davison LLP, Calgary, Alta.
Transfer Agents - Computershare Trust Company of Canada Inc., Toronto, Ont.
Profile - (Alta. 2008 amalg.) Invests in U.S. real estate with a focus on student housing and multi-family residential properties. Also holds legacy oil and gas assets.

The company will make investments in equity investments as well as direct or indirect real property acquisitions, mezzanine financing, debt and distressed asset investments and other transactional structures. It plans to build its real estate investment portfolio and business through joint venture development projects, management optimization projects, renovation projects, project financing, strategic investment services and debt financings.

Holds a preferred equity ownership position of 21.85% in a 154-unit student housing development project in Amherst, N.Y. (Auden project), and a preferred equity ownership position of 15.56% in a six-storey multi-family mixed commercial housing development project in Albany, N.Y. (Air Albany project). The company has been guaranteed a 10% preferred return on its investment within 12 months of its initial investment.

Previously explored for, developed and produced oil and gas in Alberta and Saskatchewan, with a focus on oil. Areas of interest were Bodo, Provost and Lloydminster in Alberta; and Dee Valley, Lashburn and Maidstone in Saskatchewan. At June 30, 2022, the company held interests in 20 oil wells, five gas wells, one water disposal well and a storage battery, all of which it plans to divest.

Periods ended:	12m Dec. 31/21	12m Dec. 31/20
Avg. oil prod., bbl/d	6	2
Avg. light oil price, $/bbl	60.35	38.41
Avg. heavy oil price, $/bbl	69.61	n.a.
Oil reserves, net, mbbl	16	111

Predecessor Detail - Name changed from Sahara Energy Ltd., Dec. 22, 2021.
Directors - Yachao Peng, chr., Wuhan, Hubei, People's Republic of China; Panwen (Michelle) Gao, CEO, New York, N.Y.; Luogang (Kevin) Chen, B.C.; Fei Gao, Ont.; Qingshou Gao, Wuhan, Hubei, People's Republic of China; Tao Gao, Wuhan, Hubei, People's Republic of China; Liqun Hao, Wuhan, Hubei, People's Republic of China; Jennifer Li, N.Y.; Zhaohui (John) Liang, N.Y.; Songxian Tan, United States; Jinglin Yang, B.C.
Other Exec. Officers - Yanfeng Liu, CFO & corp. sec.; Shu (Fiona) Wang, v-p, opers.

Capital Stock

	Authorized (shs.)	Outstanding (shs.)[1]
Preferred	unlimited	nil
Common	unlimited	289,684,072

[1] At Aug. 29, 2022

Major Shareholder - JK Investment (Hong Kong) Co., Limited held 69.04% interest and China Great United Petroleum Investment Co. Limited held 16.9% interest at Nov. 1, 2021.

Price Range - CAI/TSX-VEN

Year	Volume	High	Low	Close
2022	1,654,600	$0.03	$0.01	$0.01
2021	828,222	$0.03	$0.02	$0.03
2020	3,816,872	$0.03	$0.01	$0.02
2019	3,400,603	$0.03	$0.02	$0.02
2018	24,562,660	$0.05	$0.02	$0.02

Recent Close: $0.02

Wholly Owned Subsidiaries

GC Capital Holdings Inc., Del.

Financial Statistics

Periods ended:	12m Dec. 31/21^A		12m Dec. 31/20^oA
	$000s	%Chg	$000s
Salaries & benefits	308		163
General & admin expense	445		175
Operating expense	**752**	**+122**	**338**
Operating income	**(752)**	**n.a.**	**(338)**
Deprec., depl. & amort.	103		8
Finance costs, gross	10		nil
Write-downs/write-offs	(1,054)		(1,733)
Pre-tax income	**(1,714)**	**n.a.**	**(2,050)**
Net income	**(1,714)**	**n.a.**	**(2,050)**
Cash & equivalent	1,998		1,118
Current assets	9,076		9,495
Fixed assets, net	641		1,643
Total assets	**9,718**	**-13**	**11,138**
Accts. pay. & accr. liabs	511		446
Current liabilities	1,034		483
Shareholders' equity	8,605		10,297
Cash from oper. activs	**(526)**	**n.a.**	**(369)**
Cash from fin. activs	(105)		40
Cash from invest. activs	1,443		812
Net cash position	**1,998**	**+79**	**1,118**
Capital disposals	75		nil
	$		$
Earnings per share*	(0.01)		(0.01)
Cash flow per share*	(0.00)		(0.00)
	shs		shs
No. of shs. o/s*	289,684,072		289,684,072
Avg. no. of shs. o/s*	289,684,072		289,684,072
	%		%
Net profit margin	n.a.		n.a.
Return on equity	(18.14)		(18.11)
Return on assets	(16.34)		(16.74)

* Common
^o Restated
^A Reported in accordance with IFRS

Latest Results

Periods ended:	6m June 30/22^A		6m June 30/21^oA
	$000s	%Chg	$000s
Net income	4	n.a.	(499)
	$		$
Earnings per share*	nil		(0.00)

* Common
^o Restated
^A Reported in accordance with IFRS

Historical Summary
(as originally stated)

Fiscal Year	Oper. Rev.	Net Inc. Bef. Disc.	EPS*
	$000s	$000s	$
2021^A	nil	(1,714)	(0.01)
2020^A	26	(2,050)	(0.01)
2019^A	153	(450)	(0.00)
2018^A	158	(669)	(0.00)
2017^A	50	(628)	(0.00)

* Common
^A Reported in accordance with IFRS

C.66 Caplink Ventures Inc.

Symbol - CAPL.P **Exchange** - TSX-VEN **CUSIP** - 14065G
Head Office - 15718 39A Ave, Surrey, BC, V3Z 0L1 **Telephone** - (604) 825-4778
Email - bob@thast.ca
Investor Relations - Robert L. Thast (604) 825-4778
Auditors - De Visser Gray LLP C.A., Vancouver, B.C.
Lawyers - Clark Wilson LLP, Vancouver, B.C.
Transfer Agents - Odyssey Trust Company, Vancouver, B.C.
Profile - (B.C. 2021) Capital Pool Company.
Common listed on TSX-VEN, Nov. 3, 2022.
Directors - Robert L. (Bob) Thast, CEO & CFO, Surrey, B.C.; Jaclyn Thast, corp. sec., Surrey, B.C.; Ali Sodagar, Vancouver, B.C.

Capital Stock

	Authorized (shs.)	Outstanding (shs.)[1]
Common	unlimited	8,000,100

[1] At May 30, 2023

Major Shareholder - Robert L. (Bob) Thast held 50% interest and Jaclyn Thast held 22.5% interest at Nov. 3, 2022.

Price Range - CAPL.P/TSX-VEN

Year	Volume	High	Low	Close
2022	20,000	$0.14	$0.13	$0.13

Recent Close: $0.14
Capital Stock Changes - On Nov. 3, 2022, an initial public offering of 2,000,000 common shares was completed at 10¢ per share.

C.67 Capstone Infrastructure Corporation

CUSIP - 14069Q
Head Office - RBC Centre, 2930-155 Wellington St W, Toronto, ON, M5V 3H1 **Telephone** - (416) 649-1300 **Toll-free** - (855) 649-1300 **Fax** - (416) 649-1335
Website - www.capstoneinfrastructure.com
Email - mhunter@capstoneinfra.com
Investor Relations - Megan Hunter (416) 649-1325
Auditors - PricewaterhouseCoopers LLP C.A., Toronto, Ont.
Lawyers - Blake, Cassels & Graydon LLP, Toronto, Ont.
Transfer Agents - Computershare Trust Company of Canada Inc., Montréal, Qué.
FP500 Revenue Ranking - 601
Employees - 154 at Dec. 31, 2022
Profile - (B.C. 2010) Owns and operates wind, gas cogeneration, hydro, solar and biomass power generation facilities across Canada.

At Mar. 31, 2023, the company owned interests in and operated clean and renewable energy projects with a net installed capacity of 824 MW across 31 facilities in Canada, consisting of 22 wind facilities in Ontario (16), Nova Scotia (3), Quebec and Saskatchewan; three solar facilities in Alberta (2) and Ontario; four hydro facilities in Ontario (2) and British Columbia; a biomass facility in Alberta; and a natural gas power plant in Ontario.

On July 14, 2022, the Ganaraska Wind Facility, the Grey Highlands ZEP Wind Facility, the Snowy Ridge Wind Facility and the Settlers Landing Wind Facility (SLGR Wind Facilities) in Ontario were reorganized. As part of the reorganization, wholly owned **Capstone Power Corp.** acquired 1% of the conversion option held by an affiliate of **Concord Green Energy Inc.** under a debenture and such Concord affiliate exercised its right to convert the debenture into a 49% equity interest in the SLGR Wind Facilities, resulting in the company and such Concord affiliate having 51% and 49% ownership of the SLGR Wind Facilities, respectively.

Common delisted from TSX, May 5, 2016.

Predecessor Detail - Name changed from Macquarie Power and Infrastructure Corporation, Apr. 15, 2011, pursuant to the internalization of management functions previously provided by Macquarie Power Management Ltd.

Directors - Paul R. Smith, chr., Edinburgh, Midlothian, United Kingdom; David Eva, CEO, Ont.; Andrew Kennedy, CFO, Ont.; Richard L. (Rick) Knowles, Toronto, Ont.; Paul Malan, London, Middx., United Kingdom; Adèle S. Malo, Ont.; Janet P. Woodruff, West Vancouver, B.C.

Other Exec. Officers - Patrick Leitch, sr. v-p, opers.; Aileen Gien, gen. counsel & corp. sec.

Capital Stock

	Authorized (shs.)	Outstanding (shs.)[1]
Preferred	unlimited	
Series A		3,000,000
Class A	unlimited	304,609,155
Common	unlimited	nil

[1] At May 10, 2023

Preferred Series A - Entitled to cumulative annual dividends of $0.9256 payable quarterly to July 30, 2026, and thereafter at a rate reset every five years equal to the five-year Government of Canada yield plus 2.71%. Redeemable on July 31, 2026, and on July 31 every five years thereafter at $25 per share plus declared and unpaid dividends. Convertible at the holder's option on July 31, 2026, and on July 31 every five years thereafter, into floating rate first preferred series B shares on a share-for-share basis, subject to certain conditions. The series B shares would pay a quarterly dividend equal to the 90-day Canadian Treasury bill rate plus 2.71%. Non-voting.

Class A - 1.01 votes per share.

Common - One vote per share.

Major Shareholder - iCON Infrastructure Partners III, L.P. held 100% interest at Mar. 21, 2023.

Capital Stock Changes - There were no changes to capital stock from 2018 to 2022, inclusive.

Dividends

CSE.PR.A pfd A cum. red. exch. Adj. Ra $0.9255 pa Q est. Nov. 1, 2021

Wholly Owned Subsidiaries

Capstone Power Corp., Toronto, Ont.
Cardinal Power of Canada, L.P., Del.
Chi-Wiikwedong Holdings LP, Ont.
Erie Shores Wind Farm Limited Partnership, Ont.
Glace Bay Lingan Wind Power Ltd., Glace Bay, N.S.
Glen Dhu Wind Energy Limited Partnership, N.S.
Grey Highlands Clean Energy Development LP, Ont.
Helios Solar Star A-1 Partnership, Canada.
MPT Hydro LP, Ont.
Riverhurst Wind Farm LP, Ont.
SWNS Wind LP, Ont.
Sky Generation LP, Ont.
Watford Wind LP, Ont.
Whitecourt Power Limited Partnership, Alta.
Wild Rose 2 Wind LP, Canada.

Subsidiaries

75% int. in **Buffalo Atlee 4 Wind LP**, Ont.
75% int. in **Buffalo Atlee 1 Wind LP**, Ont.
75% int. in **Buffalo Atlee 3 Wind LP**, Ont.
75% int. in **Buffalo Atlee 2 Wind LP**, Ont.
51% int. in **Chi-Wiikwedong LP**, Ont.
51% int. in **Claresholm Solar LP**, Ont.
75% int. in **Kneehill Solar LP**, Alta.
75% int. in **Michichi Solar LP**, Alta.
51% int. in **Parc Eolien Saint-Philémon S.E.C.**, Qué.
51% int. in **SLGR Wind LP**
51% int. in **SP Amherst Wind Power LP**, Ont.

Investments

50% int. in **Obra Maestra Renewables, LLC**, United States.

Note: The preceding list includes only the major related companies in which interests are held.

Financial Statistics

Periods ended:	12m Dec. 31/22[A]		12m Dec. 31/21[A]
	$000s	%Chg	$000s
Operating revenue	**255,022**	**+15**	**222,567**
Cost of sales	70,712		56,366
General & admin expense	16,179		12,440
Operating expense	**86,891**	**+26**	**68,806**
Operating income	**168,131**	**+9**	**153,761**
Deprec., depl. & amort.	96,282		93,901
Finance income	3,113		998
Finance costs, gross	46,261		42,695
Investment income	695		nil
Pre-tax income	**43,582**	**+117**	**20,082**
Income taxes	12,234		3,611
Net income	**31,348**	**+90**	**16,471**
Net inc. for equity hldrs	**25,108**	**+176**	**9,110**
Net inc. for non-cont. int	**6,240**	**-15**	**7,361**
Cash & equivalent	124,897		57,376
Inventories	1,979		1,740
Accounts receivable	47,890		30,916
Current assets	232,598		131,780
Long-term investments	6,492		nil
Fixed assets, net	954,922		1,022,361
Intangibles, net	137,811		151,286
Total assets	**1,550,435**	**+13**	**1,369,491**
Accts. pay. & accr. liabs	53,976		55,405
Current liabilities	143,619		208,225
Long-term debt, gross	915,419		865,652
Long-term debt, net	827,557		716,179
Long-term lease liabilities	35,309		36,425
Preferred share equity	72,020		72,020
Shareholders' equity	310,274		208,037
Non-controlling interest	119,040		96,129
Cash from oper. activs	**117,457**	**-5**	**123,558**
Cash from fin. activs	181,720		91,989
Cash from invest. activs	(231,656)		(229,332)
Net cash position	**124,897**	**+118**	**57,376**
Capital expenditures	(239,095)		(201,883)
	$		$
Earnings per share*	0.07		0.02
Cash flow per share*	0.39		0.41
	shs		shs
No. of shs. o/s*	304,609,000		304,609,000
	%		%
Net profit margin	12.29		7.40
Return on equity	11.88		4.92
Return on assets	4.43		3.95
No. of employees (FTEs)	154		130

* Class A
[A] Reported in accordance with IFRS

Latest Results

Periods ended:	3m Mar. 31/23[A]		3m Mar. 31/22[A]
	$000s	%Chg	$000s
Operating revenue	58,379	-1	59,200
Net income	(22,892)	n.a.	21,319
Net inc. for equity hldrs	(18,813)	n.a.	19,342
Net inc. for non-cont. int	(4,079)		1,977
	$		$
Earnings per share*	(0.06)		0.06

* Class A
[A] Reported in accordance with IFRS

Historical Summary
(as originally stated)

Fiscal Year	Oper. Rev. $000s	Net Inc. Bef. Disc. $000s	EPS* $
2022[A]	255,022	31,348	0.07
2021[A]	222,567	16,471	0.02
2020[A]	181,503	979	(0.01)
2019[A]	185,338	4,226	(0.00)
2018[A]	183,629	3,897	(0.00)

* Class A
[A] Reported in accordance with IFRS

C.68 Captiva Verde Wellness Corp.

Symbol - PWR **Exchange** - CSE **CUSIP** - 14076P
Head Office - 632 Foster Ave, Coquitlam, BC, V3J 2L7 **Telephone** - (949) 903-5906
Email - westernwind@shaw.ca
Investor Relations - Jeffrey J. Ciachurski (949) 903-5906
Auditors - Davidson & Company LLP C.A., Vancouver, B.C.
Lawyers - McMillan LLP, Vancouver, B.C.
Transfer Agents - Computershare Trust Company of Canada Inc., Vancouver, B.C.
Profile - (B.C. 2015) Has real estate interests in California and New Brunswick.

Holds option to earn 50% net profit interest in Sage Ranch, a 995-unit sustainable housing project under development in Tehachapi, Calif.

Also holds 200 acres of agricultural land and 36,000 sq. ft. of buildings and processing facilities in New Brunswick. **Solargram Farms Corporation** operates outdoor cannabis cultivation and processing operations on the property, and the company is seeking to recover funds previously advanced to Solargram.

Recent Merger and Acquisition Activity

Status: terminated **Revised:** Oct. 31, 2022
UPDATE: Captiva determined that they would no longer pursue the transaction. PREVIOUS: Captiva Verde Land Corp. agreed to acquire Salud Esmeralda de Mexico S.A. de C.V., which holds a pharmaceutical licence to sell, market and distribute over 300 psychoactive and non-psychoactive drugs including cannabis products in Mexico, for issuance of 80,000,000 common shares. Jeff Ciachurski, CEO of Captiva Verde, is a shareholder of Salud Esmeralda.

Predecessor Detail - Name changed from Captiva Verde Land Corp., May 21, 2021.

Directors - Jeffrey J. (Jeff) Ciachurski, CEO, Coquitlam, B.C.; J. Michael (Mike) Boyd, Tucson, Ariz.; Orest Kostecki, Kitchener, Ont.

Other Exec. Officers - Anthony Balic, CFO

Capital Stock

	Authorized (shs.)	Outstanding (shs.)[1]
Common	unlimited	205,116,067

[1] At Apr. 13, 2023

Major Shareholder - Widely held at Apr. 13, 2023.

Price Range - PWR/CSE

Year	Volume	High	Low	Close
2022	53,902,440	$0.09	$0.02	$0.03
2021	35,408,862	$0.40	$0.04	$0.04
2020	55,782,300	$0.75	$0.16	$0.28
2019	33,604,178	$0.30	$0.08	$0.30
2018	8,700,051	$0.22	$0.06	$0.10

Recent Close: $0.03

Capital Stock Changes - In December 2022, private placement of 20,000,000 units (1 common share & 1 warrant) at 2¢ per unit was completed, with warrants exercisable at 5¢ per share for two years. In April 2023, private placement of up to 80,000,000 units (1 common share & 1 warrant) at $0.032 per unit was announced, with warrants exercisable at 5¢ per share for five years.

In November 2021, private placement of 12,000,000 units (1 common share & 1 warrant) at 6¢ per unit was completed. In February 2022, 27,000,000 common shares were issued to settle debt of $1,350,000. Also during fiscal 2022, 2,000,000 common shares were issued on exercise of options.

Financial Statistics

Periods ended:	12m Oct. 31/22[A]		12m Oct. 31/21[A]
	$000s	%Chg	$000s
General & admin expense	1,146		982
Stock-based compensation	184		nil
Operating expense	**1,331**	**+36**	**982**
Operating income	**(1,331)**	**n.a.**	**(982)**
Deprec., depl. & amort.	nil		36
Finance costs, gross	34		13
Write-downs/write-offs	(1,472)		(2,885)
Pre-tax income	**(3,625)**	**n.a.**	**(3,769)**
Net income	**(3,625)**	**n.a.**	**(3,769)**
Cash & equivalent	16		87
Current assets	16		163
Fixed assets, net	9,740		9,714
Total assets	**9,757**	**-14**	**11,301**
Bank indebtedness	834		1,870
Accts. pay. & accr. liabs	995		600
Current liabilities	1,829		2,504
Long-term lease liabilities	nil		36
Shareholders' equity	7,928		8,760
Cash from oper. activs	**(469)**	**n.a.**	**(305)**
Cash from fin. activs	578		1,778
Cash from invest. activs	(180)		(1,410)
Net cash position	**16**	**-82**	**87**
Capital expenditures	(126)		(708)
	$		$
Earnings per share*	(0.02)		(0.03)
Cash flow per share*	(0.00)		(0.00)
	shs		shs
No. of shs. o/s*	184,491,067		143,491,067
Avg. no. of shs. o/s*	174,384,218		141,977,425
	%		%
Net profit margin	n.a.		n.a.
Return on equity	(43.44)		(38.92)
Return on assets	(34.11)		(30.40)

* Common
[A] Reported in accordance with IFRS

Latest Results

Periods ended:	3m Jan. 31/23^A		3m Jan. 31/22^A
	$000s	%Chg	$000s
Net income	(267)	n.a.	2,399
	$		$
Earnings per share*	(0.00)		0.02

* Common
^A Reported in accordance with IFRS

Historical Summary
(as originally stated)

Fiscal Year	Oper. Rev.	Net Inc. Bef. Disc.	EPS*
	$000s	$000s	$
2022^A	nil	(3,625)	(0.02)
2021^A	nil	(3,769)	(0.03)
2020^A	nil	(1,891)	(0.02)
2019^A	nil	(1,569)	(0.02)
2018^A	nil	(197)	(0.00)

* Common
^A Reported in accordance with IFRS

C.69 Captor Capital Corp.

Symbol - CPTR **Exchange** - CSE **CUSIP** - 14075H
Head Office - 401-4 King St W, Toronto, ON, M5H 1B6 **Telephone** - (416) 504-3978 **Fax** - (416) 504-3982
Website - www.captorcapital.com
Email - johnz@captorcapital.com
Investor Relations - John Zorbas (866) 437-9551
Auditors - Clearhouse LLP C.A., Mississauga, Ont.
Lawyers - Berkowitz Cohen & Rennett LLC, Beverly Hills, Calif.; Cassels Brock & Blackwell LLP, Toronto, Ont.
Transfer Agents - Capital Transfer Agency Inc., Toronto, Ont.
Profile - (Ont. 2003) Distributes and retails cannabis in California.
Subsidiary **Captor Retail Group Inc.** (51% owned, **Three Habitat Consulting Holdco Inc.** 49%) owns and operates nine One Plant branded cannabis dispensaries in Santa Cruz, Antioch, El Sobrante, Salinas, Lompoc, Goleta, Atwater, Palm Springs and Castroville, Calif., as well as a supplementary direct-to-consumer delivery business which also operates under the One Plant brand.

Recent Merger and Acquisition Activity

Status: terminated **Revised:** July 26, 2023
UPDATE: The transaction was terminated. PREVIOUS: Captor Capital Corp. entered into a binding letter of intent to acquire 64.11% interest in U.K.-based Rimstock Holdings Limited for US$31,745,208 in a reverse takeover transaction. Rimstock designs and manufactures lightweight, forged alloy wheels for the automotive market at its facility in West Bromwich, U.K., and operates sales and marketing subsidiaries in Germany and the U.S. The purchase price consists of US$2,500,000 in cash as a non-refundable deposit which would be converted into shares of Rimstock on closing, and US$22,245,208 in shares of Captor Capital at a deemed value Cdn$0.25 per share and US$7,000,000 in cash on closing. Upon completion, Captor Capital would have a 2-year option to acquire the remaining 35.89% interest in Rimstock based on a valuation of Rimstock to be determined by mutual agreement but not less than US$49,520,000.
Status: terminated **Revised:** June 21, 2022
UPDATE: The transaction was terminated. PREVIOUS: Captor Capital Corp. agreed to acquire the remaining 49% interest in Captor Retail Group Inc., which owns nine cannabis dispensaries in California, by way of the acquisition of partner Three Habitat Consulting Holdco Inc. for $29,720,223, to be paid issuance of 27,018,384 common shares of Captor Capital at $1.10 per share.
Predecessor Detail - Name changed from NWT Uranium Corp., June 2, 2017.
Directors - Brady Cobb, interim chr., Fort Lauderdale, Fla.; John Zorbas, pres. & CEO, Athens, Greece; Kyle Appleby, Toronto, Ont.; Mark Klein, Tel Aviv, Israel; Bryan Reyhani, New York, N.Y.; Alexander (Alex) Spiro, New York, N.Y.
Other Exec. Officers - Jing Peng, CFO

Capital Stock

	Authorized (shs.)	Outstanding (shs.)[1]
Common	unlimited	52,095,600

[1] At July 29, 2022

Major Shareholder - SOL Global Investments Corp. held 16.1% interest at Feb. 11, 2022.

Price Range - CPTR/CSE

Year	Volume	High	Low	Close
2022	5,928,814	$1.00	$0.26	$0.40
2021	23,379,538	$2.10	$0.25	$0.95
2020	8,581,180	$0.30	$0.11	$0.26
2019	15,185,778	$2.10	$0.24	$0.26
2018	15,333,966	$17.80	$0.75	$1.25

Recent Close: $0.15
Capital Stock Changes - In April 2021, private placement of 12,800,861 units (1 common share & ½ warrant) at 95¢ per unit was completed. Also during fiscal 2022, 765,000 common shares were issued on exercise of options.

Wholly Owned Subsidiaries

Captor Cash Management Inc., Calif.
Fesanta Investments Ltd., Cyprus.
- 100% int. in **Captor Acquisition Corp.**, United States.
  - 100% int. in **CAC Consumer Group LLC**, Calif.
  - 100% int. in **CAC Consumer Services LLC**, Del.

I-5 Holdings Ltd., Vancouver, B.C.
- 100% int. in **ICH Holdings Ltd.**, United States.
  - 100% int. in **ICH Washington Holdings Ltd.**, United States. Inactive.

Mellow Extracts, LLC, Calif.
Northwest Minerals Mexico, S.A. de C.V., Mexico. Inactive.

Subsidiaries

51% int. in **Captor Retail Group Inc.**, Calif.

Investments

MedMen Enterprises Inc., Culver City, Calif. (see separate coverage)

Financial Statistics

Periods ended:	12m Mar. 31/22^A		12m Mar. 31/21^A
	$000s	%Chg	$000s
Operating revenue	**32,737**	**+102**	**16,217**
Cost of sales	20,430		10,920
General & admin expense	12,289		9,286
Stock-based compensation	3,165		469
Operating expense	**35,884**	**+74**	**20,675**
Operating income	**(3,147)**	**n.a.**	**(4,458)**
Deprec., depl. & amort.	3,106		1,643
Finance income	22		19
Finance costs, gross	1,265		989
Investment income	nil		(167)
Write-downs/write-offs	(5,329)		(698)
Pre-tax income	**(16,189)**	**n.a.**	**(6,389)**
Income taxes	2,212		673
Net inc. bef. disc. opers	**(18,401)**	**n.a.**	**(7,063)**
Income from disc. opers	nil		71
Net income	**(18,401)**	**n.a.**	**(6,992)**
Net inc. for equity hldrs	**(14,450)**	**n.a.**	**(5,867)**
Net inc. for non-cont. int	**(3,951)**	**n.a.**	**(1,125)**
Cash & equivalent	20,318		17,363
Inventories	2,038		1,404
Accounts receivable	2,568		842
Current assets	27,743		24,095
Fixed assets, net	3,201		2,900
Right-of-use assets	7,179		8,874
Intangibles, net	17,398		23,671
Total assets	**56,417**	**-6**	**60,310**
Accts. pay. & accr. liabs	6,799		8,453
Current liabilities	10,641		10,774
Long-term debt, gross	546		476
Long-term debt, net	168		284
Long-term lease liabilities	7,071		8,325
Shareholders' equity	27,864		26,857
Non-controlling interest	8,514		12,465
Cash from oper. activs	**(6,639)**	**n.a.**	**(2,788)**
Cash from fin. activs	10,086		(1,651)
Cash from invest. activs	(604)		2,910
Net cash position	**20,318**	**+17**	**17,363**
Capital expenditures	(1,178)		(1,632)
	$		$
Earnings per share*	(0.28)		(0.15)
Cash flow per share*	(0.13)		(0.07)
	shs		shs
No. of shs. o/s*	52,095,600		38,529,739
Avg. no. of shs. o/s*	51,729,893		38,594,986
	%		%
Net profit margin	(56.21)		(43.55)
Return on equity	(52.81)		(19.20)
Return on assets	(29.06)		(11.32)
Foreign sales percent	100		100

* Common
^A Reported in accordance with IFRS

Historical Summary
(as originally stated)

Fiscal Year	Oper. Rev.	Net Inc. Bef. Disc.	EPS*
	$000s	$000s	$
2022^A	32,737	(18,401)	(0.28)
2021^A	16,217	(7,063)	(0.15)
2020^A	12,495	(32,874)	(0.84)
2019^A	5,866	(46,436)	(1.23)
2018^A	5,150	3,781	0.40

* Common
^A Reported in accordance with IFRS
Note: Adjusted throughout for 1-for-20 cons. in Oct. 2018

C.70 Carbeeza Inc.

Symbol - AUTO **Exchange** - TSX-VEN **CUSIP** - 140772
Head Office - 620-10180 101 St, Edmonton, AB, T5J 3S4 **Toll-free** - (855) 216-8802
Website - www.carbeeza.com
Email - sandroauto@carbeeza.com
Investor Relations - Sandro A. Torrieri (855) 216-8802
Auditors - MNP LLP C.A., Calgary, Alta.
Transfer Agents - TSX Trust Company, Toronto, Ont.
Profile - (Alta. 2021; orig. Ont., 2012) Developing an automotive sales platform powered by artificial intelligence for consumers and automotive dealers to meet and transact the purchase of any type of vehicle. The platform allows consumers to research vehicles, find financing options and negotiate the lowest prices for their preferred vehicle from anywhere in the world.
At December 2021, the company's automotive platform was live in British Columbia and Alberta. The company plans to focus on onboarding dealerships in western Canada and Ontario followed by dealerships in Quebec and Atlantic Canada by early 2022 then dealerships in the United States.
Predecessor Detail - Name changed from Hit Technologies Inc., July 14, 2021, pursuant to the reverse takeover acquisition of Carbeeza Ltd., and concurrent amalgamation of Carbeeza Ltd. and wholly owned 2330654 Alberta Ltd.; basis 1 new for 2.5 old shs.
Directors - Sandro A. Torrieri, pres. & CEO, Edmonton, Alta.; Evan Baptie, Edmonton, Alta.; Dr. Ibrahim Gedeon, Alta.; Niel Hiscox, Toronto, Ont.; Ron S. Hozjan, Calgary, Alta.; Maria Nathanail, Calgary, Alta.
Other Exec. Officers - Joanna Hampton, interim CFO; Breton Gaunt, corp. sec.

Capital Stock

	Authorized (shs.)	Outstanding (shs.)[1]
Common	unlimited	70,143,124

[1] At May 29, 2023

Major Shareholder - David Feraco held 16.49% interest, Sandro A. Torrieri held 16.49% interest, Devin Vandenberg held 16.49% interest and Nicolas Samaha held 11.6% interest at Aug. 18, 2022.

Price Range - AUTO/TSX-VEN

Year	Volume	High	Low	Close
2022	3,124,998	$0.40	$0.09	$0.18
2021	2,383,190	$1.80	$0.41	$0.45
2020	346,879	$0.75	$0.25	$0.25
2019	952,744	$2.25	$0.25	$0.50
2018	3,321,181	$6.00	$0.75	$1.25

Consolidation: 1-for-2.5 cons. in July 2021; 1-for-20 cons. in July 2020
Recent Close: $0.18
Capital Stock Changes - In February 2023, private placement of 6,250,000 units (1 common share & 1 warrant) at 20¢ per unit was completed, with warrants exercisable at 25¢ per share for 2.5 years.

Wholly Owned Subsidiaries

Carbeeza Ltd., Stony Plain, Alta.

C.71 Carbon Streaming Corporation

Symbol - NETZ **Exchange** - NEO **CUSIP** - 14116K
Head Office - 1240-155 University Ave, Toronto, ON, M5H 3B7 **Telephone** - (647) 846-7765
Website - www.carbonstreaming.com
Email - anne@carbonstreaming.com
Investor Relations - Anne Walters (647) 846-7765
Auditors - Deloitte LLP C.A., Vancouver, B.C.
Transfer Agents - Odyssey Trust Company, Vancouver, B.C.
Employees - 18 at Mar. 28, 2023
Profile - (B.C. 2004) Acquires carbon credit streaming and royalty arrangements on projects which include nature-based solutions, the distribution of fuel-efficient cookstoves and water filtration devices, waste avoidance and energy efficiency, agricultural methane avoidance and biochar carbon removal in North America, South America, Africa and Asia.
Has streaming and royalty arrangements related to more than 20 projects around the world to scale high-integrity carbon credit projects to accelerate global climate action and advance the United Nations Sustainable Development Goals.
Carbon credit projects include Rimba Raya, a REDD+ (Reducing Emissions from Deforestation and Forest Degradation) project in Indonesia; Magdalena Bay Blue Carbon Conservation project in Mexico; Cerrado Biome REDD+ project in Brazil; construction of a biochar product facility in Waverly, Va.; two sustainable community projects in Quebec and Ontario; Community Carbon project, which consists of seven cookstoves and water filtration projects in Uganda, Mozambique, Tanzania, Zambia and Malawi; Nalgonda rice farming project in India; construction of a biochar pyrolysis pilot facility in Enfield, Me.; two carbon credit projects within the Bonobo Peace Forest located in the Democratic Republic of Congo; and four REDD+ projects in the Amazon, Brazil.
The company will make ongoing delivery payments to project partners for each carbon credit that is sold under the respective streams.
The company changed its year end to December 31 from June 30, effective Dec. 31, 2022.
On July 6, 2022, the company invested additional $1,350,000 in **Carbon Fund Advisors Inc.** As a result, the company's interest in Carbon Fund increased to 50% from 18.6%. The investment supported Carbon Fund's launch of the Carbon Strategy ETF, an actively managed thematic exchange-traded fund that aims to provide investors exposure to the growing compliance carbon markets.
Predecessor Detail - Name changed from Mexivada Mining Corp., June 15, 2020; basis 1 new for 100 old shs.
Directors - Maurice J. Swan, chr., Mississauga, Ont.; Justin Cochrane, CEO, Burlington, Ont.; Dr. R. Marc Bustin, Vancouver, B.C.; Saurabh Handa, Vancouver, B.C.; Candace J. MacGibbon, Toronto, Ont.; Alice Schroeder, Conn.; Andy Tester, Ore.; Jeanne Usonis, Calif.

Other Exec. Officers - Geoff Smith, pres. & COO; Conor Kearns, CFO; Michael Psihogios, chief invest. officer; Anne Walters, gen. counsel & corp. sec.

Capital Stock

	Authorized (shs.)	Outstanding (shs.)[1]
Common	unlimited	47,083,951

[1] At May 12, 2023

Major Shareholder - Widely held at Sept. 30, 2021.

Price Range - NETZ/NEO

Year	Volume	High	Low	Close
2022............	1,850,900	$16.70	$1.96	$2.63
2021............	711,540	$16.79	$7.55	$16.61

Recent Close: $1.22

Capital Stock Changes - During the six-month period ended Dec. 31, 2022, common shares were issued as follows: 138,113 on vesting of restricted share units and 10,000 on exercise of warrants.

On Oct. 25, 2021, common shares were consolidated on a 1-for-5 basis. In November 2021, 20,980,250 units (1 post-consolidated common share & 1 warrant) were issued without further consideration on exchange of special warrants sold previously by private placement at US$5.00 each. Also during fiscal 2022, post-consolidated common shares were issued as follows: 4,539,180 for services, 533,913 on exercise of warrants, 20,000 on exercise of options and 57,745 on conversion of restricted share units.

Wholly Owned Subsidiaries

1253661 B.C. Ltd., B.C.

Investments

50% int. in **Carbon Fund Advisors Inc.**, Del.

Financial Statistics

Periods ended:	6m Dec. 31/22[A]		12m June 30/22[A]
	US$000s	%Chg	US$000s
Operating revenue	**1,086**	**n.a.**	**147**
Cost of goods sold	625		126
Salaries & benefits	4,250		6,206
General & admin expense	4,742		6,564
Stock-based compensation	1,590		3,945
Operating expense	**11,207**	**n.a.**	**16,841**
Operating income	**(10,121)**	**n.a.**	**(16,694)**
Deprec., depl. & amort.	51		nil
Finance income	176		nil
Pre-tax income	**2,355**	**n.a.**	**(12,900)**
Net income	**2,355**	**n.a.**	**(12,900)**
Cash & equivalent	70,345		93,238
Inventories	1,019		1,644
Accounts receivable	323		341
Current assets	72,254		96,024
Long-term investments	1,597		nil
Right-of-use assets	333		nil
Total assets	**158,489**	**n.a.**	**163,467**
Accts. pay. & accr. liabs.	1,856		3,155
Current liabilities	9,781		20,433
Long-term lease liabilities	330		nil
Shareholders' equity	146,640		142,635
Cash from oper. activs.	**(8,523)**	**n.a.**	**(13,688)**
Cash from fin. activs.	29		35,132
Cash from invest. activs.	(13,212)		(35,396)
Net cash position	**70,345**	**n.a.**	**93,238**
	US$		US$
Earnings per share*	0.05		(0.34)
Cash flow per share*	(0.18)		(0.36)
	shs		shs
No. of shs. o/s*	46,952,032		46,803,919
Avg. no. of shs. o/s*	46,834,795		37,732,846
	%		%
Net profit margin	...		n.m.
Return on equity	...		(10.28)
Return on assets	...		(9.44)
No. of employees (FTEs)	n.a.		16

* Common
[A] Reported in accordance with IFRS

Latest Results

Periods ended:	3m Mar. 31/23[A]		3m Mar. 31/22[oA]
	US$000s	%Chg	US$000s
Operating revenue	21	n.a.	nil
Net income	(972)	n.a.	49
	US$		US$
Earnings per share*	(0.02)		1.05

* Common
[o] Restated
[A] Reported in accordance with IFRS

Historical Summary
(as originally stated)

Fiscal Year	Oper. Rev.	Net Inc. Bef. Disc.	EPS*
	US$000s	US$000s	US$
2022[A1]	1,086	2,355	0.05
2022[A]	147	(12,900)	(0.34)
	$000s	$000s	$
2021[A]	nil	(5,714)	(0.71)
2020[A]	nil	(109)	(0.43)
2019[A]	nil	(11)	(0.10)

* Common
[A] Reported in accordance with IFRS
[1] 6 months ended Dec. 31, 2022.

Note: Adjusted throughout for 1-for-5 cons. in Oct. 2021; 1-for-100 cons. in June 2020

C.72 CarbonTech Capital Corp.

Symbol - CT.P **Exchange** - TSX-VEN **CUSIP** - 14133L
Head Office - 2700-161 Bay St, Toronto, ON, M5J 2S1 **Telephone** - (416) 532-2200
Email - ashapack@mohawkmedical.ca
Investor Relations - Andrew Shapack (416) 532-2200
Auditors - McGovern Hurley LLP C.A., Toronto, Ont.
Lawyers - Dentons Canada LLP, Toronto, Ont.
Transfer Agents - TSX Trust Company, Toronto, Ont.
Profile - (Ont. 2021) Capital Pool Company.

In March 2023, the company entered into an agreement for the Qualifying Transaction of **Happi Ventures Inc.**, for issuance of 13,933,332 common shares at a deemed price of $0.15 per share. Happi markets and distribution accessory dwelling units used as backyard homes.

In March 2023, the company's proposed acquisition of a residential property in Toronto, Ont., which would have constituted its Qualifying Transaction, for $1,900,000, was terminated. The existing home was to be demolished and replaced with a pre-fabricated net zero rental housing project, consisting of a two-storey house, a basement unit and a garden suite.

Directors - Jonathan Westeinde, CEO, Ont.; Andrew Shapack, CFO, Toronto, Ont.; Nicole Bacsalmasi, corp. sec., Calgary, Alta.; Seldon (Jamie) James, Toronto, Ont.; Cleo Kirkland, Ont.; Richard Michaeloff, Toronto, Ont.

Capital Stock

	Authorized (shs.)	Outstanding (shs.)[1]
Common	unlimited	17,308,439

[1] At June 9, 2022

Major Shareholder - Andrew Shapack held 11.56% interest and Jonathan Westeinde held 11.56% interest at June 9, 2022.

Price Range - CT.P/TSX-VEN

Year	Volume	High	Low	Close
2022............	103,615	$0.15	$0.10	$0.15

Recent Close: $0.15

Capital Stock Changes - On June 9, 2022, an initial public offering of 5,000,000 common shares was completed at 10¢ per share.

C.73 Carcetti Capital Corp.

Symbol - CART.H **Exchange** - TSX-VEN **CUSIP** - 141385
Head Office - 3300-205 5 Ave SW, Calgary, AB, T2P 2V7 **Toll-free** - (832) 499-6009
Email - gkumoi@shaw.ca
Investor Relations - Glenn Y. Kumoi (778) 892-2502
Auditors - Davidson & Company LLP C.A., Vancouver, B.C.
Lawyers - Morton Law, LLP, Vancouver, B.C.
Transfer Agents - Odyssey Trust Company
Profile - (Can. 2012; orig. Ont., 2008) Pursuing new business opportunities.

Formerly had oil and gas and power generation operations in western Ukraine.

On Dec. 30, 2022, the company completed a reorganization of its share capital to permit the payment of a special distribution of Cdn$0.03 per share on Jan. 5, 2023, to shareholders of record on Dec. 23, 2022.

In August 2022, the company sold wholly owned **3P International Limited** and its wholly owned **Tysagaz LLC** and **3P Energy Consulting LLC** for a nominal consideration and assumption of all the 3P's and Tysagaz' liabilities, contingent and otherwise. 3P and Tysagaz held producing Rusko-Komarivske (RK) gas field and Stanivske gas field, respectively, both in Transcarpathian Basin of western Ukraine.

Periods ended:	12m Dec. 31/21	12m Dec. 31/20
Avg. NGL prod., bbl/d	n.a.	21
Avg. gas prod., mcf/d	154	3,588
Avg. BOE prod., bbl/d	26	619
Avg. NGL price, US$/bbl	n.a.	41.07
Avg. gas price, US$/mcf	9.73	3.79
Oil reserves, net, mbbl	n.a.	7
NGL reserves, net, mbbl	n.a.	9
Gas reserves, net, mmcf	3,391	2,613
BOE reserves, net, mbbl	565	451

Predecessor Detail - Name changed from Cub Energy Inc., Dec. 30, 2022; basis 1 new for 300 old shs.

Directors - Glenn Y. Kumoi, CEO & CFO, B.C.; Richard S. Silas, Vancouver, B.C.; Kenneth J. (Ken) Taylor, Delta, B.C.

Capital Stock

	Authorized (shs.)	Outstanding (shs.)[1]
Common	unlimited	1,047,384

[1] At Apr. 24, 2023

Major Shareholder - Pelicourt Limited held 39.5% interest and Fergava Finance Inc. held 14.1% interest at Nov. 8, 2022.

Price Range - CART.H/TSX-VEN

Year	Volume	High	Low	Close
2022............	178,343	$9.00	$4.50	$7.50
2021............	169,389	$10.50	$4.50	$6.00
2020............	100,290	$22.50	$3.00	$6.00
2019............	182,432	$40.50	$6.00	$18.00
2018............	86,096	$16.50	$7.50	$7.50

Consolidation: 1-for-300 cons. in Jan. 2023
Recent Close: $0.12

Capital Stock Changes - On Jan. 4, 2023, class B common shares were consolidated on a 1-for-300 basis.

On Dec. 30, 2022, a new class of class B common shares was created and existing common shares were exchanged for class B common shares on a one-for-one basis.

Dividends

CART.H com N.S.R.
1-for-300 cons eff. Jan. 4, 2023
$0.03◆i................ Jan. 5/23
Paid in 2023: $0.03◆i 2022: n.a. 2021: n.a.

◆ Special **i** Initial Payment

Wholly Owned Subsidiaries

Gastek LLC, Calif.

Financial Statistics

Periods ended:	12m Dec. 31/21[A]		12m Dec. 31/20[A]
	US$000s	%Chg	US$000s
Operating revenue	**9,699**	**+66**	**5,860**
Cost of sales	5,558		4,399
Salaries & benefits	758		1,430
General & admin expense	892		1,092
Operating expense	**7,208**	**+4**	**6,921**
Operating income	**2,491**	**n.a.**	**(1,061)**
Deprec., depl. & amort.	65		nil
Finance costs, net	67		154
Investment income	879		(1,049)
Write-downs/write-offs	(1,793)		nil
Pre-tax income	**8,259**	**n.a.**	**(2,109)**
Net income	**8,259**	**n.a.**	**(2,109)**
Cash & equivalent	7,368		4,424
Accounts receivable	77		38
Current assets	12,239		4,578
Long-term investments	nil		2,805
Fixed assets, net	nil		1,423
Right-of-use assets	nil		116
Total assets	**12,239**	**+25**	**9,781**
Accts. pay. & accr. liabs.	170		3,331
Current liabilities	4,111		10,163
Long-term debt, gross	1,526		6,805
Long-term debt, net	288		nil
Long-term lease liabilities	nil		91
Shareholders' equity	(7,456)		(786)
Cash from oper. activs.	**5,881**	**n.m.**	**182**
Cash from fin. activs.	(3,052)		(200)
Cash from invest. activs.	275		(1,635)
Net cash position	**7,368**	**+67**	**4,424**
Capital expenditures	(375)		(1,423)
Capital disposals	nil		155
	US$		US$
Earnings per share*	9.00		(3.00)
Cash flow per share*	5.61		0.18
	shs		shs
No. of shs. o/s*	1,047,384		1,047,384
Avg. no. of shs. o/s*	1,047,384		1,047,384
	%		%
Net profit margin	85.15		(35.99)
Return on equity	n.m.		n.m.
Return on assets	75.01		(18.56)
Foreign sales percent	100		100

* Common
[A] Reported in accordance with IFRS

Latest Results

Periods ended:	9m Sept. 30/22[A]		9m Sept. 30/21[oA]
	US$000s	%Chg	US$000s
Net inc. bef. disc. opers	(423)	n.a.	(668)
Income from disc. opers	268		2,806
Net income	(155)	n.a.	2,138
	US$		US$
Earns. per sh. bef. disc. opers.*	(0.39)		(0.63)
Earnings per share*	(0.39)		3.00

* Common
[o] Restated
[A] Reported in accordance with IFRS

Historical Summary
(as originally stated)

Fiscal Year	Oper. Rev. US$000s	Net Inc. Bef. Disc. US$000s	EPS* US$
2021[A]	9,699	8,259	9.00
2020[A]	5,860	(2,109)	(3.00)
2019[A]	11,633	(11,060)	(12.00)
2018[A]	20,532	3,078	3.00
2017[A]	13,116	(14,342)	(15.00)

* Common
[A] Reported in accordance with IFRS
Note: Adjusted throughout for 1-for-300 cons. in Jan. 2023

C.74 CardioComm Solutions, Inc.

Symbol - EKG **Exchange** - TSX-VEN (S) **CUSIP** - 14159N
Head Office - 305-18 Wynford Dr, North York, ON, M3C 3S2 **Telephone** - (416) 977-9425 **Toll-free** - (877) 977-9425 **Fax** - (866) 576-4493
Website - www.cardiocommsolutions.com
Email - egrima@cardiocommsolutions.com
Investor Relations - Etienne Grima (877) 977-9425
Auditors - Buckley Dodds C.P.A., Vancouver, B.C.
Lawyers - Beadle Raven LLP, Vancouver, B.C.; Torkin Manes LLP, Toronto, Ont.
Transfer Agents - Computershare Trust Company of Canada Inc., Vancouver, B.C.
Profile - (B.C. 1989) Researches, develops, manufactures and markets patented and proprietary information technology products that record, transmit, view, analyze and store electrocardiograms (ECGs) for diagnosis and management of cardiac patients worldwide.

The company's software enables ECG data to be transmitted, received and managed anywhere in the world using standard computers, wireless devices, enterprise networks, telephones or the Internet. Products include software, hardware, software modules and application service provider (ASP) services.

Software products are all cleared as Class II medical devices in Canada and the United States and are electronic medical record (EMR) compatible. Software versions include GEMS™ WIN for cardiac event monitoring and continuous ECG monitoring; GlobalCardio™ 12 Lead (GC 12), a portable, web-enabled ECG device for local and remote 12 lead ECG monitoring use; GEMS™ Lite, an electric ECG receiving system for managing patient's information by capturing transmitted ECG data and storing it in the database; and GEMS™ Mobile, a consumer use mobile app version of GEMS™ and GEMS™ Home, a PC desktop application, all of which enables users to monitor themselves using small, portable and wireless or USB-connected ECG devices sold under the HeartCheck™ brand of personal ECG monitors.

Hardware products include HeartCheck™ CardiBeat, a small handheld wirelessly connected ECG monitor that works with GEMS™ Mobile; HeartCheck™ PEN, a handheld ECG device which is a USB connectable device for use with the PC-based GEMS™ Home desktop application; HeartCheck™ handheld ECG monitor, a portable ECG device that can store up to 200 thirty second ECG readings; and GEMS™ Sirona ECG Recorder, for automatic arrhythmia detection.

Software modules consist of GEMS™ WIN Air, a live wireless ECG monitoring solution; Auto Attendant™, an automated system which enables patients to download their ECG and submit their symptoms; GEMS™ HL7 & EMR interface, a module which streamlines the volume of patient data; and GlobalCardio™ EMR integration, a module enables bidirectional movement of data including patient information, reports and links to the patients ECGs from inside the EMR.

ASP services include C4™ ECG Management Service for cardiac event loop monitoring; GlobalCardio™ 12 Lead; and HeartCheck™ SMART Monitoring, whereby users can upload their heart readings using the BT connected HeartCheck™ PEN device or the USB connected HeartCheck™ ECG PEN device. ECGs managed through the SMART Monitoring platform may be reviewed by a patient's physician or an independent ECG reading or research service or the company's own service.

Common suspended from TSX-VEN, May 8, 2023.
Predecessor Detail - Name changed from CardioComm Solutions Inc., Nov. 26, 2007; basis 1 new for 5 old shs.
Directors - Robert Caines, chr., N.Y.; Etienne Grima, CEO, CFO & corp. sec., Ont.; Dr. John Foote, Ont.; Daniel Grima, Oakville, Ont.

Capital Stock

	Authorized (shs.)	Outstanding (shs.)[1]
Common	unlimited	150,915,138

[1] At Sept. 30, 2022

Major Shareholder - Dr. Anatoly Langer held 25.72% interest at Nov. 15, 2022.

Price Range - EKG/TSX-VEN (S)

Year	Volume	High	Low	Close
2022	9,177,695	$0.04	$0.01	$0.03
2021	23,523,229	$0.10	$0.03	$0.03
2020	36,889,689	$0.11	$0.03	$0.06
2019	56,040,478	$0.13	$0.03	$0.04
2018	33,546,262	$0.07	$0.04	$0.04

Recent Close: $0.01

Financial Statistics

Periods ended:	12m Dec. 31/21[A]		12m Dec. 31/20[oA]
	$000s	%Chg	$000s
Operating revenue	**683**	**-18**	**835**
Cost of sales	45		100
Salaries & benefits	288		370
Research & devel. expense	11		nil
General & admin expense	515		411
Stock-based compensation	7		7
Operating expense	**866**	**-2**	**888**
Operating income	**(183)**	**n.a.**	**(53)**
Deprec., depl. & amort.	29		24
Finance costs, gross	32		59
Write-downs/write-offs	19		nil
Pre-tax income	**nil**	**n.a.**	**(64)**
Net income	**nil**	**n.a.**	**(64)**
Cash & equivalent	108		122
Inventories	50		87
Accounts receivable	259		110
Current assets	434		327
Fixed assets, net	11		15
Right-of-use assets	38		15
Intangibles, net	5		4
Total assets	**486**	**+35**	**361**
Accts. pay. & accr. liabs	242		474
Current liabilities	889		1,031
Long-term debt, gross	400		290
Long-term lease liabilities	21		nil
Shareholders' equity	(423)		(670)
Cash from oper. activs	**(121)**	**n.a.**	**39**
Cash from fin. activs	109		17
Cash from invest. activs	(3)		(16)
Net cash position	**108**	**-11**	**122**
Capital expenditures	(3)		(16)
	$		$
Earnings per share*	0.00		(0.00)
Cash flow per share*	(0.00)		0.00
	shs		shs
No. of shs. o/s*	150,343,398		141,489,754
Avg. no. of shs. o/s*	149,152,154		141,168,154
	%		%
Net profit margin	n.a.		(7.66)
Return on equity	n.m.		n.m.
Return on assets	n.m.		(1.46)
Foreign sales percent	61		52

* Common
[o] Restated
[A] Reported in accordance with IFRS

Latest Results

Periods ended:	9m Sept. 30/22[A]		9m Sept. 30/21[oA]
	$000s	%Chg	$000s
Operating revenue	758	+84	413
Net income	55	n.a.	(228)
	$		$
Earnings per share*	0.00		(0.00)

* Common
[o] Restated
[A] Reported in accordance with IFRS

Historical Summary
(as originally stated)

Fiscal Year	Oper. Rev. $000s	Net Inc. Bef. Disc. $000s	EPS* $
2021[A]	683	nil	0.00
2020[A]	835	(64)	(0.00)
2019[A]	875	(1,062)	(0.01)
2018[A]	1,076	(577)	(0.00)
2017[A]	1,740	40	0.00

* Common
[A] Reported in accordance with IFRS

C.75 Cardiol Therapeutics Inc.

Symbol - CRDL **Exchange** - TSX **CUSIP** - 14161Y
Head Office - 602-2265 Upper Middle Rd E, Oakville, ON, L6H 0G5
Telephone - (289) 910-0850
Website - www.cardiolrx.com
Email - trevor.burns@cardiolrx.com
Investor Relations - Trevor Burns (289) 910-0855
Auditors - BDO Canada LLP C.A., Toronto, Ont.
Transfer Agents - Computershare Trust Company of Canada Inc., Toronto, Ont.
Profile - (Ont. 2017) Researches and develops anti-inflammatory and anti-fibrotic therapies for the treatment of heart disease.

Lead product is CardiolRx™, an oral cannabidiol (CBD) formulation in Phase II clinical trials for recurrent pericarditis and acute myocarditis (ARCHER trial). CardiolRx™ is eligible for U.S. FDA orphan drug and European Medicines Agency orphan medicine designations for recurrent pericarditis and acute myocarditis. Also developing CRD-38, a subcutaneously administered drug formulation of cannabidiol intended for use in heart failure.

Pure pharmaceutical CBD is being supplied by **Dalton Pharma Services** and **Purisys, LLC.**, which the company uses for producing CardiolRx and in research programs to develop nanotherapeutics and other anti-inflammatory drugs.

In October 2022, the company discontinued the LANCER trial, designed to investigate the cardioprotective properties of CardiolRx™ in patients hospitalized with COVID-19 who have a prior history of, or risk factors for, cardiovascular disease, due to lack of eligible patients to support recruitment. The company would prioritize its Phase II clinical programs focusing on the development of CardiolRx™ for the treatment of acute myocarditis and recurrent pericarditis.

Directors - Dr. Guillermo Torre-Amione, chr., Monterrey, N.L., Mexico; David G. Elsley, pres. & CEO, Oakville, Ont.; Christopher J. (Chris) Waddick, CFO & corp. sec., Georgetown, Ont.; Jennifer M. Chao, New York, N.Y.; Teri Loxam, Pa.; Peter Pekos, Ont.; Colin Stott, Southport, N.C.; Michael J. Willner, Fla.
Other Exec. Officers - Bernard Lim, COO; Dr. Andrew Hamer, CMO; Thomas Moffatt, chief comml. officer

Capital Stock

	Authorized (shs.)	Outstanding (shs.)[1]
Class A Common	unlimited	64,097,536

[1] At May 12, 2023

Major Shareholder - Widely held at May 12, 2023.

Price Range - CRDL/TSX

Year	Volume	High	Low	Close
2022	42,517,891	$2.95	$0.65	$0.69
2021	62,731,125	$6.19	$2.25	$2.33
2020	19,270,469	$5.00	$1.87	$2.78
2019	13,310,256	$8.49	$2.21	$4.58
2018	248,531	$4.88	$4.15	$4.45

Recent Close: $1.35

Capital Stock Changes - During 2022, class A common shares were issued as follows: 1,000,000 under performance share unit plan, 503,672 on exercise of warrants, 376,622 under restricted share unit plan and 239,243 for services.

Wholly Owned Subsidiaries

Cardiol Therapeutics USA Inc., Del.

Financial Statistics

Periods ended:	12m Dec. 31/22[A]		12m Dec. 31/21[□A]
	$000s	%Chg	$000s
Operating revenue	**nil**	**n.a.**	**79**
Research & devel. expense	10,331		10,271
General & admin expense	17,772		19,754
Stock-based compensation	5,013		8,498
Operating expense	**33,116**	**-14**	**38,523**
Operating income	**(33,116)**	**n.a.**	**(38,444)**
Deprec., depl. & amort.	220		220
Finance income	1,238		106
Pre-tax income	**(30,931)**	**n.a.**	**(31,638)**
Net income	**(30,931)**	**n.a.**	**(31,638)**
Cash & equivalent	59,470		83,899
Accounts receivable	480		407
Current assets	61,438		87,140
Fixed assets, net	296		356
Intangibles, net	295		379
Total assets	**62,029**	**-29**	**87,876**
Accts. pay. & accr. liabs.	9,334		4,859
Current liabilities	9,805		11,565
Long-term lease liabilities	22		73
Shareholders' equity	52,202		76,238
Cash from oper. activs.	**(27,220)**	**n.a.**	**(23,540)**
Cash from fin. activs.	(54)		93,438
Cash from invest. activs.	(75)		(13)
Net cash position	**59,470**	**n.a.**	**(83,899)**
Capital expenditures	(13)		(13)
	$		$
Earnings per share*	(0.49)		(0.73)
Cash flow per share*	(0.44)		(0.54)
	shs		shs
No. of shs. o/s*	64,042,536		61,922,999
Avg. no. of shs. o/s*	62,505,982		43,222,819
	%		%
Net profit margin	n.a.		n.m.
Return on equity	(48.16)		(70.69)
Return on assets	(41.27)		(60.98)
No. of employees (FTEs)	n.a.		11

* Cl.A Common
[□] Restated
[A] Reported in accordance with IFRS

Latest Results

Periods ended:	3m Mar. 31/23[A]		3m Mar. 31/22[A]
	$000s	%Chg	$000s
Net income	(7,089)	n.a.	(8,954)
	$		$
Earnings per share*	(0.11)		(0.14)

* Cl.A Common
[A] Reported in accordance with IFRS

Historical Summary
(as originally stated)

Fiscal Year	Oper. Rev. $000s	Net Inc. Bef. Disc. $000s	EPS* $
2022[A]	nil	(30,931)	(0.49)
2021[A]	79	(31,638)	(0.73)
2020[A]	nil	(20,641)	(0.69)
2019[A]	nil	(13,684)	(0.53)
2018[A]	nil	(15,894)	(1.03)

* Cl.A Common
[A] Reported in accordance with IFRS

C.76 Carebook Technologies Inc.

Symbol - CRBK **Exchange** - TSX-VEN **CUSIP** - 14168C
Head Office - 1400-2045 rue Stanley, Montréal, QC, H3A 2V4 **Telephone** - (514) 499-2848 **Fax** - (514) 845-9178
Website - carebook.com
Email - ir@carebook.com
Investor Relations - Olivier Giner (514) 502-1135
Auditors - MNP LLP C.A., Montréal, Qué.
Transfer Agents - TSX Trust Company, Toronto, Ont.

Profile - (Can. 2021; orig. B.C., 2018) Develops and commercializes mobile health management and health risk assessment systems for individuals, their families, pharmacies, employers, insurers and clinics.

The company's primary products include:

Wellness Checkpoint® is a platform for employers and their employees that identify trends and risks within a group through assessments of various factors including lifestyle habits, psychological well-being, stress levels and sleep patterns.

CoreHealth is a platform offered to corporate wellness and group benefit providers to power programs and engage employees with various interventions like coaching, group challenges and habit trackers. CoreHealth offers services in the form of Application Programming Interface including scheduling, teleconferencing, questionnaires, content feeds and messaging.

Also offers large primary retailers an all-in-one platform (mobile and web apps) that brings together medication management (fill/refill prescriptions), the ability for individuals, families and caregivers to manage their health information in one spot, health assessments and recommendations based on the results to help reduce risk of chronic diseases. The app also connects pharmacy customers to health services and integrates retail services like loyalty programs, rewards and e-commerce.

Predecessor Detail - Name changed from Pike Mountain Minerals Inc., Oct. 1, 2020, pursuant to the reverse takeover acquisition of Carebook Technologies Inc. and concurrent amalgamation of (old) Carebook with wholly owned 12235978 Canada Ltd. to continue as Carebook Technologies (2020) Inc.; basis 1 new for 13.187 old shs.

Directors - Dr. Sheldon Elman, exec. chr., Westmount, Qué.; Anne-Marie Boucher, Qué.; The Hon. Dr. Philippe Couillard, Qué.; Stuart M. Elman, Westmount, Qué.; Domenic Pilla, Toronto, Ont.; Alasdair Younie, Hamilton, Bermuda

Other Exec. Officers - Michael Peters, CEO; Olivier Giner, CFO; Charles Martin, chief tech. officer; Ruby Bhullar, v-p, client success; Stéphanie Saheb, v-p, opers.; Zev Zelman, corp. sec.

Capital Stock

	Authorized (shs.)	Outstanding (shs.)[1]
Common	unlimited	90,252,356

[1] At May 30, 2023

Major Shareholder - MedTech Investment, L.P. held 53.8% interest and UIL Limited held 26.6% interest at May 12, 2023.

Price Range - CRBK/TSX-VEN

Year	Volume	High	Low	Close
2022	2,049,993	$0.38	$0.06	$0.08
2021	8,441,163	$1.54	$0.25	$0.38
2020	7,831,923	$2.85	$0.26	$1.40
2019	37,840	$1.98	$1.32	$1.32

Consolidation: 1-for-13.187 cons. in Oct. 2020
Recent Close: $0.07

Capital Stock Changes - In March 2023, private placement of 12,500,000 units (1 common share & 0.015 warrant) at 10¢ per unit was completed, with warrants exercisable at 15¢ per share for two years. In May 2023, private placement of 12,500,000 units (1 common share & 0.015 warrant) at 10¢ per unit was completed, with warrants exercisable at 15¢ per share for two years.

In May 2022, 30,000,000 common shares were issued pursuant to a rights offering at $0.15 per share.

Wholly Owned Subsidiaries

Carebook Technologies (US), Inc., Del.
CoreHealth Technologies Inc., Kelowna, B.C.
InfoTech Inc., Winnipeg, Man.

Financial Statistics

Periods ended:	12m Dec. 31/22[A]		12m Dec. 31/21[A]
	$000s	%Chg	$000s
Operating revenue	**9,254**	**+61**	**5,735**
Cost of sales	1,617		613
Salaries & benefits	8,352		9,429
Research & devel. expense	858		1,104
General & admin expense	2,515		2,741
Stock-based compensation	40		888
Operating expense	**13,382**	**-9**	**14,775**
Operating income	**(4,128)**	**n.a.**	**(9,040)**
Deprec., depl. & amort.	2,109		1,285
Finance costs, gross	1,082		733
Pre-tax income	**(19,098)**	**n.a.**	**(19,688)**
Income taxes	(1,280)		(399)
Net income	**(17,818)**	**n.a.**	**(19,289)**
Cash & equivalent	740		1,455
Accounts receivable	767		1,376
Current assets	1,770		3,256
Fixed assets, net	244		389
Right-of-use assets	436		549
Intangibles, net	6,806		21,246
Total assets	**9,256**	**-64**	**25,593**
Accts. pay. & accr. liabs.	3,161		4,227
Current liabilities	9,590		13,456
Long-term debt, gross	7,807		8,000
Long-term debt, net	3,646		1,000
Long-term lease liabilities	580		721
Equity portion of conv. debs.	572		nil
Shareholders' equity	(6,359)		6,413
Cash from oper. activs.	**(2,749)**	**n.a.**	**(7,262)**
Cash from fin. activs.	4,205		17,305
Cash from invest. activs.	(2,171)		(12,216)
Net cash position	**740**	**-49**	**1,455**
Capital expenditures	nil		(131)
	$		$
Earnings per share*	(0.27)		(0.50)
Cash flow per share*	(0.04)		(0.19)
	shs		shs
No. of shs. o/s*	77,752,356		47,752,356
Avg. no. of shs. o/s*	66,492,082		38,904,801
	%		%
Net profit margin	(192.54)		(336.34)
Return on equity	n.m.		n.m.
Return on assets	(96.46)		n.a.

* Common
[A] Reported in accordance with IFRS

Latest Results

Periods ended:	3m Mar. 31/23[A]		3m Mar. 31/22[A]
	$000s	%Chg	$000s
Operating revenue	2,518	+5	2,397
Net income	(459)	n.a.	(1,803)
	$		$
Earnings per share*	(0.01)		(0.04)

* Common
[A] Reported in accordance with IFRS

Historical Summary
(as originally stated)

Fiscal Year	Oper. Rev. $000s	Net Inc. Bef. Disc. $000s	EPS* $
2022[A]	9,254	(17,818)	(0.27)
2021[A]	5,735	(19,289)	(0.50)
2020[A1]	3,530	(10,893)	(0.45)
2020[A]	nil	(504)	(0.66)
2019[A2]	nil	(141)	(0.40)

* Common
[A] Reported in accordance with IFRS
[1] Results reflect the Oct. 1, 2020, reverse takeover acquisition of Carebook Technologies Inc.
[2] Results pertain to Pike Mountain Minerals Inc.
Note: Adjusted throughout for 1-for-13.187 cons. in Oct. 2020

C.77 CareRx Corporation

Symbol - CRRX **Exchange** - TSX **CUSIP** - 14173C
Head Office - 1200-320 Bay St, Toronto, ON, M5H 4A6 **Telephone** - (647) 361-4499 **Toll-free** - (800) 265-9197 **Fax** - (416) 927-8405
Website - www.carerx.ca
Email - info@carerx.ca
Investor Relations - Andrew Mok (416) 927-8400
Auditors - Ernst & Young LLP C.A., Toronto, Ont.
Transfer Agents - TSX Trust Company, Toronto, Ont.
FP500 Revenue Ranking - 520
Employees - 1,444 at Dec. 31, 2022

Profile - (Can. 2001) Provides pharmacy and other healthcare services to Canadian seniors.

Operates a national network of pharmacy fulfillment centres that service more than 94,000 residents in more than 1,600 long-term care facilities, retirement homes, assisted living facilities and group homes.

In May 2022, the company acquired private Cambridge, Ont.-based **Hogan Pharmacy Partners Ltd.** for issuance of 481,400 common shares valued at $2,200,000 and a $2,200,000 vendor take-back note, of which $1,000,000 is repayable after 18 months, $400,000 is repayable after 36 months and $800,000 is repayable after 48 months with the final repayment subject to downward adjustment to the extent that certain expected additional bed growth is not achieved by the fourth anniversary of closing. Hogan is a long-term care pharmacy serving 725 residents in long-term care and retirement homes in Ontario.

Predecessor Detail - Name changed from Centric Health Corporation, June 22, 2020; basis 1 new for 20 old shs.

Directors - Kevin Dalton, chr., Toronto, Ont.; Puneet Khanna, pres. & CEO, Ont.; Ralph Desando, Ont.; Keith McIntosh, Ont.; Bruce Moody, Markham, Ont.; Maria Perrella, Ont.; Jeff Watson, Ont.

Other Exec. Officers - Andrew Mok, CFO; Paul Rakowski, chief privacy officer, sr. v-p, corp. devel., gen. counsel & corp. sec.; Adrianne Sullivan-Campeau, chief people & culture officer; Travis Featherstone, v-p, IT

Capital Stock

	Authorized (shs.)	Outstanding (shs.)[1]
Common	unlimited	57,654,727[2]

[1] At Apr. 17, 2023

[2] Excludes 2,880 common shares held in escrow.

Major Shareholder - Yorkville Asset Management Inc. held 27% interest, Polar Asset Management Partners Inc. held 10.9% interest and Bruce Moody held 10% interest at Apr. 17, 2023.

Price Range - CRRX/TSX

Year	Volume	High	Low	Close
2022	8,776,881	$5.64	$2.25	$2.56
2021	14,376,626	$6.94	$3.47	$5.69
2020	5,096,183	$6.20	$2.00	$3.84
2019	2,508,977	$7.80	$2.00	$3.10
2018	3,959,651	$12.00	$4.00	$5.90

Consolidation: 1-for-20 cons. in June 2020

Recent Close: $1.92

Capital Stock Changes - In January 2023, bought deal public offering of 2,998,000 common shares, including 35,000 common shares issued on partial exercise of over-allotment option, and concurrent private placement of 1,481,500 common shares all at $2.70 per share were completed.

During 2022, common shares were issued as follows: 2,092,332 on conversion of debentures, 1,119,923 from treasury as contingent consideration, 701,823 pursuant to the acquisition of Hogan Pharmacy Partners Ltd., 425,542 under restricted share unit plan, 228,247 on exercise of warrants and 146,143 by private placement.

Wholly Owned Subsidiaries

CareRx Equity Corporation, Ont.
- 100% int. in **CareRx Holdings Inc.**, Ont.
  - 100% int. in **CareRx Corporate Holdings Inc.**, B.C.

CareRx Pharmacy Corp., Ont.
- 100% int. in **CareRx Enterprises Ltd.**, B.C.

Centric Health Pharmacy B.C. Ltd., B.C.

Pharmacy West Limited, Sask.

Note: The preceding list includes only the major related companies in which interests are held.

Financial Statistics

Periods ended:	12m Dec. 31/22[A]		12m Dec. 31/21[A]
	$000s	%Chg	$000s
Operating revenue	**381,727**	**+45**	**262,630**
Cost of goods sold	271,793		187,351
General & admin expense	77,667		52,410
Stock-based compensation	4,569		2,665
Operating expense	**354,029**	**+46**	**242,426**
Operating income	**27,698**	**+37**	**20,204**
Deprec., depl. & amort.	20,065		15,393
Finance income	278		58
Finance costs, gross	15,221		17,354
Write-downs/write-offs	(24,330)		nil
Pre-tax income	**(35,896)**	**n.a.**	**(23,735)**
Income taxes	(1,543)		(1,005)
Net inc bef disc ops, eqhldrs	(34,353)		(22,730)
Net income	**(34,353)**	**n.a.**	**(22,730)**
Cash & equivalent	28,371		35,625
Inventories	20,303		17,992
Accounts receivable	36,400		36,118
Current assets	89,176		95,245
Long-term investments	nil		2,713
Fixed assets, net	52,393		38,171
Intangibles, net	122,966		146,687
Total assets	**264,535**	**-6**	**282,816**
Accts. pay. & accr. liabs	50,245		46,313
Current liabilities	63,887		52,973
Long-term debt, gross	106,780		112,699
Long-term debt, net	99,372		111,966
Long-term lease liabilities	25,846		18,199
Equity portion of conv. debs	6,566		7,125
Shareholders' equity	64,457		82,287
Cash from oper. activs	**22,333**	**+207**	**7,269**
Cash from fin. activs	(12,989)		101,910
Cash from invest. activs	(16,598)		(93,177)
Net cash position	**28,371**	**-20**	**35,625**
Capital expenditures	(10,042)		(5,351)
Capital disposals	3		67
	$		$
Earnings per share*	(0.72)		(0.65)
Cash flow per share*	0.47		0.21
	shs		shs
No. of shs. o/s*	51,003,993		46,289,983
Avg. no. of shs. o/s*	47,596,000		34,858,000
	%		%
Net profit margin	(9.00)		(8.65)
Return on equity	(46.82)		(48.57)
Return on assets	(7.23)		(2.78)
No. of employees (FTEs)	1,444		1,378

* Common

[A] Reported in accordance with IFRS

Latest Results

Periods ended:	3m Mar. 31/23[A]		3m Mar. 31/22[A]
	$000s	%Chg	$000s
Operating revenue	91,404	-2	93,176
Net income	(2,149)	n.a.	(2,762)
	$		$
Earnings per share*	(0.04)		(0.06)

* Common

[A] Reported in accordance with IFRS

Historical Summary
(as originally stated)

Fiscal Year	Oper. Rev. $000s	Net Inc. Bef. Disc. $000s	EPS* $
2022[A]	381,727	(34,353)	(0.72)
2021[A]	262,630	(22,730)	(0.65)
2020[A]	162,196	(18,183)	(0.90)
2019[A]	124,626	(45,677)	(4.20)
2018[A]	123,742	(34,388)	(3.40)

* Common

[A] Reported in accordance with IFRS

Note: Adjusted throughout for 1-for-20 cons. in June 2020

C.78 CareSpan Health, Inc.

Symbol - CSPN **Exchange** - TSX-VEN **CUSIP** - 14174J

Head Office - Royal Centre, 1500-1055 Georgia St W, Vancouver, BC, V6E 4N7 **Telephone** - (416) 434-8903 **Toll-free** - (888) 337-5889

Website - dev.carespanhealth.com

Email - lmarkow@carespanhealth.com

Investor Relations - Leslie N. Markow (416) 402-3694

Auditors - MNP LLP C.A.

Transfer Agents - Computershare Trust Company of Canada Inc., Toronto, Ont.

Profile - (B.C. 2018) Provides CareSpan® Clinic, a cloud-based, clinical workflow-driven platform for the remote delivery of primary medical care and mental health services in the U.S.

The CareSpan® Clinic platform integrates remote patient monitoring, diagnostic tools, patient electronic health records, care collaboration capabilities, patient engagement, e-prescribing and lab ordering.

The company's revenue consists primarily of service fees to its two networks, **American Advanced Practice Network, P.C.** (American-APN) and **American MedPsych Network, P.A.** (American-MedPsych). Both are technology enabled medical organizations that deliver care utilizing CareSpan® Clinic platform, with a focus on underserved areas of the U.S.

American-APN and American MedPsych are professional corporations which cannot have lay ownership, and their shares may only be owned by nurse practitioners and licensed medical doctors, respectively. The company controls American-APN and American MedPsych through stock transfer agreements which provide that shares transferred to new clinician-owners must be approved by the company. At Mar. 31, 2023, there were under 100 practitioners practicing across the two networks.

Predecessor Detail - Name changed from Dynamo Capital Corp., Nov. 17, 2021, pursuant to the Qualifying Transaction reverse takeover acquisition of CareSpan Holdings, Inc.; basis 1 new for 4.66667 old shs.

Directors - Rembert de Villa, chr. & CEO, New York, N.Y.; Holger Micheel-Sprenger, Germany; Dr. Sam Toney

Other Exec. Officers - Darrell Messersmith, COO; Leslie N. Markow, CFO; Rajeev (Raj) Dewan, corp. sec.

Capital Stock

	Authorized (shs.)	Outstanding (shs.)[1]
Common	unlimited	46,179,771

[1] At Mar. 31, 2023

Major Shareholder - Rembert de Villa held 14.03% interest at Dec. 28, 2022.

Price Range - CSPN/TSX-VEN

Year	Volume	High	Low	Close
2022	2,339,281	$0.60	$0.06	$0.11
2021	199,931	$0.65	$0.30	$0.45
2020	20,678	$0.42	$0.26	$0.30
2019	78,964	$0.70	$0.26	$0.26
2018	30,321	$0.93	$0.47	$0.47

Consolidation: 1-for-4.66667 cons. in Nov. 2021

Recent Close: $0.10

Capital Stock Changes - In April 2022, private placement of 3,385,714 common shares was completed at Cdn$0.35 per share. In September 2022, private placement of 2,740,899 units (1 common share & 1 warrant) at 25¢ per unit was completed. In December 2022, private placement of 11,000,000 units (1 common share & ½ warrant) at 10¢ per unit was completed. Also during 2022, common shares were issued as follows: 717,194 on conversion of debt and 91,464 as share-based compensation.

Wholly Owned Subsidiaries

CareSpan Holdings, Inc., New York, N.Y.
- 15% int. in **CareSpan Asia Inc.**, Manila, Philippines.
- 98% int. in **CareSpan Integrated Networks Inc.**, Nev. 100% voting interest.
- 100% int. in **CareSpan International Inc.**, Panama. Inactive
- 100% int. in **CareSpan USA, Inc.**, Nev.
- 15% int. in **Smart Care GmbH**, Germany.

Financial Statistics

Periods ended:	12m Dec. 31/22[A]		12m Dec. 31/21[A]
	US$000s	%Chg	US$000s
Operating revenue	**4,543**	**-21**	**5,757**
Salaries & benefits	1,500		1,280
General & admin expense	1,351		1,330
Stock-based compensation	nil		405
Other operating expense	4,980		6,468
Operating expense	**7,831**	**-17**	**9,483**
Operating income	**(3,288)**	**n.a.**	**(3,726)**
Deprec., depl. & amort.	12		4
Finance costs, gross	28		1,444
Write-downs/write-offs	(1,048)		nil
Pre-tax income	**(3,141)**	**n.a.**	**(6,861)**
Net income	**(3,141)**	**n.a.**	**(6,861)**
Net inc. for equity hldrs	**(2,891)**	**n.a.**	**(6,532)**
Net inc. for non-cont. int.	**(250)**	**n.a.**	**(329)**
Cash & equivalent	394		949
Accounts receivable	985		1,619
Current assets	1,379		2,631
Fixed assets, net	nil		66
Total assets	**1,379**	**-49**	**2,697**
Accts. pay. & accr. liabs	2,031		2,655
Current liabilities	2,264		3,397
Shareholders' equity	(885)		(365)
Non-controlling interest	nil		(334)
Cash from oper. activs	**(2,294)**	**n.a.**	**(2,907)**
Cash from fin. activs	1,797		2,447
Cash from invest. activs	(58)		(43)
Net cash position	**394**	**-58**	**949**
Capital expenditures	nil		(66)
	US$		US$
Earnings per share*	(0.10)		(0.79)
Cash flow per share*	(0.07)		(0.35)
	shs		shs
No. of shs. o/s*	44,868,482		26,933,211
Avg. no. of shs. o/s*	30,725,686		8,234,851
	%		%
Net profit margin	(69.14)		(119.18)
Return on equity	n.m.		n.m.
Return on assets	(152.75)		(210.08)

* Common

[A] Reported in accordance with IFRS

Latest Results

Periods ended:	3m Mar. 31/23[A]		3m Mar. 31/22[A]
	US$000s	%Chg	US$000s
Operating revenue	904	-49	1,765
Net income	(520)	n.a.	(670)
Net inc. for equity hldrs	(520)	n.a.	(569)
Net inc. for non-cont. int.	nil		(102)
	US$		US$
Earnings per share*	(0.01)		(0.02)

* Common

[A] Reported in accordance with IFRS

Historical Summary

(as originally stated)

Fiscal Year	Oper. Rev.	Net Inc. Bef. Disc.	EPS*
	US$000s	US$000s	US$
2022[A]	4,543	(3,141)	(0.10)
2021[A]	5,757	(6,861)	(0.79)
2020[A1]	3,439	(5,906)	n.a.
2019[A]	49	(962)	n.a.

* Common

[A] Reported in accordance with IFRS

[1] Results for 2020 and prior periods pertain to CareSpan Holdings, Inc.

Note: Adjusted throughout for 1-for-4.66667 cons. in Nov. 2021

C.79 Cargojet Inc.*

Symbol - CJT **Exchange** - TSX **CUSIP** - 14179V

Head Office - 2281 Sheridan Way N, Mississauga, ON, L5K 2S3 **Telephone** - (905) 501-7373 **Toll-free** - (800) 753-1051 **Fax** - (905) 501-8228

Website - www.cargojet.com

Email - pdhillon@cargojet.com

Investor Relations - Pauline Dhillon (905) 501-7373 ext. 1135

Auditors - PricewaterhouseCoopers LLP C.A., Toronto, Ont.

Lawyers - Stikeman Elliott LLP, Toronto, Ont.

Transfer Agents - Computershare Trust Company of Canada Inc., Toronto, Ont.

FP500 Revenue Ranking - 348

Employees - 1,802 at Dec. 31, 2022

Profile - (Ont. 2010) Operates daily domestic time-sensitive overnight air cargo services between 16 Canadian cities; scheduled international routes for multiple cargo customers in the U.S., Bermuda, the U.K., Germany and Mexico; and dedicated charter service across North America and other international destinations.

Operates transportation network from coast to coast which transports an average of more than 1,300,000 lbs. of volumetric time sensitive air cargo to 16 major Canadian cities each business night utilizing a fleet of 34 all-cargo aircraft. Customers include courier companies, retailers, freight forwarders, manufacturers, specialty shippers and international airlines requiring next day delivery. Provides dedicated aircraft to customers on an aircraft, crew, maintenance and insurance basis in which it operates between points in Canada, the United States, Mexico and Europe; and operates scheduled international routes for multiple cargo customers between the United States and Bermuda, between Canada, the U.K. and Germany, and between Canada and Mexico. Also offers a dedicated charter service which transports livestock, military equipment, emergency relief supplies and any large shipment requiring immediate delivery across North America, Mexico, South America, the Caribbean and Europe, where flights are typically in the daytime and on weekends.

At June 30, 2023, the company's operating fleet was made up of 18 Boeing 767-300, 15 Boeing 757-200 and four Boeing 767-200.

During the six-month period ended June 30, 2023, the company acquired two Boeing 757-200 aircraft and a Boeing 767-300 aircraft for an undisclosed amount.

In March 2022, the company entered into a strategic agreement with **DHL Aviation (Netherlands) B.V.**, an affiliate of **Deutsche Post DHL Group**, in conjunction with DHL's consolidated charter agreement to provide air transportation services including aircraft, crew maintenance and insurance for DHL's global network for a term of five years with a renewable option for an additional two years. Under the agreement, the company would issue warrants to DHL to purchase variable voting shares that would vest based on the achievement of commercial milestones related to DHL's business with the company.

Recent Merger and Acquisition Activity

Status: pending **Revised:** June 30, 2023

UPDATE: Cargojet completed the sale of one Boeing 777-300 aircraft for Cdn$36,000,000. PREVIOUS: Cargojet Inc. entered into a letter of intent to sell two Boeing 777-300 aircraft for US$53,500,000. The transaction was expected to be completed in the second quarter of 2023.

Predecessor Detail - Succeeded Cargojet Income Fund, Jan. 1, 2011, pursuant to plan of arrangement whereby Cargojet Inc. was formed to facilitate the conversion of the fund into a corporation and fund was subsequently dissolved.

Directors - Dr. Ajay K. Virmani, founder, pres. & CEO, Oakville, Ont.; Paul V. Godfrey, chr., Toronto, Ont.; Arlene Dickinson, Calgary, Alta.; Mary Traversy, Ottawa, Ont.; John P. Webster, Toronto, Ont.

Other Exec. Officers - Scott D. Calver, CFO; Pauline Dhillon, chief corp. officer; Jamie B. Porteous, chief strategy officer; Vito Cerone, sr. v-p, sales & cust. experience; Fernando Garcia, sr. v-p, legal & corp. governance; Gord Johnston, sr. v-p, strategic partnership sales; Paul Rinaldo, sr. v-p, eng. & maint.; George Sugar, sr. v-p, regulatory compliance; Shane Workman, sr. v-p, flight opers.

Capital Stock

	Authorized (shs.)	Outstanding (shs.)[1]
Preferred	unlimited	nil
Common & Varible Vtg.	unlimited	17,209,499

[1] At June 30, 2023

Common - Held by qualified Canadians pursuant to the Canada Transportation Act (CTA). Automatically convertible into variable voting shares on a one-for-one basis if they become held by a non-qualified Canadians. Convertible at option of holder if an offer is made for all or substantially all of the variable voting shares. This conversion right is only exercisable for the purpose of depositing the resulting variable voting shares in response to the offer. One vote per share.

Variable Voting - Held by non-Canadians as defined in the CTA. Automatically convertible into common shares on a one-for-one basis if such share become held by a Canadian or holder becomes a member of any class of persons which are not restricted under the laws of Canada from owning shares or holding a specified percentage of the company's shares. Convertible at option of holder if an offer is made for all or substantially all of the common shares. This conversion right is only exercisable for the purpose of depositing the resulting common shares in response to the offer. Entitled to one vote per share, unless: (i) the number of variable voting shares outstanding, as a percentage of the total common and variable voting outstanding exceeds 49%; or (ii) the total number of votes cast by variable voting shareholders exceeds 49% of the total number of votes cast. If either of the above noted thresholds is surpassed at any time, the vote attached to each variable voting share will decrease automatically without further act or formality such that: (i) the variable voting shares as a class do not carry more than 49% of the total votes attached to all issued and outstanding common and variable voting shares; and (ii) the total number of votes cast by variable voting shareholders do not exceed 49% of the total number of votes cast. In addition, the votes attached to variable voting shares are subject to an automatic reduction in the event that any single non-Canadian or the aggregate of non-Canadian air carriers hold more than 25% of the votes.

Options - At Dec. 31, 2022, options were outstanding to purchase 60,545 common and variable voting shares at a weighted average exercise price of $132.95 per share.

Major Shareholder - Widely held at Feb. 14, 2023.

Price Range - CJT/TSX

Year	Volume	High	Low	Close
2022	16,050,366	$194.19	$109.69	$116.35
2021	22,771,180	$225.31	$159.74	$166.57
2020	16,818,309	$250.01	$67.87	$214.83
2019	11,033,805	$109.00	$66.32	$103.33
2018	6,069,295	$88.58	$57.14	$70.79

Recent Close: $99.55

Capital Stock Changes - During 2022, 1,760 common voting and/or variable voting shares were issued under restricted share unit plan and 123,832 common voting and/or variable voting shares were repurchased under a Normal Course Issuer Bid.

Dividends

CJT com & var vtg Ra $1.144 pa Q est. July 5, 2022

Prev. Rate: $1.04 est. Apr. 5, 2021

Prev. Rate: $0.936 est. Apr. 5, 2019

Long-Term Debt - Outstanding at Dec. 31, 2022:

Credit facilities[1]	$308,400,000
Sr. unsecured debs.:	
5.75% due April 2024	85,200,000
5.75% due April 2025	112,600,000
5.25% due June 2026	111,800,000
	307,200,000
Less: Current portion	nil
	618,000,000

[1] Consist of borrowings under a US$400,000,000 non-revolving term loan due July 2027, bearing interest at prime or U.S. base rate plus 20 basis points to 250 basis points.

Wholly Owned Subsidiaries

Cargojet Airways Ltd., Ont.

- 100% int. in **Aeroship Handling Ltd.**, Ont.
- 100% int. in **2422311 Ontario Inc.**, Ont.

Investments

25% int. in **21Air LLC**, Greensboro, N.C.

Financial Statistics

Periods ended:	12m Dec. 31/22[A]		12m Dec. 31/21[oA]
	$000s	%Chg	$000s
Operating revenue	**979,900**	**+29**	**757,800**
Salaries & benefits	127,500		104,000
General & admin expense	32,900		32,600
Other operating expense	501,000		336,900
Operating expense	**664,800**	**+42**	**468,500**
Operating income	**315,100**	**+9**	**289,300**
Deprec., depl. & amort.	142,200		116,400
Finance costs, gross	33,600		30,900
Pre-tax income	**220,000**	**+10**	**200,800**
Income taxes	29,400		33,400
Net income	**190,600**	**+14**	**167,400**
Cash & equivalent	6,100		94,700
Inventories	3,300		2,200
Accounts receivable	95,600		75,000
Current assets	116,100		199,900
Long-term investments	7,400		9,400
Fixed assets, net	1,643,600		1,159,900
Intangibles, net	50,300		50,300
Total assets	**1,986,300**	**+33**	**1,489,600**
Accts. pay. & accr. liabs	100,400		71,500
Current liabilities	150,500		98,000
Long-term debt, gross	618,000		307,200
Long-term debt, net	618,000		307,200
Long-term lease liabilities	57,600		69,400
Shareholders' equity	831,500		676,400
Cash from oper. activs	**282,500**	**+22**	**231,200**
Cash from fin. activs	244,000		140,200
Cash from invest. activs	(615,100)		(280,400)
Net cash position	**6,100**	**-94**	**94,700**
Capital expenditures	(611,200)		(277,600)
Capital disposals	700		300
	$		$
Earnings per share*	11.04		9.73
Cash flow per share*	16.36		13.47
Cash divd. per share*	1.12		1.04
	shs		shs
No. of shs. o/s*	17,202,186		17,324,258
Avg. no. of shs. o/s*	17,266,000		17,170,000
	%		%
Net profit margin	19.45		22.09
Return on equity	25.28		39.31
Return on assets	12.64		14.24
No. of employees (FTEs)	1,802		1,496

* Com. & var. vtg.

[o] Restated

[A] Reported in accordance with IFRS

Latest Results

Periods ended:	6m June 30/23[A]		6m June 30/22[A]
	$000s	%Chg	$000s
Operating revenue	441,600	-8	480,200
Net income	61,700	-41	104,600
	$		$
Earnings per share*	3.59		6.04

* Com. & var. vtg.

[A] Reported in accordance with IFRS

Historical Summary
(as originally stated)

Fiscal Year	Oper. Rev. $000s	Net Inc. Bef. Disc. $000s	EPS* $
2022^A	979,900	190,600	11.04
2021^A	757,800	167,400	9.73
2020^A	668,500	(87,800)	(5.63)
2019^A	486,600	11,600	0.86
2018^A	454,900	20,200	1.51

* Com. & var. vtg.
^A Reported in accordance with IFRS

C.80 Caribbean Utilities Company, Ltd.

Symbol - CUP.U **Exchange** - TSX **CUSIP** - G1899E
Head Office - 457 North Sound Rd, PO Box 38, Grand Cayman, Cayman Islands, KY1 1101 **Telephone** - (345) 949-5200 **Fax** - (345) 949-5203
Website - www.cuc-cayman.com
Email - llawrence@cuc.ky
Investor Relations - Letitia T. Lawrence (345) 914-1124
Auditors - Deloitte LLP C.A., St. John's, N.L.
Bankers - The Bank of Nova Scotia
Lawyers - Appleby, George Town, Cayman Islands
Transfer Agents - TSX Trust Company, Toronto, Ont.
Employees - 253 at Dec. 31, 2022
Profile - (Cayman Islands 1966) Generates, transmits and distributes electricity as well as provides telecommunication services in Grand Cayman, Cayman Islands.

The company is the sole supplier of electricity on Grand Cayman under a 20-year exclusive transmission and distribution licence and a 25-year non-exclusive generation licence from the Government of the Cayman Islands which expire in 2028 and 2039, respectively. Electricity is produced using diesel generation with an installed generating capacity of 166 MW and distributed to over 33,119 customers as at Dec. 31, 2022. During 2022, a peak load of 113.6 MW was reached (2021: 111.2 MW).

Wholly owned **Datalink Ltd.** provides fibre optic infrastructure and other information and communication technology services to telecommunication providers.

Periods ended:	12m Dec. 31/22	12m Dec. 31/21
Electric sales, GWh	674	661
Generating capacity, MW	166	161
Electric gen., GWh	681	662
Electric. customers	33,119	32,185

Directors - J. F. Richard Hew, pres. & CEO, Grand Cayman, Cayman Islands; Jennifer P. Dilbert, Grand Cayman, Cayman Islands; Sheree L. Ebanks, Grand Cayman, Cayman Islands; Woodrow S. Foster, Grand Cayman, Cayman Islands; Jennifer Frizzelle, Grand Cayman, Cayman Islands; Karen J. Gosse, St. John's, N.L.; Susan M. Gray, Ariz.; Sophia A. Harris, Grand Cayman, Cayman Islands; Mark Macfee, Grand Cayman, Cayman Islands; Kay Menzies, Belize; Gary J. Smith, St. John's, N.L.
Other Exec. Officers - Letitia T. Lawrence, v-p, fin., corp. srvcs. & CFO; Sacha N. Tibbetts, v-p, cust. srvc. & tech.; Claire Stafford, corp. sec. & data protection officer

Capital Stock

	Authorized (shs.)	Outstanding (shs.)[1]	Par
9% Cl.B Preference	250,000	249,500	CI$0.84
Cl.C Preference	419,666	nil	CI$0.84
Cl.D Preference	1	nil	CI$0.56
Cl.A Ordinary	60,000,000	37,664,742	CI$0.05

[1] At Mar. 13, 2023

9% Class B Preference - Entitled to fixed cumulative preferential dividends at a rate of 9% per annum of the par value and premium on such shares. If the dividend payable in any year on class A ordinary shares exceeds US$0.18 per share, each class B preference share is entitled to the equivalent of four times the excess. The company is entitled to redeem all or any class B preference shares at any time. Participating. Non-voting.
Class C Preference - Participating. Non-voting.
Class D Preference - Participating. Non-voting.
Class A Ordinary - One vote per share.
Major Shareholder - Fortis Inc. held 59% interest at Mar. 13, 2023.

Price Range - CUP.U/TSX

Year	Volume	High	Low	Close
2022	636,758	US$15.75	US$12.50	US$13.00
2021	490,229	US$15.78	US$14.01	US$15.00
2020	634,729	US$17.12	US$13.26	US$14.75
2019	933,777	US$17.60	US$12.25	US$16.38
2018	488,723	US$14.01	US$11.75	US$12.25

Recent Close: US$12.85
Capital Stock Changes - During 2022, 295,246 class A ordinary shares were issued on exercise of options.

Dividends

CUP.U cl A Ra US$0.72 pa Q est. June 15, 2023**
Prev. Rate: US$0.70 est. June 15, 2018
** Reinvestment Option

Wholly Owned Subsidiaries

Datalink Ltd., Cayman Islands.

Financial Statistics

Periods ended:	12m Dec. 31/22^A		12m Dec. 31/21^A
	US$000s	%Chg	US$000s
Operating revenue	**267,336**	**+35**	**198,478**
Cost of sales	179,733		114,179
General & admin expense	10,446		9,147
Other operating expense	6,098		5,792
Operating expense	**196,277**	**+52**	**129,118**
Operating income	**71,059**	**+2**	**69,360**
Deprec., depl. & amort.	38,991		39,137
Finance costs, gross	4,775		4,808
Pre-tax income	**33,179**	**+9**	**30,319**
Net income	**33,179**	**+9**	**30,319**
Cash & equivalent	7,948		7,360
Inventories	7,951		5,277
Accounts receivable	21,635		11,343
Current assets	83,447		53,268
Fixed assets, net	636,952		576,703
Right-of-use assets	1,951		222
Intangibles, net	4,180		3,947
Total assets	**726,539**	**+15**	**634,150**
Accts. pay. & accr. liabs	42,059		26,295
Current liabilities	77,016		55,752
Long-term debt, gross	357,511		293,291
Long-term debt, net	338,030		277,733
Long-term lease liabilities	766		141
Preferred share equity	250		250
Shareholders' equity	308,234		297,878
Cash from oper. activs	**56,188**	**-9**	**62,009**
Cash from fin. activs	41,591		(37,107)
Cash from invest. activs	(97,191)		(63,128)
Net cash position	**7,948**	**+8**	**7,360**
Capital expenditures	(96,018)		(62,038)
Capital disposals	33		78
Unfunded pension liability	1,848		1,894
	US$		US$
Earnings per share*	0.86		0.79
Cash flow per share*	1.50		1.67
Cash divd. per share*	0.70		0.70
	shs		shs
No. of shs. o/s*	37,664,724		37,369,478
Avg. no. of shs. o/s*	37,481,959		37,199,456
	%		%
Net profit margin	12.41		15.28
Return on equity	10.96		10.00
Return on assets	5.58		5.54
Foreign sales percent	100		100
No. of employees (FTEs)	253		232

* Cl.A ord.
^A Reported in accordance with U.S. GAAP

Historical Summary
(as originally stated)

Fiscal Year	Oper. Rev. US$000s	Net Inc. Bef. Disc. US$000s	EPS* US$
2022^A	267,336	33,179	0.86
2021^A	198,478	30,319	0.79
2020^A	177,450	26,065	0.74
2019^A	203,246	29,100	0.84
2018^A	194,578	26,770	0.78

* Cl.A ord.
^A Reported in accordance with U.S. GAAP

C.81 Cascades Inc.*

Symbol - CAS **Exchange** - TSX **CUSIP** - 146900
Head Office - 404 boul Marie-Victorin, Kingsey Falls, QC, J0A 1B0 **Telephone** - (819) 363-5100 **Fax** - (819) 363-5155
Website - www.cascades.com/en/
Email - jennifer_aitken@cascades.com
Investor Relations - Jennifer Aitken (514) 282-2697
Auditors - PricewaterhouseCoopers LLP C.A., Montréal, Qué.
Transfer Agents - Computershare Trust Company of Canada Inc., Montréal, Qué.
FP500 Revenue Ranking - 129
Employees - 10,000 at Dec. 31, 2022
Profile - (Que. 1964) Manufactures, converts and markets packaging including containerboard, paperboard, corrugating medium and linerboard, as well as household and sanitary paper products made from primarily recycled fibre. Manufactures and markets various types of plastic and moulded pulp containers and dividers, primarily for the food industry. Operations are conducted in Canada, and the United States.

Operations are integrated both upstream and downstream and are conducted through two operating sectors: the Packaging Products sector, which consists of the Containerboard Packaging Group, and the Specialty Products Group; and the Tissue Papers sector, which operates units that manufacture and convert tissue paper for the away-from-home and consumer products markets.

Packaging Products

The Containerboard Packaging Group produces products sold regionally and nationally to customers in a variety of industries including food, beverage and consumer products. The Group operates six linerboard and corrugated medium mills with a combined total annual production capacity of 1,575,000 short tons and are located in Quebec (2), Ontario (2) and New York (2), and 19 converting and servicing plants located across Canada and the northeastern U.S. The company holds 86.35% interest in **Greenpac Mill, LLC**, a manufacturer of lightweight linerboard with a mill in Niagara Falls, N.Y., that has an annual production capacity of 540,000 short tons. Also owns Bear Island newsprint manufacturing facility in Ashland, Va., which would be reconfigured to produce recycled lightweight linerboard and medium.

The Specialty Products Group operates in Canada and the U.S. in two sectors:

(i) The industrial packaging sector operates through jointly owned **Cascades Sonoco US Inc.** and **Cascades Sonoco Inc.** which convert uncoated paperboard into industrial packaging materials for the paper and food industries such as roll headers and wrappers from plants in Kingsey Falls and Berthierville, Que., Birmingham, Ala., and Tacoma, Wash. The Cascades Multi-Pro division, located in Drummondville, Que., manufactures laminated paperboards and specialty containers used in many industrial sectors such as furniture backing and food packaging. The Cascades Enviropac division manufactures honeycomb paperboard at a plant in each of Berthierville, Que., Grand Rapids, Mich., York, Pa., and Tacoma, Wash., and uncoated paperboard partitions for the beer, wine and spirits segments at a plant in each of St. Césaire, Que., and Aurora, Ill. The Cascades Papier Kingsey Falls division in Kingsey Falls, Que., produces uncoated recycled paperboard used primarily by packaging converters and industrial users of headers and wrappers for the paper industry. Combined capacity of the plants, including 100% of joint ventures, is 430,131 tonnes.

(ii) The consumer products packaging sector includes the Cascades Forma-Pak division in Kingsey Falls, Que., Brook, Ind., and Clarion, Iowa, and wholly owned Cascades Moulded Pulp, Inc. of Rockingham, N.C., which manufacture egg filler flats for egg processors and four-cup carriers for the quick-service restaurant industry. The Plastiques Cascades division in Kingsey Falls, Que., and wholly owned Cascades Plastics Inc. of Warrenton, Mo., manufacture polystyrene foam and rigid plastic packaging, primarily for the food industry, processors and retailers. The Cascades Inopak division in Drummondville, Que., specializes in plastic food packaging. Wholly owned **Cascades Flexible Packaging Inc.** in Mississauga, Ont., specializes in manufacturing of flexible film packaging for customers primarily in the frozen foods, bakery and ice industries.

Tissue Papers

The Tissue Group manufactures, converts and markets a wide variety of tissue paper products made primarily from recycled fibre. Products include bathroom tissue, facial tissue, paper towels, paper hand towels, paper napkins and other related products, which are sold in Canada and the U.S. under the labels Cascades PRO Signature™, Cascades PRO Perform™, Cascades PRO Select™, Cascades PRO Tandem™ and Cascades PRO Tuff-Job™ for the commercial and industrial markets, and under the labels Cascades Fluff®, Cascades Tuff® Satin Soft®, Velvet® and Tackle® brands for the consumer products market. The Group operates three manufacturing facilities in St. Helens Ore., Rockingham, N.C., and Mechanicville, N.Y.; five converting facilities in Granby, Que., Wagram and Kinston, N.C., Brownsville, Tenn., and Scappoose Ore.; and six facilities in Candiac, Lachute and Kingsey Falls, Que., Barnwell, S.C., Pryor, Okla., and Eau Claire, Wisc., with manufacturing and converting capabilities.

Shipments

Year ended Dec. 31	2022	2021
Packaging products[1 2]	1,506,000	1,521,000
Tissue papers[1]	521,000	554,000
Capacity utilization	89%	90%

[1] Short tons.
[2] Includes boxboard Europe, containerboard and specialty products.

The company also provides services to recover and process discarded materials for the municipal, industrial, commercial, and institutional sectors through 18 recovery facilities across Canada and the northeastern U.S. The facilities handled more than 3,000,000 short tons of recyclable materials in 2022.

In April 2023, the company announced the closure, beginning in July 2023, of its tissue products plants in Barnwell, S.C., and Scappoose, Ore., as well as the virgin paper tissue machine at its plant in St. Helens, Ore. The equipment slated for closure, which have a combined total annual rated capacity of 92,000 short tons of tissue paper and 10,000,000 cases of converted product, have been operating below capacity producing 56,000 short tons of tissue paper and 5,000,000 cases of converted product in 2022, mostly on the West coast. Closure costs, including severance, were expected to total $20,00,000 to $25,000,000. The closures impact 300 employees.

Recent Merger and Acquisition Activity

Status: completed **Announced:** Dec. 31, 2022
Cascades Inc. sold land and building related to a closed plant in Canada under its Specialty Products segment for $16,000,000.

Directors - Alain Lemaire, co-founder & exec. chr., Kingsey Falls, Qué.; Mario Plourde, pres. & CEO, Kingsey Falls, Qué.; Michelle A. Cormier†, Montréal, Qué.; Alex N. Blanco, Fla.; Mélanie Dunn, Montréal, Qué.; Nelson Gentiletti, Kirkland, Qué.; Hubert T. Lacroix, Westmount, Qué.; Patrick Lemaire, Kingsey Falls, Qué.; Sylvie Lemaire, Otterburn Park, Qué.; Elif Lévesque, Montréal, Qué.; Sylvie Vachon, Longueuil, Qué.
Other Exec. Officers - Dominic Doré, chief supply chain & info. officer; Maryse Fernet, chief HR officer; Robert F. Hall, chief of strategy, legal affairs; Thierry Trudel, chief experience officer; Hugo D'Amours, v-p, commun., public affairs & sustainability; Riko Gaudreault, v-p, corp. devel.; Allan Hogg, v-p, fin. & CFO; Mario Nepton, v-p, corp. srvcs.;

Michael Guerra, corp. sec.; Charles Malo, pres. & COO, containerboard packaging grp.; Jérôme Porlier, pres. & COO, specialty products grp.; Jean-David Tardif, pres. & COO, tissue grp.
† Lead director

Capital Stock

	Authorized (shs.)	Outstanding (shs.)[1]
Common	unlimited	100,669,311

[1] At Aug. 2, 2023

Options - At Dec. 31, 2022, options were outstanding to purchase 2,794,344 common shares at a weighted average exercise price of $10.01 per share expiring to 2032.

Major Shareholder - Laurent Lemaire held 12.4% interest and Letko, Brosseau & Associates Inc. held 10.2% interest at Mar. 15, 2023.

Price Range - CAS/TSX

Year	Volume	High	Low	Close
2022	69,723,329	$14.22	$7.71	$8.46
2021	84,718,675	$18.48	$12.82	$13.97
2020	74,120,456	$17.62	$9.94	$14.55
2019	47,151,060	$13.44	$7.55	$11.21
2018	54,832,304	$16.67	$9.15	$10.23

Recent Close: $12.47

Capital Stock Changes - During 2022, 355,686 common shares were issued on exercise of options and 854,421 common shares were repurchased under a Normal Course Issuer Bid.

Dividends

CAS com Ra $0.48 pa Q est. Sept. 2, 2021
Prev. Rate: $0.32 est. Sept. 6, 2019

Long-Term Debt - Outstanding at Dec. 31, 2022:

Revolv. credit facility[1]	$350,000,000
Term loan due 2027[2]	352,000,000
5.125% sr. notes due 2025[3]	175,000,000
5.125% sr. notes due 2026[4]	279,000,000
5.375% sr. notes due 2028[5]	610,000,000
Lease liabs.	208,000,000
Other debts[6]	100,000,000
Less: Unamort. fin. costs	9,000,000
	2,065,000,000
Less: Current portion	134,000,000
	1,931,000,000

[1] Bearing interest at an average rate of 6.18% and due July 2026.
[2] US$260,000,000. Bearing interest rate of 6.42% at Dec. 31, 2022.
[3] $175,000,000.
[4] US$206,000,000.
[5] US$445,000,000.
[6] Consists of $31,000,000 with recourse to the company and $69,000,000 without recourse to the company.

Wholly Owned Subsidiaries

Barcelona Cartonboard S.A.U., Barcelona, Spain.
Cascades Canada ULC, Alta.
Cascades Enviropac HPM, LLC, Grand Rapids, Mich.
Cascades Flexible Packaging Inc., Mississauga, Ont.
Cascades Holding U.S. Inc.
- 100% int. in **Cascades Tissue Group - North Carolina Inc.**, N.C.
- 100% int. in **Cascades Tissue Group - Oregon Inc.**, Ore.
- 100% int. in **Cascades Tissue Group - Wisconsin Inc.**, Wis.

Cascades Moulded Pulp, Inc., Rockingham, N.C.
Cascades Plastics Inc., Warrenton, Mo.
Cascades Tissue Group - New York Inc., United States.
Cascades Tissue Group - Tennessee Inc.
Cascades USA Inc., Del.
Plastiques Cascades une Division de Cascades Canada ULC, Kingsey Falls, Qué.

Subsidiaries

86.35% int. in **Greenpac Mill, LLC**, Niagara Falls, N.Y.

Investments

50% int. in **Cascades Sonoco inc.**, Canada.
50% int. in **Cascades Sonoco US Inc.**, Birmingham, Ala.
40% int. in **Maritime Paper Products Limited Partnership**, Dartmouth, N.S.
33.3% int. in **Tencorr Holdings Corporation**, Brampton, Ont.

Financial Statistics

Periods ended:	12m Dec. 31/22[A]		12m Dec. 31/21[A]
	$000s	%Chg	$000s
Operating revenue	**4,466,000**	**+13**	**3,956,000**
Cost of sales	2,836,000		2,517,000
Salaries & benefits	992,000		981,000
General & admin expense	262,000		71,000
Operating expense	**4,090,000**	**+15**	**3,569,000**
Operating income	**376,000**	**-3**	**387,000**
Deprec., depl. & amort.	252,000		252,000
Finance income	nil		1,000
Finance costs, gross	88,000		90,000
Investment income	19,000		18,000
Write-downs/write-offs	(102,000)		(89,000)
Pre-tax income	**(36,000)**	**n.a.**	**(38,000)**
Income taxes	(22,000)		9,000
Net inc. bef. disc. opers	**(14,000)**	**n.a.**	**(47,000)**
Income from disc. opers	nil		234,000
Net income	**(14,000)**	**n.a.**	**187,000**
Net inc. for equity hldrs	**(34,000)**	**n.a.**	**162,000**
Net inc. for non-cont. int	**20,000**	**-20**	**25,000**
Cash & equivalent	102,000		174,000
Inventories	587,000		494,000
Accounts receivable	556,000		510,000
Current assets	1,265,000		1,198,000
Long-term investments	94,000		87,000
Fixed assets, net	2,945,000		2,522,000
Intangibles, net	561,000		561,000
Total assets	**5,053,000**	**+11**	**4,566,000**
Bank indebtedness	3,000		1,000
Accts. pay. & accr. liabs	746,000		707,000
Current liabilities	917,000		822,000
Long-term debt, gross	2,065,000		1,524,000
Long-term debt, net	1,931,000		1,450,000
Shareholders' equity	1,871,000		1,879,000
Non-controlling interest	57,000		48,000
Cash from oper. activs	**144,000**	**-32**	**211,000**
Cash from fin. activs	272,000		(529,000)
Cash from invest. activs	(486,000)		(247,000)
Net cash position	**102,000**	**-41**	**174,000**
Capital expenditures	(501,000)		(286,000)
Capital disposals	19,000		53,000
Unfunded pension liability	65		79
	$		$
Earns. per sh. bef disc opers*	(0.34)		(0.59)
Earnings per share*	(0.34)		1.60
Cash flow per share*	1.43		2.07
Cash divd. per share*	0.48		0.40
	shs		shs
No. of shs. o/s*	100,361,627		100,860,362
Avg. no. of shs. o/s*	100,647,972		102,000,000
	%		%
Net profit margin	(0.31)		(1.19)
Return on equity	(1.81)		(3.96)
Return on assets	0.42		1.29
Foreign sales percent	52		55
No. of employees (FTEs)	10,000		10,000

* Common
[A] Reported in accordance with IFRS

Latest Results

Periods ended:	6m June 30/23[A]		6m June 30/22[A]
	$000s	%Chg	$000s
Operating revenue	2,302,000	+7	2,157,000
Net income	(40,000)	n.a.	3,000
Net inc. for equity hldrs	(53,000)	n.a.	(5,000)
Net inc. for non-cont. int	13,000		8,000
	$		$
Earnings per share*	(0.53)		(0.05)

* Common
[A] Reported in accordance with IFRS

Historical Summary
(as originally stated)

Fiscal Year	Oper. Rev.	Net Inc. Bef. Disc.	EPS*
	$000s	$000s	$
2022[A]	4,466,000	(14,000)	(0.34)
2021[A]	3,956,000	(47,000)	(0.59)
2020[A]	5,157,000	234,000	2.04
2019[A]	4,996,000	97,000	0.74
2018[A]	4,649,000	94,000	0.62

* Common
[A] Reported in accordance with IFRS

C.82 Cascadia Blockchain Group Corp.

Symbol - CK **Exchange** - CSE **CUSIP** - 14739C
Head Office - Richmond Centre, 6060 Minoru Blvd, PO Box 43166, Richmond, BC, V6Y 3Y3 **Telephone** - (604) 773-5180
Website - www.cascadiacorp.com
Email - echen@cascadiacorp.com
Investor Relations - Cong Chen (604) 773-5180
Auditors - Mao & Ying LLP C.A., Vancouver, B.C.
Lawyers - Dentons Canada LLP
Transfer Agents - Computershare Trust Company of Canada Inc., Vancouver, B.C.

Profile - (B.C. 2011) Develops and commercializes its proprietary trading platform technology for selected blockchain-based digital assets and utility tokens. Also planning to develop blockchain technology enterprise solutions and to provide related services for various industry sectors.

Wholly owned **CK Fintech Corp.** has developed a trading platform to provide various transaction capabilities for selected blockchain technology-based digital assets, utility tokens and cryptocurrencies.

Wholly owned **CK Blockchain Lab Corp.** and **Cascadia Blockchain Lab (U.K.) Limited** plan to focus on the development of blockchain technology and its application to various industries and sectors across markets globally.

In September 2022, the company announced plans to wind up affiliate **Eurasia BlockChain Fintech Group Limited.**

Predecessor Detail - Name changed from Cascadia Consumer Electronics Corp., Sept. 10, 2018.

Directors - Di (Danny) Deng, chr., pres. & CEO, Beijing, People's Republic of China; Hanxuan Wu, Beijing, Beijing, People's Republic of China; Shanshan Zhu, Beijing, People's Republic of China

Other Exec. Officers - Cong (Eason) Chen, v-p, fin., interim CFO & corp. sec.

Capital Stock

	Authorized (shs.)	Outstanding (shs.)[1]
Common	unlimited	73,376,692

[1] At Nov. 18, 2022

Major Shareholder - Di (Danny) Deng held 47.19% interest at Nov. 18, 2022.

Price Range - CK/CSE

Year	Volume	High	Low	Close
2022	1,659,441	$0.09	$0.01	$0.02
2021	20,381,967	$0.38	$0.06	$0.08
2020	7,624,284	$0.36	$0.05	$0.23
2019	399,814	$0.38	$0.02	$0.06
2018	19,300	$0.47	$0.30	$0.38

Recent Close: $0.03

Wholly Owned Subsidiaries

CK Blockchain Lab Corp., Canada.
CK Fintech Corp., Canada.
- 43.99% int. in **Eurasia Blockchain Fintech Group Limited**, Kazakhstan.

Cascadia Blockchain Lab (U.K.) Limited, United Kingdom.
Tianjin Bocui Technology Limited, Tianjin, People's Republic of China. Inactive.

Financial Statistics

Periods ended:	12m Jan. 31/22[A]		12m Jan. 31/21[A]
	$000s	%Chg	$000s
Salaries & benefits	311		425
General & admin expense	476		494
Operating expense	**787**	**-14**	**919**
Operating income	**(787)**	**n.a.**	**(919)**
Deprec., depl. & amort.	6		26
Finance costs, gross	6		4
Investment income	(98)		nil
Pre-tax income	**(70)**	**n.a.**	**(924)**
Net income	**(70)**	**n.a.**	**(924)**
Net inc. for equity hldrs	**(56)**	**n.a.**	**(912)**
Net inc. for non-cont. int	**(13)**	**n.a.**	**(11)**
Cash & equivalent	391		589
Accounts receivable	3		4
Current assets	395		593
Long-term investments	560		nil
Fixed assets, net	nil		17
Total assets	**954**	**+57**	**609**
Accts. pay. & accr. liabs	524		166
Current liabilities	524		166
Long-term debt, gross	40		40
Long-term debt, net	40		40
Shareholders' equity	390		413
Non-controlling interest	nil		9
Cash from oper. activs	**(370)**	**n.a.**	**(494)**
Cash from fin. activs	96		(17)
Cash from invest. activs	120		459
Net cash position	**183**	**-46**	**337**
	$		$
Earnings per share*	(0.00)		(0.01)
Cash flow per share*	(0.01)		(0.01)
	shs		shs
No. of shs. o/s*	73,376,692		71,977,438
Avg. no. of shs. o/s*	73,185,103		71,977,438
	%		%
Net profit margin	n.a.		n.a.
Return on equity	(14.20)		(120.37)
Return on assets	(8.19)		(101.55)

* Common
[A] Reported in accordance with IFRS

Latest Results

Periods ended:	6m July 31/22[A]		6m July 31/21[A]
	$000s	%Chg	$000s
Net income	(704)	n.a.	(434)
Net inc. for equity hldrs	(704)	n.a.	(425)
Net inc. for non-cont. int	nil		(9)
	$		$
Earnings per share*	(0.01)		(0.01)

* Common
[A] Reported in accordance with IFRS

Historical Summary
(as originally stated)

Fiscal Year	Oper. Rev.	Net Inc. Bef. Disc.	EPS*
	$000s	$000s	$
2022[A]	nil	(70)	(0.00)
2021[A]	nil	(924)	(0.01)
2020[A]	nil	(458)	(0.01)
2019[A]	203	(3,608)	(0.05)
2018[A]	nil	(3,373)	(0.06)

* Common
[A] Reported in accordance with IFRS

C.83 Castlebar Capital Corp.

Symbol - CBAR.P **Exchange** - TSX-VEN **CUSIP** - 14852T
Head Office - 600-1090 Georgia St W, Vancouver, BC, V6E 3V7 **Telephone** - (778) 549-6714 **Fax** - (604) 357-1030
Email - lucasbirdsall@gmail.com
Investor Relations - Lucas C. Birdsall (778) 549-6714
Auditors - Dale Matheson Carr-Hilton LaBonte LLP C.A., Vancouver, B.C.
Transfer Agents - Computershare Trust Company of Canada Inc., Vancouver, B.C.
Profile - (B.C. 2018) Capital Pool Company.
Directors - Lucas C. Birdsall, CEO & corp. sec., Vancouver, B.C.; Gerald Kelly, Vancouver, B.C.; Robert Meister, North Vancouver, B.C.; Brian P. Morrison, North Vancouver, B.C.; Kostantinos (Kosta) Tsoutsis, Vancouver, B.C.
Other Exec. Officers - Patrick O'Flaherty, CFO

Capital Stock

	Authorized (shs.)	Outstanding (shs.)[1]
Common	unlimited	2,329,908

[1] At Mar. 27, 2023

Major Shareholder - Lucas C. Birdsall held 22.53% interest at June 23, 2021.

Price Range - CBAR.P/TSX-VEN

Year	Volume	High	Low	Close
2020	28,000	$0.21	$0.19	$0.19
2019	35,500	$0.27	$0.21	$0.21

Recent Close: $0.04

C.84 Castlecap Capital Inc.

Symbol - CSTL.P **Exchange** - TSX-VEN **CUSIP** - 14843W
Head Office - 2032 45 Ave SW, Calgary, AB, T2T 2P5 **Telephone** - (403) 680-8511
Email - charleschebry@outlook.com
Investor Relations - Charles R. Chebry (403) 680-8511
Auditors - Kenway Mack Slusarchuk Stewart LLP C.A., Calgary, Alta.
Lawyers - Borden Ladner Gervais LLP, Calgary, Alta.
Transfer Agents - TSX Trust Company, Calgary, Alta.
Profile - (Alta. 2018) Capital Pool Company.

Recent Merger and Acquisition Activity

Status: pending **Revised:** Aug. 26, 2022
UPDATE: A definitive agreement was entered into. CCI would issue 55,000,000 post-consolidated common shares at a deemed price of Cdn$1.00 per share (following a 1-for-3 share consolidation). Upon completion, CCI would change its name to ATH Health Ltd. As part of the transaction, CCI would also acquire 2217317 Alberta Ltd. and CCI Finco Limited, both established for purposes of completing a Canadian and Australian financing, respectively, on a share-for-share basis. PREVIOUS: Castlecap Capital Inc. (CCI) entered into a letter of intent for the reverse takeover acquisition of ATH (Australia) Pty Ltd., which has developed an at-home urine test known as CellHealthTest for the detection of abnormal cell activity in the human body. Terms of the transaction would be provided upon execution of a definitive agreement.
Directors - Charles R. Chebry, chr., pres., CEO, CFO & corp. sec., Calgary, Alta.; Sandra Dosdall, Calgary, Alta.; Travis A. Rhodes, Calgary, Alta.; Antonio (Tony) Ruggieri, Calgary, Alta.

Capital Stock

	Authorized (shs.)	Outstanding (shs.)[1]
Class A Common	unlimited	4,000,000

[1] At May 30, 2022

Major Shareholder - Charles R. Chebry held 12.5% interest, Travis A. Rhodes held 12.5% interest, Antonio (Tony) Ruggieri held 12.5% interest and Sandra Dosdall held 10% interest at Apr. 26, 2022.

Price Range - CSTL.P/TSX-VEN

Year	Volume	High	Low	Close
2022	239,000	$0.13	$0.09	$0.11
2021	423,294	$0.20	$0.07	$0.12
2020	143,000	$0.10	$0.02	$0.06

C.85 Cathedra Bitcoin Inc.

Symbol - CBIT **Exchange** - TSX-VEN **CUSIP** - 14919F
Head Office - 320-638 Broughton St, Vancouver, BC, V6G 3K3 **Telephone** - (604) 477-9997
Website - www.cathedra.com
Email - ir@cathedra.com
Investor Relations - Sean Ty (604) 477-9997
Auditors - Kingston Ross Pasnak LLP C.A., Edmonton, Alta.
Transfer Agents - Computershare Trust Company of Canada Inc., Vancouver, B.C.
Profile - (B.C. 2018; orig. Ont., 2011) Engages in Bitcoin mining.

Has two Bitcoin mines powered by grid electricity that produce a total of 129 petahashes per second (PH/s), which consist of a 2-MW Bitcoin mining facility (the legacy Washington mine) in Moses Lake with 88 PH/s and a 2.5-MW Bitcoin mining facility (the new Washington mine) with 41 PH/s; and hosts Bitcoin mining machines at five third-party data centers in Kentucky and Tennessee that produce 214 PH/s. The company also expected to add approximately 35 PH/s to its second Washington facility with expected completion by the end of 2023. Has also developed Bitcoin mining Rovers, the company's proprietary mobile data centers that allow for rapid deployment of Bitcoin mining operations in on or off-grid environments.

In September 2022, the company ceased operations in North Dakota. The company tendered four out of its 12 Bitcoin mining containers to **Great American Mining** in exchange for waived power and generator expenses.

In May 2022, the company sold all shares held in **The Good Shepherd Land and Livestock Company Limited** to **Silvermoon Inc.** for issuance of 35,000,000 common shares, representing a 23% interest in Silvermoon.

Predecessor Detail - Name changed from Fortress Technologies Inc., Dec. 8, 2021.
Directors - Antonin (AJ) Scalia, CEO, Mont.; Thomas (Drew) Armstrong, pres., COO & chr., Va.; Marcus Dent, Austin, Tex.; David Jaques, Los Altos, Calif.
Other Exec. Officers - Sean Ty, CFO & corp. sec.; Rete Browning, chief tech. officer; Isaac Fithian, chief field opers. & mfg. officer

Capital Stock

	Authorized (shs.)	Outstanding (shs.)[1]
Common	unlimited	137,522,563

[1] At July 14, 2023

Major Shareholder - Widely held at July 14, 2023.

Price Range - CBIT/TSX-VEN

Year	Volume	High	Low	Close
2022	44,536,040	$0.70	$0.04	$0.04
2021	226,683,356	$1.01	$0.19	$0.51
2020	48,501,190	$0.28	$0.09	$0.24
2019	13,020,467	$0.21	$0.10	$0.12
2018	38,556,672	$0.24	$0.10	$0.13

Recent Close: $0.11

Capital Stock Changes - In April 2023, 18,518,518 common shares were issued for settlement of $2,500,000 of debt.

In June and May 2022, private placement of 25,916,667 units (1 common share and ¾ warrant) at 36¢ was completed. Also during 2022, common shares were issued as follows: 3,492,347 under restricted share unit plan, 1,900,000 on exercise of options and 1,000,000 on acquisition of five Bitmain S17 Miners equipment and financial assets.

Wholly Owned Subsidiaries

Fortress Blockchain Holdings Corp., Vancouver, B.C.
- 100% int. in **Fortress Blockchain (US) Holdings Corp.**, Wash.
  - 100% int. in **Cathedra Lease Co LLC**, N.H.
  - 100% int. in **Chronos SPV LLC**, Wash.
  - 100% int. in **Entelechy Bitcoin SPV LLC**, Wash.
  - 100% int. in **Standard Resources LLC**, Wash.
    - 100% int. in **Portage Resource Holdings LLC**, Ohio

Hash Stream Inc., Ont.

Investments

Low Time Preference Fund II, LLC
23% int. in **Silvermoon Inc.**

Financial Statistics

Periods ended:	12m Dec. 31/22[A]		12m Dec. 31/21[oA]
	$000s	%Chg	$000s
Operating revenue	**8,809**	**+13**	**7,801**
Cost of sales	6,389		3,684
Salaries & benefits	1,262		66
General & admin expense	2,045		1,788
Stock-based compensation	5,767		1,024
Operating expense	**15,464**	**+136**	**6,562**
Operating income	**(6,655)**	**n.a.**	**1,240**
Deprec., depl. & amort.	7,710		2,287
Finance income	26		36
Finance costs, gross	3,767		96
Write-downs/write-offs	(26,661)		nil
Pre-tax income	**(46,107)**	**n.a.**	**1,957**
Income taxes	(1,118)		1,131
Net inc. bef. disc. opers	**(44,989)**	**n.a.**	**826**
Income from disc. opers	(42)		(108)
Net income	**(45,031)**	**n.a.**	**718**
Net inc. for equity hldrs	**(44,989)**	**n.a.**	**826**
Net inc. for non-cont. int	**(42)**	**n.a.**	**(108)**
Cash & equivalent	3,264		19,368
Accounts receivable	158		90
Current assets	8,470		38,397
Long-term investments	3,014		nil
Fixed assets, net	13,713		18,716
Right-of-use assets	nil		553
Intangibles, net	nil		5
Total assets	**25,764**	**-56**	**58,368**
Accts. pay. & accr. liabs	2,315		2,484
Current liabilities	2,464		4,634
Long-term debt, gross	18,345		19,255
Long-term debt, net	18,196		18,699
Long-term lease liabilities	329		448
Shareholders' equity	4,775		34,587
Cash from oper. activs	**2,549**	**n.a.**	**(19,231)**
Cash from fin. activs	6,188		34,450
Cash from invest. activs	(13,238)		(12,392)
Net cash position	**3,225**	**-66**	**9,444**
Capital expenditures	(25,326)		(16,114)
	$		$
Earnings per share*	(0.43)		0.01
Cash flow per share*	0.02		(0.24)
	shs		shs
No. of shs. o/s*	118,531,698		86,222,684
Avg. no. of shs. o/s*	105,035,160		81,223,535
	%		%
Net profit margin	(510.72)		10.59
Return on equity	(228.38)		3.69
Return on assets	(98.21)		2.30
Foreign sales percent	100		100

* Common
[o] Restated
[A] Reported in accordance with IFRS

Latest Results

Periods ended:	3m Mar. 31/23[A]		3m Mar. 31/22[A]
	$000s	%Chg	$000s
Operating revenue	2,017	-35	3,108
Net income	(2,240)	n.a.	(3,861)
	$		$
Earnings per share*	(0.02)		(0.04)

* Common
[A] Reported in accordance with IFRS

Historical Summary
(as originally stated)

Fiscal Year	Oper. Rev.	Net Inc. Bef. Disc.	EPS*
	$000s	$000s	$
2022[A]	8,809	(44,989)	(0.43)
2021[A]	7,801	718	0.01
2020[A]	1,026	5,054	0.07
2019[A]	1,683	(1,061)	(0.01)
2018[A1]	2,307	(11,360)	(0.17)

* Common
[A] Reported in accordance with IFRS
[1] Results reflect the Aug. 16, 2018, Qualifying Transaction reverse takeover acquisition of (old) Fortress Blockchain Corp.

C.86 Cathedral Energy Services Ltd.*

Symbol - CET **Exchange** - TSX **CUSIP** - 14916J
Head Office - 6030 3 St SE, Calgary, AB, T2H 1K2 **Telephone** - (403) 265-2560 **Toll-free** - (866) 276-8201 **Fax** - (403) 262-4682
Website - www.cathedralenergyservices.com
Email - tconnors@cathedralenergyservices.com
Investor Relations - Thomas J. Connors (866) 276-8201
Auditors - KPMG LLP C.A., Calgary, Alta.

Bankers - The Toronto-Dominion Bank; HSBC Bank Canada; Canadian Western Bank; ATB Financial, Calgary, Alta.

Lawyers - DS Lawyers Canada LLP, Calgary, Alta.

Transfer Agents - Odyssey Trust Company

FP500 Revenue Ranking - 565

Employees - 302 at Dec. 31, 2022

Profile - (Alta. 1994) Provides horizontal and directional drilling services to oil and gas exploration and production companies under the name Cathedral Energy Services in western Canada and under the names Discovery Downhole Services and Altitude Energy Partners in the U.S.

Offers drilling services, including the supply and rental of drilling tools and equipment, drilling optimization and well planning. Tools and equipment supplied by the company consist of measurement-while-drilling (MWD) systems which include the proprietary RapidFire and FUSION systems; positive displacement mud motors including the proprietary nDurance motor series; rotary steerable systems (RSS); drilling jars; shock subs; and drill collars. At Dec. 31, 2022, the company had a fleet of 90 active MWD kits across North America, 1,525 mud motors in Canada (800) and the U.S. (725) and 16 RSS tools.

Engineering and manufacturing operations are conducted at a facility in Nisku, Alta. Repair, service, maintenance and logistics facilities are located in Calgary, Alta.; Casper, Wyo.; Dickinson, N.D.; and Conroe, Midland and Houston, Tex.

In July 2022, the company acquired the remaining 9.02% shares of **LEXA Drilling Technologies Inc.** from a director of the company, Rod Maxwell, for issuance of 159,836 common shares.

In April 2022, the company sold a building and land for $2,150,000.

Recent Merger and Acquisition Activity

Status: completed **Announced:** July 11, 2023
Cathedral Energy Services Ltd. acquired Fort Worth, Tex.-based Rime Downhole Technologies, LLC, which manufactures building products for the downhole-while-drilling (MWD) industry, including pulsers, pulser drivers, shock isolators and gamma modules, for US$21,000,000 cash and US$20,000,000 in subordinated exchangeable promissory notes that are exchangeable into a maximum of 24,570,000 Cathedral common shares.

Status: completed **Announced:** Oct. 26, 2022
Cathedral Energy Services Ltd. acquired the operating assets and personnel of Ensign Energy Services Inc.'s Canadian directional drilling business for a purchase price of $5,000,000 satisfied by the issuance of 7,017,988 common shares. As part of the transaction, Cathedral and Ensign entered into a marketing and technology alliance to further help support and expand the customer base of both companies in the Canadian market.

Status: completed **Revised:** July 14, 2022
UPDATE: The transaction was completed. Cathedral acquired Altitude Energy Partners and issued 67,031,032 common shares for the share consideration. PREVIOUS: Cathedral Energy Services Ltd. agreed to acquire the directional drilling services business unit of Altitude Energy Partners, LLC, a portfolio company of Black Bay Energy Capital, LLC, for a purchase price of US$100,000,000 payable in a combination of US$62,675,000 cash and issuance of 67,031,167 common shares at a deemed price of Cdn$0.7127 per share. Altitude is a privately-held, U.S.-based, directional drilling services business with headquarters in Wyoming and significant operations in Texas, primarily in the Permian Basin. Cathedral plans to operate under the Altitude name and brand in the U.S.

Status: completed **Announced:** June 22, 2022
Cathedral Energy Services Ltd. acquired the operating assets of Compass Directional Services Ltd. for $9,500,000 satisfied by $4,000,000 in cash and issuance of 7,643,139 common shares at a deemed price of $0.72 per share. Compass is a privately-owned, Canadian directional drilling business operating in the Western Canadian Sedimentary Basin.

Status: completed **Announced:** June 20, 2022
Cathedral Energy Services Ltd. acquired 90.98% of LEXA Drilling Technologies Inc., a Calgary, Alta. -based, downhole technology company, for issuance of 1,612,891 common shares. The remaining 9.02% of LEXA is held by Cathedral director Rod Maxwell. Cathedral plans to purchase the remaining shares prior to year-end from Mr. Maxwell on the same terms and conditions. LEXA is focused on the development and commercialization of high data rate positive pulse MWD (measurement-while-drilling) technology.

Predecessor Detail - Name changed from SemBioSys Genetics Inc., Dec. 18, 2009, pursuant conversion of Cathedral Energy Services Income Trust into a corporation whereby all SemBioSys assets and liabilities were transferred to 1491265 Alberta Ltd. which subsequently amalgamated with 1491277 Alberta Ltd. to form a new co. also named SemBioSys Genetics Ltd.; basis 1 Cathedral sh. for 1 Cathedral trust unit and 1 new SemBioSys sh. for 1 old SemBioSys sh.

Directors - Roderick D. (Rod) Maxwell, exec. chr., Calgary, Alta.; Thomas J. (Tom) Connors, pres. & CEO, Calgary, Alta.; Scott D. Sarjeant†, Calgary, Alta.; James R. (JR) Boyles, Casper, Wyo.; Ian S. Brown, Calgary, Alta.; Shuja U. Goraya, Houston, Tex.; Dale E. Tremblay, Philippines

Other Exec. Officers - P. Scott MacFarlane, interim CFO; Vaughn Spengler, sr. v-p, Cdn. opers.; W. Lee Harns, pres., Altitude Energy Partners, LLC; Fawzi Irani, pres., Discovery Downhole Services div.

† Lead director

Capital Stock

	Authorized (shs.)	Outstanding (shs.)[1]
Preferred	unlimited	nil
Common	unlimited	243,200,173

[1] At July 11, 2023

Options - At Dec. 31, 2022, options were outstanding to purchase 20,671,568 common shares at a weighted average exercise price of 61¢ per share with a weighted average remaining life of 2.36 years.

Warrants - At Dec. 31, 2022, warrants were outstanding exercisable for 20,362,350 common shares at a weighted average exercise price of 81¢ per share.

Normal Course Issuer Bid - The company plans to make normal course purchases of up to 12,160,008 common shares representing 5% of the total outstanding. The bid commenced on July 17, 2023, and expires on July 16, 2024.

Major Shareholder - Wilks Brothers, LLC held 10.84% interest at Mar. 28, 2023.

Price Range - CET/TSX

Year	Volume	High	Low	Close
2022	68,475,342	$1.41	$0.39	$1.26
2021	10,024,302	$0.55	$0.16	$0.38
2020	12,071,486	$0.35	$0.06	$0.19
2019	9,833,521	$0.86	$0.21	$0.30
2018	16,604,649	$1.84	$0.66	$0.71

Recent Close: $0.88

Capital Stock Changes - In May 2023, 18,837,888 common shares were issued on exercise of warrants.

In February 2022, private placement of 14,659,000 common shares was completed at 44¢ per share and 5,254,112 common shares were issued on the acquisition of the operating assets of Discovery Downhole Services. In April 2022, bought deal public offering of 37,786,700 units (1 common share & ½ warrant) at 70¢ per unit was completed, including 4,928,700 units on exercise of over-allotment option. In June 2022, 7,643,139 and 1,612,891 common shares were issued on the acquisitions of the operating assets of Compass Directional Services Ltd. and 90.98% interest in LEXA Drilling Technologies Inc., respectively. In July 2022, 67,031,032 and 159,836 common shares were issued on the acquisitions of Altitude Energy Partners, LLC and the remaining 9.02% interest in LEXA, respectively. In November 2022, 7,017,988 common shares were issued on the acquisition of Ensign Energy Services Inc.'s Canadian directional drilling business. Also during 2022, common shares were issued as follows: 1,653,265 on exercise of options and 1,106,000 on exercise of warrants.

Long-Term Debt - Outstanding at Dec. 31, 2022:

Syndicated oper. facility due 2023[1]	$13,000,000
Syndicated term facility due 2025[2]	66,600,000
4% HASCAP loan	935,000
	80,535,000
Less: Current portion	15,735,000
	64,800,000

[1] Borrowings under a $12,000,000 operating facility and $14,250,000 term loan, both bearing interest at prime plus 1.75% to 3.25% or bankers' acceptance rate plus 3% to 4.25%.

[2] Borrowings under a $74,000,000 term loan, $15,000,000 syndicated revolving facility and $10,000,000 operating facility, all bearing interest at prime plus 1.5% to 2.25% or bankers' acceptance rate plus 2.5% to 3.25%.

Wholly Owned Subsidiaries

Altitude Energy HoldCo, LLC, Del.
Altitude Energy Partners, LLC, Wyo.
CET Flight Holdco, Inc., Del.
Cathedral Energy Services Inc., Del.

Note: The preceding list includes only the major related companies in which interests are held.

Financial Statistics

Periods ended:	12m Dec. 31/22[A]		12m Dec. 31/21[◻A]
	$000s	%Chg	$000s
Operating revenue	**298,401**	**+377**	**62,524**
Cost of sales	214,110		51,095
General & admin expense	27,933		7,782
Stock-based compensation	1,387		241
Other operating expense	1,271		747
Operating expense	**244,701**	**+309**	**59,865**
Operating income	**53,700**	**n.m.**	**2,659**
Deprec., depl. & amort.	31,696		12,907
Finance costs, gross	6,074		990
Write-downs/write-offs	(107)		614
Pre-tax income	**22,961**	**n.a.**	**(8,626)**
Income taxes	4,614		nil
Net income	**18,347**	**n.a.**	**(8,626)**
Cash & equivalent	11,175		2,898
Inventories	26,195		8,423
Accounts receivable	113,477		15,609
Current assets	155,376		28,368
Fixed assets, net	108,530		35,044
Right-of-use assets	12,178		10,520
Intangibles, net	77,906		1,491
Total assets	**353,990**	**+369**	**75,423**
Accts. pay. & accr. liabs	90,389		11,069
Current liabilities	110,664		14,251
Long-term debt, gross	80,535		6,035
Long-term debt, net	64,800		5,035
Long-term lease liabilities	14,249		13,633
Shareholders' equity	153,897		42,504
Cash from oper. activs	**23,960**	**n.a.**	**(3,499)**
Cash from fin. activs	97,578		4,494
Cash from invest. activs	(115,804)		877
Net cash position	**11,175**	**+286**	**2,898**
Capital expenditures	(30,894)		(5,617)
Capital disposals	21,795		3,553
	$		$
Earnings per share*	0.11		(0.13)
Cash flow per share*	0.15		(0.05)
	shs		shs
No. of shs. o/s*	224,124,116		80,200,153
Avg. no. of shs. o/s*	162,550,576		65,030,795
	%		%
Net profit margin	6.15		(13.80)
Return on equity	18.68		(20.92)
Return on assets	10.81		(10.93)
Foreign sales percent	61		26
No. of employees (FTEs)	302		155

* Common
◻ Restated
[A] Reported in accordance with IFRS

Latest Results

Periods ended:	3m Mar. 31/23[A]		3m Mar. 31/22[A]
	$000s	%Chg	$000s
Operating revenue	127,665	+271	34,385
Net income	794	-65	2,243
	$		$
Earnings per share*	0.00		0.02

* Common
[A] Reported in accordance with IFRS

Historical Summary
(as originally stated)

Fiscal Year	Oper. Rev.	Net Inc. Bef. Disc.	EPS*
	$000s	$000s	$
2022[A]	298,401	18,347	0.11
2021[A]	62,524	(8,626)	(0.13)
2020[A]	40,574	(27,731)	(0.56)
2019[A]	120,276	(19,187)	(0.39)
2018[A]	160,827	(17,061)	(0.34)

* Common
[A] Reported in accordance with IFRS

C.87 Cavalry Capital Corp.

Symbol - CVY.P **Exchange** - TSX-VEN **CUSIP** - 13151N

Head Office - 910-800 Pender St W, Vancouver, BC, V6C 2V6

Telephone - (604) 999-4136

Email - brandon@boni.ca

Investor Relations - Brandon Bonifacio (604) 337-4997

Auditors - Dale Matheson Carr-Hilton LaBonte LLP C.A., Vancouver, B.C.

Lawyers - Capiche Legal LLP, Vancouver, B.C.

Transfer Agents - Computershare Trust Company of Canada Inc., Vancouver, B.C.

Profile - (B.C. 2021) Capital Pool Company.

Recent Merger and Acquisition Activity

Status: pending **Revised:** July 11, 2023

UPDATE: The companies entered into a definitive agreement whereby a three-cornered amalgamation would be completed where Home Run would amalgamate with 2515862 Alberta Ltd., wholly owned by Cavalry. On closing, Cavalry would change its name to Canadian Home Run Energy Corporation. Concurrently with the completion of the Qualifying Transaction, Cavalry was expected to complete a private placement of at least 15,000,000 units at a price of $0.10 per unit for aggregate gross proceeds to Cavalry of at least $1,500,000. PREVIOUS: Cavalry Capital Corp. entered into a letter of intent for the Qualifying Transaction reverse takeover acquisition of private Calgary, Alta.-based Home Run Oil & Gas Inc., which explores for and develops oil and gas in west-central Alberta, on the basis of 2.4157 Cavalry common shares for each Home Run share held, which would result in the issuance of 60,000,000 Cavalry common shares. Home Run holds a 100% working interest in 42.5 sections of lands, leases and licences, totaling 10,880 hectares, in the Ante Creek North, Ante Creek, Simonette, Clairmont and Kaybob South areas.

Directors - Brandon Bonifacio, CEO, Vancouver, B.C.; Giulio T. Bonifacio, Vancouver, B.C.; Brock Daem, Vancouver, B.C.; John D. MacPhail, North Vancouver, B.C.

Other Exec. Officers - Adam Garvin, CFO & corp. sec.

Capital Stock

	Authorized (shs.)	Outstanding (shs.)[1]
Common	unlimited	6,462,500

[1] At May 4, 2022

Major Shareholder - Widely held at May 4, 2022.

Price Range - CVY.P/TSX-VEN

Year	Volume	High	Low	Close
2022............	239,461	$0.29	$0.10	$0.10

Recent Close: $0.10

Capital Stock Changes - On May 4, 2022, an initial public offering of 3,962,500 common shares was completed at 10¢ per share.

C.88 Ceapro Inc.

Symbol - CZO **Exchange** - TSX-VEN **CUSIP** - 149907
Head Office - 7824 51 Ave NW, Edmonton, AB, T6E 6W2 **Telephone** - (780) 421-4555 **Fax** - (780) 421-1320
Website - www.ceapro.com
Email - sprefontaine@ceapro.com
Investor Relations - Stacy Prefontaine (780) 421-4555
Auditors - Grant Thornton LLP C.A., Edmonton, Alta.
Bankers - The Toronto-Dominion Bank
Lawyers - Bryan & Company LLP, Edmonton, Alta.
Transfer Agents - Computershare Trust Company of Canada Inc., Toronto, Ont.

Profile - (Can. 2002; orig. Alta., 1997 amalg.) Develops and commercializes natural products for personal care, cosmetic, human and animal health industries.

Has a commercial line of natural active ingredients, including beta glucan, avenanthramides (colloidal oat extract), oat powder, oat oil, oat peptides and lupin peptides which are marketed to the personal care, cosmetic, medical and animal health industries through distribution partners and direct sales. Through wholly owned **Juvente[DC] Inc.**, markets natural anti-aging skincare products which utilizes active ingredients including beta glucan and avenanthramides to the cosmeceutical industry. Also markets veterinary therapeutic products, including an oat shampoo, an ear cleanser and a dermal complex/conditioner, to veterinarians in Japan and Asia as well as an inhalable therapeutic product for COVID-19 patients, which contains PGX yeast beta glucan. Has a bioprocessing plant in Edmonton, Alta.

Other products and technologies under research and development or pre-commercial stage include a potential platform using the company's beta glucan technology to deliver compounds used for treatments in both personal and healthcare sectors; a variety of enabling technologies including Pressurized Gas eXpanded (PGX) drying technology; and the development of a new oat variety and certain technologies. Also received approval from Health Canada Controlled Substances and Cannabis Branch for a five year research licence with medical cannabis for the formulation of unique solid cannabinoid delivery systems using PGX technology.

Has received patents in Europe and the U.S. for its technology which increases concentration of avenanthramides in oats and in Canada, the U.S., Europe and India for its PGX technology.

Predecessor Detail - Formed from Vexco Healthcare Inc. in Alberta, Jan. 1, 1997, on amalgamation with Ceapro Developments Inc., constituting a reverse takeover by Ceapro; basis 1 new for 2 Ceapro shs. and 1 new for 4.5 Vexco shs.

Directors - Ronald W. (Ronnie) Miller, chr., Oakville, Ont.; Gilles R. Gagnon, pres. & CEO, Sherbrooke, Qué.; Geneviève Foster, Laval, Qué.; Dr. Ulrich Kosciessa, Pinneberg, Germany; Dr. William W. Li, Holliston, Mass.; Glenn R. Rourke, Westmount, Qué.

Other Exec. Officers - Stacy Prefontaine, CFO & corp. sec.; Sigrun Watson, chief revenue officer; Michel (Mitch) Regnier, sr. v-p, technical opers.; Leoni DeJoya, v-p, bioprocessing bus. unit

Capital Stock

	Authorized (shs.)	Outstanding (shs.)[1]
Class A Common	unlimited	78,253,177
Class B Common	unlimited	nil

[1] At May 23, 2023

Major Shareholder - Widely held at Apr. 19, 2023.

Price Range - CZO/TSX-VEN

Year	Volume	High	Low	Close
2022............	8,252,786	$0.82	$0.40	$0.59
2021............	9,854,948	$0.92	$0.50	$0.61
2020............	13,884,489	$0.98	$0.14	$0.66
2019............	7,367,183	$0.50	$0.27	$0.32
2018............	13,145,236	$0.67	$0.32	$0.39

Recent Close: $0.43

Capital Stock Changes - During 2022, 547,334 class A common shares were issued on exercise of options.

Wholly Owned Subsidiaries

Ceapro (P.E.I.) Inc., P.E.I.
JuventeDC Inc., Montmagny, Qué.

Financial Statistics

Periods ended:	12m Dec. 31/22[A]		12m Dec. 31/21[oA]
	$000s	%Chg	$000s
Operating revenue........................	**18,840**	**+10**	**17,195**
Cost of goods sold..........................	7,822		6,728
Research & devel. expense.............	1,789		3,878
General & admin expense...............	1,819		1,406
Operating expense.......................	**11,429**	**-5**	**12,012**
Operating income........................	**7,410**	**+43**	**5,183**
Deprec., depl. & amort....................	1,911		1,881
Finance costs, gross........................	185		207
Pre-tax income............................	**5,777**	**+75**	**3,298**
Income taxes..................................	1,379		(67)
Net income..................................	**4,398**	**+31**	**3,365**
Cash & equivalent...........................	13,811		7,781
Inventories......................................	3,757		2,324
Accounts receivable........................	2,820		2,093
Current assets................................	20,588		12,407
Fixed assets, net.............................	16,202		17,500
Intangibles, net...............................	13		16
Total assets.................................	**37,734**	**+22**	**31,051**
Accts. pay. & accr. liabs.................	1,730		682
Current liabilities............................	2,101		972
Long-term lease liabilities................	2,249		2,359
Shareholders' equity........................	32,289		27,720
Cash from oper. activs..................	**6,637**	**+89**	**3,510**
Cash from fin. activs........................	(218)		(308)
Cash from invest. activs..................	(389)		(791)
Net cash position.........................	**13,811**	**+77**	**7,781**
Capital expenditures........................	(341)		(709)
	$		$
Earnings per share*.........................	0.06		0.04
Cash flow per share*.......................	0.09		0.05
	shs		shs
No. of shs. o/s*...............................	78,233,177		77,685,843
Avg. no. of shs. o/s*........................	77,961,714		77,673,804
	%		%
Net profit margin.............................	23.34		19.57
Return on equity..............................	14.79		12.93
Return on assets.............................	13.30		11.87
Foreign sales percent......................	100		100

* Cl.A com.
[o] Restated
[A] Reported in accordance with IFRS

Latest Results

Periods ended:	3m Mar. 31/23[A]		3m Mar. 31/22[oA]
	$000s	%Chg	$000s
Operating revenue...........................	3,495	-43	6,172
Net income......................................	(385)	n.a.	1,813
	$		$
Earnings per share*.........................	(0.00)		0.02

* Cl.A com.
[o] Restated
[A] Reported in accordance with IFRS

Historical Summary
(as originally stated)

Fiscal Year	Oper. Rev.	Net Inc. Bef. Disc.	EPS*
	$000s	$000s	$
2022[A]...................	18,840	4,398	0.06
2021[A]...................	17,195	2,842	0.04
2020[A]...................	15,121	1,856	0.02
2019[A]...................	12,880	(1,133)	(0.01)
2018[A]...................	11,593	(316)	(0.00)

* Cl.A com.
[A] Reported in accordance with IFRS

C.89 Celestial Acquisition Corp.

Symbol - CES.P **Exchange** - TSX-VEN **CUSIP** - 15102Q
Head Office - 1800-181 Bay St, Toronto, ON, M5J 2T9 **Telephone** - (647) 558-5537
Website - www.celestialgrowth.com
Email - info@celestialgrowth.com
Investor Relations - Jared Bottoms (647) 558-5537
Auditors - MNP LLP C.A., Toronto, Ont.
Transfer Agents - Odyssey Trust Company, Calgary, Alta.

Profile - (Ont. 2022) Capital Pool Company.

Common listed on TSX-VEN, Dec. 22, 2022.

Directors - Jared Bottoms, CEO, Vancouver, B.C.; Jonathan Leong, CFO, Toronto, Ont.; Gary Lifshits, Toronto, Ont.; Marek Lorenc, Toronto, Ont.; Tahir Merali, Calgary, Alta.; Mark Russell, Wash.

Capital Stock

	Authorized (shs.)	Outstanding (shs.)[1]
Common	unlimited	9,250,000

[1] At Dec. 22, 2022

Major Shareholder - Widely held at Dec. 22, 2022.

Recent Close: $0.07

Capital Stock Changes - On Dec. 22, 2022, an initial public offering of 5,000,000 common shares was completed at 10¢ per share.

C.90 Celestica Inc.*

Symbol - CLS **Exchange** - TSX **CUSIP** - 15101Q
Head Office - 1900-5140 Yonge St, PO Box 42, Toronto, ON, M2N 6L7 **Telephone** - (416) 448-5800 **Toll-free** - (888) 899-9998 **Fax** - (416) 448-4810
Website - www.celestica.com
Email - clsir@celestica.com
Investor Relations - Mandeep Chawla (888) 899-9998
Auditors - KPMG LLP C.A., Toronto, Ont.
Lawyers - Blake, Cassels & Graydon LLP, Toronto, Ont.
Transfer Agents - Computershare Trust Company, Inc., Golden, Colo.; Computershare Trust Company of Canada Inc., Toronto, Ont.
FP500 Revenue Ranking - 63
Employees - 20,611 at Dec. 31, 2022

Profile - (Ont. 1996) Provides end-to-end electronics manufacturing services as well as other related services and customer support activities to original equipment manufacturers (OEMs), cloud-based and other service providers, and other companies in a wide range of industries worldwide through facilities in North America, Europe and Asia.

Offers a range of product manufacturing and related supply chain services, including design and development, new product introduction, engineering services, component sourcing, electronics manufacturing and assembly, testing, complex mechanical assembly, systems integration, precision machining, order fulfillment, logistics, asset management, product licensing, and after-market repair and return services.

Operations are carried out through two segments: Advanced Technology Solutions; and Connectivity and Cloud Solutions.

The **Advanced Technology Solutions** segment consists of aerospace and defence, industrial, healthtech and capital equipment businesses including manufacturing and electronic services; semiconductor and display equipment; industrial automation, controls, test and measurement devices; product development in telematics, human machine interfaces, Internet-of-Things; advanced solutions for surgical instruments, diagnostic imaging and patient monitoring; and managing and monitoring energy and power industries. Customers include **Applied Materials Inc.**, **Honeywell Inc.** and **Lam Research Corporation**.

The **Connectivity and Cloud Solutions** segment consists of communication and enterprise end markets, including servers and storage businesses. Also offers hardware platform solutions, which includes firmware/software enablement across all primary information technology infrastructure data center technologies and aftermarket services. Customers include **Amazon Fulfillment Services Inc.**, **Ciena Corporation**, **Dell Technologies**, **Google Inc.**, **Hewlett-Packard Enterprise**, **Hewlett-Packard Inc.**, **IBM Corporation**, **Juniper Networks Inc.**, **Meta Platforms Inc.**, **NEC Corporation**, and **Polycom Inc.**

Recent Merger and Acquisition Activity

Status: completed **Revised:** Aug. 4, 2023
UPDATE:The offering was completed for net proceeds of US$133,000,000. On closing, Onex no longer held any shares in Celestica. PREVIOUS: Onex Corporation announced a secondary offering of 6,757,198 subordinate voting shares (SVS) of Celestica Inc., substantially all of which would be issued upon conversion of a corresponding number of Celestica's multiple voting shares into SVS.

Status: completed **Revised:** June 8, 2023
UPDATE: The transaction was completed. PREVIOUS: Onex Corporation announced a secondary offering of 12,000,000 subordinate voting shares (SVS) of Celestica Inc. at US$12.40 per share for gross proceeds of US$148,800,000. Of the SVS to be sold, 11,800,000 SVS would be issued upon conversion of a corresponding number of Celestica's multiple voting shares into SVS. Onex holds about 18,600,000 Celestica MVS, representing a 15% equity interest and an 82% voting interest. The offering was expected to close on June 8, 2023.

Directors - Michael M. (Mike) Wilson, chr., Bragg Creek, Alta.; Robert A. Mionis, pres. & CEO, Hampton, N.H.; Robert A. Cascella, Boca Raton, Fla.; Deepak Chopra, Toronto, Ont.; Françoise Colpron, Mich.; Daniel P. (Dan) DiMaggio, Duluth, Ga.; Jill Kale, Md.; Laurette T. Koellner, Merritt Island, Fla.; Dr. Luis A. Müller, San Diego, Calif.; Tawfiq Popatia, Toronto, Ont.

Other Exec. Officers - Mandeep Chawla, CFO; Yann Etienvre, chief opers. officer; Leila Wong, chief HR officer; Todd C. Cooper, pres., advanced tech. solutions; Jason Phillips, pres., connectivity & cloud solutions

Capital Stock

	Authorized (shs.)	Outstanding (shs.)[1]
Preferred	unlimited	nil
Multiple Vtg.	unlimited	nil
Subordinate Vtg.	unlimited	119,328,962

[1] At Aug. 4, 2023

Multiple Voting - Convertible at any time, at the holder's option, into subordinate voting shares on a share-for-share basis. 25 votes per share.

Subordinate Voting - One vote per share.

Options - At Dec. 31, 2022, options were outstanding to purchase 400,000 subordinate voting shares at exercise prices ranging from US$10.58 to US$12.93 per share (weighted average exercise price of US$12.38 per share) expiring over a weighted average remaining contractual life of up to 4.1 years.

Normal Course Issuer Bid - The company plans to make normal course purchases of up to 8,776,134 subordinate voting shares representing 10% of the public float. The bid commenced on Dec. 13, 2022, and expires on Dec. 12, 2023.

Major Shareholder - Widely held at Aug. 4, 2023.

Price Range - CLS/TSX

Year	Volume	High	Low	Close
2022	52,663,974	$17.00	$11.28	$15.26
2021	56,070,692	$14.87	$8.94	$14.10
2020	66,471,275	$12.27	$3.83	$10.27
2019	53,949,946	$13.08	$7.76	$10.77
2018	64,964,850	$16.50	$11.68	$11.96

Recent Close: $29.67

Capital Stock Changes - During 2022, subordinate voting shares were issued as follows: 50,000 on vesting of restricted and performance share units and 20,000 on exercise of options; 3,140,000 subordinate voting shares were repurchased under a Normal Course Issuer Bid.

Long-Term Debt - Outstanding at Dec. 31, 2022:

Term loans due 2025[1]	US$627,200,000
Lease obligs.	162,400,000
Less: Unamort. debt issue costs	3,500,000
	786,100,000
Less: Current portion	52,200,000
	733,900,000

[1] Drawn from a US$350,000,000 term loan bearing interest at LIBOR plus 2.125%; and a US$365,000,000 incremental term loan bearing interest at LIBOR plus 2% and a US$600,000,000 revolving credit facility bearing interest either at LIBOR, base rate, prime rate, alternative currency daily rate or alternative currency term rate plus a specified margin.

Wholly Owned Subsidiaries

Celestica Cayman Holdings 1 Limited, Cayman Islands.
Celestica Holdings Pte Limited, Singapore.
Celestica LLC, Del. Formerly Celestica Corporation
Celestica (Thailand) Limited, Thailand.
Celestica (USA) Inc., Del.
PCI Limited, Singapore.
2480333 Ontario Inc., Ont.

Note: The preceding list includes only the major related companies in which interests are held.

Financial Statistics

Periods ended:	12m Dec. 31/22[A]		12m Dec. 31/21[A]
	US$000s	%Chg	US$000s
Operating revenue	**7,250,000**	**+29**	**5,634,700**
Cost of sales	6,488,800		5,033,900
Research & devel. expense	46,300		38,400
General & admin expense	249,200		224,700
Stock-based compensation	51,000		33,400
Operating expense	**6,835,300**	**+28**	**5,330,400**
Operating income	**414,700**	**+36**	**304,300**
Deprec., depl. & amort.	144,700		126,300
Finance costs, gross	59,700		31,700
Pre-tax income	**203,600**	**+50**	**136,000**
Income taxes	58,100		32,100
Net income	**145,500**	**+40**	**103,900**
Cash & equivalent	374,500		394,000
Inventories	2,350,300		1,697,000
Accounts receivable	1,393,500		1,260,300
Current assets	4,327,000		3,435,300
Fixed assets, net	371,500		338,700
Right-of-use assets	138,800		113,800
Intangibles, net	668,300		706,200
Total assets	**5,628,000**	**+21**	**4,666,900**
Accts. pay. & accr. liabs	1,440,800		1,238,300
Current liabilities	3,055,200		2,253,500
Long-term debt, gross	786,100		794,400
Long-term debt, net	733,900		742,900
Shareholders' equity	1,677,700		1,463,000
Cash from oper. activs	**297,900**	**+31**	**226,800**
Cash from fin. activs	(208,500)		67,700
Cash from invest. activs	(108,900)		(364,300)
Net cash position	**374,500**	**-5**	**394,000**
Capital expenditures	(109,000)		(52,200)
Capital disposals	100		2,600
Unfunded pension liability	6,000		15,600
	US$		US$
Earnings per share*	1.18		0.82
Cash flow per share*	2.41		1.79
	shs		shs
No. of shs. o/s*	121,600,000		124,700,000
Avg. no. of shs. o/s*	123,500,000		126,700,000
	%		%
Net profit margin	2.01		1.84
Return on equity	9.27		7.24
Return on assets	3.66		3.08
Foreign sales percent	95		93
No. of employees (FTEs)	20,611		18,643

* M.V. & S.V.
[A] Reported in accordance with IFRS

Latest Results

Periods ended:	6m June 30/23[A]		6m June 30/22[A]
	US$000s	%Chg	US$000s
Operating revenue	3,777,200	+15	3,284,100
Net income	80,200	+40	57,400
	US$		US$
Earnings per share*	0.66		0.46

* M.V. & S.V.
[A] Reported in accordance with IFRS

Historical Summary
(as originally stated)

Fiscal Year	Oper. Rev. US$000s	Net Inc. Bef. Disc. US$000s	EPS* US$
2022[A]	7,250,000	145,500	1.18
2021[A]	5,634,700	103,900	0.82
2020[A]	5,748,100	60,600	0.47
2019[A]	5,888,300	70,300	0.54
2018[A]	6,633,200	98,900	0.71

* M.V. & S.V.
[A] Reported in accordance with IFRS

C.91 Cematrix Corporation

Symbol - CVX **Exchange** - TSX-VEN **CUSIP** - 15120R
Head Office - 9727 40 St SE, Calgary, AB, T2C 2P4 **Telephone** - (403) 219-0484 **Toll-free** - (888) 876-0484 **Fax** - (403) 243-9839
Website - www.cematrix.com
Email - jeff@cematrix.com
Investor Relations - Jeffrey N. Kendrick (888) 876-0484
Auditors - MNP LLP C.A., Calgary, Alta.
Lawyers - McLeod Law LLP, Calgary, Alta.
Transfer Agents - Computershare Trust Company of Canada Inc., Vancouver, B.C.
Employees - 63 at Dec. 31, 2022

Profile - (Alta. 2005) Manufactures and supplies cellular concrete for various applications primarily in the geotechnical field, in multiple construction markets throughout North America.

Cellular concrete is a cement slurry-based product that is combined with air to form a lightweight, foamed concrete-like material with thermal insulating properties and moderate structural strength used as a replacement for rigid and other types of insulation as a lightweight fill or void fill. Products are used for various insulating or void fill/grouting applications in the infrastructure, industrial and commercial construction markets, including insulation of road bases, permafrost protection under buildings, utilities, roads and runways, insulation of shallow utility installations, industrial and commercial floor bases, replacement of weak and/or unstable soils and soils that are subject to seismic conditions, mechanical stabilized earth (MSE) panels, retaining wall backfill, grouting and tunnel backfill.

The company has a fleet of production equipment consisting of 10 dry mix units that can produce up to 230 m^3 per hour of cellular concrete and eight wet mix units with the capability of producing from 50 m^3 to 100 m^3 per hour of cellular concrete. The fleet is mobile and can be moved to any site in North America.

Predecessor Detail - Name changed from Moonshoot Capital Corp., Apr. 11, 2006, following Qualifying Transaction reverse takeover acquisition of Cematrix Corporation.

Directors - Minaz H. Lalani, chr., Calgary, Alta.; Jeffrey N. (Jeff) Kendrick, pres. & CEO, Calgary, Alta.; Robert L. Benson, Victoria, B.C.; Stephen E. (Steve) Bjornson, Calgary, Alta.; Patrick N. (Rick) Breen, Calgary, Alta.; Anna-Maria Cuglietta, Calgary, Alta.; John M. Kim, Toronto, Ont.

Other Exec. Officers - Randy Boomhour, CFO; Steve Bent, v-p & gen. mgr., Cematrix Canada; Patrick (Pat) Stephens, pres., Pacific International Grout Co.; Jordan Wolfe, pres., MixOnSite USA, Inc.

Capital Stock

	Authorized (shs.)	Outstanding (shs.)[1]
Common	unlimited	134,381,452

[1] At May 10, 2023

Major Shareholder - Widely held at May 10, 2023.

Price Range - CVX/TSX-VEN

Year	Volume	High	Low	Close
2022	23,528,972	$0.34	$0.14	$0.22
2021	87,957,554	$0.86	$0.30	$0.33
2020	49,233,751	$0.84	$0.27	$0.72
2019	7,142,474	$0.34	$0.16	$0.34
2018	3,775,673	$0.29	$0.15	$0.18

Recent Close: $0.20

Capital Stock Changes - During 2022, 8,772 common shares were issued on vesting of restricted share units.

Wholly Owned Subsidiaries

CEMATRIX (Canada) Inc., Calgary, Alta.
- 100% int. in **Cematrix (USA) Inc.**, Nev.
  - 100% int. in **MixOnSite USA Inc.**, Buffalo Grove, Ill.
  - 100% int. in **Pacific International Grout Co.**, Bellingham, Wash.

Canadian Cellular Concrete Services Inc., B.C.
Cematrix (Calgary) Ltd., Canada.

Investments

Glavel Inc., Burlington, Vt.

Financial Statistics

Periods ended:	12m Dec. 31/22[A]		12m Dec. 31/21[○A]
	$000s	%Chg	$000s
Operating revenue	**29,003**	**+28**	**22,601**
Cost of sales	24,941		17,287
General & admin expense	6,945		5,560
Stock-based compensation	610		274
Operating expense	**32,496**	**+41**	**23,121**
Operating income	**(3,493)**	**n.a.**	**(520)**
Deprec., depl. & amort.	1,856		2,486
Finance costs, gross	1,146		1,305
Investment income	(34)		nil
Write-downs/write-offs	nil		(768)
Pre-tax income	**(6,441)**	**n.a.**	**(2,700)**
Income taxes	(880)		(845)
Net income	**(5,561)**	**n.a.**	**(1,855)**
Cash & equivalent	10,682		19,945
Inventories	1,010		718
Accounts receivable	7,337		4,911
Current assets	19,561		26,437
Long-term investments	2,382		nil
Fixed assets, net	11,577		10,534
Right-of-use assets	1,128		1,637
Intangibles, net	6,148		5,754
Total assets	**40,817**	**-8**	**44,389**
Accts. pay. & accr. liabs	5,139		3,204
Current liabilities	10,165		4,659
Long-term debt, gross	6,411		6,710
Long-term debt, net	1,975		5,833
Long-term lease liabilities	574		1,106
Shareholders' equity	27,742		31,581
Cash from oper. activs	**(3,205)**	**n.a.**	**(833)**
Cash from fin. activs	(2,312)		18,954
Cash from invest. activs	(4,037)		(619)
Net cash position	**10,682**	**-47**	**20,231**
Capital expenditures	(1,882)		(673)
Capital disposals	86		55
	$		$
Earnings per share*	(0.04)		(0.02)
Cash flow per share*	(0.02)		(0.01)
	shs		shs
No. of shs. o/s*	133,948,710		133,939,938
Avg. no. of shs. o/s*	133,943,783		133,939,938
	%		%
Net profit margin	(19.17)		(8.21)
Return on equity	(18.75)		(11.50)
Return on assets	(10.73)		(2.62)
Foreign sales percent	74		58
No. of employees (FTEs)	63		53

* Common
○ Restated
[A] Reported in accordance with IFRS

Latest Results

Periods ended:	3m Mar. 31/23[A]		3m Mar. 31/22[A]
	$000s	%Chg	$000s
Operating revenue	7,182	+40	5,122
Net income	(1,669)	n.a.	(2,211)
	$		$
Earnings per share*	(0.01)		(0.02)

* Common
[A] Reported in accordance with IFRS

Historical Summary
(as originally stated)

Fiscal Year	Oper. Rev.	Net Inc. Bef. Disc.	EPS*
	$000s	$000s	$
2022[A]	29,003	(5,561)	(0.04)
2021[A]	22,601	(1,855)	(0.02)
2020[A]	26,564	(9,776)	(0.16)
2019[A]	22,551	(254)	(0.01)
2018[A]	17,561	(1,092)	(0.03)

* Common
[A] Reported in accordance with IFRS

C.92 Century Global Commodities Corporation

Symbol - CNT **Exchange** - TSX **CUSIP** - G2029R
Head Office - Unit 905-6, 9/F Houston Centre, 63 Mody Road Tsim Sha Tsui, Hong Kong, People's Republic of China **Overseas Tel** - 852-3951-8700 **Overseas Fax** - 852-3101-9302
Website - www.centuryglobal.ca
Email - ir@centuryglobal.ca
Investor Relations - Sandy C. K. Chim (416) 977-3188
Auditors - PricewaterhouseCoopers LLP C.A., Toronto, Ont.
Transfer Agents - TSX Trust Company, Toronto, Ont.
Employees - 26 at Mar. 31, 2023

Profile - (Cayman Islands 2016; orig. Can., 2007) Has iron prospects in Newfoundland and Labrador and Quebec. Also distributes eggs, egg products and meats in Hong Kong and Macau.

Operations are organized into two segments: Mining Operations; and Food Business.

Mining Operations

Straddling the Labrador/Quebec border, holds 91.6% interest in Joyce Lake iron project, 17,050 hectares, 20 km northeast of Schefferville. An updated feasibility study completed in October 2022 proposed an open-pit mine which would produce up to 2,500,000 tonnes annually of direct shipping iron ore (DSO) products over a 7-year mine life. Initial capital costs were estimated at $270,400,000. Proven and probable reserves were 17,370,000 tonnes grading 59.94% iron, 11.28% silicon dioxide, 0.55% aluminum dioxide and 0.76% manganese. Also holds nearby Hayot Lake iron project, 6,508 hectares 22 km north of Schefferville, with inferred resource of 1.723 billion tonnes grading 31.25% iron at September 2012.

In Quebec, holds Full Moon (Rainy Lake) iron project, 8,421 hectares, 80 km northwest of Schefferville, with indicated resource of 7.260 billion tonnes grading 30.18% iron at October 2012. A preliminary economic assessment effective Mar. 2, 2015, on Full Moon proposed an open-pit mine with a 30-year mine life. Four options were proposed for Full Moon: high silica content concentrates (preferred), low silica content concentrates, high silica content pellets and low silica content pellets. The preferred option assumes annual production of 20,000,000 tonnes of high silica content concentrate with an estimated initial capital cost of $7,207 billion. In addition, holds 68% interest (**Automotive Finco Corp.** 32%) in Duncan Lake iron property, 4,361 hectares, 40 km south of Radisson, with measured and indicated resource of 1.05 billion tonnes grading 24.42% iron at August 2012. A preliminary economic assessment released in May 2013 for Duncan Lake iron property contemplated pellet production of 12,000,000 tonnes per year over a 20-year mine life. Initial capital costs were estimated at $3.881 billion. Also holds Black Bird (formerly Lac Le Fer) iron project, 1,870 hectares, 65 km northwest of Schefferville, with indicated resource of 1,550,000 tonnes grading 59.93% iron, 7.23% silicon dioxide, 0.87% aluminum dioxide and 1.68% manganese at March 2015; and Tricor gold prospect, 547, hectares, 35 km north of Val-d'Or.

Food Business

The company distributes eggs, egg products and meats to customers including major retail chains, caterers, gourmet shops, hotels and restaurants in Hong Kong and Macau.

Predecessor Detail - Name changed from Century Iron Mines Corporation, Nov. 16, 2015.

Directors - Sandy C. K. Chim, chr., pres. & CEO, Hong Kong, Hong Kong, People's Republic of China; Dwight Ball, v-chr., N.L.; Howard Bernier†, Repentigny, Qué.; Yiyan Chen, Shanghai, People's Republic of China; John Gravelle, Ont.; Jionghui Wang, Beijing, Beijing, People's Republic of China; Gloria Wong, Hong Kong, Hong Kong, People's Republic of China; Jianlong Yang, Shanghai, Shanghai, People's Republic of China; Tak Wai (Wien) Yu, Shanghai, Shanghai, People's Republic of China

Other Exec. Officers - Wai Sze (Bonnie) Leung, CFO & co-sec.; Chun Wa (Ivan) Wong, sr. v-p, corp. fin. & project devel.; Alan Sin, v-p, food opers.; Denis S. Frawley, co-sec.
† Lead director

Capital Stock

	Authorized (shs.)	Outstanding (shs.)[1]	Par
Ordinary	5,000,000,000	118,205,485	$0.001

[1] At July 19, 2023

Major Shareholder - Leung Lee Chan held 25.07% interest, WISCO International Resources Development & Investment Limited held 23.5% interest and Sandy C. K. Chim held 18.3% interest at May 31, 2023.

Price Range - CNT/TSX

Year	Volume	High	Low	Close
2022	1,651,460	$0.42	$0.07	$0.08
2021	2,150,273	$0.40	$0.14	$0.15
2020	1,545,254	$0.28	$0.05	$0.17
2019	1,520,242	$0.25	$0.07	$0.07
2018	583,888	$0.29	$0.11	$0.17

Recent Close: $0.03

Capital Stock Changes - In July 2023, 19,700,914 common shares were issued under a rights offering at $0.02 per share.

There were no changes to capital stock from fiscal 2020 to fiscal 2023, inclusive.

Wholly Owned Subsidiaries

Century Food Global Inc., British Virgin Islands.
- 85% int. in **Century Food International Holdings Limited**, British Virgin Islands.
  - 100% int. in **Century Food Company Limited**, Hong Kong, People's Republic of China.

Century Iron Ore Holdings Inc., B.C.
- 100% int. in **Century Duncan Mining Inc.**, B.C.
- 100% int. in **Century Sunny Lake Iron Mines Limited**, B.C.
- 100% int. in **Labec Century Iron Ore Inc.**, B.C.
  - 91.6% int. in **Joyce Direct Iron Inc.**, B.C.

Trudeau Metals Inc., B.C.

Note: The preceding list includes only the major related companies in which interests are held.

Financial Statistics

Periods ended:	12m Mar. 31/23[A]		12m Mar. 31/22[A]
	$000s	%Chg	$000s
Operating revenue	**11,259**	**+29**	**8,718**
Cost of sales	8,070		6,519
Salaries & benefits	2,602		2,459
General & admin expense	1,981		2,082
Stock-based compensation	72		84
Other operating expense	57		273
Operating expense	**12,782**	**+12**	**11,416**
Operating income	**(1,523)**	**n.a.**	**(2,698)**
Deprec., depl. & amort.	257		269
Finance income	98		49
Finance costs, gross	10		14
Pre-tax income	**(1,499)**	**n.a.**	**(2,761)**
Income taxes	125		11
Net income	**(1,624)**	**n.a.**	**(2,771)**
Net inc. for equity hldrs	**(1,686)**	**n.a.**	**(2,698)**
Net inc. for non-cont. int.	**63**	**n.a.**	**(73)**
Cash & equivalent	6,526		10,273
Inventories	2,533		1,349
Accounts receivable	2,054		1,677
Current assets	11,561		13,807
Long-term investments	981		1,007
Fixed assets, net	51		60
Right-of-use assets	165		367
Explor./devel. properties	10,248		9,035
Total assets	**23,005**	**-5**	**24,322**
Accts. pay. & accr. liabs	2,223		1,571
Current liabilities	3,201		2,477
Long-term lease liabilities	65		171
Shareholders' equity	18,897		20,895
Non-controlling interest	843		780
Cash from oper. activs	**(1,961)**	**n.a.**	**(2,382)**
Cash from fin. activs	(215)		1,662
Cash from invest. activs	(42)		(566)
Net cash position	**2,205**	**-47**	**4,157**
Capital expenditures	(1,296)		(2,006)
	$		$
Earnings per share*	(0.02)		(0.03)
Cash flow per share*	(0.02)		(0.02)
	shs		shs
No. of shs. o/s*	98,504,571		98,504,571
Avg. no. of shs. o/s*	98,504,571		98,504,571
	%		%
Net profit margin	(14.42)		(31.78)
Return on equity	(8.48)		(12.41)
Return on assets	(6.82)		(11.10)
No. of employees (FTEs)	26		29

* Ordinary
[A] Reported in accordance with IFRS

Historical Summary
(as originally stated)

Fiscal Year	Oper. Rev.	Net Inc. Bef. Disc.	EPS*
	$000s	$000s	$
2023[A]	11,259	(1,624)	(0.02)
2022[A]	8,718	(2,771)	(0.03)
2021[A]	8,803	(1,763)	(0.02)
2020[A]	8,095	(5,595)	(0.05)
2019[A]	6,084	(5,539)	(0.05)

* Ordinary
[A] Reported in accordance with IFRS

C.93 Ceres Global Ag Corp.

Symbol - CRP **Exchange** - TSX **CUSIP** - 156770
Head Office - 701 Xenia Ave S, Suite 400, Minneapolis, MN, United States, 55416 **Telephone** - (952) 746-6802 **Fax** - (952) 746-6819
Website - www.ceresglobalagcorp.com
Email - cpaz@ceresglobalag.com
Investor Relations - Carlos Paz (952) 746-6808
Auditors - Baker Tilly WM LLP C.A., Vancouver, B.C.
Lawyers - Skadden, Arps, Slate, Meagher & Flom LLP; Blake, Cassels & Graydon LLP
Transfer Agents - TSX Trust Company, Toronto, Ont.
FP500 Revenue Ranking - 286
Employees - 192 at June 30, 2022

Profile - (Ont. 2007) Provides procurement, storage, handling, trading, and merchandising of commodity and specialty grains and oilseeds; provides logistic services and transloading for commodities and industrial products; and processes soybeans for meal and oil distribution, blending and producing specialty crops into birdfeed products, and distributing seed products in western Canada.

Operations are organized into three business segments: Grain; Supply Chain; and Seed and Processing.

The **Grain** segment is engaged in the procurement, storage, handling, trading and merchandising of commodity and specialty grains and oilseeds including hard red spring wheat, durum wheat, oats, barley, rye, canola and pulses through 12 grain storage and handling facilities in Minnesota, Saskatchewan, Ontario and Manitoba with a total storage capacity of 30,800,000 bushels. Two of the grain storage facilities are located at deep-water ports in the Great Lakes allowing access to vessels, and another facility is located at the Minnesota River with capacity to load barges for shipment down the Mississippi River to export terminals in New Orleans, combining to provide the company with efficient access to export and import flows of its core grains and oilseed to global markets.

The **Supply Chain** segment utilizes the company's Northgate Logistics Centre facility to provide logistics services, storage and transloading for commodities and industrial products. Northgate sits on 1,300 acres of land in Northgate, Sask., which is designed to utilize two rail loops, each capable of handling unit trains up to 120 railcars and three ladder tracks capable of handling up to 65 railcars. Northgate is capable of handling numerous commodities and is connected to the Burlington Northern Santa Fe Railway. The company continues to expand products transloaded at the Northgate facility including but not limited to barite, bentonite, solvents, drilling pipe, lumber, oriented strand board and magnesium chloride.

The **Seed and Processing** segment consists of a soybean crush facility, and seed production and distribution of Ceres Global Seeds brand products under an agreement with **Sevita International Corporation** and **Horizon Seeds Canada Inc.** Operations for this segment are primarily located in Manitoba.

Also holds 50% interest (**Steel Reef Infrastructure Corp.** 50%) in Gateway Energy Terminal for transloading of hydrocarbon products for movement between the U.S. and Canada; 50% interest (**Consolidated Grain and Barge Co.** 50%) in **Savage Riverport, LLC**, which operates a grain handling and storage facility in Savage, Minn.; 50% interest (**Farmer's Cooperative Grain and Seed Association** 50%) in **Farmers Grain, LLC**, which merchandises grain and operates a grain handling and storage facility in Thief River Falls, Minn.; 50% interest in **Berthold Farmers Elevator, LLC**, a grain originator and merchandiser with locations in Berthold and Carpio, N.D.; 25% interest in **Stewart Southern Railway Inc.** (SSR), which operates a 132-km short-line railway extending from Richardson to Stoughton, Sask., that offers a rail car storage program for shippers; and 17% interest in **Canterra Seed Holdings Ltd.**, a Canadian-based seed development company.

In February 2023, the company sold its grain storage and handling facility in Port Colborne, Ont., to **London Agricultural Commodities** for US$4,000,000.

On Oct. 14, 2021, the company entered into a purchase agreement with a vendor to supply equipment for the planned canola crush plant to be located at the company's Northgate, Sask., location. On June 24, 2022, the company suspended the project, and recognized an impairment of US$25,904,000 on the project during fiscal 2022 as a result.

Recent Merger and Acquisition Activity

Status: completed **Announced:** June 20, 2022
Ceres Global Ag Corp. sold its specialty crop blending and bird food packaging facility in Ste. Agathe, Man., along with related inventory and open contracts, for US$6,000,000.

Status: completed **Revised:** June 3, 2022
UPDATE: The transaction was completed. PREVIOUS: Ceres Global Ag Corp., through wholly owned Riverland Ag Corp., agreed to acquire 50% interest in Berthold Farmer Elevator, LLC, a grain originator and merchandiser with locations in Berthold and Carpio, N.D., for US$12,000,000.

Directors - James T. (Jim) Vanasek, chr., Sydney, N.S.W., Australia; Carlos Paz, pres. & CEO, Shorewood, Minn.; Harvey T. Joel, Toronto, Ont.; David Rotenberg, Chicago, Ill.; Harold M. Wolkin, Toronto, Ont.

Other Exec. Officers - Blake Amundson, CFO; Dusty Clevenger, v-p, strategy & bus. devel.; Holly Dammer, v-p, HR; Pat Gathman, v-p, opers.; Jennifer Henderson, v-p, gen. counsel & corp. sec.; James D. Mowbray, v-p & dir., opers.

Capital Stock

	Authorized (shs.)	Outstanding (shs.)[1]
Common	unlimited	31,094,144

[1] At Feb. 13, 2023

Major Shareholder - James T. (Jim) Vanasek held 54.4% interest and Cowan Asset Management Ltd. held 15.6% interest at Sept. 27, 2022.

Price Range - CRP/TSX

Year	Volume	High	Low	Close
2022	911,074	$5.70	$2.12	$2.31
2021	1,047,461	$5.98	$3.81	$5.58
2020	2,003,098	$4.21	$2.22	$4.03
2019	751,571	$4.88	$3.58	$3.69
2018	752,261	$5.16	$3.07	$4.48

Recent Close: $2.29

Capital Stock Changes - During fiscal 2022, 27,752 common shares were issued on exercise of options.

Wholly Owned Subsidiaries

Ceres US Holding Corp., Del.
- 100% int. in **Riverland Ag Corp.**, Del.
  - 50% int. in **Berthold Farmers Elevator, LLC**, Del.
  - 39% int. in **Ceres Global AG Corp Mexico S.A. De C.V.**, Mexico.
  - 50% int. in **Farmers Grain, LLC**, Minn.
  - 100% int. in **Nature's Organic Grist, LLC**, Minn.
  - 50% int. in **Savage Riverport LLC**, Minn.

Delmar Commodities, Ltd., Winkler, Man.

Subsidiaries

61% int. in **Ceres Global AG Corp Mexico S.A. De C.V.**, Mexico.

Investments

17% int. in **Canterra Seeds Holdings, Ltd.**, Canada.
25% int. in **Stewart Southern Railway Inc.**, Canada.

Financial Statistics

Periods ended:	12m June 30/22[A]		12m June 30/21[A]
	US$000s	%Chg	US$000s
Operating revenue	**1,060,941**	**+42**	**748,204**
Cost of sales	998,692		717,242
General & admin expense	31,316		15,402
Operating expense	**1,048,077**	**+43**	**732,644**
Operating income	**12,864**	**-17**	**15,560**
Deprec., depl. & amort.	7,223		6,957
Finance costs, net	4,965		5,600
Write-downs/write-offs	(25,904)		nil
Pre-tax income	**(2,115)**	**n.a.**	**2,645**
Income taxes	5,906		(9,768)
After-tax income (expense)	(802)		(369)
Net income	**(8,823)**	**n.a.**	**12,044**
Cash & equivalent	17,218		4,214
Inventories	66,541		112,019
Accounts receivable	44,061		38,111
Current assets	189,418		188,528
Long-term investments	26,131		14,933
Fixed assets, net	105,597		114,581
Right-of-use assets	3,083		3,886
Intangibles, net	6,611		6,978
Total assets	**333,948**	**-1**	**338,590**
Bank indebtedness	54,676		80,760
Accts. pay. & accr. liabs	53,197		41,472
Current liabilities	135,361		149,349
Long-term debt, gross	47,506		28,877
Long-term debt, net	45,168		27,557
Long-term lease liabilities	2,659		3,171
Shareholders' equity	149,505		156,918
Cash from oper. activs	**54,462**	**n.a.**	**(25,938)**
Cash from fin. activs	(8,160)		47,485
Cash from invest. activs	(33,298)		(18,029)
Net cash position	**17,218**	**+309**	**4,214**
Capital expenditures	(3,208)		(9,616)
Capital disposals	6,179		59
	US$		US$
Earnings per share*	(0.29)		0.39
Cash flow per share*	1.77		(0.84)
	shs		shs
No. of shs. o/s*	30,800,597		30,772,845
Avg. no. of shs. o/s*	30,793,602		30,772,845
	%		%
Net profit margin	(0.83)		1.61
Return on equity	(5.76)		7.98
Return on assets	(2.62)		4.06
No. of employees (FTEs)	192		193

* Common
[A] Reported in accordance with IFRS

Note: Total revenue includes realized and unrealized gains (losses).

Latest Results

Periods ended:	6m Dec. 31/22[A]		6m Dec. 31/21[A]
	US$000s	%Chg	US$000s
Operating revenue	543,139	+6	513,166
Net income	(4,855)	n.a.	12,802
	US$		US$
Earnings per share*	(0.16)		0.42

* Common
[A] Reported in accordance with IFRS

Historical Summary
(as originally stated)

Fiscal Year	Oper. Rev.	Net Inc. Bef. Disc.	EPS*
	US$000s	US$000s	US$
2022[A]	1,060,941	(8,823)	(0.29)
2021[A]	748,204	12,044	0.39
2020[A]	581,713	4,337	0.14
2019[A]	438,396	(16,871)	(0.60)
2018[A]	411,122	(556)	(0.02)

* Common
[A] Reported in accordance with IFRS

C.94 Ceridian HCM Holding Inc.

Symbol - CDAY **Exchange** - TSX **CUSIP** - 15677J
Head Office - 3311 East Old Shakopee Rd, Minneapolis, MN, United States, 55425 **Telephone** - (952) 853-8100
Website - www.ceridian.com
Email - william.mcdonald@ceridian.com
Investor Relations - William McDonald (844) 829-9499
Auditors - KPMG LLP C.P.A., Minneapolis, Minn.
Lawyers - Goodmans LLP; Weil, Gotshal & Manges LLP
Transfer Agents - TSX Trust Company, Toronto, Ont.; American Stock Transfer & Trust Company, LLC, New York, N.Y.
Employees - 8,526 at Dec. 31, 2022
Profile - (Del. 2013) Offers cloud-based human capital management (HCM) software products.

The company's flagship cloud HCM platform, Dayforce, provides human resources, payroll and tax, benefits, workforce management and talent intelligence functionality. Also offers Powerpay, a cloud human resources and payroll solution for the Canadian small businesses with fewer than 100 employees.

In addition, continues to maintain and update its Bureau solutions, a payroll and payroll-related service using legacy technology. Sales of Bureau solutions to new customers were ceased in 2012 and existing customers continue to be migrated to Dayforce. The company intends to stop actively selling its acquired Bureau payroll solutions to new customers on a stand-alone basis.

Directors - David D. Ossip, chr. & co-CEO, Toronto, Ont.; Leagh E. Turner, co-CEO, Toronto, Ont.; Gerald C. (Gerry) Throop†, Toronto, Ont.; Brent B. Bickett, Nev.; Ronald F. Clarke; Deborah Farrington, New York, N.Y.; Thomas M. Hagerty, Mass.; Linda P. Mantia, Toronto, Ont.; Ganesh B. Rao, Mass.; Andrea S. Rosen, Toronto, Ont.

Other Exec. Officers - Brendan Reid, chief mktg. officer; Chris Armstrong, exec. v-p & COO; Noémie C. Heuland, exec. v-p & CFO; Joe Korngiebel, exec. v-p & chief product & tech. officer; William (Bill) McDonald, exec. v-p, gen. counsel & corp. sec.; Warren Perlman, exec. v-p & chief digital officer; Susan Tohyama, exec. v-p & chief HR officer; Erik Zimmer, exec. v-p & head, M&A; Justine Janssen, sr. v-p, strategic initiatives; Wendy Muirhead, v-p, Ceridian Europe; Steve Holdridge, pres., cust. & revenue opers.

† Lead director

Capital Stock

	Authorized (shs.)	Outstanding (shs.)[1]	Par
Preferred	10,000,000	nil	US$0.01
Common	500,000,000	152,696,838	US$0.01

[1] At Mar. 1, 2023

Major Shareholder - T. Rowe Price Associates, Inc. held 15.4% interest, George S. Leoning held 11.9% interest and The Vanguard Group, Inc. held 10.9% interest at Mar. 1, 2023.

Price Range - CDAY/TSX

Year	Volume	High	Low	Close
2022	5,263,358	$132.14	$56.00	$86.77
2021	3,415,484	$161.59	$97.82	$132.21
2020	5,615,382	$143.47	$55.08	$135.82
2019	2,661,163	$89.33	$45.08	$88.09
2018	808,292	$57.61	$37.02	$47.05

Recent Close: $96.96

Capital Stock Changes - During 2022, common shares were issued as follows: 945,571 on exercise of options, 504,586 on vesting of restricted stock units, 243,043 under the employee stock purchase plan and 168,414 on vesting of performance stock units.

Wholly Owned Subsidiaries

ADAM HCM MEXICO, S. de R.L. de C.V., Mexico.
ATI ROW, LLC, Tex.
Ascender Capital (Thailand) Co., Ltd., Thailand.
Ascender Cloud Services Pty Ltd., Australia.
Ascender HCM Asia Pte Ltd., Singapore.
Ascender HCM Australia Pty Ltd., Australia.
Ascender HCM Holdings Pty Ltd., Australia.
Ascender HCM Malaysia Sdn. Bhd., Malaysia.
Ascender HCM New Zealand Limited, New Zealand.
Ascender HCM PS Pty Ltd., Australia.
Ascender HCM Pty Limited, Australia.
Ascender HK Limited, Hong Kong, People's Republic of China.
Ascender India Private Limited, India.
Ascender Japan KK, Japan.
Ascender Korea Limited, South Korea.
Ascender PST Pty Ltd., Australia.
Ascender Pay ANZ Pty Ltd., Australia.
Ascender Pay Pty Ltd., Australia.
Ascender PeopleStreme Australia Pty Ltd., Australia.
Ascender PeopleStreme Pty Ltd., Australia.
Ascender PeopleStreme Software Pty Ltd., Australia.
Ascender (Thailand) Co., Ltd., Thailand.
The Association for Payroll Specialists Pty Ltd., Australia.
Australian Payroll Services Pty Ltd., Australia.
Ceredian Dayforce New Zealand Limited, New Zealand.
Ceridian APJ ACQ Pty Ltd., Australia.
Ceridian APJ Pty Ltd., Australia.
Ceridian Dayforce HK Limited, People's Republic of China.
Ceridian Dayforce Holding (Thailand) Co., Ltd., Thailand.
Ceridian Dayforce Japan K.K., Japan.
Ceridian Dayforce Korea Limited, South Korea.
Ceridian Dayforce Singapore Pte. Ltd., Singapore.
Ceridian Dayforce (Thailand) Co., Ltd., Thailand.
Ceridian Dayforce Vietnam Co. Ltd., Vietnam.
Ceridian HCM, Inc., Del.
- 100% int. in **ABR Properties LLC**, Fla.
- 100% int. in **Ceridian Cares U.S.**, Minn.
- 100% int. in **Ceridian Dayforce Licensing LLC**, Del.
  - 100% int. in **Dayforce Receivables LLC**, Del.
- 100% int. in **Ceridian Global Holding Company Inc.**, Del.
- 100% int. in **Ceridian Global UK Holding Company Limited**, United Kingdom.
  - 100% int. in **Ceridian Australia Pty Ltd.**, Australia.
    - 100% int. in **Ceridian New Zealand Limited**, New Zealand.
    - 100% int. in **Lusworth Holding Pty Ltd.**, Australia.
      - 100% int. in **RITEQ Limited**, United Kingdom.
      - 100% int. in **RITEQ New Zealand Limited**, New Zealand.

- 100% int. in **RITEQ Pty Ltd.**, Australia.
- 100% int. in **Vadelem Pty. Ltd.**, Australia.
- 100% int. in **Ceridian Canada Ltd.**, Markham, Ont.
  - 100% int. in **Ceridian Acquistionco ULC**, B.C.
    - 100% int. in **Ceridian Dayforce Corporation**, Ont.
      - 100% int. in **Ceridian Dayforce Inc.**, Ont.
  - 100% int. in **Ceridian Canada Services Ltd.**, Canada.
  - 100% int. in **Ceridian Cares**, Canada.
- 100% int. in **Ceridian Dayforce Germany GmbH**, Germany.
- 100% int. in **Ceridian Dayforce Ireland Limited**, Ireland.
- 100% int. in **Ceridian Dayforce Mexico, S. de R.L. de C.V.**, Mexico.
- 100% int. in **Ceridian Europe Limited**, United Kingdom.
- 100% int. in **Ceridian Holdings UK Limited**, United Kingdom.
  - 100% int. in **Ceridian (Mauritius) Ltd.**, Mauritius.
    - 100% int. in **Ceridian (Mauritius) Learning Center Ltd.**, Mauritius.
    - 100% int. in **Ceridian (Mauritius) Technology Ltd.**, Mauritius.
- 100% int. in **Excelity Global Solutions Pte. Ltd.**, Singapore.
  - 100% int. in **Excelity Australia Pty. Ltd.**, Australia.
  - 100% int. in **Excelity HCM Solutions Sdn. Bhd.**, Malaysia.
  - 100% int. in **Excelity Philippines, Inc.**, Philippines.
  - 100% int. in **Excelity Singapore Pte. Ltd.**, Singapore.
  - 100% int. in **Payfront Technologies India Private Limited**, India.
  - 100% int. in **Pinfeng (Shanghai) Infomation Technology Co. Ltd.**, People's Republic of China.
    - 100% int. in **Yi Sai (Shanghai) Human Resources Management Co., Ltd.**, People's Republic of China.
- 100% int. in **Dayforce Talent LLC**, Del.

Ceridian National Trust Bank, United States.
Ceridian Services LLC, Del.
Ceridian Tax Service, Inc., Del.
i-Zapp Cebu Corporation, Philippines.
Ideal Canada Talent Systems Employee OpCo Ltd., Canada.
Ideal Canada Talent Systems HoldCo Ltd., Canada.
Ideal US Talent Systems Employee OpCo LLC, Del.
Ideal US Talent Systems Holdco LLC, Del.
iZapper Sdn. Bhd., Malaysia.
NIS Holdings Australia Pty Ltd., Australia.
NIS Operations Australia Pty Ltd., Australia.
Neller Employer Services Pty Ltd., Australia.
05 Systems, Inc., Toronto, Ont.
Pacific Payroll Australia Holdings Pty Ltd., Australia.
Pacific Payroll Finance Pty Ltd., Australia.
Pacific Payroll Holdings Pty Ltd., Australia.
Pacific Payroll Holdings Trust, Australia.
Pacific Payroll International Holdings Pty Ltd., Australia.
Pacific Payroll International Holdings Trust, Australia.
Pacific Payroll International Pty Ltd., Australia.
Pacific Payroll International Trust, Australia.
Pacific Payroll Partners Pty Ltd., Australia.
Pacific Payroll Partners Singapore Pte Ltd., Singapore.
Preceda Holdings Pty Ltd., Australia.
Talent2 HRBPO Corporation, Philippines.
Zapper Philippines BPO Inc., Philippines.
Zapper Services Consultancy (Shanghai) Limited, People's Republic of China.
Zapper (Vietnam) Co., Ltd., Vietnam.

Financial Statistics

Periods ended:	12m Dec. 31/22[A]		12m Dec. 31/21[A]
	US$000s	%Chg	US$000s
Operating revenue	**1,246,200**	**+22**	**1,024,200**
Cost of sales	718,000		591,000
General & admin expense	499,000		417,800
Operating expense	**1,217,000**	**+21**	**1,008,800**
Operating income	**29,200**	**+90**	**15,400**
Deprec., depl. & amort.	55,000		50,900
Finance costs, net	28,600		35,900
Pre-tax income	**(62,900)**	**n.a.**	**(90,300)**
Income taxes	10,500		(14,900)
Net income	**(73,400)**	**n.a.**	**(75,400)**
Cash & equivalent	431,900		367,500
Accounts receivable	180,100		146,300
Current assets	4,894,000		4,144,100
Fixed assets, net	174,900		128,200
Right-of-use assets	24,300		29,400
Intangibles, net	2,561,600		2,656,100
Total assets	**7,917,200**	**+10**	**7,166,200**
Accts. pay. & accr. liabs	78,300		76,400
Current liabilities	4,533,500		3,741,900
Long-term debt, gross	1,221,200		1,132,700
Long-term debt, net	1,213,400		1,124,400
Long-term lease liabilities	23,700		32,700
Shareholders' equity	2,109,400		2,227,500
Cash from oper. activs	**132,600**	**+172**	**48,800**
Cash from fin. activs	870,100		407,500
Cash from invest. activs	(342,500)		(711,100)
Net cash position	**2,604,900**	**+33**	**1,952,800**
Capital expenditures	(20,200)		(11,500)
Capital disposals	nil		37,900
	US$		US$
Earnings per share*	(0.48)		(0.50)
Cash flow per share*	0.87		0.32
	shs		shs
No. of shs. o/s*	153,856,645		151,995,031
Avg. no. of shs. o/s*	152,940,299		150,402,321
	%		%
Net profit margin	(5.89)		(7.36)
Return on equity	(3.38)		(3.49)
Return on assets	(0.97)		(1.09)
Foreign sales percent	77		75
No. of employees (FTEs)	8,526		7,462

* Common
[A] Reported in accordance with U.S. GAAP

Historical Summary
(as originally stated)

Fiscal Year	Oper. Rev.	Net Inc. Bef. Disc.	EPS*
	US$000s	US$000s	US$
2022[A]	1,246,200	(73,400)	(0.48)
2021[A]	1,024,200	(75,400)	(0.50)
2020[A]	842,500	(4,000)	(0.03)
2019[A]	824,100	78,700	0.55
2018[A]	746,400	(38,100)	(0.33)

* Common
[A] Reported in accordance with U.S. GAAP

C.95 Cerrado Gold Inc.

Symbol - CERT **Exchange** - TSX-VEN **CUSIP** - 156788
Head Office - 3205-200 Bay St, Toronto, ON, M5J 2J2 **Telephone** - (647) 796-0023
Website - www.cerradogold.com
Email - mmcallister@cerradogold.com
Investor Relations - Michael McAllister (647) 805-5662
Auditors - KPMG LLP C.A., Toronto, Ont.
Transfer Agents - TSX Trust Company, Toronto, Ont.
FP500 Revenue Ranking - 765

Profile - (Ont. 2018) Has gold interests in Argentina, Brazil and Quebec.

In Argentina, holds Minera Don Nicolás (MDN) gold-silver project, 333,400 hectares, 2,000 km south of Buenos Aires, which includes producing MDN open-pit gold-silver mine, Las Calandrias heap leach project, and a 1,000-tonne-per-day carbon-in-leach (CIL) gold recovery plant, targeted to produce 50,000 to 90,000 oz. gold doré per year. Operations at the MDN mine are focused on two mining areas, La Paloma and Martinetas, with material processed at a central plant facility. At Aug. 31, 2020, measured and indicated resource at MDN mine was 1,126,200 tonnes grading 5.49 g/t gold and 8.37 g/t silver. Construction of the Martinetas heap leach project was expected to commence in late 2023, with production expected in 2024. At October 2018, indicated resources at Las Calandrias were as follows: 7,424,000 tonnes grading 1.33 g/t gold and 24.65 g/t silver at Calandria Sur deposit (within constraining shell); 604,000 tonnes grading 3.12 g/t gold and 8.20 g/t silver at Calandria Norte deposit (within constraining shell); and 131,000 tonnes grading 2.82 g/t gold and 6.30 g/t silver at Calandria Norte deposit (below constraining shell). Construction of the Las Calandrias heap leach project was completed during the first quarter of 2023, with first gold pour completed in early July 2023. Also holds Michelle gold-silver property, 37,400 hectares, 90 km southwest of Martinetas mining area; and adjacent Los Cisnes gold-silver property, Santa Cruz province.

In Brazil, holds Monte do Carmo gold project, 82,541 hectares, 39 km east of Porto Nacional, including Serra Alta and Gogo Da Onca deposits. An updated preliminary economic assessment released in September 2021 proposed an open-pit operation with an average annual production of 131,000 oz. of gold over a 8-year mine life. Initial capital costs were estimated at US$126,000,000. At July 2021, indicated resource at Serra Alta deposit was 9,108,000 tonnes grading 1.85 g/t gold. Construction was expected to commence in the fourth quarter of 2023, with production targeted in the second quarter of 2025.

In Quebec, holds Mont Sorcier vanadium-iron-titanium prospect, 3,196 hectares, 18 km east of Chibougamau, including option to acquire additional 24 claims, requiring payment of $1,000,0000 over five years from December 2026 to 2031. An updated preliminary economic assessment released in July 2022 for Mont Sorcier proposed an open-pit mine with an annual production of 5,000,000 tonnes of iron over a 21-year mine life. Initial capital costs were estimated at US$574,000,000. At June 2022, indicated resource was 678,500,000 tonnes grading 25.5% iron.

In March 2023, the company entered into an amended and restated metals purchase and sale agreement with **Sprott Private Resource Streaming and Royalty (Collector), LP**, to include the concessions acquired by the company in its acquisition of **Minera Mariana Argentina S.A.** in 2020, broadening the stream area including production from the Las Calandrias heap leach project. Under the agreement, Sprott would provide an additional US$10,000,000 in funding, which was an increase from the original amount of US$15,000,000, in the form of an additional deposit against future production, and the step-down trigger was increased to 29,500 gold equivalent oz. from 21,500 gold equivalent oz.

In March 2022, the company entered into a gold and silver streaming agreement with **Sprott Resource Streaming and Royalty Corp.** for its Monte do Carmo gold project in Brazil for US$20,000,000. Under the agreement, the company would sell and deliver to Sprott 2.25% of all gold and silver produced from the project, of which the company has the ability to buy back 50% of the stream for up to US$13,500,000.

Periods ended:	12m Dec. 31/22	12m Dec. 31/21
Tonnes mined	375,140	411,640
Gold prod., oz	52,504	42,267
Gold sales, oz	50,668	38,839
Avg real. gold price, US$/oz	1,742	1,747
Gold cash cost, US$/oz	1,192	1,247
Silver prod., oz	95,803	94,092
Silver sales, oz	95,795	88,093

Recent Merger and Acquisition Activity

Status: completed **Revised:** May 31, 2023
UPDATE: The transaction was completed. PREVIOUS: Cerrado Gold Inc. agreed to acquire Voyager Metals Inc. on the basis of 0.1667 Cerrado common share for each Voyager common share held. The exchange ratio implies a consideration value of Cdn$0.1523 per Voyager common share. Voyager's key asset is the Mont Sorcier iron-vanadium prospect in Quebec. A private placement of common shares for proceeds of up to Cdn$4,725,000 would be completed by Voyager prior to closing, with Cerrado subscribing for $3,700,000 of the shares. Mar. 15, 2023 - Cerrado acquired 24,294,156 Voyager common shares via private placement, giving it a 19.6% ownership interest.

Predecessor Detail - Name changed from BB1 Acquisition Corp., Feb. 22, 2021, pursuant to the Qualifying Transaction reverse takeover acquisition of (old) Cerrado Gold Inc. and concurrent amalgamation of (old) Cerrado with wholly owned 2787735 Ontario Inc., with (old) Cerrado then immediately amalgamated into the company.; basis 1 new for 8.31 old shs.

Directors - Mark P. Brennan, chr. & CEO, Toronto, Ont.; Kurt Menchen, pres., Brazilian opers., Candeleria, Brazil; Maria V. Anzola, Oakville, Ont.; Robert A. (Andy) Campbell, Burlington, Ont.; Christopher B. (Chris) Jones, Toronto, Ont.; Elmer P. Salomao, Brasilia, Brazil; Jad Salomão, Brazil; Robert M. (Bob) Sellars, Oakville, Ont.

Other Exec. Officers - Clifford (Cliff) Hale-Sanders, pres.; Casper Groenewald, COO; Jason J. Brooks, CFO; Mauricio Coletti, chief min. engineer; Mauro De Silva, chief processing engineer; Clinton Swemmer, chief technical officer; David Ball, v-p, bus. devel.; Carl Calandra, v-p, gen. counsel & corp. sec.; Dr. Sergio Gelcich, v-p, explor.; Michael (Mike) McAllister, v-p, IR; Alonso Sotomayor, contr.; Veronica Nohara, pres., Argentina opers.

Capital Stock

	Authorized (shs.)	Outstanding (shs.)[1]
Common	unlimited	97,088,992

[1] At June 12, 2023.

Major Shareholder - Monte Sinai Mineração Ltda. held 11.93% interest at June 12, 2023.

Price Range - CERT/TSX-VEN

Year	Volume	High	Low	Close
2022	19,119,422	$1.96	$0.69	$0.88
2021	23,284,176	$1.89	$0.93	$1.41
2020	3,670	$0.83	$0.42	$0.42

Consolidation: 1-for-8.31 cons. in Feb. 2021
Recent Close: $0.62

Capital Stock Changes - On May 31, 2023, 16,618,000 common shares were issued pursuant to acquisition of Voyager Metals Inc.

During 2022, common shares were issued as follows: 1,632,809 on vesting of restricted share units, 265,112 on exercise of warrants and 250,000 on vesting of deferred share unit plan.

Dividends

CERT com N.S.R.
1-for-8 cons eff. Feb. 25, 2021
stk.[1] .... Aug. 31/22
Paid in 2023: n.a. 2022: stk. 2021: n.a.

[1] Stk. divd. of 0.57413 PlantExt Ltd units for ea. 1 sh. held. Each unit is comprised of 1 PlantExt com. sh. and 1 PlantExt sh. pur. wt. The Dividend will be paid upon the earlier of either (i) PlantEx completing a going public transaction, or (ii) August 31, 2022.

Wholly Owned Subsidiaries

Minera Don Nicolás S.A., Argentina.
Minera Mariana Argentina S.A., Argentina.
Serra Alta Participações Imobiliarias S.A., Brazil.
Sierra Alta Mineração Ltda., Brazil.
Voyager Metals Inc., Toronto, Ont.

Financial Statistics

Periods ended:	12m Dec. 31/22[A]		12m Dec. 31/21[□A]
	US$000s	%Chg	US$000s
Operating revenue	**80,924**	**+29**	**62,659**
Cost of sales	53,070		43,234
Salaries & benefits	2,428		2,534
General & admin expense	2,621		2,703
Stock-based compensation	2,823		3,338
Other operating expense	1,326		2,490
Operating expense	**62,268**	**+15**	**54,299**
Operating income	**18,656**	**+123**	**8,360**
Deprec., depl. & amort.	8,477		5,767
Finance income	463		148
Finance costs, gross	8,559		6,277
Pre-tax income	**(818)**	**n.a.**	**(4,697)**
Income taxes	5,090		1,602
Net income	**(5,908)**	**n.a.**	**(6,299)**
Cash & equivalent	7,364		1,755
Inventories	9,099		8,726
Accounts receivable	8,502		9,166
Current assets	66,695		46,017
Long-term investments	704		658
Fixed assets, net	38,158		31,685
Explor./devel. properties	44,861		26,692
Total assets	**162,646**	**+48**	**109,813**
Accts. pay. & accr. liabs	19,861		21,900
Current liabilities	78,333		59,560
Long-term debt, gross	13,093		1,986
Long-term debt, net	7,032		1,295
Shareholders' equity	13,354		15,122
Cash from oper. activs	**15,198**	**+126**	**6,723**
Cash from fin. activs	25,290		9,596
Cash from invest. activs	(36,109)		(21,156)
Net cash position	**5,921**	**+243**	**1,726**
Capital expenditures	(26,185)		(14,305)
	US$		US$
Earnings per share*	(0.08)		(0.09)
Cash flow per share*	0.20		0.10
	shs		shs
No. of shs. o/s*	78,628,660		76,480,739
Avg. no. of shs. o/s*	77,521,216		69,933,771
	%		%
Net profit margin	(7.30)		(10.05)
Return on equity	(41.49)		(65.33)
Return on assets	41.04		2.39
Foreign sales percent	100		100

* Common
□ Restated
[A] Reported in accordance with IFRS

Latest Results

Periods ended:	3m Mar. 31/23[A]		3m Mar. 31/22[A]
	US$000s	%Chg	US$000s
Operating revenue	24,439	0	24,474
Net income	(7,438)	n.a.	3,352
	US$		US$
Earnings per share*	(0.09)		0.04

* Common
[A] Reported in accordance with IFRS

Historical Summary
(as originally stated)

Fiscal Year	Oper. Rev. US$000s	Net Inc. Bef. Disc. US$000s	EPS* US$
2022[A]	80,924	(5,908)	(0.08)
2021[A1]	62,659	(6,299)	(0.09)
2020[A2]	28,100	(12,569)	(0.28)
2019[A]	nil	(2,895)	(0.07)
2018[A]	nil	(1,578)	(0.08)

* Common
[A] Reported in accordance with IFRS
[1] Results reflect the Feb. 22, 2021, Qualifying Transaction reverse takeover acquisition of (old) Cerrado Gold Inc.
[2] Results for 2020 and prior periods pertain to (old) Cerrado Gold Inc.
Note: Adjusted throughout for 1-for-8.31 cons. in Feb. 2021

C.96 Certive Solutions Inc.

Symbol - CBP **Exchange** - CSE **CUSIP** - 15707X
Head Office - 8149 N. 87 Place, Scottsdale, AZ, United States, 85258 **Toll-free** - (877) 698-2858
Email - sthomas@certive.com
Investor Relations - Scott Thomas (480) 922-5327
Auditors - Davidson & Company LLP C.A., Vancouver, B.C.
Bankers - Bank of Montreal, Vancouver, B.C.
Transfer Agents - Computershare Trust Company of Canada Inc., Toronto, Ont.

Profile - (B.C. 2010) Provides cloud-based business process management solutions with a focus on revenue cycle management and cybersecurity in the United States healthcare industry.

Wholly owned **Certive Health Inc.** provides revenue cycle services which assist hospitals with the reimbursement process and improve their financial and quality performance by using proprietary workflow document management and analytics tools including lost charge recovery services, diagnosis related groups accuracy reviews and chart review solutions. Also offers a suite of cyber security products which allow health care providers to protect their networks, data and patients from malicious agents and aggressors.

Common reinstated on CSE, Jan. 13, 2023.
Common suspended from CSE, Oct. 6, 2022.

Predecessor Detail - Name changed from VisualVault Corporation, Oct. 1, 2013; basis 1 new for 2 old shs.

Directors - Thomas (Tom) Marreel, chr. & CEO, Chandler, Ariz.; Timothy (Tim) Hyland, CFO & treas., Scottsdale, Ariz.; Scott Thomas, v-p, IR, Tempe, Ariz.; Sheila Schweitzer, Vero Beach, Fla.; Jeff Wareham, Goderich, Ont.

Other Exec. Officers - Brian Diver, COO; Michael J. Miller, chief legal officer & corp. sec.; Van H. Potter, chief mktg. officer; Timothy Tolchin, chief growth officer; Michael Groeger, v-p, sales; Ann Fierro, pres., Omega Technology Solutions Inc.

Capital Stock

	Authorized (shs.)	Outstanding (shs.)[1]
Preferred	unlimited	nil
Common	unlimited	159,827,576

[1] At Dec. 21, 2022

Major Shareholder - Widely held at Sept. 3, 2021.

Price Range - CBP/CSE

Year	Volume	High	Low	Close
2022	2,008,281	$0.10	$0.04	$0.05
2021	8,327,775	$0.17	$0.04	$0.07
2020	2,213,816	$0.07	$0.03	$0.04
2019	4,292,882	$0.06	$0.02	$0.06
2018	9,372,109	$0.12	$0.01	$0.03

Recent Close: $0.02

Capital Stock Changes - During fiscal 2022, 15,019,341 common shares were issued on conversion of debt.

Wholly Owned Subsidiaries

Advantive Information Systems Inc., Ariz. Inactive.
Certive Health Inc., Scottsdale, Ariz.
- 100% int. in **Certive Health Compliance Solutions Inc.**, Ariz.
- 100% int. in **Certive Health Revenue Solutions Inc.**, Ariz.

Financial Statistics

Periods ended:	12m May 31/22[A]		12m May 31/21[□A]
	US$000s	%Chg	US$000s
Operating revenue	**1,201**	**-32**	**1,756**
Cost of sales	1,406		1,611
Salaries & benefits	946		796
General & admin expense	646		424
Stock-based compensation	299		9
Operating expense	**3,297**	**+16**	**2,831**
Operating income	**(2,096)**	**n.a.**	**(1,075)**
Deprec., depl. & amort.	78		84
Finance costs, gross	894		768
Write-downs/write-offs	(85)		(229)
Pre-tax income	**(2,479)**	**n.a.**	**(2,043)**
Net income	**(2,479)**	**n.a.**	**(2,043)**
Cash & equivalent	13		39
Accounts receivable	202		404
Current assets	605		483
Intangibles, net	53		131
Total assets	**748**	**+5**	**710**
Bank indebtedness	808		916
Accts. pay. & accr. liabs	3,871		2,618
Current liabilities	9,463		8,302
Long-term debt, gross	5,028		4,687
Long-term debt, net	243		150
Equity portion of conv. debs	881		619
Shareholders' equity	(8,958)		(7,742)
Cash from oper. activs	**(1,363)**	**n.a.**	**(1,182)**
Cash from fin. activs	1,248		1,144
Cash from invest. activs	5		10
Net cash position	**10**	**+400**	**2**
	US$		US$
Earnings per share*	(0.01)		(0.01)
Cash flow per share*	(0.01)		(0.01)
	shs		shs
No. of shs. o/s*	159,424,033		144,404,692
Avg. no. of shs. o/s*	146,168,102		139,701,472
	%		%
Net profit margin	(206.41)		(116.34)
Return on equity	n.m.		n.m.
Return on assets	(217.42)		(160.38)

* Common
□ Restated
[A] Reported in accordance with IFRS

Latest Results

Periods ended:	3m Aug. 31/22[A]		3m Aug. 31/21[A]
	US$000s	%Chg	US$000s
Operating revenue	303	+15	264
Net income	(573)	n.a.	(524)
	US$		US$
Earnings per share*	(0.00)		(0.00)

* Common
[A] Reported in accordance with IFRS

Historical Summary
(as originally stated)

Fiscal Year	Oper. Rev. US$000s	Net Inc. Bef. Disc. US$000s	EPS* US$
2022[A]	1,201	(2,479)	(0.01)
2021[A]	1,756	(2,043)	(0.01)
2020[A]	1,406	(2,000)	(0.02)
2019[A]	1,110	(1,110)	(0.01)
2018[A]	1,436	(5,164)	(0.07)

* Common
[A] Reported in accordance with IFRS

C.97 Chalice Brands Ltd.

Symbol - CHAL **Exchange** - CSE (S) **CUSIP** - 15756R
Head Office - 13315 NE Airport Way, Suite 700, Portland, OR, United States, 97230 **Telephone** - (503) 384-2141
Website - chalicebrandsltd.com
Email - ir@chalicebrandsltd.com
Investor Relations - Jeffrey B. Yapp (971) 371-2685
Auditors - M&K CPAS, PLLC C.P.A., Houston, Tex.
Transfer Agents - Odyssey Trust Company, Vancouver, B.C.

Profile - (Ont. 2015; orig. B.C., 2011) Cultivates, produces and distributes cannabis products in Oregon, California, Nevada and Washington.

Operations include retail; production, supply chain and wholesale; and cultivation.

Retail - Owns and operates 16 retail dispensaries in Oregon, six of which operate under the flagship Chalice Farms brand, one under the Left Coast Connections brand, five under the Homegrown Oregon brand and four under the Cannabliss & Co. brand.

Production, supply chain and wholesale - Produces branded products through its owned production facilities in Oregon and through manufacturing agreements in other states. Primary products include distillate vaporizer cartridges under the Private Stash™ brand; high dosage single serve fruit chew blast product under the Golden™ and Chalice™ brands; ethanol extract products under the RXO brand; and live resin and distillate vaporizer cartridge under the Elysium fields brand. In addition, manufactures oil products which are sold under the Chalice™, Golden™, Private Stash™, Elysium Fields™ and Jackpot™ brands. Products are sold in licensed dispensaries throughout Oregon, as well as in several dispensaries in Nevada and California. Also distributes the RSO Go+™ brand of ethanol extract products in Washington through its royalty and consulting agreements with its contract manufacturer.

Cultivation - Operates a 10,000-sq.ft. greenhouse facility (Bald Peak) in Yamhill cty., Ore., that has an annual capacity of over 2,000 lbs. of dry cannabis flower.

Wholly owned **Tozmoz, LLC** offers multiple extraction processes including CO_2, hydrocarbon and ethanol, and both short path and wiped film distillation and also provides product manufacturing and formulation, as well as packaging services.

Subsidiary **Fifth & Root, Inc.** offers CBD skincare products which omits toxins and irritants including toxic chemicals, synthetics, GMO's, parabens, phthalates, harsh preservatives, skin-stripping sulfates and animal byproducts.

On May 23, 2023, the company obtained an order from the Ontario Superior Court of Justice granting protection under the Companies' Creditors Arrangement Act (CCAA), as well as commenced a process in the Circuit Court of the State of Oregon for an order granting the appointment of an Oregon state receiver over certain of the company's subsidiaries.

In September 2022, the company terminated the proposed acquisitions of two retail stores in Bend and Corvallis, Ore., from **Miracle Greens, Inc.** for US$2,063,999; and two outdoor cultivation assets in Grants Pass, Ore., from **Totem Farms, LLC** for US$563,587.

On July 5, 2022, the company acquired **Acreage Holdings, Inc.**'s four Oregon retail dispensaries branded as Cannabliss & Co. for US$6,200,000, consisting of US$350,000 cash and issuance of a US$5,850,000 promissory note. The acquisition increased the company's retail dispensaries in Oregon from 12 to 16.

Common suspended from CSE, May 9, 2022.

Predecessor Detail - Name changed from Golden Leaf Holdings Ltd., May 25, 2021; basis 1 new for 23 old shs.

Directors - Jeffrey B. (Jeff) Yapp, pres. & CEO, Ore.; Karl R. (Rick) Miller Jr.†, Ore.; Larry H. Martin, N.Y.; Scott Lawrence Secord, Toronto, Ont.; Gary Zipfel, Ill.

Other Exec. Officers - Meghan Miller, COO; John Ford, chief revenue officer; Ginger Mollo, chief integration officer & gen. mgr., Fifth & Root; Karen Morgan, chief mktg. officer; Jane Sullivan, chief people officer; Joel Klobas, v-p, prod.; John Magliana, gen. counsel

† Lead director

Capital Stock

	Authorized (shs.)	Outstanding (shs.)[1]
Common	unlimited	84,415,725

[1] At Oct. 19, 2022

Major Shareholder - Widely held at Oct. 19, 2022.

Price Range - CHAL/CSE (S)

Year	Volume	High	Low	Close
2022	4,717,622	$0.64	$0.22	$0.23
2021	31,644,434	$2.53	$0.32	$0.37
2020	12,240,208	$0.81	$0.23	$0.58
2019	13,187,344	$4.72	$0.35	$0.46
2018	37,783,920	$14.95	$2.07	$3.11

Consolidation: 1-for-23 cons. in May 2021

Wholly Owned Subsidiaries

CF Greenpoint CA, Inc., Calif.
CF US Franchising Inc., Ore. Inactive.
CFA Retail LLC, Ore.
Greenpoint CBD, LLC, Nevada City, Calif.
Greenpoint Equipment Leasing, LLC, Ore.
Greenpoint Holdings Delaware, Inc., Del.
- 100% int. in **GL Management, Inc.**, Nev.
- 100% int. in **Greenpoint Oregon, Inc.**, Ore.
- 100% int. in **Greenpoint Real Estate LLC**, Ore.

Greenpoint Nevada Inc., Nev.
Greenpoint Workforce, Inc., Ore.
SMS Ventures, LLC, Ore. dba Homegrown Oregon.
Tozmoz, LLC, Ore.

Subsidiaries

80% int. in **Fifth & Root, Inc.**, California, Md.

C.98 Champion Gaming Group Inc.

Symbol - WAGR **Exchange** - TSX-VEN **CUSIP** - 158498
Head Office - 552 E Market St, Suite 201, Louisville, KY, United States, 40202
Website - championgaming.com
Email - cwickham@championgaming.com
Investor Relations - Cameron Wickham (905) 330-1602
Auditors - DNTW Toronto LLP C.A., Toronto, Ont.
Transfer Agents - TSX Trust Company, Toronto, Ont.

Profile - (Ont. 2004) Provides predictive and prescriptive analytical models and win probability applications and statistics in the sports industry for teams, media, fans and bettors.

Product offerings include: a fully customized probability engine; interactive sports matchup models; spread and over/under distributions; and sports statistics and historical data statistics. Using proprietary algorithms and databases, offers a suite of sports wagering tools, as well as content, news and information, all designed to assist its customers in making educated choices related to their sports wagering activities in an engaging and entertaining manner. Its primary focus has been on building and offering tools centred around the National Football League.

Through wholly owned **EdjSports, LLC**, the company markets and sells its content and subscription-based offerings to consumers and businesses online via its principal websites the www.footballoutsiders.com, www.edjsports.com and www.edjvarsity.com domains. EdjSports' primary focus has been building and offering tools and content centred on the NFL and has been expanding into sports such as such the National Basketball Association (NBA),the Women's National Basketball Association (WNBA), the National Hockey League (NHL), Major League Baseball (MLB), global soccer, professional golf and tennis, motor sports and combat sports.

Predecessor Detail - Name changed from Prime City One Capital Corp., Nov. 30, 2021, pursuant to the reverse takeover acquisition of Champion Gaming Inc.; basis 1 new for 4 old shs.

Directors - Kenneth Hershman, co-founder & v-chr., N.Y.; J. Graham Simmonds, CEO, Toronto, Ont.; Cameron Wickham, interim CFO & interim corp. sec., Collingwood, Ont.; Ishwara Glassman Chrein; David Lubotta, Toronto, Ont.; Sean O'Leary, Ky.

Other Exec. Officers - Casey Ramage, chief mktg. officer

Capital Stock

	Authorized (shs.)	Outstanding (shs.)[1]
Common	unlimited	72,245,840

[1] At June 30, 2023

Major Shareholder - EdjSports, Inc. held 19.28% interest at Dec. 2, 2021.

Price Range - WAGR/TSX-VEN

Year	Volume	High	Low	Close
2022	4,939,458	$0.34	$0.07	$0.08
2021	2,745,415	$0.41	$0.25	$0.26
2020	30,775	$0.30	$0.10	$0.26
2019	162,007	$0.44	$0.12	$0.16
2018	204,309	$0.50	$0.10	$0.16

Consolidation: 1-for-4 cons. in Dec. 2021
Recent Close: $0.09

Capital Stock Changes - In December 2023, private placement of 4,100,000 units (1 common share & 1 warrant) at $0.075 per unit was completed. Also during 2022, 1,600,00 common shares were issued for debt settlement.

Wholly Owned Subsidiaries

Champion Gaming Inc., Toronto, Ont.
- 100% int. in **Champion Gaming USA Inc.**, Nev.
  - 100% int. in **EdjSports, LLC**, Ky.

Financial Statistics

Periods ended:	12m Dec. 31/22[A]		12m Dec. 31/21[A1]
	$000s	%Chg	$000s
Operating revenue	**11,335**	**+465**	**2,005**
Salaries & benefits	2,532		3,559
General & admin expense	2,315		3,975
Stock-based compensation	1,779		169
Operating expense	**6,626**	**-14**	**7,703**
Operating income	**4,709**	**n.a.**	**(5,698)**
Deprec., depl. & amort.	196		120
Finance income	nil		1
Finance costs, gross	218		289
Write-downs/write-offs	(483)		nil
Pre-tax income	**(6,162)**	**n.a.**	**(9,129)**
Net income	**(6,162)**	**n.a.**	**(9,129)**
Cash & equivalent	48		967
Accounts receivable	13		25
Current assets	61		1,255
Fixed assets, net	4		74
Right-of-use assets	196		812
Total assets	**261**	**-88**	**2,140**
Bank indebtedness	1,239		756
Accts. pay. & accr. liabs.	1,797		624
Current liabilities	3,638		1,908
Long-term debt, gross	722		nil
Long-term debt, net	722		nil
Long-term lease liabilities	475		641
Shareholders' equity	(4,574)		(409)
Cash from oper. activs.	**(2,039)**	**n.a.**	**(5,190)**
Cash from fin. activs.	1,212		6,126
Cash from invest. activs.	nil		(39)
Net cash position	**48**	**-95**	**967**
Capital expenditures	nil		(39)
	$		$
Earnings per share*	(0.09)		(0.26)
Cash flow per share*	(0.03)		(0.15)
	shs		shs
No. of shs. o/s*	71,645,840		65,945,840
Avg. no. of shs. o/s*	67,189,437		35,152,676
	%		%
Net profit margin	(54.36)		(455.31)
Return on equity	n.m.		n.m.
Return on assets	n.a.		(817.01)

* Cl.A com.
[A] Reported in accordance with IFRS
[1] Results reflect the Nov. 30, 2021, reverse takeover acquisition of Champion Gaming Inc.

Latest Results

Periods ended:	3m Mar. 31/23[A]		3m Mar. 31/22[A]
	$000s	%Chg	$000s
Operating revenue	257	-35	398
Net income	(611)	n.a.	(2,561)
	$		$
Earnings per share*	(0.01)		(0.04)

* Cl.A com.
[A] Reported in accordance with IFRS

Historical Summary
(as originally stated)

Fiscal Year	Oper. Rev.	Net Inc. Bef. Disc.	EPS*
	$000s	$000s	$
2022[A]	11,335	(6,162)	(0.09)
2021[A]	2,005	(9,129)	(0.26)
2020[A1]	nil	(36)	(0.01)
2019[A]	nil	(83)	(0.03)
2018[A]	nil	(160)	(0.17)

* Cl.A com.
[A] Reported in accordance with IFRS
[1] Results for 2020 and prior periods pertain to Prime City Capital Corp.
Note: Adjusted throughout for 1-for-4 cons. in Dec. 2021

C.99 Char Technologies Ltd.

Symbol - YES **Exchange** - TSX-VEN **CUSIP** - 15957L
Head Office - 403-789 Don Mills Rd, Toronto, ON, M3C 1T5
Telephone - (416) 828-2077 **Toll-free** - (866) 521-3654
Website - www.chartechnologies.com
Email - m.korol@chartechnologies.com
Investor Relations - Mark Korol (866) 521-3654
Auditors - Dale Matheson Carr-Hilton LaBonte LLP C.A.
Transfer Agents - TSX Trust Company, Toronto, Ont.

Profile - (Ont. 2013) Develops and commercializes clean technologies and solutions using High Temperature Pyrolysis (HTP). Also offers custom equipment for industrial water treatment and services in environmental compliance, environmental management, site investigation and remediation, engineering and resource efficiency assessment.

Provides modular HTP systems which convert wood-based biomass and organic waste streams such as unaerobic digestion sludge into high value outputs including renewable natural gas, green hydrogen and biocoal by heating the materials at high temperatures in the absence of oxygen. Also offers SulfaCHAR™, a charcoal-like material used to filter hydrogen sulfide (H_2S) from gas streams. The passive system directs untreated biogas, landfill gas and odour through a vessel containing SulfaCHAR™ media, which absorbs H_2S onto its surface and clean biogas and odour-free air exits the system; and CleanFyre™, a carbon-neutral and sustainable biofuel which offers similar chemical composition of coal. In addition, provides property diligence and remediation; and compliance and permitting services to a wide range of manufacturing sectors across Ontario and elsewhere in Canada, including the food and beverage, steel processing, natural resources, electronics, automotive and aerospace sectors, to help clients meet their environmental, social and governance targets and improve compliance while reducing risks.

In December 2022, the company received $11,300,000 of investment from the Government of Canada and Ontario for the expansion of the facility in Thorold, Ont., to produce renewable natural gas and biocarbon.

Predecessor Detail - Name changed from Cleantech Capital Inc., Mar. 31, 2016, following Qualifying Transaction reverse takeover acquisition of Char Technologies Inc.

Directors - William B. (Bill) White, chr., Palm Coast, Fla.; Hugh Cleland, Oakville, Ont.; Nik Nanos, Ont.; James J. Sbrolla, Toronto, Ont.; Anton Szpitalak

Other Exec. Officers - Andrew White, CEO & corp. sec.; John Nicholson, pres.; Robert Sinyard, COO; Mark Korol, CFO; Lewis Smith, chief comml. officer; Ken Goodboy, v-p, pyrolysis R&D

Capital Stock

	Authorized (shs.)	Outstanding (shs.)[1]
Common	unlimited	88,140,737

[1] At May 29, 2023

Major Shareholder - Widely held at Feb. 21, 2023.

Price Range - YES/TSX-VEN

Year	Volume	High	Low	Close
2022	10,345,154	$0.75	$0.24	$0.38
2021	17,399,738	$1.15	$0.30	$0.72
2020	4,652,418	$0.40	$0.05	$0.33
2019	1,313,100	$0.22	$0.08	$0.15
2018	1,084,876	$0.27	$0.15	$0.19

Recent Close: $0.57

Capital Stock Changes - In March 2022, private placement of 10,877,514 units (1 common share & ½ warrant) at 45¢ per unit was completed. Also during fiscal 2022, common shares were issued as follows: 556,000 on exercise of options and 63,900 on exercise of warrants.

Wholly Owned Subsidiaries

Altech Environmental Consulting Ltd. dba CharTech Solutions.
Char Biocarbon Inc., Toronto, Ont.
Char Technologies Thorold Inc., Canada.
Char Technologies (USA) LLC, Del.

Financial Statistics

Periods ended:	12m Sept. 30/22^A		12m Sept. 30/21^A
	$000s	%Chg	$000s
Operating revenue	**1,459**	**+6**	**1,378**
Cost of sales	817		669
Research & devel. expense	660		242
General & admin expense	4,182		2,076
Stock-based compensation	1,341		1,006
Operating expense	**7,000**	**+75**	**3,993**
Operating income	**(5,541)**	**n.a.**	**(2,615)**
Deprec., depl. & amort.	1,804		845
Write-downs/write-offs	nil		(264)
Pre-tax income	**(6,904)**	**n.a.**	**(3,262)**
Net income	**(6,904)**	**n.a.**	**(3,262)**
Cash & equivalent	460		3,001
Inventories	324		270
Accounts receivable	1,192		693
Current assets	2,206		4,248
Fixed assets, net	3,773		1,388
Right-of-use assets	44		96
Intangibles, net	3,927		4,591
Total assets	**9,949**	**-4**	**10,323**
Accts. pay. & accr. liabs	3,093		3,275
Current liabilities	4,417		3,898
Long-term debt, gross	838		206
Long-term debt, net	210		203
Long-term lease liabilities	15		55
Shareholders' equity	4,698		5,544
Cash from oper. activs	**(5,032)**	**n.a.**	**(2,207)**
Cash from fin. activs	5,282		6,627
Cash from invest. activs	(2,790)		(1,548)
Net cash position	**460**	**-85**	**3,001**
Capital expenditures	(2,783)		(716)
	$		$
Earnings per share*	(0.09)		(0.05)
Cash flow per share*	(0.06)		(0.03)
	shs		shs
No. of shs. o/s*	83,003,165		71,505,751
Avg. no. of shs. o/s*	77,860,982		63,984,821
	%		%
Net profit margin	(473.20)		(236.72)
Return on equity	(134.82)		(95.21)
Return on assets	(68.11)		(47.51)

* Common
^A Reported in accordance with IFRS

Latest Results

Periods ended:	6m Mar. 31/23^A		6m Mar. 31/22^A
	$000s	%Chg	$000s
Operating revenue	901	+17	773
Net income	(3,134)	n.a.	(3,294)
	$		$
Earnings per share*	(0.03)		(0.04)

* Common
^A Reported in accordance with IFRS

Historical Summary
(as originally stated)

Fiscal Year	Oper. Rev.	Net Inc. Bef. Disc.	EPS*
	$000s	$000s	$
2022^A	1,459	(6,904)	(0.09)
2021^A	1,378	(3,262)	(0.05)
2020^A	1,760	(704)	(0.02)
2019^A	1,623	(821)	(0.02)
2018^A	1,042	(1,392)	(0.03)

* Common
^A Reported in accordance with IFRS

C.100 Charbone Hydrogen Corporation

Symbol - CH **Exchange** - TSX-VEN **CUSIP** - 15956X
Head Office - 1080-5005 boul Lapinièr, Brossard, QC, J4Z 0N5 **Telephone** - (450) 678-7171
Website - www.charbone.com/en/accueil
Email - bv@charbone.com
Investor Relations - Benoit Veilleux (450) 678-7171
Auditors - KPMG LLP C.A., Montréal, Qué.
Transfer Agents - TSX Trust Company, Montréal, Qué.

Profile - (Can. 2018) Plans to produce and distribute green hydrogen using water and hydropower, as well as acquires, owns and operates small-scale hydroelectric power generation plants in North America.

Developing a 0.5-MW hydrogen facility on 36,296 m² of land in Sorel-Tracy, Que. The Sorel-Tracy facility is expected to commence production at the beginning of 2023. A plan to develop another hydrogen production facility in Manitoba is underway. The company intends to generate green hydrogen through electrolysis using water and energy generated from its own hydropower plants, ensuring a sustainable and dependable energy source.

Acquires existing hydroelectric power plants ranging from 0.25MW to 25 MW in targeted markets where there is a strong demand for renewable energy and a need for base load power supply. Also acquires semi-operational and non-operational hydroelectric plants that the company optimizes or refurbishes, as well as short-term development projects of new power plants. At February 2023, the company owned a 0.2-MW plant in Vermont; a 700-KW plant in Shawano, Wisc.; and 560-KW, 1,200-KW and 1,000-KW plants in Michigan (under agreements to purchase).

In July 2023, the proposed acquisition of all general partner and limited partner interests of **Tower Kleber Limited Partnership** and **Black River Limited Partnership** (collectively, Limited Partnerships) from **Northwoods Hydropower Inc.** for US$3,600,000 was terminated. The private U.S.-based Limited Partnerships own three operating hydroelectric plants in the Onaway area of Michigan, each with a capacity of 560 KW, 1,200 KW and 1,000 KW. The company plans to focus all of its resources on hydrogen.

In December 2022, the company entered into a memorandum of understanding with **Groupe Filgo-Sonic** for mutual cooperation in the development, design, construction and operation of green hydrogen filling stations in Quebec on existing sites owned by Filgo-Sonic. The company would use the expertise of **Resato B.V.** in the manufacturing and installation of filling stations, while Filgo-Sonic would use its expertise in the operation of service stations and refuelling stations for heavy vehicles. Previously, the company entered into a term sheet with Resato for the exclusive sales, marketing, distribution and servicing of hydrogen refuelling station technologies for the Canadian market.

On Dec. 1, 2022, the company acquired all general partner and limited partner interests of private U.S.-based **Wolf River Hydro Limited Partnership** from **Northwoods Hydropower Inc.** for US$700,000. Wolf River owns an operational 700-KW hydroelectric plant in Shawano, Wisc.

In October 2022, the company terminated an investment term sheet with **Gaussin S.A.** to acquire an exclusive licence of GAUSSIN's technology for the manufacturing, commercialization, marketing, distribution and sale of logistic off-road vehicles in Canada.

In May 2022, **Superior Plus Corp.** signed a definitive agreement with the company to provide green hydrogen to commercial and industrial customers initially in Quebec. The company would provide the company with green hydrogen from its facility in Sorel-Tracy, Que., with initial deliveries expected in the third quarter of 2022. Superior Plus would deliver hydrogen directly from the company's facility to its customers.

Recent Merger and Acquisition Activity

Status: completed **Revised:** Apr. 22, 2022

UPDATE: The transaction was completed. PREVIOUS: Orletto Capital II Inc. entered into a letter of intent for the Qualifying Transaction reverse takeover acquisition of private Brossard, Que.-based Charbone Corporation. The transaction would be completed by way of an amalgamation of Charbone and a wholly owned subsidiary of Orletto. Charbone has a 0.2-MW hydropower plant located in Vermont, plans to build a 0.5-MW hydrogen plant in Sorel-Tracy, Que., as well as plans to acquire hydropower plants in the United States. Charbone plans to use its hydropower plants to supply clean energy to its green hydrogen production plants. A private placement of subscription receipts for minimum proceeds of $5,000,000 was to be completed by Charbone. Oct. 22, 2021 - Orletto and Charbone announced private placement of up to 15,000,000 subscription receipts at a price of $0.40 per subscription receipt. Mar. 17, 2022 - Private placement of 11,270,000 subscription receipts was completed at $0.40 per receipt.

Predecessor Detail - Name changed from Orletto Capital II Inc., Apr. 14, 2022, pursuant to the Qualifying Transaction reverse takeover acquisition of Charbone Corporation; basis 1 new for 1.07937 old shs.

Directors - David B. (Dave) Gagnon, chr. & CEO, Verdun, Qué.; Mena Beshay, Richmond, B.C.; Brigitte Chabarekh, Longueuil, Qué.; Frederic (Fred) Lecoq, Outremont, Qué.; Francois Vitez, North Vancouver, B.C.

Other Exec. Officers - Daniel Charette, COO; Benoit Veilleux, CFO; Samuel Boudaux, v-p, market devel. & strategic devel.; Johann Bureau, v-p, Hydrogen; Laetitia Fiére, v-p; Richard Provencher, corp. sec.

Capital Stock

	Authorized (shs.)	Outstanding (shs.)[1]
Common	unlimited	47,257,283

[1] At Nov. 23, 2022

Major Shareholder - David B. (Dave) Gagnon held 15.2% interest, Daniel Charette held 12.63% interest and Stephane Dallaire held 10.05% interest at Aug. 18, 2022.

Price Range - CH/TSX-VEN

Year	Volume	High	Low	Close
2022	10,769,813	$0.55	$0.10	$0.13
2019	86,161	$0.12	$0.07	$0.07
2018	111,639	$0.22	$0.11	$0.11

Consolidation: 1-for-1.07937 cons. in May 2022

Recent Close: $0.07

Capital Stock Changes - In January 2023, private placement of 9,980,004 units (1 common share & 1 warrant) at 12¢ per unit was completed, with warrants exercisable at 20¢ per share for two years.

On Apr. 22, 2022, 29,311,285 post-consolidated common shares were issued pursuant to the Qualifying Transaction reverse takeover acquisition of Charbone Corporation and 11,270,000 post-consolidated units (1 common share & ½ warrant) were issued without further consideration on exchange of subscription receipts sold previously by private placement at 40¢ each. In addition, 250,000 post-consolidated common shares were issued for financing fees. On May 3, 2022, common shares were consolidated on a 1-for-1.079365 basis.

Wholly Owned Subsidiaries

Charbone Corporation USA, United States.
• 100% int. in **Stuwe & Davenport Partnership, LLC**, United States.
Charbone Hydrogen Manitoba Inc.

Charbone Hydrogen Québec Inc., Qué.
Charbone Systems Inc.

Financial Statistics

Periods ended:	12m Dec. 31/21[A1]		12m Dec. 31/20[A]
	$000s	%Chg	$000s
Salaries & benefits	3		nil
General & admin expense	2,098		345
Operating expense	**2,101**	**+509**	**345**
Operating income	**(2,101)**	**n.a.**	**(345)**
Deprec., depl. & amort.	40		nil
Finance costs, gross	1,866		44
Pre-tax income	**(4,031)**	**n.a.**	**(389)**
Net income	**(4,031)**	**n.a.**	**(389)**
Cash & equivalent	nil		1
Current assets	218		1
Fixed assets, net	731		nil
Right-of-use assets	1,253		nil
Intangibles, net	110		nil
Total assets	**2,806**	**n.m.**	**140**
Bank indebtedness	5		275
Accts. pay. & accr. liabs	1,897		129
Current liabilities	2,036		452
Long-term debt, gross	4,102		301
Long-term debt, net	3,969		301
Long-term lease liabilities	1,225		nil
Shareholders' equity	(4,424)		(613)
Cash from oper. activs	**(546)**	**n.a.**	**(28)**
Cash from fin. activs	1,418		133
Cash from invest. activs	(878)		(105)
Net cash position	**(5)**	**n.a.**	**1**
Capital expenditures	(465)		nil
	$		$
Earnings per share*	(0.17)		(0.02)
	shs		shs
No. of shs. o/s	n.a.		n.a.
Avg. no. of shs. o/s*	24,412,781		18,089,564
	%		%
Net profit margin	n.a.		n.a.
Return on equity	n.m.		n.m.
Return on assets	(146.98)		n.a.

* Common
[A] Reported in accordance with IFRS
[1] Results for 2021 and prior periods pertain to Charbone Corporation.

Latest Results

Periods ended:	9m Sept. 30/22[A]		9m Sept. 30/21[A]
	$000s	%Chg	$000s
Net income	(6,117)	n.a.	(2,746)
	$		$
Earnings per share*	(0.17)		(0.11)

* Common
[A] Reported in accordance with IFRS
Note: Adjusted throughout for 1-for-1.079365 cons. in May 2022

C.101 Charlotte's Web Holdings, Inc.*

Symbol - CWEB **Exchange** - TSX **CUSIP** - 16106R
Head Office - 700 Tech Crt, Louisville, CO, United States, 80027
Telephone - (720) 487-9508 **Toll-free** - (855) 790-8169
Website - www.charlottesweb.com
Email - cory.pala@charlottesweb.com
Investor Relations - Cory Pala (720) 484-8930
Auditors - Ernst & Young LLP C.P.A., Denver, Colo.
Lawyers - DLA Piper (Canada) LLP
Transfer Agents - Odyssey Trust Company, Vancouver, B.C.
FP500 Revenue Ranking - 775
Employees - 170 at Dec. 31, 2022
Profile - (B.C. 2018) Produces and distributes hemp-based cannibidiol (CBD) wellness products in the U.S.

The company's products are made from proprietary strains of whole-plant hemp extracts containing a full spectrum of phytocannabinoids, terpenes, flavonoids and other beneficial hemp compounds. Product categories include oil tinctures, capsules, gummies, sprays, topicals, canine-focused pet products and NSF Certified for Sports tinctures. Products are distributed through own and third-party e-commerce websites, select distributors, health practitioners and retail outlets across the U.S. Brands include Charlotte's Web™, CBDMEDIC™, Harmony Hemp™, CBD CLINIC™ and ReCreate™.

The company grows its proprietary hemp on farms leased in northeastern Colorado and sources hemp through contract farming operations in Arizona, Kentucky, Oregon and Canada. Manufacturing, extraction, research and development, and distribution operations are conducted at the company's 136,610-sq.-ft. leased facility in Louisville, Colo.

In April 2023, the company formed a joint venture with **AJNA BioSciences PBC**, a botanical drug development company focused on mental health and neurological disorders, and a subsidiary of **British American Tobacco PLC** (BAT). AJNA is partially owned and was co-founded by Joel Stanley, the former CEO and chairman of the board of the company together with certain other founding members of the company. BAT contributed US$10,000,000 for preferred units representing a 20% interest in the joint venture. The company and AJNA each hold 40% of the joint venture's voting common units. The joint venture would pursue FDA-approval for a novel botanical drug to target a neurological condition identified by the joint venture leadership team, which consist of the company, AJNA and BAT representatives. This novel botanical drug would be developed from certain proprietary hemp genetics of the company. The joint venture plans to engage with the FDA to file an Investigational New Drug application and commence Phase I clinical development in 2024. BAT holds a US$56,800,000 convertible debenture of the company, which is convertible into 19.9% ownership of the common shares of the company at a conversion price of Cdn$2.00 per share.

In November 2022, the company entered into an agreement with **Tilray Brands, Inc.** to license, manufacture and distribute Charlotte's Web™ full spectrum CBD products in Canada. First availability was expected in early 2023 for hemp extract oil tinctures, followed by gummies and topicals. Tilray would acquire and extract the company's proprietary hemp biomass, harvested from Canadian-grown hemp cultivars, and manufacture into final product at its production facilities in Canada.

In October 2022, the company entered into a promotional rights agreement with Major League Baseball (MLB) pursuant to which the company entered into an exclusive partnership with MLB to promote the company's new NSF-Certified for Sport® product line. As consideration, the company has paid and is committed to pay 4% of the company's fully diluted outstanding common shares; US$30,500,000 cash from 2022 through 2025; and 10% royalty on the company's gross revenue from the sale of MLB branded products after cumulative gross sales of all such branded products exceed US$18,000,000.

Predecessor Detail - Name changed from Stanley Brothers Holdings Inc., July 13, 2018.

Directors - John Held, chr., Austin, Tex.; Jacques Tortoroli, CEO, New York, N.Y.; Jonathan P. Atwood; Thomas Lardieri; Alicia Morga, Calif.; Susan Vogt, River Forest, Ill.

Other Exec. Officers - Jared Stanley, co-founder & COO; Jessica Saxton, CFO; Dr. Marcel Bonn-Miller, chief scientific officer; Andrew Shafer, chief mktg. officer; Stephen Rogers, sr. v-p, gen. counsel & corp. sec.

Capital Stock

	Authorized (shs.)	Outstanding (shs.)[1]
Preferred	unlimited	nil
Common	unlimited	152,951,994
Proportionate Voting	unlimited	nil

[1] At Aug. 8, 2023

Preferred - Issuable in series. Non-voting.
Common - One vote per share.
Options - At Dec. 31, 2022, options were outstanding to purchase 3,957,027 common shares at a weighted average exercise price of US$1.52 per share with a weighted average remaining contractual life of 8.37 years.
Major Shareholder - Widely held at Apr. 21, 2023.

Price Range - CWEB/TSX

Year	Volume	High	Low	Close
2022	44,033,815	$2.01	$0.49	$0.73
2021	102,713,728	$8.88	$1.28	$1.28
2020	94,486,757	$11.83	$3.08	$4.19
2019	105,345,917	$33.77	$9.55	$9.94
2018	46,001,031	$18.70	$9.05	$15.17

Recent Close: $0.31

Capital Stock Changes - During 2022, common shares were issued as follows: 6,119,121 pursuant to a licence and media agreement, 947,396 on vesting of restricted share units, 239,500 under an at-the-market equity program and 169,045 as contingent equity compensation.

Long-Term Debt - At Dec. 31, 2022, outstanding long-term debt totaled US$37,421,000 (none current) and consisted entirely of Cdn$75,300,000 principal amount of 5% convertible debentures due November 2029, convertible into common shares at Cdn$2.00 per share.

Wholly Owned Subsidiaries

Abacus Products, Inc., Toronto, Ont.
- 100% int. in **Abacus Health Products, Inc.**, Woonsocket, R.I.
  - 100% int. in **Abacus Wellness, Inc.**, Del.
  - 100% int. in **CBD Pharmaceuticals Ltd.**, Tel Aviv, Israel.

Charlotte's Web, Inc., Del.

Financial Statistics

Periods ended:	12m Dec. 31/22[A]		12m Dec. 31/21[A]
	US$000s	%Chg	US$000s
Operating revenue	**74,139**	**-23**	**96,092**
Cost of goods sold	51,323		44,529
General & admin expense	63,955		89,594
Operating expense	**115,278**	**-14**	**134,123**
Operating income	**(41,139)**	**n.a.**	**(38,031)**
Deprec., depl. & amort.	8,968		11,025
Finance costs, gross	542		n.a.
Write-downs/write-offs	(1,837)		(98,003)[1]
Pre-tax income	**(59,222)**	**n.a.**	**(137,579)**
Income taxes	91		143
Net income	**(59,313)**	**n.a.**	**(137,722)**
Cash & equivalent	66,963		19,494
Inventories	26,953		52,077
Accounts receivable	1,847		4,882
Current assets	103,761		95,807
Fixed assets, net	29,330		36,085
Right-of-use assets	16,519		20,679
Intangibles, net	28,642		2,843
Total assets	**187,642**	**+9**	**171,513**
Accts. pay. & accr. liabs	10,917		14,619
Current liabilities	21,427		20,170
Long-term debt, gross	37,421		nil
Long-term debt, net	37,421		nil
Long-term lease liabilities	17,905		20,500
Shareholders' equity	77,505		130,446
Cash from oper. activs	**(5,315)**	**n.a.**	**(29,559)**
Cash from fin. activs	52,389		8,039
Cash from invest. activs	395		(11,789)
Net cash position	**66,963**	**+244**	**19,494**
Capital expenditures	(265)		(4,918)
Capital disposals	660		13
	US$		US$
Earnings per share*	(0.40)		(0.98)
Cash flow per share*	(0.04)		(0.21)
	shs		shs
No. of shs. o/s	152,135,026		144,659,964
Avg. no. of shs. o/s*	146,631,767		140,769,247
	%		%
Net profit margin	(80.00)		(143.32)
Return on equity	(57.05)		(71.60)
Return on assets	(32.73)		(57.10)
Foreign sales percent	100		100
No. of employees (FTEs)	170		257

* Common
[A] Reported in accordance with U.S. GAAP
[1] Includes US$76,039,000 and US$19,750,000 full impairment of goodwill and intangible assets, respectively, related to wholly owned Abacus Products, Inc.

Latest Results

Periods ended:	6m June 30/23[A]		6m June 30/22[A]
	US$000s	%Chg	US$000s
Operating revenue	33,016	-14	38,234
Net income	(67)	n.a.	(16,496)
	US$		US$
Earnings per share*	(0.00)		(0.11)

* Common
[A] Reported in accordance with U.S. GAAP

Historical Summary
(as originally stated)

Fiscal Year	Oper. Rev.	Net Inc. Bef. Disc.	EPS*
	US$000s	US$000s	US$
2022[A]	74,139	(59,313)	(0.40)
2021[A]	96,092	(137,722)	(0.98)
2020[B]	95,226	(47,186)	(0.38)
2019[B]	94,594	(15,567)	(0.16)
2018[B1]	69,501	11,808	0.14

* Common
[A] Reported in accordance with U.S. GAAP
[B] Reported in accordance with IFRS
[1] Results prior to Aug. 30, 2018, pertain to CWB Holdings, Inc.

C.102 Chartwell Retirement Residences*

Symbol - CSH.UN **Exchange** - TSX **CUSIP** - 16141A
Head Office - 7070 Derrycrest Dr, Mississauga, ON, L5W 0G5
Telephone - (905) 501-9219 **Toll-free** - (888) 584-2386 **Fax** - (905) 501-0813
Website - www.chartwell.com
Email - vvolodarski@chartwell.com
Investor Relations - Vlad Volodarski (905) 501-9219
Auditors - KPMG LLP C.A., Toronto, Ont.
Lawyers - Osler, Hoskin & Harcourt LLP, Toronto, Ont.
Transfer Agents - Computershare Trust Company of Canada Inc., Toronto, Ont.

FP500 Revenue Ranking - 402
Employees - 15,928 at Dec. 31, 2022
Profile - (Ont. 2003) Owns, operates and manages a portfolio of seniors housing residences in four Canadian provinces.
Through subsidiaries, the trust indirectly holds a portfolio of seniors housing facilities consisting of independent supportive living facilities, assisted living facilities (retirement homes) and long-term care (LTC) facilities in Ontario, Quebec, Alberta and British Columbia. In addition to managing its own properties, the trust provides management and advisory services to third party owners of seniors housing facilities.
At Mar. 31, 2023, the trust's portfolio of seniors housing facilities owned or managed on behalf of others consisted of interests in 29,464 suites/beds in 191 facilities which are operating, under construction or in various stages of development. The trust's portfolio of owned communities consisted of interests in 26,501 suites/beds in 179 facilities, of which 130 are 100%-owned and 49 are partially owned. The trust's portfolio of managed properties consisted of 2,963 suites/beds in 12 facilities.

Suites/Beds	Retirement	LTC
Owned properties:		
100%-owned[1]	14,178	2,776
Partially owned[2]	9,547	nil
	23,725	2,776
Managed properties[3]	2,355	608
Total	26,080	3,384

[1] Represents 110 retirement facilities and 20 LTC facilities. Two of the retirement facilities (225 suites) completed operational closure during the first quarter of 2023, and have been removed from the trust's available capacity effective Jan. 1, 2023. The LTC facilities include one retirement residence (64 suites) connected to an LTC home and 11 retirement suites at another LTC home.
[2] Represents 49 retirement facilities.
[3] Represents eight retirement facilities and four LTC facilities.

Recent Merger and Acquisition Activity

Status: completed **Revised:** Mar. 24, 2023
UPDATE: The transaction was completed. PREVIOUS: Chartwell Retirement Residences agreed to sell an 82-suite retirement home in Ontario for $5,000,000. The property was one of three Ontario retirement residences the trust closed to new admissions during the fourth quarter of 2022.
Status: completed **Revised:** Dec. 7, 2022
UPDATE: The transaction was completed. PREVIOUS: Chartwell Retirement Residences agreed to sell two long-term care homes in British Columbia, totaling 264 beds, to AgeCare Health Services Inc. and Axium Infrastructure Inc. for $112,000,000, including assumption of $26,000,000 of property specific debt.
Status: completed **Announced:** Apr. 1, 2022
Chartwell Retirement Residences acquired three retirement residences in Collingwood, Barrie and Bowmanville, Ont., totaling 467 suites, for $228,000,000, which was settled by assumption of in place mortgages on two of the properties, cash on hand and the utilization of available credit facilities.
Status: pending **Announced:** Mar. 31, 2022
Chartwell Retirement Residences agreed to sell 16 long-term care homes in Ontario (of which one has an adjacent retirement residence), as well as its management platform and another home under development, to AgeCare Health Services Inc. and Axium Infrastructure Inc. and its affiliates for $446,500,000. The transaction was expected to close in the first half of 2023.
Predecessor Detail - Name changed from Chartwell Seniors Housing Real Estate Investment Trust, Jan. 11, 2013.
Trustees - J. Huw Thomas, chr., Oakville, Ont.; V. Ann Davis, Toronto, Ont.; James D. (Jamie) Scarlett, Toronto, Ont.
Oper. Subsid./Mgt. Co. Officers - Vlad Volodarski, CEO; Karen Sullivan, pres. & COO; Jonathan M. Boulakia, interim CFO, chief invest. officer, chief legal officer & corp. sec.

Capital Stock

	Authorized (shs.)	Outstanding (shs.)[1]
Trust Unit	unlimited	238,254,970
Class B LP Unit	unlimited	1,530,360[2 3]
Special Voting Unit	unlimited	1,530,360

[1] At May 4, 2023
[2] Classified as debt.
[3] Securities of Chartwell Master Care LP

Trust Unit - The trust intends to make monthly cash distribution equal to, on an annual basis, about 90% of its distributable income, subjecting to a minimum of 80%. Redeemable at any time at a price per trust unit equal to the lesser of: (i) 90% of the weighted average price per trust unit on the TSX during the 10-trading-day period ending immediately prior to the redemption date; and (ii) an amount equal to: (a) the closing price of the trust units on the TSX if there was a trade on the redemption date and the TSX provides a closing price; (b) the average of the highest and lowest prices of trust units on TSX if there was trading on the redemption date and the TSX provides only the highest and lowest prices of the trust units traded on that date; or (c) the average of the last bid and ask prices of the trust units if there was no trading on the redemption date. One vote per trust unit.
Special Voting Unit - Issued to holders of class B limited partnership units of subsidiary Chartwell Master Care LP. Each special voting unit entitles the holder to a number of votes at unitholder meetings equal to the number of trust units into which the class B limited partnership units are exchangeable.
Class B Limited Partnership Unit - Entitled to distributions equal to those provided to trust units. Exchangeable into trust units on a 1-for-1 basis at any time by holder. All held by non-controlling interests. Classified as financial liabilities under IFRS.
Major Shareholder - Widely held at Mar. 31, 2023.

Price Range - CSH.UN/TSX

Year	Volume	High	Low	Close
2022	120,190,486	$13.25	$7.58	$8.44
2021	96,307,411	$13.76	$10.45	$11.82
2020	148,747,843	$14.62	$6.25	$11.19
2019	73,212,604	$15.79	$13.42	$13.90
2018	62,435,255	$16.47	$13.43	$13.67

Recent Close: $10.39
Capital Stock Changes - During 2022, trust units were issued as follows: 3,388,122 under distribution reinvestment plan and 137,940 under executive unit purchase plan.

Dividends

CSH.UN unit Ra $0.612 pa M est. Apr. 15, 2020**
Prev. Rate: $0.60 est. Apr. 15, 2019
** Reinvestment Option

Long-Term Debt - Outstanding at Dec. 31, 2022:

Credit facility due 2024	$184,000,000
3.95% term loan due 2024	125,000,000
4.44% term loan due 2027	13,600,000
Fixed rate mtges.[1]	1,668,444,000
Variable rate mtges.[2]	33,224,000
3.786% ser.A sr. deb. due 2023	200,000,000
4.211% ser.B sr. deb. due 2025	150,000,000
Cl.B limited partnership units	12,916,000
Mark-to-mkt. mtge. adj.	2,265,000
Less: Financing costs	50,229,000
	2,339,220,000
Less: Current portion	391,134,000
	1,948,086,000

[1] Bear interest at rates ranging from 1.31% to 5.68%.
[2] Bear interest at bankers' acceptance plus 0.975% to the higher of prime plus 0.55% or 3.25%.

Wholly Owned Subsidiaries

CSH Trust, Ont.
- 100% int. in **Chartwell Benco Inc.**, Ont.
  - 100% int. in **GP M Trust**, Ont.
- 52% int. in **Chartwell Master Care LP**, Man.

Chartwell Master Care Corporation, Ont.

Investments

48% int. in **Chartwell Master Care LP**, Man.

Financial Statistics

Periods ended:	12m Dec. 31/22[A]		12m Dec. 31/21[oA]
	$000s	%Chg	$000s
Total revenue	**707,992**	**+4**	**677,734**
Rental operating expense	464,704		423,884
General & admin. expense	49,641		44,364
Operating expense	**514,345**	**+10**	**468,248**
Operating income	**193,647**	**-8**	**209,486**
Investment income	(3,309)		(8,376)
Deprec. & amort.	156,136		157,861
Finance costs, gross	85,091		80,931
Write-downs/write-offs	nil		(850)
Pre-tax income	**41,519**	**+496**	**6,966**
Income taxes	14,131		984
Net inc. bef. disc. opers	**27,388**	**+358**	**5,982**
Income from disc. opers	22,143		4,150
Net income	**49,531**	**+389**	**10,132**
Cash & equivalent	28,469		95,486
Accounts receivable	20,465		18,668
Current assets	280,416		146,864
Long-term investments	16,773		16,963
Income-producing props	4,050,650		4,042,147
Properties under devel.	96,415		64,546
Properties for future devel.	23,065		21,324
Property interests, net	3,176,045		3,222,779
Intangibles, net	28,135		72,503
Total assets	**3,510,342**	**+3**	**3,417,253**
Accts. pay. & accr. liabs	177,101		165,579
Current liabilities	744,634		509,420
Long-term debt, gross	2,339,220		2,353,065
Long-term debt, net	1,948,086		2,051,471
Long-term lease liabilities	7,473		11,585
Shareholders' equity	769,802		826,111
Cash from oper. activs	**137,709**	**-12**	**156,323**
Cash from fin. activs	(39,114)		(94,507)
Cash from invest. activs	(165,612)		(36,487)
Net cash position	**28,469**	**-70**	**95,486**
Capital expenditures	(111,361)		(115,344)
Capital disposals	87,732		79,917
Increase in property	(141,426)		(7,462)
	$		$
Earnings per share*	n.a.		n.a.
Cash flow per share*	0.59		0.68
Funds from opers. per sh.*	0.53		0.59
Cash divd. per share*	0.61		0.61
Total divd. per share*	**0.61**		**0.61**
	shs		shs
No. of shs. o/s*	234,752,609		231,226,547
	%		%
Net profit margin	3.87		0.88
Return on equity	3.43		0.77
Return on assets	2.41		2.19
No. of employees (FTEs)	15,928		15,589

* Trust unit
[o] Restated
[A] Reported in accordance with IFRS

Latest Results

Periods ended:	3m Mar. 31/23[A]		3m Mar. 31/22[A]
	$000s	%Chg	$000s
Total revenue	178,287	+5	169,904
Net inc. bef. disc. opers	(12,590)	n.a.	(11,862)
Income from disc. opers	3,337		8,546
Net income	(9,253)	n.a.	(3,316)
	$		$
Earnings per share*	n.a.		n.a.

[A] Reported in accordance with IFRS

Historical Summary
(as originally stated)

Fiscal Year	Total Rev.	Net Inc. Bef. Disc.	EPS*
	$000s	$000s	$
2022[A]	707,992	27,388	n.a.
2021[A]	906,469	10,132	n.a.
2020[A]	928,587	14,879	n.a.
2019[A]	915,312	1,067	n.a.
2018[A]	866,654	18,519	n.a.

* Trust unit
[A] Reported in accordance with IFRS

C.103 Chemistree Technology Inc.

Symbol - CHM **Exchange** - CSE **CUSIP** - 16383D
Head Office - 208-828 Harbourside Dr, North Vancouver, BC, V7P 3R9 **Telephone** - (604) 678-8941 **Fax** - (604) 689-7442
Website - www.chemistree.ca
Email - doug@pemgroup.ca
Investor Relations - Douglas E. Ford (604) 973-2200
Auditors - Davidson & Company LLP C.A., Vancouver, B.C.

Transfer Agents - Computershare Trust Company of Canada Inc., Vancouver, B.C.

Profile - (B.C. 2008) Invests in private and public companies operating in various industries, such as cannabis, technology, health care, biotechnology, medical technology or related consumer products.

The company's investment portfolio may include equity investments, secured or unsecured loans, warrants and options, hybrid instruments, royalties, streaming arrangements, net profit interests, asset acquisitions, majority ownership, joint ventures and licensing arrangements.

Holdings consist of sublease and licensing agreements with a third party, which subleases and operates the company's assets and leased facility in Sedro Woolley, Wash., for use in cannabis cultivation and processing under the Sugarleaf brand; equity interest in and gross sales royalty on North American sales of Vancouver, B.C.-based **ImmunoFlex Therapeutics Inc.**, which develops natural health products to enhance the immune system; equity interest in **ReVolve Renewable Power Limited**, which is focused on the development of wind and solar projects in the United States and Mexican markets; and 10% preferred membership interest in **Applied Cannabis Sciences**, a New Jersey-based applicant of medical cannabis cultivation, manufacturing and dispensary permits, carried at nil value.

In October 2022, the company agreed to sell wholly owned **Chemistree Washington Ltd.**, which owns assets used in cannabis cultivation, production, distribution as well as operating under Sugarleaf brand, an established cannabis brand within Washington state that is sold in over 120 retail locations, for US$500,000.

Predecessor Detail - Name changed from Whattozee Networks Inc., Aug. 4, 2017.

Directors - Karl Kottmeier, pres. & CEO, West Vancouver, B.C.; Douglas E. (Doug) Ford, CFO & corp. sec., West Vancouver, B.C.; Sheldon Aberman, chief cannabis officer, Ariz.; Gina Dickson, Nev.; Nicholas J. Zitelli, N.J.

Capital Stock

	Authorized (shs.)	Outstanding (shs.)[1]
Common	unlimited	49,978,811

[1] At Nov. 28, 2022

Price Range - CHM/CSE

Year	Volume	High	Low	Close
2022	11,396,721	$0.07	$0.01	$0.01
2021	68,095,559	$0.22	$0.03	$0.03
2020	51,480,726	$0.30	$0.03	$0.08
2019	17,345,991	$0.75	$0.10	$0.12
2018	9,681,872	$0.88	$0.31	$0.55

Recent Close: $0.01

Capital Stock Changes - During fiscal 2022, common shares were issued as follows: 7,796,416 for debt settlement and 2,836,000 on conversion of debenture.

Wholly Owned Subsidiaries

American CHM Investments Inc., Del.
- 100% int. in **Chemistree Washington Ltd.**, Wash.

Financial Statistics

Periods ended:	12m June 30/22[A]		12m June 30/21[A]
	$000s	%Chg	$000s
General & admin expense	1,006		1,467
Operating expense	**1,006**	**-31**	**1,467**
Operating income	**(1,006)**	**n.a.**	**(1,467)**
Deprec., depl. & amort.	94		105
Finance income	nil		45
Finance costs, gross	1,448		1,910
Write-downs/write-offs	(808)		(1,142)
Pre-tax income	**(2,884)**	**n.a.**	**(4,534)**
Income taxes	(204)		nil
Net income	**(2,681)**	**n.a.**	**(4,534)**
Cash & equivalent	1,041		396
Accounts receivable	nil		71
Current assets	2,004		2,301
Long-term investments	73		500
Fixed assets, net	nil		943
Total assets	**2,077**	**-45**	**3,743**
Accts. pay. & accr. liabs	68		65
Current liabilities	446		8,643
Long-term debt, gross	7,594		8,815
Long-term debt, net	7,594		444
Equity portion of conv. debs	1,119		672
Shareholders' equity	(5,964)		(5,409)
Cash from oper. activs	**(1,349)**	**n.a.**	**(2,451)**
Cash from fin. activs	(41)		92
Cash from invest. activs	2,035		(493)
Net cash position	**1,041**	**+163**	**396**
Capital expenditures	nil		(59)
Capital disposals	2,216		66
	$		$
Earnings per share*	(0.06)		(0.12)
Cash flow per share*	(0.03)		(0.06)
	shs		shs
No. of shs. o/s*	49,666,846		39,034,430
Avg. no. of shs. o/s*	41,632,319		38,440,868
	%		%
Net profit margin	n.a.		n.a.
Return on equity	n.m.		n.m.
Return on assets	(45.89)		(46.87)

* Common
[A] Reported in accordance with IFRS

Latest Results

Periods ended:	3m Sept. 30/22[A]		3m Sept. 30/21[A]
	$000s	%Chg	$000s
Net income	(413)	n.a.	(16)
	$		$
Earnings per share*	(0.01)		(0.00)

* Common
[A] Reported in accordance with IFRS

Historical Summary
(as originally stated)

Fiscal Year	Oper. Rev.	Net Inc. Bef. Disc.	EPS*
	$000s	$000s	$
2022[A]	nil	(2,681)	(0.06)
2021[A]	nil	(4,534)	(0.12)
2020[A]	161	(5,453)	(0.14)
2019[A]	318	(4,665)	(0.13)
2018[A]	nil	(738)	(0.04)

* Common
[A] Reported in accordance with IFRS

C.104 Chemtrade Logistics Income Fund*

Symbol - CHE.UN **Exchange** - TSX **CUSIP** - 16387P

Head Office - 300-155 Gordon Baker Rd, Toronto, ON, M2H 3N5 **Telephone** - (416) 496-5856 **Toll-free** - (866) 887-8805 **Fax** - (416) 496-9414

Website - www.chemtradelogistics.com

Email - rbhardwaj@chemtradelogistics.com

Investor Relations - Rohit Bhardwaj (866) 313-1872

Auditors - KPMG LLP C.A., Toronto, Ont.

Lawyers - Covington & Burling LLP; Osler, Hoskin & Harcourt LLP, Toronto, Ont.

Transfer Agents - Computershare Trust Company of Canada Inc., Toronto, Ont.

FP500 Revenue Ranking - 234

Employees - 1,410 at Dec. 31, 2022

Profile - (Ont. 2001) Operates diversified businesses that provide industrial chemicals and services to customers in North America and worldwide.

Operations are carried out through two segments: Sulphur & Water Chemicals; and Electrochemicals.

The **Sulphur & Water Chemicals** segment manufactures, markets or processes a range of sulphur-based products including sulphuric acid, ultrapure sulphuric acid, liquid sulphur dioxide (SO_2), sulphur, sodium bisulphite (SBS), sodium nitrite, sodium hydrosulphite (SHS), phosphorus pentasulphide sulphides as well as provides spent acid regeneration services to customers primarily in North America. The segment also processes scrubber effluent to produce ammonium sulphate in its Fort McMurray, Alta., facility and prilling of molten sulphur in its Mount Vernon, Wa., facility. Most of the sulphuric acid sales are to customers in the pulp and paper, refineries, semiconductor production, chemicals manufacturing, automotive, textiles, kaolin clay, water treatment and mining industries. Regen acid is primarily sold to oil refineries. In addition, the segment also manufactures and markets a variety of inorganic coagulants used in water treatment, including aluminum sulphate, aluminum chlorohydrate, polyaluminum chloride and ferric sulphate, which are marketed primarily to North American municipal and industrial customers.

The **Electrochemicals** segment manufactures and markets sodium chlorate and chlor-alkali products (caustic soda, chlorine and hydrochloric acid) from manufacturing facilities in Brandon, Man.; Espirito Santo, Brazil; Prince George, B.C.; and North Vancouver, B.C. Sodium chlorate is used for production of bleached pulp, agricultural herbicides, defoliants, perchlorates and in water treatment applications. Caustic soda is used in various industries including pulp and paper, soaps and detergents, aluminum, oil and gas exploration and refining, as well as for a variety of chemical processes. Chlorine is used in a variety of chemical processes primarily in the production of polyvinyl chloride (PVC) and also used to produce hydrochloric acid which is required in numerous applications such as oil and gas drilling and steel manufacturing. Almost 70% of the caustic soda produced at North Vancouver facility is consumed by pulp mills in western Canada and the Pacific Northwest. All of caustic soda produced in Brazil is sold to a neighbouring pulp mill owned by a major customer.

The fund operates more than 55 production facilities globally as at Dec. 31, 2022.

In June 2023, the company and its joint venture partner **Kanto Chemical Holdings, Inc.** made the decision to put the project to build a high purity sulphuric acid plant in Casa Grande, Ariz., on hold due to rising costs. The high purity production process would be based on Kanto Chemical's technology, which is in use in Taiwan and Japan supplying the semiconductor producers in Asia. The plant would have a total annual capacity of 100,000 tonnes of electronic grade acid. The project costs were estimated to range between US$300,000,000 and US$380,000,000 up from the original estimate of between US$175,000,000 and US$250,000,000. The fund and Kanto Chemical would own 51% and 49% interest, respectively, in the joint venture.

In February 2023, the fund announced the suspension of its plan to sell a parcel of land at its north Vancouver, B.C., site through a sale-leaseback process due to the decline in the real estate sector. The portion of the fund's north Vancouver operating facility that would have been offered for sale includes 16 hectares of industrial zoned and rail served land.

In November 2022, the fund completed the closure of its sodium chlorate facility in Beauharnois, Que. Products previously sold from the Beauharnois, Que., facility were absorbed into the existing production capacity of the fund's sodium chlorate facilities in Brandon, Man., and Prince George, B.C.

Recent Merger and Acquisition Activity

Status: completed **Announced:** Apr. 4, 2022
Chemtrade Logistics Income Fund sold its idled Augusta, Ga., sulphuric acid plant for US$10,000,000.

Trustees - Dr. Douglas W. (Doug) Muzyka, chr., Philadelphia, Pa.; Scott W. Rook, pres. & CEO, Toronto, Ont.; Lucio Di Clemente, Toronto, Ont.; Daniella E. Dimitrov, Toronto, Ont.; Luc Doyon, Montréal, Qué.; Dr. Emily Moore, Mississauga, Ont.; David Mutombo, Oakville, Ont.; Katherine A. Rethy, Huntsville, Ont.

Oper. Subsid./Mgt. Co. Officers - Rohit Bhardwaj, CFO; Tim Montgomery, grp. v-p, mfg. & eng.; Emily Powers, grp. v-p, HR & responsible care; Alan Robinson, grp. v-p, comml.; Tejinder Kaushik, v-p, IT; Susan M. Paré, gen. counsel & corp. sec.

Capital Stock

	Authorized (shs.)	Outstanding (shs.)[1]
Trust Unit	unlimited	115,845,845

[1] At May 9, 2023

Trust Unit - Each unit is transferable and represents an equal undivided beneficial interest in any distributions from the fund, whether of net income, net realized capital gains or other amounts, and in the net assets of the fund in the event of termination or winding up of the fund. Distributions are paid monthly. One vote per trust unit.

Major Shareholder - Widely held at Mar. 10, 2023.

Price Range - CHE.UN/TSX

Year	Volume	High	Low	Close
2022	92,108,237	$9.92	$6.65	$8.97
2021	110,578,780	$8.70	$5.66	$7.40
2020	124,613,247	$11.45	$3.26	$5.83
2019	107,437,057	$12.00	$8.01	$11.03
2018	47,401,131	$19.44	$10.03	$10.48

Recent Close: $8.29

Capital Stock Changes - In August 2022, bought deal public offering of 10,005,000 trust units at $8.65 per unit was completed, including 1,306,358 trust units on exercise of over-allotment. Also during 2022, 1,309,106 common shares were issued under the dividend reinvestment plan.

Dividends

CHE.UN tr unit Ra $0.60 pa M est. Apr. 30, 2020**
Prev. Rate: $1.20 est. Feb. 28, 2007
** Reinvestment Option

Long-Term Debt - Outstanding at Dec. 31, 2022:

Revolv. credit facility[1]	$370,024,000
Conv. debs.[2]	533,218,000
	903,242,000
Less: Current portion	nil
	903,242,000

[1] Consists of a $370,024,000 senior credit facility due December 2026, with a weighted average effective rate of 3.1% at Dec. 31, 2022 (Dec. 31, 2021 - 4.4%).

[2] Consists of $201,115,000 principal amount of 4.75% debentures due May 31, 2024, convertible into trust units at $26.70 per unit; $86,250,000 principal amount of 8.5% debentures due Sept. 30, 2025, convertible into trust units at $7.35 per unit; $100,000,000 principal amount of 6.5% debentures due Oct. 31, 2026, convertible into trust units at $15.80 per unit; and $130,000,000 principal amount of 6.25% debentures due Aug. 31, 2027, convertible into trust units at $10.00 per unit.

Note - In March 2023, bought deal offering of $110,000,000 principal amount of 7% convertible debentures due June 30, 2028, was completed. The debentures are convertible into trust units at $12.85 per unit. In May 2023, $100,000,000 principal amount of 4.75% convertible unsecured subordinated debentures due May 31, 2024, were redeemed. On June 30, 2023, all remaining $101,115,000 principal amount of 4.75% convertible unsecured subordinated debentures were redeemed.

Wholly Owned Subsidiaries

Chemtrade Logistics Inc., North York, Ont.
- 100% int. in **Chemtrade Electrochem Inc.**, Calgary, Alta.
  - 100% int. in **Chemtrade Brasil Ltda.**, Brazil.
  - 100% int. in **Chemtrade Electrochem U.S. Inc.**, Del.
- 100% int. in **Chemtrade Holdco US Inc.**, Del.
  - 100% int. in **Chemtrade Chemicals Corporation**, Del.
    - 100% int. in **Chemtrade Chemicals US LLC**, Del.
      - 100% int. in **Chemtrade Solutions LLC**, Del.
  - 100% int. in **Chemtrade Logistics (U.S.), Inc.**, Del.
  - 100% int. in **Chemtrade Refinery Services Inc.**, Del. Formerly Peak Sulfur, Inc.
  - 100% int. in **Chemtrade Refinery Solutions Limited Partnership**, Del.
- 100% int. in **Chemtrade Pulp Chemicals Limited Partnership**, Ont.
- 100% int. in **Chemtrade West Limited Partnership**, Ont.

Note: The preceding list includes only the major related companies in which interests are held.

Financial Statistics

Periods ended:	12m Dec. 31/22^A	%Chg	12m Dec. 31/21^A
	$000s	%Chg	$000s
Operating revenue	**1,813,383**	**+33**	**1,368,479**
Cost of sales	1,244,976		1,006,041
Salaries & benefits	62,983		65,504
General & admin expense	47,915		5,677
Stock-based compensation	20,971		25,693
Operating expense	**1,376,845**	**+25**	**1,102,915**
Operating income	**436,538**	**+64**	**265,564**
Deprec., depl. & amort.	216,950		239,622
Finance income	2,395		716
Finance costs, gross	52,364		116,898
Investment income	(436)		nil
Write-downs/write-offs	nil		(130,000)
Pre-tax income	**169,183**	**n.a.**	**(220,240)**
Income taxes	60,068		14,969
Net income	**109,115**	**n.a.**	**(235,209)**
Cash & equivalent	72,569		13,908
Inventories	147,380		111,742
Accounts receivable	123,214		96,371
Current assets	360,869		230,974
Long-term investments	5,495		nil
Fixed assets, net	957,606		940,574
Right-of-use assets	127,603		140,435
Intangibles, net	586,455		604,573
Total assets	**2,157,073**	**+5**	**2,048,970**
Accts. pay. & accr. liabs.	316,437		229,985
Current liabilities	390,635		437,857
Long-term debt, gross	903,242		1,043,704
Long-term debt, net	903,242		899,810
Long-term lease liabilities	94,071		100,863
Shareholders' equity	566,207		379,848
Cash from oper. activs.	**369,191**	**+69**	**219,039**
Cash from fin. activs.	(203,004)		(314,124)
Cash from invest. activs.	(108,877)		96,533
Net cash position	**72,569**	**+422**	**13,908**
Capital expenditures	(115,440)		(86,141)
Capital disposals	12,494		182,674
	$		$
Earnings per share*	1.01		(2.31)
Cash flow per share*	3.40		2.15
Cash divd. per share*	0.60		0.60
	shs		shs
No. of shs. o/s*	115,536,668		104,222,562
Avg. no. of shs. o/s*	108,445,732		101,730,342
	%		%
Net profit margin	6.02		(17.19)
Return on equity	23.07		(47.73)
Return on assets	6.79		(4.85)
Foreign sales percent	68		68
No. of employees (FTEs)	1,410		1,363

* Trust unit
^A Reported in accordance with IFRS

Latest Results

Periods ended:	3m Mar. 31/23^A	%Chg	3m Mar. 31/22^A
	$000s	%Chg	$000s
Operating revenue	471,245	+21	390,345
Net income	79,533	+644	10,686
	$		$
Earnings per share*	0.69		0.10

* Trust unit
^A Reported in accordance with IFRS

Historical Summary
(as originally stated)

Fiscal Year	Oper. Rev. $000s	Net Inc. Bef. Disc. $000s	EPS* $
2022^A	1,813,383	109,115	1.01
2021^A	1,368,479	(235,209)	(2.31)
2020^A	1,379,639	(167,478)	(1.81)
2019^A	1,532,855	(99,654)	(1.08)
2018^A	1,595,747	(131,517)	(1.42)

* Trust unit
^A Reported in accordance with IFRS

C.105 Chesswood Group Limited

Symbol - CHW **Exchange** - TSX **CUSIP** - 16550A
Head Office - 603-1133 Yonge St, Toronto, ON, M4T 2Y7 **Telephone** - (416) 386-3099 **Fax** - (416) 386-3085
Website - www.chesswoodgroup.com
Email - trajchel@chesswoodgroup.com
Investor Relations - Tobias Rajchel (416) 386-3072
Auditors - Ernst & Young LLP C.A., Toronto, Ont.
Lawyers - McCarthy Tétrault LLP, Toronto, Ont.
Transfer Agents - TSX Trust Company, Toronto, Ont.
FP500 Revenue Ranking - 579
Employees - 476 at Dec. 31, 2022

Profile - (Ont. 2010) Provides commercial equipment, automotive and home improvement financing as well as asset management solutions in the U.S. and Canada.

U.S. Equipment Financing

Wholly owned **Pawnee Leasing Corporation** provides micro and small-ticket equipment leases and loans of up to US$350,000 to small and medium-sized businesses in the U.S., ranging from start-ups to established businesses, in the prime and non-prime credit markets, through a network of hundreds of equipment finance broker firms.

Wholly owned **Tandem Finance Inc.** provides micro and small-ticket equipment financing to businesses of all credit profiles through equipment manufacturers, distributors and dealers in the U.S.

Canadian Equipment Financing

Subsidiary **Vault Credit Corporation** (51% owned) offers equipment leases and commercial loans to small and medium-sized businesses in various credit tiers and industries across Canada. Vault Credit operate through a nationwide network of over 60 independent brokers.

Subsidiary **Vault Home Credit Corporation** (51% owned) provides home improvement and other consumer financing solutions in Canada.

Canadian Auto Financing

Wholly owned **Rifco National Auto Finance Corporation** provides consumer financing for motor vehicle purchasers through select automotive dealerships across Canada except for Quebec.

Asset Management

Wholly owned **Waypoint Investment Partners Inc.**, **Chesswood Capital Management Inc.**, and **Chesswood Capital Management USA Inc.** offer private credit alternatives to investors seeking exposure to lease and loan receivables originated by the company's financing subsidiaries.

Portfolio at Mar. 31, 2023:

	U.S. Equip.	Cdn. Equip.	Cdn. Auto
No. of leases & loans	24,585	33,886	15,143
Gross lease & loan receiv.[1]	US$1,140,121	Cdn$852,549	Cdn$398,187

[1] In thousands.

On Oct. 1, 2022, wholly owned **Blue Chip Leasing Corporation** was amalgamated into wholly owned **Vault Credit Corporation**.

On Aug. 11, 2022, wholly owned **Pawnee Leasing Corporation** completed its fourth marketed U.S. securitization in the amount of US$347,000,000.

On May 25, 2022, the company acquired Toronto, Ont.-based **Waypoint Investment Partners Inc.**, an investment fund manager, for $1,589,610 cash and issuance of 150,983 common shares.

In March 2022, the company entered into a forward purchase agreement with **Castlelake, L.P.**, a global alternative investment manager, whereby investment entities managed by Castlelake would acquire up to US$400,000,000 of small ticket equipment loan and lease receivables originated by wholly owned **Pawnee Leasing Corporation** and **Tandem Finance Inc.**

Predecessor Detail - Succeeded Chesswood Income Fund, Jan. 1, 2011, pursuant to plan of arrangement whereby Chesswood Group Limited was formed to facilitate the conversion of the fund into a corporation and the fund was subsequently dissolved.

Directors - Frederick W. Steiner, co-founder, Toronto, Ont.; Edward Sonshine, chr., Toronto, Ont.; Ryan Marr, pres. & CEO, Ont.; Catherine Barbaro, Ont.; Raghunath (Rags) Davloor, Pickering, Ont.; Robert J. Day, Nev.; Jeff Fields, N.Y.; Daniel Wittlin, Toronto, Ont.

Other Exec. Officers - Tobias Rajchel, CFO & corp. sec.

Capital Stock

	Authorized (shs.)	Outstanding (shs.)[1]
Common	unlimited	17,817,351
Special Voting	unlimited	1,478,537
Class B Common	unlimited	1,274,601
Class C Common	unlimited	203,936

[1] At Mar. 31, 2023

Note: Class B and C common shares are securities of Chesswood U.S. Acquisition Co Limited.

Common - One vote per share.

Special Voting Share - Issued to holders of class B and C common shares of Chesswood U.S. Acquisition Co Limited. Each special voting share entitles the holder to a number of votes at shareholder meetings equal to the number of common shares into which the class B or class C common shares are exchangeable.

Class B Common - Entitles the holder to a per share dividend equal to the dividend paid on the common shares. Exchangeable for common shares at any time on a 1-for-1 basis. Dividends are restricted if certain minimum dividends on common shares have not been made. Classified as non-controlling interest.

Class C Common - Entitles the holder to a per share dividend equal to the dividend paid on the common shares. Exchangeable for common shares at any time on a 1-for-1 basis. Classified as non-controlling interest.

Normal Course Issuer Bid - The company plans to make normal course purchases of up to 1,033,781 common shares representing 10% of the public float. The bid commenced on Jan. 25, 2023, and expires on Jan. 24, 2024.

Major Shareholder - Daniel Wittlin held 12.44% interest and Edward Sonshine held 10.31% interest at Mar. 29, 2023.

Price Range - CHW/TSX

Year	Volume	High	Low	Close
2022	2,303,633	$15.25	$10.70	$11.44
2021	5,619,153	$14.55	$8.38	$14.39
2020	6,711,161	$10.93	$3.33	$9.11
2019	5,305,264	$12.45	$8.41	$10.19
2018	4,759,282	$12.59	$8.81	$10.39

Recent Close: $6.87

Capital Stock Changes - In January 2022, 498,605 common shares were issued pursuant to the acquisition of Rifco Inc. In May 2022, 150,983 common shares were issued pursuant to the acquisition of Waypoint Investment Partners Inc. Also during 2022, common shares were issued as follows: 533,332 pursuant to the merger of Blue Chip Leasing Corporation and Vault Credit Corporation, 192,100 on exercise of restricted share units, 123,389 on exercise of options; 453,612 common shares were repurchased under a Normal Course Issuer Bid.

Dividends

CHW com Ra $0.60 pa M est. Feb. 15, 2023[1]
Prev. Rate: $0.48 est. Apr. 18, 2022
Prev. Rate: $0.36 est. Dec. 15, 2021
[1] Monthly divd normally payable in June/20 has been omitted.

Wholly Owned Subsidiaries

Chesswood Holdings Ltd., Ont.
- 51% int. in **CHW/Vault Holdco Corp.**, Ont.
  - 100% int. in **Vault Credit Corporation**, Toronto, Ont.
- 100% int. in **Case Funding Inc.**, Del.
- 100% int. in **Chesswood Capital Management Inc.**, Ont.
  - 100% int. in **Chesswood Capital Management USA Inc.**, Colo.
  - 100% int. in **Waypoint Investment Partners Inc.**, Toronto, Ont.
    - 100% int. in **Chesswood Canadian ABS GP Inc.**, Ont.
    - 99% int. in **Waypoint Private Credit GP Inc.**, Ont.
- 100% int. in **Chesswood U.S. Acquisition Co Limited**, Del.
  - 100% int. in **Pawnee Leasing Corporation**, Fort Collins, Colo.
  - 100% int. in **Tandem Finance Inc.**, Houston, Tex.
- 51% int. in **Vault Home Credit Corporation**, Ont.

Lease-Win Limited, Downsview, Ont.
1000390232 Ontario Inc., Ont.
Rifco Inc., Red Deer, Alta.
- 100% int. in **Rifco National Auto Finance Corporation**, Red Deer, Alta.

Windset Capital Corporation, Del.

Investments

1% int. in **Waypoint Private Credit GP Inc.**, Ont.
Note: The preceding list includes only the major related companies in which interests are held.

Financial Statistics

Periods ended:	12m Dec. 31/22[A]		12m Dec. 31/21[□A]
	$000s	%Chg	$000s
Total revenue	**276,365**	**+100**	**138,083**
Salaries & benefits	59,322		32,269
Stock-based compensation	3,683		3,544
Other operating expense	45,823		26,450
Operating expense	**108,828**	**+75**	**62,263**
Operating income	**167,537**	**+121**	**75,820**
Deprec. & amort.	4,200		2,900
Provision for loan losses	44,315		188
Finance costs, gross	73,379		31,671
Pre-tax income	**44,179**	**+5**	**42,071**
Income taxes	13,763		10,902
Net income	**30,416**	**-2**	**31,169**
Net inc. for equity hldrs	**28,548**	**-1**	**28,796**
Net inc. for non-cont. int.	**1,868**	**-21**	**2,373**
Cash & equivalent	8,120		12,379
Investments	2,330,258		1,418,260
Fixed assets, net	2,926		2,348
Right-of-use assets	3,826		2,089
Intangibles, net	75,586		70,081
Total assets	**2,534,196**	**+58**	**1,602,583**
Accts. pay. & accr. liabs.	19,847		15,499
Debt	2,221,649		1,337,310
Lease liabilities	4,673		2,522
Shareholders' equity	211,682		173,323
Non-controlling interest	16,723		14,659
Cash from oper. activs.	**(591,169)**	**n.a.**	**(470,003)**
Cash from fin. activs.	591,676		499,818
Cash from invest. activs.	(443)		15,922
Net cash position	**103,476**	**+5**	**98,551**
Capital expenditures	(911)		(1,003)
	$		$
Earnings per share*	1.63		1.75
Cash flow per share*	(33.70)		(28.53)
Cash divd. per share*	0.46		0.32
	shs		shs
No. of shs. o/s*	17,619,661		16,574,864
Avg. no. of shs. o/s*	17,540,296		16,473,934
	%		%
Net profit margin	11.01		22.57
Return on equity	14.83		19.05
Return on assets	3.91		4.50
Foreign sales percent	55		76
No. of employees (FTEs)	476		299

* Common
[□] Restated
[A] Reported in accordance with IFRS

Historical Summary
(as originally stated)

Fiscal Year	Total Rev. $000s	Net Inc. Bef. Disc. $000s	EPS* $
2022[A]	276,365	30,416	1.63
2021[A]	138,083	31,169	1.75
2020[A]	117,056	(8,525)	(0.48)
2019[A]	126,975	12,691	0.72
2018[A]	110,586	23,343	1.31

* Common
[A] Reported in accordance with IFRS

C.106 Chicane Capital I Corp.

Symbol - CCIC.P **Exchange** - TSX-VEN **CUSIP** - 168273
Head Office - 4100-66 Wellington St W, Toronto, ON, M5K 1B7 **Telephone** - (416) 861-1100
Email - bghirmai@4frontcapitalpartners.com
Investor Relations - Benhur Ghirmai (416) 861-1100
Auditors - MNP LLP C.A., Toronto, Ont.
Lawyers - WeirFoulds LLP, Toronto, Ont.
Transfer Agents - TSX Trust Company, Toronto, Ont.
Profile - (Ont. 2022) Capital Pool Company.
Common listed on TSX-VEN, Dec. 14, 2022.
Directors - John Travaglini, CEO, Toronto, Ont.; Benhur (Ben) Ghirmai, CFO & corp. sec., Toronto, Ont.; James Allan, Toronto, Ont.; David S. Brown, Toronto, Ont.; Paul Wood, Toronto, Ont.

Capital Stock

	Authorized (shs.)	Outstanding (shs.)[1]
Common	unlimited	5,988,000

[1] At Dec. 14, 2022

Major Shareholder - John Travaglini held 10.02% interest at Dec. 14, 2022.
Recent Close: $0.05
Capital Stock Changes - On Dec. 14, 2022, an initial public offering of 3,088,000 common shares was completed at 10¢ per share.

C.107 China Education Resources Inc.

Symbol - CHN.H **Exchange** - TSX-VEN (S) **CUSIP** - 16938U
Head Office - 300-515 Pender St W, Vancouver, BC, V6B 6H5 **Telephone** - (604) 331-2388 **Fax** - (604) 682-8131
Website - www.chinaeducationresources.com
Email - admin@chinaeducationresources.com
Investor Relations - Cheng Feng Zhou (604) 331-2388
Auditors - MSLL CPA LLP C.P.A., Vancouver, B.C.
Bankers - Canadian Imperial Bank of Commerce, Vancouver, B.C.
Lawyers - Lawson Lundell LLP, Vancouver, B.C.
Transfer Agents - Computershare Trust Company of Canada Inc., Vancouver, B.C.
Profile - (B.C. 2000 amalg.) Provides kindergarten to grade 12 (K-12) education resources and services in the People's Republic of China through its national Internet portal, China Education Resources and Services Platform (CERSP), and offers its commercial service, Education Services Portal (ESP).

The CERSP, www.cersp.com, is a primary venue for teacher training in schools, districts, cities and provinces across China, and is an aggregator for subject matter experts in all K-12 subject areas. The company launched the first version of the mobile app for teacher training in 2015. The app allows users to participate in teacher training programs using their smartphones such as watch user friendly video content, discuss and communicate with other teachers on the training topics in virtue classrooms, get experts help, read training calendar, complete homework of the training program, read newsletters from the training program, retrieve personal training status report, share photos with other teachers, have social networking with other teachers, etc.

The ESP is a commercial service for the K-12 education market that extends the reach and relevance of the CERSP portal at the school and individual level. It supports the administrative, teaching, learning, testing, and assessment needs of an individual school, and it does so in a way that is standardized, allowing for combined results to the district, city, province, or national level. ESP provides school platform services, online tutoring program and digital education products.

The company also distributes third party textbooks and supplementary materials in China.

Common suspended from TSX-VEN, July 8, 2022.
Predecessor Detail - Name changed from China Ventures Inc., Dec. 16, 2004; basis 1 new for 5 old shs.
Directors - Cheng Feng Zhou, chr. & CEO, Vancouver, B.C.; Chi Tak (Danny) Hon, CFO, Vancouver, B.C.; Li Wang, Beijing, Beijing, People's Republic of China; Ansheng Zheng

Capital Stock

	Authorized (shs.)	Outstanding (shs.)[1]
Preferred	20,000,000	nil
Common	unlimited	47,364,982

[1] At Aug. 22, 2023

Major Shareholder - Cheng Feng Zhou held 13.72% interest at Apr. 15, 2021.

Price Range - CHN.H/TSX-VEN (S)

Year	Volume	High	Low	Close
2022	2,245,258	$0.04	$0.02	$0.02
2021	17,433,641	$0.36	$0.03	$0.03
2020	3,649,940	$0.08	$0.02	$0.04
2019	6,232,835	$0.08	$0.03	$0.05
2018	4,956,249	$0.15	$0.04	$0.04

Wholly Owned Subsidiaries

CEN China Education Network Ltd., Vancouver, B.C. Inactive.
CEN China Education Overseas Corporation, British Virgin Islands. Inactive.
China Educational International Inc., British Virgin Islands. Inactive.
The Winning Edge Ltd., People's Republic of China. Inactive.
- 100% int. in **CEN Smart Networks Ltd.**, People's Republic of China. Inactive.
  - 100% int. in **Today's Teachers Technology and Culture Ltd.**
    - 60% int. in **Zhong Yu Cheng Yuan Education Technology Ltd.**, People's Republic of China.

C.108 China Keli Electric Company Ltd.

Symbol - ZKL.H **Exchange** - TSX-VEN (S) **CUSIP** - 168930
Head Office - 850-1095 Pender St W, Vancouver, BC, V6E 2M6 **Telephone** - (604) 893-7007 **Fax** - (604) 677-6621
Website - www.zkl.cc
Email - philip3336@126.com
Investor Relations - Tsz Fung Lo (604) 893-7007
Auditors - K. R. Margetson Ltd. C.A., Vancouver, B.C.
Lawyers - CMJC Law Corporation, Burnaby, B.C.
Transfer Agents - Odyssey Trust Company, Vancouver, B.C.
Profile - (B.C. 2005) Pursuing acquisition of nickel extraction technology company.
Common suspended from TSX-VEN, Jan. 9, 2023.
Predecessor Detail - Name changed from HSF Capital Corporation, May 5, 2010, pursuant to Qualifying Transaction reverse takeover acquisition of Creative Grace Ltd.
Directors - Tsz Fung (Philip) Lo, CEO, CFO & corp. sec., Hong Kong, Hong Kong, People's Republic of China; Alan P. Chan, Calgary, Alta.; Yee Man Cheung, Hong Kong, Hong Kong, People's Republic of China; Sean Webster, Hong Kong, People's Republic of China

Capital Stock

	Authorized (shs.)	Outstanding (shs.)[1]
Common	unlimited	12,110,026

[1] At Aug. 31, 2022

Major Shareholder - Sean Webster held 14.4% interest at Nov. 25, 2022.

Price Range - ZKL.H/TSX-VEN (S)

Year	Volume	High	Low	Close
2021	429,913	$4.70	$0.30	$0.37
2018	410,768	$1.90	$0.20	$0.30

Consolidation: 1-for-20 cons. in May 2021
Capital Stock Changes - On May 5, 2021, common shares were consolidated on a 1-for-20 basis. In August 2021, private placement of 4,347,826 post-consolidated common shares was completed at 23¢ per share. Also during fiscal 2022, 3,241,439 post-consolidated common shares were issued for debt settlement.

Wholly Owned Subsidiaries

Hydrotech Energy Metals Limited

Financial Statistics

Periods ended:	12m Apr. 30/22[A]		12m Apr. 30/21[A]
	$000s	%Chg	$000s
General & admin expense	263		235
Operating expense	**263**	**+12**	**235**
Operating income	**(263)**	**n.a.**	**(235)**
Finance costs, net	19		40
Pre-tax income	**(282)**	**n.a.**	**(226)**
Net income	**(282)**	**n.a.**	**(226)**
Cash & equivalent	276		8
Accounts receivable	7		12
Current assets	363		20
Total assets	**363**	**n.m.**	**20**
Bank indebtedness	nil		746
Accts. pay. & accr. liabs.	49		69
Current liabilities	200		1,268
Shareholders' equity	163		(1,248)
Cash from oper. activs.	**(376)**	**n.a.**	**(327)**
Cash from fin. activs.	644		316
Net cash position	**276**	**n.m.**	**8**
	$		$
Earnings per share*	(0.03)		(0.05)
Cash flow per share*	(0.04)		(0.07)
	shs		shs
No. of shs. o/s*	12,110,026		4,520,761
Avg. no. of shs. o/s*	10,093,153		4,520,761
	%		%
Net profit margin	n.a.		n.a.
Return on equity	n.m.		n.m.
Return on assets	(147.26)		(922.45)

* Common
[A] Reported in accordance with IFRS

Latest Results

Periods ended:	3m July 31/22^A		3m July 31/21^A
	$000s	%Chg	$000s
Net income	(13)	n.a.	(76)
	$		$
Earnings per share*	(0.00)		(0.02)

* Common
^A Reported in accordance with IFRS

Historical Summary
(as originally stated)

Fiscal Year	Oper. Rev.	Net Inc. Bef. Disc.	EPS*
	$000s	$000s	$
2022^A	nil	(282)	(0.03)
2021^A	nil	(226)	(0.05)
2020^A	nil	1,980	0.44
2019^A	nil	(255)	(0.06)
2018^A	11,263	(9,161)	(2.02)

* Common
^A Reported in accordance with IFRS
Note: Adjusted throughout for 1-for-20 cons. in May 2021

C.109 ChitogenX Inc.

Symbol - CHGX **Exchange** - CSE **CUSIP** - 169916
Head Office - 16667 boul Hymus, Kirkland, QC, H9H 4R9 **Telephone** - (514) 782-0951 **Fax** - (514) 694-0865
Website - www.chitogenx.com
Email - dumais@chitogenx.com
Investor Relations - Frederic Dumais (514) 693-8847
Auditors - Guimond Lavallée Inc. C.A., Brossard, Qué.
Transfer Agents - Computershare Trust Company of Canada Inc., Toronto, Ont.
Profile - (Can. 2015) Developing therapeutic soft tissue repair technologies to improve the success rate of orthopaedic and sports medicine surgeries.

The company's proprietary biopolymer has been specifically designed to augment and accelerate the regeneration of new tissue in occupational and sports related injuries to ligaments, tendons, meniscus and cartilage. Products under development include Ortho-R for rotator cuff injuries, Ortho-M for meniscus tears, Ortho-C for cartilage repair and Ortho-V for osteoarthritis pain.

Predecessor Detail - Name changed from Ortho Regenerative Technologies Inc., Sept. 12, 2022.
Directors - Philippe Deschamps, pres. & CEO, Pa.; Tim Cunningham, Mass.; Pierre Laurin, Qué.; Dr. H. B. Brent Norton, Collingwood, Ont.; Patrick T. O'Donnell, Mass.; Steven (Steve) Saviuk, Beaconsfield, Qué.; Howard P. Walthall, Ala.
Other Exec. Officers - Luc Mainville, sr. v-p & CFO; Dr. Jonathan Sackier, sr. v-p, medical affairs; Guy-Paul Allard, v-p, legal affairs & corp. sec.

Capital Stock

	Authorized (shs.)	Outstanding (shs.)[1]
Class AA Preferred	unlimited	nil
Class B Preferred	unlimited	nil
Class A Common	unlimited	51,038,776

[1] At July 31, 2022

Major Shareholder - Manitex Capital Inc. held 11% interest at June 16, 2022.

Price Range - CHGX/CSE

Year	Volume	High	Low	Close
2022	8,139,453	$0.39	$0.17	$0.26
2021	15,067,286	$0.93	$0.31	$0.33
2020	8,852,849	$0.99	$0.19	$0.66
2019	2,765,992	$0.43	$0.16	$0.21
2018	4,034,408	$0.89	$0.19	$0.24

Recent Close: $0.14

Capital Stock Changes - On Apr. 5, 2022, private placement of 16,000,000 units (1 class A common share & 1 warrant) at 20¢ per unit was completed, with warrants exercisable at 35¢ per share for two years.

Wholly Owned Subsidiaries

OR4102022 Inc., Pa.

Financial Statistics

Periods ended:	12m Jan. 31/22^A		12m Jan. 31/21^{oA}
	$000s	%Chg	$000s
Research & devel. expense	1,480		1,067
General & admin expense	1,471		1,492
Stock-based compensation	237		282
Operating expense	**3,188**	**+12**	**2,841**
Operating income	**(3,188)**	**n.a.**	**(2,841)**
Deprec., depl. & amort.	69		89
Finance costs, gross	1,307		842
Pre-tax income	**(4,921)**	**n.a.**	**(3,772)**
Net income	**(4,921)**	**n.a.**	**(3,772)**
Cash & equivalent	313		2,379
Current assets	722		2,840
Fixed assets, net	69		73
Intangibles, net	332		364
Total assets	**1,123**	**-66**	**3,277**
Accts. pay. & accr. liabs	607		291
Current liabilities	1,869		2,311
Long-term debt, gross	5,710		4,615
Long-term debt, net	4,776		2,767
Equity portion of conv. debs	nil		469
Shareholders' equity	(7,104)		(1,801)
Cash from oper. activs	**(3,220)**	**n.a.**	**(2,981)**
Cash from fin. activs	1,164		5,051
Cash from invest. activs	(33)		(3)
Net cash position	**313**	**-87**	**2,379**
Capital expenditures	(33)		(3)
	$		$
Earnings per share*	(0.14)		(0.13)
Cash flow per share*	(0.09)		(0.10)
	shs		shs
No. of shs. o/s*	34,956,093		34,567,600
Avg. no. of shs. o/s*	34,897,265		28,748,551
	%		%
Net profit margin	n.a.		n.a.
Return on equity	n.m.		n.m.
Return on assets	(164.27)		(128.40)

* Cl.A Common
^o Restated
^A Reported in accordance with IFRS

Latest Results

Periods ended:	6m July 31/22^A		6m July 31/21^A
	$000s	%Chg	$000s
Net income	(2,213)	n.a.	(2,146)
	$		$
Earnings per share*	(0.05)		(0.06)

* Cl.A Common
^A Reported in accordance with IFRS

Historical Summary
(as originally stated)

Fiscal Year	Oper. Rev.	Net Inc. Bef. Disc.	EPS*
	$000s	$000s	$
2022^A	nil	(4,921)	(0.14)
2021^A	nil	(3,772)	(0.13)
2020^A	nil	(2,488)	(0.10)
2019^A	nil	(2,399)	(0.10)
2018^A	nil	(2,022)	(0.12)

* Cl.A Common
^A Reported in accordance with IFRS

C.110 Choice Properties Real Estate Investment Trust*

Symbol - CHP.UN **Exchange** - TSX **CUSIP** - 17039A
Head Office - The Weston Centre, 700-22 St. Clair Ave E, Toronto, ON, M4T 2S5 **Telephone** - (416) 628-7771 **Toll-free** - (855) 322-2122 **Fax** - (416) 628-7777
Website - www.choicereit.ca
Email - mario.barrafato@choicereit.ca
Investor Relations - Mario Barrafato (416) 628-7872
Auditors - PricewaterhouseCoopers LLP C.A., Toronto, Ont.
Lawyers - Torys LLP, Toronto, Ont.
Transfer Agents - TSX Trust Company, Montréal, Qué.
FP500 Subsidiary Revenue Ranking - 59
Employees - 285 at Dec. 31, 2022
Profile - (Ont. 2013) Owns, manages and develops a diversified real estate portfolio of more than 700 retail, industrial, mixed-use and residential properties across Canada.

The retail portfolio is primarily focused on necessity-based retail tenants. The industrial portfolio is centered around large, purpose-built distribution facilities for **Loblaw Companies Limited** and high-quality generic industrial assets that readily accommodate the diverse needs of a broad range of tenants. The mixed-use and residential portfolio consists of both newly developed purpose-built residential rental buildings and residential-focused mixed-use communities that are transit accessible and located in Canada's largest cities, as well as mixed-use properties which include assets with an office component.

At June 30, 2023, the trust's portfolio consisted of 702 income-producing properties totaling 63,800,000 sq. ft. of gross leasable area (GLA). Loblaw, the trust's largest tenant, represented 57.4% of the total GLA at June 30, 2023.

Geographic diversification at June 30, 2023:

	Retail	Ind.	Other[1]
British Columbia	41	4	nil
Alberta	78	46	3
Saskatchewan	16	nil	nil
Manitoba	14	nil	nil
Ontario	241	44	7
Quebec	104	4	nil
Newfoundland	8	1	nil
New Brunswick	26	2	nil
Prince Edward Island	4	nil	nil
Nova Scotia	44	15	nil
	576	116	10

[1] Includes mixed-use and residential.

Asset mix at June 30, 2023:

Sector	Props.	Owned Sq. ft.[1]
Retail	576	44,300,000
Industrial	116	17,500,000
Other[2]	10	2,000,000
	702	63,800,000

[1] GLA.
[2] Includes mixed-use and residential.

The trust also has 20 active developments consisting of 14 retail, four industrial and two residential projects, which are expected to deliver 268,000 sq. ft. of retail space, 2,472,000 sq. ft. of industrial space and 348 residential units upon completion (on a proportionate share basis).

In March and May 2023, the trust sold excess lands at retail properties in Courtenay, B.C., and Scarborough, Ont., for $4,613,000 and $3,557,000, respectively.

In April 2023, the trust acquired a 1,800-sq.-ft. retail property in Toronto, Ont., for $1,915,000.

During 2022, the trust sold a 50% interest in development land in Edmonton, Alta., for $3,643,000 (August 2022); and a 4,410-sq.-ft. retail property in Beaverton, Ont., for $1,000,000 (December 2022).

In October 2022, the trust acquired a 1,600-sq.-ft. retail property in Toronto, Ont., for $1,488,000, and sold a 50% interest in a 24,773-sq.-ft. parcel on a retail property in Quebec, Que., for $4,325,000.

In July 2022, the trust acquired a retail property in Toronto, Ont., for $687,000. Also, the trust sold a parcel on a retail property in Dartmouth, N.S., for $117,000; and a 50% interest in a 6,238-sq.-ft. parcel on a retail property in Edmonton, Alta., for $2,000,000.

In March 2022, the trust acquired a 15,526-sq.-ft. retail property in Montreal, Que., from **Loblaw Companies Limited** for $2,343,000. The property was leased back by Loblaw.

Recent Merger and Acquisition Activity

Status: completed **Announced:** June 19, 2023
Choice Properties Real Estate Investment Trust sold a 50% interest in a 103,546-sq.-ft. office property in Dartmouth, N.S., for $13,360,000, including a $5,700,000 vendor take-back mortgage.

Status: completed **Announced:** June 14, 2023
Choice Properties Real Estate Investment Trust sold a 125,000-sq.-ft. data centre in Brampton, Ont., for $74,200,000, including a $51,000,000 vendor take-back mortgage.

Status: completed **Announced:** Apr. 21, 2023
Choice Properties Real Estate Investment Trust sold a 127,000-sq.-ft. retail property in Cornwall, Ont., for $10,000,000.

Status: completed **Announced:** Mar. 30, 2023
Choice Properties Real Estate Investment Trust completed an exchange of office properties in Calgary, Alta., with a partner, whereby Choice sold its 50% interest in Calgary Place in exchange for the partner's 50% interest in Altius Centre and a vendor take-back mortgage of $13,500,000.

Status: completed **Announced:** Mar. 24, 2023
Choice Properties Real Estate Investment Trust acquired a 46,512-sq.-ft. retail property in Whitby, Ont., for $17,876,000.

Status: completed **Announced:** Mar. 16, 2023
Choice Properties Real Estate Investment Trust acquired the remaining 50% interest in the industrial project at Horizon Business Park in Edmonton, Alta., from its partner for $32,090,000, consisting of $6,523,000 cash, assumption of $15,995,000 of debt, settlement of $5,385,000 of mortgage receivable and $4,187,000 in assumed liabilities. The acquired interest includes the partner's share of a completed building and a building under development.

Status: completed **Announced:** Feb. 24, 2023
Choice Properties Real Estate Investment Trust acquired a 19,735-sq.-ft. retail property in Toronto, Ont., as a land assembly to Choice's Golden Mile mixed-use development project. Total consideration was $23,049,000.

Status: completed **Announced:** Feb. 21, 2023
Choice Properties Real Estate Investment Trust sold a 104,286-sq.-ft. retail property in Kingston, Ont., for $23,000,000.

Status: completed **Announced:** Jan. 31, 2023
Choice Properties Real Estate Investment Trust acquired three retail properties, totaling 354,671 sq. ft., in Vernon, B.C., and Calgary (2), Alta., from Loblaw Companies Limited for a total of $99,149,000. Loblaw leased back the two Calgary properties.

Status: completed **Announced:** Dec. 28, 2022

Choice Properties Real Estate Investment Trust sold a 223,723-sq.-ft. office property in Halifax, N.S., for $40,000,000, consisting of $12,000,000 cash and a $28,000,000 mortgage receivable.
Status: completed **Announced:** Dec. 5, 2022
Choice Properties Real Estate Investment Trust acquired a 22,388-sq.-ft. retail property in Vaughan, Ont., for $19,750,000.
Status: completed **Announced:** Dec. 1, 2022
Choice Properties Real Estate Investment Trust acquired an 89,690-sq.-ft. retail property in Toronto, Ont., for $53,315,000.
Status: completed **Announced:** Sept. 13, 2022
Choice Properties Real Estate Investment Trust sold a 293,195-sq.-ft. office property in Montreal, Que., for $27,000,000.
Status: completed **Announced:** Sept. 1, 2022
Choice Properties Real Estate Investment Trust acquired a 34,177-sq.-ft. retail property in Toronto, Ont., for $19,180,000, consisting of $19,049,000 cash and $131,000 in assumed liabilities.
Status: completed **Announced:** July 18, 2022
Choice Properties Real Estate Investment Trust sold a 20,728-sq.-ft. retail property in Calgary, Alta., for $6,550,000.
Status: completed **Announced:** June 28, 2022
Choice Properties Real Estate Investment Trust sold a 136,084-sq.-ft. retail property in Swift Current, Sask., for $6,500,000.
Status: completed **Announced:** June 23, 2022
Choice Properties Real Estate Investment Trust sold a 50% interest in a retail property under development in Brampton, Ont., for $10,125,000.
Status: completed **Announced:** June 17, 2022
Choice Properties Real Estate Investment Trust acquired a 98,125-sq.-ft. retail property in Halifax, N.S., from Loblaw Companies Limited for $15,228,000, including $2,034,000 of assumed debt. The property was leased back by Loblaw.
Status: completed **Announced:** May 31, 2022
Choice Properties Real Estate Investment Trust acquired a 75% interest in 154 developable acres of industrial land in East Gwillimbury in the Greater Toronto Area for $52,800,000, by exercising the equity conversion right on a mezzanine loan advanced to Rice Group. Choice plans to develop the property into a multi-phase industrial park with the potential for 1,800,000 sq. ft. of new generation logistics space. For the first phase of the development, Choice and Loblaw Companies Limited entered into a 100-acre land lease where Loblaw plans to build a 1,200,000-sq.-ft. automated, multi-temperature industrial facility. The Loblaw facility was expected to be operational in the first quarter of 2024.
Status: completed **Announced:** May 2, 2022
Choice Properties Real Estate Investment Trust acquired a 131,473-sq.-ft. retail property in Burlington, Ont., for $42,059,000.
Status: completed **Announced:** Apr. 19, 2022
Choice Properties Real Estate Investment Trust acquired an 85% interest in an additional 97-acre parcel of land in Caledon, Ont., part of an existing industrial development project, for $86,741,000.
Status: completed **Announced:** Apr. 7, 2022
Choice Properties Real Estate Investment Trust acquired the remaining 50% interest in an 89,978-sq.-ft. industrial property in Edmonton, Alta., for $14,461,000.
Status: completed **Revised:** Mar. 31, 2022
UPDATE: The transaction was completed. PREVIOUS: Choice Properties Real Estate Investment Trust agreed to sell six urban office properties to Allied Properties Real Estate Investment Trust for $733,810,000, consisting of the issuance of $550,660,000 (11,809,145) of class B limited partnership units of a subsidiary limited partnership at $46.63 per unit and a $200,000,000 promissory note. The properties were located at 110 Yonge Street (50% interest), 525 University Avenue and 175 Bloor Street East (50% interest) in Toronto, Ont.; 1508 West Broadway and 1185 West Georgia Street in Vancouver, B.C.; and 1010 Sherbrooke Street West in Montreal, Que.
Status: completed **Announced:** Mar. 1, 2022
Choice Properties Real Estate Investment Trust acquired a parcel of industrial development land in Ottawa, Ont., from Loblaw Companies Limited for $27,218,000.

Trustees - Gordon A. M. Currie, chr., Toronto, Ont.; Rael L. Diamond, pres. & CEO, Toronto, Ont.; Graeme M. Eadie‡, Toronto, Ont.; L. Jay Cross, Houston, Tex.; Diane A. Kazarian, Toronto, Ont.; Karen A. Kinsley, Ottawa, Ont.; R. Michael Latimer, Toronto, Ont.; Nancy H. O. Lockhart, Toronto, Ont.; Dale R. Ponder, Toronto, Ont.; Qi Tang, Toronto, Ont.; Cornell C. V. Wright, Toronto, Ont.

Other Exec. Officers - Ana Radic, COO; Mario Barrafato, CFO; Niall Collins, exec. v-p, devel. & const.; Mario Fatica, sr. v-p, comml. devel.; Andrew Reial, sr. v-p, office & ind.; Evan Williams, sr. v-p, retail leasing; Marcus Bertagnolli, v-p, IT solutions; Amy Chan, v-p, devel., design & eng.; Simone Cole, v-p, gen. counsel & corp. sec.; Carla Fedele, v-p, retail asset mgt., western Canada; Adam Flekser, v-p, devel.; Salman Hirani, v-p, retail asset mgt., Ont.; Erin Johnston, v-p, fin.; Sandra Liepkalns, v-p, info. security; Jennifer Maccarone, v-p, HR; Farid Malek, v-p, technical opers. & capital projects; Sharon Mitchell, v-p, bus. process optimization; Claudia Nemi, v-p, natl. prop. mgt.; Julie Robinson, v-p, const.; Joe Svec, v-p, devel. & planning; Nicole Vicano, v-p, retail, asset mgt.

‡ Lead trustee

Capital Stock

	Authorized (shs.)	Outstanding (shs.)[1]
Trust Unit	unlimited	327,859,972
Special Vtg. Unit	unlimited	395,786,525
Class A LP Unit	unlimited	n.a
Class B LP Unit	unlimited	395,786,525[2]

[1] At June 30, 2023
[2] Classified as debt.

Note: All limited partnership units are issued by subsidiary Choice Properties Limited Partnership. Class B limited partnership units are held by George Weston Limited.

Trust Unit - The trust will endeavour to make monthly cash distributions. One vote per unit.

Special Voting Unit - Only issued in tandem with class B limited partnership units and are not transferable separately from the class B limited partnership units to which they relate and, upon any valid transfer of class B limited partnership units, such special voting units will automatically be transferred to the transferee of the class B limited partnership units. As class B limited partnership units are exchanged for trust units or redeemed or purchased for cancellation, the corresponding special voting units will be cancelled for no consideration. Holders are not entitled to any economic interest in the trust, or to any interest or share in the trust, any of its distributions or in any of its net assets in the event of the termination or winding-up of the trust. Entitles the holder thereof with a right to vote on matters respecting the trust equal to the number of trust units that may be obtained upon the exchange of the class B limited partnership units for which each special voting unit is attached.

Class A Limited Partnership Unit - Held by the trust.

Class B Limited Partnership Unit - Economically equivalent to trust units. Receive distributions equal to the distributions paid on the trust units. Exchangeable, at the holder's option, into trust units on a one-for-one basis. Classified as debt.

Options - At Dec. 31, 2022, options were outstanding to purchase 253,154 trust units at prices ranging from $11.92 to $14.21 per unit expiring in 2024 and 2025.

Normal Course Issuer Bid - The company plans to make normal course purchases of up to 27,566,522 trust units representing 10% of the public float. The bid commenced on Nov. 21, 2022, and expires on Nov. 20, 2023.

Major Shareholder - George Weston Limited held 61.7% interest at June 30, 2023.

Price Range - CHP.UN/TSX

Year	Volume	High	Low	Close
2022	101,424,821	$15.91	$12.18	$14.76
2021	109,829,049	$15.40	$12.53	$15.19
2020	144,329,981	$15.14	$10.58	$13.01
2019	119,579,295	$14.75	$11.31	$13.91
2018	125,604,821	$13.46	$11.19	$11.52

Recent Close: $13.20

Capital Stock Changes - During 2022, 404,449 trust units were issued under unit-based compensation arrangement and 222,147 trust units were repurchased under a Normal Course Issuer Bid.

Dividends

CHP.UN unit Ra $0.75 pa M est. Apr. 17, 2023[1]
Prev. Rate: $0.74 est. June 15, 2017
[1] Distribution reinvestment plan suspended eff. May 2018.

Long-Term Debt - Outstanding at Dec. 31, 2022:

Revolv. credit facility[1]	$257,617,000
Sr. unsecured debs.[2]	5,308,928,000
Mtges. pay.[3]	945,959,000
Construction loans[4]	39,214,000
Cl.B exchangeable units	5,841,809,000
	12,393,527,000

[1] Borrowings under a $1.5 billion revolving credit facility, bearing interest at prime plus 0.2% or bankers' acceptance rate plus 1.2% and due Sept. 1, 2027.
[2] Had a weighted average effective interest rate of 3.79% and a weighted average term to maturity of 5.2 years (Dec. 31, 2021 - 3.56% and 5.4 years, respectively)
[3] Had a weighted average effective interest rate of 3.92% and a weighted average term to maturity of 5.0 years (Dec. 31, 2021 - 3.75% and 5.2 years, respectively).
[4] Had a weighted average effective interest rate of 3.54% and a weighted average term to maturity of 5.5 years which are due on demand (Dec. 31, 2021 - 2.08% and 6.0 years, respectively).

Note - In March 2023, offering of $550,000,000 principal amount of 5.4% series S senior unsecured debentures due Mar. 1, 2033, was completed. In August 2023, private placement of $350,000,000 principal amount of 5.699% series T senior unsecured debentures due Feb. 28, 2034, was completed.

Wholly Owned Subsidiaries

CPH Master Limited Partnership, Ont.
Choice Properties GP Inc., Canada.

Investments

45.3% int. in **Choice Properties Limited Partnership**, Ont. Class A limited partnership units.

Note: The preceding list includes only the major related companies in which interests are held.

Financial Statistics

Periods ended:	12m Dec. 31/22[A]		12m Dec. 31/21[A]
	$000s	%Chg	$000s
Total revenue	**1,264,594**	**-2**	**1,292,321**
Rental operating expense	363,953		380,306
General & admin. expense	46,620		39,623
Operating expense	**410,573**	**-2**	**419,929**
Operating income	**854,021**	**-2**	**872,392**
Investment income	369,362		66,952
Deprec. & amort.	2,201		2,294
Finance income	27,360		20,079
Finance costs, gross	536,857		534,525
Pre-tax income	**744,136**	**n.m.**	**22,329**
Income taxes	(117)		(679)
Net income	**744,253**	**n.m.**	**23,008**
Cash & equivalent	64,736		84,304
Accounts receivable	69,965		63,353
Long-term investments	1,978,611		919,279
Income-producing props.	14,119,000		14,707,000
Properties under devel.	325,000		223,000
Residential inventory	18,785		10,142
Property interests, net	14,462,785		14,940,142
Right-of-use assets	2,029		1,956
Intangibles, net	21,369		28,000
Total assets	**16,819,527**	**+4**	**16,172,603**
Accts. pay. & accr. liabs.	307,654		307,039
Long-term debt, gross	12,393,527		12,242,007
Long-term lease liabilities	1,960		1,920
Shareholders' equity	3,824,153		3,310,191
Cash from oper. activs.	**633,154**	**-5**	**669,428**
Cash from fin. activs.	(35,992)		(728,221)
Cash from invest. activs.	(616,730)		(64,122)
Net cash position	**64,736**	**-23**	**84,304**
Increase in property	(342,725)		(193,009)
Decrease in property	109,281		254,322
	$		$
Earnings per share*	n.a.		n.a.
Cash flow per share*	1.93		2.04
Funds from opers. per sh.*	0.96		0.95
Adj. funds from opers. per sh.*	0.80		0.81
Cash divd. per share*	0.74		0.74
Total divd. per share*	**0.74**		**0.74**
	shs		shs
No. of shs. o/s*	327,771,149		327,588,847
	%		%
Net profit margin	58.85		1.78
Return on equity	20.86		0.67
Return on assets	7.77		3.61
No. of employees (FTEs)	285		298

* Trust unit
[A] Reported in accordance with IFRS

Latest Results

Periods ended:	6m June 30/23[A]		6m June 30/22[A]
	$000s	%Chg	$000s
Total revenue	654,984	+2	641,130
Net income	806,472	+115	375,176
	$		$
Earnings per share*	n.a.		n.a.

[A] Reported in accordance with IFRS

Historical Summary
(as originally stated)

Fiscal Year	Total Rev.	Net Inc. Bef. Disc.	EPS*
	$000s	$000s	$
2022[A]	1,264,594	744,253	n.a.
2021[A]	1,292,321	23,008	n.a.
2020[A]	1,270,614	450,685	n.a.
2019[A]	1,288,554	(581,357)	n.a.
2018[A]	1,148,273	649,577	n.a.

* Trust unit
[A] Reported in accordance with IFRS

C.111 Choom Holdings Inc.

Symbol - CHOO **Exchange** - CSE (S) **CUSIP** - 17040B
Head Office - 191 2 Ave W, Vancouver, BC, V5Y 1B8 **Telephone** - (604) 683-2509 **Toll-free** - (866) 683-2505 **Fax** - (604) 683-2506
Email - investors@choom.ca
Investor Relations - Terese J. Gieselman (866) 683-2505
Auditors - Smythe LLP C.A., Vancouver, B.C.
Lawyers - McMillan LLP, Vancouver, B.C.
Transfer Agents - Computershare Trust Company of Canada Inc., Vancouver, B.C.

Profile - (B.C. 2006) Owns and operates cannabis retail stores and an e-commerce website under the Choom brand in Canada.

At August 2022, the company had one operational store in Niagara Falls, Ont.

On Apr. 22, 2022, the company and certain of its subsidiaries obtained an order of the Supreme Court of British Columbia providing protection from their creditors pursuant to the Companies' Creditors Arrangement Act (CCAA). Under the order, the company and its subsidiaries are authorized to enter into an interim financing term sheet with **Aurora Cannabis Inc.** pursuant to which Aurora agreed to advance up to $800,000 to fund ongoing operations and the CCAA proceedings. **Ernst & Young Inc.** was appointed as monitor.

Common suspended from CSE, June 6, 2022.

Recent Merger and Acquisition Activity

Status: completed **Revised:** Sept. 1, 2022

UPDATE: The sale of the Ontario store was completed for $1,100,000, consisting of $300,000 cash and issuance of 364,185 common shares. PREVIOUS: Choom Holdings Inc. agreed to sell nine operating retail cannabis stores in British Columbia (2), Alberta (6) and Ontario (1) to High Tide Inc. for $5,100,000 to be satisfied by the issuance of High Tide common shares. The sale represents substantially all of Choom's operations. The transaction was the result of the sale and investment solicitation process permitted under Choom's previously announced proceedings under the Companies' Creditors Arrangement Act (Canada). Aug. 4, 2022 - The sale of the British Columbia and Alberta stores was completed for $4,200,000 satisfied through the issuance of 1,782,838 common shares. The sale of the Ontario operations was expected to close in September 2022.

Predecessor Detail - Name changed from Standard Graphite Corporation, Nov. 17, 2017, following acquisition of Medi-Can Health Solutions Ltd.

Other Exec. Officers - Erik Collings, v-p, store & community devel.; Daphne Kao, v-p, people & culture; Richard (Rick) Mather, v-p, opers.; Terese J. Gieselman, corp. sec.

Capital Stock

	Authorized (shs.)	Outstanding (shs.)[1]
Preferred	unlimited	nil
Common	unlimited	466,973,142

[1] At Aug. 22, 2023

Major Shareholder - Aurora Cannabis Inc. held 19.19% interest at Mar. 31, 2023.

Price Range - SGH/TSX-VEN (D)

Year	Volume	High	Low	Close
2022	79,554,680	$0.04	$0.01	$0.01
2021	203,504,112	$0.18	$0.03	$0.04
2020	94,430,782	$0.24	$0.06	$0.07
2019	141,231,971	$0.87	$0.14	$0.18
2018	267,644,389	$1.47	$0.38	$0.43

Capital Stock Changes - In July 2021, public offering of 43,750,000 units (1 common share & ½ warrant) at 8¢ per unit was completed, with warrants exercisable at 12¢ per share for three years. In addition, 79,754,843 common shares were issued on conversion of debenture.

Wholly Owned Subsidiaries

Arbutus Brands Inc., Vancouver, B.C.
- 9.8% int. in **Sitka Weed Works Inc.**, Sooke, B.C.

Choom BC Retail Holdings Inc., B.C.
Choom Holdings USA Inc., United States.
Concord Medical Centre Inc., B.C.
835148 Yukon Inc., Yuk.
Island Green Cure Ltd., Vancouver, B.C.
Medi-Can Health Solutions Inc., B.C.
102047851 Saskatchewan Ltd., Sask.
1165962 B.C. Ltd., B.C.
Phivida Holdings Inc., Vancouver, B.C.
- 100% int. in **Phivida Organics Inc.**, B.C.
- 100% int. in **Wikala.com Inc.**, Canada.
  - 100% int. in **Platform WD d.o.o.**, Serbia.
  - 100% int. in **Wikala Holdings Inc.**, Canada.

2150639 Alberta Ltd., Calgary, Alta.
2150647 Alberta Ltd., Calgary, Alta.
2151414 Alberta Ltd., Calgary, Alta.
2168698 Alberta Ltd., Alta.
2660837 Ontario Ltd., Toronto, Ont.
2668667 Ontario Ltd., Ont.
2688412 Ontario Inc., Ont.
Universal Cannabis Coaching Inc., B.C.
Western Cannabis Coaching Centre Inc., B.C.

Financial Statistics

Periods ended:	12m June 30/21[A]		12m June 30/20[□A]
	$000s	%Chg	$000s
Operating revenue	**22,048**	**+200**	**7,358**
Cost of sales	13,912		5,107
Salaries & benefits	4,218		2,530
General & admin expense	4,041		5,851
Stock-based compensation	844		1,321
Operating expense	**23,015**	**+55**	**14,809**
Operating income	**(967)**	**n.a.**	**(7,451)**
Deprec., depl. & amort.	3,912		1,711
Finance income	27		295
Finance costs, gross	5,078		3,654
Write-downs/write-offs	(8,377)[1]		(6,197)[2]
Pre-tax income	**(20,129)**	**n.a.**	**(20,187)**
Income taxes	86		(167)
Net inc. bef. disc. opers	**(20,216)**	**n.a.**	**(20,020)**
Income from disc. opers	(1,407)		(326)
Net income	**(21,623)**	**n.a.**	**(20,346)**
Cash & equivalent	315		508
Inventories	909		1,002
Accounts receivable	357		351
Current assets	2,291		2,932
Long-term investments	715		1,905
Fixed assets, net	4,477		7,132
Right-of-use assets	7,367		8,096
Intangibles, net	10,780		11,089
Total assets	**26,206**	**-20**	**32,621**
Bank indebtedness	nil		1,093
Accts. pay. & accr. liabs	5,911		3,987
Current liabilities	12,387		6,640
Long-term debt, gross	21,470		17,847
Long-term debt, net	17,361		17,847
Long-term lease liabilities	6,653		6,590
Equity portion of conv. debs	5,739		5,739
Shareholders' equity	(11,156)		583
Cash from oper. activs	**472**	**n.a.**	**(4,783)**
Cash from fin. activs	(1,588)		4,322
Cash from invest. activs	924		(3,894)
Net cash position	**269**	**-42**	**461**
Capital expenditures	(1,043)		(4,309)
Capital disposals	469		1,092
	$		$
Earnings per share*	(0.07)		(0.10)
Cash flow per share*	0.00		(0.02)
	shs		shs
No. of shs. o/s*	325,504,273		225,753,870
Avg. no. of shs. o/s*	292,871,775		205,122,695
	%		%
Net profit margin	(91.69)		(272.08)
Return on equity	n.m.		(263.75)
Return on assets	(51.39)		(53.31)
No. of employees (FTEs)	40		51

* Common
□ Restated
[A] Reported in accordance with IFRS
[1] Includes impairment of $3,633,623 for property and equipment, $1,974,993 for intangible assets and $1,835,430 for goodwill.
[2] Includes $5,340,511 impairment of goodwill.

Latest Results

Periods ended:	3m Sept. 30/21[A]		3m Sept. 30/20[□A]
	$000s	%Chg	$000s
Operating revenue	4,841	-19	5,985
Net inc. bef. disc. opers	5,103	n.a.	(1,917)
Income from disc. opers	(35)		(1,062)
Net income	5,069	n.a.	(2,979)
	$		$
Earnings per share*	0.01		(0.01)

* Common
□ Restated
[A] Reported in accordance with IFRS

Historical Summary
(as originally stated)

Fiscal Year	Oper. Rev.	Net Inc. Bef. Disc.	EPS*
	$000s	$000s	$
2021[A]	22,048	(20,216)	(0.07)
2020[A]	7,945	(20,241)	(0.10)
2019[A]	268	(11,431)	(0.06)
2018[A]	nil	(6,575)	(0.07)
2017[A]	nil	(686)	(0.01)

* Common
[A] Reported in accordance with IFRS

C.112 Chorus Aviation Inc.*

Symbol - CHR **Exchange** - TSX **CUSIP** - 17040T
Head Office - 380-3 Spectacle Lake Dr, Dartmouth, NS, B3B 1W8 **Telephone** - (902) 873-5000
Website - www.chorusaviation.com
Email - tcotie@chorusaviation.com
Investor Relations - Tyrone D. Cotie (902) 873-5641
Auditors - PricewaterhouseCoopers LLP C.A., Halifax, N.S.
Lawyers - Osler, Hoskin & Harcourt LLP, Toronto, Ont.
Transfer Agents - Computershare Trust Company of Canada Inc.; TSX Trust Company, Halifax, N.S.
FP500 Revenue Ranking - 257
Employees - 4,829 at Dec. 31, 2022

Profile - (Can. 2010) Provides a full suite of regional and specialty aviation services including aircraft acquisition and leasing, aircraft refurbishment, engineering, modification, repurposing and transition, contract flying, aircraft and component maintenance, disassembly, parts provisioning and pilot training.

The company's operations are grouped into two segments: Regional Aviation Services; and Regional Aircraft Leasing.

Regional Aviation Services

Wholly owned **Jazz Aviation LP** operates an integral part of **Air Canada**'s domestic and transborder network under the Air Canada Express brand. The companies are parties to a capacity purchase agreement (CPA) under which Jazz provides service to and from lower density markets as well as higher density markets at off-peak times throughout Canada and to and from certain destinations in the U.S. Jazz operates flights on behalf of Air Canada, and Air Canada controls and is responsible for the covered aircraft fuel, scheduling, pricing, product distribution, seat inventories, marketing, advertising and customer service handling at certain airports.

Under the CPA, Air Canada purchases substantially all of the company's fleet capacity based on predetermined rates. The company earns a fixed fee based on an agreed number of covered aircraft operated during the term of the CPA, as well as incentive payments for successfully achieving certain performance levels related to controllable on-time performance, controllable flight completion, baggage handling performance and other customer satisfaction measures related to in-flight and check-in experience. In addition, the company is paid controllable revenue rates based on controllable costs, with the variance between revenue and cost being limited to $2,000,000 annually. Controllable costs include wages and benefits, depreciation and amortization, aircraft maintenance, materials and supplies, operating leases and other general overhead expenses. The company is also paid pass-through revenue based on pass-through costs such as airport and navigation fees, and certain aircraft maintenance, materials and supplies. Aircraft leasing revenue is also earned from certain owned aircraft and spare engines. The CPA specifies that Air Canada and Jazz will jointly agree on a seasonal operating plan prior to the start of each summer and winter schedule period which includes Air Canada's forecast regarding block hours and departures by aircraft type, available seat miles and passenger volume, and the airports to which Jazz will operate scheduled flights.

Jazz Operating Statistics:

Year ended Dec. 31	2022	2021
No. of departures	159,624	90,564
Block hours	264,174	144,999
No. of oper. aircraft[1]	114	114

[1] Covered aircraft in the CPA.

Charter flights are operated for a variety of customers through wholly owned **Voyageur Aviation Corp.** and through Jazz. Voyageur also provides specialized contract flying operations such as medical, logistical and humanitarian flights to international and Canadian customers. Through its Jazz Technical Services division, Jazz offers maintenance, repair and overhaul, part sales and technical services. Voyageur, through its Voyageur Aerotech division, also provides specialty, maintenance, repair and overhaul services, as well as engineering services.

At Dec. 31, 2022, the Regional Aviation Services segment had a fleet of 145 owned or leased aircraft, including 48 owned aircraft covered under the CPA, 58 leased aircraft covered under the CPA, 22 Voyageur aircraft and 17 non-operational aircraft.

Regional Aircraft Leasing

Operations consist of leasing owned aircraft and its asset management business. Earnings from owned aircraft include lease income from leasing aircraft to third-party air operators; and income from the trade and sale of aircraft. Earnings from managed aircraft includes asset management fees for managing aircraft on behalf of fund investors and other third-party aircraft investors and/or aircraft owners; co-investment returns from equity investment in managed funds of wholly owned **Falko Regional Aircraft Limited**; and incentive fees from funds it manages where the returns generated exceed the fund's investment performance targets. At Dec. 31, 2022, the portfolio consisted of 124 wholly or majority-owned owned aircraft and 88 aircraft managed by Falko.

Also provides pilot training through **Cygnet Aviation Academy LP**, which enables cadets to attain an integrated airline transport pilot license (ATPL) to prepare pilots for direct entry into airlines and acquire an airline-specific rating over a 20-month program consisting of training methods, scenario-based flight simulation training and airline pilot mentorship.

On Mar. 28, 2023, the company and **CAE Inc.** launched **Cygnet Aviation Academy LP**, a pilot academy in Kingston, Ont. which offers integrated airline transport pilot license (ATPL) and airline-specific rating training programs and simulations for cadet pilots. Cygnet was held through wholly owned **Jazz Aviation LP**.

Recent Merger and Acquisition Activity

Status: completed **Announced:** Dec. 31, 2022
Chorus Aviation Inc. sold 12 aircraft to a third party for $271,136,000, net of security deposits of $2,066,000.

Status: completed **Revised:** May 3, 2022
UPDATE: The transaction was completed. PREVIOUS: Chorus Aviation Inc. agreed to acquire Falko Regional Aircraft Limited, a regional aircraft lessor, and the equity interests in certain entities and aircraft which are ultimately owned by funds managed by Fortress Investment Group LLC and managed by Falko. The total consideration is US$855,000,000 consisting of US$445,000,000 of cash consideration and US$410,000,000 of existing indebtedness. The transaction includes Falko's asset management platform and Fortress' equity interests in 126 owned and managed regional aircraft. The combined company would have a total of 353 owned, operated, and managed regional aircraft. Upon closing, Chorus anticipates having 32 airline customers in 23 countries. Brookfield Asset Management Inc., through its Special Investments program, and together with institutional partners, has agreed to make an equity investment in Chorus consisting of US$300,000,000 of series 1 preferred shares and US$74,000,000 of class A variable voting and/or class B voting shares. The preferred shares will be non-convertible and would initially pay a dividend of 8.75% annually in cash, or 9.5% in kind, at Chorus' option, with step-ups after the sixth anniversary. The transaction was expected to close in the second quarter of 2022.

Predecessor Detail - Succeeded Jazz Air Income Fund, Dec. 31, 2010, pursuant to plan of arrangement whereby Chorus Aviation Inc. was formed to facilitate the conversion of the fund into a corporation and the fund was subsequently dissolved.

Directors - Paul C. Rivett, chr., Toronto, Ont.; Colin L. Copp, pres., CEO & pres., Chorus Aviation Services, Kelowna, B.C.; Karen Cramm, Halifax, N.S.; Gail Hamilton, St. John's, N.L.; R. Stephen Hannahs, Corona del Mar, Calif.; Alan Jenkins, Limerick, Ireland; Amos S. Kazzaz, Saint-Laurent, Qué.; David Levenson, Ont.; Marie-Lucie Morin, Ottawa, Ont.; Frank Yu, N.Y.

Other Exec. Officers - Gary Osborne, CFO; M. Jolene Mahody, exec. v-p & chief strategy officer; Dennis Lopes, sr. v-p, chief legal officer & corp. sec.; Laurel Clark, v-p, corp. HR & sustainability; Tyrone D. Cotie, v-p, treasury & IR; Chris Kelly, v-p, finl. planning & analysis & internal audit; Jim Murphy, v-p, corp. strategy; Colleen Purcell, v-p, corp. reporting; Jeremy Barnes, pres., Chorus Aircraft Leasing & CEO, Falko Regional Aircraft Limited; Cory Cousineau, pres., Voyageur Aviation Corp.; Randolph deGooyer, pres., Jazz Aviation LP; Steven A. (Steve) Ridolfi, pres., Chorus Aviation Capital Corp.

Capital Stock

	Authorized (shs.)	Outstanding (shs.)[1]
Preferred	80,750,000	nil
Series 1		300,000
Class A Variable Vtg.	unlimited	n.a
Class B Vtg.	unlimited	n.a
Class A & B	unlimited	194,715,595

[1] At July 24, 2023

Series 1 Preferred - Issued to Brookfield Special Investments Fund L.P., an entity controlled by Brookfield Corporation. Entitled to an annual dividend of 8.75% in cash or 9.5% in kind, increasing each year by 1% per annum in cash, 1.5% per annum in kind, starting on the sixth anniversary of the issuance (May 3, 2028) up to a cap of 14.75% per annum in cash and 15.5% per annum in kind. Non-voting.

Class A Variable Voting - Held by individuals who are not Canadians as defined in the Canada Transportation Act (CTA). Automatically convertible into class B voting shares on a one-for-one basis if the shares become held by a qualified Canadian or foreign ownership restrictions in the CTA are repealed and not replaced with similar provisions. Convertible at option of holder into class B shares if an offer is made for all or substantially all of the class B shares. This conversion right is only exercisable for the purpose of depositing the resulting class B shares in response to the offer. Entitled to one vote per share, unless: (i) a single non-Canadian holder or non-Canadians authorized to provide air service hold more than 25% of all class A and class B shares outstanding or votes that would be cast by or on behalf of a single non-Canadian or non-Canadians authorized to provide air service would exceed 25% of the total number of votes that would be cast at any meeting; and (ii) class A shares outstanding would exceed 49% of all class A and class B shares outstanding or votes that would be cast by or on behalf of class A shareholders would exceed 49% of the total number of votes that would be cast at any meeting. If either of these thresholds is exceeded, the vote attached to each class A share will decrease proportionately and automatically such that: (i) a single non-Canadian holder or non-Canadians authorized to provide air service do not carry more than 25% of all class A and class B shares outstanding or votes that would be cast by or on behalf of a single non-Canadian or non-Canadians authorized to provide air service would not exceed 25% of the total number of votes that would be cast at any meeting; and (ii) all class A shareholders do not carry more than 49% of the total number of all class A and class B shares outstanding or votes that would be cast by or on behalf of class A shareholders would not exceed 49% of the total number of votes that would be cast at any meeting.

Class B Voting - Held by qualified Canadians under the CTA. Automatically convertible into class A variable voting shares on a one-for-one basis if the shares become held by a non-qualified Canadian unless the foreign ownership restrictions of the CTA are repealed and not replaced with similar restrictions. Convertible at option of holder into class A shares if an offer is made for all or substantially all of the class A shares. This conversion right is only exercisable for the purpose of depositing the resulting class A shares in response to the offer. One vote per share.

Warrants - At Dec. 31, 2022, warrants were outstanding exercisable for 18,642,772 class A or B shares at $4.60 per share expiring on May 3, 2029.

Normal Course Issuer Bid - The company plans to make normal course purchases of up to 15,928,236 class A or B shares representing 10% of the public float. The bid commenced on Nov. 14, 2022, and expires on Nov. 13, 2023.

Major Shareholder - Brookfield Corporation held 12.9% interest at Mar. 24, 2023.

Price Range - CHR/TSX

Year	Volume	High	Low	Close
2022	119,952,358	$4.54	$2.24	$3.24
2021	158,306,636	$5.34	$3.16	$3.32
2020	288,140,353	$8.45	$1.80	$3.70
2019	83,268,049	$8.30	$5.43	$8.09
2018	107,136,657	$9.86	$4.54	$5.64

Recent Close: $2.65

Capital Stock Changes - In May 2022, private placement of 25,400,000 class B voting shares at Cdn$3.70 per share and 300,000 series 1 preferred shares at US$1,000 per share was completed with Brookfield Corporation (formerly Brookfield Asset Management Inc.) Also during 2022, 1,718,972 class A variable voting or class B voting shares were repurchased under a Normal Course Issuer Bid.

Long-Term Debt - Outstanding at Dec. 31, 2022:

Unsecured revolv. credit facility[1]	$101,580,000
Warehouse credit facility[2]	85,847,000
Term loans, secured by engines[3]	4,507,000
Term loans, secured by aircraft[4]	1,293,761,000
5.75% unsec. debs. due Dec. 2024	86,250,000
6% conv. debs. due June 2026[5]	72,500,000
5.75% unsec. debs. due June 2027	85,000,000
3.33% term loan due Aug. 2027	5,000,000
Asset backed securitization[6]	309,665,000
Less: Deferred fin. costs	12,816,000
Less: Accretion discount	12,327,000
	2,018,967,000
Less: Current portion	340,308,000
	1,678,659,000

[1] Bears interest at U.S. dollar LIBOR plus 5% and matures in April 2024.
[2] Bears interest at a weighted average rate of 5.07% and matures in January 2025.
[3] Bear interest at a weighted average rate of 4.29% and due between December 2024 and May 2028.
[4] Bear interest at a weighted average rate of 3.87% and due between May 2023 and February 2033.
[5] An equity component of $2,683,000 was included as part of shareholders' equity.
[6] Represents a majority interest in an equity note issued by Regional 2021-1 Limited in connection with an asset backed securitization of 39 regional aircraft.

Note - In January and May 2023, maturity of the unsecured revolving credit facility was extended to April 2026 from April 2024 and principal amount increased from $100,000,000 to $150,000,000, respectively. The facility bears interest at prime plus 1.5% to 2.5% or banker's acceptance rate plus 2.5% to 3.5% and for U.S. advances: U.S. base rate plus 1.5% to 2.5% or SOFR plus 2.5% to 3.5%.

Wholly Owned Subsidiaries

Adare Aircraft Leasing Limited, Ireland.
Antrim Aircraft Leasing Limited, Ireland.
Aviation General Partner Inc., Ont.
Bloom Aircraft Leasing Limited, Ireland.
Cavan Aircraft Leasing Limited, Ireland.
Chorus Aviation Capital Corp., Canada.
• 100% int. in **Jazz Leasing Inc.**, Canada.
Chorus Aviation Holdings GP Inc., Canada.
Chorus Aviation Investment Holdings LP, Ont.
Chorus Aviation Leasing Inc., Canada.
Clare Aircraft Leasing Limited, Ireland.
Clontarf Aircraft Leasing Limited, Ireland.
Commuter Aircraft Leasing Limited, Ireland.
Commuter Aircraft Leasing 2017 I Limited, Ireland.
Commuter Aircraft Leasing 2017 II Limited, United Kingdom.
Commuter Aircraft Leasing 2017 III Limited, Ireland.
Commuter Aircraft Leasing 2017 IV Limited, Ireland.
Commuter Aircraft Leasing 2017 V Limited, Ireland.
Commuter Aircraft Leasing 2017 VI Limited, Ireland.
Commuter Aircraft Leasing 2017 VII Limited, Ireland.
Commuter Aircraft Leasing 2017 VIII Limited, Ireland.
Cork Aircraft Leasing Limited, Ireland.
Cygnet Aviation Academy LP, Kingston, Ont.
DB Avo AC DAC, Ireland.
DB Avo AZ DAC, Ireland.
DB Avo GP LLC, Del.
DB Avo Holdings LP, Cayman Islands.
DB Avo US LLC, Del.
Dedalus Q400 Leasing Limited, Ireland.
Donegal Q400 Leasing Limited, Ireland.
Falko Asset Management DAC, Ireland.
Falko (Ireland) Limited, Ireland.
Falko RAOF GP II Limited, Jersey.
Falko RAOF GP III Limited, Jersey.
Falko RAOF GP Limited, Jersey.
Falko Regional Aircraft Limited, Hereford., United Kingdom.
Galway Aircraft Leasing Limited, Ireland.
Jazz Aviation LP, Ont.
Kerry ATR72 Leasing Limited, Ireland.
Kilkenny Aircraft Leasing Limited, Ireland.
Limerick Aircraft Leasing Limited, Ireland.
Malahide Aircraft Leasing Limited, Ireland.
Mayo Aircraft Leasing Limited, Ireland.
Newgrange Aircraft Leasing Limited, Ireland.
Portlaoise Aircraft Leasing Limited, Ireland.
Sandycove Aircraft Leasing Limited, Ireland.
Slane Aircraft Leasing Limited, Ireland.
Tipperary Aircraft Leasing Limited, Ireland.
Triangle Aviation Holdings LP, Ont.
Triangle Aviation Ireland DAC, Ireland.
Triangle Aviation Jersey Limited, Jersey.
Triangle Aviation (UK) Holdings Limited, United Kingdom.
Triangle 415 Leasing LLC, Del.
Triangle (Funding One) Limited, United Kingdom.
Triangle Holdings GP Inc., Del.
Triangle Holdings LP, Cayman Islands.
Triangle Regional Aircraft Leasing Limited, United Kingdom.
Triangle Symber Leasing DAC, Ireland.
Trident Aviation Leasing Services (Jersey) Limited, Jersey.
Trident Aviation Leasing Services (UK) Limited, United Kingdom.
Trident Jet (Jersey) Limited, Jersey.
Trident Turboprop (Dublin) DAC, Ireland.
Voyageur Aviation Corp., Ont.
Waterford Aircraft Leasing Limited, Ireland.
Westmeath Aircraft Leasing Limited, Ireland.

Subsidiaries

67.45% int. in **Ravelin Aviation Ireland DAC**, Ireland.
67.45% int. in **Ravelin Aviation Leasing Services DAC**, Ireland.
67.45% int. in **Ravelin Aviation Leasing Services 3 DAC**, Ireland.
67.45% int. in **Ravelin Aviation Leasing Services 2 DAC**, Ireland.
67.45% int. in **Ravelin Holdings GP LLC**, Del.
67.45% int. in **Ravelin Holdings LP**, Cayman Islands.

Financial Statistics

Periods ended:	12m Dec. 31/22[A]		12m Dec. 31/21[oA]
	$000s	%Chg	$000s
Operating revenue	**1,595,804**	**+56**	**1,023,275**
Salaries & benefits	500,670		366,095
Other operating expense	704,255		385,075
Operating expense	**1,204,925**	**+60**	**751,170**
Operating income	**390,879**	**+44**	**272,105**
Deprec., depl. & amort.	202,613		201,126
Finance income	4,047		880
Finance costs, gross	104,890		97,213
Pre-tax income	**73,850**	**n.a.**	**(27,880)**
Income taxes	21,933		(7,395)
Net income	**51,917**	**n.a.**	**(20,485)**
Net inc. for equity hldrs	**48,890**	**n.a.**	**(20,485)**
Net inc. for non-cont. int	**3,027**	**n.a.**	**nil**
Cash & equivalent	167,911		178,446
Inventories	113,820		76,235
Accounts receivable	197,364		140,091
Current assets	503,748		409,573
Long-term investments	26,008		nil
Fixed assets, net	3,282,008		2,589,087
Intangibles, net	27,890		8,831
Total assets	**4,055,909**	**+28**	**3,180,517**
Accts. pay. & accr. liabs	346,296		217,804
Current liabilities	732,689		451,675
Long-term debt, gross	2,018,967		1,903,677
Long-term debt, net	1,678,659		1,677,168
Long-term lease liabilities	6,268		6,336
Equity portion of conv. debs	2,683		5,664
Shareholders' equity	1,179,573		690,469
Non-controlling interest	88,850		nil
Cash from oper. activs	**279,512**	**+51**	**184,984**
Cash from fin. activs	(71,459)		(180,925)
Cash from invest. activs	(231,369)		(27,810)
Net cash position	**167,911**	**-6**	**178,446**
Capital expenditures	(62,280)		(74,707)
Capital disposals	271,307		1,725
Pension fund surplus	40,199		84,975
	$		$
Earnings per share*	0.13		(0.12)
Cash flow per share*	1.44		1.07
	shs		shs
No. of shs. o/s*	201,332,016		177,650,988
Avg. no. of shs. o/s*	194,440,593		173,542,862
	%		%
Net profit margin	3.25		(2.00)
Return on equity	2.78		(3.08)
Return on assets	3.47		1.56
Foreign sales percent	16		13
No. of employees (FTEs)	4,829		4,426

* Class A & B
[o] Restated
[A] Reported in accordance with IFRS

Latest Results

Periods ended:	6m June 30/23^A		6m June 30/22^A
	$000s	%Chg	$000s
Operating revenue	812,027	+11	734,723
Net income	52,337	n.a.	(17,496)
Net inc. for equity hldrs	50,580	n.a.	(17,935)
Net inc. for non-cont. int	1,757		439
	$		$
Earnings per share*	0.17		(0.13)

* Class A & B
A Reported in accordance with IFRS

Historical Summary
(as originally stated)

Fiscal Year	Oper. Rev.	Net Inc. Bef. Disc.	EPS*
	$000s	$000s	$
2022^A	1,595,804	51,917	0.13
2021^A	1,023,275	(20,485)	(0.12)
2020^A	948,721	41,486	0.26
2019^A	1,366,447	133,160	0.85
2018^A	1,451,194	66,988	0.49

* Class A & B
A Reported in accordance with IFRS
Note: Per share figures based on fund units prior to 2009.

C.113 Christina Lake Cannabis Corp.

Symbol - CLC **Exchange** - CSE **CUSIP** - 17104U
Head Office - 810-789 Pender St W, Vancouver, BC, V6C 1H2 **Telephone** - (604) 687-2038 **Fax** - (604) 687-3141
Website - christinalakecannabis.com
Email - jamie@clcannabis.com
Investor Relations - Jamie Frawley (888) 410-0304
Auditors - Dale Matheson Carr-Hilton LaBonte LLP C.A., Vancouver, B.C.
Transfer Agents - National Securities Administrators Ltd., Vancouver, B.C.
Profile - (B.C. 2014) Produces cannabis flower, oil cannabinoids, as well as hemp-based extracts and derivatives.

The company has a 32-acre property in Christina Lake, B.C., which includes more than 950,000 sq. ft. of outdoor grow space, propagation and drying rooms, research facilities and a facility for processing and extraction; it also owns an adjacent 99-acre parcel of land. Its extracts include distilled and winterized oils, kief and, additional products for sale to other licensed producers.

Predecessor Detail - Name changed from Cervantes Capital Corp., Dec. 21, 2018.
Directors - James (Jay) McMillan, chr., Ottawa, Ont.; Nicco Dehaan, COO, Grand Forks, B.C.; Mervin Boychuk, Medicine Hat, Alta.; Joel S. Dumaresq, Vancouver, B.C.; Salvatore Milia, Vancouver, B.C.; Gilbert E. (Gil) Playford, Vero Beach, Fla.
Other Exec. Officers - Mark Aiken, CEO; Ryan Smith, CFO; Milan Stefancik, v-p, sales & mktg.; Ray Baterina, corp. sec.

Capital Stock

	Authorized (shs.)	Outstanding (shs.)[1]
Class B Preferred	unlimited	nil
Common	unlimited	129,892,173

[1] At Aug. 2, 2022

Class B Preferred - Entitled to cumulative dividends over four years (to August 2024) which accrue and become payable in arrears on a monthly basis based on the achievement of certain cumulative aggregate product revenue thresholds. Non-voting.
Common - One vote per share.
Major Shareholder - Widely held at July 21, 2022.

Price Range - CLC/CSE

Year	Volume	High	Low	Close
2022	6,232,376	$0.28	$0.06	$0.08
2021	32,136,510	$1.10	$0.20	$0.24
2020	16,139,876	$0.89	$0.36	$0.75

Recent Close: $0.05
Capital Stock Changes - On Mar. 29, 2022, all 2,000,000 class B preferred shares outstanding were redeemed at $1 per share.

Financial Statistics

Periods ended:	12m Nov. 30/21^A		12m Nov. 30/20^A
	$000s	%Chg	$000s
Operating revenue	**3,633**	**n.a.**	**nil**
Cost of sales	1,430		nil
Salaries & benefits	1,182		912
Research & devel. expense	21		19
General & admin expense	2,453		1,707
Stock-based compensation	1,161		2,371
Operating expense	**6,247**	**+25**	**5,009**
Operating income	**(2,614)**	**n.a.**	**(5,009)**
Deprec., depl. & amort	336		142
Finance costs, gross	841		572
Write-downs/write-offs	(3,861)		nil
Pre-tax income	**(7,143)**	**n.a.**	**(2,853)**
Net income	**(7,143)**	**n.a.**	**(2,853)**
Cash & equivalent	1,076		1,844
Inventories	7,153		6,223
Accounts receivable	1,073		72
Current assets	9,424		8,269
Fixed assets, net	9,545		9,535
Total assets	**18,969**	**+7**	**17,804**
Accts. pay. & accr. liabs	560		671
Current liabilities	7,391		1,815
Long-term debt, gross	8,635		7,644
Long-term debt, net	1,808		6,529
Long-term lease liabilities	nil		5
Equity portion of conv. debs	418		557
Shareholders' equity	9,739		9,455
Cash from oper. activs	**(4,621)**	**n.a.**	**(3,317)**
Cash from fin. activs	5,057		9,203
Cash from invest. activs	(1,205)		(4,783)
Net cash position	**1,076**	**-42**	**1,844**
Capital expenditures	(1,229)		(4,783)
Capital disposals	25		nil
	$		$
Earnings per share*	(0.07)		(0.04)
Cash flow per share*	(0.04)		(0.04)
	shs		shs
No. of shs. o/s*	115,891,174		90,440,315
Avg. no. of shs. o/s*	108,245,854		80,152,075
	%		%
Net profit margin	(196.61)		n.a.
Return on equity	(74.43)		(37.45)
Return on assets	(34.28)		(19.00)

* Common
A Reported in accordance with IFRS

Latest Results

Periods ended:	6m May 31/22^A		6m May 31/21^A
	$000s	%Chg	$000s
Operating revenue	3,774	n.m.	279
Net income	(794)	n.a.	(4,130)
	$		$
Earnings per share*	(0.01)		(0.04)

* Common
A Reported in accordance with IFRS

Historical Summary
(as originally stated)

Fiscal Year	Oper. Rev.	Net Inc. Bef. Disc.	EPS*
	$000s	$000s	$
2021^A	3,633	(7,143)	(0.07)
2020^A	nil	(2,853)	(0.04)
2019^A	nil	(2,162)	(0.04)
2018^A	nil	(585)	(0.05)

* Common
A Reported in accordance with IFRS

C.114 Cielo Waste Solutions Corp.

Symbol - CMC **Exchange** - TSX-VEN **CUSIP** - 17178G
Head Office - 2500-605 5 Ave SW, Calgary, AB, T2P 3H5 **Telephone** - (403) 348-2972 **Fax** - (403) 343-3572
Website - www.cielows.com
Email - investors@cielows.com
Investor Relations - Jasdeep K. Dhaliwal (403) 248-2972
Auditors - KPMG LLP C.A., Calgary, Alta.
Lawyers - DLA Piper (Canada) LLP, Calgary, Alta.
Transfer Agents - Computershare Trust Company of Canada Inc., Vancouver, B.C.
Profile - (B.C. 2011) Developing a technology for refining landfill, municipal and commercial waste into renewable diesel.

The company's proprietary technology can convert household, commercial and construction or demolition garbage, including feedstocks of municipal solid waste and cellulosic materials such as wet organics (compost), all plastics, paper, tires, cardboard, sawdust and wood into high cetane, ultra-low sulfur renewable diesel, kerosene and naphtha fuels through thermal catalytic depolymerization. The company built a research and development facility (R&D site)in Aldersyde, Alta., which was commissioned in April 2023. The R&D site is a scaled-down facility that will serve as a blueprint for a planned full-scale commercial waste-to-fuel facility that would be located in Dunmore, Alta.

In May 2023, the company agreed to restructure the nature of **Renewable U Energy Inc.**'s investment in the company's commercialization efforts, which resulted in the termination of various memorandum of understanding (MOU) entered in 2018 to 2021 regarding the formation of a joint venture to build refineries in nine territories including Medicine Hat, Grande Prairie, Calgary, Lethbridge, Kamloops, Winnipeg, Toronto, Halifax and a location in the U.S. Pursuant to the previous MOUs, Renewable U has delivered $250,000 fee per territory (totaling $2,250,000) to the company. For the repayment of $1,000,000 fees for four territories, the company has now agreed to issue 16,666,667 common shares at 6¢ per share. For the repayment of fees for five territories, which is now valued at $2,000,000 (value for fees received for Medicine Hat increased to $1,000,000), the company agreed to exchange it for a participation interest in an entity that would operate the planned commercial facility in Dunmore, Alta. The repayment of $2,000,000 fees is subject to the acceptance by Renewable U of a proposal from the company setting out the terms for the repayment. If the company failed to submit a proposal on or before Oct. 28, 2023, the company would pay the $2,000,000 in cash within 60 days.

In August 2022, the company decommissioned its first bio-diesel refinery (first facility) in Aldersyde, Alta., which was capable of converting wood derivative waste materials into a distillate. The first facility was used to prove the concept for the company's proprietary technology, and data obtained from the process will be used for the design and fabrication of a planned scaled down research and development facility and future full-scale facilities.

Recent Merger and Acquisition Activity

Status: pending **Announced:** May 1, 2023
Cielo Waste Solutions Corp. agreed to acquire land in Dunmore, Alta., on which Cielo plans to build a full-scale commercial waste-to-fuel facility, from Renewable U Energy Inc. for $5,200,000.

Predecessor Detail - Name changed from Cielo Gold Corp., Aug. 14, 2013.
Directors - Sheila A. Leggett, chr., Calgary, Alta.; Ryan Jackson, CEO, Medicine Hat, Alta.; The Hon. Peter MacKay, Kings Head, N.S.; Larry Schafran, New York, N.Y.
Other Exec. Officers - Donald (Don) Allan, chr., emeritus; Jasdeep K. Dhaliwal, CFO & corp. sec.; Ryan Carruthers, exec. v-p, opers.; Stuart McCormick, v-p, envir.; Michael Yeung, v-p, bus. devel. & capital markets; Anna Cheong, contr.

Capital Stock

	Authorized (shs.)	Outstanding (shs.)[1]
Preferred	unlimited	nil
Common	unlimited	1,133,441,461

[1] At June 20, 2023

Major Shareholder - Widely held at Sept. 1, 2022.

Price Range - CMC/TSX-VEN

Year	Volume	High	Low	Close
2022	606,300,090	$0.46	$0.04	$0.08
2021	1,540,197,537	$1.65	$0.08	$0.20
2020	204,210,151	$0.14	$0.01	$0.09
2019	82,674,103	$0.18	$0.06	$0.08
2018	54,155,117	$0.30	$0.10	$0.12

Recent Close: $0.04
Capital Stock Changes - In May 2023, 16,666,667 common shares were issued for debt settlement.

In July 2022, public offering of 139,642,856 units (1 common share & 1 warrant) at 7¢ per unit was completed, including 18,214,285 units on exercise of over-allotment option. Also during fiscal 2023, common shares were issued as follows: 91,269,841 for debt settlement and 300,000 on exercise of warrants.

During fiscal 2022, common shares were issued as follows: 24,339,474 on exercise of warrants, 15,662,500 on conversion of debentures, 10,000,000 pursuant to the termination of a licence agreement and 645,000 on exercise of options.

Wholly Owned Subsidiaries

Cielo Fort Saskatchewan Corp., Alta.

Financial Statistics

Periods ended:	12m Apr. 30/23[A]		12m Apr. 30/22[◻A]
	$000s	%Chg	$000s
Salaries & benefits	2,584		4,806
Research & devel. expense	1,107		3,758
General & admin expense	2,052		3,567
Stock-based compensation	464		1,762
Operating expense	**6,206**	**-55**	**13,893**
Operating income	**(6,206)**	**n.a.**	**(13,893)**
Deprec., depl. & amort.	634		443
Finance costs, gross	2,418		1,516
Write-downs/write-offs	(25,630)[1]		(205)
Pre-tax income	**(36,182)**	**n.a.**	**(15,319)**
Income taxes	nil		(874)
Net income	**(36,182)**	**n.a.**	**(14,445)**
Cash & equivalent	1,333		2,681
Inventories	132		394
Accounts receivable	89		118
Current assets	2,020		4,138
Fixed assets, net	25,308		46,938
Right-of-use assets	151		453
Intangibles, net	1,887		2,002
Total assets	**29,366**	**-45**	**53,531**
Accts. pay. & accr. liabs.	1,394		1,951
Current liabilities	14,507		2,974
Long-term debt, gross	9,861		14,279
Long-term debt, net	nil		14,279
Long-term lease liabilities	61		430
Shareholders' equity	14,798		33,599
Cash from oper. activs.	**(4,753)**	**n.a.**	**(16,377)**
Cash from fin. activs.	8,314		21,521
Cash from invest. activs.	(5,064)		(19,664)
Net cash position	**1,153**	**-57**	**2,656**
Capital expenditures	(4,217)		(19,583)
	$		$
Earnings per share*	(0.04)		(0.02)
Cash flow per share*	(0.01)		(0.03)
	shs		shs
No. of shs. o/s*	893,542,609		662,329,912
Avg. no. of shs. o/s*	804,505,449		651,753,286
	%		%
Net profit margin	n.a.		n.a.
Return on equity	(149.52)		(49.72)
Return on assets	(81.46)		(26.37)

* Common

◻ Restated

[A] Reported in accordance with IFRS

[1] Represents impairment as a result of the decommissioning of its first bio-diesel refinery in Aldersyde, Alta.

Historical Summary
(as originally stated)

Fiscal Year	Oper. Rev. $000s	Net Inc. Bef. Disc. $000s	EPS* $
2023[A]	nil	(36,182)	(0.04)
2022[A]	nil	(14,445)	(0.02)
2021[A]	4	(39,709)	(0.11)
2020[A]	3	(6,155)	(0.03)
2019[A]	3	(2,766)	(0.02)

* Common

[A] Reported in accordance with IFRS

C.115 Cinaport Acquisition Corp. III

Symbol - CAC.P **Exchange** - TSX-VEN **CUSIP** - 17185C
Head Office - 635-333 Bay St, Toronto, ON, M5H 2R2 **Telephone** - (416) 213-8118 **Fax** - (416) 213-8666
Email - agrewal@cinaport.com
Investor Relations - Avininder Grewal (416) 213-8118 ext. 210
Auditors - MNP LLP C.A., Toronto, Ont.
Transfer Agents - TSX Trust Company, Toronto, Ont.
Profile - (Ont. 2018) Capital Pool Company.
Directors - Donald A. (Don) Wright, chr., Toronto, Ont.; Avininder (Avi) Grewal, pres., CEO & corp. sec., Mississauga, Ont.; Dr. Seshadri (Sesh) Chari, Toronto, Ont.; John O'Sullivan, Toronto, Ont.; Patrick A. Ryan, Toronto, Ont.
Other Exec. Officers - Grant Kehrli, CFO

Capital Stock

	Authorized (shs.)	Outstanding (shs.)[1]
Common	unlimited	16,095,000

[1] At Apr. 21, 2022

Major Shareholder - John O'Sullivan held 18.64% interest and Donald A. (Don) Wright held 18.64% interest at May 10, 2022.

Price Range - CAC.P/TSX-VEN

Year	Volume	High	Low	Close
2022	1,449,398	$0.13	$0.05	$0.05
2021	58,000	$0.05	$0.03	$0.05
2020	1,113,000	$0.07	$0.03	$0.06
2019	1,086,500	$0.15	$0.05	$0.05
2018	241,299	$0.20	$0.10	$0.10

Recent Close: $0.03

C.116 Cineplex Inc.*

Symbol - CGX **Exchange** - TSX **CUSIP** - 172454
Head Office - 1303 Yonge St, Toronto, ON, M4T 2Y9 **Telephone** - (416) 323-6600 **Toll-free** - (800) 333-0061 **Fax** - (416) 323-6683
Website - www.cineplex.com
Email - investorrelations@cineplex.com
Investor Relations - Mahsa Rejali (416) 323-6600
Auditors - PricewaterhouseCoopers LLP C.A., Toronto, Ont.
Lawyers - Goodmans LLP, Toronto, Ont.
Transfer Agents - TSX Trust Company, Toronto, Ont.
FP500 Revenue Ranking - 294
Employees - 12,000 at Dec. 31, 2022
Profile - (Ont. 2010) Owns, operates and has joint venture interests in 157 movie theatres with 1,625 screens throughout all ten Canadian provinces under the brands Cineplex Odeon, Cineplex Cinemas, Cineplex VIP Cinemas, Galaxy Cinemas, SilverCity and Scotiabank Theatres, as well as 13 location-based entertainment (LBE) venues in Ontario, Alberta, Manitoba, Newfoundland and Labrador, British Columbia and Nova Scotia under the brands The Rec Room and Playdium. Also operates digital commerce, alternative programming, cinema media, digital place-based media and amusement businesses.

Film Entertainment and Content

The company is an exhibitor of digital, 3D and IMAX projection technologies in Canada. At Mar. 31, 2023, the theatre network included 1,625 screens and 806 3D digital screens in 157 theatres, 25 IMAX screens, 95 UltraAVX screens, 99 VIP auditoriums, 100 D-BOX auditoriums, 283 recliner auditoriums and 27 other screen locations. Alternative programming is also featured at the company's theatres including ethnic and foreign language films, live showings of The Metropolitan Opera, sporting events, concerts and dedicated event screens.

Food service includes the company's concession sales at theatres and specialty food menus at VIP Cinemas. Theatres also feature proprietary food brands Outtakes and Melt as well as fast food retail branded outlets including Starbucks. Digital commerce operations consist of the company's e-commerce site CineplexStore.com, which rents and sells video-on-demand and premium electronic sell-through movies; movie entertainment information website cineplex.com; and the company's mobile application.

Media

These operations include cinema media, which incorporates advertising mediums related to theatre exhibition, including show-time, pre-show, digital lobby advertising as well as online and mobile advertising; and digital place-based media, which uses digital signage optimization software and offers in-store retail media networks in shopping centers, restaurants, retailers and entertainment destinations.

Amusement and Leisure

This business unit consists of wholly owned **Player One Amusement Group Inc.** (P1AG), an operator and distributor of amusement, gaming and vending equipment in North America. Operations also include 44 XSCAPE Entertainment Centres, as well as arcade games in select Cineplex theatres, LBE venues and a Junxion location, with all of the games supplied and serviced by P1AG.

Location-based Entertainment

This business unit consists of The Rec Room, a social entertainment and dining destination featuring dining, amusement gaming and live entertainment experiences all under one roof with 10 locations in Ontario, Alberta, Manitoba, Newfoundland and Labrador, and British Columbia; and Playdium, a tech-infused entertainment complex offering games and attractions for teens and families with two locations in Ontario and one in Nova Scotia.

In addition, the company offers the Scene+ customer loyalty program in partnership with **The Bank of Nova Scotia** and **Empire Company Limited**. The program offers members discounts and the opportunity to earn and redeem points for purchases at Cineplex's theatres, at its location-based entertainment establishments, as well as at locations operated by select program partners. Members also can earn and redeem points at a variety of popular retailers, including Empire's family of brands, and redeem points as credits on certain Scotiabank products, as well as book flexible travel. The company also offers CineClub, a movie subscription program which provides members with benefits accessible across Cineplex theatres, the Cineplex Store and LBE venues.

On Dec. 16, 2022, subsidiary **Canadian Digital Cinemas Partnership** (CDCP), a joint venture of the company and **Empire Theatres Limited**, wound up its operations and distributed its assets to its partners.

In December 2022, the company opened its first Junxion location at Cineplex Junxion Kildonan in Winnipeg, Man. In addition, a second location at the Erin Mills Town Centre in Mississauga, Ont., was scheduled to open during the second quarter of 2023. Cineplex Junxion is an entertainment concept which brings together movies, amusement gaming, dining and live performances in one venue.

In September 2022, **Cineworld Group plc** commenced bankruptcy proceedings in the United States. The Ontario Superior Court of Justice ruled on Dec. 14, 2021, in favour of the company following the trial of its action against Cineworld Group. The court found that Cineworld repudiated the transaction to acquire the company and awarded damages for breach of contract to the company in the amount of $1.24 billion. The court also denied Cineworld's counterclaim against the company. On Jan. 12, 2022, Cineworld filed a Notice of Appeal with the Court of Appeal for Ontario, with the company subsequently filing its Notice of Cross Appeal on Jan. 27, 2022. The company would explore all avenues available to advance its claim against Cineworld, and would actively pursue all available alternatives in the best interests of the company and its stakeholders.

Recent Merger and Acquisition Activity

Status: completed **Announced:** June 7, 2022
Empire Company Limited announced the acquisition of an ownership interest in Scene+ loyalty rewards program, making it a co-owner with Cineplex Inc. and The Bank of Nova Scotia. Terms were not disclosed. Scene+ rollout in Empire banners would begin with stores in Atlantic Canada in August 2022, and then continue across the country, culminating in early 2023. Scene+ has over 10,000,000 members and offers an assortment of opportunities to earn and redeem points across a broad spectrum of partners. AIR MILES collectors would continue to earn and redeem in Empire store until the Scene+ program is available in that region.

Predecessor Detail - Succeeded Cineplex Galaxy Income Fund, Jan. 4, 2011, pursuant to plan of arrangement whereby Cineplex Inc. was formed to facilitate the conversion of the fund into a corporation and the fund was subsequently dissolved.

Directors - Phyllis Yaffe, chr., Toronto, Ont.; Ellis Jacob, pres. & CEO, Toronto, Ont.; Jordan R. Banks, Toronto, Ont.; Robert W. (Rob) Bruce, Toronto, Ont.; Joan T. Dea, Ross, Calif.; Janice R. Fukakusa, Toronto, Ont.; Donna M. Hayes, Toronto, Ont.; The Hon. Sarabjit S. (Sabi) Marwah, Toronto, Ont.; Nadir H. Mohamed, Toronto, Ont.

Other Exec. Officers - Dan McGrath, COO; Gord Nelson, CFO; Scott Hughes, exec. v-p & chief digital & tech. officer; Sara Moore, exec. v-p & chief mktg. officer; Fabrizio Stanghieri, exec. v-p, CDM & media; Kevin Watts, exec. v-p, exhibition & location based entertainment; Robert Cousins, sr. v-p, film; Allison Dell, sr. v-p & head, HR; Thomas Santram, sr. v-p, gen. counsel & corp. sec.

Capital Stock

	Authorized (shs.)	Outstanding (shs.)[1]
Preferred	10,000,000	nil
Common	unlimited	63,375,640

[1] At Apr. 6, 2023

Options - At Dec. 31, 2022, options were outstanding to purchase 2,102,818 common shares at a weighted average exercise price of $18.90 per share with a weighted average remaining contractual life of seven years.

Major Shareholder - Widely held at Apr. 19, 2023.

Price Range - CGX/TSX

Year	Volume	High	Low	Close
2022	83,910,238	$14.10	$7.30	$8.05
2021	199,405,433	$16.76	$8.65	$13.61
2020	268,626,921	$34.06	$4.32	$9.27
2019	68,147,217	$34.39	$22.25	$33.85
2018	74,440,124	$38.42	$22.88	$25.44

Recent Close: $8.04

Capital Stock Changes - During 2022, common shares were issued as follows: 20,009 on exercise of options and 11,093 under a stock-based compensation plan.

Long-Term Debt - Outstanding at Dec. 31, 2022:

Revolving facility due 2024[1]	$327,000,000
5.75% conv. debs. due 2025[2]	252,078,000
7.5% notes payable due 2026	245,810,000
	824,888,000
Less: Current portion	nil
	824,888,000

[1] Bears interest at floating rate based on the Canadian dollar prime rate, U.S. base rate, SOFR or bankers' acceptance rate plus, in each case, an applicable margin to those rates. At Dec. 31, 2022, the average interest rate on borrowings under the facility was 6.9%.

[2] Convertible into common shares at $10.94 per share.

Wholly Owned Subsidiaries

Cineplex Entertainment Corporation, Man.
Cineplex Entertainment Limited Partnership, Toronto, Ont.
- 78.2% int. in **Canadian Digital Cinema Partnership**, Toronto, Ont.
- 100% int. in **DDC Group International Inc.**, Ont.
  - 100% int. in **Cineplex Digital Media Inc.**, Ont.
- 100% int. in **Famous Players Limited Partnership**, Man.
- 100% int. in **Galaxy Entertainment Inc.**, Ont.
  - 50% int. in **Scene GP (Ontario)**, Ont.
  - 33.33% int. in **Scene LP (Ontario)**, Ont.
  - 33.33% int. in **Scene+ GP Co. Inc.**, Canada.
- 100% int. in **Player One Amusement Group Inc.**, Toronto, Ont.
- 50% int. in **Scene IP Corporation**

Note: The preceding list includes only the major related companies in which interests are held.

Financial Statistics

Periods ended:	12m Dec. 31/22[A]		12m Dec. 31/21[A]
	$000s	%Chg	$000s
Operating revenue	**1,268,562**	**+93**	**656,669**
Cost of sales	326,599		156,357
Salaries & benefits	253,397		150,251
Other operating expense	434,580		289,131
Operating expense	**1,014,576**	**+70**	**595,739**
Operating income	**253,986**	**+317**	**60,930**
Deprec., depl. & amort.	200,714		215,289
Finance income	277		232
Finance costs, gross	122,668		123,728
Investment income	(2,608)		(755)
Write-downs/write-offs	20,119[1]		(3,889)
Pre-tax income	**1,310**	**n.a.**	**(245,383)**
Income taxes	1,197		3,339
Net inc bef disc ops, eqhldrs	113		(248,722)
Net income	**113**	**n.a.**	**(248,722)**
Cash & equivalent	34,674		26,938
Inventories	36,916		24,899
Accounts receivable	107,088		80,679
Current assets	205,363		147,865
Long-term investments	650		7,423
Fixed assets, net	449,495		464,439
Right-of-use assets	772,978		768,675
Intangibles, net	716,562		717,196
Total assets	**2,150,454**	**+2**	**2,114,838**
Accts. pay. & accr. liabs	195,296		157,950
Current liabilities	515,652		562,222
Long-term debt, gross	824,888		739,211
Long-term debt, net	824,888		739,211
Long-term lease liabilities	1,004,546		1,004,465
Shareholders' equity	(211,814)		(219,723)
Cash from oper. activs	**107,148**	**+76**	**61,004**
Cash from fin. activs	(43,347)		(91,126)
Cash from invest. activs	(55,749)		40,451
Net cash position	**34,674**	**+29**	**26,938**
Capital expenditures	(64,317)		(23,627)
Capital disposals	1,843		63,215
Unfunded pension liability	6,970		9,973
	$		$
Earnings per share*	0.00		(3.93)
Cash flow per share*	1.69		0.96
	shs		shs
No. of shs. o/s*	63,375,400		63,344,298
Avg. no. of shs. o/s*	63,359,240		63,339,239
	%		%
Net profit margin	0.01		(37.88)
Return on equity	n.m.		n.m.
Return on assets	0.50		(5.54)
Foreign sales percent	9		13
No. of employees (FTEs)	12,000		11,000

* Common

[A] Reported in accordance with IFRS

[1] Includes reversal of $10,204 impairment of property, equipment and leaseholds and $9,676 impairment of right-of-use assets.

Latest Results

Periods ended:	3m Mar. 31/23[A]		3m Mar. 31/22[A]
	$000s	%Chg	$000s
Operating revenue	340,957	+49	228,723
Net income	(30,173)	n.a.	(42,225)
	$		$
Earnings per share*	(0.48)		(0.67)

* Common

[A] Reported in accordance with IFRS

Historical Summary
(as originally stated)

Fiscal Year	Oper. Rev.	Net Inc. Bef. Disc.	EPS*
	$000s	$000s	$
2022[A]	1,268,562	113	0.00
2021[A]	656,669	(248,722)	(3.93)
2020[A]	418,263	(624,001)	(9.85)
2019[A]	1,665,146	36,516	0.58
2018[A]	1,614,823	76,956	1.22

* Common

[A] Reported in accordance with IFRS

C.117 Cipher Pharmaceuticals Inc.

Symbol - CPH **Exchange** - TSX **CUSIP** - 17253X

Head Office - 404-5750 Explorer Dr, Mississauga, ON, L4W 0A9 **Telephone** - (905) 602-5840 **Fax** - (905) 602-0628

Website - www.cipherpharma.com

Email - james.bowen@loderockadvisors.com

Investor Relations - James Bowen (416) 519-9442

Auditors - Ernst & Young LLP C.A., Toronto, Ont.

Lawyers - Goodmans LLP, Toronto, Ont.

Transfer Agents - Computershare Trust Company of Canada Inc., Toronto, Ont.

Employees - 6 at Dec. 31, 2022

Profile - (Ont. 2004) Develops and commercializes prescription medications that utilize advanced drug delivery technologies, with a focus on dermatology.

The company's strategy is to in-license products that incorporate proven drug delivery technologies and advance them through the clinical development and regulatory approval stages, after which the products are out-licensed to international partners. Licensed drug delivery technologies include Oral Lidose® Technology, whereby active ingredients are incorporated in semi-solid or liquid compositions contained in capsules; and Oral Controlled-Released Bead Technology, which is based on unique extrusion and spheronization methods, and produces beads containing up to 80% active ingredient. Both technologies are licensed by **Galephar Pharmaceutical Research, Inc.**

The company's lead dermatology drug is CIP-Isotretinoin for the treatment of severe acne. CIP-Isotretinoin has been approved in the U.S. and Canada under the trademarks Absorica™ and Absorica LD™, and Epuris®, respectively. CIP-Isotretinoin was also approved in Brazil and Mexico. Other FDA-approved drugs include CIP-Fenofibrate for the treatment of hyperlipidemia, a cholesterol disorder, and approved in the U.S. under the trademark Lipofen®; and CIP-Tramadol ER for the management of moderate to moderately severe pain, and approved in the U.S. and Canada under the trademarks Conzip® and Durela®, respectively, as well as in 18 Latin American countries. Other dermatology products include Beteflam® Patch, a self-adhesive medicated plaster for the treatment of inflammatory skin conditions such as plaque psoriasis; Actikerall™, a treatment of actinic keratosis approved in Canada; Vaniqa™, a prescription cream for reducing the growth of unwanted facial hair in women; and Ozanex™, a topical antibiotic treatment for adult and paediatric patients with impetigo approved in Canada and with exclusive worldwide rights (except China, Japan, Korea and Taiwan).

Also holds the Canadian rights to Brinavess® (Vernakalant IV), a product for the rapid conversion of recent onset atrial fibrillation to sinus rhythm; and Aggrastat®, a reversible GP IIb/IIIa inhibitor (an intravenous anti-platelet drug) for use in acute coronary syndrome (ACS) patients. Brinavess® and Aggrastat® were both approved for sale in Canada in June 2017. Pre-commercial products include CF101 (Piclidenoson), a novel chemical entity for moderate to severe plaque psoriasis and rheumatoid arthritis; MOB-015, a topical formulation of terbinafine for treatment of onychomycosis; and DTR-001 a tattoo removal cream under pre-clinical development. In addition, the company together with Galephar is developing a drug for severe hand eczema to be sold in the U.S. market.

Directors - Craig Mull, chr. & interim CEO, Ont.; Harold M. Wolkin†, Toronto, Ont.; Douglas N. (Doug) Deeth, Oakville, Ont.; Dr. Hubert Walinski, Ont.

Other Exec. Officers - Bryan Jacobs, CFO & corp. sec.; Dr. Diane Gajewczyk, v-p, scientific & medical affairs

† Lead director

Capital Stock

	Authorized (shs.)	Outstanding (shs.)[1]
Preference	unlimited	nil
Common	unlimited	25,336,518

[1] At May 11, 2023

Normal Course Issuer Bid - The company plans to make normal course purchases of up to 1,403,293 common shares representing 10% of the public float. The bid commenced on Sept. 22, 2022, and expires on Sept. 21, 2023.

Major Shareholder - Craig Mull held 40.59% interest at May 10, 2023.

Price Range - CPH/TSX

Year	Volume	High	Low	Close
2022	7,240,740	$4.07	$1.66	$3.84
2021	13,396,508	$2.80	$0.70	$1.77
2020	10,256,785	$1.55	$0.38	$0.93
2019	8,464,729	$2.35	$0.87	$1.50
2018	8,870,042	$5.28	$1.62	$1.71

Recent Close: $3.83

Capital Stock Changes - During 2022, common shares were issued as follows: 102,000 under restricted and performance share unit plan, 91,000 on exercise of options and 25,000 under share purchase plan; 1,093,000 common shares were repurchased under a Normal Course Issuer Bid.

Wholly Owned Subsidiaries

Cipher US Holdings Inc., Del.
- 100% int. in **Cipher Pharmaceuticals US HoldCo LLC**, Del.
  - 100% int. in **Cipher Pharmaceuticals US LLC**, Del.

Financial Statistics

Periods ended:	12m Dec. 31/22[A]		12m Dec. 31/21[A]
	US$000s	%Chg	US$000s
Operating revenue	**20,675**	**-6**	**21,943**
Cost of goods sold	3,992		3,684
Salaries & benefits	1,501		1,443
Research & devel. expense	98		88
General & admin expense	2,642		2,822
Stock-based compensation	403		146
Operating expense	**8,636**	**+6**	**8,183**
Operating income	**12,039**	**-13**	**13,760**
Deprec., depl. & amort.	989		701
Finance income	473		12
Finance costs, gross	6		92
Pre-tax income	**11,479**	**+4**	**11,059**
Income taxes	(15,157)		3,301
Net income	**26,636**	**+243**	**7,758**
Cash & equivalent	28,836		20,548
Inventories	2,152		1,650
Accounts receivable	6,802		6,658
Current assets	38,161		29,327
Fixed assets, net	481		501
Intangibles, net	18,460		19,353
Total assets	**73,776**	**+43**	**51,651**
Accts. pay. & accr. liabs	4,107		5,555
Current liabilities	9,369		12,294
Long-term lease liabilities	327		460
Shareholders' equity	64,080		38,897
Cash from oper. activs	**10,575**	**-23**	**13,814**
Cash from fin. activs	(1,914)		(2,470)
Cash from invest. activs	(81)		nil
Net cash position	**28,836**	**+40**	**20,548**
	US$		US$
Earnings per share*	1.05		0.29
Cash flow per share*	0.42		0.52
	shs		shs
No. of shs. o/s*	25,062,980		25,936,641
Avg. no. of shs. o/s*	25,376,290		26,597,842
	%		%
Net profit margin	128.83		35.36
Return on equity	51.73		21.69
Return on assets	42.49		16.31
Foreign sales percent	40		48
No. of employees (FTEs)	6		5

* Common

[A] Reported in accordance with IFRS

Latest Results

Periods ended:	3m Mar. 31/23[A]		3m Mar. 31/22[A]
	US$000s	%Chg	US$000s
Operating revenue	4,886	-10	5,416
Net income	2,626	+22	2,149
	US$		US$
Earnings per share*	0.10		0.08

* Common

[A] Reported in accordance with IFRS

Historical Summary
(as originally stated)

Fiscal Year	Oper. Rev.	Net Inc. Bef. Disc.	EPS*
	US$000s	US$000s	US$
2022[A]	20,675	26,636	1.05
2021[A]	21,943	7,758	0.29
2020[A]	21,607	4,386	0.16
2019[A]	22,451	2,639	0.10
2018[A]	22,749	1,201	0.04

* Common

[A] Reported in accordance with IFRS

C.118 Ciscom Corp.

Symbol - CISC **Exchange** - CSE **CUSIP** - 17282B

Head Office - 1110-20 Bay St, Toronto, ON, M5J 2N8 **Telephone** - (416) 366-9727 **Fax** - (416) 352-5094

Website - ciscomcorp.com

Email - mpepin@ciscomcorp.com

Investor Relations - P. Michel Pepin (416) 366-9727

Auditors - SRCO Professional Corporation C.A., Richmond Hill, Ont.

Lawyers - CP LLP, Toronto, Ont.

Transfer Agents - TSX Trust Company, Toronto, Ont.

Profile - (Ont. 2020) Invests in and acquires companies operating in the information, communications and technology (ICT) sector and assumes an active role in the management of these companies.

Principal subsidiaries are wholly owned **Market Focus Direct Inc.** and indirect wholly owned **Prospect Media Group Ltd.**, which provide marketing products and services in five main categories: consumer data and analytics; print flyer management; digital media management; broadcast and out of home; and integrated media strategy.

Common listed on CSE, June 30, 2023.

Recent Merger and Acquisition Activity

Status: completed **Revised:** Sept. 30, 2022
UPDATE: The transaction was completed. PREVIOUS: Ciscom Corp. agreed to acquire private Toronto, Ont.-based 1883713 Ontario Inc., which provides marketing services, including consumer data and analytics, media planning and buying for advertisers, to major retail clients across Canada, for $12,488,481, consisting of $5,800,000 cash, a $1,163,521 short-term loan payable, an earn-out of $689,710, issuance of a $1,400,000 convertible debenture and issuance of 7,633,889 common shares at a deemed price of 45¢ per share.

Directors - Drew Reid, chr. & CEO, Toronto, Ont.; P. Michel Pepin, pres., CFO & corp. sec., Brantford, Ont.; Paul Gaynor, Oro-Medonte, Ont.; Josh Howard, London, Ont.; Eric R. Klein, Toronto, Ont.; David Mathews, Toronto, Ont.; Shaun Power, Burlington, Ont.; Julia Robinson, Toronto, Ont.

Capital Stock

	Authorized (shs.)	Outstanding (shs.)[1]
Cl.A Preferred	unlimited	nil
Cl.B Preferred	unlimited	nil
Common	unlimited	51,563,831

[1] At June 30, 2023

Major Shareholder - Paul Gaynor held 20.96% interest and David Mathews held 14.8% interest at June 30, 2023.

Recent Close: $0.19

Capital Stock Changes - On Sept. 30, 2022, 7,633,889 common shares were issued pursuant to the acquisition of 1883713 Ontario Inc. Also during 2022, common shares were issued as follows: 2,420,014 by private placement and 800,000 on conversion of debenture and loan.

Wholly Owned Subsidiaries

Market Focus Direct Inc., Markham, Ont.
1883713 Ontario Inc., Toronto, Ont.
- 100% int. in **Prospect Media Group Ltd.**, Toronto, Ont.

Financial Statistics

Periods ended:	12m Dec. 31/22[A]		12m Dec. 31/21[A]
	$000s	%Chg	$000s
Operating revenue	**14,766**	**n.m.**	**1,132**
Cost of sales	12,468		941
Salaries & benefits	1,582		177
General & admin expense	1,086		478
Stock-based compensation	328		12
Operating expense	**15,465**	**+862**	**1,608**
Operating income	**(698)**	**n.a.**	**(476)**
Deprec., depl. & amort.	818		178
Finance costs, gross	250		25
Write-downs/write-offs	nil		(1,653)
Pre-tax income	**(1,761)**	**n.a.**	**(2,055)**
Income taxes	(216)		(44)
Net income	**(1,545)**	**n.a.**	**(2,011)**
Cash & equivalent	1,053		1,006
Accounts receivable	7,331		623
Current assets	9,149		1,768
Fixed assets, net	44		5
Right-of-use assets	1		8
Intangibles, net	14,609		2,842
Total assets	**23,804**	**+415**	**4,622**
Bank indebtedness	2,436		nil
Accts. pay. & accr. liabs	7,296		864
Current liabilities	12,080		1,117
Long-term debt, gross	4,161		1,132
Long-term debt, net	2,994		889
Shareholders' equity	5,912		1,858
Cash from oper. activs	**(891)**	**n.a.**	**(837)**
Cash from fin. activs	5,724		2,469
Cash from invest. activs	(4,786)		(632)
Net cash position	**1,053**	**+5**	**1,006**
Capital expenditures	(1)		nil
	$		$
Earnings per share*	(0.03)		(0.07)
Cash flow per share*	(0.02)		(0.03)
	shs		shs
No. of shs. o/s*	51,108,882		40,254,979
Avg. no. of shs. o/s*	44,491,060		26,901,595
	%		%
Net profit margin	(10.46)		(177.65)
Return on equity	(39.77)		n.m.
Return on assets	(9.33)		(85.37)

* Common
[A] Reported in accordance with IFRS

Latest Results

Periods ended:	3m Mar. 31/23[A]		3m Mar. 31/22[A]
	$000s	%Chg	$000s
Operating revenue	7,254	n.m.	403
Net income	(575)	n.a.	(377)
	$		$
Earnings per share*	(0.01)		(0.01)

* Common
[A] Reported in accordance with IFRS

Historical Summary
(as originally stated)

Fiscal Year	Oper. Rev. $000s	Net Inc. Bef. Disc. $000s	EPS* $
2022[A]	14,766	(1,545)	(0.03)
2021[A]	1,132	(2,011)	(0.07)
2020[A1]	nil	(224)	(0.22)

* Common
[A] Reported in accordance with IFRS
[1] 27 weeks ended Dec. 31, 2020.

C.119 Citadel Income Fund

Symbol - CTF.UN **Exchange** - TSX **CUSIP** - 17286A
Head Office - c/o Artemis Investment Management Limited, 200-1325 Lawrence Ave E, Toronto, ON, M3A 1C6 **Telephone** - (416) 934-7455 **Fax** - (416) 934-7459
Website - www.artemisfunds.ca
Email - tmaunder@artemisfunds.ca
Investor Relations - Trevor W. Maunder (647) 477-4884
Auditors - KPMG LLP C.A., Toronto, Ont.
Lawyers - McMillan LLP, Toronto, Ont.; Aird & Berlis LLP, Toronto, Ont.
Transfer Agents - TSX Trust Company, Toronto, Ont.
Trustees - Artemis Investment Management Limited, Toronto, Ont.
Investment Managers - Vestcap Investment Management Inc., Toronto, Ont.
Managers - Artemis Investment Management Limited, Toronto, Ont.
Profile - (Ont. 2005) Invests in a diversified portfolio of income-producing securities consisting of equity securities of principally larger capitalization companies traded on a recognized stock exchange, debt securities with a minimum of 80% of debt security investments in investment grade debt rated BBB or higher, and income funds and trust with a market capitalization of $400,000,000.

The fund does not have a fixed termination date but may be terminated by the manager upon approval of the unitholders. The fund's net assets will be distributed to unitholders on a pro rata basis.

Top 10 holdings at Mar. 31, 2023 (as a percentage of total net assets):

Holding	Percentage
Adobe Inc.	7.04%
Microsoft Corp.	5.88%
UnitedHealth Group Inc.	5.17%
iShares 0-3 Month Treasury Bond ETF	5.07%
Procter & Gamble Co.	4.80%
Linamar Corp.	4.25%
Apple Inc.	4.12%
Blackstone Inc.	3.97%
Advanced Micro Devices Inc.	3.75%
Loblaw Cos Ltd.	3.53%

Predecessor Detail - Name changed from Crown Hill Fund, Dec. 2, 2009, pursuant to merger with Citadel Premium Income Fund, Citadel S-1 Income Trust Fund, Citadel Stable S-1 Income Fund, Citadel HYTES Fund and Equal Weight Plus Fund, with Crown Hill Fund the deemed acquiror.

Oper. Subsid./Mgt. Co. Directors - Trevor W. Maunder, CEO, CFO & corp. sec., Toronto, Ont.; Gavin Swartzman, Toronto, Ont.

Oper. Subsid./Mgt. Co. Officers - Sean Lawless, man. dir. & chief compliance officer

Capital Stock

	Authorized (shs.)	Outstanding (shs.)[1]
Trust Unit	unlimited	10,243,626

[1] At Dec. 31, 2022

Trust Unit - Entitled to monthly cash distributions of 1¢ per unit. Retractable on the second last business day of each November at an amount equal to the net asset value per trust unit. Retractable on the last business day of each month at a price equal to the lesser of: (i) 90% of the weighted average trading price per trust unit on the TSX during the 15 preceding trading days; and (ii) the closing market price on the TSX, less any retraction costs. One vote per trust unit.

Major Shareholder - Saba Capital Management, L.P. held 21.22% interest at Mar. 30, 2023.

Price Range - CTF.UN/TSX

Year	Volume	High	Low	Close
2022	1,438,313	$3.65	$2.21	$2.35
2021	2,769,152	$3.90	$2.81	$3.56
2020	1,649,475	$3.49	$1.66	$2.83
2019	1,899,059	$3.56	$3.08	$3.23
2018	1,838,978	$3.61	$2.99	$3.12

Recent Close: $3.13

Capital Stock Changes - During 2022, 51,895 trust units were issued under distribution reinvestment plan and 951,850 trust units were retracted.

Dividends

CTF.UN unit red. Ra $0.12 pa M est. Mar. 17, 2014**
** Reinvestment Option

Financial Statistics

Periods ended:	12m Dec. 31/22[A]		12m Dec. 31/21[A]
	$000s	%Chg	$000s
Realized invest. gain (loss)	(1,653)		4,396
Unrealized invest. gain (loss)	(11,705)		5,609
Total revenue	**(12,201)**	**n.a.**	**10,663**
General & admin. expense	1,393		1,692
Operating expense	**1,393**	**-18**	**1,692**
Operating income	**(13,594)**	**n.a.**	**8,971**
Finance costs, gross	3		9
Pre-tax income	**(13,597)**	**n.a.**	**8,961**
Income taxes	24		45
Net income	**(13,621)**	**n.a.**	**8,917**
Cash & equivalent	8,921		309
Accounts receivable	35		53
Investments	27,679		54,556
Total assets	**36,648**	**-33**	**54,947**
Accts. pay. & accr. liabs	195		192
Shareholders' equity	36,303		54,576
Cash from oper. activs	**12,627**	**+174**	**4,602**
Cash from fin. activs	(4,661)		(7,733)
Net cash position	**8,921**	**n.m.**	**309**
	$		$
Earnings per share*	(1.23)		0.73
Cash flow per share*	1.14		0.38
Net asset value per share*	3.54		4.90
Cash divd. per share*	0.12		0.12
	shs		shs
No. of shs. o/s*	10,243,626		11,143,581
Avg. no. of shs. o/s*	11,080,158		12,259,664
	%		%
Net profit margin	n.m.		83.63
Return on equity	(29.98)		16.52
Return on assets	(29.74)		16.43

* Trust unit
[A] Reported in accordance with IFRS

Note: Net income reflects increase/decrease in net assets from operations.

Historical Summary
(as originally stated)

Fiscal Year	Total Rev. $000s	Net Inc. Bef. Disc. $000s	EPS* $
2022[A]	(12,201)	(13,621)	(1.23)
2021[A]	10,663	8,917	0.73
2020[A]	5,038	3,396	0.25
2019[A]	6,237	4,437	0.29
2018[A]	(5,443)	(7,508)	(0.45)

* Trust unit
[A] Reported in accordance with IFRS

C.120 City View Green Holdings Inc.

Symbol - CVGR **Exchange** - CSE **CUSIP** - 178718
Head Office - 132-1173 Dundas St E, Toronto, ON, M4M 3P1 **Telephone** - (416) 722-4994
Website - www.cityviewgreen.ca
Email - rob@cityviewgreen.ca
Investor Relations - Roberto Fia (416) 722-4994
Auditors - Zeifmans LLP C.A., Toronto, Ont.
Transfer Agents - Computershare Trust Company of Canada Inc., Toronto, Ont.
Profile - (B.C. 2011 amalg.) Cultivates, produces and sells medical or recreational cannabis products with focus on extraction, edibles and distribution. Also holds an interest in cannabis retailer **Budd Hutt Inc.**

The company has a 40,000-sq.-ft. cannabis production facility in Brantford, Ont., which manufactures baked goods, protein bars, chews, gummies, chocolates and sugar confectionary for licensed cannabis retailers. The company also produces hemp-based dog treats under its brands Thera-Snax™ and Pawsperity™, which is available in over 600 stores in Canada.

Affiliate **Budd Hutt Inc.** has retail cannabis licences from Alberta Gaming, Liquor and Cannabis (AGLC) for four stores in Morinville, Grande Cache, Vermilion and Leduc, Alta., and three stores planned for Cold Lake, Red Water and Whitecourt, Alta. Budd Hutt is also pursuing other retail opportunities across Canada and has access to cannabis cultivation and production licences in Alberta.

Predecessor Detail - Name changed from Icon Exploration Inc., Feb. 27, 2019, pursuant to reverse takeover acquisition of 2590672 Ontario Inc. (dba City View Green); basis 1 new for 1.25 old shs.

Directors - A. Timothy (Tim) Peterson, chr., Toronto, Ont.; Roberto (Rob) Fia, pres. & CEO, Toronto, Ont.; Joseph (Joe) Heng, Toronto, Ont.

Other Exec. Officers - Randy Macleod, COO; Sung Min (Eric) Myung, CFO

Capital Stock

	Authorized (shs.)	Outstanding (shs.)[1]
Class A Common	unlimited	294,274,054

[1] At June 30, 2022

Major Shareholder - Quinsam Capital Corporation held 10.9% interest and Budd Hutt Inc. held 10.2% interest at May 13, 2022.

Price Range - CVGR/CSE

Year	Volume	High	Low	Close
2022	45,278,713	$0.07	$0.01	$0.01
2021	48,438,038	$0.16	$0.04	$0.08
2020	25,683,283	$0.19	$0.02	$0.07
2019	33,789,327	$0.47	$0.05	$0.06
2018	9,542,140	$1.05	$0.31	$0.51

Consolidation: 1-for-1.25 cons. in Mar. 2019

Recent Close: $0.01

Capital Stock Changes - In February 2023, private placement of 21,666,668 common shares was completed at $0.15 per share.

In March 2022, private placement of 9,600,000 units (1 class A common share & 1 warrant) at 5¢ per unit was completed, with warrants exercisable at 10¢ per share for two years.

Wholly Owned Subsidiaries

2590672 Ontario Inc., Brantford, Ont.
- 27.5% int. in **Budd Hutt Inc.**, Ont.

Financial Statistics

Periods ended:	12m Dec. 31/21[A]		12m Dec. 31/20[oA]
	$000s	%Chg	$000s
General & admin expense	1,317		1,411
Stock-based compensation	232		3,482
Operating expense	**1,549**	**-68**	**4,893**
Operating income	**(1,549)**	**n.a.**	**(4,893)**
Deprec., depl. & amort.	989		433
Finance income	23		32
Finance costs, gross	469		675
Investment income	(140)		133
Write-downs/write-offs	(1,475)		nil
Pre-tax income	**(4,623)**	**n.a.**	**(5,612)**
Net income	**(4,623)**	**n.a.**	**(5,612)**
Cash & equivalent	43		153
Accounts receivable	88		276
Current assets	573		1,113
Long-term investments	nil		1,233
Fixed assets, net	2,027		629
Right-of-use assets	2,496		2,826
Intangibles, net	nil		1,887
Total assets	**5,096**	**-34**	**7,687**
Bank indebtedness	236		nil
Accts. pay. & accr. liabs	1,531		1,061
Current liabilities	2,177		1,626
Long-term debt, gross	274		468
Long-term debt, net	40		40
Long-term lease liabilities	2,802		2,958
Shareholders' equity	78		3,063
Cash from oper. activs	**(118)**	**n.a.**	**(897)**
Cash from fin. activs	2,110		1,597
Cash from invest. activs	(2,102)		(553)
Net cash position	**43**	**-72**	**153**
Capital expenditures	(1,727)		(439)
	$		$
Earnings per share*	(0.02)		(0.03)
Cash flow per share*	(0.00)		(0.00)
	shs		shs
No. of shs. o/s*	283,412,270		247,461,530
Avg. no. of shs. o/s*	269,456,802		214,609,930
	%		%
Net profit margin	n.a.		n.a.
Return on equity	(294.36)		n.m.
Return on assets	(64.99)		n.a.

* Common
[o] Restated
[A] Reported in accordance with IFRS

Latest Results

Periods ended:	6m June 30/22[A]		6m June 30/21[A]
	$000s	%Chg	$000s
Operating revenue	112	n.a.	nil
Net income	(1,224)	n.a.	(1,196)
	$		$
Earnings per share*	(0.00)		(0.00)

* Common
[A] Reported in accordance with IFRS

Historical Summary
(as originally stated)

Fiscal Year	Oper. Rev. $000s	Net Inc. Bef. Disc. $000s	EPS* $
2021[A]	nil	(4,623)	(0.02)
2020[A]	nil	(5,612)	(0.03)
2019[A1]	nil	(24,558)	(0.14)
2018[A2]	nil	(960)	(0.04)
2017[A]	nil	(310)	(0.01)

* Common
[A] Reported in accordance with IFRS
[1] Results reflect the Feb. 27, 2019, reverse takeover acquisition of 2590672 Ontario Inc. (dba City View Green).
[2] Results for 2018 and prior years pertain to Icon Exploration Inc.

Note: Adjusted throughout for 1-for-1.25 cons. in Mar. 2019

C.121 Civeo Corporation

Symbol - CVEO **Exchange** - NYSE **CUSIP** - 17878Y

Head Office - Three Allen Center, 333 Clay St, Suite 4980, Houston, TX, United States, 77002 **Telephone** - (713) 510-2400 **Fax** - (713) 510-2499

Website - www.civeo.com

Email - ir@civeo.com

Investor Relations - Carolyn J. Stone (713) 510-2400

Auditors - Ernst & Young LLP C.P.A., Houston, Tex.

Transfer Agents - Computershare Trust Company of Canada Inc., Vancouver, B.C.

FP500 Revenue Ranking - 360

Employees - 1,400 at Dec. 31, 2022

Profile - (B.C. 2015; orig. Del., 2013) Provides workforce accommodations, logistics and facility management services to the natural resource industry.

The company's scalable facilities provide long-term and workforce accommodations where traditional accommodations and related infrastructure often are not accessible, sufficient or cost effective. Once facilities are deployed in the field, the company also provides hospitality services such as lodging, food services, housekeeping and maintenance, as well as day-to-day operations such as laundry, facility management and maintenance, water and wastewater treatment, power generation, communications systems, security and logistics. Hospitality services support workforces in the Canadian oil sands and in a variety of oil and natural gas drilling, mining and related natural resource applications in Canada, Australia and the United States. The company's activity drivers are development and production activity in the Canadian oil sands region in western Canada, the met coal region of Australia's Bowen Basin and the U.S. shale formations in the Permian Basin.

Accommodations are divided into two primary types: lodges and villages, and mobile assets. The company is principally focused on hospitality services at lodges and villages, and has 27 lodges and villages in operation in Canada, Australia and the U.S., totaling over 28,000 rooms.

Lodges and Villages

At Dec. 31	2021	2020
Canada[1]		
Avg. available rooms	18,947	19,024
Avg. daily rates, US$	99	95
Australia[2]		
Avg. available rooms	9,046	9,046
Avg. daily rates, US$	79	73
United States[1]		
Avg. available rooms	535	925
Avg. daily rates, US$	n.a.	n.a.

[1] Represents lodges.
[2] Represents villages.

Directors - Richard A. Navarre, chr., United States; Bradley J. Dodson, pres. & CEO, Tex.; C. Ronald Blankenship, United States; Jagdish K. (Jay) Grewal, Man.; Martin A. Lambert, Calgary, Alta.; Michael Montelongo; Constance B. Moore, United States; Charles Szalkowski, United States; Timothy O. Wall

Other Exec. Officers - Peter L. McCann, sr. v-p, Australia; Allan D. Schoening, sr. v-p, Canada; Carolyn J. Stone, sr. v-p, CFO & treas.

Capital Stock

	Authorized (shs.)	Outstanding (shs.)[1]
Class A Preferred	n.a.	
Series 1	50,000,000	nil
Class B Preferred	n.a.	nil
Common	46,000,000	15,086,701

[1] At Mar. 20, 2023

Class A Preferred Series 1 - Entitled to a 2% annual dividend on the liquidation preference of US$10,000, payable quarterly in cash or, at the company's option, by increasing the liquidation preference, or by any combination thereof. Redeemable at US$10,000 per share plus accrued and unpaid dividends. Convertible into common shares at US$3.30 per share and mandatorily convertible on or after Apr. 2, 2023. The company has the right to convert the preferred shares if the 15-day volume weighted average price of the common shares is equal to or exceeds US$3.30. Automatically converted into common shares upon a change of control of the company. Non-voting.

Common - One vote per share.

Major Shareholder - Horizon Kinetics LLC held 25.7% interest at Mar. 20, 2023.

Price Range - CVEO/NYSE

Year	Volume	High	Low	Close
2022	2,629,924	US$32.06	US$18.97	US$31.10
2021	2,447,512	US$25.20	US$13.50	US$19.17
2020	2,332,373	US$18.42	US$4.10	US$13.90
2019	1,758,167	US$34.20	US$9.12	US$15.48
2018	3,495,055	US$55.68	US$13.56	US$17.16

Consolidation: 1-for-12 cons. in Nov. 2020

Wholly Owned Subsidiaries

Action Industrial Catering, Perth, W.A., Australia.
Civeo Canada Limited Partnership, Alta.
Civeo Holding Company 1 Pty Ltd., Australia.
Civeo Holding Company 2 Pty Ltd., Australia.
Civeo Management LLC, Del.
Civeo Pty Ltd., Australia.
Noralta Lodge Ltd., Nisku, Alta.

Financial Statistics

Periods ended:	12m Dec. 31/22[‡A]		12m Dec. 31/21[A]
	US$000s	%Chg	US$000s
Operating revenue	**697,052**	**+17**	**594,463**
Cost of sales	...		436,462
General & admin expense	...		50,700
Stock-based compensation	...		9,900
Operating expense	**...**	**n.a.**	**497,062**
Operating income	**...**	**n.a.**	**97,401**
Deprec., depl. & amort.	...		83,101
Finance income	...		2
Finance costs, gross	11,474		12,964
Write-downs/write-offs	...		(7,935)
Pre-tax income	**...**	**n.a.**	**5,873**
Income taxes	...		3,376
Net income	**6,330**	**+154**	**2,497**
Net inc. for equity hldrs	**3,997**	**+196**	**1,350**
Net inc. for non-cont. int	**2,333**	**+103**	**1,147**
Cash & equivalent	...		6,282
Inventories	...		6,468
Accounts receivable	...		114,859
Current assets	153,549		157,193
Fixed assets, net	...		389,996
Right-of-use assets	...		18,327
Intangibles, net	...		101,846
Total assets	**566,184**	**-16**	**672,734**
Accts. pay. & accr. liabs	...		82,885
Current liabilities	128,257		136,918
Long-term debt, gross	130,953		173,178
Long-term debt, net	102,505		142,602
Long-term lease liabilities	...		15,429
Preferred share equity	nil		61,941
Shareholders' equity	300,139		361,499
Non-controlling interest	3,562		1,612
Cash from oper. activs	**...**	**n.a.**	**88,534**
Cash from fin. activs	...		(86,507)
Cash from invest. activs	...		(706)
Net cash position	**...**	**n.a.**	**6,282**
Capital expenditures	...		(15,571)
Capital disposals	...		14,306
	US$		US$
Earnings per share*	0.16		(0.04)
Cash flow per share*	...		6.22
	shs		shs
No. of shs. o/s*	15,217,501		14,111,221
Avg. no. of shs. o/s*	14,002,000		14,232,000
	%		%
Net profit margin	0.91		0.42
Return on equity	0.74		(0.19)
Return on assets	n.m.		1.13
Foreign sales percent	43		46
No. of employees (FTEs)	1,400		1,100

* Common
‡ Preliminary
[A] Reported in accordance with U.S. GAAP

Historical Summary
(as originally stated)

Fiscal Year	Oper. Rev. US$000s	Net Inc. Bef. Disc. US$000s	EPS* US$
2022[‡A]	697,052	6,330	0.16
2021[A]	594,463	2,497	(0.04)
2020[A]	529,729	(132,780)	(9.64)
2019[A]	527,555	(58,334)	(4.32)
2018[A]	466,692	(81,847)	(10.08)

* Common
‡ Preliminary
[A] Reported in accordance with U.S. GAAP

Note: Adjusted throughout for 1-for-12 cons. in Nov. 2020

C.122 Clairvest Group Inc.*

Symbol - CVG **Exchange** - TSX **CUSIP** - 17965L
Head Office - 1700-22 St. Clair Ave E, Toronto, ON, M4T 2S3 **Telephone** - (416) 925-9270 **Fax** - (416) 925-5753
Website - www.clairvest.com
Email - stephaniel@clairvest.com
Investor Relations - Stephanie Lo (416) 925-9270
Auditors - Ernst & Young LLP C.A., Toronto, Ont.
Transfer Agents - TSX Trust Company, Montréal, Qué.
FP500 Revenue Ranking - 505
Employees - 47 at Mar. 31, 2023
Profile - (Ont. 1987) Invests its own capital, and that of third parties, in emerging and established companies with potential to generate superior returns. At Mar. 31, 2023, the company's corporate investment portfolio consisted of 24 investments in 12 different industries and five countries.

The company invests its own capital, and that of the third parties, through **Clairvest Equity Partners III Limited Partnership** (CEP III), **Clairvest Equity Partners IV Limited Partnership** (CEP IV), **Clairvest Equity Partners IV-A Limited Partnership** (CEP IV-A), **Clairvest Equity Partners V Limited Partnership** (CEP V), **CEP V HI India Investment Limited Partnership** (CEP V India), **Clairvest Equity Partners V-A Limited Partnership** (CEP V-A), **Clairvest Equity Partners VI Limited Partnership** (CEP VI), **Clairvest Equity Partners VI-A Limited Partnership** (CEP VI-A) and **Clairvest Equity Partners VI-B Limited Partnership** (CEP VI-B).

The company together with CEP III invested in **Chilean Gaming Holdings**, a limited partnership that owns a 50% interest in Casino Marina del Sol in Concepcion, Chile, 50% interest in Casino Chillán in Chillán, Chile, 73.8% interest in Casino Osorno in Osorno, Chile, and 73.8% interest in Casino Sol Calama in Calama, Chile.

Investments made together with CEP IV and CEP IV-A consist of entities that hold real estate surrounding a casino in Davenport, Iowa; **10671541 Canada Inc.** (Northco), a specialty aviation services company operating across Canada and in select international locations; **Top Aces Inc.**, a provider of advanced adversary services across three continents; **Momentum Decisive Solutions Canada Inc.**, an interconnected network of logistical support companies; and **New Meadowlands Racetrack, LLC**, an operator of a standardbred horse racing track in East Rutherford, N.J.

Investments made together with CEP V, CEP V India and CEP V-A consist of **Abra Health Group** (formerly **The Childsmiles Group LLC**), a multi-specialty dental practice provider with offices in New Jersey and Pennsylvania; **Accel Entertainment, Inc.**, a licensed video gaming terminal operator in the U.S.; **Digital Media Solutions, Inc.**, which operates as a lead generation engine for companies in a variety of industries; **Durante Rentals, LLC**, a construction equipment rental provider in the New York Metropolitan area; **FSB Technology (UK) Ltd.**, a business-to-business sports and Internet gaming technology supplier; **Head Digital Works Pvt. Ltd.**, an Internet-based technology and gaming company in India; **Meriplex Communications, Ltd.**, a provider of managed networking, cybersecurity and information technology (IT) services for mid-market customers throughout the U.S.; and **Winters Bros. Waste Systems of Long Island Holdings, LLC**, a provider of commercial, industrial and residential waste collection services across Long Island, N.Y.

Investments made together with CEP VI, CEP VI-A and CEP VI-B consist of **Acera Insurance Services Ltd.**, an insurance broker which offers property and casualty and group benefits insurance products; **Arrowhead Environmental Partners, LLC**, a non-hazardous waste-by-rail operator in northeastern U.S. markets; **Bluetree Dental LLC**, a multi-specialty, paediatric and orthodontics-focused dental service organization in the Mountain West region of the U.S.; **Boca Biolistics, LLC**, a biosamples company in Florida; **Brunswick Bierworks Inc.**, a contract manufacturer of specialty beverages serving Canadian and the U.S. markets; **Delaware Park**, a casino and racetrack business in Wilmington, Del., which serves the Delaware, Maryland, New Jersey and Pennsylvania markets; **F12.net Inc.**, a provider of a suite of managed IT support and services to small and medium enterprises across Canada; New Hampshire Gaming, an investment vehicle created to acquire and operate existing gaming locations in southern New Hampshire with plans to build a large-scale historical horse racing facility in Nashua, N.H.; **NovaSource Power Services**, a solar operations and maintenance company serving commercial and residential sectors globally; and **Star Waste Systems, LLC** (dba Boston Carting Services), a solid waste management company serving the Greater Boston area of Massachusetts with a focus on providing residential, commercial and roll-off container waste collection.

The company also holds investment in Grey Eagle Casino, a charitable casino on Tsuu T'ina First Nation reserve lands, near Calgary, Alta.; and residual interest in various Wellington Financial funds which are being wound up.

In addition, the company provides advisory services to its investment partners which may include evaluation of business prospects, strategic planning, marketing, and financial advice and tax strategy.

On June 30, 2023, the company announced the initial closing of **Clairvest Equity Partners VII**, a successor fund to **Clairvest Equity Partners VI**, with equity commitments of US$1 billion. The company's commitment to the fund is US$300,000,000 alongside US$700,000,000 from third party investors. The company will be the single largest investor in the fund.

Recent Merger and Acquisition Activity

Status: completed **Announced:** May 1, 2023
Clairvest Group Inc. (CVG), together with Clairvest Equity Partners VI Limited Partnership, and Franklin, Ky.-based gaming operator ECL Entertainment, LLC, acquired NHCG, LLC for an undisclosed amount. NHCG owns and operates the Lucky Moose Casino and Tavern and The River Casino & Sports Bar in Nashua, N.H. CVG and ECL would operate the existing the gaming locations with plans to build a large-scale historical horse racing facility.

Status: completed **Announced:** Mar. 1, 2023
Clairvest Group Inc. (CVG), together with Clairvest Equity Partners VI Limited Partnership, acquired a 30% interest in Reno, Nev.-based Bluetree Dental LLC for US$32,200,000 (Cdn$43,800,000), with CVG's portion being US$8,700,000 (Cdn$11,800,000) in the form of 4,134,866 units, representing 8.1% interest. Bluetree operates dental clinics specializing in paediatric dentistry and orthodontics in the Mountain West region of the U.S.

Status: completed **Announced:** Feb. 21, 2023
Clairvest Group Inc. (CVG), together with Clairvest Equity Partners VI Limited Partnership, acquired a 65% interest in Pompano Beach, Fla.-based Boca Biolistics, LLC for US$25,100,000 (Cdn$33,900,000), with CVG's portion being US$6,800,000 (Cdn$9,200,000) in the form of 6,789,426 units, representing 17.6% interest. Boca Biolistics operates as a clinical research organization (CRO) and biomaterials company focused on the procurement, storage and sale of human biological samples (specializing in infectious diseases and oncology) used for clinical trials and diagnostic development.

Status: completed **Announced:** Dec. 1, 2022
Clairvest Group Inc. and Clairvest Equity Partner V sold their shareholdings in DTG Enterprises, Inc., a provider of waste hauling and recycling services in the greater Seattle-Tacoma area of Washington, to a fund managed by Macquarie Group Limited for US$178,000,000, of which US$53,400,000 was Clairvest's portion.

Status: completed **Announced:** Sept. 21, 2022
Clairvest Group Inc. (CVG), together with Clairvest Equity Partners VI Limited Partnership, acquired a 21.1% interest in Calgary, Alta.-based Acera Insurance Services Ltd. for $100,000,000, with CVG's portion being $27,100,000 in the form of 27,058,823 class A convertible preferred shares, representing 5.7% interest. Acera provides brokerage services for property and casualty and insurance products and group benefits in Canada, with offices in Alberta, British Columbia, Ontario and Yukon. Acera is the resulting entity from the merger of Rogers Insurance Ltd. and CapriCMW Insurance Services Ltd. on Sept. 20, 2022.

Status: completed **Announced:** July 18, 2022
Clairvest Group Inc. (CVG), together with Clairvest Equity Partners V Limited Partnership (CEP V), sold a portion of its interest in Houston, Tex.-based Meriplex Communications, Ltd. to Vitruvian Partners LLP for US$160,000,000 cash (US$48,000,000 for CVG). CVG and CEP V retained 18% interest in Meriplex. Meriplex provides managed networking, cybersecurity and information technology (IT) services for mid-market customers throughout the U.S.

Status: completed **Announced:** July 1, 2022
Clairvest Group Inc., together with Clairvest Equity Partners VI Limited Partnership, acquired a 67.8% interest in Boston, Mass.-based Star Waste Systems, LLC (dba Boston Carting Services), a solid waste management company serving the Greater Boston area of Massachusetts with a focus on providing residential, commercial and roll-off container waste collection, for US$40,000,000. Clairvest's portion of the investment was US$10,800,000 for an 18.3% ownership interest.

Predecessor Detail - Name changed from Roy-L Merchant Group Inc., Dec. 4, 1991.

Directors - Michael D. Bregman, chr., Toronto, Ont.; B. Jeffrey (Jeff) Parr, v-chr. & man. dir., Toronto, Ont.; Kenneth B. (Ken) Rotman, CEO & man. dir., Toronto, Ont.; Michael A. Wagman, pres. & man. dir., Toronto, Ont.; John R. Barnett, North Palm Beach, Fla.; Anne-Mette de Place Filippini, Toronto, Ont.; Joseph E. Fluet III, Washington, D.C.; G. John Krediet, Delfstrahuizen, Netherlands; William F. (Bill) Morneau Jr., Toronto, Ont.; Lionel H. Schipper, Toronto, Ont.; Rick Watkin, Toronto, Ont.; Peter Zemsky, France

Other Exec. Officers - Daniel Cheng, CFO; James H. Miller, gen. counsel & corp. sec.

Capital Stock

	Authorized (shs.)	Outstanding (shs.)[1]
Preference	unlimited	nil
First Series	10,000,000	nil
Second Series	1,000,000	nil
Common	unlimited	15,024,001

[1] At June 26, 2023

Normal Course Issuer Bid - The company plans to make normal course purchases of up to 760,135 common shares representing 5% of the total outstanding. The bid commenced on Mar. 8, 2023, and expires on Mar. 7, 2024.

Major Shareholder - Kenneth B. (Ken) Rotman held 33.5% interest, JLR Estate Voting Trust held 17.5% interest and G.R. Heffernan & Associates Ltd. held 11.7% interest at June 26, 2023.

Price Range - CVG/TSX

Year	Volume	High	Low	Close
2022	120,700	$80.05	$55.00	$72.30
2021	69,772	$68.59	$52.00	$61.00
2020	201,878	$55.25	$39.75	$51.00
2019	174,820	$54.29	$45.30	$52.30
2018	188,467	$51.75	$39.36	$45.00

Recent Close: $82.58

Capital Stock Changes - During fiscal 2023, 28,300 common shares were repurchased under a Normal Course Issuer Bid.

During fiscal 2022, 6,100 common shares were repurchased under a Normal Course Issuer Bid.

Dividends

CVG com Ra $0.10 pa A est. June 24, 1992
$0.7105◆ July 27/23 $0.6833◆ July 28/22
$0.4696◆ July 23/21
Paid in 2023: $0.10 + $0.7105◆ 2022: $0.10 + $0.6833◆ 2021: $0.10 + $0.4696◆
◆ Special

Long-Term Debt - At Mar. 31, 2023, the company had no long-term debt.

Wholly Owned Subsidiaries

CEP MIP GP Corporation
Clairvest GP (GP LP) Inc.
Clairvest GP Manageco Inc.
Clairvest General Partner III Limited Partnership
Clairvest General Partner IV Limited Partnership
Clairvest General Partner Limited Partnership
Clairvest USA Limited

Note: The preceding list includes only the major related companies in which interests are held.

Financial Statistics

Periods ended:	12m Mar. 31/23[A]	%Chg	12m Mar. 31/22[A]
	$000s	%Chg	$000s
Realized invest. gain (loss)	75,041		94,620
Unrealized invest. gain (loss)	(137,191)		261,000
Total revenue	**130,183**	**-69**	**421,057**
Salaries & benefits	15,496		22,825
General & admin. expense	11,464		3,967
Stock-based compensation	28,578		13,081
Operating expense	**55,538**	**+39**	**39,873**
Operating income	**74,645**	**-80**	**381,184**
Deprec. & amort.	1,170		1,144
Finance costs, gross	n.a.		705
Finance costs, net	(1,577)		n.a.
Pre-tax income	**63,684**	**-83**	**375,013**
Income taxes	11,315		44,806
Net income	**52,369**	**-84**	**330,207**
Cash & equivalent	390,832		348,795
Accounts receivable	49,423		47,959
Investments	891,709		849,073
Fixed assets, net	6,577		7,295
Total assets	**1,429,651**	**+6**	**1,353,143**
Accts. pay. & accr. liabs	13,834		6,852
Shareholders' equity	1,217,727		1,179,087
Cash from oper. activs	**13,634**	**-67**	**41,015**
Cash from fin. activs	(13,729)		(8,927)
Cash from invest. activs	(452)		(466)
Net cash position	**217,870**	**0**	**218,417**
Capital expenditures, net	(452)		(466)
	$		$
Earnings per share*	3.48		21.93
Cash flow per share*	0.91		2.72
Cash divd. per share*	0.10		0.10
Extra divd. - cash*	0.68		0.47
Total divd. per share*	**0.78**		**0.57**
	shs		shs
No. of shs. o/s*	15,024,001		15,052,301
Avg. no. of shs. o/s*	15,036,381		15,055,594
	%		%
Net profit margin	40.23		78.42
Return on equity	4.37		32.42
Return on assets	3.76		28.30
No. of employees (FTEs)	47		43

* Common
[A] Reported in accordance with IFRS

Historical Summary
(as originally stated)

Fiscal Year	Total Rev. $000s	Net Inc. Bef. Disc. $000s	EPS* $
2023[A]	130,183	52,369	3.48
2022[A]	421,057	330,207	21.93
2021[A]	177,723	104,839	6.96
2020[A]	129,298	69,498	4.60
2019[A]	204,207	119,242	7.87

* Common
[A] Reported in accordance with IFRS

C.123 Clarke Inc.*

Symbol - CKI **Exchange** - TSX **CUSIP** - 181901
Head Office - 106-145 Hobson's Lake Dr, Halifax, NS, B3S 0H9 **Telephone** - (902) 442-3000 **Fax** - (902) 442-0187
Website - www.clarkeinc.com
Email - tcasey@clarkeinc.com
Investor Relations - Tom Casey (902) 442-3415
Auditors - PricewaterhouseCoopers LLP C.A., Halifax, N.S.
Bankers - HSBC Bank Canada, Toronto, Ont.
Lawyers - Bennett Jones LLP, Toronto, Ont.
Transfer Agents - Computershare Trust Company of Canada Inc., Montréal, Qué.

Employees - 620 at Dec. 31, 2022

Profile - (Can. 1997) Holds a portfolio of strategic investments and owns hotel company **Holloway Lodging Corporation**.

Wholly owned Holloway Lodging Corporation owns and acquires hotel properties in secondary, tertiary and suburban markets in Canada, and provides hotel management services to third parties. At Dec. 31, 2022, Holloway owned and operated 17 hotels across Canada. Hotels are operated with international, national or regional franchise affiliation agreements under the banners: Travelodge, Super 8®, Holiday Inn®, Quality Inn®, DoubleTree®, Sternwheeler and Standard Inn & Suites.

The company also owns a development project under construction in Ottawa, Ont., which involves a multi-building residential apartment complex with ground-floor retail space; a 33.33% interest in a real estate development project under construction located in downtown Montreal, Que., which involves a 38-storey building with seniors' housing, rental units and luxury condominiums; three vacant office properties in Houston, Tex., held for redevelopment; a parcel of land in Forestville, Que.; and a passenger/car ferry operating on the St. Lawrence River.

During 2022, the company sold its marketable securities to **Clarke Inc. Master Trust**, which holds the units of the pension plans administered by the company, for $3,025,000. In addition, the company sold a parcel of vacant land for $376,000.

Recent Merger and Acquisition Activity

Status: pending **Revised:** June 30, 2023

UPDATE: Clarke elected to exit the COA and expects to receive a preferred return on its aggregate investment of 6% up to Feb. 28, 2023, and a preferred return of 12% on its aggregate investment from Mar. 1, 2023, until the expected closing date of Nov. 1, 2023. PREVIOUS: Clarke Inc. exercised its right to sell its one-third interest in the real estate development project, which is under construction and located at 1111 Atwater Avenue in Westmount, Que., to its co-investors for consideration equal to Clarke's investment plus a 6% return. Clarke's initial investment includes $21,121,000 cash and the assumption of Clarke's proportionate share of the construction financing of $16,000,0000. The project is planned for a 38-storey building that includes seniors' housing, rental units and luxury condominiums. The transaction was expected to close on Mar. 31, 2023. Mar. 31, 2023 - Clarke was in negotiation to potentially amend and extend its co-ownership agreement (COA) with its partners on the 1111 Atwater Avenue development.

Status: completed **Announced:** June 13, 2022

Clarke Inc., through wholly owned Holloway Lodging Corporation, acquired the 206-room Stanford Inn & Suites in Grande Prairie, Alta., for $11,600,000 cash, which were funded from revolving credit facilities.

Directors - George S. Armoyan, chr., pres. & CEO, Halifax, N.S.; Blair A. Cook, St. John's, N.L.; Charles Pellerin, Victoriaville, Qué.; Jane Rafuse, Halifax, N.S.; Marc L. Staniloff, Calgary, Alta.

Other Exec. Officers - Tom Casey, CFO & co-pres. & CFO, Holloway Lodging Corporation; Tomer Cohen, v-p, invests.; Robert Sherman, co-pres. & COO, Holloway Lodging Corporation

Capital Stock

	Authorized (shs.)	Outstanding (shs.)[1]
First Preferred	unlimited	nil
Second Preferred	unlimited	nil
Common	unlimited	13,985,157

[1] At Aug. 11, 2023

Normal Course Issuer Bid - The company plans to make normal course purchases of up to 699,232 common shares representing 5% of the total outstanding. The bid commenced on July 4, 2023, and expires on July 3, 2024.

Major Shareholder - George S. Armoyan held 74.2% interest and Letko, Brosseau & Associates Inc. held 12.8% interest at Apr. 3, 2023.

Price Range - CKI/TSX

Year	Volume	High	Low	Close
2022	586,205	$14.07	$9.77	$12.48
2021	779,000	$10.32	$6.41	$10.32
2020	2,679,872	$13.75	$3.75	$6.68
2019	685,815	$13.91	$11.98	$12.44
2018	1,037,156	$12.75	$10.17	$12.50

Recent Close: $13.45

Capital Stock Changes - During 2021, 342,825 common shares were repurchased under a Normal Course Issuer Bid.

Long-Term Debt - Outstanding at Dec. 31, 2022:

Term loan due 2023[1]	$11,135,000
Mtges.[2]	42,039,000
Construction mtge.[3]	45,178,000
6.25% conv. debs. due 2028[4]	34,146,000
	132,498,000
Less: Current portion	77,423,000
	55,075,000

[1] Bears interest at prime plus 1.50%.

[2] Bear interest at a weighted average rate of 5.25% and maturing on various dates from October 2023 to February 2030.

[3] Bear interest at a 30-day Canadian Dollar Offered Rate plus 2.60%, subject to minimum rate of 4.25%.

[4] Convertible into common shares at $13.74 per share. Bear interest rate of 6.25% until Apr. 29, 2023 and 5.5% thereafter. Interest rate decreases from 6.25% to 5.5%, for the period from and including Apr. 30, 2023, to but excluding Jan. 1, 2028.

Note - In February 2023, the company repaid its $11,042,000 term loan due 2023. In July 2023, all $35,000,000 principal amount of 5.5% convertible debentures due 2028 were redeemed for $1,013.41 for each $1,000 principal amount of debentures.

Wholly Owned Subsidiaries

Holloway Lodging Corporation, Halifax, N.S.

Financial Statistics

Periods ended:	12m Dec. 31/22[A]		12m Dec. 31/21[◻A]
	$000s	%Chg	$000s
Realized invest. gain (loss)	641		30,959
Unrealized invest. gain (loss)	(322)		(8,646)
Total revenue	**65,321**	**+5**	**62,438**
General & admin. expense	2,852		2,506
Stock-based compensation	123		42
Other operating expense	42,800		27,573
Operating expense	**45,775**	**+52**	**30,121**
Operating income	**19,546**	**-40**	**32,317**
Deprec. & amort.	9,570		10,143
Finance costs, gross	6,495		6,008
Pre-tax income	**5,330**	**-73**	**19,726**
Income taxes	2,104		3,347
Net income	**3,226**	**-80**	**16,379**
Cash & equivalent	1,090		21,196
Inventories	119		78
Accounts receivable	8,041		9,346
Current assets	80,852		32,864
Long-term investments	80,885		48,849
Fixed assets, net	221,704		178,797
Properties	nil		53,704
Total assets	**416,121**	**+8**	**384,629**
Bank indebtedness	26,086		nil
Accts. pay. & accr. liabs.	22,758		12,745
Current liabilities	130,882		54,065
Long-term debt, gross	132,498		135,784
Long-term debt, net	55,075		98,033
Long-term lease liabilities	560		730
Shareholders' equity	214,970		208,619
Cash from oper. activs.	**3,402**	**n.a.**	**(7,213)**
Cash from fin. activs.	16,095		(7,820)
Cash from invest. activs.	(36,830)		30,726
Net cash position	**1,090**	**-94**	**18,423**
Capital expenditures	(19,053)		(6,768)
Capital disposals	nil		28
Pension fund surplus	75,405		54,306
	$		$
Earnings per share*	0.23		1.12
Cash flow per share*	0.24		(0.49)
	shs		shs
No. of shs. o/s*	14,069,144		14,411,969
Avg. no. of shs. o/s*	14,238,000		14,673,000
	%		%
Net profit margin	4.94		26.23
Return on equity	1.52		8.68
Return on assets	1.79		6.14
No. of employees (FTEs)	620		550

* Common

◻ Restated

[A] Reported in accordance with IFRS

Latest Results

Periods ended:	6m June 30/23[A]		6m June 30/22[A]
	$000s	%Chg	$000s
Total revenue	33,364	+34	24,875
Net income	(2,194)	n.a.	(1,979)
	$		$
Earnings per share*	(0.16)		(0.14)

* Common

[A] Reported in accordance with IFRS

Historical Summary
(as originally stated)

Fiscal Year	Total Rev.	Net Inc. Bef. Disc.	EPS*
	$000s	$000s	$
2022[A]	65,321	3,226	0.23
2021[A]	62,438	16,379	1.12
2020[A]	43,425	(19,210)	(1.21)
2019[A]	98,878	38,655	2.90
2018[A]	6,150	(564)	(0.04)

* Common

[A] Reported in accordance with IFRS

C.124 Clean Seed Capital Group Ltd.

Symbol - CSX **Exchange** - TSX-VEN **CUSIP** - 18451F

Head Office - 7541 Conway Ave, Unit 14, Burnaby, BC, V5E 2P7 **Telephone** - (604) 566-9895 **Fax** - (604) 566-9896

Website - www.cleanseedcapital.com

Email - mtommasi@cleanseedcapital.com

Investor Relations - Mark Tommasi (604) 566-9895

Auditors -

Transfer Agents - Computershare Investor Services Inc.

Profile - (B.C. 2010) Develops, manufactures and sells advanced precision no-till seeding equipments for agricultural markets.

The company owns and develops the SMART Seeder technology which enables the seeder, farmer and agronomists to plant different products including seeds and fertilizers at each square foot of the field to match changing soil conditions. Through the SMART Seeder technology, the company together with **Norwood Sales Inc.** have developed the SMART Seeder MAX™, which is built through SMART Seeder technology with the capabilities to seed all crops used by the seeders and planters; SMART Seeder MAX-S™, which include a proprietary motor drive (known as Cushion Drive Meter™) and control system (known as Seed Sync™); and MINI-MAX™, a scaled-down model of SMART Seeder MAX™ for developing countries.

The company's Smart Seeder technology has patents with expiry dates ranging from 2033 to 2037 for issued patents and has made further patent applications that, if successful, would provide patent coverage until 2041.

Has a 16,000-sq.-ft. operations and assembly facility in Saskatoon, Sask.

Directors - Graeme Lempriere, chr. & CEO, B.C.; Colin M. Rush, pres. & COO, Sask.; Gary Anderson, Winnipeg, Man.; Glenn Gatcliffe, Ont.; Steve Sommerfeld, Sask.; Ulrich Trogele, Calif.

Other Exec. Officers - Steven (Steve) Brassard, CFO & corp. sec.; Manmohanjit (Jeet) Jheetey, v-p, opers. & product devel.; Noel Lempriere, v-p, mktg.; Donald (Butch) Sinclair, v-p, sales & cust. experience; Kyle Takeuchi, contr.

Capital Stock

	Authorized (shs.)	Outstanding (shs.)[1]
Common	unlimited	89,685,645

[1] At Nov. 29, 2022

Major Shareholder - Jason Schultz held 10.32% interest at Nov. 15, 2022.

Price Range - CSX/TSX-VEN

Year	Volume	High	Low	Close
2022	5,524,858	$0.41	$0.13	$0.17
2021	11,360,503	$0.67	$0.26	$0.31
2020	6,295,256	$0.47	$0.19	$0.39
2019	14,020,063	$0.47	$0.14	$0.19
2018	11,410,341	$0.66	$0.34	$0.36

Recent Close: $0.14

Capital Stock Changes - During fiscal 2022, common shares were issued as follows: 8,892,145 by private placement and 293,000 on exercise of options.

Wholly Owned Subsidiaries

Clean Seed Agricultural Technologies Ltd., B.C.

Seed Sync Systems Ltd., B.C.

Investments

50% int. in **Clean Seed Agriculture Limited Partnership**

50% int. in **10055342 Manitoba Ltd.**, Man.

Financial Statistics

Periods ended:	12m June 30/22[A]		12m June 30/21[A]
	$000s	%Chg	$000s
Operating revenue	**1,266**	**n.m.**	**7**
Salaries & benefits	703		704
Research & devel. expense	302		78
General & admin expense	983		840
Stock-based compensation	110		323
Operating expense	**2,098**	**+8**	**1,945**
Operating income	**(832)**	**n.a.**	**(1,938)**
Deprec., depl. & amort.	1,042		940
Finance costs, gross	360		226
Pre-tax income	**(2,640)**	**n.a.**	**(3,271)**
Net income	**(2,640)**	**n.a.**	**(3,271)**
Cash & equivalent	94		302
Inventories	266		180
Accounts receivable	60		32
Current assets	523		663
Long-term investments	4,124		2,416
Fixed assets, net	799		308
Intangibles, net	9,708		9,563
Total assets	**15,155**	**+17**	**12,950**
Accts. pay. & accr. liabs.	1,952		1,186
Current liabilities	4,310		2,601
Shareholders' equity	9,302		9,258
Cash from oper. activs.	**(1,250)**	**n.a.**	**(1,584)**
Cash from fin. activs.	2,976		879
Cash from invest. activs.	(1,936)		(2,101)
Net cash position	**94**	**-69**	**302**
Capital expenditures	(133)		(69)
	$		$
Earnings per share*	(0.03)		(0.04)
Cash flow per share*	(0.02)		(0.02)
	shs		shs
No. of shs. o/s*	89,185,645		80,000,500
Avg. no. of shs. o/s*	82,875,093		77,063,267
	%		%
Net profit margin	(208.53)		n.m.
Return on equity	(28.45)		(32.84)
Return on assets	(16.22)		(22.39)

* Common

[A] Reported in accordance with IFRS

Latest Results

Periods ended:	3m Sept. 30/22[A]		3m Sept. 30/21[A]
	$000s	%Chg	$000s
Net income	(1,049)	n.a.	(898)
	$		$
Earnings per share*	(0.01)		(0.01)

* Common
[A] Reported in accordance with IFRS

Historical Summary
(as originally stated)

Fiscal Year	Oper. Rev.	Net Inc. Bef. Disc.	EPS*
	$000s	$000s	$
2022[A]	1,266	(2,640)	(0.03)
2021[A]	7	(3,271)	(0.04)
2020[A]	5,202	2,091	0.03
2019[A]	nil	(3,771)	(0.06)
2018[A]	nil	(6,204)	(0.12)

* Common
[A] Reported in accordance with IFRS

C.125 CleanGo Innovations Inc.

Symbol - CGII **Exchange** - CSE **CUSIP** - 18453D
Head Office - 422-234 5149 Country Hills Blvd NW, Calgary, AB, T3A 5K8 **Telephone** - (403) 401-2912
Website - cleangogreengo.ca
Email - anthony@cleangogreengo.com
Investor Relations - Anthony Sarvucci (403) 401-2912
Auditors - Davidson & Company LLP C.A., Vancouver, B.C.
Transfer Agents - TSX Trust Company, Vancouver, B.C.

Profile - (B.C. 2014) Manufactures and sells green, non-toxic and biodegradable cleaning products for retail, commercial and industrial markets in Canada and the U.S.

Products, which are manufactured under the CleanGo GreenGo brand, include Industrial Strength used for cleaning shops, garage and industrial yard; Total Purpose for cleaning mirrors, kitchen, bathroom and windows; Fabric & Carpet for cleaning any carpet or fabric stain; gel hand sanitizers; sanitary wipes; and concentrates.

In September 2021, the company signed a letter of intent to acquire private Alberta-based **Dakota Supplies Inc.**, which offers the MOPPITT hands-free cleaning unit for the global aviation and transportation sanitation industry, for $2,000,000. As at May 2023, the transaction was still pending.

In April 2022, the company entered into a letter of intent with **HAST Group International GmbH**, which operates PROWIN, a retail distribution arm in Ellerau Germany. The agreement is designed to help introduce the company's retail products into the European market for retail distribution as well as for white labelling and distribution throughout European Union.

Predecessor Detail - Name changed from Softlab9 Technologies Inc., Sept. 8, 2021, pursuant to the reverse takeover acquisition of CleanGo GreenGo Inc.

Directors - Anthony Sarvucci, pres. & CEO, Calgary, Alta.; Eugene Chen, Calgary, Alta.; Dr. Darren Clark, Calgary, Alta.; Morgan Rebrinsky, Calgary, Alta.

Other Exec. Officers - Paula Pearce-Sarvucci, interim CFO & corp. sec.

Capital Stock

	Authorized (shs.)	Outstanding (shs.)[1]
Common	unlimited	2,546,483

[1] At May 2, 2023

Major Shareholder - Anthony Sarvucci held 21.58% interest at Oct. 3, 2022.

Price Range - CGII/CSE

Year	Volume	High	Low	Close
2022	351,485	$5.25	$0.23	$0.55
2021	212,907	$9.40	$2.00	$3.50
2020	422,064	$38.80	$1.80	$9.40
2019	206,325	$58.50	$1.70	$4.00
2018	43,723	$97.50	$31.20	$42.90

Consolidation: 1-for-5 cons. in Jan. 2023; 1-for-4 cons. in Dec. 2021; 1-for-13 cons. in Aug. 2019; 1-for-1.5 cons. in Mar. 2019
Recent Close: $0.50

Capital Stock Changes - On Jan. 13, 2023, common shares were consolidated on a 1-for-5 basis.

During 2022, 1,260,775 common shares were issued for debt settlement.

Wholly Owned Subsidiaries

CleanGo GreenGo Inc., Calgary, Alta.
- 100% int. in **CleanGo GreenGo, Inc.**, Nev.

Financial Statistics

Periods ended:	12m Dec. 31/22[A]		12m Dec. 31/21[◻A]
	$000s	%Chg	$000s
Operating revenue	**114**	**-22**	**147**
Cost of sales	229		128
General & admin expense	1,010		691
Stock-based compensation	719		nil
Operating expense	**1,957**	**+139**	**819**
Operating income	**(1,843)**	**n.a.**	**(672)**
Deprec., depl. & amort.	80		28
Finance income	21		nil
Finance costs, gross	13		22
Write-downs/write-offs	(413)		(11)
Pre-tax income	**(1,978)**	**n.a.**	**(6,947)**
Net income	**(1,978)**	**n.a.**	**(6,947)**
Cash & equivalent	14		296
Inventories	70		209
Accounts receivable	116		149
Current assets	212		1,034
Fixed assets, net	66		79
Right-of-use assets	315		7
Total assets	**592**	**-47**	**1,120**
Accts. pay. & accr. liabs	820		930
Current liabilities	1,528		1,441
Long-term debt, gross	39		43
Long-term debt, net	39		43
Long-term lease liabilities	223		nil
Shareholders' equity	(1,198)		(364)
Cash from oper. activs	**(216)**	**n.a.**	**(1,198)**
Cash from fin. activs	(65)		358
Cash from invest. activs	nil		924
Net cash position	**14**	**-95**	**296**
	$		$
Earnings per share*	(0.85)		(4.49)
Cash flow per share*	(0.09)		(0.78)
	shs		shs
No. of shs. o/s*	2,506,483		2,254,328
Avg. no. of shs. o/s*	2,338,560		1,545,680
	%		%
Net profit margin	n.m.		n.m.
Return on equity	n.m.		n.m.
Return on assets	(229.56)		(587.86)
Foreign sales percent	1		10

* Common
[◻] Restated
[A] Reported in accordance with IFRS

Latest Results

Periods ended:	3m Mar. 31/23[A]		3m Mar. 31/22[A]
	$000s	%Chg	$000s
Operating revenue	12	-70	40
Net income	(179)	n.a.	(267)
	$		$
Earnings per share*	(0.07)		(0.15)

* Common
[A] Reported in accordance with IFRS

Historical Summary
(as originally stated)

Fiscal Year	Oper. Rev.	Net Inc. Bef. Disc.	EPS*
	$000s	$000s	$
2022[A]	114	(1,978)	(0.85)
2021[A1]	147	(6,947)	(4.50)
2020[A2]	nil	(2,352)	(3.80)
2019[A]	nil	(2,152)	(7.40)
2018[A3]	44	(5,051)	(35.10)

* Common
[A] Reported in accordance with IFRS
[1] Results reflect the Sept. 7, 2021, reverse takeover acquisition of CleanGo GreenGo Inc.
[2] Results for 2020 and prior years pertain to Softlab9 Technologies Inc.
[3] Results reflect the Mar. 2, 2018, reverse takeover acquisition of RewardDrop Software Inc.

Note: Adjusted throughout for 1-for-5 cons. in Jan. 2023; 1-for-4 cons. in Dec. 2021; 1-for-13 cons. in Aug. 2019; 1-for-1.5 cons. in Mar. 2019

C.126 Cleantech Power Corp.

Symbol - PWWR **Exchange** - NEO (S) **CUSIP** - 18453N
Head Office - 810-789 Pender St W, Vancouver, BC, V6C 1H2 **Telephone** - (604) 687-2038 **Fax** - (604) 687-3141
Website - www.cleantechpower.ca
Email - fcarnevale@cleantechpower.ca
Investor Relations - Frank Carnevale (647) 531-8264
Auditors - Dale Matheson Carr-Hilton LaBonte LLP C.A., Vancouver, B.C.
Transfer Agents - Endeavor Trust Corporation, Vancouver, B.C.

Profile - (B.C. 1987) Designs, develops, produces and commercializes micro-combined and combined heat and power systems and generators based on advanced alkaline fuel cell technology for residential, industrial and commercial markets worldwide.

Operations are organized into two business units: Fuel Cell Power; and PWWR Flow Streams.

Fuel Cell Power - This includes wholly owned **Fuel Cell Power N.V.**, which develops, produces and commercializes micro-combined heat and power (micro-CHP) systems and off-grid and back up power generation based on advanced alkaline fuel cell technology that generates zero CO_2 emissions. A fuel cell is a clean electrical power conversion/generation system and represents small power stations that provide electricity and an equivalent amount of heat for various purposes. The company's micro-CHP heat and power system based on alkaline fuel cell technology was expected to be available for commercial applications by the end of 2024.

PWWR Flow Streams - Develops, owns and operates combined heat and power (CHP) assets sold under the PWWR Flow brand. PWWR Flow assets deliver efficiency improvements of over 20% with reduced costs to customers in multi-residential and commercial applications. PWWR Flow has contracted existing CHP assets in Toronto, and has an additional pipeline of potential contracts valued at over $50,000,000 in development.

Common suspended from NEO, June 2, 2023.

Recent Merger and Acquisition Activity

Status: completed **Revised:** Apr. 22, 2022

UPDATE: The transaction was completed. PREVIOUS: Alkaline Fuel Cell Power Corp. agreed to acquire the Combined Heat and Power (CHP) generation business of AI Renewable 2018-I Limited Partnership, AI Renewable 2020-I Limited Partnership and 2191 Yonge Ltd. (collectively AI) for $3,000,000 cash and issuance of 22,575,758 common shares. AI uses a clean and renewable single fuel source energy technology that generates both electricity and heat. AI's pipeline consisted of more than 30 potential CHP projects at various stages of development.

Predecessor Detail - Name changed from Alkaline Fuel Cell Power Corp., May 4, 2023.

Directors - Joel S. Dumaresq, CFO & corp. sec., Vancouver, B.C.; Matthew J. Fish, Toronto, Ont.; Troy J. Grant, Bedford, N.S.; Maciej (Magic) Lis, Toronto, Ont.; Dr. Richard Lu, Toronto, Ont.

Other Exec. Officers - Frank Carnevale, CEO; Jo Verstappen, COO

Capital Stock

	Authorized (shs.)	Outstanding (shs.)[1]
Preferred	unlimited	nil
Common	unlimited	168,057,561

[1] At July 19, 2021

Major Shareholder - Widely held at Sept. 16, 2022.

Price Range - BIT/TSX-VEN (D)

Year	Volume	High	Low	Close
2022	6,871,000	$0.23	$0.06	$0.07
2021	7,155,000	$0.92	$0.16	$0.20
2018	412,033	$0.70	$0.25	$0.40

Consolidation: 1-for-10 cons. in July 2019
Recent Close: $0.03

Capital Stock Changes - In December 2022, private placement of up to 20,000,000 units (1 common share & 1 warrant) at 6¢ per unit was arranged, with warrants exercisable at 15¢ per share for two years.

Wholly Owned Subsidiaries

AI 1275 McPherson Ltd., Canada.
AI 2181 Ltd., Canada.
AI 2191 Yonge Ltd., Canada.
FCP Fuel Cell Power UNIP Lda., Portugal.
Fuel Cell Power N.V., Belarus.
Fuel Cell Power s.r.o., Czech Republic.
PWWR Flow 83 Borough Corp., Canada.

Financial Statistics

Periods ended:	12m Dec. 31/21[A]		12m Dec. 31/20[A]
	$000s	%Chg	$000s
Salaries & benefits	270		nil
General & admin expense	5,989		84
Stock-based compensation	2,973		nil
Operating expense	**9,232**	**n.m.**	**84**
Operating income	**(9,232)**	**n.a.**	**(84)**
Finance costs, gross	39		1
Pre-tax income	**(9,313)**	**n.a.**	**(85)**
Net income	**(9,313)**	**n.a.**	**(85)**
Cash & equivalent	5,869		14
Current assets	6,567		15
Fixed assets, net	158		nil
Right-of-use assets	184		n.a.
Total assets	**8,968**	**n.m.**	**15**
Bank indebtedness	80		87
Accts. pay. & accr. liabs	327		219
Current liabilities	454		306
Long-term lease liabilities	143		n.a.
Shareholders' equity	8,372		(291)
Cash from oper. activs	**(6,754)**	**n.a.**	**(20)**
Cash from fin. activs	15,078		nil
Cash from invest. activs	(2,242)		nil
Net cash position	**5,869**	**n.m.**	**14**
Capital expenditures	(182)		nil
	$		$
Earnings per share*	(0.06)		(0.01)
Cash flow per share*	(0.04)		(0.00)
	shs		shs
No. of shs. o/s*	168,257,571		11,618,177
Avg. no. of shs. o/s*	152,090,499		11,618,177
	%		%
Net profit margin	n.a.		n.a.
Return on equity	n.m.		n.m.
Return on assets	(206.48)		(316.98)

* Common
[A] Reported in accordance with IFRS

Latest Results

Periods ended:	9m Sept. 30/22[A]		9m Sept. 30/21[A]
	$000s	%Chg	$000s
Operating revenue	135	n.a.	nil
Net income	(4,232)	n.a.	(8,031)
	$		$
Earnings per share*	(0.02)		(0.05)

* Common
[A] Reported in accordance with IFRS

Historical Summary
(as originally stated)

Fiscal Year	Oper. Rev.	Net Inc. Bef. Disc.	EPS*
	$000s	$000s	$
2021[A]	nil	(9,313)	(0.06)
2020[A]	nil	(85)	(0.01)
2019[A]	nil	(93)	(0.00)
2018[A]	nil	(34)	(0.20)
2017[A]	nil	(154)	(0.10)

* Common
[A] Reported in accordance with IFRS
Note: Adjusted throughout for 1-for-10 cons. in July 2019

C.127 Cleantek Industries Inc.

Symbol - CTEK **Exchange** - TSX-VEN **CUSIP** - 18453K
Head Office - 3200-500 4 Ave SW, Calgary, AB, T2P 2V6 **Telephone** - (403) 567-8700
Website - www.cleantekinc.com
Email - mgowanlock@cleantekinc.com
Investor Relations - Matt Gowanlock (403) 567-8700 ext. 1102
Auditors - KPMG LLP C.A., Calgary, Alta.
Bankers - Bank of Montreal, Calgary, Alta.; HSBC Bank Canada, Calgary, Alta.
Lawyers - Torys LLP, Calgary, Alta.
Transfer Agents - Odyssey Trust Company, Calgary, Alta.
Profile - (Alta. 1993) Designs, manufactures, rents and services dehydration units for the treatment and disposal of wastewater at the point of collection as well as rents lighting towers and lighting systems for the oil and gas and construction industries in western Canada and the United States. Also manufactures and sells horizontal pumps and wellbore separators to oil and gas drilling companies to insert into drill holes to optimize fluid extraction.

Has developed and commercialized its patented wastewater dehydration technology, the ZeroE, which it rents to its customers for use at gas processing facilities and on drilling rigs. The ZeroE technology separates wastewater into clean water which is evaporated and returned to the natural hydrological cycle and concentrated brine which is disposed of using traditional means. The ZeroE technology is powered by the waste heat generated from the engine exhaust of gas plants and drilling rigs. It has a fleet of more than 70 DZeroE mobile dehydration units and has constructed and installed one contracted PZeroE system in northern Alberta. Also has a fleet of more than 200 mobile light tower systems and 120 Halo™ crown-mounted lighting systems. Complimenting the company's ZeroE™ technology is a suite of low carbon LED Lighting & Optics systems including its patented Solar Hybrid lighting systems and HALO™ Crown mounted lighting systems.

Other product solutions that are expected to utilize existing asset base of the company include SecureTek, the company's line of remote security services which is offered as a stand-alone system or integrated with the company's sustainable lighting products; and Mobile GZeroE, a new waste-gas powered, wastewater treatment and dehydration system which is currently under construction and is expected to use waste-gas as its primary energy source that allows deployment of the ZeroE system into areas without a waste-heat source.

The company's Raise Production business has three systems that can be used independently or in combination in horizontal wellbores: the Raise Efficient Artificial Lift (REAL™), which provides an artificial lift solution for the build and vertical section of a horizontal wellbore; the High Angle Reciprocating Pump (HARP™), which includes certain downhole tools, such as horizontal separation, sand control, velocity flow tubes and pack off assemblies for flow control; and the Horizontal Artificial Recovery Technology (HART™), a development stage product which provides an artificial lift solution for the lateral section of a horizontal wellbore which consists of multiple pumps running in parallel along the horizontal wellbore to access trapped or stranded reserves and draw fluid from the toe area of the wellbore.

Predecessor Detail - Name changed from Raise Production Inc., Oct. 29, 2021, pursuant to reverse takeover acquisition of private Calgary, Alta.-based CleanTek Industries Inc.; basis 1 new for 58.3 old shs.

Directors - Richard F. (Rick) McHardy, chr., Calgary, Alta.; Matt Gowanlock, pres. & CEO, Canada; Paul Colucci, United Kingdom; Reginald J. (Reg) Greenslade, Calgary, Alta.; Phillip R. (Phil) Knoll, Calgary, Alta.; Chris Lewis, Calgary, Alta.; Albert J. (Al) Stark, Calgary, Alta.

Other Exec. Officers - Chris Murray, COO; Orson A. Ross, CFO; Janan Paskaran, corp. sec.

Capital Stock

	Authorized (shs.)	Outstanding (shs.)[1]
Preferred	unlimited	nil
Class A Common	unlimited	27,645,380

[1] At May 18, 2023

Major Shareholder - Paul Colucci held 27.54% interest and Lyle Wood Contracting Limited held 11.89% interest at May 15, 2023.

Price Range - CTEK/TSX-VEN

Year	Volume	High	Low	Close
2022	1,705,804	$1.12	$0.18	$0.23
2021	603,394	$3.50	$0.91	$1.00
2020	75,816	$9.91	$1.75	$2.04
2019	78,770	$11.37	$2.92	$7.58
2018	134,063	$27.40	$7.87	$9.62

Consolidation: 1-for-58.3 cons. in Nov. 2021
Recent Close: $0.19
Capital Stock Changes - There were no changes to capital stock during 2022.

Wholly Owned Subsidiaries

Apollo Lighting Solutions Inc., Del.
Horizon Oilfield Manufacturing Inc., Alta.

Financial Statistics

Periods ended:	12m Dec. 31/22[A]		12m Dec. 31/21[A1]
	$000s	%Chg	$000s
Operating revenue	**13,146**	**+49**	**8,819**
Cost of sales	3,025		2,337
Salaries & benefits	4,449		3,589
Research & devel. expense	nil		(868)
General & admin expense	4,967		9,158
Stock-based compensation	471		1,425
Other operating expense	nil		317
Operating expense	**12,912**	**-19**	**15,958**
Operating income	**234**	**n.a.**	**(7,139)**
Deprec., depl. & amort	3,160		2,534
Finance income	nil		13
Finance costs, gross	1,229		902
Write-downs/write-offs	nil		3,171
Pre-tax income	**(3,587)**	**n.a.**	**(6,783)**
Income taxes	nil		(828)
Net income	**(3,587)**	**n.a.**	**(5,955)**
Cash & equivalent	724		1,871
Accounts receivable	2,509		1,931
Current assets	3,774		4,771
Fixed assets, net	11,139		11,279
Right-of-use assets	483		647
Intangibles, net	521		459
Total assets	**15,917**	**-7**	**17,156**
Accts. pay. & accr. liabs	2,921		2,825
Current liabilities	12,122		4,236
Long-term debt, gross	10,771		8,489
Long-term debt, net	1,853		7,444
Long-term lease liabilities	268		431
Shareholders' equity	1,628		4,988
Cash from oper. activs	**653**	**n.a.**	**(2,769)**
Cash from fin. activs	831		4,501
Cash from invest. activs	(2,649)		(459)
Net cash position	**724**	**-61**	**1,871**
Capital expenditures	(2,698)		(396)
Capital disposals	175		103
	$		$
Earnings per share*	(0.13)		(0.32)
Cash flow per share*	0.02		(0.15)
	shs		shs
No. of shs. o/s*	27,645,380		27,645,380
Avg. no. of shs. o/s*	27,645,380		18,361,786
	%		%
Net profit margin	(27.29)		(67.52)
Return on equity	n.m.		n.m.
Return on assets	n.a.		(57.61)

* Cl. A com.
[A] Reported in accordance with IFRS
[1] Results reflect the July 12, 2021, reverse takeover acquisition of Cleantek Industries Inc.

Latest Results

Periods ended:	3m Mar. 31/23[A]		3m Mar. 31/22[A]
	$000s	%Chg	$000s
Operating revenue	3,833	+22	3,147
Net income	180	n.a.	(734)
	$		$
Earnings per share*	0.01		(0.03)

* Cl. A com.
[A] Reported in accordance with IFRS

Historical Summary
(as originally stated)

Fiscal Year	Oper. Rev.	Net Inc. Bef. Disc.	EPS*
	$000s	$000s	$
2022[A]	13,146	(3,587)	(0.13)
2021[A]	8,819	(5,955)	(0.32)
2020[A1]	606	(1,675)	(0.58)
2019[A]	1,101	(9,629)	(4.66)
2018[A]	335	(2,548)	(1.17)

* Cl. A com.
[A] Reported in accordance with IFRS
[1] Results for 2020 and prior years pertain to Raise Production Inc.
Note: Adjusted throughout for 1-for-58.3 cons. in Nov. 2021

C.128 Clear Blue Technologies International Inc.

Symbol - CBLU **Exchange** - TSX-VEN **CUSIP** - 18453C
Head Office - Unit 7, 30 Lesmill Rd, Toronto, ON, M3B 2T6 **Telephone** - (647) 748-4822 **Toll-free** - (855) 733-0119 **Fax** - (289) 277-1853
Website - www.clearbluetechnologies.com
Email - miriam@clearbluetechnologies.com
Investor Relations - Miriam G. Tuerk (855) 733-0119
Auditors - Davidson & Company LLP C.A., Vancouver, B.C.
Transfer Agents - Computershare Trust Company of Canada Inc.
Profile - (Ont. 2018; orig. B.C., 2014) Develops and sells Smart Off-Grid controllers and systems, and provides cloud-based

management software and Energy-as-a-Service (EaaS) management services to power, control, monitor, manage and proactively service solar and hybrid-powered systems such as street lights, security systems, telecommunications systems, emergency power, satellite Wi-Fi and Internet of Things (IoT) devices.

The company's Smart Off-Grid technology and services allow devices to be installed anywhere, powered by clean energy, and monitored, managed and controlled over the Internet. Products and services consist of Smart Off-Grid controllers, which enable manufacturers to manage solar, hybrid solar and wind-powered systems such as streetlights, telecommunications systems, security systems, mobile power, lighting and signage and electronic charging stations; telecom solar and nano-grid power packs, which deliver a highly reliable source of power using solar and hybrid solar systems, with built-in communications; Illumience, a cloud-based management software that remotely controls, monitors and manages the devices using Smart Off-Grid controllers and power packs; Energy-as-a-Service, a subscription-based service that provides clean, wireless and managed energy to power critical systems; and smart Pico-Grid, a smart off-grid power system, that includes solar, batteries and smart controls, which is specifically designed for the ultra-low-power requirements of satellite Wi-Fi and IoT application.

Primary markets are Canada, the U.S., Middle East and Africa. The company has completed installations in 37 countries.

Predecessor Detail - Name changed from Dagobah Ventures Ltd., July 10, 2018, following reverse takeover acquistion of Clear Blue Technologies Inc. and amalgamation of Clear Blue Technologies with a wholly owned subsidiary of Dagobah Ventures Ltd.

Directors - Miriam G. Tuerk, CEO, Toronto, Ont.; John P. Tuerk, chief power officer, Toronto, Ont.; Mark S. Windrim, chief tech. officer, Toronto, Ont.; Jane Kearns, Toronto, Ont.; Steven E. (Steve) Parry, Tiny, Ont.

Other Exec. Officers - Farrukh Anwar, CFO; Paul Desjardins, sr. v-p, sales & bus. devel.; Jason Woerner, sr. v-p, solutions; Kang Lan, v-p, prod. eng.; Natalie Smith, v-p, mktg.

Capital Stock

	Authorized (shs.)	Outstanding (shs.)[1]
Preferred	unlimited	nil
Common	unlimited	67,014,242

[1] At Mar. 31, 2022

Major Shareholder - Miriam and John Tuerk held 10% interest at May 19, 2021.

Price Range - CBLU/TSX-VEN

Year	Volume	High	Low	Close
2022	16,879,951	$0.33	$0.07	$0.07
2021	35,877,256	$0.80	$0.22	$0.30
2020	32,421,138	$0.75	$0.09	$0.54
2019	12,378,590	$0.39	$0.10	$0.11
2018	9,127,606	$0.86	$0.29	$0.40

Recent Close: $0.05

Capital Stock Changes - In April and May 2022, private placement of 9,726,336 units (1 common share & ½ warrant) at 17¢ per unit was completed, with warrants exercisable at 22¢ per share for two years.

Wholly Owned Subsidiaries

Clear Blue Technologies Inc., Toronto, Ont.
Clear Blue Technologies Kenya Ltd., Kenya.
Clear Blue Technologies US Corp., United States.

Financial Statistics

Periods ended:	12m Dec. 31/21[A]		12m Dec. 31/20[A]
	$000s	%Chg	$000s
Operating revenue	**8,149**	**+103**	**4,024**
Cost of sales	5,893		2,757
Salaries & benefits	1,869		738
Research & devel. expense	24		1,494
General & admin expense	2,260		1,890
Stock-based compensation	644		298
Operating expense	**10,690**	**+49**	**7,176**
Operating income	**(2,541)**	**n.a.**	**(3,152)**
Deprec., depl. & amort.	147		139
Finance income	23		nil
Finance costs, gross	734		477
Write-downs/write-offs	(210)		(71)
Pre-tax income	**(3,667)**	**n.a.**	**(3,824)**
Income taxes	(255)		nil
Net income	**(3,411)**	**n.a.**	**(3,824)**
Cash & equivalent	2,117		3,507
Inventories	3,344		1,551
Accounts receivable	1,682		1,755
Current assets	7,769		7,757
Fixed assets, net	152		213
Intangibles, net	2,857		nil
Total assets	**11,168**	**+33**	**8,398**
Bank indebtedness	924		1,000
Accts. pay. & accr. liabs	1,782		1,023
Current liabilities	4,343		3,200
Long-term debt, gross	7,265		3,073
Long-term debt, net	6,204		2,955
Long-term lease liabilities	nil		50
Equity portion of conv. debs	879		100
Shareholders' equity	(215)		1,245
Cash from oper. activs	**(3,900)**	**n.a.**	**(3,146)**
Cash from fin. activs	5,365		6,568
Cash from invest. activs	(2,856)		24
Net cash position	**2,117**	**-40**	**3,507**
Capital expenditures	(86)		(30)
Capital disposals	1		nil
	$		$
Earnings per share*	(0.05)		(0.08)
Cash flow per share*	(0.06)		(0.07)
	shs		shs
No. of shs. o/s*	66,954,241		62,876,662
Avg. no. of shs. o/s*	64,450,673		47,930,564
	%		%
Net profit margin	(41.86)		(95.03)
Return on equity	n.m.		n.m.
Return on assets	(27.89)		(48.84)
Foreign sales percent	95		90

* Common
[A] Reported in accordance with IFRS

Latest Results

Periods ended:	3m Mar. 31/22[A]		3m Mar. 31/21[A]
	$000s	%Chg	$000s
Operating revenue	1,225	-65	3,459
Net income	(1,370)	n.a.	(433)
	$		$
Earnings per share*	(0.02)		(0.01)

* Common
[A] Reported in accordance with IFRS

Historical Summary
(as originally stated)

Fiscal Year	Oper. Rev. $000s	Net Inc. Bef. Disc. $000s	EPS* $
2021[A]	8,149	(3,411)	(0.05)
2020[A]	4,024	(3,824)	(0.08)
2019[A]	3,971	(5,102)	(0.12)
2018[A1]	3,780	(8,099)	(0.29)
2017[A2]	2,323	(3,371)	n.a.

* Common
[A] Reported in accordance with IFRS
[1] Results reflect the July 13, 2018, reverse takeover acquisition of Clear Blue Technologies Inc.
[2] Results for 2017 and 2016 pertain to Clear Blue Technologies Inc.

C.129 Clearmind Medicine Inc.

Symbol - CMND **Exchange** - CSE **CUSIP** - 185053
Head Office - 101-1220 6 Ave W, Vancouver, BC, V6H 1A5 **Telephone** - (604) 689-2646 **Fax** - (604) 689-1289
Website - www.clearmindmedicine.com
Email - invest@clearmindmedicine.com
Investor Relations - Alan Rootenberg (604) 260-1566
Auditors - Brightman Almagor Zohar & Co. C.P.A.
Transfer Agents - Computershare Trust Company of Canada Inc., Vancouver, B.C.

Profile - (B.C. 2017) Researches and develops novel psychedelic-based compounds including medicines, foods and supplements to solve health problems with a focus on treatment for alcohol use disorders including binge drinking and eating disorders.

Flagship drug candidate is CMND-100, a MEAI-based molecule treatment for alcohol use disorder which is under Phase I/IIa clinical study. Other proprietary drug candidates include treatments for binge eating, depression and treatment-resistant depression, drug-assisted psychotherapy, other binge behaviours and mental health issues.

Common listed on NASDAQ, Nov. 15, 2022.

Predecessor Detail - Name changed from Cyntar Ventures Inc., Mar. 24, 2021, pursuant to change of business from resource company to psychedelic drug discovery company.

Directors - Amitay Weiss, chr., Petah Tikva, Israel; Oz Adler, Rishon LeZion, Israel; Asaf Itzhaik, Ramat Gan, Israel; Yehonatan Shachar, Tel Aviv, Israel

Other Exec. Officers - Dr. Adi Zuloff-Shani, CEO; Oz Locker, COO; Alan Rootenberg, CFO; Mark Haden, v-p, bus. devel.; Sonny Chew, corp. sec. & treas.

Capital Stock

	Authorized (shs.)	Outstanding (shs.)[1]
Common	unlimited	2,473,617

[1] At Nov. 23, 2022

Major Shareholder - Widely held at Nov. 28, 2022.

Price Range - CMND/CSE

Year	Volume	High	Low	Close
2022	207,957	$19.20	$4.20	$4.44
2021	172,865	$29.70	$15.00	$17.40
2020	13,266	$6.30	$3.15	$5.55
2019	36,116	$3.15	$2.10	$3.15
2018	5,083	$4.50	$2.40	$2.40

Consolidation: 1-for-30 cons. in Sept. 2022
Recent Close: $0.55

Capital Stock Changes - In November 2022, public offering of 1,153,847 common shares was completed at US$6.50 per share.

In February 2022, private placement of 39,747 units (1 post-consolidated common share & 1 warrant) at 24¢ per unit was completed. On Sept. 30, 2022, common shares were consolidated on a 1-for-30 basis. Also during fiscal 2022, post-consolidated common shares were issued as follows: 26,498 on acquisition of interest in Medigus Ltd. and 2,667 for services.

Wholly Owned Subsidiaries

Clearmind Labs Ltd., Canada. Inactive
Clearmindmed Ltd., Israel.

Investments

7.7% int. in **Medigus Ltd.**

Financial Statistics

Periods ended:	12m Oct. 31/22[A]		12m Oct. 31/21[◻A]
	$000s	%Chg	$000s
Salaries & benefits	126		406
Research & devel. expense	3,894		646
General & admin expense	2,817		1,775
Stock-based compensation	1,583		846
Operating expense	**8,419**	**+129**	**3,673**
Operating income	**(8,419)**	**n.a.**	**(3,673)**
Deprec., depl. & amort.	113		3
Finance costs, gross	20		nil
Pre-tax income	**(9,370)**	**n.a.**	**(3,720)**
Income taxes	41		nil
Net income	**(9,411)**	**n.a.**	**(3,720)**
Cash & equivalent	440		4,599
Accounts receivable	70		161
Current assets	593		4,920
Fixed assets, net	18		21
Right-of-use assets	49		nil
Intangibles, net	178		198
Total assets	**1,128**	**-78**	**5,159**
Accts. pay. & accr. liabs	1,907		349
Current liabilities	2,638		357
Shareholders' equity	(1,510)		4,802
Cash from oper. activs	**(5,084)**	**n.a.**	**(2,835)**
Cash from fin. activs	698		7,356
Cash from invest. activs	(8)		(251)
Net cash position	**176**	**-96**	**4,599**
Capital expenditures	(8)		(33)
	$		$
Earnings per share*	(7.24)		(4.01)
Cash flow per share*	(3.91)		(3.06)
	shs		shs
No. of shs. o/s*	1,319,770		1,250,833
Avg. no. of shs. o/s*	1,300,050		927,345
	%		%
Net profit margin	n.a.		n.a.
Return on equity	n.m.		(140.35)
Return on assets	(298.74)		(131.17)

* Common
◻ Restated
[A] Reported in accordance with IFRS

Historical Summary
(as originally stated)

Fiscal Year	Oper. Rev.	Net Inc. Bef. Disc.	EPS*
	$000s	$000s	$
2022[A]	nil	(9,411)	(7.24)
2021[A]	nil	(3,899)	(4.20)
2020[A]	nil	(233)	(0.30)
2019[A]	nil	(105)	(0.30)
2018[A]	nil	(195)	(0.60)

* Common
[A] Reported in accordance with IFRS
Note: Adjusted throughout for 1-for-30 cons. in Sept. 2022

C.130 Clever Leaves Holdings Inc.

Symbol - CLVR **Exchange** - NASDAQ **CUSIP** - 186760
Head Office - 6501 Congress Ave, Suite 240, Boca Raton, FL, United States, 33487 **Telephone** - (561) 634-7430
Website - cleverleaves.com
Email - clvr@gatewayir.com
Investor Relations - Cody Slach (949) 574-3860
Auditors - BDO Canada LLP C.A., Vancouver, B.C.
Transfer Agents - Computershare Trust Company of Canada Inc., Vancouver, B.C.
Employees - 400 at Dec. 31, 2022
Profile - (B.C. 2020) Operates both medical cannabinoid and non-cannabinoid businesses.

Cannabinoid Business - Cultivates, extracts, manufactures and commercializes cannabinoid products. Owns 18 greenhouses which include 1,800,000 sq. ft. of greenhouse cultivation space, as well as a pharmaceutical-grade extraction facility that is capable of processing 108,000 kg of dry flower per year. With 6,000,000 sq. ft. of leased and owned land, the company's greenhouse cultivation can be expanded to 2,500,000 sq. ft. at its existing operating site. Also has agricultural land in Portugal which the company intends to sell following the cessation of its Portugal operation. Cannabinoid products are primarily sold in Australia, Germany, Israel and Brazil. Also exports shipments to Argentina, Canada, Chile, Czech Republic, Denmark, Italy, Netherlands and New Zealand. The company's cannabinoid brands include IQANNA, which launched in Germany in 2021.

Non-Cannabinoid Business - Through wholly owned **Herbal Brands, Inc.**, formulates, manufactures, markets, distributes and commercializes nutraceutical and other natural remedies, and wellness products to more than 20,000 retail locations across the United States. Herbal Brands leases a 45,000-sq.-ft. manufacturing and processing facility and office in Tempe, Ariz.

On July 5, 2023, the company sold its cannabis processing facility in Setúbal, Portugal, including 900 m^2 of factory space and 750 m^2 of warehousing space, to **Curaleaf International Holdings Limited** for €2,500,000.

In January 2023, the company approved the wind-down of its entire Portuguese operations. As of June 30, 2023, the company has completed the cessation of its Portuguese flower cultivation, post-harvest processes and manufacturing activities. The post harvest facility has been sold subsequently in July 2023, and the company intends to sell the farm land in Portugal by Dec. 31, 2023.

During the second quarter of 2022, the company sold a portion of its minority interest in **Cansativa GmbH**, which is a European Union certified and established importer and distributor of cannabis flowers and other products produced by third parties, for €2,300,000 of pre-tax proceeds, reducing the company's interest in Cansativa to 9%.

Directors - George Schultze, chr.; Andrés Fajardo, pres. & CEO; Elizabeth DeMarse; Gary M. Julien; William Muecke
Other Exec. Officers - Gustavo Escobar, COO; Henry R. (Hank) Hague III, CFO; Julián Wilches, chief regulatory officer; Marta Pinto Leite, gen. counsel & corp. sec.

Capital Stock

	Authorized (shs.)	Outstanding (shs.)[1]
Common	unlimited	45,726,599

[1] At Aug. 10, 2023

Major Shareholder - Widely held at Mar. 22, 2022.

Price Range - CLVR/NASDAQ

Year	Volume	High	Low	Close
2022	2,391,099	US$119.40	US$8.70	US$9.27
2021	1,030,768	US$582.90	US$89.70	US$93.00
2020	65,297	US$420.00	US$263.10	US$267.00

Consolidation: 1-for-30 cons. in Aug. 2023
Capital Stock Changes - During 2022, common shares were issued as follows: 14,994,765 under an at-the-market offering, 1,507,000 on conversion of debt, 377,527 on vesting of restricted share units and 151,694 on exercise of options.

Wholly Owned Subsidiaries

Clever Leaves II Portugal Cultivation S.A., Portugal.
Clever Leaves Australia Pvt. Ltd.
Clever Leaves Germany GmbH, Frankfurt am Main, Germany.
Clever Leaves International Inc., B.C.
Clever Leaves Portugal Unipessoal Lda., Portugal.
Clever Leaves UK Limited, London, Middx., United Kingdom.
Clever Leaves US, Inc., Rye Brook, N.Y.
Eagle Canada Holdings, Inc., B.C.
Ecomedics S.A.S., Bogota, Colombia.
Herbal Brands, Inc., Del.
Herbal Brands, Ltd., London, Middx., United Kingdom.
NS Herbal Brands International, Inc., B.C.
NS US Holdings, Inc., Del.
Nordschwan Holdings, Inc., B.C.
Northern Swan Deutschland Holdings, Inc., B.C.
Northern Swan Europe, Inc., B.C.
Northern Swan International, Inc., B.C.
Northern Swan Management, Inc., B.C.
Northern Swan Portugal Holdings, Inc., B.C.
1255096 B.C. Ltd., B.C.

Financial Statistics

Periods ended:	12m Dec. 31/22[A]		12m Dec. 31/21[A]
	US$000s	%Chg	US$000s
Operating revenue	**17,800**	**+16**	**15,374**
Cost of sales	7,121		3,617
Salaries & benefits	14,665		14,309
Research & devel. expense	1,719		1,546
General & admin expense	12,704		16,434
Stock-based compensation	2,343		11,451
Operating expense	**38,552**	**-19**	**47,357**
Operating income	**(20,752)**	**n.a.**	**(31,983)**
Deprec., depl. & amort.	3,672		3,508
Finance costs, net	2,702		6,818
Write-downs/write-offs	(23,736)		(21,716)
Pre-tax income	**(72,455)**	**n.a.**	**(44,681)**
Income taxes	(6,354)		950
After-tax income (expense)	(64)		(95)
Net income	**(66,165)**	**n.a.**	**(45,726)**
Cash & equivalent	12,449		37,226
Inventories	8,399		15,408
Accounts receivable	2,252		2,222
Current assets	26,247		60,393
Long-term investments	5,679		1,458
Fixed assets, net	15,463		30,932
Intangibles, net	3,354		23,117
Total assets	**52,098**	**-55**	**116,160**
Accts. pay. & accr. liabs	2,299		3,981
Current liabilities	9,426		27,245
Long-term debt, gross	1,530		25,095
Long-term debt, net	1,065		7,587
Long-term lease liabilities	1,087		nil
Shareholders' equity	40,408		72,770
Cash from oper. activs	**(29,066)**	**n.a.**	**(36,233)**
Cash from fin. activs	3,289		1,834
Cash from invest. activs	1,192		(7,280)
Net cash position	**12,888**	**-66**	**37,699**
Capital expenditures	(1,306)		(7,280)
	US$		US$
Earnings per share*	(51.60)		(53.40)
Cash flow per share*	(22.71)		(42.31)
	shs		shs
No. of shs. o/s*	1,454,559		886,860
Avg. no. of shs. o/s*	1,279,746		856,337
	%		%
Net profit margin	(371.71)		(297.42)
Return on equity	(116.92)		(54.43)
Return on assets	(78.65)		(32.43)
No. of employees (FTEs)	400		560

* Common
[A] Reported in accordance with U.S. GAAP

Latest Results

Periods ended:	6m June 30/23[A]		6m June 30/22[◻A]
	US$000s	%Chg	US$000s
Operating revenue	8,959	-2	9,141
Net inc. bef. disc. opers	(7,412)	n.a.	(11,968)
Income from disc. opers	(264)		(5,218)
Net income	(7,676)	n.a.	(17,186)
	US$		US$
Earns. per sh. bef. disc. opers.*	(5.10)		(10.50)
Earnings per share*	(5.40)		(15.30)

* Common
◻ Restated
[A] Reported in accordance with U.S. GAAP

Historical Summary
(as originally stated)

Fiscal Year	Oper. Rev.	Net Inc. Bef. Disc.	EPS*
	US$000s	US$000s	US$
2022[A]	17,800	(66,165)	(51.60)
2021[A]	15,374	(45,726)	(53.40)
2020[A]	12,117	(25,895)	(100.20)
2019[A1]	7,834	(45,980)	n.a.
2018[A1]	nil	6,531	n.a.

* Common
[A] Reported in accordance with U.S. GAAP
[1] Results pertain to Clever Leaves International Inc.
Note: Adjusted throughout for 1-for-30 cons. in Aug. 2023

C.131 Cliffside Capital Ltd.

Symbol - CEP **Exchange** - TSX-VEN **CUSIP** - 186824
Head Office - 200-11 Church St, Toronto, ON, M5E 1W1 **Telephone** - (647) 226-4894 **Fax** - (416) 861-0177
Website - www.cliffsidecapital.ca
Email - pgupta@cliffsidecapital.ca
Investor Relations - Praveen Gupta (647) 776-5810
Auditors - PricewaterhouseCoopers LLP C.A.
Lawyers - Aird & Berlis LLP, Toronto, Ont.
Transfer Agents - Computershare Trust Company of Canada Inc., Toronto, Ont.
Profile - (Ont. 2013) Acquires interests in loans and other financial assets in Canada.

Holds an 85% limited partnership interest in **CAL LP**, 60% limited partnership interest in **ACC LP** and 75% limited partnership interest **C.A.R. LP I**, which invest in fully serviced non-prime automobile loans, originated and serviced in Canada by **CanCap Management Inc.** (formerly **AutoCapital Canada Management Inc.**).

In June 2022, **C.A.R. LP I** redeemed for cancellation 1,250 outstanding units for $1,875,000. As a result, the company's holding in C.A.R. LP I was increased to 75% from 60% interest.

Directors - Michael L. Stein, chr., Toronto, Ont.; Stephen R. Malone, CEO, Toronto, Ont.; Mark H. Newman, Toronto, Ont.; Keith L. Ray, Toronto, Ont.; Todd C. Skinner, Toronto, Ont.; Richard Valade, Ont.
Other Exec. Officers - Praveen Gupta, CFO & corp. sec.

Capital Stock

	Authorized (shs.)	Outstanding (shs.)[1]
Common	unlimited	97,266,667

[1] At May 23, 2023

Major Shareholder - Michael L. Stein held 28.79% interest and Mark H. Newman held 16.06% interest at May 23, 2023.

Price Range - CEP/TSX-VEN

Year	Volume	High	Low	Close
2022	1,368,177	$0.30	$0.08	$0.13
2021	1,059,317	$0.22	$0.07	$0.22
2020	597,950	$0.14	$0.05	$0.05
2019	938,459	$0.30	$0.10	$0.14
2018	3,798,674	$0.35	$0.08	$0.18

Recent Close: $0.09
Capital Stock Changes - There were no changes to capital stock during 2022.

Dividends

CEP com Ra $0.01 pa Q est. Nov. 1, 2021
$0.0025**i** Nov. 1/21
i Initial Payment

Subsidiaries

60% int. in **ACC LP**, Ont.
85% int. in **CAL LP**, Ont.
75% int. in **C.A.R. LP I**, Ont.

Financial Statistics

Periods ended:	12m Dec. 31/22[A]		12m Dec. 31/21[A]
	$000s	%Chg	$000s
Total revenue	**22,243**	**+62**	**13,694**
General & admin. expense	2,222		1,817
Stock-based compensation	92		133
Operating expense	**2,314**	**+19**	**1,950**
Operating income	**19,929**	**+70**	**11,744**
Finance costs, gross	9,840		6,107
Pre-tax income	**(2,030)**	**n.a.**	**1,609**
Income taxes	(540)		323
Net income	**(1,491)**	**n.a.**	**1,286**
Net inc. for equity hldrs	**(1,508)**	**n.a.**	**1,058**
Net inc. for non-cont. int	**18**	**-92**	**229**
Cash & equivalent	10,676		12,426
Accounts receivable	184,956		149,784
Total assets	**199,820**	**+22**	**164,285**
Accts. pay. & accr. liabs	661		1,111
Shareholders' equity	8,240		11,058
Non-controlling interest	2,415		4,237
Cash from oper. activs	**(36,985)**	**n.a.**	**(39,271)**
Cash from fin. activs	35,235		46,388
Net cash position	**10,676**	**-14**	**12,426**
	$		$
Earnings per share*	(0.02)		0.01
Cash flow per share*	(0.38)		(0.46)
Cash divd. per share*	0.01		0.00
	shs		shs
No. of shs. o/s*	97,266,667		97,266,667
Avg. no. of shs. o/s*	97,266,667		85,246,119
	%		%
Net profit margin	(6.70)		9.39
Return on equity	(15.64)		12.44
Return on assets	3.15		4.48

* Common
[A] Reported in accordance with IFRS

Latest Results

Periods ended:	3m Mar. 31/23^A		3m Mar. 31/22^A
	$000s	%Chg	$000s
Total revenue	4,418	-20	5,516
Net income	(385)	n.a.	646
Net inc. for equity hldrs	(336)	n.a.	422
Net inc. for non-cont. int	(49)		224
	$		$
Earnings per share*	(0.00)		0.00

* Common
A Reported in accordance with IFRS

Historical Summary
(as originally stated)

Fiscal Year	Total Rev. $000s	Net Inc. Bef. Disc. $000s	EPS* $
2022^A	22,243	(1,491)	(0.02)
2021^A	13,694	1,286	0.01
2020^A	14,090	2,040	0.02
2019^A	14,820	(2,599)	(0.03)
2018^A	9,708	(1,081)	(0.01)

* Common
A Reported in accordance with IFRS

C.132 Clip Money Inc.

Symbol - CLIP **Exchange** - TSX-VEN **CUSIP** - 188834
Head Office - 96 Riverdale Ave, Ottawa, ON, K1S 1R2 **Toll-free** - (844) 593-2547
Website - clipmoney.com
Email - jarrage@clipmoney.com
Investor Relations - Joseph Arrage (844) 593-2547
Auditors - MNP LLP C.A., Winnipeg, Man.
Transfer Agents - TSX Trust Company
Employees - 8 at May 20, 2022
Profile - (Can. 2022; orig. B.C., 2021) Operates a proprietary cash deposit network to businesses and financial institutions in metropolitan areas across Canada and the U.S.

The company operates a multi-bank self-service deposit system for businesses through its network of ClipDrop Boxes that give users the capability of making deposits outside of their bank branch at top retailers and shopping malls. Rather than having to go to their bank branch or employ a cash pickup service, businesses can deposit their cash at any ClipDrop Box located near them. After being deposited, the funds are automatically credited to the business' bank account almost instantaneously. The physical deposit network is accompanied by an end-to-end system, which includes user registration, location services, bar code and RFID tracking of deposit bags, secure processing of deposits, and payment processing.

The network consisted of 339 ClipDrop deposit units at May 2023. Mall operator and big-box retailer partners included **Brookfield Properties Retail, Inc.**, **Simon Property Group, L.P.** and **Staples Inc.**

Directors - Daren Trousdell, co-founder, Jupiter, Fla.; Joseph Arrage, CEO & co-founder, Ottawa, Ont.; John Desmond, Woodbury, N.Y.; Peter A. Dorsman, Saratoga Springs, N.Y.; J. Jeffrey Gibson, Kanata, Ont.

Other Exec. Officers - Brian Bailey, pres.; Andrew Tussing, CFO; Roger Dalal, chief tech. officer

Capital Stock

	Authorized (shs.)	Outstanding (shs.)[1]
Common	unlimited	76,134,066

[1] At May 30, 2023

Major Shareholder - Joseph Arrage held 20.88% interest, Daren Trousdell held 19.6% interest and J. Jeffrey Gibson held 11.67% interest at May 9, 2023.

Price Range - CLIP/TSX-VEN

Year	Volume	High	Low	Close
2022	1,750,530	$1.02	$0.45	$0.45

Recent Close: $0.24

Capital Stock Changes - In February 2023, private placement of 3,883,760 units (1 common share & 1 warrant) at 45¢ per unit was completed, with warrants exercisable at 65¢ per share for three years.

In December 2022, private placement of 4,524,637 units (1 common share & 1 warrant) at 45¢ per unit was completed.

Wholly Owned Subsidiaries

Clip Money (USA) Inc., Del.

Financial Statistics

Periods ended:	12m Dec. 31/22^A		12m Dec. 31/21^□A
	$000s	%Chg	$000s
Operating revenue	**36**	**n.m.**	**2**
Cost of sales	1,652		129
Salaries & benefits	4,986		2,834
General & admin expense	1,667		928
Operating expense	**3,319**	**-15**	**3,891**
Operating income	**(3,283)**	**n.a.**	**(3,889)**
Deprec., depl. & amort	2,111		754
Finance income	18		1
Finance costs, gross	1,754		361
Pre-tax income	**(15,767)**	**n.a.**	**(5,492)**
Net income	**(15,767)**	**n.a.**	**(5,492)**
Cash & equivalent	2,008		1,220
Current assets	2,229		1,524
Fixed assets, net	1,051		295
Right-of-use assets	7,185		5,666
Intangibles, net	2,884		2,398
Total assets	**13,348**	**+35**	**9,883**
Accts. pay. & accr. liabs	2,119		1,229
Current liabilities	3,592		3,894
Long-term debt, gross	nil		1,437
Long-term lease liabilities	6,907		5,377
Shareholders' equity	2,792		555
Cash from oper. activs	**(6,422)**	**n.a.**	**(2,610)**
Cash from fin. activs	9,351		2,089
Cash from invest. activs	(2,180)		(1,423)
Net cash position	**2,008**	**+65**	**1,220**
Capital expenditures	(910)		(283)
	$		$
Earnings per share*	(0.28)		(0.14)
Cash flow per share*	(0.12)		(0.07)
	shs		shs
No. of shs. o/s*	70,754,831		38,204,387
Avg. no. of shs. o/s*	55,592,136		38,057,990
	%		%
Net profit margin	n.m.		n.m.
Return on equity	(942.16)		(200.91)
Return on assets	(120.64)		(67.41)
Foreign sales percent	70		66

* Common
□ Restated
A Reported in accordance with IFRS

Latest Results

Periods ended:	3m Mar. 31/23^A		3m Mar. 31/22^A
	$000s	%Chg	$000s
Operating revenue	31	n.m.	2
Net income	(2,478)	n.a.	(1,673)
	$		$
Earnings per share*	(0.03)		(0.04)

* Common
A Reported in accordance with IFRS

Historical Summary
(as originally stated)

Fiscal Year	Oper. Rev. $000s	Net Inc. Bef. Disc. $000s	EPS* $
2022^A	36	(15,767)	(0.28)
2021^A	2	(5,492)	(0.14)
2020^A	nil	(2,538)	(0.07)

* Common
A Reported in accordance with IFRS

C.133 Cloud DX Inc.

Symbol - CDX **Exchange** - TSX-VEN **CUSIP** - 18912D
Head Office - 100-72 Victoria St S, Kitchener, ON, N2G 4Y9 **Toll-free** - (888) 543-0944
Website - www.clouddx.com
Email - jay.bedard@clouddx.com
Investor Relations - Jay Bedard (888) 543-0944
Auditors - MNP LLP C.A., Waterloo, Ont.
Transfer Agents - Odyssey Trust Company, Calgary, Alta.
Profile - (Alta. 2019) Provides remote patient monitoring hardware, software and recurring revenue services for healthcare providers in Canada and the United States.

Has developed and cleared through regulatory agencies a family of proprietary medical devices, each of which collects multiple vital signs. Customers purchase Connected Health in order to remotely monitor patients with serious chronic illness including chronic obstructive pulmonary disease (COPD) and congestive heart failure (CHF), patients recovering from surgery, as well as COVID-19 patients outside of hospitals. Typical customers include academic institutions, large hospitals and provincial health authorities in Canada, and physician practices and hospitals in the United States.

Cloud DX Connected Health Kits include the proprietary Pulsewave® wrist cuff blood pressure monitor, the Cloud DX Bluetooth pulse oximeter, the Cloud DX wireless weight scale and optionally, a digital thermometer and digital wireless glucose meter from third party suppliers. These devices, combined with customized tablet computers and mobile Connected Health apps, form the patient-facing part of Connected Health. A secure online Clinician Portal allows medical professionals to remotely monitor the health of patients. Clinical support software detects when certain triggers are reached in a patient's vital signs and generates a notification to providers. With in-app text messaging, nurses can contact patients and initiate a telemedicine video conference, all within the Cloud DX platform. Patient data are aggregated into large sets of unique raw data that can be analyzed using machine learning algorithms to detect patterns that may predict future health outcomes, both on a personal level and in larger populations.

Maintains an office and technology centre in Kitchener, Ont., and manages United States operations and logistics from an office in Brooklyn, N.Y.

Predecessor Detail - Name changed from Roosevelt Capital Group Inc., pursuant to reverse takeover acquisition of (old) Cloud DX, inc., which completed a share exchange with its wholly owned subsidiary 12632926 Canada Ltd. (Cloud Canada), and concurrent amalgamation of Cloud Canada and wholly owned 12686163 Canada Inc. (continued as 12632926 Canada Inc.); basis 1 new for 4.8123 old shs.

Directors - Robert Kaul, co-founder, chr., pres. & CEO, Brooklyn, N.Y.; William A. (Bill) Charnetski, Toronto, Ont.; Neil Fraser, B.C.; Michele Middlemore, Toronto, Ont.; Brad Miller, Vancouver, B.C.; Dr. Gaurav Puri, Ont.; Dr. Constantine Zachos, Aurora, Ont.

Other Exec. Officers - Anthony Kaul, co-founder & COO; Simon Selkrig, CFO

Capital Stock

	Authorized (shs.)	Outstanding (shs.)[1]
Preferred	unlimited	nil
Common	unlimited	72,094,396

[1] At Sept. 30, 2022

Major Shareholder - Brad Miller held 11.2% interest at June 8, 2022.

Price Range - CDX/TSX-VEN

Year	Volume	High	Low	Close
2022	8,685,105	$0.39	$0.11	$0.15
2021	21,575,108	$0.80	$0.14	$0.38
2019	138,935	$1.93	$0.96	$1.44

Consolidation: 1-for-4.8123 cons. in Apr. 2021
Recent Close: $0.10

Wholly Owned Subsidiaries

Cloud DX, Inc., Brooklyn, N.Y.
- 100% int. in **12632926 Canada Ltd.**, Canada.
  - 100% int. in **Cloud Diagnostics (Canada) ULC**, B.C.

Financial Statistics

Periods ended:	12m Dec. 31/21[A]		12m Dec. 31/20[□A]
	$000s	%Chg	$000s
Operating revenue	**782**	**-33**	**1,164**
Cost of sales	491		733
Salaries & benefits	5,737		3,572
Research & devel. expense	474		551
General & admin expense	3,049		2,175
Stock-based compensation	1,018		335
Operating expense	**10,770**	**+46**	**7,365**
Operating income	**(9,988)**	**n.a.**	**(6,201)**
Deprec., depl. & amort.	433		349
Finance costs, gross	709		732
Pre-tax income	**(11,355)**	**n.a.**	**(5,812)**
Income taxes	(98)		nil
Net income	**(11,257)**	**n.a.**	**(5,812)**
Cash & equivalent	79		1,071
Inventories	685		560
Accounts receivable	404		419
Current assets	1,334		2,359
Fixed assets, net	171		163
Right-of-use assets	1,149		755
Intangibles, net	395		545
Total assets	**3,222**	**-16**	**3,822**
Accts. pay. & accr. liabs	1,544		1,570
Current liabilities	2,312		5,431
Long-term debt, gross	1,824		4,575
Long-term debt, net	1,635		2,046
Equity portion of conv. debs	79		nil
Shareholders' equity	(1,728)		(4,290)
Cash from oper. activs	**(9,181)**	**n.a.**	**(3,528)**
Cash from fin. activs	8,111		3,999
Cash from invest. activs	577		149
Net cash position	**79**	**-88**	**638**
Capital expenditures	(95)		(110)
	$		$
Earnings per share*	(0.18)		(3.10)
Cash flow per share*	(0.14)		(1.88)
	shs		shs
No. of shs. o/s*	72,094,396		n.a.
Avg. no. of shs. o/s*	64,276,113		1,877,702
	%		%
Net profit margin	n.m.		(499.31)
Return on equity	n.m.		n.m.
Return on assets	(299.68)		(176.62)

* Common
[□] Restated
[A] Reported in accordance with IFRS

Latest Results

Periods ended:	9m Sept. 30/22[A]		9m Sept. 30/21[A]
	$000s	%Chg	$000s
Operating revenue	1,072	+38	776
Net income	(6,957)	n.a.	(8,788)
	$		$
Earnings per share*	(0.10)		(0.14)

* Common
[A] Reported in accordance with IFRS

Historical Summary
(as originally stated)

Fiscal Year	Oper. Rev.	Net Inc. Bef. Disc.	EPS*
	$000s	$000s	$
2021[A]	782	(11,257)	(0.18)
	US$000s	US$000s	US$
2020[A1]	868	(4,337)	(2.31)
2019[A1]	963	(3,822)	(2.60)
2018[A]	181	(5,224)	(3.95)

* Common
[A] Reported in accordance with IFRS
[1] Results for 2020 and prior periods pertain to (old) DX Cloud, Inc.
Note: Adjusted throughout for 1-for-4.8123 cons. in Apr. 2021

C.134 CloudMD Software & Services Inc.

Symbol - DOC **Exchange** - TSX-VEN **CUSIP** - 18912C
Head Office - HSBC Building, 2200-885 Georgia St W, Vancouver, BC, V6C 3E8 **Telephone** - (778) 370-1413
Website - cloudmd.ca
Email - julia@cloudmd.ca
Investor Relations - Julia Becker (604) 785-0850
Auditors - KPMG LLP C.A., Vancouver, B.C.
Lawyers - McMillan LLP, Vancouver, B.C.; Cassels Brock & Blackwell LLP, Toronto, Ont.
Transfer Agents - Endeavor Trust Corporation, Vancouver, B.C.
FP500 Revenue Ranking - 751
Profile - (B.C. 2013) Delivers employer healthcare solutions through a workplace health and wellness platform for corporations, educational institutions, insurers and advisors. Also develops and markets healthcare technology solutions.

Operations consist of two divisions: Health & Wellness Services; and Health & Productivity Solutions.

Health & Wellness Services

Provides organizations with a comprehensive workplace health and wellness program, Kii, to support employees' and their dependents' mental, physical and social issues. Kii delivers a suite of healthcare services digitally (mobile application and online), in-person and by phone led by nurses and supported by doctors and specialists. Nurses conduct initial intake and assessment as well as serve as a guide and support throughout the personalized treatment plans within Kii, from creating care plans with the appropriate specialists and therapists to navigating options and ensuring patients stay on track. Kii offers mental health support solutions, including Employee and Family Assistance Program (EFAP), mental health coaching, therapy and treatment, Therapist Assisted Internet-based cognitive behavioural therapy (TAiCBT) and virtual medical care, that address crisis, episodic, short-term, long-term, chronic and specialized services such as trauma, substance use and addiction; rehabilitation and assessment services, including independent medical assessments, return to work support, functional capacity evaluations, rehabilitation support and job demand analysis; and absence management and occupational health solutions, including absentee management, short-term and long-term disability, workers' compensation claims management, mental health assessment and evaluation services focused on prevention, accommodation and recovery. Kii services are utilized by a wide range of customers including employers, individuals, disability case managers, life and health insurers, and property and casualty insurers.

Health & Productivity Solutions

Offers healthcare technology solutions that support the healthcare offerings of companies, insurers, clinics and pharmacies. Solutions include electronic health records (EHR), practice management (PM) and remote patient monitoring (RPM) software platforms and services, as well as outsourced IT services for medical practices in the U.S. through **Benchmark Systems, Inc.** (87.5% owned); MyHealthAccess, an online patient portal which allows online appointment booking and virtual care visits, accessed by patients in Juno EMR, a cloud-based electronic medical records (EMR) solution licensed from **WELL Health Technologies Corp.**; Real Time Intervention and Prevention Platform, a software used in substance use disorder and the company's Health and Wellness Network application which is designed to enable an automated real time inquiry of data from multiple disparate sources, identify indicators and compute risks scores so that the appropriate personnel can be alerted when the risk level of at-risk individuals is above a pre-determined level signalling intervention may be required; Health and Wellness Network, an application that enables healthcare providers to be in constant connection with their patients and provides services including curated education, peer support capability and health vitals monitoring; Medical reference library, a health education platform which provides peer-reviewed resources, including PDFs, videos and images, used by healthcare professional to provide credible medical information; and VisionPros, an online vision care platform providing contact lenses direct to customers across North America.

On July 25, 2022, the company sold its 51% interest in **West Mississauga Medical Ltd.**, a medical clinic in Ontario, for $175,000.

Recent Merger and Acquisition Activity

Status: completed **Revised:** Dec. 16, 2022
UPDATE: The acquisition of the two pharmacies in British Columbia was completed. PREVIOUS: Neighbourly Pharmacy Inc. agreed to acquire six community pharmacies in New Brunswick and Nova Scotia and two pharmacies in British Columbia for a total of $15,500,000, which would be funded from cash on hand and drawings on a credit facility. The B.C. pharmacies, Cloverdale Pharmacy Ltd. and Steveston Health Centre Ltd., located in Surrey and Richmond, B.C., respectively, would be purchased from CloudMD Software & Services Inc. for $3,800,000. Nov. 7, 2022 - The acquisition of the six pharmacies in Atlantic Canada was completed.

Status: completed **Revised:** Nov. 2, 2022
UPDATE: The transaction was completed. PREVIOUS: CloudMD Software & Services Inc. agreed to sell its British Columbia-based primary care clinics and Cloud Practice, its cloud-based electronic medical records (EMR) and practice management software, to WELL Health Technologies for $5,750,000. CloudMD's brick-and-mortar primary care clinics are HealthVue (Richmond [2], B.C.) and South Surrey Medical (Surrey, B.C.). Cloud Practice includes Juno EMR and ClinicAid. CloudMD would retain ownership of its online patient portal, MyHealthAccess, and the right (under a licence granted by WELL at closing of the transaction) to use Juno EMR. CloudMD plans to focus on its core businesses, Enterprise Health Solutions and Digital Health Solutions. The transaction was expected to close in the fourth quarter of 2022.

Predecessor Detail - Name changed from Premier Health Group Inc., Feb. 24, 2020.

Directors - Graeme H. McPhail, chr., Toronto, Ont.; Karen Adams, pres. & CEO, Stouffville, Ont.; A. Duncan Hannay, Toronto, Ont.; John A. Hill, Calgary, Alta.; Scott Milligan, Toronto, Ont.; Larry A. Shumka, Edmonton, Alta.; Gaston A. Tano, Toronto, Ont.

Other Exec. Officers - Prakash Patel, CFO; Dhruv Chandra, chief tech. officer; Dr. Luciano Michael (Lu) Barbuto, exec. v-p & pres., EHS; Aida Begovic, exec. v-p, product; Nathan Lane, exec. v-p, health & productivity solutions & U.S. opers.; Bram Lowsky, exec. v-p & head, health & wellness srvcs.; John Plunkett, exec. v-p, corp. devel.; Melissa Alvares, sr. v-p, mktg.; Julia Becker, v-p, IR; Dr. Amit Mathur, pres., U.S. opers.

Capital Stock

	Authorized (shs.)	Outstanding (shs.)[1]
Common	unlimited	301,687,788

[1] At May 29, 2023

Major Shareholder - Widely held at Oct. 31, 2022.

Price Range - DOC/TSX-VEN

Year	Volume	High	Low	Close
2022	94,635,714	$1.20	$0.17	$0.20
2021	238,527,790	$3.25	$1.11	$1.17
2020	361,098,803	$3.43	$0.35	$2.38
2019	22,441,433	$1.02	$0.25	$0.36
2018	13,542,087	$1.15	$0.05	$0.90

Recent Close: $0.14

Capital Stock Changes - In January 2022, 54,820,961 common shares were issued pursuant to the acquisition of MindBeacon Holdings Inc. Also during 2022, common shares were issued as follows: 12,020,041 as contingent consideration, 354,289 on exercise of warrants, 100,000 on exercise of options and 92,467 for services; 44,444 common shares were returned on sale of investment.

Wholly Owned Subsidiaries

Aspiria Corp., Markham, Ont.
CloudMD Holdings Corporation (Delaware) Inc., Del.
- 87.5% int. in **Benchmark Systems, Inc.**, Lynchburg, Va.

First Health Care Services of Canada Inc., Ont.
- 100% int. in **HumanaCare Organizational Resources Inc.**, Markham, Ont.

iMD Health Global Corp., Etobicoke, Ont.
Livecare Health Canada Inc., Vancouver, B.C.
- 100% int. in **Coast Medical Clinic Ltd.**, B.C.

Medical Confidence Inc., Canada.
MindBeacon Holdings Inc., Toronto, Ont.
- 100% int. in **Harmony Healthcare, Inc.**, Las Vegas, Nev.

Oncidium Inc., Woodbridge, Ont.
1143556 B.C. Ltd., B.C.
11533046 B.C. Ltd., B.C.
Re:Function Health Group Inc., B.C.
Rx Infinity Inc., Mississauga, Ont.
- 100% int. in **Rxi Health Solutions Inc.**, Canada.
- 100% int. in **Rxi Pharmacy Inc.**, Canada.

Snapclarity Inc., Ottawa, Ont.
Tetra Ventures, LLC, East Brunswick, N.J.
0869316 B.C. Ltd., B.C.

Financial Statistics

Periods ended:	12m Dec. 31/22[A]		12m Dec. 31/21[◻A]
	$000s	%Chg	$000s
Operating revenue	**114,456**	**+63**	**70,055**
Cost of sales	74,258		43,397
Research & devel. expense	3,954		1,604
General & admin expense	48,081		28,767
Stock-based compensation	1,273		5,223
Operating expense	**127,566**	**+65**	**77,387**
Operating income	**(13,110)**	**n.a.**	**(7,332)**
Deprec., depl. & amort.	14,106		5,687
Finance costs, gross	2,052		1,089
Investment income	6		32
Write-downs/write-offs	(119,593)		(6,878)
Pre-tax income	**(153,670)**	**n.a.**	**(23,501)**
Income taxes	(4,779)		355
Net inc. bef. disc. opers	**(148,891)**	**n.a.**	**(23,856)**
Income from disc. opers	(8,800)		(6,882)
Net income	**(157,691)**	**n.a.**	**(30,738)**
Net inc. for equity hldrs	**(157,927)**	**n.a.**	**(30,726)**
Net inc. for non-cont. int	**236**	**n.a.**	**(12)**
Cash & equivalent	24,058		45,082
Inventories	979		3,424
Accounts receivable	19,759		24,718
Current assets	48,991		75,382
Long-term investments	nil		407
Fixed assets, net	7,751		11,319
Intangibles, net	126,342		224,744
Total assets	**186,991**	**-40**	**312,090**
Accts. pay. & accr. liabs	21,023		30,586
Current liabilities	30,828		49,465
Long-term debt, gross	19,847		24,568
Long-term debt, net	17,690		22,130
Long-term lease liabilities	4,290		6,912
Shareholders' equity	114,646		209,573
Non-controlling interest	1,027		791
Cash from oper. activs	**(28,924)**	**n.a.**	**(21,862)**
Cash from fin. activs	(10,681)		77,068
Cash from invest. activs	18,581		(69,908)
Net cash position	**24,058**	**-47**	**45,082**
Capital expenditures	(324)		(595)
	$		$
Earns. per sh. bef disc opers*	(0.52)		(0.11)
Earnings per share*	(0.55)		(0.15)
Cash flow per share*	(0.10)		(0.10)
	shs		shs
No. of shs. o/s*	294,048,103		226,704,789
Avg. no. of shs. o/s*	288,190,051		211,234,308
	%		%
Net profit margin	(130.09)		(34.05)
Return on equity	(88.92)		(15.08)
Return on assets	(57.12)		(10.49)
Foreign sales percent	20		28

* Common
◻ Restated
[A] Reported in accordance with IFRS

Latest Results

Periods ended:	3m Mar. 31/23[A]		3m Mar. 31/22[◻A]
	$000s	%Chg	$000s
Operating revenue	26,139	-16	31,048
Net inc. bef. disc. opers	(7,003)	n.a.	(5,139)
Income from disc. opers	(143)		(509)
Net income	(7,146)	n.a.	(5,648)
Net inc. for equity hldrs	(7,145)	n.a.	(5,657)
Net inc. for non-cont. int	(1)		9
	$		$
Earnings per share*	(0.02)		(0.02)

* Common
◻ Restated
[A] Reported in accordance with IFRS

Historical Summary
(as originally stated)

Fiscal Year	Oper. Rev.	Net Inc. Bef. Disc.	EPS*
	$000s	$000s	$
2022[A]	114,456	(148,891)	(0.52)
2021[A]	102,331	(30,738)	(0.15)
2020[A]	15,016	(12,327)	(0.11)
2019[A]	6,769	(4,555)	(0.06)
2018[A]	1,202	(2,597)	(0.06)

* Common
[A] Reported in accordance with IFRS

C.135 Clover Leaf Capital Corp.

Symbol - CLVR.P **Exchange** - TSX-VEN **CUSIP** - 18915K
Head Office - Unit 1, 15782 Marine Dr, White Rock, BC, V4B 1E6 **Telephone** - (604) 536-2711
Email - ben@gocs.ca
Investor Relations - Ben Meyer (604) 536-2711
Auditors - Davidson & Company LLP C.A., Vancouver, B.C.
Transfer Agents - Odyssey Trust Company, Vancouver, B.C.
Profile - (B.C. 2021) Capital Pool Company.

Recent Merger and Acquisition Activity

Status: pending **Revised:** May 30, 2023
UPDATE: North Shore entered into an option agreement with Skyharbour Resources Ltd. to acquire the 42,900 hectare South Falcon property, thus increasing the size of the Falcon property to 55,700 hectares. PREVIOUS: Clover Leaf Capital Corp. entered into a letter of intent for the Qualifying Transaction reverse takeover acquisition of private British Columbia-based North Shore Energy Metals Ltd. on a share-for-share basis, which would result in the issuance of 16,725,000 Clover Leaf common shares. North Shore holds options to acquire 12,791-hectare Falcon uranium prospect and earn 75% interest in 4,511-hectare West Bear uranium prospect, both in the Athabasca Basin area of northern Saskatchewan. Dec. 23, 2022 - A definitive agreement was entered into. Mar. 31, 2023 - The deadline for completion of the transaction was extended from Apr. 30, 2023, to June 30, 2023.

Directors - Alain V. Fontaine, chr., Hong Kong, People's Republic of China; Tsend Tseren, pres. & CEO, Ulaanbaatar, Mongolia; J. Morgan Hay, Vancouver, B.C.; Doris A. Meyer, Vancouver, B.C.; Alexander A. (Alex) Molyneux, Taipei, Republic of China; Blake A. Steele, Hong Kong, Hong Kong, People's Republic of China

Other Exec. Officers - Daniel (Dan) O'Brien, CFO; Ben Meyer, corp. sec.

Capital Stock

	Authorized (shs.)	Outstanding (shs.)[1]
Common	unlimited	11,850,000

[1] At May 30, 2023

Major Shareholder - Widely held at May 8, 2022.

Price Range - CLVR.P/TSX-VEN

Year	Volume	High	Low	Close
2022	125,662	$0.14	$0.09	$0.09

Capital Stock Changes - On Mar. 22, 2022, an initial public offering of 4,650,000 common shares was completed at 10¢ per share.

C.136 Co-operators General Insurance Company

CUSIP - 189906
Head Office - 130 Macdonell St, PO Box 3608 Stn Main, Guelph, ON, N1H 6P8 **Telephone** - (519) 824-4400 **Toll-free** - (800) 265-2662 **Fax** - (519) 824-0599
Website - www.cooperators.ca
Email - lesley_christodoulou@cooperators.ca
Investor Relations - Lesley Christodoulou (519) 767-3909 ext. 302493
Auditors - PricewaterhouseCoopers LLP C.A., Toronto, Ont.
Transfer Agents - Computershare Trust Company of Canada Inc., Toronto, Ont.
FP500 Subsidiary Revenue Ranking - 19
Employees - 4,383 at Dec. 31, 2022
Profile - (Can. 1983 amalg.) Provides property and casualty insurance, including automobile, home, farm and commercial insurance products to individuals and commercial clients across Canada supported by a dedicated financial advisor network with 2,808 licensed insurance representatives.

Wholly owned **The Sovereign General Insurance Company** writes complex commercial and special risk insurance through independent brokers across Canada.

Wholly owned **CUMIS General Insurance Company** provides personal and commercial insurance products for credit unions and their members.

The company also offers automobile and home insurance to employer, association and affinity groups across Canada.

The company insures about 888,000 homes, 42,000 farms, 279,000 businesses and more than 1,500,000 vehicles across all regions of Canada.

On Jan. 12, 2023, the company acquired private Saint-Jean-sur-Richelieu, Que.-based **Assurances Oligny Inc.** for an undisclosed amount. Assurances Oligny provides brokerage services for home, automobile and commercial insurance products in Quebec.

Directors - John S. Harvie, chr., Moncton, N.B.; Alexandra Wilson, v-chr., Ottawa, Ont.; Robert (Rob) Wesseling, pres. & CEO, Guelph, Ont.; Michael Barrett, Ont.; Phil Baudin, Vancouver, B.C.; Louis-H. Campagna, Québec, Qué.; Brent Clode, Ont.; Hazel Corcoran, Calgary, Alta.; Mike Csversko, Dauphin, Man.; Pierre Dorval, Moonbeam, Ont.; Kate Hill, Calgary, Alta.; Chris Johnson, Chesterville, Ont.; Lorna Knudson, Sask.; Jim Laverick, Spruce Grove, Alta.; Jim MacFarlane, Upper Tantallon, N.S.; Shelley McDade, Campbell River, B.C.; Robert Moreau, Caraquet, N.B.; Jessica Provencher, Québec, Qué.; Christie Stephenson, Vancouver, B.C.; Jennifer Uhren, Sask.; Nicole Waldron, Toronto, Ont.; Jack Wilkinson, Belle Vallee, Ont.; Rod Wilson, Man.

Other Exec. Officers - Kevin Daniel, exec. v-p & chief client officer; Emmie Fukuchi, exec. v-p & chief digital & mktg. officer; Lisa Guglietti, exec. v-p & COO, property & casualty mfg.; Paul Hanna, exec. v-p, mbr. rel., governance & corp. srvcs.; Karen Higgins, exec. v-p, fin. & CFO; Laura Mably, exec. v-p & chief HR officer; Harry Pickett, exec. v-p & CIO; Kathleen A. Howie, sr. v-p, gen. counsel & assoc. sec.; Lesley Christodoulou, v-p, corp. fin. srvcs.

Capital Stock

	Authorized (shs.)	Outstanding (shs.)[1]
Senior Preference		
Class A Series B	unlimited	946,670
Class B	unlimited	29,162
Class E Series A	unlimited	nil
Class E Series B	unlimited	nil
Class E Series C	unlimited	4,000,000
Class E Series D	unlimited	nil
Class E Series E	unlimited	nil
Junior Preference		
Class C	unlimited	nil
Class C Series A	100,000	nil
Class D Series A	unlimited	13,797
Class D Series B	unlimited	42,535
Class D Series C	unlimited	43,184
Class F Series A	unlimited	488,624
Class G Series A	unlimited	14,984
Class H	unlimited	nil
Class I	unlimited	nil
Class J	unlimited	nil
Common	unlimited	26,942,059

[1] At Dec. 31, 2022

Senior Preference:

Class A, B and E preference shares rank equally and in priority to all other classes of preference and common shares. Non-voting.

Class A Series B - Entitled to non-cumulative dividend subject to minimum of 5% of redemption value and redeemable at $100, with a stated value of $100.

Class B - Entitled to non-cumulative dividend subject to minimum of 5% of redemption value. Redeemable at $50, with a stated value of $25, and convertible to class G shares series A preference shares.

Class E Series C - Entitled to non-cumulative dividend, if declared, at 5% per annum, payable quarterly. Redeemable at $25 per share.

Junior Preference:

Class C - Issuable in series.

Class D Series A, B & C - Entitled to non-cumulative dividend and redeemable at $100, with a stated value of $100.

Class F Series A - Entitled to non-cumulative dividend subject to a minimum rate of 5% if declared and redeemable at $37.50, with a stated value of $25.

Class G Series A - Entitled to non-cumulative dividend subject to minimum of 5% and redeemable at $50, with a stated value of $25.

Common - One vote per share.

Major Shareholder - The Co-operators Group Limited held 100% interest at Dec. 31, 2022.

Capital Stock Changes - During 2022, 89,512 class B preference shares and 6 class D preference series A shares were redeemed. Also during 2022, 118,264 class B preference shares and 148,926 common shares were issued.

Dividends

CCS.PR.C pfd E ser C red. exch. Ra $1.25 pa Q

Wholly Owned Subsidiaries

CUMIS General Insurance Company, Burlington, Ont.
Co-operators Insurance Agencies Limited, Canada.
Co-operators Investment Limited Partnership, Canada.
Co-operators Strategic Growth Corporation, Canada.
The Sovereign General Insurance Company, Calgary, Alta.
Note: The preceding list includes only the major related companies in which interests are held.

Financial Statistics

Periods ended:	12m Dec. 31/22[A]		12m Dec. 31/21[A]
	$000s	%Chg	$000s
Net premiums earned	3,983,565		3,790,223
Net investment income	114,414		237,872
Total revenue	**4,106,655**	**+2**	**4,034,298**
Policy benefits & claims	2,271,171		2,071,531
Commissions	588,554		586,733
Salaries & benefits	493,564		465,692
Premium taxes	138,178		131,918
Other operating expense	128,200		93,061
Operating expense	**3,619,667**	**+183**	**1,277,404**
Operating income	**(1,784,183)**	**n.a.**	**685,363**
Deprec. & amort.	10,231		12,300
Finance costs, gross	966		1,236
Pre-tax income	**476,701**	**-29**	**672,613**
Income taxes	100,988		160,202
Net income	**375,713**	**-27**	**512,411**
Cash & equivalent	315,809		537,406
Securities investments	5,302,464		5,461,502
Mortgages	667,918		659,365
Total investments	5,970,382		6,120,867
Total assets	**8,969,627**	**0**	**9,008,509**
Accts. pay. & accr. liabs	371,195		392,483
Claims provisions	3,621,718		3,627,561
Long-term lease liabilities	32,179		32,864
Preferred share equity	220,094		217,218
Shareholders' equity	2,355,908		2,394,768
Cash from oper. activs	**300,654**	**-62**	**795,584**
Cash from fin. activs	(101,307)		(327,103)
Cash from invest. activs	(420,944)		(199,918)
Net cash position	**315,809**	**-41**	**537,406**
Capital expenditures	(5,338)		(5,316)
Capital disposals	501		nil
	$		$
Earnings per share*	13.56		18.74
Cash flow per share*	11.19		29.73
Cash divd. per share*	3.06		11.72
	shs		shs
No. of shs. o/s*	26,942,059		26,793,133
Avg. no. of shs. o/s*	26,868,000		26,756,000
	%		%
Net profit margin	9.15		12.70
Return on equity	16.90		24.53
Return on assets	4.19		5.94
No. of employees (FTEs)	4,383		4,301

* Common
[A] Reported in accordance with IFRS

Historical Summary
(as originally stated)

Fiscal Year	Total Rev. $000s	Net Inc. Bef. Disc. $000s	EPS* $
2022[A]	4,106,655	375,713	13.56
2021[A]	4,034,298	512,411	18.74
2020[A]	3,879,527	290,443	10.49
2019[A]	3,556,058	174,026	6.40
2018[A]	2,962,014	(37,107)	(2.03)

* Common
[A] Reported in accordance with IFRS

C.137 Cogeco Communications Inc.*

Symbol - CCA **Exchange** - TSX **CUSIP** - 19239C
Head Office - c/o COGECO Inc., 3301-1 Place Ville-Marie, Montréal, QC, H3B 3N2 **Telephone** - (514) 764-4600 **Toll-free** - (877) 846-7863 **Fax** - (514) 874-2625
Website - corpo.cogeco.com
Email - andre-gilles.frigon@cogeco.com
Investor Relations - André-Gilles Frigon (514) 764-4795
Auditors - Deloitte LLP C.A., Montréal, Qué.
Lawyers - Stikeman Elliott LLP, Montréal, Qué.
Transfer Agents - Computershare Trust Company of Canada Inc., Montréal, Qué.
FP500 Subsidiary Revenue Ranking - 33
Employees - 4,700 at Aug. 31, 2022
Profile - (Can. 1992) Provides Internet, video and phone services to residential and business customers in Quebec, Ontario and 13 U.S. states.

Operations are organized into two segments: Canadian telecommunications; and American telecommunications.

Canadian telecommunications

High-speed Internet, digital television and Internet protocol (IP) phone services are offered to about 1,800,000 primary service units in Quebec and Ontario under the Cogeco Connexion brand. Also offers advanced network connectivity services delivered over fibre optic connection to larger businesses in its footprint.

American telecommunications

Operating under the Breezeline brand (formerly Atlantic Broadband), the company provides high-speed Internet, television and phone services to more than 1,100,000 primary service units in Massachusetts, Pennsylvania, Florida, Maryland, Delaware, South Carolina, Connecticut, Maine, New Hampshire, New York, Virginia, West Virginia and Ohio.

Periods ended:	12m Aug. 31/22	12m Aug. 31/21
Video service customers	975,628	982,708
Internet service customers	1,480,554	1,436,201
Telephony service customers	551,139	553,164

Recent Merger and Acquisition Activity

Status: completed **Revised:** Mar. 3, 2023
UPDATE: The transaction was completed for $100,000,000. PREVIOUS: Cogeco Communications Inc. agreed to acquire the telecommunications operation of Montreal, Que.-based 9303-4338 Québec inc. (dba Oxio), an Internet service provider. Oxio provides Internet and telecommunications services to 48,000 residential customers in Quebec, Ontario and western provinces. Oxio would continue to operate independently and serve its customers using its brand. Terms were not disclosed.

Predecessor Detail - Name changed from Cogeco Cable Inc., Jan. 13, 2016.

Directors - Louis Audet, chr., Westmount, Qué.; Philippe Jetté, pres. & CEO, Montréal, Qué.; James C. Cherry†, Brockville, Ont.; Colleen Abdoulah, Denver, Colo.; Mary-Ann Bell, Montréal, Qué.; Robin A. Bienenstock, Toronto, Ont.; Pippa Dunn, London, Middx., United Kingdom; Joanne S. Ferstman, Toronto, Ont.; Normand Legault, Lac-Brome, Qué.; Bernard Lord, Moncton, N.B.

Other Exec. Officers - Linda Gillespie, sr. v-p & chief HR officer; Christian Jolivet, sr. v-p, corp. affairs, chief legal officer & corp. sec.; Marie-Hélène Labrie, sr. v-p & chief public affairs, commun. & strategy officer; Dr. Zouheir Mansourati, sr. v-p & chief tech. officer; Patrice Ouimet, sr. v-p & CFO; Antoine Shiu, sr. v-p, corp. project; Elizabeth Alves, v-p, enterprise strategy & sustainability; Paul Beaudry, v-p, regulatory affairs; France De Blois, v-p, fin.; Chantal Frappier, v-p, internal audit; David Gorgas, v-p, IT & digital strategy; Martin Grenier, v-p, procurement; Julie Laviolette, v-p & treas.; Marie Ginette Lepage, v-p, wireless solutions & innovation; François-Philippe Lessard, v-p, corp. devel.; Frédéric Perron, pres., Cogeco Connexion Inc.; Frank van der Post, pres., Breezeline
† Lead director

Capital Stock

	Authorized (shs.)	Outstanding (shs.)[1]
Class A Preference	unlimited	nil
Class B Preference	unlimited	nil
Multiple Voting	unlimited	15,691,100
Subordinate Voting	unlimited	28,793,378

[1] At June 30, 2023

Class A Preference - Issuable in series and non-voting.
Class B Preference - Issuable in series and non-voting.
Multiple Voting - Ten votes per share.
Subordinate Voting - One vote per share.
Options - At Aug. 31, 2022, options were outstanding to purchase 874,165 subordinate voting shares at prices ranging from $38.08 to $118.42 per share with a weighted average remaining contractual life of 6.26 years.
Normal Course Issuer Bid - The company plans to make normal course purchases of up to 1,776,125 subordinate voting shares representing 10% of the public float. The bid commenced on May 4, 2023, and expires on May 3, 2024.
Major Shareholder - COGECO Inc. held 85% interest at May 31, 2023.

Price Range - CCA/TSX

Year	Volume	High	Low	Close
2022	23,180,370	$114.66	$62.35	$76.79
2021	20,802,018	$123.07	$95.71	$100.73
2020	34,378,907	$132.00	$87.57	$97.86
2019	23,663,151	$120.20	$65.21	$113.20
2018	18,940,701	$88.25	$61.68	$65.78

Recent Close: $63.03
Capital Stock Changes - During fiscal 2022, 75,794 subordinate voting shares were issued on exercise of options, 1,149,025 subordinate voting shares were repurchased under a Normal Course Issuer Bid and 5,991 (net) subordinate voting shares held in trust were distributed.

Dividends

CCA com S.V. Ra $3.104 pa Q est. Nov. 24, 2022
Prev. Rate: $2.82 est. Dec. 9, 2021
Prev. Rate: $2.56 est. Nov. 24, 2020

Long-Term Debt - Outstanding at Aug. 31, 2022:

Cogeco Communications Inc.	
4.18% ser.4 sr. debs. due 2023	$299,730,000
3.72% revolving loan due 2027[1]	106,199,000
4.14% ser.A sr. notes due 2024[2]	32,742,000
4.3% sr. notes due 2025[3]	281,450,000
4.29% ser.B sr. notes due 2026[4]	196,313,000
2.99% sr. notes due 2031	496,993,000
Lease liabs	43,627,000
Subsidiaries:	
4.52% sr. term facility tr. 1 due 2025[5]	2,060,614,000
5.02% sr. term facility tr. 2 due 2028[6]	1,155,801,000
	4,673,469,000
Less: Current portion	339,096,000
	4,334,373,000

[1] US$81,000,000.
[2] US$25,000,000.
[3] US$215,000,000.
[4] US$150,000,000.
[5] US$1.593 billion.
[6] US$895,500,000.

Note - In February 2023, offering of $300,000,000 principal amount of 5.299% senior secured notes due Feb. 16, 2033, was completed.

Wholly Owned Subsidiaries

Cogeco Connexion Inc., Canada.
- 79% int. in **Cogeco Communications (U.S.A.) Inc.**, Del.
  - 100% int. in **Cogeco US (CT), LLC**, Del.
  - 100% int. in **Cogeco US (Delmar), LLC**, Del.
  - 100% int. in **Cogeco US (Miami), LLC**, Del.
  - 100% int. in **Cogeco US (NH-ME) LLC**, Del.
  - 100% int. in **Cogeco US (OH), LLC**, Del.
  - 100% int. in **Cogeco US (PENN), LLC**, Del.
  - 100% int. in **Cogeco US (SC), LLC**, Del.

Note: The preceding list includes only the major related companies in which interests are held.

Financial Statistics

Periods ended:	12m Aug. 31/22[A]		12m Aug. 31/21[oA]
	$000s	%Chg	$000s
Operating revenue	**2,900,654**	**+16**	**2,510,453**
Salaries & benefits	439,609		398,977
Other operating expense	1,067,983		905,820
Operating expense	**1,507,592**	**+16**	**1,304,797**
Operating income	**1,393,062**	**+16**	**1,205,656**
Deprec., depl. & amort.	621,084		510,376
Finance costs, gross	187,617		124,163
Pre-tax income	**549,419**	**-2**	**562,373**
Income taxes	95,663		130,726
Net inc bef disc ops, eqhldrs	423,299		401,517
Net inc bef disc ops, NCI	30,457		30,130
Net income	**453,756**	**+5**	**431,647**
Net inc. for equity hldrs	**423,299**	**+5**	**401,517**
Net inc. for non-cont. int	**30,457**	**+1**	**30,130**
Cash & equivalent	370,899		549,054
Accounts receivable	108,444		78,346
Current assets	528,010		667,220
Fixed assets, net	3,027,640		2,357,845
Intangibles, net	5,553,719		4,216,061
Total assets	**9,278,509**	**+26**	**7,351,692**
Bank indebtedness	8,633		4,460
Accts. pay. & accr. liabs	380,461		270,497
Current liabilities	987,120		751,715
Long-term debt, gross	4,673,469		3,272,216
Long-term debt, net	4,334,373		3,046,872
Shareholders' equity	2,751,080		2,415,144
Non-controlling interest	438,051		391,183
Cash from oper. activs	**1,240,282**	**+22**	**1,019,059**
Cash from fin. activs	981,925		(27,408)
Cash from invest. activs	(2,407,514)		(801,298)
Net cash position	**370,899**	**-32**	**549,054**
Capital expenditures	(744,655)		(537,660)
Capital disposals	2,906		2,458
Unfunded pension liability	389		3,059
	$		$
Earnings per share*	9.16		8.47
Cash flow per share*	26.83		21.50
Cash divd. per share*	2.82		2.56
	shs		shs
No. of shs. o/s*	45,600,984		46,668,224
Avg. no. of shs. o/s*	46,228,842		47,391,520
	%		%
Net profit margin	15.64		17.19
Return on equity	16.39		17.15
Return on assets	7.32		7.44
Foreign sales percent	50		45
No. of employees (FTEs)	4,700		3,854

* M.V. & S.V.
[o] Restated
[A] Reported in accordance with IFRS

Latest Results

Periods ended:	9m May 31/23[A]		9m May 31/22[A]
	$000s	%Chg	$000s
Operating revenue	2,240,731	+3	2,175,208
Net income	326,175	-5	341,927
Net inc. for equity hldrs	305,774	-4	318,362
Net inc. for non-cont. int	20,401		23,565
	$		$
Earnings per share*	6.83		6.87

* M.V. & S.V.
[A] Reported in accordance with IFRS

Historical Summary
(as originally stated)

Fiscal Year	Oper. Rev. $000s	Net Inc. Bef. Disc. $000s	EPS* $
2022[A]	2,900,654	453,756	9.16
2021[A]	2,510,453	431,647	8.47
2020[A]	2,384,283	396,591	7.74
2019[A]	2,331,820	356,908	6.89
2018[A]	2,423,549	356,341	7.04

* M.V. & S.V.
[A] Reported in accordance with IFRS

C.138 Cognetivity Neurosciences Ltd.

Symbol - CGN **Exchange** - CSE **CUSIP** - 19243C
Head Office - 2250-1055 Hastings St W, Vancouver, BC, V6E 2E9 **Telephone** - (604) 688-9588 **Fax** - (778) 329-9361
Website - www.cognetivity.com
Email - info@cognetivity.com
Investor Relations - Dr. Sina Habibi (604) 688-9588
Auditors - MNP LLP C.A., Vancouver, B.C.
Transfer Agents - TSX Trust Company, Vancouver, B.C.
Profile - (B.C. 2015) Developing cognitive testing software for medical, commercial and consumer use.

The company's products include Integrated Cognitive Assessment (ICA), which uses artificial intelligence and machine learning techniques to help detect the earliest signs of cognitive impairment by testing the performance of large areas of the brain to support diagnosis of Alzheimer's disease, dementia and other neurological conditions; and OptiMind, an iOS mobile application that measures the user's everyday cognitive performance.

ICA software is available for clinical use in the United States, the United Kingdom and Europe with regulatory approval anticipated elsewhere in the world.

Directors - Dr. Sina Habibi, co-founder & CEO, London, Middx., United Kingdom; Dr. Thomas Sawyer, COO, CFO & corp. sec., London, Middx., United Kingdom; Dr. Christos (Chris) Kalafatis, CMO, London, Middx., United Kingdom; Dr. Mark A. Phillips, chief compliance officer, London, Middx., United Kingdom; Desmond M. (Des) Balakrishnan, legal counsel, Vancouver, B.C.; Karimah Es Sabar; David Velisek, Vancouver, B.C.
Other Exec. Officers - Seyed-Mahdi Khaligh-Razavi, co-founder & chief innovation officer; Jonathan El-Sharkawy, chief tech. officer

Capital Stock

	Authorized (shs.)	Outstanding (shs.)[1]
Class C Preferred	unlimited	15,525,786
Common	unlimited	85,049,178
Class B	unlimited	nil

[1] At Dec. 16, 2022

Class C Preferred - Not entitled to dividends. Non-transferable. Convertible into common shares on a one-for-one basis. Redeemable, at the holder's option, beginning Oct. 26, 2023, at 58¢ per share. Non-voting.
Common - One vote per share.
Class B - Not entitled to dividends. Will automatically convert into one common share upon the company attaining the CE Marketing approval for the cognitive assessment tool kit as a medical device. Non-voting.
Major Shareholder - Dr. Sina Habibi held 10.4% interest at Nov. 5, 2021.

Price Range - CGN/CSE

Year	Volume	High	Low	Close
2022	18,490,262	$0.57	$0.15	$0.24
2021	32,138,439	$1.35	$0.48	$0.55
2020	16,654,391	$0.64	$0.09	$0.64
2019	19,049,723	$0.52	$0.09	$0.22
2018	12,314,247	$0.63	$0.25	$0.36

Recent Close: $0.14
Capital Stock Changes - In February 2022, private placement of 4,812,416 units (1 common share & ½ warrant) at 55¢ per unit was completed, with warrants exercisable at 85¢ per share for three years. On Oct. 26, 2022, private placement of 15,525,786 class C preferred shares was completed at 29¢ per share.

Wholly Owned Subsidiaries

Cognetivity Ltd., United Kingdom.
• 100% int. in **Cognetivity FZ-LLC**, Dubai, United Arab Emirates.

Financial Statistics

Periods ended:	12m Jan. 31/22[A]		12m Jan. 31/21[A]
	$000s	%Chg	$000s
Salaries & benefits	4,019		1,116
Research & devel. expense	491		71
General & admin expense	4,844		1,184
Stock-based compensation	3,679		76
Operating expense	**13,033**	**+433**	**2,446**
Operating income	**(13,033)**	**n.a.**	**(2,446)**
Deprec., depl. & amort.	25		11
Finance costs, gross	61		63
Pre-tax income	**(13,127)**	**n.a.**	**(1,926)**
Income taxes	nil		2
Net income	**(13,127)**	**n.a.**	**(1,928)**
Cash & equivalent	1,377		1,360
Accounts receivable	221		nil
Current assets	1,856		1,751
Fixed assets, net	63		44
Intangibles, net	85		32
Total assets	**2,005**	**+10**	**1,828**
Bank indebtedness	1,295		nil
Accts. pay. & accr. liabs	1,754		637
Current liabilities	5,555		965
Long-term debt, gross	nil		314
Equity portion of conv. debs	nil		35
Shareholders' equity	(5,675)		863
Cash from oper. activs	**(3,215)**	**n.a.**	**(1,959)**
Cash from fin. activs	3,332		2,791
Cash from invest. activs	(100)		(50)
Net cash position	**1,377**	**+1**	**1,360**
Capital expenditures	(61)		(18)
	$		$
Earnings per share*	(0.18)		(0.03)
Cash flow per share*	(0.04)		(0.03)
	shs		shs
No. of shs. o/s*	79,402,556		70,487,707
Avg. no. of shs. o/s*	73,057,477		58,675,419
	%		%
Net profit margin	n.a.		n.a.
Return on equity	n.m.		n.m.
Return on assets	(681.76)		(144.79)

* Common
[A] Reported in accordance with IFRS

Latest Results

Periods ended:	6m July 31/22[A]		6m July 31/21[A]
	$000s	%Chg	$000s
Net income	(3,074)	n.a.	(1,901)
	$		$
Earnings per share*	(0.04)		(0.03)

* Common
[A] Reported in accordance with IFRS

Historical Summary
(as originally stated)

Fiscal Year	Oper. Rev. $000s	Net Inc. Bef. Disc. $000s	EPS* $
2022[A]	nil	(13,127)	(0.18)
2021[A]	nil	(1,928)	(0.03)
2020[A]	nil	(2,645)	(0.06)
2019[A]	nil	(4,193)	(0.10)
2018[A]	nil	(1,496)	(0.05)

* Common
[A] Reported in accordance with IFRS

C.139 Coho Collective Kitchens Inc.

Symbol - COHO **Exchange** - TSX-VEN **CUSIP** - 19249T
Head Office - 1370 Georgia St E, Vancouver, BC, V5L 2A8 **Telephone** - (604) 423-3784
Website - www.cohocommissary.com
Email - andrew@cohocommissary.com
Investor Relations - Andrew Barnes (778) 877-6513
Auditors - BDO Canada LLP C.A., Vancouver, B.C.
Lawyers - Fasken Martineau DuMoulin LLP, Vancouver, B.C.
Transfer Agents - Computershare Trust Company of Canada Inc., Vancouver, B.C.
Employees - 25 at May 27, 2022
Profile - (B.C. 2019) Provides and rents out commercial commissary (shared) kitchens to food-based businesses in Canada.

Provides private and shared kitchens as well as production space for food-based businesses, from start-ups to restaurant groups, to avoid costly buildouts of physical facilities. Services include access to share-kitchen facilities, marketing services, pre-negotiated deals with suppliers and business consultation. Available locations include Vancouver (5), Victoria (2), White Rock and Gibsons, B.C.

Has more than 100 customers across multiple food production categories, including farmers' markets, vendors, bakers, consumer packaged goods producers and restaurants. Customers that operate as virtual-only restaurants sell their products through third party delivery partners such as UberEats, DoorDash and SkipTheDishes.

Recent Merger and Acquisition Activity

Status: pending **Revised:** Aug. 9, 2023
UPDATE: The completion date was extended to Aug. 31, 2023. PREVIOUS: Coho Collective Kitchens Inc. agreed to acquire bakery and cafe business Purebread Bakery Inc. for $10,000,000 in cash and issuance of common shares valued at $220,000. Purebread operates six bakery cafe locations under the Purebread brand in Vancouver, Whistler and Squamish, B.C. The transaction was expected to close by July 31, 2023.

Directors - Andrew Barnes, CEO, B.C.; Amrit Maharaj, COO, B.C.; Yuri Fulmer, West Vancouver, B.C.; Alexander (Alex) Macdonald, Toronto, Ont.; Justin Morel, B.C.
Other Exec. Officers - Michael Yam, interim CFO; Wing Hein (Jennifer) Chan, chief mktg. officer; Bernadette D'Silva, corp. sec.

Capital Stock

	Authorized (shs.)	Outstanding (shs.)[1]
Common	unlimited	84,285,042

[1] At July 31, 2023

Major Shareholder - Andrew Barnes held 14.25% interest and Amrit Maharaj held 12.47% interest at Sept. 28, 2022.

Price Range - COHO/TSX-VEN

Year	Volume	High	Low	Close
2022	5,103,655	$0.30	$0.10	$0.13

Recent Close: $0.23
Capital Stock Changes - In July 2023, private placement of up to 27,272,727 units (1 common share & ½ warrant) at 22¢ per unit was arranged, with warrants exercisable at 40¢ per share for three years.

On June 9, 2022, an initial public offering of 16,666,670 common shares was completed at 30¢ per share. Also during fiscal 2023, common shares were issued as follows: 167,148 for finder's fee and 100,000 for financing fee.

Wholly Owned Subsidiaries

The Block at Coho Collective Kitchens Inc., Vancouver, B.C.
Café Coho Inc., B.C.
Coho Commissary Inc., Vancouver, B.C.
Coho Creekside Commissary Inc., North Vancouver, B.C.
Phantom Kitchen Inc., B.C.
Richmond by Coho Collective Kitchens Inc., B.C.
Sunshine by Coho Collective Kitchens Inc., B.C.
Victoria by Coho Collective Kitchens Inc., B.C.

Financial Statistics

Periods ended:	12m Mar. 31/23[A]		15m Mar. 31/22[A1]
	$000s	%Chg	$000s
Operating revenue	**2,551**	**n.a.**	**2,348**
Cost of sales	344		235
Salaries & benefits	2,855		1,992
General & admin expense	2,863		2,135
Stock-based compensation	289		346
Operating expense	**6,351**	**n.a.**	**4,708**
Operating income	**(3,800)**	**n.a.**	**(2,360)**
Deprec., depl. & amort.	1,327		753
Finance costs, gross	952		595
Write-downs/write-offs	(34)		nil
Pre-tax income	**(6,071)**	**n.a.**	**(10,438)**
Net income	**(6,071)**	**n.a.**	**(10,438)**
Cash & equivalent	250		111
Accounts receivable	207		123
Current assets	711		572
Fixed assets, net	4,718		2,888
Right-of-use assets	7,206		3,527
Total assets	**12,992**	**+80**	**7,208**
Bank indebtedness	nil		646
Accts. pay. & accr. liabs	2,242		1,380
Current liabilities	5,373		2,813
Long-term debt, gross	3,482		786
Long-term debt, net	1,232		540
Long-term lease liabilities	7,697		3,854
Shareholders' equity	(1,310)		1
Cash from oper. activs	**(3,139)**	**n.a.**	**(2,142)**
Cash from fin. activs	5,219		2,398
Cash from invest. activs	(1,942)		(394)
Net cash position	**250**	**+125**	**111**
Capital expenditures	(2,087)		(1,692)
	$		$
Earnings per share*	(0.07)		(0.19)
Cash flow per share*	(0.04)		(0.04)
	shs		shs
No. of shs. o/s*	84,285,042		67,351,224
Avg. no. of shs. o/s*	81,037,460		54,933,500
	%		%
Net profit margin	(237.99)		...
Return on equity	n.m.		...
Return on assets	(50.68)		...

* Common
[A] Reported in accordance with IFRS
[1] Shares and per share figures adjusted to reflect 1-for-2 share consolidation effective Feb. 17, 2022.

Historical Summary
(as originally stated)

Fiscal Year	Oper. Rev.	Net Inc. Bef. Disc.	EPS*
	$000s	$000s	$
2023[A]	2,551	(6,071)	(0.07)
2022[A1,2]	2,348	(10,438)	(0.19)
2020[A2]	975	(479)	(0.29)
2019[A2]	401	(297)	(0.19)

* Common
[A] Reported in accordance with IFRS
[1] 15 months ended Mar. 31, 2022.
[2] Shares and per share figures adjusted to reflect 1-for-2 share consolidation effective Feb. 17, 2022.

C.140 CoinAnalyst Corp.

Symbol - COYX **Exchange** - CSE (S) **CUSIP** - 19260U
Head Office - 801-1 Adelaide St E, Toronto, ON, M5C 2V9
Website - coinanalyst.tech/en
Email - p.lauria@coinanalyst.tech
Investor Relations - Pascal Lauria 49-69-264-8485-20
Auditors - Bassi & Karimjee LLP C.A., Brampton, Ont.
Transfer Agents - Odyssey Trust Company, Toronto, Ont.
Profile - (B.C. 2007) Provides an artificial intelligence (AI)-based big data analytics platform that enables traders in the cryptocurrency asset sector and other industries to access a dashboard which monitors and analyzes real-time data from the cryptocurrency and initial coin offering (ICO) market.

The software monitors news sources, tracks influencers, scans online social media, and provides sentiment analysis, forecast and trade signals on the top 300 digital assets. The software system also provides news and price quotes, as well as messaging capabilities.

The platform is accessed through a monthly subscription model and is sold to business-to-consumer (B2C) and through business-to-business-to-consumer (B2C2C).

In April 2022, the company acquired private **RockStock Equities Inc.** for issuance of 3,750,000 common shares at a deemed price of 25¢ per share. RockStock was developing an artist/fan utility that would facilitate and empower artists through an app platform to allow them to directly monetize their music, create pay-per-view performances and participate in non-fungible token (NFT) revenue generation.

Common suspended from CSE, Dec. 6, 2022.

Predecessor Detail - Name changed from Brandenburg Energy Corp., Aug. 26, 2021, pursuant to the reverse takeover acquisition of Germany-based Coin Analyst UG.

Directors - Pascal Lauria, co-founder, CEO & corp. sec., Frankfurt am Main, Germany; Daniel Nauth, Toronto, Ont.; Jeffrey (Jeff) Paolone, Ont.; Richard Paolone Jr., Toronto, Ont.

Other Exec. Officers - Aaron Meckler, CFO

Capital Stock

	Authorized (shs.)	Outstanding (shs.)[1]
Preferred	unlimited	nil
Common	unlimited	77,685,003

[1] At May 30, 2022

Major Shareholder - Pascal Lauria held 47.99% interest and activeInternet Invest UG held 11.69% interest at Nov. 1, 2021.

Price Range - BBM.H/TSX-VEN (D)

Year	Volume	High	Low	Close
2022	13,395,267	$0.21	$0.01	$0.01
2021	9,841,368	$0.31	$0.14	$0.16

Consolidation: 1-for-78.99 cons. in June 2021
Recent Close: $0.01
Capital Stock Changes - In April 2022, 3,750,000 common shares were issued pursuant to the acquisition of RockStock Equities Inc.

Wholly Owned Subsidiaries

Coin Analyst UG, Germany.
RockStock Equities Inc.
2828329 Ontario Inc., Toronto, Ont.

Financial Statistics

Periods ended:	12m Dec. 31/21[A1]		12m Aug. 31/21[A2]
	$000s	%Chg	$000s
Operating revenue	**263**	**n.a.**	**nil**
General & admin expense	1,367		109
Operating expense	**1,367**	**n.a.**	**109**
Operating income	**(1,104)**	**n.a.**	**(109)**
Deprec., depl. & amort.	93		nil
Pre-tax income	**(2,482)**	**n.a.**	**(109)**
Net income	**(2,482)**	**n.a.**	**(109)**
Cash & equivalent	1,181		16
Current assets	1,710		29
Fixed assets, net	1,185		nil
Total assets	**2,895**	**n.a.**	**29**
Accts. pay. & accr. liabs	511		nil
Current liabilities	1,171		101
Shareholders' equity	1,723		(72)
Cash from oper. activs	**739**	**n.a.**	**(71)**
Cash from fin. activs	1,661		nil
Cash from invest. activs	nil		(10)
Net cash position	**1,181**	**n.a.**	**16**
	$		$
Earnings per share*	(0.04)		(0.03)
Cash flow per share*	0.01		(0.02)
	shs		shs
No. of shs. o/s*	73,440,000		3,750,225
Avg. no. of shs. o/s*	57,703,589		3,286,174
	%		%
Net profit margin	(943.73)		n.a.
Return on equity	n.m.		n.m.
Return on assets	(169.77)		(186.32)
Foreign sales percent	100		n.a.

* Common
[A] Reported in accordance with IFRS
[1] Results reflect the Oct. 26, 2021, reverse takeover acquisition of Coin Analyst UG.
[2] Results for fiscal 2021 and prior fiscal years pertain to Brandenburg Energy Corp.

Latest Results

Periods ended:	3m Mar. 31/22[A]		3m Mar. 31/21[A]
	$000s	%Chg	$000s
Operating revenue	55	-92	671
Net income	(697)	n.a.	231
	$		$
Earnings per share*	(0.01)		0.01

* Common
[A] Reported in accordance with IFRS

Historical Summary
(as originally stated)

Fiscal Year	Oper. Rev.	Net Inc. Bef. Disc.	EPS*
	$000s	$000s	$
2021[A]	263	(2,482)	(0.04)
2021[A]	nil	(109)	(0.03)
2020[A]	nil	(230)	(0.79)
2019[A]	nil	(9)	(0.04)
2018[A]	nil	nil	nil

* Common
[A] Reported in accordance with IFRS
Note: Adjusted throughout for 1-for-78.99 cons. in June 2021

C.141 Colabor Group Inc.

Symbol - GCL **Exchange** - TSX **CUSIP** - 192667
Head Office - 1620 boul de Montarville, Boucherville, QC, J4B 8P4
Telephone - (450) 449-4911 **Fax** - (450) 449-6180
Website - www.colabor.com
Email - pascal.rodier@colabor.com
Investor Relations - Pascal Rodier (450) 449-4911
Auditors - PricewaterhouseCoopers LLP C.A., Montréal, Qué.
Bankers - National Bank of Canada, Montréal, Qué.
Lawyers - De Grandpré Chait LLP, Montréal, Qué.; McCarthy Tétrault LLP, Montréal, Qué.
Transfer Agents - Computershare Investor Services Inc.
FP500 Revenue Ranking - 442
Employees - 691 at Dec. 31, 2022
Profile - (Can. 2006) Operates as a distributor and wholesaler of food and related products to the foodservice and retail markets primarily in Quebec, Ontario and Atlantic Canada.

The company purchases and distributes food, food-related and non-food products to wholesalers who redistribute the products to foodservice and retail markets. Foodservice customers include hotels, restaurants as well as institutions specifically healthcare, government and educational institutions while retail customers include supermarkets and fish markets. Products are sold either directly from its distribution centre or through direct delivery from manufacturers and suppliers to the warehouses of wholesale distributors.

Distribution Segment

The **Colabor Division** distributes nearly 10,000 products from its two Quebec-based warehouses located in Levis and Rimouski, which cover 170,000-sq.-ft and 105,000-sq.-ft., respectively, to about 5,000 customers including restaurants, foodservice operators, specialty food stores, institutions and retail customers in Quebec and New Brunswick. Product line includes frozen products, dry staples, dairy products, meat, seafood, fruits, vegetables, disposables and sanitation products.

The **Norref Division** operates a 40,000-sq.-ft. distribution centre in Montreal, Que., and imports and distributes fresh and frozen fish and seafood products to supermarkets, restaurants, hotels, caterers and fish stores.

The **Lauzon Meats Division** operates a 68,000-sq.-ft. plant in Montreal, Que., and distributes high profile beef brands such as Boeuf Quebec, Excel Premium Beef and Menu™, the company's private brand, as well as prepares and processes meat products for the restaurant and hotel industries and institutional sector throughout Quebec and Ontario.

Wholesale Segment

The **Boucherville Division** operates a 371,000-sq.-ft. distribution centre in Boucherville, Que., and distributes about 10,000 products sourced from 600 suppliers and manufacturers to over 25,000 customers operating in Quebec, Ontario and Atlantic Canada.

In December 2022, wholly owned **Colabor Management Inc.** and **Colabor Limited Partnership** were liquidated.

In April 2022, the company acquired **Le Groupe Resto-Achats Inc.**, which provides access to group business terms for food supply and other services related to restaurants in Quebec, for $4,500,000; and certain assets related to food service activities in the Outaouais and Laurentians region in Quebec from **Ben Deshaies Inc.** for $442,000.

Predecessor Detail - Name changed from ConjuChem Biotechnologies Inc., Aug. 28, 2009, pursuant to plan of arrangement resulting in Colabor Income Fund becoming a wholly owned subsid. of Colabor Group Inc., with trust units of Colabor Income Fund and exch. LP units of subsidiary Colabor Limited Partnership exchanged for common shares of Colabor Group Inc. on a 1-for-1 basis. All assets and liabilities of (old) ConjuChem Biotechnologies Inc. were transferred to (new) ConjuChem Biotechnologies Inc. which was spun out as a new public entity on a sh.-for-sh. basis.

Directors - Warren J. White, chr., Dollard-des-Ormeaux, Qué.; Marc Beauchamp, Outremont, Qué.; Daniéle Bergeron, Lorraine, Qué.; Jean Gattuso, Montréal, Qué.; Robert B. Johnston, Isle of Palms, S.C.; Denis Mathieu, Longueuil, Qué.; François R. Roy, Montréal, Qué.

Other Exec. Officers - Louis Frenette, pres. & CEO; Pierre Blanchette, sr. v-p & CFO; Bernard Carrier, v-p, opers.; Michel Delisle, v-p, IT; Mathieu Dumulong, v-p, sales; Elisabeth Tremblay, v-p, HR & commun.; Daniel Valiquette, v-p, central procurement & private labels; Pascal Rodier, gen. counsel & corp. sec.; Marie-France Laberge, contr.

Capital Stock

	Authorized (shs.)	Outstanding (shs.)[1]
Preferred	unlimited	nil
Series A		
Common	unlimited	101,954,885

[1] At May 1, 2023

Series A Preferred - Non-voting.
Common - One vote per share.
Major Shareholder - The Article 6 Marital Trust created under the First Amended and Restated Jerry Zucker Revocable Trust dated 4-2-07 held 12.35% interest and Robert J. Briscoe held 11.77% interest at Mar. 22, 2023.

Price Range - GCL/TSX

Year	Volume	High	Low	Close
2022	6,726,218	$0.95	$0.65	$0.74
2021	18,677,088	$1.28	$0.65	$0.68
2020	22,824,363	$0.95	$0.20	$0.72
2019	33,907,439	$1.08	$0.43	$0.57
2018	20,306,578	$0.82	$0.35	$0.43

Recent Close: $1.10
Capital Stock Changes - There were no changes to capital stock during fiscal 2022.

Wholly Owned Subsidiaries

Le Groupe Resto-Achats Inc., Qué.
Les Pêcheries Norref Québec Inc., Qué.
Transport Paul-Emile Dubé Ltée, Canada.

Financial Statistics

Periods ended:	53w Dec. 31/22[A]		52w Dec. 25/21[DA]
	$000s	%Chg	$000s
Operating revenue	**574,071**	**+20**	**477,004**
Cost of goods sold	470,559		396,933
Salaries & benefits	52,815		42,537
General & admin expense	12,237		8,915
Other operating expense	9,867		3,502
Operating expense	**545,478**	**+21**	**451,887**
Operating income	**28,593**	**+14**	**25,117**
Deprec., depl. & amort.	16,082		14,088
Finance costs, gross	4,780		5,109
Pre-tax income	**6,377**	**-34**	**9,688**
Income taxes	1,826		1,435
Net inc. bef. disc. opers	**4,551**	**-45**	**8,253**
Income from disc. opers	(486)		(411)
Net income	**4,065**	**-48**	**7,842**
Cash & equivalent	nil		2,006
Inventories	45,084		38,692
Accounts receivable	45,776		45,745
Current assets	92,780		88,364
Fixed assets, net	8,247		5,568
Right-of-use assets	38,057		33,471
Intangibles, net	95,151		93,668
Total assets	**240,691**	**+5**	**229,434**
Bank indebtedness	1,275		nil
Accts. pay. & accr. liabs	42,060		43,667
Current liabilities	59,760		54,707
Long-term debt, gross	46,375		49,989
Long-term debt, net	43,375		46,989
Long-term lease liabilities	30,480		27,471
Shareholders' equity	10,894		97,590
Cash from oper. activs	**19,299**	**+3**	**18,752**
Cash from fin. activs	(16,511)		(23,917)
Cash from invest. activs	(6,061)		(1,842)
Net cash position	**(1,275)**	**n.a.**	**2,006**
Capital expenditures	(4,973)		(1,727)
Capital disposals	50		8
Unfunded pension liability	2,279		2,658
	$		$
Earnings per share*	0.04		0.08
Cash flow per share*	0.19		0.18
	shs		shs
No. of shs. o/s*	101,954,885		101,954,885
Avg. no. of shs. o/s*	101,954,885		101,893,919
	%		%
Net profit margin	0.79		1.73
Return on equity	8.39		8.87
Return on assets	3.39		5.44
No. of employees (FTEs)	691		636

* Common
[D] Restated
[A] Reported in accordance with IFRS

Latest Results

Periods ended:	12w Mar. 31/23[A]		12w Mar. 19/22[A]
	$000s	%Chg	$000s
Operating revenue	133,923	+38	97,169
Net inc. bef. disc. opers	(160)	n.a.	(1,653)
Income from disc. opers	nil		(53)
Net income	(160)	n.a.	(1,706)
	$		$
Earnings per share*	(0.00)		(0.02)

* Common
[A] Reported in accordance with IFRS

Historical Summary
(as originally stated)

Fiscal Year	Oper. Rev. $000s	Net Inc. Bef. Disc. $000s	EPS* $
2022[A1]	574,071	4,551	0.04
2021[A]	475,761	8,253	0.08
2020[A]	461,319	3,798	0.04
2019[A]	1,060,071	654	0.01
2018[A]	1,202,916	(4,387)	(0.04)

* Common
[A] Reported in accordance with IFRS
[1] 53 weeks ended Dec. 31, 2022.

C.142 Colliers International Group Inc.*

Symbol - CIGI **Exchange** - TSX **CUSIP** - 194693
Head Office - 4000-1140 Bay St, Toronto, ON, M5S 2B4 **Telephone** - (416) 960-9500 **Fax** - (416) 960-5333
Website - www.colliers.com
Email - christian.mayer@colliers.com
Investor Relations - Christian Mayer (416) 960-9176
Auditors - PricewaterhouseCoopers LLP C.A., Toronto, Ont.

Bankers - Wells Fargo Bank, N.A.; U.S. Bank National Association; National Bank of Canada; Canadian Imperial Bank of Commerce; Bank of America Canada; Bank of Montreal; The Toronto-Dominion Bank; Royal Bank of Canada; J.P. Morgan Chase Bank (Canada); HSBC Bank Canada; The Bank of Nova Scotia
Lawyers - Torys LLP, Toronto, Ont.; Fogler, Rubinoff LLP, Toronto, Ont.
Transfer Agents - TSX Trust Company, Toronto, Ont.
FP500 Revenue Ranking - 104
Employees - 18,450 at Dec. 31, 2022
Profile - (Ont. 1988 amalg.) Provides commercial real estate services to corporate and institutional clients in 34 countries worldwide (66 countries including affiliates and franchisees). Primary services are sales brokerage, lease brokerage, debt finance, outsourcing and advisory, and investment management.

The company provides services to occupiers, owners and investors in office, industrial, retail, multi-family hospitality, health care and other commercial real estate assets. Operates from 382 offices in 34 countries worldwide with over 18,000 employees. In markets where there are not company-owned operations, the company operates through affiliates and franchises operating under the Colliers International brand and trademarks. Including affiliates and franchisees, the company operates in 65 countries.

Operations are divided into four service lines: Capital Markets &Leasing, Outsourcing & Advisory; and Investment Management.

Capital Markets & Leasing services include transaction brokerage services in sales and leasing for commercial clients as well as debt finance services related to the origination and sale of multifamily and commercial mortgage loans. The company's advisors assist buyers and sellers in connection with the acquisition or disposition of real estate; assist landlords and tenants with lease opportunities and assist borrowers and lenders with the placement of debt capital on commercial real estate assets.

Outsourcing & Advisory services include corporate and workplace solutions, property and facility management, project management, engineering and design, appraisal and valuation, and loan and research for commercial real estate clients. The company partners with large corporations in managing their overall real estate portfolios and transactions to reduce costs, improve execution across multiple markets and increase operational efficiency. The business has about 7,700 professional staff globally.

Investment Management services are primarily conducted through 75%-owned **Harrison Street Real Estate Capital, LLC**, a real estate investment manager offering private real estate funds exclusively focused on the areas of education, healthcare and storage as well as social and utility infrastructure in the U.S., Europe, and Canada with almost US$56.1 billion in assets under management (AUM) at Dec. 31, 2022. Harrison together with the company's existing Investment Management platforms had AUM of US$97.7 billion at Dec. 31, 2022.

In June 2023, the company exited part of its operations in Peru.

In December 2022, the company acquired a majority interest in **BelSquare S.R.L.**, a Belgian commercial real estate advisor with offices in Brussels and Antwerp. Belsquare would be rebranded as Colliers and merged with the company's existing operations in Belgium.

During the second quarter of 2022, the company sold two individually insignificant operations, Morocco and Panama. Terms were not disclosed.

In May 2022, the company acquired a majority interest in the U.K.-based **Paragon Building Consultancy Holdings Limited**, which provides building surveying, project management, environmental assessments, and energy & sustainability consulting to owners, investors, and users of real estate, for an undisclosed amount.

In March 2022, the company discontinued and sold its business in Russia and Belarus, effective immediately, after more than 28 years of operations, to local management for an undisclosed amount.

On Mar. 7, 2022, the company announced the acquisition of Colliers Greater Cincinnati and Colliers Cleveland, which were previously affiliate operations. Terms were not disclosed.

Recent Merger and Acquisition Activity

Status: completed **Announced:** May 9, 2023
Colliers International Group Inc., through its Colliers Engineering & Design (CED) division, acquired HILGARTWILSON, LLC, an Arizona-based engineering, planning and survey firm. Terms were not disclosed. The business would rebranded and integrated into CED's operations. HILGARTWILSON employs 200 engineers, licensed surveyors, and other professionals operating from three offices in the Phoenix metropolitan area. Its services provided included civil engineering, surveying, land use planning, construction management, and environmental services.

Status: completed **Announced:** May 2, 2023
Colliers International Group Inc. acquired a controlling interest in Sydney, N.S.W.-based Craig & Rhodes Pty Ltd., a multi-discipline engineering, design and survey firm. Terms of the transaction were not disclosed. Craig & Rhodes has four offices in Australia specializing in surveying, project management, planning, engineering and advisory services for development industries, urban planners, local councils, state governments and agencies in New South Wales, Australian Capital Territory and Victoria, Australia. Craig & Rhodes would rebrand as Colliers Engineering & Design and be integrated into Colliers' existing Australian operations.

Status: completed **Announced:** Apr. 12, 2023
Colliers International Group Inc. acquired a controlling interest in Auckland, New Zealand-based Greenstone Group Limited, a commercial property management firm. Terms of the transaction were not disclosed. Greenstone provides project management and property advisory services to commercial, residential, retail, industrial, government, education and infrastructure sectors across New Zealand. Greenstone would rebrand as Colliers Project Leaders and be integrated into Colliers' existing New Zealand operations.

Status: completed **Revised:** Dec. 2, 2022
UPDATE: The transaction was completed. Pangea would merge with Colliers' existing company-owned operations in Sweden. PREVIOUS: Colliers International Group Inc. agreed to acquire a controlling interest in Pangea Property Partners AS, a capital markets advisor in Sweden and Norway. The terms of the transaction were not disclosed. Pangea would merge with Colliers' existing company-owned operations in Sweden, become the new company-owned operation in Norway, and re-brand as Colliers. Pangea's partners, together with the existing leadership team of Colliers Sweden, would retain a significant equity stake in the combined business.

Status: completed **Revised:** Oct. 12, 2022
UPDATE: The transaction was completed. PREVIOUS: Colliers International Group Inc. agreed to acquire a 75% equity interest in U.S. alternative real asset management firm Versus Capital Advisors LLC for US$356,000,000. Denver, Colo.-based Versus has US$6 billion of assets under management through actively managed, perpetual-life funds. The transaction was expected to close in the fourth quarter of 2022.

Status: completed **Announced:** Oct. 6, 2022
Colliers International Group Inc. acquired a controlling interest in Phoenix, Ariz.-based Arcadia Management Group, Inc., a commercial property management firm focused in southwestern U.S., for US$13,100,000. Arcadia provides property management, property accounting services and project management to over 60,000,000 sq. ft. of office, retail and industrial properties in 24 U.S. states.

Status: completed **Announced:** Aug. 2, 2022
Colliers International Group Inc. acquired a controlling interest in Spring Hill, Qld.-based PEAKURBAN Pty Limited, a civil engineering, infrastructure, water and planning firm, for US$26,648,000. PEAKURBAN has five offices in Australia specializing in planning, due diligence and engineering and design services for residential and mixed-use developments, civil infrastructure, water and wastewater and industrial sectors. PEAKURBAN would rebrand as Colliers Engineering & Design and be integrated into Colliers' existing Australian operations.

Status: completed **Revised:** July 6, 2022
UPDATE: The transaction was completed. PREVIOUS: Colliers International Group Inc. agreed to acquire a 65% interest in New York-based Rockwood Capital, LLC, a U.S. real estate investment management firm with more than US$12 billion of assets under management, for an initial price of US$195,000,000. The transaction was expected to close in the third quarter of 2022.

Status: completed **Revised:** June 2, 2022
UPDATE: The transaction was completed. PREVIOUS: Colliers International Group Inc. agreed to acquire a 75% interest in London, U.K.-based Basalt Infrastructure Partners LLP, a transatlantic infrastructure investment management firm with more than US$8.5 billion of assets under management. Terms were not disclosed. The transaction was expected to close in the second half of 2022.

Status: completed **Revised:** Apr. 4, 2022
UPDATE: The transaction was completed. PREVIOUS: Colliers International Group Inc. agreed to acquire a controlling interest in Colliers International Italia S.p.A., Colliers Real Estate Services Italia S.r.l. and Colliers Real Estate Management Services Italia S.r.l. (collectively, Colliers Italy), which was previously an affiliate operation. Terms of the transaction were not disclosed. The transaction was expected to close by the end of the first quarter of 2022.

Status: completed **Revised:** Apr. 4, 2022
UPDATE: The transaction was completed. PREVIOUS: Colliers International Group Inc. agreed to acquire a controlling interest in Italy-based Antirion SGR S.p.A., a real estate investment management firm with assets throughout Western Europe with more than €3.8 billion of assets under management (AUM). Terms of the transaction were not disclosed. The transaction was subject to customary closing conditions and was expected to be completed by the end of the first quarter of 2022.

Predecessor Detail - Name changed from FirstService Corporation, June 1, 2015, following spin-out of the Residential Real Estate Services and Property Services business segments to (new) FirstService Corporation.

Directors - Jay S. Hennick, chr. & CEO, Toronto, Ont.; John P. (Jack) Curtin Jr.†, Toronto, Ont.; Christopher Galvin, Ill.; P. Jane Gavan, Toronto, Ont.; The Rt. Hon. Stephen J. Harper, Alta.; Katherine M. Lee, Toronto, Ont.; Prof. Poonam Puri, Toronto, Ont.; Benjamin F. Stein, N.Y.; L. Frederick Sutherland, Pa.; Edward J. (Ed) Waitzer, Toronto, Ont.

Other Exec. Officers - Christian Mayer, CFO; Rebecca (Becky) Finley, chief brand & people officer; Robert D. Hemming, sr. v-p & chief acctg. officer; Matthew Hawkins, v-p, legal counsel & corp. sec.; Yanlin Liao, v-p, tax; Gil Borok, pres. & CEO, U.S.A.; Brian Rosen, pres. & CEO, Canada; Lynda Cralli, asst. sec. & mgr., bus.; Davoud (Dav) Amel-Azizpour, CEO, Europe, Middle East & Africa; John Kenny, CEO, Asia Pacific; Chris R. McLernon, CEO, real estate srvcs., global; Christopher Merrill, co-founder, chr. & CEO, Harrison Street; Zachary Michaud, co-chief invest. officer; Elias Mulamoottil, co-chief invest. officer; Scott Nelson, CEO, occupier srvcs. global
† Lead director

Capital Stock

	Authorized (shs.)	Outstanding (shs.)[1]
Preference	unlimited	
Series 1	2,500	nil
7% series 1	unlimited	nil
Multiple Voting	unlimited	1,325,694
Subordinate Voting	unlimited	45,853,682

[1] At Aug. 4, 2023

Multiple Voting - Convertible at any time into subordinate voting shares on a 1-for-1 basis. Twenty votes per share.

Subordinate Voting - One vote per share.

Options - At Dec. 31, 2022, options were outstanding to purchase 3,053,000 subordinate voting shares at a weighted average exercise price of US$94.30 per share with a weighted average remaining contractual life of 3.1 years.

Normal Course Issuer Bid - The company plans to make normal course purchases of up to 4,000,000 subordinate voting shares representing 10% of the public float. The bid commenced on July 20, 2023, and expires on July 19, 2024.

Major Shareholder - Jay S. Hennick held 45.9% interest at Feb. 16, 2023.

Price Range - CIGI/TSX

Year	Volume	High	Low	Close
2022	22,183,855	$200.51	$115.90	$124.38
2021	13,009,820	$190.63	$106.70	$188.38
2020	21,360,898	$122.01	$49.11	$113.28
2019	18,374,546	$103.38	$71.01	$101.10
2018	18,043,422	$109.87	$69.00	$75.29

Recent Close: $150.88

Capital Stock Changes - During 2022, 305,125 subordinate voting shares were issued on exercise of options and 1,426,713 subordinate voting shares were repurchased under a Normal Course Issuer Bid.

Dividends

CIGI com S.V. Ra US$0.30 pa S est. Jan. 12, 2022

Prev. Rate: US$0.10 est. July 8, 2016

Long-Term Debt - Outstanding at Dec. 31, 2022:

Credit facility	US$930,042,000
4% conv. sr. notes due 2025[1]	226,534,000
Sr. notes due to 2031[2]	506,533,000
Other debt due to 2025	1,044,000
Finance lease obligs.	1,480,000
	1,665,633,000
Less: Current portion	1,360,000
	1,664,273,000

[1] Convertible into subordinate voting shares at US$57.81 per share.

[2] Consists of €210,000,000 principal amount of 2.23% senior notes due 2028; US$150,000,000 principal amount of 3.02% senior notes due 2031; and €125,000,000 principal amount of 1.52% senior notes due 2031.

Minimum long-term debt repayments, excluding convertible senior notes, were reported as follows:

2023	US$1,360,000
2024	821,000
2025	242,000
2026	102,000
Thereafter	1,436,574,000

Note - In June 2023, all outstanding US$230,000,000 principal amount of 4% convertible senior subordinated notes due June 1, 2025, were redeemed.

Wholly Owned Subsidiaries

CI Holdings (USA) LLC, Del.
Colliers International EMEA Holdings Ltd., United Kingdom.
Colliers International Holdings Limited, British Virgin Islands.
Colliers International Holdings (USA), Inc., Del.
Colliers International USA, LLC, Del.
Colliers International WA, LLC, Del.
Colliers Investment Management Holdings, Inc., Del.
Colliers Macaulay Nicolls (Cyprus) Limited, Cyprus.
Colliers Macaulay Nicolls Inc., Vancouver, B.C.

Subsidiaries

75% int. in **Harrison Street Real Estate Capital, LLC**, Chicago, Ill.

Investments

Craig & Rhodes Pty Ltd., Australia.
Greenstone Group Limited, Auckland, New Zealand.

Note: The preceding list includes only the major related companies in which interests are held.

Financial Statistics

Periods ended:	12m Dec. 31/22[A]		12m Dec. 31/21[◻A]
	US$000s	%Chg	US$000s
Operating revenue	**4,459,487**	**+9**	**4,089,129**
Cost of sales	2,749,485		2,519,866
General & admin expense	1,096,107		1,022,734
Other operating expense	77,144		532,936
Operating expense	**3,922,736**	**-4**	**4,075,536**
Operating income	**536,751**	**n.m.**	**13,593**
Deprec., depl. & amort.	177,421		145,094
Finance costs, net	48,587		31,819
Investment income	6,677		6,190
Pre-tax income	**289,554**	**n.a.**	**(152,047)**
Income taxes	95,010		85,510
Net income	**194,544**	**n.a.**	**(237,557)**
Net inc. for equity hldrs	**46,253**	**n.a.**	**(390,338)**
Net inc. for non-cont. int	**148,291**	**-3**	**152,781**
Cash & equivalent	173,661		396,745
Accounts receivable	577,879		502,416
Current assets	1,213,426		1,571,007
Long-term investments	52,567		42,160
Fixed assets, net	164,493		144,755
Right-of-use assets	341,623		316,517
Intangibles, net	3,152,489		1,655,336
Total assets	**5,098,177**	**+32**	**3,873,730**
Bank indebtedness	24,286		162,911
Accts. pay. & accr. liabs	1,128,754		1,082,774
Current liabilities	1,341,582		1,537,255
Long-term debt, gross	1,665,633		756,268
Long-term debt, net	1,664,273		754,810
Long-term lease liabilities	322,496		296,633
Shareholders' equity	489,697		581,599
Non-controlling interest	3,677		3,670
Cash from oper. activs	**67,031**	**+132**	**28,890**
Cash from fin. activs	612,917		18,601
Cash from invest. activs	(872,844)		(49,414)
Net cash position	**199,042**	**-56**	**452,271**
Capital expenditures	(228,723)		(89,025)
Capital disposals	137,578		10,080
	US$		US$
Earnings per share*	1.07		(9.09)
Cash flow per share*	1.54		0.67
Cash divd. per share*	0.30		0.20
	shs		shs
No. of shs. o/s*	42,933,156		44,054,744
Avg. no. of shs. o/s*	43,409,265		42,920,089
	%		%
Net profit margin	4.36		(5.81)
Return on equity	8.63		(67.07)
Return on assets	4.34		(6.63)
Foreign sales percent	90		89
No. of employees (FTEs)	18,450		16,780

* M.V. & S.V.

[◻] Restated

[A] Reported in accordance with U.S. GAAP

Latest Results

Periods ended:	6m June 30/23[A]		6m June 30/22[A]
	US$000s	%Chg	US$000s
Operating revenue	2,043,941	-4	2,128,758
Net income	34,094	-61	88,048
Net inc. for equity hldrs	(27,003)	n.a.	11,721
Net inc. for non-cont. int	61,097		76,327
	US$		US$
Earnings per share*	(0.61)		0.27

* M.V. & S.V.

[A] Reported in accordance with U.S. GAAP

Historical Summary
(as originally stated)

Fiscal Year	Oper. Rev.	Net Inc. Bef. Disc.	EPS*
	US$000s	US$000s	US$
2022[A]	4,459,487	194,544	1.07
2021[A]	4,089,129	(237,557)	(9.09)
2020[A]	2,786,857	94,489	1.23
2019[A]	3,045,811	137,585	2.60
2018[A]	2,825,427	128,574	2.49

* M.V. & S.V.

[A] Reported in accordance with U.S. GAAP

C.143 Coloured Ties Capital Inc.

Symbol - TIE **Exchange** - TSX-VEN **CUSIP** - 19682H
Head Office - 10589 Ladner Trunk Rd, Delta, BC, V4G 1K2 **Telephone** - (604) 398-3638 **Toll-free** - (877) 483-7531 **Fax** - (604) 565-3332
Website - www.colouredtiescapital.com
Email - kal@bullruncapital.ca
Investor Relations - Kulwant Malhi (604) 805-4602
Auditors - Reliant CPA PC C.P.A.
Bankers - The Bank of Nova Scotia
Lawyers - McMillan LLP
Transfer Agents - Computershare Trust Company of Canada Inc., Toronto, Ont.

Profile - (B.C. 2020; orig. Alta., 2008 amalg.) Invests primarily in equity and derivative securities of private and public companies in a variety of industries, and has mineral interest in Quebec.

The company's investment portfolio at June 30, 2022:

Type	Fair Value
Private company investments	$1,916,000
Public company investments	8,317,000
	$10,233,000

Also holds Mazerac lithium prospect, 108 claims, 50 km southwest of Val-d'Or, Que.

In August 2022, an agreement to acquire a 1% NSR royalty on the Arnett Creek gold property in Idaho operated by **Revival Gold Inc.** for US$2,500,000 was terminated.

Recent Merger and Acquisition Activity

Status: pending **Announced:** May 9, 2023

First Responder Technologies Inc. entered into an agreement for the reverse takeover acquisition of Quebec Pegmatite Corp. (QPC), a wholly owned subsidiary of Coloured Ties Capital Inc. It is intended that First Responder Shares would be issued to QPC shareholders on a one-for-one basis at a deemed price of $0.42 per First Responder share resulting in the issuance of 11,000,000 First Responder common shares to QPC shareholders. First Responder is expected to change its name to Quebec Pegmatite Holdings Corp. after closing of the transaction. QPC plans to raise up to $1,250,000 via a private placement of shares at $0.25 per QPC share. QPC has two lithium properties in the James Bay and Mazérac regions of Quebec.

Predecessor Detail - Name changed from GrowMax Resources Corp., Nov. 29, 2021; basis 1 new for 10 old shs.

Directors - Kulwant (Kal) Malhi, chr. & CEO, Vancouver, B.C.; Desmond M. (Des) Balakrishnan, Vancouver, B.C.; Christopher R. (Chris) Cooper, Vancouver, B.C.; Bala Reddy Udumala, Vancouver, B.C.

Other Exec. Officers - Zahara (Zara) Kanji, CFO; Sheona Docksteader, corp. sec.

Capital Stock

	Authorized (shs.)	Outstanding (shs.)[1]
Preferred	unlimited	nil
Common	unlimited	17,369,552

[1] At June 12, 2023

Major Shareholder - Rauni Malhi held 12.83% interest at Aug. 12, 2022.

Price Range - TIE/TSX-VEN

Year	Volume	High	Low	Close
2022	7,571,317	$0.62	$0.26	$0.60
2021	3,027,012	$0.60	$0.35	$0.36
2019	4,602,483	$1.30	$0.75	$0.85
2018	11,383,746	$1.90	$0.70	$0.80

Consolidation: 1-for-10 cons. in Nov. 2021

Recent Close: $0.97

Capital Stock Changes - In January 2023, 3,375,000 common shares were repurchased under a Substantial Issuer Bid.

On Nov. 29, 2021, common shares were consolidated on a 1-for-10 basis.

Wholly Owned Subsidiaries

Quebec Pegmatite Corp., Qué.

Subsidiaries

95% int. in **Growmax Agri Corp.**, Alta.

Investments

Algernon Pharmaceuticals Inc., Vancouver, B.C. (see separate coverage)
AuAg Exploration Inc., Vancouver, B.C.
Beyond Medical Technologies Inc., Richmond, B.C. (see separate coverage)
Canaccord Genuity Group Inc., Vancouver, B.C. (see separate coverage)
Canagold Resources Ltd., Vancouver, B.C. (see Survey of Mines)
Cannabix Technologies Inc., Burnaby, B.C. (see separate coverage)
First Responder Technologies Inc., Vancouver, B.C. (see separate coverage)
First Uranium Resources Ltd., Vancouver, B.C. (see Survey of Mines)
Garibaldi Resources Corp., Vancouver, B.C. (see Survey of Mines)
Graphite One Inc., Vancouver, B.C. (see Survey of Mines)
Hempfusion Wellness Inc., Denver, Colo.
Hertz Lithium Corp., Vancouver, B.C.
Intrepid Metals Corp., Vancouver, B.C. (see Survey of Mines)
LQWD Technologies Corp., Vancouver, B.C. (see separate coverage)
Manning Ventures Inc., Vancouver, B.C. (see Survey of Mines)
Maverix Metals Inc., Vancouver, B.C.
Patriot Battery Metals Inc., Vancouver, B.C. (see Survey of Mines)
Quality Green Inc., Hamilton, Ont.
Red Lake Gold Inc., Vancouver, B.C. (see Survey of Mines)
Revival Gold Inc., Toronto, Ont. (see Survey of Mines)
Ride Vision Ltd., Herzliya, Israel.
Southern Energy Corp., Calgary, Alta. (see Survey of Mines)

Financial Statistics

Periods ended:	12m Sept. 30/21[A]		9m Sept. 30/20[oA]
	$000s	%Chg	$000s
Salaries & benefits	126		82
General & admin expense	778		332
Operating expense	**904**	**n.a.**	**414**
Operating income	**(904)**	**n.a.**	**(414)**
Finance income	15		50
Investment income	12		nil
Pre-tax income	**(5,051)**	**n.a.**	**6,697**
Net inc. bef. disc. opers	**(5,051)**	**n.a.**	**6,697**
Income from disc. opers	1,885		(64)
Net income	**(3,166)**	**n.a.**	**6,633**
Net inc. for equity hldrs	**(3,271)**	**n.a.**	**6,634**
Net inc. for non-cont. int	**105**	**n.a.**	**(1)**
Cash & equivalent	14,273		13,506
Current assets	21,944		27,542
Total assets	**21,944**	**-20**	**27,542**
Accts. pay. & accr. liabs	244		128
Current liabilities	244		1,038
Shareholders' equity	21,589		23,649
Non-controlling interest	111		2,855
Cash from oper. activs	**(1,711)**	**n.a.**	**(1,868)**
Cash from fin. activs	1,224		nil
Cash from invest. activs	1,254		(1,220)
Net cash position	**14,273**	**+6**	**13,506**
	$		$
Earns. per sh. bef disc opers*	(0.23)		0.31
Earnings per share*	(0.15)		0.31
Cash flow per share*	(0.08)		(0.09)
	shs		shs
No. of shs. o/s*	23,275,641		21,392,565
Avg. no. of shs. o/s*	21,748,543		21,392,565
	%		%
Net profit margin	n.a.		...
Return on equity	(22.79)		...
Return on assets	(20.41)		...

* Common
[o] Restated
[A] Reported in accordance with IFRS

Latest Results

Periods ended:	9m June 30/22[A]		9m June 30/21[A]
	$000s	%Chg	$000s
Net income	(4,550)	n.a.	(3,854)
Net inc. for equity hldrs	(4,550)	n.a.	(3,798)
Net inc. for non-cont. int	nil		(56)
	$		$
Earnings per share*	(0.20)		(0.20)

* Common
[A] Reported in accordance with IFRS

Historical Summary
(as originally stated)

Fiscal Year	Oper. Rev.	Net Inc. Bef. Disc.	EPS*
	$000s	$000s	$
2021[A]	nil	(5,051)	(0.23)
2020[A1]	nil	6,633	0.30
2019[A]	nil	(6,581)	(0.30)
2018[A]	nil	(54,289)	(2.40)
2017[A]	nil	(8,882)	(0.40)

* Common
[A] Reported in accordance with IFRS
[1] 9 months ended Sept. 30, 2020.
Note: Adjusted throughout for 1-for-10 cons. in Nov. 2021

C.144 Columbia Care Inc.

Symbol - CCHW **Exchange** - NEO **CUSIP** - 197309
Head Office - 680 Fifth Ave, 24th Flr, New York, NY, United States, 10019 **Telephone** - (212) 634-7100
Website - www.columbia.care
Email - levans@col-care.com
Investor Relations - Lee Ann Evans (212) 271-0915
Auditors - Davidson & Company LLP C.A., Vancouver, B.C.
Lawyers - Stikeman Elliott LLP, Toronto, Ont.
Transfer Agents - Odyssey Trust Company, Calgary, Alta.
FP500 Revenue Ranking - 414
Employees - 2,278 at Mar. 23, 2023
Profile - (B.C. 2019; orig. Ont., 2018) A fully-integrated medical and adult use cannabis operator in the U.S.

The company has interests in cultivation, product development, manufacturing, home delivery and dispensary operations, with 125 discrete facilities (at Aug. 14, 2023) that are in various stages of operation and development, consisting of 31 cultivation and manufacturing facilities and 94 dispensaries located in 16 U.S. states (Arizona, California, Colorado, Delaware, Florida, Illinois, Maryland, Massachusetts, New Jersey, New York, Ohio, Pennsylvania, Utah, Virginia, Washington, D.C. and West Virginia). Retail brands include Cannabist, Columbia Care, The Green Solution and Medicine Man. Product brands include Seed & Strain, Triple Seven, Hedy, gLeaf, Classix, Press and Amber and Hedy.

In July 2023, the company sold its facility in downtown Los Angeles, Calif., which consisted of a dispensary and 36,000 sq. ft. of cultivation space, for US$9,000,000. In addition, the company announced a 52-person headcount reduction, primarily from gLeaf corporate redundancy, as well as facility rightsizing and dispositions.

In March 2023, the company agreed to sell its operations in Missouri, which consisted of a 12,630-sq.-ft. manufacturing facility in Columbia and a dispensary in Hermann, for US$7,000,000.

In February 2023, the company sold its 25,486-sq.-ft. cultivation and manufacturing facility in Cidra, Puerto Rico, for an undisclosed amount. Operations in Puerto Rico were suspended in May 2020.

On Jan. 19, 2023, the company announced restructuring initiatives which included the reduction and closure of cultivation operations in six markets, primarily California, Colorado and Pennsylvania; closure of four unprofitable dispensaries in Colorado (3) and California; and elimination of 25% of corporate positions.

During 2022, the company exercised an option to acquire a 24-acre cultivation site in Vineland, N.J., for US$9,750,000.

Also during 2022, the company closed its European operations (effective May 2022), which supplied the company's products in the U.K. and European Union, as well as exited its CBD business.

In November 2021, the company acquired Colorado-based **Futurevision Holdings, Inc.** and **Futurevision 2020, LLC** (dba Medicine Man), a vertically integrated cannabis operator serving the Denver metro area, for US$42,000,000, consisting of US$8,400,000 cash and issuance of 5,840,229 common shares valued at US$33,600,000. Medicine Man's assets include a 35,000-sq.-ft. cultivation facility in Denver and three dispensaries in Aurora, Denver and Thornton. The transaction included an option to acquire **Medicine Man Longmont, LLC**, a dispensary in Longmont, Colo., for US$5,900,000. The option was exercised by the company in August 2022, following the sale of its The Green Solution Longmont location.

In April 2022, the company acquired **VentureForth Holdings, LLC**, operator of a 7,100-sq.-ft. cultivation facility and a dispensary in Washington D.C., for US$26,000,000 cash and issuance of 18,755,082 common shares. The company previously had a management services agreement with VentureForth.

Common delisted from CSE, Aug. 3, 2023.

Recent Merger and Acquisition Activity

Status: terminated **Revised:** July 31, 2023
UPDATE: The transaction was terminated. PREVIOUS: Cresco Labs Inc. agreed to acquire Columbia Care Inc. on the basis of 0.5579 Cresco subordinate voting shares for each Columbia Care common share held, representing total consideration enterprise value of U$2 billion. Columbia Care is a fully-integrated medical and adult use cannabis operator in the U.S. and Europe. The agreement includes a US$65,000,000 termination fee payable to Cresco Labs under certain circumstances. The combined entity would have over 130 retail stores in 18 markets and over US$1.1 billion in annual revenue. The transaction was expected to close in the fourth quarter of 2022. May 16, 2022 - Hart–Scott–Rodino Antitrust Improvements Act waiting period expired. July 8, 2022 - Columbia Care shareholders approved the proposed business combination. July 15, 2022 - Approval from the Supreme Court of British Columbia was received.

Status: terminated **Revised:** July 28, 2023
UPDATE: The transaction was terminated. PREVIOUS: Cresco Labs Inc. and Columbia Care Inc. agreed to sell certain assets in New York, Illinois and Massachusetts to an entity owned and controlled by Sean "Diddy" Combs for up to US$185,000,000, consisting of US$110,000,000 cash and US$45,000,000 of seller notes on closing, with the remainder payable post-closing upon achievement of certain short-term, objective and market-based milestones. The divestiture was required for Cresco to close its previously announced acquisition of Columbia Care. The combination of Cresco and Columbia Care assets to be divested include: retail assets in Brooklyn, Manhattan, New Hartford and Rochester and a production asset in Rochester, all New York; retail assets in Jefferson Park and Villa Park and a production asset in Aurora, all Illinois; and retail assets in Greenfield, Worcester and Leicester and a production asset in Leicester, all Massachusetts. The transaction was expected to close concurrently with Cresco's acquisition of Columbia Care.

Predecessor Detail - Name changed from Canaccord Genuity Growth Corp., Apr. 26, 2019, pursuant to the Qualifying Acquisition of Columbia Care LLC.

Directors - Michael Abbott, chr., N.Y.; Nicholas Vita, CEO, Conn.; Jonathan P. May†, N.Y.; Jeff Clarke, Calif.; Julie Hill, Calif.; James A. C. Kennedy, Md.; Frank Savage, Conn.; Alison Worthington, Calif.

Other Exec. Officers - David Hart, pres. & COO; Derek Watson, CFO; Jesse Channon, chief comml. officer; Guy Hussussian, chief data officer; Dr. Rosemary Mazanet, chief scientific officer; Bryan Olson, chief people & administrative officer; David Sirolly, chief legal officer & gen. counsel
† Lead director

Capital Stock

	Authorized (shs.)	Outstanding (shs.)[1]
Preferred	unlimited	nil
Common	unlimited	396,823,519
Proportionate Voting	unlimited	9,955,661[2]

[1] At June 30, 2023
[2] On an as converted basis.

Preferred - Non-voting.
Common - One vote per share.
Proportionate Voting - Equal in all respects with common shares. Common and proportionate voting shares are treated as if they were a single class. Convertible into common shares on a 100-for-1 basis. One hundred votes per share.

Major Shareholder - Widely held at Mar. 23, 2023.

Price Range - CCHW/NEO

Year	Volume	High	Low	Close
2022	48,243,729	$4.29	$0.92	$0.98
2021	48,785,215	$9.80	$3.53	$3.62
2020	10,445,219	$7.90	$1.79	$7.73
2019	1,318,500	$11.07	$2.61	$3.30

Recent Close: $0.58

Capital Stock Changes - During 2022, common shares were issued as follows: 22,858,845 on vesting of restricted share units, 4,693,780 on conversion of proportionate voting shares, 2,082,589 for acquisitions and 180,000 on exercise of warrants. In addition, 260.37 proportionate voting shares were cancelled.

Wholly Owned Subsidiaries

Columbia Care LLC, New York, N.Y.
- 49.9% int. in **Access Bryant SPC**, Calif.
- 100% int. in **Beacon Holdings, LLC**, Colo.
  - 100% int. in **The Green Solution, LLC**, Denver, Colo.
  - 100% int. in **Infuzionz, LLC**, Colo.
  - 100% int. in **Rocky Mountain Tillage, LLC**, Colo.
- 100% int. in **CCPA Industrial Hemp LLC**, Pa.
- 94.5% int. in **CCUT Pharmacy LLC**, Utah
- 100% int. in **CannAscend Alternative, LLC**, Ohio
- 100% int. in **CannAscend Alternative Logan, LLC**, Ohio
- 100% int. in **Columbia Care CO Inc.**, Colo.
- 100% int. in **Columbia Care DC LLC**, Del.
- 92.75% int. in **Columbia Care Eastern Virginia LLC**, Va.
- 100% int. in **Columbia Care Florida LLC**, Fla.
- 100% int. in **Columbia Care Industrial Hemp LLC**, N.Y.
- 96% int. in **Columbia Care MD LLC**, Md.
- 100% int. in **Columbia Care NY LLC**, N.Y.
- 92.5% int. in **Columbia Care New Jersey LLC**, N.J.
- 100% int. in **Columbia Care OH LLC**, Ohio
- 100% int. in **Columbia Care Pennsylvania LLC**, Pa.
- 100% int. in **Columbia Care UT LLC**, Utah
- 100% int. in **Columbia Care WV Industrial Hemp LLC**, W.Va.
- 100% int. in **Columbia Care WV LLC**, W.Va.
- 100% int. in **Corsa Verde, LLC**, Ohio
- 100% int. in **Curative Health Cultivation LLC**, Ill.
- 100% int. in **Curative Health LLC**, Ill.
- 100% int. in **Focused Health LLC**, Calif.
- 100% int. in **Futurevision, Ltd.**, Colo.
- 100% int. in **Green Leaf Medical, LLC**, Md.
- 100% int. in **The Healing Center of San Diego, Inc.**, Calif.
- 100% int. in **Mission Bay, LLC**, Calif.
- 100% int. in **PHC Facilities, Inc.**, Calif.
- 100% int. in **Patriot Care Corp.**, Mass.
- 100% int. in **Resource Referral Services, Inc.**, Calif.
- 100% int. in **VentureForth LLC**, D.C.
- 100% int. in **The Wellness Earth Energy Dispensary, Inc.**, Calif.

Note: The preceding list includes only the major related companies in which interests are held.

Financial Statistics

Periods ended:	12m Dec. 31/22^A		12m Dec. 31/21^A
	US$000s	%Chg	US$000s
Operating revenue	**511,578**	**+11**	**460,080**
Cost of sales	285,049		249,384
General & admin expense	189,930		170,713
Stock-based compensation	27,930		25,018
Operating expense	**502,909**	**+13**	**445,115**
Operating income	**8,669**	**-42**	**14,965**
Deprec., depl. & amort.	84,788		53,002
Finance costs, net	53,897		30,014
Write-downs/write-offs	(340,121)[1]		(74,328)[2]
Pre-tax income	**(432,694)**	**n.a.**	**(146,714)**
Income taxes	(11,213)		139
Net income	**(421,481)**	**n.a.**	**(146,853)**
Net inc. for equity hldrs	**(416,005)**	**n.a.**	**(143,097)**
Net inc. for non-cont. int	**(5,476)**	**n.a.**	**(3,756)**
Cash & equivalent	48,154		82,198
Inventories	127,905		94,567
Accounts receivable	10,087		18,302
Current assets	237,177		226,439
Long-term investments	775		776
Fixed assets, net	357,993		339,692
Right-of-use assets	219,895		245,541
Intangibles, net	164,539		551,805
Total assets	**994,726**	**-28**	**1,376,512**
Accts. pay. & accr. liabs	88,349		170,961
Current liabilities	203,118		243,997
Long-term debt, gross	329,020		160,901
Long-term debt, net	281,705		159,017
Long-term lease liabilities	224,898		246,272
Shareholders' equity	213,284		571,391
Non-controlling interest	(6,381)		(20,568)
Cash from oper. activs	**(111,401)**	**n.a.**	**(523)**
Cash from fin. activs	153,684		202,437
Cash from invest. activs	(75,327)		(191,350)
Net cash position	**49,489**	**-40**	**82,533**
Capital expenditures	(72,741)		(117,506)
Capital disposals	358		386
	US$		US$
Earnings per share*	(1.06)		(0.42)
Cash flow per share*	(0.28)		(0.00)
	shs		shs
No. of shs. o/s*	401,248,303[3]		376,152,906
Avg. no. of shs. o/s*	392,571,102		338,754,694
	%		%
Net profit margin	(82.39)		(31.92)
Return on equity	(106.03)		(31.35)
Return on assets	(35.55)		(13.54)
Foreign sales percent	100		100
No. of employees (FTEs)	2,505		2,586

* Common

^A Reported in accordance with U.S. GAAP

[1] Includes impairment of US$170,642,000 on goodwill and US$169,479,000 on intangible assets of Green Leaf (primarily Pennsylvania) and Colorado reporting units.

[2] Includes US$72,328,000 goodwill impairment.

[3] Includes proportionate voting shares on an as converted basis.

Latest Results

Periods ended:	6m June 30/23^A		6m June 30/22^A
	US$000s	%Chg	US$000s
Operating revenue	253,779	0	252,658
Net income	(65,609)	n.a.	(82,161)
Net inc. for equity hldrs	(66,203)	n.a.	(80,464)
Net inc. for non-cont. int	594		(1,697)
	US$		US$
Earnings per share*	(0.16)		(0.21)

* Common

^A Reported in accordance with U.S. GAAP

Historical Summary
(as originally stated)

Fiscal Year	Oper. Rev.	Net Inc. Bef. Disc.	EPS*
	US$000s	US$000s	US$
2022^A	511,578	(421,481)	(1.06)
2021^A	460,080	(146,853)	(0.42)
2020^B	179,503	(133,200)	(0.48)
2019^B1	77,459	(106,728)	(0.49)
2018^B2	39,328	(39,660)	n.a.

* Common

^A Reported in accordance with U.S. GAAP

^B Reported in accordance with IFRS

[1] Results reflect the Apr. 26, 2019, Qualifying Acquisition of Columbia Care LLC.

[2] Results for 2018 and prior periods pertain to Columbia Care LLC.

C.145 Comet Industries Ltd.

Symbol - CMU **Exchange** - TSX-VEN **CUSIP** - 200348
Head Office - 1710-1177 Hastings St W, Vancouver, BC, V6E 2K3 **Telephone** - (604) 640-6357 **Fax** - (604) 681-0139
Email - rick_angus@msn.com
Investor Relations - Richard J. Angus (604) 640-6357
Auditors - Manning Elliott LLP C.A., Vancouver, B.C.
Lawyers - Tupper Jonsson & Yeadon, Vancouver, B.C.
Transfer Agents - Computershare Trust Company of Canada Inc.
Profile - (B.C. 1950) Holds commercial property and land and mineral interests in British Columbia.

Owns a two-storey, 8,632-sq.-ft. commercial building in Gastown area of Vancouver; several land parcels in Pender Harbour; and two undeveloped land parcels in Terrace. The company has no plans for development of the Pender Harbour and Terrace lands.

Also holds 40% interest (**Initial Developers Ltd.** 30% and **DVO Industries Ltd.** 30%) in Iron Mask prospect, 77 hectares, southwest of Kamloops; 40% interest in Nelson Island prospect, 87 hectares, Nelson Island; and 10% net profits royalty interest in adjacent Abacus copper-silver prospect, 2,500 hectares. The company amended the official community plan for Iron Mask to allow for an industrial park development consisting of 150 sellable acres of properties in Kamloops.

Predecessor Detail - Name changed from Comet-Krain Mining Corp Ltd., Aug. 1970.

Directors - Michael O'Reilly, pres. & CEO, Kamloops, B.C.; Richard J. Angus, CFO, Vancouver, B.C.; Jesus (Jess) Alfonso, Vancouver, B.C.; Andrew Rennison, Vancouver, B.C.; Burton W. Wiley, Kamloops, B.C.

Other Exec. Officers - Carl R. Jonsson, corp. sec.

Capital Stock

	Authorized (shs.)	Outstanding (shs.)[1]
Common	50,000,000	5,038,995

[1] At July 22, 2022

Major Shareholder - Primex Investments Ltd. held 22.3% interest and Initial Developers Ltd. held 14.88% interest at July 22, 2022.

Price Range - CMU/TSX-VEN

Year	Volume	High	Low	Close
2022	51,001	$4.75	$2.90	$4.40
2021	86,940	$4.00	$2.00	$3.50
2020	101,950	$3.40	$2.60	$2.90
2019	141,100	$3.60	$2.75	$3.50
2018	383,017	$3.60	$2.60	$3.05

Recent Close: $4.00

Investments

26.6% int. in **DVO Industries Ltd.**
35.8% int. in **Initial Developers Limited**, Vancouver, B.C.

Financial Statistics

Periods ended:	12m Jan. 31/22^A		12m Jan. 31/21^A
	$000s	%Chg	$000s
Operating revenue	**425**	**+37**	**310**
Salaries & benefits	61		66
General & admin expense	444		388
Operating expense	**505**	**+11**	**454**
Operating income	**(80)**	**n.a.**	**(144)**
Deprec., depl. & amort.	1		1
Finance costs, gross	30		34
Investment income	(2)		(2)
Write-downs/write-offs	(33)		(17)
Pre-tax income	**360**	**n.a.**	**(68)**
Net income	**360**	**n.a.**	**(68)**
Cash & equivalent	827		312
Accounts receivable	nil		9
Current assets	851		344
Long-term investments	236		237
Fixed assets, net	1,506		1,354
Explor./devel. properties	nil		24
Total assets	**2,652**	**+11**	**2,395**
Bank indebtedness	nil		2
Accts. pay. & accr. liabs	171		229
Current liabilities	217		275
Long-term debt, gross	738		782
Long-term debt, net	692		738
Shareholders' equity	1,742		1,382
Cash from oper. activs	**(41)**	**n.a.**	**(6)**
Cash from fin. activs	(51)		247
Cash from invest. activs	608		nil
Net cash position	**827**	**+166**	**311**
	$		$
Earnings per share*	0.08		(0.01)
Cash flow per share*	(0.01)		(0.00)
	shs		shs
No. of shs. o/s*	4,666,901		4,666,901
Avg. no. of shs. o/s*	4,649,299		4,649,299
	%		%
Net profit margin	84.71		(21.94)
Return on equity	23.05		(5.56)
Return on assets	15.45		(1.49)

* Common

^A Reported in accordance with IFRS

Latest Results

Periods ended:	3m Apr. 30/22^A		3m Apr. 30/21^A
	$000s	%Chg	$000s
Operating revenue	160	+93	83
Net income	63	+62	39
	$		$
Earnings per share*	0.01		0.01

* Common

^A Reported in accordance with IFRS

Historical Summary
(as originally stated)

Fiscal Year	Oper. Rev.	Net Inc. Bef. Disc.	EPS*
	$000s	$000s	$
2022^A	425	360	0.08
2021^A	310	(68)	(0.01)
2020^A	516	50	0.01
2019^A	558	35	0.01
2018^A	525	nil	nil

* Common

^A Reported in accordance with IFRS

C.146 Compass Venture Inc.

Symbol - CVI.P **Exchange** - TSX-VEN **CUSIP** - 20454F
Head Office - #02-07 Hight Street Centre, 1 North Bridge Road, Singapore, Singapore, 179094 **Overseas Tel** - 65-6332-4649 **Overseas Fax** - 65-6265-6615
Email - kmlim@geneoasis.com
Investor Relations - Dr. Kah Meng Lim 65-6842-1142
Auditors - Manning Elliott LLP C.A., Vancouver, B.C.
Transfer Agents - Computershare Trust Company of Canada Inc., Vancouver, B.C.
Profile - (B.C. 2020) Capital Pool Company.
Directors - Dr. Kah Meng Lim, CEO, Singapore, Singapore; Chee Keong (Joshua) Siow, CFO & corp. sec., Singapore, Singapore; Goon Chau (Patricia) Chow, Singapore, Singapore

Capital Stock

	Authorized (shs.)	Outstanding (shs.)[1]
Common	unlimited	10,450,000

[1] At Oct. 20, 2022

Major Shareholder - Goon Chau (Patricia) Chow held 16.27% interest at Oct. 25, 2021.

Price Range - CVI.P/TSX-VEN

Year	Volume	High	Low	Close
2022	194,000	$0.17	$0.08	$0.09
2021	128,040	$0.30	$0.15	$0.17

Recent Close: $0.06

Capital Stock Changes - There were no changes to capital stock during fiscal 2022.

C.147 Composite Alliance Group Inc.

Symbol - CAG **Exchange** - TSX-VEN **CUSIP** - 20459W
Head Office - 800-333 7 Ave SW, Calgary, AB, T2P 2Z1 **Telephone** - (403) 870-7383 **Fax** - (403) 242-7479
Email - dburstall@dsavocats.ca
Investor Relations - V. E. Dale Burstall (403) 264-1915
Auditors - MNP LLP C.A.
Transfer Agents - Olympia Trust Company, Calgary, Alta.
Profile - (Alta. 2008) Designs and manufactures moulding machines and processes for sale to customers in the aerospace and automotive sectors for fabrication of composite components.

Provides composite manufacturing solutions for various processes and for different functions such as preforming, compaction, moulding, unmoulding, transfer/handling/unmolding and completion. Machines are designed and then assembled to meet clients' customary needs and specifications. Services include engineering, automation and robotization, manufacturing optimization, prototyping, commission and after-sales support. Also provides moulding presses, moulds, lay-up equipment and tool products. In, addition, the company distributes **Magnum Venus Products**, which manufactures fluid movement and production solutions for industrial applications in composites and adhesives markets, in Hong Kong and Macau, People's Republic of China.

Predecessor Detail - Name changed from CanAsia Financial Inc., Feb. 15, 2019, pursuant to reverse takeover acquisition of Techni Modul Engineering S.A.; basis 1 new for 5 old shs.

Directors - Sicheng Zhang, chr., Malta; Serge Luquain, pres. & CEO, France; V. E. Dale Burstall, corp. sec., Calgary, Alta.; JianYong (Bill) Cui, Calgary, Alta.; Ronald (Ron) Love, Calgary, Alta.

Other Exec. Officers - Vishwa Mootooveeren, CFO

Capital Stock

	Authorized (shs.)	Outstanding (shs.)[1]
Preferred	unlimited	
Series B		nil
Series C		nil
Series D		19,200,000
Common	unlimited	110,233,610

[1] At May 4, 2023

Series D Preferred - Non-voting.
Common - One vote per share.

Major Shareholder - Sicheng Zhang held 43.3% interest and Serge Luquain held 34.4% interest at June 15, 2021.

Price Range - CAG/TSX-VEN

Year	Volume	High	Low	Close
2022	476,525	$0.06	$0.02	$0.02
2021	740,509	$0.09	$0.04	$0.05
2020	736,356	$0.20	$0.04	$0.05
2019	607,294	$0.30	$0.07	$0.19
2018	1,097,408	$2.50	$0.08	$0.13

Consolidation: 1-for-5 cons. in Feb. 2019
Recent Close: $0.02

Wholly Owned Subsidiaries

Composite Alliance Asia, Hong Kong, People's Republic of China. Inactive.
Techni Modul Engineering S.A., France.
- 100% int. in **Composite Alliance Corp.**, Dallas, Tex.

Financial Statistics

Periods ended:	12m Dec. 31/21[A]		12m Dec. 31/20[A]
	$000s	%Chg	$000s
Operating revenue	**5,887**	**-13**	**6,779**
Cost of sales	2,729		3,770
Salaries & benefits	2,293		2,656
General & admin expense	1,328		1,476
Stock-based compensation	(1,204)		668
Operating expense	**5,146**	**-40**	**8,571**
Operating income	**741**	**n.a.**	**(1,792)**
Deprec., depl. & amort.	960		1,127
Finance costs, gross	228		633
Pre-tax income	**(36)**	**n.a.**	**(3,381)**
Net income	**(36)**	**n.a.**	**(3,381)**
Net inc. for equity hldrs	**(18)**	**n.a.**	**(3,381)**
Net inc. for non-cont. int	**(19)**	**n.a.**	**1**
Cash & equivalent	2,071		2,930
Accounts receivable	5,405		5,241
Current assets	8,315		9,491
Fixed assets, net	561		911
Intangibles, net	984		1,180
Total assets	**10,216**	**-15**	**11,968**
Accts. pay. & accr. liabs	2,910		4,274
Current liabilities	3,814		5,939
Long-term debt, gross	8,002		7,560
Long-term debt, net	7,591		6,407
Long-term lease liabilities	335		471
Equity portion of conv. debs	459		553
Shareholders' equity	(1,824)		(1,606)
Non-controlling interest	nil		(56)
Cash from oper. activs	**(1,416)**	**n.a.**	**774**
Cash from fin. activs	1,408		1,537
Cash from invest. activs	(558)		(166)
Net cash position	**2,071**	**-29**	**2,930**
Capital expenditures	(65)		(94)
	$		$
Earnings per share*	(0.00)		(0.03)
Cash flow per share*	(0.01)		0.01
	shs		shs
No. of shs. o/s*	110,233,610		110,233,610
Avg. no. of shs. o/s*	110,233,610		110,233,610
	%		%
Net profit margin	(0.61)		(49.87)
Return on equity	n.m.		n.m.
Return on assets	1.73		(23.15)

* Cl.A com.
[A] Reported in accordance with IFRS

Latest Results

Periods ended:	6m June 30/22[A]		6m June 30/21[A]
	$000s	%Chg	$000s
Operating revenue	1,573	-40	2,611
Net income	(1,704)	n.a.	267
Net inc. for equity hldrs	(1,704)	n.a.	279
Net inc. for non-cont. int	nil		(12)
	$		$
Earnings per share*	(0.02)		0.00

* Cl.A com.
[A] Reported in accordance with IFRS

Historical Summary
(as originally stated)

Fiscal Year	Oper. Rev. $000s	Net Inc. Bef. Disc. $000s	EPS* $
2021[A]	5,887	(36)	(0.00)
2020[A]	6,779	(3,381)	(0.03)
2019[A1]	14,735	(3,082)	(0.03)
2018[A2]	nil	(574)	(0.03)
2017[A]	nil	(107)	(0.01)

* Cl.A com.
[A] Reported in accordance with IFRS
[1] Results reflect the Feb. 12, 2019, reverse takeover acquisition of Techni Modul Engineering S.A.
[2] Results for 2018 and prior periods pertain to CanAsia Financial Inc.
Note: Adjusted throughout for 1-for-5 cons. in Feb. 2019

C.148 Comprehensive Healthcare Systems Inc.

Symbol - CHS **Exchange -** TSX-VEN **CUSIP -** 204663
Head Office - 2025 Lincoln Hwy, State Rte 27, Suite 340, Edison, NJ, United States, 08817 **Telephone -** (732) 362-2010
Website - www.comphealthcare.com
Email - toni.haugh@comphealthcare.com
Investor Relations - Toni Haugh (914) 573-8859
Auditors - McGovern Hurley LLP C.A., Toronto, Ont.
Transfer Agents - TSX Trust Company, Calgary, Alta.
Profile - (Alta. 2018) Provides healthcare administrative software to unions and insured funds, insurance companies, third party administrators, hospitals, doctors, dentists and practitioners and healthcare consumers.

Operations are conducted through wholly owned subsidiaries: **Health Plan Systems, Inc.** (trade name HPS), a provider of healthcare and benefit administrative software including HPS NOVUS Healthcare Welfare and Benefits Administration (HPS NOVUS) platform; **New York Medical Management Inc.** (trade name Sterling MM), a provider of a comprehensive medical management program that includes pre-certification of services and admissions, concurrent review, retrospective review, case management and disease management; and **Health Plan Systems Services Corporation** (trade name LionGen), a third party administrator that manages different functions of benefits such as: claims processing, utilization review, membership functions; including the processing of retirement plans and flexible spending accounts.

In September 2022, the company agreed to acquire **Benefit Administrators West, LLC**, which provides third party administrator services in the healthcare and benefits industry.

Predecessor Detail - Name changed from Greenstone Capital Corp., Sept. 29, 2021, pursuant to the Qualifying Transaction reverse takeover acquisition of (old) Comprehensive Healthcare Systems Inc.; basis 1 new for 3.53226 old shs.

Directors - Chris Cosgrove, chr., pres. & CEO; Mariam Cather, chief strategy officer & corp. sec., Brooklyn, N.Y.; Amit Durra, India; Dr. Fiona Gupta, New York, N.Y.; Vikas Ranjan, Toronto, Ont.

Other Exec. Officers - Kevin Waters, interim CFO; Marcos Domiciano, chief cust. officer; Toni Haugh, chief mktg. officer; Satish Kurian, CIO; Dr. Mark Lewandowski, chief opers. officer; Patrick Mescall, chief revenue officer; Dr. Hassan Mohaideen, CMO

Capital Stock

	Authorized (shs.)	Outstanding (shs.)[1]
Common	unlimited	104,303,956

[1] At Jan. 30, 2023

Major Shareholder - Dr. Hassan Mohaideen held 25.6% interest and Karan Pal Singh and Himangini Singh held 15.5% interest at Oct. 18, 2021.

Price Range - CHS/TSX-VEN

Year	Volume	High	Low	Close
2022	9,346,508	$0.29	$0.05	$0.09
2021	1,653,413	$0.45	$0.20	$0.23
2020	50,392	$0.35	$0.07	$0.23
2019	91,333	$0.57	$0.18	$0.18

Consolidation: 1-for-3.53226 cons. in Oct. 2021
Recent Close: $0.03

Capital Stock Changes - From October to December 2022, private placement of 34,800,000 units (1 common share & 1 warrant) at Cdn$0.05 per unit was completed, with warrants exercisable at Cdn$0.10 per share for one year and Cdn$0.15 per share in the second year.

In January 2023, private placement of 19,719,546 units (1 common share & 1 warrant) at Cdn$0.05 per unit was completed, with warrants exercisable at Cdn$0.10 per share for one year and Cdn$0.15 per share in the second year.

Wholly Owned Subsidiaries

Comprehensive Healthcare Systems Inc., Edison, N.J.
- 100% int. in **Health Plan Systems, Inc.**, United States. trade name HPS.
- 100% int. in **Health Plan Systems Services Corporation**, United States. trade name LionGen.
- 100% int. in **New York Medical Management Inc.**, United States. trade name Sterling MM.
- 100% int. in **Sterling Health Services Inc.**, United States.

Financial Statistics

Periods ended:	12m Dec. 31/21[A1]		12m Dec. 31/20[A2]
	US$000s	%Chg	US$000s
Operating revenue	**4,496**	**-5**	**4,737**
Cost of sales	3,130		2,668
Research & devel. expense	389		498
General & admin expense	3,335		1,784
Operating expense	**6,854**	**+38**	**4,950**
Operating income	**(2,358)**	**n.a.**	**(213)**
Deprec., depl. & amort.	98		101
Finance income	7		nil
Finance costs, gross	2,108		417
Write-downs/write-offs	(184)		(26)
Pre-tax income	**(4,926)**	**n.a.**	**(221)**
Net income	**(4,926)**	**n.a.**	**(221)**
Cash & equivalent	3,395		2,060
Accounts receivable	195		239
Current assets	3,768		2,319
Fixed assets, net	32		31
Right-of-use assets	306		395
Total assets	**4,106**	**+50**	**2,745**
Accts. pay. & accr. liabs	1,369		1,057
Current liabilities	3,199		5,194
Long-term debt, gross	1,361		2,510
Long-term lease liabilities	304		394
Preferred share equity	nil		77
Shareholders' equity	603		(3,563)
Cash from oper. activs	**(3,271)**	**n.a.**	**(645)**
Cash from fin. activs	4,391		2,706
Cash from invest. activs	215		(5)
Net cash position	**3,395**	**+65**	**2,060**
Capital expenditures	(10)		(5)
	US$		US$
Earnings per share*	(0.16)		n.a.
Cash flow per share*	(0.11)		n.a.
	shs		shs
No. of shs. o/s*	68,303,956		n.a.
Avg. no. of shs. o/s*	30,211,127		n.a.
	%		%
Net profit margin	(109.56)		(4.67)
Return on equity	n.m.		n.m.
Return on assets	(82.27)		11.58

* Common
[A] Reported in accordance with IFRS
[1] Results reflect the Sept. 30, 2021, Qualifying Transaction reverse takeover acquisition of (old) Comprehensive Healthcare Systems Inc.
[2] Results for 2020 and prior periods pertain to (old) Comprehensive Healthcare Systems Inc.

Latest Results

Periods ended:	9m Sept. 30/22[A]		9m Sept. 30/21[oA]
	US$000s	%Chg	US$000s
Operating revenue	3,282	-9	3,594
Net income	(3,216)	n.a.	(2,749)
	US$		US$
Earnings per share*	(0.05)		(0.39)

* Common
[o] Restated
[A] Reported in accordance with IFRS

Historical Summary
(as originally stated)

Fiscal Year	Oper. Rev. US$000s	Net Inc. Bef. Disc. US$000s	EPS* US$
2021[A]	4,496	(4,926)	(0.16)
2020[A]	4,737	(221)	n.a.
2019[A]	4,237	(748)	n.a.

* Common
[A] Reported in accordance with IFRS
Note: Adjusted throughout for 1-for-3.5322575 cons. in Oct. 2021

C.149 Computer Modelling Group Ltd.

Symbol - CMG **Exchange -** TSX **CUSIP -** 205249
Head Office - 3710 33 St NW, Calgary, AB, T2L 2M1 **Telephone -** (403) 531-1300 **Fax -** (403) 289-8502
Website - www.cmgl.ca
Email - sandra.balic@cmgl.ca
Investor Relations - Sandra Balic (403) 531-1300
Auditors - KPMG LLP C.A., Calgary, Alta.
Lawyers - Norton Rose Fulbright Canada LLP, Calgary, Alta.
Transfer Agents - Odyssey Trust Company
Employees - 184 at May 24, 2023
Profile - (Alta. 1996) Develops and licenses advanced process reservoir modelling software and provides professional services for the oil and gas industry worldwide.

Principal products include Builder, a software that gathers and organizes large volume of data, imported from a variety of methods, for the simulator; WinProp, a program that determines the behaviour and properties of reservoir fluids; STARS, a four-phase 3D thermal and chemical processes reservoir simulator used to model recovery from heavy oil, oil sands and chemically stimulated reservoirs; GEM, an Equation-of-State (EoS) compositional reservoir simulator which models primary, secondary and tertiary recovery processes in conventional and unconventional reservoirs as well as CO2 enhanced oil recovery/sequestration and VAPEX gas injection in heavy oil reserves; IMEX, a three-phase, five-component 3D reservoir simulator to model black oil and unconventional reservoirs; iSegWell, an analytical wellbore modelling tool that works with IMEX to simultaneously optimize well design and reservoir productivity by modelling flow and pressure changes from the perforations to the surface; Results, a program that provides visualization and animation for STARS, GEM and IMEX in a variety of formats; CMOST, a program that helps clients perform history matching of measured field performance data, optimize future production or net present value, and assess the risk of making capital and operating expenditures due to the inherent uncertainty of reservoir parameters; and CoFlow, a fully implicit, multi-user and multi-disciplinary Integrated Reservoir and Production System Modelling (IPSM) software which provides a unified solution for integrated asset modelling by combining reservoir, production networks and geomechanics in one environment and allows reservoir and production engineers to make informed decisions on large integrated oil and gas projects.

Professional services provided consist of support, consulting, training and contract research activities. Consulting services include routine and non-routine specialized advanced applications of the company's technology and center around reservoir engineering for field design, production optimization, operation and analysis. Contract research services are provided to address client's specialized needs in the company's reservoir simulators.

Sales and technical support offices are located in Calgary, Alta.; Houston, Tex.; London, U.K.; Bogota, Colombia; Dubai, U.A.E.; and Kuala Lumpur, Malaysia.

In February 2023, the company acquired certain assets of **Unconventional Subsurface Integration LLC** for an undisclosed amount. Under the transaction, the assets included an early-stage patented artificial intelligence (AI)-based data analytics technology targeting the development and optimization of shale reservoirs which has been used commercially in several U.S. basins. The company would assume the ongoing development of the technology.

Directors - Mark R. Miller, chr., Oakville, Ont.; Kenneth M. (Ken) Dedeluk, v-chr., Calgary, Alta.; Pramod Jain, CEO, Calgary, Alta.; Christine M. (Tina) Antony, Calgary, Alta.; Judith J. Athaide, Calgary, Alta.; John E. Billowits, Toronto, Ont.; Christopher L. Fong, Calgary, Alta.; Peter H. Kinash, Calgary, Alta.; Kiren Singh, Canmore, Alta.

Other Exec. Officers - John Mortimer, chief tech. officer; Daniel Edelshaim, head, legal; Krisztina (Kris) Howery, head, mktg.; Rahul Jain, head, bus. opers.; Mohammad Khalaf, head, corp. devel.; Kristina Mysev, head, people & culture; Sandra Balic, v-p, fin. & CFO; Sheldon Harbinson, v-p, Americas; R. David Hicks, v-p, Eastern Hemisphere; Anjani Kumar, v-p, cust. success & cons.; Dr. Long X. Nghiem, v-p, R&D & chief scientist; Kirsten (Kirsty) Sklar, corp. sec.

Capital Stock

	Authorized (shs.)	Outstanding (shs.)[1]
Preferred	unlimited	nil
Non-voting	unlimited	nil
Common	unlimited	80,667,634

[1] At May 24, 2023

Major Shareholder - EdgePoint Investment Group Inc. held 26.71% interest and Burgundy Asset Management Ltd. held 11.82% interest at May 17, 2023.

Price Range - CMG/TSX

Year	Volume	High	Low	Close
2022	17,804,974	$6.16	$4.10	$5.83
2021	25,056,382	$6.74	$3.83	$4.26
2020	28,351,524	$8.48	$3.42	$4.88
2019	31,135,522	$8.79	$5.25	$8.22
2018	26,531,497	$10.44	$5.40	$6.09

Recent Close: $8.27

Capital Stock Changes - During fiscal 2023, common shares were issued as follows: 235,000 on exercise of stock options and 67,000 on exercise of restricted share units.

During fiscal 2022, 49,000 common shares were issued on exercise of restricted share units.

Dividends

CMG com Ra $0.20 pa Q est. June 15, 2020
Prev. Rate: $0.80 est. June 13, 2014

Wholly Owned Subsidiaries

CMG (Europe) Limited, United Kingdom.
CMG Middle East FZ LLC, United Arab Emirates.
CMGL Services Corporation, Alta.
Computer Modelling Group, Inc., Colo.

Financial Statistics

Periods ended:	12m Mar. 31/23[A]		12m Mar. 31/22[A]
	$000s	%Chg	$000s
Operating revenue	**73,846**	**+12**	**66,202**
Research & devel. expense	15,870		13,941
General & admin expense	28,467		21,983
Operating expense	**44,337**	**+23**	**35,924**
Operating income	**29,509**	**-3**	**30,278**
Deprec., depl. & amort.	3,649		4,198
Finance costs, net	(788)		2,059
Pre-tax income	**26,648**	**+11**	**24,021**
Income taxes	6,851		5,616
Net income	**19,797**	**+8**	**18,405**
Cash & equivalent	66,850		59,660
Accounts receivable	23,910		17,507
Current assets	92,264		78,918
Fixed assets, net	10,366		10,908
Right-of-use assets	30,733		33,113
Intangibles, net	1,321		nil
Total assets	**137,128**	**+10**	**125,148**
Accts. pay. & accr. liabs	9,883		6,819
Current liabilities	46,542		38,912
Long-term lease liabilities	36,151		37,962
Shareholders' equity	52,450		46,718
Cash from oper. activs	**25,879**	**-10**	**28,715**
Cash from fin. activs	(16,641)		(17,420)
Cash from invest. activs	(2,048)		(703)
Net cash position	**66,850**	**+12**	**59,660**
Capital expenditures	(708)		(703)
	$		$
Earnings per share*	0.25		0.23
Cash flow per share*	0.32		0.36
Cash divd. per share*	0.20		0.20
	shs		shs
No. of shs. o/s*	80,637,000		80,335,000
Avg. no. of shs. o/s*	80,464,000		80,316,000
	%		%
Net profit margin	26.81		27.80
Return on equity	39.93		40.84
Return on assets	15.10		14.86
Foreign sales percent	71		70
No. of employees (FTEs)	165		175

* Common
[A] Reported in accordance with IFRS

Historical Summary
(as originally stated)

Fiscal Year	Oper. Rev. $000s	Net Inc. Bef. Disc. $000s	EPS* $
2023[A]	73,846	19,797	0.25
2022[A]	66,202	18,405	0.23
2021[A]	67,363	20,190	0.25
2020[A]	75,786	23,485	0.29
2019[A]	74,857	22,135	0.28

* Common
[A] Reported in accordance with IFRS

C.150 Conifex Timber Inc.

Symbol - CFF **Exchange** - TSX **CUSIP** - 207324
Head Office - 980-700 Georgia St W, PO Box 10070, Vancouver, BC, V7Y 1B6 **Telephone** - (604) 216-2949 **Toll-free** - (866) 301-2949 **Fax** - (604) 301-2949
Website - www.conifex.com
Email - trevor.pruden@conifex.com
Investor Relations - Trevor Pruden (604) 216-2949
Auditors - PricewaterhouseCoopers LLP C.A., Vancouver, B.C.
Lawyers - Sangra Moller LLP, Vancouver, B.C.
Transfer Agents - Computershare Trust Company of Canada Inc., Vancouver, B.C.
FP500 Revenue Ranking - 627
Employees - 258 at Dec. 31, 2022

Profile - (Can. 2007) Manufactures and markets softwood forest products, primarily lumber, wood chips and value added lumber finishing, and produces renewable energy in the interior region of British Columbia.

The company operates a two-line sawmill in Mackenzie, B.C., with a total annual production capacity of 240 mmfbm of lumber. Forestry licences are held in and around Mackenzie with an allowable annual cut (AAC) of 632,500 m^3, and through a 50% interest in a joint venture which holds a forest licence with an AAC of 300,000 m^3 in the same area. Lumber products are sold for the construction markets primarily in the U.S., Canada and Japan.

A 36-MW biomass power generation facility is located adjacent to the Mackenzie mill site. Primary feedstock for the facility is sourced from a portion of the residuals and former waste products produced at the company's lumber manufacturing and log harvesting operations. Power produced provides the company's electricity needs at Mackenzie with the balance of the power produced sold to **British Columbia Hydro and Power Authority**.

In April 2023, the company filed a petition in the Supreme Court of British Columbia to seek a judicial review of the Lieutenant Governor In Council of British Columbia's Order in Council 692/2022 (OIC). The OIC directed the British Columbia Utilities Commission to issue orders relieving the **British Columbia Hydro and Power Authority** of its obligation to supply service regarding cryptocurrency mining projects for 18 months. As a result, the OIC effectively paused two of the company's high-performance computing projects with Tsay Key Dene Nation.

Periods ended:	12m Dec. 31/22	12m Dec. 31/21
Lumber prod., mfbm	165,900	184,100
Lumber sales, mfbm	184,900	190,700

Predecessor Detail - Name changed from West Fourth Capital Inc., June 3, 2010, pursuant to Qualifying Transaction reverse takeover acquisition of DTR Wood Acquisitionco Ltd.; basis 1 new for 27.5 old shs.

Directors - Kenneth A. (Ken) Shields, chr. & CEO, Vancouver, B.C.; Michael Costello†, B.C.; Charles P. Miller, Tex.; Janine M. North, B.C.; David E. Roberts, St. Catharines, Ont.

Other Exec. Officers - Andrew McLellan, pres. & COO; Trevor Pruden, CFO

† Lead director

Capital Stock

	Authorized (shs.)	Outstanding (shs.)[1]
Class B Preferred	unlimited	nil
Common	unlimited	39,751,011

[1] At May 16, 2023

Normal Course Issuer Bid - The company plans to make normal course purchases of up to 2,461,754 common shares representing 10% of the public float. The bid commenced on Sept. 1, 2022, and expires on Aug. 31, 2023.

Major Shareholder - Polar Asset Management Partners Inc. held 19.65% interest and Blue Wolf Capital Partners LLC held 14.83% interest at May 16, 2023.

Price Range - CFF/TSX

Year	Volume	High	Low	Close
2022	5,378,586	$2.28	$1.50	$1.65
2021	16,763,926	$2.85	$1.38	$2.07
2020	12,423,991	$1.80	$0.26	$1.43
2019	13,975,809	$2.28	$0.20	$0.70
2018	15,757,677	$6.99	$1.50	$1.71

Recent Close: $1.25

Capital Stock Changes - During 2022, 45,000 common shares were issued under share-based compensation plan and 443,100 common shares were repurchased under a Normal Course Issuer Bid.

Dividends

CFF com Ra $0.20
$0.20◆ Aug. 8/22
Paid in 2023: n.a. 2022: $0.20◆ 2021: n.a.

◆ Special

Wholly Owned Subsidiaries

Conifex Fibre Marketing Inc., B.C.
DTR Wood Acquisitionco Ltd., Vancouver, B.C.
- 100% int. in **Conifex Mackenzie Forest Products Inc.**, B.C.
  - 20.8% int. in **Conifex Power Limited Partnership**, B.C.
- 100% int. in **Conifex Power Inc.**, B.C.
  - 100% int. in **Conifex Power Limited Partnership**, B.C.

Subsidiaries

52.5% int. in **Conifex Power Limited Partnership**, B.C.

Financial Statistics

Periods ended:	12m Dec. 31/22[A]		12m Dec. 31/21[A]
	$000s	%Chg	$000s
Operating revenue	**231,267**	**-8**	**250,533**
Cost of goods sold	148,606		156,457
Salaries & benefits	4,443		3,163
General & admin expense	42,358		41,664
Operating expense	**195,407**	**-3**	**201,283**
Operating income	**35,860**	**-27**	**49,250**
Deprec., depl. & amort.	8,397		10,788
Finance costs, gross	4,326		4,580
Pre-tax income	**33,985**	**-7**	**36,397**
Income taxes	9,493		9,201
Net income	**24,493**	**-10**	**27,195**
Cash & equivalent	8,439		6,354
Inventories	49,218		40,345
Accounts receivable	10,381		8,770
Current assets	93,284		77,741
Long-term investments	29,109		22,648
Fixed assets, net	129,912		125,428
Intangibles, net	4,958		5,016
Total assets	**257,263**	**+11**	**231,462**
Accts. pay. & accr. liabs	17,183		18,762
Current liabilities	34,177		30,398
Long-term debt, gross	56,301		59,384
Long-term debt, net	51,561		54,762
Shareholders' equity	146,267		129,832
Cash from oper. activs	**24,834**	**-7**	**26,736**
Cash from fin. activs	(9,944)		(25,734)
Cash from invest. activs	(12,809)		(5,807)
Net cash position	**8,439**	**+33**	**6,354**
Capital expenditures	(13,526)		(6,401)
Capital disposals	51		40
	$		$
Earnings per share*	0.61		0.60
Cash flow per share*	0.62		0.59
Extra divd. - cash*	0.20		...
	shs		shs
No. of shs. o/s*	39,751,000		40,149,000
Avg. no. of shs. o/s*	40,109,000		45,202,000
	%		%
Net profit margin	10.59		10.85
Return on equity	17.74		22.09
Return on assets	11.30		13.66
Foreign sales percent	71		81
No. of employees (FTEs)	258		287

* Common

[A] Reported in accordance with IFRS

Latest Results

Periods ended:	3m Mar. 31/23[A]		3m Mar. 31/22[A]
	$000s	%Chg	$000s
Operating revenue	39,941	-44	71,821
Net income	(8,058)	n.a.	11,440
	$		$
Earnings per share*	(0.20)		0.28

* Common

[A] Reported in accordance with IFRS

Historical Summary
(as originally stated)

Fiscal Year	Oper. Rev. $000s	Net Inc. Bef. Disc. $000s	EPS* $
2022[A]	231,267	24,493	0.61
2021[A]	250,533	27,195	0.60
2020[A]	128,711	(6,768)	(0.14)
2019[A]	157,404	(30,441)	(0.65)
2018[A]	669,919	(7,054)	(0.19)

* Common

[A] Reported in accordance with IFRS

C.151 Consolidated Firstfund Capital Corp.

Symbol - FFP **Exchange** - TSX-VEN **CUSIP** - 20921F

Head Office - 304-837 Hastings St W, Vancouver, BC, V6C 3N6 **Telephone** - (604) 683-6611 **Fax** - (604) 662-8524

Email - dgrant@firstfund.ca

Investor Relations - W. Douglas Grant (604) 683-6611

Auditors - HLB Cinnamon, Jang, Willoughby & Company C.A., Burnaby, B.C.

Bankers - Bank of Montreal, Vancouver, B.C.

Lawyers - MacNeill Law, Vancouver, B.C.

Transfer Agents - Computershare Trust Company of Canada Inc., Toronto, Ont.

Profile - (Can. 1983) Conducts venture capital activities and develops and manages real estate properties in Washington State.

Holds an investment in **Vitality Products Inc.**, which manufactures, markets and distributes natural health products, including vitamins, minerals and nutritional supplements.

In Washington State, the company manages 18,600 sq. ft. of retail space at Ocean Breezes, 19,400 sq. ft. of retail space at Sandcastle Resort, 10 acres of property to be developed including 2-acre Beachcomber RV Park, a 68-unit condominium totaling 100,000 sq. ft., with 7,600 sq. ft. of retail, and a 160-acre subdivision and commercial development, all in Birch Bay; and 61 acres of commercial property, along Interstate 5, a 6.7-acre RV park and an additional 7.9-acre property, all in Whatcom cty.

Predecessor Detail - Name changed from Firstfund Capital (1986) Corp., Oct. 31, 1988; basis 1 new for 10 old shs.

Directors - Stuart E. Pennington, chr., Blaine, Wash.; W. Douglas Grant, pres. & CEO, Vancouver, B.C.; Cheryl A. Grant, v-p, CFO & corp. sec., Vancouver, B.C.; Bruce J. McDonald, Surrey, B.C.

Capital Stock

	Authorized (shs.)	Outstanding (shs.)[1]
Series B Preference	10,000	4,000[2]
Common	unlimited	6,171,703

[1] At Apr. 24, 2023

[2] Classified as debt.

Series B Preference - Entitled to 6% annual cumulative dividend. Dividend arrears at Dec. 31, 2021, were $69,600. Redeemable and retractable at $10 per share. Convertible into common shares at $5.00 per share. Non-voting.

Common - One vote per share.

Major Shareholder - The estate of William N. Grant held 72.86% interest at Apr. 24, 2023.

Price Range - FFP/TSX-VEN

Year	Volume	High	Low	Close
2022	17,100	$0.28	$0.20	$0.28
2021	34,000	$0.46	$0.35	$0.35
2020	10,585	$0.36	$0.36	$0.36
2019	500	$0.32	$0.32	$0.32
2018	3,600	$0.30	$0.28	$0.30

Recent Close: $0.08

Wholly Owned Subsidiaries

Costar Marketing Corp.

ILP Marketing Ltd.

Investments

16.9% int. in **Vitality Products Inc.**, Vancouver, B.C. (see separate coverage)

Financial Statistics

Periods ended:	12m Dec. 31/21[A]		12m Dec. 31/20[A]
	$000s	%Chg	$000s
Unrealized invest. gain (loss)	(210)		(350)
Total revenue	**105**	**n.a.**	**(19)**
Salaries & benefits	104		129
General & admin. expense	137		132
Operating expense	**241**	**-8**	**261**
Operating income	**(136)**	**n.a.**	**(280)**
Deprec. & amort.	nil		1
Finance costs, gross	5		2
Pre-tax income	**(144)**	**n.a.**	**(285)**
Income taxes	(28)		(61)
Net income	**(115)**	**n.a.**	**(224)**
Cash & equivalent	208		109
Accounts receivable	5		7
Current assets	216		120
Long-term investments	809		1,019
Fixed assets, net	5		6
Total assets	**1,116**	**-7**	**1,202**
Accts. pay. & accr. liabs	76		39
Current liabilities	256		227
Long-term debt, gross	110		107
Shareholders' equity	860		975
Cash from oper. activs	**49**	**-31**	**71**
Cash from fin. activs	50		(40)
Net cash position	**208**	**+91**	**109**
	$		$
Earnings per share*	(0.02)		(0.04)
Cash flow per share*	0.01		0.01
	shs		shs
No. of shs. o/s*	6,171,703		6,171,703
Avg. no. of shs. o/s*	6,171,703		6,171,703
	%		%
Net profit margin	(109.52)		n.m.
Return on equity	(12.53)		(20.61)
Return on assets	(9.57)		(16.59)

* Common

[A] Reported in accordance with IFRS

Latest Results

Periods ended:	3m Mar. 31/22[A]		3m Mar. 31/21[A]
	$000s	%Chg	$000s
Total revenue	(59)	n.a.	1,270
Net income	(125)	n.a.	1,205
	$		$
Earnings per share*	(0.02)		0.19

* Common

[A] Reported in accordance with IFRS

Historical Summary
(as originally stated)

Fiscal Year	Total Rev. $000s	Net Inc. Bef. Disc. $000s	EPS* $
2021[A]	105	(115)	(0.02)
2020[A]	(19)	(224)	(0.04)
2019[A]	(23)	(264)	(0.04)
2018[A]	1,270	891	0.14
2017[A]	495	208	0.03

* Common

[A] Reported in accordance with IFRS

C.152 Constellation Capital Corp.

Symbol - CNST.P **Exchange** - TSX-VEN **CUSIP** - 21036W

Head Office - 202 Garrison Square SW, Calgary, AB, T2T 6B3 **Telephone** - (403) 650-7718

Email - roger.jewett@gmail.com

Investor Relations - Roger M. Jewett (403) 650-7718

Auditors - MNP LLP C.A., Calgary, Alta.

Transfer Agents - Alliance Trust Company, Calgary, Alta.

Profile - (Alta. 2022) Capital Pool Company.

Common listed on TSX-VEN, July 20, 2023.

Directors - Dayton R. Marks, pres. & CEO, Ont.; Roger M. Jewett, CFO & corp. sec., Calgary, Alta.; Chaim D. Goldreich, Toronto, Ont.; Oliver B. Holmes, Abbotsford, B.C.; Robert J. Quinn, Kingwood, Tex.

Capital Stock

	Authorized (shs.)	Outstanding (shs.)[1]
Common	unlimited	12,000,000

[1] At July 20, 2023

Major Shareholder - Dayton R. Marks held 15.83% interest at July 20, 2023.

Recent Close: $0.10

Capital Stock Changes - On July 20, 2023, an initial public offering of 6,800,000 common shares was completed at 10¢ per share.

C.153 Constellation Software Inc.*

Symbol - CSU **Exchange** - TSX **CUSIP** - 21037X

Head Office - 1200-20 Adelaide St E, Toronto, ON, M5C 2T6 **Telephone** - (416) 861-2279 **Fax** - (416) 861-2287

Website - www.csisoftware.com

Email - jbaksh@csisoftware.com

Investor Relations - Jamal Baksh (416) 861-9677

Auditors - KPMG LLP C.A., Toronto, Ont.

Lawyers - McCarthy Tétrault LLP, Toronto, Ont.

Transfer Agents - Computershare Trust Company of Canada Inc., Toronto, Ont.

FP500 Revenue Ranking - 73

Employees - 41,000 at Dec. 31, 2022

Profile - (Ont. 1995) Acquires, manages and builds vertical market software businesses which provide software solutions and services to a select group of public and private sector markets.

Operations are organized into six groups: Volaris, Harris, Topicus.com, Jonas, Perseus (formerly Homebuilder) and Vela.

The **Volaris Operating Group** serves vertical markets primarily in North America, Continental Europe, the U.K., Australia, South America and Africa including agri-food, bio sciences, cultural collections management, education, justice, marine, people transportation, retail, asset management and logistics, communications and media, drinks, financial services, library management, non-profit and rental management.

The **Harris Operating Group** serves vertical markets in North America, Continental Europe, the U.K., and Australia including utilities, public safety and justice, education, healthcare, local and county government and property management.

The **Topicus.com Operating Group** serves vertical markets in North America, Continental Europe and the U.K. including government, real estate, healthcare, automotive, finance, retail and legal.

The **Jonas Operating Group** serves vertical markets in North America, Continental Europe, the U.K., and Australia including hospitality, clubs and resorts, spa and fitness, construction, moving and storage, and payments.

The **Perseus Operating Group** serves vertical markets in North America and the U.K. including homebuilders, dealerships, real estate brokers and agents, pulp and paper, leasing and financing and pharmaceutical manufacturing.

The **Vela Operating Group** serves vertical markets in North America, Continental Europe, the U.K., Australia and South America including mining, oil and gas, aerospace, manufacturing and supply chain, public housing, financial services, travel and retail and dealerships.

The company's head office is located in Toronto, Ont., with offices worldwide including the U.S., Brazil, Italy, Germany, Switzerland, the

U.K., Romania, Denmark, Slovenia, Croatia, France, the Netherlands, Australia, Pakistan, Israel, India, Austria, Sweden, Iceland, New Zealand, South Africa, Poland, Portugal and Spain.

On May 16, 2023, the company, through its Perseus operating group, completed the acquisition of **Winklevoss Technologies, LLC**, a provider of defined benefit pension plan valuation and administration software. Terms were not disclosed.

On Feb. 23, 2023, all of the company's shareholders of record Feb. 16, 2023, received a dividend-in-kind of 3.0003833 subordinate voting shares of **Lumine Group Inc.** for each common share of the company held. This resulted to a distribution of 63,582,706 subordinate voting shares, with a remaining six subordinate voting shares retained by the company. The company also received 63,582,712 non-voting preferred shares and 1 super voting share of Lumine Group. As a result, held 50.1% of the votes attached to all outstanding voting shares and an indirect 60.05% ownership interest in the Lumine Group on a fully-diluted basis. Lumine Group holds a global portfolio of 22 communications and media software companies, including **WideOrbit Inc.** Trading of the subordinate voting shares of Lumine Group on the TSX Venture Exchange commenced Mar. 24, 2023.

During 2022, the company completed a number of acquisitions for total cash consideration of US$1.633 billion plus cash holdbacks of US$189,000,000 and contingent consideration with an estimated fair value of US$53,000,000. More than 50% of the total businesses acquired were acquisitions of shares and the remainder were asset acquisitions.

In June 2022, Lumine Group, a division of Volaris Group, acquired TOMIA, a provider of global connectivity monetization solutions. Terms were not disclosed.

In March 2022, the company, through indirect wholly owned **Aquila Software Inc.**, acquired **Lead Envy, LLC**, a fintech provider offering underwriting and decisioning software solutions in the consumer lending industry. Terms were not disclosed.

Recent Merger and Acquisition Activity

Status: completed **Revised:** Feb. 22, 2023
UPDATE: The transaction was completed. PREVIOUS: Constellation Software Inc. agreed to acquire San Francisco, Calif.-based WideOrbit Inc., which develops sales, traffic, billing and broadcast automation software for media companies. Upon completion, WideOrbit would merge with Constellation's subsidiary Lumine Group Inc., which would then be spun off into a separate business, with Constellation retaining a majority shareholding, but would distribute a dividend-in-kind, nominal value subordinate voting shares of Lumine Group to shareholders. The purchase price would include an undisclosed cash payment and the issuance of a 14% interest in Lumine Group. WideOrbit's annual gross revenues were US$167,000,000. The transaction was expected to be completed in the first quarter of 2023. Feb. 6, 2023 - Constellation filed a final prospectus for the proposed spin-out of Lumine Group and it would pay a special dividend-in-kind of subordinate voting shares of Lumine Group to Constellation shareholders on or about Feb. 23, 2023, on a 3.0003833-for-1 basis to shareholders of record on Feb. 16, 2023.

Status: completed **Revised:** Nov. 10, 2022
UPDATE: The transaction was completed. PREVIOUS: Constellation Software Inc., through wholly owned N. Harris Computer Corp., agreed to acquire NexJ Systems Inc. for Cdn$0.55 cash per share, in a transaction valued at Cdn$12,000,000. NexJ provides intelligent customer management software solutions to the financial services industry which improve productivity and client engagement with users in more than 60 countries. The transaction was expected to be completed in the fourth quarter of 2022.

Status: completed **Announced:** July 6, 2022
Modaxo Inc. acquired private Atlanta, Ga.-based Routematch Software, LLC from Uber Technologies, Inc. for an undisclosed amount. Routematch develops applications that provide trip planning, vehicle tracking, payment and other tools for fixed route transit and paratransit services. Routematch serves more than 350 transit agencies across North America and Australia, helping them to transform rider experiences and manage operational costs. Routematch would become part of Modaxo's TripSpark solution offering.

Status: completed **Revised:** May 2, 2022
UPDATE: The transaction was completed. PREVIOUS: Constellation Software Inc., through its Harris operating group, acquired the net assets of Allscripts Healthcare Solutions, Inc.'s Hospitals and Large Physician Practices business, which serves prestigious medical groups and hospitals in the U.S. and internationally, for US$700,000,000 cash including a contingent consideration of up to US$30,000,000 based on performance of the business during two years after the transaction. The acquisition included Sunrise™, a comprehensive platform of health for hospitals and health systems; Paragon®, an integrated clinical, financial and administrative electronic health records (EHR) solution; Allscripts TouchWorks®, an EHR solution for larger single and multispecialty practices; Allscripts® Opal, an electronic document management solution; and dbMotion™ solutions, an EHR-agnostic, flexible and interoperable platform. Allscripts' Hospitals and Large Physician Practices business gross revenue for the period ended Dec. 31, 2021 was US$928,000,000. The assets of Allscripts' Veradigm business segment, which offers payer and life sciences solutions to coordinated community care organizations, health plans and payors, life sciences companies and small to mid-size physician practices, are not included in this transaction and would continue to be owned by Allscripts. The transaction was expected to close during the second quarter of 2022.

Status: completed **Announced:** Mar. 3, 2022
Modaxo Inc. acquired Ramat HaSharon, Israel-based Pcentra Limited for an undisclosed amount. Pcentra provides cloud-based smart ticketing platform which enables passengers to purchase tickets online, on mobile device or through an extensive point-of-sale network.

Directors - Mark Leonard, founder & pres., Toronto, Ont.; John E. Billowits, chr., Toronto, Ont.; Mark R. Miller, COO, CEO, Volaris operating grp. & CEO, Trapeze operating grp., Oakville, Ont.; Barry Symons, CEO, Jonas operating grp., Toronto, Ont.; Jeff Bender, Ottawa, Ont.; Susan S. Gayner, Richmond, Va.; Claire M. C. Kennedy, Toronto, Ont.; Robert T. Kittel, Toronto, Ont.; Lori M. O'Neill, Ottawa, Ont.; Donna Parr, Toronto, Ont.; Andrew Pastor, Toronto, Ont.; Laurie Schultz, Vancouver, B.C.; Robin Van Poelje, Netherlands

Other Exec. Officers - Jamal Baksh, CFO; Bernard Anzarouth, chief invest. officer; Farley Noble, sr. v-p, large acq. grp.; Mark Dennison, gen. counsel & corp. sec.; Daniel Zinman, pres., Perseus operating grp.; Damian McKay, CEO, Vela software grp.

Capital Stock

	Authorized (shs.)	Outstanding (shs.)[1]
Preferred	unlimited	nil
Common	unlimited	21,191,530

[1] At May 15, 2023

Major Shareholder - Widely held at Mar. 27, 2023.

Price Range - CSU/TSX

Year	Volume	High	Low	Close
2022	8,394,635	$2,380.99	$1,783.98	$2,113.96
2021	8,065,991	$2,385.80	$1,530.35	$2,346.94
2020	12,631,864	$1,789.63	$1,076.34	$1,652.92
2019	11,161,179	$1,440.86	$824.81	$1,261.16
2018	11,539,781	$1,134.30	$722.44	$873.86

Recent Close: $2,723.35

Capital Stock Changes - There were no changes to capital stock from 2013 to 2022, inclusive.

Dividends

CSU com Ra US$4.00 pa Q est. Apr. 2, 2012
stk.[1]◆ Jan. 4/21
Paid in 2023: US$4.00 + stk. 2022: US$4.00 2021: US$4.00 + stk.◆

[1] Stk. divd. of 1.8598178 Topicus.com Inc sub vtg shs. for ea. 1 sh. held.
◆ Special

Long-Term Debt - Outstanding at Dec. 31, 2022:

Revolving credit facility due 2026[1]	US$321,000,000
Term loan	78,000,000
Debs. due 2040[2]	208,000,000
Debt without recourse to the co.[3]	902,000,000
	1,509,000,000
Less: Current portion	637,000,000
	872,000,000

[1] Bears variable interest rate calculated at standard United States and Canadian reference rates plus interest rate spreads based on a leverage table.

[2] The rate from Mar. 31, 2022, to Mar. 30, 2023 is 9.9%. Thereafter, the interest rate will be reset on March 31 of each year at a rate equal to the annual average percentage change in the All-items Consumer Price Index during the prior calendar year plus 6.5%, subject to a minimum interest rate of 0%. Redeemable on March 31 in the year that is five years following the year in which notice is given, at principal plus accrued and unpaid interest.

[3] Includes term debt facilities and revolving credit facilities of the company's subsidiaries that the company does not guarantee. The credit facilities typically bear interest at a rate calculated using an interest rate index plus a margin.

Note - The interest rate on the debentures would be reset on Mar. 31, 2023, to 13.3% from 9.9%.

Wholly Owned Subsidiaries

A&W Software GmbH, Germany.
ACCEO Solutions Inc., Montréal, Qué.
AEP Ticketing Solutions s.r.l., Italy.
AMT-Sybex Limited, United Kingdom.
AMT-Sybex (Software) Limited, Ireland.
ASA Automotive Systems Inc., Del.
ASC Automotive Solutions Center Schweiz AG, Switzerland.
Acceo Solutions Limited, United Kingdom.
Acceo Solutions, LP, Ont.
Acceo Technologies Inc., Canada.
Accovia France S.A.R.L., France.
acQuire Technology Solutions Pty Ltd, Australia.
Across Systems GmbH, Germany.
Adpat IT (Pty) Ltd., South Africa.
Advanced Management Systems Limited, New Zealand.
Aislelabs Inc., Ont.
AixConcept GmbH, Germany.
Akuiteo S.A.S., France.
Allscript Healthcare IT (Singapore) Pte. Ltd., Singapore.
Allscripts Healthcare (Australia) Pty Ltd., Australia.
Allscripts Healthcare (IT) UK Ltd., United Kingdom.
Allscripts (India) LLP, India.
The Alpha School System Pty Ltd., Australia.
Altera Digital Health Inc., Del.
Apdata Do Brasil Software Ltda., Brazil.
Apparel 21 Pty Ltd., Australia.
Application Oriented Designs Inc., Fla.
Asesorias Computacionales NeoSoft S.p.A., Chile.
Asset InterTech, Inc., Tex.
AssetWorks LLC, Del.
Atex Global Media S.A.R.L., France.
Atex Media Command AB, Sweden.
Atex Media Limited, United Kingdom.
Atex Pty Ltd., Australia.
Aurum Software Ltda., Brazil.
Automatic Netware Limited, Ireland.
BBT Software AG, Switzerland.
Baseplan North America, Inc., Del.
Baseplan Software Pty Ltd., Australia.
Bibliocommons Corp., Calif.
Binary System S.r.l., Italy.
Bizmatics, Inc., Calif.
Bluestar Software Limited, United Kingdom.
Bravura Security Inc., Alta.
C Systems Software Inc., Tex.
CAE Datamine Peru S.A., Peru.
CAKE Software Inc., Del.
CCSI, Global Inc., Ill.
CPR Vision Management Pte. Ltd., Singapore.
CRB Solutions Limited, United Kingdom.
CSI USA Inc., Del.
Capital Computer Associates, Inc., N.Y.
Capitol Appraisal Group, LLC, Tex.
Caretracker Inc., Del.
Catertrax Inc., Del.
Charity Dynamics, Inc., Del.
Charter Software Solutions Inc., Del.
Clinical Computer Systems, Inc., Ill.
Clinical Computing Inc., Ohio
Cogsdale Corporation, Charlottetown, P.E.I.
Commerce Decisions Limited, United Kingdom.
Common CENTS Solutions, Inc., Jackson, Miss.
Compusense Inc., Ohio
Computer Engineering Inc., Mo.
Computer Software Innovations, Inc., Del.
Computrition, Inc., Chatsworth, Calif.
Connecture Inc., Del.
Constellation Canadian Holdings Inc., Ont.
Constellation Enterprise Online Inc., Del.
Constellation Homebuilder Systems Inc., Del.
Constellation Hungary Financing Kft., Cyprus.
Constellation Mortgage Solutions, Inc., Del.
Constellation Netherlands Financing B.V., Netherlands.
Constellation R.O. Writer Inc., Del.
Constellation Software Australia Pty Ltd, Australia.
Constellation Software Cyprus Financing Ltd., Cyprus.
Constellation Software UK Holdco Ltd., United Kingdom.
Constellation Web Solutions Inc., Del.
Contour Software (Private) Limited, Pakistan.
Courtview Justice Solutions Inc., Del.
Creditron Canada, Inc., Ont.
CrescentOne, Inc., Del.
Criterions Software, Inc., Del.
Cultura Technologies Ltd., United Kingdom.
Cultura Technologies LLC, Del.
Cunningham Cash Registers Limited, United Kingdom.
Datamine Africa (Pty) Limited, South Africa.
Datamine Australia Pty Ltd., Australia.
Datamine Brasil Solucoes em Technologia Ltda., Brazil.
Datamine Corporate Limited, Beds., United Kingdom.
Datamine International Limited, United Kingdom.
Datapro, Inc., Fla.
dbMotion Ltd., Israel.
Dealer Information Systems Corporation, Wash.
Decideware, Inc., Calif.
Delta Computer Systems Inc., Miss.
DestinationRx, Inc., Del.
Diamond Touch Inc., Tex.
Digichart, Inc., Del.
Dynatouch Corporation, Tex.
EZ Facility Inc., Del.
Easit, AB, Sweden.
Emphasys Computer Solutions, Inc., Mich.
EnvisionWare Inc., Georgia.
eScholar LLC, N.Y.
Eureka Technology S.A.S., France.
Everwin Groupe SAS, France.
Everwin Holdings SAS, France.
Everwin SAS, France.
FACTON Gmbh, Germany.
FACTON Inc., Del.
FacilityForce, Inc., Del.
Financial Risk Solutions Limited, Ireland.
First Pacific Corporation, Ore.
Four J's Development Tools Europe Limited, Ireland.
Four J's Development Tools Inc., Wash.
Freestyle Software Inc., Del.
Friedman Corporation, Ill.
Friedman Software Canada Inc., Ont.
Future Business Systems Pty Ltd., Australia.
G1440 Inc., Del.
GXC S.A., Uruguay.
Gallery Systems Inc., N.Y.
Gary Jonas Computing Ltd., Ont.
Gateway Electronic Medical Management Systems Inc., Del.
Gladstone Limited, United Kingdom.
Gladstone MRM Limited, United Kingdom.
Global Outsource Services, LLC, Fla.
Globys, Inc., Del.
Greycon Limited, United Kingdom.

Greycon North America Inc., Ala.
Grosvenor Systems Limited, United Kingdom.
Gtechna USA Corporation, Del.
Halcom d.d., Slovenia.
Happen Business Pty Ltd., Australia.
Harris Computer Germany Gmbh, Germany.
Harris Local Government Solutions Inc., Del.
Harris Systems USA Inc., Del.
Harris (US) Computer Corporation, Del.
Helm Operations Software Inc., Ont.
Holocentric Pty Ltd., Australia.
Hospedia Limited, United Kingdom.
IDS Software Inc., N.C.
IGEA d.o.o., Croatia.
I.M.D. Parent Ltd., Israel.
I.M.D. Soft Inc., Nev.
I.M.D. Soft Ltd., Israel.
IMDSoft GmbH, Germany.
IN2 d.o.o., Croatia.
ITS Computing Limited, United Kingdom.
Iatric Systems, Inc., Del.
Ibcos Holding Limited, United Kingdom.
Icorp S.A., Uruguay.
Ideal Computer Systems Inc., Iowa
Imperial Civil Enforcement Solutions Limited, United Kingdom.
Impos Solutions International Pty Ltd., Australia.
IN2data d.o.o., Croatia.
incadea (Beijing) Information and Technology Co. Ltd., People's Republic of China.
Incadea GmbH, Germany.
Incom S.A.S., France.
Independent Solutions Pty Ltd., Australia.
Ineo Financial Solutions, LLC, Colo.
Ineo Intermediate Holdings LLC, Del.
Ineo LLC, Colo.
Ineo Management, LLC, Fla.
Ineo Tax Services, LLC, Conn.
Infinity Software Inc., Del.
Infocon Corporation, Pa.
Infogate AG, Switzerland.
Ingenious Med, Inc., Georgia.
Innosoft Canada Inc., Ont.
InReach LLC, Del.
Intellicence Inc., Del.
Intempo Software Inc., Del.
InterAct911 Corporation, Del.
Intranote A/S, Denmark.
JR3 Websmart, LLC, Tex.
Jobillico, Inc., Qué.
Jonas Collection and Recovery Inc., Del.
Jonas Computing (UK) Ltd., United Kingdom.
Jonas Fitness Inc., Del.
Jonas Holdings LLC, Del.
Jonas Software NZ Limited, New Zealand.
Jonas Software USA LLC, Del.
Juniper Consulting, S.L., Spain.
Juniper Technologies Corporation, Fla.
Just Associates Inc., Colo.
K2 Medical Systems Holding Limited, United Kingdom.
K2 Medical Systems Limited, United Kingdom.
Kestral Computing Pty Limited, Australia.
Kinetic Solutions Limited, United Kingdom.
Kitomba Australia Pty Ltd., Australia.
Kurier Tecnologia Em Informacao S.A., Brazil.
Lean Software Services, Inc., Ont.
Logan Systems, Inc., Mich.
London & Zurich Limited, United Kingdom.
MCR Systems Limited, United Kingdom.
Magalink S.A., Uruguay.
Magic Pulse Ltd., New Zealand.
Majiq Inc., Del.
Manatron, Inc., Del.
Markinson Business Solutions Pty Ltd., Australia.
Markinson Services Pty Ltd., Australia.
Markinson Software Solutions Pty Ltd., Australia.
Medaptus Solutions Inc., Del.
MEDfx Corporation, R.I.
Media-X Systems, Inc., Canada.
Medisolution (2009) Inc., Canada.
Megabus Software Pty Ltd., Australia.
Metafile Information Systems Limited, Minn.
Metech Holding Pty Ltd., Australia.
Micros South Africa (Pty) Ltd., South Africa.
Mid America Computer Corporation, Neb.
Mitchell & McCormick Inc., Ga.
Monteiro Braga Informatica Ltda., Brazil.
Morcare, LLC, Ill.
Motiondata Vector Deutschland Gmbh, Germany.
Motiondata Vector Schweiz Gmbh, Switzerland.
Motiondata Vector Software Gmbh, Austria.
N. Harris Computer Corporation, Ottawa, Ont.
NedGraphics Inc., Del.
Nedsense Nedgraphics B.V., Netherlands.
New Ultimate Billing, LLC, N.Y.
Northpointe Inc., Del.
Novatech AS, Norway.
Onhand Schools, Inc., Pa.
Optitex Ltd., Israel.
PG Govern Inc., Qué.
PG Solutions Inc., Canada.
POMS Corporation, Del.
PT Datamine Software Indonesia, Indonesia.
Pcentra Limited, Israel.
Perseus Group Software Corp., Ont.
Petrosys Pty Ltd., Australia.
Picis Clinical Solutions Inc., Del.
PLANit Sweden AB, Sweden.
Policy Processing Systems Technology Corporation, Del.
Polopoly AB, Sweden.
Portfolio+ Incorporated, Ont.
Privredno drustvo Halcom AD, Serbia.
Proenco AS, Norway.
ProShip Inc., Del.
ProSoft Technologies, Inc., Pa.
QuadraMed Canada Corporation, N.S.
QuadraMed Corporation, Del.
Quantitative Medical Systems, Inc., United States.
Quintessential School Systems, Calif.
RayenSalud S.p.A., Chile.
Reprise Software, Inc., Del.
Resolve Software Group Pty Ltd., Australia.
ReverseVision, Inc., Del.
Ricardo Simulation Inc., Mich.
Routematch Software, LLC, Atlanta, Ga.
SIV Bulgaria EOOD, Bulgaria.
SIV - Service für Informationsverarbeitung Aktiengesellschaft, Germany.
SIV Utility Service Gmbh, Germany.
SMS Software Holdings LLC, Del.
SSP Asia Pacific Pty Limited, Australia.
SSP Holdings Limited, United Kingdom.
SSP Midco 2 Limited, United Kingdom.
Saatmann GmbH & Co. KG, Germany.
Salar Inc., Md.
Salon Software Solutions Limited, United Kingdom.
Sansio Inc., Del.
Selectapension (2013) Limited, United Kingdom.
Selectapension Limited, United Kingdom.
Shipnet Asia Pte Ltd., Singapore.
Shipnet USA, Inc., Del.
Shortcuts Software Inc., Del.
Shortcuts Software Pty Limited, Australia.
Shortcuts Software (UK) Limited, United Kingdom.
SmartCOP Inc., Fla.
Smartrak Australia Pty Ltd., Australia.
Smartrak Limited, New Zealand.
Smartrak Systems Limited, New Zealand.
La Société Informatique de Gestion Maintenance Assistance, France.
Softlink Australia Pty Ltd., Australia.
Software Company AMIC GmbH, Germany.
Software Solutions Partners Africa (Propreitary) Limited, South Africa.
SpecTec Group Holding Limited, Cyprus.
SpecTec Group Holdings Limited, Cyprus.
SpecTec Ltd., United Kingdom.
SpecTec S.p.A., Italy.
Sympro, Inc., Oakland, Calif.
Syscon Justice Systems Canada Ltd., Richmond, B.C.
Systems & Software Incorporated, Vt.
Systemtechnik Gmbh, Germany.
TAC 10 Inc., Iowa
TPF Software Inc., N.J.
TTG Technology (Europe) Limited, United Kingdom.
Taranto Systems Limited, United Kingdom.
Tecplot Inc., Wash.
Tensibur S.A., Uruguay.
Tibersoft Technologies Inc., Del.
Top Producer Software Corp., Ont.
Trapeze-Elgeba GmbH, Germany.
Trapeze Germany GmbH, Germany.
Trapeze Group Asia Pacific Pty Ltd., Australia.
Trapeze Group Singapore Ltd., Singapore.
Trapeze Group (UK) Limited, United Kingdom.
Trapeze Software Group Inc., Del.
Trapeze Software ULC, Alta.
Trapeze Switzerland GmbH, Switzerland.
Travis Software Inc., Del.
Tribute Inc., Ohio
Tune, Inc., Del.
Unique Business Systems Corporation, Calif.
Uniware Systems Limited, United Kingdom.
Varsity Logistics, Inc., San Francisco, Calif.
Vela Netherlands Holding B.V., Netherlands.
Vela Software International Inc., Ont.
Vela Software Ireland Limited, Ireland.
Volaris Brasil Tecnologia Ltda., Brazil.
Volaris Group Inc., Mississauga, Ont.
WiFiSPARK Limited, United Kingdom.
Wellington Computer Systems Limited, Ireland.
Windward Software Systems Inc., B.C.
Winklevoss Technologies, LLC
Wynne Systems, Inc., Calif.
XN Leisure Systems Limited, United Kingdom.
Youbill Inc., Jenkintown, Pa.
Z57, Inc., Calif.
Zurple, Inc., Del.

Subsidiaries

65.97% int. in **AdaptIT Holdings Limited**, South Africa.
60% int. in **Constellation Software Japan Inc.**, Japan.

Investments

Lumine Group Inc., Mississauga, Ont. Owns 100% of the super voting shares and nominal subordinate voting shares. Total voting interest is 50.10%. (see separate coverage)

48.13% int. in **Topicus.com Inc.**, Toronto, Ont. Owns 100% of the super voting shares and 48.13% of the subordinate voting shares. Total voting interest is 74.12%. (see separate coverage)

Financial Statistics

Periods ended:	12m Dec. 31/22[A]		12m Dec. 31/21[A]
	US$000s	%Chg	US$000s
Operating revenue	**6,622,000**	**+30**	**5,106,000**
Salaries & benefits	3,539,000		2,695,000
General & admin expense	1,384,000		899,000
Operating expense	**4,923,000**	**+37**	**3,594,000**
Operating income	**1,699,000**	**+12**	**1,512,000**
Deprec., depl. & amort.	819,000		639,000
Finance income	nil		6,000
Finance costs, gross	110,000		68,000
Investment income	nil		1,000
Pre-tax income	**725,000**	**+94**	**374,000**
Income taxes	174,000		205,000
Net income	**551,000**	**+226**	**169,000**
Net inc. for equity hldrs	**512,000**	**+65**	**310,000**
Net inc. for non-cont. int	**39,000**	**n.a.**	**(141,000)**
Cash & equivalent	811,000		763,000
Inventories	48,000		35,000
Accounts receivable	876,000		600,000
Current assets	2,461,000		1,835,000
Long-term investments	3,000		2,000
Fixed assets, net	128,000		93,000
Right-of-use assets	283,000		245,000
Intangibles, net	4,679,000		3,428,000
Total assets	**7,882,000**	**+37**	**5,766,000**
Accts. pay. & accr. liabs	1,080,000		832,000
Current liabilities	3,768,000		2,461,000
Long-term debt, gross	1,509,000		723,000
Long-term debt, net	872,000		663,000
Long-term lease liabilities	217,000		190,000
Shareholders' equity	1,712,000		1,061,000
Non-controlling interest	221,000		460,000
Cash from oper. activs	**1,297,000**	**0**	**1,300,000**
Cash from fin. activs	483,000		(41,000)
Cash from invest. activs	(1,694,000)		(1,238,000)
Net cash position	**811,000**	**+6**	**763,000**
Capital expenditures	(41,000)		(29,000)
	US$		US$
Earnings per share*	24.18		14.65
Cash flow per share*	61.20		61.35
Cash divd. per share*	4.00		4.00
	shs		shs
No. of shs. o/s*	21,191,530		21,191,530
Avg. no. of shs. o/s*	21,191,530		21,191,530
	%		%
Net profit margin	8.32		3.31
Return on equity	36.93		29.40
Return on assets	9.30		3.94
Foreign sales percent	90		89
No. of employees (FTEs)	41,000		32,000

* Common
[A] Reported in accordance with IFRS

Latest Results

Periods ended:	3m Mar. 31/23[A]		3m Mar. 31/22[A]
	US$000s	%Chg	US$000s
Operating revenue	1,919,000	+34	1,431,000
Net income	(83,000)	n.a.	111,000
Net inc. for equity hldrs	94,000	-4	98,000
Net inc. for non-cont. int	(177,000)		13,000
	US$		US$
Earnings per share*	4.44		4.63

* Common
[A] Reported in accordance with IFRS

Historical Summary
(as originally stated)

Fiscal Year	Oper. Rev. US$000s	Net Inc. Bef. Disc. US$000s	EPS* US$
2022^A	6,622,000	551,000	24.18
2021^A	5,106,000	169,000	14.65
2020^A	3,969,000	436,000	20.59
2019^A	3,490,000	333,000	15.73
2018^A	3,060,100	379,300	17.90

* Common
^A Reported in accordance with IFRS

C.154 Contagious Gaming Inc.

Symbol - CNS **Exchange** - TSX-VEN **CUSIP** - 210737
Head Office - 800-789 Pender St W, Vancouver, BC, V6C 1H2 **Telephone** - (416) 846-5580 **Fax** - (604) 648-8105
Website - www.contagiousgaming.com
Email - craig.loverock@contagiousgaming.com
Investor Relations - Craig Loverock (647) 984-1244
Auditors - Paul J. Rozek Professional Corporation C.A., Calgary, Alta.
Lawyers - McMillan LLP, Vancouver, B.C.
Transfer Agents - Computershare Trust Company of Canada Inc., Vancouver, B.C.
Profile - (B.C. 1993) Develops software for regulated gaming and lottery markets worldwide with a focus on monetizing its digital lottery content.

The company has developed an integrated end-to-end platform for regulated gaming markets. The web-based platform provides remote access to all of the major functions and services required by online gaming operators, financial managers and player support team, It can be deployed as a stand-alone system or as part of a full-solution. The platform manages all aspects of real-money gaming, including gaming engine, player management tools, game application interface, payment system interface, data feed handler, affiliate management, presentation layer and centralized eWallet, which allows players the flexibility to deposit once, then distribute funds to different gaming operators.

Also offers web-based and mobile content for instant lottery, real money and social gaming and Goal Time, an in-play, pari-mutuel lottery style sports betting platform.

The platforms can be used in a variety of gaming scenarios including sports betting, casino, bingo and online lottery.

Predecessor Detail - Name changed from Kingsman Resources Inc., Sept. 19, 2014, following reverse takeover acquisition of Contagious Sports Limited and Telos Entertainment Inc.; basis 1 new for 2 old shs.
Directors - Desmond M. (Des) Balakrishnan, Vancouver, B.C.; Justin Barragan; Victor A. Wells, Oakville, Ont.
Other Exec. Officers - Manish Grigo, CEO; Craig Loverock, CFO & corp. sec.

Capital Stock

	Authorized (shs.)	Outstanding (shs.)[1]
Common	unlimited	47,006,835

[1] At Feb. 22, 2023

Major Shareholder - Justin Barragan held 14.91% interest at Nov. 8, 2021.

Price Range - CNS/TSX-VEN

Year	Volume	High	Low	Close
2022	4,431,817	$0.04	$0.01	$0.01
2021	23,050,562	$0.19	$0.02	$0.03
2020	3,401,418	$0.12	$0.01	$0.05
2019	1,396,976	$0.06	$0.02	$0.02
2018	3,076,823	$0.35	$0.04	$0.05

Recent Close: $0.01
Capital Stock Changes - In September 2022, private placement of up to 8,700,000 units (1 common share & 1 warrant) at $0.015 per unit was completed, with warrants exercisable at $0.05 per share for two years.

There were no changes to capital stock during fiscal 2022.

Wholly Owned Subsidiaries

Telos Entertainment Inc., Charlottetown, P.E.I.

Financial Statistics

Periods ended:	12m Mar. 31/22^A		12m Mar. 31/21^A
	$000s	%Chg	$000s
General & admin expense	438		517
Operating expense	**438**	**-15**	**517**
Operating income	**(438)**	**n.a.**	**(517)**
Finance costs, gross	24		24
Pre-tax income	**(453)**	**n.a.**	**(953)**
Net income	**(453)**	**n.a.**	**(953)**
Cash & equivalent	11		34
Accounts receivable	11		11
Current assets	23		47
Total assets	**23**	**-51**	**47**
Accts. pay. & accr. liabs	949		830
Current liabilities	1,926		1,497
Long-term debt, gross	300		300
Shareholders' equity	(1,902)		(1,449)
Cash from oper. activs	**(333)**	**n.a.**	**(159)**
Cash from fin. activs	310		50
Net cash position	**11**	**-68**	**34**
	$		$
Earnings per share*	(0.01)		(0.03)
Cash flow per share*	(0.01)		(0.01)
	shs		shs
No. of shs. o/s*	37,784,835		37,784,835
Avg. no. of shs. o/s*	37,784,835		29,937,394
	%		%
Net profit margin	n.a.		n.a.
Return on equity	n.m.		n.m.
Return on assets	n.m.		(910.78)

* Common
^A Reported in accordance with IFRS

Latest Results

Periods ended:	3m June 30/22^A		3m June 30/21^A
	$000s	%Chg	$000s
Net income	(106)	n.a.	(104)
	$		$
Earnings per share*	(0.00)		(0.00)

* Common
^A Reported in accordance with IFRS

Historical Summary
(as originally stated)

Fiscal Year	Oper. Rev. $000s	Net Inc. Bef. Disc. $000s	EPS* $
2022^A	nil	(453)	(0.01)
2021^A	nil	(953)	(0.03)
2020^A	85	(563)	(0.02)
2019^A	397	(631)	(0.02)
2018^A	281	(1,212)	(0.10)

* Common
^A Reported in accordance with IFRS

C.155 Converge Technology Solutions Corp.*

Symbol - CTS **Exchange** - TSX **CUSIP** - 21250C
Head Office - 2325-161 Bay St, Toronto, ON, M5J 2T6 **Telephone** - (416) 360-1495
Website - www.convergetp.com
Email - avjit.kamboj@convergetp.com
Investor Relations - Avjit Kamboj (416) 360-1495
Auditors - Ernst & Young LLP C.A., Toronto, Ont.
Lawyers - Blake, Cassels & Graydon LLP, Toronto, Ont.
Transfer Agents - Computershare Trust Company of Canada Inc., Vancouver, B.C.
FP500 Revenue Ranking - 209
Employees - 3,000 at Dec. 31, 2022
Profile - (Can. 2020; orig. B.C., 2018) Provides integrated information technology (IT) design, consulting and managed services solutions to corporate and government institutions throughout the U.S., Canada and Europe.

Operates through 35 acquired businesses in North America and Europe that provide integrated hardware, software and managed services solutions, with focus on advanced analytics, cloud services, cybersecurity, digital infrastructure, managed services and talent solutions.

Products - Offers customers a variety of products and services across its focus areas including data centres, which involves networking, virtualization, storage, disaster recovery and continuous replication of critical applications, infrastructure, data and systems; cloud solutions, which involve assessment, design, architecture and optimization of both public and private cloud options; unified communications, which include email, voice and video communications technologies such as phone systems and teleconferencing; networking and storage products, which include enterprise networking, security and infrastructure products that help clients meet growing bandwidth, security and storage demands; desktops, laptops, computing peripherals and other computing products; mobile and handheld devices; and the Trust platform, which consists of software solutions for privacy, access and identity management.

Services - Provides professional and managed services including managed and hosted services which involves secure, direct, aggregated and managed interconnections to multiple cloud providers; cybersecurity services, which involves the design and implementation of security solutions; cloud computing and analytics which involves the design and implementation of cloud solutions that include private, public and managed clouds as wells as data analytics and analysis; systems architecture, which consists of solutions to simplify and optimize complex infrastructures and heterogeneous operating system environments; professional services which involves administering and monitoring of a client's vendor contracts, including identifying technological needs and delivering procurement services; staffing services which involves provision of contract, contract-to-hire, and placement services for technical staffing solutions; and lifecycle and desktop recovery services, which provides break or fix, troubleshooting, maintenance and management services as well as warranty support. Managed and hosted service offerings consist of managed end-user, managed infrastructure, managed security and managed application services. Cybersecurity service offerings consist of security consulting, identity and data protection, incident management, security intelligence and analytics, and security remediation. Cloud computing and analytics solutions consist of application development, artificial intelligence, business analytics, data and performance management. Systems architecture solutions consist of next generation data centre, storage and visualization, intelligent networking and security, end-user computing and customer experience.

On May 9, 2023, the company announced the conclusion of its strategic review process, which was first announced on Nov. 22, 2022. The company concluded that none of the proposals for transactions received in the course of the strategic review process would be in the best interests of the company. The company would continue to execute its business plans as an independent publicly held company.

On Mar. 15, 2023, the company acquired the remaining 25% interest in Mainz, Germany-based **REDNET AG**, which provides information technology (IT) services by selecting, procuring, supporting and rolling out tailor-made IT solutions for the education, healthcare and government/public sectors. Terms were not disclosed.

In June 2022, subsidiary **Portage CyberTech Inc.** acquired Montreal, Que.-based **Notarius.** for $54,843,000 consisting of $44,876,000 in cash, a working capital adjustment of $4,975,000 and a promissory note of $4,992,000. Notarius offers secured digital signatures, trusted electronic signatures and reliable signature tools.

In March 2022, subsidiary **Portage CyberTech Inc.** acquired Victoria, B.C.-based **1CRM Systems Corp.** for $3,000,000 cash plus an up to $2,000,000 in earn-out payments over two years based on the achievement of certain milestones. 1CRM specializes in cloud software solutions that equip small and medium-sized organizations with integrated business information while improving their cost model and streamlining their internal business processes.

Recent Merger and Acquisition Activity

Status: completed **Revised:** Nov. 7, 2022
UPDATE: The transaction was completed. PREVIOUS: Converge Technology Solutions Corp. agreed to acquire United Kingdom-based Stone Technologies Group Limited, a provider of Information and Communications Technology (ICT) services to U.K. public sector and private sector organizations of all sizes. Pursuant to the terms, certain key management personnel of Stone reinvested a portion of the proceeds from sale of their shares into a new Converge UK holding company, representing an aggregate minority interest of 11%. Consideration would consist of Cdn$59,600,000 cash in exchange for the 89% interest in Stone. During the 12-months ended July 31, 2022, Stone generated gross revenues of €140,100,000.

Status: completed **Announced:** Sept. 12, 2022
Converge Technology Solutions Corp. acquired Toronto, Ont.-based Newcomp Analytics 2021 Inc., which offers advisory and development services, along with managed analytics and analytic bootcamps, for $18,285,000.

Status: completed **Revised:** Aug. 1, 2022
UPDATE: The transaction was completed. PREVIOUS: Converge Technology Solutions Corp. agreed to acquire San Diego, Calif.-based PC Specialists, Inc. (dba Technology Integration Group), which provides software and hardware procurement, discovery assessments, strategic planning, deployment, data centre optimization, IT asset management and cloud computing, for US$74,000,000.

Status: completed **Revised:** July 29, 2022
UPDATE: The transaction was completed for €40,264,000 ($72,588,000). PREVIOUS: Converge Technology Solutions Corp. agreed to acquire Germany-based organizations Gesellschaft für digitale Bildung, (GfdB, Society for Digital Education), Institut für modern Bildung (IfmB, Institute for Modern Education) and DEQSTER GmbH. Terms were not disclosed. GfdB and IfmB are full-service IT suppliers for education, while DEQSTER specializes in the development of production of equipment for digital learning and working.

Status: completed **Revised:** May 2, 2022
UPDATE: The transaction was completed. PREVIOUS: Converge Technology Solutions Corp. agreed to acquire Edmonton Alta.-based Interdynamix Systems Corp. (IDX) for a purchase price of $32,300,000 in cash. IDX offers solution engineering and business consulting services. The transaction was expected to close in the second quarter of 2022.

Status: completed **Announced:** Apr. 1, 2022
Converge Technology Solutions Corp. acquired private Ferndale, Mich.-based Creative Breakthroughs, Inc. (CBI) for US$47,000,000 plus working capital in excess of US$3,000,000 paid in cash at closing, and

earn-out payments of up to US$17,000,000 payable over three years. CBI provides cybersecurity solutions ranging from security programs to architecture, and integration to managed security across the U.S.

Predecessor Detail - Name changed from Norwick Capital Corp., Nov. 6, 2018, pursuant to the Qualifying Transaction reverse takeover acquisition of Converge Technology Partners Inc. and concurrent amalgamation of Converge with wholly owned Norwick Acquisition Corp.; basis 1 new for 3.2 old shs.

Directors - Thomas Volk, chr., Munich, Germany; Shaun Maine, grp. CEO, Bermuda; Brian Phillips†, Vancouver, B.C.; Nathan Chan, Toronto, Ont.; Ralph Garcea, Caledon, Ont.; Darlene Kelly, Ottawa, Ont.; Dr. Toni Rinow, Laval, Qué.

Other Exec. Officers - Cory Reid, COO & CIO; Avjit Kamboj, CFO; Julianne Belaga, chief legal officer; John G. Teltsch, chief revenue officer; Greg Berard, grp. pres. & CEO; David Luftig, exec. v-p, software & solutions; Rhonda Hanes, v-p, people opers.; Cari Hash, v-p, global integration & deployment srvcs., North America; Elizabeth Herrera, v-p, advanced analytics; Rochelle Manns, v-p, cloud platforms; Sohil Merchant, v-p, digital infrastructure & workplace; David Pacific, v-p, advanced analytics; Andrew Tenaglia, v-p, app modernization; Karie Timion, v-p, mktg.; Barbara Weitzel, pres., REDNET GmbH; Don Cuthbertson, CEO, Portage CyberTech Inc.

† Lead director

Capital Stock

	Authorized (shs.)	Outstanding (shs.)[1]
Common	unlimited	209,133,903

[1] At May 9, 2023

Normal Course Issuer Bid - The company plans to make normal course purchases of up to 19,427,276 common shares representing 10% of the public float. The bid commenced on Aug. 11, 2023, and expires on Aug. 10, 2024.

Major Shareholder - Widely held at May 5, 2023.

Price Range - CTS/TSX

Year	Volume	High	Low	Close
2022	206,123,030	$11.59	$3.60	$4.59
2021	218,524,020	$13.09	$4.58	$10.87
2020	72,989,890	$5.15	$0.75	$4.97
2019	17,675,829	$1.72	$0.48	$1.40
2018	1,115,375	$1.02	$0.55	$0.55

Recent Close: $2.66

Capital Stock Changes - During 2022, 978,567 common shares were issued on exercise of exchange rights related to the Software Information Systems, LLC and VSS Holdings, LLC, and 6,562,718 common shares repurchased under a Normal Course Issuer Bid.

Dividends

CTS com Ra $0.04 pa Q est. June 16, 2023
Listed Feb 11/21.
$0.01**i**.................. June 16/23
i Initial Payment

Long-Term Debt - Outstanding at Dec. 31, 2022:

Revolving credit facility[1]	$420,439,000
Other credit facilities due 2023[2]	1,289,000
5.57% note due 2024	194,000
4% note due 2032	1,648,000
	423,570,000
Less: Current	421,728,000
	1,842,000

[1] Bearing interest at SOFR plus 1.25% to 2.25%, with an effective interest rate of 5.1% as at Dec. 31, 2022.
[2] Consists of various credit agreements with third parties. Bearing interest between 5% to 9%.

Note - In February 2023, the borrowing capacity under the revolving credit facility was increased to $600,000,000 from $500,000,000.

Wholly Owned Subsidiaries

Converge Technology Hybrid IT Solutions Europe Ltd., Ireland.
- 100% int. in **Converge Technology Solutions Finance Ltd.**, Ireland.
  - 100% int. in **Converge Technology Solutions Holdings GmbH**, Germany.
    - 100% int. in **Converge Technology Solutions Germany GmbH**, Germany.
      - 100% int. in **DEQSTER GmbH**, Hamburg, Germany.
      - 100% int. in **Institut für modern Bildung GmbH**, Germany.
      - 100% int. in **REDNET GmbH**, Germany.
      - 100% int. in **Visucom GmbH**, Germany.
- 100% int. in **Converge Technology Solutions Holdings UK Ltd.**, United Kingdom.
  - 88.71% int. in **Converge Technology Solutions UK Limited**, United Kingdom.
    - 100% int. in **Stone Technologies Group Limited**, United Kingdom.
      - 100% int. in **Granite One Hundred Holdings Ltd.**, United Kingdom.
        - 100% int. in **Stone Computers Ltd.**, United Kingdom.
        - 100% int. in **Stone Technologies Ltd.**, United Kingdom.
          - 100% int. in **Compusys Ltd.**, United Kingdom.
- 100% int. in **Converge Technology Solutions Switzerland GmbH**, Germany.

Converge Technology Partners Inc., Toronto, Ont.
- 100% int. in **Converge Canada Finance Corp.**, Ont.
- 100% int. in **Converge Technology Solutions US, LLC**, Del.
  - 100% int. in **Accudata Systems, Inc.**, Houston, Tex.
  - 100% int. in **CarpeDatum LLC**, Denver, Colo.
  - 100% int. in **Converge Acquisition HoldCo, LLC**, Del.
    - 1% int. in **ExactlyIT Service Company S. de R.L. de C.V.**, Mexico.
  - 100% int. in **Creative Breakthroughs, Inc.**, Mich.
  - 100% int. in **Dasher Technologies, Inc.**, Campbell, Calif.
  - 100% int. in **Essex Acquisition, LLC**, Del.
    - 100% int. in **Essex Commercial Finance, LLC**, Del.
    - 100% int. in **Essex Technology Group, Inc.**, Saddle Brook, N.J.
  - 100% int. in **ExactlyIT, Inc.**, Morrisville, N.C.
    - 99% int. in **ExactlyIT Service Company S. de R.L. de C.V.**, Mexico.
  - 100% int. in **Infinity Systems Software, Inc.**, New York, N.Y.
  - 100% int. in **OHC International, LLC**, Ga.
    - 100% int. in **Corus 360 Limited**, United Kingdom.
  - 100% int. in **PC Specialists, Inc.**, San Diego, Calif.
    - 100% int. in **Itex, Inc.**, Ont.
    - 100% int. in **TIG Asia Limited**, Hong Kong, People's Republic of China.
    - 100% int. in **Technology Integration Group Hong Kong Limited**, Hong Kong, People's Republic of China.
      - 100% int. in **TIG (Shanghai) Co., Ltd.**, People's Republic of China.
  - 100% int. in **PDS Holding Company**, Del.
    - 100% int. in **Paragon Development Systems, Inc.**, Wis.
    - 100% int. in **Paragon Staffing, LLC**, Wis.
    - 100% int. in **Works Computing, LLC**, Minn.
  - 100% int. in **Unique Digital Technology, Inc.**, Houston, Tex.
  - 100% int. in **Unique Property Holdings, LLC**, Tex.
  - 100% int. in **VSS Holdings, LLC**, Madison, Miss.
    - 100% int. in **Information Insights, LLC**, Nev.
    - 100% int. in **VSS, LLC**, Jackson, Miss.
  - 100% int. in **Vicom Infinity, Inc.**, Farmingdale, N.Y.
- 100% int. in **Newcomp Analytics Inc.**, Ont.
  - 100% int. in **Newcomp Analytics Inc.**, Bahamas.
- 100% int. in **Northern Micro Inc.**, Ottawa, Ont.
- 100% int. in **1176524 Alberta Ltd.**, Alta.
  - 24% int. in **IDX Systems Corp.**, Alta.
- 100% int. in **1190422 Alberta Ltd.**, Alta.
  - 18% int. in **IDX Systems Corp.**, Alta.
- 100% int. in **1245720 Alberta Ltd.**, Alta.
  - 58% int. in **IDX Systems Corp.**, Alta.
- 100% int. in **P.C.D. Consultation Inc.**, Saint-Laurent, Qué.
- 51% int. in **Portage CyberTech Inc.**, Gatineau, Qué.
  - 100% int. in **OPIN Digital Inc.**, Ont.
    - 100% int. in **OPIN Digital Corp.**, Del.
  - 100% int. in **10084182 Canada Inc.**, Ottawa, Ont. Operating as Becker-Carroll.
  - 100% int. in **1CRM Systems Corp.**, B.C.
  - 100% int. in **Solutions Notarius Inc.**, Qué.
  - 100% int. in **Vivvo Application Studios Ltd.**, Regina, Sask.
- 100% int. in **Solutions P.C.D. Inc.**, Saint-Laurent, Qué.
- 100% int. in **2771381 Ontario Inc.**, Ont.

Financial Statistics

Periods ended:	12m Dec. 31/22[A]		12m Dec. 31/21[oA]
	$000s	%Chg	$000s
Operating revenue	**2,164,647**	**+63**	**1,329,737**
Cost of sales	1,608,929		980,919
Salaries & benefits	351,004		218,565
General & admin expense	62,640		36,240
Stock-based compensation	5,594		2,325
Operating expense	**2,028,167**	**+64**	**1,238,049**
Operating income	**136,480**	**+49**	**91,688**
Deprec., depl. & amort.	80,064		39,587
Finance costs, net	19,860		7,801
Pre-tax income	**18,785**	**-22**	**23,974**
Income taxes	(4,059)		7,608
Net income	**22,844**	**+40**	**16,366**
Net inc. for equity hldrs	**27,283**	**+71**	**15,946**
Net inc. for non-cont. int	**(4,439)**	**n.a.**	**420**
Cash & equivalent	159,890		248,193
Inventories	158,430		104,254
Accounts receivable	781,683		416,499
Current assets	1,128,279		780,708
Fixed assets, net	88,352		30,642
Intangibles, net	1,027,599		556,870
Total assets	**2,248,876**	**+64**	**1,368,837**
Accts. pay. & accr. liabs	824,924		519,434
Current liabilities	1,437,906		591,215
Long-term debt, gross	423,570		1,546
Long-term debt, net	1,842		730
Long-term lease liabilities	37,842		10,950
Shareholders' equity	599,910		613,489
Non-controlling interest	30,900		35,339
Cash from oper. activs	**41,586**	**-52**	**87,065**
Cash from fin. activs	336,310		371,384
Cash from invest. activs	(463,426)		(277,802)
Net cash position	**159,890**	**-36**	**248,193**
Capital expenditures	(23,942)		(6,310)
Capital disposals	299		187
	$		$
Earnings per share*	0.13		0.09
Cash flow per share*	0.20		0.47
	shs		shs
No. of shs. o/s*	208,812,218		214,396,369
Avg. no. of shs. o/s*	213,103,919		185,810,548
	%		%
Net profit margin	1.06		1.23
Return on equity	4.50		4.46
Return on assets	1.26		1.57
Foreign sales percent	82		80
No. of employees (FTEs)	3,000		1,815

* Common
[o] Restated
[A] Reported in accordance with IFRS

Latest Results

Periods ended:	3m Mar. 31/23[A]		3m Mar. 31/22[oA]
	$000s	%Chg	$000s
Operating revenue	678,198	+37	494,040
Net income	(3,361)	n.a.	(2,408)
Net inc. for equity hldrs	(1,957)	n.a.	(1,794)
Net inc. for non-cont. int	(1,404)		(614)
	$		$
Earnings per share*	(0.01)		(0.01)

* Common
[o] Restated
[A] Reported in accordance with IFRS

Historical Summary
(as originally stated)

Fiscal Year	Oper. Rev.	Net Inc. Bef. Disc.	EPS*
	$000s	$000s	$
2022[A]	2,164,647	22,844	0.13
2021[A]	1,527,841	16,366	0.09
2020[A]	948,799	(4,175)	(0.04)
2019[A]	687,796	(10,840)	(0.14)
2018[A1]	459,193	(18,236)	(0.28)

* Common
[A] Reported in accordance with IFRS
[1] Results prior to Nov. 7, 2018, pertain to and reflect the Qualifying Transaction reverse takeover acquisition of Converge Technology Partners Inc.

C.156 Copland Road Capital Corporation

Symbol - CRCC **Exchange** - CSE **CUSIP** - 217413
Head Office - 401-217 Queen St W, Toronto, ON, M5V 0R2 **Telephone** - (647) 242-4258
Website - copland-road.com
Email - langstaff@copland-road.com
Investor Relations - Bruce Langstaff (647) 242-4258

Auditors - Dale Matheson Carr-Hilton LaBonte LLP C.A., Vancouver, B.C.

Transfer Agents - Odyssey Trust Company, Vancouver, B.C.

Profile - (B.C. 2019; orig. Can., 2002 amalg.) Seeking new investment opportunities.

Previously invested primarily in cannabis-related assets in the United States.

On Jan. 31, 2023, a plan of arrangement was completed whereby shares of five wholly owned subsidiaries were distributed to the company's shareholders on the basis of 0.25 common share of each subsidiary for each common share of the company held. The five companies are **Bothwell Road Capital Corporation**, **Broomloan Road Capital Corporation**, **Edmiston Drive Capital Corporation**, **Goram Capital Corporation** and **James Bell Capital Corporation**. Each entity would pursue an acquisition. The company retained 1,253,250 common shares of each subsidiary, representing a 37.5% interest in each.

Predecessor Detail - Name changed from Nabis Holdings Inc., Jan. 14, 2022.

Directors - Bruce Langstaff, exec. chr., Toronto, Ont.; Jared Carroll, Toronto, Ont.; Scott M. Kelly, Toronto, Ont.; Jennifer Law, Toronto, Ont.

Other Exec. Officers - Joanne Groszek, CFO

Capital Stock

	Authorized (shs.)	Outstanding (shs.)[1]
Common	unlimited	8,217,500

[1] At Jan. 30, 2023

Major Shareholder - Scott M. Kelly held 13.9% interest and Bruce Langstaff held 11.6% interest at Nov. 11, 2022.

Price Range - CRCC/CSE

Year	Volume	High	Low	Close
2022	1,963,218	$0.33	$0.09	$0.23
2021	21,545,467	$1.10	$0.01	$0.30

Recent Close: $0.20

Capital Stock Changes - In January 2023, private placement of 2,713,500 common shares was completed at $0.25 per share

Wholly Owned Subsidiaries

Nabis AZ, LLC, United States.
Nabis Holdings California, LLC, United States.
Nabis Holdings Oklahoma Inc., United States.
Nabis Oklahoma Patient Care Inc., United States.
Nabis (US) Corp., United States.

Investments

37.5% int. in **Bothwell Road Capital Corporation**
37.5% int. in **Broomloan Road Capital Corporation**
37.5% int. in **Edmiston Drive Capital Corporation**
37.5% int. in **Goram Capital Corporation**
37.5% int. in **James Bell Capital Corporation**

Financial Statistics

Periods ended:	12m Dec. 31/21[A]		12m Dec. 31/20[□A]
	$000s	%Chg	$000s
Salaries & benefits	209		1,420
General & admin expense	1,214		3,804
Stock-based compensation	nil		244
Operating expense	**1,423**	**-74**	**5,467**
Operating income	**(1,423)**	**n.a.**	**(5,467)**
Deprec., depl. & amort.	493		1,475
Finance income	74		127
Finance costs, gross	5,063		7,403
Write-downs/write-offs	(132)		(5,760)
Pre-tax income	**3,016**	**n.a.**	**(18,891)**
Net inc. bef. disc. opers	**3,016**	**n.a.**	**(18,891)**
Income from disc. opers	18,405		518
Net income	**21,421**	**n.a.**	**(18,373)**
Cash & equivalent	1,317		1,539
Inventories	nil		657
Accounts receivable	nil		26
Current assets	1,399		2,735
Fixed assets, net	nil		687
Right-of-use assets	nil		65
Intangibles, net	nil		17,123
Total assets	**1,399**	**-93**	**20,610**
Bank indebtedness	nil		10,673
Accts. pay. & accr. liabs	202		3,724
Current liabilities	202		43,476
Long-term debt, gross	nil		29,013
Shareholders' equity	1,197		(22,866)
Cash from oper. activs	**(4,336)**	**n.a.**	**(4,792)**
Cash from fin. activs	(23,948)		(464)
Cash from invest. activs	28,867		4,107
Net cash position	**1,317**	**-14**	**1,539**
Capital expenditures	nil		(1,526)
Capital disposals	154		5,842
	$		$
Earns. per sh. bef disc opers*	0.24		(0.16)
Earnings per share*	1.72		(0.17)
Cash flow per share*	(0.35)		(0.04)
	shs		shs
No. of shs. o/s*	7,775,000		121,729,441
Avg. no. of shs. o/s*	12,397,621		119,692,280
	%		%
Net profit margin	n.a.		n.a.
Return on equity	n.m.		n.m.
Return on assets	73.42		(39.53)

* Common
[□] Restated
[A] Reported in accordance with IFRS

Latest Results

Periods ended:	6m June 30/22[A]		6m June 30/21[A]
	$000s	%Chg	$000s
Net inc. bef. disc. opers	(210)	n.a.	19,749
Income from disc. opers	nil		543
Net income	(210)	n.a.	20,291
	$		$
Earns. per sh. bef. disc. opers.*	(0.03)		0.97
Earnings per share*	(0.03)		0.10

* Common
[A] Reported in accordance with IFRS

Historical Summary
(as originally stated)

Fiscal Year	Oper. Rev.	Net Inc. Bef. Disc.	EPS*
	$000s	$000s	$
2021[A]	nil	3,016	0.24
2020[A]	13,915	(18,373)	(0.15)
2019[A1]	2,232	(26,291)	(0.24)
2018[A]	nil	(5,154)	(0.21)
2017[A]	nil	(308)	(0.02)

* Common
[A] Reported in accordance with IFRS
[1] 14 months ended Dec. 31, 2019.

C.157 Copperleaf Technologies Inc.

Symbol - CPLF **Exchange** - TSX **CUSIP** - 21766N

Head Office - 140-2920 Virtual Way, Vancouver, BC, V5M 0C4 **Telephone** - (604) 639-9700 **Toll-free** - (888) 465-5353 **Fax** - (604) 639-9699

Website - www.copperleaf.com

Email - investors@copperleaf.com

Investor Relations - Christopher F. Allen (604) 639-9700

Auditors - KPMG LLP C.A., Vancouver, B.C.

Lawyers - Fasken Martineau DuMoulin LLP, Vancouver, B.C.

Transfer Agents - Odyssey Trust Company, Vancouver, B.C.

Employees - 486 at Dec. 31, 2022

Profile - (Can. 2004; orig. B.C., 2000) Provides artificial intelligence (AI)-powered decision analytics for companies managing critical infrastructure, including physical and digital assets.

Offers a portfolio of enterprise software products that provide predictive analytics, risk modeling and analysis, financial and performance modeling, investment portfolio optimization, budgeting, plan approvals, performance management and scenario analysis, at scale. Primary products are Copperleaf Portfolio™, an investment portfolio management solution for creating, managing and communicating investment plans; Copperleaf Asset, an asset management solution for forecasting sustainment needs and managing infrastructure risk; and Copperleaf Value, a value framework management solution used to build, visualize, communicate and modify a client's decision-making framework, including strategic goals, risk definitions, value measures and value models.

Solutions are used to manage an estimated $2.8 trillion of client infrastructure across multiple industry sectors worldwide, including electricity, natural gas, water, oil and gas, pharmaceuticals and transportation.

Directors - Amos Michelson, chr., B.C.; Judith M. (Judi) Hess, v-chr. & chief strategist, Vancouver, B.C.; Paul Sakrzewski, CEO, Vancouver, B.C.; Manuel Alba, San Jose, Calif.; Michael Calyniuk, Vancouver, B.C.; Rolf Dekleer, Vancouver, B.C.; Eric MacDonald, Singapore, Singapore

Other Exec. Officers - Phil Jones, man. dir., Americas; Stefan Sadnicki, man. dir., Europe, Middle East & Africa; Rob Tanner, man. dir., Asia Pacific & Japan; Christopher F. (Chris) Allen, CFO; Michael Joy, v-p, product devel.; Linda M. Lupini, v-p, employee experience; Sandra R. MacKay, v-p, legal & corp. sec.; Dawen Nozdryn-Plotnicki, v-p, global growth office; Barry Quart, v-p, mktg.

Capital Stock

	Authorized (shs.)	Outstanding (shs.)[1]
Common	unlimited	71,932,736

[1] At May 10, 2023

Major Shareholder - Amos Michelson held 11.72% interest and PenderFund Capital Management Ltd. held 11.38% interest at May 10, 2023.

Price Range - CPLF/TSX

Year	Volume	High	Low	Close
2022	17,823,213	$24.34	$3.23	$5.74
2021	2,701,256	$26.10	$17.25	$23.85

Recent Close: $5.60

Capital Stock Changes - During 2022, 2,298,770 common shares were issued on exercise of options.

Wholly Owned Subsidiaries

Copperleaf Japan Technologies GK, Japan.
Copperleaf Technologies (AU) Pty Ltd., Australia.
Copperleaf Technologies (Asia) Pte. Ltd., Singapore.
Copperleaf Technologies B.V., Netherlands.
Copperleaf Technologies Denmark APS, Denmark.
Copperleaf Technologies FZE LLC, United Arab Emirates.
Copperleaf Technologies (Malaysia) Sdn. Bhd., Malaysia.
Copperleaf Technologies (ROK) Korea Limited, South Korea.
Copperleaf Technologies UK Limited, United Kingdom.
Copperleaf Technologies (USA) Inc., Del.

Financial Statistics

Periods ended:	12m Dec. 31/22^A		12m Dec. 31/21^A
	$000s	%Chg	$000s
Operating revenue	**73,385**	**+6**	**69,283**
Cost of sales	4,626		2,936
Salaries & benefits	74,240		53,427
Research & devel. expense	2,731		550
General & admin expense	16,678		13,056
Stock-based compensation	4,402		2,306
Operating expense	**102,677**	**+42**	**72,275**
Operating income	**(29,292)**	**n.a.**	**(2,992)**
Deprec., depl. & amort.	2,159		2,115
Finance income	2,687		157
Finance costs, gross	1,013		786
Pre-tax income	**(28,284)**	**n.a.**	**(6,277)**
Income taxes	(82)		247
Net income	**(28,202)**	**n.a.**	**(6,524)**
Cash & equivalent	149,458		161,432
Accounts receivable	21,232		32,252
Current assets	178,929		200,260
Fixed assets, net	1,901		2,010
Right-of-use assets	730		1,324
Intangibles, net	1,407		1,106
Total assets	**185,693**	**-10**	**206,042**
Accts. pay. & accr. liabs.	12,232		13,182
Current liabilities	41,369		35,063
Long-term lease liabilities	259		1,234
Shareholders' equity	133,027		155,018
Cash from oper. activs.	**(12,271)**	**n.a.**	**(4,277)**
Cash from fin. activs.	601		151,013
Cash from invest. activs.	(1,760)		(745)
Net cash position	**149,458**	**-7**	**161,432**
Capital expenditures	(871)		(572)
	$		$
Earnings per share*	(0.41)		(0.24)
Cash flow per share*	(0.18)		(0.15)
	shs		shs
No. of shs. o/s*	70,717,375		68,418,605
Avg. no. of shs. o/s*	69,602,130		27,693,445
	%		%
Net profit margin	(38.43)		(9.42)
Return on equity	(19.58)		(9.59)
Return on assets	(13.88)		(4.40)
Foreign sales percent	84		83
No. of employees (FTEs)	486		389

* Common
^A Reported in accordance with IFRS

Latest Results

Periods ended:	3m Mar. 31/23^A		3m Mar. 31/22^A
	$000s	%Chg	$000s
Operating revenue	19,966	+28	15,569
Net income	(11,790)	n.a.	(10,906)
	$		$
Earnings per share*	(0.17)		(0.16)

* Common
^A Reported in accordance with IFRS

Historical Summary
(as originally stated)

Fiscal Year	Oper. Rev.	Net Inc. Bef. Disc.	EPS*
	$000s	$000s	$
2022^A	73,385	(28,202)	(0.41)
2021^A	69,283	(6,524)	(0.24)
2020^A1	44,520	(9,083)	(0.60)
2019^A1	36,935	(10,318)	(0.74)
2018^A1	33,634	1,581	0.03

* Common
^A Reported in accordance with IFRS
^1 As shown in the prospectus dated Oct. 6, 2021.

C.158 Corby Spirit and Wine Limited*

Symbol - CSW.A **Exchange** - TSX **CUSIP** - 218349
Head Office - 1100-225 King St W, Toronto, ON, M5V 3M2 **Telephone** - (416) 479-2400 **Fax** - (416) 369-9612
Website - www.corby.ca
Email - investors.corby@pernod-ricard.com
Investor Relations - Juan Alonso (416) 479-2400
Auditors - Deloitte LLP C.A., Toronto, Ont.
Bankers - The Bank of Nova Scotia, Toronto, Ont.
Lawyers - McCarthy Tétrault LLP, Toronto, Ont.
Transfer Agents - Computershare Trust Company of Canada Inc., Toronto, Ont.
FP500 Revenue Ranking - 697
Employees - 205 at June 30, 2022
Profile - (Can. 1924, via letters patent) Markets domestically produced and imported spirits and wines; and represents selected non-owned international beverage alcohol brands in the Canadian marketplace.

Case Goods segment derives its revenue from the production and distribution of its owned beverage alcohol brands in Canada, including J.P. Wiser's®, Lot No. 40®, Pike Creek® and Gooderham & Worts® Canadian whiskies, Lamb's® rum, Polar Ice® vodka, McGuinness® liqueurs, Ungava® Premium Canadian gin, Chic Choc® spiced rum, Coureur des Bois®/Cabot Trail® maple-based liqueurs, and Foreign Affair® wines, as well as in sales to international markets. Through 90%-owned **Ace Beverage Group Inc.**, produces ready-to-drink alcohol beverages the Cottage Springs, Ace Hill, Cabana Coast and Liberty Village brands.

Commissions segment earns commission income from the representation of non-owned beverage alcohol brands in Canada. Through its affiliation with **Pernod Ricard S.A.** of Paris, France, the company represents international brands such as ABSOLUT® vodka, Chivas Regal®, The Glenlivet® and Ballantine's® Scotch whiskies, Jameson® Irish whiskey, Beefeater® gin, Malibu® rum, Kahlúa® liqueur, Mumm® champagne, and Jacob's Creek®, Wyndham Estate®, Stoneleigh®, Campo Viejo® and Kenwood® wines.

The majority of the production (90%) is sourced from the company's parent, **Hiram Walker & Sons Limited** (an indirect wholly owned subsidiary of Pernod Ricard), which is located in Windsor, Ont. The balance of production is sourced from wholly owned **Ungava Spirits Co. Ltd.**, which operates a production facility in Cowansville, Que.; wholly owned **The Foreign Affair Winery Limited**, which operates a winery and vineyard in Niagara, Ont.; and various third party vendors including a manufacturer in the United Kingdom. The U.K. site blends and bottles Lamb's products for sale in countries located outside North America.

Recent Merger and Acquisition Activity

Status: completed **Revised:** July 4, 2023
UPDATE: The transaction was completed. PREVIOUS: Corby Spirit and Wine Limited agreed to acquire a 90% interest in Toronto, Ont.-based Ace Beverage Group Inc. for $148,500,000. Ace produces ready-to-drink alcohol beverages under the Cottage Springs, Ace Hill, Cabana Coast and Liberty Village brands. The remaining 10% interest continues to be primarily held by certain Ace founders and Corby holds call options exercisable in 2025 and 2028 to acquire the remaining shares of Ace.

Predecessor Detail - Name changed from Corby Distilleries Limited, Nov. 7, 2013.

Directors - George F. McCarthy, chr., Conn.; Nicolas Krantz, pres. & CEO, Ont.; Juan Alonso, v-p & CFO, Toronto, Ont.; Dr. Claude Boulay, Montréal, Qué.; Lucio Di Clemente, Toronto, Ont.; Lani Montoya, N.J.; Patricia L. Nielsen, Mississauga, Ont.; Helga Reidel, Kingsville, Ont.; Kate Thompson, Surrey, United Kingdom

Other Exec. Officers - Caroline Begley, v-p, mktg.; Stéphane Côté, v-p, new bus. ventures; Ryan Smith, v-p, sales; Marc A. Valencia, v-p, public affairs, gen. counsel & corp. sec.

Capital Stock

	Authorized (shs.)	Outstanding (shs.)^1
Class A Common	unlimited	24,274,320
Class B Common	unlimited	4,194,536

^1 At May 8, 2023

Class A Common - One vote per share.
Class B Common - Non-voting.
Major Shareholder - Pernod Ricard S.A. held 51.61% interest at Sept. 30, 2022.

Price Range - CSW.A/TSX

Year	Volume	High	Low	Close
2022	3,424,370	$19.98	$15.95	$16.37
2021	2,560,757	$19.10	$16.50	$16.77
2020	3,247,200	$17.50	$13.46	$16.90
2019	2,759,546	$19.70	$15.00	$15.38
2018	1,932,591	$23.24	$17.25	$18.55

Recent Close: $14.98

Capital Stock Changes - There were no changes to capital stock from fiscal 2008 to fiscal 2022, inclusive.

Dividends

CSW.A cl A Ra $0.84 pa Q est. Mar. 3, 2023
Prev. Rate: $0.88 est. Dec. 9, 2022
Prev. Rate: $0.96 est. Dec. 10, 2021
Prev. Rate: $0.84 est. Mar. 5, 2021
Prev. Rate: $0.88 est. Dec. 11, 2020
CSW.B cl B N.V. Ra $0.84 pa Q est. Mar. 3, 2023
Prev. Rate: $0.88 est. Dec. 9, 2022
Prev. Rate: $0.96 est. Dec. 10, 2021
Prev. Rate: $0.84 est. Mar. 5, 2021
Prev. Rate: $0.88 est. Dec. 11, 2020

Long-Term Debt - At June 30, 2022, the company had no long-term debt.

Wholly Owned Subsidiaries

Alfred Lamb International Limited, United Kingdom.
The Foreign Affair Winery Limited, Ont.
J.P. Wiser Distillery Limited, Toronto, Ont.
Meaghers Distillery Limited, Canada.
Ungava Spirits Co. Ltd., Cowansville, Qué.

Subsidiaries

90% int. in **Ace Beverage Group Inc.**, Toronto, Ont.

Financial Statistics

Periods ended:	12m June 30/22^A		12m June 30/21^oA
	$000s	%Chg	$000s
Operating revenue	**159,393**	**0**	**159,778**
Cost of sales	49,102		50,390
General & admin expense	61,150		56,365
Operating expense	**110,252**	**+3**	**106,755**
Operating income	**49,141**	**-7**	**53,023**
Deprec., depl. & amort.	14,252		11,680
Finance income	379		633
Finance costs, gross	254		580
Write-downs/write-offs	(2,130)		nil
Pre-tax income	**32,795**	**-21**	**41,540**
Income taxes	9,393		10,949
Net income	**23,402**	**-24**	**30,591**
Cash & equivalent	52,459		94,399
Inventories	61,090		60,785
Accounts receivable	35,845		35,717
Current assets	152,483		192,213
Fixed assets, net	20,601		18,419
Right-of-use assets	3,644		4,322
Intangibles, net	70,021		27,583
Total assets	**253,513**	**0**	**254,225**
Accts. pay. & accr. liabs.	53,403		43,965
Current liabilities	54,618		47,946
Long-term lease liabilities	2,488		2,976
Shareholders' equity	183,205		187,810
Cash from oper. activs.	**45,518**	**+12**	**40,761**
Cash from fin. activs.	(27,796)		(25,468)
Cash from invest. activs.	(17,722)		(15,293)
Capital expenditures	(4,414)		(2,753)
Capital disposals	32		616
Unfunded pension liability	778		n.a.
Pension fund surplus	6,497		10,150
	$		$
Earnings per share*	0.82		1.07
Cash flow per share*	1.60		1.43
Cash divd. per share*	0.93		0.84
	shs		shs
No. of shs. o/s*	28,468,856		28,468,856
Avg. no. of shs. o/s*	28,468,856		28,468,856
	%		%
Net profit margin	14.68		19.15
Return on equity	12.61		16.97
Return on assets	9.29		12.70
Foreign sales percent	10		9
No. of employees (FTEs)	205		192

* Cl.A & B com.
^o Restated
^A Reported in accordance with IFRS

Latest Results

Periods ended:	9m Mar. 31/23^A		9m Mar. 31/22^A
	$000s	%Chg	$000s
Operating revenue	118,731	0	118,230
Net income	20,332	0	20,267
	$		$
Earnings per share*	0.71		0.71

* Cl.A & B com.
^A Reported in accordance with IFRS

Historical Summary
(as originally stated)

Fiscal Year	Oper. Rev.	Net Inc. Bef. Disc.	EPS*
	$000s	$000s	$
2022^A	159,393	23,402	0.82
2021^A	159,778	30,591	1.07
2020^A	153,356	26,652	0.94
2019^A	149,938	25,694	0.90
2018^A	146,595	25,681	0.90

* Cl.A & B com.
^A Reported in accordance with IFRS

C.159 CordovaCann Corp.

Symbol - CDVA **Exchange** - CSE **CUSIP** - 21864T
Head Office - 401-217 Queen St W, Toronto, ON, M4V 0R2 **Telephone** - (416) 523-3350
Website - www.cordovacann.com
Email - ashish@cordovacann.com
Investor Relations - Ashish Kapoor (416) 523-3350
Auditors - Kreston GTA LLP C.A., Markham, Ont.
Transfer Agents - TSX Trust Company, Toronto, Ont.
Profile - (Can. 2006; orig. Ont., 1997 amalg.) Has retail cannabis stores in Canada and cannabis cultivation and manufacturing operation in Oregon, Washington State and California.

Has a partnership with U.S. cannabis retailer **Star Buds Inc.** which gives the company the exclusive rights to own and operate retail cannabis stores under the Star Buds Cannabis Co. brand across Canada.

Has interests in eight stores in Ontario, three in Manitoba, two in Alberta and one in British Columbia.

Owns a 10,900 sq.-ft. manufacturing facility in Bremerton, Wash. with capacity for 3,000 litres of distillate production; and a 5,000 sq.-ft. manufacturing and distribution facility in Costa Mesa, Calif. with capacity for 3,000 litres of distillate production.

Wholly owned **Cannabilt Farms, LLC** owns a six-acre site that hosts a licensed cannabis cultivation facility in Clackamas cty., Ore., with capacity for 3,400 lbs. of flower and over 3,000 litres of distillate production.

The company also provides cannabis operators in Oregon, Washington and California a variety of resources and services including capital commitments, strategic positioning, brand developments, best operating practices, access to intellectual property, administrative assistance and general business consulting.

In June 2022, the company acquired the assets of **AuBio Labs, LLC** for US$700,000. The assets include licenses, equipment and a leased facility to provide cannabis extraction services and manufactured products to licensed cannabis retailers in California.

Predecessor Detail - Name changed from LiveReel Media Corporation, Jan. 3, 2018.

Directors - Thomas M. (Taz) Turner Jr., chr. & CEO, Wrightsville Beach, N.C.; Tom Bushey; Ben Higham; Dale Rasmussen; Jakob Ripshtein, Toronto, Ont.

Other Exec. Officers - Ashish Kapoor, CFO & corp. sec.

Capital Stock

	Authorized (shs.)	Outstanding (shs.)[1]
Common	unlimited	109,502,853

[1] At Nov. 29, 2022

Major Shareholder - Ashish Kapoor held 14.7% interest and Thomas M. (Taz) Turner Jr. held 14.45% interest at June 30, 2019.

Price Range - CDVA/CSE

Year	Volume	High	Low	Close
2022	5,187,630	$0.45	$0.12	$0.20
2021	9,821,722	$0.55	$0.20	$0.45
2020	8,926,334	$0.50	$0.12	$0.25
2019	3,148,221	$0.98	$0.15	$0.18
2018	556,022	$2.00	$0.80	$0.89

Recent Close: $0.18

Capital Stock Changes - During fiscal 2022, common shares were issued as follows: 8,245,100 by private placement, 5,354,400 on conversion of debentures, 1,852,280 for debt settlement, 700,000 on exercise of warrants and 200,000 on exercise of options.

Wholly Owned Subsidiaries

Cordova Investments Canada, Inc., Ont.
- 60.45% int. in **2734158 Ontario Inc.**, Ont.

CordovaCann Holdings Canada, Inc., Ont.

CordovaCann Holdings, Inc., Del.
- 100% int. in **CDVA Enterprises, LLC**, Calif.
- 100% int. in **Cannabilt Holdings, Inc.**, Ore.
  - 100% int. in **Cannabilt Farms, LLC**, Ore.
  - 100% int. in **Cannabilt OR Retail, LLC**, Ore.
  - 100% int. in **Future Processing, LLC**, Ore.
- 100% int. in **Cordova CA Holdings, LLC**, Calif.
- 100% int. in **Cordova CO Holdings, LLC**, Colo.
- 100% int. in **Cordova OR Holdings, LLC**, Ore.
  - 100% int. in **Cordova OR Operations, LLC**, Ore.

Extraction Technologies, LLC, Wash.

Subsidiaries

51% int. in **10062771 Manitoba Ltd.**, Man.

Financial Statistics

Periods ended:	12m June 30/22[A]		12m June 30/21[A]
	$000s	%Chg	$000s
Operating revenue	**13,526**	**+31**	**10,319**
Cost of sales	9,798		6,827
Salaries & benefits	2,184		1,031
General & admin expense	3,423		3,117
Stock-based compensation	2		942
Operating expense	**15,407**	**+29**	**11,916**
Operating income	**(1,881)**	**n.a.**	**(1,597)**
Deprec., depl. & amort.	1,292		960
Finance costs, gross	902		1,015
Write-downs/write-offs	(212)		(665)
Pre-tax income	**(3,984)**	**n.a.**	**(4,485)**
Income taxes	40		302
Net income	**(4,023)**	**n.a.**	**(4,787)**
Net inc. for equity hldrs	**(3,957)**	**n.a.**	**(5,155)**
Net inc. for non-cont. int	**(67)**	**n.a.**	**368**
Cash & equivalent	715		1,058
Inventories	724		505
Accounts receivable	81		8
Current assets	3,211		2,130
Fixed assets, net	3,440		6,060
Right-of-use assets	4,451		3,170
Intangibles, net	5,649		5,814
Total assets	**16,751**	**-3**	**17,274**
Accts. pay. & accr. liabs	3,557		3,326
Current liabilities	5,696		6,851
Long-term debt, gross	1,170		2,584
Long-term lease liabilities	4,312		2,890
Equity portion of conv. debs	690		307
Shareholders' equity	5,861		6,492
Non-controlling interest	725		826
Cash from oper. activs	**(2,072)**	**n.a.**	**(221)**
Cash from fin. activs	721		1,571
Cash from invest. activs	2,065		(872)
Net cash position	**1,748**	**+65**	**1,058**
Capital expenditures	(662)		(741)
Capital disposals	2,727		39
	$		$
Earnings per share*	(0.04)		(0.06)
Cash flow per share*	(0.02)		(0.00)
	shs		shs
No. of shs. o/s*	109,502,853		93,151,074
Avg. no. of shs. o/s*	100,632,038		81,683,228
	%		%
Net profit margin	(29.74)		(46.39)
Return on equity	(64.05)		(85.13)
Return on assets	(18.29)		(23.17)

* Common

[A] Reported in accordance with IFRS

Latest Results

Periods ended:	3m Sept. 30/22[A]		3m Sept. 30/21[A]
	$000s	%Chg	$000s
Operating revenue	3,696	-2	3,775
Net income	(734)	n.a.	(648)
Net inc. for equity hldrs	(757)	n.a.	(669)
Net inc. for non-cont. int	22		21
	$		$
Earnings per share*	(0.01)		(0.01)

* Common

[A] Reported in accordance with IFRS

Historical Summary
(as originally stated)

Fiscal Year	Oper. Rev.	Net Inc. Bef. Disc.	EPS*
	$000s	$000s	$
2022[A]	13,526	(4,023)	(0.04)
2021[A]	10,319	(4,787)	(0.06)
2020[A]	167	(4,651)	(0.10)
2019[A]	nil	(5,837)	(0.15)
2018[A]	nil	(4,866)	(0.15)

* Common

[A] Reported in accordance with IFRS

C.160 Core One Labs Inc.

Symbol - COOL **Exchange** - CSE **CUSIP** - 21872J

Head Office - 800-1199 Hastings St W, Vancouver, BC, V6E 3T5 **Telephone** - (604) 609-6142 **Toll-free** - (866) 347-5058 **Fax** - (604) 609-6145

Website - core1labs.com

Email - investorrelations@core1labs.com

Investor Relations - Joel Shacker (866) 347-5058

Auditors - BF Borgers CPA PC C.P.A., Lakewood, Colo.

Lawyers - McMillan LLP, Vancouver, B.C.

Transfer Agents - Computershare Trust Company of Canada Inc., Toronto, Ont.

Profile - (B.C. 2010) Produces CannaStrips™ for the oral delivery of cannabis and researching this technology for the delivery of psilocybin. Also pursuing the research and development of psychedelics for the treatment of mental health issues and has interests in walk-in medical clinics in British Columbia.

Concentrates & CannaStrips™

The company has developed a patent pending thin film oral delivery strip which dissolves instantly when placed in the mouth. Its flagship product CannaStrips™ infuses tetrahydrocannabinol (THC) or cannabidiol (CBD) into the strips that provide an exact and consistent dosage. The company is pursuing the application of its technology to the delivery of psilocybin, which could be used as a psychedelic treatment for mental health disorders.

Bio-Pharma Research and Development

Wholly owned **Vocan Biotechnologies Inc.** is a genetic engineering and biosynthesis research company developing a fermentation system for the production of psilocybin API; wholly owned **Akome Biotech Ltd.** develops psychedelic-based pharmaceuticals for the treatment of rare diseases and mental disorders including cluster headaches, Parkinson's disease, Alzheimer's disease and depression; wholly owned **New Path Laboratories Inc.**, develops and licenses natural health products and dietary supplements which contains functional and non-psychedelic mushroom to help support daily biological functions and maintain good health; and wholly owned **Awakened Biosciences Inc.** develops and researches novel technologies for the production of synthetic psylocybin psilocin analogues and for the manufacturing of various non-psychoactive psilocybin-based prodrugs which enables clients to produce resultant compounds at scale and at reduced costs.

Medical Clinics

Wholly owned **Rejuva Alternative Medicine Research Centre Inc.** and affiliate **Shahcor Health Services Inc.** operate walk-in medical clinics located in Vancouver and West Vancouver, B.C., and maintains a database of over 200,000 patients. Rejuva is in the process of opening a specialized medical clinic within Shahcor's downtown Vancouver clinic. and is building out an educational platform and developing a research program to collecting information from qualified patients of Shahcor related to psilocybin. Wholly owned **Bluejay Mental Health Group Inc.** has a specialty medical clinic located in Langley, B.C., which has an integrated telehealth platform and wholly owned **Ketamine Infusion Centers of Texas LLC** has a health and wellness clinic located in Woodlands, Tex., that was established to address treatment-resistant depression and other mental health disorders, through the delivery of ketamine infusion treatments.

Cannabis Cultivation & Processing Operations

Wholly owned **Rainy Daze Cannabis Corp.** has a long-term lease for a building under construction in British Columbia, which would house a micro-cultivation facility consisting of 2,210 sq. ft. of canopy space and 3,500 sq. ft. of operational-purpose-built building. The company plans to sell Rainy Daze once the lease for the facility commences and Rainy Day is in a potion to apply for a micro-cultivation licence from Health Canada.

Predecessor Detail - Name changed from Lifestyle Delivery Systems Inc., Sept. 6, 2019; basis 1 new for 6 old shs.

Directors - Joel Shacker, CEO, Vancouver, B.C.; Geoffrey (Geoff) Balderson, CFO & corp. sec., Vancouver, B.C.; Dr. Santiago Ferro, CMO; Ryan D. Hoggan, Lehi, Utah; Patrick C. T. (Pat) Morris, Vancouver, B.C.

Capital Stock

	Authorized (shs.)	Outstanding (shs.)[1]
Common	unlimited	30,881,637

[1] At Aug. 29, 2022

Major Shareholder - Widely held at Sept. 21, 2021.

Price Range - COOL/CSE

Year	Volume	High	Low	Close
2022	33,067,338	$2.32	$0.29	$0.67
2021	19,860,867	$11.84	$0.46	$0.70
2020	3,163,238	$8.72	$2.08	$7.12
2019	1,206,979	$65.28	$5.92	$6.40
2018	1,412,250	$147.84	$26.40	$27.84

Consolidation: 1-for-8 cons. in July 2021; 1-for-2 cons. in July 2020; 1-for-6 cons. in Sept. 2019

Recent Close: $0.43

Wholly Owned Subsidiaries

Akome Biotech Ltd., Vancouver, B.C.
Awakened Biosciences Inc., Victoria, B.C.
Bluejay Mental Health Group Inc., B.C.
Canna Delivery Systems Inc., Nev.
Frontier Mycology Corp., B.C.
Ketamine Infusions Centers of Texas, LLC, Tex.
Lifestyle Capital Corporation, Calif.
New Path Laboratories Inc., B.C.
Omni Distribution Inc., Calif.
Optimus Prime Design Corp., B.C.
Rainy Daze Cannabis Corp., B.C.
Rejuva Alternative Medicine Research Centre Inc., Vancouver, B.C.
Vocan Biotechnologies Inc., Victoria, B.C.

Investments

Plant-Based Investment Corp., Toronto, Ont.
25% int. in **Shahcor Health Services Inc.**, Vancouver, B.C.

Financial Statistics

Periods ended:	12m Dec. 31/21[A]		12m Dec. 31/20[A]
	$000s	%Chg	$000s
Operating revenue	**432**	**n.a.**	**nil**
Salaries & benefits	654		nil
Research & devel. expense	627		98
General & admin expense	5,435		4,334
Stock-based compensation	5,981		2,168
Operating expense	**12,697**	**+92**	**6,599**
Operating income	**(12,265)**	**n.a.**	**(6,599)**
Deprec., depl. & amort.	39		nil
Finance costs, gross	22		16
Investment income	567		(4,259)
Write-downs/write-offs	(25,288)		(36,832)
Pre-tax income	**(37,055)**	**n.a.**	**(46,904)**
Net inc. bef. disc. opers	**(37,055)**	**n.a.**	**(46,904)**
Income from disc. opers	nil		(7,895)
Net income	**(37,055)**	**n.a.**	**(54,799)**
Net inc. for equity hldrs	**(37,055)**	**n.a.**	**(54,619)**
Net inc. for non-cont. int	**nil**	**n.a.**	**(180)**
Cash & equivalent	920		1,898
Inventories	3		nil
Accounts receivable	185		2,972
Current assets	1,162		4,987
Fixed assets, net	155		447
Intangibles, net	5,702		4,089
Total assets	**7,610**	**-20**	**9,524**
Accts. pay. & accr. liabs	2,954		3,283
Current liabilities	3,302		3,703
Long-term debt, gross	nil		428
Long-term debt, net	nil		428
Shareholders' equity	4,309		5,393
Cash from oper. activs	**(4,642)**	**n.a.**	**(2,325)**
Cash from fin. activs	3,585		4,433
Cash from invest. activs	1,292		(315)
Net cash position	**763**	**+45**	**528**
Capital expenditures	(9)		nil
	$		$
Earns. per sh. bef disc opers*	(2.57)		(8.80)
Earnings per share*	(2.57)		(10.24)
Cash flow per share*	(0.32)		(0.22)
	shs		shs
No. of shs. o/s*	21,447,037		11,837,813
Avg. no. of shs. o/s*	14,419,549		5,319,010
	%		%
Net profit margin	n.m.		n.a.
Return on equity	(763.86)		(740.30)
Return on assets	(432.28)		(343.16)

* Common

[A] Reported in accordance with IFRS

Latest Results

Periods ended:	6m June 30/22[A]		6m June 30/21[A]
	$000s	%Chg	$000s
Operating revenue	268	n.a.	nil
Net income	(12,008)	n.a.	(30,153)
	$		$
Earnings per share*	(0.43)		(18.24)

* Common

[A] Reported in accordance with IFRS

Historical Summary
(as originally stated)

Fiscal Year	Oper. Rev. $000s	Net Inc. Bef. Disc. $000s	EPS* $
2021[A]	432	(37,055)	(2.57)
2020[A]	nil	(46,904)	(8.80)
2019[A]	5,042	(21,652)	(15.24)
2018[A]	4,081	(13,153)	(11.52)
2017[A]	191	(13,164)	(18.24)

* Common

[A] Reported in accordance with IFRS

Note: Adjusted throughout for 1-for-8 cons. in July 2021; 1-for-2 cons. in July 2020; 1-for-6 cons. in Sept. 2019

C.161 Corus Entertainment Inc.*

Symbol - CJR.B **Exchange** - TSX **CUSIP** - 220874
Head Office - Corus Quay, 25 Dockside Dr, Toronto, ON, M5A 0B5
Telephone - (416) 479-7000 **Fax** - (416) 479-7006
Website - www.corusent.com
Email - heidi.kucher@corusent.com
Investor Relations - Heidi Kucher (416) 479-6055
Auditors - Ernst & Young LLP C.A., Toronto, Ont.
Bankers - The Toronto-Dominion Bank, Toronto, Ont.
Lawyers - Osler, Hoskin & Harcourt LLP, Toronto, Ont.
Transfer Agents - TSX Trust Company, Montréal, Qué.
FP500 Revenue Ranking - 256
Employees - 3,336 at Aug. 31, 2022

Profile - (Alta. 1999; orig. Can., 1998) Develops and delivers brands and content across platforms for the Canadian and international markets. Operations include interests in specialty television networks and conventional television stations, radio stations, the production and distribution of films and television programs, merchandise licensing, book publishing, animation software, digital and streaming assets, a social media digital agency, a social media creator network, and technology and media services.

Business activities are conducted through two segments: Television and Radio.

Television

Specialty Television - The company's 33 specialty networks provide programming across Canada and include ABC Spark, Adult Swim, BC 1, Cartoon Network Canada, Cooking Channel Canada (71% interest), CMT Canada (80% interest), Crime + Investigation, DejaView, Disney Channel Canada, Disney Junior Canada, Disney XD Canada, Magnolia Network Canada (67% interest), DTOUR, Food Network Canada (71% interest), HGTV Canada (67% interest), Historia, The HISTORY Channel, H2, La chaîne Disney, Lifetime, OWN: Oprah Winfrey Network Canada, MovieTime, National Geographic (50% interest), Nat Geo Wild (50% interest), Nickelodeon Canada, Séries+, Showcase, Slice, TELETOON/TÉLÉTOON, Treehouse, W Network and YTV.

Conventional Television - The company owns and operates 15 conventional basic carriage television stations in British Columbia (2), Alberta (3), Saskatchewan (2), Manitoba, Ontario (4), Quebec, New Brunswick and Nova Scotia under the Global Television brand. Global Television includes the stand-alone news brand, Global News.

Content - The company produces and distributes films and television programs; licenses merchandise; publishes books; and develops and distributes animation software. The company creates, produces and distributes programs based on its owned and third party brands through wholly owned **Nelvana Limited**, which focuses on children's animated and live action content and related consumer products; Corus Studios, which focuses on unscripted lifestyle and factual programming; and **Aircraft Pictures Limited** (51% owned), a producer of scripted content for kids, families and young adults. Content is delivered worldwide through the company's multiple platforms, such as linear television, online and mobile platforms, over-the-top (OTT) services, and sold to international broadcasters and distributors, media companies and digital service providers. Nelvana's merchandising business involves the licensing of owned and third party brands for use in consumer products such as toys, apparel, book publishing and interactive products. Wholly owned **Kids Can Press Limited** publishes children's and young adult books. Wholly owned **Toon Boom Animation Inc.** supplies animation and storyboard software solutions for studios, professionals, students, educators and schools.

Other - The company operates digital media assets, a social digital agency and a social creator network, and provides technology and media services. Digital media assets consist of the companion websites and other digital platforms, including mobile applications, related to its brands as well as streaming services such as STACKTV, TELETOON+ and Global TV App. The company also owns so.da, a full-service social digital agency which provides strategy, content production, creatives, analytics and public relations to various brands; Kin Community Canada, a creator media studio which represents lifestyle creators and works with brands to develop and execute social media campaigns and content using Kin's network of creators; and Quay Media Services, which provides various technology and media service offerings including studio and production facilities, post-production services, full and live captioning, described video, subtitling, content ingest, signal origination, master control playout, content delivery, transcoding and media asset management.

Radio

This segment consists of 39 radio stations (29 FM and 10 AM stations) primarily in high-growth urban centres in English Canada, with a concentration in southern Ontario. Content is primarily distributed through over-the-air, analog transmission, with additional delivery methods including HD radio, online and mobile platforms, and podcasts. The company owns a 50% interest in Canadian Broadcast Sales (CBS) in partnership with **Rogers Communications Inc.** CBS is a national radio sales organization representing 43 broadcasters and more than 400 radio stations in 222 Canadian markets.

On Sept. 1, 2022, Nick+, the company's kids and family streaming service, was transitioned to TELETOON+.

On Mar. 28, 2022, the company launched Magnolia Network in Canada, becoming the first broadcaster outside of the U.S. to launch the channel. Magnolia Network Canada, a joint venture with **Discovery, Inc.**, was the rebrand of DIY Network Canada (67% owned by the company).

Recent Merger and Acquisition Activity

Status: pending **Announced:** July 13, 2023

Corus Entertainment Inc. agreed to sell wholly owned Toon Boom Animation Inc., which supplies animation and storyboard software solutions for studios, professionals, students, educators and schools, to Integrated Media Company for $147,500,000.

Directors - Heather A. Shaw, exec. chr., Calgary, Alta.; Julie M. Shaw, v-chr., Calgary, Alta.; Douglas D. (Doug) Murphy, pres. & CEO, Toronto, Ont.; Fernand Bélisle†, Luskville, Qué.; Michael T. Boychuk, Baie-d'Urfé, Qué.; Stephanie L. Coyles, Toronto, Ont.; Charmaine Crooks, Vancouver, B.C.; Michael D'Avella, Calgary, Alta.; Sameer Deen, North Miami, Fla.; Mark Hollinger, Washington, D.C.; Barry L. James, Edmonton, Alta.; Margaret O'Brien, Toronto, Ont.

Other Exec. Officers - Colin Bohm, exec. v-p, content & corp. strategy; Cheryl Fullerton, exec. v-p, people & commun.; John R. Gossling, exec. v-p & CFO; Shawn Kelly, exec. v-p, tech.; Jennifer (Jenn) Lee, exec. v-p, gen. counsel & corp. sec.; Gregory G. (Greg) McLelland, exec. v-p & chief revenue officer; Troy Reeb, exec. v-p, broadcast networks

† Lead director

Capital Stock

	Authorized (shs.)	Outstanding (shs.)[1]
Preferred	unlimited	
Class A		nil
Class 1		nil
Class 2		nil
Class A Voting	unlimited	3,371,526
Class B Non-voting	unlimited	196,068,632

[1] At May 31, 2023

Class A Voting - Convertible into class B non-voting shares on a 1-for-1 basis. One vote per share.

Class B Non-Voting - Convertible into class A voting shares on a 1-for-1 basis in limited circumstances. Non-voting.

Options - At Aug. 31, 2022, options were outstanding to purchase 7,583,100 class B non-voting shares at prices ranging from $3.38 to $17.58 per share with a weighted average remaining contractual life of 3.7 years.

Major Shareholder - Shaw Family Living Trust held 85.59% interest and Catherine M. (Cathy) Roozen held 10.18% interest at Nov. 30, 2022.

Price Range - CJR.B/TSX

Year	Volume	High	Low	Close
2022	285,044,384	$5.42	$1.92	$2.16
2021	223,377,651	$6.54	$4.21	$4.76
2020	270,333,882	$6.00	$1.78	$4.28
2019	183,287,052	$8.11	$4.69	$5.32
2018	220,161,180	$11.85	$3.62	$4.76

Recent Close: $1.31

Capital Stock Changes - During fiscal 2022, 40,866 class B non-voting shares were issued on conversion of a like number of class A voting shares and 8,706,900 class B non-voting shares were repurchased under a Normal Course Issuer Bid.

Dividends

CJR.B cl B N.V. Ra $0.12 pa Q est. Mar. 31, 2023**[1]
Prev. Rate: $0.24 est. Dec. 28, 2018

[1] Divds. paid monthly prior December/18.

** Reinvestment Option

Long-Term Debt - Outstanding at Aug. 31, 2022:

Bank loans due Mar. 2027[1]	$505,577,000
5% sr. notes due May 2028	500,000,000
6% sr. notes due Feb. 2030	250,000,000
Interim production financing[2]	15,574,000
Less: Def. fin. charges	9,501,000
	1,261,650,000
Less: Current portion	15,574,000
	1,246,076,000

[1] Interest rates fluctuate with Canadian bankers' acceptances. Effective interest rate averaged 4.5% for fiscal 2022.

[2] Revolving demand loans as interim financing for film or TV productions. Bear interest at prime plus an applicable margin.

Wholly Owned Subsidiaries

Corus Media Holdings Inc., Toronto, Ont.
Corus Radio Inc., Toronto, Ont.
Corus Sales Inc., Toronto, Ont.
Corus Television Limited Partnership, Canada.
History Television Inc., Toronto, Ont.
Kids Can Press Limited, Toronto, Ont.
Nelvana Limited, Toronto, Ont.
Showcase Television Inc., Canada.
TELETOON Canada Inc., Toronto, Ont.
Toon Boom Animation Inc., Montréal, Qué.
W Network Inc., Canada.
YTV Canada, Inc., Canada.

Subsidiaries

51% int. in **Aircraft Pictures Limited**, Toronto, Ont.
71% int. in **Food Network Canada Inc.**, Toronto, Ont. Represents an 80.2% voting interest.
67% int. in **HGTV Canada Inc.**, Canada. Represents an 80.2% voting interest.

Note: The preceding list includes only the major related companies in which interests are held.

Financial Statistics

Periods ended:	12m Aug. 31/22^A		12m Aug. 31/21^A
	$000s	%Chg	$000s
Operating revenue	**1,598,586**	**+4**	**1,543,483**
Other operating expense	571,204		512,340
Operating expense	**571,204**	**+11**	**512,340**
Operating income	**1,027,382**	**0**	**1,031,143**
Deprec., depl. & amort.	740,676		658,780
Finance costs, gross	107,108		104,078
Investment income	41		40
Write-downs/write-offs	(352,204)[1]		nil
Pre-tax income	**(191,883)**	**n.a.**	**263,333**
Income taxes	40,355		68,760
Net income	**(232,238)**	**n.a.**	**194,573**
Net inc. for equity hldrs	**(245,058)**	**n.a.**	**172,550**
Net inc. for non-cont. int.	**12,820**	**-42**	**22,023**
Cash & equivalent	54,912		43,685
Accounts receivable	311,015		325,587
Current assets	404,530		398,975
Long-term investments	30,862		61,320
Fixed assets, net	294,026		316,226
Intangibles, net	2,597,826		2,928,466
Total assets	**3,502,480**	**-9**	**3,856,617**
Accts. pay. & accr. liabs.	499,796		482,601
Current liabilities	551,013		552,347
Long-term debt, gross	1,261,650		1,349,293
Long-term debt, net	1,246,076		1,313,965
Long-term lease liabilities	119,737		128,809
Shareholders' equity	752,041		1,067,534
Non-controlling interest	151,940		152,829
Cash from oper. activs.	**216,835**	**-21**	**274,493**
Cash from fin. activs.	(230,780)		(247,182)
Cash from invest. activs.	25,172		(29,526)
Net cash position	**54,912**	**+26**	**43,685**
Capital expenditures	(17,810)		(19,554)
Capital disposals	299		316
Pension fund surplus	30,653		31,741
	$		$
Earnings per share*	(1.19)		0.83
Cash flow per share*	1.05		1.32
Cash divd. per share*	0.24		0.24
	shs		shs
No. of shs. o/s*	199,660,158		208,367,058
Avg. no. of shs. o/s*	205,905,000		208,367,058
	%		%
Net profit margin	(14.53)		12.61
Return on equity	(26.94)		17.54
Return on assets	(2.79)		6.94
Foreign sales percent	5		5
No. of employees (FTEs)	3,336		3,295

* Class A & B
^A Reported in accordance with IFRS
[1] Includes $350,000,000 goodwill impairment charge in the television segment.

Latest Results

Periods ended:	9m May 31/23^A		9m May 31/22^A
	$000s	%Chg	$000s
Operating revenue	1,172,397	-7	1,258,992
Net income	(471,473)	n.a.	133,869
Net inc. for equity hldrs.	(479,136)	n.a.	122,007
Net inc. for non-cont. int.	7,663		11,862
	$		$
Earnings per share*	(2.40)		0.59

* Class A & B
^A Reported in accordance with IFRS

Historical Summary
(as originally stated)

Fiscal Year	Oper. Rev.	Net Inc. Bef. Disc.	EPS*
	$000s	$000s	$
2022^A	1,598,586	(232,238)	(1.19)
2021^A	1,543,483	194,573	0.83
2020^A	1,511,236	(607,707)	(2.98)
2019^A	1,687,482	180,667	0.74
2018^A	1,647,347	(758,163)	(3.77)

* Class A & B
^A Reported in accordance with IFRS

C.162 CoTec Holdings Corp.

Symbol - CTH **Exchange** - TSX-VEN **CUSIP** - 22165A
Head Office - 428-755 Burrard St, Vancouver, BC, V6Z 1X6 **Telephone** - (604) 992-5600 **Fax** - (604) 770-1300
Website - www.cotec.ca
Email - braamjonker@gmail.com
Investor Relations - Abraham Jonker (604) 992-5600
Auditors - PricewaterhouseCoopers LLP C.A., Vancouver, B.C.
Bankers - Bank of Montreal, Vancouver, B.C.
Lawyers - Baker & McKenzie LLP; Towers & Hamlins LLP, London, Middx. United Kingdom; Dentons Canada LLP, Vancouver, B.C.
Transfer Agents - Computershare Trust Company of Canada Inc., Vancouver, B.C.

Profile - (B.C. 1986) Invest in disruptive technologies in the mineral extraction industry that are expected to result in much lower greenhouse gas emissions than existing processes.

The company plans to acquire interests in a selection of technologies and then apply these interests and rights to various commodity assets ranging from traditional mines to waste dumps and recycled scrap as owners, joint venture partners or licensors.

At June 2023, the company's investment portfolio included **Binding Solutions Limited**, a green pelletization technology company; **Mkango Resources Ltd.**, which has mineral interests in Malawi; **MagIron LLC**, which holds a dormant iron ore concentrator known as Plant 4 in Grand Rapids, Minn., along with land package surrounding the plant; **Maginito Limited**, a downstream rare earth technology company which holds an interest in a U.K. rare earth neodymium (NdFeB) magnet recycler; and **Ceibo Inc.**, an inorganic leaching technology company. Also holds the right to co-invest directly in underlying assets with the fund.

Also holds an option to acquire Lac Jeannine property, 31 claims, Côte-Nord region, Que.

In April 2022, the company completed a change of business from mineral exploration to an investment issuer with a focus on investing in innovative technologies that fundamentally change the manner in which minerals and commodities are extracted. Concurrently, the company completed an initial US$2,000,000 equity investment in **Binding Solutions Limited** (BSL) and signed an agreement for a capital commitment of between A$$2,000,000 and A$10,000,000 in **Basic Industries Venture Fund I, LP**. (BIVF). United Kingdom-based BSL has developed a proprietary cold agglomeration technology for the production of high-quality clean pellets from primary materials, waste dumps and stockpiles. Australian-based BIVF is a venture capital fund that is focused on investments in industrial technologies for heavy industries.

Predecessor Detail - Name changed from EastCoal Inc., Aug. 27, 2021.

Directors - Raffaele (Lucio) Genovese, chr., Zug, Switzerland; Julian A. Treger, pres. & CEO, London, Middx., United Kingdom; Thomas (Tom) Albanese, Hillsborough, N.J.; John J. Conlon, Toronto, Ont.; Sharon Fay, N.Y.; Margot Naudie, Toronto, Ont.

Other Exec. Officers - John Singleton, COO; Abraham (Braam) Jonker, CFO & corp. sec.; Eugene Hercun, v-p, fin. & corp. devel.

Capital Stock

	Authorized (shs.)	Outstanding (shs.)[1]
Common	unlimited	54,627,430

[1] At Aug. 11, 2023

Major Shareholder - Abraham (Braam) Jonker held 18.63% interest, Kings Chapel International Limited held 16.65% interest and John J. Conlon held 15.8% interest at Sept. 23, 2022.

Price Range - CTH/TSX-VEN

Year	Volume	High	Low	Close
2022	1,491,016	$0.80	$0.30	$0.47
2021	823,378	$0.68	$0.10	$0.64
2020	2,005	$0.10	$0.09	$0.10
2019	2,640,255	$0.10	$0.05	$0.09
2018	119,558	$0.30	$0.10	$0.11

Recent Close: $0.78

Capital Stock Changes - From January to March 2023, private placement of 14,874,006 units (1 common share & 1 warrant) at 50¢ per unit was completed, with warrants exercisable at 75¢ per share for one year.

In April 2022, 11,390,593 units (1 common share & 1 warrant) were issued without further consideration on exchange of subscription receipts sold previously by private placement at 55¢ each. In December 2022, 1,264,108 units (1 common share & 1 warrant) were issued without further consideration on exchange of subscription receipts sold previously by private placement at 50¢ each. Also during 2022, 4,040,404 common shares were issued exercise of warrants.

Wholly Owned Subsidiaries

CoTec USA Corp., Del.
1391621 B.C. Ltd.

Investments

3% int. in **Binding Solutions Limited**, United Kingdom.
3% int. in **Ceibo Inc.**, Del.
10% int. in **Maginito Limited**, British Virgin Islands.
16.94% int. in **MagIron LLC**, United States.

Financial Statistics

Periods ended:	12m Dec. 31/22^A		12m Dec. 31/21^A
	$000s	%Chg	$000s
General & admin expense	2,039		518
Stock-based compensation	434		88
Operating expense	**2,473**	**+308**	**606**
Operating income	**(2,473)**	**n.a.**	**(606)**
Finance costs, gross	n.a.		1
Finance costs, net	(60)		n.a.
Pre-tax income	**1,489**	**n.a.**	**(607)**
Income taxes	nil		1
Net income	**1,489**	**n.a.**	**(608)**
Cash & equivalent	239		400
Current assets	341		463
Long-term investments	9,234		nil
Total assets	**12,403**	**n.m.**	**463**
Accts. pay. & accr. liabs.	1,497		543
Current liabilities	1,497		543
Long-term debt, gross	1,554		nil
Long-term debt, net	1,554		nil
Shareholders' equity	9,221		(79)
Cash from oper. activs.	**(1,128)**	**n.a.**	**(103)**
Cash from fin. activs.	8,969		500
Cash from invest. activs.	(8,002)		nil
Net cash position	**239**	**-40**	**400**
	$		$
Earnings per share*	0.05		(0.03)
Cash flow per share*	(0.03)		(0.01)
	shs		shs
No. of shs. o/s*	39,753,424		23,058,319
Avg. no. of shs. o/s*	32,496,000		20,290,919
	%		%
Net profit margin	n.a.		n.a.
Return on equity	n.m.		n.m.
Return on assets	23.15		(256.66)

* Common
^A Reported in accordance with IFRS

Latest Results

Periods ended:	6m June 30/23^A		6m June 30/22^A
	$000s	%Chg	$000s
Net income	9,854	+416	1,911
	$		$
Earnings per share*	0.19		0.07

* Common
^A Reported in accordance with IFRS

Historical Summary
(as originally stated)

Fiscal Year	Oper. Rev.	Net Inc. Bef. Disc.	EPS*
	$000s	$000s	$
2022^A	nil	1,489	0.05
2021^A	nil	(608)	(0.03)
2020^A	nil	(103)	(0.01)
2019^A	nil	(90)	(0.01)
2018^A	nil	(95)	(0.01)

* Common
^A Reported in accordance with IFRS

C.163 Covalon Technologies Ltd.

Symbol - COV **Exchange** - TSX-VEN **CUSIP** - 22282D
Head Office - Unit 5, 1660 Tech Ave, Mississauga, ON, L4W 5S7 **Telephone** - (905) 568-8400 **Toll-free** - (877) 711-6055 **Fax** - (905) 568-5200
Website - www.covalon.com
Email - bpedlar@covalon.com
Investor Relations - Brian E. Pedlar (877) 711-6055
Auditors - PricewaterhouseCoopers LLP C.A., Oakville, Ont.
Lawyers - Stikeman Elliott LLP, Toronto, Ont.
Transfer Agents - TSX Trust Company, Toronto, Ont.

Profile - (Ont. 2004) Provides patented medical technologies and products for advanced wound care, infection prevention, and medical device coatings, with options for patients to heal with less infections, less pain and better outcomes.

The company has developed proprietary technologies consisting of: (i) collagen matrix; (ii) antimicrobial silicone adhesive; (iii) medical coating technology (CovaCoat™); and (iv) CovaGuard antimicrobial sanitizing technology. These platform technologies are protected by patents, patent applications and patents pending, patented and proprietary manufacturing processes, and trade secrets, brands, trademarks and trade names.

Products derived from the platform technologies consist of the following:

Advanced wound care dressings consist of collagen-based wound products for the treatment of chronic and infected wounds including diabetic ulcers, pressure ulcers, venous ulcers, donor and graft sites, traumatic wounds healing by secondary intention, dehisced surgical wounds, and first and second degree burns. Products are sold under the ColActive®, ColActive® Plus, ColActive® Transfer, CovaWound™ and CovaView brands.

Surgical and peri-operative products include SurgiClear™, an antimicrobial clear silicone adhesive dressing with chlorhexidine and silver used to cover and protect wound sites and wound closure devices as well as secure other primary dressings; MediClear™ Pre-Op, an antimicrobial silicone film used to cover and protect pre-operative or pre-insertion skin; and MediClear™ silicone dressings for the prevention and management of hypertrophic and keloid scars.

Infection management products include IV Clear™, an antimicrobial clear silicone adhesive dressing with chlorhexidine and silver used to cover and protect insertion sites and to secure intravenous devices to skin; SilverCoat™, an antimicrobial silicone foley catheter used in hospitals, ambulatory surgical centres and home health care situations to catheterize patients for extended periods of time; and VALGuard, which helps protect line-to-line connections, luer locks & access ports from environmental contamination.

Antimicrobial sanitizing technology platform incorporates Benzalkonium Chloride (BAC) into aunique lipid delivery system that can be applied to a variety of surfaces (porous and non-porous), and skin,to provide immediate and sustained kill of viruses and bacteria. Products include CovaGuard hand sanitizer and CovaGuard mask.

The majority of the company's products are sold through independent distributors to various healthcare providers. These products require regulatory clearances and are sold on a prescription basis in the United States, Canada, the Middle East, Europe, Asia, Latin America and other international countries. Also licenses its products and technologies to both large and start-up companies.

On Jan. 17, 2023, the company made an application in the United Kingdom to wind down its operations as at Sept. 30, 2022, and was expected to be completed in 2023.

During fiscal 2022, wholly owned **Covalon Medical Device Shanghai Co., Ltd.** was dissolved.

Predecessor Detail - Name changed from Seder Capital Corp., Dec. 24, 2004, following Qualifying Transaction reverse takeover acquisition of Covalon Technologies Inc.

Directors - Amir Boloor, chr., B.C.; Brian E. Pedlar, pres. & CEO, Ont.; Joseph Cordiano, Toronto, Ont.; Martin Goldfarb, Toronto, Ont.; Dr. Samantha Nutt, Ont.; Abraham (Abe) Schwartz, Toronto, Ont.; Ronald E. (Ron) Smith, Yarmouth, N.S.

Other Exec. Officers - Jason F. Gorel, interim CFO; Dr. Valerio (Val) DiTizio, chief scientific officer; Mark Doolittle, sr. v-p, comml. opers.; Ronald Hebert, sr. v-p, mktg.; Greg Leszczynski, v-p, HR; Elaine Zhang, v-p, opers.; Simon Smith, CEO, Covalon Technologies (Europe) Ltd.

Capital Stock

	Authorized (shs.)	Outstanding (shs.)[1]
Common	unlimited	25,009,677

[1] At Feb. 22, 2023

Major Shareholder - Abraham (Abe) Schwartz held 32.56% interest and The Goldfarb Corporation held 16.4% interest at Jan. 18, 2023.

Price Range - COV/TSX-VEN

Year	Volume	High	Low	Close
2022............	1,482,241	$2.79	$1.94	$2.34
2021............	2,218,600	$3.15	$1.11	$2.65
2020............	2,917,447	$2.10	$0.70	$1.15
2019............	2,828,118	$5.78	$1.20	$1.99
2018............	6,806,590	$9.45	$3.22	$4.10

Recent Close: $1.72

Capital Stock Changes - During fiscal 2022, common shares were issued as follows: 30,000 on exercise of options and 30,000 on exercise of warrants; 640,900 common shares were repurchased under a Normal Course Issuer Bid.

Wholly Owned Subsidiaries

Covalon Technologies (Europe) Limited
Covalon Technologies Inc.
Covalon Technologies (Israel) Ltd., Israel.
Covalon Technologies (USA) Ltd.

Financial Statistics

Periods ended:	12m Sept. 30/22[A]		12m Sept. 30/21[A]
	$000s	%Chg	$000s
Operating revenue........................	**18,146**	**-7**	**19,561**
Cost of sales..................................	10,401		9,582
Salaries & benefits.........................	11,560		5,512
Research & devel. expense.............	1,061		1,111
General & admin expense...............	3,234		1,818
Operating expense........................	**26,256**	**+46**	**18,022**
Operating income.........................	**(8,110)**	**n.a.**	**1,539**
Deprec., depl. & amort....................	1,033		700
Finance costs, gross.......................	112		419
Pre-tax income.............................	**(9,254)**	**n.a.**	**419**
Net inc. bef. disc. opers................	**(9,254)**	**n.a.**	**419**
Income from disc. opers..................	(409)		23,058
Net income....................................	**(9,663)**	**n.a.**	**23,477**
Cash & equivalent...........................	14,062		22,947
Inventories......................................	4,966		4,702
Accounts receivable........................	4,732		6,396
Current assets................................	27,228		37,438
Fixed assets, net.............................	1,216		1,257
Right-of-use assets.........................	657		852
Intangibles, net...............................	1,277		898
Total assets...................................	**30,378**	**-25**	**40,582**
Accts. pay. & accr. liabs..................	3,720		4,040
Current liabilities............................	4,539		4,996
Long-term lease liabilities................	1,559		2,049
Shareholders' equity........................	24,229		33,375
Cash from oper. activs..................	**(7,994)**	**n.a.**	**621**
Cash from fin. activs........................	(2,186)		(8,252)
Cash from invest. activs..................	(843)		(279)
Net cash position..........................	**14,062**	**-39**	**22,947**
Capital expenditures........................	(600)		(176)
Capital disposals.............................	102		nil
	$		$
Earns. per sh. bef disc opers*..........	(0.36)		0.02
Earnings per share*.........................	(0.38)		0.91
Cash flow per share*........................	(0.31)		0.02
	shs		shs
No. of shs. o/s*................................	25,287,777		25,868,677
Avg. no. of shs. o/s*.........................	25,759,555		25,821,239
	%		%
Net profit margin.............................	(51.00)		2.14
Return on equity..............................	(32.13)		1.97
Return on assets..............................	(25.77)		2.23
Foreign sales percent......................	100		99

* Common
[A] Reported in accordance with IFRS

Latest Results

Periods ended:	3m Dec. 31/22[A]		3m Dec. 31/21[A]
	$000s	%Chg	$000s
Operating revenue..........................	6,185	+25	4,936
Net inc. bef. disc. opers..................	(381)	n.a.	(1,108)
Income from disc. opers..................	nil		(409)
Net income.....................................	(381)	n.a.	(1,517)
	$		$
Earns. per sh. bef. disc. opers.*........	(0.02)		(0.04)
Earnings per share*.........................	(0.02)		(0.06)

* Common
[A] Reported in accordance with IFRS

Historical Summary
(as originally stated)

Fiscal Year	Oper. Rev.	Net Inc. Bef. Disc.	EPS*
	$000s	$000s	$
2022[A]....................	18,146	(9,254)	(0.36)
2021[A]....................	19,561	419	0.02
2020[A]....................	25,800	(6,952)	(0.27)
2019[A]....................	34,005	(9,138)	(0.41)
2018[A]....................	26,723	1,618	0.08

* Common
[A] Reported in accordance with IFRS

C.164 Coveo Solutions Inc.

Symbol - CVO **Exchange** - TSX **CUSIP** - 22289D
Head Office - 200-3175 ch des Quatre-Bourgeois, Québec, QC, G1W 2K7 **Telephone** - (418) 263-1111
Website - www.coveo.com/en
Email - bnussey@coveo.com
Investor Relations - Brandon Nussey (514) 375-0126
Auditors - PricewaterhouseCoopers LLP C.A., Québec, Qué.
Lawyers - Norton Rose Fulbright Canada LLP
Transfer Agents - TSX Trust Company, Montréal, Qué.
FP500 Revenue Ranking - 763
Employees - 743 at Mar. 31, 2023
Profile - (Can. 2004) Provides a cloud-based software-as-a-service (SaaS) platform (Coveo Relevance Cloud™) which utilizes artificial intelligence (AI) and intelligent search technologies to personalize digital experiences for customers, partners, dealers and employees.

The Coveo Relevance Cloud™ platform offers: unified content, which is synchronized from multiple disparate data sources and helps provide search recommendations; behavioural analyticals, such as searches, refinements, clicks, pages loads, add-to-cart and purchases, which is used to power dashboards and analytics in the platform; intelligence, in which the behavioural data provides the company's platforms with signals to feed its traditional machine learning and deep learning models that allows for the build of profiles for each user and anonymous personalization; and search and recommendations, which are embedded into multiple touchpoints within an organization, including communities, support portals and contact centres, allowing users to connect and discover content, products and services by matching inferred intent with results. Solutions are provided for e-commerce, service, website and workplace applications.

Wholly owned **Qubit Digital Ltd.** operates the Qubit Commerce AI platform which provides AI-powered personalization solutions, including product recommendations, badging and personalized content, for merchandising teams. Customers include those in the luxury, fashion, beauty and cosmetics, home and garden, travel and tourism, fast food, grocery retail, gaming and online betting industries.

Also has established strategic relationships with leading global technology platforms, including with Salesforce as a Salesforce Summit ISVforce Partner, SAP as an SAP® Endorsed App, and Adobe as an Adobe Accelerate Exchange Partner.

As of Mar. 31, 2023, the company's platforms supported more than 650 SaaS subscription customers worldwide in the technology, healthcare, manufacturing, financial services and retail verticals.

Predecessor Detail - Name changed from Copernic Business Solutions Inc., Oct. 13, 2004.

Directors - Laurent Simoneau, co-founder, pres. & chief tech. officer, Qué.; Louis Têtu, chr. & CEO, Québec, Qué.; J. Alberto Yépez†, Calif.; Shanti Ariker, Calif.; Fay Sien Goon, Calif.; Isaac Kim, Calif.; Frederic Lalonde, Montréal, Qué.; Valéry Zamuner, Montréal, Qué.

Other Exec. Officers - Marc Sanfaçon, co-founder & sr. v-p, tech.; Richard Tessier, co-founder & sr. v-p, products; Guy Gauvin, COO; Brandon Nussey, CFO & corp. sec.; Nicolas Darveau-Garneau, chief growth & strategy officer; Nicholas (Nick) Goode, chief corp. devel. officer; Dominic Lajoie, CIO; Tom Melzl, chief revenue officer; Sheila Morin, chief mktg. officer; Alain Bouchard, sr. v-p, professional srvcs. & technical support; Elaine Cobb, sr. v-p, cust. success; Karine Hamel, sr. v-p, fin.; Martin Laporte, sr. v-p, R&D; Benoît Leclerc, sr. v-p, comml. & intl. sales; Nicolas Pelletier, sr. v-p, R&D; Mike Raley, sr. v-p, growth opers.; Anne Thériault, v-p, legal, chief info. security officer, data privacy officer & asst. sec.; Claude-Antoine (C.A.) Tremblay, v-p, HR

† Lead director

Capital Stock

	Authorized (shs.)	Outstanding (shs.)[1]
Preferred	unlimited	nil
Multiple Vtg.	unlimited	51,033,529
Subord. Vtg.	unlimited	51,184,943

[1] At July 10, 2023

Preferred - Issuable in series.

Multiple Voting - Convertible into subordinate voting shares on a one-for-one basis. 10 votes per share.

Subordinate Voting - Non-convertible. One vote per share.

Normal Course Issuer Bid - The company plans to make normal course purchases of up to 2,559,247 subordinate voting shares representing 5% of the total outstanding. The bid commenced on July 17, 2023, and expires on July 16, 2024.

Major Shareholder - Fonds de solidarité des travailleurs du Québec (F.T.Q.) held 24% interest, Investissement Québec held 19% interest, Al-Rayyan Holding LLC held 13% interest and OGE Holdings Inc. held 12% interest at Mar. 31, 2023.

Price Range - CVO/TSX

Year	Volume	High	Low	Close
2022............	14,747,854	$16.84	$4.81	$9.08
2021............	3,742,176	$18.00	$14.82	$16.50

Recent Close: $10.92

Capital Stock Changes - In July 2023, 3,706,194 subordinate voting shares were issued under a Substantial Issuer Bid.

During fiscal 2023, 7,475,883 multiple voting shares were converted into subordinate voting shares on a one-for-one basis, 1,101,508 multiple voting shares were issued on exercise of options, 633,296 subordinate voting shares were issued under restricted share unit plan and 9,160 subordinate voting shares were issued under deferred share unit plan.

Immediately prior to the initial public offering, a capital reorganization was completed whereby common shares were redesignated as multiple voting shares, all existing preferred shares were converted into 63,356,738 multiple voting shares on a one-for-one basis, all existing classes of preferred shares were deleted from authorized share capital, and new classes of preferred shares and subordinate voting shares were created. On Nov. 24, 2021, an initial public offering of 14,340,000 subordinate voting shares and private placement of 129,996 subordinate voting shares were completed and 857,122 multiple voting shares were issued as a donation to charities, all at Cdn$15 per share; an additional 2,151,000 subordinate voting shares were issued on exercise of over-allotment option in December 2021. Also during fiscal 2022, 391,266 multiple voting shares were issued on exercise of options, 34,826 subordinate voting shares were issued under restricted stock plans and 27,671,832 multiple voting shares were converted into subordinate voting shares on a one-for-one basis.

Wholly Owned Subsidiaries

Coveo Europe B.V., Netherlands.

Coveo Software Corp., Del.
Qubit Digital Ltd., United Kingdom.

Financial Statistics

Periods ended:	12m Mar. 31/23A		12m Mar. 31/22A
	US$000s	%Chg	US$000s
Operating revenue	**112,002**	**+30**	**86,488**
Cost of sales	26,674		21,456
Research & devel. expense	35,025		30,099
General & admin expense	86,142		84,530
Operating expense	**147,841**	**+9**	**136,085**
Operating income	**(35,839)**	**n.a.**	**(49,597)**
Deprec., depl. & amort.	8,580		7,661
Finance income	5,243		127
Finance costs, gross	630		12,628
Pre-tax income	**(39,527)**	**n.a.**	**229,307**
Income taxes	205		(188,969)
Net income	**(39,732)**	**n.a.**	**418,276**
Cash & equivalent	198,452		223,072
Accounts receivable	24,233		25,476
Current assets	238,534		264,852
Fixed assets, net	6,846		8,704
Right-of-use assets	7,645		9,255
Intangibles, net	40,749		47,315
Total assets	**308,818**	**-11**	**345,500**
Accts. pay. & accr. liabs	21,435		22,910
Current liabilities	78,624		74,705
Long-term lease liabilities	8,940		11,169
Shareholders' equity	218,533		255,436
Cash from oper. activs	**(6,257)**	**n.a.**	**(35,424)**
Cash from fin. activs	(2,428)		163,402
Cash from invest. activs	(2,265)		36,618
Net cash position	**198,452**	**-11**	**223,072**
Capital expenditures	(1,585)		(1,385)
	US$		US$
Earnings per share*	(0.38)		8.23
Cash flow per share*	(0.06)		(0.70)
	shs		shs
No. of shs. o/s*	105,491,290		103,747,326
Avg. no. of shs. o/s*	104,572,190		50,811,216
	%		%
Net profit margin	(35.47)		483.62
Return on equity	(16.77)		n.m.
Return on assets	(11.95)		163.59
Foreign sales percent	94		95
No. of employees (FTEs)	743		747

* M.V. & S.V.
A Reported in accordance with IFRS

Historical Summary
(as originally stated)

Fiscal Year	Oper. Rev.	Net Inc. Bef. Disc.	EPS*
	US$000s	US$000s	US$
2023A	112,002	(39,732)	(0.38)
2022A	86,488	418,276	8.23
2021A	64,857	(600,025)	(32.64)
2020A1	55,476	(61,810)	(3.52)
2019A1	44,330	(133,572)	(7.90)

* M.V. & S.V.
A Reported in accordance with IFRS
1 As shown in the prospectus dated Nov. 17, 2021.

C.165 Craftport Cannabis Corp.

Symbol - CFT **Exchange** - CSE (S) **CUSIP** - 224130
Head Office - 4715 Paradise Valley Dr, Peachland, BC, V0H 1X3 **Telephone** - (604) 238-0009
Website - craftportcannabis.com
Email - info@craftportcannabis.com
Investor Relations - Feng Lu (604) 238-0009
Auditors - MNP LLP C.A.
Transfer Agents - TSX Trust Company, Toronto, Ont.
Profile - (Alta. 2009) Cultivates, produces and sells medical and recreational cannabis under licences from Health Canada.
Wholly owned **Potanicals Green Growers Inc.** holds a licence to cultivate, produce and sell medical and recreational cannabis under the Cannabis Act from a 12,700-sq.-ft. indoor facility in Peachland, B.C.
Through 51%-owned **1139000 B.C. Ltd.**, holds a 174,240-sq.-ft. greenhouse facility in Pitt Meadows, B.C., classified as held for sale.
Common suspended from CSE, May 9, 2023.
Predecessor Detail - Name changed from Benchmark Botanics Inc., Nov. 1, 2021; basis 1 new for 10 old shs.
Directors - George G. Dorin, chr., Surrey, B.C.; Feng Lu, CEO & interim CFO, B.C.; Yuan Gao, corp. sec., B.C.; Terry Wang, Ont.; Wenjie Zhang
Other Exec. Officers - Honggao Yu, v-p, bus. devel. & intl. market expansion

Capital Stock

	Authorized (shs.)	Outstanding (shs.)1
Common	unlimited	40,241,343

1 At Oct. 28, 2022
Major Shareholder - Widely held at Oct. 28, 2022.

Price Range - KYU/TSX-VEN (D)

Year	Volume	High	Low	Close
2022	1,092,541	$0.32	$0.02	$0.02
2021	778,086	$1.35	$0.11	$0.30
2020	814,980	$4.30	$0.50	$1.20
2019	559,153	$12.00	$1.60	$4.40
2018	614,206	$21.40	$2.20	$2.45

Consolidation: 1-for-10 cons. in Nov. 2021
Recent Close: $0.05
Capital Stock Changes - In May and July 2022, private placement of 37,500,000 common shares was completed at 8¢ per share.

Wholly Owned Subsidiaries
Potanicals Green Growers Inc., B.C.

Subsidiaries
51% int. in **1139000 B.C. Ltd.**, B.C.
- 65% int. in **Canada Bond Biotechnology Co., Ltd.**, B.C.
- 51% int. in **1161750 B.C. Ltd.**, B.C.

Financial Statistics

Periods ended:	12m Dec. 31/21A		12m Dec. 31/20oA
	$000s	%Chg	$000s
Operating revenue	**1,009**	**+18**	**852**
Cost of sales	936		767
Salaries & benefits	1,332		1,077
General & admin expense	1,549		2,036
Stock-based compensation	(56)		88
Operating expense	**3,761**	**-5**	**3,968**
Operating income	**(2,752)**	**n.a.**	**(3,116)**
Deprec., depl. & amort.	561		661
Finance income	nil		196
Finance costs, gross	666		254
Investment income	nil		(1,364)
Write-downs/write-offs	(10,133)		(11,836)
Pre-tax income	**(13,849)**	**n.a.**	**(15,048)**
Income taxes	nil		(714)
Net income	**(13,849)**	**n.a.**	**(14,334)**
Net inc. for equity hldrs	**(10,062)**	**n.a.**	**(10,105)**
Net inc. for non-cont. int.	**(3,788)**	**n.a.**	**(4,229)**
Cash & equivalent	122		250
Inventories	30		473
Accounts receivable	17		258
Current assets	264		1,185
Fixed assets, net	6,043		11,468
Right-of-use assets	nil		1,250
Intangibles, net	nil		4,564
Total assets	**6,522**	**-65**	**18,791**
Accts. pay. & accr. liabs	2,274		2,647
Current liabilities	9,701		6,971
Long-term debt, gross	7,427		4,099
Long-term lease liabilities	nil		1,093
Shareholders' equity	121		10,240
Non-controlling interest	(3,300)		488
Cash from oper. activs	**(2,731)**	**n.a.**	**(3,047)**
Cash from fin. activs	2,819		2,707
Cash from invest. activs	(217)		(285)
Net cash position	**122**	**-51**	**250**
Capital expenditures	(6)		(339)
Capital disposals	4		nil
	$		$
Earnings per share*	(0.49)		(0.55)
Cash flow per share*	(0.13)		(0.17)
	shs		shs
No. of shs. o/s*	20,361,202		20,361,222
Avg. no. of shs. o/s*	20,361,202		18,477,172
	%		%
Net profit margin	n.m.		n.m.
Return on equity	(194.21)		(81.88)
Return on assets	(104.16)		(83.51)

* Common
o Restated
A Reported in accordance with IFRS

Note: Cost of sales consists of production costs, fair value changes in biological assets included in inventory sold and other inventory changes, unrealized gain on changes in fair value of biological assets and write-off of inventory.

Latest Results

Periods ended:	6m June 30/22A		6m June 30/21A
	$000s	%Chg	$000s
Operating revenue	23	-96	640
Net income	(1,909)	n.a.	(5,329)
Net inc. for equity hldrs	(1,688)	n.a.	(3,413)
Net inc. for non-cont. int.	(222)		(1,916)
	$		$
Earnings per share*	(0.08)		(0.26)

* Common
A Reported in accordance with IFRS

Historical Summary
(as originally stated)

Fiscal Year	Oper. Rev.	Net Inc. Bef. Disc.	EPS*
	$000s	$000s	$
2021A	1,009	(13,849)	(0.49)
2020A	852	(14,334)	(0.50)
2019A	236	(3,698)	(0.20)
2018A	nil	(6,078)	(0.40)
2017A1	nil	(4,438)	(1.10)

* Common
A Reported in accordance with IFRS
1 Results reflect the Nov. 2, 2017 reverse takeover acquisition of Potanicals Green Growers Inc.
Note: Adjusted throughout for 1-for-10 cons. in Nov. 2021

C.166 Cranstown Capital Corp.

Symbol - CRAN.P **Exchange** - TSX-VEN **CUSIP** - 22459L
Head Office - Park Place, 2800-666 Burrard St, Vancouver, BC, V6C 2Z7 **Telephone** - (604) 609-3355
Email - tobypierce@hotmail.com
Investor Relations - Toby R. Pierce (604) 609-3355
Auditors - De Visser Gray LLP C.A., Vancouver, B.C.
Lawyers - DLA Piper (Canada) LLP, Vancouver, B.C.
Transfer Agents - Computershare Trust Company of Canada Inc., Vancouver, B.C.
Profile - (B.C. 2021) Capital Pool Company.
Predecessor Detail - Name changed from Torrent Capital Corp., May 3, 2021.
Directors - Toby R. Pierce, CEO, Vancouver, B.C.; Mark E. Goodman, Toronto, Ont.; Dimitry Serov, Richmond Hill, Ont.
Other Exec. Officers - Chris Beltgens, CFO; Robbie Grossman, corp. sec.

Capital Stock

	Authorized (shs.)	Outstanding (shs.)1
Common	unlimited	8,404,000

1 At July 28, 2022
Major Shareholder - Toby R. Pierce held 11.9% interest at July 8, 2021.

Price Range - CRAN.P/TSX-VEN

Year	Volume	High	Low	Close
2022	212,200	$0.17	$0.07	$0.08
2021	404,035	$0.40	$0.15	$0.19

Recent Close: $0.06
Capital Stock Changes - On July 8, 2021, an initial public offering of 4,154,000 common shares was completed at 10¢ per share.

C.167 Crescita Therapeutics Inc.

Symbol - CTX **Exchange** - TSX **CUSIP** - 225847
Head Office - 2805 Place Louis R Renaud, Laval, QC, H7V 0A3 **Toll-free** - (800) 361-0352
Website - www.crescitatherapeutics.com
Email - lkisa@crescitatx.com
Investor Relations - Linda Kisa (450) 680-4722
Auditors - Ernst & Young LLP C.A., Toronto, Ont.
Transfer Agents - TSX Trust Company, Toronto, Ont.
Employees - 78 at Dec. 31, 2022
Profile - (Ont. 2016, amalg.) Develops, manufactures, markets and licenses prescription and non-prescription skincare and drug products for the treatment and care of skin conditions and diseases and their symptoms.
Operations are organized into three segments: Commercial Skincare; Licensing & Royalties; and Manufacturing & Services.
Commercial Skincare - Manufactures and sells prescription and non-prescription skincare products. Prescription products include Pliaglis®, the company's only U.S. FDA approved prescription product, a topical local anaesthetic cream that provides safe and effective local dermal anaesthesia on intact skin prior to superficial dermatological procedures such as dermal filler injection, non-ablative laser facial resurfacing and pulsed dye laser therapy. Other prescription products include CTX-101 (formerly MiCal 1) for plaque psoriasis under Phase III clinical studies and CTX-102 (formerly MiCal 2) for dermatological skin treatment with a completed Phase II clinical study, being developed through a joint venture with a contract research organization and **Ferndale Laboratories, Inc.** Non-prescription products include Laboratoire Dr Renaud®, Pro-Derm™ and Alyria®, which provide solutions for a wide range of skin concerns such as aging, acne, hydration, pigmentation and rosacea. In Canada, also distributes ART-FILLER® range of injectables, New Cellular Treatment Factor® (NCTF) Boost 135 HA and Obagi Medical® skin care products. The non-prescription skin care products are primarily sold through spas, medispas and medical aesthetic clinics, through online platforms and international distributors. Its manufacturing facility is located in Laval, Que.
Licensing & Royalties - This segment includes the licensing of intellectual property related to the development and commercialization of the company's Pliaglis®, which the company holds distribution rights for in Canada and Mexico. Licensing agreements include **Taro Pharmaceuticals Inc.** for the U.S.; **Joyou-Biotechnology Co. Ltd.** for mainland China; **Pelpharma Handels GmbH** for Austria; **MINOS Labs** for Mexico; **Industrial Farmaceutica Cantabria, S.A.** (dba Cantabria Labs) for Italy, Portugal, France and Spain; **Croma Pharma GmbH** for Germany, the United Kingdom, Ireland, Switzerland, Brazil, Romania, Belgium, the Netherlands and Luxembourg; and **TADA MENA DWC-LLC**

for Saudi Arabia, the United Arab Emirates, Kuwait, Oman, Qatar, Bahrain, Jordan, Lebanon, Egypt, Algeria, Morocco, Tunisia, Iraq, Libya and Yemen. Cantabria Labs received an approval for a manufacturing facility in Spain to supply European countries. Pliaglis® is also available in Argentina and Brazil. The company also earns revenue for the use of the company's multiple drug delivery platforms that support the development of patented formulations that can deliver actives into or through the skin including MMPE™ (Multiplexed molecular penetration enhancers) technology, which uses synergistic combinations of pharmaceutical excipients included on the FDA's Inactive Ingredient Guide to improve topical delivery of active ingredients into or through the skin; DuraPeel™, a self-occluding, film-forming cream/gel formulation that provides extended release delivery for up to 12 hours to the site of application.

Manufacturing & Services - The company provides contract development and manufacturing services to develop topicals either under a private label or a brand name and may use a combination of the company's existing formulations or novel formulations, with or without the utilization of the company's transdermal delivery technologies.

Directors - Daniel N. (Dan) Chicoine, chr., Port Sydney, Ont.; Serge Verreault, pres. & CEO, Qué.; Anthony E. Dobranowski†, Ont.; John C. London, Ont.; Deborah Shannon-Trudeau, Montréal, Qué.

Other Exec. Officers - Jose DaRocha, CFO; François Lafortune, exec. v-p & gen. mgr.; Wade Hull, v-p, R&D; Ivonne Medina, v-p, bus. devel.; Isabelle Villeneuve, v-p, strategy, quality & innovation

† Lead director

Capital Stock

	Authorized (shs.)	Outstanding (shs.)[1]
Preferred	unlimited	nil
Common	unlimited	20,334,153

[1] At May 9, 2023

Major Shareholder - Widely held at Apr. 24, 2023.

Price Range - CTX/TSX

Year	Volume	High	Low	Close
2022	3,007,245	$0.83	$0.58	$0.66
2021	4,492,360	$1.01	$0.55	$0.65
2020	8,147,564	$1.00	$0.40	$0.70
2019	10,491,307	$1.23	$0.46	$0.93
2018	8,258,985	$0.90	$0.35	$0.45

Recent Close: $0.65

Capital Stock Changes - During 2022, 15,001 common shares were issued on exercise of options and 663,600 common shares were repurchased under a Normal Course Issuer Bid.

Wholly Owned Subsidiaries

Crescita Skin Sciences Inc., Montréal, Qué.
Dimethaid Immunology Inc., Canada.
Nuvo Research AG, Switzerland.
- 100% int. in **Nuvo Research GmbH**, Germany.

Nuvo Research America Inc., Del.
- 100% int. in **Nuvo Research U.S., Inc.**, Del.
- 100% int. in **ZARS Pharma, Inc.**, Del.
  - 100% int. in **ZARS (U.K.) Limited**, United Kingdom.

Investments

Akyucorp Ltd.

Financial Statistics

Periods ended:	12m Dec. 31/22[A]		12m Dec. 31/21[A]
	$000s	%Chg	$000s
Operating revenue	**23,525**	**+40**	**16,769**
Cost of goods sold	7,943		5,596
Salaries & benefits	8,722		5,649
Research & devel. expense	68		116
General & admin expense	4,648		4,582
Stock-based compensation	144		166
Operating expense	**21,525**	**+34**	**16,109**
Operating income	**2,000**	**+203**	**660**
Deprec., depl. & amort.	1,471		1,379
Finance income	260		182
Finance costs, gross	158		236
Investment income	57		(8)
Pre-tax income	**404**	**n.a.**	**(1,009)**
Income taxes	(458)		96
Net income	**862**	**n.a.**	**(1,105)**
Cash & equivalent	8,238		11,331
Inventories	5,646		4,392
Accounts receivable	4,561		2,107
Current assets	20,516		20,092
Long-term investments	342		338
Fixed assets, net	791		766
Right-of-use assets	1,517		1,810
Intangibles, net	2,866		3,740
Total assets	**28,484**	**-2**	**28,923**
Accts. pay. & accr. liabs.	5,602		5,332
Current liabilities	6,057		6,725
Long-term debt, gross	nil		976
Long-term lease liabilities	1,208		1,525
Shareholders' equity	21,096		20,526
Cash from oper. activs.	**(1,020)**	**n.a.**	**(1,597)**
Cash from fin. activs.	(1,846)		(500)
Cash from invest. activs.	(290)		(846)
Net cash position	**8,238**	**-27**	**11,331**
Capital expenditures	(229)		(346)
	$		$
Earnings per share*	0.04		(0.05)
Cash flow per share*	(0.05)		(0.08)
	shs		shs
No. of shs. o/s*	20,334,153		20,982,752
Avg. no. of shs. o/s*	20,690,875		20,755,290
	%		%
Net profit margin	3.66		(6.59)
Return on equity	4.14		(5.30)
Return on assets	4.18		(3.04)
Foreign sales percent	58		43
No. of employees (FTEs)	78		69

* Common
[A] Reported in accordance with IFRS

Latest Results

Periods ended:	3m Mar. 31/23[A]		3m Mar. 31/22[A]
	$000s	%Chg	$000s
Operating revenue	4,602	-7	4,951
Net income	(273)	n.a.	(474)
	$		$
Earnings per share*	(0.01)		(0.02)

* Common
[A] Reported in accordance with IFRS

Historical Summary
(as originally stated)

Fiscal Year	Oper. Rev. $000s	Net Inc. Bef. Disc. $000s	EPS* $
2022[A]	23,525	862	0.04
2021[A]	16,769	(1,105)	(0.05)
2020[A]	15,640	37	0.00
2019[A]	22,337	1,855	0.09
2018[A]	16,628	2,422	0.12

* Common
[A] Reported in accordance with IFRS

C.168 Cresco Labs Inc.

Symbol - CL **Exchange** - CSE **CUSIP** - 22587M
Head Office - 400 W. Erie St, Suite 110, Chicago, IL, United States, 60654 **Telephone** - (312) 929-0993
Website - www.crescolabs.com
Email - investors@crescolabs.com
Investor Relations - Megan Kulick (312) 929-0993
Auditors - Marcum LLP C.P.A., Chicago, Ill.
Transfer Agents - Odyssey Trust Company, Calgary, Alta.
FP500 Revenue Ranking - 326
Employees - 3,200 at Dec. 31, 2022
Profile - (B.C. 1990) Owns and operates cannabis cultivation, manufacturing and retail dispensary businesses across the United States.

Operates in nine U.S. states with 14 cultivation, processing, manufacturing and distribution facilities (at Aug. 16, 2023) in Illinois (3), Pennsylvania (1), Ohio (1), California (2), Arizona (1), Massachusetts (3), New York (1), Michigan (1) and Florida (1), including both indoor and hybrid greenhouses totaling 900,000 sq. ft. of cultivation space. These facilities allow the company to produce cannabis products across several product categories, with a portfolio of more than 500 unique products sold through company-owned as well as third-party dispensaries under owned consumer brands including Cresco, High Supply, Mindy's, Good News, Remedi, Wonder Wellness Co. and FloraCal Farms. At Aug. 16, 2023, the company operated 69 dispensaries under the Sunnyside banner in Illinois (10), Pennsylvania (13), Ohio (5), Arizona (1), Massachusetts (4), New York (4) and Florida (32).

During the second quarter of 2023, the company sold its processing centre in Maryland for US$3,300,000, and a cultivation and manufacturing facility in Florida for an undisclosed amount.

During 2022, the company shut down a cultivation facility in Arizona and restructured certain operations and activities in California, including the shut down of cultivation, manufacturing and distribution facilities.

In September 2022, the company completed a sale-and-leaseback transaction for its 135,000-sq.-ft. cultivation, manufacturing and production facility in Brookville, Pa., with **Aventine Property Group, Inc.** for US$45,000,000.

In March 2022, the company sold **2766563 Ontario Inc.** to **Delota Corp.** (formerly **Spyder Cannabis Inc.**) for Cdn$3,000,000, paid by issuance of 12,000,001 Delota common shares at Cdn$0.25 per share. 2766563 Ontario held a promissory note of Cdn$11,129,171 issued to the company by Spyder in March 2021 pursuant to its acquisition of 180 Smoke.

Recent Merger and Acquisition Activity

Status: terminated **Revised:** July 31, 2023
UPDATE: The transaction was terminated. PREVIOUS: Cresco Labs Inc. agreed to acquire Columbia Care Inc. on the basis of 0.5579 Cresco subordinate voting shares for each Columbia Care common share held, representing total consideration enterprise value of US$2 billion. Columbia Care is a fully-integrated medical and adult use cannabis operator in the U.S. and Europe. The agreement includes a US$65,000,000 termination fee payable to Cresco Labs under certain circumstances. The combined entity would have over 130 retail stores in 18 markets and over US$1.1 billion in annual revenue. The transaction was expected to close in the fourth quarter of 2022. May 16, 2022 - Hart–Scott–Rodino Antitrust Improvements Act waiting period expired. July 8, 2022 - Columbia Care shareholders approved the proposed business combination. July 15, 2022 - Approval from the Supreme Court of British Columbia was received.

Status: terminated **Revised:** July 28, 2023
UPDATE: The transaction was terminated. PREVIOUS: Cresco Labs Inc. and Columbia Care Inc. agreed to sell certain assets in New York, Illinois and Massachusetts to an entity owned and controlled by Sean "Diddy" Combs for up to US$185,000,000, consisting of US$110,000,000 cash and US$45,000,000 of seller notes on closing, with the remainder payable post-closing upon achievement of certain short-term, objective and market-based milestones. The divestiture was required for Cresco to close its previously announced acquisition of Columbia Care. The combination of Cresco and Columbia Care assets to be divested include: retail assets in Brooklyn, Manhattan, New Hartford and Rochester and a production asset in Rochester, all New York; retail assets in Jefferson Park and Villa Park and a production asset in Aurora, all Illinois; and retail assets in Greenfield, Worcester and Leicester and a production asset in Leicester, all Massachusetts. The transaction was expected to close concurrently with Cresco's acquisition of Columbia Care.

Predecessor Detail - Name changed from Randsburg International Gold Corp., Nov. 30, 2018, following reverse takeover acquisition of Cresco Labs, LLC.; basis 1 new for 812.63 old shs.

Directors - Thomas J. (Tom) Manning, chr., Evanston, Ill.; Charles Bachtell, CEO, Chicago, Ill.; Tarik Brooks, Los Angeles, Calif.; Gerald F. Corcoran, Winnetka, Ill.; Marc Lustig, Vancouver, B.C.; Randy D. Podolsky, Lincolnshire, Ill.; Michele Roberts, New York, N.Y.; Robert M. Sampson, Downers Grove, Ill.; Carol A. Vallone, Manchester, Mass.; John R. Walter, Naples, Fla.

Other Exec. Officers - Dennis Olis, CFO; Gregory F. (Greg) Butler, chief transformation officer; Angie Demchenko, chief people officer; Jason Erkes, chief commun. officer; Zach Marburger, CIO; John Schetz, gen. counsel

Capital Stock

	Authorized (shs.)	Outstanding (shs.)[1]
Subordinate Vtg.	unlimited	317,224,906
Proportionate Vtg.	unlimited	121,434
Super Vtg.	500,000	500,000
Special Subordinate Vtg.	unlimited	158,940,757
Redeemable	n.a.	99,249,208[2]

[1] At Aug. 15, 2023
[2] Represents share capital of indirect subsidiary Cresco Labs, LLC.

Subordinate Voting - Entitled to dividends. One vote per share.

Proportionate Voting - Entitled to dividends. Convertible into subordinate voting shares on a 200-for-1 basis. 200 votes per share.

Super Voting - Not entitled to dividends. Non-convertible. 2,000 votes per share.

Special Subordinate Voting - Entitled to dividends. Convertible into subordinate voting shares on a 0.00001-for-1 basis. 0.00001 votes per share.

Redeemable - Represents share capital of indirect subsidiary Cresco Labs, LLC. Convertible into proportionate voting shares on a 1-for-200 basis (with such shares convertible into subordinate voting shares on a 200-for-1 basis). Non-voting.

Major Shareholder - Charles Bachtell held 30.5% interest, Brian McCormack held 15.2% interest, Robert M. Sampson held 15.2% interest and Dominic A. Sergi held 15.2% interest at May 16, 2023.

Price Range - CL/CSE

Year	Volume	High	Low	Close
2022	75,833,168	$10.36	$2.29	$2.45
2021	114,435,599	$22.20	$7.80	$8.39
2020	87,547,208	$13.79	$2.81	$12.55
2019	65,995,523	$18.37	$5.90	$8.93
2018	3,200,890	$16.25	$4.06	$9.25

Recent Close: $1.43

Capital Stock Changes - During 2022, subordinate voting shares were issued as follows: 5,339,000 for contingent consideration pertaining to an acquisition, 3,335,000 on redemption of a like number of redeemable units, 1,279,000 on exercise of options and warrants, 585,000 on conversion of 2,925 proportionate voting shares, 337,000 under restricted share unit plan and 148,000 in relation to taxes on certain share-based payments.

Wholly Owned Subsidiaries

Bluma Wellness Inc., Fort Lauderdale, Fla.
- 100% int. in **CannCure Investments Inc.**, Ont.
  - 100% int. in **Cannabis Cures Investments, LLC**, Fla.
    - 100% int. in **3 Boys Farms, LLC**, Albany, Ga.
      - 100% int. in **Farm to Fresh Holdings, LLC**, Fla.

CRHC Holdings Corp., Ont.
- 100% int. in **Cannroy Delaware Inc.**, Del.

Cali-AntiFragile Corp., Calif.
- 100% int. in **Cub City LLC**, Santa Rosa, Calif.
- 100% int. in **River Distributing Co., LLC**, Calif.
- 100% int. in **Sonoma's Finest**, Calif.

Cresco U.S. Corp., Ill.
- 100% int. in **CMA Holdings, LLC**, Ill.
  - 100% int. in **BL Real Estate, LLC**, Mass.
  - 100% int. in **Cultivate Licensing LLC**, Mass.
    - 100% int. in **Cultivate Burncoat, Inc.**, Mass.
    - 100% int. in **Cultivate Cultivation, LLC**, Mass.
    - 100% int. in **Cultivate Framingham, Inc.**, Mass.
    - 100% int. in **Cultivate Leicester, Inc.**, Mass.
    - 100% int. in **Cultivate Worcester, Inc.**, Mass.
- 100% int. in **CP Pennsylvania Holdings, LLC**, Ill.
  - 100% int. in **Bay Asset Management, LLC**, Pa.
  - 100% int. in **Bay, LLC**, Pa.
  - 100% int. in **Ridgeback, LLC**, Colo.
- 60% int. in **Cresco Labs, LLC**, Chicago, Ill.
  - 100% int. in **Cresco Labs Notes Issuer, LLC**, Ill.
    - 100% int. in **Cresco Edibles, LLC**, Ill.
      - 75% int. in **TSC Cresco, LLC**, Ill.
    - 100% int. in **Cresco HHH, LLC**, Mass.
    - 100% int. in **Cresco Labs Arizona, LLC**, Ariz.
      - 100% int. in **Arizona Facilities Supply, LLC**, Ariz.
    - 100% int. in **Cresco Labs Joliet, LLC**, Ill.
    - 100% int. in **Cresco Labs Kankakee, LLC**, Ill.
    - 100% int. in **Cresco Labs Logan, LLC**, Ill.
    - 99% int. in **Cresco Labs Ohio, LLC**, Ohio
    - 100% int. in **Cresco Labs PA, LLC**, Ill.
      - 100% int. in **Cresco Yeltrah, LLC**, Pa.
    - 100% int. in **Cresco Labs Phoenix Farms, LLC**, Ill.
      - 100% int. in **Phoenix Farms of Illinois, LLC**, Ill.
    - 100% int. in **Cresco Labs SLO, LLC**, Calif.
      - 80% int. in **SLO Cultivation, Inc.**, Calif.
    - 100% int. in **Cresco Labs Tinad, LLC**, Ill.
      - 100% int. in **PDI Medical III, LLC**, Ill.
    - 100% int. in **JDC Chillicothe, LLC**, Ohio
      - 100% int. in **Verdant Creations Chillicothe, LLC**, Ohio
    - 100% int. in **JDC Columbus, LLC**, Ohio
      - 100% int. in **Care Med Associates, LLC**, Ohio
    - 100% int. in **JDC Elmwood, LLC**, Ill.
      - 100% int. in **FloraMedex, LLC**, Ill.
    - 100% int. in **JDC Marion, LLC**, Ohio
      - 100% int. in **Verdant Creations Marion, LLC**, Ohio
    - 100% int. in **JDC Newark, LLC**, Ohio
      - 100% int. in **Verdant Creations Newark, LLC**, Ohio
    - 100% int. in **Wellbeings, LLC**, Del.
- 85% int. in **Cresco Labs Michigan, LLC**, Mich.
- 100% int. in **Encanto Green Cross Dispensary, LLC**, Ariz.
- 100% int. in **Gloucester Street Capital, LLC**, Purchase, N.Y.
  - 100% int. in **Valley Agriceuticals, LLC**, N.Y.
- 100% int. in **Good News Holdings, LLC**, Ill.
- 100% int. in **MedMar, Inc.**, Ill.
  - 88% int. in **MedMar Lakeview, LLC**, Ill.
  - 75% int. in **MedMar Rockford, LLC**, Ill.
- 100% int. in **Wonder Holdings, LLC**, Ill.

Laurel Harvest Labs, LLC, Pa.
- 100% int. in **JDRC Mount Joy, LLC**, Ill.
- 100% int. in **JDRC Scranton, LLC**, Ill.

Financial Statistics

Periods ended:	12m Dec. 31/22[A]		12m Dec. 31/21[A]
	US$000s	%Chg	US$000s
Operating revenue	**842,681**	**+3**	**821,682**
Cost of goods sold	404,373		398,297
Salaries & benefits	157,034		133,143
General & admin expense	153,320		138,071
Stock-based compensation	19,664		24,988
Operating expense	**734,391**	**+6**	**694,499**
Operating income	**108,290**	**-15**	**127,183**
Deprec., depl. & amort.	51,930		38,640
Finance income	679		938
Finance costs, gross	58,516		52,149
Investment income	nil		(1,196)
Write-downs/write-offs	(140,655)[1]		(305,894)[2]
Pre-tax income	**(126,905)**	**n.a.**	**(256,727)**
Income taxes	88,938		40,107
Net income	**(215,843)**	**n.a.**	**(296,834)**
Net inc. for equity hldrs	**(212,047)**	**n.a.**	**(319,597)**
Net inc. for non-cont. int.	**(3,796)**	**n.a.**	**22,763**
Cash & equivalent	121,510		226,102
Inventories	134,608		136,643
Accounts receivable	56,492		43,379
Current assets	326,046		421,755
Long-term investments	1,228		5,912
Fixed assets, net	379,722		369,092
Right-of-use assets	128,264		88,017
Intangibles, net	738,145		884,411
Total assets	**1,583,692**	**-11**	**1,780,463**
Accts. pay. & accr. liabs	93,254		127,720
Current liabilities	280,866		288,394
Long-term debt, gross	487,867		485,007
Long-term debt, net	469,055		465,079
Long-term lease liabilities	156,180		118,936
Shareholders' equity	627,039		755,554
Non-controlling interest	(39,356)		42,182
Cash from oper. activs	**18,741**	**+29**	**14,487**
Cash from fin. activs	(86,643)		235,005
Cash from invest. activs	(36,577)		(163,933)
Net cash position	**121,510**	**-46**	**226,102**
Capital expenditures	(83,026)		(93,875)
Capital disposals	49,236		33,157
	US$		US$
Earnings per share*	(0.71)		(1.22)
Cash flow per share*	0.06		0.06
	shs		shs
No. of shs. o/s*	301,730,609		291,201,115
Avg. no. of shs. o/s*	298,161,665		262,326,138
	%		%
Net profit margin	(25.61)		(36.13)
Return on equity	(30.67)		(48.06)
Return on assets	(6.92)		(15.19)
Foreign sales percent	100		100
No. of employees (FTEs)	3,200		3,500

* Subord. Vtg.

[A] Reported in accordance with U.S. GAAP

[1] Includes US$117,024,000 goodwill impairment and US$21,800,000 intangible asset impairment in the California, Arizona, Massachusetts and Maryland reporting units.

[2] Pertains primarily to goodwill and intangibles impairment charge in the California reporting unit.

Latest Results

Periods ended:	6m June 30/23[A]		6m June 30/22[A]
	US$000s	%Chg	US$000s
Operating revenue	392,089	-9	432,617
Net income	(71,275)	n.a.	(31,971)
Net inc. for equity hldrs	(62,585)	n.a.	(40,922)
Net inc. for non-cont. int.	(8,690)		8,951
	US$		US$
Earnings per share*	(0.20)		(0.14)

* Subord. Vtg.

[A] Reported in accordance with U.S. GAAP

Historical Summary
(as originally stated)

Fiscal Year	Oper. Rev.	Net Inc. Bef. Disc.	EPS*
	US$000s	US$000s	US$
2022[A]	842,681	(215,843)	(0.71)
2021[A]	821,682	(296,834)	(1.22)
2020[B]	476,251	(36,562)	(0.39)
2019[B]	128,534	(65,302)	(0.37)
2018[B1]	43,252	3,093	(0.03)

* Subord. Vtg.

[A] Reported in accordance with U.S. GAAP

[B] Reported in accordance with IFRS

[1] Results reflect the Nov. 30, 2018, reverse takeover acquisition of Cresco Labs, LLC.

C.169 Critical Infrastructure Technologies Ltd.

Symbol - CTTT **Exchange** - CSE **CUSIP** - 226740
Head Office - 1480-885 Georgia St W, Vancouver, BC, V6E 3X1
Website - citech.com.au
Email - brenton.s@citech.com.au
Investor Relations - Brenton Scott 61-8-6706-6031
Auditors - Davidson & Company LLP C.A., Vancouver, B.C.
Transfer Agents - Odyssey Trust Company, Vancouver, B.C.

Profile - (B.C. 2021) Developing communications infrastructure products for critical applications in mining, emergency services, defence and government sectors.

Lead product under development is the NEXUS 16 Self-Deploying Platform, a mobile platform that supports high-capacity radio equipment and many other technology payloads. The NEXUS 16 combines a 16-metre retractable tower, multiple equipment enclosures, batteries, generators and solar panels on a self-deploying platform that can be moved around on-site or between sites by any truck that can accommodate a 20-ft. shipping container. The platform can be transported, deployed and operational in under 30 minutes.

At February 2023, the company had completed $^1/_5$ and $^1/_2$ scale prototypes and was prepared to begin phase one of its buildout of two full-scale pre-production client trial units that can be deployed to customer sites for compliance and acceptance testing.

Common listed on CSE, Feb. 28, 2023.

Predecessor Detail - Name changed from 1319275 B.C. Ltd., Feb. 13, 2023, pursuant to the acquisition of Critical Infrastructure Technologies Pty Ltd.

Directors - Imants Kins, chr., Fremantle, W.A., Australia; Brenton Scott, CEO, Perth, W.A., Australia; Eugene A. Hodgson, CFO & corp. sec., Vancouver, B.C.; Andrew Hill, chief tech. officer, Perth, W.A., Australia; Richard Paolone Jr., Toronto, Ont.

Capital Stock

	Authorized (shs.)	Outstanding (shs.)[1]
Common	unlimited	83,147,899

[1] At Feb. 28, 2023

Major Shareholder - Brenton Scott held 25.47% interest at Feb. 28, 2023.

Recent Close: $0.35

Capital Stock Changes - In February 2023, 48,135,399 common shares were issued for acquisition of Critical Infrastructure Technologies Pty Ltd.

Wholly Owned Subsidiaries

Critical Infrastructure Technologies Pty Ltd., Australia.

Financial Statistics

Periods ended:	12m June 30/22[A1]		12m June 30/21[A]
	A$000s	%Chg	A$000s
General & admin expense	140		237
Operating expense	**140**	**-41**	**237**
Operating income	**(140)**	**n.a.**	**(237)**
Deprec., depl. & amort.	376		112
Finance costs, gross	91		11
Pre-tax income	**(607)**	**n.a.**	**(360)**
Net income	**(607)**	**n.a.**	**(360)**
Cash & equivalent	169		22
Current assets	1,180		452
Intangibles, net	1,017		338
Total assets	**2,285**	**+189**	**790**
Accts. pay. & accr. liabs	499		369
Current liabilities	1,856		1,149
Long-term debt, gross	1,357		780
Shareholders' equity	428		(360)
Cash from oper. activs	**(591)**	**n.a.**	**(296)**
Cash from fin. activs	1,794		781
Cash from invest. activs	(1,056)		(463)
Net cash position	**169**	**+668**	**22**
Capital expenditures	nil		(13)
	A$		A$
Earnings per share*	n.a.		n.a.
	shs		shs
No. of shs. o/s	n.a.		n.a.
	%		%
Net profit margin	n.a.		n.a.
Return on equity	n.m.		n.m.
Return on assets	(33.56)		n.a.

[A] Reported in accordance with IFRS

[1] Results for fiscal 2022 and prior periods pertain to Critical Infrastructure Technologies Pty Ltd.

C.170 Crombie Real Estate Investment Trust

Symbol - CRR.UN **Exchange** - TSX **CUSIP** - 227107
Head Office - 200-610 East River Rd, New Glasgow, NS, B2H 3S2
Telephone - (902) 755-8100 **Toll-free** - (800) 463-2407 **Fax** - (902) 755-6477
Website - www.crombie.ca
Email - investing@crombie.ca
Investor Relations - Ruth Martin (902) 755-8100 ext. 3006
Auditors - PricewaterhouseCoopers LLP C.A., Halifax, N.S.
Lawyers - Stewart McKelvey LLP, Halifax, N.S.
Transfer Agents - TSX Trust Company, Montréal, Qué.

FP500 Revenue Ranking - 506
Employees - 303 at Dec. 31, 2022
Profile - (Ont. 2006) Acquires, owns and manages income-producing grocery-anchored retail, retail-related industrial, mixed-use residential and office properties across Canada.

The trust's focus is primarily on the acquisition and development of grocery and drugstore-anchored retail properties. The trust's portfolio at Mar. 31, 2023, consisted of 280 retail and mixed-used properties, six retail-related industrial properties and five office properties, totaling 18,550,000 sq. ft. of gross leasable area (GLA). **Empire Company Limited** (including **Sobeys Inc.** and all other Empire's subsidiaries) is the trust's largest tenant, representing 58.1% of annual minimum rent at Mar. 31, 2023.

At Mar. 31, 2023, the trust had 27 development projects totaling 1,171,000 and 9,768,000 sq. ft. of GLA for commercial and residential use, respectively.

Geographic diversification at Dec. 31, 2022:

Location	Props.	GLA[1]
Alberta	58	3,370
British Columbia	43	1,707
Quebec	45	2,170
Ontario	45	2,572
Nova Scotia	35	4,595
New Brunswick	21	1,543
Manitoba	18	658
Newfoundland & Labrador	13	1,283
Saskatchewan	9	439
Prince Edward Island	2	108
	289	18,445

[1] 000s of sq. ft.

On Jan. 19, 2023, the trust acquired a 21,000-sq.-ft. retail property in Mount Forest, Ont. for $2,122,000.

In August 2022, the trust sold a 6,000-sq.-ft. retail property in Montreal, Que. for $1,125,000 and a 9,000-sq.-ft. retail property in Cambridge, Ont. for $1,900,000.

On July 7, 2022, the trust acquired a 4,000-sq.-ft. retail property in New Waterford, N.S. for $1,350,000,.

On May 30, 2022, the trust acquired a parcel of land in Martensville, Sask., for $4,939,000.

Recent Merger and Acquisition Activity

Status: completed **Announced:** May 1, 2023
Crombie Real Estate Investment Trust acquired a 57,000-sq.-ft. retail property for $9,760,000.

Status: completed **Announced:** Feb. 27, 2023
Crombie Real Estate Investment Trust acquired a 60,000-sq.-ft. retail property in Red Deer, Alta., for $14,600,000.

Status: completed **Announced:** Nov. 16, 2022
Crombie Real Estate Investment Trust sold a 191,000-sq.-ft. retail property in Halifax, N.S., for $26,331,000.

Status: completed **Announced:** Nov. 1, 2022
Crombie Real Estate Investment Trust sold a 62,000-sq.-ft. retail property in Surrey, B.C., for $87,087,000.

Status: completed **Announced:** Sept. 15, 2022
Crombie Real Estate Investment Trust sold a 29,000-sq.-ft. retail property in Grimsby, Ont., for $7,300,000.

Status: completed **Announced:** Sept. 8, 2022
Crombie Real Estate Investment Trust sold an 11,000-sq.-ft. retail property in Burlington, Ont., for $7,600,000.

Status: completed **Announced:** Aug. 26, 2022
Crombie Real Estate Investment Trust sold a parcel of land in Halifax, N.S., for $7,701,000.

Status: completed **Announced:** Aug. 8, 2022
Crombie Real Estate Investment Trust sold a 74,000-sq.-ft. retail property in Red Deer, Alta., for $26,500,000.

Status: completed **Announced:** June 14, 2022
Crombie Real Estate Investment Trust sold a 19,000-sq.-ft. retail property in Kelowna, B.C., for $10,250,000.

Status: completed **Announced:** May 3, 2022
Crombie Real Estate Investment Trust acquired a 67,000-sq.-ft. retail property in Kitchener, Ont., for $11,000,000.

Status: completed **Announced:** Mar. 24, 2022
Crombie Real Estate Investment Trust acquired a 38,000-sq.-ft. retail property in Edmonton, Alta., for $10,520,000.

Trustees - J. Michael (Mike) Knowlton, chr., Toronto, Ont.; Mark Holly, pres. & CEO, Whitby, Ont.; Paul V. Beesley, Halifax, N.S.; Dr. A. Jane Craighead, Ont.; James M. (Jim) Dickson, Halifax, N.S.; Heather Grey-Wolf, Toronto, Ont.; Heidi Jamieson-Mills, Pictou, N.S.; Jason P. Shannon, Bedford, N.S.; Paul D. Sobey, N.S.; Michael H. Vels, Hillsburgh, Ont.; Michael Waters, Ottawa, Ont.; Karen H. Weaver, Clarksburg, Ont.

Other Exec. Officers - Clinton Keay, CFO & corp. sec.; John Barnoski, exec. v-p, corp. devel.; Arie Bitton, exec. v-p, leasing & opers.; Daniel Bourque, v-p, sustainability; Aaron Bryant, v-p, design & const., eastern Canada; Kara Cameron, v-p, acctg. & finl. reporting; Terry Doran, v-p, office props.; Cheryl Fraser, v-p, commun. & chief talent officer; Ashley Harrison, v-p, people & culture; Nathan Hines, v-p, opers. & portfolio mgt.; Brady Landry, v-p, finl. analysis & treasury; Jelena Plecas, v-p, corp. devel. strategy; Sid Schraeder, v-p, const. & design, western Canada; Jennifer Sieber, v-p, invests.; Andrew Watt, v-p, leasing; Fred Santini, gen. counsel

Capital Stock

	Authorized (shs.)	Outstanding (shs.)[1]
Trust Unit	unlimited	105,795,491
Special Voting Unit	unlimited	73,392,022
Class B LP Unit	unlimited	73,392,022[2]

[1] At Apr. 30, 2023

[2] Securities of subsidiary Crombie Limited Partnership.

Trust Unit - The trust will endeavour to make monthly cash distributions equal to approximately 80% of the trust's distributable income on an annual basis. Puttable instruments classified as financial liabilities under IFRS. One vote per trust unit.

Special Voting Unit - Issued to holders of class B limited partnership units of subsidiary Crombie Limited Partnership. Each special voting unit entitles the holder to a number of votes at unitholder meetings equal to the number of trust units into which the class B limited partnership units are exchangeable.

Class B Limited Partnership Unit - Entitled to distributions equal to those provided to trust units. Directly exchangeable into trust units on a 1-for-1 basis at any time by holder. All held by Empire Company Limited. Puttable instruments classified as financial liabilities under IFRS.

Major Shareholder - Empire Company Limited held 41.5% interest at Mar. 14, 2023.

Price Range - CRR.UN/TSX

Year	Volume	High	Low	Close
2022	43,324,731	$18.91	$13.68	$15.86
2021	37,132,227	$19.09	$13.93	$18.62
2020	66,696,994	$16.71	$9.26	$14.35
2019	42,015,700	$16.33	$12.40	$15.94
2018	33,854,879	$13.79	$12.14	$12.52

Recent Close: $13.08

Capital Stock Changes - In January 2022, bought deal public offering of 6,705,000 trust units at $17.45 per unit and private placement of 4,756,446 Crombie Limited Partnership class B limited partnership units at $17.45 per unit were completed. Also during 2022, 1,215,032 trust units and 860,958 Crombie Limited Partnership class B limited partnership units were issued under distribution reinvestment plan and 36,487 trust units were issued under unit-based compensation plan.

Dividends

CRR.UN unit Ra $0.89004 pa M est. June 16, 2008**
** Reinvestment Option

Subsidiaries

59.1% int. in **Crombie Limited Partnership**, N.S.
- 50% int. in **Broadview Property Holdings Limited**, N.S.
- 100% int. in **Bronte Property Holdings Limited**, N.S.
- 50% int. in **Bronte Village General Partner Limited**, Canada.
- 50% int. in **Bronte Village Limited Partnership**, Ont.
- 100% int. in **CDTL Investment Partnership**, N.S.
- 100% int. in **CDTL Property Partnership**, N.S.
- 100% int. in **Crombie Bedford South Limited**, N.S.
- 100% int. in **Crombie Burnaby Property Holdings Limited**, N.S.
- 100% int. in **Crombie Danforth Property Holdings Limited**, N.S.
- 100% int. in **Crombie Davie Street Limited Partnership**, Man.
  - 100% int. in **1600 Davie Commercial Holdings Inc.**, B.C.
  - 50% int. in **1600 Davie GP Inc.**, B.C.
  - 50% int. in **1600 Davie Limited Partnership**, B.C.
  - 50% int. in **1600 Davie Residential Holdings Inc.**, B.C.
- 100% int. in **Crombie Developments Limited**, Canada.
- 50% int. in **Crombie FC Properties Limited**, N.S.
- 100% int. in **Crombie 4250 Albert Street Regina Inc.**, N.S.
- 100% int. in **Crombie General Partner Limited**, N.S.
- 100% int. in **Crombie King George Developments Limited Partnership**, Man.
  - 100% int. in **4326664 Nova Scotia Limited**, N.S.
- 100% int. in **Crombie Kitchener Property Holdings Limited**, N.S.
- 100% int. in **Crombie Management Limited**, N.S.
- 100% int. in **Crombie McCowan Road Holdings Limited**, N.S.
- 100% int. in **Crombie Nelson Property Holdings Limited**, N.S.
- 50% int. in **Crombie Northam Properties Limited**, N.S.
- 11% int. in **Crombie OSR Property Holdings (I) Limited**, N.S.
- 11% int. in **Crombie OSR Property Holdings (II) Limited**, N.S.
- 100% int. in **Crombie Peakview Way Holdings Limited**, N.S.
- 100% int. in **Crombie Penhorn Mall (2011) Limited**, N.S.
- 100% int. in **Crombie Properties II Partnership**, N.S.
  - 50% int. in **1700 East Broadway GP Inc.**, B.C.
  - 50% int. in **1700 East Broadway Limited Partnership**, B.C.
    - 50% int. in **1304193 B.C. Ltd.**, B.C.
- 100% int. in **Crombie Properties Holdings II Limited**, N.S.
- 100% int. in **Crombie Property Holdings II Limited**, Canada.
- 100% int. in **Crombie Southdale Holdings Limited**, N.S.
- 100% int. in **Crombie Yonge Street Holdings Limited**, N.S.
- 50% int. in **Duke Street Limited Partnership**, Qué.
- 50% int. in **The Duke Street Properties General Partner Limited**, Canada.
- 100% int. in **4427131 Canada Inc.**, Canada.
- 100% int. in **4541511 Canada Inc.**, Canada.
- 100% int. in **Jacklin Property Limited**, N.S.
- 100% int. in **Marché St-Augustin Properties Inc.**, Canada.
- 100% int. in **Marché St-Charles-de-Drummond Properties Inc.**, Canada.
- 50% int. in **140 CPN Holdings Limited**, Ont.
- 100% int. in **1600 Davie Commercial Holdings Inc.**, B.C.
- 100% int. in **Penhorn Plaza Holdings Limited**, N.S.
- 50% int. in **Penhorn Residential Holdings GP Limited**, N.S.
- 50% int. in **Penhorn Residential Holdings Limited Partnership**, N.S.
- 100% int. in **Snowcat Beltline Developments Inc.**, N.S.
- 100% int. in **Snowcat Kensington Developments Inc.**, N.S.
- 100% int. in **Snowcat Mission Developments Inc.**, N.S.
- 100% int. in **Snowcat Property Holdings Limited**, N.S.
- 50% int. in **2526042 Ontario Inc.**, Ont.
- 100% int. in **2761304 Ontario Inc.**, Ont.

Financial Statistics

Periods ended:	12m Dec. 31/22[A]		12m Dec. 31/21[oA]
	$000s	%Chg	$000s
Total revenue	**419,591**	**+3**	**408,892**
Rental operating expense	137,773		125,861
Salaries & benefits	12,590		19,178
General & admin. expense	6,957		6,306
Operating expense	**157,320**	**+4**	**151,345**
Operating income	**262,271**	**+2**	**257,547**
Investment income	(4,954)		(2,941)
Deprec. & amort.	79,836		75,763
Finance income	562		548
Finance costs, gross	83,576		93,336
Write-downs/write-offs	(10,400)		(2,539)
Pre-tax income	**167,804**	**+8**	**155,566**
Income taxes	4		165
Net income	**167,800**	**+8**	**155,401**
Cash & equivalent	6,117		3,915
Accounts receivable	19,317		24,441
Current assets	53,642		69,278
Long-term investments	40,397		44,210
Fixed assets	14,152		13,484
Income-producing props.	4,202,628		4,052,042
Properties under devel.	67,144		109,787
Property interests, net	3,559,707		3,518,275
Intangibles, net	40,869		39,451
Total assets	**4,078,398**	**+1**	**4,023,041**
Current liabilities	366,156		465,406
Long-term debt, gross	2,045,973		2,218,250
Long-term debt, net	1,799,015		1,893,755
Long-term lease liabilities	34,057		34,420
Cash from oper. activs	**233,545**	**+3**	**226,365**
Cash from fin. activs	(184,059)		(302,712)
Cash from invest. activs	(47,284)		18,490
Net cash position	**6,117**	**+56**	**3,915**
Capital expenditures	(256)		(194)
Increase in property	(219,706)		(141,075)
Decrease in property	171,702		144,014
Unfunded pension liability	5,428		6,021
	$		$
Earnings per share*	n.a.		n.a.
Cash flow per share*	1.31		1.37
Funds from opers. per sh.*	1.16		1.14
Adj. funds from opers. per sh.*	1.01		0.97
Cash divd. per share*	0.89		0.89
Total divd. per share*	**0.89**		**0.89**
	shs		shs
No. of shs. o/s*	178,376,896		164,802,973
	%		%
Net profit margin	39.99		38.01
Return on equity	n.m.		n.m.
Return on assets	6.21		6.12
No. of employees (FTEs)	303		294

* Trust unit
[o] Restated
[A] Reported in accordance with IFRS

Latest Results

Periods ended:	3m Mar. 31/23[A]		3m Mar. 31/22[A]
	$000s	%Chg	$000s
Total revenue	107,551	+2	104,946
Net income	25,173	0	25,248
	$		$
Earnings per share*	n.a.		n.a.

[A] Reported in accordance with IFRS

Historical Summary
(as originally stated)

Fiscal Year	Total Rev. $000s	Net Inc. Bef. Disc. $000s	EPS* $
2022[A]	419,591	167,800	n.a.
2021[A]	408,892	155,401	n.a.
2020[A]	388,733	67,608	n.a.
2019[A]	398,741	161,875	n.a.
2018[A]	414,649	107,407	n.a.

* Trust unit
[A] Reported in accordance with IFRS

C.171 Cronos Group Inc.*

Symbol - CRON **Exchange** - TSX **CUSIP** - 22717L
Head Office - 300-111 Peter St, Toronto, ON, M5V 2H1 **Telephone** - (416) 504-0004
Website - www.thecronosgroup.com
Email - investor.relations@thecronosgroup.com
Investor Relations - Shayne Laidlaw (416) 504-0004
Auditors - KPMG LLP C.A., Vaughan, Ont.
Lawyers - Dentons Canada LLP, Toronto, Ont.
Transfer Agents - TSX Trust Company, Toronto, Ont.

FP500 Revenue Ranking - 742

Employees - 447 at Dec. 31, 2022

Profile - (B.C. 2020; orig. Ont., 2012) Cultivates, manufactures and markets cannabis and cannabis-derived products for the medical and adult-use markets in Canada and internationally. Brands include Spinach®, PEACE NATURALS® and Lord Jones®.

Has an 84,000-sq.-ft. GMP-compliant fermentation and manufacturing facility in Winnipeg, Man., which operates as Cronos Fermentation consisting of fully equipped laboratories, two large scale microbial fermentation production areas and three downstream processing plants with a combined production capacity of 102,000 litres.

Also operates four fully operational licensed production facilities and a greenhouse totaling 67,000 sq. ft., and an additional 286,000 sq. ft. partially licensed, near Stayner, Ont., which operate as Peace Naturals Campus with an estimated annual capacity of 40,000 kg. Following its planned exit of Peace Naturals Campus at the end of 2022, the company announced in February 2023 a shift in its strategic plans instead for the realignment of business, with the intent to retain select components of operations at the campus, namely distribution and warehousing, certain R&D activities and manufacturing of certain proprietary innovation products, while seeking to lease the remaining portions of the campus to third parties.

Manufactures, markets and distributes hemp-derived CBD consumer products under the Lord Jones brand through e-commerce, retail and hospitality partner channels in the United States. Products include CBD oil, tinctures, gel capsules, bath salts, gumdrops, body lotions and creams.

Through 50%-owned **Cronos Growing Company Inc.**, a joint venture with a Canadian large-scale greenhouse operator Bert Mucci, the company operates an 850,000-sq.-ft. purpose-built greenhouse on 100 acres of land in Kingsville, Ont., with a production capacity of up to 70,000 kg of cannabis annually.

In Israel, through a joint venture with Kibbutz Gan Shmuel, the company holds the required certifications from the Medical Cannabis Unit of the Israeli Ministry of Health to produce, manufacture and distribute medical cannabis in Israel. The joint venture has built a 45,000-sq.-ft. greenhouse facility with a production capacity of 5,000 kg per year; and a 17,000-sq.-ft. manufacturing facility for analytics, formulation development and research purposes. The joint venture has been distributing PEACE NATURALS branded cannabis products to the Israeli medical cannabis market since the second quarter of 2020.

In addition, the company held 10% interest in **Vitura Health Limited** (formerly **Cronos Australia Limited**), which owns a medicinal cannabis company; and 13.7% interest in **NatuEra S.A.R.L**, a joint venture with **Agroidea S.A.S.**, whereby the company received a licence to cultivate psychoactive cannabis for the production of seeds for cultivation, production of grain, and manufacture of derivative products, and has a marijuana cultivation and manufacturing facility in Cundinamarca, Colombia.

On May 31, 2023, the company announced it was winding down and exiting its U.S. hemp-derived CBD operations by the end of the second quarter of 2023. Also plans to launch its adult-use Lord Jones® brand in Canada in the fourth quarter of 2023.

In December 2022, affiliate **NatuEra S.A.R.L.**, has entered into a convertible bridge loan agreement with its joint venture partner **Agroidea SAS** and a new investment group, whereby Agroidea and the new investment group provided $9,500,000 in exchange for convertible notes that were converted into equity immediately following the closing of the loan. Agroidea is a Colombian agricultural services provider which owned the remaining 50% of Natuera's common shares. As a result, the company's ownership interest in NatuEra decreased to 13.7% from 50%.

During 2022, the company ceased producing and distributing products under the Happy Dance and PEACE+ brands. Happy Dance and PEACE+ were brands focused on the production and distribution of U.S. hemp-derived cannabinoid products.

On Dec. 2, 2022, the company and **Vitura Health Limited** (formerly **Cronos Australia Limited**) agreed to terminate the intellectual property license that granted Vitura the right to use certain intellectual property of the company, including, but not limited to, the Cronos name and the PEACE NATURALS brand.

Predecessor Detail - Name changed from PharmaCan Capital Corp., Mar. 1, 2017.

Directors - Michael (Mike) Gorenstein, chr., pres. & CEO, Miami, Fla.; James D. (Jim) Rudyk†, Oakville, Ont.; Jason M. Adler, Pacific Palisades, Calif.; Kendrick F. Ashton Jr., McLean, Va.; Kamran Khan, Richmond, Va.; Dominik Meier, Richmond, Va.; Elizabeth Seegar, Richmond, Va.

Other Exec. Officers - James Holm, CFO; Jeffrey (Jeff) Jacobson, chief growth officer; Shannon Buggy, sr. v-p & global head, people; Terry Doucet, sr. v-p, legal & regulatory affairs, gen. counsel & corp. sec.; Anna Shlimak, sr. v-p, corp. affairs & strategy; Arye Weigensberg, sr. v-p & head, R&D; Carlos Cortez, v-p & contr.; Ran Gorelik, gen. mgr., Cronos Israel

† Lead director

Capital Stock

	Authorized (shs.)	Outstanding (shs.)[1]
Common	unlimited	380,815,921

[1] At Apr. 27, 2023

Options - At Dec. 31, 2022, options were outstanding to purchase 5,350,600 common shares at a weighted average exercise price of Cdn$10.57 per share with a weighted average remaining contractual term of 0.73 years.

Major Shareholder - Altria Group, Inc. held 41% interest at Mar. 31, 2023.

Price Range - CRON/TSX

Year	Volume	High	Low	Close
2022	84,819,737	$5.36	$3.32	$3.44
2021	141,697,079	$20.08	$4.86	$4.98
2020	262,835,011	$11.85	$5.82	$8.84
2019	358,433,262	$32.95	$7.97	$9.97
2018	470,914,906	$19.81	$5.96	$14.38

Recent Close: $2.29

Capital Stock Changes - During 2022, common shares were issued as follows: 4,157,888 as research and development milestones payment and 1,464,822 under a share-based compensation plan.

Long-Term Debt - At Dec. 31, 2022, the company had no long-term debt.

Wholly Owned Subsidiaries

Hortican Inc., Toronto, Ont.
- 100% int. in **Cronos Canada Holdings Inc.**, Canada.
- 100% int. in **Cronos Global Holdings Inc.**, Canada.
  - 13.7% int. in **NatuEra S.A.R.L.**, Colombia.
  - 10% int. in **Vitura Health Limited**, Melbourne, Vic., Australia.
- 100% int. in **Cronos Group USA Holdings Company Limited**, B.C.
- 70% int. in **Cronos Israel G.S. Cultivations Ltd.**, Israel.
- 90% int. in **Cronos Israel G.S. Manufacturing Ltd.**, Israel.
- 90% int. in **Cronos Israel G.S. Pharmacies Ltd.**, Israel.
- 90% int. in **Cronos Israel G.S. Store Ltd.**, Israel.
- 100% int. in **Cronos Research Labs Ltd.**, Israel.
- 100% int. in **Cronos USA Client Services LLC**, Del.
- 100% int. in **Cronos USA Holdings Inc.**, Del.
- 100% int. in **The Peace Naturals Project Inc.**, Stayner, Ont.
- 100% int. in **Redwood IP Holding, LLC**, Del.
- 100% int. in **Redwood Operations CA, LLC**, Calif.
- 100% int. in **Redwood Retail, LLC**, Calif.
- 100% int. in **Redwood Wellness, LLC**, Del.
- 100% int. in **Thanos Holdings Ltd.**, B.C.
- 100% int. in **Zeus Cannabinoids LLC**, Del.

Note: The preceding list includes only the major related companies in which interests are held.

Financial Statistics

Periods ended:	12m Dec. 31/22[A]		12m Dec. 31/21[A]
	US$000s	%Chg	US$000s
Operating revenue	**91,904**	**+23**	**74,435**
Cost of sales	79,935		91,969
Research & devel. expense	13,381		23,331
General & admin expense	93,460		141,419
Stock-based compensation	15,115		10,151
Other operating expense	5,333		nil
Operating expense	**207,224**	**-22**	**266,870**
Operating income	**(115,320)**	**n.a.**	**(192,435)**
Deprec., depl. & amort.	6,025		4,484
Finance income	22,550		9,098
Finance costs, gross	13		27
Investment income	3,114		(6,313)
Write-downs/write-offs	(64,885)		(363,675)
Pre-tax income	**(134,559)**	**n.a.**	**(397,135)**
Income taxes	34,175		(431)
Net inc. bef. disc. opers	**(168,734)**	**n.a.**	**(396,704)**
Income from disc. opers	nil		(500)
Net income	**(168,734)**	**n.a.**	**(397,204)**
Net inc. for equity hldrs	**(168,734)**	**n.a.**	**(396,107)**
Net inc. for non-cont. int	**nil**	**n.a.**	**(1,097)**
Cash & equivalent	877,721		1,004,657
Inventories	37,559		32,802
Accounts receivable	23,113		22,067
Current assets	960,156		1,079,718
Long-term investments	89,748		135,156
Fixed assets, net	60,557		74,070
Right-of-use assets	2,273		8,882
Intangibles, net	27,737		19,177
Total assets	**1,213,009**	**-13**	**1,397,738**
Accts. pay. & accr. liabs	66,771		37,287
Current liabilities	68,116		54,373
Long-term lease liabilities	2,546		7,095
Shareholders' equity	1,143,885		1,337,243
Non-controlling interest	(2,921)		(2,967)
Cash from oper. activs	**(88,948)**	**n.a.**	**(153,616)**
Cash from fin. activs	(2,897)		(13,442)
Cash from invest. activs	(1,842)		(28,898)
Net cash position	**764,644**	**-14**	**886,973**
Capital expenditures, net	(3,451)		(11,144)
	US$		US$
Earnings per share*	(0.45)		(1.07)
Cash flow per share*	(0.24)		(0.41)
	shs		shs
No. of shs. o/s*	380,575,403		374,952,693
Avg. no. of shs. o/s*	376,961,797		370,390,965
	%		%
Net profit margin	(183.60)		(532.95)
Return on equity	(13.60)		(25.95)
Return on assets	(12.92)		(23.87)
Foreign sales percent	39		32
No. of employees (FTEs)	447		n.a.

* Common

[A] Reported in accordance with U.S. GAAP

Latest Results

Periods ended:	3m Mar. 31/23[A]		3m Mar. 31/22[A]
	US$000s	%Chg	US$000s
Operating revenue	20,144	-20	25,033
Net income	(19,257)	n.a.	(32,653)
Net inc. for equity hldrs	(19,169)	n.a.	(32,638)
Net inc. for non-cont. int	(88)		(15)
	US$		US$
Earnings per share*	(0.05)		(0.09)

* Common

[A] Reported in accordance with U.S. GAAP

Historical Summary

(as originally stated)

Fiscal Year	Oper. Rev.	Net Inc. Bef. Disc.	EPS*
	US$000s	US$000s	US$
2022[A]	91,904	(168,734)	(0.45)
2021[A]	74,435	(396,704)	(1.07)
2020[A]	46,719	(74,620)	(0.21)
2019[A]	23,750	1,165,574	3.76
	$000s	$000s	$
2018[B]	15,703	(19,205)	(0.11)

* Common

[A] Reported in accordance with U.S. GAAP

[B] Reported in accordance with IFRS

C.172 Crossover Acquisitions Inc.

Symbol - CRSS.P **Exchange** - TSX-VEN **CUSIP** - 22767T

Head Office - 700-77 King St W, Toronto, ON, M5K 1G8 **Telephone** - (416) 574-4818

Email - dmitchell@stillbridge.com

Investor Relations - David Mitchell (416) 574-4818
Auditors - Wasserman Ramsay C.A., Markham, Ont.
Transfer Agents - TSX Trust Company, Toronto, Ont.
Profile - (Ont. 2019) Capital Pool Company.

Recent Merger and Acquisition Activity

Status: pending **Revised:** Mar. 21, 2023

UPDATE: The companies have entered into an agreement that provides for a transaction by way of three-cornered amalgamation of Resolute and a wholly owned subsidiary of Crossover. Each Resolute class A share would be exchanged for one post-consolidated common share of Crossover (following a 1-for-2 share consolidation). A total of 42,068,200 post-consolidated common shares were expected to be issued to Resolute shareholders. An additional 16,000,000 post-consolidated common shares would be issued on exchange of subscription receipts to be issued by Resolute under a minimum $4,000,000 private placement. Crossover plans to change its name to Resolute Resources Ltd.PREVIOUS: Crossover Acquisitions Inc. entered into a letter of intent for the Qualifying Transaction reverse takeover acquisition of Resolute Resources Ltd., which explores for and develops oil and gas in Alberta and British Columbia.

Directors - David Mitchell, CEO, CFO & corp. sec., Mississauga, Ont.; Matthew Goldman, Toronto, Ont.; Lawrence Guy, Toronto, Ont.; Kiernan Lynch, Toronto, Ont.; Terrence (Terry) Lynch, Nassau, Bahamas

Capital Stock

	Authorized (shs.)	Outstanding (shs.)[1]
Common	unlimited	16,500,000

[1] At May 19, 2022

Major Shareholder - Widely held at Oct. 15, 2021.

Price Range - CRSS.P/TSX-VEN

Year	Volume	High	Low	Close
2022............	2,767,500	$0.20	$0.07	$0.07
2021............	1,328,373	$0.20	$0.12	$0.15

Recent Close: $0.07

C.173 Crown Capital Partners Inc.

Symbol - CRWN **Exchange** - TSX **CUSIP** - 22821L
Head Office - 19-131 700 2 St SW, Calgary, AB, T2P 2W2 **Telephone** - (403) 775-2554
Website - www.crowncapital.ca
Email - craig.armitage@crowncapital.ca
Investor Relations - Craig Armitage (416) 347-8954
Auditors - KPMG LLP C.A., Calgary, Alta.
Lawyers - Torys LLP, Calgary, Alta.
Transfer Agents - TSX Trust Company, Calgary, Alta.
Profile - (Can. 1999) Provides specialty financing solutions operating mainly in the telecommunications infrastructure, distribution services and distributed power markers.

Operations are organized into six segments: Network services; Distribution services; Distributed power; Specialty finance; Real estate; and Corporate and other.

The **Network services** segment provides network connectivity to customers in otherwise underserved markets. Revenue earned by the segment includes network services revenue, which consists of contractual revenue related to the access and usage of telecommunications infrastructure in addition to revenue from professional services, network support, maintenance and repair services, and hardware sales.

The **Distribution services** segment includes wholly owned **Go Direct Global Inc.**, which provides end-to-end integrated e-commerce and business-to-business fulfillment and distribution services. Revenue earned by the segment includes provision of distribution services which consists of inventory storage, inventory management, order fulfillment, freight management, customer service and information technology support.

The **Distributed power** segment is managed through 43.2%-owned **Crown Capital Power Limited Partnership** (Crown Power) which invests in on-site power generation assets that provide electricity under long-term contracts to mid to large-scale electricity users, such as manufacturers, commercial properties and condominiums. Design, construction and operation of the distributed power projects is conducted by partners, in which the company and Crown Power holds ownership interests.

The **Specialty finance** segment consists of 28% interest in **Crown Capital Partner Funding, LP** (Crown Partners Fund), an investment fund which offers special situations financing solutions to businesses for transitory capital requirements, generally in the form of short- and medium-term senior or subordinated loans. Also includes investments in corporate loans to **PenEquity Realty Corporation** and a 12.5% interest in **Crown Private Credit Partners Inc.** (CPCP), which holds investment management contracts in respect of Crown Partners Fund and **Crown Capital Fund IV Investment, LP**.

The **Real estate** segment includes wholly owned **PRC Stoney Creek Corp.**, which owns a grocery-anchored community retail plaza in Hamilton, Ont.; and wholly owned **PRC Barrie Corp.**, which owns a medium to high-density residential project in Barrie, Ont.

The **Corporate and other** segment includes wholly owned **Lumbermens Credit Group Ltd.**, a construction credit reporting company whose assets primarily include property and equipment and credit reporting customer contracts. The segment also includes assets, liabilities, revenues and expenses that aren't directly related to any of the other four reportable segments.

On June 24, 2022, the company acquired **Go Direct Global Inc.**, which provides end-to-end integrated e-commerce fulfillment and distribution services, in exchange for the extinguishment of a $3,895,000 investment in a Canadian debt security.

Directors - Christopher A. (Chris) Johnson, co-founder, pres. & CEO, Toronto, Ont.; Alan M. Rowe, chr., Toronto, Ont.; John A. Brussa, Calgary, Alta.; C. Robert Gillis, Brooklyn, N.S.; Steven Sharpe, Toronto, Ont.

Other Exec. Officers - Michael Overvelde, sr. v-p, fin. & CFO; Daniella Gan, v-p, fin.; Adam Jenkins, v-p; Christopher Roberts, v-p, opers.; Shane Melanson, contr.

Capital Stock

	Authorized (shs.)	Outstanding (shs.)[1]
Common	unlimited	5,633,946

[1] At May 10, 2023

Normal Course Issuer Bid - The company plans to make normal course purchases of up to 280,000 common shares representing 5% of the total outstanding. The bid commenced on Apr. 13, 2023, and expires on Apr. 12, 2024.

Major Shareholder - EdgePoint Investment Group Inc. held 20% interest, Christopher A. (Chris) Johnson held 13.3% interest and Portland Investment Counsel Inc. held 11% interest at Apr. 5, 2023.

Price Range - CRWN/TSX

Year	Volume	High	Low	Close
2022............	655,565	$9.00	$7.00	$9.00
2021............	830,483	$7.50	$4.54	$7.50
2020............	1,828,489	$8.04	$3.14	$4.93
2019............	1,108,365	$10.48	$6.81	$7.59
2018............	2,031,889	$10.55	$9.01	$10.40

Recent Close: $7.65

Capital Stock Changes - During 2022, 1,450,556 common shares were repurchased under a Normal Courser Issuer Bid.

Wholly Owned Subsidiaries

Community Network Partners Inc.
Crown Capital Fund III Management Inc., Canada.
Crown Capital Funding Corporation, Canada.
- 19.8% int. in **Crown Capital Fund IV Investment, LP**, Alta.
  - 5.6% int. in **Crown Capital Partner Funding, LP**, Canada.
- 26.8% int. in **Crown Capital Partner Funding, LP**, Canada. Previously Crown Capital Fund IV, LP.
- 43.2% int. in **Crown Capital Power Limited Partnership**, Canada.
- 100% int. in **Crown Capital Private Credit Fund, LP**, Alta.
  - 100% int. in **PenEquity Development Limited**
    - 100% int. in **Lumberness Credit Group Ltd.**
    - 100% int. in **PRC Barrie Corp.**, Ont.
      - 100% int. in **Penady (North Barrie) Limited**
    - 100% int. in **PRC Stoney Creek Corp.**, Ont.
      - 100% int. in **Penady (Stoney Creek) Ltd.**, Ont.

Crown Capital LP Partner Funding Inc., Canada. Formerly Crown Capital Fund IV Management Inc.
Crown Capital Private Credit Management Inc., Canada.
Galaxy Broadband Communications Inc., Mississauga, Ont.
Go Direct Global Inc., Mississauga, Ont.
- 100% int. in **Go Direct America Inc.**, United States.
- 100% int. in **Go Direct Supply Chain Solutions Inc.**, Canada.

10824356 Canada Inc., Canada. Crown Power GP.
PenEquity Development GP Inc.
WireIE Holdings International Inc., Ont.
- 100% int. in **WireIE (Canada) Inc.**, Canada.
- 100% int. in **WireIE (Development) Inc.**, Canada.

WireIE Inc.

Subsidiaries

85.8% int. in **Onsite Power Partners Ltd.**

Financial Statistics

Periods ended:	12m Dec. 31/22[A]		12m Dec. 31/21[¤A]
	$000s	%Chg	$000s
Realized invest. gain (loss)...............	(1,268)		86
Unrealized invest. gain (loss)............	1,270		(322)
Total revenue.................................	**40,181**	**-15**	**47,396**
Salaries & benefits..........................	8,756		9,741
General & admin. expense...............	29,541		16,480
Stock-based compensation.............	530		803
Operating expense........................	**38,827**	**+44**	**27,029**
Operating income.........................	**1,354**	**-93**	**20,367**
Deprec. & amort.............................	6,175		3,880
Finance costs, gross........................	3,635		4,075
Write-downs/write-offs....................	(3,653)		(751)
Pre-tax income.............................	**(9,588)**	**n.a.**	**2,381**
Income taxes..................................	(2,113)		371
Net income...................................	**(7,475)**	**n.a.**	**2,010**
Cash & equivalent...........................	7,244		10,842
Inventories......................................	1,458		1,108
Accounts receivable........................	14,195		6,056
Current assets................................	28,128		26,658
Long-term investments....................	36,658		49,970
Fixed assets, net.............................	35,219		14,279
Intangibles......................................	7,344		6,159
Total assets...................................	**166,662**	**+19**	**140,115**
Bank indebtedness..........................	11,900		12,450
Accts. pay. & accr. liabs...................	12,302		6,931
Current liabilities............................	50,632		24,459
Long-term debt, gross.....................	40,821		19,762
Long-term debt, net.........................	20,991		19,150
Long-term lease liabilities................	16,753		644
Equity portion of conv. debs............	483		483
Shareholders' equity........................	50,670		69,075
Cash from oper. activs...................	**3,101**	**-82**	**17,471**
Cash from fin. activs........................	9,674		(65,796)
Cash from invest. activs..................	(16,377)		48,206
Net cash position..........................	**7,244**	**-33**	**10,842**
Capital expenditures........................	(2,602)		(1,196)
	$		$
Earnings per share*.........................	(1.26)		0.23
Cash flow per share*.......................	0.52		2.00
	shs		shs
No. of shs. o/s*...............................	5,642,546		7,093,102
Avg. no. of shs. o/s*........................	5,912,105		8,735,781
	%		%
Net profit margin.............................	(18.60)		4.24
Return on equity..............................	(12.48)		2.67
Return on assets..............................	(3.03)		2.36

* Common
[¤] Restated
[A] Reported in accordance with IFRS

Latest Results

Periods ended:	3m Mar. 31/23[A]		3m Mar. 31/22[A]
	$000s	%Chg	$000s
Total revenue..................................	17,055	+137	7,209
Net income......................................	(712)	n.a.	(2,550)
	$		$
Earnings per share*.........................	(0.13)		(0.38)

* Common
[A] Reported in accordance with IFRS

Historical Summary
(as originally stated)

Fiscal Year	Total Rev.	Net Inc. Bef. Disc.	EPS*
	$000s	$000s	$
2022[A]...................	40,181	(7,475)	(1.26)
2021[A]...................	47,396	2,010	0.23
2020[A]...................	44,824	(13,295)	(1.43)
2019[A]...................	25,207	(209)	(0.02)
2018[A]...................	32,666	20,276	0.74

* Common
[A] Reported in accordance with IFRS

C.174 Cryptoblox Technologies Inc.

Symbol - BLOX **Exchange** - CSE **CUSIP** - 22906X
Head Office - 2400-1055 Georgia St W, Vancouver, BC, V6E 3P3 **Telephone** - (236) 259-0279
Website - cryptoblox.ca
Email - info@cryptoblox.ca
Investor Relations - Akshay Sood (236) 259-0279
Auditors - NVS Chartered Accountants Professional Corporation C.A., Markham, Ont.
Transfer Agents - Odyssey Trust Company, Vancouver, B.C.
Profile - (B.C. 2015) Combines proprietary blockchain technology with patented artificial intelligence (AI)-driven battery management system (BMS) to provide products and services for the Electric Vehicle (EV) and Energy Storage Solution (ESS) markets.

ESS products include the IoniX Pro Home SmartWall, which stores energy captured by solar panels or from the grid and keeps it in reserve to enable owners to customize system energy usage while monitoring energy expenditure in real-time with cloud-based battery management technology; TITAN EnergyCore, which is an ESS designed for self-recovery, battery self-repair, and AI-powered operations and maintenance for industrial and commercial markets; RV Freedom, which was built to power electric devices within a recreational vehicle (RV) and manage these with proprietary blockchain management system; EV Smart Charger, which was created to outperform existing charging stations with remote monitoring, drawing from the battery during peak rate times and recharging during off-peak hours; Smart Miner, which is an ESS capable of using a carbon negative process to mine the renewable obligation base energy economy (ROBe^2) protocol cryptocurrency; and IoniX Pro Smart Station, which is an EV charging solution consisting of the EV Smart Charger and TITAN series SmartCore, a large scale ESS, to power over 100 EVs per day.

Also offers the Smart Command™ system and application (app), which is integrated into the entire IoniX Pro suite of ESS products, allowing for complete power management and smart grid communications; and is developing a blockchain-based app for smartphones that will allow electric vehicle drivers to make crypto payments at charging stations.

Wholly owned **Optimal CP Inc.** is developing large-scale cryptocurrency mining facilities in Alberta.

Wholly owned **Red Water Acquisition Corp.** specializes in air-cooled data centres and advanced heat recapture products. Red Water has obtained development rights in Sturgeon cty., Alta., for its operations.

The company has exclusive North and South American, European and African distribution rights to a broad set of applied technologies and solutions for battery management systems, energy storage technology applications and battery safety applications developed by **Jiangsu RichPower New Energy Co. Ltd.**, a battery management system and energy storage system company in the People's Republic of China as well as exclusive worldwide rights to create its own branded line of electric vehicles based on Daymak Spiritus by **Daymak International Inc.**, a distributor of light electric vehicles in Canada.

In October 2022, wholly owned **GRT Technologies Inc.** was dissolved.

Recent Merger and Acquisition Activity

Status: completed **Revised:** June 29, 2023

UPDATE: The transaction was completed. Cryptoblox issued a total of 118,280,800 common shares on closing, with the remaining 101,719,200 common shares to be issued upon the completion of certain milestones being met by Red Water. PREVIOUS: Cryptoblox Technologies Inc. agreed to acquire private Red Water Acquisition Corp., which specializes in air-cooled data centres and advanced heat recapture products, for issuance of 220,000,000 common shares at a deemed price of 5¢ per share.

Status: terminated **Revised:** Feb. 2, 2023

UPDATE: The transaction was terminated. PREVIOUS: Cryptoblox Technologies Inc. agreed to acquire private Calgary, Alta.-based CryptoTherm Manufacturing Inc. from 1289048 B.C. Ltd. for issuance of 400,000,000 common share sat a deemed price of 5¢ per share. CryptoTherm designs and builds liquid-cooled data centres, specifically designed for cryptocurrency mining, and advanced heat recapture products.

Predecessor Detail - Name changed from Extreme Vehicle Battery Technologies Corp., Mar. 3, 2022.

Directors - Akshay Sood, CEO; Victor Hui-Fai Ho, B.C.; Taryn Stemp, B.C.

Other Exec. Officers - Maryam Amin-Shanjani, CFO

Capital Stock

	Authorized (shs.)	Outstanding (shs.)[1]
Common	unlimited	664,055,092

[1] At June 29, 2023

Major Shareholder - Widely held at June 14, 2022.

Price Range - BLOX/CSE

Year	Volume	High	Low	Close
2022	197,720,227	$0.15	$0.01	$0.01
2021	1,034,610,543	$0.95	$0.04	$0.14
2020	110,035,406	$0.08	$0.00	$0.05
2019	27,252,000	$0.03	$0.00	$0.00
2018	67,213,672	$0.78	$0.01	$0.02

Split: 6-for-1 split in Oct. 2020; 1-for-10 cons. in Jan. 2019

Recent Close: $0.01

Capital Stock Changes - On June 29, 2023, 118,280,800 common shares were issued pursuant to the acquisition of Red Water Acquisition Corp.

Wholly Owned Subsidiaries

CryptoPlug Technologies Inc., Canada.

1Linx Ltd., N.Y.

Optimal CP Inc., Canada.

Red Water Acquisition Corp., Canada.

Investments

25% int. in **IoniX Pro Battery Technologies Inc.**, Canada.

Financial Statistics

Periods ended:	12m Jan. 31/22[A]		12m Jan. 31/21[A]
	$000s	%Chg	$000s
Salaries & benefits	80		510
Research & devel. expense	381		nil
General & admin expense	21,292		1,081
Stock-based compensation	8		43
Operating expense	**21,791**	**n.m.**	**1,634**
Operating income	**(21,791)**	**n.a.**	**(1,634)**
Deprec., depl. & amort.	100		40
Finance costs, gross	6		2
Pre-tax income	**(21,748)**	**n.a.**	**(1,654)**
Net income	**(21,748)**	**n.a.**	**(1,654)**
Cash & equivalent	1,002		438
Accounts receivable	441		nil
Current assets	3,830		554
Intangibles, net	6,860		960
Total assets	**10,690**	**+606**	**1,514**
Bank indebtedness	45		44
Accts. pay. & accr. liabs	599		1,137
Current liabilities	1,308		2,302
Long-term debt, gross	47		42
Long-term debt, net	47		42
Shareholders' equity	9,336		(1,230)
Cash from oper. activs	**(11,385)**	**n.a.**	**(1,214)**
Cash from fin. activs	11,948		1,500
Net cash position	**1,002**	**+129**	**438**
	$		$
Earnings per share*	(0.05)		(0.01)
Cash flow per share*	(0.03)		(0.00)
	shs		shs
No. of shs. o/s*	538,306,991		314,102,540
Avg. no. of shs. o/s*	412,634,428		274,257,241
	%		%
Net profit margin	n.a.		n.a.
Return on equity	n.m.		n.m.
Return on assets	(356.31)		(198.20)

* Common

[A] Reported in accordance with IFRS

Latest Results

Periods ended:	9m Oct. 31/22[A]		9m Oct. 31/21[A]
	$000s	%Chg	$000s
Net income	(209)	n.a.	(6,883)
	$		$
Earnings per share*	(0.00)		(0.02)

* Common

[A] Reported in accordance with IFRS

Historical Summary
(as originally stated)

Fiscal Year	Oper. Rev. $000s	Net Inc. Bef. Disc. $000s	EPS* $
2022[A]	nil	(21,748)	(0.05)
2021[A]	nil	(1,654)	(0.01)
2020[A]	20	(751)	(0.01)
2019[A]	77	(8,656)	(0.18)
2018[A]	76	(3,518)	(0.13)

* Common

[A] Reported in accordance with IFRS

Note: Adjusted throughout for 6-for-1 split in Oct. 2020; 1-for-10 cons. in Jan. 2019

C.175 CryptoStar Corp.

Symbol - CSTR **Exchange** - TSX-VEN **CUSIP** - 22905W

Head Office - 4400-181 Bay St, Toronto, ON, M5J 2T3 **Telephone** - (416) 368-6200

Website - www.cryptostar.com

Email - david.jellins@cryptostar.com

Investor Relations - David Jellins (416) 368-6200

Auditors - Kingston Ross Pasnak LLP C.A., Edmonton, Alta.

Lawyers - CP LLP, Toronto, Ont.

Transfer Agents - TSX Trust Company, Toronto, Ont.

Profile - (Ont. 2017) Has cryptocurrency mining operations with data centres in the U.S. and Canada and provides equipment hosting services worldwide.

The company primarily mines Bitcoin and Ethereum in Utah, Alberta, Quebec and Newfoundland and Labrador. At Aug. 29, 2022, the company had an aggregate hashrate of 125,550 megahashes per second (MH/s) from GPU miners and 94.4 petahashes per second (PH/s) from ASIC miners running at its data centres. At June 20, 2022, the company had equipment hosting agreements for a total mining capacity of 12 MW at its Utah data centre facilities.

Predecessor Detail - Name changed from Aumento Capital VI Corporation, Sept. 26, 2018, following Qualifying Transaction reverse takeover acquisition of CryptoStar Inc. and concurrent amalgamation of CryptoStar with wholly owned 2626694 Ontario Inc.

Directors - David Jellins, pres. & CEO, Sydney, N.S.W., Australia; Amelia Jones, chief comml. officer, Sydney, N.S.W., Australia; Christopher N. Malone, Aurora, Ont.; Aurelio Useche, Verdun, Qué.

Other Exec. Officers - Jing Peng, CFO; Lawrence Liu, contr.

Capital Stock

	Authorized (shs.)	Outstanding (shs.)[1]
Common	unlimited	429,016,069

[1] At Aug. 26, 2022

Major Shareholder - David Jellins held 12.07% interest and Amelia Jones held 12.07% interest at Dec. 8, 2021.

Price Range - CSTR/TSX-VEN

Year	Volume	High	Low	Close
2022	113,361,140	$0.13	$0.02	$0.02
2021	1,291,919,609	$0.84	$0.08	$0.13
2020	250,873,605	$0.18	$0.02	$0.12
2019	50,077,915	$0.26	$0.01	$0.05
2018	28,415,855	$0.08	$0.01	$0.02

Recent Close: $0.03

Wholly Owned Subsidiaries

CryptoStar Holdings Inc., Toronto, Ont.
- 100% int. in **CryptoStar USA, Inc.**, Del.

Neuro Digital Inc., Qué.

Financial Statistics

Periods ended:	12m Dec. 31/21[A]		12m Dec. 31/20[oA]
	US$000s	%Chg	US$000s
Operating revenue	**4,742**	**+788**	**534**
Cost of sales	465		660
Salaries & benefits	702		363
General & admin expense	1,188		889
Stock-based compensation	1,105		255
Operating expense	**3,460**	**+60**	**2,167**
Operating income	**1,282**	**n.a.**	**(1,633)**
Deprec., depl. & amort.	3,862		3,296
Finance income	7		nil
Finance costs, gross	248		248
Pre-tax income	**(3,457)**	**n.a.**	**(5,203)**
Income taxes	6		nil
Net income	**(3,463)**	**n.a.**	**(5,203)**
Cash & equivalent	12,211		404
Current assets	15,336		705
Fixed assets, net	15,703		5,153
Right-of-use assets	1,574		1,899
Intangibles, net	1,506		2,724
Total assets	**36,708**	**+248**	**10,549**
Accts. pay. & accr. liabs	795		1,394
Current liabilities	5,346		1,573
Long-term debt, gross	nil		3,569
Long-term debt, net	nil		3,569
Long-term lease liabilities	1,849		2,065
Shareholders' equity	29,463		3,242
Cash from oper. activs	**(3,391)**	**n.a.**	**(1,097)**
Cash from fin. activs	24,925		1,490
Cash from invest. activs	(14,885)		(105)
Net cash position	**7,050**	**n.m.**	**402**
Capital expenditures	(11,294)		(430)
Capital disposals	15		325
	US$		US$
Earnings per share*	(0.01)		(0.02)
Cash flow per share*	(0.01)		(0.01)
	shs		shs
No. of shs. o/s*	425,077,804		242,793,300
Avg. no. of shs. o/s*	375,487,991		213,344,044
	%		%
Net profit margin	(73.03)		(974.34)
Return on equity	(21.18)		(117.96)
Return on assets	(13.60)		(43.44)
Foreign sales percent	37		80

* Common

[o] Restated

[A] Reported in accordance with IFRS

Latest Results

Periods ended:	6m June 30/22[A]		6m June 30/21[A]
	US$000s	%Chg	US$000s
Operating revenue	2,970	+356	652
Net income	(6,001)	n.a.	(3,359)
	US$		US$
Earnings per share*	(0.01)		(0.01)

* Common

[A] Reported in accordance with IFRS

Historical Summary
(as originally stated)

Fiscal Year	Oper. Rev. US$000s	Net Inc. Bef. Disc. US$000s	EPS* US$
2021[A]	4,742	(3,463)	(0.01)
2020[A]	504	(5,203)	(0.02)
2019[A]	9,927	(2,136)	(0.01)
2018[A1]	15,011	(20,079)	(0.10)
2017[A2]	10,326	3,686	0.03

* Common
[A] Reported in accordance with IFRS
[1] Results reflect the Sept. 26, 2018, Qualifying Transaction reverse takeover acquisition of CryptoStar Holdings Inc.
[2] 51 weeks ended Dec. 31, 2017.

C.176 CubicFarm Systems Corp.

Symbol - CUB **Exchange** - TSX **CUSIP** - 22968P
Head Office - 7170 Grover Rd, Langley, BC, V2Y 2R1 **Toll-free** - (888) 280-9076
Website - www.cubicfarms.com
Email - investors@cubicfarms.com
Investor Relations - Investor Relations (888) 280-9076
Auditors -
Transfer Agents - Computershare Trust Company of Canada Inc., Vancouver, B.C.
Employees - 49 at May 2, 2023
Profile - (B.C. 2015) Builds and sells automated onsite commercial-scale fresh agricultural produce and livestock feed technologies.

The company operates in two segments: Feed Division and Fresh Division.

Feed Division

Operates using Hydrogen Automated Vertical Pastures™, a smart farming equipment that uses a unique process to sprout grains such as wheat and barley, in a controlled environment to efficiently produce a high-performance feed ingredient for livestock 365 days a year. It has an automated seeder that spreads half an inch of small grain seed on the growing surface. A fine mist of water is sprayed from above to initiate growth, followed by a gentle-rain automated irrigation system to feed the plants as they sprout. After six days, fresh green feed on the growing surface is rolled off and harvested at the push of a button on the touchscreen control panel. HydroGreen products are manufactured at a 21,620-sq.-ft. warehouse and office space in Sioux Falls, S.D., and research and development, product testing, customer visits, partner training and feed trials are housed within a 12,000-sq.-ft. Innovation centre in Sioux Falls.

Fresh Division

Operates using CubicFarm™ System for growing leafy greens, tomatoes, flowers, herbs, and microgreens consists of growing machines, a germination machine and an irrigation and nutrient system, with each machine built within an insulated stainless-steel container. The growing machines and germination machines use a conveyor to cycle the crops within trays. These crops are bathed in lights as they cycle through the machine and are dosed with nutrient rich water as crop trays reach the bottom return track. The machines open into a centralized, climate controlled clean work area where crops are planted, harvested and packaged. In addition, it manages FreshHub, an out-of-container climate-controlled environment to provide a growing system for commercial scale lettuce programs. CubicFarm™ Systems are manufactured in the People's Republic of China with a research and development facility in Langley, B.C.

Directors - Daniel A. Burns, chr., Vancouver, B.C.; G. David Cole, Ont.; Michael McCarthy, B.C.; Janet Wood, B.C.
Other Exec. Officers - John de Jonge, interim CEO & pres., HYDROGREEN, INC.; Michael B. Kyne, interim CFO

Capital Stock

	Authorized (shs.)	Outstanding (shs.)[1]
Class A Preferred	unlimited	nil
Class B Preferred	unlimited	nil
Common	unlimited	263,163,774

[1] At May 15, 2023

Major Shareholder - Ospraie AG Science, LLC held 13.57% interest at Mar. 15, 2023.

Price Range - CUB/TSX

Year	Volume	High	Low	Close
2022	36,367,265	$1.33	$0.06	$0.08
2021	41,268,151	$1.82	$0.91	$1.17
2020	15,969,584	$1.24	$0.12	$0.95
2019	5,578,201	$1.70	$0.29	$0.39

Recent Close: $0.04

Capital Stock Changes - In March 2023, public offering of 56,027,000 units (1 common share & 1 warrant) at 5¢ per unit was completed, with warrants exercisable at 10¢ per share for three years.

In June 2022, public offering of 7,361,000 common shares was completed at 55¢ per share. In December 2022, public offering of 21,428,570 units (1 common share & 1 warrant) at $0.063 per unit was completed. Also during 2022, 253,800 common shares were issued on exercise of options and warrants.

Wholly Owned Subsidiaries

CubicFarm Systems (Shanghai) Corp., Shanghai, Shanghai, People's Republic of China.
CubicFarm Systems U.S. Corp., Del.
• 100% int. in **HYDROGREEN, INC.**, S.D.
CubicFarm Manufacturing Corp., B.C.
CubicFarm Produce (Canada) Corp., B.C.

Investments

20% int. in **1241876 B.C. Ltd.**, B.C.
Note: The preceding list includes only the major related companies in which interests are held.

Financial Statistics

Periods ended:	12m Dec. 31/22[A]		12m Dec. 31/21[A]
	$000s	%Chg	$000s
Operating revenue	**3,636**	**-31**	**5,273**
Cost of sales	10,098		5,264
Research & devel. expense	10,420		7,518
General & admin expense	19,311		21,299
Operating expense	**39,829**	**+17**	**34,082**
Operating income	**(36,193)**	**n.a.**	**(28,809)**
Deprec., depl. & amort.	1,915		1,654
Finance income	13		511
Finance costs, gross	1,606		492
Write-downs/write-offs	(21,022)[1]		506
Pre-tax income	**(61,164)**	**n.a.**	**(29,353)**
Income taxes	(793)		4
Net income	**(60,370)**	**n.a.**	**(29,357)**
Cash & equivalent	2,945		21,381
Inventories	13,311		8,433
Accounts receivable	1,897		2,127
Current assets	20,878		35,347
Fixed assets, net	1,006		9,432
Right-of-use assets	1,945		2,629
Intangibles, net	nil		7,246
Total assets	**23,778**	**-57**	**54,677**
Accts. pay. & accr. liabs.	7,515		4,530
Current liabilities	22,746		9,780
Long-term debt, gross	10,708		2,157
Long-term debt, net	8,627		1,785
Long-term lease liabilities	2,250		1,888
Shareholders' equity	(9,968)		41,091
Cash from oper. activs.	**(28,006)**	**n.a.**	**(30,467)**
Cash from fin. activs.	14,790		43,535
Cash from invest. activs.	(5,208)		(7,810)
Net cash position	**2,945**	**-86**	**21,381**
Capital expenditures	(4,845)		(7,169)
Capital disposals	37		nil
	$		$
Earnings per share*	(0.33)		(0.19)
Cash flow per share*	(0.15)		(0.20)
	shs		shs
No. of shs. o/s*	207,136,774		178,093,404
Avg. no. of shs. o/s*	183,540,231		154,480,753
	%		%
Net profit margin	n.m.		(556.74)
Return on equity	n.m.		(93.45)
Return on assets	(149.86)		(64.56)
No. of employees (FTEs)	69		159

* Common
[A] Reported in accordance with IFRS
[1] Includes $16,393,709 impairment loss to non-current assets of the Feed division and $4,053,527 impairment loss to non-current assets of Fresh division.

Latest Results

Periods ended:	3m Mar. 31/23[A]		3m Mar. 31/22[A]
	$000s	%Chg	$000s
Operating revenue	455	+86	244
Net income	(4,672)	n.a.	(8,760)
	$		$
Earnings per share*	(0.02)		(0.05)

* Common
[A] Reported in accordance with IFRS

Historical Summary
(as originally stated)

Fiscal Year	Oper. Rev. $000s	Net Inc. Bef. Disc. $000s	EPS* $
2022[A]	3,636	(60,370)	(0.33)
2021[A]	5,273	(29,357)	(0.19)
2020[A1]	625	(10,126)	(0.08)
2020[A]	5,168	(10,092)	(0.11)
2019[A]	5,356	(7,631)	(0.11)

* Common
[A] Reported in accordance with IFRS
[1] 6 months ended Dec. 31, 2020.

C.177 Curaleaf Holdings, Inc.

Symbol - CURA **Exchange** - CSE **CUSIP** - 23126M
Head Office - 420 Lexington Ave, Suite 2035, New York, NY, United States, 10170 **Telephone** - (781) 451-0150
Website - www.curaleaf.com
Email - ir@curaleaf.com
Investor Relations - Camilo Lyon (781) 451-0150
Auditors - PKF O'Connor Davies, LLP C.P.A., New York, N.Y.
Transfer Agents - Odyssey Trust Company, Calgary, Alta.
FP500 Revenue Ranking - 239
Employees - 5,931 at Dec. 31, 2022
Profile - (B.C. 2014) Operates a vertically integrated cannabis business, including cultivation sites, processing facilities and dispensaries for medical and adult-use markets across the U.S. and Europe.

In the United States, the company cultivates, processes, markets and sells a wide-range of permitted cannabis products across its operating markets, including flower, pre-rolls and flower pods, dry-herb vapourizer cartridges, concentrates for vapourizing such as pre-filled vapourizer cartridges and disposable vapourizer pens, concentrates for dabbing such as distillate droppers, mints, topical balms and lotions, tinctures, lozenges, capsules and edibles, as well as hemp-derived products. The company sells medical and adult-use cannabis via retail and wholesale channels under the Curaleaf, Select and Grassroots brands. At June 30, 2023, the company actively operated in 17 states, with a focus on limited licence states including Arizona, Connecticut, Florida, Illinois, Maryland, Massachusetts, Nevada, New York, New Jersey, North Dakota and Pennsylvania. Operations consisted of 150 retail dispensaries in 16 states, 21 cultivation sites (totaling 1,800,000 sq. ft.) in 15 states and 23 processing sites in 16 states. The company's dispensaries also offer home delivery services in certain states, and drive-thru service at select locations in Nevada, Utah and Florida.

In Europe, subsidiary **Curaleaf International Holdings Limited** conducts a fully integrated medical cannabis business consisting of cultivation facilities in Portugal; four processing and manufacturing facilities in Spain, Portugal, the U.K. and Germany; distribution operations in the U.K., Germany and Switzerland; an online pharmacy and a clinic network in the U.K.; and wholesale supply across the region.

On July 5, 2023, subsidiary **Curaleaf International Holdings Limited** acquired a processing facility in Setúbal, Portugal, including 900 m^2 of factory space and 750 m^2 of warehousing space, from **Clever Leaves Holdings Inc.** for €2,500,000.

On July 1, 2023, the company agreed to sell its operations in Oregon, which consisted of a dispensary, a processing facility and a cultivation site, to **Hotbox Farms LLC** for an undisclosed amount.

During the second quarter of 2023, the company sold a cultivation facility in Colorado for an undisclosed amount.

In April 2023, the company acquired **Deseret Wellness LLC**, a cannabis retail operator in Utah with three dispensaries in Park City, Provo and Payson, for US$20,000,000 in cash and subordinate voting shares.

On Jan. 26, 2023, the company announced the closure of the majority of its operations in California, Colorado and Oregon and the consolidation of cultivation and processing operations in Massachusetts to a single facility in Webster, Mass., resulting in the closure of its Amesbury, Mass., facility. These three markets contributed less than US$50,000,000 in revenue to the company last year.

During the third quarter of 2022, the company sold a dispensary in Little Rock, Ark., for an undisclosed amount.

On Sept. 16, 2022, subsidiary **Curaleaf International Holdings Limited** acquired a 55% interest in Paderborn, Germany-based **Four 20 Pharma GmbH**, a manufacturer and distributor of medical cannabis, for €19,700,000 in cash and subordinate voting shares of the company.

On Sept. 1, 2022, the company acquired **Pueblo West Organics, LLC** (PWO) for US$6,000,000. PWO operates a 75,960-sq.-ft. indoor cultivation and processing facility, a 12,000-sq.-ft. dispensary and cultivation facility and a 2.1-acre outdoor cultivation facility, all in Pueblo West, Colo.

During the second quarter of 2022, the company sold its operations in Oklahoma, which consisted mainly of wholesale supply of its Select-branded products. Terms were not disclosed.

On May 12, 2022, the company acquired **NRPC Management, LLC**, which manages **Natural Remedy Patient Center, LLC**, a dispensary in Safford, Ariz., pursuant to a management services agreement. Total consideration was US$10,700,000, consisting of US$9,900,000 cash and issuance of 164,098 subordinate voting shares.

During the first quarter of 2022, the company entered into letters of intent to sell its operations in Vermont, which consisted of two dispensaries and a 13,000-sq.-ft. cultivation and processing facility. Terms were not disclosed.

Recent Merger and Acquisition Activity

Status: completed **Revised:** Oct. 5, 2022
UPDATE: The transaction was completed. Total consideration was US$181,000,000, consisting of US$10,000,000 cash and issuance of 2,700,000 subordinate voting shares on closing, as well as US$75,000,000 cash and issuance of 16,500,000 subordinate voting shares to be paid in three instalments on the first, second and third anniversaries of the closing. PREVIOUS: Curaleaf Holdings, Inc. agreed to acquire Tryke Companies, LLC (dba Reef Dispensaries), a vertically integrated multi-state cannabis operator with cultivation, processing and retail assets in Arizona, Nevada and Utah, for US$280,000,000, consisting of US$40,000,000 cash on closing as well as additional US$75,000,000 cash and issuance of 17,000,000 subordinate voting shares, both payable in three equal instalments on the first, second and third anniversaries of the closing of the transaction. Tryke's assets

include six retail dispensaries under the Reef brand in Arizona (2) and Nevada (4), and cultivation and processing facilities in Nevada, Arizona and Utah. The transaction was expected to close in the second half of 2022.

Predecessor Detail - Name changed from Lead Ventures Inc., Oct. 25, 2018, following reverse takeover acquisition of Curaleaf, Inc.

Directors - Boris Jordan, exec. chr., Miami Beach, Fla.; Joseph F. (Joe) Lusardi, exec. v-chr., Newburyport, Mass.; Michelle Bodner, N.Y.; Peter Derby, N.Y.; Dr. Jaswinder Grover, Las Vegas, Nev.; Karl Johansson, Minn.; Mitchell Kahn, Ill.; Shasheen Shah, N.M.

Other Exec. Officers - Matt Darin, CEO; Edward (Ed) Kremer, CFO; Peter Clateman, chief legal officer; Camilo Lyon, chief invest. officer; Tyneeha Rivers, chief people officer; James (Jim) Shorris, chief compliance officer; Joe Holland, exec. v-p, opers.; Kate Lynch, exec. v-p, mktg.; Tracy Brady, sr. v-p, corp. commun.; Jessie Kater, sr. v-p, innovation, R&D

Capital Stock

	Authorized (shs.)	Outstanding (shs.)[1]
Multiple Vtg.	unlimited	93,970,705
Subord. Vtg.	unlimited	631,026,947

[1] At Aug. 8, 2023

Multiple Voting - All held by Boris Jordan. Convertible into subordinate voting shares on a 1-for-1 basis at any time. Automatically convert into subordinate voting shares upon the earlier of: (i) transfer or disposition of the multiple voting shares by Mr. Jordan to one or more third parties which are not permitted holders; (ii) Mr. Jordan or his permitted holders no longer beneficially owning, directly or indirectly and in total, at least 5% of the subordinate voting and multiple voting shares; and (iii) the first business day following the first annual shareholders' meeting following the subordinate voting shares being listed for trading on a U.S. national securities exchange. 15 votes per share.

Subordinate Voting - One vote per share.

Major Shareholder - Boris Jordan held 70% interest at Dec. 31, 2022.

Price Range - CURA/CSE

Year	Volume	High	Low	Close
2022	108,843,179	$11.53	$4.86	$5.83
2021	131,946,573	$23.30	$10.37	$11.30
2020	113,330,853	$16.73	$3.72	$15.24
2019	178,654,027	$15.75	$5.93	$8.18
2018	38,048,760	$11.49	$5.12	$6.46

LEAD/CSE (D)

Year	Volume	High	Low	Close
2018	473,520	$1.00	$0.14	$0.25

Recent Close: $3.95

Capital Stock Changes - During 2022, subordinate voting shares were issued as follows: 7,392,857 for business acquisitions, 2,585,129 on exercise of options and 152,508 as share-based compensation; 980,098 subordinate voting shares were cancelled.

Wholly Owned Subsidiaries

Curaleaf, Inc., Wakefield, Mass.
- 100% int. in **CLF AZ, Inc.**, Ariz.
- 100% int. in **CLF Holdings Alabama, Inc.**, Ala.
- 100% int. in **CLF MD Employer, LLC**, Md.
- 100% int. in **CLF Maine, Inc.**, Me.
- 100% int. in **CLF NY, Inc.**, N.Y.
- 100% int. in **CLF Oregon, LLC**, Ore.
- 100% int. in **CLF Sapphire Holdings, Inc.**, Ore.
- 100% int. in **Cura CO LLC**, Colo.
- 100% int. in **Curaleaf CA, Inc.**, Calif.
- 100% int. in **Curaleaf Columbia, LLC**, Md.
- 100% int. in **Curaleaf Compassionate Care VA, LLC**, Va.
- 100% int. in **Curaleaf KY, Inc.**, Ky.
- 100% int. in **Curaleaf Maine Dispensary, Inc.**, Me.
- 100% int. in **Curaleaf Massachusetts, Inc.**, Mass.
- 100% int. in **Curaleaf MD, LLC**, Md.
- 100% int. in **Curaleaf NJ II, Inc.**, Del.
- 100% int. in **Curaleaf OGT, Inc.**, Ohio
- 100% int. in **Curaleaf PA, LLC**, Pa.
- 100% int. in **Curaleaf Processing, Inc.**, Mass.
- 100% int. in **Curaleaf Stamford, Inc.**, Conn.
- 100% int. in **Curaleaf UT, LLC**, Utah
- 100% int. in **Focused Employer, Inc.**, Mass.
- 100% int. in **Focused Investment Partners, LLC**, Mass.
- 100% int. in **GR Companies, Inc.**, Highland Park, Ill. dba Grassroots
- 100% int. in **MI Health, LLC**, Md.
- 100% int. in **PT Nevada, Inc.**, Nev.
- 100% int. in **PalliaTech CT, Inc.**, Conn.
- 100% int. in **PalliaTech Florida, Inc.**, Fla.
- 100% int. in **Virginia's Kitchen, LLC**, Denver, Colo.

Subsidiaries

68.5% int. in **Curaleaf International Holdings Limited**, Guernsey.

Note: The preceding list includes only the major related companies in which interests are held.

Financial Statistics

Periods ended:	12m Dec. 31/22[A]		12m Dec. 31/21[□A]
	US$000s	%Chg	US$000s
Operating revenue	**1,336,342**	**+12**	**1,195,987**
Cost of goods sold	709,390		590,752
General & admin expense	447,538		386,637
Stock-based compensation	28,017		39,481
Operating expense	**1,184,945**	**+17**	**1,016,870**
Operating income	**151,397**	**-15**	**179,117**
Deprec., depl. & amort.	163,769		120,544
Finance income	137		629
Finance costs, gross	93,330		78,512
Write-downs/write-offs	(144,461)[1]		(14,573)
Pre-tax income	**(226,429)**	**n.a.**	**(62,197)**
Income taxes	150,502		152,445
Net income	**(376,931)**	**n.a.**	**(214,642)**
Net inc. for equity hldrs	**(370,098)**	**n.a.**	**(205,940)**
Net inc. for non-cont. int.	**(6,833)**	**n.a.**	**(8,702)**
Cash & equivalent	163,177		299,329
Inventories	250,643		248,146
Accounts receivable	52,162		60,427
Current assets	605,334		726,623
Long-term investments	2,797		4,401
Fixed assets, net	618,165		525,825
Right-of-use assets	279,514		179,083
Intangibles, net	1,842,321		1,641,888
Total assets	**3,397,919**	**+9**	**3,105,073**
Accts. pay. & accr. liabs.	197,798		113,717
Current liabilities	491,079		316,240
Long-term debt, gross	622,820		459,883
Long-term debt, net	570,856		457,917
Long-term lease liabilities	283,133		175,210
Shareholders' equity	1,279,704		1,546,121
Non-controlling interest	121,113		118,972
Cash from oper. activs.	**46,401**	**n.a.**	**(58,280)**
Cash from fin. activs.	50,539		449,119
Cash from invest. activs.	(228,623)		(163,974)
Net cash position	**163,177**	**-45**	**299,329**
Capital expenditures, net	(138,362)		(171,955)
	US$		US$
Earnings per share*	(0.52)		(0.29)
Cash flow per share*	0.07		(0.08)
	shs		shs
No. of shs. o/s*	717,490,830		708,340,434
Avg. no. of shs. o/s*	711,159,444		698,759,274
	%		%
Net profit margin	(28.21)		(17.95)
Return on equity	(25.02)		(14.09)
Return on assets	(6.66)		2.05
Foreign sales percent	100		100
No. of employees (FTEs)	5,931		5,138

* Subord. Vtg.
□ Restated
[A] Reported in accordance with U.S. GAAP
[1] Includes impairment of US$92,600,000 on goodwill and US$37,200,000 on intangible assets.

Latest Results

Periods ended:	6m June 30/23[A]		6m June 30/22[□A]
	US$000s	%Chg	US$000s
Operating revenue	675,076	+8	623,031
Net inc. bef. disc. opers.	(115,235)	n.a.	(51,252)
Income from disc. opers.	(15,726)		(8,774)
Net income	(130,961)	n.a.	(60,026)
Net inc. for equity hldrs	(125,622)	n.a.	(58,378)
Net inc. for non-cont. int.	(5,339)		(1,648)
	US$		US$
Earns. per sh. bef. disc. opers.*	(0.15)		(0.07)
Earnings per share*	(0.17)		(0.08)

* Subord. Vtg.
□ Restated
[A] Reported in accordance with U.S. GAAP

Historical Summary
(as originally stated)

Fiscal Year	Oper. Rev. US$000s	Net Inc. Bef. Disc. US$000s	EPS* US$
2022[A]	1,336,342	(376,931)	(0.52)
2021[B]	1,195,990	(118,773)	(0.16)
2020[B]	626,637	(61,328)	(0.11)
2019[B]	221,018	(69,848)	(0.15)
2018[B1]	77,057	(61,877)	(0.14)

* Subord. Vtg.
[A] Reported in accordance with U.S. GAAP
[B] Reported in accordance with IFRS
[1] Results reflect the Oct. 26, 2018, reverse takeover acquisition of Curaleaf, Inc.

C.178 Currency Exchange International, Corp.

Symbol - CXI **Exchange** - TSX **CUSIP** - 23131B
Head Office - 6675 Westwood Blvd, Suite 300, Orlando, FL, United States, 32821 **Telephone** - (407) 240-0224 **Toll-free** - (888) 998-3948 **Fax** - (407) 240-0217
Website - www.ceifx.com
Email - bill.mitoulas@ceifx.com
Investor Relations - Bill Mitoulas (407) 240-0224
Auditors - Grant Thornton LLP C.A., Burlington, Ont.
Transfer Agents - Computershare Trust Company of Canada Inc., Toronto, Ont.
Employees - 251 at Oct. 31, 2022

Profile - (Fla. 1998) Provides currency exchange, wire transfer and cheque cashing services from locations in the United States and Canada.

Primary products and services include the exchange of foreign currencies, foreign currency-related international payments, purchase and sale of foreign bank drafts, and foreign cheque. Key market cities include Boston, Mass.; Chicago, Ill.; Honolulu, Hawaii; Miami and Orlando, Fla.; New York, N.Y.; Los Angeles, San Diego and San Francisco, Calif.; Seattle, Wash.; and Washington, D.C. The company has 2,586 wholesale company relationships and services; and 18,406 transacting locations as at Oct. 31, 2022. In addition, products and services are catered to corporate customers such as hotels, resorts and tourist attractions; money service businesses; financial institutions; and retail customers through a dedicated sales force and 37 company-owned retail branch outlets located in New York, Virginia, Maryland, Florida, California, Colorado, Massachusetts, New Jersey, Hawaii, Illinois and Washington. Operations in Canada are limited to the exchange of foreign currencies for financial institutions and corporate customers in the money services industry, as well as international payment services for financial institutions and certain corporate customers. Also provides services to international financial institutions from selected countries.

The company's proprietary web-based software, CXIFX, is used by the company's wholly owned branches as well as approved corporate and financial institution clients of the company and their customers. CXIFX automates the exchange of foreign currencies, wire transfer and electronic payments, purchase and sale of foreign bank drafts, and foreign cheque clearing; and serves as a regulatory compliance and risk management tool. It also includes OnlineFx, an e-commerce platform that markets foreign exchange products directly to consumers.

During fiscal 2022, the company closed one of its retail locations in San Francisco, Calif.

Directors - Chirag J. Bhavsar, chr., Fla.; Randolph W. Pinna, pres. & CEO, Ont.; Joseph A. August, Ont.; Chitwant S. Kohli, Ont.; Mark D. Mickleborough, Ont.; Stacey Mowbray, Ont.; Carol Poulsen, Burlington, Ont.; V. James Sardo, Fla.; Daryl Yeo, Mississauga, Ont.

Other Exec. Officers - Matthew A. Schillo, COO; Gerhard S. Barnard, CFO; Dennis Winkel, chief risk officer & chief privacy officer; Khatuna Bezhitashvili, v-p, HR; Christopher Johnson, v-p, finl. institutions; Paul Ohm, v-p, IT; Irene Vomvolakis, v-p, opers.; Ian Zarac, v-p, finl. institutions; Margaret Kingerski, corp. sec.; Katie Davis, treas.

Capital Stock

	Authorized (shs.)	Outstanding (shs.)[1]	Par
Preferred	2,000,000	nil	
Common	100,000,000	6,435,790	US$1.00

[1] At Jan. 31, 2023

Major Shareholder - Randolph W. Pinna held 21.38% interest at Feb. 10, 2023.

Price Range - CXI/TSX

Year	Volume	High	Low	Close
2022	981,449	$22.19	$12.36	$22.19
2021	1,591,852	$14.77	$10.60	$13.50
2020	1,396,017	$18.24	$8.80	$11.05
2019	1,121,823	$30.19	$17.00	$18.00
2018	836,104	$31.77	$22.50	$26.75

Recent Close: $24.21

Capital Stock Changes - During fiscal 2022, 14,553 common shares were issued on exercise of options.

Wholly Owned Subsidiaries

Exchange Bank of Canada, Toronto, Ont.
eZforex.com, Inc., Tex.

Financial Statistics

Periods ended:	12m Oct. 31/22[A]		12m Oct. 31/21[□A]
	US$000s	%Chg	US$000s
Operating revenue	**66,283**	**+117**	**30,566**
Salaries & benefits	25,415		17,691
General & admin expense	18,604		9,797
Stock-based compensation	1,094		979
Operating expense	**45,113**	**+58**	**28,467**
Operating income	**21,170**	**+909**	**2,099**
Deprec., depl. & amort.	3,273		3,328
Finance income	112		27
Finance costs, gross	3,510		2,250
Write-downs/write-offs	nil		(24)
Pre-tax income	**14,213**	**n.a.**	**(176)**
Income taxes	2,429		955
Net income	**11,783**	**n.a.**	**(1,132)**
Cash & equivalent	88,559		66,528
Accounts receivable	14,274		16,521
Current assets	112,439		91,168
Fixed assets, net	711		515
Right-of-use assets	4,096		3,440
Intangibles, net	6,470		7,519
Total assets	**125,529**	**+22**	**102,923**
Bank indebtedness	5,930		4,037
Accts. pay. & accr. liabs.	32,773		29,344
Current liabilities	52,060		41,287
Long-term lease liabilities	2,985		2,812
Shareholders' equity	69,306		58,016
Cash from oper. activs.	**25,519**	**+219**	**8,011**
Cash from fin. activs.	214		(1,486)
Cash from invest. activs.	(1,291)		(764)
Net cash position	**88,559**	**+33**	**66,528**
Capital expenditures	(564)		(131)
	US$		US$
Earnings per share*	1.83		(0.18)
Cash flow per share*	3.97		1.25
	shs		shs
No. of shs. o/s*	6,429,489		6,429,489
Avg. no. of shs. o/s*	6,429,489		6,414,936
	%		%
Net profit margin	17.78		(3.70)
Return on equity	18.51		(1.95)
Return on assets	12.89		14.13
Foreign sales percent	74		76
No. of employees (FTEs)	251		205

* Common
□ Restated
A Reported in accordance with IFRS

Historical Summary
(as originally stated)

Fiscal Year	Oper. Rev. US$000s	Net Inc. Bef. Disc. US$000s	EPS* US$
2022[A]	66,283	11,783	1.83
2021[A]	30,264	(1,132)	(0.18)
2020[A]	25,013	(8,524)	(1.33)
2019[A]	41,784	2,925	0.46
2018[A]	39,098	4,227	0.67

* Common
A Reported in accordance with IFRS

C.179 Current Water Technologies Inc.

Symbol - WATR **Exchange** - TSX-VEN **CUSIP** - 23131M
Head Office - Unit 4, 70 Southgate Dr, Guelph, ON, N1G 4P5 **Telephone** - (519) 836-6155 **Toll-free** - (800) 811-6216 **Fax** - (519) 836-5683
Website - www.currentwatertechnologies.com
Email - gshelp@currentwatertechnologies.com
Investor Relations - Dr. Gene S. Shelp (519) 836-6155
Auditors - Wasserman Ramsay C.A., Markham, Ont.
Transfer Agents - TSX Trust Company, Toronto, Ont.
Profile - (Ont. 1996) Develops technologies that are sold individually or in integrated turnkey systems to treat contaminated waste and drinking water for the mining, metal processing, agricultural, chemical, municipal and waste management industries, and to recover nickel and other valuable metals from waste mill sulphide tailings.

The company's proprietary electrochemical technologies include: Electro-Static Deionization, a system that lowers the concentration of total dissolved solids in water containing arsenic, nitrate, fluoride, perchlorate, ammonia, sulfate, metals or other ionic compounds; AmmEL, a treatment process for removal of dissolved ammonia from industrial and municipal water without producing the carcinogen nitrate and the greenhouse gas nitrous oxide; NitrEL, an electrochemical water treatment process that reduces nitrate concentrations in contaminated drinking water, groundwater and industrial process wastewater streams by converting the nitrate directly to environmentally friendly nitrogen gas; AmdEL, an electrochemical system that prevents the oxidation of sulphide minerals in tailings or waste rock, in situ, preventing the formation of acid mine drainage; and ExtrEL, a hydrometallurgical alternative for the recovery of metals from sulphide tailings and ore, which works by enhancing the oxidation of sulphide minerals and the subsequent solubility of metals.

Wholly owned **Pumptronics Incorporated** manufactures integrated pump stations specializing in custom design and automation.

Predecessor Detail - Name changed from ENPAR Technologies Inc., Jan. 2, 2018.

Directors - Dr. Gene S. Shelp, pres. & CEO, Guelph, Ont.; Dr. Barry J. Shelp, corp. sec., Guelph, Ont.; Nizar Kammourie, Montréal, Qué.; Alexander Kaszuba, Mississauga, Ont.

Other Exec. Officers - Edward P. W. (Ed) Tsang, CFO

Capital Stock

	Authorized (shs.)	Outstanding (shs.)[1]
Preferred	unlimited	nil
Common	unlimited	212,275,038

[1] At Apr. 28, 2023

Major Shareholder - Widely held at Nov. 10, 2022.

Price Range - WATR/TSX-VEN

Year	Volume	High	Low	Close
2022	52,843,093	$0.06	$0.03	$0.04
2021	339,437,060	$0.16	$0.02	$0.05
2020	17,911,017	$0.04	$0.02	$0.02
2019	29,568,129	$0.06	$0.03	$0.04
2018	39,144,439	$0.23	$0.04	$0.05

Recent Close: $0.03

Capital Stock Changes - There were no changes to capital stock during 2022.

Wholly Owned Subsidiaries

Pumptronics Incorporated, Canada.

Financial Statistics

Periods ended:	12m Dec. 31/22[A]		12m Dec. 31/21[A]
	$000s	%Chg	$000s
Operating revenue	**2,158**	**+83**	**1,182**
Cost of sales	2,027		1,813
Salaries & benefits	124		112
General & admin expense	508		529
Stock-based compensation	371		114
Operating expense	**3,030**	**+18**	**2,568**
Operating income	**(872)**	**n.a.**	**(1,386)**
Deprec., depl. & amort.	164		158
Finance costs, gross	16		27
Write-downs/write-offs	nil		3
Pre-tax income	**(1,053)**	**n.a.**	**(1,569)**
Net income	**(1,053)**	**n.a.**	**(1,569)**
Cash & equivalent	119		635
Inventories	459		384
Accounts receivable	37		84
Current assets	669		1,105
Fixed assets, net	123		160
Right-of-use assets	106		234
Intangibles, net	4		2
Total assets	**903**	**-40**	**1,501**
Accts. pay. & accr. liabs.	587		200
Current liabilities	1,248		1,051
Long-term debt, gross	120		124
Long-term debt, net	120		120
Long-term lease liabilities	nil		113
Shareholders' equity	(465)		217
Cash from oper. activs.	**(377)**	**n.a.**	**(1,006)**
Cash from fin. activs.	(137)		1,602
Cash from invest. activs.	(3)		(93)
Net cash position	**119**	**-81**	**635**
Capital expenditures	nil		(99)
Capital disposals	nil		6
	$		$
Earnings per share*	(0.00)		(0.01)
Cash flow per share*	(0.00)		(0.00)
	shs		shs
No. of shs. o/s*	212,275,038		212,275,038
Avg. no. of shs. o/s*	212,275,038		205,689,889
	%		%
Net profit margin	(48.80)		(132.74)
Return on equity	n.m.		n.m.
Return on assets	(86.27)		(108.71)
Foreign sales percent	14		4

* Common
A Reported in accordance with IFRS

Latest Results

Periods ended:	3m Mar. 31/23[A]		3m Mar. 31/22[A]
	$000s	%Chg	$000s
Operating revenue	1,002	+45	689
Net income	329	n.a.	(65)
	$		$
Earnings per share*	0.00		(0.01)

* Common
A Reported in accordance with IFRS

Historical Summary
(as originally stated)

Fiscal Year	Oper. Rev. $000s	Net Inc. Bef. Disc. $000s	EPS* $
2022[A]	2,158	(1,053)	(0.01)
2021[A]	1,182	(1,569)	(0.01)
2020[A]	1,412	(308)	(0.00)
2019[A]	2,404	20	0.00
2018[A]	2,435	(4,791)	(0.03)

* Common
A Reported in accordance with IFRS

C.180 Currie Rose Resources Inc.

Symbol - CUI **Exchange** - TSX-VEN **CUSIP** - 231900
Head Office - 2704-401 Bay St, PO Box 4, Toronto, ON, M5H 2Y4 **Telephone** - (905) 688-9115 **Fax** - (905) 688-5615
Website - www.currierose.com
Email - mike@currierose.com
Investor Relations - Michael R. Griffiths (905) 688-9115
Auditors - Jones & O'Connell LLP C.A., St. Catharines, Ont.
Bankers - Royal Bank of Canada, St. Catharines, Ont.
Lawyers - DuMoulin Black LLP, Vancouver, B.C.
Transfer Agents - Capital Transfer Agency Inc., Toronto, Ont.
Profile - (B.C. 2006; orig. Ont., 1973) Has mineral interests and develops hydrogen solutions in Australia.

Holds North Queensland vanadium-molybdenum project, 1,246 km^2, 450 km west of Townsville, consisting of Toolebuc and Flinders River deposits. At October 2022, indicated resource at North Queensland was 61,330,000 tonnes grading 0.34% vanadium and 234.6 ppm molybdenum.

Also develops exportable hydrogen technology, including storage and transport solutions.

In June 2023, the company acquired Australia-based private **WA Hydrogen Pty Ltd.**, which develops exportable hydrogen technology, including storage and transport solutions, for issuance of 50,000,000 common shares at a deemed value of 5¢ per share and a 5% royalty on future revenues.

Directors - Simon Coyle, pres. & CEO; Michael R. (Mike) Griffiths, v-p, explor., Perth, W.A., Australia; Stephen Coates, Toronto, Ont.; Caroline Keats, Perth, W.A., Australia; Nicole Morcombe; Ryan J. Smith, St. Catharines, Ont.

Other Exec. Officers - David Bhumgara, CFO; Namrata Malhotra, corp. sec.

Capital Stock

	Authorized (shs.)	Outstanding (shs.)[1]
Common	unlimited	224,525,233

[1] At June 19, 2023

Major Shareholder - Accelerate Resources Limited held 12.81% interest at May 9, 2022.

Price Range - CUI/TSX-VEN

Year	Volume	High	Low	Close
2022	6,707,324	$0.08	$0.02	$0.03
2021	15,610,188	$0.15	$0.03	$0.07
2020	4,355,912	$0.06	$0.02	$0.04
2019	4,071,720	$0.08	$0.02	$0.03
2018	3,008,262	$0.20	$0.06	$0.06

Recent Close: $0.09

Capital Stock Changes - In June 2023, 50,000,000 common shares were issued pursuant to the acquisition of WA Hydrogen Pty Ltd.

In January and August 2022, private placement of 16,360,894 units (1 common share & 1 warrant) at 5¢ per unit was completed. In August 2022, 25,000,000 common shares were issued on acquisition of North Queensland project. In October 2022, private placement of 79,000,001 units (1 common share & ½ warrant) at 3¢ per unit was completed.

Wholly Owned Subsidiaries

Currie Rose Vanadium Pty Ltd., Australia.
WA Hydrogen Pty Ltd., Australia.

Investments

MacDonald Mines Exploration Ltd., Toronto, Ont. (see Survey of Mines)

Financial Statistics

Periods ended:	12m Dec. 31/22[A]		12m Dec. 31/21[A]
	$000s	%Chg	$000s
General & admin expense	467		298
Stock-based compensation	187		nil
Operating expense	**654**	**+119**	**298**
Operating income	**(654)**	**n.a.**	**(298)**
Finance income	12		nil
Write-downs/write-offs	nil		(1,500)
Pre-tax income	**(705)**	**n.a.**	**(1,943)**
Net income	**(705)**	**n.a.**	**(1,943)**
Cash & equivalent	2,304		145
Accounts receivable	16		10
Current assets	2,335		161
Explor./devel. properties	1,051		nil
Total assets	**3,386**	**n.m.**	**161**
Accts. pay. & accr. liabs	316		466
Current liabilities	316		466
Shareholders' equity	3,070		(305)
Cash from oper. activs	**(622)**	**n.a.**	**(65)**
Cash from fin. activs	2,989		159
Cash from invest. activs	(182)		(108)
Net cash position	**2,287**	**n.m.**	**66**
Capital expenditures	(182)		(153)
	$		$
Earnings per share*	(0.01)		(0.04)
Cash flow per share*	(0.01)		(0.00)
	shs		shs
No. of shs. o/s*	174,525,233		54,164,338
Avg. no. of shs. o/s*	94,209,470		46,273,927
	%		%
Net profit margin	n.a.		n.a.
Return on equity	n.m.		n.m.
Return on assets	(39.75)		(200.41)

* Common
[A] Reported in accordance with IFRS

Historical Summary
(as originally stated)

Fiscal Year	Oper. Rev.	Net Inc. Bef. Disc.	EPS*
	$000s	$000s	$
2022[A]	nil	(705)	(0.01)
2021[A]	nil	(1,943)	(0.04)
2020[A]	nil	(432)	(0.01)
2019[A]	nil	(71)	(0.00)
2018[A]	nil	(324)	(0.01)

* Common
[A] Reported in accordance with IFRS

C.181 Cuspis Capital II Ltd.

Symbol - CCII.P **Exchange** - TSX-VEN **CUSIP** - 23169N
Head Office - 700-77 King St W, Toronto, ON, M5K 1G8 **Telephone** - (416) 214-4810
Email - will@cuspiscapital.com
Investor Relations - William W. Ollerhead (416) 214-0876
Auditors - McGovern Hurley LLP C.A., Toronto, Ont.
Transfer Agents - TSX Trust Company, Toronto, Ont.
Profile - (Ont. 2019) Capital Pool Company.

Recent Merger and Acquisition Activity

Status: terminated **Revised:** July 6, 2023
UPDATE: The letter of intent expired. PREVIOUS: Cuspis Capital II Ltd. entered into a letter of intent for the Qualifying Transaction reverse takeover acquisition of private Toronto, Ont.-based Peninsula Capital Corp., which owns a portfolio of affordable single family rental housing in U.S. markets. Cuspis would issue post-consolidated common shares on a to-be-determined basis. A condition of completion of the transaction was that Peninsula would complete a private placement of a minimum of $20,000,000. The transaction was expected to be completed no later than Dec. 1, 2022. Dec. 15, 2022 - The deadline to complete the transaction was extended to June 30, 2023.
Status: terminated **Revised:** May 6, 2022
UPDATE: The transaction was terminated. PREVIOUS: Cuspis Capital II Ltd. entered into a letter of intent for the Qualifying Transaction reverse takeover acquisition of private Winnipeg, Man.-based Cytophage Technologies Inc., which was developing bacteriophage products as an alternative to antibiotics and vaccines, to prevent and treat bacterial and viral infections that affect human health, animal health and food safety. Cuspis would issue post-consolidated common shares on a to-be-determined basis. As condition of completion of the transaction was that Cytophage would complete a private placement of a minimum of $10,000,000 and a maximum of $15,000,000.
Directors - William W. (Will) Ollerhead, chr. & CEO, Toronto, Ont.; J. Grant McCutcheon, CFO & corp. sec., Toronto, Ont.; C. Fraser Elliott, Toronto, Ont.; Jack Schoenmakers, Kitchener, Ont.

Capital Stock

	Authorized (shs.)	Outstanding (shs.)[1]
Common	unlimited	12,500,000

[1] At Nov. 28, 2022
Major Shareholder - Widely held at Dec. 11, 2020.

Price Range - CCII.P/TSX-VEN

Year	Volume	High	Low	Close
2022	165,285	$0.35	$0.30	$0.30
2021	1,025,950	$0.45	$0.16	$0.40
2020	326,000	$0.25	$0.20	$0.20

Recent Close: $0.35
Capital Stock Changes - There were no changes to capital stock during fiscal 2022.

C.182 Cuspis Capital III Ltd.

Symbol - CIII.P **Exchange** - TSX-VEN **CUSIP** - 23168Y
Head Office - 700-77 King St W, Toronto, ON, M5K 1G8 **Telephone** - (416) 214-4810
Email - will@ollerheadcapital.com
Investor Relations - William W. Ollerhead (416) 214-4810
Auditors - McGovern Hurley LLP C.A., Toronto, Ont.
Lawyers - CP LLP, Toronto, Ont.
Transfer Agents - TSX Trust Company, Toronto, Ont.
Profile - (Ont. 2019) Capital Pool Company.

Recent Merger and Acquisition Activity

Status: pending **Announced:** May 31, 2023
Cuspis Capital III Ltd. entered into a letter of intent for the Qualifying Transaction reverse takeover acquisition of private Winnipeg, Man.-based Cytophage Technologies Inc., which was developing bacteriophage products as an alternative to antibiotics and vaccines, to prevent and treat bacterial and viral infections that affect human health, animal health and food safety. Cuspis would issue post-consolidated common shares on a basis anticipated to be between 1-for-2 and 1-for-5. As condition of completion of the transaction was that Cytophage would complete a private placement of a minimum of $3,000,000 and a maximum of $5,000,000.
Directors - William W. (Will) Ollerhead, CEO, Toronto, Ont.; J. Grant McCutcheon, CFO & corp. sec., Toronto, Ont.; C. Fraser Elliott, Toronto, Ont.; Jack Schoenmakers, Kitchener, Ont.

Capital Stock

	Authorized (shs.)	Outstanding (shs.)[1]
Common	unlimited	35,000,000

[1] At May 30, 2022
Major Shareholder - Widely held at Feb. 1, 2022.

Price Range - CIII.P/TSX-VEN

Year	Volume	High	Low	Close
2022	1,240,840	$0.27	$0.07	$0.11

Recent Close: $0.17
Capital Stock Changes - On Feb. 1, 2022, an initial public offering of 25,000,000 common shares was completed at 20¢ per share.

C.183 Cybeats Technologies Corp.

Symbol - CYBT **Exchange** - CSE **CUSIP** - 23249F
Head Office - 202-65 International Blvd, Toronto, ON, M9W 6L9 **Toll-free** - (888) 832-9232
Website - www.cybeats.com
Email - james@cybeats.com
Investor Relations - James Van Staveren (888) 713-7266
Auditors - Jackson & Co., LLP C.A., Etobicoke, Ont.
Transfer Agents - TSX Trust Company, Toronto, Ont.
Employees - 48 at Nov. 21, 2022
Profile - (B.C. 2021; orig. Idaho, 1916) Provides Cybeats, an Internet of Things (IoT) cybersecurity platform designed to secure and protect high-valued connected devices and eliminates device downtime due to cyberattacks.
Principal products consist of: the software bill of materials (SBOM) studio, a software management platform which assures enterprises their products are built with and remain secured, compliant and proactive to cybersecurity threats; and the IoT runtime device security protection (RDSP) solution, an embedded security solution installed on devices by IoT device manufacturers. The solutions improve software security through software bill of materials analysis of vulnerabilities and monitoring active software and IoT devices through continuous real-time assessment.
Customers include software developers and consumers, and downstream companies selling connected IoT devices. Consumer-facing products for connected IoT devices include medical devices, critical infrastructure, consumer electronics, automotive and aerospace.
Common listed on CSE, Nov. 21, 2022.

Recent Merger and Acquisition Activity

Status: completed **Revised:** Nov. 11, 2022
UPDATE: The transaction was completed. PREVIOUS: Scryb Inc. entered into a letter of intent to sell wholly owned Cybeats Technologies Inc., which provides a cybersecurity platform designed to secure and protect high-valued connected devices, to private Toronto, Ont.-based Pima Zinc Corp. Terms of the transaction were to be subsequently disclosed. Aug. 11, 2022 - A definitive agreement was entered into. Pima would issue 60,000,000 common shares at a deemed price of 50¢ per share. Upon completion, Cybeats would amalgamate with Pima's wholly owned 2635212 Ontario Inc., and Pima would change its name to Cybeats Technologies Corp.
Predecessor Detail - Name changed from Pima Zinc Corp., Nov. 9, 2022, pursuant to the reverse takeover acquisition of Cybeats Technologies Inc. and concurrent amalgamation of (old) Cybeats with wholly owned 2635212 Ontario Inc.
Directors - Yoav Raiter, chr. & CEO, Toronto, Ont.; Greg Falck, B.C.; Justin Leger, B.C.; Michael Minder, Bermuda; Medhanie Tekeste, Ont.
Other Exec. Officers - Josh Bald, CFO; Bob Lyle, chief revenue officer; Dmitry Raidman, chief tech. officer; Chris Blask, v-p, strategy; Julia Cherry, v-p, cust. success; Gonda Lamberink, v-p, sales

Capital Stock

	Authorized (shs.)	Outstanding (shs.)[1]
Common	unlimited	99,545,939

[1] At May 30, 2023
Major Shareholder - Widely held at Jan. 18, 2023.

Price Range - CYBT/CSE

Year	Volume	High	Low	Close
2022	970,008	$1.65	$1.19	$1.53

Recent Close: $0.70
Capital Stock Changes - In May 2023, private placement of 6,221,000 units (1 common share & ½ warrant) at $1 per unit was completed, with warrants exercisable at $1.40 per share for two years.
In April 2022, 14,250,000 common shares were issued for debt settlement. On Nov. 11, 2022, 60,000,000 common shares were issued pursuant to the reverse takeover acquisition of Cybeats Technologies Inc. Also during 2022, common shares were issued as follows: 16,734,800 by private placement and 200,000 on exercise of warrants.

Financial Statistics

Periods ended:	12m Dec. 31/22[A1]		12m Dec. 31/21[oA]
	$000s	%Chg	$000s
Operating revenue	**115**	**n.a.**	**nil**
Salaries & benefits	451		nil
General & admin expense	2,603		146
Stock-based compensation	4,523		nil
Operating expense	**7,578**	**n.m.**	**146**
Operating income	**(7,463)**	**n.a.**	**(146)**
Deprec., depl. & amort.	29		nil
Finance costs, gross	37		nil
Pre-tax income	**(7,534)**	**n.a.**	**(146)**
Net income	**(7,534)**	**n.a.**	**(146)**
Cash & equivalent	379		13
Accounts receivable	389		nil
Current assets	1,178		13
Fixed assets, net	19		nil
Right-of-use assets	181		nil
Total assets	**1,379**	**n.m.**	**13**
Accts. pay. & accr. liabs	1,334		403
Current liabilities	1,909		403
Long-term debt, gross	558		nil
Long-term debt, net	558		nil
Long-term lease liabilities	86		nil
Shareholders' equity	(1,175)		(390)
Cash from oper. activs	**(15,425)**	**n.a.**	**5**
Cash from fin. activs	16,021		(6)
Cash from invest. activs	(230)		nil
Net cash position	**379**	**n.m.**	**13**
Capital expenditures	(230)		nil
	$		$
Earnings per share*	(0.33)		(0.10)
Cash flow per share*	(0.71)		0.00
	shs		shs
No. of shs. o/s*	92,451,939		n.a.
Avg. no. of shs. o/s*	21,695,194		1,267,139
	%		%
Net profit margin	n.m.		n.a.
Return on equity	n.m.		n.m.
Return on assets	(975.54)		(39.51)

* Common
[o] Restated
[A] Reported in accordance with IFRS
[1] Results reflect the Nov. 11, 2022, reverse takeover acquisition of Cybeats Technologies Inc.

Latest Results

Periods ended:	3m Mar. 31/23[A]		3m Mar. 31/22[oA]
	$000s	%Chg	$000s
Operating revenue	218	n.a.	nil
Net income	(1,188)	n.a.	(50)
	$		$
Earnings per share*	(0.01)		(0.04)

* Common
[o] Restated
[A] Reported in accordance with IFRS

Historical Summary
(as originally stated)

Fiscal Year	Oper. Rev.	Net Inc. Bef. Disc.	EPS*
	$000s	$000s	$
2022[A]	115	(7,534)	(0.33)
2021[A1]	52	(1,443)	(0.16)
2020[A1]	2	(801)	(0.09)

* Common
[A] Reported in accordance with IFRS
[1] Results pertain to Cybeats Technologies Inc.

C.184 CyberCatch Holdings, Inc.

Symbol - CYBE **Exchange** - TSX-VEN **CUSIP** - 23250C
Head Office - 4445 Eastgate Mall, Suite 200, San Diego, CA, United States, 92121 **Toll-free** - (866) 753-2923
Website - cybercatch.com
Email - info@cybercatch.com
Investor Relations - Sai Huda (866) 753-2923
Auditors - Hay & Watson C.A., Vancouver, B.C.
Transfer Agents - Computershare Trust Company of Canada Inc., Vancouver, B.C.
Employees - 12 at Mar. 31, 2023
Profile - (B.C. 2021) Has developed a proprietary Software-as-a-Service cybersecurity platform product for continuous compliance, security and cyber risk mitigation for small and medium-sized businesses (SMBs) in the United States.

The cloud-native platform solution first helps a SMB implement a baseline of cybersecurity controls in accordance with a regulation, standard or framework, then automatically and continuously tests the controls to identify control deficiencies and non-compliance with cybersecurity requirements, so the SMB can take prompt action to remediate the control deficiency, regain compliance with cybersecurity requirements and avoid creating a security weakness that an attacker can exploit to commit a data theft or ransomware attack.

Recent Merger and Acquisition Activity

Status: completed **Revised:** Apr. 13, 2023
UPDATE: The transaction was completed. (old) Cyber Catch Holdings amalgamated with a wholly owned subsidiary of Hopefield and continued as CyberCatch Global, Inc. PREVIOUS: Hopefield Ventures Inc. entered into a letter of intent for the Qualifying Transaction reverse takeover acquisition of private Vancouver, B.C.-based CyberCatch Holdings, Inc., a cybersecurity company that provides a software-as-a-service (SaaS) platform solution for continuous compliance, security and cyber risk mitigation. Dec. 8, 2022 - A definitive agreement was entered into whereby CyberCatch would amalgamate with a wholly owned subsidiary of Hopefield. Hopefield would consolidate its common shares on 1-for-3.87 basis and change its name to CyberCatch Holdings, Inc., and CyberCatch would change its name to CyberCatch Global, Inc. A total of 42,320,000 post-consolidated common shares were expected to be issued to CyberCatch shareholders. Feb. 27, 2023 - Conditional TSX Venture Exchange approval was received.

Status: terminated **Revised:** Sept. 29, 2022
UPDATE: The transaction was terminated. PREVIOUS: Hopefield Ventures Inc. entered into a letter of intent for the Qualifying Transaction reverse takeover acquisition of private Vancouver, B.C.-based Madali Ventures Corporation on the basis of 3.81 Hopefield post-consolidated common shares for each Madali share held (following a 1-for-1.76 share consolidation), which would result in the issuance of 20,000,000 Hopefield post-consolidated common shares. Hopefield provides financial applications and platform infrastructure using blockchain technology and decentralized finance (DeFi) to consumers and organizations such as financial institutions, banks and companies involved in financial transactions. Feb. 1, 2022 - The parties entered into a definitive agreement.

Predecessor Detail - Name changed from Hopefield Ventures Inc., Apr. 12, 2023, pursuant to the Qualifying Transaction reverse takeover acquisition of (old) CyberCatch Holdings, Inc. (renamed CyberCatch Global, Inc.); basis 1 new for 3.87 old shs.
Directors - Sai Huda, chr. & CEO, San Diego, Calif.; Gary Evans, San Diego, Calif.; Kay Nichols, Ponte Vedra Beach, Fla.; Pierre L. Soulard, Toronto, Ont.
Other Exec. Officers - Darren Tindale, CFO & corp. sec.; Katherine Atmar, chief mktg. officer; Andrew Kim, chief info. security officer; Bryan Rho, chief tech. officer; Ranell Gonzales, v-p & head, global sales; Franklin Jackson, v-p & CIO

Capital Stock

	Authorized (shs.)	Outstanding (shs.)[1]
Common	unlimited	55,354,993

[1] At Apr. 24, 2023

Major Shareholder - Sai Huda held 28.9% interest at Apr. 24, 2023.

Price Range - CYBE/TSX-VEN

Year	Volume	High	Low	Close
2022............	578,837	$0.39	$0.23	$0.33
2021............	2,726,188	$1.53	$0.66	$1.35

Consolidation: 1-for-3.87 cons. in Apr. 2023
Recent Close: $0.20
Capital Stock Changes - In April 2023, common shares were consolidated on a 1-for-3.87 basis and 42,234,992 post-consolidated common shares were issued pursuant to the Qualifying Transaction reverse takeover acquisition of (old) CyberCatch Holdings, Inc. (renamed CyberCatch Gobal, Inc.) In addition, 250,000 post-consolidated common shares were issued as finder's fee and private placement of 2,870,000 post-consolidated units (1 common share & ½ warrant) at $0.50 per unit was completed, with warrants exercisable at $0.70 per share for three years.

On Aug. 5, 2021, Hopefield Ventures Inc. completed an initial public offering of 25,000,000 common shares at 10¢ per share.

Wholly Owned Subsidiaries

CyberCatch Global, Inc., San Diego, Calif.
- 100% int. in **CyberCatch, Inc.**, San Diego, Calif.

Financial Statistics

Periods ended:	12m July 31/22[A1]		12m July 31/21[A]
	$000s	%Chg	$000s
Operating revenue	**102**	**+750**	**12**
Cost of sales	141		24
Salaries & benefits	2,223		304
General & admin expense	1,266		607
Stock-based compensation	nil		1
Operating expense	**3,630**	**+298**	**912**
Operating income	**(3,528)**	**n.a.**	**(900)**
Finance costs, gross	198		63
Pre-tax income	**(4,647)**	**n.a.**	**(614)**
Net income	**(4,647)**	**n.a.**	**(614)**
Cash & equivalent	171		1,142
Accounts receivable	54		2
Current assets	255		1,149
Fixed assets, net	47		34
Total assets	**916**	**-31**	**1,322**
Bank indebtedness	256		nil
Accts. pay. & accr. liabs	488		97
Current liabilities	3,636		1,681
Long-term debt, gross	2,773		1,574
Shareholders' equity	(2,720)		(359)
Cash from oper. activs	**(3,273)**	**n.a.**	**(437)**
Cash from fin. activs	2,874		1,712
Cash from invest. activs	(591)		(148)
Net cash position	**171**	**-85**	**1,142**
Capital expenditures	(23)		(36)
	$		$
Earnings per share*	n.a.		n.a.
	shs		shs
No. of shs. o/s	n.a.		n.a.
	%		%
Net profit margin	n.m.		n.m.
Return on equity	n.m.		n.m.
Return on assets	(397.59)		n.a.

[A] Reported in accordance with IFRS
[1] Results for fiscal 2022 and prior periods pertain to (old) CyberCatch Holdings, Inc.
Note: Adjusted throughout for 1-for-3.87 cons. in Apr. 2023

C.185 Cybin Inc.

Symbol - CYBN **Exchange** - NEO **CUSIP** - 23256X
Head Office - 5600-100 King St W, Toronto, ON, M5X 1C9 **Toll-free** - (866) 292-4601
Website - cybin.com
Email - doug@cybin.com
Investor Relations - Douglas Drysdale (866) 292-4601
Auditors - Zeifmans LLP C.A., Toronto, Ont.
Transfer Agents - Odyssey Trust Company, Calgary, Alta.
Employees - 50 at June 27, 2023
Profile - (Ont. 2020; orig. B.C., 2016) Researches and develops psychedelic-based therapeutics for psychiatric and neurological conditions.

Pharmaceutical products under development include CYB003, a deuterated psilocybin analog for the treatment of major depressive disorder (MDD) and alcohol use disorder; CYB004, a deuterated version of dimethyltryptamine (DMT) for the treatment of anxiety disorders; and CYB005, a phenethylamine derivative for the treatment of neuroinflammation. The products are planned to be delivered through innovative drug delivery systems including sublingual films, orally disintegrating tablets (ODT) and via inhalation. CYB003 is undergoing Phase 1/2a clinical trial, and CYB004 is undergoing Phase 1 clinical trial.

Also pursuing the development of a patient digital therapy platform, which would help patients undergoing psychedelic therapies to memorialize the learning from their treatment sessions and to assist with the integration of such learnings into the patient's psychotherapy program.

In September 2022, the company agreed to sell an exclusive licence for an extensive targeted class of tryptamine-based molecules from **Mindset Pharma Inc.** for a licence fee of US$500,000, plus additional payments totaling up to US$9,500,000 payable by cash and common shares upon achievement of certain clinical development milestones.

In July 2022, the company acquired a Phase 1 N,N-dimethyltryptamine (DMT) study from **Entheon Biomedical Corp.** for $1,000,000. The study would be used to accelerate the development path for CYB004, the company's proprietary deuterated DMT molecule for the treatment of anxiety disorders. In connection, the company and Entheon entered into a data licence agreement, permitting Entheon to access certain data.

Predecessor Detail - Name changed from Clarmin Explorations Inc., Nov. 4, 2020, following reverse takeover acquisition of Cybin Corp. and concurrent amalgamation of Cybin Corp. with wholly owned 2762898 Ontario Inc.
Directors - Eric So, chr. & pres., Toronto, Ont.; Paul Glavine, chief growth officer, Toronto, Ont.; Theresa S. Firestone†, Toronto, Ont.; Grant B. Froese, Toronto, Ont.; Dr. Eric Hoskins, Toronto, Ont.; Mark A. Lawson, Toronto, Ont.
Other Exec. Officers - Douglas (Doug) Drysdale, CEO; Aaron Bartlone, COO; Greg Cavers, CFO; Lori Challenger, chief compliance, ethics & admin. officer; Gabriel Fahel, chief legal officer; Dr. Amir Inamdar, CMO, European opers.; Dr. Alex Nivorozhkin, chief scientific officer; Dr. Kenneth Avery, sr. v-p, chemistry & mfg.; Allison House-Gecewicz, sr. v-p, clinical opers.; Erica Olson, v-p & contr.; Robert Mino, gen. counsel
† Lead director

Capital Stock

	Authorized (shs.)	Outstanding (shs.)[1]
Preferred	unlimited	nil
Common	unlimited	208,325,846
Class B Common	n.a.	530,542

[1] At June 27, 2023

Common - One vote per share.
Class B Common - Issued by wholly owned Cybin US Holdings Inc. Convertible into common shares on a 10-for-1 basis. Non-voting.
Major Shareholder - Widely held at July 11, 2022.

Price Range - CYBN/NEO

Year	Volume	High	Low	Close
2022............	2,579,100	$1.52	$0.38	$0.42
2021............	23,721,700	$4.00	$1.20	$1.45
2020............	4,699,400	$2.49	$0.05	$1.90
2019............	2,019,015	$0.17	$0.08	$0.08
2018............	2,549,294	$0.50	$0.10	$0.15

Recent Close: $0.40
Capital Stock Changes - During fiscal 2023, common shares were issued as follows: 20,754,120 under an at-the-market offering and 1,164,638 on exercise of warrants. In addition, 360,374.2 class B common shares were issued for milestone payments and 876,967.2 class B common shares were converted into 8,769,672 common shares.

In August 2021, public offering of 10,147,600 common shares was completed at $3.40 per share, including 1,323,600 common shares on exercise of over-allotment option. Also during fiscal 2022, common shares were issued as follows: 3,231,261 on exercise of warrants and 1,588,300 on exercise of options. In addition, 269,007.8 class B common shares were issued for milestone payments and 184,116 class B common shares were converted into 1,841,160 common shares.

Wholly Owned Subsidiaries

Cybin Corp., Toronto, Ont.
- 100% int. in **Cybin IRL Limited**, Dublin, Ireland.
- 100% int. in **Cybin US Holdings Inc.**, Nev.
  - 100% int. in **Adelia Therapeutics Inc.**, Boston, Mass.
- 100% int. in **Natures Journey Inc.**, Ont.
- 100% int. in **Serenity Life Sciences Inc.**, Ont.

Financial Statistics

Periods ended:	12m Mar. 31/23[A]		12m Mar. 31/22[A]
	$000s	%Chg	$000s
Research & devel. expense	25,491		17,586
General & admin expense	21,090		28,054
Stock-based compensation	4,686		18,030
Operating expense	**51,267**	**-19**	**63,670**
Operating income	**(51,267)**	**n.a.**	**(63,670)**
Deprec., depl. & amort.	251		168
Finance income	603		241
Pre-tax income	**(47,490)**	**n.a.**	**(67,631)**
Net income	**(47,490)**	**n.a.**	**(67,631)**
Cash & equivalent	16,633		53,641
Accounts receivable	3,050		2,102
Current assets	23,185		58,355
Long-term investments	nil		242
Fixed assets, net	450		491
Intangibles, net	30,262		24,975
Total assets	**53,897**	**-36**	**84,063**
Accts. pay. & accr. liabs	5,663		5,262
Current liabilities	5,663		7,908
Shareholders' equity	48,234		76,155
Cash from oper. activs	**(47,431)**	**n.a.**	**(45,207)**
Cash from fin. activs	13,564		35,777
Cash from invest. activs	(3,309)		(770)
Net cash position	**16,633**	**-69**	**53,641**
Capital expenditures	(142)		(105)
	$		$
Earnings per share*	(0.26)		(0.40)
Cash flow per share*	(0.26)		(0.27)
	shs		shs
No. of shs. o/s*	200,634,154		175,111,654
Avg. no. of shs. o/s*	185,428,767		167,287,240
	%		%
Net profit margin	n.a.		n.a.
Return on equity	(76.36)		n.m.
Return on assets	(68.85)		n.a.

* Common
[A] Reported in accordance with IFRS

Historical Summary
(as originally stated)

Fiscal Year	Oper. Rev. $000s	Net Inc. Bef. Disc. $000s	EPS* $
2023[A]	nil	(47,490)	(0.26)
2022[A]	nil	(67,631)	(0.40)
2021[A1]	864	(32,220)	(0.32)
2020[A2]	nil	(189)	(0.01)
2019[A]	nil	(101)	(0.01)

* Common
[A] Reported in accordance with IFRS
[1] Results reflect the Nov. 5, 2020, reverse takeover acquisition of Cybin Corp.
[2] Results for fiscal 2020 and prior periods pertain to Clarmin Explorations Inc.

C.186 Cymat Technologies Ltd.

Symbol - CYM **Exchange** - TSX-VEN **CUSIP** - 23257A
Head Office - 2-6320 Danville Rd, Mississauga, ON, L5T 2L7 **Telephone** - (905) 696-9900 **Fax** - (905) 696-9300
Website - www.cymat.com
Email - liik@cymat.com
Investor Relations - Michael M. Liik (905) 696-2427
Auditors - Grant Thornton LLP C.A., Mississauga, Ont.
Lawyers - McMillan LLP, Toronto, Ont.
Transfer Agents - TSX Trust Company, Toronto, Ont.
Profile - (Ont. 2006) Produces ultra-light stabilized aluminum foam (SAF), a metallic foam that is manufactured by bubbling gas into molten-alloyed aluminum containing a dispersion of fine ceramic particles to create foam that is then cast into either flat panels or near-net shapes.

Has exclusive worldwide rights, through patents and licences from **Alcan International Inc.** and **Hydro Aluminum AS**, to manufacture and market SAF, with a focus on producing products for four major markets: automotive, architecture, defence and general industrial markets seeking energy management systems.

Products include Alusion™, which are flat light-weight architectural panels offering multiple product variations used for facades, wall cladding, ceiling tiles or dropped ceilings, restaurants, bars, offices, apartment buildings, showroom displays, Terrazzo flooring, signage, lighting fixtures, exhibits and other applications in the architectural and design market; and SmartMetal™, which are manufactured into large dimensional panels of both interior and exterior blast attenuating systems as well as near-net shaped castings and are effective at absorbing large amounts of energy in an efficient, light-weight and recyclable package for the defence and military, and automotive markets.

SAF is manufactured and marketed from a 26,000-sq.-ft. facility in Mississauga, Ont.

Predecessor Detail - Name changed from Cymat Corp., Aug. 8, 2006, pursuant to plan of arrangement whereby Cymat Corp. transferred to newly created Cymat Technologies Ltd. all assets and liabilities except future tax assets, plus $1,600,000 in cash. Cymat Corp. shldrs. received 1 Cymat Technologies sh. for each sh. held.

Directors - Michael M. Liik, exec. chr. & CEO, Toronto, Ont.; Alar Kongats; Martin J. Mazza, Ont.

Other Exec. Officers - Mario DeAngelis, COO; Darryl Kleebaum, CFO; Vince Benincasa, chief comml. officer; Angie Deyannis, v-p, bus. devel., Alusion; Jim Johnson, v-p, SmartMetal sales & opers.

Capital Stock

	Authorized (shs.)	Outstanding (shs.)[1]
Common	unlimited	59,085,612

[1] At Aug. 29, 2022

Major Shareholder - Widely held at Dec. 7, 2021.

Price Range - CYM/TSX-VEN

Year	Volume	High	Low	Close
2022	11,550,427	$0.80	$0.30	$0.39
2021	21,674,662	$1.05	$0.16	$0.67
2020	5,145,788	$0.34	$0.17	$0.20
2019	6,243,330	$0.43	$0.19	$0.31
2018	4,758,224	$0.33	$0.17	$0.24

Recent Close: $0.28

Capital Stock Changes - In May 2021, private placement of 7,719,725 units (1 common share & ½ warrant) at 65¢ per unit was completed. Also during fiscal 2022, common shares were issued as follows: 1,771,984 on exercise of warrants and 1,650,000 on exercise of options.

Wholly Owned Subsidiaries

ALU-MMC Hungary, Zrt., Hungary.

Financial Statistics

Periods ended:	12m Apr. 30/22[A]		12m Apr. 30/21[A]
	$000s	%Chg	$000s
Operating revenue	**3,124**	**-25**	**4,152**
Research & devel. expense	181		131
General & admin expense	4,774		1,761
Other operating expense	2,328		2,029
Operating expense	**7,284**	**+86**	**3,921**
Operating income	**(4,160)**	**n.a.**	**231**
Deprec., depl. & amort.	178		168
Finance costs, gross	337		627
Pre-tax income	**(4,747)**	**n.a.**	**(543)**
Net income	**(4,747)**	**n.a.**	**(543)**
Cash & equivalent	2,466		5,018
Inventories	1,180		263
Accounts receivable	838		165
Current assets	4,750		5,470
Fixed assets, net	1,081		1,085
Total assets	**6,172**	**-6**	**6,583**
Accts. pay. & accr. liabs	1,416		1,499
Current liabilities	2,151		1,959
Long-term debt, gross	136		120
Long-term debt, net	124		120
Long-term lease liabilities	770		880
Shareholders' equity	2,343		2,876
Cash from oper. activs	**(4,318)**	**n.a.**	**433**
Cash from fin. activs	2,301		4,365
Cash from invest. activs	(535)		(31)
Net cash position	**2,466**	**-51**	**5,018**
Capital expenditures	(215)		(31)
	$		$
Earnings per share*	(0.09)		(0.01)
Cash flow per share*	(0.08)		0.01
	shs		shs
No. of shs. o/s*	55,488,612		44,346,903
Avg. no. of shs. o/s*	53,697,922		43,196,098
	%		%
Net profit margin	(151.95)		(13.08)
Return on equity	(181.91)		n.m.
Return on assets	(69.15)		1.99

* Common
[A] Reported in accordance with IFRS

Historical Summary
(as originally stated)

Fiscal Year	Oper. Rev. $000s	Net Inc. Bef. Disc. $000s	EPS* $
2022[A]	3,124	(4,747)	(0.09)
2021[A]	4,152	(543)	(0.01)
2020[A]	1,687	(1,815)	(0.04)
2019[A]	2,644	(1,359)	(0.04)
2018[A]	3,046	(1,116)	(0.03)

* Common
[A] Reported in accordance with IFRS

C.187 Cymbria Corporation

Symbol - CYB **Exchange** - TSX **CUSIP** - 23257X
Head Office - 500-150 Bloor St W, Toronto, ON, M5S 2X9 **Telephone** - (416) 963-9353 **Toll-free** - (866) 757-7207 **Fax** - (416) 963-5060
Website - www.cymbria.com
Email - farmer@edgepointwealth.com
Investor Relations - Patrick Farmer (416) 963-9353
Auditors - KPMG LLP C.A., Toronto, Ont.
Lawyers - Stikeman Elliott LLP, Toronto, Ont.
Transfer Agents - Computershare Trust Company of Canada Inc., Toronto, Ont.
Investment Advisors - EdgePoint Investment Group Inc., Toronto, Ont.
Managers - EdgePoint Investment Group Inc., Toronto, Ont.
Profile - (Ont. 2008) Invests in a managed portfolio of globally diversified equity securities and **EdgePoint Wealth Management Inc.**, an investment manager which offers mutual funds and institutional and other investment products through financial advisors.

Top 10 holdings at June 30, 2023 (as a percentage of portfolio):

Holding	Percentage
EdgePoint Wealth Management Inc.	16.15%
Restaurant Brands International Inc.	3.75%
Mattel, Inc.	3.64%
Berry Global Group Inc.	3.49%
Dollar Tree, Inc.	3.38%
SAP SE	2.97%
Osisko Gold Royalties Ltd.	2.61%
DSM-Firmenich AG	2.41%
Elevance Health Inc.	2.32%
Computer Modelling Group Ltd.	2.27%

Directors - Patrick Farmer, co-founder & chr., Bolton, Ont.; Ugo Bizzarri, Toronto, Ont.; Reena Carter, Etobicoke, Ont.; James S. A. (Jim) MacDonald, Toronto, Ont.; Edward J. (Ed) Waitzer, Toronto, Ont.

Other Exec. Officers - Tye Bousada, co-founder & co-CEO; Geoff MacDonald, co-founder & co-CEO; Norman Tang, CFO; Diane Rossi, corp. sec.

Capital Stock

	Authorized (shs.)	Outstanding (shs.)[1]
Class A	unlimited	16,279,603
Class J	unlimited	6,413,442
Common	unlimited	100

[1] At Aug. 10, 2023

Class A - The net asset value of each class A share is equal to the value of the assets of the company allocated to class A less the company's liabilities allocated to class A divided by the number of class A shares outstanding. The manager charges a monthly management fee at an annual rate of 1.00% of the daily net average asset values of the class A shares, excluding the value of EdgePoint Wealth Management Inc. Rank equal to class J shares with respect to payment of dividends and repayment of capital. Non-voting.

Class J - Exchangeable for class A shares at an exchange ratio based on relative net asset values. The net asset value of each class J share is equal to the value of the assets of the company allocated to class J less the company's liabilities allocated to class J divided by the number of class J shares outstanding. The manager charges the holders of class J shares a monthly management fee at an annual rate of 0.5% of the daily net average asset values of the class J shares, excluding the value of EdgePoint Wealth Management Inc. Non-voting.

Common - Redeemable and retractable at $1.00 per share. One vote per share.

Normal Course Issuer Bid - The company plans to make normal course purchases of up to 1,616,273 class A shares representing 10% of the public float. The bid commenced on May 25, 2023, and expires on May 24, 2024.

Major Shareholder - EdgePoint Investment Group Inc. held 100% interest at Mar. 30, 2023.

Price Range - CYB/TSX

Year	Volume	High	Low	Close
2022	1,314,450	$63.94	$51.61	$57.00
2021	1,600,696	$67.99	$49.51	$63.51
2020	2,684,784	$55.51	$36.40	$52.50
2019	2,024,544	$57.35	$51.27	$55.24
2018	1,240,300	$62.31	$51.52	$57.49

Recent Close: $59.50

Capital Stock Changes - During 2022, 36,200 class J shares were converted to 40,442 class A shares and 9,600 class A shares were repurchased under a Normal Course Issuer Bid.

Investments

20.7% int. in **EdgePoint Wealth Management Inc.**, Toronto, Ont.

Financial Statistics

Periods ended:	12m Dec. 31/22[A]		12m Dec. 31/21[A]
	$000s	%Chg	$000s
Realized invest. gain (loss)	(428)		118,566
Unrealized invest. gain (loss)	(117,707)		145,589
Total revenue	**(79,089)**	**n.a.**	**303,339**
General & admin. expense	16,203		16,727
Operating expense	**16,203**	**-3**	**16,727**
Operating income	**(95,292)**	**n.a.**	**286,612**
Finance costs, gross	1,490		395
Pre-tax income	**(96,782)**	**n.a.**	**286,217**
Income taxes	(16,149)		32,644
Net income	**(80,633)**	**n.a.**	**253,573**
Cash & equivalent	104,535		97,423
Accounts receivable	1,772		1,453
Investments	1,315,158		1,417,533
Total assets	**1,438,044**	**-5**	**1,516,409**
Bank indebtedness	5,050		2,550
Accts. pay. & accr. liabs	399		97
Debt	30,050		nil
Shareholders' equity	1,364,512		1,445,670
Cash from oper. activs	**(20,096)**	**n.a.**	**53,091**
Cash from fin. activs	26,975		(3,471)
Net cash position	**104,535**	**+7**	**97,423**
	$		$
Earnings per share*	(3.49)		10.66
Earnings per share**	(3.67)		12.35
Cash flow per share***	(0.88)		2.33
Net asset value per share*	58.01		61.50
	shs		shs
No. of shs. o/s***	22,763,545		22,768,903
	%		%
Net profit margin	n.m.		83.59
Return on equity	(5.74)		19.23
Return on assets	(5.37)		18.44

* Class A
** Class J
*** Class A & Class J
[A] Reported in accordance with IFRS

Latest Results

Periods ended:	6m June 30/23[A]		6m June 30/22[A]
	$000s	%Chg	$000s
Total revenue	110,743	n.a.	(190,714)
Net income	89,035	n.a.	(172,273)
	$		$
Earnings per share*	3.76		(7.36)
Earnings per share**	4.32		(8.08)

* Class A
** Class J
[A] Reported in accordance with IFRS

Historical Summary
(as originally stated)

Fiscal Year	Total Rev. $000s	Net Inc. Bef. Disc. $000s	EPS* $
2022[A]	(79,089)	(80,633)	(3.49)
2021[A]	303,339	253,573	10.66
2020[A]	(9,545)	(13,799)	(0.62)
2019[A]	204,297	170,459	7.15
2018[A]	34,674	21,744	0.80

* Class A
[A] Reported in accordance with IFRS

C.188 Cypher Metaverse Inc.

Symbol - CODE **Exchange** - CSE **CUSIP** - 23267C
Head Office - 1780-355 Burrard St, Vancouver, BC, V6C 2G8 **Telephone** - (778) 806-5150 **Toll-free** - (877) 806-2633
Website - www.cypher-meta.com
Email - tkovaleva@ktbusiness2010.com
Investor Relations - Tatiana Kovaleva (604) 343-2977
Auditors - PKF Antares Professional Corporation C.A., Calgary, Alta.
Transfer Agents - Odyssey Trust Company, Calgary, Alta.
Profile - (B.C. 2013) Invests in blockchain, non-fungible tokens (NFT), crypto-technologies, cannabidiol (CBD) wellness and medical marijuana companies. Also engages in Bitcoin mining.

The company either invests, acquires or forms partnerships and joint ventures with companies that develop blockchain technologies to help accelerate its implementation in cryptographic tokens and transactional cryptocurrencies, enterprise grade smart contracts, global data management, media distribution and ownership, and supply chain auditing.

Portfolio of investments include: **InstaCoin Technologies Ltd.** (50% interest), which is developing a NFT platform; **Glanis Pharmaceuticals Inc.** (49% interest), which holds patents for transdermal delivery and oral mucosal delivery of chloroquine and hydroxychloroquine; and 30% interest in Arcology, a blockchain platform being developed by **Capital Blocktech Inc.** Also holds interests in **Aerosax Research and Technology Ltd.**, which developed Trad3r, a virtual immersive social platform application that allows users to trade a wide range of options from celebrities and sportsteams to Instagram stories and stocks with real money, in exchange for rewards; and **Love Hemp Group plc**, which invests in and/or acquires CBD wellness and medical marijuana companies.

Also has a Bitcoin mining facility in New York that produce 10,350 terahashes per second (TH/s).

During the third quarter of 2022, the company agreed to sell its Bitcoin mining equipment to an arm's length party for $60,000 and wholly owned **360 Blockchain USA Inc.** and **SV CryptoLab Inc.** were wound up. The company was evaluating alternative opportunities to generate crypto asset revenue streams.

Recent Merger and Acquisition Activity

Status: pending **Announced:** May 19, 2023
Cypher Metaverse Inc. entered into a letter of intent for the reverse takeover acquisition of Agapi Luxury Brands Inc. on the basis of 0.7601 Cypher common share for each Agapi share held. Agapi produces and sells premium luxury branded cigars sold under the brand Freud Cigar Co. Agapi plans to complete an equity financing of Agapi common shares for gross proceeds of up to $750,000.

Predecessor Detail - Name changed from Codebase Ventures Inc., Mar. 23, 2022.
Directors - George Tsafalas, pres. & CEO, Vancouver, B.C.; Brian D. Keane, New York, N.Y.; Harrison Ross, Vancouver, B.C.
Other Exec. Officers - Tatiana Kovaleva, CFO; Jeff Koyen, chief strategy officer; Kyle Maron, v-p, bus. devel.

Capital Stock

	Authorized (shs.)	Outstanding (shs.)[1]
Common	unlimited	15,571,906

[1] At May 18, 2023

Major Shareholder - Widely held at June 7, 2022.

Price Range - CODE/CSE

Year	Volume	High	Low	Close
2022	4,818,171	$1.25	$0.10	$0.11
2021	19,893,104	$7.50	$1.00	$1.05
2020	6,503,430	$3.50	$0.40	$2.10
2019	1,387,558	$6.00	$1.50	$2.00
2018	2,444,786	$28.00	$2.00	$2.50

Consolidation: 1-for-10 cons. in Dec. 2022; 1-for-10 cons. in June 2020
Recent Close: $0.11

Capital Stock Changes - In February and March 2022, private placement of 15,749,999 units (1 common share & 1 warrant) at 7¢ per unit was completed, with warrants exercisable at 9¢ for two years. On Dec. 20, 2022, common shares were consolidated on a 1-for-10 basis.

Investments

Aerosax Research and Technology Ltd.
30% int. in **Capital Blocktech Inc.**, Alta.
49% int. in **Glanis Pharmaceuticals Inc.**, B.C.
50% int. in **InstaCoin Technologies Ltd.**, United Kingdom.
Love Hemp Group plc, United Kingdom.

Financial Statistics

Periods ended:	12m Dec. 31/21[A]		12m Dec. 31/20[A]
	$000s	%Chg	$000s
Realized invest. gain (loss)	nil		(353)
Unrealized invest. gain (loss)	(161)		(1,153)
Total revenue	**(70)**	**n.a.**	**(1,365)**
General & admin. expense	3,625		1,946
Stock-based compensation	6,207		700
Other operating expense	206		nil
Operating expense	**10,038**	**+279**	**2,646**
Operating income	**(10,108)**	**n.a.**	**(4,011)**
Deprec. & amort.	410		nil
Write-downs/write-offs	(2,685)		nil
Pre-tax income	**(13,293)**	**n.a.**	**(4,020)**
Net income	**(13,293)**	**n.a.**	**(4,020)**
Net inc. for equity hldrs	**(13,293)**	**n.a.**	**(4,027)**
Net inc. for non-cont. int	**nil**	**n.a.**	**7**
Cash & equivalent	3,607		895
Accounts receivable	4		28
Investments	563		2,138
Fixed assets, net	94		nil
Intangibles, net	57		nil
Total assets	**4,375**	**+40**	**3,125**
Accts. pay. & accr. liabs	162		158
Shareholders' equity	4,213		2,956
Non-controlling interest	10		10
Cash from oper. activs	**(4,284)**	**n.a.**	**(1,877)**
Cash from fin. activs	7,333		3,152
Cash from invest. activs	(839)		(460)
Net cash position	**3,104**	**+247**	**895**
Capital expenditures	(640)		nil
	$		$
Earnings per share*	(1.20)		(0.90)
Cash flow per share*	(0.37)		(0.41)
	shs		shs
No. of shs. o/s*	13,077,906		7,943,973
Avg. no. of shs. o/s*	11,469,503		4,586,942
	%		%
Net profit margin	n.m.		n.m.
Return on equity	(370.85)		(162.28)
Return on assets	(354.48)		(150.39)

* Common
[A] Reported in accordance with IFRS

Latest Results

Periods ended:	9m Sept. 30/22[A]		9m Sept. 30/21[A]
	$000s	%Chg	$000s
Total revenue	(386)	n.a.	994
Net income	(2,744)	n.a.	(6,756)
	$		$
Earnings per share*	(0.20)		(0.60)

* Common
[A] Reported in accordance with IFRS

Historical Summary
(as originally stated)

Fiscal Year	Total Rev. $000s	Net Inc. Bef. Disc. $000s	EPS* $
2021[A]	(70)	(13,293)	(1.20)
2020[A]	(1,365)	(4,020)	(0.90)
2019[A]	5	(4,961)	(2.00)
2018[A]	(392)	(6,515)	(3.00)
2017[A]	(543)	(2,621)	(3.00)

* Common
[A] Reported in accordance with IFRS
Note: Adjusted throughout for 1-for-10 cons. in Dec. 2022; 1-for-10 cons. in June 2020

C.189 Cypherpunk Holdings Inc.

Symbol - HODL **Exchange** - CSE **CUSIP** - 232662
Head Office - 401-217 Queen St W, Toronto, ON, M5V 0R2 **Telephone** - (416) 599-8547 **Fax** - (416) 599-4959
Website - cypherpunkholdings.com
Email - veronika@cypherpunkholdings.com
Investor Relations - Veronika Oswald (647) 946-1300
Auditors - Kingston Ross Pasnak LLP C.A., Edmonton, Alta.
Lawyers - Crowell & Moring LLP, Washington, D.C.; Davies Ward Phillips & Vineberg LLP, Toronto, Ont.
Transfer Agents - TSX Trust Company, Toronto, Ont.
Profile - (Ont. 2002) Invests and holds cryptocurrency, makes equity investments in early stage companies in the privacy, gaming, DeFi (Decentralized finance) and blockchain sectors and enrages in leasing IPv4 addresses and bitcoin mining.

At Dec. 31, 2021, the company's cryptocurrency holdings consisted of 400.78 Bitcoin and 361.61 Ethereum with market values of $23,400,000 and $1,700,000, respectively.

Investments include interests in **Streetside Development, LLC**, which has developed Samourai Wallet, an advanced and secure mobile bitcoin wallet, and has other privacy technologies including Open Exploration Tool, Ricochet, Stonewall, Whirlpool and Dojo; **NGRAVE.IO**, which has developed ZERO, a fully offline hardware wallet that features the world's highest security certification, EAL7, for its secure operating system; **zkSnacks Limited**, which offers products including Wasabi Wallet, an opensource, non-custodial, privacy-focused bitcoin wallet for desktop use; **Chia Network Inc.**, a company that builds blockchains based on proofs of space and time to make cryptocurrency more secure; **Animoca Brands Corporation Limited**, which operates and invests in the digital entertainment, blockchain and gamification sectors; **GOAT Gaming Pte Ltd.**, which offers a play-to-earn gaming platform; and **Panxora Management Corporation**, a portfolio management and advisory company.

Predecessor Detail - Name changed from Khan Resources Inc., Feb. 4, 2019.
Directors - Antanas (Tony) Guoga, exec. chr., interim pres. & interim CEO, Lithuania; Mohammed (Moe) Adham, chief invest. officer, Ottawa, Ont.; Jon Matonis, chief economist, London, Middx., United Kingdom; Rubsun Ho, Toronto, Ont.; Peter Tutlys, Newmarket, Ont.; Leah Wald, Nashville, Tenn.
Other Exec. Officers - Douglas (Doug) Harris, CFO

Capital Stock

	Authorized (shs.)	Outstanding (shs.)[1]
Common	unlimited	157,110,718

[1] At Mar. 1, 2023

Normal Course Issuer Bid - The company plans to make normal course purchases of up to 8,003,535 common shares representing 5% of the total outstanding. The bid commenced on Jan. 25, 2023, and expires on Jan. 24, 2024.
Major Shareholder - Antanas (Tony) Guoga held 14.63% interest at May 10, 2021.

Price Range - HODL/CSE

Year	Volume	High	Low	Close
2022	37,717,895	$0.19	$0.07	$0.07
2021	230,304,719	$0.50	$0.13	$0.17
2020	68,187,820	$0.22	$0.03	$0.19
2019	43,152,037	$0.11	$0.03	$0.04
2018	19,972,059	$0.18	$0.05	$0.06

Recent Close: $0.10

Wholly Owned Subsidiaries

Khan Resources B.V., Netherlands.

Investments

Animoca Brands Corporation Limited, Hong Kong, Hong Kong, People's Republic of China.
Chia Network Inc., Del.
GOAT Gaming Pte Ltd., Singapore.
NGRAVE.IO, Brussels, Belgium.
Panxora Management Corporation, Bahamas.
Streetside Development, LLC, Wyo.
4.5% int. in **zkSnacks Limited**, Gibraltar.

Financial Statistics

Periods ended:	12m Sept. 30/21^A		12m Sept. 30/20^A
	$000s	%Chg	$000s
Realized invest. gain (loss)	(4)		283
Unrealized invest. gain (loss)	251		1,019
Total revenue	**407**	**-69**	**1,326**
General & admin. expense	1,684		579
Stock-based compensation	664		366
Operating expense	**2,348**	**+148**	**945**
Operating income	**(1,941)**	**n.a.**	**381**
Deprec. & amort.	75		nil
Pre-tax income	**(2,360)**	**n.a.**	**379**
Income taxes	(1,186)		nil
Net income	**(1,174)**	**n.a.**	**379**
Cash & equivalent	877		485
Inventories	n.a.		3,927
Accounts receivable	242		18
Investments	4,620		2,412
Intangibles, net	24,356		nil
Total assets	**31,231**	**+356**	**6,856**
Accts. pay. & accr. liabs	322		186
Debt	1,186		nil
Shareholders' equity	27,842		6,670
Cash from oper. activs	**(1,635)**	**n.a.**	**(1,651)**
Cash from fin. activs	14,102		493
Cash from invest. activs	(12,075)		(100)
Net cash position	**877**	**+81**	**485**
	$		$
Earnings per share*	(0.01)		0.00
Cash flow per share*	(0.01)		(0.02)
	shs		shs
No. of shs. o/s*	159,970,718		100,266,482
Avg. no. of shs. o/s*	134,200,366		91,104,733
	%		%
Net profit margin	(288.45)		28.58
Return on equity	(6.80)		6.26
Return on assets	(6.16)		6.11

* Common
^A Reported in accordance with IFRS

Latest Results

Periods ended:	3m Dec. 31/21^A		3m Dec. 31/20^A
	$000s	%Chg	$000s
Total revenue	4,649	-23	6,028
Net income	3,687	-34	5,594
	$		$
Earnings per share*	0.02		0.06

* Common
^A Reported in accordance with IFRS

Historical Summary
(as originally stated)

Fiscal Year	Total Rev. $000s	Net Inc. Bef. Disc. $000s	EPS* $
2021^A	407	(1,174)	(0.01)
2020^A	1,326	379	0.00
2019^A	(2,216)	(2,914)	(0.03)
2018^A	1,392	792	0.01
2017^A	nil	(1,465)	(0.02)

* Common
^A Reported in accordance with IFRS

D

D.1 D-BOX Technologies Inc.

Symbol - DBO **Exchange** - TSX **CUSIP** - 23305P
Head Office - 2172 rue de la Province, Longueuil, QC, J4G 1R7 **Telephone** - (450) 442-3003 **Toll-free** - (888) 442-3269 **Fax** - (450) 442-3230
Website - www.d-box.com
Email - smailhot@d-box.com
Investor Relations - Sébastien Mailhot (450) 912-2036
Auditors - Ernst & Young LLP C.A., Montréal, Qué.
Bankers - National Bank of Canada, Montréal, Qué.
Lawyers - BCF LLP, Montréal, Qué.
Transfer Agents - Computershare Investor Services Inc.
Employees - 94 at Sept. 30, 2022

Profile - (Can. 1998) Designs, manufactures and commercializes haptic systems for the home entertainment and commercial segments.

The company's computer programmed software haptic effects, D-BOX Haptic Code or D-BOX HaptiCode is precisely synchronized with the linear content, such as movies, TV series and recorded music, or it is integrated within the game, application or software when the content is interactive.

D-BOX software products, including the D-BOX HaptiCode, are either embedded in the film, video game, virtual reality content or other content distributed by a third party, or electronically distributed by the company to its customers.

The company markets the D-BOX haptic systems to the home entertainment segment which consists of the following sub-markets: video game peripherals including video game chairs, video game controllers and sim racing rigs; virtual reality systems; and furniture including recliner and love seats. The company also markets its products to the commercial markets which consists of projects related to location-based entertainment centres, theme parks, arcades, museums, planetariums and commercial theatres as well as the simulation and training segment.

At Oct. 27, 2022, 850 screens worldwide were equipped with D-BOX haptic systems in commercial theaters.

Predecessor Detail - Name changed from Altitude Venture Capital Corp., Dec. 27, 2000.

Directors - Denis Chamberland, chr., Sutton, Qué.; Sébastien Mailhot, pres. & CEO, Boucherville, Qué.; Louis P. Bernier, Mont-Royal, Qué.; Brigitte Bourque, Montréal, Qué.; Zrinka Dekic, Los Angeles, Calif.; Luc Martin, Laval, Qué.; Jean-Pierre Trahan, Brossard, Qué.

Other Exec. Officers - David Montpetit, CFO; Sébastien Boire-Lavigne, chief tech. officer; Sébastien Côté, v-p, HR; Robert Desautels, v-p, bus. devel. & strategic partnerships; Karen Mendoza, v-p, sales; Stéphane Vidal, v-p, product & brand

Capital Stock

	Authorized (shs.)	Outstanding (shs.)[1]
Class B Preferred	unlimited	nil
Class A Common	unlimited	220,225,573

[1] At Nov. 11, 2022

Major Shareholder - Fidelity Management & Research Company held 12% interest at July 27, 2022.

Price Range - DBO/TSX

Year	Volume	High	Low	Close
2022	25,539,730	$0.14	$0.07	$0.09
2021	77,483,202	$0.16	$0.08	$0.10
2020	182,594,160	$0.27	$0.03	$0.11
2019	19,716,355	$0.19	$0.10	$0.10
2018	27,389,876	$0.32	$0.15	$0.17

Recent Close: $0.11

Capital Stock Changes - There were no changes to capital stock during fiscal 2022.

Wholly Owned Subsidiaries

D-BOX USA INC., Del.
D-BOX Entertainment Technology (Shanghai) Co. Ltd., People's Republic of China.

Financial Statistics

Periods ended:	12m Mar. 31/22[A]		12m Mar. 31/21[oA]
	$000s	%Chg	$000s
Operating revenue	**21,313**	**+92**	**11,080**
Cost of goods sold	8,868		5,987
Research & devel. expense	2,174		1,769
General & admin expense	9,349		6,492
Stock-based compensation	192		154
Operating expense	**20,583**	**+43**	**14,402**
Operating income	**730**	**n.a.**	**(3,322)**
Deprec., depl. & amort.	1,972		2,349
Finance income	9		13
Finance costs, gross	405		501
Write-downs/write-offs	(179)		(209)
Pre-tax income	**(1,867)**	**n.a.**	**(6,226)**
Income taxes	nil		(34)
Net income	**(1,867)**	**n.a.**	**(6,192)**
Cash & equivalent	3,937		9,134
Inventories	5,163		4,547
Accounts receivable	6,441		2,341
Current assets	16,361		16,828
Fixed assets, net	3,051		3,762
Intangibles, net	2,162		2,229
Total assets	**22,350**	**-6**	**23,736**
Accts. pay. & accr. liabs	4,135		3,518
Current liabilities	7,183		7,864
Long-term debt, gross	3,451		2,041
Long-term debt, net	2,850		1,641
Long-term lease liabilities	483		700
Shareholders' equity	11,834		13,531
Cash from oper. activs	**(3,323)**	**n.a.**	**(242)**
Cash from fin. activs	(744)		5,640
Cash from invest. activs	(1,124)		(425)
Net cash position	**3,937**	**-57**	**9,134**
Capital expenditures	(415)		(13)
	$		$
Earnings per share*	(0.01)		(0.04)
Cash flow per share*	(0.02)		(0.00)
	shs		shs
No. of shs. o/s*	220,225,573		220,225,573
Avg. no. of shs. o/s*	220,225,573		179,225,710
	%		%
Net profit margin	(8.76)		(55.88)
Return on equity	(14.72)		(44.42)
Return on assets	(6.34)		(22.50)
Foreign sales percent	77		77
No. of employees (FTEs)	90		91

* Cl.A com.
[o] Restated
[A] Reported in accordance with IFRS

Latest Results

Periods ended:	6m Sept. 30/22[A]		6m Sept. 30/21[A]
	$000s	%Chg	$000s
Operating revenue	13,255	+51	8,764
Net income	(714)	n.a.	(1,765)
	$		$
Earnings per share*	(0.00)		(0.01)

* Cl.A com.
[A] Reported in accordance with IFRS

Historical Summary
(as originally stated)

Fiscal Year	Oper. Rev.	Net Inc. Bef. Disc.	EPS*
	$000s	$000s	$
2022[A]	21,313	(1,867)	(0.01)
2021[A]	11,080	(6,192)	(0.04)
2020[A]	25,895	(6,250)	(0.04)
2019[A]	34,164	(1,705)	(0.01)
2018[A]	35,478	(1,761)	(0.01)

* Cl.A com.
[A] Reported in accordance with IFRS

D.2 D2L Inc.

Symbol - DTOL **Exchange** - TSX **CUSIP** - 23344V
Head Office - 560-137 Glasgow St, Kitchener, ON, N2G 4X8 **Telephone** - (519) 772-0325 **Toll-free** - (888) 772-0325 **Fax** - (519) 772-0324
Website - d2l.com
Email - ir@d2l.com
Investor Relations - Craig Armitage (416) 347-8954
Auditors - KPMG LLP C.A., Vaughan, Ont.
Transfer Agents - Computershare Trust Company of Canada Inc., Toronto, Ont.
FP500 Revenue Ranking - 637

Profile - (Can. 2014; orig. Ont., 2011) Offers D2L Brightspace, a cloud-based software platform for supporting learning in the classroom, online learning and professional development and training, to kindergarten to grade 12 (K-12) schools, higher education institutions and private sector enterprises.

The platform's functionality is extended through Performance+, an analytics package which provides native reporting abilities with predictive analytics, additional report visualizations and adaptive learning engine; and Creator+, which provides easy-to-use authoring tools and engages learners through add-on solutions such as adaptive video, widgets and interactive tools to help instructors create engaging, video-based training and courses. Primarily sold through direct sales force in North America, Europe and Australia, as well as through indirect channel partners in other countries around the world. Customers include 570 colleges and universities, 160 K-12 schools and districts, 420 businesses, healthcare institutions and governments, as well as 80 professional associations and industry partners in more than 40 countries. Solutions are sold via a subscription model, often with a service component, and are typically structured with a minimum user level commitment. The majority of customers enter into contracts with terms of three to five years with no right of termination for convenience.

Predecessor Detail - Name changed from D2L Holdings Inc., June 20, 2014.

Directors - John Baker, chr. & CEO, Ont.; John (Ian) Giffen†, Toronto, Ont.; Tim Connor, Calif.; Robert G. (Bob) Courteau, Toronto, Ont.; Tracy Edkins, B.C.; The Rt. Hon. David L. Johnston, Ashton, Ont.; Heather Zynczak, Utah

Other Exec. Officers - Stephen Laster, pres.; Josh Huff, CFO; Puneet Arora, chief revenue officer; Jeremy Auger, chief strategy officer; Anna Forgione, chief legal officer; Nicolas (Nick) Oddson, chief tech. officer; Jennifer Ogden-Reese, chief mktg. officer; Yvonne Bell, sr. v-p, people & culture; Mudit Garg, sr. v-p, rev.; Elliot Gowans, sr. v-p, intl.; Adam Moore, sr. v-p, strategic accounts; Christian Pantel, sr. v-p, user experience design & product devel.; Al Patel, sr. v-p, professional srvcs. & support; Lee Poteck, sr. v-p, sales & customer success; Ira Stuchberry, sr. v-p & deputy gen. counsel; Rajesh Talpade, sr. v-p, product mgt.

† Lead director

Capital Stock

	Authorized (shs.)	Outstanding (shs.)[1]
Multiple Vtg.	unlimited	27,390,588
Subordinate Vtg.	unlimited	25,908,112

[1] At Apr. 26, 2023

Multiple Voting - All held by the company's founder, chair and CEO John Baker. Convertible into subordinate voting shares on a one-for-one basis at any time at the option of the holder and automatically in certain other circumstances. Ten votes per share.

Subordinate Voting - One vote per share.

Major Shareholder - John Baker held 91.52% interest at Apr. 26, 2023.

Price Range - DTOL/TSX

Year	Volume	High	Low	Close
2022	4,577,337	$15.88	$5.08	$6.48
2021	3,432,523	$17.20	$11.66	$13.75

Recent Close: $7.96

Capital Stock Changes - During fiscal 2023, subordinate voting shares were issued as follows: 120,224 on exercise of options and 113,804 on settlement of restricted share units.

Wholly Owned Subsidiaries

D2L Commerce Inc.
D2L Corporation, Kitchener, Ont.
- 100% int. in **D2L Asia Pte. Ltd.**, Singapore.
- 100% int. in **D2L Australia Pty Ltd.**, Vic., Australia.
- 100% int. in **D2L Brasil Soluções de Tecnologia para Educação Ltda.**, Brazil.
- 100% int. in **D2L Europe Ltd.**, United Kingdom.
  - 100% int. in **D2L EU B.V.**, Netherlands.
- 100% int. in **D2L Ltd.**, Md.

Desire2Learn LLC

Financial Statistics

Periods ended:	12m Jan. 31/23[A]		12m Jan. 31/22[A]
	US$000s	%Chg	US$000s
Operating revenue	**168,396**	**+11**	**151,880**
Cost of sales	60,626		63,933
Research & devel. expense	43,068		46,599
General & admin expense	76,386		112,562
Operating expense	**179,716**	**-19**	**223,095**
Operating income	**(11,320)**	**n.a.**	**(71,215)**
Deprec., depl. & amort.	4,244		3,499
Finance income	1,336		170
Finance costs, gross	716		295
Write-downs/write-offs	(4,474)		nil
Pre-tax income	**(17,943)**	**n.a.**	**(97,817)**
Income taxes	434		(164)
Net income	**(18,377)**	**n.a.**	**(97,653)**
Cash & equivalent	110,732		114,675
Accounts receivable	20,895		26,156
Current assets	146,404		154,726
Fixed assets, net	4,287		2,324
Right-of-use assets	11,205		1,323
Intangibles, net	7,359		13,012
Total assets	**176,610**	**-1**	**179,213**
Accts. pay. & accr. liabs	23,451		24,340
Current liabilities	110,241		111,720
Long-term lease liabilities	11,879		694
Shareholders' equity	54,091		66,380
Cash from oper. activs	**3,779**	**n.m.**	**112**
Cash from fin. activs	(1,630)		79,078
Cash from invest. activs	(3,672)		(10,215)
Net cash position	**110,732**	**-3**	**114,675**
Capital expenditures	(3,672)		(796)
	US$		US$
Earnings per share*	(0.35)		(2.88)
Cash flow per share*	0.07		0.00
	shs		shs
No. of shs. o/s*	53,146,530		52,912,502
Avg. no. of shs. o/s*	53,029,605		33,918,112
	%		%
Net profit margin	(10.91)		(64.30)
Return on equity	(30.51)		n.m.
Return on assets	(9.92)		(73.50)
Foreign sales percent	75		73
No. of employees (FTEs)	n.a.		1,100

* S.V. & M.V.
[A] Reported in accordance with IFRS

Historical Summary
(as originally stated)

Fiscal Year	Oper. Rev.	Net Inc. Bef. Disc.	EPS*
	US$000s	US$000s	US$
2023[A]	168,396	(18,377)	(0.35)
2022[A]	151,880	(97,653)	(2.88)
2021[A]	126,372	(41,496)	(1.57)
2020[A]	109,485	(5,718)	(0.22)

* S.V. & M.V.
[A] Reported in accordance with IFRS

D.3 DATA Communications Management Corp.

Symbol - DCM **Exchange** - TSX **CUSIP** - 23761M
Head Office - 9195 Torbram Rd, Brampton, ON, L6S 6H2 **Telephone** - (905) 791-3151 **Toll-free** - (800) 268-0128 **Fax** - (905) 791-3277
Website - www.datacm.com
Email - jlorimer@datacm.com
Investor Relations - James E. Lorimer (905) 791-3151 ext. 4101
Auditors - PricewaterhouseCoopers LLP C.A., Toronto, Ont.
Lawyers - McCarthy Tétrault LLP, Toronto, Ont.
Transfer Agents - Computershare Trust Company of Canada Inc., Toronto, Ont.
FP500 Revenue Ranking - 585
Employees - 910 at Mar. 1, 2023
Profile - (Ont. 2011) Provides printing, marketing and communications products and services to a diversified client base including financial services, retail, healthcare, energy and the public sector.

Products and services include technology-enabled **Workflow Management Solutions**, which help clients manage the complexity of their marketing and communications workflows through its DCMFlex workflow management, multimedia campaign management (MCM), regulatory communications, and retail campaign management platforms; **Digital Asset Management Solutions**, which allow users to store, locate, and share digital brand assets as part of their overall marketing workflow process through its ASMBL platform; **Personalized Video Platform**, which is an end-to-end solution for personalized video content production which delivers and executes personalized messaging; **Marketing, Strategy and Creative Services Solutions**, which includes marketing and brand strategy, creative, online and offline marketing communications, packaging design, marketing campaign execution, and environmental design; and **Print and Communications Management Solutions**, which include commercial print, business cards, letterheads, and envelopes, business forms, custom Point-of-Sale (POS) transaction rolls, direct mail services, e-forms and e-presentment, personalized email, finishing (binding, cutting, folding and lamination), gift and loyalty cards, kitting and delivery services, primary/marketing labels, lottery rolls and selection slips, secure print products, variable print and personalization, and wide/large/grand format products. Also offers support services which include analytics, barcode and radio frequency identification (RFID) solutions, outsourced program management, and resale of product/services from third party to the company's clients.

Key operations are located in Drummondville, Que.; Toronto, Burlington and Brampton, Ont.; and Calgary, Alta. Small specialty manufacturing/warehousing facilities are located in Niles, Ill. In addition, the company manages three on-demand digital print centres located across Canada. At Mar. 1, 2023, the company had 14 leased facilities located across Canada and in Illinois, for manufacturing/warehousing, on-demand digital print centres as well as sales/administrative and creative services offices.

Has 40 trademark registrations in Canada; 13 trademark applications; eight patent registrations; and two copyrighted works on which security interests have been registered. Also has two trademark registrations, 11 trademark applications and one patent registration in the U.S.

Recent Merger and Acquisition Activity

Status: completed **Revised:** June 8, 2023
UPDATE: The transaction was completed. PREVIOUS: DATA Communications Management Corp. entered into the agreement for the sale and lease-back of an RR Donnelley Canada site in Oshawa, Ont., for net proceeds of $23,000,000. The transaction was expected to close before the end of the second quarter of 2023.

Status: completed **Revised:** Apr. 25, 2023
UPDATE: The transaction was completed. PREVIOUS: DATA Communications Management Corp. (DCM) agreed to acquire Moore Canada Corporation (dba RR Donnelley Canada), the Canadian operations of R.R. Donnelley & Sons Company, for a total cash purchase price of $123,000,000, subject to working capital and other customary post-closing adjustments. RRD Canada provides print and related services to thousands of customers across Canada, including financial institutions, retailers, insurance providers, transportation companies, government organizations and other regulated industries. RRD Canada generated revenue of $250,000,000 in 2022 and has 1,000 employees. Included in the purchase price, DCM would acquire three sites currently owned by RRD Canada at an implied net value of $30,000,000 and plans to enter into a sale and lease-back arrangement for each site. The transaction was expected to close in the second quarter of 2023. Mar. 29, 2023 - DCM received a "no-action letter" indicating the Commissioner of Competition does not intend to challenge DCM's acquisition of the Canadian operations of R.R. Donnelley & Sons Company.

Predecessor Detail - Name changed from DATA Group Ltd., July 4, 2016; basis 1 new for 100 old shs.

Directors - J. R. Kingsley Ward, chr., Toronto, Ont.; Gregory J. (Greg) Cochrane, v-chr., Toronto, Ont.; Richard C. Kellam, pres. & CEO, Toronto, Ont.; Merri L. Jones, Toronto, Ont.; James J. Murray, Toronto, Ont.; Michael G. Sifton, Ont.; Alison Simpson, Toronto, Ont.; Derek J. Watchorn, King City, Ont.

Exec. Officers - James E. Lorimer, CFO & corp. sec.; Rael Fisher, chief integration officer; Shelly Anwyll, sr. v-p, North America, emerging markets; Steve Livingstone, sr. v-p, digital; Sharad Verma, sr. v-p, strategy; Patrick Aussant, v-p, IT opers.; Christine Custodio, v-p, opers.; Barbara Franovic-Wilkins, v-p, mktg.; Geneviéve Gravel, v-p, people & culture; Asem Moqbel, v-p, procurement; Karen Redfern, v-p, cust. tech. solutions; Jason Sharpe, v-p, comml. acceleration

Capital Stock

	Authorized (shs.)	Outstanding (shs.)[1]
Common	unlimited	45,710,988

[1] At May 10, 2023

Major Shareholder - KST Industries Inc. held 11.3% interest at May 10, 2023.

Price Range - DCM/TSX

Year	Volume	High	Low	Close
2022	8,223,590	$1.51	$1.01	$1.45
2021	21,930,702	$1.51	$0.55	$1.28
2020	13,263,812	$0.82	$0.09	$0.63
2019	6,864,577	$1.60	$0.22	$0.24
2018	6,215,680	$2.02	$1.04	$1.33

Recent Close: $3.04

Capital Stock Changes - In May 2023, private placement of 8,333,333 common shares was arranged at $3.00 per share. Agents hold an option to sell up to an additional 1,666,666 shares.

There were no changes to capital stock during 2022.

Wholly Owned Subsidiaries

DATA Communications Management (US) Corp., Del.
Moore Canada Corporation, Mississauga, Ont.

Financial Statistics

Periods ended:	12m Dec. 31/22[A]		12m Dec. 31/21[oA]
	$000s	%Chg	$000s
Operating revenue	**273,804**	**+16**	**235,331**
Cost of sales	132,871		108,210
Salaries & benefits	91,040		86,691
Research & devel. expense	1,015		nil
General & admin expense	10,644		11,709
Operating expense	**235,570**	**+14**	**206,610**
Operating income	**38,234**	**+33**	**28,721**
Deprec., depl. & amort.	11,160		15,143
Finance costs, gross	5,309		7,253
Pre-tax income	**19,895**	**+652**	**2,644**
Income taxes	5,929		1,079
Net income	**13,966**	**+792**	**1,565**
Cash & equivalent	4,208		901
Inventories	20,220		12,133
Accounts receivable	54,630		51,567
Current assets	82,057		68,041
Fixed assets, net	6,779		8,416
Right-of-use assets	33,505		33,476
Intangibles, net	19,480		21,015
Total assets	**149,481**	**+7**	**140,084**
Accts. pay. & accr. liabs	44,133		37,589
Current liabilities	69,479		62,845
Long-term debt, gross	27,047		36,299
Long-term debt, net	15,380		24,556
Long-term lease liabilities	33,011		32,976
Shareholders' equity	22,847		8,041
Cash from oper. activs	**22,675**	**-16**	**26,945**
Cash from fin. activs	(17,931)		(23,413)
Cash from invest. activs	(1,476)		(3,222)
Net cash position	**4,208**	**+367**	**901**
Capital expenditures	(1,475)		(1,832)
Capital disposals	70		nil
Unfunded pension liability	3,705		4,968
	$		$
Earnings per share*	0.32		0.04
Cash flow per share*	0.51		0.61
	shs		shs
No. of shs. o/s*	44,062,831		44,062,831
Avg. no. of shs. o/s*	44,062,831		43,993,494
	%		%
Net profit margin	5.10		0.67
Return on equity	90.43		17.39
Return on assets	12.22		3.85
No. of employees (FTEs)	910		925

* Common
[o] Restated
[A] Reported in accordance with IFRS

Latest Results

Periods ended:	3m Mar. 31/23[A]		3m Mar. 31/22[A]
	$000s	%Chg	$000s
Operating revenue	76,077	+10	69,257
Net income	(2,431)	n.a.	3,713
	$		$
Earnings per share*	(0.06)		0.08

* Common
[A] Reported in accordance with IFRS

Historical Summary
(as originally stated)

Fiscal Year	Oper. Rev.	Net Inc. Bef. Disc.	EPS*
	$000s	$000s	$
2022[A]	273,804	13,966	0.32
2021[A]	235,331	1,565	0.04
2020[A]	259,314	11,506	0.27
2019[A]	282,876	(13,987)	(0.65)
2018[A]	322,769	2,249	0.11

* Common
[A] Reported in accordance with IFRS

D.4 DAVIDsTEA INC.

Symbol - DTEA **Exchange** - TSX-VEN **CUSIP** - 238661
Head Office - 5430 rue Ferrier, Mount Royal, QC, H4P 1M2 **Telephone** - (514) 739-0006 **Toll-free** - (888) 873-0006 **Fax** - (514) 739-0200
Website - www.davidstea.com
Email - f.zitella@davidstea.com
Investor Relations - Frank Zitella (514) 739-0006
Auditors - Ernst & Young LLP C.A., Montréal, Qué.
Transfer Agents - American Stock Transfer & Trust Company, LLC, New York, N.Y.; TSX Trust Company
FP500 Revenue Ranking - 790
Employees - 124 at Apr. 28, 2023
Profile - (Can. 2008) Retails a specialty branded selection of proprietary loose-leaf teas, pre-packaged teas, tea sachets, and tea-related gifts and accessories through its website, the Amazon

Marketplace, wholesale customers including more than 3,800 grocery stores and pharmacies, and 18 company-owned mall-based stores and one kiosk in Canada.

Offers different flavours of loose-leaf tea spanning eight different tea categories: white, green, oolong, black, pu'erh, mate, rooibos and herbal tea. The company works with vendors who source ingredients for the company's teas and tea blends from all over the world, including the People's Republic of China, South Korea, Japan, Taiwan, Vietnam, India, Nepal, Kenya, Sri Lanka, South Africa and Thailand. The company's tea merchandise is sourced from a number of suppliers who manufactures the company's unique and proprietary designs. Tea-related gifts offered include special edition seasonal and holiday gift packages, as well as novelty themed gifts that continue to innovate with new themes, seasonal collections and visually-appealing gift boxes. Tea accessories offered include tea mugs, travel mugs, teacup sets, teapots, tea makers, kettles, infusers, filters, frothers, tins and spoons. On-the-go craft tea beverages are also offered in the company's retail stores.

The company also has agreement with **Loblaw Companies Limited** which allows select products of the company to be available in more than 1,250 Loblaw grocery and pharmacy storefronts across Canada, thereby enhancing its offering in communities across the Atlantic provinces, Ontario, Manitoba, Saskatchewan, Alberta and British Columbia, with new products available in Real Canadian Superstore® and Atlantic Superstore® locations.

Finished goods are assembled in a production and assembly facility in Montreal, Que. Products are distributed from distribution centres in Sherbrooke, Que., that ships to Canadian customers, and Champlain, N.Y., that ships to U.S. customers.

Common delisted from NASDAQ, Apr. 17, 2023.

Common listed on TSX-VEN, Apr. 3, 2023.

Directors - Jane Silverstone Segal, chr., Montréal, Qué.; Sarah Segal, CEO & chief brand officer, Montréal, Qué.; Pat De Marco†, Montréal, Qué.; Susan L. Burkman, Bromont, Qué.; Peter Robinson, Mayne Island, B.C.

Other Exec. Officers - Frank Zitella, pres., COO, CFO & corp. sec.; Laura Wordingham, head, tea & mdsg.; Joe Bongiorno, v-p, fin.

† Lead director

Capital Stock

	Authorized (shs.)	Outstanding (shs.)[1]
Common	unlimited	26,624,108

[1] At May 1, 2023

Major Shareholder - Herschel H. Segal held 45.1% interest and DOMO Capital Management, LLC held 11.4% interest at May 1, 2023.

Price Range - DTEA/NASDAQ (D)

Year	Volume	High	Low	Close
2022	1,768,700	US$3.85	US$0.65	US$0.79
2021	14,898,813	US$7.43	US$2.14	US$3.10
2020	12,381,711	US$3.25	US$0.32	US$2.41
2019	8,277,140	US$2.30	US$1.12	US$1.46
2018	19,486,017	US$5.30	US$1.08	US$1.18

Recent Close: $0.50

Capital Stock Changes - During the 52-week ended Jan. 28, 2023, 199,351 common shares were issued under restricted share unit plan.

Wholly Owned Subsidiaries

DAVIDsTEA (USA) Inc., Del.

Financial Statistics

Periods ended:	52w Jan. 28/23[A]		52w Jan. 29/22[◻A]
	$000s	%Chg	$000s
Operating revenue	**83,026**	**-20**	**104,073**
Cost of sales	52,262		60,871
Salaries & benefits	14,117		10,222
General & admin expense	25,777		26,978
Stock-based compensation	1,413		1,405
Operating expense	**93,569**	**-6**	**99,476**
Operating income	**(10,543)**	**n.a.**	**4,597**
Deprec., depl. & amort.	3,495		4,318
Finance income	414		143
Finance costs, gross	730		152
Write-downs/write-offs	257		nil
Pre-tax income	**(14,868)**	**n.a.**	**77,127**
Income taxes	nil		(1,000)
Net income	**(14,868)**	**n.a.**	**78,127**
Cash & equivalent	22,440		25,107
Inventories	19,522		31,048
Accounts receivable	3,258		3,209
Current assets	51,059		63,506
Fixed assets, net	510		775
Right-of-use assets	9,345		12,087
Intangibles, net	1,679		2,234
Total assets	**62,593**	**-20**	**78,602**
Accts. pay. & accr. liabs	12,310		12,300
Current liabilities	20,216		20,098
Long-term lease liabilities	7,682		10,189
Shareholders' equity	34,695		48,315
Cash from oper. activs	**488**	**n.a.**	**(4,241)**
Cash from fin. activs	(3,026)		(797)
Cash from invest. activs	(129)		(52)
Net cash position	**22,440**	**-11**	**25,107**
Capital expenditures	(129)		(52)
	$		$
Earnings per share*	(0.56)		2.97
Cash flow per share*	0.02		(0.16)
	shs		shs
No. of shs. o/s*	26,623,068		26,423,717
Avg. no. of shs. o/s*	26,530,443		26,323,469
	%		%
Net profit margin	(17.91)		75.07
Return on equity	(35.82)		n.m.
Return on assets	(20.03)		97.95
Foreign sales percent	18		21
No. of employees (FTEs)	159		204

* Common

◻ Restated

[A] Reported in accordance with IFRS

Historical Summary
(as originally stated)

Fiscal Year	Oper. Rev.	Net Inc. Bef. Disc.	EPS*
	$000s	$000s	$
2023[A]	83,026	(14,868)	(0.56)
2022[A]	104,073	78,127	2.97
2021[A]	121,686	(55,932)	(2.14)
2020[A]	196,462	(31,197)	(1.20)
2019[A]	212,753	(33,539)	(1.29)

* Common

[A] Reported in accordance with IFRS

D.5 DGL Investments No.1 Inc.

Symbol - DGL.P **Exchange** - TSX-VEN **CUSIP** - 25240Y

Head Office - 480-1500 Georgia St W, Vancouver, BC, V6G 2Z6 **Telephone** - (604) 684-4535 **Fax** - (888) 829-4124

Email - gsangha2x4@hotmail.com

Investor Relations - Gurpreet S. Sangha (778) 245-2282

Auditors - Davidson & Company LLP C.A., Vancouver, B.C.

Transfer Agents - Computershare Trust Company of Canada Inc., Vancouver, B.C.

Profile - (B.C. 2021) Capital Pool Company.

Directors - Gurpreet S. Sangha, pres. & CEO, Surrey, B.C.; Alnesh P. Mohan, CFO, Vancouver, B.C.; Larry K. Doan, Vancouver, B.C.; Luis H. Goyzeuta, Spain

Other Exec. Officers - David W. Smalley, corp. sec.

Capital Stock

	Authorized (shs.)	Outstanding (shs.)[1]
Common	unlimited	5,000,000

[1] At Feb. 22, 2022

Major Shareholder - Luis H. Goyzeuta held 12% interest, Alnesh P. Mohan held 12% interest and Gurpreet S. Sangha held 12% interest at Aug. 26, 2021.

Price Range - DGL.P/TSX-VEN

Year	Volume	High	Low	Close
2022	40,400	$0.11	$0.06	$0.07
2021	10,000	$0.12	$0.12	$0.12

Recent Close: $0.12

D.6 DGTL Holdings Inc.

Symbol - DGTL **Exchange** - TSX-VEN **CUSIP** - 23343T

Head Office - 801-1 Adelaide St E, Toronto, ON, M5C 2V9 **Toll-free** - (877) 879-3485

Website - dgtlinc.com

Email - john@consciencecapitalcorp.com

Investor Relations - John-David A. Belfontaine (877) 879-3485

Auditors - Zeifmans LLP C.A., Toronto, Ont.

Lawyers - Garfinkle Biderman LLP, Toronto, Ont.

Transfer Agents - Computershare Trust Company of Canada Inc.

Profile - (Can. 2018) Acquires and accelerates transformative digital media, marketing and advertising software technologies, powered by artificial intelligence. Also provides micro-influencer marketing for brands of all sizes and across all industries through a proprietary software-as-a-service (SaaS)/content-as-a service platform.

The company specializes in accelerating commercialized enterprise level SaaS companies in the sectors of content, analytics and distribution via a range of unique capitalization structures including investment, mergers and acquisitions, earnouts and licensing structures. The company is targeting social media, gaming and streaming technologies for mergers and acquisitions and licensing.

Wholly owned **Engagement Labs Inc.** provides intelligent data, insights and recommendations to marketers and organizations through its proprietary TotalSocial® platform. TotalSocial® combines online (social media) and offline (word of mouth) data for its predictive analytics engine, which uses proprietary algorithms and artificial intelligence/machine learning, to forecast future sales and provide marketers with better insights, improved marketing return on investment and increased sales.

In addition, the company offers a content management system built on proprietary artificial intelligence and machine learning technology through its Total Influence platform. The Total Influence platform provides an end-to-end social influence marketing solution to brands and agencies by generating data and analytics, searching for appropriate creators, managing content process and campaigns and reporting results and recommendations. The company serves numerous global brands including DraftKings, Publicis Groupe, Budweiser, Stella Artois, Veritone, Shein, Hoegaarden, ExpressVPN, Mitsubishi Motors, Montejo, Doordash, Syneos Health, Michelob Ultra and Patagonia.

In July 2022, the company commenced the wind down and dissolution of wholly owned **Hashoff LLC**, which offered a content management system built on proprietary artificial intelligence and machine learning technology.

Recent Merger and Acquisition Activity

Status: completed **Revised:** Mar. 2, 2022

UPDATE: The transaction was completed. PREVIOUS: DGTL Holdings Inc. agreed to acquire Engagement Labs Inc. on the basis of 0.1136 DGTL common shares for each Engagement Labs share held, which would result in the issuance of 5,320,000 DGTL common shares. Engagement Labs provides intelligent data, insights and recommendations to marketers and organizations through its proprietary TotalSocial® platform. The boards of directors of both companies unanimously approved the transaction, which was expected to be completed in early 2022. Feb. 14, 2022 - Engagement Labs shareholders approved the transaction.

Predecessor Detail - Name changed from Conscience Capital Inc., July 30, 2020, pursuant to Qualifying Transaction reverse takeover of Hashoff LLC.

Directors - John-David A. Belfontaine, chr. & CEO, Toronto, Ont.; David M. Beck, Toronto, Ont.; George Kovalyov, Richmond, B.C.

Other Exec. Officers - Christopher (Chris) Foster, CFO; Steven M. Brown, chief comml. officer; Tom Jessiman, co-CEO, Hashoff LLC; Joel Wright, co-CEO, Hashoff LLC

Capital Stock

	Authorized (shs.)	Outstanding (shs.)[1]
Class A Preferred	unlimited	4,178,100
Common	unlimited	45,242,266

[1] At Oct. 28, 2022

Class A Preferred - Entitled to cumulative dividends of 4% per annum. Convertible into common shares on a one-for-one basis, subject to adjustment, until April 2025. Redeemable at any time, at the company's option, at Cdn$0.70 per share plus accrued and unpaid dividends. Non-voting.

Common - One vote per share.

Major Shareholder - John-David A. Belfontaine held 11.49% interest at Oct. 14, 2022.

Price Range - DGTL/TSX-VEN

Year	Volume	High	Low	Close
2022	10,705,606	$0.25	$0.04	$0.04
2021	27,596,450	$1.03	$0.15	$0.22
2020	11,567,996	$0.64	$0.18	$0.62
2019	808,000	$0.20	$0.10	$0.10

Recent Close: $0.02

Capital Stock Changes - In March 2022, 5,419,173 common shares were issued on acquisition of Engagement Labs Inc. Also during fiscal 2022, common shares were issued as follows: 2,130,826 on conversion of a like number of class A preferred shares, 280,000 for services and 158,385 on exercise of options; 34,091 common shares were cancelled.

Wholly Owned Subsidiaries

Engagement Labs Inc., Toronto, Ont.

Engagement Labs Ltd., United Kingdom.

Engagement Labs Services Inc., Ont.

Hashoff LLC, New York, N.Y.
Keller Fay Group LLC, N.J.

Financial Statistics

Periods ended:	12m May 31/22[A]		12m May 31/21[A]
	$000s	%Chg	$000s
Operating revenue	**2,515**	**-37**	**3,977**
Cost of sales	1,605		2,907
Salaries & benefits	970		1,476
General & admin expense	1,994		2,518
Stock-based compensation	nil		1,178
Operating expense	**4,569**	**-43**	**8,078**
Operating income	**(2,054)**	**n.a.**	**(4,101)**
Deprec., depl. & amort.	759		713
Finance income	182		172
Finance costs, gross	89		107
Write-downs/write-offs	(3,091)		(3,708)
Pre-tax income	**(4,929)**	**n.a.**	**(7,264)**
Income taxes	(438)		(439)
Net income	**(4,491)**	**n.a.**	**(6,825)**
Cash & equivalent	1,411		1,111
Accounts receivable	624		468
Current assets	2,627		2,465
Fixed assets, net	10		7
Intangibles, net	1,880		3,701
Total assets	**4,517**	**-27**	**6,172**
Accts. pay. & accr. liabs.	2,219		1,510
Current liabilities	3,175		2,036
Long-term debt, gross	1,276		171
Long-term debt, net	1,276		104
Preferred share equity	1,964		2,965
Shareholders' equity	(188)		3,103
Cash from oper. activs.	**(1,163)**	**n.a.**	**(2,419)**
Cash from fin. activs.	1,020		2,761
Cash from invest. activs.	478		(320)
Net cash position	**1,411**	**+27**	**1,111**
Capital expenditures	(174)		(5)
	$		$
Earnings per share*	(0.11)		(0.23)
Cash flow per share*	(0.03)		(0.01)
	shs		shs
No. of shs. o/s*	45,242,266		37,287,973
Avg. no. of shs. o/s*	40,425,022		29,816,520
	%		%
Net profit margin	(178.57)		(171.61)
Return on equity	n.m.		(386.14)
Return on assets	(82.51)		(83.58)
Foreign sales percent	76		100

* Common
[A] Reported in accordance with IFRS

Latest Results

Periods ended:	3m Aug. 31/22[A]		3m Aug. 31/21[A]
	$000s	%Chg	$000s
Operating revenue	490	-13	566
Net income	(33)	n.a.	(511)
	$		$
Earnings per share*	(0.00)		(0.01)

* Common
[A] Reported in accordance with IFRS

Historical Summary
(as originally stated)

Fiscal Year	Oper. Rev.	Net Inc. Bef. Disc.	EPS*
	$000s	$000s	$
2022[A]	2,515	(4,491)	(0.11)
2021[A]	3,977	(6,825)	(0.23)
2020[A]	503	(643)	(0.03)

* Common
[A] Reported in accordance with IFRS

D.7 DIRTT Environmental Solutions Ltd.

Symbol - DRT **Exchange** - TSX **CUSIP** - 25490H
Head Office - 7303 30 St SE, Calgary, AB, T2C 1N6 **Telephone** - (403) 723-5000 **Toll-free** - (800) 605-6707 **Fax** - (403) 723-6644
Website - www.dirtt.net
Email - nsomayaji@dirtt.net
Investor Relations - Nandini Somayaji (403) 671-7152
Auditors - PricewaterhouseCoopers LLP C.A., Calgary, Alta.
Lawyers - Torys LLP
Transfer Agents - Computershare Trust Company of Canada Inc.
FP500 Revenue Ranking - 633
Employees - 922 at Dec. 31, 2022
Profile - (Alta. 2003) Provides industrialized construction solutions for interior spaces using its system of physical products and digital tools that enables organizations, together with construction and design leaders, to build high-performing and adaptable interior environments.

Operating in the workplace, healthcare, education and public sector markets, the company's system provides total design freedom, and greater certainty in cost, schedule and outcomes.

The company's proprietary design integration software, ICE®, translates the vision of architects and designers into a 3D model that also acts as manufacturing information. ICE is also licensed to unrelated companies and construction partners of the company. The software serves as the engine for the company's industrialized construction system which enables solutions to be designed, visualized, organized, configured, priced and manufactured off-site, with final assembly and installation completed at the job site.

Interior DIRTT solutions offered are solid walls, which include extensive options with 4", 6", and 2" furring wall offerings that connect seamlessly to other products in the construction system and enable unique finishes, colours and configurations; glass walls, which are available as double pane, classic center-mount or Inspire™ profiles that accommodate base building variance and acoustic requirements; combination walls, which can be combined for a mix of privacy and transparency, and customized and configured to fit any design; Leaf Folding Walls®, the retractable modular wall system which adds functionality with an effortless solution to quickly adapt space, and customize dimensions and finishes; headwalls, the modular, multi-trade healthcare headwall system which is an efficient, adaptable approach to healthcare construction, and can be customized to meet unique healthcare compliance requirements; doors, which include swing doors, sliding doors and pivot doors, that integrate seamlessly with solid and glass wall assemblies, and meet smoke-rating and acoustic requirements; casework, which offers custom cabinets, closets and storage solutions with consistent quality and efficient installation, as well as precision-manufactured casework which is delivered with predictable lead times; timber, a traditional craftsmanship which meets advanced, custom manufacturing to create striking designs and structural elements, and can be integrated with broader scopes to bring natural elements to spaces with rapid assembly on-site; modular electrical system (pre-wired distribution system), including pre-mounted and terminated device boxes installed at the factory to reduce project time and cost on-site, which supports connected infrastructure needs and has plug-in connections that allow quick installations and easy modifications; fibre to the edge networks, which deliver unlimited bandwidth capability and longer-reaching signal strength while reducing supporting infrastructure needs and material costs; and Access floors (low-profile, fixed-height), which provides an adaptable foundation for connected infrastructure with long-term accessibility for easy moves, additions and changes. The company's system also enables integrations with technology, custom graphics, writable surfaces and Breathe® Living Walls.

At Dec. 31, 2022, the company had 67 construction partners and 46 sales representatives across North America. In addition, the company also has four company-operated DIRTT Experience Center (DXC) across North America. Construction partners were required to invest in their own DXC's to effectively showcase DIRTT solutions.

Clients range from small owner-managed businesses to large multi-national companies in a variety of industries including healthcare, education, financial services, government and military, manufacturing, non-profit, energy, professional services, retail, technology and hospitality.

Manufacturing facilities are located in Calgary, Alta.; Rock Hill, S.C.; and Savannah, Ga. The company has temporarily suspended operations at the Rock Hill facility, shifting related manufacturing to its Calgary facility.

During 2022, the company discontinued the Reflect wall product line. In April 2022, the company has completed the closing of its manufacturing facility in Phoenix, Ariz., which includes the transfer of certain manufacturing equipment to its facilities in Calgary, Alta., and Rockhill, S.C.

Directors - Kenneth D. Sanders, chr., San Francisco, Calif.; Benjamin Urban, CEO, Calgary, Alta.; Douglas A. Edwards, Charlotte, N.C.; Aron A. English, Seattle, Wash.; Shaun Noll, Menlo Park, Calif.; Scott L. Robinson, New York, N.Y.; Scott C. Ryan, Phoenix, Ariz.

Other Exec. Officers - Richard Hunter, COO; Fareeha Khan, CFO; Mark Greffen, chief tech. officer; Nandini Somayaji, sr. v-p, talent, gen. counsel & corp. sec.

Capital Stock

	Authorized (shs.)	Outstanding (shs.)[1]
Preferred	unlimited	
Common	unlimited	98,750,453

[1] At Apr. 10, 2023

Major Shareholder - 22NW Fund, L.P. held 19.5% interest and 726 BC LLC held 18.3% interest at Apr. 10, 2023.

Price Range - DRT/TSX

Year	Volume	High	Low	Close
2022	18,308,186	$2.95	$0.34	$0.69
2021	27,334,801	$5.99	$2.09	$2.75
2020	51,143,746	$4.45	$1.02	$3.11
2019	33,458,117	$9.30	$3.97	$4.25
2018	56,832,337	$7.29	$4.39	$6.11

Recent Close: $0.40

Capital Stock Changes - In November 2022, private placement of 8,667,449 common shares was completed at US$0.32 per share. Also during 2022, common shares were issued as follows: 2,995,045 on vesting of restricted share units, 720,901 under employee share purchase plan and 154,016 as share-based compensation.

Wholly Owned Subsidiaries

DIRTT Environmental Solutions, Inc., Colo.

Financial Statistics

Periods ended:	12m Dec. 31/22[A]		12m Dec. 31/21[A]
	US$000s	%Chg	US$000s
Operating revenue	**172,161**	**+17**	**147,593**
Cost of sales	128,882		109,620
General & admin expense	52,412		61,636
Stock-based compensation	4,277		4,713
Other operating expense	30,514		17,606
Operating expense	**216,085**	**+12**	**193,575**
Operating income	**(43,924)**	**n.a.**	**(45,982)**
Deprec., depl. & amort.	15,119		14,513
Finance income	51		77
Finance costs, gross	5,160		3,131
Write-downs/write-offs	nil		(1,443)
Pre-tax income	**(54,942)**	**n.a.**	**(53,872)**
Income taxes	21		(204)
Net income	**(54,963)**	**n.a.**	**(53,668)**
Cash & equivalent	10,821		60,313
Inventories	22,251		18,457
Accounts receivable	21,810		17,540
Current assets	62,125		103,804
Fixed assets, net	41,522		51,697
Right-of-use assets	30,490		30,880
Intangibles, net	4,406		7,395
Total assets	**143,653**	**-28**	**199,439**
Accts. pay. & accr. liabs.	19,881		22,751
Current liabilities	35,998		37,087
Long-term debt, gross	65,435		70,642
Long-term debt, net	62,129		67,319
Long-term lease liabilities	27,534		27,267
Shareholders' equity	17,992		67,766
Cash from oper. activs.	**(44,260)**	**n.a.**	**(31,210)**
Cash from fin. activs.	(874)		62,452
Cash from invest. activs.	(4,024)		(14,138)
Net cash position	**14,239**	**-78**	**63,408**
Capital expenditures	(2,394)		(11,781)
Capital disposals	227		18
	US$		US$
Earnings per share*	(0.63)		(0.63)
Cash flow per share*	(0.50)		(0.37)
	shs		shs
No. of shs. o/s*	97,882,844		85,345,433
Avg. no. of shs. o/s*	87,662,000		85,027,000
	%		%
Net profit margin	(31.93)		(36.36)
Return on equity	(128.18)		(58.24)
Return on assets	(29.03)		(26.43)
Foreign sales percent	85		88
No. of employees (FTEs)	922		989

* Common
[A] Reported in accordance with U.S. GAAP

Historical Summary
(as originally stated)

Fiscal Year	Oper. Rev.	Net Inc. Bef. Disc.	EPS*
	US$000s	US$000s	US$
2022[A]	172,161	(54,963)	(0.63)
2021[A]	147,593	(53,668)	(0.63)
2020[A]	171,507	(11,298)	(0.13)
2019[A]	247,735	(4,396)	(0.05)
	$000s	$000s	$
2018[B]	356,679	2,997	0.04

* Common
[A] Reported in accordance with U.S. GAAP
[B] Reported in accordance with IFRS

D.8 DLC Holdings Corp.

Symbol - DLC **Exchange** - TSX-VEN **CUSIP** - 255884
Head Office - 1600-609 Granville St, Vancouver, BC, V7Y 1C3 **Telephone** - (604) 669-1322 **Fax** - (604) 669-3877
Email - mp@desmondandcompany.com
Investor Relations - Mark Pajak (604) 669-1322
Auditors - Davidson & Company LLP C.A., Vancouver, B.C.
Transfer Agents - Computershare Trust Company of Canada Inc.
Profile - (B.C. 2011) Invests in agricultural land and in the food processing industry focusing on acquiring and operating real assets in partnership with local family owned operators and entrepreneurs.

Wholly owned **Superior Macadamias (Pty) Ltd.** processes and distributes macadamia nuts sourced from local farmers in South Africa and sells their product to the international markets. Operations are conducted from a plant in White River, South Africa, with a processing capacity of 1,800 tonnes of wet nut in shell (WNS).

Wholly owned **Craven House Industries Ltd.** has sole ownership rights for four adjacent properties, totaling 500 hectares, in Bahia, Brazil with a total of 7.5 km of ocean and water frontage which has no operations. Also owns a plot of development land in Salta, Argentina.

Subsidiary **Ceniako Ltd.** has sole ownership rights for five adjacent properties, totaling 2,000 hectares, in Bahia, Brazil with a total of 2 km of ocean frontage which has no operations. The company plans to find a joint venture partner for which it would provide the land for cultivation and the partner would bear the cost of plantation and cultivation or lease the land to an agricultural company in exchange for rent and a percentage of the profits from the cultivation of the land.

Predecessor Detail - Name changed from Desmond Investments Ltd., Feb. 7, 2017.

Directors - Mark Pajak, pres., CEO & corp. sec., London, Middx., United Kingdom; Barry J. Allen, Vancouver, B.C.; Balbir S. Bindra, Hong Kong, Hong Kong, People's Republic of China; Craig Goldenberger, Kirkland, Wash.

Other Exec. Officers - Tamra Spink, CFO

Capital Stock

	Authorized (shs.)	Outstanding (shs.)[1]
Class A Preferred	unlimited	4,545,455
Class B Preferred	unlimited	51,071,397
Common	unlimited	29,033,375

[1] At Nov. 23, 2022

Class A Preferred - Convertible into common shares on a 1-for-1 basis. Non-voting.

Class B Preferred - Convertible into common shares on a 1-for-1 basis. One vote per share.

Common - One vote per share.

Price Range - DLC/TSX-VEN

Year	Volume	High	Low	Close
2022	35,200	$0.18	$0.04	$0.10
2021	254,515	$0.19	$0.01	$0.03
2020	61,700	$0.18	$0.05	$0.16
2019	353,965	$0.29	$0.01	$0.14
2018	792,000	$0.32	$0.04	$0.26

Recent Close: $0.15

Wholly Owned Subsidiaries

Craven House Industries Ltd., Ireland.
- 50.1% int. in **Finishtec Acabamentos Tecnicos Em Metais Ltda.**, Brazil.
- 99.9% int. in **Universal Properties Brasil Administracao de Imoveis Ltda**, Brazil.

DLC North America LLC, United States.
Desmond Agricultural Products Ltd., Ireland.
- 100% int. in **Superior Macadamias (Pty) Ltd.**, South Africa.

Subsidiaries

60.5% int. in **Ceniako Ltd.**, Cyprus.
- 100% int. in **Woodford Empreendimentos Imobiliarios Ltda.**, Brazil.

Financial Statistics

Periods ended:	12m Dec. 31/21[A]		12m Dec. 31/20[A]
	$000s	%Chg	$000s
General & admin expense	104		103
Operating expense	**104**	**+1**	**103**
Operating income	**(104)**	**n.a.**	**(103)**
Deprec., depl. & amort.	17		24
Finance income	nil		18
Finance costs, gross	51		52
Pre-tax income	**1,333**	**n.a.**	**(4,985)**
Net income	**1,333**	**n.a.**	**(4,985)**
Net inc. for equity hldrs	**1,317**	**n.a.**	**(3,683)**
Net inc. for non-cont. int.	**16**	**n.a.**	**(1,302)**
Cash & equivalent	161		235
Accounts receivable	4		6
Current assets	165		241
Long-term investments	11,704		11,240
Fixed assets, net	854		907
Total assets	**12,738**	**+3**	**12,404**
Accts. pay. & accr. liabs	146		203
Current liabilities	241		358
Long-term debt, gross	1,109		1,060
Long-term debt, net	1,109		1,060
Shareholders' equity	8,712		8,100
Non-controlling interest	2,677		2,887
Cash from oper. activs	**(127)**	**n.a.**	**(68)**
Cash from fin. activs	4		72
Cash from invest. activs	nil		189
Net cash position	**128**	**-39**	**211**
	$		$
Earnings per share*	0.02		(0.06)
Cash flow per share*	(0.00)		(0.00)
	shs		shs
No. of shs. o/s*	29,033,375		29,033,375
Avg. no. of shs. o/s*	29,033,375		29,033,375
	%		%
Net profit margin	n.a.		n.a.
Return on equity	15.67		(38.44)
Return on assets	11.01		(34.24)

* Common
[A] Reported in accordance with IFRS

Latest Results

Periods ended:	9m Sept. 30/22[A]		9m Sept. 30/21[A]
	$000s	%Chg	$000s
Net income	2,112	n.a.	(166)
Net inc. for equity hldrs	1,603	n.a.	(194)
Net inc. for non-cont. int.	509		28
	$		$
Earnings per share*	0.02		(0.00)

* Common
[A] Reported in accordance with IFRS

Historical Summary
(as originally stated)

Fiscal Year	Oper. Rev. $000s	Net Inc. Bef. Disc. $000s	EPS* $
2021[A]	nil	1,333	0.02
2020[A]	nil	(4,985)	(0.06)
2019[A]	nil	(478)	(0.02)
2018[A1]	nil	(5,953)	(0.09)
2017[A]	nil	(267)	(0.01)

* Common
[A] Reported in accordance with IFRS
[1] Results reflect the Apr. 24, 2018, reverse takeover acquisition of 60.5% of Oceania Ltd. and 100% of Craven House Industries Ltd.

D.9 DMG Blockchain Solutions Inc.

Symbol - DMGI **Exchange** - TSX-VEN **CUSIP** - 23345B
Head Office - 4193 104 St, Delta, BC, V4K 3N3 **Telephone** - (778) 300-6115
Website - www.dmgblockchain.com
Email - sheldon@dmgblockchain.com
Investor Relations - Sheldon Bennett (604) 710-7269
Auditors - Kingston Ross Pasnak LLP C.A., Edmonton, Alta.
Transfer Agents - Computershare Trust Company of Canada Inc., Vancouver, B.C.

Profile - (B.C. 2011) Operates a cryptocurrency mining facility and develops and licenses proprietary blockchain and cryptocurrecny software.

Operations are focused on two business segments: Core (infrastructure operations); and Core+ (software and services).

Core: Infrastructure Operations - Owns and operates a 27,000-sq.-ft. data centre in Christina Lake, B.C., with a power capacity of 85 MW, where the company mines cryptocurrencies and provides hosting and management services to third party clients. Also offers consulting services to other parties related to developing and setting up of data centre operations as well as supplies crypto-mining hardware.

Core+: Software and Services - Develops and licenses blockchain and cryptocurrency software products as well provides services. Software products operate under the Blockseer brand and are focused on crypto regulatory and compliance issues and safety and security. Regulatory and compliance platforms include Walletscore, a risk-scoring tool which measures the propensity of a crypto wallet to engage in criminal activity, enabling to meet anti-money laundering (AML) and anti-fraud compliance obligations; Helm, a platform which monitors key metrics, including temperature, humidity, individual and pooled hashrates, as well as real-time switching and routing, allowing any mining facility's staff to make real-time adjustments and repairs; Mining pools which consist of Blockseer pool, a North American-based audited bitcoin mining pool, providing real-time AML and a new standard in mining compliance and governance and Terra pool, in partnership with **Argo Blockchain plc**, dedicated to decentralizing the bitcoin network hashrate and providing more transparency in the crypto-mining industry; and Petra, a business-to-business software under development which allows financial institutions to transact in bitcoin while ensuring regulatory and compliance requirements. Safety and security platforms include Explorer/Intelligence, an analytics platform that enables tracking of cryptocurrency transactions on both bitcoin and Ethereum blockchains; Exchange, a portal for the Bosonic Network which eliminates counterparty risk; Freeze, a software product under development which would provide custody solution to securely manage digital assets with the choice of single or multiple signatures to execute a crypto transaction; and Breeze, to equitably distribute earned rewards from mined blocks to Terra Pool members. Services include audit of cryptocurrency mining operations, digital asset valuation, forensics investigation and technical due diligence which are provided primarily to audit, accountancy, legal and law enforcement organizations.

Predecessor Detail - Name changed from Aim Explorations Ltd., Feb. 8, 2018, pursuant to Qualifying Transaction reverse takeover acquisition of and amalgamation of (old) DMG Blockchain Solutions Inc. with a wholly owned subsidiary.

Directors - Sheldon Bennett, CEO, Coquitlam, B.C.; Heather Sim, CFO, B.C.; John D. (J.D.) Abouchar, Calif.; John M. Place, Ottawa, Ont.

Other Exec. Officers - Steven Eliscu, COO; Adrian Glover, chief tech. officer; Catherine Cox, corp. sec.

Capital Stock

	Authorized (shs.)	Outstanding (shs.)[1]
Common	unlimited	167,681,377

[1] At May 30, 2023

Major Shareholder - Widely held at Apr. 26, 2023.

Price Range - DMGI/TSX-VEN

Year	Volume	High	Low	Close
2022	80,949,858	$0.85	$0.13	$0.13
2021	628,164,330	$5.34	$0.50	$0.79
2020	167,385,064	$0.90	$0.04	$0.60
2019	32,503,057	$0.25	$0.07	$0.09
2018	66,248,802	$1.98	$0.13	$0.15

Recent Close: $0.30

Capital Stock Changes - During fiscal 2022, common shares were issued as follows: 259,375 on exercise of warrants and 110,000 on exercise of options.

Wholly Owned Subsidiaries

DMG Blockchain Services Inc., Tex.
DMG-US, Inc., United States.
- 100% int. in **Datient, Inc.**, Calif.

1132517 B.C. Ltd., Canada.
1141559 B.C. Ltd., Canada.

Investments

15% int. in **Black Box Manufacturing Inc.**, Vancouver, B.C.
Brane Inc., Ottawa, Ont.

Financial Statistics

Periods ended:	12m Sept. 30/22[A]		12m Sept. 30/21[oA]
	$000s	%Chg	$000s
Operating revenue	**43,236**	**+323**	**10,218**
Research & devel. expense	2,365		826
General & admin expense	3,428		3,123
Stock-based compensation	3,077		4,149
Other operating expense	13,033		6,558
Operating expense	**21,903**	**+49**	**14,666**
Operating income	**21,333**	**n.a.**	**(4,448)**
Deprec., depl. & amort.	19,825		2,053
Finance income	111		105
Finance costs, gross	19		324
Write-downs/write-offs	(1,309)		(19)
Pre-tax income	**(16,975)**	**n.a.**	**(9,552)**
Net income	**(16,975)**	**n.a.**	**(9,552)**
Net inc. for equity hldrs	**(16,975)**	**n.a.**	**(9,550)**
Net inc. for non-cont. int.	**nil**	**n.a.**	**(3)**
Cash & equivalent	1,649		20,173
Accounts receivable	6,321		3,301
Current assets	17,585		49,790
Long-term investments	75		5,678
Fixed assets, net	58,083		31,196
Intangibles, net	nil		58
Total assets	**96,902**	**-13**	**111,128**
Accts. pay. & accr. liabs	3,901		4,123
Current liabilities	5,382		5,740
Long-term debt, gross	292		292
Long-term lease liabilities	93		73
Shareholders' equity	91,428		105,315
Cash from oper. activs	**15,186**	**n.a.**	**(29,834)**
Cash from fin. activs	(126)		93,703
Cash from invest. activs	(33,500)		(45,447)
Net cash position	**1,248**	**-94**	**19,687**
Capital expenditures	(2,646)		(20,284)
Capital disposals	3,856		4,560
	$		$
Earnings per share*	(0.10)		(0.07)
Cash flow per share*	0.09		(0.22)
	shs		shs
No. of shs. o/s*	167,256,377		166,887,002
Avg. no. of shs. o/s*	167,180,278		136,160,785
	%		%
Net profit margin	(39.26)		(93.48)
Return on equity	(17.26)		(15.58)
Return on assets	(16.30)		(13.91)

* Common
[o] Restated
[A] Reported in accordance with IFRS

Latest Results

Periods ended:	6m Mar. 31/23[A]		6m Mar. 31/22[A]
	$000s	%Chg	$000s
Operating revenue	14,798	-43	26,159
Net income	(9,427)	n.a.	5,093
	$		$
Earnings per share*	(0.06)		0.03

* Common
[A] Reported in accordance with IFRS

Historical Summary
(as originally stated)

Fiscal Year	Oper. Rev.	Net Inc. Bef. Disc.	EPS*
	$000s	$000s	$
2022[A]	43,236	(16,975)	(0.10)
2021[A]	10,218	(9,552)	(0.07)
2020[A]	7,404	(2,828)	(0.03)
2019[A]	10,103	(7,752)	(0.05)
2018[A1]	11,466	(25,511)	(0.25)

* Common
[A] Reported in accordance with IFRS
[1] Results reflect the Feb. 9, 2018, Qualifying Transaction reverse takeover acquisition of (old) DMG Blockchain Solutions Inc.

D.10 DREAM Unlimited Corp.

Symbol - DRM **Exchange** - TSX **CUSIP** - 26153M
Head Office - State Street Financial Centre, 301-30 Adelaide St E, Toronto, ON, M5C 3H1 **Telephone** - (416) 365-3535 **Toll-free** - (877) 365-3535 **Fax** - (416) 365-6565
Website - www.dream.ca
Email - dstarkman@dream.ca
Investor Relations - Deborah J. Starkman (877) 365-3536
Auditors - PricewaterhouseCoopers LLP C.A., Toronto, Ont.
Lawyers - Osler, Hoskin & Harcourt LLP, Toronto, Ont.
Transfer Agents - Computershare Trust Company of Canada Inc., Toronto, Ont.
FP500 Revenue Ranking - 542
Employees - 263 at Dec. 31, 2022
Profile - (Ont. 2013, amalg.) Develops and owns mixed-used properties, condominiums, commercial properties, residential lands, and multi-family and housing properties; and provides real estate asset management and advisory services.

The company's reporting segments consist of Recurring Income and Development.

The **Recurring Income** segment consists of the company's contracts to provide asset management and development management services to **Dream Industrial Real Estate Investment Trust, Dream Impact Trust, Dream Residential Real Estate Investment Trust** (Dream Residential REIT), **Dream Office Real Estate Investment Trust** (Dream Office REIT) and on behalf of various institutional/third-party real estate partnerships, including the company's private fund business Dream Real Estate Private Equity (formerly Dream Equity Partners); 37% and 12% equity interest in Dream Office REIT and Dream Residential REIT, respectively, both of which generate monthly distributions for the company; Dream Impact's lending portfolio, consisting of loans secured by various types of residential and commercial real estate properties; and income-producing office, retail, residential, mixed-use, hotel and recreational properties in the Greater Toronto Area (GTA) and Ottawa, Ont., Gatineau, Que., Saskatchewan, Alberta and the U.S., with 6,899,000 sq. ft. of commercial/retail gross leasable area (GLA) and 8,205 residential/hotel units at Mar. 31, 2023. At Mar. 31, 2023, assets under management totaled $24 billion, including fee-earning assets under management of about $17 billion.

The **Development** segment consists of urban development assets in the GTA and Ottawa-Gatineau; and community development assets in western Canada. Urban development assets consist of condominium, purpose-built rental and mixed-use developments. These include Forma Condos, Quayside, Riverside Square, West Don Lands and Canary District in downtown Toronto, as well as Zibi and Dream LeBreton in Ottawa-Gatineau region. At Mar. 31, 2023, the company had interests in 25,629 residential units and 4,023,000 sq. ft. of commercial/retail GLA in various stages of planning, construction or redevelopment. Western Canada community development consists of land, housing, multi-family and retail/commercial assets within the company's master-planned communities in Saskatoon and Regina, Sask., and Calgary and Edmonton, Alta. At Mar. 31, 2023, the company owned 8,897 acres of land in western Canada, of which 8,500 acres were in nine large master-planned communities at various stages of approval; and 227 purpose-built rental units and 74,000 sq. ft. of commercial/retail GLA in planning and construction stage. The segment also includes Dream Impact's investment in the Virgin Hotels Las Vegas in Nevada.

Recent Merger and Acquisition Activity

Status: completed **Announced:** Mar. 31, 2023
DREAM Unlimited Corp. acquired an additional 12.5% interest in the Distillery District, an income property in Toronto, Ont., with 395,000 sq. ft. of commercial and retail area, for $27,000,000, consisting of $14,000,000 cash on closing and a $13,000,000 promissory note. As a result, DREAM's interest increased to 62.5% from 50%.

Status: completed **Announced:** May 6, 2022
Dream Residential Real Estate Investment Trust acquired 16 multi-residential properties, totaling 3,432 units, located in three markets across the Sunbelt and Midwest regions of the United States for total consideration of US$388,347,000. Vendors included DREAM Unlimited Corp. and Pauls Capital, LLC.

Status: completed **Announced:** Apr. 29, 2022
DREAM Unlimited Corp. (33.33%) and Dream Impact Trust (33.33%), together with Dream Impact Fund LP (33.33%), acquired Dream LeBreton, a 2.7-acre development land which would serve as the site of the first phase of the Building LeBreton project in Ottawa, Ont. Dream LeBreton was expected to have 600 rental housing units. Terms were not disclosed.

Status: completed **Announced:** Mar. 15, 2022
DREAM Unlimited Corp. (33.33%) and Dream Impact Trust (33.33%), together with Dream Impact Fund LP (33.33%), acquired 177 St. George Street, a 57-unit apartment building in Toronto, Ont., for $22,500,000.

Directors - Joanne S. Ferstman, chr., Toronto, Ont.; Michael J. Cooper, pres. & chief responsible officer, Toronto, Ont.; P. Jane Gavan, pres., asset mgt., Toronto, Ont.; James G. Eaton, Toronto, Ont.; Richard N. Gateman, Calgary, Alta.; Duncan N. R. Jackman, Toronto, Ont.; Jennifer (Jen) Lee Koss, Toronto, Ont.; Vincenza Sera, Toronto, Ont.
Other Exec. Officers - Jason Lester, v-chr., devel.; Deborah J. Starkman, CFO; Jay Jiang, exec. v-p, corp. devel. & strategy; Brian D. Pauls, exec. v-p, ind.; Gordon Wadley, exec. v-p, comml. properties; Tsering Yangki, exec. v-p, real estate fin. & devel.; Meaghan Peloso, sr. v-p, impact; Alexander Sannikov, sr. v-p, ind.; Bruce Traversy, sr. v-p, ind.; Robert Hughes, gen. counsel & corp. sec.

Capital Stock

	Authorized (shs.)	Outstanding (shs.)[1]
First Preference	unlimited	nil
Class A Subordinate Voting	unlimited	41,244,327
Class B Common	unlimited	1,557,353

[1] At May 9, 2023

Class A Subordinate Voting - Convertible into class B common shares on a 1-for-1 basis in the event of an offer to purchase the class B common shares by a third party, and in certain circumstances. One vote per share.
Class B Common - Convertible into class A subordinate voting shares on a 1-for-1 basis at any time. 100 votes per share.
Normal Course Issuer Bid - The company plans to make normal course purchases of up to 2,231,143 class A subordinate voting shares representing 10% of the public float. The bid commenced on Sept. 21, 2022, and expires on Sept. 20, 2023.
Major Shareholder - Michael J. Cooper held 88% interest at Apr. 14, 2023.

Price Range - DRM/TSX

Year	Volume	High	Low	Close
2022	12,882,611	$50.71	$22.01	$25.43
2021	20,973,946	$38.94	$20.36	$38.83
2020	19,300,511	$27.56	$13.84	$21.25
2019	8,464,769	$23.92	$13.40	$23.40
2018	10,470,662	$20.92	$13.08	$13.68

Consolidation: 1-for-2 cons. in July 2020
Recent Close: $20.40
Capital Stock Changes - During 2022, class A subordinate voting shares were issued as follows: 117,618 on vesting of restricted share units and 10,599 on vesting of performance share units; 376,546 class A subordinate voting shares were repurchased under a Normal Course Issuer Bid.

Dividends

DRM com Ra $0.50 pa Q est. Mar. 31, 2023
Prev. Rate: $0.40 est. Dec. 31, 2021
Prev. Rate: $0.28 est. Mar. 31, 2021
Prev. Rate: $0.12 est. Mar. 31, 2020
$0.05◆ Dec. 30/22
Paid in 2023: $0.375 2022: $0.40 + $0.05◆ 2021: $0.31
◆ Special

Wholly Owned Subsidiaries

DREAM Asset Management Corporation, Toronto, Ont.
- 41% int. in **Dream Impact Fund LP**, Ont.
- 100% int. in **Dream Impact Master GP Inc.**, Ont.
- 32% int. in **Dream Impact Trust**, Toronto, Ont. (see separate coverage)
- 100% int. in **Dundee Resort Development, LLC**, Colo.
- 100% int. in **LDL Properties**, Ont.

Investments

37% int. in **Dream Office Real Estate Investment Trust**, Toronto, Ont. (see separate coverage)
12% int. in **Dream Residential Real Estate Investment Trust**, Toronto, Ont. (see separate coverage)
Note: The preceding list includes only the major related companies in which interests are held.

Financial Statistics

Periods ended:	12m Dec. 31/22[A]		12m Dec. 31/21[A]
	$000s	%Chg	$000s
Total revenue	**343,768**	**+5**	**325,922**
Rental operating expense	76,748		51,589
Salaries & benefits	27,103		21,928
General & admin. expense	33,407		17,640
Other operating expense	153,413		183,193
Operating expense	**290,671**	**+6**	**274,350**
Operating income	**53,097**	**+3**	**51,572**
Investment income	56,093		90,721
Deprec. & amort.	7,525		6,434
Finance income	8,724		9,966
Finance costs, gross	51,803		26,675
Pre-tax income	**197,291**	**+57**	**125,875**
Income taxes	32,846		15,214
Net income	**164,445**	**+49**	**110,661**
Net inc. for equity hldrs	**164,445**	**+49**	**110,030**
Net inc. for non-cont. int	**nil**	**n.a.**	**631**
Cash & equivalent	47,633		52,564
Accounts receivable	268,037		234,541
Long-term investments	1,067,499		1,029,629
Fixed assets	11,900		8,109
Income-producing props.	1,490,571		1,175,935
Properties under devel.	618,388		615,708
Residential inventory	395,125		324,535
Property interests, net	2,515,984		2,124,287
Right-of-use assets	1,931		1,409
Intangibles, net	13,576		13,576
Total assets	**3,956,494**	**+13**	**3,488,674**
Bank indebtedness	3,062		1,534
Accts. pay. & accr. liabs	186,021		141,545
Long-term debt, gross	1,612,571		1,293,695
Long-term lease liabilities	11,836		11,602
Shareholders' equity	1,553,692		1,422,213
Cash from oper. activs	**(66,353)**	**n.a.**	**67,023**
Cash from fin. activs	198,468		277,591
Cash from invest. activs	(137,046)		(477,171)
Net cash position	**47,633**	**-9**	**52,564**
Increase in property	(190,705)		(486,757)
	$		$
Earnings per share*	3.86		2.52
Cash flow per share*	(1.56)		1.53
Funds from opers. per sh.*	3.99		n.a.
Cash divd. per share*	0.40		0.31
Extra divd. - cash*	0.05		nil
Total divd. per share*	**0.45**		**0.31**
	shs		shs
No. of shs. o/s*	42,587,702		42,836,031
Avg. no. of shs. o/s*	42,601,025		43,685,083
	%		%
Net profit margin	47.84		33.95
Return on equity	11.05		7.82
Return on assets	5.58		4.24
Foreign sales percent	n.a.		10
No. of employees (FTEs)	263		236

* Class A & B
[A] Reported in accordance with IFRS

Latest Results

Periods ended:	3m Mar. 31/23[A]		3m Mar. 31/22[A]
	$000s	%Chg	$000s
Total revenue	72,196	+36	53,214
Net income	34,601	-18	42,173
	$		$
Earnings per share*	0.81		0.99

* Class A & B
[A] Reported in accordance with IFRS

Historical Summary
(as originally stated)

Fiscal Year	Total Rev.	Net Inc. Bef. Disc.	EPS*
	$000s	$000s	$
2022[A]	343,768	164,445	3.86
2021[A]	325,922	110,661	2.52
2020[A]	347,623	159,638	3.37
2019[A]	580,430	331,745	6.25
2018[A]	339,873	192,053	3.52

* Class A & B
[A] Reported in accordance with IFRS
Note: Adjusted throughout for 1-for-2 cons. in July 2020

D.11 DRI Healthcare Trust

Symbol - DHT.UN **Exchange** - TSX **CUSIP** - 23344H
Head Office - 1 First Canadian Place, 7250-100 King St W, PO Box 62, Toronto, ON, M5X 1B1 **Telephone** - (416) 863-1865
Website - drihealthcare.com
Email - ir@drihealthcare.com
Investor Relations - Dave Levine (416) 324-5738

Auditors - Deloitte LLP C.A., Toronto, Ont.
Lawyers - Osler, Hoskin & Harcourt LLP, Toronto, Ont.
Transfer Agents - Computershare Trust Company of Canada Inc., Toronto, Ont.
FP500 Revenue Ranking - 753
Employees - 35 at Dec. 31, 2022
Profile - (Ont. 2020) Owns and acquires pharmaceutical royalties.

Holds a portfolio of 24 royalty streams on 20 pharmaceutical products that address medically necessary therapeutic areas such as oncology, neurology, ophthalmology, endocrinology, hemato-oncology, dermatology, as well as lysosomal storage disorders, autoimmune and respiratory diseases and influenza

Royalty assets include Empaveli/Syfovre (hemato-oncology/ophthalmology), Spinraza (neurology), Xolair (respiratory), Eylea I and II (ophthalmology), Ilaris (autoimmune disease), Natpara (endocrinology), Omidria (ophthalmology), Oracea (dermatology), Orserdu (oncology), Rydapt (oncology), Simponi and Stelara (autoimmune disease), Vonjo (hemato-oncology), Xenpozyme (lysosomal storage disorder), Xolair (respiratory disease), Zejula (oncology) and Zytiga (oncology).

Products are marketed by global pharmaceutical companies including **Apellis Pharmaceuticals Inc.**, **GSK plc**, **Menari Group**, **Rayner Surgical Inc.**, **Sanofi S.A.**, **Swedish Orphan Biovitrum AB**, **Johnson & Johnson**, **AstraZeneca PLC**, **Novartis International AG**, **Galderma S.A.**, **Biogen Inc.**, **Merck & Co.**, **Mitsubishi Tanabe Pharma Corporation**, **Roche Holding AG** and **Regeneron Pharmaceuticals, Inc.**

In April 2023, the trust acquired an additional royalty stream on Empaveli/Syfovre for US$3,700,000.

During 2022, wholly owned **ROC Royalties S.a.r.l.** and **DRC Springing III LLC** were dissolved.

Recent Merger and Acquisition Activity

Status: completed **Announced:** Aug. 14, 2023
DRI Healthcare Trust acquired a second royalty interest in Orserdu™ (elacestrant) from Radius Health Inc. for US$130,000,000. Orserdu™ is an oral, selective estrogen receptor degrader used in the treatment of postmenopausal women or adult men with ESR1-mutated ER+/HER2-metastatic breast cancer.

Status: completed **Announced:** July 7, 2023
DRI Healthcare Trust acquired an additional royalty interest in Vonjo® (pacritinib) from S*Bio Pte. Ltd. for US$66,000,000. Vonjo is a drug for the treatment of adults with intermediate or high-risk primary or secondary (post-polycythemia vera or post-essential thrombocythemia) myelofibrosis.

Status: completed **Announced:** June 30, 2023
DRI Healthcare Trust acquired a royalty interest in Orserdu™ (elacestrant) from Eisai Co., Ltd. for US$85,000,000. Orserdu™ is an oral, selective estrogen receptor degrader used in the treatment of postmenopausal women or adult men with ESR1-mutated ER+/HER2-metastatic breast cancer.

Status: completed **Announced:** Apr. 27, 2023
DRI Healthcare Trust sold its TZIELD™ royalty interest to Sanofi S.A. for US$210,000,000. TZIELD is a biologic drug indicated to delay the onset of stage 3 type 1 diabetes in adults and paediatric patients.

Status: completed **Announced:** Mar. 8, 2023
DRI Healthcare Trust acquired MacroGenics, Inc.'s royalty interest in the worldwide sales of TZIELD (teplizumab-mzwv) for an up-front purchase price of US$100,000,000. TZIELD is a biologic drug indicated to delay the onset of stage 3 type 1 diabetes in adults and paediatric patients.

Status: completed **Announced:** Nov. 28, 2022
DRI Healthcare Trust acquired a royalty interest in Xenpozyme® (olipudase alfa), which is a product for the treatment of non-central nervous system manifestations of acid sphingomyelinase deficiency, for US$30,000,000. Xenpozyme® was approved in Japan in March 2022, by the European Commission in June 2022 and by the U.S. Food and Drug Administration (FDA) in August 2022.

Status: completed **Announced:** Oct. 3, 2022
DRI Healthcare Trust acquired a royalty interest in OMIDRIA® (phenylephrine and ketorolac), a bisulfite-free and preservative-free product that is indicated for intracameral irrigation during cataract surgery or intraocular lens replacement to maintain pupil dilation and reduce postoperative pain, from Omeros Corporation for US$125,000,000. OMIDRIA® was approved by the U.S. Food and Drug Administration (FDA) in May 2014 and the European Medicines Agency in July 2015. The royalty was subject to annual caps, and would be paid until 2030.

Status: completed **Announced:** Sept. 12, 2022
DRI Healthcare Trust acquired a royalty interest in Zejula (niraparib), a once-daily oral prescription treatment for both first-line and recurrent ovarian cancer, from AnaptysBio, Inc. for US$35,000,000. An additional milestone payment of US$10,000,000 would be paid should Zejula be approved by the U.S. Food and Drug Administration (FDA) for the treatment of endometrial cancer on or before Dec. 31, 2025. The royalty was expected to continue for at least 10 years worldwide (to at least the end of 2033).

Status: completed **Announced:** July 21, 2022
DRI Healthcare Trust acquired a royalty interest (less than 1%) in the worldwide sales of pegcetacoplan, an active molecule in the first targeted C3 therapy for use in adults with paroxysmal nocturnal hemoglobinuria, for US$24,500,000, with an option to increase its interest in pegcetacoplan in the future. Pegcetacoplan was approved by the U.S. Food and Drug Administration (FDA) and the European Medicines Agency in 2021. Pegcetacoplan was marketed in the U.S. under the brand name Empaveli®, and outside the U.S. under the brand name Aspaveli®. The royalty was expected to expire in the U.S. in the fourth quarter of 2031 and in the European Union in the second quarter of 2032.

Status: completed **Announced:** Mar. 4, 2022
DRI Healthcare Trust acquired a royalty interest in Vonjo (pacritinib), a drug for the treatment of adults with intermediate or high-risk primary or secondary (post-polycythemia vera or post-essential thrombocythemia) myelofibrosis, for US$60,000,000. Under the agreement, DRI would receive 9.6% of the first US$125,000,000 annual U.S. net sales, 4.5% of annual net U.S. sales between US$125,000,000 and US$175,000,000, and 0.5% of annual U.S. net sales between US$175,000,000 and US$400,000,000, with no entitlement above US$400,000,000 of annual U.S. net sales.

Trustees - Gary M. Collins, chr., Vancouver, B.C.; Behzad Khosrowshahi, pres. & CEO, Toronto, Ont.; Ali G. Hedayat, Toronto, Ont.; Kevin Layden, Vancouver, B.C.; Dr. Paul Mussenden, United Kingdom; Prof. Poonam Puri, Toronto, Ont.; Sandra J. Stuart, Vancouver, B.C.; Dr. Tamara Vrooman, Vancouver, B.C.
Oper. Subsid./Mgt. Co. Officers - Chris Anastasopoulos, CFO

Capital Stock

	Authorized (shs.)	Outstanding (shs.)[1]
Preferred	unlimited	nil
Trust Unit	unlimited	46,717,980

[1] At Aug. 14, 2023

Normal Course Issuer Bid - The company plans to make normal course purchases of up to 2,493,280 trust units representing 10% of the public float. The bid commenced on Nov. 14, 2022, and expires on Nov. 13, 2023.

Major Shareholder - Mackenzie Financial Corporation held 17.2% interest, CIBC Asset Management Inc. held 12.8% interest and Dixon Mitchell Investment Counsel Inc. held 10.3% interest at Mar. 29, 2023.

Price Range - DHT.UN/TSX

Year	Volume	High	Low	Close
2022	10,253,985	$9.22	$5.83	$7.89
2021	9,248,783	$12.57	$6.05	$6.75

Recent Close: $12.68

Capital Stock Changes - In July 2023, bought deal public offering of 9,223,000 trust units was completed at Cdn$10.60 per unit, including 1,203,000 trust units on exercise of over-allotment option. Net proceeds would be used to fund royalty transactions or to repay indebtedness drawn on secured credit facility to fund royalty transactions.

During 2022, 99,155 common shares were issued on vesting of restricted units and 1,388,440 common shares were repurchased under a Normal Course Issuer Bid.

Dividends

DHT.UN unit Ra US$0.30 pa Q est. Jan. 20, 2022
Listed Feb 11/21.
Prev. Rate: US$0.15 est. July 20, 2021
Prev. Rate: US$0.0668 est. Apr. 20, 2021
US$0.5334◆......... July 20/23 stk.[1]◆**g**........... Jan. 20/23
US$0.22◆............ Jan. 20/22 US$0.0167**i**....... Apr. 20/21
Paid in 2023: US$0.30 + US$0.5334◆ + stk.◆**g** 2022: US$0.30 + US$0.22◆ 2021: US$0.0917**i**

DHT.U unit Ra US$0.30 pa Q est. Jan. 20, 2022
Listed Feb 11/21.
Prev. Rate: US$0.15 est. July 20, 2021
Prev. Rate: US$0.0668 est. Apr. 20, 2021
US$0.5334◆......... July 20/23 stk.◆**g**............. Jan. 20/23
US$0.22◆............ Jan. 20/22 US$0.0167**i**....... Apr. 20/21
Paid in 2023: US$0.30 + US$0.5334◆ + stk.◆**g** 2022: US$0.30 + US$0.22◆ 2021: US$0.0917**i**

[1] Distribution will be automatically reinvested and the units will be consolidated immediately after distribution. Equiv to US$0.1655.
◆ Special **g** Capital Gain **i** Initial Payment

Wholly Owned Subsidiaries

DRC Management III LLC 1, Del.
DRC Management III LLC 2, Del.
DRC Management LLC 2, Del.
DRC Springing III LLC, Del.
DRI Healthcare ICAV, Ireland.
- 100% int. in **DRI Healthcare LP 2**, Del.
  - 100% int. in **Drug Royalty LP 1**, Del.
  - 100% int. in **Drug Royalty LP 3**, Cayman Islands.
- 100% int. in **DRI Healthcare L.P.**, Del.
  - 100% int. in **DRI Healthcare Acquisitions LP 1**, Del.
  - 100% int. in **DRI Healthcare Acquisitions L.P.**, Del.
  - 100% int. in **DRI Healthcare GP, LLC**, Del.

TCD Royalty Sub, LP, Del.

Financial Statistics

Periods ended:	12m Dec. 31/22[A]		12m Dec. 31/21[A]
	US$000s	%Chg	US$000s
Operating revenue	**87,273**	**+9**	**79,860**
Research & devel. expense	3,228		2,252
General & admin expense	6,532		7,351
Stock-based compensation	1,191		473
Other operating expense	4,589		5,414
Operating expense	**15,540**	**0**	**15,490**
Operating income	**71,733**	**+11**	**64,370**
Deprec., depl. & amort.	59,266		41,837
Finance income	5,761		1,905
Finance costs, gross	6,630		2,236
Pre-tax income	**11,598**	**-46**	**21,563**
Net income	**11,598**	**-46**	**21,563**
Cash & equivalent	36,686		61,712
Accounts receivable	27,748		30,148
Current assets	64,903		92,427
Intangibles, net	518,134		293,658
Total assets	**633,419**	**+45**	**436,695**
Accts. pay. & accr. liabs.	5,542		1,557
Current liabilities	50,096		18,973
Long-term debt, gross	244,988		43,921
Long-term debt, net	210,417		38,600
Shareholders' equity	372,341		378,985
Cash from oper. activs	**77,469**	**-16**	**91,864**
Cash from fin. activs	171,173		342,183
Cash from invest. activs	(273,668)		(372,335)
Net cash position	**36,686**	**-41**	**61,712**
	US$		US$
Earnings per share*	0.30		0.62
Cash flow per share*	2.01		2.65
Cash divd. per share*	$0.30		$0.17
Extra divd. - cash*	$nil		$0.22
Extra stk. divd. - cash equiv.*	$0.17		$...
Total divd. per share*	**$0.47**		**$0.39**
	shs		shs
No. of shs. o/s*	37,790,395		39,079,680
Avg. no. of shs. o/s*	38,570,499		34,646,277
	%		%
Net profit margin	13.29		27.00
Return on equity	3.09		n.m.
Return on assets	3.41		n.a.
No. of employees (FTEs)	35		35

* Trust Unit
[A] Reported in accordance with IFRS

Latest Results

Periods ended:	6m June 30/23[A]		6m June 30/22[A]
	US$000s	%Chg	US$000s
Operating revenue	49,499	+20	41,253
Net income	73,910	+741	8,791
	US$		US$
Earnings per share*	1.96		0.23

* Trust Unit
[A] Reported in accordance with IFRS

D.12 DXI Capital Corp.

Symbol - DXI.H **Exchange** - TSX-VEN **CUSIP** - 267473
Head Office - 404-999 Canada Pl, Vancouver, BC, V6C 3E2 **Telephone** - (604) 638-5050 **Toll-free** - (866) 888-8230 **Fax** - (604) 638-5051
Website - www.dxicap.com
Email - rhodgkinson@dxicap.com
Investor Relations - Robert L. Hodgkinson (866) 888-8230
Auditors - Davidson & Company LLP C.A., Vancouver, B.C.
Lawyers - Farris LLP, Vancouver, B.C.; Dorsey & Whitney LLP, Denver, Colo.
Transfer Agents - Computershare Trust Company, N.A., Denver, Colo.; Computershare Trust Company of Canada Inc., Vancouver, B.C.
Profile - (B.C. 2005; orig. Ont., 1968) Seeking new business opportunities.
Predecessor Detail - Name changed from DXI Energy Inc., Sept. 11, 2020; basis 1 new for 100 old shs.
Directors - Robert L. (Bob) Hodgkinson, chr. & CEO, Vancouver, B.C.; Ronnie (Ron) Bozzer, B.C.; Dr. A. Ross Gorrell, Delta, B.C.
Other Exec. Officers - Sean P. Hodgins, COO & CFO

Capital Stock

	Authorized (shs.)	Outstanding (shs.)[1]
First Preferred	unlimited	nil
Second Preferred	unlimited	nil
Common	unlimited	12,000,000

[1] At Mar. 21, 2022

Major Shareholder - Robert L. (Bob) Hodgkinson held 45% interest and Charles Hodgkinson held 37.8% interest at Oct. 23, 2020.

Price Range - DXI.H/TSX-VEN

Year	Volume	High	Low	Close
2022............	45,921	$0.38	$0.17	$0.18
2021............	251,597	$0.88	$0.32	$0.32
2020............	209,847	$3.50	$0.41	$0.49
2019............	232,332	$11.00	$3.00	$3.00
2018............	305,544	$13.50	$1.50	$4.00

Consolidation: 1-for-100 cons. in Sept. 2020
Recent Close: $0.12

Wholly Owned Subsidiaries

0855524 B.C. Ltd., B.C. Inactive.

Financial Statistics

Periods ended:	12m Dec. 31/21[A]		12m Dec. 31/20[A]
	$000s	%Chg	$000s
Operating revenue........................	**nil**	**n.a.**	**295**
Cost of sales..................................	nil		436
General & admin expense...............	216		470
Stock-based compensation............	nil		6
Operating expense........................	**216**	**-76**	**912**
Operating income..........................	**(216)**	**n.a.**	**(617)**
Deprec., depl. & amort....................	1		73
Finance costs, gross.......................	36		384
Write-downs/write-offs....................	nil		(1,201)
Pre-tax income.............................	**(243)**	**n.a.**	**6,199**
Net income...................................	**(243)**	**n.a.**	**6,199**
Cash & equivalent...........................	19		73
Accounts receivable........................	nil		2
Current assets................................	25		81
Fixed assets, net.............................	1		2
Total assets..................................	**26**	**-69**	**83**
Accts. pay. & accr. liabs..................	171		100
Current liabilities............................	661		475
Shareholders' equity........................	(635)		(392)
Cash from oper. activs..................	**(169)**	**n.a.**	**(419)**
Cash from fin. activs........................	115		299
Net cash position..........................	**19**	**-74**	**73**
Capital expenditures........................	nil		(6)
	$		$
Earnings per share*.........................	(0.02)		1.45
Cash flow per share*.......................	(0.01)		(0.10)
	shs		shs
No. of shs. o/s*..............................	11,966,024		11,610,130
Avg. no. of shs. o/s*........................	11,821,716		4,282,646
	%		%
Net profit margin.............................	n.a.		n.m.
Return on equity..............................	n.m.		n.m.
Return on assets.............................	(379.82)		612.37

* Common
[A] Reported in accordance with IFRS

Historical Summary
(as originally stated)

Fiscal Year	Oper. Rev. $000s	Net Inc. Bef. Disc. $000s	EPS* $
2021[A]...................	nil	(243)	(0.02)
2020[A]...................	295	6,199	1.45
2019[A]...................	1,128	(5,221)	(3.00)
2018[A]...................	1,744	(11,632)	(11.00)
2017[A]...................	2,480	(5,209)	(8.00)

* Common
[A] Reported in accordance with IFRS
Note: Adjusted throughout for 1-for-100 cons. in Sept. 2020

D.13 DXStorm.com Inc.

Symbol - DXX **Exchange** - TSX-VEN **CUSIP** - 26745P
Head Office - 824 Winston Churchill Blvd, Oakville, ON, L6J 7X2 **Telephone** - (905) 842-8262 **Toll-free** - (877) 397-8676 **Fax** - (905) 842-3255
Website - www.dxstorm.com
Email - zoran@dxstorm.com
Investor Relations - Zoran Popovic (877) 397-8676
Auditors - MS Partners LLP C.A., Toronto, Ont.
Transfer Agents - Computershare Trust Company of Canada Inc., Vancouver, B.C.
Profile - (Ont. 2000; orig. B.C., 1993) Provides products and services including medical application software development, custom programming, e-commerce and Internet-based solutions, web hosting, hardware resale and management services for clients in Canada, the U.S. and Sint Maarten.
The company offers e-commerce services, which include an e-commerce hosting service for businesses through ClicShop; custom developed e-commerce solutions including a complete storefront and online ticketing systems through 5Click Solutions; DXshop, a turnkey e-store solution for small to medium-sized retail businesses; DXcart, an e-commerce enabler for websites on any platform; DXweb, a website development and hosting service for companies of any size; DXcustom, an enterprise class web systems and software for companies of any size; and online payment solutions for businesses through DXGreenGate.
Other solutions include medical image analysis software with a picture archiving and communication system (PACS) through subsidiary **Medical Diagnostic Exchange Corporation** (dba MDX); web hosting and mail services through subsidiary **ACEnetx Inc.** and wholly owned **Clic.net Telecommunications Inc.**; and retail payment solutions through DXCard.
Predecessor Detail - Name changed from West Park Resources Inc., June 19, 2000, following reverse takeover acquisition of DXStorm Inc.
Directors - Zoran Popovic, pres., CEO & corp. sec., Oakville, Ont.; Steven (Steve) Smashnuk, CFO & chief tech. officer, Oakville, Ont.; Douglas Jovanovic; John JC. Kim; John A. Ryan, Puslinch, Ont.

Capital Stock

	Authorized (shs.)	Outstanding (shs.)[1]
Common	unlimited	23,586,650

[1] At Nov. 28, 2022
Major Shareholder - Zoran Popovic held 67% interest at Nov. 19, 2021.

Price Range - DXX/TSX-VEN

Year	Volume	High	Low	Close
2022............	69,000	$0.04	$0.01	$0.01
2021............	306,320	$0.08	$0.03	$0.03
2020............	912,335	$0.17	$0.03	$0.05
2019............	100,500	$0.04	$0.02	$0.02
2018............	504,411	$0.05	$0.04	$0.04

Recent Close: $0.01
Capital Stock Changes - In April 2022, private placement of 2,857,142 units (1 common share & 1 warrant) at $0.035 per unit was completed.

Wholly Owned Subsidiaries

Clic.net Connexion Inc. Inactive
Clic.net Telecommunications, Inc.
DXStorm Inc. Inactive
Elan Informatique Inc. Inactive
3697932 Canada Inc., Vancouver, B.C. Operating as 5Click. Inactive

Subsidiaries

76% int. in **ACEnetx Inc.**, Thornhill, Ont.
67% int. in **Medical Diagnostic Exchange Corporation** Inactive

Financial Statistics

Periods ended:	12m June 30/22[A]		12m June 30/21[A]
	$000s	%Chg	$000s
Operating revenue........................	**111**	**-24**	**146**
Research & devel. expense.............	131		95
General & admin expense...............	206		266
Operating expense........................	**337**	**-7**	**361**
Operating income..........................	**(226)**	**n.a.**	**(214)**
Deprec., depl. & amort....................	2		2
Write-downs/write-offs....................	nil		(2)
Pre-tax income.............................	**(228)**	**n.a.**	**(200)**
Net income...................................	**(228)**	**n.a.**	**(200)**
Cash & equivalent...........................	29		7
Accounts receivable........................	3		62
Current assets................................	38		72
Fixed assets, net.............................	4		5
Total assets..................................	**42**	**-45**	**77**
Bank indebtedness..........................	nil		10
Accts. pay. & accr. liabs..................	557		448
Current liabilities............................	565		473
Long-term debt, gross.....................	40		40
Long-term debt, net.........................	40		40
Shareholders' equity........................	(563)		(436)
Cash from oper. activs..................	**(68)**	**n.a.**	**(40)**
Cash from fin. activs........................	90		nil
Net cash position..........................	**29**	**+314**	**7**
	$		$
Earnings per share*.........................	(0.01)		(0.01)
Cash flow per share*.......................	(0.00)		(0.00)
	shs		shs
No. of shs. o/s*..............................	23,856,650		29,729,508
Avg. no. of shs. o/s*........................	23,586,650		20,729,508
	%		%
Net profit margin.............................	(205.41)		(136.99)
Return on equity..............................	n.m.		n.m.
Return on assets.............................	(383.19)		(181.82)
Foreign sales percent......................	1		1

* Common
[A] Reported in accordance with IFRS

Latest Results

Periods ended:	3m Sept. 30/22[A]		3m Sept. 30/21[A]
	$000s	%Chg	$000s
Operating revenue...........................	40	-2	41
Net income......................................	(50)	n.a.	(55)
	$		$
Earnings per share*.........................	(0.00)		(0.00)

* Common
[A] Reported in accordance with IFRS

Historical Summary
(as originally stated)

Fiscal Year	Oper. Rev. $000s	Net Inc. Bef. Disc. $000s	EPS* $
2022[A]...................	111	(228)	(0.01)
2021[A]...................	146	(200)	(0.01)
2020[A]...................	373	(181)	(0.01)
2019[A]...................	503	(128)	(0.01)
2018[A]...................	554	(307)	(0.01)

* Common
[A] Reported in accordance with IFRS

D.14 Danavation Technologies Corp.

Symbol - DVN **Exchange** - CSE **CUSIP** - 23585V
Head Office - 21 Roybridge Gate, Woodbridge, ON, L4H 1E6 **Telephone** - (905) 605-6702 **Toll-free** - (833) 386-8800
Website - danavation.com
Email - jricci@danavation.com
Investor Relations - John M. Ricci (833) 386-8800
Auditors - Kreston GTA LLP C.A., Markham, Ont.
Transfer Agents - Computershare Trust Company of Canada Inc., Vancouver, B.C.
Profile - (B.C. 2007) Provides micro e-paper displays and software in North America which enable retailers, grocers and other users to automate labelling, price, product information and promotions in real-time.
The company's Digital Smart Labels™ are powered by Internet of Things (IoT) automation technology and proprietary software platform. Customers include retailers, big box and boutique grocers, healthcare providers, pet shelters, manufacturing and logistics companies.
Also developing new proprietary products including Radio Frequency ID/Near Frequency Communication (NFC) tags, IoT sensors for compliance, video analytics and biometric systems.
Common reinstated on CSE, Dec. 28, 2022.
Common suspended from CSE, Dec. 5, 2022.
Predecessor Detail - Name changed from Wolf's Den Capital Corp., Jan. 6, 2021, pursuant to the reverse takeover acquisition of Danavation Technologies Inc.; basis 1 new for 30 old shs.
Directors - John M. Ricci, pres. & CEO, Kleinburg, Ont.; Frank Borges, v-p, Toronto, Ont.; Michael Della Fortuna, Woodbridge, Ont.; Riccardo Forno, Toronto, Ont.; Vivek Jain, Regina, Sask.; Jorge Martínez, Vancouver, B.C.
Other Exec. Officers - Kyle Nazareth, CFO; Michael D. Tran, chief tech. officer; Jo-Anne Archibald, corp. sec.

Capital Stock

	Authorized (shs.)	Outstanding (shs.)[1]
Preferred	unlimited	nil
Common	unlimited	114,174,850

[1] At Dec. 28, 2022
Major Shareholder - Frank Borges held 19.67% interest and John M. Ricci held 19.67% interest at Feb. 18, 2022.

Price Range - DVN/CSE

Year	Volume	High	Low	Close
2022............	16,636,885	$0.37	$0.18	$0.20
2021............	118,147,210	$0.78	$0.26	$0.38

Consolidation: 1-for-30 cons. in Jan. 2021
Recent Close: $0.06
Capital Stock Changes - From August to October 2022, private placement of 6,892,000 units (1 common share & ½ warrant) at 25¢ per unit was completed, with warrants exercisable at 35¢ per share for two years.
During fiscal 2022, common shares were issued as follows: 590,000 by private placement, 400,000 on exercise of options and 91,863 on exercise of warrants.

Wholly Owned Subsidiaries

Danavation Technologies Inc., Toronto, Ont.
0890810 BC Ltd., B.C.

Financial Statistics

Periods ended:	12m July 31/22[A]		12m July 31/21[◻A]
	$000s	%Chg	$000s
Operating revenue	**1,154**	**+255**	**325**
Cost of goods sold	813		203
Salaries & benefits	1,720		1,777
General & admin expense	2,958		2,799
Stock-based compensation	649		996
Operating expense	**6,140**	**+6**	**5,775**
Operating income	**(4,986)**	**n.a.**	**(5,450)**
Deprec., depl. & amort.	248		250
Finance costs, gross	758		84
Pre-tax income	**(6,180)**	**n.a.**	**(5,685)**
Net income	**(6,180)**	**n.a.**	**(5,685)**
Cash & equivalent	14		6
Inventories	454		108
Accounts receivable	277		595
Current assets	881		1,087
Fixed assets, net	647		684
Right-of-use assets	1,911		2,130
Total assets	**3,454**	**-11**	**3,901**
Bank indebtedness	750		nil
Accts. pay. & accr. liabs	1,089		753
Current liabilities	2,773		1,512
Long-term debt, gross	3,358		nil
Long-term debt, net	3,358		nil
Long-term lease liabilities	1,828		1,968
Shareholders' equity	(4,506)		421
Cash from oper. activs	**(4,117)**	**n.a.**	**(3,635)**
Cash from fin. activs	4,241		3,283
Cash from invest. activs	(116)		(341)
Net cash position	**14**	**+133**	**6**
Capital expenditures	(103)		(716)
	$		$
Earnings per share*	(0.06)		(0.06)
Cash flow per share*	(0.04)		(0.04)
	shs		shs
No. of shs. o/s*	104,282,850		103,200,987
Avg. no. of shs. o/s*	103,586,235		92,671,393
	%		%
Net profit margin	(535.53)		n.m.
Return on equity	n.m.		n.m.
Return on assets	n.a.		n.a.

* Common
◻ Restated
[A] Reported in accordance with IFRS

Latest Results

Periods ended:	3m Oct. 31/22[A]		3m Oct. 31/21[A]
	$000s	%Chg	$000s
Operating revenue	428	+210	138
Net income	(1,301)	n.a.	(1,524)
	$		$
Earnings per share*	(0.01)		(0.01)

* Common
[A] Reported in accordance with IFRS

Historical Summary
(as originally stated)

Fiscal Year	Oper. Rev. $000s	Net Inc. Bef. Disc. $000s	EPS* $
2022[A]	1,154	(6,180)	(0.06)
2021[A1]	190	(5,820)	(0.06)
2020[A2]	nil	(360)	(1.80)
2019[A]	nil	(7,523)	(3.60)
2018[A3]	nil	(18)	(2.10)

* Common
[A] Reported in accordance with IFRS
[1] Results reflect the Jan. 8, 2021, reverse takeover acquisition of Danavation Technologies Inc.
[2] Results for 2020 and prior periods pertain to Wolf's Den Capital Corp.
[3] Results adjusted to reflect 1-for-100 share consolidation on July 18, 2019.
Note: Adjusted throughout for 1-for-30 cons. in Jan. 2021

D.15 Darelle Online Solutions Inc.

Symbol - DAR **Exchange** - TSX-VEN **CUSIP** - 237205
Head Office - 527-2818 Main St, Vancouver, BC, V5T 0C1 **Telephone** - (778) 840-3325
Website - www.darelle.com
Email - dbethune@darelle.com
Investor Relations - Dean Bethune (778) 840-3325
Auditors - MNP LLP C.A., Vancouver, B.C.
Lawyers - Holmes & King LLP, Vancouver, B.C.
Transfer Agents - Computershare Trust Company of Canada Inc.
Profile - (B.C. 2005) Provides online raffle lottery system which enables charitable and non-profit organizations to create, sell, deliver and manage their raffle ticket and 50/50 draws online.

The company is also offering a "Chase the Ace" raffle service which is a combination of a traditional and a progressive 50/50 raffle where one participant will win a percentage of the proceeds from the primary draw and the opportunity to draw a card to win the progressive portion.
Predecessor Detail - Name changed from Free Energy International Inc., Apr. 18, 2016, following the acquisition of Darelle Media Inc.
Directors - Dean Bethune, chr., pres. & CEO, B.C.; A. Scott Hamilton, CFO, Calgary, Alta.; Michael Ellis, Vancouver, B.C.; John Newman, Calgary, Alta.
Other Exec. Officers - Kyle Kotapski, pres., Darelle Media Inc.

Capital Stock

	Authorized (shs.)	Outstanding (shs.)[1]
Class A Preferred	unlimited	nil
Common	unlimited	73,708,147

[1] At Nov. 30, 2022
Major Shareholder - Dean Bethune held 11.5% interest and Kyle Kotapski held 10.9% interest at Sept. 21, 2021.

Price Range - DAR/TSX-VEN

Year	Volume	High	Low	Close
2022	3,099,273	$0.02	$0.01	$0.01
2021	4,192,692	$0.04	$0.01	$0.01
2019	1,661,312	$0.03	$0.01	$0.01
2018	5,800,633	$0.05	$0.02	$0.02

Recent Close: $0.01
Capital Stock Changes - There were no changes to capital stock from fiscal 2019 to fiscal 2022, inclusive.

Wholly Owned Subsidiaries
Darelle Media Inc., B.C.
0639305 B.C. Ltd., Richmond, B.C.

Financial Statistics

Periods ended:	12m Aug. 31/22[A]		12m Aug. 31/21[A]
	$000s	%Chg	$000s
Operating revenue	**145**	**-44**	**258**
Salaries & benefits	101		132
General & admin expense	226		289
Operating expense	**327**	**-22**	**421**
Operating income	**(182)**	**n.a.**	**(163)**
Finance costs, gross	4		3
Pre-tax income	**(184)**	**n.a.**	**(128)**
Net income	**(184)**	**n.a.**	**(128)**
Cash & equivalent	82		93
Accounts receivable	46		104
Current assets	128		200
Total assets	**128**	**-36**	**200**
Accts. pay. & accr. liabs	70		71
Current liabilities	1,124		1,016
Long-term debt, gross	39		35
Long-term debt, net	39		35
Shareholders' equity	(1,035)		(851)
Cash from oper. activs	**(11)**	**n.a.**	**(18)**
Cash from fin. activs	nil		60
Net cash position	**82**	**-12**	**93**
	$		$
Earnings per share*	(0.00)		(0.00)
Cash flow per share*	(0.00)		(0.00)
	shs		shs
No. of shs. o/s*	73,708,147		73,708,147
Avg. no. of shs. o/s*	73,708,147		73,708,147
	%		%
Net profit margin	(126.90)		(49.61)
Return on equity	n.m.		n.m.
Return on assets	(109.76)		(87.72)

* Common
[A] Reported in accordance with IFRS

Latest Results

Periods ended:	3m Nov. 30/22[A]		3m Nov. 30/21[A]
	$000s	%Chg	$000s
Operating revenue	9	-68	28
Net income	(48)	n.a.	(79)
	$		$
Earnings per share*	(0.00)		(0.00)

* Common
[A] Reported in accordance with IFRS

Historical Summary
(as originally stated)

Fiscal Year	Oper. Rev. $000s	Net Inc. Bef. Disc. $000s	EPS* $
2022[A]	145	(184)	(0.00)
2021[A]	258	(128)	(0.00)
2020[A]	145	(396)	(0.01)
2019[A]	131	(529)	(0.01)
2018[A]	124	(450)	(0.01)

* Common
[A] Reported in accordance with IFRS

D.16 Dash Capital Corp.

Symbol - DCX.P **Exchange** - TSX-VEN **CUSIP** - 23753H
Head Office - 4000-421 7 Ave SW, Calgary, AB, T2P 4K9 **Telephone** - (403) 651-9009
Email - darrellgdenney@gmail.com
Investor Relations - Darrell Denney (403) 651-9009
Auditors - BDO Canada LLP C.A., Calgary, Alta.
Transfer Agents - Odyssey Trust Company, Calgary, Alta.
Profile - (Alta. 2021) Capital Pool Company.

Recent Merger and Acquisition Activity
Status: pending **Revised:** June 15, 2023
UPDATE: The transaction remained pending, with the completion date having been extended to Aug. 15, 2023. The extension represented the sixth amendment to the completion date. PREVIOUS: Dash Capital Corp. entered into a letter of intent for the Qualifying Transaction reverse takeover acquisition of private Calgary, Alta.-based Simply Solventless Concentrates Ltd. (SSC), which manufactures solventless concentrates for cannabis users through contract manufacturing agreements with Canadian licence producers. Dash would issue post-consolidated common shares on a to-be-determined basis, which would result in SSC shareholders holding 90% of Dash's issued and outstanding shares upon completion. Aug. 6, 2021 - A definitive agreement was entered into. The basis of share exchange would be 1-for-1 (following a 1-for-3 share consolidation), with post-consolidated common shares having a deemed value of 29¢ per share. Upon completion, SSC would amalgamate with Dash's wholly owned 2366191 Alberta Ltd., and Dash would change its name to Simply Solventless Concentrates Ltd.
Directors - Darrell Denney, CEO, Calgary, Alta.; Stephen E. (Steve) Bjornson, CFO, Calgary, Alta.; Todd L. McAllister, Alta.; Murray K. Scalf, Calgary, Alta.
Other Exec. Officers - Gordon Cameron, corp. sec.

Capital Stock

	Authorized (shs.)	Outstanding (shs.)[1]
Common	unlimited	11,000,000

[1] At Mar. 31, 2023
Major Shareholder - Widely held at May 14, 2021.

Price Range - DCX.P/TSX-VEN

Year	Volume	High	Low	Close
2021	85,000	$0.18	$0.13	$0.13

D.17 Datable Technology Corporation

Symbol - DAC **Exchange** - TSX-VEN **CUSIP** - 23803L
Head Office - 301-1062 Homer St, Vancouver, BC, V6B 2W9 **Telephone** - (604) 639-5440 **Toll-free** - (877) 623-8437
Website - www.datablecorp.com
Email - rcraig@3tierlogic.com
Investor Relations - Robert Craig (604) 639-5441
Auditors - Dale Matheson Carr-Hilton LaBonte LLP C.A., Vancouver, B.C.
Lawyers - McMillan LLP, Vancouver, B.C.
Transfer Agents - TSX Trust Company
Profile - (B.C. 2011) Provides consumer lifecyle and data management platform used by consumer brands to access new consumer communities and engage them while collecting, analyzing and managing their first-party data.

Core product is PLATFORM^3, a Software-as-a-Service (SaaS) consumer marketing platform which enables consumer packaged goods companies and consumer brands to build and launch promotions and special offers on mobile devices and online. These promotions are presented to consumers before they enter into a store or when they are in the store aisle through incorporation of proprietary algorithms to send targeted email and text messages to consumers once they engage with a brand. Brands can use different modules of PLATFORM^3 to launch promotions, special offers or contest to engage and activate consumers, and to collect detailed data including consumer demographics and purchasing behaviour. PLATFORM^3 also includes a rewards portal which connects consumers to 300 gift cards including Virtual Visa, Amazon, Best Buy and others, whereby the company earns breakage fees from consumers who fail to redeem their gift cards earned as rewards for participating in promotions launched by brands on the platform.

The company is also developing Flexxi Rewards Network, a consumer data platform that enables consumer to collect, store and secure their data in a form of a digital asset/profile (Data Wallet).

Recent Merger and Acquisition Activity
Status: terminated **Revised:** Mar. 3, 2022
UPDATE: The transaction was terminated. PREVIOUS: Datable Technology Corporation agreed to acquire Adjoy, Inc (dba Dabbl) for issuance of 70,888,887 common shares at a deemed price of 15¢ per share and issuance of 4,200,000 common shares at a deemed price of 12¢ per share for the purchase of US$400,000 debt of Adjoy. Adjoy operates Dabbl, a mobile shopper engagement platform which allows users to complete quick tasks to earn gift cards from brands.
Predecessor Detail - Name changed from 3TL Technologies Corp., May 18, 2018.
Directors - Kim D. M. Oishi, exec. chr. & interim CFO, Vancouver, B.C.; Robert (Rob) Craig, pres. & CEO, Surrey, B.C.; Yucai (Rick) Huang, Richmond, B.C.; Adam R. Kniec, 150 Mile House, B.C.
Other Exec. Officers - Federico De Giuli, chief tech. officer; Hussein Hallak, v-p, product & strategy; Patrick Pharris, v-p, sales & mktg.

Capital Stock

	Authorized (shs.)	Outstanding (shs.)[1]
Preferred	unlimited	nil
Common	unlimited	182,472,436

[1] At Sept. 21, 2022

Major Shareholder - Widely held at July 18, 2022.

Price Range - DAC/TSX-VEN

Year	Volume	High	Low	Close
2022	47,676,912	$0.06	$0.01	$0.02
2021	184,914,995	$0.16	$0.06	$0.06
2020	148,779,219	$0.14	$0.02	$0.13
2019	42,069,493	$0.13	$0.02	$0.03
2018	26,513,988	$0.22	$0.05	$0.07

Recent Close: $0.01

Capital Stock Changes - In June 2022, private placement of 18,500,000 units (1 common share & 1 warrant) at 2¢ per unit was completed, with warrants exercisable at 5¢ per share for two years.

Financial Statistics

Periods ended:	12m Dec. 31/21[A]		12m Dec. 31/20[A]
	$000s	%Chg	$000s
Operating revenue	**3,532**	**+79**	**1,969**
Cost of sales	1,885		633
Salaries & benefits	2,730		1,620
General & admin expense	2,652		1,958
Stock-based compensation	489		193
Operating expense	**7,755**	**+76**	**4,404**
Operating income	**(4,223)**	**n.a.**	**(2,435)**
Deprec., depl. & amort.	109		124
Finance costs, net	(285)		50
Pre-tax income	**(4,588)**	**n.a.**	**(2,457)**
Net income	**(4,588)**	**n.a.**	**(2,457)**
Cash & equivalent	1,243		1,374
Accounts receivable	260		258
Current assets	2,249		1,983
Fixed assets, net	24		32
Right-of-use assets	182		54
Total assets	**2,455**	**+19**	**2,070**
Accts. pay. & accr. liabs.	824		638
Current liabilities	2,492		2,267
Long-term debt, gross	48		26
Long-term debt, net	28		26
Shareholders' equity	(2,947)		(222)
Cash from oper. activs.	**(3,515)**	**n.a.**	**(1,654)**
Cash from fin. activs.	3,465		2,574
Cash from invest. activs.	(82)		(7)
Net cash position	**1,243**	**-10**	**1,374**
Capital expenditures	(17)		(7)
	$		$
Earnings per share*	(0.03)		(0.03)
Cash flow per share*	(0.03)		(0.02)
	shs		shs
No. of shs. o/s*	148,598,162		129,473,856
Avg. no. of shs. o/s*	137,720,541		91,532,036
	%		%
Net profit margin	(129.90)		(124.78)
Return on equity	n.m.		n.m.
Return on assets	(202.78)		(167.26)
Foreign sales percent	87		82

* Common

[A] Reported in accordance with IFRS

Latest Results

Periods ended:	6m June 30/22[A]		6m June 30/21[A]
	$000s	%Chg	$000s
Operating revenue	1,729	+31	1,320
Net income	(2,162)	n.a.	(1,979)
	$		$
Earnings per share*	(0.01)		(0.02)

* Common

[A] Reported in accordance with IFRS

Historical Summary
(as originally stated)

Fiscal Year	Oper. Rev.	Net Inc. Bef. Disc.	EPS*
	$000s	$000s	$
2021[A]	3,532	(4,588)	(0.03)
2020[A]	1,969	(2,457)	(0.03)
2019[A]	1,561	(2,214)	(0.04)
2018[A]	1,421	(2,179)	(0.07)
2017[A]	1,193	(2,040)	(0.14)

* Common

[A] Reported in accordance with IFRS

D.18 DataMetrex AI Limited

Symbol - DM **Exchange** - TSX-VEN **CUSIP** - 23809L
Head Office - 2802-2300 Yonge St, Toronto, ON, M4P 1E4 **Telephone** - (416) 482-3282
Website - www.datametrex.com
Email - mgunter@datametrex.com
Investor Relations - J. Marshall Gunter (514) 295-2300
Auditors - Baker Tilly WM LLP C.A., Vancouver, B.C.
Transfer Agents - TSX Trust Company, Toronto, Ont.
Employees - 30 at Aug. 18, 2022

Profile - (Ont. 2011) Collects, analyzes and presents structured and unstructured data using machine learning and artificial intelligence and operates health security businesses, including concierge medical and telemedicine. Also installs electric vehicle (EV) charging stations and offers mobile EV charging services.

Operations are organized into three segments: Artificial Intelligence (AI), Machine Learning (ML) and Business Intelligence (BI); Health Technology and Security; and EV Services.

AI, ML and BI - This segment provides products including NexaSecurity, an analytics platform which captures, structures and visualizes unstructured social media data from Twitter, Facebook, Tumblr, blogs, web forums, online news sites, Google Alerts and RSS feeds allowing for better decisions by pinpointing specific trends, risks and opportunities taking place; NexaSMART, an automated reporting application which uses generated visualizations from NexaSecurity to create reports based on algorithms and features scheduled reporting which allows users to structure reporting based on regular schedule that the user needs or in response to triggering events in the data itself; and AnalyticsGPT, a combination of NexaSMART and Generative Pre-trained Transformer (GPT) which eliminates the entry barrier to predictive analytics, providing access to advanced AI technology utilized by governments and large corporations easily.

Health Technology and Security - This segment includes Medi-Call, a subscription-based Software-as-a-Service mobile application which offers on-demand medical services through connecting patients with physicians via geo-location in real-time and features mental care services including virtual counselling, support, medical attention and prescription services. Also operates two health centres in Calgary and Edmonton, Alta., which provides services such as primary care, pharmacy, physiotherapy, nutrition counselling, preventative health, corporate health care, cosmetic and occupational health care.

EV Services - This segment installs EV charging stations in Vancouver, B.C., and Toronto, Ont.; offers emergency fast charging roadside assistance service and premium-on-demand mobile EV charging services in the Greater Metro Vancouver area; and provides a proprietary mobile application which allows clients to reserve its roadside EV charging service. Also developing Mobile Charging Cart, a wireless electric vehicle charger which can be freely moved to various locations for use in commercial plazas and shopping malls in Vancouver.

In July 2023, the company announced it is considering a possible spin out of its healthcare division, including wholly owned **Medi-Call Inc.**, **Imagine Health Medical Clinics Ltd.**, **Imagine Health Pharmacies & Research Ltd.** and **Imagine Health Physio Ltd.**, with a distribution of shares to existing shareholders of the company.

In November 2022, the company acquired **Imagine Health Medical Clinics Ltd.**, **Imagine Health Pharmacies & Research Ltd.** and **Imagine Health Physio Ltd.** (collectively as Imagine Health) including two health centres in Edmonton and Calgary, Alta. for $1,300,000 and issuance of 5,000,000 common shares at a deemed price of 10¢ per share. Imagine Health offers collaborative, multidisciplinary health services to ensure patients receive quality, accessible healthcare from expert clinical teams.

Recent Merger and Acquisition Activity

Status: completed **Announced:** June 8, 2022
DataMetrex AI Limited acquired private Ontario-based EV Connect Solutions Inc., which was developing a mobile application that allows clients to reserve its roadside assistance electric vehicle (EV) charging service drivers, for issuance of 66,666,667 common shares at a deemed price of 15¢ per share. EV Connect was targeting the beta test of the mobile application for the third quarter of 2022, and planned to have the charging vehicles on the road by the end of 2022.

Predecessor Detail - Name changed from Everfront Ventures Corp., Sept. 27, 2017, following Qualifying Transaction reverse takeover of Datametrex Limited and subsequent amalgamation of Datametrex with wholly owned Everfront Acquisition Corp,.

Directors - Paul Haber, chr., Toronto, Ont.; J. Marshall Gunter, CEO, Ont.; Benjamin (Benj) Gallander, Toronto, Ont.; The Hon. James S. (Jim) Peterson, Toronto, Ont.

Other Exec. Officers - Charles Park, COO; Dong H. (Don) Shim, CFO; Maxime Martineau, chief tech. officer; Dr. Omar Sharif, CMO

Capital Stock

	Authorized (shs.)	Outstanding (shs.)[1]
Common	unlimited	393,884,701

[1] At Mar. 31, 2023

Major Shareholder - Widely held at June 28, 2022.

Price Range - DM/TSX-VEN

Year	Volume	High	Low	Close
2022	161,451,871	$0.29	$0.07	$0.08
2021	479,976,780	$0.37	$0.14	$0.16
2020	608,058,107	$0.22	$0.01	$0.14
2019	107,575,677	$0.06	$0.01	$0.02
2018	241,964,871	$0.44	$0.04	$0.04

Recent Close: $0.07

Capital Stock Changes - On June 8, 2022, 66,666,667 common shares were issued pursuant to the acquisition of EV Connect Solutions Inc. On Nov. 28, 2022, common shares were issued pursuant to the acquisition of Imagine Health Medical Clinics Ltd., Imagine Health Pharmacies & ResearchLtd., and Imagine Health Physio Ltd. Also during 2022, 1,250,000 common shares were issued on exercise of options and 17,807,500 common shares were repurchased under a Normal Course Issuer Bid.

Wholly Owned Subsidiaries

Datametrex Blockchain Limited
- 100% int. in **Datametrex Korea Limited**, South Korea.
- 7.2% int. in **Graph Blockchain Inc.**, Toronto, Ont. (see separate coverage)

Datametrex Electric Vehicle Solutions Inc., Ont.
Datametrex Limited, Toronto, Ont. Inactive.
Imagine Health Medical Clinics Ltd., Alta.
Imagine Health Pharmacies & Research Ltd., Alta.
Imagine Health Physio Ltd., Alta.
Medi-Call Inc., B.C.
9225-6965 Quebec, Qué.
- 55.9% int. in **9172-8766 Quebec Inc.**, Montréal, Qué.

Ronin Blockchain Corp., Vancouver, B.C. Inactive.

Investments

8.65% int. in **Justera Health Ltd.**, Toronto, Ont. (see separate coverage)
44.1% int. in **9172-8766 Quebec Inc.**, Montréal, Qué.

Financial Statistics

Periods ended:	12m Dec. 31/22[A]		12m Dec. 31/21[A]
	$000s	%Chg	$000s
Operating revenue	**30,489**	**-38**	**49,029**
Cost of sales	20,294		28,000
Salaries & benefits	3,929		4,251
General & admin expense	5,103		2,556
Stock-based compensation	nil		1,710
Other operating expense	772		nil
Operating expense	**30,098**	**-18**	**36,516**
Operating income	**391**	**-97**	**12,513**
Deprec., depl. & amort.	2,792		1,512
Finance income	102		nil
Finance costs, gross	18		3
Investment income	nil		(13)
Write-downs/write-offs	(6,745)		nil
Pre-tax income	**(16,270)**	**n.a.**	**11,766**
Income taxes	989		2,676
Net income	**(17,259)**	**n.a.**	**9,090**
Cash & equivalent	9,413		17,985
Accounts receivable	3,412		5,664
Current assets	15,619		23,775
Fixed assets, net	2,920		71
Right-of-use assets	3,784		227
Intangibles, net	13,677		18,567
Total assets	**36,000**	**-16**	**42,641**
Accts. pay. & accr. liabs.	2,120		4,700
Current liabilities	9,403		9,437
Long-term debt, gross	745		30
Long-term debt, net	225		30
Long-term lease liabilities	3,330		120
Shareholders' equity	22,769		32,489
Cash from oper. activs.	**(249)**	**n.a.**	**11,453**
Cash from fin. activs.	(2,403)		2,192
Cash from invest. activs.	(3,792)		(234)
Net cash position	**8,935**	**-42**	**15,400**
Capital expenditures	(2,032)		(31)
	$		$
Earnings per share*	(0.04)		0.03
Cash flow per share*	(0.00)		0.04
	shs		shs
No. of shs. o/s*	410,275,201		355,166,034
Avg. no. of shs. o/s*	387,153,455		323,104,628
	%		%
Net profit margin	(56.61)		18.54
Return on equity	(62.47)		50.87
Return on assets	(43.84)		34.55
Foreign sales percent	7		7
No. of employees (FTEs)	n.a.		30

* Common

[A] Reported in accordance with IFRS

Latest Results

Periods ended:	3m Mar. 31/23[A]		3m Mar. 31/22[A]
	$000s	%Chg	$000s
Operating revenue	3,832	-64	10,714
Net income	(1,251)	n.a.	1,353
	$		$
Earnings per share*	(0.01)		0.01

* Common

[A] Reported in accordance with IFRS

Historical Summary
(as originally stated)

Fiscal Year	Oper. Rev. $000s	Net Inc. Bef. Disc. $000s	EPS* $
2022[A]	30,489	(17,259)	(0.04)
2021[A]	49,029	9,090	0.03
2020[A]	12,378	(5,006)	(0.02)
2019[A]	3,401	(2,783)	(0.01)
2018[A]	2,230	(19,399)	(0.10)

* Common
[A] Reported in accordance with IFRS

D.19 Daura Capital Corp.

Symbol - DUR.P **Exchange** - TSX-VEN **CUSIP** - 23833V
Head Office - 501-543 Granville St, Vancouver, BC, V6C 1X8 **Telephone** - (604) 669-0660 **Fax** - (604) 688-1157
Email - btsang@seabordservices.com
Investor Relations - To Ping Tsang (604) 669-0660
Auditors - Davidson & Company LLP C.A., Vancouver, B.C.
Lawyers - Northwest Law Group, Vancouver, B.C.
Transfer Agents - Computershare Trust Company of Canada Inc., Vancouver, B.C.
Profile - (B.C. 2018) Capital Pool Company.
In November 2022, the company's proposed Qualifying Transaction acquisition of private **Estrella Gold S.A.C.**, which holds 15 exploration concessions covering 9,927 hectares and option to acquire 900-hectare Antonella gold prospect in Peru, for issuance of 3,000,000 common shares was terminated.
Directors - Mark D. Sumner, CEO, Lake Oswego, Ore.; Christina Cepeliauskas, Vancouver, B.C.; Dr. Nicholas M. Lindsay, Perth, W.A., Australia; Duncan Quinn-Smith, New York, N.Y.
Other Exec. Officers - To Ping (William) Tsang, CFO & corp. sec.

Capital Stock

	Authorized (shs.)	Outstanding (shs.)[1]
Common	unlimited	7,054,668

[1] At Aug. 29, 2022
Major Shareholder - EMX Royalty Corporation held 17.01% interest, Mark D. Sumner held 17.01% interest and Jason Surratt held 10.87% interest at Oct. 29, 2021.

Price Range - DUR.P/TSX-VEN

Year	Volume	High	Low	Close
2019	29,333	$0.15	$0.10	$0.10

Recent Close: $0.03

D.20 Deal Pro Capital Corporation

Symbol - DPCC.P **Exchange** - TSX-VEN **CUSIP** - 242274
Head Office - Scotia Plaza, 2100-40 King St W, Toronto, ON, M5H 3C2 **Telephone** - (416) 543-8289
Email - harold.wolkin@sympatico.ca
Investor Relations - Harold M. Wolkin (416) 543-8289
Auditors - RSM Canada LLP C.A., Toronto, Ont.
Transfer Agents - TSX Trust Company, Toronto, Ont.
Profile - (Ont. 2021) Capital Pool Company.
Directors - Harold M. Wolkin, CEO, CFO & corp. sec., Toronto, Ont.; Vassilios (Bill) Mitoulas, v-p, commun., Toronto, Ont.; Norman Levine, Toronto, Ont.
Other Exec. Officers - Ralph Garcea, v-p, bus. devel.; Lorne Gertner, v-p

Capital Stock

	Authorized (shs.)	Outstanding (shs.)[1]
Common	unlimited	8,207,001

[1] At May 31, 2022
Major Shareholder - Ralph Garcea held 12.18% interest, Steve Kaszas held 12.18% interest, Vassilios (Bill) Mitoulas held 12.18% interest and Harold M. Wolkin held 12.18% interest at Oct. 28, 2021.

Price Range - DPCC.P/TSX-VEN

Year	Volume	High	Low	Close
2022	163,501	$0.20	$0.05	$0.15
2021	161,000	$0.20	$0.10	$0.10

Recent Close: $0.02

D.21 Decibel Cannabis Company Inc.

Symbol - DB **Exchange** - TSX-VEN **CUSIP** - 243437
Head Office - 1440-140 4 Ave SW, Calgary, AB, T2P 3N3 **Telephone** - (403) 570-4798 **Toll-free** - (844) 993-4769
Website - www.decibelcc.com
Email - stuart.boucher@decibelcc.com
Investor Relations - Stuart Boucher (780) 619-0310
Auditors - KPMG LLP C.A., Calgary, Alta.
Transfer Agents - Odyssey Trust Company, Calgary, Alta.
Profile - (Alta. 2018; orig. B.C., 1992) Produces, distributes and sells cannabis products for the Canadian and international markets.
Production operations include The Qwest Estate, a 26,000-sq.-ft. indoor cultivation, processing and distributing facility in Creston, B.C., with 14,000 sq. ft. of dedicated grow areas and 12,000 sq. ft. of production support areas; Thunderchild Cultivation, an 80,000-sq.-ft. indoor cultivation, packaging and processing facility in Battleford, Sask.; and The Plant, a 60,000-sq.-ft. extraction, processing and manufacturing centre in Calgary, Alta., with 24,000 sq. ft. of licensed extraction and product development space.
Retail operations include six cannabis stores (at Mar. 31, 2023), operating under the Prairie Records banner, in Saskatoon (2) and Warman, Sask., and Calgary (2) and Edmonton, Alta., as well as an e-commerce platform in Saskatchewan. The company also supplies and distributes its products to licensed producers and provincial wholesalers and retailers in British Columbia, Alberta, Saskatchewan, Manitoba, Ontario, Prince Edward Island and New Brunswick, as well as to distribution partners in Israel.
Products include cannabis flower, pre-rolls, edibles, vapes and concentrates under the brands Qwest, Qwest Reserve, Blendcraft by Qwest, Pressed by Qwest and General Admission.
Predecessor Detail - Name changed from Westleaf Inc., Mar. 1, 2020.
Directors - Shawn Dym, chr., Toronto, Ont.; Paul D. Wilson, CEO, Calgary, Alta.; Manjit K. Minhas, Calgary, Alta.; Jakob Ripshtein, Toronto, Ont.; Nadia Vattovaz, Toronto, Ont.
Other Exec. Officers - Kris Newell, COO; Stuart Boucher, CFO; Adam Coates, chief revenue officer; Warren Matzelle, chief product devel. & mktg. officer

Capital Stock

	Authorized (shs.)	Outstanding (shs.)[1]
Preferred	unlimited	nil
Common	unlimited	408,814,808

[1] At June 2, 2023
Major Shareholder - Widely held at June 2, 2023.

Price Range - DB/TSX-VEN

Year	Volume	High	Low	Close
2022	49,542,447	$0.17	$0.07	$0.10
2021	100,209,795	$0.37	$0.08	$0.15
2020	48,192,474	$0.23	$0.04	$0.07
2019	75,776,594	$4.00	$0.17	$0.20
2018	86,897	$0.73	$0.29	$0.56

Consolidation: 1-for-2.9233 cons. in Jan. 2019
Recent Close: $0.16
Capital Stock Changes - During 2022, common shares were issued as follows: 601,665 on exercise of restricted share units and 24,522 on exercise of options.

Wholly Owned Subsidiaries

dB Retail Holdings Inc., Alta.
- 0.2% int. in **dB Retail L.P.**, Alta.

Decibel Labs Holdings Inc., Alta.
- 100% int. in **Westleaf Labs Inc.**, Alta.
  - 0.2% int. in **Westleaf Labs L.P.**, Alta.

Thunderchild Holdings Inc., Alta.
- 100% int. in **dB Thunderchild Cultivation Inc.**, Alta.
  - 0.2% int. in **dB Thunderchild Cultivation L.P.**, Alta.

We Grow B.C. Ltd., B.C.
- 100% int. in **1070582 B.C. Ltd.**, B.C.
  - 100% int. in **R. Spetifore & Sons Ltd.**, B.C.

Westleaf Retail Inc., Alta.
- 99.8% int. in **dB Retail L.P.**, Alta.

Subsidiaries

99.8% int. in **dB Thunderchild Cultivation L.P.**, Alta.
99.8% int. in **Westleaf Labs L.P.**, Alta.

Financial Statistics

Periods ended:	12m Dec. 31/22[A]		12m Dec. 31/21[A]
	$000s	%Chg	$000s
Operating revenue	**79,326**	**+51**	**52,453**
Cost of goods sold	52,896		24,280
Salaries & benefits	11,120		7,484
General & admin expense	10,541		8,558
Stock-based compensation	1,814		2,426
Operating expense	**76,371**	**+79**	**42,748**
Operating income	**2,955**	**-70**	**9,705**
Deprec., depl. & amort.	3,669		3,737
Finance costs, gross	3,158		4,090
Pre-tax income	**(4,462)**	**n.a.**	**1,743**
Net income	**(4,462)**	**n.a.**	**1,743**
Cash & equivalent	2,966		1,919
Inventories	45,424		34,656
Accounts receivable	16,612		12,839
Current assets	69,773		56,630
Fixed assets, net	57,924		58,864
Right-of-use assets	4,620		3,343
Intangibles, net	4,622		4,680
Total assets	**140,880**	**+12**	**125,929**
Accts. pay. & accr. liabs	44,325		24,961
Current liabilities	53,880		47,115
Long-term debt, gross	43,733		45,479
Long-term debt, net	35,046		24,057
Long-term lease liabilities	3,793		3,689
Equity portion of conv. debs	nil		1,938
Shareholders' equity	47,211		50,735
Cash from oper. activs	**8,258**	**n.a.**	**(17,146)**
Cash from fin. activs	(3,447)		18,470
Cash from invest. activs	(3,764)		(3,225)
Net cash position	**2,966**	**+55**	**1,919**
Capital expenditures	(3,266)		(2,960)
Capital disposals	47		nil
	$		$
Earnings per share*	(0.01)		0.01
Cash flow per share*	0.02		(0.05)
	shs		shs
No. of shs. o/s*	404,654,387		404,028,200
Avg. no. of shs. o/s*	404,154,231		365,778,015
	%		%
Net profit margin	(5.62)		3.32
Return on equity	(9.11)		4.14
Return on assets	(0.98)		5.43

* Common
[A] Reported in accordance with IFRS

Latest Results

Periods ended:	3m Mar. 31/23[A]		3m Mar. 31/22[A]
	$000s	%Chg	$000s
Operating revenue	27,141	+63	16,650
Net income	(569)	n.a.	(4,372)
	$		$
Earnings per share*	(0.00)		(0.01)

* Common
[A] Reported in accordance with IFRS

Historical Summary
(as originally stated)

Fiscal Year	Oper. Rev. $000s	Net Inc. Bef. Disc. $000s	EPS* $
2022[A]	79,326	(4,462)	(0.01)
2021[A]	52,453	1,743	0.01
2020[A]	29,930	(9,210)	(0.03)
2019[A1]	6,235	(6,531)	(0.10)
2018[A2]	nil	(7,173)	(0.13)

* Common
[A] Reported in accordance with IFRS
[1] Results reflect the Dec. 20, 2019, reverse takeover acquisition of We Grow B.C. Ltd.
[2] Results reflect the Dec. 28, 2018, reverse takeover acquisition of Westleaf Cannabis Inc.
Note: Adjusted throughout for 1-for-2.9233 cons. in Jan. 2019

D.22 Decisive Dividend Corporation

Symbol - DE **Exchange** - TSX-VEN **CUSIP** - 24345T
Head Office - 260-1855 Kirschner Rd, Kelowna, BC, V1Y 4N7 **Telephone** - (250) 870-9146 **Fax** - (250) 870-9149
Website - www.decisivedividend.com
Email - rick@decisivedividend.com
Investor Relations - Rick Torriero (250) 870-9146
Auditors - PricewaterhouseCoopers LLP C.A., Vancouver, B.C.
Lawyers - Pushor Mitchell LLP, Kelowna, B.C.; MLT Aikins LLP, Winnipeg, Man.
Transfer Agents - Computershare Trust Company of Canada Inc., Vancouver, B.C.
Employees - 341 at Dec. 31, 2022

Profile - (B.C. 2012) Acquires profitable, well-established, high quality manufacturing companies.

Operations are focused on two business segments: Finished Product; and Component Manufacturing.

Finished Product operations

The company's **Blaze King** division designs and produces wood burning stoves, wood burning fireplace inserts, gas stoves, gas fireplaces and gas fireplace inserts. Products are manufactured from its facilities in Penticton, B.C., and Walla Walla, Wash., and are distributed worldwide.

Wholly owned **Slimline Manufacturing Ltd.** designs, manufactures and distributes agricultural air blast sprayers and industrial wastewater evaporators from its facility in Penticton, B.C. Sprayers are marketed under the Turbo Mist brand and are used primarily in the agriculture industry for application of treatments to crops; wastewater evaporators are sold under the EcoMister name and are primarily used in the mining, oil and gas and waste management industries. Also manufactures custom products and sells various, sprayers, evaporator and other industrial parts.

Wholly owned **Marketing Impact Limited** designs, manufactures and distributes a comprehensive range of merchandising products, systems and solutions at its facility in Concord, Ont., for retail customers in North America, including grocery stores, convenience stores and pharmacies. Products include product pusher systems, loss prevention solutions, merchandising bins and accessories, shelf management systems and sign holder systems. Also designs and manufactures store displays for consumer-packaged goods customers.

Wholly owned **ACR Heat Products Limited** manufactures and sells wood burning, multifuel, gas and electric stoves, electric fireplaces and outdoor pizza ovens primarily in the U.K.

Wholly owned **Capital I Industries Inc.** and **Irving Machine Inc.** design, manufacture and distribute road maintenance and construction equipment including dozer blades, snow blades and wings, slopers, gravel reclaimers, gravel groomers, lifts, mulchers and mowers, that are used in the construction and maintenance of gravel roads.

Component Manufacturing operations

Wholly owned **Unicast Inc.** produces and distributes industrial wear parts and valves for the mining, aggregate and cement industries. Wear parts are parts for machinery that wear out quickly when processing cement and crushing rock. Products are shipped from its facility in Kelowna, B.C., to dealers and customers worldwide.

Wholly owned **Hawk Machine Works Ltd.** offers manufacturing, machine work, assembly and testing of custom precision machined metal products for different industries in North America. Products and services include general machining, hydraulic fracturing tools, ground and subsurface tools, rods and couplings, reconditioning services and resale parts. Operations are conducted from its manufacturing site in Linden, Alta.

Wholly owned **Northside Industries Inc.** offers full-service welding and fabrication solutions to various industries across North America, with a focus on the commercial vehicle and forestry sectors. Products produced include truck and automotive components, fuel-hydraulic fluid tanks, j-brackets and straps, bumpers, truck chassis components, cab panels, tanks, architectural components, tool and battery boxes and steel under-decking. Also globally distributes Hydrau-Flo, a fast fuel filling valve system that is also aimed at preventing overfilling, spillage and fuel tank rupture. Products are manufactured from its facility in West Kelowna, B.C.

Wholly owned **Micon Industries Ltd.** designs, manufactures and distributes radiator seals and grommets to fit radiators designed for the demanding cooling systems of the mining and road construction industries.

Wholly owned **Procore International Radiators Ltd.** designs, manufactures and distributes radiators for cooling systems found in the heavy duty equipment used in the mining, oil and gas and road construction industries.

Recent Merger and Acquisition Activity

Status: completed **Announced:** Apr. 18, 2023
Decisive Dividend Corporation acquired three businesses for $17,200,000. The acquired companies, which are Tisdale, Sask.-based Capital I Industries Inc. and its sister company, Irving Machine Inc. (together Capital I), Merritt, B.C.-based Micon Industries Ltd., and Merritt, B.C.-based Procore International Radiators Ltd., manufacture and sell a range of products that support non-cyclical road maintenance and construction customers, as well as heavy equipment maintenance customers across multiple industries and geographies.

Status: completed **Announced:** Oct. 3, 2022
Decisive Dividend Corporation acquired Birmingham, U.K.-based ACR Heat Products Limited, which manufactures and sells woodburning, multifuel and gas stoves primarily in the U.K., for $8,300,000, consisting of $7,600,000 cash and issuance of 166,790 common shares valued at $700,000. The cash portion was funded with proceeds from a recently completed private placement.

Status: completed **Announced:** Apr. 14, 2022
Decisive Dividend Corporation acquired Vaughan, Ont.-based Marketing Impact Limited for $10,000,000, consisting of $9,000,000 cash and issuance of 235,294 common shares at $4.25 per share. Up to an additional $1,500,000 would be paid by Decisive Dividend contingent on Marketing Impact achieving certain earnings targets over the next three years. Marketing Impact designs, manufactures and distributes merchandising products, systems and solutions for retail customers, including grocery stores, convenience stores and pharmacies, as well as store displays for consumer-packaged goods customers in North America.

Directors - James Paterson, chr., Kelowna, B.C.; Jeff Schellenberg, CEO, Kelowna, B.C.; G. Terence (Terry) Edwards, COO & corp. sec., Kelowna, B.C.; Timothy Pirie†, Kelowna, B.C.; M. Bruce Campbell, Kelowna, B.C.; Michael Conway, West Kelowna, B.C.; Peter D. Jeffrey, Kelowna, B.C.; Chief Robert Louie, West Kelowna, B.C.; Warren Matheos, Calgary, Alta.

Other Exec. Officers - Rick Torriero, CFO; Daryll Lowry, pres., Slimline Manufacturing Ltd.; Alan Murphy, pres., Valley Comfort Systems Inc.; Tim Stewart, pres., Hawk Machine Works Ltd.; Mark Watson, pres., Unicast Inc.; Cooper Harrison, asst. v-p, fin.

† Lead director

Capital Stock

	Authorized (shs.)	Outstanding (shs.)[1]
Common	unlimited	13,375,081

[1] At May 10, 2023

Normal Course Issuer Bid - The company plans to make normal course purchases of up to 746,800 common shares representing 5% of the total outstanding. The bid commenced on Feb. 16, 2023, and expires on Feb. 15, 2024.

Major Shareholder - Waratah Capital Advisors Ltd. held 18.6% interest at May 10, 2023.

Price Range - DE/TSX-VEN

Year	Volume	High	Low	Close
2022	1,619,819	$5.22	$3.92	$5.02
2021	2,504,283	$4.49	$2.12	$4.04
2020	4,199,801	$3.87	$1.15	$2.22
2019	2,054,091	$4.39	$3.39	$3.70
2018	1,513,072	$4.49	$3.28	$3.87

Recent Close: $8.31

Capital Stock Changes - In April 2023, offering of 1,964,488 units (1 common share & ½ warrant) at $5.91 per unit was completed, with warrants exercisable at $7.09 per share for two years.

On Apr. 4, 2022, 235,294 common shares were issued pursuant to the acquisition of Marketing Impact Limited. In September 2022, private placement of 1,848,364 units (1 common share & ½ warrant) at $4.12 per unit was completed. On Oct. 3, 2022, 166,790 common shares were issued pursuant to the acquisition of ACR Heat Products Limited. Also during 2022, common shares were issued as follows: 299,754 on exercise of options, 188,787 under the dividend reinvestment plan and 70,694 under the employee share purchase plan; 14,775 common shares were repurchased under a Normal Course Issuer Bid.

Dividends

DE com Ra $0.48 pa M est. Aug. 15, 2023**
Prev. Rate: $0.42 est. Apr. 14, 2023
Prev. Rate: $0.36 est. May 13, 2022
Prev. Rate: $0.30 est. Sept. 15, 2021
Prev. Rate: $0.24 est. May 14, 2021
Prev. Rate: $0.36 est. Apr. 14, 2017
** Reinvestment Option

Wholly Owned Subsidiaries

ACR Heat Products Limited, Birmingham, Warks., United Kingdom.
Capital I Industries Inc., Tisdale, Sask.
• 100% int. in **Irving Machine Inc.**, Tisdale, Sask.
Hawk Machine Works Ltd., Alta.
Marketing Impact Limited, Vaughan, Ont.
Micon Industries Ltd., Merritt, B.C.
Northside Industries Inc., West Kelowna, B.C.
Procore International Radiators Ltd., Merritt, B.C.
Slimline Manufacturing Ltd., Penticton, B.C.
Unicast Inc., Kelowna, B.C.
Valley Comfort Systems Inc., B.C.
• 100% int. in **Blaze King Industries Canada Ltd.**, Penticton, B.C.
• 100% int. in **Blaze King Industries, Inc.**, Wash.

Financial Statistics

Periods ended:	12m Dec. 31/22[A]		12m Dec. 31/21[oA]
	$000s	%Chg	$000s
Operating revenue	**98,587**	**+58**	**62,491**
Cost of goods sold	64,137		39,643
Salaries & benefits	13,157		8,752
General & admin expense	8,703		5,554
Stock-based compensation	143		256
Operating expense	**86,140**	**+59**	**54,205**
Operating income	**12,447**	**+50**	**8,286**
Deprec., depl. & amort.	4,884		366
Finance income	20		408
Finance costs, gross	2,524		2,079
Write-downs/write-offs	(22)		(27)
Pre-tax income	**5,687**	**+93**	**2,940**
Income taxes	1,603		658
Net income	**4,084**	**+79**	**2,282**
Cash & equivalent	4,734		2,143
Inventories	14,940		10,106
Accounts receivable	16,380		10,646
Current assets	38,487		23,883
Fixed assets, net	12,299		7,586
Intangibles, net	47,648		28,828
Total assets	**98,434**	**+63**	**60,297**
Accts. pay. & accr. liabs.	18,022		7,852
Current liabilities	20,558		11,130
Long-term debt, gross	32,669		22,590
Long-term debt, net	32,669		22,590
Long-term lease liabilities	5,059		1,533
Shareholders' equity	34,130		22,222
Cash from oper. activs.	**8,427**	**+116**	**3,908**
Cash from fin. activs.	11,063		(2,982)
Cash from invest. activs.	(17,197)		(1,753)
Net cash position	**4,734**	**+121**	**2,143**
Capital expenditures	(2,140)		(1,844)
Capital disposals	40		91
	$		$
Earnings per share*	0.31		0.19
Cash flow per share*	0.65		0.33
Cash divd. per share*	0.35		0.21
	shs		shs
No. of shs. o/s*	14,888,021		12,093,113
Avg. no. of shs. o/s*	13,033,000		11,925,000
	%		%
Net profit margin	4.14		3.65
Return on equity	14.49		10.49
Return on assets	7.43		6.68
Foreign sales percent	52		58
No. of employees (FTEs)	341		267

* Common
[o] Restated
[A] Reported in accordance with IFRS

Latest Results

Periods ended:	3m Mar. 31/23[A]		3m Mar. 31/22[A]
	$000s	%Chg	$000s
Operating revenue	30,854	+65	18,689
Net income	1,966	+284	512
	$		$
Earnings per share*	0.13		0.04

* Common
[A] Reported in accordance with IFRS

Historical Summary
(as originally stated)

Fiscal Year	Oper. Rev.	Net Inc. Bef. Disc.	EPS*
	$000s	$000s	$
2022[A]	98,587	4,084	0.31
2021[A]	62,491	2,282	0.19
2020[A]	48,457	(736)	(0.06)
2019[A]	47,390	759	0.07
2018[A]	37,993	550	0.07

* Common
[A] Reported in accordance with IFRS

D.23 DeepMarkit Corp.

Symbol - MKT **Exchange** - TSX-VEN **CUSIP** - 24380K
Head Office - 100-750 11 St SW, Calgary, AB, T2P 3N7 **Telephone** - (403) 537-0067
Website - www.deepmarkit.com
Email - corp@deepmarkit.com
Investor Relations - Ranjeet Sundher (403) 537-0067
Auditors - SRCO Professional Corporation C.A., Richmond Hill, Ont.
Transfer Agents - Odyssey Trust Company, Calgary, Alta.

Profile - (Alta. 2007) Operates MintCarbon.io, a web-based software-as-a-service platform that facilitates the minting of carbon credits into non-fungible tokens (NFTs).

In September 2022, the company changed its year end to June 30 from December 31.

Predecessor Detail - Name changed from Challenger Deep Resources Corp., Oct. 29, 2015.

Directors - Ranjeet Sundher, interim CEO, North Vancouver, B.C.; Steven E. (Steve) Vanry, pres., Calgary, Alta.; J. Garnet (Garry) Clark, Thunder Bay, Ont.; Paul T. McKenzie, Vancouver, B.C.

Other Exec. Officers - Curtis Smith, CFO; Jack Bogart, chief tech. officer; Alex Parken, corp. sec.

Capital Stock

	Authorized (shs.)	Outstanding (shs.)[1]
Preferred	unlimited	nil
Common	unlimited	4,246,571

[1] At June 22, 2023

Major Shareholder - Ranjeet Sundher held 24.49% interest at Sept. 2, 2022.

Price Range - MKT/TSX-VEN

Year	Volume	High	Low	Close
2022	908,634	$9.12	$0.80	$1.40
2021	63,598	$6.80	$1.25	$6.00
2020	52,977	$2.50	$0.50	$1.25
2019	67,748	$11.00	$0.50	$1.50
2018	314,523	$82.50	$5.00	$5.00

Consolidation: 1-for-40 cons. in June 2023; 4-for-1 split in May 2022; 1-for-5 cons. in Apr. 2021; 1-for-10 cons. in Oct. 2019

Recent Close: $0.15

Capital Stock Changes - On June 22, 2023, common shares were consolidated on a 1-for-40 basis.

On Feb. 18, 2022, 60,000,000 post-split common shares were issued pursuant to the acquisition of First Carbon Corp. and private placement of 17,340,000 units (1 post-split common share & 1 warrant) at 13¢ per unit was completed. In March 2022, private placement of 9,800,000 units (1 post-split common share & 1 warrant) at 21¢ per unit was completed. In May 2022, common shares were split on a 4-for-1 basis. Also during the six-month period ended June 30, 2022, 448,000 post-split common shares were issued as finders' fees.

Wholly Owned Subsidiaries

DeepMarkit AI Corp.
DeepMarkit Digital Corp. Inactive.
First Carbon Corp., Vancouver, B.C.

Financial Statistics

Periods ended:	6m June 30/22[A]		12m Dec. 31/21[□A]
	$000s	%Chg	$000s
Operating revenue	**1**	**n.a.**	**3**
Salaries & benefits	110		175
General & admin expense	1,977		170
Stock-based compensation	1,987		nil
Operating expense	**4,074**	**n.a.**	**346**
Operating income	**(4,073)**	**n.a.**	**(343)**
Deprec., depl. & amort.	1		3
Finance costs, net	nil		237
Write-downs/write-offs	2,124		nil
Pre-tax income	**(6,209)**	**n.a.**	**(4,765)**
Net income	**(6,209)**	**n.a.**	**(4,765)**
Cash & equivalent	1,949		501
Accounts receivable	170		24
Current assets	535		609
Fixed assets, net	5		6
Intangibles, net	5,336		nil
Total assets	**7,994**	**n.a.**	**648**
Bank indebtedness	nil		35
Accts. pay. & accr. liabs	453		337
Current liabilities	453		372
Long-term debt, gross	37		nil
Long-term debt, net	37		nil
Shareholders' equity	7,504		276
Cash from oper. activs	**(2,583)**	**n.a.**	**(314)**
Cash from fin. activs	3,950		721
Cash from invest. activs	81		nil
Net cash position	**1,949**	**n.a.**	**501**
	$		$
Earnings per share*	(1.72)		(7.44)
Cash flow per share*	(0.71)		(0.49)
	shs		shs
No. of shs. o/s*	4,246,570		2,056,870
Avg. no. of shs. o/s*	3,621,293		640,876
	%		%
Net profit margin	...		n.m.
Return on equity	...		n.m.
Return on assets	...		n.m.

* Common
□ Restated
[A] Reported in accordance with IFRS

Latest Results

Periods ended:	3m Sept. 30/22[A]		3m Sept. 30/21[□A]
	$000s	%Chg	$000s
Operating revenue	nil	n.a.	1
Net income	(1,351)	n.a.	(145)
	$		$
Earnings per share*	(0.32)		(0.40)

* Common
□ Restated
[A] Reported in accordance with IFRS

Historical Summary
(as originally stated)

Fiscal Year	Oper. Rev. $000s	Net Inc. Bef. Disc. $000s	EPS* $
2022[A1]	1	(6,209)	(1.72)
2021[A]	3	(4,765)	(7.30)
2020[A]	6	(610)	(1.50)
2019[A]	8	(685)	(2.50)
2018[A]	3	(1,912)	(8.40)

* Common
[A] Reported in accordance with IFRS
[1] 6 months ended June 30, 2022.

Note: Adjusted throughout for 1-for-40 cons. in June 2023; 4-for-1 split in May 2022; 1-for-5 cons. in Apr. 2021; 1-for-10 cons. in Oct. 2019

D.24 DeepSpatial Inc.

Symbol - DSAI **Exchange** - CSE **CUSIP** - 24381D
Head Office - 3000-77 King St W, Toronto, ON, M5K 1G8 **Telephone** - (416) 304-1231
Website - www.deepspatial.ai
Email - rahul.kushwahphd@gmail.com
Investor Relations - Dr. Rahul Kushwah (416) 543-9617
Auditors - Kreston GTA LLP C.A., Markham, Ont.
Transfer Agents - Computershare Trust Company of Canada Inc., Toronto, Ont.

Profile - (Can. 2010) Offers artificial intelligence (AI)-powered solutions that provide enterprise insight using geospatial data, geographic information systems and machine learning.

The company uses AI to create robust location intelligence solutions for transforming existing location data into business outcomes. Location data can be anything from addresses and latitude or longitude coordinates, buildings, monuments or alike and when this data is correlated with internal business data, it creates business context to improve decision making backed by data driven analytics.

The company's technology unites business data with business operations to help it understand customer personas; inventory consumption and link it to effective supply chains and warehouse planning; expand existing markets by locating potential customers analogous to existing clients; and to promote targeted pricing and discount strategies on a geospatial basis.

The technology is targeted towards companies in the manufacturing, retail, food and beverage, and transportation sectors.

Predecessor Detail - Name changed from Aylen Capital Inc., Dec. 21, 2020, pursuant to the reverse takeover acquisition of Loc8 Corp. (dba Deepspatial AI) and concurrent amalgamation of Loc8 with wholly owned 2774951 Ontario Limited (and continued as DeepSpatial (Ontario) Inc.).

Directors - Sheldon Kales, chr., Toronto, Ont.; Dr. Rahul Kushwah, CEO, Toronto, Ont.; Nandan Mishra, India; Tomas (Tom) Sipos, Toronto, Ont.

Other Exec. Officers - Rakesh Malhotra, CFO & corp. sec.; Himanshu U. Singh, chief tech. officer; Ardhendu Mishra, v-p, ind. eng.; Rahul Pandey, v-p, bus. devel.; Debojyoti (Deb) Purkayastha, v-p, global bus. devel.; Vaibhav Sharma, v-p, enterprise solutions

Capital Stock

	Authorized (shs.)	Outstanding (shs.)[1]
Preferred	unlimited	nil
Common	unlimited	94,030,509

[1] At Nov. 29, 2022

Major Shareholder - Algo8 AI Private Limited held 22.9% interest, Sheldon Kales held 16.1% interest and Dr. Rahul Kushwah held 12.9% interest at Jan. 21, 2022.

Price Range - DSAI/CSE

Year	Volume	High	Low	Close
2022	6,156,578	$0.18	$0.03	$0.04
2021	13,392,961	$0.50	$0.10	$0.15
2020	631,816	$0.34	$0.02	$0.14
2019	395,808	$0.12	$0.04	$0.04
2018	390,224	$0.22	$0.06	$0.08

Consolidation: 1-for-4 cons. in Dec. 2020

Recent Close: $0.08

Capital Stock Changes - During fiscal 2022, common shares were issued as follows: 376,000 on vesting of restricted share units and 250,000 for services.

Wholly Owned Subsidiaries

DeepSpatial Asia Private Limited, India.
DeepSpatial (Ontario) Inc., Toronto, Ont.

Financial Statistics

Periods ended:	12m June 30/22[A]		12m June 30/21[A1]
	$000s	%Chg	$000s
Research & devel. expense	116		6
General & admin expense	512		376
Stock-based compensation	746		121
Other operating expense	288		1,916
Operating expense	**1,662**	**-31**	**2,419**
Operating income	**(1,662)**	**n.a.**	**(2,419)**
Deprec., depl. & amort.	306		306
Pre-tax income	**(1,968)**	**n.a.**	**(2,726)**
Net income	**(1,968)**	**n.a.**	**(2,726)**
Cash & equivalent	171		1,024
Current assets	352		1,140
Intangibles, net	1,284		1,591
Total assets	**1,636**	**-40**	**2,731**
Accts. pay. & accr. liabs	165		81
Current liabilities	171		81
Shareholders' equity	1,435		2,620
Cash from oper. activs	**(853)**	**n.a.**	**(733)**
Cash from fin. activs	nil		554
Net cash position	**171**	**-83**	**1,024**
	$		$
Earnings per share*	(0.02)		(0.03)
Cash flow per share*	(0.01)		(0.01)
Extra divd. - cash*	nil		0.08
	shs		shs
No. of shs. o/s*	94,030,509		93,404,509
Avg. no. of shs. o/s*	93,600,279		83,236,984
	%		%
Net profit margin	n.a.		n.a.
Return on equity	(97.07)		n.m.
Return on assets	(90.13)		n.a.

* Common
[A] Reported in accordance with IFRS
[1] Results reflect the Dec. 22, 2020, reverse takeover acquisition of Loc8 Corp.

Latest Results

Periods ended:	3m Sept. 30/22[A]		3m Sept. 30/21[A]
	$000s	%Chg	$000s
Net income	(352)	n.a.	(480)
	$		$
Earnings per share*	(0.00)		(0.00)

* Common
[A] Reported in accordance with IFRS

Historical Summary
(as originally stated)

Fiscal Year	Oper. Rev. $000s	Net Inc. Bef. Disc. $000s	EPS* $
2022[A]	nil	(1,968)	(0.02)
2021[A]	nil	(2,726)	(0.03)
2020[A1,2]	nil	(523)	(0.01)
2019[A3]	608	(214)	(0.05)
2018[A]	561	740	0.18

* Common
[A] Reported in accordance with IFRS
[1] 43 weeks ended June 30, 2020.
[2] Results pertain to Loc8 Corp.
[3] Results for 2019 and prior years pertain to Aylen Capital Inc.

Note: Adjusted throughout for 1-for-4 cons. in Dec. 2020

D.25 Defence Therapeutics Inc.

Symbol - DTC **Exchange** - CSE **CUSIP** - 24463V
Head Office - 1680-200 Burrard St, Vancouver, BC, V6C 3L6 **Telephone** - (514) 947-2272 **Fax** - (604) 357-1704
Website - defencetherapeutics.com
Email - splouffe@defencetherapeutics.com
Investor Relations - Sébastien Plouffe (514) 947-2272
Auditors - Crowe MacKay LLP C.A., Vancouver, B.C.
Transfer Agents - Computershare Trust Company of Canada Inc., Toronto, Ont.

Profile - (B.C. 2020; orig. Que., 2017) Engages in research and development with a focus on enhancing intracellular delivery of biological/biosimilar therapeutic drugs targeting cancer and infectious diseases.

The company's Accum™ technology enables efficient intracellular access to a given biological while maintaining target cell specificity. Its product pipeline focuses on effective intracellular access by different types of vaccine (DNA, RNA and protein) and by protein-delivery systems such as monoclonal antibody (mAb)-based therapies. The company is focused on research, development and advancement of products using its proprietary Accum™ technology.

Products under development include the addition of Accum-linked antigens to allogeneic dendritic cells to enhance the therapeutic efficacy of vaccines to treat melanoma, lymphoma, colon and breast cancer cells in vitro; a new protein-based vaccine formulation against COVID and infectious diseases; antibody drug conjugates targeting various cancers including the enhancing of ADC Kadcyla (T-DM1) to specifically treat breast cancer; the AccuTOX program, which consists of over 50 Accum variants that are currently being tested for their therapeutic efficacy against breast, colon, melanoma and lymphoma cancers; and cervical cancer vaccine whereby a protein-based anti-cervical cancer vaccine is being attached to the E7 protein to protect and control cervical cancer growth.

Predecessor Detail - Name changed from ACCUM Therapeutics Inc., Mar. 26, 2020.

Directors - Sébastien Plouffe, pres. & CEO, Montréal, Qué.; P. Joseph Meagher, CFO, Vancouver, B.C.; Dr. Moutih Rafei, v-p, R&D, Vaudreuil-Dorion, Qué.; Kwin Grauer; Dr. Raimar Löbenberg, Edmonton, Alta.; Dr. Sarkis Meterissian, Mont-Royal, Qué.

Other Exec. Officers - Dr. Simon Beaudoin, co-founder & chief tech. science officer; Carrie Cesarone, corp. sec.

Capital Stock

	Authorized (shs.)	Outstanding (shs.)[1]
Class A Common	unlimited	37,849,174
Class B Common	unlimited	nil
Class C Common	unlimited	nil
Class A Special	unlimited	nil
Class C Special	unlimited	nil
Class D Special	unlimited	nil

[1] At Nov. 28, 2022

Major Shareholder - Widely held at Nov. 3, 2022.

Price Range - DTC/CSE

Year	Volume	High	Low	Close
2022	1,924,183	$5.65	$1.45	$2.60
2021	2,650,673	$8.15	$1.75	$5.40

Recent Close: $2.71

Capital Stock Changes - During fiscal 2022, 1,412,400 common shares were issued on exercise of warrants.

Financial Statistics

Periods ended:	12m June 30/22[A]		12m June 30/21[A]
	$000s	%Chg	$000s
Research & devel. expense	3,760		1,159
General & admin expense	3,189		1,095
Stock-based compensation	371		606
Operating expense	**7,320**	**+156**	**2,860**
Operating income	**(7,320)**	**n.a.**	**(2,860)**
Pre-tax income	**(7,344)**	**n.a.**	**(2,859)**
Net income	**(7,344)**	**n.a.**	**(2,859)**
Cash & equivalent	507		5,453
Current assets	674		5,563
Intangibles, net	46		46
Total assets	**720**	**-87**	**5,609**
Accts. pay. & accr. liabs	1,107		122
Current liabilities	1,107		122
Shareholders' equity	(388)		5,487
Cash from oper. activs	**(6,044)**	**n.a.**	**(2,290)**
Cash from fin. activs	1,098		5,877
Net cash position	**507**	**-91**	**5,453**
	$		$
Earnings per share*	(0.20)		(0.11)
Cash flow per share*	(0.17)		(0.09)
	shs		shs
No. of shs. o/s*	36,633,174		35,220,774
Avg. no. of shs. o/s*	36,077,323		26,596,154
	%		%
Net profit margin	n.a.		n.a.
Return on equity	n.m.		(77.79)
Return on assets	(232.07)		(76.03)

* Common

[A] Reported in accordance with IFRS

Latest Results

Periods ended:	3m Sept. 30/22[A]		3m Sept. 30/21[A]
	$000s	%Chg	$000s
Net income	(1,703)	n.a.	(1,530)
	$		$
Earnings per share*	(0.05)		(0.04)

* Common

[A] Reported in accordance with IFRS

Historical Summary
(as originally stated)

Fiscal Year	Oper. Rev.	Net Inc. Bef. Disc.	EPS*
	$000s	$000s	$
2022[A]	nil	(7,344)	(0.20)
2021[A]	nil	(2,859)	(0.11)
2020[A]	nil	(673)	(0.71)
2019[A]	nil	(2)	(19.46)

* Common

[A] Reported in accordance with IFRS

D.26 DeFi Technologies Inc.

Symbol - DEFI **Exchange** - NEO **CUSIP** - 244916

Head Office - 198 Davenport Rd, Toronto, ON, M5R 1J2 **Telephone** - (416) 309-2696 **Fax** - (416) 861-8165

Website - valour.com

Email - ryanp@fmfinancialgroup.com

Investor Relations - Ryan Ptolemy (416) 861-5882

Auditors - BF Borgers CPA PC C.P.A., Lakewood, Colo.

Transfer Agents - TSX Trust Company, Toronto, Ont.

Employees - 5 at Mar. 31, 2022

Profile - (Ont. 2009; orig. B.C., 1986) Provides investors exposure across the decentralized finance (DeFi) ecosystem through development and listing of exchange traded products and participation in decentralized blockchain networks by running nodes that contribute to network security and stability, governance and transaction validation. Also invests in tokens of DeFi companies in early-stage ventures.

The company has three distinct business lines: DeFi ETPs, DeFi Ventures and DeFi Infrastructure.

DeFi ETPs - Through wholly owned **Valour Inc.**, develops Exchange Traded Notes (ETNs) that synthetically track the value of a single DeFi protocol or a basket of protocols. ETNs simplify the ability for retail and institutional investors to gain exposure to DeFi protocols or basket of protocols as it removes the need to manage a wallet, two-factor authentication, various logins and other intricacies that are linked to managing a DeFi protocol portfolio.

DeFi Venture - Invests in various companies and leading protocols across the DeFi ecosystem to build a diversified portfolio of DeFi assets.

DeFi Infrastructure - Offers governance services and products within the DeFi ecosystem. Node management of decentralized protocols are offered to support governance, security and transaction validation for their networks.

The company's existing product range includes Valour Uniswap (UNI), Cardano (ADA), Polkadot (DOT), Solana (SOL), Avalanche (AVAX), Cosmos (ATOM) and Enjin (ENJ) ETPs, as well as flagship Bitcoin Zero and Valour Ethereum Zero products.

Predecessor Detail - Name changed from Valour Inc., July 10, 2023.

Directors - Olivier F. Roussy Newton, exec. chr. & CEO, Zug, Switzerland; Suzanne (Sue) Ennis, Toronto, Ont.; Stefan Hascoet, Geneva, Switzerland; William C. (Con) Steers, Toronto, Ont.; Mikael Tandetnik, Geneva, Switzerland; Krisztian Tóth, Toronto, Ont.

Other Exec. Officers - Ryan Ptolemy, CFO; James R. N. (Russell) Starr, head, capital markets; Kenny Choi, corp. sec.

Capital Stock

	Authorized (shs.)	Outstanding (shs.)[1]
Potash Stream Preferred	20,000,000	4,500,000
Common	unlimited	219,010,501

[1] At Mar. 31, 2023

Potash Stream Preferred - Entitled to receive a 9% cumulative preferential cash dividend, payable annually on the last day of January until the January following the first year of initial potash production. In and each succeeding year, a dividend is payable quarterly on the last day of the month following the quarter, at a rate equal to the total amount of net potash revenue for the quarter divided by 20,000,000. Non-voting.

Common - One vote per share.

Major Shareholder - Widely held at Mar. 29, 2022.

Price Range - DEFI/NEO

Year	Volume	High	Low	Close
2022	17,643,300	$3.14	$0.10	$0.13
2021	29,848,643	$4.37	$0.48	$2.99
2020	32,721,852	$0.79	$0.02	$0.66
2019	7,512,069	$0.08	$0.03	$0.04
2018	8,381,950	$0.43	$0.05	$0.06

Recent Close: $0.10

Capital Stock Changes - In October 2022, private placement of up to 25,000,000 units (1 common share & ½ warrant) at 20¢ per unit was arranged, with warrants exercisable at 30¢ per share for two years.

Wholly Owned Subsidiaries

DeFi Capital Inc.

DeFi Holdings (Bermuda) Ltd., Bermuda.
- 100% int. in **Valour Management Limited**, United Kingdom.

Electrum Streaming Inc., Ont.
- 100% int. in **Crypto 21 AB**, Sweden.

Valour Inc., Cayman Islands.
- 100% int. in **DeFi Europe AG**, Switzerland.

Financial Statistics

Periods ended:	12m Dec. 31/21[A]		12m Dec. 31/20[oA]
	$000s	%Chg	$000s
Operating revenue	**15,081**	**+411**	**2,951**
General & admin expense	14,954		600
Stock-based compensation	42,035		116
Operating expense	**56,989**	**n.m.**	**716**
Operating income	**(41,908)**	**n.a.**	**2,235**
Deprec., depl. & amort.	3,640		nil
Finance costs, gross	1,186		nil
Write-downs/write-offs	(17,483)		nil
Pre-tax income	**(71,495)**	**n.a.**	**2,074**
Net income	**(71,495)**	**n.a.**	**2,074**
Cash & equivalent	9,161		332
Inventories	177,617		637
Accounts receivable	33		nil
Current assets	379,360		1,776
Long-term investments	10,258		5,520
Fixed assets, net	33,569		nil
Right-of-use assets	6		nil
Intangibles, net	68,436		nil
Total assets	**459,691**	**n.m.**	**7,296**
Accts. pay. & accr. liabs	4,412		992
Current liabilities	367,904		992
Preferred share equity	4,321		4,321
Shareholders' equity	91,781		6,304
Cash from oper. activs	**(326,919)**	**n.a.**	**(2,195)**
Cash from fin. activs	332,009		2,680
Cash from invest. activs	3,779		(142)
Net cash position	**9,161**	**n.m.**	**332**
Capital expenditures	(31)		nil
	$		$
Earnings per share*	(0.37)		0.04
Cash flow per share*	(1.70)		(0.03)
	shs		shs
No. of shs. o/s*	211,102,552		103,405,361
Avg. no. of shs. o/s*	192,626,463		55,836,068
	%		%
Net profit margin	(474.07)		70.28
Return on equity	(159.87)		n.m.
Return on assets	(30.11)		52.29

* Common

[o] Restated

[A] Reported in accordance with IFRS

Latest Results

Periods ended:	3m Mar. 31/22[A]		3m Mar. 31/21[A]
	$000s	%Chg	$000s
Operating revenue	1,821	-44	3,261
Net income	(12,319)	n.a.	(6,851)
	$		$
Earnings per share*	(0.06)		(0.04)

* Common

[A] Reported in accordance with IFRS

Historical Summary
(as originally stated)

Fiscal Year	Oper. Rev.	Net Inc. Bef. Disc.	EPS*
	$000s	$000s	$
2021[A]	15,081	(71,495)	(0.37)
2020[A]	(47)	2,074	0.04
2019[A]	(834)	(1,507)	(0.04)
2018[A]	(6,197)	(9,794)	(0.24)
2017[A]	3,974	4,090	0.17

* Common

[A] Reported in accordance with IFRS

D.27 Definity Financial Corporation*

Symbol - DFY **Exchange** - TSX **CUSIP** - 24477T

Head Office - 111 Westmount Rd S, PO Box 2000, Waterloo, ON, N2J 4S4 **Telephone** - (519) 570-8500 **Toll-free** - (800) 265-2180

Website - www.definityfinancial.com

Email - dennis.westfall@definityfc.com

Investor Relations - Dennis Westfall (416) 435-5568

Auditors - Ernst & Young LLP C.A., Waterloo, Ont.

Transfer Agents - Computershare Trust Company of Canada Inc., Toronto, Ont.

FP500 Revenue Ranking - 163

Employees - 3,555 at Dec. 31, 2022

Profile - (Ont. 2021) Provides property and casualty (P&C) insurance throughout Canada in two business lines: personal insurance, including automobile, property, liability and pet insurance products to individual customers; and commercial insurance, including automobile, property, liability and specialty insurance products to businesses.

Insurance products are offered primarily through four wholly owned companies: **Definity Insurance Company** (formerly **Economical Mutual Insurance Company**), a provider of automobile, property, liability and specialty insurance to individuals and businesses, as well as group insurance, small businesses and mid-market insurance, and specialty offerings for large enterprises, with solutions offered under the Economical brand through brokers; **Sonnet Insurance Company**, a fully digital direct insurance platform serving individuals, corporate groups and affinity members with automobile, home, condo, tenant, landlord and pet insurance; **Family Insurance Solutions Inc.**, a distributor of Definity Insurance home and optional automobile personal insurance products on an exclusive basis through brokers in British Columbia; and **Petline Insurance Company**, a pet health insurer operating through brands Petsecure and Peppermint on a direct basis online and through branding partners.

The company has active relationships with a network of more than 700 independent brokerage firms and a broker base of more than 29,000 individual brokers. Digital platforms are Sonnet Insurance and Vyne, the company's digital broker platform.

At Dec. 31, 2022, the company's investment portfolio totaled $4.898 billion, excluding investments in associates.

In March 2022, the company announced a strategic partnership with **APOLLO Insurance Solutions Ltd.**, a Canadian online insurance broker and managing general agent specializing in commercial insurance. The strategic partnership included a distribution relationship between wholly owned **Definity Insurance Company** and APOLLO, and an initial minority equity investment by the company in APOLLO.

Recent Merger and Acquisition Activity

Status: completed **Announced:** Oct. 3, 2022
Definity Financial Corporation acquired an additional 50% interest in McDougall Insurance Brokers Limited for $217,000,000, increasing its interest to 75%. The purchase price was funded with cash on hand. McDougall is an Ontario-based property and casualty insurance brokerage, representing more than 50 insurance companies and with operations across over 40 branches with more than 450 employees.

Status: completed **Announced:** Oct. 3, 2022
Definity Financial Corporation acquired Guelph, Ont.-based insurance brokerages T.G Colley & Sons Limited (dba Colley Insurance) and Integrisure Group Insurance Inc. for $13,000,000, funded with cash on hand. Colley Insurance provides personal home and automobile insurance products as well as business insurance products, and Integrisure specializes in providing group home and automobile insurance products to employer groups.

Directors - John H. Bowey, chr., Conestogo, Ont.; Rowan Saunders, pres. & CEO, Toronto, Ont.; Elizabeth L. (Betty) DelBianco, Toronto, Ont.; Daniel J. Fortin, Pickering, Ont.; Barbara H. Fraser, Toronto, Ont.; Richard M. (Dick) Freeborough, Oakville, Ont.; Sabrina Geremia, Toronto, Ont.; Dr. Micheal J. Kelly, Waterloo, Ont.; Robert G. McFarlane, Vancouver, B.C.; Adrian Mitchell, Toronto, Ont.; J. Susan Monteith, Toronto, Ont.; Edouard Schmid, Zurich, Switzerland; Michael P. Stramaglia, Toronto, Ont.

Other Exec. Officers - Liam McFarlane, chief risk & actuarial officer; Paul MacDonald, exec. v-p, personal insce. & digital channels; Philip (Phil) Mather, exec. v-p & CFO; Fabian Richenberger, exec. v-p, comml. insce. & insce. opers.; Innes Dey, sr. v-p, legal & strategy; Roger Dunbar, sr. v-p, Sonnet insce.; Donna Ince, sr. v-p & chief underwriting officer, personal insce.; Tatjana Lalkovic, sr. v-p & chief tech. officer; Brigid V. Pelino, sr. v-p & chief people & culture officer; Obaid Rahman, sr. v-p & chief underwriting officer, comml. insce.; Thomas (Tom) Reikman, sr. v-p & chief distrib. officer; Michael Padfield, gen. counsel & corp. sec.

Capital Stock

	Authorized (shs.)	Outstanding (shs.)[1]
Preferred	unlimited	nil
Common	unlimited	115,900,000

[1] At Aug. 2, 2023

Normal Course Issuer Bid - The company plans to make normal course purchases of up to 3,476,781 common shares representing 3% of the total outstanding. The bid commenced on May 31, 2023, and expires on May 30, 2024.

Major Shareholder - Healthcare of Ontario Pension Plan held 19.9% interest at Apr. 4, 2023.

Price Range - DFY/TSX

Year	Volume	High	Low	Close
2022	50,805,178	$40.95	$27.00	$38.48
2021	14,653,910	$30.27	$26.00	$29.53

Recent Close: $37.81

Capital Stock Changes - During 2022, 1,500,000 common shares were purchased and held in trust.

Dividends

DFY com Ra $0.55 pa Q est. Mar. 28, 2023
Listed Nov 18/21.
Prev. Rate: $0.50 est. Sept. 28, 2022
Prev. Rate: $0.70 est. Mar. 28, 2022
$0.175i .... Mar. 28/22
i Initial Payment

Long-Term Debt - At Dec. 31, 2022, outstanding debt totaled $39,100,000 and consisted entirely of demand loans.

Wholly Owned Subsidiaries

Definity Insurance Company, Waterloo, Ont. formerly Economical Mutual Insurance Company
- 100% int. in **Integrisure Group Insurance Inc.**, Guelph, Ont.
- 100% int. in **McConville Omni Insurance Brokers Ltd.**, Ont.
- 78% int. in **McDougall Insurance Brokers Limited**, Belleville, Ont.
- 100% int. in **The Missisquoi Insurance Company**, Canada.
- 100% int. in **The Perth Insurance Company**, Canada.
- 100% int. in **Petline Insurance Company**, Canada.
- 100% int. in **Sonnet Insurance Company**, Canada.
- 100% int. in **TEIG Investment Partnership**, Ont.
- 100% int. in **T.G Colley & Sons Limited**, Guelph, Ont.
- 100% int. in **Waterloo Insurance Company**, Kitchener, Ont.
- 100% int. in **Westmount Financial Inc.**, Ont.
  - 100% int. in **Family Insurance Solutions Inc.**, Canada.

Financial Statistics

Periods ended:	12m Dec. 31/22[A]		12m Dec. 31/21[A]
	$000s	%Chg	$000s
Net premiums earned	3,248,600		2,833,600
Net investment income	(95,200)		76,000
Total revenue	**3,180,700**	**+9**	**2,917,800**
Policy benefits & claims	1,987,900		1,721,500
Commissions	520,400		426,500
Premium taxes	120,400		106,900
Other operating expense	435,000		392,400
Operating expense	**1,075,800**	**+16**	**925,800**
Operating income	**117,000**	**-57**	**270,500**
Pre-tax income	**305,200**	**+9**	**281,200**
Income taxes	52,600		68,000
Net income	**252,600**	**+18**	**213,200**
Net inc. for equity hldrs	**252,000**	**+18**	**213,200**
Net inc. for non-cont. int	**600**	**n.a.**	**nil**
Cash & equivalent	200,500		387,300
Accounts receivable	1,463,800		1,255,100
Securities investments	4,739,400		5,210,000
Total investments	4,934,600		5,442,900
Total assets	**8,316,800**	**+5**	**7,891,400**
Accts. pay. & accr. liabs	198,100		191,700
Claims provisions	3,254,300		3,336,100
Debt	39,100		nil
Long-term lease liabilities	31,700		18,900
Policy liabilities & claims	1,765,400		1,599,200
Shareholders' equity	2,371,900		2,396,300
Non-controlling interest	108,500		nil
Cash from oper. activs	**305,800**	**-53**	**655,200**
Cash from fin. activs	73,400		376,800
Cash from invest. activs	(374,700)		(1,044,200)
Net cash position	**502,600**	**+1**	**498,100**
Pension fund surplus	40,300		21,400
	$		$
Earnings per share*	2.19		2.03
Cash flow per share*	2.66		6.23
Cash divd. per share*	0.55		nil
	shs		shs
No. of shs. o/s*	114,400,000		115,900,000
Avg. no. of shs. o/s*	115,100,000		105,200,000
	%		%
Net profit margin	7.94		7.31
Return on equity	10.57		10.12
Return on assets	3.12		2.94
No. of employees (FTEs)	3,555		3,065

* Common
[A] Reported in accordance with IFRS

Latest Results

Periods ended:	6m June 30/23[A]		6m June 30/22[◻A]
	$000s	%Chg	$000s
Total revenue	2,032,700	+55	1,310,700
Net income	174,300	n.a.	(109,800)
Net inc. for equity hldrs	172,500	n.a.	(109,800)
Net inc. for non-cont. int	1,800		nil
	$		$
Earnings per share*	1.50		(0.95)

* Common
◻ Restated
[A] Reported in accordance with IFRS

Historical Summary
(as originally stated)

Fiscal Year	Total Rev.	Net Inc. Bef. Disc.	EPS*
	$000s	$000s	$
2022[A]	3,180,700	252,600	2.19
2021[A]	2,917,800	213,200	2.03
2020[A1]	2,696,300	153,900	n.a.
2019[A]	2,527,000	17,400	n.a.
2018[A]	2,421,500	(73,000)	n.a.

* Common
[A] Reported in accordance with IFRS
[1] Results for 2020 and prior periods pertain to Definity Insurance Company (formerly Economical Mutual Insurance Company).

D.28 Delivra Health Brands Inc.

Symbol - DHB **Exchange** - TSX-VEN **CUSIP** - 24703H
Head Office - 404-999 Canada Pl, Vancouver, BC, V6C 3E2 **Telephone** - (604) 449-9280
Website - delivrahealthbrands.com
Email - jtasse@delivrahealth.com
Investor Relations - Jack Z. Tasse (877) 915-7934
Auditors - Davidson & Company LLP C.A., Vancouver, B.C.
Transfer Agents - Computershare Trust Company of Canada Inc., Vancouver, B.C.

Profile - (B.C. 2008) Develops and distributes cannabis infused and non-infused health, wellness and self-care products, with a focus on sleep and pain.

Portfolio of brands consist of Dream Water™, which are non-cannabis-infused sleep aid products available in liquid shots, gummies and powder packet formats; and LivRelief™, a line of cannabis-infused and non-infused topical creams for joint and muscle pain, nerve pain, varicose veins, wound healing and sports performance. Dream Water™ products are sold online and in various retailers throughout the U.S., Canada, Europe and Africa and LivRelief™ products are available online and in major retailers and provincial dispensaries across Canada and Africa.

In December 2022, wholly owned **United Greeneries Holdings Ltd.** sold its 68,000-sq.-ft. Lucky Lake indoor facility in Saskatchewan for a total consideration of $3,000,000.

Predecessor Detail - Name changed from Harvest One Cannabis Inc., Sept. 8, 2022.

Directors - Frank A. Holler, exec. chr., Summerland, B.C.; Gord Davey, pres. & CEO, Hamilton, Ont.; Andrew (Andy) Bayfield, Etobicoke, Ont.; Jason Bednar, Calgary, Alta.

Other Exec. Officers - Jack Z. Tasse, CFO & corp. sec.; Matthew Wagar, sr. v-p, mktg. & innovation

Capital Stock

	Authorized (shs.)	Outstanding (shs.)[1]
Preferred	unlimited	nil
Common	unlimited	252,617,854

[1] At Nov. 28, 2022

Major Shareholder - Hygrovest Limited held 21.99% interest at Jan. 27, 2022.

Price Range - DHB/TSX-VEN

Year	Volume	High	Low	Close
2022	29,140,414	$0.07	$0.02	$0.02
2021	151,774,132	$0.58	$0.06	$0.07
2020	71,712,439	$0.20	$0.05	$0.07
2019	106,811,213	$1.15	$0.16	$0.19
2018	230,346,313	$2.20	$0.33	$0.39

Recent Close: $0.02

Capital Stock Changes - There were no changes to capital stock during fiscal 2022.

Wholly Owned Subsidiaries

Delivra Corp., Hamilton, Ont.
- 100% int. in **Delivra Inc.**, Ont.
  - 100% int. in **Delivra Pharmaceuticals Inc.**, Ont.
  - 100% int. in **LivCorp Inc.**, Ont.
    - 100% int. in **LivCorp International Inc.**, Ont.
    - 100% int. in **PortaPack Ltd.**, P.E.I.
  - 100% int. in **LivVet Inc.**, Ont.

Dream Products Inc., Canada.
- 100% int. in **Dream Products USA Inc.**, Del.
  - 100% int. in **Sarpes Beverages, LLC**, United States.

United Greeneries Holdings Ltd., Duncan, B.C.
United Greeneries Operations Ltd., Duncan, B.C.

Investments

Cann Group Limited, Melbourne, Vic., Australia.

Financial Statistics

Periods ended:	12m June 30/22^A		12m June 30/21^A
	$000s	%Chg	$000s
Operating revenue	**8,139**	**+2**	**7,956**
Cost of sales	4,759		5,048
Research & devel. expense	nil		72
General & admin expense	6,145		8,314
Stock-based compensation	352		577
Operating expense	**11,256**	**-20**	**14,011**
Operating income	**(3,117)**	**n.a.**	**(6,055)**
Deprec., depl. & amort.	2,119		2,216
Finance costs, net	635		(41)
Write-downs/write-offs	(1,174)		(13,101)
Pre-tax income	**(7,009)**	**n.a.**	**(22,672)**
Net inc. bef. disc. opers	**(7,009)**	**n.a.**	**(22,672)**
Income from disc. opers	nil		(5,866)
Net income	**(7,009)**	**n.a.**	**(28,538)**
Cash & equivalent	1,110		5,142
Inventories	220		2,279
Accounts receivable	1,576		2,020
Current assets	7,485		9,835
Fixed assets, net	270		2,908
Intangibles, net	3,675		6,032
Total assets	**11,585**	**-39**	**19,063**
Accts. pay. & accr. liabs	6,105		6,924
Current liabilities	6,541		7,236
Long-term debt, gross	2,107		2,162
Long-term debt, net	1,671		1,850
Shareholders' equity	3,373		9,977
Cash from oper. activs	**(4,441)**	**n.a.**	**(9,647)**
Cash from fin. activs	(309)		446
Cash from invest. activs	1,350		12,269
Net cash position	**1,084**	**-76**	**4,431**
Capital expenditures	(10)		(33)
Capital disposals	104		25
	$		$
Earns. per sh. bef disc opers*	(0.03)		(0.10)
Earnings per share*	(0.03)		(0.13)
Cash flow per share*	(0.02)		(0.04)
	shs		shs
No. of shs. o/s*	252,617,854		252,617,854
Avg. no. of shs. o/s*	252,617,854		225,961,186
	%		%
Net profit margin	(86.12)		(284.97)
Return on equity	(105.00)		(104.25)
Return on assets	(45.74)		(58.96)
Foreign sales percent	56		55

* Common
^A Reported in accordance with IFRS

Latest Results

Periods ended:	3m Sept. 30/22^A		3m Sept. 30/21^A
	$000s	%Chg	$000s
Operating revenue	1,729	-19	2,130
Net income	(381)	n.a.	(1,454)
	$		$
Earnings per share*	(0.00)		(0.01)

* Common
^A Reported in accordance with IFRS

Historical Summary
(as originally stated)

Fiscal Year	Oper. Rev.	Net Inc. Bef. Disc.	EPS*
	$000s	$000s	$
2022^A	8,139	(7,009)	(0.03)
2021^A	7,956	(22,672)	(0.10)
2020^A	8,384	(62,771)	(0.29)
2019^A	11,465	(27,965)	(0.15)
2018^A	726	(12,607)	(0.11)

* Common
^A Reported in accordance with IFRS

D.29 Delota Corp.

Symbol - LOTA **Exchange** - CSE **CUSIP** - 24713H
Head Office - Unit 2, 7941 Jane St, Concord, ON, L4K 2M7 **Telephone** - (905) 330-1602 **Toll-free** - (888) 504-7737
Website - delota.com
Email - info@delota.com
Investor Relations - Cameron Wickham (888) 504-7737
Auditors - Stern & Lovrics LLP C.A., Toronto, Ont.
Transfer Agents - Capital Transfer Agency Inc., Toronto, Ont.
Employees - 147 at Jan. 31, 2023
Profile - (Alta. 2014) Sells vape, cannabis and other related products through retail stores in Ontario and e-commerce sites.

Owns and operates 28 nicotine vape stores across Ontario under the 180 Smoke name, and five licensed cannabis dispensaries under the Offside Cannabis name with stores in Niagara Falls, Pickering, Hamilton, Blue Mountains and Port Perry, Ont. Also owns and operates e-commerce sites www.180smoke.ca and www.offsidecannabis.ca.

In March 2022, the company acquired **2766563 Ontario Inc.** from **Cresco Labs Inc.** for $3,000,000, satisfied through the issuance of 12,000,001 common shares at a deemed price of 25¢ per share. 2766563 Ontario held a promissory note of $11,129,171 issued by the company to Cresco in March 2021 pursuant to its acquisition of **180 Smoke LLC**.

Common delisted from TSX-VEN, May 17, 2023.
Common listed on CSE, May 15, 2023.
Predecessor Detail - Name changed from Spyder Cannabis Inc., Nov. 17, 2021.
Directors - Mark Pelchovitz, exec. chr., Richmond Hill, Ont.; Cameron Wickham, exec. v-chr., CEO & corp. sec., Collingwood, Ont.; Daniel (Dan) Pelchovitz, CEO, cannabis div., Brampton, Ont.; Marc Askenasi, Toronto, Ont.; Steven Glaser, Toronto, Ont.
Other Exec. Officers - Christina Pan, COO; Ankit Gosain, CFO

Capital Stock

	Authorized (shs.)	Outstanding (shs.)[1]
Preferred	unlimited	nil
Common	unlimited	26,809,615

[1] At May 15, 2023

Major Shareholder - Mark Pelchovitz held 16.59% interest and Saimi Pelchovitz held 11.26% interest at June 6, 2021.

Price Range - LOTA/TSX-VEN (D)

Year	Volume	High	Low	Close
2022	3,685,442	$0.30	$0.11	$0.16
2021	21,385,954	$1.95	$0.13	$0.29
2020	3,055,476	$0.43	$0.08	$0.15
2019	1,768,494	$0.73	$0.15	$0.23
2018	46,300	$0.65	$0.25	$0.40

Consolidation: 1-for-5 cons. in Sept. 2021
Recent Close: $0.10
Capital Stock Changes - In March 2022, 12,000,001 common shares were issued pursuant to the acquisition of 2766563 Ontario Inc.

Wholly Owned Subsidiaries

180 VFC Inc., Canada.
SPDR (USA) Corporation, United States.
Spyder Cannabis Subco Inc., Ont.
- 100% int. in **The Green Spyder Inc.**, Alta.
  - 100% int. in **The Green Spyder IP Inc.**, Ont.
  - 100% int. in **The Green Spyder (Lundys) Inc.**, Ont.
  - 100% int. in **The Green Spyder (Pickering) Inc.**, Ont.
- 100% int. in **Spyder Vapes (Appleby) Inc.**, Burlington, Ont.
- 100% int. in **Spyder Vapes (East) Inc.**, Scarborough, Ont.
- 100% int. in **Spyder Vapes Inc.**, Ont.

2360149 Ontario Inc., Ont.
- 100% int. in **420 Wellness Inc.**, Alta.
- 100% int. in **180 Smoke LLC**, Del.

2488004 Ontario Inc., Ont.
2766563 Ontario Inc., Ont.

Financial Statistics

Periods ended:	12m Jan. 31/22^A		12m Jan. 31/21^A
	$000s	%Chg	$000s
Operating revenue	**17,686**	**n.m.**	**1,276**
Cost of goods sold	9,873		891
Salaries & benefits	4,211		302
General & admin expense	3,450		769
Stock-based compensation	181		nil
Operating expense	**17,353**	**+784**	**1,962**
Operating income	**333**	**n.a.**	**(686)**
Deprec., depl. & amort.	1,235		242
Finance costs, gross	812		194
Write-downs/write-offs	(7,251)		(330)
Pre-tax income	**(8,898)**	**n.a.**	**(1,310)**
Income taxes	(53)		nil
Net income	**(8,845)**	**n.a.**	**(1,310)**
Cash & equivalent	1,010		298
Inventories	1,465		171
Current assets	3,502		543
Fixed assets, net	1,035		219
Right-of-use assets	5,038		470
Intangibles, net	3,830		nil
Total assets	**13,405**	**+988**	**1,232**
Accts. pay. & accr. liabs	2,077		746
Current liabilities	15,103		1,729
Long-term debt, gross	749		1,105
Long-term debt, net	749		179
Long-term lease liabilities	5,490		552
Shareholders' equity	(8,515)		(1,228)
Cash from oper. activs	**965**	**n.a.**	**(316)**
Cash from fin. activs	(167)		720
Cash from invest. activs	(86)		(234)
Net cash position	**1,010**	**+239**	**298**
Capital expenditures	(98)		(234)
Capital disposals	12		nil
	$		$
Earnings per share*	(0.65)		(0.15)
Cash flow per share*	0.07		(0.04)
	shs		shs
No. of shs. o/s*	14,809,614		9,418,235
Avg. no. of shs. o/s*	13,695,315		8,984,964
	%		%
Net profit margin	(50.01)		(102.66)
Return on equity	n.m.		n.m.
Return on assets	(109.83)		(81.67)

* Common
^A Reported in accordance with IFRS

Latest Results

Periods ended:	9m Oct. 31/22^A		9m Oct. 31/21^A
	$000s	%Chg	$000s
Operating revenue	19,025	+57	12,108
Net income	7,873	n.a.	(1,470)
	$		$
Earnings per share*	0.32		(0.11)

* Common
^A Reported in accordance with IFRS

Historical Summary
(as originally stated)

Fiscal Year	Oper. Rev.	Net Inc. Bef. Disc.	EPS*
	$000s	$000s	$
2022^A	17,686	(8,845)	(0.65)
2021^A	1,276	(1,310)	(0.15)
2020^A1	757	(2,179)	(0.35)
2019^A2	972	(620)	n.a.
2018^A2	740	(362)	n.a.

* Common
^A Reported in accordance with IFRS
[1] Results reflect the May 31, 2019, Qualifying Transaction reverse takeover acquisition of Spyder Vapes Inc.
[2] Results pertain to Spyder Vapes Inc.
Note: Adjusted throughout for 1-for-5 cons. in Sept. 2021

D.30 DelphX Capital Markets Inc.

Symbol - DELX **Exchange** - TSX-VEN **CUSIP** - 24721L
Head Office - 15 Prince Arthur Ave, Toronto, ON, M5R 1B2 **Telephone** - (416) 347-0197
Website - www.delphx.com
Email - simon.selkrig@delphx.com
Investor Relations - Simon Selkrig (416) 904-4134
Auditors - Davidson & Company LLP C.A., Vancouver, B.C.
Transfer Agents - Computershare Trust Company of Canada Inc., Vancouver, B.C.
Profile - (B.C. 2016) Develops and distributes private placement securities that provide default protection and risk mitigation on underlying corporate, municipal and sovereign securities.

Has developed three proprietary securities: Collateralized Put Option™ (CPO), which provides secured default protection for underlying corporate, municipal and sovereign securities, with each CPO strike price equalling the par value of its underlying security; Collateralized Reference Note™ (CRN), which enables credit investors to take on the default exposure of a single underlying security or optionally participate in a pool of diversified risks that broadly diffuses the impact of credit events; and Credit Rating Security (CRS), which provides bond holders and traders protection against potential rating changes on existing bonds. The securities are developed by the company and are to be issued by wholly owned **Quantem Capital LLC.**

Predecessor Detail - Name changed from Seaside Exploration Partners Corp., Apr. 25, 2018, following Qualifying Transaction reverse takeover acquisition of DelphX Corporation.

Directors - Patrick Wood, pres. & CEO, Ont.; Alexander G. Jardin, chief actuary & risk officer, Burlington, Ont.; Salim Hasham, N.Y.; Steven J. (Steve) Mannik, Fla.

Other Exec. Officers - Shant V. Harootunian, COO; Simon Selkrig, CFO

Capital Stock

	Authorized (shs.)	Outstanding (shs.)[1]
Common	unlimited	139,016,489

[1] At May 26, 2023

Major Shareholder - Larry Fondren held 17.98% interest and Keith Ainsworth held 14.66% interest at Aug. 16, 2022.

Price Range - DELX/TSX-VEN

Year	Volume	High	Low	Close
2022	16,800,732	$0.54	$0.08	$0.08
2021	20,736,950	$0.88	$0.07	$0.46
2020	5,437,633	$0.19	$0.04	$0.12
2019	7,620,556	$0.40	$0.03	$0.14
2018	9,548,863	$1.13	$0.34	$0.37

Recent Close: $0.09

Capital Stock Changes - In June 2023, private placement of 5,425,000 units (1 common share & 1 warrant) at 8¢ per unit was completed, with warrants exercisable at 15¢ per share for two years.

In May 2022, private placement of 4,982,727 units (1 common share & 1 warrant) at 22¢ per unit was complete. In December 2022, private placement of 5,422,221 units (1 common share & 1 warrant) at 9¢ per unit was completed. Also during 2022, common shares were issued as follows: 4,825,715 by private placement, 250,000 on exercise of options, 47,617 for services and 20,000 on exercise of warrants.

Wholly Owned Subsidiaries

DelphX Corporation, Malvern, Pa.
- 100% int. in **DelphX Data Corporation**, Ont.
- 100% int. in **DelphX Services Corporation**, Del.
- 100% int. in **Quantem Capital Corporation Ltd.**, Bermuda.
- 100% int. in **Quantem Capital LLC**, Del.

Financial Statistics

Periods ended:	12m Dec. 31/22[A]		12m Dec. 31/21[A]
	$000s	%Chg	$000s
Salaries & benefits	1,297		291
General & admin expense	2,662		1,484
Stock-based compensation	528		2,359
Operating expense	**4,487**	**+9**	**4,134**
Operating income	**(4,487)**	**n.a.**	**(4,134)**
Deprec., depl. & amort.	142		106
Finance costs, gross	18		104
Write-downs/write-offs	(38)		(61)
Pre-tax income	**(4,666)**	**n.a.**	**(3,252)**
Net income	**(4,666)**	**n.a.**	**(3,252)**
Cash & equivalent	264		1,473
Current assets	475		1,665
Right-of-use assets	nil		142
Total assets	**475**	**-74**	**1,807**
Accts. pay. & accr. liabs	3,366		2,583
Current liabilities	3,366		2,773
Long-term lease liabilities	nil		60
Shareholders' equity	(2,891)		(1,026)
Cash from oper. activs	**(3,361)**	**n.a.**	**(1,399)**
Cash from fin. activs	2,042		2,664
Net cash position	**264**	**-82**	**1,473**
	$		$
Earnings per share*	(0.04)		(0.03)
Cash flow per share*	(0.03)		(0.01)
	shs		shs
No. of shs. o/s*	133,514,823		117,966,543
Avg. no. of shs. o/s*	133,514,823		118,966,543
	%		%
Net profit margin	n.a.		n.a.
Return on equity	n.m.		n.m.
Return on assets	(407.36)		(267.57)

* Common

[A] Reported in accordance with IFRS

Latest Results

Periods ended:	3m Mar. 31/23[A]		3m Mar. 31/22[A]
	$000s	%Chg	$000s
Net income	(826)	n.a.	(1,118)
	$		$
Earnings per share*	(0.01)		(0.01)

* Common

[A] Reported in accordance with IFRS

Historical Summary

(as originally stated)

Fiscal Year	Oper. Rev.	Net Inc. Bef. Disc.	EPS*
	$000s	$000s	$
2022[A]	nil	(4,666)	(0.04)
2021[A]	nil	(3,252)	(0.03)
2020[A]	nil	(2,618)	(0.03)
2019[A]	nil	(4,858)	(0.06)
2018[A1]	nil	(8,505)	(0.12)

* Common

[A] Reported in accordance with IFRS

[1] Results reflect the Apr. 25, 2018, Qualifying Transaction reverse takeover acquisition of DelphX Corporation.

D.31 Delta CleanTech Inc.

Symbol - DELT **Exchange** - CSE **CUSIP** - 24747L

Head Office - 2-2305 Victoria Ave, Regina, SK, S4P 0S7 **Telephone** - (306) 352-6132 **Fax** - (306) 545-3262

Website - deltacleantech.ca

Email - jallison@deltacleantech.ca

Investor Relations - Jeffrey Allison (306) 352-6132

Auditors - Ernst & Young LLP C.A., Calgary, Alta.

Bankers - Royal Bank of Canada

Lawyers - Gowling WLG (Canada) LLP, Calgary, Alta.; McDougall Gauley LLP, Regina, Sask.

Transfer Agents - Odyssey Trust Company, Calgary, Alta.

Profile - (Alta. 2020) Provides clean energy products and services including CO_2 capture, solvent and ethanol purification, hydrogen production, carbon credit certification and trading, and methane collection and destruction to CO_2 industrial gas emitters and other target customers.

CO_2 Capture - Offers solutions for CO_2 enhanced heavy oil production, food grade CO_2 markets and industrial CO_2 applications. Its LCDesign® CO_2 capture system has been engineered on a skid using oil field fabrication techniques to reduce capital and operating costs for CO_2 production while feasibility of a project is determined and prior to the construction of a full-sized fixed CO_2 producing facility. The LCDesign® technology also includes the PDOengine® (Process Design Optimization Engine). This computer modeling software allows the company to accurately predict the plants production performance and capital costing prior to plant construction.

Solvent and Ethanol Purification - The company utilizes its patented Delta Reclaimer® purification technology to service the CO_2 capture and other large chemical production facilities that seek to reclaim, recycle and reuse the extracted solvents and alcohols, rather than have these contaminated fluids disposed underground. Products include Delta Solvent Reclaiming System™, which reclaims hydrocarbon-based and other solvents for use in natural gas processing, ethanol-based solvents and post-combustion CO_2 capturing processes; and Delta Glycol Reclaiming System™, which reclaims and purifies glycols, such as mono-ethylene glycol and tri-ethylene glycol, used for natural gas dehydration processes.

Hydrogen Production - Has developed and is in the early stages of commercializing technologies to produce hydrogen from crude ethanol and other bio-sources such as grains and cellulous.

Carbon Credit Certification and Trading - Subsidiary **Carbon Rx Inc.** is engaged in the origination, validation, digitization and streaming of carbon credits. Carbon Rx is a platform for the trading of carbon credits and facilitates the trading of such carbon credits on various carbon credit exchanges around the world. Carbon Rx also holds 50% interest in **Viridius Trading, LLC**, which would operate as a decentralized autonomous organization (DAO) on the Ethereum network, created to build a modern and community-driven carbon credit registry, to promote and catalyze carbon credit projects, with a focus on regenerative agriculture and related nature-based solutions.

Methane Collection and Destruction - Carbon Rx holds a licence for a methane destruction technology that would destruct methane and other benzene, toluene and xylene (BTX) gases creating CO_2 equivalent carbon credits.

The company's revenues from contracts with customers are derived from engineering, processing, design and consulting services.

In November 2022, the management team of wholly owned **Carbon Rx Inc.** exercised their options to purchase class A common shares in Carbon Rx. As a result, the company's ownership in Carbon decreased to 83%.

Directors - Wayne L. Bernakevitch, chr., Regina, Sask.; Jeffrey (Jeff) Allison, pres. & CEO, Calgary, Alta.; Garth Fredrickson, Regina, Sask.; Lionel P. Kambeitz, Regina, Sask.

Other Exec. Officers - Jacelyn Case, CFO & corp. sec.; Dr. Ahmed Aboudheir, chief tech. officer

Capital Stock

	Authorized (shs.)	Outstanding (shs.)[1]
Common	unlimited	63,823,100

[1] At Mar. 31, 2023

Major Shareholder - HTC Purenergy Inc. held 13.6% interest at June 7, 2022.

Price Range - DELT/CSE

Year	Volume	High	Low	Close
2022	14,919,755	$0.42	$0.03	$0.03
2021	5,310,845	$0.90	$0.38	$0.40

Recent Close: $0.03

Wholly Owned Subsidiaries

CO2 Technologies Pty Ltd., Australia.

Subsidiaries

83% int. in **Carbon Rx Inc.**
- 50% int. in **Viridius Trading, LLC**, Del.

Financial Statistics

Periods ended:	12m Dec. 31/21[A]
	$000s
Operating revenue	**375**
Salaries & benefits	442
Research & devel. expense	988
General & admin expense	1,171
Stock-based compensation	1,043
Other operating expense	90
Operating expense	**3,734**
Operating income	**(3,359)**
Deprec., depl. & amort.	282
Finance income	16
Finance costs, gross	2
Pre-tax income	**(4,258)**
Net income	**(4,258)**
Cash & equivalent	4,260
Accounts receivable	20
Current assets	4,360
Long-term investments	198
Fixed assets, net	32
Right-of-use assets	52
Intangibles, net	2,891
Total assets	**7,533**
Accts. pay. & accr. liabs	326
Current liabilities	375
Long-term lease liabilities	4
Shareholders' equity	7,154
Cash from oper. activs	**(2,616)**
Cash from fin. activs	7,069
Cash from invest. activs	(3,694)
Net cash position	**760**
Capital expenditures	(36)
	$
Earnings per share*	(0.07)
Cash flow per share*	(0.05)
	shs
No. of shs. o/s*	58,523,100
Avg. no. of shs. o/s*	54,293,526
	%
Net profit margin	n.m.
Return on equity	n.m.
Return on assets	n.a.

* Common

[A] Reported in accordance with IFRS

Latest Results

Periods ended:	9m Sept. 30/22[A]		9m Sept. 30/21[A]
	$000s	%Chg	$000s
Operating revenue	598	+59	375
Net income	(2,214)	n.a.	(2,238)
	$		$
Earnings per share*	(0.04)		(0.06)

* Common

[A] Reported in accordance with IFRS

D.32 Delta 9 Cannabis Inc.

Symbol - DN **Exchange** - TSX **CUSIP** - 247754

Head Office - PO Box 68096 Osborne Village, Winnipeg, MB, R3L 2V9 **Telephone** - (204) 898-7722 **Toll-free** - (855) 245-1259

Website - invest.delta9.ca

Email - ian.chadsey@delta9.ca

Investor Relations - Ian Chadsey (204) 898-7722

Auditors - Baker Tilly HMA LLP C.A., Winnipeg, Man.

Lawyers - MLT Aikins LLP, Winnipeg, Man.

Transfer Agents - Computershare Trust Company of Canada Inc., Vancouver, B.C.

Profile - (B.C. 2001) Retails, produces and distributes cannabis and cannabis-related products in Canada. Also manufactures and sells modular cannabis cultivation Grow Pods.

Retail operations are conducted through **Delta 9 Lifestyle Cannabis Clinic Inc.** (68.78% owned) and wholly owned **Delta 9 Cannabis Store Inc.**, which operate retail cannabis stores under the names Delta 9 Cannabis Store, Discounted Cannabis, Garden Variety and Uncle Sam's Cannabis in Winnipeg (12), Brandon (2), Selkirk and Thompson, Man.; Edmonton (19), Calgary and Grande Prairie, Alta.; and Lloydminster, Sask. as at Sept. 30, 2022. Delta 9 Lifestyle also operates a medical clinic in Winnipeg, Man., which markets Delta 9 branded products and provides consultation services to patients seeking medical recommendation for a cannabis prescription.

Cultivation and processing operations are conducted at an 80,000-sq.-ft. facility in Winnipeg, Man., which produces medical and recreational cannabis products. Cultivation at the facility uses the company's proprietary grow pod system. Grow pods are modular, scalable and stackable production units which are built from retrofitted 40-foot shipping containers designed for the production of cannabis.

Also distributes cannabis and cannabis-related products to authorized provincial and territorial distributors and retailers in Manitoba, Saskatchewan, Alberta, British Columbia, Ontario and Newfoundland and Labrador.

In addition, manufactures and sells Grow Pods, which are retrofitted shipping containers for the production of cannabis and non-production plants. At Nov. 14, 2022, the company had 297 Grow Pods fully licensed and approved by Health Canada in service, consisting of 262 Grow Pods used for the production of cannabis and 35 Grow Pods used for non-production plants, plant harvesting, processing and packaging activities or laboratory and testing activities.

In September 2022, the company acquired all or substantially all of **10552763 Canada Corp.**'s assets relating to the operation of three Garden Variety branded retail cannabis stores Manitoba for $3,250,000 including issuance of 17,944,785 common shares at $0.163 per share and 1,993,865 common shares to be issued in six months. Two of the stores are located in Winnipeg and one is in Brandon.

Recent Merger and Acquisition Activity

Status: completed **Announced:** Mar. 31, 2022

Delta 9 Cannabis Inc. acquired substantially all of Uncle Sam's Cannabis Ltd.'s assets relating to the operation of 17 retail cannabis stores in Alberta from Uncle Sam's Cannabis Ltd. and Wissam El Annan for a purchase price of $12,500,000.

Predecessor Detail - Name changed from SVT Capital Corp., Oct. 31, 2017, following reverse takeover acquisition and amalgamation of Delta 9 Bio-Tech Inc. (deemed acquiror) with wholly owned 10240907 Canada Corp.

Directors - Nitin Kaushal, chr., Richmond Hill, Ont.; John W. Arbuthnot IV, CEO, Winnipeg, Man.; Hugh H. Aird, Toronto, Ont.; J. William (Bill) Arbuthnot III, Winnipeg, Man.; Stuart Starkey

Other Exec. Officers - Mark Jonker, COO; James (Jim) Lawson, CFO; Marshall Posner, chief mktg. officer; Ian Chadsey, v-p, corp. affairs; Dan Rogers, v-p, opers.

Capital Stock

	Authorized (shs.)	Outstanding (shs.)[1]
Common	unlimited	149,009,432

[1] At Nov. 14, 2022

Major Shareholder - J. William (Bill) Arbuthnot III held 15.82% interest and John W. Arbuthnot IV held 14.78% interest at May 20, 2022.

Price Range - DN/TSX

Year	Volume	High	Low	Close
2022	21,466,689	$0.34	$0.06	$0.06
2021	33,867,952	$0.75	$0.29	$0.29
2020	29,501,663	$0.80	$0.33	$0.51
2019	30,730,003	$1.85	$0.37	$0.70
2018	68,097,595	$2.94	$0.95	$1.22

Recent Close: $0.05

Capital Stock Changes - In April 2022, private placement of 2,038,217 common shares was completed $0.314 per share. In June 2022, offering of 8,800,027 units (1 common share & 1 warrant) at $0.22 per unit was completed, with warrants exercisable at $0.255 per share for three years.

Wholly Owned Subsidiaries

Delta 9 Bio-Tech Inc., Winnipeg, Man.
- 68.78% int. in **Delta 9 Lifestyle Cannabis Clinic Inc.**, Man.

Delta 9 Cannabis Store Inc., Canada.
Delta 9 Logistics Inc.

Subsidiaries

53% int. in **Blue Horseshoe Manufacturing Inc.**, Man.

Investments

Oceanic Releaf Inc., N.L.
50% int. in **10007705 Manitoba Ltd.**, Man.
Vitreous Cannabis Inc., Canada.

Financial Statistics

Periods ended:	12m Dec. 31/21[A]		12m Dec. 31/20[A]
	$000s	%Chg	$000s
Operating revenue	**62,291**	**+20**	**52,047**
Cost of sales	44,972		34,049
General & admin expense	17,168		14,036
Stock-based compensation	1,462		1,620
Operating expense	**63,602**	**+28**	**49,705**
Operating income	**(1,311)**	**n.a.**	**2,342**
Deprec., depl. & amort.	6,328		5,110
Finance income	31		44
Finance costs, gross	3,899		3,198
Pre-tax income	**(11,543)**	**n.a.**	**(5,084)**
Income taxes	(401)		401
Net income	**(11,142)**	**n.a.**	**(5,485)**
Net inc. for equity hldrs	**(11,177)**	**n.a.**	**(6,418)**
Net inc. for non-cont. int.	**35**	**-96**	**932**
Cash & equivalent	943		8,077
Inventories	20,383		15,260
Accounts receivable	4,569		5,055
Current assets	30,720		32,522
Long-term investments	533		925
Fixed assets, net	28,208		30,710
Right-of-use assets	11,990		10,918
Intangibles, net	3,061		814
Total assets	**74,781**	**-2**	**76,401**
Accts. pay. & accr. liabs.	10,991		5,673
Current liabilities	40,299		15,770
Long-term debt, gross	24,538		25,035
Long-term debt, net	2,482		22,925
Long-term lease liabilities	5,528		3,603
Shareholders' equity	24,669		32,008
Non-controlling interest	610		927
Cash from oper. activs.	**(775)**	**n.a.**	**1,508**
Cash from fin. activs.	(3,498)		7,041
Cash from invest. activs.	(2,860)		(6,318)
Net cash position	**943**	**-88**	**8,077**
Capital expenditures	(2,580)		(5,838)
	$		$
Earnings per share*	(0.11)		(0.07)
Cash flow per share*	n.a.		0.02
	shs		shs
No. of shs. o/s*	105,657,268		101,940,350
Avg. no. of shs. o/s*	103,343,876		89,425,996
	%		%
Net profit margin	(17.89)		(10.54)
Return on equity	(39.44)		(19.32)
Return on assets	(9.76)		(2.85)
No. of employees (FTEs)	210		190

* Common
[A] Reported in accordance with IFRS

Latest Results

Periods ended:	9m Sept. 30/22[A]		9m Sept. 30/21[A]
	$000s	%Chg	$000s
Operating revenue	45,669	+1	45,171
Net income	(16,629)	n.a.	(5,983)
Net inc. for equity hldrs	(16,383)	n.a.	(6,795)
Net inc. for non-cont. int.	(245)		813
	$		$
Earnings per share*	(0.14)		(0.07)

* Common
[A] Reported in accordance with IFRS

Historical Summary
(as originally stated)

Fiscal Year	Oper. Rev.	Net Inc. Bef. Disc.	EPS*
	$000s	$000s	$
2021[A]	62,291	(11,142)	(0.11)
2020[A]	52,047	(5,485)	(0.07)
2019[A]	31,766	13,516	0.16
2018[A]	7,569	(8,585)	(0.10)
2017[A1]	944	(7,924)	(0.16)

* Common
[A] Reported in accordance with IFRS
[1] Results reflect the Nov. 1, 2017, reverse takeover acquisition of Delta 9 Bio-Tech Inc.

D.33 dentalcorp Holdings Ltd.

Symbol - DNTL **Exchange** - TSX **CUSIP** - 24874B
Head Office - 2600-181 Bay St, Toronto, ON, M5J 2T3 **Telephone** - (416) 558-8338
Website - www.dentalcorp.ca
Email - sebastien.bouchard@dentalcorp.ca
Investor Relations - Sebastien Bouchard (416) 558-8338 ext. 229
Auditors - Ernst & Young LLP C.A., Toronto, Ont.
Transfer Agents - TSX Trust Company, Toronto, Ont.
FP500 Revenue Ranking - 298
Employees - 9,750 at Mar. 31, 2023

Profile - (B.C. 2018) Operates a network of more than 542 dental practices and 8,550 team members across Canada.

The company's network of dental practices across Canada includes more than 1,800 dentists, more than 2,100 hygienists and more than 4,650 auxiliary dental health professionals. When acquiring a dental practice, the company generally acquires all of the equipment and other major assets of the practice, other than certain intangible assets, which are acquired by the dentist through a professional corporation using secured debt provided by the company on arm's length terms. Partner dentists are responsible for the operational oversight of, and provision of dental services, at one or more of the company's practice locations pursuant to services agreements with the company.

Practices are provided with hellodent, the company's proprietary patient acquisition platform, and dc engage, its exclusive AI driven customer relationship management platform.

During 2022, the company acquired 47 dental practices compared with 61 during 2021.

In November 2022, the company announced commencement of review and evaluation of strategic alternatives that may be available to the company to unlock shareholder value.

Directors - Graham L. Rosenberg, chr. & CEO, Toronto, Ont.; Jeffrey L. Rosenthal†, Ont.; Sandra Bosela, Toronto, Ont.; Stacey Mowbray, Ont.; Rajan Shah, Conn.; Andrew C. Taub, N.Y.; Gino Volpacchio, Conn.; Robert T. Wolf, Toronto, Ont.

Other Exec. Officers - Guy Amini, pres. & corp. sec.; Matthew Miclea, COO; Nate Tchaplia, CFO; Nicola Deall, chief people officer; Martin M. Fecko, chief mktg. officer; Jeff Forbes, chief tech. officer; Dr. Gary Glassman, chief dental officer; Julian Perez, chief legal officer; Jennifer Callahan, sr. v-p, practice devel.; Julia Croll, sr. v-p, corp. brand & commun.; Richard Maisel, sr. v-p & treas.; Michelle McAra, sr. v-p, corp. devel.; Lizelle Peterson, sr. v-p, fin.; Joe Spagnuolo, sr. v-p, opers.; Milen Arora, v-p, performance mktg.; Brett Dunlop, v-p, finl. reporting; Sean Grant-Young, v-p, corp. devel.; Ryan McArthur, v-p, real estate; Stuart M. (Stu) Miller, v-p & deputy gen. counsel; Nick Pakkidis, v-p, procurement; Rebecca Sampson, v-p, mktg.; Vikas Sharma, v-p, opers.

† Lead director

Capital Stock

	Authorized (shs.)	Outstanding (shs.)[1]
Preferred	unlimited	nil
Subordinate Vtg.	unlimited	178,079,763
Multplie Vtg.	unlimited	9,183,822

[1] At Apr. 5, 2023

Subordinated Voting - One vote per share.

Multiple Voting - All controlled by Graham Rosenberg. Convertible anytime into subordinated voting shares on a one-for-one basis at anytime and automatically in certain other circumstances. 10 votes per share.

Normal Course Issuer Bid - The company plans to make normal course purchases of up to 3,500,000 subordinate voting shares representing 2% of the total outstanding. The bid commenced on May 16, 2023, and expires on May 15, 2024.

Major Shareholder - Graham L. Rosenberg held 34.3% interest and L Catterton Management Limited held 27.3% interest at Apr. 5, 2023.

Price Range - DNTL/TSX

Year	Volume	High	Low	Close
2022	43,432,467	$17.08	$5.65	$8.90
2021	23,561,988	$18.68	$13.80	$16.27

Recent Close: $6.66

Capital Stock Changes - In January 2022, bought deal public offering of 7,055,250 subordinated voting shares was completed at $16.30 per share, including 920,250 shares on exercise of over-allotment option. Also during 2022, subordinated voting shares were issued as follows: 10,916,024 on acquisition of dental practices, 273,518 in settlement of contingent consideration, 38,841 to partner and associate dentists, and 13,142 on vesting of restricted share units; 88,650 subordinated voting shares were cancelled.

Wholly Owned Subsidiaries

dentalcorp Health Services Ltd., B.C.
- 100% int. in **DCC Health Services (Quebec) Inc.**, Qué.

Note: The preceding list includes only the major related companies in which interests are held.

Financial Statistics

Periods ended:	12m Dec. 31/22[A]		12m Dec. 31/21[A]
	$000s	%Chg	$000s
Operating revenue	**1,250,300**	**+21**	**1,030,800**
Cost of sales	638,400		535,400
Salaries & benefits	261,800		216,800
General & admin expense	141,700		126,400
Stock-based compensation	12,500		75,200
Operating expense	**1,054,400**	**+11**	**953,800**
Operating income	**195,900**	**+154**	**77,000**
Deprec., depl. & amort.	190,300		158,500
Finance income	2,300		1,200
Finance costs, gross	70,300		116,200
Pre-tax income	**(77,400)**	**n.a.**	**(171,200)**
Income taxes	(60,800)		(10,800)
Net income	**(16,600)**	**n.a.**	**(160,400)**
Cash & equivalent	110,500		141,800
Inventories	35,800		35,500
Accounts receivable	96,300		75,300
Current assets	259,200		263,800
Long-term investments	100		300
Fixed assets, net	196,300		167,400
Right-of-use assets	282,600		238,300
Intangibles, net	2,525,300		2,155,400
Total assets	**3,375,200**	**+19**	**2,837,800**
Accts. pay. & accr. liabs.	133,100		108,500
Current liabilities	182,700		171,200
Long-term debt, gross	1,060,000		894,100
Long-term debt, net	1,060,000		894,100
Long-term lease liabilities	283,700		236,600
Shareholders' equity	1,787,700		1,514,000
Cash from oper. activs.	**138,600**	**+152**	**55,100**
Cash from fin. activs.	247,500		248,100
Cash from invest. activs.	(419,800)		(262,900)
Net cash position	**110,500**	**-22**	**141,800**
Capital expenditures	(31,200)		(18,000)
	$		$
Earnings per share*	(0.09)		(1.22)
Cash flow per share*	0.76		0.42
	shs		shs
No. of shs. o/s*	186,348,451		168,140,326
Avg. no. of shs. o/s*	181,583,471		131,790,084
	%		%
Net profit margin	(1.33)		(15.56)
Return on equity	(1.01)		(15.29)
Return on assets	(0.05)		(1.91)
No. of employees (FTEs)	8,550		7,300

* S.V. & M.V.
[A] Reported in accordance with IFRS

Historical Summary
(as originally stated)

Fiscal Year	Oper. Rev.	Net Inc. Bef. Disc.	EPS*
	$000s	$000s	$
2022[A]	1,250,300	(16,600)	(0.09)
2021[A]	1,030,800	(160,400)	(1.22)
2020[A]	666,237	(157,151)	(1.76)
2019[A]	767,492	(63,911)	(0.73)

* S.V. & M.V.
[A] Reported in accordance with IFRS

D.34 Departure Bay Capital Corp.

Symbol - DBC.P **Exchange** - TSX-VEN **CUSIP** - 24951D
Head Office - 228-1122 Mainland St, Vancouver, BC, V6B 5L1 **Telephone** - (778) 870-5028
Email - trevortreweeke@gmail.com
Investor Relations - Trevor Treweeke (778) 870-5028
Auditors - Crowe MacKay LLP C.A., Vancouver, B.C.
Lawyers - AFG Law LLP, Vancouver, B.C.
Transfer Agents - TSX Trust Company, Vancouver, B.C.
Profile - (B.C. 2022) Capital Pool Company.
Common listed on TSX-VEN, Oct. 26, 2022.
Directors - Trevor Treweeke, CEO & corp. sec., Nanaimo, B.C.; Alan C. Savage, CFO, West Vancouver, B.C.; Paul Andreola, Vancouver, B.C.; Jake Bouma, Vancouver, B.C.

Capital Stock

	Authorized (shs.)	Outstanding (shs.)[1]
Preferred	unlimited	nil
Common	unlimited	4,500,000

[1] At Jan. 18, 2023

Major Shareholder - Paul Andreola held 11.11% interest, Jake Bouma held 11.11% interest, Alan C. Savage held 11.11% interest and Trevor Treweeke held 11.11% interest at Oct. 26, 2022.

Price Range - DBC.P/TSX-VEN

Year	Volume	High	Low	Close
2022	20,000	$0.15	$0.12	$0.14

Recent Close: $0.11
Capital Stock Changes - On Oct. 26, 2022, an initial public offering of 2,000,000 common shares was completed at 10¢ per share.

D.35 The Descartes Systems Group Inc.*

Symbol - DSG **Exchange** - TSX **CUSIP** - 249906
Head Office - 120 Randall Dr, Waterloo, ON, N2V 1C6 **Telephone** - (519) 746-8110 **Toll-free** - (800) 419-8495 **Fax** - (519) 747-0082
Website - www.descartes.com
Email - lmccauley@descartes.com
Investor Relations - Laurie McCauley (800) 419-8495
Auditors - KPMG LLP C.A., Toronto, Ont.
Lawyers - Morgan, Lewis & Bockius LLP; Blake, Cassels & Graydon LLP, Toronto, Ont.
Transfer Agents - Computershare Trust Company, Inc., Lakewood, Colo.; Computershare Trust Company of Canada Inc., Toronto, Ont.
FP500 Revenue Ranking - 423
Employees - 2,027 at Jan. 31, 2023
Profile - (Can. 2006; orig. Ont., 1981) Provides cloud, device and data content-based solutions focused on improving the productivity, performance, security and sustainability of logistics-intensive businesses.

Customers use the company's modular, Software-as-a-Service (SaaS) solutions to route, track and help improve the safety, performance and compliance of delivery resources; plan, allocate and execute shipments; rate, audit and pay transportation invoices; access global trade data; file customs and security documents for imports and exports; and complete numerous other logistics processes by participating in a large, collaborative multi-modal logistics community.

Principal products and services include the Logistics Technology Platform, which digitally combines its logistics network with an array of logistics management applications and a comprehensive offering of global trade related intelligence. Applications consist of routing, mobile and telematics, transportation management, e-commerce shipping and fulfillment, customs and regulatory compliance, global logistics network services, broker and forwarder enterprise systems and global trade intelligence solutions. Also provides consulting, implementation and training services which include project management and consulting services that assist in the configuration, implementation and deployment of the solutions; and customer support and maintenance services, which is provided worldwide 24 hours a day via telephone, online customer portal or email.

Solutions are offered on either subscription, transactional or perpetual licence basis. Solutions are developed and marketed primarily for transportation providers (air, ocean, rail and truck modes); logistics service providers (including third-party logistics providers, freight forwarders, non-vessel owning common carriers [NVOCCs] and customs brokers); and logistics-intensive manufacturers, retailers, distributors and mobile service providers. Other customers include government customs and census agencies, manufacturers, retailers, consumer products suppliers, wholesale distributors, and companies in industries such as healthcare, recycling/waste management, pharmaceuticals, and oil and gas.

The company is headquartered in Waterloo, Ont., with representative offices in Toronto, Ottawa and Windsor, Ont.; and Sorel-Tracy and Montreal, Que. Primary representative offices are located across the U.S., Europe, South America and Asia Pacific.

Recent Merger and Acquisition Activity

Status: completed **Announced:** Apr. 20, 2023
The Descartes Systems Group Inc. acquired Melbourne, Australia-based Localz Pty Ltd., which provides a technology platform that combines real-time vehicle location tracking and communications to deliver safe, transparent, customer centric Software-as-a-Service solutions that transform the customer delivery experience, for US$6,200,000 cash.

Status: completed **Announced:** Feb. 14, 2023
The Descartes Systems Group Inc. acquired Minneapolis, Minn.-based Windigo Logistics, Inc., which provides GroundCloud, a cloud-based software system offering final-mile carrier solutions and road safety compliance tools, for US$138,000,000, which was satisfied with cash on hand. A performance-based earn-out payment of up to US$80,000,000 would be paid based on the combined business achieving revenue-based targets in each of the first two years post-acquisition, with any earn-out expected to be paid in fiscal 2025 and fiscal 2026.

Status: completed **Announced:** Jan. 6, 2023
The Descartes Systems Group Inc. acquired Phoenix, Ariz.-based Supply Vision, a provider of shipment management software for North American Logistics Services Providers (LSPs), for up front cash consideration of US$12,000,000 plus potential performance-based earnout of up to US$3,000,000.

Status: completed **Announced:** June 6, 2022
The Descartes Systems Group Inc. acquired Utah-based XPS Technologies, LLC, a provider of e-commerce multi-carrier parcel shipping solutions, for upfront consideration of US$65,000,000 plus potential performance-based consideration. The maximum amount payable under the all-cash performance-based earnout is US$75,000,000, based on XPS achieving revenue-based targets in each of the first two years post-acquisition.Any earnout is expected to be paid in fiscal 2024 and fiscal 2025.

Status: completed **Announced:** Apr. 21, 2022
The Descartes Systems Group Inc. acquired San Francisco, Calif.-based Foxtrot Systems Inc., a provider of machine learning-based mobile route execution solutions for US$4,000,000. Foxtrot's advanced machine learning algorithms leverage millions of data points collected from vehicles in the field, helping customers reduce last-mile costs, improve customer service and learn service factors that improve route efficiency and on-time performance.

Directors - Eric A. Demirian, chr., Toronto, Ont.; Edward J. Ryan, CEO, Fort Washington, Pa.; Deepak Chopra, Toronto, Ont.; Deborah Close, Calgary, Alta.; Sandra L. Hanington, Toronto, Ont.; Kelley Irwin, Pickering, Ont.; Dennis Maple, Malvern, Pa.; Chris E. Muntwyler, Baech, Switzerland; Jane A. O'Hagan, Calgary, Alta.; John J. Walker, Wyckoff, N.J.
Other Exec. Officers - J. Scott Pagan, pres. & COO; Allan J. Brett, CFO; Andrew Roszko, chief comml. officer; Raimond Diederick, exec. v-p, info. srvcs.; Edward (Ed) Gardner, exec. v-p, corp. devel.; Chris Jones, exec. v-p, industry & srvcs.; Chad Murphy, exec. v-p, professional srvcs.; Robert (Bob) Parker, exec. v-p, cust. support & client srvcs.; Kenneth Wood, exec. v-p, product mgt.; Maija Michell, sr. v-p, HR; Peter V. Nguyen, sr. v-p, legal, gen. counsel & corp. sec.

Capital Stock

	Authorized (shs.)	Outstanding (shs.)[1]
Common	unlimited	85,078,029

[1] At May 31, 2023

Options - At Jan. 31, 2023, options were outstanding to purchase 1,593,433 common shares at prices ranging from US$18.95 to US$68.49 per share with a weighted average remaining contractual life of 4.1 years.
Major Shareholder - T. Rowe Price Associates, Inc. held 11.7% interest at May 2, 2023.

Price Range - DSG/TSX

Year	Volume	High	Low	Close
2022	51,235,734	$102.62	$72.94	$94.39
2021	29,859,558	$115.29	$68.61	$104.62
2020	46,123,593	$82.40	$38.65	$74.45
2019	36,686,999	$58.11	$33.96	$55.50
2018	35,535,628	$46.61	$31.39	$36.03

Recent Close: $100.04
Capital Stock Changes - During fiscal 2023, 63,890 common shares were issued on exercise of options.
Long-Term Debt - At Jan. 31, 2023, the company had no long-term debt.

Wholly Owned Subsidiaries

Descartes Systems (Belgium) NV, Belgium.
Descartes Systems (Germany) GmbH, Germany.
Descartes Systems (Sweden) AB, Sweden.
Descartes Systems UK Limited, United Kingdom.
Descartes Systems (USA) LLC, Del.
Descartes Visual Compliance Inc., Canada.
Descartes Visual Compliance (USA) LLC, Del.
MacroPoint, LLC, Cleveland, Ohio.
NetCHB, LLC, Ariz.
12268761 Canada Inc., Canada.
XPS Technologies, LLC, Cottonwood Heights, Utah.
Note: The preceding list includes only the major related companies in which interests are held.

Financial Statistics

Periods ended:	12m Jan. 31/23^A		12m Jan. 31/22^A
	US$000s	%Chg	US$000s
Operating revenue	**486,014**	**+14**	**424,690**
Cost of sales	112,386		101,078
Research & devel. expense	68,565		61,151
General & admin expense	90,119		77,354
Stock-based compensation	13,667		11,017
Operating expense	**284,737**	**+14**	**250,600**
Operating income	**201,277**	**+16**	**174,090**
Deprec., depl. & amort.	65,402		64,228
Finance income	4,461		299
Finance costs, gross	1,167		1,123
Pre-tax income	**133,728**	**+30**	**102,610**
Income taxes	31,492		16,328
Net income	**102,236**	**+18**	**86,282**
Cash & equivalent	276,385		213,437
Inventories	759		868
Accounts receivable	56,831		55,780
Current assets	358,651		292,059
Fixed assets, net	11,434		10,817
Right-of-use assets	6,774		10,571
Intangibles, net	905,455		838,370
Total assets	**1,316,044**	**+11**	**1,185,431**
Accts. pay. & accr. liabs	90,878		67,008
Current liabilities	169,595		133,433
Long-term lease liabilities	3,923		7,382
Shareholders' equity	1,099,391		999,819
Cash from oper. activs	**192,395**	**+9**	**176,138**
Cash from fin. activs	(4,603)		1,516
Cash from invest. activs	(121,632)		(95,107)
Net cash position	**276,385**	**+29**	**213,437**
Capital expenditures	(6,071)		(4,829)
	US$		US$
Earnings per share*	1.21		1.02
Cash flow per share*	2.27		2.08
	shs		shs
No. of shs. o/s*	84,820,100		84,756,210
Avg. no. of shs. o/s*	84,791,000		84,591,000
	%		%
Net profit margin	21.04		20.32
Return on equity	9.74		9.03
Return on assets	8.25		7.76
Foreign sales percent	93		91
No. of employees (FTEs)	2,027		1,813

* Common
^A Reported in accordance with U.S. GAAP

Latest Results

Periods ended:	3m Apr. 30/23^A		3m Apr. 30/22^A
	US$000s	%Chg	US$000s
Operating revenue	136,614	+17	116,395
Net income	29,353	+27	23,115
	US$		US$
Earnings per share*	0.35		0.27

* Common
^A Reported in accordance with U.S. GAAP

Historical Summary
(as originally stated)

Fiscal Year	Oper. Rev.	Net Inc. Bef. Disc.	EPS*
	US$000s	US$000s	US$
2023^A	486,014	102,236	1.21
2022^A	424,690	86,282	1.02
2021^A	348,664	52,100	0.62
2020^A	325,791	36,997	0.45
2019^A	275,171	31,277	0.41

* Common
^A Reported in accordance with U.S. GAAP

D.36 Desert Mountain Energy Corp.

Symbol - DME **Exchange** - TSX-VEN **CUSIP** - 25043D

Head Office - 250-750 Pender St W, Vancouver, BC, V6C 2T7 **Telephone** - (604) 788-0300

Website - www.desertmountainenergy.com

Email - don@desertmountainenergy.com

Investor Relations - Donald A. Mosher (604) 617-5448

Auditors - Crowe MacKay LLP C.A., Calgary, Alta.

Lawyers - Fasken Martineau DuMoulin LLP, Vancouver, B.C.

Transfer Agents - TSX Trust Company, Vancouver, B.C.

Profile - (B.C. 2008) Provides trucking services for oil and gas production equipment and has helium and oil and gas interests in Arizona.

Through wholly owned **Dessert Mountain Trucking LLC**, the company earns revenue from providing trucking services for moving oil field and production equipment for customers.

Also holds Holbrook Basin helium and oil and gas project, 100,000 acres, Holbrook Basin area, including South Winslow and Gunnar Dome prospects, and McCauley helium processing facility. Commercial production of hydrogen and other noble gases were expected to occur by the end of July or early August 2023.

In August 2022, the company acquired a 40-acre parcel of land in Navajo cty., Ariz., for an undisclosed amount. The land would be used for future facilities.

Predecessor Detail - Name changed from African Queen Mines Ltd., Mar. 22, 2018; basis 1 new for 4 old shs.

Directors - Robert Rohlfing, exec. chr. & CEO, Ariz.; Donald A. (Don) Mosher, pres., North Vancouver, B.C.; Dr. James Cronoble, v-p, explor., Colo.; Jessica Davey, v-p, land, Colo.; Michael O'Shea; Jenaya Rohlfing, Tex.; Weldon Stout, Okla.; Dr. Kelli Ward, Ariz.

Other Exec. Officers - Valorie Farley, CFO; Marta H. Wasko, v-p, geol.; Frances Murphy, corp. sec.

Capital Stock

	Authorized (shs.)	Outstanding (shs.)[1]
Preferred	unlimited	nil
Common	unlimited	90,258,109

[1] At May 30, 2023

Major Shareholder - Widely held at Mar. 20, 2023.

Price Range - DME/TSX-VEN

Year	Volume	High	Low	Close
2022	15,067,974	$4.43	$1.70	$2.77
2021	29,195,549	$4.95	$1.31	$2.05
2020	25,263,339	$2.11	$0.14	$1.50
2019	7,104,774	$0.31	$0.13	$0.23
2018	12,717,386	$0.27	$0.08	$0.21

Recent Close: $0.41

Capital Stock Changes - In March 2023, bought deal public offering of 11,845,000 units (1 common share & 1 warrant) was completed at $1.95 per unit, with warrants exercisable at $2.70 per share for two years.

In September 2022, private placement of 2,149,461 units (1 common share & 1 warrant) at $2.60 per unit was completed. Also during fiscal 2022, common shares were issued as follows; 3,228,400 on exercise of warrants, 867,500 on exercise of options, 182,383 on exercise of share appreciation rights and 119,477 as finder's fees.

Wholly Owned Subsidiaries

Desert Energy Corp., Nevada City, Calif.
Desert Mountain Trucking LLC, Ariz.
PAM Botswana (Pty) Ltd., Botswana. Inactive.
Saguaro Family Land Company, Ariz.

Subsidiaries

99.97% int. in **AQ Kenya Gold Limited**, Kenya. Inactive.
99% int. in **PAM Moçambique, Limitada**, Mozambique. Inactive.

Investments

Brixton Metals Corporation, Vancouver, B.C. (see Survey of Mines)

Financial Statistics

Periods ended:	12m Sept. 30/22^A		12m Sept. 30/21^A
	$000s	%Chg	$000s
Operating revenue	**444**	**n.a.**	**nil**
Cost of sales	200		nil
Salaries & benefits	177		nil
General & admin expense	3,187		1,568
Stock-based compensation	3,452		5,436
Operating expense	**7,016**	**0**	**7,004**
Operating income	**(6,572)**	**n.a.**	**(7,004)**
Deprec., depl. & amort.	152		5
Finance income	136		n.a.
Write-downs/write-offs	nil		(603)
Pre-tax income	**(7,528)**	**n.a.**	**(7,895)**
Net income	**(7,528)**	**n.a.**	**(7,895)**
Cash & equivalent	12,521		26,819
Accounts receivable	412		19
Current assets	13,363		27,139
Fixed assets, net	10,401		461
Intangibles, net	nil		12
Explor./devel. properties	15,086		6,845
Total assets	**40,019**	**+16**	**34,521**
Accts. pay. & accr. liabs	2,325		502
Current liabilities	2,348		517
Shareholders' equity	37,318		33,854
Cash from oper. activs	**(3,522)**	**n.a.**	**(1,602)**
Cash from fin. activs	6,996		22,314
Cash from invest. activs	(17,858)		(4,185)
Net cash position	**12,230**	**-54**	**26,614**
Capital expenditures, net	(15,943)		(4,185)
	$		$
Earnings per share*	(0.10)		(0.12)
Cash flow per share*	(0.05)		(0.03)
	shs		shs
No. of shs. o/s*	77,584,895		71,037,674
Avg. no. of shs. o/s*	73,722,688		63,766,154
	%		%
Net profit margin	n.m.		n.a.
Return on equity	(21.15)		(33.37)
Return on assets	(20.20)		(32.85)
Foreign sales percent	100		n.a.

* Common
^A Reported in accordance with IFRS

Latest Results

Periods ended:	6m Mar. 31/23^A		6m Mar. 31/22^A
	$000s	%Chg	$000s
Operating revenue	1,002	n.a.	nil
Net income	(3,735)	n.a.	(3,258)
	$		$
Earnings per share*	(0.05)		(0.05)

* Common
^A Reported in accordance with IFRS

Historical Summary
(as originally stated)

Fiscal Year	Oper. Rev.	Net Inc. Bef. Disc.	EPS*
	$000s	$000s	$
2022^A	444	(7,528)	(0.10)
2021^A	nil	(7,895)	(0.12)
2020^A	nil	(1,503)	(0.04)
2019^A	nil	(339)	(0.01)
2018^A	nil	(636)	(0.02)

* Common
^A Reported in accordance with IFRS

D.37 Destiny Media Technologies Inc.

Symbol - DSY **Exchange** - TSX-VEN **CUSIP** - 25063G

Head Office - 428-1575 Georgia St W, Vancouver, BC, V6G 2V3 **Telephone** - (604) 609-7736 **Toll-free** - (800) 833-7846 **Fax** - (604) 609-0611

Website - www.dsny.com

Email - fredv@dsny.com

Investor Relations - Frederick W. Vandenberg (604) 609-7736 ext. 236

Auditors - Smythe LLP C.A., Vancouver, B.C.

Transfer Agents - TSX Trust Company

Profile - (Nev. 2014; orig. Colo., 1998) Develops and markets proprietary software that enables distribution and promotion of digital media content in the music industry over the Internet.

The company's primary technology is Play MPE®, a cloud-based Software-as-a-Service solution for promoting and distributing audio, video, images, promotional information and other digital content primarily for the music industry. The platform consists of Caster, a full-service distribution management system which allows record labels and artists to create music promotional campaigns and market, promote and deliver music releases directly to targeted recipients; and Player, a web-based music player and mobile application which enables recipients to discover, download, stream and review music releases as well as provide access to promotional content and unique metadata, including ISRC codes, photos, tour dates and artist contact information. Play MPE® is a permissions-only access system such that only recipients designated or targeted to receive content obtain access to that content. Music on the platform is protected by proprietary watermarking technologies which contain tracking information so that the source of unauthorized copies can be traced. The Play MPE® platform is currently used by the recording industry for transferring pre-release music, radio shows and music videos to recipients such as radio stations, media reviewers, VIPs, DJs, film and TV personnel, sports stadiums and retailers. Customers include small independent artists, small to large independent record labels, promoters and major record labels, including **Universal Music Group**, **Warner Music Group** and **Sony Music Entertainment**.

Under development is MTR™, a service which would provide airplay monitoring of digital broadcasts of music.

The company also has a legacy business, the Clipstream® online video platform, a self-service system for encoding, hosting and reporting on video playback which can be embedded in third party websites or emails.

Directors - Hyonmyong (Hoch) Cho, chr., Vancouver, B.C.; Frederick W. (Fred) Vandenberg, pres., CEO & corp. sec., Vancouver, B.C.; S. Jay Graber, Vancouver, B.C.; David Mossberg, Vancouver, B.C.; Dr. David Summers, Vancouver, B.C.

Other Exec. Officers - Olya Massalitina, CFO

Capital Stock

	Authorized (shs.)	Outstanding (shs.)[1]	Par
Common	20,000,000	10,116,576	US$0.001

[1] At July 11, 2023

Normal Course Issuer Bid - The company plans to make normal course purchases of up to 506,213 common shares representing 5% of the total outstanding. The bid commenced on May 5, 2023, and expires on May 4, 2024.

Major Shareholder - Mark A. Graber held 20.61% interest at Nov. 14, 2022.

Price Range - DSY/TSX-VEN

Year	Volume	High	Low	Close
2022	420,165	$2.00	$0.49	$0.65
2021	1,186,655	$3.28	$0.95	$1.52
2020	1,075,071	$1.50	$0.69	$0.95
2019	888,810	$2.28	$1.00	$1.18
2018	394,093	$2.00	$0.80	$1.25

Consolidation: 1-for-5 cons. in Sept. 2019

Recent Close: $1.13

Capital Stock Changes - During fiscal 2022, 143,100 common shares were repurchased under a Normal Course Issuer Bid.

Wholly Owned Subsidiaries

Destiny Software Productions Inc., B.C.
- 100% int. in **Sonox Digital Inc.**, B.C.

MPE Distribution Inc., Nev.
Tonality Inc., Nev.

Financial Statistics

Periods ended:	12m Aug. 31/22[A]		12m Aug. 31/21[A]
	US$000s	%Chg	US$000s
Operating revenue	**4,024**	**-4**	**4,172**
Cost of sales	657		394
Research & devel. expense	1,100		1,195
General & admin expense	1,889		2,078
Operating expense	**3,646**	**-1**	**3,667**
Operating income	**378**	**-25**	**505**
Deprec., depl. & amort.	143		105
Finance income	9		4
Write-downs/write-offs	(84)		(15)
Pre-tax income	**153**	**-60**	**383**
Income taxes	4		nil
Net income	**149**	**-61**	**383**
Cash & equivalent	2,096		2,753
Accounts receivable	444		380
Current assets	2,725		3,310
Fixed assets, net	312		143
Right-of-use assets	nil		190
Intangibles, net	530		188
Total assets	**3,567**	**-8**	**3,866**
Accts. pay. & accr. liabs	436		513
Current liabilities	457		748
Shareholders' equity	3,110		3,118
Cash from oper. activs	**307**	**-42**	**529**
Cash from fin. activs	(191)		(260)
Cash from invest. activs	(693)		591
Net cash position	**2,096**	**-24**	**2,753**
Capital expenditures	(326)		(45)
	US$		US$
Earnings per share*	0.01		0.04
Cash flow per share*	0.03		0.05
	shs		shs
No. of shs. o/s*	10,122,261		10,265,361
Avg. no. of shs. o/s*	10,169,426		10,415,105
	%		%
Net profit margin	3.70		9.18
Return on equity	4.78		12.81
Return on assets	4.01		9.98
No. of employees (FTEs)	n.a.		34

* Common
[A] Reported in accordance with U.S. GAAP

Latest Results

Periods ended:	9m May 31/23[A]		9m May 31/22[A]
	US$000s	%Chg	US$000s
Operating revenue	2,988	-1	3,030
Net income	364	n.a.	(40)
	US$		US$
Earnings per share*	0.04		(0.00)

* Common
[A] Reported in accordance with U.S. GAAP

Historical Summary
(as originally stated)

Fiscal Year	Oper. Rev. US$000s	Net Inc. Bef. Disc. US$000s	EPS* US$
2022[A]	4,024	149	0.01
2021[A]	4,172	383	0.04
2020[A]	3,825	169	0.02
2019[A]	3,809	611	0.06
2018[A]	3,606	656	0.05

* Common
[A] Reported in accordance with U.S. GAAP
Note: Adjusted throughout for 1-for-5 cons. in Sept. 2019

D.38 Deveron Corp.

Symbol - FARM **Exchange** - TSX-VEN **CUSIP** - 25162L
Head Office - 1702-141 Adelaide St W, Toronto, ON, M5H 3L5
Telephone - (647) 963-2429
Website - deveron.com
Email - plinton@deveron.com
Investor Relations - Philip Linton (647) 622-0076
Auditors - Grant Thornton LLP C.A., Toronto, Ont.
Lawyers - Irwin Lowy LLP, Toronto, Ont.
Transfer Agents - TSX Trust Company, Toronto, Ont.
Employees - 127 at Apr. 14, 2022
Profile - (Ont. 2011) Provides data collection and data insights services to the farming sector in North America, with a focus on the United States and Canada.

Services provided include soil fertility sampling services, carbon sampling, fertility and carbon analysis, and other laboratory tests, as well as agronomic insights. By leveraging a digital process that uses farm-collected data, the company is able to offer unbiased interpretation of production decisions, ultimately providing recommendations on optimizing farm input usage. The company has a team of agronomists and data scientists, as well as a network of data technicians that are deployed to collect various types of farm data. Moreover, the company acquires and operates local farm field service providers and soil laboratories, who then leverage the company's standardized data solutions and technology platforms to grow their businesses.

On Oct. 27, 2022, the company acquired all of the assets of Clear Lake, Iowa-based **Frontier Labs Inc.** for US$825,000 cash on closing, US$412,500 payable on each of the first two anniversaries of closing date, issuance of 746,570 common shares at 50¢ per share upon receipt of the approval of the acquisition and issuance of 373,285 common shares at 50¢ per share on each of the first two anniversaries following the signing of the definitive agreement on Oct. 4, 2023. Frontier Labs provides soil testing and precision agriculture services.

In July 2022, the company acquired the assets of **Agri-Labs, Inc.** for US$425,000 cash upon signing of agreement, an aggregate of US$210,000 cash on each of the first two anniversaries of the signing of the agreement, issuance of US$180,000 of common shares upon TSX Venture Exchange approval and issuance of US$90,000 of common shares on each of the first two anniversaries of the signing of the agreement. Agri-Labs provides digital dependent consulting services for the agricultural industry that provides fertility recommendations and other ag related services to individual growers and fertilizer dealers in Indiana, Michigan, and Ohio with 45,000 soil samples processed annually.

Recent Merger and Acquisition Activity

Status: completed **Revised:** May 24, 2022
UPDATE: The transaction was completed. Consideration consisted of $37,800,000 in cash, $4,900,000 in promissory notes and 13,688,182 common shares at a deemed issue price of $0.55 per share. PREVIOUS: Deveron Corp. agreed to acquire a 67% interest in London, Ont.-based A&L Canada Laboratories East, Inc. one of the largest soil and tissue laboratories in Canada processing 435,000 soil samples annually, for $50,300,000 consisting of $42,800,000 in cash and $7,500,000 in Deveron common shares. A&L operates a 54,500-sq.-ft. laboratory, including a large R&D group that has produced patented, crop specific yield and disease solutions. Deveron and A&L have cooperated in Canadian soil testing and analysis since 2019 and jointly own and operate Wood's End Laboratory in the United States. Deveron would also have an option to purchase the remaining 33% of A&L following the three-year anniversary of the closing of the acquisition. During the 12- month period ended Dec. 31, 2021, A&L had unaudited revenue of $26,700,000. May 11, 2022 - The agreement was amended whereby consideration would now consists of $34,800,000 in cash, $8,000,000 in promissory notes and $7,500,000 in common shares.

Predecessor Detail - Name changed from Deveron UAS Corp., Sept. 3, 2020.

Directors - William (Bill) Linton, chr., Toronto, Ont.; David A. MacMillan, pres., CEO & corp. sec., Toronto, Ont.; Tim Close, Toronto, Ont.; Roger Dent, Toronto, Ont.; Joelle Faulkner, Ont.; Christopher O. (Chris) Irwin, Toronto, Ont.; Greg Patterson

Other Exec. Officers - Carmelo (Carm) Marrelli, CFO; Craig Hogan, v-p, fin.; Scott Jackman, v-p, sales; Pranay Joshi, v-p, eng.; Philip Linton, v-p, corp. devel.; Mike Wilson, v-p, data collection

Capital Stock

	Authorized (shs.)	Outstanding (shs.)[1]
Special	unlimited	nil
Common	unlimited	155,930,423

[1] At June 16, 2023

Major Shareholder - Widely held at June 19, 2023.

Price Range - FARM/TSX-VEN

Year	Volume	High	Low	Close
2022	17,829,926	$0.87	$0.37	$0.47
2021	16,828,244	$0.96	$0.38	$0.78
2020	7,690,242	$0.44	$0.11	$0.42
2019	6,909,437	$0.32	$0.14	$0.19
2018	8,905,880	$0.45	$0.10	$0.19

Recent Close: $0.35

Capital Stock Changes - In May 2023, private placement of 16,774,194 common shares was completed at $0.31 per share.

In February 2022, public offering of 16,428,573 units (1 common share & ½ warrant) at $0.70 per unit was completed. In May 2022, 13,688,182 common shares were issued on acquisition of 67% interest in A&L Canada Laboratories East, Inc. Also during 2022, common shares were issued as follows: 6,257,143 by private placement, 5,793,733 on exercise of warrants, 2,477,522 on exercise of options, 750,000 on acquisition of assets of Agri-Labs, Inc., 746,570 on acquisition of Frontier Labs Inc., 594,717 on acquisition of the assets of Stealth Ag, Inc., 524,691 on acquisition of the assets of Agronomic Solutions, Inc., 98,039 on acquisition of FD Agro Technologies LLC (Farm Dog) and 55,335 on acquisition of Tana Ag Solutions Group LLP.

Wholly Owned Subsidiaries

Deveron USA, LLC, Mo.
- 100% int. in **Tru Agronomy, LLC**, Minn.
- 51% int. in **Woods East Laboratories, LLC**, Del.

FD Agro Technologies LLC
Veritas Farm Management Inc., Chatham, Ont.

Subsidiaries

67% int. in **A&L Canada Laboratories East, Inc.**, London, Ont.

Financial Statistics

Periods ended:	12m Dec. 31/22[A]		12m Dec. 31/21[oA]
	$000s	%Chg	$000s
Operating revenue	**28,923**	**+236**	**8,598**
Cost of sales	8,971		2,770
Salaries & benefits	11,396		5,741
General & admin expense	10,922		3,428
Stock-based compensation	1,147		666
Operating expense	**32,437**	**+157**	**12,605**
Operating income	**(3,514)**	**n.a.**	**(4,007)**
Deprec., depl. & amort.	4,830		914
Finance income	59		15
Finance costs, gross	3,368		111
Pre-tax income	**(8,175)**	**n.a.**	**(5,020)**
Income taxes	399		nil
Net income	**(8,574)**	**n.a.**	**(5,020)**
Net inc. for equity hldrs	**(9,086)**	**n.a.**	**(5,177)**
Net inc. for non-cont. int	**512**	**+226**	**157**
Cash & equivalent	5,825		6,867
Accounts receivable	6,495		2,518
Current assets	13,872		9,677
Fixed assets, net	17,778		1,508
Right-of-use assets	4,805		1,783
Intangibles, net	79,667		9,800
Total assets	**116,727**	**+413**	**22,767**
Bank indebtedness	4,927		nil
Accts. pay. & accr. liabs	4,969		1,913
Current liabilities	15,227		4,086
Long-term debt, gross	38,763		216
Long-term debt, net	36,033		nil
Long-term lease liabilities	4,089		1,193
Equity portion of conv. debs	1,740		nil
Shareholders' equity	19,286		14,678
Non-controlling interest	24,716		1,633
Cash from oper. activs	**(9,998)**	**n.a.**	**(3,923)**
Cash from fin. activs	52,406		8,975
Cash from invest. activs	(43,451)		(4,402)
Net cash position	**5,825**	**-15**	**6,867**
Capital expenditures	(5,492)		(513)
Capital disposals	212		nil
	$		$
Earnings per share*	(0.07)		(0.07)
Cash flow per share*	(0.09)		(0.05)
	shs		shs
No. of shs. o/s*	136,421,107		89,006,602
Avg. no. of shs. o/s*	116,387,677		76,992,311
	%		%
Net profit margin	(29.64)		(58.39)
Return on equity	(53.50)		(45.14)
Return on assets	(7.23)		(30.55)
Foreign sales percent	40		73
No. of employees (FTEs)	...		102

* Common
[o] Restated
[A] Reported in accordance with IFRS

Latest Results

Periods ended:	3m Mar. 31/23[A]		3m Mar. 31/22[A]
	$000s	%Chg	$000s
Operating revenue	5,359	+281	1,407
Net income	(6,134)	n.a.	(3,550)
Net inc. for equity hldrs	(5,732)	n.a.	(3,551)
Net inc. for non-cont. int	(402)		1
	$		$
Earnings per share*	(0.04)		(0.04)

* Common
[A] Reported in accordance with IFRS

Historical Summary
(as originally stated)

Fiscal Year	Oper. Rev. $000s	Net Inc. Bef. Disc. $000s	EPS* $
2022[A]	28,923	(8,574)	(0.07)
2021[A]	8,598	(5,020)	(0.07)
2020[A]	2,869	(1,762)	(0.04)
2019[A]	2,055	(1,937)	(0.05)
2018[A]	501	(1,529)	(0.05)

* Common
[A] Reported in accordance with IFRS

D.39 Devonian Health Group Inc.

Symbol - GSD **Exchange** - TSX-VEN **CUSIP** - 251834
Head Office - 360 rue des Entrepreneurs, Montmagny, QC, G5V 4T1
Telephone - (450) 937-6696
Website - www.groupedevonian.com
Email - pmontanaro@groupedevonian.com
Investor Relations - Pierre J. Montanaro (450) 434-9707
Auditors - PricewaterhouseCoopers LLP C.A., Montréal, Qué.

Bankers - Bank of Montreal
Lawyers - Stein Monast LLP, Québec, Qué.
Transfer Agents - TSX Trust Company, Montréal, Qué.
Employees - 6 at July 31, 2022
Profile - (Can. 2017 amalg.; orig. Can., 2013) Develops botanical drugs for the treatment of inflammatory-autoimmune diseases, including ulcerative colitis and atopic dermatitis (eczema); and manufactures and commercializes a line of botanical cosmeceutical skin care products.
The company has developed a platform named The Supra Molecular Complex Extraction and Stabilisation Technology (SUPREX™) which involves a process of extracting, purifying, stabilising and conditioning of products from the active photosynthesis machinery of plants and algae.
Products made from this technology include Thykamine™, which is being studied and developed as a prescription rectal enema for the treatment of active mild-to-moderate distal ulcerative colitis and as a cream for the treatment of mild-to-moderate atopic dermatitis; and R-Spinasome®, an active ingredient in the company's line of anti-aging product consisting of day, night and eye creams under the Purgenesis™ brand or as private labels through marketing partners. Organic baby spinach is the primary raw material being used to produce Thykamine™ and R-Spinasome®, which has immunomodulatory, antioxidant and anti-inflammatory properties. A Canadian Phase 3 clinical study in paediatric patients for Thykamine™ for atopic dermatitis would begin in early 2023. Other pharmaceutical applications of Thykamine™ are hand and foot syndrome associated to chemotherapy, radiation dermatitis associated with radiotheraphy and inflammatory acne.
Thykamine™ would be produced at the company's 1,625-m^2 facility in Montmagny, Que., and then transferred to pharmaceutical subcontractors for the manufacturing of the finished dosage forms of the drug. The company also holds a licence from Health Canada to research and develop cannabinoid-based pharmaceutical products at its facility in Montmagny, Que.
Through wholly owned **Altius Healthcare Inc.**, imports, markets and distributes generic and brand name medicines in Canada, including pantoprazole magnesium for the relief of acid reflux symptoms or gastroesophageal reflux disease (GERD); and Cleo-35®, which is used to treat hormonal acne in women.
Predecessor Detail - Formed from Orletto Capital Inc. in Canada, May 12, 2017, pursuant to Qualifying Transaction reverse takeover acquisition of and amalgamation with (old) Devonian Health Group Inc.; basis 1 new for 2.75 old shs.
Directors - Pierre J. Montanaro, pres. & CEO, Qué.; Dr. André P. Boulet, chief science officer, Blainville, Qué.; Ashish B. Chabria, New York, N.Y.; Dr. Louis Flamand, Qué.; Jean Forcione, Qué.; Luc Grégoire, New York, N.Y.
Other Exec. Officers - Colette Laurin, interim CFO & contr.

Capital Stock

	Authorized (shs.)	Outstanding (shs.)[1]
Multiple Vtg.	unlimited	nil
Subord. Vtg.	unlimited	136,366,475
Subord. Exch. Vtg.	unlimited	nil

[1] At Feb. 3, 2023

Multiple Voting - Exchangeable into subordinate voting shares on a one-for-one basis at option of holders and automatically in certain other circumstances. Six votes per share.
Subordinate Voting - One vote per share.
Major Shareholder - Dr. André P. Boulet held 14.73% interest at Feb. 15, 2023.

Price Range - GSD/TSX-VEN

Year	Volume	High	Low	Close
2022	1,289,060	$0.68	$0.28	$0.34
2021	4,748,034	$0.70	$0.14	$0.58
2020	2,454,141	$0.24	$0.09	$0.13
2019	2,118,847	$0.44	$0.12	$0.17
2018	2,558,465	$0.70	$0.25	$0.32

Recent Close: $0.20
Capital Stock Changes - In September 2021, private placement of 2,415,090 units (1 subordinate voting share & 1 warrant) at 44¢ per unit was completed. In November 2021, private placement of 32,897,662 units (1 subordinate voting share & 1 warrant) at 30¢ per unit was completed. On Apr. 19, 2022, all 19,966,523 multiple voting shares were converted into a like number of subordinate voting shares. Also during fiscal 2022, subordinate voting shares were issued as follows: 1,311,553 for debt settlement, 700,000 on exercise of warrants and 353,642 for interest.

Wholly Owned Subsidiaries

Altius Healthcare Inc., Ont.

Financial Statistics

Periods ended:	12m July 31/22[A]		12m July 31/21[A]
	$000s	%Chg	$000s
Operating revenue	**2,305**	**+56**	**1,475**
Cost of sales	1,744		1,716
Research & devel. expense	779		610
General & admin expense	1,298		342
Stock-based compensation	533		83
Operating expense	**4,354**	**+58**	**2,750**
Operating income	**(2,049)**	**n.a.**	**(1,276)**
Deprec., depl. & amort.	864		1,030
Finance income	40		nil
Finance costs, gross	575		1,086
Pre-tax income	**(3,448)**	**n.a.**	**(3,346)**
Net income	**(3,448)**	**n.a.**	**(3,346)**
Cash & equivalent	7,805		345
Inventories	155		28
Accounts receivable	315		219
Current assets	8,417		664
Fixed assets, net	2,885		3,067
Intangibles, net	10,284		10,877
Total assets	**21,586**	**+48**	**14,608**
Accts. pay. & accr. liabs.	1,035		1,809
Current liabilities	1,041		1,814
Long-term debt, gross	4,257		5,258
Long-term debt, net	4,257		5,258
Long-term lease liabilities	16		13
Shareholders' equity	16,273		7,523
Cash from oper. activs.	**(2,872)**	**n.a.**	**(1,833)**
Cash from fin. activs.	10,411		1,279
Cash from invest. activs.	(5,079)		(14)
Net cash position	**2,805**	**+713**	**345**
Capital expenditures	(74)		(14)
	$		$
Earnings per share*	(0.03)		(0.04)
Cash flow per share*	(0.02)		(0.02)
	shs		shs
No. of shs. o/s*	131,138,635		93,460,688
Avg. no. of shs. o/s*	119,027,954		88,842,565
	%		%
Net profit margin	(149.59)		(226.85)
Return on equity	(28.98)		(39.58)
Return on assets	(15.88)		(14.44)
No. of employees (FTEs)	6		n.a.

* Common
[A] Reported in accordance with IFRS

Latest Results

Periods ended:	3m Oct. 31/22[A]		3m Oct. 31/21[A]
	$000s	%Chg	$000s
Operating revenue	410	-7	440
Net income	(1,196)	n.a.	(848)
	$		$
Earnings per share*	(0.01)		(0.01)

* Common
[A] Reported in accordance with IFRS

Historical Summary
(as originally stated)

Fiscal Year	Oper. Rev. $000s	Net Inc. Bef. Disc. $000s	EPS* $
2022[A]	2,305	(3,448)	(0.03)
2021[A]	1,475	(3,346)	(0.04)
2020[A]	2,143	(4,375)	(0.06)
2019[A]	5,938	(2,979)	(0.04)
2018[A]	3,200	(3,187)	(0.05)

* Common
[A] Reported in accordance with IFRS

D.40 DevvStream Holdings Inc.

Symbol - DESG **Exchange** - NEO **CUSIP** - 25189R
Head Office - 2133-1177 Hastings St W, Vancouver, BC, V6E 2K3 **Telephone** - (778) 799-2019
Website - devvstream.com
Email - info@devvstream.com
Investor Relations - David Goertz (778) 799-2019
Auditors - MNP LLP C.A., Ottawa, Ont.
Transfer Agents - Odyssey Trust Company, Vancouver, B.C.
Profile - (B.C. 2021) Invests in carbon credit generating projects.
Invests in and partners with companies having green technologies that generate renewable energy, improve energy efficiencies, eliminate or reduce emissions, and sequester carbon directly from the air.
Provides upfront capital for sustainability projects in exchange for carbon credit rights, and through these rights, generates and manages carbon credits by utilizing a blockchain-based platform developed and operated by **Devvio, Inc.**
Common listed on NEO, Jan. 17, 2023.

Recent Merger and Acquisition Activity

Status: completed **Revised:** Nov. 4, 2022
UPDATE: The transaction was completed. A total of 4,650,000 multiple voting shares and 26,000,001 subordinate voting shares were issued. The name of 1319738 B.C. was changed to DevvStream Holdings Inc. PREVIOUS: 1319738 B.C. Ltd. entered into a letter of intent for the reverse takeover acquisition of private Vancouver, B.C.-based DevvESG Streaming, Inc., which invests in carbon credit generating projects, on a share-for-share basis. Dec. 17, 2021 - A definitive agreement was entered into. Feb. 1, 2022 - DevvESG changed its name to DevvStream Inc.
Predecessor Detail - Name changed from 1319738 B.C. Ltd., Nov. 4, 2022, pursuant to the reverse takeover acquisition of DevvStream Inc.
Directors - Tom Anderson, chr., Albuquerque, N.M.; Dr. Michael Max Bühler; Stephen Kukucha, Vancouver, B.C.; Jamila Piracci, Richmond, Tex.; Ray Quintana, Albuquerque, N.M.
Other Exec. Officers - Sunny Trinh, CEO; Chris Merkel, COO & corp. sec.; David Goertz, CFO; Dr. Destenie Nock, chief sustainability officer; Bryan Went, chief revenue officer

Capital Stock

	Authorized (shs.)	Outstanding (shs.)[1]
Multiple Voting	unlimited	4,650,000
Subordinate Voting	unlimited	27,249,794

[1] At Jan. 17, 2023

Multiple Voting - Each convertible, at the holder's option, into 10 subordinate voting shares. 10 votes per share.
Subordinate Voting - One vote per share.
Major Shareholder - Devvio, Inc. held 63.05% interest at Jan. 17, 2023.
Recent Close: $1.06
Capital Stock Changes - On Nov. 4, 2022, 4,650,000 multiple voting shares and 26,000,001 subordinate voting shares were issued pursuant to the reverse takeover acquisition of DevvStream Inc.

Wholly Owned Subsidiaries

DevvStream Inc., Vancouver, B.C.

Financial Statistics

Periods ended:	48w July 31/22[A1]
	$000s
Salaries & benefits	643
General & admin expense	3,141
Stock-based compensation	1,201
Operating expense	**4,986**
Operating income	**(4,986)**
Deprec., depl. & amort.	1
Write-downs/write-offs	(2,288)
Pre-tax income	**(7,581)**
Net income	**(7,581)**
Cash & equivalent	4,816
Accounts receivable	6
Current assets	5,389
Fixed assets, net	6
Total assets	**5,396**
Accts. pay. & accr. liabs.	257
Current liabilities	4,390
Shareholders' equity	1,005
Cash from oper. activs.	**(4,406)**
Cash from fin. activs.	10,858
Cash from invest. activs.	(1,635)
Net cash position	**4,816**
Capital expenditures	(7)
	$
Earnings per share*	(0.40)
Cash flow per share*	(0.23)
	shs
No. of shs. o/s	n.a.
Avg. no. of shs. o/s*	19,024,798
	%
Net profit margin	n.a.
Return on equity	n.m.
Return on assets	n.a.

* M.V. & S.V.
[A] Reported in accordance with IFRS
[1] Results pertain to DevvStream Inc.

D.41 Dexterra Group Inc.*

Symbol - DXT **Exchange** - TSX **CUSIP** - 252371
Head Office - Airway Centre, 425-5915 Airport Rd, Mississauga, ON, L4V 1T1 **Telephone** - (416) 483-5152 **Toll-free** - (866) 305-6565
Website - www.dexterra.com
Email - drew.knight@dexterra.com
Investor Relations - R. Drew Knight (866) 305-6565
Auditors - PricewaterhouseCoopers LLP C.A., Calgary, Alta.
Lawyers - Blake, Cassels & Graydon LLP, Calgary, Alta.
Transfer Agents - TSX Trust Company, Calgary, Alta.
FP500 Subsidiary Revenue Ranking - 70
Employees - 8,949 at Dec. 31, 2022
Profile - (Alta. 2006 amalg.) Provides facilities management and operations services, workforce accommodation solutions, forestry

services, modular building capabilities and other support services for diverse clients in the public and private sectors across Canada.

Has three operating divisions: Integrated Facilities Management; Workforce Accommodations, Forestry & Energy Services; and Modular Solutions.

Integrated Facilities Management - Provides operations and maintenance solutions for built assets and infrastructure in the public and private sectors, including aviation, defence, retail, healthcare, business and industry, education, rail, hotels and leisure, and government. Services for space and infrastructure include maintenance, repair and operations; management of building utilities and energy performance; asset management including planning, budgeting and lifecycle management; and project management and delivery of renovations, modifications, refits and upgrades. Services for people and organizations include customer care; cleaning and environmental services including waste management; food services; management of parking and security services; material handling and logistical services; and 24/7 client help desk solutions.

Workforce Accommodations, Forestry & Energy Services - Provides full service workforce accommodation, camp management and catering services to customers working on projects in remote regions of Canada's provinces and northern territories where the local infrastructure does not provide such facilities. In addition, provides forestry services including tree planting, forest clearing and thinning and Type-2 firefighting services to public and private sector customers in Quebec, Ontario, Saskatchewan and Alberta.

This division also includes the energy services business which consists of relocatable structure (office units, lavatory units, mine dry units, wellsite units and associated equipment), access mat rentals, equipment sales and installation, transportation, service, and other revenue associated with the rentals, sales, and soil stabilization.

Modular Solutions - This division includes the design, manufacturing, transportation and installation of residential, retail and commercial modular buildings. Modular units are designed and manufactured at a 73,870-sq.-ft. facility in Kamloops, B.C.; an 87,000-sq.-ft. manufacturing space in Calgary, Alta.; a 46,792-sq.-ft. facility in Grimsby, Ont.; and a 144,130-sq.-ft. facility in Cambridge, Ont.

In February 2023, the company acquired **VCI CONTROLS Inc.**, which supplies building technologies and services that improve comfort, safety, energy efficiency and occupant productivity, for total consideration of $4,800,000 consisting of $3,820,000 in cash on closing with a holdback of $980,000 being subject to release over the 12-month period following closing upon meeting certain milestones.

Predecessor Detail - Name changed from Horizon North Logistics Inc., Nov. 13, 2020.

Directors - R. William (Bill) McFarland, chr., Richmond Hill, Ont.; Mark Becker, CEO, Calgary, Alta.; Tabatha Bull, Ont.; Mary Garden, Victoria, B.C.; The Rt. Hon. David L. Johnston, Ashton, Ont.; Dr. Simon Landy, Toronto, Ont.; Kevin D. Nabholz, Calgary, Alta.; Russell A. Newmark, Inuvik, N.W.T.; Antonia (Toni) Rossi, Toronto, Ont.

Other Exec. Officers - R. Drew Knight, CFO; Cindy G. McArthur, chief HR officer; Christos Gazeas, exec. v-p, legal, gen. counsel & corp. sec.; Lee-Anne Lyon-Bartley, exec. v-p, health, safety, envir. & quality; Roderick (JD) MacCuish, exec. v-p, strategy & corp. planning; Sanjay Gomes, pres., integrated facilities mgt.; Robert (Rob) Johnston, pres., NRB modular solutions; Jeff Litchfield, pres., workforce accommodations, forestry & energy srvcs.

Capital Stock

	Authorized (shs.)	Outstanding (shs.)[1]
Preferred	unlimited	nil
Common	unlimited	64,951,694

[1] At Aug. 4, 2023

Options - At Dec. 31, 2022, options were outstanding to purchase 1,632,000 common shares at prices ranging from $3.05 to $8.5 per share with weighted average remaining contractual life of 3.2 years.

Normal Course Issuer Bid - The company plans to make normal course purchases of up to 1,300,000 common shares representing 2% of the total outstanding. The bid commenced on May 15, 2023, and expires on May 14, 2024.

Major Shareholder - Fairfax Financial Holdings Limited held 49% interest and Polar Asset Management Partners Inc. held 13% interest at Mar. 21, 2023.

Price Range - DXT/TSX

Year	Volume	High	Low	Close
2022	10,620,874	$8.75	$5.02	$5.53
2021	11,717,535	$9.46	$5.72	$8.59
2020	15,032,760	$6.55	$1.28	$6.49
2019	13,262,531	$12.20	$4.50	$6.15
2018	19,608,104	$16.35	$7.40	$9.00

Consolidation: 1-for-5 cons. in July 2020

Recent Close: $5.85

Capital Stock Changes - During 2022, 90,545 common shares were issued on exercise of options.

Dividends

DXT com Ra $0.35 pa Q est. Oct. 15, 2021[1]

[1] Quarterly divd normally payable in Apr/20 has been omitted.

Long-Term Debt - At Dec. 31, 2022, outstanding long-term debt totaled $94,045,000 (none current and net of $777,000 unamortized financing costs) and consisted entirely of borrowings under a $200,000,000 credit facility due on Sept. 7, 2024, bearing interest at prime plus 0.5% to 1.75% or bankers' acceptance rate plus 1.5% to 2.75%.

Wholly Owned Subsidiaries

Dexterra Group USA Inc., Del.
Dexterra Services LLC, Del.
Horizon North Camp & Catering Inc., Alta.
- 0.1% int. in **Horizon North Camp & Catering Partnership**, Alta.

Horizon North Kapewin Inc., Canada.
NRB Inc., Grimsby, Ont.
Pioneer Site Service Ltd., Canada.
Powerful Group of Companies Inc.
VCI CONTROLS Inc., Toronto, Ont.

Subsidiaries

99.99% int. in **Dana Hospitality GP Inc.**, Canada.
- 0.01% int. in **Dana Hospitality LP**, Oakville, Ont.

99.99% int. in **FCPI Dana Investment Inc.**, Ont.
- 99.99% int. in **Dana Hospitality LP**, Oakville, Ont.
  - 100% int. in **Marek Hospitality Inc.**, Canada.

99.9% int. in **Horizon North Camp & Catering Partnership**, Alta.

Investments

49% int. in **Acden Horizon North Limited Partnership**, Canada.
49% int. in **Acho Horizon North Camp Services Limited Partnership**, Canada.
49% int. in **Big Spring Lodging Limited Partnership**
49% int. in **Deninu Kue Horizon North Camp & Catering Limited Partnership**, Canada.
40% int. in **Eclipse Camp Solutions Incorporated**, Canada.
49% int. in **Gitxaala Horizon North Services L.P.**
49% int. in **Halfway River Horizon North Camp Services Limited Partnership**, Canada.
49% int. in **Kitikmeot Camp Solutions Limited**, Canada.
49% int. in **Secwepemc Camp & Catering Limited Partnership**, Canada.
49% int. in **Sekui Limited Partnership**, Canada.
49% int. in **Skin Tyee Horizon North Camp Services Limited Partnership**, Canada.
49% int. in **Tahitan Horizon North Services Inc.**, Canada.
49% int. in **Tangmaarvik Inland Camp Services Inc.**
49% int. in **Two Lakes Horizon North Camp Services Limted Partnership**, Canada.

Note: The preceding list includes only the major related companies in which interests are held.

Financial Statistics

Periods ended:	12m Dec. 31/22[A]		12m Dec. 31/21[◻A]
	$000s	%Chg	$000s
Operating revenue	**971,517**	**+32**	**733,380**
Cost of sales	528,716		383,977
Salaries & benefits	375,334		259,938
General & admin expense	18,019		13,775
Stock-based compensation	1,112		2,099
Operating expense	**923,181**	**+40**	**659,789**
Operating income	**48,336**	**-34**	**73,591**
Deprec., depl. & amort.	38,605		38,061
Finance costs, gross	8,953		5,101
Investment income	2,025		2,482
Pre-tax income	**3,220**	**-90**	**33,336**
Income taxes	(495)		8,708
Net income	**3,715**	**-85**	**24,628**
Net inc. for equity hldrs	**3,433**	**-86**	**24,355**
Net inc. for non-cont. int.	**282**	**+3**	**273**
Inventories	26,045		16,998
Accounts receivable	211,397		184,776
Current assets	242,766		208,935
Long-term investments	15,000		17,100
Fixed assets, net	156,608		161,981
Right-of-use assets	23,363		22,057
Intangibles, net	163,982		120,417
Total assets	**611,401**	**+15**	**533,629**
Accts. pay. & accr. liabs	170,629		121,868
Current liabilities	197,977		136,437
Long-term debt, gross	94,045		65,320
Long-term debt, net	94,045		65,320
Long-term lease liabilities	20,311		17,722
Shareholders' equity	286,790		304,348
Non-controlling interest	193		(31)
Cash from oper. activs	**63,991**	**-1**	**64,486**
Cash from fin. activs	(14,154)		(56,495)
Cash from invest. activs	(49,837)		(7,991)
Capital expenditures	(6,940)		(5,860)
Capital disposals	709		749
	$		$
Earnings per share*	0.05		0.37
Cash flow per share*	0.98		0.99
Cash divd. per share*	0.35		0.33
	shs		shs
No. of shs. o/s*	65,241,628		65,151,083
Avg. no. of shs. o/s*	65,205,182		65,074,508
	%		%
Net profit margin	0.38		3.36
Return on equity	1.16		n.m.
Return on assets	2.46		n.a.
No. of employees (FTEs)	8,949		6,248

* Common
◻ Restated
[A] Reported in accordance with IFRS

Latest Results

Periods ended:	6m June 30/23[A]		6m June 30/22[A]
	$000s	%Chg	$000s
Operating revenue	535,917	+17	457,856
Net income	13,177	+835	1,410
Net inc. for equity hldrs	13,058	+983	1,206
Net inc. for non-cont. int.	119		204
	$		$
Earnings per share*	0.20		0.02

* Common
[A] Reported in accordance with IFRS

Historical Summary
(as originally stated)

Fiscal Year	Oper. Rev.	Net Inc. Bef. Disc.	EPS*
	$000s	$000s	$
2022[A]	971,517	3,715	0.05
2021[A]	733,380	24,628	0.37
2020[A1]	471,246	64,479	1.25
2019[A2]	458,096	(84,786)	(2.55)
2018[A]	394,245	(8,196)	(0.25)

* Common
[A] Reported in accordance with IFRS
[1] Results reflect the May 29, 2020, reverse takeover acquisition of 10647802 Canada Limited.
[2] Results for 2019 and prior years pertain to Horizon North Logistics Inc.

Note: Adjusted throughout for 1-for-5 cons. in July 2020

D.42 DiagnaMed Holdings Corp.

Symbol - DMED **Exchange** - CSE **CUSIP** - 25245D
Head Office - 2900-550 Burrard St, Vancouver, BC, V6C 0A3
Website - www.diagnamed.com
Email - info@diagnamed.com
Investor Relations - Jing Peng (416) 800-2684
Auditors - Clearhouse LLP C.A., Mississauga, Ont.
Transfer Agents - Marrelli Trust Company Limited, Vancouver, B.C.

Profile - (B.C. 2021) Developing a platform of software-based prescription digital therapeutic devices for detecting brain age and tremors for neurological disorders.

The company is developing two products:

BrainYear™ is an at-home electroencephalogram (EEG) machine learning solution to detect an individual's brain age. The difference between one's chronological age and one's "brain age" is called the "brain-age gap". Potential applications for BrainYear™ include being used as screening tool for identifying brain-age gaps that suggests Parkinson's disease or Alzheimer's disease that can be followed up with specific neurological diagnostic tests; or as a tool for researchers who wish to test potential interventions for slowing or reversing neurological aging and age-related neurological diseases.

BrainTremor™ is a wearable device to detect tremors and brain activity for neurological disorders by EEG. A proof of concept study of BrainTremor was expected to commence in the fourth quarter of 2022 and be completed in the second quarter of 2023.

Common listed on CSE, Nov. 8, 2022.

Predecessor Detail - Name changed from Wolf Acquisitions 2.0 Corp., Dec. 21, 2021.

Directors - Fabio A. Chianelli, pres. & CEO, Toronto, Ont.; Ming Jang, Vancouver, B.C.; Elyssia Patterson, Vancouver, B.C.; Carlo Sansalone, Vaughan, Ont.

Other Exec. Officers - Jing Peng, CFO & corp. sec.; Dr. Bassma Ghali, v-p, product

Capital Stock

	Authorized (shs.)	Outstanding (shs.)[1]
Common	unlimited	76,222,085

[1] At Nov. 8, 2022

Major Shareholder - Widely held at Nov. 8, 2022.

Price Range - DMED/CSE

Year	Volume	High	Low	Close
2022	5,708,920	$0.10	$0.02	$0.04

Recent Close: $0.04

Wholly Owned Subsidiaries

DiagnaMed Inc., Toronto, Ont.

Financial Statistics

Periods ended:	51w Sept. 30/21[A1]
	$000s
Research & devel. expense	202
General & admin expense	482
Operating expense	**684**
Operating income	**(684)**
Pre-tax income	**(1,948)**
Net income	**(1,948)**
Cash & equivalent	2,358
Accounts receivable	32
Current assets	2,390
Total assets	**2,390**
Accts. pay. & accr. liabs	150
Current liabilities	150
Shareholders' equity	2,240
Cash from oper. activs	**(566)**
Cash from fin. activs	2,889
Cash from invest. activs	34
Net cash position	**2,358**
	$
Earnings per share*	(0.03)
Cash flow per share*	(0.01)
	shs
No. of shs. o/s*	75,600,085
Avg. no. of shs. o/s*	55,768,041
	%
Net profit margin	n.a.
Return on equity	n.m.
Return on assets	n.a.

* Common

[A] Reported in accordance with IFRS

[1] Results reflect the Aug. 11, 2021, reverse takeover acquisition of DiagnaMed Inc.

Latest Results

Periods ended:	9m June 30/22[A]
	$000s
Net income	(828)
	$
Earnings per share*	(0.01)

* Common

[A] Reported in accordance with IFRS

D.43 Diagnos Inc.

Symbol - ADK **Exchange** - TSX-VEN **CUSIP** - 252442

Head Office - 265-7005 boul Taschereau, Brossard, QC, J4Z 1A7 **Telephone** - (450) 678-8882 **Toll-free** - (877) 678-8882 **Fax** - (450) 678-8119

Website - www.diagnos.ca

Email - mmassue@diagnos.ca

Investor Relations - Marc-André Massue (877) 678-8882

Auditors - Raymond Chabot Grant Thornton LLP C.A., Montréal, Qué.

Lawyers - Borden Ladner Gervais LLP, Montréal, Qué.

Transfer Agents - Computershare Trust Company of Canada Inc., Montréal, Qué.

Profile - (Can. 1996) Provides an Artificial Intelligence (AI) software which enhances digital images to assist health specialists in the early detection of critical health issues, including diabetic retinopathy and stroke.

The company has developed FLAIRE, an AI platform used to assist health specialists in interpreting medical images for the early detection of critical health problems. Computer Assisted Retinal Analysis (CARA), a proprietary web-based application based on FLAIRE, provides sharper, clearer and easier-to-analyze retinal images to help detect diabetic retinopathy. CARA integrates fundus cameras with an image processing engine, allowing eye care specialists to more clearly visualize both normal retinal landmarks (optic nerve, vascular system, macula and fovea), as well as pathological changes (exudates, haemorrhages, micro-aneurisms and neo-vascularisation). CARA is approved for sale in Canada, in the U.S., Mexico, the U.A.E., Saudi Arabia, Costa Rica and countries of the European Union.

The company is also developing CARA-ST (CARA Stroke), which is the use of CARA software tool in the detection of stroke through the inspection and analysis of the retina. CARA-ST is under clinical trial in the U.S.

Predecessor Detail - Name changed from Goths Resources Inc., Sept. 26, 2000.

Directors - André M. Larente, pres. & CEO, Saint-Jean-sur-Richelieu, Qué.; Dr. Francis Bellido, Qué.; Vincent Duhamel, Westmount, Qué.; Robert Dunn, Montréal, Qué.

Other Exec. Officers - Yves-Stéphane Couture, v-p, sales; Riadh Kobbi, v-p, bus. intelligence; Marc-André Massue, v-p, fin., CFO & corp. sec.; Guillermo Moreno Robles, v-p, sales

Capital Stock

	Authorized (shs.)	Outstanding (shs.)[1]
Common	unlimited	70,610,514

[1] At Mar. 31, 2023

Major Shareholder - Tristram R. (Tris) Coffin held 11.58% interest at July 13, 2022.

Price Range - ADK/TSX-VEN

Year	Volume	High	Low	Close
2022	19,725,187	$0.40	$0.13	$0.28
2021	26,980,909	$0.77	$0.33	$0.34
2020	33,220,365	$0.70	$0.14	$0.59
2019	16,358,507	$0.50	$0.10	$0.22
2018	9,640,749	$1.55	$0.30	$0.35

Consolidation: 1-for-10 cons. in Apr. 2019

Recent Close: $0.52

Capital Stock Changes - During fiscal 2023, 1,136,363 common shares were issued on conversion of debentures.

During fiscal 2022, common shares were issued as follows: 1,320,169 on exercise of warrants and 850,000 on exercise of options.

Subsidiaries

99.74% int. in **Diagnos Healthcare (India) Pvt. Ltd.**, Mumbai, India. Inactive.

99.8% int. in **Diagnos Internacional S.A. de C.V.**, Mexico. Inactive.

Financial Statistics

Periods ended:	12m Mar. 31/23[A]		12m Mar. 31/22[A]
	$000s	%Chg	$000s
Operating revenue	**486**	**+11**	**439**
Cost of sales	793		857
General & admin expense	1,828		2,129
Operating expense	**2,620**	**-12**	**2,986**
Operating income	**(2,134)**	**n.a.**	**(2,547)**
Deprec., depl. & amort	101		106
Finance costs, gross	271		48
Write-downs/write-offs	nil		3
Pre-tax income	**(2,481)**	**n.a.**	**(2,608)**
Net income	**(2,481)**	**n.a.**	**(2,608)**
Cash & equivalent	297		921
Accounts receivable	263		346
Current assets	575		1,289
Fixed assets, net	248		253
Total assets	**823**	**-47**	**1,542**
Bank indebtedness	169		125
Accts. pay. & accr. liabs	460		463
Current liabilities	719		659
Long-term debt, gross	1,900		832
Long-term debt, net	1,900		832
Long-term lease liabilities	153		164
Shareholders' equity	(1,948)		(114)
Cash from oper. activs	**(1,884)**	**n.a.**	**(2,038)**
Cash from fin. activs	1,285		1,596
Cash from invest. activs	475		504
Net cash position	**297**	**-29**	**421**
Capital expenditures	(24)		(31)
	$		$
Earnings per share*	(0.04)		(0.04)
Cash flow per share*	(0.03)		(0.03)
	shs		shs
No. of shs. o/s*	70,610,514		69,474,151
Avg. no. of shs. o/s*	69,617,364		68,734,973
	%		%
Net profit margin	(510.49)		(594.08)
Return on equity	n.m.		n.m.
Return on assets	(186.89)		(146.62)
Foreign sales percent	6		7

* Common

[A] Reported in accordance with IFRS

Historical Summary (as originally stated)

Fiscal Year	Oper. Rev. $000s	Net Inc. Bef. Disc. $000s	EPS* $
2023[A]	486	(2,481)	(0.04)
2022[A]	439	(2,608)	(0.04)
2021[A]	267	(2,051)	(0.03)
2020[A]	332	(3,383)	(0.08)
2019[A]	326	(3,839)	(0.20)

* Common

[A] Reported in accordance with IFRS

Note: Adjusted throughout for 1-for-10 cons. in Apr. 2019

D.44 Dialogue Health Technologies Inc.

Symbol - CARE **Exchange** - TSX **CUSIP** - 25249F

Head Office - 200-390 rue Notre-Dame O, Montréal, QC, H2Y 1T9 **Telephone** - (438) 940-2635

Website - www.dialogue.co

Email - investors@dialogue.co

Investor Relations - Jean Marc Ayas (438) 940-2635

Auditors - Deloitte LLP C.A., Montréal, Qué.

Transfer Agents - Computershare Trust Company of Canada Inc., Montréal, Qué.

Profile - (Can. 2016) Offers virtual primary care, mental health, employee assistance programs (EAP) in Canada and an Internet-based cognitive behavioural therapy (iCBT) program in Australia, all through an Integrated Health Platform™.

The Integrated Health Platform™ is a one-stop healthcare hub that centralizes all the company's programs in a single, user-friendly application, providing access to services 24 hours per day, 365 days per year from the convenience of a smartphone, computer or tablet. The platform leverages a multidisciplinary team of over 600 providers across 12 clinical specialties and other non-clinical specialties in Canada.

Customers include employers, insurers and organizations who offer access to the platform to their members. Has more than 48,000 customers in Canada. Revenue is generated from customers through a per-member-per-month subscription model under one to three-year contracts. At Dec. 31, 2022, 5,000,000 Canadian members and their dependents had access to the virtual platform.

On Dec. 31, 2022, the company sold wholly owned **ARGUMED Consulting Group GmbH**, which provides occupational health and safety service program in Germany, for €1,875,000.

Recent Merger and Acquisition Activity

Status: pending **Announced:** July 26, 2023

Sun Life Financial Inc. agreed to acquire all issued common shares of Dialogue Health Technologies Inc., other than certain common shares currently owned by Sun Life's affiliates and members of Dialogue executive management, for $5.15 per share in cash for a total equity value of $365,000,000. Dialogue's executive management would maintain a minority interest in Dialogue following closing. Dialogue would operate as a standalone entity of Sun Life Canada. The directors and certain members of Dialogue executive management, owning 8.7% of the common shares, and Portag3 Ventures LP, Portag3 Ventures II Investments LP and WSC IV LP, collectively holding 21%, have entered into customary support and voting agreements to vote in favour of the transaction. Certain members of Dialogue executive management have also agreed to roll a portion of their equity in Dialogue and would remain as Dialogue shareholders, owning a 3% interest with Sun Life owning the remaining 97%. The transaction was expected to close in the fourth quarter of 2023.

Status: completed **Revised:** Apr. 30, 2022

UPDATE: The transaction was completed. PREVIOUS: Dialogue Health Technologies Inc. agreed to acquire London, U.K.-based Tictrac Ltd. for $56,000,000 (£35,000,000) total consideration consisting of $24,000,000 (£15,000,000) cash and up to $32,000,000 (£20,000,000) earnout payment upon achievement of certain revenue milestones. The earnout consideration, at its maximum, would be paid 54% in cash and 46% in Dialogue common shares. Tictrac provides global health and wellness platform which supports employers and insurance partners to engage with their communities to improve overall health and wellness.

Predecessor Detail - Name changed from Dialogue Technologies Inc., Nov. 23, 2020.

Directors - Cherif Habib, co-founder & CEO, Montréal, Qué.; Paul Desmarais III, chr., Montréal, Qué.; Norma Beauchamp, Toronto, Ont.; Timothy E. (Tim) Hodgson, Toronto, Ont.; Melissa J. Kennedy, Toronto, Ont.; Paul Lepage, Bromont, Qué.; Jean-François Marcoux, Montréal, Qué.

Other Exec. Officers - Jean-Nicolas Guillemetter, COO; Navaid Mansuri, CFO; Darryl Campbell, chief info. security officer; Alexis Smirnov, chief tech. officer; Jennifer Buckley, sr. v-p, comml.; Benjamin (Benny) Axt, v-p, strategy; Gabriella Baciu, v-p, cust. success; Sylvain Beauséjour, v-p, talent & culture; Martin Blinder, v-p & gen. mgr., U.K.; Valentina De Castris, v-p, strategic projects; Jennifer Foubert, v-p, strategic partnerships & comml. opers.; Lilian Lau, v-p, mktg.; John McCalla, v-p, software eng.; Cameron Moore, v-p, product & design; Stephanie Panetta, v-p, fin.; Randy Wetmore, v-p, sales

Capital Stock

	Authorized (shs.)	Outstanding (shs.)[1]
Common	unlimited	65,895,332

[1] At Mar. 31, 2023

Major Shareholder - Sun Life Financial Inc. held 22.86% interest and White Star Capital, L.P. held 12.97% interest at Apr. 13, 2023.

Price Range - CARE/TSX

Year	Volume	High	Low	Close
2022	13,262,598	$7.39	$2.05	$2.32
2021	16,239,199	$20.35	$5.72	$7.29

Recent Close: $5.11

Capital Stock Changes - During 2022, 713,591 common shares were issued as share-based compensation.

Wholly Owned Subsidiaries

Dialogue Health Technologies Australia Pty Ltd., Australia.
- 100% int. in **e-Hub Health Pty Ltd.**, Australia.

Optima Global Health Inc., Montréal, Qué.

Tictrac Ltd., United Kingdom.

Financial Statistics

Periods ended:	12m Dec. 31/22^A		12m Dec. 31/21^oA
	$000s	%Chg	$000s
Operating revenue	**87,132**	**+35**	**64,534**
Cost of sales	43,788		38,067
Research & devel. expense	10,524		9,287
General & admin expense	51,768		35,716
Stock-based compensation	3,470		2,061
Operating expense	**109,550**	**+29**	**85,131**
Operating income	**(22,418)**	**n.a.**	**(20,597)**
Deprec., depl. & amort.	2,745		2,621
Finance income	1,233		753
Finance costs, gross	239		391
Pre-tax income	**(24,976)**	**n.a.**	**(248,272)**
Income taxes	(467)		(322)
Net inc. bef. disc. opers	**(24,509)**	**n.a.**	**(247,949)**
Income from disc. opers	(1,444)		(3,402)
Net income	**(25,953)**	**n.a.**	**(251,351)**
Cash & equivalent	62,697		104,296
Accounts receivable	16,264		12,727
Current assets	82,330		119,767
Fixed assets, net	936		1,137
Right-of-use assets	784		1,568
Intangibles, net	30,823		12,781
Total assets	**119,388**	**-12**	**135,253**
Accts. pay. & accr. liabs.	6,728		3,820
Current liabilities	19,865		11,260
Long-term debt, gross	1,107		1,474
Long-term debt, net	707		1,074
Long-term lease liabilities	343		911
Shareholders' equity	97,351		119,941
Cash from oper. activs	**(15,569)**	**n.a.**	**(23,279)**
Cash from fin. activs	(1,155)		89,712
Cash from invest. activs	(24,660)		(4,956)
Net cash position	**62,697**	**-40**	**104,296**
Capital expenditures	(454)		(651)
	$		$
Earns. per sh. bef disc opers*	(0.37)		(4.42)
Earnings per share*	(0.39)		(4.48)
Cash flow per share*	(0.24)		(0.41)
	shs		shs
No. of shs. o/s*	66,543,148		65,829,557
Avg. no. of shs. o/s*	66,136,237		56,109,012
	%		%
Net profit margin	(28.13)		(384.21)
Return on equity	(22.56)		n.m.
Return on assets	(19.07)		(245.56)

* Common
^o Restated
^A Reported in accordance with IFRS

Latest Results

Periods ended:	3m Mar. 31/23^A		3m Mar. 31/22^oA
	$000s	%Chg	$000s
Operating revenue	24,532	+26	19,537
Net inc. bef. disc. opers	(2,655)	n.a.	(6,679)
Income from disc. opers	nil		(389)
Net income	(2,655)	n.a.	(7,068)
	$		$
Earns. per sh. bef. disc. opers.*	(0.04)		(0.10)
Earnings per share*	(0.04)		(0.11)

* Common
^o Restated
^A Reported in accordance with IFRS

Historical Summary
(as originally stated)

Fiscal Year	Oper. Rev.	Net Inc. Bef. Disc.	EPS*
	$000s	$000s	$
2022^A	87,132	(24,509)	(0.37)
2021^A	68,049	(251,351)	(4.48)
2020^A	35,802	(20,231)	(1.81)
2019^A	10,089	(12,043)	(1.13)

* Common
^A Reported in accordance with IFRS

D.45 DiaMedica Therapeutics Inc.

Symbol - DMAC **Exchange** - NASDAQ **CUSIP** - 25253X
Head Office - c/o DiaMedica USA Inc., 301 Carlson Pky, Suite 210, Minneapolis, MN, United States, 55305 **Telephone** - (763) 496-5454 **Fax** - (763) 710-4456
Website - www.diamedica.com
Email - skellen@diamedica.com
Investor Relations - Scott Kellen (763) 496-5118
Auditors - Baker Tilly US, LLP C.P.A., Minneapolis, Minn.
Lawyers - Fillmore Riley LLP, Winnipeg, Man.
Transfer Agents - Computershare Trust Company of Canada Inc., Toronto, Ont.

Profile - (B.C. 2019; orig. Man., 2000) Develops therapeutic treatments from novel recombinant proteins, focusing on the treatment of acute ischemic stroke and chronic kidney disease.

The company's lead product under development is DM199, a recombinant form of human KLK1 protein, targeted to activate Bradykinin (BK), a peptide that causes blood vessels to enlarge and causes many beneficial effects such as anti-inflammation, cell repair and decrease in brain cell death. This mechanism is targeted to treat chronic kidney disease (Phase II), which would result in improvement of blood flow in the kidney, promote regeneration of new blood vessels, support structural integrity of the kidney by reducing scar tissue formation, oxidative stress and inflammation, and activates mechanisms that upregulates T regulatory cells, improve insulin sensitization, glucose uptake, glycogen synthesis and lower blood pressure; and acute ischemic stroke (Phase II/III), which would result in an improvement of cerebral blood flow and activity balance, regeneration of new blood vessels and neurons, and decrease the death of brain cells. Other indication include vascular dementia, hypertension and type II diabetes. Also identified a potential novel new treatment for inflammatory diseases, DM300, which is currently in the pre-clinical stage of development.

Predecessor Detail - Name changed from DiaMedica Inc., Dec. 29, 2016.

Directors - Richard D. Pilnik, chr., Indianapolis, Ind.; Rick Pauls, pres. & CEO, Minneapolis, Minn.; Dr. Michael Giuffre, Calgary, Alta.; Tanya N. Lewis; James T. Parsons, Mississauga, Ont.; Dr. Charles Semba, San Francisco, Calif.

Other Exec. Officers - Scott Kellen, CFO & corp. sec.; Dominic Cundari, chief comml. officer; Kirsten Gruis, CMO; Ed Rady, chief comml. advisor; Dr. Harry Alcorn Jr., sr. v-p, clinical opers.; Paul Papi, v-p, bus. devel.

Capital Stock

	Authorized (shs.)	Outstanding (shs.)[1]
Common	unlimited	26,443,067

[1] At May 3, 2022

Major Shareholder - Widely held at Mar. 22, 2022.

Price Range - DMAC/NASDAQ

Year	Volume	High	Low	Close
2022	3,755,903	US$3.91	US$1.13	US$1.58
2021	10,642,311	US$10.88	US$3.01	US$3.73
2020	6,051,127	US$10.40	US$1.96	US$10.14
2019	3,673,247	US$5.90	US$1.71	US$4.85

DMA/TSX-VEN (D)

Year	Volume	High	Low	Close
2019	86,045	$5.05	$3.89	$4.63
2018	2,606,990	$18.00	$3.33	$4.10

Wholly Owned Subsidiaries

DiaMedica Australia Pty Ltd., Australia.
DiaMedica USA Inc., Minneapolis, Minn.

Financial Statistics

Periods ended:	12m Dec. 31/21^A		12m Dec. 31/20^A
	US$000s	%Chg	US$000s
Research & devel. expense	8,278		7,755
General & admin expense	3,786		3,080
Stock-based compensation	1,558		1,843
Operating expense	**13,622**	**+7**	**12,678**
Operating income	**(13,622)**	**n.a.**	**(12,678)**
Deprec., depl. & amort.	24		21
Pre-tax income	**(13,564)**	**n.a.**	**(12,265)**
Income taxes	28		27
Net income	**(13,592)**	**n.a.**	**(12,292)**
Cash & equivalent	45,112		27,507
Accounts receivable	130		340
Current assets	45,439		27,921
Fixed assets, net	70		74
Right-of-use assets	42		100
Total assets	**45,551**	**+62**	**28,095**
Accts. pay. & accr. liabs.	1,475		1,963
Current liabilities	1,524		2,028
Long-term lease liabilities	3		53
Shareholders' equity	44,024		26,014
Cash from oper. activs	**(12,252)**	**n.a.**	**(9,185)**
Cash from fin. activs	30,087		28,845
Cash from invest. activs	(20,537)		(16,134)
Net cash position	**4,707**	**-36**	**7,409**
Capital expenditures, net	(20)		(31)
	US$		US$
Earnings per share*	(0.65)		(0.78)
Cash flow per share*	(0.59)		(0.59)
	shs		shs
No. of shs. o/s*	26,443,067		18,746,157
Avg. no. of shs. o/s*	20,773,399		15,680,320
	%		%
Net profit margin	n.a.		n.a.
Return on equity	(38.81)		(73.10)
Return on assets	(36.91)		(66.18)
No. of employees (FTEs)	15		11

* Common
^A Reported in accordance with U.S. GAAP

Latest Results

Periods ended:	3m Mar. 31/22^A		3m Mar. 31/21^A
	US$000s	%Chg	US$000s
Net income	(3,508)	n.a.	(3,622)
	US$		US$
Earnings per share*	(0.13)		(0.19)

* Common
^A Reported in accordance with U.S. GAAP

Historical Summary
(as originally stated)

Fiscal Year	Oper. Rev.	Net Inc. Bef. Disc.	EPS*
	US$000s	US$000s	US$
2021^A	nil	(13,592)	(0.65)
2020^A	nil	(12,292)	(0.78)
2019^A	nil	(10,649)	(0.89)
2018^A	500	(5,734)	(0.74)
2017^B	nil	(4,175)	(0.80)

* Common
^A Reported in accordance with U.S. GAAP
^B Reported in accordance with IFRS
Note: Adjusted throughout for 1-for-20 cons. in Nov. 2018

D.46 Diamond Estates Wines & Spirits Inc.

Symbol - DWS **Exchange** - TSX-VEN **CUSIP** - 252593
Head Office - 1067 Niagara Stone Rd, Niagara-on-the-Lake, ON, L0S 1J0 **Telephone** - (905) 641-1042 **Fax** - (905) 641-9879
Website - www.lakeviewwineco.com
Email - rconte@diamondwines.com
Investor Relations - Ryan Conte
Auditors - MNP LLP C.A., Burlington, Ont.
Bankers - Bank of Montreal
Transfer Agents - TSX Trust Company, Toronto, Ont.

Profile - (Ont. 2011) Produces, markets and distributes Canadian and international wines and ciders, as well as spirits and beer, to liquor boards and licensed establishments throughout Canada.

Operates five production facilities wineries, four in Ontario and one in British Columbia. The company's family of brands include 20 Bees, Creekside, EastDell, Lakeview Cellars, Mindful, Queenston Mile, Shiny Apple Cider, Fresh, Proud Pour, Red Tractor, Seasons, Serenity, Persona and Backyard Vineyards.

Through wholly owned **Trajectory Beverage Partners**, the company is the sales agent for international brands in all regions of Canada as well as a distributor in the western provinces. These brands include Josh wines from California; FatBastard, Meffre, Pierre Chavin and Andre Lurton wines from France; Brimincourt Champagne from France; Merlet and Larsen Cognacs from France; Kaiken wines from Argentina; Blue Nun and Erben wines from Germany; Calabria Family Estate Wines and McWilliams Wines from Australia; Saint Clair Family Estate Wines and Yealands Family Wines from New Zealand; Redemption Bourbon and Rye whiskies from the U.S.; Gray Whale Gin from California; Storywood and Cofradia Tequilas from Mexico; Magnum Cream Liqueur from Scotland; Talamonti and Cielo wines from Italy; Catedral and Cabeca de Toiro wines from Portugal; Waterloo Beer & Radlers from Canada; Landshark Lager from the U.S.; Edinburgh Gin, Tamdhu, Glengoyne and Smokehead single-malt Scotch whiskies from Scotland; Islay Mist, Grand MacNish and Waterproof whiskies from Scotland; C. Mondavi & Family wines including C.K Mondavi & Charles Krug from Napa; Wize Spirits, Hounds Vodka and Valley of Mother of God Gins from Canada; Bols Vodka from Amsterdam; Koyle Family Wines from Chile; and Pearse Lyons whiskies and gins from Ireland.

On Apr. 1, 2022, wholly owned **Equity Wine Group Inc.**, **Creekside Estate Winery Inc.**, **26101636 Ontario Inc.** and **1314102 Ontario Ltd.** were amalgamated into wholly owned **Diamond Estates Wines & Spirits Ltd.**.

Predecessor Detail - Name changed from WhiteKnight Acquisitions II Inc., Sept. 20, 2013, pursuant to Qualifying Transaction reverse takeover acquisition of Diamond Estates Wines & Spirits Ltd.

Directors - David Beutel, chr., Toronto, Ont.; Andrew Howard, pres. & CEO, Thornbury, Ont.; Guy Blanchette, Saint-Bruno, Qué.; John De Sousa, Oakville, Ont.; Claude Gilbert, Brossard, Qué.; Keith R. Harris, Collingwood, Ont.; John W. W. Hick, Toronto, Ont.; Ronald (Ron) McEachern, Toronto, Ont.

Other Exec. Officers - Ryan Conte, CFO; Tim McChesney, sr. v-p, mktg. & strategy; Thomas (Tom) Green, v-p, winemaking & winery opers. & corp. sec.

Capital Stock

	Authorized (shs.)	Outstanding (shs.)[1]
Common	unlimited	27,875,978

[1] At Mar. 31, 2023

Major Shareholder - Lassonde Industries Inc. held 19.2% interest at Dec. 31, 2022.

Price Range - DWS/TSX-VEN

Year	Volume	High	Low	Close
2022	2,854,514	$1.50	$0.45	$0.56
2021	3,873,209	$2.15	$1.31	$1.40
2020	3,577,918	$2.40	$0.80	$1.30
2019	3,405,680	$2.50	$1.40	$2.20
2018	3,554,864	$3.80	$2.10	$2.30

Consolidation: 1-for-10 cons. in Nov. 2021
Recent Close: $0.39

Capital Stock Changes - There were no changes to capital stock during 2023.

In October 2021, 1,049,534 post-consolidated common shares were issued to extinguish $1,889,162 of 10% debentures, 3,055,556 post-consolidated common shares were issued on acquisition of Equity Wine Group Inc., and private placement of 3,770,398 (1 post-consolidated common share & ½ warrant) at $1.80 per unit was completed. On Nov. 15, 2021, common shares were consolidated on a 1-for-10 basis.

Wholly Owned Subsidiaries

Backyard Vineyards Corp., Langley, B.C.
Diamond Estates Wines & Spirits Ltd., Toronto, Ont.
• 100% int. in **De Sousa Wines Toronto Inc.**, Ont.
10028088 Ontario Inc., Canada.
Trajectory Beverage Partners, Ont.

Financial Statistics

Periods ended:	12m Mar. 31/23[A]		12m Mar. 31/22[A]
	$000s	%Chg	$000s
Operating revenue	**31,723**	**+6**	**29,986**
Cost of sales	21,112		18,938
Salaries & benefits	6,871		6,310
General & admin expense	8,204		6,465
Stock-based compensation	502		546
Operating expense	**36,690**	**+14**	**32,260**
Operating income	**(4,967)**	**n.a.**	**(2,274)**
Deprec., depl. & amort.	1,557		1,653
Finance costs, gross	2,379		1,468
Pre-tax income	**(8,526)**	**n.a.**	**(2,473)**
Net income	**(8,526)**	**n.a.**	**(2,473)**
Inventories	26,289		28,914
Accounts receivable	3,159		4,105
Current assets	29,790		34,503
Fixed assets, net	25,141		25,893
Right-of-use assets	2,555		2,878
Intangibles, net	4,483		4,891
Total assets	**61,969**	**-9**	**68,165**
Accts. pay. & accr. liabs.	6,709		8,800
Current liabilities	37,773		35,199
Long-term debt, gross	30,017		25,950
Long-term lease liabilities	1,906		2,308
Shareholders' equity	22,290		30,313
Cash from oper. activs.	**(4,248)**	**n.a.**	**(2,327)**
Cash from fin. activs.	4,543		5,435
Cash from invest. activs.	(295)		(3,108)
Capital expenditures	(295)		(393)
	$		$
Earnings per share*	(0.31)		(0.11)
Cash flow per share*	(0.15)		(0.11)
	shs		shs
No. of shs. o/s*	27,875,978		27,875,978
Avg. no. of shs. o/s*	27,875,978		21,979,998
	%		%
Net profit margin	(26.88)		(8.25)
Return on equity	(32.42)		(10.20)
Return on assets	(9.45)		(1.70)
Foreign sales percent	4		8

* Common
[A] Reported in accordance with IFRS

Historical Summary
(as originally stated)

Fiscal Year	Oper. Rev.	Net Inc. Bef. Disc.	EPS*
	$000s	$000s	$
2023[A]	31,723	(8,526)	(0.31)
2022[A]	29,986	(2,473)	(0.11)
2021[A]	25,553	(2,635)	(0.13)
2020[A]	26,794	(4,186)	(0.20)
2019[A]	28,123	(3,271)	(0.20)

* Common
[A] Reported in accordance with IFRS
Note: Adjusted throughout for 1-for-10 cons. in Nov. 2021

D.47 Digicann Ventures Inc.

Symbol - DCNN **Exchange** - CSE **CUSIP** - 25380E
Head Office - 810-789 Pender St W, Vancouver, BC, V6C 1H2 **Telephone** - (604) 687-2038 **Toll-free** - (800) 783-6056 **Fax** - (604) 685-6905
Website - digicann.io
Email - ir@digicann.io
Investor Relations - Nicholas Kuzyk (800) 783-6056
Auditors - Baker Tilly WM LLP C.A., Vancouver, B.C.
Transfer Agents - Endeavor Trust Corporation, Vancouver, B.C.
Profile - (B.C. 2004) Distributes medical cannabis as well as cannabidiol (CBD) and tetrahydrocannabinol (THC) test kits in Europe.

Wholly owned **Farmako GmbH** is a wholesale distributor of medical cannabis and offers test kits of THC CBD to pharmacies in Germany. The test kits facilitate the identity testing of different types of cannabis medicines and active pharmaceutical ingredients.

In June 2023, the company exited its joint venture **Propagation Services Canada Inc.** (dba Boundary Bay Cannabis), which owns and operates a 2,200,000-sq.-ft. greenhouse complex in Delta, B.C., of which 130,000 sq. ft. was utilized. The company settled it its debt receivable and sold its 70% equity interest in Propagation Services Canada to its joint venture partner for $250,000.

Predecessor Detail - Name changed from Agra Ventures Ltd., Aug. 2, 2023; basis 1 new for 25 old shs.

Directors - Nicholas (Nick) Kuzyk, interim CEO, Calgary, Alta.; Fiona Fitzmaurice, CFO, Ont.; Anthony Carnevale, Ont.; Jonathan Hirsh

Capital Stock

	Authorized (shs.)	Outstanding (shs.)[1]
Common	unlimited	6,531,785

[1] At Aug. 8, 2023

Major Shareholder - Widely held at May 20, 2022.

Price Range - DCNN/CSE

Year	Volume	High	Low	Close
2022	4,480,011	$19.50	$0.13	$0.25
2021	271,781	$356.25	$12.25	$14.50
2020	179,556	$450.00	$56.25	$112.50
2019	168,011	$3,225.00	$356.25	$356.25
2018	161,358	$1,567.50	$292.50	$862.50

Consolidation: 1-for-25 cons. in Aug. 2023; 1-for-150 cons. in Aug. 2021

Recent Close: $0.03

Capital Stock Changes - On Aug. 8, 2023, common shares were consolidated on a 1-for-25 basis.

Wholly Owned Subsidiaries

AgraFlora Europe GmbH, Germany.
• 100% int. in **Farmako GmbH**, Frankfurt am Main, Germany.
AgraFlora Holdings Corp., Canada.
Canutra Naturals Ltd., B.C.
1180782 B.C. Ltd., Toronto, Ont.
Sanna Health Corp., Toronto, Ont.
Trichome Cannabrands Inc., Ont.

Subsidiaries

80% int. in **11122347 Canada Corp.**, Canada.
80% int. in **11353675 Canada Corp.**, Canada.
80% int. in **11353705 Canada Corp.**, Canada.
80% int. in **11406426 Canada Corp.**, Canada.
80% int. in **Potluck Potions and Edibles Inc.**, Canada.

Investments

50% int. in **Eurasia Infused Cosmetics Inc.**, Canada.
Note: The preceding list includes only the major related companies in which interests are held.

Financial Statistics

Periods ended:	12m Dec. 31/21[A]		12m Dec. 31/20[oA]
	$000s	%Chg	$000s
Operating revenue	**928**	**-38**	**1,492**
Cost of goods sold	523		966
Salaries & benefits	579		1,292
Research & devel. expense	nil		395
General & admin expense	4,799		12,718
Stock-based compensation	nil		3,397
Operating expense	**5,901**	**-69**	**18,767**
Operating income	**(4,973)**	**n.a.**	**(17,275)**
Deprec., depl. & amort.	369		1,019
Finance income	650		102
Finance costs, gross	6,626		5,728
Investment income	(4,165)		(4,732)
Write-downs/write-offs	(569)		(73,070)[1]
Pre-tax income	**(2,414)**	**n.a.**	**(103,203)**
Net income	**(2,414)**	**n.a.**	**(103,203)**
Net inc. for equity hldrs	**(5,096)**	**n.a.**	**(102,856)**
Net inc. for non-cont. int.	**2,682**	**n.a.**	**(347)**
Cash & equivalent	4,343		274
Inventories	99		111
Accounts receivable	224		149
Current assets	5,663		562
Long-term investments	23,439		30,004
Fixed assets, net	1,258		16,700
Intangibles, net	906		1,167
Total assets	**46,217**	**-25**	**61,733**
Accts. pay. & accr. liabs.	1,667		8,489
Current liabilities	25,858		53,464
Long-term debt, gross	23,781		30,723
Long-term debt, net	nil		29,826
Long-term lease liabilities	1,302		3,052
Shareholders' equity	19,219		4,747
Non-controlling interest	(171)		(1,019)
Cash from oper. activs.	**(6,219)**	**n.a.**	**(4,690)**
Cash from fin. activs.	1,136		12,319
Cash from invest. activs.	7,843		(11,431)
Net cash position	**3,093**	**n.m.**	**274**
Capital expenditures	(8)		(5,617)
Capital disposals	nil		407
	$		$
Earnings per share*	(10.71)		(295.76)
Cash flow per share*	(13.07)		...
	shs		shs
No. of shs. o/s*	535,540		401,648
Avg. no. of shs. o/s*	475,768		348,919
	%		%
Net profit margin	(260.13)		n.m.
Return on equity	(42.53)		(287.64)
Return on assets	7.80		(115.12)

* Common
[o] Restated
[A] Reported in accordance with IFRS
[1] Includes $33,685,650 impairment of PP&E, intangible assets and goodwill, $29,210,673 write-off of convertible loan receivable from Transnational Cannabis Ltd. and $8,459,815 impairment of investments.

Latest Results

Periods ended:	6m June 30/22[A]		6m June 30/21[A]
	$000s	%Chg	$000s
Operating revenue	319	-46	592
Net income	(2,679)	n.a.	(1,365)
	$		$
Earnings per share*	(3.50)		(3.00)

* Common
[A] Reported in accordance with IFRS

Historical Summary
(as originally stated)

Fiscal Year	Oper. Rev.	Net Inc. Bef. Disc.	EPS*
	$000s	$000s	$
2021[A]	928	(2,414)	(10.71)
2020[A]	1,492	(103,203)	(294.75)
2019[A]	4	(101,691)	(581.63)
2018[A]	nil	(5,820)	(70.88)
2017[A]	nil	(2,120)	(35.47)

* Common
[A] Reported in accordance with IFRS
Note: Adjusted throughout for 1-for-25 cons. in Aug. 2023; 1-for-150 cons. in Aug. 2021; 5-for-1 split in Nov. 2018

D.48 Digihost Technology Inc.

Symbol - DGHI **Exchange** - TSX-VEN **CUSIP** - 25381D
Head Office - 2830 Produce Row, Houston, TX, United States, 77023
Website - www.digihost.ca
Email - michel@digihostblockchain.com
Investor Relations - Michel Amar (818) 280-9758

Auditors - Raymond Chabot Grant Thornton LLP C.A., Montréal, Qué.
Lawyers - Peterson McVicar LLP, Toronto, Ont.
Transfer Agents - Marrelli Transfer Services Corp., Toronto, Ont.
Employees - 20 at Mar. 31, 2023
Profile - (B.C. 2017) Engages in cryptocurrency mining and provides hosting services. Also operates a 60-MW power plant in North Tonawanda.

The company primarily mines Bitcoin and Ethereum at their facilities located in Buffalo and North Tonawanda in upper New York State as well as a facility in Columbiana, Alabama. Current hash rate (at Mar. 31, 2023) is 900 petahashes per hour.

Also provides rental of land and sale of energy to third parties. Operates a 60-MW natural gas fired power plant with infrastructure that includes both company-owned miners as well as third-party hosting.

On Feb. 8, 2023, the company acquired a 60-MW power plant in North Tonawanda, N.Y., for US$3,500,000 cash and issuance of 437,318 common shares with a deemed value of US$750,000.

During the second quarter of 2022, the company acquired 25 acres of land in North Carolina in order to access a 200-MW power infrastructure program. The company is currently in discussions with potential joint venture partners to utilize the property.

On July 28, 2022, shareholders approved a change of continuance into Ontario.

In June 2022, the company acquired a 160,000-sq.-ft. property in Alabama from **Grede II, LLC** for US$1,500,000 and US$1,250,000 paid in 25 equal monthly instalments. The property has a total power capacity of 55 MW.

Predecessor Detail - Name changed from HashChain Technology Inc., Feb. 20, 2020, pursuant to reverse takeover acquisition of Digihost International, Inc.; basis 1 new for 40 old shs.

Directors - Michel Amar, chr. & CEO, Los Angeles, Calif.; Alec Amar, pres., Los Angeles, Calif.; Zhichao Li, New York, N.Y.; Adam Rossman, Los Angeles, Calif.; Gerry Rotonda, New York, N.Y.

Other Exec. Officers - Paul Ciullo, CFO; Luke Marchiori, chief renewable energy officer; Daniel Rotunno, v-p, opers.

Capital Stock

	Authorized (shs.)	Outstanding (shs.)[1]
Subordinate Voting	unlimited	28,566,243
Proportionate Voting	unlimited	3,333

[1] At June 15, 2023

Subordinate Voting - One vote per share.
Proportionate Voting - Convertible into subordinate voting shares on a 200-for-1 basis. 200 votes per share.
Major Shareholder - Michel Amar held 20.18% interest at June 15, 2023.

Price Range - DGHI/TSX-VEN

Year	Volume	High	Low	Close
2022	7,152,947	$6.20	$0.42	$0.47
2021	39,007,766	$17.61	$1.65	$5.97
2020	4,561,474	$3.60	$0.27	$2.97
2019	607,333	$6.00	$0.60	$1.20
2018	3,681,140	$220.80	$2.40	$3.60

Consolidation: 1-for-3 cons. in Oct. 2021; 1-for-40 cons. in Feb. 2020
Recent Close: $1.30
Capital Stock Changes - In March 2022, private placement of 2,729,748 units (1 subordinate voting share & 1 warrant) at Cdn$4.40 per unit was completed. Also during 2022, subordinate voting shares were issued as follows: 300,000 on exercise of warrants, 19,391 for debt settlement and 2,100 for cash; 165,200 subordinate voting shares were repurchased under a Normal Course Issuer Bid.

Wholly Owned Subsidiaries

DGX Holdings, LLC
Digihost International, Inc., Buffalo, N.Y.
World Generation X, LLC

Financial Statistics

Periods ended:	12m Dec. 31/22[A]		12m Dec. 31/21[A]
	US$000s	%Chg	US$000s
Operating revenue	**24,190**	**-3**	**24,952**
Cost of sales	20,278		10,542
General & admin expense	5,055		2,841
Stock-based compensation	3,296		7,804
Operating expense	**28,630**	**+35**	**21,187**
Operating income	**(4,440)**	**n.a.**	**3,765**
Deprec., depl. & amort	10,709		3,281
Finance costs, gross	254		333
Pre-tax income	**2,792**	**+8**	**2,590**
Income taxes	(1,537)		2,301
Net income	**4,329**	**n.m.**	**289**
Cash & equivalent	4,651		34,408
Current assets	6,130		36,216
Fixed assets, net	41,811		38,142
Right-of-use assets	2,538		2,079
Intangibles, net	1,314		2,790
Total assets	**52,600**	**-34**	**80,027**
Accts. pay. & accr. liabs	2,345		2,273
Current liabilities	3,255		5,519
Long-term debt, gross	877		nil
Long-term debt, net	389		nil
Long-term lease liabilities	448		nil
Shareholders' equity	47,175		70,205
Cash from oper. activs	**(3,411)**	**n.a.**	**(8,860)**
Cash from fin. activs	18,859		44,469
Cash from invest. activs	(14,513)		(34,725)
Net cash position	**1,851**	**+102**	**916**
Capital expenditures	(14,685)		(33,925)
Capital disposals	795		nil
	US$		US$
Earnings per share*	0.16		0.01
Cash flow per share*	(0.13)		(0.41)
	shs		shs
No. of shs. o/s*	27,842,204		24,956,165
Avg. no. of shs. o/s*	27,227,284		21,781,806
	%		%
Net profit margin	17.90		1.16
Return on equity	7.38		n.m.
Return on assets	7.12		n.a.

* Subord. Vtg.
[A] Reported in accordance with IFRS

Latest Results

Periods ended:	3m Mar. 31/23[A]		3m Mar. 31/22[oA]
	US$000s	%Chg	US$000s
Operating revenue	4,104	-44	7,312
Net income	(9,093)	n.a.	12,015
	US$		US$
Earnings per share*	(0.32)		0.05

* Subord. Vtg.
[o] Restated
[A] Reported in accordance with IFRS

Historical Summary
(as originally stated)

Fiscal Year	Oper. Rev.	Net Inc. Bef. Disc.	EPS*
	US$000s	US$000s	US$
2022[A]	24,190	4,329	0.16
2021[A]	24,952	289	0.01
2020[A1]	3,553	(5,191)	(0.45)
	$000s	$000s	$
2019[A2]	11,503	(8,548)	(3.60)
2018[A]	3,370	(28,488)	(29.69)

* Subord. Vtg.
[A] Reported in accordance with IFRS
[1] Results reflect the Feb. 14, 2020, reverse takeover acquisition of Digihost International, Inc.
[2] Results for fiscal 2019 and prior fiscal years pertain to HashChain Technology Inc.
Note: Adjusted throughout for 1-for-3 cons. in Oct. 2021; 1-for-40 cons. in Feb. 2020

D.49 Direct Communication Solutions, Inc.

Symbol - DCSI **Exchange** - CSE **CUSIP** - 25460P
Head Office - 11021 Via Frontera, Suite C, San Diego, CA, United States, 92127 **Telephone** - (858) 798-7100
Website - www.dcsbusiness.com
Email - cbursey@dcsbusiness.com
Investor Relations - Chris Bursey (858) 525-2483
Auditors - Davidson & Company LLP C.A., Vancouver, B.C.
Lawyers - Fang & Associates, Vancouver, B.C.
Transfer Agents - TSX Trust Company, Vancouver, B.C.
Profile - (Del. 2017; orig. Fla., 2006) Designs, develops and deploys solutions for the Internet of Things (IoT) market.

Provides software-as-a-service (SaaS) solutions including MiFleet, which provides fleet and vehicle SaaS telematics; MiSensors, a machine-to-machine device management and service enablement for wireless sensors; and MiFailover, which provides high-speed wireless Internet failover to small and medium-sized businesses as a redundancy solution to continue to run their business in the event the Internet is not available. Also developing BrewSee, a management and monitoring system for the hospitality industry.

Also offers MiConnectivity platform which provides wireless data connectivity for global connectivity through the company's fully integrated SIM management platform; MiEbike which is a mobile app designed to track E-bikes in real time; and MiServices™ to provide managed services solution that includes all-inclusive device readiness program and engineering support. Services include software development, hardware integration and logistics support from SIM to shipment, including device preparation, custom labelling, packaging, configuration confirmation, and system-side checks. In addition, also resells IoT telematics devices such as GPS devices, modems, embedded modules and routers.

Directors - Chris Bursey, founder, chr., pres. & CEO, Calif.; David Diamond, Calif.; William (Bill) Espley, Vancouver, B.C.; Julie Hajduk, Vancouver, B.C.; John Hubler, N.J.; Michael Ueland; Mike Zhou, Vancouver, B.C.

Other Exec. Officers - Dave Scowby, COO; Konstantin Lichtenwald, CFO; Eric Placzek, chief tech. officer; Michael T. Lawless, exec. v-p, bus. devel.

Capital Stock

	Authorized (shs.)	Outstanding (shs.)[1]	Par
Common	40,000,000	2,305,079	US$0.00001

[1] At June 30, 2023

Major Shareholder - Chris Bursey held 40.3% interest at Aug. 8, 2022.

Price Range - DCSI/CSE

Year	Volume	High	Low	Close
2022	449,727	$12.04	$2.10	$8.19
2021	749,072	$18.69	$2.10	$3.08
2020	335,899	$15.75	$3.50	$14.35

Consolidation: 1-for-7 cons. in Feb. 2023
Recent Close: $1.89
Capital Stock Changes - On Feb. 10, 2023, common shares were consolidated on a 1-for-7 basis.

During 2022, 499,996 common shares were issued for services.

Wholly Owned Subsidiaries

Direct Communication Solutions (Canada) Inc., B.C. Inactive.

Financial Statistics

Periods ended:	12m Dec. 31/22[A]		12m Dec. 31/21[oA]
	US$000s	%Chg	US$000s
Operating revenue	**22,586**	**+37**	**16,526**
Cost of sales	16,218		12,144
Research & devel. expense	553		1,158
General & admin expense	7,011		5,340
Operating expense	**23,783**	**+28**	**18,643**
Operating income	**(1,197)**	**n.a.**	**(2,117)**
Deprec., depl. & amort.	432		246
Finance costs, gross	772		417
Write-downs/write-offs	(225)		(95)
Pre-tax income	**(2,234)**	**n.a.**	**(1,995)**
Net income	**(2,234)**	**n.a.**	**(1,995)**
Cash & equivalent	3,211		2,507
Inventories	793		2,224
Accounts receivable	3,374		3,903
Current assets	8,554		8,664
Fixed assets, net	41		79
Right-of-use assets	689		869
Intangibles, net	420		630
Total assets	**9,755**	**-5**	**10,297**
Bank indebtedness	nil		1,671
Accts. pay. & accr. liabs.	6,502		4,660
Current liabilities	7,416		7,233
Long-term debt, gross	1,469		275
Long-term debt, net	1,194		275
Long-term lease liabilities	584		662
Shareholders' equity	(2,563)		(828)
Cash from oper. activs.	**1,353**	**n.a.**	**(1,032)**
Cash from fin. activs.	(288)		2,078
Cash from invest. activs.	(4)		(12)
Net cash position	**3,567**	**+42**	**2,507**
Capital expenditures	(4)		(12)
	US$		US$
Earnings per share*	(0.97)		(0.90)
Cash flow per share*	0.59		(0.47)
	shs		shs
No. of shs. o/s*	2,305,091		2,233,663
Avg. no. of shs. o/s*	2,299,989		2,218,456
	%		%
Net profit margin	(9.89)		(12.07)
Return on equity	n.m.		n.m.
Return on assets	(14.69)		(21.35)
Foreign sales percent	95		98

* Common
[o] Restated
[A] Reported in accordance with IFRS

Latest Results

Periods ended:	6m June 30/23[A]		6m June 30/22[oA]
	US$000s	%Chg	US$000s
Operating revenue	7,782	-43	13,598
Net income	(2,349)	n.a.	695
	US$		US$
Earnings per share*	(1.02)		0.30

* Common
[o] Restated
[A] Reported in accordance with IFRS

Historical Summary
(as originally stated)

Fiscal Year	Oper. Rev. US$000s	Net Inc. Bef. Disc. US$000s	EPS* US$
2022[A]	22,586	(2,234)	(0.97)
2021[A]	16,526	(1,772)	(0.77)
2020[A]	14,257	(1,948)	(0.98)
2019[A]	16,064	(1,096)	(0.77)
2018[A1]	15,956	63	0.07

* Common
[A] Reported in accordance with IFRS
[1] As shown in the prospectus dated Dec. 20, 2019.
Note: Adjusted throughout for 1-for-7 cons. in Feb. 2023

D.50 Divergent Energy Services Corp.

Symbol - DVG **Exchange** - TSX-VEN **CUSIP** - 255051
Head Office - 2020-715 5 Ave SW, Calgary, AB, T2P 2X6 **Telephone** - (403) 543-0060 **Fax** - (403) 543-0069
Website - www.divergentenergyservices.com
Email - ken.olson@divergentenergyservices.com
Investor Relations - Kenneth E. Olson (403) 543-0060
Auditors - MNP LLP C.A., Calgary, Alta.
Bankers - HSBC Bank Canada, Calgary, Alta.
Lawyers - DS Lawyers Canada LLP, Calgary, Alta.
Transfer Agents - Computershare Trust Company of Canada Inc., Calgary, Alta.
Profile - (Alta. 1999 amalg.) Provides electric submersible water pumps and related services to the oil and gas industry primarily in the U.S.
The company's Electric Submersible Pump System is designed to lift large volumes of fluid from both oil and gas wells which features abrasion resistance through heavy-duty materials and coatings for bearings, bushings and other components subjected to sand, sand management within the pump using wide-vane technology and gas separation to break up gas slugs and free gas that interferes with operations.
Operations are carried out through its Artificial Lift Systems segment which services Wyoming and Colorado from its facility in Gillette, Wyo.
Predecessor Detail - Name changed from Canadian Oilfield Solutions Corp., June 9, 2014.
Directors - Cameron Barton, exec. chr., Alta.; Ken Berg, pres. & CEO, Alta.; Kenneth M. (Ken) Bagan†, Calgary, Alta.; Geoff Bury, Alta.; Robert Riecken, Calgary, Alta.
Other Exec. Officers - Kenneth E. (Ken) Olson, CFO & corp. sec.
† Lead director

Capital Stock

	Authorized (shs.)	Outstanding (shs.)[1]
Preferred	unlimited	nil
Common	unlimited	33,004,912

[1] At May 10, 2023
Major Shareholder - Donald R. Luft held 15.32% interest and Murray L. Cobbe held 15.04% interest at May 2, 2023.

Price Range - DVG/TSX-VEN

Year	Volume	High	Low	Close
2022	5,686,546	$0.18	$0.07	$0.10
2021	9,960,959	$0.25	$0.04	$0.07
2020	4,169,846	$0.25	$0.05	$0.10
2019	500,491	$0.65	$0.15	$0.15
2018	2,055,127	$1.10	$0.15	$0.15

Consolidation: 1-for-10 cons. in Jan. 2021
Recent Close: $0.06
Capital Stock Changes - There were no changes to capital stock during 2022.

Wholly Owned Subsidiaries

American Oilfield Solutions Corp., United States.
Extreme Pump Solutions LLC, Gillette, Wyo.
FlexTek Oilfield Supply LLC, Houston, Tex. Inactive.
Karlington Artificial Lift LLC, United States. Inactive.

Financial Statistics

Periods ended:	12m Dec. 31/22[A]		12m Dec. 31/21[A]
	US$000s	%Chg	US$000s
Operating revenue	**12,506**	**+50**	**8,362**
Cost of sales	9,702		6,264
General & admin expense	1,802		1,639
Stock-based compensation	44		31
Other operating expense	40		(181)
Operating expense	**11,588**	**+49**	**7,753**
Operating income	**918**	**+51**	**609**
Deprec., depl. & amort.	208		211
Finance costs, net	(149)		1,839
Pre-tax income	**561**	**-77**	**2,462**
Net income	**561**	**-77**	**2,462**
Cash & equivalent	556		607
Inventories	680		711
Accounts receivable	1,114		877
Current assets	2,484		2,299
Fixed assets, net	171		133
Right-of-use assets	457		535
Total assets	**3,112**	**+5**	**2,967**
Accts. pay. & accr. liabs.	1,566		1,438
Current liabilities	2,323		1,993
Long-term debt, gross	2,915		2,957
Long-term debt, net	2,458		2,741
Long-term lease liabilities	257		353
Shareholders' equity	(1,926)		(2,120)
Cash from oper. activs.	**925**	**-32**	**1,352**
Cash from fin. activs.	(899)		(835)
Cash from invest. activs.	(77)		27
Net cash position	**556**	**-8**	**607**
Capital expenditures	(77)		nil
Capital disposals	nil		27
	US$		US$
Earnings per share*	0.02		0.08
Cash flow per share*	0.03		0.04
	shs		shs
No. of shs. o/s*	33,004,912		33,004,912
Avg. no. of shs. o/s*	33,004,912		32,256,624
	%		%
Net profit margin	4.49		29.44
Return on equity	n.m.		n.m.
Return on assets	18.46		80.14
Foreign sales percent	100		100

* Common
[A] Reported in accordance with IFRS

Latest Results

Periods ended:	3m Mar. 31/23[A]		3m Mar. 31/22[A]
	US$000s	%Chg	US$000s
Operating revenue	3,103	+19	2,616
Net income	168	n.m.	11
	US$		US$
Earnings per share*	0.01		0.00

* Common
[A] Reported in accordance with IFRS

Historical Summary
(as originally stated)

Fiscal Year	Oper. Rev. US$000s	Net Inc. Bef. Disc. US$000s	EPS* US$
2022[A]	12,506	561	0.02
2021[A]	8,362	2,462	0.08
2020[A]	4,332	129	0.01
2019[A]	8,178	(2,644)	(0.20)
2018[A]	7,535	71	0.01

* Common
[A] Reported in accordance with IFRS
Note: Adjusted throughout for 1-for-10 cons. in Jan. 2021

D.51 Diversified Royalty Corp.

Symbol - DIV **Exchange** - TSX **CUSIP** - 255331
Head Office - 330-609 Granville St, PO Box 10033, Vancouver, BC, V7Y 1A1 **Telephone** - (604) 235-3146 **Fax** - (604) 685-9970
Website - www.diversifiedroyaltycorp.com
Email - greg@diversifiedroyaltycorp.com
Investor Relations - Greg Gutmanis (236) 521-8471
Auditors - KPMG LLP C.A., Vancouver, B.C.
Lawyers - Farris LLP, Vancouver, B.C.
Transfer Agents - Computershare Trust Company of Canada Inc., Toronto, Ont.
Profile - (B.C. 2020; orig. Can., 1992) Acquires royalty streams from multi-location businesses and franchisors in North America.

Mr. Lube Royalty

The company owns the Canadian trademarks and certain other intellectual property used by **Mr. Lube Canada Limited Partnership** in the operation of its quick service oil change and automotive maintenance franchise business across Canada.
Subsidiary **ML Royalties Limited Partnership** has granted Mr. Lube a 99-year licence, expiring Aug. 19, 2114, to the Mr. Lube trademarks and intellectual property in exchange for a monthly royalty equal to 7.95% of the non-tire system sales and 2.5% for system sales on tires and rims of the Mr. Lube locations in the royalty pool (the royalty pool is adjusted on May 1 of each year). The royalty rate may be increased in 0.5% increments (other than in respect of tire sales) four times during the life of the royalty. At June 30, 2023, Mr. Lube had 166 locations, of which 144 were in the royalty pool.

Sutton Group Real Estate Royalty

The company owns the Canadian and U.S. trademarks and certain other intellectual property used by **Sutton Group Realty Services Ltd.** in the operation of its residential real estate brokerage franchising business which has about 6,300 real estate agents across Canada.
Subsidiary **SGRS Royalties Limited Partnership** has granted Sutton a 99-year licence, expiring Dec. 31, 2114, to the Sutton trademarks and intellectual property in exchange for a royalty equal to $65.906 per agent in the royalty pool per month (effective July 1, 2023). The royalty rate increases by 2% on July 1 each year and may be increased in 10% increments four times during the life of the royalty. At June 30, 2023, 5,400 agents were in the royalty pool.

AIR MILES® Royalty

The company owns the Canadian trademarks and certain other intellectual property used by an affiliate of **Bank of Montreal** (BMO) in the operation of its AIR MILES® reward program, a full service outsourced coalition loyalty program that allow consumers to earn reward miles, which can be redeemed for multiple reward choices, as they shop across a broad range of retailers and other sponsors participating in the reward program.
Wholly owned **AM Royalties Limited Partnership** has granted BMO the exclusive right and licence to use the AIR MILES® trademarks and intellectual property for an indefinite term in exchange for 1% of gross billings from the program, payable quarterly.

Mr. Mikes Restaurant Royalty

The company owns the worldwide trademarks and certain other intellectual property used by **Mr. Mikes Restaurants Corporation** in the operation of its casual steakhouse restaurant business across western Canada.
Subsidiary **MRM Royalties Limited Partnership** has granted Mr. Mikes a 99-year licence, expiring May 20, 2118, to the Mr. Mikes trademarks and intellectual property in exchange for a royalty, payable every four weeks, equal to 4.35% of gross sales of the Mr. Mikes locations in the royalty pool (the royalty pool is adjusted on April 1 of each year). The royalty rate may be increased in 0.25% increments six times during the life of the royalty. At June 30, 2023, Mr. Mikes had 46 restaurants, of which 44 were in the royalty pool.

Nurse Next Door Royalty

The company owns the worldwide trademarks and certain other intellectual property rights used by **Nurse Next Door Professional Homecare Services Inc.** (NND) in its home care business, with more than 250 corporate and franchised locations in Canada, the U.S. and Australia.

Subsidiary **NND Royalties Limited Partnership** has granted NND a 99-year licence, expiring Nov. 15, 2118, to the NND trademarks and intellectual property in exchange for a monthly royalty payment equal to the greater of (i) 6% of gross sales from franchise and corporate locations for such month, and (ii) $425,722 (or $5,108,664 annually), which increases at a fixed rate of 2% on October 1 of each year.

Oxford Education Royalty

The company owns the worldwide trademarks and certain other intellectual property rights used by **Oxford Learning Centres, Inc.** in its pre-school, elementary and secondary school and post-secondary supplemental education business. Oxford operates in Canada, the U.S., and internationally under the Grade Power brand in the U.S. and under the Oxford Learning Centres brand elsewhere.

Subsidiary **OX Royalties Limited Partnership** has granted Oxford a 99-year licence, expiring Feb. 20, 2119, to use the Oxford trademarks and intellectual property in exchange for a monthly royalty of 7.67% of gross sales from franchise and corporate locations included in the royalty pool (the royalty pool is adjusted on May 1 of each year). The royalty rate may be increased in 0.25% increments six times during the life of the royalty. At June 30, 2023, Oxford had 156 locations, of which 146 were in the royalty pool.

Stratus Royalty

The company owns the worldwide trademarks and certain other intellectual property used by **SBS Franchising, LLC** (Stratus) in the operation of its commercial cleaning services and building maintenance services franchise business under Stratus Business Solutions name.

Wholly owned **Strat-B Royalties Limited Partnership** has granted Stratus a 50-year licence, expiring Nov. 15, 2072, to the Stratus trademarks and intellectual property in exchange for an annual royalty payment equal to US$6,000,000, which automatically increases by 5% on November 15 in 2023, 2024, 2025 and 2026 and by 4% on November 15 each year thereafter. The royalty rate may also increase on April 1 of each year. At June 30, 2023, Stratus had 68 master franchise businesses in the U.S. and Canada.

In addition to royalties, the company also receives management fees from Mr. Lube, Sutton, Mr. Mikes, NND and Oxford.

On June 1, 2023, **Bank of Montreal** (BMO) completed the acquisition of the AIR MILES Reward Program business from **LoyaltyOne, Co.** Wholly owned **AM Royalties Limited Partnership** (AM LP) owns the Canadian AIR MILES trademarks and certain related Canadian intellectual property rights. Prior to the AIR MILES acquisition, AM LP licensed the AIR MILES rights to LoyaltyOne, Co. for use in the AIR Miles Reward Program business in Canada. In connection with the AIR MILES acquisition, the AIR MILES licences were assigned to, and assumed by, an affiliate of BMO, and remain in full force and effect.

In November 2022, the company and subsidiary **MRM Royalties Limited Partnership** (MRM LP) amended the royalty agreement with **Mr. Mikes Restaurants Corporation** pursuant to which Mr. Mikes would pay, effective June 13, 2022, a royalty to MRM LP equal to 4.35% of the actual system sales of Mr. Mikes locations in the royalty pool. Previously, the royalty rate was 4.35% of the notional system sales of Mr. Mikes locations in the royalty pool.

Recent Merger and Acquisition Activity

Status: completed **Revised:** Nov. 15, 2022

UPDATE: The transaction was completed. PREVIOUS: Diversified Royalty Corp. agreed to acquire the trademarks and certain other intellectual property rights utilized by North Hollywood, Calif.-based SBS Franchising, LLC in its business of offering, managing and operating master franchises for commercial cleaning services and building maintenance care in the United States and Canada as Stratus Building Solutions. The purchase price was US$59,400,000, subject to adjustment if certain conditions are met, to be funded with drawings from acquisition and credit facilities. On closing, Diversified would license these rights in the United States, Canada, Australia, New Zealand and the United Kingdom back to Stratus for 50 years, in exchange for an initial annual royalty of US$6,000,000. The initial royalty automatically increases by 5% on each anniversary of the closing date in calendar years 2023, 2024, 2025 and 2026 and by 4% on each anniversary of the closing date thereafter.

Predecessor Detail - Name changed from BENEV Capital Inc., Sept. 26, 2014.

Directors - Paula Rogers, chr., North Vancouver, B.C.; Roger J. Chouinard, Toronto, Ont.; Johnny Ciampi, Vancouver, B.C.; Garry P. Herdler, King of Prussia, Pa.; Kevin Smith, North Vancouver, B.C.

Other Exec. Officers - Sean Morrison, pres. & CEO; Greg Gutmanis, v-p, acqs., CFO & corp. sec.; Adrian Law, contr.

Capital Stock

	Authorized (shs.)	Outstanding (shs.)[1]
Common	unlimited	143,132,308
ML Royalties LP		
Class B LP Unit		90,127,485
Class E LP Unit		100,000,000
Class F LP Unit		100,000,000
SGRS Royalties LP		
Class A LP Unit		99,544,608
Class B LP Unit		100,000,000
Class C LP Unit		100,000,000
Class D LP Unit		100,000,000
Class E LP Unit		100,000,000
MRM Royalties LP		
Class B LP Unit		1,000,000,000
Class C LP Unit		1,000,000,000
NND Royalties LP		
Class B LP Unit		1,000,000,000
OX Royalties LP		
Class B LP Unit		100,000,000
Class C LP Unit		100,000,000
Class D LP Unit		100,000,000
Class E LP Unit		100,000,000
Class F LP Unit		100,000,000
Class G LP Unit		100,000,000
Class H LP Unit		100,000,000

[1] At Aug. 14, 2023

Common - One vote per share.

ML Royalties Limited Partnership Class B, E and F LP Unit - All held by Mr. Lube Canada Limited Partnership. Class B LP units are convertible into common shares on May 1 of each year upon the addition of new Mr. Lube locations into the royalty pool. Class E and F LP units are convertible into common shares if royalty rate is increased in respective 0.5% increments.

SGRS Royalties Limited Partnership Class A, B, C, D and E LP Unit - All held by Sutton Group Realty Services Ltd. Class A LP units are convertible into common shares on July 1 of each year upon the addition of new agents into the royalty pool. Class B, C, D and E LP units are convertible into common shares if royalty rate is increased in respective 10% increments.

MRM Royalties Limited Partnership Class B and C LP Unit - All held by Mr. Mikes Restaurants Corporation. Class B LP units are convertible into common shares on April 1 of each year upon the addition of new Mr. Mikes locations into the royalty pool. Class C LP units are convertible into common shares if royalty rate is increased in respective 0.25% increments.

NND Royalties Limited Partnership Class B LP Unit - All held by Nurse Next Door Professional Homecare Services Inc. Convertible into common shares on February 1 of each year if royalty rate is increased by 2%.

OX Royalties Limited Partnership Class B, C, D, E, F, G and H LP Unit - All held by Oxford Learning Centres, Inc. Class B LP units are convertible into common shares on May 1 of each year upon the addition of new Oxford locations into the royalty pool. Class C, D, E, F, G and H LP units are convertible into common shares if the distribution entitlement is increased.

Major Shareholder - Widely held at May 9, 2023.

Price Range - DIV/TSX

Year	Volume	High	Low	Close
2022	78,378,772	$3.39	$2.51	$2.98
2021	76,548,267	$2.99	$2.31	$2.82
2020	83,617,554	$3.44	$1.17	$2.38
2019	41,714,419	$3.28	$2.58	$3.14
2018	42,519,617	$3.74	$2.55	$2.83

Recent Close: $2.81

Capital Stock Changes - In November 2022, bought deal public offering of 16,428,900 common shares was completed at $2.80 per share, including 2,142,900 common shares on exercise of over-allotment option. Also during 2022, common shares were issued as follows: 1,270,057 under dividend reinvestment plan, 1,083,063 for Mr. Lube royalty pool adjustment and 81,582 on vesting of restricted share units.

Dividends

DIV com Ra $0.24 pa M est. Jan. 31, 2023**
Prev. Rate: $0.235 est. Oct. 31, 2022
Prev. Rate: $0.22 est. Nov. 30, 2021
Prev. Rate: $0.21 est. Aug. 31, 2021
Prev. Rate: $0.20 est. Apr. 30, 2020
** Reinvestment Option

Wholly Owned Subsidiaries

AM Royalties GP Inc., B.C.
AM Royalties Limited Partnership, B.C.
ML Royalties Limited Partnership, B.C. Represents ownership of all ordinary LP units.
MRM Royalties Limited Partnership, B.C. Represents ownership of all ordinary LP units.
NND Holdings GP Inc., B.C.
- 99% int. in **NND Royalties GP Inc.**, B.C.

NND Holdings Limited Partnership, B.C.
- 100% int. in **NND Royalties Limited Partnership**, B.C. Represents ownership of all class A and C LP units.

OX Royalties GP Inc., B.C.
SGRS Royalties Limited Partnership, B.C. Represents ownership of all ordinary LP units.
Strat-B Royalties GP Inc., B.C.
Strat-B Royalties Limited Partnership, B.C.

Subsidiaries

99% int. in **ML Royalties GP Inc.**, B.C.
99% int. in **MRM Royalties GP Inc.**, B.C.
99.9% int. in **OX Royalties Limited Partnership**, B.C. Represents ownership of ordinary LP units.
99% int. in **SGRS Royalties GP Inc.**, B.C.

Financial Statistics

Periods ended:	12m Dec. 31/22[A]		12m Dec. 31/21[A]
	$000s	%Chg	$000s
Operating revenue	**45,183**	**+21**	**37,281**
Salaries & benefits	2,271		1,968
General & admin expense	1,301		1,086
Stock-based compensation	1,176		1,031
Operating expense	**4,748**	**+16**	**4,085**
Operating income	**40,435**	**+22**	**33,196**
Deprec., depl. & amort.	100		90
Finance income	168		29
Finance costs, gross	12,379		9,073
Write-downs/write-offs	(7,553)		1,724
Pre-tax income	**23,499**	**-28**	**32,684**
Income taxes	7,938		9,166
Net income	**15,561**	**-34**	**23,518**
Cash & equivalent	7,409		8,939
Accounts receivable	5,591		4,922
Current assets	15,513		14,158
Long-term investments	42,339		44,467
Right-of-use assets	801		897
Intangibles, net	398,592		320,595
Total assets	**458,450**	**+20**	**380,764**
Accts. pay. & accr. liabs	5,376		2,544
Current liabilities	6,862		61,617
Long-term debt, gross	199,009		168,827
Long-term debt, net	199,009		112,859
Long-term lease liabilities	770		829
Equity portion of conv. debs	5,127		2,938
Shareholders' equity	233,888		191,525
Cash from oper. activs	**28,377**	**+2**	**27,815**
Cash from fin. activs	49,369		(11,138)
Cash from invest. activs	(79,308)		(16,956)
Net cash position	**7,409**	**-17**	**8,939**
Capital expenditures	(4)		(244)
	$		$
Earnings per share*	0.12		0.19
Cash flow per share*	0.23		0.23
Cash divd. per share*	0.22		0.21
	shs		shs
No. of shs. o/s*	141,422,794		122,559,192
Avg. no. of shs. o/s*	125,607,078		121,866,677
	%		%
Net profit margin	34.44		63.08
Return on equity	7.32		12.34
Return on assets	5.66		8.13
Foreign sales percent	2		n.a.

* Common
[A] Reported in accordance with IFRS

Latest Results

Periods ended:	6m June 30/23[A]		6m June 30/22[A]
	$000s	%Chg	$000s
Operating revenue	26,490	+27	20,822
Net income	15,784	+18	13,339
	$		$
Earnings per share*	0.11		0.11

* Common
[A] Reported in accordance with IFRS

Historical Summary
(as originally stated)

Fiscal Year	Oper. Rev. $000s	Net Inc. Bef. Disc. $000s	EPS* $
2022[A]	45,183	15,561	0.12
2021[A]	37,281	23,518	0.19
2020[A]	30,496	(8,885)	(0.07)
2019[A]	30,463	14,044	0.13
2018[A]	26,709	10,120	0.09

* Common
[A] Reported in accordance with IFRS

D.52 Dividend 15 Split Corp.

Symbol - DFN **Exchange** - TSX **CUSIP** - 25537R
Head Office - c/o Quadravest Capital Management Inc., 2510-200 Front St W, PO Box 51, Toronto, ON, M5V 3K2 **Telephone** - (416) 304-4440 **Toll-free** - (877) 478-2372
Website - www.quadravest.com
Email - info@quadravest.com
Investor Relations - Shari Payne (877) 478-2372

Auditors - PricewaterhouseCoopers LLP C.A., Toronto, Ont.
Lawyers - Blake, Cassels & Graydon LLP, Toronto, Ont.
Transfer Agents - Computershare Trust Company of Canada Inc., Toronto, Ont.
Investment Managers - Quadravest Capital Management Inc., Toronto, Ont.
Managers - Quadravest Capital Management Inc., Toronto, Ont.
Profile - (Ont. 2004) Invests in a portfolio primarily consisting of dividend-paying common shares of 15 Canadian public companies.

The company's actively managed portfolio will include common shares of **Bank of Montreal**, **The Bank of Nova Scotia**, **BCE Inc.**, **Canadian Imperial Bank of Commerce**, **CI Financial Corp.**, **Enbridge Inc.**, **Manulife Financial Corporation**, **National Bank of Canada**, **Royal Bank of Canada**, **Sun Life Financial Inc.**, **TELUS Corporation**, **TC Energy Corporation**, **Thomson Reuters Corporation**, **The Toronto-Dominion Bank** and **TransAlta Corporation**, each of whose securities will generally represent no less than 4% and no more than 8% of the net asset value of the company. Up to 15% of the net asset value may be invested in equity securities of issuers other than the companies above.

To supplement the dividends received on the investment portfolio and to reduce risk, the company will, from time to time, write covered call options in respect of all or part of the common shares in the portfolio.

The investment manager receives a management fee at an annual rate equal to 0.65% of the net asset value of the company calculated and payable monthly in arrears. In addition, the manager receives an administration fee at an annual rate equal to 0.1% of the net asset value of the company calculated and payable monthly in arrears, as well as service fee payable to dealers on the class A shares at a rate of 0.5% per annum.

The company will terminate on Dec. 1, 2024, or earlier at the discretion of the manager if the class A or preferred shares are delisted by the TSX or if the net asset value of the company declines to less than $5,000,000. At such time all outstanding class A and preferred shares will be redeemed. The termination date may be extended beyond Dec. 1, 2024, for a further five years and thereafter for additional successive periods of five years as determined by the board of directors.

Top 10 holdings at Feb. 28, 2023 (as a percentage of net assets):

Holdings	Percentage
Royal Bank of Canada	8.5%
The Toronto-Dominion Bank	6.7%
Manulife Financial Corporation	6.3%
Bank of Montreal	5.9%
BCE Inc.	5.6%
TC Energy Corporation	5.6%
Sun Life Financial Inc.	5.4%
Enbridge Inc.	5.2%
Canadian Imperial Bank of Commerce	5.1%
Suncor Energy Inc.	5.1%

Directors - S. Wayne Finch, chr., pres. & CEO, Caledon, Ont.; Laura L. Johnson, corp. sec., Oakville, Ont.; Peter F. Cruickshank, Oakville, Ont.; Michael W. Sharp, Toronto, Ont.; John D. Steep, Stratford, Ont.
Other Exec. Officers - Silvia Gomes, CFO

Capital Stock

	Authorized (shs.)	Outstanding (shs.)[1]
Preferred	unlimited	115,475,852[2]
Class B	3,000	1,000[2]
Class A	unlimited	119,705,352

[1] At May 15, 2023
[2] Classified as debt.

Preferred - Entitled to receive fixed cumulative preferential monthly dividends of $0.04583 per share. Under a regular monthly retraction, a shareholder will receive, for each preferred share, an amount equal to the lesser of: (i) $10; and (ii) 96% of the net asset value (NAV) per unit (1 preferred share and 1 class A share) less the cost to the company of purchasing a class A share in the market for cancellation. Under a concurrent annual retraction on the August valuation date of each year, a shareholder will receive, for each unit, an amount equal to the NAV per unit less any costs (to a maximum of 1% of the NAV per unit) related to liquidating the portfolio to pay such amount. All outstanding preferred shares will be redeemed on Dec. 1, 2024, at a price per share equal to $10. Rank in priority to the class A and B shares with respect to the payment of dividends and the repayment of capital on the dissolution, liquidation or winding-up of the company. Non-voting.
Class B - Not entitled to receive dividends. Retractable and redeemable at any time at $1.00 per share. Rank subsequent to preferred shares and prior to class A shares with respect to entitlement on the dissolution, liquidation or winding-up of the company. One vote per share.
Class A - The company will endeavour to pay monthly cash distributions of 10¢ per share (to yield 8% per annum on the original issue price). If, after such dividends are paid, any amounts remain available, a special dividend of such amount will be made to shareholders in November of each year. No regular monthly dividends will be paid in any year so long as any dividends on the preferred shares are then in arrears or so long as the NAV per unit is equal to or less than $15. Additionally, no special year-end dividends will be paid if after payment of such a dividend the NAV per unit would be less than $25.00. Under a regular monthly retraction, a shareholder will receive, for each class A share, the amount by which 96% of the NAV per unit exceeds the cost to the company of purchasing a preferred share in the market. Under a concurrent annual retraction on the August valuation date of each year, a shareholder will receive, for each unit, an amount equal to the NAV per unit less any costs (to a maximum of 1% of the NAV per unit) related to liquidating the portfolio to pay such amount. All outstanding class A shares will be redeemed on Dec. 1, 2024, at a price per share equal to $15. Class A shareholders are also entitled to receive the balance, if any, of the value of the investment portfolio remaining after returning the original issue price to preferred and class A shareholders. Rank subsequent to the preferred shares and class B shares with respect to the payment of dividends and the repayment of capital on the dissolution, liquidation or winding-up of the company. Non-voting.
Normal Course Issuer Bid - The company plans to make normal course purchases of up to 11,528,622 preferred shares representing 10% of the public float. The bid commenced on May 29, 2023, and expires on May 28, 2024.

The company plans to make normal course purchases of up to 11,962,416 class A shares representing 10% of the public float. The bid commenced on May 29, 2023, and expires on May 28, 2024.
Major Shareholder - Quadravest Capital Management Inc. held 100% interest at Feb. 23, 2023.

Price Range - DFN/TSX

Year	Volume	High	Low	Close
2022	72,767,436	$8.83	$6.36	$7.53
2021	61,525,915	$8.47	$6.60	$8.00
2020	60,099,248	$8.93	$3.55	$6.76
2019	24,114,040	$9.44	$7.58	$8.58
2018	29,670,184	$11.00	$6.17	$7.72

Recent Close: $4.89
Capital Stock Changes - On Sept. 20, 2022, bought deal public offering of 4,610,000 preferred shares and 2,230,000 class A shares was completed at $9.65 and $7.75 per share, respectively. Also during fiscal 2022, 9,353,900 preferred shares and 12,369,400 class A shares were issued under an at-the-market equity program.

Dividends

DFN cl A N.V. omitted pa M[1]
DFN.PR.A pfd cum. ret. Ra $0.55 pa M
[1] No set frequency divd normally payable in Nov/20 has been omitted.

Financial Statistics

Periods ended:	12m Nov. 30/22[A]		12m Nov. 30/21[A]
	$000s	%Chg	$000s
Realized invest. gain (loss)	14,672		(19,866)
Unrealized invest. gain (loss)	(6,062)		221,507
Total revenue	**75,515**	**-69**	**247,274**
General & admin. expense	14,066		12,693
Other operating expense	2,582		2,763
Operating expense	**16,648**	**+8**	**15,455**
Operating income	**58,867**	**-75**	**231,819**
Finance costs, gross	60,570		47,544
Pre-tax income	**(1,703)**	**n.a.**	**184,275**
Net income	**(1,703)**	**n.a.**	**184,275**
Cash & equivalent	286,407		150,585
Accounts receivable	4,296		4,224
Investments	1,445,089		1,433,509
Total assets	**1,735,792**	**+9**	**1,588,318**
Accts. pay. & accr. liabs.	1,295		2,013
Debt	1,050,526		910,897
Shareholders' equity	654,462		661,341
Cash from oper. activs.	**59,891**	**n.a.**	**(408,843)**
Cash from fin. activs.	75,931		454,254
Net cash position	**286,407**	**+90**	**150,585**
	$		$
Earnings per share*	(0.02)		2.47
Cash flow per share*	0.61		(5.48)
Net asset value per share*	6.19		7.26
Cash divd. per share*	1.20		1.20
	shs		shs
No. of shs. o/s*	105,688,952		91,089,552
Avg. no. of shs. o/s*	97,637,135		74,672,640
	%		%
Net profit margin	(2.26)		74.52
Return on equity	(0.26)		37.77
Return on assets	3.54		18.59

* Class A
[A] Reported in accordance with IFRS

Note: Net income reflects increase/decrease in net assets from operations.

Historical Summary
(as originally stated)

Fiscal Year	Total Rev. $000s	Net Inc. Bef. Disc. $000s	EPS* $
2022[A]	75,515	(1,703)	(0.02)
2021[A]	247,274	184,275	2.47
2020[A]	(56,829)	(96,887)	(1.77)
2019[A]	126,947	90,310	1.83
2018[A]	(15,745)	(48,305)	(1.10)

* Class A
[A] Reported in accordance with IFRS

D.53 Dividend 15 Split Corp. II

Symbol - DF **Exchange** - TSX **CUSIP** - 25537W
Head Office - c/o Quadravest Capital Management Inc., 2510-200 Front St W, PO Box 51, Toronto, ON, M5V 3K2 **Telephone** - (416) 304-4440 **Toll-free** - (877) 478-2372
Website - www.quadravest.com
Email - info@quadravest.com
Investor Relations - Shari Payne (877) 478-2372
Auditors - PricewaterhouseCoopers LLP C.A., Toronto, Ont.
Lawyers - Blake, Cassels & Graydon LLP, Toronto, Ont.
Transfer Agents - Computershare Trust Company of Canada Inc., Toronto, Ont.
Investment Managers - Quadravest Capital Management Inc., Toronto, Ont.
Managers - Quadravest Capital Management Inc., Toronto, Ont.
Profile - (Ont. 2006) Invests in a portfolio primarily consisting of dividend-paying common shares of 15 Canadian public companies.

The company's actively managed portfolio will include common shares of **Manulife Financial Corporation**, **The Bank of Nova Scotia**, **The Toronto-Dominion Bank**, **TELUS Corporation**, **Royal Bank of Canada**, **Canadian Imperial Bank of Commerce**, **BCE Inc.**, **Sun Life Financial Inc.**, **CI Financial Corp.**, **National Bank of Canada**, **Thomson Reuters Corporation**, **TC Energy Corporation**, **Enbridge Inc.**, **Bank of Montreal** and **TransAlta Corporation**, each of whose securities will generally represent no less than 4% and no more than 8% of the net asset value of the company. Up to 15% of the net asset value may be invested in equity securities of issuers other than the companies above.

To supplement the dividends received on the investment portfolio and to reduce risk, the company will, from time to time, write covered call options in respect of all or part of the common shares in the portfolio.

The investment manager receives a management fee at an annual rate equal to 0.65% of the net asset value of the company calculated and payable monthly in arrears. In addition, the manager receives an administration fee at an annual rate equal to 0.1% of the net asset value of the company calculated and payable monthly in arrears, as well as service fee payable to dealers on the class A shares at a rate of 0.5% per annum.

The company will terminate on Dec. 1, 2024, or earlier at the discretion of the manager if the class A or preferred shares are delisted by the TSX or if the net asset value of the company declines to less than $5,000,000. At such time all outstanding class A and preferred shares will be redeemed. The termination date may be extended beyond Dec. 1, 2024, for a further five years and thereafter for additional successive periods of five years as determined by the board of directors.

Top 10 holdings at Feb. 28, 2023 (as a percentage of net assets):

Holdings	Percentage
Royal Bank of Canada	8.5%
Bank of Montreal	6.9%
Manulife Financial Corporation	6.7%
Sun Life Financial Inc.	6.7%
Toronto-Dominion Bank	6.7%
BCE Inc.	6.1%
TC Energy Corporation	6.1%
Thomson Reuters Corporation	6.0%
Canadian Imperial Bank of Commerce	5.7%
National Bank of Canada	5.4%

Oper. Subsid./Mgt. Co. Directors - S. Wayne Finch, chr., pres. & CEO, Caledon, Ont.; Laura L. Johnson, corp. sec., Oakville, Ont.; Peter F. Cruickshank, Oakville, Ont.; Michael W. Sharp, Toronto, Ont.; John D. Steep, Stratford, Ont.
Other Exec. Officers - Silvia Gomes, CFO

Capital Stock

	Authorized (shs.)	Outstanding (shs.)[1]
Preferred	unlimited	31,069,049[2]
Class B	1,000	1,000[2]
Class A	unlimited	31,069,049

[1] At May 15, 2023
[2] Classified as debt.

Preferred - Entitled to receive fixed cumulative preferential monthly dividends of $0.04792 per share (to yield 5.75% per annum on the original $10 issue price). Under a regular monthly retraction, a shareholder will receive, for each preferred share, an amount equal to the lesser of: (i) $10; and (ii) 96% of the net asset value (NAV) per unit (1 class A share and 1 preferred share) less the cost to the company of purchasing a class A share in the market for cancellation. Under a concurrent annual retraction on the August valuation date of each year, a shareholder will receive, for each unit, an amount equal to the NAV per unit less any costs (to a maximum of 1% of the NAV per unit) related to liquidating the portfolio to pay such amount. All outstanding preferred shares will be redeemed on Dec. 1, 2024, at a price per share equal to $10. Rank in priority to the class A and B shares with respect to the payment of dividends and the repayment of capital on the dissolution, liquidation or winding-up of the company. Non-voting.
Class B - Not entitled to receive dividends. Retractable and redeemable at any time at $1.00 per share. Rank subsequent to preferred shares and prior to class A shares with respect to entitlement on the dissolution, liquidation or winding-up of the company. One vote per share.
Class A - The company will endeavour to pay monthly cash distributions of 10¢ per share (to yield 8% per annum on the original issue price). If, after such dividends are paid, any amounts remain available, a special dividend of such amount will be made to shareholders in November of each year. No regular monthly dividends will be paid in any year so long as any dividends on the preferred shares are then in arrears or so long as the NAV per unit is equal to or less than $15. Additionally, no special year-end dividends will be paid if after payment of such a dividend the NAV per unit would be less than $25.00. Under a regular monthly retraction, a shareholder will receive, for each class A share, the amount by which 96% of the NAV per unit exceeds the cost to the company of purchasing a preferred share in the market. Under a concurrent annual retraction on the August valuation date of each year, a shareholder will receive, for each unit, an amount equal to the NAV per unit less any costs (to a maximum of 1% of the

NAV per unit) related to liquidating the portfolio to pay such amount. All outstanding class A shares will be redeemed on Dec. 1, 2024, at a price per share equal to $15. Class A shareholders are also entitled to receive the balance, if any, of the value of the investment portfolio remaining after returning the original issue price to preferred and class A shareholders. Rank subsequent to the preferred shares and class B shares with respect to the payment of dividends and the repayment of capital on the dissolution, liquidation or winding-up of the company. Non-voting.

Normal Course Issuer Bid - The company plans to make normal course purchases of up to 3,106,904 preferred shares representing 10% of the public float. The bid commenced on May 29, 2023, and expires on May 28, 2024.

The company plans to make normal course purchases of up to 3,098,274 class A shares representing 10% of the public float. The bid commenced on May 29, 2023, and expires on May 28, 2024.

Major Shareholder - Dividend 15 Split Corp. II Holding Trust held 100% interest at Feb. 23, 2023.

Price Range - DF/TSX

Year	Volume	High	Low	Close
2022	40,103,312	$6.60	$3.33	$3.85
2021	24,951,575	$6.55	$2.88	$6.24
2020	8,107,634	$6.00	$2.07	$2.94
2019	11,159,441	$5.64	$3.20	$5.09
2018	18,627,446	$9.00	$2.59	$3.45

Recent Close: $3.36

Capital Stock Changes - During fiscal 2022, 7,221,200 preferred shares and 7,963,300 class A shares were issued under an at-the-market equity program, and 422,300 preferred shares and 1,164,400 class A shares were retracted.

Dividends

DF cl A N.V. omitted [1]

$0.10	June 10/22	$0.10	May 10/22
$0.10	Apr. 8/22	$0.10	Mar. 10/22

Paid in 2023: n.a. 2022: $0.60 2021: $0.80

DF.PR.A pfd cum. ret. Ra $0.575 pa M

[1] Monthly divd normally payable in July/22 has been omitted.

Financial Statistics

Periods ended:	12m Nov. 30/22[A]		12m Nov. 30/21[A]
	$000s	%Chg	$000s
Realized invest. gain (loss)	2,377		1,921
Unrealized invest. gain (loss)	(6,056)		40,172
Total revenue	**13,389**	**-71**	**46,782**
General & admin. expense	3,920		2,345
Other operating expense	848		635
Operating expense	**4,768**	**+60**	**2,980**
Operating income	**8,621**	**-80**	**43,802**
Finance costs, gross	18,855		11,501
Pre-tax income	**(10,234)**	**n.a.**	**32,301**
Net income	**(10,234)**	**n.a.**	**32,301**
Cash & equivalent	59,810		63,353
Accounts receivable	1,225		896
Investments	398,569		312,025
Total assets	**459,604**	**+22**	**376,274**
Accts. pay. & accr. liabs	363		506
Debt	311,118		243,130
Shareholders' equity	145,251		128,854
Cash from oper. activs	**(77,108)**	**n.a.**	**(96,134)**
Cash from fin. activs	73,565		146,638
Net cash position	**59,810**	**-6**	**63,353**
	$		$
Earnings per share*	(0.34)		2.02
Cash flow per share*	(2.53)		(6.01)
Net asset value per share*	4.67		5.30
Cash divd. per share*	0.60		0.80
	shs		shs
No. of shs. o/s*	31,111,849		24,312,949
Avg. no. of shs. o/s*	30,446,403		15,985,732
	%		%
Net profit margin	(76.44)		69.05
Return on equity	(7.47)		36.93
Return on assets	2.06		15.57

* Class A

[A] Reported in accordance with IFRS

Note: Net income reflects increase/decrease in net assets from operations.

Historical Summary
(as originally stated)

Fiscal Year	Total Rev. $000s	Net Inc. Bef. Disc. $000s	EPS* $
2022[A]	13,389	(10,234)	(0.34)
2021[A]	46,782	32,301	2.02
2020[A]	(13,210)	(23,238)	(1.67)
2019[A]	36,026	24,946	1.52
2018[A]	(4,760)	(15,837)	(0.96)

* Class A

[A] Reported in accordance with IFRS

D.54 Dividend Growth Split Corp.

Symbol - DGS **Exchange** - TSX **CUSIP** - 25537Y

Head Office - c/o Brompton Group Limited, Bay Wellington Tower, Brookfield Place, 2930-181 Bay St, PO Box 793, Toronto, ON, M5J 2T3 **Telephone** - (416) 642-9061 **Toll-free** - (866) 642-6001 **Fax** - (416) 642-6001

Website - www.bromptongroup.com

Email - wong@bromptongroup.com

Investor Relations - Ann P. Wong (866) 642-6001

Auditors - PricewaterhouseCoopers LLP C.A., Toronto, Ont.

Transfer Agents - TSX Trust Company, Toronto, Ont.

Managers - Brompton Funds Limited, Toronto, Ont.

Portfolio Managers - Brompton Funds Limited, Toronto, Ont.

Profile - (Ont. 2011 amalg.; orig. Ont., 2007) Invests in a portfolio consisting primarily of equity securities of Canadian dividend growth companies.

Investments in the portfolio have a market capitalization of at least $2 billion and a history of dividend growth or, in the manager's view, a high potential for future dividend growth. The portfolio may contain more or less than 20 investments but not less than 15 investments. The portfolio is rebalanced to an approximately equally weighted basis, at least annually, to adjust for changes in the market values of investments, to remove a company that ceases to pay or suspends its dividends, or to reflect the impact of a merger, acquisition or other significant corporate action or event affecting portfolio constituents. Up to 20% of the portfolio may be invested in global dividend growth companies.

To generate additional income, the company may write covered call or put options in respect of common shares held in the portfolio. The company will terminate on Sept. 27, 2024, subject to extension for periods of up to five years, as determined by the board of directors.

The manager receives a management fee at an annual rate equal to 0.6% of the net asset value calculated and payable monthly in arrears.

Top 10 holdings at Mar. 31, 2023 (as a percentage of net asset value):

Holdings	Percentage
Brompton Global Dividend Growth ETF	9.6%
Dollarama Inc.	5.1%
Restaurant Brands International Inc.	4.4%
Tourmaline Oil Corp.	4.3%
Thomson Reuters Corporation	4.2%
Canadian Pacific Railway Ltd.	4.1%
Canadian Natural Resources Ltd.	4.1%
Imperial Oil Ltd.	4.0%
Sun Life Financial Inc.	3.8%
Royal Bank of Canada	3.7%

Oper. Subsid./Mgt. Co. Directors - Mark A. Caranci, pres. & CEO, Toronto, Ont.; Ann P. Wong, CFO & chief compliance officer, Toronto, Ont.; Christopher S. L. Hoffmann, Toronto, Ont.; Raymond R. Pether, Toronto, Ont.

Oper. Subsid./Mgt. Co. Officers - Laura Lau, chief invest. officer; Kathryn A. H. Banner, sr. v-p & corp. sec.; Michael D. Clare, sr. v-p & sr. portfolio mgr.; Christopher Cullen, sr. v-p; Manith (Manny) Phanvongsa, sr. v-p; Michelle L. Tiraborelli, sr. v-p

Capital Stock

	Authorized (shs.)	Outstanding (shs.)[1]
Preferred	unlimited	48,116,733[2]
Class A	unlimited	48,116,733
Class J	unlimited	150

[1] At Apr. 12, 2023

[2] Classified as debt.

Preferred - Entitled to receive fixed cumulative preferential quarterly dividends of $0.1375 per share, effective Dec. 13, 2019 (to yield 5.5% per annum on the original $10 issue price). Retractable monthly at a price equal to 96% of the lesser of: (i) the net asset value (NAV) per unit (1 class A share and 1 preferred share) less the cost to the company of purchasing a class A share for cancellation; and (ii) $10. Under a concurrent quarterly retraction (February, May, August and November of each year), a shareholder will receive, for each unit, an amount equal to the NAV per unit less any costs associated with the retraction. All outstanding preferred shares will be redeemed on Sept. 27, 2024, at a price per share equal to the lesser of: (i) $10 plus any accrued and unpaid distributions; and (ii) the NAV per share. Rank in priority to the class A and class J shares with respect to the payment of dividends and the repayment of capital on the dissolution, liquidation or winding-up of the company. Non-voting.

Class A - Entitled to monthly non-cumulative cash distributions of 10¢ per share (to yield 8% per annum on the original $15 issue price). No distributions will be paid if the distributions payable on the preferred shares are in arrears or in respect of a cash distribution, after payment of the distribution, the NAV per unit (1 class A share and 1 preferred share) would be less than $15. In addition, no distributions in excess of 10¢ per month would be paid on the class A shares if, after payment of the distribution, the NAV per unit would be less than $25 unless the company has to make such distributions to fully recover refundable taxes. Retractable monthly at a price per class A share equal to 96% of the difference between: (i) the NAV per unit, and (ii) cost to the company of purchasing a preferred share for cancellation. Under a concurrent quarterly retraction, a shareholder will receive, for each unit, an amount equal to the NAV per unit less any costs related to liquidating any portion of the portfolio to fund such retraction. All outstanding class A shares will be redeemed on Sept. 27, 2024, at a price equal to the greater of: (i) the NAV per unit minus $10 plus any accrued and unpaid distributions on a preferred share; and (ii) nil. Rank subsequent to the preferred shares but in priority to the class J shares with respect to the payment of dividends and the repayment of capital on the dissolution, liquidation or winding-up of the company. Non-voting.

Class J - Not entitled to dividends. Redeemable and retractable at $1.33 per share. Rank subsequent to both the preferred and class A shares with respect to the payment of dividends and the repayment of capital on the dissolution, liquidation or winding-up of the company. One vote per share.

Major Shareholder - DGS Trust held 100% interest at Mar. 23, 2023.

Price Range - DGS/TSX

Year	Volume	High	Low	Close
2022	62,388,010	$7.35	$4.51	$5.74
2021	50,028,756	$7.48	$3.35	$6.81
2020	23,379,298	$6.19	$2.45	$3.40
2019	25,719,430	$6.18	$3.35	$5.27
2018	40,346,421	$8.27	$2.60	$3.61

Recent Close: $4.28

Capital Stock Changes - In March 2022, public offering of 3,989,500 preferred shares and 3,989,500 class A shares was completed at $10 and $6.80 per share, respectively. Also during 2022, 46,673 preferred shares and 46,673 class A shares were retracted.

Dividends

DGS cl A omitted **[1]

$0.10	May 12/23	$0.10	Feb. 14/23
$0.10	Jan. 16/23	$0.10	Dec. 14/22

Paid in 2023: $0.30 2022: $1.00 2021: $0.90

DGS.PR.A pfd cum. red. ret. Ra $0.55 pa Q

[1] Monthly divd normally payable in Mar/23 has been omitted.

** Reinvestment Option

Financial Statistics

Periods ended:	12m Dec. 31/22[A]		12m Dec. 31/21[A]
	$000s	%Chg	$000s
Realized invest. gain (loss)	7,561		28,631
Unrealized invest. gain (loss)	(36,271)		90,841
Total revenue	**(3,819)**	**n.a.**	**138,104**
General & admin. expense	5,094		3,860
Operating expense	**5,094**	**+32**	**3,860**
Operating income	**(8,913)**	**n.a.**	**134,244**
Finance costs, gross	27,369		23,889
Pre-tax income	**(36,284)**	**n.a.**	**110,353**
Net income	**(36,284)**	**n.a.**	**110,353**
Cash & equivalent	2,505		2,463
Accounts receivable	2,763		2,930
Investments	711,649		729,153
Total assets	**716,981**	**-2**	**734,560**
Accts. pay. & accr. liabs	45		240
Debt	481,167		441,739
Shareholders' equity	228,096		285,963
Cash from oper. activs	**(18,149)**	**n.a.**	**(198,485)**
Cash from fin. activs	18,191		196,201
Net cash position	**2,505**	**+2**	**2,463**
	$		$
Earnings per share*	(0.76)		3.20
Cash flow per share*	(0.38)		(5.76)
Net asset value per share*	4.74		6.47
Cash divd. per share*	1.00		1.00
	shs		shs
No. of shs. o/s*	48,116,733		44,173,906
Avg. no. of shs. o/s*	47,467,906		34,455,423
	%		%
Net profit margin	n.m.		79.91
Return on equity	(14.12)		54.17
Return on assets	(1.23)		23.11

* Class A

[A] Reported in accordance with IFRS

Note: Net income reflects increase/decrease in net assets from operations.

Historical Summary
(as originally stated)

Fiscal Year	Total Rev. $000s	Net Inc. Bef. Disc. $000s	EPS* $
2022[A]	(3,819)	(36,284)	(0.76)
2021[A]	138,104	110,353	3.20
2020[A]	(12,873)	(33,304)	(1.04)
2019[A]	113,572	90,268	2.50
2018[A]	(73,911)	(98,231)	(2.67)

* Class A

[A] Reported in accordance with IFRS

D.55 Dividend Select 15 Corp.

Symbol - DS **Exchange** - TSX **CUSIP** - 255380

Head Office - c/o Quadravest Capital Management Inc., 2510-200 Front St W, PO Box 51, Toronto, ON, M5V 3K2 **Telephone** - (416) 304-4440 **Toll-free** - (877) 478-2372

Website - www.quadravest.com

Email - info@quadravest.com

Investor Relations - Shari Payne (877) 478-2372

Auditors - PricewaterhouseCoopers LLP C.A., Toronto, Ont.

Lawyers - Blake, Cassels & Graydon LLP, Toronto, Ont.

Transfer Agents - Computershare Trust Company of Canada Inc., Toronto, Ont.

Investment Managers - Quadravest Capital Management Inc., Toronto, Ont.

Managers - Quadravest Capital Management Inc., Toronto, Ont.

Portfolio Advisors - Quadravest Capital Management Inc., Toronto, Ont.

Profile - (Ont. 2010) Invests in a portfolio of dividend paying common shares of 15 Canadian public companies.

The investment portfolio will be selected from among the following 20 companies: **Bank of Montreal**, **BCE Inc.**, **Canadian Imperial Bank of Commerce**, **Cenovus Energy Inc.**, **CI Financial Corp.**, **Enbridge Inc.**, **Great-West Lifeco Inc.**, **Loblaw Companies Limited**, **National Bank of Canada**, **Ovintiv Inc.**, **Power Corporation of Canada**, **Royal Bank of Canada**, **Sun Life Financial Inc.**, **TC Energy Corporation**, **TELUS Corporation**, **The Bank of Nova Scotia**, **The Toronto-Dominion Bank**, **Thomson Reuters Corporation**, **TMX Group Inc.** and **TransAlta Corporation**.

To supplement the dividends received on the investment portfolio and to reduce risk, the company may, from time to time, write covered call options in respect of all or part of the common shares in the portfolio.

The manager is entitled to a management fee at an annual rate equal to 1.10% of the company's net asset value calculated at the month-end valuation date, from which a service fee of 0.40% is payable by the manager to dealers.

The company may be terminated at the discretion of the manager upon 60 days' prior written notice if the equity shares are delisted by the TSX, or if the net asset value of the company decreases to less than $5,000,000. At such time all equity shares will be redeemed.

Top 10 holdings at Feb. 28, 2023 (as a percentage of net assets):

Holdings	Percentage
Thomson Reuters Corporation	8.8%
Enbridge Inc.	8.6%
Sun Life Financial Inc.	8.5%
Royal Bank of Canada	8.4%
National Bank of Canada	7.3%
The Toronto-Dominion Bank	7.1%
TELUS Corporation	5.8%
Cenovus Energy Inc.	5.6%
Canadian Imperial Bank of Commerce	5.4%
BCE Inc.	5.2%

Directors - S. Wayne Finch, chr., pres. & CEO, Caledon, Ont.; Laura L. Johnson, corp. sec., Oakville, Ont.; Peter F. Cruickshank, Oakville, Ont.; Michael W. Sharp, Toronto, Ont.; John D. Steep, Stratford, Ont.

Other Exec. Officers - Silvia Gomes, CFO

Capital Stock

	Authorized (shs.)	Outstanding (shs.)[1]
Equity	unlimited	8,350,141
Class B	1,000	1,000[2]

[1] At Feb. 23, 2023

[2] Classified as debt.

Equity - Entitled to monthly cash distributions determined by applying a 10% annualized rate on the volume weighted average market price of the shares over the last three trading days of the preceding month. Retractable in March of each year at a price equal to the net asset value per share, less any costs to fund the retraction. Retractable monthly at a price equal to the lessor of: (i) 95% of the weighted average price of the shares on TSX for the 10 business days prior to the retraction date; (ii) the closing price per share; and (iii) 95% of the net asset value per share, less any costs to fund the retraction. Non-voting except in certain circumstances.

Class B - Not entitled to receive dividends. Retractable at 2¢ per share and are entitled to liquidation value of 2¢ per share. Rank prior to Equity shares with respect to entitlement on the dissolution, liquidation or winding-up of the company. One vote per share.

Major Shareholder - Dividend Select 15 Holding Trust held 100% interest at Feb. 23, 2023.

Price Range - DS/TSX

Year	Volume	High	Low	Close
2022	2,766,848	$10.15	$7.50	$7.73
2021	2,715,536	$10.27	$6.41	$10.01
2020	2,338,249	$7.75	$3.47	$6.45
2019	2,507,017	$7.55	$6.69	$7.40
2018	3,545,625	$9.14	$6.21	$6.81

Recent Close: $6.25

Capital Stock Changes - During fiscal 2022, 2,199,400 equity shares were issued under an at-the-market equity program.

Dividends

DS equity sh N.V. Var. Ra pa M

$0.05492	Sept. 8/23	$0.05475	Aug. 10/23
$0.05558	July 10/23	$0.05967	June 9/23

Paid in 2023: $0.54341 2022: $0.87516 2021: $0.77942

Financial Statistics

Periods ended:	12m Nov. 30/22[A]		12m Nov. 30/21[A]
	$000s	%Chg	$000s
Realized invest. gain (loss)	401		(19)
Unrealized invest. gain (loss)	(741)		10,533
Total revenue	**1,628**	**-87**	**12,221**
General & admin. expense	760		666
Other operating expense	199		154
Operating expense	**959**	**+17**	**820**
Operating income	**669**	**-94**	**11,401**
Pre-tax income	**669**	**-94**	**11,401**
Net income	**669**	**-94**	**11,401**
Cash & equivalent	8,222		1,005
Accounts receivable	175		117
Investments	52,223		45,242
Total assets	**60,620**	**+31**	**46,364**
Accts. pay. & accr. liabs	92		99
Shareholders' equity	58,465		45,736
Cash from oper. activs	**(4,909)**	**n.a.**	**4,195**
Cash from fin. activs	12,126		(6,313)
Net cash position	**8,222**	**+718**	**1,005**
	$		$
Earnings per share*	0.09		1.87
Cash flow per share*	(0.67)		0.69
Net asset value per share*	7.10		7.58
Cash divd. per share*	0.88		0.78
	shs		shs
No. of shs. o/s*	8,230,741		6,031,341
Avg. no. of shs. o/s*	7,365,637		6,112,974
	%		%
Net profit margin	41.09		93.29
Return on equity	1.28		26.34
Return on assets	1.25		25.97

* Equity

[A] Reported in accordance with IFRS

Historical Summary
(as originally stated)

Fiscal Year	Total Rev.	Net Inc. Bef. Disc.	EPS*
	$000s	$000s	$
2022[A]	1,628	669	0.09
2021[A]	12,221	11,401	1.87
2020[A]	(3,862)	(4,675)	(0.69)
2019[A]	9,145	8,155	0.97
2018[A]	(1,811)	(2,941)	(0.30)

* Equity

[A] Reported in accordance with IFRS

D.56 Docebo Inc.

Symbol - DCBO **Exchange** - TSX **CUSIP** - 25609L

Head Office - 701-366 Adelaide St W, Toronto, ON, M5V 1R9 **Telephone** - (416) 456-5868 **Toll-free** - (800) 681-4601

Website - www.docebo.com

Email - mike.mccarthy@docebo.com

Investor Relations - Mike McCarthy (416) 283-9930

Auditors - KPMG LLP C.A., Vaughan, Ont.

Lawyers - Goodmans LLP, Toronto, Ont.

Transfer Agents - TSX Trust Company, Toronto, Ont.

FP500 Revenue Ranking - 672

Employees - 880 at Dec. 31, 2022

Profile - (Ont. 2016) Provides a suite of artificial intelligence (AI)-based corporate e-learning software and services to various enterprises and industries worldwide.

Learning suite offered includes Docebo Learn LMS, a cloud-based learning management system (LMS) that allows customers to deliver scalable and flexible personalized learning programs, from formal training to social learning, to multiple internal, external and blended audiences; Docebo Shape, an AI-based content creation tool that transforms internal and external resources in various formats into multilingual e-learning content in minutes; Docebo Content, which allows customers to access a library of thousands of off-the-shelf and mobile-ready learning courses covering a range of topics; Docebo Learning Impact, a learning measurement tool to evaluate the effectiveness of learning programs; Docebo Learning Analytics, a business intelligence tool that allows customers to retrieve, analyze and transform the data from their learning programs into useful business insights; Docebo Connect, a module acting as a connector between the customer's platform and third-party software-as-a-service (SaaS) systems to manage automated workflows shared among systems; and Docebo Flow, which allows the customer's trainees to access relevant training content as they work on a platform thereby eliminating switching back and forth between software.

Additional products include Docebo for Salesforce, which allows customers to embed the company's LMS with the third-party Salesforce customer relationship management (CRM) platform; Docebo Embed (OEM), which allows OEMs to embed and re-sell Docebo as part of their human capital management (HCM), risk management and retail/hospitality SaaS suites; Docebo Mobile App Publisher, an on-demand app builder which allows customers to create their own branded mobile application based on the company's Docebo Go.Learn mobile learning application and publish it as their own in the Apple App Store, the Google Play Store or in their own Apple Enterprise store; Docebo Extended Enterprise, which allows customers to train multiple external audiences with a single LMS solution; and Docebo Discover, Coach & Share, which provides learners access to social learning with the sharing of knowledge through informal, social, interactive and experiential learning.

The company is headquartered in Toronto, Ont., with offices in Biassono, Italy; Athens, Ga.; London, U.K.; Paris, France; Munich, Germany; Dubai, U.A.E.; and Melbourne, Australia.

In April 2023, the company acquired PeerBoard, a plug and play community-as-a-service platform which integrates directly to websites and custom built environments, from **Circles Collective Inc.** The acquisition would expand the company's external training offering and enhance social learning capabilities. Terms were not disclosed.

Directors - Jason Chapnik, chr., Toronto, Ont.; Claudio Erba, CEO, Italy; Steven E. (Steve) Spooner†, Kanata, Ont.; William Anderson, Toronto, Ont.; Kristin Halpin Perry, Shelburne, Vt.; James Merkur, Toronto, Ont.; Trisha Price, Wilmington, N.C.

Other Exec. Officers - Alessio Artuffo, pres. & COO; Sukaran Mehta, CFO; Martino Bagini, chief corp. devel. officer; Francesca Bossi, chief HR officer; Ryan Brock, chief mktg. officer; Domenic Di Sisto, chief legal officer & corp. sec.; Fabio Pirovano, chief product officer; Nina Simosko, chief sales officer; Nicole Williams, sr. v-p, rev. strategy & opers.; Mike McCarthy, v-p, IR; Giuseppe Tomasello, v-p, AI

† Lead director

Capital Stock

	Authorized (shs.)	Outstanding (shs.)[1]
Preferred	unlimited	nil
Common	unlimited	33,013,459

[1] At May 10, 2023

Normal Course Issuer Bid - The company plans to make normal course purchases of up to 1,650,672 common shares representing 5% of the total outstanding. The bid commenced on May 18, 2023, and expires on May 17, 2024.

Major Shareholder - Jason Chapnik held 41.26% interest and Cat Rock Capital Management LP held 16.34% interest at Apr. 10, 2023.

Price Range - DCBO/TSX

Year	Volume	High	Low	Close
2022	18,925,954	$86.01	$31.66	$44.74
2021	26,048,903	$117.55	$47.22	$84.87
2020	14,910,315	$84.61	$10.30	$82.75
2019	4,524,708	$16.99	$11.29	$16.99

Recent Close: $61.28

Capital Stock Changes - During 2022, common shares were issued as follows: 20,814 under the employee share purchase plan, 15,364 as an earn-out payment pursuant to the acquisition of forMetris Société par Actions Simplifiée, 14,840 on exercise of options and 5,515 on releasing of restricted share units.

Wholly Owned Subsidiaries

Docebo Australia Pty Ltd., Australia.

Docebo DACH GmbH, Germany.

Docebo EMEA FZ-LLC, United Arab Emirates.

Docebo France Société par Actions Simplifiée, Paris, France.

Docebo Ireland Limited, Ireland.

Docebo NA, Inc., Nev.

Docebo S.p.A., Italy.

Docebo UK Limited, United Kingdom.

Financial Statistics

Periods ended:	12m Dec. 31/22^A		12m Dec. 31/21^{□A}
	US$000s	%Chg	US$000s
Operating revenue	**142,912**	**+37**	**104,242**
Cost of sales	28,178		20,786
Research & devel. expense	24,778		20,363
General & admin expense	89,837		71,789
Stock-based compensation	4,713		2,261
Operating expense	**147,506**	**+28**	**115,199**
Operating income	**(4,594)**	**n.a.**	**(10,957)**
Deprec., depl. & amort.	2,333		2,019
Finance income	3,912		437
Finance costs, gross	400		502
Pre-tax income	**7,782**	**n.a.**	**(13,429)**
Income taxes	764		172
Net income	**7,018**	**n.a.**	**(13,601)**
Cash & equivalent	216,293		215,323
Accounts receivable	37,527		27,685
Current assets	263,585		251,588
Fixed assets, net	2,624		2,645
Right-of-use assets	2,038		3,059
Intangibles, net	7,132		6,877
Total assets	**283,669**	**+6**	**268,222**
Accts. pay. & accr. liabs	26,025		22,851
Current liabilities	84,362		69,272
Long-term lease liabilities	1,692		2,690
Shareholders' equity	192,211		190,656
Cash from oper. activs	**2,288**	**n.a.**	**(3,254)**
Cash from fin. activs	1,579		422
Cash from invest. activs	(2,152)		(1,145)
Net cash position	**216,293**	**0**	**215,323**
Capital expenditures	(1,081)		(1,145)
	US$		US$
Earnings per share*	0.21		(0.41)
Cash flow per share*	0.07		(0.10)
	shs		shs
No. of shs. o/s*	32,913,955		32,857,422
Avg. no. of shs. o/s*	33,067,716		32,867,801
	%		%
Net profit margin	4.91		(13.05)
Return on equity	3.67		(6.95)
Return on assets	2.67		(5.01)
No. of employees (FTEs)	880		726

* Common
□ Restated
A Reported in accordance with IFRS

Latest Results

Periods ended:	3m Mar. 31/23^A		3m Mar. 31/22^A
	US$000s	%Chg	US$000s
Operating revenue	41,459	+29	32,055
Net income	1,245	n.a.	(6,959)
	US$		US$
Earnings per share*	0.04		(0.21)

* Common
A Reported in accordance with IFRS

Historical Summary
(as originally stated)

Fiscal Year	Oper. Rev. US$000s	Net Inc. Bef. Disc. US$000s	EPS* US$
2022^A	142,912	7,018	0.21
2021^A	104,242	(13,601)	(0.41)
2020^A	62,917	(7,654)	(0.26)
2019^A	41,443	(11,914)	(0.49)
2018^{A1}	27,075	(11,651)	(0.52)

* Common
A Reported in accordance with IFRS
1 As shown in the prospectus dated Oct. 1, 2019.

D.57 Dollarama Inc.*

Symbol - DOL **Exchange** - TSX **CUSIP** - 25675T
Head Office - 5805 av Royalmount, Montréal, QC, H4P 0A1 **Telephone** - (514) 737-1006 **Toll-free** - (888) 755-1006 **Fax** - (514) 940-6169
Website - www.dollarama.com
Email - jp.towner@dollarama.com
Investor Relations - Jean-Philippe Towner (514) 737-1006 ext. 1237
Auditors - PricewaterhouseCoopers LLP C.A., Montréal, Qué.
Transfer Agents - Computershare Trust Company of Canada Inc., Montréal, Qué.
FP500 Revenue Ranking - 113
Employees - 24,945 at Jan. 29, 2023
Profile - (Can. 2004) Operates 1,507 general merchandise retail dollar stores across Canada (at Apr. 30, 2023) under the Dollarama® banner. Also holds a 50.1% interest in **Central American Retail Sourcing, Inc.**, parent company of Latin American value retailer Dollarcity.

Offers broad assortment of consumable products, general merchandise and seasonal items, including private label and nationally branded products, that are sold in individual or multiple units at select fixed price points up to Cdn$5.00. Consumable products include paper, plastics, foils, cleaning supplies, basic health and beauty care products, pet food, confectionery, drinks, snacks and other food products. General merchandise include party supplies, office supplies, arts and craft supplies, greeting cards and stationery, giftware, household wares, kitchenware, glassware, hardware, electronics, toys and apparel. Seasonal items include Valentine's Day, St. Patrick's Day, Easter, Halloween and the winter holidays merchandise, along with seasonal summer and winter merchandise. The company owns and operates all of its store locations which average 10,469 sq. ft. and are located in high-traffic places in metropolitan areas, mid-sized cities and small towns. In addition, the company operates an online store and mobile application that allows customers to pay in-store, purchase or redeem e-gift cards, scan products for price and availability, and search store location. Also has partnerships with third-party delivery platforms such as Instacart, Uber Eats and Doordash to provide same-day delivery to its customers. Warehouses (7) and distribution centre (1) are all located in the Montreal, Que., area.

Also has operations in Latin America through its 50.1% interest in Dollarcity, offering consumable products, general merchandise and seasonal items at select fixed price points up to US$4.00 (or the equivalent in local currency) in El Salvador, Guatemala, Colombia and Peru. At Mar. 31, 2023, Dollarcity operated 448 stores in Colombia (267), El Salvador (66), Guatemala (91) and Peru (24).

Canadian store breakdown at Jan. 29, 2023:

Province	Stores
British Columbia	132
Alberta	154
Saskatchewan	44
Manitoba	47
Ontario	590
Quebec	399
New Brunswick	44
Nova Scotia	43
Prince Edward Island	5
Nfld. & Labrador	26
Northwest Territories	1
Yukon	1
	1,486

During fiscal 2023, 65 net new stores were opened.

Recent Merger and Acquisition Activity

Status: pending **Announced:** Dec. 7, 2022
Dollarama agreed to acquire three adjacent properties in Mount Royal, Que., for cash of consideration of $87,300,000. The properties are situated near Dollarama's centralized logistics operations and adjacent to its distribution centre. Dollarama plans to redevelop the site to support future logistics. The transaction was expected to close in the first half of Dollarama's fiscal year ending Jan. 28, 2024.

Directors - Stephen K. Gunn, chr., Toronto, Ont.; Neil Rossy, pres. & CEO, Montréal, Qué.; Joshua (Josh) Bekenstein, Wayland, Mass.; Gregory David, Toronto, Ont.; Elisa D. Garcia, Fla.; Kristin W. Mugford, Mass.; Nicholas G. (Laki) Nomicos, Mass.; Samira Sakhia, Montréal, Qué.; Thecla Sweeney, Ont.; J. Huw Thomas, Oakville, Ont.

Other Exec. Officers - Johanne Choinière, COO; Jean-Philippe (J.P.) Towner, CFO; Nicolas Hien, CIO; Mark Di Pesa, sr. v-p, HR; Laurence L'Abbé, sr. v-p, legal affairs & corp. sec.; Geoffrey Robillard, sr. v-p, import div.; John Assaly, v-p, global procurement

Capital Stock

	Authorized (shs.)	Outstanding (shs.)[1]
Common	unlimited	283,376,026

1 At June 30, 2023

Options - At Jan. 29, 2023, options were outstanding to purchase 3,358,385 common shares at prices ranging from $12.02 to $73.79 per share with a weighted average remaining life of 63 months.

Normal Course Issuer Bid - The company plans to make normal course purchases of up to 13,695,242 common shares representing 4.8% of the total outstanding. The bid commenced on July 7, 2023, and expires on July 6, 2024.

Major Shareholder - Widely held at Apr. 11, 2023.

Price Range - DOL/TSX

Year	Volume	High	Low	Close
2022	167,190,902	$85.88	$60.34	$79.19
2021	160,799,066	$64.49	$46.56	$63.31
2020	222,226,016	$55.45	$34.70	$51.88
2019	192,600,043	$52.12	$31.20	$44.63
2018	279,410,211	$56.67	$30.70	$32.47

Recent Close: $85.81

Capital Stock Changes - During fiscal 2023, 608,150 common shares were issued on exercise of options and 8,916,071 common shares were repurchased under a Normal Course Issuer Bid.

Dividends

DOL com Ra $0.2832 pa Q est. May 5, 2023
Prev. Rate: $0.2212 est. May 6, 2022
Prev. Rate: $0.2012 est. May 7, 2021
Prev. Rate: $0.188 est. Feb. 5, 2021
Prev. Rate: $0.176 est. May 10, 2019

Long-Term Debt - Outstanding at Jan. 29, 2023:

3.55% sr. notes due 2023	$500,000,000
5.084% sr. notes due 2025	250,000,000
1.871% sr. notes due 2026	375,000,000
1.505% sr. notes due 2027	300,000,000
2.443% sr. notes due 2029	375,000,000
5.165% sr. notes due 2030	450,000,000
Accrued int. on notes	17,177,000
Less: Unamort. debt issue costs	9,107,000
Less: Adj. on int. swap	6,167,000
	2,251,903,000
Less: Current portion	510,315,000
	1,741,588,000

Wholly Owned Subsidiaries

Dollarama International Inc., Montréal, Qué.
• 50.1% int. in **Central American Retail Sourcing, Inc.**, Panama.
Dollarama L.P., Montréal, Qué.

Note: The preceding list includes only the major related companies in which interests are held.

Financial Statistics

Periods ended:	52w Jan. 29/23^A		52w Jan. 30/22^{□A}
	$000s	%Chg	$000s
Operating revenue	**5,052,741**	**+17**	**4,330,761**
Cost of sales	2,854,535		2,428,536
Salaries & benefits	540,380		501,953
General & admin expense	158,209		134,583
Stock-based compensation	14,187		8,617
Operating expense	**3,574,847**	**+16**	**3,081,368**
Operating income	**1,477,894**	**+18**	**1,249,393**
Deprec., depl. & amort.	331,792		297,960
Finance costs, gross	115,394		91,216
Investment income	45,399		33,184
Pre-tax income	**1,076,107**	**+20**	**893,401**
Income taxes	274,244		230,232
Net income	**801,863**	**+21**	**663,169**
Cash & equivalent	101,261		71,058
Inventories	957,172		590,927
Accounts receivable	56,290		26,260
Current assets	1,156,947		717,367
Long-term investments	267,768		211,926
Fixed assets, net	802,750		761,876
Right-of-use assets	1,699,755		1,480,255
Intangibles, net	892,436		891,848
Total assets	**4,819,656**	**+19**	**4,063,562**
Bank indebtedness	nil		89,386
Accts. pay. & accr. liabs	336,862		283,125
Current liabilities	1,162,874		911,891
Long-term debt, gross	2,251,903		1,796,914
Long-term debt, net	1,741,588		1,539,240
Long-term lease liabilities	1,741,936		1,526,564
Shareholders' equity	28,410		(66,034)
Cash from oper. activs	**869,043**	**-25**	**1,159,218**
Cash from fin. activs	(682,291)		(1,368,631)
Cash from invest. activs	(156,549)		(158,673)
Net cash position	**101,261**	**+43**	**71,058**
Capital expenditures	(134,049)		(136,772)
Capital disposals	278		839
	$		$
Earnings per share*	2.77		2.19
Cash flow per share*	3.00		3.83
Cash divd. per share*	0.22		0.20
	shs		shs
No. of shs. o/s*	284,505,648		292,813,569
Avg. no. of shs. o/s*	289,412,000		302,963,000
	%		%
Net profit margin	15.87		15.31
Return on equity	n.m.		n.m.
Return on assets	19.99		17.64
No. of employees (FTEs)	24,945		23,350

* Common
□ Restated
A Reported in accordance with IFRS

Latest Results

Periods ended:	13w Apr. 30/23^A		13w May 1/22^A
	$000s	%Chg	$000s
Operating revenue	1,294,549	+21	1,072,884
Net income	179,873	+24	145,502
	$		$
Earnings per share*	0.63		0.50

* Common
A Reported in accordance with IFRS

Historical Summary
(as originally stated)

Fiscal Year	Oper. Rev.	Net Inc. Bef. Disc.	EPS*
	$000s	$000s	$
2023[A]	5,052,741	801,863	2.77
2022[A]	4,330,761	663,169	2.19
2021[A]	4,026,259	564,348	1.82
2020[A]	3,787,291	564,039	1.80
2019[A1]	3,548,503	548,874	1.69

* Common
[A] Reported in accordance with IFRS
[1] 53 weeks ended Feb. 3, 2019.

D.58 Doman Building Materials Group Ltd.

Symbol - DBM **Exchange** - TSX **CUSIP** - 25703L
Head Office - 1600-1100 Melville St, PO Box 39, Vancouver, BC, V6E 4A6 **Telephone** - (604) 432-1400 **Fax** - (604) 436-6670
Website - domanbm.com
Email - ali.mahdavi@domanbm.com
Investor Relations - Ali Mahdavi (416) 962-3300
Auditors - KPMG LLP C.A., Vancouver, B.C.
Lawyers - DLA Piper (Canada) LLP, Vancouver, B.C.; Goodmans LLP, Toronto, Ont.
Transfer Agents - TSX Trust Company, Vancouver, B.C.
FP500 Revenue Ranking - 169
Employees - 2,052 at Dec. 31, 2022
Profile - (Can. 2010; orig. B.C., 2009) Distributes, produces and treats lumber as well as related building materials, and provides other value-add services across Canada and the U.S., servicing the new home construction, home renovation and industrial markets.

Operates through four divisions: CanWel Building Materials; CanWel Treating; Doman U.S.; and CanWel Fibre.

The **CanWel Building Materials** division warehouses and distributes lumber, treated lumber, panel boards (plywood, wafer board and oriented strand board), specialty industrial products, siding, roofing, insulation, engineered wood products, mouldings, milled items, paneling, ceiling tiles, storage items (shelving and closet lining), caulking, adhesives, locks, fasteners, forms and drainage, decking, cedar products, fencing, railings and reinforcement bars. Products are sold to big box warehouse stores, large independent chains, large co-operatives and smaller independent chains, stores and yards through distribution centres in 16 locations across Canada.

The **CanWel Treating** division provides pressure treating services for consumer lumber as well as wood products used by construction companies, public utilities and retailers. The treatment process protects wood and wood products against decay and pests. Treating plants are located in Maskinongé, Que., Cambridge and Hagersville, Ont., and Surrey and Abbotsford, B.C.

The **Doman U.S.** division consists of Cascade Group, which includes California Cascade and the Cascade Treating, which operates distribution, manufacturing and treating facilities in California and Oregon, as well as warehouses and distributes a variety of items including lumber, poles, posts, shakes, shingles and other forest products, engineered wood, decking, fencing, specialty-branded products and accessories and related products; Honsador, which operates in Hawaii with 11 distribution facilities, four manufacturing and treating facilities and a buying/logistics office in Oregon that provides building materials, distribution, treating services, truss manufacturing, electrical products supply and value added services; and Hixson Lumber, which operates in central United States with 19 treating plants, two specialty planing mills and five specialty sawmills in eight U.S. states, as well as distributes, produces and treats lumber, fencing and building materials.

The **CanWel Fibre** division's operations consist of ownership and management of private timberlands (117,000 acres are owned in the Kootenay and Hazelton, B.C., area) and crown forest licenses, full service logging and trucking operations, post-peeling and wood treatment operations for the agricultural and specialty lumber markets in western Canada and the western U.S. It also conducts select operations in central Canada and lumber trading in North America through **Lignum Forest Products LLP**. Production facilities are located in Cranbrook, Prince George and Edgewater, B.C.; Prince Albert, Sask.; and Combermere, Ont.

Predecessor Detail - Name changed from CanWel Building Materials Group Ltd., May 31, 2021.

Directors - Amar S. Doman, chr. & CEO, West Vancouver, B.C.; Ian M. Baskerville, Toronto, Ont.; Kelvin P. M. Dushnisky, Toronto, Ont.; Sam Fleiser, Toronto, Ont.; Marie Meisenbach Graul, Ill.; Michelle M. Harrison, Sacramento, Calif.; Harry Rosenfeld, West Vancouver, B.C.; Siegfried J. Thoma, Portland, Ore.

Other Exec. Officers - James Code, CFO; Stephen W. Marshall, v-p, treated wood, CanWel treating div.; R. S. (Rob) Doman, gen. counsel & corp. sec.; Marc Séguin, pres., CanWel Building Materials Ltd.

Capital Stock

	Authorized (shs.)	Outstanding (shs.)[1]
Preferred	unlimited	nil
Common	unlimited	86,890,538

[1] At May 11, 2023

Major Shareholder - Amar S. Doman held 19.18% interest at Mar. 31, 2023.

Price Range - DBM/TSX

Year	Volume	High	Low	Close
2022	58,050,806	$8.82	$5.30	$5.75
2021	78,420,892	$10.83	$6.13	$7.77
2020	51,719,981	$7.86	$2.73	$7.67
2019	35,569,647	$5.71	$4.24	$5.36
2018	45,372,108	$7.50	$4.19	$4.56

Recent Close: $7.63

Capital Stock Changes - During 2022, common shares were issued as follows: 222,808 under employee common share ownership plan and 74,694 under restricted equity common share plan.

Dividends

DBM com Ra $0.56 pa Q est. Jan. 14, 2022
Prev. Rate: $0.48 est. Oct. 15, 2020
$0.04†................. Apr. 15/21
Paid in 2023: $0.42 2022: $0.56 2021: $0.48 + $0.04†

† Extra

Wholly Owned Subsidiaries

CanWel Building Materials Ltd., Vancouver, B.C.
- 100% int. in **California Cascade Industries Inc.**, Calif.
- 100% int. in **CanWel Fibre Corp.**, Vancouver, B.C.
  - 100% int. in **Aallcann Wood Suppliers Inc.**, Prince Albert, Sask.
  - 100% int. in **CanWel Forest Products Ltd.**, B.C.
    - 100% int. in **Kispiox River Timber Ltd.**, B.C.
  - 100% int. in **CanWel Timber Ltd.**, B.C.
  - 50% int. in **Fernie Wilderness Adventures Inc.**, B.C.
  - 100% int. in **Kootenay Wood Preservers Ltd.**, B.C.
    - 100% int. in **Palmer Bar Holdings Inc.**, B.C.
  - 100% int. in **WoodEx Industries Ltd.**, B.C.
    - 100% int. in **Lignum Forest Products LLP**, B.C.
    - 100% int. in **NWWT General Partner Inc.**, B.C.
    - 100% int. in **Northwest Wood Treaters Limited Partnership**, Man.
    - 100% int. in **PPWP General Partner Inc.**, B.C.
    - 100% int. in **Pastway Planing and Wood Preserving Limited Partnership**, Man.
- 100% int. in **EWP General Partner Inc.**, B.C.
- 100% int. in **Eastern Wood Preservers Limited Partnership**, Man.
- 100% int. in **Fontana Wood Treating, Inc.**, Del.
  - 100% int. in **L.A. Lumber Treating, Ltd.**, Del.
- 100% int. in **Hixson Lumber Company**, Tex.
  - 100% int. in **Hixson Property Holdings, LLC**, Del.
- 100% int. in **Honsador Acquisition Corp.**, Del.
  - 100% int. in **Alpha Supply, LLC**, Del.
  - 100% int. in **Ariel Truss LLC**, Del.
  - 100% int. in **Honolulu Wood Treating LLC**, Del.
  - 100% int. in **Honsador Lumber LLC**, Del.
  - 100% int. in **Island Truss Holdings, LLC**, Del.
- 100% int. in **NAWP General Partner Inc.**, B.C.
- 100% int. in **North American Wood Preservers Limited Partnership**, Man.
- 100% int. in **Oregon Cascade Building Materials, Inc.**, Del.
- 100% int. in **QWP General Partner Inc.**, B.C.
- 100% int. in **Quebec Wood Preservers Limited Partnership**, Man.
- 100% int. in **TFI General Partner Inc.**, B.C.
- 100% int. in **Total Forest Industries Limited Partnership**, Man.
- 100% int. in **WCW General Partner Inc.**, B.C.
- 100% int. in **Western Cleanwood Preservers Limited Partnership**, Man.
- 100% int. in **Woodland Wood Preservers, Ltd.**, Del.

Financial Statistics

Periods ended:	12m Dec. 31/22[A]		12m Dec. 31/21[A]
	$000s	%Chg	$000s
Operating revenue	**3,039,017**	**+19**	**2,543,674**
Cost of sales	2,630,222		2,152,675
General & admin expense	205,696		164,065
Operating expense	**2,835,918**	**+22**	**2,316,740**
Operating income	**203,099**	**-11**	**226,934**
Deprec., depl. & amort.	66,877		55,063
Finance costs, gross	37,574		27,138
Pre-tax income	**98,717**	**-29**	**138,464**
Income taxes	19,977		31,955
Net income	**78,740**	**-26**	**106,509**
Cash & equivalent	1,400		2,333
Inventories	374,182		405,667
Accounts receivable	156,140		213,132
Current assets	554,208		636,349
Fixed assets, net	139,741		151,808
Right-of-use assets	144,967		151,954
Intangibles, net	553,695		544,908
Total assets	**1,445,193**	**-6**	**1,538,163**
Bank indebtedness	5,636		3,034
Accts. pay. & accr. liabs	137,807		156,696
Current liabilities	249,607		217,645
Long-term debt, gross	535,693		669,013
Long-term debt, net	473,562		665,332
Long-term lease liabilities	133,016		138,582
Shareholders' equity	568,488		497,709
Cash from oper. activs	**222,204**	**+351**	**49,293**
Cash from fin. activs	(224,780)		454,479
Cash from invest. activs	(4,491)		(503,290)
Net cash position	**(4,236)**	**n.a.**	**(701)**
Capital expenditures	(6,792)		(6,865)
Capital disposals	2,301		1,901
Unfunded pension liability	851		1,701
	$		$
Earnings per share*	0.91		1.27
Cash flow per share*	2.56		0.59
Cash divd. per share*	0.56		0.50
Extra divd. - cash*	nil		0.04
Total divd. per share*	**0.56**		**0.54**
	shs		shs
No. of shs. o/s*	86,991,660		86,694,158
Avg. no. of shs. o/s*	86,885,617		83,554,517
	%		%
Net profit margin	2.59		4.19
Return on equity	14.77		25.41
Return on assets	7.29		10.59
Foreign sales percent	58		47
No. of employees (FTEs)	2,052		2,125

* Common
[A] Reported in accordance with IFRS

Latest Results

Periods ended:	3m Mar. 31/23[A]		3m Mar. 31/22[A]
	$000s	%Chg	$000s
Operating revenue	609,119	-28	851,300
Net income	14,911	-65	42,028
	$		$
Earnings per share*	0.17		0.48

* Common
[A] Reported in accordance with IFRS

Historical Summary
(as originally stated)

Fiscal Year	Oper. Rev.	Net Inc. Bef. Disc.	EPS*
	$000s	$000s	$
2022[A]	3,039,017	78,740	0.91
2021[A]	2,543,674	106,509	1.27
2020[A]	1,613,804	59,587	0.77
2019[A]	1,334,201	17,219	0.22
2018[A]	1,291,295	30,015	0.39

* Common
[A] Reported in accordance with IFRS

D.59 Dominion Lending Centres Inc.

Symbol - DLCG **Exchange** - TSX **CUSIP** - 257414
Head Office - 2215 Coquitlam Ave, Port Coquitlam, BC, V3B 1J6 **Toll-free** - (888) 806-8080
Website - www.dlcg.ca
Email - rburpee@dlcg.ca
Investor Relations - Robin Burpee (403) 455-9670
Auditors - Ernst & Young LLP C.A., Calgary, Alta.
Transfer Agents - Computershare Trust Company of Canada Inc., Edmonton, Alta.
Employees - 158 at Dec. 31, 2022
Profile - (Alta. 2021 amalg.) Provides mortgage brokerage franchising and mortgage broker data connectivity services across Canada.

Mortgage brokerage franchising and mortgage broker data connectivity services across Canada is conducted through three Ontario-based wholly owned subsidiaries: **Mortgage Architects Inc.**, **MCC Mortgage Centre Canada Inc.** and **Newton Connectivity Systems Inc.** Newton provides Velocity, a secure all-in-one operating platform that connects mortgage brokers to lenders and third parties by automating the entire mortgage application, approval, underwriting and funding process. Services include training, technology, recruitment and operational support to its franchises and brokers as well as expertise related to property purchases, mortgage refinancing and renewals, credit lines and other borrowing needs. At Mar. 31, 2023, the company had 7,856 brokers, 539 franchises and more than 1,000 locations across Canada, with $9.355 billion funded mortgage volumes at the three-month period ended Mar. 31, 2023.

Also holds 52% interest in **Cape Communications International Inc.**, operating as Impact Radio Accessories™, a designer, manufacturer and retailer of unique radio communication products for public safety, military, security, retail and hospitality applications.

Recent Merger and Acquisition Activity

Status: completed **Announced:** Aug. 31, 2022
Dominion Lending Centres Inc. sold its 58.4% interest in Surrey, B.C.-based Club16 Limited Partnership, which operates 16 fitness clubs in Vancouver, B.C., under the Club16 Trevor Linden Fitness and She's FIT! Health banners, for $16,500,000 cash and $1,500,000 promissory note.

Predecessor Detail - Formed from Founders Advantage Capital Corp. in Alberta, Jan. 1, 2021, pursuant to amalgamation with (old) Dominion Lending Centres Inc., following acquistion of remainder of Dominion Lending Centres Limited Partnership.

Directors - Gary Mauris, exec. chr. & CEO, Vancouver, B.C.; Chris Kayat, exec. v-chr., B.C.; James G. M. Bell, co-pres., Calgary, Alta.; Ron Gratton†, Calgary, Alta.; Trevor Bruno, B.C.; Dennis F. Sykora, Calgary, Alta.; J. R. Kingsley Ward, Toronto, Ont.

Other Exec. Officers - Eddy Cocciollo, co-pres.; Dong Lee, COO; Robin Burpee, co-CFO; Geoff Hague, co-CFO; Slawomir Kownacki, chief tech. officer; Joe Pinheiro, v-p, corp. devel.; Kate Brady, pres., Dominion Media Corp.; Rich Spence, pres., MMC Mortgage Centre Canada Inc.; Geoff Willis, pres. & CEO, Newton Connectivity Systems Inc.; Dustan Woodhouse, pres., Mortgage Architects Inc.

† Lead director

Capital Stock

	Authorized (shs.)	Outstanding (shs.)[1]
Class B Preferred	unlimited	nil
Series 1		26,774,054[2]
Class A Common	unlimited	48,286,091

[1] At May 23, 2023

[2] Classified as debt.

Series 1 Class B Preferred - Non-convertible. Non-voting. Entitled to nominate 40% of the company's directors.

Common - One vote per share.

Normal Course Issuer Bid - The company plans to make normal course purchases of up to 1,000,000 class A common shares representing 2% of the total outstanding. The bid commenced on May 29, 2023, and expires on May 28, 2024.

Major Shareholder - Gary Mauris and Chris Kayat collectively held 37.8% interest and Trevor Bruno held 30.3% interest at Apr. 6, 2023.

Price Range - DLCG/TSX

Year	Volume	High	Low	Close
2022	4,234,017	$4.50	$2.25	$3.20
2021	10,653,566	$4.55	$2.81	$3.75
2020	10,871,455	$3.20	$0.58	$3.07
2019	4,764,885	$1.35	$0.95	$1.30
2018	8,538,285	$2.40	$1.13	$1.25

Recent Close: $1.99

Capital Stock Changes - On Feb. 28, 2022, 1,853,247 class A common shares were issued pursuant to the acquisition of the remaining 30% interest in 10017078 Canada Inc. Also during 2022, class A common shares were issued as follows: 2,078,568 on exercise of warrants and 75,000 on exercise of options; 1,781,790 class A common shares were repurchased under a Substantial Issuer Bid and 230,135 class A common shares were repurchased under a Normal Course Issuer Bid.

Dividends

DLCG cl A Var. Ra pa Q[1]
Listed Feb 3/22.

$0.03	Sept. 15/23	$0.03	June 15/23
$0.03	Mar. 15/23	$0.03	Dec. 15/22

Paid in 2023: $0.09 2022: $0.09 2021: n.a.

[1] Quarterly divd normally payable in Apr/19 has been omitted.

Wholly Owned Subsidiaries

MCC Mortgage Centre Canada Inc., Mississauga, Ont.
Mortgage Architects Inc., Mississauga, Ont.
10017078 Canada Inc., Canada.
- 100% int. in **Newton Connectivity Systems Inc.**, Toronto, Ont.

Subsidiaries

52% int. in **Cape Communications International Inc.**, Kelowna, B.C.

Financial Statistics

Periods ended:	12m Dec. 31/22[A]		12m Dec. 31/21[A]
	$000s	%Chg	$000s
Operating revenue	**70,720**	**-10**	**78,816**
Cost of sales	10,704		9,845
Salaries & benefits	17,586		16,689
General & admin expense	12,163		9,658
Stock-based compensation	(104)		1,107
Operating expense	**40,349**	**+8**	**37,299**
Operating income	**30,371**	**-27**	**41,517**
Deprec., depl. & amort.	3,985		4,130
Finance costs, gross	4,752		33,351
Investment income	817		(99)
Write-downs/write-offs	(4,778)		nil
Pre-tax income	**18,993**	**+292**	**4,845**
Income taxes	6,707		8,788
Net income	**12,286**	**n.a.**	**(3,943)**
Net inc. for equity hldrs	**12,061**	**n.a.**	**(5,508)**
Net inc. for non-cont. int	**225**	**-86**	**1,565**
Cash & equivalent	9,214		20,886
Accounts receivable	14,063		17,990
Current assets	26,558		40,783
Long-term investments	8,025		28,763
Fixed assets, net	241		352
Right-of-use assets	1,961		1,859
Intangibles, net	185,743		181,866
Total assets	**223,937**	**-12**	**253,925**
Accts. pay. & accr. liabs	26,570		46,884
Current liabilities	38,409		64,590
Long-term debt, gross	142,673		154,926
Long-term debt, net	135,978		138,785
Long-term lease liabilities	1,753		1,860
Shareholders' equity	31,958		31,740
Non-controlling interest	231		2,081
Cash from oper. activs	**15,873**	**-59**	**39,061**
Cash from fin. activs	(36,640)		(23,745)
Cash from invest. activs	9,100		(4,759)
Net cash position	**9,214**	**-56**	**20,886**
Capital expenditures	(1)		(134)
Capital disposals	13		28
	$		$
Earnings per share*	0.25		(0.12)
Cash flow per share*	0.33		0.84
Cash divd. per share*	0.09		nil
	shs		shs
No. of shs. o/s*	48,352,731		46,357,841
Avg. no. of shs. o/s*	47,458,420		46,578,984
	%		%
Net profit margin	17.37		(5.00)
Return on equity	37.87		(13.57)
Return on assets	6.43		(12.09)
No. of employees (FTEs)	158		138

* Cl.A Common
[A] Reported in accordance with IFRS

Latest Results

Periods ended:	3m Mar. 31/23[A]		3m Mar. 31/22[A]
	$000s	%Chg	$000s
Operating revenue	11,638	-32	17,029
Net income	(47)	n.a.	(22,490)
Net inc. for equity hldrs	(57)	n.a.	(22,679)
Net inc. for non-cont. int	10		189
	$		$
Earnings per share*	(0.00)		(0.50)

* Cl.A Common
[A] Reported in accordance with IFRS

Historical Summary
(as originally stated)

Fiscal Year	Oper. Rev.	Net Inc. Bef. Disc.	EPS*
	$000s	$000s	$
2022[A]	70,720	12,286	0.25
2021[A]	78,816	(3,943)	(0.12)
2020[A1]	52,413	23,871	0.44
2019[A]	90,322	2,468	(0.09)
2018[A]	133,541	(20,377)	(0.55)

* Cl.A Common
[A] Reported in accordance with IFRS
[1] Results reflect 100% ownership of Dominion Lending Centres Limited Partnership effective Dec. 31, 2020.

D.60 Dominus Acquisitions Corp.

Symbol - DAQ.P **Exchange** - TSX-VEN **CUSIP** - 25756D
Head Office - 1430-800 Pender St W, Vancouver, BC, V6C 2V6
Telephone - (604) 363-0411
Email - kevin@calibrecapital.ca
Investor Relations - Kevin Ma (604) 363-0411
Auditors - Dale Matheson Carr-Hilton LaBonte LLP C.A., Vancouver, B.C.
Transfer Agents - Odyssey Trust Company, Calgary, Alta.
Profile - (B.C. 2020) Capital Pool Company.
Directors - Kevin Ma, pres., CEO, CFO & corp. sec., Vancouver, B.C.; Desmond M. (Des) Balakrishnan, Vancouver, B.C.; Braden (Brady) Fletcher, B.C.; Ali Pejman, B.C.

Capital Stock

	Authorized (shs.)	Outstanding (shs.)[1]
Common	unlimited	9,300,000

[1] At Aug. 31, 2022

Major Shareholder - Desmond M. (Des) Balakrishnan held 10% interest, Kevin Ma held 10% interest and Ali Pejman held 10% interest at Feb. 10, 2022.

Price Range - DAQ.P/TSX-VEN

Year	Volume	High	Low	Close
2022	265,000	$0.12	$0.10	$0.11

Recent Close: $0.12

Capital Stock Changes - On Feb. 10, 2022, an initial public offering of 5,000,000 common shares was completed at 10¢ per share.

D.61 Dorel Industries Inc.*

Symbol - DII.B **Exchange** - TSX **CUSIP** - 25822C
Head Office - 300-1255 av Greene, Westmount, QC, H3Z 2A4
Telephone - (514) 934-3034
Website - www.dorel.com
Email - ir@dorel.com
Investor Relations - Jeffrey Schwartz (514) 934-3034
Auditors - KPMG LLP C.A., Montréal, Qué.
Lawyers - Fasken Martineau DuMoulin LLP, Montréal, Qué.; Schiff Hardin & Waite, Chicago, Ill.
Transfer Agents - Computershare Trust Company of Canada Inc., Toronto, Ont.
FP500 Revenue Ranking - 218
Employees - 4,000 at May 24, 2023
Profile - (Que. 1962) Designs, manufactures and distributes ready-to-assemble furniture and home furnishings, as well as juvenile products and accessories.

Products are distributed through mass merchant discount chains, department stores, club format outlets, hardware/home centres, and Internet retailers consisting of mass merchant sites such as Walmart.com and pure Internet retailers such as Amazon. Operations are carried out through two business segments: Juvenile and Home.

Juvenile

Manufactures and distributes infant car seats, strollers, high chairs, playpens, swings, developmental toys, and infant health and safety aids. This segment operates in North America, Europe, Latin America, Australia, New Zealand, Israel and The People's Republic of China. Products are exported to more than 100 countries around the world.

U.S. operations are carried out through wholly owned **Dorel Juvenile Group, Inc.** (Dorel Juvenile U.S.A.), headquartered in Foxboro, Mass., with facilities in Columbus, Ind., and Ontario, Calif. Canadian operations are headquartered in Toronto, Ont. Principal brand names in North America are Cosco, Safety 1st, Tiny Love and Maxi-Cosi.

Dorel Juvenile Europe's headquarters and major product design facilities are located in Helmond, the Netherlands. Sales operations, and manufacturing and assembly facilities are located in the Netherlands and Portugal, while sales and/or distribution subsidiaries are in France, Italy, Spain, the United Kingdom, Germany, Belgium, Switzerland and Poland. Key brand names in Europe include Maxi-Cosi, BebeConfort, Safety 1st and Tiny Love.

In Latin America, wholly owned **Companhia Dorel Brasil Produtos Infantis** (Dorel Juvenile Brazil) manufactures car seats locally and imports other juvenile products in Brazil, such as strollers, under local brands Infanti and Voyage, as well as the company's international brands such as Safety 1st, Cosco and Maxi-Cosi. Dorel Juvenile Chile distributes juvenile products in Chile, Bolivia, Peru and Argentina under the Infanti brand, and operates close to 83 retail stores in Chile and Peru under the Infanti brand. Dorel Juvenile Chile also sells via company-owned e-commerce websites, to major omni-channel retailers, and into Bolivia, Argentina, Colombia, Panama and other Caribbean countries through local distributors. The company's global brands are also available to customers in Mexico.

In Australia and New Zealand, wholly owned **Dorel Australia Pty Ltd.** (Dorel Juvenile Australia) assembles and distributes products under the global brands, as well as the local brand Mother's Choice.

In Israel, wholly owned **Tiny Love Ltd.** sells developmental toys for babies and toddlers in 80 countries under the Tiny Love brand.

Home

This segment consists of five operating divisions: Ameriwood Home, headquartered in Wright City, Mo., which specializes in both domestically manufactured and imported ready-to-assemble furniture with manufacturing and distribution facilities in Tiffin, Ohio, and Cornwall, Ont.; Cosco Home & Office, located in Columbus, Ind., which specializes in folding furniture, step stools, hand trucks, specialty ladders and outdoor furniture; DHP Furniture, based in Montreal, Que., which manufactures and imports futons, mattresses and bedroom furniture, as well as imports upholstery, kitchen, nursery and dining room furniture; and Dorel Home Europe (Notio Living), based in Denmark with warehouse and locations in the United Kingdom and Denmark, distributes an assortment of imported furniture including bedroom, office, upholstered, audio visual, kitchen, living, and dining room furniture in the U.K. and mainland Europe. Major distribution facilities of Ameriwood Home, Cosco Home & Office and DHP Furniture are located in California, Georgia, Michigan and Quebec. Notio living distributes primarily through e-commerce channels. The company markets its products under generic retail house brand names as well as branded products including Ameriwood, Altra, System Build, Ridgewood, DHP, Dorel Fine Furniture, Dorel Living, Signature Sleep, Cosmo Living, Novagratz, Little Seeds, Queer Eye, Cosco and Alphason.

Recent Merger and Acquisition Activity

Status: completed **Announced:** Oct. 1, 2022
Dorel Industries Inc. completed the sale and leaseback of its Dorel Home ready-to-assemble manufacturing facility in Cornwall, Ont., for US$33,408,000.

Directors - Norman M. Steinberg, co-chr., Côte Saint-Luc, Qué.; Maurice Tousson, co-chr., Toronto, Ont.; Martin Schwartz, pres. & CEO, Westmount, Qué.; Alan Schwartz, exec. v-p, opers., Montréal, Qué.; Jeffrey Schwartz, exec. v-p, CFO & corp. sec., Toronto, Ont.; Jeff A. Segel, exec. v-p, sales & mktg., Westmount, Qué.; Alain S. Benedetti, Sainte-Anne-des-Lacs, Qué.; Brad A. Johnson, Wellesley, Mass.; Sharon M. Ranson, Qué.

Other Exec. Officers - Nicolas Duran, grp. pres. & CEO, Dorel Juvenile; Frank Rana, sr. v-p, fin. & asst. sec.; Edward (Ed) Wyse, sr. v-p, global procurement; Norman Braunstein, CEO, Dorel Home

Capital Stock

	Authorized (shs.)	Outstanding (shs.)[1]
Preferred	unlimited	nil
Class A	unlimited	4,149,085
Class B	unlimited	28,388,532

[1] At May 11, 2023

Preferred - Issuable in series and non-voting.

Class A Multiple Voting - Rank equally with class B subordinate voting shares with respect to dividends and distribution of assets on dissolution. Convertible at any time at the option of the holder into class B subordinate voting shares on a one-for-one basis. Ten votes per share.

Class B Subordinate Voting - Convertible into class A multiple voting shares on a one-for-one basis under certain circumstances if a takeover bid is made for class A multiple voting shares. One vote per share.

Major Shareholder - Martin Schwartz, Alan Schwartz, Jeffrey Schwartz and Jeff Segel, collectively, held 60.18% interest at Apr. 11, 2023.

Price Range - DII.B/TSX

Year	Volume	High	Low	Close
2022	34,009,573	$28.43	$4.39	$5.20
2021	28,688,353	$24.35	$10.37	$20.49
2020	40,253,516	$15.95	$1.25	$14.93
2019	18,738,193	$18.45	$4.65	$5.98
2018	12,119,093	$33.10	$14.70	$17.64

Recent Close: $5.89

Capital Stock Changes - During 2022, class B subordinate voting shares were issued as follows: 98,586 due to settlement of deferred share units and 355 on conversion of a like number of class A multiple voting shares; 69,600 class B subordinate voting shares were repurchased under a Normal Course Issuer Bid.

Dividends

DII.B cl B S.V. N.S.R. [1]
US$12.00◆ Feb. 1/22
Paid in 2023: n.a. 2022: US$12.00◆ 2021: n.a.

DII.A cl A M.V. N.S.R. [1]
US$12.00◆ Feb. 1/22
Paid in 2023: n.a. 2022: US$12.00◆ 2021: n.a.

[1] Quarterly divd normally payable in Jan/20 has been omitted.
◆ Special

Long-Term Debt - Outstanding at Dec. 30, 2022:

Revolv. credit facility[1]	US$208,420,000
Balance of bus. acquisition[2]	5,666,666
Debt financing lease	33,703,000
Other	8,941,000
	256,730,000
Less: Current portion	6,591,000
	250,139,000

[1] Senior secured asset-based facility. Bears interest at various rates averaging 4.16%. Matures on June 11, 2026.

[2] Pertains to remaining balance from US$16,964,000 total consideration on acquisition of Notio Living A/S. Non-interest bearing. Payable in two instalments: US$2,833,000 in February 2023 and US$2,833,000 in February 2024.

Wholly Owned Subsidiaries

AMPA 2P S.A.S., France.
Alphason Designs Limited, United Kingdom.
Ameriwood Home China Co., Ltd., People's Republic of China.
Angel Juvenile Products (Zhongshan) Co., Ltd., People's Republic of China.
BABY ART B.V.B.A., Belgium.
Companhia Dorel Brasil Produtos Infantis, Brazil.
DJGM, S.A. de C.V., Mexico.
DS Canada Limited Partnership, Vancouver, B.C.
Dorel Asia S.r.l., Christ Church, Barbados.
Dorel Australia Pty Ltd., Australia.
Dorel Belgium S.A., Belgium.
Dorel China America, Inc., Del.
Dorel Finance Limited, Barbados.
Dorel France Holding S.A.S., France.
Dorel France S.A.S., Cholet, France.
Dorel Germany GmbH, Frechen, Germany.
Dorel Global (MCO) Limited, Macau, People's Republic of China.
Dorel Hispania S.A., Barcelona, Spain.
Dorel Home Furnishings Europe Limited, United Kingdom.
Dorel Home Furnishings, Inc., Tiffin, Ohio.
Dorel Home Furnishings, Inc., Del.
Dorel Home Furnishings, Inc., Mich.
Dorel International Trade Limited, Barbados.
Dorel Italia S.p.A., Telgate, Italy.
Dorel Juvenile Canada Inc., Canada.
Dorel Juvenile Group, Inc., Foxboro, Mass.
Dorel Juvenile Switzerland S.A., Crissier, Switzerland.
Dorel Limited, Barbados.
Dorel Luxembourg S.A.R.L., Luxembourg.
Dorel Polska Sp z.o.o., Poland.
Dorel Portugal Artigos para bébé Unipessoal, Lda., Arvore, Portugal.
Dorel Sports Luxembourg S.A.R.L., Luxembourg.
Dorel (U.K.) Limited, Borehamwood, Herts., United Kingdom.
IGC Dorel New Zealand Limited, New Zealand.
Loft24 GmbH, Germany.
Maxi Miliaan B.V., Helmond, Netherlands.
Notio Living A/S, Denmark.
Shanghai Dorel Juvenile Product Co., Ltd., People's Republic of China.
Tiny Love Ltd., Tel Aviv, Israel.

Subsidiaries

70% int. in **Best Brands Group S.A.**, Panama.
70% int. in **Comercial e Industrial Silfa S.A.**, Chile.
70% int. in **Comexa Comercializadora Extranjera S.A.**, Panama.
70% int. in **Comexa Distribution Limited**, Barbados.
70% int. in **Dorel Colombian Holdings Limited**, Barbados.
70% int. in **Dorel Sports Chile S.A.**, Chile.
70% int. in **Dorel Sports Peru S.R.L.**, Peru.
70% int. in **Ofir S.A.**, Panama.

Note: The preceding list includes only the major related companies in which interests are held.

Financial Statistics

Periods ended:	12m Dec. 30/22[A]		12m Dec. 30/21[A]
	US$000s	%Chg	US$000s
Operating revenue	**1,570,274**	**-11**	**1,758,705**
Cost of sales	1,325,230		1,426,468
Research & devel. expense	16,701		16,910
General & admin expense	247,420		246,231
Operating expense	**1,589,351**	**-6**	**1,689,609**
Operating income	**(19,077)**	**n.a.**	**69,096**
Deprec., depl. & amort.	71,218		68,694
Finance costs, gross	28,999		38,268
Write-downs/write-offs	(239)		308
Pre-tax income	**(127,978)**	**n.a.**	**(53,540)**
Income taxes	(9,065)		58,295
Net inc. bef. disc. opers	**(118,913)**	**n.a.**	**(111,835)**
Income from disc. opers	254,876		80,211
Net income	**135,963**	**n.a.**	**(31,624)**
Cash & equivalent	32,409		52,166
Inventories	421,478		364,684
Accounts receivable	193,030		258,501
Current assets	681,837		1,527,779
Fixed assets, net	87,350		87,541
Right-of-use assets	142,427		84,077
Intangibles, net	112,292		127,091
Total assets	**1,060,448**	**-43**	**1,851,068**
Bank indebtedness	11,946		3,783
Accts. pay. & accr. liabs	279,620		343,145
Current liabilities	375,084		834,978
Long-term debt, gross	256,730		438,337
Long-term debt, net	250,139		433,836
Long-term lease liabilities	129,601		72,709
Shareholders' equity	281,144		469,000
Cash from oper. activs	**(133,013)**	**n.a.**	**19,819**
Cash from fin. activs	(608,380)		(23,691)
Cash from invest. activs	734,895		14,141
Net cash position	**32,409**	**-38**	**52,166**
Capital expenditures	(19,933)		(28,683)
Capital disposals	106		55,242
Unfunded pension liability	7,327		15,087
	US$		US$
Earns. per sh. bef disc opers*	(3.65)		(3.44)
Earnings per share*	4.18		(0.97)
Cash flow per share*	(4.09)		0.61
Extra divd. - cash*	12.00		...
	shs		shs
No. of shs. o/s*	32,537,617		32,508,631
Avg. no. of shs. o/s*	32,536,991		32,505,967
	%		%
Net profit margin	(7.57)		(6.36)
Return on equity	(31.70)		(23.17)
Return on assets	(6.32)		(1.79)
Foreign sales percent	93		92

* Class A & B
[A] Reported in accordance with IFRS

Latest Results

Periods ended:	3m Mar. 30/23[A]		3m Mar. 31/22[A]
	US$000s	%Chg	US$000s
Operating revenue	333,197	-22	428,035
Net inc. bef. disc. opers	(31,509)	n.a.	(27,218)
Income from disc. opers	nil		261,713
Net income	(31,509)	n.a.	234,495
	US$		US$
Earns. per sh. bef. disc. opers.*	(0.97)		(0.84)
Earnings per share*	(0.97)		7.20

* Class A & B
[A] Reported in accordance with IFRS

Historical Summary
(as originally stated)

Fiscal Year	Oper. Rev.	Net Inc. Bef. Disc.	EPS*
	US$000s	US$000s	US$
2022[A]	1,570,274	(118,913)	(3.65)
2021[A]	1,758,705	(111,835)	(3.44)
2020[A]	2,762,485	(43,403)	(1.34)
2019[A]	2,634,646	(10,453)	(0.32)
2018[A]	2,619,513	(444,343)	(13.70)

* Class A & B
[A] Reported in accordance with IFRS

D.62 Doseology Sciences Inc.

Symbol - MOOD **Exchange** - CSE **CUSIP** - 258484
Head Office - 197-116 5100 Anderson Way, Vernon, BC, V1T 0C4
Telephone - (236) 349-0064
Website - doseology.com
Email - investor@doseology.com
Investor Relations - Shawn Balaghi (236) 349-0064
Auditors - Dale Matheson Carr-Hilton LaBonte LLP C.A., Vancouver, B.C.
Lawyers - TingleMerrett LLP, Calgary, Alta.
Transfer Agents - Endeavor Trust Corporation, Vancouver, B.C.

Profile - (B.C. 2019) Develops, sells and researches psychedelic and non-psychedelic products and compounds, including tinctures and powders, to improve mental health and well-being in Canada and the U.S.

Products include medical mushroom tinctures and powders for focus, mood, energy, immune support and sleep which are sold and marketed through several Canadian retail stores; and online through the company's website, Amazon.ca and Well.ca.

Also has pending licence approval from Health Canada to conduct research and development on psychedelic compounds for scientific purposes, which would permit the laboratory analysis of psilocybin and psilocin from mushrooms, as well as the possession, processing, sale, sending, transportation and delivery of such psychedelic compounds; and plans to open a clinic which offers treatment for mental illness and pain relief using psychedelic compounds in Canada and the U.S.

Effective Mar. 17, 2022, the company's common shares commenced trading on the Frankfurt Stock Exchange under the symbol VU7.

Predecessor Detail - Name changed from Pcybin Therapeutics Inc., Jan. 28, 2020.

Directors - Daniel Vice, co-founder, Milwaukie, Ore.; Shawn Balaghi, interim CEO & interim CFO, Coquitlam, B.C.; Scott M. Reeves, Calgary, Alta.

Other Exec. Officers - Lindsay Hamelin-Vendel, corp. sec.

Capital Stock

	Authorized (shs.)	Outstanding (shs.)[1]
Common	unlimited	41,100,300

[1] At Oct. 28, 2022

Major Shareholder - Shane Gordon held 16.19% interest at Nov. 15, 2021.

Price Range - MOOD/CSE

Year	Volume	High	Low	Close
2022	6,169,820	$0.27	$0.02	$0.04
2021	2,057,303	$0.40	$0.16	$0.18

Recent Close: $0.02

Capital Stock Changes - In November 2021, 5,942,500 units (1 common share & 1 warrant) were issued without further consideration on exchange of subscription receipts sold previously by private placement at 40¢ each. Also during fiscal 2022, 100,300 common shares were issued as finder's fees.

Wholly Owned Subsidiaries

Dose Labs Inc., B.C.

Financial Statistics

Periods ended:	12m June 30/22[A]		12m June 30/21[A]
	$000s	%Chg	$000s
Salaries & benefits	473		75
Research & devel. expense	62		112
General & admin expense	877		1,176
Stock-based compensation	86		20
Other operating expense	31		92
Operating expense	**1,529**	**+4**	**1,474**
Operating income	**(1,529)**	**n.a.**	**(1,474)**
Deprec., depl. & amort.	140		93
Finance income	7		3
Finance costs, gross	76		68
Pre-tax income	**(1,939)**	**n.a.**	**(1,627)**
Net income	**(1,939)**	**n.a.**	**(1,627)**
Cash & equivalent	1,874		3,734
Inventories	10		129
Accounts receivable	85		28
Current assets	2,973		5,002
Fixed assets, net	883		907
Intangibles, net	14		81
Total assets	**3,869**	**-35**	**5,990**
Accts. pay. & accr. liabs	125		417
Current liabilities	219		2,755
Long-term lease liabilities	653		659
Shareholders' equity	2,998		2,577
Cash from oper. activs	**(1,711)**	**n.a.**	**(2,368)**
Cash from fin. activs	(140)		5,787
Cash from invest. activs	(8)		(26)
Net cash position	**1,874**	**-50**	**3,734**
Capital expenditures	(6)		(146)
	$		$
Earnings per share*	(0.05)		(0.06)
Cash flow per share*	(0.04)		(0.08)
	shs		shs
No. of shs. o/s*	41,100,300		35,057,500
Avg. no. of shs. o/s*	39,097,070		27,888,468
	%		%
Net profit margin	n.a.		n.a.
Return on equity	(69.56)		(89.20)
Return on assets	(37.79)		(43.61)

* Common

[A] Reported in accordance with IFRS

Historical Summary
(as originally stated)

Fiscal Year	Oper. Rev.	Net Inc. Bef. Disc.	EPS*
	$000s	$000s	$
2022[A]	nil	(1,939)	(0.05)
2021[A]	nil	(1,627)	(0.06)
2020[A1]	nil	(432)	(0.51)

* Common

[A] Reported in accordance with IFRS

[1] 49 weeks ended June 30, 2020.

D.63 Draganfly Inc.

Symbol - DPRO **Exchange** - CSE **CUSIP** - 26142Q
Head Office - 2108 St. George Ave, Saskatoon, SK, S7M 0K7 **Telephone** - (306) 955-9907 **Toll-free** - (800) 979-9794
Website - www.draganfly.com
Email - paul.sun@draganfly.com
Investor Relations - Paul Sun (800) 979-9794
Auditors - Dale Matheson Carr-Hilton LaBonte LLP C.A., Vancouver, B.C.
Lawyers - DLA Piper (Canada) LLP, Vancouver, B.C.
Transfer Agents - Endeavor Trust Corporation, Vancouver, B.C.
Employees - 55 at Dec. 31, 2022
Profile - (B.C. 2018) Manufactures drones, provides contract engineering and flight services and offers software and artificial intelligence (AI) systems for public safety, agriculture, industrial inspections, and mapping and surveying markets.

Operations are conducted through the following subsidiaries:

Wholly owned **Draganfly Innovations Inc.** and **Draganfly Innovations USA, Inc.** engineer and manufacture commercial UAV (Unmanned Aerial Vehicles), RPAS (Remotely Piloted Aircraft System), UVS (Unmanned Vehicle Systems) and software for public safety, agriculture, industrial inspections, and mapping and surveying markets.

Wholly owned **Dronelogics Systems Inc.** integrates solutions for custom robotics, hardware and software which provides a wide scope of services including sales, training, rentals, maintenance, flying and data processing services.

Also offers products including quad-copters, fixed-wing aircrafts, ground based robots, handheld controllers, flight training and software used for tracking, live streaming, data collection and health monitoring. Services offered include sanitary spraying services to any indoor or outdoor public gathering space such as sports auditoriums and fields. In addition, the company has a health/telehealth platform with an initial focus on COVID-19 screening.

In March 2023, the company expanded its production facility in Burnaby, B.C. to enable the production and manufacturing of UAV (Unmanned Aerial Vehicles) systems and components including Draganfly Heavy Lift and Commander 3XL.

In January 2023, the company entered into a strategic agreement with India-based Remote Sensing Instruments (RSI), a geospatial technology company in India, to develop, manufacture and distribute the company's drones in India. RSI provides geospatial informational data analysis products, services and analytics with a focus on satellite and drone-sourced data in the South Asian markets.

In December 2022, the company launched Draganfly UAS A.I.R. Space, a flight facility which provides a control site for the design, validation and optimization of standard operating procedures, sensor selection and data collection techniques, in Spring Branch, Tex. In addition, the facility would enable remote sensor testing from drones for various mines and other unexploded ordinances on and below the surface.

Predecessor Detail - Name changed from Drone Acquisition Corp., Aug. 15, 2019, pursuant reverse takeover acquisition of Draganfly Innovations Inc.

Directors - Cameron Chell, co-founder, pres. & CEO, Bowen Island, B.C.; John M. Mitnick, chr., Va.; Scott Larson†, Burnaby, B.C.; Olen Aasen, Vancouver, B.C.; Andrew Hill (Andy) Card Jr., N.H.; Denis G. Silva, Burnaby, B.C.; Julie M. Wood, Va.

Other Exec. Officers - Paul Mullen, COO; Paul Sun, CFO & corp. sec.; Deborah R. Greenberg, chief legal officer & corp. services officer

† Lead director

Capital Stock

	Authorized (shs.)	Outstanding (shs.)[1]
Common	unlimited	43,147,965

[1] At May 9, 2023

Major Shareholder - Widely held at May 9, 2023.

Price Range - DPRO/CSE

Year	Volume	High	Low	Close
2022	7,329,712	$4.80	$0.65	$1.00
2021	24,738,063	$21.25	$2.05	$2.08
2020	8,532,659	$5.75	$2.00	$4.05
2019	582,558	$4.45	$2.50	$3.10

Consolidation: 1-for-5 cons. in July 2021
Recent Close: $1.22

Capital Stock Changes - In March 2023, public offering of 8,000,000 common shares was completed at US$1.00 per share.

During 2022, common shares were issued as follows: 1,072,595 on vesting of restricted share units, 16,538 on exercise of warrants and 12,500 on exercise of options.

Wholly Owned Subsidiaries

Draganfly Innovations Inc., Saskatoon, Sask.
Draganfly Innovations USA, Inc., Del.
Dronelogics Systems Inc., Vancouver, B.C.

Financial Statistics

Periods ended:	12m Dec. 31/22[A]		12m Dec. 31/21[A]
	$000s	%Chg	$000s
Operating revenue	**7,605**	**+8**	**7,054**
Cost of sales	6,814		4,411
Salaries & benefits	6,105		2,768
Research & devel. expense	651		511
General & admin expense	16,861		14,379
Stock-based compensation	3,311		3,953
Operating expense	**33,742**	**+30**	**26,021**
Operating income	**(26,137)**	**n.a.**	**(18,966)**
Deprec., depl. & amort.	773		311
Finance costs, net	44		5
Write-downs/write-offs	(226)		nil
Pre-tax income	**(27,654)**	**n.a.**	**(16,203)**
Net income	**(27,654)**	**n.a.**	**(16,203)**
Cash & equivalent	7,895		23,076
Inventories	1,056		3,391
Accounts receivable	2,089		1,407
Current assets	13,517		33,559
Long-term investments	193		291
Fixed assets, net	405		297
Right-of-use assets	345		468
Intangibles, net	180		6,534
Total assets	**14,639**	**-65**	**42,113**
Accts. pay. & accr. liabs	2,817		799
Current liabilities	3,348		6,722
Long-term debt, gross	87		93
Long-term debt, net	5		87
Long-term lease liabilities	245		379
Shareholders' equity	11,041		34,926
Cash from oper. activs	**(16,349)**	**n.a.**	**(22,005)**
Cash from fin. activs	(48)		46,267
Cash from invest. activs	769		(3,306)
Net cash position	**7,895**	**-66**	**23,076**
Capital expenditures	(80)		(213)
	$		$
Earnings per share*	(0.82)		(0.61)
Cash flow per share*	(0.49)		(0.79)
	shs		shs
No. of shs. o/s*	34,270,579		33,168,946
Avg. no. of shs. o/s*	33,556,969		27,787,348
	%		%
Net profit margin	(363.63)		(229.70)
Return on equity	(120.32)		(83.58)
Return on assets	(97.46)		(65.85)
No. of employees (FTEs)	55		44

* Common

[A] Reported in accordance with IFRS

Latest Results

Periods ended:	3m Mar. 31/23[A]		3m Mar. 31/22[A]
	$000s	%Chg	$000s
Operating revenue	1,601	-22	2,045
Net income	(7,068)	n.a.	(6,204)
	$		$
Earnings per share*	(0.20)		(0.19)

* Common

[A] Reported in accordance with IFRS

Historical Summary
(as originally stated)

Fiscal Year	Oper. Rev.	Net Inc. Bef. Disc.	EPS*
	$000s	$000s	$
2022[A]	7,605	(27,654)	(0.82)
2021[A]	7,054	(16,203)	(0.61)
2020[A]	4,364	(8,016)	(0.50)
2019[A1]	1,380	(11,095)	(1.15)
2018[A]	1,387	(602)	(0.15)

* Common

[A] Reported in accordance with IFRS

[1] Results prior to Aug. 15, 2019, pertain to and reflect the reverse takeover acquisition of Draganfly Innovations Inc.

Note: Adjusted throughout for 1-for-5 cons. in July 2021

D.64 Draxos Capital Corp.

Symbol - DRAX.P **Exchange** - TSX-VEN **CUSIP** - 26150W
Head Office - 2200-145 King St W, Toronto, ON, M5H 4G2 **Telephone** - (416) 504-5805
Email - gprekupec@dipchand.com
Investor Relations - Gregory M. Prekupec (416) 504-5805
Auditors - Segal GCSE LLP C.A., Toronto, Ont.
Lawyers - Minden Gross LLP, Toronto, Ont.
Transfer Agents - Odyssey Trust Company, Calgary, Alta.
Profile - (Ont. 2021) Capital Pool Company.
Directors - Gregory M. Prekupec, CEO, Ont.; Jason Atkinson, corp. sec., Ont.; Robert W. C. Becher, Caledon, Ont.; William A. (Bill) Kanters, Calgary, Alta.

Other Exec. Officers - Ronald (Ron) Love, CFO

Capital Stock

	Authorized (shs.)	Outstanding (shs.)[1]
Common	unlimited	3,233,470

[1] At May 29, 2023

Major Shareholder - Jason Atkinson held 10.3% interest, Robert W. C. Becher held 10.3% interest, William A. (Bill) Kanters held 10.3% interest and Gregory M. Prekupec held 10.3% interest at Feb. 24, 2022.

Price Range - DRAX.P/TSX-VEN

Year	Volume	High	Low	Close
2022............	52,500	$0.30	$0.14	$0.20

Recent Close: $0.12

Capital Stock Changes - On Feb. 24, 2022, an initial public offering of 1,500,000 common shares was completed at 15¢ per share.

D.65 Dream Impact Trust

Symbol - MPCT.UN **Exchange** - TSX **CUSIP** - 26154L
Head Office - 301-30 Adelaide St E, Toronto, ON, M5C 3H1 **Telephone** - (416) 365-3535 **Fax** - (416) 365-6565
Website - www.dreamimpacttrust.ca
Email - klefever@dream.ca
Investor Relations - Kimberly Lefever (877) 365-3535
Auditors - PricewaterhouseCoopers LLP C.A., Toronto, Ont.
Lawyers - Osler, Hoskin & Harcourt LLP, Toronto, Ont.
Transfer Agents - Computershare Trust Company of Canada Inc., Toronto, Ont.
Managers - DREAM Asset Management Corporation, Toronto, Ont.
Profile - (Can. 2014) Invests in real estate assets that generate strong financial returns and provide positive social and environmental impacts.

Real estate assets are reported under two segments: Recurring Income, and Development and Investment Holdings.

Recurring Income - Includes a portfolio of 17 income-producing office and commercial properties, totaling 1,400,000 sq. ft. of gross leasable area, as well as 14 multi-family rental properties, totaling 1,592 units, located in the Greater Toronto Area (GTA) and Ottawa, Ont., and Gatineau, Que.; the District Energy System, also known as Zibi Community Utility, which provides heating, cooling and domestic hot water for the Zibi community in Ottawa/Gatineau; and a lending portfolio consisting of loans secured by various types of residential and commercial real estate properties.

Development and Investment Holdings - Consists of investments in residential and mixed-use development projects in the GTA, downtown Toronto and Ottawa/Gatineau; 10% interest in Virgin Hotels Las Vegas, a hotel and casino resort in Las Vegas, Nev.; and development loans secured by two residential projects (Empire Lakeshore and Empire Brampton) in the GTA. Primary development projects include Zibi, a 34-acre mixed-use waterfront community situated along the Ottawa River in Ottawa and Gatineau, which would include 1,900 residential units, more than 2,000,000 sq. ft. of commercial space and eight acres of riverfront parks and plazas; West Don Lands, a purpose-built, multi-family rental apartment community in Toronto, expected to include more than 2,000 rental units as well as ancillary retail and office components; Dream LeBreton, the first phase of the Building LeBreton project in Ottawa, Ont., which would consist of two residential buildings with a total of 608 rental units; Canary Block 10, a mixed-use project in the Canary District of downtown Toronto, which is being developed in partnership with Anishnawbe Health Toronto (AHT) and would include a 238-unit multi-family rental building, a 206-unit condominium and a purpose-built five-storey Indigenous Hub; and Brightwater, a 72-acre mixed-used waterfront community being developed on the site of a former oil refinery in Port Credit, Ont., which would include 3,000 residential units, more than 350,000 sq. ft. of retail and commercial space and 18 acres of parks and green space.

In March 2022, the trust acquired a 3% interest in 673 Warden, a 30,000-sq.-ft. commercial building in Scarborough, Ont., for an undisclosed amount.

Recent Merger and Acquisition Activity

Status: completed **Revised:** Mar. 1, 2023
UPDATE: Dream Impact Fund, Dream Impact Trust and Great Gulf Group completed the acquisition of phase one of Quayside, consisting of 4.5 acres. PREVIOUS: Dream Impact Fund LP (37.5%), Dream Impact Trust (12.5%) and Great Gulf Group of Companies Inc. (50%) agreed to acquire Quayside, a 12-acre waterfront development site in downtown Toronto, Ont., for an undisclosed amount. Upon full build-out, Quayside was expected to provide more than 4,000 residential units and 3.5 acres of public green space.

Status: completed **Announced:** Sept. 29, 2022
Dream Impact Trust acquired four office properties as part of the Berkeley land assembly in Toronto, Ont., for $11,300,000.

Status: completed **Announced:** July 11, 2022
Dream Impact Trust and Dream Impact Fund LP each acquired a 50% interest in 70 Park, a 210-unit multi-family rental building in Mississauga, Ont., including an adjacent land. Total purchase price was $105,500,000, of which $25,000,000 was allocated to the land slated for redevelopment on the site.

Status: completed **Announced:** June 28, 2022
Dream Impact Trust and Dream Impact Fund LP each acquired a 50% interest in 111 Cosburn, a 23-unit multi-family rental building in Toronto, Ont., for $8,200,000.

Status: completed **Announced:** Apr. 29, 2022
DREAM Unlimited Corp. (33.33%) and Dream Impact Trust (33.33%), together with Dream Impact Fund LP (33.33%), acquired Dream LeBreton, a 2.7-acre development land which would serve as the site of the first phase of the Building LeBreton project in Ottawa, Ont. Dream LeBreton was expected to have 600 rental housing units. Terms were not disclosed.

Status: completed **Announced:** Mar. 15, 2022
DREAM Unlimited Corp. (33.33%) and Dream Impact Trust (33.33%), together with Dream Impact Fund LP (33.33%), acquired 177 St. George Street, a 57-unit apartment building in Toronto, Ont., for $22,500,000.

Predecessor Detail - Name changed from Dream Hard Asset Alternatives Trust, Oct. 26, 2020.
Trustees - Amar Bhalla, chr., Toronto, Ont.; Dr. Catherine Brownstein, Brookline, Mass.; Robert G. (Rob) Goodall, Toronto, Ont.; Jennifer (Jen) Lee Koss, Toronto, Ont.; Karine L. MacIndoe, Toronto, Ont.
Oper. Subsid./Mgt. Co. Officers - Meaghan Peloso, CFO

Capital Stock

	Authorized (shs.)	Outstanding (shs.)[1]
Preferred Unit	unlimited	nil
Special Trust Unit	unlimited	nil
Trust Unit	unlimited	17,134,554

[1] At June 20, 2023

Normal Course Issuer Bid - The company plans to make normal course purchases of up to 4,648,812 trust units representing 10% of the public float. The bid commenced on Feb. 1, 2023, and expires on Jan. 31, 2024.

Major Shareholder - DREAM Unlimited Corp. held 32% interest at May 9, 2023.

Price Range - MPCT.UN/TSX

Year	Volume	High	Low	Close
2022............	3,231,928	$25.40	$15.32	$16.12
2021............	2,643,772	$27.72	$22.60	$24.60
2020............	4,889,961	$31.76	$15.08	$24.12
2019............	2,570,811	$31.40	$24.20	$31.00
2018............	2,543,003	$28.36	$23.60	$24.96

Consolidation: 1-for-4 cons. in June 2023
Recent Close: $9.53

Capital Stock Changes - On June 20, 2023, trust units were consolidated on a 1-for-4 basis.

During 2022, trust units were issued as follows: 1,517,828 in settlement of asset management fees, 563,382 under distribution reinvestment plan and 82,642 on exchange of deferred units; 193,100 trust units were repurchased under a Normal Course Issuer Bid.

Dividends

MPCT.UN unit Ra $0.64 pa M est. Mar. 15, 2023**
1-for-4 cons eff. June 20, 2023
Prev. Rate: $0.40 est. Aug. 15, 2014
** Reinvestment Option

Subsidiaries

99.99% int. in **Dream Impact Master LP**, Toronto, Ont.

Financial Statistics

Periods ended:	12m Dec. 31/22[A]		12m Dec. 31/21[oA]
	$000s	%Chg	$000s
Total revenue..............................	**27,300**	**-5**	**28,625**
Salaries & benefits..........................	3,316		4,064
General & admin. expense..............	9,204		9,155
Other operating expense.................	7,235		6,690
Operating expense.........................	**19,755**	**-1**	**19,909**
Operating income..........................	**7,545**	**-13**	**8,716**
Provision for loan losses..................	nil		1,465
Finance costs, gross........................	9,286		4,680
Pre-tax income..............................	**(45,997)**	**n.a.**	**20,249**
Income taxes....................................	(2,443)		(1,201)
Net income....................................	**(43,554)**	**n.a.**	**21,450**
Cash & equivalent............................	2,244		8,431
Accounts receivable.........................	3,353		1,834
Current assets..................................	14,607		20,103
Long-term investments....................	401,852		401,303
Properties...	303,855		276,285
Total assets...................................	**724,169**	**+3**	**701,702**
Accts. pay. & accr. liabs..................	9,047		11,413
Current liabilities.............................	78,429		93,720
Long-term debt, gross......................	220,889		133,150
Long-term debt, net.........................	159,189		55,748
Shareholders' equity.........................	478,732		536,931
Cash from oper. activs..................	**(7,424)**	**n.a.**	**15,425**
Cash from fin. activs.........................	61,950		11,205
Cash from invest. activs....................	(60,713)		(128,870)
Net cash position...........................	**2,244**	**-73**	**8,431**
Capital expenditures.........................	(16,624)		(36,784)
	$		$
Earnings per share*.........................	(2.64)		1.32
Cash flow per share*........................	(0.45)		0.95
Net asset value per share*...............	33.00		37.24
Cash divd. per share*......................	1.60		1.60
	shs		shs
No. of shs. o/s*................................	16,760,629		16,267,941
Avg. no. of shs. o/s*.........................	16,479,235		16,249,149
	%		%
Net profit margin.............................	(159.54)		74.93
Return on equity..............................	(8.58)		3.98
Return on assets..............................	(4.88)		3.91

* Trust Unit
[o] Restated
[A] Reported in accordance with IFRS

Latest Results

Periods ended:	3m Mar. 31/23[A]		3m Mar. 31/22[oA]
	$000s	%Chg	$000s
Total revenue..................................	4,053	-49	8,008
Net income.......................................	(3,357)	n.a.	349
	$		$
Earnings per share*.........................	(0.20)		0.04

* Trust Unit
[o] Restated
[A] Reported in accordance with IFRS

Historical Summary
(as originally stated)

Fiscal Year	Total Rev. $000s	Net Inc. Bef. Disc. $000s	EPS* $
2022[A]....................	27,300	(43,554)	(2.64)
2021[A]....................	22,153	21,450	1.32
2020[A]....................	33,892	16,339	0.96
2019[A]....................	56,766	27,977	1.67
2018[A]....................	60,462	13,902	0.73

* Trust Unit
[A] Reported in accordance with IFRS
Note: Adjusted throughout for 1-for-4 cons. in June 2023

D.66 Dream Industrial Real Estate Investment Trust*

Symbol - DIR.UN **Exchange** - TSX **CUSIP** - 26153W
Head Office - State Street Financial Centre, 301-30 Adelaide St E, Toronto, ON, M5C 3H1 **Telephone** - (416) 365-3535 **Toll-free** - (877) 365-3535 **Fax** - (416) 365-6565
Website - www.dream.ca/investors/industrial/
Email - lquan@dream.ca
Investor Relations - Lenis W. Quan (416) 365-2353
Auditors - PricewaterhouseCoopers LLP C.A., Toronto, Ont.
Lawyers - Osler, Hoskin & Harcourt LLP, Toronto, Ont.
Transfer Agents - Computershare Trust Company of Canada Inc., Toronto, Ont.
FP500 Revenue Ranking - 527
Employees - 108 at Dec. 31, 2022
Profile - (Ont. 2012) Owns, manages and operates industrial properties in key markets across Canada, Europe and the U.S. At June 30, 2023, the trust co-owned and managed 321 assets (536 industrial buildings)

totaling 70,305,000 sq. ft., including 10% interest in **Dream Summit Industrial LP**.

DREAM Asset Management Corporation, a wholly owned subsidiary of **DREAM Unlimited Corp.**, provides asset management services to the trust and wholly owned **Dream Industrial Management LP** is the trust's property manager.

Geographic breakdown at June 30, 2023:

	Assets[1,2]	Bldg.[1]	Area[3]
Western Canada	42	80	5,069,000
Ontario	65	103	9,065,000
Quebec	35	48	6,128,000
Europe	90	102	17,390,000
U.S.	24	38	9,726,000
Dream Summit Ind. LP	65	165	22,927,000
	321	536	70,305,000

[1] Includes owned and managed properties and excludes assets held for sale.

[2] Consists of a building, or a cluster of buildings in close proximity to one another, attracting similar tenants.

[3] Owned and managed gross leasable area (sq. ft.).

Building type breakdown at June 30, 2023:

Buildings type	Assets[1]	Bldg.
Distribution	191	300
Urban logistics	92	178
Light industrial	38	58
	321	536

[1] Consists of a building, or a cluster of buildings in close proximity to one another, attracting similar tenants.

In May 2023, bought deal secondary offering of 12,500,000 trust units of the trust by selling shareholder **Dream Office Real Estate Investment Trust** at $14.20 per unit was completed. On closing, Dream Office REIT held 4.9% of the issued and outstanding voting units of the trust (previously 9.4%).

In March 2023, the trust sold a 35,000-sq.-ft. industrial property in Hilversum, Netherlands, for $3,801,000.

In February 2023, the trust acquired Rail Spur Land, a 0.35-acre parcel of land adjacent to an owned property in Edmonton, Alta., for $150,000.

In December 2022, the trust sold a 41,000-sq.-ft. industrial property in Renswoude, Netherlands, for $3,976,000, and a 12,000-sq.-ft. industrial property in Hoorn, Netherlands, for $1,446,000.

Recent Merger and Acquisition Activity

Status: completed **Revised:** Feb. 17, 2023
UPDATE: The transaction was completed. GIC and DIR have formed a limited partnership, Dream Summit Industrial LP, with an ownership structure of 90% and 10%, respectively. PREVIOUS: A joint venture between GIC Pte. Ltd., Singapore's sovereign wealth fund, and Dream Industrial Real Estate Investment Trust (DIR) agreed to acquire Summit Industrial Income REIT for $5.9 billion in cash, including assumption of debt. Summit unitholders would receive $23.50 per unit in cash by way of a special distribution and a redemption of units. The joint venture would be a limited partnership owned 10% by DIR and 90% by GIC. A subsidiary of Dream Asset Management Corporation would be the asset manager for the joint venture and DIR's interest in the joint venture. Upon closing, DIR would manage 69,000,000 sq. ft. across Canada, the U.S. and Europe, including 32,000,000 sq. ft. on behalf of its institutional clients in North America. GIC and DIR have also agreed to pursue additional acquisition opportunities in major industrial markets in Canada. Summit owns 160 industrial properties in Canada totaling nearly 21,600,000 sq. ft. The transaction was expected to close in the first quarter of 2023. Dec. 14, 2022 - Summit's unitholders approved the transaction. Dec. 20, 2022 - Court approval was received. Feb. 7, 2023 - Summit announced the receipt of approval under the Investment Canada Act. The transaction was expected to close on Feb. 17, 2023.

Status: completed **Announced:** Oct. 20, 2022
Dream Industrial Real Estate Investment Trust acquired a 217,000-sq.-ft. industrial property in Etobicoke, Ont., for $66,500,000.

Status: completed **Announced:** Aug. 13, 2022
Dream Industrial Real Estate Investment Trust acquired a 63,000-sq.-ft. single-tenant distribution facility in Burkau, Germany, for $13,920,000.

Status: completed **Revised:** July 20, 2022
UPDATE: The transaction was completed. PREVIOUS: Dream Industrial Real Estate Investment Trust agreed to acquire a 213,000-sq.-ft. single-tenant distribution facility in Gütersloh, Germany, for €17,500,000.

Status: completed **Announced:** June 21, 2022
Dream Industrial Real Estate Investment Trust acquired an 81,000-sq.-ft. industrial property in Burlington, Ont., for $26,900,000.

Status: completed **Announced:** June 17, 2022
Dream Industrial Real Estate Investment Trust acquired a 25,000-sq.-ft. industrial property in Cambridge, Ont., for $5,400,000.

Status: completed **Announced:** June 9, 2022
Dream Industrial Real Estate Investment Trust acquired a 106,000-sq.-ft. industrial property in Bemmel, Netherlands, for $36,401,000.

Status: completed **Revised:** June 2, 2022
UPDATE: The transaction was completed. PREVIOUS: Dream Industrial Real Estate Investment Trust agreed to acquire a 119,000-sq.-ft. single-tenant logistics facility in Burgbernheim, Germany, for €19,000,000. The facility is being acquired through a sale-leaseback transaction and includes 3.2 acres of excess land.

Status: completed **Announced:** June 1, 2022
Dream Industrial Real Estate Investment Trust acquired a 43,000-sq.-ft. industrial property in Montreal, Que., for $9,910,000.

Status: completed **Revised:** June 1, 2022
UPDATE: The transaction was completed. PREVIOUS: Dream Industrial Real Estate Investment Trust agreed to acquire a 472,000-sq.-ft. single-tenant logistics facility in Minden, Germany, for €48,500,000.

Status: completed **Announced:** May 24, 2022
Dream Industrial Real Estate Investment Trust acquired a 90,000-sq.-ft. industrial property in Richmond Hill, Ont., for $25,850,000.

Status: completed **Announced:** May 20, 2022
Dream Industrial Real Estate Investment Trust acquired a 189,000-sq.-ft. industrial property in Triptis, Germany, for $14,693,000.

Status: completed **Announced:** May 19, 2022
Dream Industrial Real Estate Investment Trust acquired a 105,000-sq.-ft. industrial property in Houten, Netherlands, for $19,238,000.

Status: completed **Announced:** May 17, 2022
Dream Industrial Real Estate Investment Trust acquired a 29,000-sq.-ft. industrial property in Kitchener, Ont., for $6,250,000.

Status: completed **Announced:** Apr. 28, 2022
Dream Industrial Real Estate Investment Trust sold two parcels of development land, the 30-acre Brampton East Lands site in Brampton, Ont., and the 28-acre Maple Grove Road site in Cambridge, Ont., for $70,500,000 and $27,500,000, respectively. The properties were sold to a newly formed joint venture (JV), owned 25% by Dream with the remaining 75% interest held by a global sovereign wealth fund. The JV was formed to buy well-located development sites in the Greater Toronto Area and other select markets within the Greater Golden Horseshoe Area to build industrial assets with the intention to hold the properties following stabilization.

Status: completed **Announced:** Apr. 28, 2022
Dream Industrial Real Estate Investment Trust acquired an 86,000-sq.-ft. industrial property in Richmond Hill, Ont., for $30,000,000.

Status: completed **Announced:** Apr. 26, 2022
Dream Industrial Real Estate Investment Trust acquired a 137,000-sq.-ft. industrial property in Cambridge, Ont., for $31,800,000.

Status: completed **Announced:** Apr. 20, 2022
Dream Industrial Real Estate Investment Trust acquired a 56,000-sq.-ft. industrial property in Düsseldorf, Germany, for $6,170,000.

Status: completed **Announced:** Apr. 19, 2022
Dream Industrial Real Estate Investment Trust acquired a 141,000-sq.-ft. industrial property in De Lier, Netherlands, for $30,793,000.

Status: completed **Announced:** Apr. 8, 2022
Dream Industrial Real Estate Investment Trust acquired Cross Roads Commercial, a 19.5-acre development land in Balzac, Alta., for $12,000,000.

Status: completed **Announced:** Mar. 31, 2022
Dream Industrial Real Estate Investment Trust acquired a 94,000-sq.-ft. industrial property in Burlington, Ont., for $17,900,000.

Status: completed **Announced:** Mar. 24, 2022
Dream Industrial Real Estate Investment Trust acquired a 147,000-sq.-ft. single-tenant logistics facility in Wijchen, Netherlands, for €19,200,000.

Status: completed **Announced:** Mar. 16, 2022
Dream Industrial Real Estate Investment Trust acquired a 128,000-sq.-ft. single-tenant distribution facility in Bodegraven, Netherlands, for €26,000,000. The acquisition included an adjacent 2.5-acre development-ready site.

Predecessor Detail - Name changed from Dundee Industrial Real Estate Investment Trust, May 8, 2014.

Trustees - Vincenza Sera, chr., Toronto, Ont.; Brian D. Pauls, CEO, Denver, Colo.; Dr. R. Sacha Bhatia, Toronto, Ont.; Michael J. Cooper, Toronto, Ont.; J. Michael (Mike) Knowlton, Toronto, Ont.; Ben Mulroney, Toronto, Ont.; Vicky L. Schiff, Los Angeles, Calif.; Jennifer Scoffield, Mississauga, Ont.

Other Exec. Officers - Alexander Sannikov, pres. & COO; Lenis W. Quan, CFO; Joe Iadeluca, sr. v-p, portfolio mgt., Que. & eastern Canada; Bruce Traversy, sr. v-p & head, invests.

Capital Stock

	Authorized (shs.)	Outstanding (shs.)[1]
Preferred Unit	unlimited	nil
Trust Unit	unlimited	267,601,816
Special Trust Unit	unlimited	13,346,572
Class B LP Unit	unlimited	13,346,572[2 3]

[1] At July 31, 2023

[2] Classified as debt.

[3] Securities of subsidiary Dream Industrial LP.

Trust Unit - Entitled to monthly cash distributions of $0.05833 per unit. One vote per trust unit.

Special Trust Unit - Issued to holders of class B limited partnership units of wholly owned Dream Industrial LP. Each special voting unit entitles the holder to a number of votes at unitholder meetings equal to the number of trust units into which the class B limited partnership units are exchangeable.

Major Shareholder - Widely held at Apr. 14, 2023.

Price Range - DIR.UN/TSX

Year	Volume	High	Low	Close
2022	186,859,482	$17.40	$10.25	$11.69
2021	144,153,013	$17.60	$12.61	$17.22
2020	135,449,059	$14.31	$6.89	$13.15
2019	110,506,031	$14.13	$9.32	$13.14
2018	58,018,552	$10.98	$8.79	$9.52

Recent Close: $13.56

Capital Stock Changes - In March 2022, bought deal public offering of 14,110,500 trust units was completed at $16.30 per unit, including 1,840,500 trust units on exercise of over-allotment option. Also during 2022, trust units were issued as follows: 5,477,800 under at-the-market equity program, 3,025,530 under distribution reinvestment plan, 123,449 for vested deferred trust units and 2,083 under unit purchase plan.

Dividends

DIR.UN unit Ra $0.70 pa M est. May 15, 2013**
** Reinvestment Option

Long-Term Debt - Outstanding at Dec. 31, 2022:

Revolving credit facility[1]	$50,742,000
U.S. term loan	338,057,000
Mtges.	529,600,000
Unsecured debs.[2]	1,494,549,000
Subsidiary redeemable units	216,871,000
	2,629,819,000
Less: Current portion	275,536,000
	2,354,283,000

[1] Consists of $500,000,000 unsecured revolving credit facility maturing Jan. 31, 2026. Net of unamortized financing costs and unamortized fair value adjustments.

[2] Consists of $200,000,000 principal amount of 1.662% series A debentures due Dec. 22, 2025, $200,000,000 principal amount of three-month CDOR plus 0.35% series B debentures due June 17, 2024, $400,000,000 principal amount of 2.057% series C debentures due June 17, 2027, $250,000,000 principal amount of 2.539% series D debentures due Dec. 7, 2026, and $200,000,000 principal amount of 3.968% series E debentures due Apr. 13, 2026.

Subsidiary Redeemable Units - Class B limited partnership units of Dream Industrial LP, of which there were 18,551,855 outstanding at Dec. 31, 2022. Together with the accompanying special trust units, the subsidiary redeemable units have economic and voting rights equivalent to the trust units. Entitled to a distribution equal to distributions declared on trust units. May be surrendered or indirectly exchanged on a 1-for-1 basis at the option of the holder, subject to certain restrictions, for trust units.

Minimum principal debt repayments were reported as follows:

2023	$271,168,000
2024	307,277,000
2025	846,470,000
2026	501,801,000
2027	400,000,000
2028-2030	69,118,000

Note - In March 2023, private placement of $200,000,000 principal amount of 5.383% series F senior unsecured debentures due Mar. 22, 2028, was completed.

Wholly Owned Subsidiaries

Dream Industrial LP, Ont.
- 100% int. in **Dream Industrial International Sub-Trust**
  - 100% int. in **Dream Industrial International Europe Inc.**
    - 0.1% int. in **Dream Industrial Europe Advisors Cooperatieve U.A.**, Netherlands.
  - 100% int. in **Dream Industrial International Holdings LP**
    - 99.9% int. in **Dream Industrial Europe Advisors Cooperatieve U.A.**, Netherlands.
- 100% int. in **Dream Industrial Management LP**, Ont.
  - 100% int. in **Dream Industrial Management Corp.**, Ont.
- 100% int. in **Dream Industrial US Holdings Inc.**, Del.
  - 100% int. in **Dream Industrial 2017 USHoldings LLC**, Del.

Dream Industrial Property Management Trust, Ont.

Investments

10% int. in **Dream Summit Industrial LP**, Ont.
- 100% int. in **Summit Industrial Income REIT**, Markham, Ont.

Financial Statistics

Periods ended:	12m Dec. 31/22^A		12m Dec. 31/21^oA
	$000s	%Chg	$000s
Total revenue	**369,567**	**+28**	**289,815**
Rental operating expense	87,980		71,916
General & admin. expense	30,264		22,807
Operating expense	**118,244**	**+25**	**94,723**
Operating income	**251,323**	**+29**	**195,092**
Investment income	38,482		39,270
Finance income	674		2,587
Finance costs, gross	33,865		69,375
Pre-tax income	**725,366**	**+14**	**638,602**
Income taxes	19,481		30,257
Net income	**705,885**	**+16**	**608,345**
Cash & equivalent	83,802		164,015
Accounts receivable	27,673		7,857
Current assets	115,525		176,739
Long-term investments	313,527		139,355
Income-producing props	6,652,838		5,618,966
Properties for future devel	106,587		77,641
Property interests, net	6,759,425		5,696,607
Total assets	**7,280,493**	**+20**	**6,053,566**
Accts. pay. & accr. liabs	73,816		82,101
Current liabilities	368,823		134,845
Long-term debt, gross	2,629,819		2,364,459
Long-term debt, net	2,354,283		2,326,110
Shareholders' equity	4,452,741		3,499,423
Cash from oper. activs	**218,394**	**+25**	**174,391**
Cash from fin. activs	487,953		(1,764,496)
Cash from invest. activs	(780,358)		1,503,005
Net cash position	**83,802**	**-49**	**164,015**
Capital expenditures	(147,615)		(45,964)
Increase in property	(615,438)		(1,986,202)
Decrease in property	73,578		281,983
	$		$
Earnings per share*	n.a.		n.a.
Cash flow per share*	0.85		0.75
Funds from opers. per sh.*	0.89		0.81
Cash divd. per share*	0.70		0.70
Total divd. per share*	**0.70**		**0.70**
	shs		shs
No. of shs. o/s*	256,604,207		233,864,845
	%		%
Net profit margin	191.00		209.91
Return on equity	17.75		22.51
Return on assets	11.08		14.09
No. of employees (FTEs)	108		94

* Trust Unit
[o] Restated
[A] Reported in accordance with IFRS

Latest Results

Periods ended:	6m June 30/23^A		6m June 30/22^A
	$000s	%Chg	$000s
Total revenue	217,283	+22	177,387
Net income	62,622	-90	614,369
	$		$
Earnings per share*	n.a.		n.a.

[A] Reported in accordance with IFRS

Historical Summary
(as originally stated)

Fiscal Year	Total Rev. $000s	Net Inc. Bef. Disc. $000s	EPS* $
2022^A	369,567	705,885	n.a.
2021^A	289,815	608,345	n.a.
2020^A	235,946	200,155	n.a.
2019^A	195,331	176,773	n.a.
2018^A	193,548	157,528	n.a.

* Trust Unit
[A] Reported in accordance with IFRS

D.67 Dream Office Real Estate Investment Trust*

Symbol - D.UN **Exchange** - TSX **CUSIP** - 26153P
Head Office - State Street Financial Centre, 301-30 Adelaide St E, Toronto, ON, M5C 3H1 **Telephone** - (416) 365-3535 **Fax** - (416) 365-6565
Website - www.dream.ca
Email - jjiang@dream.ca
Investor Relations - Jay Jiang (877) 365-3535
Auditors - PricewaterhouseCoopers LLP C.A., Toronto, Ont.
Lawyers - Osler, Hoskin & Harcourt LLP, Toronto, Ont.
Transfer Agents - Computershare Trust Company of Canada Inc., Toronto, Ont.
FP500 Revenue Ranking - 660
Employees - 256 at Dec. 31, 2022
Profile - (Ont. 2003) Owns central business district office properties primarily in downtown Toronto, Ont.

The trust provides property management services to its tenants and other businesses through subsidiary **Dream Office Management LP**.

The trust's property portfolio consists of ownership interests in 26 office properties totaling 5,017,000 sq. ft. of gross leasable area and two properties totaling 87,000 sq. ft. under development. In addition, the trust owns a 50% interest in an 11,000-sq.-ft. boutique office property in Toronto, Ont., held through a joint venture arrangement. The portfolio includes central business district and suburban office properties concentrated in major urban centres, primarily in Toronto, Ont.

Geographic diversification

Region	Area[1]
Toronto - downtown	3,154,000
Non-core markets[2]	1,863,000
	5,017,000

[1] Owned gross leasable area (sq. ft.).
[2] Includes properties in Calgary, Alta.; Saskatoon and Regina, Sask.; Mississauga and Scarborough, Ont.; and Kansas.

In May 2023, bought deal secondary offering of 12,500,000 trust units of **Dream Industrial Real Estate Investment Trust** held by the trust at $14.20 per unit was completed. As a result, the trust's interest in Dream Industrial decreased to 4.9% from 9.4% of the issued and outstanding voting units.

In February 2023, the trust sold 565,000 trust units of **Dream Industrial Real Estate Investment Trust** for net proceeds of $8,305,500.

Recent Merger and Acquisition Activity

Status: completed **Revised:** Jan. 30, 2023
UPDATE: The transaction was completed. PREVIOUS: Dream Office Real Estate Investment Trust agreed to sell 720 Bay Street, a 248,000-sq.-ft. office building in Toronto, Ont., for gross proceeds of $135,000,000. The transaction was expected to close in the first quarter of 2023, subject to customary closing conditions.
Status: completed **Announced:** Sept. 1, 2022
Dream Office Real Estate Investment Trust sold Princeton Tower, a 136,000-sq.-ft. office property in Saskatoon, Sask., for $14,000,000.

Predecessor Detail - Name changed from Dundee Real Estate Investment Trust, May 13, 2014.

Trustees - Michael J. Cooper, chr. & CEO, Toronto, Ont.; Donald K. (Don) Charter‡, Toronto, Ont.; Amar Bhalla, Toronto, Ont.; P. Jane Gavan, Toronto, Ont.; The Hon. Dr. Khristinn (Kelllie) Leitch, Madison, Miss.; Karine L. MacIndoe, Toronto, Ont.; Qi Tang, Toronto, Ont.

Other Exec. Officers - Gordon Wadley, COO; Jay Jiang, CFO
‡ Lead trustee

Capital Stock

	Authorized (shs.)	Outstanding (shs.)[1]
REIT Unit, Series A	unlimited	32,623,208
REIT Unit, Series B	unlimited	nil
Special REIT Unit	unlimited	5,233,823[2]
Subsid. Redeem Unit	unlimited	5,233,823[2 3]

[1] At Aug. 4, 2023
[2] Classified as debt.
[3] Securities of Dream Office LP.

REIT Unit - One vote per REIT unit. Issuable in two series: REIT units, series A, and REIT units, series B. Redeemable at any time at a price equal to the lesser of 90% of a 20-day weighted average market price prior to the redemption date and 100% of the market price on the redemption date. No preference or priority over any other units. **Series A** - Entitled to receive cash distributions from the trust derived from its investment in Dream Office OTA LP. **Series B** - Entitled to receive cash distributions from the trust derived from its investment in Dream Office OTB LP. Convertible at any time into REIT units, series A, on a one-for-one basis.

Special REIT Unit - Only issuable to holders of Dream Office LP class B units, series 1. Non-transferable separately from the LP class B units, series 1, to which they relate and will be automatically redeemed for a nominal amount and cancelled upon surrender or exchange (one-for-one) of such limited partnership class B units, series 1. One vote per special REIT unit.

Normal Course Issuer Bid - The company plans to make normal course purchases of up to 2,538,524 REIT units, series A representing 10% of the public float. The bid commenced on Aug. 21, 2023, and expires on Aug. 20, 2024.

Major Shareholder - Michael J. Cooper held 39.6% interest and Artis Real Estate Investment Trust held 11.2% interest at May 4, 2023.

Price Range - D.UN/TSX

Year	Volume	High	Low	Close
2022	39,766,448	$30.53	$14.48	$14.94
2021	40,232,553	$24.63	$19.12	$24.63
2020	55,974,463	$36.80	$15.21	$19.80
2019	37,522,110	$31.43	$21.89	$31.13
2018	48,175,500	$26.01	$20.72	$22.29

Recent Close: $13.15

Capital Stock Changes - In June 2023, a 1-for-2 consolidation of REIT units and special REIT units was approved and 12,500,000 REIT units, series A were repurchased under a Substantial Issuer Bid.

During 2022, 61,390 REIT units, series A were issued on exchange of deferred units and 1,985,551 REIT units, series A were repurchased under a Normal Course Issuers Bid.

Dividends

D.UN unit Ra $1.00 pa M est. Aug. 15, 2017**
stk.[1]◆g................ June 16/23
Paid in 2023: $0.74997 + stk.◆g 2022: $0.99996 2021: $0.99996

[1] Distribution will be automatically reinvested and the units will be consolidated immediately after distribution. Equiv to $4.55.
** Reinvestment Option ◆ Special **g** Capital Gain

Long-Term Debt - Outstanding at Dec. 31, 2022:

Credit facilities[1]	$319,696,000
Mtges. due to 2029	1,056,817,000
Subsidiary redeemable units	78,193,000
Less: Financing costs	3,730,000
	1,450,976,000
Less: Current portion	265,967,000
	1,185,009,000

[1] Consists of borrowings under a $375,000,000 revolving credit facility, bearing interest at banker's acceptance rate plus 1.7% or prime plus 0.7%, due September 2025; a $20,000,000 revolving credit facility, bearing interest at prime plus 0.85%, due March 2025; and a $112,870,000 non-revolving credit facility, bearing interest at 2.15%, due March 2027.

Subsidiary Redeemable Units - Class B limited partnership units, series 1, of Dream Office LP, of which there were 5,233,823 outstanding at Dec. 31, 2022. Together with the accompanying special trust units, the subsidiary redeemable units have economic and voting rights equivalent to the REIT units, series A. Entitled to a distribution equal to distributions declared on REIT units, series B, or if no such distribution is declared, on REIT units, series A. May be surrendered or indirectly exchanged on a 1-for-1 basis at the option of the holder, subject to certain restrictions, for REIT units, series B.

Minimum principal debt repayments were reported as follows:

2023	$267,271,000
2024	86,685,000
2025	544,606,000
2026	86,879,000
2027	172,757,000
Thereafter	218,315,000

Note - In February 2023, the company entered into a new $20,000,000 credit facility due on demand, bearing interest at banker's acceptance rate plus 2% or prime plus 0.5%. During the second quarter of 2023, principal amount of the revolving credit facility decreased to $10,000,000 from $20,000,000.

Wholly Owned Subsidiaries

Dream Office OTA (GP) Inc.
Dream Office OTA LP
- 45% int. in **Dream Office LP**, Ont.
  - 50% int. in **Dream Office Management LP**, Ont.
    - 50% int. in **Dream Office Management Corp.**, Ont.

Dream Office OTB (GP) Inc.
Dream Office OTB LP
- 45% int. in **Dream Office LP**, Ont.
  - 50% int. in **Dream Office Management LP**, Ont.
    - 50% int. in **Dream Office Management Corp.**, Ont.

Investments

4.9% int. in **Dream Industrial Real Estate Investment Trust**, Toronto, Ont. (see separate coverage)

Note: The preceding list includes only the major related companies in which interests are held.

Financial Statistics

Periods ended:	12m Dec. 31/22[A]		12m Dec. 31/21[A]
	$000s	%Chg	$000s
Total revenue	**196,273**	**0**	**195,932**
Rental operating expense	90,149		88,798
Salaries & benefits	3,514		3,254
General & admin. expense	6,464		6,557
Operating expense	**100,127**	**+2**	**98,609**
Operating income	**96,146**	**-1**	**97,323**
Investment income	59,705		90,305
Deprec. & amort.	430		897
Finance income	2,189		1,605
Finance costs, gross	57,374		48,573
Pre-tax income	**64,313**	**-59**	**155,109**
Income taxes	672		(203)
Net inc. bef. disc. opers	**63,641**	**-59**	**155,312**
Income from disc. opers	nil		(1,105)
Net income	**63,641**	**-59**	**154,207**
Cash & equivalent	8,018		8,763
Accounts receivable	12,265		9,937
Current assets	160,089		24,773
Long-term investments	479,626		431,640
Fixed assets	9,517		9,522
Income-producing props	2,305,215		2,533,478
Properties under devel.	64,809		23,078
Property interests, net	2,370,305		2,557,268
Total assets	**3,066,892**	**0**	**3,065,560**
Accts. pay. & accr. liabs	51,838		65,586
Current liabilities	321,647		146,128
Long-term debt, gross	1,450,976		1,412,182
Long-term debt, net	1,185,009		1,335,643
Long-term lease liabilities	4,057		4,108
Shareholders' equity	1,532,174		1,548,328
Cash from oper. activs	**76,669**	**-20**	**95,807**
Cash from fin. activs	(58,593)		(70,739)
Cash from invest. activs	(19,241)		(29,376)
Net cash position	**8,018**	**-9**	**8,763**
Capital expenditures	nil		(3)
Increase in property	(46,820)		(42,560)
Decrease in property	14,087		(811)
	$		$
Earnings per share*	n.a.		n.a.
Cash flow per share*	1.45		1.71
Funds from opers. per sh.*	1.52		1.56
Cash divd. per share*	1.00		1.00
Total divd. per share*	**1.00**		**1.00**
	shs		shs
No. of shs. o/s*	51,344,416		53,268,577
Avg. no. of shs. o/s*	52,916,000		55,971,000
	%		%
Net profit margin	32.42		79.27
Return on equity	4.13		10.19
Return on assets	3.93		6.85
No. of employees (FTEs)	256		234

* REIT unit
[A] Reported in accordance with IFRS

Latest Results

Periods ended:	6m June 30/23[A]		6m June 30/22[A]
	$000s	%Chg	$000s
Total revenue	95,228	-3	97,771
Net income	(48,328)	n.a.	118,204
	$		$
Earnings per share*	n.a.		n.a.

[A] Reported in accordance with IFRS

Historical Summary
(as originally stated)

Fiscal Year	Total Rev. $000s	Net Inc. Bef. Disc. $000s	EPS* $
2022[A]	196,273	63,641	n.a.
2021[A]	195,932	155,312	n.a.
2020[A]	206,585	177,250	n.a.
2019[A]	229,018	125,886	n.a.
2018[A]	285,207	157,778	n.a.

* REIT unit
[A] Reported in accordance with IFRS

D.68 Dream Residential Real Estate Investment Trust

Symbol - DRR.U **Exchange** - TSX **CUSIP** - 26154C
Head Office - c/o DREAM Unlimited Corp., State Street Financial Centre, 301-30 Adelaide St E, Toronto, ON, M5C 3H1 **Telephone** - (416) 365-3535 **Toll-free** - (877) 365-3535 **Fax** - (416) 365-6565
Website - dream.ca/investors/dream-residential-reit
Email - dlau@dream.ca
Investor Relations - Derrick Lau (416) 365-2364
Auditors - PricewaterhouseCoopers LLP C.A., Toronto, Ont.
Lawyers - Osler, Hoskin & Harcourt LLP, Toronto, Ont.
Transfer Agents - Computershare Trust Company of Canada Inc., Toronto, Ont.
Employees - 95 at Dec. 31, 2022
Profile - (Ont. 2022) Acquires, owns and operates multi-residential properties in the United States.

At Mar. 31, 2023, the trust owned a portfolio of 15 garden-style apartment complexes and one townhome community, totaling 3,432 units, in Oklahoma, Texas, Ohio, Kansas and Kentucky.

Region	Props.	Units
Greater Oklahoma City region[1]	6	1,431
Greater Dallas-Fort Worth region	4	1,049
Greater Cincinnati region[2]	6	952

[1] Includes a 132-unit property in Wichita, Kan.
[2] Includes a 144-unit property in Georgetown, Ky.

Dream DRR Asset Management LP, owned by **Dream Unlimited Corp.**, and **Pauls Realty Services, LLC**, owned by **Pauls Capital, LLC**, are the trust's asset managers.

Recent Merger and Acquisition Activity

Status: completed **Announced:** May 6, 2022
Dream Residential Real Estate Investment Trust acquired 16 multi-residential properties, totaling 3,432 units, located in three markets across the Sunbelt and Midwest regions of the United States for total consideration of US$388,347,000. Vendors included DREAM Unlimited Corp. and Pauls Capital, LLC.

Trustees - Vicky L. Schiff, chr., Los Angeles, Calif.; Brian D. Pauls, CEO, Denver, Colo.; Leonard M. Abramsky, Toronto, Ont.; P. Jane Gavan, Toronto, Ont.; Fahad Khan, Toronto, Ont.
Oper. Subsid./Mgt. Co. Officers - Scott Schoeman, COO; Derrick Lau, CFO; Robert Hughes, gen. counsel & corp. sec.

Capital Stock

	Authorized (shs.)	Outstanding (shs.)[1]
Preferred Unit	unlimited	nil
Trust Unit	unlimited	12,702,900
Class B Unit	unlimited	7,011,203[2]

[1] At May 3, 2023
[2] Securities of subsidiary DRR Holdings LLC.

Trust Unit - Entitled to monthly cash distributions as determined by the trust. Redeemable at any time at a price equal to the lesser of 90% of a 20-day weighted average closing market price prior to the redemption date and 100% of the market price on the redemption date. One vote per trust unit.
Class B Unit - Issued by subsidiary DRR Holdings LLC. Economically equivalent to the trust units and redeemable under certain circumstances by the holder for cash or trust units on a 1-for-1 basis. Entitled to distributions from DRR Holdings equal to distributions as those paid to holders of trust units. Holders of class B units include DREAM Unlimited Corp., Pauls Capital, LLC and Strategic Consolidated Income Fund LLC. Non-voting. Classified as financial liabilities.
Normal Course Issuer Bid - The company plans to make normal course purchases of up to 973,418 trust units representing 10% of the public float. The bid commenced on Jan. 6, 2023, and expires on Jan. 5, 2024.
Major Shareholder - Widely held at Apr. 14, 2023.

Price Range - DRR.U/TSX

Year	Volume	High	Low	Close
2022	3,671,706	US$12.15	US$6.55	US$6.80

Recent Close: US$7.49
Capital Stock Changes - On May 6, 2022, an initial public offering of 9,620,000 trust units was completed at US$13 per unit. Also during the 44-week period ended Dec. 31, 2022, trust units were issued as follows: 2,948,627 on redemption and exchange of a like number of DRR Holdings LLC class B units, 169,230 as advisory fee and 38,461 on acquisition of properties.

Dividends

DRR.U tr unit Ra US$0.42 pa M est. July 15, 2022
Listed May 6/22.
Prev. Rate: US$0.3528 est. June 15, 2022
US$0.0294i.......... June 15/22
i Initial Payment

Wholly Owned Subsidiaries

DRR Holdings Inc., Del.
- 100% int. in **DRR Holdings LLC**, Del. Represents class A units.

Financial Statistics

Periods ended:	44w Dec. 31/22[A]		12m Dec. 31/21[§A]
	US$000s	%Chg	US$000s
Total revenue	**29,102**	**-28**	**40,198**
Rental operating expense	16,296		21,032
Salaries & benefits	419		n.a.
General & admin. expense	1,747		3,143
Operating expense	**18,462**	**-24**	**24,175**
Operating income	**10,640**	**-34**	**16,023**
Finance income	134		nil
Finance costs, gross	7,346		9,804
Pre-tax income	**112,826**	**+220**	**35,232**
Net income	**112,826**	**+220**	**35,232**
Cash & equivalent	11,645		14,752
Accounts receivable	920		214
Current assets	13,615		15,844
Income-producing props	418,230		378,441
Property interests, net	418,230		378,441
Total assets	**432,504**	**+10**	**394,851**
Accts. pay. & accr. liabs	6,385		12,215
Current liabilities	56,437		12,215
Long-term debt, gross	184,298		277,669
Long-term debt, net	136,621		277,669
Shareholders' equity	239,291		104,967
Cash from oper. activs	**11,052**	**n.a.**	**n.a.**
Cash from fin. activs	100,561		n.a.
Cash from invest. activs	(99,968)		n.a.
Net cash position	**11,645**	**n.a.**	**n.a.**
Capital expenditures	(5,271)		n.a.
	US$		US$
Earnings per share*	n.a.		n.a.
Cash flow per share*	0.87		n.a.
Funds from opers. per sh.*	0.40		n.a.
Cash divd. per share*	0.27		n.a.
Total divd. per share*	**0.27**		**n.a.**
	shs		shs
No. of shs. o/s*	12,776,418		n.a.
	%		%
Net profit margin	...		87.65
Return on equity	...		n.m.
Return on assets	...		n.a.
Foreign sales percent	100		n.a.
No. of employees (FTEs)	95		n.a.

* Trust Unit
§ Pro forma
[A] Reported in accordance with IFRS

Latest Results

Periods ended:	3m Mar. 31/23[A]
	US$000s
Total revenue	11,639
Net income	(10,868)
	US$
Earnings per share*	n.a.

[A] Reported in accordance with IFRS

D.69 Drone Delivery Canada Corp.

Symbol - FLT **Exchange** - TSX-VEN **CUSIP** - 26210W
Head Office - 6-6221 Hwy 7, Vaughan, ON, L4H 0K8 **Telephone** - (647) 501-3290
Website - www.dronedeliverycanada.com
Email - billm@dronedeliverycanada.com
Investor Relations - Bill Mitoulas (416) 837-7147
Auditors - D & H Group LLP C.A., Vancouver, B.C.
Lawyers - Irwin Lowy LLP, Toronto, Ont.
Transfer Agents - Computershare Trust Company of Canada Inc., Toronto, Ont.
Employees - 50 at Mar. 30, 2023
Profile - (B.C. 2011) Designs, develops and implements a commercially viable drone-based logistics systems for government and corporate organizations globally.

The company provides a turnkey logistics solution which includes hardware, a proprietary software system and professional services. The company has one operating drone deemed fully compliant (Sparrow), and has two other drones under development (Canary, and Condor). The company's flight management software, FLYTE, allows secure autonomous operations by monitoring commercial air traffic (manned and unmanned), weather and other sensor data which are presented to the operators in the company's Operations Control Centre in Vaughan, Ont. In addition to the control centre, the company also has an engineering lab, a commercialization centre and a flight test range in Vaughan.

The company was awarded a Compliant Operator Status Certificate by Transport Canada and was granted a domestic cargo licence under the Canada Transportation Act and Air Transport Regulations (Canada). Also met Transport Canada's compliant unmanned aircraft standards for its delivery drone.

During the first quarter of 2022, the company received approval from Transport Canada for the implementation of dangerous goods transportation with the **DSV Air & Sea Inc.** (DSV) route.

Predecessor Detail - Name changed from Asher Resources Corporation, June 6, 2016, following reverse takeover acquisition of Drone Delivery Canada Inc.; basis 1 new for 4 old shs.

Directors - Michael Della Fortuna, chr., Woodbridge, Ont.; Debbie Fischer, Toronto, Ont.; Christopher O. (Chris) Irwin, Toronto, Ont.; Vijay J. Kanwar, Toronto, Ont.; Kevin D. Sherkin, Toronto, Ont.; Larry D. Taylor, Toronto, Ont.

Other Exec. Officers - Steve Magirias, CEO; Manish Arora, CFO; Mark Wuennenberg, v-p, regulatory affairs

Capital Stock

	Authorized (shs.)	Outstanding (shs.)[1]
Common Vtg. & Variable Vtg.	unlimited	224,199,312

[1] At May 15, 2023

Variable Voting - Held by individuals who are not Canadians as defined in the Canada Transportation Act (CTA). Automatically convertible into common voting shares on a one-for-one basis if the shares become held by a qualified Canadian or foreign ownership restrictions in the CTA are repealed and not replaced with similar provisions. Convertible at option of holder into common voting shares if an offer is made for all or substantially all of the common voting shares. This conversion right is only exercisable for the purpose of depositing the resulting common voting shares in response to the offer. Entitled to one vote per share, unless: (i) a single non-Canadian holder or non-Canadians authorized to provide air service hold more than 25% of all variable voting and common voting shares outstanding or votes that would be cast by or on behalf of a single non-Canadian or non-Canadians authorized to provide air service would exceed 25% of the total number of votes that would be cast at any meeting; and (ii) variable voting shares outstanding would exceed 49% of all variable and common voting shares outstanding or votes that would be cast by or on behalf of variable voting shareholders would exceed 49% of the total number of votes that would be cast at any meeting. If either of these thresholds is exceeded, the vote attached to each variable voting share will decrease proportionately and automatically such that: (i) a single non-Canadian holder or non-Canadians authorized to provide air service do not carry more than 25% of all variable and common voting shares outstanding or votes that would be cast by or on behalf of a single non-Canadian or non-Canadians authorized to provide air service would not exceed 25% of the total number of votes that would be cast at any meeting; and (ii) all variable voting shareholders do not carry more than 49% of the total number of all variable and common voting shares outstanding or votes that would be cast by or on behalf of variable voting shareholders would not exceed 49% of the total number of votes that would be cast at any meeting.

Common Voting - Held by qualified Canadians under the CTA. Automatically convertible into variable voting shares on a one-for-one basis if the shares become held by a non-qualified Canadian unless the foreign ownership restrictions of the CTA are repealed and not replaced with similar restrictions. Convertible at option of holder into variable voting shares if an offer is made for all or substantially all of the variable shares. This conversion right is only exercisable for the purpose of depositing the resulting variable voting share in response to the offer. One vote per share.

Major Shareholder - Widely held at May 1, 2023.

Price Range - FLT/TSX-VEN

Year	Volume	High	Low	Close
2022	31,397,567	$0.82	$0.21	$0.28
2021	290,639,172	$2.55	$0.74	$0.75
2020	135,541,842	$1.10	$0.50	$0.82
2019	85,710,272	$1.74	$0.62	$0.83
2018	90,379,125	$2.26	$0.88	$1.40

Recent Close: $0.28

Capital Stock Changes - Effective June 21, 2022, amendments to the company's share capital were implemented to create two new class of shares, variable voting shares and common voting shares and eliminate common shares. Each common share held by a non-Canadian was converted into one variable voting share and each common share held by a Canadian was converted into common voting share. Also during 2022, 300 variable voting shares and/or common voting shares were issued on exercise of warrants.

Wholly Owned Subsidiaries

Drone Delivery USA Inc., N.Y. Inactive

Financial Statistics

Periods ended:	12m Dec. 31/22[A]	%Chg	12m Dec. 31/21[A]
	$000s	%Chg	$000s
Operating revenue	**826**	**+147**	**335**
Salaries & benefits	5,813		4,838
Research & devel. expense	1,955		1,628
General & admin expense	4,856		6,461
Stock-based compensation	1,167		1,353
Operating expense	**13,791**	**-3**	**14,280**
Operating income	**(12,964)**	**n.a.**	**(13,945)**
Deprec., depl. & amort.	1,007		856
Finance income	297		62
Finance costs, gross	46		55
Write-downs/write-offs	(59)		(72)
Pre-tax income	**(13,414)**	**n.a.**	**(14,700)**
Net income	**(13,414)**	**n.a.**	**(14,700)**
Cash & equivalent	15,299		27,675
Inventories	119		nil
Accounts receivable	487		421
Current assets	16,248		28,602
Fixed assets, net	2,443		3,079
Right-of-use assets	179		359
Intangibles, net	878		920
Total assets	**19,748**	**-40**	**32,959**
Accts. pay. & accr. liabs.	910		1,390
Current liabilities	1,213		1,970
Long-term lease liabilities	20		227
Shareholders' equity	18,515		30,762
Cash from oper. activs.	**(11,943)**	**n.a.**	**(11,887)**
Cash from fin. activs.	(256)		16,785
Cash from invest. activs.	(177)		(687)
Net cash position	**15,299**	**-45**	**27,675**
Capital expenditures	(177)		(597)
	$		$
Earnings per share*	(0.06)		(0.07)
Cash flow per share*	(0.05)		(0.05)
	shs		shs
No. of shs. o/s*	224,199,312		224,199,012
Avg. no. of shs. o/s*	224,199,176		222,139,166
	%		%
Net profit margin	n.m.		n.m.
Return on equity	(54.44)		(50.81)
Return on assets	(50.73)		(46.99)
No. of employees (FTEs)	46		50

* Var. & com. vtg.

[A] Reported in accordance with IFRS

Latest Results

Periods ended:	3m Mar. 31/23[A]	%Chg	3m Mar. 31/22[A]
	$000s	%Chg	$000s
Operating revenue	575	+302	143
Net income	(2,539)	n.a.	(3,589)
	$		$
Earnings per share*	(0.01)		(0.02)

* Var. & com. vtg.

[A] Reported in accordance with IFRS

Historical Summary
(as originally stated)

Fiscal Year	Oper. Rev.	Net Inc. Bef. Disc.	EPS*
	$000s	$000s	$
2022[A]	826	(13,414)	(0.06)
2021[A]	335	(14,700)	(0.07)
2020[A]	265	(14,130)	(0.08)
2019[A]	nil	(15,597)	(0.09)
2018[A]	nil	(19,612)	(0.12)

* Var. & com. vtg.

[A] Reported in accordance with IFRS

Note: Results for 2015 and prior years pertain to Asher Resources Corporation.

D.70 Drummond Ventures Corp.

Symbol - DVX.P **Exchange** - TSX-VEN **CUSIP** - 262302

Head Office - 1400-400 Burrard St, Vancouver, BC, V6C 3A6 **Telephone** - (604) 336-8192

Email - craigvrollins@gmail.com

Investor Relations - Craig Rollins (236) 788-6817

Auditors - MNP LLP C.A., Vancouver, B.C.

Transfer Agents - Computershare Trust Company of Canada Inc., Vancouver, B.C.

Profile - (B.C. 2018) Capital Pool Company.

Directors - Craig Rollins, CEO, CFO & corp. sec., Vancouver, B.C.; Marcel H. de Groot, Vancouver, B.C.; David E. De Witt, Vancouver, B.C.

Capital Stock

	Authorized (shs.)	Outstanding (shs.)[1]
Common	unlimited	5,125,000

[1] At Nov. 29, 2022

Major Shareholder - Marcel H. de Groot held 26.02% interest, David DeWitt held 26.02% interest and Craig Rollins held 26.02% interest at Nov. 17, 2022.

Price Range - DVX.P/TSX-VEN

Year	Volume	High	Low	Close
2022	64,600	$0.50	$0.12	$0.15
2021	125,000	$0.40	$0.21	$0.25
2019	209,000	$0.35	$0.15	$0.35
2018	5,000	$0.15	$0.15	$0.15

Recent Close: $0.17

Capital Stock Changes - There were no changes to capital stock from fiscal 2020 to fiscal 2022, inclusive.

D.71 Dundee Corporation*

Symbol - DC.A **Exchange** - TSX **CUSIP** - 264901

Head Office - 2000-80 Richmond St W, Toronto, ON, M5H 2A4 **Telephone** - (416) 350-3388 **Toll-free** - (888) 332-2661 **Fax** - (416) 363-4536

Website - dundeecorporation.com

Email - ir@dundeecorporation.com

Investor Relations - Mark Pereira (416) 365-5172

Auditors - PricewaterhouseCoopers LLP C.A., Toronto, Ont.

Lawyers - Stikeman Elliott LLP, Toronto, Ont.

Transfer Agents - Computershare Trust Company of Canada Inc., Toronto, Ont.

Profile - (Ont. 1984) Owns and manages a portfolio of publicly listed and privately held businesses, with a focus on the mining sector.

The company primarily operates as a mining investment and merchant bank business. Merchant banking operations are conducted mainly through wholly owned **Goodman & Company, Investment Counsel Inc.** (GCIC), a portfolio manager and exempt market dealer across Canada, and an investment fund manager in Ontario, Quebec and Newfoundland. At Mar. 31, 2023, assets under management totaled $42,547,000.

Significant mining investments include **Ausgold Limited** and **Saturn Metals Limited**, which has mineral interests in Australia; **Borborema Inc.**, which holds Borborema gold project in northeastern Brazil; **Maritime Resources Corp.** and **Magna Mining Inc.**, which has mineral interests in Canada; **Reunion Gold Corporation**, which has gold interests in French Guiana and Guyana; **Centaurus Metals Limited**, which has mineral interests in Brazil; and **Dundee Sustainable Technologies Inc.**, which develops and commercializes environment-friendly technologies for the extraction of precious and base metals.

The company also holds a legacy investment portfolio which includes the management of assets, both domestic and international, consisting of physical assets and debt or equity securities in various sectors, including resource and real estate. Legacy investments include 84% interest in **United Hydrocarbon International Corp.**, which has royalty interest on oil and gas exploration and development activities in the Republic of Chad; 90% interest in**AgriMarine Holdings Inc.**, which develops proprietary aquaculture technologies; wholly owned **Dundee 360 Real Estate Corporation**, which offers management services in the development and project administration of recreational real estate assets, as well as financial reporting services to hotels; 20% interest in **Android Industries, LLC**, a high technology-enabled assembler and sequencer of complex assemblies for the automotive industry; and 3.2% interest in **TauRx Pharmaceuticals Ltd.**, a neuroscience company focused on the discovery, development and commercialization of products for the diagnosis and treatment of neuro-degenerative diseases caused through protein aggregation.

In March 2023, wholly owned **AgriMarine Holdings Inc.** sold its wholly owned **West Coast Fishculture (Lois Lake) Ltd.**, which owns and operates a steelhead fish farm in Powell River, B.C. Terms were not disclosed. Upon completion of the transaciton, the company awarded a 10% interest in AgriMarine to a former executive, reducing the company's interest in AgriMarine from 100% to 90%.

In March 2023, the company acquired 3,025,000 units (1 common share & 1 warrant) of **Viva Gold Corp.** at a price of 14¢ per share. As a result, the company's interest in Viva increased to 19.98% from 19.94%.

In January 2023, the company acquired 1,363,600 **Magna Mining Inc.** common shares for $1,500,000 pursuant to a private placement. Following the closing of the private placement, the company's interest in Magna decreased to 21% from 22%.

During 2022, the company acquired 100,00 common shares of **Blue Goose Capital Corp.** from Blue Goose minority shareholders, thereby increasing the company's interest to 97% from 96%. Terms were not disclosed.

In December 2022, the company shut down the operations of Dundee Goodman Merchant Partners (DGMP), a division of the company's wholly owned **Goodman & Company, Investment Counsel Inc.**, due to market conditions and capital allocation priorities. DGMP previously offered services to mining companies, including financing, capital raising, merger and acquisitions advisory, fairness opinions, due diligence and technical services.

In September 2022, the company acquired 18,518,518 subscription receipts of **Magna Mining Inc.** for $5,000,000, which were subsequently exchanged for 18,518,518 common shares and 9,259,259 warrants of Magna. As a result, the company's interest in Magna increased to 22% from 19%.

In July 2022, the company sold its remaining 20% interest in **Dundee Securities Europe Limited** for £30,000.

In February 2022, the company invested $5,040,000 in **Reunion Gold Corporation** to acquire 28,573,907 Reunion common shares at $0.175 per share by way of a private placement. Subsequently in July 2022, the company invested a further $6,100,000 in Reunion to acquire 23,500,000 units (1 common share & ½ warrant) at 26¢ per unit.

In May 2022, the company acquired 18,300,000 common shares of **Viva Gold Corp.** at 12¢ per share for total consideration of $2,196,000. On closing, the company held 19.98% of the outstanding common shares of Viva Gold.

Recent Merger and Acquisition Activity

Status: completed **Revised:** Sept. 21, 2022

UPDATE: The transaction was completed. Dundee holds 20% interest in Borborema Inc., a newly formed holding company, which holds Big River Gold Limited. PREVIOUS: Aura Minerals Inc., through a subsidiary (Aura BidCo), agreed to acquire Big River Gold Limited for A$0.36 per share in cash. Aura would hold its interest in Aura BidCo through an intermediate holding company (Aura JVCo) and Dundee Resources Limited, which holds 19.3% interest in Big River, has agreed, subject to certain limited conditions, to receive shares in Aura JVCo in lieu of the cash consideration in order to indirectly maintain a 20% equity interest in Big River. The offer values Big River at A$79,300,000 (A$91,700,000 on a fully diluted basis). Big River's material asset is Borborema gold project in Brazil, which is expected to operate as an open-pit gold project. Dundee Resources is wholly owned by Dundee Corporation. Copulos Group, which holds an 18.8% interest in Big River, plans to vote in favour of the transaction. The transaction was expected to close in or around late July or early August 2022. Sept. 2, 2022 - Big River shareholders approved the transaction.

Predecessor Detail - Name changed from Dundee Bancorp Inc., Dec. 21, 2004.

Directors - Peter B. Nixon, chr., Niagara-on-the-Lake, Ont.; Jonathan C. Goodman, pres. & CEO, Toronto, Ont.; Tanya Covassin, Ont.; Isabel Meharry, Ont.; Andrew T. Molson, Westmount, Qué.; Allen J. Palmiere, Toronto, Ont.; A. Murray Sinclair Jr., Vancouver, B.C.

Other Exec. Officers - Steven Sharpe, exec. v-chr.; Lila A. Manassa Murphy, exec. v-p & CFO; Darcy Donelle, v-p, fin.; Perina Montesano, v-p, internal audit; Mark Pereira, v-p & corp. sec.

Capital Stock

	Authorized (shs.)	Outstanding (shs.)[1]
First Preference	unlimited	
Series 2	5,200,000	1,149,162
Series 3	5,200,000	1,817,522
Second Preference	unlimited	nil
Third Preference	unlimited	nil
Class A Subordinate Voting	unlimited	85,313,622[2]
Class B Common	unlimited	3,114,491[3]

[1] At Mar. 31, 2023

[2] At May 10, 2023.

[3] At May 1, 2023.

First Preference Series 2 - Entitled to fixed preferential cumulative annual dividends of $1.321 payable quarterly to Sept. 30, 2024, and thereafter at a rate reset every five years equal to the five-year Government of Canada bond yield plus 4.1%. Redeemable on Sept. 30, 2024, and on September 30 every five years thereafter at $25 per share plus declared and unpaid dividends. Convertible on Sept. 30, 2024, and on September 30 every five years thereafter, into first preference series 3 shares on a share-for-share basis, subject to certain conditions.

First Preference Series 3 - Entitled to cumulative preferential annual dividends payable quarterly equal to the 90-day Canadian Treasury bill rate plus 4.1%. Redeemable on Sept. 30, 2024, and on September 30 every five years thereafter at $25 per share plus declared and unpaid dividends. Redeemable on any date that is not a conversion date at $25.50 per share plus declared and unpaid dividends. Convertible on Sept. 30, 2024, and on September 30 every five years thereafter, into first preference series 2 shares on a share-for-share basis, subject to certain conditions.

Class A Subordinate Voting - Convertible into class B common shares on a 1-for-1 basis in the event of an offer to purchase the class B common shares by a third party, and in certain circumstances. One vote per share.

Class B Common - Convertible into class A subordinate voting shares on a 1-for-1 basis at any time. One hundred votes per share.

Options - At Dec. 31, 2022, options were outstanding to purchase 4,230,000 class A subordinate voting shares at a weighted average exercise price of $1.13 per share with a weighted average remaining contractual life of up to 5.27 years.

Normal Course Issuer Bid - The company plans to make normal course purchases of up to 7,571,650 class A subordinate voting shares representing 10% of the public float. The bid commenced on Apr. 12, 2023, and expires on Apr. 11, 2024.

The company plans to make normal course purchases of up to 114,916 first preference series 2 shares representing 10% of the public float. The bid commenced on Apr. 12, 2023, and expires on Apr. 11, 2024.

The company plans to make normal course purchases of up to 181,752 first preference series 3 shares representing 10% of the public float. The bid commenced on Apr. 12, 2023, and expires on Apr. 11, 2024.

Major Shareholder - Ned and Anita Goodman Joint Partner Trust held 78.6% interest at May 1, 2023.

Price Range - DC.A/TSX

Year	Volume	High	Low	Close
2022............	10,531,420	$1.63	$1.07	$1.42
2021............	18,183,830	$1.82	$1.23	$1.42
2020............	21,167,786	$1.60	$0.60	$1.39
2019............	15,499,295	$1.51	$0.80	$1.19
2018............	19,951,964	$2.70	$1.01	$1.28

Recent Close: $1.24

Capital Stock Changes - During 2022, 317,419 class A subordinate voting shares were issued under the share incentive plan and 46,692 class A subordinate voting shares were repurchased under a Normal Course Issuer Bid.

Dividends

DC.PR.B pfce 1st ser 2 cum. red. exch. Adj. Ra $1.321 pa Q est. Dec. 31, 2019

DC.PR.D pfce 1st ser 3 cum. red. exch. Fltg. Ra pa Q

$0.5457...............	Oct. 2/23	$0.53977..........	June 30/23
$0.50733.............	Mar. 31/23	$0.46756..........	Jan. 3/23

Paid in 2023: $2.06036 2022: $0.90656 2021: $1.05505

Long-Term Debt - At Dec. 31, 2022, outstanding debt totaled $5,730,000 and consisted entirely of borrowings from loan facilities by subsidiary Dundee Sustainable Technologies Inc.

Wholly Owned Subsidiaries

Dundee Agricultural Corporation, Ont.
- 90% int. in **AgriMarine Holdings Inc.**, Vancouver, B.C.
- 97% int. in **Blue Goose Capital Corporation**, Toronto, Ont.

Dundee Global Investment Management Inc., Ont.
- 100% int. in **Goodman & Company, Investment Counsel Inc.**, Toronto, Ont.

Dundee Resources Limited, Ont.
- **Almonty Industries Inc.**, Toronto, Ont. (see Survey of Mines)
- 12.5% int. in **Ausgold Limited**, Perth, W.A., Australia.
- 20% int. in **Borborema Inc.**, British Virgin Islands.
  - 100% int. in **Big River Gold Limited**, Perth, W.A., Australia.
- 5.1% int. in **Centaurus Metals Limited**, West Perth, W.A., Australia.
- 78% int. in **Dundee Sustainable Technologies Inc.**, Montréal, Qué. 84% voting interest. (see Survey of Mines)
- 20.8% int. in **Magna Mining Inc.**, Dowling, Ont. (see Survey of Mines)
- **Mako Gold Limited**, Australia.
- 19.8% int. in **Maritime Resources Corp.**, Toronto, Ont. (see Survey of Mines)
- **Moneta Gold Inc.**, Timmins, Ont. (see Survey of Mines)
- 15.93% int. in **Reunion Gold Corporation**, Longueuil, Qué. (see Survey of Mines)
- 16.5% int. in **SPC Nickel Corp.**, Sudbury, Ont. (see Survey of Mines)
- 17.2% int. in **Saturn Metals Limited**, West Perth, W.A., Australia.
- 84% int. in **United Hydrocarbon International Corp.**, Canada.

Dundee 360 Real Estate Corporation, Montréal, Qué.
- 45% int. in **Sotarbat 360 S.A.S.**, France.

Subsidiaries

98% int. in **Dundee Acquisition Ltd.**, Toronto, Ont. Class B common shares.

Investments

20% int. in **Android Industries, LLC**, Mich.

50% int. in **Dundee Sarea Acquisition I Limited Partnership**

3.2% int. in **TauRx Pharmaceuticals Ltd.**

19.98% int. in **Viva Gold Corp.**, Langley, B.C. (see Survey of Mines)

Financial Statistics

Periods ended:	12m Dec. 31/22[A]		12m Dec. 31/21[◻A]
	$000s	%Chg	$000s
Total revenue................................	**66,499**	**n.a.**	**(22,702)**
General & admin. expense..............	21,951		21,291
Stock-based compensation............	3,384		2,546
Other operating expense................	3,072		3,385
Operating expense........................	**28,407**	**+4**	**27,222**
Operating income.........................	**38,092**	**n.a.**	**(49,924)**
Deprec. & amort............................	1,060		1,730
Finance costs, gross......................	1,027		1,896
Write-downs/write-offs..................	(783)		(771)
Pre-tax income.............................	**34,622**	**n.a.**	**(88,822)**
Income taxes.................................	5,629		3,084
Net inc bef disc ops, eqhldrs...........	30,113		(84,473)
Net inc bef disc ops, NCI................	(1,120)		(7,433)
Net inc. bef. disc. opers................	**28,993**	**n.a.**	**(91,906)**
Disc. opers., equity hldrs................	(13,006)		(8,542)
Disc. opers., NCI...........................	nil		(450)
Income from disc. opers.................	(13,006)		(8,992)
Net income....................................	**15,987**	**n.a.**	**(100,898)**
Net inc. for equity hldrs................	**17,107**	**n.a.**	**(93,015)**
Net inc. for non-cont. int..............	**(1,120)**	**n.a.**	**(7,883)**
Cash & equivalent..........................	47,181		93,853
Accounts receivable.......................	6,146		10,810
Investments....................................	297,912		217,170
Fixed assets, net.............................	1,441		7,156
Right-of-use assets........................	2,072		4,227
Intangibles, net...............................	4,977		6,222
Total assets..................................	**374,222**	**+4**	**358,188**
Accts. pay. & accr. liabs..................	10,320		16,089
Debt..	5,730		5,002
Lease liabilities..............................	2,941		4,205
Preferred share equity....................	78,090		78,090
Shareholders' equity.......................	354,140		335,290
Non-controlling interest..................	(3,736)		(2,398)
Cash from oper. activs..................	**(20,914)**	**n.a.**	**(10,666)**
Cash from fin. activs.......................	(5,180)		(69,596)
Cash from invest. activs..................	(20,388)		51,545
Net cash position.........................	**47,181**	**-50**	**93,853**
Capital expenditures, net................	(526)		(121)
	$		$
Earns. per sh. bef disc opers*..........	0.30		(0.99)
Earnings per share*........................	0.15		(1.09)
Cash flow per share*......................	(0.24)		(0.12)
	shs		shs
No. of shs. o/s*...............................	88,082,581		87,811,854
Avg. no. of shs. o/s*........................	87,996,643		88,668,021
	%		%
Net profit margin............................	43.60		n.m.
Return on equity.............................	9.69		(27.75)
Return on assets.............................	8.15		(20.04)

* Class A & B

◻ Restated

A Reported in accordance with IFRS

Latest Results

Periods ended:	3m Mar. 31/23[A]		3m Mar. 31/22[◻A]
	$000s	%Chg	$000s
Total revenue..................................	(8,357)	n.a.	49,072
Net inc. bef. disc. opers..................	(11,431)	n.a.	31,756
Income from disc. opers.................	(248)		(801)
Net income.....................................	(11,679)	n.a.	30,955
Net inc. for equity hldrs..................	(11,368)	n.a.	31,126
Net inc. for non-cont. int.................	(311)		(171)
	$		$
Earns. per sh. bef. disc. opers.*........	(0.14)		0.35
Earnings per share*........................	(0.14)		0.34

* Class A & B

◻ Restated

A Reported in accordance with IFRS

Historical Summary
(as originally stated)

Fiscal Year	Total Rev.	Net Inc. Bef. Disc.	EPS*
	$000s	$000s	$
2022[A]..................	66,499	28,993	0.30
2021[A]..................	(15,851)	(97,066)	(1.05)
2020[A]..................	107,975	(88,074)	(0.69)
2019[A]..................	79,074	(19,408)	(0.24)
2018[A]..................	22,928	(212,622)	(3.52)

* Class A & B

A Reported in accordance with IFRS

D.72 Dye & Durham Limited*

Symbol - DND **Exchange** - TSX **CUSIP** - 267488
Head Office - 1100-25 York St, Toronto, ON, M5J 2V5 **Telephone** - (416) 640-7100 **Toll-free** - (800) 268-7580
Website - www.dyedurham.com
Email - charlie.maccready@dyedurham.com
Investor Relations - Charlie MacCready (416) 640-7100 ext. 3470
Auditors - Ernst & Young LLP C.A., Toronto, Ont.
Transfer Agents - Computershare Trust Company of Canada Inc., Toronto, Ont.
FP500 Revenue Ranking - 480
Employees - 1,381 at Sept. 28, 2022
Profile - (Ont. 2020) Provides cloud-based software and technology services that improve productivity and efficiency for law firms, financial service institutions and government organizations in Canada, Australia, the U.K. and Ireland.

The company is structured into three core verticals: **Real estate and practice management**, which enables customers to execute transactions securely and easily in real estate and legal practice and case management workflow; **Data insights and due diligence**, which involves due diligence searches by aggregating data and public records into a comprehensive set of insights to allow customers to evaluate corporations or real estate in connection with mergers and acquisitions, financing and restructuring transactions, transferring ownership in real property, mortgaging real property and registering claims and liens against real property; and **Payments infrastructure**, which facilitates the transfer of money through payment processing, settlement (interbank netting and clearing of funds) and payment remittance services, primarily for bill and tax payments and remittances and real estate payments.

On Mar. 27, 2023, the company announced it has engaged **Raymond James Financial International Limited** and **INFOR Financial Inc.** to act as financial advisors in respect of a sale of **TM Group (UK) Limited**, as has been mandated by the United Kingdom's Competition and Markets Authority. The sale of TM Group to a third party remains the company's preferred option and has engaged with multiple bidders as part of an auction process. The company is also exploring a potential admission of TM Group to AIM, a market operated by the **London Stock Exchange plc.** which would need to be proceeded by a spin-out of TM Group to its shareholders and then seek admission of TM Group to AIM market.

Recent Merger and Acquisition Activity

Status: pending **Announced:** July 10, 2023
Dye & Durham Limited agreed to sell wholly owned TM Group (UK) Limited, which provides technology-enabled real estate due diligence solutions used by law firms and conveyancers to complete both residential and commercial real estate transactions across the U.K., to Germany-based Aurelius Group for £50,000,000 at closing, and up to £41,000,000 in potential additional earn-out payments between 2023 and 2026. Dye & Durham acquired TM Group in July 2021, and was ordered by the United Kingdom's Competition and Markets Authority (CMA) to sell TM Group after it found it would substantially lessen competition in property serach reports in the U.K. Following completion, Dye & Durham was planning to seek new merger and acquisition opportunities in the U.K.

Status: completed **Announced:** May 23, 2023
Dye & Durham Limited acquired Cape Town, South Africa-based GhostPractice Inc., which provides cloud-based software designed to help manage law firms, organize cases and collaborate with clients. Terms of the transaction were not disclosed.

Status: completed **Announced:** Jan. 23, 2023
Dye & Durham Limited acquired Insight Legal Software Ltd., a provider of legal practice management software throughout the United Kingdom. Terms were not disclosed.

Status: terminated **Revised:** Sept. 23, 2022
UPDATE: The transaction was terminated. PREVIOUS: Dye & Durham Limited agreed to acquire Australian Securities Exchange-listed Link Administration Holdings Limited, a Sydney, Australia-based provider of mission critical software, servicing more than 6,000 clients worldwide across the financial services and corporate business segments, for Cdn$3.2 billion (representing A$5.50 cash per Link ordinary share). Dye & Durham would fund the transaction through a combination of debt and equity. Link's Corporate Markets division connects issuers to their stakeholders through its software platform, providing shareholder management and analytics, stakeholder engagement and employee share plan products worldwide; and Retirement and Superannuation Solutions business provides comprehensive financial data solutions, including data management and member engagement products to Superannuation funds in Australia, New Zealand and the U.K. Link's board of directors unanimously recommended that shareholders vote in favour of the transaction. June 27, 2022 - Dye & Durham revised its offer to A$4.30 cash per share. July 6, 2022 - Dye & Durham revised its offer to A$4.70 cash per share, consisting of base consideration of A$4.57 per share and up to A$0.13 per share for the proceeds from the sale of Link's Banking and Credit Management business. July 21, 2022 - Dye & Durham and Link agreed to an amended offer price of A$4.81 cash per share. Link's board of directors unanimously recommended that shareholders vote in favour of the revised price. Aug. 22, 2022 - Link's shareholders voted in favour of the transaction. Sept. 8, 2022 - Link received confirmation that The Australian Competition and Consumer Commission (ACCC) would not oppose the proposed transaction after accepting a court-enforceable undertaking from Dye & Durham to divest its existing Australian business (formerly GlobalX Information Pty Ltd. and SAI Global's property division). Link also confirmed it obtained approval from the Central Bank of Ireland in respect of the transaction. Sept. 12, 2022 - The U.K. Financial Conduct Authority (FCA) delivered a warning notice to Dye & Durham stating that it was proposing to approve its acquisition of Link Fund Solutions Limited (LFS) subject to conditions. The current proposed conditions provided that the FCA would not approve the proposed acquisition unless Dye & Durham undertook to cover any shortfall in the value of the assets of LFS, up to a maximum of £306,096,527 (A$523,000,000 or Cdn$465,000,000) in relation to any restitution and/or redress payments that the FCA may levy on LFS in relation to its management of the LF Woodford Equity and Income Fund, which was a £3 billion (A$5.13 billion or Cdn$4.56 billion) investment fund that collapsed in 2019 after it was unable to repay investors. Sept. 14, 2022 - Dye & Durham received written confirmation from Australia's Foreign Investment Review Board (FIRB) that the Commonwealth Government had no objection to the proposed acquisition. Sept. 18, 2022 - Dye & Durham made a revised proposal whereby it would maintain the A$4.81 cash per share consideration, but would pay A$3.81 per share upon completion of the transaction, with the remaining A$1.00 per share payable upon a final and binding conclusion of the U.K. FCA's active enforcement investigation into LFS within two years of the transaction's completion. Sept. 19, 2022 - Link rejected Dye & Durham's proposed offer following the U.K. FCA's decision.

Directors - Brian L. Derksen, chr., Dallas, Tex.; Matthew Proud, CEO, Toronto, Ont.; Mario Di Pietro, Toronto, Ont.; David L. MacDonald, Markham, Ont.; Leslie A. O'Donoghue, Calgary, Alta.; Edward D. (Ted) Prittie, Dubai, United Arab Emirates; Ronnie Wahi, Vancouver, B.C.
Other Exec. Officers - Martha Vallance, COO; Frank Di Liso, CFO; Wojtek Dabrowski, chief commun. officer; John Sulja, CIO; Charlie MacCready, exec. v-p, chief legal officer & corp. sec.

Capital Stock

	Authorized (shs.)	Outstanding (shs.)[1]
Common	unlimited	54,896,646

[1] At June 21, 2023

Options - At June 30, 2022, options were outstanding to purchase 3,618,000 common shares at prices ranging from less than $19.99 to $51 per share with a weighted average remaining contractual life of 3.89 years.
Normal Course Issuer Bid - The company plans to make normal course purchases of up to 3,457,508 common shares representing 5% of the total outstanding. The bid commenced on Sept. 30, 2022, and expires on Sept. 29, 2023.
Major Shareholder - Mawer Investment Management Limited held 16.31% interest, Plantro Ltd. held 11.99% interest, The Capital Group Companies, Inc. held 11.54% interest and Invesco Canada Ltd. held 10.82% interest at Nov. 10, 2022.

Price Range - DND/TSX

Year	Volume	High	Low	Close
2022	79,985,245	$45.89	$11.62	$16.41
2021	66,533,910	$53.13	$35.51	$44.88
2020	26,442,673	$53.68	$11.25	$50.52

Recent Close: $17.53
Capital Stock Changes - In December 2022, 10,344,827 common shares were repurchased under a Substantial Issuer Bid. In June 2023, 882,352 common shares were repurchased under a Substantial Issuer Bid.

During fiscal 2022, common shares were issued as follows: 405,000 on exercise of options, 127,000 by private placement and 106,000 pursuant to the acquisition of GlobalX Information Pty Ltd.

Dividends

DND com Ra $0.075 pa Q est. Dec. 14, 2020
Long-Term Debt - At June 30 2022, outstanding long-term debt totaled $1,156,828,000 ($19,564,000 current) and consisted of $876,484,000 drawn on credit facilities and $276,000,000 of 3.75% convertible debentures due Mar. 1, 2026; convertible into common shares at $73.23 per share.
Substantial Issuer Bid - The company is making an offer for up to $52,000,000 principal amount of its 3.75% convertible debentures due 2026 at between $500 and $650 per $1,000 principal amount. The bid commenced on July 26, 2023, and expires on Aug. 30, 2023.

Wholly Owned Subsidiaries

Dye & Durham Corporation, Toronto, Ont.
- 100% int. in **Dye & Durham Holdings Pty Ltd.**, Australia.
  - 100% int. in **Dye & Durham Australia Pty Limited**, Australia.
    - 100% int. in **Dye & Durham Information Pty Ltd.**, Australia.
- 100% int. in **Dye & Durham Mercury Ltd.**, Ont.
- 100% int. in **Dye & Durham (UK) Limited**, United Kingdom.
  - 100% int. in **Easy Convey Limited**, Lightwater, Surrey, United Kingdom.
  - 100% int. in **Future Climate Info Limited**, Kent, United Kingdom.
  - 100% int. in **Index Franchising Limited**, United Kingdom.
  - 100% int. in **Index Insure Limited**, United Kingdom.
  - 100% int. in **Insight Legal Software Ltd.**, Farnborough, Hants., United Kingdom.
  - 100% int. in **R-Squared Bidco Limited**, Reading, Berks., United Kingdom.
  - 100% int. in **Stanley Davis Group Limited**, London, Middx., United Kingdom.
  - 100% int. in **TM Group (UK) Limited**, United Kingdom.
  - 100% int. in **Terrafirma IDC Ltd**, Bristol, Gloucs., United Kingdom.

Note: The preceding list includes only the major related companies in which interests are held.

Financial Statistics

Periods ended:	12m June 30/22[A]		12m June 30/21[A]
	$000s	%Chg	$000s
Operating revenue	**474,808**	**+127**	**208,945**
Cost of sales	57,558		27,921
General & admin expense	66,028		23,441
Stock-based compensation	23,962		26,008
Other operating expense	84,292		41,311
Operating expense	**231,840**	**+95**	**118,681**
Operating income	**242,968**	**+169**	**90,264**
Deprec., depl. & amort.	132,932		49,411
Finance costs, gross	42,377		57,299
Pre-tax income	**18,087**	**n.a.**	**(42,103)**
Income taxes	10,246		(1,254)
Net income	**7,841**	**n.a.**	**(40,849)**
Net inc. for equity hldrs	**7,665**	**n.a.**	**(40,849)**
Net inc. for non-cont. int	**176**	**n.a.**	**nil**
Cash & equivalent	223,619		429,335
Accounts receivable	70,365		47,077
Current assets	306,064		484,506
Fixed assets, net	3,005		3,290
Right-of-use assets	9,668		9,360
Intangibles, net	1,927,140		1,058,609
Total assets	**2,250,442**	**+44**	**1,558,366**
Accts. pay. & accr. liabs	117,970		59,931
Current liabilities	161,214		106,620
Long-term debt, gross	1,156,808		589,560
Long-term debt, net	1,137,244		572,153
Long-term lease liabilities	7,118		7,229
Shareholders' equity	763,424		750,917
Non-controlling interest	5		nil
Cash from oper. activs	**185,437**	**+134**	**79,354**
Cash from fin. activs	535,297		1,138,806
Cash from invest. activs	(923,582)		(790,672)
Net cash position	**223,619**	**-48**	**429,335**
Capital expenditures	(1,172)		(1,588)
	$		$
Earnings per share*	0.11		(0.72)
Cash flow per share*	2.69		1.41
Cash divd. per share*	0.08		0.06
	shs		shs
No. of shs. o/s*	69,149,000		68,511,000
Avg. no. of shs. o/s*	68,911,000		56,423,000
	%		%
Net profit margin	1.65		(19.55)
Return on equity	1.01		n.m.
Return on assets	1.38		1.71
Foreign sales percent	45		39

* Common
[A] Reported in accordance with IFRS

Latest Results

Periods ended:	9m Mar. 31/23[A]		9m Mar. 31/22[A]
	$000s	%Chg	$000s
Operating revenue	330,912	-4	345,136
Net income	(81,464)	n.a.	11,096
Net inc. for equity hldrs	(81,464)	n.a.	10,970
Net inc. for non-cont. int	nil		126
	$		$
Earnings per share*	(1.27)		0.16

* Common
[A] Reported in accordance with IFRS

Historical Summary
(as originally stated)

Fiscal Year	Oper. Rev.	Net Inc. Bef. Disc.	EPS*
	$000s	$000s	$
2022[A]	474,808	7,841	0.11
2021[A]	208,945	(40,849)	(0.72)
2020[A1]	65,510	(11,237)	(0.55)
2019[A]	43,845	710	0.03
2018[A]	32,541	1,236	0.05

* Common
[A] Reported in accordance with IFRS
[1] Results for fiscal 2020 and prior periods pertain to Dye & Durham Corporation.

d.73 dynaCERT Inc.

Symbol - DYA **Exchange** - TSX **CUSIP** - 26780A
Head Office - 101-501 Alliance Ave, Toronto, ON, M6N 2J1 **Telephone** - (416) 766-9691 **Fax** - (416) 766-9889
Website - www.dynacert.com
Email - jpayne@dynacert.com
Investor Relations - Murray James Payne (416) 766-9691 ext. 2
Auditors - HDCPA Professional Corporation C.A., Mississauga, Ont.
Lawyers - TingleMerrett LLP, Calgary, Alta.
Transfer Agents - TSX Trust Company, Toronto, Ont.
Employees - 30 at Mar. 24, 2023

Profile - (Ont. 2004 amalg.) Manufactures and distributes carbon emission reduction technologies globally for use with internal combustion engines.

The company's lead product, HydraGEN™, is an electrolysis system which produces measured amounts of pure hydrogen and oxygen that are introduced into any internal combustion engine air intake, in front of the turbo charger to create a homogeneous mixture with the injected fuel that is consumed during the combustion process, resulting in fuel savings and emission reductions. Target markets for HydraGEN™ include diesel engines used in on-road vehicles, refrigerated trailers, off-road construction, power generation, mining and forestry equipment, marine vessels and railroad locomotives. The HydraGEN™ technology is employed throughout the company's product lines.

Other products include HG145, which targets 10 to 15-litre diesel engines; HG2, which is designed to be appropriate for those smaller displacement diesel engines used in buses, class 2 to class 7 trucks, refrigerator trailers and containers, mobile construction equipment, small generators and smaller trucks commonly found outside of North America; HG4C, which targets 40 to 60-litre engines; and HG6C, which targets 60 to 90-litre engines. Multiple units may be combined together for a single engine that is larger than 100 Liters.

Also offers HydraLytica™, a telematics device software which enables dealers and clients to easily access fuel saving and carbon emission reduction reports from diesel-powered vehicles and machinery equipped with the company's HydraGEN™ technology as well as FreighTech, a suite of software applications essential for modern fleet management, offered to both users and non-users of HydraGEN™.

Operations are carried out from a 29,700-sq.ft. building in Toronto, Ont., which includes an assembly plant, a research and development facility, inventory storage and office premises.

In February 2023, the company entered into a collaboration agreement with Ont.-based **Cipher Neutron Inc.** (CN) to develop, produce and market hydrogen technology, including AEM electrolyser technology which is designed to produce green hydrogen for world-wide large infrastructure projects, and reversible fuel cell technology to emergency preparedness and efficient storage of hydrogen as a long-term source of power. Under the agreement, the company has options to acquire common shares of CN at various expiry dates up to July 31, 2025, which if fully exercised could result of up to 50% ownership interest in CN, for a total exercise price of $17,500,000. The company has committed to exercise certain of its CN options in amounts ranging up to 50% of the net proceeds of any equity financing by the company up to a maximum of $5,000,000 at favourable seed capital exercise prices of CN equity to the company. Once options exercised, the company would own 25% of CN on an undiluted basis.

Predecessor Detail - Name changed from Dynamic Fuel Systems Inc., Dec. 18, 2012.

Directors - Wayne Hoffman, chr., Brantford, Ont.; Murray James (Jim) Payne, pres. & CEO, Caledon, Ont.; Jean-Pierre Colin, exec. v-p, interim CFO & corp. sec., Collingwood, Ont.; Bruce Barnaby, Ont.; Amir Farahi, Ont.; Brian Warner, Ont.; Tracy Weslosky, Ont.; Jeffery (Jeff) Zajac, Ont.

Other Exec. Officers - Enrico Schläepfer, v-p, global sales

Capital Stock

	Authorized (shs.)	Outstanding (shs.)[1]
Common	unlimited	380,512,515

[1] At May 14, 2023

Major Shareholder - Widely held at May 10, 2023.

Price Range - DYA/TSX

Year	Volume	High	Low	Close
2022	45,553,491	$0.33	$0.08	$0.18
2021	121,438,689	$0.86	$0.19	$0.21
2020	242,905,938	$1.25	$0.33	$0.59
2019	115,363,403	$0.79	$0.19	$0.71
2018	50,585,479	$0.50	$0.17	$0.19

Recent Close: $0.20

Capital Stock Changes - During 2022, 333,335 common shares were issued on exercise of options.

Wholly Owned Subsidiaries

dynaCERT GmbH, Germany.

dynaCERT International Strategic Holdings Inc.

Financial Statistics

Periods ended:	12m Dec. 31/22[A]		12m Dec. 31/21[A]
	$000s	%Chg	$000s
Operating revenue	**1,149**	**+52**	**757**
Cost of goods sold	2,290		2,218
Salaries & benefits	1,784		2,728
Research & devel. expense	1,345		2,847
General & admin expense	2,995		3,105
Stock-based compensation	1,792		2,861
Operating expense	**10,207**	**-26**	**13,761**
Operating income	**(9,058)**	**n.a.**	**(13,004)**
Deprec., depl. & amort.	1,031		895
Finance income	34		312
Finance costs, gross	nil		8
Write-downs/write-offs	(1,193)		nil
Pre-tax income	**(10,956)**	**n.a.**	**(16,325)**
Net income	**(10,956)**	**n.a.**	**(16,325)**
Cash & equivalent	156		8,338
Inventories	2,636		2,777
Accounts receivable	183		190
Current assets	3,343		12,048
Fixed assets, net	1,619		2,108
Right-of-use assets	1,278		1,701
Intangibles, net	886		958
Total assets	**7,125**	**-58**	**16,814**
Accts. pay. & accr. liabs.	1,168		1,328
Current liabilities	2,046		1,892
Long-term lease liabilities	968		1,408
Shareholders' equity	4,111		13,515
Cash from oper. activs.	**(7,878)**	**n.a.**	**(8,660)**
Cash from fin. activs.	(207)		(430)
Cash from invest. activs.	(97)		(1,409)
Net cash position	**156**	**-98**	**8,338**
Capital expenditures	nil		(620)
	$		$
Earnings per share*	(0.03)		(0.04)
Cash flow per share*	(0.02)		(0.02)
	shs		shs
No. of shs. o/s*	381,817,515		381,484,180
Avg. no. of shs. o/s*	381,580,334		381,264,702
	%		%
Net profit margin	(953.52)		n.m.
Return on equity	(124.32)		(81.91)
Return on assets	(91.53)		(73.65)

* Common

[A] Reported in accordance with IFRS

Latest Results

Periods ended:	3m Mar. 31/23[A]		3m Mar. 31/22[A]
	$000s	%Chg	$000s
Operating revenue	73	-26	98
Net income	(1,457)	n.a.	(2,257)
	$		$
Earnings per share*	(0.00)		(0.01)

* Common

[A] Reported in accordance with IFRS

Historical Summary
(as originally stated)

Fiscal Year	Oper. Rev.	Net Inc. Bef. Disc.	EPS*
	$000s	$000s	$
2022[A]	1,149	(10,956)	(0.03)
2021[A]	757	(16,325)	(0.04)
2020[A]	468	(13,725)	(0.04)
2019[A]	1,065	(12,666)	(0.04)
2018[A]	92	(11,413)	(0.04)

* Common

[A] Reported in accordance with IFRS

E

E.1 E-L Financial Corporation Limited*

Symbol - ELF **Exchange** - TSX **CUSIP** - 268575
Head Office - 1000-165 University Ave, Toronto, ON, M5H 3B8 **Telephone** - (416) 947-2578 **Fax** - (416) 362-2592
Website - www.e-lfinancial.ca
Email - cartyr@e-lfinancial.com
Investor Relations - Richard B. Carty (416) 947-2578
Auditors - PricewaterhouseCoopers LLP C.A., Toronto, Ont.
Transfer Agents - Computershare Trust Company of Canada Inc., Toronto, Ont.
Employees - 1,089 at Dec. 31, 2022
Profile - (Ont. 1968) Operates as an investment and insurance holding company through indirect subsidiary **The Empire Life Insurance Company** and its E-L Corporate segment, which includes the oversight of investments in global equities held through direct and indirect holdings of common shares, investment funds, closed-end investment companies and other private companies.

Indirect subsidiary **The Empire Life Insurance Company**'s major product lines include wealth management, which consists of segregated fund products, guaranteed interest rate products and mutual funds; individual insurance, which consists of term life insurance, whole life insurance (participating and non-participating), health and disability insurance, and universal life insurance; and group solutions, which consist of life, short and long-term disability, extended health, dental, critical illness, and accidental death and dismemberment, as well as creditor insurance products. Empire Life serves more than 592,000 individual customers (including organizations), more than 14,000 group customers with over 250,000 certificate-holders, and 900 group retirement plans (pension and registered savings plans) at December 2022. It has relationships with more than 34,000 professional financial advisors through a network of independent financial advisors, managing general agents, national account firms and employee benefit brokers and representatives.

Other significant investments include **United Corporations Limited** (54.9% interest) and **Economic Investment Trust Limited** (24.7% interest), closed-end investment companies with portfolios of global investments; and **Algoma Central Corporation** (36.8% interest), a shipping company.

On Mar. 10, 2022, subsidiary **The Empire Life Insurance Company** acquired 100% of the shares of six financial services firms and amalgamated them into one wholly owned subsidiary under the name **TruStone Financial Inc.** for $57,910,000 cash. The six acquired agencies were **Life Management Financial Group Ltd.**, **LMF Investor Services Inc.**, **Paradigm Financial Advisors (North) Inc.**, **Paradigm Financial Advisors Inc.**, **Dwight Goertz & Associates Insurance Agency Limited** and **Pacific Place Financial Services Inc.**

Directors - Duncan N. R. Jackman, chr., pres. & CEO, Toronto, Ont.; M. Victoria D. Jackman, Toronto, Ont.; Peter J. Levitt, Ont.; Elizabeth M. Loach, Ont.; Clive P. Rowe, Delray Beach, Fla.; Stephen J. R. Smith, Toronto, Ont.; Mark M. Taylor, Mississauga, Ont.

Other Exec. Officers - Richard B. Carty, v-p, gen. counsel & corp. sec.; Scott F. Ewert, v-p & CFO; Fahad Khan, v-p & chief invest. officer; Susan C. Clifford, treas.

Capital Stock

	Authorized (shs.)	Outstanding (shs.)[1]
First Preference	unlimited	
Series 1		4,000,000
Series 2		4,000,000
Series 3		4,000,000
Preference	402,733	
Series A		258
Common	unlimited	3,552,390

[1] At June 30, 2023

First Preference - Issuable in series. Rank in priority to the series A preference and common shares with respect to the payment of dividends. Non-voting.

Series 1 - Entitled to non-cumulative preferential annual dividends of $1.325 per share payable quarterly. Redeemable at $25 per share plus declared and unpaid dividends. Convertible into common shares, determined by dividing the then applicable redemption price per share plus declared and unpaid dividends by the greater of $1.00 and 95% of the weighted average trading price of the common shares for the 20 consecutive trading days ending on the fourth day prior to the conversion date.

Series 2 - Entitled to non-cumulative preferential annual dividends of $1.1875 per share payable quarterly. Redeemable at $25 per share plus declared and unpaid dividends. Convertible into common shares, determined by dividing the then applicable redemption price per share plus declared and unpaid dividends by the greater of $1.00 and 95% of the weighted average trading price of the common shares for the 20 consecutive trading days ending on the fourth day prior to the conversion date.

Series 3 - Entitled to non-cumulative preferential annual dividends of $1.375 per share payable quarterly. Redeemable at $25 per share plus declared and unpaid dividends. Convertible into common shares, determined by dividing the then applicable redemption price per share plus declared and unpaid dividends by the greater of $1.00 and 95% of the weighted average trading price of the common shares for the 20 consecutive trading days ending on the fourth day prior to the conversion date.

Series A Preference - Entitled to non-cumulative preferential annual dividends of 50¢ per share payable quarterly. Rank senior to common shares in respect to dividend payments. Convertible into common shares on a share-for-share basis. Allowed to participate equally with the common shares in the event of liquidation, dissolution or winding-up. Provision is made for adjustment in the event of subdivision or consolidation of the common shares. One vote per share.

Common - One vote per share.

Normal Course Issuer Bid - The company plans to make normal course purchases of up to 177,854 common shares representing 5% of the total outstanding. The bid commenced on Mar. 9, 2023, and expires on Mar. 8, 2024.

Major Shareholder - Dominion and Anglo Investment Corporation Limited held 41% interest, Canadian & Foreign Securities Co. Limited held 15.1% interest and Economic Investment Trust Limited held 10.9% interest at Mar. 2, 2023.

Price Range - ELF/TSX

Year	Volume	High	Low	Close
2022	119,477	$947.85	$780.01	$894.00
2021	116,496	$989.99	$762.56	$909.49
2020	295,165	$840.00	$485.00	$765.00
2019	187,909	$828.95	$720.05	$828.95
2018	148,180	$834.00	$734.03	$740.01

Recent Close: $922.00

Capital Stock Changes - In September 2022, 103,626 common shares were repurchased under a Substantial Issuer Bid. Also during 2022, 40,660 common shares were repurchased under a Normal Course Issuer Bid.

Dividends

ELF com Ra $15.00 pa Q est. Apr. 17, 2023
Prev. Rate: $10.00 est. July 16, 2021
Prev. Rate: $5.00 est. Apr. 15, 2016
$25.00◆ Apr. 14/22 $80.00◆ Sept. 24/21
Paid in 2023: $13.75 2022: $10.00 + $25.00◆ 2021: $7.50 + $80.00◆

ELF.PR.F pfd 1st ser 1 red. cv Ra $1.325 pa Q
ELF.PR.G pfd 1st ser 2 red. cv Ra $1.1875 pa Q
ELF.PR.H pfd 1st ser 3 red. cv Ra $1.375 pa Q
◆ Special

Long-Term Debt - Outstanding at Dec. 31, 2022:

Margin loan[1]	$55,000,000
Operating facility[2]	50,000,000
Series 2017-1 subord. debs.[3]	199,964,000
Series 2021-1 subord. debs.[4]	199,165,000
4% sr. notes due 2050	198,786,000
	702,915,000

[1] Bears interest at the three-month CDOR plus 0.4%.
[2] Bears interest at the prime rate of the bank minus 0.25%.
[3] Bears interest at 3.664% to Mar. 15, 2023, and at the three-month CDOR plus 1.53% thereafter. Due 2028.
[4] Bears interest at 2.024% to Sept. 24, 2026, and at the three-month CDOR plus 0.67% thereafter. Due 2031.

Wholly Owned Subsidiaries

E-L Financial Services Limited, Canada.
- 98.3% int. in **The Empire Life Insurance Company**, Kingston, Ont.
  - 100% int. in **TruStone Financial Inc.**, Ont.

Subsidiaries

54.9% int. in **United Corporations Limited**, Toronto, Ont. (see separate coverage)

Investments

36.8% int. in **Algoma Central Corporation**, St. Catharines, Ont. (see separate coverage)
24.7% int. in **Economic Investment Trust Limited**, Toronto, Ont. (see separate coverage)
1.1% int. in **The Empire Life Insurance Company**, Kingston, Ont.

Financial Statistics

Periods ended:	12m Dec. 31/22[A]		12m Dec. 31/21[A]
	$000s	%Chg	$000s
Net premiums earned	1,042,554		915,543
Net investment income	481,037		457,546
Total revenue	**(647,372)**	**n.a.**	**2,482,476**
Policy benefits & claims	(827,846)		481,099
Commissions	249,363		233,778
Salaries & benefits	118,881		111,645
Premium taxes	22,359		18,229
Other operating expense	106,020		94,218
Operating expense	**496,623**	**+8**	**457,870**
Operating income	**(316,149)**	**n.a.**	**1,543,507**
Deprec. & amort.	10,894		14,412
Finance costs, gross	27,986		31,753
Pre-tax income	**(355,029)**	**n.a.**	**1,497,342**
Income taxes	(27,716)		215,350
Net income	**(327,313)**	**n.a.**	**1,281,992**
Net inc. for equity hldrs	**(174,363)**	**n.a.**	**1,152,961**
Net inc. for non-cont. int	**(154,242)**	**n.a.**	**116,182**
Net inc. for partic policyhldrs	**1,292**	**-90**	**12,849**
Cash & equivalent	302,946		636,101
Accounts receivable	81,083		48,700
Securities investments	13,556,794		16,015,949
Mortgages	119,556		153,564
Total investments	14,275,008		16,711,053
Segregated fund assets	8,565,675		9,257,298
Total assets	**23,493,593**	**-12**	**26,790,622**
Accts. pay. & accr. liabs	98,250		73,326
Debt	702,915		602,158
Policy liabilities & claims	5,667,588		7,118,925
Segregated fund liabilities	8,565,675		9,257,298
Partic. policyhldrs.' equity	56,065		58,212
Preferred share equity	300,001		300,001
Shareholders' equity	6,656,997		7,257,420
Non-controlling interest	1,030,156		1,279,377
Cash from oper. activs	**397,831**	**+14**	**348,104**
Cash from fin. activs	(293,749)		(342,669)
Cash from invest. activs	(437,237)		202,909
Net cash position	**302,946**	**-52**	**636,101**
Unfunded pension liability	n.a.		17,130
Pension fund surplus	23,063		n.a.
	$		$
Earnings per share*	(53.47)		314.67
Cash flow per share*	112.00		96.31
Cash divd. per share*	10.00		8.75
Extra divd. - cash*	25.00		80.00
Total divd. per share*	**35.00**		**88.75**
	shs		shs
No. of shs. o/s*	3,557,090		3,701,376
Avg. no. of shs. o/s*	3,552,062		3,614,578
	%		%
Net profit margin	n.m.		51.64
Return on equity	(2.85)		17.32
Return on assets	(1.20)		5.06
No. of employees (FTEs)	1,089		895

* Common
[A] Reported in accordance with IFRS

Latest Results

Periods ended:	6m June 30/23[A]		6m June 30/22[oA]
	$000s	%Chg	$000s
Total revenue	1,734,575	n.a.	(2,184,520)
Net income	591,769	n.a.	(957,994)
Net inc. for equity hldrs	489,156	n.a.	(732,966)
Net inc. for non-cont. int	97,920		(218,000)
Net inc. for partic policyhldrs	4,693		(7,028)
	$		$
Earnings per share*	139.08		(206.24)

* Common
[o] Restated
[A] Reported in accordance with IFRS

Historical Summary
(as originally stated)

Fiscal Year	Total Rev. $000s	Net Inc. Bef. Disc. $000s	EPS* $
2022[A]	(647,372)	(327,313)	(53.47)
2021[A]	2,482,476	1,281,992	314.67
2020[A]	2,536,041	603,512	128.21
2019[A]	2,930,093	861,682	185.67
2018[A]	1,076,692	57,001	3.96

* Common
[A] Reported in accordance with IFRS

E.2 E Split Corp.

Symbol - ENS **Exchange** - TSX **CUSIP** - 26916F
Head Office - c/o Middlefield Limited, 1 First Canadian Place, 5800-100 King St W, PO Box 192, Toronto, ON, M5X 1A6 **Telephone** - (416) 362-0714 **Toll-free** - (888) 890-1868 **Fax** - (416) 362-7925
Website - www.middlefield.com
Email - sroberts@middlefield.com
Investor Relations - Sarah Roberts (416) 847-5355
Auditors - Deloitte LLP C.A., Toronto, Ont.
Lawyers - Fasken Martineau DuMoulin LLP, Toronto, Ont.
Transfer Agents - TSX Trust Company
Managers - Middlefield Limited, Calgary, Alta.
Portfolio Advisors - Middlefield Capital Corporation, Toronto, Ont.
Profile - (Ont. 2018) Holds common shares of **Enbridge Inc.** in order to provide preferred shareholders with quarterly cash distributions on a fixed, cumulative and preferential basis and class A shareholders with non-cumulative monthly cash distributions and the opportunity for capital appreciation through exposure to the performance of the Enbridge common shares.

At Dec. 31, 2022, the company held 7,710,000 common shares of **Enbridge Inc.** with a market value of $408,013,200.

The company has a scheduled termination date of June 30, 2028, subject to extension for successive terms of up to five years.

In May 2023, an extension of the maturity date of the company for an additional five-year term to June 30, 2028, was approved.

Directors - Dean Orrico, pres. & CEO, Vaughan, Ont.; Craig Rogers, CFO & corp. sec., Toronto, Ont.; Jeremy T. Brasseur, Toronto, Ont.; Wendy Teo, Toronto, Ont.

Capital Stock

	Authorized (shs.)	Outstanding (shs.)[1]
Preferred	unlimited	21,485,524[2]
Class A	unlimited	20,431,324
Class M	unlimited	100

[1] At June 27, 2023
[2] Classified as debt.

Preferred - Entitled to fixed cumulative preferential quarterly cash distributions of $0.13125 per share to yield 5.25% per annum on the original $10 issue price. Retractable monthly for a price per share equal to 96% of the lesser of: (i) the net asset value (NAV) per unit (1 class A share and 1 preferred share) less the cost to the company for purchasing a class A share in the market for cancellation; and (ii) $10. Retractable in January of each year together with a class A share for a price equal to the NAV per unit less any retraction costs, including commissions. All outstanding preferred shares will be redeemed on June 30, 2028, at a price per share equal to the lesser of: (i) the NAV per share; and (ii) $10 plus accrued and unpaid dividends. Rank in priority to the class A and class M shares with respect to the payment of distributions and the repayment of capital on the dissolution, liquidation or winding-up of the company. Non-voting.

Class A - Entitled to non-cumulative monthly cash distributions of 13¢ per share. No distributions will be paid if the distributions payable on the preferred shares are in arrears or in respect of a cash distribution, after payment of the distribution, the NAV per unit would be less than $15. Retractable monthly for a price equal to 96% of the difference between: (i) the NAV per unit; and (ii) the cost to the company of purchasing a preferred share in the market for cancellation. If the NAV per unit is less than $10, plus accrued and unpaid dividends on a preferred share, the class A retraction price will be nil. Retractable in January of each year together with a preferred share for a price equal to the NAV per unit less any retraction costs, including commissions. All outstanding class A shares will be redeemed on June 30, 2028, at a price per share equal to the greater of: (i) the NAV per unit minus the sum of $10 plus accrued dividends and unpaid dividends per preferred share; and (ii) nil. Rank subsequent to the preferred shares but in priority to the class M shares with respect to the payment of distributions and the repayment of capital on the dissolution, liquidation or winding-up of the company. Non-voting.

Class M - Not entitled to receive distributions. Retractable and redeemable at any time at 10¢ per share. Rank subsequent to both preferred and class A shares with respect to distributions on the dissolution, liquidation or winding-up of the company. One vote per share.

Major Shareholder - E Split Corp. Holding Trust held 100% interest at Mar. 31, 2023.

Price Range - ENS/TSX

Year	Volume	High	Low	Close
2022	13,083,933	$16.98	$13.90	$15.14
2021	16,093,202	$16.19	$11.45	$14.22
2020	2,959,371	$16.94	$8.25	$11.65
2019	1,876,016	$15.91	$10.90	$15.30
2018	1,094,960	$15.28	$10.45	$10.85

Recent Close: $13.30

Capital Stock Changes - On June 6, 2023, public offering of 4,382,200 preferred shares at $10 per share was completed. On June 27, 2023, public offering of 3,328,000 preferred shares at $10 per share was completed.

During 2022, 11 preferred shares and 11 class A shares were retracted.

Dividends

ENS cl A Ra $1.56 pa M est. June 14, 2019**[1]
ENS.PR.A pref cum. Ra $0.525 pa Q
[1] Dividend reinvestment plan implemented eff. October 31, 2018.
** Reinvestment Option

Financial Statistics

Periods ended:	12m Dec. 31/22[A]		12m Dec. 31/21[A]
	$000s	%Chg	$000s
Realized invest. gain (loss)	872		(88)
Unrealized invest. gain (loss)	26,548		27,686
Total revenue	**54,293**	**+25**	**43,487**
General & admin. expense	4,313		2,377
Other operating expense	20		198
Operating expense	**4,333**	**+68**	**2,575**
Operating income	**49,960**	**+22**	**40,912**
Finance costs, gross	8,979		6,036
Pre-tax income	**40,981**	**+18**	**34,876**
Net income	**40,981**	**+18**	**34,876**
Cash & equivalent	9,740		18,991
Accounts receivable	7		8
Investments	408,013		384,657
Total assets	**417,761**	**+3**	**403,655**
Accts. pay. & accr. liabs	251		167
Debt	171,033		171,033
Shareholders' equity	242,008		227,987
Cash from oper. activs	**17,709**	**n.a.**	**(232,237)**
Cash from fin. activs	(26,960)		249,228
Net cash position	**9,740**	**-49**	**18,991**
	$		$
Earnings per share*	2.40		3.49
Cash flow per share*	1.04		(23.24)
Net asset value per share*	14.15		13.33
Cash divd. per share*	1.56		1.56
	shs		shs
No. of shs. o/s*	17,103,324		17,103,335
Avg. no. of shs. o/s*	17,103,335		9,992,550
	%		%
Net profit margin	75.48		80.20
Return on equity	17.44		24.42
Return on assets	12.16		15.68

* Class A
[A] Reported in accordance with IFRS

Note: Net income reflects increase/decrease in net assets from operations.

Historical Summary
(as originally stated)

Fiscal Year	Total Rev. $000s	Net Inc. Bef. Disc. $000s	EPS* $
2022[A]	54,293	40,981	2.40
2021[A]	43,487	34,876	3.49
2020[A]	(11,481)	(15,046)	(3.60)
2019[A]	20,268	17,476	5.47
2018[A1]	(2,846)	(4,360)	(1.36)

* Class A
[A] Reported in accordance with IFRS
[1] 6 months ended Dec. 31, 2018.

E.3 ECC Ventures 4 Corp.

Symbol - ECCF.P **Exchange** - TSX-VEN **CUSIP** - 268275
Head Office - c/o Emprise Capital Corporation, 1600-609 Granville St, PO Box 10068 Pacific Centre, Vancouver, BC, V7Y 1C3 **Telephone** - (778) 331-8505 **Fax** - (866) 824-8321
Email - dmcfaul@emprisecapital.com
Investor Relations - Douglas McFaul (778) 331-8505
Auditors - Davidson & Company LLP C.A., Vancouver, B.C.
Lawyers - Cassels Brock & Blackwell LLP, Vancouver, B.C.
Transfer Agents - Endeavor Trust Corporation, Vancouver, B.C.
Profile - (B.C. 2021) Capital Pool Company.
Directors - Douglas (Doug) McFaul, pres., CEO, CFO & corp. sec., Coquitlam, B.C.; Brent Ackerman, Mayne Island, B.C.; Rick Cox, B.C.

Capital Stock

	Authorized (shs.)	Outstanding (shs.)[1]
Common	unlimited	5,650,000

[1] At June 21, 2023

Major Shareholder - Douglas (Doug) McFaul held 15.9% interest at June 21, 2023.

Price Range - ECCF.P/TSX-VEN

Year	Volume	High	Low	Close
2022	6,500	$0.17	$0.16	$0.16
2021	160,000	$0.13	$0.13	$0.13

Recent Close: $0.14

Capital Stock Changes - There were no changes to capital stock during 2022.

E.4 ECC Ventures 5 Corp.

Symbol - ECCV.P **Exchange** - TSX-VEN **CUSIP** - 268274
Head Office - c/o Emprise Capital Corporation, 1600-609 Granville St, PO Box 10068 Pacific Centre, Vancouver, BC, V7Y 1C3 **Telephone** - (778) 331-8505 **Fax** - (778) 508-9923
Email - dmcfaul@emprisecapital.com
Investor Relations - Douglas McFaul (778) 331-8505
Auditors - Davidson & Company LLP C.A., Vancouver, B.C.
Lawyers - Cassels Brock & Blackwell LLP, Vancouver, B.C.
Transfer Agents - Endeavor Trust Corporation, Vancouver, B.C.
Profile - (B.C. 2021) Capital Pool Company.

Recent Merger and Acquisition Activity

Status: pending **Revised:** May 12, 2022
UPDATE: A definitive agreement was entered into. PREVIOUS: ECC Ventures 5 Corp. (ECC5) entered into a letter of intent for the Qualifying Transaction reverse takeover acquisition of Tel Aviv, Israel-based Shelfie-Tech Ltd. for issuance of 87,338,348 post-consolidated ECC5 common shares at 42¢ per share (following a 1-for-1.5 share consolidation). Shelfie is developing an artificial intelligence (AI) powered shelf inventory analytics robotic platform's solution which consists of a digital image capturing system and centralized management system that provides real-time visibility into the retail shelf supply, pinpointing products running low on inventory. Upon completion, Shelfie would amalgamate with ECC5's wholly owned 1360621 B.C. Ltd., and ECC5 would change its name to Shelfie-Tech Ltd.

Directors - Douglas (Doug) McFaul, pres., CEO, CFO & corp. sec., Coquitlam, B.C.; David Bremner, Vancouver, B.C.; Peter Dickie, West Vancouver, B.C.

Capital Stock

	Authorized (shs.)	Outstanding (shs.)[1]
Common	unlimited	5,650,000

[1] At June 21, 2023

Major Shareholder - Douglas (Doug) McFaul held 31.9% interest at June 21, 2023.

Price Range - ECCV.P/TSX-VEN

Year	Volume	High	Low	Close
2022	4,000	$0.15	$0.15	$0.15
2021	160,000	$0.13	$0.13	$0.13

Capital Stock Changes - There were no changes to capital stock during 2022.

Wholly Owned Subsidiaries

1360621 B.C. Ltd., B.C.

E.5 ECC Ventures 6 Corp.

Symbol - ECCS.P **Exchange** - TSX-VEN **CUSIP** - 26827M
Head Office - c/o Emprise Capital Corporation, 1600-609 Granville St, PO Box 10068 Pacific Centre, Vancouver, BC, V7Y 1C3 **Telephone** - (778) 331-8505 **Fax** - (778) 508-9923
Investor Relations - Peter Dickie (778) 331-8505
Auditors - Davidson & Company LLP C.A., Vancouver, B.C.
Transfer Agents - Endeavor Trust Corporation, Vancouver, B.C.
Profile - (B.C. 2021) Capital Pool Company.
Directors - Peter Dickie, pres., CEO, CFO & corp. sec., West Vancouver, B.C.; Charles Desjardins, Vancouver, B.C.; Nathan Dumo, Vancouver, B.C.

Capital Stock

	Authorized (shs.)	Outstanding (shs.)[1]
Common	unlimited	5,650,000

[1] At June 21, 2023

Major Shareholder - Nathan Dumo held 31.9% interest at June 21, 2023.

Price Range - ECCS.P/TSX-VEN

Year	Volume	High	Low	Close
2022	6,500	$0.16	$0.14	$0.16
2021	160,000	$0.14	$0.14	$0.14

Recent Close: $0.16

Capital Stock Changes - There were no changes to capital stock during 2022.

E.6 ECN Capital Corp.

Symbol - ECN **Exchange** - TSX **CUSIP** - 26829L
Head Office - 2800-161 Bay St, Toronto, ON, M5J 2S1 **Telephone** - (416) 646-4710 **Fax** - (844) 402-1074
Website - www.ecncapitalcorp.com
Email - jwimsatt@ecncapitalcorp.com
Investor Relations - John Wimsatt (561) 717-4772
Auditors - Ernst & Young LLP C.A., Toronto, Ont.
Transfer Agents - Computershare Trust Company of Canada Inc., Toronto, Ont.
FP500 Revenue Ranking - 597
Employees - 560 at Dec. 31, 2022
Profile - (Ont. 2016) Originates, manages and advises on consumer loans on behalf of U.S. banks, credit unions, life insurance companies, pension funds and institutional investors.

Operations are conducted through three operating companies: **Triad Financial Services, Inc.**, which represents the manufactured housing finance segment; and **Source One Financial Services, LLC** and

Intercoastal Financial Group, LLC, representing the recreational vehicles and marine finance segment.

Triad originates and manages longer duration secured consumer loan portfolios. These loans are primarily prime and super-prime loans to consumers for the purchase of manufactured homes throughout the U.S. with limited recourse. Originations are sourced through a national network of 3,000 dealers and manufacturers. Triad also assists third parties in servicing, underwriting and originating manufactured housing loan transactions, and provides floor plan financing for select dealers and manufacturers.

Source One provides consumer lending programs and outsourced finance and insurance solutions for the recreational vehicle and marine industries through more than 2,000 dealers in 38 U.S. states. Intercoastal Financial Group originates prime and super-prime loans to consumers to facilitate the purchase of recreational and marine vehicles through a network of sales representatives across the U.S.

Year ended Dec. 31	2022	2021
	US$000	US$000
Originations	2,197,325	1,042,878
Avg. earning assets, owned	421,066	196,251
Avg. earning assets, managed	3,712,017	2,856,522

On Mar. 7, 2023, the company announced it has initiated a review of strategic alternatives to maximize shareholder value. Alternatives would include a sale of the company or one of its business units, strategic funding arrangements and capital relationships as well as other options.

On Jan. 31, 2023, the company acquired Lodi, Calif.-based **Wake Lending, LLC**, which originates prime and super-prime recreational vehicle and marine loans through dealers and sales representatives primarily on the western coast of the U.S., for US$2,500,000.

Recent Merger and Acquisition Activity

Status: completed **Revised:** Oct. 4, 2022

UPDATE: The transaction was completed. PREVIOUS: ECN Capital Corp. agreed to sell wholly owned ECN Kessler Holdco LLC, which holds Kessler Financial Services, LLC, to funds managed by Stone Point Capital LLC for cash proceeds of US$210,000,000. Kessler manages, advises and structures consumer credit card portfolios and other financial products for credit card issuers, banks, credit unions and payment networks. It has US$28 billion in managed credit card portfolios.

Status: completed **Announced:** July 1, 2022

ECN Capital Corp. acquired Fort Pierce, Fla.-based Intercoastal Financial Group, LLC (IFG), a marine and recreational vehicle finance company, for total consideration of US$74,161,000, including US$55,814,000 in cash and deferred consideration of US$18,347,000 to be paid over the next two years. IFG originates prime and super-prime loans on behalf of more than 18 bank partners through a network of sales representatives nationwide. IFG, together with Source One Financial Services, LLC, would form ECN's new operating segment, marine and recreational vehicles finance.

Directors - William W. (Bill) Lovatt, chr., Winnipeg, Man.; Steven K. Hudson, CEO, Palm Beach, Fla.; Carol E. Goldman, Des Peres, Mo.; Karen L. Martin, Toronto, Ont.; David D. Morris, Montréal, Qué.; Paul J. Stoyan, Toronto, Ont.

Other Exec. Officers - Michael Lepore, CFO; Algis Vaitonis, chief credit officer; John Wimsatt, chief invest. officer; Matthew (Matt) Nelson, pres. & CEO, Source One Financial Services, LLC; Michael Tolbert, pres., Triad Financial Services, Inc.; Hans Kraaz, CEO, Intercoastal Financial Group, LLC

Capital Stock

	Authorized (shs.)	Outstanding (shs.)[1]
Preferred	unlimited	nil
Series A		nil
Series B		nil
Series C		3,712,400
Series D		nil
Common	unlimited	245,779,995

[1] At May 16, 2023

Preferred Series C - Entitled to cumulative annual dividends of Cdn$1.9843 per share payable quarterly to June 30, 2027, and thereafter at a rate reset every five years equal to the five-year Government of Canada yield plus 5.19%. Redeemable on June 30, 2027, and on June 30 every five years thereafter at Cdn$25 per share plus declared and unpaid dividends. Convertible at the holder's option on June 30, 2027, and on June 30 every five years thereafter, into floating rate preferred series D shares on a share-for-share basis, subject to certain conditions. The series D shares would pay a quarterly dividend equal to the 90-day Canadian Treasury bill rate plus 5.19%. Non-voting.

Common - One vote per share.

Normal Course Issuer Bid - The company plans to make normal course purchases of up to 22,170,050 common shares representing 10% of the public float. The bid commenced on Sept. 19, 2022, and expires on Sept. 18, 2023.

The company plans to make normal course purchases of up to 371,040 series C preferred shares representing 10% of the public float. The bid commenced on Sept. 19, 2022, and expires on Sept. 18, 2023.

Major Shareholder - North Peak Capital Management, LLC held 15.22% interest and Voss Capital LLC held 13.08% interest at May 16, 2023.

Price Range - ECN/TSX

Year	Volume	High	Low	Close
2022	165,557,172	$7.29	$2.60	$2.78
2021	151,907,414	$12.24	$4.60	$5.34
2020	130,672,851	$6.60	$2.67	$6.47
2019	125,309,901	$5.19	$3.40	$4.79
2018	298,347,834	$3.97	$3.13	$3.45

Recent Close: $2.69

Capital Stock Changes - During 2022, common shares were issued as follows: 1,416,395 by private placement, 388,919 on vesting of restricted share units and 8,916 on exercise of options. In addition, 2,550,200 common shares were repurchased under a Normal Course Issuer Bid.

Dividends

ECN com Ra $0.04 pa Q est. Mar. 31, 2022
Prev. Rate: $0.12 est. Mar. 31, 2021
Prev. Rate: $0.10 est. Jan. 15, 2020
$3.36◆ Dec. 22/21 $4.14◆r Dec. 22/21
Paid in 2023: $0.03 2022: $0.04 2021: $0.09 + $3.36◆ + $4.14◆r

ECN.PR.C pfd ser C cum. red. exch. Adj. Ra $1.98425 pa Q est. Oct. 3, 2022

pfd ser A cum. red. exch. Adj. Ra $1.625 pa Q est. Mar. 31, 2017[1]
$0.40625f Dec. 31/21

[1] Redeemed Dec. 31, 2021 at $25 per sh.

◆ Special **f** Final Payment **r** Return of Capital

Wholly Owned Subsidiaries

ECN (U.S.) Holdings Corp., Del.
- 100% int. in **ECN Platinum LLC**, Del.
  - 100% int. in **Intercoastal Financial Group, LLC**, Fort Pierce, Fla.
  - 100% int. in **Source One Financial Services, LLC**, Lakeville, Minn.
- 100% int. in **Triad Financial Services, Inc.**, Jacksonville, Fla.

Note: The preceding list includes only the major related companies in which interests are held.

Financial Statistics

Periods ended:	12m Dec. 31/22[A]		12m Dec. 31/21[oA]
	US$000s	%Chg	US$000s
Total revenue	**199,012**	**+58**	**126,250**
Salaries & benefits	62,208		46,746
General & admin. expense	41,508		37,668
Stock-based compensation	12,189		24,194
Operating expense	**115,905**	**+7**	**108,608**
Operating income	**83,107**	**+371**	**17,642**
Deprec. & amort.	12,944		9,373
Finance costs, gross	43,652		21,072
Pre-tax income	**17,258**	**n.a.**	**(23,374)**
Income taxes	10,538		(7,405)
Net inc. bef. disc. opers	**6,720**	**n.a.**	**(15,969)**
Income from disc. opers	9,171		985,765
Net income	**15,891**	**-98**	**969,796**
Cash & equivalent	15,292		47,239
Inventories	nil		7,950
Accounts receivable	203,385		148,902
Investments	712,215		246,430
Fixed assets, net	50,083		44,460
Right-of-use assets	19,098		17,758
Intangibles, net	229,925		368,590
Total assets	**1,416,331**	**+24**	**1,146,115**
Accts. pay. & accr. liabs	76,823		176,033
Debt	1,007,998		274,597
Lease liabilities	21,145		19,176
Preferred share equity	67,052		67,052
Shareholders' equity	193,675		218,627
Cash from oper. activs	**(877,090)**	**n.a.**	**(1,272)**
Cash from fin. activs	721,744		(1,833,097)
Cash from invest. activs	116,276		1,697,939
Net cash position	**15,292**	**-68**	**47,239**
Capital expenditures	(26,553)		(7,091)
Capital disposals	36,742		nil
	US$		US$
Earns. per sh. bef disc opers*	0.01		(0.13)
Earnings per share*	0.04		3.92
Cash flow per share*	(3.56)		(0.01)
Cash divd. per share*	$0.04		$4.23
Extra divd. - cash*	$nil		$7.50
Total divd. per share*	**$0.04**		**$11.73**
	shs		shs
No. of shs. o/s*	245,382,585		246,118,555
Avg. no. of shs. o/s*	246,496,920		243,732,318
	%		%
Net profit margin	3.38		(12.65)
Return on equity	1.21		(7.38)
Return on assets	1.85		(0.11)
Foreign sales percent	100		100
No. of employees (FTEs)	560		462

* Common
[o] Restated
[A] Reported in accordance with IFRS

Latest Results

Periods ended:	3m Mar. 31/23[A]		3m Mar. 31/22[oA]
	US$000s	%Chg	US$000s
Total revenue	47,843	+39	34,532
Net inc. bef. disc. opers	(19,522)	n.a.	(36)
Income from disc. opers	nil		5,506
Net income	(19,522)	n.a.	5,470
	US$		US$
Earns. per sh. bef. disc. opers.*	(0.09)		(0.00)
Earnings per share*	(0.09)		0.02

* Common
[o] Restated
[A] Reported in accordance with IFRS

Historical Summary
(as originally stated)

Fiscal Year	Total Rev.	Net Inc. Bef. Disc.	EPS*
	US$000s	US$000s	US$
2022[A]	199,012	6,720	0.01
2021[A]	221,376	4,969	(0.04)
2020[A]	263,609	15,824	0.03
2019[A]	247,956	10,382	0.00
2018[A]	203,965	(2,635)	(0.04)

* Common
[A] Reported in accordance with IFRS

E.7 EF EnergyFunders Ventures, Inc.

Symbol - EFV **Exchange** - TSX-VEN **CUSIP** - 26843R
Head Office - 716 S. Frio St, Suite 201, San Antonio, TX, United States, 78207 **Telephone** - (254) 699-0975
Website - www.energyfunders.com
Email - laura@energyfunders.com
Investor Relations - Laura Pommer Fidler (254) 699-0975
Auditors - Fruci & Associates II, PLLC C.P.A., Spokane, Wash.
Bankers - Royal Bank of Canada, Toronto, Ont.
Lawyers - DLA Piper (Canada) LLP
Transfer Agents - TSX Trust Company, Toronto, Ont.

Profile - (B.C. 2019; orig. Que., 1945) Has oil and gas interests in Alberta, Louisiana and Texas. Also owns a financial technology platform.

In Alberta, holds 45% interest (**Viking Investments Group, Inc.** 50%, **EnergyFunders Yield Fund I GP LLC** 5%) in Joffre D-3 Oil Unit No. 1.

In Louisiana, holds interests in Middlebrooks and Savoy wells in St. Landry Parish and Acadia Parish, respectively.

In Texas, holds 50% interest in non-producing well and certain lease holdings totaling 200,000 acres, Polk and Tyler ctys., including the Woodbine, Eagle Ford and Yegua sandstones.

At Dec. 31, 2021, the company had 3 gross (0.6 net) producing oil wells, 1 gross (0.7 net) producing gas well and 10 gross (5.4 net) non-producing oil and gas wells.

In addition, wholly owned **EF Resources, Inc.** (EFR) owns the EnergyFunders financial technology platform that allows individuals and entities to invest directly into energy investments. EFR manages investment portfolio companies, charging a carried interest on production income as well as a management fee on portfolio companies as well as receives reimbursement income from the portfolio companies for soft costs incurred. EFR does not invest directly in the portfolio companies.

Periods ended:	12m Dec. 31/21	12m Dec. 31/20
Avg. oil & NGL prod., bbl/d	394	nil
Avg. gas prod., mcf/d	3	399
Avg. BOE prod., bbl/d	68	67
Avg. oil & NGL price, $/bbl	45.07	n.a.
Avg. gas price, $/mcf	4.63	2.51
Oil reserves, net, mbbl	156	173
Gas reserves, net, mmcf	719	915
BOE reserves, net, mbbl	280	326

Predecessor Detail - Name changed from Paleo Resources, Inc., Mar. 7, 2022.

Directors - Roger S. Braugh Jr., exec. chr., Corpus Christi, Tex.; Laura Pommer Fidler, CEO; Garrett Glass, CFO & contr.; Paul Sewell, Tex.

Other Exec. Officers - Casey Minshew, chief comml. officer; Virginia U. Light, v-p, reservoir eng. & regulatory affairs & corp. sec.

Capital Stock

	Authorized (shs.)	Outstanding (shs.)[1]
Common	unlimited	543,284,697

[1] At Mar. 31, 2022

Major Shareholder - Roger S. Braugh Jr. held 27.55% interest, Christopher J. (Chris) Pettit held 25.03% interest and Todo Gato Holdings, LLC held 11.58% interest at Nov. 4, 2021.

Price Range - EFV/TSX-VEN

Year	Volume	High	Low	Close
2022	7,244,663	$0.03	$0.01	$0.01
2021	16,414,358	$0.04	$0.01	$0.01
2020	13,292,377	$0.04	$0.01	$0.01
2019	6,543,266	$0.10	$0.01	$0.03
2018	5,725,355	$0.14	$0.03	$0.08

Recent Close: $0.01

Wholly Owned Subsidiaries

EF Resources Inc., Houston, Tex.
- 100% int. in **EF Advisor, LLC**, Tex.

- 100% int. in **EF Equity Holdings LLC**
- 100% int. in **EF Funding Portal, LLC**, Tex.
- 100% int. in **EF GP, LLC**, Tex.
- 100% int. in **EF Manager, LLC**
- 100% int. in **EF Managment Holding, LLC**
- 100% int. in **EF VC2, LLC**, Tex.
- 100% int. in **EF VC6, LLC**, Tex.
- 100% int. in **EnergyFunders, LLC**, Tex.

Paleo Resources (USA), Inc., United States.
- 100% int. in **Tanager Chalk, Inc.** Inactive.

Tanager Energy GP, LLC Inactive.
Tanager Energy, LP Inactive.

Financial Statistics

Periods ended:	12m Dec. 31/21^A		12m Dec. 31/20^A
	US$000s	%Chg	US$000s
Operating revenue	**906**	**+163**	**344**
Cost of sales	173		121
General & admin expense	1,050		698
Operating expense	**1,223**	**+49**	**819**
Operating income	**(317)**	**n.a.**	**(475)**
Deprec., depl. & amort.	405		270
Finance costs, gross	472		322
Investment income	nil		21
Write-downs/write-offs	nil		(9,767)
Pre-tax income	**(148)**	**n.a.**	**(10,729)**
Net income	**(148)**	**n.a.**	**(10,729)**
Net inc. for equity hldrs	**(220)**	**n.a.**	**(10,712)**
Net inc. for non-cont. int	**72**	**n.a.**	**(17)**
Cash & equivalent	129		147
Accounts receivable	177		41
Current assets	322		218
Long-term investments	498		nil
Intangibles, net	439		439
Explor./devel. properties	1,313		970
Total assets	**2,822**	**+51**	**1,875**
Accts. pay. & accr. liabs	2,557		2,217
Current liabilities	5,235		8,023
Long-term debt, gross	705		2,271
Long-term debt, net	325		453
Shareholders' equity	(3,521)		(6,986)
Non-controlling interest	11		(6)
Cash from oper. activs	**54**	**n.a.**	**(603)**
Cash from fin. activs	629		663
Cash from invest. activs	(694)		(97)
Net cash position	**129**	**-12**	**147**
Capital expenditures	(276)		(122)
	US$		US$
Earnings per share*	(0.00)		(0.04)
Cash flow per share*	0.00		(0.00)
	shs		shs
No. of shs. o/s*	543,284,697		313,179,813
Avg. no. of shs. o/s*	435,375,979		277,541,099
	%		%
Net profit margin	(16.34)		n.m.
Return on equity	n.m.		n.m.
Return on assets	13.80		(167.80)
Foreign sales percent	95		100

* Common
^A Reported in accordance with U.S. GAAP

Latest Results

Periods ended:	3m Mar. 31/22^A		3m Mar. 31/21^A
	US$000s	%Chg	US$000s
Operating revenue	236	+83	129
Net income	(201)	n.a.	(295)
Net inc. for equity hldrs	(201)	n.a.	(294)
Net inc. for non-cont. int	nil		(1)
	US$		US$
Earnings per share*	(0.00)		(0.00)

* Common
^A Reported in accordance with U.S. GAAP

Historical Summary
(as originally stated)

Fiscal Year	Oper. Rev.	Net Inc. Bef. Disc.	EPS*
	US$000s	US$000s	US$
2021^A	906	(148)	(0.00)
2020^A	344	(10,729)	(0.04)
2019^A	262	1,480	0.01
	$000s	$000s	$
2018^B	760	(3,170)	(0.02)
2017^B	379	(9,718)	(0.09)

* Common
^A Reported in accordance with U.S. GAAP
^B Reported in accordance with IFRS

E.8 EGF Theramed Health Corp.

Symbol - TMED **Exchange** - CSE **CUSIP** - 268469
Head Office - 1600-609 Granville St, PO Box 10068 Pacific Centre, Vancouver, BC, V7Y 1C3 **Telephone** - (778) 331-4303 **Toll-free** - (888) 425-3126
Website - www.egftheramedhealth.com
Email - dmcfaul@emprisecapital.com
Investor Relations - Doug McFaul (778) 331-8505
Auditors - Dale Matheson Carr-Hilton LaBonte LLP C.A., Vancouver, B.C.
Bankers - Bank of Montreal, Vancouver, B.C.
Transfer Agents - Endeavor Trust Corporation, Vancouver, B.C.
Profile - (B.C. 2011) Developing technologies, products and diagnostic tools for personalized medical care, including research with natural health and wellness products, as well as researches and develops commercial exploitation of psychedelic and psychedelic-based products.

Through wholly owned **Seedadelic Med Corp.**, distributes psychedelic plant seeds that contains LSA (d-lysergic acid amide) such as Argyreia Nervosa (Hawaiian Baby Woodrose) and Ipomoea Violacea (Morning Glory) and plans to operate a web-based and mobile application, allowing users to register and purchase psychedelic plant seed products on-line; wholly owned **Hemp Extraction Technology Corp.**, manufactures medical grade oil from industrial hemp using its proprietary extraction technology; wholly owned **Medical Green Natural List Corp.**, develops and operates a software and portal for a medical marketplace app to connect buyers with sellers; and 50%-owned **Western Agri Supply Solutions Ltd.**, provides supply sourcing and supply chain management to the industrial hemp market.

In August 2022, the company entered into a non-binding agreement to acquire B.C.-based **Reefer Keeper Delivery Corp.** for issuance of 8,000,000 common shares at a deemed price of 13¢ per share. Reefer Keeper offers a delivery application and web-based platforms for obtaining cannabis products from local dispensaries.

Predecessor Detail - Name changed from Theramed Health Corporation, Oct. 24, 2019; basis 1 new for 100 old shs.
Directors - Usama (Sam) Chaudhry, CFO, Vancouver, B.C.; George Anstey, B.C.
Other Exec. Officers - Connor Yuen, CEO

Capital Stock

	Authorized (shs.)	Outstanding (shs.)[1]
Common	unlimited	10,491,161

[1] At Nov. 29, 2022

Major Shareholder - Widely held at Mar. 24, 2021.

Price Range - TMED/CSE

Year	Volume	High	Low	Close
2022	908,604	$1.15	$0.08	$0.62
2021	1,349,107	$5.40	$0.50	$0.70
2020	1,232,478	$40.00	$1.10	$3.40
2019	19,628	$480.00	$12.80	$16.00
2018	3,809	$1,480.00	$340.00	$340.00

Consolidation: 1-for-20 cons. in July 2022; 1-for-100 cons. in Oct. 2019
Recent Close: $0.31
Capital Stock Changes - On July 11, 2022, common shares were consolidated on a 1-for-20 basis.

In July 2021, private placement of 2,083,334 units (1 common share & ½ warrant) at 12¢ per unit was completed.

Wholly Owned Subsidiaries

Hemp Extraction Technology Corp., Canada.
Medical Green Natural List Corp., Canada.
Seedadelic Med Corp., Ont.

Investments

33.06% int. in **Pharmadelic Labs Inc.**, Las Vegas, Nev. Inactive.
50% int. in **Western Agri Supply Solutions Corp.**, Canada.

Financial Statistics

Periods ended:	12m June 30/22^A		12m June 30/21^A
	$000s	%Chg	$000s
General & admin expense	989		1,037
Stock-based compensation	nil		71
Operating expense	**989**	**-11**	**1,108**
Operating income	**(989)**	**n.a.**	**(1,108)**
Finance income	1		5
Finance costs, gross	16		66
Write-downs/write-offs	(346)		452
Pre-tax income	**(1,364)**	**n.a.**	**(744)**
Net income	**(1,364)**	**n.a.**	**(744)**
Net inc. for equity hldrs	**(1,350)**	**n.a.**	**(974)**
Net inc. for non-cont. int	**(14)**	**n.a.**	**229**
Cash & equivalent	15		703
Accounts receivable	155		139
Current assets	176		849
Intangibles, net	nil		346
Total assets	**179**	**-85**	**1,197**
Accts. pay. & accr. liabs	1,244		1,233
Current liabilities	2,514		2,408
Long-term debt, gross	3		3
Equity portion of conv. debs	26		26
Shareholders' equity	(1,020)		91
Non-controlling interest	(1,315)		(1,302)
Cash from oper. activs	**(993)**	**n.a.**	**(784)**
Cash from fin. activs	306		712
Cash from invest. activs	nil		410
Net cash position	**15**	**-98**	**702**
	$		$
Earnings per share*	(0.63)		(1.00)
Cash flow per share*	(0.46)		(0.73)
	shs		shs
No. of shs. o/s*	2,157,849		2,053,683
Avg. no. of shs. o/s*	2,155,260		1,073,459
	%		%
Net profit margin	n.a.		n.a.
Return on equity	n.m.		n.m.
Return on assets	(195.93)		(79.44)

* Common
^A Reported in accordance with IFRS

Latest Results

Periods ended:	3m Sept. 30/22^A		3m Sept. 30/21^A
	$000s	%Chg	$000s
Net income	(294)	n.a.	(161)
Net inc. for equity hldrs	(279)	n.a.	(161)
Net inc. for non-cont. int	(15)		nil
	$		$
Earnings per share*	(0.03)		(0.07)

* Common
^A Reported in accordance with IFRS

Historical Summary
(as originally stated)

Fiscal Year	Oper. Rev.	Net Inc. Bef. Disc.	EPS*
	$000s	$000s	$
2022^A	nil	(1,364)	(0.63)
2021^A	nil	(744)	(1.00)
2020^A	nil	(21,620)	(124.20)
2019^A	nil	(14,395)	(375.40)
2018^A	nil	(936)	(80.00)

* Common
^A Reported in accordance with IFRS

Note: Adjusted throughout for 1-for-20 cons. in July 2022; 1-for-100 cons. in Oct. 2019

E.9 EQ Inc.

Symbol - EQ **Exchange** - TSX-VEN **CUSIP** - 26884V
Head Office - 401-1235 Bay St, Toronto, ON, M5R 3K4 **Telephone** - (416) 597-8889 **Toll-free** - (866) 962-9764 **Fax** - (416) 597-2345
Website - www.eqworks.com
Email - peter.kanniah@eqworks.com
Investor Relations - Peter Kanniah (416) 260-4326
Auditors - RSM Canada LLP C.A., Toronto, Ont.
Lawyers - Gowling WLG (Canada) LLP, Toronto, Ont.
Transfer Agents - TSX Trust Company, Toronto, Ont.
Employees - 42 at Dec. 31, 2022
Profile - (Ont. 2000 amalg.) Provides actionable intelligence for businesses to attract, retain and grow the customer base using unique data sets, advanced analytics, machine learning and artificial intelligence.

Focuses on targeted advertising and incorporates advertising technologies, data analytics and programmatic media buying capabilities into a single system.

The company's Software-as-a-Service technology platforms consist of LOCUS, ATOM, Paymi and Clear Lake. LOCUS is an automated data processing technology that provides customized audiences and reporting data on-demand through capturing data about places people go. ATOM is a programmatic media buying platform that enables the company to purchase targeted media for its clients to influence consumer behaviour. Focusing specifically on mobile networks, ATOM allows clients to target its advertising initiatives through various demographic, geographic, and behavioural profiles. Paymi is a cloud-based marketing platform that uses card linking technology to enable consumers to receive cash-back rewards for credit and debit card transactions and offer merchant partners the ability to understand more about their customers to drive greater sales and increase market share. Customers include medium to large scale businesses, with physical locations, advertising agencies and research firms who want to better understand their customers and potential customers. Clear Lake is a consumer insight platform which provides users with real-time access in consumer purchasing panels and incorporates aggregated transactional spend data, geospatial insights on consumer location, other proprietary and exclusive data.

Predecessor Detail - Name changed from Cyberplex Inc., June 13, 2013.

Directors - Vernon Lobo, chr., Toronto, Ont.; Geoffrey A. Rotstein, pres. & CEO, Toronto, Ont.; James Beriker, San Francisco, Calif.

Other Exec. Officers - Peter Kanniah, CFO & corp. sec.; Mark Finney, chief revenue officer; Dilshan Kathriarachchi, chief tech. officer; Mark Ditkofsky, exec. v-p, data platforms & strategy

Capital Stock

	Authorized (shs.)	Outstanding (shs.)[1]
Common	unlimited	69,468,957

[1] At May 19, 2023

Major Shareholder - Widely held at Apr. 28, 2023.

Price Range - EQ/TSX-VEN

Year	Volume	High	Low	Close
2022	3,931,052	$1.29	$0.99	$1.20
2021	6,501,532	$1.90	$1.10	$1.20
2020	8,455,779	$1.67	$0.73	$1.63
2019	3,822,142	$0.94	$0.62	$0.94
2018	5,810,201	$0.77	$0.54	$0.73

Recent Close: $0.95

Capital Stock Changes - There were no changes to capital stock during 2022.

Wholly Owned Subsidiaries

CX Digital Media U.S.A Inc., Del.
- 100% int. in **CX U.S.A. Pacific, Inc.**, Calif.
- 100% int. in **CX U.S.A. Southwest, Inc.**, Tex.

EQ Advertising Group Ltd., Ont.
Integrated Reward Inc., Ont.
Tapped Networks Inc., Toronto, Ont.

Financial Statistics

Periods ended:	12m Dec. 31/22[A]		12m Dec. 31/21[A]
	$000s	%Chg	$000s
Operating revenue	**10,979**	**-9**	**12,086**
Salaries & benefits	4,725		4,629
General & admin expense	11,586		10,799
Stock-based compensation	230		643
Operating expense	**16,541**	**+3**	**16,071**
Operating income	**(5,562)**	**n.a.**	**(3,985)**
Deprec., depl. & amort.	710		586
Finance income	43		66
Finance costs, gross	89		153
Pre-tax income	**(6,435)**	**n.a.**	**(5,955)**
Net income	**(6,435)**	**n.a.**	**(5,955)**
Cash & equivalent	1,253		8,763
Accounts receivable	3,535		4,687
Current assets	5,022		13,838
Fixed assets, net	55		101
Right-of-use assets	nil		6
Intangibles, net	5,070		5,107
Total assets	**10,147**	**-47**	**19,052**
Accts. pay. & accr. liabs.	3,488		4,514
Current liabilities	4,908		7,531
Long-term debt, gross	79		77
Long-term debt, net	nil		77
Shareholders' equity	5,239		11,444
Cash from oper. activs.	**(5,623)**	**n.a.**	**(3,090)**
Cash from fin. activs.	(45)		9,996
Cash from invest. activs.	(1,883)		(1,363)
Net cash position	**1,253**	**-86**	**8,763**
Capital expenditures	(21)		(58)
	$		$
Earnings per share*	(0.09)		(0.09)
Cash flow per share*	(0.08)		(0.05)
	shs		shs
No. of shs. o/s*	69,435,624		69,435,624
Avg. no. of shs. o/s*	69,435,624		67,266,224
	%		%
Net profit margin	(58.61)		(49.27)
Return on equity	(77.14)		(74.47)
Return on assets	(43.47)		(39.96)
Foreign sales percent	1		1
No. of employees (FTEs)	42		58

* Common
[A] Reported in accordance with IFRS

Latest Results

Periods ended:	3m Mar. 31/23[A]		3m Mar. 31/22[A]
	$000s	%Chg	$000s
Operating revenue	1,691	-38	2,714
Net income	(1,388)	n.a.	(1,859)
	$		$
Earnings per share*	(0.02)		(0.03)

* Common
[A] Reported in accordance with IFRS

Historical Summary
(as originally stated)

Fiscal Year	Oper. Rev.	Net Inc. Bef. Disc.	EPS*
	$000s	$000s	$
2022[A]	10,979	(6,435)	(0.09)
2021[A]	12,086	(5,955)	(0.09)
2020[A]	10,421	(3,427)	(0.06)
2019[A]	8,965	(1,914)	(0.04)
2018[A]	5,868	(1,830)	(0.05)

* Common
[A] Reported in accordance with IFRS

E.10 EQB Inc.*

Symbol - EQB **Exchange** - TSX **CUSIP** - 26886R
Head Office - Equitable Bank Tower, 700-30 St. Clair Ave W, Toronto, ON, M4V 3A1 **Telephone** - (416) 515-7000 **Toll-free** - (866) 407-0004 **Fax** - (416) 515-7001
Website - eqbank.investorroom.com/home
Email - investor_enquiry@eqbank.ca
Investor Relations - Richard Gill (416) 513-3638
Auditors - KPMG LLP C.A., Toronto, Ont.
Transfer Agents - Computershare Trust Company of Canada Inc., Toronto, Ont.
FP500 Revenue Ranking - 247
Employees - 1,685 at Dec. 31, 2022

Profile - (Ont. 2004) Through wholly owned **Equitable Bank**, a Schedule I Canadian bank, provides savings and lending products and trust services to more than 488,000 personal and commercial customers and 200 credit unions across Canada through a digital, branchless business model, under the Equitable Bank, EQ Bank, Bennington Financial and Concentra Trust brands.

Personal Banking - Offers deposit products including guaranteed investment certificates (GICs) and high-interest savings accounts (HISAs), as well as single-family loans, home equity lines of credit and wealth decumulation solutions, such as reverse mortgages and insurance lending solutions (cash surrender value lines of credit and immediate financing arrangements). Savings products are offered through the digital banking platform **EQ Bank**, wholly owned **Equitable Bank** and **Equitable Trust**, and a network of independent financial planners and brokers. Personal loan products are originated through a network of brokers, business partners and other third party distribution agents.

Commercial Banking - Offers commercial real estate lending, specialized financing solutions and equipment loans, as well as provides credit union and trust services. Operations are conducted through the following business lines: **Business Enterprise Solutions**, which provides commercial real estate loans to entrepreneurs and small and medium-sized enterprises (SMEs); **Commercial Finance Group**, which offers loans, including bridge loans, construction loans and asset repositioning transactions, to medium-sized institutional and corporate investors; **Multi-Unit Insured**, which focuses on multi-unit residential mortgages insured by Canada Mortgage and Housing Corporation; **Specialized Finance**, which provides secured lending solutions to mortgage investment corporations and other specialty lenders; **Equipment Financing**, which operates through wholly owned **Bennington Financial Corp.**, a provider of commercial vehicle and equipment leasing to small and established business customers with a focus on transportation, construction and food service; **Credit Union**, which primarily provides term and demand deposit products as well as leasing and lending products to credit unions; and **Concentra Trust**, which provides registered plan trustee services to credit union and corporate clients, personal trust and estate services to high-net-worth personal trusts, and corporate trust services with a focus on Indigenous trust relationships. Commercial products are distributed through a network of mortgage and leasing brokers, lending partners and other financial institutions.

At Dec. 31	2022	2021
	$000	$000
Deposits	31,051,813	20,856,383
Principal personal loans	32,042,693	22,302,540
Principal comml. loans	14,541,396	10,499,700

In February 2023, the company changed its fiscal year end to October 31 from December 31, effective Oct. 31, 2023.

Recent Merger and Acquisition Activity

Status: completed **Revised:** Nov. 1, 2022
UPDATE: The transaction was completed. PREVIOUS: Equitable Group Inc., through wholly owned Equitable Bank, agreed to acquire Concentra Bank for $470,000,000. The consideration would be partially funded with proceeds from a subscription receipt offering. Equitable would acquire Credit Union Central of Saskatchewan's (SaskCentral) 84% interest in Concentra, with the remaining 16% interest acquired from Concentra shareholders. Concentra was a Saskatoon, Sask.-based Schedule I chartered bank which had $11.3 billion in assets at Nov. 30, 2021. The boards of directors of Equitable, Concentra and SaskCentral unanimously approved the transaction, which was expected to be completed in the second half of 2022, subject to satisfaction of customary closing conditions and receipt of required regulatory approvals, including those required under the Bank Act (Canada), the Trust and Loan Companies Act (Canada) and the Competition Act (Canada). Sept. 29, 2022 - Approval was obtained from the federal Minister of Finance. The transaction was expected to be completed in fourth quarter of 2022, potentially as early as Nov. 1, 2022.

Predecessor Detail - Name changed from Equitable Group Inc., June 6, 2022.

Directors - Michael S. Hanley, chr., Mont-Royal, Qué.; Andrew R. G. Moor, pres. & CEO, Toronto, Ont.; Michael R. Emory, Toronto, Ont.; Susan Ericksen, Cumming, Ga.; Kishore (Kish) Kapoor, Toronto, Ont.; Yongah Kim, Toronto, Ont.; Marcos A. Lopez, Calgary, Alta.; Rowan Saunders, Toronto, Ont.; Carolyn M. Schuetz, Toronto, Ont.; Vincenza Sera, Toronto, Ont.; Michael P. Stramaglia, Toronto, Ont.

Other Exec. Officers - Daniel (Dan) Broten, sr. v-p & chief tech. officer; Darren Lorimer, sr. v-p & grp. head, comml. banking; Mahima Poddar, sr. v-p & grp. head, personal banking; Gavin Stanley, sr. v-p & chief HR officer; Ronald (Ron) Tratch, sr. v-p & chief risk officer; Chadwick Westlake, sr. v-p & CFO

Capital Stock

	Authorized (shs.)	Outstanding (shs.)[1]	Par
Preferred	unlimited		
Series 3		2,911,800	$25
Class A Series 1		3,888,500[2]	$25
Class A Series 2		551,000[3]	$25
Common	unlimited	37,729,584	n.p.v.

[1] At June 30, 2023
[2] Securities of wholly owned Concentra Bank.
[3] Securities of wholly owned Concentra Bank.

Preferred Series 3 - Entitled to non-cumulative annual dividends of $1.4923 per share payable quarterly to Sept. 30, 2024, and thereafter at a rate reset every five years equal to the five-year Government of Canada bond yield plus 4.78%. Redeemable on Sept. 30, 2024, and on September 30 every five years thereafter at $25 per share plus declared and unpaid dividends. Convertible at the holder's option, on Sept. 30, 2024, and on September 30 every five years thereafter, into floating rate preferred series 4 shares on a share-for-share basis, subject to certain conditions. The series 4 shares would pay a quarterly dividend equal to the 90-day Canadian Treasury bill rate plus 4.78%.

Class A Preferred Series 1 - Issued by wholly owned Concentra Bank. Entitled to non-cumulative annual dividends of 99¢ per share payable quarterly to Jan. 31, 2026, and thereafter at a rate reset every five years equal to the five-year Government of Canada bond yield plus 3.59%. Redeemable at $25 per share plus declared and unpaid dividends, subject to the approval of the Office of the Superintendent of Financial Institutions Canada (OSFI)and the requirement of the Bank Act (Canada). Convertible at the holder's option, on Jan. 31, 2026, and on January 31 every five years thereafter, into floating rate class A preferred series 2 shares on a share-for-share basis. Upon occurrence of a Non-Viability Contingent Capital (NVCC) trigger event, the shares would immediately be cancelled for no consideration and the stated capital in respect of the shares would immediately be reduced to nil.

Class A Preferred Series 2 - Issued by wholly owned Concentra Bank. Entitled to non-cumulative dividends payable quarterly equal to the 90-day Canadian Treasury bill rate plus 3.59%. Redeemable at $25 per share plus declared and unpaid dividends, subject to the approval of OSFI and the requirement of the Bank Act (Canada). Convertible at the holder's option, on Jan. 31, 2026, and on January 31 every five years thereafter, into fixed rate class A preferred series 1 shares on a share-for-share basis. Upon occurrence of a Non-Viability Contingent Capital (NVCC) trigger event, the shares would immediately be cancelled for no consideration and the stated capital in respect of the shares would immediately be reduced to nil.

Common - One vote per share.

Options - At Dec. 31, 2022, options were outstanding to purchase 1,229,851 common shares at prices ranging from $26.58 to $80.86 per share with a weighted average remaining contractual life of up to 6.6 years.

Normal Course Issuer Bid - The company plans to make normal course purchases of up to 1,150,000 common shares representing 3.8% of the public float. The bid commenced on Dec. 23, 2022, and expires on Dec. 22, 2023.

The company plans to make normal course purchases of up to 288,680 preferred series 3 shares representing 10% of the public float. The bid commenced on Dec. 23, 2022, and expires on Dec. 22, 2023.

Major Shareholder - Stephen J. R. Smith held 17.42% interest and Oakwest Corporation Limited held 10.19% interest at Mar. 24, 2023.

Price Range - EQB/TSX

Year	Volume	High	Low	Close
2022	19,806,773	$78.68	$44.81	$56.73
2021	12,512,514	$84.78	$50.55	$68.91
2020	29,839,294	$56.67	$22.29	$50.50
2019	18,472,434	$60.94	$29.23	$54.68
2018	15,056,122	$36.49	$26.01	$29.56

Split: 2-for-1 split in Oct. 2021
Recent Close: $75.49

Capital Stock Changes - On Nov. 1, 2022, 3,266,000 common shares were issued without further consideration on exchange of subscription receipts sold previously by bought deal public offering at $70.50 each. Also during 2022, common shares were issued as follows: 118,970 on exercise of options and 108,334 under the dividend reinvestment plan.

In addition, 7,600 preferred series 3 shares were repurchased under a Normal Course Issuer Bid.

Dividends

EQB com Ra $1.52 pa Q est. Sept. 29, 2023**
Prev. Rate: $1.48 est. June 30, 2023
Prev. Rate: $1.40 est. Mar. 31, 2023
Prev. Rate: $1.32 est. Dec. 30, 2022
Prev. Rate: $1.24 est. Sept. 30, 2022
Prev. Rate: $1.16 est. June 30, 2022
Prev. Rate: $1.12 est. Mar. 31, 2022
2-for-1 split eff. Oct. 26, 2021
Prev. Rate: $1.48 est. Mar. 27, 2020
EQB.PR.C pfd ser 3 red. exch. Adj. Ra $1.49225 pa Q est. Dec. 31, 2019
sub rcpt Ra $1.16 pa Q est. June 30, 2022
Delisted Nov 2/22.
Prev. Rate: $1.12 est. Mar. 31, 2022
$0.28i.................. Mar. 31/22
** Reinvestment Option i Initial Payment

Long-Term Debt - At Dec. 31, 2022, the company had no subordinated debt.

Wholly Owned Subsidiaries

Equitable Bank, Toronto, Ont.
- 100% int. in **Bennington Financial Corp.**, Oakville, Ont.
- 100% int. in **Concentra Bank**, Saskatoon, Sask.
- 100% int. in **Concentra Trust**, Canada.
- 100% int. in **EQB Covered Bond (Legislative) GP Inc.**, Toronto, Ont.
- 100% int. in **EQB Covered Bond (Legislative) Guarantor Limited Partnership**, Ont.
- 100% int. in **Equitable Trust**, Toronto, Ont.

Financial Statistics

Periods ended:	12m Dec. 31/22[A]		12m Dec. 31/21[A]
	$000s	%Chg	$000s
Interest income	**1,616,231**	**+46**	**1,107,320**
Interest expense	882,826		524,711
Net interest income	**733,405**	**+26**	**582,609**
Other income	48,781		60,298
Salaries & pension benefits	183,605		128,965
Non-interest expense	376,471		260,176
Pre-tax income	**368,457**	**-6**	**390,405**
Income taxes	98,276		97,875
Net income	**270,181**	**-8**	**292,530**
Cash & equivalent	495,106		773,251
Securities	2,863,505		1,791,357
Net non-performing loans	131,662		88,380
Total loans	46,510,215		32,900,762
Fixed assets, net	27,646		14,100
Total assets	**51,144,957**	**+41**	**36,159,070**
Deposits	31,051,813		20,856,383
Other liabilities	17,558,189		13,350,053
Preferred share equity	181,411		70,607
Shareholders' equity	2,534,955		1,952,634
Cash from oper. activs	**29,885**	**-96**	**693,258**
Cash from fin. activs	458,738		(19,504)
Cash from invest. activs	(766,768)		(458,246)
	$		$
Earnings per share*	7.63		8.49
Cash flow per share*	0.86		20.42
Cash divd. per share*	1.21		0.74
	shs		shs
No. of shs. o/s*	37,564,114		34,070,810
Avg. no. of shs. o/s*	34,688,502		33,946,749
	%		%
Basel III Common Equity Tier 1	13.70		13.30
Basel III Tier 1	14.70		13.90
Basel III Total	15.10		14.20
Net profit margin	34.54		45.50
Return on equity	12.49		16.67
Return on assets	0.62		0.87
No. of employees (FTEs)	1,685		1,161

* Common
[A] Reported in accordance with IFRS

Latest Results

Periods ended:	6m June 30/23[A]		6m June 30/22[A]
	$000s	%Chg	$000s
Net interest income	492,496	+50	328,829
Net income	230,444	+57	146,783
	$		$
Earnings per share*	6.00		4.24

* Common
[A] Reported in accordance with IFRS

Historical Summary
(as originally stated)

Fiscal Year	Int. Inc. $000s	Net Inc. Bef. Disc. $000s	EPS* $
2022[A]	1,616,231	270,181	7.63
2021[A]	1,107,320	292,530	8.49
2020[A]	1,121,665	223,804	6.52
2019[A]	1,116,810	206,479	6.05
2018[A]	860,063	165,626	4.87

* Common
[A] Reported in accordance with IFRS

Note: Adjusted throughout for 2-for-1 split in Oct. 2021

E.11 ESE Entertainment Inc.

Symbol - ESE **Exchange** - TSX-VEN **CUSIP** - 26906P
Head Office - 1000-409 Granville St, Vancouver, BC, V6C 1T2 **Telephone** - (778) 238-4988
Website - esegaming.com/
Email - investors@ese.gg
Investor Relations - Konrad Wasiela (778) 238-4988
Auditors - Crowe MacKay LLP C.A., Vancouver, B.C.
Transfer Agents - Endeavor Trust Corporation, Vancouver, B.C.

Profile - (B.C. 2018) Operates multiple assets in the gaming and eSports industries including physical infrastructure, broadcasting, global distribution for gaming and eSports-related content, advertising, sponsorship support and eSport teams.

Operations are organized as follows:

Technology and Data - Provides gaming technology and data services to video game developers, looking for insight on new users through its subsidiaries.

Esports Professional Teams - Operates three professional eSports teams who compete on the world stage with other international teams, in games such as League of Legends, Apex Legends and FIFA 20.

Simulation racing and Digital Motorsport Solutions - Provides simulation racing and digital motorsports services including 3D laser scanning of the facility and the adjacent area, aerial photography, preparation of documentation with architectural standards, creation of multimedia animations (virtual tour), development of 3D models for the game Assetto Corsa or Factor 2, creating promotional video clips, and creating a model for virtual reality presentations.

E-commerce - Owns and develops e-commerce platforms through online e-commerce websites where customers can purchase goods directly including motorsports.com, an online store focused on simulation racing equipment and hardware; and K1CK.com, which sells branded eSports and gaming merchandise.

Digital Events - Organizes events competitions, tournaments, leagues and more for the gaming industry.

Esports Events Broadcasting - Provides contents hosted by the company and other event organizers on multiple media outlets through purchasing license to broadcast from game publishers such as Riot Games, Activision Blizzard, EA, and more. Competitions will be broadcasted on third party media outlets including Twitch and YouTube that allows revenue generated by sponsors and/or the fans and viewers, on a subscription or one-time basis.

Esports and Gaming Infrastructure - Provides outsourced network services including B2B and B2C services and operates a global telecom network.

Virtual Pitstop - Provides technology services for video game developers, racing fans, and gamers to engage in motorsports-related eSports including precise design of cars and tracks using 3D laser scanning technology; development of 3D models of real-life racetracks, which can be implemented into video games; development of virtual reality (VR) and augmented reality (AR) racing content; creation of animations, skins, visualizations for promotional or architectural purposes; and the organization and execution of international digital motorsport events.

On June 6, 2023, common shares were listed on the OTCQX Best Market under the symbol ENTEF.

Recent Merger and Acquisition Activity

Status: terminated **Revised:** Apr. 30, 2023
UPDATE: The transaction was terminated. PREVIOUS: ESE Entertainment Inc. entered into a letter of intent to sell wholly owned Dublin, Ireland-based Auto Simulation Limited (dba Digital Motorsports; DMS) and Poland-based Frenzy Sp.zo.o. to a NASDAQ-listed U.S. special purpose acquisition company for issuance of common shares valued at Cdn$41,000,000. DMS provides infrastructure, technology and support for eSports worldwide, particularly in the simulation racing sector. Frenzy creates and executes eSports and gaming events, broadcasts and media content as well as operates professional mobile, automated television equipment, allowing it to produce reality shows from every part of the globe.

Predecessor Detail - Name changed from Kepler Acquisition Corp., Aug. 17, 2020, pursuant to reverse takeover of (old) ESE Entertainment Inc.; basis 1.5 new for 1 old sh.

Directors - Konrad Wasiela, CEO, B.C.; Roderick W. (Rick) Brace, Collingwood, Ont.; Rajeev (Raj) Dewan, Richmond Hill, Ont.; Ravinder (Robert) Kang, Vancouver, B.C.; Ron Segev, B.C.

Other Exec. Officers - Eric Jodoin, COO; Andrea Lieuwen, CFO

Capital Stock

	Authorized (shs.)	Outstanding (shs.)[1]
Common	unlimited	80,370,803

[1] At June 27, 2023

Major Shareholder - Konrad Wasiela held 24% interest at Nov. 1, 2022.

Price Range - ESE/TSX-VEN

Year	Volume	High	Low	Close
2022	18,657,056	$1.56	$0.30	$0.35
2021	46,808,066	$4.58	$0.93	$1.28
2020	24,678,568	$1.97	$0.17	$1.26
2019	392,250	$0.13	$0.09	$0.10

Split: 1.5-for-1 split in Aug. 2020
Recent Close: $0.18

Capital Stock Changes - In January 2023, private placement of 5,000,502 units (1 common share & ½ warrant) at 40¢ per unit was completed, with warrants exercisable at 70¢ per share for three years.

During fiscal 2022, common shares were issued as follows: 6,497,959 as deferred compensation shares issued to 9327-7358 Quebec Inc. (dba GameAddik), 1,412,250 on acquisition of Auto Simulation Limited (dba Digital Motorsports), 1,112,500 on exercise of stocks, 879,184 pursuant to the acquisition of GameAddik, 681,860 as earn-out shares, 656,606 pursuant to the acquisition of Frenzy Sp.zo.o, 469,874 for services and 26,822 on exercise of warrants.

Wholly Owned Subsidiaries

Auto Simulation Limited, Dublin, Ireland. dba Digital Motorsports.
ESE Entertainment Holdings Inc., B.C.
- 100% int. in **ESE Europe Sp. z o.o**, Poland.
- 100% int. in **Frenzy Sp.zo.o.**, Poland.

9327-7358 Quebec Inc., Qué.

Subsidiaries

51% int. in **World Performance Group Ltd.**, Ont.
- 99% int. in **Foresight Resolutions S.R.L.**, Romania.
- 99% int. in **WPG Racing Solutions S.R.L.**, Romania.

Financial Statistics

Periods ended:	12m Oct. 31/22[A]		12m Oct. 31/21[oA]
	$000s	%Chg	$000s
Operating revenue	**58,819**	**+417**	**11,385**
Cost of sales	51,120		10,235
Salaries & benefits	3,665		2,338
General & admin expense	5,943		4,106
Stock-based compensation	13,235		9,630
Operating expense	**73,963**	**+181**	**26,308**
Operating income	**(15,144)**	**n.a.**	**(14,923)**
Deprec., depl. & amort.	828		39
Finance costs, gross	545		n.a.
Write-downs/write-offs	(13,042)		(3,756)
Pre-tax income	**(29,393)**	**n.a.**	**(18,663)**
Income taxes	444		1
Net income	**(29,838)**	**n.a.**	**(18,664)**
Net inc. for equity hldrs	**(29,396)**	**n.a.**	**(17,216)**
Net inc. for non-cont. int	**(442)**	**n.a.**	**(1,448)**
Cash & equivalent	812		4,825
Accounts receivable	9,572		844
Current assets	11,788		6,524
Intangibles, net	6,874		8,320
Total assets	**21,451**	**+38**	**15,502**
Bank indebtedness	1,534		nil
Accts. pay. & accr. liabs	6,977		1,001
Current liabilities	13,937		1,307
Long-term debt, gross	858		nil
Long-term debt, net	358		nil
Long-term lease liabilities	941		nil
Shareholders' equity	2,707		14,025
Cash from oper. activs	**(1,749)**	**n.a.**	**(4,490)**
Cash from fin. activs	4,998		11,203
Cash from invest. activs	(7,216)		(2,340)
Net cash position	**812**	**-83**	**4,825**
Capital expenditures	(569)		(18)
	$		$
Earnings per share*	(0.46)		(0.38)
Cash flow per share*	(0.03)		(0.10)
	shs		shs
No. of shs. o/s*	72,505,504		60,768,449
Avg. no. of shs. o/s*	64,182,300		45,500,947
	%		%
Net profit margin	(50.73)		(163.94)
Return on equity	(340.82)		(237.64)
Return on assets	(156.62)		(228.39)
No. of employees (FTEs)	nil		70

* Common
[o] Restated
[A] Reported in accordance with IFRS

Latest Results

Periods ended:	6m Apr. 30/23[A]		6m Apr. 30/22[A]
	$000s	%Chg	$000s
Operating revenue	24,910	+8	23,028
Net income	(5,007)	n.a.	(3,720)
Net inc. for equity hldrs	(4,785)	n.a.	(3,774)
Net inc. for non-cont. int	(222)		54
	$		$
Earnings per share*	(0.06)		(0.06)

* Common
[A] Reported in accordance with IFRS

Historical Summary
(as originally stated)

Fiscal Year	Oper. Rev.	Net Inc. Bef. Disc.	EPS*
	$000s	$000s	$
2022[A]	58,819	(29,838)	(0.46)
2021[A]	11,385	(18,664)	(0.38)
2020[A1]	390	(3,802)	(0.14)
2019[A2]	nil	(184)	n.a.

* Common
[A] Reported in accordance with IFRS
[1] Results prior to Aug. 12, 2020, pertain to and reflect the Qualifying Transaction reverse takeover acquisition of (old) ESE Entertainment Inc.
[2] 19 weeks ended Oct. 31, 2019.
Note: Adjusted throughout for 1.5-for-1 split in Aug. 2020

E.12 ESSA Pharma Inc.

Symbol - EPIX **Exchange** - NASDAQ **CUSIP** - 29668H
Head Office - 720-999 Broadway W, Vancouver, BC, V5Z 1K5 **Telephone** - (778) 331-0962 **Fax** - (888) 308-8974
Website - www.essapharma.com
Email - dwood@essapharma.com
Investor Relations - David S. Wood (778) 331-0962
Auditors - Davidson & Company LLP C.A., Vancouver, B.C.
Lawyers - Blake, Cassels & Graydon LLP, Vancouver, B.C.
Transfer Agents - Computershare Trust Company of Canada Inc., Vancouver, B.C.
Employees - 50 at Dec. 13, 2022
Profile - (B.C. 2009) Developing small molecule drugs for the treatment of prostate cancer.

The company is developing drugs to expand the interval of time in which patients suffering from castrate-resistant prostate cancer (CRPC) can benefit from hormone-based therapies by disrupting the androgen receptor (AR) signaling pathway, which drives prostate cancer growth, by preventing AR through selective binding to the N-terminal domain of the AR.

Lead product candidate is EPI-7386, a novel drug candidate that inhibits the N-terminal domain of the androgen receptor. An investigational new drug (IND) application for its EPI-7386 for the treatment of metastatic castration resistant prostate cancer (mCRPC) was filed and accepted by the FDA, and a clinical trial application (CTA) was also filed and authorized by Health Canada. The FDA has granted Fast Track Designation to EPI-7386 for the treatment of adult male patients with mCRPC resistant to standard-of-care treatment. EPI-7386 is under going a phase 1a study as a monotherapy for the treatment of adult male patients with CRPC resistant to standard-of-care treatments and phase 1/2 trials in combination with approved second-generation antiandrogen therapies as an earlier line of treatment for patients with mCRPC. These trials of combination therapies are in collaboration pharmaceutical companies in the prostate cancer space, including **Janssen Research & Development, LLC**, **Astellas Pharma Inc.** and **Bayer Consumer Care AG**.

In October 2022, the company announced that **Janssen Research & Development, LLC** would suspend its enrollment into the Phase I clinical study of EPI-7386 with apalutamide or EPI-7386 with abiraterone and prednisone in metastatic castration-resistant prostate cancer patients due to operational recruitment challenges.

During fiscal 2022, wholly owned **Realm Therapeutics Inc.** and **Realm Therapeutics plc** were liquidated and dissolved.

Directors - Dr. Richard M. Glickman, chr., Victoria, B.C.; Dr. David R. Parkinson, pres. & CEO, Calif.; Franklin M. Berger, New York, N.Y.; Philip Kantoff, Boston, Mass.; Alex Martin, N.J.; Lauren Merendino; Scott Requadt, Mass.; Gary Sollis, B.C.; Marella Thorell, Pa.; Sanford (Sandy) Zweifach, Calif.

Other Exec. Officers - David S. Wood, CFO; Dr. Alessandra Cesano, CMO; Peter Virsik, exec. v-p & COO; Dr. Han-Jie Zhou, sr. v-p, chemistry & chemistry mfg. & control; Dr. Raymond Andersen, corp. sec.

Capital Stock

	Authorized (shs.)	Outstanding (shs.)[1]
Class A Preferred	unlimited	nil
Common	unlimited	44,092,374

[1] At Feb. 7, 2023

Major Shareholder - BVF Partners L.P. held 26.5% interest and BB Biotech AG held 17.9% interest at Jan. 10, 2023.

Price Range - EPIX/NASDAQ

Year	Volume	High	Low	Close
2022	33,710,780	US$14.88	US$1.40	US$2.52
2021	19,818,401	US$35.45	US$7.42	US$14.20
2020	4,075,085	US$12.32	US$3.00	US$11.93

EPI/TSX (D)

Year	Volume	High	Low	Close
2020	657,438	$11.34	$4.00	$8.20
2019	632,043	$8.45	$1.90	$7.04
2018	484,360	$7.15	$2.50	$2.71

Capital Stock Changes - During fiscal 2022, common shares were issued as follows: 72,910 on exercise of options and 15,820 under stock-based compensation plan.

Wholly Owned Subsidiaries

ESSA Pharmaceuticals Corp., Houston, Tex.

Financial Statistics

Periods ended:	12m Sept. 30/22[A]		12m Sept. 30/21[A]
	US$000s	%Chg	US$000s
Salaries & benefits	5,784		4,769
Research & devel. expense	18,019		18,884
General & admin expense	5,004		3,905
Stock-based compensation	7,888		9,476
Operating expense	**36,695**	**-1**	**37,034**
Operating income	**(36,695)**	**n.a.**	**(37,034)**
Deprec., depl. & amort	265		109
Finance income	1,737		235
Finance costs, gross	14		22
Pre-tax income	**(35,215)**	**n.a.**	**(36,840)**
Income taxes	(112)		(34)
Net income	**(35,103)**	**n.a.**	**(36,805)**
Cash & equivalent	167,238		194,927
Accounts receivable	6		489
Current assets	169,059		197,598
Right-of-use assets	186		308
Total assets	**169,505**	**-14**	**198,166**
Accts. pay. & accr. liabs	2,177		3,809
Current liabilities	2,310		3,930
Long-term lease liabilities	76		210
Shareholders' equity	167,118		194,006
Cash from oper. activs	**(28,704)**	**n.a.**	**(25,416)**
Cash from fin. activs	253		141,991
Cash from invest. activs	(52,348)		35,015
Net cash position	**57,076**	**-59**	**137,825**
	US$		US$
Earnings per share*	(0.80)		(0.96)
Cash flow per share*	(0.65)		(0.66)
	shs		shs
No. of shs. o/s*	44,073,076		43,984,346
Avg. no. of shs. o/s*	44,038,241		38,480,378
	%		%
Net profit margin	n.a.		n.a.
Return on equity	(19.44)		(26.94)
Return on assets	(19.09)		(26.39)
No. of employees (FTEs)	50		30

* Common
[A] Reported in accordance with U.S. GAAP

Latest Results

Periods ended:	3m Dec. 31/22[A]		3m Dec. 31/21[A]
	US$000s	%Chg	US$000s
Net income	(6,742)	n.a.	(9,098)
	US$		US$
Earnings per share*	(0.15)		(0.21)

* Common
[A] Reported in accordance with U.S. GAAP

Historical Summary
(as originally stated)

Fiscal Year	Oper. Rev.	Net Inc. Bef. Disc.	EPS*
	US$000s	US$000s	US$
2022[A]	nil	(35,103)	(0.80)
2021[A]	nil	(36,805)	(0.96)
2020[A]	nil	(23,445)	(1.04)
2019[B]	nil	(10,442)	(1.24)
2018[B]	nil	(11,629)	(2.55)

* Common
[A] Reported in accordance with U.S. GAAP
[B] Reported in accordance with IFRS

E.13 EV Technology Group Ltd.

Symbol - EVTG **Exchange** - NEO **CUSIP** - 269276
Head Office - 198 Davenport Rd, Toronto, ON, M5R 1J2 **Telephone** - (416) 861-2267 **Fax** - (416) 861-8165
Website - evtgroup.com
Email - wouter@evtgroup.com
Investor Relations - Wouter Witvoet (416) 861-2267
Auditors - McGovern Hurley LLP C.A., Toronto, Ont.
Transfer Agents - TSX Trust Company
Profile - (Ont. 2013; orig. Alta., 1998) Acquires and owns iconic automotive brands that are transitioning to electric and operates a complimentary set of business lines. Distributes MOKE electric vehicles in France and operates a MOKE rental business in St. Tropez, France.

Through wholly owned **Moke France S.A.S.**, the company is a dealer and distributor in France of MOKE electric vehicles for **MOKE International Limited** (MIL), which is the manufacturer of MOKE vehicles. Beginning in the summer of 2022, MOKE France plans to sell these vehicles to hotels, clubs, restaurants, and notable personalities in the South of France, as well as open retail sales. Also opening a flagship store in Saint Tropez from which it plans to operate a rental business offering MOKE electric vehicles during the summer season. Other sources of revenue will include offering a full set of planned experiences for customers, including tours of beaches in Saint Tropez and MOKEs with ready fitted picnics and merchandise and selling MOKE merchandise, particularly items for the beach.

The company is working with MIL to roll out MOKE electric vehicles across Europe and internationally.

On Apr. 4, 2022, the company sold wholly owned **Sonoro Energy Iraq B.V.**, to a third party for nominal consideration. Sonoro Energy held Salah ad Din licence covering 24,363 km^2 in Iraq for bitumen exploration and asphalt production.

Recent Merger and Acquisition Activity

Status: completed **Revised:** Apr. 7, 2022
UPDATE: The transaction was completed. EVT amalgamated with a wholly owned subsidiary of Blue Sky to continue as EV Experiences Inc. Blue Sky changed its name to EV Technology Group Ltd. PREVIOUS: Blue Sky Energy Inc. entered into a letter of intent for the reverse takeover acquisition of private Toronto, Ont.-based EV Technology Group Inc. (EVT), which invests in and operates electric vehicle (EV) brands and assembly in niche markets, for issuance of 90,000,000 post-consolidated common shares at a deemed price of $1.00 per share (following a 1-for-4 share consolidation). Jan. 19, 2022 - The companies entered into a definitive agreement. The transaction would be completed by way of an amalgamation of EVT and a wholly owned subsidiary of Blue Sky. On closing, Blue Sky would change its name to EV Technology Group Ltd. Shares of the resulting issuer would be listed on the NEO exchange. Mar. 15, 2022 - EVT completed the first tranche of a private placement consisting of 5,400,000 subscription receipts at $1.00 per receipt.

Predecessor Detail - Name changed from Blue Sky Energy Inc., Apr. 5, 2022, pursuant to the reverse takeover acquisition of EV Technology Group Inc.; basis 1 new for 4 old shs.

Directors - Wouter Witvoet, chr. & CEO, Zug, Switzerland; Olivier F. Roussy Newton, pres., Zug, Switzerland; Wijnand Donkers; Jon Foster, Calif.; Manpreet Singh, Washington, D.C.; Kent P. Thexton, Toronto, Ont.

Other Exec. Officers - David Maher, COO; Ryan Ptolemy, CFO; Dan Burge, chief product officer; Kenny Choi, corp. sec.

Capital Stock

	Authorized (shs.)	Outstanding (shs.)[1]
First Preferred	unlimited	nil
Second Preferred	unlimited	nil
Common	unlimited	106,298,050

[1] At Apr. 12, 2022

Major Shareholder - Wouter Witvoet held 10.7% interest at Apr. 12, 2022.

Price Range - EVTG/NEO

Year	Volume	High	Low	Close
2022	457,900	$5.02	$0.17	$0.17
2021	260,222	$1.20	$0.44	$1.04
2020	797,521	$1.00	$0.30	$0.44

Consolidation: 1-for-4 cons. in Apr. 2022
Recent Close: $0.02
Capital Stock Changes - In April 2022, common shares were consolidated on a 1-for-4 basis, 2,5013,340 post-consolidated common shares were issued for satisfaction of $2,633,294 of liabilities. 90,263,970 post-consolidated common shares were issued pursuant to the reverse takeover acquisition of EV Technology Group Inc. (old EVT) and 5,811,500 post-consolidated common shares were issued were issued without further consideration on exchange of subscription receipts sold previously by private placement by old EVT at $1.00 each.

Wholly Owned Subsidiaries

EV Experiences Inc., Toronto, Ont.
- 100% int. in **MOKE France S.A.S.**, France.

E.14 EVP Capital Inc.

Symbol - EVP.P **Exchange** - TSX-VEN **CUSIP** - 26929F
Head Office - c/o Meretsky Law Firm, 2150-121 King St W, Toronto, ON, M5H 3T9 **Telephone** - (416) 943-0808
Email - jason@meretsky.com
Investor Relations - Jason D. Meretsky (416) 943-0808 ext. 4
Auditors - MNP LLP C.A., Toronto, Ont.
Transfer Agents - TSX Trust Company, Toronto, Ont.
Profile - (Ont. 2021) Capital Pool Company.
Common listed on TSX-VEN, Aug. 4, 2023.
Predecessor Detail - Name changed from EVP CPC Inc., Apr. 25, 2023.
Directors - Lorne M. Sugarman, CEO & corp. sec., Toronto, Ont.; Jason Baibokas, Toronto, Ont.; Mark Dickinson, Toronto, Ont.; Jason D. Meretsky, Toronto, Ont.
Other Exec. Officers - Edward Jonasson, CFO

Capital Stock

	Authorized (shs.)	Outstanding (shs.)[1]
Common	unlimited	8,545,200

[1] At Aug. 4, 2023

Major Shareholder - Widely held at Aug. 4, 2023.

Capital Stock Changes - On Aug. 4, 2023, an initial public offering of 4,600,000 common shares was completed at 10¢ per share.

E.15 EXMceuticals Inc.

Symbol - EXM **Exchange** - CSE (S) **CUSIP** - 30207T

Head Office - 3000-421 7 Ave SW, Calgary, AB, T2P 4K9 **Telephone** - (403) 554-1562

Website - www.exmceuticals.com

Email - investors@exmceuticals.com

Investor Relations - Jonathan Summers (403) 554-1562

Auditors - Dale Matheson Carr-Hilton LaBonte LLP C.A., Vancouver, B.C.

Transfer Agents - Odyssey Trust Company

Profile - (B.C. 2008) Seeking new business opportunities.

In April 2022, the company sold wholly owned **EXMceuticals Portugal, Lda.** for €80,000, following the cease of all of its in January 2022. EXMceuticals Portugal had operated a cannabis research and development laboratory in Lisbon, Portugal, which contained a pilot-scale refinery for developing cannabis-based products. The company was seeking alternative business opportunities.

Common suspended from CSE, Nov. 4, 2021.

Predecessor Detail - Name changed from Orofino Minerals Inc., Dec. 7, 2018, pursuant to reverse takeover acquisition of EXM Ceuticals Inc.; basis 1 new for 7 old shs.

Directors - Jonathan Summers, chr., United Kingdom; Michael W. (Mike) Kinley, CFO, Halifax, N.S.; Marc Bernier

Other Exec. Officers - Julie Lemieux, CEO & corp. sec.; Paulo Martins, CEO & country dir., Portugal

Capital Stock

	Authorized (shs.)	Outstanding (shs.)[1]
Common	100,000,000	75,167,510

[1] At Aug. 22, 2023

Major Shareholder - Jonathan Summers held 16.51% interest and Michael Cohen held 11.13% interest at July 24, 2020.

Price Range - ORR.H/TSX-VEN (D)

Year	Volume	High	Low	Close
2021	1,741,197	$0.27	$0.13	$0.20
2020	3,066,809	$0.60	$0.11	$0.18
2019	4,984,561	$1.97	$0.47	$0.50
2018	19,476	$1.30	$0.77	$0.95

Wholly Owned Subsidiaries

Ceuticals Farming Limited, Malawi. Inactive.
EMX Management Ltd., United Kingdom. Inactive.
EXMceuticals Holdings B.V., Netherlands.
- 100% int. in **EXMceuticals Portugal, Lda.**, Portugal.
- 100% int. in **EXMceuticals Portugal II, Unipessoal Lda.**, Portugal.

Note: The preceding list includes only the major related companies in which interests are held.

E.16 Earth Alive Clean Technologies Inc.

Symbol - EAC **Exchange** - TSX-VEN **CUSIP** - 27031Q

Head Office - 1560-1050 Côte du Beaver Hall, Montréal, QC, H2Z 1S4 **Telephone** - (438) 333-1680

Website - earthalivect.com

Email - nsofronis@earthalivect.com

Investor Relations - Nikolaos Sofronis (438) 316-3562

Auditors - PricewaterhouseCoopers LLP C.A., Montréal, Qué.

Transfer Agents - Computershare Trust Company of Canada Inc.

Employees - 24 at Dec. 31, 2022

Profile - (Can. 2014 amalg.) Develops, manufactures and distributes microbial technology-based products for farming operations, industrial applications and dust control in mining.

Operates through two segments: Mines-Infrastructure; and Agriculture.

The **Mines-Infrastructure** segment consists of EA-1™, a biodegradable microbial dust suppression technology primarily for the mining industry which is patented in Canada, Australia, Brazil, Chile and Peru. EA-1™ keeps the dust from becoming airborne while helping to retain moisture in the soil, reducing the formation of ripples on the road, provides soil stabilization, and improves traction. Also offers RapidAll™, a biodegradable industrial cleaner used to clean and eliminate organic materials such as fats, grease, oil and synthetics, heavy dirt and grime.

The **Agriculture** segment consists of Soil Activator®, a Canadian Food Inspection Agency (CFIA)-approved organic microbial biofertilizer for organic and non-organic farms, and consists of a blend of naturally-occurring soil microorganisms; Medagri™ and Medfer™ are solid products based on beneficial bacteria which helps plant growth and health; Bactifer™, a solid product based on rhizobacteria to invigorate crops and soils. Other products include Big Blue Fish™ Hydrolysate, which improves germination and root development, and builds trace elements in the soil; Big Blue Wave™, a sea mineral solution derived from ocean water; Alga™, a liquid seaweed which helps plants efficiently regulate their hydration; and Mineralized Seaweed™, a blend of liquid seaweed extract and nutrient dense low-sodium ionic sea mineral solution.

Products are distributed in Canada, the U.S., Central and South America, and Europe through sales representatives, industrial business-to-business model, retailers and online through e-commerce websites.

Directors - Robert Blain, chr., Montréal, Qué.; Nikolaos Sofronis, pres. & CEO, Luxembourg, Luxembourg; Richard Boomer, Brussels, Belgium; David Colon, Versailles, France; Valérie Renard, Liège, Belgium; Nicolas Schlumberger, Beijing, Beijing, People's Republic of China; Dr. Viviane Yargeau, Saint-Basile-le-Grand, Qué.

Other Exec. Officers - Jean-Philippe Lejeune, CFO; Eric Paul-Hus, chief legal officer & corp. sec.; Claudia Toussaint, chief tech. officer; Paola Correal, v-p, opers. & bus. admin.

Capital Stock

	Authorized (shs.)	Outstanding (shs.)[1]
Common	unlimited	518,355,857

[1] At May 29, 2023

Major Shareholder - Groupe Lune Rouge Inc. held 11.93% interest at May 7, 2023.

Price Range - EAC/TSX-VEN

Year	Volume	High	Low	Close
2022	22,457,720	$0.07	$0.02	$0.03
2021	38,953,604	$0.18	$0.06	$0.06
2020	24,683,655	$0.16	$0.06	$0.13
2019	22,020,906	$0.30	$0.06	$0.10
2018	44,876,602	$0.45	$0.12	$0.20

Recent Close: $0.02

Capital Stock Changes - In May 2023, private placement of 175,000,000 units (1 common share & 1 warrant) at 2¢ per unit was completed, with warrants exercisable at 5¢ per share for five years.

In April 2022, private placement of 101,866,666 units (1 common share & ½ warrant) at 6¢ per unit was completed.

Wholly Owned Subsidiaries

Earth Alive Chile S.p.A., Chile.
Earth Alive Europe S.L., Spain.

Financial Statistics

Periods ended:	12m Dec. 31/22[A]		12m Dec. 31/21[oA]
	$000s	%Chg	$000s
Operating revenue	**2,313**	**-35**	**3,570**
Cost of goods sold	1,601		2,643
Salaries & benefits	1,980		1,636
Research & devel. expense	424		83
General & admin expense	2,022		909
Stock-based compensation	74		602
Operating expense	**6,101**	**+4**	**5,873**
Operating income	**(3,788)**	**n.a.**	**(2,303)**
Deprec., depl. & amort.	533		28
Finance income	146		8
Finance costs, gross	25		7
Pre-tax income	**(4,115)**	**n.a.**	**(2,329)**
Net income	**(4,115)**	**n.a.**	**(2,329)**
Cash & equivalent	6,706		3,915
Inventories	278		547
Accounts receivable	1,152		763
Current assets	8,192		5,242
Fixed assets, net	187		138
Right-of-use assets	761		nil
Intangibles, net	4		6
Total assets	**9,145**	**+70**	**5,386**
Accts. pay. & accr. liabs	1,619		635
Current liabilities	1,824		675
Long-term debt, gross	40		40
Long-term lease liabilities	604		nil
Shareholders' equity	6,716		4,712
Cash from oper. activs	**(2,667)**	**n.a.**	**(1,592)**
Cash from fin. activs	5,983		4,946
Cash from invest. activs	(6,525)		(4)
Net cash position	**706**	**-82**	**3,915**
Capital expenditures	(525)		(4)
	$		$
Earnings per share*	(0.01)		(0.01)
Cash flow per share*	(0.01)		(0.01)
	shs		shs
No. of shs. o/s*	343,355,857		241,489,191
Avg. no. of shs. o/s*	316,474,376		241,489,191
	%		%
Net profit margin	(177.91)		(65.24)
Return on equity	(72.02)		(75.08)
Return on assets	(56.29)		(64.09)
Foreign sales percent	90		92
No. of employees (FTEs)	24		15

* Common
[o] Restated
[A] Reported in accordance with IFRS

Latest Results

Periods ended:	3m Mar. 31/23[A]		3m Mar. 31/22[A]
	$000s	%Chg	$000s
Operating revenue	387	-32	573
Net income	(1,263)	n.a.	(561)
	$		$
Earnings per share*	(0.00)		(0.00)

* Common
[A] Reported in accordance with IFRS

Historical Summary
(as originally stated)

Fiscal Year	Oper. Rev.	Net Inc. Bef. Disc.	EPS*
	$000s	$000s	$
2022[A]	2,313	(4,115)	(0.01)
2021[A]	3,570	(2,329)	(0.01)
2020[A]	2,780	(1,416)	(0.01)
2019[A]	2,178	(2,662)	(0.01)
2018[A]	1,432	(3,512)	(0.03)

* Common
[A] Reported in accordance with IFRS

E.17 EarthLabs Inc.

Symbol - SPOT **Exchange** - TSX-VEN **CUSIP** - 27034B

Head Office - 1010-69 Yonge St, Toronto, ON, M5E 1K3 **Telephone** - (416) 941-8900

Website - earthlabs.com

Email - denis@earthlabs.com

Investor Relations - Denis Laviolette (647) 345-7768

Auditors - MNP LLP C.A., Toronto, Ont.

Transfer Agents - Computershare Trust Company of Canada Inc., Toronto, Ont.

Profile - (Can. 2017) Holds a portfolio of software-as-a-service (SaaS) tools and services (CEO.CA and DigiGeoData) and invests in the securities of junior mining companies.

The product portfolio includes CEO.CA, an investment social network for resource investors to share knowledge and track stocks in real-time; CEO.CA PRO, a platform for real-time stock price monitoring and live market depth which is offered on a monthly subscription; DigiGeoAtlas, a software-as-a-service based online geographic information system (GIS) interactive mapping interface that spatially links and displays data; and DigiGeoMaps, the industry standard maps which provide an overview both on a global/country scale or a more focused regional basis.

At Mar. 31, 2023, the company held an investment portfolio consisting of 93 positions, in primarily resource companies, with a fair value of $27,515,239; and a 27.5% interest in **Golden Planet Mining Corp.** (GPM), a private gold exploration company, with a fair value of $2,199,574. Also holds net smelter return royalties (NSR) and options to acquire NSRs on 21 properties, including a 0.2% NSR on **New Found Gold Corp.**'s Queensway gold project in Newfoundland.

Recent Merger and Acquisition Activity

Status: completed **Revised:** Dec. 1, 2022

UPDATE: The transaction was completed. PREVIOUS: EarthLabs Inc. agreed to sell its exploration consulting and technology division to Brisbane, Australia-based ALS Limited, a provider of laboratory testing, inspection, certification and verification solutions, in exchange for $24,000,000 in cash and assumption of up to $6,000,000 in specified liabilities, subject to working capital adjustments. The business includes wholly owned Ridgeline Exploration Services Inc. and Geotic Inc., which are EarthLabs' exploration software-as-a-service and global consulting services and field services divisions.

Predecessor Detail - Name changed from GoldSpot Discoveries Corp., Sept. 2, 2022.

Directors - Vincent Dubé-Bourgeois, co-founder & pres., Qué.; Denis Laviolette, co-founder, exec. chr. & CEO, Toronto, Ont.; Gerald M. (Gerry) Feldman, Thornhill, Ont.; Jay Sujir, Vancouver, B.C.

Other Exec. Officers - Binh Quach, CFO & corp. sec.; Dr. Shawn Hood, chief tech. officer; Cejay Kim, chief bus. officer; Mathew Wilson, chief invest. officer

Capital Stock

	Authorized (shs.)	Outstanding (shs.)[1]
Common	unlimited	137,388,527

[1] At May 25, 2023

Major Shareholder - Eric S. Sprott held 17.3% interest at Dec. 30, 2022.

Price Range - SPOT/TSX-VEN

Year	Volume	High	Low	Close
2022	24,849,451	$0.94	$0.20	$0.22
2021	52,092,215	$1.55	$0.32	$0.92
2020	39,421,739	$0.50	$0.13	$0.40
2019	22,808,792	$0.58	$0.08	$0.14
2018	109,500	$0.64	$0.40	$0.44

Consolidation: 1-for-2 cons. in Feb. 2019

Recent Close: $0.23

Capital Stock Changes - During 2022, 2,803,738 common shares were issued on acquisition of DigiGeoData Inc., and 346,495 common shares were issued on exercise of options.

Wholly Owned Subsidiaries

CEO.CA Technologies Ltd., Calif.

DigiGeoData Inc., Canada.
Resource Quantamental Corp., Canada.

Investments

27.5% int. in **Golden Planet Mining Corp.**, North Vancouver, B.C.

Financial Statistics

Periods ended:	12m Dec. 31/22^A		12m Dec. 31/21^oA
	$000s	%Chg	$000s
Realized invest. gain (loss)	(3,289)		6,966
Unrealized invest. gain (loss)	(7,774)		173
Total revenue	**(6,552)**	**n.a.**	**7,663**
Salaries & benefits	2,367		2,319
General & admin. expense	2,840		1,422
Stock-based compensation	1,825		717
Operating expense	**8,199**	**+84**	**4,458**
Operating income	**(14,751)**	**n.a.**	**3,205**
Deprec. & amort.	1,173		297
Finance costs, gross	14		14
Write-downs/write-offs	(9,415)		nil
Pre-tax income	**(29,675)**	**n.a.**	**2,237**
Income taxes	(3,064)		(30)
Net inc. bef. disc. opers	**(26,611)**	**n.a.**	**2,267**
Income from disc. opers	19,766		8,774
Net income	**(6,845)**	**n.a.**	**11,041**
Cash & equivalent	25,346		6,559
Accounts receivable	116		1,288
Current assets	52,809		52,468
Fixed assets, net	146		1,652
Intangibles	10,316		19,016
Total assets	**63,272**	**-13**	**73,125**
Accts. pay. & accr. liabs	1,002		2,477
Current liabilities	3,517		8,723
Long-term lease liabilities	87		90
Shareholders' equity	58,096		58,096
Cash from oper. activs	**18,655**	**n.a.**	**(10,436)**
Cash from fin. activs	(74)		19,915
Cash from invest. activs	206		(7,387)
Net cash position	**25,346**	**+286**	**6,559**
Capital expenditures	(5)		nil
	$		$
Earns. per sh. bef disc opers*	(0.20)		0.02
Earnings per share*	(0.05)		0.10
Cash flow per share*	0.14		(0.09)
	shs		shs
No. of shs. o/s*	136,555,193		133,404,960
Avg. no. of shs. o/s*	136,236,146		112,512,143
	%		%
Net profit margin	n.m.		29.58
Return on equity	(44.68)		5.94
Return on assets	(39.00)		4.71

* Common
^o Restated
^A Reported in accordance with IFRS

Latest Results

Periods ended:	3m Mar. 31/23^A		3m Mar. 31/22^A
	$000s	%Chg	$000s
Total revenue	4,769	+32	3,607
Net income	2,266	n.a.	(619)
	$		$
Earnings per share*	0.02		(0.00)

* Common
^A Reported in accordance with IFRS

Historical Summary
(as originally stated)

Fiscal Year	Total Rev.	Net Inc. Bef. Disc.	EPS*
	$000s	$000s	$
2022^A	(6,552)	(26,611)	(0.20)
2021^A	16,370	3,381	0.03
2020^A	17,460	10,440	0.11
2019^A1	2,312	(4,689)	(0.06)
2018^A	1,243	(1,291)	n.a.

* Common
^A Reported in accordance with IFRS
[1] Results reflect the Feb. 8, 2019, Qualifying Transaction reverse takeover acquisition of GoldSpot Discoveries Inc.
Note: Adjusted throughout for 1-for-2 cons. in Feb. 2019

E.18 EarthRenew Inc.

Symbol - ERTH **Exchange** - CSE **CUSIP** - 27034F
Head Office - PO Box 1186 Stn Main, Okotoks, AB, T1S 1B1 **Telephone** - (403) 809-9232 **Fax** - (403) 452-5697
Website - replenishnutrients.com/investors
Email - matthew.greenberg@replenishnutrients.com
Investor Relations - Matthew Greenberg (403) 809-9232
Auditors - PricewaterhouseCoopers LLP C.A., Calgary, Alta.
Transfer Agents - TSX Trust Company, Toronto, Ont.
Employees - 19 at May 2, 2022

Profile - (Ont. 2014; orig. Que., 1990 amalg.) Through wholly owned **Replenish Nutrients Ltd.**, manufactures and distributes regenerative agriculture fertilizer and other crop inputs to organic farming and horticultural communities in Canada and the United States.

Sells dry macronutrient products consisting of potash, phosphate, sulphur, organic carbon material and bio-actives in blended or granular form. Has a manufacturing facility in Beiseker, Alta., which can produce 20,000 tonnes of regenerative fertilizer and an additional 46,000 tonnes of blended product. Facilities under development include a 50,000-tonne fertilizer blending facility in Debolt, Alta., with commissioning expected to commence in 2024; and a 200,000-tonne granulation facility at the **K+S Potash Canada General Partnership** potash mine in Bethune, Sask. Has also entered into a letter of intent with **Diamond Feeders LLC** to develop its first facility in Colorado which would produce 40,000 tonnes of organic fertilizer pellets per year for distribution in the United States.

In June 2022, a name change to **Replenish Nutrients Holding Corp.** was approved.

During the first quarter of 2022, the company has decided to halt the restart of the Strathmore production facility in Alberta to focus on development of the Beiseker, Debolt and Bethune fertilizer production facilities. The Strathmore Plant has the capacity to generate 4 MW of electricity from an industrial-sized gas turbine. The electricity was previously sold to Alberta's power grid during supply shortages or demand spikes, or to cryptocurrency miners, which can co-locate on site. The company also used the exhausted heat from the turbine to dry manure feedstock to produce high-value organic fertilizer.

Predecessor Detail - Name changed from Valencia Ventures Inc., Jan. 10, 2019, pursuant to reverse takeover acquisition of 2292055 Ontario Inc. (dba EarthRenew).

Directors - Catherine Stretch, chr., Toronto, Ont.; Neil Weins, CEO, chief tech. officer, head, sales & pres., Replenish Nutrients Ltd., Okotoks, Alta.; Chris Best, Calgary, Alta.; Brad Orr, Calgary, Alta.; Lucas A. Tomei, Alta.

Other Exec. Officers - Kevin Erickson, COO; Matthew Greenberg, CFO & corp. sec.; Gerard Philpott, chief comml. officer

Capital Stock

	Authorized (shs.)	Outstanding (shs.)[1]
Common	unlimited	141,883,762

[1] At May 9, 2023

Major Shareholder - Neil Weins held 11.49% interest at May 9, 2023.

Price Range - ERTH/CSE

Year	Volume	High	Low	Close
2022	95,858,598	$0.40	$0.11	$0.13
2021	33,284,895	$0.57	$0.15	$0.19
2020	32,023,026	$0.43	$0.15	$0.26
2019	18,440,116	$0.44	$0.06	$0.33

Consolidation: 1-for-3 cons. in June 2020
Recent Close: $0.09

Capital Stock Changes - In June 2022, public offering of 41,804,500 units (1 common share & 1 warrant) at 25¢ per unit was completed, including 951,125 units on exercise of over-allotment option. Also during 2022, common shares were issued as follows: 7,100,000 on exercise of warrants, 600,000 by private placement and 50,000 on exercise of options.

Wholly Owned Subsidiaries

EarthRenew Strathmore Inc., Ont.
Replenish Nutrients Ltd., Alta.
- 100% int. in **Replenish Nutrients US Inc.**, Colo.

Financial Statistics

Periods ended:	12m Dec. 31/22^A		12m Dec. 31/21^oA
	$000s	%Chg	$000s
Operating revenue	**17,270**	**+40**	**12,300**
Cost of sales	15,120		8,999
Research & devel. expense	282		155
General & admin expense	3,106		4,178
Stock-based compensation	614		841
Operating expense	**19,122**	**+35**	**14,173**
Operating income	**(1,852)**	**n.a.**	**(1,873)**
Deprec., depl. & amort.	1,903		1,210
Finance income	14		1
Finance costs, gross	171		115
Write-downs/write-offs	(2,634)		652
Pre-tax income	**(7,735)**	**n.a.**	**(4,634)**
Income taxes	(650)		70
Net income	**(7,085)**	**n.a.**	**(4,703)**
Cash & equivalent	3,632		1,275
Inventories	11,927		926
Accounts receivable	4,057		3,030
Current assets	19,713		5,335
Fixed assets, net	9,304		8,791
Intangibles, net	9,758		12,666
Total assets	**38,775**	**+45**	**26,792**
Accts. pay. & accr. liabs	12,236		5,205
Current liabilities	16,251		7,728
Long-term debt, gross	3,499		3,152
Long-term debt, net	2,977		2,563
Long-term lease liabilities	525		434
Shareholders' equity	14,917		10,536
Cash from oper. activs	**(6,279)**	**n.a.**	**(375)**
Cash from fin. activs	10,953		4,546
Cash from invest. activs	(2,317)		(3,850)
Net cash position	**3,632**	**+185**	**1,275**
Capital expenditures	(2,422)		(1,966)
Capital disposals	105		nil
	$		$
Earnings per share*	(0.06)		(0.06)
Cash flow per share*	(0.05)		(0.00)
	shs		shs
No. of shs. o/s*	141,883,762		92,329,262
Avg. no. of shs. o/s*	120,094,804		74,599,990
	%		%
Net profit margin	(41.02)		(38.24)
Return on equity	(55.67)		(61.80)
Return on assets	(21.13)		(28.28)
No. of employees (FTEs)	...		15

* Common
^o Restated
^A Reported in accordance with IFRS

Latest Results

Periods ended:	3m Mar. 31/23^A		3m Mar. 31/22^A
	$000s	%Chg	$000s
Operating revenue	2,490	-19	3,064
Net income	(264)	n.a.	(1,364)
	$		$
Earnings per share*	(0.00)		(0.01)

* Common
^A Reported in accordance with IFRS

Historical Summary
(as originally stated)

Fiscal Year	Oper. Rev.	Net Inc. Bef. Disc.	EPS*
	$000s	$000s	$
2022^A	17,270	(7,085)	(0.06)
2021^A	12,300	(4,703)	(0.06)
2020^A	507	(3,877)	(0.08)
2019^A	183	(1,374)	(0.06)
2018^A1	nil	(4,517)	(0.24)

* Common
^A Reported in accordance with IFRS
[1] Results reflect the Dec. 21, 2018, reverse takeover acquisition of 2292055 Ontario Inc.
Note: Adjusted throughout for 1-for-3 cons. in June 2020

E.19 Earthworks Industries Inc.

Symbol - EWK **Exchange** - TSX-VEN **CUSIP** - 27032K
Head Office - 615-800 Pender St W, Vancouver, BC, V6C 2V6 **Telephone** - (604) 669-3143 **Toll-free** - (800) 422-5141 **Fax** - (604) 669-3107
Website - www.earthworksinc.com
Email - david@earthworksinc.com
Investor Relations - David B. Atkinson (800) 422-5141
Auditors - Crowe MacKay LLP C.A., Vancouver, B.C.
Bankers - Royal Bank of Canada
Lawyers - Tupper Jonsson & Yeadon, Vancouver, B.C.
Transfer Agents - Computershare Investor Services Inc.

Employees - 3 at June 3, 2022
Profile - (B.C. 1984) Proposes to design, construct and operate an integrated waste management project on a portion of the Cortina Indian Rancheria in Colusa cty., Calif.
The company has completed an environmental impact study of a landfill project in California through wholly owned **Cortina Integrated Waste Management, Inc.** (CIWM). The leased land would be developed and operated as the Cortina integrated landfill project. CIWM has a lease to 2032 and renewable for an additional 25 years to 2057. The landfill encompasses 200 acres of the 443-acre leased area. The lease also allows the use of the property for material recovery, composting and soil bioremediation.
In March 2019, wholly owned **Cortina Integrated Waste Management, Inc.** (CIWM) received a second letter from the United States Department of the Interior - Bureau of Indian Affairs (BIA) advising that its lease covering the site of the proposed Cortina integrated landfill project had been terminated. In August 2019, CIWM filed all appeal requirements with the U.S. Department of the Interior Board of Indian Appeals (IBIA), which automatically suspended the termination of the lease. The lease would remain in good standing, pending disposition of the appeal.
Predecessor Detail - Name changed from Procordia Explorations Ltd., Sept. 15, 1993; basis 1 new for 5 old shs.
Directors - David B. Atkinson, pres. & CEO, Vancouver, B.C.; David Russell, CFO, Vancouver, B.C.; David F. Andrews, Vancouver, B.C.; Richard D. (Rick) Powell, Santa Rosa, Calif.; Calvin Woroniak, Comox, B.C.
Other Exec. Officers - Carl R. Jonsson, corp. sec.

Capital Stock

	Authorized (shs.)	Outstanding (shs.)[1]
Common	unlimited	98,810,832

[1] At June 2, 2023
Major Shareholder - Widely held at June 2, 2023.

Price Range - EWK/TSX-VEN

Year	Volume	High	Low	Close
2022	4,868,021	$0.35	$0.14	$0.20
2021	7,727,493	$0.50	$0.19	$0.30
2020	12,228,081	$0.38	$0.06	$0.29
2019	16,025,570	$0.11	$0.03	$0.11
2018	15,178,629	$0.23	$0.04	$0.05

Recent Close: $0.32
Capital Stock Changes - In May 2023, private placement of 4,500,000 units (1 common share & 1 warrant) at 20¢ per unit was completed, with warrants exercisable at 40¢ per share for one year.
During fiscal 2022, common shares were issued as follows: 2,500,000 by private placement, 2,050,000 on exercise of options and 1,270,000 for debt settlement.

Wholly Owned Subsidiaries
Cortina Integrated Waste Management, Inc., Calif.

Financial Statistics

Periods ended:	12m Nov. 30/22[A]		12m Nov. 30/21[A]
	$000s	%Chg	$000s
Salaries & benefits	44		48
General & admin expense	419		386
Stock-based compensation	918		173
Operating expense	**1,381**	**+128**	**607**
Operating income	**(1,381)**	**n.a.**	**(607)**
Deprec., depl. & amort.	1		1
Finance income	58		nil
Finance costs, gross	594		439
Pre-tax income	**(1,841)**	**n.a.**	**(1,046)**
Net income	**(1,841)**	**n.a.**	**(1,046)**
Cash & equivalent	209		288
Accounts receivable	6		7
Current assets	255		424
Fixed assets, net	nil		1
Explor./devel. properties	11,850		10,802
Total assets	**12,105**	**+8**	**11,228**
Bank indebtedness	973		853
Accts. pay. & accr. liabs	457		449
Current liabilities	2,524		2,038
Equity portion of conv. debs	290		290
Shareholders' equity	2,383		2,109
Cash from oper. activs	**(377)**	**n.a.**	**(553)**
Cash from fin. activs	722		895
Cash from invest. activs	(425)		(123)
Net cash position	**209**	**-27**	**288**
	$		$
Earnings per share*	(0.02)		(0.01)
Cash flow per share*	(0.00)		(0.01)
	shs		shs
No. of shs. o/s*	94,310,832		88,490,832
Avg. no. of shs. o/s*	90,650,996		80,935,113
	%		%
Net profit margin	n.a.		n.a.
Return on equity	(81.97)		(52.95)
Return on assets	(10.69)		(5.48)

* Common
[A] Reported in accordance with IFRS

Latest Results

Periods ended:	3m Feb. 28/23[A]		3m Feb. 28/22[A]
	$000s	%Chg	$000s
Net income	(272)	n.a.	(202)
	$		$
Earnings per share*	(0.00)		(0.00)

* Common
[A] Reported in accordance with IFRS

Historical Summary
(as originally stated)

Fiscal Year	Oper. Rev. $000s	Net Inc. Bef. Disc. $000s	EPS* $
2022[A]	nil	(1,841)	(0.02)
2021[A]	nil	(1,046)	(0.01)
2020[A]	nil	(1,019)	(0.01)
2019[A]	nil	(936)	(0.01)
2018[A]	nil	(1,150)	(0.02)

* Common
[A] Reported in accordance with IFRS

E.20 East Side Games Group Inc.

Symbol - EAGR **Exchange** - TSX **CUSIP** - 275255
Head Office - 3104-1055 Dunsmuir St, Vancouver, BC, V7X 1G4 **Telephone** - (604) 288-4417
Website - eastsidegamesgroup.com
Email - darcy@eastsidegamesgroup.com
Investor Relations - Darcy Taylor (604) 288-4418
Auditors - KPMG LLP C.A., Vancouver, B.C.
Transfer Agents - Odyssey Trust Company, Vancouver, B.C.
FP500 Revenue Ranking - 748
Employees - 175 at Mar. 31, 2023
Profile - (B.C. 2018) Develops, operates and publishes free-to-play, casual mobile games.
Games are developed and published on digital platforms by the company's studios, East Side Games and LDRLY Games, which specialize in free-to-play, casual mobile games that include evolving narrative and strategies and could be played in a few minutes or run by itself for long periods of time suitable for play on a wide range of devices, including mobile phones and tablets.
East Side Games' portfolio includes Archer: Danger Phone; Dragon Up: Idle Adventure; The Goldbergs: Back to the 80s; It's Always Sunny: The Gang Goes Mobile; Trailer Park Boys: Grea$y Money; The Office: Somehow We Manage; RuPaul's Drag Race: Superstar; Star Trek: Lower Decks - the Badgey Directive; Milk Farm Tycoon; and Doctor Who: Lost in Time. LDRLY Games' portfolio has a general cannabis theme and targeted to mature audiences which include Bud Farm Idle Tycoon; Bud Farm 420; Bud Farm Grass Roots; Cheech & Chong Bud Farm; Bud Farm Quest for Buds; Potfarm Legacy; and B-Real Monster Buds. Games are available worldwide in the Apple App Store and Google Play. Revenue is generated primarily from in-app purchases and the balance from the sale of in-game advertising to third parties.
Predecessor Detail - Name changed from Leaf Mobile Inc., May 25, 2022.
Directors - Jason Bailey, exec. chr. & CEO, Vancouver, B.C.; Derek Lew, corp. sec., Vancouver, B.C.; Michael S. (Mike) Edwards, Whistler, B.C.; Darcy Taylor, West Vancouver, B.C.; Birgit Troy, Port Moody, B.C.
Other Exec. Officers - Lisa Shek, COO; Jason Chan, interim CFO; Elin Jonsson, chief bus. officer; Wally Nguyen, chief revenue officer; Jim Wagner, chief of product

Capital Stock

	Authorized (shs.)	Outstanding (shs.)[1]
Common	unlimited	81,536,436

[1] At Mar. 31, 2023
Major Shareholder - Jason Bailey held 50.13% interest at Mar. 24, 2023.

Price Range - EAGR/TSX

Year	Volume	High	Low	Close
2022	8,234,352	$4.27	$0.55	$0.72
2021	12,921,808	$5.80	$2.19	$3.56
2020	1,533,553	$4.80	$1.90	$2.25
2019	13,474	$2.00	$1.50	$1.55

Consolidation: 1-for-10 cons. in Aug. 2021
Recent Close: $0.50
Capital Stock Changes - During 2022, common shares were issued as follows: 4,444,444 for achievement of a performance milestone, 419,389 on acquisition of Funko Pop! Blitz mobile game, 41,250 on exercise of warrants and 11,027 on exercise of options.

Wholly Owned Subsidiaries
Eastside Games Inc., Vancouver, B.C.
• 100% int. in **Keh Kaw Games Inc.**, B.C.
Eastside Games (Ontario) Inc., Ont.
Eastside Games USA Inc., United States.
1182533 B.C. Ltd., Vancouver, B.C.
• 100% int. in **LDRLY (Technologies) Inc.**, Vancouver, B.C.
Note: The preceding list includes only the major related companies in which interests are held.

Financial Statistics

Periods ended:	12m Dec. 31/22[A]		12m Dec. 31/21[oA]
	$000s	%Chg	$000s
Operating revenue	**116,280**	**+25**	**93,187**
Cost of sales	43,767		32,472
Research & devel. expense	16,324		13,062
General & admin expense	48,698		39,974
Stock-based compensation	2,528		4,005
Operating expense	**111,317**	**+24**	**89,513**
Operating income	**4,963**	**+35**	**3,674**
Deprec., depl. & amort.	12,801		7,781
Finance costs, gross	478		1,720
Investment income	546		370
Write-downs/write-offs	(195)		nil
Pre-tax income	**9,954**	**n.a.**	**(3,081)**
Income taxes	(802)		(263)
Net income	**10,756**	**n.a.**	**(2,817)**
Cash & equivalent	5,707		9,242
Accounts receivable	8,720		10,146
Current assets	18,450		22,097
Long-term investments	1,057		950
Fixed assets, net	545		681
Intangibles, net	56,107		53,906
Total assets	**80,248**	**-1**	**80,790**
Bank indebtedness	870		nil
Accts. pay. & accr. liabs	15,874		10,634
Current liabilities	19,784		31,681
Shareholders' equity	48,521		24,199
Cash from oper. activs	**10,022**	**+122**	**4,522**
Cash from fin. activs	(9,490)		(4,207)
Cash from invest. activs	(4,116)		4,512
Net cash position	**5,658**	**-39**	**9,242**
Capital expenditures	(201)		(343)
	$		$
Earnings per share*	0.13		(0.04)
Cash flow per share*	0.12		0.01
	shs		shs
No. of shs. o/s*	81,536,436		76,620,326
Avg. no. of shs. o/s*	80,506,952		73,469,877
	%		%
Net profit margin	9.25		(3.02)
Return on equity	29.65		(16.09)
Return on assets	13.87		(2.44)

* Common
[o] Restated
[A] Reported in accordance with IFRS

Latest Results

Periods ended:	3m Mar. 31/23[A]		3m Mar. 31/22[oA]
	$000s	%Chg	$000s
Operating revenue	24,294	-32	35,608
Net income	(1,024)	n.a.	25
	$		$
Earnings per share*	(0.01)		0.00

* Common
[o] Restated
[A] Reported in accordance with IFRS

Historical Summary
(as originally stated)

Fiscal Year	Oper. Rev. $000s	Net Inc. Bef. Disc. $000s	EPS* $
2022[A]	116,280	10,756	0.13
2021[A]	93,187	(1,881)	(0.03)
2020[A1]	31,085	(4,335)	(0.23)
2019[A]	nil	(472)	(0.04)

* Common
[A] Reported in accordance with IFRS
[1] Results reflect the Apr. 17, 2020, Qualifying Transaction reverse takeover acquisition of 1182533 B.C. Ltd. (dba Leaf Digital Studios).
Note: Adjusted throughout for 1-for-10 cons. in Aug. 2021

E.21 Eastower Wireless Inc.

Symbol - ESTW.H **Exchange** - TSX-VEN (S) **CUSIP** - 27777L
Head Office - 8000 N Federal Hwy, Boca Raton, FL, United States, 33847 **Telephone** - (561) 549-9070 **Fax** - (561) 549-9054
Website - www.eastower.com
Email - investor@eastowerwireless.com
Investor Relations - Vlado P. Hreljanovic (561) 549-9070
Auditors - McGovern Hurley LLP C.A., Toronto, Ont.
Transfer Agents - TSX Trust Company, Toronto, Ont.
Profile - (B.C. 2022; orig. Can., 2016) Ceased business operations. Previously provided wireless communications infrastructure and related services in the southeast region of the United States.
In January 2023, the company ceased business operations as a result of an inability to complete an equity or debt financing. The company was in process of identifying and evaluating businesses or assets to complete a change of business or reverse takeover.

Common suspended from TSX-VEN, May 9, 2023.

Recent Merger and Acquisition Activity

Status: completed **Revised:** Mar. 19, 2022

UPDATE: The transaction was completed. EasTower Group amalgamated with EasTower Acquisition Corporation, a wholly owned subsidiary of OV2. PREVIOUS: OV2 Investment 1 Inc. entered into a letter of intent for the Qualifying Transaction reverse takeover acquisition of Boca Raton, Fla.-based EasTower Group, Inc. and Delaware incorporated EGI Investments, Inc. on a share-for-share basis (following a 0.79730908-for-1 share consolidation). EasTower Group and EGI shareholders would be issued 15,450,141 and 8,443,533 OV2 post-consolidated common shares, respectively. The fully diluted combined valuation of EasTower and EGI was agreed to be $6,000,000. EasTower Group provides wireless communications infrastructure and related services in the U.S., specializing in the construction, installation, upgrades and maintenance of wireless communications systems. EGI's sold asset was convertible debt in EasTower Group. Apr. 23, 2021 - A definitive agreement was entered into. Upon completion, EasTower would amalgamate with OV2's wholly owned EasTower Acquisition Corporation, and OV2 would change its name and continue its incorporation into British Columbia from Canada. Aug. 31, 2020 - EGI was no longer a party to the transaction. July 21, 2021 - EasTower Group completed a private placement of 3,510,000 units (1 common share & ½ warrant) at 25¢ per share, with warrants exercisable at 40¢ per share for two years.

Predecessor Detail - Name changed from OV2 Investment 1 Inc., Mar. 11, 2022, pursuant to the Qualifying Transaction reverse takeover acquisition of EasTower Group, Inc., and cocurrent amalgamation of EasTower Group wtih wholly owned EasTower Acquisition Corporation; basis 0.797309 new for 1 old sh.

Directors - Vlado P. Hreljanovic, pres. & CEO, Boynton Beach, Fla.; Joel Liebman, Garden City, N.Y.; Margaret Perialas, West Palm Beach, Fla.

Other Exec. Officers - Kyle Appleby, CFO

Capital Stock

	Authorized (shs.)	Outstanding (shs.)[1]
Common	unlimited	104,754,307

[1] At Mar. 20, 2023

Major Shareholder - Donna E. Anderson held 16.49% interest and Vlado P. Hreljanovic held 13.31% interest at Mar. 20, 2023.

Price Range - ESTW.H/TSX-VEN (S)

Year	Volume	High	Low	Close
2022............	22,646,427	$0.25	$0.01	$0.01

Consolidation: 0.797309-for-1 cons. in Mar. 2022

Recent Close: $0.01

Capital Stock Changes - In March 2023, debt conversions of a total of 34,248,045 common shares at Cdn$0.01 per share for settlement of US$255,659 of debt were completed. Also in March 2023, additional debt conversions of a total of 82,723,464 common shares at Cdn$0.005 per share for settlement of US$301,163 of debt were announced.

In March 2022, common shares were consolidated on a 1-for-0.7973091 basis, 30,563,213 post-consolidated common shares were issued pursuant to the Qualifying Transaction reverse takeover acquisition of EasTower Group, Inc., 10,463,177 post-consolidated common shares were issued on conversion of EasTower Group convertible debentures, and 2,500,000 post-consolidated common shares were issued as finder's fees. In addition, 8,659,000 units (1 post-consolidated common share & ½ warrant) were issued without further consideration on exchange of subscription receipts sold previously by private placement at 25¢ each. In August 2022, private placement of 10,320,872 units (1 post-consolidated common share & 1 warrant) at 5¢ per unit was completed, with warrants exercisable at 10¢ per share for two years.

Wholly Owned Subsidiaries

EasTower Group, Inc., Boca Raton, Fla.
- 100% int. in **EasTower Communications Inc.**, United States.

Financial Statistics

Periods ended:	12m Dec. 31/21[A1]		12m Dec. 31/20[A]
	US$000s	%Chg	US$000s
Operating revenue........................	**1,493**	**-48**	**2,895**
Cost of sales....................................	852		1,674
General & admin expense...............	2,255		2,683
Operating expense........................	**3,107**	**-29**	**4,357**
Operating income..........................	**(1,614)**	**n.a.**	**(1,462)**
Deprec., depl. & amort....................	192		198
Finance costs, gross........................	278		375
Pre-tax income.............................	**(1,195)**	**n.a.**	**(2,035)**
Net income....................................	**(1,195)**	**n.a.**	**(2,035)**
Cash & equivalent............................	104		23
Accounts receivable........................	122		504
Current assets.................................	226		527
Fixed assets, net.............................	46		114
Right-of-use assets.........................	307		117
Total assets....................................	**598**	**-24**	**782**
Accts. pay. & accr. liabs..................	672		815
Current liabilities............................	2,565		3,741
Long-term debt, gross.....................	3,617		2,992
Long-term debt, net.........................	1,866		1,137
Long-term lease liabilities................	202		91
Preferred share equity.....................	37		37
Shareholders' equity........................	(4,374)		(4,629)
Cash from oper. activs..................	**(342)**	**n.a.**	**(2,345)**
Cash from fin. activs........................	477		2,333
Cash from invest. activs...................	(54)		(10)
Net cash position..........................	**104**	**+352**	**23**
Capital expenditures........................	(54)		(10)
	US$		US$
Earnings per share*.........................	(0.04)		(0.14)
	shs		shs
No. of shs. o/s.................................	n.a.		n.a.
	%		%
Net profit margin.............................	(80.04)		(70.29)
Return on equity..............................	n.m.		n.m.
Return on assets.............................	(132.90)		(152.22)
Foreign sales percent......................	100		100

* Common

[A] Reported in accordance with IFRS

[1] Results for 2021 and prior periods pertain to EasTower Group, Inc.

Latest Results

Periods ended:	9m Sept. 30/22[A]		9m Sept. 30/21[A]
	US$000s	%Chg	US$000s
Operating revenue...........................	1,185	+9	1,092
Net income......................................	(3,457)	n.a.	(1,021)
	US$		US$
Earnings per share*.........................	(0.06)		(0.04)

* Common

[A] Reported in accordance with IFRS

Historical Summary
(as originally stated)

Fiscal Year	Oper. Rev. US$000s	Net Inc. Bef. Disc. US$000s	EPS* US$
2021[A]...................	1,493	(1,195)	(0.04)
2020[A]...................	2,895	(2,035)	(0.14)
2019[A]...................	2,783	(2,924)	(0.34)

* Common

[A] Reported in accordance with IFRS

Note: Adjusted throughout for 0.7973091-for-1 cons. in Mar. 2022

E.22 EastWest Bioscience Inc.

Symbol - EAST.H **Exchange** - TSX-VEN (S) **CUSIP** - 27783V

Head Office - 260 Okanagan Ave E, Penticton, BC, V2A 3J7 **Telephone** - (778) 683-5522 **Toll-free** - (800) 409-1930

Website - www.eastwestbioscience.com

Email - ciska@eastwestscience.com

Investor Relations - Ciska Asriel (800) 409-1930

Auditors - Dale Matheson Carr-Hilton LaBonte LLP C.A., Vancouver, B.C.

Transfer Agents - Computershare Trust Company of Canada Inc., Calgary, Alta.

Profile - (Alta. 2014) Owns, produces, manufactures and manages various brands in retail, manufacturing, supply chain, storage and distribution.

Operations are organized into six segments: Manufacturing; Retail; Intellectual Property; Real Estate; Self-storage; and Consumer Goods.

Manufacturing - This segment includes wholly owned **Orchard Vale Natural Inc.** (OVN), which owns and operates a Health Canada licensed manufacturing and warehouse facility in Penticton B.C., totaling 34,000 sq. ft., for encapsulating, packaging and labelling health supplements for the company and third parties under contract manufacturing agreements.

Retail - This segment includes Sangster's Health Centres, which own the brand rights and manage the franchisor-franchisee distribution relationships as well as sells supplements and wellness products through its 14 franchise locations and its online e-commerce platform; Sangster's Corporate Stores, which own and manage Sangster's corporate owned stores across Canada and maintained a corporate retail presence in Saskatoon, Sask.; and Sangster's Leases, which hold the head lease for certain franchise and corporate store locations with landlord and subleases to franchisees and corporate stores.

Intellectual Property - This segment includes wholly owned **1123573 B.C. Ltd.**, which holds the Health Canada licences to 187 natural product numbers (NPN) certified by Health Canada. These NPNs are mandatory for supplement products to be marketed in Canada and are valuable assets for any companies that are manufacturing, distributing and marketing supplements in Canada.

Real Estate - This segment includes wholly owned **1123568 B.C. Ltd.**, which owns and manages the land and building at Penticton, B.C. The land and building is a 34,000-sq.-ft. facility located off the main street in Penticton. It is equipped with two loading docks, ample parking and is fully secured. Current tenants include wholly owned OVN, Sangster's and EWS.

Self-storage - This segment includes affiliate **1290185 B.C. Ltd.** (dba Spare Room Co), which owns and manages five self-storage sites located in Oliver, Penticton, South Okanagan, Merritt and Duncan, all in British Columbia.

Consumer Goods - This segment includes wholly owned **EastWest Science Ltd.**, which distributes hemp-based consumer goods to business-to-business clients, wholesalers, distributors and end consumers.

In addition, the company through a joint venture with licensed hemp processor **Azema Sciences Inc.**, wholly owned **EastWest Science USA Inc.** has access to 9,000 sq. ft. of Azema's 18,000-sq.-ft. cannabidiol (CBD) processing facility in Lebanon, Ky. EastWest USA plans to manufacture CBD infused products.

Products include natural health supplements; pet food and pet supplements; food products such as raw hemp seeds and granola; and hair care, skin care and body care products.

Common suspended from TSX-VEN, Dec. 2, 2022.

Predecessor Detail - Name changed from Harbour Star Capital Inc., Nov. 30, 2018.

Directors - Rodney Gelineau, co-founder, pres. & CEO, Penticton, B.C.; Jeff Bierman, Chicago, Ill.; Nathan Lidder, Vancouver, B.C.; Paul Mandl, Jakarta, Indonesia

Other Exec. Officers - Ciska Asriel, co-founder, COO & interim CFO; Scott M. Reeves, corp. sec.; Carlo Bevilacqua, pres., Sangsters Health Centres

Capital Stock

	Authorized (shs.)	Outstanding (shs.)[1]
Preferred	unlimited	nil
Common	unlimited	100,664,323

[1] At June 29, 2022

Major Shareholder - Rodney Gelineau held 16.9% interest and Ciska Asriel held 12.4% interest at Feb. 7, 2022.

Price Range - EAST.H/TSX-VEN (S)

Year	Volume	High	Low	Close
2022............	15,227,204	$0.04	$0.02	$0.03
2021............	71,368,659	$0.06	$0.02	$0.02
2020............	96,972,701	$0.09	$0.01	$0.02
2019............	63,601,725	$0.16	$0.02	$0.03
2018............	74,882,999	$0.39	$0.11	$0.15

Recent Close: $0.03

Wholly Owned Subsidiaries

EastWest Science Ltd., B.C.
EastWest Science USA Inc., Ky.
1011705 B.C. Ltd., Richmond, B.C.
102064495 Saskatchewan Inc., Sask. Operating as Sangster's.
102064509 Saskatchewan Inc., Sask. Operating as Sangster's Corporate Stores.
102064512 Saskatchewan Inc., Sask. Operating as SHC Leasing.
1123568 B.C. Ltd., B.C.
1123573 B.C. Ltd., B.C.
Orchard Vale Naturals Inc., B.C.
Orchard Valley Naturals Inc., B.C.

Investments

40% int. in **1290185 B.C. Ltd.**, B.C.

Financial Statistics

Periods ended:	12m July 31/21[A]		12m July 31/20[A]
	$000s	%Chg	$000s
Operating revenue	**1,058**	**-19**	**1,306**
Cost of goods sold	480		695
Salaries & benefits	548		547
Research & devel. expense	9		3
General & admin expense	1,299		1,287
Stock-based compensation	186		74
Operating expense	**2,522**	**-3**	**2,606**
Operating income	**(1,464)**	**n.a.**	**(1,300)**
Deprec., depl. & amort.	118		127
Finance costs, gross	257		223
Investment income	11		(23)
Write-downs/write-offs	(235)		21
Pre-tax income	**(1,628)**	**n.a.**	**(1,132)**
Net income	**(1,628)**	**n.a.**	**(1,132)**
Net inc. for equity hldrs	**(1,605)**	**n.a.**	**(1,132)**
Net inc. for non-cont. int	**(22)**	**n.a.**	**nil**
Cash & equivalent	1,056		107
Inventories	205		211
Accounts receivable	59		89
Current assets	1,354		691
Long-term investments	49		26
Fixed assets, net	2,126		2,242
Intangibles, net	194		225
Total assets	**3,722**	**+17**	**3,184**
Accts. pay. & accr. liabs	982		770
Current liabilities	3,420		3,010
Long-term debt, gross	2,417		2,268
Long-term debt, net	368		220
Shareholders' equity	(66)		(46)
Non-controlling interest	372		nil
Cash from oper. activs	**(688)**	**n.a.**	**(324)**
Cash from fin. activs	1,616		310
Cash from invest. activs	21		67
Net cash position	**1,056**	**+887**	**107**
Capital expenditures	(9)		(1)
Capital disposals	30		94
	$		$
Earnings per share*	(0.02)		(0.01)
Cash flow per share*	(0.01)		(0.00)
	shs		shs
No. of shs. o/s*	97,569,279		92,605,775
Avg. no. of shs. o/s*	94,728,670		83,770,859
	%		%
Net profit margin	(153.88)		(86.68)
Return on equity	n.m.		n.m.
Return on assets	(39.70)		(26.15)

* Common
[A] Reported in accordance with IFRS

Latest Results

Periods ended:	9m Apr. 30/22[A]		9m Apr. 30/21[A]
	$000s	%Chg	$000s
Operating revenue	667	-29	935
Net income	956	n.a.	(671)
Net inc. for equity hldrs	1,043	n.a.	(671)
Net inc. for non-cont. int	(87)		nil
	$		$
Earnings per share*	0.01		(0.01)

* Common
[A] Reported in accordance with IFRS

Historical Summary
(as originally stated)

Fiscal Year	Oper. Rev.	Net Inc. Bef. Disc.	EPS*
	$000s	$000s	$
2021[A]	1,058	(1,628)	(0.02)
2020[A]	1,306	(1,132)	(0.01)
2019[A]	1,752	(3,649)	(0.05)
2018[A1]	208	(3,286)	(0.06)
2017[A]	24	(840)	n.a.

* Common
[A] Reported in accordance with IFRS
[1] Results prior to July 23, 2018, pertain to and reflect the Qualifying Transaction reverse takeover acquisition of 1011705 B.C. Ltd. (dba EastWest Science).

E.23 Eastwood Bio-Medical Canada Inc.

Symbol - EBM **Exchange** - TSX-VEN **CUSIP** - 27783W
Head Office - Unit 1130, 4871 Shell Rd, Richmond, BC, V6X 3Z6
Telephone - (604) 247-2100 **Fax** - (604) 247-2101
Website - www.eleotin.ca
Email - info@eastwoodcos.com
Investor Relations - Yunji Kim (604) 247-1000
Auditors - Saturna Group Chartered Accountants LLP C.A., Vancouver, B.C.
Transfer Agents - Computershare Trust Company of Canada Inc., Vancouver, B.C.
Profile - (B.C. 2010) Markets and distributes Eleotin® natural health products in Canada, the United States and Asia.

The company is a licensed distributor of **Eastwood Bio-Medical Research Inc.**'s Eleotin® line of products, which include formulations based on natural ingredients that are presented in tea or capsule form. Eleotin® product formulations have been granted Health Canada approval as natural health products including products for diabetes, general health maintenance, obesity management and hypertension. The company is the exclusive distributor of Eleotin® products in Canada and the non-exclusive distributor in the United States, and distributes certain Eleotin® products to selected sub-distributors in Asia.

The company's licensed products which have secured Health Canada product license numbers include Eleotin® A 700, for spleen deficiency, lack of appetite, and fatigue; Eleotin® AL88, laxative; Eleotin® Cal20, for bone and teeth maintenance; Eleotin® V3D, for development and maintenance of bones, teeth and good health; Eleotin® G2000, for cardiovascular health; Eleotin® H55 for sedative and tension relief; Eleotin® Zn330 for tissue formation and metabolism; Eleotin® Bentley, for healthy glucose level; and Eleotin® LBM, for hypertension relief.

Directors - Dr. Youngsoo Kim, CEO, B.C.; Yunji Kim, pres., CFO & corp. sec., Vancouver, B.C.; Dr. Marcus Kuypers, Wash.; Ian M. Mallmann, Richmond, B.C.; Dr. Terrance G. Owen, Abbotsford, B.C.

Capital Stock

	Authorized (shs.)	Outstanding (shs.)[1]
Common	unlimited	68,885,969

[1] At May 23, 2023

Major Shareholder - Eastwood Bio-Medical Research Inc. held 69.38% interest at May 31, 2023.

Price Range - EBM/TSX-VEN

Year	Volume	High	Low	Close
2022	235,199	$2.00	$0.50	$1.00
2021	1,225,548	$2.72	$0.99	$1.40
2020	920,305	$2.88	$0.96	$2.00
2019	2,017,811	$6.00	$0.85	$2.49
2018	16,917,242	$8.49	$0.07	$5.50

Recent Close: $0.75

Capital Stock Changes - There were no changes to capital stock from fiscal 2018 to fiscal 2022, inclusive.

Financial Statistics

Periods ended:	12m Oct. 31/22[A]		12m Oct. 31/21[A]
	$000s	%Chg	$000s
Operating revenue	**1,300**	**+33**	**981**
Cost of sales	397		523
Salaries & benefits	454		472
General & admin expense	472		497
Operating expense	**1,322**	**-11**	**1,491**
Operating income	**(22)**	**n.a.**	**(510)**
Deprec., depl. & amort.	107		105
Finance costs, gross	11		3
Write-downs/write-offs	(5)		(5)
Pre-tax income	**(150)**	**n.a.**	**(604)**
Net income	**(150)**	**n.a.**	**(604)**
Cash & equivalent	40		21
Accounts receivable	15		6
Current assets	103		58
Fixed assets, net	302		371
Right-of-use assets	90		179
Total assets	**513**	**-26**	**691**
Bank indebtedness	28		nil
Accts. pay. & accr. liabs	103		53
Current liabilities	1,018		834
Long-term debt, gross	35		31
Long-term debt, net	35		31
Shareholders' equity	(294)		(144)
Cash from oper. activs	**(4)**	**n.a.**	**(116)**
Cash from fin. activs	26		20
Cash from invest. activs	(3)		(6)
Net cash position	**40**	**+90**	**21**
Capital expenditures	(3)		(6)
	$		$
Earnings per share*	(0.00)		(0.01)
Cash flow per share*	(0.00)		(0.00)
	shs		shs
No. of shs. o/s*	68,885,969		68,885,969
Avg. no. of shs. o/s*	68,885,969		68,885,969
	%		%
Net profit margin	(11.54)		(61.57)
Return on equity	n.m.		n.m.
Return on assets	(23.09)		(74.01)
Foreign sales percent	84		80

* Common
[A] Reported in accordance with IFRS

Latest Results

Periods ended:	6m Apr. 30/23[A]		6m Apr. 30/22[A]
	$000s	%Chg	$000s
Operating revenue	552	-13	634
Net income	(245)	n.a.	(40)
	$		$
Earnings per share*	(0.01)		(0.01)

* Common
[A] Reported in accordance with IFRS

Historical Summary
(as originally stated)

Fiscal Year	Oper. Rev.	Net Inc. Bef. Disc.	EPS*
	$000s	$000s	$
2022[A]	1,300	(150)	(0.00)
2021[A]	981	(604)	(0.01)
2020[A]	718	(852)	(0.01)
2019[A]	1,293	(577)	(0.01)
2018[A]	744	(862)	(0.01)

* Common
[A] Reported in accordance with IFRS

E.24 Eat & Beyond Global Holdings Inc.

Symbol - EATS **Exchange** - CSE **CUSIP** - 27785T
Head Office - 1570-505 Burrard St, Vancouver, BC, V7X 1M5
Telephone - (604) 416-4099
Website - eatandbeyond.com
Email - kelvin@eatandbeyond.com
Investor Relations - Kelvin Lee (604) 961-0296
Auditors - Crowe MacKay LLP C.A., Vancouver, B.C.
Lawyers - McMillan LLP, Vancouver, B.C.
Transfer Agents - Olympia Trust Company, Vancouver, B.C.
Employees - 1 at July 18, 2022
Profile - (B.C. 2019) Invests in global plant-based, fermented and cultured protein companies that are developing and commercializing innovative food technology as well as alternative food products.

Investments in publicly traded companies include: **good natured Products Inc.**, which designs, produces and distributes high-performance plant-based bioplastics for use in packaging and durable product applications; **The Very Good Food Company Inc.**, which develops, produces, distributes and sells plant-based meat, cheese and other food alternatives under the The Very Good Butchers and The Very Good Cheese Co. brands; **Zoglo's Incredible Food Corp.**, which designs, develops, produces, distributes and sells plant-based meat alternative products; and **Plantfuel Life Inc.**, which manufactures plant-based supplements and nutritional products.

Private companies include **Mylk Brands Inc.**, which owns **Fresh Start Beverage Company** (dba Banana Wave), which produces beverages made from oats and real bananas; **TurtleTree Labs Pte. Ltd.**, which develops dairy milk and infant nutrition using cell-based technology through business-to-business (B2B) partnerships; **Eat Just Inc.**, which develops and sells plant-based alternatives, conventionally produced eggs and cultivated meat products; **11270702 Canada Inc.** (dba Daydream Drinks), which offers adaptogen-infused sparkling water with no sugar or caffeine; **Plant Power Restaurant Group, LLC**, which offers quick service restaurant food in plant-based biodegradable packaging including burgers, fries, shakes and chicken tenders; **Beyond Moo Ltd.**, which manufactures and sells oat-based yogurt, kefir and butter; and **Circular Solutions Inc.**, which is a container sharing platform for takeout food from restaurants, cafe and grocery stores, eliminating single-use plastic containers.

In August 2022, the company changed its year end to July 31 from December 31.

Recent Merger and Acquisition Activity

Status: completed **Revised:** Apr. 1, 2022
UPDATE: The transaction was completed. PREVIOUS: Eat Beyond Global Holdings Inc. entered into a letter of intent for the acquisition of private British Columbia-based Mylk Brands Inc. for issuance of 14,470,588 common shares at a deemed price of 80¢ per share. Mylk, through wholly owned Boca Raton, Fla.-based Fresh Start Beverage Company (dba Banana Wave), produces a non-dairy banana milk made from fibre-rich oats and real bananas. Jan. 24, 2022 - A definitive agreement was entered into.

Predecessor Detail - Name changed from Eat Beyond Global Holdings Inc., Mar. 29, 2022.

Directors - Young Bann, CEO; Ravinder (Robert) Kang, Vancouver, B.C.; Alexander (Alex) Somjen, Toronto, Ont.

Other Exec. Officers - Geoffrey (Geoff) Balderson, CFO & corp. sec.; Justin Osbourne, v-p, sales

Capital Stock

	Authorized (shs.)	Outstanding (shs.)[1]
Common	unlimited	17,063,698

[1] At June 29, 2023

Major Shareholder - Widely held at June 16, 2022.

Price Range - EATS/CSE

Year	Volume	High	Low	Close
2022	1,842,997	$4.97	$0.18	$0.21
2021	6,610,641	$31.92	$2.52	$2.98
2020	3,893,447	$21.28	$3.71	$16.59

Consolidation: 1-for-7 cons. in Mar. 2023
Recent Close: $0.07

Capital Stock Changes - On Mar. 9, 2023, common shares were consolidated on a 1-for-7 basis.

In April 2022, 22,115,310 common shares were issued on acquisition of Mylk Brands Inc. Also during the seven months ended Aug. 31, 2022, 500,000 common shares were issued for debt settlement.

Wholly Owned Subsidiaries

Mylk Brands Inc., B.C.
- 100% int. in **Fresh Start Beverage Company**, Fla.

Investments

32% int. in **Beyond Moo Ltd.**, Mississauga, Ont.

Financial Statistics

Periods ended:	7m July 31/22[A]		12m Dec. 31/21[A]
	$000s	%Chg	$000s
Realized invest. gain (loss)	152		627
Total revenue	**(5,412)**	**n.a.**	**769**
Salaries & benefits	227		156
General & admin. expense	787		2,664
Stock-based compensation	1,162		508
Operating expense	**2,176**	**n.a.**	**3,328**
Operating income	**(7,588)**	**n.a.**	**(2,559)**
Write-downs/write-offs	nil		(153)
Pre-tax income	**(7,439)**	**n.a.**	**(2,730)**
Net income	**(7,439)**	**n.a.**	**(2,730)**
Cash & equivalent	6,932		4,017
Accounts receivable	76		nil
Total assets	**7,436**	**n.a.**	**4,120**
Accts. pay. & accr. liabs	643		433
Shareholders' equity	6,794		3,688
Cash from oper. activs	**(813)**	**n.a.**	**(2,941)**
Cash from fin. activs	nil		2,782
Net cash position	**121**	**n.a.**	**934**
	$		$
Earnings per share*	(1.12)		(0.63)
Cash flow per share*	(0.12)		(0.65)
	shs		shs
No. of shs. o/s*	8,090,731		4,859,972
Avg. no. of shs. o/s*	6,683,727		4,545,147
	%		%
Net profit margin	...		(355.01)
Return on equity	...		(80.26)
Return on assets	...		(74.38)

* Common
[A] Reported in accordance with IFRS

Historical Summary
(as originally stated)

Fiscal Year	Total Rev. $000s	Net Inc. Bef. Disc. $000s	EPS* $
2022[A1]	(5,412)	(7,439)	(1.12)
2021[A]	769	(2,730)	(0.63)
2020[A]	1,468	(1,960)	(0.98)
2020[A2,3]	nil	(147)	(0.14)
2019[A]	nil	(45)	n.a.

* Common
[A] Reported in accordance with IFRS
[1] 7 months ended July 31, 2022.
[2] 51 weeks ended Aug. 31, 2020.
[3] As shown in the prospectus dated Nov. 6, 2020.
Note: Adjusted throughout for 1-for-7 cons. in Mar. 2023

E.25 Eat Well Investment Group Inc.

Symbol - EWG **Exchange** - CSE (S) **CUSIP** - 27786T
Head Office - 1305-1090 Georgia St W, Vancouver, BC, V6E 3V7
Telephone - (604) 315-1237 **Fax** - (604) 683-1585
Website - www.eatwellgroup.com
Email - ir@eatwellgroup.com
Investor Relations - Marc Aneed (604) 685-9316
Auditors - CM3 Advisory C.P.A., San Diego, Calif.
Lawyers - McMillan LLP, Vancouver, B.C.
Transfer Agents - Computershare Trust Company of Canada Inc., Toronto, Ont.

Profile - (B.C. 2007) Owns and manages a portfolio of investments focusing on high-growth companies in the agribusiness, food-tech, plant-based, and environmental, social and governance (ESG) sectors.

The investment portfolio includes wholly owned **Belle Pulses Ltd.**, a processor of pulses such as yellow and green peas, faba beans and chickpeas intended for human and pet consumption, and distributed to 35 countries; wholly owned **Sapientia Technologies LLC**, which develops intellectual property primarily in the savory snacking sector with secondary focus on pet treats, toddler snacks and meal staples such as plant-protein based pulses; and 51% interest in **PataFoods Inc.** (dba Amara), which manufactures and distributes healthy, organic, non-GMO, plant-based and convenient baby and children's food that are sold throughout major North American retailers.

Common suspended from CSE, July 10, 2023.

Predecessor Detail - Name changed from Rockshield Capital Corp., Sept. 2, 2021.

Directors - Marc Aneed, pres. & CEO, Irvine, Calif.; Patrick (Pat) Dunn, CFO; Desmond M. (Des) Balakrishnan, Vancouver, B.C.; Daniel Brody, Cayman Islands; Matthew J. Fish, Toronto, Ont.; Nick Grafton, Toronto, Ont.

Other Exec. Officers - Mark Coles, chief invest. officer; Barry Didato, v-p, strategy; Nick DeMare, corp. sec.

Capital Stock

	Authorized (shs.)	Outstanding (shs.)[1]
Common	unlimited	155,590,547

[1] At July 29, 2022

Major Shareholder - Widely held at Sept. 13, 2021.

Price Range - CUA/TSX-VEN (D)

Year	Volume	High	Low	Close
2022	35,679,795	$0.73	$0.16	$0.22
2021	75,176,340	$1.24	$0.11	$0.62
2020	7,976,193	$0.13	$0.03	$0.11
2019	14,151,828	$0.14	$0.04	$0.05
2018	78,845,763	$0.84	$0.10	$0.10

Recent Close: $0.17

Capital Stock Changes - In February 2022, private placement of 6,690,666 units (1 common share & ½ warrant) at $0.75 per unit was completed, with warrants exercisable at $1.00 per share for three years. In April 2022, 10,403,995 units (1 common share & ½ warrant) were issued without further consideration on exchange of special warrants sold in December 2021 at $0.55 each, with warrants exercisable at $0.75 per share for three years.

Wholly Owned Subsidiaries

10111404 Saskatchewan Ltd., Sask.
- 58.75% int. in **Belle Pulses Ltd.**, Sask.

10111406 Saskatchewan Ltd., Sask.
- 35% int. in **Belle Pulses Ltd.**, Sask.

1325242 B.C. ULC, B.C.
Rockshield Capital Management Corp., United States.
Rockshield Plywood Corp., Canada. Inactive.
Sapientia Technology Inc., Hong Kong, People's Republic of China.

Subsidiaries

51% int. in **PataFoods, Inc.**, San Francisco, Calif.

Investments

6.25% int. in **Belle Pulses Ltd.**, Sask.

Latest Results

Periods ended:	6m May 31/22[A]		6m May 31/21[A]
	$000s	%Chg	$000s
Total revenue	144	-87	1,088
Net income	(8,629)	n.a.	(1,659)
	$		$
Earnings per share*	(0.06)		(0.02)

* Common
[A] Reported in accordance with IFRS

E.26 Ecolomondo Corporation

Symbol - ECM **Exchange** - TSX-VEN **CUSIP** - 27900T
Head Office - 3435 boul Pitfield, Saint-Laurent, QC, H4S 1H7
Telephone - (450) 587-5999 **Fax** - (514) 328-2955
Website - www.ecolomondo.com
Email - esorella@ecolomondocorp.com
Investor Relations - Elio Sorella (450) 587-5999
Auditors - Raymond Chabot Grant Thornton LLP C.A., Montréal, Qué.
Bankers - Canadian Imperial Bank of Commerce, Montréal, Qué.
Lawyers - BCF LLP, Montréal, Qué.
Transfer Agents - Computershare Trust Company of Canada Inc., Montréal, Qué.

Profile - (Can. 2015) Commercializing a green technology which converts/recycles hydrocarbon waste into marketable commodity end-products.

The company's Thermal Decomposition Process (TDP) is a closed loop, slow pyrolysis technology which operates in an oxygen-free environment using batch rotary reactor that recovers high value re-usable commodities from scrap tire waste, notably recovered carbon black, oil, gas, fibre and steel.

The company is commercializing its technology through the sale and operation of turnkey facilities based on the TDP platform, including operation of wholly owned or joint venture turnkey facilities. TDP turnkey facilities may consist of two to eight reactors. The company has built a two-reactor TDP facility in Hawkesbury, Ont., which has commenced its ramp-up phase in the fourth quarter of 2022. The Hawkesbury facility covers 46,200 sq. ft. and has four main production departments, namely tire shredding, thermal decomposition, recycled carbon black refining and oil fractionation. The Hawkesbury facility is estimated to process at least 14,000 tons of tire waste per year and produce 5,300 tons of recovered carbon black, 42,700 barrels of oil, 1,800 tons of steel, 1,600 tons of process gas and 850 tons of fibre. The company also proposed a six-reactor TDP facility to be situated on a 137-acre parcel of land in Shamrock, Tex. The proposed facility is estimated to process 42,000 tons of tire waste per year and produce 15,900 tons of recovered carbon black, 128,100 barrels of oil, 5,400 tons of steel, 4,800 tons of syngas and 2,550 tons of fibre. Construction of the facility is expected to begin by the end of the fourth quarter of 2023.

Operates a two-reactor, industrial-sized pilot plant in Contrecoeur, Que., which the company was assessing the role of the pilot plant and how it would contribute to the company's strategic goal.

Predecessor Detail - Name changed from Cortina Capital Corp., Oct. 20, 2017, pursuant to Qualifying Transaction reverse takeover acquisition of private Saint-Laurent, Que.-based Ecolomondo Corporation Inc. on the basis of 5.5 Cortina common shares for each Ecolomondo share held.

Directors - Elio Sorella, chr., pres. & CEO, Laval, Qué.; Donald Prinksy, CFO, Montréal, Qué.; Brigitte Gauthier, corp. sec., Montréal, Qué.; Alain Denis, Laval-sur-le-Lac, Qué.; Suzanne Desrosiers, Laval, Qué.; Mario Girard, Québec, Qué.; Michelle Rosa, Beloeil, Qué.; Joseph Sorella, Laval, Qué.

Other Exec. Officers - Jean-François Labbé, COO

Capital Stock

	Authorized (shs.)	Outstanding (shs.)[1]
Common	unlimited	188,765,150

[1] At May 17, 2023

Major Shareholder - Elio Sorella held 74.81% interest at May 17, 2023.

Price Range - ECM/TSX-VEN

Year	Volume	High	Low	Close
2022	5,003,738	$0.70	$0.37	$0.41
2021	6,364,234	$1.48	$0.20	$0.58
2020	1,015,378	$0.40	$0.20	$0.35
2019	1,192,583	$0.36	$0.21	$0.30
2018	1,976,046	$0.40	$0.25	$0.37

Recent Close: $0.39

Capital Stock Changes - In January 2023, private placement of 2,222,336 units (1 common share & 1 warrant) at 45¢ per unit was completed, with warrants exercisable at 55¢ per share for six months.

During 2022, 2,928,571 common shares were issued on exercise of options.

Wholly Owned Subsidiaries

Ecolomondo Environmental (Contrecoeur) Inc., Saint-Laurent, Qué. formerly Ecolomondo Corporation Inc.
- 100% int. in **9083-5018 Quebec Inc.**, Montréal, Qué.

Ecolomondo Environmental (Hawkesbury) Inc., Montréal, Qué.
Ecolomondo Process Technologies Inc., Canada.

Investments

Ecolomondo Corporation USA Inc., Del.

Financial Statistics

Periods ended:	12m Dec. 31/22[A]		12m Dec. 31/21[A]
	$000s	%Chg	$000s
Research & devel. expense	198		106
General & admin expense	475		1,368
Operating expense	**673**	**-54**	**1,473**
Operating income	**(673)**	**n.a.**	**(1,473)**
Deprec., depl. & amort.	720		729
Finance income	17		14
Finance costs, gross	71		77
Pre-tax income	**(1,130)**	**n.a.**	**(826)**
Income taxes	(93)		(176)
Net income	**(1,037)**	**n.a.**	**(650)**
Cash & equivalent	105		4,405
Accounts receivable	209		145
Current assets	593		5,201
Fixed assets, net	43,241		36,327
Right-of-use assets	123		60
Total assets	**43,958**	**+6**	**41,588**
Accts. pay. & accr. liabs	1,840		1,065
Current liabilities	6,307		5,175
Long-term debt, gross	33,760		31,832
Long-term debt, net	32,919		31,182
Long-term lease liabilities	78		20
Shareholders' equity	2,610		2,646
Cash from oper. activs	**(45)**	**n.a.**	**(1,484)**
Cash from fin. activs	864		13,261
Cash from invest. activs	(5,119)		(11,179)
Net cash position	**105**	**-98**	**4,405**
Capital expenditures	(5,119)		(11,329)
	$		$
Earnings per share*	(0.01)		(0.00)
Cash flow per share*	(0.00)		(0.01)
	shs		shs
No. of shs. o/s*	186,542,814		183,614,243
Avg. no. of shs. o/s*	184,845,358		178,966,491
	%		%
Net profit margin	n.a.		n.a.
Return on equity	(39.46)		(39.23)
Return on assets	(2.27)		(1.62)

* Common
[A] Reported in accordance with IFRS

Latest Results

Periods ended:	3m Mar. 31/23[A]		3m Mar. 31/22[A]
	$000s	%Chg	$000s
Net income	(261)	n.a.	(170)
	$		$
Earnings per share*	(0.00)		(0.00)

* Common
[A] Reported in accordance with IFRS

Historical Summary
(as originally stated)

Fiscal Year	Oper. Rev.	Net Inc. Bef. Disc.	EPS*
	$000s	$000s	$
2022A	nil	(1,037)	(0.01)
2021A	nil	(650)	(0.00)
2020A	nil	(1,829)	(0.01)
2019A	1	(1,118)	(0.01)
2018A	21	(1,702)	(0.01)

* Common
A Reported in accordance with IFRS

E.27 Economic Investment Trust Limited*

Symbol - EVT **Exchange** - TSX **CUSIP** - 278893
Head Office - c/o E-L Financial Corporation Limited, 1000-165 University Ave, Toronto, ON, M5H 3B8 **Telephone** - (416) 947-2578 **Fax** - (416) 362-2592
Website - www.evt.ca
Email - glosnekf@e-lfinancial.com
Investor Relations - Frank J. Glosnek (416) 947-2578
Auditors - PricewaterhouseCoopers LLP C.A., Toronto, Ont.
Bankers - The Bank of Nova Scotia, Toronto, Ont.
Transfer Agents - Computershare Trust Company of Canada Inc., Toronto, Ont.
Profile - (Can. 1927, via Dominion charter) Invests in a portfolio of common equities, consisting of a mix of high yielding and low yielding Canadian and foreign investments.

The company manages a portion of the Canadian investments in the portfolio whose performance is primarily derived from investments in **E-L Financial Corporation Limited**, **The Bank of Nova Scotia** and **Algoma Central Corporation**. The balance of the investment portfolio is managed by **Neuberger Berman Canada ULC**, including all of the company's foreign equity investments. All of the Canadian investments, other than those that may be part of the Neuberger portfolio from time to time, are long-term investments. At June 30, 2023, 50.4% of the investment portfolio was held in long-term investments and 49.6% was managed by Neuberger.

Geographic mix of investment portfolio at June 30, 2023 (as a percentage of fair value):

	Fair Value	Percentage
Canada	$568,253,000	52.4%
United States	316,870,000	29.2%
Europe (excluding U.K.)	73,304,000	6.8%
Emerging Markets	60,246,000	5.6%
Japan	30,565,000	2.8%
United Kingdom	19,565,000	1.8%
Australia	15,928,000	1.4%
Total	1,084,731,000	100%

Directors - Duncan N. R. Jackman, chr., pres. & CEO, Toronto, Ont.; M. Victoria D. Jackman, Toronto, Ont.; Jonathan Simmons, Ont.; Mark M. Taylor, Mississauga, Ont.; Kevin J. Warn-Schindel, Bahamas; Stuart D. Waugh, Toronto, Ont.
Other Exec. Officers - Scott F. Ewert, v-p; Richard B. Carty, corp. sec.; Frank J. Glosnek, treas.

Capital Stock

	Authorized (shs.)	Outstanding (shs.)[1]
Preferred	200,000	
Series A	100,000	nil
Common	unlimited	5,461,428

[1] At June 30, 2023

Normal Course Issuer Bid - The company plans to make normal course purchases of up to 273,231 common shares representing 5% of the total outstanding. The bid commenced on Mar. 9, 2023, and expires on Mar. 8, 2024.
Major Shareholder - Dominion and Anglo Investment Corporation Limited held 27.5% interest, E-L Financial Corporation Limited held 24.67% interest, Canadian & Foreign Securities Co. Limited held 13.13% interest and Dondale Investments Limited held 12.66% interest at Feb. 22, 2023.

Price Range - EVT/TSX

Year	Volume	High	Low	Close
2022	100,427	$136.00	$112.00	$130.00
2021	72,381	$127.01	$107.01	$127.00
2020	105,834	$111.76	$81.99	$109.01
2019	96,922	$117.14	$99.80	$109.00
2018	51,994	$118.00	$97.91	$100.60

Recent Close: $132.09
Capital Stock Changes - In September 2022, 103,007 common shares were repurchased under a Substantial Issuer Bid. Also during 2022, 17,900 common shares were repurchased under a Normal Course Issuer Bid.

Dividends
EVT com Ra $1.20 pa Q est. Mar. 31, 2017
$4.98† Mar. 31/23 $8.69◆ Mar. 31/22
$4.07◆ Mar. 31/21
Paid in 2023: $0.90 + $4.98† 2022: $1.20 + $8.69◆ 2021: $1.20 + $4.07◆
† Extra ◆ Special

Long-Term Debt - At Dec. 31, 2022, outstanding debt totaled $14,500,000 and consisted entirely of amounts drawn on an operating facility, bearing interest at prime rate minus 0.25%.

Note - In January 2023, all outstanding balance on the operating facility was repaid.

Investments
47.7% int. in **TGV Holdings Limited**, Toronto, Ont.

Financial Statistics

Periods ended:	12m Dec. 31/22A		12m Dec. 31/21A
	$000s	%Chg	$000s
Realized invest. gain (loss)	(78,291)		193,428
Unrealized invest. gain (loss)	18,505		(13,008)
Total revenue	**(17,010)**	**n.a.**	**241,347**
General & admin. expense	2,596		4,397
Operating expense	**2,596**	**-41**	**4,397**
Operating income	**(19,606)**	**n.a.**	**236,950**
Finance costs, gross	219		nil
Pre-tax income	**(19,825)**	**n.a.**	**236,950**
Income taxes	(2,366)		25,142
Net income	**(17,459)**	**n.a.**	**211,808**
Cash & equivalent	12,831		46,110
Investments	1,073,307		1,146,035
Total assets	**1,099,261**	**-8**	**1,194,545**
Accts. pay. & accr. liabs	284		151
Debt	14,500		nil
Shareholders' equity	1,008,877		1,098,092
Cash from oper. activs	**23,977**	**-63**	**64,571**
Cash from fin. activs	(57,256)		(29,707)
Net cash position	**12,831**	**-72**	**46,110**
	$		$
Earnings per share*	(3.15)		37.92
Cash flow per share*	4.32		11.56
Net asset value per share*	184.62		196.60
Cash divd. per share*	1.20		1.20
Extra divd. - cash*	8.69		4.07
Total divd. per share*	**9.89**		**5.27**
	shs		shs
No. of shs. o/s*	5,464,628		5,585,535
Avg. no. of shs. o/s*	5,547,739		5,586,384
	%		%
Net profit margin	n.m.		87.76
Return on equity	(1.66)		21.03
Return on assets	(1.51)		19.38

* Common
A Reported in accordance with IFRS

Latest Results

Periods ended:	6m June 30/23A		6m June 30/22A
	$000s	%Chg	$000s
Total revenue	54,861	n.a.	(117,220)
Net income	46,074	n.a.	(102,377)
	$		$
Earnings per share*	8.43		(18.34)

* Common
A Reported in accordance with IFRS

Historical Summary
(as originally stated)

Fiscal Year	Total Rev.	Net Inc. Bef. Disc.	EPS*
	$000s	$000s	$
2022A	(17,010)	(17,459)	(3.15)
2021A	241,347	211,808	37.92
2020A	35,501	30,100	5.38
2019A	134,354	113,510	20.21
2018A	(42,001)	(39,671)	(7.06)

* Common
A Reported in accordance with IFRS

E.28 EcoSynthetix Inc.

Symbol - ECO **Exchange** - TSX **CUSIP** - 27923D
Head Office - 3365 Mainway, Burlington, ON, L7M 1A6 **Telephone** - (905) 335-5669 **Fax** - (289) 337-9780
Website - www.ecosynthetix.com
Email - rhaire@ecosynthetix.com
Investor Relations - Robert Haire (289) 288-5011
Auditors - PricewaterhouseCoopers LLP C.A., Toronto, Ont.
Lawyers - Cassels Brock & Blackwell LLP, Toronto, Ont.
Transfer Agents - TSX Trust Company, Toronto, Ont.
Employees - 26 at Feb. 28, 2023
Profile - (Ont. 2011) Develops and commercializes environmentally friendly, bio-based technologies as replacement solutions for synthetic, petrochemical-based adhesives and other related products in the Americas, Europe, Middle East and Africa, and Asia Pacific.

Two bio-based technology platforms have been developed with broad applications across industries: (i) a biopolymer nanosphere technology; and (ii) a bio-based sugar macromer technology.

Products developed based on the technology platforms include: EcoSphere® biolatex® binders, derived from the biopolymer platform which performs as an alternative to petroleum-based latex and targets applications in the coated paper and paperboard industry; DuraBind™ binders, which are fully compatible with existing resin formulations and can be substituted in current formulations for use in the building materials sector such as wood composites and insulation; Bioform™, derived from biopolymer platform which performs as an alternative to petroleum-based polyvinylpyrrolidone (PVP) and acts as a fixative agent in the personal care market that are commercially used in hair gel formulations; Surflock™, derived from biopolymer platform which are utilized in various paperboard, tissue and paper applications to increase fiber to fiber interactions resulting in increased dry strength of end products; EcoMer®, sugar-based macromers that are available to polymer manufacturers as bio-based building blocks to create new waterborne sugar-acrylic polymers and resins, capable of partially replacing a wide variety of petrochemical monomers and can be customized using different sugars and alcohols into a variety of grades and viscosity levels, from a resinous solid to a liquid; and EcoStix® smart waterborne pressure-sensitive adhesives, which incorporate EcoMer® biomonomer to address specific end-use needs such as wash-off labels for recyclable packaging and fruit labelling, repulpable tapes, paper labels and postage stamps which do not interfere in paper recycling, high temperature resistant labels for automotive and biodegradation for adhesion to materials that are compostable such as bio-based plastic films as well as paper.

Products are manufactured from natural polysaccharide feedstocks, such as corn starch, in a patented process and can be created pre-dispersed in water or as a dry powder.

Products are manufactured at a facility in Dyersburg, Tenn., with annualized capacity of 80,000,000 lbs.; and a plant in Oosterhout, Netherlands, with annualized capacity of 80,000,000 lbs.

In February 2023, the company announced that it plans to internalize its North American manufacturing operations at its Centre of Innovations and corporate headquarters in Burlington, Ont. and install in-house manufacturing asset with annualized capacity of up to 30,000,000 lbs. As a result, the company plans to cease production at the facility in Dyersburg, Tenn., by the end of 2023. In addition, the company announced plans to invest in its manufacturing infrastructure in Oosterhout, Netherlands to enable flexibility in supply chain options and reduce manufacturing costs.

Directors - Paul Lucas, chr., Oakville, Ont.; Jeffrey (Jeff) MacDonald, CEO, King City, Ont.; Susan Allen, Mississauga, Ont.; Sara C. Elford, Shawnigan Lake, B.C.; Jeffrey M. Nodland, Tex.
Other Exec. Officers - Robert (Rob) Haire, CFO & corp. sec.; Edward (Ted) van Egdom, sr. v-p, opers.; Ralph De Jong, v-p, R&D & cust. solutions

Capital Stock

	Authorized (shs.)	Outstanding (shs.)[1]
Common	unlimited	59,224,759

[1] At May 1, 2023

Normal Course Issuer Bid - The company plans to make normal course purchases of up to 3,867,436 common shares representing 10% of the total outstanding. The bid commenced on May 13, 2023, and expires on May 12, 2024.
Major Shareholder - Lions Investment Ltd. held 17.49% interest and TD Waterhouse Canada Inc. held 14.37% interest at Mar. 27, 2023.

Price Range - ECO/TSX

Year	Volume	High	Low	Close
2022	10,748,017	$7.20	$3.50	$4.12
2021	17,662,134	$6.44	$3.69	$5.86
2020	20,613,210	$3.91	$1.46	$3.69
2019	25,101,810	$3.45	$1.73	$2.65
2018	12,667,446	$2.40	$1.52	$1.94

Recent Close: $4.24
Capital Stock Changes - During 2022, common shares were issued as follows: 846,355 on exercise of options and 115,466 on conversion of restricted share units; 626,400 common shares were repurchased under a Normal Course Issuer Bid.

Wholly Owned Subsidiaries
EcoSynthetix Corporation, Ont.
• 100% int. in **EcoSynthetix B.V.**, Netherlands.
EcoSynthetix Ltd., Mich.

Financial Statistics

Periods ended:	12m Dec. 31/22[A]		12m Dec. 31/21[A]
	US$000s	%Chg	US$000s
Operating revenue	**19,035**	**+5**	**18,162**
Cost of sales	14,172		13,403
Research & devel. expense	1,493		1,238
General & admin expense	5,135		5,382
Operating expense	**20,800**	**+4**	**20,023**
Operating income	**(1,765)**	**n.a.**	**(1,861)**
Deprec., depl. & amort.	1,137		1,381
Finance income	528		62
Pre-tax income	**(2,375)**	**n.a.**	**(3,180)**
Net income	**(2,375)**	**n.a.**	**(3,180)**
Cash & equivalent	4,809		42,227
Inventories	5,317		2,074
Accounts receivable	2,912		1,912
Current assets	34,196		46,312
Long-term investments	10,139		nil
Fixed assets, net	3,859		4,670
Total assets	**48,194**	**-5**	**50,982**
Accts. pay. & accr. liabs.	2,320		2,108
Current liabilities	2,595		2,364
Long-term lease liabilities	544		820
Shareholders' equity	45,055		47,798
Cash from oper. activs.	**(4,896)**	**n.a.**	**474**
Cash from fin. activs.	(1,515)		474
Cash from invest. activs.	(31,153)		24,687
Net cash position	**4,809**	**-89**	**42,227**
Capital expenditures	(273)		(380)
	US$		US$
Earnings per share*	(0.04)		(0.06)
Cash flow per share*	(0.08)		0.01
	shs		shs
No. of shs. o/s*	59,264,660		58,929,239
Avg. no. of shs. o/s*	58,898,673		57,410,885
	%		%
Net profit margin	(12.48)		(17.51)
Return on equity	(5.12)		(6.54)
Return on assets	(4.79)		(6.19)
Foreign sales percent	85		85

* Common
[A] Reported in accordance with IFRS

Historical Summary
(as originally stated)

Fiscal Year	Oper. Rev.	Net Inc. Bef. Disc.	EPS*
	US$000s	US$000s	US$
2022[A]	19,035	(2,375)	(0.04)
2021[A]	18,162	(3,180)	(0.06)
2020[A]	13,663	(2,402)	(0.04)
2019[A]	18,447	(1,454)	(0.02)
2018[A]	22,799	(2,531)	(0.04)

* Common
[A] Reported in accordance with IFRS

E.29 Eddy Smart Home Solutions Ltd.

Symbol - EDY **Exchange** - TSX-VEN (S) **CUSIP** - 279369
Head Office - 900-5255 Yonge St, Toronto, ON, M2N 6P4 **Toll-free** - (877) 388-3339
Website - eddysolutions.com
Email - bbaril@eddysolutions.com
Investor Relations - Boris Baril (877) 388-3339
Auditors - KPMG LLP C.A., Hamilton, Ont.
Transfer Agents - TSX Trust Company, Toronto, Ont.
Profile - (Ont. 2020) Produces and sells smart water metering products for homes and buildings that protect against water damage with intelligent technology and real time data.

The company's product and service offerings consist of the rental, sale, monitoring, and installation of water leak detection systems designed to detect and prevent water leaks in multi-unit residential buildings, single family homes and commercial properties.

Product and service offering consists of a hardware and software component that work together to provide comprehensive water protection. The primary hardware components include equipment such as water meters that measure the flow of water through pipes, wireless sensors that detect the presence of water leaks, shutoff valves that can turn off water flow in the building, and gateways which allow the devices to communicate with each other and with the company's monitoring centre. The monitoring centre has 24/7 availability to respond to alerts by contacting the subscriber or subscriber's building manager and remotely activating shutoff valves.

At June 30, 2022, the company had 1,734 subscribers in the single-family homes segment (Dec. 31, 2021 - 1,794), 9,153 subscribers in the multi-residential buildings segment (Dec. 31, 2021 - 8,561), and 349,201 sq. ft. managed in the commercial and industrial segment (Dec. 31, 2021 - 38,343).

Common suspended from TSX-VEN, July 7, 2023.

Recent Merger and Acquisition Activity

Status: completed **Revised:** May 4, 2022
UPDATE: The transaction was completed for issuance of 12,266,000 common shares valued at $7,359,600. PREVIOUS: Eddy Smart Home Solutions Ltd. agreed to acquire Reed Controls Inc. for a purchase price of $7,300,000. Reed has developed a water management technology platform of hardware & cloud software to manage water related risk, conserve water & accelerate IoT adoption among global plumbing manufacturers

Predecessor Detail - Name changed from Aumento Capital VIII Corp., Jan. 11, 2022, pursuant to the reverse takeover acquisition of (old) Eddy Smart Home Solutions Inc.

Directors - Mark L. Silver, exec. chr. & CEO, Toronto, Ont.; Gary M. Goodman, Toronto, Ont.; Chris Gower, Edmonton, Alta.; William Jones, Toronto, Ont.; George Krieser, Toronto, Ont.; Paul Pathak, Toronto, Ont.

Other Exec. Officers - Sajid Khan, pres. & COO; Boris Baril, CFO & corp. sec.; Adam Bartman, exec. v-p, opers.; June Thomson, exec. v-p, sales & mktg.; Avi Yurman, exec. v-p; Shkya Ghanbarian, v-p, sales; Avishai Moscovich, v-p, mktg. & bus. devel.; Elliot Samuel, v-p, sales & proptech

Capital Stock

	Authorized (shs.)	Outstanding (shs.)[1]
Common	unlimited	53,485,043

[1] At June 30, 2022

Major Shareholder - Mark L. Silver held 14.7% interest at June 24, 2022.

Price Range - EDY/TSX-VEN (S)

Year	Volume	High	Low	Close
2022	7,130,839	$0.60	$0.08	$0.10
2021	60,901	$1.00	$0.55	$0.55

Recent Close: $0.04

Capital Stock Changes - In January 2022, 65,262,619 common shares were issued pursuant to the reverse takeover acquisition of (old) Eddy Smart Home Solutions Inc., including 20,713,449 common shares issued without further consideration on exchange of subscription receipts sold previously by (old) Eddy at 59¢ each. On May 4, 2022, 12,266,000 common shares were issued pursuant to the acquisition of Reed Controls Inc.

Wholly Owned Subsidiaries

Eddy Smart Home Solutions Inc., Toronto, Ont.
- 100% int. in **2865357 Ontario Inc.**, Ont.
  - 100% int. in **1000080686 Ontario Inc.**, Ont.
    - 100% int. in **Eddy Home Distribution Inc.**, Ont.
    - 100% int. in **Eddy Home Inc.**, Ont.
    - 100% int. in **Municipal Water Savings California Corp.**, Calif.

Reed Controls Inc., Concord, Ont.

Financial Statistics

Periods ended:	12m Dec. 31/21[A1]		12m Dec. 31/20[oA]
	$000s	%Chg	$000s
Operating revenue	**1,223**	**+30**	**944**
Cost of sales	558		1,288
General & admin expense	7,332		3,613
Stock-based compensation	284		2
Operating expense	**7,890**	**+61**	**4,901**
Operating income	**(6,667)**	**n.a.**	**(3,957)**
Deprec., depl. & amort.	321		408
Finance income	4		4
Finance costs, gross	1,004		60
Pre-tax income	**(8,011)**	**n.a.**	**(4,412)**
Net income	**(8,011)**	**n.a.**	**(4,412)**
Cash & equivalent	111		193
Inventories	1,649		1,444
Accounts receivable	699		145
Current assets	4,600		2,082
Fixed assets, net	280		318
Right-of-use assets	470		578
Total assets	**6,308**	**+94**	**3,255**
Bank indebtedness	3,103		nil
Accts. pay. & accr. liabs.	3,344		896
Long-term debt, gross	2,556		280
Long-term debt, net	40		30
Long-term lease liabilities	584		718
Shareholders' equity	(5,427)		683
Cash from oper. activs.	**(5,846)**	**n.a.**	**(3,243)**
Cash from fin. activs.	5,798		2,878
Cash from invest. activs.	(33)		(11)
Net cash position	**111**	**-42**	**193**
Capital expenditures	(33)		(11)
	$		$
Earnings per share*	(0.13)		(0.08)
Cash flow per share*	(0.10)		n.a.
	shs		shs
No. of shs. o/s	n.a.		n.a.
Avg. no. of shs. o/s*	61,222,853		n.a.
	%		%
Net profit margin	(655.03)		(467.37)
Return on equity	n.m.		n.m.
Return on assets	(146.54)		(115.67)
Foreign sales percent	28		47

* Common
[o] Restated
[A] Reported in accordance with IFRS
[1] Results for 2021 and prior periods pertain to Eddy Smart Home Solutions Inc.

Latest Results

Periods ended:	6m June 30/22[A]		6m June 30/21[A]
	$000s	%Chg	$000s
Operating revenue	889	+29	688
Net income	(5,756)	n.a.	(2,868)
	$		$
Earnings per share*	(0.08)		(0.05)

* Common
[A] Reported in accordance with IFRS

Historical Summary
(as originally stated)

Fiscal Year	Oper. Rev.	Net Inc. Bef. Disc.	EPS*
	$000s	$000s	$
2021[A]	1,223	(8,011)	(0.13)
2020[A]	944	(4,412)	(0.08)
2019[A]	784	(5,210)	(0.49)

* Common
[A] Reported in accordance with IFRS

E.30 Edesa Biotech, Inc.

Symbol - EDSA **Exchange** - NASDAQ **CUSIP** - 27966L
Head Office - 100 Spy Crt, Markham, ON, L3R 5H6 **Telephone** - (289) 800-9600
Website - www.edesabiotech.com
Email - investors@edesabiotech.com
Investor Relations - Dr. Pardeep Nijhawan (289) 800-9600
Auditors - MNP LLP C.A., Toronto, Ont.
Lawyers - Fasken Martineau DuMoulin LLP, Toronto, Ont.
Transfer Agents - Computershare Trust Company of Canada Inc., Vancouver, B.C.
Employees - 16 at Dec. 14, 2022
Profile - (B.C. 2009; orig. Can., 2007) Acquires, develops and commercializes clinical-stage drugs for inflammatory and immune-related diseases with clear unmet medical needs.

Lead product is EB05, a monoclonal antibody developed for acute and chronic disease indications that involve dysregulated innate immunity responses. EB05 is being evaluated in a Phase 3 trial as a potential treatment for Acute Respiratory Distress Syndrome (ARDS), a life-threatening form of respiratory failure.

Also developing EB01, a topical vanishing cream for the treatment of moderate-to-severe chronic allergic contact dermatitis (ACD). In Canada, has received approval for a clinical trial application for its EB06 monoclonal antibody candidate to conduct a future Phase 2 study in vitiligo, a common autoimmune disorder that causes the skin to lose its colour in patches. In the U.S., the company is preparing an investigational new drug application (IND) for a future Phase 2 study of EB07 for treatment of systemic sclerosis (SSc), an autoimmune rheumatic disorder that causes fibrosis (scarring/hardening) of skin and internal organs.

Predecessor Detail - Name changed from Stellar Biotechnologies Inc., June 7, 2019, pursuant to reverse takeover acquisition of (old) Edesa Biotech Inc.; basis 1 new for 6 old shs.

Directors - Sean MacDonald, chr., Ont.; Dr. Pardeep (Par) Nijhawan, CEO & corp. sec., Ont.; Jennifer M. Chao, New York, N.Y.; Lorin K. Johnson, Calif.; Frank R. Oakes, Port Hueneme, Calif.; Paul W. Pay, United Kingdom; Carlo Sistilli, Ont.

Other Exec. Officers - Michael Brooks, pres.; Stephen L. Lemieux, CFO; Rajan (Raj) Puri, sr. v-p, mfg.; Blair Gordon, v-p, R&D; Gary Koppenjan, v-p, IR & commun.

Capital Stock

	Authorized (shs.)	Outstanding (shs.)[1]
Preferred	unlimited	
Common	unlimited	20,058,665

[1] At Feb. 9, 2023

Major Shareholder - Dr. Pardeep (Par) Nijhawan held 22.1% interest at Dec. 14, 2022.

Price Range - EDSA/NASDAQ

Year	Volume	High	Low	Close
2022	6,387,126	US$6.10	US$0.77	US$2.16
2021	43,840,746	US$11.99	US$4.07	US$5.63
2020	31,897,772	US$19.10	US$1.58	US$4.25
2019	9,564,679	US$17.28	US$3.36	US$4.01
2018	2,644,022	US$45.78	US$4.56	US$5.46

Consolidation: 1-for-6 cons. in June 2019

Capital Stock Changes - During fiscal 2022, common shares were issued as follows: 2,166,884 by private placement and 1,199,727 on exercise of pre-funded warrants.

Wholly Owned Subsidiaries

Edesa Biotech Research, Inc., Ont.
Edesa Biotech USA, Inc., Calif. formerly Stellar Biotechnologies, Inc.

Financial Statistics

Periods ended:	12m Sept. 30/22[A]		12m Sept. 30/21[A]
	US$000s	%Chg	US$000s
Research & devel. expense	13,335		17,947
General & admin expense	2,657		2,420
Stock-based compensation	2,261		3,195
Operating expense	**18,253**	**-23**	**23,562**
Operating income	**(18,253)**	**n.a.**	**(23,562)**
Deprec., depl. & amort.	118		119
Finance income	64		11
Pre-tax income	**(17,548)**	**n.a.**	**(13,342)**
Income taxes	1		1
Net income	**(17,549)**	**n.a.**	**(13,343)**
Cash & equivalent	7,091		7,839
Accounts receivable	1,255		3,303
Current assets	9,092		12,091
Fixed assets, net	13		15
Right-of-use assets	18		97
Intangibles, net	2,281		2,382
Total assets	**11,576**	**-21**	**14,585**
Accts. pay. & accr. liabs	2,122		1,380
Current liabilities	2,141		1,459
Long-term debt, gross	44		47
Long-term debt, net	44		47
Long-term lease liabilities	nil		21
Shareholders' equity	9,391		13,058
Cash from oper. activs	**(12,279)**	**n.a.**	**(13,665)**
Cash from fin. activs	11,630		14,175
Cash from invest. activs	(6)		(6)
Net cash position	**7,091**	**-10**	**7,839**
Capital expenditures	(6)		(6)
	US$		US$
Earnings per share*	(1.05)		(1.10)
Cash flow per share*	(0.74)		(1.13)
	shs		shs
No. of shs. o/s*	16,662,014		13,295,403
Avg. no. of shs. o/s*	16,662,014		12,077,822
	%		%
Net profit margin	n.a.		n.a.
Return on equity	(156.35)		(120.39)
Return on assets	(134.16)		(105.28)

* Common
[A] Reported in accordance with U.S. GAAP

Latest Results

Periods ended:	3m Dec. 31/22[A]		3m Dec. 31/21[A]
	US$000s	%Chg	US$000s
Net income	(2,335)	n.a.	(4,379)
	US$		US$
Earnings per share*	(0.13)		(0.33)

* Common
[A] Reported in accordance with U.S. GAAP

Historical Summary
(as originally stated)

Fiscal Year	Oper. Rev.	Net Inc. Bef. Disc.	EPS*
	US$000s	US$000s	US$
2022[A]	nil	(17,549)	(1.05)
2021[A]	nil	(13,343)	(1.10)
2020[A]	329	(6,364)	(0.74)
2019[A1,2]	411	(2,777)	(0.55)
2018[A3]	212	(5,039)	(10.56)

* Common
[A] Reported in accordance with U.S. GAAP
[1] 9 months ended Sept. 30, 2019.
[2] Results reflect the June 7, 2019, reverse takeover acquisition of Edesa Biotech Inc.
[3] Results for fiscal 2018 and prior fiscal years pertain to Stellar Biotechnologies Inc.
Note: Adjusted throughout for 1-for-6 cons. in June 2019

E.31 Edge Total Intelligence Inc.

Symbol - CTRL **Exchange** - TSX-VEN **CUSIP** - 279874
Head Office - 2600-1066 Hastings St W, Vancouver, BC, V6E 3X1 **Toll-free** - (888) 771-3343
Website - edgeti.com
Email - ir@edgeti.com
Investor Relations - James Barrett (888) 771-3343
Auditors - MNP LLP C.A.
Transfer Agents - TSX Trust Company, Vancouver, B.C.
Profile - (B.C. 2019) Develops, markets and sells network management software and provides maintenance and support services for customers of its software. Also offers systems engineering and business consulting services.
The principal product is edgeCore™, a software that extracts and aggregates operational and management data from disconnected systems while providing automated pipelines to orchestrate specific tasks across various business and information technology systems. The platform presents the progress, status and results of tasks in the context of user's role and assignment.
Revenue model consists of Software-as-a-Service (SaaS) annual subscription fees, user licences, implementation services for software product customization and advisory services.
In March 2022, common shares were listed on the Frankfurt Stock Exchange under the stock symbol Q5i.
Predecessor Detail - Name changed from Aphelion Capital Corp., Dec. 24, 2021, pursuant to the Qualifying Transaction reverse takeover acquisition of (old) Edge Technologies, Inc.
Directors - James (Jim) Barrett, CEO, S.C.; Jason E. James, Calgary, Alta.; Seth Kay, Vancouver, B.C.; Edward Mede, Ill.; Steven Owings, S.C.; Brett Paulson; David Roman, Mass.
Other Exec. Officers - Geremy Connor, CFO; Jacques Jarman, chief revenue officer; Scott Lesley, chief tech. officer; Nick Brigman, v-p, products; John Palmer, v-p, cust. success; Joshua Armstrong, corp. sec.

Capital Stock

	Authorized (shs.)	Outstanding (shs.)[1]
Preferred Multiple Vtg.	unlimited	26,600
Subordinate Vtg,	unlimited	19,025,459

[1] At Mar. 31, 2023
Preferred Multiple Voting - Convertible into subordinate voting shares on a 1000-for-1 basis. 1,000 votes per share.
Subordinate Voting - One vote per share.
Major Shareholder - Lotus Domaine III, L.P. held 26.63% interest and James (Jim) Barrett held 11.26% interest at June 10, 2022.

Price Range - CTRL/TSX-VEN

Year	Volume	High	Low	Close
2022	453,820	$0.75	$0.58	$0.64
2020	775,000	$0.28	$0.08	$0.26

Split: 2-for-1 split in Dec. 2021
Recent Close: $0.72
Capital Stock Changes - During 2022, common shares were issued as follows: 1,577,815 on conversion of debentures, 396,000 on exercise of warrants and 100,000 on exercise of options.

Wholly Owned Subsidiaries

Edge Technologies, Inc., Arlington, Va.
- 100% int. in **Edge Technologies d.o.o.**, Serbia.

Financial Statistics

Periods ended:	12m Dec. 31/22[A]		12m Dec. 31/21[oA1]
	US$000s	%Chg	US$000s
Operating revenue	**3,571**	**-13**	**4,088**
Cost of sales	524		533
Salaries & benefits	322		621
Research & devel. expense	1,618		1,128
General & admin expense	3,294		2,970
Operating expense	**5,758**	**+10**	**5,252**
Operating income	**(2,187)**	**n.a.**	**(1,164)**
Deprec., depl. & amort.	1,040		1,455
Finance costs, gross	980		1,033
Pre-tax income	**(6,227)**	**n.a.**	**(10,667)**
Income taxes	4		2
Net income	**(6,232)**	**n.a.**	**(10,669)**
Cash & equivalent	480		3,792
Accounts receivable	931		139
Current assets	1,484		4,036
Fixed assets, net	28		16
Right-of-use assets	53		121
Intangibles, net	2,010		5,812
Total assets	**3,575**	**-64**	**9,986**
Bank indebtedness	1,299		2,499
Accts. pay. & accr. liabs	974		1,227
Current liabilities	10,112		5,640
Long-term debt, gross	7,695		6,372
Long-term debt, net	1,740		5,872
Long-term lease liabilities	nil		64
Shareholders' equity	(8,277)		(3,153)
Cash from oper. activs	**(3,735)**	**n.a.**	**(1,237)**
Cash from fin. activs	679		5,796
Cash from invest. activs	(256)		(876)
Net cash position	**480**	**-87**	**3,792**
Capital expenditures	(17)		(15)
	US$		US$
Earnings per share*	(0.34)		(1.30)
	shs		shs
No. of shs. o/s*	18,993,459		16,919,644
Avg. no. of shs. o/s*	18,457,066		8,227,913
	%		%
Net profit margin	(174.52)		(260.98)
Return on equity	n.m.		n.m.
Return on assets	(77.45)		(94.42)

* Sub. Vtg.
[o] Restated
[A] Reported in accordance with IFRS
[1] Results reflect the Dec. 24, 2021, reverse takeover acquisition of Edge Technologies, Inc.

Latest Results

Periods ended:	3m Mar. 31/23[A]		3m Mar. 31/22[A]
	US$000s	%Chg	US$000s
Operating revenue	914	-4	957
Net income	(588)	n.a.	(1,367)
	US$		US$
Earnings per share*	(0.03)		(0.08)

* Sub. Vtg.
[A] Reported in accordance with IFRS

Historical Summary
(as originally stated)

Fiscal Year	Oper. Rev.	Net Inc. Bef. Disc.	EPS*
	US$000s	US$000s	US$
2022[A]	3,571	(6,232)	(0.34)
2021[A]	4,088	(10,669)	(1.30)
2020[A]	6,116	1,936	0.03
2019[A]	6,974	(6,895)	(0.10)

* Sub. Vtg.
[A] Reported in accordance with IFRS
Note: Adjusted throughout for 2-for-1 split in Dec. 2021

E.32 Edgewater Wireless Systems Inc.

Symbol - YFI **Exchange** - TSX-VEN **CUSIP** - 280359
Head Office - 202-11 Hines Rd, Kanata, ON, K2K 2X1 **Telephone** - (613) 271-3710 **Fax** - (613) 271-1152
Website - www.edgewaterwireless.com
Email - andrews@edgewaterwireless.com
Investor Relations - Andrew Skafel (613) 271-3710
Auditors - KPMG LLP C.A., Ottawa, Ont.
Transfer Agents - Computershare Trust Company of Canada Inc., Calgary, Alta.
Profile - (Can. 1987; orig. B.C., 1980) Develops and commercializes Wi-Fi spectrum slicing technologies and intellectual property for the wireless communications market.
The company's patented spectrum slicing technology allows a frequency to be divided or sliced into multiple concurrent channels to enable more radios to operate in a single coverage area. The technology allows more capacity from a single, Wi-Fi complaint radio in order to support a high density of users and devices with reduced latency and contention.
Spectrum slicing solutions consist of MCSR™ (Multi-Channel, Single Radio) silicon solutions, which include chips and modules; aera™ access points solutions; and intellectual property licensing. Target clients include original equipment manufacturers (OEM), original design manufacturers (ODM), service providers and silicon manufacturers for the residential and enterprise Wi-Fi markets.
Predecessor Detail - Name changed from Kik Polymers Inc., Feb. 1, 2012, pursuant to reverse takeover acquisition of Edgewater Wireless Systems, Ltd.
Directors - Brian Imrie, chr., Ont.; Andrew Skafel, pres. & CEO, Ottawa, Ont.; Ralph Garcea, Caledon, Ont.
Other Exec. Officers - Chris Olney, CFO & corp. sec.; Eric Smith, v-p, product

Capital Stock

	Authorized (shs.)	Outstanding (shs.)[1]
Preferred Series 1	1,600,000	nil
Preferred Series 2	unlimited	nil
Common	unlimited	186,963,263

[1] At Oct. 31, 2022
Major Shareholder - Widely held at Oct. 18, 2022.

Price Range - YFI/TSX-VEN

Year	Volume	High	Low	Close
2022	23,721,644	$0.11	$0.05	$0.05
2021	135,451,656	$0.24	$0.05	$0.07
2020	20,501,343	$0.08	$0.03	$0.05
2019	32,610,612	$0.15	$0.07	$0.07
2018	57,684,338	$0.81	$0.08	$0.11

Recent Close: $0.05
Capital Stock Changes - There were no changes to capital stock during fiscal 2022.

Wholly Owned Subsidiaries

7781911 Canada Ltd., Ottawa, Ont. formerly Edgewater Wireless Systems, Ltd.
- 100% int. in **Edgewater Wireless do Brasil Technologia Ltda.**, Brazil.

Financial Statistics

Periods ended:	12m Apr. 30/22[A]		12m Apr. 30/21[A]
	$000s	%Chg	$000s
Operating revenue	**11**	**n.a.**	**nil**
Cost of sales	1		nil
Research & devel. expense	96		7
General & admin expense	910		755
Other operating expense	42		53
Operating expense	**1,049**	**+29**	**815**
Operating income	**(1,038)**	**n.a.**	**(815)**
Deprec., depl. & amort.	4		10
Finance income	2		nil
Finance costs, gross	nil		26
Pre-tax income	**(1,058)**	**n.a.**	**(773)**
Net income	**(1,058)**	**n.a.**	**(773)**
Cash & equivalent	178		1,499
Accounts receivable	13		17
Current assets	353		1,562
Fixed assets, net	3		3
Right-of-use assets	51		nil
Total assets	**407**	**-74**	**1,565**
Bank indebtedness	149		13
Accts. pay. & accr. liabs	1,541		2,015
Current liabilities	1,979		2,284
Long-term debt, gross	nil		33
Long-term debt, net	nil		33
Long-term lease liabilities	37		nil
Shareholders' equity	(1,609)		(774)
Cash from oper. activs	**(1,417)**	**n.a.**	**(515)**
Cash from fin. activs	100		1,986
Cash from invest. activs	(3)		(11)
Net cash position	**168**	**-89**	**1,488**
Capital expenditures	(3)		nil
	$		$
Earnings per share*	(0.01)		(0.00)
Cash flow per share*	(0.01)		(0.00)
	shs		shs
No. of shs. o/s*	186,963,263		186,963,263
Avg. no. of shs. o/s*	186,963,263		171,061,091
	%		%
Net profit margin	n.m.		n.a.
Return on equity	n.m.		n.m.
Return on assets	(107.30)		(83.46)

* Common
[A] Reported in accordance with IFRS

Latest Results

Periods ended:	6m Oct. 31/22[A]		6m Oct. 31/21[A]
	$000s	%Chg	$000s
Operating revenue	2	-50	4
Net income	(447)	n.a.	(567)
	$		$
Earnings per share*	(0.00)		(0.00)

* Common
[A] Reported in accordance with IFRS

Historical Summary
(as originally stated)

Fiscal Year	Oper. Rev.	Net Inc. Bef. Disc.	EPS*
	$000s	$000s	$
2022[A]	11	(1,058)	(0.01)
2021[A]	nil	(773)	(0.01)
2020[A]	2	(2,038)	(0.01)
2019[A]	421	(2,806)	(0.02)
2018[A]	73	(3,867)	(0.03)

* Common
[A] Reported in accordance with IFRS

E.33 Eguana Technologies Inc.

Symbol - EGT **Exchange** - TSX-VEN **CUSIP** - 282365
Head Office - 3636 7 St SE, Calgary, AB, T2G 2Y8 **Telephone** - (403) 508-7177 **Fax** - (403) 205-2509
Website - www.eguanatech.com
Email - justin.holland@eguanatech.com
Investor Relations - Justin Holland (647) 258-0343 ext. 103
Auditors - KPMG LLP C.A., Calgary, Alta.
Lawyers - Dentons Canada LLP, Calgary, Alta.
Transfer Agents - TSX Trust Company, Toronto, Ont.
Profile - (Alta. 1996) Designs, markets, manufactures and sells residential and commercial energy storage systems and micro inverter products for solar self-consumption, grid services and demand charge applications based on proprietary power control technology.

The company's fully integrated energy storage system (ESS) consists of the software controller, or energy management system (EMS), the battery, and the advanced power control technology which allows for charging and discharging of batteries in a seamless bi-directional conversion process. Products are designed and delivered as a value-added, factory-assembled ESS with pre-integrated lithium batteries that are certified for grid connection in major global markets. Features of the ESS include flexible capacity, simple installation processes, remote diagnostic and update capabilities, and remote battery recovery. In addition, the company offers a suite of micro inverter products which are integrated with its ESS platform.

The systems are available in multiple size configurations under the brands Evolve, Enduro, Elevate and Enfuse. Sales channel development is focused on the U.S. market, particularly California and Hawaii. The company's products are certified for use in Germany, the U.K., France, Australia and North America.

In March 2023, the company acquired Adelaide, Australia-based **Solarlab Pty Ltd.** for A$250,000. Solar delivers and supplies design, sales, installation and monitoring services in energy storage and residential and commercial solar markets in Australia.

In November 2022, wholly owned **EGT Markets Limited Partnership** was dissolved.

In May 2022, the company changed its fiscal year end to December 31 from September 30.

Predecessor Detail - Name changed from Sustainable Energy Technologies Ltd., Nov. 1, 2013.

Directors - George W. Powlick, chr., Ariz.; Justin Holland, CEO, Ont.; Michael Carten, Calgary, Alta.; Karen Hayward, Calif.; Robert D. Penner, Calgary, Alta.; Graeme Stening, United Kingdom

Other Exec. Officers - Brent Harris, founder & COO; Hansine Ullberg, CFO; Daljit Ghotra, chief tech. officer

Capital Stock

	Authorized (shs.)	Outstanding (shs.)[1]
First Preferred	unlimited	nil
Series 8		1[2]
Common	unlimited	424,075,928

[1] At May 29, 2023
[2] Classified as debt.

First Preferred, Series 8 - Issued to the subscriber of first preferred series 7 shares. Entitled to designate a representative to the board of directors of the company so long as the holder owns in the aggregate more than 10% of the issued and outstanding common shares on a fully diluted basis. Retractable at $1.00.

Common - One vote per share.

Major Shareholder - DHCT II Luxembourg S.A.R.L. held 21.6% interest at May 1, 2023.

Price Range - EGT/TSX-VEN

Year	Volume	High	Low	Close
2022	52,025,373	$0.57	$0.21	$0.25
2021	121,670,403	$0.64	$0.21	$0.48
2020	47,358,201	$0.25	$0.06	$0.22
2019	32,721,674	$0.24	$0.05	$0.06
2018	58,251,212	$0.35	$0.15	$0.19

Recent Close: $0.12

Capital Stock Changes - Effective Dec. 17, 2021, all 434,860 first preferred shares, series A were converted into 18,119,167 common shares. Also during the fifteen-month period ended Dec. 31, 2022, common shares were issued as follows: 15,095,580 on exercise of warrants, 1,326,986 for dividends and 205,000 on exercise of options.

Wholly Owned Subsidiaries

Eguana Americas Inc., Del.
Eguana GmbH, Germany.
Eguana Inc., Calgary, Alta.
Eguana Pty Ltd., Australia.
SET Overseas Ltd.
Solarlab Pty Ltd., Adelaide, S.A., Australia.
Sustainable Energy Europa S.L.

Financial Statistics

Periods ended:	15m Dec. 31/22[A]		12m Sept. 30/21[A]
	$000s	%Chg	$000s
Operating revenue	**16,827**	**n.a.**	**7,175**
Cost of goods sold	16,594		6,705
Research & devel. expense	4,297		1,954
General & admin expense	7,206		4,883
Stock-based compensation	1,455		1,531
Operating expense	**29,552**	**n.a.**	**15,073**
Operating income	**(12,725)**	**n.a.**	**(7,898)**
Deprec., depl. & amort.	682		323
Finance costs, gross	4,044		2,236
Write-downs/write-offs	(22)		(20)
Pre-tax income	**(18,773)**	**n.a.**	**(10,400)**
Income taxes	(1,945)		nil
Net income	**(16,828)**	**n.a.**	**(10,400)**
Cash & equivalent	15,035		4,604
Inventories	7,040		5,894
Accounts receivable	13,517		2,512
Current assets	44,794		13,940
Fixed assets, net	1,446		498
Right-of-use assets	1,044		317
Intangibles, net	119		158
Total assets	**47,403**	**n.a.**	**14,914**
Accts. pay. & accr. liabs	4,229		3,094
Current liabilities	11,126		11,234
Long-term debt, gross	35,342		5,480
Long-term debt, net	31,771		nil
Long-term lease liabilities	883		189
Preferred share equity	nil		567
Equity portion of conv. debs	7,311		nil
Shareholders' equity	3,623		3,491
Cash from oper. activs	**(33,697)**	**n.a.**	**(14,838)**
Cash from fin. activs	44,609		19,357
Cash from invest. activs	(1,071)		(351)
Net cash position	**15,035**	**n.a.**	**4,604**
Capital expenditures	(1,190)		(193)
	$		$
Earnings per share*	(0.04)		(0.03)
Cash flow per share*	(0.09)		(0.05)
	shs		shs
No. of shs. o/s*	403,166,645		368,419,912
Avg. no. of shs. o/s*	393,376,220		299,257,088
	%		%
Net profit margin	...		(144.95)
Return on equity	...		n.m.
Return on assets	...		(87.29)
Foreign sales percent	100		100

* Common
[A] Reported in accordance with IFRS

Latest Results

Periods ended:	3m Mar. 31/23[A]		3m Mar. 31/22[¤A]
	$000s	%Chg	$000s
Operating revenue	5,855	n.m.	285
Net income	(5,314)	n.a.	(2,403)
	$		$
Earnings per share*	(0.01)		(0.01)

* Common
[¤] Restated
[A] Reported in accordance with IFRS

Historical Summary
(as originally stated)

Fiscal Year	Oper. Rev.	Net Inc. Bef. Disc.	EPS*
	$000s	$000s	$
2022[A1]	16,827	(16,828)	(0.04)
2021[A]	7,175	(10,400)	(0.03)
2020[A]	7,952	(8,239)	(0.04)
2019[A]	3,428	(9,141)	(0.04)
2018[A]	3,897	(4,786)	(0.02)

* Common
[A] Reported in accordance with IFRS
[1] 15 months ended Dec. 31, 2022.

E.34 Electrameccanica Vehicles Corp.

Symbol - SOLO **Exchange** - NASDAQ **CUSIP** - 284849
Head Office - 8057 North Fraser Way, Burnaby, BC, V5J 5M8 **Telephone** - (604) 428-7656 **Toll-free** - (888) 457-7676
Website - www.electrameccanica.com
Email - bal@electrameccanica.com
Investor Relations - Baljinder K. Bhullar (888) 457-7676
Auditors - KPMG LLP C.A., Vancouver, B.C.
Lawyers - Kerr, Russell & Weber, PLC; McMillan LLP, Vancouver, B.C.
Transfer Agents - VStock Transfer. LLC, Woodmere, N.Y.
Employees - 216 at Mar. 22, 2022
Profile - (B.C. 2015) Designs and manufactures electric vehicles and high-end specialty cars.

The company has designed and built the all-electric, three-wheeled SOLO, a single-seater electric vehicle with range of up to 100 miles and a top speed of 80 mph. Production of SOLO commenced on Aug. 26, 2020 and initial deliveries commenced on Oct. 4, 2021. 61 SOLOs and 12 high-end custom build cars were delivered in 2021.

Under early design development stage is Tofino, a two-seater electric roadster; and in prototype phase is e-Roadster, a two-seater sports car with modern information and entertainment system and a vintage look.

Has a manufacturing agreement with Chongqing, People's Republic of China-based **Zongshen Industrial Group Ltd.** to produce SOLO vehicles.

Head office is located in Burnaby, B.C.; retail stores are located in California, Arizona and Oregon; service and distribution centre is in Los Angeles and Huntington Beach, Calif.; and an engineering centre in Burnaby, B.C. Also has a temporary office and an assembly facility in Mesa, Ariz., with a production capacity of up to 20,000 vehicles per year.

Directors - Jerry Kroll, co-founder, Vancouver, B.C.; Steven A. Sanders, chr., New York, N.Y.; Susan E. Docherty, CEO & interim COO, Ariz.; Luisa Ingargiola, Tampa, Fla.; Dietmar Ostermann, Detroit, Mich.; William G. (Bill) Quigley III, Mich.; Michael Richardson, Fla.; Dave Shemmans, Sussex, United Kingdom; Joanne F. Q. Yan, Vancouver, B.C.

Other Exec. Officers - Mark Orsmond, CFO; Baljinder K. (Bal) Bhullar, chief compliance officer; Kim Brink, chief revenue officer; Isaac Moss, CAO; Tony Dent, gen. counsel & corp. sec.

Capital Stock

	Authorized (shs.)	Outstanding (shs.)[1]
Common	unlimited	118,611,498

[1] At June 9, 2022

Major Shareholder - Widely held at June 9, 2022.

Price Range - SOLO/NASDAQ

Year	Volume	High	Low	Close
2022	65,372,467	US$2.53	US$0.57	US$0.60
2021	289,858,187	US$9.73	US$2.21	US$2.28
2020	356,967,648	US$13.59	US$0.90	US$6.19
2019	53,122,677	US$6.71	US$1.06	US$2.15
2018	10,982,062	US$7.47	US$0.90	US$1.08

Wholly Owned Subsidiaries

EMV Automotive Technology (Chongqing) Inc., Chongqing, People's Republic of China.
EMV Automotive USA Inc., Nev.
- 100% int. in **ElectraMeccanica USA, LLC**, Ariz.

Intermeccanica International Inc., New Westminster, B.C.
SOLO EV LLC, Mich.

Financial Statistics

Periods ended:	12m Dec. 31/21[A]		12m Dec. 31/20[A]
	US$000s	%Chg	US$000s
Operating revenue	**2,101**	**+269**	**569**
Cost of goods sold	4,335		699
Salaries & benefits	26,320		9,867
Research & devel. expense	2,367		2,384
General & admin expense	20,444		6,964
Stock-based compensation	5,178		6,261
Operating expense	**58,645**	**+124**	**26,175**
Operating income	**(56,544)**	**n.a.**	**(25,607)**
Deprec., depl. & amort.	4,251		1,604
Finance income	270		170
Pre-tax income	**(41,326)**	**n.a.**	**(63,079)**
Income taxes	1		(33)
Net income	**(41,327)**	**n.a.**	**(63,047)**
Cash & equivalent	221,928		129,451
Inventories	3,580		609
Accounts receivable	372		213
Current assets	240,309		135,312
Fixed assets, net	10,124		9,290
Intangibles, net	966		969
Total assets	**252,851**	**+73**	**145,754**
Accts. pay. & accr. liabs	6,811		3,461
Current liabilities	7,854		4,556
Long-term lease liabilities	1,495		500
Shareholders' equity	243,138		122,679
Cash from oper. activs	**(60,418)**	**n.a.**	**(22,487)**
Cash from fin. activs	157,682		138,927
Cash from invest. activs	(4,787)		(1,399)
Net cash position	**221,928**	**+71**	**129,451**
Capital expenditures	(4,639)		(1,400)
	US$		US$
Earnings per share*	(0.37)		(1.08)
Cash flow per share*	(0.54)		(0.39)
	shs		shs
No. of shs. o/s*	117,338,964		89,309,563
Avg. no. of shs. o/s*	111,720,726		58,352,766
	%		%
Net profit margin	n.m.		n.m.
Return on equity	(22.59)		(96.55)
Return on assets	(20.74)		(78.35)

* Common
[A] Reported in accordance with IFRS

Note: Share and earnings per share figures for 2016 and 2017 were adjusted to reflect a 1-for-2 share consolidation completed on May 15, 2018.

Latest Results

Periods ended:	3m Mar. 31/22[A]		3m Mar. 31/21[A]
	US$000s	%Chg	US$000s
Operating revenue	1,039	+465	184
Net income	(17,832)	n.a.	(181)
	US$		US$
Earnings per share*	(0.15)		(0.00)

* Common
[A] Reported in accordance with IFRS

Historical Summary
(as originally stated)

Fiscal Year	Oper. Rev.	Net Inc. Bef. Disc.	EPS*
	US$000s	US$000s	US$
2021[A]	2,101	(41,327)	(0.37)
2020[A]	569	(63,047)	(1.08)
	$000s	$000s	$
2019[A]	776	(30,742)	(0.85)
2018[A]	777	(10,038)	(0.38)
2017[A]	109	(11,366)	(0.52)

* Common
[A] Reported in accordance with IFRS

Note: Earnings per share figures for 2016 and 2017 were adjusted to reflect a 1-for-2 share consolidation completed on May 15, 2018.

E.35 Electrovaya Inc.

Symbol - ELVA **Exchange** - TSX **CUSIP** - 28617B
Head Office - 6688 Kitimat Rd, Mississauga, ON, L5N 1P8 **Telephone** - (905) 855-4610 **Toll-free** - (800) 388-2865 **Fax** - (905) 822-7953
Website - www.electrovaya.com
Email - jroy@electrovaya.com
Investor Relations - Jason Roy (800) 388-2865
Auditors - Goodman & Associates LLP C.A., Toronto, Ont.
Lawyers - Fasken Martineau DuMoulin LLP, Toronto, Ont.
Transfer Agents - TSX Trust Company, Toronto, Ont.
Employees - 77 at Sept. 30, 2022
Profile - (Ont. 1996) Designs, develops and manufactures lithium ion batteries, battery systems and battery-related products for the materials handling electric vehicles (MHEV), buses, trucks and other electric transportation applications, as well as for electric stationary storage and other battery markets.

Main businesses include Lithium Ion Battery systems for powering buses, trucks and MHEV, which includes fork-lifts and automated guided vehicles as well as accessories such as battery chargers; electromotive power products for electric trucks, buses and other electric transportation applications; industrial energy storage products; specialty applications which require complex power solutions, including competencies in building systems for third parties; and electrodes, cells and modules.

Also offers EVISION, an internally developed and proprietary remote monitoring system that is able to track battery operational usage in company-powered applications such as lift trucks or electric buses in real-time. The system monitors battery health, utilization and charging to provide customers with optimized fleet and charging management. EVISION subscriptions generate recurring and trailing revenue to the company. In addition, the company also conducts research into next generation cells and batteries in the areas of solid-state cells, electrode production and higher energy density batteries.

Operations are carried out at a 62,000-sq.-ft. battery and battery systems research and manufacturing facility in Mississauga, Ont., which also serves as the company's headquarters.

Common listed on NASDAQ, July 6, 2023.

Predecessor Detail - Name changed from Electrofuel Inc., Aug. 13, 2002.

Directors - Dr. Sankar Das Gupta, co-founder & exec. chr., Mississauga, Ont.; Dr. James K. Jacobs, co-founder, Toronto, Ont.; Dr. Rajshekar (Raj) Das Gupta, CEO, Mississauga, Ont.; Dr. Carolyn M. Hansson, Waterloo, Ont.; Kartick Kumar, San Francisco, Calif.

Other Exec. Officers - John Gibson, CFO & corp. sec.; Dr. Jeremy Dang, v-p, bus. & project devel.

Capital Stock

	Authorized (shs.)	Outstanding (shs.)[1]
Common	unlimited	32,967,267

[1] At June 16, 2023

Major Shareholder - Dr. Sankar Das Gupta held 31.33% interest at Feb. 21, 2023.

Price Range - ELVA/TSX

Year	Volume	High	Low	Close
2022	4,080,076	$6.60	$2.65	$5.00
2021	13,205,995	$12.50	$4.00	$4.65
2020	13,105,719	$9.05	$0.80	$7.45
2019	5,032,577	$1.75	$0.70	$0.93
2018	7,044,565	$3.10	$0.70	$0.70

Consolidation: 1-for-5 cons. in June 2023
Recent Close: $4.96
Capital Stock Changes - In November 2022, private placement of 3,508,680 units (1 post-consolidated common share & ½ warrant) at Cdn$4.2305 per unit was completed, with warrants exercisable at Cdn$5.30 per share for three years. On June 16, 2023, common shares were consolidated on a 1-for-5 basis.

During fiscal 2022, common shares were issued as follows: 1,174,286 for financing fees and 71,666 on exercise of options.

Wholly Owned Subsidiaries

Electrovaya Corporation, Ont.
Miljobil Grenland AS, Porsgrunn, Norway. Inactive.

Financial Statistics

Periods ended:	12m Sept. 30/22[A]		12m Sept. 30/21[A]
	US$000s	%Chg	US$000s
Operating revenue	**19,823**	**+71**	**11,584**
Cost of goods sold	14,847		7,660
Research & devel. expense	3,899		4,555
General & admin expense	3,836		3,931
Stock-based compensation	1,358		541
Other operating expense	87		58
Operating expense	**24,027**	**+43**	**16,745**
Operating income	**(4,204)**	**n.a.**	**(5,161)**
Deprec., depl. & amort.	399		319
Finance costs, gross	2,700		2,669
Pre-tax income	**(6,547)**	**n.a.**	**(7,534)**
Net income	**(6,547)**	**n.a.**	**(7,534)**
Cash & equivalent	626		4,202
Inventories	4,477		4,666
Accounts receivable	6,309		1,341
Current assets	15,681		12,028
Fixed assets, net	2,312		2,870
Total assets	**18,081**	**+21**	**14,977**
Bank indebtedness	16,580		8,642
Accts. pay. & accr. liabs	4,147		3,248
Current liabilities	21,371		13,453
Long-term lease liabilities	2,235		2,603
Shareholders' equity	(5,919)		(1,696)
Cash from oper. activs	**(11,815)**	**n.a.**	**(8,116)**
Cash from fin. activs	9,516		10,916
Cash from invest. activs	(423)		(560)
Net cash position	**626**	**-85**	**4,202**
Capital expenditures	(49)		(560)
	US$		US$
Earnings per share*	(0.20)		(0.25)
Cash flow per share*	(0.40)		(0.29)
	shs		shs
No. of shs. o/s*	29,437,372		29,188,182
Avg. no. of shs. o/s*	29,344,623		27,978,771
	%		%
Net profit margin	(33.03)		(65.04)
Return on equity	n.m.		n.m.
Return on assets	(23.27)		(37.98)
Foreign sales percent	90		81
No. of employees (FTEs)	77		51

* Common
[A] Reported in accordance with IFRS

Historical Summary
(as originally stated)

Fiscal Year	Oper. Rev. US$000s	Net Inc. Bef. Disc. US$000s	EPS* US$
2022[A]	19,823	(6,547)	(0.20)
2021[A]	11,584	(7,534)	(0.25)
2020[A]	14,525	1,112	0.05
2019[A]	4,891	(2,837)	(0.15)
2018[A]	5,633	(10,172)	(0.52)

* Common
[A] Reported in accordance with IFRS
Note: Adjusted throughout for 1-for-5 cons. in June 2023

E.36 Element Fleet Management Corp.*

Symbol - EFN **Exchange** - TSX **CUSIP** - 286181
Head Office - TD Canada Trust Tower, Brookfield Place, 3600-161 Bay St, Toronto, ON, M5J 2S1 **Telephone** - (416) 386-1067 **Toll-free** - (877) 534-0019 **Fax** - (888) 772-8129
Website - www.elementfleet.com
Email - mbarrett@elementcorp.com
Investor Relations - Michael Barrett (416) 646-5698
Auditors - Ernst & Young LLP C.A., Toronto, Ont.
Lawyers - Blake, Cassels & Graydon LLP, Toronto, Ont.
Transfer Agents - Computershare Trust Company of Canada Inc., Toronto, Ont.
FP500 Revenue Ranking - 226
Employees - 2,500 at Dec. 31, 2022
Profile - (Ont. 2011 amalg.) Operates as a global fleet management company providing services and financing solutions for commercial vehicle and equipment fleets across North America, Australia and New Zealand.

The company provides vehicle fleet leasing and fleet management solutions and related service programs to corporate, government and not-for-profit clients. It offers services across many asset types, including cars and light duty vehicles, medium and heavy duty trucks, and material handling equipment. Service offerings include acquisition, financing, title, licensing and registration, telematics, risk and safety, accident management, tolls, violations and compliance, fuel services, managed maintenance, personal usage and expense tracking, rental services, remarketing and Arc by Element, which is an end-to-end electric vehicle (EV) solutions that includes assistance in selecting best fit-for-use EVs, facilitating the deployment of appropriate charging infrastructure and supporting clients to pilot and manage the integration of EVs seamlessly into their fleets.

Through its alliance with **Arval**, the company's operations include more than 1,500,000 vehicles under management across 56 countries including the U.S., Canada, Mexico, Australia and New Zealand.

Fleet management portfolio distribution[1]

At Dec. 31	2022	2021
Region	$000s	$000s
U.S. & Canada	4,710,263	5,212,719
Australia & N.Z.	1,597,736	1,570,941
Mexico	2,054,569	1,381,535
Total	8,362,568	8,165,195

[1] Includes net finance receivables and equipment under operating leases.

Predecessor Detail - Name changed from Element Financial Corporation, Oct. 3, 2016, pursuant to plan of arrangement whereby ECN Capital Corp. was spun off as a separate publicly traded company.
Directors - David F. Denison, chr., Toronto, Ont.; Laura L. Dottori-Attanasio, pres. & CEO, Toronto, Ont.; Virginia C. Addicott, Cleveland, Ohio; Andrew C. Clarke, Austin, Tex.; G. Keith Graham, Chatham, Ont.; Dr. Joan Lamm-Tennant, New York, N.Y.; Rubin J. McDougal, Alpine, Utah; Arielle Meloul-Wechsler, Montréal, Qué.; Andrea S. Rosen, Toronto, Ont.
Other Exec. Officers - David Colman, exec. v-p, gen. counsel & corp. sec.; Chris Gittens, exec. v-p & chief digital officer; Jim Halliday, exec. v-p & COO; Israel (Izzy) Kaufman, exec. v-p & treas.; David Madrigal, exec. v-p & chief comml. officer; Jacqueline A. T. (Jacqui) McGillivray, exec. v-p & chief people & social impact officer; Frank Ruperto, exec. v-p & CFO; Michael Barrett, v-p, IR

Capital Stock

	Authorized (shs.)	Outstanding (shs.)[1]
Preferred	unlimited	
Series A		4,600,000
Series C		5,126,400
Series E		5,321,900
Common	unlimited	389,623,243

[1] At Aug. 8, 2023

Preferred - Issuable in series. Non-voting.
Series A - Entitled to fixed cumulative preferential annual dividends of $1.7333 per share payable quarterly to Dec. 31, 2023, and thereafter at a rate reset every five years equal to the five-year Government of Canada yield plus 4.71%. Redeemable on Dec. 31, 2023, and on December 31 every five years thereafter at $25 per share plus declared and unpaid dividends. Convertible at the holder's option on Dec. 31, 2023, and on December 31 every five years thereafter, into floating rate preferred series B shares on a share-for-share basis, subject to certain conditions. The preferred series B shares would pay a quarterly dividend equal to the 90-day Canadian Treasury bill rate plus 4.71%.
Series C - Entitled to fixed cumulative preferential annual dividends of $1.5525 per share payable quarterly to June 30, 2024, and thereafter at a rate reset every five years equal to the five-year Government of Canada yield plus 4.81%. Redeemable on June 30, 2024, and on June 30 every five years thereafter at $25 per share plus declared and unpaid dividends. Convertible at the holder's option on June 30, 2024, and on June 30 every five years thereafter, into floating rate preferred series D shares on a share-for-share basis, subject to certain conditions. The preferred series D shares would pay a quarterly dividend equal to the 90-day Canadian Treasury bill rate plus 4.81%.
Series E - Entitled to fixed cumulative preferential annual dividends of $1.4758 per share payable quarterly to Sept. 30, 2024, and thereafter at a rate reset every five years equal to the five-year Government of Canada yield plus 4.72%. Redeemable on Sept. 30, 2024, and on September 30 every five years thereafter at $25 per share plus declared and unpaid dividends. Convertible at the holder's option on Sept. 30, 2024, and on September 30 every five years thereafter, into floating rate preferred series F shares on a share-for-share basis, subject to certain conditions. The preferred series F shares would pay a quarterly dividend equal to the 90-day Canadian Treasury bill rate plus 4.72%.
Common - One vote per share.
Options - At Dec. 31, 2022, employee options were outstanding to purchase 3,809,948 common shares at a weighted average exercise price of $7.17 per share with a weighted average remaining life of 2.15 years.
Preferred Series I (old) - Were entitled to fixed cumulative preferential annual dividends of $1.4375 per share payable quarterly to June 30, 2022. Redeemed on June 30, 2022, at $25 per share.
Normal Course Issuer Bid - The company plans to make normal course purchases of up to 39,228,719 common shares representing 10% of the public float. The bid commenced on Nov. 15, 2022, and expires on Nov. 14, 2023.
Major Shareholder - Widely held at Mar. 15, 2023.

Price Range - EFN/TSX

Year	Volume	High	Low	Close
2022	218,267,404	$19.64	$10.99	$18.45
2021	214,587,148	$15.28	$11.72	$12.88
2020	312,473,981	$13.82	$6.96	$13.38
2019	226,236,651	$11.97	$6.68	$11.09
2018	535,298,936	$9.76	$3.21	$6.91

Recent Close: $20.48
Capital Stock Changes - On June 30, 2022, all 6,000,000 series I preferred shares were redeemed at $25 per share. Also during 2022, common shares were issued as follows: 1,301,758 on exercise of options and 22,502 on conversion of debentures; 13,906,200 common shares were repurchased under a Normal Course Issuer Bid.

Dividends

EFN com Ra $0.40 pa Q est. Jan. 13, 2023**[1]
Prev. Rate: $0.31 est. Jan. 14, 2022
Prev. Rate: $0.26 est. Jan. 15, 2021
EFN.PR.A pfd ser A cum. red. exch. Adj. Ra $1.73325 pa Q est. Mar. 29, 2019
EFN.PR.C pfd ser C cum. red. exch. Adj. Ra $1.5525 pa Q est. Sept. 30, 2019
EFN.PR.E pfd ser E cum. red. exch. Adj. Ra $1.47575 pa Q est. Dec. 31, 2019
pfd ser I cum. red. exch. Adj. Ra $1.4375 pa Q est. Oct. 2, 2017[2]
$0.359375f.......... June 30/22
[1] Dividend reinvestment plan implemented eff. Oct. 1, 2018.
[2] Redeemed June 30, 2022 at $25 per sh.
** Reinvestment Option f Final Payment

Long-Term Debt - Outstanding at Dec. 31, 2022:

Sr. revolv. credit facilities[1]	$1,893,323,000
4.25% conv. debs. due 2024[2]	163,933,000
2.60% sr. notes due 2024	1,219,032,000
Vehicle mgt. asset-backed debt:	
Term facilities due to 2023[3]	387,034,000
Term notes, amort. due to 2023[4]	1,115,459,000
Variable funding notes[5]	4,120,361,000
Other[6]	83,639,000
Less: Deferred fin. costs	19,227,000
Less: Hedge accounting fair value adj.	45,935,000
Add: Continuing involvement liability	54,173,000
	8,971,792,000

[1] Bear interest at a weighted average interest rate of 6.61% at Dec. 31, 2022.
[2] Convertible into common shares at $11.91 per share. An equity component of convertible debentures totaling $13,799,000 was included in shareholders' equity.
[3] Bear interest at a weighted average interest rate of 5.30% at Dec. 31, 2022.
[4] Bear interest at a weighted average interest rate of 1.50% at Dec. 31, 2022.
[5] Bear interest at a weighted average interest rate of 5.04% at Dec. 31, 2022.
[6] Bear interest at a weighted average interest rate of 4.08% at Dec. 31, 2022.

Note - In April 2023, the company issued US$750,000,000 of vehicle management asset-backed term notes .
Note - In June 2023, private offering of US$750,000,000 principal amount of 6.271% senior notes due June 26, 2026, was arranged.

Wholly Owned Subsidiaries

EFN (Netherlands) International B.V., Netherlands.
- 100% int. in **EFN (Australia) Pty Limited**, Australia.
  - 100% int. in **EFN (New Zealand) Limited**, New Zealand.
    - 100% int. in **Custom Fleet N.Z.**, New Zealand.
  - 100% int. in **Element Financial (Australia) Pty Limited**, Australia.
    - 100% int. in **Element Fleet Services Australia Pty Ltd.**, Australia.
      - 100% int. in **Custom Fleet Pty Ltd.**, Australia.
- 100% int. in **EFN (Netherlands) B.V.**, Netherlands.
  - 100% int. in **Element Fleet Holding Mexico S.A. de C.V.**, Mexico.
    - 100% int. in **Element Fleet Management Corporation Mexico S.A. de C.V.**, Mexico.
- 100% int. in **EFN (Netherlands) 2 B.V.**, Netherlands.
  - 100% int. in **Element Fleet Management (US) Holdings Inc.**, Del.
    - 81% int. in **Element Fleet Management (US) Corp.**, Del.
      - 100% int. in **Element Vehicle Management Services Group LLC**, Del.
        - 100% int. in **Element Fleet Corporation**, Del.
          - 100% int. in **Chesapeake Finance Holdings II LLC**, Del.

Element Fleet Management Inc., Ont.
- 100% int. in **FLR LP Inc.**, Man.
  - 100% int. in **Element Fleet Lease Receivables L.P.**, Canada.

Investments

19% int. in **Element Fleet Management (US) Corp.**, Del.
Note: The preceding list includes only the major related companies in which interests are held.

Financial Statistics

Periods ended:	12m Dec. 31/22[A]		12m Dec. 31/21[A]
	$000s	%Chg	$000s
Total revenue	**1,959,793**	**+18**	**1,656,951**
Salaries & benefits	322,886		306,884
General & admin. expense	124,848		104,401
Stock-based compensation	31,303		24,120
Other operating expense	48,031		45,539
Operating expense	**527,068**	**+10**	**480,944**
Operating income	**1,432,725**	**+22**	**1,176,007**
Deprec. & amort.	603,179		536,106
Provision for loan losses	(25)		(5,535)
Finance costs, gross	276,666		196,449
Pre-tax income	**549,553**	**+20**	**457,676**
Income taxes	139,910		101,670
Net income	**409,643**	**+15**	**356,006**
Cash & equivalent	68,876		45,271
Accounts receivable	215,817		204,873
Investments	10,876,227		9,733,457
Fixed assets, net	80,899		93,872
Intangibles, net	2,159,699		2,050,999
Total assets	**14,332,218**	**+10**	**12,973,412**
Accts. pay. & accr. liabs	1,465,198		1,206,550
Debt	8,971,792		8,198,035
Preferred share equity	365,113		511,869
Equity portion of conv. debs	13,799		13,829
Shareholders' equity	3,680,973		3,450,949
Cash from oper. activs	**229,631**	**-91**	**2,512,102**
Cash from fin. activs	(7,594)		(2,390,228)
Cash from invest. activs	(65,610)		(85,949)
Net cash position	**68,876**	**+52**	**45,271**
Capital expenditures	(3,866)		(6,036)
Capital disposals	1,933		761
	$		$
Earnings per share*	0.96		0.76
Cash flow per share*	0.58		5.94
Cash divd. per share*	0.33		0.27
	shs		shs
No. of shs. o/s*	392,495,287		405,077,227
Avg. no. of shs. o/s*	396,907,113		423,070,096
	%		%
Net profit margin	20.90		21.49
Return on equity	12.20		10.42
Return on assets	4.51		3.64
No. of employees (FTEs)	2,500		2,500

* Common
[A] Reported in accordance with IFRS

Note: Total revenue is the sum of interest income, before provision for credit losses; gross rental revenue; and service and other revenue, gross.

Latest Results

Periods ended:	6m June 30/23[A]		6m June 30/22[A]
	$000s	%Chg	$000s
Total revenue	1,208,089	+31	920,557
Net income	226,515	+11	204,724
	$		$
Earnings per share*	0.55		0.47

* Common
[A] Reported in accordance with IFRS

Historical Summary
(as originally stated)

Fiscal Year	Total Rev. $000s	Net Inc. Bef. Disc. $000s	EPS* $
2022[A]	1,959,793	409,643	0.96
2021[A]	1,656,951	356,006	0.76
2020[A]	1,781,972	287,092	0.56
2019[A]	2,020,153	97,701	0.12
2018[A]	1,770,180	(199,104)	(0.62)

* Common
[A] Reported in accordance with IFRS

E.37 Element Lifestyle Retirement Inc.

Symbol - ELM **Exchange** - TSX-VEN **CUSIP** - 28619G
Head Office - 438 King Edward Ave W, Vancouver, BC, V5Y 0M5 **Telephone** - (604) 676-1418
Website - www.elementlifestyleretirement.com
Email - michaeldiao@elementliving.com
Investor Relations - Bo Jun Diao (604) 676-1418
Auditors - MNP LLP C.A., Vancouver, B.C.
Lawyers - Boughton Law Corporation, Vancouver, B.C.
Transfer Agents - Computershare Trust Company of Canada Inc.
Profile - (B.C. 2007) Develops and manages retirement communities in British Columbia for third party owners and independent operators.

The company provides two primary services: development services, which includes property selection, assembly and acquisition, building and community design, municipal approval and land entitlement processes, financing, marketing, sales and leasing, and construction project management; and management services, which includes the administration, operation and financing of retirement communities and physical facilities. The company operates the communities that it develops under management contracts for terms of 20 years or longer.

Clients consist of **Care Pacific Holdings Ltd.**, which owns the OPAL Project in Vancouver, and the OASIS Project in Langley; and **Aquara Limited Partnership**, which owns the AQUARA Project in Victoria.

The OPAL Project is a 142,000-sq.-ft. lifestyle retirement community with 44 seniors residential condominium units, 56 seniors rental units and 30 seniors licensed care units. OPAL was open for operation in December 2019. The OASIS Project is intended to be a master-planned community on 17 acres of land consisting of 721,000 sq. ft. of gross floor area for residential use with 835 residential units and 26,000 sq. ft. of gross floor area for commercial use. The development of OASIS would be completed in phases. The AQUARA Project is part of a master-planned community which includes several existing high rise residential towers. The property is a five-storey development consisting of 153,000 sq. ft. of gross floor area with 155 units with a mixture of condo, rental and licensed care units.

Predecessor Detail - Name changed from Sonoma Resources Inc., Dec. 2, 2015.

Directors - Bo Jun (Michael) Diao, CEO, Coquitlam, B.C.; Ernest (Ernie) Hee, exec. v-p & interim CFO, Vancouver, B.C.; Teresa Sun, corp. sec., B.C.; Dr. John H. V. Gilbert, Vancouver, B.C.; Scott A. Young, Vancouver, B.C.

Other Exec. Officers - Wendy Ho, v-p, project devel.

Capital Stock

	Authorized (shs.)	Outstanding (shs.)[1]
Common	unlimited	70,478,299

[1] At Oct. 26, 2022

Major Shareholder - Hua Min Chen held 24.4% interest and Ke Fei Deng held 11.35% interest at Apr. 28, 2022.

Price Range - ELM/TSX-VEN

Year	Volume	High	Low	Close
2022	903,014	$0.08	$0.01	$0.02
2021	4,051,388	$0.15	$0.03	$0.07
2020	2,581,974	$0.10	$0.01	$0.10
2019	2,065,992	$0.16	$0.06	$0.08
2018	1,082,471	$0.19	$0.08	$0.12

Recent Close: $0.03

Capital Stock Changes - There were no changes to capital stock from fiscal 2020 to fiscal 2022, inclusive.

Wholly Owned Subsidiaries

Aquara GP Ltd., B.C.
Element Lifestyle Management Inc., Vancouver, B.C.
Element Lifestyle Retirement (Hong Kong) Ltd., Hong Kong, Hong Kong, People's Republic of China.
Element Medical Equipment Inc., Vancouver, B.C.

Investments

50% int. in **Element Lifestyle (Vic Harbour West) Inc.**, Victoria, B.C.

Financial Statistics

Periods ended:	12m May 31/22[A]		12m May 31/21[oA]
	$000s	%Chg	$000s
Operating revenue	**2,093**	**+548**	**323**
Salaries & benefits	872		786
General & admin expense	620		497
Operating expense	**1,492**	**+16**	**1,284**
Operating income	**601**	**n.a.**	**(961)**
Deprec., depl. & amort.	62		209
Finance income	70		24
Finance costs, gross	661		398
Pre-tax income	**(22)**	**n.a.**	**(1,528)**
Net income	**(22)**	**n.a.**	**(1,528)**
Cash & equivalent	232		102
Accounts receivable	931		35
Current assets	1,228		1,760
Fixed assets, net	25		82
Intangibles, net	27		27
Total assets	**2,174**	**+10**	**1,984**
Accts. pay. & accr. liabs	200		187
Current liabilities	200		235
Long-term debt, gross	2,444		2,197
Long-term debt, net	2,444		2,197
Equity portion of conv. debs	678		678
Shareholders' equity	(470)		(448)
Cash from oper. activs	**(669)**	**n.a.**	**(1,132)**
Cash from fin. activs	805		905
Cash from invest. activs	(6)		(7)
Net cash position	**232**	**+127**	**102**
Capital expenditures	(6)		(7)
	$		$
Earnings per share*	(0.00)		(0.02)
Cash flow per share*	(0.01)		(0.02)
	shs		shs
No. of shs. o/s*	70,478,299		70,478,299
Avg. no. of shs. o/s*	70,478,299		70,478,299
	%		%
Net profit margin	(1.05)		(473.07)
Return on equity	n.m.		n.m.
Return on assets	30.74		(42.13)

* common
[o] Restated
[A] Reported in accordance with IFRS

Latest Results

Periods ended:	3m Aug. 31/22[A]		3m Aug. 31/21[A]
	$000s	%Chg	$000s
Operating revenue	264	+108	127
Net income	(214)	n.a.	(320)
	$		$
Earnings per share*	(0.01)		(0.01)

* common
[A] Reported in accordance with IFRS

Historical Summary
(as originally stated)

Fiscal Year	Oper. Rev. $000s	Net Inc. Bef. Disc. $000s	EPS* $
2022[A]	2,093	(22)	(0.00)
2021[A]	323	(1,528)	(0.02)
2020[A]	120	(2,361)	(0.03)
2019[A]	949	(1,422)	(0.02)
2018[A]	1,810	(963)	(0.01)

* common
[A] Reported in accordance with IFRS

E.38 Element Nutritional Sciences Inc.

Symbol - ELMT **Exchange** - CSE **CUSIP** - 28619R
Head Office - 401-1100 Walkers Line, Burlington, ON, L7N 2G3 **Toll-free** - (855) 348-1970
Website - elmtinc.com
Email - slowther@elementnutrition.com
Investor Relations - Stuart Lowther (855) 348-1970
Auditors - SRCO Professional Corporation C.A., Richmond Hill, Ont.
Transfer Agents - Endeavor Trust Corporation, Vancouver, B.C.
Profile - (B.C. 2018) Develops science based-nutritional products under the Rejuvenate™ brand for the ageing demographic 45 and over and offers protein powders and other nutritional supplements for the sports nutrition market under the JAKTRX™ brand in Canada and the United States.

The company's flagship brand is Rejuvenate™, a muscle health product designed to help slow and/or prevent muscle loss due to aging. The initial product is a single serve powdered product sold in a carton holding 30 single serve pouches. These Rejuvenate™ products are sold at Loblaws, Shoppers Drug Mart and Rexall stores in Canada and in Walgreens, CVS, Walmart and Meijer stores in the United States. Online, the products are available on the company's own e-commerce platform as well as Amazon.com and Amazon.ca. Under development is an organic plant-based, single serve liquid ready to drink beverage version in chocolate, vanilla and mocha flavours sold in tetra packs. In the United States, the company commenced retail sales of the beverage product on its e-commerce platform in early 2021 and expects to commence sales in stores in the third quarter of 2021. In Canada, initial sales were expected to commence on the company's e-commerce platform Rejuvenate.ca and Amazon.ca in the first quarter of 2022.

Contract manufacturers are utilized to produce all products. New products are developed using a patented method of administering a formulation of essential amino acids. The company plans to launch up to 12 more beverage products under the Rejuvenate™ brand over the next three to five years. Other powdered formulations will also be developed.

Also offers the JAKTRX™ product line of protein powders and other nutritional supplements targeting the sports nutrition market.

Predecessor Detail - Name changed from PJ1 Capital Corp., Aug. 31, 2020, pursuant to the reverse takeover acquisition of Element Nutrition Inc.

Directors - Stuart Lowther, chr., pres. & CEO, Halton Hills, Ont.; Shaun Power, CFO & corp. sec., Burlington, Ont.; Sean Bromley, Vancouver, B.C.; Gregory J. (Greg) Cochrane, Toronto, Ont.; Lino Fera, Halton Hills, Ont.

Other Exec. Officers - Stephen Brown, COO; Janice Day, chief sales officer; Vito Sanzone, chief mktg. officer; John Duffy, v-p, U.S. sales

Capital Stock

	Authorized (shs.)	Outstanding (shs.)[1]
Common	unlimited	113,333,147

[1] At June 14, 2023

Major Shareholder - Stuart Lowther held 15.28% interest at Jan. 17, 2023.

Price Range - ELMT/CSE

Year	Volume	High	Low	Close
2022	36,655,149	$0.45	$0.07	$0.08
2021	29,104,353	$0.94	$0.27	$0.44

Recent Close: $0.13

Capital Stock Changes - In May 2022, public offering of 14,000,000 common shares was completed at 25¢ per share.

Wholly Owned Subsidiaries

Element Nutrition Inc., Ont.
- 100% int. in **Element Nutrition Ltd.**, United States.
- 100% int. in **JAKTRX Inc.**, Ont.

Hammock Pharmaceuticals, Inc., United States.

Financial Statistics

Periods ended:	12m Dec. 31/21‡A		12m Dec. 31/20ºA
	$000s	%Chg	$000s
Operating revenue	**2,357**	**+141**	**980**
Cost of sales	...		817
Salaries & benefits	...		1,168
General & admin expense	...		2,553
Other operating expense	...		43
Operating expense	**...**	**n.a.**	**4,581**
Operating income	**...**	**n.a.**	**(3,601)**
Deprec., depl. & amort.	...		149
Finance costs, gross	...		53
Write-downs/write-offs	...		(2,181)
Pre-tax income	**(8,780)**	**n.a.**	**(7,716)**
Net income	**(8,780)**	**n.a.**	**(7,716)**
Cash & equivalent	492		87
Inventories	...		341
Accounts receivable	...		627
Current assets	4,919		1,133
Fixed assets, net	77		68
Right-of-use assets	nil		99
Total assets	**4,996**	**+284**	**1,300**
Bank indebtedness	219		500
Accts. pay. & accr. liabs.	2,971		2,432
Long-term debt, gross	503		765
Long-term debt, net	29		52
Long-term lease liabilities	nil		52
Shareholders' equity	1,304		(2,505)
Cash from oper. activs.	**(9,942)**	**n.a.**	**(2,152)**
Cash from fin. activs.	10,549		221
Cash from invest. activs.	(37)		1,848
Net cash position	**492**	**+466**	**87**
Capital expenditures	(37)		(10)
	$		$
Earnings per share*	(0.10)		(0.36)
Cash flow per share*	(0.12)		(0.10)
	shs		shs
No. of shs. o/s*	96,573,916		56,933,162
Avg. no. of shs. o/s*	83,623,532		21,469,605
	%		%
Net profit margin	(372.51)		(787.35)
Return on equity	n.m.		n.m.
Return on assets	(278.91)		(671.31)

* Common
‡ Preliminary
º Restated
A Reported in accordance with IFRS

Latest Results

Periods ended:	9m Sept. 30/22A		9m Sept. 30/21A
	$000s	%Chg	$000s
Operating revenue	4,132	+100	2,063
Net income	(5,448)	n.a.	(7,488)
	$		$
Earnings per share*	(0.05)		(0.09)

* Common
A Reported in accordance with IFRS

Historical Summary
(as originally stated)

Fiscal Year	Oper. Rev.	Net Inc. Bef. Disc.	EPS*
	$000s	$000s	$
2021‡A	2,357	(8,780)	(0.10)
2020A1	980	(7,716)	(0.36)
2019A	1,674	(1,497)	(0.11)

* Common
‡ Preliminary
A Reported in accordance with IFRS
[1] Results prior to Aug. 31, 2020, pertain to and reflect the reverse takeover acquisition of Element Nutrition Inc.

E.39 Elixxer Ltd.

Symbol - ELXR **Exchange** - TSX-VEN (S) **CUSIP** - 28660W
Head Office - 700-1100 boul René-Lévesque O, Montréal, QC, H3B 4N4 **Telephone** - (514) 788-1499 **Fax** - (514) 397-2375
Website - www.elixxer.com
Email - ferras@elixxer.com
Investor Relations - Ferras Zalt
Auditors - Kreston GTA LLP C.A., Markham, Ont.
Lawyers - Fasken Martineau DuMoulin LLP, Montréal, Qué.
Transfer Agents - Computershare Trust Company of Canada Inc., Toronto, Ont.

Profile - (Can. 2004) Invests primarily in companies engaged in the legal global cannabis market, with investments in Australia, Jamaica, Switzerland, Italy and Canada.

Primary investments include various interests in **Little Green Pharma Limited** (formerly **Habi Pharma Pty Ltd.**), which produces and sells medical cannabis products in Australia and exports to Germany; **Global Canna Labs Limited**, which produces medical cannabis from an over 270,000 sq. ft. cultivation facility in Montego Bay, Jamaica; **Viridi Unit S.A.**, which produces, processes and distributes high-cannabidiol legal cannabis products under its ONE Premium Cannabis brand in over 500 retail locations across Switzerland; **Evolution Bnk S.r.l.**, which has indoor cannabis production facilities in Pavia, Italy; **Freia Farmaceutici S.r.l.**, which develops and markets hemp-based pharmaceutical products authorized by the Italian Ministry of Health and licensed for sale throughout the European Union; and **Tricho-Med Corporation** (dba AAA Trichomes), which produces a premium low-cost medical cannabis products in Canada.

In addition, holds 5% royalty streams on net sales of Tricho-Med, Global Canna Labs, Evolution and Viridi.

In March 2022, the company agreed to sell its 18.4% interest in **Viridi Unit S.A.**, which produces, processes and distributes high-cannabidiol legal cannabis products under its ONE Premium Cannabis brand in more than 500 retail locations across Switzerland, to **Global A Brands, Inc.** for $1,000,000.

Common suspended from TSX-VEN, May 11, 2022.

Predecessor Detail - Name changed from LGC Capital Ltd., Aug. 6, 2019.

Directors - Ferras Zalt, exec. chr. & interim CEO, London, Middx., United Kingdom; Tarik Alhaidary, London, Middx., United Kingdom; Jayahari (Jay) Balasubramaniam, Toronto, Ont.; Jeremy Green; Rafi Hazan, Dollard-des-Ormeaux, Qué.; Alexey (Alex) Kanayev, Toronto, Ont.

Other Exec. Officers - Kym No, interim CFO & contr.; Richard Widmann, exec. v-p, comml.; Faisal Dajani, v-p, bus. devel.; Guy Charette, legal counsel; Michael Kozub, corp. sec.

Capital Stock

	Authorized (shs.)	Outstanding (shs.)[1]
Preferred	unlimited	
Common	unlimited	11,349,687

[1] At May 30, 2022

Major Shareholder - Arlington Capital L.P. held 31.01% interest and AIP Convertible Private Debt Fund LP held 26.67% interest at Sept. 30, 2021.

Price Range - ELXR/TSX-VEN (S)

Year	Volume	High	Low	Close
2022	763,202	$2.00	$1.00	$1.15
2021	2,145,251	$3.50	$0.50	$1.50
2020	1,996,511	$5.50	$0.50	$1.50
2019	1,618,319	$15.00	$3.50	$5.00
2018	5,320,146	$103.00	$7.50	$9.00

Consolidation: 1-for-100 cons. in Feb. 2022

Wholly Owned Subsidiaries

LGC Capital EU OU, Estonia.
LGC Capital Spain S.L., Spain.
LGC Finance Limited, British Virgin Islands.

Investments

Freia Farmaceutici S.R.L., Italy.
Little Green Pharma Limited, Perth, W.A., Australia.
18.4% int. in **Viridi Unit S.A.**, Switzerland.

Financial Statistics

Periods ended:	12m Dec. 31/21A		12m Dec. 31/20A
	$000s	%Chg	$000s
Realized invest. gain (loss)	nil		75
Unrealized invest. gain (loss)	169		6,393
Total revenue	**212**	**-97**	**6,706**
Salaries & benefits	693		371
General & admin. expense	1,372		2,507
Stock-based compensation	1		413
Operating expense	**2,447**	**-26**	**3,291**
Operating income	**(2,235)**	**n.a.**	**3,415**
Deprec. & amort.	2		2
Finance costs, gross	1,755		3,305
Write-downs/write-offs	(29)		(2,168)
Pre-tax income	**(3,663)**	**n.a.**	**(9,783)**
Net income	**(3,663)**	**n.a.**	**(9,783)**
Cash & equivalent	13,586		2,103
Investments	2,820		18,121
Fixed assets, net	nil		6
Total assets	**16,836**	**-19**	**20,814**
Bank indebtedness	6,114		11,970
Accts. pay. & accr. liabs.	1,910		2,963
Debt	431		1,123
Shareholders' equity	8,381		4,759
Cash from oper. activs.	**(4,019)**	**n.a.**	**(3,013)**
Cash from fin. activs.	32		3,130
Cash from invest. activs.	2,186		1,061
Net cash position	**302**	**-86**	**2,103**
	$		$
Earnings per share*	(0.42)		(2.00)
Cash flow per share*	(0.46)		(0.52)
	shs		shs
No. of shs. o/s*	11,126,100		6,335,080
Avg. no. of shs. o/s*	8,803,918		5,769,236
	%		%
Net profit margin	n.m.		(145.88)
Return on equity	(55.75)		(109.08)
Return on assets	(10.14)		(28.94)

* Common
A Reported in accordance with IFRS

Latest Results

Periods ended:	3m Mar. 31/22A		3m Mar. 31/21A
	$000s	%Chg	$000s
Total revenue	2,381	-29	3,336
Net income	(3,145)	n.a.	1,995
	$		$
Earnings per share*	(0.29)		0.31

* Common
A Reported in accordance with IFRS

Historical Summary
(as originally stated)

Fiscal Year	Total Rev.	Net Inc. Bef. Disc.	EPS*
	$000s	$000s	$
2021A	212	(3,663)	(0.42)
2020A	6,706	(9,783)	(2.00)
2019A1	(6,069)	(23,681)	(5.00)
2018A	828	(16,530)	(5.00)
2017A	394	(5,048)	(2.00)

* Common
A Reported in accordance with IFRS
[1] 15 months ended Dec. 31, 2019.
Note: Adjusted throughout for 1-for-100 cons. in Feb. 2022

E.40 Else Nutrition Holdings Inc.

Symbol - BABY **Exchange** - TSX **CUSIP** - 290257
Head Office - 1048 165 St, Surrey, BC, V4A 9A2 **Telephone** - (604) 603-7787
Website - www.elsenutrition.com
Email - sokhiep@elsenutrition.com
Investor Relations - Sokhie S. Puar (604) 603-7787
Auditors - Kost Forer Gabbay & Kasierer C.A., Tel Aviv, Israel
Transfer Agents - Computershare Trust Company of Canada Inc., Vancouver, B.C.
Employees - 32 at Mar. 31, 2023

Profile - (B.C. 2011) Develops, manufactures, markets and sells organic, vegan, natural, clean-label and gluten-free dairy and soy free alternatives to baby, toddler, kids and adult nutrition and foods. Also sells baby snacks and baby feeding accessories.

Products include Else Super Cereal, a plant-based, organic and non-GMO cereal for babies; Else™ Toddler Omega, a nutrition drink with added Omega 3 and Omega 6 fatty acids for toddlers; plant-based protein shakes for children between 3 to 12 years old which can be used as a milk alternative, meal replacement or serve alongside meals and mixed into recipes such as smoothies, pancakes and muffins; baby feeding accessories including sterile and non-sterile bottles, and disposable sterile nipples (teats) which are both sold exclusively in Israel; and vegan-friendly snacks for the babies and toddlers under the HEART brand.

Products under development include plant-based, non-dairy and non-soy nutrition formula consisting of baby formula products which are substitute for breast milk for infants that are 12 months and under; and variations of Else formula intended for use by babies 6 months and older. The company is also developing a series of plant-based, clean label, whole balanced meal products in different food categories.

Predecessor Detail - Name changed from ASB Capital Inc., June 12, 2019, pursuant to Qualifying Transaction reverse takeover acquisition of Else Nutrition GH Ltd.; basis 1 new for 5 old shs.

Directors - Uriel Kesler, co-founder & COO, Yehud, Israel; Hamutal Yitzhak, chr., co-founder & CEO, Tel Aviv, Israel; Akash Bedi, Hong Kong, People's Republic of China; Yaki Lutski, Israel; Satwinder Mann, Abbotsford, B.C.; Sokhie S. Puar, Vancouver, B.C.; Eli Ronen, Israel

Other Exec. Officers - Shay Shamir, CFO & corp. sec.; Michael Azar, chief tech. officer & co-founder; Mike Glick, v-p, North America & gen. mgr., U.S.; Reuben Halevi, v-p, sales opers.; Avi B. Markus, v-p & country mgr., Canada

Capital Stock

	Authorized (shs.)	Outstanding (shs.)[1]
Common	unlimited	113,322,224

[1] At May 15, 2023

Major Shareholder - Uriel Kesler held 11.67% interest and Hamutal Yitzhak held 11.67% interest at May 8, 2023.

Price Range - BABY/TSX

Year	Volume	High	Low	Close
2022	22,230,399	$1.66	$0.49	$0.55
2021	38,222,430	$4.50	$1.06	$1.14
2020	79,654,724	$5.07	$0.45	$3.91
2019	9,018,096	$0.75	$0.29	$0.53
2018	81,600	$0.83	$0.30	$0.30

Consolidation: 1-for-5 cons. in June 2019

Recent Close: $0.50

Capital Stock Changes - In June 2022, bought deal public offering of 7,004,000 units (1 common share & 1 warrant) was completed at $1.05 per unit. Also during 2022, 1,400,000 common shares were issued on exercise of warrants.

Wholly Owned Subsidiaries

Else Nutrition Australia Pty Ltd., Australia.
Else Nutrition Canada Inc., Vancouver, B.C.
Else Nutrition GH Ltd., Israel.
Else Nutrition USA, Inc., Del.

Financial Statistics

Periods ended:	12m Dec. 31/22[A]		12m Dec. 31/21[A]
	$000s	%Chg	$000s
Operating revenue	**8,527**	**+82**	**4,687**
Cost of sales	7,216		3,944
Salaries & benefits	6,029		4,073
Research & devel. expense	2,564		1,966
General & admin expense	11,663		9,839
Stock-based compensation	1,094		2,201
Operating expense	**28,566**	**+30**	**22,023**
Operating income	**(20,039)**	**n.a.**	**(17,336)**
Deprec., depl. & amort.	496		384
Pre-tax income	**(17,614)**	**n.a.**	**(1,618)**
Net income	**(17,614)**	**n.a.**	**(1,618)**
Cash & equivalent	15,381		24,276
Inventories	5,910		4,546
Accounts receivable	1,542		799
Current assets	24,789		31,138
Fixed assets, net	533		484
Right-of-use assets	578		956
Intangibles, net	263		344
Total assets	**26,163**	**-21**	**32,922**
Accts. pay. & accr. liabs	3,122		2,958
Current liabilities	3,369		3,317
Long-term debt, gross	2,807		nil
Long-term debt, net	2,807		nil
Long-term lease liabilities	320		590
Shareholders' equity	15,595		26,772
Cash from oper. activs	**(20,911)**	**n.a.**	**(15,763)**
Cash from fin. activs	11,689		16,850
Cash from invest. activs	170		1,141
Net cash position	**14,564**	**-37**	**23,047**
Capital expenditures	(160)		(287)
	$		$
Earnings per share*	(0.16)		(0.02)
Cash flow per share*	(0.19)		(0.16)
	shs		shs
No. of shs. o/s*	112,600,220		104,196,220
Avg. no. of shs. o/s*	108,684,822		97,463,350
	%		%
Net profit margin	(206.57)		(34.52)
Return on equity	(83.15)		(8.52)
Return on assets	(59.62)		(5.20)

* Common
[A] Reported in accordance with IFRS

Latest Results

Periods ended:	3m Mar. 31/23[A]		3m Mar. 31/22[A]
	$000s	%Chg	$000s
Operating revenue	2,914	+82	1,601
Net income	(7,903)	n.a.	(7,234)
	$		$
Earnings per share*	(0.07)		(0.07)

* Common
[A] Reported in accordance with IFRS

Historical Summary
(as originally stated)

Fiscal Year	Oper. Rev.	Net Inc. Bef. Disc.	EPS*
	$000s	$000s	$
2022[A]	8,527	(17,614)	(0.16)
2021[A]	4,687	(1,618)	(0.02)
2020[A]	1,482	(24,104)	(0.30)
2019[A1]	554	(5,378)	(0.11)
2018[A2,3]	nil	(154)	n.a.

* Common
[A] Reported in accordance with IFRS
[1] Results reflect the June 13, 2019, reverse takeover acquisition of Else Nutrition GH Ltd.
[2] 7 months ended Dec. 31, 2018.
[3] Results pertain to Else Nutrition GH Ltd.
Note: Adjusted throughout for 1-for-5 cons. in June 2019

E.41 Elysee Development Corp.

Symbol - ELC **Exchange** - TSX-VEN **CUSIP** - 290737
Head Office - 900-1021 Hastings St W, Vancouver, BC, V6E 0C3 **Telephone** - (778) 373-1562 **Fax** - (604) 648-8665
Website - www.elyseedevelopment.com
Email - gcloetens@elyseedevelopment.com
Investor Relations - Guido Cloetens (778) 373-1562
Auditors - Lancaster & David C.A., Vancouver, B.C.
Lawyers - MLT Aikins LLP, Vancouver, B.C.
Transfer Agents - Computershare Trust Company of Canada Inc., Vancouver, B.C.

Profile - (Alta. 1996) Invests in private and public companies with a focus on publicly traded resource companies.

At Mar. 31, 2023, the company's most significant investments held included **Arizona Sonoran Copper Company Inc.**, **Oceanagold Corporation**, **Western Copper and Gold Corp.**, **Copper Mountain Mining Corp.**, **Dundee Precious Metals Inc.**, **Agnico Eagle Mines Limited**, **Green Impact Partners Inc.**, **Spartan Delta Corp.**, **Minera Alamos Inc.** and **SSR Mining Inc.**

Predecessor Detail - Name changed from Alberta Star Development Corp., July 15, 2015.

Directors - Martin A. Burian, chr., Vancouver, B.C.; Guido Cloetens, pres. & CEO, Belgium; Thibaut Lepouttre; Gaston J. Reymenants, Belgium

Other Exec. Officers - Gordon (Gord) Steblin, CFO

Capital Stock

	Authorized (shs.)	Outstanding (shs.)[1]
Preferred	unlimited	nil
Common	unlimited	28,450,613

[1] At May 3, 2023

Normal Course Issuer Bid - The company plans to make normal course purchases of up to 1,422,530 common shares representing 5% of the total outstanding. The bid commenced on May 11, 2023, and expires on May 10, 2024.

Major Shareholder - Guido Cloetens held 17.46% interest at Oct. 1, 2021.

Price Range - ELC/TSX-VEN

Year	Volume	High	Low	Close
2022	3,032,863	$0.83	$0.49	$0.53
2021	7,257,389	$0.88	$0.50	$0.80
2020	3,852,605	$0.54	$0.28	$0.50
2019	2,492,313	$0.42	$0.33	$0.36
2018	1,886,920	$0.40	$0.28	$0.35

Recent Close: $0.41

Capital Stock Changes - During 2022, 250,000 common shares were issued on exercise of options and 125,500 common shares were repurchased under a Normal Course Issuer Bid.

Dividends

ELC com N.S.R.
$0.01 Apr. 11/23 $0.02 Mar. 31/22
$0.03 Mar. 3/21
Paid in 2023: $0.01 2022: $0.02 2021: $0.03

Wholly Owned Subsidiaries

Elysee Development (U.S.), Inc., United States.

Note: The preceding list includes only the major related companies in which interests are held.

Financial Statistics

Periods ended:	12m Dec. 31/22[A]		12m Dec. 31/21[A]
	$000s	%Chg	$000s
Realized invest. gain (loss)	759		4,210
Unrealized invest. gain (loss)	2,686		3,844
Total revenue	**(1,573)**	**n.a.**	**546**
General & admin. expense	558		500
Stock-based compensation	193		5
Operating expense	**751**	**+49**	**505**
Operating income	**(2,324)**	**n.a.**	**41**
Finance costs, gross	4		3
Pre-tax income	**(2,328)**	**n.a.**	**38**
Net income	**(2,328)**	**n.a.**	**38**
Cash & equivalent	11,036		15,220
Accounts receivable	62		171
Current assets	11,769		15,397
Long-term investments	3,768		2,829
Total assets	**15,537**	**-15**	**18,226**
Accts. pay. & accr. liabs	66		48
Current liabilities	141		138
Shareholders' equity	15,396		18,088
Cash from oper. activs	**(284)**	**n.a.**	**(1,583)**
Cash from fin. activs	(556)		(400)
Net cash position	**790**	**-52**	**1,629**
	$		$
Earnings per share*	(0.08)		0.00
Cash flow per share*	(0.01)		(0.06)
Cash divd. per share*	0.02		0.03
	shs		shs
No. of shs. o/s*	28,497,113		28,372,613
Avg. no. of shs. o/s*	28,453,034		27,980,051
	%		%
Net profit margin	n.m.		6.96
Return on equity	(13.91)		0.21
Return on assets	(13.77)		0.22

* Common
[A] Reported in accordance with IFRS

Latest Results

Periods ended:	3m Mar. 31/23[A]		3m Mar. 31/22[A]
	$000s	%Chg	$000s
Total revenue	716	-14	837
Net income	575	-21	728
	$		$
Earnings per share*	0.02		0.03

* Common
[A] Reported in accordance with IFRS

Historical Summary
(as originally stated)

Fiscal Year	Total Rev.	Net Inc. Bef. Disc.	EPS*
	$000s	$000s	$
2022[A]	(1,573)	(2,328)	(0.08)
2021[A]	546	38	0.00
2020[A]	4,797	4,019	0.15
2019[A1]	2,441	1,817	0.07
2018[A]	1,893	1,289	0.06

* Common
[A] Reported in accordance with IFRS
[1] 13 months ended Dec. 31, 2019.

E.42 Emera Incorporated*

Symbol - EMA **Exchange** - TSX **CUSIP** - 290876
Head Office - 5151 Terminal Rd, Halifax, NS, B3J 1A1 **Telephone** - (902) 450-0507 **Toll-free** - (888) 450-0507
Website - www.emera.com
Email - dave.bezanson@emera.com
Investor Relations - Dave Bezanson (800) 358-1995
Auditors - Ernst & Young LLP C.A., Halifax, N.S.
Lawyers - Osler, Hoskin & Harcourt LLP
Transfer Agents - TSX Trust Company
FP500 Revenue Ranking - 85
Employees - 7,122 at Dec. 31, 2022

Profile - (N.S. 1998) Generates, transmits and distributes electricity, transmits and distributes gas, and provides utility energy services in Canada, the United States and in three Caribbean countries.

The company's operations are organized into five segments: Florida Electric Utility; Canadian Electric Utilities; Other Electric Utilities; Gas Utilities and Infrastructure; and Other.

Florida Electric Utility

Wholly owned **Tampa Electric Company** owns 6,549 MW of generating capacity, 2,171 km of transmission facilities and 19,916 km of distribution facilities that provide electric services to about 827,000 customers in west central Florida.

Canadian Electric Utilities

Operations include wholly owned **Nova Scotia Power Incorporated**, which provides electricity generation, transmission and distribution services to 541,000 customers throughout Nova Scotia with 2,420 MW of generating capacity, 5,000 km of transmission facilities and 28,000 of distribution facilities; wholly owned **NSP Maritime Link Inc.**, which owns and operates Maritime Link, which consists of two 170-km subsea transmission cables connecting Newfoundland and Nova Scotia; and 31.9% interest in the partnership capital of **Labrador-Island Link Limited Partnership**, a $3.7 billion electricity transmission project to enable the transmission of Muskrat Falls energy between Labrador and the island of Newfoundland.

Other Electric Utilities

Operations include wholly owned **Emera (Caribbean) Incorporated** and its wholly owned **Barbados Light & Power Company Limited**, an electric utility operator on the Caribbean island of Barbados serving 133,000 customers with 276 MW of generating capacity, 188 km of transmission lines and 3,789 km of distribution lines; wholly owned **Grand Bahama Power Company Limited**, an electric utility operator on Grand Bahama Island serving 19,000 customers with 98 MW of generating capacity, 90 km of transmission lines and 670 km of distribution lines; and 19.5% interest in **St. Lucia Electricity Services Limited**, an electric utility operator serving customers on the Caribbean island of St. Lucia.

Gas Utilities and Infrastructure

Operations include wholly owned **Peoples Gas System, Inc.**, which purchases, distributes and sells natural gas for about 468,000 customers in Florida through 24,300 km of natural gas mains and 13,500 km of service lines; wholly owned **New Mexico Gas Company, Inc.**, which purchases, transmits, distributes and sells natural gas for 545,000 customers in New Mexico through 2,426 km of transmission lines and 17,781 km of distributions lines; wholly owned **SeaCoast Gas Transmission, LLC**, an intrastate natural gas transmission service provider in Florida; wholly owned **Emera Brunswick Pipeline Company Ltd.**, which owns a 145-km pipeline that delivers re-gasified liquified natural gas from Saint John, N.B., to the United States border; and 12.9% interest in **Maritimes & Northeast Pipeline Limited Partnership**, a 1,400-km pipeline which transports natural gas throughout markets in Atlantic Canada and the northeastern United States.

Other

Includes wholly owned **Emera Energy Services, Inc.**, which purchases and sells natural gas and electricity, and provides related energy asset management services; wholly owned **Brooklyn Power Corporation**, which owns a 30-MW biomass co-generation electricity facility in Brooklyn, N.S.; and 50% interest in **Bear Swamp Power Company, LLC**, a 660-MW pumped storage hydroelectric facility in northwestern Massachusetts.

In March 31, 2022, the company sold 51.9% interest in subsidiary **Dominica Electricity Services Ltd.** (Domlec) to the Government of the Commonwealth of Dominica for an undisclosed amount. Domlec owns 26.7 MW of generating capacity, of which 75% is oil-fired and 25% is hydro. Domlec also owns 475 km of transmission facilities and 709 km of distribution facilities.

Predecessor Detail - Name changed from NS Power Holdings Incorporated, July 10, 2000.

Directors - M. Jacqueline (Jackie) Sheppard, chr., Calgary, Alta.; Scott C. Balfour, pres. & CEO, Halifax, N.S.; James V. (Jim) Bertram, Calgary, Alta.; Henry E. Demone, Lunenburg, N.S.; Paula Y. Gold-Williams, San Antonio, Tex.; Kent M. Harvey, New York, N.Y.; B. Lynn Loewen, Westmount, Qué.; Ian E. Robertson, Oakville, Ont.; Andrea S. Rosen, Toronto, Ont.; Karen H. Sheriff, Picton, Ont.; Jochen E. Tilk, Toronto, Ont.

Other Exec. Officers - Gregory W. (Greg) Blunden, CFO; Chris Heck, chief digital officer; Bruce A. Marchand, chief risk & sustainability officer; R. Michael (Mike) Roberts, chief HR officer; Michael R. Barrett, exec. v-p, legal & gen. counsel; Karen E. Hutt, exec. v-p, bus. devel. & strategy; Daniel P. Muldoon, exec. v-p, project devel. & opers. support; Stephen D. Aftanas, corp. sec.; Robert R. (Rob) Bennett, pres. & CEO, Emera Technologies LLC; Archie Collins, pres. & CEO, Tampa Electric Company; Dave McGregor, pres., Grand Bahama Power Company Limited & COO, Emera Caribbean Inc.; Ryan Shell, pres., New Mexico Gas Company; Judy A. Steele, pres. & COO, Emera Energy Incorporated; Helen J. Wesley, pres., Peoples Gas System

Capital Stock

	Authorized (shs.)	Outstanding (shs.)[1]
First Preferred	unlimited	
Series A		4,866,814
Series B		1,133,186
Series C		10,000,000
Series E		5,000,000
Series F		8,000,000
Series H		12,000,000
Series J		8,000,000
Series L		9,000,000
Second Preferred	unlimited	nil
Common	unlimited	273,000,000

[1] At Aug. 8, 2023

First Preferred - Issuable in series and non-voting.

Series A - Entitled to fixed non-cumulative annual dividends of $0.5456 per share payable quarterly to Aug. 15, 2025, and thereafter at a rate reset every five years equal to the five-year Government of Canada yield plus 1.84%. Redeemable on Aug. 15, 2025, and on August 15 every five years thereafter at $25 per share plus declared and unpaid dividends. Convertible at the holder's option on Aug. 15, 2025, and on August 15 every five years thereafter, into floating rate first preferred series B shares on a share-for-share basis, subject to certain conditions.

Series B - Entitled to floating rate non-cumulative annual dividends equal to the 90-day Canadian Treasury bill rate plus 1.84%. Redeemable on Aug. 15, 2025, and on August 15 every five years thereafter at $25 per share plus declared and unpaid dividends. Convertible at the holder's option on Aug. 15, 2025, and on August 15 every five years thereafter, into first preferred series A shares on a share-for-share basis, subject to certain conditions.

Series C - Entitled to fixed non-cumulative annual dividends of $0.40213 per share payable quarterly to Aug. 15, 2028, and thereafter at a rate reset every five years equal to the five-year Government of Canada yield plus 2.65%. Redeemable on Aug. 15, 2028, and on August 15 every five years thereafter at $25 per share plus declared and unpaid dividends. Convertible at the holder's option on Aug. 15, 2028, and on August 15 every five years thereafter, into floating rate first preferred series D shares on a share-for-share basis, subject to certain conditions. The series D shares would pay a quarterly dividend equal to the 90-day Canadian Treasury bill rate plus 2.65%.

Series E - Entitled to fixed cumulative annual dividends of $1.125 per share payable quarterly. Redeemable at $25 per share.

Series F - Entitled to fixed cumulative annual dividends of $1.05052 per share payable quarterly to Feb. 15, 2025, and thereafter at a rate reset every five years equal to the five-year Government of Canada yield plus 2.63%. Redeemable on Feb. 15, 2025, and on February 15 every five years thereafter at $25 per share plus declared and unpaid dividends. Convertible at the holder's option on Feb. 15, 2025, and on February 15 every five years thereafter, into floating rate first preferred series G shares on a share-for-share basis, subject to certain conditions. The series G shares would pay a quarterly dividend equal to the 90-day Canadian Treasury bill rate plus 2.63%.

Series H - Entitled to fixed cumulative annual dividends of $0.39525 per share payable quarterly to Aug. 15, 2028, and thereafter at a rate reset every five years equal to the five-year Government of Canada yield plus 2.54%, provided that such rate shall not be less than 4.9%. Redeemable on Aug. 15, 2028, and on August 15 every five years thereafter at $25 per share plus declared and unpaid dividends. Convertible at the holder's option on Aug. 15, 2028, and on August 15 every five years thereafter, into floating rate first preferred series I shares on a share-for-share basis, subject to certain conditions. The series I shares would pay a quarterly dividend equal to the 90-day Canadian Treasury bill rate plus 2.54%.

Series J - Entitled to fixed cumulative annual dividends of $1.0625 per share payable quarterly to May 15, 2026, and thereafter at a rate reset every five years equal to the five-year Government of Canada yield plus 3.28%, provided that such rate shall not be less than 4.25%. Redeemable on May 15, 2026, and on May 15 every five years thereafter at $25 per share plus declared and unpaid dividends. Convertible at the holder's option on May 15, 2026, and on May 15 every five years thereafter, into floating rate first preferred series K shares on a share-for-share basis, subject to certain conditions. The series K shares would pay a quarterly dividend equal to the 90-day Canadian Treasury bill rate plus 3.28%.

Series L - Entitled to fixed cumulative preferential annual dividends of $1.15 payable quarterly. Redeemable at $26 per share on or after Nov. 15, 2026, and declining by 25¢ per share annually to Nov. 15, 2030, and at $25 per share thereafter.

Second Preferred - Issuable in series and non-voting.

Common - One vote per share.

Options - At Dec. 31, 2022, options were outstanding to purchase 2,853,879 common shares at a weighted average exercise price of $50.41 per share.

Reserved - At Dec. 31, 2022, there were 6,000,000 common shares reserved for issuance under the senior management common share option plan and 2,700,000 common shares reserved for issuance under the employee common share purchase plan.

Major Shareholder - Widely held at Mar. 20, 2023.

Price Range - EMA/TSX

Year	Volume	High	Low	Close
2022	321,142,557	$65.23	$48.63	$51.75
2021	225,595,173	$63.71	$49.66	$63.22
2020	279,279,641	$60.94	$42.12	$54.10
2019	240,199,314	$58.89	$42.82	$55.79
2018	182,790,890	$47.57	$38.09	$43.71

Recent Close: $50.74

Capital Stock Changes - During 2022, common shares were issued as follows: 4,072,469 under an at-the-market offering, 4,210,000 under the dividend reinvestment plan and 600,000 on exercise of options.

Dividends

EMA com Ra $2.76 pa Q est. Nov. 15, 2022**
Prev. Rate: $2.65 est. Nov. 15, 2021
Prev. Rate: $2.55 est. Nov. 16, 2020
EMA.PR.A pfd 1st ser A cum. red. exch. Adj. Ra $0.5455 pa Q est. Nov. 16, 2020
EMA.PR.C pfd 1st ser C cum. red. exch. Adj. Ra $1.6085 pa Q est. Nov. 15, 2018
EMA.PR.E pfd 1st ser E cum. red. Adj. Ra $1.125 pa Q est. Aug. 15, 2013
EMA.PR.F pfd 1st ser F cum. red. exch. Adj. Ra $1.0505 pa Q est. May 15, 2020
EMA.PR.B pfd 1st ser B cum. red. exch. Fltg. Ra pa Q

$0.3955	Aug. 15/23	$0.3777	May 15/23
$0.357	Feb. 15/23	$0.2543	Nov. 15/22

Paid in 2023: $1.1302 2022: $0.6869 2021: $0.4873

EMA.PR.H pfd 1st ser H cum. red. exch. Adj. Ra $1.581 pa Q est. Aug. 15, 2018
EMA.PR.J pfd 1st ser J red. exch. Adj. Ra $1.0625 pa Q est. Aug. 16, 2021
Listed Apr 6/21.
EMA.PR.L pfd 1st ser L cum. red. Ra $1.15 pa Q
Listed Sep 24/21.
$0.1638**i** Nov. 15/21
** Reinvestment Option **i** Initial Payment

Long-Term Debt - Outstanding at Dec. 31, 2022:

B.A. & LIBOR loans due 2027	$403,000,000
2.9% notes due to 2023	500,000,000
6.75% US$ subord. notes due 2076	1,625,000,000
Tampa Electric notes & bonds	4,341,000,000
Peoples Gas System notes & bonds	772,000,000
New Mexico Gas notes & bonds	832,000,000
Emera U.S. Finance LP notes	3,725,000,000
Nova Scotia Power debt	3,546,000,000
Emera Brunswick Pipeline credit facility	249,000,000
Emera (Caribbean) Incorporated	449,000,000
Fair market value adjustment	2,000,000
Less: Debt issuance costs	126,000,000
	16,318,000,000
Less: Current portion	574,000,000
	15,744,000,000

Minimum long-term debt repayments were reported as follows:

2023	$574,000,000
2024	1,613,000,000
2025	262,000,000
2026	3,110,000,000
2027	946,000,000
Thereafter	9,937,000,000

Note - In March 2023, Nova Scotia Power Incorporated completed an offering of $300,000,000 principal amount of 4.951% series 2023-1 unsecured notes due Nov. 15, 2032 and $200,000,000 principal amount of 5.355% series 2023-2 unsecured notes due Mar, 24, 2053. In May 2023, offering of $500,000,000 principal amount of 4.838% senior unsecured notes due may 2, 2030, Series 2023-1 was completed.

Wholly Owned Subsidiaries

Emera Brunswick Pipeline Company Ltd., N.B.
Emera (Caribbean) Incorporated, Barbados.
- 100% int. in **Barbados Light & Power Company Limited**, Barbados.
- 100% int. in **Grand Bahama Power Company Limited**, Bahamas.
- 19.5% int. in **St. Lucia Electricity Services Limited**, Saint Lucia.

Emera Energy Incorporated, Halifax, N.S.
- 50% int. in **Bear Swamp Power Company, LLC**, Mass.
- 100% int. in **Brooklyn Power Corporation**, Brooklyn, N.S.
- 100% int. in **Emera Energy Services, Inc.**, Halifax, N.S.

Emera Energy LP, N.S.
Emera Newfoundland & Labrador Holdings Inc., Labrador City, N.L.
- 100% int. in **ENL Island Link Inc.**, N.L.
- 31.9% int. in **Labrador-Island Link Limited Partnership**, N.L.
- 100% int. in **NSP Maritime Link Inc.**, N.L.

Emera Reinsurance Limited, Barbados.
Emera Technologies LLC
Emera U.S. Finance LP, United States.
Emera U.S. Holdings Inc., United States.
- 100% int. in **TECO Energy, Inc.**, Tampa, Fla.
  - 100% int. in **New Mexico Gas Company, Inc.**, Albuquerque, N.M.
  - 100% int. in **SeaCoast Gas Transmission, LLC**, Del.
  - 100% int. in **TECO Finance Inc.**
  - 100% int. in **TECO Gas Operations, Inc.**, Fla.
    - 100% int. in **Peoples Gas System, Inc.**, Tampa, Fla.
  - 100% int. in **Tampa Electric Company**, Tampa, Fla.

Nova Scotia Power Incorporated, Halifax, N.S. (see separate coverage)

Investments

12.9% int. in **Maritimes & Northeast Pipeline Limited Partnership**, Halifax, N.S.

Note: The preceding list includes only the major related companies in which interests are held.

Financial Statistics

Periods ended:	12m Dec. 31/22[A]		12m Dec. 31/21[A]
	$000s	%Chg	$000s
Operating revenue	**7,588,000**	**+32**	**5,765,000**
Other operating expense	4,934,000		3,933,000
Operating expense	**4,934,000**	**+25**	**3,933,000**
Operating income	**2,654,000**	**+45**	**1,832,000**
Deprec., depl. & amort.	952,000		902,000
Finance costs, net	709,000		611,000
Investment income	129,000		143,000
Write-downs/write-offs	(73,000)[1]		nil
Pre-tax income	**1,194,000**	**+115**	**555,000**
Income taxes	185,000		(6,000)
Net income	**1,009,000**	**+80**	**561,000**
Net inc. for equity hldrs	**1,008,000**	**+80**	**560,000**
Net inc. for non-cont. int	**1,000**	**0**	**1,000**
Cash & equivalent	332,000		417,000
Inventories	769,000		538,000
Accounts receivable	1,503,000		1,064,000
Current assets	4,896,000		3,136,000
Long-term investments	1,418,000		1,382,000
Fixed assets, net	22,996,000		20,353,000
Right-of-use assets	58,000		58,000
Intangibles, net	6,012,000		5,696,000
Total assets	**39,742,000**	**+16**	**34,244,000**
Bank indebtedness	2,726,000		1,742,000
Accts. pay. & accr. liabs	2,199,000		1,642,000
Current liabilities	7,287,000		4,878,000
Long-term debt, gross	16,318,000		14,658,000
Long-term debt, net	15,744,000		14,196,000
Long-term lease liabilities	59,000		59,000
Preferred share equity	1,422,000		1,422,000
Shareholders' equity	11,427,000		10,116,000
Non-controlling interest	14,000		34,000
Cash from oper. activs	**913,000**	**-23**	**1,185,000**
Cash from fin. activs	1,555,000		1,311,000
Cash from invest. activs	(2,569,000)		(2,332,000)
Net cash position	**332,000**	**-20**	**417,000**
Capital expenditures	(2,596,000)		(2,359,000)
Capital disposals	n.a.		3,000
Pension fund surplus	5,000		78,000
	$		$
Earnings per share*	3.56		1.98
Cash flow per share*	3.43		4.61
Cash divd. per share*	2.68		2.58
	shs		shs
No. of shs. o/s*	269,950,000		261,070,000
Avg. no. of shs. o/s*	266,000,000		257,200,000
	%		%
Net profit margin	13.30		9.73
Return on equity	10.11		6.04
Return on assets	2.73		1.71
Foreign sales percent	77		73
No. of employees (FTEs)	7,122		7,140

* Common
[A] Reported in accordance with U.S. GAAP
[1] Consists entirely of goodwill impairment for wholly owned Grand Bahama Power Company Limited that is driven by the effects of macro-economic factors on discount rate calculations, including the risk-free rate assumption.

Latest Results

Periods ended:	6m June 30/23[A]		6m June 30/22[A]
	$000s	%Chg	$000s
Operating revenue	3,851,000	+13	3,395,000
Net income	620,000	+90	326,000
	$		$
Earnings per share*	2.17		1.12

* Common
[A] Reported in accordance with U.S. GAAP

Historical Summary
(as originally stated)

Fiscal Year	Oper. Rev. $000s	Net Inc. Bef. Disc. $000s	EPS* $
2022[A]	7,588,000	1,009,000	3.56
2021[A]	5,765,000	561,000	1.98
2020[A]	5,506,000	984,000	3.78
2019[A]	6,111,000	710,000	2.76
2018[A]	6,524,000	747,000	3.05

* Common
[A] Reported in accordance with U.S. GAAP

E.43 Emerge Commerce Ltd.

Symbol - ECOM **Exchange** - TSX-VEN **CUSIP** - 29104G
Head Office - 400-355 Adelaide St W, Toronto, ON, M5V 1S2 **Telephone** - (416) 479-9590
Website - www.emerge-commerce.com
Email - investor@emerge-brands.com
Investor Relations - Jonathan Leong (416) 479-9590
Auditors - MNP LLP C.A., Toronto, Ont.
Lawyers - CP LLP, Toronto, Ont.
Transfer Agents - TSX Trust Company, Toronto, Ont.
Profile - (Ont. 2017) Operates online shopping websites in Canada and the U.S., providing access to pet supplies, meat subscriptions and apparel, groceries, golf experiences and products, nearby escapes and family offers.

The company's main operating e-commerce brands include wholesalepet.com, which offers pet supplies for pet boutiques, stores, and service businesses; trulocal.ca, a locally sourced meat subscription service and apparel store; underpar.com and justgolfstuff.ca, which offer golf experiences and products; carnivoreclub.co., which offers premium artisanal meat subscriptions; wagjag.com, which offers local restaurant, spas and other experiences for family audiences; berightback.ca., which offers deals on hotels, bed and breakfast and others; and wanlow.com, which offers outdoor playing and learning about nature for kids.

Other brands include buytopia.ca and shop.ca., which the company continues to operate with the primary purpose of driving online traffic to its other online shopping portals.

In July 2024, the company agreed to sell substantially all of the assets related to its WagJag and BeRightBack business to **15124174 Canada Inc.** for $1,000,000 in cash. WagJag and BeRight Back are a daily deals e-commerce business in Canada for discounted vouchers. Closing is expected to occur on or prior to Aug. 25, 2023.

Recent Merger and Acquisition Activity

Status: completed **Revised:** Apr. 28, 2023
UPDATE: The transaction was completed. PREVIOUS: Emerge Commerce Ltd. agreed to sell indirect wholly owned BattlBox, LLC to Battlbrands Holdings, Inc. for US$7,170,203, consisting of US$6,008,666 cash and the assumption of US$1,161,537 of outstanding liabilities. Battlebrands would assume the BattlBox brand, which offers survival, outdoor and camping goods subscriptions. The transaction excluded Carnivore Club, which offers premium artisanal meat subscriptions; Carnivore Club would remain an EMERGE brand.

Predecessor Detail - Name changed from Aumento Capital VII Corporation, Dec. 7, 2020, pursuant to the Qualifying Transaction reverse takeover acquisition of EMERGE Commerce Inc. and concurrent amalgamation of EMERGE with wholly owned 1260383 B.C. Ltd.; basis 1 new for 1.33333 old shs.

Directors - Drew Green, chr., Vancouver, B.C.; Ghassan Halazon, pres. & CEO, Toronto, Ont.; John M. Kim, Toronto, Ont.; Ian M. McKinnon, Toronto, Ont.; Jonson Sun, Toronto, Ont.

Other Exec. Officers - Fazal Khaishgi, COO; Jonathan Leong, CFO; Maurice Finn, v-p, sales

Capital Stock

	Authorized (shs.)	Outstanding (shs.)[1]
Common	unlimited	106,722,652

[1] At May 26, 2023

Major Shareholder - Ghassan Halazon held 10.03% interest at June 6, 2022.

Price Range - ECOM/TSX-VEN

Year	Volume	High	Low	Close
2022	28,453,962	$0.90	$0.07	$0.08
2021	45,990,421	$1.72	$0.58	$0.62
2020	10,299,999	$1.74	$0.67	$1.14
2019	18,000	$0.67	$0.67	$0.67
2018	30,750	$0.73	$0.67	$0.67

Consolidation: 1-for-1.33333 cons. in Dec. 2020
Recent Close: $0.04
Capital Stock Changes - In July 2023, private placement of 14,960,000 units (1 common share & 1 warrant) at 5¢ per unit was completed, with warrants exercisable at 10¢ per share for two years.

Wholly Owned Subsidiaries

Carnivore Club Subscription Box Canada Inc., Canada.
EMERGE Brands Inc., Toronto, Ont.
- 100% int. in **Athletesvideo Ltd.**, Ont.
  - 100% int. in **2161184 Ontario Inc.**, Toronto, Ont.
    - 100% int. in **UnderPar Golf LLC**, Calif.
      - 100% int. in **Just Golf Stuff LLC**, Calif.
- 100% int. in **Evandale Caviar Inc.**, Ont.
- 100% int. in **2785160 Ontario Inc.**, Ont.

Emerge US Holdings LLC, United States.
- 100% int. in **Carnivore Club, LLC**, United States.
- 100% int. in **Retail Store Networks, Inc.**, United States.

truLOCAL Inc., Kitchener, Ont.
- 100% int. in **Farmbox Inc.**, Ont.
- 100% int. in **truLOCAL (US) Inc.**, Del.

Financial Statistics

Periods ended:	12m Dec. 31/21[A]		12m Dec. 31/20[oA]
	$000s	%Chg	$000s
Operating revenue	**34,829**	**+278**	**9,204**
Cost of goods sold	19,718		2,031
Salaries & benefits	6,122		1,979
General & admin expense	7,750		4,387
Stock-based compensation	1,599		1,774
Operating expense	**35,189**	**+246**	**10,170**
Operating income	**(360)**	**n.a.**	**(966)**
Deprec., depl. & amort.	3,976		1,555
Finance costs, gross	1,849		1,640
Pre-tax income	**(6,987)**	**n.a.**	**(4,220)**
Income taxes	(427)		210
Net income	**(6,561)**	**n.a.**	**(4,430)**
Cash & equivalent	7,767		12,395
Inventories	4,720		897
Accounts receivable	1,928		1,302
Current assets	16,424		15,219
Fixed assets, net	685		44
Right-of-use assets	140		144
Intangibles, net	62,893		27,765
Total assets	**80,275**	**+85**	**43,456**
Bank indebtedness	24,324		7,471
Accts. pay. & accr. liabs	11,862		10,615
Current liabilities	43,007		21,463
Long-term lease liabilities	32		101
Shareholders' equity	27,004		18,075
Cash from oper. activs	**(3,431)**	**n.a.**	**(186)**
Cash from fin. activs	26,179		9,545
Cash from invest. activs	(27,336)		(5,605)
Net cash position	**7,767**	**-37**	**12,395**
Capital expenditures	(36)		(8)
	$		$
Earnings per share*	(0.07)		(0.07)
Cash flow per share*	(0.04)		(0.00)
	shs		shs
No. of shs. o/s*	103,578,529		88,367,301
Avg. no. of shs. o/s*	95,035,845		62,869,392
	%		%
Net profit margin	(18.84)		(48.13)
Return on equity	(29.11)		(38.79)
Return on assets	(7.80)		(7.47)

* Common
[o] Restated
[A] Reported in accordance with IFRS

Latest Results

Periods ended:	6m June 30/22[A]		6m June 30/21[A]
	$000s	%Chg	$000s
Operating revenue	30,837	+122	13,910
Net income	(3,646)	n.a.	(4,237)
	$		$
Earnings per share*	(0.04)		(0.05)

* Common
[A] Reported in accordance with IFRS

Historical Summary
(as originally stated)

Fiscal Year	Oper. Rev. $000s	Net Inc. Bef. Disc. $000s	EPS* $
2021[A]	34,829	(6,561)	(0.07)
2020[A1]	9,203	(4,430)	(0.07)
2019[A2]	4,160	(3,050)	(0.07)
2018[A2]	3,968	(487)	(0.01)

* Common
[A] Reported in accordance with IFRS
[1] Results reflect the Dec. 7, 2020, reverse takeover acquisition of EMERGE Commerce Inc.
[2] Results pertain to EMERGE Commerce Inc.
Note: Adjusted throughout for 1-for-1.333333 cons. in Dec. 2020

E.44 Emergence Global Enterprises Inc.

Symbol - EMRG **Exchange** - CSE (S) **CUSIP** - 29103M
Head Office - 14 Centre St, Essex, ON, N8M 1N9 **Toll-free** - (855) 438-3674 **Fax** - (519) 776-8161
Website - www.emergenceglobalinc.com
Email - joe@emergenceglobalinc.com
Investor Relations - Joseph A. Byrne (519) 257-0460
Auditors - Olayinka Oyebola & Co. C.A., Lagos, Nigeria
Bankers - Bank of Montreal, Vancouver, B.C.
Lawyers - Bennett Jones LLP
Transfer Agents - Computershare Trust Company of Canada Inc., Vancouver, B.C.
Profile - (B.C. 2011) Acquires, creates and builds reputable natural health consumer foods, products and brands.

Wholly owned **Nubreed Nutrition, Inc.** develops and distributes branded sports and nutrition specialty supplements in the U.S., Canada,

Australia and other jurisdictions. Products include Metadyne, Tenacity and Phantom XS powders and capsules for weight loss; Notorious pre-workout powder supplements; Myoblast protein powder blend; and Helix BCAA++ recovery and amino acid powder.

Wholly owned **ProDynn Distribution, LLC** distributes branded all-natural foods, sports and nutrition specialty supplements throughout North America, with FitnessONE.com as its flagship retail outlet.

Wholly owned **Edge Nutrition (Canada) Inc.** offers protein powders, vitamins, supplements and herbal remedies under more than 40 different brands and targets healthy and active lifestyles, keto, paleo, vegan and fasting conscious consumers. Edge Nutrition has a retail location in Windsor, Ont., as well as an e-commerce platform on www.edgenutrition.com.

Wholly owned **Well & Wild Superfoods Ltd.** develops and provides advanced health products including Cleansify™, a natural tonic that helps improve circulation and provides all natural relief from bloating, digestive upset, heartburn and gas. Cleansify is available at Whole Foods Canada, Healthy Planet, Organic Garage, Nature's Emporium, Nature's Source, Choices Market, select Foodland (Sobeys) locations and online through WELL.ca.

Wholly owned **Coastal Rock Trading LLC** develops health and sport nutrition brands and supplies new and advanced health products to consumers, distributors and retailers in Australia, New Zealand, Hong Kong, Taiwan, Vietnam, UAE, Peru, India, Canada, the U.S., Puerto Rico and the Dominican Republic.

Wholly owned **O'Grow Investments Inc.** owns Complete Commercial Automated growing systems with vertical technologies and innovations for indoor farming.

Also develops tinctures from specialty herbs such as Echinacea Augustifolia and others. This specialty herbs are grown on a farm near Sherwood Park, Alta.

In December 2022, the company acquired intellectual property, technology and patents from **Alvera Inc.** for issuance of 18,000,000 common shares at a deemed value of Cdn$0.05 per share. Alvera, a private Alberta-based health and wellness company, focuses on targeted delivery systems and unique technologies focused on the human endocannabinoid system.

On Apr. 12, 2022, the company acquired **O'Grow Investments Inc.**, including Complete Commercial Automated growing systems with vertical technologies and innovations for indoor farming, for issuance of 10,850,000 common shares (issued on Apr. 19, 2022).

On Mar. 31, 2022, the company acquired certain vertical farming assets in Strathcona cty., Alta., from **J-CAL Investments Inc.** for issuance of 6,469,306 common shares (issued on Apr. 7, 2022).

Common suspended from CSE, Mar. 9, 2023.

Predecessor Detail - Name changed from Velocity Data Inc., Feb. 15, 2020.

Directors - Joseph A. (Joe) Byrne, chr. & CEO, Essex, Ont.; Diego F. Rodriguez, v-p & treas., Bogota, Colombia; Alex Tarrabain, compt.; Cameron Canzellarini, Old Saybrook, Conn.; Christian J. Gallant, Tilbury, Ont.; David McLoughlin, N.J.; Rick Purdy, Edmonton, Alta.

Other Exec. Officers - Harvey Panesar, pres.; Raju Kalsi, CFO; Harold A. Aubrey de Lavenu, contr., opers.

Capital Stock

	Authorized (shs.)	Outstanding (shs.)[1]
Preferred	unlimited	nil
Common	unlimited	80,042,748

[1] At July 31, 2022

Major Shareholder - Joseph A. (Joe) Byrne held 18.75% interest at July 8, 2022.

Price Range - GTR/TSX-VEN (D)

Year	Volume	High	Low	Close
2022	899,764	$0.30	$0.03	$0.09
2021	885,317	$1.62	$0.16	$0.17
2020	927,194	$2.60	$0.22	$0.50
2019	640,539	$0.49	$0.01	$0.15
2018	433,990	$0.16	$0.01	$0.01

Recent Close: $0.05

Capital Stock Changes - In December 2022, 18,000,000 common shares were issued pursuant to the acquisition of intellectual property, technology and patents of multiple technologies.

In April 2022, 6,469,306 common shares were issued pursuant to the acquisition of certain vertical farming assets and 10,850,000 common shares were issued pursuant to the acquisition of O'Grow Investments Inc.

Wholly Owned Subsidiaries

Coastal Rock Trading LLC, Del.
Edge Nutrition (Canada) Inc., Canada.
Nubreed Nutrition, Inc., Troy, Mich.
O'Grow Investments Inc., Canada.
ProDynn Distribution, LLC, Wis.
Well & Wild Superfoods Ltd., Canada.

Financial Statistics

Periods ended:	12m Oct. 31/21[A]		12m Oct. 31/20[oA]
	US$000s	%Chg	US$000s
Operating revenue	**1,926**	**n.a.**	**nil**
Cost of sales	1,438		nil
General & admin expense	676		304
Operating expense	**2,114**	**+595**	**304**
Operating income	**(188)**	**n.a.**	**(304)**
Finance costs, net	95		38
Pre-tax income	**(283)**	**n.a.**	**6,576**
Net inc. bef. disc. opers	**(283)**	**n.a.**	**6,576**
Income from disc. opers	nil		(221)
Net income	**(283)**	**n.a.**	**6,355**
Cash & equivalent	208		3
Inventories	521		nil
Accounts receivable	87		nil
Current assets	978		3
Fixed assets, net	142		nil
Intangibles, net	3,937		nil
Total assets	**5,058**	**n.m.**	**3**
Accts. pay. & accr. liabs	336		237
Current liabilities	1,463		569
Long-term debt, gross	1,630		627
Long-term debt, net	776		374
Shareholders' equity	2,818		(940)
Cash from oper. activs	**(710)**	**n.a.**	**(57)**
Cash from fin. activs	1,002		66
Cash from invest. activs	(191)		nil
Net cash position	**208**	**n.m.**	**3**
Capital expenditures	(191)		nil
	US$		US$
Earnings per share*	(0.01)		0.39
Cash flow per share*	(0.03)		(0.00)
	shs		shs
No. of shs. o/s*	20,681,971		16,156,971
Avg. no. of shs. o/s*	20,681,974		16,146,521
	%		%
Net profit margin	(14.69)		n.a.
Return on equity	n.m.		n.m.
Return on assets	(11.18)		n.m.

* Common
[o] Restated
[A] Reported in accordance with IFRS

Latest Results

Periods ended:	9m July 31/22[A]		9m July 31/21[A]
	US$000s	%Chg	US$000s
Operating revenue	1,524	+38	1,104
Net income	(23)	n.a.	(165)
	US$		US$
Earnings per share*	(0.00)		(0.02)

* Common
[A] Reported in accordance with IFRS

Historical Summary
(as originally stated)

Fiscal Year	Oper. Rev. US$000s	Net Inc. Bef. Disc. US$000s	EPS* US$
2021[A]	1,926	(283)	(0.01)
2020[A]	nil	6,576	0.39
2019[A]	nil	(124)	(0.01)
2018[A]	nil	(156)	(0.01)
2017[A]	1,346	(712)	(0.07)

* Common
[A] Reported in accordance with IFRS

E.45 Emergia Inc.

Symbol - EMER **Exchange** - CSE (S) **CUSIP** - 29102V
Head Office - 402-185 av Dorval, Dorval, QC, H9S 5J9 **Telephone** - (514) 420-1414 **Toll-free** - (888) 520-1414 **Fax** - (866) 285-4823
Website - www.emergia.com
Email - hpetit@emergia.com
Investor Relations - Henri Petit (888) 520-1414 ext. 231
Auditors - Raymond Chabot Grant Thornton LLP C.A., Montréal, Qué.
Bankers - Royal Bank of Canada; Canadian Imperial Bank of Commerce; The Toronto-Dominion Bank
Lawyers - BCF LLP, Montréal, Qué.
Transfer Agents - TSX Trust Company, Toronto, Ont.
Profile - (Can. 2018; orig. B.C., 2015 amalg.) Develops, acquires and manages multi-purpose real estate, including retail, multi-suite residential, industrial and office buildings as well as land for future development.

The company focuses on small to medium-sized portfolios of mixed-use properties in Ontario, Quebec and Greece. Properties are classified into revenue-generating properties, which are held directly by Emergia and through joint venture arrangements including 25%-owned **12028735 Canada Inc.** and 30%-owned retail plazas in Ontario; properties held for development; and properties held for sale.

At June 30, 2022, the property portfolio included nine properties consisting of six retail plazas in Ontario and three retail and office properties in Quebec; five properties held for development consisting of three mixed-use properties in Quebec (2) and Ontario, a multi-family property in Quebec and a hospitality property in Greece; and one property held for sale in Quebec.

Common suspended from CSE, July 20, 2023.

Recent Merger and Acquisition Activity

Status: completed **Revised:** Mar. 31, 2022
UPDATE: The transaction was completed. Total consideration was $41,031,152, consisting of the assumption of $28,968,732 of existing mortgages, issuance of 9,776,800 class A common shares at $1.00 per share and $2,285,620 cash. PREVIOUS: Emergia Inc. agreed to acquire 31% of the total value of a portfolio consisting of six retail plazas in six Ontario cities for $40,690,000, consisting of cash, assumption of debt and issuance of 10,140,000 class A common shares at a deemed price of $1.00 per share. The portfolio included 568,000 sq. ft. of gross leasable area (GLA), with an additional development potential of 196,000 sq. ft. of GLA.

Status: completed **Announced:** June 21, 2021
UPDATE: The transaction was terminated. PREVIOUS: Emergia Inc. agreed to acquire 85% interests in a portfolio of income producing properties in Ontario, for $121,300,000, consisting of $89,300,000 payable by assumption of debt and $32,000,000 of combined cash and Emergia shares. The portfolio consists of six retail plazas having an aggregate gross leasable area (GLA) of 550,000 sq. ft. and a land to develop an additional 200,000 sq. ft. of GLA, part of which is currently in development. The transaction is expected to close in the third quarter of 2021. In addition, Emergia is in advanced discussions for the acquisition of the remaining 15% interest in the portfolio.

Predecessor Detail - Name changed from The Delma Group Inc., Jan. 21, 2020.

Directors - Henri Petit, chr., pres. & CEO, Lorraine, Qué.; François Castonguay†, Carignan, Qué.; Joseph Cianci, Laval, Qué.; Panagiotis Mitropoulos, Greece; Faraj M. Nakhleh, Montréal, Qué.; Roy Scaini, Woodbridge, Ont.; Lou Valeriati, Richmond Hill, Ont.

Other Exec. Officers - Ratha Siv, CFO & treas.; Stéphane Beaudoin, v-p, opers.; Isabelle Lamy, v-p, legal affairs & corp. sec.
† Lead director

Capital Stock

	Authorized (shs.)	Outstanding (shs.)[1]
Class A Common	unlimited	44,505,065
Class B Common	unlimited	4,510,891

[1] At June 30, 2022

Class A Common - One vote per share.

Class B Common - Automatically convertible into class A common shares on Mar. 23, 2023, on a 1-for-1 basis. 100 votes per share.

Major Shareholder - Henri Petit held 19.38% interest at May 28, 2022.

Price Range - EMER/CSE (S)

Year	Volume	High	Low	Close
2022	6,141,656	$1.35	$0.20	$0.33
2021	1,313,576	$1.25	$0.55	$0.95
2020	802,800	$1.55	$0.50	$1.00
2019	347,109	$2.50	$0.51	$1.00
2018	57,733	$7.25	$1.05	$1.70

Recent Close: $0.19

Capital Stock Changes - In March 2022, 9,776,800 class A common shares were issued pursuant to the acquisition of an interest in six Ontario retail plazas.

Wholly Owned Subsidiaries

Bromont I Limited Partnership
Emergia Asset Management Quebec Inc., Qué.
Emergia Canada Inc., Canada.
Emergia Pure Bromont Inc., Bromont, Qué.
Emergia Real Estate Ontario Inc., Ont.
Emergia Real Estate Quebec Inc., Qué.
- 100% int. in **Aux 22 Sentiers Inc.**, Canada.
- 100% int. in **Emergia Real Estate Inc.**, Canada.
- 100% int. in **GHP Real Estate Corporation Inc.**, Canada.
- 100% int. in **Lupa Investments Inc.**, Dorval, Qué.

NTA Development Corporation
9216-3583 Québec Inc., Qué.
9335-5709 Quebec Inc., Canada.

Investments

25% int. in **12028735 Canada Inc.**, Canada.

Note: The preceding list includes only the major related companies in which interests are held.

Financial Statistics

Periods ended:	12m Dec. 31/21[A]		12m Dec. 31/20[oA]
	$000s	%Chg	$000s
Total revenue	**555**	**-80**	**2,733**
Rental operating expense	201		1,509
General & admin. expense	2,172		2,388
Operating expense	**2,373**	**-39**	**3,897**
Operating income	**(1,818)**	**n.a.**	**(1,164)**
Investment income	642		13
Deprec. & amort.	nil		2
Finance costs, gross	2,748		4,882
Write-downs/write-offs	nil		(368)
Pre-tax income	**36,998**	**n.a.**	**(27,149)**
Income taxes	4,351		44
Net income	**32,647**	**n.a.**	**(27,193)**
Cash & equivalent	438		82
Accounts receivable	91		148
Current assets	7,016		2,185
Long-term investments	3,306		2,915
Fixed assets	3		3
Income-producing props	120,975		51,139
Properties under devel.	nil		18,115
Property interests, net	1,772		69,257
Total assets	**131,300**	**+70**	**77,036**
Accts. pay. & accr. liabs	5,952		6,563
Current liabilities	13,956		33,384
Long-term debt, gross	50,771		42,815
Long-term debt, net	43,074		16,038
Shareholders' equity	69,274		27,239
Cash from oper. activs	**(2,867)**	**n.a.**	**(1,139)**
Cash from fin. activs	11,955		800
Cash from invest. activs	(8,733)		465
Net cash position	**438**	**+434**	**82**
Increase in property	10,113		nil
Decrease in property	1,380		465
	$		$
Earnings per share*	1.10		(1.43)
Cash flow per share*	(0.10)		(0.06)
	shs		shs
No. of shs. o/s*	32,904,085		24,350,265
Avg. no. of shs. o/s*	29,714,699		18,981,561
	%		%
Net profit margin	n.m.		(994.99)
Return on equity	67.65		(87.21)
Return on assets	33.68		(23.49)

* Class A & B
[o] Restated
[A] Reported in accordance with IFRS

Latest Results

Periods ended:	6m June 30/22[A]		6m June 30/21[A]
	$000s	%Chg	$000s
Total revenue	259	-9	284
Net income	2,892	n.m.	166
	$		$
Earnings per share*	0.06		0.01

* Class A & B
[A] Reported in accordance with IFRS

Historical Summary
(as originally stated)

Fiscal Year	Total Rev.	Net Inc. Bef. Disc.	EPS*
	$000s	$000s	$
2021[A]	555	32,647	1.10
2020[A]	2,733	(27,193)	(1.43)
2019[A]	2,911	(5,984)	(0.43)
2018[A1]	1,515	(19,116)	(1.78)
2017[A2]	15	(460)	(4.00)

* Class A & B
[A] Reported in accordance with IFRS
[1] Results reflect the Mar. 23, 2018, reverse takeover acquisition of the Delma Group.
[2] Results for 2017 and prior years pertain to Aydon Income Properties Inc.

Note: Adjusted throughout for 1-for-200 cons. in Mar. 2018

E.46 Empatho Holdings Inc.

Symbol - EMPH **Exchange** - CSE **CUSIP** - 29158D
Head Office - 2600-222 Bay St, PO Box 37, Toronto, ON, M5K 1B7 **Telephone** - (416) 710-0664
Website - www.empatho.com
Email - yan@empatho.com
Investor Relations - Yan Namer (416) 710-0064
Auditors - MNP LLP C.A., Toronto, Ont.
Transfer Agents - Capital Transfer Agency Inc., Toronto, Ont.
Profile - (B.C. 2021; orig. Sask., 1981) Offers a smart solution powered by proprietary PsychAI™ artificial intelligence allowing patients to manage their own health and achieve wellness goals.

Predecessor Detail - Name changed from Shane Resources Ltd., Dec. 3, 2021, pursuant to the reverse takeover acquisition of Empatho Corp. and subsequent amalgamation of Empatho with wholly owned 13348776 Canada Inc.

Directors - Dr. Rakesh Jetly, chr., Ottawa, Ont.; Terri Clouse, Nashville, Tenn.

Other Exec. Officers - Yan Namer, CEO & corp. sec.; John C. Ross, CFO; Hamid Boland, chief tech. officer; Dr. Joshua (Josh) Granek, chief science officer

Capital Stock

	Authorized (shs.)	Outstanding (shs.)[1]
Common	unlimited	72,552,000

[1] At Dec. 29, 2021

Major Shareholder - Hybrid Financial Ltd. held 19.16% interest at Dec. 29, 2021.

Price Range - EMPH/CSE

Year	Volume	High	Low	Close
2022	19,515,333	$0.25	$0.01	$0.01
2021	50,943	$0.40	$0.25	$0.25

Recent Close: $0.01

Capital Stock Changes - On Dec. 14, 2021, 64,352,000 common shares were issued pursuant to the reverse takeover acquisition of Empatho Corp. and 4,000,000 common shares were issued as finder's fee.

Wholly Owned Subsidiaries

Empatho Corp., Toronto, Ont.
- 100% int. in **Empatho Labs Inc.**, Toronto, Ont.

Financial Statistics

Periods ended:	49w Oct. 31/21[A1]		12m Dec. 31/20[A2]
	$000s	%Chg	$000s
Research & devel. expense	1,152		n.a.
General & admin expense	1,162		53
Stock-based compensation	181		n.a.
Operating expense	**2,495**	**n.a.**	**53**
Operating income	**(2,495)**	**n.a.**	**(53)**
Pre-tax income	**(2,496)**	**n.a.**	**(53)**
Net income	**(2,496)**	**n.a.**	**(53)**
Cash & equivalent	231		19
Accounts receivable	n.a.		11
Current assets	3,386		30
Total assets	**3,386**	**n.a.**	**30**
Accts. pay. & accr. liabs	1,431		20
Current liabilities	1,431		20
Shareholders' equity	(1,183)		10
Cash from oper. activs	**(901)**	**n.a.**	**(56)**
Cash from fin. activs	4,150		75
Net cash position	**3,249**	**n.a.**	**19**
	$		$
Earnings per share*	(0.06)		(0.00)
Cash flow per share*	(0.02)		(0.00)
	shs		shs
No. of shs. o/s	n.a.		n.a.
Avg. no. of shs. o/s*	43,699,420		n.a.
	%		%
Net profit margin	n.a.		n.a.
Return on equity	n.m.		n.m.
Return on assets	(146.14)		(321.21)

* Common
[A] Reported in accordance with IFRS
[1] Results pertain to Empatho Corp.
[2] Results for 2020 and prior years pertain to Shane Resources Ltd.

Historical Summary
(as originally stated)

Fiscal Year	Oper. Rev.	Net Inc. Bef. Disc.	EPS*
	$000s	$000s	$
2021[A1]	nil	(2,496)	(0.06)
2020[A]	nil	(53)	(0.00)
2019[A]	nil	(88)	(0.00)

* Common
[A] Reported in accordance with IFRS
[1] 49 weeks ended Oct. 31, 2021.

E.47 Empire Company Limited*

Symbol - EMP.A **Exchange** - TSX **CUSIP** - 291843
Head Office - 115 King St, Stellarton, NS, B0K 1S0 **Telephone** - (902) 752-8371 **Fax** - (902) 755-6477
Website - www.empireco.ca
Email - investor.relations@empireco.ca
Investor Relations - Katie Brine (905) 238-7124 ext. 2092
Auditors - PricewaterhouseCoopers LLP C.A., Halifax, N.S.
Lawyers - Stewart McKelvey LLP, Halifax, N.S.
Transfer Agents - TSX Trust Company, Montréal, Qué.
FP500 Revenue Ranking - 20
Employees - 67,000 at May 6, 2023
Profile - (N.S. 1963 amalg.) Conducts food retailing operations through wholly owned **Sobeys Inc.**, which has more than 1,600 retail stores as well as more than 350 retail fuel locations across Canada, and holds investments in **Crombie Real Estate Investment Trust** and Genstar real estate partnerships.

Food Retailing - Wholly owned **Sobeys Inc.** carries on business in the retail food and food distribution industry through company-owned stores, franchised stores and affiliated stores in all 10 Canadian provinces. Operations include various food store formats, pharmacies, fuel locations, liquor stores and wholesale business. At May 6, 2023, retail banners consisted of Sobeys (240), Safeway (138), IGA (192), IGA extra (138), Farm Boy (47), Longo's (37), Thrifty Foods (26), Foodland (215), Marché Bonichoix (50), Les Marchés Tradition (78), Pete's Frootique & Fine Foods (2), FreshCo/Chalo! FreshCo (142), Lawtons (77), Rachelle-Béry (10), Needs (80), Boni-Soir (4), Voisin (4), Kim Phat (3), Cash & Carry (6) and IGA Express (1). The retail network also included 389 retail fuel sites under the FastFuel, Shell, Safeway, Irving and Petro-Canada banners, many of which are co-located within the company's grocery and convenience stores (excluding 38 Safeway co-located stations or 17 co-branded convenience fuel stations); and 103 liquor stores under the Sobeys Liquor, Safeway Liquor and Thrifty Foods Liquor banners. In addition to retail stores, the company operates grocery e-commerce businesses under the banners Voilà, Grocery Gateway, IGA.net and ThriftyFoods.com. The retail network is serviced through 28 distribution centres located across Canada.

Investments & Other Operations - This segment consists of a 41.5% interest in **Crombie Real Estate Investment Trust**; and a 40.7% interest in **Genstar Development Partnership**, a 48.6% interest in **Genstar Development Partnership #2**, a 39% interest in each of **GDC Investments 4, L.P.** and **GDC Investments 7, L.P.**, a 37.1% interest in **GDC Investments 8, L.P.** and a 49% interest in **The Fraipont Partnership** (collectively Genstar). Genstar is a residential property developer with operations in select markets in Canada and the U.S.

In March 2023, the company announced that the Longo's e-commerce business, Grocery Gateway, would be merged into e-commerce platform Voilà in July 2023.

Recent Merger and Acquisition Activity

Status: completed **Announced:** June 12, 2023
Marlin Spring Investments Limited and Greybrook Capital Inc., through its real estate investment and asset management division, Greybrook Realty Partners Inc., acquired development land located at 40 to 60 St. Lawrence Avenue in Toronto, Ont., from Sobeys Inc. for an undisclosed amount. A rezoning application was submitted to construct three condominium towers on the site, which is zoned industrial. The towers would range in storeys from the mid-20s to the low-40s, and would have commercial and retail space below, an underground parking, and a package of interior and exterior amenities. The transaction was effective on May 1, 2023.

Status: pending **Announced:** Dec. 15, 2022
Empire Company Limited agreed to sell all 56 retail fuel sites in western Canada to Canadian Mobility Services Limited, wholly owned by Shell Canada Limited, for $100,000,000.

Status: completed **Announced:** June 7, 2022
Empire Company Limited announced the acquisition of an ownership interest in Scene+ loyalty rewards program, making it a co-owner with Cineplex Inc. and The Bank of Nova Scotia. Terms were not disclosed. Scene+ rollout in Empire banners would begin with stores in Atlantic Canada in August 2022, and then continue across the country, culminating in early 2023. Scene+ has over 10,000,000 members and offers an assortment of opportunities to earn and redeem points across a broad spectrum of partners. AIR MILES collectors would continue to earn and redeem in Empire store until the Scene+ program is available in that region.

Directors - James M. (Jim) Dickson, chr., Halifax, N.S.; Michael B. Medline, pres. & CEO, Toronto, Ont.; Michelle Banik, Toronto, Ont.; Cynthia J. Devine, Toronto, Ont.; Sharon R. Driscoll, Vancouver, B.C.; Gregory Josefowicz, Fennville, Mich.; Susan (Sue) Lee, Vancouver, B.C.; William (Bill) Linton, Toronto, Ont.; Martine Reardon, New York, N.Y.; Frank C. Sobey, Pictou, N.S.; John R. Sobey, Pictou, N.S.; Karl R. Sobey, Halifax, N.S.; Paul D. Sobey, N.S.; Robert G. C. (Rob) Sobey, Stellarton, N.S.; Martine Turcotte, Verdun, Qué.

Other Exec. Officers - Simon Gagné, exec. v-p & chief HR officer; Douglas B. (Doug) Nathanson, exec. v-p, chief devel. officer, gen. counsel & corp. sec.; Matt Reindel, exec. v-p & CFO; Vivek Sood, exec. v-p, related businesses; Pierre St-Laurent, exec. v-p & COO

Capital Stock

	Authorized (shs.)	Outstanding (shs.)[1]	Par
2002 Pref.	991,980,000	nil	$25
Cl.A Non-vtg.	745,160,121	152,894,388	n.p.v.
Cl.B Common	122,400,000	98,138,079	n.p.v.

[1] At July 7, 2023

2002 Preferred - Issuable in series. Each series rank equally with the 2002 preferred shares of every other series in respect to the payment of dividends and in the distribution of assets. The company may not create or issue any shares ranking in priority or on a parity to the 2002 preferred shares as to the payment of dividends or the distribution of assets without the approval of two thirds of the preferred shareholders. Non-voting.

Class A Non-Voting & Class B Common - Rank equally, share for share with each other, except that class A shares are non-voting and class B shares are entitled to one vote per share; and directors may declare dividends on the class A shares without being obliged to declare an equal or any dividend on the class B shares. Class B shares are convertible into class A shares at any time on a share-for-share basis. Under certain circumstances, where an offer is made to purchase class B shares, holders of the class A shares shall be entitled to receive a follow-up offer at the highest price per share paid to class B shareholders.

Options - At May 6, 2023, options were outstanding to purchase 4,222,832 class A non-voting shares at prices ranging from $18.70 to $42.60 per share with a weighted average remaining life of 4.67 years.

Normal Course Issuer Bid - The company plans to make normal course purchases of up to 12,600,000 class A non-voting shares representing 9% of the public float. The bid commenced on July 2, 2023, and expires on July 1, 2024.

Major Shareholder - Sobey family held 94.49% interest at July 7, 2023.

Price Range - EMP.A/TSX

Year	Volume	High	Low	Close
2022	112,730,091	$46.04	$33.09	$35.66
2021	125,250,513	$42.93	$34.50	$38.54
2020	147,667,231	$40.87	$23.88	$34.79
2019	125,858,860	$37.43	$27.61	$30.46
2018	117,118,307	$29.82	$22.35	$28.83

Recent Close: $35.08

Capital Stock Changes - During fiscal 2023, 46,130 class A non-voting shares were issued on exercise of options, 9,444,902 class A non-voting shares were repurchased under a Normal Course Issuer Bid and 14,993 (net) class A non-voting shares held in trust were released.

In May 2021, 3,187,348 class A non-voting shares were issued pursuant to the acquisition of 51% interest in Longo Brothers Fruit Markets Inc. Also during fiscal 2022, 432,014 class A non-voting shares were issued on exercise of options, 6,378,983 class A non-voting shares were repurchased under a Normal Course Issuer Bid and 7,485 (net) class A non-voting shares held in trust were released.

Dividends

EMP.A cl A N.V. Ra $0.73 pa Q est. July 31, 2023
Prev. Rate: $0.66 est. July 29, 2022
Prev. Rate: $0.60 est. July 30, 2021
Prev. Rate: $0.52 est. July 31, 2020

Long-Term Debt - Outstanding at May 6, 2023:

Credit facility due on demand[1]	$44,500,000
Credit facilities due 2027[2]	355,700,000
5.11% first mtge. loan due 2033	3,700,000
Medium-term notes:	
Ser.D 6.06% due 2035	175,000,000
Ser.E 5.79% due 2036	125,000,000
Ser.F 6.64% due 2040	150,000,000
Notes payable & other debt	160,300,000
Less: Unamortized trans. costs	1,900,000
	1,012,300,000
Less: Current portion	101,000,000
	911,300,000

[1] Borrowings under an operating line of credit, bearing interest at a floating rate tied to prime rate.

[2] Borrowings under revolving term credit facilities, bearing interest at floating rates tied to prime rate or bankers' acceptance rates.

Principal debt retirement for the next five fiscal years:

2024	$101,000,000
2025	8,900,000
2026	7,100,000
2027	6,300,000
2028	323,700,000
Thereafter	567,200,000

Wholly Owned Subsidiaries

ECL Properties Limited, Stellarton, N.S. Formerly Crombie Properties Limited
- 100% int. in **ECL Developments Ltd.**, N.S.
  - 41.5% int. in **Crombie Real Estate Investment Trust**, New Glasgow, N.S. (see separate coverage)
- 49% int. in **The Fraipont Partnership**, Alta.
- 37.1% int. in **GDC Investments 8, L.P.**, Del.
- 39% int. in **GDC Investments 4, L.P.**, Ga.
- 39% int. in **GDC Investments 7, L.P.**, Ga.
- 40.7% int. in **Genstar Development Partnership**, Alta.
- 48.6% int. in **Genstar Development Partnership #2**, Alta.

Sobeys Inc., Stellarton, N.S.
- 100% int. in **Sobeys Capital Incorporated**, N.S.
  - 88% int. in **Farm Boy Company Inc.**, N.S.
  - 51% int. in **Longo Brothers Fruit Markets Inc.**, Vaughan, Ont.

Note: The preceding list includes only the major related companies in which interests are held.

Financial Statistics

Periods ended:	52w May 6/23[A]		53w May 7/22[A]
	$000s	%Chg	$000s
Operating revenue	**30,478,100**	**+1**	**30,162,400**
Cost of sales	22,685,400		22,502,700
General & admin expense	5,678,200		5,508,800
Operating expense	**28,363,600**	**+1**	**28,011,500**
Operating income	**2,114,500**	**-2**	**2,150,900**
Deprec., depl. & amort.	1,030,600		967,100
Finance income	26,200		29,500
Finance costs, gross	293,200		311,600
Investment income	87,700		93,100
Pre-tax income	**965,400**	**-11**	**1,081,600**
Income taxes	237,700		270,300
Net income	**727,700**	**-10**	**811,300**
Net inc. for equity hldrs	**686,000**	**-8**	**745,800**
Net inc. for non-cont. int	**41,700**	**-36**	**65,500**
Cash & equivalent	221,300		812,300
Inventories	1,743,300		1,591,500
Accounts receivable	683,400		558,800
Current assets	2,955,000		3,212,700
Long-term investments	1,455,700		1,380,700
Fixed assets, net	3,338,100		3,159,200
Right-of-use assets	4,860,900		4,999,700
Intangibles, net	3,443,400		3,397,500
Total assets	**16,483,700**	**-1**	**16,593,600**
Accts. pay. & accr. liabs	3,028,600		2,988,900
Current liabilities	3,857,500		4,239,700
Long-term debt, gross	1,012,300		1,176,700
Long-term debt, net	911,300		595,700
Long-term lease liabilities	5,620,900		5,775,900
Shareholders' equity	5,200,400		4,991,500
Non-controlling interest	136,300		142,400
Cash from oper. activs	**1,605,300**	**-24**	**2,107,100**
Cash from fin. activs	(1,511,600)		(1,293,900)
Cash from invest. activs	(684,700)		(891,400)
Net cash position	**221,300**	**-73**	**812,300**
Capital expenditures	(574,200)		(633,000)
Capital disposals	48,900		165,600
Unfunded pension liability	79,600		89,400
	$		$
Earnings per share*	2.65		2.81
Cash flow per share*	6.20		7.95
Cash divd. per share*	0.66		0.60
	shs		shs
No. of shs. o/s*	253,278,953		262,662,732
Avg. no. of shs. o/s*	258,824,231		265,170,624
	%		%
Net profit margin	2.39		2.69
Return on equity	13.46		15.93
Return on assets	5.74		6.58
No. of employees (FTEs)	67,000		67,000

* Class A & B

[A] Reported in accordance with IFRS

Historical Summary
(as originally stated)

Fiscal Year	Oper. Rev.	Net Inc. Bef. Disc.	EPS*
	$000s	$000s	$
2023[A]	30,478,100	727,700	2.65
2022[A1]	30,162,400	811,300	2.81
2021[A]	28,268,300	764,200	2.61
2020[A]	26,588,200	612,800	2.16
2019[A]	25,142,000	416,400	1.42

* Class A & B

[A] Reported in accordance with IFRS

[1] 53 weeks ended May 7, 2022.

E.48 Empower Clinics Inc.

Symbol - EPW **Exchange** - CSE (S) **CUSIP** - 29246V
Head Office - 505-1771 Robson St, Vancouver, BC, V6G 1C9
Telephone - (604) 789-2146 **Toll-free** - (855) 855-9058
Website - empowerclinics.com
Email - s.mcauley@empowerclinics.com
Investor Relations - Steven J. McAuley (855) 855-9058
Auditors - Zeifmans LLP C.A., Toronto, Ont.
Transfer Agents - Olympia Trust Company, Calgary, Alta.

Profile - (Can. 2008; orig. Nev., 1997) Provides integrated healthcare and diagnostics solutions in Canada and the U.S., through operation of multidisciplinary clinics, manufacturing and marketing of medical devices and at-home testing products, operation of a medical diagnostics laboratory, and provision of testing services.

Operations are organized into two business units: Health and Wellness, and Diagnostics and Technology.

Health and Wellness - Operates six clinics under The Medi-Collective banner, along with digital and telemedicine services, located in Etobicoke (2), Kitchener, London, Toronto and Thornhill, Ont., which offer primary care, paramedical, specialty and wellness services.

Diagnostics and Technology - Operations include wholly owned **Medi + Sure Canada Inc.**, which manufactures, distributes and sells medical devices and at-home testing products in Canada, including diabetes care devices and test kits for influenza and vitamin D; MediSure Laboratory, a medical diagnostics laboratory in Dallas, Tex., which provides diagnostic services and testing solutions, including COVID-19, vitamin and hormone testing, at testing sites and client locations in Texas and surrounding states, as well as sells direct-to-consumer at-home COVID-19 test kits in the U.S. and Canada; and provision of COVID-19 testing solutions in British Columbia through three testing sites near Port of Vancouver, B.C., and a concierge mobile service.

In December 2022, the company changed its fiscal year end to March 31 from December 31, effective Dec. 20, 2022.

Effective Sept. 1, 2022, the company closed two of its The Medi-Collective clinics located in Hamilton and Mississauga, Ont.

In March 2022, the company sold wholly owned **Sun Valley Health Holdings, LLC, Sun Valley Health Franchising, LLC, Sun Valley Health, LLC, Sun Valley Health West, LLC, Sun Valley Health Tucson, LLC, Sun Valley Health Mesa, LLC, Sun Valley Alternative Health Centers NV, LLC** to former owners for US$181,664. These subsidiaries operated medical cannabis clinics under the Sun Valley Health banner in Arizona, Oregon and Washington.

Common suspended from CSE, Aug. 15, 2023.

Common reinstated on CSE, Nov. 9, 2022.

Predecessor Detail - Name changed from Adira Energy Ltd., Apr. 19, 2018, following the reverse takeover acquisition of SMAART Holdings Inc.; basis 1 new for 6.72625 old shs.

Directors - Steven J. McAuley, chr., pres., CEO & interim CFO, Vancouver, B.C.; Andrejs Bunkse, Phoenix, Ariz.; Alexis Wukich

Capital Stock

	Authorized (shs.)	Outstanding (shs.)[1]
Common	unlimited	88,465,505

[1] At June 21, 2023

Major Shareholder - Widely held at July 7, 2021.

Price Range - ADL/TSX-VEN (D)

Year	Volume	High	Low	Close
2022	33,810,636	$2.18	$0.10	$0.15
2021	181,537,472	$12.50	$1.00	$1.55
2020	109,944,256	$2.00	$0.13	$1.43
2019	5,821,216	$1.13	$0.13	$0.20
2018	3,314,153	$2.55	$0.33	$0.48

Consolidation: 1-for-5 cons. in June 2023

Recent Close: $0.04

Capital Stock Changes - On June 21, 2023, common shares were consolidated on a 1-for-5 basis.

In January 2022, private placement of 5,500,000 units (1 common share & 1 warrant) at Cdn$0.20 per unit was completed, with warrants exercisable at Cdn$0.30 per share for two years. In December 2022, private placement of 16,850,000 units (1 common share & 1 warrant) at Cdn$0.05 per unit was completed, with warrants exercisable at Cdn$0.075 per share for two years.

Wholly Owned Subsidiaries

Empower Healthcare Assets Inc., Del.
- 100% int. in **Kai Medical Laboratory, LLC**, Dallas, Tex.

Kai Medical Canada Corp., Canada.
Lawrence Park Health and Wellness Clinic Inc., Canada.
Medi + Sure Canada Inc., Canada.
Medi-Collective: Brown's Line FHO Inc., Canada.
Medi Collective Corp., Canada.
11000900 Canada Inc., Canada.
S.M.A.A.R.T. Holdings Co., United States. Inactive.
- 100% int. in **Empower Healthcare Corp.**, Canada.
- 100% int. in **Empower Healthcare Corp.**, United States.
  - 100% int. in **The Hemp & Cannabis Company**, Wash. Inactive.
  - 100% int. in **SMAART Inc.**, Ore. Inactive.
  - 100% int. in **THCF Access Points, Inc.**, Ore. Inactive.

Financial Statistics

Periods ended:	12m Dec. 31/21[A]		12m Dec. 31/20[oA]
	US$000s	%Chg	US$000s
Operating revenue	**4,369**	**+355**	**961**
Cost of sales	3,020		527
Salaries & benefits	1,691		517
General & admin expense	3,782		3,092
Stock-based compensation	777		324
Operating expense	**9,270**	**+108**	**4,460**
Operating income	**(4,901)**	**n.a.**	**(3,499)**
Deprec., depl. & amort.	540		179
Finance income	nil		8
Finance costs, gross	185		524
Write-downs/write-offs	(9,565)[1]		(588)
Pre-tax income	**(31,736)**	**n.a.**	**(16,696)**
Net inc. bef. disc. opers	**(31,736)**	**n.a.**	**(16,696)**
Income from disc. opers	(520)		(370)
Net income	**(32,256)**	**n.a.**	**(17,066)**
Cash & equivalent	866		4,890
Inventories	205		18
Accounts receivable	566		265
Current assets	3,160		5,254
Fixed assets, net	1,132		1,590
Intangibles, net	nil		2,386
Total assets	**5,037**	**-45**	**9,230**
Accts. pay. & accr. liabs	3,725		3,443
Current liabilities	7,703		7,001
Long-term debt, gross	1,561		3,041
Long-term debt, net	1,054		1,140
Long-term lease liabilities	2,650		255
Shareholders' equity	(6,393)		(5,490)
Cash from oper. activs	**(4,070)**	**n.a.**	**(1,750)**
Cash from fin. activs	2,952		6,770
Cash from invest. activs	(2,946)		(310)
Net cash position	**866**	**-82**	**4,890**
Capital expenditures	(2,152)		(3)
	US$		US$
Earnings per share*	(0.50)		(0.45)
Cash flow per share*	(0.06)		(0.05)
	shs		shs
No. of shs. o/s*	67,889,004		56,762,381
Avg. no. of shs. o/s*	65,601,740		36,466,323
	%		%
Net profit margin	(726.39)		n.m.
Return on equity	n.m.		n.m.
Return on assets	(442.29)		(299.87)
Foreign sales percent	68		100

* Common
[o] Restated
[A] Reported in accordance with IFRS
[1] Includes property and equipment impairment of US$4,699,802 and full impairment of intangible assets and goodwill totaling US$403,213 and US$4,461,607, respectively.

Latest Results

Periods ended:	9m Sept. 30/22[A]		9m Sept. 30/21[A]
	US$000s	%Chg	US$000s
Operating revenue	4,235	+31	3,226
Net inc. bef. disc. opers	(590)	n.a.	(27,052)
Income from disc. opers	134		(513)
Net income	(456)	n.a.	(27,565)
	US$		US$
Earns. per sh. bef. disc. opers.*	(0.01)		(0.40)
Earnings per share*	(0.01)		(0.45)

* Common
[A] Reported in accordance with IFRS

Historical Summary
(as originally stated)

Fiscal Year	Oper. Rev. US$000s	Net Inc. Bef. Disc. US$000s	EPS* US$
2021[A]	4,369	(31,736)	(0.50)
2020[A]	3,209	(17,066)	(0.45)
2019[A]	2,032	(4,302)	(0.20)
2018[A1]	1,091	(3,790)	(0.30)
2017[A2]	nil	(75)	(0.15)

* Common
[A] Reported in accordance with IFRS
[1] Results reflect the Apr. 27, 2018, reverse takeover acquisition of S.M.A.A.R.T Holdings Inc.
[2] Results for 2017 and prior years pertain to Adira Energy Ltd.
Note: Adjusted throughout for 1-for-5 cons. in June 2023; 1-for-6.726254 cons. in Apr. 2018

E.49 Enablence Technologies Inc.

Symbol - ENA **Exchange** - TSX-VEN **CUSIP** - 292483
Head Office - 119-390 March Rd, Ottawa, ON, K2K 0G7 **Telephone** - (613) 656-2850 **Fax** - (613) 656-2855
Website - www.enablence.com
Email - paul.rowland@enablence.com
Investor Relations - T. Paul Rowland (613) 656-2850
Auditors - MNP LLP C.A., Ottawa, Ont.
Lawyers - Fasken Martineau DuMoulin LLP, Ottawa, Ont.
Transfer Agents - Computershare Trust Company of Canada Inc., Toronto, Ont.

Profile - (Can. 2006; orig. B.C., 1995) Designs, manufactures and sells planar lightwave circuit (PLC) optical chips primarily for the data centre infrastructure and light detection and ranging (LiDAR) end markets.

Products consist of a series of compact PLC optical chips which function as multiplexers (mux) and demultiplexers (demux) in multi-channel optical transceivers primarily used in the data communications market and optical chip sets for use in LiDAR. The company is also developing optical chips for use for advanced vision applications, including medical devices (optical coherence tomography), and virtual and augmented reality devices.

Facilities include a non-captive optical chip fabrication plant in Fremont, Calif., and a research and development centre in Ottawa, Ont. These facilities enable the company to also manufacture chips designed by third party customers and provide custom designing, engineering and fabrication services.

Predecessor Detail - Name changed from Pacific Northwest Partners Limited, July 24, 2006, following reverse takeover acquisition of Enablence Inc.

Directors - Dr. Derek H. Burney, chr., Colo.; Derek J. Burney; Louis De Jong, Toronto, Ont.; Daniel Huff; Oded Tal

Other Exec. Officers - Dr. Ashok Balakrishnan, co-founder & chief tech. officer; Todd Haugen, CEO; T. Paul Rowland, CFO

Capital Stock

	Authorized (shs.)	Outstanding (shs.)[1]
Preferred	unlimited	nil
Common	unlimited	18,590,000

[1] At Feb. 15, 2023

Major Shareholder - Daniel J. Bordessa held 31.8% interest and David Roland held 10.4% interest at Nov. 2, 2022.

Price Range - ENA/TSX-VEN

Year	Volume	High	Low	Close
2022	317,501	$2.40	$0.79	$1.80
2021	437,792	$5.40	$0.71	$1.04
2020	32,947	$2.40	$0.60	$1.80
2019	173,687	$4.80	$0.60	$2.40
2018	354,034	$7.20	$3.00	$4.20

Consolidation: 1-for-120 cons. in Nov. 2021
Recent Close: $1.80

Capital Stock Changes - On Nov. 22, 2021, common shares were consolidated on a 1-for-120 basis. During fiscal 2022, post-consolidated common shares were issued as follows: 11,376,000 for debt settlement, 1,170,000 for services and 694,440 by private placement.

Wholly Owned Subsidiaries

Enablence Canada Inc., Ottawa, Ont.
Enablence (HK) Limited, Hong Kong, People's Republic of China.
- 100% int. in **Suzhou Enablence Optoelectronic Technologies Co., Ltd**, People's Republic of China.

Enablence USA Inc., Del.
- 100% int. in **Enablence USA Components Inc.**, Fremont, Calif.

Financial Statistics

Periods ended:	12m June 30/22[A]		12m June 30/21[A]
	US$000s	%Chg	US$000s
Operating revenue	**1,978**	**-22**	**2,521**
Cost of goods sold	2,311		2,733
Research & devel. expense	1,356		1,466
General & admin expense	2,664		2,505
Stock-based compensation	1,365		2
Operating expense	**7,696**	**+15**	**6,706**
Operating income	**(5,718)**	**n.a.**	**(4,185)**
Deprec., depl. & amort.	140		152
Finance income	nil		1,380
Finance costs, gross	2,055		3,097
Write-downs/write-offs	74		41
Pre-tax income	**11,489**	**n.a.**	**(5,041)**
Income taxes	(204)		nil
Net income	**11,693**	**n.a.**	**(5,041)**
Cash & equivalent	191		194
Inventories	262		301
Accounts receivable	436		427
Current assets	1,165		1,093
Fixed assets, net	269		298
Total assets	**1,434**	**+3**	**1,391**
Accts. pay. & accr. liabs	4,990		5,666
Current liabilities	5,733		41,130
Long-term debt, gross	5,979		35,242
Long-term debt, net	5,493		nil
Shareholders' equity	(9,792)		(39,739)
Cash from oper. activs	**(5,052)**	**n.a.**	**(2,340)**
Cash from fin. activs	5,071		2,677
Cash from invest. activs	(56)		(64)
Net cash position	**191**	**-2**	**194**
Capital expenditures	(111)		(64)
Capital disposals	55		nil
	US$		US$
Earnings per share*	0.91		(1.20)
Cash flow per share*	(0.39)		(0.43)
	shs		shs
No. of shs. o/s*	18,590,000		5,349,391
Avg. no. of shs. o/s*	12,793,000		5,349,391
	%		%
Net profit margin	591.15		(199.96)
Return on equity	n.m.		n.m.
Return on assets	975.89		(129.34)

* Common
[A] Reported in accordance with IFRS

Latest Results

Periods ended:	6m Dec. 31/22[A]		6m Dec. 31/21[A]
	US$000s	%Chg	US$000s
Operating revenue	976	-2	997
Net income	(4,039)	n.a.	14,940
	US$		US$
Earnings per share*	(0.22)		2.40

* Common
[A] Reported in accordance with IFRS

Historical Summary
(as originally stated)

Fiscal Year	Oper. Rev. US$000s	Net Inc. Bef. Disc. US$000s	EPS* US$
2022[A]	1,978	11,693	0.91
2021[A]	2,521	(5,041)	(1.20)
2020[A]	1,101	(9,557)	(1.20)
2019[A1]	1,424	(10,355)	(2.40)
2018[A]	3,388	(10,377)	(2.40)

* Common
[A] Reported in accordance with IFRS
[1] Amended.
Note: Adjusted throughout for 1-for-120 cons. in Nov. 2021

E.50 Enbridge Inc.*

Symbol - ENB **Exchange** - TSX **CUSIP** - 29250N
Head Office - Fifth Avenue Place, 200-425 1 St SW, Calgary, AB, T2P 3L8 **Telephone** - (403) 231-3900 **Toll-free** - (800) 481-2804 **Fax** - (403) 231-3920
Website - www.enbridge.com
Email - investor.relations@enbridge.com
Investor Relations - Rebecca Morley (800) 481-2804
Auditors - PricewaterhouseCoopers LLP C.A., Calgary, Alta.
Lawyers - Sullivan & Cromwell LLP, New York, N.Y.; McCarthy Tétrault LLP, Calgary, Alta.
Transfer Agents - Computershare Trust Company of Canada Inc., Calgary, Alta.
FP500 Revenue Ranking - 9
Employees - 11,100 at Dec. 31, 2022
Profile - (Can. 1949, via Special Act of Parliament) Provides energy transportation, distribution and generation. Operations include

transportation and storage of crude oil, natural gas and natural gas liquids, gathering, processing and distribution of natural gas, and energy marketing in North America; and renewable energy generation in Canada, the U.S., the U.K., Germany and France.

Operations are conducted through five business segments: Liquids Pipelines; Gas Transmission and Midstream; Gas Distribution and Storage; Renewable Power Generation; and Energy Services.

Liquids Pipelines

This segment consists of pipelines and related terminals in Canada and the U.S. that transport and export various grades of crude oil and other liquid hydrocarbons. Assets include the Mainline System, Regional Oil Sands System, Gulf Coast and Mid-Continent pipelines and related assets, and other assets.

The Mainline System consists of the Canadian Mainline System and the Lakehead System. The Canadian Mainline System transports various grades of crude oil and other liquid hydrocarbons within western Canada and from western Canada to the Canada/U.S. border near Gretna, Man., and Neche, N.D., and from the U.S./Canada border near Port Huron, Mich., and Sarnia, Ont., to eastern Canada and the northeastern U.S. The Lakehead System is the portion of the Mainline System in the U.S., which transports crude oil and liquid petroleum from western Canada to the U.S.

The Regional Oil Sands System includes five intra-Alberta long haul pipelines (88.43% interest in Athabasca, Waupisoo and Wood Buffalo Extension/Athabasca Twin; 38.43% interest in Woodland; and 58.43% interest in Norlite) and two large terminals (Athabasca and Cheecham) which provide access to production from 12 producing oil sands projects in Alberta.

The Gulf Coast and Mid-Continent pipelines and related assets include 50% interest in the 1,078-km, 950,000-bbl-per-day Seaway Pipeline, including an 805-km long-haul system from Cushing, Okla., to Freeport, Tex., the Texas City Terminal and Distribution System that serve refineries in Houston and Texas City areas, and 8,800,000 bbl of crude oil tankage on the Texas Gulf Coast; the 950-km, 660,000-bbl-per-day Flanagan South Pipeline, which extends from the company's terminal at Flanagan, Ill., to Cushing, Okla.; the 938-km, 193,000-bbl-per-day Spearhead Pipeline, which extends from Flanagan, Ill., to Cushing, Okla.; 68.5% interest in the 1,368-km, 900,000-bbl-per-day Gray Oak Pipeline, which runs from the Permian Basin in West Texas to the U.S. Gulf Coast; the Enbridge Ingleside Energy Center, a crude oil storage and export terminal in Ingleside, Tex., with 15,600,000 bbl of storage and 1,500,000 bbl per day of export capacity; 30% interest in the 925-km, 670,000-bbl-per-day Cactus II Pipeline, which extends from Wink to Corpus Christi, Tex.; the 50-km, 300,000-bbl-per-day Viola Pipeline in the Corpus Christi area; the 350,000-bbl Taft Terminal near Corpus Christi, Tex.; and 26,000,000-bbl crude oil storage terminals at Cushing, Okla. (Cushing Terminal).

Other assets include Southern Lights Pipeline, the Express-Platte System, the Bakken System, and feeder pipelines and other. The 180,000-bbl-per-day Southern Lights Pipeline transports diluent from the Manhattan Terminal near Chicago, Ill., to three delivery facilities at the Edmonton and Hardisty Terminals in Alberta and the Kerrobert Terminal in Saskatchewan. The Express-Platte System consists of the 310,000-bbl-per-day Express and 145,000 to 164,000-bbl-per-day Platte crude oil pipelines totaling 2,736 km which run from Hardisty, Alta., to Wood River, Ill., and 5,600,000 bbl of crude oil storage. The Bakken System consists of the North Dakota System, which services the Bakken in North Dakota and includes a gathering system that provides delivery to Clearbrook, Minn., and a transportation system extending from Berthold, N.D., into Cromer, Man.; and 27.6% interest in the Bakken Pipeline System, which consists of the Dakota Access Pipeline from the Bakken area in North Dakota to Patoka, Ill., and the Energy Transfer Crude Oil Pipeline from Patoka, Ill., to Nederland, Tex. Feeder pipelines and other include Hardisty Contract Terminal and Hardisty Storage Caverns near Hardisty, Alta.; 65% interest in the 300,000-bbl-per-day Southern Access Extension pipeline from Flanagan to Patoka, Ill.; the 480,000-bbl Patoka storage in Illinois; the 101,000-bbl-per-day Toledo pipeline system which connects with the Lakehead System and delivers to Ohio and Michigan; and the 45,000-bbl-per-day Norman Wells System which transports crude oil from Norman Wells, N.W.T., to Zama, Alta.

Gas Transmission and Midstream

This segment consists of investments in natural gas pipelines and gathering and processing facilities in Canada and the U.S., including U.S. Gas Transmission, Canadian Gas Transmission, U.S. Midstream and other assets.

U.S. Gas Transmission transmits and stores natural gas through interstate pipeline systems for customers in various regions of the midwestern, northeastern and southern U.S. Assets include the 13,765-km, 12.04-bcf-per-day Texas Eastern system, which extends from producing fields in the Gulf Coast region of Texas and Louisiana to Ohio, Pennsylvania, New Jersey and New York; the 1,820-km, 3.09-bcf-per-day Algonquin system, which connects with the Texas Eastern system in New Jersey and extends through New Jersey, New York, Connecticut, Rhode Island and Massachusetts; 78% interest in the Maritimes & Northeast (M&N) system that consists of the 552-km, 0.83-bcf-per-day M&N U.S. system, which extends from northeastern Massachusetts to the border of Canada near Baileyville, Me., and the 885-km, 0.55-bcf-per-day M&N Canada system, which extends from Goldboro, N.S., to the U.S. border near Baileyville, Me., connecting to M&N U.S.; East Tennessee system, which has capacity of 1.86 bcf per day and consists of two mainline systems totaling 2,449 km of pipeline in Tennessee, Georgia, North Carolina and Virginia, a liquefied natural gas (LNG) storage facility near Kingsport, Tenn., and storage facilities in Saltville, Va.; 50% interest in the 1,199-km, 1.39-bcf-per-day Gulfstream system, which transports natural gas from Mississippi, Alabama, Louisiana and Texas, crossing the Gulf of Mexico to markets in central and southern Florida; 50% interest in the 832-km, 1-bcf-per-day Sabal Trail system, which extends through Alabama, Georgia and Florida; 50% interest in the 414-km, 1.4-bcf-per-day NEXUS system, which transports natural gas from the Texas Eastern system in Ohio to the Vector pipeline in Michigan; the 285-km, 2.6-bcf-per-day Valley Crossing system, which runs from Agua Dulce, Tex., to the Gulf of Mexico, east of Brownsville, Tex., providing supply to Mexico's state-owned utility **Comisión Federal de Electricidad**; 50% interest in the 462-km, 1.1-bcf-per-day Southeast Supply Header system, which extends from the Perryville Hub in northeastern Louisiana through Mississippi and Alabama; 60% interest in the 560-km, 1.745-bcf-per-day Vector pipeline, which extends from Joliet, Ill., to Dawn, Ont.; and certain other gas pipeline and storage assets.

Canadian Gas Transmission includes the 2,950-km, 3.6-bcf-per-day British Columbia Pipeline, which stretches from Fort Nelson, B.C., and from Gordondale, Alta., to the Canada/U.S. border at Huntingdon (Abbotsford), B.C., and Sumas, Wash.; 50% interest in the Alliance Pipeline, which has capacity of 1.8 bcf per day and consists of a 3,000-km natural gas transmission pipeline and 860 km of lateral pipelines and related infrastructure, transporting liquids-rich natural gas from northeastern British Columbia, northwestern Alberta and the Bakken area in North Dakota to the Alliance Chicago gas exchange hub downstream of **Aux Sable Liquid Products LP**'s natural gas liquid (NGL) extraction and fractionation plant at Channahon, Ill.; and certain other midstream gas gathering pipelines.

U.S. Midstream includes 42.7% interest in Aux Sable Liquid Products LP, which owns and operates an NGL extraction and fractionation plant at Channahon, Ill.; 42.7% interest in **Aux Sable Midstream LLC**, which owns and operates the Palermo Conditioning Plant and the Prairie Rose Pipeline in the Bakken area of North Dakota; and 50% interest in **Aux Sable Canada LP**, which has interests in the Septimus Pipeline in the Montney area of British Columbia and a facility which processes refinery/upgrader offgas in Fort Saskatchewan, Alta. Aux Sable's facilities are connected to the Alliance Pipeline to facilitate deliveries of liquids-rich gas for processing at the Channahon plant. U.S. Midstream also includes 13.2% interest in **DCP Midstream, LP**, which gathers, compresses, treats, processes, transports, stores and sells natural gas; produces, fractionates, transports, stores and sells NGL; and recovers and sells condensate. DCP owns and operates more than 36 plants and 86,905 km of natural gas and NGL pipelines, with operations in nine states across major producing regions.

Other assets consist primarily of offshore pipelines including 11 natural gas gathering and regulated transmission pipelines and four oil pipelines in the Gulf of Mexico, with 2,100 km of underwater pipe and onshore facilities with total capacity of 6.5 bcf per day.

Gas Distribution and Storage

This segment consists of natural gas utility operations in Ontario and Quebec. Wholly owned **Enbridge Gas Inc.**, a rate-regulated natural gas utility, serves 3,900,000 residential, commercial and industrial customers in Ontario. Enbridge Gas owns and operates 149,000 km of distribution pipelines, 5,500 km of transmission pipelines and five associated mainline compressor stations, and 284 bcf of integrated underground storage facilities (Tecumseh Gas Storage facility and Dawn Hub in southwestern Ontario). Wholly owned **Gazifère Inc.** distributes natural gas to 44,000 customers in western Quebec.

Renewable Power Generation

This segment consists of investments in renewable energy assets with 2,185 MW of net power generating capacity. Assets include 23 wind farms, totaling 1,968 MW of net generating capacity, consisting of 16 onshore wind farms in North America located in Alberta, Ontario, Quebec, Colorado, Texas, Indiana and West Virginia, one offshore wind farm in the U.K. (Rampion), two offshore wind farms in Germany (Hohe See and Albatros) and four offshore wind projects in France, of which three are under construction/active development (Saint-Nazaire, Fécamp, Calvados and Provence Grand Large); seven solar facilities in Ontario (3), Alberta, Nevada, New Jersey and Pennsylvania totaling 93 MW of net generating capacity and an additional 97 MW in 10 solar projects under construction; five waste heat recovery facilities in Saskatchewan (4) and Alberta with 17 MW of net generating capacity; a geothermal plant in Oregon with 8.8 MW of net generating capacity; and a hydroelectric facility in Ontario with 0.8 MW of net generating capacity. Also includes 25% interest in the 450-MW East-West Tie transmission line in northwestern Ontario.

Energy Services

This segment provides commodity marketing and logistical services to North American refiners, producers and other customers. Crude oil, condensate, natural gas, NGL and power marketing services are offered and include transportation, storage, supply management and product exchanges.

Operating Statistics

Year ended Dec. 31	2022	2021
Liquids Pipeline Deliveries:		
Mainline system, bbl/d[1]..............	2,957,000	2,764,000
Regional Oil Sands system, bbl/d[2]..	n.a.	1,929,000
Gas Distribution & Storage:		
Enbridge Gas Inc.		
Volume, bcf................................	2,162	1,943
No. of active customers..............	3,900,000	3,800,000

[1] Represents deliveries ex-Gretna, Man., which is made up of United States and eastern Canada deliveries originating from western Canada.

[2] Volumes are for the Athabasca, Waupisoo, Woodland and Wood Buffalo pipelines, and exclude laterals on the Regional Oil Sands system.

In November 2022, the company announced a $3.6 billion expansion of the T-South section of the British Columbia Pipeline, which would add 300 mmcf per day of capacity; a regulatory application was expected to be filed in 2024, with 2028 targeted as the in-service date. The company also launched an open season to gauge shipper interest in a potential 500-mmcf-per-day expansion of the T-North segment of the British Columbia Pipeline; capital cost of such expansion was estimated at up to $1.9 billion.

During the third quarter of 2022, the 11-MW SunBridge wind farm in Saskatchewan was decommissioned following the end of the power purchase agreement with **Saskatchewan Power Corporation**. The facility began operations in February 2002 and was 50/50 owned by the company and **Suncor Energy Inc.**

On Aug. 17, 2022, the company and Houston, Tex.-based **Phillips 66 Company** swapped interests in two U.S. assets in a joint venture merger transaction, whereby a single joint venture, **DCP Midstream, LLC**, held both the company's and Phillips 66's indirect ownership interests in **Gray Oak Pipeline, LLC** (totaling 65%) and **DCP Midstream, LP** (totaling 56.51%). **Gray Oak Holdings, LLC**, a joint venture between the company and Phillipps 66, was merged with and into DCP Midstream, LLC.

As a result, the company's indirect economic interest in Gray Oak increased to 58.5% from 22.75% and its indirect economic interest in DCP Midstream, LP decreased to 13.2% from 28.26%. Phillips 66's indirect economic interest in Gray Oak decreased to 6.5% from 42.25% and its indirect economic interest in DCP Midstream, LP increased to 43.31% from 28.26%. Phillips 66 paid the company US$404,000,000 (Cdn$522,000,000) as part of the transaction.

Recent Merger and Acquisition Activity

Status: pending **Announced:** May 1, 2023
Enbridge Inc. agreed to acquire FortisBC Midstream Inc., which holds 93.8% interest in the Aitken Creek and 100% interest in the Aitken Creek North underground natural gas storage facilities in British Columbia, from Fortis Inc. for $400,000,000. The underground reservoir was located 120 km northeast of Fort St. John, B.C., in the Montney production region, and had 77 bcf of working gas capacity. The storage facilities connect to all three major long-haul natural gas transportation lines in western Canada, including Enbridge's Westcoast and Alliance pipelines. The transaction was expected to be completed in late 2023, subject to receipt of customary regulatory approvals and closing conditions.

Status: completed **Revised:** Apr. 3, 2023
UPDATE: The transaction was completed. PREVIOUS: Enbridge Inc. agreed to acquire Tres Palacios Holdings LLC, which owns and operates a natural gas storage facility in Markham, Tex., from Crestwood Equity Partners LP, Brookfield Infrastructure Partners L.P. (BIP LP) and BIP LP's institutional partners for US$335,000,000. Crestwood owns 50.1% in Tres Palacios, and BIP LP and its partners own 49.9%. Tres Palacios consists of three natural gas storage salt caverns with a total working gas capacity of 35 bcf and an integrated 62-mile natural gas header pipeline system, with eleven inter- and intrastate natural gas pipeline connections, including Enbridge's Texas Eastern pipeline.

Status: pending **Announced:** Mar. 1, 2023
Enbridge Inc. agreed to acquire a 10% interest in Concord, Mass.-based Divert, Inc. for US$80,000,000. Divert develops and provides advanced technologies, logistics and anaerobic digestion facilities to reduce and prevent food waste. Enbridge and Divert also announced a Cdn$1 billion infrastructure agreement to support the development of wasted-food-to-renewable-natural-gas facilities across North America.

Status: completed **Announced:** Jan. 9, 2023
Enbridge Inc. acquired Diamondback Energy, Inc.'s 10% interest in the 900,000-bbl-per-day Gray Oak Pipeline, which runs from the Permian Basin in West Texas to the U.S. Gulf Coast, for US$172,000,000. As a result, Enbridge's ownership in Gray Oak increased to 68.5% from 58.5%.

Status: completed **Revised:** Nov. 29, 2022
UPDATE: The transaction was completed. PREVIOUS: Enbridge Inc. agreed to acquire a 30% interest in the Woodfibre liquefied natural gas (LNG) project, a 2,100,000-tonne-per-year LNG export facility with 250,000 cubic metres of floating storage capacity being developed near Squamish, B.C., from Pacific Energy Corporation Limited for $533,000,000. Pacific Energy would retain the remaining 70% stake in the facility. Capital for the project was estimated at $5.1 billion, with an in-service date targeted in 2027.

Status: completed **Announced:** Nov. 2, 2022
Enbridge Inc. acquired an additional 10% interest in the 670,000-bbl-per-day Cactus II Pipeline, which extends from Wink to Corpus Christi, Tex., from Western Midstream Partners, LP for US$177,000,000. As a result, Enbridge's non-operating ownership in Cactus II increased to 30% from 20%.

Status: completed **Revised:** Oct. 5, 2022
UPDATE: The transaction was completed. PREVIOUS: Enbridge Inc. agreed to sell an 11.57% non-operating interest in seven pipelines in the Athabasca region of northern Alberta to a group of 23 First Nation and Métis communities for $1.12 billion. The pipelines consisted of Athabasca, Wood Buffalo Extension/Athabasca Twin and associated tanks, Norlite (70% owned by Enbridge), Waupisoo, Wood Buffalo, Woodland (50% owned by Enbridge) and Woodland Extension.

Status: completed **Announced:** Sept. 27, 2022
Enbridge Inc. acquired Dallas, Tex.-based Tri Global Energy, LLC (TGE), a U.S. renewable energy project developer, for US$270,000,000 in cash and assumed debt. An additional US$50,000,000 in payments could be made contingent on successful execution of TGE's project portfolio. TGE had a development portfolio of wind and solar projects representing more than 7 GW of renewable generation capacity.

Status: completed **Announced:** Aug. 2, 2022
Enbridge Inc. acquired a 10% interest in Oakville, Ont.-based Oakville Enterprises Corporation, a provider of energy and infrastructure solutions including electricity distribution, infrastructure services, energy services and electricity generation to municipal, commercial and residential clients across Canada. Terms were not disclosed.

Predecessor Detail - Name changed from IPL Energy Inc., Oct. 7, 1998.

Directors - Pamela L. Carter, chr., Franklin, Tenn.; Gregory L. (Greg) Ebel, pres. & CEO, Houston, Tex.; Mayank M. (Mike) Ashar, Calgary, Alta.; Gaurdie E. Banister Jr., Houston, Tex.; Susan M. Cunningham, Houston, Tex.; Jason B. Few, Westport, Conn.; Teresa S. Madden, Boulder, Colo.; Stephen S. Poloz, Orleans, Ont.; S. Jane Rowe, Toronto, Ont.; Dan C. Tutcher, Houston, Tex.; Steven W. (Steve) Williams, Calgary, Alta.

Other Exec. Officers - Matthew A. Akman, exec. v-p, corp. strategy & pres., power; Colin K. Gruending, exec. v-p & pres., liquids pipelines; Cynthia L. Hansen, exec. v-p & pres., gas transmission & midstream; Michele E. Harradence, exec. v-p & pres., gas distrib. & storage; Patrick R. (Pat) Murray, exec. v-p & CFO; Byron C. Neiles, exec. v-p & CAO; Robert R. (Bob) Rooney, exec. v-p & chief legal officer; Phillip M. Anderson, sr. v-p, bus. devel.; David W. Bryson, sr. v-p & chief opers. officer, gas transmission & midstream; Allen C. Capps, sr. v-p & chief comml. officer, gas transmission & midstream; Maximilian G. (Max) Chan, sr. v-p, corp. devel.; Michael A. (Mike) Fernandez, sr. v-p & chief commun. officer; Bhushan N. Ivaturi, sr. v-p & CIO; Melissa Y. Moye, sr. v-p & chief HR officer; Dean C. Patry, sr. v-p, opers. & eng., liquid pipelines; Laura J. Sayavedra, sr. v-p, safety & reliability, projects & unify; R. Thomas Schwartz, sr. v-p & gen. counsel; Marc N. Weil, sr. v-p, comml., liquids pipelines; Michelle R. George, v-p, new energy tech.; Jonathan E. Gould, v-p, treasury, risk & pensions; Christopher J. (Chris) Johnston, v-p, fin. & contr.; Robert J. Jozwiak, v-p, power opers.; Leigh D. Kelln, v-p, power strategy & comml.; Vikesh B. Kohli, v-p, safety & reliability; Cathleen A. (Cathy) Larson Ward, v-p, sustained bus. optimization; Leslie A. O'Leary, v-p, enterprise tax; Maistran B. Pillay, v-p, ERP & enterprise applications; Peter V. Sheffield, v-p & chief sustainability officer; Michael F. Spencer, v-p, corp. devel.; Jennifer M. H. Strain, v-p, corp. law; Phil Teijeira, v-p & chief supply chain officer; Karen K. L. Uehara, v-p & corp. sec.; Bruce J. Webster, v-p & chief audit exec.; Collette D. Wetter, v-p, unify lead & sustainment; Lisa D. Wilson, v-p & chief compliance officer; Bryan E. Ysebaert, v-p, enterprise asset & work mgt.

Capital Stock

	Authorized (shs.)	Outstanding (shs.)[1]
Preferred	unlimited	
5.5% Series A		5,000,000
5.2% Series B		20,000,000
Series C		nil
5.41% Series D		18,000,000
4.69% Series F		18,172,305[2]
Series G		1,827,695[3]
4.38% Series H		14,000,000
4.89% Series J		nil
5.86% Series L		16,000,000
5.09% Series N		18,000,000
4.38% Series P		16,000,000
4.07% Series R		16,000,000
5.95% Series 1		16,000,000
3.74% Series 3		24,000,000
5.38% Series 5		8,000,000
4.45% Series 7		10,000,000
4.1% Series 9		11,000,000
3.94% Series 11		20,000,000
3.04% Series 13		14,000,000
2.98% Series 15		11,000,000
5.15% Series 17		nil
6.21% Series 19		20,000,000
Common	unlimited	2,024,676,423

[1] At Apr. 28, 2023

[2] At June 1, 2023.

[3] At June 1, 2023.

Preferred - Issuable in series. Non-voting.

5.5% Series A - Entitled to fixed cumulative preferential annual dividends of Cdn$1.375 per share payable quarterly. Redeemable any time in whole or in part at Cdn$25 per share plus accrued and unpaid dividends.

5.2% Series B - Entitled to fixed cumulative preferential annual dividends of Cdn$1.3005 per share payable quarterly prior to June 1, 2027, and thereafter at a rate reset every five years equal to the five-year Government of Canada bond yield plus 2.4%. Redeemable on June 1, 2027, and on June 1 every five years thereafter at Cdn$25 per share plus accrued and unpaid dividends. Convertible into preferred shares, series C, subject to certain conditions, on June 1, 2027, and on June 1 every five years thereafter. The preferred shares, series C would pay a quarterly dividend equal to the 90-day Canadian Treasury bill rate plus 2.4%.

5.41% Series D - Entitled to fixed cumulative preferential annual dividends of Cdn$1.353 per share payable quarterly prior to Mar. 1, 2028, and thereafter at a rate reset every five years equal to the five-year Government of Canada bond yield plus 2.37%. Redeemable on Mar. 1, 2028, and on March 1 every five years thereafter at Cdn$25 per share plus accrued and unpaid dividends. Convertible into preferred shares, series E, subject to certain conditions, on Mar. 1, 2028, and on March 1 every five years thereafter. The preferred shares, series E would pay a quarterly dividend equal to the 90-day Canadian Treasury bill rate plus 2.37%.

4.69% Series F - Entitled to fixed cumulative preferential annual dividends of Cdn$1.3845 per share payable quarterly prior to June 1, 2028, and thereafter at a rate reset every five years equal to the five-year Government of Canada bond yield plus 2.51%. Redeemable on June 1, 2028, and on June 1 every five years thereafter at Cdn$25 per share plus accrued and unpaid dividends. Convertible into preferred shares, series G, subject to certain conditions, on June 1, 2028, and on June 1 every five years thereafter. The preferred shares, series G would pay a quarterly dividend equal to the 90-day Canadian Treasury bill rate plus 2.51%.

Series G - Entitled to floating cumulative preferential annual dividends payable quarterly equal to the 90-day Canadian Treasury bill rate plus 2.51%. Redeemable on June 30, 2028, and on June 30 every five years thereafter at $25 per share or at $25.50 per share on any other non-conversion date, plus declared and unpaid dividends on both cases. Convertible at the holder's option, on June 30, 2028, and on June 30 every five years thereafter, into preferred series F shares on a share-for-share basis, subject to certain conditions.

4.38% Series H - Entitled to fixed cumulative preferential annual dividends of Cdn$1.094 per share payable quarterly prior to Sept. 1, 2023, and thereafter at a rate reset every five years equal to the five-year Government of Canada bond yield plus 2.12%. Redeemable on Sept. 1, 2023, and on September 1 every five years thereafter at Cdn$25 per share plus accrued and unpaid dividends. Convertible into preferred shares, series I, subject to certain conditions, on Sept. 1, 2023, and on September 1 every five years thereafter. The preferred shares, series I would pay a quarterly dividend equal to the 90-day Canadian Treasury bill rate plus 2.12%.

5.86% Series L - Entitled to fixed cumulative preferential annual dividends of US$1.4645 per share payable quarterly prior to Sept. 1, 2027, and thereafter at a rate reset every five years equal to the five-year U.S. Government bond yield plus 3.15%. Redeemable on Sept. 1, 2027, and on September 1 every five years thereafter at US$25 per share plus accrued and unpaid dividends. Convertible into preferred shares, series M, subject to certain conditions, on Sept. 1, 2027, and on September 1 every five years thereafter. The preferred shares, series M would pay a quarterly dividend equal to the 90-day U.S. Treasury bill rate plus 3.15%.

5.09% Series N - Entitled to fixed cumulative preferential annual dividends of Cdn$1.2715 per share payable quarterly prior to Dec. 1, 2023, and thereafter at a rate reset every five years equal to the five-year Government of Canada bond yield plus 2.65%. Redeemable on Dec. 1, 2023, and on December 1 every five years thereafter at Cdn$25 per share plus accrued and unpaid dividends. Convertible into preferred shares, series O, subject to certain conditions, on Dec. 1, 2023, and on December 1 every five years thereafter. The preferred shares, series O would pay a quarterly dividend equal to the 90-day Canadian Treasury bill rate plus 2.65%.

4.38% Series P - Entitled to fixed cumulative preferential annual dividends of Cdn$1.0948 per share payable quarterly prior to Mar. 1, 2024, and thereafter at a rate reset every five years equal to the five-year Government of Canada bond yield plus 2.5%. Redeemable on Mar. 1, 2024, and on March 1 every five years thereafter at Cdn$25 per share plus accrued and unpaid dividends. Convertible into preferred shares, series Q, subject to certain conditions, on Mar. 1, 2024, and on March 1 every five years thereafter. The preferred shares, series Q would pay a quarterly dividend equal to the 90-day Canadian Treasury bill rate plus 2.5%.

4.07% Series R - Entitled to fixed cumulative preferential annual dividends of Cdn$1.0183 per share payable quarterly prior to June 1, 2024, and thereafter at a rate reset every five years equal to the five-year Government of Canada bond yield plus 2.5%. Redeemable on June 1, 2024, and on June 1 every five years thereafter at Cdn$25 per share plus accrued and unpaid dividends. Convertible into preferred shares, series S, subject to certain conditions, on June 1, 2024, and on June 1 every five years thereafter. The preferred shares, series S would pay a quarterly dividend equal to the 90-day Canadian Treasury bill rate plus 2.5%.

5.95% Series 1 - Entitled to fixed cumulative preferential annual dividends of US$1.4873 per share payable quarterly prior to June 1, 2023, and thereafter at a rate reset every five years equal to the five-year U.S. Government bond yield plus 3.14%. Redeemable on June 1, 2023, and on June 1 every five years thereafter at US$25 per share plus accrued and unpaid dividends. Convertible into preferred shares, series 2, subject to certain conditions, on June 1, 2023, and on June 1 every five years thereafter. The preferred shares, series 2 would pay a quarterly dividend equal to the 90-day U.S. Treasury bill rate plus 3.14%.

3.74% Series 3 - Entitled to fixed cumulative preferential annual dividends of Cdn$0.9343 per share payable quarterly prior to Sept. 1, 2024, and thereafter at a rate reset every five years equal to the five-year Government of Canada bond yield plus 2.38%. Redeemable on Sept. 1, 2024, and on September 1 every five years thereafter at Cdn$25 per share plus accrued and unpaid dividends. Convertible into preferred shares, series 4, subject to certain conditions, on Sept. 1, 2024, and on September 1 every five years thereafter. The preferred shares, series 4 would pay a quarterly dividend equal to the 90-day Canadian Treasury bill rate plus 2.38%.

5.38% Series 5 - Entitled to fixed cumulative preferential annual dividends of US$1.3438 per share payable quarterly prior to Mar. 1, 2024, and thereafter at a rate reset every five years equal to the five-year U.S. Government bond yield plus 2.82%. Redeemable on Mar. 1, 2024, and on March 1 every five years thereafter at US$25 per share plus accrued and unpaid dividends. Convertible into preferred shares, series 6, subject to certain conditions, on Mar. 1, 2024, and on March 1 every five years thereafter. The preferred shares, series 6 would pay a quarterly dividend equal to the 90-day U.S. Treasury bill rate plus 2.82%.

4.45% Series 7 - Entitled to fixed cumulative preferential annual dividends of Cdn$1.1122 per share payable quarterly prior to Mar. 1, 2024, and thereafter at a rate reset every five years equal to the five-year Government of Canada bond yield plus 2.57%. Redeemable on Mar. 1, 2024, and on March 1 every five years thereafter at Cdn$25 per share plus accrued and unpaid dividends. Convertible into preferred shares, series 8, subject to certain conditions, on Mar. 1, 2024, and on March 1 every five years thereafter. The preferred shares, series 8 would pay a quarterly dividend equal to the 90-day Canadian Treasury bill rate plus 2.57%.

4.1% Series 9 - Entitled to fixed cumulative preferential annual dividends of Cdn$1.0242 per share payable quarterly prior to Dec. 1, 2024, and thereafter at a rate reset every five years equal to the five-year Government of Canada bond yield plus 2.66%. Redeemable on Dec. 1, 2024, and on December 1 every five years thereafter at Cdn$25 per share plus accrued and unpaid dividends. Convertible into preferred shares, series 10, subject to certain conditions, on Dec. 1, 2024, and on December 1 every five years thereafter. The preferred shares, series 10 would pay a quarterly dividend equal to the 90-day Canadian Treasury bill rate plus 2.66%.

3.94% Series 11 - Entitled to fixed cumulative preferential annual dividends of Cdn$0.9845 per share payable quarterly prior to Mar. 1, 2025, and thereafter at a rate reset every five years equal to the five-year Government of Canada bond yield plus 2.64%. Redeemable on Mar. 1, 2025, and on March 1 every five years thereafter at Cdn$25 per share plus accrued and unpaid dividends. Convertible into preferred shares, series 12, subject to certain conditions, on Mar. 1, 2025, and on March 1 every five years thereafter. The preferred shares, series 12 would pay a quarterly dividend equal to the 90-day Canadian Treasury bill rate plus 2.64%.

3.04% Series 13 - Entitled to fixed cumulative preferential annual dividends of Cdn$0.7608 per share payable quarterly prior to June 1, 2025, and thereafter at a rate reset every five years equal to the five-year Government of Canada bond yield plus 2.66%. Redeemable on June 1, 2025, and on June 1 every five years thereafter at Cdn$25 per share plus accrued and unpaid dividends. Convertible into preferred shares, series 14, subject to certain conditions, on June 1, 2025, and on June 1 every five years thereafter. The preferred shares, series 14 would pay a quarterly dividend equal to the 90-day Canadian Treasury bill rate plus 2.66%.

2.98% Series 15 - Entitled to fixed cumulative preferential annual dividends of Cdn$0.7458 per share payable quarterly prior to Sept. 1, 2025, and thereafter at a rate reset every five years equal to the five-year Government of Canada bond yield plus 2.68%. Redeemable on Sept. 1, 2025, and on September 1 every five years thereafter at Cdn$25 per share plus accrued and unpaid dividends. Convertible into preferred shares, series 16, subject to certain conditions, on Sept. 1, 2025, and on September 1 every five years thereafter. The preferred shares, series 16 would pay a quarterly dividend equal to the 90-day Canadian Treasury bill rate plus 2.68%.

6.21% Series 19 - Entitled to fixed cumulative preferential annual dividends of Cdn$1.553 per share payable quarterly prior to Mar. 1, 2028, and thereafter at a rate reset every five years equal to the five-year Government of Canada bond yield plus 3.17%, provided that, in any event, such rate shall not be less than 4.9% per annum. Redeemable on Mar. 1, 2028, and on March 1 every five years thereafter at Cdn$25 per share plus accrued and unpaid dividends. Convertible into preferred shares, series 20, subject to certain conditions, on Mar. 1, 2028, and on March 1 every five years thereafter. The preferred shares, series 20 would pay a quarterly dividend equal to the 90-day Canadian Treasury bill rate plus 3.17%.

Common - One vote per share.

Options - At Dec. 31, 2022, options were outstanding to purchase 27,624,000 common shares at a weighted average exercise price of Cdn$48.46 per share with a weighted average remaining life of 5.7 years.

Preferred 5.15% Series 17 (old) - Were entitled to fixed cumulative preferential annual dividends of Cdn$1.2875 per share payable quarterly prior to Mar. 1, 2022. Redeemed on Mar. 1, 2022, at Cdn$25 per share.

Preferred Series C (old) - Were entitled to cumulative preferential annual dividends payable quarterly equal to the 90-day Canadian Treasury bill rate plus 2.4%. Converted into preferred shares, series B on a 1-for-1 basis on June 1, 2022.

Preferred 4.89% Series J (old) - Were entitled to fixed cumulative preferential annual dividends of US$1.2216 per share payable quarterly prior to June 1, 2022. Redeemed on June 1, 2022, at US$25 per share.

Normal Course Issuer Bid - The company plans to make normal course purchases of up to 27,938,163 common shares representing 1.4% of the total outstanding. The bid commenced on Jan. 6, 2023, and expires on Jan. 5, 2024.

Major Shareholder - Widely held at Mar. 2, 2023.

Price Range - ENB/TSX

Year	Volume	High	Low	Close
2022	2,299,493,836	$59.69	$48.88	$52.92
2021	2,116,679,624	$54.00	$40.63	$49.41
2020	1,839,303,647	$57.32	$33.06	$40.71
2019	1,196,886,718	$52.17	$41.64	$51.63
2018	944,721,121	$51.04	$37.36	$42.41

Recent Close: $46.83

Capital Stock Changes - On June 1, 2023, 1,827,695 reset preferred shares, series F were converted into a like number of floating preferred shares, series G.

On Mar. 1, 2022, all 30,000,000 reset preferred shares, series 17 were redeemed at Cdn$25 per share. On June 1, 2022, all 1,730,188 floating preferred shares, series C were converted into a like number of reset preferred shares, series B and all 8,000,000 reset preferred shares, series J were redeemed at US$25 per share. Also during 2022, 2,000,000 common shares were issued on exercise of options and 3,000,000 common shares were repurchased under a Normal Course Issuer Bid.

Dividends

ENB com Ra $3.55 pa Q est. Mar. 1, 2023[1]
Prev. Rate: $3.44 est. Mar. 1, 2022
Prev. Rate: $3.34 est. Mar. 1, 2021
Prev. Rate: $3.24 est. Mar. 1, 2020
ENB.PR.A pfd ser A cum. red. Ra $1.375 pa Q
ENB.PR.B pfd ser B cum. red. exch. Adj. Ra $1.255 pa Q est. Sept. 1, 2022
ENB.PR.D pfd ser D cum. red. exch. Adj. Ra $1.353 pa Q est. June 1, 2023
ENB.PR.F pfd ser F cum. red. exch. Adj. Ra $1.3845 pa Q est. Sept. 1, 2023
ENB.PR.H pfd ser H cum. red. exch. Adj. Ra $1.094 pa Q est. Dec. 1, 2018
ENB.PF.U pfd ser L cum. red. exch. Adj. Ra US$1.46975 pa Q est. Dec. 1, 2022
ENB.PR.N pfd ser N cum. red. exch. Adj. Ra $1.2715 pa Q est. Mar. 1, 2019
ENB.PR.P pfd ser P cum. red. exch. Adj. Ra $1.09475 pa Q est. June 1, 2019
ENB.PR.T pfd ser R cum. red. exch. Adj. Ra $1.01825 pa Q est. Sept. 1, 2019
ENB.PR.V pfd ser 1 cum. red. exch. Adj. Ra US$1.675925 pa Q est. Sept. 1, 2023
ENB.PR.Y pfd ser 3 cum. red. exch. Adj. Ra $0.93425 pa Q est. Dec. 1, 2019
ENB.PF.V pfd ser 5 cum. red. exch. Adj. Ra US$1.343825 pa Q est. June 1, 2019
ENB.PR.J pfd ser 7 cum. red. exch. Adj. Ra $1.11225 pa Q est. June 1, 2019
ENB.PF.A pfd ser 9 cum. red. exch. Adj. Ra $1.02425 pa Q est. Mar. 1, 2020
ENB.PF.C pfd ser 11 cum. red. exch. Adj. Ra $0.9845 pa Q est. June 1, 2020
ENB.PF.E pfd ser 13 cum. red. exch. Adj. Ra $0.76075 pa Q est. Sept. 1, 2020
ENB.PF.G pfd ser 15 cum. red. exch. Adj. Ra $0.74575 pa Q est. Dec. 1, 2020
ENB.PF.K pfd ser 19 cum. red. exch. Adj. Ra $1.553 pa Q est. June 1, 2023
ENB.PR.G pfd ser G cum. red. exch. Fltg. Ra pa Q
Listed Jun 1/23.
$0.43858**i**............ Sept. 1/23
pfd ser J cum. red. exch. Adj. Ra US$1.22175 pa Q est. Sept. 1, 2017[2]
US$0.3054**f**.......... June 1/22
pfd ser 17 cum. red. exch. Adj. Ra $1.2875 pa Q est. Mar. 1, 2017[3]
$0.321875**f**.......... Mar. 1/22
pfd ser C cum. red. exch. Fltg. Ra pa Q
Delisted Jun 2/22.

$0.184..............	June 1/22	$0.15719..........	Mar. 1/22
$0.16081..............	Dec. 1/21	$0.15753..........	Sept. 1/21

Paid in 2023: n.a. 2022: $0.34119 2021: $0.62684

[1] Dividend reinvestment plan suspended eff. Dec. 1, 2018.
[2] Redeemed June 1, 2022 at $25 per sh.
[3] Redeemed March 1, 2022 at $25 per sh.
f Final Payment **i** Initial Payment

Long-Term Debt - Outstanding at Dec. 31, 2022:

Enbridge Inc.:	
Comml. paper & cr. facility due 2023-2027	$7,984,000,000
Floating rate notes due 2023-2024[1]	1,491,000,000
US$ sr. notes due 2023-2051[2]	12,060,000,000
Med.-term notes due 2023-2064[3]	8,223,000,000
Sustain.-linked bonds due 2032-2033[4]	3,355,000,000
Subord. term notes due 2077-2078[5]	6,736,000,000
Subord. term notes due 2080-2083[6]	3,596,000,000
Other debt[7]	15,000,000
Subsidiary debt:	
Enbridge (U.S.) Inc. debt	4,206,000,000
Enbridge Energy Partners, L.P. sr. notes	3,320,000,000
Enbridge Gas Inc. debt	11,746,000,000
Enbridge Pipe. (Southern Lights) sr. notes	921,000,000
Enbridge Pipelines Inc. debt	5,937,000,000
Enbridge Southern Lights LP sr. notes	222,000,000
Spectra Energy Capital, LLC sr. notes	234,000,000
Algonquin Gas Transmission, LLC sr. notes	1,152,000,000
East Tennessee Natural Gas, LLC sr. notes	258,000,000
Texas Eastern Transmission, LP sr. notes	3,455,000,000
Spectra Energy Partners, LP sr. notes	4,336,000,000
Tri Global Energy, LLC sr. notes	18,000,000
Westcoast Energy Inc. notes & debs	1,500,000,000
Fair value adj.	608,000,000
Less: Debt disc., premiums & issue costs	393,000,000
Less: Short-term borrowings	1,996,000,000
	78,984,000,000
Less: Current portion	6,045,000,000
	72,939,000,000

[1] Bear interest equal to SOFR plus 0.4% to 0.63%.
[2] Bear a weighted average interest rate of 3.5%.
[3] Bear a weighted average interest rate of 3.8%.
[4] Bear a weighted average interest rate of 2%.
[5] Bear a weighted average interest rate of 5.9%.
[6] Bear a weighted average interest rate of 4.1%.
[7] Consists primarily of finance lease obligations.

Wholly Owned Subsidiaries

Enbridge Energy Management L.L.C., United States.
Enbridge Income Fund, Calgary, Alta.
Enbridge Pipelines (Athabasca) Inc., Alta.
Enbridge Pipelines Inc., Edmonton, Alta.
Enbridge Pipelines (NW) Inc, Calgary, Alta.
- 100% int. in **Enbridge Gas Inc.**, Toronto, Ont.

Enbridge Pipelines (Southern Lights) L.L.C.
Enbridge Southern Lights LP, Calgary, Alta.
Enbridge US Holdings Inc., Canada.
- 100% int. in **Enbridge Energy Company, Inc.**, Del.
  - 100% int. in **Enbridge Energy Partners, L.P.**, Houston, Tex.
    - 100% int. in **Enbridge Energy, Limited Partnership**, Del.
    - 25% int. in **Enbridge Holdings (DakTex) L.L.C.**, Del.
- 100% int. in **Midcoast Energy Partners, L.P.**, United States.

Gazifère Inc., Gatineau, Qué.
IPL System Inc., Alta.
Spectra Energy Capital, LLC, Del.
- 100% int. in **Spectra Energy DEFS Holding, LLC**, Del.
- 100% int. in **Spectra Energy Transmission, LLC**, Del.
  - 100% int. in **Spectra Energy Partners, LP**, Houston, Tex.
    - 100% int. in **East Tennessee Natural Gas, LLC**, Tenn.
    - 50% int. in **Gulfstream Natural Gas System, LLC**, United States.
    - 78% int. in **Maritimes & Northeast Pipeline Limited Partnership**, Halifax, N.S.
    - 78% int. in **Maritimes & Northeast Pipeline, LLC**, Del.
    - 50% int. in **NEXUS Gas Transmission, LLC**, United States.
    - 50% int. in **Sabal Trail Transmission, LLC**, Del.
    - 50% int. in **Southeast Supply Header, LLC**, United States.
    - 100% int. in **Spectra Energy Transmission II, LLC**, Del.
      - 100% int. in **Texas Eastern Transmission, LP**, Del.
    - 50% int. in **Steckman Ridge, L.P.**, United States.
    - 100% int. in **Tri Global Energy, LLC**, Dallas, Tex.
- 100% int. in **Westcoast Energy Inc.**, Calgary, Alta.

Tidal Energy Marketing Inc., Calgary, Alta.
Tidal Energy Marketing (U.S.) LLC, Del.
Valley Crossing Pipeline, LLC, Del.

Subsidiaries

51% int. in **EIH S.à.r.l.**, Luxembourg.
- 50% int. in **Eolien Maritime France S.A.S.**, France.

75% int. in **Enbridge Holdings (DakTex) L.L.C.**, Del.
51% int. in **Enbridge Renewable Infrastructure Investments S.A.R.L.**, Luxembourg.
65% int. in **Illinois Extension Pipeline Company, L.L.C.**, United States.
75% int. in **MarEn Bakken Company LLC**, Del.
60% int. in **Vector Pipeline Limited Partnership**, Canada.
60% int. in **Vector Pipeline L.P.**, United States.

Investments

50% int. in **Alliance Pipeline L.P.**, Del.
50% int. in **Alliance Pipeline Limited Partnership**, Calgary, Alta.
50% int. in **Aux Sable Canada LP**, Alta.
42.7% int. in **Aux Sable Liquid Products L.P.**, Del.
42.7% int. in **Aux Sable Midstream LLC**, Del.
30% int. in **Cactus II Pipeline, LLC**, Tex.
DCP Midstream, LLC, Denver, Colo. The company holds 23.4% interest in class A units to represent ownership in DCP Midstream, LP and 90% interest in class B units to represent ownership in Gray Oak Pipeline, LLC.
- 56.51% int. in **DCP Midstream, LP**, Denver, Colo. The company holds a 13.2% economic interest.
- 76.11% int. in **Gray Oak Pipeline, LLC**, United States. The company holds a 68.5% economic interest.

24.9% int. in **Rampion Offshore Wind Limited**, United Kingdom.
50% int. in **Seaway Crude Pipeline Company**, Oklahoma City, Okla.
30% int. in **Woodfibre LNG Limited Partnership**, B.C.
Note: The preceding list includes only the major related companies in which interests are held.

Financial Statistics

Periods ended:	12m Dec. 31/22[A]		12m Dec. 31/21[A]
	$000s	%Chg	$000s
Operating revenue	**53,309,000**	**+13**	**47,071,000**
Other operating expense	40,808,000		35,414,000
Operating expense	**40,808,000**	**+15**	**35,414,000**
Operating income	**12,501,000**	**+7**	**11,657,000**
Deprec., depl. & amort.	4,317,000		3,852,000
Finance costs, gross	3,179,000		2,655,000
Investment income	2,056,000		1,711,000
Write-downs/write-offs	(3,006,000)		(111,000)
Pre-tax income	**4,542,000**	**-41**	**7,729,000**
Income taxes	1,604,000		1,415,000
Net income	**2,938,000**	**-53**	**6,314,000**
Net inc. for equity hldrs	**3,003,000**	**-51**	**6,189,000**
Net inc. for non-cont. int	**(65,000)**	**n.a.**	**125,000**
Cash & equivalent	861,000		286,000
Inventories	2,255,000		1,670,000
Accounts receivable	5,616,000		4,957,000
Current assets	12,147,000		8,959,000
Long-term investments	16,529,000		13,954,000
Fixed assets, net	104,460,000		100,067,000
Right-of-use assets	680,000		645,000
Intangibles, net	36,458,000		36,783,000
Total assets	**179,608,000**	**+6**	**168,864,000**
Bank indebtedness	1,996,000		1,515,000
Accts. pay. & accr. liabs	6,172,000		5,314,000
Current liabilities	20,301,000		18,229,000
Long-term debt, gross	78,984,000		74,125,000
Long-term debt, net	72,939,000		67,961,000
Long-term lease liabilities	716,000		645,000
Preferred share equity	6,818,000		7,747,000
Shareholders' equity	59,887,000		60,826,000
Non-controlling interest	3,511,000		2,542,000
Cash from oper. activs	**11,230,000**	**+21**	**9,256,000**
Cash from fin. activs	(5,428,000)		1,236,000
Cash from invest. activs	(5,270,000)		(10,657,000)
Net cash position	**907,000**	**+183**	**320,000**
Capital expenditures	(4,647,000)		(7,818,000)
Unfunded pension liability	n.a.		88,000
Pension fund surplus	655,000		n.a.
	$		$
Earnings per share*	1.28		2.87
Cash flow per share*	5.55		4.58
Cash divd. per share*	3.44		3.34
	shs		shs
No. of shs. o/s*	2,025,000,000		2,026,000,000
Avg. no. of shs. o/s*	2,025,000,000		2,023,000,000
	%		%
Net profit margin	5.51		13.41
Return on equity	4.88		10.90
Return on assets	2.87		5.15
Foreign sales percent	48		57
No. of employees (FTEs)	11,100		10,900

* Common
[A] Reported in accordance with U.S. GAAP

Latest Results

Periods ended:	3m Mar. 31/23[A]		3m Mar. 31/22[A]
	$000s	%Chg	$000s
Operating revenue	12,075,000	-20	15,097,000
Net income	1,866,000	-9	2,057,000
Net inc. for equity hldrs	1,817,000	-10	2,029,000
Net inc. for non-cont. int	49,000		28,000
	$		$
Earnings per share*	0.86		0.95

* Common
[A] Reported in accordance with U.S. GAAP

Historical Summary
(as originally stated)

Fiscal Year	Oper. Rev.	Net Inc. Bef. Disc.	EPS*
	$000s	$000s	$
2022[A]	53,309,000	2,938,000	1.28
2021[A]	47,071,000	6,314,000	2.87
2020[A]	39,087,000	3,416,000	1.48
2019[A]	50,069,000	5,827,000	2.64
2018[A]	46,378,000	3,333,000	1.46

* Common
[A] Reported in accordance with U.S. GAAP

E.51 Endurance Capital Corp.

Symbol - ECAP.P **Exchange** - TSX-VEN **CUSIP** - 29290G
Head Office - 835-1100 Melville St, Vancouver, BC, V6E 4A6
Telephone - (604) 493-2004
Email - info@endurcap.com
Investor Relations - Darren Seed (604) 493-2004
Auditors - PricewaterhouseCoopers LLP C.A., Vancouver, B.C.
Transfer Agents - Olympia Trust Company, Vancouver, B.C.

Profile - (B.C. 2021) Capital Pool Company.
Directors - Darren Seed, CEO, CFO & corp. sec., Vancouver, B.C.; David R. Demers, Vancouver, B.C.; Issa Nakhleh, Vancouver, B.C.

Capital Stock

	Authorized (shs.)	Outstanding (shs.)[1]
Common	unlimited	13,600,000

[1] At May 19, 2023

Major Shareholder - Widely held at June 8, 2022.

Price Range - ECAP.P/TSX-VEN

Year	Volume	High	Low	Close
2022............	777,500	$0.20	$0.09	$0.09
2021............	97,500	$0.20	$0.15	$0.15

Recent Close: $0.05
Capital Stock Changes - There were no changes to capital stock during 2022.

E.52 Enerflex Ltd.

Symbol - EFX **Exchange** - TSX **CUSIP** - 29269R
Head Office - 904-1331 MacLeod Trail SE, Calgary, AB, T2G 0K3 **Telephone** - (403) 387-6377 **Toll-free** - (800) 242-3178 **Fax** - (403) 720-4385
Website - www.enerflex.com
Email - ir@enerflex.com
Investor Relations - Stefan Ali (403) 717-4953
Auditors - Ernst & Young LLP C.A., Calgary, Alta.
Bankers - The Bank of Nova Scotia, Toronto, Ont.; The Toronto-Dominion Bank, Calgary, Alta.
Lawyers - Burnet, Duckworth & Palmer LLP, Calgary, Alta.
Transfer Agents - TSX Trust Company, Calgary, Alta.
FP500 Revenue Ranking - 236
Employees - 4,900 at Dec. 31, 2022
Profile - (Can. 2011 amalg.) Provides energy infrastructure and energy transition products to customers in the global natural gas, energy transition and water treatment markets. Product offerings includes processing, cryogenic, compression, electric power and produced water solutions.

Operations are conducted in Canada, the U.S., Argentina, Bolivia, Brazil, Colombia, Ecuador, Mexico, Peru, the U.K., Netherlands, the U.A.E., Oman, Bahrain, Egypt, Kuwait, India, Iraq, Nigeria, Pakistan, Saudi Arabia, Australia, People's Republic of China, Indonesia, Singapore Malaysia and Thailand, and are organized into three segments: North America, Latin America, and Eastern Hemisphere. Operations of each of the three geographic segments are structured along three main product lines: Energy Infrastructure; Engineered Systems; and After-Market Service.

Energy Infrastructure - Provides solutions and comprehensive contract operations for natural gas compression, processing, produced water and electric power equipment across Canada, the U.S., Bahrain, Oman, Indonesia, Nigeria, Pakistan, Argentina, Bolivia, Brazil, Colombia, Mexico, and Peru. Includes critical infrastructure that the company owns, operates, and manages under contract to its customers' operations.

Engineered Systems - The company engineers, designs, fabricates and assembles modular natural gas-handling and low carbon solutions including oil and gas processing, gas compression systems, energy transition, produced water handling and treatment and electric power generation. Oil and gas processing systems include dehydration and natural gas liquids recovery, refrigeration, cryogenic processing, condensate stabilization, dew point control, and amine sweetening. Compression systems are used in natural gas gathering compression, gas lift compression, inlet and residue compression in processing facilities, compression for natural gas storage and pipeline compression. Energy translation solutions include carbon capture utilization and storage, renewable natural gas, electrification and hydrogen projects. Produced water handling and treatment includes lab-scale testing, research and development, and build-own-operate-maintain solutions. Electric power generation systems provides field construction, installation and commissioning of electric powers solutions in the oil and gas, industrial, institutional, greenhouse, data centres, mining, renewables, and agriculture sectors worldwide. Manufacturing facilities are located in Calgary, Alta., Houston, Tex., Broken Arrow, Okla., Sharjah, U.A.E., Brisbane, Australia and Singapore. The company also provides retrofit solutions which re-engineers, reconfigures and repackages existing compression equipment for various field applications.

After-Market Services - Provides after-market mechanical services, parts distribution, operations and maintenance solutions, equipment optimization and maintenance programs, manufacturer warranties, exchange components, long-term service agreements, and technical services to global customers.

Effective Oct. 13, 2022, the company's common shares commenced trading on the New York Stock Exchange (NYSE) under the symbol EFXT. The listing was in conjunction with the company's acquisition of Houston, Tex.-based **Exterran Corporation**.

Common listed on NYSE, Oct. 13, 2022.

Recent Merger and Acquisition Activity

Status: completed **Revised:** Oct. 13, 2022
UPDATE: The transaction was completed. Enerflex issued 34,013,055 common shares. PREVIOUS: Enerflex Ltd. agreed to acquire Houston, Tex.-based Exterran Corporation on the basis of 1.021 Enerflex common shares for each Exterran common share held, in a transaction valued at US$735,000,000. Exterran offers natural gas processing and treatment and compression products and services, providing critical midstream infrastructure solutions to customers through operations in 25 countries. Upon completion, Exterran would amalgamate with Enerflex's wholly owned Enerflex US Holdings Inc. The boards of directors of both companies unanimously approved the transaction, which was expected to be completed in the second half of 2022.

Directors - Kevin J. Reinhart, chr., Calgary, Alta.; Marc E. Rossiter, pres. & CEO, Calgary, Alta.; Fernando R. Assing, Houston, Tex.; Joanne L. Cox, Calgary, Alta.; W. Byron Dunn, Dallas, Tex.; Laura W. Folse, Tex.; James C. Gouin, Belle River, Ont.; Mona Hale, Edmonton, Alta.; Juan Carlos Villegas, Santiago, Chile; Michael A. Weill, Houston, Tex.
Other Exec. Officers - Patricia Martinez, chief energy transition officer; Rodney D. Gray, sr. v-p & CFO; David H. Izett, sr. v-p & gen. counsel; Robert G. Mitchell, sr. v-p & CAO; Matthew Lemieux, v-p, corp. devel. & treasury; Roger George, pres., water solutions; Mauricio Meineri, pres., Latin America; Philip A. J. Pyle, pres., eastern hemisphere; Gregory (Greg) Stewart, pres., U.S.A.; Helmuth Witulski, pres., Canada

Capital Stock

	Authorized (shs.)	Outstanding (shs.)[1]
Preferred	unlimited	nil
Common	unlimited	123,739,020

[1] At Apr. 30, 2023

Major Shareholder - Widely held at Mar. 10, 2023.

Price Range - EFX/TSX

Year	Volume	High	Low	Close
2022............	86,419,166	$9.70	$4.99	$8.54
2021............	67,933,764	$11.12	$6.43	$7.66
2020............	105,442,318	$12.39	$4.18	$6.56
2019............	49,181,747	$20.38	$10.05	$12.23
2018............	53,193,655	$18.72	$13.55	$15.98

Recent Close: $8.08
Capital Stock Changes - On Oct. 13, 2022, 34,013,055 common shares were issued pursuant to the acquisition of Exterran Corporation. Also during 2022, 47,120 common shares were issued on exercise of options.

Dividends

EFX com Var. Ra pa Q

$0.025.................	Oct. 12/23	$0.025.............	July 6/23
$0.025.................	Apr. 6/23	$0.025.............	Jan. 12/23

Paid in 2023: $0.10 2022: $0.10 2021: $0.08

Wholly Owned Subsidiaries

Enerflex Energy Systems (Australia) Pty Ltd., Australia.
- 70% int. in **Enerflex Middle East LLC**, Oman.
- 100% int. in **Enerflex Middle East WLL**, Bahrain.

Enerflex Holding Company NL B.V., Netherlands.
- 100% int. in **Exterran Middle East LLC**, Oman.

Enerflex Inc., Del.
- 100% int. in **Enerflex Energy Systems Inc.**, Del.
- 100% int. in **Enerflex US Holdings Inc.**, Houston, Tex.
  - 100% int. in **Exterran Energy Solutions, LP**, Del.

Enerflex International Holdings Ltd., Barbados.

Financial Statistics

Periods ended:	12m Dec. 31/22[A]		12m Dec. 31/21[¤A]
	$000s	%Chg	$000s
Operating revenue........................	**1,777,798**	**+85**	**960,156**
Cost of goods sold..........................	1,345,865		670,466
General & admin expense................	235,979		134,303
Stock-based compensation............	16,162		12,937
Operating expense........................	**1,598,006**	**+95**	**817,706**
Operating income........................	**179,792**	**+26**	**142,450**
Deprec., depl. & amort....................	128,287		87,622
Finance income..............................	10,484		3,286
Finance costs, gross........................	49,407		20,281
Investment income..........................	4,719		671
Write-downs/write-offs....................	(49,233)		(537)
Pre-tax income............................	**(79,733)**	**n.a.**	**38,102**
Income taxes..................................	21,210		56,557
Net income...................................	**(100,943)**	**n.a.**	**(18,455)**
Cash & equivalent...........................	253,776		172,758
Inventories......................................	369,298		172,687
Accounts receivable........................	456,578		212,206
Current assets.................................	1,446,050		709,707
Long-term investments....................	34,977		27,064
Fixed assets, net.............................	1,402,843		706,742
Right-of-use assets.........................	78,372		49,887
Intangibles, net...............................	782,150		576,388
Total assets.................................	**4,269,589**	**+95**	**2,191,442**
Accts. pay. & accr. liabs..................	610,579		234,212
Current liabilities............................	1,138,947		355,401
Long-term debt, gross.....................	1,390,325		331,422
Long-term debt, net.........................	1,363,237		331,422
Long-term lease liabilities...............	72,908		43,108
Shareholders' equity........................	1,542,908		1,353,754
Cash from oper. activs..................	**19,768**	**-91**	**208,194**
Cash from fin. activs........................	11,854		(80,456)
Cash from invest. activs..................	4,328		(48,861)
Net cash position..........................	**253,776**	**+47**	**172,758**
Capital expenditures.......................	(115,480)		(57,341)
Capital disposals.............................	16,323		4,890
	$		$
Earnings per share*........................	(1.04)		(0.21)
Cash flow per share*........................	0.20		2.32
Cash divd. per share*......................	0.10		0.09
	shs		shs
No. of shs. o/s*................................	123,739,020		89,678,845
Avg. no. of shs. o/s*........................	97,045,917		89,678,845
	%		%
Net profit margin.............................	(5.68)		(1.92)
Return on equity..............................	(6.97)		(1.34)
Return on assets..............................	(1.19)		(1.29)
Foreign sales percent......................	85		82
No. of employees (FTEs)..................	4,900		2,000

* Common
[¤] Restated
[A] Reported in accordance with IFRS

Latest Results

Periods ended:	3m Mar. 31/23[A]		3m Mar. 31/22[A]
	$000s	%Chg	$000s
Operating revenue...........................	825,044	+155	323,069
Net income......................................	12,524	n.a.	(369)
	$		$
Earnings per share*.........................	0.11		(0.00)

* Common
[A] Reported in accordance with IFRS

Historical Summary
(as originally stated)

Fiscal Year	Oper. Rev.	Net Inc. Bef. Disc.	EPS*
	$000s	$000s	$
2022[A]..................	1,777,798	(100,943)	(1.04)
2021[A]..................	960,156	(18,455)	(0.21)
2020[A]..................	1,217,052	88,257	0.98
2019[A]..................	2,045,422	152,128	1.70
2018[A]..................	1,703,273	101,416	1.14

* Common
[A] Reported in accordance with IFRS

E.53 Energy Plug Technologies Corp.

Symbol - PLUG **Exchange** - CSE **CUSIP** - 29280V
Head Office - 400-1681 Chestnut St, Vancouver, BC, V6J 4M6 **Telephone** - (604) 283-1262
Website - energyplugcorp.com
Email - paul@energyplugcorp.com
Investor Relations - Paul E. Dickson (604) 283-1262
Auditors - Davidson & Company LLP C.A., Vancouver, B.C.
Transfer Agents - Computershare Trust Company of Canada Inc., Toronto, Ont.

Profile - (B.C. 2018; orig. Ont., 2010) Provides virtual private network (VPN) services to the retail market and small and medium-sized enterprises (SMEs). Also developed an analytics and solutions technology for storage of hydrogen as an energy carrier.

Offers VPN Logix, an Android mobile application enabling instant virtual private network (VPN) protection which secures and encrypts internet connection with no technical knowledge or configuration required. Users of VPN Logix may receive LOGIX Tokens, which are tokens on the TRON network and are redeemable for products, services and upgrades.

Wholly owned **Greentech Hydrogen Innovations Corp.** has developed the Hydrogen-of-Things™ (HoT) smart hydrogen storage and distribution sensor technology, a hardware device with an integrated electronic chipset and software installations running algorithms operating wirelessly at hydrogen production plants, transport fleets and commercial end-user facilities to collect data for determining various metrics in using hydrogen as an energy carrier. The device is in the prototype and testing stage.

During the first quarter of fiscal 2023, wholly owned **Mobilman Management Inc.** was dissolved.

Predecessor Detail - Name changed from VPN Technologies Inc., June 1, 2023.

Directors - Paul E. Dickson, pres. & CEO, B.C.; Connie Hang, CFO, Vancouver, B.C.; Lindsay Hamelin-Vendel, Vancouver, B.C.; Bernard O'Brien

Other Exec. Officers - Curtis Ingleton, chief technical officer; Robert Young, chief mktg. officer; Patrick Butler, v-p, shareholder commun.; Rosie Hausler, v-p, mktg.; Jan Urata, corp. sec.

Capital Stock

	Authorized (shs.)	Outstanding (shs.)[1]
Common	unlimited	52,227,780

[1] At June 1, 2023

Major Shareholder - Widely held at July 6, 2022.

Price Range - PLUG/CSE

Year	Volume	High	Low	Close
2022	2,162,150	$0.10	$0.02	$0.04
2021	5,320,041	$0.35	$0.08	$0.13
2020	2,229,509	$0.23	$0.03	$0.06
2019	2,771,445	$0.55	$0.05	$0.08
2018	2,207,747	$2.50	$0.40	$0.40

Consolidation: 1-for-10 cons. in Nov. 2019

Recent Close: $0.09

Capital Stock Changes - In May 2023, private placement of 15,900,000 units (1 common share & ½ warrant) at $0.05 per unit was completed, with warrants exercisable at $0.075 per share for one year.

There were no changes to capital stock during fiscal 2022.

Wholly Owned Subsidiaries

Greentech Hydrogen Innovators Corp., Vancouver, B.C.

Financial Statistics

Periods ended:	12m June 30/22[A]		12m June 30/21[oA]
	$000s	%Chg	$000s
Operating revenue	**nil**	**n.a.**	**14**
Research & devel. expense	79		14
General & admin expense	387		664
Stock-based compensation	nil		358
Operating expense	**466**	**-55**	**1,036**
Operating income	**(466)**	**n.a.**	**(1,022)**
Deprec., depl. & amort.	nil		52
Pre-tax income	**(438)**	**n.a.**	**(1,047)**
Net income	**(438)**	**n.a.**	**(1,047)**
Cash & equivalent	546		1,046
Current assets	613		1,099
Total assets	**613**	**-44**	**1,099**
Accts. pay. & accr. liabs	54		123
Current liabilities	103		151
Shareholders' equity	510		948
Cash from oper. activs	**(516)**	**n.a.**	**(212)**
Cash from fin. activs	16		1,248
Cash from invest. activs	nil		8
Net cash position	**546**	**-48**	**1,046**
Capital expenditures	nil		(19)
Capital disposals	nil		27
	$		$
Earnings per share*	(0.01)		(0.05)
Cash flow per share*	(0.01)		(0.01)
	shs		shs
No. of shs. o/s*	35,807,780		35,807,780
Avg. no. of shs. o/s*	35,807,780		19,154,986
	%		%
Net profit margin	n.a.		n.m.
Return on equity	(60.08)		n.m.
Return on assets	(51.17)		(184.66)

* Common

[o] Restated

[A] Reported in accordance with IFRS

Historical Summary

(as originally stated)

Fiscal Year	Oper. Rev.	Net Inc. Bef. Disc.	EPS*
	$000s	$000s	$
2022[A]	nil	(438)	(0.01)
2021[A]	14	(1,047)	(0.05)
2020[A]	25	(579)	(0.07)
2019[A]	11	(965)	(0.20)
2018[A]	nil	(759)	(0.20)

* Common

[A] Reported in accordance with IFRS

Note: Adjusted throughout for 1-for-10 cons. in Nov. 2019

E.54 Enghouse Systems Limited*

Symbol - ENGH **Exchange** - TSX **CUSIP** - 292949

Head Office - 800-80 Tiverton Crt, Markham, ON, L3R 0G4 **Telephone** - (905) 946-3200 **Fax** - (905) 946-3201

Website - www.enghouse.com

Email - investor@enghouse.com

Investor Relations - Sam Anidjar (905) 946-3200

Auditors - Ernst & Young LLP C.A., Toronto, Ont.

Bankers - Royal Bank of Canada, Toronto, Ont.

Transfer Agents - TSX Trust Company, Toronto, Ont.

FP500 Revenue Ranking - 500

Employees - 1,729 at Oct. 31, 2022

Profile - (Ont. 1984) Develops and provides enterprise software solutions focusing on contact centres, video communications, virtual healthcare, telecommunications networks, public safety and transit markets worldwide.

Operations are organized into two business segments: Interactive Management and Asset Management.

Interactive Management - This segment specializes in contact centre and interaction software and services designed to facilitate remote work, enhance customer service, increase efficiency and manage customer communications across multiple types of interactions including voice, email, social channels, web chats, text and video. Core technologies include contact center, video collaboration, interactive voice response, artificial intelligence, outbound dialers, attendant console, agent performance optimization, customer survey, business intelligence and analytics that may be deployed in private cloud, multi-tenant cloud or on-premise environments. Customers include small to large enterprises including financial services companies, telecoms, business process service providers, as well as technology and health care providers.

Asset Management - This segment provides a portfolio of software and services solutions to cable operators, network telecommunication providers, media, transit, defence, utilities and public safety companies, as well as transit e-ticketing, automated fare collection, fleet routing, dispatch, scheduling, communications and emergency control centre solutions for the transportation, government, first responders, distribution and security sectors. Customers are primarily large companies that are often government-owned or regulated in their respective jurisdictions. Also includes software solutions that enable video service providers to deploy next-generation, advanced video services for all screens.

The segment has two operating groups: Enghouse Networks and Enghouse Transportation. Enghouse Networks offers software technology solutions for telecommunication service providers and defence companies. Products include Network Infrastructure, Business Support Systems, Operations Support Systems and Digital Transformation. Enghouse Transportation develops and implements integrated software solutions for planning and managing public and private transportation operations, and also provides and delivers end-to-end emergency and non-emergency public safety control centre and dispatch systems.

The company is headquartered in Markham, Ont., and has offices around the world including Canada, the U.S., the U.K., Sweden, Norway, Denmark, the Netherlands, Australia, Austria, New Zealand, Israel, Croatia, Hungary, Germany, France, Italy, Lebanon, Ireland, Romania, Belgium, Spain, Columbia, Malaysia, the Unite Arab Emirates, Japan, India, Pakistan, People's Republic of China, Brazil, Portugal and Kenya.

Recent Merger and Acquisition Activity

Status: completed **Revised:** Aug. 1, 2023

UPDATE: The transaction was completed for a purchase price of US$20,700,000, subject to adjustments. Lifesize would be integrated within the Enghouse Interactive Management Group. PREVIOUS: Enghouse Systems Limited agreed to acquire the assets of Texas-based Lifesize Inc., a global provider of video conferencing and omnichannel contact centre products and services. Lifesize has voluntarily filed for Chapter 11 Bankruptcy in the United States. Brands to be acquired include Lifesize, Kaptivo, ProScheduler, Serenova and Telstrat. Terms were not disclosed.

Status: completed **Announced:** Feb. 9, 2023

Enghouse Systems Limited acquired São Paulo, Brazil-based Mobi All Tecnologia S.A. (dba Navita), a developer of Software-as-a-Service (SaaS)-based enterprise mobility management software solutions focused on managing and controlling critical mobile assets as well as telecommunications and information technology expense management. Terms of the transaction were not disclosed.

Status: completed **Revised:** Feb. 8, 2023

UPDATE: The transaction was completed. Qumu would join Enghouse's Interactive Management Group. PREVIOUS: Enghouse Systems Limited agreed to acquire Qumu Corporation, a Minneapolis, Minn.-based, NASDAQ-listed company which provides cloud-based enterprise video technology that creates, manages, secures, distributes and measures the success of live and on-demand video within the enterprise, for US$0.90 cash per share, for a total equity value of US$18,000,000. Common use cases for Qumu's products included executive webcasts, virtual events, employee collaboration and training. Upon completion, Qumu would amalgamate with a wholly owned subsidiary of Enghouse. The boards of directors of both companies unanimously approved the transaction, which was expected to be completed in February 2023.

Status: completed **Announced:** Sept. 6, 2022

Enghouse Systems Limited acquired Rochester, N.Y.-based VoicePort LLC, a provider of Software-as-a-Service automated solutions. Voiceport software products include inbound and outbound IVR, AI-powered chatbots and provide full web chat capability. Terms of the transaction were not disclosed.

Status: completed **Announced:** July 6, 2022

Enghouse Systems Limited acquired Innsbruck, Austria-based NTW Software GmbH, provides a suite of products ranging from attendant console to contact centers for organizations of all sizes primarily within the Cisco market segment. Terms of the transaction were not disclosed.

Status: completed **Announced:** June 23, 2022

Enghouse Systems Limited acquired Stockholm, Sweden-based Competella AB, a provider of Software-as-a-Service and On-Premise contact center and attendant console solutions. Competella offers a complete contact center platform created to enhance the offerings of Microsoft Teams. Terms of the transaction were not disclosed.

Directors - Stephen J. Sadler, chr. & CEO, Ont.; Pierre Lassonde†, Toronto, Ont.; Eric A. Demirian, Toronto, Ont.; Jane Mowat, Toronto, Ont.; Melissa Sonberg, Montréal, Qué.; Paul J. Stoyan, Toronto, Ont.

Other Exec. Officers - Vincent Mifsud, pres.; Lynette Corbett, chief admin. & HR officer; Sam Anidjar, v-p, corp. devel.; Sam Castiglione, v-p, corp. devel.; Todd M. May, v-p & gen. counsel; Robert (Rob) Medved, v-p, fin. & corp. sec.; Tim Peters, v-p, global demand generation

† Lead director

Capital Stock

	Authorized (shs.)	Outstanding (shs.)[1]
Class A Preference	unlimited	nil
Class B Preference	unlimited	nil
Common	unlimited	55,270,239

[1] At June 12, 2023

Options - At Oct. 31, 2022, options were outstanding to purchase 1,463,500 common shares at prices ranging from $25 to $62 per share with a weighted average remaining contractual life of 3.99 years.

Normal Course Issuer Bid - The company plans to make normal course purchases of up to 3,000,000 common shares representing 7% of the public float. The bid commenced on May 2, 2023, and expires on May 1, 2024.

Major Shareholder - Mawer Investment Management Limited held 12.62% interest, Stephen J. Sadler held 11.9% interest and Pierre Lassonde held 10.22% interest at Jan. 16, 2023.

Price Range - ENGH/TSX

Year	Volume	High	Low	Close
2022	24,467,054	$48.51	$23.96	$35.97
2021	28,082,469	$66.66	$43.31	$48.43
2020	37,792,149	$80.91	$35.87	$61.65
2019	16,626,515	$51.21	$30.97	$48.18
2018	20,039,786	$43.50	$29.89	$33.21

Split: 2-for-1 split in Jan. 2019

Recent Close: $29.47

Capital Stock Changes - During fiscal 2022, 40,000 common shares were issued on exercise of options and 343,185 common shares were repurchased under a Normal Course Issuer Bid.

Dividends

ENGH com Ra $0.88 pa Q est. May 31, 2023
Prev. Rate: $0.74 est. May 31, 2022
Prev. Rate: $0.64 est. May 31, 2021
Prev. Rate: $0.54 est. May 29, 2020
$1.50◆ Feb. 16/21
Paid in 2023: $0.625 2022: $0.715 2021: $0.615 + $1.50◆

◆ Special

Long-Term Debt - At Oct. 31, 2022, the company had no long-term debt.

Wholly Owned Subsidiaries

CDRator A/S, Denmark.
Dialogic Group Inc., Parsippany, N.J.
Enghouse Holdings (UK) Limited, United Kingdom.
Enghouse Interactive AB, Sweden.
Enghouse Interactive Inc., Del.
Enghouse Interactive, S.L.U., Spain.
Enghouse Interactive (U.K.) Limited, United Kingdom.
- 100% int. in **Gamma Projects Limited**, United Kingdom.

Espial Group Inc., Ottawa, Ont.
- 100% int. in **Espial Corporation**, Del.
- 100% int. in **Espial DE, Inc.**
- 100% int. in **Espial Group Limited**
- 100% int. in **Espial Limited**
- 100% int. in **Espial Limited**
- 100% int. in **Espial S.A.S.**, France.
- 100% int. in **Espial (UK) Limited**, Cambs., United Kingdom.
- 100% int. in **Espial Unipessoal LDA**

Qumu Corporation, Minneapolis, Minn.
Tollgrade Communications, Inc., Cranberry, Pa.
Vidyo, Inc., Hackensack, N.J.

Note: The preceding list includes only the major related companies in which interests are held.

Financial Statistics

Periods ended:	12m Oct. 31/22[A]		12m Oct. 31/21[A]
	$000s	%Chg	$000s
Operating revenue	**427,585**	**-8**	**467,177**
Cost of sales	130,097		129,627
Research & devel. expense	72,262		77,197
General & admin expense	82,895		89,818
Stock-based compensation	1,708		2,026
Operating expense	**286,962**	**-4**	**298,668**
Operating income	**140,623**	**-17**	**168,509**
Deprec., depl. & amort.	46,727		54,793
Finance income	1,192		214
Finance costs, gross	824		1,122
Pre-tax income	**96,238**	**-10**	**107,418**
Income taxes	1,740		14,624
Net income	**94,498**	**+2**	**92,794**
Cash & equivalent	228,054		198,834
Accounts receivable	93,104		89,374
Current assets	334,498		303,660
Fixed assets, net	4,186		6,246
Right-of-use assets	20,063		25,943
Intangibles, net	315,904		324,843
Total assets	**704,998**	**+5**	**674,624**
Accts. pay. & accr. liabs.	60,525		71,506
Current liabilities	163,873		174,538
Long-term lease liabilities	13,055		17,660
Shareholders' equity	508,165		454,311
Cash from oper. activs	**103,181**	**-13**	**118,460**
Cash from fin. activs	(54,868)		(119,507)
Cash from invest. activs	(21,090)		(37,615)
Net cash position	**225,104**	**+15**	**195,890**
Capital expenditures	(919)		(3,333)
Unfunded pension liability	1,821		2,663
	$		$
Earnings per share*	1.70		1.67
Cash flow per share*	1.86		2.14
Cash divd. per share*	0.69		0.59
Extra divd. - cash*	nil		1.50
Total divd. per share*	**0.69**		**2.09**
	shs		shs
No. of shs. o/s*	55,250,239		55,553,424
Avg. no. of shs. o/s*	55,465,000		55,450,000
	%		%
Net profit margin	22.10		19.86
Return on equity	19.64		19.52
Return on assets	13.82		13.04
Foreign sales percent	94		95
No. of employees (FTEs)	1,729		1,813

* Common
[A] Reported in accordance with IFRS

Latest Results

Periods ended:	6m Apr. 30/23[A]		6m Apr. 30/22[A]
	$000s	%Chg	$000s
Operating revenue	219,896	+1	217,414
Net income	29,559	-25	39,468
	$		$
Earnings per share*	0.53		0.71

* Common
[A] Reported in accordance with IFRS

Historical Summary
(as originally stated)

Fiscal Year	Oper. Rev. $000s	Net Inc. Bef. Disc. $000s	EPS* $
2022[A]	427,585	94,498	1.70
2021[A]	467,177	92,794	1.67
2020[A]	503,778	98,590	1.79
2019[A]	385,853	70,849	1.30
2018[A]	342,845	57,745	1.06

* Common
[A] Reported in accordance with IFRS
Note: Adjusted throughout for 2-for-1 split in Jan. 2019

E.55 Enlighta Inc.

Symbol - NLTA.H **Exchange** - TSX-VEN **CUSIP** - G3066B
Head Office - 30 DeCastro St, Wickhams Cay 1, PO Box 4519, Road Town, Tortola, British Virgin Islands
Website - enlightahealth.com
Email - yzhu@enlightahealth.com
Investor Relations - Yun Zhu (604) 200-8028
Auditors - Dale Matheson Carr-Hilton LaBonte LLP C.A., Vancouver, B.C.
Transfer Agents - Computershare Trust Company of Canada Inc., Calgary, Alta.
Profile - (British Virgin Islands 2019; orig. B.C., 2016 amalg.) Enters into joint ventures and intellectual property and licensing agreements in the healthcare, medical, green and clean technologies and related asset digitization sectors.

The company's portfolio includes the Fischer Institute of Asia, a joint venture with Arizona-based Fischer Institute of Physical Therapy and Performance, which provides the Asian market with licensed partner clinic facilities for orthopaedic post-surgery and/or post-treatment recovery, sports-related trauma treatment, orthopaedic, spinal and degenerative treatment and treatment of professional athletes; and a global master licence for automated bioprocessing systems for adipose tissue which could be used in clinical fields including cosmetic and aesthetic medicine, wound management, conditions of hair loss, cardiovascular and heart diseases, gastrointestinal diseases, peripheral arterial disease, female pelvic medicine, critical limb ischemia, osteoarthritis, hepatic and kidney disease, urology, neurodegenerative diseases, ophthalmology, spinal cord injuries, respiratory medicine and autoimmune diseases.

Predecessor Detail - Name changed from HooXi Network Inc., July 23, 2019.

Directors - John F. Wallace, chr.; Yun (Avis) Zhu, CEO, Beijing, Beijing, People's Republic of China; Norman (Norm) Tsui, pres., Richmond, B.C.; Dr. Chaofan (Christina) Gong; Bing (Ben) Wu, New York, N.Y.
Other Exec. Officers - Jing Chen, CFO

Capital Stock

	Authorized (shs.)	Outstanding (shs.)[1]
Preferred	unlimited	nil
Common	unlimited	17,080,529

[1] At Sept. 30, 2022

Major Shareholder - Dr. Bruno Wu held 24.8% interest at Apr. 4, 2022.

Price Range - NLTA.H/TSX-VEN

Year	Volume	High	Low	Close
2022	228,273	$0.28	$0.02	$0.07
2021	536,123	$0.28	$0.07	$0.09
2020	233,479	$0.20	$0.02	$0.16
2019	191,648	$1.12	$0.10	$0.21
2018	320,491	$4.35	$0.50	$1.01

Recent Close: $0.02

Capital Stock Changes - In June 2022, private placement of up to 11,800,000 common shares at $0.055 per share was announced.

There were no changes to capital stock from fiscal 2021 to fiscal 2022, inclusive.

Wholly Owned Subsidiaries

Beijing Pan Asia Consulting Co., Ltd.
Brilliance International Auto Company Limited
CTC Life Sciences Inc., New York, N.Y.
Cloud Medical Group Inc., Canada.
Orchard Road Management Corp.

Financial Statistics

Periods ended:	12m June 30/22[A]		12m June 30/21[oA]
	$000s	%Chg	$000s
Salaries & benefits	272		325
Research & devel. expense	39		nil
General & admin expense	329		136
Stock-based compensation	nil		57
Operating expense	**640**	**+24**	**518**
Operating income	**(640)**	**n.a.**	**(518)**
Deprec., depl. & amort.	315		315
Write-downs/write-offs	(2,669)		nil
Pre-tax income	**(3,627)**	**n.a.**	**(837)**
Net income	**(3,627)**	**n.a.**	**(837)**
Cash & equivalent	42		60
Current assets	46		61
Intangibles, net	nil		2,961
Total assets	**46**	**-98**	**3,045**
Bank indebtedness	1,940		1,566
Accts. pay. & accr. liabs.	601		348
Current liabilities	2,541		1,914
Shareholders' equity	(2,495)		1,131
Cash from oper. activs	**(380)**	**n.a.**	**(437)**
Cash from fin. activs	362		437
Net cash position	**42**	**-30**	**60**
	$		$
Earnings per share*	(0.21)		(0.05)
Cash flow per share*	(0.02)		(0.03)
	shs		shs
No. of shs. o/s*	17,080,529		17,080,529
Avg. no. of shs. o/s*	17,080,529		17,080,529
	%		%
Net profit margin	n.a.		n.a.
Return on equity	n.m.		(55.03)
Return on assets	(219.69)		(25.29)

* Common
[o] Restated
[A] Reported in accordance with IFRS

Latest Results

Periods ended:	3m Sept. 30/22[A]		3m Sept. 30/21[A]
	$000s	%Chg	$000s
Net income	(154)	n.a.	(243)
	$		$
Earnings per share*	(0.01)		(0.01)

* Common
[A] Reported in accordance with IFRS

Historical Summary
(as originally stated)

Fiscal Year	Oper. Rev. $000s	Net Inc. Bef. Disc. $000s	EPS* $
2022[A]	nil	(3,627)	(0.21)
2021[A]	nil	(837)	(0.05)
2020[A]	nil	(5,267)	(0.31)
2019[A]	nil	(2,959)	(0.25)
2018[A]	nil	(8,946)	(1.05)

* Common
[A] Reported in accordance with IFRS
Note: Adjusted throughout for 1-for-15 cons. in July 2018

E.56 Ensign Energy Services Inc.*

Symbol - ESI **Exchange** - TSX **CUSIP** - 293570
Head Office - 1000-400 5 Ave SW, Calgary, AB, T2P 0L6 **Telephone** - (403) 262-1361 **Fax** - (403) 262-8215
Website - www.ensignenergy.com
Email - michael.gray@ensignenergy.com
Investor Relations - Michael R. Gray (403) 267-6234
Auditors - PricewaterhouseCoopers LLP C.A., Calgary, Alta.
Bankers - Bank of Montreal; HSBC Bank Canada, Calgary, Alta.
Lawyers - Burnet, Duckworth & Palmer LLP, Calgary, Alta.
Transfer Agents - Computershare Trust Company of Canada Inc., Calgary, Alta.
FP500 Revenue Ranking - 258
Employees - 4,772 at Dec. 31, 2022
Profile - (Alta. 1987) Provides a wide range of oilfield services, including drilling and well servicing, oil sands coring, directional drilling, underbalanced and managed pressure drilling, equipment rentals and transportation. Operations are conducted in three geographic areas: Canada, the U.S. and International.

In Canada, operations and services are carried out through wholly owned **Ensign Drilling Inc.** through six operating divisions: Ensign Canadian Drilling, Encore Coring & Drilling, Ensign Well Servicing, Enhanced Drill Systems and Chandel Equipment Rentals, with a fleet of 123 drilling rigs, 21 specialty oil sands/coring rigs, 47 well servicing rigs, underbalanced and managed pressure drilling units, directional drilling kits and oilfield rental assets operating throughout western Canada, Yukon and the Northwest Territories.

In the U.S., contract drilling and well servicing operations are carried out through wholly owned **Ensign United States Drilling Inc.**, with a fleet of 17 drilling rigs, 22 well servicing rigs and directional drilling kits and oilfield rental assets in the Rocky Mountain region; wholly owned **Ensign United States Drilling (California) Inc.**, with a fleet of 17 drilling rigs and 25 well servicing rigs in California; and wholly owned **Ensign US Southern Drilling LLC**, with a fleet of 55 drilling rigs, based in Houston, Tex., and serving the Southern region, New Mexico and Pennsylvania.

International contract drilling and workover services are carried out through the following wholly owned subsidiaries: **Ensign Australia Pty Limited**, with a fleet of 14 drilling and workover rigs in Australia; **Ensign International Energy Services LLC** (70% owned) and **Ensign Bahrain Drilling WLL**, with a fleet of six drilling and workover rigs in Oman and Bahrain; **Ensign Argentina S.A.**, with a fleet of four drilling and workover rigs in Argentina; **Ensign de Venezuela C.A.**, with a fleet of eight drilling and workover rigs in Venezuela; and **Trinidad Drilling International Luxembourg S.A.R.L.**, with a fleet of two drilling rigs in Bahrain, Kuwait and Mexico.

Utilization Rate

Year ended Dec. 31	2022	2021
Drilling		
Canada	27.1%	18.5%
U.S.	38.7%	24.7%
International	23.7%	19.3%
Well Servicing		
Canada	24.9%	19.1%
U.S.	70.8%	71.7%

Periods ended:	12m Dec. 31/22	12m Dec. 31/21
No. of drill rigs	246	262
Drill rig operating days	35,490	24,795
No. of service rigs	94	100
Service rig operating hrs	171,304	161,170

Recent Merger and Acquisition Activity

Status: completed **Announced:** Oct. 26, 2022
Cathedral Energy Services Ltd. acquired the operating assets and personnel of Ensign Energy Services Inc.'s Canadian directional drilling business for a purchase price of $5,000,000 satisfied by the issuance of 7,017,988 common shares. As part of the transaction, Cathedral and Ensign entered into a marketing and technology alliance to further help support and expand the customer base of both companies in the Canadian market.
Status: completed **Announced:** Mar. 4, 2022

Ensign Energy Services Inc. sold two 3,000-hp AC drilling rigs that were cold-stacked in Mexico for US$34,000,000 cash.

Predecessor Detail - Name changed from Ensign Resource Service Group Inc., May 19, 2005.

Directors - N. Murray Edwards, chr., Switzerland; Robert H. (Bob) Geddes, pres. & COO, Calgary, Alta.; Len O. Kangas†, Red Deer, Alta.; Gary W. Casswell, Montgomery, Tex.; Darlene J. Haslam, Calgary, Alta.; James B. (Jim) Howe, Calgary, Alta.; Cary A. Moomjian Jr., Frisco, Tex.; Gail D. Surkan, Red Deer, Alta.; Barth E. Whitham, Denver, Colo.

Other Exec. Officers - Michael R. (Mike) Gray, CFO; Brent J. Conway, exec. v-p, intl. opers.; Michael R. Nuss, exec. v-p, U.S. opers.; Eldon Culshaw, sr. v-p, Cdn. opers.; Jonathan Baskeyfield, v-p, tax; Jehad (Jake) Hamdan, v-p, eng.; Ahmed Iqbal, v-p & contr.; Patrick Kearley, v-p, global HSE & field training; Rick Pingel, v-p, global supply chain; Cathy Robinson, v-p, global HR; Trevor Russell, v-p, fin.; Ron Tolton, v-p, IT; Justin Louie, gen. counsel & corp. sec.

† Lead director

Capital Stock

	Authorized (shs.)	Outstanding (shs.)[1]
Preferred	unlimited	nil
Common	unlimited	183,693,722

[1] At Aug. 3, 2023

Options - At Dec. 31, 2022, options were outstanding to purchase 4,287,410 common shares at prices ranging from $0.54 to $6.02 per share (weighted average exercise price of $2.57 per share) with an average remaining life of 2.75 years.

Major Shareholder - N. Murray Edwards held 23.36% interest and Fairfax Financial Holdings Limited held 11.83% interest at Mar. 17, 2023.

Price Range - ESI/TSX

Year	Volume	High	Low	Close
2022	134,917,374	$5.00	$1.70	$3.41
2021	133,265,639	$2.50	$0.90	$1.68
2020	240,003,801	$3.08	$0.22	$0.91
2019	98,309,735	$6.45	$2.25	$2.85
2018	61,057,811	$7.83	$4.14	$4.79

Recent Close: $2.76

Capital Stock Changes - In June 2022, 21,142,857 common shares were issued on conversion of $37,000,000 of convertible debentures. Also during 2022, 46,050 common shares were issued on exercise of options and the total of unvested common shares held in trust for stock-based compensation plans was increased by 300,738 common shares.

Long-Term Debt - Outstanding at Dec. 31, 2022:

Credit facility[1]	$882,686,000
9.25% sr. notes due April 2024[2]	565,344,000
Less: Def. financing costs	8,455,000
	1,439,575,000
Less: Current portion	882,686,000
	556,889,000

[1] Consist of a $900,000,000 revolving credit facility, bearing interest at Canadian prime rate plus 1.25% to 3.75% or U.S. base/prime rate plus 1.25% to 3.75% or commitment rate of 0.56% to 1.19% or bankers' acceptance rate plus 2.25% to 4.75% or LIBOR and letters of credit rate plus 2.25% to 4.75%. Matures in the earlier of: (i) six months prior to maturity date of 9.25% sr. notes due Apr. 15, 2024; and (ii) Nov. 25, 2024.

[2] US$700,000,000.

Wholly Owned Subsidiaries

Ensign Argentina S.A., Buenos Aires, Argentina.
Ensign Australia Pty Limited, Australia.
Ensign Bahrain Drilling WLL, Bahrain.
Ensign (Barbados) Holdings Inc., Barbados.
Ensign de Venezuela C.A., Venezuela.
Ensign Drilling Inc., Alta.
Ensign International Energy Services Pty Limited, Adelaide, S.A., Australia.
Ensign US Southern Drilling LLC, Del.
Ensign United States Drilling (California) Inc., Bakersfield, Calif.
Ensign United States Drilling Inc., Denver, Colo.
OFS Global Inc., Nev.
TDL Bahrain WLL, Bahrain.
TDL Kuwait for Oil Rigs and Natural Gas Extraction Activities, Services and Facilities S.P.C., Kuwait.

Subsidiaries

70% int. in **Ensign International Energy Services LLC**, Oman.

Note: The preceding list includes only the major related companies in which interests are held.

Financial Statistics

Periods ended:	12m Dec. 31/22[A]		12m Dec. 31/21[A]
	$000s	%Chg	$000s
Operating revenue	**1,577,329**	**+58**	**995,594**
General & admin expense	48,628		38,226
Stock-based compensation	19,711		6,377
Other operating expense	1,155,083		744,195
Operating expense	**1,223,422**	**+55**	**788,798**
Operating income	**353,907**	**+71**	**206,796**
Deprec., depl. & amort.	281,137		288,188
Finance income	nil		7,431
Finance costs, gross	128,077		108,415
Pre-tax income	**(6,373)**	**n.a.**	**(194,462)**
Income taxes	(14,859)		(38,454)
Net inc. bef. disc. opers	**8,486**	**n.a.**	**(156,008)**
Income from disc. opers	nil		(3,452)
Net income	**8,486**	**n.a.**	**(159,460)**
Net inc. for equity hldrs	**8,128**	**n.a.**	**(159,475)**
Net inc. for non-cont. int	**358**	**n.m.**	**15**
Cash & equivalent	49,880		13,305
Accounts receivable	359,933		226,807
Current assets	470,611		289,864
Fixed assets, net	2,516,923		2,512,953
Total assets	**3,183,904**	**+7**	**2,977,054**
Accts. pay. & accr. liabs	268,243		177,932
Current liabilities	1,178,411		185,636
Long-term debt, gross	1,439,575		1,453,884
Long-term debt, net	556,889		1,453,884
Long-term lease liabilities	5,948		4,327
Equity portion of conv. debs	nil		2,380
Shareholders' equity	1,288,770		1,192,662
Cash from oper. activs	**319,962**	**+79**	**178,642**
Cash from fin. activs	(162,045)		(35,032)
Cash from invest. activs	(121,457)		(174,586)
Net cash position	**49,880**	**+275**	**13,305**
Capital expenditures	(174,393)		(183,180)
Capital disposals	47,544		7,228
	$		$
Earns. per sh. bef disc opers*	0.05		(0.96)
Earnings per share*	0.05		(0.98)
Cash flow per share*	1.82		1.10
	shs		shs
No. of shs. o/s*	183,459,123		161,969,478
Avg. no. of shs. o/s*	175,578,024		162,541,464
	%		%
Net profit margin	0.54		(15.67)
Return on equity	0.66		(12.20)
Return on assets	(5.26)		(2.29)
Foreign sales percent	72		75
No. of employees (FTEs)	4,772		4,160

* Common
[A] Reported in accordance with IFRS

Latest Results

Periods ended:	6m June 30/23[A]		6m June 30/22[A]
	$000s	%Chg	$000s
Operating revenue	916,822	+35	676,799
Net income	14,785	n.a.	(21,470)
Net inc. for equity hldrs	14,543	n.a.	(21,551)
Net inc. for non-cont. int	242		81
	$		$
Earnings per share*	0.08		(0.13)

* Common
[A] Reported in accordance with IFRS

Historical Summary
(as originally stated)

Fiscal Year	Oper. Rev.	Net Inc. Bef. Disc.	EPS*
	$000s	$000s	$
2022[A]	1,577,329	8,486	0.05
2021[A]	995,594	(156,008)	(0.96)
2020[A]	936,818	(66,740)	(0.41)
2019[A]	1,592,247	(163,454)	(1.02)
2018[A]	1,156,357	58,664	0.37

* Common
[A] Reported in accordance with IFRS

E.57 Enterprise Group, Inc.

Symbol - E **Exchange** - TSX **CUSIP** - 29373A
Head Office - 2-64 Riel Dr, St. Albert, AB, T8N 4A4 **Telephone** - (780) 418-4400 **Toll-free** - (888) 303-3361 **Fax** - (780) 418-1941
Website - www.enterprisegrp.ca
Email - des.okell@enterprisegrp.ca
Investor Relations - Desmond O'Kell (888) 303-3361
Auditors - Grant Thornton LLP C.A., Edmonton, Alta.
Lawyers - Borden Ladner Gervais LLP, Calgary, Alta.
Transfer Agents - Odyssey Trust Company, Calgary, Alta.
Employees - 90 at Dec. 31, 2022

Profile - (Alta. 2004) Provides specialty equipment rentals and services for the build-out of infrastructure for the energy, pipeline and construction industry.

Wholly owned **Artic Therm International Ltd.** (ATI) provides flameless heat technology to the broad based construction and oil and gas industries in western Canada. ATI owns a fleet of over 200 flameless heaters ranging in heat output from 375,000 British Thermal Units (BTUs) to 3,300,000 BTUs.

Wholly owned **Hart Oilfield Rentals Ltd.** provides oilfield infrastructure site services and rentals to its oil and gas customers. It designs, manufactures, and assembles modular/combo equipment, including fuel, generator, light stand, sewage treatment, medic security, and truck trailer combos. Hart's rental equipment fleet consists of 2,000 pieces of equipment designed to provide one-stop on-site infrastructure in support of drilling and completion operations. Hart services highly active plays of west-central Alberta and northeastern British Columbia, including Cardium, Duvernay, Montney and the Deep Basin from four service locations in Drayton Valley, Whitecourt and Grande Prairie, Alta.

Wholly owned **Westar Oilfield Rentals Inc.** provides oilfield and infrastructure site services and rentals to a variety of oil and gas customers, servicing the Fort St. John area with more than 600 pieces of owned equipment.

Wholly owned **Evolution Power Projects Inc.** provides low-emission mobile power systems and associated surface infrastructure to the energy, resource and industrial sectors, delivering real-time emission metrics. Evolution Power owns a fleet of turbine and compression engine power plants along with micro grid transmission infrastructure.

The company is headquartered in St. Albert, Alta., and has field offices in Morinville, Edmonton, Drayton Valley, Fort McMurray, Whitecourt and Grande Prairie, Alta.; Pouce Coupe and Fort St. John, B.C.

On Jan. 23, 2023, the company's common shares commenced trading on the OTCQB Venture Market under the ticker symbol ETOLF.

In May 2022, the company sold its office and yard facility in Pouce Coupe, B.C., for $530,000.

Predecessor Detail - Name changed from Enterprise Oilfield Group, Inc., July 30, 2012.

Directors - Leonard D. Jaroszuk, chr., pres. & CEO, St. Albert, Alta.; Desmond (Des) O'Kell, sr. v-p & corp. sec., St. Albert, Alta.; N. John Campbell†, Vancouver, B.C.; Neil Darling, Calgary, Alta.; John H. C. Pinsent, Edmonton, Alta.

Other Exec. Officers - Warren M. Cabral, CFO

† Lead director

Capital Stock

	Authorized (shs.)	Outstanding (shs.)[1]
Preferred	unlimited	nil
Common	unlimited	49,694,874

[1] At May 9, 2023

Normal Course Issuer Bid - The company plans to make normal course purchases of up to 2,401,064 common shares representing 10% of the public float. The bid commenced on Aug. 30, 2022, and expires on Aug. 29, 2023.

Major Shareholder - Leonard D. Jaroszuk held 29.1% interest at May 2, 2023.

Price Range - E/TSX

Year	Volume	High	Low	Close
2022	12,911,524	$0.46	$0.28	$0.39
2021	14,680,870	$0.37	$0.18	$0.31
2020	10,244,451	$0.34	$0.10	$0.22
2019	14,411,606	$0.31	$0.15	$0.20
2018	10,133,656	$0.63	$0.17	$0.23

Recent Close: $0.44

Capital Stock Changes - During 2022, 4,881,000 common shares were issued on exercise of options and 1,799,000 common shares were repurchased under a Normal Course Issuer Bid.

Wholly Owned Subsidiaries

E One Limited, Alta.
- 100% int. in **Artic Therm International Ltd.**, Edmonton, Alta.
- 100% int. in **Evolution Power Projects Inc.**, Alta.
- 100% int. in **Hart Oilfield Rentals Ltd.**, Grande Prairie, Alta.
- 100% int. in **Westar Oilfield Rentals Inc.**, Fort St. John, B.C.

Note: The preceding list includes only the major related companies in which interests are held.

Financial Statistics

Periods ended:	12m Dec. 31/22[A]		12m Dec. 31/21[A]
	$000s	%Chg	$000s
Operating revenue	**26,892**	**+44**	**18,732**
Cost of sales	16,012		12,101
General & admin expense	2,733		1,764
Stock-based compensation	102		25
Operating expense	**18,847**	**+36**	**13,890**
Operating income	**8,045**	**+66**	**4,842**
Deprec., depl. & amort.	4,521		5,856
Finance costs, gross	1,478		1,202
Pre-tax income	**2,274**	**n.a.**	**(2,418)**
Income taxes	(1)		(43)
Net income	**2,275**	**n.a.**	**(2,376)**
Cash & equivalent	1,062		877
Inventories	327		296
Accounts receivable	7,457		5,133
Current assets	9,988		7,153
Fixed assets, net	41,823		40,947
Intangibles, net	498		553
Total assets	**55,372**	**+8**	**51,147**
Accts. pay. & accr. liabs.	2,015		1,633
Current liabilities	2,620		2,858
Long-term debt, gross	15,509		14,799
Long-term debt, net	14,904		13,574
Shareholders' equity	34,786		32,222
Cash from oper. activs.	**5,911**	**+69**	**3,501**
Cash from fin. activs.	(1,373)		(937)
Cash from invest. activs.	(4,352)		(2,471)
Net cash position	**1,062**	**+21**	**877**
Capital expenditures	(5,569)		(3,845)
Capital disposals	1,217		1,375
	$		$
Earnings per share*	0.05		(0.05)
Cash flow per share*	0.12		0.07
	shs		shs
No. of shs. o/s*	50,965,874		47,883,874
Avg. no. of shs. o/s*	49,118,044		48,717,533
	%		%
Net profit margin	8.46		(12.68)
Return on equity	6.79		(7.07)
Return on assets	7.05		(2.31)
No. of employees (FTEs)	90		80

* Common
[A] Reported in accordance with IFRS

Latest Results

Periods ended:	3m Mar. 31/23[A]		3m Mar. 31/22[A]
	$000s	%Chg	$000s
Operating revenue	10,008	+31	7,629
Net income	2,801	+67	1,678
	$		$
Earnings per share*	0.06		0.04

* Common
[A] Reported in accordance with IFRS

Historical Summary
(as originally stated)

Fiscal Year	Oper. Rev.	Net Inc. Bef. Disc.	EPS*
	$000s	$000s	$
2022[A]	26,892	2,275	0.05
2021[A]	18,732	(2,376)	(0.05)
2020[A]	15,520	(4,445)	(0.10)
2019[A]	19,522	(5,036)	(0.09)
2018[A]	20,480	(8,366)	(0.15)

* Common
[A] Reported in accordance with IFRS

E.58 Enthusiast Gaming Holdings Inc.

Symbol - EGLX **Exchange** - TSX **CUSIP** - 29385B
Head Office - 805-90 Eglinton Ave E, Toronto, ON, M4P 2Y3 **Telephone** - (416) 623-9360
Website - www.enthusiastgaming.com
Email - alex@enthusiastgaming.com
Investor Relations - Alexander Macdonald (416) 623-9360
Auditors - KPMG LLP C.A., Vaughan, Ont.
Lawyers - Norton Rose Fulbright Canada LLP, Toronto, Ont.
Transfer Agents - Computershare Trust Company of Canada Inc., Vancouver, B.C.
FP500 Revenue Ranking - 651
Employees - 240 at Dec. 31, 2022

Profile - (B.C. 2018) Operates a gaming network through the provision of gaming-related content and media, management of eSports teams, influencers and content creators, and organization of gaming and eSports events.

Operations are organized into three segments: Media & Content; eSports & Entertainment; and Subscription.

Media & Content - Offers content through more than 50 wholly owned or affiliated websites which provides news, reviews, videos, live streams, blog posts, tips, chats, message boards and other video-gaming related content and casual games. Also produces and programs over 20 weekly shows across Advertising Video On Demand (AVOD) and Over-the-Top (OTT) channels and represents over 500 gaming influencers across YouTube and Twitch. In addition, owns gaming and pop culture content brands including BBC Gaming, a Fortnite community channel; Arcade Cloud, a gaming channel which features comedic animations revolved around certain games; and Wisecrack, an educational channel which produces web series and podcast focused on analysis of pop culture, movies, television and games.

eSports & Entertainment - Provides management and support services to players involved in professional gaming, as well as owns and manages several eSports teams which compete globally in Apex Legends, Overwatch, World of Warcraft, Rainbow Six Siege, PlayerUnknown's Battlegrounds (PUBG), Super Smash Bros., Rocket League and Call of Duty: Mobile, including Vancouver Titans of the Overwatch League and the Seattle Surge of the Call of Duty® eSports league as well as teams of gaming content creators on Youtube, Twitch and TikTok.

In addition, operates over 25 video game networking events across 11 countries, including Enthusiast Pocket Gamer Party, Top 50 Developer Guide, Mobile Mixers, the Mobile Games Awards and Pocket Gamer Connects.

Subscription - Offers subscription-based web and video properties including The Sims Resource, Icy Veins, Tabstat website, Tabwire Twitch channel, GameKnot, Addicting Games, Shockwave, TeachMe, TypeRacer, Little Big Snake, Fantasy Football Scout and LiveFPL websites and U.GG.

In January 2023, wholly owned **Enthusiast Gaming (TSR) Inc.** was amalgamated into wholly owned **Enthusiast Gaming Media Holdings Inc.** In addition, wholly owned **Hexagon Games Corp.** and **Enthusiast Gaming Media Holdings Inc.** were amalgamated into wholly owned **Enthusiast Gaming Inc.**

In April 2022, the company acquired **Fantasy Media Ltd.** and **Fantasy Football Scout Limited** for a total consideration of $4,627,600 in cash and common shares and earnout cash consideration of $804,800 upon renewal of the Fantasy League agreement. Fantasy owns and operates the web properties consisting of FantasyFootballScout.co.uk, which provides weekly scout report newsletters, integrated live rank data, data visualizations and three player comparison tools to the football community; and livefpl.net, which tracks the Premier League rankings of the members in real time, both overall and mini-leagues.

Recent Merger and Acquisition Activity

Status: completed **Announced:** Sept. 29, 2022
Enthusiast Gaming Holdings Inc. sold certain video game editorial websites for $6,800,000. The assets include Destructoid.com, Siliconera.com, Upcomer.com, PCInvasion.com, Operationsports.com and EscapistMagazine.com, as well as their social media handles and the rights of Enthusiast to certain legacy domains and related content such as NintendoEnthusiast.com.

Predecessor Detail - Name changed from J55 Capital Corp., Sept. 5, 2019, pursuant to Qualifying Transaction acquisition of Aquilini GameCo Inc., and concurrent acquisition of (old) Enthusiast Gaming Holdings Inc.; basis 1 new for 8 old shs.

Directors - Adrian T. Montgomery, chr., Toronto, Ont.; Nicolas (Nick) Brien, CEO, Los Angeles, Calif.; John L. Albright, Toronto, Ont.; Michael J. Beckerman, Toronto, Ont.; Scott M. O'Neil, Pa.

Other Exec. Officers - Bill Karamouzis, pres.; Alexander (Alex) Macdonald, CFO; Tara Fournier, chief people officer; Alan Liang, chief tech. officer; Shinggo Lu, chief product officer; Matt Goodman, exec. v-p, strategic partnerships; Amanda Rubin, exec. v-p, brand solutions; Scotty Tidwell, exec. v-p, content & creators; JB Elliott, sr. v-p, legal & gen. counsel

Capital Stock

	Authorized (shs.)	Outstanding (shs.)[1]
Preferred	unlimited	nil
Common	unlimited	151,767,243

[1] At May 25, 2023

Major Shareholder - Widely held at May 30, 2023.

Price Range - EGLX/TSX

Year	Volume	High	Low	Close
2022	121,953,941	$4.80	$0.70	$0.74
2021	140,480,406	$11.10	$3.50	$3.72
2020	47,283,415	$4.84	$1.15	$4.53
2019	22,630,885	$5.20	$1.54	$2.07
2018	750	$2.70	$2.70	$2.70

Consolidation: 1-for-8 cons. in Sept. 2019; 1-for-1.25 cons. in Aug. 2019

Recent Close: $0.57

Capital Stock Changes - During 2022, common shares were issued as follows: 16,280,103 for settlement of deferred liability, 1,098,325 for debt settlement, 760,938 on exercise of options, 42,838 on vesting of restricted share units and 35,770 on acquisition of Outplayed, Inc.

Wholly Owned Subsidiaries

Aquilini GameCo Inc., Toronto, Ont.
- 25% int. in **AIG eSports Canada Holdings Ltd.**, Canada.
- 25% int. in **AIG eSports USA Intermediate Holdings, LLC**, United States.
- 100% int. in **GameCo eSports USA Inc.**, United States.
- 100% int. in **Luminosity Gaming Inc.**, Ont.
- 100% int. in **Luminosity Gaming (USA), LLC**, Calif.

Enthusiast Gaming Properties Inc., Toronto, Ont.
- 100% int. in **Enthusiast Gaming Inc.**, Toronto, Ont.
  - 100% int. in **Enthusiast Gaming Live Inc.**, Toronto, Ont.
  - 100% int. in **Enthusiast Gaming Media (US) Inc.**, Wilmington, Del.
    - 100% int. in **Addicting Games, Inc.**, Los Angeles, Calif.
      - 100% int. in **TeachMe, Inc.**, Del.
    - 100% int. in **GameKnot LLC**, Calif.
    - 100% int. in **Outplayed, Inc.**, Austin, Tex.
    - 100% int. in **Storied Talent, LLC**, United States.
    - 100% int. in **Tabwire LLC**, Chicago, Ill.
  - 100% int. in **Enthusiast Gaming (PG) Inc.**, Canada.
  - 100% int. in **Steel Media Limited**, Bath, Somt., United Kingdom.
    - 100% int. in **Fantasy Football Scout Limited**, United Kingdom.
    - 100% int. in **Fantasy Media Ltd.**, United Kingdom.

Omnia Media Inc., Culver City, Calif.
Vedatis S.A.S., Lyon, France.

Financial Statistics

Periods ended:	12m Dec. 31/22[A]		12m Dec. 31/21[A]
	$000s	%Chg	$000s
Operating revenue	**202,836**	**+21**	**167,364**
Cost of sales	139,371		129,590
Salaries & benefits	36,493		25,140
General & admin expense	50,294		33,822
Stock-based compensation	7,751		18,918
Operating expense	**233,909**	**+13**	**207,470**
Operating income	**(31,073)**	**n.a.**	**(40,106)**
Deprec., depl. & amort.	16,708		9,158
Finance income	36		64
Finance costs, gross	3,620		2,845
Investment income	1,242		(267)
Write-downs/write-offs	(31,281)		nil
Pre-tax income	**(78,882)**	**n.a.**	**(52,986)**
Income taxes	(2,051)		(939)
Net income	**(76,831)**	**n.a.**	**(52,047)**
Cash & equivalent	7,541		22,786
Accounts receivable	37,868		33,802
Current assets	47,844		59,266
Long-term investments	2,450		885
Fixed assets, net	181		248
Right-of-use assets	2,100		2,886
Intangibles, net	288,583		324,236
Total assets	**341,438**	**-12**	**387,783**
Accts. pay. & accr. liabs.	32,823		34,391
Current liabilities	59,040		68,448
Long-term debt, gross	17,587		9,829
Long-term debt, net	145		7,695
Long-term lease liabilities	1,478		2,214
Shareholders' equity	254,651		262,768
Cash from oper. activs.	**(26,640)**	**n.a.**	**(23,679)**
Cash from fin. activs.	6,498		76,015
Cash from invest. activs.	4,343		(33,944)
Net cash position	**7,416**	**-67**	**22,654**
Capital expenditures	(11)		(3)
	$		$
Earnings per share*	(0.54)		(0.43)
Cash flow per share*	(0.19)		(0.20)
	shs		shs
No. of shs. o/s*	151,767,243		133,549,269
Avg. no. of shs. o/s*	143,535,305		121,002,659
	%		%
Net profit margin	(37.88)		(31.10)
Return on equity	(29.70)		(25.73)
Return on assets	(20.11)		(16.15)
Foreign sales percent	98		99
No. of employees (FTEs)	240		260

* Common
[A] Reported in accordance with IFRS

Historical Summary
(as originally stated)

Fiscal Year	Oper. Rev.	Net Inc. Bef. Disc.	EPS*
	$000s	$000s	$
2022[A]	202,836	(76,831)	(0.54)
2021[A]	167,364	(52,047)	(0.43)
2020[A]	72,963	(26,852)	(0.32)
2019[A1]	12,209	(78,546)	(2.07)
2018[§A]	14,818	(28,582)	n.a.

* Common
§ Pro forma
[A] Reported in accordance with IFRS
[1] Results reflect the Aug. 30, 2019, Qualifying Transaction reverse takeover acquisition of Aquilini GameCo Inc.

Note: Adjusted throughout for 1-for-8 cons. in Sept. 2019; 1-for-1.25 cons. in Aug. 2019

E.59 Entourage Health Corp.

Symbol - ENTG **Exchange** - TSX-VEN **CUSIP** - 293861
Head Office - 200-276 Queen St W, Toronto, ON, M5V 2A1 **Toll-free** - (844) 933-3636 **Fax** - (844) 933-3637
Website - entouragehealthcorp.com
Email - marianella@entouragecorp.com
Investor Relations - Marianella delaBarrera (844) 933-3636
Auditors - MNP LLP C.A.
Transfer Agents - TSX Trust Company, Toronto, Ont.
Profile - (Ont. 2014) Produces and sells cannabis products in Canada.

Operates a 158-acre property in Strathroy, Ont., with 522,720 sq. ft. of indoor greenhouse cultivation facility , 27 acres of outdoor cultivation and a 50,000 sq. ft. of processing facility; a 26,000 sq. ft. indoor facility in Aylmer, Ont., used for cannabis extraction, processing, product development and fullfillment; and a 10,000 sq. ft. micropropagation and specialty extraction facility in Guelph, Ont.

Medical cannabis products are sold directly to patients, including through the company's Starseed Medicinal online marketplace, supply agreements with Shoppers Drug Mart and union groups; and recreational cannabis are distributed through wholesale agreements with provincial agencies and licensed retailers and distributors in Ontario, Alberta, British Columbia, Nova Scotia, Manitoba, Saskatchewan, Quebec and New Brunswick. Products are marketed under the brands Starseed, WeedMD and Mary's Medicinals for the medical market, and Mary's Medicinals, Color Cannabis®, Saturday Cannabis® and Royal City Cannabis Co. for the adult-use market.

Predecessor Detail - Name changed from WeedMD Inc., July 13, 2021.

Directors - George Scorsis, exec. chr. & CEO, Toronto, Ont.; Gail Paech†, Toronto, Ont.; Jason Alexander, Ont.; Lu Cacioppo, Ont.; Bruce R. Croxon, Ont.

Other Exec. Officers - James Afara, COO; Vaani Maharaj, CFO; Dr. Peter M. Blecher, CMO; Vincent Doré, chief legal officer & corp. sec.; Joseph Mele, chief comml. officer; Deborah Sikkema, chief people officer; Pat Scanlon, head, cultivation; Marianella delaBarrera, sr. v-p, communs. & corp. affairs; Jeff Keyes, sr. v-p, opers.; Norman Wright, v-p, sales, adult use

† Lead director

Capital Stock

	Authorized (shs.)	Outstanding (shs.)[1]
Common	unlimited	306,744,396

[1] At Aug. 29, 2022

Major Shareholder - The Labourers' Pension Fund of Central and Eastern Canada held 24.47% interest at May 25, 2021.

Price Range - ENTG/TSX-VEN

Year	Volume	High	Low	Close
2022............	33,040,103	$0.14	$0.02	$0.02
2021............	140,148,637	$0.99	$0.07	$0.08
2020............	60,951,127	$0.89	$0.23	$0.25
2019............	112,191,690	$2.15	$0.78	$0.86
2018............	205,986,655	$3.25	$0.99	$1.31

Recent Close: $0.02

Wholly Owned Subsidiaries

CannTx Life Sciences Inc., Guelph, Ont.
Entourage Brands Corp., Aylmer, Ont.
- 100% int. in **2686912 Ontario Limited**, Ont.
- 100% int. in **2686913 Ontario Inc.**, Ont.

Starseed Holdings Inc., Toronto, Ont.
- 100% int. in **North Star Wellness Inc.**, Ont.

Subsidiaries

50.1% int. in **Pioneer Cannabis Corp.**

Note: The preceding list includes only the major related companies in which interests are held.

Financial Statistics

Periods ended:	12m Dec. 31/21[A]		12m Dec. 31/20[A]
	$000s	%Chg	$000s
Operating revenue........................	**42,272**	**+44**	**29,434**
Cost of goods sold..........................	53,987		53,640
Salaries & benefits..........................	11,947		12,495
Research & devel. expense.............	397		834
General & admin expense...............	16,385		13,349
Stock-based compensation............	860		2,638
Operating expense........................	**83,575**	**+1**	**82,956**
Operating income........................	**(41,303)**	**n.a.**	**(53,522)**
Deprec., depl. & amort....................	2,737		2,153
Finance income..............................	nil		66
Finance costs, gross.......................	11,025		5,909
Write-downs/write-offs....................	(31,165)		(35,764)
Pre-tax income..........................	**(78,935)**	**n.a.**	**(89,607)**
Net income....................................	**(78,935)**	**n.a.**	**(89,607)**
Cash & equivalent..........................	22,347		22,554
Inventories......................................	29,641		30,665
Accounts receivable.......................	7,677		2,253
Current assets................................	61,425		66,789
Fixed assets, net.............................	81,700		96,906
Right-of-use assets.........................	nil		3,136
Intangibles, net...............................	nil		4,498
Total assets..................................	**144,224**	**-16**	**171,329**
Accts. pay. & accr. liabs..................	17,437		15,559
Current liabilities............................	116,393		21,729
Long-term debt, gross.....................	102,420		78,306
Long-term debt, net.........................	4,571		74,319
Long-term lease liabilities................	1,834		1,191
Equity portion of conv. debs............	1,626		1,514
Shareholders' equity.......................	21,426		74,090
Cash from oper. activs..................	**(30,008)**	**n.a.**	**(35,539)**
Cash from fin. activs........................	24,064		51,261
Cash from invest. activs...................	1,841		(1,401)
Net cash position..........................	**21,516**	**-16**	**25,618**
Capital expenditures.......................	(449)		(1,182)
Capital disposals.............................	337		nil
	$		$
Earnings per share*........................	(0.32)		(0.43)
Cash flow per share*.......................	(0.12)		(0.17)
	shs		shs
No. of shs. o/s*...............................	303,976,702		210,261,715
Avg. no. of shs. o/s*........................	249,012,535		208,047,322
	%		%
Net profit margin............................	(186.73)		(304.43)
Return on equity.............................	(165.28)		(85.28)
Return on assets............................	(43.04)		(43.92)

* Common
[A] Reported in accordance with IFRS

Latest Results

Periods ended:	6m June 30/22[A]		6m June 30/21[A]
	$000s	%Chg	$000s
Operating revenue..........................	22,115	+6	20,883
Net income......................................	(17,791)	n.a.	(16,959)
	$		$
Earnings per share*........................	(0.06)		(0.08)

* Common
[A] Reported in accordance with IFRS

Historical Summary
(as originally stated)

Fiscal Year	Oper. Rev.	Net Inc. Bef. Disc.	EPS*
	$000s	$000s	$
2021[A]..................	42,272	(78,935)	(0.32)
2020[A]..................	29,434	(89,607)	(0.43)
2019[A]..................	20,820	(10,392)	(0.09)
2018[A]..................	7,955	(895)	(0.01)
2017[A1].................	1,451	(8,805)	(0.15)

* Common
[A] Reported in accordance with IFRS
[1] Results reflect the April 2017 Qualifying transaction reverse takeover acquisition of WeedMD Rx Inc.

E.60 Environmental Waste International Inc.

Symbol - EWS **Exchange** - TSX-VEN **CUSIP** - 29411G
Head Office - 1-1751 Wentworth St, Whitby, ON, L1N 8R6 **Telephone** - (905) 686-8689 **Toll-free** - (800) 399-2366 **Fax** - (905) 428-8730
Website - www.ewi.ca
Email - kelli.harrington@ewi.ca
Investor Relations - Kelli Harrington (780) 429-1900
Auditors - Jones & O'Connell LLP C.A., St. Catharines, Ont.
Transfer Agents - TSX Trust Company, Toronto, Ont.
Profile - (Ont. 1987) Researches, designs, develops, sells and maintains technologically advanced systems based on the patented Reverse Polymerization™ process, associated proprietary microwave delivery system and hybrid microwave process for the break down of tires and other rubber waste.

The Reverse Polymerization™ process applies high energy microwaves to organic waste to break molecular bonds of materials to have simpler chemical components. The company's pilot plant tire system breaks the molecular bonds in tires and other rubber products, reducing them to their base components of carbon black, oil, steel and hydrocarbon vapours. The carbon black can be recycled for tires, rubber compounding, weather stripping and other rubber products. In addition to tires, the company has designed solutions for the safe disposal, recycling and/or recapture of useable by-products including liquid biological waste, food waste, and medical and animal waste. The company has a waste tire facility in Sault Ste. Marie, Ont.

Recent Merger and Acquisition Activity

Status: terminated **Revised:** Mar. 28, 2023
UPDATE: The transaction was terminated. PREVIOUS: Environmental Waste International Inc. (EWS) agreed to sell a 70% interest in wholly owned Ellsin Environmental Ltd., which owns a waste tire pilot plant in Sault Ste. Marie, Ont., to private Ontario-based Torreco Inc. Under the agreement, Torreco would invest $7,000,000, in exchange for a 70% interest in Ellsin, to convert the pilot plant into a commercial scale recycling plant utilizing EWS's microwave technology. Torreco has made an initial share purchase in Ellsin of $400,000 and has committed to invest an additional $6,600,000 over the next five months. EWS would also receive a royalty in perpetuity on the revenue generated from the sale of valuable commodities produced from its tire recycling process at the plant. Torreco processes used tires through a microwave system which deconstructs used tires into their base components, carbon black, steel, oil and syngas. Apr. 8, 2021 - Torreco made an additional $600,000 investment, resulting to a 10% ownership in Ellsin.

Predecessor Detail - Name changed from E.W.M.C. International Inc., Sept. 27, 2001.

Directors - Emanuel Gerard, chr., New York, N.Y.; Sam Geist, Toronto, Ont.; Paul E. Orlin, New York, N.Y.

Other Exec. Officers - Kelli Harrington, pres. & CEO; Gary Nobrega, CFO; Steve Kantor, chief tech. officer

Capital Stock

	Authorized (shs.)	Outstanding (shs.)[1]
Common	unlimited	279,909,886

[1] At May 25, 2023

Major Shareholder - EWI Investors, LLC held 15% interest and Paul E. Orlin held 10.1% interest at May 19, 2023.

Price Range - EWS/TSX-VEN

Year	Volume	High	Low	Close
2022............	17,163,918	$0.12	$0.02	$0.03
2021............	61,736,329	$0.57	$0.10	$0.11
2020............	35,996,112	$0.29	$0.03	$0.24
2019............	3,478,001	$0.07	$0.03	$0.06
2018............	10,471,195	$0.09	$0.04	$0.05

Recent Close: $0.03

Capital Stock Changes - In May 2023, private placement of 13,240,943 units (1 common share & 1 warrant) at 5¢ per unit was completed, with warrants exercisable at 10¢ per share for two years. In addition, an up to 1-for-20 share consolidation was proposed.

During 2022, 8,250,000 common shares were issued by private placement.

Wholly Owned Subsidiaries

EWI Rubber Inc.
Environmental Waste Management Corporation, Ajax, Ont.
Jaguar Carbon Sales Limited
2228641 Ontario Limited, Ont.

Subsidiaries

90% int. in **Ellsin Environmental Ltd.**, Ont.

Financial Statistics

Periods ended:	12m Dec. 31/22^A		12m Dec. 31/21^A
	$000s	%Chg	$000s
Operating revenue	**nil**	**n.a.**	**112**
Research & devel. expense	496		629
General & admin expense	988		866
Stock-based compensation	431		343
Other operating expense	122		116
Operating expense	**2,036**	**+4**	**1,954**
Operating income	**(2,036)**	**n.a.**	**(1,841)**
Deprec., depl. & amort.	115		116
Finance costs, gross	205		214
Pre-tax income	**(2,291)**	**n.a.**	**(1,315)**
Net income	**(2,291)**	**n.a.**	**(1,315)**
Net inc. for equity hldrs	**(2,260)**	**n.a.**	**(1,273)**
Net inc. for non-cont. int	**(32)**	**n.a.**	**(41)**
Cash & equivalent	54		297
Accounts receivable	nil		103
Current assets	213		516
Fixed assets, net	2,483		2,031
Right-of-use assets	88		118
Total assets	**2,784**	**+4**	**2,666**
Accts. pay. & accr. liabs	938		513
Current liabilities	4,248		3,319
Long-term debt, gross	4,116		3,265
Long-term debt, net	838		587
Shareholders' equity	(3,304)		(2,296)
Non-controlling interest	927		959
Cash from oper. activs	**(1,149)**	**n.a.**	**(1,613)**
Cash from fin. activs	1,442		2,400
Cash from invest. activs	(536)		(1,110)
Net cash position	**54**	**-82**	**297**
Capital expenditures	(536)		(1,110)
	$		$
Earnings per share*	(0.01)		(0.01)
Cash flow per share*	(0.00)		(0.01)
	shs		shs
No. of shs. o/s*	266,668,943		258,418,943
Avg. no. of shs. o/s*	264,910,746		253,961,717
	%		%
Net profit margin	n.a.		n.m.
Return on equity	n.m.		n.m.
Return on assets	(76.55)		(47.71)
Foreign sales percent	n.a.		68

* Common
^A Reported in accordance with IFRS

Latest Results

Periods ended:	3m Mar. 31/23^A		3m Mar. 31/22^A
	$000s	%Chg	$000s
Net income	(507)	n.a.	(473)
Net inc. for equity hldrs	(499)	n.a.	(465)
Net inc. for non-cont. int	(8)		(8)
	$		$
Earnings per share*	(0.00)		(0.00)

* Common
^A Reported in accordance with IFRS

Historical Summary
(as originally stated)

Fiscal Year	Oper. Rev.	Net Inc. Bef. Disc.	EPS*
	$000s	$000s	$
2022^A	nil	(2,291)	(0.01)
2021^A	112	(1,315)	(0.01)
2020^A	113	(2,417)	(0.02)
2019^A	222	(2,772)	(0.02)
2018^A	221	(1,143)	(0.01)

* Common
^A Reported in accordance with IFRS

E.61 EnWave Corporation

Symbol - ENW **Exchange** - TSX-VEN **CUSIP** - 29410K
Head Office - Unit 1, 1668 Derwent Way, Delta, BC, V3M 6R9 **Telephone** - (604) 806-6110
Website - www.enwave.net
Email - bcharleton@enwave.net
Investor Relations - Brent Charleton (778) 378-9616
Auditors - PricewaterhouseCoopers LLP C.A., Vancouver, B.C.
Lawyers - McMillan LLP, Vancouver, B.C.
Transfer Agents - Computershare Trust Company of Canada Inc., Vancouver, B.C.
Employees - 67 at Sept. 30, 2022
Profile - (Can. 1999 amalg.) Licenses, designs, builds, sells and installs its patented Radiant Energy Vacuum (REV™) dehydration platforms for applications in the food, cannabis and pharmaceutical sectors. Also manufactures, markets and sells dried cheese products.

The proprietary REV™ dehydration platforms apply microwave energy under vacuum in a low temperature environment above or below freezing levels to dehydrate product loads in a very gentle, homogenous and efficient way. REV™ platforms are suitable to produce commercial applications in multiple markets, including fruits and vegetables, dairy products, ready-to-eat meals, baked goods, cannabis products, nutraceuticals and pharmaceuticals. Commercial REV™ platforms include nutraREV®, a drum-based system which is designed for the dehydration of discrete food pieces including fruits, vegetables, herbs, dairy products, meats and seafood; and quantaREV®, a tray-based or belt-based system which is designed for high-volume dehydration of solid, liquid, granular or encapsulated food or cannabis products. The company has also developed freezeREV®, a pilot-scale technology designed for the dehydration of biomaterial and pharmaceutical products below the freezing point in vials. The company has partnered with **GEA Lyophil GmbH** to further develop and commercialize freezeREV®. REV™ systems are assembled and tested at the company's manufacturing facility in Delta, B.C. Also operates REVworx™, a vacuum-microwave toll drying facility located in Delta, which has received Safe Quality Food (SQF) certification that allows the company to offer toll drying services to food producing partners around the globe. The facility houses both a batch 10 KW and 60 KW continuous vacuum-microwave line to accelerate the commercialization of products utilizing its REV™ technology on behalf of third party clients.

In addition, wholly owned **NutraDried Food Company, LLC** manufactures and sells Moon Cheese®, a dried cheese snack produced using REV™; Protein Blitz Mix, which is a mix of cheese and nuts; and Moon Cheese® Crunchy Sticks. NutraDried products are sold online and in retail locations across Canada and the U.S. NutraDried also co-manufactures REV™-dried cheese for sale in bulk as an ingredient or inclusion for third party brands. Products are manufactured at its facility in Ferndale, Wash.

Predecessor Detail - Formed from Commonwealth Assisted Living Inc. in Canada, July 14, 1999, on amalgamation with DRI Dehydration Research Inc., constituting a reverse takeover by DRI; basis 1.86 new for 1 DRI sh. and 1 new for 1 Commonwealth sh.

Directors - John P. A. Budreski, exec. chr., Vancouver, B.C.; Brent Charleton, pres. & CEO, B.C.; Pablo Cussatti, N.Y.; Mary C. Ritchie, Edmonton, Alta.; Stephen Sanford, Wash.; Patrick Turpin, Utah

Other Exec. Officers - Mark T. Alev, COO; Dylan Murray, CFO & corp. sec.; Mehmet Sucu, chief engineer; Dr. John Zhang, chief scientific officer; Brad Lahrman, CEO, NutraDried Food Company, LLC

Capital Stock

	Authorized (shs.)	Outstanding (shs.)[1]
Preferred	unlimited	nil
Common	unlimited	110,695,055

[1] At Aug. 24, 2023

Normal Course Issuer Bid - The company plans to make normal course purchases of up to 10,798,644 common shares representing 10% of the public float. The bid commenced on Nov. 24, 2022, and expires on Nov. 23, 2023.

Major Shareholder - Widely held at Feb. 14, 2023.

Price Range - ENW/TSX-VEN

Year	Volume	High	Low	Close
2022	10,274,625	$1.01	$0.40	$0.42
2021	25,727,561	$1.82	$0.85	$0.96
2020	31,880,388	$1.87	$0.56	$1.15
2019	38,570,737	$2.66	$1.25	$1.68
2018	22,456,544	$1.72	$0.97	$1.31

Recent Close: $0.28

Capital Stock Changes - During fiscal 2022, 235,000 on vesting of restricted share units.

Wholly Owned Subsidiaries

EnWave USA Corporation, Del.
- 100% int. in **NutraDried Food Company, LLC**, Ferndale, Wash.

REV Technology Corporation, Del.

Financial Statistics

Periods ended:	12m Sept. 30/22^A		12m Sept. 30/21^A
	$000s	%Chg	$000s
Operating revenue	**23,703**	**-10**	**26,476**
Cost of sales	17,412		19,309
Research & devel. expense	2,175		1,876
General & admin expense	7,394		7,446
Stock-based compensation	1,132		824
Operating expense	**37,576**	**+28**	**29,455**
Operating income	**(13,873)**	**n.a.**	**(2,979)**
Deprec., depl. & amort.	2,684		2,512
Finance costs, net	26		(7)
Write-downs/write-offs	(46)		(5)
Pre-tax income	**(6,955)**	**n.a.**	**(4,832)**
Income taxes	(28)		(707)
Net income	**(6,927)**	**n.a.**	**(4,125)**
Cash & equivalent	6,199		11,790
Inventories	6,622		5,722
Accounts receivable	1,960		2,130
Current assets	18,000		24,131
Fixed assets, net	5,539		4,538
Right-of-use assets	1,968		1,405
Intangibles, net	21		207
Total assets	**25,847**	**-16**	**30,641**
Accts. pay. & accr. liabs	4,476		4,421
Current liabilities	6,616		6,618
Long-term debt, gross	224		191
Long-term debt, net	220		191
Long-term lease liabilities	1,383		839
Shareholders' equity	17,628		22,988
Cash from oper. activs	**(2,263)**	**n.a.**	**2,037**
Cash from fin. activs	(939)		(2,934)
Cash from invest. activs	(2,522)		(1,824)
Net cash position	**6,199**	**-47**	**11,790**
Capital expenditures	(2,691)		(1,990)
Capital disposals	99		75
	$		$
Earnings per share*	(0.06)		(0.04)
Cash flow per share*	(0.02)		0.02
	shs		shs
No. of shs. o/s*	110,440,055		110,205,055
Avg. no. of shs. o/s*	110,351,301		111,572,716
	%		%
Net profit margin	(29.22)		(15.58)
Return on equity	(34.11)		(16.07)
Return on assets	(24.53)		(11.57)
No. of employees (FTEs)	67		85

* Common
^A Reported in accordance with IFRS

Historical Summary
(as originally stated)

Fiscal Year	Oper. Rev.	Net Inc. Bef. Disc.	EPS*
	$000s	$000s	$
2022^A	23,703	(6,927)	(0.06)
2021^A	26,476	(4,125)	(0.04)
2020^A	32,883	(4,441)	(0.04)
2019^A	42,842	(1,986)	(0.02)
2018^A	22,825	(945)	(0.01)

* Common
^A Reported in accordance with IFRS

E.62 EonX Technologies Inc.

Symbol - EONX **Exchange** - CSE **CUSIP** - 29415K
Head Office - 1183 Toorak Rd, Melbourne, VIC, Australia, 3124 **Overseas Tel** - 61-1300-134-418
Website - eonx.com
Email - andrew.kallen@eonx.com
Investor Relations - Andrew Kallen 61-1300-134-418
Auditors - MNP LLP C.A., Toronto, Ont.
Lawyers - Joanne S. McClusky, Vancouver, B.C.
Transfer Agents - Endeavor Trust Corporation, Vancouver, B.C.
Profile - (B.C. 2020) Provides financial technology products for enterprise clients including payment processor, e-wallets, identity and security for know-your-client (KYC) and anti-money laundering (AML), loyalty points solutions and an e-commerce store.

Provides clients with a branded web and mobile platform to engage with their customers using payment and loyalty solutions. Solutions include a payment processor, e-wallets, inventory of online loyalty cards and an online store marketplace. Clients integrate the EONX platform with their existing website and end user customers are then invited into the white label platform that leads to payment processing and sale of products, vouchers and gift cards and other services. End user customers earn reward points on every transaction. The company charges an annual platform fee plus transaction fees to its clients and charges either a monthly fee or a fee on every transaction generated in its platform.

Plans to expand operations to the United States and Canada.

Directors - Anoosh Manzoori, chr., Melbourne, Vic., Australia; Andrew Kallen, CEO, Vic., Australia; Pavel Zagaria, chief tech. officer; Justin A. Hanka, Vic., Australia

Other Exec. Officers - John Dinan, CFO & corp. sec.

Capital Stock

	Authorized (shs.)	Outstanding (shs.)[1]
Common	unlimited	38,175,671

[1] At Nov. 30, 2022

Major Shareholder - Andrew Kallen held 77.71% interest at Jan. 17, 2022.

Price Range - EONX/CSE

Year	Volume	High	Low	Close
2022	1,026,266	$1.75	$0.20	$0.20
2021	1,552,952	$0.84	$0.40	$0.82

Recent Close: $0.10

Capital Stock Changes - During fiscal 2021, common shares were issued as follows: 4,666,471 for debt settlement and 4,109,200 on exercise of options.

Wholly Owned Subsidiaries

Eonx Corporation, United States.
Eonx Services UK Ltd., United Kingdom.
EonX Services Pty Ltd., Australia.

Note: The preceding list includes only the major related companies in which interests are held.

Financial Statistics

Periods ended:	12m June 30/22[A]		12m June 30/21[oA]
	A$000s	%Chg	A$000s
Operating revenue	**8,167**	**+49**	**5,474**
Salaries & benefits	6,418		2,575
Research & devel. expense	3,373		1,837
General & admin expense	1,818		944
Stock-based compensation	3,365		386
Operating expense	**14,974**	**+161**	**5,742**
Operating income	**(6,807)**	**n.a.**	**(268)**
Deprec., depl. & amort.	326		332
Finance costs, gross	187		86
Pre-tax income	**(7,319)**	**n.a.**	**(4,000)**
Income taxes	120		704
Net income	**(7,439)**	**n.a.**	**(4,704)**
Cash & equivalent	1,301		5,126
Inventories	1,935		698
Accounts receivable	3,109		702
Current assets	8,954		8,921
Fixed assets, net	71		76
Right-of-use assets	307		468
Total assets	**11,423**	**+20**	**9,556**
Accts. pay. & accr. liabs.	7,300		2,965
Current liabilities	14,258		7,867
Long-term debt, gross	7,533		7,994
Long-term debt, net	2,500		5,433
Long-term lease liabilities	247		503
Shareholders' equity	(5,582)		(4,246)
Cash from oper. activs.	**(3,832)**	**n.a.**	**(1,551)**
Cash from fin. activs.	2,008		5,610
Cash from invest. activs.	(2,000)		nil
Net cash position	**1,301**	**-75**	**5,126**
	A$		A$
Earnings per share*	(0.20)		(0.41)
Cash flow per share*	(0.10)		(0.14)
	shs		shs
No. of shs. o/s*	38,175,791		29,400,120
Avg. no. of shs. o/s*	37,021,490		11,391,736
	%		%
Net profit margin	(91.09)		(85.93)
Return on equity	n.m.		n.m.
Return on assets	(69.11)		(57.02)
Foreign sales percent	100		100

* Common
[o] Restated
[A] Reported in accordance with IFRS

Latest Results

Periods ended:	3m Sept. 30/22[A]		3m Sept. 30/21[oA]
	A$000s	%Chg	A$000s
Operating revenue	5,175	n.m.	178
Net income	(1,674)	n.a.	(1,120)
	A$		A$
Earnings per share*	(0.04)		(0.08)

* Common
[o] Restated
[A] Reported in accordance with IFRS

Historical Summary
(as originally stated)

Fiscal Year	Oper. Rev.	Net Inc. Bef. Disc.	EPS*
	A$000s	A$000s	A$
2022[A]	8,167	(7,439)	(0.20)
2021[A1]	5,474	(4,704)	(0.41)
2020[A2]	8,230	91	n.a.

* Common
[A] Reported in accordance with IFRS
[1] Results reflect the Mar. 23, 2021, reverse takeover acquisition of EonX Services Pty Ltd.
[2] Results pertain to EonX Services Pty Ltd.

E.63 ePlay Digital Inc.

Symbol - EPY **Exchange** - CSE **CUSIP** - 26885W
Head Office - 2464-246 Stewart Green Dr SW, Calgary, AB, T3H 3C8 **Telephone** - (403) 775-9475
Website - www.eplaydigital.com
Email - info@eplaydigital.com
Investor Relations - Trevor Doerksen (403) 775-9475
Auditors - Charlton & Company C.A., Vancouver, B.C.
Transfer Agents - Endeavor Trust Corporation, Vancouver, B.C.

Profile - (B.C. 2013) Develops and publishes mobile game applications, specializing in sports and entertainment augmented reality.

The company offers a social game engine and content marketing platform to engage audiences. Its solutions integrate artificial Intelligence (AI), TV, VOD, 3D holograms, and sports, daily fantasy and social games to create multi-platform destinations and campaigns for brands, sports teams and venues. The platform features the Klocked Sports World metaverse, with automated virtual production for sports and mass participation events, as well as Fan Freak, a sports gaming application.

Also publishes augmented reality mobile games with in-app rewards, including Big Shot Basketball and the Howie's Games series, as well as its augmented reality fitness application, Klocked.run.

Subsidiary **Mobovivo Inc.** (96.7% owned) specializes in augmented reality, mobile game and metaverse development.

Common reinstated on CSE, July 12, 2023.

Common suspended from CSE, May 10, 2023.

Predecessor Detail - Name changed from Network Life Sciences Inc., Oct. 16, 2016.

Directors - Trevor Doerksen, pres. & CEO, Calgary, Alta.; David Gratton; Manfred G. von Nostitz, Kuala Lumpur, Malaysia

Other Exec. Officers - Dong H. (Don) Shim, CFO & corp. sec.

Capital Stock

	Authorized (shs.)	Outstanding (shs.)[1]
Preferred	unlimited	nil
Common	unlimited	98,965,819

[1] At May 31, 2023

Major Shareholder - Widely held at Apr. 28, 2022.

Price Range - EPY/CSE

Year	Volume	High	Low	Close
2022	79,850,629	$0.15	$0.01	$0.02
2021	313,046,473	$0.36	$0.03	$0.09
2020	46,776,749	$0.10	$0.02	$0.04
2019	45,267,656	$0.15	$0.03	$0.04
2018	70,193,961	$0.26	$0.07	$0.08

Recent Close: $0.02

Capital Stock Changes - There were no changes to capital stock during 2022.

Wholly Owned Subsidiaries

Emerald Oncology Limited, Ireland. Inactive.
Holo3D Technologies Inc., Canada.

Subsidiaries

96.7% int. in **MoboVivo Inc.**, Calgary, Alta.

Financial Statistics

Periods ended:	12m Dec. 31/22[A]		12m Dec. 31/21[A]
	$000s	%Chg	$000s
Operating revenue	**54**	**+38**	**39**
Research & devel. expense	421		266
General & admin expense	388		693
Stock-based compensation	...		573
Operating expense	**809**	**-47**	**1,532**
Operating income	**(755)**	**n.a.**	**(1,493)**
Deprec., depl. & amort.	3		3
Finance costs, gross	4		5
Write-downs/write-offs	(2)		(12)
Pre-tax income	**(716)**	**n.a.**	**(4,238)**
Net income	**(716)**	**n.a.**	**(4,238)**
Net inc. for equity hldrs	**(697)**	**n.a.**	**(4,220)**
Net inc. for non-cont. int.	**(19)**	**n.a.**	**(18)**
Cash & equivalent	31		606
Accounts receivable	2		nil
Current assets	51		625
Intangibles, net	4		7
Total assets	**55**	**-91**	**632**
Bank indebtedness	1,262		20
Accts. pay. & accr. liabs.	332		197
Current liabilities	1,594		217
Long-term debt, gross	40		1,279
Long-term debt, net	40		1,279
Shareholders' equity	(1,465)		(768)
Non-controlling interest	(115)		(96)
Cash from oper. activs.	**(576)**	**n.a.**	**(764)**
Cash from fin. activs.	nil		1,305
Cash from invest. activs.	nil		64
Net cash position	**31**	**-95**	**606**
	$		$
Earnings per share*	(0.01)		(0.05)
Cash flow per share*	(0.01)		(0.01)
	shs		shs
No. of shs. o/s*	98,965,819		98,965,819
Avg. no. of shs. o/s*	98,965,819		89,526,206
	%		%
Net profit margin	n.m.		n.m.
Return on equity	n.m.		n.m.
Return on assets	(207.28)		n.m.

* Common
[A] Reported in accordance with IFRS

Historical Summary
(as originally stated)

Fiscal Year	Oper. Rev.	Net Inc. Bef. Disc.	EPS*
	$000s	$000s	$
2022[A]	54	(716)	(0.01)
2021[A]	39	(4,238)	(0.05)
2020[A]	54	(328)	(0.00)
2019[A]	27	(3,233)	(0.05)
2018[A]	205	(447)	(0.01)

* Common
[A] Reported in accordance with IFRS

E.64 Essential Energy Services Ltd.

Symbol - ESN **Exchange** - TSX **CUSIP** - 29669R
Head Office - Livingston Place West, 1100-250 2 St SW, Calgary, AB, T2P 0C1 **Telephone** - (403) 263-6778 **Fax** - (403) 263-6737
Website - www.essentialenergy.ca
Email - gamundson@essentialenergy.ca
Investor Relations - Garnet K. Amundson (403) 263-6778
Auditors - KPMG LLP C.A., Calgary, Alta.
Bankers - ATB Financial, Calgary, Alta.; Canadian Western Bank, Calgary, Alta.; National Bank of Canada, Calgary, Alta.
Lawyers - Fasken Martineau DuMoulin LLP, Calgary, Alta.
Transfer Agents - Computershare Trust Company of Canada Inc., Calgary, Alta.
FP500 Revenue Ranking - 706
Employees - 332 at Dec. 31, 2022

Profile - (Alta. 2010) Provides completion, production and wellsite restoration to oil and gas exploration and production companies in western Canada and the U.S.

Services are provided through two operating segments: Essential Coil Well Service and Tryton Tool Services.

The **Essential Coil Well Service** segment provides completion, stimulation and work-over services on long-reach horizontal wells with a fleet of coiled tubing rigs and fluid and nitrogen pumpers. Coiled tubing rigs are used on the pre-fracturing, fracturing and post-fracturing stages of well development. The coiled tubing rigs are supported by a fleet of fluid and nitrogen pumpers. Fluid pumpers are used to maintain downhole circulation, provide ancillary acid/solvent treatments and inject friction reducers and other chemicals into the wellbore. Nitrogen pumpers are used to pump inert nitrogen gas into the wellbore for stimulation or work-over operations and to purge the coiled tubing of fluids once the coiled tubing work has been completed.

The **Tryton Tool Services** segment includes downhole tool sales and rentals including the Tryton Multi-Stage Fracturing System® (which allows producers to isolate and fracture intervals of a horizontal section of a well separately and continuously), conventional packers, tubing anchors, bridge plugs, sub-surface safety valves, cement retainers and related accessories which are used in production, abandonment and wellsite restoration activities. Also offers oilfield service equipment rentals including specialty drill pipe and various other tools and handling equipment. Operations are carried out across the Western Canadian Sedimentary Basin and in Texas, Oklahoma and Kansas.

Equipment

Year ended Dec. 31	2022	2021
Coiled tubing rigs	19	25
Fluid pumpers	11	13
Nitrogen pumpers	5	6

Predecessor Detail - Succeeded Essential Energy Services Trust, May 5, 2010, pursuant to plan of arrangement whereby Essential Energy Services Ltd. was formed to facilitate the conversion of the trust into a corporation.

Directors - James A. Banister, chr., Calgary, Alta.; Garnet K. Amundson, pres. & CEO, Calgary, Alta.; Felicia B. Bortolussi, Calgary, Alta.; Robert T. (Bob) German, Calgary, Alta.; Sophia J. Langlois, Calgary, Alta.; Robert B. (Bob) Michaleski, Calgary, Alta.

Other Exec. Officers - Laura Ingram, CFO; Jeffrey B. (Jeff) Newman, sr. v-p; Karen D. Perasalo, v-p, fin. & corp. sec.; Jade Iluk, dir., HR

Capital Stock

	Authorized (shs.)	Outstanding (shs.)[1]
Preferred	unlimited	nil
Common	unlimited	132,690,097

[1] At Mar. 23, 2023

Normal Course Issuer Bid - The company plans to make normal course purchases of up to 12,965,027 common shares representing 10% of the public float. The bid commenced on Dec. 23, 2022, and expires on Dec. 22, 2023.

Major Shareholder - Widely held at Mar. 3, 2023.

Price Range - ESN/TSX

Year	Volume	High	Low	Close
2022	39,175,498	$0.56	$0.26	$0.39
2021	33,472,931	$0.46	$0.21	$0.39
2020	38,668,283	$0.40	$0.12	$0.22
2019	50,097,046	$0.49	$0.25	$0.38
2018	25,629,850	$0.82	$0.24	$0.30

Recent Close: $0.36

Capital Stock Changes - During 2022, 8,490,216 common shares were repurchased under a Normal Course Issuer Bid.

Wholly Owned Subsidiaries

Essential Coil Well Service Ltd., Alta.
- 0.01% int. in **Essential Coil Well Service Limited Partnership**, Alta.

Essential Energy Services USA Inc., Del.
- 100% int. in **Essential Well Service USA Inc.**, Del.
- 100% int. in **Tryton Tools USA Inc.**, Tex.
  - 100% int. in **Sam's Packer and Supply, LLC**, Kan.

Tryton Ltd., Alta.
- 0.01% int. in **Tryton Tool Services Limited Partnership**, Alta.

Subsidiaries

99.99% int. in **Essential Coil Well Service Limited Partnership**, Alta.
99.99% int. in **Tryton Tool Services Limited Partnership**, Alta.

Financial Statistics

Periods ended:	12m Dec. 31/22[A]		12m Dec. 31/21[A]
	$000s	%Chg	$000s
Operating revenue	**150,097**	**+24**	**121,208**
Cost of sales	79,778		66,222
Salaries & benefits	48,508		36,855
General & admin expense	3,755		2,950
Stock-based compensation	4,203		7,653
Operating expense	**136,244**	**+20**	**113,680**
Operating income	**13,853**	**+84**	**7,528**
Deprec., depl. & amort.	16,793		17,874
Finance costs, gross	917		1,071
Pre-tax income	**(1,723)**	**n.a.**	**(11,386)**
Income taxes	32		11
Net income	**(1,755)**	**n.a.**	**(11,397)**
Cash & equivalent	2,063		6,462
Inventories	34,617		31,111
Accounts receivable	27,086		29,341
Current assets	66,029		68,740
Fixed assets, net	76,180		81,532
Right-of-use assets	8,317		8,814
Total assets	**150,526**	**-5**	**159,086**
Accts. pay. & accr. liabs	14,307		14,399
Current liabilities	21,295		23,450
Long-term debt, gross	950		nil
Long-term debt, net	950		nil
Long-term lease liabilities	5,542		6,622
Shareholders' equity	117,382		122,826
Cash from oper. activs	**10,243**	**-13**	**11,823**
Cash from fin. activs	(8,256)		(5,325)
Cash from invest. activs	(6,390)		(6,109)
Net cash position	**2,063**	**-68**	**6,462**
Capital expenditures	(9,745)		(7,580)
Capital disposals	3,310		1,351
	$		$
Earnings per share*	(0.01)		(0.08)
Cash flow per share*	0.07		0.08
	shs		shs
No. of shs. o/s*	133,366,597		141,856,813
Avg. no. of shs. o/s*	139,294,000		141,856,813
	%		%
Net profit margin	(1.17)		(9.40)
Return on equity	(1.46)		(8.87)
Return on assets	(0.53)		(6.47)
No. of employees (FTEs)	332		299

* Common
[A] Reported in accordance with IFRS

Historical Summary
(as originally stated)

Fiscal Year	Oper. Rev. $000s	Net Inc. Bef. Disc. $000s	EPS* $
2022[A]	150,097	(1,755)	(0.01)
2021[A]	121,208	(11,397)	(0.08)
2020[A]	96,173	(16,810)	(0.12)
2019[A]	141,133	(1,556)	(0.01)
2018[A]	189,894	(8,778)	(0.06)

* Common
[A] Reported in accordance with IFRS

E.65 Esstra Industries Inc.

Symbol - ESS **Exchange** - TSX-VEN **CUSIP** - 29730R
Head Office - 40440 Thunderbird Ridge, Squamish, BC, V8B 0G1
Telephone - (604) 377-0403
Email - virginia@volnick.com
Investor Relations - Virginia Olnick (604) 785-1425
Auditors - Davidson & Company LLP C.A., Vancouver, B.C.
Lawyers - McLennan Ross LLP, Edmonton, Alta.
Transfer Agents - Computershare Trust Company of Canada Inc., Toronto, Ont.

Profile - (B.C. 2018; orig. Alta., 1996) Invests in marketable securities, real estate ventures and real estate developments.

Holds investment in **ExSorbtion Inc.**, a Nevada-based company involved in developing lithium extraction technology, which is carried at nominal value.

Directors - Virginia Olnick, CEO & corp. sec., Vancouver, B.C.; David B. Atkinson, CFO, Vancouver, B.C.; Peter G. Dickson, Edmonton, Alta.; Greg Kuenzel

Capital Stock

	Authorized (shs.)	Outstanding (shs.)[1]
Preferred Class I	unlimited	nil
Preferred Class II	unlimited	nil
Preferred Class III	unlimited	nil
Common	unlimited	8,202,501

[1] At Sept. 22, 2022

Major Shareholder - Peter Damouri held 12.03% interest, Wynne Olnick held 11.89% interest and Glenn Olnick held 11.53% interest at Nov. 5, 2021.

Price Range - ESS/TSX-VEN

Year	Volume	High	Low	Close
2022	54,011	$0.20	$0.10	$0.10
2021	500	$0.20	$0.20	$0.20
2020	189,000	$0.65	$0.10	$0.40
2019	57,100	$0.18	$0.12	$0.12
2018	93,500	$0.25	$0.10	$0.18

Recent Close: $0.10

Capital Stock Changes - There were no changes to capital stock during fiscal 2022.

Wholly Owned Subsidiaries

412688 B.C. Ltd., B.C.

Investments

5% int. in **ExSorbtion Inc.**, Nev.

Financial Statistics

Periods ended:	12m May 31/22[A]		12m May 31/21[A]
	$000s	%Chg	$000s
Realized invest. gain (loss)	5		nil
Unrealized invest. gain (loss)	(82)		29
Total revenue	**(74)**	**n.a.**	**29**
General & admin. expense	96		171
Operating expense	**96**	**-44**	**171**
Operating income	**(170)**	**n.a.**	**(142)**
Write-downs/write-offs	(352)		nil
Pre-tax income	**(520)**	**n.a.**	**(146)**
Net income	**(520)**	**n.a.**	**(146)**
Cash & equivalent	125		286
Current assets	125		286
Long-term investments	nil		352
Total assets	**125**	**-80**	**638**
Accts. pay. & accr. liabs	82		76
Current liabilities	82		76
Shareholders' equity	42		562
Cash from oper. activs	**(85)**	**n.a.**	**(111)**
Cash from fin. activs	nil		300
Cash from invest. activs	7		(277)
Net cash position	**64**	**-55**	**142**
	$		$
Earnings per share*	(0.06)		(0.02)
Cash flow per share*	(0.01)		(0.01)
	shs		shs
No. of shs. o/s*	8,202,501		8,202,501
Avg. no. of shs. o/s*	8,202,501		7,927,159
	%		%
Net profit margin	n.m.		(503.45)
Return on equity	(172.19)		(30.10)
Return on assets	(136.30)		(27.57)

* Common
[A] Reported in accordance with IFRS

Historical Summary
(as originally stated)

Fiscal Year	Total Rev. $000s	Net Inc. Bef. Disc. $000s	EPS* $
2022[A]	(74)	(520)	(0.06)
2021[A]	29	(146)	(0.02)
2020[A]	33	(28)	(0.00)
2019[A]	(112)	(197)	(0.03)
2018[A]	(6)	(58)	(0.01)

* Common
[A] Reported in accordance with IFRS

E.66 Ether Capital Corporation

Symbol - ETHC **Exchange** - NEO **CUSIP** - 29764T
Head Office - 3100-130 Adelaide St W, Toronto, ON, M5H 3P5
Telephone - (416) 347-2740
Website - ethcap.co
Email - ian@ethcap.co
Investor Relations - Ian McPherson (416) 347-2740
Auditors - Ernst & Young LLP C.A., Toronto, Ont.
Lawyers - McCarthy Tétrault LLP
Transfer Agents - TSX Trust Company, Toronto, Ont.

Profile - (Ont. 2018; orig. B.C., 2009) Invests in the cryptocurrency Ether as well as in projects, protocols and technologies that leverage the Ethereum ecosystem.

The company allocates a material portion of its Ether to a developing activity within the Ethereum 2.0 network called staking which generates revenue on the Ether allocated and committed to validating the continuous transactions (blocks) on the Ethereum beacon blockchain, thus allowing the company to generate a yield on its assets to supplement its passive price exposure to Ether. Staked Ether is not freely tradable future until after the expected merger of the Ethereum main blockchain and the Ethereum 2.0 beacon chain.

At Mar. 31, 2023, the company held 8,364 Ether valued at $20,669,729, 36,000 Staked Ether valued at $82,263,551 and 1,203 Staked Ether Rewards valued at $2,563,542.

Also holds a minority interest in **Wyre, Inc.**, a digital currency payment processor that provides payment application programming interfaces (APIs) to power fintech applications built on Ethereum and other blockchains.

On May 31, 2022, wholly owned **Ethereum Capital Inc.** was dissolved.
During the first quarter of 2022, the company divested its non-core digital assets, Maker (MKR) and Uniswap (UNI) tokens, for total proceeds of about $5,800,000.

Predecessor Detail - Name changed from Movit Media Corp., Apr. 17, 2018, pursuant to reverse takeover acquisition of Ethereum Capital Inc.; basis 1 new for 12.5 old shs.

Directors - Som Seif, exec. chr. & co-CIO, Toronto, Ont.; Brian Mosoff, CEO, Ont.; Camillo O. (Cam) di Prata, Toronto, Ont.; Liam Horne, Waterloo, Ont.; Colleen M. McMorrow, Oakville, Ont.; John Ruffolo, Toronto, Ont.; Boris Wertz, Vancouver, B.C.

Other Exec. Officers - Ian McPherson, pres. & CFO; Jillian Friedman, COO

Capital Stock

	Authorized (shs.)	Outstanding (shs.)[1]
Common	unlimited	34,103,620

[1] At Apr. 27, 2023

Normal Course Issuer Bid - The company plans to make normal course purchases of up to 2,566,662 common shares representing 7.5% of the total outstanding. The bid commenced on July 1, 2023, and expires on June 30, 2024.

Major Shareholder - MMCAP International Inc. held 14.66% interest at Apr. 27, 2023.

Price Range - ETHC/NEO

Year	Volume	High	Low	Close
2022	998,800	$4.64	$1.15	$1.54
2021	3,835,000	$5.80	$2.13	$4.51
2020	1,664,300	$3.35	$0.18	$3.30
2019	1,094,500	$0.84	$0.20	$0.20
2018	311,634	$2.63	$0.40	$0.42

Recent Close: $1.74

Capital Stock Changes - During 2022, common shares were issued as follows: 169,407 on exercise of options and 137,578 on exercise of warrants; 378,900 common shares were repurchased under a Normal Course Issuer Bid.

Investments

3.96% int. in **Wyre, Inc.**, San Francisco, Calif.

Financial Statistics

Periods ended:	12m Dec. 31/22[A]		12m Dec. 31/21[oA]
	$000s	%Chg	$000s
Operating revenue	**3,690**	**+146**	**1,502**
Salaries & benefits	1,469		395
General & admin expense	1,627		1,294
Stock-based compensation	806		326
Operating expense	**3,902**	**+94**	**2,015**
Operating income	**(212)**	**n.a.**	**(513)**
Write-downs/write-offs	(65,470)[1]		(2,836)[2]
Pre-tax income	**(62,950)**	**n.a.**	**(3,180)**
Income taxes	(4,572)		(4,687)
Net income	**(58,378)**	**n.a.**	**1,507**
Cash & equivalent	2,887		3,410
Accounts receivable	103		290
Current assets	2,990		3,699
Long-term investments	nil		6,200
Fixed assets, net	8		nil
Intangibles, net	73,140		210,423
Total assets	**76,137**	**-65**	**220,322**
Accts. pay. & accr. liabs	505		503
Current liabilities	505		503
Shareholders' equity	75,632		204,185
Cash from oper. activs	**(1,620)**	**n.a.**	**(46)**
Cash from fin. activs	(617)		27,226
Cash from invest. activs	(732)		(24,185)
Net cash position	**441**	**-87**	**3,410**
	$		$
Earnings per share*	(1.73)		0.05
Cash flow per share*	(0.05)		(0.00)
	shs		shs
No. of shs. o/s*	33,705,737		33,825,535
Avg. no. of shs. o/s*	33,705,737		31,968,941
	%		%
Net profit margin	n.m.		100.33
Return on equity	(39.52)		1.27
Return on assets	(39.38)		1.19

* Common
[o] Restated
[A] Reported in accordance with IFRS
[1] Includes impairment of digital intangible assets of $63,465,485 and impairment on investment of $2,004,900.
[2] Pertains to impairment of digital intangible assets.

Latest Results

Periods ended:	3m Mar. 31/23[A]		3m Mar. 31/22[A]
	$000s	%Chg	$000s
Operating revenue	1,154	-2	1,172
Net income	(18,678)	n.a.	(7,759)
	$		$
Earnings per share*	(0.55)		(0.23)

* Common
[A] Reported in accordance with IFRS

Historical Summary
(as originally stated)

Fiscal Year	Oper. Rev.	Net Inc. Bef. Disc.	EPS*
	$000s	$000s	$
2022[A]	3,690	(58,378)	(1.73)
2021[A]	1,502	(3,180)	(0.10)
2020[A]	nil	22,432	0.97
2019[A]	89	(1,471)	(0.06)
2018[A1]	nil	(35,232)	(2.05)

* Common
[A] Reported in accordance with IFRS
[1] Results reflect the Apr. 18, 2018, reverse takeover acquisition of Ethereum Capital Inc.

E.67 The Ether Fund

Symbol - QETH.UN **Exchange** - TSX **CUSIP** - 29764L
Head Office - 2700-161 Bay St, Toronto, ON, M5J 2S1 **Telephone** - (416) 639-2130
Website - 3iq.ca
Email - john.loeprich@3iq.ca
Investor Relations - John Loeprich (416) 639-2130
Auditors - Raymond Chabot Grant Thornton LLP C.A., Montréal, Qué.
Lawyers - Renno & Co., Montréal, Qué.
Transfer Agents - TSX Trust Company, Toronto, Ont.
Trustees - 3iQ Corp., Toronto, Ont.
Managers - 3iQ Corp., Toronto, Ont.
Profile - (Ont. 2020) Invests in the digital currency ether (ETH).

The fund invests in ETH purchased from reputable digital asset trading platforms and over-the-counter counterparties. Digital asset trading platforms are spot markets on which ETH can be exchanged for U.S. dollars. These platforms are not regulated as securities exchanges or commodity futures exchanges under the securities or commodity futures laws of Canada, the United States or other global jurisdictions.

The value of ETH held by the fund is based on the MVIS CryptoCompare Ethereum Benchmark Rate Index maintained by **MV Index Solutions GmbH** (MVIS). Prior to May 2, 2022, the fund's ETH was valued based on MVIS CryptoCompare Institutional Ethereum Index maintained by MVIS.

The manager is entitled to a management fee at an annual rate of 1.95% of net asset value, calculated daily and payable monthly plus taxes. The fund does not have a fixed termination date but may be terminated at the discretion of the manager without unitholder approval.

Directors - Frederick T. (Fred) Pye, chr. & CEO, Pointe-Claire, Qué.; John Loeprich, CFO, Moffat, Ont.; Anthony Cox, exec. v-p, Toronto, Ont.

Oper. Subsid./Mgt. Co. Officers - Pascal St-Jean, pres.; Diana Escobar Bold, chief compliance officer

Capital Stock

	Authorized (shs.)	Outstanding (shs.)[1]
Class A Unit	unlimited	4,278,182
Class F Unit	unlimited	nil

[1] At Aug. 9, 2023

Class A & F Units - Denominated in U.S. dollars. The fund does not intend to pay distributions. Class F units are designed for fee-based investors and/or institutional accounts. Retractable in June of each year at a price equal to the net asset value (NAV) per unit on first business day following June 15, less any costs and expenses associated with the retraction. Payment of proceeds of annual redemption will be made in U.S. dollars or, at the request of a unitholder who is redeeming at least 20,000 units, in ether. In connection with annual redemption, unitholders may elect to convert their units on a NAV basis to units of 3iQ CoinShares Ether ETF. Class A units are retractable monthly at a price equal to 95% of closing market price per class A unit, less any costs and expenses associated with the retraction. The class A retraction price will not be an amount that is more than 95% of the NAV per class A unit. Class F units issued are reclassified immediately as class A units on a 1-for-1 basis. Class F units may be issued in the future that may not be reclassified immediately as class A units and as such, there may be outstanding class F units in the future. One vote per unit.

Normal Course Issuer Bid - The company plans to make normal course purchases of up to 481,436 class A units representing 10% of the public float. The bid commenced on Mar. 1, 2023, and expires on Feb. 29, 2024.

Major Shareholder - Widely held at Dec. 31, 2022.

Price Range - QETH.UN/TSX

Year	Volume	High	Low	Close
2022	5,529,628	$82.00	$20.50	$23.31
2021	17,004,176	$101.11	$26.79	$76.19

QETH.U/TSX

Year	Volume	High	Low	Close
2021	21,468,585	US$81.07	US$18.15	US$59.95
2020	2,969,226	US$15.95	US$10.57	US$15.95

Recent Close: $34.39

Capital Stock Changes - During 2022, 5,070,724 class A units were retracted and 102,100 class A units were repurchased under a Normal Course Issuer Bid.

Financial Statistics

Periods ended:	12m Dec. 31/22[A]		12m Dec. 31/21[A]
	US$000s	%Chg	US$000s
Realized invest. gain (loss)	77,614		13,017
Unrealized invest. gain (loss)	(488,833)		494,270
Total revenue	**(411,220)**	**n.a.**	**507,288**
General & admin. expense	7,805		12,990
Operating expense	**7,805**	**-40**	**12,990**
Operating income	**(419,025)**	**n.a.**	**494,298**
Finance costs, gross	nil		33
Pre-tax income	**(419,025)**	**n.a.**	**494,265**
Net income	**(419,025)**	**n.a.**	**494,265**
Cash & equivalent	41		77
Investments	114,254		686,117
Total assets	**114,295**	**-83**	**686,194**
Accts. pay. & accr. liabs	65		245
Shareholders' equity	114,010		684,549
Cash from oper. activs	**6,556**	**n.a.**	**(55,468)**
Cash from fin. activs	(6,592)		55,248
Net cash position	**41**	**-47**	**77**
	US$		US$
Earnings per share*	(53.52)		47.20
Cash flow per share*	0.84		(5.30)
Net asset value per share*	20.15		63.20
	shs		shs
No. of shs. o/s*	5,657,805		10,830,629
Avg. no. of shs. o/s*	7,829,156		10,471,936
	%		%
Net profit margin	n.m.		97.43
Return on equity	(104.95)		n.m.
Return on assets	(104.69)		n.a.

* Class A
[A] Reported in accordance with IFRS

E.68 Eupraxia Pharmaceuticals Inc.

Symbol - EPRX **Exchange** - TSX **CUSIP** - 29842P
Head Office - 201-2067 Cadboro Bay Rd, Victoria, BC, V8R 5G4 **Telephone** - (250) 590-3968 **Fax** - (250) 590-2588
Website - eupraxiapharma.com
Email - degan@eupraxiapharma.com
Investor Relations - Danielle Egan (778) 401-3302
Auditors - Baker Tilly WM LLP C.A., Vancouver, B.C.
Lawyers - Blake, Cassels & Graydon LLP, Vancouver, B.C.
Transfer Agents - TSX Trust Company, Vancouver, B.C.
Employees - 21 at Dec. 31, 2022
Profile - (B.C. 2011) Develops locally delivered, extended-release alternatives to currently approved drugs that address therapeutic areas with high unmet medical need.

Lead product candidates are EP-104IAR, which is in Phase 2 development for the treatment of pain due to knee osteoarthritis; and EP104GI, which is in Phase 1b/2a development for the treatment of eosinophilic esophagitis, a rarely disease that restricts the ability to swallow food.

An earlier-stage pipeline of potential product candidates include a range of drugs for indications such as post-surgical pain (EP-105) and post-surgical site infections (EP-201), each designed to improve on the activity and tolerability of approved drugs.

Also developing a formulation of EP-104IAR modified for use in canine and equine osteoarthritis. The company continues to seek a partner for the development, regulatory approval and commercialization of the veterinary version of EP-104IAR.

The company is headquartered in Victoria, B.C., with manufacturing operations carried out in Canada, the U.S., Italy and the U.K.

Directors - Dr. Simon N. Pimstone, chr., Vancouver, B.C.; Dr. James A. Helliwell, CEO, Vancouver, B.C.; Paul L. Geyer, Vancouver, B.C.; Dr. Richard M. Glickman, Victoria, B.C.; John S. Montalbano, Vancouver, B.C.; Dr. Michael Wilmink, Phoenix, Ariz.

Other Exec. Officers - Dr. Amanda Malone, co-founder & chief scientific officer; Bruce G. Cousins, pres. & CFO; Paul A. Brennan, chief bus. officer; Dr. Mark Kowalski, CMO; Ash Bassett, v-p, fin.; Vik Peck, v-p, program mgt., regulatory & quality affairs; Dr. Murray Webb, v-p, translational science

Capital Stock

	Authorized (shs.)	Outstanding (shs.)[1]
Preferred	unlimited	nil
Common	unlimited	21,769,745

[1] At May 10, 2023

Major Shareholder - Manchester Management Company LLC held 12.8% interest at Apr. 18, 2023.

Price Range - EPRX/TSX

Year	Volume	High	Low	Close
2022	5,687,066	$4.85	$0.80	$3.65
2021	3,291,191	$7.75	$1.72	$2.45

Recent Close: $7.53

Capital Stock Changes - In April 2022, public offering of 7,150,550 units (1 common share & ½ warrant) at $2.05 per unit was completed.

Also during 2022, 200,000 common shares were issued on exercise of warrants.

Wholly Owned Subsidiaries

Eupraxia Pharmaceuticals Australia Pty Ltd., Australia.

Subsidiaries

95% int. in **AMDM Holdings Inc.**, Wash.
95% int. in **Eupraxia Pharma, Inc.**, Del.
- 100% int. in **Eupraxia Holdings, Inc.**, Del.
  - 100% int. in **Eupraxia Pharmaceuticals USA, LLC**, Del.

Financial Statistics

Periods ended:	12m Dec. 31/22[A]		12m Dec. 31/21[A]
	$000s	%Chg	$000s
Salaries & benefits	2,148		2,357
Research & devel. expense	17,203		9,679
General & admin expense	1,639		2,316
Stock-based compensation	2,020		4,215
Operating expense	**23,010**	**+24**	**18,566**
Operating income	**(23,010)**	**n.a.**	**(18,566)**
Deprec., depl. & amort.	193		112
Finance income	569		66
Finance costs, gross	1,588		1,297
Pre-tax income	**(23,917)**	**n.a.**	**(23,370)**
Net income	**(23,917)**	**n.a.**	**(23,370)**
Net inc. for equity hldrs	**(23,259)**	**n.a.**	**(22,990)**
Net inc. for non-cont. int	**(658)**	**n.a.**	**(380)**
Cash & equivalent	24,736		29,901
Accounts receivable	122		430
Current assets	25,177		30,602
Fixed assets, net	601		445
Right-of-use assets	95		144
Total assets	**25,876**	**-17**	**31,222**
Accts. pay. & accr. liabs	3,966		2,113
Current liabilities	4,142		2,268
Long-term debt, gross	10,408		9,359
Long-term debt, net	10,300		9,264
Long-term lease liabilities	69		138
Shareholders' equity	11,364		19,553
Non-controlling interest	1,492		834
Cash from oper. activs	**(18,776)**	**n.a.**	**(14,642)**
Cash from fin. activs	13,523		49,915
Cash from invest. activs	8,701		(14,450)
Net cash position	**24,736**	**+18**	**20,892**
Capital expenditures	(308)		(432)
	$		$
Earnings per share*	(1.21)		(1.85)
Cash flow per share*	(0.97)		(1.18)
	shs		shs
No. of shs. o/s*	21,593,145		14,242,595
Avg. no. of shs. o/s*	19,285,447		12,405,838
	%		%
Net profit margin	n.a.		n.a.
Return on equity	(150.46)		n.m.
Return on assets	(78.21)		(135.10)
No. of employees (FTEs)	21		19

* Common
[A] Reported in accordance with IFRS

Latest Results

Periods ended:	3m Mar. 31/23[A]		3m Mar. 31/22[A]
	$000s	%Chg	$000s
Net income	(5,042)	n.a.	(3,760)
Net inc. for equity hldrs	(4,960)	n.a.	(3,691)
Net inc. for non-cont. int	(82)		(69)
	$		$
Earnings per share*	(0.23)		(0.26)

* Common
[A] Reported in accordance with IFRS

Historical Summary
(as originally stated)

Fiscal Year	Oper. Rev. $000s	Net Inc. Bef. Disc. $000s	EPS* $
2022[A]	nil	(23,917)	(1.21)
2021[A]	nil	(23,370)	(1.85)
2020[A]	nil	(4,011)	(0.65)
2019[A1]	nil	(7,241)	(1.17)
2018[A1]	nil	(14,833)	(2.16)

* Common
[A] Reported in accordance with IFRS
[1] As shown in the prospectus dated Mar. 3, 2021. Shares and per share figures adjusted to reflect 1-for-4 share consolidation effective immediately prior to the initial public offering completed on Mar. 9, 2021.

E.69 Eureka Capital Corp.

Symbol - EBCD.P **Exchange** - TSX-VEN **CUSIP** - 298528
Head Office - 1214-12 Royal Visa Way NW, Calgary, AB, T3R 0N2 **Telephone** - (587) 435-0542
Email - khalid@besure.com
Investor Relations - Khalid Karmali (587) 435-0542
Auditors - Buchanan Barry LLP C.A., Calgary, Alta.
Transfer Agents - Odyssey Trust Company, Calgary, Alta.
Profile - (Alta. 2022) Capital Pool Company.
Common listed on TSX-VEN, Mar. 9, 2023.
Directors - Minaz H. Lalani, CEO & CFO, Calgary, Alta.; Khalid Karmali, corp. sec., Calgary, Alta.; Stephen E. (Steve) Bjornson, Calgary, Alta.; Karim Lalani, Victoria, B.C.

Capital Stock

	Authorized (shs.)	Outstanding (shs.)[1]
Common	unlimited	9,700,000

[1] At Mar. 9, 2023

Major Shareholder - Minaz H. Lalani held 30.92% interest at Mar. 9, 2023.
Recent Close: $0.13
Capital Stock Changes - On Mar. 9, 2023, an initial public offering of 5,900,000 common shares was completed at 10¢ per share.

E.70 European Residential Real Estate Investment Trust

Symbol - ERE.UN **Exchange** - TSX **CUSIP** - 29880W
Head Office - 401-11 Church St, Toronto, ON, M5E 1W1 **Telephone** - (416) 861-9404
Website - www.eresreit.com
Email - j.chou@eresreit.com
Investor Relations - Jenny Chou (416) 354-0188
Auditors - Ernst & Young LLP C.A., Toronto, Ont.
Lawyers - Stikeman Elliott LLP, Toronto, Ont.
Transfer Agents - TSX Trust Company, Toronto, Ont.
Profile - (Ont. 2016) Owns and invests in multi-residential properties in Europe, with a focus on the Netherlands.

The trust's portfolio (at Mar. 31, 2023) consists of 158 residential properties in the Netherlands, representing 6,900 residential suites; and 450,911 sq. ft. of gross leasable area across a commercial property in each of Germany and Belgium, as well as ancillary retail space in the Netherlands.

Canadian Apartment Properties Real Estate Investment Trust (CAPREIT) acts as asset manager of the trust. **European Residential Management B.V.**, owned by CAPREIT, and **Maple Knoll Capital Ltd.** manage the trust's residential and two commercial properties, respectively.

In August 2022, the trust sold a single-family home in the Randstad region of the Netherlands for €900,000.

Recent Merger and Acquisition Activity

Status: completed **Announced:** May 2, 2022
European Residential Real Estate Investment Trust acquired five multi-residential properties in Rotterdam, Netherlands, consisting of 110 suites, for €23,000,000.

Status: completed **Revised:** Mar. 31, 2022
UPDATE: The transaction was completed. PREVIOUS: European Residential Real Estate Investment Trust agreed to acquire FiftyOne property in Arnhem, Netherlands, consisting of 201 residential apartments, for €45,000,000, which would be financed via a long-term mortgage and a promissory note.

Predecessor Detail - Name changed from European Commercial Real Estate Investment Trust, Mar. 29, 2019, following acquisition of a portfolio of multi-residential properties in the Netherlands.
Trustees - Dr. Gina P. Cody, chr., Toronto, Ont.; Mark Kenney, CEO, Newmarket, Ont.; Jan Arie Breure, Monaco; Harold Burke, Toronto, Ont.; Ira Gluskin, Toronto, Ont.; Gervais Levasseur, Dollard-des-Ormeaux, Qué.
Oper. Subsid./Mgt. Co. Officers - Jenny Chou, CFO

Capital Stock

	Authorized (shs.)	Outstanding (shs.)[1]
Trust Unit	unlimited	90,510,807
Special Voting Unit	unlimited	142,040,821
Class B LP Unit		142,040,821[2 3]

[1] At Apr. 5, 2023
[2] Classified as debt.
[3] Units of subsidiary ERES Limited Partnership.

Note: All class B LP units are held by Canadian Apartment Properties Real Estate Investment Trust

Trust Unit - Retractable at a price equal to the lesser of: (i) 90% of the market price of the trust units on the principal market on which the trust units are traded during the 10 trading days immediately preceding the retraction date; and (ii) 100% of the closing market price of the trust units on the principal market on which the trust units traded on the retraction date. One vote per trust unit.
Special Voting Unit - Issued to holders of class B limited partnership units of subsidiary ERES Limited Partnership. Each special voting unit entitles the holder to a number of votes at unitholder meetings equal to the number of trust units into which the class B limited partnership units are exchangeable.
Class B Limited Partnership Unit - Entitled to distributions equal to those provided to trust units. Directly exchangeable into trust units on a 1-for-1 basis at any time by the holder. Classified as long-term debt under IFRS.
Major Shareholder - Canadian Apartment Properties Real Estate Investment Trust held 65% interest at Apr. 5, 2023.

Price Range - ERE.UN/TSX

Year	Volume	High	Low	Close
2022	23,300,668	$5.06	$2.70	$3.03
2021	20,038,622	$4.82	$4.09	$4.51
2020	25,462,185	$5.37	$2.81	$4.17
2019	17,182,586	$5.19	$3.71	$4.65
2018	5,104,378	$4.25	$3.33	$3.75

Recent Close: $2.54
Capital Stock Changes - During 2022, trust units were issued as follows: 944,185 under distribution reinvestment plan and 31,817 on exercise of options.

Dividends

ERE.UN unit Ra □0.12 pa M est. Aug. 15, 2023[1]
Prev. Rate: □0.12 est. July 17, 2023
Prev. Rate: □0.12 est. Mar. 15, 2023
Prev. Rate: □0.12 est. Feb. 15, 2023
Prev. Rate: □0.12 est. Jan. 16, 2023
Prev. Rate: □0.12 est. Apr. 18, 2022
Prev. Rate: □0.11 est. Apr. 15, 2021
Prev. Rate: □0.105 est. July 15, 2019
[1] Effective July 2019, distributions declared in Euros and paid in Cdn$ based on the exchange rate on the date of payment.

Wholly Owned Subsidiaries

ERES General Partner Corp., Ont.

Investments

35% int. in **ERES Limited Partnership**, Ont. Represents voting interest through ownership of class A limited partnership units.
- 100% int. in **ERES Hong Kong Limited**, Hong Kong, People's Republic of China.
- 100% int. in **ERES NL Holding B.V.**, Netherlands.

Financial Statistics

Periods ended:	12m Dec. 31/22[A]		12m Dec. 31/21[A]
	€000s	%Chg	€000s
Total revenue	**89,252**	**+16**	**76,872**
Rental operating expense	17,836		15,163
General & admin. expense	9,669		8,949
Stock-based compensation	(1,592)		761
Property taxes	2,436		2,191
Operating expense	**28,349**	**+5**	**27,064**
Operating income	**60,903**	**+22**	**49,808**
Finance costs, gross	33,207		28,009
Pre-tax income	**109,703**	**-28**	**151,880**
Income taxes	(6,713)		55,742
Net income	**116,416**	**+21**	**96,138**
Cash & equivalent	10,889		10,348
Accounts receivable	3,462		2,150
Current assets	15,444		13,963
Income-producing props	1,897,060		1,859,600
Intangibles, net	nil		10,541
Total assets	**1,939,206**	**+3**	**1,887,685**
Accts. pay. & accr. liabs	4,177		3,411
Current liabilities	111,452		79,327
Long-term debt, gross	1,261,971		1,330,475
Long-term debt, net	1,200,089		1,278,371
Shareholders' equity	550,147		441,765
Cash from oper. activs	**58,815**	**+9**	**54,122**
Cash from fin. activs	54,743		136,717
Cash from invest. activs	(113,007)		(191,216)
Net cash position	**10,889**	**+5**	**10,348**
Capital expenditures	(23,994)		(19,427)
Increase in property	(89,018)		(171,628)
Decrease in property	880		309
	€		€
Earnings per share*	n.a.		n.a.
Cash flow per share*	0.66		0.61
Funds from opers. per sh.*	$0.17		$0.15
Adj. funds from opers. per sh.*	$0.15		$0.14
Cash divd. per share*	$0.16		$0.16
Total divd. per share*	**$0.16**		**$0.16**
	shs		shs
No. of shs. o/s*	90,262,833		89,286,831
Avg. no. of shs. o/s*	89,738,000		88,991,000
	%		%
Net profit margin	130.44		125.06
Return on equity	23.47		24.17
Return on assets	7.93		6.72
Foreign sales percent	100		100

* Trust Unit
[A] Reported in accordance with IFRS

Latest Results

Periods ended:	3m Mar. 31/23[A]		3m Mar. 31/22[A]
	€000s	%Chg	€000s
Total revenue	23,380	+10	21,254
Net income	(106,348)	n.a.	(31,729)
	€		€
Earnings per share*	n.a.		n.a.

[A] Reported in accordance with IFRS

Historical Summary
(as originally stated)

Fiscal Year	Total Rev.	Net Inc. Bef. Disc.	EPS*
	€000s	€000s	€
2022A	89,252	116,416	n.a.
2021A	76,872	96,138	n.a.
2020A	69,880	118,657	n.a.
2019A1	41,481	(16,806)	n.a.
	$000s	$000s	$
2018A	12,160	8,232	n.a.

* Trust Unit
A Reported in accordance with IFRS
1 Results reflect the Mar. 29, 2019, reverse takeover acquisition of multi-residential properties in the Netherlands from Canadian Apartment Properties Real Estate Investment Trust.

E.71 Eve & Co Incorporated

Symbol - EVE.H **Exchange** - TSX-VEN (S) **CUSIP** - 29970Q
Head Office - 2941 Napperton Dr, Strathroy, ON, N7G 3H8 **Toll-free** - (855) 628-6337
Website - www.evecannabis.ca
Email - invest@evecannabis.ca
Investor Relations - Melinda Rombouts (855) 628-6337
Auditors - Davidson & Company LLP C.A., Vancouver, B.C.
Transfer Agents - TSX Trust Company, Toronto, Ont.
Profile - (Ont. 2014) Produces and sells cannabis products including dried cannabis, cannabis plants and cannabis oil in Canada.

Wholly owned **Natural MedCo Ltd.** is a licensed producer under the Cannabis Act from a 1,000,000-sq.-ft. greenhouse facility in Strathroy, Ont., and has received EU-GMP certification. An additional 7,300-sq.ft. of processing area was approved by Health Canada. Natural MedCo is also authorized to sell cannabis extracts, edibles and topicals.

The company plans to operate in the female-focused recreational cannabis market under the Eve brand. It would continue to operate under the Natural MedCo brand in the medical cannabis market.

On Mar. 25, 2022, the company filed for protection under the Companies' Creditors Arrangement Act (CCAA) and **BDO Canada Limited** was appointed monitor.

Common suspended from TSX-VEN, Mar. 30, 2022.

Predecessor Detail - Name changed from Carlaw Capital V Corp., June 28, 2018, following Qualifying Transaction reverse takeover acquisition of 1600978 Ontario Inc. (Natural MedCo) by way of an amalgamation with a wholly owned subsidiary; basis 2 new for 1 old sh.

Directors - Melinda Rombouts, pres. & CEO, Strathroy, Ont.

Other Exec. Officers - Kim Arnel, interim CFO; Ivan R. Vrána, v-p, govt. rel. & bus. devel.; Ruth Chun, corp. sec.; David Burch, dir., Natural MedCo Ltd.

Capital Stock

	Authorized (shs.)	Outstanding (shs.)1
Common	unlimited	36,754,100

1 At Aug. 22, 2023

Major Shareholder - Melinda Rombouts held 20.15% interest at May 14, 2021.

Price Range - EVE.H/TSX-VEN (S)

Year	Volume	High	Low	Close
2022	1,080,990	$0.16	$0.10	$0.10
2021	13,872,227	$0.70	$0.11	$0.12
2020	11,375,169	$2.05	$0.36	$0.42
2019	22,838,212	$6.30	$1.25	$1.90
2018	16,314,899	$6.60	$1.55	$2.40

Consolidation: 1-for-10 cons. in Dec. 2020

Capital Stock Changes - In February 2022, 5,189,607 common shares were issued for settlement of $657,000 of debt.

Wholly Owned Subsidiaries

Eve & Co International Holdings Ltd., Canada.
Natural MedCo Ltd., Strathroy, Ont.

E.72 EverGen Infrastructure Corp.

Symbol - EVGN **Exchange** - TSX-VEN **CUSIP** - 30008P
Head Office - 390-1050 Homer St, Vancouver, BC, V6B 2W9 **Telephone** - (604) 202-7004
Website - www.evergeninfra.com
Email - mischa@evergeninfra.com
Investor Relations - Mischa Zajtmann (604) 202-7004
Auditors - PricewaterhouseCoopers LLP C.A., Calgary, Alta.
Transfer Agents - TSX Trust Company, Vancouver, B.C.
Profile - (B.C. 2020) Acquires, develops, builds, owns and operates a portfolio of renewable natural gas (RNG), waste to energy and related infrastructure projects.

The company owns and operates organic waste conversion processing facilities in British Columbia, Alberta and Ontario which processes inbound organics, yard waste and biosolids and produces organic compost and soils for farmers, gardeners and developers. These organics are intended to be converted to biogas via anaerobic digestion. The biogas would then be upgraded to RNG and sold to gas utilities under long term contracts. The company plans to become the dominant supplier of RNG in the form of purified biomethane to **FortisBC Energy Inc.**, a local gas utility, and expand its operations in North America, including actively pursuing the development of project clusters similar to the one in British Columbia, Alberta, Ontario and Québec.

On Sept. 14, 2022 common shares were listed on the OTCQX® Best Market under the symbol EVGIF.

In July 2022, the company acquired 67% interest in **Grow the Energy Circle Ltd.**, a farm scale biogas facility in Lethbridge, Alta., for $2,100,000 and issuance of 600,000 common shares. The company also agreed to work with GrowTEC to develop and expand the renewable natural gas (RNG) output at the facility.

In May 2022, the company acquired a 50% interest in Project Radius, a portfolio of three late-development stage renewable natural gas (RNG) development projects in Ontario which is capable of producing approximately 550,000 GJ of RNG annually, for $1,500,000.

Directors - Chase Edgelow, CEO, B.C.; Djenane Cameron, Ont.; Mary C. Hemmingsen, Vancouver, B.C.; Ford G. Nicholson, Vancouver, B.C.; Jon Ozturgut, Wash.

Other Exec. Officers - Mischa Zajtmann, pres., corp. sec. & COO; Sean Hennessy, CFO; Jamie Betts, v-p, opers.

Capital Stock

	Authorized (shs.)	Outstanding (shs.)1
Common	unlimited	13,307,000

1 At June 30, 2022

Major Shareholder - Widely held at Sept. 19, 2022.

Price Range - EVGN/TSX-VEN

Year	Volume	High	Low	Close
2022	5,413,474	$5.20	$1.86	$2.05
2021	3,293,620	$6.48	$3.74	$4.10

Recent Close: $2.77

Capital Stock Changes - During 2022, 600,000 common shares were issued pursuant to the acquisition of 67% interest in Grow the Energy Circle Ltd. and 163,000 common shares were repurchased under a Normal Course Issuer Bid.

Wholly Owned Subsidiaries

Fraser Valley Biogas Ltd., Abbotsford, B.C.
1000208169 Ontario Inc., Vancouver, B.C.
- 50% int. in **Radius RNG Limited Partnership**, Canada.

Pacific Coast Renewables Corp., Abbotsford, B.C.
Sea to Sky Soils and Composting Inc., Pemberton, B.C.

Subsidiaries

67% int. in **Grow the Energy Circle Ltd.**, Alta.

Financial Statistics

Periods ended:	12m Dec. 31/22A		12m Dec. 31/21¤A
	$000s	%Chg	$000s
Operating revenue	**7,459**	**-22**	**9,564**
Cost of goods sold	5,169		3,733
Salaries & benefits	2,789		2,648
General & admin expense	3,003		2,617
Stock-based compensation	433		1,389
Operating expense	**10,961**	**+6**	**10,387**
Operating income	**(3,502)**	**n.a.**	**(823)**
Deprec., depl. & amort.	3,187		2,760
Finance costs, gross	596		458
Pre-tax income	**(4,850)**	**n.a.**	**(2,382)**
Income taxes	(740)		(429)
Net income	**(4,110)**	**n.a.**	**(1,953)**
Net inc. for equity hldrs	**(4,099)**	**n.a.**	**(1,953)**
Net inc. for non-cont. int.	**(11)**	**n.a.**	**nil**
Cash & equivalent	8,852		19,597
Accounts receivable	3,325		3,325
Current assets	13,236		25,019
Long-term investments	1,112		nil
Fixed assets, net	29,789		17,007
Intangibles, net	41,819		38,584
Total assets	**85,956**	**+7**	**80,610**
Accts. pay. & accr. liabs	3,547		3,197
Current liabilities	7,111		4,474
Long-term debt, gross	5,759		6,458
Long-term debt, net	5,059		5,758
Long-term lease liabilities	5,238		2,999
Shareholders' equity	58,916		61,372
Non-controlling interest	2,466		nil
Cash from oper. activs	**(1,347)**	**n.a.**	**(1,919)**
Cash from fin. activs	(1,923)		34,189
Cash from invest. activs	(7,475)		(17,357)
Net cash position	**8,852**	**-55**	**19,597**
Capital expenditures	(7,669)		(1,590)
Capital disposals	81		3
	$		$
Earnings per share*	(0.30)		(0.18)
Cash flow per share*	(0.10)		(0.17)
	shs		shs
No. of shs. o/s*	13,809,000		13,367,000
Avg. no. of shs. o/s*	13,593,000		11,029,000
	%		%
Net profit margin	(55.10)		(20.42)
Return on equity	(6.82)		(4.19)
Return on assets	(4.33)		(2.41)

* Common
¤ Restated
A Reported in accordance with IFRS

Latest Results

Periods ended:	3m Mar. 31/23A		3m Mar. 31/22A
	$000s	%Chg	$000s
Operating revenue	1,683	+18	1,427
Net income	(996)	n.a.	(219)
Net inc. for equity hldrs	(907)	n.a.	(219)
Net inc. for non-cont. int.	(89)		nil
	$		$
Earnings per share*	(0.07)		(0.02)

* Common
A Reported in accordance with IFRS

Historical Summary
(as originally stated)

Fiscal Year	Oper. Rev.	Net Inc. Bef. Disc.	EPS*
	$000s	$000s	$
2022A	7,459	(4,110)	(0.30)
2021A	9,564	(1,953)	(0.18)
2020A1	nil	(2,233)	n.a.

* Common
A Reported in accordance with IFRS
1 33 weeks ended Dec. 31, 2020.

E.73 Evertz Technologies Limited*

Symbol - ET **Exchange** - TSX **CUSIP** - 30041N
Head Office - 5292 John Lucas Dr, Burlington, ON, L7L 5Z9 **Telephone** - (905) 335-3700 **Toll-free** - (877) 995-3700 **Fax** - (905) 335-3573
Website - www.evertz.com
Email - dmoore@evertz.com
Investor Relations - Douglas Moore (905) 335-7580
Auditors - BDO Canada LLP C.A., Oakville, Ont.
Lawyers - WeirFoulds LLP, Toronto, Ont.
Transfer Agents - Computershare Trust Company of Canada Inc., Toronto, Ont.
FP500 Revenue Ranking - 495
Employees - 1,950 at Apr. 30, 2023
Profile - (Can. 1981) Designs, manufactures and markets video and audio infrastructure solutions for the television, telecommunications, professional audio-visual (AV) and new media industries.

The company provides software, equipment and technology solutions used in the production, post-production and transmission of television content for content creators, broadcasters, specialty channels, television service providers, telecommunications, professional AV and new media companies. Operations are located in Canada, the U.S., the U.K., Europe, Asia and the Middle East. Products are designed, assembled, manufactured, developed, tested, packaged and shipped from facilities in Burlington, Ont., the U.S. and the U.K.

Core products work together in integrated systems, and are categorized as follows:

Infrastructure Solutions - These solutions are used across the broadcasting industry for various signal processing, routing and distribution functions, such as conversion from analog to digital, electrical to optical, from standard definition (SD) to high definition (HD) to 3Gb/s (3G) and 12Gb/s 4K/8K Ultra HD serial digital interfaces (SDI).

Visualization and Monitoring Solutions - These products enable users to view, monitor and manage a large number of broadcast signals locally or across geographically dispersed infrastructure. Products include multi-image display processors for network control centres, and Internet Protocol (IP) monitoring and Simple Network Management Protocol (SNMP)-based network management products for facility monitoring environment.

Playout and Content Management Solutions - These solutions enable customers to improve operational workflow by providing a scalable, feature-rich and cost-effective solution for both baseband and file based playout.

Compression and Media Transport Solutions - These products allow broadcasters and service providers to deliver video and audio content over small and large geographical distances by enabling Ultra HD, 3G, HD and SD video and audio signals to be delivered over IP networks using compression techniques such as MPEG-2, H.264, HEVC, JPEG2000 and JPEG XS.

Software Defined Video Networking - This solution is developed up to 400Gbps ethernet core, offering a flexible format agnostic IP infrastructure that supports Ultra HD and 8K video, and the use of virtualized services.

Live Production - DreamCatcher™ consists of instant replay system and live media production suite of tools to create content for multiple platforms with features including content ingest/capture, production playout, slo-motion replay, quick turnaround editing, content management and collaborative production for formats up to Ultra HD and 8K.

Direct-to-Consumer - These solutions enable content owners and rights holders to monetize content by offering Software-as-a-Service solutions to deliver content across new distribution platforms and increase user engagement with gamification.

Professional AV Solutions - These are end-to-end solutions for the professional AV market, including solutions for Networked Based AV distribution and visualization, routing, KVM, video wall technology, and video record, capture and playback. Target markets include education, government, medical and corporate communications.

Recent Merger and Acquisition Activity

Status: terminated **Revised:** Apr. 15, 2023
UPDATE: Haivision rejected the revised offer. PREVIOUS: Evertz Technologies Limited delivered an expression of interest letter to Haivision Systems Inc. outlining a proposal to acquire all of the issued and outstanding common shares of Haivision for $4.50 per share. Any formal, binding offer would be subject to completion of due diligence procedures by Evertz. Apr. 14, 2023 - Evertz submitted a revised offer of $4.75 per share. Mar. 23, 2023 - Haivision rejected the offer.

Predecessor Detail - Name changed from Evertz Microsystems Inc., June 6, 1997.

Directors - Douglas A. (Doug) DeBruin, exec. chr. & exec. v-p, admin., Burlington, Ont.; Romolo Magarelli, pres. & CEO, Kleinburg, Ont.; Rakesh Patel, chief tech. officer, Mississauga, Ont.; Christopher M. Colclough, Mississauga, Ont.; Dr. Ian L. McWalter, Ont.; Brian Piccioni, Ont.; Dr. Thomas V. Pistor, San Francisco, Calif.

Other Exec. Officers - Simon Reed, man. dir., Evertz UK Ltd.; Douglas (Doug) Moore, CFO & corp. sec.; Brian Campbell, exec. v-p, bus. devel.; Jeremy Blythe, v-p, eng., media distrib.; Eric Fankhauser, v-p, advanced eng.; Paulo Francisco, v-p, eng., Evertz AV div.; Marsha Garner, v-p, inside sales & admin.; Orest Holyk, v-p, sales, U.S.A.; Jeff Marks, v-p, mfg.; Robert Peter, v-p, intl. opers.; Vince Silvestri, v-p, software sys.; Daniel (Dan) Turow, v-p, file-based solutions & CIO

Capital Stock

	Authorized (shs.)	Outstanding (shs.)[1]
Preferred	unlimited	nil
Common	unlimited	76,145,758

[1] At Apr. 30, 2023

Options - At Apr. 30, 2023, options were outstanding to purchase 4,788,500 common shares at prices ranging from $12.28 to $17.98 per share with a weighted average remaining contractual life of 2.1 years.

Normal Course Issuer Bid - The company plans to make normal course purchases of up to 3,809,810 common shares representing 5% of the total outstanding. The bid commenced on Nov. 14, 2022, and expires on Nov. 13, 2023.

Major Shareholder - Douglas A. (Doug) DeBruin held 31.7% interest and Romolo Magarelli held 31.7% interest at Aug. 30, 2022.

Price Range - ET/TSX

Year	Volume	High	Low	Close
2022............	3,580,801	$16.54	$10.99	$12.77
2021............	5,525,592	$15.90	$12.35	$13.14
2020............	6,455,544	$18.65	$9.69	$13.22
2019............	4,787,110	$19.27	$15.47	$17.86
2018............	5,486,699	$18.46	$14.68	$16.19

Recent Close: $12.28

Capital Stock Changes - During fiscal 2023, 83,938 common shares were repurchased under a Normal Course Issuer Bid.

During fiscal 2022, 54,670 common shares were repurchased under a Normal Course Issuer Bid.

Dividends

ET com Ra $0.76 pa Q est. Dec. 22, 2022
Prev. Rate: $0.72 est. Dec. 23, 2020

Long-Term Debt - At Apr. 30, 2023, the company had no long-term debt.

Wholly Owned Subsidiaries

Evertz Microsystems Ltd., Ont.
Evertz U.K. Ltd., United Kingdom.
Evertz USA Inc., Manassas, Va.
Holdtech Kft., Hungary.
Quintech Electronics & Communications, Inc., Indiana, Pa.
Tech Digital Manufacturing Limited, Canada.

Subsidiaries

73% int. in **Ease Live AS**, Bergen, Norway.
75% int. in **Truform Metal Fabrication Ltd.**, Canada.

Investments

20% int. in **Ddsports, Inc.**, Overland Park, Kan.

Note: The preceding list includes only the major related companies in which interests are held.

Financial Statistics

Periods ended:	12m Apr. 30/23[A]		12m Apr. 30/22[A]
	$000s	%Chg	$000s
Operating revenue........................	**454,578**	**+3**	**441,016**
Cost of goods sold............................	178,968		178,100
Research & devel. expense.............	98,965		84,684
General & admin expense...............	61,518		60,884
Stock-based compensation............	4,662		5,028
Operating expense........................	**344,113**	**+5**	**328,696**
Operating income........................	**110,465**	**-2**	**112,320**
Deprec., depl. & amort....................	16,803		17,582
Finance income................................	376		309
Finance costs, gross........................	3,718		2,445
Investment income...........................	(5,364)		(1,493)
Pre-tax income.............................	**87,810**	**-10**	**97,912**
Income taxes....................................	23,255		25,235
Net income....................................	**64,555**	**-11**	**72,677**
Net inc. for equity hldrs.................	**64,032**	**-11**	**71,745**
Net inc. for non-cont. int..............	**523**	**-44**	**932**
Cash & equivalent............................	12,468		33,902
Inventories.......................................	202,479		177,268
Accounts receivable........................	106,871		100,020
Current assets..................................	343,169		323,518
Long-term investments....................	8,160		5,474
Fixed assets, net...............................	34,730		37,877
Right-of-use assets..........................	20,396		24,637
Intangibles, net................................	23,458		24,350
Total assets....................................	**436,652**	**+4**	**420,979**
Bank indebtedness...........................	5,928		nil
Accts. pay. & accr. liabs..................	75,521		68,405
Current liabilities.............................	171,741		164,571
Long-term lease liabilities...............	18,827		22,760
Shareholders' equity.........................	243,099		230,938
Non-controlling interest....................	2,985		2,710
Cash from oper. activs..................	**53,814**	**-22**	**68,673**
Cash from fin. activs.........................	(58,023)		(137,516)
Cash from invest. activs....................	(17,119)		(4,963)
Net cash position..........................	**12,468**	**-63**	**33,902**
Capital expenditures.........................	(6,572)		(5,478)
Capital disposals..............................	60		515
	$		$
Earnings per share*..........................	0.84		0.94
Cash flow per share*........................	0.71		0.90
Cash divd. per share*.......................	0.74		0.72
	shs		shs
No. of shs. o/s*................................	76,145,758		76,229,696
Avg. no. of shs. o/s*.........................	76,200,428		76,266,341
	%		%
Net profit margin..............................	14.20		16.48
Return on equity...............................	27.02		27.40
Return on assets..............................	15.69		17.07
Foreign sales percent.......................	93		95
No. of employees (FTEs)..................	1,950		1,767

* Common
[A] Reported in accordance with IFRS

Historical Summary
(as originally stated)

Fiscal Year	Oper. Rev.	Net Inc. Bef. Disc.	EPS*
	$000s	$000s	$
2023[A]....................	454,578	64,555	0.84
2022[A]....................	441,016	72,677	0.94
2021[A]....................	342,888	41,960	0.55
2020[A]....................	436,592	69,172	0.90
2019[A]....................	443,556	78,504	1.02

* Common
[A] Reported in accordance with IFRS

E.74 Everybody Loves Languages Corp.

Symbol - ELL **Exchange** - TSX-VEN **CUSIP** - 30042G
Head Office - 1100-20 Bay St, Toronto, ON, M5J 2N8 **Telephone** - (416) 927-7000 **Toll-free** - (866) 927-7011 **Fax** - (416) 927-1222
Website - www.everybodyloveslanguages.com
Email - kqureshi@lingomedia.com
Investor Relations - Khurram R. Qureshi (866) 927-7011
Auditors - RSM Canada LLP C.A., Toronto, Ont.
Lawyers - WeirFoulds LLP, Toronto, Ont.
Transfer Agents - Computershare Trust Company of Canada Inc., Toronto, Ont.

Profile - (Ont. 1998; orig. Alta., 1996) Provides online and print-based education products and services focused on English language learning worldwide.

Wholly owned **Everybody Loves Languages Inc.** (formerly **ELL Technologies Ltd.**) provides Software-as-a-Service-based eLearning solutions for English language which includes assessments, online and offline content, real-time reports, speech recognition technology and white-label tools. ELL's suite of web-based language learning products and applications include Winnie's World, English Academy, Campus, English for Success, Master and Business, as well as online courses to learn French, Mandarin, Spanish and Portuguese languages. Products are sold and marketed in Latin America, Asia, Europe and the U.S. through a network of distributors. ELL earns revenues from online and offline licensing fees from these products and applications. ELL also owns 51% interest in **Everybody Loves Languages Ltd.**, a joint venture with **Row-9 Digital** which develops and sells language learning programs that teach reading, writing, speaking and listening skills using clips from popular Hollywood films such as Soul, Lightyear, Encanto and West Side Story. The joint venture has ready-to-use movie-based lessons that are aligned with the Common European Framework of Reference for Languages (CEFR) framework and has contents for learning English, Spanish, Portugese, French and Mandarin.

Wholly owned **Lingo Learning Inc.** is a print-based publisher of English language learning textbook programs in the People's Republic of China and has an established market of over 300,000,000 students and co-published more than 831,000,000 units from its library of program titles.Subsidiary Everybody Loves Languages Ltd. (ELLL) develops and sells language learning programs that teach reading, writing, speaking and listening skills using clips from popular Hollywood films such as Soul, Lightyear, Encanto and West Side Story. ELLL has ready-to-use movie-based lessons that are aligned with the Common European Framework of Reference for Languages (CEFR) framework and has contents for learning English, Spanish, Portugese, French and Mandarin.

In September 2022, the company entered into a partnership with **Row-9 Digital** to combine the company's learning management system and content with Row-9 Digital's AcadaMe+ to offer language learning programs that teach reading, writing, speaking and listening skills using clips from popular Hollywood films. The AcadaMe+ platform transforms movies into academic tools and offers features including interactive lessons, smart lesson creator to aid teachers, student performance report and teachers' community zone. This new business unit would operate under **Everybody Loves Languages Ltd.**, which would be 51%-owned by the company and 49%-owned by Row-9 Digital.

Predecessor Detail - Name changed from Lingo Media Corporation, Oct. 17, 2022.

Directors - Gali Bar-Ziv, pres. & CEO, Toronto, Ont.; Khurram R. Qureshi, CFO, Toronto, Ont.; Weibing (Tommy) Gong, Toronto, Ont.; Laurent Mareschal, Toronto, Ont.; Robert Martellacci, Ont.

Capital Stock

	Authorized (shs.)	Outstanding (shs.)[1]
Preferred	unlimited	nil
Common	unlimited	35,609,192

[1] At Aug. 29, 2022

Major Shareholder - Widely held at Sept. 1, 2022.

Price Range - ELL/TSX-VEN

Year	Volume	High	Low	Close
2022............	4,855,526	$0.13	$0.07	$0.08
2021............	6,885,650	$0.13	$0.06	$0.06
2020............	5,357,886	$0.16	$0.01	$0.08
2019............	7,753,387	$0.18	$0.05	$0.10
2018............	5,809,497	$0.19	$0.05	$0.08

Recent Close: $0.04

Wholly Owned Subsidiaries

Everybody Loves Languages Inc., United Kingdom.
Lingo Group Limited, Ont.
Lingo Learning Inc., Toronto, Ont. Formerly Lingo Media Ltd.
Parlo Corporation, Ont.
Speak2Me Inc., People's Republic of China.
Vizualize Technologies Corporation, Ont.

Subsidiaries

51% int. in **Everybody Loves Languages Ltd.**

Financial Statistics

Periods ended:	12m Dec. 31/21[A]		12m Dec. 31/20[A]
	$000s	%Chg	$000s
Operating revenue	**2,640**	**+26**	**2,102**
Cost of sales	318		329
Research & devel. expense	243		266
General & admin expense	1,036		74
Stock-based compensation	56		23
Operating expense	**1,653**	**+139**	**693**
Operating income	**987**	**-30**	**1,409**
Deprec., depl. & amort.	22		31
Finance costs, gross	14		7
Write-downs/write-offs	nil		(32)
Pre-tax income	**968**	**-26**	**1,304**
Income taxes	189		193
Net income	**779**	**-30**	**1,110**
Cash & equivalent	1,881		1,213
Accounts receivable	1,102		974
Current assets	3,079		2,356
Fixed assets, net	17		24
Right-of-use assets	nil		17
Total assets	**3,097**	**+29**	**2,396**
Accts. pay. & accr. liabs	179		221
Current liabilities	367		459
Long-term debt, gross	80		70
Long-term debt, net	80		70
Shareholders' equity	2,650		1,867
Cash from oper. activs	**650**	**-11**	**728**
Cash from fin. activs	20		44
Cash from invest. activs	(2)		(2)
Net cash position	**1,881**	**+55**	**1,213**
Capital expenditures	(2)		(2)
	$		$
Earnings per share*	0.02		0.03
Cash flow per share*	0.02		0.02
	shs		shs
No. of shs. o/s*	35,529,192		35,529,192
Avg. no. of shs. o/s*	35,529,192		35,529,192
	%		%
Net profit margin	29.51		52.81
Return on equity	34.49		84.31
Return on assets	28.77		51.33
Foreign sales percent	100		100

* Common
[A] Reported in accordance with IFRS

Latest Results

Periods ended:	6m June 30/22[A]		6m June 30/21[A]
	$000s	%Chg	$000s
Operating revenue	1,140	-3	1,180
Net income	218	-24	288
	$		$
Earnings per share*	0.01		0.01

* Common
[A] Reported in accordance with IFRS

Historical Summary
(as originally stated)

Fiscal Year	Oper. Rev.	Net Inc. Bef. Disc.	EPS*
	$000s	$000s	$
2021[A]	2,640	779	0.02
2020[A]	2,102	1,110	0.03
2019[A]	1,956	163	0.00
2018[A]	1,940	(104)	(0.00)
2017[A]	2,777	(6,261)	(0.18)

* Common
[A] Reported in accordance with IFRS

E.75 Everyday People Financial Corp.

Symbol - EPF **Exchange** - TSX-VEN **CUSIP** - 30042D
Head Office - 450-11150 Jasper Ave, Edmonton, AB, T5K 0C7
Toll-free - (888) 825-9808
Website - everydaypeoplefinancial.com
Email - letsconnect@epfinancial.ca
Investor Relations - Barret J. Reykdal (888) 825-9808
Auditors - RSM Alberta LLP C.A., Edmonton, Alta.
Transfer Agents - Odyssey Trust Company, Calgary, Alta.

Profile - (Alta. 2022; orig. B.C., 2020) Provides credit collection services to customers in the U.K. and Canada, and offers credit and payment cards, and home ownership facilitation programs Canada.

Operates in three segments: Collection Services, Financial Services and EP Homes.

Collection Services - Operates debt collection agencies specializing in the collection of consumer and commercial debt through wholly owned **BPO Collections Limited** in the U.K. and wholly owned **General Credit Services Inc.** and **Groupe Solution Collect Solu Inc.** in Canada.

Financial Services - Offers secured credit cards and operates business lines that offer distinct credit products branded towards specific credit and payment markets in Canada. The company operates in partnership with **Directcash Bank**, a Schedule 1 Canadian Chartered Bank and credit card issuer with access to Visa®, MasterCard®, Interac® and Swift® networks, to provide credit and payment card programs directly to consumers. Currently offered is the EP Secured Credit Card, which is designed to assist clients in the process of rebuilding or establishing their credit.

EP Homes - Wholly owned **Everyday People Homes Inc.** is a home ownership facilitator that acquires new homes directly from homebuilders and offers eligible clients in Canada the ability to acquire a new home through a structured lease and dedicated down payment accumulation program. EP Homes offers the Bridge to Homeownership™ program which targets affordable homes for consumers with household income of $110,000 or more and average to excellent credit scores.

In November 2022, the company changed its fiscal year end to December 31 from September 30, effective Oct. 1, 2022.

Recent Merger and Acquisition Activity

Status: completed **Announced:** Mar. 31, 2023
Everyday People Financial Corp., through wholly owned General Credit Services Inc., acquired Montreal, Que.-based Groupe Solution Collect Solu Inc., which provides accounts receivable management solutions and debt collection services to enterprise clients in Quebec. Consideration was $3,400,000 cash and a $759,900 promissory note; contingent consideration of $1,400,000 in cash or shares is payable upon attainment of certain performance milestones.

Status: completed **Revised:** Dec. 30, 2022
UPDATE: The transaction was completed. PREVIOUS: Everyday People Financial Corp. entered into a letter of intent to acquire private Vancouver, B.C.-based General Credit Services Inc., a Canadian account receivable management company, for issuance of up to 8,900,000 common shares at a deemed price of $1.00 per share. Dec. 9, 2022 - A definitive agreement was entered into. Total consideration would be $6,583,998, consisting of $5,344,455 cash, issuance of 1,781,485 common shares valued at $703,687 and contingent consideration of $535,856 (representing an additional 1,781,485 common shares to be issued if General Credit's EBITDA was equal to or greater than $1,781,485 in any one year before Dec. 31, 2025).

Status: completed **Revised:** Aug. 31, 2022
UPDATE: The transaction was completed. Justify issued a total of 108,415,054 common shares at a deemed price of $1.00 per share. PREVIOUS: Justify Capital Corp. entered into a letter of intent for the Qualifying Transaction reverse takeover acquisition of private Edmonton, Alta.-based Everyday People Financial Inc., which specializes in credit cards, lending, payment processing, home ownership facilitation and a collections agency, on a share-for-share basis, which would result in the issuance of 85,688,456 Justify common shares. Dec. 6, 2021 - A definitive agreement was entered into. Upon completion, Everyday would amalgamate with a wholly owned subsidiary of Justify, and Justify would change its name to Everyday People Financial Corp. and continue its incorporation into Alberta from British Columbia. The Justify common shares issued would have a deemed price of $1.00 per share.

Predecessor Detail - Name changed from Justify Capital Corp., Aug. 31, 2022, pursuant to the Qualifying Transaction reverse takeover acquisition of Everyday People Financial Inc.

Directors - Gordon J. Reykdal, exec. chr., Edmonton, Alta.; Graham Rankin, co-CEO, Ayr., United Kingdom; Barret J. Reykdal, co-CEO, Alta.; Nitin Kaushal, Richmond Hill, Ont.; Robert S. (Rob) Pollock, Toronto, Ont.; Scott Sinclair, Vancouver, B.C.; Amy ter Haar, Ont.

Other Exec. Officers - Mayank Mahajan, CFO; Renata Berlingo, sr. v-p, opers. & corp. sec.; Adelhardt Glombick, v-p, fin.; Peter Sorrentino, pres., General Credit Services Inc.

Capital Stock

	Authorized (shs.)	Outstanding (shs.)[1]
Preferred	unlimited	nil
Common	unlimited	113,976,539

[1] At June 20, 2023

Major Shareholder - Carrie Reykdal held 20.2% interest at June 20, 2023.

Price Range - EPF/TSX-VEN

Year	Volume	High	Low	Close
2022	10,178,124	$0.80	$0.20	$0.40
2021	137,150	$0.50	$0.38	$0.45
2020	225,200	$0.46	$0.22	$0.41

Recent Close: $0.32

Capital Stock Changes - On Aug. 31, 2022, 108,415,054 common shares were issued pursuant to the Qualifying Transaction reverse takeover acquisition of Everyday People Financial Inc. On Dec. 30, 2022, 1,781,485 common shares were issued pursuant to the acquisition of General Credit Services Inc. Also during the 15 months ended Dec. 31, 2022, 320,000 common shares were issued on exercise of options and 100,000 common shares were issued on exercise of warrants.

Wholly Owned Subsidiaries

BPO Collections Limited, Ayr., United Kingdom.
Climb Credit Inc., Mississauga, Ont.
EP Security Capital Inc., Canada.
EP Travel Card Inc., Canada.
Everyday People Care Inc., Canada.
- 50% int. in **Smart Everyday People Inc.**, Canada.

Everyday People Financial Ltd., United Kingdom.
Everyday People Homes Inc., Alta.
- 100% int. in **EP Homes I Inc.**, Alta.
- 100% int. in **EP Homes II Inc.**, Alta.
- 100% int. in **EP Homes III Inc.**, Alta.
- 100% int. in **EP Homes IV Inc.**, Alta.

Everyday People Prepaid Card Inc., Alta.
General Credit Services Inc., Vancouver, B.C.
- 100% int. in **Groupe Solution Collect Solu Inc.**, Montréal, Qué.

Subsidiaries

71% int. in **EP Card ehf.**, Iceland.
51% int. in **iKort ehf.**, Iceland.

Financial Statistics

Periods ended:	15m Dec. 31/22[A1]		12m Sept. 30/21[□A2]
	$000s	%Chg	$000s
Operating revenue	**22,474**	**n.a.**	**13,646**
Cost of sales	9,568		6,118
Salaries & benefits	8,939		5,543
General & admin expense	8,060		3,774
Stock-based compensation	931		737
Other operating expense	1,518		505
Operating expense	**29,016**	**n.a.**	**16,677**
Operating income	**(6,542)**	**n.a.**	**(3,031)**
Deprec., depl. & amort.	2,251		1,538
Finance costs, gross	1,945		876
Write-downs/write-offs	(29,365)		(12)
Pre-tax income	**(44,962)**	**n.a.**	**(4,757)**
Income taxes	725		178
Net income	**(45,687)**	**n.a.**	**(4,934)**
Cash & equivalent	1,187		2,313
Accounts receivable	2,343		1,304
Current assets	16,961		15,464
Long-term investments	387		1,525
Fixed assets, net	574		483
Right-of-use assets	1,412		1,612
Intangibles, net	20,145		42,059
Total assets	**46,246**	**n.a.**	**63,625**
Bank indebtedness	nil		1,344
Accts. pay. & accr. liabs	5,363		3,281
Current liabilities	18,425		15,203
Long-term debt, gross	8,684		6,155
Long-term debt, net	5,031		1,510
Long-term lease liabilities	1,500		1,463
Shareholders' equity	11,006		43,608
Cash from oper. activs	**(8,877)**	**n.a.**	**(365)**
Cash from fin. activs	14,608		2,947
Cash from invest. activs	(6,114)		(1,516)
Net cash position	**1,187**	**n.a.**	**2,313**
Capital expenditures	(226)		(106)
	$		$
Earnings per share*	(0.44)		(0.06)
Cash flow per share*	(0.08)		(0.00)
	shs		shs
No. of shs. o/s*	113,976,539		n.a.
Avg. no. of shs. o/s*	105,307,937		86,401,756
	%		%
Net profit margin	...		(36.16)
Return on equity	...		(13.00)
Return on assets	...		(6.72)
Foreign sales percent	78		75
No. of employees (FTEs)	...		139

* Common
□ Restated
[A] Reported in accordance with IFRS
[1] Results reflect the Aug. 31, 2022, reverse takeover acquisiion of Everyday People Financial Inc.
[2] Results pertain to Everyday People Financial Inc.

Latest Results

Periods ended:	3m Mar. 31/23[A]		3m Mar. 31/22[□A]
	$000s	%Chg	$000s
Operating revenue	8,000	+76	4,534
Net income	(1,114)	n.a.	(1,088)
	$		$
Earnings per share*	(0.01)		(0.02)

* Common
□ Restated
[A] Reported in accordance with IFRS

Historical Summary
(as originally stated)

Fiscal Year	Oper. Rev.	Net Inc. Bef. Disc.	EPS*
	$000s	$000s	$
2022[A1,2]	22,474	(45,687)	(0.44)
2021[A3]	13,646	(4,934)	(0.06)
2020[A3]	18,941	(4,572)	(0.05)

* Common
[A] Reported in accordance with IFRS
[1] 15 months ended Dec. 31, 2022.
[2] Results reflect the Aug. 31, 2022, reverse takeover acquisiion of Everyday People Financial Inc.
[3] Results pertain to Everyday People Financial Inc.

E.76 EvokAI Creative Labs Inc.

Symbol - OKAI **Exchange** - TSX-VEN **CUSIP** - 30053J
Head Office - 1600-609 Granville St, PO Box 10068, Pacific Centre, Vancouver, BC, V7Y 1C3 **Telephone** - (778) 331-8505 **Fax** - (866) 824-8938
Website - www.evokailabs.com
Email - sackerman@emprisecapital.com
Investor Relations - Scott Ackerman (778) 331-8505
Auditors - Dale Matheson Carr-Hilton LaBonte LLP C.A., Vancouver, B.C.
Transfer Agents - Endeavor Trust Corporation, Vancouver, B.C.
Profile - (B.C. 2017; orig. Ont., 2011) Develops and deploys machine learning models to search medical data and uncover insights to help improve health outcomes, patient experiences, drug development, preclinical and clinical decisions, and provide more accurate diagnoses.
Customers are those in the medical sector, consisting of neuroscience partners in fields such as pharma, neurology, psychology, neuropsychiatry and rehabilitation.
In April 2023, the company agreed to acquire Finland-based **Head Instruments Oy**, which creates smart medical devices and solutions to improve patients' quality of life and provide support to medical professionals, for issuance of €3,157,565 (Cdn$4,643,000) of common shares.

Recent Merger and Acquisition Activity

Status: completed **Revised:** Apr. 11, 2023
UPDATE: The transaction was completed. Sebastiani issued a total of 58,166,667 post-consolidated common shares at a deemed price of Cdn$0.75 per share. (New) EvokAI's common shares commenced trading on the TSX Venture Exchange effective Apr. 14, 2023. PREVIOUS: Sebastiani Ventures Corp. entered into a letter of intent for the reverse takeover acquisition of Switzerland-based EvokAI Creative Labs Inc., which develops and deploys machine learning models to search medical data and uncover insights to help improve health outcomes, patient experiences, drug development, preclinical and clinical decisions, and provide more accurate diagnoses, on the basis of 4.752230256 Sebastiani post-consolidated common shares for each EvokAI share held (following a 1-for-2.6628503 share consolidation), which would result in the issuance of 70,000,000 Sebastiani post-consolidated common shares. Upon completion, EvokAI would amalgamate with Sebastiani's wholly owned Sebastiani Mergerco Inc. to form EvokAI Innovation Corp., and Sebastiani would change its name to (new) EvokAI Creative Labs Inc. A condition to completing the acquisition was (old) EvokAI completing a private placement of a minimum of 5,000,000 subscription receipts at Cdn$1.00 per receipt. Sept. 22, 2022 - A definitive agreement was entered into. Dec. 22, 2022 - (Old) EvokAI completed a private placement of 6,666,667 subscription receipts at Cdn$0.75 per receipt. Each subscription receipt would automatically convert into 1 (new) EvokAI post-consolidated common share upon completion of the transaction.
Predecessor Detail - Name changed from Sebastiani Ventures Corp., Apr. 11, 2023, pursuant to the reverse takeover acquisition of Switzerland-based (old) EvokAI Creative Labs Inc. and concurrent amalgamation of (old) EvokAI with wholly owned Sebastiani Mergerco Inc. (and continued as EvokAI Innovation Corp.); basis 1 new for 2.66285 old shs.
Directors - Alejandro Antalich, CEO, Montevideo, Uruguay; Scott Ackerman, CFO & corp. sec., Surrey, B.C.; Rick Cox, B.C.; Peter Dickie, West Vancouver, B.C.

Capital Stock

	Authorized (shs.)	Outstanding (shs.)[1]
Preferred	unlimited	nil
Common	unlimited	66,580,953

[1] At Apr. 27, 2023

Major Shareholder - Juan Sartori held 60.88% interest at Apr. 14, 2023.

Price Range - OKAI/TSX-VEN

Year	Volume	High	Low	Close
2022	68,983	$0.48	$0.24	$0.43
2021	44,261	$0.31	$0.23	$0.27
2020	22,108	$0.51	$0.31	$0.31
2019	24,539	$0.52	$0.37	$0.52
2018	52,600	$0.53	$0.36	$0.37

Consolidation: 1-for-2.66285 cons. in Apr. 2023
Recent Close: $1.77
Capital Stock Changes - On Apr. 11, 2023, common shares were consolidated on a 1-for-2.6628503 basis (effective on the TSX Venture Exchange on Apr. 14, 2023) and 58,166,667 post-consolidated common shares were issued pursuant to the reverse takeover acquisition of (old) EvokAI Creative Labs Inc.
In June 2022, Sebastiani Ventures Corp. completed a private placement of 3,333,333 units (1 common share & 1 warrant) at $0.075 per unit.

Wholly Owned Subsidiaries

EvokAI Innovation Corp., Switzerland.
- 96% int. in **Advancience AG**, Switzerland.

Financial Statistics

Periods ended:	12m Dec. 31/22[A1]		12m Dec. 31/21[A]
	$000s	%Chg	$000s
General & admin expense	473		86
Operating expense	**473**	**+450**	**86**
Operating income	**(473)**	**n.a.**	**(86)**
Pre-tax income	**(472)**	**n.a.**	**(86)**
Net income	**(472)**	**n.a.**	**(86)**
Cash & equivalent	4		42
Accounts receivable	8		2
Current assets	15		45
Total assets	**15**	**-67**	**45**
Bank indebtedness	46		nil
Accts. pay. & accr. liabs	170		18
Current liabilities	215		18
Shareholders' equity	(200)		27
Cash from oper. activs	**(328)**	**n.a.**	**(90)**
Cash from fin. activs	290		nil
Net cash position	**4**	**-90**	**42**
	$		$
Earnings per share*	(0.06)		(0.01)
Cash flow per share*	(0.04)		(0.01)
	shs		shs
No. of shs. o/s*	8,414,286		7,162,495
Avg. no. of shs. o/s*	7,899,851		7,162,495
	%		%
Net profit margin	n.a.		n.a.
Return on equity	n.m.		(122.86)
Return on assets	n.m.		(96.63)

* Common
[A] Reported in accordance with IFRS
[1] Results for 2022 and prior years pertain to Sebastiana Ventures Corp.

Historical Summary
(as originally stated)

Fiscal Year	Oper. Rev.	Net Inc. Bef. Disc.	EPS*
	$000s	$000s	$
2022[A]	nil	(472)	(0.06)
2021[A]	nil	(86)	(0.01)
2020[A]	nil	(89)	(0.01)
2019[A]	nil	(81)	(0.01)
2018[A]	nil	(96)	(0.01)

* Common
[A] Reported in accordance with IFRS
Note: Adjusted throughout for 1-for-2.6628503 cons. in Apr. 2023

E.77 Exchange Income Corporation*

Symbol - EIF **Exchange** - TSX **CUSIP** - 301283
Head Office - 101-990 Lorimer Blvd, Winnipeg, MB, R3P 0Z9 **Telephone** - (204) 982-1857 **Fax** - (204) 982-1855
Website - exchangeincomecorp.ca
Email - mpyle@eig.ca
Investor Relations - Michael C. Pyle (204) 982-1850
Auditors - PricewaterhouseCoopers LLP C.A., Winnipeg, Man.
Bankers - Bank of America Canada; Raymond James Finance Company of Canada Ltd.; Wells Fargo Bank, N.A.; Royal Bank of Canada; HSBC Bank Canada; Laurentian Bank of Canada; ATB Financial; Bank of Montreal; The Bank of Nova Scotia; The Toronto-Dominion Bank; Canadian Imperial Bank of Commerce; National Bank of Canada
Lawyers - MLT Aikins LLP, Winnipeg, Man.
Transfer Agents - TSX Trust Company, Calgary, Alta.
FP500 Revenue Ranking - 216
Employees - 5,775 at Dec. 31, 2022
Profile - (Can. 2009; orig. Can., 2002) Provides aerospace and aviation services including scheduled passenger, charter and freight services, emergency medical services, sales of aircraft, engines and aftermarket parts, aerospace special mission operations and pilot training services; and manufactures niche specialty products including unitized window wall systems and temporary access solutions.

Aerospace & Aviation

Wholly owned **Provincial Aerospace Ltd.** operates an aerospace division through wholly owned **PAL Aerospace Ltd.**, a scheduled airline with fixed base operations through wholly owned **PAL Airlines Ltd.**, and a flight training business through wholly owned **CANLink Aviation Inc.** PAL Aerospace provides customized and integrated special mission aircraft solutions to governments/militaries and industry customers primarily in Canada, the Caribbean, the Netherlands and the Middle East, which are provided via mission systems design and integration, aircraft modifications, intelligence, surveillance and reconnaissance operations, software development, logistics and in-service support. PAL Aerospace also performs fixed-wing medevac services for the government in Newfoundland and Labrador and Nova Scotia. PAL Airlines provides passenger, charter and freight services to communities throughout Newfoundland and Labrador, New Brunswick, Nova Scotia and Quebec. CANLink Aviation operates Moncton Flight College, which provides a full range of domestic and international flight training services to over 350 students at its two bases in Moncton and Fredericton, N.B.
Wholly owned **Regional One, Inc.** purchases, leases and sells aircraft, aircraft parts, engines and engine parts, and other related support items applicable to regional and commuter aircraft for customers worldwide. Has a portfolio of aircraft, engines and spares parts including avionics, hydraulic and fuel system rotables, maintenance line-replacement-units, landing gears, propellers and insurance spares such as flight controls.
Wholly owned **Calm Air International LP** provides scheduled passenger and freight services to isolated communities throughout northern Manitoba and Nunavut, and on-demand charter services to third parties with destinations throughout Canada and the U.S. from its main bases at Winnipeg, Thompson and Churchill, Man., and Rankin Inlet, Nunavut.
Wholly owned **Perimeter Aviation LP** provides regular scheduled passenger airline service under the Perimeter Airlines and Bearskin Airlines brands, medevac operations and freight services to locations in Manitoba and northern Ontario, and on-demand charter services to third parties with destinations throughout Canada and the U.S. Owns and operates a terminal at the Winnipeg James Armstrong Richardson International Airport; and maintains a hangar and cargo facility in Thunder Bay, Ont., and northern service bases in Thompson, Man., and Sioux Lookout, Ont.
Wholly owned **Keewatin Air LP** provides aeromedical transport, secure governmental and general charter services to locations in Nunavut, the Northwest Territories and northern Manitoba. Operates facilities at Rankin Inlet, Iqaluit, Cambridge Bay and Igloolik, Nunavut; Yellowknife, N.W.T.; and Winnipeg and Churchill, Man. Keewatin Air operations include **Advanced Paramedic Ltd.**, which provides air and ground ambulance services throughout Alberta for primary care, community care, provincial and federal governments, First Nations and industrial customers.
Wholly owned **Custom Helicopters Ltd.** provides rotary wing-related services from several bases in Manitoba, Nunavut, British Columbia, Ontario, and Newfoundland and Labrador. Also performs seasonal field operations throughout Canada. Services include mineral exploration, wildlife surveys, aerial inspection and emergency related services.
Wholly owned **Carson Air Ltd.** provides fixed wing air ambulance services in British Columbia and air cargo services in British Columbia and Alberta as well as operates a flight school, Southern Interior Flight Centre. Services are provided from three bases in Kelowna and Vancouver, B.C., and Calgary, Alta.
Wholly owned **Crew Training International, Inc.** delivers training solutions for its customers across an array of aviation platforms and has in-depth experience in training pilots and sensor operators on both manned and unmanned aircraft for the U.S. Government and commercial applications. Customers include the U.S. Air Force, U.S. Navy, and U.S. Marine Corps. Training solutions are being delivered for these customers by 525 employees on military bases throughout the U.S.

Manufacturing

Wholly owned **Quest Window Systems Inc.** designs, manufactures and installs the ECOWALL advanced unitized window wall system used primarily in high-rise multi-residential developments in Canada and the U.S. Operates two adjacent manufacturing facilities in Mississauga, Ont., totaling 180,000 sq. ft., and a 329,000-sq.-ft. manufacturing facility in Dallas/Fort Worth, Tex. Quest operations include **Window Installation Specialists, Inc.** and **Advanced Window, Inc.**
Wholly owned **BVGlazing Systems Ltd.**, designs, engineers, manufactures and supplies window, door and railing systems for mid-rise and high-rise building projects in Canada and the U.S. Manufactures unitized and stick curtain wall systems and rail systems in addition to window wall glazing systems. Has manufacturing facilities in Niagara Falls and Concord, Ont.
Wholly owned **WesTower Communications Ltd.** engineers, designs, fabricates, constructs, maintains and services wireless and wireline infrastructure for telecommunications carriers and independent tower operators throughout Canada. WesTower operations include **Telcon Datvox Inc.** and **Ryko Telecommunications Inc.**
Wholly owned **Stainless Fabrication, Inc.** designs and manufactures specialized stainless steel tanks, vessels, and processing equipment for the pharmaceutical, ethanol, chemical, food, dairy, beverage, health and cosmetics industries. Operates two manufacturing facilities, with 85,000 sq. ft. of production space and 7,000 sq. ft. of warehouse space, in Springfield, Mo.
Wholly owned **Ben Machine Products Company Incorporated** manufactures complex, precision-machined components and assemblies primarily for the aerospace and defence industry in Canada and the U.S. Services offered include computer numerically controlled milling and turning, sheet metal fabrication, welding, complex assembly and various finishing services. Operates manufacturing facilities totaling 100,000 sq. ft. located in Vaughan and Mississauga, Ont. Ben Machine operations include **Macfab Manufacturing Inc.**
Wholly owned **L.V. Control Mfg. Ltd.** designs and manufactures electrical distribution equipment and automation systems for the agricultural industry in Canada, with a focus on grain handling, crop input, feed processing and seed cleaning and processing. Products are manufactured at a 15,000-sq.-ft. facility in Winnipeg, Man.
Wholly owned **Water Blast Manufacturing LP** is the exclusive dealer for Hotsy hot and cold water pressure washers, parts washers, replacement parts, cleaning compounds and accessories in Alberta, British Columbia, the Northwest Territories, Saskatchewan and North Dakota. Also manufactures and sells specialized heavy-duty pressure washer, steam systems, automatic parts washers, caustic dip tanks, wash water recycle systems, and customized tanks and trailers.
Wholly owned **Overlanders Manufacturing LP** provides fabrication and manufacturing of precision sheet metal and tubular products for companies in British Columbia, Alberta and the Pacific Northwest region of the U.S. The fabrication of metal includes processes such as punching, cutting, bending, welding, laser cutting and stamping. Also provides value added services such as sub-assembly, prototyping, powder coating, manufacturing and design for diverse products.
Wholly owned **Northern Mat & Bridge Limited Partnership** manufactures, sells and offers rentals and lease to own options on

construction mats including access mats, rig mats and crane mats, as well as temporary bridges including standard portable bridges with and without modular decks and all steel low profile bridges. Also offers planning and consultation, delivery, installation, maintenance, relocation, removal, reclamation, cleaning and disposal of their products.

Wholly owned **Hansen Industries Ltd.** provides custom fabrication of precision metal components and assemblies using automated equipment from its facilities in Richmond, B.C., with more than 30 CNC (computer numerical control) equipped machines used to produce components within its two key divisions, metal and machining. Also has a high-volume metal stamping shop. Services are provided to customers primarily located in western Canada, supporting such customers through the product conceptualization, prototyping, production and service phases of their product life cycle.

On May 30, 2023, wholly owned **PAL Airlines Ltd.** signed a letter of intent with **Air Canada** to acquire up to six additional Dash 8-400 aircraft which would be operated of Air Canada under its Express brand. The aircraft would be operated on routes in eastern Canada for a term of up to five years. PAL would operate these routes on top of its existing network in eastern Canada.

Recent Merger and Acquisition Activity

Status: completed **Revised:** May 1, 2023
UPDATE: The transaction was completed. PREVIOUS: Exchange Income Corporation agreed to acquire to BVGlazing Systems Ltd., for a purchase price of $95,000,000 payable by $72,000,000 in cash and the issuance of $23,000,000 of common shares. BVGlazing designs, engineers, manufactures and supplies window, door and railing systems for mid-rise and high-rise building projects in Canada and the U.S. Has manufacturing facility in Niagara Falls and Concord, Ont. The transaction was expected to close in the second quarter of 2023.

Status: completed **Announced:** Apr. 3, 2023
Exchange Income Corporation (EIC) acquired private Richmond, B.C.-based Hansen Industries Ltd., which provides custom fabrication of precision metal components and assemblies using automated equipment, for $42,500,000, consisting of $38,000,000 cash and issuance of $4,500,000 of common shares. The cash component was funded from EIC's credit facility. Hansen had more than 30 CNC (computer numerical control) equipped machines used to produce components within its two key divisions, metal and machining, as well as a high-volume metal stamping shop.

Status: completed **Announced:** May 10, 2022
Exchange Income Corporation (EIC) acquired private Calgary, Alta.-based Northern Mat & Bridge Limited Partnership from TriWest Capital Partners Inc. for $325,000,000, including issuance of $35,000,000 of common shares. Northern Mat & Bridge offers wooden construction mats including access mats, rig mats and crane mats, as well as temporary bridges including standard portable bridges with and without modular decks and all steel low profile bridges. Northern Mat would be reported within EIC's manufacturing segment.

Status: completed **Announced:** May 10, 2022
Exchange Income Corporation (EIC) acquired private Peace River, Alta.-based Advanced Paramedics Ltd. (APL), a provider of air and ground ambulance services throughout Alberta, for $15,000,000, including issuance of $2,000,000 of common shares. APL would be reported within EIC's aerospace & aviation segment.

Directors - Donald W. (Don) Streuber, chr., Winnipeg, Man.; Duncan D. Jessiman Jr., exec. v-chr., Winnipeg, Man.; Michael C. (Mike) Pyle, CEO, Winnipeg, Man.; W. J. Brad Bennett, Kelowna, B.C.; Gary J. Buckley, Winnipeg, Man.; Polly Craik, Winnipeg, Man.; Barb Gamey, Winnipeg, Man.; Bruce W. J. Jack, Winnipeg, Man.; Melissa Sonberg, Montréal, Qué.; Edward L. Warkentin, Winnipeg, Man.

Other Exec. Officers - Carmele N. Peter, pres.; Darwin R. Sparrow, COO; Richard Wowryk, CFO; Curtis Anderson, chief tech. officer; Travis Muhr, CAO; Steven Stennett, chief legal officer; Adam S. Terwin, chief corp. devel. officer; David White, exec. v-p, aviation; Dianne Spencer, mgr., compliance & corp. sec.; Doron Marom, CEO, Regional One, Inc.

Capital Stock

	Authorized (shs.)	Outstanding (shs.)[1]
Common	unlimited	46,444,727

[1] At June 14, 2023.

Normal Course Issuer Bid - The company plans to make normal course purchases of up to 3,958,307 common shares representing 10% of the public float. The bid commenced on Mar. 15, 2023, and expires on Mar. 14, 2024.

Major Shareholder - Widely held at Apr. 6, 2023.

Price Range - EIF/TSX

Year	Volume	High	Low	Close
2022	23,272,226	$53.46	$37.79	$52.63
2021	23,856,246	$47.77	$35.12	$42.14
2020	46,483,101	$45.86	$12.57	$36.64
2019	22,967,969	$46.10	$27.60	$44.69
2018	21,015,121	$35.74	$25.58	$28.26

Recent Close: $47.50

Capital Stock Changes - In June 2023, bought deal public offering of 3,306,250 common shares was completed at $52.25 per share, including 431,250 common shares on exercise of over-allotment option. Net proceeds would be used to fund growth initiatives, including partially funding the investments associated with the recent announcements at Carson Air Ltd. and PAL Airlines Ltd., and for general corporate purposes.

In September 2022, bought deal public offering of 2,362,100 common shares was completed at $48.70 per share, including 308,100 common shares on exercise of over-allotment option. Also during 2022, common shares were issued as follows: 863,256 pursuant to the acquisition of Northern Mat & Bridge Limited Partnership, 350,172 under dividend reinvestment plan, 56,505 under employee share purchase plan, 55,121 under deferred share plan, 49,326 pursuant to the acquisition of Advanced Paramedics Ltd., 2,039 under First Nations community partnership agreements and 155 on conversion of debentures.

Dividends

EIF com Ra $2.52 pa M est. Sept. 15, 2022**
Prev. Rate: $2.40 est. June 15, 2022
Prev. Rate: $2.28 est. Sept. 13, 2019
** Reinvestment Option

Long-Term Debt - Outstanding at Dec. 31, 2022:

Revolv. credit facility due May 2026	$1,218,326,000
Conv. debs.:	
5.35% due June 2025[1]	78,215,000
5.75% due Mar. 2026[2]	84,384,000
5.25% due July 2028[3]	138,699,000
5.25% due January 2029[4]	110,683,000
Less: Unamort. trans. costs & disc.	16,100,000
	1,614,207,000
Less: Current portion	nil
	1,614,207,000

[1] Convertible into common shares at $49 per share. An equity component of $3,866,000 was classified as part of shareholders' equity.
[2] Convertible into common shares at $49 per share. An equity component of $2,497,000 was classified as part of shareholders' equity.
[3] Convertible into common shares at $52.70 per share. An equity component of $4,241,000 was classified as part of shareholders' equity.
[4] Convertible into common shares at $60 per share. An equity component of $3,413,000 was classified as part of shareholders' equity.

Normal Course Issuer Bid - The company plans to make normal course purchases of up to $8,038,000 principal amount of its 5.35% convertible debentures due June 2025, up to $8,625,000 principal amount of its 5.75% convertible debentures due March 2026, up to $14,375,000 principal amount of its 5.25% convertible debentures due July 2028 and up to $11,500,000 principal amount of its 5.25% convertible debentures due January 2029, all representing 10% of the public float. The bid commenced on Mar. 15, 2023, and expires no later than Mar. 14, 2024.

Note - In May 2023, the credit facility was amended whereby the maximum amount was increased to $2 billion and the maturity was extended to May 2027.

Wholly Owned Subsidiaries

Advanced Paramedics Ltd., Peace River, Alta.
BVGlazing Systems Ltd., Concord, Ont.
Ben Machine Products Company Incorporated, Vaughan, Ont.
- 100% int. in **Alliance Maintenance L.P.**, Man.
- 100% int. in **Central Point Procurement Inc.**, Canada.
- 100% int. in **8900973 Canada Ltd.**, Canada.
  - 100% int. in **EIC Aircraft Leasing Limited**, Dublin, Ireland.
    - 100% int. in **R1 Lease Services Limited**, Ireland.
  - 100% int. in **EIC Luxembourg S.A.R.L.**, Luxembourg.

Calm Air International LP, Thompson, Man.
Carson Air Ltd., Kelowna, B.C.
- 100% int. in **Southern Interior Flight Centre (1993) Ltd.**, B.C.

Custom Helicopters Ltd., Man.
EIC Holdings Corporation, Canada.
EIIF Management USA, Inc., Del.
- 100% int. in **Advanced Window, Inc.**, Frederick, Md.
- 100% int. in **Crew Training International, Inc.**, Memphis, Tenn.
- 100% int. in **Dallas Sailer Enterprises, Inc.**, N.D.
- 100% int. in **EIC Communications USA Inc.**, Del.
- 100% int. in **EIC US Aerospace and Defence Holdings Inc.**, Del.
- 60% int. in **EIIF CRJ Aero Investment, LLC**
- 100% int. in **Exchange Technology Services USA Inc.**, Del.
- 100% int. in **Quest USA, Inc.**, Del.
- 100% int. in **Regional One, Inc.**, Miami, Fla.
  - 100% int. in **R1 GP Inc.**, Man.
- 100% int. in **Stainless Fabrication, Inc.**, Springfield, Mo.
- 100% int. in **Team J.A.S., Inc.**, Jacksonville, Fla.
- 100% int. in **Window Installation Specialists, Inc.**, Seattle, Wash.

Hansen Industries Ltd., Richmond, B.C.
Keewatin Air LP, Winnipeg, Man.
L.V. Control Mfg. Ltd., Winnipeg, Man.
Macfab Manufacturing Inc., Mississauga, Ont.
Northern Mat Holdings Corporation, Canada.
- 99.99% int. in **NMB Holdings Limited Partnership**, Alta.
  - 100% int. in **Northern Mat & Bridge Limited Partnership**, Calgary, Alta.
    - 100% int. in **NMB Access Services Ltd.**, Alta.
    - 100% int. in **Northern Mat & Bridge (East) Limited Partnership**, Ont.
      - 100% int. in **2415794 Ontario Ltd.**, Ont.

Overlanders Manufacturing LP, B.C.
Perimeter Aviation LP, Winnipeg, Man.
- 51% int. in **7078650 Canada Ltd.**, Winnipeg, Man.

Provincial Aerospace Ltd., St. John's, N.L.
- 100% int. in **CANLink Aviation Inc.**, Canada.
- 100% int. in **PAL Aero Services Ltd.**, N.L.
- 100% int. in **PAL Aerospace Ltd.**, N.L.
  - 49% int. in **Airpro Sar Services Incorporated**, Canada.
  - 100% int. in **Atlantic Avionics Inc.**, Canada.
  - 100% int. in **CarteNav Solutions Inc.**, Halifax, N.S.
  - 100% int. in **DECA Aviation Engineering Ltd.**, Ont.
  - 100% int. in **ISR Support Europe B.V.**, Netherlands.
  - 49% int. in **PAL Aerospace Services Aircraft Maintenance LLC**, United Arab Emirates.
  - 100% int. in **PAL Middle East FZ-LLC**, United Arab Emirates.
  - 100% int. in **Provincial Aerospace Netherlands B.V.**, Netherlands.
  - 100% int. in **Provincial Airlines (Curacao) Limited B.V.**, Curacao.
- 100% int. in **PAL Airlines Ltd.**, N.L.
  - 33.33% int. in **Air Borealis Inc.**, N.L.
  - 33.33% int. in **Air Borealis Limited Partnership**, N.L.

Quest Window Systems Inc., Mississauga, Ont.
Ryko Telecommunications Inc., Regina, Sask.
7328010 Canada Ltd., Churchill, Man.
Telcon Datvox Inc., St. Catharines, Ont.
Water Blast Manufacturing LP, Edmonton, Alta.
WesTower Communications Ltd., Canada.

Financial Statistics

Periods ended:	12m Dec. 31/22[A]		12m Dec. 31/21[A]
	$000s	%Chg	$000s
Operating revenue	**2,059,373**	**+46**	**1,413,146**
General & admin expense	254,611		190,960
Other operating expense	1,348,320		892,306
Operating expense	**1,602,931**	**+48**	**1,083,266**
Operating income	**456,442**	**+38**	**329,880**
Deprec., depl. & amort.	219,708		186,385
Finance costs, gross	78,418		52,198
Pre-tax income	**151,469**	**+61**	**94,263**
Income taxes	41,800		25,675
Net income	**109,669**	**+60**	**68,588**
Cash & equivalent	139,896		75,408
Inventories	335,060		255,451
Accounts receivable	434,956		301,767
Current assets	1,045,932		700,458
Long-term investments	109,080		58,827
Fixed assets, net	1,284,409		1,070,573
Right-of-use assets	157,319		83,439
Intangibles, net	926,715		667,539
Total assets	**3,548,836**	**+37**	**2,588,667**
Accts. pay. & accr. liabs.	451,906		267,635
Current liabilities	580,451		475,350
Long-term debt, gross	1,614,207		1,199,827
Long-term debt, net	1,614,207		1,101,019
Long-term lease liabilities	133,181		69,397
Equity portion of conv. debs.	14,017		17,607
Shareholders' equity	1,019,054		800,275
Cash from oper. activs.	**335,119**	**+18**	**285,047**
Cash from fin. activs.	380,968		79,421
Cash from invest. activs.	(655,451)		(357,942)
Net cash position	**139,896**	**+86**	**75,408**
Capital expenditures	(359,634)		(274,421)
Capital disposals	85,010		52,293
	$		$
Earnings per share*	2.72		1.84
Cash flow per share*	8.31		7.65
Cash divd. per share*	2.41		2.28
	shs		shs
No. of shs. o/s*	42,479,063		38,740,389
Avg. no. of shs. o/s*	40,348,003		37,265,034
	%		%
Net profit margin	5.33		4.85
Return on equity	12.06		9.23
Return on assets	5.42		4.37
Foreign sales percent	39		40
No. of employees (FTEs)	5,775		5,400

* Common
[A] Reported in accordance with IFRS

Latest Results

Periods ended:	3m Mar. 31/23[A]		3m Mar. 31/22[A]
	$000s	%Chg	$000s
Operating revenue	526,844	+32	400,226
Net income	6,861	+83	3,753
	$		$
Earnings per share*	0.16		0.10

* Common
[A] Reported in accordance with IFRS

Historical Summary
(as originally stated)

Fiscal Year	Oper. Rev.	Net Inc. Bef. Disc.	EPS*
	$000s	$000s	$
2022[A]	2,059,373	109,669	2.72
2021[A]	1,413,146	68,588	1.84
2020[A]	1,149,629	28,055	0.80
2019[A]	1,341,374	83,636	2.58
2018[A]	1,203,392	70,769	2.25

* Common
[A] Reported in accordance with IFRS

E.78 Exco Technologies Limited*

Symbol - XTC **Exchange** - TSX **CUSIP** - 30150P
Head Office - 200-130 Spy Crt, Markham, ON, L3R 5H6 **Telephone** - (905) 477-3065 **Fax** - (905) 477-2449
Website - www.excocorp.com

Email - dkirk@excocorp.com
Investor Relations - Darren M. Kirk (905) 477-3065 ext. 7233
Auditors - Ernst & Young LLP C.A., Toronto, Ont.
Transfer Agents - TSX Trust Company, Toronto, Ont.
FP500 Revenue Ranking - 474
Employees - 4,902 at Sept. 30, 2022
Profile - (Ont. 1986 amalg.) Designs, develops and manufactures dies, moulds, components and assemblies, and consumable equipment for the die-casting, extrusion and automotive industries. Operations consist of 20 strategic locations in Canada, the U.S., Mexico, Colombia, Brazil, Thailand, Morocco, Italy and Germany.

Operations are carried out through two business segments: Casting and Extrusion Technology; and Automotive Solutions.

Casting and Extrusion Technology - This segment consists of three business lines: Extrusion technology, which involves the designing and manufacturing of aluminum extrusion dies which are supplied to aluminum extruders in North America, Central and South America, the Far East and Europe; Casting technology, which involves the designing and manufacturing of die-cast moulds used to produce aluminum, magnesium and structural aluminum high pressure die-castings; and Castool, which involves the designing and manufacturing of consumable tooling components and related capital equipment for light metal die-cast machines and extrusion presses. Production facilities are located in Markham, Newmarket and Uxbridge Ont.; Chesterfield, Mich.; Toledo, Ohio; Wylie, Tex.; Queretaro, Mexico (2); Medellin, Colombia; Sorocaba, Brazil; Kenitra, Morocco; Chonburi, Thailand; and Aldenhoven and Weissenburg, Germany; and Brescia, Italy (2).

Automotive Solutions - This segment designs, develops and manufactures automotive interior trim components and assemblies primarily for passenger and light truck vehicles. Operations consist of four divisions: Polytech, Polydesign, Neocon and AFX Industries (AFX). Polytech and Polydesign manufacture flexible storage systems, flexible restraint systems, plastic injection moulded consoles, gearshift boots and componentry, and other interior trim products. Polydesign also has additional product lines which include the cutting and sewing of seat covers, headrests, instrument panels, sun visors and door panels. Neocon designs and manufactures cargo organizer, and flooring and protective systems for original equipment manufacturers (OEMs) and electronic vehicle (EV) manufacturers. AFX manufactures die cut leather and other interior trim material, fabricating interior trim components and plastic injection moulded interior trim componentry. Automotive Solutions has manufacturing facilities in Dartmouth, N.S.; Matamoros, Mexico (2); and Tangier, Morocco.

Recent Merger and Acquisition Activity

Status: completed **Revised:** May 2, 2022
UPDATE: The transaction was completed. PREVIOUS: Exco Technologies Limited agreed to acquire Halex® Extrusion Dies business from Halex Holdings GmbH (Halex), which manufactures aluminum extrusion dies and provides heat treatment services in Europe, for €40,000,000 (Cdn$58,000,000). Halex has four manufacturing facilities for extrusion dies located in Germany (2) and Italy (2).

Directors - Brian A. Robbins, exec. chr., Aurora, Ont.; Darren M. Kirk, pres. & CEO, Mississauga, Ont.; Paul E. Riganelli, exec. v-p, Niagara-on-the-Lake, Ont.; Robert B. Magee†, Caledon, Ont.; Edward H. Kernaghan, Toronto, Ont.; Colleen M. McMorrow, Oakville, Ont.

Other Exec. Officers - Jeff Blackburn, v-p & gen. mgr., castings technologies grp.; Nick Gnatyuk, v-p & gen. mgr., extrusion grp.; Matthew Posno, v-p, fin., CFO & corp. sec.; Paul Robbins, v-p & gen. mgr., Castool div.; William Schroers, pres. & CEO, automotive solutions grp.

† Lead director

Capital Stock

	Authorized (shs.)	Outstanding (shs.)[1]
Preferred	unlimited	nil
Common	unlimited	38,912,464
Special	275	nil

[1] At June 30, 2023

Options - At Sept. 30, 2022, options were outstanding to purchase 1,046,500 common shares at prices ranging from $8.29 to $10.15 per share with a weighted average remaining contractual life of 2.98 years.

Normal Course Issuer Bid - The company plans to make normal course purchases of up to 1,785,000 common shares representing 10% of the public float. The bid commenced on Feb. 20, 2023, and expires on Feb. 19, 2024.

Major Shareholder - Brian A. Robbins held 25.54% interest and Edward J. Kernaghan held 25.17% interest at Dec. 6, 2022.

Price Range - XTC/TSX

Year	Volume	High	Low	Close
2022	9,985,291	$10.57	$6.80	$7.70
2021	11,190,234	$11.50	$9.06	$10.31
2020	10,514,329	$9.45	$4.72	$9.23
2019	7,796,266	$10.49	$7.00	$7.93
2018	11,411,948	$10.48	$8.50	$9.03

Recent Close: $7.89

Capital Stock Changes - During fiscal 2022, 27,000 common shares were issued on exercise of options and 385,033 common shares were repurchased under a Normal Course Issuer Bid.

Dividends

XTC com Ra $0.42 pa Q est. Mar. 31, 2022
Prev. Rate: $0.40 est. Mar. 31, 2021
Prev. Rate: $0.38 est. Mar. 30, 2020

Long-Term Debt - At Sept. 30, 2022, outstanding long-term debt totaled $95,000,000 (none current) and consisted entirely of revolving credit facility due February 2025, bearing interest based on prime, bankers' acceptance, CDOR or Euribor base rates plus a relevant margin depending on the level of the company's net leverage ratio.

Wholly Owned Subsidiaries

AFX Industries LLC, Port Huron, Mich.
Automotive Solutions Neocon USA, Inc., Ala.
Automotive Solutions Polytech
• 100% int. in **Automotive Solutions Polydesign S.A.R.L.**, Morocco.
Castool 90 S.A.R.L., Morocco.
Castool 180 Co. Ltd., Thailand.
Exco Brazil Tooling Solutions Ltd., Brazil.
Exco Extrusion Dies, Inc., Mich.
Exco Extrusion Dies (Texas) Inc., Tex.
Exco Tooling Solutions S.A.S., Medellín, Colombia.
Excoeng de Mexico S. de R.L. de C.V., Qro., Mexico.
Halex - Aldenhoven GmbH, Germany.
Halex - Gussago S.p.A., Italy.
Halex - Verdello S.r.l., Italy.
Halex - Weissenburg GmbH, Germany.

Financial Statistics

Periods ended:	12m Sept. 30/22[A]		12m Sept. 30/21[□A]
	$000s	%Chg	$000s
Operating revenue	**489,943**	**+6**	**461,171**
Cost of sales	392,673		351,960
General & admin expense	44,048		38,874
Stock-based compensation	384		371
Operating expense	**437,105**	**+12**	**391,205**
Operating income	**52,838**	**-24**	**69,966**
Deprec., depl. & amort.	25,372		21,082
Finance income	29		23
Finance costs, gross	2,475		428
Pre-tax income	**25,199**	**-48**	**48,577**
Income taxes	6,233		10,157
Net income	**18,966**	**-51**	**38,420**
Cash & equivalent	17,024		24,098
Inventories	97,962		77,759
Accounts receivable	113,940		83,130
Current assets	244,428		191,692
Fixed assets, net	207,103		149,474
Intangibles, net	123,145		87,644
Total assets	**576,316**	**+34**	**430,127**
Bank indebtedness	12,363		5,540
Accts. pay. & accr. liabs	85,900		59,040
Current liabilities	107,877		73,330
Long-term debt, gross	95,000		nil
Long-term debt, net	95,000		nil
Long-term lease liabilities	6,650		420
Shareholders' equity	348,509		345,058
Cash from oper. activs	**23,473**	**-51**	**47,790**
Cash from fin. activs	79,976		(16,875)
Cash from invest. activs	(110,356)		(38,332)
Net cash position	**17,024**	**-29**	**24,098**
Capital expenditures	(52,112)		(38,426)
Capital disposals	765		381
	$		$
Earnings per share*	0.49		0.98
Cash flow per share*	0.60		1.22
Cash divd. per share*	0.42		0.40
	shs		shs
No. of shs. o/s*	38,912,464		39,270,497
Avg. no. of shs. o/s*	39,084,977		39,269,959
	%		%
Net profit margin	3.87		8.33
Return on equity	5.47		11.37
Return on assets	4.14		9.23
Foreign sales percent	93		94
No. of employees (FTEs)	4,902		4,876

* Common
[□] Restated
[A] Reported in accordance with IFRS

Latest Results

Periods ended:	9m June 30/23[A]		9m June 30/22[A]
	$000s	%Chg	$000s
Operating revenue	459,151	+31	349,532
Net income	17,074	+27	13,397
	$		$
Earnings per share*	0.44		0.34

* Common
[A] Reported in accordance with IFRS

Historical Summary
(as originally stated)

Fiscal Year	Oper. Rev.	Net Inc. Bef. Disc.	EPS*
	$000s	$000s	$
2022[A]	489,943	18,966	0.49
2021[A]	461,171	38,420	0.98
2020[A]	412,309	27,424	0.69
2019[A]	507,348	26,632	0.65
2018[A]	575,554	42,270	1.00

* Common
[A] Reported in accordance with IFRS

E.79 eXeBlock Technology Corporation

Symbol - XBLK.X **Exchange** - CSE **CUSIP** - 30151G
Head Office - 280-1090 Georgia St W, Vancouver, BC, V6E 3V7
Telephone - (604) 899-0106 **Fax** - (604) 684-5973
Website - www.exeblock.ca
Email - rrandall@exeblock.ca
Investor Relations - Robert Randall (604) 899-0106
Auditors - Manning Elliott LLP C.A., Vancouver, B.C.
Transfer Agents - National Securities Administrators Ltd., Vancouver, B.C.

Profile - (B.C. 2015) Pursuing acquisition of a company that offers digital security solutions for global enterprises including development and delivery of non-fungible tokens (NFTs).

Directors - Ian M. Klassen, interim pres. & interim CEO, Vancouver, B.C.; Robert (Rob) Randall, CFO & corp. sec., Halifax, N.S.; Paul Thomson, Bedford, N.S.

Capital Stock

	Authorized (shs.)	Outstanding (shs.)[1]
Common	unlimited	53,539,031

[1] At Jan. 20, 2022

Major Shareholder - Wade K. Dawe held 11.5% interest at Jan. 6, 2021.

Price Range - XBLK.X/CSE

Year	Volume	High	Low	Close
2022	2,050,047	$0.10	$0.02	$0.02
2020	6,432,011	$0.11	$0.02	$0.07
2019	9,116,675	$0.10	$0.03	$0.04
2018	32,626,297	$1.10	$0.03	$0.04

Recent Close: $0.03

Wholly Owned Subsidiaries

eXeBlock Technology Inc., Debert, N.S.

Financial Statistics

Periods ended:	12m Aug. 31/21[A]		12m Aug. 31/20[A]
	$000s	%Chg	$000s
General & admin expense	318		319
Operating expense	**318**	**0**	**319**
Operating income	**(318)**	**n.a.**	**(319)**
Finance income	3		19
Pre-tax income	**(315)**	**n.a.**	**(300)**
Net income	**(315)**	**n.a.**	**(300)**
Cash & equivalent	947		1,289
Accounts receivable	67		32
Current assets	1,027		1,337
Total assets	**1,027**	**-23**	**1,337**
Accts. pay. & accr. liabs	65		60
Current liabilities	65		60
Shareholders' equity	962		1,277
Cash from oper. activs	**(343)**	**n.a.**	**(275)**
Cash from fin. activs	nil		103
Net cash position	**947**	**-27**	**1,289**
	$		$
Earnings per share*	(0.01)		(0.01)
Cash flow per share*	(0.01)		(0.01)
	shs		shs
No. of shs. o/s*	53,539,031		53,539,031
Avg. no. of shs. o/s*	53,539,031		51,583,894
	%		%
Net profit margin	n.a.		n.a.
Return on equity	(28.14)		(21.81)
Return on assets	(26.65)		(20.76)

* Common
[A] Reported in accordance with IFRS

Latest Results

Periods ended:	3m Nov. 30/21[A]		3m Nov. 30/20[A]
	$000s	%Chg	$000s
Net income	(54)	n.a.	(80)
	$		$
Earnings per share*	(0.00)		(0.00)

* Common
[A] Reported in accordance with IFRS

Historical Summary
(as originally stated)

Fiscal Year	Oper. Rev.	Net Inc. Bef. Disc.	EPS*
	$000s	$000s	$
2021A	nil	(315)	(0.01)
2020A	nil	(300)	(0.01)
2019A	nil	(435)	(0.01)
2018A	nil	(4,846)	(0.08)
2017A	nil	(162)	(0.02)

* Common
A Reported in accordance with IFRS

E.80 Exelerate Capital Corp.

Symbol - XCAP.P **Exchange** - TSX-VEN **CUSIP** - 30163L
Head Office - c/o Fasken Martineau LLP, 2900-550 Burrard St, Vancouver, BC, V6C 0A3
Email - mkohler@exelerate.ca
Investor Relations - Mark W. Kohler (416) 209-8016
Auditors - RSM Canada LLP C.A., Toronto, Ont.
Lawyers - Fasken Martineau DuMoulin LLP, Vancouver, B.C.
Transfer Agents - Capital Transfer Agency Inc., Toronto, Ont.
Profile - (B.C. 2018) Capital Pool Company.
Predecessor Detail - Name changed from Exelerate Health Inc., Feb. 19, 2019.
Directors - Mark W. Kohler, chr. & CEO, Toronto, Ont.; Michael Boyd, Ont.; Sheldon M. Pollack, Toronto, Ont.; Barry C. Richards, Toronto, Ont.
Other Exec. Officers - Sean Carr, CFO & corp. sec.

Capital Stock

	Authorized (shs.)	Outstanding (shs.)[1]
Common	unlimited	17,560,250

[1] At July 26, 2022

Major Shareholder - Widely held at Dec. 20, 2021.

Price Range - XCAP.P/TSX-VEN

Year	Volume	High	Low	Close
2022	628,010	$0.11	$0.04	$0.04
2021	220,250	$0.35	$0.10	$0.16
2020	177,500	$0.14	$0.10	$0.14
2019	459,334	$0.17	$0.05	$0.10

Recent Close: $0.05

E.81 Exro Technologies Inc.

Symbol - EXRO **Exchange** - TSX **CUSIP** - 30222R
Head Office - 12-21 Highfield Cir SE, Calgary, AB, T2G 5N6 **Telephone** - (587) 619-1517
Website - www.exro.com
Email - dbishop@exro.com
Investor Relations - Darrell Bishop (604) 674-7746
Auditors - PricewaterhouseCoopers LLP C.A., Calgary, Alta.
Transfer Agents - TSX Trust Company
Employees - 129 at Mar. 30, 2023
Profile - (B.C. 2014) Developing power control electronics technology for optimizing the cost, performance and efficiency of motors and batteries.

Power electronics are what control and convert electric power. The company's core technologies are Coil Driver™ for motor control and Cell Driver™ for battery control. The Coil Driver™ is an adaptive electric vehicle traction inverter that replaces the standard inverter in electric vehicles. The patented Coil Driver™ technology applies coil switching to increase torque at low speeds and enhance power and efficiency at high speeds. The Cell Driver™ is a fully integrated battery energy storage system designed to optimize performance and reduce costs for stationary commercial and industrial energy storage applications. Cell Driver™ extends batteries into a second life by enabling next-generation battery management with cell-level control. It is equipped with the company's proprietary Battery Control System™ (BCS). The company also provides end-to-end electric vehicle design and engineering services through its vehicle systems division.

The company has licensing and strategic agreements with **LAND Electric Motorcycles, Inc.**, **Heinzmann GmbH & Co. KG**, **Potencia Industrial, S.A. de C.V.**, **Zero Motorcycles Inc.**, **ev Transportation Services Inc.**, **Linamar Corporation**, **SEA Electric Pty Ltd.**, **Vicinity Motor Corp.**, **Traktionssysteme Austria GmbH** and **Wolong Electric Group Ltd.**, as well as European and Brazil non-disclosure agreement (NDA) partners, for the integration of the company's systems to different markets such as scooters, electric bikes, recreational, light electric cars and motorcycles, fleet vans; electric buses; passenger vehicles, long-haul trucks; and industrial vehicles. Also has distribution agreements with **Greentech Renewables Southwest**, **Inferno Solar Ltd.**, **Photovoltaics California**, **ProSolar America**, **Shaw Solar** and **High Point Electric**, which supports the company's go-to-market strategy for its Cell Driver™ stationary energy storage system for the commercial and industrial market.

In May 2023, the company announced a definitive commercialization agreement with **Linamar Corporation** following the continued successful testing and validation by Linamar of the co-developed integrated electric axle (eAxle) utilizing the company's Coil Driver™ traction inverter. The agreement is set for an initial five-year term to build a demonstration vehicle containing the eAxle product to be utilized as a joint marketing asset for the medium duty commercial vehicle market. The agreement contemplates the start of series production by the fourth quarter of 2024 and includes annual commercial volume targets that build to 25,000 units per annum by 2027. Linamar is granted exclusivity to the company's Coil Driver™ product for use in medium duty Class 3-6 electric beam axle applications.

Predecessor Detail - Name changed from BioDE Ventures Ltd., Aug. 16, 2017, following reverse takeover acquisition of (old) Exro Technologies Inc. and concurrent amalgamation of (old) Exro with wholly owned 1089001 B.C. Ltd.
Directors - Rodney (Rod) Copes, chr., Sanibel, Fla.; Sue Ozdemir, CEO, Gilbert, Ariz.; Anita Ganti, Los Gatos, Calif.; Terence Johnsson, Berlin, Germany; Aleksandra (Aleks) Miziolek, Detroit, Mich.; Frank P. Simpkins, Pa.
Other Exec. Officers - Simon Strawbridge, COO; W. John Meekison, CFO; Darrell Bishop, chief invest. officer; Spyros Gorgogiannis, chief eng. officer; Eric Hustedt, chief tech. officer; Josh Sobil, chief comml. officer; Raymond Millien, v-p, legal & corp. sec.; Brian Van Batavia, pres., Exro Vehicle Systems Inc.

Capital Stock

	Authorized (shs.)	Outstanding (shs.)[1]
Common	unlimited	167,841,877

[1] At May 23, 2023

Major Shareholder - Widely held at May 23, 2023.

Price Range - EXRO/TSX

Year	Volume	High	Low	Close
2022	62,582,862	$3.10	$0.73	$2.10
2021	90,546,867	$7.55	$2.56	$2.91
2020	137,302,846	$5.15	$0.22	$4.38
2019	24,569,809	$0.38	$0.18	$0.34
2018	20,411,376	$0.57	$0.20	$0.36

Recent Close: $1.98

Capital Stock Changes - In May 2023, bought deal public offering of 15,525,000 common shares was completed at $2.25 per share, including 2,025,000 shares on exercise of over-allotment option. Net proceeds would be used to meet the capital expenditure and working capital obligations associated with the definitive commercialization agreement with Linamar Corporation and for general working capital purposes.

In February 2022, bought deal public offering of 12,722,450 units (1 common share & ½ warrant), including 1,659,450 units on exercise of over-allotment option, was completed at $1.60 per unit. In September 2022, public offering of 7,920,000 units (1 common share & 1 warrant) and concurrent private placement of 1,403,756 units (1 common share & 1 warrant) all at $1.05 per unit were completed. Also during 2022, common shares were issued as follows: 2,096,250 on exercise of warrants and 1,786,500 on exercise of options.

Wholly Owned Subsidiaries

DPM Technologies Inc., B.C.
Exro Technologies USA, Inc., United States.
- 100% int. in **Exro Vehicle Systems Inc.**, Del.

Financial Statistics

Periods ended:	12m Dec. 31/22A		12m Dec. 31/21A
	$000s	%Chg	$000s
Operating revenue	**2,185**	**n.a.**	**nil**
Cost of sales	1,901		nil
Salaries & benefits	13,787		7,341
Research & devel. expense	8,766		7,408
General & admin expense	11,119		5,398
Stock-based compensation	2,605		9,789
Operating expense	**38,178**	**+28**	**29,936**
Operating income	**(35,992)**	**n.a.**	**(29,936)**
Deprec., depl. & amort.	2,245		701
Finance costs, net	863		123
Pre-tax income	**(40,025)**	**n.a.**	**(24,579)**
Net income	**(40,025)**	**n.a.**	**(24,579)**
Cash & equivalent	17,444		15,349
Inventories	2,175		174
Accounts receivable	965		135
Current assets	21,472		17,829
Fixed assets, net	26,216		15,505
Total assets	**60,879**	**+32**	**45,995**
Accts. pay. & accr. liabs.	5,507		3,005
Current liabilities	7,964		3,658
Long-term debt, gross	11,552		48
Long-term debt, net	11,552		48
Long-term lease liabilities	5,946		4,516
Shareholders' equity	35,417		37,774
Cash from oper. activs.	**(31,337)**	**n.a.**	**(20,235)**
Cash from fin. activs.	43,664		3,111
Cash from invest. activs.	(9,510)		(15,795)
Net cash position	**17,444**	**+14**	**15,349**
Capital expenditures	(10,238)		(10,077)
	$		$
Earnings per share*	(0.29)		(0.20)
Cash flow per share*	(0.23)		(0.17)
	shs		shs
No. of shs. o/s*	146,834,230		120,905,274
Avg. no. of shs. o/s*	137,685,067		120,133,748
	%		%
Net profit margin	n.m.		n.a.
Return on equity	(109.37)		(57.31)
Return on assets	(74.90)		(51.12)
No. of employees (FTEs)	125		76

* Common
A Reported in accordance with IFRS

Latest Results

Periods ended:	3m Mar. 31/23A		3m Mar. 31/22A
	$000s	%Chg	$000s
Operating revenue	325	+212	104
Net income	(8,163)	n.a.	(10,116)
	$		$
Earnings per share*	(0.05)		(0.08)

* Common
A Reported in accordance with IFRS

Historical Summary
(as originally stated)

Fiscal Year	Oper. Rev.	Net Inc. Bef. Disc.	EPS*
	$000s	$000s	$
2022A	2,185	(40,025)	(0.29)
2021A	nil	(24,579)	(0.20)
2020A	nil	(10,969)	(0.12)
2019A	nil	(4,665)	(0.07)
2018A	nil	(3,127)	(0.06)

* Common
A Reported in accordance with IFRS

E.82 Extendicare Inc.*

Symbol - EXE **Exchange** - TSX **CUSIP** - 30224T
Head Office - 400-3000 Steeles Ave E, Markham, ON, L3R 4T9 **Telephone** - (905) 470-4000 **Fax** - (905) 470-5588
Website - www.extendicare.com
Email - jfountain@extendicare.com
Investor Relations - Jillian E. Fountain (905) 470-5534
Auditors - KPMG LLP C.A., Toronto, Ont.
Lawyers - Bennett Jones LLP
Transfer Agents - Computershare Trust Company of Canada Inc., Toronto, Ont.
FP500 Revenue Ranking - 302
Employees - 18,000 at Dec. 31, 2022
Profile - (Ont. 2012) Owns and operates or provides contract services to 103 long-term care homes with capacity for 13,258 residents, and provides publicly-funded home health care services in Canada. Also provides management and consulting services to third-party owners of long-term care facilities and group purchasing services to third-party clients.

Owns and operates 53 long-term care (LTC) centres and manages 50 LTC homes and retirement communities for third parties in Ontario (80),

Alberta (16) and Manitoba (7). Also provides management and consulting services, and home health care services. Also holds 15% managed interest in a portfolio of 25 long-term care homes (LTC), consisting of 3,100 funded LTC beds, in Ontario and Manitoba held in a joint venture partnership with an affiliate of **Axium Infrastructure Inc.**

Long-Term Care Services - LTC centres are designed for individuals primarily seniors who cannot be cared for at home or in another setting, due to factors such as physical limitations and cognitive impairment, and for those who require professional nursing care on a daily basis and 24 hours supervision. In addition to providing accommodation and meals, residents receive assistance with activities of daily living and continuing care.

Home Health Care Services - Through wholly owned **ParaMed Inc.**, the company provides care and support services to clients through its 49 locations in Alberta (2), Manitoba (1), Ontario (45), and Nova Scotia (1). ParaMed's professionals and staff members provide complex nursing care, occupational, physical and speech therapy, as well as assistance with daily activities.

Management & Consulting Services - Through its Extendicare Assist division, wholly owned **Extendicare (Canada) Inc.** (ECI) manages long-term care centres, retirement communities and an Ontario-based chronic care unit for not-for-profit and for-profit organizations, hospitals and municipalities seeking to improve their management practices, levels of care and operating efficiencies. Most of these contracts include financial administration, record keeping, regulatory compliance and purchasing.

Group Purchasing Services - Through SGP Purchasing Partner Network division, ECI offers purchasing contracts for food, capital equipment, furnishings, cleaning and nursing supplies, and office products to third-party clients representing 111,772 seniors across Canada at Mar. 31, 2023.

LTC homes and retirement communities at Mar. 31, 2023:

	No. of facilities	Capacity
Owned/leased	53	7,299
Managed	50	5,959
	103	13,258

On Mar. 1, 2022, the company announced it would form a joint venture with **Axium Infrastructure Inc.** for the redevelopment of class C retirement homes owned by the company. The joint venture would be owned 85% by Axium and 15% by the company. The joint venture was expected to close by Sept. 30, 2023.

Recent Merger and Acquisition Activity

Status: completed **Revised:** Aug. 1, 2023
UPDATE: The transaction was completed. Total cash consideration for the Revera was $32,600,000, net of holdbacks, plus the assumption of $37,100,000 in debt. PREVIOUS: Extendicare Inc. agreed to acquire a 15% managed interest in 18 class A long-term care homes in Ontario and six homes in Manitoba from Revera Inc. The remaining 85% interest will continue to be owned by an affiliate of Axium Infrastructure Inc. On closing, Extendicare would enter into management contracts with Revera to manage all of Revera's other long-term care homes, which consist of 31 class C homes in Ontario and one personal care home in Manitoba. The Revera transactions would add 56 long-term care homes to the 108 long-term care homes Extendicare currently operates (58 owned, 50 managed). These homes would also join the SGP Purchasing Partner Network. Total cash consideration is $36,000,000 plus the assumption of $34,000,000 in debt.

Status: completed **Announced:** Oct. 9, 2022
Extendicare Inc. sold its long-term care homes in Saskatchewan to the Saskatchewan Health Authority (SHA) for $13,100,000 cash. The transaction was in relation to the completion of the transition of operations and delivery of long-term care services of Extendicare to SHA.

Status: completed **Revised:** May 16, 2022
UPDATE: The transaction was completed. PREVIOUS: Extendicare Inc. agreed to sell its Espirt retirement living operations consisting of 1,050 retirement living suites across 11 retirement communities in Ontario (7) and Saskatchewan (4), to Sienna-Sabra LP, a 50/50 partnership formed between Sienna Senior Living Inc. and Irvine, Calif.-based Sabra Health Care REIT, Inc., for a purchase price of $307,500,000, subject to customary closing adjustments. Sienna would partially fund its portion of the acquisition price with proceeds from a proposed bought deal public offering. The portfolio consisted of 840 independent living suites, 51 assisted living suites and 157 memory care suites. Extendicare plans to focus on its long-term care and home health care segments.

Predecessor Detail - Succeeded Extendicare Real Estate Investment Trust, July 1, 2012, pursuant to plan of arrangement whereby Extendicare Inc. was formed to facilitate the conversion of the trust into a corporation.

Directors - Alan D. Torrie, chr., Toronto, Ont.; Dr. Michael Guerriere, pres. & CEO, Toronto, Ont.; Norma Beauchamp, Toronto, Ont.; Sandra L. Hanington, Toronto, Ont.; Alan R. Hibben, Yorks., United Kingdom; Brent Houlden, Toronto, Ont.; Donna E. Kingelin, Ont.; Samir A. Manji, West Vancouver, B.C.; Aladin W. (Al) Mawani, Thornhill, Ont.

Exec. Officers - Dr. Matthew Morgan, CMO; David Bacon, sr. v-p & CFO; Steve Paraskevopoulos, sr. v-p, ParaMed & chief tech. officer; Leslie Sarauer, sr. v-p & chief HR officer; John Toffoletto, sr. v-p, chief legal officer & corp. sec.; Kathryn Bradley, v-p, strategy & performance; Maura Dyer, v-p, HR; Elaine E. Everson, v-p, corp. devel.; Jillian E. Fountain, v-p, IR; Lavernne Hudson, v-p, prop. devel. & constr.; Katie LeMoyne, v-p, IT; Lisa Pearson, v-p, public affairs; Norman Quesnel, v-p, labour & employee rel.; Mark Trenholm, v-p, fin.

Capital Stock

	Authorized (shs.)	Outstanding (shs.)[1]
Common	unlimited	84,351,546

[1] At June 16, 2023

Normal Course Issuer Bid - The company plans to make normal course purchases of up to 7,273,707 common shares representing 10% of the public float. The bid commenced on June 30, 2023, and expires on June 29, 2024.

Major Shareholder - Samir A. Manji held 12.86% interest and Global Alpha Capital Management Ltd. held 10.7% interest at Apr. 6, 2023.

Price Range - EXE/TSX

Year	Volume	High	Low	Close
2022	40,026,601	$8.00	$6.47	$6.56
2021	59,672,537	$8.71	$5.80	$7.30
2020	95,789,460	$8.85	$4.90	$6.64
2019	51,253,480	$9.60	$6.30	$8.44
2018	51,255,902	$9.15	$5.95	$6.35

Recent Close: $6.54

Capital Stock Changes - During 2022, 177,425 common shares were issued as share-based compensation and 5,011,180 common shares were repurchased under a Normal Course Issuer Bid.

Dividends

EXE com Ra $0.48 pa M est. June 17, 2013**
** Reinvestment Option

Long-Term Debt - Outstanding at Dec. 31, 2022:

Construction loans due to 2024[1]	$33,288,000
5% conv. debs. due 2025[2]	123,719,000
Mtges. due 2025[3]	22,121,000
Mtges. due to 2037[4]	43,498,000
Mtges. due to 2038[5]	103,248,000
Lease liabs.	63,502,000
Less: Def. fin. costs	4,402,000
	383,974,000
Less: Current portion	19,239,000
	364,735,000

[1] Bearing interest at a prime rate plus 1.25% or CDOR plus 2.75%.
[2] Convertible into common shares at $12.25 per share. An equity component of $7,085,000 was classified as part of shareholders' equity.
[3] Bear interest at a variable rate based on the lenders cost of funds plus 2.25%.
[4] Bear interest at rates ranging from 2.65% to 7.70%.
[5] Bear interest at rates ranging from 3.49% to 5.64%.

Principal repayments on long-term debt were reported as follows:

2023	$24,280,000
2024	56,994,000
2025	184,567,000
2026	20,663,000
2027	38,048,000
Thereafter	78,029,000

Wholly Owned Subsidiaries

Extendicare (Canada) Inc., Toronto, Ont.
ParaMed Inc., Canada.

Note: The preceding list includes only the major related companies in which interests are held.

Financial Statistics

Periods ended:	12m Dec. 31/22[A]		12m Dec. 31/21[oA]
	$000s	%Chg	$000s
Operating revenue	**1,221,577**	**+5**	**1,166,987**
Cost of sales	1,113,048		1,034,017
General & admin expense	51,075		52,431
Operating expense	**1,164,123**	**+7**	**1,086,448**
Operating income	**57,454**	**-29**	**80,539**
Deprec., depl. & amort.	31,559		30,831
Finance income	5,018		1,867
Finance costs, gross	21,456		22,621
Write-downs/write-offs	(4,942)		(14,969)
Pre-tax income	**(4,496)**	**n.a.**	**13,985**
Income taxes	15		6,481
Net inc. bef. disc. opers	**(4,511)**	**n.a.**	**7,504**
Income from disc. opers	74,065		4,000
Net income	**69,554**	**+505**	**11,504**
Cash & equivalent	167,281		104,627
Accounts receivable	61,166		69,435
Current assets	258,038		224,920
Fixed assets, net	388,719		535,600
Intangibles, net	97,064		92,484
Total assets	**781,579**	**-13**	**900,323**
Accts. pay. & accr. liabs	250,140		192,994
Current liabilities	274,985		281,912
Long-term debt, gross	383,974		536,851
Long-term debt, net	364,735		463,274
Equity portion of conv. debs	7,085		7,085
Shareholders' equity	100,701		101,923
Cash from oper. activs	**98,714**	**+67**	**59,077**
Cash from fin. activs	(191,859)		(74,836)
Cash from invest. activs	155,644		(59,386)
Net cash position	**167,281**	**+60**	**104,627**
Capital expenditures	(101,629)		(65,176)
Unfunded pension liability	26,081		33,754
	$		$
Earns. per sh. bef disc opers*	(0.05)		0.10
Earnings per share*	0.78		0.13
Cash flow per share*	1.11		0.66
Cash divd. per share*	0.48		0.48
	shs		shs
No. of shs. o/s*	84,728,744		89,562,499
Avg. no. of shs. o/s*	89,008,792		89,989,803
	%		%
Net profit margin	(0.37)		0.64
Return on equity	(4.45)		6.52
Return on assets	2.02		2.11
No. of employees (FTEs)	18,000		20,000

* Common
[o] Restated
[A] Reported in accordance with IFRS

Latest Results

Periods ended:	3m Mar. 31/23[A]		3m Mar. 31/22[A]
	$000s	%Chg	$000s
Operating revenue	324,712	+6	305,710
Net inc. bef. disc. opers	11,580	+186	4,045
Income from disc. opers	nil		75
Net income	11,580	+181	4,120
	$		$
Earnings per share*	0.14		0.04

* Common
[A] Reported in accordance with IFRS

Historical Summary
(as originally stated)

Fiscal Year	Oper. Rev.	Net Inc. Bef. Disc.	EPS*
	$000s	$000s	$
2022[A]	1,221,577	(4,511)	(0.05)
2021[A]	1,216,758	9,012	0.10
2020[A]	1,158,293	42,586	0.47
2019[A]	1,131,950	17,051	0.19
2018[A]	1,120,007	8,084	0.09

* Common
[A] Reported in accordance with IFRS

F

F.1 FG Acquisition Corp.

Symbol - FGAA.U **Exchange** - TSX **CUSIP** - 30327L
Head Office - 1800-510 Georgia St W, Vancouver, BC, V6B 0M3
Website - www.fgacquisition.com
Email - hbaqar@sequoiafin.com
Investor Relations - Hassan R. Baqar (847) 791-6817
Auditors - MNP LLP C.A., Toronto, Ont.
Lawyers - Norton Rose Fulbright Canada LLP, Toronto, Ont.
Transfer Agents - TSX Trust Company, Toronto, Ont.

Profile - (B.C. 2021) A Special Purpose Acquisition Corporation formed for the purpose of effecting an acquisition of one or more businesses or assets by way of a merger, share exchange, asset acquisition, share purchase, reorganization or any other similar business combination involving the company.

The company has until July 5, 2024, to complete a Qualifying Acquisition, which could be extended to up to 36 months with class A restricted voting shareholder approval. The company plans to execute a Qualifying Acquisition in the financial services sector by leveraging **FGAC Investors LLC**'s and **CG Investments VII Inc.**'s (the sponsors) network to find one or more attractive investment opportunities. However, the company's search for a Qualifying Acquisition is not limited to a particular industry or geographic region.

In July 2023, the permitted timeline by which the company has to consummate a Qualifying Acquisition was extended from July 5, 2023, to July 5, 2024.

Recent Merger and Acquisition Activity

Status: pending **Announced:** May 12, 2023
FG Acquisition Corp. announced the proposed Qualifying Acquisition of Think Financial Group Holdings Limited (ThinkMarkets), which operates multi-asset online brokerage ThinkMarkets. The agreement values ThinkMarkets at $160,000,000. Terms are to be entered into. On closing, FG plans to change its name to ThinkMarkets Group Holdings Limited. A private placement of convertible debentures for proceeds of up to $20,000,000 was planned by FG. The transaction was expected to close in July 2023.

Directors - D. Kyle Cerminara, chr., N.C.; Larry G. Swets Jr., CEO, Fla.; Hassan R. Baqar, CFO & corp. sec., Ill.; Dr. Richard E. Govignon Jr., N.J.; Pete Huitsing, Calif.; Andrew B. McIntyre, Ont.

Capital Stock

	Authorized (shs.)	Outstanding (shs.)[1]
Cl.A Restricted Vtg.	unlimited	11,500,000[2]
Class B	unlimited	2,875,000

[1] At Apr. 26, 2023
[2] Classified as debt.

Class A Restricted Voting - Automatically convertible into common shares upon closing of Qualifying Acquisition on a 1-for-1 basis. Not permitted to redeem more than 15% of class A restricted voting shares outstanding. Automatically redeemable if no Qualifying Acquisition is completed. One vote per share on all matters requiring shareholder approval including a proposed Qualifying Acquisition but not on the election and/or removal of directors and auditors.

Class B - Non-redeemable. Automatically convertible into proportionate voting shares upon closing of Qualifying Acquisition on the basis of 1 proportionate voting share for 100 class B shares. One vote per share.

Common - Not issuable prior to closing of Qualifying Acquisition. One vote per share.

Proportionate Voting - Not issuable prior to closing of Qualifying Acquisition. Would be convertible, at the holder's option, into common shares on the basis of 100 common shares for 1 proportionate share. 100 votes per share.

Major Shareholder - FGAC Investors LLC held 17.78% interest at May 26, 2023.

Price Range - FGAA.U/TSX

Year	Volume	High	Low	Close
2022............	498,303	US$9.90	US$9.51	US$9.90

Recent Close: US$10.25

Capital Stock Changes - In June 2023, certain changes to the articles of corporation were approved including: (i) class B shares automatically converting into common shares, rather than proportionate voting shares, upon closing of Qualifying Acquisition; (ii) creation of a class of preferred shares, issuable in series; and (iii) removal of class A restricted voting shares, class B shares and proportionate voting shares upon closing of Qualifying Acquisition. In July 2023, 11,398,742 class A restricted voting shares were redeemed.

On Apr. 5, 2022, an initial public offering of 10,000,000 units (1 class A restricted voting share & ½ warrant) at US$10 per unit was completed. Subsequently, 1,500,000 units were issued on exercise of over-allotment option.

F.2 FLINT Corp.

Symbol - FLNT **Exchange** - TSX **CUSIP** - 33944M
Head Office - Bow Valley Square 2, 3500-205 5 Ave SW, Calgary, AB, T2P 2V7 **Telephone** - (587) 318-0997 **Toll-free** - (855) 410-1112 **Fax** - (587) 475-2181
Website - flintcorp.com
Email - mdesrosiers@flintcorp.com
Investor Relations - Murray J. Desrosiers (855) 891-8451
Auditors - Ernst & Young LLP C.A., Toronto, Ont.
Lawyers - Norton Rose Fulbright Canada LLP, Toronto, Ont.
Transfer Agents - Computershare Trust Company of Canada Inc., Toronto, Ont.
FP500 Revenue Ranking - 431
Employees - 3,100 at Dec. 31, 2022

Profile - (Alta. 2022; orig. Ont., 2011) Provides asset integrity services including maintenance and turnarounds, wear technologies and weld overlays, fabrication, modularization and machining, facility construction, pipeline installation and integrity, high voltage construction, electrical and instrumentation, workforce supply, heavy equipment operators and environmental services across Western Canada.

Operates through three divisions: Maintenance and Construction; Wear Technologies; and Flint Environmental Services.

Maintenance and Construction services includes pipeline and facility maintenance and management, which consists of planning and scheduling, cost control, procurement, regulatory compliance, logistics and material management, warehousing and the supply of skilled plant operators and trade professionals; supplemental and operational maintenance, which consists of complete plant and field support, quality control, field operations and safety management systems personnel; facility construction, pipeline installation and integrity, electrical and instrumentation, high voltage construction; fabrication, machining and modular assembly; and workforce supply.

Wear Technologies division manufactures and distributes a range of products and services, including overlay pipe spools, pipe bends, wear plates, custom overlay solutions, and chrome white iron spools, all under the AssetArmor™ brand, which provides asset protection against abrasion, corrosion, and erosion. The division also offers fabrication services, such as piping, specialty alloys, custom-designed components, structural steel assemblies and pressure vessel fabrication. Manufacturing facilities are located in Sherwood Park (2), Lloydminster and Airdrie, Alta.

Flint Environmental Services provides environmental consulting and field services to clients across various end markets, such as oil and gas, pipeline, forestry, mining, power and government. The environmental services business complements the fabrication, construction and maintenance service offerings, enabling the company to provide its customers with services that span the full project lifecycle, from construction to decommissioning.

Customers include oil and gas (upstream, midstream and downstream), petrochemical, mining, power, agriculture, forestry, infrastructure and water treatment industries.

Predecessor Detail - Name changed from ClearStream Energy Services Inc., Dec. 1, 2022.

Directors - Sean D. McMaster, chr., Calgary, Alta.; Jordan L. Bitove, Toronto, Ont.; Herbert Fraser Clarke, St. John's, N.L.; Katrisha (Trisha) Gibson; Karl R. Johannson, Calgary, Alta.; Dean T. MacDonald, St. John's, N.L.

Other Exec. Officers - Barry Card, CEO; Neil Wotton, COO; Jennifer Stubbs, CFO; Murray J. Desrosiers, sr. v-p, legal & corp. devel.; James Healey, v-p, fin. & corp. controlling; Deloris Hetherington, v-p, HR; Brad Naeth, v-p, wear & envirl. srvcs.; Herb Thomas, v-p, opers.; Angela Thompson, v-p, corp. srvcs.; Clint Tisnic, v-p, operational fin.

Capital Stock

	Authorized (shs.)	Outstanding (shs.)[1]
Preferred	n.a.	
Series 1	n.a.	127,732
Series 2	n.a.	40,111
Common	unlimited	110,001,239

[1] At May 1, 2023

Preferred Series 1- Total authorized amount is equal to not more than one-half of the issued and outstanding common shares at the time of issuance. Entitled to 10% fixed cumulative dividends payable when the company have sufficient monies to be able to do so. Convertible into common shares, at the holder's option, at a price of 35¢ per share. Redeemable by the company at $1,100 per share plus accrued and unpaid dividends. Non-voting.

Preferred Series 2 - Total authorized amount is equal to not more than one-half of the issued and outstanding common shares at the time of issuance. Entitled to 10% fixed cumulative dividends payable when the company have sufficient monies to be able to do so. Convertible into common shares, at the holder's option, at a price of 10¢ per share. Redeemable by the company at $1,100 per share plus accrued and unpaid dividends. Non-voting.

Common - One vote per share.

Major Shareholder - Canso Investment Counsel Ltd. held 16% interest at May 1, 2023.

Price Range - FLNT/TSX

Year	Volume	High	Low	Close
2022............	37,994,569	$0.08	$0.03	$0.04
2021............	201,652,485	$0.15	$0.03	$0.06
2020............	15,777,562	$0.06	$0.01	$0.03
2019............	98,963,522	$0.11	$0.01	$0.05
2018............	26,541,092	$0.10	$0.01	$0.01

Recent Close: $0.03

Capital Stock Changes - During 2022, 8,571 common shares were issued on conversion of 3 preferred series 1 shares.

Wholly Owned Subsidiaries

Clearwater Energy Services GP Inc., Alta.
- 0.01% int. in **Clearwater Energy Services LP**

Flint Asset GP Ltd., Alta.
- 0.01% int. in **Flint Equipment LP**, Alta.
- 0.01% int. in **Flint Real Estate L.P.**, Alta.

Flint GP Inc., Alta.
- 0.01% int. in **Flint Energy Services Limited Partnership**, Sherwood Park, Alta.

Flint Wear Technologies GP Inc., Alta.
- 0.01% int. in **Flint Wear Technologies LP**

Subsidiaries

99.99% int. in **Clearwater Energy Services LP**
99.99% int. in **Flint Energy Services Limited Partnership**, Sherwood Park, Alta.
99.99% int. in **Flint Equipment LP**, Alta.
99.99% int. in **Flint Real Estate L.P.**, Alta.
99.99% int. in **Flint Wear Technologies LP**

Financial Statistics

Periods ended:	12m Dec. 31/22[A]		12m Dec. 31/21[A]
	$000s	%Chg	$000s
Operating revenue........................	**604,673**	**+55**	**389,402**
Cost of sales..................................	541,540		349,066
Salaries & benefits..........................	24,562		17,461
General & admin expense................	12,642		8,837
Stock-based compensation.............	3,061		2,239
Operating expense........................	**581,805**	**+54**	**377,603**
Operating income.........................	**22,868**	**+94**	**11,799**
Deprec., depl. & amort.....................	11,039		12,893
Finance costs, gross........................	16,903		15,934
Investment income..........................	141		534
Write-downs/write-offs....................	(3,652)		(8,270)
Pre-tax income..............................	**(12,431)**	**n.a.**	**(9,296)**
Net inc. bef. disc. opers.................	**(12,431)**	**n.a.**	**(9,296)**
Income from disc. opers..................	(548)		(12)
Net income....................................	**(12,979)**	**n.a.**	**(9,308)**
Cash & equivalent............................	3,134		21,680
Inventories......................................	5,729		5,532
Accounts receivable........................	159,371		107,178
Current assets.................................	170,675		136,451
Long-term investments...................	469		678
Fixed assets, net.............................	53,689		54,965
Intangibles, net................................	9,145		13,360
Total assets...................................	**233,978**	**+14**	**205,454**
Accts. pay. & accr. liabs..................	57,893		34,869
Current liabilities.............................	70,591		84,735
Long-term debt, gross......................	182,682		165,751
Long-term debt, net.........................	181,245		123,878
Long-term lease liabilities................	21,884		23,852
Preferred share equity.....................	141,930		141,933
Shareholders' equity........................	(42,229)		(29,250)
Cash from oper. activs...................	**(15,987)**	**n.a.**	**2,217**
Cash from fin. activs........................	(1,165)		(9,790)
Cash from invest. activs...................	(1,394)		(1,224)
Net cash position...........................	**3,134**	**-86**	**21,680**
Capital expenditures........................	(2,099)		(1,500)
Capital disposals.............................	788		1,678
	$		$
Earnings per share*.........................	(0.11)		(0.08)
Cash flow per share*.......................	(0.15)		0.02
	shs		shs
No. of shs. o/s*................................	110,001,239		109,992,668
Avg. no. of shs. o/s*.........................	110,000,472		109,992,668
	%		%
Net profit margin.............................	(2.06)		(2.39)
Return on equity..............................	n.m.		n.m.
Return on assets.............................	2.04		3.15
No. of employees (FTEs)..................	3,100		2,400

* Common
[A] Reported in accordance with IFRS

Latest Results

Periods ended:	3m Mar. 31/23[A]		3m Mar. 31/22[A]
	$000s	%Chg	$000s
Operating revenue...........................	150,479	+37	109,848
Net inc. bef. disc. opers...................	(3,325)	n.a.	(7,783)
Income from disc. opers..................	nil		(13)
Net income......................................	(3,325)	n.a.	(7,796)
	$		$
Earnings per share*.........................	(0.03)		(0.07)

* Common
[A] Reported in accordance with IFRS

Historical Summary
(as originally stated)

Fiscal Year	Oper. Rev. $000s	Net Inc. Bef. Disc. $000s	EPS* $
2022^A	604,673	(12,431)	(0.11)
2021^A	389,402	(9,296)	(0.08)
2020^A	393,121	3,469	0.03
2019^A	464,252	(6,652)	(0.06)
2018^A	378,332	(30,072)	(0.28)

* Common
^A Reported in accordance with IFRS

F.3 FLYHT Aerospace Solutions Ltd.

Symbol - FLY **Exchange** - TSX-VEN **CUSIP** - 30252U
Head Office - 500-1212 31 Ave NE, Calgary, AB, T2E 7S8 **Telephone** - (403) 250-9956 **Toll-free** - (866) 250-9956 **Fax** - (403) 291-9717
Website - www.flyht.com
Email - aforbes@flyht.com
Investor Relations - Alana Forbes (866) 250-9956
Auditors - KPMG LLP C.A., Calgary, Alta.
Lawyers - TingleMerrett LLP, Calgary, Alta.
Transfer Agents - Odyssey Trust Company
Profile - (Can. 2003 amalg.) Designs, develops and provides real-time monitoring, management and reporting information systems and safety products for the aerospace industry.

The company's airborne hardware products include Automated Flight Information Reporting System (AFIRS™) Family, a collection of avionics installed on aircrafts that captures and monitors hundreds of essential functions from aircraft including data recorded by the aircraft's black box. AFIRS™ transmits this information in real-time to the company's servers to power solutions such as real-time fleet visualizations and fleet wide actionable intelligence. AFIRS™ Family includes AFIRS 228™, AFIRS Edge™ and AFIRS Controller. Hardware products also include Water Vapour Sensing System (FLYHT-WVSS-II), an externally mounted aircraft sensor that detects and reports water vapour as relative humidity; and Tropospheric Airborne Meteorological Data Reporting system (TAMDAR), a unique sensor device installed on aircraft that captures temperature, atmospheric pressure, winds aloft, icing, turbulence and relative humidity.

The company also offers actionable intelligence solutions that use the data collected by the AFIRS™ avionics systems to provide valuable business intelligence for aircraft operators to use in streamlining and optimizing operations and proactively enhancing safety. Offerings include aircraft health monitoring solution that supports real-time monitoring of operational status of an entire fleet of aircraft, as well as prognostics, diagnostics and maintenance recommendations for aircrafts; Auxiliary Power Unit (APU) management, which provide real-time data on APU usage and notifications of APU over-use to be able to make real-time adjustments; FuelSense™, an application that provides insight to an airline's management and usage of fuel; FleetWatch™, which is used by airlines for real-time fleet management to allow global tracking and alerting and to track aircraft through the entire flight; ClearPort™, which provides a clear view into the status of an aircraft in a turn; AviationDW, a managed data warehouse, tailor-made for use with the client's backend system, allowing for the generation of key performance indicators and data analysis based on historical data; Aircraft Fleet View, a native application that gives a real-time view of airline fleet status; and AirCraft Systems Investigation Software (ACSIS), an aircraft maintenance, troubleshooting and engineering tool that alerts the client's maintenance personnel about any problem experienced by the fleet's systems or components and helps them find a solution.

The company also provides two-way text messaging to the flight deck through the multi-control display unit (MCDU) or an iPad application where updated crew assignments, crew repositioning and tail swaps can be sent to the aircraft directly and in real-time. The company's latest auxiliary hardware products provide both power and connectivity to the devices used by pilots to create a secure, reliable platform for Electronic Flight Bags (EFBs). The AFIRS™ voice solution uses the Iridium satellite constellation with global coverage and an onboard satellite phone to provide a rapid and reliable private satcom channel to the flight deck. The company's communication solutions also include long range satellite communication (satcom), as well as Air Traffic Safety (ATS) Services voice, providing a higher performance alternative to that of legacy High Frequency (HF) communications. The AFIRS 228™ TSO is a TSO-C159b certified Iridium satcom solution providing the aircraft with reliable FANS 1/A, ADS-C, CPDLC and ACARS over Iridium messaging Capabilities. The AFIRS Edge™ includes 5G/4G/3G cellular capabilities, a modular Iridium Certus satcom, and the ability to integrate with existing onboard broadband solutions.

Through wholly owned **CrossConsense GmbH & Co. KG**, assists the aviation industry in using and applying SWISS Aviation's comprehensive Aircraft Maintenance and Engineering Operating System (AMOS) software solution for maintenance, engineering and logistics needs, including required hardware, database and 1st and 2nd level application support. In addition to maintenance system software solutions, CrossConsense provides data migration services for customers transitioning from other maintenance, repair and overhaul (MRO) platforms to AMOS, business intelligence and customization services, and consulting services.

In March 2022, the company acquired Frankfurt, Germany-based **CrossConsense GmbH & Co. KG**, which develops and markets software to support commercial aviation maintenance management, for $1,250,000 cash and issuance of 1,900,000 common shares. CrossConsense's products include a predictive maintenance troubleshooting and engineering tool; software to support aircraft maintenance, repair and data migration; and live data dashboards to assist aircraft maintenance teams. CrossConsense also offers consulting and support services as well as hosting, database operation and performance monitoring of commercial aircraft maintenance applications.

Predecessor Detail - Name changed from AeroMechanical Services Ltd., May 17, 2012.

Directors - Capt. Mary I. McMillan, chr., Grass Valley, Calif.; Michael W. (Mike) Brown, Nanaimo, B.C.; Dr. Peter (Pete) Large, Westminster, Calif.; Douglas G. (Doug) Marlin, Calgary, Alta.; Brent Rosenthal, Livingston, N.J.; Paul Takalo, Calgary, Alta.; Nancy N. Young, Chevy Chase, Md.

Other Exec. Officers - Kent Jacobs, pres. & interim CEO; Alana Forbes, CFO; Gurjot Bhullar, v-p, opers.; Scott Chambers, v-p, sales & mktg.; Darryl Deane, v-p, solutions; Michael Fang, v-p, China opers.; Murray Skelton, v-p, bus. devel.; Derek Taylor, v-p, strategic opportunities

Capital Stock

	Authorized (shs.)	Outstanding (shs.)[1]
Class A Preferred	unlimited	nil
Class B Preferred	unlimited	nil
Class C Preferred	unlimited	nil
Common	unlimited	38,806,774

[1] At May 10, 2023

Major Shareholder - Bleichroeder LP held 16.74% interest at Apr. 6, 2023.

Price Range - FLY/TSX-VEN

Year	Volume	High	Low	Close
2022	4,422,811	$1.19	$0.60	$1.15
2021	7,764,286	$1.14	$0.56	$0.74
2020	11,867,177	$1.88	$0.39	$0.68
2019	4,854,939	$1.90	$0.97	$1.30
2018	7,041,775	$2.05	$0.94	$1.00

Recent Close: $0.80

Capital Stock Changes - During 2022, common shares were issued as follows: 1,900,000 pursuant to the acquisition of CrossConsense GmbH & Co. KG and 487,598 on exercise of options.

Wholly Owned Subsidiaries

AeroMechanical Services USA Inc., United States. Inactive.
CrossConsense GmbH & Co. KG, Germany.
CrossConsense Services GmbH, Germany.
FLYHT Germany GmbH, Germany.
Flyht Corp., Canada. Inactive.
Flyht Inc., United States.
Flyht India Corp., Canada. Inactive.

Financial Statistics

Periods ended:	12m Dec. 31/22^A	%Chg	12m Dec. 31/21^A
	$000s	%Chg	$000s
Operating revenue	**23,879**	**+111**	**11,319**
Cost of sales	8,673		4,849
Salaries & benefits	10,208		8,740
Research & devel. expense	60		(47)
General & admin expense	4,508		2,121
Stock-based compensation	179		194
Operating expense	**23,628**	**+49**	**15,857**
Operating income	**251**	**n.a.**	**(4,538)**
Deprec., depl. & amort.	660		693
Finance income	40		104
Finance costs, gross	624		732
Pre-tax income	**(1,003)**	**n.a.**	**(5,859)**
Net income	**(1,003)**	**n.a.**	**(5,859)**
Cash & equivalent	2,648		4,521
Inventories	1,385		1,683
Accounts receivable	5,127		1,590
Current assets	9,630		8,323
Fixed assets, net	2,839		2,813
Intangibles, net	2,754		264
Total assets	**16,540**	**+25**	**13,250**
Accts. pay. & accr. liabs	2,736		1,703
Current liabilities	5,311		3,351
Long-term debt, gross	4,878		4,456
Long-term debt, net	4,049		3,792
Long-term lease liabilities	2,273		2,129
Shareholders' equity	4,895		3,965
Cash from oper. activs	**(1,238)**	**n.a.**	**(5,150)**
Cash from fin. activs	851		5,130
Cash from invest. activs	(1,523)		(598)
Net cash position	**2,648**	**-41**	**4,521**
Capital expenditures	(81)		(369)
	$		$
Earnings per share*	(0.03)		(0.19)
Cash flow per share*	(0.03)		(0.16)
	shs		shs
No. of shs. o/s*	38,804,474		36,416,876
Avg. no. of shs. o/s*	38,151,602		31,415,175
	%		%
Net profit margin	(4.20)		(51.76)
Return on equity	(22.64)		(171.57)
Return on assets	(2.54)		(38.00)
Foreign sales percent	88		83

* Common
^A Reported in accordance with IFRS

Latest Results

Periods ended:	3m Mar. 31/23^A	%Chg	3m Mar. 31/22^A
	$000s	%Chg	$000s
Operating revenue	4,757	-5	5,031
Net income	(1,657)	n.a.	(1,284)
	$		$
Earnings per share*	(0.04)		(0.03)

* Common
^A Reported in accordance with IFRS

Historical Summary
(as originally stated)

Fiscal Year	Oper. Rev. $000s	Net Inc. Bef. Disc. $000s	EPS* $
2022^A	23,879	(1,003)	(0.03)
2021^A	11,319	(5,859)	(0.19)
2020^A	13,653	(3,237)	(0.12)
2019^A	21,171	(747)	(0.04)
2018^A	13,591	(1,967)	(0.09)

* Common
^A Reported in accordance with IFRS

F.4 FP Newspapers Inc.

Symbol - FP **Exchange** - TSX-VEN **CUSIP** - 302586
Head Office - 2900-650 Georgia St W, PO Box 11583, Vancouver, BC, V6B 4N8 **Telephone** - (604) 681-8817 **Fax** - (604) 681-8861
Website - www.fpnewspapers.com
Email - dave.kreklewetz@freepress.mb.ca
Investor Relations - Dave Kreklewetz (204) 771-1897
Auditors - PricewaterhouseCoopers LLP C.A., Winnipeg, Man.
Transfer Agents - TSX Trust Company, Toronto, Ont.
Employees - 364 at May 18, 2023
Profile - (Can. 2010) Holds interests in Manitoba based news and media publications that are available in both print and digital formats.

Through its 49% investment in **FP Canadian Newspapers Limited Partnership** (FPLP), interests are held in the Winnipeg Free Press, along with several other Manitoba based news and media publications that are available in both print and digital formats.

Newspapers and related businesses include the Winnipeg Free Press which publishes six days a week for delivery to subscribers and single copy sales, and publishes a single copy edition on Sundays; the Brandon

Sun which publishes six days a week, serving Brandon and the surrounding area of southwestern Manitoba; the Canstar Community News which publishes two community newspapers weekly in Winnipeg; and the Carillon which is a weekly paid newspaper serving Steinbach and southeastern Manitoba.

Predecessor Detail - Succeeded FP Newspapers Income Fund, Dec. 31, 2010, pursuant to plan of arrangement whereby FP Newspapers Inc. was formed to facilitate the conversion of the fund into a corporation and the fund was subsequently dissolved.

Directors - Robert (Bob) Silver, chr., Winnipeg, Man.; G. Stephen Dembroski, Toronto, Ont.; Daniel Friedman, Man.; Darryl E. Levy, Winnipeg, Man.; Aldo Santin, Winnipeg, Man.; Deanna Traa, Winnipeg, Man.

Other Exec. Officers - Michael (Mike) Power, pres. & CEO; Dave Kreklewetz, v-p, fin. & CFO

Capital Stock

	Authorized (shs.)	Outstanding (shs.)[1]
Preferred	1	1
Common	unlimited	6,902,592

[1] At Apr. 19, 2023

Preferred - Held by FPCN Media Management Inc. Entitled to elect one-third of the company's board of directors. Redeemable at $1.00 per share if Canstar Publications Ltd. and Kimberley Anne Holdings Inc. cease to own at least 10% of FP Canadian Newspapers Limited Partnership. One vote per share.

Common - One vote per share.

Major Shareholder - Ronald N. Stern held 29% interest at Apr. 19, 2023.

Price Range - FP/TSX-VEN

Year	Volume	High	Low	Close
2022	904,758	$1.48	$0.70	$0.76
2021	628,383	$1.50	$0.54	$1.38
2020	412,075	$0.66	$0.20	$0.62
2019	582,942	$0.59	$0.07	$0.38
2018	1,364,759	$0.14	$0.08	$0.10

Recent Close: $0.80

Capital Stock Changes - There were no changes to capital stock from 2011 to 2022, inclusive.

Investments

49% int. in **FP Canadian Newspapers Limited Partnership**, B.C.
• 100% int. in **Derksen Printers Ltd.**, Steinbach, Man.
49% int. in **FPCN General Partner Inc.**, Canada.

Financial Statistics

Periods ended:	12m Dec. 30/22[A]		12m Dec. 30/21[A]
	$000s	%Chg	$000s
Total revenue	**887**	**-14**	**1,027**
General & admin. expense	196		180
Operating expense	**196**	**+9**	**180**
Operating income	**691**	**-18**	**847**
Pre-tax income	**691**	**-18**	**847**
Income taxes	387		(19)
Net income	**304**	**-65**	**866**
Cash & equivalent	106		289
Accounts receivable	3		3
Current assets	130		299
Long-term investments	8,328		8,486
Total assets	**8,458**	**-4**	**8,785**
Accts. pay. & accr. liabs	49		49
Current liabilities	49		680
Shareholders' equity	8,117		7,813
Cash from oper. activs	**(183)**	**n.a.**	**228**
Net cash position	**106**	**-63**	**289**
	$		$
Earnings per share*	0.04		0.13
Cash flow per share*	(0.03)		0.03
	shs		shs
No. of shs. o/s*	6,902,592		6,902,592
Avg. no. of shs. o/s*	6,902,592		6,902,592
	%		%
Net profit margin	34.27		84.32
Return on equity	3.82		11.73
Return on assets	3.53		10.21

* Common
[A] Reported in accordance with IFRS

Latest Results

Periods ended:	3m Mar. 30/23[A]		3m Mar. 31/22[A]
	$000s	%Chg	$000s
Total revenue	(3,909)	n.a.	605
Net income	(3,950)	n.a.	297
	$		$
Earnings per share*	(0.57)		0.04

* Common
[A] Reported in accordance with IFRS

Historical Summary
(as originally stated)

Fiscal Year	Total Rev.	Net Inc. Bef. Disc.	EPS*
	$000s	$000s	$
2022[A]	887	304	0.04
2021[A]	1,027	866	0.13
2020[A]	5,609	3,984	0.58
2019[A]	2,176	1,444	0.21
2018[A]	1,187	(1,965)	(0.28)

* Common
[A] Reported in accordance with IFRS

F.5 FRNT Financial Inc.

Symbol - FRNT **Exchange** - TSX-VEN **CUSIP** - 30322H
Head Office - Unit 200, 49 Wellington St E, Toronto, ON, M5E 1C9
Toll-free - (833) 222-3768
Website - www.frnt.io
Email - jackie.kelly@frnt.io
Investor Relations - Jackie Kelly (833) 222-3768
Auditors - Baker Tilly WM LLP C.A., Vancouver, B.C.
Transfer Agents - Odyssey Trust Company, Toronto, Ont.

Profile - (Can. 2018) Provides a capital markets trading platform for institutional investors to access alternative trade opportunities, such as cryptocurrency.

FRNT is a next generation institutional sales and trading platform. The company plans to present a new set of opportunities, primarily through synthetic exposure to cryptocurrency, targeted to institutional investors. Offers the following products/services: OTC derivatives; technology licensing around deliverable services; and research and consulting.

OTC Derivatives - The company plans to offer bilateral OTC contracts and trading services to institutional investors, in the form of fully-collateralized contracts for difference (CFDs) exclusively on specific indices. A CFD is an accepted derivatives product that allows clients to become economically exposed to the price movement of an underlying instrument, asset, or sector (such as a share, index, market sector, currency pair, treasury, or commodity) without the need for ownership and physical settlement of the underlying instrument or asset.

Licensing of Deliverable Trading Technology - The company enters into licensing agreements with a variety of different trading firms to licence front and back-end trading technology. Trading firms then utilize the technology to operate their trading desks and the company typically receives a fixed or floating rate based on the amount of notional trading volume transacted through such platforms.

Research and Consulting - The company engages in agreements where it allows firms to reproduce and distribute its research.

On May 12, 2022, common shares were listed on the Frankfurt Stock Exchange under the symbol XZ3.

Directors - Stéphane Ouellette, co-founder & CEO, Ont.; Adam Rabie, co-founder, Nassau, Bahamas; R. Geoffrey (Geoff) Browne, Toronto, Ont.; Daniel (Dan) Cristall, Calgary, Alta.; Eric Richmond, Ont.

Other Exec. Officers - Dr. David Washburn, pres.; Alexander (Alex) McAulay, CFO & corp. sec.; Brandon Collins, co-chief tech. officer; Stephen Vo Van, co-chief tech. officer

Capital Stock

	Authorized (shs.)	Outstanding (shs.)[1]
Common	unlimited	35,149,329

[1] At Nov. 28, 2022

Major Shareholder - Stéphane Ouellette held 30.75% interest, Adam Rabie held 22.15% interest and Coinsquare Ltd. held 11.43% interest at July 8, 2022.

Price Range - FRNT/TSX-VEN

Year	Volume	High	Low	Close
2022	2,949,496	$2.37	$0.30	$0.34

Recent Close: $0.35

Capital Stock Changes - On Apr. 19, 2022, an initial public offering of 4,000,000 common shares was completed at $1.50 per share.

Wholly Owned Subsidiaries

FRNT Asset Management Inc., Ont.
FRNT Financial UK Limited, United Kingdom.

Investments

2.47% int. in **Paradox Fund**, Cayman Islands.

Financial Statistics

Periods ended:	12m June 30/22[A]		12m June 30/21[A]
	$000s	%Chg	$000s
Operating revenue	**293**	**+166**	**110**
Salaries & benefits	1,007		487
General & admin expense	1,625		668
Stock-based compensation	635		1,826
Operating expense	**3,267**	**+10**	**2,981**
Operating income	**(2,974)**	**n.a.**	**(2,871)**
Deprec., depl. & amort.	53		2
Finance costs, gross	25		10
Write-downs/write-offs	nil		(54)
Pre-tax income	**(2,727)**	**n.a.**	**(2,066)**
Net income	**(2,727)**	**n.a.**	**(2,066)**
Cash & equivalent	5,109		5,428
Accounts receivable	3,006		44
Current assets	8,310		5,496
Fixed assets, net	29		7
Right-of-use assets	276		nil
Total assets	**8,639**	**+57**	**5,503**
Accts. pay. & accr. liabs	264		323
Current liabilities	558		543
Long-term debt, gross	263		255
Long-term debt, net	35		35
Shareholders' equity	7,870		4,926
Cash from oper. activs	**(3,243)**	**n.a.**	**(777)**
Cash from fin. activs	5,004		3,643
Cash from invest. activs	146		(2,010)
Net cash position	**3,404**	**+127**	**1,498**
Capital expenditures	(29)		(9)
	$		$
Earnings per share*	(0.09)		(0.08)
Cash flow per share*	(0.10)		(0.03)
	shs		shs
No. of shs. o/s*	35,149,329		31,149,329
Avg. no. of shs. o/s*	32,015,082		27,225,524
	%		%
Net profit margin	(930.72)		n.m.
Return on equity	(42.62)		(63.49)
Return on assets	(38.21)		(55.30)
Foreign sales percent	2		n.a.

* Common
[A] Reported in accordance with IFRS

Latest Results

Periods ended:	3m Sept. 30/22[A]		3m Sept. 30/21[A]
	$000s	%Chg	$000s
Operating revenue	191	+582	28
Net income	(477)	n.a.	(100)
	$		$
Earnings per share*	(0.01)		(0.00)

* Common
[A] Reported in accordance with IFRS

Historical Summary
(as originally stated)

Fiscal Year	Oper. Rev.	Net Inc. Bef. Disc.	EPS*
	$000s	$000s	$
2022[A]	293	(2,727)	(0.09)
2021[A]	110	(2,066)	(0.08)
2020[A]	104	(359)	(0.01)

* Common
[A] Reported in accordance with IFRS

F.6 FRX Innovations Inc.

Symbol - FRXI **Exchange** - TSX-VEN **CUSIP** - 30326X
Head Office - 200 Turnpike Rd, Chelmsford, MA, United States, 01824
Telephone - (978) 244-9500 **Fax** - (978) 250-4533
Website - www.frx-innovations.com
Email - mlebel@frxpolymers.com
Investor Relations - Marc-Andre Lebel (508) 335-5215
Auditors - MNP LLP C.A., Toronto, Ont.
Transfer Agents - Odyssey Trust Company, Toronto, Ont.
Employees - 21 at Nov. 25, 2022

Profile - (Can. 2020) Has developed Nofia®, a patented technology that produces halogen-free, non-leaching flame retardant additives used in textiles, automotive interiors, consumer electronics and next generation recyclable plastic.

Nofia® products are manufactured at a facility in Antwerp, Belgium. Product types include: Nofia® homopolymers which are transparent and high flowing polymers used in polyesters; Nofia® copolymers which are polyphosphonate-co-carbonates with good impact resistance used for consumer electronics; and Nofia® oligomers which are phosphorus based additives with phenolic end groups used for flame retarding thermoset resins such as printed circuit boards and dispersion in coatings.

On Sept. 1, 2022, common shares were listed on the Frankfurt Stock Exchange under the symbol W2A.

Common reinstated on TSX-VEN, July 18, 2023.

Common suspended from TSX-VEN, July 13, 2023.

Recent Merger and Acquisition Activity

Status: completed **Revised:** May 16, 2022

UPDATE: The transaction was completed. Good2GoRTO issued a total of 77,709,391 post-consolidated common shares. PREVIOUS: Good2GoRTO Corp. entered into a letter of intent for the Qualifying Transaction reverse takeover acquisition of Chemlsford, Mass.-based FRX Polymers, Inc., which manufactures halogen-free, polymeric flame retardent for used in textiles, automotive interiors, consumer electronics and next generation recyclable plastic. The basis of share consideration would be subsequently disclosed upon entering into a definitive agreement. Nov. 2, 2021 - A definitive agreement was entered into. The basis of share consideration was 1.0767 Good2GoRTO post-consolidated common shares for each FRX share held (following a proposed 1-for-3.5 share consolidation). Upon completion, FRX would amalgamate with Good2GoRTO's wholly owned 13448061 Canada Inc., and Good2GoRTO would change its name to FRX Innovations Inc.

Predecessor Detail - Name changed from Good2GoRTO Corp., May 16, 2022, pursuant to the Qualifying Transaction reverse takeover acquisition of FRX Polymers, Inc. and concurrent amalgamation of FRX with wholly owned 13448061 Canada Inc.; basis 1 new for 3.5 old shs.

Directors - Ross Haghighat, chr., Mass.; Marc-Andre Lebel, pres. & CEO, Orleans, Mass.; Mark Lotz, CFO & corp. sec., Vancouver, B.C.; James C. (Jim) Cassina, Nassau, Bahamas; Frank R. Hallam, Burnaby, B.C.; Dr. Bernhard Mohr, Germany; Ekaterina Terskin, Gaithersburg, Md.; Fanglu Wang, Hong Kong, People's Republic of China

Other Exec. Officers - Dr. Mike Goode, chief comml. officer; Dr. Ulrich Girrbach, v-p, fiber & textiles; Ina Jiang, v-p, sales & mktg.; Dr. Xiudong Sun, v-p, research & applications

Capital Stock

	Authorized (shs.)	Outstanding (shs.)[1]
Common	unlimited	79,994,865

[1] At Sept. 30, 2022

Major Shareholder - CITIC Capital Silk Road Fund, LP held 26.04% interest and Evonik Industries AG held 12.39% interest at May 24, 2022.

Price Range - FRXI/TSX-VEN

Year	Volume	High	Low	Close
2022	2,958,938	$0.75	$0.22	$0.26

Recent Close: $0.17

Capital Stock Changes - On May 16, 2022, common shares were consolidated on a 1-for-3.5 basis (effective on the TSX Venture Exchange May 24, 2022), 77,709,391 post-consolidated common shares were issued pursuant to the Qualifying Transaction reverse takeover acquisition of FRX Polymers, Inc. and 636,781 units (1 post-consolidated common share & ½ warrant) were issued as finder's fee, with warrants exercisable at Cdn$1.15 per share for two years.

Wholly Owned Subsidiaries

FRX Polymer (Canada) Inc., Canada.

FRX Polymers, Inc., Chelmsford, Mass.

- 100% int. in **FRX Polymer (Europe) N.V.**, Belgium.
- 100% int. in **FRX (Shanghai) Consulting Co. Ltd.**, People's Republic of China.

Financial Statistics

Periods ended:	12m Dec. 31/21[A1]		12m Dec. 31/20[B]
	US$000s	%Chg	US$000s
Operating revenue	**6,120**	**+16**	**5,277**
Cost of goods sold	7,109		6,598
Research & devel. expense	763		841
General & admin expense	1,914		853
Operating expense	**9,786**	**+18**	**8,293**
Operating income	**(3,666)**	**n.a.**	**(3,016)**
Deprec., depl. & amort.	1,098		1,145
Finance income	nil		8
Finance costs, gross	1,417		1,177
Write-downs/write-offs	(25)		(194)
Pre-tax income	**(8,732)**	**n.a.**	**(6,187)**
Net income	**(8,732)**	**n.a.**	**(6,187)**
Cash & equivalent	453		547
Inventories	1,419		1,159
Accounts receivable	2,270		2,663
Current assets	4,446		4,728
Fixed assets, net	19,143		21,822
Right-of-use assets	510		569
Intangibles, net	803		760
Total assets	**21,021**	**-25**	**27,879**
Accts. pay. & accr. liabs	1,974		1,529
Current liabilities	4,099		2,786
Long-term debt, gross	26,800		22,736
Long-term debt, net	25,530		22,699
Long-term lease liabilities	504		564
Shareholders' equity	(7,644)		384
Non-controlling interest	(539)		(545)
Cash from oper. activs	**(3,379)**	**n.a.**	**(2,911)**
Cash from fin. activs	3,368		906
Cash from invest. activs	(122)		(145)
Net cash position	**453**	**-17**	**547**
Capital expenditures	(17)		(55)
	US$		US$
Earnings per share*	(0.35)		(0.26)
Cash flow per share*	(0.14)		(0.12)
	shs		shs
No. of shs. o/s	n.a.		n.a.
Avg. no. of shs. o/s*	24,931,780		23,949,685
	%		%
Net profit margin	(142.68)		(117.24)
Return on equity	n.m.		(167.94)
Return on assets	(29.92)		(17.58)

* Common

[A] Reported in accordance with IFRS

[B] Reported in accordance with U.S. GAAP

[1] Results prior to May 16, 2022, pertain to and reflect the Qualifying Transaction reverse takeover acquisition of FRX Polymers, Inc.

Latest Results

Periods ended:	9m Sept. 30/22[A]		9m Sept. 30/21[A]
	US$000s	%Chg	US$000s
Operating revenue	2,803	-30	3,978
Net income	(10,948)	n.a.	(5,724)
	US$		US$
Earnings per share*	(0.29)		(0.24)

* Common

[A] Reported in accordance with IFRS

Historical Summary
(as originally stated)

Fiscal Year	Oper. Rev. US$000s	Net Inc. Bef. Disc. US$000s	EPS* US$
2021[A]	6,120	(8,732)	(0.35)
2020[B]	5,277	(6,187)	(0.26)
2019[B]	5,627	(8,068)	(0.34)

* Common

[A] Reported in accordance with IFRS

[B] Reported in accordance with U.S. GAAP

Note: Adjusted throughout for 1-for-3.5 cons. in May 2022

F.7 FSD Pharma Inc.

Symbol - HUGE **Exchange** - CSE **CUSIP** - 35954B

Head Office - 4000-199 Bay St, Toronto, ON, M5L 1A9 **Telephone** - (289) 677-0806 **Fax** - (905) 373-0303

Website - www.fsdpharma.com

Email - zsaeed@fsdpharma.com

Investor Relations - Zeeshan Saeed (416) 854-8884

Auditors - MNP LLP C.A., Toronto, Ont.

Lawyers - Blake, Cassels & Graydon LLP

Transfer Agents - Marrelli Trust Company Limited, Vancouver, B.C.

Employees - 17 at Dec. 31, 2022

Profile - (Ont. 1998 amalg.) Researches and develops therapeutics for neurodegenerative diseases, and proprietary formulation of natural ingredients, vitamins and minerals to help with liver and brain function for quickly relieving effects of alcohol consumption.

Pipeline of drug candidates include: Lucid-MS (Lucid-21-302), a patented, proprietary neuroprotective new chemical entity (NCE) that has demonstrated in preclinical models the potential to reverse and prevent myelin degradation, an underlying cause of multiple sclerosis and other neurodegenerative disorders; Lucid-PSYCH (Lucid-201), a novel psychedelic compound under preclinical studies for the treatment of major depressive disorder (MDD); and UNBUZZD™, a proprietary formulation of natural ingredients, vitamins, and minerals to help with liver and brain function for the purposes of potentially quickly relieving from the effects of alcohol consumption, such as inebriation, and restoring normal lifestyle.

In August 2023, the company has signed a definitive agreement with **Celly Nutrition Inc.** (Celly Nu), whereby the company has granted Celly Nu an exclusive rights to recreational applications for the company's alcohol misuse technology and launch UNBUZZD™ which is a revolutionary rapid alcohol detoxification drink.

In June 2023, the company terminated the clinical development of ultra-micronized palmitoylethanolamide (PEA) or FSD-PEA (also known as FSD-201) for the treatment of inflammatory diseases and put on hold any further clinical development of Lucid-PSYCH for mental health disorder as part of a strategic decision to focus efforts and allocate capital to the advancement of Lucid-MS and UNBUZZD™.

On Apr. 12, 2023, the company announced plans to complete a spin-out transaction via a plan of arrangement whereby shares of a newly formed wholly owned subsidiary would be separated into an independent public company. The spin-out transaction was expected to be completed in July 2023. Post-closing, the company would complete a reverse takeover transaction with a business that has yet to be identified. Subsequently on May 12, 2023, the company announced its continuous work towards the spin-out transaction and would schedule a special meeting to approve the spin-out separate from the June 29, 2023 shareholders meeting as one of its proposed assets to be included in the spin-out transaction which is necessary documentation for shareholder approval would not be ready in time for mailing deadline for the June 29, 2023 shareholders meeting.

In March 2023, wholly owned **FSD Pharma Australia Pty Ltd.** received certificate of approval from The Alfred Ethics Committee in Australia to proceed with a Phase 1 clinical trial of Lucid-201 (Lucid-Psych) as a novel drug candidate for the potential treatment of major depressive disorder.

In November 2022, the company created new subsidiary **FSD Pharma Australia Pty Ltd.**, which would be used to facilitate the company's development of certain compounds through Australian clinical trials.

In May 2022, the company created new subsidiary **FSD Strategic Investments Inc.**, which would focus on generating returns and cash flow through the issuance of loans secured by residential or commercial property, with FSD Strategic Investments having a first collateral mortgage on the secured property.

Recent Merger and Acquisition Activity

Status: completed **Revised:** May 6, 2022

UPDATE: The transaction was completed for Cdn$16,400,000. PREVIOUS: FSD Pharma Inc. agreed to sell its 620,000-sq.-ft. former Kraft® food manufacturing plant in Cobourg, Ont., together with the 64.43-acre property on which the facility is located, for Cdn$16,500,000. Of the total building space, 25,000 sq. ft. was operational and licensed for cannabis cultivation and processing. FSD Pharma, through wholly owned FV Pharma Inc., ceased its cannabis operations in September 2020.

Predecessor Detail - Name changed from Century Financial Capital Group Inc., May 24, 2018, following reverse takeover acquistion of FV Pharma Inc. and concurrent amalgamation of FV Pharma with wholly owned 2620756 Ontario Inc.

Directors - Anthony J. Durkacz, exec. co-chr., Toronto, Ont.; Zeeshan Saeed, exec. co-chr., pres. & CEO, Mississauga, Ont.; Dr. Lakshmi P. Kotra, pres., Lucid Psycheceuticals Inc., Ont.; Adnan Bashir, Ont.; Dr. Eric Hoskins, Toronto, Ont.; Nitin Kaushal, Richmond Hill, Ont.; Michael (Zappy) Zapolin, Mass.

Other Exec. Officers - Donal V. Carroll, COO; Nathan Coyle, CFO

Capital Stock

	Authorized (shs.)	Outstanding (shs.)[1]
Class A Multiple Vtg.	unlimited	72
Class B Subord. Vtg.	unlimited	39,040,614

[1] At July 20, 2023

Class A Multiple Voting - Entitled to dividends. Convertible, at any time at the holder's option, into class B subordinate voting shares on a one-for-one basis. 276,660 votes per share.

Class B Subordinate Voting - Entitled to dividends. Non-convertible. One vote per share.

Normal Course Issuer Bid - The company plans to make normal course purchases of up to 1,925,210 class B subordinate voting shares representing 5% of the total outstanding. The bid commenced on Jan. 18, 2023, and expires on Jan. 17, 2024.

Major Shareholder - Zeeshan Saeed held 15.06% interest, Anthony J. Durkacz held 13.78% interest and Dr. Raza Bokhari held 11.27% interest at May 15, 2023.

Price Range - HUGE/CSE

Year	Volume	High	Low	Close
2022	11,344,551	$1.41	$0.92	$1.04
2021	19,242,216	$5.25	$1.26	$1.32
2020	10,007,619	$15.10	$1.70	$1.99
2019	7,635,491	$89.45	$4.40	$7.11
2018	13,005,676	$188.94	$15.08	$57.29

Consolidation: 1-for-201 cons. in Oct. 2019

Recent Close: $1.68

Capital Stock Changes - During 2022, class B subordinate voting shares were issued as follows: 400,000 on conversion of performance share units and 158,144 as share-based compensation; 2,504,688 class B subordinate voting shares were cancelled.

Wholly Owned Subsidiaries

FSD Biosciences Inc., Toronto, Ont.
• 100% int. in **Prismic Pharmaceuticals Inc.**, Scottsdale, Ariz.
FSD Pharma Australia Pty Ltd., Australia.
FSD Strategic Investments Inc., Ont.
FV Pharma Inc., Cobourg, Ont.
Lucid Psycheceuticals Inc., Canada.

Investments

A2ZCryptocap Inc., Calgary, Alta. (see separate coverage)
Solarvest BioEnergy Inc., Vancouver, B.C. (see separate coverage)

Financial Statistics

Periods ended:	12m Dec. 31/22[A]		12m Dec. 31/21[A]
	US$000s	%Chg	US$000s
Salaries & benefits	2,782		2,529
Research & devel. expense	6,911		6,328
General & admin expense	12,991		13,544
Stock-based compensation	1,531		7,444
Operating expense	**24,215**	**-19**	**29,845**
Operating income	**(24,215)**	**n.a.**	**(29,845)**
Deprec., depl. & amort.	4,537		4,046
Finance costs, gross	49		69
Pre-tax income	**(26,704)**	**n.a.**	**(33,938)**
Net inc. bef. disc. opers	**(26,704)**	**n.a.**	**(33,938)**
Income from disc. opers	3,097		(1,347)
Net income	**(23,607)**	**n.a.**	**(35,285)**
Cash & equivalent	16,980		35,418
Accounts receivable	374		501
Current assets	17,850		45,933
Long-term investments	828		660
Fixed assets, net	106		nil
Right-of-use assets	155		168
Intangibles, net	12,040		16,202
Total assets	**38,411**	**-39**	**62,963**
Bank indebtedness	301		301
Accts. pay. & accr. liabs	7,108		7,511
Current liabilities	7,830		8,701
Long-term lease liabilities	38		131
Shareholders' equity	30,542		54,131
Cash from oper. activs	**(28,333)**	**n.a.**	**(20,746)**
Cash from fin. activs	(2,069)		38,212
Cash from invest. activs	12,123		269
Net cash position	**16,980**	**-52**	**35,260**
	US$		US$
Earns. per sh. bef disc opers*	(0.69)		(0.97)
Earnings per share*	(0.61)		(1.01)
Cash flow per share*	(0.73)		(0.59)
	shs		shs
No. of shs. o/s*	38,504,210		40,450,754
Avg. no. of shs. o/s*	38,732,381		34,945,210
	%		%
Net profit margin	n.a.		n.a.
Return on equity	(63.08)		(75.05)
Return on assets	(52.59)		(64.56)
No. of employees (FTEs)	17		10

* Cl.B Subord. Vtg.
[A] Reported in accordance with IFRS

Latest Results

Periods ended:	6m June 30/23[A]		6m June 30/22[A]
	US$000s	%Chg	US$000s
Net inc. bef. disc. opers	(15,448)	n.a.	(13,426)
Income from disc. opers	nil		3,097
Net income	(15,448)	n.a.	(10,330)
	US$		US$
Earns. per sh. bef. disc. opers.*	(0.39)		(0.34)
Earnings per share*	(0.39)		(0.26)

* Cl.B Subord. Vtg.
[A] Reported in accordance with IFRS

Historical Summary
(as originally stated)

Fiscal Year	Oper. Rev.	Net Inc. Bef. Disc.	EPS*
	US$000s	US$000s	US$
2022[A]	nil	(26,704)	(0.69)
2021[A]	nil	(33,938)	(0.97)
2020[A]	nil	(28,452)	(2.36)
	$000s	$000s	$
2019[A]	257	(52,013)	(7.37)
2018[A1]	nil	(22,711)	(3.82)

* Cl.B Subord. Vtg.
[A] Reported in accordance with IFRS
[1] Results reflect the May 24, 2018, reverse takeover acquisition of FV Pharma Inc.
Note: Adjusted throughout for 1-for-201 cons. in Oct. 2019

F.8 FTI Foodtech International Inc.

Symbol - FTI **Exchange** - TSX-VEN **CUSIP** - 30264T
Head Office - 156 Abbeywood Trail, Toronto, ON, M3B 3B7 **Telephone** - (416) 444-1058 **Fax** - (416) 444-9524
Website - www.fti-foodtech.com
Email - info@fti-foodtech.com
Investor Relations - William A. Hullah (416) 444-1058
Auditors - NVS Chartered Accountants Professional Corporation C.A., Markham, Ont.
Lawyers - Robert M. Isles, Toronto, Ont.
Transfer Agents - Computershare Trust Company of Canada Inc., Vancouver, B.C.
Profile - (Can. 2008; orig. B.C., 1978) Resells liquidation merchandise through barter exchanges and aims to integrate blockchain technology with the barter and food industries.
The company exchanges surplus goods inventory or liquidation goods on barter exchanges for which transactions are tendered using barter exchange dollars (barter credits).
Also sell personal protective equipment (PPE) such as disposable and fabric face masks, face shields, goggles, hand sanitizers, thermometers and safety supplies aimed to minimize the spared of Covid-19 virus. In addition, the company also markets and sells Covid-19 Antibody Test Kit worldwide.
Predecessor Detail - Name changed from Cold Lake Resources Inc., Dec. 11, 1985.
Directors - William A. Hullah, founder, pres. & CEO, Don Mills, Ont.; Dr. Linda Lakats, v-p & CFO, Toronto, Ont.; Joanne Strongman, West Vancouver, B.C.
Other Exec. Officers - Robert Isles, corp. sec.

Capital Stock

	Authorized (shs.)	Outstanding (shs.)[1]
Preferred	unlimited	nil
Common	unlimited	14,968,863

[1] At Mar. 1, 2023
Major Shareholder - William A. Hullah held 23.25% interest at Aug. 25, 2021.

Price Range - FTI/TSX-VEN

Year	Volume	High	Low	Close
2022	837,103	$0.18	$0.06	$0.09
2021	4,125,657	$0.18	$0.08	$0.10
2020	8,730,622	$0.52	$0.04	$0.14
2019	848,254	$0.15	$0.05	$0.07
2018	1,896,032	$0.80	$0.08	$0.08

Recent Close: $0.09
Capital Stock Changes - In November 2021, private placement of 1,000,000 units (1 common share & 1 warrant) at 10¢ per unit was completed.

Financial Statistics

Periods ended:	12m Mar. 31/22[A]		12m Mar. 31/21[A]
	$000s	%Chg	$000s
Operating revenue	**160**	**-18**	**195**
Cost of sales	76		149
General & admin expense	45		61
Stock-based compensation	nil		78
Operating expense	**120**	**-58**	**288**
Operating income	**40**	**n.a.**	**(93)**
Write-downs/write-offs	(24)		(3)
Pre-tax income	**21**	**n.a.**	**(85)**
Net income	**21**	**n.a.**	**(85)**
Cash & equivalent	25		49
Inventories	10		34
Accounts receivable	2		2
Current assets	209		198
Total assets	**321**	**+27**	**252**
Accts. pay. & accr. liabs	36		19
Current liabilities	36		19
Shareholders' equity	99		(22)
Cash from oper. activs	**(55)**	**n.a.**	**(70)**
Cash from fin. activs	31		91
Net cash position	**25**	**-49**	**49**
	$		$
Earnings per share*	0.00		(0.01)
Cash flow per share*	(0.00)		(0.00)
	shs		shs
No. of shs. o/s*	14,968,863		13,968,863
Avg. no. of shs. o/s*	14,968,863		13,968,863
	%		%
Net profit margin	13.13		(43.59)
Return on equity	n.m.		n.m.
Return on assets	7.33		(39.72)

* Common
[A] Reported in accordance with IFRS

Historical Summary
(as originally stated)

Fiscal Year	Oper. Rev.	Net Inc. Bef. Disc.	EPS*
	$000s	$000s	$
2022[A]	160	21	0.00
2021[A]	195	(85)	(0.01)
2020[A]	37	(12)	(0.00)
2019[A]	125	(279)	(0.02)
2018[A]	22	(406)	(0.03)

* Common
[A] Reported in accordance with IFRS

F.9 Fab-Form Industries Ltd.

Symbol - FBF **Exchange** - TSX-VEN **CUSIP** - 302735
Head Office - Unit 19, 1610 Derwent Way, Delta, BC, V3M 6W1 **Telephone** - (604) 596-3278 **Toll-free** - (888) 303-3278
Website - www.fab-form.com
Email - rick@fab-form.com
Investor Relations - Richard N. Fearn (604) 596-3278 ext. 101
Auditors - Culver & Co. C.A., Vancouver, B.C.
Lawyers - Preston Law, Vancouver, B.C.
Transfer Agents - Computershare Trust Company of Canada Inc., Vancouver, B.C.
Profile - (B.C. 1995) Develops, manufactures and distributes proprietary fabric forming systems used to form concrete footings, columns, foundations and walls for residential and commercial building structures in Canada and the U.S.
Products include Fastfoot®, which is made of high density polyethylene fabric that is used to replace lumber and plywood in forming concrete footings; Fast-Tube™, a fabric column form for forming round concrete columns; Monopour, a method that uses insulated concrete form (ICF) block to form the footing, thereby eliminating the need for footing forming lumber, stakes, cold joint and double pour; and Zont Twist™ Bracing, a bracing system that keeps ICF walls horizontally and vertically straight. The company's bracing system has various components including Zont Twist™ bracket, which is used to lock horizontal walers and vertical strongbacks in position to flatten the wall; Zuckle™ Wall Aligner, which is designed specifically for ICF walls and can be quickly adjusted using electric drill; ZAT, a bracket used in installing catwalk around the foundation forms; ZEE, an alternative bracket over T-Blocks; Zeveler, a bracket used to level up ICF wall on top of an uneven footing; and ZOTE, a durable steel bin that are ideal for moving Zonts, Zuckles and Zevelers around the jobsite.
Predecessor Detail - Name changed from Fastfoot Industries Ltd., Dec. 14, 2001; basis 1 new for 3 old shs.
Directors - Don Russell, acting chr. & CFO, Vancouver, B.C.; Richard N. (Rick) Fearn, pres. & CEO, White Rock, B.C.; Joey Fearn, COO, Vancouver, B.C.; Nigel Protter, Pemberton, B.C.
Other Exec. Officers - Vishwanath Kumar, corp. sec. & contr.

Capital Stock

	Authorized (shs.)	Outstanding (shs.)[1]
Preferred	100,000,000	nil
Common	100,000,000	9,084,036

[1] At June 30, 2022
Major Shareholder - Richard N. (Rick) Fearn held 34.88% interest at Apr. 25, 2022.

Price Range - FBF/TSX-VEN

Year	Volume	High	Low	Close
2022	1,102,394	$1.80	$0.85	$1.75
2021	1,660,208	$0.99	$0.38	$0.85
2020	1,122,390	$0.55	$0.16	$0.39
2019	1,117,868	$0.55	$0.27	$0.40
2018	1,407,136	$0.99	$0.33	$0.37

Recent Close: $1.56

Financial Statistics

Periods ended:	12m Dec. 31/21^A		12m Dec. 31/20^{oA}
	$000s	%Chg	$000s
Operating revenue	**4,424**	**+68**	**2,635**
Cost of sales	2,853		1,787
Salaries & benefits	191		229
General & admin expense	311		307
Operating expense	**3,356**	**+45**	**2,318**
Operating income	**1,068**	**+237**	**317**
Deprec., depl. & amort.	30		31
Finance costs, net	7,615		n.a.
Pre-tax income	**1,038**	**+244**	**302**
Income taxes	272		81
Net income	**766**	**+248**	**220**
Cash & equivalent	1,516		1,300
Inventories	801		547
Accounts receivable	449		213
Current assets	2,766		2,060
Fixed assets, net	71		70
Right-of-use assets	523		519
Intangibles, net	4		4
Total assets	**3,391**	**+27**	**2,664**
Accts. pay. & accr. liabs	142		335
Current liabilities	254		429
Long-term lease liabilities	418		426
Shareholders' equity	2,719		1,809
Cash from oper. activs	**356**	**-31**	**519**
Cash from fin. activs	(108)		(98)
Cash from invest. activs	(31)		1
Net cash position	**1,516**	**+17**	**1,300**
Capital expenditures	(14)		(15)
Capital disposals	nil		19
	$		$
Earnings per share*	0.09		0.03
Cash flow per share*	0.04		0.06
	shs		shs
No. of shs. o/s*	9,084,036		8,822,065
Avg. no. of shs. o/s*	8,867,991		8,822,065
	%		%
Net profit margin	17.31		8.35
Return on equity	33.83		12.95
Return on assets	25.30		9.54
Foreign sales percent	26		28

* Common
° Restated
^A Reported in accordance with IFRS

Latest Results

Periods ended:	6m June 30/22^A		6m June 30/21^A
	$000s	%Chg	$000s
Operating revenue	3,012	+50	2,002
Net income	654	+103	322
	$		$
Earnings per share*	0.07		0.04

* Common
^A Reported in accordance with IFRS

Historical Summary
(as originally stated)

Fiscal Year	Oper. Rev.	Net Inc. Bef. Disc.	EPS*
	$000s	$000s	$
2021^A	4,424	766	0.09
2020^A	2,635	220	0.03
2019^A	2,892	347	0.04
2018^A	2,820	337	0.04
2017^A	2,410	212	0.03

* Common
^A Reported in accordance with IFRS

F.10 Faction Investment Group Corp.

Symbol - FINV.P **Exchange** - TSX-VEN **CUSIP** - 303044
Head Office - 2160-650 Georgia St W, Vancouver, BC, V6B 4N7 **Telephone** - (778) 945-3948
Email - juppal@mackcapgroup.com
Investor Relations - Jeffrey Uppal (778) 945-3948
Auditors - Dale Matheson Carr-Hilton LaBonte LLP C.A., Vancouver, B.C.
Transfer Agents - Computershare Trust Company of Canada Inc., Vancouver, B.C.
Profile - (B.C. 2021) Capital Pool Company.
A proposed Qualifying Transaction reverse takeover acquisition of **IO Charge Innovations Inc.** was terminated in February 2023.
Common listed on TSX-VEN, Sept. 12, 2022.
Directors - Brandon Bonifacio, Vancouver, B.C.; Christopher (Chris) Mackay, Vancouver, B.C.; Craig Rollins, Vancouver, B.C.
Other Exec. Officers - Jeffrey Uppal, pres. & CEO; Geoffrey (Geoff) Lee, CFO & corp. sec.

Capital Stock

	Authorized (shs.)	Outstanding (shs.)[1]
Common	unlimited	9,900,000

[1] At June 19, 2023
Major Shareholder - Christopher (Chris) Mackay held 16.06% interest, Brandon Bonifacio held 10.1% interest and Jeffrey Uppal held 10% interest at June 19, 2023.

Price Range - FINV.P/TSX-VEN

Year	Volume	High	Low	Close
2022	101,000	$0.13	$0.07	$0.10

Recent Close: $0.10
Capital Stock Changes - On Sept. 12, 2022, an initial public offering of 2,500,000 common shares was completed at 10¢ per share.

F.11 Faircourt Gold Income Corp.

Symbol - FGX **Exchange** - NEO **CUSIP** - 30376T
Head Office - c/o Faircourt Asset Management Inc., 2107-120 Adelaide St W, Toronto, ON, M5H 1T1 **Telephone** - (416) 364-8989 **Toll-free** - (800) 831-0304
Website - www.faircourtassetmgt.com
Email - ctaerk@faircourtassetmgt.com
Investor Relations - Charles Taerk (800) 831-0304
Auditors - PricewaterhouseCoopers LLP C.A., Toronto, Ont.
Bankers - The Bank of Nova Scotia; Canadian Imperial Bank of Commerce
Lawyers - Stikeman Elliott LLP, Toronto, Ont.
Transfer Agents - TSX Trust Company, Toronto, Ont.
Managers - Faircourt Asset Management Inc., Toronto, Ont.
Profile - (Ont. 2007) Invests in common shares of companies included in the S&P/TSX Global Gold Index.
The company does not have a fixed termination date but may be terminated at any time by the manager with approval from shareholders.
The manager is entitled to a management fee at an annual rate of 1.10% of net asset value, calculated and payable monthly.
The company's top 10 long positions at Dec. 31, 2022 (as a percentage of net asset value):

Holding	Percentage
Agnico Eagle Mines Limited	11.33%
Barrick Gold Corporation	11.29%
Franco-Nevada Corporation	9.77%
K92 Mining Inc.	7.19%
Wheaton Precious Metals Corp.	7.01%
Endeavour Mining Corporation	6.47%
Dundee Precious Metals Inc.	5.38%
Alamos Gold Inc.	5.28%
SSR Mining Inc.	4.68%
Eldorado Gold Corporation	4.54%

Oper. Subsid./Mgt. Co. Directors - Charles Taerk, pres. & CEO, Toronto, Ont.; Douglas Waterson, CFO & portfolio mgr., Thornhill, Ont.

Capital Stock

	Authorized (shs.)	Outstanding (shs.)[1]
Class A	unlimited	2,774,104
Common	unlimited	100

[1] At Dec. 31, 2022
Class A - Entitled to a monthly distribution of $0.024 per share. Retractable in April of each year for a price equal to the net asset value per share less the amount which is the lesser of: (i) 25¢ per share; and (ii) the pro rata share of the aggregate of all brokerage fees, commissions and other costs. Retractable in any other month for a price equal to the lesser of: (i) 94% of the market price per share; and (ii) the closing market price per share less, in each case, the lesser of: (a) 25¢ per share; and (b) the pro rata share of the aggregate of all brokerage fees, commissions and other costs. Non-voting.
Common - Not entitled to dividends. Redeemable and retractable at $1.00 per share. Rank subsequent to class A shares with respect to distributions on the dissolution, liquidation or winding-up of the company. One vote per share.
Major Shareholder - FGX Trust held 100% interest at Mar. 27, 2023.

Price Range - FGX/NEO

Year	Volume	High	Low	Close
2022	97,700	$4.44	$2.80	$3.00
2021	67,800	$4.88	$3.50	$3.72
2020	67,300	$5.40	$1.70	$4.61
2019	65,800	$3.53	$2.51	$3.48
2018	1,280,855	$3.58	$2.32	$2.60

Recent Close: $2.65
Capital Stock Changes - During 2022, 190,700 class A shares were retracted.

Dividends

FGX cl A Ra $0.288 pa M est. July 16, 2018

Financial Statistics

Periods ended:	12m Dec. 31/22^A		12m Dec. 31/21^A
	$000s	%Chg	$000s
Realized invest. gain (loss)	(164)		1,803
Unrealized invest. gain (loss)	(1,140)		(4,363)
Total revenue	**(552)**	**n.a.**	**(1,687)**
General & admin. expense	343		419
Operating expense	**343**	**-18**	**419**
Operating income	**(895)**	**n.a.**	**(2,106)**
Finance costs, gross	84		65
Pre-tax income	**(979)**	**n.a.**	**(2,171)**
Net income	**(979)**	**n.a.**	**(2,171)**
Cash & equivalent	2,006		2,666
Investments	9,094		11,354
Total assets	**11,128**	**-21**	**14,129**
Accts. pay. & accr. liabs	265		187
Debt	1,700		2,200
Shareholders' equity	9,068		11,638
Cash from oper. activs	**1,436**	**-65**	**4,079**
Cash from fin. activs	(2,096)		(2,999)
Net cash position	**2,006**	**-25**	**2,666**
	$		$
Earnings per share*	(0.35)		(0.71)
Cash flow per share*	0.51		1.33
Net asset value per share*	3.27		3.93
Cash divd. per share*	0.24		0.29
	shs		shs
No. of shs. o/s*	2,774,104		2,964,804
Avg. no. of shs. o/s*	2,835,755		3,066,655
	%		%
Net profit margin	n.m.		n.m.
Return on equity	(9.46)		(15.65)
Return on assets	(7.09)		(12.61)

* Class A
^A Reported in accordance with IFRS

Note: Note: Net income reflects increase/decrease in net assets from operations.

Historical Summary
(as originally stated)

Fiscal Year	Total Rev.	Net Inc. Bef. Disc.	EPS*
	$000s	$000s	$
2022^A	(552)	(979)	(0.35)
2021^A	(1,687)	(2,171)	(0.71)
2020^A	5,488	4,939	1.43
2019^A	5,225	4,686	1.17
2018^A	(1,546)	(2,071)	(0.46)

* Class A
^A Reported in accordance with IFRS

F.12 Faircourt Split Trust

Symbol - FCS.UN **Exchange** - NEO **CUSIP** - 30376N
Head Office - c/o Faircourt Asset Management Inc., 2107-120 Adelaide St W, Toronto, ON, M5H 1T1 **Telephone** - (416) 364-8989 **Toll-free** - (800) 831-0304
Website - www.faircourtassetmgt.com
Email - ctaerk@faircourtassetmgt.com
Investor Relations - Charles Taerk (800) 831-0304
Auditors - PricewaterhouseCoopers LLP C.A., Toronto, Ont.
Bankers - The Bank of Nova Scotia; Canadian Imperial Bank of Commerce
Lawyers - Stikeman Elliott LLP, Toronto, Ont.
Transfer Agents - TSX Trust Company, Toronto, Ont.
Investment Advisors - Faircourt Asset Management Inc., Toronto, Ont.
Managers - Faircourt Asset Management Inc., Toronto, Ont.
Profile - (Ont. 2006) Invests in North American equities and income producing securities including common shares, income trusts, limited partnerships, real estate investment trusts, corporate and convertible bonds, preferred shares, other income funds and other yield generating investments.
The manager receives a management fee at an annual rate equal to 1.1% of the net asset value calculated daily and payable monthly in arrears and a service fee at an annual rate equal to 0.40% of the net asset value.
Top 10 long positions at Dec. 31, 2022 (as a percentage of net assets):

Holdings	Percentage
Waste Connections Inc.	9.54%
InterRent REIT	8.17%
Brookfield Infrastructure Partners LP	7.81%
Rexford Industrial Realty Inc.	6.56%
Dream Industrial REIT	5.80%
Fortis Inc.	5.38%
Invesco DB US$ Index Bullish Fund	5.34%
Brookfield Corporation, class A	5.28%
Costco Wholesale Corporation	4.39%
Walmart Inc.	3.41%

Oper. Subsid./Mgt. Co. Directors - Charles Taerk, pres. & CEO, Toronto, Ont.; Douglas Waterson, CFO & portfolio mgr., Thornhill, Ont.

Capital Stock

	Authorized (shs.)	Outstanding (shs.)[1]
Trust Unit	unlimited	816,092

[1] At Dec. 31, 2022

Trust Unit - Entitled to monthly cash distributions of 6¢ per unit. Retractable in June of each year for an amount equal to the net asset value per unit, less any costs associated with the retraction. One vote per trust unit.

Major Shareholder - Widely held at Mar. 27, 2023.

Price Range - FCS.UN/NEO

Year	Volume	High	Low	Close
2022	19,900	$6.50	$2.94	$3.10
2021	14,500	$5.90	$5.11	$5.50
2020	7,000	$6.17	$5.15	$5.31
2019	23,700	$6.25	$4.65	$5.59
2018	462,285	$6.22	$4.05	$4.05

Recent Close: $3.02

Capital Stock Changes - There were no changes to capital stock during 2022.

Dividends

FCS.UN unit Ra $0.18 pa M est. Aug. 4, 2022
Prev. Rate: $0.72 est. Apr. 6, 2017

Financial Statistics

Periods ended:	12m Dec. 31/22[A]		12m Dec. 31/21[A]
	$000s	%Chg	$000s
Realized invest. gain (loss)	67		317
Unrealized invest. gain (loss)	(864)		102
Total revenue	**(762)**	**n.a.**	**514**
General & admin. expense	205		228
Operating expense	**205**	**-10**	**228**
Operating income	**(967)**	**n.a.**	**286**
Finance costs, gross	5		16
Pre-tax income	**(973)**	**n.a.**	**269**
Net income	**(973)**	**n.a.**	**269**
Cash & equivalent	789		738
Accounts receivable	8		18
Investments	1,793		2,910
Total assets	**3,081**	**-32**	**4,563**
Accts. pay. & accr. liabs	134		125
Debt	113		228
Shareholders' equity	2,821		4,161
Cash from oper. activs	**570**	**-60**	**1,431**
Cash from fin. activs	(519)		(1,250)
Net cash position	**789**	**+7**	**738**
	$		$
Earnings per share*	(1.19)		0.33
Cash flow per share*	0.70		1.75
Net asset value per share*	3.46		5.10
Cash divd. per share*	0.33		0.72
	shs		shs
No. of shs. o/s*	816,092		816,092
Avg. no. of shs. o/s*	816,092		819,605
	%		%
Net profit margin	n.m.		52.33
Return on equity	(27.87)		6.20
Return on assets	(25.33)		5.63

* Trust unit
[A] Reported in accordance with IFRS

Note: Net income reflects increase/decrease in net assets resulting from operations.

Historical Summary
(as originally stated)

Fiscal Year	Total Rev.	Net Inc. Bef. Disc.	EPS*
	$000s	$000s	$
2022[A]	(762)	(973)	(1.19)
2021[A]	514	269	0.33
2020[A]	778	510	0.56
2019[A]	3,834	2,994	2.89
2018[A]	(624)	(1,897)	(1.72)

* Trust unit
[A] Reported in accordance with IFRS

F.13 Fairfax Financial Holdings Limited*

Symbol - FFH **Exchange** - TSX **CUSIP** - 303901
Head Office - 800-95 Wellington St W, Toronto, ON, M5J 2N7
Telephone - (416) 367-4941 **Fax** - (416) 367-4946
Website - www.fairfax.ca
Email - dbulas@fairfax.ca
Investor Relations - Derek Bulas (416) 367-4941
Auditors - PricewaterhouseCoopers LLP C.A., Toronto, Ont.
Lawyers - Torys LLP, Toronto, Ont.
Transfer Agents - Computershare Trust Company of Canada Inc., Toronto, Ont.; Computershare Trust Company, N.A., Canton, Mass.
FP500 Revenue Ranking - 17
Employees - 47,040 at Dec. 31, 2022

Profile - (Can. 1951) Provides property and casualty insurance and reinsurance, and investment management through subsidiaries in Canada, the U.S., Asia and internationally.

Insurance and Reinsurance

Northbridge Financial Corporation (100% owned) - Offers commercial property and casualty insurance products in Canada through wholly owned **Northbridge General Insurance Corporation** and **Federated Insurance Company of Canada**, under the Northbridge Insurance, Federated Insurance and TruShield Insurance brands.

Crum & Forster Holdings Corp. (100% owned) - A national commercial property and casualty insurance group in the U.S. which writes a broad range of coverages, including admitted property and casualty, accident and health, specialty and excess and surplus lines.

Zenith National Insurance Corp. (100% owned) - Primarily provides workers' compensation insurance in the U.S.

Odyssey Group Holdings, Inc. (90.01% owned) - Underwrites treaty and facultative reinsurance and specialty insurance globally, with principal locations in the U.S., Toronto, Ont., London, U.K., Paris, France, Singapore and Latin America.

Brit Limited (86.2% owned) - A global specialty insurer and reinsurer in London, U.K.

Allied World Assurance Company Holdings, Ltd. (82.87% owned) - Provides property, casualty and specialty insurance and reinsurance solutions globally, with principal locations in the U.S., Bermuda, the U.K., Singapore and Canada.

Group Re - Consists of the participation of wholly owned **CRC Reinsurance Limited**, **Wentworth Insurance Company Ltd.** and **Connemara Reinsurance Company Ltd.**, all based in Barbados, in the reinsurance of the company's subsidiaries as the third party reinsurers. Group Re also writes third party business.

Bryte Insurance Company Limited (100% owned) - Writes property and casualty insurance in South Africa and Botswana.

Eurolife FFH General Insurance Single Member S.A. (80% owned) - Writes property and casualty insurance in Greece and Romania.

Fairfax Asia - Wholly owned **Falcon Insurance Company (Hong Kong) Ltd.** writes property and casualty insurance to niche markets in Hong Kong. **The Pacific Insurance Berhad** (85% owned) writes all classes of general and medical insurance in Malaysia. **PT Asuransi Multi Artha Guna Tbk.** (80.31% owned) writes all classes of general insurance in Indonesia. **Fairfirst Insurance Limited** (78% owned) writes general insurance in Sri Lanka, specializing in automobile and personal accident lines of business. Wholly owned **Singapore Reinsurance Corporation Limited** underwrites general property and casualty reinsurance in Asia.

Fairfax Central and Eastern Europe - Wholly owned **Colonnade Insurance S.A.** writes general insurance through its branches in the Czech Republic, Hungary, Slovakia, Bulgaria, Poland and Romania and through its Ukrainian insurance company. Wholly owned **Polskie Towarzystwo Reasekuracji S.A.** writes reinsurance in central and eastern European regions. **FFH Ukraine Holdings** (69.97% owned) writes property and casualty insurance in Ukraine through subsidiaries **ARX Insurance Company** and **Universalna.**

Fairfax Latin America - Wholly owned **Fairfax Brasil Seguros Corporativos S.A.** writes general insurance in Brazil. Wholly owned **Fairfax Latin America Ltd.** writes property and casualty insurance through its operating companies in Chile, Colombia, Argentina and Uruguay.

Other insurance and reinsurance investments include 49% interest in **Go Digit Infoworks Services Private Limited**, 47.1% interest in **Thai Reinsurance Public Company Limited**, 43.7% interest in **Gulf Insurance Group K.S.C.P.**, 41.2% interest in **Falcon Insurance PLC**, 35% interest in **Bank for Investment and Development of Vietnam Insurance Joint Stock Corporation** (BIC Insurance) and 15% interest in **Alltrust Insurance Company of China Ltd.**

Life Insurance and Run-off - **Eurolife FFH Life Insurance Single Member S.A.** (80% owned) writes primarily life insurance in Greece and Romania. Wholly owned **TIG Insurance Company** manages run-off businesses in the U.S.

Non-insurance

This segment consists of the company's wholly owned **Praktiker Hellas Trading Single Member S.A.**, a retailer of do-it-yourself and home improvement goods in Greece; **William Ashley China Corporation**, a Canadian retailer of tableware, giftware, kitchenware and home decorations; and **FAIRVentures Inc.**, which focuses on developing and investing in innovations and technologies to support the Fairfax group businesses. Also includes the company's interests in **Sporting Life Group Limited** (88.52% owned), a retail business investor, and its wholly owned **Sporting Life Inc.**, a retailer of sporting goods and apparel, and **Golf Town Limited**, a retailer of golf equipment, apparel and accessories; **Recipe Unlimited Corporation** (84.03% owned), a franchiser, owner and operator of restaurants across Canada and internationally; **Grivalia Hospitality S.A.** (78.4% owned), a hospitality real estate investor, developer and manager with assets in Greece, Cyprus and Panama; **Thomas Cook (India) Limited** (73.35% owned), a provider of integrated travel and travel-related financial services, and its wholly owned **Sterling Holiday Resorts Limited**, an owner and operator of holiday resorts; **Trooh Media Inc.** (65% owned), a provider of out-of-home advertising services in North America; **Farmers Edge Inc.** (61.29% owned), a provider of advanced digital tools for agriculture; **AGT Food and Ingredients Inc.** (59.56% owned), an originator, processor and distributor of value-added pulses and staple foods; **Boat Rocker Media Inc.** (44.93% economic interest, 56.09% voting interest), a creator, producer and distributor of entertainment content for all platforms; **Kitchen Stuff Plus, Inc.** (55% owned), a retailer of housewares and home decorations; **McEwan Enterprises Inc.** (55% owned), an operator of restaurants and grocery stores, as well as provider of catering services in Canada; **Dexterra Group Inc.** (48.72% owned), a provider of infrastructure support services; **EXCO Resources, Inc.** (44.4% owned), an explorer, developer and producer of oil and gas in the U.S.; **Atlas Corp.** (43.2% owned), a global asset management firm with interests in maritime shipping and energy sectors; **Peak Achievement Athletics Inc.** (42.6% owned), a retailer of sports equipment, apparel and accessories; **Fairfax India Holdings Corporation** (41.64% economic interest, 94.98% voting interest), an investor in public and private Indian businesses or other businesses with customers, suppliers or business primarily conducted in, or dependent on, India; **Helios Fairfax Partners Corporation** (formerly **Fairfax Africa Holdings Corporation**; 34.48% economic interest, 53.35% voting interest), an investor in public and private African businesses or other businesses with customers, suppliers or business primarily conducted in, or dependent on, Africa; **Eurobank Ergasias Services and Holdings S.A.** (32.2% owned), a financial services provider in Europe; **Quess Corp Limited** (30.9% owned), an integrated business services provider in India; **Astarta Holding N.V.** (30% owned), a holding company with businesses in the farming, sugar production, milk and cattle, soybean crushing and bio-energy industries in Ukraine; and **Stelco Holdings Inc.** (23.6% owned), a producer of steel products, pig iron and metallurgical coke used primarily in the construction, automotive and energy industries in Canada and the United States.

Investment Management

Wholly owned **Hamblin Watsa Investment Counsel Ltd.** provides investment management to the insurance, reinsurance and run-off subsidiaries of the company.

On June 5, 2023, the company agreed to invest US$200,000,000 in global real investment company **Kennedy-Wilson Holdings, Inc.** via the acquisition of perpetual preferred stock that carries a 6% annual dividend rate and is callable by Kennedy Wilson at any time. The company also acquired seven-year warrants for 12,300,000 common shares with an initial exercise price of US$16.21 per share. The investment was expected to close during the second quarter of 2023.

On May 11, 2023, **Amynta Agency Inc.** (dba Amynta Group) acquired **Ambridge Group** from **Brit Limited**, 86.2% owned by the company, for US$400,000,000, consisting of US$275,000,000 cash and a US$125,000,000 promissory note. In addition, a multi-year agreement was entered into for Brit to be a significant capacity partner to Ambridge. The transaction included Ambridge in the U.S., and international units in the U.K. and Germany. Ambridge is a global Managing General Underwriter (MGU), offering a broad range of transactional, specialty casualty, cyber, professional liability and reinsurance coverages. Ambridge places more than US$600,000,000 of gross premium written on behalf of Brit and a number of global insurers. Amynta Group is an insurance services company with more than US$3.5 billion in total managed premium and 2,000 associates across North America, Europe and Australia.

On Apr. 26, 2022, the company converted Cdn$11,050,000 principal amount of convertible debentures of **Ensign Energy Services Inc.** into 6,314,286 common shares of Ensign at a price of Cdn$1.75 per share. As a result, the company held 21,800,886 Ensign common shares, representing a 12.87% equity interest, and no longer owned or controlled any convertible debentures.

On Mar. 17, 2022, the company converted certain of its preferred shares in **Thomas Cook (India) Limited** to common shares, which increased the company's interest to 71.7% from 66.8%.

Recent Merger and Acquisition Activity

Status: pending **Announced:** June 5, 2023
Fairfax Financial Holdings Limited agreed with Kennedy-Wilson Holdings, Inc.to acquire an interest of 95% in certain of the real estate construction loans that Kennedy Wilson has agreed to acquire from Pacific Western Bank, which is owned by PacWest Bancorp. The total purchase price US$2.1 billion, of which Fairfax would fund 95% (US$2 billion). The aggregate principal balance currently outstanding under the loans is US$2.3 billion. Fairfax would also assume approximately 95% of all future funding obligations under the loans. The transaction was expected to close in multiple tranches during the second and early part of the third quarter of 2023.

Status: pending **Announced:** Apr. 19, 2023
Fairfax Financial Holdings Limited agreed to acquire an additional 46.32% interest in Gulf Insurance Group K.S.C.P. from Kuwait Projects Company (Holding) K.S.C.P. (KIPCO) and certain of its affiliates for 263,653,200 Kuwaiti Dinar (US$860,000,000), representing a price per share of 2.00 Kuwaiti Dinar (US$6.53) per share, subject to a reduction by the amount of any dividends received by the KIPCO sellers after Jan. 1, 2023. On closing, Fairfax's equity interest in GIG would increase from 43.69% to 90.01%.

Status: completed **Revised:** Mar. 28, 2023
UPDATE: The transaction was completed. PREVIOUS: A consortium consisting of David L. Sokol, chairman of Atlas Corp., certain affiliates of Fairfax Financial Holdings Limited, the Washington family, and Ocean Network Express Pte. Ltd., a global container, transportation and shipping company, announced a proposal to acquire all of the outstanding common shares of Atlas that the consortium does not already own or control for US$14.45 per share in cash. Fairfax, the Washington family and Sokol own or control 68% of the fully-diluted outstanding common shares of Atlas and would continue their ownership in Atlas as part of the consortium. Atlas owns, operates and manages businesses in the maritime shipping and energy sectors. Sept. 26, 2022 - The consortium increased the bid price to US$15.50 per share in cash. Nov. 1, 2022 - Poseidon Acquisition Corp., an entity formed by certain affiliates of Fairfax Financial Holdings Limited, certain affiliates of the Washington family, David L. Sokol and Ocean Network Express Pte. Ltd., entered into a definitive agreement to acquire Atlas for an enterprise value of US$10.9 billion. Poseidon would acquire all outstanding common shares of Atlas not owned by Fairfax, Washington and Sokol for US$15.50 per share in cash. Fairfax, Washington and

Sokol own 68% of the outstanding common shares of Atlas, with Fairfax's interest being 36.7%.

Status: completed **Revised:** Mar. 1, 2023

UPDATE: The transaction was completed. PREVIOUS: Paper Excellence B.V., through wholly owned Domtar Corporation, agreed to acquire Resolute Forest Products Inc. for US$20.50 per share, together with a contractual contingent value right (CVR) entitling the holder to a share of future softwood lumber duty deposit refunds. The transaction represents an enterprise value of US$2.7 billion. The transaction would be carried out by way of a merger of Resolute with Terra Acquisition Sub Inc., a Delaware-based newly created wholly owned subsidiary of Domtar. Resolute owns or operates over 40 facilities, producing market pulp, tissue, wood products and papers, as well as power generation facilities in the U.S. and Canada. Resolute's board of directors unanimously approved the transaction, which was expected to be completed in the first half of 2023, and was subject to Resolute shareholders approval, receipt of the required regulatory approvals and other customary closing conditions. Fairfax Financial Holdings Limited, which owns a 39.8% interest in Resolute, entered into a voting and support agreement to vote in favour of the transaction. Oct. 31, 2022 - Resolute's shareholders approved the transaction.

Status: completed **Revised:** Oct. 31, 2022

UPDATE: The transaction was completed. PREVIOUS: Fairfax Financial Holdings Limited agreed to sell its global pet insurance operations to JAB Holding Company S.A.R.L's Pet Insurance business and Fairfax would also make a US$200,000,000 investment in JCP V, JAB's newest consumer fund. Fairfax would receive US$1.4 billion, consisting of US$1.15 billion cash and US$250,000,000 in seller notes. The businesses to be acquired are Crum & Forster Pet Insurance Group™ and Pethealth Inc. The transaction was expected to close in the second half of 2022.

Status: completed **Revised:** Oct. 28, 2022

UPDATE: The transaction was competed. PREVIOUS: Recipe Unlimited Corporation entered into a letter of intent to be taken private by Hamblin Watsa Investment Counsel Ltd., investment manager on behalf of certain affiliates of Fairfax Financial Holdings Limited. A newly formed wholly owned subsidiary of the buying group consisting of certain affiliates of Fairfax would acquire all of the multiple voting shares (MVS) and subordinate voting shares of Recipe, other than those shares owned by Fairfax or its affiliates and a maximum of 4,000,000 MVS owned by Cara Holdings Limited, at a purchase price of Cdn$20.73 cash per share. Cara is controlled by the Phelan family, which holds 12,740,077 MVS of Recipe. Fairfax holds 5,657,435 subordinate voting shares and 21,314,747 MVS of Recipe. The transaction was expected to close in the fourth quarter of 2022. Sept. 1, 2022 - A definitive agreement was entered into. Sept. 26, 2022 - Recipe's board of directors unanimously recommended that shareholders vote in favour of the transaction.

Status: completed **Announced:** Sept. 27, 2022

Fairfax Financial Holdings Limited acquired an additional 12% interest in Pembroke, Bermuda-based Allied World Assurance Company Holdings, Ltd. for US$733,500,000, including the fair value of a call option exercised and an accrued dividend paid. As a result, Fairfax increased its interest in Allied World to 82.9% from 70.9%. Allied World, through subsidiaries, provides property, casualty and specialty insurance and reinsurance products globally, with principal locations in the U.S., Bermuda, the U.K., Singapore and Canada.

Status: completed **Announced:** July 5, 2022

Fairfax Financial Holdings Limited acquired an additional 44.9% interest in Athens, Greece-based Grivalia Hospitality S.A. for US$194,600,000 (€190,000,000) cash. As a result, Fairfax increased its interest in Grivalia to 78.4% from 33.5%. Grivalia acquires, develops and manages hospitality real estate in Greece, Cyprus and Panama on behalf of its shareholders.

Predecessor Detail - Name changed from Markel Financial Holdings Limited, May 8, 1987.

Directors - V. Prem Watsa, chr. & CEO, Toronto, Ont.; R. William (Bill) McFarland†, Richmond Hill, Ont.; Robert J. Gunn, Toronto, Ont.; The Rt. Hon. David L. Johnston, Ashton, Ont.; Karen L. Jurjevich, Toronto, Ont.; Christine N. McLean, Toronto, Ont.; Brian J. Porter, Toronto, Ont.; Timothy R. Price, Toronto, Ont.; Brandon W. Sweitzer, Stuart, Fla.; Lauren C. Templeton, Lookout Mountain, Tenn.; Benjamin P. Watsa, Toronto, Ont.; William C. Weldon, North Palm Beach, Fla.

Other Exec. Officers - Peter S. Clarke, pres. & COO; Jennifer Allen, v-p & CFO; Bryan Bailey, v-p, tax; Derek Bulas, v-p & chief legal officer; Jean Cloutier, v-p, intl. opers.; Vinodh Loganadhan, v-p, admin. srvcs.; Bradley P. (Brad) Martin, v-p, strategic invests.; Olivier Quesnel, v-p & chief actuary; Thomas Rowe, v-p, corp. affairs; Eric P. Salsberg, v-p & corp. sec.; John C. Varnell, v-p, corp. devel.; Michael (Mike) Wallace, v-p, insce. opers.; Marc Adee, pres., Crum & Forster Holdings Corp.; Gobinath Athappan, pres., The Pacific Insurance Berhad; Andrew A. Barnard, pres., Fairfax Insurance Group; Nicholas C. Bentley, pres., RiverStone Group LLC; Wade Burton, pres., Hamblin Watsa Investment Counsel Ltd.; Bruno Camargo, pres., Fairfax Brasil Seguros Corporativos S.A.; Fabricio Campos, pres., Fairfax Latin America; Peter Csakvari, pres., Colonnade Insurance S.A.; Lou Iglesias, pres., Allied World Assurance Company Holdings, Ltd.; Bijan Khosrowshahi, pres., Fairfax International; Jacek Kugacz, pres., Polskie Towarzystwo Reasekuracji S.A.; Oleksiy Muzychko, pres., Universalna Insurance; Edwyn O'Neill, pres., Bryte Insurance Company Limited; Andrey Peretyazhko, pres., ARX Insurance Company; Alexander Sarrigeorgiou, pres., Eurolife FFH Insurance Group; Martin Thompson, pres. & CEO, Brit Limited; Kari L. Van Gundy, pres., Zenith National Insurance Corp.; Brian D. Young, pres. & CEO, Odyssey Group Holdings, Inc.; Ramaswamy Athappan, CEO, Fairfax Asia

† Lead director

Capital Stock

	Authorized (shs.)	Outstanding (shs.)[1]
Preferred	unlimited	
Series C		7,515,642
Series D		2,484,358
Series E		5,440,132
Series F		2,099,046
Series G		7,719,843
Series H		2,280,157
Series I		10,420,101
Series J		1,579,899
Series K		9,500,000
Series M		9,200,000
Multiple Voting	unlimited	1,548,000
Subordinate Voting	unlimited	22,479,769

[1] At Mar. 31, 2023

Note: Multiple voting and subordinate voting shares include 799,230 shares held through ownership in shareholder.

Preferred - Issuable in one or more series. Rank prior to the multiple and subordinate voting shares in the payment of dividends and in the event of liquidation, dissolution or winding up of the company. Non-voting.

Series C - Entitled to cumulative preferential annual dividends of Cdn$1.1775 per share payable quarterly to Dec. 31, 2024, and thereafter at a rate reset every five years equal to the five-year Government of Canada yield plus 3.15%. Redeemable on Dec. 31, 2024, and on December 31 every five years thereafter at Cdn$25 per share plus accrued and unpaid dividends. Convertible at the holder's option on Dec. 31, 2024, and on December 31 every five years thereafter, into floating rate series D preferred shares on a share-for-share basis, subject to certain conditions.

Series D - Entitled to cumulative preferential dividends payable quarterly equal to the 90-day Canadian Treasury bill rate plus 3.15%. Redeemable on Dec. 31, 2024, and on December 31 every five years thereafter at Cdn$25 per share plus accrued and unpaid dividends. Convertible at the holder's option on Dec. 31, 2024, and on December 31 every five years thereafter, into series C preferred shares on a share-for-share basis, subject to certain conditions.

Series E - Entitled to cumulative preferential annual dividends of Cdn$0.7958 per share payable quarterly to Mar. 31, 2025, and thereafter at a rate reset every five years equal to the five-year Government of Canada yield plus 2.16%. Redeemable on Mar. 31, 2025, and on March 31 every five years thereafter at Cdn$25 per share plus accrued and unpaid dividends. Convertible at the holder's option on Mar. 31, 2025, and on March 31 every five years thereafter, into floating rate series F preferred shares on a share-for-share basis, subject to certain conditions.

Series F - Entitled to cumulative preferential dividends payable quarterly equal to the 90-day Canadian Treasury bill rate plus 2.16%. Redeemable on Mar. 31, 2025, and on March 31 every five years thereafter at Cdn$25 per share plus accrued and unpaid dividends. Convertible at the holder's option on Mar. 31, 2025, and on March 31 every five years thereafter, into series E preferred shares on a share-for-share basis, subject to certain conditions.

Series G - Entitled to cumulative preferential dividends of Cdn$0.7405 per share payable quarterly to Sept. 30, 2025, and thereafter at a rate reset every five years equal to the five-year Government of Canada yield plus 2.56%. Redeemable on Sept. 30, 2025, and on September 30 every five years thereafter at Cdn$25 per share plus accrued and unpaid dividends. Convertible at the holder's option on Sept. 30, 2025, and on September 30 every five years thereafter, into floating rate series H preferred shares on a share-for-share basis, subject to certain conditions.

Series H - Entitled to cumulative preferential dividends payable quarterly equal to the 90-day Canadian Treasury bill rate plus 2.56%. Redeemable on Sept. 30, 2025, and on September 30 every five years thereafter at Cdn$25 per share plus accrued and unpaid dividends. Convertible at the holder's option on Sept. 30, 2025, and on September 30 every five years thereafter, into series G preferred shares on a share-for-share basis, subject to certain conditions.

Series I - Entitled to cumulative preferential annual dividends of Cdn$0.83175 per share payable quarterly to Dec. 31, 2025, and thereafter at a rate reset every five years equal to the five-year Government of Canada yield plus 2.85%. Redeemable on Dec. 31, 2025, and on December 31 every five years thereafter at Cdn$25 per share plus accrued and unpaid dividends. Convertible at the holder's option on Dec. 31, 2025, and on December 31 every five years thereafter, into floating rate series J preferred shares on a share-for-share basis, subject to certain conditions.

Series J - Entitled to cumulative preferential dividends payable quarterly equal to the 90-day Canadian Treasury bill rate plus 2.85%. Redeemable on Dec. 31, 2025, and on December 31 every five years thereafter at Cdn$25 per share plus accrued and unpaid dividends. Convertible at the holder's option on Dec. 31, 2025, and on December 31 every five years thereafter, into series I preferred shares on a share-for-share basis, subject to certain conditions.

Series K - Entitled to cumulative preferential annual dividends of Cdn$1.2613 per share payable quarterly to Mar. 31, 2027, and thereafter at a rate reset every five years equal to the five-year Government of Canada yield plus 3.51%. Redeemable on Mar. 31, 2027, and on March 31 every five years thereafter at Cdn$25 per share plus accrued and unpaid dividends. Convertible at the holder's option, on Mar. 31, 2027, and on March 31 every five years thereafter, into floating rate series L preferred shares on a share-for-share basis, subject to certain conditions. The series L shares would pay a quarterly dividend equal to the 90-day Canadian Treasury bill rate plus 3.51%.

Series M - Entitled to cumulative preferential annual dividends of Cdn$1.2508 per share payable quarterly to Mar. 31, 2025, and thereafter at a rate reset every five years equal to the five-year Government of Canada yield plus 3.98%. Redeemable on Mar. 31, 2025, and on March 31 every five years thereafter at Cdn$25 per share plus accrued and unpaid dividends. Convertible at the holder's option, on Mar. 31, 2025, and on March 31 every five years thereafter, into floating rate series N preferred shares on a share-for-share basis, subject to certain conditions. The series N shares would pay a quarterly dividend equal to the 90-day Canadian Treasury bill rate plus 3.98%.

Multiple Voting - Convertible into subordinate voting shares on a share-for-share basis. Entitled to 50 votes per share, except when the voting power exceeds 41.8% of the votes attached to all voting shares. The shares are automatically and permanently reduced to one vote per share if (i) the number of the multiple voting shares held by the major shareholders falls below 1,548,000 shares, unless this results from a sale to purchasers who make an equivalent unconditional offer to purchase all outstanding subordinate voting shares; or (ii) the number of multiple voting shares held by purchasers falls below 1,548,000.

Subordinate Voting - One vote per share.

Normal Course Issuer Bid - The company plans to make normal course purchases of up to 2,381,484 subordinate voting shares representing 10% of the public float. The bid commenced on Sept. 30, 2022, and expires on Sept. 29, 2023.

The company plans to make normal course purchases of up to 751,034 series C preferred shares representing 10% of the public float. The bid commenced on Sept. 30, 2022, and expires on Sept. 29, 2023.

The company plans to make normal course purchases of up to 543,613 series E preferred shares representing 10% of the public float. The bid commenced on Sept. 30, 2022, and expires on Sept. 29, 2023.

The company plans to make normal course purchases of up to 771,984 series G preferred shares representing 10% of the public float. The bid commenced on Sept. 30, 2022, and expires on Sept. 29, 2023.

The company plans to make normal course purchases of up to 1,042,010 series I preferred shares representing 10% of the public float. The bid commenced on Sept. 30, 2022, and expires on Sept. 29, 2023.

The company plans to make normal course purchases of up to 950,000 series K preferred shares representing 10% of the public float. The bid commenced on Sept. 30, 2022, and expires on Sept. 29, 2023.

The company plans to make normal course purchases of up to 178,415 series D preferred shares representing 10% of the public float. The bid commenced on Sept. 30, 2022, and expires on Sept. 29, 2023.

The company plans to make normal course purchases of up to 919,600 series M preferred shares representing 10% of the public float. The bid commenced on Sept. 30, 2022, and expires on Sept. 29, 2023.

The company plans to make normal course purchases of up to 179,629 series F preferred shares representing 10% of the public float. The bid commenced on Sept. 30, 2022, and expires on Sept. 29, 2023.

The company plans to make normal course purchases of up to 228,015 series H preferred shares representing 10% of the public float. The bid commenced on Sept. 30, 2022, and expires on Sept. 29, 2023.

The company plans to make normal course purchases of up to 157,989 series J preferred shares representing 10% of the public float. The bid commenced on Sept. 30, 2022, and expires on Sept. 29, 2023.

Major Shareholder - V. Prem Watsa held 43.9% interest at Mar. 10, 2023.

Price Range - FFH/TSX

Year	Volume	High	Low	Close
2022............	14,497,975	$815.01	$569.62	$802.07
2021............	17,637,633	$636.08	$427.49	$622.24
2020............	20,040,367	$637.11	$319.37	$433.85
2019............	10,625,586	$667.23	$542.70	$609.74
2018............	10,789,646	$788.88	$565.99	$600.98

Recent Close: $1,132.93

Capital Stock Changes - During 2022, 142,969 subordinate voting shares were issued on reissue of treasury shares, 387,790 subordinate voting shares were repurchased under a Normal Course Issuer Bid and 295,474 subordinate voting shares were acquired for treasury.

Dividends

FFH com S.V. Ra US$10.00 pa A est. Jan. 26, 2011
FFH.U com S.V. Ra US$10.00 pa A est. Jan. 27, 2015
FFH.PR.C pfd ser C cum. red. exch. Adj. Ra $1.17725 pa Q est. Mar. 31, 2020
FFH.PR.E pfd ser E cum. red. exch. Adj. Ra $0.79575 pa Q est. June 30, 2020
FFH.PR.G pfd ser G cum. red. exch. Adj. Ra $0.7405 pa Q est. Dec. 31, 2020
FFH.PR.I pfd ser I cum. red. exch. Adj. Ra $0.83175 pa Q est. Mar. 31, 2021
FFH.PR.K pfd ser K cum. red. exch. Adj. Ra $1.26125 pa Q est. June 30, 2022
FFH.PR.D pfd ser D cum. red. exch. Fltg. Ra pa Q

$0.4808................	June 29/23	$0.45394..........	Mar. 30/23
$0.40314..............	Dec. 29/22	$0.29157..........	Sept. 29/22

Paid in 2023: $0.93474 2022: $1.13169 2021: $0.81743

FFH.PR.M pfd ser M cum. red. exch. Adj. Ra $1.25075 pa Q est. June 30, 2020
FFH.PR.F pfd ser F cum. red. exch. Fltg. Ra pa Q

$0.4191................	June 29/23	$0.39223..........	Mar. 30/23
$0.34144..............	Dec. 29/22	$0.22918..........	Sept. 29/22

Paid in 2023: $0.81133 2022: $0.88487 2021: $0.56992

FFH.PR.H pfd ser H cum. red. exch. Fltg. Ra pa Q

$0.44403	June 29/23	$0.41717	Mar. 30/23
$0.36637	Dec. 29/22	$0.25439	Sept. 29/22

Paid in 2023: $0.8612 2022: $0.9846 2021: $0.66992

FFH.PR.J pfd ser J cum. red. exch. Fltg. Ra pa Q

$0.46211	June 29/23	$0.43524	Mar. 30/23
$0.38444	Dec. 29/22	$0.27266	Sept. 29/22

Paid in 2023: $0.89735 2022: $1.0569 2021: $0.74242

Long-Term Debt - Outstanding at Dec. 31, 2022:

Fairfax debt:	
4.875% sr. notes due 2024	US$281,600,000
4.95% sr. notes due 2025[1]	257,200,000
8.3% sr. notes due 2026	91,700,000
4.7% sr. notes due 2026[2]	331,000,000
4.25% sr. notes due 2027[3]	478,600,000
2.75% sr. notes due 2028[4]	792,200,000
4.85% sr. notes due 2028	596,900,000
4.23% sr. notes due 2029[5]	367,700,000
4.625% sr. notes due 2030	646,400,000
3.375% sr. notes due 2031	586,800,000
3.95% sr. notes due 2031[6]	623,200,000
5.625% sr. notes due 2032	743,600,000
7.75% sr. notes due 2037	90,700,000
Subsidiary debt:	
Allied World debt	522,700,000
Zenith National debs	38,300,000
Brit Limited debt	172,400,000
Fairfax India debt	561,100,000
Recipe Unlimited debt	461,500,000
AGT debt	508,400,000
Boat Rocker debt	155,200,000
Other subsidiary debt	317,700,000
	8,624,900,000

[1] Cdn$350,000,000.
[2] Cdn$450,000,000.
[3] Cdn$650,000,000.
[4] €750,000,000.
[5] Cdn$500,000,000.
[6] Cdn$850,000,000.

Minimum debt repayments are due as follows:

2023	US$372,100,000
2024	1,031,000,000
2025	802,300,000
2026	455,100,000
2027	510,400,000
Thereafter	5,502,600,000

Wholly Owned Subsidiaries

Bryte Insurance Company Limited, South Africa.
CRC Reinsurance Limited, Barbados. Formerly CRC (Bermuda) Reinsurance Limited
Colonnade Insurance S.A., Luxembourg.
Connemara Reinsurance Company Ltd., Barbados.
Crum & Forster Holdings Corp., Morristown, N.J.
- 100% int. in **United States Fire Insurance Company**, N.Y.
  - 100% int. in **First Mercury Insurance Company**, Ill.
  - 100% int. in **The North River Insurance Company**, N.J.
    - 100% int. in **Seneca Insurance Company, Inc.**, N.Y.

FAIRVentures Inc., Ont.
Fairfax Brasil Seguros Corporativos S.A., São Paulo, Brazil.
Fairfax Latin America Ltd., Miami, Fla.
- 99.99% int. in **La Meridional Compañía Argentina de Seguros S.A.**, Argentina.
- 100% int. in **SBI Seguros Uruguay S.A.**, Montevideo, Uruguay.
- 100% int. in **SBS Seguros Colombia S.A.**, Colombia.
- 100% int. in **Southbridge Compañía de Seguros Generales S.A.**, Chile.

Falcon Insurance Company (Hong Kong) Ltd., Hong Kong, Hong Kong, People's Republic of China.
Hamblin Watsa Investment Counsel Ltd., Toronto, Ont.
Northbridge Financial Corporation, Toronto, Ont.
- 100% int. in **Federated Insurance Company of Canada**, Winnipeg, Man.
- 100% int. in **Northbridge General Insurance Corporation**, Toronto, Ont.
  - 100% int. in **Verassure Insurance Company**, Toronto, Ont.

Polskie Towarzystwo Reasekuracji S.A., Warsaw, Poland.
Praktiker Hellas Trading Single Member S.A., Greece.
Singapore Reinsurance Corporation Limited, Singapore.
TIG Insurance Company, Calif.
Wentworth Insurance Company Ltd., Barbados.
William Ashley China Corporation, Toronto, Ont.
Zenith National Insurance Corp., Woodland Hills, Calif.
- 100% int. in **Zenith Insurance Company**, Calif.

Subsidiaries

59.56% int. in **AGT Food and Ingredients Inc.**, Regina, Sask.
82.87% int. in **Allied World Assurance Company Holdings, Ltd.**, Pembroke, Bermuda.
- 100% int. in **Allied World Assurance Company, Ltd.**, Bermuda.
  - 100% int. in **Allied World Assurance Company, AG**, Switzerland.
  - 100% int. in **Allied World Assurance Company (Europe) DAC**, Ireland.
- 100% int. in **Allied World Assurance Holdings (U.S.) Inc.**, Del.
  - 100% int. in **Allied World Insurance Company**, N.H.
    - 100% int. in **Allied World Assurance Company (U.S.) Inc.**, Del.
    - 100% int. in **Allied World Specialty Insurance Company**, Del.
      - 100% int. in **Allied World Surplus Lines Insurance Company**, Ark.
      - 100% int. in **Vantapro Specialty Insurance Company**, Ark.
  - 100% int. in **Allied World National Assurance Company**, N.H.

86.2% int. in **Brit Limited**, London, Middx., United Kingdom.
- 100% int. in **Brit Insurance Holdings Limited**, United Kingdom.
  - 100% int. in **Brit Reinsurance (Bermuda) Limited**, Bermuda.
  - 100% int. in **Brit Syndicates Limited**, United Kingdom.

80% int. in **Eurolife FFH General Insurance Single Member S.A.**, Greece.
80% int. in **Eurolife FFH Life Insurance Single Member S.A.**, Greece.
69.97% int. in **FFH Ukraine Holdings**, Ukraine.
- 99.98% int. in **ARX Insurance Company**, Ukraine.
- 99.98% int. in **ARX Life Insurance Company**, Ukraine.
- 99.99% int. in **Universalna**, Ukraine.

78% int. in **Fairfirst Insurance Limited**, Colombo, Sri Lanka.
61.2% int. in **Farmers Edge Inc.**, Winnipeg, Man. (see separate coverage)
78.4% int. in **Grivalia Hospitality S.A.**, Athens, Greece.
55% int. in **Kitchen Stuff Plus, Inc.**, Toronto, Ont.
55% int. in **McEwan Enterprises Inc.**, Ont.
90.01% int. in **Odyssey Group Holdings, Inc.**, Stamford, Conn.
- 100% int. in **Odyssey Reinsurance Corporation**, Conn.
  - 100% int. in **Greystone Insurance Company**, Conn.
  - 100% int. in **Hudson Insurance Company**, Del.
  - 100% int. in **Newline Holdings UK Limited**, United Kingdom.
    - 100% int. in **Newline Corporate Name Limited**, United Kingdom.
    - 100% int. in **Newline Europe Versicherung AG**, Cologne, Germany.
    - 100% int. in **Newline Insurance Company Limited**, United Kingdom.
  - 100% int. in **Odyssey Re Europe Holdings S.A.S.**, France.
    - 100% int. in **Odyssey Re Europe S.A.**, France.

80.31% int. in **PT Asuransi Multi Artha Guna Tbk.**, Jakarta, Indonesia.
85% int. in **The Pacific Insurance Berhad**, Malaysia.
84.03% int. in **Recipe Unlimited Corporation**, Vaughan, Ont.
88.52% int. in **Sporting Life Group Limited**, Canada.
- 100% int. in **Golf Town Limited**, Canada.
- 100% int. in **Sporting Life Inc.**, Toronto, Ont.

73.35% int. in **Thomas Cook (India) Limited**, India.
- 100% int. in **Sterling Holiday Resorts Limited**, India.

65% int. in **Trooh Media Inc.**, Del.

Investments

14% int. in **Altius Minerals Corporation**, St. John's, N.L. (see Survey of Mines)
30% int. in **Astarta Holding N.V.**, Ukraine.
43.2% int. in **Atlas Corp.**, Hong Kong, Hong Kong, People's Republic of China.
44.93% int. in **Boat Rocker Media Inc.**, Toronto, Ont. Holds 56.09% voting interest. (see separate coverage)
48.72% int. in **Dexterra Group Inc.**, Mississauga, Ont. (see separate coverage)
44.4% int. in **EXCO Resources, Inc.**, Dallas, Tex.
32.2% int. in **Eurobank Ergasias Services and Holdings S.A.**, Greece.
41.64% int. in **Fairfax India Holdings Corporation**, Toronto, Ont. Holds 94.98% voting interest. (see separate coverage)
17.2% int. in **Foran Mining Corporation**, Vancouver, B.C. (see Survey of Mines)
43.69% int. in **Gulf Insurance Group K.S.C.P.**, Kuwait City, Kuwait.
32.6% int. in **Helios Fairfax Partners Corporation**, Toronto, Ont. Holds 53.3% voting interest. (see separate coverage)
42.6% int. in **Peak Achievement Athletics Inc.**, Canada.
30.9% int. in **Quess Corp Limited**, India.
23.6% int. in **Stelco Holdings Inc.**, Hamilton, Ont. (see separate coverage)
16.09% int. in **ZoomerMedia Limited**, Toronto, Ont. (see separate coverage)

Note: The preceding list includes only the major related companies in which interests are held.

Financial Statistics

Periods ended:	12m Dec. 31/22[A]		12m Dec. 31/21[A]
	US$000s	%Chg	US$000s
Net premiums earned	21,006,100		16,558,000
Net investment income	(772,100)		4,085,900
Total revenue	**28,050,000**	**+6**	**26,467,900**
Policy benefits & claims	13,851,900		10,740,500
Commissions	3,454,900		2,787,900
Other operating expense	3,057,500		2,946,100
Operating expense	**6,512,400**	**+14**	**5,734,000**
Operating income	**7,685,700**	**-23**	**9,993,400**
Finance costs, gross	452,800		513,900
Pre-tax income	**1,712,000**	**-61**	**4,392,600**
Income taxes	425,200		726,000
Net income	**1,286,800**	**-65**	**3,666,600**
Net inc. for equity hldrs	**1,147,200**	**-66**	**3,401,100**
Net inc. for non-cont. int	**139,600**	**-47**	**265,500**
Cash & equivalent	1,345,800		1,478,300
Accounts receivable	21,023,300		18,973,700
Securities investments	7,462,300		7,874,800
Real estate	51,300		119,600
Total investments	54,322,900		51,697,400
Total assets	**92,125,100**	**+6**	**86,645,400**
Accts. pay. & accr. liabs	8,822,100		8,163,200
Claims provisions	40,507,800		36,908,800
Debt	8,624,900		7,753,000
Long-term lease liabilities	1,094,000		1,140,700
Preferred share equity	1,335,500		1,335,500
Shareholders' equity	16,676,200		16,385,100
Non-controlling interest	3,659,600		4,930,200
Cash from oper. activs	**(4,419,900)**	**n.a.**	**6,641,000**
Cash from fin. activs	(1,294,600)		(1,189,300)
Cash from invest. activs	384,800		1,838,600
Net cash position	**6,119,600**	**-48**	**11,685,400**
Capital expenditures, net	(334,200)		(326,900)
Unfunded pension liability	69,200		56,200
	US$		US$
Earnings per share*	46.62		129.33
Cash flow per share*	(186.98)		255.88
Cash divd. per share*	10.00		10.00
	shs		shs
No. of shs. o/s*	24,124,535		24,664,830
Avg. no. of shs. o/s*	23,637,824		25,953,114
	%		%
Net profit margin	4.59		13.85
Return on equity	7.25		24.35
Return on assets	1.82		5.10
Foreign sales percent	89		87
No. of employees (FTEs)	47,040		39,040

* M.V. & S.V.
[A] Reported in accordance with IFRS

Latest Results

Periods ended:	3m Mar. 31/23[A]		3m Mar. 31/22[oA]
	US$000s	%Chg	US$000s
Total revenue	9,325,600	+36	6,858,800
Net income	1,404,000	+101	698,800
Net inc. for equity hldrs	1,250,000	+112	588,700
Net inc. for non-cont. int	154,000		110,100
	US$		US$
Earnings per share*	53.17		24.23

* M.V. & S.V.
[o] Restated
[A] Reported in accordance with IFRS

Historical Summary
(as originally stated)

Fiscal Year	Total Rev. US$000s	Net Inc. Bef. Disc. US$000s	EPS* US$
2022[A]	28,050,000	1,286,800	46.62
2021[A]	26,467,900	3,666,600	129.33
2020[A]	19,794,900	37,400	6.59
2019[A]	21,532,800	1,971,200	72.80
2018[A]	17,757,700	817,900	12.03

* M.V. & S.V.
[A] Reported in accordance with IFRS

F.14 Fairfax India Holdings Corporation

Symbol - FIH.U **Exchange** - TSX **CUSIP** - 303897
Head Office - 800-95 Wellington St W, Toronto, ON, M5J 2N7 **Telephone** - (416) 367-4941 **Fax** - (416) 367-4946
Website - www.fairfaxindia.ca
Email - j_varnell@fairfax.ca
Investor Relations - John C. Varnell (416) 367-4941
Auditors - PricewaterhouseCoopers LLP C.A., Toronto, Ont.
Lawyers - Torys LLP, Toronto, Ont.
Transfer Agents - Computershare Trust Company of Canada Inc., Toronto, Ont.

Portfolio Advisors - Hamblin Watsa Investment Counsel Ltd., Toronto, Ont.

Employees - 10 at Dec. 31, 2022

Profile - (Can. 2014) Invests in public and private equity securities and debt instruments in India and Indian businesses or other businesses with customers, suppliers or business primarily conducted in, or dependent on, India.

The company is controlled by **Fairfax Financial Holdings Limited** (FFH). **Fairbridge Capital Private Limited** is the sub-advisor to portfolio advisor **Hamblin Watsa Investment Counsel Ltd.**, both of which are wholly owned by FFH.

Holdings and investments consist of **IIFL Finance Limited**, which offers home loans, gold loans, loans against property, digital loans, microfinancing, construction and real estate financing, and capital market financing services; **IIFL Securities Limited**, which provides retail and institutional brokerage and investment advisory services and products such as financial planning, equity, commodities and currency brokering, depository participant services, investment banking, portfolio management and distribution of mutual funds, bonds and other products; **CSB Bank Limited** (formerly **The Catholic Syrian Bank Limited**), which provides retail banking, non-resident Indian banking services, small-to-medium enterprise and wholesale banking services across India; **Fairchem Organics Limited**, which manufactures oleochemicals used in the paints, inks and adhesives industries, as well as intermediate nutraceutical and health products; **5paisa Capital Limited**, which provides an online platform and mobile applications for trading securities on the **BSE Limited** (formerly Bombay Stock Exchange) and the **National Stock Exchange of India Ltd.**; **Bangalore International Airport Limited**, which operates the Kempegowda International Airport Bengaluru; **Sanmar Chemicals Group**, which manufactures suspension polyvinyl chloride (PVC), caustic soda, calcium chloride, chloromethanes, refrigerant gases, industrial salt and specialty chemical intermediates with an operational presence in India and Egypt; **Seven Islands Shipping Limited**, which owns and operates 24 vessels that transport liquid and gas cargo along the Indian coast and in international waters; **National Commodities Management Services Limited** (formerly **National Collateral Management Services Limited**), which offers grain procurement, storage and preservation, testing and certification, collateral management, commodity and weather intelligence, commodity management and financing as well as construction and operation of silo projects primarily for the agricultural sector; **Maxop Engineering Company Private Limited**, which provides precision aluminum die casting and machining solutions for the automotive and industrial sectors in Asia, North America and Europe; **Saurashtra Freight Private Limited**, which operates a container freight station in Mundra port; **Jaynix Engineering Private Limited**, which manufactures non-ferrous electrical connectors and electrical assemblies and serves as a Tier 1 supplier to major electrical OEMs in North America and Europe; **National Stock Exchange of India Limited**, which operates India's largest stock exchange; and **India Housing Fund**, which invests in equity, debt and equity-linked instruments of real estate and construction companies involved in projects or ventures with expected growth potential.

During the first and second quarter of 2023, the company sold the remaining 2.5% interest in Mumbai, India-based **360 ONE WAM Limited** (formerly **IIFL Wealth Management Limited**) for US$45,974,000. 360 ONE WAM operates wealth management and asset management businesses.

In June 2023, wholly owned **FIH Private Investments Ltd.** acquired an additional 3% interest in **Bangalore International Airport Limited** (BIAL) from **Siemens AG**'s wholly owned **Siemens Project Ventures GmbH** for US$75,000,000 (Rs6.2 billion). As a result, the company interest in BIAL increased to 57% (FIH Private 13.4%, subsidiary **Anchorage Infrastructure Investments Holdings Limited** 43.6%).

In addition, the company agreed to acquire an additional 7% interest in BIAL for US$175,000,000, upon achievement of certain performance conditions by BIAL subsequent to Oct. 31, 2023.

In December 2022, the company sold a 1.3% interest in Mumbai, India-based **IIFL Wealth Management Limited** for US$25,600,000 (Rs2.1 billion). As a result, the company's equity interest in IIFL Wealth decreased to 2.5% from 3.8%. IIFL Wealth Management operates wealth management and asset management businesses.

In November 2022, the company sold a 9.8% interest in Mumbai, India-based **IIFL Wealth Management Limited** to **Bain Capital, L.P.** for US$172,000,000 (Rs14 billion). As a result, the company's equity interest in IIFL Wealth decreased to 3.8% from 13.6%. IIFL Wealth Management operates wealth management and asset management businesses.

Recent Merger and Acquisition Activity

Status: completed **Revised:** Sept. 6, 2022

UPDATE: The second transaction was completed for Rs1.75 billion (US$22,100,000). PREVIOUS: Fairfax India Holdings Corporation agreed to acquire a 67% interest in New Delhi, India-based Maxop Engineering Company Private Limited for up to Rs4.88 billion (US$66,000,000) in two transactions. Fairfax India would acquire an initial 51% interest in Maxop for Rs2.22 billion (US$30,000,000), and an additional 16% interest for up to Rs2.66 billion (US$36,000,000) in the second transaction. Maxop provides precision aluminum die casting and machining solutions for aluminum die casting components used by the automotive and industrial sectors, with customers in Asia, North America and Europe. Maxop operates four plants in Manesar and two plants in Jaipur, all in India. Nov. 30, 2021 - The initial transaction was completed for Rs2.22 billion (US$29,500,000).

Directors - V. Prem Watsa, founder & chr., Toronto, Ont.; Chandran Ratnaswami, CEO, Toronto, Ont.; Gopalakrishnan Soundarajan, COO, Toronto, Ont.; Christopher D. (Chris) Hodgson†, Markham, Ont.; Sharmila Karve, Mumbai, India; The Hon. Jason T. Kenney, Calgary, Alta.; Sumit Maheshwari, Mumbai, India; R. William (Bill) McFarland, Richmond Hill, Ont.; Satish Rai, Pickering, Ont.; Lauren C. Templeton, Lookout Mountain, Tenn.; Benjamin P. Watsa, Toronto, Ont.

Exec. Officers - Amy Sherk, CFO; Jennifer Allen, v-p; John C. Varnell, v-p, corp. affairs; Jennifer E. Pankratz, gen. counsel & corp. sec.; Amy Tan, CEO, FIH Mauritius Investments Ltd. & FIH Private Investments Ltd.

† Lead director

Capital Stock

	Authorized (shs.)	Outstanding (shs.)[1]
Preference	unlimited	nil
Multiple Voting	unlimited	30,000,000
Subordinate Voting	unlimited	106,698,971

[1] At June 30, 2023

Multiple Voting - Convertible into subordinate voting shares on a share-for-share basis, under certain circumstances. All held by Fairfax Financial Holdings Limited. Fifty votes per share.

Subordinate Voting - One vote per share.

Normal Course Issuer Bid - The company plans to make normal course purchases of up to 5,863,570 subordinate voting shares representing 10% of the public float. The bid commenced on Sept. 30, 2022, and expires on Sept. 29, 2023.

Major Shareholder - Fairfax Financial Holdings Limited held 95.05% interest at Mar. 10, 2023.

Price Range - FIH.U/TSX

Year	Volume	High	Low	Close
2022	9,655,077	US$13.12	US$9.25	US$12.28
2021	13,924,804	US$14.90	US$9.65	US$12.61
2020	15,849,974	US$13.86	US$5.28	US$9.60
2019	11,034,033	US$14.48	US$11.01	US$12.80
2018	15,178,133	US$18.49	US$12.12	US$13.13

Recent Close: US$13.51

Capital Stock Changes - During 2022, 2,964,452 subordinate voting shares were repurchased under a Normal Course Issuer Bid.

Wholly Owned Subsidiaries

FIH Mauritius Investments Ltd., Mauritius.
- 88.5% int. in **Anchorage Infrastructure Investments Holdings Limited**, India.
  - 43.6% int. in **Bangalore International Airport Limited**, Bangalore, India.
- 100% int. in **FIH Private Investments Ltd.**, Mauritius.
  - 13.4% int. in **Bangalore International Airport Limited**, Bangalore, India.
  - 49.7% int. in **CSB Bank Limited**, Thrissur, India.
  - 52.8% int. in **Fairchem Organics Limited**, Ahmedabad, India.
  - 25% int. in **5paisa Capital Limited**, Mumbai, India.
  - 20.9% int. in **IIFL Finance Limited**, Mumbai, India.
  - 27.7% int. in **IIFL Securities Limited**, Mumbai, India.
  - 70% int. in **Jaynix Engineering Private Limited**, Vadodara, India.
  - 67% int. in **Maxop Engineering Company Private Limited**, New Delhi, India.
  - 91% int. in **National Commodities Management Services Limited**, Gurgaon, India.
  - 1% int. in **National Stock Exchange of India Limited**, Mumbai, India.
  - 42.9% int. in **Sanmar Chemicals Group**, Chennai, India.
  - 51% int. in **Saurashtra Freight Private Limited**, Mumbai, India.
  - 48.5% int. in **Seven Islands Shipping Limited**, Mumbai, India.

Financial Statistics

Periods ended:	12m Dec. 31/22[A]		12m Dec. 31/21[A]
	US$000s	%Chg	US$000s
Realized invest. gain (loss)	95,882		227,193
Unrealized invest. gain (loss)	153,656		438,935
Total revenue	**237,526**	**-66**	**693,539**
Salaries & benefits	1,163		921
General & admin. expense	12,307		4,605
Other operating expense	2,560[1]		125,968
Operating expense	**16,030**	**-88**	**131,494**
Operating income	**221,496**	**-61**	**562,045**
Finance costs, gross	25,521		28,515
Pre-tax income	**195,975**	**-63**	**533,530**
Income taxes	4,487		39,030
Net income	**191,488**	**-61**	**494,500**
Net inc. for equity hldrs	**191,439**	**-61**	**494,514**
Net inc. for non-cont. int	**49**	**n.a.**	**(14)**
Cash & equivalent	197,140		30,376
Accounts receivable	5,599		5,339
Investments	3,160,916		3,546,332
Total assets	**3,365,569**	**-6**	**3,584,346**
Accts. pay. & accr. liabs	1,143		866
Debt	497,306		496,785
Shareholders' equity	2,642,036		2,774,792
Non-controlling interest	114,737		127,642
Cash from oper. activs	**152,344**	**+149**	**61,089**
Cash from fin. activs	(35,582)		(51,298)
Net cash position	**147,448**	**+385**	**30,376**
	US$		US$
Earnings per share*	1.38		3.38
Cash flow per share*	1.10		0.42
	shs		shs
No. of shs. o/s*	138,270,900		141,235,352
Avg. no. of shs. o/s*	139,066,682		146,379,346
	%		%
Net profit margin	80.62		71.30
Return on equity	7.07		18.94
Return on assets	6.23		15.65
Foreign sales percent	100		100
No. of employees (FTEs)	10		9

* Subord. Vtg.

[A] Reported in accordance with IFRS

[1] Includes recovery of performance fee amounting to US$36,428,000.

Latest Results

Periods ended:	6m June 30/23[A]		6m June 30/22[A]
	US$000s	%Chg	US$000s
Total revenue	207,351	n.a.	(30,805)
Net income	114,108	n.a.	(13,772)
Net inc. for equity hldrs	103,848	n.a.	(13,748)
Net inc. for non-cont. int	10,260		(24)
	US$		US$
Earnings per share*	0.75		(0.10)

* Subord. Vtg.

[A] Reported in accordance with IFRS

Historical Summary

(as originally stated)

Fiscal Year	Total Rev. US$000s	Net Inc. Bef. Disc. US$000s	EPS* US$
2022[A]	237,526	191,488	1.38
2021[A]	693,539	494,500	3.38
2020[A]	(12,972)	(41,476)	(0.27)
2019[A]	712,689	516,338	3.38
2018[A]	166,518	96,432	0.63

* Subord. Vtg.

[A] Reported in accordance with IFRS

F.15 Fairplay Ventures Inc.

Symbol - FPY.P **Exchange** - TSX-VEN **CUSIP** - 30556L

Head Office - 401-10 Four Seasons Pl, Toronto, ON, M9B 6H7

Telephone - (905) 483-0561 **Fax** - (866) 245-3454

Email - nmeyer@canadianlifesettlements.com

Investor Relations - Nicholas Meyer (905) 483-0561

Auditors - Clearhouse LLP C.A., Mississauga, Ont.

Transfer Agents - Computershare Trust Company of Canada Inc.

Profile - (Ont. 2019) Capital Pool Company.

Directors - Mark Scarrow, CFO, Ont.; Bruno Amadi, Toronto, Ont.; Jason F. Gorel, Ont.

Other Exec. Officers - Nicholas Meyer, CEO & corp. sec.

Capital Stock

	Authorized (shs.)	Outstanding (shs.)[1]
Common	unlimited	8,500,000

[1] At July 12, 2023

Major Shareholder - Bruno Amadi held 11.76% interest at Mar. 10, 2023.

Capital Stock Changes - There were no changes to capital stock during 2022.

F.16 Fandifi Technology Corp.

Symbol - FDM **Exchange** - CSE **CUSIP** - 302437
Head Office - 830-1100 Melville St, Vancouver, BC, V6E 4A6
Telephone - (604) 256-6990
Website - www.fandomesports.com
Email - info@fandomesports.com
Investor Relations - David Vinokurov (604) 256-6990
Auditors - Dale Matheson Carr-Hilton LaBonte LLP C.A., Vancouver, B.C.
Transfer Agents - Computershare Investor Services Inc.
Profile - (B.C. 2006) Develops and provides a prediction fan engagement platform for sports and eSports enthusiasts.

The Fandifi fan engagement platform is a prediction engine which facilitates real time predictions in events ranging from eSports, sports, scripted, programing and live streamed broadcasts and provides prediction actions to viewers to assist content creators in extending peak viewership metrics and to generate new revenue streams through in platform purchases. The platform is a module-based architecture using a proprietary technology which is able to generate a customizable mobile enabled application capable of including only the particular functionalities required by a specific target audience. It uses the DataBionix™ platform that allows real-time data organization and extraction of meaningful insights, including but not limited to, in-games statistics, teams related forecasts, gamers past and predicted performances.

Also operates www.fandomart.com, a non-fungible token (NFT) marketplace where rewards can be bought, sold or traded on a interoperable blockchain agnostic platform.

In April 2022, the company entered into a letter of intent with **Yoruba Media Labs**, a developer of original content/IP that can play out in the tech, gaming and ad spaces, whereby Yoruba would be facilitating business collaborations for the company with celebrity eSports tournaments, globally recognized awards shows, original scripted programming and live music events and venues.

Predecessor Detail - Name changed from Fandom Sports Media Corp., Apr. 12, 2022.

Directors - Zhengquan (Philip) Chen, chr., Toronto, Ont.; David Vinokurov, pres. & CEO, Toronto, Ont.; Tristan Brett, Vancouver, B.C.; Andra Enescu, Etobicoke, Ont.

Other Exec. Officers - Lyle Strachan, CFO; Christian Gravel, chief strategy officer; Stan Yazhemsky, chief tech. officer

Capital Stock

	Authorized (shs.)	Outstanding (shs.)[1]
Common	unlimited	82,105,133

[1] At June 29, 2022

Major Shareholder - Widely held at Sept. 15, 2021.

Price Range - FDM/CSE

Year	Volume	High	Low	Close
2022	29,590,176	$0.26	$0.05	$0.05
2021	114,939,959	$0.83	$0.10	$0.18
2020	50,776,260	$0.59	$0.04	$0.17
2019	9,735,181	$1.15	$0.10	$0.15
2018	24,034,054	$3.55	$0.65	$1.00

Consolidation: 1-for-10 cons. in Feb. 2020
Recent Close: $0.02

Wholly Owned Subsidiaries

Bridarias Limited, Cyprus.
Fandom Esports Curacao N.V., Curacao.

Financial Statistics

Periods ended:	12m Jan. 31/22[A]		12m Jan. 31/21[A]
	$000s	%Chg	$000s
Research & devel. expense	963		234
General & admin expense	1,901		1,090
Stock-based compensation	778		1,753
Operating expense	**3,642**	**+18**	**3,077**
Operating income	**(3,642)**	**n.a.**	**(3,077)**
Deprec., depl. & amort.	121		nil
Finance costs, gross	16		6
Pre-tax income	**(3,777)**	**n.a.**	**(3,051)**
Net income	**(3,777)**	**n.a.**	**(3,051)**
Cash & equivalent	3,445		735
Current assets	4,012		793
Fixed assets, net	28		nil
Intangibles, net	890		nil
Total assets	**4,930**	**+522**	**793**
Accts. pay. & accr. liabs	140		105
Current liabilities	140		105
Shareholders' equity	4,789		688
Cash from oper. activs	**(2,736)**	**n.a.**	**(1,265)**
Cash from fin. activs	5,483		1,999
Cash from invest. activs	(38)		nil
Net cash position	**3,445**	**+369**	**735**
Capital expenditures	(38)		nil
	$		$
Earnings per share*	(0.05)		(0.09)
Cash flow per share*	(0.04)		(0.04)
	shs		shs
No. of shs. o/s*	82,105,133		49,834,283
Avg. no. of shs. o/s*	75,937,683		33,924,670
	%		%
Net profit margin	n.a.		n.a.
Return on equity	(137.92)		n.m.
Return on assets	(131.43)		(752.78)

* Common
[A] Reported in accordance with IFRS

Latest Results

Periods ended:	3m Apr. 30/22[A]		3m Apr. 30/21[A]
	$000s	%Chg	$000s
Net income	(796)	n.a.	(1,313)
	$		$
Earnings per share*	(0.01)		(0.02)

* Common
[A] Reported in accordance with IFRS

Historical Summary
(as originally stated)

Fiscal Year	Oper. Rev. $000s	Net Inc. Bef. Disc. $000s	EPS* $
2022[A]	nil	(3,777)	(0.05)
2021[A]	nil	(3,051)	(0.09)
2020[A]	nil	(2,202)	(1.50)
2019[A]	nil	(4,130)	(0.30)
2018[A]	nil	(4,297)	(0.50)

* Common
[A] Reported in accordance with IFRS

Note: Adjusted throughout for 1-for-10 cons. in Feb. 2020

F.17 FansUnite Entertainment Inc.

Symbol - FANS **Exchange** - TSX **CUSIP** - 30727R
Head Office - 303-780 Beatty St, Vancouver, BC, V6B 2M1 **Telephone** - (604) 329-8669
Website - www.fansunite.com
Email - graeme@fansunite.com
Investor Relations - Graeme Moore (604) 329-8669
Auditors - KPMG LLP C.A., Vancouver, B.C.
Transfer Agents - Odyssey Trust Company, Vancouver, B.C.
Employees - 97 at Dec. 31, 2022
Profile - (B.C. 2018) Operates an omni-channel customer acquisition company focused on North American sport betting affiliate and online gaming market. Also develops and operates a technology platform for business-to-business (B2B) online gaming and interactive entertainment markets.

Through wholly owned **American AffiliateCo LLC** engages and educates new retail and digital customers to register, deposit and bet on the mobile sportsbooks of many major licensed iGaming operators in the U.S. Affiliate services are delivered through Betting Hero, which offers in-person activations, quality assurance testing, competitive analysis and consulting, as well as providing support through their hotlines; and Props.com brands, which offers high quality journalism with influencer content driving multi-platform engagement.

Also offers Chameleon, a white label B2B gaming platform that allows independent operators to launch their own platforms. The platform includes a suite of products and solutions for eSports betting, traditional sports betting, eSports daily fantasy, casino-style games, cryptocurrency wallet and news content. In addition, owns and operates Askott Games, a developer of RNG (random number generator) casino games with eSports and video game themes, targeting players ages 21-35, for online sportsbooks and casinos.

In May 2023, the company entered into a definitive agreement to sell its wholly owned **McBookie Ltd.**, a Scottish-focused sportsbook and online casino company in the U.K., for total consideration of US$4,016,544.

In February 2023, the company sold BetPrep, a sports betting and iGaming brand, to **Stram Entertainment Limited** (dba BestOdds) for a 30% revenue share for three years subject to a minimum monthly guarantee.

In December 2022, wholly owned **American AffiliateCo LLC** agreed to transfer all the intellectual property and intangible assets under Wagers, a sports betting and iGaming brand, to **404 LLC** for the return and cancellation of 5,000,000 from Christopher Grove, director of the company and controller of 404.

In December 2022, the company was granted a license by the Ohio Casino Control Commission to begin operations in Ohio starting on Jan. 1, 2023.

In April 2022, the company was granted a licence by Alcohol and Gaming Commission of Ontario to begin operations in Ontario.

Recent Merger and Acquisition Activity

Status: pending **Announced:** May 8, 2023
FansUnite Entertainment Inc. entered into a definitive agreement with Betr Holdings Inc. to sell the source code of Chameleon iGaming platform for $3,000,000 cash, $2,000,000 Betr Series A2 preferred shares, to be settled through warrants at a price of US$0.01 per share and up to $5,000,000 in milestone payments payable over 12 months after closing of the transaction, payable as to $3,000,000 cash and $2,000,000 Betr Series A2 preferred shares, to be settled through warrants at a price of US$0.01 per share. Chameleon is an iGaming platform that enables companies to launch their own sports and related gambling brands. FansUnite would retain the use of Chameleon and source code to further develop and maintain the platform, and the ability to sell such use.

Predecessor Detail - Name changed from HIC Horizon Investments Capital Ltd., Mar. 27, 2020, pursuant to the reverse takeover acquisition of (old) FansUnite Entertainment Inc. and concurrent amalgamation of (old) FansUnite with wholly owned 1209080 B.C. Ltd. to form FansUnite Holdings Inc.

Directors - Scott Burton, CEO, Vancouver, B.C.; Chris Grove, Las Vegas, Nev.; James Keane, Vancouver, B.C.; Quinton Singleton, Las Vegas, Nev.

Other Exec. Officers - Ian Winter, COO; Graeme Moore, CFO & corp. sec.; Jeremy Hutchings, chief technical officer

Capital Stock

	Authorized (shs.)	Outstanding (shs.)[1]
Common	unlimited	357,572,305

[1] At Aug. 14, 2023

Normal Course Issuer Bid - The company plans to make normal course purchases of up to 17,898,515 common shares representing 5% of the total outstanding. The bid commenced on June 20, 2023, and expires on June 19, 2024.

Major Shareholder - Widely held at May 4, 2023.

Price Range - FANS/TSX

Year	Volume	High	Low	Close
2022	93,698,424	$0.48	$0.06	$0.07
2021	340,105,441	$2.37	$0.37	$0.42
2020	119,827,294	$1.22	$0.19	$1.10

Recent Close: $0.06

Capital Stock Changes - In March 2023, private placement of 37,976,242 units (1 common share & 1 warrant) at 8¢ per unit was completed, with warrants exercisable at 12¢ per share for three years.

During 2022, common shares were issued as follows: 38,017,883 pursuant to the acquisition of American AffiliateCo LLC, 2,750,000 on vesting of restricted share units, 877,698 for services, 201,867 on exercise of warrants and 8,332 on exercise of options; 5,000,000 common shares were cancelled and 227,000 common shares were repurchased under a Normal Course Issuer Bid.

Wholly Owned Subsidiaries

AmAff Canada Affiliates Inc., B.C.
American AffiliateCo LLC, Las Vegas, Nev.
Askott Entertainment Inc., Vancouver, B.C.
- 100% int. in **Askott Services Ltd.**, United Kingdom.
- 100% int. in **E.G.G. Limited**, Malta.

FansUnite Media Inc., Vancouver, B.C.

Investments

Cash Live Entertainment Inc., Vancouver, B.C.

Financial Statistics

Periods ended:	12m Dec. 31/22[A]		12m Dec. 31/21[A]
	$000s	%Chg	$000s
Operating revenue	**27,301**	**+387**	**5,603**
Cost of sales	12,454		2,724
Salaries & benefits	14,379		4,391
General & admin expense	9,063		8,500
Stock-based compensation	6,693		2,248
Operating expense	**42,589**	**+138**	**17,864**
Operating income	**(15,288)**	**n.a.**	**(12,261)**
Deprec., depl. & amort.	21,276		3,977
Finance income	nil		71
Finance costs, gross	12,370		1,378
Write-downs/write-offs	(71,658)		nil
Pre-tax income	**(60,121)**	**n.a.**	**(17,734)**
Income taxes	1,147		(685)
Net income	**(61,268)**	**n.a.**	**(17,049)**
Cash & equivalent	2,914		4,893
Accounts receivable	4,711		6,803
Current assets	8,877		22,314
Long-term investments	63		77
Fixed assets, net	67		60
Right-of-use assets	359		109
Intangibles, net	68,055		155,156
Total assets	**77,453**	**-56**	**177,945**
Bank indebtedness	8,233		nil
Accts. pay. & accr. liabs	4,509		7,108
Current liabilities	25,170		29,551
Long-term lease liabilities	153		39
Shareholders' equity	42,983		83,285
Cash from oper. activs	**(6,733)**	**n.a.**	**(8,156)**
Cash from fin. activs	7,418		17,698
Cash from invest. activs	(11,894)		(76)
Net cash position	**2,914**	**-79**	**13,974**
Capital expenditures	(56)		(76)
	$		$
Earnings per share*	(0.20)		(0.08)
Cash flow per share*	(0.02)		(0.04)
	shs		shs
No. of shs. o/s*	319,379,446		282,750,666
Avg. no. of shs. o/s*	309,637,689		200,121,900
	%		%
Net profit margin	(224.42)		(304.28)
Return on equity	(97.04)		(32.11)
Return on assets	(38.11)		(15.48)
Foreign sales percent	100		100
No. of employees (FTEs)	97		n.a.

* Common
[A] Reported in accordance with IFRS

Latest Results

Periods ended:	6m June 30/23[A]		6m June 30/22[oA]
	$000s	%Chg	$000s
Operating revenue	13,036	-2	13,237
Net inc. bef. disc. opers	(11,031)	n.a.	(25,217)
Income from disc. opers	4,407		143
Net income	(6,624)	n.a.	(25,074)
	$		$
Earns. per sh. bef. disc. opers.*	(0.03)		(0.09)
Earnings per share*	(0.02)		(0.09)

* Common
[o] Restated
[A] Reported in accordance with IFRS

Historical Summary
(as originally stated)

Fiscal Year	Oper. Rev.	Net Inc. Bef. Disc.	EPS*
	$000s	$000s	$
2022[A]	27,301	(61,268)	(0.20)
2021[A1]	5,603	(17,049)	(0.08)
2020[A1]	1,558	(13,463)	(0.14)
2019[A2]	nil	(2,909)	(0.08)
2018[A2]	8	(3,255)	(0.12)

* Common
[A] Reported in accordance with IFRS
[1] Results reflect the Mar. 26, 2020, reverse takeover acquisition of (old) FansUnite Entertainment Inc.
[2] Results pertain to (old) FansUnite Entertainment Inc.

F.18 Farmers Edge Inc.

Symbol - FDGE **Exchange** - TSX **CUSIP** - 30957Q
Head Office - 25 Rothwell Rd, Winnipeg, MB, R3P 2M5 **Telephone** - (204) 997-7006 **Toll-free** - (866) 724-3343 **Fax** - (888) 825-7576
Website - www.farmersedge.ca
Email - laura.workman@farmersedge.ca
Investor Relations - Laura Workman (866) 724-3343
Auditors - PricewaterhouseCoopers LLP C.A., Winnipeg, Man.
Lawyers - McCarthy Tétrault LLP
Transfer Agents - Computershare Trust Company of Canada Inc., Toronto, Ont.
Employees - 417 at Dec. 31, 2022
Profile - (Can. 2022; orig. Man., 2014 amalg.) Offers FarmCommand®, a proprietary, cloud-based analytics software platform that provides farmers with real-time monitoring, alerts, predictive models and outcome-based data recommendations. Also sells crop insurance products and carbon offsets.

Through FarmCommand®, data is integrated from multiple field-level sources including weather stations, soil moisture probes, telematics devices, location tracking devices, grain cart weighing devices, soil sampling, irrigation monitoring and satellite imagery. Growers may also access the company's e-commerce platform to purchase the company's suite of solution products and other crop inputs available through this online marketplace.

FarmCommand® is sold on a subscription basis, per acre per year, and primarily through a network of agriculture industry channel partners consisting of global crop input manufacturers and retailers, seed and crop protection companies, equipment manufacturers, grain companies and food manufacturers. Partnerships have also been formed with global insurance, reinsurance and other large agriculture industry participants, some of whom would serve as agents to sell the company's products, as well as help enhance the products to sell to these verticals.

Through its Managing General Agency DigiAg Risk Management offers insurance products including canola heat blast yield protection and group benefits targeting farmers.

Also offers Smart Carbon, a program which provides the company's grower customers the opportunity to generate carbon offsets creating a new revenue stream for growers.

The company is headquartered in Winnipeg, Man., and has additional regional head office locations in Lincoln, Neb.; Ridgehaven, S.A.; and Campinas, Brazil.

On Aug. 15, 2022, the company continued into the jurisdiction of the Canada Business Corporations Act from Manitoba.

During the first quarter of 2022, the company completed the closure of operations in Ukraine and Russia.

Directors - R. William (Bill) McFarland, chr., Richmond Hill, Ont.; Vibhore Arora, CEO, Surrey, B.C.; James Borel, Naples, Fla.; Natacha Mainville, Saint-Léonard, Qué.; Quinn McLean, Toronto, Ont.; Steven R. Mills, St. Louis, Mo.

Other Exec. Officers - Jay Jung, CFO; Colleen Coates, exec. v-p, people & culture; Matt Hesse, exec. v-p, global opers.; Rob Meijer, exec. v-p, corp. devel.; Matt Anderson, v-p, global opers.; Michelle Batista, v-p, sales, Canada; Jay Kinnaird, v-p, enterprise tech.; Darren Peters, v-p, global insce.; Amit Pradhan, v-p, strategy; Manoj Regmi, v-p, tech.; Laura Workman, gen. counsel & corp. sec.

Capital Stock

	Authorized (shs.)	Outstanding (shs.)[1]
Preferred	unlimited	nil
Common	unlimited	42,008,554

[1] At Mar. 31, 2023

Major Shareholder - Fairfax Financial Holdings Limited held 61.2% interest at Mar. 31, 2023.

Price Range - FDGE/TSX

Year	Volume	High	Low	Close
2022	6,808,072	$4.03	$0.23	$0.28
2021	11,096,362	$21.00	$3.11	$3.16

Recent Close: $0.20

Capital Stock Changes - During 2022, 51,757 common shares were issued on vesting of restricted share units.

Wholly Owned Subsidiaries

DigiAg Risk Management Inc., Canada.
Farmers Edge Australia Pty Ltd., Australia.
Farmers Edge LLC, Russia.
Farmers Edge (US), Inc., Minn.
- 100% int. in **CommoditAg, LLC**, United States.
- 100% int. in **DigiAg Risk Management (US), LLC**, United States.
- 100% int. in **Smart Farm, LLC**, Minn.

Farmers Edge Ukraine LLC, Ukraine.
7050160 Manitoba Inc., Man.
- 1% int. in **Farmers Edge (Brasil) Consultoria Em Atvidades Agricolas Ltda.**, Brazil.

Subsidiaries

99% int. in **Farmers Edge (Brasil) Consultoria Em Atvidades Agricolas Ltda.**, Brazil.

Financial Statistics

Periods ended:	12m Dec. 31/22[A]		12m Dec. 31/21[A]
	$000s	%Chg	$000s
Operating revenue	**32,771**	**-9**	**36,172**
Cost of sales	38,159		34,872
Research & devel. expense	5,554		7,900
General & admin expense	40,773		33,359
Stock-based compensation	1,716		3,627
Other operating expense	15,600		6,276
Operating expense	**101,802**	**+18**	**86,034**
Operating income	**(69,031)**	**n.a.**	**(49,862)**
Deprec., depl. & amort.	16,910		18,414
Finance costs, gross	1,714		7,707
Pre-tax income	**(86,883)**	**n.a.**	**(66,351)**
Net income	**(86,883)**	**n.a.**	**(66,351)**
Cash & equivalent	20,788		54,720
Inventories	2,766		2,517
Accounts receivable	11,683		19,480
Current assets	36,731		78,958
Fixed assets, net	33,193		31,608
Intangibles, net	17,094		25,217
Total assets	**87,018**	**-36**	**135,783**
Accts. pay. & accr. liabs	12,416		17,464
Current liabilities	24,327		26,435
Long-term debt, gross	38,919		nil
Long-term debt, net	38,583		nil
Long-term lease liabilities	3,533		3,466
Shareholders' equity	20,489		104,034
Cash from oper. activs	**(59,701)**	**n.a.**	**(62,201)**
Cash from fin. activs	36,001		128,750
Cash from invest. activs	(10,368)		(17,777)
Net cash position	**20,788**	**-62**	**54,720**
Capital expenditures	(7,073)		(7,975)
Capital disposals	1,415		368
	$		$
Earnings per share*	(2.07)		(1.81)
Cash flow per share*	(1.42)		(1.70)
	shs		shs
No. of shs. o/s*	41,959,882		41,908,125
Avg. no. of shs. o/s*	41,959,882		36,602,325
	%		%
Net profit margin	(265.12)		(183.43)
Return on equity	(139.55)		n.m.
Return on assets	(76.45)		(54.48)
Foreign sales percent	64		51
No. of employees (FTEs)	417		584

* Common
[A] Reported in accordance with IFRS

Latest Results

Periods ended:	3m Mar. 31/23[A]		3m Mar. 31/22[A]
	$000s	%Chg	$000s
Operating revenue	6,298	-26	8,561
Net income	(18,692)	n.a.	(22,182)
	$		$
Earnings per share*	(0.44)		(0.53)

* Common
[A] Reported in accordance with IFRS

Historical Summary
(as originally stated)

Fiscal Year	Oper. Rev.	Net Inc. Bef. Disc.	EPS*
	$000s	$000s	$
2022[A]	32,771	(86,883)	(2.07)
2021[A]	36,172	(66,351)	(1.81)
2020[A]	45,880	(84,633)	(8.01)
2019[A1]	23,802	(117,960)	(11.97)
2018[A1]	18,141	(106,159)	(10.82)

* Common
[A] Reported in accordance with IFRS
[1] As shown in the prospectus dated Feb. 24, 2021. Shares and per share figures adjusted to reflect 1-for-7 consolidation effective immediately prior to the initial public offering completed on Mar. 3, 2021.

F.19 Farstarcap Investment Corp.

Symbol - FRS.P **Exchange** - TSX-VEN **CUSIP** - 311736
Head Office - 1100-1199 Hastings St W, Vancouver, BC, V6E 3T5 **Telephone** - (604) 639-4521 **Fax** - (604) 684-0642
Email - rgm@malaspinaconsultants.com
Investor Relations - Robert G. McMorran (604) 313-9940
Auditors - Baker Tilly WM LLP C.A., Vancouver, B.C.
Transfer Agents - Computershare Trust Company of Canada Inc., Vancouver, B.C.
Profile - (B.C. 2016) Capital Pool Company.
Directors - Konstantine (Kon) Tsakumis, pres. & CEO, Richmond, B.C.; Robert G. (Rob) McMorran, CFO & corp. sec., Vancouver, B.C.; Neil MacRae, Port Coquitlam, B.C.; Mark St. John Wright, Surrey, B.C.

Capital Stock

	Authorized (shs.)	Outstanding (shs.)[1]
Common	unlimited	5,610,001

[1] At May 29, 2023

Major Shareholder - Mark St. John Wright held 10.69% interest at Oct. 25, 2022.

Price Range - FRS.P/TSX-VEN

Year	Volume	High	Low	Close
2022	230,000	$0.13	$0.05	$0.07
2021	100,000	$0.12	$0.08	$0.12
2020	50,000	$0.13	$0.05	$0.05
2019	613,750	$0.20	$0.07	$0.14

Recent Close: $0.04

Capital Stock Changes - There were no changes to capital stock from fiscal 2020 to fiscal 2022, inclusive.

Wholly Owned Subsidiaries

1299840 B.C. Ltd., Canada.

F.20 FendX Technologies Inc.

Symbol - FNDX **Exchange** - CSE **CUSIP** - 314460
Head Office - 200-2010 Winston Park Dr, Oakville, ON, L6H 5R7 **Toll-free** - (800) 344-9868
Website - fendxtech.com
Email - carolyn@fendxtech.com
Investor Relations - Dr. Carolyn Myers (800) 344-9868
Auditors - Dale Matheson Carr-Hilton LaBonte LLP C.A., Vancouver, B.C.
Transfer Agents - Endeavor Trust Corporation, Vancouver, B.C.
Employees - 2 at Mar. 15, 2023
Profile - (B.C. 2020) Developing surface protection products that protect surfaces from pathogen contamination.

Holds an exclusive worldwide licence to several patent applications and certain technology to research, develop and commercialize surface protection coating products using a patent-pending nanotechnology licensed from McMaster University in Hamilton, Ont.

First product under development is REPELWRAP™, a surface coating film that repels bacteria, viruses and liquids. Once developed, the product will be targeted to areas prone to high levels of surface contamination including healthcare settings, such as hospitals, long-term care, senior's residences and clinics; and high traffic public touchpoints, such as transportation, hospitality, stadiums/arenas/malls, restaurants, schools and business offices. REPELWRAP™ is expected to be launched in the Canadian market in the first half of 2024.

Common listed on CSE, Mar. 20, 2023.

Directors - Dr. Carolyn Myers, pres. & CEO, N.J.; Stephen D. Randall, Toronto, Ont.; Pierre L. Soulard, Toronto, Ont.

Other Exec. Officers - Andrea Mulder, COO; Rose Zanic, CFO & corp. sec.

Capital Stock

	Authorized (shs.)	Outstanding (shs.)[1]
Common	unlimited	51,913,453

[1] At Mar. 20, 2023

Major Shareholder - Widely held at Mar. 20, 2023.

Recent Close: $0.30

Capital Stock Changes - In March 2023, 13,138,000 units (1 common share & ½ warrant) were issued without further consideration on exchange of subscription receipts sold previously by private placement at 30¢ each, with warrants exercisable at 50¢ per share for two years.

Financial Statistics

Periods ended:	12m Dec. 31/21[A1]		22w Dec. 31/20[A1]
	$000s	%Chg	$000s
Research & devel. expense	109		nil
General & admin expense	1,022		337
Operating expense	**1,131**	**n.a.**	**337**
Operating income	**(1,131)**	**n.a.**	**(337)**
Pre-tax income	**(1,123)**	**n.a.**	**(337)**
Net income	**(1,123)**	**n.a.**	**(337)**
Cash & equivalent	1,084		357
Accounts receivable	15		nil
Current assets	1,243		357
Fixed assets, net	4		nil
Total assets	**1,247**	**+249**	**357**
Accts. pay. & accr. liabs	388		330
Current liabilities	388		330
Shareholders' equity	859		27
Cash from oper. activs	**(945)**	**n.a.**	**(7)**
Cash from fin. activs	1,677		364
Cash from invest. activs	(5)		nil
Net cash position	**1,084**	**+204**	**357**
Capital expenditures	(5)		nil
	$		$
Earnings per share*	(0.07)		n.a.
Cash flow per share*	(0.06)		n.a.
	shs		shs
No. of shs. o/s*	35,857,773		n.a.
Avg. no. of shs. o/s*	17,172,990		n.a.
	%		%
Net profit margin	n.a.		...
Return on equity	(253.50)		...
Return on assets	(140.02)		...

* Common
[A] Reported in accordance with IFRS
[1] As shown in the prospectus dated Jan. 31, 2023.

F.21 Fennec Pharmaceuticals Inc.

Symbol - FRX **Exchange** - TSX **CUSIP** - 31447P
Head Office - 68 TW Alexander Dr, PO Box 13628, Research Triangle Park, NC, United States, 27709 **Telephone** - (919) 636-4530 **Fax** - (919) 890-0490
Website - www.fennecpharma.com
Email - randrade@fennecpharma.com
Investor Relations - Robert C. Andrade (919) 246-5299
Auditors - Haskell & White LLP C.P.A., Irvine, Calif.
Lawyers - LaBarge Weinstein LLP
Transfer Agents - Computershare Trust Company of Canada Inc.
Employees - 36 at Dec. 31, 2022
Profile - (B.C. 2011; orig. Can., 1998) Develops and commercializes PEDMARK™ (sodium thiosulfate) to reduce the risk of platinum-induced ototoxicity in paediatric patients with cancer, and has royalty interest in Eniluracil.

PEDMARK™ is a sodium thiosulfate anhydrous injection, which acts as a chemoprotectant and a protectant against hearing loss often caused by platinum-based anti-cancer agents in children. The company has licensed from Oregon Health & Science University intellectual property rights for use of PEDMARK™. Two Phase III clinical trials of survival and reduction of ototoxicity have been completed. The drug was commercially launched in the U.S. in October 2022 and received Orphan Drug designation by U.S. FDA in 2004. Marketing authorization for PEDMARK™, which is known as Pedmarqsi™ in Europe Union, was granted by the European Medicines Agency in June 2023.

Also holds 5% royalty interest for the sale of Eniluracil, which was sold by the company to **Elion Oncology, LLC**.

Predecessor Detail - Name changed from Adherex Technologies Inc., Sept. 3, 2014; basis 1 new for 3 old shs.

Directors - Dr. Khalid Islam, chr., Lugano, Switzerland; Rostislav C. (Rosty) Raykov, CEO, Oakville, Ont.; Adrian Haigh, COO, Sintra, Portugal; Robert C. Andrade, CFO, Tex.; Dr. Marco Brughera, Milan, Italy; Dr. Jodi A. Cook, S.C.; Shubh Goel, N.J.; Chris A. Rallis, N.C.

Other Exec. Officers - Mark Gowland, contr.

Capital Stock

	Authorized (shs.)	Outstanding (shs.)[1]
Common	unlimited	26,411,000

[1] At Mar. 31, 2023

Major Shareholder - Southpoint Capital Advisors LP held 15.43% interest and Essetifin S.p.A. held 15.12% interest at Apr. 24, 2023.

Price Range - FRX/TSX

Year	Volume	High	Low	Close
2022	196,955	$13.80	$5.35	$13.09
2021	272,978	$13.25	$4.95	$5.60
2020	356,786	$14.08	$6.29	$9.09
2019	241,072	$10.00	$4.35	$8.45
2018	606,787	$18.86	$7.22	$8.55

Recent Close: $11.10

Capital Stock Changes - During 2022, common shares were issued as follows: 273,000 on exercise of options and 74,000 on vesting of restricted share units.

Wholly Owned Subsidiaries

Cadherin Biomedical Inc., Canada. Inactive.
Fennec Pharmaceuticals (EU) Limited, Ireland. Inactive
Fennec Pharmaceuticals, Inc., Del.
Oxiquant, Inc., Del. Inactive.

Financial Statistics

Periods ended:	12m Dec. 31/22[A]		12m Dec. 31/21[A]
	US$000s	%Chg	US$000s
Operating revenue	**1,535**	**n.a.**	**nil**
Cost of goods sold	86		nil
Research & devel. expense	3,531		4,981
General & admin expense	20,507		12,242
Operating expense	**24,038**	**+40**	**17,223**
Operating income	**(22,503)**	**n.a.**	**(17,223)**
Deprec., depl. & amort.	149		16
Finance income	195		54
Finance costs, gross	978		126
Pre-tax income	**(23,714)**	**n.a.**	**(17,346)**
Net income	**(23,714)**	**n.a.**	**(17,346)**
Cash & equivalent	23,774		21,100
Inventories	576		nil
Accounts receivable	1,545		nil
Current assets	26,728		22,387
Total assets	**26,939**	**+20**	**22,414**
Accts. pay. & accr. liabs	4,609		1,654
Current liabilities	4,609		1,654
Long-term debt, net	25,000		5,000
Shareholders' equity	(2,569)		15,772
Cash from oper. activs	**(18,058)**	**n.a.**	**(14,222)**
Cash from fin. activs	20,732		4,978
Net cash position	**23,774**	**+13**	**21,100**
	US$		US$
Earnings per share*	(0.90)		(0.67)
Cash flow per share*	(0.69)		(0.55)
	shs		shs
No. of shs. o/s*	26,361,000		26,014,000
Avg. no. of shs. o/s*	26,275,000		26,006,000
	%		%
Net profit margin	n.m.		n.a.
Return on equity	n.m.		(77.36)
Return on assets	(92.14)		(63.98)
No. of employees (FTEs)	36		10

* Common
[A] Reported in accordance with U.S. GAAP

Latest Results

Periods ended:	6m June 30/23[‡A]		6m June 30/22[A]
	US$000s	%Chg	US$000s
Operating revenue	5,002	n.a.	nil
Net income	(11,496)	n.a.	(8,768)
	US$		US$
Earnings per share*	(0.44)		(0.34)

* Common
‡ Preliminary
[A] Reported in accordance with U.S. GAAP

Historical Summary
(as originally stated)

Fiscal Year	Oper. Rev.	Net Inc. Bef. Disc.	EPS*
	US$000s	US$000s	US$
2022[A]	1,535	(23,714)	(0.90)
2021[A]	nil	(17,346)	(0.67)
2020[A]	170	(18,109)	(0.76)
2019[A]	nil	(12,775)	(0.64)
2018[A]	nil	(9,888)	(0.52)

* Common
[A] Reported in accordance with U.S. GAAP

F.22 Fibre-Crown Manufacturing Inc.

Symbol - FBR.H **Exchange** - TSX-VEN **CUSIP** - 315673
Head Office - 605-369 Terminal Ave, Vancouver, BC, V6A 4C4 **Telephone** - (604) 605-0166 **Fax** - (604) 692-0117
Email - morgan@nitalakelodge.com
Investor Relations - Morgan Pickering (604) 605-0166
Auditors - Crowe MacKay LLP C.A., Vancouver, B.C.
Transfer Agents - Computershare Trust Company of Canada Inc., Vancouver, B.C.
Profile - (B.C. 2003 amalg.; orig. B.C., 2002) No current operations.

Predecessor Detail - Formed from Tulane Capital Corp. in British Columbia, May 22, 2003, following Qualifying Transaction reverse takeover acquisition of and amalgamation with Fibre-Crown Manufacturing Inc. and was considered a recapitalization of Tulane.

Directors - Morgan Pickering, pres., CEO & CFO, Pemberton, B.C.; Jatinder S. (Jack) Bal, Delta, B.C.; Bradley N. (Brad) Scharfe, Vancouver, B.C.; Walter Schultz, Vancouver, B.C.

Capital Stock

	Authorized (shs.)	Outstanding (shs.)[1]
Common	unlimited	7,107,764

[1] At Mar. 31, 2023

Major Shareholder - Michael C. Scholz held 42.81% interest at Aug. 2, 2022.

Price Range - FBR.H/TSX-VEN

Year	Volume	High	Low	Close
2022	96,330	$0.20	$0.05	$0.07
2021	27,800	$0.15	$0.10	$0.15
2020	601,000	$0.14	$0.13	$0.13
2019	355,000	$0.18	$0.09	$0.17
2018	51,500	$0.15	$0.10	$0.10

Recent Close: $0.05

Financial Statistics

Periods ended:	12m Dec. 31/22[A]		12m Dec. 31/21[A]
	$000s	%Chg	$000s
General & admin expense	59		56
Operating expense	**59**	**+5**	**56**
Operating income	**(59)**	**n.a.**	**(56)**
Finance income	58		52
Pre-tax income	**(1)**	**n.a.**	**(3)**
Net income	**(1)**	**n.a.**	**(3)**
Cash & equivalent	411		421
Current assets	912		921
Total assets	**912**	**-1**	**921**
Accts. pay. & accr. liabs	11		20
Current liabilities	11		20
Shareholders' equity	901		902
Cash from oper. activs	**(9)**	**n.a.**	**2**
Net cash position	**411**	**-2**	**421**
	$		$
Earnings per share*	(0.00)		(0.00)
Cash flow per share*	(0.00)		0.00
	shs		shs
No. of shs. o/s*	7,107,764		7,107,764
Avg. no. of shs. o/s*	7,107,764		7,107,764
	%		%
Net profit margin	n.a.		n.a.
Return on equity	(0.11)		(0.33)
Return on assets	(0.11)		(0.33)

* Common

[A] Reported in accordance with IFRS

Latest Results

Periods ended:	3m Mar. 31/23[A]		3m Mar. 31/22[A]
	$000s	%Chg	$000s
Net income	nil	n.a.	2
	$		$
Earnings per share*	nil		0.00

* Common

[A] Reported in accordance with IFRS

Historical Summary
(as originally stated)

Fiscal Year	Oper. Rev.	Net Inc. Bef. Disc.	EPS*
	$000s	$000s	$
2022[A]	nil	(1)	(0.00)
2021[A]	nil	(3)	(0.00)
2020[A]	nil	nil	nil
2019[A]	nil	7	0.00
2018[A]	nil	16	0.00

* Common

[A] Reported in accordance with IFRS

F.23 Field Trip Health & Wellness Ltd.

Symbol - FTHW.H **Exchange** - TSX-VEN (S) **CUSIP** - 31656Q

Head Office - 401-30 Duncan St, Toronto, ON, M5V 2C3 **Toll-free** - (833) 833-1967

Website - www.fieldtriphealth.com

Email - paula@fieldtriphealth.com

Investor Relations - Paula Amy Hewitt (416) 617-6277

Auditors - Ernst & Young LLP C.A., Toronto, Ont.

Transfer Agents - Computershare Trust Company, N.A., Canton, Mass.; Computershare Trust Company of Canada Inc., Calgary, Alta.

Profile - (Can. 2022) Develops and delivers psychedelic therapies through health centres, as well as offers digital teletherapy tools.

Owns and operates clinics that offer psychedelic therapies, including ketamine-assisted psychotherapies (KAP) and psychedelic-assisted therapy (PAT), to address mental health and mood disorders including severe depression, anxiety and post-traumatic stress disorder (PTSD). Owns 12 clinics, of which 11 perform KAP and one performs PAT, which are located in Toronto, Ont.; Fredericton, N.B.; Vancouver, B.C.; New York, N.Y.; Santa Monica and San Diego, Calif.; Chicago, Ill.; Atlanta, Ga.; Seattle, Wash.; Houston, Tex.; Washington, D.C.; and Amsterdam, Netherlands.

Has developed the Trip mobile application, which provides users with self-directed consciousness-expanding activities and features mood tracking, personalized music, trip record keeping, guided journaling, voice recording and mindfulness content; and the Portal patient application, a digital health platform which provides ongoing support and education to patients participating in psychedelic therapies at the clinics.

Also researches and develops psilocybin-producing mushrooms and other related fungi conducted at a research and cultivation facility in Mona, Jamaica, in collaboration with the University of West Indies.

On Mar. 22, 2023, the company filed for protection under the Companies' Creditors Arrangement Act (CCAA) and **PricewaterhouseCoopers Inc.** was appointed monitor.

In March 2023, the company announced the closure of five clinics in Chicago, Ill., Washington, D.C., Seattle, Wash., San Diego, Calif., and Fredericton, N.B.

The company was incorporated on Apr. 28, 2022, as a wholly owned subsidiary of **Field Trip Health Ltd.** to facilitate the transfer of Field Trip's clinic, digital and botanical research operations to the company. The transfer was completed on Aug. 11, 2022, and Field Trip spun out the company to its shareholders on the basis of 0.85983356 common shares of the company for each Field Trip share held; Field Trip shareholders received a total of 50,055,011 common shares of the company. In conjunction, Field Trip changed its name to **Reunion Neuroscience Inc.**

Common suspended from TSX-VEN, Mar. 27, 2023.

Directors - Keith Merker, chief restructuring officer, London, Ont.; Dr. Araba Chintoh, Ont.; Barry Fishman, Thornhill, Ont.; Alexander Shoghi, Tex.

Other Exec. Officers - Mujeeb Jafferi, pres.; Donna Wong, CFO; Amardeep Manhas, chief tech. officer; Vicki Reed, chief mktg. officer; Dr. Michael Verbora, sr. v-p & medical dir.; Michael Coupland, v-p, occupational health; Edgar M. Diaz, v-p, clinical opers., Canada; Paula Amy Hewitt, v-p, chief privacy officer & gen. counsel; Chet Lakhani, v-p, digital strategy & product; Dr. Elizabeth Wolfson, v-p, clinical srvcs., USA

Capital Stock

	Authorized (shs.)	Outstanding (shs.)[1]
Common	unlimited	89,814,231

[1] At Aug. 17, 2022

Major Shareholder - Reunion Neuroscience Inc. held 21.84% interest and Oasis Investments II Master Fund Ltd. held 19.99% interest at Aug. 17, 2022.

Price Range - FTHW.H/TSX-VEN (S)

Year	Volume	High	Low	Close
2022	2,239,476	$0.60	$0.06	$0.08

Recent Close: $0.06

Capital Stock Changes - On Aug. 11, 2022, 50,055,011 common shares were issued pursuant to the transfer of former parent Field Trip Health Ltd.'s (renamed Reunion Neuroscience Inc.) clinic, digital and botanical research operations to the company, private placement of 35,559,220 common shares was completed at 50¢ per share and 4,200,000 common shares were issued without further consideration on exchange of subscription receipts sold previously by private placement at 50¢ each.

Wholly Owned Subsidiaries

Field Trip Health Holdings Inc., Canada.
- 100% int. in **Field Trip at Home Inc.**, Del.
- 100% int. in **Field Trip Digital Canada Inc.**, Canada.
  - 100% int. in **Field Trip Digital USA Inc.**, Del.
    - 100% int. in **Field Trip Digital LLC**, Del.
- 100% int. in **Field Trip Health B.V.**, Netherlands.
- 100% int. in **Field Trip Health Canada Inc.**, Canada.
- 100% int. in **Field Trip Health USA Inc.**, Del.
- 100% int. in **Field Trip Natural Products Ltd.**, Kingston, Jamaica.
- 100% int. in **Field Trip Training USA Inc.**, Del.

Financial Statistics

Periods ended:	12m Mar. 31/22[A1]		12m Mar. 31/21[A1]
	$000s	%Chg	$000s
Operating revenue	**4,860**	**+406**	**961**
Salaries & benefits	18,529		6,945
Research & devel. expense	97		168
General & admin expense	15,208		5,924
Stock-based compensation	5,645		2,880
Operating expense	**39,479**	**+148**	**15,917**
Operating income	**(34,619)**	**n.a.**	**(14,956)**
Deprec., depl. & amort	3,603		1,394
Finance income	28		19
Finance costs, gross	1,096		303
Pre-tax income	**(40,058)**	**n.a.**	**(17,877)**
Net income	**(40,058)**	**n.a.**	**(17,877)**
Cash & equivalent	1,999		1,304
Accounts receivable	1,053		730
Current assets	4,442		3,331
Fixed assets, net	4,462		2,199
Right-of-use assets	27,285		7,182
Intangibles, net	483		427
Total assets	**37,348**	**+174**	**13,621**
Accts. pay. & accr. liabs	4,049		2,111
Current liabilities	6,634		3,223
Long-term debt, gross	31		23
Long-term debt, net	31		23
Long-term lease liabilities	26,714		6,403
Shareholders' equity	3,968		3,972
Cash from oper. activs	**(14,524)**	**n.a.**	**(4,019)**
Cash from fin. activs	18,781		7,599
Cash from invest. activs	(3,625)		(2,523)
Net cash position	**2,775**	**+47**	**1,892**
Capital expenditures	(2,980)		(1,979)
	$		$
Earnings per share*	(0.81)		(0.63)
Cash flow per share*	(0.29)		(0.14)
	shs		shs
No. of shs. o/s	n.a.		n.a.
Avg. no. of shs. o/s*	49,656,441		28,432,833
	%		%
Net profit margin	(824.24)		n.m.
Return on equity	(1,009.02)		n.m.
Return on assets	(152.89)		n.a.

* Common

[A] Reported in accordance with IFRS

[1] Results were prepared on a carve-out basis representing former parent Field Trip Health Ltd.'s (renamed Reunion Neuroscience Inc.) clinic, digital and botanical research operations.

F.24 Fiera Capital Corporation*

Symbol - FSZ **Exchange** - TSX **CUSIP** - 31660A

Head Office - 1500-1981 av McGill College, Montréal, QC, H3A 0H5 **Telephone** - (514) 954-3300 **Toll-free** - (800) 361-3499 **Fax** - (514) 954-9692

Website - www.fieracapital.com

Email - mguay@fieracapital.com

Investor Relations - Marie-France Guay (514) 294-5878

Auditors - Deloitte LLP C.A., Montréal, Qué.

Lawyers - Davis Polk & Wardwell LLP; Fasken Martineau DuMoulin LLP

Transfer Agents - Computershare Trust Company of Canada Inc., Toronto, Ont.

FP500 Revenue Ranking - 409

Employees - 856 at Dec. 31, 2022

Profile - (Ont. 1955) Provides asset management services to institutional, financial intermediary and private wealth clients across North America, Europe and key markets in Asia.

At Dec. 31, 2022, the company had $158.5 billion in assets under management (AUM), consisting of institutional clients (53.2% of the AUM), financial intermediary clients (38% of the AUM) and private wealth clients (8.8% of the AUM).

Investment strategies span public and private markets globally. Public market asset classes include small to large cap equities, fixed income and liquid alternatives; and private market investments include real estate, infrastructure, private credit, agriculture, private equity and diversified private markets.

Institutional - Provides portfolio management solutions to pension funds of corporations and financial institutions, endowments, foundations, first nations communities, religious and charitable organizations, and public sector funds of major municipalities and universities. Client accounts are managed by the company on a segregated and pooled basis.

Financial Intermediaries - Has relationships with institutional and private wealth clients that are managed through strategic financial intermediary partners, such as banks and their affiliates, insurance companies and independent financial advisor networks. Also acts as sub-advisor on behalf of financial partners and intermediaries in the management of their mutual funds, pooled funds and exchange-traded funds provided to retail, mass affluent and high net worth investors.

Private Wealth - Provides asset management services and counsel to high net worth individuals, family offices, family foundations, trusts, estates and endowments.

Assets Under Management

At Dec. 31	2022 $millions	2021 $millions
Public markets:		
Institutional	70,823	82,625
Finl. intermediaries	59,113	77,453
Private wealth	10,329	12,370
	140,265	172,448
Private markets:		
Institutional	13,507	11,980
Finl. intermediaries	1,162	1,034
Private wealth	3,572	2,852
	18,241	15,866
Total AUM	158,506	188,314

Recent Merger and Acquisition Activity

Status: completed **Revised:** Aug. 3, 2022

UPDATE: Fiera Capital acquired the remaining 3.28% interest in Fiera Real Estate UK for £2,208,000 (Cdn$3,476,000). PREVIOUS: Fiera Capital Corporation acquired an additional 16.72% interest in London, U.K.-based Fiera Real Estate UK Limited for £11,285,000 (Cdn$18,183,000), thereby increasing its ownership to 96.72% from 80%. Fiera Real Estate UK invests in and provides a range of services, such as property, financial, legal and advisory, to property companies across the U.K.

Predecessor Detail - Name changed from Fiera Sceptre Inc., Apr. 16, 2012.

Directors - Jean-Guy Desjardins, chr. & CEO, Westmount, Qué.; Réal Bellemare, Montréal, Qué.; John Braive, Ont.; Annick Charbonneau, Qué.; Gary M. Collins, Vancouver, B.C.; Lucie Martel, Montréal, Qué.; Guy Masson, Qué.; Jean C. Monty, Montréal, Qué.; François Olivier, Montréal, Qué.; Norman M. Steinberg, Côte Saint-Luc, Qué.

Other Exec. Officers - Gabriel Castiglio, exec. dir., chief legal officer & corp. sec.; Jean Michel, exec. dir. & pres. & chief invest. officer, Fiera public markets; Lucas Pontillo, exec. dir. & CFO; Klaus Schuster, exec. dir. & CEO, EMEA; Peter Stock, exec. dir. & pres., Fiera private wealth; John Valentini, exec. dir. & pres. & CEO, Fiera private markets; Sebastian Blandizzi, chief tech. & opers. officer; Lyne Lamothe, chief HR officer; Jonathan Moncrieff, chief compliance officer; Wenzel R. B. Hoberg, global head, real estate; Michael Quigley, global head, distrib.

Capital Stock

	Authorized (shs.)	Outstanding (shs.)[1]
Preferred	unlimited	nil
Class A Subord. Vtg.	unlimited	85,694,246[2]
Class B Special Vtg.	unlimited	19,212,401

[1] At June 20, 2023

[2] At Aug. 3, 2023.

Class A Subordinate Voting - Entitled to elect one-third of the board of directors. One vote per share.

Class B Special Voting - Participate equally with class A subordinate voting shares with respect to dividends and in the event of any liquidation, dissolution or winding-up, etc. May not be issued to any person other than Fiera Capital L.P. Convertible into class A subordinate voting shares on a 1-for-1 basis at any time and automatically convertible upon disposition by Fiera Capital L.P. or 20 days following the occurrence of a class B termination date. A class B termination date is the earlier of (i) 90 days after the date Fiera Capital L.P. ceases to own and control at least 20% of the total class A subordinate voting and class B special voting shares or (ii) control of Fiera Capital L.P. is acquired by a person other than an employee, officer or director of the company or other entity wholly owned by Fédération des caisses Desjardins du Québec. Entitled to elect two-thirds of the board of directors. One vote per share.

Options - At Dec. 31, 2022, options were outstanding to purchase 3,865,505 class A subordinate voting shares at a weighted average exercise price of $11.33 per share with a weighted average remaining contractual life of 6.73 years.

Normal Course Issuer Bid - The company plans to make normal course purchases of up to 4,000,000 class A subordinate voting shares representing 4.7% of the total outstanding. The bid commenced on Aug. 16, 2023, and expires on Aug. 15, 2024.

Major Shareholder - Fiera Capital L.P. held 20.9% interest at May 11, 2023.

Price Range - FSZ/TSX

Year	Volume	High	Low	Close
2022	62,539,670	$10.77	$8.17	$8.68
2021	59,552,636	$11.83	$9.80	$10.49
2020	56,409,816	$13.18	$4.77	$10.68
2019	33,290,093	$12.78	$9.73	$11.71
2018	22,474,586	$13.37	$10.50	$11.29

Recent Close: $5.82

Capital Stock Changes - During 2022, class A subordinate voting shares were issued as follows: 1,305,127 on vesting of performance share units and 50,590 on exercise of options; 3,560,000 class A subordinate voting shares were repurchased under a Normal Course Issuer Bid.

Dividends

FSZ cl A S.V. Ra $0.86 pa Q est. Dec. 21, 2021**
Prev. Rate: $0.84 est. May 1, 2019
** Reinvestment Option

Long-Term Debt - Outstanding at Dec. 31, 2022:

Revolv. credit facility due 2026[1]	$445,490,000
5.6% hybrid debs. due 2024	108,260,000
6% hybrid debs. due 2027	99,351,000
Less: Def. fin. costs	1,492,000
	651,609,000
Less: Current portion	nil
	651,609,000

[1] Bears interest payable monthly at Canadian prime rate plus 0% to 1.5%, bankers' acceptance rate plus 1% to 2.5%, U.S. base rate plus 0% to 1.5% or adjusted term SOFR plus 1% to 2.5%.

Note - In June 2023, bought deal offering of $65,000,000 principal amount of 8.25% senior subordinated unsecured debentures due Dec. 31, 2026, was completed. Also in June 2023, all $110,000,000 000,000 principal amount of 5.6% senior subordinated debentures due July 31, 2024, were called for redemption on July 31, 2024.

Wholly Owned Subsidiaries

Fiera Capital (Europe) Limited, London, Middx., United Kingdom.
- 100% int. in **Fiera Capital (IOM) Limited**, Isle of Man.
- 100% int. in **Fiera Capital (UK) Limited**, United Kingdom.

Fiera Private Debt Inc., Canada.
Fiera Real Estate Investments Limited, Halifax, N.S.
- 100% int. in **Fiera Real Estate UK Limited**, London, Middx., United Kingdom.

Fiera US Holdings Inc., United States.
- 100% int. in **Fiera Capital Inc.**, United States.

Subsidiaries

60.4% int. in **Fiera Comox Partners Inc.**
75% int. in **Fiera Infrastructure Inc.**, Canada.

Investments

11.9% int. in **Fiera Capital (Asia) Inc.**
- 100% int. in **Fiera Capital (Asia) Hong Kong Limited**, Hong Kong, People's Republic of China.
- 100% int. in **Fiera Capital (Asia), L.P.**, Hong Kong, Hong Kong, People's Republic of China.
- 100% int. in **Fiera Capital (Asia) Singapore Pte. Ltd.**, Singapore.

Note: The preceding list includes only the major related companies in which interests are held.

Financial Statistics

Periods ended:	12m Dec. 31/22[A]		12m Dec. 31/21[A]
	$000s	%Chg	$000s
Total revenue	**681,439**	**-9**	**749,871**
Salaries & benefits	267,105		380,160
General & admin. expense	106,153		93,168
Stock-based compensation	20,639		32,764
Other operating expense	116,343		28,841
Operating expense	**510,240**	**-5**	**534,933**
Operating income	**171,199**	**-20**	**214,938**
Deprec. & amort.	57,622		67,622
Finance costs, gross	42,005		32,074
Write-downs/write-offs	nil		(3,625)
Pre-tax income	**41,645**	**-58**	**98,835**
Income taxes	10,123		22,214
Net income	**31,522**	**-59**	**76,621**
Net inc. for equity hldrs	**25,353**	**-66**	**73,532**
Net inc. for non-cont. int	**6,169**	**+100**	**3,089**
Cash & equivalent	68,213		111,983
Accounts receivable	146,747		216,454
Current assets	250,277		349,349
Long-term investments	21,180		21,061
Fixed assets, net	23,726		26,273
Right-of-use assets	67,150		77,763
Intangibles	911,036		934,582
Total assets	**1,329,331**	**-10**	**1,472,128**
Accts. pay. & accr. liabs	158,811		207,529
Current liabilities	225,893		300,023
Long-term debt, gross	651,609		603,653
Long-term debt, net	651,609		603,653
Long-term lease liabilities	78,699		91,641
Equity portion of conv. debs	nil		3,339
Shareholders' equity	341,045		415,313
Non-controlling interest	5,836		2,835
Cash from oper. activs	**113,310**	**-34**	**171,286**
Cash from fin. activs	(148,150)		(179,351)
Cash from invest. activs	(6,340)		43,553
Net cash position	**62,199**	**-39**	**102,594**
Capital expenditures, net	(4,921)		(16,136)
	$		$
Earnings per share*	0.25		0.71
Cash flow per share*	1.11		1.65
Cash divd. per share*	0.86		0.85
	shs		shs
No. of shs. o/s*	102,640,479		104,844,762
Avg. no. of shs. o/s*	102,447,711		103,839,056
	%		%
Net profit margin	4.63		10.22
Return on equity	6.70		16.65
Return on assets	4.52		6.81
Foreign sales percent	39		47
No. of employees (FTEs)	856		844

* Cl. A & B
[A] Reported in accordance with IFRS

Latest Results

Periods ended:	3m Mar. 31/23[A]		3m Mar. 31/22[A]
	$000s	%Chg	$000s
Total revenue	157,091	-9	172,343
Net income	(748)	n.a.	5,453
Net inc. for equity hldrs	(2,517)	n.a.	3,419
Net inc. for non-cont. int	1,769		2,034
	$		$
Earnings per share*	(0.02)		0.03

* Cl. A & B
[A] Reported in accordance with IFRS

Historical Summary
(as originally stated)

Fiscal Year	Total Rev. $000s	Net Inc. Bef. Disc. $000s	EPS* $
2022[A]	681,439	31,522	0.25
2021[A]	749,871	76,621	0.71
2020[A]	695,145	2,027	(0.03)
2019[A]	657,170	(10,706)	(0.14)
2018[A]	540,285	(4,755)	(0.05)

* Cl. A & B
[A] Reported in accordance with IFRS

F.25 Fife Capital Corp.

Symbol - FFC.P **Exchange** - TSX-VEN **CUSIP** - 31660L
Head Office - 1703-595 Burrard St, Vancouver, BC, V7X 1J1
Telephone - (604) 488-5427 **Fax** - (604) 681-4692
Email - lee@earlston.ca
Investor Relations - Sandra Lee (604) 488-5427
Auditors - Davidson & Company LLP C.A., Vancouver, B.C.
Transfer Agents - Computershare Trust Company of Canada Inc., Vancouver, B.C.

Profile - (B.C. 2020) Capital Pool Company.

Directors - A. Murray Sinclair Jr., pres., CEO, CFO & corp. sec., Vancouver, B.C.; Robert M. (Bob) Buchan, Toronto, Ont.; Edward (Ted) Hirst, West Vancouver, B.C.

Capital Stock

	Authorized (shs.)	Outstanding (shs.)[1]
Common	unlimited	3,530,000

[1] At Dec. 5, 2022

Major Shareholder - Robert M. (Bob) Buchan held 13.03% interest, Edward (Ted) Hirst held 13.03% interest and A. Murray Sinclair Jr. held 13.03% interest at Apr. 26, 2022.

Price Range - FFC.P/TSX-VEN

Year	Volume	High	Low	Close
2022	71,500	$0.50	$0.28	$0.28
2021	74,700	$0.45	$0.34	$0.40

Recent Close: $0.28

Capital Stock Changes - There were no changes to capital stock during fiscal 2022.

F.26 Filament Health Corp.

Symbol - FH **Exchange** - NEO **CUSIP** - 31685W
Head Office - 210-4475 Wayburne Dr, Burnaby, BC, V5G 4X4
Telephone - (604) 500-2407
Website - filament.health
Email - anna@filament.health
Investor Relations - Anna Cordon (604) 500-2407
Auditors - MNP LLP C.A., Calgary, Alta.
Lawyers - Fasken Martineau DuMoulin LLP, Vancouver, B.C.
Transfer Agents - Computershare Trust Company of Canada Inc., Vancouver, B.C.
Employees - 10 at June 27, 2023

Profile - (B.C. 2021 amalg.) Discovers, extracts, manufactures and commercializes psychedelic medicines to treat mental health conditions.

Drug candidates consist of PEX010, a proprietary psilocybin formulation administered orally, which is under a Phase II trial and tested on subjects experiencing major depressive disorder and methamphetamine use disorder; and PEX020 and PEX030, a proprietary formulation of non-psilocybin mushroom compound, administered orally and through a non-ingestive route, respectively, under a Phase I clinical trial designed to compare the effects to those of PEX010. Other clinical trials for PEX010 include treatment of alcohol use disorder, addiction and chronic pain. In addition, the company develops AEX010, an ayahuasca formulation, and AEX020, a standardized monoamine oxidase inhibitor, which are both in the pre-clinical stage of development.

Operates a 3,416-sq.-ft. manufacturing, research and development facility in Burnaby, B.C., which allows for the propagation of psychedelic plants, conducting of genetic research, performance of extraction procedures, running of in-house trials, and distribution of intellectual property and drug candidates to drug developers, researchers and other licensed parties.

In January 2023, the company (40%) entered into a joint venture agreement with **Jaguar Health Inc.** (40%) and **One Small Planet Capital LLC** (20%) to establish U.S.-based **Magdalena Biosciences Inc.** The joint venture aims to develop natural prescription drugs derived from plants for mental health indications, including attention deficit hyperactivity disorder (ADHD) in adults. One Small Planet would provide initial funding of US$1,000,000 for the purchase of 2,000,000 common shares at a price of 50¢ per share. Jaguar Health is a San Francisco,

Calif.-based pharmaceuticals company that develops plant-based prescription medicines for people and animals with gastrointestinal distress. One Small Planet is a Boulder, Colo.-based capital group that creates new global systems informed by the principles of the natural world.

In June 2022, the company entered into a collaboration agreement with **Jaguar Health, Inc.** to develop botanical prescription drugs for specific psychoactive target indications in the U.S. Under the agreement, Jaguar would be responsible for the identification of plants that may offer novel mechanisms of action as well as for botanical drug development and raw material supply chain while the company would be responsible for the developing and manufacturing required to produce the drug candidates.

Recent Merger and Acquisition Activity

Status: pending **Announced:** July 19, 2023

Filament Health Corp. and Jupiter Acquisition Corporation, a Special Purpose Acquisition Company, entered into an agreement for a business combination to create a new public holding (Pubco) company representing the combined business that is expected to be listed on NASDAQ. The proposed business combination reflects a pro forma enterprise valuation of US$210,000,000. Consideration would be in the form of shares in Pubco, and the proposed business combination was expected to provide at least US$5,000,000 of net proceeds to Pubco. At closing, the holders of outstanding Filament shares would receive equity in Pubco valued at US$0.85 per share (subject to adjustments). The transaction would be carried out as follows: Juipter would merge with and into a wholly owned subsidiary of Pubco and Filament would amalgamate with another wholly owned subsidiary of Pubco. The closing was expected in the fourth quarter of 2023.

Predecessor Detail - Formed from 1287396 B.C. Limited in British Columbia, June 22, 2021, pursuant to the reverse takeover acquisition of and amalgamation with Filament Ventures Corp. (deemed acquiror); basis 1 new com. sh. for 1 com. sh. of both 1287396 B.C. and Filament Ventures.

Directors - Benjamin (Ben) Lightburn, co-founder, chr. & CEO, West Vancouver, B.C.; Jon Conlin, corp. sec., North Vancouver, B.C.; Dr. Konstantin Adamsky, Tel Aviv, Israel; Maureen O'Connell, N.Y.; Chris Wagner, West Vancouver, B.C.

Other Exec. Officers - Lisa Ranken, COO; Warren Duncan, CFO; Ryan Moss, chief science officer; Andry Tjahyana, v-p, bus. devel.

Capital Stock

	Authorized (shs.)	Outstanding (shs.)[1]
Common	unlimited	174,948,813

[1] At June 27, 2023

Major Shareholder - Benjamin (Ben) Lightburn held 41.2% interest and Tom Kineshanko held 12.1% interest at Dec. 31, 2022.

Price Range - FH/NEO

Year	Volume	High	Low	Close
2022	689,000	$0.30	$0.05	$0.05
2021	530,500	$0.50	$0.22	$0.28

Recent Close: $0.17

Capital Stock Changes - In July 2022, private placement of 9,616,000 units (1 common share & 1 warrant) at 13¢ per unit was completed. Also during 2022, common shares were issued as follows: 270,000 on exercise of options, 206,100 for services and 99,844 for debt settlement.

Wholly Owned Subsidiaries

Psilo Scientific Ltd., Vancouver, B.C.

Investments

40% int. in **Magdalena Biosciences Inc.**, Del.

Financial Statistics

Periods ended:	12m Dec. 31/22[A]		12m Dec. 31/21[A1]
	$000s	%Chg	$000s
Operating revenue	**365**	**n.a.**	**nil**
Salaries & benefits	1,277		903
Research & devel. expense	839		477
General & admin expense	2,467		4,965
Stock-based compensation	1,095		2,754
Operating expense	**5,678**	**-38**	**9,099**
Operating income	**(5,313)**	**n.a.**	**(9,099)**
Deprec., depl. & amort.	201		172
Finance income	21		nil
Finance costs, gross	185		40
Write-downs/write-offs	(10,872)[2]		nil
Pre-tax income	**(16,537)**	**n.a.**	**(9,291)**
Income taxes	(71)		(38)
Net income	**(16,466)**	**n.a.**	**(9,254)**
Cash & equivalent	2,847		4,629
Accounts receivable	212		126
Current assets	3,172		5,344
Fixed assets, net	525		557
Right-of-use assets	488		624
Intangibles, net	460		11,142
Total assets	**4,741**	**-73**	**17,842**
Bank indebtedness	nil		281
Accts. pay. & accr. liabs	294		369
Current liabilities	417		755
Long-term debt, gross	719		nil
Long-term debt, net	719		nil
Long-term lease liabilities	411		535
Shareholders' equity	3,193		16,553
Cash from oper. activs	**(3,867)**	**n.a.**	**(5,407)**
Cash from fin. activs	2,155		9,424
Cash from invest. activs	(71)		(266)
Net cash position	**2,847**	**-38**	**4,629**
Capital expenditures	(32)		(130)
	$		$
Earnings per share*	(0.10)		(0.06)
Cash flow per share*	(0.02)		(0.04)
	shs		shs
No. of shs. o/s*	174,948,813		164,756,869
Avg. no. of shs. o/s*	169,464,834		147,037,695
	%		%
Net profit margin	n.m.		n.a.
Return on equity	(166.78)		(106.57)
Return on assets	(144.20)		(98.42)
No. of employees (FTEs)	11		11

* Common

[A] Reported in accordance with IFRS

[1] Results reflect the June 22, 2021, reverse takeover acquisition of and amalgamation with Filament Ventures Corp.

[2] Pertains to impairment of goodwill for $10,682,334 and bad debt expsense for $190,067

Latest Results

Periods ended:	3m Mar. 31/23[A]		3m Mar. 31/22[A]
	$000s	%Chg	$000s
Net income	(1,316)	n.a.	(1,595)
Net inc. for equity hldrs	(1,254)	n.a.	(1,595)
Net inc. for non-cont. int	(62)		nil
	$		$
Earnings per share*	(0.01)		(0.01)

* Common

[A] Reported in accordance with IFRS

Historical Summary
(as originally stated)

Fiscal Year	Oper. Rev.	Net Inc. Bef. Disc.	EPS*
	$000s	$000s	$
2022[A]	365	(16,466)	(0.10)
2021[A]	nil	(9,254)	(0.06)
2020[A1,2]	nil	(111)	(0.00)

* Common

[A] Reported in accordance with IFRS

[1] 30 weeks ended Dec. 31, 2020.

[2] Results pertain to Filament Ventures Corp.

F.27 Financial 15 Split Corp.

Symbol - FTN **Exchange** - TSX **CUSIP** - 317504

Head Office - c/o Quadravest Capital Management Inc., 2510-200 Front St W, PO Box 51, Toronto, ON, M5V 3K2 **Telephone** - (416) 304-4440 **Toll-free** - (877) 478-2372

Website - www.quadravest.com

Email - info@quadravest.com

Investor Relations - Shari Payne (877) 478-2372

Auditors - PricewaterhouseCoopers LLP C.A., Toronto, Ont.

Lawyers - Blake, Cassels & Graydon LLP, Toronto, Ont.

Transfer Agents - Computershare Trust Company of Canada Inc., Toronto, Ont.

Investment Managers - Quadravest Capital Management Inc., Toronto, Ont.

Managers - Quadravest Capital Management Inc., Toronto, Ont.

Profile - (Ont. 2003) Invests in a portfolio primarily consisting of common shares of 10 Canadian and five U.S. financial services companies.

The Canadian financial services companies include **Bank of Montreal**, **The Bank of Nova Scotia**, **Canadian Imperial Bank of Commerce**, **Royal Bank of Canada**, **The Toronto-Dominion Bank**, **National Bank of Canada**, **Manulife Financial Corporation**, **Sun Life Financial Inc.**, **Great-West Lifeco Inc.** and **CI Financial Corp.** The U.S. financial services companies include **Bank of America Corp.**, **Citigroup Inc.**, **Goldman Sachs Group Inc.**, **J.P. Morgan Chase & Co.** and **Wells Fargo & Co.** Shares held within the portfolio are expected to range between 4% and 8% in weight but may vary from time to time. The portfolio may hold up to 15% of its net asset value in equity securities of other issuers.

To supplement the dividends received on the investment portfolio and to reduce risk, the company may, from time to time, write covered call options in respect of all or part of the common shares in the portfolio.

The company will terminate on Dec. 1, 2025, or earlier at the discretion of the manager if the preferred or class A shares are delisted by the TSX or if the net asset value of the company declines to less than $5,000,000. At such time, all outstanding preferred and class A shares will be redeemed. The termination date may be extended beyond Dec. 1, 2025, for a further five years and thereafter for additional successive periods of five years as determined by the board of directors.

The investment manager receives a management fee at an annual rate equal to 0.65% of the net asset value of the company calculated and payable monthly in arrears. In addition, the manager receives an administration fee at an annual rate equal to 0.1% of the net asset value of the company calculated and payable monthly in arrears, as well a service fee payable to dealers on the class A shares at a rate of 0.5% per annum.

Top 10 holdings at Feb. 28, 2023 (as a percentage of net assets):

Holdings	Percentage
J.P. Morgan Chase & Co.	9.1%
Goldman Sachs Group Inc.	7.7%
Bank of America Corp.	7.5%
Royal Bank of Canada	6.8%
Wells Fargo & Co.	6.5%
The Toronto-Dominion Bank	5.6%
Citigroup Inc.	5.6%
National Bank of Canada	5.3%
Manulife Financial Corporation	5.1%
Canadian Imperial Bank of Commerce	4.3%

Directors - S. Wayne Finch, chr., pres. & CEO, Caledon, Ont.; Laura L. Johnson, corp. sec., Oakville, Ont.; Peter F. Cruickshank, Oakville, Ont.; Michael W. Sharp, Toronto, Ont.; John D. Steep, Stratford, Ont.

Other Exec. Officers - Silvia Gomes, CFO

Capital Stock

	Authorized (shs.)	Outstanding (shs.)[1]
Preferred	unlimited	40,093,727[2]
Class B	1,000	1,000[2]
Class A	unlimited	40,174,417

[1] At May 15, 2023

[2] Classified as debt.

Preferred - Entitled to receive fixed cumulative preferential monthly dividends of $0.05625 per share (to yield 6.75% per annum on the original $10 issue price). Retractable at any time at a price per share equal to the lesser of: (i) $10; and (ii) 98% of the net asset value (NAV) per unit (one preferred share and one class A share) less the cost to the company of purchasing one class A share in the market for cancellation. Shareholders who concurrently retract one unit in October of each year are entitled to receive an amount equal to the NAV per unit less any expenses (to a maximum of 1% of the NAV per unit) related to liquidating the portfolio to pay such redemption. All outstanding preferred shares will be redeemed on Dec. 1, 2025, at $10 per share. Rank in priority to class A and class B shares with respect to the payment of dividends and the repayment of capital. Non-voting.

Class B - Not entitled to dividends. Retractable at $1.00 per share and are entitled to liquidation value of $1.00 per share. Rank subsequent to preferred shares and prior to class A shares with respect to the repayment of capital on the dissolution, liquidation or winding-up of the company. One vote per share.

Class A - The company will endeavour to pay monthly cash dividends targeted to be $0.1257 per share (to yield 8% per annum on the original $15 issue price). If, after such dividends are paid, any amounts remain available, a special dividend of such amount will be made to shareholders in November of each year. Retractable at any time at a price per share equal to 98% of the NAV per unit less the cost to the company of purchasing one preferred share in the market for cancellation. Shareholders who concurrently retract one unit in October of each year are entitled to receive an amount equal to the NAV per unit less any expenses (to a maximum of 1% of the NAV per unit) related to liquidating the portfolio to pay such redemption. All outstanding class A shares will be redeemed on Dec. 1, 2025, at $15 per share. Class A shareholders are also entitled to receive the balance, if any, of the value of the investment portfolio remaining after returning the original issue price to preferred and class A shareholders. Rank subordinate to preferred and class B shares with respect to payment of dividends and the repayment of capital. Non-voting.

Normal Course Issuer Bid - The company plans to make normal course purchases of up to 4,007,080 preferred shares representing

10% of the public float. The bid commenced on May 29, 2023, and expires on May 28, 2024.

The company plans to make normal course purchases of up to 4,017,102 class A shares representing 10% of the public float. The bid commenced on May 29, 2023, and expires on May 28, 2024.

Major Shareholder - Quadravest Capital Management Inc. held 100% interest at Feb. 23, 2023.

Price Range - FTN/TSX

Year	Volume	High	Low	Close
2022	31,904,197	$12.42	$8.30	$9.23
2021	18,657,955	$12.24	$9.19	$11.49
2020	20,426,792	$18.48	$6.00	$9.74
2019	19,703,786	$22.45	$12.45	$17.55
2018	19,041,174	$26.53	$8.18	$14.63

Consolidation: 0.4-for-1 cons. in Dec. 2020

Recent Close: $8.82

Capital Stock Changes - In March 2022, public offering of 2,558,000 preferred shares and 2,558,000 class A shares was completed at $10.35 and $11.85 per share, respectively. In August 2022, public offering of 3,292,000 preferred shares and 2,292,000 class A shares was completed at $10 and $9.50 per share, respectively. Also during fiscal 2022, 5,176,500 preferred shares and 6,630,000 class A shares were issued under an at-the-market program.

Dividends

FTN cl A N.V. Ra $1.5084 pa M est. June 9, 2023
FTN.PR.A pfd cum. ret. Ra $0.75 pa M
Prev. Rate: $0.675

Financial Statistics

Periods ended:	12m Nov. 30/22^A		12m Nov. 30/21^A
	$000s	%Chg	$000s
Realized invest. gain (loss)	2,877		2,878
Unrealized invest. gain (loss)	(20,382)		102,692
Total revenue	**1,587**	**-99**	**119,165**
General & admin. expense	4,840		4,885
Other operating expense	2,701		1,506
Operating expense	**7,541**	**+18**	**6,391**
Operating income	**(5,954)**	**n.a.**	**112,774**
Finance costs, gross	21,153		14,793
Pre-tax income	**(27,107)**	**n.a.**	**97,980**
Net income	**(27,107)**	**n.a.**	**97,980**
Cash & equivalent	129,120		28,116
Accounts receivable	1,287		741
Investments	539,181		480,133
Total assets	**670,924**	**+32**	**508,991**
Accts. pay. & accr. liabs	504		703
Debt	346,488		236,224
Shareholders' equity	309,903		267,437
Cash from oper. activs	**(59,684)**	**n.a.**	**(34,409)**
Cash from fin. activs	160,748		(178,376)
Net cash position	**129,120**	**+359**	**28,116**
	$		$
Earnings per share*	(0.95)		4.45
Cash flow per share*	(2.09)		(1.56)
Net asset value per share*	8.83		11.32
Cash divd. per share*	1.51		1.51
	shs		shs
No. of shs. o/s*	35,102,317		23,622,317
Avg. no. of shs. o/s*	28,541,192		22,023,390
	%		%
Net profit margin	n.m.		82.22
Return on equity	(9.39)		47.77
Return on assets	(1.01)		20.79

* Class A
^A Reported in accordance with IFRS

Note: Net income reflects increase/decrease in net assets from operations.

Historical Summary
(as originally stated)

Fiscal Year	Total Rev.	Net Inc. Bef. Disc.	EPS*
	$000s	$000s	$
2022^A	1,587	(27,107)	(0.95)
2021^A	119,165	97,980	4.45
2020^A	(81,278)	(112,249)	(6.38)
2019^A	90,650	59,111	3.50
2018^A	(17,244)	(47,041)	(3.13)

* Class A
^A Reported in accordance with IFRS

Note: Adjusted throughout for 0.4-for-1 cons. in Dec. 2020

F.28 FinCanna Capital Corp.

Symbol - CALI.X **Exchange** - CSE **CUSIP** - 31773B
Head Office - 550-800 Pender St W, Vancouver, BC, V6C 2V6 **Telephone** - (778) 327-5799 **Fax** - (778) 327-6675
Email - vvipul@wealthstewards.ca
Investor Relations - Vern Vipul (416) 545-9103
Auditors - Davidson & Company LLP C.A., Vancouver, B.C.
Transfer Agents - National Securities Administrators Ltd., Vancouver, B.C.

Profile - (B.C. 2011) Provides capital to licensed medical cannabis companies in the U.S., with a focus on the California market.

The company holds the former software assets of **Green Compliance, Inc.**, an enterprise compliance and point-of-sale software solution for licensed cannabis dispensaries as assets held for sale.

In August 2022, the company wrote off its 20% perpetual royalty licence in **QVI, Inc.** (dba West County Brands, formerly known as The Galley), a cannabis infused product manufacturer based in California, subsequent to QVI announcing it plans to suspend operations indefinitely.

Predecessor Detail - Name changed from Astar Minerals Ltd., Dec. 29, 2017, pursuant to reverse takeover acquisition of private company FinCanna Capital Corp. and amalgamation of FinCanna with a wholly owned subsidiary of Astar.

Directors - Vern Vipul, CEO; James Blackwell; Michael Coner

Other Exec. Officers - Sung Min (Eric) Myung, CFO; Enrico Moretti, corp. sec.

Capital Stock

	Authorized (shs.)	Outstanding (shs.)[1]
Common	unlimited	62,544,343

[1] At Oct. 31, 2022

Major Shareholder - Widely held at Sept. 1, 2020.

Price Range - CALI.X/CSE

Year	Volume	High	Low	Close
2022	22,621,958	$0.28	$0.01	$0.01
2021	5,417,249	$2.00	$0.11	$0.30
2020	2,217,832	$1.25	$0.35	$0.80
2019	3,510,103	$1.95	$0.75	$1.25
2018	7,072,665	$14.50	$0.80	$1.10

Consolidation: 1-for-10 cons. in Dec. 2021

Recent Close: $0.01

Capital Stock Changes - On Dec. 9, 2021, common shares were consolidated on a 1-for-10 basis. In April 2022, private placement of 29,055,000 post-consolidated units (1 common share & 1 warrant) at 10¢ per unit was completed. During fiscal 2022, 1,590,245 common shares were issued on conversion of debentures.

Wholly Owned Subsidiaries

FCC Holdings Ltd., Canada.
FCC Ventures, Inc.
FinCanna Holdings Corp., B.C.

Financial Statistics

Periods ended:	12m Apr. 30/22^A		12m Apr. 30/21^A
	$000s	%Chg	$000s
Operating revenue	**nil**	**n.a.**	**142**
Research & devel. expense	nil		171
General & admin expense	1,701		2,147
Operating expense	**1,701**	**-27**	**2,318**
Operating income	**(1,701)**	**n.a.**	**(2,176)**
Deprec., depl. & amort	173		403
Finance costs, gross	1,180		756
Write-downs/write-offs	(5,831)		(7,848)
Pre-tax income	**(8,858)**	**n.a.**	**(11,289)**
Net income	**(8,858)**	**n.a.**	**(11,289)**
Cash & equivalent	1,179		1,629
Accounts receivable	17		138
Current assets	1,348		3,315
Long-term investments	nil		2,469
Fixed assets, net	10		129
Intangibles, net	230		383
Total assets	**1,588**	**-75**	**6,397**
Accts. pay. & accr. liabs	473		301
Current liabilities	7,437		354
Long-term debt, gross	6,616		6,337
Long-term debt, net	nil		6,337
Long-term lease liabilities	nil		64
Shareholders' equity	(5,850)		(358)
Cash from oper. activs	**(1,341)**	**n.a.**	**(2,128)**
Cash from fin. activs	2,707		3,664
Cash from invest. activs	(1,816)		(2,554)
Net cash position	**1,179**	**-28**	**1,629**
Capital expenditures	nil		(109)
	$		$
Earnings per share*	(0.71)		(1.10)
Cash flow per share*	(0.11)		(0.21)
	shs		shs
No. of shs. o/s*	42,468,850		11,823,605
Avg. no. of shs. o/s*	12,510,413		10,280,293
	%		%
Net profit margin	n.a.		n.m.
Return on equity	n.m.		n.m.
Return on assets	(192.31)		(106.61)

* Common
^A Reported in accordance with IFRS

Latest Results

Periods ended:	6m Oct. 31/22^A		6m Oct. 31/21^A
	$000s	%Chg	$000s
Operating revenue	nil	n.a.	79
Net income	(1,664)	n.a.	(1,550)
	$		$
Earnings per share*	(0.04)		(0.10)

* Common
^A Reported in accordance with IFRS

Historical Summary
(as originally stated)

Fiscal Year	Oper. Rev.	Net Inc. Bef. Disc.	EPS*
	$000s	$000s	$
2022^A	nil	(8,858)	(0.71)
2021^A	142	(11,289)	(1.10)
2020^A	777	(11,684)	(1.20)
2019^A	1,883	210	0.02
2018^A1	838	(12,696)	(3.10)

* Common
^A Reported in accordance with IFRS
[1] Results reflect the Dec. 27, 2017, reverse takeover acquisition of (old) Fincanna Capital Corp.

Note: Adjusted throughout for 1-for-10 cons. in Dec. 2021

F.29 Findev Inc.

Symbol - FDI **Exchange** - TSX-VEN **CUSIP** - 31773A
Head Office - 200-10 Wanless Ave, Toronto, ON, M4N 1V6 **Telephone** - (416) 481-2222
Website - www.findev.ca
Email - sweinreb@findev.ca
Investor Relations - Yisroel Weinreb (877) 848-8790
Auditors - Dale Matheson Carr-Hilton LaBonte LLP C.A.
Lawyers - Norton Rose Fulbright Canada LLP, Ottawa, Ont.
Transfer Agents - Computershare Trust Company of Canada Inc., Toronto, Ont.

Profile - (Can. 2004) Provides loan financing to residential and retail development real estate projects within Toronto, Ont.

Targets real estate projects that are identified as uniquely positioned to generate above average returns within a two-year to three-year timeframe including condominiums, purpose-built rentals, townhouses, low-rise/subdivisions and retail developments. Loans are generally for a period of one to five years, bridging projects through their development cycle. The mortgage and loan investments are secured by mortgages registered on title and/or other forms of security, including, but not limited to, floating charge debentures, general security agreements, postponement of specific claims, and joint and several guarantees.

Predecessor Detail - Name changed from TransGaming Inc., Sept. 16, 2016, following the sale of GameTree TV business resulting in a change-of-business; basis 1 new for 35 old shs.

Directors - Brice N. Scheschuk, chr., Toronto, Ont.; Yisroel (Sruli) Weinreb, CEO, Toronto, Ont.; Devon Cranson, Toronto, Ont.; Niall Finnegan, Toronto, Ont.; Anthony Heller, Toronto, Ont.; David Roff, Toronto, Ont.

Other Exec. Officers - Claude Ayache, CFO

Capital Stock

	Authorized (shs.)	Outstanding (shs.)[1]
Class B Preferred	unlimited	nil
Common	unlimited	28,647,441

[1] At May 25, 2023

Major Shareholder - Anthony Heller held 48.31% interest at May 19, 2023.

Price Range - FDI/TSX-VEN

Year	Volume	High	Low	Close
2022	663,472	$0.52	$0.40	$0.41
2021	1,544,593	$0.60	$0.40	$0.47
2020	1,319,006	$0.50	$0.30	$0.49
2019	718,508	$0.57	$0.35	$0.42
2018	771,167	$0.62	$0.35	$0.50

Recent Close: $0.40

Capital Stock Changes - There were no changes to capital stock from 2017 to 2022, inclusive.

Dividends

FDI com Ra $0.03 pa Q est. Jan. 6, 2017

Wholly Owned Subsidiaries

Findev Lending Inc.

Financial Statistics

Periods ended:	12m Dec. 31/22A		12m Dec. 31/21A
	$000s	%Chg	$000s
Total revenue	**3,045**	**+14**	**2,662**
General & admin. expense	279		258
Operating expense	**279**	**+8**	**258**
Operating income	**2,766**	**+15**	**2,404**
Finance costs, gross	2		2
Pre-tax income	**2,242**	**-6**	**2,387**
Income taxes	735		(3,013)
Net income	**1,507**	**-72**	**5,400**
Cash & equivalent	286		280
Investments	21,386		19,990
Total assets	**23,953**	**+3**	**23,288**
Accts. pay. & accr. liabs	86		69
Shareholders' equity	23,652		23,004
Cash from oper. activs	**865**	**+2**	**852**
Cash from fin. activs	(859)		(859)
Net cash position	**286**	**+2**	**280**
	$		$
Earnings per share*	0.05		0.19
Cash flow per share*	0.03		0.03
Cash divd. per share*	0.03		0.03
	shs		shs
No. of shs. o/s*	28,647,441		28,647,441
Avg. no. of shs. o/s*	28,647,441		28,647,441
	%		%
Net profit margin	49.49		202.85
Return on equity	6.46		26.04
Return on assets	6.39		25.73

* Common
A Reported in accordance with IFRS

Latest Results

Periods ended:	3m Mar. 31/23A		3m Mar. 31/22A
	$000s	%Chg	$000s
Total revenue	809	+8	749
Net income	538	0	537
	$		$
Earnings per share*	0.02		0.02

* Common
A Reported in accordance with IFRS

Historical Summary
(as originally stated)

Fiscal Year	Total Rev.	Net Inc. Bef. Disc.	EPS*
	$000s	$000s	$
2022A	3,045	1,507	0.05
2021A	2,662	5,400	0.19
2020A	2,225	1,931	0.07
2019A	1,998	1,671	0.06
2018A	1,761	1,505	0.05

* Common
A Reported in accordance with IFRS

F.30 Fineqia International Inc.

Symbol - FNQ **Exchange** - CSE **CUSIP** - 31788W
Head Office - 760-777 Hornby St, Vancouver, BC, V6Z 1S4 **Telephone** - (778) 654-2324
Website - www.fineqia.com
Email - bundeep.rangar@fineqia.com
Investor Relations - Bundeep S. Rangar (778) 654-2324
Auditors - Baker Tilly WM LLP C.A., Toronto, Ont.
Transfer Agents - National Securities Administrators Ltd., Vancouver, B.C.
Profile - (B.C. 2006) Provides a platform and associated services to place and administer debt and equity securities issuances in an alternative area of finance known as crowdfunding.

The platform distributes and markets debt instruments (known as minibonds) to the crowd, and allows investors to discover and invest in high yield securities, as well as transparently highlighting the risks and objectively outlining opportunities involved. The platform also allows to bypass much of the cost overhead inherent in large financial institutions, which results in higher yields.

In addition, holds a portfolio of equity and debt investments on companies engaged in the development of blockchain, fintech and cryptocurrency technology. Portfolio includes Estonia-based **Black Syndicate Holdings Limited** (Black Insurance), a digital insurance start-up company; U.K.-based **Nivaura Limited** which offers a capital markets platform that is licensed to clients on a white label basis; California-based **Wave Financial Group, LLC** which offers early-stage investment, asset management, treasury management and strategy consulting; Texas-based **Phunware, Inc.** which offers an enterprise cloud platform for mobile that provides products, solutions, data and services for brands worldwide; and Massachusetts-based **IDEO CoLab Ventures Fund**, which invests in early stage blockchain and crypto start-up companies, and **IDEO CoLab Forte Series A LLC**, which operates a blockchain gaming platform.

Predecessor Detail - Name changed from Nanostruck Technologies Inc., Aug. 2, 2016.
Directors - Martin Graham, chr., London, Middx., United Kingdom; Bundeep S. Rangar, pres. & CEO, London, Middx., United Kingdom; Brij P. S. Chadda, Mississauga, Ont.
Other Exec. Officers - Stephen J. (Steve) McCann, interim CFO; Michael Coletta, chief strategy officer

Capital Stock

	Authorized (shs.)	Outstanding (shs.)[1]
Preferred	unlimited	nil
Common	unlimited	1,214,635,464

[1] At Jan. 4, 2023

Major Shareholder - Bundeep S. Rangar held 16.9% interest and Andrew John Scott Walton-Green held 11.95% interest at Oct. 21, 2020.

Price Range - FNQ/CSE

Year	Volume	High	Low	Close
2022	55,636,206	$0.01	$0.01	$0.01
2021	426,557,715	$0.06	$0.01	$0.01
2020	10,408,931	$0.01	$0.01	$0.01
2019	37,587,584	$0.02	$0.01	$0.01
2018	83,906,474	$0.06	$0.01	$0.01

Recent Close: $0.01
Capital Stock Changes - In April 2023, private placement of up to 100,000,000 units (1 common share & 1 warrant) at 1¢ per unit was announced, with warrants exercisable at 5¢ per share for three years.

From August to December 2022, private placement of 482,460,590 units (1 common share & 1 warrant) at 1¢ per unit was completed, with warrants exercisable at 5¢ per share for three years. In addition, 50,697,500 units (same terms) were issued on conversion of debt.

Wholly Owned Subsidiaries

Blue Gold Tailing Technologies Ltd., Mississauga, Ont. Inactive.
Fineqia AG mvK, Liechtenstein.
Fineqia Investments Limited, Malta.
- **Black Syndicate Holdings Limited**, Tallinn, Estonia.
- **IDEO CoLab Forte Series A LLC**, Calif.
- **IDEO CoLab Ventures Fund**, United States.
- **Nivaura Limited**, United Kingdom.
- **Phunware, Inc.**, Austin, Tex.
- **Wave Financial Group, LLC**, Los Angeles, Calif.

Fineqia Limited, United Kingdom.

F.31 Finning International Inc.*

Symbol - FTT **Exchange** - TSX **CUSIP** - 318071
Head Office - 19100 94 Ave, Surrey, BC, V4N 5C3 **Telephone** - (604) 691-6444 **Toll-free** - (888) 346-6464 **Fax** - (604) 871-8231
Website - www.finning.com
Email - ilona.rojkova@finning.com
Investor Relations - Ilona Rojkova (604) 331-4865
Auditors - Deloitte LLP C.A., Vancouver, B.C.
Lawyers - Borden Ladner Gervais LLP, Vancouver, B.C.
Transfer Agents - Computershare Trust Company of Canada Inc., Vancouver, B.C.
FP500 Revenue Ranking - 66
Employees - 14,246 at Dec. 31, 2022
Profile - (Can. 1986; orig. B.C., 1933) Sells, rents and provides parts and customer support services for **Caterpillar Inc.** equipment and engines and complementary equipment in western Canada, Chile, Argentina, Bolivia, the U.K. and Ireland. Also operates 4Refuel, a mobile on-site refuelling business in most of Canadian provinces and Texas.

Operations consist of five principal activities: product support; new equipment sales; used equipment sales; equipment rental; and refuelling. Principal markets include mining, construction (including pipeline and oil field development), power generation and forestry. Customers include private enterprise and government. The company operates in Canada (British Columbia, Yukon, Alberta, Saskatchewan, the Northwest Territories and a portion of Nunavut); South America (Chile, Argentina and Bolivia); and U.K. and Ireland (England, Scotland, Wales, Northern Ireland and the Republic of Ireland).

Product Support - Provides replacement parts and maintenance and repair services for the products it sells. To provide customers with a convenient access to a supply of parts, the company maintains parts inventory throughout its locations in western and northern Canada, South America, and the U.K. and Ireland. All major parts distribution centres within each geographic area are connected through information systems, which provide immediate information on both the company and Caterpillar parts inventories. In addition to in-shop capability, on-site services are also provided with specialized personnel and equipment sent at customer locations. Also offers equipment rebuilds, allowing customers to extend their fleets' operating life by remanufacturing and exchanging major components. Remanufactured components sourced from Caterpillar are extensively used to meet continuing demand for component replacement in Caterpillar products. Also operates centralized component remanufacturing centres that can dismantle, test, repair and replace worn components, as well as a hydraulic hose replacement and repair company that provides on-site mobile hose services including hose replacement, assembly and fitting, oil replenishment and general hydraulic servicing. The hydraulic hose company also sells hydraulic and fluid power products and parts via a network of branches and through online channels. Furthermore, maintenance and repair contracts are offered for preventive maintenance, planned and guaranteed component replacement and guaranteed cost per hour contracts. Digital dealer services are also offered through the CUBIQ™ performance solutions platform, which combines live data with the data collected from thousands of pieces of equipment and technical experts to offer equipment insights, condition monitoring and other value-added services.

New Equipment Sales - Distributes Caterpillar products including tractors, off-highway trucks, drills, electric rope shovels, hydraulic excavators and drag lines, backhoe loaders, excavators, forklifts, articulated trucks, loaders, log loaders, tree harvesters, skidders, motor graders, paving products, compactors, wheel tractor-scrapers, pipe layers, extensive underground equipment and products complementary to Caterpillar-branded products. Also sells and rents Caterpillar-branded and non-branded engines and power systems for use in electric power generation, oil and gas, marine and industrial applications, and supplies complete or partial power systems engineering projects to customers.

Used Equipment Sales - Buys and sells used equipment domestically and internationally, with a focus on the product and types of equipment for which the company is a dealer. Machines are accepted in trade, received from the rental fleet, and purchased from customers and others on the open market. Some of this equipment is reconditioned or rebuilt in the company's service shops or rebuild centres and resold under a warranty program. Also purchases and sells entire fleets of used equipment and sells used equipment on consignment or through auctions.

Equipment Rental - Offers rental agreements for equipment ranging from short-term arrangements to longer term arrangements. Also provides equipment under rental agreements that include an option to purchase.

Finning Canada division operates three rental fleets. The heavy rental fleet is operated through the dealership network and focuses mainly on mid to large size Caterpillar earth moving equipment, such as track type tractors, articulated trucks, wheel loaders and excavators, primarily for the construction, oil and gas industries. The power generation rental fleet services a wide variety of customers for larger temporary power generation applications. Also offers rental products that are complementary to customers under its The CAT Rental Store banner. These include smaller Caterpillar earth moving equipment and forklifts, work platforms, light towers, power generation and distribution equipment, heat products, air compressors and various other non-Caterpillar branded equipment.

Finning South America division maintains a rental fleet consisting of motor graders, compactors, excavators, backhoe loaders, tractors, compressors, power generators and light towers. The rental business mainly serves customers in the construction and mining industries. Also offers Caterpillar products, as well as select non-Caterpillar products, under The CAT Rental Store banner and through selected dealership branches.

Finning UK & Ireland division maintains a fleet of rental equipment for rental contracts which are normally more long-term in nature. The fleet consists mainly of larger equipment such as wheel loaders, and articulated and rigid chassis dump trucks. Customers served include quarrying and construction companies, waste and recycling customers, as well as a wide variety of customers in larger power generation applications which are on a mid to long-term basis contracts.

Refuelling - Provides mobile on-site refuelling services through wholly owned **4Refuel Canada LP** and serves customers in construction, transportation, oil and gas, power generation and other industrial sectors in British Columbia, Alberta, Saskatchewan, Manitoba, Ontario, Québec, New Brunswick, Nova Scotia and Texas. 4Refuel also holds a 54.5% interest in **Compression Technology Corporation** (dba ComTech Energy), which develops alternative energy infrastructure and provides proprietary mobile fuelling solutions for low-carbon fuels, including compressed natural gas, renewable natural gas and hydrogen, in North America.

On Dec. 30, 2022, 31.4%-owned **Energyst B.V.** was dissolved. The company received a final distribution of $1,000,000 in relation to this liquidation.

Recent Merger and Acquisition Activity

Status: completed **Announced:** Mar. 22, 2022
Finning International Inc. acquired United Kingdom-based Hydraquip Hose & Hydraulics Ltd. and Hoses Direct Ltd. (collectively Hydraquip), an onsite mobile hydraulic hose replacement and repair company, for £65,000,000. Hydraquip has 270 employees serving more than 4,000 customers across a diverse range of industries, including construction, power systems, transportation, waste management, utilities, manufacturing and materials handling.

Predecessor Detail - Name changed from Finning Ltd., Apr. 25, 1997; basis 2 new for 1 old sh.
Directors - Harold N. (Hal) Kvisle, chr., Calgary, Alta.; Kevin Parkes, pres. & CEO, Edmonton, Alta.; Vicki L. Avril-Groves, Cape Coral, Fla.; James E. C. (Jim) Carter, Edmonton, Alta.; Jacynthe Côté, Candiac, Qué.; Nicholas (Nicky) Hartery, Limerick, Ireland; Mary Lou Kelley, South Bend, Ind.; Andrés J. Kuhlmann, Santiago, Chile; Stuart L. (Stu) Levenick, Naples, Fla.; Christopher W. (Chris) Patterson, Greensboro, N.C.; Charles F. Ruigrok, Calgary, Alta.; Edward R. (Ted) Seraphim, North Vancouver, B.C.; Manjit K. Sharma, Toronto, Ont.; Nancy G. Tower, Calgary, Alta.
Other Exec. Officers - Tim Ferwerda, man. dir., Finning U.K & Ireland; Alexandre De Moraes Zanelatto, exec. v-p, global supply chain; Kieran C. Holm, exec. v-p, global used equip.; H. Jane Murdoch, exec. v-p, chief HR officer & gen. counsel; Greg Palaschuk, exec. v-p & CFO; Anna P. Marks, sr. v-p & contr.; Dori C. Assaly, corp. sec.; Juan Pablo Amar, pres., Finning South America; David F. N. Primrose, pres., Finning Canada

Capital Stock

	Authorized (shs.)	Outstanding (shs.)[1]
Preferred	unlimited	
Series A	600,000	nil
Series B	600,000	nil
Series C	400,000	nil
Series D	500,000	nil
Series E	1,000,000	nil
Series F	1,300,000	nil
Common	unlimited	145,991,533

[1] At July 31, 2023

Options - At Dec. 31, 2022, options were outstanding to purchase 1,567,168 common shares at prices ranging from $17.75 to $34.02 per share with a weighted average remaining life of 4.38 years.

Normal Course Issuer Bid - The company plans to make normal course purchases of up to 14,900,895 common shares representing 10% of the public float. The bid commenced on May 13, 2023, and expires on May 12, 2024.

Major Shareholder - Widely held at Mar. 16, 2023.

Price Range - FTT/TSX

Year	Volume	High	Low	Close
2022	117,717,449	$40.20	$23.46	$33.66
2021	98,101,472	$40.22	$26.56	$31.88
2020	103,494,001	$28.28	$10.59	$27.03
2019	110,575,520	$26.49	$21.17	$25.30
2018	112,047,676	$36.48	$22.46	$23.80

Recent Close: $41.10

Capital Stock Changes - During 2022, 174,187 common shares were issued on exercise of options and 6,941,039 common shares were repurchased under a Normal Course Issuer Bid.

Dividends

FTT com Ra $1.00 pa Q est. June 8, 2023
Prev. Rate: $0.944 est. June 9, 2022
Prev. Rate: $0.90 est. Sept. 2, 2021
Prev. Rate: $0.82 est. June 6, 2019

Long-Term Debt - Outstanding at Dec. 31, 2022:

Medium-term notes:	
3.40% due 2023, Ser.F[1]	$114,000,000
4.08% due 2024, Ser.B[2]	135,000,000
4.28% due 2024, Ser.D[3]	68,000,000
2.626% due 2026	184,000,000
4.53% due 2027, Ser.E[4]	271,000,000
5.077% due 2042	149,000,000
Other term loans	8,000,000
	929,000,000
Less: Current portion	114,000,000
	815,000,000

[1] £70,000,000.
[2] US$100,000,000.
[3] US$50,000,000.
[4] US$200,000,000.

Note - In May 2023, offering of $350,000,000 principal amount of 4.445% senior unsecured notes due May 16, 2028, was completed. Net proceeds were used to repay all outstanding principal amount of its 3.4% medium term notes due May 2023.

Wholly Owned Subsidiaries

Finning Argentina S.A., Resistencia, Argentina. Formerly Macrosa Del Plata S.A.
Finning Bolivia S.A., Bolivia. Formerly Matreq Ferreyros S.A.
Finning Chile S.A., Chile.
Finning (Ireland) Limtied, Ireland.
Finning Soluciones Mineras S.A., Argentina. Formerly Servicios Mineras S.A.
Finning (U.K.) Ltd., United Kingdom.
4Refuel Canada LP, Oakville, Ont.
• 54.5% int. in **Compression Technology Corporation**, Milton, Ont.
Moncouver S.A., Uruguay.
OEM Remanufacturing Company Inc., Edmonton, Alta.

Investments

20% int. in **Agriterra Equipment**, Alta.
25% int. in **PipeLine Machinery International ULC**, Houston, Tex.

Note: The preceding list includes only the major related companies in which interests are held.

Financial Statistics

Periods ended:	12m Dec. 31/22[A]		12m Dec. 31/21[A]
	$000s	%Chg	$000s
Operating revenue	**9,279,000**	**+27**	**7,294,000**
Cost of sales	6,723,000		5,174,000
General & admin expense	1,422,000		1,230,000
Stock-based compensation	36,000		36,000
Operating expense	**8,181,000**	**+27**	**6,440,000**
Operating income	**1,098,000**	**+29**	**854,000**
Deprec., depl. & amort.	333,000		319,000
Finance costs, gross	95,000		75,000
Investment income	3,000		2,000
Pre-tax income	**673,000**	**+41**	**477,000**
Income taxes	172,000		114,000
Net inc bef disc ops, eqhldrs	503,000		364,000
Net inc bef disc ops, NCI	(2,000)		(1,000)
Net income	**501,000**	**+38**	**363,000**
Net inc. for equity hldrs	**503,000**	**+38**	**364,000**
Net inc. for non-cont. int	**(2,000)**	**n.a.**	**(1,000)**
Cash & equivalent	288,000		502,000
Inventories	2,461,000		1,687,000
Accounts receivable	1,129,000		839,000
Current assets	4,781,000		3,619,000
Long-term investments	83,000		84,000
Fixed assets, net	1,442,000		1,348,000
Intangibles, net	758,000		643,000
Total assets	**7,269,000**	**+22**	**5,971,000**
Bank indebtedness	1,068,000		374,000
Accts. pay. & accr. liabs	1,373,000		908,000
Current liabilities	3,401,000		2,155,000
Long-term debt, gross	929,000		1,111,000
Long-term debt, net	815,000		921,000
Long-term lease liabilities	255,000		241,000
Shareholders' equity	2,443,000		2,323,000
Non-controlling interest	18,000		20,000
Cash from oper. activs	**1,000**	**-100**	**425,000**
Cash from fin. activs	(13,000)		(300,000)
Cash from invest. activs	(268,000)		(151,000)
Net cash position	**288,000**	**-43**	**502,000**
Capital expenditures	(171,000)		(133,000)
Capital disposals	nil		8,000
Pension fund surplus	23,000		128,000
	$		$
Earnings per share*	3.25		2.26
Cash flow per share*	0.01		2.64
Cash divd. per share*	0.93		0.86
	shs		shs
No. of shs. o/s*	151,041,250		157,808,102
Avg. no. of shs. o/s*	154,740,313		161,088,129
	%		%
Net profit margin	5.40		4.98
Return on equity	21.11		16.07
Return on assets	8.64		7.35
Foreign sales percent	44		46
No. of employees (FTEs)	14,246		12,452

* Common
[A] Reported in accordance with IFRS

Latest Results

Periods ended:	6m June 30/23[A]		6m June 30/22[A]
	$000s	%Chg	$000s
Operating revenue	5,159,000	+22	4,242,000
Net income	281,000	+29	217,000
Net inc. for equity hldrs	282,000	+29	218,000
Net inc. for non-cont. int	(1,000)		(1,000)
	$		$
Earnings per share*	1.89		1.39

* Common
[A] Reported in accordance with IFRS

Historical Summary
(as originally stated)

Fiscal Year	Oper. Rev. $000s	Net Inc. Bef. Disc. $000s	EPS* $
2022[A]	9,279,000	501,000	3.25
2021[A]	7,294,000	363,000	2.26
2020[A]	6,196,000	232,000	1.43
2019[A]	7,817,000	242,000	1.48
2018[A]	6,996,000	232,000	1.38

* Common
[A] Reported in accordance with IFRS

F.32 Fintech Select Ltd.

Symbol - FTEC **Exchange** - TSX-VEN **CUSIP** - 31810H
Head Office - 227-1600 Steeles Ave W, Concord, ON, L4K 4M2
Telephone - (905) 752-0352 **Toll-free** - (800) 691-4422 **Fax** - (905) 669-5363
Website - www.fintechselect.com
Email - mabuleil@fintechselect.com
Investor Relations - Mohammad Abuleil (800) 584-8819
Auditors - Wasserman Ramsay C.A., Markham, Ont.
Transfer Agents - TSX Trust Company, Toronto, Ont.

Profile - (Ont. 2004) Provides payment services, including prepaid card programs, mobile banking solutions, cryptocurrency point-of-sale (POS), and e-wallet and online payment solutions, and related customer care services.

The company offers prepaid MasterCard and Visa card programs for government and corporate organizations; its Twifty mobile banking solution, which is interconnected to its prepaid card programs and offers many features including credit card processing, e-commerce processing, corporate disbursements, fraud and risk management, invoice management, peer-to-peer micro lending and transaction dispute resolution; and Selectcoin, a proprietary solution that allows any POS terminal to operate as a cryptocurrency exchange allowing anyone to buy and sell cryptocurrencies in a streamlined and simplified manner. The company provides 24/7 call support for its clients within Canada and the U.S., and offers Call-Center-as-a-Service to third parties which can be scaled to support any sized customer service program.

The company has also developed a prepaid closed-loop card solution for its Libyan partner, **Raseed**, that can be used by Raseed's clients and regional Libyan banks, which allows banks and other clients to load funds on their cards, which can then be used within the POS closed network.

The company's legacy business is the sale of wireless prepaid mobile and long-distance airtime.

Predecessor Detail - Name changed from Selectcore Ltd., Aug. 25, 2017.

Directors - Mujir A. Muneeruddin, chr., Oakville, Ont.; Mohammad Abuleil, pres. & CEO, Waterloo, Ont.; Naveed Ul-Hassan, Toronto, Ont.

Exec. Officers - Yu (Wendell) Zhang, CFO

Capital Stock

	Authorized (shs.)	Outstanding (shs.)[1]
Common	unlimited	80,049,515

[1] At May 30, 2023

Major Shareholder - Widely held at Nov. 21, 2022.

Price Range - FTEC/TSX-VEN

Year	Volume	High	Low	Close
2022	12,434,324	$0.07	$0.02	$0.02
2021	71,006,229	$0.19	$0.04	$0.04
2020	49,484,906	$0.14	$0.02	$0.09
2019	20,231,838	$0.08	$0.02	$0.02
2018	71,300,230	$0.42	$0.03	$0.03

Recent Close: $0.03

Capital Stock Changes - During 2022, 7,425,000 common shares were issued in settlement of directors' fees and management compensation.

Wholly Owned Subsidiaries

Local Fone Services Inc., Windsor, Ont.
1382285 Ontario Ltd.
SelectCore USA, LLC
2143436 Ontario Ltd.
2314606 Ontario Ltd.

Financial Statistics

Periods ended:	12m Dec. 31/22A		12m Dec. 31/21A
	$000s	%Chg	$000s
Operating revenue	**2,588**	**-7**	**2,771**
Cost of sales	187		243
Salaries & benefits	2,623		2,211
General & admin expense	244		187
Stock-based compensation	nil		71
Operating expense	**3,054**	**+13**	**2,712**
Operating income	**(466)**	**n.a.**	**59**
Deprec., depl. & amort.	125		127
Finance costs, gross	15		28
Write-downs/write-offs	(382)		nil
Pre-tax income	**1,196**	**n.a.**	**(113)**
Net income	**1,196**	**n.a.**	**(113)**
Cash & equivalent	148		364
Inventories	16		17
Accounts receivable	145		155
Current assets	321		559
Fixed assets, net	90		107
Right-of-use assets	57		154
Intangibles, net	14		402
Total assets	**483**	**-61**	**1,223**
Bank indebtedness	4		137
Accts. pay. & accr. liabs.	1,316		3,558
Current liabilities	1,893		3,850
Long-term lease liabilities	nil		57
Shareholders' equity	(1,409)		(2,684)
Cash from oper. activs.	**(244)**	**n.a.**	**124**
Cash from fin. activs.	212		(87)
Cash from invest. activs.	(5)		(2)
Net cash position	**36**	**-50**	**72**
Capital expenditures	(5)		(2)
	$		$
Earnings per share*	0.02		(0.00)
Cash flow per share*	(0.00)		0.00
	shs		shs
No. of shs. o/s*	80,049,515		72,624,515
Avg. no. of shs. o/s*	79,520,611		72,391,443
	%		%
Net profit margin	46.21		(4.08)
Return on equity	n.m.		n.m.
Return on assets	141.97		(6.84)

* Common
A Reported in accordance with IFRS

Latest Results

Periods ended:	3m Mar. 31/23A		3m Mar. 31/22A
	$000s	%Chg	$000s
Operating revenue	1,374	+83	750
Net income	455	-77	1,993
	$		$
Earnings per share*	0.01		0.03

* Common
A Reported in accordance with IFRS

Historical Summary
(as originally stated)

Fiscal Year	Oper. Rev.	Net Inc. Bef. Disc.	EPS*
	$000s	$000s	$
2022A	2,588	1,196	0.01
2021A	2,771	(113)	(0.00)
2020A	2,885	405	0.01
2019A	3,275	(254)	(0.00)
2018A	3,025	765	0.01

* Common
A Reported in accordance with IFRS

F.33 Firan Technology Group Corporation*

Symbol - FTG **Exchange** - TSX **CUSIP** - 318093
Head Office - 250 Finchdene Sq, Toronto, ON, M1X 1A5 **Telephone** - (416) 299-4000 **Toll-free** - (800) 258-5396 **Fax** - (416) 299-1140
Website - www.ftgcorp.com
Email - jamiecrichton@ftgcorp.com
Investor Relations - James Crichton (800) 258-5396
Auditors - MNP LLP C.A., Toronto, Ont.
Lawyers - Blake, Cassels & Graydon LLP, Toronto, Ont.
Transfer Agents - TSX Trust Company, Toronto, Ont.
FP500 Revenue Ranking - 787
Employees - 462 at Nov. 30, 2022
Profile - (Can. 2003 amalg.) Designs, manufactures and supplies aerospace and defence electronics products and subsystems to customers worldwide.

Operates through two divisions: wholly owned **FTG Circuits Inc.**, which manufactures high reliability printed circuit boards for the aviation, defence and high technology industries; and wholly owned **FTG Aerospace Inc.**, which designs, manufactures and repairs illuminated cockpits panels, keyboards, bezel, sub-assemblies and assemblies for original equipment manufacturers of avionic products and airframe manufacturers. These products are interactive devices that display information and contain buttons and switches that can be used to input signals into an avionics box or aircraft.

Manufacturing operations are located in Toronto, Ont.; Chatsworth, Calif.; Fredericksburg, Va.; Minnetonka, Minn.; Haverhill, Mass; and Tianjin, People's Republic of China.

In April 2023, the company acquired Haverhill, Mass.-based **IMI, Inc.**, a manufacturer of specialty RF circuit boards focused on the aerospace and defence markets, for $1,800,000.

During fiscal 2022, wholly owned **Firan Technology Group (Barbados) 1 Corporation** was dissolved.

Recent Merger and Acquisition Activity

Status: completed **Revised:** Apr. 28, 2023
UPDATE: The transaction was completed. PREVIOUS: Firan Technology Group Corporation to acquire Holaday Circuits, Inc., a Minnetonka, Minn.-based manufacturer of high technology circuit boards focused on the aerospace and defence markets, for $24,000,000 plus an earnout provision of up to $6,000,000 based on future performance.

Predecessor Detail - Name changed from Circuit World Corporation, May 18, 2004.

Directors - Edward C. (Ed) Hanna, chr., Beaufort, N.C.; Bradley C. (Brad) Bourne, pres. & CEO, Mississauga, Ont.; Michael L. (Mike) Andrade, Toronto, Ont.; Robert J. Beutel, Toronto, Ont.; David F. Masotti, Etobicoke, Ont.; Amy F. Rice, Jacksonville, Fla.

Other Exec. Officers - James (Jamie) Crichton, v-p, CFO & corp. sec.; Peter P. Dimopoulos, v-p, bus. devel.; Hardeep S. Heer, v-p, eng. & chief tech. officer; Hitesh Talati, v-p, gen. mgr., FTG Circuits Toronto & gen. mgr., FTG Circuits Fredicksburg; M. Shawn Thompson, v-p & gen. mgr., FTG Circuits Chatsworth & v-p & gen. mgr., FTG Aerospace Chatsworth; Randy Drake, gen. mgr., FTG Aerospace Toronto div.; Brandon Kuecker, gen. mgr., FTG Aerospace Tianjin Inc.

Capital Stock

	Authorized (shs.)	Outstanding (shs.)[1]
Preferred	unlimited	
Series 1		nil
Common	unlimited	23,911,002

[1] At June 2, 2023

Normal Course Issuer Bid - The company plans to make normal course purchases of up to 1,195,550 common shares representing 5% of the total outstanding. The bid commenced on June 5, 2023, and expires on June 4, 2024.

Major Shareholder - Oakwest Corporation Limited held 20.1% interest, Bradley C. (Brad) Bourne held 11.4% interest and TD Waterhouse Canada Inc. held 10% interest at Feb. 28, 2023.

Price Range - FTG/TSX

Year	Volume	High	Low	Close
2022	6,864,739	$3.01	$1.75	$2.35
2021	12,192,302	$3.50	$1.87	$2.65
2020	7,165,548	$4.37	$1.45	$2.05
2019	5,806,403	$4.16	$2.10	$4.07
2018	4,308,816	$3.88	$1.93	$2.11

Recent Close: $3.40

Capital Stock Changes - During fiscal 2022, 564,300 common shares were repurchased under a Normal Course Issuer Bid.

Long-Term Debt - At Nov. 30, 2022, outstanding long-term debt totaled $1,398,000 ($913,000 current and net of $47,000 deferred financing charges) and consisted entirely of five-year bank term loans, bearing interest at LIBOR plus 2% and LIBOR plus 2.15%.

Wholly Owned Subsidiaries

Firan Technology Group (Barbados) 2 Corporation, Barbados.
- 100% int. in **FTG Aeropace Tianjin Inc.**, Tianjin, Tianjin, People's Republic of China.

Firan Technology Group (USA) Corporation, Chatsworth, Calif.
- 100% int. in **FTG Aerospace Inc.**, Calif.
- 100% int. in **FTG Circuits Fredericksburg Inc.**, Va.
- 100% int. in **FTG Circuits Inc.**, Chatsworth, Calif.

Holaday Circuits, Inc., Minnetonka, Minn.
IMI, Inc., Haverhill, Mass.

Subsidiaries

60% int. in **FTG Printronics Circuit Ltd.**, Tianjin, People's Republic of China.

Financial Statistics

Periods ended:	12m Nov. 30/22A		12m Nov. 30/21ᴰA
	$000s	%Chg	$000s
Operating revenue	**89,624**	**+13**	**79,365**
Cost of sales	62,991		56,494
Research & devel. expense	5,851		5,351
General & admin expense	12,678		10,950
Stock-based compensation	128		66
Operating expense	**81,648**	**+12**	**72,861**
Operating income	**7,976**	**+23**	**6,504**
Deprec., depl. & amort.	5,733		6,289
Finance costs, gross	n.a.		582
Finance costs, net	443		n.a.
Pre-tax income	**2,342**	**-9**	**2,578**
Income taxes	1,574		2,408
Net income	**768**	**+352**	**170**
Net inc. for equity hldrs	**698**	**+173**	**256**
Net inc. for non-cont. int.	**70**	**n.a.**	**(86)**
Cash & equivalent	15,666		20,196
Inventories	19,664		16,953
Accounts receivable	16,615		16,014
Current assets	53,947		57,144
Fixed assets, net	10,718		11,078
Right-of-use assets	9,463		1,098
Intangibles, net	215		327
Total assets	**83,746**	**+5**	**79,452**
Accts. pay. & accr. liabs.	14,906		13,760
Current liabilities	23,137		17,171
Long-term debt, gross	3,328		2,262
Long-term debt, net	2,415		1,327
Long-term lease liabilities	8,899		9,123
Shareholders' equity	48,330		50,145
Non-controlling interest	965		940
Cash from oper. activs.	**11,261**	**+48**	**7,634**
Cash from fin. activs.	(1,731)		(2,697)
Cash from invest. activs.	(12,022)		(2,950)
Net cash position	**15,666**	**-22**	**20,196**
Capital expenditures	(12,311)		(2,900)
	$		$
Earnings per share*	0.03		0.01
Cash flow per share*	0.46		0.31
	shs		shs
No. of shs. o/s*	23,926,901		24,491,201
Avg. no. of shs. o/s*	24,319,499		24,491,201
	%		%
Net profit margin	0.86		0.21
Return on equity	1.42		0.51
Return on assets	0.94		0.25
Foreign sales percent	90		90
No. of employees (FTEs)	462		450

* Common
ᴰ Restated
A Reported in accordance with IFRS

Latest Results

Periods ended:	6m June 2/23A		6m June 3/22A
	$000s	%Chg	$000s
Operating revenue	58,598	+37	42,779
Net income	6,553	n.a.	(698)
Net inc. for equity hldrs	6,475	n.a.	(719)
Net inc. for non-cont. int.	78		21
	$		$
Earnings per share*	0.27		(0.03)

* Common
A Reported in accordance with IFRS

Historical Summary
(as originally stated)

Fiscal Year	Oper. Rev.	Net Inc. Bef. Disc.	EPS*
	$000s	$000s	$
2022A	89,624	768	0.03
2021A	79,365	170	0.01
2020A	102,435	1,262	0.06
2019A	112,653	5,982	0.27
2018A	109,420	2,865	0.13

* Common
A Reported in accordance with IFRS

F.34 Firm Capital Mortgage Investment Corporation

Symbol - FC **Exchange** - TSX **CUSIP** - 318323
Head Office - 163 Cartwright Ave, Toronto, ON, M6A 1V5 **Telephone** - (416) 635-0221 **Fax** - (416) 635-1713
Website - www.firmcapital.com/fcmic/
Email - spoklar@firmcapital.com
Investor Relations - Sandy I. Poklar (416) 635-0221
Auditors - RSM Canada LLP C.A., Toronto, Ont.
Lawyers - Miller Thomson LLP, Toronto, Ont.

Transfer Agents - Computershare Trust Company of Canada Inc., Toronto, Ont.
Managers - FC Treasury Management Inc., Toronto, Ont.
Employees - 1 at Dec. 31, 2022
Profile - (Ont. 2010) Provides short-term residential and commercial real estate finance through mortgage banker **Firm Capital Corporation**.
The company focuses on market niches underserviced by the larger, more traditional financial institutions. Properties financed include single family dwellings, multi-family residential properties, condominiums (single and multiple units), commercial/industrial properties, investment properties, land and development sites, and development and construction projects. The types of financing include: bridge financing, equity and participating mortgage loans, joint venture financing for builders and developers, mezzanine and subordinated mortgage debt for investment properties, partnership capital and distressed mortgage debt purchases.
The company qualifies as a Mortgage Investment Corporation (MIC) under the Income Tax Act (Canada). MICs are special purpose entities that are entitled to deduct in computing its income all taxable dividends (other than capital gains dividends) it pays to shareholders in the year and in the first 90 days of the following taxation year, provided that such dividends are not deductible in the preceding taxation year. As a result, an MIC is able to operate as a flow-through entity. In order to qualify as an MIC, at least 50% of the company's assets must consist of residential mortgages or cash, the company must not hold any foreign assets nor engage in activities outside of investing funds, the company must have at least 20 shareholders, and no person may hold more than 25% of the company's outstanding shares. The company intends to make distributions to the extent necessary to reduce its taxable income each year to nil so that it has no tax payable under Part I of the Tax Act. To the extent that it realizes a capital gain in excess of applicable capital losses, the company intends to elect to have dividends to be capital gains dividends to the maximum extent allowable.
The investment portfolio at Mar. 31, 2023, consisting of 254 investments, was valued as follows:

Type	Value
Conventional first mtges	$540,935,841
Related debt investments	60,204,284
Conventional non-first mtges	34,735,178
Non-conventional mtges	9,631,774
Debtor in possession loan	6,306,738
	651,813,815
Less:	
Impairment provision	8,956,000
Fair value adjustment	4,700,000
Unamortized fees	948,971
	637,208,844

Predecessor Detail - Succeeded Firm Capital Mortgage Investment Trust, Jan. 1, 2011, pursuant to plan of arrangement whereby Firm Capital Mortgage Investment Corporation was formed to facilitate the conversion of the trust into a corporation and the trust was subsequently dissolved.
Directors - Stanley Goldfarb, chr., Toronto, Ont.; Eli Dadouch, pres. & CEO, Toronto, Ont.; Jonathan Mair, exec. v-p & COO, Vaughan, Ont.; Victoria Granovski, sr. v-p, credit & equity capital & corp. sec., Vaughan, Ont.; Michael Warner, sr. v-p, mtge. lending, Thornhill, Ont.; Geoffrey Bledin, Antigua and Barbuda; Morris Fischtein, Toronto, Ont.; Anthony Heller, Toronto, Ont.; The Hon. Francis J. C. (Frank) Newbould, Toronto, Ont.; The Hon. Joe Oliver, Toronto, Ont.; Keith L. Ray, Toronto, Ont.; Lawrence (Larry) Shulman, Toronto, Ont.
Other Exec. Officers - Ryan M. Lim, CFO; Sandy I. Poklar, exec. v-p & man. dir., fin.

Capital Stock

	Authorized (shs.)	Outstanding (shs.)[1]
Preferred	unlimited	nil
Common	unlimited	34,486,866

[1] At May 9, 2023

Major Shareholder - Widely held at May 9, 2023.

Price Range - FC/TSX

Year	Volume	High	Low	Close
2022	9,658,757	$14.74	$10.45	$10.69
2021	9,311,657	$15.84	$12.59	$14.35
2020	11,281,205	$15.45	$7.73	$12.73
2019	6,728,024	$15.05	$12.76	$14.72
2018	6,596,172	$13.69	$12.35	$13.15

Recent Close: $10.75
Capital Stock Changes - During 2022, common shares were issued as follows: 799,616 on conversion of debentures, 45,000 on exercise of options and 30,239 under dividend reinvestment plan.

Dividends

FC com Ra $0.936 pa M est. Feb. 15, 2019**
$0.014◆ Jan. 16/23 $0.012◆ Jan. 17/22
$0.008◆ Jan. 15/21
Paid in 2023: $0.936 + $0.014◆ 2022: $0.936 + $0.012◆ 2021: $0.936 + $0.008◆
** Reinvestment Option ◆ Special

Wholly Owned Subsidiaries

FC Finance Trust
FC Residential Mortgage Company Inc.
Firm Capital Mortgage Fund Inc.

Financial Statistics

Periods ended:	12m Dec. 31/22[A]		12m Dec. 31/21[oA]
	$000s	%Chg	$000s
Total revenue	**60,119**	**+25**	**47,905**
General & admin. expense	6,289		5,304
Stock-based compensation	1,668		71
Operating expense	**7,957**	**+48**	**5,375**
Operating income	**52,162**	**+23**	**42,530**
Provision for loan losses	2,959		(1,150)
Finance costs, gross	14,869		11,094
Pre-tax income	**32,234**	**+8**	**29,985**
Net income	**32,234**	**+8**	**29,985**
Cash & equivalent	49		54
Investments	649,742		635,352
Total assets	**656,176**	**+2**	**640,283**
Bank indebtedness	72,952		74,548
Accts. pay. & accr. liabs	2,720		2,229
Debt	178,284		177,807
Equity portion of conv. debs	7,110		4,552
Shareholders' equity	399,046		382,673
Cash from oper. activs	**51,860**	**+27**	**40,952**
Cash from fin. activs	(27,746)		40,350
Cash from invest. activs	(18,800)		(83,186)
Net cash position	**(15,236)**	**n.a.**	**(20,551)**
	$		$
Earnings per share*	0.94		0.95
Cash flow per share*	1.51		1.30
Cash divd. per share*	0.94		0.94
Extra divd. - cash*	0.01		0.01
Total divd. per share*	**0.95**		**0.95**
	shs		shs
No. of shs. o/s*	34,485,740		33,610,885
Avg. no. of shs. o/s*	34,332,947		31,560,133
	%		%
Net profit margin	53.62		62.59
Return on equity	8.25		8.26
Return on assets	7.26		6.86
No. of employees (FTEs)	1		1

* Common
o Restated
A Reported in accordance with IFRS

Latest Results

Periods ended:	3m Mar. 31/23[A]		3m Mar. 31/22[A]
	$000s	%Chg	$000s
Total revenue	19,016	+51	12,588
Net income	8,712	+11	7,862
	$		$
Earnings per share*	0.25		0.23

* Common
A Reported in accordance with IFRS

Historical Summary
(as originally stated)

Fiscal Year	Total Rev.	Net Inc. Bef. Disc.	EPS*
	$000s	$000s	$
2022[A]	60,119	32,234	0.94
2021[A]	47,905	29,985	0.95
2020[A]	44,176	26,353	0.91
2019[A]	47,343	28,002	1.01
2018[A]	47,313	25,751	0.99

* Common
A Reported in accordance with IFRS

F.35 Firm Capital Property Trust

Symbol - FCD.UN **Exchange** - TSX **CUSIP** - 318326
Head Office - 163 Cartwright Ave, Toronto, ON, M6A 1V5 **Telephone** - (416) 635-0221 **Fax** - (416) 635-1713
Website - www.firmcapital.com
Email - spoklar@firmcapital.com
Investor Relations - Sandy I. Poklar (416) 635-0221
Auditors - RSM Canada LLP C.A., Toronto, Ont.
Lawyers - Fogler, Rubinoff LLP, Toronto, Ont.
Transfer Agents - TSX Trust Company, Toronto, Ont.
Employees - 1 at Dec. 31, 2022
Profile - (Ont. 2012) Acquires and owns retail, industrial and multi-residential properties across Canada.
The trust's property portfolio at Mar. 31, 2023, consisted of 66 commercial properties, totaling 2,545,397 sq. ft. of gross leasable area, in Ontario, Quebec, Nova Scotia, New Brunswick, Saskatchewan, Manitoba and Alberta; five multi-residential complexes consisting of 599 units in Ottawa, Ont., Dartmouth and Lower Sackville, N.S., Edmonton, Alta., and Pointe-Claire, Que.; and four manufactured homes communities consisting of 536 units in Calgary, Alta., and McGregor, Trenton and Peterborough, Ont.

Commercial Property Mix

Type	Area[1]
Retail	1,137,532
Industrial	1,407,865
	2,545,397

[1] Gross leasable area (sq. ft.). Figures represent an owned interest basis.

Geographic Diversification

Region	Percentage[1]
Ontario	38%
Quebec	36%
Nova Scotia	7%
Alberta	17%
Other	2%

[1] As a percentage of net operating income.

The trust's assets and properties are managed by **Firm Capital Realty Partners Inc.** and **Firm Capital Property Management Corp.**, respectively.
In February 2023, the trust acquired 50% interests in a 56-site manufactured housing community (MHC) called SunPark Parkhill Estates in Peterborough, Ont., and a 58-site MHC called Sun Park Skyview Estates in Trenton, Ont., for $1,550,000 and $1,300,000, respectively.
In December 2022, the trust sold an 11,247-sq.-ft. retail property in Pembroke, Ont., for $2,700,000.
In March 2022, the trust acquired a 50% interest in a 34,612-sq.-ft. multi-tenant industrial property in Saint Laurent, Que., for $3,150,000.

Recent Merger and Acquisition Activity

Status: completed **Announced:** Dec. 29, 2022
Firm Capital Property Trust sold a 39,490-sq.-ft. medical office property in Barrie, Ont., for $10,700,000.
Status: completed **Revised:** Dec. 22, 2022
UPDATE: The transaction was completed. PREVIOUS: Firm Capital Property Trust (50%) and private clients affiliated with certain members of senior management and the board of trustees of Firm Capital (50%) agreed to acquire two multi-tenant industrial properties in Edmonton, Alta., totaling 68,000 sq. ft., for $6,200,000. The consideration would be financed with a new first mortgage and the assumption of an existing first mortgage, both from a Canadian Chartered Bank, as well as cash.
Status: completed **Revised:** Apr. 12, 2022
UPDATE: The transaction was completed. PREVIOUS: Firm Capital Property Trust (50%) and private clients affiliated with certain members of senior management and the board of trustees of Firm Capital (50%) agreed to acquire six multi-tenant industrial properties in Edmonton, Alta., totaling 234,424 sq. ft., for $36,300,000. The consideration would be financed with a new first mortgage from a Canadian Chartered Bank as well as cash.
Predecessor Detail - Succeeded ISG Capital Corporation, Nov. 29, 2012, pursuant to plan of arrangement whereby Firm Capital Property Trust was formed to facilitate the conversion of the corporation into a trust.
Trustees - Stanley Goldfarb, chr., Toronto, Ont.; Eli Dadouch, v-chr. & co-chief invest. officer, Toronto, Ont.; Robert McKee, pres. & CEO, Toronto, Ont.; Sandy I. Poklar, CFO, Toronto, Ont.; Victoria Granovski, corp. sec., Vaughan, Ont.; Jonathan Mair, co-chief invest. officer, Vaughan, Ont.; Geoffrey Bledin, Antigua and Barbuda; Jeffrey Goldfarb, Toronto, Ont.; Lawrence (Larry) Shulman, Toronto, Ont.; Howard Smuschkowitz, Toronto, Ont.; Manfred J. Walt, Toronto, Ont.

Capital Stock

	Authorized (shs.)	Outstanding (shs.)[1]
Trust Unit	unlimited	36,925,197
Special Voting Unit	unlimited	nil

[1] At July 4, 2023

Trust Units - The trust will endeavour to make monthly cash distributions. Retractable at a price equal to the lesser of: (i) 90% of the market price of the units on the principal market on which the trust units are traded during the 10-trading-day period immediately preceding the retraction date; and (ii) 100% of the closing market price of the trust units on the principal market on which the units traded on the unit retraction date. One vote per trust unit.
Special Voting Unit - Issued to holders of limited partnership units of subsidiary Firm Capital Property Limited Partnership. Each special voting unit entitles the holder to a number of votes at unitholder meetings equal to the number of trust units into which the limited partnership units are exchangeable.
Normal Course Issuer Bid - The company plans to make normal course purchases of up to 3,324,528 trust units representing 10% of the public float. The bid commenced on July 18, 2023, and expires on July 17, 2024.
Major Shareholder - Widely held at May 9, 2023.

Price Range - FCD.UN/TSX

Year	Volume	High	Low	Close
2022	8,213,117	$8.10	$5.20	$5.69
2021	7,628,356	$8.10	$6.07	$7.94
2020	5,936,714	$6.95	$3.99	$6.34
2019	3,916,820	$7.05	$5.61	$6.74
2018	1,360,430	$6.85	$5.27	$6.05

Recent Close: $5.25
Capital Stock Changes - In May 2022, bought deal public offering of 3,243,000 trust units was completed at $7.10 per unit, including 423,000 trust units on exercise of over-allotment option. Also during 2022, common shares were issued as follows: 295,000 on exercise of options and 380 under the distribution reinvestment plan; 449,400 common shares were repurchased under a Normal Course Issuer Bid.

Dividends

FCD.UN unit Ra $0.52 pa M est. Feb. 15, 2022**
Listed Mar 10/22.
Prev. Rate: $0.51 est. Feb. 15, 2021
Prev. Rate: $0.50 est. Feb. 17, 2020
** Reinvestment Option

Wholly Owned Subsidiaries

FCPT GP Inc., Ont.
Firm Capital Property Limited Partnership, Ont.

Financial Statistics

Periods ended:	12m Dec. 31/22[A]		12m Dec. 31/21[A]
	$000s	%Chg	$000s
Total revenue	**54,019**	**+16**	**46,430**
Rental operating expense	9,457		7,771
General & admin. expense	14,852		14,730
Stock-based compensation	(1,660)		1,729
Operating expense	**22,649**	**-7**	**24,230**
Operating income	**31,370**	**+41**	**22,200**
Finance income	149		60
Finance costs, gross	12,592		9,180
Pre-tax income	**(1,184)**	**n.a.**	**58,388**
Net income	**(1,184)**	**n.a.**	**58,388**
Cash & equivalent	4,986		5,896
Accounts receivable	1,180		2,985
Current assets	16,018		12,304
Income-producing props	616,306		563,352
Property interests, net	616,306		563,352
Total assets	**633,898**	**+10**	**576,356**
Bank indebtedness	18,726		24,798
Accts. pay. & accr. liabs	5,528		7,298
Current liabilities	101,194		56,779
Long-term debt, gross	306,781		239,913
Long-term debt, net	233,996		221,928
Long-term lease liabilities	183		222
Shareholders' equity	296,514		295,915
Cash from oper. activs	**29,970**	**+13**	**26,601**
Cash from fin. activs	49,827		21,437
Cash from invest. activs	(80,708)		(47,828)
Net cash position	**4,986**	**-15**	**5,896**
Capital expenditures	(4,015)		(4,308)
Increase in property	(81,266)		(69,344)
Decrease in property	4,573		25,825
	$		$
Earnings per share*	n.a.		n.a.
Cash flow per share*	0.81		7.84
Funds from opers. per sh.*	0.54		0.46
Adj. funds from opers. per sh.*	0.46		0.48
Cash divd. per share*	0.52		0.51
Total divd. per share*	**0.52**		**0.51**
	shs		shs
No. of shs. o/s*	37,100,097		34,011,117
	%		%
Net profit margin	(2.19)		125.75
Return on equity	(0.40)		22.48
Return on assets	1.89		12.79
No. of employees (FTEs)	1		1

* Trust Unit
[A] Reported in accordance with IFRS

Latest Results

Periods ended:	3m Mar. 31/23[A]		3m Mar. 31/22[A]
	$000s	%Chg	$000s
Total revenue	14,209	+9	13,041
Net income	5,397	+1	5,338
	$		$
Earnings per share*	n.a.		n.a.

[A] Reported in accordance with IFRS

Historical Summary
(as originally stated)

Fiscal Year	Total Rev.	Net Inc. Bef. Disc.	EPS*
	$000s	$000s	$
2022[A]	54,019	(1,184)	n.a.
2021[A]	46,430	58,388	n.a.
2020[A]	44,536	15,831	n.a.
2019[A]	36,156	35,721	n.a.
2018[A]	22,061	15,829	n.a.

* Trust Unit
[A] Reported in accordance with IFRS

F.36 First and Goal Capital Corp.

Symbol - FGCC.P **Exchange** - TSX-VEN **CUSIP** - 31861F
Head Office - 800-365 Bay St, Toronto, ON, M5H 2V1 **Telephone** - (416) 786-7690
Email - pgs@arclaure.ca
Investor Relations - Paul G. Smith (416) 786-7690
Auditors - McGovern Hurley LLP C.A., Toronto, Ont.
Transfer Agents - TSX Trust Company, Toronto, Ont.
Profile - (Ont. 2021) Capital Pool Company.
Directors - Paul G. Smith, CEO, CFO & corp. sec., Toronto, Ont.; Charles J. Gavsie, Ont.; Daiana Turcu, Ont.

Capital Stock

	Authorized (shs.)	Outstanding (shs.)[1]
Common	unlimited	15,827,500

[1] At Mar. 31, 2023

Major Shareholder - Widely held at Jan. 11, 2022.

Price Range - FGCC.P/TSX-VEN

Year	Volume	High	Low	Close
2022	14,000	$0.12	$0.10	$0.12

Recent Close: $0.04

Capital Stock Changes - On Jan. 11, 2022, an initial public offering of 5,377,500 common shares was completed at 10¢ per share.

F.37 First Capital Real Estate Investment Trust*

Symbol - FCR.UN **Exchange** - TSX **CUSIP** - 31890B
Head Office - 400-85 Hanna Ave, Toronto, ON, M6K 3S3 **Telephone** - (416) 504-4114 **Toll-free** - (866) 404-4114 **Fax** - (416) 941-1655
Website - www.fcr.ca
Email - investorrelations@fcr.ca
Investor Relations - Neil Downey (416) 530-6634
Auditors - Ernst & Young LLP C.A., Toronto, Ont.
Lawyers - Davies Ward Phillips & Vineberg LLP, Montréal, Qué.; Torys LLP, Toronto, Ont.
Transfer Agents - Computershare Trust Company of Canada Inc., Toronto, Ont.
FP500 Revenue Ranking - 406
Employees - 371 at Dec. 31, 2022
Profile - (Ont. 2019) Develops, owns and operates grocery-anchored, open-air retail centres in major urban markets across Canada, with tenants including grocery stores, pharmacies, liquor stores, banks, restaurants, cafés, fitness centres, medical, childcare facilities and professional and personal services.

The trust targets specific super urban and top-tier suburban neighbourhoods in Toronto, Montreal, Vancouver, Edmonton, Calgary and Ottawa. A super urban or top-tier suburban property is defined based on proximity to transit, "walk score" and population density. At June 30, 2023, the trust had interests in 144 properties, totaling 19,425,000 sq. ft. of owned gross leasable area.

Geographic mix of property portfolio:

Urban markets	Props.	Area[1]
Greater Toronto Area	51	6,895,000
Greater Montreal Area	27	3,580,000
Greater Calgary Area	15	2,356,000
Greater Vancouver Area	15	1,608,000
Greater Edmonton Area	10	2,219,000
Greater Ottawa Area	12	1,021,000
Kitchener/Waterloo/Guelph	5	990,000
Other	9	756,000
	144	19,425,000

[1] Owned gross leasable area (sq. ft.). Excludes residential gross leasable area of 184,000 sq. ft.

On Mar. 3, 2023, the trust entered into an agreement with **Sandpiper Group** and **Artis Real Estate Investment Trust** whereby Sandpiper and Artis withdrew their previous meeting requisition, as well as their nominees for election to the board of trustees of the trust. The annual and special meeting of unitholders that was to be held on Mar. 28, 2023, was rescheduled to Apr. 11, 2023.

During the fourth quarter of 2022, the trust acquired a 50% interest in 328 Bloor Street West, a 2,117-sq.-ft. property in Toronto, Ont., for $3,300,000.

During the third quarter of 2022, the trust acquired 64 Montgomery Avenue, a 0.1-acre property in Toronto, Ont., for $2,500,000. In addition, the trust sold its 4.1-acre parcel of land in Milton, Ont., and 0.2-acre parcel of land in Brossard, Que., for $3,305,000.

During the second quarter of 2022, the trust acquired 70 Montgomery Avenue, a 0.1-acre property in Toronto, Ont., for $3,600,000.

During the first quarter of 2022, the trust sold a 1-acre parcel of land in Saint-Hubert, Que., for $4,500,000; and acquired 66 Montgomery Avenue, a 0.1-acre property in Toronto, Ont., for $2,500,000.

Recent Merger and Acquisition Activity

Status: completed **Announced:** June 30, 2023
First Capital Real Estate Investment Trust acquired the land under its Centre Commercial Maisonneuve property in Montreal, Que., totaling 8.6 acres and 114,514 sq. ft. of leasable area, for $55,200,000.

Status: pending **Revised:** June 30, 2023
UPDATE: First Capital sold the Queen Mary Road property. PREVIOUS: First Capital Real Estate Investment Trust agreed to sell 5051 Yonge Street, a multi-level retail centre site located in North York, Ont.; a residential development site of the final phase of the intensification at Wilderton Shopping Centre in Montreal, Que.; and 5146-5164 Queen Mary Road, a small apartment building with ground floor retail, in Montreal. Total consideration was $74,000,000.

Status: completed **Revised:** June 9, 2023
UPDATE: The transaction was completed. PREVIOUS: First Capital Real Estate Investment Trust agreed to sell the 77-suite, five-star Hazelton Hotel, together with its 50% interest in ONE Restaurant, located in Toronto's Yorkville neighbourhood to Hennick & Company, Inc. for $110,000,000. Hennick & Company is a private firm that invests in high-quality real estate assets.

Status: completed **Announced:** Jan. 31, 2023
First Capital Real Estate Investment Trust acquired a 50% interest in an 8,979-sq.-ft. property adjacent to First Capital's Bloor Street & Spadina Road holdings in Toronto, Ont., for $15,700,000.

Status: completed **Announced:** Dec. 31, 2022
First Capital Real Estate Investment Trust sold its 25% interest in Yonge & Roselawn development site, a 0.5-acre parcel of land in Toronto, Ont., for $30,300,000.

Status: completed **Revised:** Dec. 31, 2022
UPDATE: The transaction was completed. PREVIOUS: First Capital Real Estate Investment Trust agreed to sell its remaining 50% non-managing interest in the residential component of King High Line in Toronto, Ont., for $149,000,000. First Capital would retain its 100% interest in the retail and commercial parking components of King High Line.

Status: completed **Announced:** Sept. 30, 2022
First Capital Real Estate Investment Trust acquired a 50% interest in 50,088-sq.-ft. Amberlea Shopping Centre in Pickering, Ont., for $23,000,000.

Status: completed **Revised:** Sept. 30, 2022
UPDATE: The transaction was completed. PREVIOUS: First Capital Real Estate Investment Trust agreed to sell its 161,496-sq.-ft. La Porte de Gatineau and 43,052-sq.-ft. Bayview Lane Plaza located in Gatineau, Que., and Markham, Ont., respectively, for $80,000,000.

Status: completed **Announced:** June 30, 2022
First Capital Real Estate Investment Trust sold the 40,000-sq.-ft. Staples Gateway retail location in Edmonton, Alta., for $10,300,000.

Status: completed **Announced:** Mar. 31, 2022
First Capital Real Estate Investment Trust acquired a 50% interest in 102 Atlantic Avenue, a 8,734-sq.-ft. property in Toronto, Ont., for $7,600,000.

Predecessor Detail - Succeeded First Capital Realty Inc., Dec. 30, 2019, pursuant to plan of arrangement whereby First Capital Real Estate Investment Trust was formed to facilitate the conversion of the corporation into a trust.

Trustees - Paul C. Douglas, chr., Toronto, Ont.; Adam E. Paul, pres. & CEO, Toronto, Ont.; Leonard M. Abramsky, Toronto, Ont.; Sheila Botting, Burlington, Ont.; Ian L. T. Clarke, Pickering, Ont.; Dayna M. Gibbs, Toronto, Ont.; Ira Gluskin, Toronto, Ont.; Annalisa King, Vancouver, B.C.; Aladin W. (Al) Mawani, Thornhill, Ont.; Richard W. Nesbitt, London, Middx., United Kingdom

Oper. Subsid./Mgt. Co. Officers - Elle Agourias, chief acctg. officer; Simon Streeter, CIO; Neil Downey, exec. v-p, enterprise strategies & CFO; Jordan Robins, exec. v-p & COO; Carmine Francella, sr. v-p, real estate srvcs.; Alison Harnick, sr. v-p, gen. counsel & corp. sec.; Michele Walkau, sr. v-p, brand & culture; Jennifer Arezes, v-p, devel.; Leigh Balgopal, v-p, legal affairs; Sarah Heppinstall, v-p, const.; Sue Klinner, v-p, bus. process & risk mgt.; Terry Ledamun, v-p, leasing central & Edmonton; Ryan Ng, v-p, fin.; Marcel Parsons, v-p, asset strategy; Eric Sherman, v-p, real estate, Yorkville; J. J. Shier, v-p, opers.; Greg Timson, v-p, leasing eastern; Ian Turnbull, v-p, special projects

Capital Stock

	Authorized (shs.)	Outstanding (shs.)[1]
Trust Unit	unlimited	212,200,000
Special Voting Unit	unlimited	60,021
Class B LP Unit	unlimited	60,021[2 3]

[1] At July 31, 2023
[2] Classified as debt.
[3] Securities of First Capital REIT Limited Partnership.

Trust Unit - The trust will endeavour to make monthly cash distributions. Retractable at a price equal to the lesser of: (i) 90% of the market price of the trust units on the principal market on which the trust units are traded during the 10 trading days immediately preceding the retraction date; and (ii) 100% of the closing market price of the trust units on the principal market on which the trust units traded on the unit retraction date. One vote per trust unit.

Special Voting Unit - Issued to holders of class B limited partnership units of subsidiary First Capital REIT Limited Partnership. Each special voting unit entitles the holder to a number of votes at unitholder meetings equal to the number of trust units into which the class B limited partnership units are exchangeable.

Class B Limited Partnership Unit - Entitled to distributions equal to those provided to trust units. Directly exchangeable into trust units on a 1-for-1 basis at any time by holder on or before Dec. 29, 2023, the date upon which all class B LP Units are expected to be automatically exchanged for trust units. Classified as long-term debt under IFRS.

Options - At Dec. 31, 2022, options were outstanding to purchase 6,275,000 trust units at a weighted average exercise price of $19.76 per unit with a weighted average remaining life of 4.9 years.

Normal Course Issuer Bid - The company plans to make normal course purchases of up to 21,148,491 trust units representing 10% of the public float. The bid commenced on May 18, 2023, and expires on May 17, 2024.

Major Shareholder - Widely held at Feb. 24, 2023.

Price Range - FCR.UN/TSX

Year	Volume	High	Low	Close
2022	123,101,167	$19.06	$14.08	$16.81
2021	133,789,557	$19.19	$13.39	$18.86
2020	247,900,876	$22.09	$11.09	$13.55
2019	117,468,546	$22.79	$18.60	$20.67

FCR/TSX (D)

Year	Volume	High	Low	Close
2019	116,426,183	$22.79	$18.60	$20.86
2018	89,138,181	$21.41	$18.28	$18.85

Recent Close: $14.04

Capital Stock Changes - During 2022, trust units were issued as follows: 172,000 on exercise of options and settlement of restricted, performance and deferred share units and 43,000 on conversion of a like number of class B limited partnership units; 6,238,000 trust units were repurchased under a Normal Course Issuer Bid.

Dividends

FCR.UN tr unit Ra $0.864 pa M est. Oct. 17, 2022**[1]
Prev. Rate: $0.43 est. May 16, 2022
Prev. Rate: $0.432 est. Feb. 15, 2021
Prev. Rate: $0.86 est. Oct. 7, 2014

[1] First Capital Realty Inc. com prior to Dec. 30, 2019. Distribution paid quarterly prior to Jan. 2020.
** Reinvestment Option

Long-Term Debt - Outstanding at Dec. 31, 2022:

Credit facilities	$1,104,614,000
Mtges.[1]	1,127,361,000
Sr. unsecured debs.:	
3.9% ser.Q due Oct. 2023	299,835,000
4.79% ser.R due Aug. 2024	300,323,000
4.32% ser.S due July 2025	300,588,000
3.6% ser.T due May 2026	300,386,000
3.46% ser.V due Jan. 2027	199,397,000
3.75% ser.U due July 2027	299,124,000
3.45% ser.A due Mar. 2028	199,171,000
Class B L.P. units	1,009,000
	4,131,808,000
Less: Current portion	556,882,000
	3,574,926,000

[1] Bear interest at a weighted average rate of 3.4% at Dec. 31, 2022, and due to 2031.

Wholly Owned Subsidiaries

First Capital REIT Limited Partnership, Toronto, Ont.
- 100% int. in **First Capital Realty Inc.**, Toronto, Ont.
  - 35.4% int. in **Aukland and Main Developments LP**, Toronto, Ont.
  - 50% int. in **College Square General Partnership**, Ottawa, Ont.
  - 20% int. in **FC Urban Properties, LP**, Toronto, Ont.
  - 78% int. in **Fashion Media Group GP Ltd.**, Toronto, Ont.
  - 100% int. in **First Capital Holdings Trust**, Ont.
    - 6.2% int. in **M+M Urban Realty LP**, Toronto, Ont.
  - 50% int. in **Green Capital Limited Partnership**, Markham, Ont.
  - 50% int. in **Lakeshore Development LP**, Toronto, Ont.
  - 67% int. in **Main and Main Developments LP**, Toronto, Ont.
    - 46.9% int. in **M+M Urban Realty LP**, Toronto, Ont.
  - 70.9% int. in **Maincore Equities Inc.**, Toronto, Ont.
    - 46.9% int. in **M+M Urban Realty LP**, Toronto, Ont.
  - 94% int. in **Stackt Properties LP**, Toronto, Ont.

Financial Statistics

Periods ended:	12m Dec. 31/22[A]		12m Dec. 31/21[A]
	$000s	%Chg	$000s
Total revenue	**693,096**	**+3**	**674,890**
Rental operating expense	267,597		262,352
General & admin. expense	45,235		38,207
Operating expense	**312,832**	**+4**	**300,559**
Operating income	**380,264**	**+2**	**374,331**
Investment income	(199)		(1,460)
Deprec. & amort.	5,673		6,018
Finance income	19,870		10,880
Finance costs, gross	150,042		152,670
Pre-tax income	**(152,564)**	**n.a.**	**499,565**
Income taxes	7,197		25,929
Net income	**(159,761)**	**n.a.**	**473,636**
Net inc. for equity hldrs	**(159,997)**	**n.a.**	**460,131**
Net inc. for non-cont. int	**236**	**-98**	**13,505**
Cash & equivalent	32,694		34,699
Accounts receivable	25,970		27,784
Current assets	473,373		556,865
Long-term investments	525,772		479,096
Fixed assets	28,215		29,971
Income-producing props	8,530,661		9,060,939
Property interests, net	8,537,276		9,068,610
Intangibles, net	3,460		2,960
Total assets	**9,581,938**	**-5**	**10,109,074**
Bank indebtedness	1,594		2,476
Accts. pay. & accr. liabs	154,144		154,237
Current liabilities	797,531		791,270
Long-term debt, gross	4,131,808		4,423,044
Long-term debt, net	3,574,926		3,854,916
Shareholders' equity	4,279,373		4,620,942
Non-controlling interest	55,922		48,140
Cash from oper. activs	**251,221**	**+1**	**249,613**
Cash from fin. activs	(387,209)		(470,245)
Cash from invest. activs	133,983		154,887
Net cash position	**32,694**	**-6**	**34,699**
Increase in property	(188,806)		(168,023)
Decrease in property	187,963		319,068
	$		$
Earnings per share*	n.a.		n.a.
Cash flow per share*	1.18		1.14
Funds from opers. per sh.*	1.21		1.14
Adj. funds from opers. per sh.*	1.04		n.a.
Cash divd. per share*	0.58		0.43
Total divd. per share*	**0.58**		**0.43**
	shs		shs
No. of shs. o/s*	213,518,000		219,541,000
	%		%
Net profit margin	(23.05)		70.18
Return on equity	(3.60)		10.40
Return on assets	(0.03)		6.14
No. of employees (FTEs)	371		341

* Trust Unit
[A] Reported in accordance with IFRS

Latest Results

Periods ended:	6m June 30/23[A]		6m June 30/22[A]
	$000s	%Chg	$000s
Total revenue	347,914	+1	345,082
Net income	20,077	+839	2,139
Net inc. for equity hldrs	19,689	+737	2,353
Net inc. for non-cont. int	388		(214)
	$		$
Earnings per share*	n.a.		n.a.

[A] Reported in accordance with IFRS

Historical Summary
(as originally stated)

Fiscal Year	Total Rev.	Net Inc. Bef. Disc.	EPS*
	$000s	$000s	$
2022[A]	693,096	(159,761)	n.a.
2021[A]	674,890	473,636	n.a.
2020[A]	672,890	7,482	n.a.
2019[A1]	746,773	414,340	n.a.
2018[A]	729,595	351,838	1.38

* Trust Unit
[A] Reported in accordance with IFRS
[1] Results prior to Dec. 30, 2019, pertain to First Capital Realty Inc.

F.38 First Growth Funds Limited

Symbol - FGFL **Exchange** - CSE **CUSIP** - Q3859T
Head Office - Level 14, 440 Collins St, Melbourne, VIC, Australia, 3000 **Overseas Tel** - 61-3-8620-6400
Website - www.firstgrowthfunds.com
Email - cosec@firstgrowthfunds.com
Investor Relations - Luke Martino 61-3-8620-6400
Auditors - Pitcher Partners BA&A Pty Ltd. C.A., Brisbane, Qld. Australia
Transfer Agents - Odyssey Trust Company, Vancouver, B.C.
Profile - (Australia 1986) Invests in various asset classes including listed equities, private equity, blockchain and digital assets and operates an advisory business providing corporate advisory, capital raising and capital markets support to its portfolio.

The company provides advisory services to listed and unlisted companies; is licensed in Australia to present investment opportunities to accredited investors in Australia and earn commission fees; and invests across a diversified portfolio of different asset classes, including equity and convertible note investments in large and small cap listed and private companies involved in Blockchain and digital currency such as cryptocurrencies Bitcoin and Ethereum.

The company's investment portfolio at Sept. 30, 2022 (based on asset allocation):

Asset type:	Percentage
Cash	9.77%
Current financial assets (listed)	67.65%
Current financial assets (unlisted)	nil
Non-current financial assets (unlisted)	20.34%
Equity accounted investments	2.24%
Total	100%

In May 2023, the company agreed to acquire a 12.7% interest in **Sienna Mining Limited**, which is pursuing a uranium deposit in southern Tanzania surrounding **Rosatom State Nuclear Energy Corporation**'s Nyota deposit.

Directors - Michael R. Clarke, chr., Adelaide, S.A., Australia; Geoff Barnes, Sydney, N.S.W., Australia; Athan Lekkas, Adelaide, S.A., Australia

Other Exec. Officers - Luke Martino, CFO & corp. sec.

Capital Stock

	Authorized (shs.)	Outstanding (shs.)[1]
Ordinary	unlimited	77,798,218

[1] At Sept. 30, 2022

Major Shareholder - Geoff Barnes held 10.89% interest at Oct. 21, 2022.

Price Range - FGFL/CSE

Year	Volume	High	Low	Close
2022	2,790,345	$0.04	$0.01	$0.01
2021	3,124,004	$0.22	$0.02	$0.04
2020	2,227,909	$0.28	$0.01	$0.11

Recent Close: $0.01

Capital Stock Changes - There were no changes to capital stock during fiscal 2020 or fiscal 2022.

Wholly Owned Subsidiaries

First Growth Advisory Pty Ltd., Australia.

Investments

50% int. in **Cryptondata Vault LLC**, United States.
Magnum Mining Exploration, Australia.
14.2% int. in **SQID Technologies Limited**, Melbourne, Vic., Australia. (see separate coverage)
24.43% int. in **Vello Technologies Inc.**, Melbourne, Vic., Australia.

Note: The preceding list includes only the major related companies in which interests are held.

Financial Statistics

Periods ended:	12m June 30/22[A]		12m June 30/21[A]
	A$000s	%Chg	A$000s
Unrealized invest. gain (loss)	(5,166)		1,748
Total revenue	**(5,021)**	**n.a.**	**2,783**
General & admin. expense	932		1,229
Operating expense	**932**	**-24**	**1,229**
Operating income	**(5,953)**	**n.a.**	**1,555**
Write-downs/write-offs	nil		103
Pre-tax income	**(5,954)**	**n.a.**	**1,658**
Income taxes	14		nil
Net income	**(5,967)**	**n.a.**	**1,658**
Cash & equivalent	3,809		9,391
Accounts receivable	19		11
Current assets	3,828		9,402
Long-term investments	989		1,360
Total assets	**4,817**	**-55**	**10,762**
Accts. pay. & accr. liabs	98		76
Current liabilities	98		76
Shareholders' equity	4,719		10,686
Cash from oper. activs	**(327)**	**n.a.**	**(3,494)**
Net cash position	**529**	**-38**	**856**
	A$		A$
Earnings per share*	(0.08)		0.02
Cash flow per share*	(0.00)		(0.04)
	shs		shs
No. of shs. o/s*	77,798,218		77,798,218
Avg. no. of shs. o/s*	77,798,218		77,798,218
	%		%
Net profit margin	n.m.		59.58
Return on equity	(77.47)		16.82
Return on assets	(76.60)		16.65

* Ordinary
[A] Reported in accordance with IFRS

Note: Total revenue includes advisory/commission income, digital currency sales, interest income, diividend income and realized and unrealized gains.

Latest Results

Periods ended:	3m Sept. 30/22[A]		3m Sept. 30/21[A]
	A$000s	%Chg	A$000s
Total revenue	14	n.a.	(3,208)
Net income	(210)	n.a.	(3,447)
	A$		A$
Earnings per share*	(0.00)		(0.04)

* Ordinary
[A] Reported in accordance with IFRS

Historical Summary
(as originally stated)

Fiscal Year	Total Rev.	Net Inc. Bef. Disc.	EPS*
	A$000s	A$000s	A$
2022[A]	(5,021)	(5,967)	(0.08)
2021[A]	2,783	1,658	0.02
2020[A1]	3,184	934	0.01
2019[A]	(624)	(5,067)	(0.07)
2018[A]	785	(823)	(0.00)

* Ordinary
[A] Reported in accordance with IFRS
[1] Comparative earnings per share, shares outstanding and weighted average shares outstanding adjusted to reflect 1-for-20 share consolidation on Dec. 2, 2019.

F.39 First Hydrogen Corp.

Symbol - FHYD **Exchange** - TSX-VEN **CUSIP** - 32057N
Head Office - 440-755 Burrard St, Vancouver, BC, V6Z 1X6 **Telephone** - (604) 601-2018 **Toll-free** - (844) 787-3398 **Fax** - (604) 688-1320
Website - firsthydrogen.com
Email - balraj@pureextraction.ca
Investor Relations - Balraj S. Mann (604) 601-2018
Auditors - Sam S. Mah Inc. C.A., Vancouver, B.C.
Transfer Agents - Computershare Trust Company of Canada Inc., Vancouver, B.C.
Profile - (B.C. 2007) Develops, engineers, manufactures and sells equipment focusing on zero-emission vehicles, green hydrogen production and distribution and supercritical carbon dioxide extractor systems in the U.K., Europe and North America.

Designing and building hydrogen-fuel-cell-powered light commercial demonstrator vehicles (LCV), which will have a range of more than 630 km. These vehicles were being trialled with an initial 16 fleet operators in the U.K. The development of LCV is under two agreements with **AVL Powertrain UK Ltd.** and **Ballard Power Systems Inc.**, with the company owning the commercial rights for the vehicle design.

Through First Hydrogen Energy division, is developing green hydrogen production projects with sites initially in the U.K. and Canada that would accommodate large refuelling stations and on-site hydrogen production. Has four green hydrogen production facilities under development in the U.K. Also has an agreement with **FEV Consulting GmbH**, the automotive consultancy of **FEV Group**, to jointly design and manufacture a prototype bespoke hydrogen refuelling station to be rolled out to the hydrogen mobility market.

Also under development are hydrogen-fuel-cell-powered supercritical carbon dioxide extractor systems that can be operated in remote locations with no electrical power grids.

Predecessor Detail - Name changed from Pure Extraction Corp., Oct. 7, 2021.
Directors - Balraj S. Mann, pres. & CEO, Richmond, B.C.; Barry Hartley, North Vancouver, B.C.; Alicia Milne, Burnaby, B.C.
Other Exec. Officers - Nancy Zhao, CFO & corp. sec.; Luisa Ferres Meyer, chief people officer; Francois Morin, v-p, corp. & bus. devel.; Robert (Rob) Campbell, CEO, energy; Steve Gill, CEO, automotive

Capital Stock

	Authorized (shs.)	Outstanding (shs.)[1]
Common	unlimited	70,610,015

[1] At July 29, 2023

Major Shareholder - Widely held at June 28, 2022.

Price Range - FHYD/TSX-VEN

Year	Volume	High	Low	Close
2022	16,049,317	$5.30	$1.67	$4.69
2021	7,591,077	$2.41	$0.20	$1.92
2020	503,591	$0.75	$0.25	$0.42
2018	64,325	$0.55	$0.15	$0.18

Recent Close: $2.54
Capital Stock Changes - In May and June 2023, private placement of 1,680,300 units (1 common share & 1 warrant) at $2.40 per unit was completed, with warrants exercisable at $2.85 per share for two years.

In April 2022, private placement of 2,245,222 units (1 common share & 1 warrant) at $2.70 per unit was completed. Also during fiscal 2023, common shares were issued as follows: 6,232,726 on exercise of warrants, 3,750,000 on conversion of debentures and 250,000 on exercise of options.

In April 2021, private placement of 7,500,000 units (1 common share & ½ warrant) at 40¢ per unit was completed. In September 2021, private placement of 2,400,000 units (1 common share & 1 warrant) at $1.25 per unit was completed. Also during fiscal 2022, common shares were issued as follows: 3,000,000 pursuant to the assignment of two letters of intents from Nova Light Capital Limited, 2,818,276 on exercise of options, 1,250,000 on conversion of debenture, 249,590 as finder's fees and 18,750 on exercise of warrants.

Wholly Owned Subsidiaries

First Hydrogen Automotive (USA) Inc.
First Hydrogen Energy (USA) Inc., United States.
First Hydrogen Limited, United Kingdom.
First Hydrogen (Quebec) Corp., Qué.
NetzeroH2 Inc.
1063136 B.C. Ltd., Valemount, B.C.
1300492 B.C. Ltd.
Pure Extraction Ltd., Vancouver, B.C.
ZeronetH2 Inc.
Note: The preceding list includes only the major related companies in which interests are held.

Financial Statistics

Periods ended:	12m Mar. 31/23[A]		12m Mar. 31/22[A]
	$000s	%Chg	$000s
Operating revenue	**160**	**n.a.**	**nil**
Cost of sales	155		nil
Salaries & benefits	4,402		366
Research & devel. expense	5,103		4,544
General & admin expense	5,236		2,803
Stock-based compensation	897		725
Operating expense	**15,793**	**+87**	**8,438**
Operating income	**(15,633)**	**n.a.**	**(8,438)**
Deprec., depl. & amort.	103		nil
Finance costs, gross	185		413
Write-downs/write-offs	(409)		(33)
Pre-tax income	**(13,716)**	**n.a.**	**(8,868)**
Net income	**(13,716)**	**n.a.**	**(8,868)**
Cash & equivalent	395		2,599
Inventories	242		564
Current assets	3,340		4,157
Fixed assets, net	8		nil
Intangibles, net	892		991
Total assets	**4,240**	**-18**	**5,149**
Accts. pay. & accr. liabs	2,997		2,057
Current liabilities	3,151		2,887
Long-term debt, gross	31		1,260
Long-term debt, net	nil		1,141
Shareholders' equity	1,089		1,121
Cash from oper. activs	**(13,636)**	**n.a.**	**(7,152)**
Cash from fin. activs	11,583		8,114
Cash from invest. activs	(12)		nil
Net cash position	**395**	**-85**	**2,599**
Capital expenditures	(12)		nil
	$		$
Earnings per share*	(0.23)		(0.18)
Cash flow per share*	(0.22)		(0.14)
	shs		shs
No. of shs. o/s*	67,526,165		55,337,855
Avg. no. of shs. o/s*	60,825,227		49,546,874
	%		%
Net profit margin	n.m.		n.a.
Return on equity	(1,241.27)		(775.51)
Return on assets	(288.23)		(217.60)

* Common
[A] Reported in accordance with IFRS

Historical Summary
(as originally stated)

Fiscal Year	Oper. Rev.	Net Inc. Bef. Disc.	EPS*
	$000s	$000s	$
2023[A]	160	(13,716)	(0.23)
2022[A]	nil	(8,868)	(0.18)
2021[A]	302	(2,461)	(0.06)
2020[A]	nil	(597)	n.a.

* Common
[A] Reported in accordance with IFRS

F.40 First National Financial Corporation

Symbol - FN **Exchange** - TSX **CUSIP** - 33564P
Head Office - 1900-16 York St, Toronto, ON, M5J 0E6 **Telephone** - (416) 593-1100 **Toll-free** - (888) 488-0794 **Fax** - (416) 593-1900
Website - www.firstnational.ca
Email - rob.inglis@firstnational.ca
Investor Relations - Robert Inglis (800) 465-0039
Auditors - Ernst & Young LLP C.A., Toronto, Ont.
Lawyers - Stikeman Elliott LLP, Toronto, Ont.
Transfer Agents - Computershare Trust Company of Canada Inc., Toronto, Ont.
FP500 Revenue Ranking - 260
Employees - 1,686 at Dec. 31, 2022
Profile - (Ont. 2011, amalg.) Originates, underwrites and services prime mortgages for single-family residential clients and multi-unit residential and commercial clients sourced from independent mortgage brokers and in-house underwriters.

At Dec. 31, 2022, mortgages under administration totaled $131 billion (2021 - $123.9 billion), of which 68% were single-family residential mortgages and 32% were multi-unit residential or commercial mortgages. Offices are located in Halifax, Montreal, Toronto, Calgary and Vancouver.

Originations by segment:

At Dec. 31	2022	2021
	$millions	$millions
Single-family[1]	26,319	29,719
Multi-unit[2]	11,797	12,405
	38,116	42,124

[1] Residential mortgages.
[2] Residential and commercial mortgages.

Predecessor Detail - Succeeded First National Financial Income Fund, Jan. 1, 2011, pursuant to plan of arrangement whereby First National Financial Corporation was formed to facilitate the conversion of the fund into a corporation and the fund was subsequently dissolved.
Directors - Stephen J. R. Smith, exec. chr., Toronto, Ont.; Jason Ellis, pres. & CEO, Toronto, Ont.; Moray Tawse, exec. v-p & corp. sec., Toronto, Ont.; Robert Mitchell†, Vancouver, B.C.; Martine M. Irman, Toronto, Ont.; Duncan N. R. Jackman, Toronto, Ont.; Barbara Palk, Toronto, Ont.; Robert W. Pearce, Oakville, Ont.; Diane Sinhuber, Mississauga, Ont.
Other Exec. Officers - Robert (Rob) Inglis, CFO; Thomas Kim, sr. v-p & man. dir., capital markets; Scott C. McKenzie, sr. v-p, residential mtges.; Jeremy Wedgbury, sr. v-p, comml. mtges.; Hilda Wong, sr. v-p, chief privacy officer, chief AML officer & gen. counsel
† Lead director

Capital Stock

	Authorized (shs.)	Outstanding (shs.)[1]	Par
Class A Preference	unlimited		
Series 1	unlimited	2,984,835	$25
Series 2	unlimited	1,015,165	$25
Common	unlimited	59,967,429	

[1] At Mar. 27, 2023

Class A Preference Series 1 - Entitled to cumulative annual dividends of $0.72375 per share payable quarterly to Mar. 31, 2026, and thereafter at a rate reset every five years equal to the five-year Government of Canada yield plus 2.07%. Redeemable on Mar. 31, 2026, and on March 31 every five years thereafter at $25 per share plus declared and unpaid dividends. Convertible at the holder's option on Mar. 31, 2026, and on March 31 every five years thereafter, into floating rate preference series 2 shares on a share-for-share basis, subject to certain conditions.
Class A Preference Series 2 - Entitled to cumulative annual dividends payable quarterly equal to the 90-day Government of Canada Treasury bill rate plus 2.07%. Redeemable on Mar. 31, 2026, and on March 31 every five years thereafter at $25 per share, or at $25.50 per share in the case of redemptions on any other date. Convertible at the holder's option on Mar. 31, 2026, and on March 31 every five years thereafter, into preference series 1 shares on a share-for-share basis, subject to certain conditions.
Common - One vote per share.
Major Shareholder - Stephen J. R. Smith held 37.4% interest and Moray Tawse held 34% interest at Mar. 27, 2023.

Price Range - FN/TSX

Year	Volume	High	Low	Close
2022	11,387,173	$45.89	$32.12	$36.42
2021	9,669,949	$53.25	$39.19	$41.56
2020	16,201,552	$41.80	$18.75	$41.48
2019	6,792,453	$44.95	$26.97	$38.08
2018	4,918,481	$29.99	$25.34	$27.46

Recent Close: $37.91
Capital Stock Changes - There were no changes to capital stock during 2022.

Dividends

FN com Ra $2.40 pa M est. Dec. 15, 2022**
Prev. Rate: $2.349996 est. June 15, 2021
Prev. Rate: $2.10 est. Dec. 15, 2020
$1.25◆ Dec. 15/21
Paid in 2023: $1.80 2022: $2.15833 2021: $2.245831 + $1.25◆
FN.PR.A pfd A ser 1 cum. red. exch. Adj. Ra $0.72375 pa Q est. July 15, 2021
FN.PR.B pfd A ser 2 cum. red. exch. Fltg. Ra pa Q
$0.413489 July 14/23 $0.382377 Apr. 14/23
$0.339518 Jan. 16/23 $0.2231 Oct. 14/22
Paid in 2023: $1.135384 2022: $0.667663 2021: $0.547448

** Reinvestment Option ◆ Special

Wholly Owned Subsidiaries

FNFC Trust
First National Financial GP Corporation, Ont.
- 100% int. in **First National Asset Management Inc.**, Ont.
- 0.01% int. in **First National Financial LP**, Toronto, Ont.

First National Mortgage Corporation, Ont.

Subsidiaries

99.99% int. in **First National Financial LP**, Toronto, Ont.

Financial Statistics

Periods ended:	12m Dec. 31/22[A]		12m Dec. 31/21[A]
	$000s	%Chg	$000s
Total revenue	**1,574,293**	**+13**	**1,394,606**
Salaries & benefits	192,989		177,038
General & admin. expense	962,591		895,656
Operating expense	**1,155,580**	**+8**	**1,072,694**
Operating income	**418,713**	**+30**	**321,912**
Deprec. & amort.	13,622		9,182
Finance costs, gross	136,009		48,909
Pre-tax income	**269,082**	**+2**	**263,821**
Income taxes	71,350		69,260
Net income	**197,732**	**+2**	**194,561**
Accounts receivable	114,675		97,602
Investments	39,727,138		38,385,435
Fixed assets, net	39,993		36,968
Right-of-use assets	49,374		52,385
Intangibles, net	29,776		29,776
Total assets	**43,763,672**	**+4**	**42,274,158**
Bank indebtedness	1,065,868		965,420
Accts. pay. & accr. liabs	74,465		72,508
Debt	399,222		398,888
Lease liabilities	51,171		52,871
Preferred share equity	97,394		97,394
Shareholders' equity	698,980		577,410
Cash from oper. activs	**509,157**	**n.a.**	**(402,894)**
Cash from fin. activs	(556,733)		133,046
Cash from invest. activs	(52,872)		(12,740)
Net cash position	**(1,065,868)**	**n.a.**	**(965,420)**
Capital expenditures	(12,380)		(31,956)
	$		$
Earnings per share*	3.25		3.20
Cash flow per share*	8.49		(6.72)
Cash divd. per share*	2.16		2.27
Extra divd. - cash*	nil		1.25
Total divd. per share*	**2.16**		**3.52**
	shs		shs
No. of shs. o/s*	59,967,429		59,967,429
Avg. no. of shs. o/s*	59,967,429		59,967,429
	%		%
Net profit margin	12.56		13.95
Return on equity	36.00		40.25
Return on assets	0.69		0.56
No. of employees (FTEs)	1,686		1,579

* Common
[A] Reported in accordance with IFRS

Historical Summary
(as originally stated)

Fiscal Year	Total Rev. $000s	Net Inc. Bef. Disc. $000s	EPS* $
2022[A]	1,574,293	197,732	3.25
2021[A]	1,394,606	194,561	3.20
2020[A]	1,380,294	190,229	3.12
2019[A]	1,326,523	177,213	2.90
2018[A]	1,181,510	166,427	2.73

* Common
[A] Reported in accordance with IFRS

F.41 First Responder Technologies Inc.

Symbol - WPN **Exchange** - CSE **CUSIP** - 33618F
Head Office - Royal Centre, 1500-1055 Georgia St W, PO Box 11117, Vancouver, BC, V6G 2Z6 **Telephone** - (604) 805-4602
Email - kal@bullruncapita.ca
Investor Relations - Kulwant Malhi (604) 805-4602
Auditors - Mao & Ying LLP C.A., Vancouver, B.C.
Transfer Agents - Computershare Trust Company of Canada Inc., Vancouver, B.C.
Profile - (B.C. 2017) Pursuing acquisition of mineral exploration company.

Previously, the company was engaged in the development of Sentinel™ WiFi Concealed Weapons Detection Unit from a WiFi-based detection technology developed by and licensed from **Rutgers University** that can be used to detect dangerous concealed weapons.

During fiscal 2021, the company decided to stop further development of its WiFi-based weapons detection technology. The licence for the technology was terminated subsequent to June 30, 2022. The company held exclusive global rights for the new WiFi technology developed by Rutgers University.

On June 14, 2022, wholly owned **First Responder Technologies (USA) Inc.** was dissolved.

Recent Merger and Acquisition Activity

Status: pending **Announced:** May 9, 2023
First Responder Technologies Inc. entered into an agreement for the reverse takeover acquisition of Quebec Pegmatite Corp. (QPC), a wholly owned subsidiary of Coloured Ties Capital Inc. It is intended that First Responder Shares would be issued to QPC shareholders on a one-for-one basis at a deemed price of $0.42 per First Responder share resulting in the issuance of 11,000,000 First Responder common shares to QPC shareholders. First Responder is expected to change its name to Quebec Pegmatite Holdings Corp. after closing of the transaction. QPC plans to raise up to $1,250,000 via a private placement of shares at $0.25 per QPC share. QPC has two lithium properties in the James Bay and Mazérac regions of Quebec.

Directors - Kulwant (Kal) Malhi, CEO, Vancouver, B.C.; Michael C. Kelly, Langley, B.C.; Milan Malhi, Whistler, B.C.; Harveer Sidhu, B.C.
Other Exec. Officers - Harpreet (Harry) Nijjar, CFO

Capital Stock

	Authorized (shs.)	Outstanding (shs.)[1]
Common	unlimited	2,714,367

[1] At Feb. 24, 2023

Major Shareholder - Kulwant (Kal) Malhi held 13.31% interest and Rutgers, The State University of New Jersey held 10.25% interest at Nov. 10, 2022.

Price Range - WPN/CSE

Year	Volume	High	Low	Close
2022	246,850	$1.00	$0.13	$0.13
2021	453,018	$3.25	$0.38	$0.38
2020	1,798,459	$9.75	$2.13	$2.75

Consolidation: 1-for-25 cons. in Dec. 2022
Recent Close: $0.42
Capital Stock Changes - On Dec. 20, 2022, common shares were consolidated on a 1-for-25 basis. In March 2023, private placement of 7,425,000 units (1 common share & 1 warrant) at $0.085 per unit was closed, with warrants exercisable at 11¢ per share for two years.

During fiscal 2022, 5,977,458 common shares were issued for debt settlement.

Financial Statistics

Periods ended:	12m June 30/22[A]		12m June 30/21[□A]
	$000s	%Chg	$000s
Research & devel. expense	nil		1,523
General & admin expense	551		1,561
Stock-based compensation	nil		(84)
Operating expense	**551**	**-82**	**3,000**
Operating income	**(551)**	**n.a.**	**(3,000)**
Deprec., depl. & amort.	nil		575
Finance income	nil		3
Finance costs, gross	122		11
Write-downs/write-offs	(41)		(1,616)
Pre-tax income	**(485)**	**n.a.**	**(5,120)**
Net income	**(485)**	**n.a.**	**(5,120)**
Cash & equivalent	101		54
Current assets	109		135
Fixed assets, net	nil		42
Total assets	**109**	**-38**	**177**
Accts. pay. & accr. liabs	806		1,483
Current liabilities	2,138		1,537
Long-term debt, gross	439		337
Long-term debt, net	nil		337
Shareholders' equity	(2,029)		(1,697)
Cash from oper. activs	**(263)**	**n.a.**	**(1,929)**
Cash from fin. activs	310		439
Cash from invest. activs	nil		(5)
Net cash position	**101**	**+87**	**54**
Capital expenditures	nil		(5)
	$		$
Earnings per share*	(0.25)		(2.00)
Cash flow per share*	(0.10)		(0.78)
	shs		shs
No. of shs. o/s*	2,714,367		2,475,269
Avg. no. of shs. o/s*	2,620,872		2,475,269
	%		%
Net profit margin	n.a.		n.a.
Return on equity	n.m.		n.m.
Return on assets	(253.85)		(238.52)

* Common
[□] Restated
[A] Reported in accordance with IFRS

Latest Results

Periods ended:	3m Sept. 30/22[A]		3m Sept. 30/21[A]
	$000s	%Chg	$000s
Net income	(105)	n.a.	42
	$		$
Earnings per share*	(0.04)		0.02

* Common
[A] Reported in accordance with IFRS

Historical Summary
(as originally stated)

Fiscal Year	Oper. Rev. $000s	Net Inc. Bef. Disc. $000s	EPS* $
2022[A]	nil	(485)	(0.25)
2021[A]	nil	(5,120)	(2.00)
2020[A]	nil	(7,143)	(3.50)
2019[A]	nil	(521)	(1.00)
2018[A]	nil	(46)	n.a.

* Common
[A] Reported in accordance with IFRS
Note: Adjusted throughout for 1-for-25 cons. in Dec. 2022

F.42 First Tidal Acquisition Corp.

Symbol - AAA.P **Exchange** - TSX-VEN **CUSIP** - 33719F
Head Office - 228-1122 Mainland St, Vancouver, BC, V6B 5L1
Email - ianbmcgavney@gmail.com
Investor Relations - Ian McGavney (506) 721-6874
Auditors - Wasserman Ramsay C.A., Markham, Ont.
Transfer Agents - Computershare Trust Company of Canada Inc., Vancouver, B.C.
Profile - (B.C. 2021) Capital Pool Company.

Recent Merger and Acquisition Activity

Status: terminated **Revised:** Sept. 28, 2022
UPDATE: The transaction was terminated. PREVIOUS: First Tidal Acquisition Corp. entered into a letter of intent for the Qualifying Transaction reverse takeover acquisition of private Montreal, Que.-based Toro Beverages Inc., which produces and sells matcha-based beverages, on a share-for-share basis (following a 1-for-3 share consolidation), which would result in the issuance of 22,877,648 First Tidal post-consolidated common shares. Completion is subject to Toro completing a private placement of subscription receipts at 50¢ per receipt, for gross proceeds of between $3,500,000 and $5,000,000. Toro's beverages include the ToroMatcha brand of energy drinks and the Matcha Colada brand of seltzers, and are sold across Canada and in the United Arab Emirates. Toro plans to expand into the U.S. and other global markets upon completion of the transaction. Mar. 29, 2022 - A definitive agreement was entered into. Upon completion, First Tidal would consolidate its common shares on a 1-for-2 basis, Toro would amalgamate with a wholly owned subsidiary of First Tidal, and First Tidal would change its name to Toro Beverages Inc.

Directors - Ian McGavney, CEO, CFO & corp. sec., Quispamsis, N.B.; James P. (Jim) Defer, North Vancouver, B.C.; Jakson Inwentash, Toronto, Ont.; Craig Taylor, Vancouver, B.C.

Capital Stock

	Authorized (shs.)	Outstanding (shs.)[1]
Cl. B Preferred	unlimited	nil
Cl. A Common	unlimited	8,000,000

[1] At July 10, 2023

Major Shareholder - Widely held at Aug. 26, 2021.

Price Range - AAA.P/TSX-VEN

Year	Volume	High	Low	Close
2022	79,500	$0.10	$0.02	$0.03
2021	181,500	$0.16	$0.11	$0.11

Recent Close: $0.05
Capital Stock Changes - There were no changes to capital stock during fiscal 2023.

F.43 FirstService Corporation*

Symbol - FSV **Exchange** - TSX **CUSIP** - 33767E
Head Office - 600-1255 Bay St, Toronto, ON, M5R 2A9 **Telephone** - (416) 960-9566 **Fax** - (647) 258-0008
Website - www.firstservice.com
Email - jrakusin@firstservice.com
Investor Relations - Jeremy Rakusin (416) 960-9566
Auditors - PricewaterhouseCoopers LLP C.A., Toronto, Ont.
Lawyers - Fogler, Rubinoff LLP, Toronto, Ont.
Transfer Agents - TSX Trust Company, Toronto, Ont.
FP500 Revenue Ranking - 115
Employees - 27,000 at Dec. 31, 2022
Profile - (Ont. 2014) Provides residential property management and services to residential and commercial customers in North America.

FirstService Residential - This division provides property management and related property services to 8,700 communities (representing over 4,000,000 residents) in three Canadian provinces and 25 U.S. states under the FirstService Residential brand. Services include on-site staffing for building engineering and maintenance, swimming pool and amenity management, security, concierge and front desk personnel, financial services (cash management, other banking transaction-related services, and specialized property insurance brokerage), energy management solutions and advisory services, and resale processing services. Clients include condominiums, co-operatives, homeowner associations, master-planned communities, active adult and lifestyle communities and other residential developments governed by common interest or multi-unit residential community associations.

FirstService Brands - This division provides essential property services to residential and commercial customers through both franchise systems and company-owned operations. Franchise operations consist of: Paul Davis Restoration, which provides water, fire and mold cleanup, construction rebuild and restoration services for the insurance industry through 338 franchises in Canada and the U.S.; CertaPro Painters, which provides residential and commercial painting services with 364 franchises in Canada and the U.S.; California Closets, which provides custom-designed and installed closet and home storage solutions with 87 franchises and 138 branded retail showrooms in Canada and the U.S.; Pillar to Post Home Inspectors, which provides home inspection services with 496 franchises in North America; and Floor Coverings International, a residential and commercial floor coverings design and installation operator with 239 franchises in North America. Company-owned operations include 21 California Closets locations, 14 Paul Davis Restoration locations and one CertaPro Painters location in the U.S. and Canada; Century Fire Protection, which provides fire protection services in the southeastern U.S.; and First Onsite, which provides commercial and large loss property restoration services in North America.

In March 2023, the company acquired a Paul Davis franchise headquartered in Houston, Tex., for an undisclosed amount.

In January 2023, the company, through its FirstService Residential segment, acquired **Charles H. Greenthal & Co.**, a residential management and leasing firm with more than 250 condominium, cooperative and rental properties under management throughout New York city, Long Island and Westchester cty., N.Y.; and **Tudor Realty Services Corp.**, which provides residential property management and brokerage services. Terms were not disclosed.

During 2022, the company acquired a business under its FirstService Residential segment and six businesses under its FirstService Brands segment for total consideration of US$52,000,000. Acquisitions include Birmingham, Ala.-based **Watermark Restoration Inc.**, which provides commercial property water and fire restoration, as well as capital improvement and renovation services across the southeast U.S.; Toronto, Ont.-based **Confra Global Solutions Inc.**, which provides commercial renovation and reconstruction services throughout southern Ontario; New Orleans, La.-based **Emergency Restoration, Inc.**, which provides emergency water mitigation and property restoration services; two Paul Davis operations in Nebraska and Utah; a California Closets franchise in Oregon; and a regional firm operating in New York city, N.Y.

Recent Merger and Acquisition Activity

Status: completed **Announced:** Apr. 4, 2023
FirstService Corporation acquired private Toronto, Ont.-based Crossbridge Condominium Services Ltd., which provides residential management services to a portfolio of condominium companies across the Greater Toronto Area of Ontario. Terms of the transaction were not disclosed. Crossbridge had been an affiliate of Brookfield Business Partners L.P.

Predecessor Detail - Name changed from New FSV Corporation, June 1, 2015.

Directors - Jay S. Hennick, founder & chr., Toronto, Ont.; D. Scott Patterson, pres. & CEO, Toronto, Ont.; Yousry Bissada, Toronto, Ont.; Elizabeth Carducci, Ont.; Steve H. Grimshaw, Tex.; Frederick F. Reichheld, Wellesley, Mass.; Joan E. Sproul, Ont.; Erin J. Wallace, Colo.

Other Exec. Officers - Jeremy Rakusin, CFO; Steve Carpenter, sr. v-p, tech. & sustainability & info. srvcs.; Douglas G. Cooke, sr. v-p, corp. sec. & contr.; Alex Nguyen, sr. v-p, strategy & corp. devel.; Patrick Tran, sr. v-p, tax; Roger M. Thompson, v-p, strategy & effectiveness; Charlie E. Chase, pres. & CEO, FirstService brands; David Diestel, CEO, FirstService Residential

Capital Stock

	Authorized (shs.)	Outstanding (shs.)[1]
Common	unlimited	44,615,127

[1] At Aug. 11, 2023

Options - At Dec. 31, 2022, options were outstanding to purchase 2,337,573 common shares at weighted average exercise price of US$120.06 per share with a weighted average remaining contractual life of 2.5 years.

Normal Course Issuer Bid - The company plans to make normal course purchases of up to 1,600,000 common shares representing 4.1% of the public float. The bid commenced on Aug. 26, 2023, and expires on Aug. 25, 2024.

Major Shareholder - Widely held at Feb. 27, 2023.

Price Range - FSV/TSX

Year	Volume	High	Low	Close
2022	22,192,924	$251.57	$145.76	$165.81
2021	17,964,031	$256.01	$168.02	$248.60
2020	22,166,786	$189.17	$83.36	$174.22
2019	12,518,395	$143.26	$88.42	$120.89
2018	11,887,327	$115.17	$78.15	$93.69

Recent Close: $199.07

Capital Stock Changes - During 2022, 213,462 common shares were issued on exercise of options.

Dividends

FSV com Ra US$0.90 pa Q est. Apr. 11, 2023
Prev. Rate: US$0.81 est. Apr. 7, 2022
Prev. Rate: US$0.73 est. Apr. 7, 2021
Prev. Rate: US$0.66 est. Apr. 7, 2020

Long-Term Debt - Outstanding at Dec. 31, 2022:

Credit facility[1]	US$568,672,000
Other l-t debt due to 2023	457,000
3.84% sr. notes due 2025	90,000,000
4.53% notes due 2032	60,000,000
Capital leases	15,334,000
	734,463,000
Less: Current portion	35,665,000
	698,798,000

[1] Borrowings under a US$1 billion revolving credit facility due February 2027, bearing interest at 0.20% to 2.5% over floating reference rates.

Wholly Owned Subsidiaries

FirstOnSite USA Holdings, Inc., Fort Worth, Tex.
FirstService CAM Holdings, Inc., Del.
FirstService Residential, Inc., Irvine, Calif.
- 100% int. in **FirstService Residential Florida, Inc.**, Fla.

FirstService Restoration, Inc., Del.

Subsidiaries

89.2% int. in **Bellwether FOS Holdco, Inc.**, Fort Worth, Tex.
- 94.8% int. in **Century Fire Holdings, LLC**, Del.
- 100% int. in **Interstate Restoration, LLC**, Fort Worth, Tex.

97.2% int. in **FS Brands, Inc.**, Del.

Note: The preceding list includes only the major related companies in which interests are held.

Financial Statistics

Periods ended:	12m Dec. 31/22[A]		12m Dec. 31/21[A]
	US$000s	%Chg	US$000s
Operating revenue	**3,745,835**	**+15**	**3,249,072**
Cost of sales	2,565,720		2,202,840
General & admin expense	846,429		733,602
Operating expense	**3,412,149**	**+16**	**2,936,442**
Operating income	**333,686**	**+7**	**312,630**
Deprec., depl. & amort.	110,140		98,965
Finance costs, net	25,191		16,036
Pre-tax income	**193,981**	**-7**	**209,005**
Income taxes	48,974		52,875
Net income	**145,007**	**-7**	**156,130**
Net inc. for equity hldrs	**121,074**	**-10**	**135,212**
Net inc. for non-cont. int	**23,933**	**+14**	**20,918**
Cash & equivalent	136,219		165,665
Inventories	242,341		161,387
Accounts receivable	635,942		551,564
Current assets	1,108,872		964,660
Fixed assets, net	167,012		138,066
Right-of-use assets	205,544		159,730
Intangibles, net	1,254,537		1,225,469
Total assets	**2,774,514**	**+11**	**2,509,023**
Accts. pay. & accr. liabs	398,313		386,529
Current liabilities	636,989		618,472
Long-term debt, gross	734,463		652,804
Long-term debt, net	698,798		595,368
Long-term lease liabilities	168,557		122,337
Shareholders' equity	907,466		799,722
Cash from oper. activs	**105,893**	**-37**	**167,269**
Cash from fin. activs	18,782		24,431
Cash from invest. activs	(160,800)		(206,320)
Net cash position	**159,348**	**-18**	**194,271**
Capital expenditures	(77,609)		(58,204)
	US$		US$
Earnings per share*	2.74		3.08
Cash flow per share*	2.40		3.82
Cash divd. per share*	0.81		0.73
	shs		shs
No. of shs. o/s*	44,226,493		44,013,031
Avg. no. of shs. o/s*	44,175,107		43,840,834
	%		%
Net profit margin	3.87		4.81
Return on equity	14.18		18.52
Return on assets	5.49		6.64
Foreign sales percent	88		88
No. of employees (FTEs)	27,000		25,000

* Common
[A] Reported in accordance with U.S. GAAP

Latest Results

Periods ended:	6m June 30/23[A]		6m June 30/22[A]
	US$000s	%Chg	US$000s
Operating revenue	2,138,179	+21	1,765,279
Net income	77,380	+30	59,327
Net inc. for equity hldrs	61,478	+26	48,651
Net inc. for non-cont. int	15,902		10,676
	US$		US$
Earnings per share*	1.38		1.10

* Common
[A] Reported in accordance with U.S. GAAP

Historical Summary
(as originally stated)

Fiscal Year	Oper. Rev.	Net Inc. Bef. Disc.	EPS*
	US$000s	US$000s	US$
2022[A]	3,745,835	145,007	2.74
2021[A]	3,249,072	156,130	3.08
2020[A]	2,772,415	109,590	2.04
2019[A]	2,407,410	(227,631)	(6.58)
2018[A]	1,931,473	90,280	1.83

* Common
[A] Reported in accordance with U.S. GAAP

F.44 5D Acquisition Corp.

Symbol - FIVD.P **Exchange** - TSX-VEN **CUSIP** - 33830F
Head Office - 220-333 Terminal Ave, Vancouver, BC, V6A 4C1
Email - mfazil@lionparkcapital.com
Investor Relations - Mohammad S. Fazil (403) 613-7310
Auditors - Dale Matheson Carr-Hilton LaBonte LLP C.A., Vancouver, B.C.
Lawyers - Pushor Mitchell LLP, Kelowna, B.C.
Transfer Agents - Olympia Trust Company, Vancouver, B.C.
Profile - (B.C. 2020) Capital Pool Company.
Common listed on TSX-VEN, Apr. 14, 2023.

Directors - Mohammad S. (Mo) Fazil, CEO, Calgary, Alta.; Alexander (Alex) McAulay, CFO & corp. sec., Vancouver, B.C.; David Labistour, North Vancouver, B.C.; Joel Primus, Agassiz, B.C.; Paul D. Wilson, Calgary, Alta.

Capital Stock

	Authorized (shs.)	Outstanding (shs.)[1]
Common	unlimited	5,629,000

[1] At Apr. 14, 2023

Major Shareholder - Mohammad S. (Mo) Fazil held 10.66% interest at Apr. 14, 2023.

Recent Close: $0.10

Capital Stock Changes - On Apr. 14, 2023, an initial public offering of 3,129,000 common shares was completed at 10¢ per share.

F.45 5N Plus Inc.*

Symbol - VNP **Exchange** - TSX **CUSIP** - 33833X
Head Office - 4385 rue Garand, Saint-Laurent, QC, H4R 2B4
Telephone - (514) 856-0644 **Fax** - (514) 856-9611
Website - www.5nplus.com
Email - invest@5nplus.com
Investor Relations - Richard Perron (514) 856-0644 ext. 2555
Auditors - PricewaterhouseCoopers LLP C.A., Montréal, Qué.
Bankers - Laurentian Bank of Canada, Montréal, Qué.; Business Development Bank of Canada; Canadian Imperial Bank of Commerce, Montréal, Qué.; The Toronto-Dominion Bank, Montréal, Qué.; HSBC Bank Canada, Montréal, Qué.; National Bank of Canada, Montréal, Qué.
Lawyers - BCF LLP
Transfer Agents - Computershare Trust Company of Canada Inc., Montréal, Qué.
FP500 Revenue Ranking - 540
Employees - 766 at Dec. 31, 2022
Profile - (Can. 2007 amalg.) Produces specialty semiconductors and performance materials for various applications in the renewable energy, security, space, pharmaceutical, medical imaging and industrial sectors.

Operates two business segments: Specialty Semiconductors and Performance Materials.

The **Specialty Semiconductors** segment manufactures and sells products associated with metals including cadmium, gallium, germanium, indium and tellurium which are sold as semiconductor compounds, semiconductor wafers, ultra high purity metals, epitaxial semiconductor substrates and solar cells used in renewable energy, space satellites and imaging applications. End markets include photovoltaics (terrestrial and spatial solar energy), medical imaging, infrared imaging, optoelectonics and advanced electronics.

The **Performance Material** segment manufactures and sells products associated with metals including bismuth, low melting alloys, cobalt, nickel, copper, iron and tin which are sold as active pharmaceutical ingredients, animal feed additives, specialized chemicals, commercial grade metals, alloys and engineered powders used in pharmaceutical and healthcare, industrial, catalytic and extractive applications.

Operations are conducted from the head office and manufacturing facilities in a 25,000-sq.-ft. building with 77,000-sq.-ft. adjoining manufacturing facilities in Montreal, Que., and 50,700-sq.-ft. adjoining facilities in Eisenhüttenstadt, Germany. The company also has a 48,500-sq.-ft. facility in Kulim, Malaysia, dedicated to recycling cadmium telluride bearing residues. Production operations are also located in Lübeck and Heilbronn, Germany; Shangyu, People's Republic of China (PRC); Vientiane, Laos; St. George, Utah; and Trumbull, Conn. The company operates a sales office in Hong Kong, PRC.

On May 11, 2022, the company announced a commercial agreement with **Rio Tinto plc** to refine the tellurium to be produced at Rio Tinto's Kennecott copper operation in Utah. The tellurium would be refined at the company's Montreal, Que., facility and primarily used for the manufacturing of thin-film photovoltaic (PV) modules by **First Solar Inc.** under an existing semiconductor supply agreement between First Solar and the company. The tellurium would also be used to manufacture ultra high purity semiconductor substrates at the company's facility in St. George, Utah, to serve clients in the security and medical imaging markets.

Recent Merger and Acquisition Activity

Status: completed **Announced:** Dec. 19, 2022
5N Plus Inc. sold wholly owned 5N Plus Belgium S.A., which owns a manufacturing facility in Tilly, Belgium that produces lead-based products and nitrate chemicals primarily used in the industrial, catalytic and extractive sectors, to Vital Materials Co., Ltd. Terms were not disclosed. 5N Plus announced in May 2022 its intention to halt production at the facility and proceed with the site's closure.

Directors - Luc Bertrand, chr., Montréal, Qué.; Gervais Jacques, pres. & CEO, Candiac, Qué.; Jean-Marie Bourassa, Montréal, Qué.; Blair Dickerson; Nathalie Le Prohon, Westmount, Qué.

Other Exec. Officers - Richard Perron, CFO; Roland Dubois, exec. v-p, specialty semiconductors & chief comml. officer; Paul Tancell, exec. v-p, performance materials

Capital Stock

	Authorized (shs.)	Outstanding (shs.)[1]
Preferred	unlimited	nil
Class B	unlimited	nil
Common	unlimited	88,454,724

[1] At Aug. 1, 2023

Options - At Dec. 31, 2022, options were outstanding to purchase 1,598,938 common shares at a weighted average exercise price of Cdn$1.91 per share expiring from February 2023 to May 2028.

Major Shareholder - Caisse de dépôt et placement du Québec held 18.3% interest and Letko, Brosseau & Associates Inc. held 11.4% interest at Apr. 4, 2023.

Price Range - VNP/TSX

Year	Volume	High	Low	Close
2022	29,677,538	$3.22	$1.03	$2.91
2021	52,439,567	$5.01	$2.06	$2.38
2020	12,537,858	$3.06	$1.01	$2.95
2019	13,905,516	$3.83	$1.92	$2.46
2018	15,934,460	$3.73	$2.22	$3.10

Recent Close: $3.55

Capital Stock Changes - There were no changes to capital stock during 2022.

Long-Term Debt - At Dec. 31, 2022, outstanding long-term debt totaled US$121,000,000 (none current) and consisted of a US$25,000,000 subordinated term loan, bearing interest at five-year U.S. swap rate plus 4.19% due March 2024; and US$96,000,000 in borrowings under a senior secured revolving facility, bearing interest at Canadian prime rate, U.S. base rate, Hong Kong base rate or SOFR, plus a margin based on the company's senior net debt to consolidated EBITDA ratio, due April 2026.

Wholly Owned Subsidiaries

AZUR SPACE Solar Power GmbH, Heilbronn, Germany.
5N Plus Lao Industrial Resources Co. Ltd., Vientiane, Laos.
5N Plus Semiconductors LLC, St. George, Utah.
5N Plus Wisconsin Inc., Trumbull, Conn.
5N PV GmbH, Eisenhüttenstadt, Germany.
5N Plus Asia Limited, Hong Kong, People's Republic of China.
5N Plus Lübeck GmbH, Lübeck, Germany.
5N Plus Shangyu Co. Ltd., Shangyu, Zhejiang, People's Republic of China.

Investments

Microbion Corporation, Bozeman, Mont.

Financial Statistics

Periods ended:	12m Dec. 31/22[A]		12m Dec. 31/21[A]
	US$000s	%Chg	US$000s
Operating revenue	**264,223**	**+26**	**209,990**
Research & devel. expense	4,638		736
General & admin expense	27,566		21,194
Stock-based compensation	999		689
Other operating expense	168,747		155,375
Operating expense	**201,950**	**+13**	**177,994**
Operating income	**62,273**	**+95**	**31,996**
Deprec., depl. & amort.	17,992		12,788
Finance costs, gross	5,234		4,131
Write-downs/write-offs	(12,478)		nil
Pre-tax income	**(18,288)**	**n.a.**	**8,740**
Income taxes	4,711		5,630
Net income	**(22,999)**	**n.a.**	**3,110**
Cash & equivalent	42,691		35,940
Inventories	86,254		95,526
Accounts receivable	32,872		42,098
Current assets	187,162		195,522
Fixed assets, net	77,951		81,526
Right-of-use assets	30,082		32,198
Intangibles, net	43,388		54,315
Total assets	**347,985**	**-7**	**373,590**
Accts. pay. & accr. liabs	40,200		46,454
Current liabilities	62,846		65,059
Long-term debt, gross	121,000		116,000
Long-term debt, net	121,000		116,000
Long-term lease liabilities	28,266		30,153
Shareholders' equity	112,776		136,247
Cash from oper. activs	**23,741**	**+131**	**10,270**
Cash from fin. activs	2,409		36,219
Cash from invest. activs	(18,994)		(49,929)
Net cash position	**42,691**	**+19**	**35,940**
Capital expenditures	(16,062)		(5,385)
Capital disposals	2,836		285
Unfunded pension liability	10,581		14,725
	US$		US$
Earnings per share*	(0.26)		0.04
Cash flow per share*	0.27		0.12
	shs		shs
No. of shs. o/s*	88,330,236		88,330,236
Avg. no. of shs. o/s*	88,330,236		82,636,023
	%		%
Net profit margin	(8.70)		1.48
Return on equity	(18.47)		2.44
Return on assets	(4.55)		1.53
Foreign sales percent	92		91
No. of employees (FTEs)	766		853

* Common
[A] Reported in accordance with IFRS

Latest Results

Periods ended:	6m June 30/23[A]		6m June 30/22[A]
	US$000s	%Chg	US$000s
Operating revenue	114,362	-16	136,809
Net income	11,597	n.a.	(7,885)
	US$		US$
Earnings per share*	0.13		(0.09)

* Common
[A] Reported in accordance with IFRS

Historical Summary
(as originally stated)

Fiscal Year	Oper. Rev. US$000s	Net Inc. Bef. Disc. US$000s	EPS* US$
2022[A]	264,223	(22,999)	(0.26)
2021[A]	209,990	3,110	0.04
2020[A]	177,192	2,186	0.03
2019[A]	195,971	1,785	0.02
2018[A]	217,995	13,972	0.17

* Common
[A] Reported in accordance with IFRS

F.46 Flagship Communities Real Estate Investment Trust

Symbol - MHC.UN **Exchange** - TSX **CUSIP** - 33843T
Head Office - 467 Erlanger Rd, Erlanger, KY, United States, 41018
Telephone - (859) 568-3390
Website - flagshipcommunities.com
Email - investor_relations@flagshipcommunities.com
Investor Relations - Eddie Carlisle (859) 568-3390
Auditors - MNP LLP C.A., Toronto, Ont.
Lawyers - Adams, Stepner, Woltermann & Dusing, PLLC, Covington, Ky.; Blake, Cassels & Graydon LLP, Toronto, Ont.
Transfer Agents - TSX Trust Company, Toronto, Ont.
Employees - 140 at Dec. 31, 2022

Profile - (Ont. 2020) Owns and acquires manufactured home communities (MHCs) and related assets in the U.S.

At Mar. 31, 2023, the trust owned a 100% interest in 68 MHCs with 12,273 lots located in Arkansas, Kentucky, Illinois, Indiana, Missouri, Ohio and Tennessee, and a fleet of 1,200 manufactured homes for lease to residents.

During the first quarter of 2023, the trust sold 34 rental homes for US$650,000.

In February 2023, the company acquired a 20-acre manufactured housing resort community in Austin, Ind., which included 94 developed lots and 26 lots for additional expansion totaling 120 homesites, for issuance of US$2,000,000 Class B units of subsidiary **Flagship Operating, LLC**.

During 2022, the trust sold 147 rental homes for US$1,827,000.

Recent Merger and Acquisition Activity

Status: completed **Announced:** May 4, 2023
Flagship Communities Real Estate Investment Trust acquired three manufactured housing communities in Arkansas, Indiana and Tennessee, which included 660 lots, for a total purchase price of US$21,000,000.

Status: completed **Revised:** Nov. 30, 2022
UPDATE: The transaction was completed. PREVIOUS: Flagship Communities Real Estate Investment Trust agreed to acquire a 20-acre resort-style manufactured housing community in Marblehead, Ohio, for US$7,800,000.

Status: completed **Revised:** Sept. 22, 2022
UPDATE: The transaction was completed. PREVIOUS: Flagship Communities Real Estate Investment Trust agreed to acquire two manufactured housing communities in Louisville, Ky., and Bloomington, Ill., which included 584 lots and 97 rental homes, for a total purchase price of US$32,300,000.

Status: completed **Announced:** May 18, 2022
Flagship Communities Real Estate Investment Trust acquired two manufactured housing communities in Florence, Ky., for US22,500,000.

Status: completed **Revised:** Apr. 29, 2022
UPDATE: The transaction was completed. PREVIOUS: Flagship Communities Real Estate Investment Trust agreed to acquire a manufactured housing community in suburban Springfield Ill., for US$6,250,000. The transaction was expected to close on or about May 29, 2022.

Trustees - Peter C. B. Bynoe, chr., Chicago, Ill.; Kurtis (Kurt) Keeney, pres. & CEO, Covington, Ky.; Nathaniel (Nathan) Smith, chief invest. officer, Fort Mitchell, Ky.; Louis M. Forbes, Toronto, Ont.; J. Susan Monteith, Toronto, Ont.; Andrew L. Oppenheim, Calgary, Alta.; Ann I. Rooney, Calgary, Alta.

Other Exec. Officers - Eddie Carlisle, CFO & corp. sec.

Capital Stock

	Authorized (shs.)	Outstanding (shs.)[1]
Trust Unit	unlimited	15,317,656
Class B Unit	unlimited	5,587,629[2]

[1] At May 9, 2023
[2] Securities of wholly owned Flagship Operating, LLC.

Trust Unit - Entitled to initial monthly cash distributions equal to approximately 65% of estimated adjusted funds from operations (AFFO), payable in U.S. dollars. One vote per trust unit.

Class B Unit - Entitled to receive distributions from wholly owned Flagship Operating, LLC on the same per unit basis as holders of trust units. Redeemable, at the holder's option, for a cash payment of equivalent value or trust units on a one-for-one basis. Non-voting.

Major Shareholder - Widely held at Mar. 16, 2023.

Price Range - MHC.UN/TSX

Year	Volume	High	Low	Close
2022	63,751	$22.25	$17.70	$21.80

MHC.U/TSX

Year	Volume	High	Low	Close
2022	2,177,117	US$20.26	US$13.07	US$16.24
2021	3,570,860	US$22.26	US$14.50	US$19.30
2020	1,136,226	US$15.51	US$13.75	US$14.76

Recent Close: $21.85

Capital Stock Changes - There were no changes to capital stock during 2022.

Dividends

MHC.U unit Ra US$0.562 pa M est. Aug. 15, 2023
Prev. Rate: US$0.562 est. Dec. 15, 2022
Prev. Rate: US$0.5352 est. Sept. 15, 2022
Prev. Rate: US$0.5355 est. July 15, 2022
Prev. Rate: US$0.5355 est. Feb. 15, 2022
Prev. Rate: US$0.5355 est. Dec. 15, 2021
Prev. Rate: US$0.51 est. Dec. 15, 2020
MHC.UN unit Ra US$0.562 pa M est. Aug. 15, 2023
Listed Jun 13/22.
Prev. Rate: US$0.562 est. May 15, 2023
Prev. Rate: US$0.5616 est. Apr. 17, 2023
Prev. Rate: US$0.562 est. Feb. 15, 2023
Prev. Rate: US$0.562 est. Dec. 15, 2022
Prev. Rate: US$0.5352 est. July 15, 2022
US$0.0446**i** July 15/22
i Initial Payment

Wholly Owned Subsidiaries

Flagship HC, Inc., Del.
- 100% int. in **Flagship Operating, LLC**, Del.
  - 100% int. in **Charlie's Homes, LLC**, Del.
  - 100% int. in **Flagship Managcco**, Del.
    - 100% int. in **Flagship TRS, LLC**, Del.

Financial Statistics

Periods ended:	12m Dec. 31/22[A]		12m Dec. 31/21[A]
	US$000s	%Chg	US$000s
Total revenue	**58,798**	**+37**	**43,075**
Rental operating expense	15,631		10,979
Salaries & benefits	8,416		6,506
General & admin. expense	3,637		2,712
Operating expense	**27,684**	**+37**	**20,197**
Operating income	**31,114**	**+36**	**22,878**
Deprec. & amort.	290		174
Finance costs, gross	14,111		10,924
Pre-tax income	**42,682**	**-29**	**60,008**
Net income	**42,682**	**-29**	**60,008**
Cash & equivalent	16,926		15,451
Accounts receivable	873		753
Current assets	22,938		19,622
Fixed assets	4,213		2,718
Income-producing props	770,043		670,523
Property interests, net	770,043		670,523
Total assets	**799,268**	**+15**	**695,125**
Bank indebtedness	10,000		nil
Accts. pay. & accr. liabs	409		978
Current liabilities	20,852		9,101
Long-term debt, gross	421,347		363,967
Long-term debt, net	420,615		363,330
Shareholders' equity	357,745		322,694
Cash from oper. activs	**31,033**	**+25**	**24,823**
Cash from fin. activs	45,891		145,756
Cash from invest. activs	(75,449)		(166,627)
Net cash position	**16,926**	**+10**	**15,451**
Capital expenditures	(1,521)		(895)
Capital disposals	10		8
Increase in property	(75,789)		(164,779)
Decrease in property	1,827		1,460
	US$		US$
Earnings per share*	n.a.		n.a.
Cash flow per share*	2.19		1.99
Funds from opers. per sh.*	1.08		1.03
Adj. funds from opers. per sh.*	0.93		0.88
Cash divd. per share*	0.32		0.51
Total divd. per share*	**0.32**		**0.51**
	shs		shs
No. of shs. o/s*	14,141,185		14,141,185
Avg. no. of shs. o/s*	14,141,185		12,495,407
	%		%
Net profit margin	72.59		139.31
Return on equity	12.55		25.59
Return on assets	7.60		12.44
No. of employees (FTEs)	140		140

* Trust Unit

[A] Reported in accordance with IFRS

Latest Results

Periods ended:	3m Mar. 31/23[A]		3m Mar. 31/22[A]
	US$000s	%Chg	US$000s
Total revenue	16,758	+22	13,693
Net income	16,215	+566	2,433
	US$		US$
Earnings per share*	n.a.		n.a.

[A] Reported in accordance with IFRS

Historical Summary
(as originally stated)

Fiscal Year	Total Rev.	Net Inc. Bef. Disc.	EPS*
	US$000s	US$000s	US$
2022[A]	58,798	42,682	n.a.
2021[A]	43,075	60,008	n.a.
2020[A1]	8,304	47,338	n.a.

* Trust Unit

[A] Reported in accordance with IFRS

[1] 20 weeks ended Dec. 31, 2020.

F.47 Flora Growth Corp.

Symbol - FLGC **Exchange** - NASDAQ **CUSIP** - 339764

Head Office - 900-65 Queen St W, Toronto, ON, M5H 2M5 **Telephone** - (416) 861-2269

Website - www.floragrowth.ca

Email - evan.veryard@floragrowth.ca

Investor Relations - Evan Veryard (416) 571-9037

Auditors - Davidson & Company LLP C.A., Vancouver, B.C.

Lawyers - Greenberg Traurig LLP

Transfer Agents - Continental Stock Transfer & Trust Company, New York, N.Y.; TSX Trust Company, Toronto, Ont.

Employees - 322 at Nov. 7, 2022

Profile - (Ont. 2019) Manufactures and distributes global cannabis products and brands, with significant outdoor operations in Colombia, and provides pharmaceutical grade medical cannabis to distribution partners, primarily in Germany.

Has five operating segments: Cannabis growth and derivative production; Consumer products; Pharmaceuticals and nutraceuticals; Food and beverage; and Corporate.

Cannabis growth and derivative production - Consists of cultivation activities on the company's 361-acre farm, of which 249 acres are licensed for cannabis cultivation, and a 10,500-sq.-ft. cannabis extraction facility (Flora Lab 1), in Bucaramanga, Colombia.

Consumer products - This segment includes **Hemp Textiles & Co LLC**, which develops, manufactures and sells hemp-based loungewear under the Stardog brand; **Vessel Brand Inc.**, which manufactures and distributes vape pen products and dry-herb accessories throughout the U.S. and internationally; and **Flora Beauty LLC**, which manufactures and sells skincare and beauty products made with ingredients such as CBD oil extract, hemp beads for exfoliators and other natural ingredients through two brands, Mind Naturals and Ô.

Pharmaceuticals and nutraceuticals - This includes the company's manufacturing and research and development centres that produce pharmaceuticals, cosmetics, nutraceuticals for domestic and international markets. This includes product lines that are private label, white label, and custom formulations. Operations consist of a 16,000-ft. facility (Flora Lab 2) in Bogota, Colombia for topicals, capsules and dietary supplements, an 18,000-sq.-ft. facility in Ft. Lauderdale, Fla. (Flora Lab 3) for ingestibles, gummies and tinctures; and a 2,300-sq. life sciences lab in Bogota (Flora Lab 4) for compound pharmaceutical grade formulas.

Food and beverage - This segment includes Mambe branded Juices and other snack products containing CBD; and Tonino Lamborghini branded CBD beverages.

Corporate - This segment includes the sale of cannabis educational course content and materials to institutions in the Colombian market.

Wholly owned **Franchise Global Health Inc.** has operations in Germany, Canada, Denmark, Colombia, Saint Vincent and the Grenadines and Portugal.

In Germany, wholly owned **ACA Müller ADAG Pharma Vertriebs GmbH** imports, exports and distributes prescription drugs and medical cannabis, with medical cannabis sold in more than 1,200 pharmacies across Germany, and has supply agreements for the supply of cannabis products for distribution primarily in Germany, as well as in Denmark, Finland, Iceland, Norway and Sweden; and wholly owned **Phatebo GmbH** distributes pharmaceutical and medical cannabis products to treat a variety of health indications including drugs related to cancer therapies, ADHD, multiple sclerosis and anti-depressants, within 18 countries worldwide (primarily in Europe).

In Canada, holds minority investment in, and has entered into a strategic partnership with, a Canadian licensed producer, whereby the licensed producer has dedicated up to 500,000 sq. ft. of cultivation capacity at its cultivation facility for the production of cannabis products on behalf of the company, for export to the company's European subsidiaries for onward distribution and sale in Europe and other markets. Also, indirect wholly owned **Alchemist Labs Ltd.** has applied for a cannabis retail licence for a 3,389-sq.-ft. retail location in Winnipeg, Man.

In Denmark, wholly owned **Rangers Pharmaceuticals A/S** has a licence to store, sell and export cannabis genetics, with a portfolio of more than 250 strains.

In Colombia, indirect wholly owned **Green CannaHealth S.A.S.** holds a licence to cultivate and process cannabidiol (CBD) and tetrahydrocannabinol (THC), as well as extract and export cannabis extracts. Cannabis is cultivated on a 100-acre leased property located 50 km from Ibagué, Tolima province.

In Saint Vincent and the Grenadines, has entered into a strategic partnership with a licensed cultivator to import low-cost, high-quality, tropical grown cannabis into Germany.

In Portugal, has entered into a strategic partnership and investment with a licensed cultivator.

In July 2022, wholly owned **Just Brand LLC** acquired the assets of **No Cap Hemp Co.**, a Florida-based manufacturer and distributor of CBD products, for US$900,000.

Recent Merger and Acquisition Activity

Status: completed **Revised:** Dec. 23, 2022

UPDATE: The transaction was completed. Franchise Global shareholders received 0.29102 Flora common share for each share held, resulting in issuance of 43,525,951 Flora common shares.. PREVIOUS: Flora Growth Corp. agreed to acquire Franchise Global Health Inc. for issuance of between 36,615,060 and 43,525,951 Flora common shares.

Status: pending **Revised:** Nov. 10, 2022

UPDATE: Prior entering into the definitive agreement, the pharmaceutical distributor asked for a re-negotiation of the terms of the LOI, which were not disclosed. PREVIOUS: Franchise Global Health Inc. entered into a letter of intent (LOI), effective May 6, 2022, for the acquisition of a Germany-based pharmaceutical and medical cannabis distributor, which offers a wide range of products for medical companies in Germany, for payment of €15,3000,000 and issuance of €2,700,000 common shares. The transaction is expected to close in the fourth quarter of 2022.

Status: completed **Revised:** Mar. 25, 2022

UPDATE: The transaction was completed. PREVIOUS: Mercury Acquisitions Corp. entered into a letter of intent for the Qualifying Transaction reverse takeover acquisition of private Toronto, Ont.-based Franchise Cannabis Corp., which operates in the medical cannabis and nutraceutical industries, with principal operations and assets in Germany, Denmark and Colombia, on a share-for-share basis (following a to-be-determined share consolidation basis). The deemed value of each Mercury share would be 18¢ (pre-consolidation basis). Oct. 14, 2021 - A definitive agreement was entered into. Mercury would issue 128,289,230 post-consolidated common shares at a deemed price of $1.80 per share (following a 1-for-10 share consolidation). Upon completion, Franchise would amalgamate with Mercury's wholly owned 2868303 Ontario Inc., and Mercury would change its name to Franchise Global Health Inc. Dec. 6, 2021 - Conditional approval from the TSX Venture Exchange was received.

Directors - Kevin R. Taylor, chr., Fort Lauderdale, Fla.; Clifford A. Starke, CEO, Panama City, Panama; Juan Carlos Gomez, Colombia; Hussein Rakine, Fla.; Thomas Solomon, Switzerland; Edward Woo, B.C.

Other Exec. Officers - Dany Vaiman, CFO; Joël Reyes, sr. v-p, global opers.; Holly Bell, v-p, regulatory affairs; Orlando Bustos, v-p, strategic fin. & finl. planning & analysis; Javier Franco, v-p, agri.; Damian Lopez, v-p, legal & corp. strategy; Evan Veryard, v-p, IR; James Williams, v-p, corp. devel.; Matthew Cohen, gen. counsel & corp. sec.

Capital Stock

	Authorized (shs.)	Outstanding (shs.)[1]
Common	unlimited	6,846,900

[1] At June 9, 2023

Major Shareholder - Widely held at Nov. 9, 2022.

Price Range - FLGC/NASDAQ

Year	Volume	High	Low	Close
2022	1,708,296	US$47.40	US$4.20	US$4.56
2021	2,917,279	US$429.00	US$33.60	US$35.60

Consolidation: 1-for-20 cons. in June 2023

Capital Stock Changes - On June 9, 2023, common shares were consolidated on a 1-for-20 basis.

In December 2022, 43,525,951 common shares were issued pursuant to the acquisition of Franchise Global Health Inc.

Wholly Owned Subsidiaries

Breeze Laboratory S.A.S., Colombia.
Cosechemos YA S.A.S., Colombia.
Flora Beauty LLC, United States.
Franchise Global Health Inc., Vancouver, B.C.
- 100% int. in **Franchise Cannabis Corp.**, Toronto, Ont.
  - 100% int. in **ACA Müller ADAG Pharma Vertriebs GmbH**, Germany.
    - 100% int. in **SATIVA Verwaltungs GmbH and Co. KG**, Germany.
    - 100% int. in **SATIVA Verwaltungs GmbH**, Germany.
  - 100% int. in **CBDMed Therapeutics Inc.**, Canada.
  - 100% int. in **Fayber Technologies Inc.**, Ont.
    - 100% int. in **Catalunia S.A.S.**, Colombia.
      - 100% int. in **Green CannaHealth S.A.S.**, Colombia.
  - 100% int. in **Harmony Health One Inc.**, Ont.
  - 100% int. in **Klokken Aarhus Inc.**, Ont.
    - 100% int. in **Rangers Pharmaceuticals A/S**, Denmark.
  - 100% int. in **1200325 B.C. Ltd.**, B.C.
    - 100% int. in **Alchemist Labs Ltd.**, Man.
  - 100% int. in **Phatebo GmbH**, Germany.

Grupo Farmacuetico Cronomed S.A.S., Colombia.
- 100% int. in **Labcofarm Laboratorios S.A.S.**, Colombia.

Hemp Textiles & Co LLC, United States.
- 100% int. in **Hemp Textiles & Co S.A.S.**, Colombia.

High Roller Private Label LLC, Hollywood, Fla.
Just Brands LLC, Fort Lauderdale, Fla.
Vessel Brand Inc., Carlsbad, Calif.

Subsidiaries

90% int. in **Kasa Wholefoods Company S.A.S.**, Colombia.
- 100% int. in **Kasa Wholefoods Company LLC**, United States.

Financial Statistics

Periods ended:	12m Dec. 31/21[A]		12m Dec. 31/20[A1]
	US$000s	%Chg	US$000s
Operating revenue	**8,980**	**n.m.**	**106**
Cost of sales	6,555		35
Research & devel. expense	132		78
General & admin expense	16,703		7,374
Stock-based compensation	1,340		4,901
Operating expense	**24,730**	**+100**	**12,388**
Operating income	**(15,750)**	**n.a.**	**(12,282)**
Deprec., depl. & amort.	765		113
Finance costs, gross	84		30
Write-downs/write-offs	(1,386)		(1,816)
Pre-tax income	**(21,459)**	**n.a.**	**(14,334)**
Income taxes	(98)		nil
Net income	**(21,361)**	**n.a.**	**(14,334)**
Net inc. for equity hldrs	**(21,249)**	**n.a.**	**(14,170)**
Net inc. for non-cont. int.	**(112)**	**n.a.**	**(164)**
Cash & equivalent	37,614		15,523
Inventories	2,993		540
Accounts receivable	5,324		922
Current assets	47,943		17,634
Long-term investments	2,670		nil
Fixed assets, net	3,750		411
Right-of-use assets	1,229		318
Intangibles, net	29,790		1,089
Total assets	**85,479**	**+339**	**19,452**
Accts. pay. & accr. liabs	5,628		1,809
Long-term debt, gross	18		320
Long-term debt, net	18		251
Long-term lease liabilities	908		251
Shareholders' equity	77,166		16,363
Cash from oper. activs	**(20,648)**	**n.a.**	**(8,421)**
Cash from fin. activs	58,106		25,816
Cash from invest. activs	(14,550)		(2,164)
Net cash position	**37,614**	**+142**	**15,523**
Capital expenditures	(3,983)		(234)
	US$		US$
Earnings per share*	(9.60)		(9.40)
Cash flow per share*	(9.40)		(5.63)
	shs		shs
No. of shs. o/s*	3,275,850		1,917,917
Avg. no. of shs. o/s*	2,197,700		1,495,067
	%		%
Net profit margin	(237.87)		n.m.
Return on equity	(45.44)		n.m.
Return on assets	(40.56)		(138.71)

* Common

[A] Reported in accordance with IFRS

[1] Shares and per share figures adjusted to reflect 1-for-3 share consolidation effective Apr. 30, 2021.

Latest Results

Periods ended:	9m Sept. 30/22[A]		9m Sept. 30/21[A]
	US$000s	%Chg	US$000s
Operating revenue	25,682	+510	4,211
Net income	(40,104)	n.a.	(8,769)
Net inc. for equity hldrs	(39,969)	n.a.	(8,705)
Net inc. for non-cont. int	(135)		(64)
	US$		US$
Earnings per share*	(10.80)		(4.20)

* Common

[A] Reported in accordance with IFRS

Historical Summary
(as originally stated)

Fiscal Year	Oper. Rev.	Net Inc. Bef. Disc.	EPS*
	US$000s	US$000s	US$
2021[A]	8,980	(21,361)	(9.60)
2020[A]	106	(14,334)	(9.40)
2019[A1]	nil	(2,844)	(1.20)

* Common

[A] Reported in accordance with IFRS

[1] 42 weeks ended Dec. 31, 2019.

Note: Adjusted throughout for 1-for-20 cons. in June 2023

F.48 Florence One Capital Inc.

Symbol - FONC.P **Exchange** - TSX-VEN **CUSIP** - 340288

Head Office - 1250-639 5 Ave SW, Calgary, AB, T2P 0M9 **Telephone** - (403) 613-7310

Email - mfazil@lionparkcapital.com

Investor Relations - Mohammad S. Fazil (403) 613-7310

Auditors - Dale Matheson Carr-Hilton LaBonte LLP C.A., Vancouver, B.C.

Lawyers - TingleMerrett LLP, Calgary, Alta.

Transfer Agents - Odyssey Trust Company, Calgary, Alta.

Profile - (Alta. 2021) Capital Pool Company.

Common listed on TSX-VEN, Sept. 12, 2022.

Directors - Mohammad S. (Mo) Fazil, pres., CEO, CFO & sec.-treas., Calgary, Alta.; Qiang (Max) Guo, Toronto, Ont.; Viswanathan (Vishy) Karamadam, Mississauga, Ont.; Emmanuel Paul, Toronto, Ont.; Scott M. Reeves, Calgary, Alta.; James C. Tworek, Calgary, Alta.

Capital Stock

	Authorized (shs.)	Outstanding (shs.)[1]
Common	unlimited	16,042,000

[1] At June 26, 2023

Major Shareholder - Widely held at Sept. 12, 2022.

Price Range - FONC.P/TSX-VEN

Year	Volume	High	Low	Close
2022	565,500	$0.17	$0.06	$0.08

Recent Close: $0.07

Capital Stock Changes - On Sept. 12, 2022, an initial public offering of 2,542,000 common shares was completed at 10¢ per share.

F.49 Flow Beverage Corp.

Symbol - FLOW **Exchange** - TSX **CUSIP** - 34344J

Head Office - Unit 7-10, 155 Industrial Pky S, Aurora, ON, L4G 3G6 **Toll-free** - (844) 356-9426

Website - investors.flowhydration.com

Email - kevin.helfand@flowhydration.com

Investor Relations - Kevin Helfand (416) 702-6746

Auditors - Ernst & Young LLP C.A., Toronto, Ont.

Transfer Agents - TSX Trust Company, Toronto, Ont.

Employees - 214 at Oct. 31, 2022

Profile - (Can. 2021; orig. Ont., 2014) Produces and markets premium alkaline spring water packaged in Tetra Paks in Canada and the United States under the Flow brand.

The premium spring water contained in the company's branded products has distinct alkalinity, mineral profile and electrolyte content, and the majority is sourced from two wholly owned springs located in Bruce cty., Ont., and Augusta cty. (Seawright Springs), Va. Products are packaged at the company's production facility in Aurora, Ont., and through a co-manufacturing agreement with **BioSteel Sports Nutrition Inc.** at the company's previously owned facility in Verona, Va.

The company distributed 30 stock keeping units (SKUs) in Canada and 25 SKUs in the U.S. at Jan. 29, 2023, including various organic flavours and collagen-infused spring waters; subsequently a line of vitamin-infused waters was introduced. Products are distributed to more than 46,000 stores across North America through a network of more than 47 distributors. Sales are also made direct to consumers through its own e-commerce sites in Canada and the U.S., and through Amazon.com and Amazon.ca. The company also co-packs other companies' beverage products in Tetra Paks at its packaging facilities.

In July 2022, the company signed an agreement with **WB Canna Co. & Wellness** to distribute Flow products across the Caribbean and Central America; and launched its Flow Vitamin-Infused Water line of products in three organic flavours: Cherry, Citrus and Elderberry.

Recent Merger and Acquisition Activity

Status: completed **Announced:** Nov. 9, 2022

Flow Beverage Corp. sold all the assets of its production facility in Verona, Va., a 144-acre spring water source, to BioSteel Sports Nutrition Inc. for US$19,500,000, consisting of US$13,200,000 cash and US$6,300,000 for the repayment of debt and the retirement of lease obligations. As part of the transaction, Flow and BioSteel entered into a co-manufacturing agreement whereby BioSteel would produce Flow's portfolio of branded water at the facility, in addition to the production of BioSteel-branded sports hydration drinks on site.

Predecessor Detail - Name changed from RG One Corp., June 29, 2021, pursuant to the reverse takeover acquisition of Flow Water Inc. (FWI), and concurrent amalgamation of FWI with wholly owned RG One Subco Inc.

Directors - Nicholas Reichenbach, exec. chr. & CEO, Innisfil, Ont.; Patrick Bousquet-Chavanne†, Southampton, N.Y.; Joe Jackman, Toronto, Ont.; Michael E. Lines, Toronto, Ont.; Stephen A. (Steve) Smith, Toronto, Ont.

Other Exec. Officers - Trent MacDonald, CFO; Kevin Helfand, chief legal & HR officer; Devan Pennell, chief strategy officer; Adrian Ross, sr. v-p, opers.

† Lead director

Capital Stock

	Authorized (shs.)	Outstanding (shs.)[1]
Multiple Vtg.	unlimited	6,214,566
Subordinate Vtg.	unlimited	49,325,522

[1] At Mar. 22, 2023

Multiple Voting - Convertible into subordinate voting shares on a 1-for-1 basis and automatically convert into subordinate voting shares upon certain transfers and other events. 10 votes per share.

Subordinate Voting - One vote per share.

Major Shareholder - Nicholas Reichenbach held 34.69% interest at Mar. 22, 2023.

Price Range - FLOW/TSX

Year	Volume	High	Low	Close
2022	8,101,047	$1.80	$0.17	$0.19
2021	13,829,918	$8.46	$1.25	$1.59

Recent Close: $0.34

Capital Stock Changes - During fiscal 2022, subordinate voting shares were issued as follows: 1,149,760 on vesting of restricted share units and 158,307 on vesting of deferred share units.

Wholly Owned Subsidiaries

Flow Water Inc., Aurora, Ont.
- 100% int. in **Flow Beverages Inc.**, United States.
- 100% int. in **Flow Beverages (Switzerland) S.A.**, Switzerland.
- 100% int. in **Flow Glow Beverages Inc.**, Canada. dormant.
- 100% int. in **2446692 Ontario Inc.**, Ont.

Financial Statistics

Periods ended:	12m Oct. 31/22[A]		12m Oct. 31/21[A1]
	$000s	%Chg	$000s
Operating revenue	**47,120**	**+10**	**42,698**
Cost of sales	37,949		31,390
Salaries & benefits	14,546		15,624
General & admin expense	27,524		25,611
Stock-based compensation	5,723		18,291
Operating expense	**85,742**	**-6**	**90,916**
Operating income	**(38,622)**	**n.a.**	**(48,218)**
Deprec., depl. & amort.	1,965		1,963
Finance costs, gross	5,680		6,268
Write-downs/write-offs	(842)		n.a.
Pre-tax income	**(47,707)**	**n.a.**	**(62,253)**
Net income	**(47,707)**	**n.a.**	**(62,253)**
Cash & equivalent	2,282		51,567
Inventories	10,061		8,934
Accounts receivable	11,901		8,693
Current assets	26,695		72,560
Fixed assets, net	11,208		32,957
Right-of-use assets	10,430		25,680
Intangibles, net	589		1,589
Total assets	**82,338**	**-38**	**132,901**
Accts. pay. & accr. liabs	12,948		15,563
Current liabilities	16,981		37,164
Long-term debt, gross	10,221		22,920
Long-term debt, net	8,211		4,645
Long-term lease liabilities	6,928		20,917
Shareholders' equity	33,096		70,175
Cash from oper. activs	**(33,044)**	**n.a.**	**(27,888)**
Cash from fin. activs	(15,261)		69,215
Cash from invest. activs	(981)		(8,005)
Net cash position	**2,281**	**-96**	**51,567**
Capital expenditures	(981)		(8,005)
	$		$
Earnings per share*	(0.88)		(1.40)
Cash flow per share*	(0.61)		(0.63)
	shs		shs
No. of shs. o/s*	54,812,594		53,504,527
Avg. no. of shs. o/s*	54,125,009		44,518,162
	%		%
Net profit margin	(101.25)		(145.80)
Return on equity	(92.39)		(154.43)
Return on assets	(39.05)		(50.25)
Foreign sales percent	50		46
No. of employees (FTEs)	214		220

* M.V. & S.V.

[A] Reported in accordance with IFRS

[1] Results prior to June 29, 2021, pertain to and reflect the reverse takeover acquisition of Flow Water Inc.

Latest Results

Periods ended:	3m Jan. 31/23[A]		3m Jan. 31/22[A]
	$000s	%Chg	$000s
Operating revenue	9,851	-17	11,888
Net income	(7,698)	n.a.	(9,913)
	$		$
Earnings per share*	(0.14)		(0.18)

* M.V. & S.V.

[A] Reported in accordance with IFRS

Historical Summary
(as originally stated)

Fiscal Year	Oper. Rev.	Net Inc. Bef. Disc.	EPS*
	$000s	$000s	$
2022[A]	47,120	(47,707)	(0.88)
2021[A]	42,698	(62,253)	(1.40)
2020[A]	22,962	(48,149)	n.a.
2019[A]	16,363	(48,992)	n.a.

* M.V. & S.V.

[A] Reported in accordance with IFRS

F.50 Flow Capital Corp.

Symbol - FW **Exchange** - TSX-VEN **CUSIP** - 343449

Head Office - 3002-1 Adelaide St E, PO Box 171, Toronto, ON, M5C 2V9 **Telephone** - (416) 777-0383 **Toll-free** - (800) 513-3868 **Fax** - (416) 760-7172

Website - www.flowcap.com

Email - alex@flowcap.com

Investor Relations - Alexander W. Baluta (416) 777-0383

Auditors - Dale Matheson Carr-Hilton LaBonte LLP C.A., Vancouver, B.C.

Bankers - Canadian Western Bank; National Bank of Canada; Royal Bank of Canada; The Toronto-Dominion Bank

Lawyers - Owens, Wright LLP, Toronto, Ont.

Transfer Agents - Computershare Trust Company of Canada Inc., Calgary, Alta.

Profile - (B.C. 2018) Invests in emerging growth companies in the United States, the United Kingdom and Canada using venture debt and royalty-based financing structures. Also provides advisory services.

Venture debt typically consists of a term loan of up three years, interest payments and warrants on the company stock. Royalty-based (or revenue-based) financing involves providing capital to businesses in exchange for a percentage of monthly revenue. The company creates shareholder value by earning stable, recurring revenues from a diverse portfolio of cash flow-oriented investments in growth companies, royalty buyouts or buydowns and realized returns from equity and warrants.

At Mar. 31, 2023, the company's active investment portfolio consisted of ten fully paying investments, four past due investment and three investments classified as delinquent, distressed or in legal process. The total carrying value of investments was $40,968,160.

In October 2022, the company invested US$1,750,000 in **Prolifiq Software, Inc.**, a provider of Software-as-a-service (Saas) solutions for structuring sales account management and opportunity planning. The company would earn a fixed interest on the investment and receive warrants at a strike price of $0.10 per share.

Predecessor Detail - Name changed from LOGiQ Asset Management Inc., June 7, 2018, following the reverse takeover acquisition of and amalgamation with Grenville Strategic Royalty Corp.; basis 1 new for 12 old shs.

Directors - Vernon Lobo, chr., Toronto, Ont.; Alexander W. (Alex) Baluta, pres. & CEO, Toronto, Ont.; Catherine E. McLeod-Seltzer, West Vancouver, B.C.; Alan D. Torrie, Toronto, Ont.; Michael Zych, Oakville, Ont.

Other Exec. Officers - Gaurav Singh, CFO; Matthew Gan, v-p; Arin Minasians, v-p, corp. devel.

Capital Stock

	Authorized (shs.)	Outstanding (shs.)[1]	Par
Common	unlimited	30,597,610	
Cl.A Preferred			
Series 1	1,811,666	406,667[2]	$3.00

[1] At May 26, 2023

[2] Classified as debt.

Class A Preferred - Non-voting and issuable in series.

Series 1 - Entitled to receive cumulative quarterly dividends of $0.069 per share. Redeemable on June 28, 2028. A holder may request the company to redeem up to one-third of the holder's shares on June 28, 2025, June 28, 2026, and June 28, 2027.

Common - One vote per share.

Normal Course Issuer Bid - The company plans to make normal course purchases of up to 2,598,100 common shares representing 10% of the public float. The bid commenced on Oct. 13, 2022, and expires on Oct. 12, 2023.

Major Shareholder - Widely held at Sept. 2, 2022.

Price Range - FW/TSX-VEN

Year	Volume	High	Low	Close
2022	3,392,535	$0.63	$0.36	$0.61
2021	4,292,741	$0.60	$0.40	$0.47
2020	8,055,824	$0.46	$0.19	$0.43
2019	9,489,046	$0.38	$0.17	$0.29
2018	8,622,570	$0.96	$0.24	$0.24

Consolidation: 1-for-2 cons. in June 2020

Recent Close: $0.56

Capital Stock Changes - During 2022, common shares were issued as follows: 187,833 on vesting of performance share units and 47,200 on exercise of warrants; 184,500 common shares were cancelled.

Wholly Owned Subsidiaries

Flow Capital Partnership Holding Corp., Ont.
Flow Capital US Corp., United States.
Flow Investment Holdings Corp., Canada.
Flow Investor Services Corp., Toronto, Ont.
LOGIQ Capital 2016, Toronto, Ont.
Tuscarora Capital Inc.

Investments

20% int. in **Flow Priority Return Fund II LP**, Canada.

Financial Statistics

Periods ended:	12m Dec. 31/22[A]		12m Dec. 31/21[oA]
	$000s	%Chg	$000s
Realized invest. gain (loss)	1,523		5,597
Total revenue	**10,296**	**-3**	**10,612**
Salaries & benefits	1,482		1,403
General & admin. expense	1,622		1,461
Stock-based compensation	196		119
Operating expense	**3,301**	**+11**	**2,983**
Operating income	**6,995**	**-8**	**7,629**
Deprec. & amort.	37		36
Finance costs, gross	1,798		1,579
Pre-tax income	**6,920**	**+6**	**6,531**
Income taxes	(7,591)		933
Net income	**14,511**	**+159**	**5,597**
Cash & equivalent	26,627		8,910
Current assets	26,792		9,278
Long-term investments	223,743		34,677
Fixed assets, net	26		63
Total assets	**58,682**	**+33**	**44,018**
Accts. pay. & accr. liabs	1,014		963
Current liabilities	13,225		4,294
Long-term debt, gross	18,937		17,842
Long-term debt, net	7,317		16,342
Long-term lease liabilities	nil		23
Shareholders' equity	38,140		23,347
Cash from oper. activs	**6,582**	**n.a.**	**(2,303)**
Cash from fin. activs	(1,633)		(1,012)
Cash from invest. activs	nil		317
Net cash position	**9,561**	**+131**	**4,145**
Capital expenditures	nil		(8)
	$		$
Earnings per share*	0.46		0.18
Cash flow per share*	0.21		(0.07)
	shs		shs
No. of shs. o/s*	31,290,610		31,240,077
Avg. no. of shs. o/s*	31,276,125		31,407,914
	%		%
Net profit margin	140.94		52.74
Return on equity	47.20		27.09
Return on assets	35.60		16.98

* Common

[o] Restated

[A] Reported in accordance with IFRS

Latest Results

Periods ended:	3m Mar. 31/23[A]		3m Mar. 31/22[A]
	$000s	%Chg	$000s
Total revenue	1,747	-55	3,868
Net income	345	-85	2,350
	$		$
Earnings per share*	0.01		0.08

* Common

[A] Reported in accordance with IFRS

Historical Summary
(as originally stated)

Fiscal Year	Total Rev.	Net Inc. Bef. Disc.	EPS*
	$000s	$000s	$
2022[A]	10,296	14,511	0.46
2021[A]	10,427	5,597	0.18
2020[A]	10,379	2,122	0.06
2019[A]	4,026	(12,223)	(0.29)
2018[A1]	4,594	3,030	0.12

* Common

[A] Reported in accordance with IFRS

[1] Results reflect the June 7, 2018, reverse takeover acquisition of Grenville Strategic Royalty Corp.

Note: Adjusted throughout for 1-for-2 cons. in June 2020

F.51 Flower One Holdings Inc.

Symbol - FONE **Exchange** - CSE (S) **CUSIP** - 34348Q
Head Office - 600-20 Richmond St E, Toronto, ON, M5C 2R9
Telephone - (416) 913-9642 **Fax** - (416) 841-5528
Website - www.flowerone.com
Email - ir@flowerone.com
Investor Relations - Kellen O'Keefe (702) 660-7775
Auditors - MNP LLP C.A., Vancouver, B.C.
Lawyers - Fasken Martineau DuMoulin LLP, Vancouver, B.C.
Transfer Agents - Odyssey Trust Company, Calgary, Alta.

Profile - (B.C. 2007) Cultivates, produces and distributes medical and recreational cannabis in Nevada.

The company owns and operates a 400,000-sq.-ft. greenhouse, with annual production capacity of 100,000 to 110,000 lbs. of dry flower; a 55,000-sq.-ft. production facility, with annual processing capacity of 1,000 lbs. of bulk and branded flower along with 3,000 to 5,000 lbs. of biomass into dozens of products; and a 25,000-sq.-ft. indoor cultivation and production facility, all in North Las Vegas, Nev. Also provides contract cultivation, production and packaging for out-of-state brands looking to enter the Nevada market.

Operations include cannabis cultivation, processing, production and high-volume packaging of medical and recreational cannabis products ranging from wholesale flower, full-spectrum oils and distillates to finished consumer packaged goods including flower, pre-rolls, concentrates, edibles, beverages, topicals and other infused products. Products are sold under Cookies, 22Red, Lift Tickets, Heavy Hitters, Kiva Confections, Old Pal, Natures Lab, Palms Premium, HUXTON, G Pen, The Clear, Miss Grass, ALTWELL, Palms and NLVO brands.

Common suspended from CSE, Dec. 6, 2022.

Predecessor Detail - Name changed from Theia Resources Ltd., Sept. 21, 2018, following reverse takeover acquisition of CNX Holdings Inc. and concurrent amalgamation of CNX with and into wholly owned Flower One Corp.; basis 1 new for 10 old shs.

Directors - Salpy Boyajian, chr. & exec. v-p, Nev.; Kellen O'Keefe, pres. & CEO, Los Angeles, Calif.; Eliza Gairard, Conn.; Thoms Gesky; Nitin Kaushal, Richmond Hill, Ont.

Other Exec. Officers - Tim Shoemake, COO; Araxie Grant, CFO

Capital Stock

	Authorized (shs.)	Outstanding (shs.)[1]
Preferred	unlimited	nil
Common	unlimited	473,098,910

[1] At June 30, 2022

Major Shareholder - Harry Ayvazian held 31.33% interest at Sept. 27, 2021.

Price Range - THH/TSX-VEN (D)

Year	Volume	High	Low	Close
2022	58,181,700	$0.07	$0.01	$0.01
2021	139,356,669	$0.47	$0.04	$0.04
2020	88,522,668	$1.05	$0.11	$0.20
2019	56,386,568	$3.75	$0.65	$1.01
2018	19,689,417	$2.00	$0.65	$1.45

Recent Close: $0.01

Wholly Owned Subsidiaries

FO Labour Management Ltd., Canada.
Flower One Corp., Toronto, Ont.

- 100% int. in **Cana Nevada Corp.**, Las Vegas, Nev.
  - 100% int. in **CN Labor Management, Inc.**, Las Vegas, Nev.
  - 100% int. in **CN Landco II, LLC**, Las Vegas, Nev.
  - 100% int. in **CN Landco III, LLC**, Nev.
  - 100% int. in **CN Landco LLC**, Las Vegas, Nev.
  - 100% int. in **CN Licenseco I, Inc.**, Las Vegas, Nev. dba Cana Nevada.
  - 100% int. in **CN Licenseco III, Inc.**, Nev.
  - 100% int. in **North Las Vegas Equipment Co. III, Inc.**, Nev.
  - 100% int. in **North Las Vegas Equipment Co., Inc.**, Las Vegas, Nev.
  - 100% int. in **North Las Vegas Services, Inc.**, Nev.

Financial Statistics

Periods ended:	12m Dec. 31/21[A]		12m Dec. 31/20[A]
	US$000s	%Chg	US$000s
Operating revenue	**58,357**	**+70**	**34,243**
Cost of sales	27,204[1]		44,768[2]
Salaries & benefits	5,200		3,521
General & admin expense	23,843		21,748
Stock-based compensation	5,321		1,153
Operating expense	**61,568**	**-14**	**71,190**
Operating income	**(3,211)**	**n.a.**	**(36,947)**
Deprec., depl. & amort.	7,127		8,625
Finance costs, gross	22,665		26,261
Write-downs/write-offs	(3,187)		(61,942)
Pre-tax income	**(24,448)**	**n.a.**	**(122,625)**
Income taxes	nil		(5,155)
Net income	**(24,448)**	**n.a.**	**(117,470)**
Cash & equivalent	868		1,056
Inventories	9,665		13,608
Accounts receivable	4,541		3,058
Current assets	17,906		21,204
Fixed assets, net	97,420		108,515
Total assets	**117,813**	**-10**	**130,202**
Bank indebtedness	6,193		12,419
Accts. pay. & accr. liabs	20,146		23,522
Current liabilities	36,138		86,026
Long-term debt, gross	48,910		59,898
Long-term debt, net	48,910		30,898
Long-term lease liabilities	20,718		21,505
Shareholders' equity	857		(11,867)
Cash from oper. activs	**(12,140)**	**n.a.**	**(22,946)**
Cash from fin. activs	12,128		18,395
Cash from invest. activs	(176)		(1,063)
Net cash position	**868**	**-18**	**1,056**
Capital expenditures	(1,074)		(1,063)
Capital disposals	898		nil
	US$		US$
Earnings per share*	(0.06)		(0.51)
Cash flow per share*	(0.03)		(0.10)
	shs		shs
No. of shs. o/s*	460,679,630		275,351,599
Avg. no. of shs. o/s*	384,063,782		231,266,541
	%		%
Net profit margin	(41.89)		(343.05)
Return on equity	n.m.		n.m.
Return on assets	(1.44)		(52.52)
Foreign sales percent	100		100

* Common

[A] Reported in accordance with IFRS

[1] Net of realized fair value adjustment on sale of inventory of $16,062,193 and unrealized gain on fair value adjustment on growth of biological assets of $15,740,123.

[2] Net of realized fair value adjustment on sale of inventory of $37,219,276 and unrealized gain on fair value adjustment on growth of biological assets of $9,791,477.

Historical Summary
(as originally stated)

Fiscal Year	Oper. Rev.	Net Inc. Bef. Disc.	EPS*
	US$000s	US$000s	US$
2021[A]	58,357	(24,448)	(0.06)
2020[A]	34,243	(117,470)	(0.51)
2019[A]	9,477	525	0.00
2018[A1]	131	(12,450)	(0.09)
	$000s	$000s	$
2018[A2]	nil	(171)	(0.10)

* Common

[A] Reported in accordance with IFRS

[1] Results reflect the Sept. 21, 2018, reverse takeover acquisition of CNX Holdings Inc.

[2] Results for fiscal 2018 and prior fiscal years pertain to Theia Resources Ltd.

Note: Adjusted throughout for 1-for-10 cons. in Oct. 2018

F.52 FluroTech Ltd.

Symbol - TEST **Exchange** - TSX-VEN **CUSIP** - 34388D
Head Office - 601-246 Stewart Green SW, Calgary, AB, T3H 3C8
Telephone - (403) 680-0644 **Toll-free** - (833) 949-8378
Website - www.flurotech.com
Email - danny@flurotech.com
Investor Relations - Danny Dalla-Longa (403) 680-0644
Auditors - Davidson & Company LLP C.A., Vancouver, B.C.
Transfer Agents - TSX Trust Company, Calgary, Alta.

Profile - (Alta. 2018 amalg.) Undergoing a reorganization.

Prior to Nov. 29, 2022, the company was developing a novel, proprietary, and highly sensitive real-time, point-of-care antigen test, which uses fluorescence spectroscopy to quantify the SARS-CoV-2 viral load in salivary samples. The Pandemic and Emerging Disease Defense platform (PEDD) was designed to process thousands of tests per hour and provide fast, accurate, secure results.

In November 2022, the company announced its exit from the pandemic and emerging disease industry immediately and halted any further expenditures on development of its Pandemic and Emerging Disease Defense Platform.

Predecessor Detail - Formed from Snow Eagle Resources Ltd. in Alberta, May 24, 2018, pursuant to Qualifying Transaction amalgamation with CannaTest Photonics Ltd. (deemed acquiror); basis 1 new for 4.5 old shs.

Directors - Sidney (Sid) Dutchak, chr., Calgary, Alta.; Danny Dalla-Longa, pres. & CEO, Calgary, Alta.; David (Dave) Majeski, Edmonton, Alta.; Dr. Brendan Miles, Calgary, Alta.

Other Exec. Officers - Curtis Smith, CFO; Dr. Joxel Garcia, CMO; Dr. Elmar J. Prenner, chief scientist; Gary P. Jones, v-p, bus. devel.; Rex H. Kary, corp. sec.

Capital Stock

	Authorized (shs.)	Outstanding (shs.)[1]
Preferred	unlimited	nil
Common	unlimited	120,685,542

[1] At Aug. 23, 2022

Major Shareholder - Alberta Biophotonics Inc. held 23.7% interest at Dec. 14, 2021.

Price Range - TEST/TSX-VEN

Year	Volume	High	Low	Close
2022	16,469,912	$0.11	$0.01	$0.01
2021	69,002,755	$0.85	$0.06	$0.10
2020	23,347,603	$0.42	$0.06	$0.12
2019	10,705,178	$0.63	$0.14	$0.17
2018	16,318,775	$0.81	$0.34	$0.40

Recent Close: $0.01

Wholly Owned Subsidiaries

FluroTest Diagnostic Systems Ltd., Alta.
- 100% int. in **FluroTest LLC**, United States.

Financial Statistics

Periods ended:	12m Dec. 31/21[A]		12m Dec. 31/20[OA]
	$000s	%Chg	$000s
Research & devel. expense	1,043		nil
General & admin expense	1,161		756
Stock-based compensation	983		101
Operating expense	**3,187**	**+272**	**856**
Operating income	**(3,187)**	**n.a.**	**(856)**
Deprec., depl. & amort.	102		43
Finance income	nil		44
Finance costs, gross	4		2
Investment income	(295)		(26)
Write-downs/write-offs	(7,020)[1]		nil
Pre-tax income	**(10,567)**	**n.a.**	**(884)**
Net inc. bef. disc. opers	**(10,567)**	**n.a.**	**(884)**
Income from disc. opers	(70)		(1,790)
Net income	**(10,637)**	**n.a.**	**(2,674)**
Cash & equivalent	551		617
Inventories	34		22
Accounts receivable	28		10
Current assets	643		675
Fixed assets, net	611		85
Total assets	**1,254**	**+66**	**757**
Accts. pay. & accr. liabs	323		268
Current liabilities	323		268
Long-term debt, gross	25		22
Long-term debt, net	25		22
Shareholders' equity	779		468
Cash from oper. activs	**(2,407)**	**n.a.**	**(1,985)**
Cash from fin. activs	4,111		40
Cash from invest. activs	(1,770)		844
Net cash position	**551**	**-11**	**617**
Capital expenditures	(353)		nil
Capital disposals	22		nil
	$		$
Earns. per sh. bef disc opers*	(0.10)		(0.02)
Earnings per share*	(0.10)		(0.05)
Cash flow per share*	(0.02)		(0.04)
	shs		shs
No. of shs. o/s*	120,685,542		54,273,815
Avg. no. of shs. o/s*	102,026,488		54,273,815
	%		%
Net profit margin	n.a.		n.a.
Return on equity	(1,694.79)		(50.37)
Return on assets	n.m.		(40.43)

* Common

[O] Restated

[A] Reported in accordance with IFRS

[1] Represents goodwill impairment related to COVID-19 rapid antigen testing system.

Latest Results

Periods ended:	6m June 30/22[A]		6m June 30/21[A]
	$000s	%Chg	$000s
Net inc. bef. disc. opers	(430)	n.a.	(1,836)
Income from disc. opers	5		(45)
Net income	(425)	n.a.	(1,881)
	$		$
Earnings per share*	(0.00)		(0.02)

* Common

[A] Reported in accordance with IFRS

Historical Summary
(as originally stated)

Fiscal Year	Oper. Rev.	Net Inc. Bef. Disc.	EPS*
	$000s	$000s	$
2021[A]	nil	(10,567)	(0.10)
2020[A]	nil	(884)	(0.02)
2019[A]	251	(4,347)	(0.02)
2018[A1]	nil	(5,128)	(0.11)
2017[A2]	nil	(508)	n.a.

* Common

[A] Reported in accordance with IFRS

[1] Results reflect the May 24, 2018, Qualifying Transaction reverse takeover acquisition of CannaTest Photonics Ltd.

[2] 4 months ended Dec. 31, 2017.

Note: Adjusted throughout for 1-for-4.5 cons. in June 2018

F.53 Fobi AI Inc.

Symbol - FOBI **Exchange** - TSX-VEN **CUSIP** - 34416F
Head Office - Unit 2 F, 541 Howe St, Vancouver, BC, V6C 2C2
Toll-free - (877) 754-5336
Website - www.fobi.ai
Email - rob@fobi.ai
Investor Relations - Robert D. Anson (778) 689-6549
Auditors - Manning Elliott LLP C.A., Vancouver, B.C.
Transfer Agents - Computershare Trust Company of Canada Inc., Vancouver, B.C.

Profile - (B.C. 2019 amalg.) Provides contactless solutions and data intelligence for delivering real-time analytics and reporting, customer engagement, promotions and loyalty, as well as for easy venue access and interactions to retail, telecom, financial services, hospitality, sports and entertainment sectors.

Solutions are organized into three segments: Connect and Analyze; Activate and Engage; and Access and Health.

The **Connect and Analyze** solutions connect disparate data points using artificial intelligence (AI) data processing to deliver real time-time analytics and reporting such as Insights for On-Premise systems, which connects data from disparate on-premise systems into one accessible Insights portal that automatically interprets the data using an AI, for real-time access and action of data; Insights for Cloud-Based systems, where an application programming interface (API) automatically aggregate and send complex data from cloud-based systems to Insights portal, where it's transformed into useful information; and Custom Development and Business Intelligence for custom data integrations visualized in one comprehensive Insights portal such as operational, historical, point-of-sale, market or environmental data.

The **Activate and Engage** solutions build customer loyalty with targeted coupons, promotions and engagement as well as execute omnichannel marketing and provide detailed segment campaigns by location, demographics and time. The segment includes PassPro, an advanced wallet pass product that expands the capabilities of the mobile wallet; Passcreator, a do-it-yourself solution that enables you to build, distribute, validate and manage your own mobile wallet passes while engaging directly with the customers through their smartphones; and Qples, an online coupon and advertising platform to deliver global consumer packaged goods (CPG) generated coupons into any retail platform.

The **Access and Health** solutions provide easy venue access and interactions, including CheckPoint, which automates the entire registration, ticketing and check-in process for venues, conference and the attendees; Smart Vital, a health and safety system that can screen, detect, protect and provide continuous action against potential threat or infectious diseases; Kai Care, a medical testing system for a variety of illness including Covid-19 and influenza A/B; ChechVax™, for businesses' fast and contactless on-site implementation and tracking of health screening sing wallet pass technology; and AltID, a digital ID verification solution for credential verification.

The company also provides Investor Relations Marketing & Advisory, which offers technology and services depending on needs and preferences for strong connections with investors; and Marketing and Coupon services.

Technologies include Fobi, a hardware device and API technology that connects data from disparate sources; Wallet Pass, a software for customer engagement and interaction; Insights Portal, where data is automatically interpreted using AI, for real-time access and action of data; Smart Tap, which validates Near Field Communication reader into one smart device, users can tap to engage using Wallet Passes, member cards, digital promotions, and more; and Smart Scan app, which scans customer's wallet passes using any smartphone or tablet camera to validate, void and record passes.

In May 2022, the company entered into a letter of intent to acquire certain intellectual properties and assets owned by Virginia-based

Grocery Shopping Labs Inc. related to the Basket application, which allows users to create grocery lists and then compare prices for products across all various local stores, online e-commerce shops and delivery companies.

Predecessor Detail - Name changed from Loop Insights Inc., June 4, 2021.

Directors - Robert D. (Rob) Anson, chr., pres. & CEO, Nanaimo, B.C.; Michael (Mike) Devine, B.C.; Peter Green, West Vancouver, B.C.; Jeffrey Hyman, N.Y.

Other Exec. Officers - Gavin G. Lee, COO; Jason Tong, CFO; Jon Haydock, chief technical officer; Colby McKenzie, chief revenue officer; Mike Canevaro, sr. v-p, bus. devel.; Richard Lee, sr. v-p, strategy & corp. devel.; Ian Cameron, v-p, mktg.; Jolie Summers, v-p, product; Kendra Low, corp. sec.

Capital Stock

	Authorized (shs.)	Outstanding (shs.)[1]
Common	unlimited	163,524,104

[1] At May 8, 2023

Major Shareholder - Robert D. (Rob) Anson held 21.39% interest at Oct. 31, 2022.

Price Range - FOBI/TSX-VEN

Year	Volume	High	Low	Close
2022	69,126,480	$1.53	$0.20	$0.28
2021	198,798,981	$3.93	$0.94	$1.39
2020	258,917,027	$2.98	$0.05	$2.05
2019	13,445,377	$0.69	$0.13	$0.17
2018	2,080,280	$0.70	$0.15	$0.20

Consolidation: 1-for-10 cons. in June 2019

Recent Close: $0.21

Capital Stock Changes - In September 2022, private placement of 3,681,595 units (1 common share & ½ warrant) at 35¢ per unit was completed, with warrants exercisable at 65¢ per share for two years.

During fiscal 2022, common shares were issued as follows: 8,616,260 on exercise of warrants, 2,817,500 on exercise of options and 1,524,031 on acquisition of intellectual properties.

Wholly Owned Subsidiaries

AlkaLi3 Resources Inc., Canada.
Fobi AI Germany GmbH, Munich, Germany. dba Passcreator
Fobi AI (USA) Inc., Nev. Inactive.
1334047 B.C. Ltd., Canada.

Financial Statistics

Periods ended:	12m June 30/22[A]		12m June 30/21[A]
	$000s	%Chg	$000s
Operating revenue	**2,036**	**n.m.**	**158**
Cost of sales	nil		36
Salaries & benefits	5,897		2,297
Research & devel. expense	nil		168
General & admin expense	5,458		3,441
Stock-based compensation	7,978		5,243
Operating expense	**19,333**	**+73**	**11,185**
Operating income	**(17,297)**	**n.a.**	**(11,027)**
Deprec., depl. & amort.	1,394		108
Finance income	11		1
Finance costs, gross	135		18
Write-downs/write-offs	(10)		nil
Pre-tax income	**(19,281)**	**n.a.**	**(11,097)**
Income taxes	(129)		nil
Net income	**(19,152)**	**n.a.**	**(11,097)**
Cash & equivalent	1,194		7,502
Inventories	120		nil
Accounts receivable	1,242		845
Current assets	2,913		8,963
Fixed assets, net	114		122
Right-of-use assets	37		38
Intangibles, net	5,477		2,366
Total assets	**8,541**	**-27**	**11,682**
Accts. pay. & accr. liabs	1,802		539
Current liabilities	2,045		684
Long-term lease liabilities	20		22
Shareholders' equity	6,333		10,704
Cash from oper. activs	**(8,892)**	**n.a.**	**(6,394)**
Cash from fin. activs	3,000		13,832
Cash from invest. activs	(571)		(111)
Net cash position	**1,031**	**-86**	**7,502**
Capital expenditures	(59)		(95)
	$		$
Earnings per share*	(0.14)		(0.09)
Cash flow per share*	(0.06)		(0.05)
	shs		shs
No. of shs. o/s*	147,820,054		134,862,263
Avg. no. of shs. o/s*	140,301,265		125,364,113
	%		%
Net profit margin	(940.67)		n.m.
Return on equity	(224.83)		n.m.
Return on assets	(188.08)		(166.04)

* Common
[A] Reported in accordance with IFRS

Latest Results

Periods ended:	3m Sept. 30/22[A]		3m Sept. 30/21[A]
	$000s	%Chg	$000s
Operating revenue	532	-8	580
Net income	(3,009)	n.a.	(4,432)
	$		$
Earnings per share*	(0.02)		(0.03)

* Common
[A] Reported in accordance with IFRS

Historical Summary
(as originally stated)

Fiscal Year	Oper. Rev.	Net Inc. Bef. Disc.	EPS*
	$000s	$000s	$
2022[A]	2,036	(19,152)	(0.14)
2021[A]	158	(11,097)	(0.09)
2020[A]	nil	(5,251)	(0.08)
2019[A1]	nil	(13,663)	(0.30)
2018[A2]	nil	(146)	(0.02)

* Common
[A] Reported in accordance with IFRS
[1] Results reflect the June 12, 2019, reverse takeover acquisition of (old) Loop Insights Inc.
[2] Results for 2018 and prior years pertain to AlkaLi3 Resources Inc.
Note: Adjusted throughout for 1-for-10 cons. in June 2019

F.54 Foraco International S.A.

Symbol - FAR **Exchange -** TSX **CUSIP -** F4269M
Head Office - 26 Plage de l'Estaque, Marseille, France, 13016
Overseas Tel - 33-496-151-360 **Overseas Fax -** 33-496-151-361
Website - www.foraco.com
Email - ir@foraco.com
Investor Relations - Fabien Sevestre (877) 795-6363
Auditors - Deloitte & Associés, Marseille, France
Lawyers - Fasken Martineau DuMoulin LLP, Vancouver, B.C.
Transfer Agents - Computershare Trust Company of Canada Inc., Toronto, Ont.
Employees - 2,860 at Mar. 31, 2023

Profile - (France 1997) Provides diversified contract drilling services primarily to the mining and water sectors, with operations carried out in Africa, the Middle East, Europe, North and South America, and Asia-Pacific.

Drilling services are offered for various mining stages including exploration, development and production. Geological sampling and testing techniques offered includes chips and cores, stabilized holes for blasting, logging, boreholes to be used for injection of water or acid, cold water injection, production boreholes and large diameter core and dual tube rotary bulk samples. Drilling capabilities extend to various mineral resources including precious metals, base metals, bulk commodities like coking coal or iron ore and others like lithium and diamonds. Also specializes in turnkey service contracts associated with mining that may include aspects related to water management or construction activities such as installation of high capacity production pumps. Drilling services are provided using the following types of drilling rigs: rotary, core diamond, combination and underground. At Mar. 31, 2023 the company operated 302 drilling rigs in 22 countries and five continents. Drilling rigs include 62 rotary, 190 core diamond, 18 combination and 32 underground.

Also drills wells for drinking water, irrigation water, industrial water, and dewatering wells, and has experience in a wide range of techniques used in water well drilling, as well as expertise in the inspection, servicing and rehabilitation of existing wells. The company can offer an integrated package of services to its customers, including turnkey contracts for water production and initial distribution systems in rural or semi-urban areas of developing countries.

Headquarters are located in Marseille, France, with the main technical and engineering base in Lunel, France. Regional offices are located in Perth, W.A., which is the primary location for Australian and Asia-Pacific activities; Lunel, France, which is the primary location for Europe and Africa and which has a sub-regional office in Abidjan, Ivory Coast; Almaty, Kazakhstan; Moscow, Russia, which supervise the Russian operations; North Bay, Ont., which manage the North American operations; and Santiago, Chile and Mendoza, Argentina, which manage the South American operations. In Brazil, operations are managed from Crixas, Goias state. The company has also established a network of local offices, each led by a country manager.

In April 2023, the company agreed to sell its 50% interest in private Russia-based **Eastern Drilling Company LLC** (EDC Russia) to its Russian partners for an undisclosed amount. In connection, the company acquired 50% interest in **EDC Kazakhstan LLC**, which was previously owned by EDC Russia. The company had been providing technical and out-of-country support services to EDC Russia until early 2022. During 2022, EDC Russia contributed US$22,700,000 and US$2,000,000 to the company's consolidated revenue and net income, respectively.

Directors - W. Warren Holmes†, Stratford, Ont.; Bruno Chabas, Amsterdam, Netherlands; Jean-Pierre M. Charmensat, Marseille, France; Jean Diercxens, Antwerp, Belgium; Jorge Hurtado, Santiago, Chile; Daniel Simoncini, Singapore, Singapore

Other Exec. Officers - Timothy (Tim) Bremner, CEO; Fabien Sevestre, CFO; Olivier Demesy, sr. v-p, Latin America, Europe & Africa; Thierry Merle, v-p, Europe & Middle East; Denis Simonin, v-p, Africa; Laurence Mahieux, gen. counsel
† Lead director

Capital Stock

	Authorized (shs.)	Outstanding (shs.)[1]
Common	unlimited	98,949,733[2]

[1] At Mar. 31, 2023
[2] Net of 302,065 common shares held by the company.

Normal Course Issuer Bid - The company plans to make normal course purchases of up to 1,000,000 common shares representing 1% of the total outstanding. The bid commenced on Oct. 4, 2022, and expires on Oct. 3, 2023.

Major Shareholder - Jean-Pierre M. Charmensat held 20.74% interest and Daniel Simoncini held 13.67% interest at Mar. 6, 2023.

Price Range - FAR/TSX

Year	Volume	High	Low	Close
2022	3,098,571	$2.33	$0.92	$1.50
2021	6,735,555	$2.45	$0.47	$1.84
2020	2,601,393	$0.62	$0.22	$0.52
2019	2,003,136	$0.57	$0.25	$0.35
2018	1,308,955	$0.54	$0.34	$0.47

Recent Close: $1.80

Capital Stock Changes - During 2022, 598,113 common shares were repurchased under a Normal Course Issuer Bid and 711,000 treasury shares were transferred pursuant to the equity investment plan.

Wholly Owned Subsidiaries

Foraco Australia Pty Ltd, Australia.
- 100% int. in **John Nitschke Drilling Pty Ltd.**, Adelaide, S.A., Australia.

Foraco Brazil S.A., Brazil.
Foraco Burkina Faso S.A., Burkina Faso.
Foraco CI S.A., Côte d'Ivoire.
Foraco Canada Ltd., Canada.
Foraco Chile S.A., Chile.
- 100% int. in **Foraco Argentina S.A.**, Argentina.

Foraco Congo S.A.R.L., Democratic Republic of Congo.
Foraco Corp Ltd., United States.
Foraco Drilling Kazakhstan LLC, Kazakhstan.
Foraco Germany, Germany.
Foraco Ghana Ltd., Ghana.
Foraco Guinée S.A.R.L., Guinea.
Foraco Holding Participações Ltda., Brazil.
Foraco Management S.A.S.U., France.
Foraco Mexico S.A., Mexico.
Foraco Niger S.A., Niger.
Foraco Peru S.A.C., Peru.
Foraco S.A.S.U., France.
Foraco Sahel S.A.R.L., Mali.
Foraco Salta, Argentina.
Foraco San Juan, Argentina.
Foraco Sénégal S.A., Senegal.
Foraco Singapore, Singapore.
Foraco Subsahara S.A., Chad.
Foraco U.K., United Kingdom.
Géode International S.A.S.U., France.
I³ Directional Drilling Solutions Ltd., Canada.

Subsidiaries

51% int. in **Foremi S.A.**, Côte d'Ivoire.

Investments

50% int. in **EDC Kazakhstan**, Kazakhstan.
50% int. in **Eastern Drilling Company LLC**, Moscow, Russia.
49% int. in **Innu Innuit Foraco GP Inc.**, Canada.

Note: The preceding list includes only the major related companies in which interests are held.

Financial Statistics

Periods ended:	12m Dec. 31/22[A1]		12m Dec. 31/21[A1]
	US$000s	%Chg	US$000s
Operating revenue	**330,555**	**+23**	**269,689**
Cost of sales	240,890		205,316
General & admin expense	23,108		21,323
Operating expense	**263,998**	**+16**	**226,639**
Operating income	**66,557**	**+55**	**43,050**
Deprec., depl. & amort.	19,830		18,681
Finance costs, net	11,800		(24,865)
Write-downs/write-offs	(343)		(242)
Pre-tax income	**34,585**	**-29**	**48,992**
Income taxes	8,805		9,982
Net income	**25,780**	**-34**	**39,010**
Net inc. for equity hldrs	**19,761**	**-44**	**35,487**
Net inc. for non-cont. int.	**6,019**	**+71**	**3,523**
Cash & equivalent	29,409		23,924
Inventories	44,030		37,057
Accounts receivable	42,439		32,237
Current assets	126,110		104,397
Long-term investments	111		103
Fixed assets, net	39,536		39,681
Intangibles, net	64,055		63,504
Total assets	**249,545**	**+9**	**228,792**
Bank indebtedness	2,323		1,913
Accts. pay. & accr. liabs	28,717		26,401
Current liabilities	83,149		64,426
Long-term debt, gross	97,937		101,685
Long-term debt, net	84,771		94,101
Long-term lease liabilities	3,276		4,684
Shareholders' equity	65,187		55,979
Non-controlling interest	10,305		6,549
Cash from oper. activs	**37,429**	**+29**	**29,018**
Cash from fin. activs	(10,678)		(7,798)
Cash from invest. activs	(20,042)		(18,586)
Net cash position	**29,409**	**+23**	**23,924**
	US$		US$
Earnings per share*	0.20		0.38
Cash flow per share*	0.38		0.41
	shs		shs
No. of shs. o/s*	98,986,225		98,873,338
Avg. no. of shs. o/s*	98,721,125		94,252,613
	%		%
Net profit margin	7.80		14.46
Return on equity	32.62		103.00
Return on assets	10.78		17.09
No. of employees (FTEs)	2,789		2,891

* Common

[A] Reported in accordance with IFRS

[1] Amended.

Latest Results

Periods ended:	3m Mar. 31/23[A]		3m Mar. 31/22[A]
	US$000s	%Chg	US$000s
Operating revenue	88,378	+30	67,740
Net income	8,001	+928	778
Net inc. for equity hldrs	6,635	n.m.	428
Net inc. for non-cont. int	1,366		350
	US$		US$
Earnings per share*	0.07		0.00

* Common

[A] Reported in accordance with IFRS

Historical Summary
(as originally stated)

Fiscal Year	Oper. Rev.	Net Inc. Bef. Disc.	EPS*
	US$000s	US$000s	US$
2022[A]	330,555	25,780	0.20
2021[A]	269,689	39,010	0.38
2020[A]	207,122	7,519	0.05
2019[A]	205,444	2,632	0.01
2018[A]	180,046	(10,630)	(0.12)

* Common

[A] Reported in accordance with IFRS

F.55 Forbidden Spirits Distilling Corp.

Symbol - VDKA **Exchange** - TSX-VEN (S) **CUSIP** - 34519R

Head Office - 4400 Wallace Hill Rd, Kelowna, BC, V1W 4C3 **Telephone** - (250) 764-6011

Website - forbiddenspirits.ca

Email - blair@forbiddenspirits.ca

Investor Relations - C. Blair Wilson (250) 317-0996

Auditors - Smythe LLP C.A.

Transfer Agents - TSX Trust Company, Calgary, Alta.

Profile - (B.C. 2021 amalg.) Manufactures and distributes alcoholic spirits which include brands such as REBEL Vodka, Forbidden Spirits Vodka, Forbidden Fire Liquor, Adam's Apple Brandy, Eve's Original Gin and Wallace Hill Whisky.

The company is a craft distillery which ferments, distils, bottles and distributes spirits with frozen apple juice concentrate as the main raw material. Operations include a distillery, tasting room and warehouse in Kelowna, B.C. Products are sold directly to retail customers from its on-site tasting room, to on-premise customers such as restaurants, pubs, hotels and golf courses from its manufacturing plant, and to off-premise customers such as private beer, wine and spirits stores. The company also sells its products in Canada through its online store, as well as throughout British Columbia through its third party contracted wholesale sales agents.

In January 2023, the company agreed to acquire Alberta-based distiller **1593688 Alberta Ltd.** for $3,200,000, consisting of $1,600,000 cash and issuance of 6,400,000 common shares at 26¢ per share.

In July 2022, the company postponed indefinitely the acquisition of Niagara Falls, Ont.-based **Niagara Falls Craft Distillers Ltd.** (NFCD). On Mar. 16, 2022, the company entered into a letter of intent to acquire NFCD, which manufactures spirits, beers, and ready-to-drink products for themselves and by contract for others, for $4,810,000, consisting of $4,000,000 cash and issuance of 1,124,898 common shares valued at 72¢ per share.

Common suspended from TSX-VEN, May 9, 2023.

Predecessor Detail - Formed from Spartan Acquisition Corp. in British Columbia, Dec. 16, 2021, pursuant to the Qualifying Transaction reverse takeover acquisition of and amalgamation with Forbidden Distillery Inc. (deemed acquiror).

Directors - C. Blair Wilson, pres. & CEO, Kelowna, B.C.; Eugene A. Hodgson, Vancouver, B.C.; Maya Kanigan, Kelowna, B.C.

Other Exec. Officers - Terese J. Gieselman, CFO; Kelly J. Wilson, corp. sec.

Capital Stock

	Authorized (shs.)	Outstanding (shs.)[1]
Preferred	unlimited	nil
Common	unlimited	61,004,024

[1] At Nov. 25, 2022

Major Shareholder - C. Blair Wilson held 22.44% interest and Kelly J. Wilson held 22.44% interest at Dec. 20, 2021.

Price Range - VDKA/TSX-VEN (S)

Year	Volume	High	Low	Close
2022	6,465,016	$0.21	$0.01	$0.01
2021	232,700	$0.30	$0.20	$0.20
2020	249,300	$0.30	$0.25	$0.25

Recent Close: $0.02

Financial Statistics

Periods ended:	12m Dec. 31/21[A1]		12m Dec. 31/20[A2]
	$000s	%Chg	$000s
Operating revenue	**593**	**+19**	**499**
Cost of sales	292		294
Salaries & benefits	512		322
Research & devel. expense	6		nil
General & admin expense	1,273		658
Stock-based compensation	288		22
Operating expense	**2,371**	**+83**	**1,296**
Operating income	**(1,778)**	**n.a.**	**(797)**
Deprec., depl. & amort.	203		253
Finance income	2		nil
Finance costs, gross	218		148
Pre-tax income	**(3,890)**	**n.a.**	**(1,131)**
Net income	**(3,890)**	**n.a.**	**(1,131)**
Cash & equivalent	1,731		5
Inventories	535		441
Accounts receivable	98		36
Current assets	2,436		639
Fixed assets, net	2,270		2,055
Right-of-use assets	522		997
Intangibles, net	81		87
Total assets	**5,309**	**+41**	**3,778**
Bank indebtedness	150		652
Accts. pay. & accr. liabs	1,012		882
Current liabilities	1,323		1,656
Long-term debt, gross	807		153
Long-term debt, net	683		139
Long-term lease liabilities	595		1,035
Shareholders' equity	2,708		948
Cash from oper. activs	**(1,162)**	**n.a.**	**(841)**
Cash from fin. activs	2,531		896
Cash from invest. activs	231		(76)
Net cash position	**1,731**	**n.m.**	**131**
Capital expenditures	(38)		(119)
Capital disposals	nil		45
	$		$
Earnings per share*	(0.09)		(0.22)
Cash flow per share*	(0.03)		(0.17)
	shs		shs
No. of shs. o/s*	59,004,024		n.a.
Avg. no. of shs. o/s*	41,064,823		5,072,516
	%		%
Net profit margin	(655.99)		(226.65)
Return on equity	(212.80)		(87.00)
Return on assets	(80.82)		(26.93)

* Common

[A] Reported in accordance with IFRS

[1] Results reflect the Dec. 16, 2021, Qualifying Transaction reverse takeover acquisition of Forbidden Distillery Inc.

[2] Results for 2020 and prior period pertain to Forbidden Distillery Inc.

Latest Results

Periods ended:	9m Sept. 30/22[A]		9m Sept. 30/21[A]
	$000s	%Chg	$000s
Operating revenue	541	+13	479
Net income	(1,431)	n.a.	(1,349)
	$		$
Earnings per share*	(0.02)		(0.26)

* Common

[A] Reported in accordance with IFRS

Historical Summary
(as originally stated)

Fiscal Year	Oper. Rev.	Net Inc. Bef. Disc.	EPS*
	$000s	$000s	$
2021[A]	593	(3,890)	(0.09)
2020[A]	499	(1,131)	(0.22)
2019[A]	207	(1,025)	(0.23)

* Common

[A] Reported in accordance with IFRS

F.56 Fortis Inc.*

Symbol - FTS **Exchange** - TSX **CUSIP** - 349553

Head Office - Fortis Place, 1100-5 Springdale St, PO Box 8837, St. John's, NL, A1B 3T2 **Telephone** - (709) 737-2800 **Fax** - (709) 737-5307

Website - www.fortisinc.com

Email - samaimo@fortisinc.com

Investor Relations - Stephanie A. Amaimo (709) 737-2900

Auditors - Deloitte LLP C.A., St. John's, N.L.

Lawyers - McInnes Cooper, St. John's, N.L.; Davies Ward Phillips & Vineberg LLP, Toronto, Ont.

Transfer Agents - Computershare Trust Company, N.A., Louisville, Ky.; Computershare Trust Company of Canada Inc., Toronto, Ont.

FP500 Revenue Ranking - 54

Employees - 9,200 at Mar. 31, 2023

Profile - (N.L. 1987; orig. Can., 1977) Provides electricity and gas through regulated electric and natural gas utility holdings in five Canadian provinces, 10 U.S. states and three Caribbean countries, as well as non-regulated energy assets located in Belize and British Columbia.

Regulated Electric & Gas Utilities

Subsidiary **ITC Holdings Corp.** owns and operates 25,800 circuit km of high-voltage lines in Michigan's Lower Peninsula and portions of Iowa, Minnesota, Illinois, Missouri, Kansas and Oklahoma that transmit electricity from generating stations to local distribution facilities connected to its transmission systems.

Wholly owned **UNS Energy Corporation**, a utility services holding company, operates through regulated utility **Tucson Electric Power Company**, which distributes electricity to 443,000 retail customers in southeastern Arizona, as well as sells wholesale electricity in western U.S.; **UNS Electric, Inc.**, which provides electricity to 102,000 customers in Mohave and Santa Cruz ctys., Ariz.; and **UNS Gas, Inc.**, which provides natural gas to 167,000 retail customers in Mohave, Yavapai, Coconino, Navajo and Santa Cruz ctys., Ariz.

Wholly owned **CH Energy Group, Inc.** owns **Central Hudson Gas & Electric Corporation**, a regulated utility serving 300,000 electric and 80,000 natural gas customers in portions of Mid-Hudson River Valley area of New York, and operates 15,100 circuit km of electric transmission and distribution lines and 2,400 km of gas transmission and distribution lines.

Wholly owned **FortisBC Holdings Inc.** (formerly **Terasen Inc.**) owns and operates 51,200 km of natural gas distribution and transmission pipelines and is the largest natural gas distributor in British Columbia. FortisBC operates through wholly owned **FortisBC Energy Inc.**, which serves 1,076,000 customers in over 135 communities, including residential, commercial and industrial and transportation customers in Lower Mainland, Vancouver Island and Whistler regions of British Columbia.

Wholly owned **FortisAlberta Inc.**, a regulated electric distribution utility in Alberta, owns and operates electric distribution system that delivers electricity generated by other market participants from high-voltage transmission substations to end-use customers in a substantial portion of southern and central Alberta. The system includes 90,200 circuit km of distribution lines, serving 584,000 customers, including residential, commercial, farm, oil and gas, and industrial consumers.

Wholly owned **FortisBC Inc.** is an integrated electric utility that owns hydroelectric generating plants, high voltage transmission lines and a network of distribution assets in the southern interior of British Columbia, including 7,300 circuit km of transmission and distribution lines, serving 188,000 customers. This segment also includes operation, maintenance and management services related to the 493-MW Waneta hydroelectric generation facility (owned by BC Hydro); the operation of the 335-MW Waneta Expansion (owned by **Columbia Power Corporation** and **Columbia Basin Trust**); and the 149-MW Brilliant hydroelectric plant, the 185-MW Arrow Lakes generating station, and the 120-MW Brilliant Expansion plant (all owned by CPC and CBT). FortisBC also owns four regulated hydroelectric generation facilities on the Kootenay River, with an aggregate capacity of 225 MW.

Subsidiary **Newfoundland Power Inc.** is the principal distributor of electricity on the island portion of Newfoundland and Labrador, serving 274,000 customers. Newfoundland Power owns and operates 11,500 circuit km of transmission and distribution lines, and operates generating facilities with a combined capacity of 143 MW.

Wholly owned **Maritime Electric Company, Limited** operates an integrated electric utility on Prince Edward Island, serving 88,000 customers, and owns and operates generating facilities with a combined capacity of 90 MW. Maritime Electric owns and operates about 6,600 circuit km of transmission and distribution lines.

Wholly owned **FortisOntario Inc.**, together with its wholly owned subsidiaries **Canadian Niagara Power Inc.**, **Cornwall Street Railway, Light and Power Company, Limited** and **Algoma Power Inc.**, owns and operates 3,500 circuit km of transmission and distribution lines, providing service to 68,000 customers in Fort Erie, Cornwall, Gananoque, Port Colborne and the district of Algoma, all in Ontario. FortisOntario also owns 10% interest in each of **Westario Power Inc.**, **Rideau St. Lawrence Holdings Inc.** and **Grimsby Power Inc.**, three regional electric distribution companies serving 40,000 customers.

Subsidiary **Caribbean Utilities Company, Ltd.** (60% owned), the sole provider of electricity on Grand Cayman, Cayman Islands, owns and operates 810 circuit km of transmission and distribution lines and 24 km of submarine cable, serving 33,000 customers. In addition, wholly owned **FortisTCI Limited** and its subsidiary **Turks and Caicos Utilities Limited** own and operate 700 km of transmission and distribution lines on the Turks and Caicos Islands, serving over 17,000 customers; and 33%-owned **Belize Electricity Limited** (BEL), an integrated electric utility, which distributes electricity in Belize.

Also holds 39% interest in **Wataynikaneyap Power Limited Partnership** which is developing 1,800 km of transmission lines in northwestern Ontario to connect 17 remote First Nations communities to the Ontario power grid. Wataynikaneyap Power is majority-owned by a partnership of 24 First Nation communities. The project is expected to be completed in 2024.

Non-Regulated Energy Infrastructure

Through 33%-owned **Belize Electric Company Limited** owns the 25-MW Mollejon, the 7-MW Chalillo and the 19-MW Vaca hydroelectric generating facilities in Belize. All of the electricity output of these facilities is sold to BEL under 50-year power purchase agreements expiring in 2055 and 2060.

In British Columbia, holds a 93.8% interest in Aitken Creek underground natural gas storage facility with a working gas capacity of 77 bcf.

Regulated - Gas Volumes

Year ended Dec. 31	2022	2021
	PJ	PJ
FortisBC Holdings	231	228
UNS Energy	16	16
Central Hudson	25	23

Regulated - Electricity Sales

Year ended Dec. 31	2022	2021
	GWh	GWh
FortisAlberta[1]	16,923	16,643
FortisBC	3,542	3,460
Other electric[2]	9,470	9,266
UNS Energy	16,059	16,842
Central Hudson	5,002	5,000

[1] Energy deliveries.

[2] Include Newfoundland Power, Maritime Electric, FortisOntario, Caribbean Utilities, and Fortis Turks and Caicos.

Non-Regulated - Energy Sales

Year ended Dec. 31	2022	2021
	GWh	GWh
Energy Infrastructure[1]	225	147

[1] Include the operations of non-regulated generation assets in Belize and British Columbia.

Recent Merger and Acquisition Activity

Status: pending **Announced:** May 1, 2023

Enbridge Inc. agreed to acquire FortisBC Midstream Inc., which holds 93.8% interest in the Aitken Creek and 100% interest in the Aitken Creek North underground natural gas storage facilities in British Columbia, from Fortis Inc. for $400,000,000. The underground reservoir was located 120 km northeast of Fort St. John, B.C., in the Montney production region, and had 77 bcf of working gas capacity. The storage facilities connect to all three major long-haul natural gas transportation lines in western Canada, including Enbridge's Westcoast and Alliance pipelines. The transaction was expected to be completed in late 2023, subject to receipt of customary regulatory approvals and closing conditions.

Directors - Jo Mark Zurel, chr., St. John's, N.L.; David G. Hutchens, pres. & CEO, Tucson, Ariz.; Tracey C. Ball, Victoria, B.C.; Pierre J. Blouin, Montréal, Qué.; Lawrence T. Borgard, Naples, Fla.; Maura J. Clark, New York, N.Y.; Lisa Crutchfield, Pa.; Margarita K. Dilley, Washington, D.C.; Julie A. Dobson, Potomac, Md.; Lisa L. Durocher, Toronto, Ont.; Gianna M. Manes, S.C.; Donald R. (Don) Marchand, Calgary, Alta.

Other Exec. Officers - Jocelyn H. Perry, exec. v-p & CFO; James R. (Jim) Reid, exec. v-p, sustainability & chief legal officer; Gary J. Smith, exec. v-p, opers. & innovation; Stuart I. Lochray, sr. v-p, capital markets & bus. devel.; Stephanie A. Amaimo, v-p, IR; Julie M. Avery, v-p & contr.; Karen J. Gosse, v-p, fin.; Ronald J. Hinsley, v-p & CIO; Karen M. McCarthy, v-p, commun. & corp. affairs; Regan P. O'Dea, v-p & gen. counsel; Kevin Woodbury, v-p, innovation & tech.; Linda H. Blair Apsey, pres. & CEO, ITC Holdings Corp.

Capital Stock

	Authorized (shs.)	Outstanding (shs.)[1]
First Preference	unlimited	
Series F		5,000,000
Series G		9,200,000
Series H		7,665,082
Series I		2,334,918
Series J		8,000,000
Series K		10,000,000
Series M		24,000,000
Second Preference	unlimited	nil
Common	unlimited	486,500,000

[1] At Aug. 1, 2023

First Preference - Issuable in series and non-voting.

Series F - Entitled to cumulative preferential annual dividends of $1.225 per share. Redeemable at $25 per share plus accrued and unpaid dividends.

Series G - Entitled to cumulative preferential annual dividends of $1.0983 per share payable quarterly to Aug. 31, 2023, and thereafter at a rate reset every five years equal to the five-year Government of Canada bond yield plus 2.13%. Redeemable on Sept. 1, 2023, and on September 1 every five years thereafter at $25 per share.

Series H - Entitled to cumulative preferential annual dividends of $0.4588 per share payable quarterly to May 31, 2025, and thereafter at a rate reset every five years equal to the five-year Government of Canada bond yield plus 1.45%. Redeemable on June 1, 2025, and on June 1 every five years thereafter at $25 per share. Convertible at the holder's option, on June 1, 2025, and on June 1 every five years thereafter, into floating rate first preference series I shares on a share-for-share basis, subject to certain conditions.

Series I - Entitled to cumulative preferential dividends payable quarterly equal to the 90-day Canadian Treasury bill rate plus 1.45%. Redeemable on June 1, 2025, and on June 1 every five years thereafter at $25 per share. Convertible at the holder's option on June 1, 2025, and on June 1 every five years thereafter, into first preference series H shares on a share-for-share basis, subject to certain conditions.

Series J - Entitled to cumulative preferential annual dividends of $1.1875 per share payable quarterly. Redeemable at $25 per share plus accrued and unpaid dividends.

Series K - Entitled to cumulative preferential annual dividends of $0.9823 per share payable quarterly to Mar. 1, 2024, and thereafter at a rate reset rate every five years equal to the five-year Government of Canada bond yield plus 2.05%. Convertible at the holder's option on Mar. 1, 2024, and on March 1 every five years thereafter, into floating rate first preference series L shares on a share-for-share basis, subject to certain conditions. The series L shares would pay a quarterly dividend equal to the 90-day Canadian Treasury bill rate plus 2.05%.

Series M - Entitled to cumulative preferential annual dividends of $0.9783 per share payable quarterly to Dec. 1, 2024, and thereafter at a rate reset every five years equal to the five-year Government of Canada bond yield plus 2.48%. Convertible at the holder's option, on Dec. 1, 2024, and on December 1 every five years thereafter, into floating rate first preference series N shares on a share-for-share basis, subject to certain conditions. The series N shares would pay a quarterly dividend equal to the 90-day Canadian Treasury bill rate plus 2.48%

Second Preference - Issuable in series and non-voting.

Common - One vote per share.

Options - At Dec. 31, 2022, options were outstanding to purchase 2,300,000 common shares at a weighted average exercise price of $47.72 per share with a weighted average expected life of 4 years.

Major Shareholder - Widely held at Mar. 17, 2023.

Price Range - FTS/TSX

Year	Volume	High	Low	Close
2022	422,290,773	$65.26	$48.45	$54.18
2021	386,670,920	$61.54	$48.97	$61.03
2020	441,457,030	$59.28	$41.52	$52.00
2019	297,490,090	$56.94	$44.00	$53.88
2018	269,283,881	$47.36	$39.38	$45.51

Recent Close: $53.43

Capital Stock Changes - During 2022, common shares were issued as follows: 6,400,000 under the dividend reinvestment plan and share purchase plan and 1,000,000 on exercise of options.

Dividends

FTS com Ra $2.26 pa Q est. Dec. 1, 2022**
Prev. Rate: $2.14 est. Dec. 1, 2021
Prev. Rate: $2.02 est. Dec. 1, 2020
FTS.PR.F pfd 1st ser F cum. red. Ra $1.225 pa Q
FTS.PR.G pfd 1st ser G cum. red. Adj. Ra $1.09825 pa Q est. Dec. 1, 2018
FTS.PR.H pfd 1st ser H cum. red. exch. Adj. Ra $0.45875 pa Q est. Sept. 1, 2020
FTS.PR.J pfd 1st ser J cum. red. Ra $1.1875 pa Q
FTS.PR.K pfd 1st ser K cum. red. exch. Adj. Ra $0.98125 pa Q est. June 1, 2019
FTS.PR.M pfd 1st ser M cum. red. exch. Adj. Ra $0.97825 pa Q est. Mar. 1, 2020
FTS.PR.I pfd 1st ser I cum. red. exch. Fltg. Ra pa Q

$0.371781	Sept. 1/23	$0.371529	June 1/23
$0.346562	Mar. 1/23	$0.267141	Dec. 1/22

Paid in 2023: $1.089872 2022: $0.66755 2021: $0.388914

** Reinvestment Option

Long-Term Debt - Outstanding at Dec. 31, 2022:

Corporate Debt:	
Credit facility borrowings	$1,657,000,000
Debs. due 2039[1]	$200,000,000
Sr. notes & prom. notes[2]	3,691,000,000
Subsidiary Debt:	
FortisBC Energy 4.61% debs. to 2052	3,295,000,000
FortisAlta. 4.49% debs. due to 2052	2,485,000,000
FortisBC debs.[3]	885,000,000
Nfld. Power 5.26% bonds due to 2060	666,000,000
Maritime Elec. 5.31% bonds due to 2061	260,000,000
FortisOnt. 4.45% sr. notes due to 2048	152,000,000
Carib. Utils. debt due to 2052[4]	745,000,000
Central Hudson prom. notes due to 2060[5]	1,526,000,000
UNS Energy bonds & notes[6]	3,573,000,000
ITC bonds & notes[7]	9,341,000,000
Finance lease obligs	338,000,000
Fair value adjustments	102,000,000
Less: Deferred fin. costs & debt disc	166,000,000
	28,750,000,000
Less: Current portion	2,483,000,000
	26,267,000,000

[1] Bear interest at weighted average fixed rate of 6.51%.

[2] Consist of $2.691 billion 3.82% unsecured senior notes and promissory notes due to 2044 and $1 billion 3.31% unsecured senior notes due 2029.

[3] Consist of $25,000,000 8.8% secured debentures due 2023 and $860,000,000 4.70% unsecured debentures due to 2052.

[4] Consists of senior notes and bonds. Bear interest at weighted average fixed and variable rate of 4.71%.

[5] Bear interest at weighted average fixed and variable rate of 4.14%.

[6] Consist of $123,000,000 4% unsecured tax-exempt bonds due to 2029 and $2.450 billion 3.58% unsecured notes due to 2052.

[7] Consist of $270,000,000 6% unsecured shareholder note due 2028, $4.541 billion 3.98% unsecured senior notes due to 2043, $1.186 billion 3.83% secured senior notes due to 2055 and $3.344 billion 4.22% secured mortgage bonds due to 2055.

Minimum long-term debt repayments were reported as follows:

2023	$2,481,000,000
2024	1,434,000,000
2025	518,000,000
2026	2,434,000,000
2027	1,977,000,000
Thereafter	19,734,000,000

Minimum finance lease obligations repayments were reported as follows:

2023	$45,000,000
2024	44,000,000
2025	41,000,000
2026	40,000,000
2027	39,000,000
Thereafter	1,020,000,000

Wholly Owned Subsidiaries

FortisBC Holdings Inc., Vancouver, B.C. Formerly Terasen Inc.
- 100% int. in **FortisBC Energy Inc.**, Vancouver, B.C. Formerly Terasen Gas Inc.
- 100% int. in **FortisBC Midstream Inc.**, B.C.

FortisOntario Inc., Fort Erie, Ont.
- 100% int. in **Algoma Power Inc.**, Sault Ste. Marie, Ont.
- 100% int. in **Canadian Niagara Power Inc.**, Fort Erie, Ont.
- 100% int. in **Cornwall Street Railway, Light and Power Company, Limited**, Cornwall, Ont.

FortisTCI Limited, Providenciales, Turks and Caicos Islands.
- 100% int. in **Turks and Caicos Utilities Limited**, Turks and Caicos Islands.

FortisUS Holdings Nova Scotia Limited, Canada.
- 100% int. in **FortisUS Inc.**, Del.
  - 100% int. in **CH Energy Group, Inc.**, Poughkeepsie, N.Y.
    - 100% int. in **Central Hudson Gas & Electric Corporation**
  - 80.1% int. in **ITC Investment Holdings Inc.**, Mich.
    - 100% int. in **ITC Holdings Corp.**, Novi, Mich.
      - 100% int. in **ITC Great Plains, LLC**, United States.
      - 100% int. in **ITC Interconnection LLC**
      - 100% int. in **ITC Midwest LLC**, United States.
      - 100% int. in **International Transmission Company**, United States.
      - 100% int. in **METC GP Holdings, Inc.**
        - 100% int. in **Michigan Transco Holdings, LLC**
          - 100% int. in **Michigan Electric Transmission Company, LLC**, Mich.
  - 100% int. in **UNS Energy Corporation**, Ariz.
    - 100% int. in **Tucson Electric Power Company**, Tucson, Ariz.
    - 100% int. in **UNS Electric, Inc.**, Ariz.
    - 100% int. in **UNS Gas, Inc.**, Ariz.

FortisWest Inc., Canada.
- 100% int. in **Fortis Pacific Holdings Inc.**, B.C.
  - 100% int. in **FortisBC Inc.**, Kelowna, B.C.
- 100% int. in **FortisAlberta Holdings Inc.**, Alta.
  - 100% int. in **FortisAlberta Inc.**, Calgary, Alta.
- 100% int. in **Maritime Electric Company, Limited**, Charlottetown, P.E.I.

Newfoundland Power Inc., St. John's, N.L.

Subsidiaries

59% int. in **Caribbean Utilities Company, Ltd.**, Grand Cayman, Cayman Islands. (see separate coverage)

Investments

33% int. in **Belize Electric Company Limited**, Belize.
39% int. in **Wataynikaneyap Power Limited Partnership**, Canada.

Note: The preceding list includes only the major related companies in which interests are held.

Financial Statistics

Periods ended:	12m Dec. 31/22[A]		12m Dec. 31/21[A]
	$000s	%Chg	$000s
Operating revenue	**11,043,000**	**+17**	**9,448,000**
Other operating expense	6,635,000		5,474,000
Operating expense	**6,635,000**	**+21**	**5,474,000**
Operating income	**4,408,000**	**+11**	**3,974,000**
Deprec., depl. & amort.	1,668,000		1,505,000
Finance income	11,000		5,000
Finance costs, gross	1,102,000		1,003,000
Investment income	n.a.		7,000
Int. charged to construction	78,000		77,000
Pre-tax income	**1,803,000**	**+10**	**1,639,000**
Income taxes	289,000		234,000
Net income	**1,514,000**	**+8**	**1,405,000**
Net inc. for equity hldrs	**1,394,000**	**+8**	**1,294,000**
Net inc. for non-cont. int.	**120,000**	**+8**	**111,000**
Cash & equivalent	209,000		131,000
Inventories	661,000		478,000
Accounts receivable	1,759,000		1,269,000
Current assets	4,269,000		2,728,000
Long-term investments	316,000		178,000
Fixed assets, net	41,663,000		37,816,000
Intangibles, net	14,012,000		13,063,000
Total assets	**64,252,000**	**+11**	**57,659,000**
Bank indebtedness	253,000		247,000
Accts. pay. & accr. liabs	2,204,000		1,782,000
Current liabilities	6,617,000		4,802,000
Long-term debt, gross	28,750,000		25,672,000
Long-term debt, net	26,267,000		24,040,000
Long-term lease liabilities	34,000		32,000
Preferred share equity	1,623,000		1,623,000
Shareholders' equity	21,030,000		19,288,000
Non-controlling interest	1,812,000		1,628,000
Cash from oper. activs	**3,074,000**	**+6**	**2,907,000**
Cash from fin. activs	1,035,000		451,000
Cash from invest. activs	(4,059,000)		(3,488,000)
Net cash position	**209,000**	**+60**	**131,000**
Capital expenditures	(3,587,000)		(3,189,000)
Unfunded pension liability	n.a.		200,000
Pension fund surplus	16,000		n.a.
	$		$
Earnings per share*	2.78		2.61
Cash flow per share*	6.42		6.17
Cash divd. per share*	2.17		2.05
	shs		shs
No. of shs. o/s*	482,200,000		474,800,000
Avg. no. of shs. o/s*	478,600,000		470,900,000
	%		%
Net profit margin	13.71		14.87
Return on equity	7.18		7.09
Return on assets	4.00		4.00
Foreign sales percent	59		57
No. of employees (FTEs)	9,242		9,095

* Common
[A] Reported in accordance with U.S. GAAP

Latest Results

Periods ended:	6m June 30/23[A]		6m June 30/22[A]
	$000s	%Chg	$000s
Operating revenue	5,913,000	+11	5,322,000
Net income	830,000	+15	723,000
Net inc. for equity hldrs	764,000	+15	666,000
Net inc. for non-cont. int	66,000		57,000
	$		$
Earnings per share*	1.51		1.33

* Common
[A] Reported in accordance with U.S. GAAP

Historical Summary
(as originally stated)

Fiscal Year	Oper. Rev. $000s	Net Inc. Bef. Disc. $000s	EPS* $
2022[A]	11,043,000	1,514,000	2.78
2021[A]	9,448,000	1,405,000	2.61
2020[A]	8,935,000	1,389,000	2.60
2019[A]	8,783,000	1,852,000	3.79
2018[A]	8,390,000	1,286,000	2.59

* Common
[A] Reported in accordance with U.S. GAAP

F.57 Forward Water Technologies Corp.

Symbol - FWTC **Exchange** - TSX-VEN **CUSIP** - 34988A
Head Office - B2-80 Birmingham St, Toronto, ON, M8V 3W6 **Telephone** - (416) 451-8155
Website - www.forwardwater.com
Email - howie.honeyman@forwardwater.com
Investor Relations - C. Howie Honeyman (416) 451-8155
Auditors - RSM Canada LLP C.A., Calgary, Alta.
Transfer Agents - TSX Trust Company, Toronto, Ont.

Profile - (Ont. 2016) Has developed a patented industrial wastewater treatment system that allows manufacturing operations to clean their wastewater.

Extracts clean water through a membrane utilizing a Forward Osmosis (FO) method. Without using applied pressure, applied energy or forced filtration, the company's FO process rejects all impurities and separates only the clean water from the waste stream. Has completed full commercial design of modular transportable containerized equipment and is prepared to deliver this equipment to end users. Targeting three sectors: industrial wastewater; brine management; and food and beverage.

Has three revenue models: Build Own Operate, where the company constructs a facility for on-site operation and operates the equipment as service; Build Operate Transfer, where the company constructs a facility for on-site operation and operates the equipment as a service and over time, operations are taken over by customer; and Licensing, where the company would license the technology with well-established equipment providers and operators.

Predecessor Detail - Name changed from Hope Well Capital Corp., Oct. 20, 2021, pursuant to the Qualifying Transaction reverse takeover acquisition of Forward Water Technologies Inc. (FWT) and concurrent amalgamation of FWTwith wholly owned 2644246 Ontario Limited.

Directors - Lea M. Ray, chr., Toronto, Ont.; C. Howie Honeyman, pres. & CEO, Toronto, Ont.; Dr. Wayne Maddever, COO, Burlington, Ont.; Gerald (Gerry) Goldberg, Toronto, Ont.; John Koehle, Toronto, Ont.; Andrew Pasternak, Toronto, Ont.

Other Exec. Officers - Michael (Mike) Willetts, CFO; Grant W. Thornley, v-p, eng. solution sales

Capital Stock

	Authorized (shs.)	Outstanding (shs.)[1]
Common	unlimited	105,911,740

[1] At Oct. 25, 2022

Major Shareholder - FirstLine Venture Partners Corporation held 25.1% interest, Sustainable Chemistry Alliance held 25.1% interest and GreenCentre Canada held 13.8% interest at Aug. 23, 2022.

Price Range - FWTC/TSX-VEN

Year	Volume	High	Low	Close
2022	15,903,006	$0.20	$0.05	$0.06
2021	1,492,047	$0.30	$0.12	$0.14

Recent Close: $0.07

Capital Stock Changes - On Oct. 25, 2021, 96,771,900 common shares were issued pursuant to the Qualifying Transaction reverse takeover acquisition of Forward Water Technologies Inc., including 32,350,000 units (1 common share & ½ warrant) issued without further consideration on exchange of subscription receipts sold previously by private placement at $1.00 each. Also during fiscal 2022, 1,103,200 common shares were issued as finder's fee.

Wholly Owned Subsidiaries

Forward Water Technologies Inc., Mississauga, Ont.

Financial Statistics

Periods ended:	12m Mar. 31/22[A1]		12m Mar. 31/21[A]
	$000s	%Chg	$000s
Operating revenue	**6**	**-86**	**42**
Salaries & benefits	335		199
Research & devel. expense	651		351
General & admin expense	1,766		412
Stock-based compensation	35		nil
Operating expense	**2,787**	**+190**	**962**
Operating income	**(2,781)**	**n.a.**	**(920)**
Deprec., depl. & amort.	265		356
Finance income	1		2
Finance costs, gross	112		390
Pre-tax income	**(4,179)**	**n.a.**	**(1,500)**
Net income	**(4,179)**	**n.a.**	**(1,500)**
Cash & equivalent	3,040		155
Accounts receivable	217		30
Current assets	3,632		294
Fixed assets, net	926		803
Total assets	**4,557**	**+315**	**1,098**
Accts. pay. & accr. liabs	464		525
Current liabilities	464		2,739
Long-term debt, gross	318		2,247
Long-term debt, net	279		264
Shareholders' equity	3,514		(2,267)
Cash from oper. activs	**(2,655)**	**n.a.**	**(200)**
Cash from fin. activs	5,473		10
Cash from invest. activs	48		nil
Net cash position	**3,012**	**n.m.**	**147**
	$		$
Earnings per share*	(0.05)		(0.14)
	shs		shs
No. of shs. o/s*	105,600,099		n.a.
Avg. no. of shs. o/s*	77,872,756		10,800,000
	%		%
Net profit margin	n.m.		n.m.
Return on equity	n.m.		n.m.
Return on assets	(143.84)		(69.79)

* Common

[A] Reported in accordance with IFRS

[1] Results prior to Oct. 25, 2021, pertain to and reflect the Qualifying Transaction reverse takeover acquisition of Forward Water Technologies Inc.

Latest Results

Periods ended:	6m Sept. 30/22[A]		6m Sept. 30/21[A]
	$000s	%Chg	$000s
Operating revenue	nil	n.a.	1
Net income	(1,066)	n.a.	(1,566)
	$		$
Earnings per share*	(0.01)		(0.14)

* Common

[A] Reported in accordance with IFRS

Historical Summary
(as originally stated)

Fiscal Year	Oper. Rev.	Net Inc. Bef. Disc.	EPS*
	$000s	$000s	$
2022[A]	6	(4,179)	(0.05)
2021[A]	42	(1,500)	(0.14)
2020[A]	31	(1,282)	(0.13)

* Common

[A] Reported in accordance with IFRS

F.58 Fountain Asset Corp.

Symbol - FA **Exchange** - TSX-VEN **CUSIP** - 35063X
Head Office - Unit 609, 3 Market St, Toronto, ON, M5E 0A3 **Telephone** - (647) 344-4425
Website - www.fountainassetcorp.com
Email - info@fountainassetcorp.com
Investor Relations - Andrew Parks (647) 344-4429
Auditors - MNP LLP C.A., Toronto, Ont.
Lawyers - Wildeboer Dellelce LLP, Toronto, Ont.
Transfer Agents - TSX Trust Company, Toronto, Ont.
Profile - (Can. 2005 amalg.) Provides a range of merchant banking services to small and mid-sized public and private companies in the manufacturing, retail, financial services, technology, cannabis, biotechnology, oil and gas, mining and cryptocurrency sectors.

Services offered include equity financing, asset-based lending, mergers and acquisitions advisory, operational management support and facilitating of debt and equity financing structures.

At Mar. 31, 2022, the company had $173,652 invested in loans and convertible debentures.

Predecessor Detail - Name changed from GC-Global Capital Corp., Aug. 31, 2015.

Directors - Morris J. Prychidny, chr., Toronto, Ont.; Andrew Parks, pres. & CEO, Toronto, Ont.; Roger Daher, Markham, Ont.; Michael B. Galloro, Toronto, Ont.; Paul A. Kelly, Toronto, Ont.

Other Exec. Officers - Matthew (Matt) Davis, CFO

Capital Stock

	Authorized (shs.)	Outstanding (shs.)[1]
Preferred	unlimited	nil
Multiple Voting	unlimited	87,760
Subordinate Voting	unlimited	61,776,702

[1] At May 27, 2022

Multiple Voting - Convertible into subordinate voting shares on a 1-for-1 basis at any time. Four votes per share.

Subordinate Voting - Convertible into multiple voting shares on a 1-for-1 basis in the event an offer is made to purchase multiple voting shares. One vote per share.

Major Shareholder - Widely held at May 27, 2022.

Price Range - FA/TSX-VEN

Year	Volume	High	Low	Close
2022	1,861,202	$0.30	$0.11	$0.14
2021	7,422,439	$0.37	$0.14	$0.32
2020	3,183,310	$0.40	$0.08	$0.23
2019	2,507,525	$0.65	$0.18	$0.35
2018	12,786,311	$0.64	$0.25	$0.58

Recent Close: $0.07

Wholly Owned Subsidiaries

Fountain Advisor's Corp., Canada.
Somersby Park General Partner Inc., United States.

Subsidiaries

73% int. in **Somersby Park 2010 Limited Partnership**, Del.

Note: The preceding list includes only the major related companies in which interests are held.

Financial Statistics

Periods ended:	12m Dec. 31/21[A]		12m Dec. 31/20[A]
	$000s	%Chg	$000s
Realized invest. gain (loss)	3,322		(9,054)
Unrealized invest. gain (loss)	(1,101)		11,026
Total revenue	**2,403**	**-12**	**2,726**
Salaries & benefits	478		305
General & admin. expense	493		683
Stock-based compensation	163		154
Operating expense	**1,134**	**-1**	**1,142**
Operating income	**1,269**	**-20**	**1,584**
Pre-tax income	**832**	**-68**	**2,577**
Income taxes	32		nil
Net income	**799**	**-69**	**2,577**
Cash & equivalent	2,999		1,063
Accounts receivable	315		1,234
Investments	17,352		15,993
Total assets	**20,833**	**+6**	**19,590**
Accts. pay. & accr. liabs	198		303
Shareholders' equity	20,220		19,257
Cash from oper. activs	**1,936**	**+182**	**687**
Net cash position	**2,959**	**+189**	**1,023**
	$		$
Earnings per share*	0.01		0.04
Cash flow per share*	0.03		0.01
	shs		shs
No. of shs. o/s*	61,864,462		61,864,462
Avg. no. of shs. o/s*	61,864,462		59,002,304
	%		%
Net profit margin	33.25		94.53
Return on equity	4.05		14.67
Return on assets	3.95		13.57

* M.V. & S.V.

[A] Reported in accordance with IFRS

Latest Results

Periods ended:	3m Mar. 31/22[A]		3m Mar. 31/21[A]
	$000s	%Chg	$000s
Total revenue	(1,801)	n.a.	5,051
Net income	(2,034)	n.a.	4,841
	$		$
Earnings per share*	(0.03)		0.08

* M.V. & S.V.

[A] Reported in accordance with IFRS

Historical Summary
(as originally stated)

Fiscal Year	Total Rev.	Net Inc. Bef. Disc.	EPS*
	$000s	$000s	$
2021[A]	2,403	799	0.01
2020[A]	2,726	2,577	0.04
2019[A]	(17,171)	(18,505)	(0.31)
2018[A]	13,241	8,584	0.15
2017[A]	5,059	3,195	0.06

* M.V. & S.V.

[A] Reported in accordance with IFRS

F.59 Fountainhall Capital Corp.

Symbol - FUN.P **Exchange** - TSX-VEN **CUSIP** - 35084J
Head Office - 1703-595 Burrard St, Vancouver, BC, V7X 1J1 **Telephone** - (604) 488-5427
Email - sinclair@earlston.ca
Investor Relations - A. Murray Sinclair Jr. (604) 488-8717
Auditors - Davidson & Company LLP C.A., Vancouver, B.C.
Transfer Agents - Computershare Trust Company of Canada Inc., Vancouver, B.C.
Profile - (B.C. 2021) Capital Pool Company.
Directors - A. Murray Sinclair Jr., pres., CEO, CFO & corp. sec., Vancouver, B.C.; Dr. Robert A. (Bob) Quartermain, Vancouver, B.C.; Arthur R. (Rick) Rule IV, Calif.

Capital Stock

	Authorized (shs.)	Outstanding (shs.)[1]
Common	unlimited	5,150,000

[1] At Oct. 31, 2022

Major Shareholder - Dr. Robert A. (Bob) Quartermain held 19.42% interest, Arthur R. (Rick) Rule IV held 19.42% interest and A. Murray Sinclair Jr. held 19.42% interest at Oct. 4, 2022.

Price Range - FUN.P/TSX-VEN

Year	Volume	High	Low	Close
2022	352,600	$0.62	$0.37	$0.60
2021	29,500	$0.46	$0.35	$0.46

Recent Close: $0.55

Capital Stock Changes - On Dec. 14, 2021, an initial public offering of 2,150,000 common shares was completed at 15¢ per share.

F.60 Four Arrows Capital Corp.

Symbol - AROW.P **Exchange** - TSX-VEN **CUSIP** - 35085L
Head Office - 1208 Rosewood Cres, North Vancouver, BC, V7P 1H4 **Telephone** - (604) 889-4790
Email - aly.nazerali@ipm.bc.ca
Investor Relations - Altaf Nazerali (604) 628-7597
Auditors - Manning Elliott LLP C.A., Vancouver, B.C.
Transfer Agents - Endeavor Trust Corporation, Vancouver, B.C.
Profile - (B.C. 2019) Capital Pool Company.
Directors - Alex Lyamport, CEO & corp. sec., Sunny Isles, Fla.; Leon A. Berker; Altaf (Aly) Nazerali, Vancouver, B.C.
Other Exec. Officers - Jaisun Garcha, CFO

Capital Stock

	Authorized (shs.)	Outstanding (shs.)[1]
Common	unlimited	13,099,664

[1] At May 29, 2023

Major Shareholder - Alex Lyamport held 32.3% interest at Mar. 29, 2022.

Price Range - AROW.P/TSX-VEN

Year	Volume	High	Low	Close
2022	674,550	$0.13	$0.05	$0.07
2021	1,020,740	$0.30	$0.12	$0.12

Recent Close: $0.04

F.61 49 North Resources Inc.

Symbol - FNR **Exchange** - TSX-VEN **CUSIP** - 34978T
Head Office - 602-224 4 Ave S, Saskatoon, SK, S7K 5M5 **Telephone** - (306) 653-2692 **Fax** - (306) 664-4483
Website - www.fnr.ca
Email - ir@fnr.ca
Investor Relations - Thomas MacNeill (306) 653-2692
Auditors - Kenway Mack Slusarchuk Stewart LLP C.A., Calgary, Alta.
Lawyers - McKercher LLP, Saskatoon, Sask.
Transfer Agents - Alliance Trust Company, Calgary, Alta.
Profile - (Sask. 2008 amalg.) Invests in common shares and other securities of resource companies.

At Mar. 31, 2023, the investment portfolio consisted of securities of 39 resource companies with a fair market value of $8,831,000.

Company type	Fair market value
Base and precious metals	$5,635,000
Diamonds	379,000
Oil & Gas	817,000
Other	2,000,000

Predecessor Detail - Name changed from 49 North Resource Fund Inc., Aug. 25, 2009.

Directors - Thomas (Tom) MacNeill, chr., pres. & CEO, Saskatoon, Sask.; Andrew B. Davidson, CFO & corp. sec., Saskatoon, Sask.; Dr. Norman M. Betts, Fredericton, N.B.; Andrew A. Cook, Toronto, Ont.

Capital Stock

	Authorized (shs.)	Outstanding (shs.)[1]
First Preferred	unlimited	
Series I		2,662,311
Series II		674,781
Second Preferred	unlimited	nil
Common	unlimited	166,271,110

[1] At May 30, 2023

First Preferred Series I & II - Entitled to 2.5% cumulative dividends payable annually. Convertible at the holder's option into common shares at 50¢ per share. Redeemable at $1.00 per share. Non-voting.

Common - One vote per share.

Major Shareholder - Thomas (Tom) MacNeill held 12.1% interest at July 16, 2021.

Price Range - FNR/TSX-VEN

Year	Volume	High	Low	Close
2022	19,678,842	$0.06	$0.02	$0.03
2021	22,999,864	$0.13	$0.03	$0.04
2020	22,544,857	$0.21	$0.02	$0.12
2019	7,810,672	$0.06	$0.02	$0.02
2018	8,751,321	$0.12	$0.02	$0.02

Recent Close: $0.03

Capital Stock Changes - During 2022, 32,800 common shares were issued on conversion of 16,236 preferred shares.

Financial Statistics

Periods ended:	12m Dec. 31/22[A]		12m Dec. 31/21[A]
	$000s	%Chg	$000s
Realized invest. gain (loss)	(35)		(121)
Unrealized invest. gain (loss)	(7,669)		(5,810)
Total revenue	**(6,900)**	**n.a.**	**(5,169)**
Salaries & benefits	44		83
General & admin. expense	881		1,043
Stock-based compensation	297		nil
Operating expense	**1,222**	**+9**	**1,126**
Operating income	**(8,122)**	**n.a.**	**(6,295)**
Deprec. & amort.	54		56
Finance costs, gross	114		188
Write-downs/write-offs	98		(54)
Pre-tax income	**(8,192)**	**n.a.**	**(6,593)**
Net inc bef disc ops, eqhldrs	(8,192)		(6,593)
Net income	**(8,192)**	**n.a.**	**(6,593)**
Cash & equivalent	8,745		16,239
Accounts receivable	34		41
Current assets	9,500		16,967
Fixed assets, net	16		21
Right-of-use assets	95		145
Total assets	**19,128**	**-28**	**26,463**
Accts. pay. & accr. liabs	2,022		1,414
Current liabilities	7,535		6,927
Long-term debt, gross	6,137		6,140
Long-term debt, net	696		699
Long-term lease liabilities	54		104
Preferred share equity	2,642		2,654
Shareholders' equity	10,843		18,733
Cash from oper. activs	**(303)**	**n.a.**	**(1,786)**
Cash from fin. activs	nil		1,607
Cash from invest. activs	15		465
Net cash position	**45**	**-86**	**333**
	$		$
Earnings per share*	(0.05)		(0.07)
Cash flow per share*	(0.00)		(0.02)
	shs		shs
No. of shs. o/s*	166,271,110		166,238,310
Avg. no. of shs. o/s*	166,269,251		93,163,064
	%		%
Net profit margin	n.m.		n.m.
Return on equity	(67.48)		(35.51)
Return on assets	(35.44)		(21.99)

* Common

[A] Reported in accordance with IFRS

Note: Net income reflects increases/decreases in net assets.

Latest Results

Periods ended:	3m Mar. 31/23[A]		3m Mar. 31/22[A]
	$000s	%Chg	$000s
Total revenue	122	n.a.	(1,381)
Net income	(129)	n.a.	(2,005)
	$		$
Earnings per share*	(0.00)		(0.01)

* Common

[A] Reported in accordance with IFRS

Historical Summary
(as originally stated)

Fiscal Year	Total Rev.	Net Inc. Bef. Disc.	EPS*
	$000s	$000s	$
2022[A]	(6,900)	(8,192)	(0.05)
2021[A]	(5,169)	(6,593)	(0.07)
2020[A]	17,859	16,032	0.19
2019[A]	3,191	191	0.00
2018[A]	(3,344)	(5,209)	(0.08)

* Common

[A] Reported in accordance with IFRS

F.62 4Front Ventures Corp.

Symbol - FFNT **Exchange** - CSE **CUSIP** - 35086B

Head Office - 7010 E. Chauncey Lane, Suite 235, Phoenix, AZ, United States, 85054 **Telephone** - (602) 633-3067

Website - www.4frontventures.com

Email - andrew.thut@4frontventures.com

Investor Relations - Andrew Thut (602) 633-3067

Auditors - Davidson & Company LLP C.A., Vancouver, B.C.

Transfer Agents - Alliance Trust Company, Calgary, Alta.

FP500 Revenue Ranking - 701

Employees - 641 at Mar. 30, 2023

Profile - (B.C. 2019) Has cannabis cultivation, production and retail operations in state-licensed markets in the U.S.

Operations are conducted through the following segments:

THC Cannabis - Operates seven cultivation and manufacturing facilities in Georgetown, Holliston and Worcester, Mass., Elk Grove, Ill., and Commerce, Watsonville and Monterey cty., Calif., which supply the company's retail operations and engage in wholesale sales to other licensed parties. A 250,000-sq.-ft. cultivation and manufacturing facility is under construction in Matteson, Ill., with commencement of operations expected in the second half of 2023. Cannabis products produced include all product categories under more than 25 different brands such as Island, Mini Budz, Legends, Private Reserve, Chewee's, Marmas, Hi-Burst, Crystal Clear and Terp Stix. Retail operations consist of six dispensaries under the Mission brand in Brookline, Georgetown and Worcester, Mass., Chicago and Calumet City, Ill., and Ann Arbor, Mich. The company also leases cannabis production facilities and sells equipment, supplies and intellectual property to cannabis producers in Washington. Facilities for lease are located in Olympia, Wash., consisting of 116,500 sq. ft. of indoor cultivation, processing and distribution; and Elma, Wash., consisting of 60,000 sq. ft. of indoor cultivation and warehouse.

CBD Wellness - Wholly owned **Pure Ratios Holdings, Inc.**, based in San Diego, Calif., produces and sells CBD products. Products are distributed and sold across the U.S. through e-commerce platforms, business-to-business channels and third party fulfilment vendors.

In March 2023, the company agreed to acquire **Euphoria, LLC**, which holds a conditional retail dispensary licence in Chicago, Ill., for US$4,500,000.

In August 2022, the company acquired California cannabis and hemp brands, Bloom Farms and Bloom Farms Wellness, which included concentrates, vapes, tinctures and topicals, for issuance of 3,750,000 class A subordinate voting shares at a deemed price of US$0.56 per share.

In April 2022, the company acquired **Island Global Holdings, Inc.** (dba Island Cannabis Co.), a premier California cannabis brand and producer of pre-rolls, flower and concentrate products with 250,000 sq. ft. of cultivation canopy throughout Santa Cruz and Monterey ctys., Calif., for issuance 8,783,716 class A subordinate voting shares and US$10,000,000 in promissory notes.

Predecessor Detail - Succeeded Cannex Capital Holdings Inc., July 31, 2019, pursuant to the amalgamation of wholly owned 1196260 B.C. Ltd. and (old) 4Front Ventures Corp. (deemed acquiror) to form (new) 4Front Ventures (resulting issuer), and the concurrent voluntary dissolution of Cannex (predecessor public company); basis 1 (new) 4Front Ventures subord. vtg. sh. for each Cannex com. sh. and 1 (new) 4Front Ventures cl.B proportionate vtg. sh. for each 80 Cannex cl.A conv. rest. shs.

Directors - Robert E. Hunt, chr., Calif.; Leonid (Leo) Gontmakher, CEO, Puerto Rico; David Daily, Austin, Tex.; Chetan Gulati, Fla.; Kristopher (Kris) Krane, Ill.; Roman Tkachenko, Redmond, Wash.

Other Exec. Officers - Tera Martin, chief of staff; Andrew Thut, chief invest. officer; Gabe Mendoza, exec. v-p, rev.; Brandon Mills, exec. v-p; Christopher Wimmer, gen. counsel; Ray Landgraf, pres., California opers.; Nicole Frederick, dir., external reporting & interim CFO

Capital Stock

	Authorized (shs.)	Outstanding (shs.)[1]
Class A Subordinate Voting	unlimited	648,583,519
Class C Multiple Voting	unlimited	1,276,208

[1] At Aug. 15, 2023

Class A Subordinate Voting - One vote per share.

Class C Multiple Voting - Convertible into class A subordinate voting shares on a 1-for-1 basis, in certain circumstances. 800 votes per share.

Major Shareholder - Trevor Pratte held 17.64% interest, Karl Chowscano held 17.48% interest and Joshua N. (Josh) Rosen held 15.98% interest at May 15, 2023.

Price Range - FFNT/CSE

Year	Volume	High	Low	Close
2022	46,083,388	$1.28	$0.26	$0.31
2021	84,847,126	$2.52	$1.12	$1.27
2020	56,961,951	$1.21	$0.25	$1.15
2019	38,605,549	$2.35	$0.37	$0.59
2018	74,495,344	$1.93	$0.50	$0.92

Recent Close: $0.13

Capital Stock Changes - In January 2022, 28,571,428 class A subordinate voting shares were issued pursuant to the acquisition of New England Cannabis Corporation, Inc. In April 2022, 8,783,716 class A subordinate voting shares were issued pursuant to the acquisition of Island Global Holdings, Inc. Also during 2022, class A subordinate voting shares were issued as follows: 6,235,512 on conversion of notes, 3,750,000 pursuant to the acquisition of Bloom Farms and Bloom Farms Wellness brands, 1,750,604 as share-based compensation, 91,436 on exercise of warrants and 51,975 on exercise of options.

Wholly Owned Subsidiaries

4Front California Capital Holdings Inc., Calif.

4Front Nevada Corp., Nev.

- 100% int. in **BrightLeaf Development LLC**, Wash.
  - 100% int. in **Ag-Grow Imports, LLC**, Wash.
  - 100% int. in **Fuller Hill Development Co, LLC**, Wash.
  - 100% int. in **Real Estate Properties LLC**, Wash.

4Front U.S. Holdings, Inc., Del.

- 100% int. in **4Front Holdings LLC**, Del.
  - 100% int. in **4Front Advisors, LLC**, Ariz.
  - 100% int. in **Linchpin Investors, LLC**, Del.
  - 100% int. in **Mission Partners USA, LLC**, Del.
    - 100% int. in **Harborside Illinois Grown Medicine, Inc.**, Ill.
    - 100% int. in **Healthy Pharms, Inc.**, Mass.
      - 100% int. in **New England Cannabis Corporation, Inc.**, Mass.
    - 100% int. in **IL Grown Medicine, LLC**, Ill.
    - 95% int. in **MMA Capital, LLC**, Mass.
    - 100% int. in **Mission MA, Inc.**, Mass.
    - 100% int. in **Mission Partners IP, LLC**, Del.
    - 100% int. in **Om of Medicine, LLC**, Mich.

Island Global Holdings, Inc., Calif.

- 100% int. in **Carousel Bay LLC**, Calif.
- 100% int. in **Gold Coast Gardens LLC**, Calif.
- 100% int. in **Isla Buena Vista LLC**, Calif.
- 100% int. in **Robot Farms Inc.**, Calif.

Pure Ratios Holdings, Inc., Del.

Financial Statistics

Periods ended:	12m Dec. 31/22[A]		12m Dec. 31/21[oA]
	US$000s	%Chg	US$000s
Operating revenue	**118,577**	**+13**	**104,566**
Cost of goods sold	72,275		53,636
General & admin expense	55,585		48,087
Stock-based compensation	7,214		10,081
Operating expense	**135,074**	**+21**	**111,804**
Operating income	**(16,497)**	**n.a.**	**(7,238)**
Deprec., depl. & amort.	8,339		6,636
Finance income	32		15
Finance costs, gross	12,685		13,704
Write-downs/write-offs	(13,184)[1]		nil
Pre-tax income	**(36,970)**	**n.a.**	**(24,358)**
Income taxes	9,907		13,931
Net income	**(46,877)**	**n.a.**	**(38,289)**
Net inc. for equity hldrs	**(46,898)**	**n.a.**	**(38,309)**
Net inc. for non-cont. int	**21**	**+5**	**20**
Cash & equivalent	15,190		22,581
Inventories	25,592		20,087
Accounts receivable	7,391		1,946
Current assets	53,267		50,874
Fixed assets, net	56,906		42,633
Right-of-use assets	138,451		100,519
Intangibles, net	84,882		49,401
Total assets	**344,732**	**+35**	**255,539**
Accts. pay. & accr. liabs	26,966		11,542
Current liabilities	77,450		48,838
Long-term debt, gross	84,165		70,813
Long-term debt, net	75,106		64,616
Long-term lease liabilities	136,185		93,111
Shareholders' equity	28,258		37,460
Non-controlling interest	93		72
Cash from oper. activs	**8,768**	**+52**	**5,777**
Cash from fin. activs	10,708		10,886
Cash from invest. activs	(26,867)		(13,014)
Net cash position	**15,190**	**-33**	**22,581**
Capital expenditures	(2,434)		(13,872)
	US$		US$
Earnings per share*	(0.07)		(0.06)
Cash flow per share*	0.01		0.01
	shs		shs
No. of shs. o/s*	643,416,275		594,181,604
Avg. no. of shs. o/s*	632,951,141		590,998,816
	%		%
Net profit margin	(39.53)		(36.62)
Return on equity	(142.72)		(96.24)
Return on assets	(10.26)		(7.28)
Foreign sales percent	100		100

* Cl.A Subord. Vtg.

[o] Restated

[A] Reported in accordance with U.S. GAAP

[1] Pertains to impairment of certain licences in Massachusetts and Illinois.

Latest Results

Periods ended:	6m June 30/23[A]		6m June 30/22[A]
	US$000s	%Chg	US$000s
Operating revenue	61,072	+12	54,487
Net income	(22,856)	n.a.	(12,440)
Net inc. for equity hldrs	(22,866)	n.a.	(12,450)
Net inc. for non-cont. int	10		10
	US$		US$
Earnings per share*	(0.04)		(0.02)

* Cl.A Subord. Vtg.

[A] Reported in accordance with U.S. GAAP

Historical Summary
(as originally stated)

Fiscal Year	Oper. Rev. US$000s	Net Inc. Bef. Disc. US$000s	EPS* US$
2022[A]	118,577	(46,877)	(0.07)
2021[A]	104,566	(38,289)	(0.06)
2020[A]	57,635	(59,992)	(0.12)
2019[B1]	31,126	(180,906)	(0.43)
2018[B2,3]	6,940	(3,701)	(0.03)

* Cl.A Subord. Vtg.
[A] Reported in accordance with U.S. GAAP
[B] Reported in accordance with IFRS
[1] Results reflect the July 31, 2019, plan of arrangement between Cannex Capital Holdings Inc. and 4Front Holdings, LLC.
[2] 7 months ended Apr. 30, 2018.
[3] Results reflect the Mar. 12, 2018, reverse takeover acquisition of Cannex Capital Group Inc.

F.63 Fraser Mackenzie Accelerator Corp.

Symbol - FMAC.P **Exchange** - TSX-VEN **CUSIP** - 35549E
Head Office - 116 Eastbourne Ave, Toronto, ON, M5P 2G3 **Telephone** - (416) 818-6163
Email - pbenson@fmmc.ca
Investor Relations - Philip Benson (416) 818-6163
Auditors - RSM Canada LLP C.A., Toronto, Ont.
Lawyers - Dentons Canada LLP, Toronto, Ont.
Transfer Agents - TSX Trust Company, Toronto, Ont.
Profile - (Ont. 2022) Capital Pool Company.
Common listed on TSX-VEN, Feb. 22, 2023.
Directors - Philip (Phil) Benson, chr., pres. & CEO, Toronto, Ont.; Donald Bent, CFO, Toronto, Ont.; Robert Eberschlag, corp. sec., Toronto, Ont.; David Iacobelli, Oakville, Ont.; Michael R. (Mike) Lambert, Calgary, Alta.; Michael M. Liik, Toronto, Ont.

Capital Stock

	Authorized (shs.)	Outstanding (shs.)[1]
Common	unlimited	20,571,000

[1] At Feb. 22, 2023

Major Shareholder - Widely held at Feb. 22, 2023.
Recent Close: $0.11
Capital Stock Changes - On Feb. 22, 2023, an initial public offering of 14,371,000 common shares was completed at 10¢ per share.

F.64 Frequency Exchange Corp.

Symbol - FREQ **Exchange** - TSX-VEN **CUSIP** - 358019
Head Office - 2050-1055 Georgia St W, Vancouver, BC, V6E 3P3 **Telephone** - (250) 732-7170
Website - frequencyexchangecorp.com
Email - stephen@frequencyexchangecorp.com
Investor Relations - Stephen L. Davis (250) 732-7170
Auditors - MNP LLP C.A., Vancouver, B.C.
Transfer Agents - Olympia Trust Company, Vancouver, B.C.
Profile - (B.C. 2019) Produces and sells wearable devices capable of transmitting frequencies to repair cell function damaged by Lyme disease and restore immunity.

The company is a cloud-based wellness service provider utilizing smart wearable technology. Its wearable wellness products use light pulse and sound frequency technology to deliver layered frequency recordings to the user. Core product is the Wave 1, a wearable device that receives specific frequency packages designed to support the body's immune system around Lyme disease.

The Wave 1 is priced at US$1,650 and manufacturing is subcontracted to **Arrow Electronics Inc.**

Predecessor Detail - Name changed from Israel Capital Canada Corp., Feb. 2, 2022, pursuant to the Qualifying Transaction reverse takeover acquisition of FREmedica Technologies Inc.
Directors - Stephen L. Davis, chr., pres. & CEO, Mill Bay, B.C.; Hari B. Varshney, CFO & corp. sec., Vancouver, B.C.; Nicole Sullivan, pres., FREmedica Technologies Inc., B.C.; Bradley (Brad) Aelicks, North Vancouver, B.C.; Dr. Keith Pyne, New York, N.Y.

Capital Stock

	Authorized (shs.)	Outstanding (shs.)[1]
Common	unlimited	36,779,553

[1] At May 30, 2023

Major Shareholder - Wave Force Electronics Inc. held 45.17% interest at June 20, 2023.

Price Range - FREQ/TSX-VEN

Year	Volume	High	Low	Close
2022	2,682,461	$0.40	$0.06	$0.10
2020	10,000	$0.38	$0.38	$0.38

Recent Close: $0.05

Wholly Owned Subsidiaries
FREmedica Technologies Inc., Victoria, B.C.

F.65 The Fresh Factory B.C. Ltd.

Symbol - FRSH **Exchange** - CSE **CUSIP** - 35805H
Head Office - 2050-1055 Georgia St W, Vancouver, BC, V6E 3P3 **Toll-free** - (877) 743-8289
Website - thefreshfactory.co
Email - john@thefreshfactory.co
Investor Relations - John Mikulich (877) 495-1638
Auditors - MNP LLP C.A., Toronto, Ont.
Transfer Agents - Olympia Trust Company
Profile - (B.C. 2018) Develops, formulates, manufactures, distributes and sells plant-based and clean-label food and beverages under its own brands and for customers.

The company produces products for several companies and for its own brand, these include: cold-pressed juice; other beverages such cold-brew teas, shakes and smoothies and speciality beverages; dips and spreads; dressings and sauces; soups; and various snack bars. Company brands are Field + Farmer and Element Pressed. Products are sold online, through distributors and through retailers across the United States.

Has manufacturing facilities in Carol Streams and West Chicago, Ill., that have various bottling lines that allow the company to produce cold-pressed juice and other bottled products; various filling capabilities for the production of dips and spreads that are filled in cups including both hot-fill and cold-fill capabilities; a bar line that allows for the production of snack bars that are packaged in sleeves; and a pouch line that allows for the production of dips and spreads that are filled in pouches.

Predecessor Detail - Name changed from 1181718 B.C. Ltd., Oct. 27, 2021, pursuant to the reverse takeover acquisition of The Fresh Factory, PBC (dba The Fresh Factory).
Directors - Nathan G. (Nate) Laurel, chr., Chicago, Ill.; Bill Besenhofer, CEO, Palatine, Ill.; Jeff Cantalupo, Hinsdale, Ill.; Lindsay Levin, Tex.; Besar Xhelili, Ont.
Other Exec. Officers - John Mikulich, CFO; Mike Weglarz, exec. v-p, commercialization; Isabella Chia, sr. v-p, mktg.

Capital Stock

	Authorized (shs.)	Outstanding (shs.)[1]
Subord. Vtg.	unlimited	10,910,211
Proportionate Vtg.	unlimited	364,195

[1] At Aug. 25, 2022

Subordinate Voting - One vote per share.
Proportionate Voting - Have the same rights, are equal in all respects of subordinate voting shares, except have 100 votes per share. Convertible into subordinate voting shares, subject to certain restrictions.
Major Shareholder - Nathan G. (Nate) Laurel held 21.54% interest at June 7, 2022.

Price Range - FRSH/CSE

Year	Volume	High	Low	Close
2022	870,044	$1.20	$0.50	$0.70
2021	770,554	$1.60	$0.85	$1.13

Recent Close: $0.70

Wholly Owned Subsidiaries
The Fresh Factory, PBC, Carol Stream, Ill.
- 100% int. in **87P LLC**, United States. dba Fresh Factory Manufacturing
- 100% int. in **Element Creations LLC**, United States. dba Element Pressed
- 100% int. in **Made Here LLC**, United States. dba Field + Farmer

Financial Statistics

Periods ended:	12m Dec. 31/21[A1]		12m Dec. 31/20[◊A]
	US$000s	%Chg	US$000s
Operating revenue	**12,799**	**+55**	**8,270**
Cost of sales	10,864		6,574
General & admin expense	3,455		1,695
Stock-based compensation	913		nil
Operating expense	**15,232**	**+84**	**8,269**
Operating income	**(2,433)**	**n.a.**	**1**
Deprec., depl. & amort.	832		670
Finance costs, gross	317		255
Write-downs/write-offs	(128)		nil
Pre-tax income	**(6,696)**	**n.a.**	**(938)**
Net income	**(6,696)**	**n.a.**	**(938)**
Cash & equivalent	6,820		323
Inventories	988		574
Accounts receivable	1,010		770
Current assets	9,206		1,889
Fixed assets, net	4,731		3,882
Intangibles, net	48		68
Total assets	**13,985**	**+140**	**5,839**
Accts. pay. & accr. liabs.	1,756		1,047
Current liabilities	2,308		4,812
Long-term debt, gross	500		3,824
Long-term debt, net	500		3,324
Long-term lease liabilities	1,350		1,524
Shareholders' equity	9,827		(997)
Cash from oper. activs.	**(1,780)**	**n.a.**	**(384)**
Cash from fin. activs.	9,667		786
Cash from invest. activs.	(1,390)		(285)
Net cash position	**6,820**	**n.m.**	**323**
Capital expenditures	(1,390)		(232)
	US$		US$
Earnings per share*	(0.20)		(0.39)
Cash flow per share*	(0.05)		n.a.
	shs		shs
No. of shs. o/s*	11,292,906		n.a.
Avg. no. of shs. o/s*	32,777,791		2,399,998
	%		%
Net profit margin	(52.32)		(11.34)
Return on equity	n.m.		n.m.
Return on assets	(64.36)		(14.04)

* Subord. Vtg,
[◊] Restated
[A] Reported in accordance with IFRS
[1] Results reflect the Oct. 27, 2021, reverse takeover acquisition of The Fresh Factory, PBC.

Latest Results

Periods ended:	6m June 30/22[A]		6m June 30/21[A]
	US$000s	%Chg	US$000s
Operating revenue	8,424	+38	6,096
Net income	(2,539)	n.a.	(1,353)
	US$		US$
Earnings per share*	(0.05)		(0.56)

* Subord. Vtg,
[A] Reported in accordance with IFRS

Historical Summary
(as originally stated)

Fiscal Year	Oper. Rev. US$000s	Net Inc. Bef. Disc. US$000s	EPS* US$
2021[A]	12,799	(6,696)	(0.20)
2020[A1]	8,270	(938)	(0.39)
2019[A]	6,849	(2,093)	(0.87)

* Subord. Vtg,
[A] Reported in accordance with IFRS
[1] Results for 2020 and prior period pertains to The Fresh Factory, PBC.

F.66 Friday's Dog Holdings Inc.

Symbol - FRDY **Exchange** - TSX-VEN **CUSIP** - 358369
Head Office - 710-1030 Georgia St W, Vancouver, BC, V6E 2Y3 **Telephone** - (604) 428-6128
Website - fridaysdog.com
Email - investors@fridaysdog.com
Investor Relations - Anthony Paterson (604) 428-6128
Auditors - Davidson & Company LLP C.A., Vancouver, B.C.
Transfer Agents - Computershare Trust Company of Canada Inc., Vancouver, B.C.
Profile - (B.C. 1987) Retails pet care products online under the Friday's Dog brand which use natural, non-toxic ingredients and cruelty-free testing.

The company's initial product portfolio has nine stock keeping units (SKU) consisting of five non-sulphide bottle shampoo and conditioner items, one oral rinse and three flavoured treat pouches. All products are free of additives and toxins, with cruelty-free testing. Products are sold directly to consumers through the company's e-commerce site fridaysdog.com, as well as on Amazon. The company also plans to sell the products on televised home shopping channels such as QVC, as well as plans to be ready for retail distribution by the first quarter of 2023. Products are produced under contract by **Synergy Labs, Inc.** in Fort Lauderdale, Fla.

Recent Merger and Acquisition Activity

Status: terminated **Revised:** July 17, 2023
ALC postponed the spin-out of its Macusani project. The transaction was terminated. PREVIOUS: American Lithium Corp. (ALC) announced a definitive agreement to spin-out its Macusani uranium project in Peru via the sale of the property to Friday's Dog Holdings Inc., a public company listed on the TSX Venture Exchange which would be renamed International Uranium Corp. ALC would receive 80,000,000 International Uranium post-consolidated common shares (following a 1-for-4.5 consolidation) in consideration for the Macusani property. The transaction would involve the transfer of wholly owned Macusani Uranium S.A.C. to International Uranium. A concurrent private placement of subscription receipts would be completed by International Uranium for gross proceeds of $15,000,000. Friday's Dog plans to spin-out wholly owned Friday's Dog Inc. (FDI), which holds its existing canine care and grooming product manufacturing business, to Friday's Dog shareholders via the distribution of 1 FDI share for each Friday's Dog share held. No securities of FDI are expected to be listed on any regulated stock exchange upon closing of the transaction.

Predecessor Detail - Name changed from Cerro Mining Corp., Mar. 4, 2022, pursuant to the revere takeover acquisition of Friday's Dog Inc. (FDI) and concurrent amalgamation of wholly owned 1308821 B.C. Ltd. and FDI.

Directors - Jeremy T. Ross, CEO, Vancouver, B.C.; Arthur H. Kwan, Calgary, Alta.; Anthony Paterson, Vancouver, B.C.; Ali Sodagar, Vancouver, B.C.; Dominic Stann, Vancouver, B.C.

Other Exec. Officers - Chelsea Rusche, pres. & COO; Ryan E. Cheung, CFO & corp. sec.; Steve Elston, chief creative officer; Ariel Foxman, chief branding strategist

Capital Stock

	Authorized (shs.)	Outstanding (shs.)[1]
Common	unlimited	91,469,352

[1] At Aug. 29, 2022

Major Shareholder - Widely held at Mar. 4, 2022.

Price Range - FRDY/TSX-VEN

Year	Volume	High	Low	Close
2022	5,148,971	$0.38	$0.07	$0.08
2020	456,618	$0.60	$0.07	$0.60
2019	169,882	$0.36	$0.07	$0.10
2018	293,433	$0.44	$0.28	$0.33

Consolidation: 1-for-2 cons. in May 2019
Recent Close: $0.08

Capital Stock Changes - In February 2022, 43,923,423 common shares were issued pursuant to the revere takeover acquisition of Friday's Dog Inc., and 18,552,000 units (1 common share & ½ warrant) were issued without further consideration on exchange of subscription receipts sold previously by private placement at $0.50 each.

Wholly Owned Subsidiaries

Friday's Dog Inc., Los Angeles, Calif.
- 100% int. in **Friday's Dog (Canada) Inc.**, Canada.
- 100% int. in **Friday's Dog (USA) Inc.**`, United States.

Financial Statistics

Periods ended:	12m Jan. 31/22[A1]		12m Jan. 31/21[A]
	$000s	%Chg	$000s
Exploration expense	nil		3
General & admin expense	446		88
Operating expense	**446**	**+390**	**91**
Operating income	**(446)**	**n.a.**	**(91)**
Finance income	10		nil
Finance costs, gross	nil		3
Pre-tax income	**(426)**	**n.a.**	**58**
Net income	**(426)**	**n.a.**	**58**
Cash & equivalent	541		283
Current assets	9,851		287
Total assets	**9,851**	**n.m.**	**287**
Accts. pay. & accr. liabs	170		51
Current liabilities	170		51
Shareholders' equity	(9,681)		(236)
Cash from oper. activs	**(336)**	**n.a.**	**(189)**
Cash from fin. activs	9,873		464
Cash from invest. activs	(9,276)		nil
Net cash position	**540**	**+94**	**278**
	$		$
Earnings per share*	(0.02)		0.00
Cash flow per share*	(0.01)		(0.01)
	shs		shs
No. of shs. o/s*	27,243,929		17,243,929
Avg. no. of shs. o/s*	24,422,011		14,375,077
	%		%
Net profit margin	n.a.		n.a.
Return on equity	n.m.		n.m.
Return on assets	(8.40)		41.22

* Common
[A] Reported in accordance with IFRS
[1] Results for fiscal 2022 and prior periods pertain to Cerro Mining Corp.

Latest Results

Periods ended:	6m June 30/22[A]		6m June 30/21[A]
	$000s	%Chg	$000s
Operating revenue	5	n.a.	nil
Net income	(17,429)	n.a.	(1,900)
	$		$
Earnings per share*	(0.24)		(0.08)

* Common
[A] Reported in accordance with IFRS

Historical Summary
(as originally stated)

Fiscal Year	Oper. Rev.	Net Inc. Bef. Disc.	EPS*
	$000s	$000s	$
2022[A]	nil	(426)	(0.02)
2021[A]	nil	58	0.00
2020[A]	nil	(140)	(0.02)
2019[A]	nil	(30)	(0.00)
2018[A]	nil	(8)	(0.00)

* Common
[A] Reported in accordance with IFRS

Note: Adjusted throughout for 1-for-2 cons. in May 2019

F.67 Frontera Energy Corporation*

Symbol - FEC **Exchange** - TSX **CUSIP** - 35905B
Head Office - 2000-222 3 Ave SW, Calgary, AB, T2P 0B9 **Telephone** - (403) 705-8814
Website - www.fronteraenergy.ca
Email - ir@fronteraenergy.ca
Investor Relations - Brent Anderson (403) 705-8827
Auditors - Ernst & Young LLP C.A., Toronto, Ont.
Lawyers - McMillan LLP
Transfer Agents - Computershare Trust Company of Canada Inc., Toronto, Ont.
FP500 Revenue Ranking - 248
Employees - 1,191 at Dec. 31, 2022

Profile - (B.C. 2007; orig. B.C., 1985) Explores for, develops and produces oil and gas in Colombia, Guyana and Ecuador.

In Colombia, principal properties include a 97.5% interest in Arrendajo, 5,730 gross (5,586 net) acres, 100% interest in Cachicamo, 10,091 acres, 100% interest in Casimena, 6,850 acres, 87.5% interest in Canaguaro, 6,290 gross (5,504 net) acres, 100% interest in Corcel, 11,188 acres, 100% interest in CPE-6, 169,626 acres, 100% interest in Cravo Viejo, 23,836 acres, 100% interest in Cubiro, 30,036 acres, 100% interest in Guatiquia, 11,086 acres, 60% interest in Quifa, 248,586 gross (149,152 net) acres, 100% interest in Sabanero, 67,897 acres, and 100% interest in Llanos 7, 55, 99 and 119, 152,675, 102,800, 134,992 and 26,956 acres, respectively, all in Llanos basin; 50% interest in VIM-1, 142,047 gross (71,024 net) acres, 100% interest in La Creciente, 16,711 acres, 100% interest in VIM-22, 412,330 acres, and 100% interest in VIM-46, 74,799 acres, all in Lower Magdalena basin; 25% interest in Abanico, 25,659 gross (6,415 net) acres, and 53.1% interest in Neiva, 2,395 gross (1,272 net) acres, both in Upper Magdalena basin; 100% interest in Cordillera-24, 619,817 acres, central Colombia; 60% interest in CR-1, 307,384 gross (184,431 net) acres, north Colombia; and 50% interest in Caguan-5, 919,321 gross (459,661 net) acres, and 60% interest in Caguan-6, 119,048 gross (71,429 net) acres, both in south Colombia. Also holds 100% interest in Enterrios and Rio Mata, 14,920 and 26,381 acres, respectively, and 100% interest in El Deficil, 33,965 gross (22,077 net) acres.

In offshore Guyana, holds 68% interest (**CGX Energy Inc.** 32%) in Corentyne offshore petroleum prospecting licence (PPL) covering 846,243 gross (575,445 net) acres.

In Ecuador, holds 50% interest (**GeoPark Limited** 50%) in Perico and Espejo Blocks, 17,718 gross (8,859 net) and 15,652 gross (7,826 net) acres, respectively.

At Dec. 31, 2022, the company had 516 gross (420 net) producing oil wells, 6 gross (5.5 net) producing gas wells, 885 gross (683.18 net) non-producing oil wells and 11 gross (10 net) non-producing gas wells. During 2022, 5 gross (3 net) oil exploration wells, 68 gross (51.7 net) oil development wells, 2 gross (1 net) service exploration wells, 138 gross (120.3 net) service development wells, 1 gross (0.68 net) stratigraphic exploration well and 2 gross (1.5 net) dry holes exploration wells were drilled. Undeveloped land holdings totaled 4,509,326 gross (3,084,366 net) acres at Dec. 31, 2022.

Also holds interests in pipelines, storage, port and other facilities relating to the distribution and exportation of crude oil products in Colombia, including a 99.8% interest in Puerto Bahia Terminal, a greenfield liquids import-export terminal with a 2,600 mbbl storage and cargo handling facility located on the Bay of Cartagena; a 35% indirect interest in **Oleoducto de los Llanos Orientales S.A.** (ODL) pipeline running from Rubiales Field to the Monterrey or Cusiana Station in Casanare with a capacity of 300,000 bbl per day; a 90.6% working interest in Guaduas-La Dorada (OGD) pipeline running from Guaduas field to La Dorada with a capacity of 40,000 bbl per day; a 5.45% working interest in Oleoducto del Alto Magdalena (OAM) pipeline running from Tenay to Vasconia with a capacity of 100,000 bbl per day; and a 1% working interest in **Oleoducto de Colombia S.A.** (ODC) pipeline running from Vasconia to Coveñas terminal in the Caribbean with a capacity of 236,000 bbl per day.

In February 2023, the company and its joint venture partner, **CGX Energy Inc.**, completed the process of relinquishing the Demerara block through a mutual termination agreement with the Government of Guyana. The joint venture plans to focus on the exploration opportunities in the Corentyne block, following the discovery at the Kawa-1 exploration well on that block.

In January 2023, **ON Energy Inc.** and the Government of Guyana finalized a surrender deed to formalize the relinquishment of the Berbice block in Guyana. The company holds a 47.73% indirect interest in Berbice block through its 76.97% interest in **CGX Energy Inc.**, which in turn holds a 62% interest in ON Energy.

On Dec. 1, 2022, the company and its joint venture partner **CGX Energy Inc.** completed an agreement, whereby CGX transferred to the company its 29.73% participating interest in the Corentyne block in exchange for the company funding the Wei-1 exploration well for up to US$130,000,000 and up to an additional US$29,000,000 for certain Kawa-1 exploration well. In addition, CGX assigned an additional 4.94% participating interest in the Corentyne block to the company as consideration for the repayment of CGX loans totaling US$54,000,000 and cash payment to CGX of US$3,800,000. As a result, CGX and the company own a 32% and 68% participating interest, respectively, in the Corentyne block.

Periods ended:	12m Dec. 31/22	12m Dec. 31/21
Avg. BOE prod., bbl/d	36,099	34,691
Avg. BOE price, US$/bbl	91.73	66.54
Oil reserves, net, mbbl	135,594	147,944
NGL reserves, net, mbbl	7,458	6,714
Gas reserves, net, mmcf	78,553	70,441
BOE reserves, net, mbbl	156,833	167,016

Recent Merger and Acquisition Activity

Status: completed **Announced:** Sept. 30, 2022
Frontera Energy Corporation acquired the remaining 40.07% interest in Pipeline Investment Ltd. for US$47,400,000. Pipeline Investment holds 35% interest in Oleoducto de los Llanos Orientales S.A., which operates the ODL pipeline in Colombia running from Rubiales Field and the Monterrey or Cusiana Station in Casanare, with a capacity of 300,000 bbl per day.

Status: completed **Revised:** Apr. 27, 2022
UPDATE: The transaction was completed. PREVIOUS: Frontera Energy Corporation agreed to acquire the remaining 35% working interest in El Dificil Block, which consists of producing gas fields in Colombia, from Petroquímica Comodoro Rivadavia S.A. for US$13,000,000. Closing was expected in the second half of 2022, subject to customary closing conditions and approval by the Agencia Nacional de Hidrocarburos.

Predecessor Detail - Name changed from Pacific Exploration & Production Corporation, June 12, 2017.

Directors - Gabriel de Alba, chr., Miami, Fla.; Orlando Cabrales Segovia, CEO, Bogota, Colombia; Luis F. Alarcon, Bogota, Colombia; Dr. W. Ellis Armstrong, London, Middx., United Kingdom; Russell Ford, Austin, Tex.; Veronique Giry, Calgary, Alta.

Other Exec. Officers - René Burgos Díaz, CFO; Luz Maria Zea, chief compliance officer; Ivan Arevalo, v-p, opers.; Alejandra Bonilla, v-p, legal & corp. sec.; Renata Campagnaro, v-p, mktg., logistics & bus. sustainability; Victor Vega, v-p, field devel., reservoir mgt. & explor.

Capital Stock

	Authorized (shs.)	Outstanding (shs.)[1]
Preferred	unlimited	nil
Common	unlimited	85,188,573

[1] At May 2, 2023

Major Shareholder - The Catalyst Capital Group Inc. held 40.82% interest and Gramercy Funds Management LLC held 12.72% interest at Mar. 30, 2023.

Price Range - FEC/TSX

Year	Volume	High	Low	Close
2022	35,191,938	$15.95	$8.53	$12.27
2021	41,442,465	$10.35	$3.16	$10.24
2020	64,990,170	$10.74	$2.01	$3.21
2019	46,576,866	$15.16	$8.64	$9.80
2018	21,973,677	$23.46	$11.06	$13.38

Recent Close: $9.95

Capital Stock Changes - During 2022, 510,147 common shares were issued as share-based compensation, 5,416,666 common shares were repurchased under a Substantial Issuer Bid and 4,197,100 common shares were repurchased under a Normal Course Issuer Bid.

Long-Term Debt - Outstanding at Dec. 31, 2022:

Loans[1]	US$12,828,000
Credit facility[2]	103,094,000
7.875% sr. notes due 2028	392,535,000
	508,457,000
Less: Current portion	115,922,000
	392,535,000

[1] Bearing interest at LIBOR plus 4.95% and due December 2023.
[2] Bearing interest at LIBOR plus 5% and due June 2025.

Wholly Owned Subsidiaries

Frontera Bahia Holding Ltd., British Virgin Islands.
- 98.33% int. in **Infrastructure Ventures Inc.**, British Virgin Islands. Formerly Pacific Infrastructure Ventures Inc.
  - 11.95% int. in **Sociedad Portuaria Puerto Bahia S.A.**, Colombia.
- 74.15% int. in **Sociedad Portuaria Puerto Bahia S.A.**, Colombia.

Frontera Energy Guyana Holding Ltd., Bermuda.
- 100% int. in **Frontera Energy Guyana Corp.**, Bahamas.

Frontera ODL Holding Corp., Bahamas.
- 100% int. in **Pipeline Investment Ltd.**, Bermuda.
  - 35% int. in **Oleoducto de los Llanos Orientales S.A.**, Panama.

Frontera Petroleum International Holdings B.V., Netherlands.
- 100% int. in **Frontera Energy Colombia AG**, Switzerland.
  - 13.86% int. in **Sociedad Portuaria Puerto Bahia S.A.**, Colombia.
- 100% int. in **Petroleos Sud Americanos S.A.**, Colombia.

Pacific Stratus Energy S.A., Panama.
- 87.6% int. in **Frontera Energy del Peru S.A.**, Peru.
- 99.99% int. in **Frontera Energy Off Shore Peru S.R.L.**, Peru.

Petro International Ltd., Bahamas.
- 100% int. in **Petrominerales Bermuda Ltd.**, Bermuda.
  - **Frontera Energy del Peru S.A.**, Peru.
  - 100% int. in **Petrominerales Peru Ltd.**, Bermuda.
    - 12.39% int. in **Frontera Energy del Peru S.A.**, Peru.

Subsidiaries

76.05% int. in **CGX Energy Inc.**, Toronto, Ont. (see Survey of Mines)

Investments

0.01% int. in **Frontera Energy Off Shore Peru S.R.L.**, Peru.

Note: The preceding list includes only the major related companies in which interests are held.

Financial Statistics

Periods ended:	12m Dec. 31/22[A]		12m Dec. 31/21[A]
	US$000s	%Chg	US$000s
Operating revenue	**1,270,758**	**+42**	**894,061**
Exploration expense	2,369		1,513
General & admin expense	55,063		52,134
Stock-based compensation	9,140		8,394
Other operating expense	568,571		412,011
Operating expense	**635,143**	**+34**	**474,052**
Operating income	**635,615**	**+51**	**420,009**
Deprec., depl. & amort.	195,419		126,692
Finance income	5,505		5,362
Finance costs, gross	52,991		51,822
Investment income	42,043		38,033
Write-downs/write-offs	205,833		559,188
Pre-tax income	**540,310**	**-15**	**637,105**
Income taxes	249,275		1,039
Net income	**291,035**	**-54**	**636,066**
Net inc. for equity hldrs	**286,615**	**-54**	**628,133**
Net inc. for non-cont. int	**4,420**	**-44**	**7,933**
Cash & equivalent	289,845		257,504
Inventories	75,109		50,076
Accounts receivable	87,948		115,515
Current assets	509,450		517,160
Long-term investments	61,846		88,366
Fixed assets, net	1,760,780		1,532,751
Explor./devel. properties	320,580		188,904
Total assets	**2,738,455**	**+5**	**2,611,080**
Accts. pay. & accr. liabs	466,580		402,595
Current liabilities	619,057		596,045
Long-term debt, gross	508,457		552,562
Long-term debt, net	392,535		405,838
Long-term lease liabilities	545		3,332
Shareholders' equity	1,579,347		1,400,966
Non-controlling interest	9,857		47,925
Cash from oper. activs	**620,479**	**+90**	**327,380**
Cash from fin. activs	(193,604)		(108,381)
Cash from invest. activs	(383,266)		(186,943)
Net cash position	**289,845**	**+13**	**257,504**
Capital expenditures	(415,660)		(311,762)
	US$		US$
Earnings per share*	3.16		6.50
Cash flow per share*	6.84		3.39
	shs		shs
No. of shs. o/s*	85,592,075		94,695,694
Avg. no. of shs. o/s*	90,743,301		96,691,579
	%		%
Net profit margin	22.90		71.14
Return on equity	19.23		59.69
Return on assets	11.95		29.42
Foreign sales percent	100		100
No. of employees (FTEs)	1,191		1,145

* Common
[A] Reported in accordance with IFRS

Latest Results

Periods ended:	3m Mar. 31/23[A]		3m Mar. 31/22[A]
	US$000s	%Chg	US$000s
Operating revenue	250,366	-2	254,627
Net income	(11,415)	n.a.	101,980
Net inc. for equity hldrs	(11,330)	n.a.	102,228
Net inc. for non-cont. int	(85)		(248)
	US$		US$
Earnings per share*	(0.13)		1.08

* Common
[A] Reported in accordance with IFRS

Historical Summary
(as originally stated)

Fiscal Year	Oper. Rev.	Net Inc. Bef. Disc.	EPS*
	US$000s	US$000s	US$
2022[A]	1,270,758	291,035	3.16
2021[A]	894,061	636,066	6.50
2020[A]	648,508	(481,912)	(5.13)
2019[A]	1,383,577	305,799	3.01
2018[A]	1,320,485	(258,761)	(2.59)

* Common
[A] Reported in accordance with IFRS

F.68 Fuelpositive Corporation

Symbol - NHHH **Exchange** - TSX-VEN **CUSIP** - 35954F
Head Office - Unit B, 99 Northland Rd, Waterloo, ON, N2V 1Y8 **Telephone** - (416) 535-8395 **Toll-free** - (877) 817-7034 **Fax** - (416) 535-4043
Website - www.fuelpositive.com
Email - ian@fuelpositive.com
Investor Relations - Ian Clifford (416) 535-8395 ext. 3
Auditors - Clearhouse LLP C.A., Mississauga, Ont.
Lawyers - Kutkevicius Kirsh, LLP, Toronto, Ont.
Transfer Agents - TSX Trust Company, Toronto, Ont.
Profile - (Ont. 2004) Developing clean energy technologies including an on-farm/onsite, containerized green ammonia (NH_3) production system as well as supercapacitor energy storage technology.

Lead product, Green Ammonia Production System, converts air, water and sustainable electricity to produce green anhydrous ammonia for multiple applications including fertilizer for farming, fuel for grain drying, fuel for internal combustion engines and solution for grid storage. Pre-sales of the product started in August 2022.

Also holds technology rights to solid-state capacitor and related energy storage technologies, which is still under development, and development milestones must be achieved before commercial viability can be fully established.

Predecessor Detail - Name changed from EEStor Corporation, Feb. 9, 2021.
Directors - Ian Clifford, founder, chr. & CEO, Qué.; Nelson Leite, COO, Ont.; Olushola (Shola) Ashiru, New York, N.Y.; Gordon D. Ellis, Ont.; Lenore Newman, B.C.
Other Exec. Officers - Jing Peng, CFO; Dr. Abhijit Paul, v-p, R&D

Capital Stock

	Authorized (shs.)	Outstanding (shs.)[1]
Preferred	unlimited	nil
Common	unlimited	463,870,000

[1] At Aug. 16, 2023

Major Shareholder - Widely held at May 15, 2023.

Price Range - NHHH/TSX-VEN

Year	Volume	High	Low	Close
2022	53,968,505	$0.23	$0.11	$0.15
2021	223,543,676	$0.40	$0.05	$0.19
2020	27,506,952	$0.08	$0.01	$0.06
2019	30,640,936	$0.18	$0.02	$0.04
2018	25,294,969	$0.54	$0.10	$0.13

Recent Close: $0.06

Capital Stock Changes - In June and July 2023, private placement of 85,313,768 units (1 common share & 1 warrant) at $0.065 per unit was completed, with warrants exercisable at 9¢ per share for three years. In August 2023, 27,393,987 units (1 common share & 1 warrant) were issued at $0.065 per unit for settlement of $1,780,609 of debt.

In October 2021, private placement of 30,434,784 units (1 common share & 1 warrant) at 23¢ per unit was completed. Also during fiscal 2022, common shares were issued as follows: 15,000,000 for intellectual property rights, 6,278,700 on exercise of warrants, 6,000,000 on conversion of debentures and 4,800,000 on exercise of options.

Wholly Owned Subsidiaries

EEStor Limited
ZENN Capital Inc.
ZMC America, Inc.

Subsidiaries

71.3% int. in **EEStor, Inc.**, Tex.

Financial Statistics

Periods ended:	12m Sept. 30/22[A]		12m Sept. 30/21[A]
	$000s	%Chg	$000s
Salaries & benefits	2,557		2,326
Research & devel. expense	62		180
General & admin expense	3,068		1,640
Stock-based compensation	988		1,681
Operating expense	**6,674**	**+15**	**5,827**
Operating income	**(6,674)**	**n.a.**	**(5,827)**
Deprec., depl. & amort.	1,834		544
Finance income	28		nil
Finance costs, gross	10		83
Pre-tax income	**(14,300)**	**n.a.**	**(6,408)**
Net income	**(14,300)**	**n.a.**	**(6,408)**
Net inc. for equity hldrs	**(13,922)**	**n.a.**	**(6,613)**
Net inc. for non-cont. int	**(378)**	**n.a.**	**206**
Cash & equivalent	2,211		5,257
Current assets	3,685		5,688
Fixed assets, net	380		7
Right-of-use assets	154		nil
Intangibles, net	9,006		14,837
Total assets	**28,843**	**-12**	**32,846**
Bank indebtedness	nil		12
Accts. pay. & accr. liabs	1,119		1,548
Current liabilities	1,129		1,560
Long-term debt, gross	60		248
Long-term debt, net	60		248
Long-term lease liabilities	102		nil
Equity portion of conv. debs	nil		87
Shareholders' equity	32,088		35,196
Non-controlling interest	(4,536)		(4,158)
Cash from oper. activs	**(7,139)**	**n.a.**	**(4,001)**
Cash from fin. activs	7,158		9,662
Cash from invest. activs	(3,066)		(414)
Net cash position	**2,211**	**-58**	**5,257**
Capital expenditures	(396)		(8)
	$		$
Earnings per share*	(0.04)		(0.03)
Cash flow per share*	(0.02)		(0.02)
	shs		shs
No. of shs. o/s*	351,219,146		288,705,662
Avg. no. of shs. o/s*	335,775,993		214,953,188
	%		%
Net profit margin	n.a.		n.a.
Return on equity	(41.38)		(25.00)
Return on assets	(46.33)		(26.40)

* Common
[A] Reported in accordance with IFRS

Latest Results

Periods ended:	6m Mar. 31/23[A]		6m Mar. 31/22[A]
	$000s	%Chg	$000s
Net income	(6,209)	n.a.	(4,696)
Net inc. for equity hldrs	(6,269)	n.a.	(4,773)
Net inc. for non-cont. int	60		77
	$		$
Earnings per share*	(0.02)		(0.01)

* Common
[A] Reported in accordance with IFRS

Historical Summary
(as originally stated)

Fiscal Year	Oper. Rev.	Net Inc. Bef. Disc.	EPS*
	$000s	$000s	$
2022[A]	nil	(14,300)	(0.04)
2021[A]	nil	(6,408)	(0.03)
2020[A]	nil	(1,459)	(0.01)
2019[A]	nil	(6,656)	(0.05)
2018[A]	nil	(5,771)	(0.05)

* Common
[A] Reported in accordance with IFRS

F.69 Full Circle Lithium Corp.

Symbol - FCLI **Exchange** - TSX-VEN **CUSIP** - 359917
Head Office - 902-18 King St E, Toronto, ON, M5C 1C4 **Telephone** - (416) 214-9672
Website - fullcirclelithium.com
Email - cvicens@fullcirclelithium.com
Investor Relations - Carlos Vicens (416) 457-6529
Auditors - MNP LLP C.A., Toronto, Ont.
Transfer Agents - Marrelli Trust Company Limited, Toronto, Ont.
Profile - (Ont. 2021) Recycles and processes specialty chemicals with a focus on lithium and battery materials reintegration to meet expected demand growth for battery-grade raw materials in the U.S.

Sources and recovers lithium and other battery materials through three business divisions: battery recycling from end-of-life lithium-ion batteries; lithium feedstock recycling from industrial and chemical feedstock; and lithium refinery from upstream feedstock.

High purity battery materials recycled and processed include lithium, copper, aluminum, nickel, cobalt, manganese, iron phosphate and graphite. Leases a fully permitted lithium processing plant in Nahunta, Ga.., which is being refurbished in order to have a processing capacity of 2,000 tonnes per year of battery-grade lithium carbonate.

Recent Merger and Acquisition Activity

Status: completed **Revised:** Apr. 25, 2023
UPDATE: The transaction was completed. ESG issued a total of 63,039,786 post-consolidated common shares, inclusive of 12,185,786 subscription receipts issued by (old) Full Circle by private placement which were each exchanged without further consideration into 1 (new) Full Circle post-consolidated common share. PREVIOUS: ESG Capital 1 Inc. entered into a letter of intent for the Qualifying Transaction reverse takeover acquisition of private Ontario-based Full Circle Lithium Inc., a battery material processing company focused on lithium and battery materials reintegration, on a share-for-share basis (following a 1-for-1.17 share consolidation). Jan. 17, 2023 - A definitive agreement was entered into. Upon completion, Full Circle would amalgamate with ESG's wholly owned 1000412731 Ontario Inc. to form Full Circle Canada Inc., and ESG would change its name to Full Circle Lithium Corp.

Predecessor Detail - Name changed from ESG Capital 1 Inc., Apr. 19, 2023, pursuant to the Qualifying Transaction reverse takeover acquisition of Full Circle Lithium Inc. and concurrent amalgamation of (old) Full Circle with wholly owned 1000412731 Ontario Inc. (and continued as Full Circle Canada Inc.); basis 1 new for 1.17 old shs.

Directors - Paul Fornazzari, chr., Toronto, Ont.; Carlos Vicens, CEO, Mississauga, Ont.; Michael (Mike) Cosic, Toronto, Ont.; Franco Mignacco, Argentina; Orlee Wertheim, Toronto, Ont.

Other Exec. Officers - Thomas Currin, COO; Omar Gonzalez, CFO & corp. sec.; Dr. William (Bill) Bourcier, chief tech. officer

Capital Stock

	Authorized (shs.)	Outstanding (shs.)[1]
Common	unlimited	68,328,786

[1] At May 1, 2023

Major Shareholder - Carlos Vicens held 10.32% interest at May 1, 2023.

Price Range - FCLI/TSX-VEN

Year	Volume	High	Low	Close
2022	15,384	$0.70	$0.70	$0.70
2021	45,491	$0.82	$0.42	$0.67

Consolidation: 1-for-1.17 cons. in May 2023

Recent Close: $0.67

Capital Stock Changes - On Apr. 25, 2023, common shares were consolidated on a 1-for-1.17 basis (effective on the TSX Venture Exchange on May 1, 2023), 63,039,786 post-consolidated common shares were issued pursuant to the Qualifying Transaction reverse takeover acquisition of Full Circle Lithium Inc. and 1,789,000 units (1 post-consolidated common share & ½ warrant) were issued without further consideration on exchange of subscription receipts sold previously by private placement at Cdn$0.70 each.

There were no changes to capital stock during 2022.

Wholly Owned Subsidiaries

Full Circle Canada Inc., Ont.
- 100% int. in **Full Circle Lithium (US) Inc.**, Ga.

Financial Statistics

Periods ended:	23w Oct. 31/22[A1]
	US$000s
General & admin expense	212
Stock-based compensation	86
Operating expense	**298**
Operating income	**(298)**
Pre-tax income	**(298)**
Net income	**(298)**
Cash & equivalent	2,384
Accounts receivable	11
Current assets	2,402
Fixed assets, net	1,117
Right-of-use assets	481
Total assets	**4,000**
Accts. pay. & accr. liabs	144
Current liabilities	150
Long-term lease liabilities	485
Shareholders' equity	3,569
Cash from oper. activs	**(61)**
Cash from fin. activs	3,710
Cash from invest. activs	(1,122)
Net cash position	**2,384**
Capital expenditures	(1,117)
	US$
Earnings per share*	(0.01)
Cash flow per share*	(0.00)
	shs
No. of shs. o/s*	50,854,000
Avg. no. of shs. o/s*	37,367,350
	%

* Common
[A] Reported in accordance with IFRS
[1] Results pertain to Full Circle Lithium Inc.
Note: Adjusted throughout for 1-for-1.17 cons. in May 2023

F.70 Fusion Pharmaceuticals Inc.

Symbol - FUSN **Exchange** - NASDAQ **CUSIP** - 36118A
Head Office - 270 Longwood Rd S, Hamilton, ON, L8P 0A6 **Telephone** - (289) 799-0891 **Toll-free** - (888) 506-4125
Website - www.fusionpharma.com
Email - cray@fusionpharma.com
Investor Relations - Amanda Cray (888) 506-4125
Auditors - PricewaterhouseCoopers LLP C.P.A., Boston, Mass.
Lawyers - Goodwin Procter LLP, Boston, Mass.; Osler, Hoskin & Harcourt LLP, Toronto, Ont.
Transfer Agents - American Stock Transfer & Trust Company, LLC, New York, N.Y.
Employees - 86 at Mar. 7, 2022

Profile - (Can. 2014) Developing radiopharmaceuticals, which are drugs that contain medical isotopes, as precision medicines for the treatment of cancer.

The company is developing targeted alpha therapies (TATs), where alpha particles emitted from medical isotopes are used to kill cancer cells by creating lethal, double stranded DNA breaks. Through its TAT platform together with its proprietary Fast-Clear linker technology, the company connects alpha particle emitting isotopes to various targeting molecules in order to selectively deliver the alpha emitting payloads to tumours.

The lead product candidate, FPI-1434 (undergoing a Phase 1 clinical trial), utilizes the Fast-Clear™ linker to connect a humanized monoclonal antibody that targets the insulin-like growth factor 1 receptor, or IGF-1R, with actinium-225, or ^{225}Ac. Other products include FPI-1966 (advancing to a Phase 1 study following the investigational new drug clearance), which targets the fibroblast growth factor receptor 3 (FGFR3); and FPI-2059, a small molecule that targets neurotensin receptor 1 (NTSR1). In addition, the company has a collaboration with **AstraZeneca UK Limited** to jointly develop novel TATs and combination programs between the company's TATs and AstraZeneca's DNA Damage Repair Inhibitors (DDRis) and immuno-oncology agents; a clinical trial collaboration with **Merck & Co., Inc.** to evaluate FPI-1434 in combination with Merck's KEYTRUDA® (Pembrolizumab) in patients with solid tumours expressing IGF-1R; and a strategic research collaboration with **48 Hour Discovery Inc.** and **Pepscan Therapeutics B.V.** to discover novel peptide-based radiopharmaceuticals for the treatment of various solid tumours.

The company has an agreement with McMaster University in Hamilton, Ont., to build a 27,000-sq.-ft. radiopharmaceutical manufacturing facility that was expected to be operational by early 2024.

Directors - Dr. John Valliant, founder & CEO, Hamilton, Ont.; Barbara Duncan, chr., New York, N.Y.; Dr. Donald A. Bergstrom, Winchester, Mass.; Dr. Pablo Cagnoni, Cambridge, Mass.; Dr. Johan Christenson, Stockholm, Sweden; Steven Gannon, Montréal, Qué.; Chau Q. Khuong, New York, N.Y.; Dr. Philina Lee, Cambridge, Mass.; Dr. Heather Preston, San Francisco, Calif.

Other Exec. Officers - Mohit Rawat, pres. & chief bus. officer; John Crowley, CFO; Dr. Dmitri Bobilev, CMO; Cara Ferreira, chief of staff; Dr. Christopher Leamon, chief scientific officer; Maria D. Stahl, chief legal officer; Eric Hoffman, sr. v-p, bus. devel.; Victor Paulus, sr. v-p, regulatory affairs

Capital Stock

	Authorized (shs.)	Outstanding (shs.)[1]
Preferred	unlimited	nil
Common	unlimited	43,342,402

[1] At Apr. 18, 2022

Major Shareholder - Widely held at Apr. 1, 2022.

Price Range - FUSN/NASDAQ

Year	Volume	High	Low	Close
2022	2,219,869	US$8.73	US$1.98	US$3.15
2021	2,767,978	US$13.30	US$4.12	US$4.17
2020	5,418,938	US$19.00	US$11.40	US$11.75

Wholly Owned Subsidiaries

Fusion Pharmaceuticals US Inc., United States.

Financial Statistics

Periods ended:	12m Dec. 31/21[A]		12m Dec. 31/20[A]
	US$000s	%Chg	US$000s
Operating revenue	**1,440**	**n.a.**	**nil**
Research & devel. expense	52,988		15,801
General & admin expense	21,230		18,284
Stock-based compensation	8,603		3,368
Operating expense	**82,821**	**+121**	**37,453**
Operating income	**(81,381)**	**n.a.**	**(37,453)**
Deprec., depl. & amort.	634		482
Finance costs, net	(381)		38,794
Pre-tax income	**(81,165)**	**n.a.**	**(75,722)**
Income taxes	(118)		2,611
Net income	**(81,047)**	**n.a.**	**(78,333)**
Cash & equivalent	200,795		222,399
Accounts receivable	357		nil
Current assets	211,762		228,164
Long-term investments	19,987		77,082
Fixed assets, net	2,967		1,967
Right-of-use assets	6,486		nil
Total assets	**252,271**	**-19**	**310,676**
Accts. pay. & accr. liabs	9,758		8,058
Current liabilities	12,511		11,857
Long-term lease liabilities	5,507		nil
Shareholders' equity	231,456		294,513
Cash from oper. activs	**(75,740)**	**n.a.**	**(29,767)**
Cash from fin. activs	347		265,507
Cash from invest. activs	37,774		(210,453)
Net cash position	**54,789**	**-41**	**92,408**
Capital expenditures	(1,491)		(1,123)
	US$		US$
Earnings per share*	(1.90)		(3.62)
Cash flow per share*	(1.78)		(1.35)
	shs		shs
No. of shs. o/s*	43,073,727		41,725,797
Avg. no. of shs. o/s*	42,598,843		22,033,269
	%		%
Net profit margin	n.m.		n.a.
Return on equity	(30.82)		n.m.
Return on assets	(28.79)		(41.22)

* Common
[A] Reported in accordance with U.S. GAAP

Latest Results

Periods ended:	3m Mar. 31/22[A]		3m Mar. 31/21[A]
	US$000s	%Chg	US$000s
Operating revenue	585	n.a.	nil
Net income	(19,909)	n.a.	(17,529)
	US$		US$
Earnings per share*	(0.46)		(0.42)

* Common
[A] Reported in accordance with U.S. GAAP

Historical Summary
(as originally stated)

Fiscal Year	Oper. Rev. US$000s	Net Inc. Bef. Disc. US$000s	EPS* US$
2021[A]	1,440	(81,047)	(1.90)
2020[A]	nil	(78,333)	(3.62)
2019[§A]	nil	(16,189)	n.a.
2018[A]	nil	(11,652)	n.a.

* Common
§ Pro forma
[A] Reported in accordance with U.S. GAAP

G

G.1 G2 Energy Corp.

Symbol - GTOO **Exchange** - CSE **CUSIP** - 40054T
Head Office - 209-1120 Hamilton St, Vancouver, BC, V6B 2S2 **Telephone** - (778) 775-4985
Website - www.g2.energy
Email - slawek@g2.energy
Investor Relations - Slawomir Smulewicz (778) 775-4985
Auditors - Dale Matheson Carr-Hilton LaBonte LLP C.A., Vancouver, B.C.
Transfer Agents - Endeavor Trust Corporation, Vancouver, B.C.
Profile - (B.C. 2014) Explores for, develops and produces oil and gas in the U.S.

Holds the Masten Unit, a 2,600-acre producing oil and gas field in the Permian basin in Levelland, Tex., with production of 72 bbl per day and 75 mcf per day from 16 active wells as at July 1, 2022. There are eight additional shut-in wells and 16 injection wells in the Masten Unit.

At July 1, 2022, net proved plus probable reserves totaled 614,000 bbl oil and 832,910 mcf gas.

In September 2022, the company agreed to acquire **Bridwell Oil Company**'s Masten lease in Texas for $270,000.

Recent Merger and Acquisition Activity

Status: terminated **Revised:** Sept. 16, 2022
UPDATE: The transaction was terminated. PREVIOUS: G2 Energy Corp. agreed to acquire additional oil and gas properties in the Permian Basin in Cochran cty., Tex., for US$7,600,000 cash and issuance of 1,002,765 common shares at a deemed price of US$0.20 per share. The properties consist of five leases totaling 4,826 gross (3,876 net) acres within the Levelland field, which were producing 130 bbl of oil per day and 35 mcf per day of gas from 54 active wells.

Status: completed **Revised:** May 31, 2022
UPDATE: The transaction was completed. PREVIOUS: G2 Technologies Corp. signed a letter of intent to acquire 30 operated producing oil wells in Cochran cty., Tex., from a group of individuals and companies for US4,000,000 cash and issuance of US$200,000 in G2 common shares. Dec. 24, 2021 - G2 signed a purchase and sales agreement with a group of individuals and companies including Texas-based Jala Capital Investments, LLC and Reagan Oil & Gas, LLC. The acquisition would result in a change of business for G2. May 20, 2022 - The transaction was amended whereby G2 would acquire combined operating producing oil and gas properites known as the Masten unit and other related assets in Texas. The consideration was US$4,000,000, consisting of US$400,000 cash, issuance of a US$1,600,000 promissory note and US$2,000,000 paid with funds raised from a debenture financing.

Predecessor Detail - Name changed from G2 Technologies Corp., June 9, 2022, following change of business from the production of residential and commercial wood pellets in Europe to a U.S.-focused oil and gas company.

Directors - Slawomir (Slawek) Smulewicz, exec. chr., CEO & corp. sec., Vancouver, B.C.; David (Dave) Whitby, pres. & COO, Amsterdam, Netherlands; Gabriel M. Queiroz, CFO; John Costigan, v-p, corp. devel., Vancouver, B.C.; Kai Hensler, B.C.; Markus Mair

Capital Stock

	Authorized (shs.)	Outstanding (shs.)[1]
Preferred	unlimited	nil
Common	unlimited	18,339,577

[1] At June 9, 2023

Major Shareholder - Widely held at June 14, 2022.

Price Range - GTOO/CSE

Year	Volume	High	Low	Close
2022	2,290,184	$1.33	$0.18	$0.28
2021	1,213,421	$1.60	$0.33	$0.40
2020	280,337	$3.00	$0.50	$0.50
2019	269,388	$9.50	$0.50	$0.50
2018	784,240	$44.50	$5.00	$8.00

Consolidation: 1-for-5 cons. in June 2023; 1-for-20 cons. in Jan. 2021

Recent Close: $0.06

Capital Stock Changes - In October 2022, private placement of 1,285,000 units (1 post-consolidated common share & ½ warrant) at 50¢ per unit was completed, with warrants exercisable at $1.00 per share for two years. On June 9, 2023, common shares were consolidated on a 1-for-5 basis.

During fiscal 2022, common shares were issued as follows: 22,329,950 by private placement, 5,000,000 on acquisition of oil and gas properties and 80,000 on exercise of warrants.

Wholly Owned Subsidiaries

G2 Energy USA Corp., Canada.
- 100% int. in **G2 Energy Holding US, Inc.**, United States.
  - 100% int. in **G2 Energy TX1, Inc.**, United States.
  - 100% int. in **G2 Energy TX2, Inc.**, United States.

Financial Statistics

Periods ended:	12m June 30/22[A]		12m June 30/21[A]
	$000s	%Chg	$000s
Operating revenue	**229**	**n.a.**	**nil**
Cost of sales	53		nil
General & admin expense	2,634		950
Stock-based compensation	136		84
Operating expense	**2,823**	**+173**	**1,034**
Operating income	**(2,594)**	**n.a.**	**(1,034)**
Deprec., depl. & amort.	17		nil
Finance costs, gross	59		27
Pre-tax income	**(3,196)**	**n.a.**	**(869)**
Net income	**(3,196)**	**n.a.**	**(869)**
Cash & equivalent	202		159
Accounts receivable	288		97
Current assets	658		258
Fixed assets, net	7,130		nil
Total assets	**7,788**	**n.m.**	**258**
Accts. pay. & accr. liabs	406		171
Current liabilities	1,442		187
Long-term debt, gross	4,433		32
Long-term debt, net	3,847		32
Shareholders' equity	1,216		40
Cash from oper. activs	**(2,158)**	**n.a.**	**(1,347)**
Cash from fin. activs	5,402		1,502
Cash from invest. activs	(3,202)		nil
Net cash position	**202**	**+27**	**159**
	$		$
Earnings per share*	(0.45)		(0.35)
Cash flow per share*	(0.30)		(0.53)
	shs		shs
No. of shs. o/s*	10,157,217		4,675,227
Avg. no. of shs. o/s*	7,124,705		2,531,127
	%		%
Net profit margin	n.m.		n.a.
Return on equity	(508.92)		n.m.
Return on assets	(77.98)		(516.56)

* Common
[A] Reported in accordance with IFRS

Latest Results

Periods ended:	3m Sept. 30/22[A]		3m Sept. 30/21[A]
	$000s	%Chg	$000s
Operating revenue	448	n.a.	nil
Net income	(222)	n.a.	(221)
	$		$
Earnings per share*	(0.02)		(0.05)

* Common
[A] Reported in accordance with IFRS

Historical Summary
(as originally stated)

Fiscal Year	Oper. Rev. $000s	Net Inc. Bef. Disc. $000s	EPS* $
2022[A]	229	(3,196)	(0.45)
2021[A]	nil	(869)	(0.35)
2020[A]	570	(741)	(1.00)
2019[A]	1,432	(1,904)	(2.00)
2018[A1]	896	(7,561)	(11.00)

* Common
[A] Reported in accordance with IFRS
[1] Results reflect the July 21, 2017, reverse takeover acquisition of (old) Green 2 Blue Energy Corp.

Note: Adjusted throughout for 1-for-5 cons. in June 2023; 1-for-20 cons. in Jan. 2021

G.2 G6 Materials Corp.

Symbol - GGG **Exchange** - TSX-VEN **CUSIP** - 361333
Head Office - 760 Koehler Ave, Unit 2, Ronkonkoma, NY, United States, 11779 **Telephone** - (631) 405-5115
Website - www.g6-materials.com
Email - daniel.stolyarov@graphene3dlab.com
Investor Relations - Dr. Daniel Stolyarov (631) 405-5116
Auditors - MNP LLP C.A.
Lawyers - Salley Bowes Harwardt Law Corp., Vancouver, B.C.
Transfer Agents - Endeavor Trust Corporation, Vancouver, B.C.
Profile - (B.C. 2011) Develops, manufactures and markets proprietary products based on graphene and other advanced materials for use in various industries including aerospace, automotive, healthcare, marine, medical prosthetics and military.

Operates in the following areas:

Air Purification and Hygiene - Has filed a provisional patent application which covers the method of manufacturing the graphene oxide-based anti-viral coating, and offers Breathe+ Pro Air Purifier, an antimicrobial graphene air filtration system that removes microbes, dust particles, smog, dander, pollen and volatile organic compounds from the air, as well as accompanying replacement filters.

Conductive Epoxies - Manufactures adhesive materials under the G6-Epoxy™ brand, which are specialty adhesive epoxies made with proprietary mix of high performance carbon fillers for the aerospace, automotive, electronics and communication industries. Products are categorized according into use: general purpose adhesives, for effective high-performance bonding, sealing and coating; flexible adhesives, which are optimized for applications requiring a soft or flexible bond; high-temperature adhesives; and room temperature adhesives, which are for bonding of sensitive components at room temperature.

High Performance Composites - Develops advanced composites formulation based on graphene additives which are used to improve performance of fibre composite laminates including carbon fibre and fibreglass composites that are used for making marine vessels and structures, construction, automotive and aerospace. The laminated composites enhanced with graphene have better fatigue resistance, better shock absorbent properties and lower water absorption.

R&D Materials - Owns Graphene Supermarket® (www.graphene-supermarket.com), an e-commerce platform which sells extensive selection of graphene and other 2D-based R&D materials including reduced graphene oxide in powder or solution form; CVD grown graphene transferred onto substrates such as silicon dioxide, glass, and quartz; and graphene on TEM grids, graphene aerogels and foams. All products can be customized and bulk quantities of which can be manufactured on demand.

Graphene Manufacturing Process - Owns a patent for an energy-efficient and chemically non-invasive process that significantly lowers the cost of preparing and separating high-quality graphene nanoplatelets that is only a few atomic layers thick.

The company has an 8,000-sq.-ft. facility in Ronkonkoma, N.Y., and a 3,895-sq.-ft. office and warehouse facility in Cerritos, Calif. In addition, the company has five U.S. patents granted and five patent applications filed.

Predecessor Detail - Name changed from Graphene 3D Lab Inc., Jan. 23, 2020.

Directors - John Gary Dyal, chr., N.Y.; Dr. Elena Polyakova, co-CEO, N.Y.; Dr. Daniel Stolyarov, pres., co-CEO & chief tech. officer, N.Y.; Guy Bourgeois

Other Exec. Officers - Kevin Cornish, CEO & CFO; Jeffrey T. (Jeff) Dare, corp. sec.; Scott Van Pelt, contr.

Capital Stock

	Authorized (shs.)	Outstanding (shs.)[1]
Common	unlimited	16,367,919

[1] At July 12, 2023

Major Shareholder - Widely held at Nov. 8, 2021.

Price Range - GGG/TSX-VEN

Year	Volume	High	Low	Close
2022	2,140,078	$1.20	$0.35	$0.40
2021	5,937,619	$4.70	$0.80	$1.10
2020	6,442,553	$1.45	$0.30	$0.75
2019	2,325,404	$1.15	$0.40	$0.45
2018	2,761,150	$2.45	$0.50	$0.65

Consolidation: 1-for-10 cons. in July 2023

Recent Close: $0.24

Capital Stock Changes - On July 12, 2023, common shares were consolidated on a 1-for-10 basis.

In August 2021, 25,000,000 common shares were issued pursuant to the acquisition of GX Technologies LLC.

Wholly Owned Subsidiaries

GX Technologies LLC, N.C.
Graphene Laboratories, Inc., Calverton, N.Y.
Graphene 3D Lab (U.S.) Inc., Calverton, N.Y.

Financial Statistics

Periods ended:	12m May 31/22[A]		12m May 31/21[A]
	US$000s	%Chg	US$000s
Operating revenue	**1,358**	**-30**	**1,940**
Cost of goods sold	755		1,422
Salaries & benefits	509		172
Research & devel. expense	179		166
General & admin expense	1,486		1,149
Stock-based compensation	180		269
Operating expense	**3,109**	**-2**	**3,177**
Operating income	**(1,751)**	**n.a.**	**(1,237)**
Deprec., depl. & amort.	196		183
Finance costs, gross	11		7
Pre-tax income	**(4,736)**	**n.a.**	**(1,130)**
Net income	**(4,736)**	**n.a.**	**(1,130)**
Cash & equivalent	2,119		4,879
Inventories	970		387
Accounts receivable	52		25
Current assets	3,360		5,432
Fixed assets, net	115		28
Right-of-use assets	112		234
Intangibles, net	175		218
Total assets	**3,762**	**-36**	**5,913**
Accts. pay. & accr. liabs	148		150
Current liabilities	262		238
Long-term lease liabilities	nil		150
Shareholders' equity	3,500		5,525
Cash from oper. activs	**(2,283)**	**n.a.**	**(1,240)**
Cash from fin. activs	(166)		5,381
Cash from invest. activs	(106)		(9)
Net cash position	**2,119**	**-57**	**4,879**
Capital expenditures	(106)		(9)
	US$		US$
Earnings per share*	(0.40)		(0.10)
Cash flow per share*	(0.18)		(0.12)
	shs		shs
No. of shs. o/s*	16,367,919		13,867,919
Avg. no. of shs. o/s*	12,835,170		10,335,170
	%		%
Net profit margin	(348.75)		(58.25)
Return on equity	(104.95)		(36.21)
Return on assets	(97.67)		(31.73)
Foreign sales percent	100		100

* Common
[A] Reported in accordance with IFRS

Latest Results

Periods ended:	3m Aug. 31/22[A]		3m Aug. 31/21[A]
	US$000s	%Chg	US$000s
Operating revenue	358	+5	341
Net income	(648)	n.a.	(571)
	US$		US$
Earnings per share*	(0.05)		(0.04)

* Common
[A] Reported in accordance with IFRS

Historical Summary
(as originally stated)

Fiscal Year	Oper. Rev. US$000s	Net Inc. Bef. Disc. US$000s	EPS* US$
2022[A]	1,358	(4,736)	(0.40)
2021[A]	1,940	(1,130)	(0.10)
2020[A]	923	(1,014)	(0.10)
2019[A]	947	(599)	(0.10)
2018[A]	910	(1,064)	(0.20)

* Common
[A] Reported in accordance with IFRS
Note: Adjusted throughout for 1-for-10 cons. in July 2023

G.3 GABY Inc.

Symbol - GABY **Exchange** - CSE **CUSIP** - 36257J
Head Office - 3414 Standish Ave, Santa Rosa, CA, United States, 95407 **Toll-free** - (800) 674-2239
Website - www.gabyinc.com
Email - ir@gabyinc.com
Investor Relations - Margot M. Micallef
Auditors - Davidson & Company LLP C.A., Vancouver, B.C.
Transfer Agents - Odyssey Trust Company, Calgary, Alta.
Profile - (Alta. 2003) Winding down operations.

Previously had cannabis retail operations in California, including Mankind cannabis dispensary in San Diego, Calif.

In August 2021, the company announced the closure of operations at wholly owned **Sonoma Pacific Distribution Inc.** in Santa Rosa, Calif., and the consolidation of its manufacturing and distribution operations at **Wild West Industries, Inc.** in San Diego, Calif. Subsequently during the second quarter of 2022, operations ceased at Wild West.

Recent Merger and Acquisition Activity

Status: terminated **Revised:** June 1, 2023

UPDATE: The transaction was terminated. PREVIOUS: Hempfusion Wellness Inc. agreed to sell wholly owned HempFusion, Inc., which formulates, markets, distributes and sells natural supplements and products derived from industrial hemp extract and other natural ingredients, to GABY Inc. for issuance of 13,011,148 GABY post-consolidated common shares (following a 1-for-20 share consolidation). The transaction would represent the sale of substantially all of Hempfusion Wellness's assets.

Predecessor Detail - Name changed from Gabriella's Kitchen Inc., Oct. 22, 2019.

Capital Stock

	Authorized (shs.)	Outstanding (shs.)[1]
Preferred	unlimited	nil
Common	unlimited	733,947,041

[1] At May 1, 2023

Major Shareholder - Ebon Johnson held 10.26% interest, Margot M. Micallef held 10.1% interest and Corriente Master Fund II, LP held 10% interest at Mar. 29, 2022.

Price Range - GABY/CSE

Year	Volume	High	Low	Close
2022	51,193,942	$0.03	$0.01	$0.01
2021	75,540,062	$0.15	$0.03	$0.03
2020	31,544,082	$0.12	$0.03	$0.05
2019	50,141,517	$0.48	$0.07	$0.10
2018	10,630,670	$0.75	$0.27	$0.27

Recent Close: $0.01

Wholly Owned Subsidiaries

GK Brands Inc., Calif.
Gabriella's Kitchen LLC, Del.
Miramar Professional Services, Inc., San Diego, Calif.
- 100% int. in **Wild West Industries, Inc.**, San Diego, Calif.

Raw Chocolate Alchemy LLC, Calif.
2Rise Naturals LLC, Ariz.

Financial Statistics

Periods ended:	12m Dec. 31/21[A]		12m Dec. 31/20[A]
	$000s	%Chg	$000s
Operating revenue	**32,435**	**+697**	**4,072**
Cost of goods sold	18,776		3,315
Salaries & benefits	6,922		3,821
General & admin expense	5,399		3,770
Stock-based compensation	1,551		637
Operating expense	**32,647**	**+183**	**11,544**
Operating income	**(212)**	**n.a.**	**(7,472)**
Deprec., depl. & amort.	1,688		350
Finance costs, gross	3,341		538
Write-downs/write-offs	(2,374)		(4,694)
Pre-tax income	**(9,785)**	**n.a.**	**(13,138)**
Income taxes	2,462		(309)
Net inc. bef. disc. opers	**(12,247)**	**n.a.**	**(12,829)**
Income from disc. opers	nil		(1,162)
Net income	**(12,247)**	**n.a.**	**(13,991)**
Cash & equivalent	4,068		103
Inventories	1,342		643
Accounts receivable	160		611
Current assets	6,660		1,527
Fixed assets, net	7,853		1,095
Intangibles, net	46,763		2,392
Total assets	**65,895**	**n.m.**	**5,037**
Bank indebtedness	19		1,656
Accts. pay. & accr. liabs	8,218		7,065
Current liabilities	14,002		9,583
Long-term debt, gross	34,741		947
Long-term debt, net	33,270		207
Long-term lease liabilities	744		569
Shareholders' equity	3,888		(5,340)
Cash from oper. activs	**116**	**n.a.**	**(1,703)**
Cash from fin. activs	5,820		993
Cash from invest. activs	(2,002)		102
Net cash position	**4,068**	**n.m.**	**103**
Capital expenditures	(40)		(7)
Capital disposals	136		110
	$		$
Earns. per sh. bef disc opers*	(0.02)		(0.05)
Earnings per share*	(0.02)		(0.06)
Cash flow per share*	0.00		(0.01)
	shs		shs
No. of shs. o/s*	683,326,319		237,793,408
Avg. no. of shs. o/s*	539,476,460		228,937,349
	%		%
Net profit margin	(37.76)		(315.05)
Return on equity	n.m.		n.m.
Return on assets	(22.74)		(98.81)
Foreign sales percent	100		100

* Common
[A] Reported in accordance with IFRS

Latest Results

Periods ended:	9m Sept. 30/22[A]		9m Sept. 30/21[¤A]
	US$000s	%Chg	US$000s
Operating revenue	16,321	-16	19,429
Net income	(5,540)	n.a.	(6,690)
	US$		US$
Earnings per share*	(0.01)		(0.01)

* Common
[¤] Restated
[A] Reported in accordance with IFRS

Historical Summary
(as originally stated)

Fiscal Year	Oper. Rev. $000s	Net Inc. Bef. Disc. $000s	EPS* $
2021[A]	32,435	(12,247)	(0.02)
2020[A]	4,072	(12,829)	(0.05)
2019[A]	11,888	(22,788)	(0.16)
2018[A1]	2,442	(7,721)	(0.12)
2017[A]	1,275	(3,760)	(0.09)

* Common
[A] Reported in accordance with IFRS
[1] Results adjusted to reflect 7-for-1 share split effective Apr. 18, 2018.
Note: Earnings per share for 2018 and 2017 adjusted to reflect 7-for-1 share split effective Apr. 18, 2018.

G.4 GBLT Corp.

Symbol - GBLT **Exchange** - TSX-VEN **CUSIP** - 36150R
Head Office - An Gut Nazareth 18 A, Duren, Germany, 52353 **Overseas Tel** - 49-2421-208-56-0 **Overseas Fax** - 49-2421-208-56-29
Website - www.gbt-international.com
Email - investor@gbltcorp.com
Investor Relations - Dr. Thilo Senst 49-2421-20856-0
Auditors - Dale Matheson Carr-Hilton LaBonte LLP C.A., Vancouver, B.C.
Transfer Agents - TSX Trust Company, Toronto, Ont.
Profile - (Ont. 2014) Manufactures and distributes mobile power batteries, storage systems, solar panels, digital displays and LED lighting products under the Avide/ENTAC, AgfaPhoto and Extravolt® brands, as well as personal protection equipment and cannabidiol (CBD) products under the Dr. Senst brand, to largest retail chains worldwide.

Avide/ENTAC licences held by the company are for commercial-grade screens and commercial LED kiosks, LED light bulbs, LED lamps, under cabinet lights and other light bulbs and lighting ballasts, battery powered generators and mobile solar panels. The company sells Avide/ENTAC branded LED light bulbs globally, with the exception of the U.S.

Manufactures and sells medical consumable portfolio under the brand Dr. Senst. The products include personal protection equipment such as face masks, disinfectants, insect repellant, protective gloves, sanitizers, oximeters and thermometers. Also offers CBD mouth drops, nebulizers and pain therapy and massage.

Holds a licence from AgfaPhoto to distribute AgfaPhoto's entire suite of mobile energy products such as batteries, rechargeable batteries and chargers, and storage solutions products globally.

Also offers private installations of solar panels for residential homes, as well as for industrial and commercial projects through subsidiary **Gebäude Technologie Center GmbH**. The company plans to manufacture and distribute its own solar panels under the Extravolt® brand in 2023.

In addition, the company manufactures mobile power batteries, storage systems, digital displays and LED lighting as well as personal protective equipment for private label products.

Products are sold in supermarkets, department stores, drugstores, convenience stores, gas stations and others. Also supplies governments, public services and large industrial customers. The company has offices and facilities located across Western and Eastern Europe, Asia, and Commonwealth and Scandinavia.

Predecessor Detail - Name changed from CUP Capital Corp., Mar. 22, 2018.

Directors - Dr. Thilo Senst, CEO, Cologne, Germany; John Denham, Toronto, Ont.; Alfred Schopf, Germany

Other Exec. Officers - Sven Carbow, COO; Kyle Appleby, CFO

Capital Stock

	Authorized (shs.)	Outstanding (shs.)[1]
Common	unlimited	113,328,090

[1] At May 30, 2023

Major Shareholder - Dr. Thilo Senst held 66.43% interest at June 9, 2022.

Price Range - GBLT/TSX-VEN

Year	Volume	High	Low	Close
2022	3,429,195	$0.16	$0.04	$0.11
2021	11,690,177	$0.43	$0.11	$0.15
2020	18,383,438	$0.26	$0.02	$0.24
2019	5,836,813	$0.35	$0.05	$0.07
2018	6,063,985	$0.60	$0.10	$0.15

Recent Close: $0.06

Capital Stock Changes - There were no changes to capital stock during 2022.

Wholly Owned Subsidiaries

GBT GmbH, Germany.
- 100% int. in **SSD Stahlservice Deutschland UG**, Germany.

Investments

25% int. in **GBLT Africa (Pty) Ltd.**

Financial Statistics

Periods ended:	12m Dec. 31/22[A]		12m Dec. 31/21[A]
	€000s	%Chg	€000s
Operating revenue	**39,712**	**+28**	**31,112**
Cost of goods sold	35,700		28,568
Salaries & benefits	1,370		733
General & admin expense	1,928		1,140
Stock-based compensation	nil		119
Operating expense	**38,998**	**+28**	**30,560**
Operating income	**714**	**+29**	**552**
Deprec., depl. & amort.	106		50
Finance costs, gross	323		156
Write-downs/write-offs	(360)		(419)
Pre-tax income	**167**	**n.a.**	**(174)**
Net income	**167**	**n.a.**	**(174)**
Net inc. for equity hldrs	**173**	**n.a.**	**(174)**
Net inc. for non-cont. int.	**(6)**	**n.a.**	**nil**
Cash & equivalent	98		580
Inventories	4,198		2,469
Accounts receivable	2,567		2,729
Current assets	7,224		6,722
Long-term investments	nil		45
Fixed assets, net	223		25
Right-of-use assets	162		189
Intangibles, net	160		nil
Total assets	**7,921**	**+11**	**7,129**
Bank indebtedness	962		959
Accts. pay. & accr. liabs	3,702		4,464
Current liabilities	7,630		7,471
Long-term debt, gross	1,538		1,324
Long-term debt, net	564		50
Long-term lease liabilities	112		138
Shareholders' equity	(448)		(576)
Cash from oper. activs	**(104)**	**n.a.**	**(811)**
Cash from fin. activs	(203)		1,031
Cash from invest. activs	(175)		(27)
Net cash position	**98**	**-83**	**580**
Capital expenditures	(175)		(15)
	€		€
Earnings per share*	0.00		(0.00)
Cash flow per share*	(0.00)		(0.01)
	shs		shs
No. of shs. o/s*	113,328,090		113,328,090
Avg. no. of shs. o/s*	113,617,612		113,062,319
	%		%
Net profit margin	0.42		(0.56)
Return on equity	n.m.		n.m.
Return on assets	6.51		(0.27)

* Common
[A] Reported in accordance with IFRS

Latest Results

Periods ended:	3m Mar. 31/23[A]		3m Mar. 31/22[A]
	€000s	%Chg	€000s
Operating revenue	5,115	-36	8,039
Net income	(369)	n.a.	(18)
	€		€
Earnings per share*	(0.00)		(0.00)

* Common
[A] Reported in accordance with IFRS

Historical Summary
(as originally stated)

Fiscal Year	Oper. Rev.	Net Inc. Bef. Disc.	EPS*
	€000s	€000s	€
2022[A]	39,712	167	0.00
2021[A]	31,112	(174)	(0.00)
2020[A]	23,797	527	0.00
2019[A]	20,429	(1,099)	(0.01)
2018[A1]	20,701	(4,147)	(0.04)

* Common
[A] Reported in accordance with IFRS
[1] Results reflect the Mar. 22, 2018, Qualifying Transaction reverse takeover acquisition of GBLT German Battery & Lighting Technologies plc.

G.5 GCC Global Capital Corporation

Symbol - GCCC.H **Exchange** - TSX-VEN **CUSIP** - 36164U
Head Office - 270-3631 3 Rd, Richmond, BC, V6X 2B9 **Telephone** - (778) 389-9960 **Fax** - (604) 620-0557
Website - www.gcccglobal.com
Email - cahu@gcccglobal.com
Investor Relations - Yonghong Hu (778) 869-8001
Auditors - MNP LLP C.A., Vancouver, B.C.
Transfer Agents - TSX Trust Company, Toronto, Ont.
Profile - (Can. 2012) Invests in natural resources, real estate and high technology industries.

The company's sole investment is a 28.57% interest in **New Age Development Ltd.**, a private company which owns a 35,884-sq.-ft. parcel of land with a 939-sq.-ft. vacant log cabin structure in Calgary, Alta. Development plans include an eight-story, mixed-use commercial and residential building on the property.

Predecessor Detail - Name changed from CWN Mining Acquisition Corp, Jan. 3, 2018, following change of business acquisition of an interest in New Age Developments Ltd.

Directors - Haijian Liu, chr., Shenzhen, Guangdong, People's Republic of China; Huijun Wang, CEO, Surrey, B.C.; Qianying (Joanna) Zhou, Vancouver, B.C.

Other Exec. Officers - Yonghong (Cathy) Hu, CFO & corp. sec.; Wenjun Chu, v-p, invest.

Capital Stock

	Authorized (shs.)	Outstanding (shs.)[1]
Common	unlimited	12,527,200

[1] At Oct. 25, 2022

Major Shareholder - Haijian Liu held 77.36% interest at Nov. 12, 2021.

Price Range - GCCC.H/TSX-VEN

Year	Volume	High	Low	Close
2022	260,386	$0.10	$0.08	$0.10
2021	536,276	$0.09	$0.05	$0.08
2020	507,706	$0.21	$0.03	$0.05
2019	48,000	$0.08	$0.03	$0.07
2018	967,020	$0.25	$0.03	$0.05

Recent Close: $0.01

Capital Stock Changes - There were no changes to capital stock from fiscal 2016 to fiscal 2022, inclusive.

Investments

28.57% int. in **New Age Development Ltd.**, Alta.

Financial Statistics

Periods ended:	12m June 30/22[A]		12m June 30/21[A]
	$000s	%Chg	$000s
Salaries & benefits	163		316
General & admin. expense	82		63
Operating expense	**244**	**-36**	**379**
Operating income	**(244)**	**n.a.**	**(379)**
Deprec. & amort.	26		42
Finance costs, gross	178		133
Pre-tax income	**(482)**	**n.a.**	**(654)**
Net income	**(482)**	**n.a.**	**(654)**
Cash & equivalent	12		11
Accounts receivable	nil		11
Current assets	15		27
Long-term investments	829		910
Fixed assets, net	26		36
Right-of-use assets	nil		16
Total assets	**870**	**-12**	**989**
Accts. pay. & accr. liabs	31		23
Current liabilities	37		51
Long-term debt, gross	1,732		1,367
Long-term debt, net	1,732		1,367
Shareholders' equity	(900)		(428)
Cash from oper. activs	**(180)**	**n.a.**	**(350)**
Cash from fin. activs	180		308
Net cash position	**12**	**+9**	**11**
	$		$
Earnings per share*	(0.04)		(0.05)
Cash flow per share*	(0.01)		(0.03)
	shs		shs
No. of shs. o/s*	12,527,200		12,527,200
Avg. no. of shs. o/s*	12,527,200		12,527,200
	%		%
Net profit margin	n.a.		n.a.
Return on equity	n.m.		n.m.
Return on assets	(32.71)		(47.78)

* Common
[A] Reported in accordance with IFRS

Historical Summary
(as originally stated)

Fiscal Year	Total Rev.	Net Inc. Bef. Disc.	EPS*
	$000s	$000s	$
2022[A]	nil	(482)	(0.04)
2021[A]	nil	(654)	(0.05)
2020[A]	nil	(683)	(0.05)
2019[A]	nil	(820)	(0.07)
2018[A]	nil	(1,063)	(0.08)

* Common
[A] Reported in accordance with IFRS

G.6 GDI Integrated Facility Services Inc.

Symbol - GDI **Exchange** - TSX **CUSIP** - 361569
Head Office - 695 av 90e, LaSalle, QC, H8R 3A4 **Telephone** - (514) 368-1504 **Fax** - (514) 368-2500
Website - www.gdi.com
Email - david.hinchey@gdi.com
Investor Relations - David Hinchey (514) 368-8690 ext. 282
Auditors - KPMG LLP C.A., Montréal, Qué.
Lawyers - Fasken Martineau DuMoulin LLP, Montréal, Qué.
Transfer Agents - TSX Trust Company, Montréal, Qué.
FP500 Revenue Ranking - 208
Employees - 26,500 at Dec. 31, 2022
Profile - (Can. 2015; orig. B.C., 1998) Provides integrated commercial facility services in Canada and the U.S. including commercial cleaning services; building system controls, repair, servicing, energy performance optimization and other facility services; and distribution of cleaning and sanitation supplies.

Services are provided to owners and managers of various facilities such as office buildings, educational facilities, industrial facilities, healthcare establishments, stadiums and event venues, hotels, shopping centres, distribution facilities, large retailers, airports and other transportation facilities.

At Dec. 31, 2022, the company operated through various facilities located in 10 Canadian provinces and in more than 30 U.S. states. Business is carried on through three business lines: Janitorial Services; Technical Services; and Complimentary Services.

Janitorial Services - Provides daily or weekly services which can include cleaning and dusting desks and tables, vacuuming carpets, cleaning floors, sanitizing kitchens and washrooms, watering plants, cleaning exterior facilities, cleaning interior parking areas and removal of garbage. Also provides less frequent services (monthly, quarterly or annually) including stripping and waxing floors, carpet cleaning, heavy dust cleaning and window cleaning. Wholly owned **Modern Cleaning Concept L.P.** operates a network of about 700 independent franchisees that provide commercial cleaning services from small to large-size facilities across Canada.

Technical Services - Through wholly owned **Ainsworth Inc.** (Ontario), **ESC Automation Inc.**, **Ainsworth Inc.** (Delaware), **The BPAC Group Inc.**, and **Gestion E.C.I. Inc.**, provides building system controls installation, repairs and servicing coast to coast in Canada and in certain U.S. states. Building system repair and servicing includes the installation, control, repairs and servicing of the mechanical and electrical systems and equipment within a facility, as well as the installation and operation of the building automation systems that control and monitor the energy usage, environment, lighting, and various other systems within the facility. Systems and equipment which the company services include heating, ventilation and air conditioning (HVAC), refrigeration, mechanical and plumbing, cabling and communications, building automation and control, security systems, real-time locating systems and power systems. Also operates one motor shop that rebuilds, rewinds, reconditions and redesigns all types of AC and DC motors, pumps and generators, and provides high voltage services for the distribution and transmission of electricity. In addition, the company offers retrofitting and renovation services as well as turn-key solutions in energy and greenhouse gas reduction as well as provides turn-key solutions in energy and greenhouse gas reduction. These services are provided to commercial, industrial, institutional, government and multi-tenant residential building clients.

Complementary Services - This business includes the manufacturing and distribution of cleaning supplies and equipment; and integrated facility services. Through wholly owned **Superior Solutions L.P.**, manufactures and distributes cleaning supplies, distributes equipment and provides rental and repair services for cleaning equipment, servicing a diverse range of clients such as commercial properties, educational and government facilities and entertainment and hospitality complexes through distribution centres located in Ontario, Québec, Nova Scotia and Kansas; wholly owned **Fuller Industries, LLC**, operates a 585,000-sq.-ft. chemical and cleaning products manufacturing facility in Kansas, and manufactures a full line of cleaning chemicals as well as a range of cleaning products such as spray bottles, plastic containers, brooms and brushes for the commercial and industrial markets; and the company's integrated facility services, which provides full range of facility services required to operate and maintain a facility through a self performance model to clients interested in consolidating outsourced suppliers under one contract throughout North America.

Recent Merger and Acquisition Activity

Status: completed **Announced:** Sept. 1, 2022
GDI Integrated Facility Services Inc. acquired Bellevue, Wash.-based Cascadian Building Maintenance, Ltd., which provides janitorial services in the U.S., for an undisclosed amount.

Status: completed **Announced:** Mar. 1, 2022
GDI Integrated Facility Services Inc. acquired Markham, Ont.-based M.T.I. Mechanical Trade Industries Ltd., which provides mechanical services and installation in commercial or industrial heating, ventilation, air conditioning, plumbing and electrical as well as provides design/build construction management and mechanical construction, for an undisclosed amount.

Predecessor Detail - Name changed from Medwell Capital Corp., May 13, 2015, following reverse takeover acquisition of and amalgamation with (old) GDI Integrated Facility Services Inc.; basis 1 new for 10.4 old shs.

Directors - David G. Samuel, chr., Toronto, Ont.; Claude Bigras, pres. & CEO, Montréal, Qué.; Michael T. Boychuk†, Baie-d'Urfé, Qué.; Suzanne Blanchet, La Prairie, Qué.; Robert J. McGuire, N.Y.; Anne Ristic, Ont.; Richard G. Roy, Verchères, Qué.; Carl M. Youngman, Newton, Mass.

Other Exec. Officers - Fred Edwards, chief mktg. officer; Christian Marcoux, chief legal officer & corp. sec.; Bob Vukovic, CIO; David Hinchey, exec. v-p, corp. devel.; Kevin Padley, exec. v-p, integrated facility srvcs. & janitorial Cdn. sales; Jocelyn Trottier, exec. v-p; Stéphane Lavigne, sr. v-p & CFO; Mike A. Boomrod, pres., GDI Services Inc.; Craig Rudin, pres. & CEO, Superior Solution GP Inc.; Craig Stanford, pres. & COO, Ainsworth Inc.; Avi Steinberg, pres., GDI Services (Quebec) L.P. & pres., Modern Cleaning Concept GP Inc.

† Lead director

Capital Stock

	Authorized (shs.)	Outstanding (shs.)[1]
Preferred	unlimited	nil
Multiple Voting	unlimited	8,741,200
Subordinte Voting	unlimited	14,672,296

[1] At Mar. 15, 2023

Multiple Voting - All held by entities of Birch Hill Equity Partners Management Inc. and Claude Bigras. Convertible at any time at the option of the holder into subordinate voting shares on a one-for-one basis. Automatically convert into subordinate voting shares, if the number of multiple voting shares held by Birch Hill or Claude Bigras falls below 10% of the total subordinate and multiple voting shares outstanding or those held by Claude Bigras if he is no longer president or director of the company. If the number votes attached to multiple voting shares exceeds 40% of the total number of subordinate and multiple voting shares outstanding, the votes attached to multiple voting shares will automatically decrease proportionately such that the multiple voting shares as a class do not carry more than 40% of the aggregate votes attached to all issued and outstanding shares. Four votes per share.

Subordinate Voting - One vote per share.

Major Shareholder - Birch Hill Equity Partners Management Inc. held 29.3% interest and Claude Bigras held 12% interest at Mar. 15, 2023.

Price Range - GDI/TSX

Year	Volume	High	Low	Close
2022	3,792,763	$59.32	$41.00	$45.50
2021	4,624,453	$60.00	$41.00	$53.81
2020	4,059,809	$47.50	$24.19	$44.47
2019	2,091,429	$37.25	$18.38	$33.83
2018	1,364,298	$19.90	$15.06	$18.48

Recent Close: $41.55

Capital Stock Changes - During 2022, subordinate voting shares were issued as follows: 340,000 on exercise of options and 100,000 in exchange for a like number of multiple voting shares; 47,000 subordinate voting shares were repurchased under a Normal Course Issuer Bid.

Wholly Owned Subsidiaries

GDI Integrated Facility Services USA Inc., Del.
- 100% int. in **Ainsworth Inc.**, Del.
  - 100% int. in **The BPAC Group, Inc.**, N.Y.
- 100% int. in **Cascadian Building Maintenance, Ltd.**, Bellevue, Wash.
- 100% int. in **GDI Services Inc.**, United States.
- 100% int. in **IH Services, Inc.**, Greenville, S.C.

Modern Cleaning Concept GP Inc., Canada.
- 0.1% int. in **Modern Cleaning Concept L.P.**, Qué.

9266135 Canada Inc., Canada.
- 100% int. in **Ainsworth Inc.**, Toronto, Ont.
  - 100% int. in **ESC Automation Inc.**, Vancouver, B.C.
  - 100% int. in **Gestion E.C.I. Inc.**, Montréal, Qué.
  - 100% int. in **M.T.I. Mechanical Trade Industries Ltd.**, Markham, Ont.
- 0.1% int. in **GDI Services (Canada) LP**, Canada.
- 0.1% int. in **GDI Services (Québec) LP**, Qué.

Super Solutions GP Inc., Canada.
- 0.1% int. in **Super Solutions L.P.**, Qué.

Subsidiaries

99.9% int. in **GDI Services (Canada) LP**, Canada.
99.9% int. in **GDI Services (Québec) LP**, Qué.
99.9% int. in **Modern Cleaning Concept L.P.**, Qué.
99.9% int. in **Super Solutions L.P.**, Qué.

Financial Statistics

Periods ended:	12m Dec. 31/22[A]		12m Dec. 31/21[A]
	$000s	%Chg	$000s
Operating revenue	**2,172,000**	**+36**	**1,597,169**
Cost of sales	1,733,000		1,257,188
General & admin expense	294,000		214,106
Operating expense	**2,027,000**	**+38**	**1,471,294**
Operating income	**145,000**	**+15**	**125,875**
Deprec., depl. & amort.	74,000		52,111
Finance costs, net	19,000		20,230
Pre-tax income	**49,000**	**-23**	**63,567**
Income taxes	13,000		20,202
Net income	**36,000**	**-17**	**43,365**
Cash & equivalent	7,000		24,315
Inventories	45,000		34,214
Accounts receivable	524,000		430,697
Current assets	606,000		514,329
Fixed assets, net	122,000		117,267
Intangibles, net	483,000		444,802
Total assets	**1,220,000**	**+12**	**1,084,658**
Bank indebtedness	10,000		2,604
Accts. pay. & accr. liabs	286,000		250,076
Current liabilities	397,000		356,897
Long-term debt, gross	388,000		327,247
Long-term debt, net	345,000		298,868
Shareholders' equity	439,000		391,028
Cash from oper. activs	**50,000**	**-57**	**116,979**
Cash from fin. activs	(10,000)		88,238
Cash from invest. activs	(63,000)		(182,041)
Net cash position	**(3,000)**	**n.a.**	**21,711**
Capital expenditures	(19,000)		(15,123)
Capital disposals	nil		956
	$		$
Earnings per share*	1.57		1.89
Cash flow per share*	2.15		5.09
	shs		shs
No. of shs. o/s*	23,414,000		23,121,000
Avg. no. of shs. o/s*	23,242,000		22,974,000
	%		%
Net profit margin	1.66		2.72
Return on equity	8.67		11.88
Return on assets	3.12		4.73
Foreign sales percent	44		34
No. of employees (FTEs)	26,500		29,500

* S.V. & M.V.
[A] Reported in accordance with IFRS

Historical Summary
(as originally stated)

Fiscal Year	Oper. Rev.	Net Inc. Bef. Disc.	EPS*
	$000s	$000s	$
2022[A]	2,172,000	36,000	1.57
2021[A]	1,597,169	43,365	1.89
2020[A]	1,411,611	47,991	2.18
2019[A]	1,285,102	6,756	0.32
2018[A]	1,103,497	12,701	0.60

* S.V. & M.V.
[A] Reported in accordance with IFRS

G.7 GFL Environmental Inc.*

Symbol - GFL **Exchange** - TSX **CUSIP** - 36168Q

Head Office - 500-100 New Park Pl, Vaughan, ON, L4K 0H9 **Telephone** - (905) 326-0101 **Fax** - (289) 695-2551

Website - www.gflenv.com

Email - pdovigi@gflenv.com

Investor Relations - Patrick Dovigi (416) 673-9385

Auditors - KPMG LLP C.A., Vaughan, Ont.

Transfer Agents - Computershare Trust Company of Canada Inc., Toronto, Ont.; Computershare Trust Company, N.A., Louisville, Ky.

FP500 Revenue Ranking - 93

Employees - 19,500 at Dec. 31, 2022

Profile - (Ont. 2007) Provides solid and liquid waste management, and soil remediation services, including collection, transportation, transfer, recycling and disposal services for municipal, residential, commercial and industrial customers in Canada and the U.S.

The company has two business lines: Solid Waste and Environmental Services.

The **Solid Waste** business line provides collection services through municipal collection contracts, residential subscription agreements and commercial customer service agreements; transfer stations for consolidation of waste from collection operations; landfill sites for disposal; and material recovery and organic processing services for segregation and preparation of recyclable materials. In addition, wholly owned **GFL Renewables LLC** develops renewable natural gas projects at the company's municipal solid waste landfills.

The **Environmental** Services business line collects, manages, transports and processes hazardous and non-hazardous industrial and commercial waste, including contaminated waste water, for treatment, recycling, recovery, disposal or beneficial use. Also resells liquid waste products including used motor oil and downstream by-products; and includes remediation and disposal of contaminated and remediated soils.

In May 2023, bought deal secondary offering of 18,176,073 subordinate voting shares of the company by selling shareholders **BCEC-GFL Borrower (Cayman) LP** (an entity affiliated with **BC Partners Advisors LP**), **OTPP Environmental Services Trust**, **GFL Borrower II (Cayman) LP** and **Poole Private Capital, LLC** at US$36.20 per share was arranged.

During 2022, the company acquired 40 businesses, including 35 solid waste management businesses, for total consideration of $1,473 billion. In addition, the company sold certain post collection assets and ancillary operation for total consideration of $117,700,000.

In April 2022, the company reached an agreement with the Canadian Competition Bureau to address concerns raised by the Bureau with the company's August 2021 acquisition of the solid waste and environmental services businesses of **Terrapure Environmental Ltd.** The company has agreed to divest four liquid waste facilities and three tank farms in western Canada. These sites were expected to generate annual aggregate revenue of $20,000,000 in 2022.

Units delisted from NYSE, Mar. 16, 2023.

Recent Merger and Acquisition Activity

Status: pending **Announced:** June 5, 2023
GFL Environmental Inc. sold its solid waste collection operations in Nashville, Tenn., (May 1, 2023), Colorado and New Mexico (June 1) and Pennsylvania , Maryland and Delaware (closing June 30, 2023). Total gross proceeds were expected to be over $1.6 billion.

Status: completed **Announced:** May 2, 2022
GFL Environmental Inc. acquired Sugar Land, Tex.-based Sprint Waste Services, LP, a vertically integrated network of solid waste assets across 16 sites in Texas (14) and Louisiana (2), including two construction and demolition (C&D) landfills in the Greater Houston Area. Terms were not disclosed. Sprint Waste operations include a fleet of more than 400 vehicles and 8,000 rental containers.

Status: completed **Revised:** Apr. 25, 2022
UPDATE: The divestiture of GFL Infrastructure was completed for $224,000,000 in cash and a 45% equity interest in GIP, an entity that is controlled by funds managed by HPS Investment Partners Inc. through a 47% equity interest. Affiliates controlled by Patrick Dovigi, the executive chair of the GIP board of directors, hold an 8% equity interest in GIP. PREVIOUS: GFL Environmental Inc. announced plans to divest its infrastructure services division (GFL Infrastructure) for cash and an equity interest in new entity Green Infrastructure Partners Inc. (GIP) in exchange for cash and equity interest in GIP. GFL's soil remediation division, which is included in its infrastructure segment, would be combined with its liquid waste segment and rebranded as environmental services. In connection with the intended acquisition of GFL Infrastructure, GIP would acquire Coco Paving, Inc. and its affiliates, a vertically integrated infrastructure services businesses with operations across Ontario , Quebec , Manitoba and Saskatchewan.

Predecessor Detail - Name changed from GFL Environmental Corporation, Nov. 3, 2013.

Directors - Patrick Dovigi, chr., pres. & CEO, Ont.; Dino Chiesa†, Toronto, Ont.; Violet A. M. (Vi) Konkle, Ont.; Sandra Levy, Toronto, Ont.; Jessica L. McDonald, Vancouver, B.C.; Arun Nayar, Naples, Fla.; Paolo Notarnicola, N.Y.; Ven Poole, N.C.; Blake Sumler, Ont.; Raymond Svider, N.Y.

Other Exec. Officers - Mindy Gilbert, exec. v-p & chief legal officer; Elizabeth J. Grahek, exec. v-p, strategic initiatives; Luke Pelosi, exec. v-p & CFO; Greg Yorston, exec. v-p & COO, solid waste

† Lead director

Capital Stock

	Authorized (shs.)	Outstanding (shs.)[1]
Preferred	unlimited	
Series A		28,571,428
Series B		8,196,721
Subordinate Vtg.	unlimited	357,354,378
Multiple Vtg.	unlimited	11,812,964

[1] At June 30, 2023

Preferred - Issuable in series. Entitled to vote on an as-converted basis for all matters on which holders of subordinate voting shares and multiple voting shares vote.

Series A - All held by HPS Investment Partners, LLC. At Dec. 31, 2022, convertible into 27,842,293 subordinate voting shares at US$25.19 per share. Subject to transfer restrictions, but can be converted into subordinate voting shares by the holder at any time. From Dec. 31, 2024, the company would have the option each quarter to redeem a number of preferred shares in the amount equal to the increase in the liquidation preference for the quarter. The initial liquidation preference is US$21 per share, accreting at a rate of 7% per annum, compounded quarterly. The redemption amount can be satisfied in either cash or subordinate voting shares; if the redemption amount for a particular quarter is paid in cash, the accretion rate for that quarter would be 6% per annum.

Series B - All held by HPS Investment Partners, LLC. At Dec. 31, 2022, convertible into 7,268,463 subordinate voting shares at US$43.91 per share. Subject to transfer restrictions, but can be converted into subordinate voting shares by the holder at any time. From Dec. 31, 2025, the company would have the option each quarter to redeem a number of preferred shares in the amount equal to the increase in the liquidation preference for the quarter. The initial liquidation preference is US$36.60 per share, accreting at a rate of 6% per annum, compounded quarterly. The redemption amount can be satisfied in either cash or subordinate voting shares; if the redemption amount for a particular quarter is paid in cash, the accretion rate for that quarter would be 5% per annum.

Subordinate Voting - One vote per share.

Multiple Voting - All controlled by Patrick Dovigi. Convertible into subordinate voting shares on a one-for-one basis. Automatically convertible into subordinate voting shares under certain circumstances, including: (i) Patrick Dovigi no longer holding at least 2% of the outstanding shares; (ii) Patrick Dovigi no longer serving as a director or officer of the company; or (iii) the twentieth anniversary of the closing of the initial public offering being Mar. 5, 2040. Ten votes per share.

Options - At Dec. 31, 2022, options were outstanding to purchase 22,128,582 subordinate voting shares at a weighted average exercise price of US$32.59 per share.

Normal Course Issuer Bid - The company plans to make normal course purchases of up to 17,867,120 subordinate voting shares representing 5% of the total outstanding. The bid commenced on May 12, 2023, and expires on May 11, 2024.

Major Shareholder - Patrick Dovigi held 23.6% interest and BC Partners Advisors LP held 21.8% interest at Apr. 3, 2023.

Price Range - GFL/TSX

Year	Volume	High	Low	Close
2022	79,768,545	$48.39	$31.57	$39.54
2021	58,372,388	$54.01	$35.28	$47.83
2020	65,563,231	$37.60	$16.85	$37.11

Recent Close: $43.96

Capital Stock Changes - On Mar. 15, 2023, 25,665,433 subordinate voting shares were issued on the automatic conversion of all outstanding tangible equity units (TEUs).

During 2022, subordinate voting shares were issued as follows: 3,976,434 pursuant to business acquisitions, 731,290 on exercise of restricted share units, 450,000 on exercise of options and 297 on conversion of tangible equity units; 8,057 subordinate voting shares were cancelled. In addition, 250,000 multiple voting shares were converted into a like number of subordinate voting shares.

Dividends

GFL sub vtg S.V. Ra US$0.052 pa Q est. Apr. 28, 2023
Prev. Rate: US$0.048 est. July 29, 2022
Prev. Rate: US$0.048 est. Apr. 29, 2022
Prev. Rate: US$0.044 est. Apr. 30, 2021
Prev. Rate: US$0.04 est. Apr. 30, 2020

Long-Term Debt - Outstanding at Dec. 31, 2022:

Revolv. credit facility	$771,800,000
Term loans[1]	2,242,700,000
4.25% US$ sr. notes due 2025	677,200,000
3.75% US$ sr. notes due 2025	1,015,800,000
5.125% US$ sr. notes due 2026	677,200,000
4% US$ sr. notes due 2028	1,015,800,000
3.5% US$ sr. notes due 2028	1,015,800,000
4.75% US$ sr. notes due 2029	1,015,800,000
4.375% US$ sr. notes due 2029	744,900,000
Other[2]	75,000,000
Derivative liability	79,900,000
Discount	(5,500,000)
Deferred finance costs	(59,600,000)
	9,266,8000,000
Less: Current portion	58,300,000
	9,208,500,000

[1] Consist of a $1,742,700,000 term loan bearing interest at LIBOR plus 3% or U.S. prime plus 2% and due May 31, 2025; and a $500,000,000 term loan bearing interest at SOFR/bankers acceptance plus 1.5% to 2.25% or Canadian/U.S. prime plus 0.5% to 1.25% and due Sept. 27, 2026.

[2] Includes $48,900,000 promissory notes with bearing interest at 3% per annum, payable quarterly and due June 14, 2027.

Note - In January 2023, maturity of the $1.743 billion term loan was extended to May 2027 from May 2025, bearing interest at SOFR plus 3% or U.S. prime plus 2%.

Wholly Owned Subsidiaries

American Waste, Inc., Kalkaska, Mich.
County Waste of Virginia, LLC, Clifton Park, N.Y.
GFL Environmental Services Inc., Ont.
GFL Environmental Services USA, Inc., Del.
GFL Environmental USA Inc., Del.
GFL Everglades Holdings LLC, Del.
Soil Safe, Inc., Columbia, Md.
WCA Waste Corporation, Houston, Tex.
Wrangler Holdco Corp., Del.

Investments

45% int. in **Green Infrastructure Partners Inc.**, Ont.

Financial Statistics

Periods ended:	12m Dec. 31/22[A]		12m Dec. 31/21[□A]
	$000s	%Chg	$000s
Operating revenue	**6,761,300**	**+32**	**5,136,600**
Cost of sales	4,472,100		3,319,500
General & admin expense	641,400		487,300
Stock-based compensation	55,100		45,700
Operating expense	**5,168,600**	**+34**	**3,852,500**
Operating income	**1,592,700**	**+24**	**1,284,100**
Deprec., depl. & amort.	1,525,500		1,525,500
Finance costs, gross	489,300		432,500
Investment income	20,700		nil
Write-downs/write-offs	(7,200)		nil
Pre-tax income	**(359,300)**	**n.a.**	**(736,200)**
Income taxes	(176,100)		(109,200)
Net inc. bef. disc. opers	**(183,200)**	**n.a.**	**(627,000)**
Income from disc. opers	(127,900)		20,200
Net income	**(311,100)**	**n.a.**	**(606,800)**
Net inc. for equity hldrs	**(311,800)**	**n.a.**	**(606,800)**
Net inc. for non-cont. int	**700**	**n.a.**	**nil**
Cash & equivalent	82,100		190,400
Inventories	84,200		82,000
Accounts receivable	1,118,100		1,134,700
Current assets	1,383,100		1,495,700
Long-term investments	326,600		nil
Fixed assets, net	6,540,300		6,010,600
Intangibles, net	11,427,400		10,831,100
Total assets	**19,767,600**	**+7**	**18,396,500**
Accts. pay. & accr. liabs	1,557,700		1,319,700
Current liabilities	2,692,100		1,522,400
Long-term debt, gross	9,266,800		8,001,800
Long-term debt, net	9,248,900		7,984,600
Long-term lease liabilities	327,300		257,400
Shareholders' equity	6,037,200		5,776,100
Non-controlling interest	6,900		nil
Cash from oper. activs	**1,096,300**	**+22**	**897,900**
Cash from fin. activs	569,000		1,964,700
Cash from invest. activs	(1,734,200)		(2,687,200)
Net cash position	**82,100**	**-57**	**190,400**
Capital expenditures	(780,100)		(647,200)
Capital disposals	364,100		259,700
	$		$
Earnings per share*	(0.73)		(1.83)
Cash flow per share*	2.99		2.48
Cash divd. per share*	US$0.05		US$0.04
	shs		shs
No. of shs. o/s*	343,442,881		375,061,066
Avg. no. of shs. o/s*	367,170,911		361,566,007
	%		%
Net profit margin	(2.71)		(12.21)
Return on equity	(4.52)		(11.88)
Return on assets	0.35		(1.52)
Foreign sales percent	60		62
No. of employees (FTEs)	19,500		18,000

* Subord. Vtg.
[□] Restated
[A] Reported in accordance with IFRS

Note: Average number of shares includes subordinate voting shares to be issued upon conversion of the prepaid stock purchase contract component of the tangible equity units.

Latest Results

Periods ended:	6m June 30/23[A]		6m June 30/22[A]
	$000s	%Chg	$000s
Operating revenue	3,742,700	+20	3,108,900
Net inc. bef. disc. opers	76,000	-65	219,600
Income from disc. opers	nil		(127,900)
Net income	76,000	-17	91,700
Net inc. for equity hldrs	75,500	-18	91,700
Net inc. for non-cont. int	500		nil
	$		$
Earns. per sh. bef. disc. opers.*	0.08		0.49
Earnings per share*	0.08		0.14

* Subord. Vtg.
[A] Reported in accordance with IFRS

Historical Summary
(as originally stated)

Fiscal Year	Oper. Rev.	Net Inc. Bef. Disc.	EPS*
	$000s	$000s	$
2022[A]	6,761,300	(183,200)	(0.73)
2021[A]	5,525,500	(606,800)	(1.83)
2020[A]	4,196,200	(994,900)	(2.80)
2019[A]	3,346,851	(451,653)	(0.12)
2018[A1,2]	1,224,797	(318,663)	(0.12)

* Subord. Vtg.
[A] Reported in accordance with IFRS
[1] 7 months ended Dec. 31, 2018.
[2] Results from June 1, 2018, pertain to successor company (following GFL Environmental Inc. [the company] amalgamating with former parent GFL Environmental Holdings Inc. and continuing under the GFL Environmental Inc. name).

G.8 GHP Noetic Science-Psychedelic Pharma Inc.

Symbol - PSYF.P **Exchange** - TSX-VEN (S) **CUSIP** - 36175A
Head Office - 18 Lumley Ave, Toronto, ON, M4G 2X5 **Telephone** - (647) 949-2663
Email - paul@npn.ca
Investor Relations - Paul Barbeau (613) 218-5319
Auditors - MNP LLP C.A., Toronto, Ont.
Lawyers - Norton Rose Fulbright Canada LLP, Toronto, Ont.
Transfer Agents - Odyssey Trust Company, Toronto, Ont.
Profile - (Ont. 2020) Capital Pool Company.
Common suspended from TSX-VEN, June 5, 2023.
Common reinstated on TSX-VEN, Sept. 16, 2022.

Recent Merger and Acquisition Activity

Status: terminated **Revised:** May 3, 2022
UPDATE: The transaction was terminated. PREVIOUS: GHP Noetic Science-Psychedelic Pharma Inc. entered into a letter of intent for the Qualifying Transaction reverse takeover acquisition of private Toronto, Ont.-based Diamond Therapeutics Inc. by way of a three-cornered amalgamation of Diamond and a wholly owned subsidiary of GHP. The transaction would be completed on the basis of 4.2221 post-consolidated GHP common shares for each Diamond share held (following a 1-for-2.2727 share consolidation), resulting in the issuance of 88,960,000 GHP post-consolidated common shares. Diamond develops drugs for mental health conditions using psychedelic compounds focusing on sub-perceptual, non-hallucinogenic treatments. Prior to closing, GHP or Diamond would complete a private placement of at least $2,000,000 of subscription receipts. GHP would change its name to Diamond Therapeutics Inc. upon completion of the transaction.

Directors - Paul Barbeau, CEO, Ottawa, Ont.; Warren Wright, CFO, Schomberg, Ont.; Sa'ad Shah, corp. sec., Toronto, Ont.; Andrew Jolley, Utah; George Main, Toronto, Ont.

Capital Stock

	Authorized (shs.)	Outstanding (shs.)[1]
Common	unlimited	10,000,000

[1] At Aug. 30, 2022

Major Shareholder - Noetic Psychedelic Fund LP held 19.6% interest at Aug. 13, 2021.

Price Range - PSYF.P/TSX-VEN (S)

Year	Volume	High	Low	Close
2022	430,804	$0.20	$0.02	$0.07
2021	133,584	$0.38	$0.21	$0.25
2020	2,375,462	$0.45	$0.13	$0.38

Recent Close: $0.06

G.9 GINSMS Inc.

Symbol - GOK **Exchange** - TSX-VEN **CUSIP** - 37611E
Head Office - 1700-421 7 Ave SW, Calgary, AB, T2P 4K9
Website - www.ginsms.com
Email - investor.relations@ginsms.com
Investor Relations - Siang Hui Chin 65-6441-1029
Auditors - RSM Hong Kong C.P.A., Hong Kong, Hong Kong People's Republic of China
Lawyers - Miller Thomson LLP, Montréal, Qué.
Transfer Agents - TSX Trust Company, Calgary, Alta.
Profile - (Can. 2009) Provides cloud-based application-to-peer (A2P) messaging services, mobile data services and solutions to mobile telecommunications industry primarily in Singapore, Indonesia, Europe and United States.

The company has two main business segments: Messaging business, and Software products & services.

The Messaging business segment, which operates through indirectly wholly owned **GIN International Ltd.**, provides A2P messaging services allowing the transmission of SMS to mobile subscribers of more than 200 mobile operators globally. A2P messaging service enables mobile application developers, SMS gateways, enterprises and financial institutions to deliver SMS worldwide without any upfront capital investment through the use of an application programming interface. Mobile application developers use A2P messaging service to deliver one-time-passwords for authentication of over-the-top mobile applications, in-app purchase confirmations or promotion of latest game releases. Enterprises and financial institutions use the A2P service in the areas of mobile marketing, mobile transactions, security, customer relationship management and enterprise resource planning.

The Software products & services segment, which operates through wholly owned **Inphosoft Group Pte. Ltd.** (IGPL), provides support and maintenance services to customers that have purchased its products and solutions. IGPL also maintains the A2P platform and develops new features to support the company's messaging business, as well as outsources technical resources to customers for the purpose of software development based on a time and material basis.

Directors - Siang Hui (Joel) Chin, CEO, Singapore; Fung Yuen (Paul) Law, Hong Kong, People's Republic of China; Man Bong (Benedict) Leung, Toronto, Ont.

Other Exec. Officers - Chee Ming Shum, interim CFO; Stephen Chan, sr. v-p, mobile advtg. & enterprise bus.; Derrick Ong, sr. v-p, telecoms & messaging bus.; Hongwei Xu, sr. v-p, mobile applications, enterprise products & solutions & chief tech. officer; Bruno Caron, corp. sec.

Capital Stock

	Authorized (shs.)	Outstanding (shs.)[1]
Preferred	unlimited	nil
Common	unlimited	187,118,368

[1] At May 25, 2023

Major Shareholder - Xinhua Holdings Limited held 52.29% interest, Siang Hui (Joel) Chin held 19.95% interest and Inphosoft Pte. Limited held 15.25% interest at May 25, 2023.

Price Range - GOK/TSX-VEN

Year	Volume	High	Low	Close
2022	550,255	$0.05	$0.01	$0.02
2021	2,997,525	$0.29	$0.03	$0.03
2020	1,356,889	$0.13	$0.01	$0.02
2019	2,533,000	$0.05	$0.02	$0.03
2018	18,600	$0.23	$0.10	$0.10

Recent Close: $0.04

Capital Stock Changes - In November 2022, 37,324,507 common shares were issued for loan repayment.

Wholly Owned Subsidiaries

Global Edge Technology Limited, British Virgin Islands.
- 100% int. in **Redstone Resources Limited**, British Virgin Islands.
  - 100% int. in **GIN International Ltd.**, Hong Kong, People's Republic of China.

Inphosoft Group Pte. Ltd., Singapore.
Inphosoft Malaysia Sdn. Bhd., Malaysia.

Subsidiaries

99% int. in **PT Inphosoft Indonesia**, Indonesia.

Financial Statistics

Periods ended:	12m Dec. 31/22^A		12m Dec. 31/21^A
	$000s	%Chg	$000s
Operating revenue	**3,024**	**+11**	**2,731**
Cost of sales	1,863		1,708
Salaries & benefits	406		251
General & admin expense	439		397
Operating expense	**2,708**	**+15**	**2,356**
Operating income	**316**	**-16**	**375**
Deprec., depl. & amort.	94		87
Finance costs, gross	6		10
Write-downs/write-offs	(133)		10
Pre-tax income	**(24)**	**n.a.**	**291**
Income taxes	8		9
Net income	**(32)**	**n.a.**	**281**
Cash & equivalent	191		184
Accounts receivable	557		601
Current assets	810		851
Fixed assets, net	62		33
Right-of-use assets	76		49
Total assets	**948**	**+2**	**933**
Bank indebtedness	580		580
Accts. pay. & accr. liabs.	601		591
Current liabilities	3,250		6,922
Shareholders' equity	(2,318)		(5,976)
Non-controlling interest	(14)		(13)
Cash from oper. activs.	**355**	**+93**	**184**
Cash from fin. activs.	(332)		(258)
Cash from invest. activs.	(60)		(18)
Net cash position	**191**	**+4**	**184**
Capital expenditures	(60)		(18)
	$		$
Earnings per share*	(0.00)		0.00
Cash flow per share*	0.00		0.00
	shs		shs
No. of shs. o/s*	187,118,368		149,793,861
Avg. no. of shs. o/s*	154,702,289		149,793,861
	%		%
Net profit margin	(1.06)		10.29
Return on equity	n.m.		n.m.
Return on assets	(2.55)		29.41
Foreign sales percent	100		100

* Common
^A Reported in accordance with IFRS

Latest Results

Periods ended:	3m Mar. 31/23^A		3m Mar. 31/22^A
	$000s	%Chg	$000s
Operating revenue	821	+13	726
Net income	72	-5	76
	$		$
Earnings per share*	0.00		0.00

* Common
^A Reported in accordance with IFRS

Historical Summary
(as originally stated)

Fiscal Year	Oper. Rev. $000s	Net Inc. Bef. Disc. $000s	EPS* $
2022^A	3,024	(32)	(0.00)
2021^A	2,731	281	0.00
2020^A	2,823	(4)	(0.00)
2019^A	2,639	(315)	(0.00)
2018^A	5,355	(1,203)	(0.01)

* Common
^A Reported in accordance with IFRS

G.10 GLG Life Tech Corporation

Symbol - GLG **Exchange** - TSX **CUSIP** - 361793
Head Office - 280-13071 Vanier Pl, Richmond, BC, V6V 2J1 **Telephone** - (604) 669-2602 **Toll-free** - (855) 454-7587 **Fax** - (604) 285-2606
Website - www.glglifetech.com
Email - simon.springett@glglifetech.com
Investor Relations - Simon Springett (604) 285-2602 ext. 101
Auditors - DNTW Toronto LLP C.A., Toronto, Ont.
Lawyers - Maitland & Company, Vancouver, B.C.
Transfer Agents - Computershare Trust Company of Canada Inc., Vancouver, B.C.

Profile - (B.C. 1998) Produces and sells natural sweeteners, including stevia and monk fruit extracts, for the food and beverage industry.

Specializes in growing, refining and producing high grade stevia, a natural zero-calorie sweetener. Stevia is extracted and processed from the stevia plant, and high-grade monk fruit extract, an all-natural sweetener extracted from monk fruit (also known as luo han guo).

Stevia operations in the People's Republic of China include three processing factories and stevia growing areas across 10 provinces. The production facilities have combined capacity to process 41,000 tonnes of raw stevia leaf annually, which produces 500 tonnes of high-grade stevia extract, and 130 tonnes of high-purity monk fruit extract.

Stevia products include ClearTaste Stevia, RebPure™, RebSweet™, AnySweetPLUS™, BlendSure™, PureSTV™, TasteBoost™ and Reb M Gold™. Monkfruit products include MonkSweet™, MonkGold™ and ClearTaste Monk Fruit. Other products include P-Pro Plus which complements the benefits of pea protein with **MycoTechnology, Inc.**'s ClearTaste™, a mushroom extract that blocks the perception of bitterness, astringency and sourness, to offer pea protein without any of taste issues; and Naturals+ line, which provides other natural ingredients to customers in the foods, dietary supplements, and cosmetic industries.

In addition, the company distributes **East West Pharma Group**'s cannabidiol products across Canada and Europe.

Predecessor Detail - Name changed from GLG Life Tech Limited, Mar. 14, 2007; basis 1 new for 3 old shs.

Directors - Dr. Yong (Luke) Zhang, chr. & CEO, Heze, Shandong, People's Republic of China; Brian A. Palmieri, v-chr., Cody, Wyo.; Simon Springett, COO, Boulder, Colo.; Sophia Leung, Vancouver, B.C.; Yingchun Liu, Heze, Shandong, People's Republic of China

Other Exec. Officers - Edward Wang, CFO & contr.; Kevin Li, v-p, innovation & quality assurance; Qibin Wang, v-p, agri. & chief agri. scientist; Yunru Zhang, v-p, China bus. devel.; Zhang Lei, gen. mgr., quality assurance; Kunzhong Pang, pres., primary processing

Capital Stock

	Authorized (shs.)	Outstanding (shs.)[1]
Common	unlimited	38,394,223

[1] At May 24, 2023

Major Shareholder - Rosa Yuan held 17% interest, Dr. Yong (Luke) Zhang held 11.5% interest and China Agriculture and Healthy Foods Co. Ltd. held 11.2% interest at May 4, 2022.

Price Range - GLG/TSX

Year	Volume	High	Low	Close
2022	4,494,150	$0.15	$0.03	$0.03
2021	8,028,771	$0.53	$0.10	$0.10
2020	2,329,847	$0.52	$0.14	$0.17
2019	1,503,211	$1.00	$0.14	$0.15
2018	1,121,889	$1.39	$0.56	$0.76

Recent Close: $0.05

Wholly Owned Subsidiaries

Agricultural High Tech Developments Limited, Marshall Islands.
GLG Life Tech U.S., Inc., United States.
Intercontinental Cannabis Corporation, B.C.

Subsidiaries

98.85% int. in **Anhui Runhai Biotechnology Company Limited**, Anhui, People's Republic of China.

Note: The preceding list includes only the major related companies in which interests are held.

Financial Statistics

Periods ended:	12m Dec. 31/21^A		12m Dec. 31/20^A
	$000s	%Chg	$000s
Operating revenue	**10,876**	**-29**	**15,290**
Cost of sales	7,051		11,008
General & admin expense	3,424		3,998
Stock-based compensation	73		360
Operating expense	**10,547**	**-31**	**15,365**
Operating income	**329**	**n.a.**	**(75)**
Deprec., depl. & amort.	1,431		2,093
Finance income	nil		129
Finance costs, gross	21,449		16,746
Write-downs/write-offs	(95)		134
Pre-tax income	**(23,870)**	**n.a.**	**28,084**
Net income	**(23,870)**	**n.a.**	**28,084**
Net inc. for equity hldrs.	**(23,704)**	**n.a.**	**16,527**
Net inc. for non-cont. int.	**(166)**	**n.a.**	**11,557**
Cash & equivalent	239		556
Inventories	2,874		3,644
Accounts receivable	2,213		1,691
Current assets	6,469		6,714
Fixed assets, net	17,671		18,299
Right-of-use assets	337		429
Total assets	**24,554**	**-3**	**25,442**
Accts. pay. & accr. liabs.	16,610		16,264
Current liabilities	172,292		147,644
Long-term debt, gross	50,443		49,128
Long-term lease liabilities	226		326
Shareholders' equity	(147,148)		(121,900)
Non-controlling interest	(816)		(628)
Cash from oper. activs.	**220**	**n.a.**	**(8,330)**
Cash from fin. activs.	(539)		(25,364)
Cash from invest. activs.	(127)		33,094
Net cash position	**239**	**-57**	**556**
Capital expenditures	(127)		(5)
Capital disposals	nil		1,532
	$		$
Earnings per share*	(0.62)		0.43
Cash flow per share*	0.01		(0.22)
	shs		shs
No. of shs. o/s*	38,394,223		38,394,223
Avg. no. of shs. o/s*	38,394,223		38,394,223
	%		%
Net profit margin	(219.47)		183.68
Return on equity	n.m.		n.m.
Return on assets	(9.68)		144.39
No. of employees (FTEs)	89		97

* Common
^A Reported in accordance with IFRS

Latest Results

Periods ended:	9m Sept. 30/22^A		9m Sept. 30/21^A
	$000s	%Chg	$000s
Operating revenue	7,885	0	7,874
Net income	(17,316)	n.a.	(15,385)
Net inc. for equity hldrs.	(17,224)	n.a.	(15,290)
Net inc. for non-cont. int.	(93)		(95)
	$		$
Earnings per share*	(0.45)		(0.40)

* Common
^A Reported in accordance with IFRS

Historical Summary
(as originally stated)

Fiscal Year	Oper. Rev. $000s	Net Inc. Bef. Disc. $000s	EPS* $
2021^A	10,876	(23,870)	(0.62)
2020^A	15,290	28,084	0.43
2019^A	10,150	(25,017)	(0.50)
2018^A	16,583	(26,463)	(0.57)
2017^A	19,388	(17,567)	(0.44)

* Common
^A Reported in accordance with IFRS

G.11 GOAT Industries Ltd.

Symbol - GOAT **Exchange** - CSE **CUSIP** - 38021J
Head Office - 810-789 Pender St W, Vancouver, BC, V6C 1H2 **Toll-free** - (833) 446-2847
Website - goatindustries.co
Email - info@goatindustries.co
Investor Relations - Lawrence Hay (833) 446-2847
Auditors - WDM Chartered Accountants C.A., Vancouver, B.C.
Transfer Agents - Endeavor Trust Corporation, Vancouver, B.C.

Profile - (B.C. 2020) Invests and acquires companies, with a focus on cellular agriculture, energy infrastructure, raw material extraction and onshore manufacturing. Also has mineral interests in British Columbia and Quebec.

The investment portfolio includes **FunGuys Beverages Inc.** (100% owned), which manufactures and distributes organic mushroom-infused cold brew coffee drinks under the KOLD™ brand; **Kojo Pet Performance Inc.** (100% owned), which offers plant and cell-based pet food; **1000288601 Ontario Inc.** (100% owned), which holds a Canadian licence for use of lithium solvent extraction technology; **Sophie's Kitchen, Inc.** (35.1% interest), which produces a line of frozen and shelf-stable plant-based "seafood" products; **The Vegetarian Butcher Inc.** (12.4% interest), which provides meat alternatives and operate retail stores in Kelowna and Vancouver, B.C.; and **Evanesce Packaging Solutions Inc.** (less than 1%), which produces eco-friendly compostable food containers made with plant-based by-products.

Also holds claims in the vicinity of **American Eagle Gold Corp.**'s NAK copper prospect, 80 km from Smithers, B.C.; lithium claims adjacent to **Power Metals Corp.**'s Case Lake lithium-cesium property; and 15 lithium claims, including six claims south of **Patriot Battery Metals Inc.**'s Corvette lithium project, James Bay, Que., and eight claims, 60 km northeast of Kangiqsualujjuaq, Que. and a claim in Southern Quebec.

In March 2023, the company agreed to acquire the 1,925-hectare Lacana-Doran uranium-lithium prospect in Quebec for issuance of 80,000,000 common shares at a deemed price of $0.011 per share.

In October 2022, the company acquired **1000288601 Ontario Inc.**, which holds a licence for use of lithium solvent extraction technology in Canada from Australia-based **Ekosolve Ltd.**, for issuance of 45,000,000 common shares at a deemed price of $0.025 per share.

In August 2022, the company acquired **Kojo Pet Performance Inc.**, which produces and markets plant and cell-based pet food offerings, for issuance of 25,000,000 common shares at a deemed price of $0.039 per share. Kojo is also eligible to earn up to an additional contingent consideration of 30,000,000 common shares subject to achievement of certain performance milestones.

Predecessor Detail - Name changed from Billy Goat Brands Ltd., Sept. 12, 2022.

Directors - Lawrence Hay, CEO, interim CFO & corp. sec., Vancouver, B.C.; Alexander (Alex) Benger, Victoria, B.C.; Mohammad Sharifi, Vancouver, B.C.

Other Exec. Officers - Zaki Mohammed, pres., FunGuys Beverages

Capital Stock

	Authorized (shs.)	Outstanding (shs.)[1]
Common	unlimited	3,281,680

[1] At July 19, 2023

Major Shareholder - Widely held at June 6, 2023.

Price Range - GOAT/CSE

Year	Volume	High	Low	Close
2022	1,935,287	$17.00	$0.50	$1.00
2021	293,282	$53.00	$11.00	$14.00

Consolidation: 1-for-100 cons. in July 2023

Recent Close: $0.12

Capital Stock Changes - On July 19, 2023, common shares were consolidated on a 1-for-100 basis.

Wholly Owned Subsidiaries

FunGuys Beverages Inc., B.C.
Kojo Pet Performance Inc.
1000288601 Ontario Inc., Canada.

Financial Statistics

Periods ended:	12m Dec. 31/21[A]		12m Dec. 31/20[A]
	$000s	%Chg	$000s
General & admin expense	3,253		37
Stock-based compensation	2,482		nil
Operating expense	**5,735**	**n.m.**	**37**
Operating income	**(5,735)**	**n.a.**	**(37)**
Finance income	103		103
Pre-tax income	**(6,083)**	**n.a.**	**(37)**
Net income	**(6,083)**	**n.a.**	**(37)**
Cash & equivalent	673		410
Current assets	2,193		410
Long-term investments	8,822		nil
Total assets	**11,015**	**n.m.**	**410**
Accts. pay. & accr. liabs	130		33
Current liabilities	130		33
Shareholders' equity	10,811		376
Cash from oper. activs	**(4,170)**	**n.a.**	**(4)**
Cash from fin. activs	10,112		414
Cash from invest. activs	(5,679)		nil
Net cash position	**(5,679)**	**n.a.**	**410**
	$		$
Earnings per share*	(9.00)		(1.19)
Cash flow per share*	(6.30)		(0.13)
	shs		shs
No. of shs. o/s*	1,021,603		40,000
Avg. no. of shs. o/s*	661,928		31,200
	%		%
Net profit margin	n.a.		n.a.
Return on equity	(108.75)		n.m.
Return on assets	(106.49)		n.a.

* Common
[A] Reported in accordance with IFRS

Latest Results

Periods ended:	9m Sept. 30/22[A]		9m Sept. 30/21[A]
	$000s	%Chg	$000s
Net income	(3,524)	n.a.	(5,148)
	$		$
Earnings per share*	(3.00)		(12.00)

* Common
[A] Reported in accordance with IFRS

Note: Adjusted throughout for 1-for-100 cons. in July 2023

G.12 GOLO Mobile Inc.

Symbol - WLTR.H **Exchange** - TSX-VEN **CUSIP** - 381721

Head Office - 920-3400 boul de Maisonneuve O, Montréal, QC, H3Z 3B8 **Telephone** - (514) 380-2700

Website - www.usewalter.com

Email - scott@mcgregorcorp.com

Investor Relations - Scott McGregor (514) 669-6065

Auditors - BF Borgers CPA PC C.P.A., Lakewood, Colo.

Transfer Agents - Odyssey Trust Company, Calgary, Alta.

Profile - (Can. 2019; orig. Alta., 2016) Seeking new business opportunities.

Previously provided smart building technology through a mobile application and web software solution, known as usewalter, that enables property managers of multi-residential buildings and commercial real estate to quickly and efficiently provide communication tools, manage Internet of Things (IoT) devices and offer a concierge service that facilitates the delivery of direct-to-home services.

Predecessor Detail - Name changed from HAW Capital Corp., June 26, 2019, pursuant to Qualifying Transaction reverse takeover acquisition of GOLO Inc. and amalgamation of GOLO Inc. with a wholly owned subsidiary.

Directors - Scott McGregor, chr. & CEO, Calgary, Alta.; Marshall Mewha, CFO, Courtney, B.C.; Jay Campbell, Calgary, Alta.; Robert McCue, Sin., Mexico

Other Exec. Officers - Eric McCutcheon, co-founder & v-p, residential sales; Thierry Skoda, co-founder & chief tech. officer; Hugo Lachance, v-p, comml. sales; Nicolas Picard, v-p, fin.

Capital Stock

	Authorized (shs.)	Outstanding (shs.)[1]
Common	unlimited	209,456,534

[1] At May 30, 2022

Major Shareholder - James McRoberts held 16.25% interest, Robert McCue held 15.37% interest, Scott McGregor held 11.05% interest, Jay Campbell held 11% interest and Marshall Mewha held 11% interest at May 26, 2022.

Price Range - WLTR.H/TSX-VEN

Year	Volume	High	Low	Close
2021	8,308,806	$0.35	$0.04	$0.04
2020	7,693,798	$0.36	$0.10	$0.12
2019	8,688,720	$0.44	$0.23	$0.36
2018	180,700	$0.41	$0.15	$0.15

Wholly Owned Subsidiaries

2150304 Alberta Ltd., Alta.

Financial Statistics

Periods ended:	12m Dec. 31/21[A]		12m Dec. 31/20[A]
	$000s	%Chg	$000s
Operating revenue	**232**	**+158**	**90**
Salaries & benefits	1,813		1,602
General & admin expense	1,852		1,702
Stock-based compensation	490		270
Operating expense	**4,156**	**+16**	**3,574**
Operating income	**(3,924)**	**n.a.**	**(3,484)**
Deprec., depl. & amort.	544		668
Finance costs, net	24		53
Write-downs/write-offs	(6,847)		nil
Pre-tax income	**(12,261)**	**n.a.**	**(4,548)**
Income taxes	(722)		(86)
Net inc. bef. disc. opers	**(11,539)**	**n.a.**	**(4,462)**
Income from disc. opers	nil		(7,902)
Net income	**(11,539)**	**n.a.**	**(12,364)**
Cash & equivalent	572		130
Accounts receivable	nil		99
Current assets	922		682
Fixed assets, net	nil		1,181
Right-of-use assets	nil		397
Intangibles, net	nil		6,649
Total assets	**922**	**-90**	**8,909**
Accts. pay. & accr. liabs	207		569
Current liabilities	207		1,090
Long-term lease liabilities	nil		513
Shareholders' equity	715		6,554
Cash from oper. activs	**(3,999)**	**n.a.**	**(4,315)**
Cash from fin. activs	4,071		2,868
Cash from invest. activs	375		(544)
Net cash position	**572**	**+340**	**130**
Capital expenditures	(144)		(41)
Capital disposals	13		267
	$		$
Earns. per sh. bef disc opers*	(0.06)		(0.03)
Earnings per share*	(0.06)		(0.09)
Cash flow per share*	(0.02)		(0.03)
	shs		shs
No. of shs. o/s*	209,456,534		156,726,326
Avg. no. of shs. o/s*	204,343,603		144,851,713
	%		%
Net profit margin	n.m.		n.m.
Return on equity	(317.49)		(53.44)
Return on assets	(234.75)		(42.39)

* Common
[A] Reported in accordance with IFRS

Latest Results

Periods ended:	3m Mar. 31/22[A]		3m Mar. 31/21[A]
	$000s	%Chg	$000s
Operating revenue	nil	n.a.	74
Net income	(138)	n.a.	(1,258)
	$		$
Earnings per share*	(0.00)		(0.01)

* Common
[A] Reported in accordance with IFRS

Historical Summary
(as originally stated)

Fiscal Year	Oper. Rev.	Net Inc. Bef. Disc.	EPS*
	$000s	$000s	$
2021[A]	232	(11,539)	(0.06)
2020[A]	90	(4,462)	(0.03)
2019[A1]	34	(14,564)	(0.16)
2018[A]	207	(8,873)	n.a.
2017[A]	126	(5,409)	n.a.

* Common
[A] Reported in accordance with IFRS
[1] Results reflect the June 26, 2019, Qualifying Transaction reverse takeover acquisition of GOLO Inc.

G.13 G2M Cap Corp.

Symbol - GTM.P **Exchange** - TSX-VEN **CUSIP** - 40054H

Head Office - 905-1111 Hastings St W, Vancouver, BC, V6E 2J3 **Telephone** - (604) 638-2545 **Fax** - (604) 638-2546

Email - martensen@slater.group

Investor Relations - Melissa Martensen (604) 638-2545

Auditors - Davidson & Company LLP C.A., Vancouver, B.C.

Lawyers - Farris LLP, Vancouver, B.C.

Transfer Agents - TSX Trust Company, Toronto, Ont.

Profile - (B.C. 2022) Capital Pool Company.

Common listed on TSX-VEN, May 25, 2023.

Directors - Hari Nesathurai, pres. & CEO, Jordan Station, Ont.; Harpal Dhillon, COO, Surrey, B.C.; Douglas J. Jamieson, CFO, Toronto, Ont.; Paul M. Doyle, St. Catharines, Ont.; Kesavan Tharmarajah, Markham, Ont.

Other Exec. Officers - Melissa Martensen, corp. sec.

Capital Stock

	Authorized (shs.)	Outstanding (shs.)[1]
Preferred	unlimited	nil
Common	unlimited	13,600,000

[1] At May 25, 2023

Major Shareholder - Harpal Dhillon held 14.71% interest, Douglas J. Jamieson held 14.71% interest, Hari Nesathurai held 14.71% interest and Ross Phillips held 14.71% interest at May 25, 2023.

Recent Close: $0.05

Capital Stock Changes - On May 25, 2023, an initial public offering of 5,000,000 common shares was completed at 10¢ per share.

G.14 GURU Organic Energy Corp.

Symbol - GURU **Exchange** - TSX **CUSIP** - 36260M
Head Office - 602-7236 rue Waverly, Montréal, QC, H2R 0C2 **Telephone** - (514) 845-4878
Website - investors.guruenergy.com/en/home
Email - ingy.sarraf@guruenergy.com
Investor Relations - Ingy Sarraf (514) 845-4878 ext. 224
Auditors - KPMG LLP C.A., Montréal, Qué.
Transfer Agents - TSX Trust Company, Toronto, Ont.
Employees - 70 at Oct. 31, 2022

Profile - (Can. 2021; orig. Ont., 2018) Produces organic energy drinks made with plant-based ingredients under the GURU brand.

The company's organic energy drinks are marketed in Canada and across the U.S. through a distribution network of more than 25,000 points of sale, and through guruenergy.com and Amazon. As at Oct. 31, 2022, GURU products were present in more than 5,000 locations in Quebec; 11,000 locations in Ontario, Western Canada and Atlantic Canada; and more than 9,000 locations in the United States.

Manufacturing is outsourced to a network of established third-party co-packers certified to manufacture organic products.

Predecessor Detail - Name changed from Mira X Acquisition Corp., Oct. 28, 2020, pursuant to Qualifying Transaction reverse takeover acquisition of 6384269 Canada Inc. (dba GURU Beverage); basis 1 new for 83.846 old shs.

Directors - Joseph Zakher, exec. chr., Montréal, Qué.; Carl Goyette, pres. & CEO, Montréal, Qué.; Alain L. Miquelon†, Montréal, Qué.; Eric Graveline, Las Vegas, Nev.; Philippe Meunier, Montréal, Qué.

Other Exec. Officers - Ingy Sarraf, CFO & corp. sec.; Rajaa Grar, chief revenue officer; Emmanuelle Ouimet, exec. v-p, mktg.; Alexis Giguère, v-p, sales, Canada; Dr. Luc-Pierre Martin-Privat, v-p, R&D & innovation
† Lead director

Capital Stock

	Authorized (shs.)	Outstanding (shs.)[1]
Common	unlimited	31,871,209

[1] At July 17, 2023

Normal Course Issuer Bid - The company plans to make normal course purchases of up to 1,593,560 common shares representing 5% of the total outstanding. The bid commenced on July 25, 2023, and expires on July 24, 2024.

Major Shareholder - Eric Graveline held 22.39% interest and Joseph Zakher held 20.18% interest at Jan. 25, 2023.

Price Range - GURU/TSX

Year	Volume	High	Low	Close
2022	3,747,842	$16.12	$2.24	$2.25
2021	5,250,470	$23.48	$12.05	$16.07
2020	4,436,506	$20.25	$2.10	$20.21
2019	3,053	$23.90	$10.48	$10.90
2018	2,767	$25.15	$11.32	$12.58

Consolidation: 1-for-83.846 cons. in Nov. 2020

Recent Close: $2.03

Capital Stock Changes - During fiscal 2022, common shares were issued as follows: 25,611 on exercise of options and 9,937 under restricted share unit plan; 158,500 were cancelled.

Wholly Owned Subsidiaries

GURU Beverage Co., United States.
GURU Beverage Inc., Canada.

Financial Statistics

Periods ended:	12m Oct. 31/22[A]		12m Oct. 31/21[A]
	$000s	%Chg	$000s
Operating revenue	**29,081**	**-4**	**30,191**
Cost of goods sold	13,388		12,308
General & admin expense	33,238		27,286
Operating expense	**46,626**	**+18**	**39,594**
Operating income	**(17,545)**	**n.a.**	**(9,403)**
Deprec., depl. & amort.	877		517
Finance income	nil		109
Finance costs, gross	(28)		159
Pre-tax income	**(17,545)**	**n.a.**	**(10,075)**
Income taxes	20		(231)
Net income	**(17,565)**	**n.a.**	**(9,844)**
Cash & equivalent	46,291		66,954
Inventories	8,518		7,338
Accounts receivable	4,995		5,455
Current assets	60,059		80,533
Fixed assets, net	1,329		1,103
Right-of-use assets	1,919		1,886
Intangibles, net	19		28
Total assets	**65,349**	**-23**	**85,005**
Accts. pay. & accr. liabs.	8,213		10,265
Current liabilities	8,664		10,683
Long-term lease liabilities	1,579		1,573
Shareholders' equity	55,085		72,545
Cash from oper. activs.	**(18,840)**	**n.a.**	**(10,156)**
Cash from fin. activs.	(1,000)		47,817
Cash from invest. activs.	(21,647)		(1,103)
Net cash position	**25,491**	**-62**	**66,954**
Capital expenditures	(566)		(1,158)
	$		$
Earnings per share*	(0.54)		(0.33)
Cash flow per share*	(0.58)		(0.34)
	shs		shs
No. of shs. o/s*	32,212,458		32,335,410
Avg. no. of shs. o/s*	32,336,701		30,172,972
	%		%
Net profit margin	(60.40)		(32.61)
Return on equity	(27.52)		(18.55)
Return on assets	(23.40)		(15.28)
Foreign sales percent	17		14
No. of employees (FTEs)	70		70

* Common
[A] Reported in accordance with IFRS

Historical Summary
(as originally stated)

Fiscal Year	Oper. Rev.	Net Inc. Bef. Disc.	EPS*
	$000s	$000s	$
2022[A]	29,081	(17,565)	(0.54)
2021[A]	30,191	(9,844)	(0.33)
2020[A]	22,100	(2,156)	(0.07)
2019[A1]	17,499	705	n.a.
2018[A]	12,240	(105)	n.a.

* Common
[A] Reported in accordance with IFRS
[1] Results for fiscal 2019 and 2018 pertain to 6384269 Canada Inc. (dba GURU Beverage)

Note: Adjusted throughout for 1-for-83.846 cons. in Nov. 2020

G.15 Gaia Grow Corp.

Symbol - GAIA **Exchange** - CSE (S) **CUSIP** - 36269A
Head Office - 303-750 Pender St W, Vancouver, BC, V6C 2T7 **Telephone** - (604) 681-0084 **Fax** - (604) 681-0094
Website - www.gaiagrow.com
Email - fp@gaiagrow.com
Investor Relations - Frederick Pels (604) 681-0084
Auditors - MSLL CPA LLP C.P.A., Vancouver, B.C.
Transfer Agents - Computershare Trust Company of Canada Inc., Vancouver, B.C.

Profile - (B.C. 2011) Extracts and sells hemp-based products in Canada and has retail cannabis stores in British Columbia.

Wholly owned **TruExtracts (Calgary) Inc.** owns a 12,500-sq.-ft. licensed extraction facility in Calgary, Alta., which would be expanded to 28,500-sq.-ft. The facility has the ability to extract using supercritical carbon dioxide, ethanol, butane and pentane, as well as solventless extraction. TruExtracts also offer white label services for various products.

The company also operates two retail cannabis stores (The Green Room) in Squamish and Nelson, B.C. In addition, the company owns two stores pending opening in Powell River, B.C. Customers can also order through the company's online portal.

In June 2022, the company disposed of all assets and liabilities of **Gaia Bio-Pharmaceuticals Inc.** for no consideration.

In May 2022, the company returned ownership of wholly owned subsidiary **Canna Stream Solutions Ltd.** to its original owners for no consideration and cancelled 12,500,000 common shares issued originally issued as consideration for its acquisition. The company also sold its 1,494-acre property in Lamont cty., Alta., for $110,000 to a third party. Canna Stream was developing technologies for storing, transportation and processing of physical and chemical cannabis waste.

Common suspended from CSE, May 9, 2023.

Predecessor Detail - Name changed from Spirit Bear Capital Corp., July 23, 2019, pursuant to the Qualifying Transaction reverse takeover acquisition of (old) Gaia Grow Corp.

Directors - Frederick (Fred) Pels, CEO, Edmonton, Alta.; James C. Tworek, pres., Calgary, Alta.; Marc A. Lowenstein, CFO, Calgary, Alta.

Other Exec. Officers - Cassandra Gee, corp. sec.

Capital Stock

	Authorized (shs.)	Outstanding (shs.)[1]
Common	unlimited	17,716,995

[1] At Nov. 8, 2022

Major Shareholder - Etienne Moshevich held 29.43% interest and Frederick (Fred) Pels held 19.52% interest at Apr. 16, 2020.

Price Range - GAIA/TSX-VEN (D)

Year	Volume	High	Low	Close
2022	15,753,558	$0.75	$0.03	$0.05
2021	7,038,316	$2.75	$0.50	$0.63
2020	2,064,248	$1.75	$0.25	$0.63
2019	1,570,774	$3.50	$0.63	$0.75
2018	4,140	$4.50	$1.58	$3.00

Consolidation: 1-for-25 cons. in Aug. 2022

Recent Close: $0.01

Capital Stock Changes - On Aug. 9, 2022, common shares were consolidated on a 1-for-25 basis.

Wholly Owned Subsidiaries

Gaia Grow Holdings Corp., Vancouver, B.C.
- 100% int. in **Gaia Bio-Pharmaceuticals Inc.**, Alta.

1193805 B.C. Ltd.
1202465 B.C. Ltd., B.C.
Patriot Cannabis Brands Inc., B.C.
Regenco Technology Inc., Alta.
TruExtracts Inc., Canada.

Financial Statistics

Periods ended:	12m Dec. 31/21[A]		12m Dec. 31/20[A]
	$000s	%Chg	$000s
Operating revenue	**7**	**n.a.**	**nil**
General & admin expense	1,966		809
Operating expense	**1,966**	**+143**	**809**
Operating income	**(1,959)**	**n.a.**	**(809)**
Deprec., depl. & amort.	188		49
Finance income	1		nil
Finance costs, gross	148		28
Write-downs/write-offs	(4,360)		(5,198)
Pre-tax income	**(6,521)**	**n.a.**	**(6,205)**
Net income	**(6,521)**	**n.a.**	**(6,205)**
Cash & equivalent	430		775
Accounts receivable	155		54
Current assets	687		884
Fixed assets, net	187		141
Right-of-use assets	1,285		236
Total assets	**2,159**	**+71**	**1,261**
Accts. pay. & accr. liabs.	357		263
Current liabilities	542		338
Long-term lease liabilities	1,174		177
Shareholders' equity	(508)		747
Cash from oper. activs.	**(1,992)**	**n.a.**	**(987)**
Cash from fin. activs.	1,647		(82)
Cash from invest. activs.	nil		(81)
Net cash position	**430**	**-45**	**775**
Capital expenditures	nil		(81)
	$		$
Earnings per share*	(0.50)		(0.75)
Cash flow per share*	(0.17)		(0.11)
	shs		shs
No. of shs. o/s*	13,661,459		9,300,079
Avg. no. of shs. o/s*	11,520,787		8,937,442
	%		%
Net profit margin	n.m.		n.a.
Return on equity	n.m.		(186.64)
Return on assets	(372.69)		(169.79)

* Common
[A] Reported in accordance with IFRS

Latest Results

Periods ended:	9m Sept. 30/22[A]		9m Sept. 30/21[A]
	$000s	%Chg	$000s
Operating revenue	129	n.m.	7
Net income	(3,337)	n.a.	(1,676)
	$		$
Earnings per share*	(0.23)		(0.25)

* Common
[A] Reported in accordance with IFRS

Historical Summary
(as originally stated)

Fiscal Year	Oper. Rev. $000s	Net Inc. Bef. Disc. $000s	EPS* $
2021[A]	7	(6,521)	(0.50)
2020[A]	nil	(6,205)	(0.75)
2019[A1]	nil	(3,492)	(0.75)
2018[A2]	nil	nil	n.a.

* Common
[A] Reported in accordance with IFRS
[1] Results reflect the July 23, 2019, Qualifying Transaction reverse takeover acquisition of (old) Gaia Grow Corp.
[2] 27 weeks ended Dec. 31, 2018.
Note: Adjusted throughout for 1-for-25 cons. in Aug. 2022

G.16 Galaxy Digital Holdings Ltd.

Symbol - GLXY **Exchange** - TSX **CUSIP** - G37092
Head Office - 300 Vesey St, New York, NY, United States, 10282
Telephone - (212) 390-9194
Website - www.galaxydigital.io
Email - francesca.donangelo@galaxydigital.io
Investor Relations - Francesca Don Angelo (212) 390-9216
Auditors - KPMG LLP C.P.A., New York, N.Y.
Transfer Agents - TSX Trust Company, Toronto, Ont.
Profile - (Cayman Islands 2018; orig. Ont., 2006 amalg.) Holds interest in a diversified financial services and investment management business dedicated to the digital assets and blockchain technology industry.

Through affiliate **Galaxy Digital Holdings LP** (controlled by Michael Novogratz and the company), operates three distinct business lines:

Global Markets - Galaxy Global Markets (GGM) provides financial products and services primarily to institutions, corporations and qualified individuals within the digital asset ecosystem. GGM operates two business units: Trading and Investment Banking.

The Trading business unit services more than 290 active counterparties globally and provides liquidity on a principal basis across a variety of centralized and decentralized exchanges, and over-the-counter (OTC) markets globally. Through GGM, counterparties can access digital asset spot and derivative trading, bespoke lending and structured products. GGM also engages in proprietary quantitative, arbitrage and macro trading strategies.

The Investment Banking business unit offers financial and strategic advisory services for the digital assets, Web3 and blockchain technology sector. This business unit helps clients execute large, complex transactions, including mergers and acquisitions (M&A) and divestitures; provides restructuring advisory services; and offers equity and debt capital market services, including project financing.

Also developing GalaxyOne, which would integrate trading, derivatives, custody, lending, margin, on-chain staking and research through a regulatory-compliant platform that utilizes robust risk-monitoring tools and transparent reporting.

Asset Management - Galaxy Asset Management (GAM) is a global asset management platform providing investors access to the digital asset ecosystem via a diverse suit of institutional-grade investment vehicles that span passive, active and venture strategies. GAM's passive strategies consist of single- and multi-asset private funds, as well as a suite of regulated spot digital asset exchange-traded funds (ETFs) through partnerships with asset managers in Brazil, Canada, Europe and the U.S. GAM's active strategies offers investors diversified, lower volatility and risk-managed access to the current and next generation of liquid digital assets via a long-biased strategy. GAM's venture strategies are organized around two investment themes: interactive ventures, which is a sector-focused venture arm managing client capital across three funds; and crypto ventures, which invests client capital across two global multi-manager venture funds and manages the partnership's balance sheet venture investments. As at June 30, 2023, GAM had US$2.489 billion of assets under management.

Digital Infrastructure Solutions - Galaxy Digital Infrastructure Solutions (GDIS) develops, operates and invests in technology that powers the digital assets ecosystem. Operations include proprietary Bitcoin and hosting services, critical network validator services, and the development of enterprise-grade custodial technology. Bitcoin mining facilities are located in Dickens cty. (Helios), and Diboll, Tex., with 3.0 EH/s in hash rate under management as at June 30, 2023.

In May 2021, the company's board of directors approved a proposed reorganization and domestication of the company and affiliate **Galaxy Digital Holdings LP** (GDH LP). Under the reorganization, the company and GDH LP would redomicile from the Cayman Islands to Delaware and complete a proposed internal restructuring whereby **Galaxy Digital Pubco Inc.** (Pubco) would be formed to become the successor of the company, with each ordinary share of the company becoming class A shares of Pubco, and control of GDH LP's general partner would be transferred to Pubco from Michael Novogratz. As at August 2023, the reorganization is still pending.

In January 2023, affiliate **Galaxy Digital Holdings LP** acquired additional shares of **Candy Digital LLC** for US$13,000,000.

In December 2022, the company acquired the Helios bitcoin mining facility and its related operations from **Argo Blockchain plc** for US$65,000,000. Helios is located in Dickens cty., Tex., which can operate up to 180 MW of mining capacity.

In August 2022, the company exercised its right to terminate its agreement to acquire Palo Alto, Calif.-based **BitGo**, a digital assets infrastructure provider, for issuance of 44,800,000 common shares of the successor to the company and US$265,000,000 cash. The transaction has an implied value of US$1.158 billion.

Recent Merger and Acquisition Activity

Status: completed **Revised:** Feb. 22, 2023
UPDATE: The transaction was completed for US$44,000,000. PREVIOUS: Galaxy Digital Holdings Ltd. was selected as the winning bidder for GK8, a secure institutional digital asset self-custody platform. Terms were not disclosed. The acquisition would be the result of a sale process executed in connection with Celsius Network LLC's Chapter 11 bankruptcy and is subject to court approvals and other closing conditions. GK8 is a technology provider for institutions looking to custody their digital assets with the highest possible security, using patented technology to safely store cryptocurrencies and execute blockchain transactions without connecting to the Internet

Predecessor Detail - Name changed from Bradmer Pharmaceuticals Inc., Aug. 1, 2018, pursuant to plan of arrangement reverse takeover acquisition of First Coin Capital Corp. and Galaxy Digital LP.; basis 1 new for 126.38 old shs.

Directors - Michael Daffey, chr., London, Middx., United Kingdom; Michael (Mike) Novogratz, CEO, N.Y.; Bill Koutsouras†, Grand Cayman, Cayman Islands; Jane Dietze, R.I.; Dominic Docherty, Dubai, United Arab Emirates; Richard Tavoso, N.J.; Damien Vanderwilt, N.Y.

Other Exec. Officers - Christopher (Chris) Ferraro, pres.; Leon Marshall, man. dir., global head of sales; Erin Brown, COO; Alex Ioffe, CFO; Sebastian Benkert, chief mktg. officer; Thomas Harrop, chief risk officer; Leinee Hornbeck, chief people officer; Kim Pillemer, chief of staff; Eddie Schwartz, chief security officer; Andrew Siegel, chief compliance officer & gen. counsel; Michael Ashe, head, invest. banking; Robert Bogucki, co-head, trading; Sam Englebardt, head, Galaxy Interactive; Amanda Fabiano, head, min.; Tim Grant, head, Europe; Tom Harrop, head, treasury; Luka Jankovic, head, lending; Danielle Johnson, global head, distrib.; Michael Jordan, co-head, principal invests.; Andrew Karos, head, electronic trading; Jonathan Kol, co-head, principal invests.; Steve Kurz, head, asset mgt.; Sam Lee, head, tax; Andrew Taubman, head, opers. tech.; Alex Thorn, head, firmwide research; Mark Toomey, head, North America asset mgt. sales; Jason Urban, co-head, trading; Alexander Field, v-p, eng.; Veronica Baird, chief diversity, equity, inclusion & culture officer; Francesca Don Angelo, deputy gen. counsel & corp. sec.
† Lead director

Capital Stock

	Authorized (shs.)	Outstanding (shs.)[1]	Par
Ordinary	2,000,000,000	106,999,897	$0.001

[1] At Aug. 4, 2023

Normal Course Issuer Bid - The company plans to make normal course purchases of up to 10,056,193 ordinary shares representing 10% of the public float. The bid commenced on May 31, 2023, and expires on May 30, 2024.

Major Shareholder - Widely held at May 19, 2023.

Price Range - GLXY/TSX

Year	Volume	High	Low	Close
2022	230,636,128	$27.49	$3.33	$3.87
2021	194,312,838	$46.70	$7.90	$22.65
2020	73,740,124	$11.67	$0.56	$10.90
2019	28,894,207	$2.91	$1.00	$1.06
2018	21,403,355	$3.18	$0.89	$1.00

Recent Close: $4.84

Capital Stock Changes - During 2022, ordinary shares were issued as follows: 10,055,909 on exchange of class B units of Galaxy Digital Holdings LP, 2,627,053 on exercise of options, 1,424,694 on vesting of restricted and deferred share units, and 23,838 on exercise of warrants; 10,596,720 ordinary shares were repurchased under a Normal Course Issuer Bid and 273,729 ordinary shares were cancelled.

Wholly Owned Subsidiaries

GDH Intermediate LLC, Del.
Galaxy Digital Inc., Del.
- 100% int. in **GDH Titan Merger Sub 1, Inc.**, Del.
- 50% int. in **GDH Titan Merger Sub 2, Inc.**, Del.

Investments

33.1% int. in **Galaxy Digital Holdings LP**, New York, N.Y.

Financial Statistics

Periods ended:	12m Dec. 31/22[A]		12m Dec. 31/21[A]
	US$000s	%Chg	US$000s
General & admin expense	nil		84
Operating expense	**nil**	**n.a.**	**84**
Operating income	**nil**	**n.a.**	**(84)**
Finance income	1,913		nil
Investment income	(333,981)		506,653
Write-downs/write-offs	(252,518)		nil
Pre-tax income	**(578,581)**	**n.a.**	**504,037**
Income taxes	(55,905)		101,955
Net income	**(522,676)**	**n.a.**	**402,082**
Cash & equivalent	10,049		26,823
Accounts receivable	669		3
Current assets	78,914		47,314
Long-term investments	257,810		841,463
Total assets	**394,275**	**-56**	**888,777**
Current liabilities	56,806		66,619
Shareholders' equity	299,308		786,293
Cash from oper. activs	**(76,774)**	**n.a.**	**(19,547)**
Cash from fin. activs	(47,400)		34,129
Cash from invest. activs	107,400		12,241
Net cash position	**10,049**	**-63**	**26,823**
	US$		US$
Earnings per share*	(4.99)		4.27
Cash flow per share*	(0.73)		(0.21)
	shs		shs
No. of shs. o/s*	104,811,539		101,550,494
Avg. no. of shs. o/s*	104,835,527		94,195,024
	%		%
Net profit margin	n.a.		n.a.
Return on equity	(96.29)		77.83
Return on assets	(81.47)		69.53

* Ordinary
[A] Reported in accordance with IFRS

Latest Results

Periods ended:	6m June 30/23[A]		6m June 30/22[A]
	US$000s	%Chg	US$000s
Net income	152,015	n.a.	(175,791)
	US$		US$
Earnings per share*	1.46		(1.68)

* Ordinary
[A] Reported in accordance with IFRS

Historical Summary
(as originally stated)

Fiscal Year	Oper. Rev. US$000s	Net Inc. Bef. Disc. US$000s	EPS* US$
2022[A]	nil	(522,676)	(4.99)
2021[A]	nil	402,082	4.27
2020[A]	nil	103,386	1.51
2019[A]	nil	(132,519)	(2.00)
2018[A1]	nil	(36,673)	(1.37)

* Ordinary
[A] Reported in accordance with IFRS
[1] Results reflect the Aug. 1, 2018, reverse takeover acquisition of Galaxy Digital LP and First Coin Capital Corp.

G.17 Galaxy Ventures Inc.

Symbol - GXY.P **Exchange** - TSX-VEN **CUSIP** - 36321X
Head Office - 615-800 Pender St W, Vancouver, BC, V6C 2V6
Telephone - (604) 780-2510
Email - jy@copsewood.ca
Investor Relations - Jonathan Younie (604) 780-2510
Auditors - Crowe MacKay LLP C.A., Vancouver, B.C.
Lawyers - Sangra Moller LLP, Vancouver, B.C.
Transfer Agents - Odyssey Trust Company, Vancouver, B.C.
Profile - (B.C. 2021) Capital Pool Company.
Common listed on TSX-VEN, Nov. 10, 2022.
Directors - Andrew Thomson, pres. & CEO, Vancouver, B.C.; Daryl Rebeck, Vancouver, B.C.; Baldev T. Sangara, Vancouver, B.C.; Scott Sinclair, Vancouver, B.C.
Other Exec. Officers - Jonathan Younie, CFO & corp. sec.

Capital Stock

	Authorized (shs.)	Outstanding (shs.)[1]
Common	unlimited	8,100,000

[1] At Nov. 10, 2022

Major Shareholder - Widely held at Nov. 10, 2022.
Recent Close: $0.10
Capital Stock Changes - On Nov. 10, 2022, an initial public offering of 5,000,000 common shares was completed at 10¢ per share.

G.18 Gamehost Inc.

Symbol - GH **Exchange** - TSX **CUSIP** - 36468B
Head Office - 104-548 Laura Ave, Red Deer County, AB, T4E 0A5 **Telephone** - (403) 346-4545 **Toll-free** - (877) 703-4545 **Fax** - (403) 340-0683
Website - www.gamehost.ca
Email - cthomas@gamehost.ca
Investor Relations - Craig M. Thomas (877) 703-4545
Auditors - Pivotal LLP C.A., Red Deer, Alta.
Bankers - Canadian Western Bank, Red Deer, Alta.
Lawyers - Lindsey MacCarthy LLP, Calgary, Alta.
Transfer Agents - Computershare Trust Company of Canada Inc.
Profile - (Alta. 2010) Owns and operates casino, hotel and entertainment assets in Alberta.

Wholly owned **Gamehost Limited Partnership** and **Deerfoot Inn & Casino Inc.** own and operate the following:

The Great Northern Casino, a 33,314-sq.-ft., casino and entertainment facility in Grand Prairie, Alta., consisting of 10 table games, 403 slot machines, 30 video lottery terminals and a three-table poker room. The non-gaming area includes a 30-seat cafe, a 290-seat showroom/lounge and office and administrative areas. Also owns the 122-room Service Plus Inns & Suites limited service hotel; a 10,530-sq.-ft. commercial multi-tenant lease facility; and the 94-room Encore Suites limited service hotel, all adjacent to the casino. A complete interior refurbishment and exterior facelift , which includes a redesign of the food and beverage amenities, was completed in December 2022.

The Rivers Casino & Entertainment Centre, a 34,663-sq.-ft. casino and entertainment facility in Fort McMurray, Alta., consisting of 10 table games, 406 slot machines, a three-table poker room and 16 electronic gaming tables. The non-gaming area includes a 40-seat restaurant, a 125-seat lounge and a 180-seat live entertainment showroom.

The Deerfoot Inn and Casino, a 188-room hotel and 67,200-sq.-ft. casino entertainment facility in Calgary, Alta., consisting of 32 table games including an 11-table private high limit room, 773 slot machines, 12 electronic gaming tables, 24 video lottery terminals and nine-table poker room. There is also a 5,300-sq.-ft. live entertainment (pay-per-view sporting events) facility, afternoon buffets, an island pub, a pub style restaurant with café and a sushi bar adjacent to the gaming floor. The hotel facility also includes 28 suites, a restaurant, a lounge, 14 conference/banquet rooms, a health and fitness centre and a full water park.

In March 2023, the company announced that Alberta Gaming, Liquor and Cannabis (AGLC), the gaming regulator in Alberta, increased the slot commission rate of the total net sales of slot operators by 2% for two years to help in the reinvestments in the facilities and for promotional activities.

On May 5, 2022, the company acquired the remaining 9% interest in the Deerfoot Inn and Casino in Calgary, Alta., for $13,600,000.

Predecessor Detail - Succeeded Gamehost Income Fund, Dec. 31, 2010, pursuant to plan of arrangement whereby Gamehost Inc. was formed to facilitate the conversion of the fund into a corporation and the fund was subsequently dissolved.

Directors - David J. Will, chr., pres. & CEO, Red Deer, Alta.; Darcy J. Will, v-p & corp. sec., Red Deer, Alta.; James R. McPherson, Red Deer, Alta.; Peter L. Miles, Vancouver, B.C.; Timothy J. (Tim) Sebastian, Calgary, Alta.; Jerry P. Van Someren, Red Deer, Alta.

Other Exec. Officers - Elston J. Noren, COO; Craig M. Thomas, CFO

Capital Stock

	Authorized (shs.)	Outstanding (shs.)[1]
Preferred	unlimited	nil
Common	unlimited	21,706,492

[1] At Aug. 10, 2023

Normal Course Issuer Bid - The company plans to make normal course purchases of up to 1,085,324 common shares representing 5% of the total outstanding. The bid commenced on Aug. 14, 2023, and expires on Aug. 13, 2024.

Major Shareholder - David J. Will held 26.6% interest and CI Investments Inc. held 11.7% interest at Apr. 4, 2023.

Price Range - GH/TSX

Year	Volume	High	Low	Close
2022	2,540,782	$9.57	$6.98	$8.16
2021	2,030,676	$8.85	$5.75	$6.94
2020	3,507,053	$8.80	$3.31	$5.81
2019	2,091,573	$10.53	$8.01	$8.48
2018	3,000,401	$12.95	$8.88	$9.32

Recent Close: $8.62

Capital Stock Changes - During 2022, 400,000 common shares were repurchased under a Normal Course Issuer Bid.

Dividends

GH com N.S.R. [1]

$0.03	Sept. 15/23	$0.03	Aug. 15/23
$0.03	July 14/23	$0.03	June 15/23

Paid in 2023: $0.27 2022: $0.27 2021: n.a.

[1] Monthly divd normally payable in May/20 has been omitted.

Wholly Owned Subsidiaries

Deerfoot Inn & Casino Inc., Calgary, Alta.
Gamehost Limited Partnership, Alta.

Financial Statistics

Periods ended:	12m Dec. 31/22^A		12m Dec. 31/21^A
	$000s	%Chg	$000s
Operating revenue	**69,700**	**+109**	**33,300**
Cost of sales	21,500		10,200
Salaries & benefits	20,700		11,300
General & admin expense	3,000		2,300
Operating expense	**45,200**	**+90**	**23,800**
Operating income	**24,500**	**+158**	**9,500**
Deprec., depl. & amort.	4,800		4,400
Finance income	100		100
Finance costs, gross	2,600		1,700
Pre-tax income	**16,300**	**+114**	**7,600**
Income taxes	3,300		1,500
Net income	**13,000**	**+113**	**6,100**
Net inc. for equity hldrs	**12,700**	**+127**	**5,600**
Net inc. for non-cont. int.	**300**	**-40**	**500**
Cash & equivalent	15,600		15,600
Inventories	700		600
Accounts receivable	2,100		4,900
Current assets	20,000		22,700
Long-term investments	1,200		1,500
Fixed assets, net	75,300		76,600
Right-of-use assets	10,000		10,700
Intangibles, net	76,900		76,900
Total assets	**183,400**	**-3**	**188,400**
Accts. pay. & accr. liabs.	4,600		3,900
Current liabilities	33,300		31,300
Long-term debt, gross	54,500		49,000
Long-term debt, net	27,200		22,300
Long-term lease liabilities	11,600		12,200
Shareholders' equity	103,900		108,000
Non-controlling interest	nil		6,500
Cash from oper. activs	**20,800**	**+93**	**10,800**
Cash from fin. activs	(18,300)		2,900
Cash from invest. activs	(2,500)		(8,400)
Net cash position	**15,600**	**0**	**15,600**
Capital expenditures	(2,500)		(8,400)
	$		$
Earnings per share*	0.56		0.24
Cash flow per share*	0.92		0.47
Cash divd. per share*	0.30		nil
	shs		shs
No. of shs. o/s*	22,300,000		22,700,000
Avg. no. of shs. o/s*	22,500,000		23,000,000
	%		%
Net profit margin	18.65		18.32
Return on equity	11.99		5.23
Return on assets	8.11		4.11

* Common
^A Reported in accordance with IFRS

Latest Results

Periods ended:	3m Mar. 31/23^A		3m Mar. 31/22^A
	$000s	%Chg	$000s
Operating revenue	19,839	+33	14,900
Net income	4,547	+107	2,200
Net inc. for equity hldrs	4,547	+127	2,000
Net inc. for non-cont. int.	nil		200
	$		$
Earnings per share*	0.21		0.09

* Common
^A Reported in accordance with IFRS

Historical Summary
(as originally stated)

Fiscal Year	Oper. Rev.	Net Inc. Bef. Disc.	EPS*
	$000s	$000s	$
2022^A	69,700	13,000	0.56
2021^A	33,300	6,100	0.24
2020^A	34,600	5,700	0.22
2019^A	68,100	16,600	0.64
2018^A	70,400	18,200	0.69

* Common
^A Reported in accordance with IFRS

G.19 Gamelancer Media Corp.

Symbol - GMNG **Exchange** - TSX **CUSIP** - 36468M
Head Office - 405-120 Carlton St, Toronto, ON, M5A 4K2 **Telephone** - (416) 457-5201
Website - gamelancer.com
Email - jon.dwyer@gamelancer.com
Investor Relations - Jonathan Dwyer (416) 627-8868
Auditors - MNP LLP C.A., Toronto, Ont.
Transfer Agents - Computershare Trust Company of Canada Inc., Vancouver, B.C.
Employees - 3 at Dec. 31, 2022

Profile - (Ont. 2023; orig. B.C., 1999) Produces short-form video content for brands, with broadcast on its owned and operated channels on TikTok, Snapchat and Instagram.

The company owns and operates a network of 44 channels where it sells direct advertising for clients and partners. The network across multiple platforms produces and distributes content to over 39,000,000 followers and subscribers, generating over 2 billion monthly video views. Subscribers are located in the U.S., Canada, the U.K., and Australia. Develops brand, agency and creator relationships through its strategic partnerships with **TikTok North America** and **Snap Inc.**, and operates a business with Snapchat where it creates Snapchat Discover shows which generate monthly recurring revenue.

On Apr. 5, 2023, the company continued from British Columbia to Ontario.

On Sept. 20, 2022, the company announced that it would take steps to write down its NFT (non-fungible token) assets and cease operating in the NFT market.

In March 2022, the company acquired **JoyBox Media Inc.** (rebranded Gamelancer Studios), a media network and marketing agency, for $131,526 and issuance of 3,333,332 common shares at a deemed price of 15¢ per share. The company would also pay up to $168,474 and issue up to $700,000 of common shares upon achieving certain milestones.

Common listed on TSX, July 19, 2023.
Common delisted from CSE, July 19, 2023.

Recent Merger and Acquisition Activity

Status: completed **Revised:** Apr. 14, 2022
UPDATE: The transaction was completed. PREVIOUS: Wondr Gaming Corp. entered into letter of intent to acquire Gamelancer, Inc. for US$10,000,000, of which US$7,500,000 was payable on closing and the balance within one year of closing. Gamelancer was the largest Gen Z social gaming network with more 24,000,000 fans and 1 billion monthly video views across 22 channels on TikTok, Instagram and Snapchat. Mar. 21, 2022 - A definitive agreement was entered into. Consideration would be the issuance of 212,338,900 Wondr common shares and US$12,000,000 cash, with US$7,000,000 payable on closing, US$2,500,000 within six months of closing and US$2,500,000 twelve months from closing. Upon completion, Wondr would change its name to Gamelancer Gaming Corp.

Predecessor Detail - Name changed from Gamelancer Gaming Corp., Sept. 27, 2022.

Directors - Jonathan (Jon) Dwyer, chr. & CEO, Mississauga, Ont.; Razvan Romanescu, chief strategy officer, Panama City, Panama; Jean-Francois (JF) Cote†, Qué.; Samuel Banks, New York, N.Y.; Paul Coffey, Ont.; Cyril M. Leeder, Ottawa, Ont.; Robert (Rob) Segal, Toronto, Ont.

Other Exec. Officers - Max Desmarais, pres.; Michael (Mike) Cotton, COO & chief bus. officer; Pooja Sharma, CFO; Tommy Callaway, chief technical officer; Rob Frohling, chief revenue officer; Zak Longo, chief creative officer; Darren Lopes, chief product officer; Gareth Hill, sr. v-p & global head, partnerships; Gopal Patel, v-p, opers.; Ian Rasmussen, v-p & head, cust. success
† Lead director

Capital Stock

	Authorized (shs.)	Outstanding (shs.)[1]
Common	unlimited	561,545,994

[1] At July 19, 2023

Major Shareholder - Razvan Romanescu held 20.42% interest, Mayfair Gaming, LLC held 10.7% interest and Darren Lopes held 10.22% interest at May 8, 2023.

Price Range - TTI.H/TSX-VEN (D)

Year	Volume	High	Low	Close
2022	69,452,524	$0.20	$0.05	$0.11
2021	53,491,041	$0.40	$0.16	$0.18

Recent Close: $0.10

Capital Stock Changes - In June 2023, private placement of 100,035,500 units (1 common share & 1 warrant) at 10¢ per unit was completed, with warrants exercisable at 15¢ per share for three years. In July 2023, 13,333,334 common shares were issued as final payment related to Gamelancer, Inc. acquisition.

In January and February 2022, private placement of 50,000,000 units (1 common share & ½ warrants) at 20¢ per unit was completed. In March 2022, 3,333,332 common shares were issued pursuant to the acquisition of JoyBox Media Inc. On Apr. 14, 2022, 212,338,900 common shares were issued pursuant to the acquisition of Gamelancer, Inc. Also during 2022, common shares were issued as follows: 10,000,000 on exercise of options, 3,000,000 for advisory services and 162,800 on exercise of warrants.

Wholly Owned Subsidiaries

Enterprise Gaming Canada Inc., Canada.
Hot Dot Media Inc.
JoyBox Media Inc., B.C.
Wondr Gaming Corporation, Mississauga, Ont.
Wondr Gaming USA Corp., Del.
- 100% int. in **Gamelancer, Inc.**, Calif.

Financial Statistics

Periods ended:	12m Dec. 31/22[A]		12m Dec. 31/21[A1]
	$000s	%Chg	$000s
Operating revenue	**3,564**	**n.m.**	**187**
Salaries & benefits	746		626
Research & devel. expense	nil		894
General & admin expense	7,629		3,910
Stock-based compensation	2,190		691
Operating expense	**10,565**	**+73**	**6,121**
Operating income	**(7,001)**	**n.a.**	**(5,934)**
Deprec., depl. & amort.	1,680		82
Finance income	3		4
Finance costs, gross	277		201
Write-downs/write-offs	(988)		(170)
Pre-tax income	**(11,295)**	**n.a.**	**(9,579)**
Income taxes	(587)		nil
Net income	**(10,708)**	**n.a.**	**(9,579)**
Cash & equivalent	557		3,753
Inventories	88		nil
Accounts receivable	1,754		367
Current assets	2,552		4,423
Fixed assets, net	2		5
Right-of-use assets	nil		22
Intangibles, net	46,956		3,343
Total assets	**49,564**	**+532**	**7,848**
Accts. pay. & accr. liabs	3,268		1,620
Current liabilities	7,953		1,697
Long-term debt, gross	3,989		nil
Long-term debt, net	3,989		nil
Shareholders' equity	32,350		6,150
Cash from oper. activs	**(5,484)**	**n.a.**	**(4,663)**
Cash from fin. activs	14,906		8,200
Cash from invest. activs	(12,600)		(48)
Net cash position	**557**	**-85**	**3,753**
Capital expenditures	(2)		(5)
	$		$
Earnings per share*	(0.03)		(0.07)
Cash flow per share*	(0.01)		(0.03)
	shs		shs
No. of shs. o/s*	443,507,494		164,672,462
Avg. no. of shs. o/s*	369,389,628		138,519,774
	%		%
Net profit margin	(300.45)		n.m.
Return on equity	n.m.		(297.35)
Return on assets	n.a.		(215.64)
No. of employees (FTEs)	3		n.a.

* Common
[A] Reported in accordance with IFRS
[1] Results reflect the May 3, 2021, reverse takeover acquisition of Wondr Gaming Corporation.

Latest Results

Periods ended:	3m Mar. 31/23[A]		3m Mar. 31/22[A]
	$000s	%Chg	$000s
Operating revenue	722	+978	67
Net income	(2,591)	n.a.	(1,674)
	$		$
Earnings per share*	(0.01)		(0.01)

* Common
[A] Reported in accordance with IFRS

Historical Summary
(as originally stated)

Fiscal Year	Oper. Rev.	Net Inc. Bef. Disc.	EPS*
	$000s	$000s	$
2022[A]	3,564	(10,708)	(0.03)
2021[A]	187	(9,579)	(0.07)
2020[A1]	nil	(1,934)	n.a.
2020[A2]	nil	136	0.03
2019[A]	nil	(27)	(0.08)

* Common
[A] Reported in accordance with IFRS
[1] Results pertain to Wondr Gaming Corporation.
[2] Results for fiscal 2020 and prior fiscal years pertain to TransGlobe Internet and Telecom Co., Ltd.
Note: Adjusted throughout for 1-for-30 cons. in Apr. 2021

G.20 GameOn Entertainment Technologies Inc.

Symbol - GET **Exchange** - CSE **CUSIP** - 36468X
Head Office - 401-750 Pender St W, Vancouver, BC, V6C 2T7 **Telephone** - (604) 428-7050 **Fax** - (604) 428-7052
Website - www.gameon.app
Email - matt@gameon.app
Investor Relations - Matthew Bailey (604) 428-7050
Auditors - MNP LLP C.A., Burlington, Ont.
Transfer Agents - Odyssey Trust Company, Vancouver, B.C.
Profile - (B.C. 2010) Provides broadcasters, TV networks, streaming platforms, leagues, tournaments, sportsbook and Non-fungible token (NFT) projects with while label prediction games, fantasy games and NFT-based games.

Proprietary products include FanClash, which creates game play around live events using a real-time fantasy technology where a fan can earn points for every pass, tackle, assist and other actions.

In June 2021, common shares were listed on the Frankfurt Stock Exchange in Germany under the symbol GET.

Predecessor Detail - Name changed from V2 Games Inc., Jan. 13, 2021.

Directors - Carey Dillen, chr., Vancouver, B.C.; Matthew (Matt) Bailey, CEO, Miami, Fla.; David Meltzer; Katrina Palanca, Tex.; Shafin D. Tejani, Vancouver, B.C.

Other Exec. Officers - Sheri Rempel, CFO; Sohail Godall, v-p, opers.; Ryan Nowack, v-p, partnerships

Capital Stock

	Authorized (shs.)	Outstanding (shs.)[1]
Common	unlimited	64,730,846

[1] At Nov. 23, 2022

Major Shareholder - Victory Square Technologies Inc. held 21.55% interest at June 30, 2022.

Price Range - GET/CSE

Year	Volume	High	Low	Close
2022	10,483,306	$0.25	$0.04	$0.05
2021	20,235,542	$0.98	$0.22	$0.23

Recent Close: $0.14

Wholly Owned Subsidiaries

V2 Games USA Inc., Del.

Financial Statistics

Periods ended:	12m Dec. 31/21[A]		12m Dec. 31/20[A]
	$000s	%Chg	$000s
Operating revenue	**13**	**+333**	**3**
Salaries & benefits	1,285		74
General & admin expense	3,987		346
Stock-based compensation	2,669		nil
Operating expense	**7,940**	**n.m.**	**421**
Operating income	**(7,927)**	**n.a.**	**(418)**
Deprec., depl. & amort.	603		633
Finance income	nil		252
Finance costs, gross	327		300
Write-downs/write-offs	(383)		(202)
Pre-tax income	**(9,121)**	**n.a.**	**(981)**
Income taxes	(51)		nil
Net income	**(9,071)**	**n.a.**	**(981)**
Cash & equivalent	1,610		135
Current assets	1,794		1,903
Long-term investments	nil		985
Intangibles, net	4,374		4,374
Total assets	**6,169**	**-16**	**7,366**
Bank indebtedness	nil		295
Accts. pay. & accr. liabs	268		161
Current liabilities	385		3,229
Long-term debt, gross	136		1,650
Long-term debt, net	41		107
Equity portion of conv. debs	428		200
Shareholders' equity	5,743		3,997
Cash from oper. activs	**(5,403)**	**n.a.**	**(500)**
Cash from fin. activs	5,179		574
Cash from invest. activs	1,698		4
Net cash position	**1,610**	**n.m.**	**135**
	$		$
Earnings per share*	(0.16)		(0.04)
Cash flow per share*	(0.10)		(0.02)
	shs		shs
No. of shs. o/s*	63,192,385		43,483,298
Avg. no. of shs. o/s*	55,463,069		28,000,000
	%		%
Net profit margin	n.m.		n.m.
Return on equity	(186.26)		(44.71)
Return on assets	(129.23)		(12.84)

* Common
[A] Reported in accordance with IFRS

Historical Summary
(as originally stated)

Fiscal Year	Oper. Rev.	Net Inc. Bef. Disc.	EPS*
	$000s	$000s	$
2021[A]	13	(9,071)	(0.16)
2020[A]	3	(981)	(0.04)
2019[A]	4	271	0.01

* Common
[A] Reported in accordance with IFRS

G.21 GameSquare Holdings, Inc.

Symbol - GAME **Exchange** - TSX-VEN **CUSIP** - 364934
Head Office - 33 Whitehall St, 8th Flr, New York, NY, United States, 10004 **Telephone** - (212) 931-1200
Website - www.enginegaming.com
Email - mmunoz@franklymedia.com
Investor Relations - Michael Munoz (212) 931-1200
Auditors - Kreston GTA LLP C.A., Markham, Ont.
Transfer Agents - Computershare Trust Company of Canada Inc., Toronto, Ont.
Profile - (B.C. 2020; orig. Ont., 2011) Operates as a gaming, eSports and media company offering eSports content, streaming technology, gaming platforms, data analytics, marketing and advertising.

Wholly owned **Code Red Esports Ltd.** operates an eSports agency which represents on-screen talent, influencers and players in Europe and throughout the world and provides eSports consultancy for brands and organizations.

Wholly owned **GCN Inc.** designs, produces and manages gaming and eSports platforms for tournaments, influencer campaigns, livestream and video-on-demand (VOD) content development.

Wholly owned **NextGen Tech, LLC** (dba as Complexity Gaming) is an eSports team made up of players from various countries which compete in several game franchises, including CS:GO, Fortnite, Valorant, APEX Legends, Hearthstone, Madden Football and FIFA Soccer.

Wholly owned **Swingman LLC** (dba Cut+Sew and Zoned) is a gaming and lifestyle marketing agency with a focus on traditional sports, gaming, emerging technology, new media, music and fashion.

Wholly owned **GameSquare Esports (USA) Inc.** (dba Fourth Frame Studios) is a creative production studio which focuses on gaming, pop culture and youth.

Wholly owned **Mission Supply Co.** provides merchandise and consumer product design, marketing and sales consultation to brands and eSports organizations.

Wholly owned **Frankly Inc.** provides a complete suite of solutions which allow broadcasters and publishers to create, manage, publish and monetize digital content across all channels. Products include an online video platform for live, video-on-demand (VOD) and live-to-VOD workflows; a content management system; and mobile applications and over-the-top (OTT) TV applications. Frankly also provides comprehensive advertising products and services, including direct sales and programmatic ad support.

Wholly owned **Stream Hatchet S.L.** provides gaming and eSports streaming data analytics software products and services for clients including streamers, eSports organizations, video game publishers and advertising agencies.

Wholly owned **Sideqik, Inc.** offers an influencer marketing platform to brands, direct marketers and agencies for discovering, connecting and executing marketing campaigns with content creators/social media influencers.

In July 2022, the company discontinued operations of WinView, a skills-based sports prediction mobile games platform for traditional sports and eSports.

In June 2022, the company completed the sale of certain assets of wholly owned **UMG Events, LLC** to **Harena Data, Inc.**, for US$100. Concurrently, the company entered into a transition services agreement with the purchaser for a total value of US$300,000 with payments beginning July 31, 2022, and the remainder to be paid in full, 12 months following the first payment. UMG offered a video gaming competition platform for eSports events, live gaming entertainment events and online play as well as created and distributed eSports content.

In April 2022, 96%-owned **Eden Games S.A.**, a gaming studio which designs and develops racing games for mobile and gaming consoles, was sold.

Recent Merger and Acquisition Activity

Status: completed **Revised:** Apr. 6, 2023
UPDATE: The transaction was completed. PREVIOUS: Engine Gaming & Media, Inc. entered into a definitive agreement for the reverse takeover of Toronto, Ont.-based Gamesquare Esports Inc., whereby Engine would issue 0.08262 Engine common shares for each common share of GameSquare. A total of 25,409,372 Engine common shares is expected to be issued to GameSquare shareholders that would result in GameSquare shareholders holding 60% interest in Engine. GameSquare operates an eSports, lifestyle and marketing agency. The transaction is expected to be completed in the first quarter of 2023.

Predecessor Detail - Name changed from Engine Gaming and Media, Inc., Apr. 11, 2023, pursuant to the reverse takeover acquisition of Gamesquare Esports Inc.; basis 1 new for 4 old shs.

Directors - Tom Rogers, exec. chr., New York, N.Y.; Justin Kenna, CEO, Los Angeles, Calif.; Louis (Lou) Schwartz, pres., Atlanta, Ga.; Travis Goff, Dallas, Tex.; Jeremi Gorman; Stuart (Stu) Porter; Thomas (Tom) Walker, Dallas, Tex.

Other Exec. Officers - Michael (Mike) Munoz, CFO; Tyler Blevins, chief innovation officer; Paolo DiPasquale, chief strategy officer; Matthew (Matt) Ehrens, chief tech. officer; Sean Horvath, chief revenue officer; Jill Peters, chief media officer; John Wilk, gen. counsel

Capital Stock

	Authorized (shs.)	Outstanding (shs.)[1]
Preferred	unlimited	nil
Common	unlimited	12,678,378

[1] At Apr. 11, 2023

Major Shareholder - Blue & Silver Ventures, Ltd. held 11.4% interest and John C. Goff held 10.4% interest at Apr. 11, 2023.

Price Range - GAME/TSX-VEN

Year	Volume	High	Low	Close
2022	499,026	$17.00	$2.72	$5.40
2021	1,962,287	$66.00	$14.48	$15.40
2020	1,426,435	$72.00	$23.40	$41.12
2019	85,476	$562.50	$30.00	$68.40
2018	11,542	$3,915.00	$225.00	$270.00

Consolidation: 1-for-4 cons. in Apr. 2023; 1-for-15 cons. in Aug. 2020; 1-for-5 cons. in Oct. 2019; 1-for-15 cons. in June 2019
Recent Close: $3.35
Capital Stock Changes - In April 2023, common shares were consolidated on a 1-for-4 basis, 6,519,996 post-consolidated common

shares were issued on acquisition of Gamesquare Esports Inc., and 1,918,250 post-consolidated common shares were issued without further consideration on exchange of subscription receipts sold previously by public offering at US$5.00 each.

During fiscal 2022, common shares were issued as follows: 203,537 on vesting of restricted share units and 57,029 for services.

Wholly Owned Subsidiaries

Frankly Inc., New York, N.Y.
- 100% int. in **Frankly Co.**, Calif.
- 100% int. in **Frankly Media LLC**, New York, N.Y.
- 100% int. in **Vemba Media Technologies Pvt. Ltd.**, India.

Gamesquare Esports Inc., Toronto, Ont.
- 100% int. in **Code Red Esports Ltd.**, London, Middx., United Kingdom.
- 100% int. in **GameSquare Esports (USA) Inc.**, Nev.
  - 100% int. in **GCN Inc.**, Los Angeles, Calif.
  - 100% int. in **NextGen Tech, LLC**, Frisco, Tex.
  - 100% int. in **Swingman LLC**, Los Angeles, Calif.
- 100% int. in **Mission Supply Co.**, Aurora, Colo.

Sideqik, Inc., Atlanta, Ga.
Stream Hatchet S.L., Terrassa, Spain.

Financial Statistics

Periods ended:	12m Aug. 31/22[A]		12m Aug. 31/21[□A]
	US$000s	%Chg	US$000s
Operating revenue	**41,883**	**+26**	**33,345**
Salaries & benefits	14,087		12,161
General & admin expense	10,644		8,840
Stock-based compensation	4,688		3,703
Other operating expense	30,090		23,289
Operating expense	**59,509**	**+1**	**58,739**
Operating income	**(17,626)**	**n.a.**	**(25,394)**
Deprec., depl. & amort.	1,242		4,891
Finance costs, gross	730		1,275
Investment income	nil		(104)
Write-downs/write-offs	(3,873)		nil
Pre-tax income	**(16,402)**	**n.a.**	**(24,552)**
Net inc. bef. disc. opers	**(16,402)**	**n.a.**	**(24,552)**
Income from disc. opers	1,988		(16,243)
Net income	**(14,413)**	**n.a.**	**(40,795)**
Net inc. for equity hldrs	**(14,479)**	**n.a.**	**(40,721)**
Net inc. for non-cont. int.	**65**	**n.a.**	**(74)**
Cash & equivalent	8,602		15,306
Accounts receivable	8,404		8,647
Current assets	22,059		31,558
Long-term investments	2,630		2,630
Fixed assets, net	127		404
Right-of-use assets	11		557
Intangibles, net	17,867		30,977
Total assets	**42,695**	**-37**	**67,463**
Bank indebtedness	772		822
Accts. pay. & accr. liabs	16,529		16,126
Current liabilities	21,825		32,495
Long-term debt, gross	7,250		10,048
Long-term debt, net	4,983		9,037
Long-term lease liabilities	nil		365
Shareholders' equity	15,887		25,422
Non-controlling interest	nil		143
Cash from oper. activs	**(20,330)**	**n.a.**	**(30,339)**
Cash from fin. activs	(327)		39,584
Cash from invest. activs	13,451		92
Net cash position	**8,602**	**-44**	**15,306**
Capital expenditures	(79)		(188)
	US$		US$
Earns. per sh. bef disc opers*	(4.20)		(8.24)
Earnings per share*	(3.72)		(13.72)
Cash flow per share*	(5.20)		(10.22)
	shs		shs
No. of shs. o/s*	3,950,969		3,885,827
Avg. no. of shs. o/s*	3,909,355		2,968,694
	%		%
Net profit margin	(39.16)		(73.63)
Return on equity	(79.73)		(192.23)
Return on assets	(28.45)		(38.51)
No. of employees (FTEs)	...		195

* Common
□ Restated
[A] Reported in accordance with IFRS

Latest Results

Periods ended:	3m Nov. 30/22[A]		3m Nov. 30/21[□A]
	US$000s	%Chg	US$000s
Operating revenue	10,270	-16	12,214
Net inc. bef. disc. opers	(5,500)	n.a.	2,136
Income from disc. opers	134		(3,464)
Net income	(5,366)	n.a.	(1,329)
Net inc. for equity hldrs	(5,366)	n.a.	(1,353)
Net inc. for non-cont. int.	nil		25
	US$		US$
Earns. per sh. bef. disc. opers.*	(1.40)		0.56
Earnings per share*	(1.36)		(0.32)

* Common
□ Restated
[A] Reported in accordance with IFRS

Historical Summary
(as originally stated)

Fiscal Year	Oper. Rev. US$000s	Net Inc. Bef. Disc. US$000s	EPS* US$
2022[A]	41,883	(16,402)	(4.20)
2021[A]	37,221	(39,171)	(13.16)
2020[A]	11,108	(32,415)	(43.84)
2019[A]	4,219	(14,097)	(376.77)
2018[A]	3,633	(11,503)	(360.00)

* Common
[A] Reported in accordance with IFRS

Note: Adjusted throughout for 1-for-4 cons. in Apr. 2023; 1-for-15 cons. in Aug. 2020; 1-for-5 cons. in Oct. 2019; 1-for-15 cons. in June 2019

G.22 Gatekeeper Systems Inc.

Symbol - GSI **Exchange** - TSX-VEN **CUSIP** - 36734X
Head Office - 301-31127 Wheel Ave, Abbotsford, BC, V2T 6H1 **Telephone** - (604) 864-6187 **Toll-free** - (888) 666-4833 **Fax** - (604) 864-8490
Website - www.gatekeeper-systems.com
Email - kchin@gatekeeper-systems.com
Investor Relations - Kelsey Chin (604) 864-6187
Auditors - Buckley Dodds C.P.A., Vancouver, B.C.
Transfer Agents - Computershare Trust Company of Canada Inc., Vancouver, B.C.

Profile - (B.C. 2010) Engineers, manufactures and distributes high-definition mobile video and data solutions for various markets including school districts, law enforcement, pubic transit authorities, as well as the U.S. military and coast guard under a Platform-as-a-Service business model.

Products include interior and exterior cameras; digital video recorders (DVRs); dashboard cameras; wireless access points; mobile wireless modules; video display mirror; and mobile WiFi system. Also offers ITSS™ (Intelligent Temperature Sensing System), an infrared body temperature sensor system that incorporates a smart panel, thermal imaging and artificial intelligence to quickly and accurately measure the body temperature of passengers who board school buses and public transportation vehicles; TIMS™ (Ticket Infraction Management System), a cloud-based software application for managing citations from school bus stop arm violations and photo enforcement systems; Student Protector™, a high-speed licence plate reading system which records licence plates of stop arm violators and issues tickets or citations; G4 Enterprise incident management software, which provides video analytics and wireless interconnectivity to the company's on-vehicle DVRs; CLARITY, an industry-first integrated video and school bus operating platform that offers a solution, including providing school districts with the scheduling and on-bus video and data analysis tools they need to efficiently manage the logistics of their school bus operations; and Automated Lane Enforcement (ALE™), a video and data analytics solution that provides automatic enforcement of transit lane violations by automating video evidence capture and processing vehicle infractions relating to bus lanes and streetcars.

Office, manufacturing and research and development activities are conducted at a 25,000-sq.-ft. facility in Abbotsford, B.C. Also has a service centre in Bristol, Pa., for its transit customer South East Pennsylvania Transit Authority. Products destined for U.S. customers are assembled in the Bristol facility.

Predecessor Detail - Name changed from Indigo Sky Capital Corp., May 28, 2013, pursuant to Qualifying Transaction reverse takeover acquisition of (old) Gatekeeper Systems Inc. (subsequently renamed GSI Systems Inc.).

Directors - Douglas A. (Doug) Dyment, chr., pres. & CEO, Chilliwack, B.C.; Charlie Bruce, N.Y.; David Stumpo, Wash.

Other Exec. Officers - Kelsey Chin, CFO & corp. sec.; Douglas M. Fraser, v-p, product mgt. & programs; Jeff Gruban, v-p, sales & bus. devel.; Jason Harris, v-p, student protector programs; Valerie Higgins, v-p, sales

Capital Stock

	Authorized (shs.)	Outstanding (shs.)[1]	Par
Class A Preferred	unlimited	nil	n.p.v.
Class B Preferred	unlimited	nil	$0.01
Class C Preferred	unlimited	nil	n.p.v.
Common	unlimited	91,399,395	n.p.v.

[1] At May 31, 2023

Major Shareholder - Douglas A. (Doug) Dyment held 10.2% interest at Nov. 14, 2022.

Price Range - GSI/TSX-VEN

Year	Volume	High	Low	Close
2022	28,531,934	$0.61	$0.19	$0.27
2021	48,132,280	$1.43	$0.47	$0.51
2020	84,765,225	$0.99	$0.12	$0.69
2019	65,985,492	$0.28	$0.09	$0.23
2018	39,587,033	$0.15	$0.08	$0.10

Recent Close: $0.33

Capital Stock Changes - During fiscal 2022, 1,095,500 common shares were issued on exercise of options.

Wholly Owned Subsidiaries

Gatekeeper Systems U.S.A. Inc., Delaware, Ont.

Note: The preceding list includes only the major related companies in which interests are held.

Financial Statistics

Periods ended:	12m Aug. 31/22[A]		12m Aug. 31/21[□A]
	$000s	%Chg	$000s
Operating revenue	**20,031**	**+16**	**17,231**
Cost of sales	10,722		9,715
Salaries & benefits	4,161		3,512
Research & devel. expense	1,445		1,353
General & admin expense	1,777		2,569
Stock-based compensation	265		12
Operating expense	**18,371**	**+50**	**12,284**
Operating income	**1,661**	**-66**	**4,947**
Deprec., depl. & amort.	366		359
Finance income	10		4
Finance costs, gross	220		137
Write-downs/write-offs	(55)		(4)
Pre-tax income	**1,443**	**n.a.**	**(683)**
Income taxes	(432)		316
Net income	**1,875**	**n.a.**	**(1,000)**
Cash & equivalent	2,604		3,601
Inventories	8,491		4,684
Accounts receivable	8,630		3,101
Current assets	20,089		11,654
Fixed assets, net	1,180		1,237
Intangibles, net	160		156
Total assets	**23,016**	**+60**	**14,402**
Accts. pay. & accr. liabs	4,808		2,196
Current liabilities	8,892		2,632
Long-term lease liabilities	738		670
Shareholders' equity	12,546		9,980
Cash from oper. activs	**(4,597)**	**n.a.**	**4,142**
Cash from fin. activs	3,624		(1,452)
Cash from invest. activs	(30)		(107)
Net cash position	**2,604**	**-28**	**3,601**
Capital expenditures	(30)		(94)
	$		$
Earnings per share*	0.02		(0.01)
Cash flow per share*	(0.05)		0.05
	shs		shs
No. of shs. o/s*	91,399,395		90,303,895
Avg. no. of shs. o/s*	90,883,613		89,804,860
	%		%
Net profit margin	9.36		(5.80)
Return on equity	15.86		(9.61)
Return on assets	11.55		(5.33)
Foreign sales percent	91		85

* Common
□ Restated
[A] Reported in accordance with IFRS

Latest Results

Periods ended:	3m Nov. 30/22[A]		3m Nov. 30/21[A]
	$000s	%Chg	$000s
Operating revenue	4,885	+81	2,700
Net income	(152)	n.a.	213
	$		$
Earnings per share*	(0.00)		0.00

* Common
[A] Reported in accordance with IFRS

Historical Summary
(as originally stated)

Fiscal Year	Oper. Rev. $000s	Net Inc. Bef. Disc. $000s	EPS* $
2022[A]	20,031	1,875	0.02
2021[A]	17,231	121	0.00
2020[A]	20,317	3,579	0.04
2019[A]	13,726	(295)	(0.00)
2018[A]	7,851	(1,323)	(0.02)

* Common
[A] Reported in accordance with IFRS

G.23 Geekco Technologies Corporation

Symbol - GKO **Exchange** - TSX-VEN **CUSIP** - 36847L
Head Office - 620-1600A boul Saint-Martin E, Laval, QC, H7G 4R8
Telephone - (450) 681-7744 **Fax** - (450) 681-8400
Email - info@flipnpik-na.com
Investor Relations - Mario Beaulieu (514) 402-6334
Auditors - Bélanger Dalcourt Randlett Fequet CPA Inc. C.A., Montréal, Qué.
Transfer Agents - Computershare Trust Company of Canada Inc., Montréal, Qué.
Profile - (Can. 2010) Operates FlipNpik mobile application, a collaborative social network for local businesses.

Holds the North American rights to use and operate the FlipNpik application. For the rest of the world, although the owner of the application, the company is the licensor of the Fliptech licence for the operation of the FlipNpik application by **FNP Technologies S.A.** (formerly **Multimicrocloud S.A**). The FlipNpik application leverages the community of consumers, content creators and influencers to stimulate local shopping and boost the visibility of local businesses. In exchange, active users who create and share digital content within the platform receive "Social Flips" that can be used to earn rewards and/or goods from strategic partners and local businesses.

Predecessor Detail - Name changed from Woden Venture Capital Corporation, Sept. 25, 2020, pursuant to the Qualifying Transaction reverse takeover acquisition of Geekco Technologies Inc.; basis 1 new for 4 old shs.

Directors - Henri Harland, chr., Rosemère, Qué.; Sylvain Aird, Montréal, Qué.; Vincenzo Guzzo, Terrebonne, Qué.; Nadira Hajjar, Laval, Qué.; Daniel Perry, Morocco

Other Exec. Officers - Mario Beaulieu, CEO & interim COO; Xavier Harland, CFO

Capital Stock

	Authorized (shs.)	Outstanding (shs.)[1]
Common	unlimited	37,501,064

[1] At Mar. 31, 2023

Major Shareholder - Henri Harland held 33.79% interest and Nadira Hajjar held 15.97% interest at Aug. 31, 2022.

Price Range - GKO/TSX-VEN

Year	Volume	High	Low	Close
2022	433,111	$0.45	$0.05	$0.08
2021	2,107,925	$0.70	$0.13	$0.40
2020	1,526,838	$0.60	$0.12	$0.55
2019	186,000	$0.20	$0.08	$0.12
2018	277,666	$0.36	$0.04	$0.12

Consolidation: 1-for-4 cons. in Oct. 2020
Recent Close: $0.03

Capital Stock Changes - During 2022, 464,501 class A common shares were issued on conversion of debentures.

Wholly Owned Subsidiaries

FlipNpik Technologies Inc., Laval, Qué.

Investments

FNP Technologies S.A., France.

Financial Statistics

Periods ended:	12m Dec. 31/22[A]		12m Dec. 31/21[oA]
	$000s	%Chg	$000s
Operating revenue	**3**	**-73**	**11**
General & admin expense	1,249		2,029
Operating expense	**1,249**	**-38**	**2,029**
Operating income	**(1,246)**	**n.a.**	**(2,018)**
Deprec., depl. & amort.	395		193
Finance income	82		90
Finance costs, gross	482		398
Pre-tax income	**(2,914)**	**n.a.**	**331**
Income taxes	nil		(97)
Net income	**(2,914)**	**n.a.**	**429**
Cash & equivalent	115		747
Accounts receivable	272		476
Current assets	482		1,320
Long-term investments	2,266		3,139
Fixed assets, net	7		9
Right-of-use assets	nil		7
Intangibles, net	2,390		2,477
Total assets	**5,438**	**-25**	**7,243**
Accts. pay. & accr. liabs	877		557
Current liabilities	2,110		565
Long-term debt, gross	1,232		979
Long-term debt, net	nil		979
Equity portion of conv. debs	191		191
Shareholders' equity	2,994		5,354
Cash from oper. activs	**(324)**	**n.a.**	**(1,141)**
Cash from fin. activs	(3)		1,163
Cash from invest. activs	(305)		(416)
Net cash position	**115**	**-85**	**747**
Capital expenditures	nil		(4)
	$		$
Earnings per share*	(0.08)		0.01
Cash flow per share*	(0.01)		(0.03)
	shs		shs
No. of shs. o/s*	36,623,876		36,159,375
Avg. no. of shs. o/s*	36,533,237		36,159,375
	%		%
Net profit margin	n.m.		n.m.
Return on equity	(71.34)		9.06
Return on assets	(39.22)		15.75

* Cl.A Common
[o] Restated
[A] Reported in accordance with IFRS

Latest Results

Periods ended:	3m Mar. 31/23[A]		3m Mar. 31/22[A]
	$000s	%Chg	$000s
Operating revenue	27	+29	21
Net income	(594)	n.a.	308
	$		$
Earnings per share*	(0.02)		0.01

* Cl.A Common
[A] Reported in accordance with IFRS

Historical Summary
(as originally stated)

Fiscal Year	Oper. Rev.	Net Inc. Bef. Disc.	EPS*
	$000s	$000s	$
2022[A]	3	(2,914)	(0.08)
2021[A]	11	250	0.01
2020[A1]	61	(1,881)	(0.18)
2019[A2]	247	(41)	n.a.
2018[A]	259	(266)	n.a.

* Cl.A Common
[A] Reported in accordance with IFRS
[1] Results reflect the October 2020 reverse takeover of Geekco Technologies Inc.
[2] Results for 2019 and 2018 pertain to Geekco Technologies Inc.
Note: Adjusted throughout for 1-for-4 cons. in Oct. 2020

G.24 Gemina Laboratories Ltd.

Symbol - GLAB **Exchange** - CSE **CUSIP** - 368650
Head Office - 302-3600 Gilmore Way, Burnaby, BC, V5G 4R8
Telephone - (604) 760-1997
Website - www.geminalabs.com
Email - investor@geminalabs.com
Investor Relations - Brian Firth (604) 760-1997
Auditors - Davidson & Company LLP C.A., Vancouver, B.C.
Transfer Agents - Computershare Trust Company of Canada Inc., Vancouver, B.C.
Employees - 5 at May 30, 2022
Profile - (B.C. 2017) Designs, builds and sells proprietary point-of-care diagnostic products for respiratory diseases.

The company develops novel surface functionalization chemistries for the detection of pathogens and biomarkers. Has developed the Generation 1 technology, which is included within the company's principal product, Legio-X™ COVID rapid antigen test. The company has also launched a prototype test for detecting and distinguishing between influenza A and B. In addition, in collaboration with **ReadyGo Diagnostics Limited**, the company plans to pair the surface chemistries with alternative diagnostic device platforms to deliver molecular assay for tuberculosis detection.

The development of chemistries may also have application for the detection of biomarkers for human wellness monitoring; detection of pathogens in the built environment; to food and potable water safety; and in veterinary medicine.

In December 2022, the company acquired 19% interest of U.K.-based **RAPIvD Limited** for £259,259 and issuance of 1,086,956 common shares. The company also has the option to acquire the remaining 81% interest for £800,000, issuance of 4,347,826 common shares, the closing balance of RAPIvD at the time of exercise of the option and earnout payments equivalent to 25% of RAPIvD profits for each year for three years after the completion of the transaction. RAPIvD is a specialized research and development contractor which optimizes and transforms rapid test prototypes into products that can be manufactured commercially.

In October 2022, the company entered into an agreement with **International Point of Care, Inc.** (IPOC) for the manufacturing, supply and licence of its Legio-X™ COVID rapid antigen test in Canada.

In May 2022, the company was awarded a European Union (EU) CE Mark under the EU's In Vitro Diagnostic Medical Device Directive (IVDD) for its Legio X Gemina COVID-19 rapid antigen test product.

Predecessor Detail - Name changed from D1 Capital Corp., Feb. 10, 2021, pursuant to the reverse takeover acquisition of Ecoscreen Solutions Inc. and concurrent amalgamation of Ecoscreen with wholly owned 1272305 B.C. Ltd.

Directors - John Davies, chr., Vancouver, B.C.; Brian Firth, CEO, United Kingdom; Robert Porter, pres., United Kingdom; Robert C. Greene, chief tech. officer, Vancouver, B.C.; Martin Cronin, Kelowna, B.C.; Dr. Bola Grace, United Kingdom; Martha Najib, Lakeway, Tex.

Other Exec. Officers - Michael Liggett, CFO & corp. sec.; Dr. Stefan Hamill, v-p, strategy; Elliot Hong, v-p, product devel.; Hugh McNaught, v-p, mktg.; LeAnn Mogerman, contr.

Capital Stock

	Authorized (shs.)	Outstanding (shs.)[1]
Common	unlimited	73,325,878

[1] At May 31, 2023

Major Shareholder - EcoMine Technologies Corporation held 60.6% interest at May 30, 2022.

Price Range - GLAB/CSE

Year	Volume	High	Low	Close
2022	2,572,859	$0.76	$0.30	$0.50
2021	614,733	$0.60	$0.31	$0.39

Recent Close: $0.50

Capital Stock Changes - In March 2023, private placement of 3,472,994 common shares was completed at $0.75 per share.

In June and July 2022, offering of 5,626,735 units (1 common share & 1 warrant) and private placement of 1,536,200 units (1 common share & 1 warrant), all at 60¢ per unit, was completed. Also during fiscal 2022, common shares were issued as follows: 2,000,001 on exercise of warrants and 1,086,956 pursuant to the acquisition of RAPIvD Limited.

Wholly Owned Subsidiaries

Ecoscreen Solutions Inc., Vancouver, B.C.
Gemina Laboratories (UK) Limited, United Kingdom.

Investments

19% int. in **RAPIvD Limited**, United Kingdom.

Financial Statistics

Periods ended:	12m Jan. 31/23[A]		12m Jan. 31/22[A]
	$000s	%Chg	$000s
Salaries & benefits	877		707
Research & devel. expense	3,355		1,728
General & admin expense	1,305		1,553
Stock-based compensation	393		702
Operating expense	**5,930**	**+26**	**4,691**
Operating income	**(5,930)**	**n.a.**	**(4,691)**
Deprec., depl. & amort.	50		44
Finance costs, net	(1)		1
Pre-tax income	**(5,979)**	**n.a.**	**(4,735)**
Net income	**(5,979)**	**n.a.**	**(4,735)**
Cash & equivalent	83		1,156
Accounts receivable	386		178
Current assets	563		1,379
Long-term investments	994		nil
Fixed assets, net	80		15
Right-of-use assets	238		26
Total assets	**1,875**	**+32**	**1,420**
Accts. pay. & accr. liabs.	1,706		430
Current liabilities	1,748		470
Long-term lease liabilities	198		5
Shareholders' equity	(72)		944
Cash from oper. activs.	**(4,510)**	**n.a.**	**(3,872)**
Cash from fin. activs.	3,941		4,138
Cash from invest. activs.	(505)		8
Net cash position	**83**	**-93**	**1,156**
Capital expenditures	(80)		(10)
	$		$
Earnings per share*	(0.10)		(0.10)
Cash flow per share*	(0.07)		(0.08)
	shs		shs
No. of shs. o/s*	65,852,884		55,602,992
Avg. no. of shs. o/s*	60,190,253		47,658,574
	%		%
Net profit margin	n.a.		n.a.
Return on equity	n.m.		(857.79)
Return on assets	(362.91)		(239.93)

* Common
[A] Reported in accordance with IFRS

Latest Results

Periods ended:	3m Apr. 30/23[A]		3m Apr. 30/22[A]
	$000s	%Chg	$000s
Net income	(1,709)	n.a.	(781)
	$		$
Earnings per share*	(0.02)		(0.01)

* Common
[A] Reported in accordance with IFRS

Historical Summary
(as originally stated)

Fiscal Year	Oper. Rev.	Net Inc. Bef. Disc.	EPS*
	$000s	$000s	$
2023[A]	nil	(5,979)	(0.10)
2022[A]	nil	(4,735)	(0.10)
2021[A1,2]	nil	(834)	(0.02)

* Common
[A] Reported in accordance with IFRS
[1] 39 weeks ended Jan. 31, 2021.
[2] Results pertain to Ecoscreen Solutions Inc.

G.25 Gencan Capital Inc.

Symbol - GCA.X **Exchange** - CSE **CUSIP** - 36869X
Head Office - 100-87 Scollard St, Toronto, ON, M5R 1G4 **Telephone** - (416) 920-0500
Email - cday@thoughtlaunch.ca
Investor Relations - Cameron Day (416) 920-0500
Auditors - BDO Canada LLP C.A., Toronto, Ont.
Bankers - Royal Bank of Canada, Toronto, Ont.
Transfer Agents - Computershare Trust Company of Canada Inc., Toronto, Ont.
Profile - (Ont. 2013) Seeking new business opportunities.
Predecessor Detail - Name changed from Genterra Energy Inc., Aug. 15, 2015.
Directors - John A. McMahon, CEO, Toronto, Ont.; Timothy (Tim) Diamond, Oakville, Ont.; Christopher J. (Chris) Hobbs, Oakville, Ont.
Other Exec. Officers - Cameron Day, CFO

Capital Stock

	Authorized (shs.)	Outstanding (shs.)[1]
Common	unlimited	16,092,284

[1] At Aug. 5, 2022

Major Shareholder - Suzerain Corporation held 18.6% interest and John A. McMahon held 12.4% interest at Aug. 5, 2022.

Price Range - GCA.X/CSE

Year	Volume	High	Low	Close
2022	484,961	$0.32	$0.15	$0.16
2021	242,524	$0.40	$0.05	$0.32
2020	129,241	$0.10	$0.03	$0.04
2019	72,835	$0.30	$0.05	$0.15
2018	96,642	$0.35	$0.03	$0.05

Recent Close: $0.10

Financial Statistics

Periods ended:	12m Sept. 30/21[A]		12m Sept. 30/20[A]
	$000s	%Chg	$000s
General & admin expense	153		116
Operating expense	**153**	**+32**	**116**
Operating income	**(153)**	**n.a.**	**(116)**
Finance income	1		4
Pre-tax income	**(152)**	**n.a.**	**(112)**
Income taxes	(30)		(30)
Net income	**(122)**	**n.a.**	**(83)**
Cash & equivalent	400		484
Accounts receivable	1		1
Current assets	432		516
Total assets	**432**	**-16**	**516**
Accts. pay. & accr. liabs.	56		18
Current liabilities	56		18
Shareholders' equity	376		498
Cash from oper. activs.	**(84)**	**n.a.**	**(72)**
Net cash position	**400**	**-17**	**484**
	$		$
Earnings per share*	(0.01)		(0.01)
Cash flow per share*	(0.01)		(0.00)
	shs		shs
No. of shs. o/s*	16,092,284		16,092,284
Avg. no. of shs. o/s*	16,092,284		16,092,284
	%		%
Net profit margin	n.a.		n.a.
Return on equity	(27.92)		(15.40)
Return on assets	(25.74)		(14.89)

* Common
[A] Reported in accordance with IFRS

Historical Summary
(as originally stated)

Fiscal Year	Oper. Rev.	Net Inc. Bef. Disc.	EPS*
	$000s	$000s	$
2021[A]	nil	(122)	(0.01)
2020[A]	nil	(83)	(0.01)
2019[A]	nil	(105)	(0.01)
2018[A]	333	610	0.04
2017[A]	474	(9)	(0.00)

* Common
[A] Reported in accordance with IFRS

G.26 General Assembly Holdings Limited

Symbol - GA **Exchange** - TSX-VEN **CUSIP** - 66981M
Head Office - 331 Adelaide St W, Toronto, ON, M5V 1R5 **Telephone** - (416) 803-1488
Website - gapizza.com
Email - eric.balshin@gapizza.com
Investor Relations - Eric Balshin (647) 892-8784
Auditors - DNTW Toronto LLP C.A., Toronto, Ont.
Transfer Agents - Odyssey Trust Company, Calgary, Alta.
Employees - 27 at May 2, 2022
Profile - (Ont. 2017) Operates a pizza restaurant, a frozen pizza subscription service and a wholesale business for frozen pizza across Canada.

The company's premium frozen pizzas are available via its direct-to-consumer (DTC) pizza subscription service, at grocers across Ontario, Alberta, Quebec and British Columbia, and at its restaurant in downtown Toronto, Ont. The restaurant serves store specific products along with its pizzas including salads, general bread, wine, beer and premium non-alcoholic drinks. The subscription service is offered through www.gapizza.com and allows customers to pay a monthly fee for a select offering of pizzas that are delivered directly to customers. Wholesale accounts include smaller independent grocers, restaurants and national grocery store chains operating in Ontario, including Summerhill Market, Fiesta Farms, Loblaws (PC Chef) and Fresh and Wild. All frozen pizza productions are done in a master production facility in Vaughan, Ont.

At June 30, 2022, production capacity was at 100,000 pizzas per month. The company plans to move the master production facility to a new 12,610-sq.-ft. facility in Mississauga, Ont., where operation was expected to commence in the fourth quarter of 2022.

Predecessor Detail - Name changed from Lalani Thompson Holdings Inc., Dec. 15, 2020.
Directors - Ali Khan Lalani, founder & pres., Toronto, Ont.; Ted Hastings, chr., Waterloo, Ont.; Kevin Ferrell, Oakville, Ont.; Glen Keleher; Iain Klugman, Kitchener, Ont.
Other Exec. Officers - Eric Balshin, interim CEO; Katharine Joakim, CFO; Ryan Donik, sr. v-p, mktg.; Eric Hacke, sr. v-p, tech.; Amy Hastings, sec.-treas.

Capital Stock

	Authorized (shs.)	Outstanding (shs.)[1]
Class A Common	unlimited	23,498,744

[1] At Aug. 29, 2022

Major Shareholder - Ali Khan Lalani held 17.77% interest at Apr. 26, 2022.

Price Range - GA/TSX-VEN

Year	Volume	High	Low	Close
2022	2,849,192	$0.79	$0.05	$0.08
2021	3,059,670	$1.35	$0.48	$0.60

Recent Close: $0.03

Wholly Owned Subsidiaries

GA CPG Limited, Toronto, Ont.
GA Subscriptions Limited, Toronto, Ont.
2499754 Ontario Limited, Toronto, Ont. dba General Assembly

Financial Statistics

Periods ended:	12m Dec. 31/21[A]		12m Dec. 31/20[oA]
	$000s	%Chg	$000s
Operating revenue	**4,637**	**+120**	**2,104**
Cost of sales	4,320		1,344
General & admin expense	9,412		1,698
Operating expense	**13,732**	**+351**	**3,042**
Operating income	**(9,095)**	**n.a.**	**(938)**
Deprec., depl. & amort.	733		336
Finance costs, gross	302		289
Pre-tax income	**(10,598)**	**n.a.**	**(1,258)**
Net income	**(10,598)**	**n.a.**	**(1,258)**
Cash & equivalent	1,259		878
Inventories	389		28
Accounts receivable	789		185
Current assets	2,644		1,110
Fixed assets, net	3,918		706
Right-of-use assets	4,708		1,257
Total assets	**11,564**	**+273**	**3,097**
Accts. pay. & accr. liabs.	2,580		962
Current liabilities	4,352		2,740
Long-term debt, gross	2,701		119
Long-term debt, net	2,669		32
Long-term lease liabilities	4,441		1,282
Shareholders' equity	103		(957)
Cash from oper. activs.	**(8,661)**	**n.a.**	**(99)**
Cash from fin. activs.	12,064		838
Cash from invest. activs.	(3,022)		(55)
Net cash position	**1,259**	**+43**	**879**
Capital expenditures	(3,022)		(55)
	$		$
Earnings per share*	(0.49)		(0.97)
Cash flow per share*	(0.40)		(0.08)
	shs		shs
No. of shs. o/s*	22,348,744		13,372,854
Avg. no. of shs. o/s*	21,603,760		1,297,857
	%		%
Net profit margin	(228.55)		(59.79)
Return on equity	n.m.		n.m.
Return on assets	(140.45)		(29.95)

* Cl.A Common
[o] Restated
[A] Reported in accordance with IFRS

Historical Summary
(as originally stated)

Fiscal Year	Oper. Rev.	Net Inc. Bef. Disc.	EPS*
	$000s	$000s	$
2021[A]	4,637	(10,598)	(0.49)
2020[A]	2,104	(1,258)	(0.97)
2019[A]	2,266	(536)	n.a.

* Cl.A Common
[A] Reported in accordance with IFRS

G.27 Generation Gold Corp.

Symbol - GEN **Exchange** - TSX-VEN **CUSIP** - 37149N
Head Office - 228-1122 Mainland St, Vancouver, BC, V6B 5L1 **Telephone** - (604) 721-9191
Email - anthonyzelen88@gmail.com
Investor Relations - Anthony Zelen (778) 388-5258
Auditors - Charlton & Company C.A., Vancouver, B.C.
Lawyers - AFG Law LLP, Vancouver, B.C.
Transfer Agents - Computershare Trust Company of Canada Inc., Vancouver, B.C.
Profile - (B.C. 2018) Holds option from **Origen Resources Inc.** to earn 60% interest in Arlington copper-silver prospect, 1,572 hectares, 17 km north of Beaverdell, B.C.

In December 2022, the company acquired an option to earn 60% interest in **Origen Resources Inc.**'s 1,572-hectare Arlington copper-silver prospect in south-central British Columbia. The acquisition constituted the company's Qualifying Transaction.

Predecessor Detail - Name changed from Jessy Ventures Corp., Dec. 13, 2022, pursuant to the Qualifying Transaction acquisition of an option on the Arlington copper-silver prospect in south-central British Columbia.

Directors - Anthony Zelen, CEO, Coldstream, B.C.; Dallas Miller, N.S.W., Australia; Christopher (Chris) Reynolds, Vancouver, B.C.; Gary D. A. Schellenberg, Vancouver, B.C.

Other Exec. Officers - Marcy Kiesman, CFO

Capital Stock

	Authorized (shs.)	Outstanding (shs.)[1]
Preferred	unlimited	nil
Common	unlimited	11,624,332

[1] At Dec. 28, 2022

Major Shareholder - Widely held at Dec. 28, 2022.

Price Range - GEN/TSX-VEN

Year	Volume	High	Low	Close
2021............	216,833	$0.20	$0.10	$0.13
2020............	35,250	$0.10	$0.10	$0.10
2019............	35,000	$0.15	$0.09	$0.10

Recent Close: $0.08

Capital Stock Changes - In December 2022, private placement of 3,800,000 units (1 common share & 1 warrant) at 10¢ per unit was completed, with warrants exercisable at $0.125 per share for three years.

In August 2021, private placement of 2,718,332 common shares was completed at 9¢ per share. Also during fiscal 2022, 6,000 common shares were issued on exercise of warrants.

G.28 Generative AI Solutions Corp.

Symbol - AICO **Exchange** - CSE **CUSIP** - 37149M

Head Office - Bentall 5, 2300-550 Burrard St, Vancouver, BC, V6C 2B5 **Telephone** - (406) 879-7632 **Toll-free** - (833) 879-7632

Website - www.genai-solutions.com

Email - ryan.selby@gmail.com

Investor Relations - Ryan Selby (833) 879-7632

Auditors - Manning Elliott LLP C.A., Vancouver, B.C.

Transfer Agents - National Securities Administrators Ltd., Vancouver, B.C.

Profile - (B.C. 2018) Developing an artificial intelligence (AI) technology that utilizes machine learning and natural language processing to improve efficiency, accuracy and decision-making across multiple industries, with an initial focus on the education industry.

Principal product under development is the Classmate application, an online AI program that would provide virtual machine-interface tutoring to high school students as well as junior-level university students.

On July 26, 2022, the company made a cash distribution to its holders equal to Cdn$0.41 per subordinate voting share and Cdn$410 per multiple voting share. The record date for the distribution was Aug. 3, 2022. This was following the sale of substantially all of the company's business undertakings on June 24, 2022, where in the company received cash proceeds of Cdn$69,200,000 (after satisfying its obligations and liabilities) from the sale, and retained Cdn$1,000,000 cash to explore new business opportunities.

During fiscal 2023, the company acquired from its Chinese manufacturing partner Poda Pod manufacturing equipment, 15 patent applications related to Poda Pod technology and three Chinese trademarks for $3,670,000 cash. The manufacturing equipment consists of all proprietary custom-built equipment for Poda Pods production capable of producing an estimated 5,000,000 Poda Pods per year. The acquired manufacturing equipment was subsequently sold as part of the sale of substantially all of the assets and properties used in the company's business of developing, manufacturing and marketing multi-substrate heated capsule technology to **Altria Group, Inc.** in June 2022.

On Mar. 1, 2022, wholly owned **Poda Technologies Ltd.** was amalgamated into the company.

Recent Merger and Acquisition Activity

Status: completed **Revised:** Apr. 17, 2023

UPDATE: The transaction was completed. PREVIOUS: Idle Lifestyle Inc. entered into a letter of intent for the reverse takeover acquisition of private Burnaby, B.C.-based Ultron Capital Corp., which was developing an artificial intelligence (AI) technology that utilizes machine learning and natural language processing to improve efficiency, accuracy and decision-making across multiple industries, with an initial focus on the education industry. Terms of the transaction would be subsequently disclosed. Feb. 4, 2023 - Idle changed its name to Generative AI Solutions Corp. Feb. 16, 2023 - A definitive agreement was entered into. Upon completion, Ultron would amalgamate with Generative AI's wholly owned 1399318 B.C. Ltd. to form Ultron Capital Inc. In conjunction, all outstanding multiple voting shares of Generative AI would be converted into subordinate voting shares on a 1,000-for-1 basis, with the subordinate voting shares redesignated as class B shares, and a new class of common shares would be created. The basis of consideration would be one-for-one, with Generative AI issuing a total of 51,176,001 common shares at a deemed price of 15¢ per share.

Status: completed **Revised:** Jan. 31, 2023

UPDATE: The transaction was completed. PREVIOUS: Ultron Capital Corp. agreed to the reverse takeover acquisition of private Vancouver, B.C.-based R&R&D Solutions Inc. for issuance of 42,801,000 common shares at a deemed price of 15¢ per share. R&R&D holds certain intellectual property rights which will be used for the development of the Classmate application, an online artificial intelligence (AI) program that would provide virtual machine-interface tutoring to high school students as well as junior-level university students.

Status: completed **Revised:** June 24, 2022

UPDATE: The transaction was completed. PREVIOUS: Poda Holdings, Inc., together with Ryan Selby and Ryan Karkairan, the co-founders and CEO and COO of Poda, respectively, agreed to sell to Altria Group, Inc. substantially all of the assets and properties used in Poda's business of developing, manufacturing and marketing multi-substrate heated capsule technology, including, without limitation, Selby's and Karkairan's patents related to such technology and Poda's exclusive perpetual licence of certain of those patents, for a total of US$100,500,000. Poda would receive US$55,275,000 of the purchase price (representing 55%), with Selby and Karkairan receiving the balance. The transaction would result in Poda selling all or substantially all of its business undertakings. A special committee of Poda's board of directors unanimously recommended the transaction, and accordingly Poda's board of directors unanimously recommended that shareholders vote in favour of the transaction.

Predecessor Detail - Name changed from Idle Lifestyle Inc., Feb. 4, 2023, pursuant to the reverse takeover acquisition of Ultron Capital Corp. and concurrent amalgamation of Ultron with wholly owned 1399318 B.C. Ltd. (and continued as Ultron Capital Inc.).

Directors - Ryan Selby, chr., CEO & corp. sec., Richmond, B.C.; Aaron Bowden, Calgary, Alta.; Patrick Gray, New York, N.Y.

Other Exec. Officers - Paul Ciullo, CFO

Capital Stock

	Authorized (shs.)	Outstanding (shs.)[1]
Common	unlimited	51,176,001
Class B	unlimited	5,549,373

[1] At Apr. 19, 2023

Common - One vote per share.

Class B - Entitled to dividends. Convertible into common shares such that, on a per-holder basis, 10% of the issued and outstanding class B shares will convert to common shares on Apr. 17, 2025 (representing two years after the completion of the reverse takeover acquisition of Ultron Capital Corp.), and 15% are to be converted every three months thereafter. One vote per share.

Major Shareholder - The Selby Family Trust 2022 held 16.92% interest at Apr. 19, 2023.

Price Range - AICO/CSE

Year	Volume	High	Low	Close
2022............	1,847,387	$12.60	$0.15	$0.15
2021............	905,938	$81.30	$9.15	$11.70

Consolidation: 1-for-30 cons. in Feb. 2023

Recent Close: $0.84

Capital Stock Changes - Pursuant to the Apr. 17, 2023, reverse takeover acquisition of Ultron Capital Corp., all 815.67 multiple voting shares were converted into 815,670 subordinate voting shares (1,000-for-1 basis), all then outstanding 5,549,373 subordinate voting shares were redesignated as class B shares, a new class of common shares was created and 51,176,001 common shares were issued pursuant to the acquisition of Ultron. In June 2023, private placement of up to 9,000,000 units (1 common share & 1 warrant) at $0.56 per unit was arranged, with warrants exercisable at $1.65 per share for two years.

On Feb. 13, 2023, subordinate voting and multiple voting shares were consolidated on a 1-for-30 basis.

Wholly Owned Subsidiaries

Ultron Capital Inc., Burnaby, B.C.
- 100% int. in **R&R&D Solutions Inc.**, Vancouver, B.C.

Financial Statistics

Periods ended:	13m Feb. 28/22[A1]		12m Jan. 31/21[A]
	$000s	%Chg	$000s
Salaries & benefits..........................	374		nil
Research & devel. expense..............	384		nil
General & admin expense................	9,633		285
Stock-based compensation.............	448		32
Operating expense........................	**10,838**	**n.m.**	**317**
Operating income..........................	**(10,838)**	**n.a.**	**(317)**
Finance costs, gross........................	76		85
Write-downs/write-offs....................	nil		(3,594)
Pre-tax income.............................	**(11,047)**	**n.a.**	**(4,025)**
Net income...................................	**(11,047)**	**n.a.**	**(4,025)**
Cash & equivalent............................	13,235		12
Current assets..................................	13,912		19
Total assets....................................	**13,912**	**n.m.**	**19**
Accts. pay. & accr. liabs..................	625		506
Current liabilities..............................	915		2,792
Long-term debt, gross......................	nil		185
Long-term debt, net.........................	nil		60
Equity portion of conv. debs............	nil		48
Shareholders' equity.........................	12,392		(3,407)
Cash from oper. activs...................	**(6,062)**	**n.a.**	**24**
Cash from fin. activs.........................	19,251		335
Cash from invest. activs...................	34		(380)
Net cash position...........................	**13,235**	**n.m.**	**12**
	$		$
Earnings per share*.........................	(7.80)		(2.70)
Cash flow per share*........................	(4.22)		0.02
	shs		shs
No. of shs. o/s*................................	1,866,908		1,426,131
Avg. no. of shs. o/s*.........................	1,435,315		1,426,131
	%		%
Net profit margin..............................	n.a.		n.a.
Return on equity...............................	n.m.		n.m.
Return on assets...............................	(157.50)		n.a.

* Common

[A] Reported in accordance with IFRS

[1] Results reflect the Apr. 27, 2021, reverse takeover acquisition of Poda Technologies Ltd.

Latest Results

Periods ended:	3m May 31/22[A]		3m May 31/21[A]
	$000s	%Chg	$000s
Net income.......................................	(2,374)	n.a.	(1,021)
	$		$
Earnings per share*.........................	(1.20)		(2.10)

* Common

[A] Reported in accordance with IFRS

Note: Adjusted throughout for 1-for-30 cons. in Feb. 2023

G.29 Genesis AI Corp.

Symbol - AIG **Exchange** - CSE **CUSIP** - 371957

Head Office - 750-1620 Dickson Ave, Kelowna, BC, V1Y 9Y2 **Telephone** - (778) 484-8028 **Fax** - (250) 868-8493

Email - rcheung@mcpa.ca

Investor Relations - Ryan E. Cheung (778) 484-8028

Auditors - De Visser Gray LLP C.A., Vancouver, B.C.

Transfer Agents - Computershare Trust Company of Canada Inc., Vancouver, B.C.

Profile - (B.C. 2005) Pursuing acquisition of a company engaged in carbon sequestration; and generative artificial intelligence intellectual property assets.

Prior to October 2018, developed and provided cybersecurity and cryptocurrency security solutions to protect businesses from external and internal cyber attacks.

In July 2023, the company entered into a term sheet to acquire certain generative artificial intelligence (AI) intellectual property assets (Woodlands.ai) from **Carbonethic Holding Inc.** for Cdn$100,000 in cash and up to Cdn$1,500,000 in royalty payments from revenue generated by the company over 36 months from closing. Woodlands.ai is a generative AI, natural resources model in development, building digital twins of real-world forests. Digital forests can be manipulated and studied in computer generated worlds, with the influence of deep machine learning, neural networks, and AI. Digital forest technology has many applications including carbon offsetting, forest and land management and wildfire protection.

In May 2022, the company entered into an option agreement with **Treelab Carbon Technologies Inc.** whereby the company would acquire Treelab for US$50,000 cash (paid on May 2022) and issuance of 20,000,000 common shares valued at Cdn$2,500,000 within three years to 2025. Treelab has a memorandum of understanding with High Bar First Nations whereby it would work together to plant new trees on indigenous lands located in the Fraser Canyon/Cariboo region in British Columbia for the purpose of carbon sequestration. The pilot project would take place on 250 acres of High Bar lands where Treelab would plant over 200,000 tress and Treelab would be working to bring the carbon credits to the compliance market.

Predecessor Detail - Name changed from Gallagher Security Corp., July 11, 2023.

Directors - Devinder (Dev) Randhawa, pres. & CEO, Kelowna, B.C.; Jamie Bannerman, Kelowna, B.C.; Jeremy P. Wiebe, B.C.

Other Exec. Officers - Ryan E. Cheung, CFO & corp. sec.

Capital Stock

	Authorized (shs.)	Outstanding (shs.)[1]	Par
Preferred	unlimited	nil	$1.00
Common	unlimited	37,615,315	n.p.v.
Convertible Common	unlimited	nil	n.p.v.

[1] At July 11, 2023

Major Shareholder - Devinder (Dev) Randhawa held 26.02% interest at Nov. 14, 2022.

Price Range - AIG/CSE

Year	Volume	High	Low	Close
2022	4,524,179	$0.20	$0.02	$0.03
2021	3,786,724	$0.30	$0.12	$0.24
2020	1,800,166	$0.20	$0.01	$0.15
2019	2,791,791	$1.05	$0.05	$0.09
2018	4,780,622	$8.70	$0.60	$0.75

Consolidation: 1-for-10 cons. in June 2019

Recent Close: $0.13

Capital Stock Changes - In July 2023, private placement of 10,000,000 units (1 common share & 1 warrant) at 5¢ per unit was completed, with warrants exercisable at 6¢ per share for three years. In July 2023, private placement of up to 21,428,571 units (1 common share & 1 warrant) at 7¢ per unit was arranged, with warrants exercisable at 11¢ per share for two years.

There were no changes to capital stock during fiscal 2022.

Financial Statistics

Periods ended:	12m June 30/22[A]		12m June 30/21[A]
	US$000s	%Chg	US$000s
Salaries & benefits	8		3
General & admin expense	242		305
Stock-based compensation	nil		170
Operating expense	**250**	**-48**	**478**
Operating income	**(250)**	**n.a.**	**(478)**
Finance income	nil		1
Finance costs, gross	nil		3
Write-downs/write-offs	nil		(601)
Pre-tax income	**742**	**n.a.**	**(942)**
Net inc bef disc ops, eqhldrs	742		(942)
Net income	**742**	**n.a.**	**(942)**
Cash & equivalent	45		183
Accounts receivable	11		16
Current assets	56		199
Total assets	**95**	**-52**	**199**
Accts. pay. & accr. liabs	289		206
Current liabilities	290		1,197
Shareholders' equity	(195)		(998)
Cash from oper. activs	**(159)**	**n.a.**	**(157)**
Cash from fin. activs	60		932
Cash from invest. activs	(39)		(600)
Net cash position	**45**	**-75**	**183**
	US$		US$
Earnings per share*	0.03		(0.05)
Cash flow per share*	(0.01)		(0.01)
	shs		shs
No. of shs. o/s*	27,651,315		27,651,315
Avg. no. of shs. o/s*	27,651,315		19,641,797
	%		%
Net profit margin	n.a.		n.a.
Return on equity	n.m.		n.m.
Return on assets	504.76		(849.77)

* Common

[A] Reported in accordance with IFRS

Latest Results

Periods ended:	3m Sept. 30/22[A]		3m Sept. 30/21[A]
	US$000s	%Chg	US$000s
Net income	(34)	n.a.	(81)
	US$		US$
Earnings per share*	(0.00)		(0.00)

* Common

[A] Reported in accordance with IFRS

Historical Summary
(as originally stated)

Fiscal Year	Oper. Rev.	Net Inc. Bef. Disc.	EPS*
	US$000s	US$000s	US$
2022[A]	nil	742	0.03
2021[A]	nil	(942)	(0.05)
2020[A]	nil	(188)	(0.02)
2019[A]	nil	(848)	(0.12)
	$000s	$000s	$
2018[A1]	119	(11,894)	(33.83)

* Common

[A] Reported in accordance with IFRS

[1] Results reflect the June 12, 2018, reverse takeover acquisition of Hill Top Security, Inc.

Note: Adjusted throughout for 1-for-10 cons. in June 2019

G.30 Genesis Acquisition Corp.

Symbol - REBL.P **Exchange** - TSX-VEN **CUSIP** - 37182V

Head Office - c/o Pushor Mitchell LLP, 301-1655 Ellis St, Kelowna, BC, V1Y 2B3 **Telephone** - (250) 317-0996 **Fax** - (250) 762-9115

Email - blair@forbiddenspirits.ca

Investor Relations - C. Blair Wilson (250) 317-0996

Auditors - MNP LLP C.A., Calgary, Alta.

Transfer Agents - TSX Trust Company, Calgary, Alta.

Profile - (B.C. 2019) Capital Pool Company.

Recent Merger and Acquisition Activity

Status: pending **Announced:** Apr. 4, 2022

Genesis Acquisition Corp. entered into a letter of intent for the Qualifying Transaction reverse takeover acquisition of private Las Vegas, Nev.-based Skybox Sports Network Inc. (dba Rise Display) on a share-for-share basis, resulting in the issuance of 32,850,000 Genesis common shares valued at $9,855,000. Rise Display manufactures and distributes digital signage for financial and sports markets throughout the U.S. and Canada. Products include LED ticker, betting boards and sportsbook sign. The transaction would be completed by way of a reverse triangular merger between Genesis, a wholly owned subsidiary of Genesis and Skybox. As part of the transaction, Skybox would complete a private placement of subscription receipts ranging from $3,000,000 to $4,500,000 at $0.30 per receipt that would ultimately be exchanged for Genesis common shares. Upon closing, Genesis would change its name to Skybox Sports Network Inc.

Directors - C. Blair Wilson, pres., CEO & CFO, Kelowna, B.C.; Karen Danard, Delta, B.C.; Eugene A. Hodgson, Vancouver, B.C.; Jason McDougall, Delta, B.C.; Joseph (Joe) Miller, Surrey, B.C.

Other Exec. Officers - Kelly J. Wilson, corp. sec.

Capital Stock

	Authorized (shs.)	Outstanding (shs.)[1]
Common	unlimited	3,650,000

[1] At Sept. 28, 2022

Major Shareholder - Widely held at Aug. 13, 2021.

Price Range - REBL.P/TSX-VEN

Year	Volume	High	Low	Close
2022	13,000	$0.15	$0.05	$0.05
2021	75,500	$0.16	$0.10	$0.15
2020	59,600	$0.30	$0.14	$0.15
2019	170,100	$0.25	$0.21	$0.21

Capital Stock Changes - There were no changes to capital stock during fiscal 2021 or fiscal 2022.

G.31 Genesis Land Development Corp.*

Symbol - GDC **Exchange** - TSX **CUSIP** - 37183V

Head Office - 6240-333 96 Ave NE, Calgary, AB, T3K 0S3 **Telephone** - (403) 265-8079 **Toll-free** - (800) 341-7211

Website - www.genesisland.com

Email - genesis@genesisland.com

Investor Relations - Wayne King (403) 265-8079

Auditors - MNP LLP C.A., Calgary, Alta.

Lawyers - Norton Rose Fulbright Canada LLP, Calgary, Alta.

Transfer Agents - Computershare Trust Company of Canada Inc., Calgary, Alta.

FP500 Revenue Ranking - 724

Employees - 85 at Dec. 31, 2022

Profile - (Alta. 1997) Acquires, develops and sells land, residential lots and homes primarily in Alberta.

The company's activities are organized into business segments: Land Development and Home Building.

The **Land Development** business segment involves the acquisition of land held for future development, and in the planning, land servicing and marketing of residential communities and commercial and industrial developments. The company primarily develops residential lots in Calgary, including Sage Meadows, Sage Hill Crest, Saddlestone, Lewiston, Logan Landing, Huxley and Hotchkiss; Airdrie, including The Canals, Bayside and Bayview; and Rocky View cty., including OMNI. During 2022, 236 lots were sold compared with 247 lots in 2021.

The **Home Building** business segment includes the acquisition of lots primarily from the land development division and the construction and sale of single-family houses and townhouses. The company is active in its residential communities of Saddlestone, Sage Hill Crest, Bayside and Bayview, and had 12 professionally designed and staged show homes at December 2022. During 2022, the company sold 169 homes compared with 191 homes in 2021.

During the second quarter of 2023, the company sold a 3.34-acre parcel of development land in Calgary, Alta., for $4,242,000; and acquired 3.56 acres of land adjacent to future residential development land (Huxley) in the Belvedere community in Calgary for $663,000.

In February 2023, the company acquired an additional 25 acres in the OMNI project in North Conrich, Alta., from **GLP5 NE Calgary Development Inc.** for $1,253,000, thereby increasing the company's interest in the project to 73% from 59%.

During 2022, subsidiaries **Genesis Limited Partnership #8, Genesis Limited Partnership #9, GP GLP9 Inc., GLP9 Subco Inc.** were wound up.

During the third quarter of 2022, the company sold a 3.22-acre multi-family site in Calgary, Alta., to **Sage Hill Estates Apartments LP** (SHEA LP) for $3,589,000 and used the proceeds to acquire a 50% interest in SHEA LP by way of a capital contribution of $3,589,000. SHEA LP plans to build a 300-unit rental apartment complex in the company's Sage Hill Crest community.

In addition, the company sold a 3.68-acre parcel of land in Calgary for $3,864,000.

In March 2022, the company sold a 3.32-acre parcel of development land in Airdrie, Alta., for $2,200,000.

Recent Merger and Acquisition Activity

Status: pending **Announced:** Mar. 31, 2023

Genesis Land Development Corp. agreed to acquire 53 residential lots in Calgary, Alta., for $6,590,000. Genesis paid an initial $1,239,000, with the balance due on closing. The transaction was expected to be completed between July 2023 and 2024.

Status: completed **Revised:** Jan. 16, 2023

UPDATE: The transaction was completed. PREVIOUS: Genesis Land Development Corp. agreed to sell a 20% interest to each of two separate Calgary, Alta.-based third-party home builders in the Genesis Lewiston development project, which was 130 acres of residential development land located in north Calgary where 915 homes would be fully developed. Each builder would pay $9,900,000, representing a total sale price of $19,800,000 for the combined 40% interest. Development of the Lewiston lands was expected to commence in the spring of 2023.

Status: completed **Announced:** July 28, 2022

Genesis Land Development Corp. acquired Genesis Limited Partnership #4 and Genesis Limited Partnership #5's combined 49% interest in three parcels of land totaling 456 acres at North Conrich in Rocky View cty., Alta., for $5,000,000. As a result, Genesis Land Development increased its ownership of the lands to 100% interest.

Status: completed **Announced:** June 30, 2022

Genesis Land Development Corp. acquired 62 residential lots in the Calgary Metropolitan area in Alberta for $11,131,000.

Status: pending **Announced:** May 2, 2022

Genesis Land Development Corp. agreed to acquire 160 acres of future residential development land in Calgary, Alta., for either $28,000,000 or $30,000,000 with the closing date being either June 15, 2023, or Jan. 31, 2025. The land was adjacent to two other approved residential projects and Genesis was planning on securing final development approvals from the City of Calgary. Upon receiving all necessary approvals, the land was expected to yield 1,100 housing units once fully developed.

Status: completed **Revised:** Apr. 4, 2022

UPDATE: The transaction was completed. PREVIOUS: Genesis Land Development Corp. agreed to acquire 157 acres of future residential development land in Calgary, Alta., for $29,150,000. The transaction was expected to be completed in April 2022.

Predecessor Detail - Name changed from Genesis Capital Corp., Nov. 19, 1998.

Directors - Stephen J. Griggs, chr., Mississauga, Ont.; Iain Stewart, pres. & CEO, Calgary, Alta.; Steven J. Glover†, Canmore, Alta.; Mark W. Mitchell, Calgary, Alta.; Calvin Younger, Toronto, Ont.

Other Exec. Officers - Wayne King, CFO; Parveshindera Sidhu, sr. v-p, home bldg. & pres., Genesis Builders Group Inc.; Brian Whitwell, sr. v-p, asset mgt.; Brendan McCashin, v-p, land devel.; Arnie Stefaniuk, v-p, regl. planning

† Lead director

Capital Stock

	Authorized (shs.)	Outstanding (shs.)[1]
Preferred	unlimited	nil
Common	unlimited	56,852,673

[1] At July 27, 2023

Normal Course Issuer Bid - The company plans to make normal course purchases of up to 2,843,166 common shares representing 5% of the total outstanding. The bid commenced on Dec. 16, 2022, and expires on Dec. 15, 2023.

Major Shareholder - Garfield R. Mitchell held 54.3% interest and Mark W. Mitchell held 19.5% interest at Mar. 31, 2023.

Price Range - GDC/TSX

Year	Volume	High	Low	Close
2022	1,900,548	$2.98	$1.83	$2.03
2021	2,975,700	$3.00	$1.97	$2.31
2020	5,598,168	$2.45	$0.81	$2.09
2019	2,605,421	$3.19	$1.96	$2.27
2018	1,888,393	$4.01	$3.10	$3.16

Recent Close: $2.21

Capital Stock Changes - There were no changes to capital stock during 2022.

Dividends

GDC com Ra $0.085

$0.085◆	June 12/23	$0.075◆	Dec. 15/22
$0.075◆	Aug. 26/22	$0.15◆	Jan. 11/21

Paid in 2023: $0.085◆ 2022: $0.15◆ 2021: $0.15◆ + rt.

◆ Special

Long-Term Debt - Outstanding at Dec. 31, 2022:

Line of credit[1]	$53,188,000
Land loans[2]	12,522,000
Less: Def. fin. fees	653,000
	65,057,000

[1] Consists of $7,364,000 drawn on an operating line of credit, bearing interest at prime plus 0.75%; $25,626,000 drawn on a revolving line of credit due February 2025, bearing interest at prime plus 1.9%; and $20,198,000 drawn on an operating line of credit due October 2025, bearing interest at prime plus 0.5%.

[2] Bears interest at prime plus 0.5%. Due between May 2024 and March 2025.

Wholly Owned Subsidiaries

GLDC Management Inc.
GP LPLP 2007 Inc.
Genesis Builders Group Inc., Alta. Formerly Reliant Homes Inc.
- 100% int. in **The Breeze Inc.**, Alta.

Genesis Keystone Ltd.
Genesis Land Development (Ricardo Ranch) Corp.
Genesis Land Development (Southeast) Corp., Calgary, Alta.
Genesis Northeast Calgary Ltd., Calgary, Alta.
Lewiston Lands GP Inc.
Polar Hedge Enhanced Income Trust, Toronto, Ont.
- 80% int. in **Genpol Inc.**, Alta.
- 80.12% int. in **Genpol LP**

Sage Hill Crest Apartments Corp.
Siseneg Holding Inc.

Subsidiaries

99.99% int. in **Genesis Sage Meadows Partnership**, Alta.
60% int. in **Lewiston Lands Limited Partnership**

Investments

GLP5 GP Inc.
GLP5 NE Calgary Development Inc.
GP RRSP 2007 Inc.
Genesis Limited Partnership #4, Alta.
Genesis Limited Partnership #5, Alta.
20% int. in **Genpol Inc.**, Alta.
19.88% int. in **Genpol LP**
50% int. in **Kinwood Communities Inc.**, Calgary, Alta.
LP RRSP Limited Partnership #1
LP RRSP Limited Partnership #2
LPLP 2007 Subco Inc.
LPLP 2007 Subco #2 Inc.
0.02% int. in **Limited Partnership Land Pool 2007**, Alta.
1504431 Alberta Ltd.
2% int. in **Sage Hill Estates Apartments GP Inc.**
49% int. in **Sage Hill Estates Apartments LP**

Financial Statistics

Periods ended:	12m Dec. 31/22[A]		12m Dec. 31/21[A]
	$000s	%Chg	$000s
Total revenue	**140,357**	**+28**	**109,761**
Cost of real estate sales	113,199		77,918
General & admin. expense	19,580		16,581
Stock-based compensation	1,021		587
Operating expense	**133,800**	**+41**	**95,086**
Operating income	**6,557**	**-55**	**14,675**
Investment income	560		562
Finance income	512		338
Finance costs, gross	1,612		1,220
Pre-tax income	**6,017**	**-58**	**14,355**
Income taxes	1,628		3,375
Net income	**4,389**	**-60**	**10,980**
Net inc. for equity hldrs	**4,520**	**-58**	**10,877**
Net inc. for non-cont. int	**(131)**	**n.a.**	**103**
Cash & equivalent	36,598		63,975
Accounts receivable	22,165		13,632
Long-term investments	10,318		6,170
Fixed assets	1,590		1,481
Properties for future devel.	225,584		180,722
Property interests, net	267,273		220,336
Right-of-use assets	562		655
Total assets	**364,140**	**+12**	**324,929**
Accts. pay. & accr. liabs	30,414		26,408
Long-term debt, gross	65,057		32,668
Long-term lease liabilities	841		842
Shareholders' equity	224,632		228,624
Non-controlling interest	2,705		7,314
Cash from oper. activs	**(43,756)**	**n.a.**	**2,388**
Cash from fin. activs	18,482		32,729
Cash from invest. activs	(2,103)		(885)
Net cash position	**36,598**	**-43**	**63,975**
Capital expenditures	(607)		(875)
	$		$
Earnings per share*	0.08		0.24
Cash flow per share*	(0.77)		0.05
Extra divd. - cash*	0.15		nil
	shs		shs
No. of shs. o/s*	56,863,335		56,863,335
Avg. no. of shs. o/s*	56,863,335		44,642,895
	%		%
Net profit margin	3.13		10.00
Return on equity	1.99		5.23
Return on assets	1.62		4.03
No. of employees (FTEs)	85		71

* Common
[A] Reported in accordance with IFRS

Latest Results

Periods ended:	6m June 30/23[A]		6m June 30/22[A]
	$000s	%Chg	$000s
Total revenue	90,537	+113	42,590
Net income	4,191	n.a.	(615)
Net inc. for equity hldrs	4,253	n.a.	(399)
Net inc. for non-cont. int	(62)		(216)
	$		$
Earnings per share*	0.07		(0.01)

* Common
[A] Reported in accordance with IFRS

Historical Summary
(as originally stated)

Fiscal Year	Total Rev. $000s	Net Inc. Bef. Disc. $000s	EPS* $
2022[A]	140,357	4,389	0.08
2021[A]	109,761	10,980	0.24
2020[A]	103,933	(205)	0.00
2019[A]	68,097	3,035	0.04
2018[A]	81,437	3,779	0.10

* Common
[A] Reported in accordance with IFRS

G.32 GeneTether Therapeutics Inc.

Symbol - GTTX **Exchange** - CSE **CUSIP** - 37187D
Head Office - 301-1665 Ellis St, Kelowna, BC, V1Y 2B3 **Toll-free** - (833) 294-4363
Website - genetether.com
Email - roland@genetether.com
Investor Relations - Roland Boivin (833) 294-4363
Auditors - Horne LLP C.P.A., Ridgeland, Miss.
Lawyers - Pushor Mitchell LLP, Kelowna, B.C.
Transfer Agents - Odyssey Trust Company, Calgary, Alta.
Profile - (B.C. 2021) Developing GeneTether™, a disruptive proprietary platform technology designed to increase the efficiency of DNA insertion into the genome for gene correction and complementation strategies.

Gene editing therapies are created based on GeneTether™, which increases the efficiency of genome editing technologies including CRISPR-Cas, TALENs and ZFNs. GeneTether™ uses a proprietary method to tether donor DNA templates to genome editing complex, making the template readily available for use during the genome editing repair stage, and is leveraged to develop curative therapies for the treatment of rare, monogenic diseases of the kidney and the skin.

Directors - Daren Graham, chr., Palm Beach, Fla.; Roland Boivin, CEO, Montréal, Qué.; André P. Fraga, Gibraltar; P. Gage Jull, Ont.

Other Exec. Officers - Jean Jen, CFO & corp. sec.; R. Geoffrey Sargent, chief scientific officer

Capital Stock

	Authorized (shs.)	Outstanding (shs.)[1]
Common	unlimited	48,178,935

[1] At Nov. 25, 2022

Major Shareholder - Dr. William J. (Bill) Garner held 48.83% interest and R. Geoffrey Sargent held 22.77% interest at Mar. 29, 2022.

Price Range - GTTX/CSE

Year	Volume	High	Low	Close
2022	474,513	$0.68	$0.03	$0.10

Recent Close: $0.04

Capital Stock Changes - On Mar. 29, 2022, an initial public offering of 7,500,000 units (1 common share & 1 warrant) at Cdn$0.60 per unit was completed, with warrants exercisable at Cdn$0.72 per share for three years.

Wholly Owned Subsidiaries

GeneTether Inc., Wilmington, Del.

Financial Statistics

Periods ended:	12m Dec. 31/21[A1]		12m Dec. 31/20[A2]
	US$000s	%Chg	US$000s
Research & devel. expense	405		59
General & admin expense	1,232		12
Stock-based compensation	875		nil
Operating expense	**1,637**	**n.m.**	**72**
Operating income	**(1,637)**	**n.a.**	**(72)**
Finance costs, gross	nil		1
Pre-tax income	**(1,638)**	**n.a.**	**(73)**
Net income	**(1,638)**	**n.a.**	**(73)**
Cash & equivalent	180		45
Current assets	370		45
Total assets	**370**	**+722**	**45**
Bank indebtedness	nil		122
Accts. pay. & accr. liabs	213		1
Current liabilities	213		123
Shareholders' equity	157		(78)
Cash from oper. activs	**(740)**	**n.a.**	**(69)**
Cash from fin. activs	875		104
Net cash position	**180**	**+300**	**45**
	US$		US$
Earnings per share*	(0.05)		(0.10)
Cash flow per share*	(0.02)		(0.10)
	shs		shs
No. of shs. o/s*	38,505,450		n.a.
Avg. no. of shs. o/s*	35,761,916		n.a.
	%		%
Net profit margin	n.a.		n.a.
Return on equity	n.m.		n.m.
Return on assets	(789.40)		(248.28)

* Common
[A] Reported in accordance with IFRS
[1] Results reflect the Nov. 30, 2021, reverse takeover acquisition of GeneTether Inc.
[2] Results pertain to GeneTether Inc.

Latest Results

Periods ended:	9m Sept. 30/22[A]		9m Sept. 30/21[A]
	US$000s	%Chg	US$000s
Net income	(1,338)	n.a.	(1,077)
	US$		US$
Earnings per share*	(0.03)		(1.15)

* Common
[A] Reported in accordance with IFRS

Historical Summary
(as originally stated)

Fiscal Year	Oper. Rev. US$000s	Net Inc. Bef. Disc. US$000s	EPS* US$
2021[A]	nil	(1,638)	(0.05)
2020[A1]	nil	(73)	(0.10)
2019[A1]	nil	(87)	(0.12)

* Common
[A] Reported in accordance with IFRS
[1] Results pertain to GeneTether Inc.

G.33 genifi inc.

Symbol - GNFI **Exchange** - TSX-VEN **CUSIP** - 37229A
Head Office - 1401-80 Richmond St W, Toronto, ON, M5H 2A4
Telephone - (416) 488-7700
Website - genifi.com

Email - andrew.hilton@genifi.com
Investor Relations - Andrew Hilton (416) 606-8833
Auditors - MNP LLP C.A., Toronto, Ont.
Transfer Agents - Computershare Trust Company of Canada Inc., Toronto, Ont.
Profile - (Can. 2008) Offers software-as-a-service (SaaS) platforms including IDVerifact™, for digital identity verification; and tunl.™, for open banking and customer chat support, coupled with seamless integration of the company's partners financial technology platforms.
Previously offered Prodigy Labs™, the company's services business, which integrates and customizes the platforms for unique enterprise customer requirements, and provides technology services for digital identity, payments, open banking and digital transformation.

Recent Merger and Acquisition Activity

Status: completed **Announced:** Dec. 30, 2022
UPDATE: The transaction was completed. PREVIOUS: Prodigy Ventures Inc. agreed to sell wholly owned TCB Corporation (dba Prodigy Labs), which provides the Prodigy Labs™ service business, to UST Global (Canada) Inc. for $8,500,000, with up to an additional $4,000,000 payable upon the achievement of certain EBITDA and revenue targets. Prodigy Labs™ integrates and customizes the IDVerifact™ and tunl.™ platforms for unique enterprise customer requirements, and provides technology services for digital identity, payments, open banking and digital transformation.
Predecessor Detail - Name changed from Prodigy Ventures Inc., July 1, 2023.
Directors - Thomas (Tom) Beckerman, chr. & CEO, Toronto, Ont.; William (Bill) Maurin, Mississauga, Ont.; Stephen T. Moore, Toronto, Ont.
Other Exec. Officers - Andrew Hilton, CFO & corp. sec.; George Colwell, sr. v-p

Capital Stock

	Authorized (shs.)	Outstanding (shs.)[1]
Common	unlimited	144,287,403

[1] At July 4, 2023

Major Shareholder - Thomas (Tom) Beckerman held 65.2% interest at May 15, 2023.

Price Range - GNFI/TSX-VEN

Year	Volume	High	Low	Close
2022	4,241,667	$0.12	$0.03	$0.04
2021	15,538,785	$0.37	$0.08	$0.10
2020	2,596,273	$0.20	$0.07	$0.09
2019	1,165,654	$0.24	$0.11	$0.17
2018	1,233,361	$0.34	$0.14	$0.17

Recent Close: $0.04
Capital Stock Changes - During 2022, 1,072,500 common shares were issued for services.

Dividends

GNFI com N.S.R.
$0.041103**r** Mar. 22/23
Paid in 2023: $0.041103**r** 2022: n.a. 2021: n.a.

r Return of Capital

Wholly Owned Subsidiaries

FICANEX Technology Inc., Canada.
IDVerifact Inc., Toronto, Ont.
13165078 Canada Inc., Canada.

Financial Statistics

Periods ended:	12m Dec. 31/22[A]		12m Dec. 31/21[¤A]
	$000s	%Chg	$000s
Operating revenue	**1,733**	**+168**	**647**
Cost of sales	582		223
Salaries & benefits	2,446		2,245
General & admin expense	1,164		935
Stock-based compensation	15		52
Operating expense	**4,207**	**+22**	**3,456**
Operating income	**(2,474)**	**n.a.**	**(2,810)**
Deprec., depl. & amort.	917		492
Finance costs, gross	10		14
Write-downs/write-offs	(4,040)		nil
Pre-tax income	**(7,441)**	**n.a.**	**(3,316)**
Income taxes	(538)		(640)
Net inc. bef. disc. opers	**(6,903)**	**n.a.**	**(2,675)**
Income from disc. opers	1,468		1,804
Net income	**(5,435)**	**n.a.**	**(872)**
Cash & equivalent	1,781		2,733
Accounts receivable	1,771		1,531
Current assets	3,989		4,874
Fixed assets, net	7		93
Right-of-use assets	12		26
Intangibles, net	nil		5,190
Total assets	**4,616**	**-55**	**10,192**
Accts. pay. & accr. liabs	1,691		1,692
Current liabilities	1,863		1,731
Long-term lease liabilities	nil		12
Shareholders' equity	2,722		8,118
Cash from oper. activs	**(624)**	**n.a.**	**(374)**
Cash from fin. activs	(14)		(155)
Cash from invest. activs	(314)		1,131
Net cash position	**1,781**	**-35**	**2,733**
Capital expenditures	(8)		(37)
Capital disposals	2		2
	$		$
Earnings per share*	(0.05)		(0.02)
Cash flow per share*	(0.00)		(0.00)
	shs		shs
No. of shs. o/s*	144,287,403		143,214,903
Avg. no. of shs. o/s*	144,166,930		128,004,224
	%		%
Net profit margin	(398.33)		(413.45)
Return on equity	(127.36)		(45.47)
Return on assets	(93.11)		(33.98)

* Common
¤ Restated
[A] Reported in accordance with IFRS

Latest Results

Periods ended:	3m Mar. 31/23[A]		3m Mar. 31/22[¤A]
	$000s	%Chg	$000s
Operating revenue	545	+23	442
Net inc. bef. disc. opers	(780)	n.a.	(693)
Income from disc. opers	6,732		390
Net income	5,952	n.a.	(303)
	$		$
Earnings per share*	(0.01)		(0.00)

* Common
¤ Restated
[A] Reported in accordance with IFRS

Historical Summary
(as originally stated)

Fiscal Year	Oper. Rev. $000s	Net Inc. Bef. Disc. $000s	EPS* $
2022[A]	1,733	(6,903)	(0.05)
2021[A]	13,462	(872)	(0.01)
2020[A]	15,969	525	0.00
2019[A]	20,330	343	0.00
2018[A]	16,943	176	0.00

* Common
[A] Reported in accordance with IFRS

G.34 Genix Pharmaceuticals Corporation

Symbol - GENX **Exchange** - TSX-VEN **CUSIP** - 37232A
Head Office - 300-1055 Hastings St W, Vancouver, BC, V6E 1J8
Telephone - (604) 609-6198
Website - genixpharm.com
Email - kbottomley@genixpharm.com
Investor Relations - Kevin J. Bottomley (604) 609-6199
Auditors - Buckley Dodds C.P.A., Vancouver, B.C.
Bankers - HSBC Bank Canada
Lawyers - McMillan LLP
Transfer Agents - Computershare Trust Company of Canada Inc., Toronto, Ont.
Profile - (Alta. 1993) Researches, develops, manufactures, sales and distributes branded and generic ophthalmic drugs and ophthalmic over-the-counter products. Also markets and sells nutraceuticals and pharmaceutical products.
Holds 30 approved generic prescription ophthalmic drugs, which require marketing approval in Canada. The company does not expect to generate revenue from these drugs until the fourth quarter of 2023 or the first quarter of 2024. Also holds the Canadian rights to distribute two herbal health supplements, Sucanon® and Rechlor®, both of which help manage blood sugar levels and improve insulin sensitivity in non-insulin dependent adults; the global rights for Flu-X®, a plant-based anti-viral, anti-flu and anti-cold virus spray; the Canadian rights to a generic version of Synthroid® (Levothyroxine sodium), a widely prescribed treatment for hypothyroidism.
Predecessor Detail - Name changed from Alta Natural Herbs & Supplements Ltd., June 21, 2019.
Directors - Sina S. Pirooz, CEO, B.C.; Mahmoud Aziz, pres. & chr., B.C.; Kevin J. Bottomley, Vancouver, B.C.; Paul Chow, Vancouver, B.C.; Jamie A. Lewin, Vancouver, B.C.
Other Exec. Officers - Danny W. K. Lee, CFO; Monita Faris, corp. sec.

Capital Stock

	Authorized (shs.)	Outstanding (shs.)[1]
Preferred	unlimited	nil
Common	unlimited	59,224,131

[1] At Apr. 11, 2023

Major Shareholder - Paul Chow held 17.28% interest, Union Venture Trading S.A. held 13.3% interest and Mahmoud Aziz held 10.84% interest at Apr. 11, 2023.

Price Range - GENX/TSX-VEN

Year	Volume	High	Low	Close
2022	2,653,385	$0.19	$0.05	$0.08
2021	5,141,758	$0.28	$0.10	$0.12
2020	10,562,907	$0.30	$0.04	$0.17
2019	626,878	$0.09	$0.01	$0.07
2018	874,708	$0.10	$0.04	$0.06

Recent Close: $0.06
Capital Stock Changes - There were no changes to capital stock from fiscal 2021 to fiscal 2022, inclusive.

Financial Statistics

Periods ended:	12m Oct. 31/22[A]		12m Oct. 31/21[A]
	$000s	%Chg	$000s
General & admin expense	208		309
Stock-based compensation	259		809
Operating expense	**467**	**-58**	**1,118**
Operating income	**(467)**	**n.a.**	**(1,118)**
Deprec., depl. & amort.	564		537
Finance income	nil		1
Finance costs, gross	12		4
Pre-tax income	**(1,074)**	**n.a.**	**(1,653)**
Net income	**(1,074)**	**n.a.**	**(1,653)**
Cash & equivalent	9		139
Inventories	171		5
Accounts receivable	17		5
Current assets	240		188
Right-of-use assets	4		32
Intangibles, net	3,999		4,549
Total assets	**4,253**	**-11**	**4,769**
Bank indebtedness	178		15
Accts. pay. & accr. liabs	235		44
Current liabilities	1,054		744
Long-term debt, gross	636		663
Long-term lease liabilities	nil		11
Shareholders' equity	3,199		4,014
Cash from oper. activs	**(220)**	**n.a.**	**(428)**
Cash from fin. activs	93		(129)
Cash from invest. activs	(3)		nil
Net cash position	**9**	**-94**	**139**
	$		$
Earnings per share*	(0.02)		(0.03)
Cash flow per share*	(0.00)		(0.01)
	shs		shs
No. of shs. o/s*	59,224,131		59,224,131
Avg. no. of shs. o/s*	59,224,131		59,224,131
	%		%
Net profit margin	n.a.		n.a.
Return on equity	(29.78)		(37.27)
Return on assets	(23.54)		(32.60)

* Common
[A] Reported in accordance with IFRS

Latest Results

Periods ended:	3m Jan. 31/23[A]		3m Jan. 31/22[A]
	$000s	%Chg	$000s
Operating revenue	2	n.a.	nil
Net income	(228)	n.a.	(338)
	$		$
Earnings per share*	(0.00)		(0.01)

* Common
[A] Reported in accordance with IFRS

Historical Summary
(as originally stated)

Fiscal Year	Oper. Rev. $000s	Net Inc. Bef. Disc. $000s	EPS* $
2022A	nil	(1,074)	(0.02)
2021A	nil	(1,653)	(0.03)
2020A	nil	(719)	(0.01)
2019A	137	(165)	(0.00)
2018A	420	(25)	(0.00)

* Common
A Reported in accordance with IFRS

G.35 Gentor Resources Inc.

Symbol - GNT.H **Exchange** - TSX-VEN **CUSIP** - G38275
Head Office - 1 First Canadian Place, 7070-100 King St W, PO Box 419, Toronto, ON, M5X 1E3 **Telephone** - (416) 366-2221 **Fax** - (416) 366-7722
Website - www.gentorresources.com
Email - info@gentorresources.com
Investor Relations - Arnold T. Kondrat (416) 361-2510
Auditors - Kreston GTA LLP C.A., Markham, Ont.
Bankers - The Toronto-Dominion Bank, Toronto, Ont.
Lawyers - Norton Rose Fulbright Canada LLP, Toronto, Ont.
Transfer Agents - Island Stock Transfer LLC, St. Petersburg, Fla.; TSX Trust Company, Toronto, Ont.
Profile - (Cayman Islands 2012; orig. Fla., 2005) Seeking new business opportunities.
Directors - Arnold T. Kondrat, pres. & CEO, Toronto, Ont.; Richard J. Lachcik, Wasaga Beach, Ont.; William R. (Bill) Wilson, Arvada, Colo.
Other Exec. Officers - Donat K. Madilo, CFO; Geoffrey G. Farr, corp. sec.

Capital Stock

	Authorized (shs.)	Outstanding (shs.)[1]	Par
Common	500,000,000	38,906,742	US$0.0008

[1] At May 31, 2023

Major Shareholder - Arnold T. Kondrat held 51.49% interest at May 31, 2023.

Price Range - GNT.H/TSX-VEN

Year	Volume	High	Low	Close
2022	121,000	$0.14	$0.04	$0.05
2021	230,875	$0.11	$0.06	$0.09
2020	136,500	$0.08	$0.03	$0.08
2019	545,597	$0.07	$0.05	$0.05
2018	720,687	$0.12	$0.06	$0.06

Recent Close: $0.05
Capital Stock Changes - In May 2023, a 1-for-2 share consolidation was proposed.
There were no changes to capital stock from 2020 to 2022, inclusive.

Wholly Owned Subsidiaries
Gentor International Limited, British Virgin Islands.

Financial Statistics

Periods ended:	12m Dec. 31/22A		12m Dec. 31/21ºA
	US$000s	%Chg	US$000s
Salaries & benefits	155		155
General & admin expense	122		157
Operating expense	**277**	**-11**	**312**
Operating income	**(277)**	**n.a.**	**(312)**
Finance costs, gross	1		1
Pre-tax income	**(258)**	**n.a.**	**21**
Net income	**(258)**	**n.a.**	**21**
Cash & equivalent	10		4
Current assets	25		20
Total assets	**25**	**+25**	**20**
Accts. pay. & accr. liabs	178		217
Current liabilities	1,067		805
Long-term debt, gross	26		25
Long-term debt, net	26		25
Shareholders' equity	(1,068)		(810)
Cash from oper. activs	**6**	**+100**	**3**
Net cash position	**10**	**+150**	**4**
	US$		US$
Earnings per share*	(0.01)		0.00
Cash flow per share*	0.00		0.00
	shs		shs
No. of shs. o/s*	38,906,742		38,906,742
Avg. no. of shs. o/s*	38,906,742		38,906,742
	%		%
Net profit margin	n.a.		n.a.
Return on equity	n.m.		n.m.
Return on assets	n.m.		122.22

* Common
º Restated
A Reported in accordance with U.S. GAAP

Historical Summary
(as originally stated)

Fiscal Year	Oper. Rev. US$000s	Net Inc. Bef. Disc. US$000s	EPS* US$
2022A	nil	(258)	(0.01)
2021A	nil	21	0.00
2020A	nil	(301)	(0.01)
2019A	nil	(296)	(0.01)
2018A	nil	(41)	(0.00)

* Common
A Reported in accordance with U.S. GAAP

G.36 Geodrill Limited

Symbol - GEO **Exchange** - TSX **CUSIP** - G3828T
Head Office - Ragnall House, 18 Peel Rd, Douglas, Isle of Man, IM1 4LZ **Overseas Tel** - 44-1624-676-585
Website - www.geodrill-gh.com
Email - jlongo@geodrill-gh.com
Investor Relations - Joanna Longo
Auditors - PricewaterhouseCoopers LLP C.A., Toronto, Ont.
Lawyers - Cassels Brock & Blackwell LLP, Toronto, Ont.
Transfer Agents - TSX Trust Company, Toronto, Ont.
Employees - 1,575 at Dec. 31, 2022
Profile - (Isle of Man 1998) Provides exploration and development drilling services, primarily to gold companies with operations in Ghana, Burkina Faso, Cote d'Ivoire, Mali, Egypt, Chile and Peru.

Specializes in reverse circulation and diamond core drilling using a fleet of multi-purpose, core, air-core, grade control, underground and water borehole drill rigs operating from workshops and supply bases at Anwiankwanta, Ghana; Ouagadougou, BurkinaFaso; Bouake, Côte d'Ivoire; Bamako, Mali; Alexandria, Egypt and Lima, Peru. At Dec. 31, 2022, the company had 80 drill rigs including four rented rigs. The company also owns drilling support equipment, including a fleet of boosters and auxiliary compressors.

On Aug. 18, 2022, ordinary shares commenced trading on the OTCQX Market under the stock symbol GEODF.

Directors - John Bingham, chr., Douglas, Isle of Man; David (Dave) Harper, pres. & CEO, Accra, Ghana; Peter Prattas, Ont.; Ronald Sellwood, Salt Lake City, Utah
Other Exec. Officers - Terry Burling, COO; Gregory G. (Greg) Borsk, CFO; Victoria Prentice, corp. sec.

Capital Stock

	Authorized (shs.)	Outstanding (shs.)[1]
Ordinary	unlimited	46,921,400

[1] At June 2, 2023

Normal Course Issuer Bid - The company plans to make normal course purchases of up to 2,343,820 ordinary shares representing 5% of the total outstanding. The bid commenced on June 7, 2023, and expires on June 6, 2024.
Major Shareholder - David (Dave) Harper held 39.5% interest and Sustainable Capital Africa Alpha Fund held 17% interest at Apr. 4, 2023.

Price Range - GEO/TSX

Year	Volume	High	Low	Close
2022	5,430,983	$2.93	$2.05	$2.63
2021	8,110,635	$2.99	$1.40	$2.11
2020	4,823,778	$2.07	$0.80	$1.56
2019	1,392,759	$1.89	$1.20	$1.44
2018	4,964,920	$2.33	$1.35	$1.42

Recent Close: $2.55
Capital Stock Changes - During 2022, 1,520,000 ordinary shares were issued on exercise of options.

Dividends
GEO ord Ra $0.08 pa S est. Apr. 10, 2023
Prev. Rate: $0.06 est. Apr. 8, 2022
Prev. Rate: $0.02 est. Apr. 9, 2021
$0.01i .... Apr. 9/21
i Initial Payment

Wholly Owned Subsidiaries
Drilling Services Malta Limited, Malta.
- 100% int. in **Vannin Resources Unipessoal Limitada**, Madeira Islands.
  - 100% int. in **Geodrill Sondagens Ltda.**, Brazil.
  - 95% int. in **Recon Drilling Chile S.p.A.**, Chile.
  - 95% int. in **Recon Drilling S.A.C.**, Peru.

Geodrill Leasing Limited, Isle of Man.
Geodrill Mauritius Limited, Mauritius.
- 100% int. in **Geodrill Cote d'Ivoire S.A.R.L.**, Côte d'Ivoire.
  - 95% int. in **Geo-Drill S.A.R.L.**, Mali.
- 100% int. in **Geodrill for Leasing and Specialized Services Freezone LLC**, Egypt.
- 100% int. in **Geodrill Ghana Limited**, Accra, Ghana.
- 100% int. in **Silver Back Egypt for Mining and Drilling Services S.A.E.**, Egypt.

Financial Statistics

Periods ended:	12m Dec. 31/22A		12m Dec. 31/21A
	US$000s	%Chg	US$000s
Operating revenue	**138,625**	**+20**	**115,214**
Cost of sales	98,048		85,116
General & admin expense	2,162		1,620
Operating expense	**141,118**	**+63**	**86,736**
Operating income	**(2,493)**	**n.a.**	**28,478**
Deprec., depl. & amort.	10,029		9,006
Finance costs, gross	691		654
Write-downs/write-offs	(768)		(616)
Pre-tax income	**27,630**	**+40**	**19,794**
Income taxes	8,712		5,676
Net income	**18,918**	**+34**	**14,118**
Net inc. for equity hldrs	**18,916**	**+34**	**14,138**
Net inc. for non-cont. int	**2**	**n.a.**	**(20)**
Cash & equivalent	14,391		9,275
Inventories	31,553		27,832
Accounts receivable	34,297		23,707
Current assets	82,868		66,659
Fixed assets, net	57,059		49,085
Right-of-use assets	1,302		812
Total assets	**141,229**	**+21**	**116,556**
Accts. pay. & accr. liabs	22,136		17,038
Current liabilities	28,332		22,301
Long-term debt, gross	4,608		6,902
Long-term debt, net	2,627		3,961
Long-term lease liabilities	620		303
Shareholders' equity	107,058		87,527
Cash from oper. activs	**25,286**	**+71**	**14,782**
Cash from fin. activs	(2,850)		2,831
Cash from invest. activs	(16,885)		(14,632)
Net cash position	**14,391**	**+55**	**9,275**
Capital expenditures	(16,885)		(14,632)
	US$		US$
Earnings per share*	0.41		0.31
Cash flow per share*	0.55		0.33
Cash divd. per share*	$0.06		$0.02
	shs		shs
No. of shs. o/s*	46,836,400		45,316,400
Avg. no. of shs. o/s*	46,322,486		45,082,449
	%		%
Net profit margin	13.65		12.25
Return on equity	19.44		17.61
Return on assets	15.04		13.57
Foreign sales percent	100		100
No. of employees (FTEs)	1,575		1,298

* Ordinary
A Reported in accordance with IFRS

Latest Results

Periods ended:	3m Mar. 31/23A		3m Mar. 31/22A
	US$000s	%Chg	US$000s
Operating revenue	37,562	+12	33,409
Net income	6,130	+3	5,951
Net inc. for equity hldrs	6,130	+3	5,952
Net inc. for non-cont. int	nil		(1)
	US$		US$
Earnings per share*	0.13		0.13

* Ordinary
A Reported in accordance with IFRS

Historical Summary
(as originally stated)

Fiscal Year	Oper. Rev. US$000s	Net Inc. Bef. Disc. US$000s	EPS* US$
2022A	138,625	18,918	0.41
2021A	115,214	14,118	0.31
2020A	82,436	7,513	0.17
2019A	87,408	3,876	0.09
2018A	88,539	662	0.02

* Ordinary
A Reported in accordance with IFRS

G.37 Gibson Energy Inc.*

Symbol - GEI **Exchange** - TSX **CUSIP** - 374825
Head Office - 1700-440 2 Ave SW, Calgary, AB, T2P 5E9 **Telephone** - (403) 206-4000 **Fax** - (403) 206-4001
Website - www.gibsonenergy.com
Email - beth.pollock@gibsonenergy.com
Investor Relations - Beth Pollock (403) 992-6472
Auditors - PricewaterhouseCoopers LLP C.A., Calgary, Alta.
Bankers - Bank of Montreal; Royal Bank of Canada, Calgary, Alta.
Lawyers - Bennett Jones LLP, Calgary, Alta.
Transfer Agents - Odyssey Trust Company, Calgary, Alta.
FP500 Revenue Ranking - 55
Employees - 475 at Dec. 31, 2022
Profile - (Alta. 2011 amalg.) Stores, processes, gathers and markets liquids and refined products in Canada and the United States.

The company has two integrated business segments as follows:

Infrastructure - Includes terminals, rail loading and unloading facilities, gathering pipelines, a diluent recovery unit (DRU), a crude oil processing facility, and other small terminals. Primary facilities consist of the owned and operated Hardisty and Edmonton Terminals, both principal hubs in Alberta for aggregating and exporting liquids and refined products out of the Western Canadian Sedimentary Basin. The Hardisty Terminal has 13,500,000 bbl of storage capacity and has connections to all major pipelines in the area, including the company's network of 500 km of crude oil pipelines which has combined capacity of 90,000 bbl per day, the Hardisty DRU (50% owned) and the Hardisty Unit Train Facility, which has the ability to load three and a half unit trains per day. The DRU, located adjacent to the Hardisty Terminal, is a facility which separates the diluent added to the raw bitumen in the production process and has a nameplate capacity of 50,000 bbl per day. The Edmonton Terminal has 1,700,000 bbl of storage capacity and also has manifest rail loading/offloading capabilities as well as connections to major pipelines, refineries and upgrading facilities in the area. During 2022, the Hardisty and Edmonton Terminals had average throughput of 1,200,000 and 155,000 bbl per day, respectively.

Operations also include a crude oil processing facility in Moose Jaw, Sask., with 1,100,000 bbl of onsite storage capacity and a throughput of up to 24,000 bbl per day, depending on crude feedstock. In the U.S., owns and operates the Gibson Wink Terminal in Wink, Tex., South Texas Gateway Terminal, a liquids terminal and export facility, in Ingleside, Tex., with 8,600,000 bbl of storage capacity, and the Pyote East, Pyote West and Flintlock Pipelines which have connections to major pipelines transporting oil from the Permian Basin to the U.S. Gulf Coast. Also holds 36% interest in a crude-by-rail and storage terminal and a pipeline connection to a common carrier crude oil pipeline in Joliet, Ill.

Marketing - Involves the purchasing, selling, storing and optimizing of hydrocarbon products, including crude oil, natural gas liquids (NGLs), road asphalt, roofing flux, frac oils, light and heavy straight run distillates, combined vacuum gas oil (CVGO) and an oil-based drilling mud product. This segment sources the crude oil used in the refining process of the Moose Jaw facility and markets the refined products produced. This segment also provides a full suite of marketing services to third parties, including integrated oil companies, producers, refineries and end-user customers. This segment's optimization opportunities are typically location, quality and time-based. Hydrocarbon products are sourced from western Canada as well as the Permian Basin and marketed throughout Canada and the U.S. During 2022, the segment marketed an average of 615,000 physical bbl per day.

In May 2022, the company placed the biofuels blending project at its Edmonton Terminal into service ahead of schedule and within budgeted capital to facilitate the storage, blending and transportation of renewable diesel.

Recent Merger and Acquisition Activity

Status: completed **Revised:** Aug. 1, 2023

UPDATE: The transaction was completed. PREVIOUS: Gibson Energy Inc. agreed to acquire South Texas Gateway Terminal LLC, which owns a newly built crude oil export facility on the Texas Gulf Coast, for US$1.1 billion. The facility has a terminalling capacity to 8,600,000 bbls of oil across 20 tanks. The transaction was expected to close in the third quarter of 2023.

Predecessor Detail - Formed from Gibson Energy Holding ULC in Alberta, June 15, 2011, following amalgamation with (old) Gibson Energy Inc. and 1441682 Alberta Ltd. (privately held).

Directors - James M. Estey, chr., Calgary, Alta.; Steven R. (Steve) Spaulding, pres. & CEO, Calgary, Alta.; Douglas P. Bloom, Coquitlam, B.C.; James J. Cleary, Colorado Springs, Colo.; Judy E. Cotte, Toronto, Ont.; Heidi L. Dutton, Saskatoon, Sask.; John L. Festival, Calgary, Alta.; Diane A. Kazarian, Toronto, Ont.; Margaret C. (Peggy) Montana, Houston, Tex.

Exec. Officers - Sean M. Brown, sr. v-p & CFO; Kyle J. DeGruchy, sr. v-p & chief comml. officer; Omar Saif, sr. v-p & COO; Sean M. Wilson, sr. v-p, chief administrative & sustainability officer & corp. sec.; Mark Chyc-Cies, v-p, strategy, planning & IR; Jessica Ferguson, v-p, legal & gen. counsel; Kelly Holtby, v-p, comml. devel.; Kamran Naseer, v-p, fin.; Beth Pollock, v-p & treas.; Krista Weir, v-p, HR

Capital Stock

	Authorized (shs.)	Outstanding (shs.)[1]
Preferred	unlimited	nil
Common	unlimited	141,600,000

[1] At July 28, 2023

Options - At Dec. 31, 2022, options were outstanding to purchase 452,677 common shares at a weighted average exercise price of $20.88 per share with a weighted average remaining contractual life of 1.2 years.

Normal Course Issuer Bid - The company plans to make normal course purchases of up to 8,760,553 common shares representing 7.5% of the public float. The bid commenced on Aug. 31, 2022, and expires on Aug. 30, 2023.

Major Shareholder - M&G Investment Management Limited held 19.91% interest at Mar. 20, 2023.

Price Range - GEI/TSX

Year	Volume	High	Low	Close
2022	128,038,436	$27.75	$21.15	$23.64
2021	107,245,515	$26.98	$18.78	$22.42
2020	157,820,835	$28.34	$10.96	$20.56
2019	103,174,994	$27.68	$18.18	$26.59
2018	89,542,967	$23.32	$15.68	$18.68

Recent Close: $19.86

Capital Stock Changes - On Aug. 1, 2023, 20,010,000 common shares were issued without further consideration on exchange of subscription receipts sold previously by bought deal offering at $20.15 each.

During 2022, common shares were issued as follows: 1,321,639 on exercise of options and 1,001,058 on equity awards; 5,988,400 common shares were repurchased under a Normal Course Issuer Bid.

Dividends

GEI com Ra $1.56 pa Q est. Apr. 17, 2023**
Prev. Rate: $1.48 est. Apr. 14, 2022
Prev. Rate: $1.40 est. Apr. 16, 2021
Prev. Rate: $1.36 est. Apr. 17, 2020
** Reinvestment Option

Long-Term Debt - Outstanding at Dec. 31, 2022:

Revolv. credit facility due 2027[1]	$255,000,000
2.45% sr. notes due 2025	325,000,000
2.85% sr. notes due 2027	325,000,000
3.6% sr. notes due 2029	500,000,000
5.25% hybrid notes due 2080[2]	250,000,000
Less: Unamort. disc. & issue costs	8,228,000
	1,646,772,000
Less: Current portion	nil
	1,646,772,000

[1] Bears interest at Canadian prime rate, U.S. base rate, U.S. LIBOR or Canadian banker's acceptance rate plus applicable margin.

[2] The interest rate will reset on Dec. 22, 2030, and on December 22 every five years thereafter, at a fixed rate equal to the five-year Government of Canada yield plus (i) 4.715% for the period from Dec. 22, 2030, to Dec. 21, 2050, and (ii) 5.465% for the period from Dec. 22, 2050, to Dec. 21, 2080. Convertible by the company into one preferred share for each $1,000 principal amount.

Note - In February 2023, maturity of the revolving credit facility was extended to February 2028 from April 2027. In July 2023, offering of $350,000,000 of 5.8% senior unsecured medium term notes due 2026, $350,000,000 of 5.75% senior unsecured medium term notes due 2033 and $200,000,000 of 6.2% senior unsecured medium term notes due 2053 was completed. The company also issued $200,000,000 of 8.7% fixed-to-fixed rate subordinated notes due 2083.

Wholly Owned Subsidiaries

Gibson Energy GP Ltd., Alta.
- 100% int. in **Gibson Energy Infrastructure Partnership**, Alta.

Gibson (U.S.) Parentco Corp., Calgary, Alta.
- 100% int. in **Gibson (U.S.) Holdco Corp.**, Del.
  - 100% int. in **Gibson (U.S.) Acquisitionco Corp.**, Del.
    - 100% int. in **Gibson Energy Corp.**, Del.
    - 100% int. in **Gibson Energy Infrastructure, LLC**, Del.
      - 36% int. in **Zenith Energy Terminals Joliet Holdings LLC**, Del.
    - 100% int. in **Gibson Energy, LLC**, Del.
  - 100% int. in **Gibson (U.S.) Finco Corp.**, Del.

Moose Jaw Refinery ULC, Alta.
- 100% int. in **Moose Jaw Refinery Partnership**, Alta.

South Texas Gateway Terminal LLC, Tex.

Investments

50% int. in **Hardisty Energy Terminal Limited Partnership**, Alta.

Note: The preceding list includes only the major related companies in which interests are held.

Financial Statistics

Periods ended:	12m Dec. 31/22[A]		12m Dec. 31/21[A]
	$000s	%Chg	$000s
Operating revenue	**11,035,411**	**+53**	**7,211,148**
Cost of sales	10,505,865		6,749,901
General & admin expense	60,980		57,870
Operating expense	**10,566,845**	**+55**	**6,807,771**
Operating income	**468,566**	**+16**	**403,377**
Deprec., depl. & amort.	144,479		173,861
Finance costs, gross	64,939		61,344
Investment income	20,926		6,083
Pre-tax income	**290,135**	**+60**	**181,237**
Income taxes	66,890		36,184
Net income	**223,245**	**+54**	**145,053**
Cash & equivalent	83,596		62,688
Inventories	257,754		255,131
Accounts receivable	460,135		663,112
Current assets	821,524		1,006,439
Long-term investments	165,111		172,715
Fixed assets, net	1,556,427		1,612,636
Right-of-use assets	47,739		52,582
Intangibles, net	391,131		394,230
Total assets	**3,194,998**	**-7**	**3,431,760**
Accts. pay. & accr. liabs	566,341		671,997
Current liabilities	685,689		796,508
Long-term debt, gross	1,646,772		1,660,609
Long-term debt, net	1,646,772		1,660,609
Long-term lease liabilities	34,504		52,031
Shareholders' equity	573,016		644,126
Cash from oper. activs	**598,312**	**+176**	**216,806**
Cash from fin. activs	(445,506)		(82,955)
Cash from invest. activs	(134,400)		(127,060)
Net cash position	**83,596**	**+33**	**62,688**
Capital expenditures	(140,381)		(117,672)
Capital disposals	8,240		19,822
Pension fund surplus	702		553
	$		$
Earnings per share*	1.53		0.99
Cash flow per share*	4.09		1.48
Cash divd. per share*	1.48		1.40
	shs		shs
No. of shs. o/s*	142,961,379		146,627,082
Avg. no. of shs. o/s*	146,221,479		146,344,843
	%		%
Net profit margin	2.02		2.01
Return on equity	36.68		21.92
Return on assets	8.25		5.97
Foreign sales percent	15		20
No. of employees (FTEs)	475		460

* Common
[A] Reported in accordance with IFRS

Latest Results

Periods ended:	6m June 30/23[A]		6m June 30/22[A]
	$000s	%Chg	$000s
Operating revenue	4,979,374	-15	5,884,156
Net income	140,277	+60	87,889
	$		$
Earnings per share*	0.99		0.60

* Common
[A] Reported in accordance with IFRS

Historical Summary
(as originally stated)

Fiscal Year	Oper. Rev.	Net Inc. Bef. Disc.	EPS*
	$000s	$000s	$
2022[A]	11,035,411	223,245	1.53
2021[A]	7,211,148	145,053	0.99
2020[A]	4,938,066	121,309	0.83
2019[A]	7,336,322	176,339	1.21
2018[A]	6,846,589	81,125	0.57

* Common
[A] Reported in accordance with IFRS

G.38 Gildan Activewear Inc.*

Symbol - GIL **Exchange** - TSX **CUSIP** - 375916

Head Office - 3300-600 boul de Maisonneuve O, Montréal, QC, H3A 3J2 **Telephone** - (514) 735-2023 **Toll-free** - (866) 755-2023 **Fax** - (514) 734-8379

Website - www.gildancorp.com

Email - jhayem@gildan.com

Investor Relations - Jessy Hayem (866) 755-2023

Auditors - KPMG LLP C.A., Montréal, Qué.

Lawyers - Norton Rose Fulbright Canada LLP, Montréal, Qué.

Transfer Agents - Computershare Trust Company, N.A., Golden, Colo.; Computershare Trust Company of Canada Inc., Montréal, Qué.

FP500 Revenue Ranking - 136

Employees - 47,000 at Apr. 2, 2023

Profile - (Can. 1984) Manufactures and markets activewear, underwear and hosiery for printwear markets and retail markets.

Manufactures broad range of basic apparel products to a customer base which includes wholesale distributors, screenprinters and embellishers in more than 60 countries across North America, Europe, the Asia-Pacific region and Latin America; and to retailers in North America including mass merchants, department stores, national chains, specialty retailers, craft stores and online retailers; and to global lifestyle brand companies who market these products under their own brands. Products include activewear, which consists of t-shirts, fleece tops and bottoms, and sport shirts; hosiery, which consists of athletic, dress, casual and workwear socks, liner socks and socks for therapeutic purposes; and underwear, which consists of men's and boys' underwear (tops and bottoms) and ladies panties. Products are sold under company-owned brands including Gildan®, Gildan Performance®, Gildan Platinum®, American Apparel®, Comfort Colors®, Gildan® Hammer™, Alsyle® , GoldToe®, PowerSox™, Signature Gold by GoldToe®, Peds®, MediPeds® and All Pro®. Also holds exclusive distribution rights in the U.S. and Canada to sell socks under the Under Armour® brand.

Manufacturing facilities are located in the U.S., Central America, the Caribbean and Bangladesh. Operates (at Jan. 1, 2023) yarn-spinning facilities in Salisbury (2), Clarkton, Mocksville, Sanford (2), and Mayodan and Eden, N.C.; textile facilities in Honduras (4), the Dominican Republic and Bangladesh; sewing facilities in Honduras (3), Nicaragua (4), the Dominican Republic (3) and Bangladesh; and garment-dyeing and hosiery manufacturing facilities in Honduras.

In February 2023, the company closed its yarn-spinning facility in Cedartown, Ga.

During fiscal 2022, the company exited the sheer panty hose, tights, leggings, ladies shapewear, intimates and accessories products, marketed under the Secret®, Silks®, Secret Silky® and Therapy Plus® brands.

Recent Merger and Acquisition Activity

Status: completed **Announced:** Apr. 2, 2023
Gildan Activewear Inc. sold and leased back a distribution centre in the U.S. for US$51,000,000.

Status: completed **Announced:** Dec. 31, 2022
Gildan Activewear Inc. sold its sheer inventory and trademarks for total proceeds of $6,400,000. Sheer business includes sheer panty hose, tights and leggings under Therapy Plus®, Secret®, Silks® and Secret Silky®.

Status: completed **Announced:** Aug. 1, 2022
Gildan Activewear Inc. sold a yarn spinning facility in Mayodan, N.C., for US$29,400,000. The facility was the smallest of the four facilities acquired as part of Gildan's acquisition of Frontier Yarns, Inc. in December 2021.

Directors - Glenn J. Chamandy, co-founder, pres. & CEO, Westmount, Qué.; Donald C. Berg, chr., Lakewood Ranch, Fla.; Maryse Bertrand, Westmount, Qué.; Dhaval Buch, India; Marcello (Marc) Caira, Toronto, Ont.; Shirley E. Cunningham, Estero, Fla.; Charles M. Herington, Miami, Fla.; Luc Jobin, Montréal, Qué.; Craig A. Leavitt, Red Hook, N.Y.; Anne Martin-Vachon, Trois-Rivières, Qué.

Other Exec. Officers - Arun D. Bajaj, exec. v-p, legal affairs & chief HR officer; Rhodri J. Harries, exec. v-p & chief finl. & admin. officer; Sophie Argiriou, v-p, investor commun.; Michelle Taylor, v-p, gen. counsel & corp. sec.; Benito A. Masi, pres., mfg.; Chuck J. Ward, pres., sales, mktg. & distrib.

Capital Stock

	Authorized (shs.)	Outstanding (shs.)[1]
First Preferred	unlimited	nil
Second Preferred	unlimited	nil
Common	unlimited	175,572,760

[1] At July 31, 2023

First Preferred - Issuable in series.
Second Preferred - Issuable in series.
Common - One vote per share.
Options - At Jan. 1, 2023, options were outstanding to purchase 746,000 common shares at prices ranging from Cdn$33.01 to Cdn$42.27 per share with remaining contractual life of up to three years, and 1,988,000 common shares at prices ranging from US$20.77 to US$30.00 per share with remaining contractual life of up to five years.
Normal Course Issuer Bid - The company plans to make normal course purchases of up to 8,778,638 common shares representing 5% of the total outstanding. The bid commenced on Aug. 9, 2023, and expires on Aug. 8, 2024.
Major Shareholder - Widely held at Mar. 6, 2023.

Price Range - GIL/TSX

Year	Volume	High	Low	Close
2022	128,542,297	$55.13	$33.83	$37.08
2021	97,317,434	$54.73	$31.72	$53.63
2020	171,250,039	$39.82	$13.64	$35.59
2019	140,926,615	$53.33	$30.81	$38.39
2018	154,515,375	$45.45	$33.03	$41.44

Recent Close: $39.45
Capital Stock Changes - During fiscal 2022, common shares were issued as follows: 490,000 on exercise of options, 229,000 on vesting of restricted share units and 48,000 under the employee share purchase plan. In addition, 13,097,000 common shares were repurchased under a Normal Course Issuer Bid and 228,000 common shares were repurchased as settlement of non-treasury restricted share units.

Dividends

GIL com N.S.R. [1]

US$0.186	Sept. 18/23	US$0.186	June 19/23
US$0.186	Apr. 10/23	US$0.169	Dec. 19/22

Paid in 2023: US$0.558 2022: US$0.676 2021: US$0.462

[1] Quarterly divd normally payable in June/20 has been omitted.

Long-Term Debt - Outstanding at Jan. 1, 2023:

Notes payable due 2023[1]	US$150,000,000
Notes payable due 2026[2]	150,000,000
Term loan due 2026[3]	300,000,000
Revolv. facility due 2027[3]	330,000,000
	930,000,000
Less: Current portion	150,000,000
	780,000,000

[1] Consist of US$100,000,000 and US$50,000,000 of notes payable bearing interest at 2.7% and U.S. LIBOR plus 1.53%, respectively.
[2] Consist of US$100,000,000 and US$50,000,000 of notes payable bearing interest at 2.91% and U.S. LIBOR plus 1.57%, respectively.
[3] Bears interest at U.S. Term Secured Overnight Financing Rate (Term SOFR) plus 1% to 3%.

Wholly Owned Subsidiaries

G.A.B. Limited, Bangladesh.
Gildan Activewear Dominican Republic Textile Company Inc., Barbados.
Gildan Activewear (Eden) Inc., N.C.
Gildan Activewear EU S.R.L., Belgium.
Gildan Activewear Honduras Textile Company, S. de R.L., Honduras.
Gildan Activewear SRL, Bridgetown, Barbados.
Gildan Activewear (UK) Limited, United Kingdom.
Gildan Charleston Inc., Del.
Gildan Choloma Textiles, S. de R. L., Honduras.
Gildan Honduras Properties, S. de R.L., Honduras.
Gildan Hosiery Rio Nance, S. de R.L., Honduras.
Gildan Mayan Textiles, S. de R.L., Honduras.
Gildan Textiles de Sula, S. de R.L., Honduras.
Gildan USA Inc., Del.
Gildan Yarns, LLC, Del.
Phoenix Sanford, LLC, N.C.
• 100% int. in **Frontier Yarns, Inc.**, N.C.
SDS International Limited, Bangladesh.
Note: The preceding list includes only the major related companies in which interests are held.

Financial Statistics

Periods ended:	12m Jan. 1/23[A]		12m Jan. 2/22[A]
	US$000s	%Chg	US$000s
Operating revenue	**3,240,482**	**+11**	**2,922,570**
Cost of sales	2,123,144		1,846,959
General & admin expense	324,108		314,171
Operating expense	**2,447,252**	**+13**	**2,161,130**
Operating income	**793,230**	**+4**	**761,440**
Deprec., depl. & amort.	124,926		135,402
Finance costs, gross	36,957		27,331
Write-downs/write-offs	(64,440)		34,076[1]
Pre-tax income	**566,428**	**-9**	**624,558**
Income taxes	24,888		17,375
Net income	**541,540**	**-11**	**607,183**
Cash & equivalent	150,417		179,246
Inventories	1,225,940		774,358
Accounts receivable	248,785		329,967
Current assets	1,726,952		1,447,233
Fixed assets, net	1,115,169		985,073
Right-of-use assets	77,958		92,447
Intangibles, net	501,628		590,445
Total assets	**3,440,214**	**+10**	**3,136,682**
Accts. pay. & accr. liabs	471,208		440,401
Current liabilities	641,673		463,603
Long-term debt, gross	930,000		600,000
Long-term debt, net	780,000		600,000
Long-term lease liabilities	80,162		93,812
Shareholders' equity	1,882,162		1,919,405
Cash from oper. activs	**413,488**	**-33**	**617,510**
Cash from fin. activs	(258,274)		(754,753)
Cash from invest. activs	(182,404)		(187,833)
Net cash position	**150,417**	**-16**	**179,246**
Capital expenditures	(239,128)		(127,457)
Capital disposals	28,607		106,358
	US$		US$
Earnings per share*	2.94		3.08
Cash flow per share*	2.25		3.13
Cash divd. per share*	0.68		0.46
	shs		shs
No. of shs. o/s*	179,709,339		192,267,273
Avg. no. of shs. o/s*	184,128,000		197,014,000
	%		%
Net profit margin	16.71		20.78
Return on equity	28.49		34.91
Return on assets	17.54		20.58
Foreign sales percent	96		96
No. of employees (FTEs)	51,000		48,000

* Common
[A] Reported in accordance with IFRS
[1] Net of a US$55,600,000 impairment reversal relating to intangible assets acquired in previous business acquisitions and a US$24,100,000 write-off of certain intangible assets relating to Hosiery operations.

Latest Results

Periods ended:	6m July 2/23[A]		6m July 3/22[A]
	US$000s	%Chg	US$000s
Operating revenue	1,543,301	-8	1,670,452
Net income	252,905	-17	304,604
	US$		US$
Earnings per share*	1.42		1.63

* Common
[A] Reported in accordance with IFRS

Historical Summary
(as originally stated)

Fiscal Year	Oper. Rev.	Net Inc. Bef. Disc.	EPS*
	US$000s	US$000s	US$
2022[A]	3,240,482	541,540	2.94
2021[A]	2,922,570	607,183	3.08
2020[A]	1,981,276	(225,282)	(1.14)
2019[A]	2,823,901	259,809	1.27

* Common
[A] Reported in accordance with IFRS

G.39 Givex Corp.

Symbol - GIVX **Exchange** - TSX **CUSIP** - 37638G
Head Office - 1400-134 Peter St, Toronto, ON, M5V 2H2 **Telephone** - (416) 350-9660 **Fax** - (416) 350-9661
Website - www.givex.com
Email - don.gray@givex.com
Investor Relations - Don Gray (416) 350-9660
Auditors - KPMG LLP C.A., Vaughan, Ont.
Transfer Agents - Odyssey Trust Company
Employees - 356 at Feb. 28, 2023
Profile - (Ont. 2022; orig. B.C., 2019) Develops and commercializes a full-suite cloud-based omni-channel software platform which facilitates commerce for merchants, primarily retail, hospitality and food service businesses.

The platform includes customer engagement solutions, such as gift cards and e-gift cards, loyalty programs, e-commerce, online ordering tools and mobile applications; enterprise point-of-sale (POS), which consists of the GivexPOS system, a cloud-based solution that can be customized to specific industries and features inventory management, kitchen display systems, menu boards, menu management, kiosks, hand-held ordering tablets and online ordering mobile applications; payments solutions through GivexPay, a payment processing product which allows users to select their preferred payment type while delivering fraud defence and customer insights; integrations solutions, which enables clients to integrate third-party POS, payment devices and online ordering applications with the company's products and solutions; and analytics, which offers clients access to standard reports containing real-time data on their gift, loyalty and promotional programs to gain both exploratory and predictive insights. The solutions can be used as a single service or in combination with one another.

The platform is deployed in more than 122,000 active client locations across over 100 countries.

In November 2022, the company continued from the jurisdiction of British Columbia to Ontario.

In August 2022, the company acquired Nottingham, U.K.-based **Counter Solutions Holdings Limited**, a provider of point-of-sale (POS) and front and back of the house technology solutions mainly for the retail and hospitality sectors. Purchase price was $5,900,000 paid as a combination of cash and contingent consideration payable.

Predecessor Detail - Name changed from Givex Information Technology Group Limited, Nov. 10, 2022.

Directors - Don Gray, chr. & CEO, Bahamas; Jim Woodside, CFO, Toronto, Ont.; Michael Carr†, Burlington, Ont.; Miles Evans, Bahamas; Divya Kulkarni, Ont.; Robert R. (Rob) Munro, Toronto, Ont.

Other Exec. Officers - Brittain Brown, pres.; Graham Campbell, COO; Mo Chaar, chief comml. officer; Debra Demeza, exec. v-p, HR; Juan Tovar, sr. v-p, corp. integrations; Jeff Hergott, corp. sec.

† Lead director

Capital Stock

	Authorized (shs.)	Outstanding (shs.)[1]
Preferred	unlimited	nil
Common	unlimited	126,465,531

[1] At May 2, 2023

Normal Course Issuer Bid - The company plans to make normal course purchases of up to 6,101,326 common shares representing 5% of the total outstanding. The bid commenced on Nov. 9, 2022, and expires on Nov. 8, 2023.

Major Shareholder - Don Gray & Debra Demeza together held 29.78% interest and JPE Trust held 14.73% interest at Mar. 17, 2023.

Price Range - GIVX/TSX

Year	Volume	High	Low	Close
2022............	11,330,932	$1.05	$0.38	$0.45
2021............	5,702,353	$1.84	$0.60	$0.85

Recent Close: $0.44

Capital Stock Changes - During 2022, common shares were issued as follows: 8,697,525 on vesting of restricted share units, 625,000 on the acquisition of 1157457 Ontario Inc. (dba Kalex Equipment Services) and 189,081 on the acquisition of Loyalty Lane, Inc.; 64,816 common shares were repurchased under a Normal Course Issuer Bid.

Wholly Owned Subsidiaries

Givex Corporation, Toronto, Ont.
- 100% int. in **Givex Australia Pty Limited**, Australia.
- 10% int. in **Givex Brasil Serviços de Cartões-Presente e Programas de Fidelidade Ltda.**, Brazil.
- 100% int. in **Givex Canada Corporation**, Ont.
  - 100% int. in **Givex Mexico, S.A. de C.V.**, Mexico City, D.F., Mexico.
  - 100% int. in **1157487 Ontario Inc.**, Toronto, Ont. dba Kalex Equipment Services.
  - 100% int. in **Owen Business Systems Ltd.**, Victoria, B.C.
- 100% int. in **Givex Europe S.A.R.L.**, Nyon, Switzerland.
- 100% int. in **Givex International Corporation**, Bahamas.
  - 90% int. in **Givex Brasil Serviços de Cartões-Presente e Programas de Fidelidade Ltda.**, Brazil.
  - 100% int. in **Givex Hong Kong Limited**, Hong Kong, Hong Kong, People's Republic of China.
    - 100% int. in **Givex Cathay Limited**, People's Republic of China.
    - 100% int. in **ValuAccess Limited**, Hong Kong, People's Republic of China.
- 100% int. in **Givex Singapore Pte. Ltd.**, Singapore.
- 100% int. in **Givex UK Corporation Limited**, United Kingdom.
  - 100% int. in **Counter Solutions Holdings Limited**, Nottingham, Notts., United Kingdom.
- 100% int. in **Givex USA Corporation**, Del.
  - 100% int. in **Loyalty Lane, Inc.**, Marietta, Ga.
    - 100% int. in **Electronic Scrip Incorporated**, Calif.
    - 100% int. in **Media Solutions Company, LLC**, Ga.

Financial Statistics

Periods ended:	12m Dec. 31/22[A]		12m Dec. 31/21[oA]
	$000s	%Chg	$000s
Operating revenue........................	**72,905**	**+32**	**55,206**
Cost of sales..................................	22,975		17,078
Salaries & benefits..........................	26,404		20,921
General & admin expense...............	17,645		8,934
Stock-based compensation.............	10,498		3,594
Operating expense........................	**77,522**	**+53**	**50,527**
Operating income.........................	**(4,617)**	**n.a.**	**4,679**
Deprec., depl. & amort.....................	5,206		4,419
Finance costs, net...........................	717		557
Pre-tax income.............................	**(10,066)**	**n.a.**	**(3,169)**
Income taxes..................................	29		869
Net income...................................	**(10,095)**	**n.a.**	**(4,038)**
Cash & equivalent...........................	24,431		36,817
Inventories......................................	4,105		2,300
Accounts receivable........................	12,411		8,425
Current assets................................	51,044		52,366
Fixed assets, net.............................	2,529		2,007
Right-of-use assets.........................	4,492		5,567
Intangibles, net...............................	19,379		5,117
Total assets...................................	**82,053**	**+16**	**70,717**
Accts. pay. & accr. liabs..................	13,696		6,685
Current liabilities............................	26,004		18,568
Long-term debt, gross.....................	7,641		5,088
Long-term debt, net.........................	4,531		762
Long-term lease liabilities................	2,594		3,962
Shareholders' equity........................	47,048		46,980
Cash from oper. activs..................	**5,528**	**-32**	**8,145**
Cash from fin. activs........................	(1,842)		16,440
Cash from invest. activs..................	(15,975)		(3,174)
Net cash position..........................	**24,431**	**-34**	**36,817**
Capital expenditures........................	(1,451)		(822)
	$		$
Earnings per share*........................	(0.09)		(0.04)
Cash flow per share*.......................	0.05		0.09
	shs		shs
No. of shs. o/s*...............................	124,555,094		115,108,304
Avg. no. of shs. o/s*........................	118,604,429		92,287,884
	%		%
Net profit margin.............................	(13.85)		(7.31)
Return on equity..............................	(21.47)		(11.23)
Return on assets.............................	(13.24)		(6.86)
Foreign sales percent......................	56		55

* Common
[o] Restated
[A] Reported in accordance with IFRS

Latest Results

Periods ended:	3m Mar. 31/23[A]		3m Mar. 31/22[A]
	$000s	%Chg	$000s
Operating revenue..........................	19,158	+17	16,332
Net income......................................	(1,234)	n.a.	(2,581)
	$		$
Earnings per share*........................	(0.01)		(0.02)

* Common
[A] Reported in accordance with IFRS

Historical Summary
(as originally stated)

Fiscal Year	Oper. Rev.	Net Inc. Bef. Disc.	EPS*
	$000s	$000s	$
2022[A]...................	72,905	(10,095)	(0.09)
2021[A1].................	55,167	(4,038)	(0.04)
2020[A]...................	51,525	2,521	0.56
2019[A]...................	49,332	(698)	(0.15)
2018[A]...................	41,464	4,145	0.92

* Common
[A] Reported in accordance with IFRS
[1] Results prior to Nov. 25, 2021, pertain to and reflect the Qualifying Transaction reverse takeover acquisition of Givex Corporation.

Note: Adjusted throughout for 1-for-9.1871 cons. in Dec. 2021

G.40 Glacier Media Inc.

Symbol - GVC **Exchange** - TSX **CUSIP** - 376394
Head Office - 2188 Yukon St, Vancouver, BC, V5Y 3P1 **Telephone** - (604) 872-8565 **Fax** - (604) 638-2453
Website - www.glaciermedia.ca
Email - osmysnuik@glaciermedia.ca
Investor Relations - Orest E. Smysnuik (604) 708-3264
Auditors - PricewaterhouseCoopers LLP C.A., Vancouver, B.C.
Transfer Agents - Computershare Trust Company of Canada Inc., Toronto, Ont.
FP500 Revenue Ranking - 685
Employees - 1,540 at Dec. 31, 2022

Profile - (Can. 2000 amalg.) Operates as an information and marketing solutions company which provides data, analytics and intelligence products and content and marketing solutions.

Has three business segments: Environmental and Property Information (EPI); Commodity Information; and Community Media.

EPI provides environmental data, property information and related products and offerings under its core brands including Environmental Risk Information Services (ERIS), which provides environmental risk data and related products for commercial and industrial real estate properties across North America to environmental consultants, commercial real estate (CRE) brokers, financial institutions and insurance companies to enable them to assess environmental risks around CRE transactions; STP ComplianceEHS, which produces digital audit guides and compliance tools for use in environmental health and safety audits across forty countries worldwide; and REW.ca, which is a residential real estate listings and property information marketplace in British Columbia.

Commodity Information serves mining industries, associated suppliers and the financial industry with a wide variety of intelligence offerings and consists of Glacier Farm Media Group and The Northern Miner Group. Glacier FarmMedia Group brands include the Western Producer; Alberta Farmer Express; Manitoba Co-Operator; Country Guide; Farmtario; Canada's Outdoor Farm Show; Ag In Motion; AgDealer; Global Auction Guide; MarketsFarm; and Weather Innovations. Resource Innovation Group brands include the Northern Miner; the Canadian Mining Journal; CostMine; edumine; Mining.com; and Global Mining Symposium.

Community Media provides a variety of news products and marketing services, including local news, general community information, classified websites, digital marketing services and newsprint operations and consists of print-based and digital operations. Digital brands include Castanet Media, a digital only media business which is a source of news and information in the Okanagan region (Kelowna, Kamloops, Penticton and Vernon, B.C.). Other core digital brands include Vancouver Is Awesome, a partial interest in Village Media and Eastward Media (targeting the Asian market). Also operates the Local News Collective, a provider of local news and information in British Columbia. The Community Media Newspaper Group reaches more than 2,000,000 readers in print in over 60 local markets in western Canada. The brands include the Victoria Times-Colonist, North ShoreNews, Tri-Cities News, Burnaby Now, Richmond News, Prince George Citizen, St. Albert Gazette, Estevan Mercury and Yorkton This Week.

Predecessor Detail - Name changed from Glacier Ventures International Corp., July 15, 2008.

Directors - Samuel (Sam) Grippo, chr., B.C.; Mark Melville, pres. & CEO, Vancouver, B.C.; Bruce W. Aunger, corp. sec., Maple Ridge, B.C.; Hugh McKinnon, Surrey, B.C.; Geoffrey L. Scott, Vancouver, B.C.

Other Exec. Officers - Orest E. Smysnuik, CFO; Craig Roberts, exec. v-p, bus. info.; Gail Ankiewicz, pres., specialty technical publishers; Simon Bray, pres., REW.ca; Alvin Brouwer, pres., Lower Mainland Publishing LP & pres., Glacier Community Media Digital; Peter Kvarnstrom, pres., community media; Carol Le Noury, pres., envirl. risk info. srvcs.; Bob Willcox, pres., Glacier FarmMedia

Capital Stock

	Authorized (shs.)	Outstanding (shs.)[1]
Special Preferred	20,000	nil
Preferred	unlimited	nil
Common	unlimited	131,131,598

[1] At May 25, 2023

Major Shareholder - Madison Venture Corporation held 53.85% interest at May 25, 2023.

Price Range - GVC/TSX

Year	Volume	High	Low	Close
2022............	8,002,753	$0.45	$0.29	$0.33
2021............	19,013,457	$0.59	$0.28	$0.39
2020............	18,865,625	$0.60	$0.18	$0.26
2019............	14,755,958	$0.77	$0.48	$0.56
2018............	3,986,055	$0.90	$0.55	$0.60

Recent Close: $0.16

Capital Stock Changes - During 2022, 1,126,130 common shares were repurchased under a Normal Course Issuer Bid.

Wholly Owned Subsidiaries

GVIC Communications Corp., Vancouver, B.C.
- 86% int. in **Aberdeen Publishing Limited Partnership**, B.C.
- 59% int. in **Alta Newspaper Group Limited Partnership**, B.C.
- 100% int. in **BIV Media Limited Partnership**, B.C.
- 100% int. in **Castanet Holdings Limited Partnership**, B.C.
- 28% int. in **Continental Newspapers Ltd.**, B.C.
- 55% int. in **ERI Environmental Risk LP**, Canada.
  - 100% int. in **ERIS Information Inc.**, Wash.
  - 100% int. in **ERIS Information Limited Partnership**, Canada.
  - 55% int. in **STP Publications Limited Partnership**, B.C.
- 50% int. in **Estevan Press Limited Partnership**, Sask.
- 100% int. in **GMD Digital Limited Partnership**, B.C.
- 97% int. in **Glacier Farm Media Limited Partnership**, B.C.
- 100% int. in **Glacier Publications Limited Partnership**, Toronto, Ont.
- 100% int. in **Glacier RIG Ltd.**, B.C.
- 50% int. in **Great West Newspapers Limited Partnership**, Alta.
- 100% int. in **Infomine USA Inc.**, Wash.
- 100% int. in **KCN Capital News Company Ltd.**, B.C.
- 50% int. in **Kodiak Press Limited Partnership**, B.C.
- 100% int. in **LMP Publication (BCNW) Limited Partnership**, B.C.
- 100% int. in **LMP Publication Limited Partnership**, B.C.
- 100% int. in **Moosejaw Express Limited Partnership**, B.C.
- 100% int. in **Northern Publishing Ltd.**, B.C.

- 35% int. in **1294739 Alberta Ltd.**, Alta.
- 100% int. in **Peak Publishing Limited Partnership**, B.C.
- 100% int. in **Prairie Newspaper Group Limited Partnership**
- 100% int. in **Prince George Citizen Limited Partnership**, B.C.
- 100% int. in **REW Digital Ltd.**, B.C.
- 50% int. in **REW Money Ltd.**, B.C.
- 48% int. in **Rhode Island Suburban Newspapers Inc.**, R.I.
- 100% int. in **Sunshine Coast Reporter Partnership**, B.C.
- 59% int. in **Swift Current Holdings Limited Partnership**, B.C.
- 23% int. in **Village Media Inc.**, B.C.
- 87% int. in **Weather Innovations Consulting Limited Partnership**, B.C.
- 97% int. in **Western Producer Publications Partnership**
- 100% int. in **Whistler Publishing Limited Partnership**, B.C.

Financial Statistics

Periods ended:	12m Dec. 31/22[A]		12m Dec. 31/21[A]
	$000s	%Chg	$000s
Operating revenue	**176,012**	**+7**	**164,562**
Cost of sales	128,680		109,497
General & admin expense	44,249		37,318
Operating expense	**172,929**	**+18**	**146,815**
Operating income	**3,083**	**-83**	**17,747**
Deprec., depl. & amort.	12,455		12,626
Finance income	590		58
Finance costs, gross	2,303		1,175
Investment income	11,829		5,467
Write-downs/write-offs	(15,525)		nil
Pre-tax income	**(35,096)**	**n.a.**	**(2,912)**
Income taxes	(6,167)		(3,758)
Net inc bef disc ops, eqhldrs	(29,553)		(4,880)
Net inc bef disc ops, NCI	624		5,726
Net income	**(28,929)**	**n.a.**	**846**
Net inc. for equity hldrs	**(29,553)**	**n.a.**	**(4,880)**
Net inc. for non-cont. int	**624**	**-89**	**5,726**
Cash & equivalent	19,636		21,744
Inventories	3,054		2,672
Accounts receivable	34,332		35,686
Current assets	59,692		62,606
Long-term investments	26,324		44,604
Fixed assets, net	30,083		31,802
Right-of-use assets	9,264		10,244
Intangibles, net	64,626		77,152
Total assets	**237,557**	**-12**	**271,120**
Accts. pay. & accr. liabs	29,515		29,624
Current liabilities	47,756		46,999
Long-term debt, gross	7,621		8,062
Long-term debt, net	7,165		7,611
Long-term lease liabilities	6,984		7,819
Shareholders' equity	150,933		178,547
Non-controlling interest	16,108		17,913
Cash from oper. activs	**7,946**	**-44**	**14,113**
Cash from fin. activs	(7,284)		(6,302)
Cash from invest. activs	(2,770)		(342)
Net cash position	**19,636**	**-10**	**21,744**
Capital expenditures	(1,612)		(5,490)
Capital disposals	nil		4,297
Unfunded pension liability	8,391		11,140
	$		$
Earnings per share*	(0.22)		(0.04)
Cash flow per share*	0.06		0.11
	shs		shs
No. of shs. o/s*	131,629,429		132,755,559
Avg. no. of shs. o/s*	132,558,408		130,895,835
	%		%
Net profit margin	(16.44)		0.51
Return on equity	(17.94)		(2.79)
Return on assets	(10.63)		0.19
Foreign sales percent	20		18
No. of employees (FTEs)	1,540		n.a.

* Common
[A] Reported in accordance with IFRS

Latest Results

Periods ended:	3m Mar. 31/23[A]		3m Mar. 31/22[A]
	$000s	%Chg	$000s
Operating revenue	39,218	-7	42,232
Net income	(8,854)	n.a.	211
Net inc. for equity hldrs	(5,217)	n.a.	(666)
Net inc. for non-cont. int	(3,637)		877
	$		$
Earnings per share*	(0.04)		(0.01)

* Common
[A] Reported in accordance with IFRS

Historical Summary
(as originally stated)

Fiscal Year	Oper. Rev. $000s	Net Inc. Bef. Disc. $000s	EPS* $
2022[A]	176,012	(28,929)	(0.22)
2021[A]	164,562	846	(0.04)
2020[A]	151,304	(14,741)	(0.12)
2019[A]	184,790	37,320	0.29
2018[A]	188,372	1,753	0.01

* Common
[A] Reported in accordance with IFRS

G.41 Glass House Brands Inc.

Symbol - GLAS.A.U **Exchange** - NEO **CUSIP** - 377130
Head Office - 3645 Long Beach Blvd, Long Beach, CA, United States, 90807 **Telephone** - (415) 233-2785
Website - www.glasshousebrands.com
Email - mvendetti@glasshousegroup.com
Investor Relations - Mark Vendetti (562) 264-5078
Auditors - Macias Gini & O'Connell LLP C.P.A., Los Angeles, Calif.
Transfer Agents - Odyssey Trust Company, Calgary, Alta.
FP500 Revenue Ranking - 744
Employees - 449 at Dec. 31, 2022
Profile - (B.C. 2019) Cultivates, manufactures, retails and wholesales cannabis products in California for both adult and medicinal use.

Cultivation operations consist of three indoor greenhouse facilities: the 5,500,000-sq.-ft. SoCal facility in Camarillo, of which 1,500,000 sq. ft. is operational; and the 150,000-sq.-ft. Casitas facility and the 350,000-sq.-ft. Padaro facility, both in Carpinteria. Extraction and manufacturing operations are conducted at a 20,000-sq.-ft. facility in Lompoc and a 12,000-sq.-ft. facility in Adelanto. The facilities produce flower, oil, concentrates, tinctures, vaporizers and edibles under the brands Glass House Farms, PLUS Products, Allswell, Forbidden Flowers and Mama Sue Wellness.

Owns and operates ten retail dispensaries under the banners Farmacy, The Pottery and Natural Healing Center.

In April 2023, the company, through wholly owned through **GHG-NHC Turlock Inc.**, acquired **NHC Turlock, LLC**, a California-based retail dispensary, on opening of the store. The consideration would be paid 80% in shares priced at the 25-day volume-weighted price (VWAP) of equity shares as at the end of its six full quarter of operations and 20% in the form of an 8% unsecured, subordinated promissory note due April 2027.

From August to December 2022, wholly owned **GH Group, Inc.** completed a private placement of 49,969 series B preferred shares at US$1,000 per share, including the exchange of all its outstanding series A preferred shares for series B preferred shares. In January 2023, GH Group completed a private placement of 4,700 series C preferred shares at US$1,000 per share. The series B and series C preferred shares would be entitled to an annual dividend at a rate of 20% for the first two years after initial issuance, 22.5% for the third year and, thereafter, 25% until the 54-month anniversary of the initial issuance, payable quarterly with an annual amount equal to 10% paid in cash and the balance paid in kind. If series B and series C preferred shares remain outstanding after the 54-month anniversary of the initial issuance, the annual dividend thereafter would be payable solely in cash at a rate of 20%.

In September 2022, the company acquired three retail dispensaries operating under the Natural Healing Center name in Grover Beach, Lemoore and Morro Bay, Calif., for total consideration of US$34,000,000, including issuance of 5,606,112 subordinate, restricted and limited voting shares at US$4.41 per share.

In July 2022, the company acquired the remaining 50% interest in The Pottery, a retail dispensary in Los Angeles, Calif., which includes an indoor cultivation facility, for issuance of 500,000 subordinate, restricted and limited voting shares at US$6.00 per share. The company elected not to acquire the remaining 50% interest in the underlying real property.

On June 30, 2022, the company sold wholly owned **2000 De La Vina LLC**, which owns the real property of the Farmacy dispensary in Santa Barbara, Calif., for US$3,060,000. The company remained as manager and retained control of 2000 De La Vina.

Recent Merger and Acquisition Activity

Status: completed **Revised:** Apr. 28, 2022
UPDATE: The transaction was completed for US$32,951,894, consisting of Cdn$20,504,851 convertible debenture notes, issuance of 2,311,213 subordinate, restricted and limited voting shares and 1,794,751 restricted share units. PREVIOUS: Glass House Brands Inc. agreed to acquire the business of Plus Products Inc. through the acquisition of Plus Products' wholly owned Plus Products Holdings Inc. for US$25,600,000, consisting of a combination of unsecured convertible debt and equity, plus additional performance-based consideration. Plus Products manufactures and distributes cannabis-infused edibles in California. Plus Products commenced proceedings under the Companies' Creditors Arrangement Act (CCAA) on Sept. 13, 2021, and had Cdn$20,504,851 of outstanding convertible debentures, including accrued interest. The convertible debt to be issued by Glass House would have a face value equal to the principal value and accrued interest of Plus Products debentures, and would be distributed to Plus Products debenture holders. The remaining consideration would be distributed to Plus Products securityholders, management and employees.

Predecessor Detail - Name changed from Mercer Park Brand Acquisition Corp., June 29, 2021, pursuant to the Qualifying Acquisition of GH Group, Inc. (dba Glass House Group, Inc.) and concurrent amalgamation of GH Group with wholly owned MPB Mergersub Corp.

Directors - Kyle Kazan, exec. chr. & CEO, Palos Verdes Estates, Calif.; Graham Farrar, pres., Santa Barbara, Calif.; Robert (Bob) Hoban, Denver, Colo.; Lameck Humble Lukanga, Los Angeles, Calif.; Robert (Jamie) Mendola, San Francisco, Calif.; George Raveling, Los Angeles, Calif.; Jocelyn Rosenwald, Costa Mesa, Calif.

Other Exec. Officers - Mark Vendetti, CFO; Hilal Tabsh, chief revenue officer; Jennifer Barry, v-p, retail; John Brebeck, v-p, IR; Jacqueline de Ginestet, v-p, sales; Will Tu, v-p & contr.; Ben Vasquez, v-p, farm opers.; Benjamin Vega, gen. counsel & corp. sec.

Capital Stock

	Authorized (shs.)	Outstanding (shs.)[1]
Preferred	unlimited	nil
Multiple Vtg.	unlimited	4,754,979
Subordinate Vtg.	unlimited	10,213,020
Restricted Vtg.	unlimited	5,458,040
Limited Vtg.	unlimited	44,894,054

[1] At July 3, 2023

Preferred - Non-voting.
Multiple Voting - 50 votes per share. Automatically redeemable on June 29, 2024, at US$0.001 per share.
Subordinate, Restricted and **Limited Voting** - One vote per share, except limited voting shares are not entitled to vote for the election of directors.
Major Shareholder - Kyle Kazan held 34.5% interest, Graham Farrar held 22.7% interest and Jamie Rosenwald held 14.8% interest at May 9, 2023.

Price Range - GLAS.A.U/NEO

Year	Volume	High	Low	Close
2022	1,401,900	US$6.52	US$1.90	US$1.96
2021	2,361,841	US$12.70	US$3.51	US$3.60
2020	72,000	US$10.08	US$9.05	US$10.08
2019	71,300	US$10.08	US$9.52	US$9.70

Recent Close: US$3.74

Capital Stock Changes - In April 2022, 2,311,213 subordinate, restricted and limited voting shares (collectively, equity shares) were issued pursuant to the acquisition of Plus Products Holdings Inc. In September 2022, 5,606,112 equity shares were issued pursuant to the acquisition of Natural Healing Center dispensaries. Also during 2022, equity shares were issued as follows: 5,936,636 on conversion of a like number of MPB Acquisition Corp. exchangeable shares, 2,162,265 under restricted share unit plan, 500,000 pursuant to the acquisition of The Pottery Inc., 347,108 for convertible debenture interest payment and 227,116 on exercise of options.

Wholly Owned Subsidiaries

MPB Acquisition Corp., Nev. 64.17% voting interest.
- 100% int. in **GH Group, Inc.**, Long Beach, Calif.
  - 100% int. in **Bud and Bloom**, Santa Ana, Calif.
  - 100% int. in **CA Manufacturing Solutions LLC**, Calif.
  - 100% int. in **East St. Gertrude 1327 LLC**, Calif.
  - 100% int. in **Farmacy SB, Inc.**, Calif.
  - 100% int. in **G&K Produce LLC**, Calif.
  - 100% int. in **GH Camarillo, LLC**, Calif.
  - 100% int. in **Glass House Camarillo Cultivation, LLC**, Calif.
  - 100% int. in **Glass House Farm LLC**, Calif.
  - 100% int. in **iCANN, LLC**, Calif.
  - 100% int. in **K&G Flowers LLC**, Calif.
  - 100% int. in **Lompoc TIC LLC**, Calif.
  - 100% int. in **Magu Farm LLC**, Calif.
  - 100% int. in **Mission Health Associates, Inc.**, Calif.
  - 100% int. in **NHC Lemoore, LLC**, Calif.
  - 100% int. in **NHC-MB LLC**, Calif.
  - 100% int. in **Natural Healing Center, LLC**, Calif.
  - 100% int. in **Plus Products Holdings Inc.**, Nev.
    - 100% int. in **Carberry LLC**, Calif.
- 100% int. in **The Pottery Inc.**, Calif.

Note: The preceding list includes only the major related companies in which interests are held.

Financial Statistics

Periods ended:	12m Dec. 31/22[A]		12m Dec. 31/21[□A1]
	US$000s	%Chg	US$000s
Operating revenue	**90,891**	**+31**	**69,447**
Cost of goods sold	69,353		53,427
General & admin expense	46,380		37,680
Stock-based compensation	12,756		8,710
Operating expense	**128,489**	**+29**	**99,817**
Operating income	**(37,598)**	**n.a.**	**(30,370)**
Deprec., depl. & amort.	12,301		4,767
Finance income	56		65
Finance costs, gross	7,608		2,737
Investment income	(2,007)		(1,089)
Write-downs/write-offs	nil		(818)
Pre-tax income	**(30,855)**	**n.a.**	**(41,067)**
Income taxes	4,742		3,298
Net income	**(35,597)**	**n.a.**	**(44,366)**
Net inc. for equity hldrs	**(35,535)**	**n.a.**	**(44,168)**
Net inc. for non-cont. int.	**(62)**	**n.a.**	**(198)**
Cash & equivalent	11,144		51,067
Inventories	12,058		6,596
Accounts receivable	5,653		2,894
Current assets	41,457		69,120
Long-term investments	4,246		7,196
Fixed assets, net	216,717		195,799
Right-of-use assets	10,848		3,078
Intangibles, net	70,460		10,549
Total assets	**348,668**	**+21**	**288,081**
Accts. pay. & accr. liabs	22,334		10,215
Current liabilities	54,247		56,747
Long-term debt, gross	62,659		44,855
Long-term debt, net	62,619		44,817
Long-term lease liabilities	9,859		2,865
Shareholders' equity	217,438		181,070
Non-controlling interest	(4,262)		(198)
Cash from oper. activs	**(40,805)**	**n.a.**	**(20,285)**
Cash from fin. activs	30,082		181,318
Cash from invest. activs	(29,201)		(111,501)
Net cash position	**14,144**	**-74**	**54,067**
Capital expenditures	(27,766)		(108,496)
	US$		US$
Earnings per share*	(0.87)		(1.14)
Cash flow per share*	(0.64)		(0.52)
	shs		shs
No. of shs. o/s*	60,408,834		43,318,384
Avg. no. of shs. o/s*	64,182,436		40,280,639
	%		%
Net profit margin	(39.16)		(63.88)
Return on equity	(17.83)		(42.60)
Return on assets	(8.42)		(23.16)
Foreign sales percent	100		100
No. of employees (FTEs)	449		458

* Subord. Vtg.
□ Restated
A Reported in accordance with U.S. GAAP
1 Results reflect the June 29, 2021, Qualifying Acquisition of GH Group, Inc. (dba Glass House Group, Inc.).

Latest Results

Periods ended:	6m June 30/23[A]		6m June 30/22[A]
	US$000s	%Chg	US$000s
Operating revenue	73,687	+142	30,446
Net income	(63,690)	n.a.	(34,018)
Net inc. for equity hldrs	(63,738)	n.a.	(33,971)
Net inc. for non-cont. int	47		(47)
	US$		US$
Earnings per share*	(0.97)		(0.59)

* Subord. Vtg.
A Reported in accordance with U.S. GAAP

Historical Summary
(as originally stated)

Fiscal Year	Oper. Rev. US$000s	Net Inc. Bef. Disc. US$000s	EPS* US$
2022[A]	90,891	(35,597)	(0.87)
2021[A]	69,447	(44,366)	(1.13)
2020[A1]	48,260	(16,659)	n.a.
2019[A1]	16,941	(10,735)	n.a.
2018[A1]	8,967	(1,311)	n.a.

* Subord. Vtg.
A Reported in accordance with U.S. GAAP
1 Results pertain to GH Group, Inc.

G.42 Global Compliance Applications Corp.

Symbol - APP **Exchange** - CSE **CUSIP** - 37960T
Head Office - 830-1100 Melville St, PO Box 43, Vancouver, BC, V6E 4A6 **Toll-free** - (800) 409-5679
Website - globalcompliance.app
Email - info@gcac.tech
Investor Relations - Bradley Moore (800) 409-5679
Auditors - Dale Matheson Carr-Hilton LaBonte LLP C.A., Vancouver, B.C.
Transfer Agents - Computershare Trust Company of Canada Inc.
Profile - (B.C. 2014) Designs and develops blockchain technologies and machine learning solutions for the medical cannabis industry.

The company's primary solution is the Efixii platform, an Ethereum layer 2 blockchain Ethereum Virtual Machine (EVM) programming functionality which addresses some of the shortcomings of current Ethereum-based smart contracts such as ecological impact, poor throughput and high transaction costs. The platform is designed to improve the capabilities of Ethereum smart contracts by boosting their speed and scalability while adding privacy and Know-Your-Customer (KYC) features, as well as allows developers to easily run unmodified EVM contracts and Ethereum transactions on a second layer while benefiting from Etehereum's layer 1 security. Other solutions include clearESG, which provides a tool to help companies pick their environmental, social and governance (ESG) commitment, record the proof, and share it with their customers, community and investors; Prescriptii patient care solution, which offers patients access to important information about medical cannabis products while also giving feedback through surveys about the experiences and effectiveness of the product; and TraceLocker, an Ethereum blockchain compliance platform for medical cannabis growers and importers which is also integrated to patient care component and its efficacy-driven algorithms, creating a complete efficacy-driven, seed-to-shop-to-seed, cannabis solution.

In November 2022, the company agreed to acquire a 33% interest in **Blue Anchor 420 SPV (Pty) Ltd.** (SPV) from **Blue Anchor Risk Solutions (Pty) Ltd.** for issuance of $200,000 in common shares. SPV is a cell captive insurance company focused on cannabis growing operations in Southern Africa.

In July 2022, the company acquired private Dayton, Ohio-based **WasteTrakr Technologies, Inc.** for issuance of 2,310,108 common shares. WasteTrakr provides recycling solutions for the waste being generated by the cannabis industry using a specialty waste software.

In June 2022, the company signed a letter of intent to form a joint venture with **COSMOL PPV Telecom** to open an online portal focused on providing Canadian veterans with Exfixii cultivated cannabis products. The company would transfer its medical cannabis licence and hold a 49% interest in the joint venture, with the remaining 51% interest to be held by COSMOL. The new entity would be incorporated and operated in New Brunswick.

Predecessor Detail - Name changed from Global Cannabis Applications Corp., July 14, 2022.

Directors - Bradley Moore, CEO, Vancouver, B.C.; Alexander B. (Alex) Helmel, interim CFO & corp. sec., Vancouver, B.C.; Jeffrey Hayzlett, Sioux Falls, S.D.

Other Exec. Officers - Alon Tzipory, COO; Hanan Gelbendorf, v-p, product devel.; Steve Peterson, pres., GCAC North America Inc.

Capital Stock

	Authorized (shs.)	Outstanding (shs.)[1]
Common	unlimited	246,277,499

1 At May 30, 2023

Major Shareholder - Widely held at July 29, 2021.

Price Range - APP/CSE

Year	Volume	High	Low	Close
2022	46,701,945	$0.08	$0.01	$0.02
2021	86,818,345	$0.41	$0.04	$0.05
2020	54,010,924	$0.15	$0.02	$0.13
2019	46,615,525	$0.15	$0.02	$0.04
2018	189,540,961	$0.99	$0.08	$0.10

Recent Close: $0.02

Capital Stock Changes - During fiscal 2022, common shares were issued as follows: 12,800,000 by private placement, 5,650,000 for debt settlement, 1,650,000 on conversion of debt and 1,007,059 on exercise of warrants.

Wholly Owned Subsidiaries

Antisocial Holdings Ltd., Vancouver, B.C. Inactive.
GCAC Europe UAB, Lithuania. Inactive.
GCAC North America Inc., United States.
Opinit LLC, Calif. Inactive.

Subsidiaries

61% int. in **Global Cannabis Apps Corporation (Australia) Pty Ltd.**, Australia. Inactive.

Investments

45.8% int. in **Citizen Green OU**, Estonia. Inactive.

Financial Statistics

Periods ended:	12m June 30/22[A]		12m June 30/21[□A]
	$000s	%Chg	$000s
Operating revenue	**7**	**+133**	**3**
Research & devel. expense	49		174
General & admin expense	1,841		2,013
Stock-based compensation	110		456
Operating expense	**2,000**	**-24**	**2,643**
Operating income	**(1,993)**	**n.a.**	**(2,640)**
Deprec., depl. & amort.	81		70
Finance costs, gross	32		33
Pre-tax income	**(2,099)**	**n.a.**	**322**
Net income	**(2,099)**	**n.a.**	**322**
Cash & equivalent	48		1,017
Current assets	322		1,092
Fixed assets, net	1		2
Intangibles, net	295		368
Total assets	**619**	**-58**	**1,462**
Bank indebtedness	475		443
Accts. pay. & accr. liabs	1,154		1,103
Current liabilities	1,644		1,556
Shareholders' equity	(1,025)		(105)
Cash from oper. activs	**(1,761)**	**n.a.**	**(1,926)**
Cash from fin. activs	799		2,978
Cash from invest. activs	(7)		(39)
Net cash position	**48**	**-95**	**1,017**
Capital expenditures	nil		(2)
	$		$
Earnings per share*	(0.01)		0.00
Cash flow per share*	(0.01)		(0.01)
	shs		shs
No. of shs. o/s*	200,252,483		179,145,424
Avg. no. of shs. o/s*	183,354,199		156,743,258
	%		%
Net profit margin	n.m.		n.m.
Return on equity	n.m.		n.m.
Return on assets	(198.65)		38.97

* Common
□ Restated
A Reported in accordance with IFRS

Latest Results

Periods ended:	3m Sept. 30/22[A]		3m Sept. 30/21[A]
	$000s	%Chg	$000s
Operating revenue	2	0	2
Net income	(466)	n.a.	(394)
	$		$
Earnings per share*	(0.00)		(0.00)

* Common
A Reported in accordance with IFRS

Historical Summary
(as originally stated)

Fiscal Year	Oper. Rev. $000s	Net Inc. Bef. Disc. $000s	EPS* $
2022[A]	7	(2,099)	(0.01)
2021[A]	3	322	0.00
2020[A]	nil	(1,665)	(0.02)
2019[A]	nil	(7,562)	(0.08)
2018[A]	nil	(5,473)	(0.09)

* Common
A Reported in accordance with IFRS

G.43 Global Crossing Airlines Group Inc.

Symbol - JET **Exchange** - NEO **CUSIP** - 37960G
Head Office - Building 5A, Miami International Airport, 4200 N.W. 36 St, Miami, FL, United States, 33166 **Telephone** - (786) 751-8550
Website - www.globalairlinesgroup.com
Email - ryan.goepel@globalairlinesgroup.com
Investor Relations - Ryan Goepel (786) 751-8503
Auditors - Rosenberg Rich Baker Berman & Company C.P.A., Somerset, N.J.
Transfer Agents - Computershare Trust Company of Canada Inc., Vancouver, B.C.
Employees - 400 at Dec. 31, 2022
Profile - (Del. 2020; orig. B.C., 1966) Operates as an ACMI (aircraft, crew, maintenance and insurance) and charter airline serving the U.S., Caribbean and Latin American markets.

Provides passenger and cargo aircraft charter services to customers including airlines, tour operators, college and professional sports teams, incentive groups, resorts and casino groups, cruise ship companies and government agencies; and ACMI services, which involve the provision of outsourced passenger aircraft operating services including aircraft, crew, maintenance and insurance. The company has three primary bases: Miami International Airport in Florida, the main base; Las Vegas Airport in Las Vegas, Nev., a flight attendant base; and San Antonio Airport at San Antonio, Tex., a base for maintenance, flight attendants and pilots. At March 2023, the company's fleet consisted of six Airbus A320s and 2.7 Airbus A321 aircraft. Also operates an A321 freighter aircraft under ACMI operations which services package operators, and freight and logistics companies.

Predecessor Detail - Name changed from Global Crossing Airlines Inc., Dec. 24, 2020.

Directors - Edward J. (Ed) Wegel, chr., pres. & CEO, Coral Gables, Fla.; T. Allen McArtor, v-chr., Va.; Ryan Goepel, exec. v-p & CFO, Fla.; Deborah Robinson†, Toronto, Ont.; Alan Bird, London, Middx., United Kingdom; Cordia Harrington, Tenn.; Prof. John Quelch, Fla.

Other Exec. Officers - Juan Nuñez, COO; George M. Hambrick, chief of staff; Mark Salvador, chief mktg. officer; Indyara Andion, v-p & gen. counsel; Varun Nandlal, v-p, cargo & security; Sheila Paine, corp. sec.

† Lead director

Capital Stock

	Authorized (shs.)	Outstanding (shs.)[1]	Par
Common	200,000,000	37,965,552	US$0.001
Cl.A Non-vtg. Common	5,537,313	5,537,313	US$0.001
Cl.B Non-vtg. Common	50,000,000	13,217,209	US$0.001

[1] At Apr. 30, 2023

Common - One vote per share.

Class A Non-voting - All held by Ascent Global Logistics, Inc. Rank equally with common and class B non-voting shares with respect to dividends and the distribution of assets in the case of liquidation, dissolution or winding-up of the company or other distribution of the company's assets. Convertible into common shares on a one-for-one basis, provided that the holder or any of its affiliates does not own in excess of 4.99% in the aggregate of the issued and outstanding shares after such conversion.

Class B Non-voting - Identical to common shares except are held by non-U.S. citizens. Non-U.S. citizens may own 49% of the company's total issued and outstanding shares. Convertible into common shares on a one-for-one basis.

Major Shareholder - Ascent Global Logistics, Inc. held 14.71% interest, Cordia Harrington held 11.72% interest and Edward J. (Ed) Wegel held 10.98% interest at Mar. 1, 2023.

Price Range - JET/NEO

Year	Volume	High	Low	Close
2022	1,607,456	$1.98	$0.68	$0.91
2021	10,723,235	$4.00	$0.86	$1.80
2020	9,777,032	$3.30	$0.40	$0.87
2019	6,907,681	$6.60	$0.35	$0.50
2018	16,321,837	$14.20	$3.55	$5.50

Consolidation: 1-for-10 cons. in June 2020

Recent Close: $1.17

Capital Stock Changes - During 2022, shares were issued as follows: 1,110,510 on exercise of warrants, 537,954 under the restricted share unit plan, 460,809 under the employee stock purchase plan and 83,333 on exercise of options.

Dividends

JET com N.S.R.
Listed Mar 16/22.
stk.[1] .... July 2/21
Paid in 2023: n.a. 2022: n.a. 2021: stk.

[1] Stk. divd. of 0.5 Canada Jetlines Operations Ltd com. shs. for ea. 1 sh. held.

Wholly Owned Subsidiaries

Capitol Airlines, LLC
Global X Air Tours, LLC
Global Crossing Airlines, Inc., Miami, Fla.

- 100% int. in **Global Crossing Airlines, LLC**, Fla.
- 100% int. in **GlobalX A320 Aircraft Acquisition Corp.**, Vancouver, B.C.
  - 100% int. in **GlobalX A321 Aircraft Acquisition Corp.**, Nev.
- 50% int. in **GlobalX Ground Team, LLC**, Fla.
- 80% int. in **GlobalX Travel Technologies, Inc.**, Del.

GlobalX Colombia S.A.S., Colombia.
LatinX Air S.A.S., Ecuador.

Investments

13% int. in **Canada Jetlines Operations Ltd.**, Mississauga, Ont. (see separate coverage)

Financial Statistics

Periods ended:	12m Dec. 31/22[A]		12m Dec. 31/21[□A]
	US$000s	%Chg	US$000s
Operating revenue	**97,110**	**+579**	**14,292**
Salaries & benefits	29,243		8,530
General & admin expense	54,072		18,491
Stock-based compensation	1,387		1,254
Other operating expense	23,035		3,143
Operating expense	**107,737**	**+243**	**31,418**
Operating income	**(10,627)**	**n.a.**	**(17,126)**
Deprec., depl. & amort.	609		34
Finance costs, gross	1,622		31
Pre-tax income	**(15,821)**	**n.a.**	**(19,996)**
Net inc. bef. disc. opers	**(15,821)**	**n.a.**	**(19,996)**
Income from disc. opers	nil		178
Net income	**(15,821)**	**n.a.**	**(19,819)**
Cash & equivalent	1,876		5,242
Accounts receivable	2,664		746
Current assets	11,724		9,671
Fixed assets, net	2,441		619
Right-of-use assets	27,953		22,668
Total assets	**51,164**	**+31**	**39,074**
Accts. pay. & accr. liabs	14,456		6,278
Current liabilities	27,866		14,702
Long-term debt, gross	6,892		1,573
Long-term debt, net	5,081		nil
Long-term lease liabilities	23,190		20,042
Shareholders' equity	(7,256)		4,246
Cash from oper. activs	**(6,848)**	**n.a.**	**(10,798)**
Cash from fin. activs	6,227		18,896
Cash from invest. activs	(1,912)		(653)
Net cash position	**5,461**	**-32**	**7,994**
Capital expenditures	(1,912)		(653)
	US$		US$
Earnings per share*	(0.30)		(0.43)
Cash flow per share*	(0.13)		(0.23)
	shs		shs
No. of shs. o/s*	53,440,482		51,237,876
Avg. no. of shs. o/s*	52,074,647		46,185,089
	%		%
Net profit margin	(16.29)		(139.91)
Return on equity	n.m.		n.m.
Return on assets	(31.47)		n.a.
No. of employees (FTEs)	400		200

* Comm., Cl.A & Cl.B
□ Restated
[A] Reported in accordance with U.S. GAAP

Latest Results

Periods ended:	3m Mar. 31/23[A]		3m Mar. 31/22[A]
	US$000s	%Chg	US$000s
Operating revenue	32,151	+96	16,380
Net income	(6,072)	n.a.	(4,780)
	US$		US$
Earnings per share*	(0.11)		(0.09)

* Comm., Cl.A & Cl.B
[A] Reported in accordance with U.S. GAAP

Historical Summary
(as originally stated)

Fiscal Year	Oper. Rev.	Net Inc. Bef. Disc.	EPS*
	US$000s	US$000s	US$
2022[A]	97,110	(15,821)	(0.30)
2021[A]	14,292	(19,996)	(0.43)
2020[A1]	nil	(2,044)	(0.11)
	$000s	$000s	$
2019[B2]	nil	(10,062)	(1.20)
2018[B]	nil	(5,686)	(0.80)

* Comm., Cl.A & Cl.B
[A] Reported in accordance with U.S. GAAP
[B] Reported in accordance with IFRS
[1] Results reflect the June 23, 2020, reverse takeover acquisition of Global Crossing Airlines, Inc.
[2] Results for 2019 and prior years pertain to Canada Jetlines Ltd.

Note: Adjusted throughout for 1-for-10 cons. in June 2020

G.44 Global Dividend Growth Split Corp.

Symbol - GDV **Exchange** - TSX **CUSIP** - 379444

Head Office - c/o Brompton Group Limited, Bay Wellington Tower, Brookfield Place, 2930-181 Bay St, PO Box 793, Toronto, ON, M5J 2T3 **Telephone** - (416) 642-9061 **Toll-free** - (866) 642-6001 **Fax** - (416) 642-6001

Website - www.bromptongroup.com

Email - wong@bromptongroup.com

Investor Relations - Ann P. Wong (416) 642-6000

Auditors - PricewaterhouseCoopers LLP C.A., Toronto, Ont.

Transfer Agents - TSX Trust Company, Toronto, Ont.

Managers - Brompton Funds Limited, Toronto, Ont.

Portfolio Managers - Brompton Funds Limited, Toronto, Ont.

Profile - (Ont. 2018) Invests in a diversified portfolio consisting of equity securities of at least 20 large capitalization global dividend growth companies.

To be included in the portfolio, an issuer must have a minimum market capitalization of US$10 billion and a history of dividend growth or, in the manager's view, a high potential for future dividend growth.

The company has a five-year term and will terminate on June 30, 2026, subject to extension for periods of up to five years, as determined by the board of directors.

The manager receives a management fee at an annual rate equal to 0.85% of the net asset value calculated and payable monthly in arrears.

Top 10 holdings at Mar. 31, 2023 (as a percentage of net asset value):

Holdings	Percentage
Microsoft Corporation	2.8%
Schneider Electric SE	2.7%
Apple Inc.	2.7%
BAE Systems plc	2.7%
L'Oreal S.A.	2.7%
Broadcom Inc.	2.7%
ASML Holding N.V.	2.7%
Motorola Solutions Inc.	2.6%
Abbvie Inc.	2.6%
Eli Lilly and Company	2.6%

Directors - Mark A. Caranci, pres. & CEO, Toronto, Ont.; Ann P. Wong, CFO & chief compliance officer, Toronto, Ont.; Christopher S. L. Hoffmann, Toronto, Ont.; Raymond R. Pether, Toronto, Ont.

Other Exec. Officers - Laura Lau, chief invest. officer; Kathryn A. H. Banner, sr. v-p & corp. sec.; Michael D. Clare, sr. v-p & sr. portfolio mgr.; Christopher Cullen, sr. v-p; Manith (Manny) Phanvongsa, sr. v-p; Michelle L. Tiraborelli, sr. v-p

Capital Stock

	Authorized (shs.)	Outstanding (shs.)[1]
Preferred	unlimited	15,312,001[2]
Class A	unlimited	15,312,001
Class J	unlimited	100[2]

[1] At Feb. 15, 2023
[2] Classified as debt.

Preferred - Entitled to fixed cumulative preferential quarterly distributions of $0.125 per share. Retractable in June of each year at a price per unit equal to the net asset value (NAV) per unit (one class A share and one preferred share), less any costs associated with the retraction. Retractable in any other month at a price per share equal to 96% of the lesser of: (i) the NAV per unit less the cost to the company to purchase a class A share for cancellation; and (ii) $10. All outstanding preferred shares will be redeemed on June 30, 2026, at a price per share equal to the lesser of: (i) $10 plus any accrued and unpaid distributions; and (ii) the NAV per preferred share. Rank in priority to class A shares and class J shares with respect to payment of distributions and repayment of capital on the dissolution, liquidation or winding-up of company. Non-voting.

Class A - Entitled to monthly non-cumulative cash distributions targeted to be 10¢ per share. No distributions will be paid if the distributions payable on the preferred shares are in arrears or in respect of a cash distribution, after payment of the distribution, the NAV per unit would be less than $15. Retractable in June of each year along with an equal number of preferred shares at a price per share equal to the NAV per unit, less any costs associated with the retraction, including commissions. Retractable in any other month at a price per share equal to 96% of the difference between: (i) the NAV per unit on the retraction date; and (ii) the cost to the company to purchase a preferred share for cancellation. All outstanding class A shares will be redeemed on June 30, 2026, at a price per share equal to the greater of: (i) the NAV per unit minus $10 and any accrued and unpaid distributions on a preferred share; and (ii) nil. Rank subsequent to preferred shares but in priority to class J shares with respect to payment of distributions and repayment of capital on the dissolution, liquidation or winding-up of company. Non-voting.

Class J - Not entitled to receive dividends. Redeemable and retractable at any time at $1.00 per share. Rank subsequent to preferred shares and class A shares with respect to distributions on dissolution, liquidation or winding-up of company. One vote per share.

Major Shareholder - Brompton Oil Split Trust held 100% interest at Mar. 23, 2023.

Price Range - GDV/TSX

Year	Volume	High	Low	Close
2022	11,114,504	$13.04	$9.23	$10.70
2021	8,011,555	$13.18	$10.25	$12.64
2020	1,764,884	$12.08	$4.71	$10.50
2019	1,910,596	$11.43	$7.97	$11.22
2018	1,084,316	$11.75	$7.11	$8.85

Recent Close: $9.26

Capital Stock Changes - In February 2023, public offering of 2,100,935 preferred shares and 2,100,935 class A shares was completed at $9.75 and $10.65 per share, respectively.

In January 2022, public offering of 1,274,700 preferred shares and 1,274,700 class A shares was completed at $10 and $12.40 per share, respectively. In March 2022, public offering of 1,588,875 preferred shares and 1,588,875 class A shares was completed at $10.05 and $11.85 per share, respectively. In April 2022, public offering of 1,434,700 preferred shares and 1,434,700 class A shares was completed at $10 and $11.65 per share, respectively.

Dividends

GDV cl A Ra $1.20 pa M est. July 16, 2018**
GDV.PR.A pfd cum. red. ret. Ra $0.50 pa Q
** Reinvestment Option

Financial Statistics

Periods ended:	12m Dec. 31/22[A]		12m Dec. 31/21[A]
	$000s	%Chg	$000s
Realized invest. gain (loss)	(27,759)		13,133
Unrealized invest. gain (loss)	(14,298)		14,518
Total revenue	**(35,255)**	**n.a.**	**30,378**
General & admin. expense	2,904		1,787
Operating expense	**2,904**	**+63**	**1,787**
Operating income	**(38,159)**	**n.a.**	**28,591**
Finance costs, gross	7,615		5,221
Pre-tax income	**(46,477)**	**n.a.**	**23,135**
Net income	**(46,477)**	**n.a.**	**23,135**
Cash & equivalent	1,518		879
Accounts receivable	626		368
Investments	233,106		203,801
Total assets	**236,749**	**+15**	**205,155**
Accts. pay. & accr. liabs	107		163
Debt	132,110		89,127
Shareholders' equity	100,919		113,356
Cash from oper. activs	**(76,645)**	**n.a.**	**(96,008)**
Cash from fin. activs	77,237		95,863
Net cash position	**1,518**	**+73**	**879**
	$		$
Earnings per share*	(3.79)		3.65
Cash flow per share*	(6.24)		(15.16)
Net asset value per share*	7.64		12.72
Cash divd. per share*	1.20		1.20
	shs		shs
No. of shs. o/s*	13,210,966		8,912,691
Avg. no. of shs. o/s*	12,273,712		6,331,670
	%		%
Net profit margin	n.m.		76.16
Return on equity	(43.38)		29.73
Return on assets	(17.59)		19.52

* Class A
† Unaudited
[A] Reported in accordance with IFRS

Historical Summary
(as originally stated)

Fiscal Year	Total Rev.	Net Inc. Bef. Disc.	EPS*
	$000s	$000s	$
2022[†A]	(35,255)	(46,477)	(3.79)
2021[A]	30,378	23,135	3.65
2020[A]	1,955	(1,281)	(0.36)
2019[A]	16,727	13,689	3.86
2018[A1]	(4,320)	(6,753)	(1.90)

* Class A
† Unaudited
[A] Reported in accordance with IFRS
[1] 6 months ended Dec. 31, 2018.

G.45 Global Education Communities Corp.

Symbol - GEC **Exchange** - TSX **CUSIP** - 37961F
Head Office - 1200-777 Broadway W, Vancouver, BC, V5Z 4J7 **Telephone** - (604) 871-9909 **Fax** - (604) 871-9919
Website - gechq.com
Email - toby@gechq.com
Investor Relations - Toby Y. C. Chu (888) 865-0901
Auditors - KPMG LLP C.A., Vancouver, B.C.
Bankers - Bank of Montreal
Lawyers - Owen Bird Law Corporation, Vancouver, B.C.
Transfer Agents - Computershare Trust Company of Canada Inc., Vancouver, B.C.
Employees - 353 at Aug. 31, 2022
Profile - (B.C. 1986) Owns and operates business, technical and language colleges in Canada and Asia, operates student recruitment centres in Asia and develops and manages student-centric rental apartments in the Metro Vancouver area of British Columbia.

Education

Sprott Shaw College offers diplomas and certificates in health care, tourism, hospitality, business, administrative, technical trades, and international studies through 16 campus locations in British Columbia. Sprott Shaw Language College and Vancouver International College provide English as a Second Language (ESL) programs to international students through campuses in Vancouver and Victoria, B.C., and Toronto, Ont.

Wholly owned **Global Education Alliance Inc.** and **A Plus Student Services Inc.** are student referral businesses that recruit kindergarten, primary, secondary school and university students from overseas for the private school sector in North America.

Wholly owned **CIBT School of Business and Technology Corp.** provides associate degree programs in automotive technical training, English teacher preparation, English as a Second Language (ESL) and accounting in the People's Republic of China.

Real Estate

Wholly owned **Global Education City Holdings Inc.** (GECH) develops and manages academic assets such as student-centric rental apartments, corporate housing, hotel and education super-centres for domestic and international students as well as working professionals in the Metro Vancouver area of British Columbia. GEC-branded locations in the Vancouver, B.C., area include GEC Viva Tower, GEC Pearson, GEC Burnaby Heights, GEC Granville Hotel and Suites, and GEC Marine Gateway. Projects under development include GEC King Edward and GEC Global Education City (Richmond). Projects which received rezoning approvals, with development and building permit approval still pending, include GEC Education Mega Center Surrey and GEC Oakridge. Project in rezoning phase includes GEC Cybercity.

Through 51%-owned **IRIX Design Group Inc.**, provides graphic design and advertising services primarily to the real estate industry.

Predecessor Detail - Name changed from CIBT Education Group Inc., Apr. 17, 2023.

Directors - Toby Y. C. Chu, chr., pres. & CEO, Vancouver, B.C.; Morris Chen, B.C.; Dr. Tony H. David, Vancouver, B.C.; Derek Feng, Manhattan Beach, Calif.; May Hsu, Calif.; Troy Rice, Scottsdale, Ariz.; Shane Weir, Hong Kong, Hong Kong, People's Republic of China

Other Exec. Officers - Victor Tesan, COO & pres., education srvcs.; Hilbert Ng, CFO & pres., Global Education City Holdings Inc.; Dr. Dennis Huang, exec. v-p, chief acctg. officer & corp. sec.; Louise Xu, v-p, corp. fin.; Steve Sohn, pres., Sprott Shaw Language College & pres., Vancouver International College

Capital Stock

	Authorized (shs.)	Outstanding (shs.)[1]
Common	150,000,000	67,521,140

[1] At Apr. 14, 2023

Normal Course Issuer Bid - The company plans to make normal course purchases of up to 3,374,877 common shares representing 5% of the total outstanding. The bid commenced on Mar. 22, 2023, and expires on Mar. 21, 2024.

Major Shareholder - Shane Corporation S.A.R.L. held 13.9% interest at Jan. 3, 2023.

Price Range - GEC/TSX

Year	Volume	High	Low	Close
2022	2,801,911	$0.67	$0.42	$0.44
2021	6,674,048	$0.84	$0.56	$0.63
2020	7,470,894	$0.72	$0.40	$0.66
2019	8,762,076	$0.76	$0.48	$0.68
2018	11,345,040	$0.87	$0.58	$0.65

Recent Close: $0.35

Capital Stock Changes - During fiscal 2022, 1,517,500 common shares were repurchased under a Normal Course Issuer Bid.

Wholly Owned Subsidiaries

A Plus Student Services Inc., B.C.
CIBT School of Business and Technology Corp., Vancouver, B.C.
- 100% int. in **Beijing Fenghua Education Consulting Co. Ltd.**, Beijing, Beijing, People's Republic of China.
- 60% int. in **CIBT Beihai International College**, People's Republic of China.
- 100% int. in **CIBT Weifang Huajia Education Managment Inc.**, People's Republic of China.

GEC Management Limited Partnership, B.C.
GEC Master GP Inc., B.C.
GEC Master 1 Limited Partnership, B.C.
- 21% int. in **GEC King Edward II Limited Partnership**, B.C.
- 39% int. in **GEC Pearson Limited Partnership**, B.C.
  - 100% int. in **0873438 Ltd.**, B.C.

GEC Master 2 Limited Partnership, B.C.
- 25% int. in **GEC Burnaby Heights Limited Partnership**, B.C.
  - 100% int. in **1089330 B.C Ltd.**, B.C.
- 21% int. in **GEC Education Mega Center Limited Partnership**, B.C.
  - 100% int. in **GEC Education Mega Center Inc.**, B.C.
- 36% int. in **GEC Education Super Center Limited Partnership**, B.C.
  - 100% int. in **1089260 B.C. Ltd.**, B.C.
- 47% int. in **GEC Granville Limited Partnership**, B.C.
  - 100% int. in **1033190 B.C. Ltd.**, B.C.
- 100% int. in **GEC Marine Gateway Limited Partnership**, B.C.
  - 100% int. in **Dorchester Properties (North) Ltd.**, B.C.
  - 100% int. in **Dorchester Properties (South) Ltd.**, B.C.
- 28% int. in **Global Education City (Richmond) Limited Partnership**, B.C.
- 20% int. in **Global Oakridge Acquisition Limited Partnership**, B.C.
  - 100% int. in **GEC Oakridge Holdings Inc.**

Global Education Alliance Inc., B.C.
Global Education City Holdings Inc., B.C.
- 100% int. in **CIBT Group Holdings Inc.**, B.C.
  - 100% int. in **GEC Burnaby Heights GP Inc.**, B.C.
  - 100% int. in **GEC EMC GP Inc.**, B.C.
  - 100% int. in **GEC ESC GP Inc.**, B.C.
  - 100% int. in **GEC Granville GP Inc.**, B.C.
  - 100% int. in **GEC King Edward II GP Inc.**, B.C.
    - 100% int. in **1022003 B.C. Ltd.**, B.C.
  - 100% int. in **GEC Marine-Gateway GP Inc.**, B.C.
  - 100% int. in **GEC Oakridge Acquisition GP Inc.**, B.C.
  - 100% int. in **GEC Pearson GP Inc.**, B.C.
  - 100% int. in **GEC (Richmond) GP Inc.**, B.C.
  - 100% int. in **GEC Viva GP Inc.**, B.C.

Sprott-Shaw College Corp., B.C.
- 100% int. in **SSC School of Advanced Education Corp.**, B.C.
- 100% int. in **Sprott Shaw Language College Inc.**, B.C.
  - 100% int. in **Sprott Shaw Language College (BC) Corp.**, B.C.
  - 100% int. in **2566422 Ontario Inc.**, Ont.
    - 100% int. in **Sprott Shaw Language College (Ontario) Corp.**, Ont.
- 80% int. in **Vancouver International College (2016) Limited Partnership**

Subsidiaries

51% int. in **IRIX Design Group Inc.**, B.C.

Investments

20% int. in **Vancouver International College (2016) Limited Partnership**

Financial Statistics

Periods ended:	12m Aug. 31/22[A]		12m Aug. 31/21[A]
	$000s	%Chg	$000s
Operating revenue	**73,235**	**+20**	**60,869**
Cost of sales	28,311		23,954
Salaries & benefits	13,855		12,960
General & admin expense	15,840		15,395
Stock-based compensation	150		108
Operating expense	**58,156**	**+11**	**52,417**
Operating income	**15,079**	**+78**	**8,452**
Deprec., depl. & amort.	6,865		6,799
Finance income	1,615		5,177
Finance costs, gross	12,092		12,892
Write-downs/write-offs	(40,000)[1]		(410)
Pre-tax income	**(56,964)**	**n.a.**	**5,708**
Income taxes	(1,194)		531
Net income	**(55,770)**	**n.a.**	**5,177**
Net inc. for equity hldrs	**(15,336)**	**n.a.**	**4,703**
Net inc. for non-cont. int	**(40,434)**	**n.a.**	**474**
Cash & equivalent	9,724		18,338
Inventories	840		852
Accounts receivable	13,857		21,173
Current assets	33,793		69,942
Long-term investments	356,335		322,606
Fixed assets, net	57,931		58,390
Right-of-use assets	12,028		11,920
Intangibles, net	13,047		12,716
Total assets	**477,733**	**-8**	**519,039**
Accts. pay. & accr. liabs	18,233		18,866
Current liabilities	226,233		204,831
Long-term debt, gross	250,561		244,250
Long-term debt, net	67,759		87,356
Long-term lease liabilities	10,813		12,283
Shareholders' equity	27,874		50,797
Non-controlling interest	134,158		152,786
Cash from oper. activs	**6,748**	**-61**	**17,106**
Cash from fin. activs	12,397		46,945
Cash from invest. activs	(27,738)		(68,716)
Net cash position	**9,724**	**-47**	**18,338**
Capital expenditures	(597)		(1,608)
	$		$
Earnings per share*	(0.22)		0.07
Cash flow per share*	0.10		0.24
	shs		shs
No. of shs. o/s*	68,460,740		69,978,240
Avg. no. of shs. o/s*	68,688,415		71,288,932
	%		%
Net profit margin	(76.15)		8.51
Return on equity	(38.99)		9.22
Return on assets	(8.81)		3.47
Foreign sales percent	5		5
No. of employees (FTEs)	353		341

* Common
[A] Reported in accordance with IFRS
[1] Pertains to impairment of the $40,000,000 deposit paid for the construction of buildings under a discontinued project of affiliate Global Education City (Richmond) Limited Partnership.

Latest Results

Periods ended:	6m Feb. 28/23[A]		6m Feb. 28/22[A]
	$000s	%Chg	$000s
Operating revenue	35,459	+5	33,792
Net income	(2,171)	n.a.	72
Net inc. for equity hldrs	(2,796)	n.a.	(47)
Net inc. for non-cont. int	625		119
	$		$
Earnings per share*	(0.04)		(0.00)

* Common
[A] Reported in accordance with IFRS

Historical Summary
(as originally stated)

Fiscal Year	Oper. Rev.	Net Inc. Bef. Disc.	EPS*
	$000s	$000s	$
2022A	73,235	(55,770)	(0.22)
2021A	60,869	5,177	0.07
2020A	62,548	(4,751)	0.02
2019A	70,997	14,932	0.03
2018A	74,900	45,371	0.25

* Common
A Reported in accordance with IFRS

G.46 Global Food and Ingredients Ltd.

Symbol - PEAS **Exchange** - TSX-VEN **CUSIP** - 37960F
Head Office - 400-43 Colborne St, Toronto, ON, M5E 1E3 **Telephone** - (416) 840-6801 **Toll-free** - (855) 434-3468
Website - www.gfiglobalfood.com
Email - bill.murray@gfiglobalfood.com
Investor Relations - William Murray (416) 840-6801
Auditors - KPMG LLP C.A., Vaughan, Ont.
Lawyers - Wildeboer Dellelce LLP, Toronto, Ont.
Transfer Agents - TSX Trust Company, Toronto, Ont.
Employees - 80 at May 30, 2022
Profile - (Ont. 2020) Processes and distributes plant-based food and ingredients with a focus on pulses and specialty crops including peas, lentils, beans, chickpeas, split peas, pea and lentil flours, and pea protein products.

Operations are organized into four primary business lines: plant-based core ingredients, value-added ingredients, plant-based pet food ingredients (for dog and cat food manufacturers) and downstream products.

Supplies are sourced from farms surrounding the company's four processing facilities in Saskatchewan (3) and Alberta (1). Products are distributed to food processors, grocery and restaurant chains, and institutional and foodservice customers, such as schools and hospitals, in the food and pet food markets worldwide. Trademarked brands include North Lily, North Lily Organic, Five Peas in Love (plant-based ready-to-eat side dishes and meals), Bentilia (plant-based pastas) and Pulsera (advanced plant-based protein ingredients). Brands and distribution network with sales office in Canada and the U.S., selling to over 37 countries have capabilities to package bulk ingredients into pouches and pillow bags to be sold under the North Lily brand or as private label products to the customers.

In July 2023, the company sold its Yofiit business, a premium plant-based milk and snack food operation, to **14901100 Canada Inc.** for total consideration of $2,978,000, consisting of $2,700,000 assumption of liabilities related to purchased assets and the remainder being set-off against the $278,000 share repurchase amount. YoFiit products include plant-based milk, snack bars and granola.

In June 2023, the company entered into a non-binding letter of intent to sell 49.9% interest of its newly created subsidiary **Pet Food Co.**, which operates pet food ingredients division, to **35 Oak Holdings Ltd.** for $3,200,000.

In March 2023, the company acquired the Bentilia business of **Export-Associates Inc.**, which sells a high protein, gluten-free pasta, for total consideration of $1,397,399, consisting of $741,469 cash, issuance of $375,000 common shares and issuance of $280,930 warrants.

Recent Merger and Acquisition Activity

Status: completed **Revised:** June 10, 2022
UPDATE: The transaction was completed. Pivotal issued a total of 62,938,505 post-consolidated common shares. (New) GFI's common shares commenced trading on the TSX Venture Exchange effective June 20, 2022. PREVIOUS: Pivotal Financial Corp. entered into a letter of intent for the Qualifying Transaction reverse takeover acquisition of private Toronto, Ont.-based Global Food and Ingredients Inc. (GFI), which processes and distributes plant-based food and ingredients, on the basis of 5 Pivotal post-consolidated common shares for each GFI share held (following a 1-for-5 share consolidation). The consideration would consist of the issuance of 56,000,000 Pivotal post-consolidated common shares at a deemed price of $1.25 per share. Nov. 5, 2021 - A definitive agreement was entered into. Upon completion, GFI would amalgamate with Pivotal's wholly owned 13476669 Canada Inc., and Pivotal would change its name to Global Food and Ingredients Ltd. May 18, 2022 - GFI completed a private placement of 2,845,200 subscription receipts at $1.25 per receipt. Each subscription receipt would automatically convert into 1 (new) GFI unit (1 common share & 1 warrant) upon completion of the transaction, with warrants exercisable at $1.75 per share for two years.

Predecessor Detail - Name changed from Pivotal Financial Corp., June 10, 2022, pursuant to the Qualifying Transaction reverse takeover acquisition of Global Food and Ingredients Inc. and concurrent amalgamation of (old) Global Food with wholly owned 13476669 Canada Inc.; basis 1 new for 5 old shs.

Directors - Robert T. Wolf, chr., Toronto, Ont.; David Hanna, pres. & CEO, Toronto, Ont.; Amber MacArthur, Toronto, Ont.; Erin L. Rooney, Dundas, Ont.; Frank van Biesen, Mississauga, Ont.; Michael (Mike) Wiener, Toronto, Ont.

Other Exec. Officers - William (Bill) Murray, CFO; Michael Moussa, v-p, ingredients; Jason Phillips, v-p, opers.; Jaime Rueda, v-p & pres., North Lily Foods Inc.; Jeffrey Gebert, corp. sec.

Capital Stock

	Authorized (shs.)	Outstanding (shs.)[1]
Common	unlimited	66,063,503

[1] At Mar. 31, 2023

Major Shareholder - David Hanna held 33.64% interest and 35 Oak Holdings Ltd. held 13.27% interest at Aug. 22, 2022.

Price Range - PEAS/TSX-VEN

Year	Volume	High	Low	Close
2022	2,018,114	$1.19	$0.34	$0.38
2021	57,892	$1.45	$0.75	$0.75

Consolidation: 1-for-5 cons. in June 2022
Recent Close: $0.28
Capital Stock Changes - On June 10, 2022, common shares were consolidated on a 1-for-5 basis (effective on the TSX Venture Exchange on June 20, 2022) and 62,938,505 post-consolidated common shares were issued pursuant to the Qualifying Transaction reverse takeover acquisition of Global Food and Ingredients Inc.

On Apr. 22, 2021, Pivotal Financial Corp. completed an initial public offering of 10,000,000 common shares at 20¢ per share.

Wholly Owned Subsidiaries

Global Food and Ingredients Inc., Toronto, Ont.
- 100% int. in **GFI Brands Inc.**
- 100% int. in **Global Food and Ingredients USA Inc.**, United States.
  - 100% int. in **North Lily Foods Inc.**, N.C.

Pet Food Co.

Financial Statistics

Periods ended:	12m Mar. 31/23A1		12m Mar. 31/22A
	$000s	%Chg	$000s
Operating revenue	**123,260**	**-1**	**124,420**
Cost of sales	116,442		120,443
Salaries & benefits	4,225		3,527
General & admin expense	2,332		1,259
Operating expense	**122,999**	**-2**	**125,229**
Operating income	**262**	**n.a.**	**(809)**
Deprec., depl. & amort.	2,098		1,004
Finance income	172		60
Finance costs, gross	2,719		2,525
Pre-tax income	**(10,494)**	**n.a.**	**(6,371)**
Income taxes	(1,865)		(114)
Net inc. bef. disc. opers	**(8,629)**	**n.a.**	**(6,256)**
Income from disc. opers	(1,776)		(34)
Net income	**(10,405)**	**n.a.**	**(6,291)**
Net inc. for equity hldrs	**(10,405)**	**n.a.**	**(4,364)**
Net inc. for non-cont. int	**nil**	**n.a.**	**(1,927)**
Cash & equivalent	483		1,793
Inventories	11,525		14,828
Accounts receivable	12,073		17,545
Current assets	27,548		35,784
Fixed assets, net	29,042		27,498
Right-of-use assets	1,122		1,035
Intangibles, net	1,102		4,587
Total assets	**59,512**	**-15**	**69,679**
Bank indebtedness	14,639		21,338
Accts. pay. & accr. liabs	9,926		9,991
Current liabilities	28,530		44,460
Long-term debt, gross	15,547		23,286
Long-term debt, net	14,912		15,078
Long-term lease liabilities	701		765
Shareholders' equity	14,299		6,144
Cash from oper. activs	**4,960**	**n.a.**	**(12,569)**
Cash from fin. activs	(5,413)		25,177
Cash from invest. activs	(808)		(12,278)
Net cash position	**483**	**-73**	**1,793**
Capital expenditures	(2,755)		(9,783)
	$		$
Earns. per sh. bef disc opers*	(0.14)		(2.35)
Earnings per share*	(0.17)		(2.35)
Cash flow per share*	0.08		(6.83)
	shs		shs
No. of shs. o/s*	66,063,503		n.a.
Avg. no. of shs. o/s*	63,328,073		1,839,320
	%		%
Net profit margin	(7.00)		(5.03)
Return on equity	(84.42)		(96.71)
Return on assets	(9.90)		(6.65)

* Common
A Reported in accordance with IFRS
[1] Results reflect the June 10, 2022, Qualifying Transaction reverse takeover acquisition of Global Food and Ingredients Inc.

Historical Summary
(as originally stated)

Fiscal Year	Oper. Rev.	Net Inc. Bef. Disc.	EPS*
	$000s	$000s	$
2023A	123,260	(8,629)	(0.14)
2022A	124,420	(6,256)	(2.35)
2021A	61,567	1,156	0.31
2020A	14,566	4,030	0.82

* Common
A Reported in accordance with IFRS
Note: Adjusted throughout for 1-for-5 cons. in June 2022

G.47 Global Health Clinics Ltd.

Symbol - MJRX **Exchange** - CSE **CUSIP** - 37958W
Head Office - 400-837 Hastings St W, Vancouver, BC, V6C 3N6 **Telephone** - (604) 283-1722 **Toll-free** - (855) 537-6272 **Fax** - (888) 241-5996
Email - dhaliwal.jat@gmail.com
Investor Relations - Jatinder Dhaliwal (855) 537-6272
Auditors - Dale Matheson Carr-Hilton LaBonte LLP C.A., Vancouver, B.C.
Transfer Agents - Computershare Trust Company of Canada Inc., Vancouver, B.C.
Profile - (B.C. 2013) Operates a virtual clinic for legal use of medicinal cannabis. Also researches and develops psilocybin products.

Wholly owned **Medicinal Cannabis Resource Centre Inc.** (MCRCI) operates a virtual clinic in British Columbia which guides patients through the process of becoming legal users of medical marijuana. Services provided include assisting patients in gathering their necessary medical files, arranging appointments with doctors affiliated with MCRCI, choosing a licensed producer of medicinal cannabis, and providing guidance in the use of medicinal cannabis.

Wholly owned **2756407 Ontario Ltd.** (dba Wonder Scientific) researches and develops psilocybin products for psychedelics research and novel drug development sectors. Wonder focuses on developing products to supply clinical trials, regulated markets and resellers, as well as creating custom active pharmaceutical formulations (API) and contract manufacturer quality agreements.

The company paused all operations related to psilocybin and research into psychedelics and novel drug development due to operational and staffing difficulties but would continue to pursue opportunities as they arise.

Predecessor Detail - Name changed from Leo Resources Inc., Aug. 20, 2018, following change of business acquisition of Green Life Clinics Ltd.

Directors - Jatinder (Jay) Dhaliwal, CEO, Vancouver, B.C.; Usama (Sam) Chaudhry, CFO, Vancouver, B.C.; Amin Lahijani, Vancouver, B.C.; Judy Su, Vancouver, B.C.

Capital Stock

	Authorized (shs.)	Outstanding (shs.)[1]
Series A Preferred	unlimited	100
Common	unlimited	9,392,113

[1] At May 1, 2023

Series A Preferred - Non-retractable. Non-redeemable without dividend. Non-voting.
Common - One vote per share.
Major Shareholder - Widely held at May 1, 2023.

Price Range - MJRX/CSE

Year	Volume	High	Low	Close
2022	993,364	$1.40	$0.08	$0.09
2021	1,306,243	$7.00	$0.70	$1.10
2020	205,587	$6.60	$1.00	$4.60
2019	30,904	$34.00	$1.00	$2.00
2018	107,744	$112.00	$15.00	$29.00

Consolidation: 1-for-20 cons. in July 2022; 1-for-10 cons. in May 2020
Recent Close: $0.08
Capital Stock Changes - In October 2021, private placement of 750,000 units (1 post-consolidated common share & 1 warrant) at $1.00 per unit was completed. On July 11, 2022, common shares were consolidated on a 1-for-20 basis. In July 2022, private placement of 5,555,557 units (1 post-consolidated common share & 1 warrant) at 9¢ per unit was completed.

Wholly Owned Subsidiaries

Anytime Health Corp., B.C.
Medicinal Cannabis Resource Centre Inc., B.C.
Patient Access Pavilions Ltd., Canada.
- 100% int. in **Green Life Clinics Ltd.**, B.C.

2756407 Ontario Ltd., Ont.
2770914 Ontario Inc., Ont.

Financial Statistics

Periods ended:	12m July 31/22[A]		12m July 31/21[A]
	$000s	%Chg	$000s
Operating revenue	**147**	**-35**	**225**
Cost of sales	31		47
Salaries & benefits	186		93
Research & devel. expense	13		42
General & admin expense	1,366		1,248
Operating expense	**1,595**	**+11**	**1,431**
Operating income	**(1,448)**	**n.a.**	**(1,206)**
Deprec., depl. & amort.	1		128
Finance income	nil		5
Finance costs, gross	17		8
Write-downs/write-offs	(1)		(2,510)
Pre-tax income	**(1,369)**	**n.a.**	**(8,479)**
Net income	**(1,369)**	**n.a.**	**(8,479)**
Cash & equivalent	497		456
Accounts receivable	9		13
Current assets	577		608
Fixed assets, net	2		3
Total assets	**579**	**-5**	**611**
Bank indebtedness	288		31
Accts. pay. & accr. liabs.	782		977
Current liabilities	1,104		1,051
Long-term debt, net	35		nil
Preferred share equity	100		100
Shareholders' equity	(560)		(440)
Cash from oper. activs.	**(1,489)**	**n.a.**	**(826)**
Cash from fin. activs.	1,529		763
Cash from invest. activs.	nil		429
Net cash position	**497**	**+9**	**456**
	$		$
Earnings per share*	(0.37)		(4.00)
Cash flow per share*	(0.40)		(0.39)
	shs		shs
No. of shs. o/s*	9,392,138		3,086,582
Avg. no. of shs. o/s*	3,744,572		2,109,634
	%		%
Net profit margin	(931.29)		n.m.
Return on equity	n.m.		n.m.
Return on assets	(227.23)		n.m.

* Common
[A] Reported in accordance with IFRS

Latest Results

Periods ended:	6m Jan. 31/23[A]		6m Jan. 31/22[A]
	$000s	%Chg	$000s
Operating revenue	57	-23	74
Net income	(844)	n.a.	(864)
	$		$
Earnings per share*	(0.09)		(0.20)

* Common
[A] Reported in accordance with IFRS

Historical Summary
(as originally stated)

Fiscal Year	Oper. Rev.	Net Inc. Bef. Disc.	EPS*
	$000s	$000s	$
2022[A]	147	(1,369)	(0.37)
2021[A]	225	(8,479)	(4.00)
2020[A]	352	(1,704)	(5.40)
2019[A]	488	(16,304)	(68.00)
2018[A]	nil	(3,144)	(20.00)

* Common
[A] Reported in accordance with IFRS

Note: Adjusted throughout for 1-for-20 cons. in July 2022; 1-for-10 cons. in May 2020

G.48 Global Hemp Group Inc.

Symbol - GHG **Exchange** - CSE **CUSIP** - 37953Y
Head Office - 106-1169 Mount Seymour Rd, North Vancouver, BC, V7H 2Y4 **Telephone** - (778) 726-2900 **Fax** - (604) 592-6882
Website - www.globalhempgroup.com
Email - info@globalhempgroup.com
Investor Relations - Curtis Huber (604) 617-0033
Auditors - Dale Matheson Carr-Hilton LaBonte LLP C.A., Vancouver, B.C.
Lawyers - Dunton Rainville LLP, Montréal, Qué.
Transfer Agents - Odyssey Trust Company, Vancouver, B.C.
Profile - (B.C. 2009) Developing projects focused on the industrial applications of hemp.

The company plans to develop and implement its concept of a Hemp Agro-Industrial Zone (HAIZ), an industrial hemp processing zone located adjacent to hemp farming areas. The model is designed to be replicated in any region where the law allows for industrial hemp cultivation. Applications of hemp that may be pursued under the HAIZ model include building materials, biocomposites, textiles and non-wovens.

Its initial project is the Colorado HAIZ in Hayden, Colo., being developed in partnership with affiliate **Western Sierra Resource Corporation**. The project would include irrigated industrial hemp cultivation; processing of hemp and on-site manufacturing of sustainable hemp-based construction products; and construction of green and affordable housing utilizing the hemp-based products produced. The project covers 874 acres consisting of 44 acres for a centralized processing and manufacturing campus (the X-West property), 166 acres for housing development and additional 664 acres for hemp farming and future housing development.

The company also has a research and development (R&D) division in Mexico, which is developing patented intellectual property that can be utilized in the Colorado HAIZ or widely marketed. R&D is focused on the development of environmentally friendly construction materials such as replacement of medium density fibreboard (MDF) with hemp-based products, nanofertilizers as an alternative to chemical fertilizers and enhanced extraction from hemp.

Common reinstated on CSE, Feb. 9, 2023.
Common suspended from CSE, Feb. 7, 2023.

Recent Merger and Acquisition Activity

Status: terminated **Revised:** Jan. 3, 2023
UPDATE: The transaction was terminated. PREVIOUS: Global Hemp Group Inc. entered into a binding letter of intent for the reverse takeover acquisition of Revitalize Earth for issuance of 360,000,000 post-consolidated common shares (following a 1-for-10 share consolidation) at 30¢ per share. revitalize Earth is a non-profit company based in Tarzana, Calif., which operates cannabis farms in the U.S. fulfilling demand both in the medical marijuana sector and the consumer market for cannabinoids. Nov. 10, 2022 - The date for entering into a definitive agreement was extended to Mar. 31, 2023.

Predecessor Detail - Name changed from Arris Holdings Inc., Mar. 25, 2014.
Directors - Curtis (Curt) Huber, chr., Burnaby, B.C.; Roger A. Johnson II, Colo.; Véronique Laberge, Laval, Qué.; Dr. Paul T. Perrault, Montréal, Qué.; Aurelio Useche, Verdun, Qué.
Other Exec. Officers - Stephen D. Barnhill Jr., pres. & CEO; Rachel Lu, CFO; Michel Lebeuf Jr., corp. sec.

Capital Stock

	Authorized (shs.)	Outstanding (shs.)[1]
Class B Preferred	unlimited	11,006,400[2]
Common	unlimited	335,693,392

[1] At May 30, 2022
[2] Classified as debt.

Class B Preferred - Entitled to annual dividend of US$0.01 per share, payable in cash or shares at the option of the holder. Convertible into common shares on a 2-for-1 basis. Redeemable at US$0.50 per share plus accrued an unpaid dividends. Mature on May 13, 2031. Non-voting. Classified as long-term debt under IFRS.
Common - One vote per share.
Major Shareholder - Widely held at Mar. 2, 2021.

Price Range - GHG/CSE

Year	Volume	High	Low	Close
2022	96,365,344	$0.04	$0.01	$0.02
2021	449,895,326	$0.11	$0.02	$0.02
2020	60,001,497	$0.05	$0.01	$0.03
2019	43,606,549	$0.14	$0.03	$0.03
2018	232,395,542	$0.37	$0.10	$0.14

Recent Close: $0.01
Capital Stock Changes - In March 2023, private placement of up to 75,000,000 units (1 common share & 1 warrant) at 1¢ per unit was arranged, with warrants exercisable at 5¢ per share for three years.

In April 2022, private placement of 30,000,000 units (1 common share & 1 warrant) at 2¢ per unit was completed, with warrants exercisable at 5¢ per share to Sept. 8, 2023.

Wholly Owned Subsidiaries

Covered Bridge Acres Ltd., Canada.
Covered Bridge Acres Ltd., Ore.
41389 Farms Ltd., Ore.

Investments

46.85% int. in **Western Sierra Resource Corporation**, Colo. Voting interest.

Financial Statistics

Periods ended:	12m Sept. 30/21[A]		12m Sept. 30/20[A]
	$000s	%Chg	$000s
Operating revenue	**nil**	**n.a.**	**29**
Cost of goods sold	nil		8
Research & devel. expense	26		29
General & admin expense	681		161
Stock-based compensation	2,168		488
Operating expense	**2,875**	**+319**	**686**
Operating income	**(2,875)**	**n.a.**	**(657)**
Deprec., depl. & amort.	41		22
Finance income	nil		1
Finance costs, gross	184		4
Investment income	nil		(482)
Write-downs/write-offs	(4,156)		3
Pre-tax income	**(8,038)**	**n.a.**	**(1,378)**
Net income	**(8,038)**	**n.a.**	**(1,378)**
Net inc. for equity hldrs.	**(8,036)**	**n.a.**	**(1,270)**
Net inc. for non-cont. int.	**(2)**	**n.a.**	**(108)**
Cash & equivalent	138		16
Accounts receivable	37		32
Current assets	193		65
Fixed assets, net	1,706		2,359
Total assets	**3,999**	**+65**	**2,424**
Bank indebtedness	nil		795
Accts. pay. & accr. liabs.	393		677
Current liabilities	1,595		1,509
Long-term debt, gross	4,086		nil
Long-term debt, net	2,996		nil
Shareholders' equity	(1,362)		957
Non-controlling interest	nil		(43)
Cash from oper. activs.	**(916)**	**n.a.**	**(60)**
Cash from fin. activs.	2,885		225
Cash from invest. activs.	(1,847)		(632)
Net cash position	**138**	**+762**	**16**
Capital expenditures	(739)		nil
Capital disposals	413		nil
	$		$
Earnings per share*	(0.03)		(0.01)
Cash flow per share*	(0.00)		(0.00)
	shs		shs
No. of shs. o/s*	307,993,392		211,660,432
Avg. no. of shs. o/s*	265,701,566		188,802,302
	%		%
Net profit margin	n.a.		n.m.
Return on equity	n.m.		(112.84)
Return on assets	(244.56)		(64.90)
Foreign sales percent	n.a.		100

* Common
[A] Reported in accordance with IFRS

Latest Results

Periods ended:	6m Mar. 31/22[A]		6m Mar. 31/21[A]
	$000s	%Chg	$000s
Net income	(32)	n.a.	(1,318)
Net inc. for equity hldrs.	(32)	n.a.	(1,317)
Net inc. for non-cont. int.	nil		(2)
	$		$
Earnings per share*	(0.00)		(0.01)

* Common
[A] Reported in accordance with IFRS

Historical Summary
(as originally stated)

Fiscal Year	Oper. Rev.	Net Inc. Bef. Disc.	EPS*
	$000s	$000s	$
2021[A]	nil	(8,038)	(0.03)
2020[A]	29	(1,378)	(0.01)
2019[A]	3	(2,918)	(0.02)
2018[A]	nil	(1,586)	(0.01)
2017[A]	nil	(814)	(0.01)

* Common
[A] Reported in accordance with IFRS

G.49 Global Investments Capital Corp.

Symbol - GLIN.P **Exchange** - TSX-VEN (S) **CUSIP** - 37956J
Head Office - 1900-520 3 Ave SW, Calgary, AB, T2P 0R3 **Telephone** - (403) 669-4848
Email - peters.trevor@gmail.com
Investor Relations - Trevor Peters (403) 669-4848
Auditors - MNP LLP C.A., Calgary, Alta.
Lawyers - Borden Ladner Gervais LLP, Calgary, Alta.
Transfer Agents - TSX Trust Company, Calgary, Alta.
Profile - (Alta. 2017) Capital Pool Company.

Common suspended from TSX-VEN, Dec. 2, 2019.

Directors - Thane Ritchie, CEO, West Vancouver, B.C.; Trevor Peters, CFO & corp. sec., Calgary, Alta.; Patrick Conway, Chicago, Ill.; Robb McNaughton, Calgary, Alta.; Paul Wolfe, Wheaton, Ill.

Capital Stock

	Authorized (shs.)	Outstanding (shs.)[1]
Preferred	unlimited	nil
Common	unlimited	9,000,000

[1] At Jan. 24, 2022

Major Shareholder - Thane Ritchie held 44.4% interest at May 7, 2021.

Price Range - GLIN.P/TSX-VEN (S)

Year	Volume	High	Low	Close
2019	106,000	$0.10	$0.05	$0.05
2018	214,030	$0.24	$0.09	$0.09

G.50 Global UAV Technologies Ltd.

Symbol - UAV **Exchange** - CSE **CUSIP** - 379433
Head Office - 488-1090 Georgia St W, Vancouver, BC, V6E 3V7 **Telephone** - (604) 678-2531 **Toll-free** - (888) 905-7011 **Fax** - (604) 678-2532
Website - www.globaluavtech.com
Email - james@globaluavtech.com
Investor Relations - James D. Rogers (604) 678-2531
Auditors - Davidson & Company LLP C.A., Vancouver, B.C.
Lawyers - Tupper Jonsson & Yeadon, Vancouver, B.C.
Transfer Agents - Computershare Trust Company of Canada Inc., Vancouver, B.C.
Profile - (B.C. 1980) No current operations.

The company was pursuing a restructuring, including the sale of its subsidiaries or its key unmanned aerial vehicles (UAV) assets. Previously produced, researched and designed professional grade UAV, as well as provided geophysics and remote surveying services and regulatory consulting management.

Predecessor Detail - Name changed from Alta Vista Ventures Ltd., May 17, 2017.

Directors - James D. Rogers, pres. & interim CEO, Vancouver, B.C.; Andrew R. Male, COO, Vancouver, B.C.; Jeffrey J. (Jeff) Stevens, Scarborough, Ont.

Other Exec. Officers - Stephen Sulis, interim CFO; Von Rowell Torres, corp. sec.; Ramiro Cotarelo, pres., High Eye Aerial Surveys

Capital Stock

	Authorized (shs.)	Outstanding (shs.)[1]
Common	unlimited	1,171,167

[1] At June 29, 2022

Price Range - UAV/CSE

Year	Volume	High	Low	Close
2022	206,122	$0.80	$0.16	$0.18
2021	2,205,416	$11.48	$0.43	$0.44
2020	1,346,570	$4.05	$0.68	$3.38
2019	460,980	$6.75	$0.68	$0.68
2018	1,628,241	$34.43	$4.05	$4.73

Consolidation: 1-for-135 cons. in Aug. 2021
Recent Close: $0.18

Wholly Owned Subsidiaries

Aerial Imaging Resources Inc., Flin Flon, Man.
High Eye Aerial Imaging Inc., Wasaga Beach, Ont.
Minera AltaVista, S.A. de C.V., Mexico. Inactive.
NOVAerial Robotics Ltd.
Pioneer Aerial Surveys Ltd., Canada.
UAV Regulatory Services Ltd., B.C.

Financial Statistics

Periods ended:	12m Oct. 31/21[A]		12m Oct. 31/20[A]
	$000s	%Chg	$000s
Operating revenue	**14**	**-97**	**493**
Cost of sales	nil		310
Salaries & benefits	nil		13
General & admin expense	312		612
Operating expense	**312**	**-67**	**935**
Operating income	**(298)**	**n.a.**	**(442)**
Deprec., depl. & amort	95		166
Finance costs, gross	nil		16
Write-downs/write-offs	nil		(113)
Pre-tax income	**142**	**n.a.**	**(597)**
Net income	**142**	**n.a.**	**(597)**
Cash & equivalent	10		67
Accounts receivable	27		24
Current assets	37		90
Fixed assets, net	282		377
Total assets	**319**	**-32**	**468**
Accts. pay. & accr. liabs	1,308		1,586
Current liabilities	1,308		1,618
Long-term debt, gross	60		40
Long-term debt, net	60		40
Shareholders' equity	(1,048)		(1,190)
Cash from oper. activs	**(77)**	**n.a.**	**(12)**
Cash from fin. activs	20		40
Cash from invest. activs	nil		24
Net cash position	**10**	**-85**	**67**
	$		$
Earnings per share*	0.14		(0.59)
Cash flow per share*	(0.08)		(0.01)
	shs		shs
No. of shs. o/s*	1,013,167		1,013,005
Avg. no. of shs. o/s*	1,013,167		1,013,005
	%		%
Net profit margin	n.m.		(121.10)
Return on equity	n.m.		n.m.
Return on assets	36.09		(76.40)

* Common
[A] Reported in accordance with IFRS

Latest Results

Periods ended:	6m Apr. 30/22[A]		6m Apr. 30/21[A]
	$000s	%Chg	$000s
Operating revenue	nil	n.a.	14
Net income	(96)	n.a.	(112)
	$		$
Earnings per share*	(0.09)		(0.11)

* Common
[A] Reported in accordance with IFRS

Historical Summary
(as originally stated)

Fiscal Year	Oper. Rev.	Net Inc. Bef. Disc.	EPS*
	$000s	$000s	$
2021[A]	14	142	0.14
2020[A]	493	(597)	(0.59)
2019[A]	1,937	(1,514)	(1.35)
2018[A]	1,816	(4,716)	(5.40)
2017[A]	1,027	(3,022)	(5.40)

* Common
[A] Reported in accordance with IFRS
Note: Adjusted throughout for 1-for-135 cons. in Aug. 2021

G.51 GlobalBlock Digital Asset Trading Limited

Symbol - BLOK.H **Exchange** - TSX-VEN **CUSIP** - 37892G
Head Office - 203-82 Richmond St E, Toronto, ON, M5C 1P1 **Telephone** - (416) 848-6865 **Fax** - (416) 361-0923
Email - stuartolley@outlook.com
Investor Relations - Stuart M. Olley (403) 618-4900
Auditors - Kingston Ross Pasnak LLP C.A., Edmonton, Alta.
Lawyers - Edwards, Kenny & Bray LLP, Vancouver, B.C.
Transfer Agents - Computershare Trust Company of Canada Inc., Vancouver, B.C.
Profile - (B.C. 1991) Seeking new business opportunities.

Formerly owned and operated a European Union-based digital asset brokerage. Also continues to own blockchain patents.

In May 2022, the company moved its digital asset brokerage and trading services business from the U.K. to Lithuania. Operations were transferred to wholly owned **GlobalBlock Europe, UAB** from wholly owned **GlobalBlock Limited**, which ceased operations effective the date of the transfer.

Recent Merger and Acquisition Activity

Status: completed **Revised:** Aug. 1, 2023
UPDATE: The transaction was completed. PREVIOUS: GlobalBlock Digital Asset Trading Limited agreed to sell wholly owned GlobalBlock Limited (GB UK) and its digital asset broker business back to the founders of GB UK in exchange for the return of the 48,450,000 common shares of GlobalBlock held by them, which were originally issued when GlobalBlock acquired GB UK in 2021. The sale represents substantially all of GlobalBlock's property. The agreement sets forth how the assets, liabilities and obligations of GlobalBlock and GB UK and its business are to be dispersed or transferred amongst GlobalBlock and GB UK effective as at Dec. 31, 2022. On closing, GlobalBlock would be seeking alternative transactions and businesses to acquire or combine with. May 15, 2023 - Shareholder approval was received.

Predecessor Detail - Name changed from Helix Applications Inc., July 22, 2021.

Directors - Rupert Williams, interim CEO, Godalming, Surrey, United Kingdom; Trevor M. Gabriel, Monte Carlo, Monaco; Stuart M. Olley, Calgary, Alta.

Other Exec. Officers - James (Jim) O'Neill, CFO; Gordon Chmilar, corp. sec.

Capital Stock

	Authorized (shs.)	Outstanding (shs.)[1]
Class A Preference	unlimited	nil
Common	unlimited	76,798,741

[1] At Aug. 1, 2023

Major Shareholder - Widely held at Aug. 1, 2023.

Price Range - BLOK.H/TSX-VEN

Year	Volume	High	Low	Close
2022	8,672,731	$0.87	$0.05	$0.07
2021	15,189,545	$1.76	$0.14	$0.62
2020	1,194,208	$0.20	$0.05	$0.15
2019	3,011,984	$0.55	$0.05	$0.10
2018	1,236,110	$0.96	$0.45	$0.45

Recent Close: $0.18

Capital Stock Changes - In May and June 2023, private placement of 20,300,000 units (1 common share & 1 warrant) at 5¢ per unit was completed, with warrants exercisable at 10¢ per share for one year. In August 2023, 48,450,000 common shares were repurchased and cancelled.

There were no changes to capital stock during 2022.

Financial Statistics

Periods ended:	12m Dec. 31/22[A]		12m Dec. 31/21[oA]
	$000s	%Chg	$000s
Salaries & benefits	76		340
General & admin expense	708		733
Stock-based compensation	112		558
Operating expense	**896**	**-45**	**1,631**
Operating income	**(896)**	**n.a.**	**(1,631)**
Finance income	nil		38
Write-downs/write-offs	nil		(150)
Pre-tax income	**(1,024)**	**n.a.**	**(4,039)**
Net inc. bef. disc. opers	**(1,024)**	**n.a.**	**(4,039)**
Income from disc. opers	(10,866)		(32,117)
Net income	**(11,889)**	**n.a.**	**(36,156)**
Cash & equivalent	3		29,829
Current assets	13,606		35,739
Fixed assets, net	nil		61
Intangibles, net	nil		8,968
Total assets	**13,606**	**-70**	**44,767**
Accts. pay. & accr. liabs	267		878
Current liabilities	12,566		31,455
Shareholders' equity	1,040		12,949
Cash from oper. activs	**(2,257)**	**n.a.**	**(3,618)**
Cash from fin. activs	nil		2,820
Cash from invest. activs	(358)		(556)
Net cash position	**90**	**-97**	**3,053**
	$		$
Earns. per sh. bef disc opers*	(0.01)		(0.05)
Earnings per share*	(0.11)		(0.47)
Cash flow per share*	(0.02)		(0.05)
	shs		shs
No. of shs. o/s*	104,948,741		104,948,741
Avg. no. of shs. o/s*	104,948,741		76,352,312
	%		%
Net profit margin	n.a.		n.a.
Return on equity	(14.64)		(46.71)
Return on assets	(3.51)		(16.42)

* Common
[o] Restated
[A] Reported in accordance with IFRS

Latest Results

Periods ended:	3m Mar. 31/23[A]		3m Mar. 31/22[oA]
	$000s	%Chg	$000s
Net inc. bef. disc. opers	1,383	n.a.	(755)
Income from disc. opers	nil		(967)
Net income	1,383	n.a.	(1,721)
	$		$
Earns. per sh. bef. disc. opers.*	0.01		(0.01)
Earnings per share*	0.01		(0.02)

* Common
[o] Restated
[A] Reported in accordance with IFRS

Historical Summary
(as originally stated)

Fiscal Year	Oper. Rev. $000s	Net Inc. Bef. Disc. $000s	EPS* $
2022A	nil	(1,024)	(0.01)
2021A	1,474	(36,156)	(0.47)
2020A	nil	(625)	(0.01)
2019A	nil	(14,184)	(0.21)
2018A	nil	(4,642)	(0.11)

* Common
A Reported in accordance with IFRS

G.52 Glorious Creation Limited

Symbol - GCIT.X **Exchange** - CSE **CUSIP** - 37960L
Head Office - 405-1328 Pender St W, Vancouver, BC, V6E 4T1 **Telephone** - (778) 889-4966
Email - teresacherry79@gmail.com
Investor Relations - Teresa M. Cherry (604) 428-7050
Auditors - Davidson & Company LLP C.A., Vancouver, B.C.
Lawyers - K MacInnes Law Group, Vancouver, B.C.
Transfer Agents - Computershare Trust Company of Canada Inc., Vancouver, B.C.
Profile - (B.C. 2018; orig. Can., 2015) Seeking new business opportunities.

Previously provided commercial services for foreign small and medium-sized enterprises (SMEs) seeking ready access to the growing market for consumer and industrial goods in Vietnam through its virtual cross-border (VCB) business platform, which was an e-commerce platform that provided all the IT services and logistics management for the execution of commerce across national borders and multiple currencies, as well as provided a business-to-business (B2B) online marketplace for linking SMEs in southern People's Republic of China and southern Vietnam.

Directors - Liam L. Corcoran, CEO, Vancouver, B.C.; Toby Lim, North Vancouver, B.C.; Nicholas Luksha, B.C.
Other Exec. Officers - Teresa M. Cherry, CFO

Capital Stock

	Authorized (shs.)	Outstanding (shs.)[1]
Common	unlimited	20,983,389

[1] At Feb. 2, 2022

Major Shareholder - Widely held at Nov. 3, 2020.

Price Range - GCIT.X/CSE

Year	Volume	High	Low	Close
2022	16,023	$0.33	$0.30	$0.31
2021	112,600	$0.60	$0.30	$0.60
2020	47,892	$4.00	$0.07	$0.65
2019	4,357	$7.00	$0.14	$0.14
2018	2,535	$9.10	$7.70	$8.40

Consolidation: 1-for-14 cons. in July 2020

Financial Statistics

Periods ended:	12m Dec. 31/21A		12m Dec. 31/20A
	$000s	%Chg	$000s
General & admin expense	221		118
Stock-based compensation	nil		18
Operating expense	**221**	**+62**	**136**
Operating income	**(221)**	**n.a.**	**(136)**
Pre-tax income	**(221)**	**n.a.**	**(136)**
Net income	**(221)**	**n.a.**	**(136)**
Cash & equivalent	291		509
Current assets	291		509
Total assets	**291**	**-43**	**509**
Accts. pay. & accr. liabs	27		24
Current liabilities	29		26
Shareholders' equity	262		483
Cash from oper. activs	**(218)**	**n.a.**	**(287)**
Cash from fin. activs	nil		784
Net cash position	**291**	**-43**	**509**
	$		$
Earnings per share*	(0.01)		(0.01)
Cash flow per share*	(0.01)		(0.03)
	shs		shs
No. of shs. o/s*	20,983,389		20,983,389
Avg. no. of shs. o/s*	20,983,389		10,799,584
	%		%
Net profit margin	n.a.		n.a.
Return on equity	(59.33)		n.m.
Return on assets	(55.25)		(52.21)

* Common
A Reported in accordance with IFRS

Historical Summary
(as originally stated)

Fiscal Year	Oper. Rev. $000s	Net Inc. Bef. Disc. $000s	EPS* $
2021A	nil	(221)	(0.01)
2020A	nil	(136)	(0.01)
2019A	7	(103)	(0.03)
2018A	70	(1,566)	(0.56)
2017A	33	(1,200)	(0.42)

* Common
A Reported in accordance with IFRS
Note: Adjusted throughout for 1-for-14 cons. in July 2020

G.53 Glow LifeTech Corp.

Symbol - GLOW **Exchange** - CSE **CUSIP** - 37989H
Head Office - 206-65 International Blvd, Toronto, ON, M9W 6L9 **Telephone** - (647) 872-9982 **Toll-free** - (844) 247-6633
Website - www.glowlifetech.com
Email - jamesv@glowlifetech.com
Investor Relations - James Van Staveren (855) 442-4569
Auditors - Jackson & Co., LLP C.A., Toronto, Ont.
Transfer Agents - Capital Transfer Agency Inc., Toronto, Ont.
Profile - (Ont. 1988 amalg.) Produces nutraceutical and cannabinoid-based products with dramatically enhanced bioavailability, absorption and effectiveness.

Pursuant to a licensing agreement with **Swiss PharmaCan AG**, the company has exclusive North American rights for the manufacturing, distribution and sale of materials using MyCell Enhanced® Technology delivery system for all cannabis and hemp compounds, as well as curcumin, vitamin K, iron and its respective derivatives and mixtures. MyCell transforms poorly absorbed natural compounds into enhanced water-compatible concentrates, unlocking the full healing potential of natural active compounds. The company has developed products enhanced by MyCell Technology including MyCell® liquid water-soluble THC and CBD ingredients, which it plans to commercialize within Canada; ArtemiC™, an oral spray containing artemisinin, curcumin, boswellia serrata and vitamin C; and Artemic Support®, a water-soluble supplement containing curcuma longa, boswellia serrata and vitamin C aimed to support the immune system. The company has built out a licensed processing space in **Medz Cannabis Inc.**'s facility in Toronto, Ont., for the MyCell® ingredients. The processing space is part of a collaborative partnership with Medz for cannabis product manufacturing where in the company would perform manufacturing services within a facility under quality and compliance control of Medz, with all products released under Medz licence.

Also has a cannabis Smart Consumption System, consisting of a suite of cloud connected hardware and software products which assist medicinal and recreational cannabis users and patients to store, journal, control, consume and manage the purchase of cannabis related products.

Predecessor Detail - Name changed from Ateba Resources Inc., Feb. 26, 2021, pursuant to the reverse takeover acquisition of Glow LifeTech Ltd. and concurrent amalgamation of Glow LifeTech with wholly owned 2760626 Ontario Inc.; basis 1 new for 1.5 old shs.

Directors - W. Clark Kent, pres. & CEO, Ont.; Roberto Carducci, chief comml. officer; Greg Falck, B.C.; Christopher O. (Chris) Irwin, Toronto, Ont.; Medhanie Tekeste, Ont.
Other Exec. Officers - Josh Bald, CFO; Dr. Tom Glawdel, chief opers. officer; James Van Staveren, corp. sec.

Capital Stock

	Authorized (shs.)	Outstanding (shs.)[1]
Common	unlimited	57,108,546

[1] At Aug. 29, 2022

Major Shareholder - Widely held at Jan. 13, 2023.

Price Range - GLOW/CSE

Year	Volume	High	Low	Close
2022	5,538,345	$0.32	$0.06	$0.09
2021	14,539,263	$0.88	$0.17	$0.28

Consolidation: 1-for-1.5 cons. in Feb. 2021
Recent Close: $0.09

Wholly Owned Subsidiaries

Glow LifeTech Ltd., Ont.
- 100% int. in **Swiss Pharma Corp.**, Switzerland.

Financial Statistics

Periods ended:	12m Dec. 31/21A1		12m Dec. 31/20A2
	$000s	%Chg	$000s
Salaries & benefits	122		nil
General & admin expense	2,495		153
Stock-based compensation	2,618		nil
Operating expense	**5,234**	**n.m.**	**153**
Operating income	**(5,234)**	**n.a.**	**(153)**
Deprec., depl. & amort	43		nil
Finance costs, gross	4		nil
Pre-tax income	**(11,314)**	**n.a.**	**(153)**
Net income	**(11,314)**	**n.a.**	**(153)**
Cash & equivalent	868		2
Inventories	100		nil
Accounts receivable	nil		1
Current assets	1,290		3
Long-term investments	1,748		nil
Fixed assets, net	393		nil
Intangibles, net	333		nil
Total assets	**3,764**	**n.m.**	**3**
Bank indebtedness	40		6
Accts. pay. & accr. liabs	176		309
Current liabilities	328		316
Shareholders' equity	3,436		(313)
Cash from oper. activs	**(3,181)**	**n.a.**	**(19)**
Cash from fin. activs	4,589		nil
Cash from invest. activs	(541)		nil
Net cash position	**868**	**n.m.**	**2**
	$		$
Earnings per share*	(0.24)		(0.05)
Cash flow per share*	(0.07)		(0.01)
	shs		shs
No. of shs. o/s*	57,108,546		3,111,103
Avg. no. of shs. o/s*	47,690,458		3,111,103
	%		%
Net profit margin	n.a.		n.a.
Return on equity	n.m.		n.m.
Return on assets	(600.48)		n.m.

* Common
A Reported in accordance with IFRS
[1] Results reflect the Mar. 3, 2021, reverse takeover acquisition of Glow LifeTech Ltd.
[2] Results for 2020 and prior years pertain to Ateba Resources Inc.

Latest Results

Periods ended:	6m June 30/22A		6m June 30/21A
	$000s	%Chg	$000s
Net income	(1,116)	n.a.	(11,554)
	$		$
Earnings per share*	(0.02)		(0.30)

* Common
A Reported in accordance with IFRS

Historical Summary
(as originally stated)

Fiscal Year	Oper. Rev. $000s	Net Inc. Bef. Disc. $000s	EPS* $
2021A	nil	(11,314)	(0.24)
2020A	nil	(153)	(0.04)
2019A	nil	(56)	(0.01)
2018A1	nil	(187)	(0.08)
2017A	nil	(449)	(0.01)

* Common
A Reported in accordance with IFRS
[1] Shares and per share figures adjusted to reflect 1-for-50 share consolidation effective July 12, 2018.
Note: Adjusted throughout for 1-for-1.5 cons. in Feb. 2021

G.54 Gnomestar Craft Inc.

Symbol - GNOM **Exchange** - CSE (S) **CUSIP** - 362006
Head Office - 8788 River Rd, Delta, BC, V4G 1B5 **Toll-free** - (866) 210-1420 **Fax** - (604) 648-9568
Website - gnomestarcannabis.com
Email - mark@vodis.ca
Investor Relations - Mark Lotz (778) 242-9677
Auditors - Kingston Ross Pasnak LLP C.A., Edmonton, Alta.
Transfer Agents - Odyssey Trust Company
Profile - (B.C. 2011) Produces and distributes medical and recreational cannabis products in British Columbia and Nunavut under the Cannabis Act.

The company holds a cultivation and processing licence from Health Canada for its 12,000-sq.-ft. indoor cannabis facility in Delta, B.C., designed for small batch production of premium craft cannabis. Cannabis products, which include Meat Breath, Red Congolese and Comatose Kush Hybrid, are marketed under the brand Gnomestar Craft Cannabis.

Common suspended from CSE, Oct. 6, 2022.

Predecessor Detail - Name changed from Vodis Pharmaceuticals Inc., Dec. 7, 2020.

Directors - Mark Lotz, interim CEO & CFO, Vancouver, B.C.

Capital Stock

	Authorized (shs.)	Outstanding (shs.)[1]
Preferred	unlimited	nil
Common	unlimited	85,410,804

[1] At Oct. 3, 2021

Price Range - GNOM/CSE (S)

Year	Volume	High	Low	Close
2022	4,599,486	$0.04	$0.01	$0.01
2021	24,763,787	$0.13	$0.03	$0.04
2020	19,466,571	$0.08	$0.02	$0.06
2019	26,214,133	$0.18	$0.03	$0.04
2018	60,363,383	$0.76	$0.07	$0.10

Recent Close: $0.01

Wholly Owned Subsidiaries

Vodis Innovative Pharmaceuticals Inc., B.C.
Vodis USA Inc., Wash.
0962559 B.C. Ltd., B.C.

Financial Statistics

Periods ended:	12m Mar. 31/21[A]		12m Mar. 31/20[A]
	$000s	%Chg	$000s
Operating revenue	**267**	**n.a.**	**nil**
Cost of sales	537[1]		nil
General & admin expense	512		846
Stock-based compensation	110		nil
Operating expense	**1,160**	**+37**	**846**
Operating income	**(893)**	**n.a.**	**(846)**
Deprec., depl. & amort.	95		268
Finance costs, gross	53		63
Pre-tax income	**(876)**	**n.a.**	**(1,303)**
Net income	**(876)**	**n.a.**	**(1,303)**
Cash & equivalent	nil		321
Inventories	75		nil
Accounts receivable	135		30
Current assets	320		400
Fixed assets, net	899		1,044
Total assets	**1,219**	**-16**	**1,444**
Accts. pay. & accr. liabs.	592		571
Current liabilities	2,359		2,381
Long-term lease liabilities	511		476
Shareholders' equity	(1,650)		(1,413)
Cash from oper. activs.	**(130)**	**n.a.**	**(279)**
Cash from fin. activs.	(53)		776
Cash from invest. activs.	(139)		(198)
Net cash position	**nil**	**n.a.**	**321**
Capital expenditures	(139)		(198)
	$		$
Earnings per share*	(0.01)		(0.02)
Cash flow per share*	(0.00)		(0.00)
	shs		shs
No. of shs. o/s*	85,410,804		79,239,504
Avg. no. of shs. o/s*	79,613,515		64,721,137
	%		%
Net profit margin	(328.09)		n.a.
Return on equity	n.m.		n.m.
Return on assets	(61.81)		(113.45)

* Common
[A] Reported in accordance with IFRS
[1] Net of fair value adjustment of biological assets.

Historical Summary
(as originally stated)

Fiscal Year	Oper. Rev.	Net Inc. Bef. Disc.	EPS*
	$000s	$000s	$
2021[A]	267	(876)	(0.01)
2020[A]	nil	(1,303)	(0.02)
2019[A]	nil	(4,208)	(0.09)
2018[A]	nil	(3,744)	(0.12)
2017[A]	10	(6,186)	(0.27)

* Common
[A] Reported in accordance with IFRS

G.55 goeasy Ltd.*

Symbol - GSY **Exchange** - TSX **CUSIP** - 380355
Head Office - 510-33 City Centre Dr, Mississauga, ON, L5B 2N5 **Telephone** - (905) 272-2788 **Fax** - (905) 272-9886
Website - www.goeasy.com
Email - investor_relations@goeasy.com
Investor Relations - Farhan Ali Khan (905) 272-2788
Auditors - Ernst & Young LLP C.A., Toronto, Ont.
Bankers - National Bank of Canada, Toronto, Ont.; The Toronto-Dominion Bank, Toronto, Ont.; Wells Fargo Bank, N.A., Toronto, Ont.; Bank of Montreal, Toronto, Ont.; Canadian Imperial Bank of Commerce, Toronto, Ont.
Lawyers - Blake, Cassels & Graydon LLP, Toronto, Ont.
Transfer Agents - TSX Trust Company, Toronto, Ont.
FP500 Revenue Ranking - 336
Employees - 2,438 at Dec. 31, 2022

Profile - (Ont. 1993 amalg.) Provides non-prime leasing and lending through easyhome, easyfinancial and LendCare brands. Financial products and services offered include unsecured and secured instalment loans, merchant financing through a variety of verticals and lease-to own merchandise.

Operations are organized into two reportable segments: easyfinancial and easyhome.

easyfinancial provides unsecured and secured consumer loans of up to $100,000 at interest rates starting at 9.9% to customers who normally would not qualify for credit from traditional sources. Unsecured loans generally range from nine to 84 months while secured loans generally range from five to 20 years. Various ancillary products are also offered including a customer protection program that provides creditor insurance; a home and auto benefits product which provides roadside assistance; a gap insurance product which covers buyer and lender from any shortfall in cases of total loss insurance claims; warranty coverage on select financial products; and a credit monitoring and optimization tool that helps customers understand the steps to take to rebuild their credit. easyfinancial, which includes easyfinancial and LendCare brands, has 304 locations across Canada, including two kiosks located within easyhome stores, three operations centres and 299 stand-alone locations as at June 30, 2023. In addition to its locations, loans are also issued to customers online and through its point-of-sale channel, which includes 8,500 merchant partners across Canada.

Geographic breakdown of the 299 easyfinancial kiosks and stand-alone locations at Dec. 31, 2022:

Province	Stores
British Columbia	36
Alberta	29
Saskatchewan	10
Manitoba	9
Ontario	125
Quebec	46
New Brunswick	13
Nova Scotia	16
Prince Edward Island	3
Nfld. & Labrador	12

easyhome provides lease-to-own financial solutions, offering customers brand-name household furniture, appliances and electronics through flexible lease agreements. Leases are offered without down payment or credit check requirements, and customers have the option to terminate their lease at any time without penalty. easyhome has 144 stores across Canada, including 34 franchised stores and 110 corporate-owned stores as at June 30, 2023.

Geographic breakdown of the 120 corporate-owned stores at Dec. 31, 2022:

Province	Stores
British Columbia	12
Alberta	18
Saskatchewan	5
Manitoba	3
Ontario	39
Quebec	9
New Brunswick	10
Nova Scotia	12
Prince Edward Island	2
Nfld. & Labrador	10

The company leases all of its branch or store locations, which are generally located in strip shopping centres, plazas or stand-alone buildings.

During 2022, the company invested $40,000,000 convertible notes of **1195407 B.C. Ltd.**, a subsidiary of online car retailer, **Canada Drives Ltd.** The notes would convert into preferred shares on defined terms. In connection, the company would also become a preferred non-bank financing provider within Canada Drives' online automotive retail platform. Canada Drives's platform allows customers to shop, purchase, finance and trade-in vehicles online.

Predecessor Detail - Name changed from easyhome Ltd., Sept. 14, 2015.

Directors - Donald K. (Don) Johnson†, chr., emeritus, Ont.; David Ingram, exec. chr., Ont.; Jason Mullins, pres. & CEO, Ont.; David Appel, Ont.; Karen Basian, Ont.; Tara Deakin, Ont.; Susan Doniz, Guelph, Ont.; The Hon. James Moore, B.C.; Sean Morrison, Vancouver, B.C.; Jonathan Tétrault, Qué.

Other Exec. Officers - Jason Appel, exec. v-p & chief risk officer; Andrea Fiederer, exec. v-p & chief mktg. officer; Jackie Foo, exec. v-p & COO; Hal Khouri, exec. v-p & CFO; Sabrina Anzini, sr. v-p & chief legal officer; David Cooper, sr. v-p & chief talent officer; Michael A. Eubanks, sr. v-p & CIO; Farhan Ali Khan, sr. v-p & chief corp. devel. officer; Steven Poole, sr. v-p, easyhome opers. & mdsg.; Ali Metel, pres., LendCare Capital Inc.

† Lead director

Capital Stock

	Authorized (shs.)	Outstanding (shs.)[1]
Preference	unlimited	nil
Common	unlimited	16,542,889

[1] At Aug. 9, 2023

Options - At Dec. 31, 2022, options were outstanding to purchase 345,000 common shares at prices ranging from $33.56 to $163.13 per share with a weighted average remaining contractual life of 2.26 years.

Normal Course Issuer Bid - The company plans to make normal course purchases of up to 1,252,730 common shares representing 10% of the public float. The bid commenced on Dec. 21, 2022, and expires on Dec. 20, 2023.

Major Shareholder - Donald K. (Don) Johnson held 17.8% interest at Mar. 21, 2023.

Price Range - GSY/TSX

Year	Volume	High	Low	Close
2022	15,493,728	$179.69	$95.00	$106.45
2021	17,107,588	$218.35	$91.20	$179.27
2020	26,788,354	$100.48	$21.08	$96.65
2019	10,461,880	$73.35	$34.53	$69.55
2018	10,678,051	$54.80	$30.42	$35.77

Recent Close: $124.27

Capital Stock Changes - In November 2022, bought deal public offering of 488,750 common shares was completed at $118.50 per share, including 63,750 common shares on exercise of over-allotment option. Also during 2022, common shares were issued as follows: 161,000 on exercise of options, 25,000 under restricted share unit plan and 21,000 under dividend reinvestment plan; 450,058 common shares were repurchased under a Normal Course Issuer Bid.

Dividends

GSY com Ra $3.84 pa Q est. Apr. 14, 2023**
Prev. Rate: $3.64 est. Apr. 8, 2022
Prev. Rate: $2.64 est. Apr. 9, 2021
Prev. Rate: $1.80 est. Apr. 10, 2020
** Reinvestment Option

Long-Term Debt - Outstanding at Dec. 31, 2022:

Revolv. secs. warehouse facility[1]	$805,825,000
Revolv. credit facility[2]	148,646,000
5.375% sr. notes due Dec. 2024	739,741,000
4.375% sr. notes due May 2026	429,256,000
Secured borrowings[3]	105,792,000
	2,229,260,000

[1] Borrowings under a $1.4 billion revolving securitization warehouse facility bearing interest at the one-month CDOR plus 1.85% and due on Aug. 30, 2024.

[2] Borrowings under a $270,000,000 senior revolving credit facility bearing interest at either lender's prime rate plus 0.75% or banker's acceptance rate plus 2.25%.

[3] Borrowings under a $105,000,000 securitization facility bearing interest at the Government of Canada Bonds (GOCB) rate, with a floor rate of 0.95%, plus 3.95%; and an $85,000,000 securitization facility bearing interest at the GOCB rate, with a floor rate of 0.25%, plus 3.25%.

Note - In March 2023, the maximum borrowing capacity under the revolving credit facility was increased to $370,000,000 from $270,000,000. In June 2023, the maturity date of the revolving securitization warehouse facility was extended to Oct. 31, 2025, from Aug. 30, 2024.

Wholly Owned Subsidiaries

easyfinancial Services Inc., Ont.
LendCare Capital Inc., Ont.
RTO Asset Management Inc., Alta.

Investments

Affirm Holdings, Inc., San Francisco, Calif.
Brim Financial Inc., Toronto, Ont.
1195407 B.C. Ltd., B.C.

Financial Statistics

Periods ended:	12m Dec. 31/22[A]		12m Dec. 31/21[A]
	$000s	%Chg	$000s
Total revenue	**1,019,336**	**+23**	**826,722**
Salaries & benefits	174,236		157,157
General & admin. expense	34,069		30,393
Stock-based compensation	10,053		8,875
Other operating expense	93,823		88,324
Operating expense	**312,181**	**+10**	**284,749**
Operating income	**707,155**	**+30**	**541,973**
Deprec. & amort.	81,306		78,886
Finance costs, gross	107,972		79,025
Write-downs/write-offs	(293,442)[1]		(182,084)
Pre-tax income	**195,776**	**-38**	**316,854**
Income taxes	55,615		71,911
Net income	**140,161**	**-43**	**244,943**
Cash & equivalent	62,654		102,479
Accounts receivable	25,697		20,769
Investments	57,304		64,441
Fixed assets, net	84,293		82,467
Right-of-use assets	65,758		57,140
Intangibles, net	319,725		340,574
Total assets	**3,302,889**	**+27**	**2,596,153**
Accts. pay. & accr. liabs	51,136		57,134
Debt	2,229,260		1,552,679
Lease liabilities	74,328		65,607
Shareholders' equity	869,688		789,913
Cash from oper. activs	**(505,881)**	**n.a.**	**(78,875)**
Cash from fin. activs	508,547		298,936
Cash from invest. activs	(42,491)		(210,635)
Net cash position	**62,654**	**-39**	**102,479**
Capital expenditures	(9,871)		(7,815)
	$		$
Earnings per share*	8.61		15.12
Cash flow per share*	(31.08)		(4.87)
Cash divd. per share*	3.64		2.64
	shs		shs
No. of shs. o/s*	16,445,000		16,199,000
Avg. no. of shs. o/s*	16,275,000		16,200,000
	%		%
Net profit margin	13.75		29.63
Return on equity	16.89		39.72
Return on assets	7.37		14.94
No. of employees (FTEs)	2,438		2,352

* Common

[A] Reported in accordance with IFRS

[1] Consists of bad debts of $272,893,000 and write-offs of intangibles of $20,549,000.

Latest Results

Periods ended:	6m June 30/23[A]		6m June 30/22[A]
	$000s	%Chg	$000s
Total revenue	590,225	+22	483,794
Net income	106,986	+66	64,396
	$		$
Earnings per share*	6.36		3.96

* Common

[A] Reported in accordance with IFRS

Historical Summary
(as originally stated)

Fiscal Year	Total Rev. $000s	Net Inc. Bef. Disc. $000s	EPS* $
2022[A]	1,019,336	140,161	8.61
2021[A]	826,722	244,943	15.12
2020[A]	652,922	136,505	9.21
2019[A]	609,383	64,349	4.40
2018[A]	506,191	53,124	3.78

* Common

[A] Reported in accordance with IFRS

G.56 Gold Flora Corporation

Symbol - GRAM **Exchange** - NEO **CUSIP** - 38090M
Head Office - 3165 Red Hill Ave, Costa Mesa, CA, United States, 62626 **Telephone** - (949) 252-1908
Website - www.goldflora.com
Email - ir@goldflora.com
Investor Relations - Marshall Minor (949) 252-1908
Auditors - Marcum LLP C.P.A., New York, N.Y.
Transfer Agents - Odyssey Trust Company, Toronto, Ont.
Profile - (Del. 2023) Cultivates, manufactures, extracts, distributes and retails cannabis and cannabis products throughout California.

Owns and operates 20 retail stores, 12 house brands, three distribution centers, and one manufacturing facility and six cultivation facilities.

Retail operations include King's Crew in Long Beach, Airfield Supply Company in San Jose and the Higher Level chain serving Hollister and Seaside. Sells and distributes several prominent brands including its own premium lines of Gold Flora, Roll Bleezy, Sword & Stoned, Aviation Cannabis and Jetfuel Cannabis products.

Operations are conducted at a 200,000-sq.-ft. cannabis campus in Desert Hot Springs, which consists of indoor cultivation, manufacturing and extraction facilities, as well as its own distribution company. The campus has the ability to be expanded to 620,000 sq. ft.

In November 2022, the company acquired **Coastal Holding Company, LLC**, a retail dispensary and delivery operator, for issuance of 24,796,902 shares of wholly owned **Coast L Acquisition Corp.**. US$3,750,000 in cash and assumption of US$1,800,000 of debt. Subsequently, an additional 106,290 shares of Coast L were issued. The Coast L shares are exchangeable into common shares of the company on a 1-for-1 basis. Coastal's operating dispensaries are located in Santa Barbara, Pasadena, West Los Angeles, Stockton and Vallejo, Calif. At Mar. 31, 2023, 18,269,094 Coast L shares have been exchanged for common shares of the company and 6,635,098 remain outstanding.

In September 2022, the company acquired the remaining 15% interest of **Calma Weho, LLC**, an operating dispensary in West Hollywood, Calif., for issuance of 1,762,495 common shares valued at US$1,500,000.

Common delisted from NEO, Oct. 7, 2022.

Common listed on NEO, Oct. 7, 2022.

Recent Merger and Acquisition Activity

Status: completed **Revised:** July 7, 2023
UPDATE: The transaction was completed. PREVIOUS: TPCO Holdings Corp. agreed to the reverse takeover acquisition of Costa Mesa, Calif.-based Gold Flora, LLC, which has cultivation, manufacturing, extraction, distribution and retail cannabis operations in California. The transaction would consist of TPCO, Stately Capital Corporation and newly formed Gold Flora Corporation amalgamating to form a new company to be named Gold Flora Corporation, which would then acquire (old) Gold Flora. (New) Gold Flora would continue its incorporation from British Columbia into Delaware. TPCO shareholders would receive common shares of (new) Gold Flora on a one-for-one basis and (old) Gold Flora shareholders would receive 1.5233 (new) Gold Flora common shares for each (old) Gold Flora unit held, which would result in the issuance of a total of 312,138,271 (new) Gold Flora common shares. TPCO and (old) Gold Flora shareholders would hold a 49% and 51% interest in (new) Gold Flora, respectively. (New) Gold Flora would have 20 retail stores, 12 house brands, three distribution centers, and one manufacturing facility and six cultivation facilities in California. (New) Gold Flora would remain a reporting issuer in Canada on the NEO Exchange.

Predecessor Detail - Succeeded TPCO Holding Corp., July 7, 2023, pursuant to the amalgamation of TPCO Holding Corp., Stately Capital Corporation and newly formed Gold Flora Corporation to form (new) Gold Flora Corporation, which concurrently acquired Costa Mesa, Calif.-based Gold Flora, LLC by reverse takeover and domesticated in the U.S. as a Delaware corporation.

Directors - Troy Datcher, chr., Calif.; Laurie Holcomb, CEO, Calif.; Mark Castaneda, Calif.; Al Foreman, New York, N.Y.; Michael W. Lau; Heather Molloy; Jeffrey Sears

Other Exec. Officers - Marshall Minor, CFO; Greg Gamet, chief opers. officer; Philip Hague, chief cultivation officer; Mark Russ, chief revenue officer

Capital Stock

	Authorized (shs.)	Outstanding (shs.)[1]
Preferred	10,000,000	nil
Common	450,000,000	312,138,271

[1] At July 10, 2023

Major Shareholder - Laurie Holcomb held 18.18% interest at July 10, 2023.

Price Range - GRAM/NEO

Year	Volume	High	Low	Close
2022	706,000	$0.75	$0.20	$0.20

Recent Close: $0.18

Capital Stock Changes - Pursuant to the July 7, 2023, amalgamation of TPCO Holding Corp., Stately Capital Corporation and Gold Flora Corporation to form Gold Flora Corporation (new) and concurrent reverse takeover acquisition of Gold Flora, LLC by Gold Flora (new), a total of 312,138,271 common shares were issued to the shareholders of TPCO (1-for-1 basis) and (old) Gold Flora (1.5233-for-1 basis).

Wholly Owned Subsidiaries

Gold Flora, LLC, Costa Mesa, Calif.
TPCO US Holding LLC, United States.

Note: The preceding list includes only the major related companies in which interests are held.

Financial Statistics

Periods ended:	12m Dec. 31/22[§A]		12m Dec. 31/21[A1]
	US$000s	%Chg	US$000s
Operating revenue	**149,297**	**-14**	**173,415**
Cost of sales	108,356		153,182
Salaries & benefits	n.a.		36,865
General & admin expense	n.a.		89,862
Stock-based compensation	n.a.		20,456
Operating expense	**108,356**	**-64**	**300,365**
Operating income	**40,941**	**n.a.**	**(126,950)**
Deprec., depl. & amort.	n.a.		27,616
Finance income	846		1,245
Finance costs, gross	22,440		10,141
Write-downs/write-offs	(130,567)		(658,994)
Pre-tax income	**(142,923)**	**n.a.**	**(589,405)**
Income taxes	(13,410)		(2,373)
Net income	**(129,513)**	**n.a.**	**(587,032)**
Net inc. for equity hldrs	**(129,314)**	**n.a.**	**(587,060)**
Net inc. for non-cont. int	**(199)**	**n.a.**	**28**
Cash & equivalent	98,915		165,311
Inventories	17,311		27,240
Accounts receivable	3,392		4,706
Current assets	138,645		224,833
Long-term investments	1,478		2,500
Fixed assets, net	41,126		23,047
Right-of-use assets	63,007		53,004
Intangibles, net	123,282		266,195
Total assets	**417,091**	**-27**	**571,455**
Accts. pay. & accr. liabs	40,184		41,625
Current liabilities	90,372		58,687
Long-term debt, gross	58,526		9,324
Long-term debt, net	28,030		1,828
Long-term lease liabilities	139,384		64,561
Shareholders' equity	132,655		361,075
Non-controlling interest	174		nil
Cash from oper. activs	**n.a.**	**n.a.**	**(128,373)**
Cash from fin. activs	n.a.		(225,633)
Cash from invest. activs	n.a.		(53,724)
Net cash position	**98,915**	**-40**	**165,311**
Capital expenditures	n.a.		(9,760)
Capital disposals	n.a.		375
	US$		US$
Earnings per share*	n.a.		(6.18)
Cash flow per share*	n.a.		(1.35)
	shs		shs
No. of shs. o/s*	n.a.		97,065,092
Avg. no. of shs. o/s*	n.a.		95,006,080
	%		%
Net profit margin	(86.75)		(338.51)
Return on equity	(52.38)		n.m.
Return on assets	(22.09)		(97.86)
No. of employees (FTEs)	n.a.		513

* Common

§ Pro forma

[A] Reported in accordance with U.S. GAAP

[1] Results for 2021 and prior year pertain to TPCO Holding Corp.

Historical Summary
(as originally stated)

Fiscal Year	Oper. Rev. US$000s	Net Inc. Bef. Disc. US$000s	EPS* US$
2022[§A]	149,297	(129,513)	n.a.
2021[A]	173,415	(587,032)	(6.18)
2020[A]	nil	(6,464)	(1.90)

* Common

§ Pro forma

[A] Reported in accordance with U.S. GAAP

G.57 Goldcliff Resource Corporation

Symbol - GCN **Exchange** - TSX-VEN **CUSIP** - 38076H
Head Office - 400-789 Pender St W, Vancouver, BC, V6C 1H2 **Telephone** - (250) 764-8879 **Toll-free** - (866) 769-4802 **Fax** - (250) 764-5134
Website - www.goldcliff.com
Email - gwsanders@gmail.com
Investor Relations - George W. Sanders (866) 769-4802
Auditors - Davidson & Company LLP C.A., Vancouver, B.C.
Bankers - Bank of Montreal, Vancouver, B.C.
Lawyers - Vector Corporate Finance Lawyers, Vancouver, B.C.
Transfer Agents - Computershare Trust Company of Canada Inc., Vancouver, B.C.
Profile - (B.C. 1986) Has mineral interests in Nevada and British Columbia. Also developing an online crowd-funding platform.

In Nevada, holds options from **Ely Gold Royalties Inc.** to acquire Nevada Rand gold-silver prospect, 25 claims; and Aurora West prospect, 51 claims, both in Mineral cty.

In British Columbia, holds formerly producing Ainsworth silver-graphite property, 1,856 hectares, west of Kootenay Lake; option to acquire nearby 2,915 hectares of mineral tenures and 295 hectares of crown grants; Panorama Ridge gold prospect, 7,655 hectares, 6 km northeast of Hedley; and option to acquire Kettle Valley gold prospect, 33 km north of Rock Creek, requiring exploration expenditures of $1,000,000 by December 2023.

The company is also developing DirectRoyalty, an online crowd-funding platform that will provide investors with direct ownership of royalties, income streams and advanced sales from precious metals production.

Directors - George W. Sanders, pres. & CEO, Kelowna, B.C.; Gary R. Moore, v-p, fin. & CFO, Delta, B.C.; Edwin R. Rockel, Vancouver, B.C.; Paul F. Saxton, Furry Creek, B.C.; Shobodian (Sam) Zastavnikovich, B.C.

Other Exec. Officers - Graham H. Scott, corp. sec.

Capital Stock

	Authorized (shs.)	Outstanding (shs.)[1]
Common	unlimited	61,911,241

[1] At Mar. 28, 2023

Major Shareholder - George W. Sanders held 33.27% interest at Mar. 28, 2023.

Price Range - GCN/TSX-VEN

Year	Volume	High	Low	Close
2022	12,174,161	$0.18	$0.03	$0.03
2021	13,171,137	$0.14	$0.07	$0.09
2020	27,496,385	$0.18	$0.07	$0.12
2019	6,040,405	$0.17	$0.05	$0.11
2018	8,475,100	$0.23	$0.05	$0.05

Recent Close: $0.03

Capital Stock Changes - During fiscal 2022, common shares were issued as follows: 1,950,000 by private placement, 1,750,000 on exercise of warrants, 700,000 for debt settlement and 251,923 on exercise of options.

Wholly Owned Subsidiaries

Goldcliff Resources (US) Inc., Nev.

Investments

Lincoln Gold Mining Inc., Vancouver, B.C. (see Survey of Mines)

Financial Statistics

Periods ended:	12m Oct. 31/22[A]		12m Oct. 31/21[A]
	$000s	%Chg	$000s
Exploration expense	549		451
General & admin expense	226		286
Stock-based compensation	179		18
Operating expense	**954**	**+26**	**755**
Operating income	**(954)**	**n.a.**	**(755)**
Write-downs/write-offs	nil		68
Pre-tax income	**(1,238)**	**n.a.**	**(814)**
Net income	**(1,238)**	**n.a.**	**(814)**
Cash & equivalent	206		870
Accounts receivable	31		26
Current assets	237		902
Explor./devel. properties	548		413
Total assets	**854**	**-38**	**1,385**
Accts. pay. & accr. liabs	58		72
Current liabilities	238		85
Shareholders' equity	616		1,300
Cash from oper. activs	**(753)**	**n.a.**	**(818)**
Cash from fin. activs	553		388
Cash from invest. activs	(133)		(154)
Net cash position	**96**	**-78**	**430**
Capital expenditures	(135)		(171)
	$		$
Earnings per share*	(0.02)		(0.02)
Cash flow per share*	(0.01)		(0.02)
	shs		shs
No. of shs. o/s*	61,561,241		56,909,318
Avg. no. of shs. o/s*	59,899,808		49,272,354
	%		%
Net profit margin	n.a.		n.a.
Return on equity	(129.23)		(54.39)
Return on assets	(110.59)		(50.40)

* Common

[A] Reported in accordance with IFRS

Historical Summary
(as originally stated)

Fiscal Year	Oper. Rev.	Net Inc. Bef. Disc.	EPS*
	$000s	$000s	$
2022[A]	nil	(1,238)	(0.02)
2021[A]	nil	(814)	(0.02)
2020[A]	nil	(934)	(0.02)
2019[A]	nil	(840)	(0.03)
2018[A]	nil	(207)	(0.01)

* Common

[A] Reported in accordance with IFRS

G.58 Golden Star Capital Ventures Inc.

Symbol - GCV.P **Exchange** - TSX-VEN **CUSIP** - 38119D

Head Office - 1510-789 Pender St W, Vancouver, BC, V6C 1H2 **Telephone** - (604) 603-8979

Email - pacificpioneer@hotmail.com

Investor Relations - George Wang (236) 888-3322

Auditors - Mao & Ying LLP C.A., Vancouver, B.C.

Transfer Agents - Odyssey Trust Company, Vancouver, B.C.

Profile - (B.C. 2021) Capital Pool Company.

Common listed on TSX-VEN, Nov. 10, 2022.

Directors - George Wang, CEO, Richmond, B.C.; Wei Kang, CFO & corp. sec., Vancouver, B.C.; Hong (Iris) Duan, West Vancouver, B.C.; Ian M. Mallmann, Richmond, B.C.

Capital Stock

	Authorized (shs.)	Outstanding (shs.)[1]
Common	unlimited	4,000,000

[1] At Nov. 10, 2022

Major Shareholder - George Wang held 25% interest, Hong (Iris) Duan held 10% interest and Wei Kang held 10% interest at Nov. 10, 2022.

Capital Stock Changes - On Nov. 10, 2022, an initial public offering of 2,000,000 common shares was completed at 10¢ per share.

G.59 GoldMoney Inc.

Symbol - XAU **Exchange** - TSX **CUSIP** - 38149A

Head Office - 307-334 Adelaide St W, Toronto, ON, M5V 1R4 **Telephone** - (647) 499-6748 **Toll-free** - (800) 854-7418 **Fax** - (647) 499-4435

Website - www.goldmoney.com

Email - mark.olson@goldmoney.com

Investor Relations - Mark Olson (647) 250-7098

Auditors - KPMG LLP C.A., Toronto, Ont.

Lawyers - Peterson McVicar LLP, Toronto, Ont.

Transfer Agents - TSX Trust Company, Toronto, Ont.

FP500 Revenue Ranking - 536

Employees - 48 at June 13, 2023

Profile - (B.C. 2019; orig. Can., 2015 amalg.) Provides precious metal investment and services including trading, delivery and storage as well as operates a precious metals payment network. Also holds an interest in **Mene Inc.**, which crafts and sells gold and platinum jewelry.

Operations are organized into three segments:

Goldmoney Holding® operates Goldmoney.com, an online platform which allows users to create an account that enables them to purchase, hold, sell and exchange weight of physical gold, silver, platinum and palladium, which are insured and securely stored in 13 vaults in seven countries. Clients can fund and purchase precious metal in nine major currencies.

Wholly owned **Schiff Gold LLC** offers the purchase and sale of physical precious metals in the form of bars, coins and wafers direct-to-consumer delivery without requiring a Goldmoney Holding®. Also provides physical sale and fulfillment services to Goldmoney Holding® owners.

Affiliate **Mene Inc.** designs, manufactures and markets 24-karat gold and platinum jewelry through a transparent pricing and e-commerce site under the Mene brand.

Predecessor Detail - Name changed from BitGold Inc., July 30, 2015.

Directors - Roy Sebag, chr., pres. & CEO, Oxford, Oxon., United Kingdom; James Turk†, London, Middx., United Kingdom; Andres Finkielsztain, Buenos Aires, Argentina; Mahendra Naik, Toronto, Ont.; Stefan Wieler, Zurich, Switzerland

Other Exec. Officers - Paul Mennega, COO; Mark Olson, CFO; Alessandro (Alex) Premoli, chief tech. officer

† Lead director

Capital Stock

	Authorized (shs.)	Outstanding (shs.)[1]
Common	unlimited	14,000,495

[1] At June 23, 2023

Normal Course Issuer Bid - The company plans to make normal course purchases of up to 1,097,557 post-consolidated common shares representing 10% of the public float. The bid commenced on Aug. 30, 2022, and expires on Aug. 29, 2023.

Major Shareholder - Roy Sebag held 23.78% interest at June 13, 2023.

Price Range - XAU/TSX

Year	Volume	High	Low	Close
2022	1,529,981	$11.35	$7.25	$8.45
2021	4,023,194	$22.00	$9.15	$9.90
2020	4,743,442	$16.50	$7.00	$12.35
2019	5,617,821	$13.25	$7.65	$9.35
2018	4,737,369	$33.25	$7.10	$8.60

Consolidation: 1-for-5 cons. in June 2023

Recent Close: $9.61

Capital Stock Changes - On June 23, 2023, common shares were consolidated on a 1-for-5 basis.

During fiscal 2023, 281,445 common shares were issued under restricted unit plan and 5,934,073 common shares were repurchased under a Normal Course Issuer Bid.

During fiscal 2022, common shares were issued as follows: 510,365 under restricted share unit plan and 5,025 on exercise of options; 474,500 common shares were repurchased under a Normal Course Issuer Bid.

Wholly Owned Subsidiaries

BlockVault Inc., Toronto, Ont.
- 100% int. in **BlockVault Holding Limited**, Jersey.

Goldmoney BVI Inc., British Virgin Islands.
- 100% int. in **Goldmoney Europe Limited**, Jersey.
  - 100% int. in **Goldmoney Wealth Limited**, Jersey.

Goldmoney IP Holdings Corp., Canada.
Goldmoney Vault Inc., Toronto, Ont.
Goldmoney Vault (UK) Ltd., United Kingdom.
Goldmoney Vault USA Inc., Del.
Goldmoney Vault USA Limited, Del.
Schiff Gold LLC, Conn.

Subsidiaries

60% int. in **Totenpass Inc**, Canada.

Investments

36.1% int. in **Mene Inc.**, Toronto, Ont. (see separate coverage)

Financial Statistics

Periods ended:	12m Mar. 31/23[A]		12m Mar. 31/22[A]
	$000s	%Chg	$000s
Operating revenue	**302,854**	**-14**	**350,246**
Cost of sales	290,013		337,056
Salaries & benefits	4,775		4,350
Research & devel. expense	708		664
General & admin expense	7,460		9,139
Stock-based compensation	565		1,457
Operating expense	**303,521**	**-14**	**352,666**
Operating income	**(667)**	**n.a.**	**(2,420)**
Deprec., depl. & amort.	1,184		1,023
Finance income	1,789		388
Finance costs, gross	nil		23
Investment income	(251)		(412)
Write-downs/write-offs	(9,500)		(13,800)
Pre-tax income	**7,884**	**n.a.**	**(5,620)**
Income taxes	1,190		442
Net income	**6,695**	**n.a.**	**(6,062)**
Net inc. for equity hldrs	**6,803**	**n.a.**	**(5,750)**
Net inc. for non-cont. int.	**(109)**	**n.a.**	**(312)**
Cash & equivalent	43,275		33,837
Inventories	53,228		54,158
Accounts receivable	1,022		887
Long-term investments	34,604		34,818
Fixed assets, net	882		1,405
Intangibles, net	29,919		40,086
Total assets	**176,051**	**-1**	**176,963**
Accts. pay. & accr. liabs	3,928		2,027
Shareholders' equity	172,544		175,249
Non-controlling interest	(421)		(312)
Cash from oper. activs	**21,817**	**n.a.**	**(7,182)**
Cash from fin. activs	(10,030)		(1,250)
Cash from invest. activs	1,930		10,550
Net cash position	**40,073**	**+54**	**26,031**
Capital expenditures	(5)		(44)
	$		$
Earnings per share*	0.45		(0.40)
Cash flow per share*	1.47		(0.47)
	shs		shs
No. of shs. o/s*	13,995,742		15,126,267
Avg. no. of shs. o/s*	14,840,111		15,152,854
	%		%
Net profit margin	2.21		(1.73)
Return on equity	3.91		(3.23)
Return on assets	3.79		(3.29)

* Common

[A] Reported in accordance with IFRS

Historical Summary
(as originally stated)

Fiscal Year	Oper. Rev.	Net Inc. Bef. Disc.	EPS*
	$000s	$000s	$
2023[A]	302,854	6,695	0.45
2022[A]	350,246	(6,062)	(0.40)
2021[A]	654,410	11,652	0.75
2020[A]	458,873	(9,713)	(0.65)
2019[A]	281,544	21,680	1.40

* Common

[A] Reported in accordance with IFRS

Note: Adjusted throughout for 1-for-5 cons. in June 2023

G.60 The Good Flour Corp.

Symbol - GFCO **Exchange** - CSE **CUSIP** - 382099

Head Office - 5791 Sidley St, Burnaby, BC, V5J 5E6 **Telephone** - (604) 568-1598

Website - goodflour.co

Email - info@goodflour.co

Investor Relations - Matthew Clayton (604) 568-1598

Auditors - Dale Matheson Carr-Hilton LaBonte LLP C.A., Vancouver, B.C.

Transfer Agents - TSX Trust Company, Vancouver, B.C.

Profile - (B.C. 2014; orig. Sask., 2009) Manufactures and distributes gluten free (GF) all-purpose baking flour and other GF products under The Good Flour Co. brand.

Other GF products include pizza and pasta flour, tempura batter mix, fish and chips batter mix, fried chicken mix, pancake and waffle mix, vanilla bean cake mix and pizza shells. Products are manufactured in Vancouver and Burnaby, B.C. Also has a co-packing partnership with a flour-milling and ingredient company in the United States for its alt-wheat flours. Products are distributed to retailers and food service clients including hotels, resorts and restaurants, and directly to customers through its website, goodflour.co. Customers are located across North America, Australia and the United Kingdom.

During fiscal 2022, the company transferred its legacy Scoot-E-Bike® assets to **Raytroniks Corporation**. The assets included intellectual property, Scoot-E-Bike® inventory and the company's ownership of Scoot-E-Bike Inc. In return, Raytroniks settled all debt claims owed to them by the company. In addition, the company sold assets to **West Hall Tech Ltd.** including scooter inventory, parts and components, all rights and logos held by the company to the unregistered trademarks "LOOPShare" and "Loop Scooters" and the loopscooters.com domain name. In return, West Hall entered into a lease agreement for the company's former premises at 131 Water Street in Vancouver, B.C., and assumed responsibility for the disposal of the assets.

Predecessor Detail - Name changed from LOOPShare Ltd., Nov. 1, 2021, pursuant to the reverse takeover acquisition of VGAN Brands Inc.

Directors - Matthew Clayton, chr., B.C.; Hamid Salimian, CEO, Vancouver, B.C.; Olen Aasen, Vancouver, B.C.; Denis G. Silva, Burnaby, B.C.; C. Paul Sparkes, Toronto, Ont.

Other Exec. Officers - Dean Golbeck, CFO; Jennifer E. (Jen) Peters, pres., VGAN Brands Inc.

Capital Stock

	Authorized (shs.)	Outstanding (shs.)[1]
Class A	unlimited	72,181,457

[1] At Mar. 1, 2023

Major Shareholder - Widely held at Oct. 27, 2022.

Price Range - GFCO/CSE

Year	Volume	High	Low	Close
2022	1,132,510	$0.82	$0.33	$0.70
2021	1,088,681	$1.90	$0.43	$0.61
2020	407,002	$7.50	$0.70	$0.70
2019	320,175	$21.50	$2.00	$3.80
2018	52,264	$8.00	$3.50	$5.50

Consolidation: 1-for-10 cons. in Mar. 2021; 1-for-10 cons. in Oct. 2019

Recent Close: $0.25

Capital Stock Changes - On Mar. 11, 2021, class A shares were consolidated on a 1-for-10 basis. In November 2021, 60,075,000 post-consolidated class A shares were issued pursuant to the reverse takeover acquisition of VGAN Brands Inc. Also during fiscal 2022, 165,000 post-consolidated class A shares were issued for debt settlement and 11 post-consolidated class A shares were cancelled.

Wholly Owned Subsidiaries

The Good Flour Milling Corp., B.C.
Good Flour USA Corp., Nev.

Financial Statistics

Periods ended:	12m June 30/22[A1]		12m June 30/21[A2]
	$000s	%Chg	$000s
Operating revenue	**481**	**n.a.**	**nil**
Cost of sales	512		nil
General & admin expense	1,703		133
Stock-based compensation	384		nil
Operating expense	**2,599**	**n.m.**	**133**
Operating income	**(2,118)**	**n.a.**	**(133)**
Deprec., depl. & amort.	71		nil
Finance costs, gross	61		nil
Write-downs/write-offs	(726)		nil
Pre-tax income	**(5,476)**	**n.a.**	**(133)**
Net inc. bef. disc. opers	**(5,476)**	**n.a.**	**(133)**
Income from disc. opers	(69)		nil
Net income	**(5,545)**	**n.a.**	**(133)**
Cash & equivalent	1,344		755
Inventories	90		nil
Current assets	1,736		836
Fixed assets, net	709		nil
Right-of-use assets	311		nil
Total assets	**2,757**	**+230**	**836**
Accts. pay. & accr. liabs	976		120
Current liabilities	1,180		120
Long-term debt, gross	533		nil
Long-term debt, net	533		nil
Long-term lease liabilities	116		nil
Shareholders' equity	928		716
Cash from oper. activs	**(3,143)**	**n.a.**	**(14)**
Cash from fin. activs	4,381		850
Cash from invest. activs	(661)		(82)
Net cash position	**1,344**	**+78**	**755**
Capital expenditures	(796)		nil
	$		$
Earnings per share*	(0.10)		(0.00)
Cash flow per share*	(0.05)		nil
	shs		shs
No. of shs. o/s*	63,284,468		n.a.
Avg. no. of shs. o/s*	63,284,468		n.a.
	%		%
Net profit margin	n.m.		n.a.
Return on equity	(666.18)		n.m.
Return on assets	(301.42)		(17.76)

* Class A
[A] Reported in accordance with IFRS
[1] Results reflect the Nov. 5, 2021, reverse takeover acquisition of VGAN Brands Inc.
[2] Results pertain to VGAN Brands Inc.

Historical Summary
(as originally stated)

Fiscal Year	Oper. Rev. $000s	Net Inc. Bef. Disc. $000s	EPS* $
2022[A]	481	(5,476)	(0.10)
2021[A]	nil	(133)	(0.00)
2020[A1]	905	(2,802)	(0.94)
2019[A]	30	(4,650)	(3.90)
2018[A]	nil	(2,734)	(6.00)

* Class A
[A] Reported in accordance with IFRS
[1] Results for 2020 and prior years pertain to LOOPShare Ltd.

Note: Adjusted throughout for 1-for-10 cons. in Mar. 2021; 1-for-10 cons. in Oct. 2019

G.61 Good Gamer Entertainment Inc.

Symbol - GOOD **Exchange** - TSX-VEN **CUSIP** - 382113
Head Office - 764-1055 Dunsmuir St, Vancouver, BC, V7X 1L3
Toll-free - (888) 337-5889
Website - goodgamer.ca
Email - info@goodgamer.gg
Investor Relations - Zahara Kanji (888) 337-5889
Auditors - BF Borgers CPA PC C.P.A., Lakewood, Colo.
Transfer Agents - Computershare Trust Company of Canada Inc., Vancouver, B.C.

Profile - (B.C. 2011) Operates a play-to-earn game discovery and entertainment platform and an online eSports skills-based, real money gaming tournament management platform in the United States and Canada. Also develops blockchain solutions for a non-fungible token-based blockchain game.

The company's PlayCash mobile application allows users to play mobile games, take surveys and watch videos to earn in-app currency that can be used on gift cards from providers including Visa, Master Card and Amazon.

The Good Gamer tournament management platform allows game developers to enable social competition in their games and host eSports tournaments for players to win real cash prizes. Players are able to enter tournaments and win prizes upon paying an entrance fee. Mobile game publishers are able to monetize their games by way of retaining a percentage of real money competitions. Two games from the company's portfolio, Balloon Protect and Lava Monster, have been converted to offer tournament play facilitated by the Good Gamer tournament management platform.

The company is also developing blockchain applications to create non-fungible tokens (NFT), artwork, characters and a NFT-based blockchain game under the Chosen Ones brand as well as developing a NFT marketplace where players can purchase and sell various NFTs to play in the game.

Predecessor Detail - Name changed from Credent Capital Corp., Oct. 14, 2021, pursuant to the Qualifying Transaction reverse takeover acquisition of Good Gamer Corp.; basis 1 new for 5 old shs.

Directors - Charlo Barbosa, CEO, North Vancouver, B.C.; Adam Hudani, v-p, opers., Maple Ridge, B.C.; Howard Donaldson, Santa Monica, Calif.; Russel H. (Russ) McMeekin, Calgary, Alta.

Other Exec. Officers - Zahara (Zara) Kanji, CFO; Shoukri Kattan, chief architect; Xing (James) Hong, v-p, opers.; Kelly Pladson, corp. sec.

Capital Stock

	Authorized (shs.)	Outstanding (shs.)[1]
Common	unlimited	42,567,756

[1] At Nov. 24, 2022

Major Shareholder - Charlo Barbosa held 30.72% interest at Nov. 10, 2022.

Price Range - GOOD/TSX-VEN

Year	Volume	High	Low	Close
2022	5,019,381	$0.84	$0.05	$0.08
2021	613,944	$0.78	$0.54	$0.65

Recent Close: $0.07

Capital Stock Changes - In October 2021, common shares were consolidated on a 1-for-5 basis and 40,414,090 post-consolidated common shares were issued pursuant to the Qualifying Transaction reverse takeover acquisition of Good Gamer Corp. (GGC), including 10,000,000 common shares on exchange of subscription receipts sold previously by GGC at 40¢ each. Also during the 15-month period ended Mar. 31, 2022, post-consolidated common shares were issued as follows: 1,000,000 as finder's fee, 212,000 for debt settlement and 91,666 on exercise of options.

Wholly Owned Subsidiaries

Good Gamer Corp., Vancouver, B.C.
- 100% int. in **Good Gamer Corp. (US)**, United States.
- 99% int. in **Good Gamer India Pvt. Ltd.**, India. Discontinued
- 100% int. in **Perk Power Corp.**, Canada.

Financial Statistics

Periods ended:	15m Mar. 31/22[A1]		12m Dec. 31/20[¤A]
	$000s	%Chg	$000s
Operating revenue	**1**	**n.a.**	**2**
Salaries & benefits	469		98
Research & devel. expense	596		nil
General & admin expense	1,767		1,675
Stock-based compensation	691		132
Operating expense	**3,523**	**n.a.**	**1,905**
Operating income	**(3,522)**	**n.a.**	**(1,903)**
Deprec., depl. & amort.	235		316
Finance costs, gross	23		41
Write-downs/write-offs	1,050		nil
Pre-tax income	**(18,301)**	**n.a.**	**(2,179)**
Net inc. bef. disc. opers	**(18,301)**	**n.a.**	**(2,179)**
Income from disc. opers	(144)		(107)
Net income	**(18,445)**	**n.a.**	**(2,286)**
Net inc. for equity hldrs	**(18,444)**	**n.a.**	**(2,286)**
Net inc. for non-cont. int	**(1)**	**n.a.**	**nil**
Cash & equivalent	1,583		798
Accounts receivable	nil		76
Current assets	2,068		1,314
Fixed assets, net	5		4
Intangibles, net	14		1,217
Total assets	**2,086**	**n.a.**	**2,583**
Accts. pay. & accr. liabs	413		628
Current liabilities	419		646
Long-term debt, gross	nil		53
Long-term debt, net	nil		53
Shareholders' equity	1,669		1,885
Non-controlling interest	(2)		nil
Cash from oper. activs	**(3,105)**	**n.a.**	**(2,061)**
Cash from fin. activs	3,829		3,270
Cash from invest. activs	(61)		(481)
Net cash position	**1,583**	**n.a.**	**798**
Capital expenditures	(2)		(3)
	$		$
Earnings per share*	(0.52)		(0.55)
Cash flow per share*	(0.09)		n.a.
	shs		shs
No. of shs. o/s*	42,582,756		n.a.
Avg. no. of shs. o/s*	35,259,022		n.a.
	%		%
Net profit margin	...		n.m.
Return on equity	...		(165.39)
Return on assets	...		(112.70)

* Common
[¤] Restated
[A] Reported in accordance with IFRS
[1] Results reflect the Oct. 18, 2021, reverse takeover acquisition of Good Gamer Corp.

Latest Results

Periods ended:	6m Sept. 30/22[A]		6m Sept. 30/21[A]
	$000s	%Chg	$000s
Operating revenue	98	n.m.	1
Net inc. bef. disc. opers	(949)	n.a.	(1,178)
Income from disc. opers	...		(85)
Net income	(949)	n.a.	(1,263)
Net inc. for equity hldrs	(949)	n.a.	(1,264)
	$		$
Earnings per share*	(0.03)		n.a.

* Common
[A] Reported in accordance with IFRS

Historical Summary
(as originally stated)

Fiscal Year	Oper. Rev. $000s	Net Inc. Bef. Disc. $000s	EPS* $
2022[A1,2]	1	(18,301)	(0.52)
2020[A3]	14	(2,286)	(0.55)
2019[A]	3	(385)	(1.50)

* Common
[A] Reported in accordance with IFRS
[1] 15 months ended Mar. 31, 2022.
[2] Results reflect the Oct. 18, 2021, reverse takeover acquisition of Good Gamer Corp.
[3] Results for 2020 and prior periods pertain to Good Gamer Corp.

Note: Adjusted throughout for 1-for-5 cons. in Oct. 2021

G.62 good natured Products Inc.

Symbol - GDNP **Exchange** - TSX-VEN **CUSIP** - 38210L
Head Office - 814-470 Granville St, Vancouver, BC, V6C 1V5
Telephone - (604) 998-4058 **Toll-free** - (877) 286-0617
Website - investor.goodnaturedproducts.com
Email - invest@goodnaturedproducts.com
Investor Relations - Spencer Churchill (877) 286-0617
Auditors - Deloitte LLP C.A., Vancouver, B.C.

Lawyers - Stikeman Elliott LLP, Vancouver, B.C.
Transfer Agents - TSX Trust Company
Employees - 196 at Dec. 31, 2022
Profile - (B.C. 2015; orig. Alta., 2014) Designs, produces and distributes high-performance plant-based bioplastics for use in packaging and durable product applications.

Offers more than 400 products and services including food packaging for baked goods, deli and prepared meals, and fruits and veggies; compostable take out containers such as hot cups and lids, plates, carry out boxes, cutlery, and soup bowls and lids; home and business products such as bins, totes and crates; commercial products such as pallet stretch wrap, rollstock and resin; and services such as custom thermoformed packaging and polymer engineering. Has more than 1,200 active national, regional and small business recurring customers across 50 states and provinces. Also offers direct purchasing through Amazon and its own e-commerce platform in the U.S. and Canada.

Through wholly owned **Shepherd Thermoforming & Packaging Inc.**, designs custom packaging including engineering, mold production and final product manufacturing for both thin gauge and heavy gauge applications.

Through wholly owned **Integrated Packaging Films GP Inc.**, manufactures rigid plastic sheets for use in thermoformed packaging of clients in the electronics, retail, industrial, food and medical packaging markets.

Through wholly owned **Ex-Tech Plastics Inc.**, produces plastic sheet and film products, including extruded roll stock sheet for thermoformed packaging.

Through wholly owned **FormTex Plastics Corporation**, manufactures custom plastic packaging for the medical, food, electronic, industrial and retail end markets using thermoforming machines.

Recent Merger and Acquisition Activity

Status: completed **Revised:** Sept. 30, 2022
UPDATE: The transaction was completed. PREVIOUS: good natured Products Inc. agreed to acquire the land and buildings at its Ayr, Ont., manufacturing location for $9,400,000, which would be funded with a capital loan and drawings from a mortgage financing. The acquisition included an existing 30,000-sq.-ft. industrial building and 2,900,000 acres of land that has potential for future expansion.

Status: completed **Revised:** July 1, 2022
UPDATE: The transaction was completed. PREVIOUS: good natured Products Inc. agreed to acquire private Houston, Tex.-based FormTex Plastics Corporation, which manufactures custom plastic packaging for the medical, food, electronic, industrial and retail end markets using thermoforming machines, for US$4,800,000. The consideration would be financed with proceeds from a proposed bought deal public offering and a term loan.

Predecessor Detail - Name changed from Solegear Bioplastic Technologies Inc., Oct. 31, 2017.

Directors - Paul Antoniadis, exec. chr. & CEO, Vancouver, B.C.; Tami Kozikowsk, Minn.; Joel Marsh, Minneapolis, Minn.; Karl Sanft, Thousand Oaks, Calif.; Keith E. Spencer, Vancouver, B.C.

Other Exec. Officers - Kerry Biggs, CFO; Dr. Michel Labonté, chief tech. officer; Stephanie Zahn, chief growth officer; Don Holmstrom, exec. v-p, corp. devel., strategic partnerships & capital planning; Kevin Leong, v-p, fin.

Capital Stock

	Authorized (shs.)	Outstanding (shs.)[1]
Preferred	unlimited	nil
Common	unlimited	241,829,971

[1] At June 5, 2023.

Major Shareholder - Widely held at June 5, 2023.

Price Range - GDNP/TSX-VEN

Year	Volume	High	Low	Close
2022	34,544,529	$0.78	$0.23	$0.26
2021	196,708,937	$1.98	$0.65	$0.73
2020	101,061,274	$1.38	$0.09	$0.90
2019	26,590,478	$0.22	$0.09	$0.17
2018	14,725,822	$0.15	$0.09	$0.10

Recent Close: $0.10

Capital Stock Changes - In October 2022, 16,402,500 units (1 common share & 1 warrant) were issued without further consideration on exchange of special warrants sold in June 2022 at 40¢ each. Also during 2022, common shares were issued as follows: 2,113,000 on vesting of restricted and performance share units, 1,989,000 on exercise of warrants, 302,000 on exercise of options and 217,000 on conversion of debt.

Wholly Owned Subsidiaries

FormTex Plastics Corporation, Houston, Tex.
good natured Products (CAD) Inc., Vancouver, B.C.
- 100% int. in **good natured Products Industrial Canada GP**, Canada.
  - 0.01% int. in **good natured Products Industrial Canada LP**, Canada.
- 99.99% int. in **good natured Products Industrial Canada LP**, Canada.
- 100% int. in **good natured Products Packaging Brampton GP**, Ont.
  - 0.01% int. in **good natured Products Packaging Brampton LP**, Ont.
- 100% int. in **good natured Products Packaging Canada GP**, Ont.
  - 0.01% int. in **good natured Products Packaging Canada LP**, Ont.
- 99.99% int. in **good natured Products Packaging Canada LP**, Ont.
  - 99.99% int. in **good natured Products Packaging Brampton LP**, Ont.
- 100% int. in **good natured Products (US) Inc.**, United States.
  - 100% int. in **good natured Products Direct LLC**, Canada.
  - 100% int. in **good natured Products (Illinois) LLC**, Ill.
    - 100% int. in **Ex-Tech Plastics Inc.**, Ill.
  - 100% int. in **good natured Products Packaging US LLC**, United States.
  - 100% int. in **good natured Products Real Estate U.S., LLC**, United States.
  - 100% int. in **good natured Products (Texas) LLC**, Tex.
- 100% int. in **Integrated Packaging Films GP Inc.**, Ont.
  - 100% int. in **IPF Holdings Inc.**, Ayr, Ont.
- 100% int. in **Mechar Amco Ltd.**, Ont.
  - 50% int. in **IPF Holdings Inc.**, Ayr, Ont.
- 100% int. in **1306187 B.C. Ltd.**, B.C.

Good Natured Real Estate Holdings (Ontario) Inc.
Shepherd Thermoforming & Packaging Inc., Brampton, Ont.

Financial Statistics

Periods ended:	12m Dec. 31/22[A]		12m Dec. 31/21[A]
	$000s	%Chg	$000s
Operating revenue	**100,966**	**+65**	**61,132**
Cost of sales	72,982		44,644
Salaries & benefits	9,488		5,700
Research & devel. expense	741		519
General & admin expense	16,884		12,965
Stock-based compensation	2,150		2,254
Operating expense	**102,245**	**+55**	**66,082**
Operating income	**(1,279)**	**n.a.**	**(4,950)**
Deprec., depl. & amort.	3,536		1,941
Finance income	15		85
Finance costs, gross	5,550		4,552
Pre-tax income	**(11,798)**	**n.a.**	**(12,821)**
Income taxes	(216)		(126)
Net income	**(11,582)**	**n.a.**	**(12,695)**
Cash & equivalent	11,860		10,655
Inventories	12,663		16,036
Accounts receivable	9,360		13,689
Current assets	34,812		41,367
Fixed assets, net	44,692		30,463
Right-of-use assets	5,001		2,164
Intangibles, net	13,489		10,809
Total assets	**104,441**	**+15**	**90,529**
Accts. pay. & accr. liabs.	18,265		17,699
Current liabilities	24,858		57,380
Long-term debt, gross	61,913		46,355
Long-term debt, net	55,320		6,674
Shareholders' equity	18,950		21,092
Cash from oper. activs.	**4,565**	**n.a.**	**(13,661)**
Cash from fin. activs.	16,463		36,387
Cash from invest. activs.	(20,522)		(20,251)
Net cash position	**11,860**	**+11**	**10,655**
Capital expenditures	(15,063)		(4,264)
Capital disposals	109		nil
	$		$
Earnings per share*	(0.05)		(0.06)
Cash flow per share*	0.02		(0.06)
	shs		shs
No. of shs. o/s*	241,707,000		220,683,000
Avg. no. of shs. o/s*	227,845,000		210,831,000
	%		%
Net profit margin	(11.47)		(20.77)
Return on equity	(57.85)		(110.85)
Return on assets	(6.29)		(11.49)
No. of employees (FTEs)	196		191

* Common
[A] Reported in accordance with IFRS

Latest Results

Periods ended:	3m Mar. 31/23[A]		3m Mar. 31/22[A]
	$000s	%Chg	$000s
Operating revenue	20,315	-22	25,936
Net income	(2,521)	n.a.	(1,592)
	$		$
Earnings per share*	(0.01)		(0.01)

* Common
[A] Reported in accordance with IFRS

Historical Summary
(as originally stated)

Fiscal Year	Oper. Rev.	Net Inc. Bef. Disc.	EPS*
	$000s	$000s	$
2022[A]	100,966	(11,582)	(0.05)
2021[A]	61,132	(12,695)	(0.06)
2020[A]	16,713	(7,187)	(0.06)
2019[A]	10,099	(3,474)	(0.03)
2018[A]	5,103	(3,106)	(0.03)

* Common
[A] Reported in accordance with IFRS

G.63 The Good Shroom Co Inc.

Symbol - MUSH **Exchange -** TSX-VEN **CUSIP -** 88338U
Head Office - 11 Beacon Rd, Kirkland, QC, J7V 5V5 **Telephone -** (514) 924-2574
Website - www.thegoodshroom.co
Email - eric@teonan.com
Investor Relations - Eric Ronsse (514) 924-2574
Auditors - Raymond Chabot Grant Thornton LLP C.A., Montréal, Qué.
Transfer Agents - TSX Trust Company, Toronto, Ont.
Profile - (Can. 2021; orig. Ont., 2011) Develops, manufactures and sells wellness beverages, cannabis and hash products.

Wholly owned **Teonan Biomedical Inc.** produces instant coffees and teas sold in ready to use powder form under the brand Teonan®, which contain a custom blend of organic functional mushrooms and a dose of probiotics. Also holds a licence from Health Canada to manufacture and sell cannabis related products under Velada™ and Nordique Royale™ brands which include cannabis-infused beverage line made with functional mushrooms; hashish products, which consist of Afghan Gold, OG Hawaiian, Le Kush X, Le Choix du Nord; and dried flower products, which consist of Sky Cuddler, Sage n' Sour and Cherry Blossom. Products are sold across Canada and the U.S. through authorized retailers and the company's own and third party online platforms.

Predecessor Detail - Name changed from Cluny Capital Corp., Apr. 15, 2021, pursuant to the Qualifying Transaction reverse takeover acquisition of Teonan Biomedical Inc., and concurrent amalgamation of Teonan Biomedical with a wholly owned subsidiary; basis 1 new for 3 old shs.

Directors - Eric Ronsse, chr. & CEO, Kirkland, Qué.; Franck Aton, Paris, France; Claude Dufresne, Mont-Tremblant, Qué.; Steven (Steve) Saviuk, Beaconsfield, Qué.

Other Exec. Officers - Scott Jardin, CFO; Anik Gendron, corp. sec.

Capital Stock

	Authorized (shs.)	Outstanding (shs.)[1]
Common	unlimited	48,624,682

[1] At Jan. 9, 2023

Major Shareholder - Eric Ronsse held 37.7% interest at Jan. 9, 2022.

Price Range - MUSH/TSX-VEN

Year	Volume	High	Low	Close
2022	12,100,104	$0.14	$0.02	$0.08
2021	13,383,361	$0.52	$0.08	$0.10
2020	353,333	$0.21	$0.09	$0.15
2019	15,500	$0.20	$0.15	$0.15
2018	107,333	$0.33	$0.15	$0.15

Consolidation: 1-for-3 cons. in Apr. 2021
Recent Close: $0.17
Capital Stock Changes - During fiscal 2022, 400,000 common shares were issued for services.

Wholly Owned Subsidiaries

Teonan Biomedical Inc., Kirkland, Qué.

Financial Statistics

Periods ended:	12m July 31/22[A]		12m July 31/21[A1]
	$000s	%Chg	$000s
Operating revenue	**1,523**	**+529**	**242**
Cost of goods sold	986		180
Salaries & benefits	493		454
General & admin expense	425		1,113
Stock-based compensation	587		580
Operating expense	**2,491**	**+7**	**2,327**
Operating income	**(968)**	**n.a.**	**(2,085)**
Deprec., depl. & amort.	61		58
Finance costs, gross	19		148
Pre-tax income	**(1,629)**	**n.a.**	**(3,849)**
Net income	**(1,629)**	**n.a.**	**(3,849)**
Cash & equivalent	752		1,689
Inventories	386		187
Accounts receivable	236		88
Current assets	1,446		2,041
Fixed assets, net	38		45
Right-of-use assets	160		214
Total assets	**1,644**	**-29**	**2,300**
Bank indebtedness	nil		100
Accts. pay. & accr. liabs.	654		117
Current liabilities	706		267
Long-term debt, gross	40		40
Long-term debt, net	40		40
Long-term lease liabilities	115		168
Shareholders' equity	763		1,804
Cash from oper. activs.	**(778)**	**n.a.**	**(1,714)**
Cash from fin. activs.	(160)		247
Cash from invest. activs.	nil		2,582
Net cash position	**682**	**-58**	**1,619**
Capital expenditures	nil		(21)
	$		$
Earnings per share*	(0.03)		(0.10)
Cash flow per share*	(0.02)		(0.04)
	shs		shs
No. of shs. o/s*	48,774,683		48,374,683
Avg. no. of shs. o/s*	48,590,987		39,176,835
	%		%
Net profit margin	(106.96)		n.m.
Return on equity	(126.92)		n.m.
Return on assets	(81.64)		(244.37)
Foreign sales percent	5		23

* Common

[A] Reported in accordance with IFRS

[1] Results prior to Apr. 15, 2021, pertain to and reflect the Qualifying Transaction reverse takeover acquisition of Teonan Biomedical Inc.

Latest Results

Periods ended:	3m Oct. 31/22[A]		3m Oct. 31/21[oA]
	$000s	%Chg	$000s
Operating revenue	823	n.m.	49
Net income	(190)	n.a.	(338)
	$		$
Earnings per share*	(0.00)		(0.01)

* Common

[o] Restated

[A] Reported in accordance with IFRS

Historical Summary
(as originally stated)

Fiscal Year	Oper. Rev.	Net Inc. Bef. Disc.	EPS*
	$000s	$000s	$
2022[A]	1,523	(1,629)	(0.03)
2021[A]	242	(3,849)	(0.10)
2020[A]	197	(420)	n.a.

* Common

[A] Reported in accordance with IFRS

Note: Adjusted throughout for 1-for-3 cons. in Apr. 2021

G.64 Goodbridge Capital Corp.

Symbol - GODB.P **Exchange** - TSX-VEN **CUSIP** - 382162
Head Office - 1500-1055 Georgia St W, Vancouver, BC, V6E 4N7 **Telephone** - (604) 689-9111 **Fax** - (604) 685-7084
Email - magbian@yahoo.com
Investor Relations - Magaly Bianchini (416) 822-8525
Auditors - Charlton & Company C.A., Vancouver, B.C.
Transfer Agents - Odyssey Trust Company, Calgary, Alta.
Profile - (B.C. 2021) Capital Pool Company.
Common listed on TSX-VEN, Feb. 22, 2023.
Directors - Anthony Viele, CEO, Woodbridge, Ont.; Magaly Bianchini, CFO & corp. sec., Toronto, Ont.; Thomas Christoff, B.C.; Dr. K. Terry Christopher, Bedford, N.S.

Capital Stock

	Authorized (shs.)	Outstanding (shs.)[1]
Common	unlimited	4,082,000

[1] At Feb. 22, 2023

Major Shareholder - Magaly Bianchini held 12.24% interest, Thomas Christoff held 12.24% interest, Dr. K. Terry Christopher held 12.24% interest and Anthony Viele held 12.24% interest at Feb. 22, 2023.
Recent Close: $0.12
Capital Stock Changes - On Feb. 22, 2023, an initial public offering of 2,082,000 common shares was completed at 10¢ per share.

G.65 Goodfellow Inc.*

Symbol - GDL **Exchange** - TSX **CUSIP** - 38216R
Head Office - 225 rue Goodfellow, Delson, QC, J5B 1V5 **Telephone** - (450) 635-6511 **Toll-free** - (800) 361-6503 **Fax** - (450) 635-3729
Website - www.goodfellowinc.com/en/
Email - cbrisebois@goodfellowinc.com
Investor Relations - Charles B. Brisebois (450) 635-6511
Auditors - KPMG LLP C.A., Montréal, Qué.
Lawyers - Fasken Martineau DuMoulin LLP, Montréal, Qué.; Bernier Beaudry Inc., Québec, Qué.
Transfer Agents - Computershare Trust Company of Canada Inc., Montréal, Qué.
FP500 Revenue Ranking - 425
Employees - 677 at Nov. 30, 2022
Profile - (Can. 1972) Remanufactures, sells and distributes lumber and wood products.

Products include remanufactured and recycled timber, pressure treated lumber, machine coated stained siding, hardwood and softwood panel products, laminated veneer lumber, engineered wood products including laminated timber, rough and dressed imported and domestic hardwoods, hardwood flooring products and softwood lumber. Other products added in its product lines are wire products and building products including foil insulation, house wrap insulation, ceiling products, trus joist, composite decking and hardware. Also offers services such as kiln facilities, paint shop for customized products, millwork, pressure treatment facilities and engineering. The company serves more than 5,000 Canadian and export customers within home centres, lumber dealers and large chains, specialty retailers, government, manufacturers and industrial industries.

Owns nine manufacturing plants and 13 distribution centres which include warehouses, wood-drying kilns and pre-dryer, re-manufacturing mills, wood staining facilities, glue lamination and wood treating plants located at its 3,500,000-sq.ft. facility in Delson, Que. In addition, the company operates wood treating plants in Elmsdale, N.S., and Deer Lake, N.L., as well as wood drying kilns and grading chains in Drummondville, Trois-Rivieres, and Mont-Tremblant, Que.

The company purchases its lumber and lumber products from more than 1,200 sawmills and remanufacturing plants in Canada, the U.S. and abroad. Distribution centres and sales offices are located in Richmond, B.C.; Calgary and Edmonton, Alta.; Saskatoon, Sask.; Winnipeg, Man.; Campbellville and Ottawa, Ont.; Quebec City, Que.; Moncton, N.B.; Dartmouth, N.S.; Deer Lake, N.L.; and Manchester, N.H. Wholly owned **Quality Hardwoods Ltd.** has manufacturing, distribution and sales facilities in Powassan, Ont.

Directors - Robert F. Hall, chr., Canton-de-Hatley, Qué.; Alain Côté, Boucherville, Qué.; David A. Goodfellow, Léry, Qué.; G. Douglas Goodfellow, Beaconsfield, Qué.; James W. (Jim) Hewitt, Dorval, Qué.; Stephen A. Jarislowsky, Westmount, Qué.; Dr. Sarah S. Prichard, Montréal, Qué.

Other Exec. Officers - Patrick Goodfellow, pres. & CEO; Charles B. Brisebois, CFO & corp. sec.; Mary Lohmus, exec. v-p, Ont. & western Canada; David (Dave) Warren, sr. v-p, Atlantic; Éric Bisson, v-p, Que.; Luc Dignard, v-p, sales, Quebec dealer sales; Harry Haslett, v-p, sales & mktg., Atlantic; Eric McNeely, v-p, bus. devel., flooring; Jeffrey (Jeff) Morrison, v-p, natl. accounts; Luc Pothier, v-p, opers.

Capital Stock

	Authorized (shs.)	Outstanding (shs.)[1]
Common	unlimited	8,530,454

[1] At July 5, 2023

Normal Course Issuer Bid - The company plans to make normal course purchases of up to 428,127 common shares representing 5% of the total outstanding. The bid commenced on Nov. 10, 2022, and expires on Nov. 9, 2023.

Major Shareholder - David A. Goodfellow held 20.5% interest, G. Douglas Goodfellow held 19.6% interest and Stephen A. Jarislowsky held 12.5% interest at Apr. 4, 2023.

Price Range - GDL/TSX

Year	Volume	High	Low	Close
2022	1,169,202	$14.10	$9.85	$12.49
2021	1,577,170	$11.80	$7.85	$9.55
2020	909,940	$8.60	$3.50	$8.14
2019	429,239	$6.45	$4.50	$5.10
2018	455,966	$8.45	$4.90	$5.30

Recent Close: $15.00

Capital Stock Changes - During fiscal 2022, 4,600 common shares were repurchased under a Normal Course Issuer Bid.

Dividends

GDL com N.S.R. [1]

$0.50	Mar. 16/23	$0.50	Nov. 10/22
$0.40	Mar. 18/22	$0.30	Nov. 19/21

Paid in 2023: $0.50 2022: $0.90 2021: $0.60

[1] First divd. since Aug/16.

Long-Term Debt - At Nov. 30, 2022, the company had no long-term debt.

Wholly Owned Subsidiaries

Goodfellow Distribution Inc., Del.
Quality Hardwoods Ltd., Powassan, Ont.

Investments

40% int. in **Lebel-Goodfellow Treating Inc.**, Canada.

Financial Statistics

Periods ended:	12m Nov. 30/22[A]		12m Nov. 30/21[A]
	$000s	%Chg	$000s
Operating revenue	**631,185**	**+2**	**615,946**
Cost of goods sold	494,227		478,605
General & admin expense	80,844		77,104
Operating expense	**575,071**	**+3**	**555,709**
Operating income	**56,114**	**-7**	**60,237**
Deprec., depl. & amort.	7,710		7,314
Finance income	5		2
Finance costs, gross	3,206		2,696
Pre-tax income	**44,716**	**-11**	**50,523**
Income taxes	12,037		12,687
Net income	**32,679**	**-14**	**37,836**
Cash & equivalent	3,420		4,253
Inventories	112,294		109,787
Accounts receivable	64,423		63,246
Current assets	185,131		181,475
Fixed assets, net	32,269		30,022
Right-of-use assets	14,999		12,262
Intangibles, net	2,096		2,650
Total assets	**246,917**	**+4**	**237,591**
Bank indebtedness	nil		9,246
Accts. pay. & accr. liabs.	36,286		37,897
Current liabilities	43,536		62,568
Long-term lease liabilities	12,537		10,924
Shareholders' equity	186,779		160,948
Cash from oper. activs.	**26,013**	**-22**	**33,278**
Cash from fin. activs.	(14,747)		(33,830)
Cash from invest. activs.	(4,853)		(1,337)
Net cash position	**3,420**	**n.a.**	**(2,993)**
Capital expenditures	(4,827)		(1,333)
Capital disposals	45		29
Pension fund surplus	11,620		10,397
	$		$
Earnings per share*	3.82		4.42
Cash flow per share*	3.04		3.89
Cash divd. per share*	0.90		0.60
	shs		shs
No. of shs. o/s*	8,557,954		8,562,554
Avg. no. of shs. o/s*	8,562,171		8,562,554
	%		%
Net profit margin	5.18		6.14
Return on equity	18.80		26.82
Return on assets	14.46		17.48
Foreign sales percent	11		11
No. of employees (FTEs)	677		683

* Common

[A] Reported in accordance with IFRS

Latest Results

Periods ended:	6m May 31/23[A]		6m May 31/22[A]
	$000s	%Chg	$000s
Operating revenue	248,251	-21	314,312
Net income	6,364	-64	17,659
	$		$
Earnings per share*	0.75		2.06

* Common

[A] Reported in accordance with IFRS

Historical Summary
(as originally stated)

Fiscal Year	Oper. Rev.	Net Inc. Bef. Disc.	EPS*
	$000s	$000s	$
2022[A]	631,185	32,679	3.82
2021[A]	615,946	37,836	4.42
2020[A]	454,103	13,811	1.61
2019[A]	449,587	3,054	0.36
2018[A]	475,207	2,571	0.30

* Common

[A] Reported in accordance with IFRS

G.66 Goodfood Market Corp.*

Symbol - FOOD **Exchange** - TSX **CUSIP** - 38217M
Head Office - 4600 rue Hickmore, Saint-Laurent, QC, H4T 1K2 **Telephone** - (514) 836-7956
Website - www.makegoodfood.ca/en/investisseurs
Email - ir@makegoodfood.ca
Investor Relations - Roslane Aouameur (855) 515-5191
Auditors - KPMG LLP C.A., Montréal, Qué.
Lawyers - Fasken Martineau DuMoulin LLP, Toronto, Ont.
Transfer Agents - TSX Trust Company, Toronto, Ont.
FP500 Revenue Ranking - 592
Employees - 1,225 at Sept. 3, 2022

Profile - (Can. 2017 amalg.; orig. Ont., 2015) Operates an online grocery subscription business which delivers grocery items, meal kits and meal solutions across Canada.

Through the company's website and mobile application, customers have the ability to build a grocery basket by selecting from a variety of grocery items, meal kits and meal solutions, based on the customer's taste preferences and personal schedules. Meal solutions include ready-to-eat products, ready-to-heat products, breakfast products and seasonal products. Orders can be delivered weekly or daily in certain geographic regions. No delivery or fulfilment fees currently apply other than fees for weekly deliveries that contain frozen products totaling less than $30. At June 3, 2023, the company had operating locations in Greater Montreal Area in Quebec, Greater Toronto Area in Ontario and Calgary, Alta., consisting of administrative offices, distribution and manufacturing centres and fulfilment facilities.

The company serves customers across British Columbia, Alberta, Saskatchewan, Manitoba, Ontario, Quebec, Nova Scotia, New Brunswick and Prince Edward Island. At June 3, 2023, the company had 119,000 active customers compared with 211,000 active customers at June 4, 2022. A customer is considered active when the customer has placed an order within the last three months.

During the fourth quarter of fiscal 2022, the company consolidated its British Columbia production facility into its Calgary facility, closed all of its micro-fulfilment centres and shut down its 30-minute on-demand offering.

Predecessor Detail - Name changed from Mira VII Acquisition Corp., May 30, 2017, pursuant to Qualifying Transaction reverse takeover acquisition of Goodfood Market Inc.; basis 1 new for 22.2222 old shs.

Directors - Jonathan Ferrari, chr. & CEO, Montréal, Qué.; Neil Cuggy, pres. & COO, Montréal, Qué.; Donald Olds†, Montréal, Qué.; John Khabbaz, N.Y.; Theresa (Terry) Yanofsky, Westmount, Qué.

Other Exec. Officers - Roslane (Ross) Aouameur, CFO; Bipasha Chiu, chief tech. officer; Simon Brown, exec. v-p, product & mdsg.; Raffi Krikorian, exec. v-p, ready-to-cook & supply chain; Jennifer Stahlke, exec. v-p, mktg. & mbr. happiness

† Lead director

Capital Stock

	Authorized (shs.)	Outstanding (shs.)[1]
Common	unlimited	76,484,064

[1] At July 17, 2023

Options - At Sept. 3, 2022, options were outstanding to purchase 3,262,799 common shares at a weighted average exercise price of $4.44 per share with a weighted average remaining life of 5.7 years.

Major Shareholder - John Khabbaz held 12.94% interest, Neil Cuggy held 11.97% interest and Jonathan Ferrari held 11.97% interest at Dec. 1, 2022.

Price Range - FOOD/TSX

Year	Volume	High	Low	Close
2022	47,249,175	$4.22	$0.26	$0.45
2021	119,367,944	$14.72	$3.58	$4.07
2020	101,880,988	$12.74	$1.49	$12.12
2019	21,555,682	$3.98	$2.51	$3.13
2018	9,853,852	$3.31	$2.10	$2.67

Recent Close: $0.40

Capital Stock Changes - In January 2023, a 1-for-10 share consolidation and creation of an authorized class of preferred shares were approved.

During fiscal 2022, common shares were issued as follows: 293,647 on conversion of debentures, 231,453 on vesting of restricted share units, 161,707 on exercise of options and 8,900 on vesting of employee share purchase units; 110,231 common shares were purchased and held in trust through employee share purchase plan.

Long-Term Debt - Outstanding at Sept. 3, 2022:

Loan due 2023[1]	$11,875,000
Conv. debs.[2]	27,469,000
Less: Unamort. financing costs	132,000
	39,212,000
Less: Current portion	11,743,000
	27,469,000

[1] Bears interest at variable bankers' acceptance rate plus 2.5%.

[2] Consists of 5.75% convertible debentures due on Mar. 31, 2025, convertible into common shares at $4.70 per share; and 5.75% convertible debentures due on Mar. 31, 2027, convertible into common shares at $4.60 per share. An equity component of $5,174,000 was classified as part of shareholders' equity.

Note - In February 2023, private placement of $12,675,000 principal amount of 12.5% convertible debentures due Feb. 6, 2028, including $10,000,000 to Investissement Québec, was completed. The debentures are convertible into common shares at $0.75 per share.

Wholly Owned Subsidiaries

Goodfood AB Inc., Canada. Inactive.
Goodfood BC Inc., Canada. Inactive.
Goodfood Ontario Inc., Canada. Inactive.
Goodfood Québec Inc., Canada. Inactive.
Yumm Meal Solutions Corp., Canada. Inactive.

Financial Statistics

Periods ended:	52w Sept. 3/22[A]		12m Aug. 31/21[A]
	$000s	%Chg	$000s
Operating revenue	**268,586**	**-29**	**379,234**
Cost of goods sold	200,531		263,140
General & admin expense	110,080		132,166
Stock-based compensation	5,876		4,230
Operating expense	**316,487**	**-21**	**399,536**
Operating income	**(47,901)**	**n.a.**	**(20,302)**
Deprec., depl. & amort.	17,295		8,820
Finance costs, net	5,233		2,170
Write-downs/write-offs	(46,085)		nil
Pre-tax income	**(123,256)**	**n.a.**	**(31,292)**
Income taxes	(1,495)		500
Net income	**(121,761)**	**n.a.**	**(31,792)**
Cash & equivalent	36,885		125,535
Inventories	6,884		14,318
Current assets	52,197		146,530
Fixed assets, net	18,408		33,367
Right-of-use assets	55,419		69,157
Intangibles, net	3,174		2,082
Total assets	**129,848**	**-49**	**255,262**
Accts. pay. & accr. liabs.	27,104		52,207
Current liabilities	52,816		63,396
Long-term debt, gross	39,212		26,974
Long-term debt, net	27,469		26,323
Long-term lease liabilities	60,741		67,668
Equity portion of conv. debs.	5,174		843
Shareholders' equity	(11,178)		97,875
Cash from oper. activs.	**(58,981)**	**n.a.**	**(16,358)**
Cash from fin. activs.	8,002		55,503
Cash from invest. activs.	(37,671)		(18,012)
Net cash position	**36,885**	**-71**	**125,535**
Capital expenditures	(35,880)		(16,651)
	$		$
Earnings per share*	(1.62)		(0.45)
Cash flow per share*	(0.79)		(0.23)
	shs		shs
No. of shs. o/s*	75,233,023		74,647,547
Avg. no. of shs. o/s*	74,982,435		70,742,923
	%		%
Net profit margin	(45.33)		(8.38)
Return on equity	n.m.		(40.91)
Return on assets	(63.23)		(15.20)
No. of employees (FTEs)	1,225		3,280

* Common
[A] Reported in accordance with IFRS

Latest Results

Periods ended:	39w June 3/23[A]		39w June 4/22[A]
	$000s	%Chg	$000s
Operating revenue	131,330	-40	218,229
Net income	(12,774)	n.a.	(63,354)
	$		$
Earnings per share*	(0.17)		(0.85)

* Common
[A] Reported in accordance with IFRS

Historical Summary
(as originally stated)

Fiscal Year	Oper. Rev.	Net Inc. Bef. Disc.	EPS*
	$000s	$000s	$
2022[A]	268,586	(121,761)	(1.62)
2021[A]	379,234	(31,792)	(0.45)
2020[A]	285,372	(4,136)	(0.07)
2019[A]	161,333	(20,937)	(0.38)
2018[A]	70,502	(9,435)	(0.19)

* Common
[A] Reported in accordance with IFRS

G.67 Goodness Growth Holdings Inc.

Symbol - GDNS **Exchange** - CSE **CUSIP** - 38238W
Head Office - 207 South 9 St, Minneapolis, MN, United States, 55402
Telephone - (612) 999-1606 **Toll-free** - (844) 484-7366
Website - www.goodnessgrowth.com
Email - samgibbons@goodnessgrowth.com
Investor Relations - Sam Gibbons (844) 484-7366
Auditors - Davidson & Company LLP C.A., Vancouver, B.C.
Lawyers - DLA Piper (Canada) LLP, Vancouver, B.C.
Transfer Agents - Odyssey Trust Company, Vancouver, B.C.
FP500 Revenue Ranking - 774
Employees - 409 at Mar. 1, 2023

Profile - (Alta. 2004) Cultivates, manufactures, distributes and sells medical and adult-use cannabis products in the United States. Also develops intellectual property for health, wellness and recreational applications.

Wholly owned **Vireo Health, Inc.** is licensed to conduct marijuana activities in seven U.S. states and Puerto Rico. Operations consist of indoor, outdoor and greenhouse cultivation and processing facilities in Arizona, Maryland, Minnesota, New Mexico and New York; wholesale distribution activities in Maryland, Minnesota, New Mexico and New York; and 18 retail dispensaries, which primarily operate under the Green Goods banner, in Arizona (1), Maryland (1), Minnesota (8), New Mexico (4) and New York (4). Products produced include flower, pre-rolls, concentrates, vaporizer pens and cartridges, syringes, ingestibles and topicals, which are marketed under various brands including Vireo Spectrum, 1937, LiteBud, Kings & Queens, Hi-Color and Amplifi.

Wholly owned **Resurgent Biosciences, Inc.** is a science incubator focused on the development and commercialization of naturally derived medicines, therapies, products and technologies, including novel product formulations, novel delivery systems and harm-mitigation processes. Resurgent holds a portfolio of intellectual property including the patent-pending TerpSafe packaging technology, which preserves the native terpene content of cannabis flower, as well as patents for harm reduction in tobacco products. Resurgent is also pursuing opportunities in psychedelics.

Recent Merger and Acquisition Activity

Status: terminated **Revised:** Oct. 14, 2022

UPDATE: Verano has provided notice to terminate the transaction. Goodness believes that Verano has no legal basis to terminate the agreement. Verano's repudiation of agreement was acknowledged by Goodness, and the transaction would not proceed. Goodness plans to immediately commence legal proceedings against Verano to seek damages. PREVIOUS: Verano Holdings Corp. entered into a definitive agreement to acquire Goodness Growth Holdings Inc. in an all-share transaction valued at about US$413,000,000. Each Goodness subordinate voting share will be exchanged for 0.22652 Verano class A subordinate voting share and each Goodness multiple voting share and super voting share will be exchanged for 22.652 Verano class A subordinate voting shares. Goodness' active operations include 18 dispensaries; five cultivation and processing facilities; a research and development facility; and the Vireo Spectrum, 1937, LiteBud, Kings & Queens, Hi-Color and Amplifi product brands. The acquisition was intended to add the New York, Minnesota and New Mexico markets to Verano's operations. The transaction was subject to the approvals of Goodness shareholders, the Supreme Court of B.C. and U.S. regulatory bodies. Goodness shareholders holding 36.7% voting interest have agreed to vote in favor of the transaction. A termination fee of US$14,875,000 would be payable by either company under certain circumstances.

Predecessor Detail - Name changed from Vireo Health International, Inc., June 9, 2021.

Directors - Dr. Kyle E. Kingsley, founder & exec. chr., Minneapolis, Minn.; Joshua N. (Josh) Rosen, interim CEO, Scottsdale, Ariz.; Amber H. Shimpa, pres., Maple Grove, Minn.; Chelsea A. Grayson, Los Angeles, Calif.; Ross M. Hussey, Minn.; Victor E. Mancebo, Miami, Fla.; Judd T. Nordquist, Deephaven, Minn.

Other Exec. Officers - John A. Heller, CFO; Dr. Stephen Dahmer, CMO; Eric Greenbaum, chief scientific officer; Harris Rabin, chief mktg. officer; J. Michael Schroeder, chief compliance officer, gen. counsel & corp. sec.; Patrick Peters, exec. v-p, retail; Sam Gibbons, v-p, IR; Albe Zakes, v-p, corp. commun.

Capital Stock

	Authorized (shs.)	Outstanding (shs.)[1]
Subordinate Voting	unlimited	86,721,030
Multiple Voting	unlimited	348,642
Super Voting	unlimited	65,411

[1] At Mar. 27, 2023

Subordinate Voting - One vote per share.

Multiple Voting - Each convertible into 100 subordinate voting shares. 100 votes per share.

Super Voting - Each convertible into 100 subordinate voting shares. 1,000 votes per share.

Major Shareholder - Dr. Kyle E. Kingsley held 39% interest at Mar. 1, 2023.

Price Range - GDNS/CSE

Year	Volume	High	Low	Close
2022	31,419,829	$3.37	$0.20	$0.22
2021	49,831,481	$4.92	$1.46	$2.16
2020	44,104,979	$2.03	$0.30	$1.86
2019	44,317,494	$6.87	$1.05	$1.38
2018	210,459	$21.34	$1.55	$2.33

Consolidation: 1-for-19.4024 cons. in Mar. 2019
Recent Close: $0.15

Wholly Owned Subsidiaries

Vireo Health, Inc., Del.
- 100% int. in **Arizona Natural Remedies, Inc.**, Ariz.
- 100% int. in **EHF Cultivation Management, LLC**, Ariz.
- 100% int. in **Elephant Head Farm, LLC**, Ariz.
- 100% int. in **MaryMed, LLC**, Md.
- 100% int. in **Minnesota Medical Solutions, LLC**, Minn.
- 100% int. in **1776 Hemp, LLC**, Del.
- 100% int. in **Resurgent Biosciences, Inc.**, Del.
- 100% int. in **Retail Management Associates, LLC**, Ariz.

- 100% int. in **Verdant Grove, LLC**, Mass.
- 100% int. in **Vireo Health of Massachusetts, LLC**, Del.
  - 100% int. in **Mayflower Botanicals, Inc.**, Mass.
- 100% int. in **Vireo Health of Nevada I, LLC**, Nev.
- 100% int. in **Vireo Health of New Mexico, LLC**, Del.
  - 100% int. in **Red Barn Growers, Inc.**, N.M.
- 100% int. in **Vireo Health of New York, LLC**, N.Y.
- 100% int. in **Vireo Health of Puerto Rico, LLC**, Del.
  - 100% int. in **Vireo Health de Puerto Rico, LLC**, Puerto Rico.
    - 100% int. in **XAAS Agro, Inc.**, Puerto Rico.
- 100% int. in **Vireo of Charm City, LLC**, Md.

Financial Statistics

Periods ended:	12m Dec. 31/22‡A		12m Dec. 31/21A
	US$000s	%Chg	US$000s
Operating revenue	**74,626**	**+37**	**54,446**
Cost of sales	...		29,365
Salaries & benefits	...		16,221
General & admin expense	...		17,435
Stock-based compensation	...		5,183
Operating expense	**...**	**n.a.**	**68,204**
Operating income	**...**	**n.a.**	**(13,758)**
Deprec., depl. & amort.	...		1,442
Finance costs, net	22,594		10,575
Write-downs/write-offs	...		(5,170)
Pre-tax income	**(36,564)**	**n.a.**	**(29,568)**
Income taxes	5,893		4,122
Net income	**(42,457)**	**n.a.**	**(33,690)**
Cash & equivalent	...		15,155
Inventories	...		20,422
Accounts receivable	...		4,502
Current assets	46,729		41,640
Fixed assets, net	...		99,489
Right-of-use assets	...		8,510
Intangibles, net	...		10,368
Total assets	**159,156**	**-5**	**166,970**
Accts. pay. & accr. liabs	...		14,805
Current liabilities	29,709		16,406
Long-term debt, gross	58,029		27,329
Long-term debt, net	46,249		27,329
Long-term lease liabilities	...		80,228
Shareholders' equity	3,441		43,006
Cash from oper. activs	**(18,073)**	**n.a.**	**(30,517)**
Cash from fin. activs	23,684		25,778
Cash from invest. activs	(5,617)		(7,211)
Net cash position	**15,149**	**0**	**15,155**
Capital expenditures	...		(18,044)
	US$		US$
Earnings per share*	(0.33)		(0.27)
Cash flow per share*	(0.14)		(0.25)
	shs		shs
No. of shs. o/s*	128,126,330		128,111,328
Avg. no. of shs. o/s*	128,126,330		123,814,521
	%		%
Net profit margin	(56.89)		(61.88)
Return on equity	(182.82)		(63.96)
Return on assets	(26.04)		(24.99)
Foreign sales percent	100		100

* Subord. Vtg.
‡ Preliminary
A Reported in accordance with U.S. GAAP

Historical Summary
(as originally stated)

Fiscal Year	Oper. Rev.	Net Inc. Bef. Disc.	EPS*
	US$000s	US$000s	US$
2022‡A	74,626	(42,457)	(0.33)
2021A	54,446	(33,690)	(0.27)
2020A	49,211	(22,942)	(0.24)
2019B1	29,956	(57,010)	(0.71)
	$000s	$000s	$
2018B2	nil	(190)	(0.39)

* Subord. Vtg.
‡ Preliminary
A Reported in accordance with U.S. GAAP
B Reported in accordance with IFRS
1 Results reflect the Mar. 18, 2019, reverse takeover acquisiton of Vireo Health, Inc.
2 Results for 2018 and prior years pertain to Darien Business Development Corp.
Note: Adjusted throughout for 1-for-19.4024 cons. in Mar. 2019

G.68 Good2Go4 Corp.

Symbol - GFOR.P **Exchange** - TSX-VEN **CUSIP** - 382145
Head Office - 1505-1 King St W, Toronto, ON, M5H 1A1 **Telephone** - (416) 364-4039
Email - cassina@bellnet.ca
Investor Relations - James C. Cassina (416) 364-4039
Auditors - MNP LLP C.A., Toronto, Ont.
Transfer Agents - TSX Trust Company, Toronto, Ont.
Profile - (Ont. 2021) Capital Pool Company.
Directors - James C. (Jim) Cassina, CEO, CFO & corp. sec., Nassau, Bahamas; Dikshant Batra, Toronto, Ont.; Sandra J. (Sandy) Hall, Oshawa, Ont.

Capital Stock

	Authorized (shs.)	Outstanding (shs.)1
Common	unlimited	6,000,000

1 At June 30, 2022
Major Shareholder - James C. (Jim) Cassina held 33.33% interest at Oct. 27, 2021.

Price Range - GFOR.P/TSX-VEN

Year	Volume	High	Low	Close
2022	55,000	$0.17	$0.08	$0.08
2021	10,000	$0.12	$0.12	$0.12

Recent Close: $0.11
Capital Stock Changes - On Oct. 27, 2021, an initial public offering of 2,150,000 common shares was completed at 10¢ per share.

G.69 Gourmet Ocean Products Inc.

Symbol - GOP.H **Exchange** - TSX-VEN **CUSIP** - 383561
Head Office - 488-1090 Georgia St W, Vancouver, BC, V6E 3V7 **Telephone** - (778) 328-8898 **Fax** - (778) 724-1108
Email - petehughes@me.com
Investor Relations - Peter R. Hughes (604) 802-7372
Auditors - Davidson & Company LLP C.A., Vancouver, B.C.
Lawyers - Bacchus Law Corporation, Vancouver, B.C.
Transfer Agents - TSX Trust Company, Vancouver, B.C.
Profile - (B.C. 2008) Seeking new business opportunities.
Formerly grew, distributed, marketed and sold specialty seafood products such as sea cucumbers, scallops and oysters to customers in Asia and Canada.
Predecessor Detail - Name changed from Megal Capital Corporation, Feb. 14, 2014, pursuant to Qualifying Transaction reverse takeover acquisition of Wen Lian Aquaculture Co., Ltd.
Directors - Peter R. Hughes, pres. & CEO, Vancouver, B.C.; George G. Dorin, Surrey, B.C.; Laizhong Qiu, Burnaby, B.C.
Other Exec. Officers - Jin Kuang, CFO & corp. sec.

Capital Stock

	Authorized (shs.)	Outstanding (shs.)1
Common	unlimited	125,068,733

1 At Jan. 28, 2022
Major Shareholder - Guonan (Bruce) Qiu held 65% interest at June 22, 2021.

Price Range - GOP.H/TSX-VEN

Year	Volume	High	Low	Close
2022	990,580	$0.02	$0.01	$0.01
2021	5,210,163	$0.07	$0.01	$0.02
2020	3,958,170	$0.03	$0.01	$0.02
2019	827,800	$0.01	$0.01	$0.01
2018	3,278,723	$0.06	$0.01	$0.01

Recent Close: $0.01

Financial Statistics

Periods ended:	12m Sept. 30/21A		12m Sept. 30/20A
	$000s	%Chg	$000s
General & admin expense	112		130
Operating expense	**112**	**-14**	**130**
Operating income	**(112)**	**n.a.**	**(130)**
Pre-tax income	**(112)**	**n.a.**	**(101)**
Net income	**(112)**	**n.a.**	**(101)**
Cash & equivalent	2		1
Current assets	8		13
Total assets	**8**	**-38**	**13**
Bank indebtedness	309		243
Accts. pay. & accr. liabs	68		27
Current liabilities	377		270
Shareholders' equity	(369)		(257)
Cash from oper. activs	**(65)**	**n.a.**	**(124)**
Cash from fin. activs	66		123
Net cash position	**2**	**+100**	**1**
	$		$
Earnings per share*	(0.00)		(0.00)
Cash flow per share*	(0.00)		(0.00)
	shs		shs
No. of shs. o/s*	125,068,733		125,068,733
Avg. no. of shs. o/s*	125,068,733		125,068,733
	%		%
Net profit margin	n.a.		n.a.
Return on equity	n.m.		n.m.
Return on assets	n.m.		(721.43)

* Common
A Reported in accordance with IFRS

Historical Summary
(as originally stated)

Fiscal Year	Oper. Rev.	Net Inc. Bef. Disc.	EPS*
	$000s	$000s	$
2021A	nil	(112)	(0.00)
2020A	nil	(101)	(0.00)
2019A	nil	921	0.01
2018A	693	(1,261)	(0.01)
2017A	1,441	(1,807)	(0.01)

* Common
A Reported in accordance with IFRS

G.70 Grand Peak Capital Corp.

Symbol - GPK **Exchange** - CSE **CUSIP** - 38611W
Head Office - 210-9648 128 St, Surrey, BC, V3T 2X9 **Telephone** - (604) 357-4725 **Fax** - (604) 592-6882
Website - www.grandpeakcapital.com
Email - sonny@grandpeakcapital.com
Investor Relations - Sonny Janda (604) 357-3741
Auditors - Dale Matheson Carr-Hilton LaBonte LLP C.A., Vancouver, B.C.
Lawyers - Sangra Moller LLP, Vancouver, B.C.
Transfer Agents - Odyssey Trust Company, Vancouver, B.C.
Profile - (B.C. 2010) Invests in real estate ventures in Canada and the U.S., marketable securities and early stage venture capital companies.
The company's investment portfolio at Mar. 31, 2023, consisted of $2,208,021 in marketable securities, $1,049,900 in investment properties and $396,533 in warrants and options.
In April 2022, the company and **COMSovereign Holding Corp.** terminated their distribution agreement, which granted the company with a non-exclusive, non-transferable right to distribute, sell, market and support COMS' inventory of telecommunications hardware and software products to customers, agents and regional distributors in Canada and India.
Common reinstated on CSE, May 17, 2023.
Common suspended from CSE, Feb. 7, 2023.
Predecessor Detail - Name changed from Black Mountain Capital Corporation, Nov. 20, 2007; basis 1 new for 5 old shs.
Directors - Sonny Janda, CEO, Vancouver, B.C.; Jatinder (Jerry) Bains, Brampton, Ont.; Tajinder Johal, Delta, B.C.
Other Exec. Officers - Navin Sandhu, interim CFO

Capital Stock

	Authorized (shs.)	Outstanding (shs.)1
Common	unlimited	108,557,940

1 At May 30, 2023
Major Shareholder - Widely held at Feb. 23, 2023.

Price Range - GPK/CSE

Year	Volume	High	Low	Close
2022	57,350	$0.40	$0.09	$0.09
2021	57,500	$0.49	$0.16	$0.20
2020	477,329	$0.75	$0.04	$0.39
2019	328,504	$0.47	$0.03	$0.03
2018	86,700	$0.17	$0.05	$0.05

Split: 3-for-1 split in May 2019
Recent Close: $0.08
Capital Stock Changes - There were no changes to capital stock from fiscal 2020 to fiscal 2022, inclusive.

Wholly Owned Subsidiaries

Fruitridge 65 LLC, United States.
Grand Peak USA, Inc., United States.

Financial Statistics

Periods ended:	12m Sept. 30/22[A]		12m Sept. 30/21[A]
	$000s	%Chg	$000s
Realized invest. gain (loss)	(247)		(3,027)
Unrealized invest. gain (loss)	(4,654)		(5,296)
Total revenue	**(4,495)**	**n.a.**	**(8,010)**
Salaries & benefits	56		60
General & admin. expense	319		217
Operating expense	**375**	**+35**	**277**
Operating income	**(4,870)**	**n.a.**	**(8,287)**
Deprec. & amort.	11		11
Finance costs, gross	14		250
Write-downs/write-offs	(261)		(9)
Pre-tax income	**(5,156)**	**n.a.**	**3,113**
Income taxes	2		nil
Net income	**(5,158)**	**n.a.**	**3,113**
Cash & equivalent	3,060		7,869
Accounts receivable	80		11
Current assets	3,140		8,934
Properties	1,050		1,331
Total assets	**4,190**	**-59**	**10,266**
Accts. pay. & accr. liabs.	140		110
Current liabilities	1,697		110
Long-term debt, gross	nil		947
Long-term debt, net	nil		947
Shareholders' equity	2,493		9,208
Cash from oper. activs.	**(14)**	**n.a.**	**51**
Cash from fin. activs.	(962)		503
Cash from invest. activs.	849		(582)
Net cash position	**271**	**-32**	**397**
	$		$
Earnings per share*	(0.05)		0.03
Cash flow per share*	(0.00)		0.00
	shs		shs
No. of shs. o/s*	108,557,940		108,557,940
Avg. no. of shs. o/s*	108,557,940		108,557,940
	%		%
Net profit margin	n.m.		(38.86)
Return on equity	(88.16)		40.68
Return on assets	(71.17)		34.25

* Common
[A] Reported in accordance with IFRS

Latest Results

Periods ended:	6m Mar. 31/23[A]		6m Mar. 31/22[A]
	$000s	%Chg	$000s
Total revenue	274	n.a.	(2,490)
Net income	(437)	n.a.	(2,676)
	$		$
Earnings per share*	(0.00)		(0.02)

* Common
[A] Reported in accordance with IFRS

Historical Summary
(as originally stated)

Fiscal Year	Total Rev.	Net Inc. Bef. Disc.	EPS*
	$000s	$000s	$
2022[A]	(4,495)	(5,158)	(0.05)
2021[A]	(8,010)	3,113	0.03
2020[A]	307	3,236	0.03
2019[A]	309	(6,694)	(0.06)
2018[A]	541	(783)	(0.01)

* Common
[A] Reported in accordance with IFRS
Note: Adjusted throughout for 3-for-1 split in May 2019

G.71 Granite Real Estate Investment Trust

Symbol - GRT.UN **Exchange** - TSX **CUSIP** - 387437
Head Office - 4010-77 King St W, PO Box 159 Toronto-Dominion Centre, Toronto, ON, M5K 1H1 **Telephone** - (647) 925-7500 **Fax** - (416) 861-1240
Website - www.granitereit.com
Email - lclarfield@granitereit.com
Investor Relations - Lawrence Clarfield (647) 925-7536
Auditors - Deloitte LLP C.A., Toronto, Ont.
Transfer Agents - Computershare Trust Company, N.A., Louisville, Ky.; Computershare Trust Company of Canada Inc., Toronto, Ont.
FP500 Revenue Ranking - 489
Employees - 69 at Dec. 31, 2022
Profile - (Ont. 2012) Acquires, develops, owns and manages logistics, warehouse and industrial properties in North America and Europe.

At Mar. 8, 2023, the property portfolio consisted of 140 distribution/e-commerce, industrial/warehouse, flex/office and special purpose properties, as well and as properties under development and land held for development, totaling 59,400,000 sq. ft. of gross leasable area (GLA), in Canada, the U.S., Austria, Germany and the Netherlands.

Magna International Inc. and its wholly owned subsidiaries represent 26% of the annual lease payments at Dec. 31, 2022.

Property portfolio at Mar. 8, 2023[1]:

	Props.	GLA[2]
Canada	37	6,500,000
U.S.	64	35,400,000
Austria	9	7,500,000
Germany	14	4,600,000
Netherlands	16	5,400,000
	140	59,400,000

[1] Includes properties under development (eight properties) and land held for development (four properties).
[2] Sq. ft.

Recent Merger and Acquisition Activity

Status: completed **Announced:** Aug. 19, 2022
Granite Real Estate Investment Trust acquired a 10.1-acre parcel of land in Brant cty, Ont., for a purchase price of Cdn$6,400,000.

Status: completed **Announced:** July 1, 2022
Granite Real Estate Investment Trust acquired a 500,000-sq.-ft. distribution facility in Tilburg, Netherlands, for a purchase price of €76,100,000.

Status: completed **Announced:** June 9, 2022
Granite Real Estate Investment Trust sold an income-producing property in Trebon, Czech Republic for a sale price of $31,500,000.

Status: completed **Announced:** May 26, 2022
Granite Real Estate Investment Trust acquired a distribution facility in Etobicoke, Ont., for a purchase price of $17,700,000.

Status: completed **Announced:** May 24, 2022
Granite Real Estate Investment Trust acquired a distribution facility in Brampton, Ont., for a purchase price of $20,850,000.

Status: completed **Announced:** May 5, 2022
Granite Real Estate Investment Trust acquired a property under development for US$11,300,000 consisting of a 200,000-sq.-ft. built-to-suit modern distribution facility to be constructed on 13.6 acres in Bolingbrook, Ill. Construction has commenced and the property was expected to be completed in the first quarter of 2023.

Status: completed **Announced:** Apr. 14, 2022
Granite Real Estate Investment Trust acquired two newly constructed modern distribution facilities, totaling 1,400,000 sq. ft., in Clayton, Ind., for $179,100,000.

Predecessor Detail - Succeeded Granite Real Estate Inc., Jan. 3, 2013, pursuant to plan of arrangement whereby Granite Real Estate Investment Trust and Granite REIT Inc. were formed to facilitate the conversion to a real estate investment trust.

Trustees - Kelly Marshall, chr., Ont.; Kevan S. Gorrie, pres. & CEO, Toronto, Ont.; Peter Aghar, Toronto, Ont.; Remco Daal, Vancouver, B.C.; Fern Grodner, Wash.; Aladin W. (Al) Mawani, Thornhill, Ont.; Gerald J. (Gerry) Miller, Kelowna, B.C.; Sheila A. Murray, Toronto, Ont.; Emily Pang, Ont.; Jennifer Warren, New York, N.Y.

Other Exec. Officers - Teresa Neto, CFO; Lawrence Clarfield, exec. v-p, gen. counsel & corp. sec.; Lorne Kumer, exec. v-p & head, global real estate; Michael A. Ramparas, exec. v-p, global real estate & head, invests.; Witsard Schaper, sr. v-p & head, Europe; Jon Sorg, sr. v-p & head, U.S.; Kristy Boys, v-p, treasury; Alison Clements, v-p, real estate; Paul Galos, v-p, fin., Europe; Bernhard Hamet, v-p, legal, Europe; Stephanie Karamarkovic, v-p, acctg. & finl. reporting; Will Miller, v-p, portfolio mgt.; Mario Pecile, v-p, const., North America; Tim Pickering, v-p, tax.; Wolfgang Sorger, v-p, const., Europe; Keith Stephen, v-p, sustainability & envir.; Frank Tozzi, v-p, const., North America

Capital Stock

	Authorized (shs.)	Outstanding (shs.)[1]
Stapled Unit	unlimited	63,743,762

[1] At May 12, 2023

Stapled Unit - Each consists of one trust unit of the REIT and one common share of Granite REIT Inc. One vote per stapled unit.

Normal Course Issuer Bid - The company plans to make normal course purchases of up to 6,349,296 stapled units representing 10% of the public float. The bid commenced on May 24, 2023, and expires on May 23, 2024.

Major Shareholder - Widely held at Mar. 31, 2023.

Price Range - GRT.UN/TSX

Year	Volume	High	Low	Close
2022	42,981,723	$105.56	$63.29	$69.08
2021	34,857,023	$105.79	$71.66	$105.40
2020	53,037,288	$80.06	$40.77	$77.90
2019	39,499,436	$69.12	$52.85	$65.98
2018	23,229,752	$57.68	$47.93	$53.21

Recent Close: $73.03

Capital Stock Changes - During 2022, stapled units were issued as follows: 136,000 under an at-the-market equity program and 44,000 in settlement of deferred stapled units; 2,166,000 stapled units were repurchased under a Normal Course Issuer Bid.

Dividends

GRT.UN stapled unit Ra $3.2004 pa M est. Jan. 17, 2023
Prev. Rate: $3.0996 est. Jan. 14, 2022
Prev. Rate: $3.00 est. Jan. 15, 2021

Wholly Owned Subsidiaries

Granite REIT Holdings Limited Partnership, Qué.
- 100% int. in **Granite Canadian Properties LP**, Ont.
- 100% int. in **Granite Real Estate Inc.**, Qué.
  - 100% int. in **Granite Europe B.V.**, Netherlands.
    - 99.74% int. in **Granite AS Holding Germany GmbH**, Germany.
      - 100% int. in **Granite AS Real Estate Germany GmbH & Co. KG**, Germany.
    - 99.74% int. in **Granite Germany Holding GmbH**, Germany.
      - 99.74% int. in **Granite Germany Real Estate GmbH & Co. KG**, Germany.
    - 100% int. in **Granite Holdings B.V.**, Netherlands.
      - 100% int. in **Granite AUT GmbH**, Austria.
        - 100% int. in **Granite Austria GmbH & Co. KG**, Austria.
        - 100% int. in **Granite Thondorf RE GmbH & Co. KG**, Austria.
    - 95% int. in **Granite Real Estate (Czech) s.r.o**, Czech Republic.
- 100% int. in **Granite US Master LP**, Del.
  - 100% int. in **Granite US Holdco LP**, Del.
    - 100% int. in **Granite REIT America Inc.**, Del.
      - 100% int. in **Granite (Houston 90) LLC**, Houston, Tex.
        - 95.27% int. in **NP-GR Houston Industrial, LLC**, Houston, Tex.
      - 100% int. in **Granite (1301 Chalk Hill) LP**, Del.
        - 100% int. in **Commerce 30 Building C, Inc.**, Del.

Financial Statistics

Periods ended:	12m Dec. 31/22[A]		12m Dec. 31/21[A]
	$000s	%Chg	$000s
Total revenue	**455,579**	**+16**	**393,488**
Rental operating expense	75,221		60,812
Salaries & benefits	18,225		17,092
General & admin. expense	11,240		21,308
Operating expense	**104,686**	**+6**	**99,212**
Operating income	**350,893**	**+19**	**294,276**
Deprec. & amort.	1,598		1,320
Finance income	1,625		3,109
Finance costs, gross	50,967		47,226
Pre-tax income	**92,157**	**-94**	**1,550,839**
Income taxes	(63,665)		240,567
Net inc bef disc ops, eqhldrs	155,768		1,309,937
Net inc bef disc ops, NCI	54		335
Net income	**155,822**	**-88**	**1,310,272**
Net inc. for equity hldrs	**155,768**	**-88**	**1,309,937**
Net inc. for non-cont. int	**54**	**-84**	**335**
Cash & equivalent	135,081		402,513
Accounts receivable	12,176		10,771
Current assets	273,594		486,529
Fixed assets	4,037		2,486
Income-producing props	8,486,105		7,727,368
Properties under devel	272,504		162,817
Properties for future devel	80,962		80,973
Property interests, net	8,843,608		7,973,644
Total assets	**9,280,354**	**+8**	**8,566,697**
Accts. pay. & accr. liabs	114,775		113,244
Current liabilities	619,318		164,375
Long-term debt, gross	3,048,477		2,444,476
Long-term debt, net	458,156		2,444,476
Long-term lease liabilities	32,977		31,645
Shareholders' equity	5,475,375		5,318,653
Non-controlling interest	4,972		2,881
Cash from oper. activs	**277,496**	**+6**	**262,264**
Cash from fin. activs	214,559		333,475
Cash from invest. activs	(766,556)		(1,025,424)
Net cash position	**135,081**	**-66**	**402,513**
Capital expenditures	(267,985)		(99,760)
Increase in property	(492,717)		(925,901)
Decrease in property	63,943		35,428
	$		$
Earnings per share*	n.a.		n.a.
Cash flow per share*	4.26		4.10
Funds from opers. per sh.*	4.44		3.93
Adj. funds from opers. per sh.*	4.05		3.68
Cash divd. per share*	3.11		3.01
Total divd. per share*	**3.11**		**3.01**
	shs		shs
No. of shs. o/s*	63,708,000		65,694,000
Avg. no. of shs. o/s*	65,200,000		64,000,000
	%		%
Net profit margin	34.20		332.99
Return on equity	2.89		28.36
Return on assets	2.71		17.63
Foreign sales percent	83		83
No. of employees (FTEs)	69		58

* Stapled Unit
[A] Reported in accordance with IFRS

Note: Comparable funds from operations (which excludes large, non-recurring items) per stapled unit was reported as $3.27 in 2014 and $3.04 in 2013.

Historical Summary
(as originally stated)

Fiscal Year	Total Rev. $000s	Net Inc. Bef. Disc. $000s	EPS* $
2022[A]	455,579	155,822	n.a.
2021[A]	393,488	1,310,272	n.a.
2020[A]	340,199	429,927	n.a.
2019[A]	273,678	382,275	n.a.
2018[A]	247,483	465,357	n.a.

* Stapled Unit
[A] Reported in accordance with IFRS

G.72 Graph Blockchain Inc.

Symbol - GBLC **Exchange** - CSE **CUSIP** - 388659
Head Office - 2802-2300 Yonge St, Toronto, ON, M4P 1E4 **Telephone** - (647) 465-3647
Website - www.graphblockchain.com
Email - phaber@graphblockchain.com
Investor Relations - Paul Haber (416) 482-3282
Auditors - Kingston Ross Pasnak LLP C.A., Edmonton, Alta.
Transfer Agents - Computershare Trust Company of Canada Inc., Vancouver, B.C.
Profile - (B.C. 1982) Provides exposure to various areas of Decentralized Finance (DeFi), particulary the cyrptocurrency and non-fungible token (NFT) markets.
Wholly owned **Babbage Mining Corp.** focuses on mining and storing altcoins, which are alternative cryptocurrencies to bitcoins, through Proof of Stake mining, a process of verifying cryptocurrency transactions in exchange for block rewards and a share of the transaction fees.
Wholly owned **Beyond the Moon Inc.** manages the process of entering crypto launchpads by helping to facilitate the access to early-stage crypto tokens which provide the first public investment round, called an Initial DEX Offering (IDO).
Wholly owned **New World Inc.** provides access to a web3-based augmented reality non-fungible token (NFT) marketplace and application which caters to artists, celebrities and the general consumer where users can create and sell digital art.
Wholly owned **Optimum Coin Analyser Inc.** provides software-as-a-service (SaaS) coin trading platform to help cryptocurrency traders better read signals and analysis to generate superior trading returns.
Wholly owned **Niftable Inc.** provides a platform for the sale and post-sale of NFTs on behalf of charities.
In July 2022, a name change to **New World Ltd.** was approved.
Predecessor Detail - Name changed from Reg Technologies Inc., Nov. 6, 2018, following reverse takeover acquisition of Graph Blockchain Limited.; basis 1 new for 10 old shs.
Directors - Paul Haber, chr. & CEO, Toronto, Ont.; Youngcho Lee, Vancouver, B.C.
Other Exec. Officers - Frank Kordy, interim CFO; Andrew El'Lithy, interim chief tech. officer

Capital Stock

	Authorized (shs.)	Outstanding (shs.)[1]
Common	unlimited	57,770,118

[1] At Dec. 12, 2022
Major Shareholder - Widely held at June 13, 2022.

Price Range - GBLC/CSE

Year	Volume	High	Low	Close
2022	25,082,343	$0.50	$0.03	$0.03
2021	106,066,232	$4.90	$0.20	$0.45
2020	17,375,114	$0.55	$0.05	$0.30
2019	7,392,969	$0.70	$0.05	$0.10
2018	1,786,003	$2.00	$0.40	$0.45

Consolidation: 1-for-10 cons. in Nov. 2022
Recent Close: $0.03
Capital Stock Changes - On Nov. 16, 2022, common shares were consolidated on a 1-for-10 basis.
In June 2021, 46,153,846 common shares were issued on acquisition of Beyond the Moon Inc. In July 2021, 46,153,846 common shares were issued on acquisition of New World Inc. In August 2021, 71,428,571 common shares were issued on acquisition of Optimum Coin Analyser Inc. On Jan. 28, 2022, 52,000,000 common shares were issued on acquisition of Niftable Inc. Also during fiscal 2022, common shares were issued as follows: 4,000,000 for services and 60,000 on exercise of warrants.

Wholly Owned Subsidiaries
Babbage Mining Corp.
Beyond the Moon Inc., Ont.
BluStem Ltd.
New World Inc., Canada.
Niftable Inc.
Optimum Coin Analyser Inc.

Financial Statistics

Periods ended:	12m Apr. 30/22[A]		12m Apr. 30/21[A]
	$000s	%Chg	$000s
Operating revenue	**45**	**-90**	**433**
Cost of sales	4		378
Salaries & benefits	404		51
General & admin expense	423		48
Stock-based compensation	781		8,352
Other operating expense	4,412		1,014
Operating expense	**6,024**	**-39**	**9,843**
Operating income	**(5,979)**	**n.a.**	**(9,410)**
Deprec., depl. & amort.	208		1
Finance income	8		nil
Finance costs, gross	nil		2
Write-downs/write-offs	(1,666)		(191)
Pre-tax income	**(24,045)**	**n.a.**	**(15,330)**
Net income	**(24,045)**	**n.a.**	**(15,330)**
Cash & equivalent	3,653		8,803
Accounts receivable	428		418
Current assets	4,530		9,342
Fixed assets, net	nil		1
Intangibles, net	5,645		nil
Total assets	**11,330**	**-4**	**11,752**
Accts. pay. & accr. liabs	895		742
Current liabilities	895		742
Long-term debt, gross	1		40
Long-term debt, net	1		40
Shareholders' equity	9,535		10,969
Cash from oper. activs	**(5,664)**	**n.a.**	**(1,152)**
Cash from fin. activs	(146)		12,447
Cash from invest. activs	661		(2,600)
Net cash position	**3,653**	**-59**	**8,803**
	$		$
Earnings per share*	(0.48)		(0.81)
Cash flow per share*	(0.11)		(0.06)
	shs		shs
No. of shs. o/s*	57,770,170		35,790,544
Avg. no. of shs. o/s*	49,977,584		18,957,389
	%		%
Net profit margin	n.m.		n.m.
Return on equity	(234.54)		n.m.
Return on assets	(208.34)		(257.83)

* Common
[A] Reported in accordance with IFRS

Latest Results

Periods ended:	6m Oct. 31/22[A]		6m Oct. 31/21[A]
	$000s	%Chg	$000s
Operating revenue	1,121	n.a.	nil
Net income	(2,257)	n.a.	(7,330)
	$		$
Earnings per share*	(0.04)		(0.16)

* Common
[A] Reported in accordance with IFRS

Historical Summary
(as originally stated)

Fiscal Year	Oper. Rev. $000s	Net Inc. Bef. Disc. $000s	EPS* $
2022[A]	45	(24,045)	(0.48)
2021[A]	433	(15,330)	(0.81)
2020[A]	nil	(759)	(0.05)
2019[A1]	2,192	(7,618)	(0.59)
2018[A2]	nil	(70)	(0.14)

* Common
[A] Reported in accordance with IFRS
[1] Results reflect the Nov. 6, 2018, reverse takeover acquisition of Graph Blockchain Limited.
[2] Results for fiscal 2018 and prior fiscal years pertain to Reg Technologies Inc.
Note: Adjusted throughout for 1-for-10 cons. in Nov. 2022; 1-for-10 cons. in Oct. 2018

G.73 Graphene Manufacturing Group Ltd.

Symbol - GMG **Exchange** - TSX-VEN **CUSIP** - Q42733
Head Office - Unit 5, 848 Boundary Rd, Brisbane, QLD, Australia, 4077 **Overseas Tel** - 61-7-3040-5716
Website - www.graphenemg.com
Email - craig.nicol@graphenemg.com
Investor Relations - Craig Nicol 61-4-1544-5223
Auditors - BDO Audit Pty Ltd., Brisbane, Qld. Australia
Lawyers - DuMoulin Black LLP, Vancouver, B.C.
Transfer Agents - Computershare Trust Company of Canada Inc., Vancouver, B.C.
Employees - 37 at Oct. 18, 2022
Profile - (Australia 2016) Researches, develops, manufactures and markets graphene-enhanced products, including coatings, automotive fluids, fuel and batteries.
Has developed a proprietary production process to produce graphene powder from natural gas (methane), not from mined graphite. This process decomposes natural gas (methane) into its elements, carbon (including as graphene), hydrogen and some residual hydrocarbon gases. Produced graphene powder may be suitable for various applications and industries, with an initial focus on energy saving and energy storage solutions.
In the energy savings segment, the company develops, manufactures and commercializes graphene-enhanced heating, ventilation and air conditioning (HVAC) coatings, lubricants and fluids. Commercial product is THERMAL-XR® coating system, a paint formulation and application system designed to improve the conductivity of heat exchange surfaces, resulting in an efficiency improvement and a potential power reduction when applied to air conditioning condenser coils or other industrial processes needing heat transfer. THERMAL-XR® is primarily targeted to the HVAC and refrigeration market and being evaluated for other applications with high energy requirements, including data centres and mining, energy and gas producers. Products under development include G™ Lubricant, G™ Coolant, G™ Fluids, and G™ Diesel and Bio-diesel.
In the energy storage segment, the company and University of Queensland are collaborating, with financial support from the Australian Government, on the research, development and commercialization of graphene aluminum-ion batteries. The company has a Battery Development Centre in Brisbane, Qld., to develop, manufacture and test battery pouch cell prototypes.
In May 2023, the company and **Rio Tinto plc** signed a joint development agreement to support the accelerated development and application of the company's graphene aluminum-ion batteries in the mining and minerals industry. Rio Tinto would contribute technical and operational performance criteria and up to A$6,000,000, in exchange for preferential access rights, over two years with payments spread over the term of the agreement. The company would retain ownership of the intellectual property of the graphene aluminum-ion batteries, with Rio Tinto having the right to procure and use the batteries in its operations.
In September 2022, the company acquired the manufacturing intellectual property and brand rights of **OzKem Pty Ltd.**'s THERMAL-XR® coating products for A$1,000,000 cash and subsequent issuance of 250,413 ordinary shares valued at A$1,000,000, conditional on a successful commercial batch blend of THERMAL-XR® by the company. OzKem developed THERMAL-XR® using the company's graphene together with OzKem's base heating, ventilation and air conditioning (HVAC) coating.
Predecessor Detail - Name changed from Graphene Manufacturing Group Pty Ltd., Apr. 2, 2021.
Directors - Craig Nicol, founder, man. dir. & CEO, Brisbane, Qld., Australia; Guy Outen, chr., London, Middx., United Kingdom; Dr. Emma FitzGerald, Somt., United Kingdom; William W. (Will) Ollerhead, Toronto, Ont.; Robert W. Shewchuk, Calgary, Alta.; Andrew Small
Other Exec. Officers - Lisa Roobottom, COO; Scott Richardson, interim CFO; Bobby Bran, chief project officer; Paul Mackintosh, chief health, safety, envir., quality, risk & sustainability officer; Anjana Reddy, corp. sec.; Deborah Appleton, contr.

Capital Stock

	Authorized (shs.)	Outstanding (shs.)[1]
Preferred	unlimited	nil
Ordinary	unlimited	81,973,169

[1] At May 24, 2023
Major Shareholder - Craig Nicol held 15.88% interest at Oct. 18, 2022.

Price Range - GMG/TSX-VEN

Year	Volume	High	Low	Close
2022	28,925,942	$5.83	$2.26	$2.37
2021	59,538,577	$7.25	$0.73	$5.44

Recent Close: $1.30
Capital Stock Changes - In August 2023, public offering of 2,029,412 units (1 ordinary share & ½ warrant) at Cdn$1.70 per unit was completed, including 264,706 units on exercise of over-allotment option, with warrants exercisable at Cdn$2.20 per share for four years.
In November 2022, bought deal public offering of 2,091,850 units (1 ordinary share & 1 warrant) at Cdn$2.75 per unit was completed, including 272,850 units on exercise of over-allotment option, with warrants exercisable at Cdn$3.35 per share for four years.
In September 2021, public offering of 5,635,000 units (1 ordinary share & ½ warrant) at Cdn$2.05 per unit, including 735,000 units on exercise of over-allotment option, and concurrent private placement of 425,000 units (1 ordinary share & ½ warrant) at Cdn$2.14 per unit were completed. Also during fiscal 2022, ordinary shares were issued as follows: 2,048,053 on exercise of warrants and 1,111,652 on exercise of options.

Financial Statistics

Periods ended:	12m June 30/22[A]		12m June 30/21[A]
	A$000s	%Chg	A$000s
Operating revenue	**54**	**-78**	**246**
Salaries & benefits	4,408		2,576
Research & devel. expense	83		63
General & admin expense	2,648		2,089
Stock-based compensation	864		108
Other operating expense	311		2,416
Operating expense	**8,314**	**+15**	**7,252**
Operating income	**(8,260)**	**n.a.**	**(7,006)**
Deprec., depl. & amort.	351		263
Finance income	2		2
Finance costs, gross	63		23
Pre-tax income	**(11,770)**	**n.a.**	**(8,110)**
Net income	**(11,770)**	**n.a.**	**(8,110)**
Cash & equivalent	12,258		3,359
Inventories	350		336
Accounts receivable	143		56
Current assets	14,481		4,671
Fixed assets, net	2,162		225
Intangibles, net	33		49
Total assets	**16,676**	**+237**	**4,944**
Accts. pay. & accr. liabs.	804		539
Current liabilities	5,578		2,910
Long-term lease liabilities	898		nil
Shareholders' equity	10,100		2,034
Cash from oper. activs.	**(6,568)**	**n.a.**	**(3,349)**
Cash from fin. activs.	16,547		4,107
Cash from invest. activs.	(1,080)		1,901
Net cash position	**12,258**	**+265**	**3,359**
Capital expenditures	(1,066)		(256)
	A$		A$
Earnings per share*	(0.15)		(0.13)
Cash flow per share*	(0.09)		(0.06)
	shs		shs
No. of shs. o/s*	78,764,797		69,545,092
Avg. no. of shs. o/s*	76,035,720		60,534,549
	%		%
Net profit margin	n.m.		n.m.
Return on equity	(194.00)		(436.14)
Return on assets	(108.30)		(236.22)

* Ordinary
[A] Reported in accordance with IFRS

Latest Results

Periods ended:	9m Mar. 31/23[A]		9m Mar. 31/22[A]
	A$000s	%Chg	A$000s
Operating revenue	114	+208	37
Net income	(7,974)	n.a.	(13,534)
	A$		A$
Earnings per share*	(0.10)		(0.18)

* Ordinary
[A] Reported in accordance with IFRS

Historical Summary
(as originally stated)

Fiscal Year	Oper. Rev.	Net Inc. Bef. Disc.	EPS*
	A$000s	A$000s	A$
2022[A]	54	(11,770)	(0.15)
2021[A]	246	(8,110)	(0.13)
2020[A]	111	(2,067)	n.a.
2019[A]	88	(1,729)	n.a.

* Ordinary
[A] Reported in accordance with IFRS

G.74 Great-West Lifeco Inc.*

Symbol - GWO **Exchange** - TSX **CUSIP** - 39138C
Head Office - 100 Osborne St N, PO Box 6000 Stn Main, Winnipeg, MB, R3C 1V3 **Telephone** - (204) 946-1190 **Fax** - (204) 946-4139
Website - www.greatwestlifeco.com
Email - deirdre.neary@canadalife.com
Investor Relations - Deirdre Neary (204) 946-1190
Auditors - Deloitte LLP C.A., Winnipeg, Man.
Lawyers - Blake, Cassels & Graydon LLP
Transfer Agents - Computershare Investor Services (Ireland) Ltd., Dublin, Ireland; Computershare Investor Services plc, Bristol, Gloucs. United Kingdom; Computershare Trust Company, N.A., Canton, Mass.; Computershare Trust Company of Canada Inc., Toronto, Ont.
FP500 Subsidiary Revenue Ranking - 3
Employees - 31,000 at Dec. 31, 2022
Profile - (Can. 1979) Provides life and health insurance, retirement and investment, asset management and reinsurance products and services in Canada, the U.S. and Europe. At Dec. 31, 2022, the company had $2.5 trillion in assets under administration.

Canada

This segment operates through wholly owned **The Canada Life Assurance Company** (Canada Life). Operations are divided into two business units: individual customer and group customer. The individual customer unit provides life, disability and critical illness insurance products as well as wealth savings and income products and services to individual clients. Products are distributed through a multi-channel network of financial security advisors, managing general agencies and national accounts, including Financial Horizons Group. The group customer unit offers life, accidental death and dismemberment, disability, critical illness, health and dental protection, creditor insurance as well as retirement savings and income and annuity products and other specialty products to group clients, with products distributed through brokers, consultants, third party administrators/payers, financial security advisors and financial institutions.

United States

This segment includes the operations of wholly owned **Empower Annuity Insurance Company of America** (formerly **Great-West Life & Annuity Insurance Company**), **Putnam Investments, LLC** and the U.S. branch operations of Canada Life. Empower Annuity provides saving, investment and advisory solutions under the Empower brand and the Empower Investments, Empower Institutional and Personal Capital sub-brands. Empower offers employer-sponsored defined contribution, defined benefit and non-qualified plans, including enrolment services, communication materials, investment options and education services, to public/non-profit and corporate clients as well as individual retirement accounts and taxable brokerage accounts to individual clients. Empower Investments offers fund management, investment and advisory services. Empower Institutional offers private label recordkeeping and administrative services for financial institutions and other providers of employer-sponsored defined contribution, defined benefit and non-qualified plans. Personal Capital offers hybrid online financial advice and wealth management products and services. Putnam provides investment management services and related administrative functions and distribution services and offers investment products, including equity, fixed income, absolute return and alternative strategies, through Putnam Funds, Putnam Exchange Traded Funds, Putnam World Trust Funds, institutional portfolios, model-based separately management accounts and model portfolios for individual and institutional investors.

Europe

This segment consists of the company's U.K., Irish and German insurance and wealth management operations. Businesses operate under the Canada Life brand in the U.K. and Germany and the Irish Life brand in Ireland. Core products offered by the U.K. business are bulk and individual payout annuities, equity release mortgages, investments (including bonds, retirement drawdown and pension) and group insurance which are distributed primarily through independent financial advisors and employee benefit consultants in the U.K. and Isle of Man. In Ireland, the company offers savings and investments, individual and group life insurance, health insurance and pension products which are distributed through independent brokers, a direct sales force and tied agent bank branches. The company also has fund management operations in Ireland, which manage assets for various institutional clients across Europe and North America; and owns a number of Irish employee benefits and wealth consultancy businesses. In Germany, core products offered are individual and group pensions and life insurance products distributed through independent brokers and multi-tied agents.

Capital and Risk Solutions

This segment includes the company's reinsurance business operating primarily in the U.S., Barbados, Bermuda and Ireland. Through subsidiaries and branches of Canada Life and Empower Annuity, the reinsurance business provides a product portfolio consisting of life, health, annuity/longevity, mortgage, surety and property catastrophe reinsurance and retrocession which are distributed directly to clients or through independent reinsurance brokers.

On Dec. 31, 2022, wholly owned **Empower Annuity Insurance Company of America** completed two separate agreements to cede, via indemnity reinsurance, $7.946 billion of insurance contract liabilities to a non-related party.

Effective Aug. 1, 2022, wholly owned **Great-West Life & Annuity Insurance Company** changed its name to **Empower Annuity Insurance Company of America**.

Recent Merger and Acquisition Activity

Status: pending **Announced:** June 13, 2023
The Canada Life Assurance Company, wholly owned by Great-West Lifeco Inc., agreed to acquire Winnipeg, Man.-based Value Partners Group Inc., an investment firm serving the wealth management needs of affluent and high-net-worth families across Canada. Terms of the transaction were not disclosed. Value Partners includes Value Partners Investments Inc., which manages nine retail mutual funds; Value Partners Investment Counsel, which provides discretionary investment management services; and LP Financial Planning Services Ltd., a mutual fund dealer. The transaction was expected to be completed in the fourth quarter of 2023, subject to regulatory and customary closing conditions.

Status: pending **Announced:** May 31, 2023
Great-West Lifeco Inc. (Lifeco) agreed to sell Putnam Investments, LLC to global asset management firm Franklin Resources, Inc. (operating as Franklin Templeton) for a purchase price of about US$925,000,000 consisting of US$825,000,000 in upfront consideration consisting of 33,330,000 common shares at closing and US$100,000,000 in cash six months after closing. In addition, Franklin Templeton would pay up to US$375,000,000 in contingent consideration between three and seven years after close, tied to revenue growth from the partnership. Lifeco would retain its controlling interest in PanAgora Asset Management, Inc., which has US$33 billion in assets under management (AUM). Lifeco, Power Corporation of Canada and Franklin Templeton also entered into a strategic partnership to distribute Franklin Templeton products for the benefit of clients, distribution partners and shareholders. Lifeco would allocate an initial US$25 billion in AUM to Franklin Templeton's specialist investment managers within 12 months of closing. Lifeco has agreed to retain shares representing a 4.9% interest in Franklin Templeton for a minimum five-year period. The transaction was expected to close in the fourth quarter of 2023.

Status: pending **Announced:** May 16, 2023
Canada Life Limited (Canada Life U.K.), wholly owned by Great-West Lifeco Inc., agreed to sell its individual onshore protection business to Countrywide Assured plc, a wholly owned subsidiary of Chesnara plc, for an undisclosed amount. About 47,000 life insurance and critical illness customer policies would be transferred to Countrywide in 2024, subject to the completion of a court-approved transfer. The transaction follows Canada Life U.K.'s announcement that it closed onshore individual protection insurance to new business in November 2022.

Status: pending **Announced:** Apr. 3, 2023
The Canada Life Assurance Company, wholly owned by Great-West Lifeco Inc., agreed to acquire Investment Planning Counsel Inc. (IPC) for $575,000,000, which would be financed with cash on hand. IPC, 95.22%-owned by IGM Financial Inc. and 4.78%-owned by IPC Management, was a wealth dealer and investment company operating both MFDA and IIROC platforms with 650 advisors who manage $32 billion in assets under management (AUM). Upon completion, Canada Life would have more than 4,000 advisor relationships and more than $85 billion in AUM. The boards of directors of Great-West Lifeco and IGM unanimously approved the transaction, which was expected to be completed by the end of 2023, subject to regulatory approvals. Great-West Lifeco and IGM were both subsidiaries of Power Corporation of Canada.

Status: completed **Revised:** Apr. 4, 2022
UPDATE: The transaction was completed. PREVIOUS: Empower Retirement, LLC, a subsidiary of Great-West Lifeco Inc. (GWL), agreed to acquire Prudential Financial, Inc.'s full-service retirement business for a total transaction value of US$3.55 billion (Cdn$4.45 billion). Prudential's full-service retirement business covers more than 4,300 workplace savings plans, about 4,000,000 participants and US$314 billion in assets under administration (AUA). The acquisition would expand Empower's business to over 16,600,000 participants, 71,000 workplace savings plans and about US$1.4 trillion in AUA. GWL expects to finance the transaction in part with issuance of US$1.15 billion of limited recourse capital notes and US$1 billion of short-term debt. The transaction was expected to close in the first quarter of 2022.

Directors - R. Jeffrey Orr, chr., Montréal, Qué.; Paul A. Mahon, pres. & CEO, Winnipeg, Man.; Michael R. Amend, Mooresville, N.C.; Deborah J. Barrett, Toronto, Ont.; Roberta A. (Robin) Bienfait, Norcross, Ga.; Heather E. Conway, Toronto, Ont.; Marcel R. Coutu, Calgary, Alta.; André Desmarais, Westmount, Qué.; Paul Desmarais Jr., Westmount, Qué.; The Hon. Gary A. Doer, Winnipeg, Man.; David G. Fuller, Toronto, Ont.; Claude Généreux, Westmount, Qué.; Paula B. Madoff, New York, N.Y.; Susan J. McArthur, Toronto, Ont.; T. Timothy Ryan Jr., Miami Beach, Fla.; Dhvani D. Shah, Fla.; Gregory D. Tretiak, Westmount, Qué.; Siim A. Vanaselja, Toronto, Ont.; Brian E. Walsh, Rye, N.Y.

Other Exec. Officers - Sharon C. Geraghty, exec. v-p & gen. counsel; Garry MacNicholas, exec. v-p & CFO; Grace M. Palombo, exec. v-p & chief HR officer; Steven M. (Steve) Rullo, exec. v-p & global CIO; Raman Srivastava, exec. v-p & global chief invest. officer; Dervla M. Tomlin, exec. v-p & chief risk officer; Amy Metzger, sr. v-p & chief compliance officer; Nancy D. Russell, sr. v-p & chief internal auditor; David B. Simmonds, sr. v-p & chief commun. & sustainability officer; Jeremy W. Trickett, sr. v-p & chief governance officer; Gordon M. (Gord) Peters, v-p, assoc. gen. counsel & corp. sec.; David M. Harney, pres. & COO, Europe; Arshil Jamal, pres. & grp. head, strategy, invests., reinsurance & corp. devel.; Jeffrey F. (Jeff) Macoun, pres. & COO, Canada; Edmund F. Murphy III, pres. & CEO, Empower Annuity Insurance Company of America; Robert L. Reynolds, pres. & CEO, Putnam Investments, LLC; Declan Bolger, CEO, Irish Life Group Limited

Capital Stock

	Authorized (shs.)	Outstanding (shs.)[1]
First Preferred	unlimited	
Series G		12,000,000
Series H		12,000,000
Series I		12,000,000
Series L		6,800,000
Series M		6,000,000
Series N		10,000,000
Series P		10,000,000
Series Q		8,000,000
Series R		8,000,000
Series S		8,000,000
Series T		8,000,000
Series Y		8,000,000
Class A Preferred	unlimited	nil
Second Preferred	unlimited	nil
Limited Recourse Capital Notes	n.a.	
Series 1		1,500,000
Common	unlimited	931,287,061

[1] At June 30, 2023

First Preferred - Issuable in series. Entitled to temporary voting rights that carry a number of votes calculated based on a formula which accounts for the number of common and first preferred shares outstanding.

Series G - Entitled to non-cumulative preferential annual dividends of $1.30 per share payable quarterly. Redeemable at $25 per share.

Series H - Entitled to non-cumulative preferential annual dividends of $1.21252 per share payable quarterly. Redeemable at $25 per share.

Series I - Entitled to non-cumulative preferential annual dividends of $1.125 per share payable quarterly. Redeemable at $25 per share.

Series L - Entitled to non-cumulative preferential annual dividends of $1.4125 per share payable quarterly. Redeemable at $25 per share.

Series M - Entitled to non-cumulative preferential annual dividends of $1.45 per share payable quarterly. Redeemable at $25 per share.

Series N - Entitled to non-cumulative preferential annual dividends of $0.43725 per share payable quarterly to Dec. 31, 2025, and thereafter at a rate reset every five years equal to the five-year Government of Canada yield plus 1.3%. Redeemable on Dec. 31, 2025, and on December 31 every five years thereafter at $25 per share. Convertible at the holder's option, on Dec. 31, 2025, and on December 31 every five years thereafter, into floating rate first preferred series O shares on a share-for-share basis, subject to certain conditions. The series O shares would pay a quarterly dividend equal to the 90-day Canadian Treasury bill rate plus 1.3%.

Series P - Entitled to non-cumulative preferential annual dividends of $1.35 per share payable quarterly. Redeemable at $25 per share.

Series Q - Entitled to non-cumulative preferential annual dividends of $1.2875 per share payable quarterly. Redeemable at $25 per share.

Series R - Entitled to non-cumulative preferential annual dividends of $1.20 per share payable quarterly. Redeemable at $25 per share.

Series S - Entitled to non-cumulative preferential annual dividends of $1.3125 per share payable quarterly. Redeemable at $25.25 per share to June 30, 2023, and at $25 per share thereafter.

Series T - Entitled to non-cumulative preferential annual dividends of $1.2875 per share payable quarterly. Redeemable at $26 per share and declining by 25¢ per share annually to June 30, 2026, and at $25 per share thereafter.

Series Y - Entitled to non-cumulative preferential annual dividends of $1.125 per share payable quarterly. Redeemable at $26 per share on or after Dec. 31, 2026, and declining by 25¢ per share annually to Dec. 31, 2030, and at $25 per share thereafter.

Class A Preferred - Issuable in series. Non-voting. Rank pari passu with first preferred shares and senior to second preferred shares.

Second Preferred - Issuable in series. Non-voting.

Limited Recourse Capital Notes (LRCN) Series 1 - Notes with recourse limited to assets held by a third party trustee in a consolidated trust. Bear interest at 3.6% per annum until Dec. 31, 2026, and thereafter at an annual rate reset every five years equal to the five-year Government of Canada yield plus 2.641% until Dec. 31, 2076. Maturing on Dec. 31, 2081. Trust assets consist of non-cumulative five-year reset first preferred series U shares.

Common - One vote per share.

Options - At Dec. 31, 2022, options were outstanding to purchase 17,093,615 common shares at prices ranging from $27.13 to $38.75 per share expiring to 2032.

Normal Course Issuer Bid - The company plans to make normal course purchases of up to 20,000,000 common shares representing 2.2% of the total outstanding. The bid commenced on Jan. 27, 2023, and expires on Jan. 26, 2024.

Major Shareholder - Power Corporation of Canada held 65% interest at Mar. 8, 2023.

Price Range - GWO/TSX

Year	Volume	High	Low	Close
2022	553,133,866	$41.50	$27.99	$31.30
2021	365,013,767	$39.73	$28.85	$37.96
2020	299,635,805	$35.60	$18.88	$30.35
2019	181,184,326	$34.42	$27.52	$33.26
2018	152,128,871	$35.59	$26.83	$28.18

Recent Close: $38.22

Capital Stock Changes - During 2022, 1,232,772 common shares were issued on exercise of options.

Dividends

GWO com Ra $2.08 pa Q est. Mar. 31, 2023
Prev. Rate: $1.96 est. Dec. 31, 2021
Prev. Rate: $1.752 est. Mar. 31, 2020
GWO.PR.G pfd 1st ser G 5.2% red. Ra $1.30 pa Q
GWO.PR.H pfd 1st ser H 4.85% red. Ra $1.2125 pa Q
GWO.PR.I pfd 1st ser I 4.5% red. Ra $1.125 pa Q
GWO.PR.L pfd 1st ser L 5.65% red. Ra $1.4125 pa Q
GWO.PR.M pfd 1st ser M 5.80% red. Ra $1.45 pa Q
GWO.PR.N pfd 1st ser N 3.65% red. exch. Adj. Ra $0.43725 pa Q est. Mar. 31, 2021
GWO.PR.P pfd 1st ser P 5.4% red. Adj. Ra $1.35 pa Q est. June 29, 2012
GWO.PR.Q pfd 1st ser Q 5.15% red. Ra $1.2875 pa Q
GWO.PR.R pfd 1st ser R 4.80% red. Ra $1.20 pa Q
GWO.PR.S pfd 1st ser S 5.25% red. Ra $1.3125 pa Q
GWO.PR.T pfd 1st ser T 5.15% red. Ra $1.2875 pa Q
GWO.PR.Y pfd 1st ser Y 4.5% red. Ra $1.125 pa Q
Listed Oct 8/21.
$0.2589i.............. Dec. 31/21
pfd 1st ser F 5.9% red. Ra $1.475 pa Q[1]
$0.36875f............ Dec. 31/21
[1] Redeemed Dec. 31, 2021 at $25 per sh.
f Final Payment **i** Initial Payment

Long-Term Debt - Outstanding at Dec. 31, 2022:

Commercial paper & other[1]	$135,000,000
LIBOR+0.7% credit facility[2]	67,000,000
Adj. term SOFR credit facility[3]	675,000,000
Sr. bonds:	
2.5% due 2023[4]	725,000,000
1.75% due 2026[4]	722,000,000
4.7% due 2029[4]	721,000,000
Sr. notes:	
0.904% due 2025[3]	672,000,000
1.357% due 2027[5]	538,000,000
4.047% due 2028[6]	403,000,000
1.776% due 2031[5]	537,000,000
4.15% due 2047[7]	930,000,000
4.581% due 2048[3]	669,000,000
3.075% due 2051[7]	935,000,000
Debs.:	
3.337% due 2028	498,000,000
6.4% due 2028	100,000,000
2.379% due 2030	597,000,000
6.74% due 2031	196,000,000
6.67% due 2033	395,000,000
5.998% due 2039	343,000,000
2.981% due 2050	494,000,000
7.529% capital trust secs. due 2052	157,000,000
	10,509,000,000

[1] Bearing interest at 4.628%.
[2] US$50,000,000.
[3] US$500,000,000.
[4] €500,000,000.
[5] US$400,000,000.
[6] US$300,000,000.
[7] US$700,000,000.

Wholly Owned Subsidiaries

The Canada Life Assurance Company, Winnipeg, Man.
- 100% int. in **Canada Life Capital Corporation Inc.**, Toronto, Ont.
  - 100% int. in **Canada Life International Holdings Limited**, Bermuda.
    - 100% int. in **The Canada Life Group (U.K.) Limited**, Potters Bar, Middx., United Kingdom.
      - 100% int. in **Canada Life Limited**, Potters Bar, Middx., United Kingdom.
        - 100% int. in **Irish Life Group Limited**, Ireland.
          - 100% int. in **Irish Life Assurance, plc**, Ireland.
- 100% int. in **Canada Life Irish Holding Company Limited**, Dublin, Ireland.
- 100% int. in **The Canada Life Insurance Company of Canada**, Winnipeg, Man.
- 100% int. in **Financial Horizons Incorporated**, Kitchener, Ont.
- 100% int. in **GWL Realty Advisors Inc.**, Winnipeg, Man.
- 100% int. in **Quadrus Investment Services Ltd.**, Ont.

Great-West Financial (Nova Scotia) Co., N.S.
- 100% int. in **Great-West Lifeco U.S. LLC**, Del.
  - 100% int. in **Empower Holdings, Inc.**, Del.
    - 100% int. in **Empower Annuity Insurance Company of America**, Greenwood Village, Colo.
      - 100% int. in **Empower Advisory Group, LLC**, Colo.
      - 100% int. in **Empower Capital Management, LLC**, Colo.
      - 100% int. in **Empower Financial Services, Inc.**, Del.
      - 100% int. in **Empower Life & Annuity Insurance Company of New York**, N.Y.
      - 100% int. in **Empower Plan Services, LLC**, Del.
      - 100% int. in **Empower Retirement, LLC**, Denver, Colo.
      - 100% int. in **Empower Trust Company, LLC**, Colo.
      - 100% int. in **Personal Capital Corporation**, Redwood City, Calif.
        - 100% int. in **Personal Capital Advisors Corporation**, Calif.
- 100% int. in **Putnam Investments, LLC**, Boston, Mass.

Investments

3.9% int. in **IGM Financial Inc.**, Winnipeg, Man. (see separate coverage)

Note: The preceding list includes only the major related companies in which interests are held.

Financial Statistics

Periods ended:	12m Dec. 31/22[A]		12m Dec. 31/21[A]
	$000s	%Chg	$000s
Net premiums earned	52,821,000		52,813,000
Net investment income	(15,757,000)		4,310,000
Total revenue	**44,662,000**	**-31**	**64,417,000**
Policy benefits & claims	29,664,000		50,295,000
Commissions	2,675,000		2,664,000
Salaries & benefits	4,614,000		4,191,000
General & admin. expense	2,266,000		1,938,000
Premium taxes	497,000		500,000
Operating expense	**10,052,000**	**+8**	**9,293,000**
Operating income	**4,946,000**	**+2**	**4,829,000**
Deprec. & amort.	558,000		523,000
Finance costs, gross	417,000		349,000
Write-downs/write-offs	(25,000)		nil
Pre-tax income	**3,768,000**	**-3**	**3,867,000**
Income taxes	234,000		304,000
Net income	**3,534,000**	**-1**	**3,563,000**
Net inc. for equity hldrs	**3,349,000**	**+3**	**3,262,000**
Net inc. for non-cont. int	**185,000**	**-39**	**301,000**
Cash & equivalent	7,290,000		6,075,000
Accounts receivable	5,271,000		5,127,000
Securities investments	173,217,000		154,214,000
Mortgages	39,529,000		28,852,000
Real estate	8,344,000		7,763,000
Total investments	230,548,000		199,729,000
Segregated fund assets	387,897,000		357,419,000
Total assets	**701,455,000**	**+11**	**630,488,000**
Bank indebtedness	274,000		407,000
Accts. pay. & accr. liabs	3,194,000		3,032,000
Debt	10,509,000		8,804,000
Long-term lease liabilities	507,000		522,000
Policy liabilities & claims	247,698,000		220,833,000
Segregated fund liabilities	387,897,000		357,419,000
Preferred share equity	4,220,000		4,220,000
Shareholders' equity	29,010,000		27,216,000
Non-controlling interest	3,308,000		3,267,000
Cash from oper. activs	**7,047,000**	**-32**	**10,373,000**
Cash from fin. activs	(620,000)		(992,000)
Cash from invest. activs	(5,493,000)		(11,212,000)
Net cash position	**7,290,000**	**+20**	**6,075,000**
Unfunded pension liability	n.a.		218,000
Pension fund surplus	466,000		n.a.
	$		$
Earnings per share*	3.46		3.37
Cash flow per share*	7.56		11.16
Cash divd. per share*	1.96		1.80
	shs		shs
No. of shs. o/s*	931,853,110		930,620,338
Avg. no. of shs. o/s*	931,682,589		929,461,348
	%		%
Net profit margin	7.91		5.53
Return on equity	13.47		14.12
Return on assets	0.59		0.63
Foreign sales percent	70		70
No. of employees (FTEs)	31,000		28,000

* Common
[A] Reported in accordance with IFRS

Latest Results

Periods ended:	6m June 30/23[A]		6m June 30/22[oA]
	$000s	%Chg	$000s
Total revenue	18,050,000	n.a.	(9,422,000)
Net inc. bef. disc. opers	1,250,000	-45	2,257,000
Income from disc. opers	(90,000)		(7,000)
Net income	1,160,000	-48	2,250,000
Net inc. for equity hldrs	1,158,000	-48	2,222,000
Net inc. for non-cont. int	2,000		28,000
	$		$
Earns. per sh. bef. disc. opers.*	1.27		2.32
Earnings per share*	1.17		2.32

* Common
[o] Restated
[A] Reported in accordance with IFRS

Historical Summary
(as originally stated)

Fiscal Year	Total Rev.	Net Inc. Bef. Disc.	EPS*
	$000s	$000s	$
2022[A]	44,662,000	3,534,000	3.46
2021[A]	64,417,000	3,563,000	3.37
2020[A]	60,583,000	3,154,000	3.17
2019[A]	44,698,000	2,507,000	2.49
2018[A]	44,032,000	3,075,000	3.00

* Common
[A] Reported in accordance with IFRS

G.75 Green Block Mining Corp.

Symbol - GBMC **Exchange** - CSE (S) **CUSIP** - 392705
Head Office - 1430-800 Pender St W, Vancouver, BC, V6C 2V6 **Toll-free** - (877) 770-6545
Website - www.linkglobal.io
Email - kevin@linkglobal.io
Investor Relations - Kevin Ma (877) 770-6545
Auditors - Dale Matheson Carr-Hilton LaBonte LLP C.A., Vancouver, B.C.
Transfer Agents - Odyssey Trust Company, Vancouver, B.C.
Profile - (B.C. 2018) Engages in cryptocurrency mining and provides all-in hosting and managed services for third party cryptocurrency miners, and sells verified emission reduction credits.

Generates revenues from cryptocurrency mining, as well as from building and managing semi-portable, self-contained power solutions (or containers) that can be rapidly deployed in virtually any environment to provide cost-effective power and infrastructure solutions to third party digital currency miners. Also mines Bitcoin with its own computing power with 18.75 MW of power onsite.

In addition, sells verified emission reduction credits.

Common suspended from CSE, July 11, 2022.

Predecessor Detail - Name changed from Link Global Technologies Inc., Mar. 25, 2022.

Directors - Daniel Feldman, CEO; Kevin Ma, Vancouver, B.C.; Michael Vogel, Coquitlam, B.C.

Other Exec. Officers - Emmery Wang, CFO & corp. sec.; Patrick Enwright, chief comml. officer; Hans Looman, chief tech. officer; Michael Shader, v-p, tech.

Capital Stock

	Authorized (shs.)	Outstanding (shs.)[1]
Common	unlimited	64,115,107

[1] At Aug. 22, 2023

Major Shareholder - Widely held at June 14, 2021.

Price Range - GBMC/CSE (S)

Year	Volume	High	Low	Close
2022	9,131,678	$0.15	$0.04	$0.05
2021	88,835,450	$1.70	$0.12	$0.13
2020	3,715,056	$0.66	$0.30	$0.61

Wholly Owned Subsidiaries

Clean Carbon Equity Inc.
Link Power Corp., Canada.

Investments

50% int. in **Pure Digital Power Corp.**, Alta.

G.76 Green Impact Partners Inc.

Symbol - GIP **Exchange** - TSX-VEN **CUSIP** - 39306L
Head Office - 400-2207 4 St SW, Calgary, AB, T2S 1X1 **Telephone** - (780) 667-8798
Website - www.greenipi.com
Email - jdouglas@greenipi.com
Investor Relations - Jesse Douglas (780) 667-8798
Auditors - Deloitte LLP C.A., Calgary, Alta.
Transfer Agents - Odyssey Trust Company, Vancouver, B.C.
FP500 Revenue Ranking - 644
Profile - (B.C. 2011) Operates water and solids treatment and recycling facilities and develops and builds renewable natural gas (RNG) and clean bio-energy projects throughout North America.

Water and Solids Treatment and Recycling

Operates water, waste and solids disposal and recycling facilities which serve a diverse customer base including municipalities, governments, utilities, infrastructure, industrial, energy and mining industries in North America. Operations include five water treatment facilities in Rycroft, Grande Cache, Cynthia, Claresholm and Mayerthorpe, Alta.; a treating facility and natural gas liquids blending facility in Swan Hills, Alta.; an industrial disposal facility in Heward, Sask.; and 80% interest in a solids recycling business that provides collection, hauling, recycling and initial processing services in Maui, Hawaii.

Clean Energy Production

Through a strategic partnership with **Amber Infrastructure Group Limited**, develops and constructs renewable energy projects in Canada and the U.S., including RNG, biofuel and hydrogen distribution. Principal projects are GreenGas RNG facility in Weld cty., Colo., which would convert organic waste from two dairy farms into RNG, generating over 360,000,000,000 British thermal units (Btu) per year of RNG; a dairy RNG project in Iowa under late-stage development which was expected to include three locations and generate 350,000,000,000 Btu per year of RNG; and Future Energy Park, a biofuel facility in Calgary, Alta., under permitting and approval stage which would use non-food grade wheat to produce RNG and ethanol estimated annually at over 3,500,000,000,000 Btu of RNG and over 300,000,000 litres of cellulosic equivalent ethanol as well as 100,000 tonnes per year of protein distillers grain (cattle feed) and 1,500,000 tonnes per year of carbon offset credits, and capture 400,000 tonnes of clean carbon dioxide. Amber holds 50% project-level equity interest in GreenGas, Iowa RNG project and Future Energy Park. Also has an early stage farm-based RNG project in southern Alberta, expected to produce up to 810,000,000,000 Btu per year of RNG.

During the second quarter of 2022, the company invested an additional $2,600,000 in **Future Energy Development Corp.** (FEDC). As a result, the company's ownership interest in FEDC increased to 35.7% from 29.4%. FEDC holds the Future Energy Park biofuel facility in Calgary, Alta.

In March 2022, the company entered into a partnership to develop a dairy renewable natural gas (RNG) project consisting of three locations in Iowa, with a targeted production of 3,500,000,000,000 British thermal units (Btu) per year of RNG. Capital costs were estimated at $100,000,000 and start of construction was targeted in early 2023 with completion in late 2024.

Recent Merger and Acquisition Activity

Status: completed **Revised:** Feb. 23, 2023
UPDATE: The transaction was completed. PREVIOUS: Green Impact Partners Inc. agreed to sell 50% project-level equity interest in GreenGas renewable natural gas (RNG) facility in Weld cty., Colo., RNG project in Iowa, and Future Energy Park, a biofuel facility in Calgary, Alta., to private London, U.K.-based Amber Infrastructure Group Limited for up to Cdn$485,000,000 for the Iowa and Future Energy Park projects and up to Cdn$60,000,000 (US$43,900,000) for the GreenGas facility, US$28,500,000 of which is payable upon closing and the rest upon potential future completion of a third-party sale of GreenGas Colorado investment tax credits.

Status: completed **Revised:** Feb. 21, 2023
UPDATE: The transaction was completed. PREVIOUS: Green Impact Partners Inc. (GIP) agreed to acquire Advanced Renewables Colorado, LLC's minority interest in GreenGas Colorado, LLC, which holds GreenGas renewable natural gas (RNG) facility in Weld cty., Colo., for US$11,200,000. As a result, GIP now owns 100% of GreenGas.

Predecessor Detail - Name changed from Blackheath Resources Inc., June 1, 2021, pursuant to reverse takeover acquisition of certain clean energy assets, renewable natural gas development projects and solids recycling facilities from Wolverine Energy and Infrastructure Inc.; basis 1 new for 48.42 old shs.

Directors - Geeta Sankappanavar, chr., Calgary, Alta.; Jesse Douglas, CEO, Nisku, Alta.; Bruce A. Chan, Whistler, B.C.; Alicia Dubois, Canmore, Alta.; Jeff D. Hunter, Houston, Tex.; Natascha Kiernan, West Vancouver, B.C.

Other Exec. Officers - Kathy Bolton, CFO; Nikolaus Kiefer, chief invest. officer; Robert J. Beekhuizen, v-p, major projects; Julia S. Ciccaglione, v-p, regulatory & envir.; Jeff MacBeath, v-p, fin.; Dorreen Miller, v-p, commun.; Greg Pecharsky, v-p, corp. devel. & capital markets; Steven Piepgrass, v-p, const.; Fred Scott, v-p, eng.; Wade Scott, v-p, opers.; Rhonda Stanley, v-p, clean energy mktg.

Capital Stock

	Authorized (shs.)	Outstanding (shs.)[1]
Common	unlimited	20,300,005

[1] At May 19, 2023

Major Shareholder - Wolverine Energy and Infrastructure Inc. held 25.4% interest and Jesse Douglas held 11.4% interest at Oct. 21, 2022.

Price Range - GIP/TSX-VEN

Year	Volume	High	Low	Close
2022	1,964,254	$9.25	$3.51	$5.08
2021	3,390,163	$12.59	$4.25	$6.00
2020	18,947	$11.38	$3.15	$11.38
2019	20,615	$14.53	$2.18	$3.63
2018	11,629	$33.89	$2.42	$2.42

Consolidation: 1-for-48.42 cons. in June 2021; 1-for-10 cons. in Dec. 2019

Recent Close: $7.29

Capital Stock Changes - In June 2023, private placement of 1,000,000 common shares was completed at $10 per share.

There were no changes to capital stock during 2022.

Wholly Owned Subsidiaries

Green Impact Operating Corp., Canada.
- 100% int. in **Akira Infra I Ltd.**, Calgary, Alta.
  - 80% int. in **Aloha Glass Recycling Inc.**, Hawaii
- 36.8% int. in **Future Energy Development Corp.**, Alta.
- 100% int. in **Transition Energy Inc.**, Victoria, B.C.

Note: The preceding list includes only the major related companies in which interests are held.

Financial Statistics

Periods ended:	12m Dec. 31/22[A]		12m Dec. 31/21[oA]
	$000s	%Chg	$000s
Operating revenue	**213,738**	**+66**	**128,972**
Cost of sales	208,337		121,607
Salaries & benefits	1,751		1,911
General & admin expense	3,655		1,868
Stock-based compensation	2,446		36
Operating expense	**216,189**	**+72**	**125,422**
Operating income	**(2,451)**	**n.a.**	**3,550**
Deprec., depl. & amort.	5,458		5,366
Finance income	nil		71
Finance costs, gross	1,086		1,041
Write-downs/write-offs	(3,001)		nil
Pre-tax income	**(10,342)**	**n.a.**	**(4,616)**
Income taxes	(981)		(3,974)
Net income	**(9,361)**	**n.a.**	**(642)**
Net inc. for equity hldrs	**(9,340)**	**n.a.**	**(796)**
Net inc. for non-cont. int.	**(21)**	**n.a.**	**154**
Cash & equivalent	2,692		4,498
Inventories	2,065		1,038
Accounts receivable	17,433		16,535
Current assets	25,742		23,560
Long-term investments	2,803		2,803
Fixed assets, net	194,267		143,795
Intangibles, net	1,695		4,782
Total assets	**226,977**	**+29**	**176,070**
Accts. pay. & accr. liabs.	21,031		21,020
Current liabilities	29,856		21,252
Long-term debt, gross	66,405		368
Long-term debt, net	66,057		136
Shareholders' equity	103,867		114,944
Non-controlling interest	13,803		12,795
Cash from oper. activs	**(2,519)**	**n.a.**	**(416)**
Cash from fin. activs	55,808		41,606
Cash from invest. activs	(55,561)		(36,734)
Net cash position	**2,692**	**-40**	**4,498**
Capital expenditures	(52,927)		(37,181)
	$		$
Earnings per share*	(0.46)		(0.05)
Cash flow per share*	(0.12)		(0.03)
	shs		shs
No. of shs. o/s*	20,300,005		20,300,005
Avg. no. of shs. o/s*	20,300,005		16,300,003
	%		%
Net profit margin	(4.38)		(0.50)
Return on equity	n.m.		n.m.
Return on assets	n.a.		n.a.

* Common
[o] Restated
[A] Reported in accordance with IFRS

Latest Results

Periods ended:	3m Mar. 31/23[A]		3m Mar. 31/22[A]
	$000s	%Chg	$000s
Operating revenue	38,498	-14	44,787
Net income	4,492	n.a.	(529)
Net inc. for equity hldrs	4,492	n.a.	(545)
Net inc. for non-cont. int.	nil		16
	$		$
Earnings per share*	0.22		(0.03)

* Common
[A] Reported in accordance with IFRS

Historical Summary
(as originally stated)

Fiscal Year	Oper. Rev. $000s	Net Inc. Bef. Disc. $000s	EPS* $
2022[A]	213,738	(9,361)	(0.46)
2021[A1]	128,972	(642)	(0.05)
2020[A2]	nil	(88)	(0.60)
2019[A]	nil	(27)	(0.26)
2018[A]	nil	(307)	(3.00)

* Common
[A] Reported in accordance with IFRS
[1] Results reflect the May 27, 2021, reverse takeover acquisition of certain clean energy assets, renewable natural gas development projects and water and solids recycling facilities from Wolverine Energy and Infrastructure Inc.
[2] Results for 2020 and prior years pertain to Blackheath Resources Inc.

Note: Adjusted throughout for 1-for-48.42 cons. in June 2021; 1-for-10 cons. in Dec. 2019

G.77 Green Panda Capital Corp.

Symbol - GPCC.P **Exchange** - TSX-VEN **CUSIP** - 393212
Head Office - TD Centre North Tower, 3000-77 King St W, PO Box 95, Toronto, ON, M5K 1G8 **Telephone** - (416) 365-3701

Email - sukin21cn@hotmail.com
Investor Relations - Richard Zhou (647) 404-8966
Auditors - Segal GCSE LLP C.A., Toronto, Ont.
Transfer Agents - TSX Trust Company, Toronto, Ont.
Profile - (Ont. 2018) Capital Pool Company.

Recent Merger and Acquisition Activity

Status: terminated **Revised:** Mar. 24, 2023
UPDATE: The transaction was terminated. PREVIOUS: Green Panda Capital Corp. entered into a letter of intent for the Qualifying Transaction reverse takeover acquisition of private B.C.-based Cobre Minerals Inc., which was pursuing the acquisition of Tron Mineral Resources MX S.A., which holds the Don Pedro copper project in Jalisco state, Mexico, on a share-for-share basis, which would result in the issuance of 12,150,000 Green Panda post-consolidated common shares (following a share consolidation on a to-be-determined basis). Upon completion, Green Panda would change its name to Cobre Minerals Inc.

Status: terminated **Revised:** July 6, 2022
UPDATE: The transaction was terminated. PREVIOUS: Green Panda Capital Corp. entered into a letter of intent for the Qualifying Transaction reverse takeover acquisition of private 1301666 B.C. Ltd., which was pursuing the acquisition of two mineral properties in Nevada, on a share-for-share basis, which would result in the issuance of 46,801,131 Green Panda post-consolidated common shares (following a share consolidation on a to-be-determined basis). Upon completion, Green Panda would change its name to Falcon Butte Minerals Corp.

Directors - Richard Zhou, pres. & CEO, Richmond Hill, Ont.; Steven Olsthoorn, CFO & corp. sec., Richmond Hill, Ont.; Yongbiao (Winfield) Ding, Toronto, Ont.; Rodney Ireland, Ont.; Andrew Skafel, Ottawa, Ont.

Capital Stock

	Authorized (shs.)	Outstanding (shs.)[1]
Common	unlimited	6,288,700

[1] At June 16, 2023

Major Shareholder - Richard Zhou held 32.12% interest and Donglei Chen held 19.08% interest at May 25, 2021.

Price Range - GPCC.P/TSX-VEN

Year	Volume	High	Low	Close
2022	4,000	$0.09	$0.08	$0.08
2021	779,070	$0.15	$0.07	$0.08
2020	246,799	$0.18	$0.04	$0.10
2019	25,650	$0.18	$0.10	$0.18

Capital Stock Changes - There were no changes to capital stock from fiscal 2020 to fiscal 2022, inclusive.

G.78 Green Rise Foods Inc.

Symbol - GRF **Exchange** - TSX-VEN **CUSIP** - 39328G
Head Office - 301-47 Colborne St, Toronto, ON, M5E 1P8 **Telephone** - (416) 294-2881
Website - www.greenrisefoods.ca
Email - vnarang@greenrisecapital.ca
Investor Relations - Vincent Narang (416) 861-9001
Auditors - RSM Canada LLP C.A., Toronto, Ont.
Transfer Agents - TSX Trust Company, Toronto, Ont.
Profile - (Ont. 2017) Grows, packages and sells tomatoes and mini peppers produced from greenhouses in Kingsville and Leamington, Ont.

The company owns three greenhouse ranges in Leamington and Kingsville (2), Ont. These include a 51-acre greenhouse (GR1) in Leamington, which produces beefsteak, medley, and piccolo tomatoes; a 21-acre greenhouse (GR2) which produces beefsteak tomatoes and a 16-acre greenhouse (GR3) which produces and packs mini peppers, both in Kingsville. GR1 is situated on an 81-acre parcel of land, with 36 acres of the range being utilized for growing tomatoes, and 15 acres being leased to an affiliate that grows organic peppers. GR2 is located on a 57-acre greenhouse property, while GR3 is on a 34-acre farm property.

On Jan. 1, 2023, wholly owned **Bull Market Farms Inc.** was amalgamated into the company.

Recent Merger and Acquisition Activity

Status: completed **Revised:** June 30, 2022
UPDATE: The transaction was completed. PREVIOUS: Green Rise Foods Inc. agreed to acquire a 16-acre greenhouse range located on a 34-acre farm in Kingsville, Ont., from 2073834 Ontario Limited for $14,826,000, which would be funded with conventional mortgage financing. 2073834 Ontario was principally owned and controlled by Adam Suder, Green Rise's chief growth officer. The greenhouse range was producing and packing high demand, high quality mini peppers.

Predecessor Detail - Name changed from Green Rise Capital Corporation, Sept. 2, 2020.

Directors - Enrico (Rick) Paolone, chr., Toronto, Ont.; Vincent Narang, CEO & corp. sec., Toronto, Ont.; Jerry A. Mancini, Ont.; Thomas A. McKee, Ont.; Stanley A. Thomas, Maple, Ont.

Other Exec. Officers - George Hatzoglou, CFO; Adam Suder, chief growth officer

Capital Stock

	Authorized (shs.)	Outstanding (shs.)[1]
Common	unlimited	46,389,066

[1] At May 25, 2023

Major Shareholder - Enrico (Rick) Paolone held 15% interest and Vincent Narang held 14.8% interest at May 12, 2023.

Price Range - GRF/TSX-VEN

Year	Volume	High	Low	Close
2022	303,958	$1.85	$0.50	$0.55
2021	1,480,131	$3.15	$1.00	$1.20
2020	1,025,794	$2.00	$0.15	$1.75
2019	717,854	$0.40	$0.15	$0.21
2018	241,380	$0.39	$0.15	$0.15

Recent Close: $0.55

Capital Stock Changes - During 2022, 1,033,332 common shares were issued on exercise of options.

Wholly Owned Subsidiaries

Mor Gro Sales Inc., Ont.

Financial Statistics

Periods ended:	12m Dec. 31/22[A]		12m Dec. 31/21[oA]
	$000s	%Chg	$000s
Operating revenue	**23,056**	**+30**	**17,711**
Cost of sales	7,743		5,917
Salaries & benefits	7,611		7,093
General & admin expense	2,148		2,014
Operating expense	**17,502**	**+16**	**15,024**
Operating income	**5,554**	**+107**	**2,687**
Deprec., depl. & amort.	8,105		5,752
Finance costs, gross	1,169		1,160
Pre-tax income	**(1,939)**	**n.a.**	**(4,225)**
Income taxes	(171)		(810)
Net income	**(1,768)**	**n.a.**	**(3,415)**
Inventories	491		802
Accounts receivable	421		1,011
Current assets	2,963		3,517
Fixed assets, net	52,818		41,731
Total assets	**55,781**	**+23**	**45,248**
Bank indebtedness	891		2,914
Accts. pay. & accr. liabs.	5,758		4,671
Current liabilities	25,821		9,767
Long-term debt, gross	44,584		31,377
Long-term debt, net	25,620		29,358
Long-term lease liabilities	89		275
Shareholders' equity	3,455		4,866
Cash from oper. activs.	**8,518**	**+165**	**3,216**
Cash from fin. activs.	10,731		14,065
Cash from invest. activs.	(19,249)		(20,338)
Capital expenditures	(249)		(591)
	$		$
Earnings per share*	(0.04)		(0.08)
Cash flow per share*	0.19		0.07
	shs		shs
No. of shs. o/s*	46,389,066		45,355,734
Avg. no. of shs. o/s*	45,718,565		45,056,648
	%		%
Net profit margin	(7.67)		(19.28)
Return on equity	(42.49)		(53.28)
Return on assets	(1.41)		(6.40)

* Common
[o] Restated
[A] Reported in accordance with IFRS

Latest Results

Periods ended:	3m Mar. 31/23[A]		3m Mar. 31/22[oA]
	$000s	%Chg	$000s
Operating revenue	158	-33	235
Net income	(569)	n.a.	(708)
	$		$
Earnings per share*	(0.01)		(0.02)

* Common
[o] Restated
[A] Reported in accordance with IFRS

Historical Summary
(as originally stated)

Fiscal Year	Oper. Rev. $000s	Net Inc. Bef. Disc. $000s	EPS* $
2022[A]	23,056	(1,768)	(0.04)
2021[A]	17,711	(3,415)	(0.08)
2020[A]	15,413	865	0.02
2019[A1]	13,697	(2,235)	(0.06)
2018[A2,3]	8,324	3,655	n.a.

* Common
[A] Reported in accordance with IFRS
[1] Results reflect the Sept. 30, 2019, Qualifying Transaction reverse takeover acquisition of Bull Market Farms Inc.
[2] 40 weeks ended Dec. 31, 2018.
[3] Results pertain to Bull Market Farms Inc.

G.79 Green River Gold Corp.

Symbol - CCR **Exchange** - CSE **CUSIP** - 39328D
Head Office - 115-6220 Fulton Rd NW, Edmonton, AB, T6A 3T4 **Telephone** - (780) 993-2193 **Fax** - (780) 482-5263
Website - greenrivergold.com
Email - perry.little@greenrivergold.ca
Investor Relations - Pearson John Little (780) 993-2193
Auditors - BDO Canada LLP C.A., Calgary, Alta.
Lawyers - Salley Bowes Harwardt Law Corp., Vancouver, B.C.
Transfer Agents - Computershare Trust Company of Canada Inc., Vancouver, B.C.
Profile - (Can. 2006) Has mineral interests in British Columbia.

Holds Fontaine gold and Quesnel nickel prospects, totaling 20,000 hectares, 12 km southwest of Barkerville; Kymar silver prospect, 1,625 hectares, 28 km west of Invermere; and KaLi lithium prospect, 1,060 hectares, 30 km northwest of Clearwater. Also holds placer mining claims along past producing creeks and rivers, including Fontaine Creek, 679 hectares; nearby Little Swift River, 896 hectares; nearby Sovereign Creek, 409 hectares; Willow River, 136 hectares, 12 km from Wells; and Swift River, 447 hectares, 40 km east of Quesnel.

In April 2023, the company acquired the 1,060-hectare KaLi lithium prospect in British Columbia for $1,859 cash.

In September 2022, the company exited the retail business with the sale of its remaining retail inventory for $75,000 to **Gold Rush Suppliers Inc.**

Predecessor Detail - Name changed from Greywacke Exploration Ltd., Aug. 25, 2017.

Directors - Pearson John (Perry) Little, pres. & CEO, Alta.; Shawn Stockdale, CFO & corp. sec., Alta.; Vern Kibblewhite, Alta.; David Upright, Alta.; Ricky James (Rick) Watters, Alta.

Capital Stock

	Authorized (shs.)	Outstanding (shs.)[1]
Common	unlimited	103,042,313

[1] At Mar. 31, 2023

Major Shareholder - Widely held at Nov. 15, 2021.

Price Range - CCR/CSE

Year	Volume	High	Low	Close
2022	19,461,793	$0.10	$0.03	$0.08
2021	28,280,855	$0.08	$0.05	$0.07
2020	14,375,047	$0.10	$0.04	$0.07
2019	3,416,400	$0.08	$0.04	$0.07
2018	6,400,720	$0.09	$0.03	$0.06

Recent Close: $0.04

Capital Stock Changes - During fiscal 2022, 37,297,792 common shares were issued by private placement.

Financial Statistics

Periods ended:	12m Sept. 30/22[A]		12m Sept. 30/21[◻A]
	$000s	%Chg	$000s
Operating revenue	**nil**	**n.a.**	**29**
General & admin expense	750		422
Stock-based compensation	441		nil
Operating expense	**1,191**	**+182**	**422**
Operating income	**(1,191)**	**n.a.**	**(393)**
Deprec., depl. & amort.	36		36
Finance costs, gross	46		45
Write-downs/write-offs	(6)		(63)
Pre-tax income	**(1,132)**	**n.a.**	**(538)**
Net inc. bef. disc. opers	**(1,132)**	**n.a.**	**(538)**
Disc. opers., equity hldrs	(177)		(494)
Disc. opers., NCI	(20)		2
Income from disc. opers	(197)		(492)
Net income	**(1,329)**	**n.a.**	**(1,030)**
Net inc. for equity hldrs	**(1,309)**	**n.a.**	**(1,032)**
Net inc. for non-cont. int	**(20)**	**n.a.**	**2**
Cash & equivalent	226		35
Inventories	nil		122
Accounts receivable	48		36
Current assets	955		990
Fixed assets, net	83		29
Right-of-use assets	7		34
Explor./devel. properties	1,395		879
Total assets	**2,512**	**+27**	**1,974**
Bank indebtedness	4		255
Accts. pay. & accr. liabs	198		285
Current liabilities	397		1,036
Long-term debt, gross	147		334
Long-term debt, net	142		84
Long-term lease liabilities	nil		7
Equity portion of conv. debs	59		28
Shareholders' equity	1,972		835
Non-controlling interest	nil		12
Cash from oper. activs	**(816)**	**n.a.**	**(376)**
Cash from fin. activs	1,769		992
Cash from invest. activs	(761)		(585)
Net cash position	**226**	**+546**	**35**
Capital expenditures	(326)		(148)
	$		$
Earns. per sh. bef disc opers*	(0.01)		(0.01)
Earnings per share*	(0.02)		(0.02)
Cash flow per share*	(0.01)		(0.01)
	shs		shs
No. of shs. o/s*	94,362,541		57,064,749
Avg. no. of shs. o/s*	77,675,000		50,873,000
	%		%
Net profit margin	n.a.		n.m.
Return on equity	(79.23)		(56.28)
Return on assets	(48.42)		(26.92)

* Common
◻ Restated
[A] Reported in accordance with IFRS

Latest Results

Periods ended:	6m Mar. 31/23[A]		6m Mar. 31/22[A]
	$000s	%Chg	$000s
Operating revenue	nil	n.a.	107
Net inc. bef. disc. opers	(358)	n.a.	(884)
Income from disc. opers	nil		(80)
Net income	(358)	n.a.	(964)
Net inc. for equity hldrs	(358)	n.a.	(944)
Net inc. for non-cont. int	nil		(20)
	$		$
Earns. per sh. bef. disc. opers.*	(0.00)		(0.01)
Earnings per share*	(0.00)		(0.01)

* Common
[A] Reported in accordance with IFRS

Historical Summary
(as originally stated)

Fiscal Year	Oper. Rev.	Net Inc. Bef. Disc.	EPS*
	$000s	$000s	$
2022[A]	nil	(1,132)	(0.01)
2021[A]	305	(1,038)	(0.02)
2020[A]	290	(396)	(0.01)
2019[A]	4	(113)	(0.01)
2018[A]	14	(72)	(0.00)

* Common
[A] Reported in accordance with IFRS

G.80 Green Scientific Labs Holdings Inc.

Symbol - GSL **Exchange** - CSE **CUSIP** - 39337P
Head Office - 4001 SW 47 Ave, Suite 208, Davie, FL, United States, 33314 **Telephone** - (561) 340-4772 **Toll-free** - (833) 837-8223
Website - www.greenscientificlabs.com
Email - info@greenscientificlabs.com
Investor Relations - Michael Richmond (561) 350-4772
Auditors - SRCO Professional Corporation C.A., Richmond Hill, Ont.
Transfer Agents - Capital Transfer Agency Inc., Toronto, Ont.
Profile - (B.C. 1980) Operates cannabis and hemp testing laboratories to provide analytical testing services to ensure product quality and consumer safety.

The company owns and operates cannabis and hemp testing laboratories in Davie, Fla., and Phoenix Ariz., which provides analytical testing services for state-licensed cannabis and hemp growers, product formulators, processors, distributors and retailers. Testing services include cannabinoid profile, terpenoid profile, microbiological analysis, pesticide analysis, residual solvent analysis, mycotoxin analysis, moisture analysis, foreign materials analysis and heavy metal analysis.

New testing laboratory facilities are planned to also be opened in Arizona, New Jersey, Michigan and Illinois.

Predecessor Detail - Name changed from Prominex Resource Corp., Nov. 15, 2021, pursuant to the the reverse takeover acquisition of Green Scientific Labs, LLC (GSL) and concurrent amalgamation of GSL with wholly owned PRC Merger Sub, Inc.; basis 1 new for 168.68 old shs.

Directors - Michael Richmond, chr. & interim CFO, Boca Raton, Fla.; Olivier Centner, Toronto, Ont.; Ed Murray, Fla.; Alexander (Alex) Spiro, New York, N.Y.

Other Exec. Officers - Rafael Bombonato, chief compliance officer & interim CEO

Capital Stock

	Authorized (shs.)	Outstanding (shs.)[1]
Cl.A Subord. Voting	unlimited	14,782,345
Cl.B Multiple Voting	unlimited	64,166

[1] At Aug. 23, 2022

Class A Subordinate Voting - One vote per share.

Class B Multiple Voting - Each convertible into 100 subordinate voting shares. 100 votes per share.

Major Shareholder - Green Scientific Labs Management Group, LLC held 20.21% interest at Nov. 15, 2021.

Price Range - GSL/CSE

Year	Volume	High	Low	Close
2022	901,512	$5.50	$0.01	$0.01
2021	270,392	$7.35	$2.55	$5.00

Consolidation: 1-for-168.68 cons. in Nov. 2021; 1-for-40 cons. in Aug. 2020

Recent Close: $0.03

Wholly Owned Subsidiaries

Green Scientific Labs, LLC, Davie, Fla.
- 100% int. in **Green Scientific Labs AZ LLC**, Ariz.
- 100% int. in **Green Scientific Labs CT, LLC**, United States.
- 100% int. in **Green Scientific Labs IL LLC**, Ill.
- 100% int. in **Green Scientific Labs Michigan LLC**, Mich.
- 100% int. in **Green Scientific Labs NJ LLC**, N.J.

Financial Statistics

Periods ended:	12m Dec. 31/21[A1]		12m Dec. 31/20[A2]
	US$000s	%Chg	US$000s
Operating revenue	**7,591**	**+25**	**6,096**
Salaries & benefits	5,558		2,509
General & admin expense	4,009		2,603
Stock-based compensation	614		480
Operating expense	**10,181**	**+82**	**5,592**
Operating income	**(2,590)**	**n.a.**	**505**
Deprec., depl. & amort.	1,246		760
Finance costs, gross	555		841
Write-downs/write-offs	(14)		(78)
Pre-tax income	**(8,524)**	**n.a.**	**(911)**
Net income	**(8,524)**	**n.a.**	**(911)**
Cash & equivalent	5,184		154
Inventories	1,004		252
Accounts receivable	721		485
Current assets	7,279		912
Fixed assets, net	3,958		1,265
Right-of-use assets	6,107		2,189
Intangibles, net	5		37
Total assets	**17,423**	**+296**	**4,402**
Accts. pay. & accr. liabs	1,973		607
Current liabilities	3,026		1,751
Long-term debt, gross	nil		702
Long-term debt, net	nil		235
Long-term lease liabilities	5,033		1,731
Shareholders' equity	9,298		488
Cash from oper. activs	**(2,832)**	**n.a.**	**493**
Cash from fin. activs	10,733		(223)
Cash from invest. activs	(2,870)		(453)
Net cash position	**5,184**	**n.m.**	**154**
Capital expenditures	(3,085)		(390)
	US$		US$
Earnings per share*	(0.75)		n.a.
Cash flow per share*	(0.25)		n.a.
	shs		shs
No. of shs. o/s*	14,701,745		n.a.
Avg. no. of shs. o/s*	11,381,454		n.a.
	%		%
Net profit margin	(112.29)		(14.94)
Return on equity	(174.21)		n.m.
Return on assets	(73.03)		n.a.
Foreign sales percent	100		100

* Cl.A Subord. Vtg.
[A] Reported in accordance with IFRS
[1] Results reflect the Nov. 15, 2021, reverse takeover acquisition of Green Scientific Labs, LLC.
[2] Results pertain to Green Scientific Labs, LLC.

Latest Results

Periods ended:	6m June 30/22[A]		6m June 30/21[A]
	US$000s	%Chg	US$000s
Operating revenue	2,347	-46	4,327
Net income	(3,411)	n.a.	(653)
	US$		US$
Earnings per share*	(0.23)		(8.10)

* Cl.A Subord. Vtg.
[A] Reported in accordance with IFRS

Historical Summary
(as originally stated)

Fiscal Year	Oper. Rev.	Net Inc. Bef. Disc.	EPS*
	US$000s	US$000s	US$
2021[A]	7,591	(8,524)	(0.75)
2020[A1]	6,096	(911)	n.a.
2019[A1]	3,620	298	n.a.

* Cl.A Subord. Vtg.
[A] Reported in accordance with IFRS
[1] Results pertain to Green Scientific Labs, LLC.

Note: Adjusted throughout for 1-for-168.68 cons. in Nov. 2021; 1-for-40 cons. in Aug. 2020

G.81 Green Thumb Industries Inc.

Symbol - GTII **Exchange** - CSE **CUSIP** - 39342L
Head Office - 325 W Huron St, Suite 700, Chicago, IL, United States, 60654 **Telephone** - (312) 471-6720
Website - www.gtigrows.com
Email - investorrelations@gtigrows.com
Investor Relations - Andrew Grossman (312) 471-6720
Auditors - Baker Tilly US, LLP C.P.A., Chicago, Ill.
Transfer Agents - Odyssey Trust Company, Vancouver, B.C.
FP500 Revenue Ranking - 288
Employees - 3,763 at Dec. 31, 2022
Profile - (B.C. 2006 amalg.) Owns, manufactures, distributes and retails branded cannabis products across the U.S.

The company's portfolio of cannabis brands include &Shine, Beboe, Dogwalkers, Doctor Solomon's, Good Green, incredibles and RYTHM, which are distributed to third-party licensed retail cannabis stores and company-owned retail cannabis stores across the U.S. Products include flower, pre-rolls, concentrates, vape, capsules, tinctures, edibles, topicals and other cannabis-related products. At June 30, 2023, the company owned and operated 18 cultivation, processing and manufacturing facilities and 83 retail stores in 15 U.S. states (California, Colorado, Connecticut, Florida, Illinois, Maryland, Massachusetts, Minnesota, Nevada, New Jersey, New York, Ohio, Pennsylvania, Rhode Island and Virginia). Company-owned stores operate under the RISE name as well as other store names, primarily where naming is subject to licensing or similar restrictions or co-ownership.

In December 2022, the company acquired land at Ocala, Fla., containing a 28-acre cultivation and processing facility, for US$5,584,000.

On Oct. 19, 2022, the company announced an agreement to lease space in Circle K convenience stores in Florida to operate RISE Express branded stores featuring medical marijuana beginning in 2023. The company plans to launch its test and learn phase of the rollout with 10 RISE Express stores adjacent to Circle K stores. Circle K, owned by **Alimentation Couche-Tard Inc.**, had 600 locations in Florida.

In September 2022, the company acquired **Maryland Health and Wellness Center, Inc.**, a dispensary in Hagerstown, Md., for US$30,000.

In March 2022, the company acquired the remaining 50% interest in **ILDISP, LLC**, owner of two dispensaries in Effingham and Charleston, Ill., for US$18,623,000 cash and issuance of 204,036 subordinate voting shares valued at US$3,785,000.

Predecessor Detail - Name changed from Bayswater Uranium Corporation, June 12, 2018, following reverse takeover acquisition of VCP23, LLC.; basis 1 new for 10 old shs.

Directors - Benjamin (Ben) Kovler, chr. & CEO, Chicago, Ill.; Anthony Georgiadis, pres., Fla.; Wendy Berger, Chicago, Ill.; Richard Drexler, Fla.; Jeffrey (Jeff) Goldman, Ill.; Ethan Nadelmann, N.Y.; Dawn Wilson Barnes, Ga.

Other Exec. Officers - Mathew Faulkner, CFO; Rachel Albert, CAO; Kate Lloyd, chief counsel, secs. & governance & asst. sec.; Andrew (Andy) Grossman, exec. v-p, capital markets & IR; Josh Barrington, sr. v-p, tech.; Kelly Dean, sr. v-p, people; Matt Ingram, sr. v-p, opers.; Ryan Marek, sr. v-p, mktg.; Matt Navarro, sr. v-p, retail; Dominic O'Brien, sr. v-p, rev.; Rebecca Brown, v-p, govt. strategy; Shannon Weaver, v-p, commun.; Bret Kravitz, gen. counsel & corp. sec.

Capital Stock

	Authorized (shs.)	Outstanding (shs.)[1]
Subordinate Voting	unlimited	207,989,463
Multiple Voting	unlimited	38,531
Super Voting	unlimited	251,690

[1] At May 1, 2023

Subordinate Voting - Entitled to dividends. One vote per share.

Multiple Voting - Entitled to dividends. Each convertible into 100 subordinate voting shares. 100 votes per share.

Super Voting - Entitled to dividends. Each convertible into one multiple voting share or 100 subordinate voting shares. 1,000 votes per share.

Major Shareholder - Benjamin (Ben) Kovler held 39.7% interest at Apr. 1, 2023.

Price Range - GTII/CSE

Year	Volume	High	Low	Close
2022	65,258,693	$28.67	$10.09	$11.98
2021	72,534,355	$49.66	$22.89	$28.20
2020	73,354,565	$31.48	$5.05	$31.18
2019	58,975,613	$22.02	$9.91	$12.79
2018	29,343,810	$32.50	$0.25	$10.95

Recent Close: $9.20

Capital Stock Changes - During 2022, subordinate voting shares were issued as follows: 3,334,100 on conversion of 33,341 super voting shares, 667,080 for contingent consideration, 441,454 on exercise of options, 433,341 on vesting of restricted share units, 204,036 pursuant to the acquisition of the remaining 50% interest in ILDISP, LLC and 142,952 for settlement of business obligation.

Wholly Owned Subsidiaries

GTI23, Inc., Del.

- 100% int. in **VCP23, LLC**, Chicago, Ill.
  - 100% int. in **For Success Holding Company**, Los Angeles, Calif.
  - 100% int. in **GTI Core, LLC**, Del.
    - 100% int. in **Advanced Grow Labs LLC**, Conn.
    - 100% int. in **Bluepoint Apothecary, LLC**, Conn.
    - 46% int. in **Bluepoint Wellness of Westport, LLC**, Conn.
    - 100% int. in **Dharma Pharmaceuticals, LLC**, Va.
    - 100% int. in **Fiorello Pharmaceuticals, Inc.**, N.Y.
    - 100% int. in **GTI-Clinic Illinois Holdings, LLC**, Ill.
    - 100% int. in **GTI Florida, LLC**, Fla.
      - 100% int. in **KSGNF, LLC**, Fla.
    - 100% int. in **GTI Maryland, LLC**, Md.
      - 100% int. in **Chesapeake Alternatives, LLC**, Md.
    - 100% int. in **GTI Nevada, LLC**, Nev.
    - 100% int. in **GTI New Jersey, LLC**, N.J.
    - 100% int. in **GTI Pennsylvania, LLC**, Pa.
    - 100% int. in **GTI Rhode Island, LLC**, R.I.
      - **Summit Medical Compassion Center, Inc.**, R.I.
    - 100% int. in **ILDISP, LLC**, Ill.
    - 100% int. in **Integral Associates CA, LLC**, Calif.
    - 100% int. in **Integral Associates, LLC**, Nev.
    - 100% int. in **JB17, LLC**, Md.
    - 100% int. in **KW Ventures Holdings, LLC**, Pa.
    - 100% int. in **LeafLine Industries, LLC**, Minn.
    - 100% int. in **Liberty Compassion, Inc.**, Mass.
    - 100% int. in **MC Brands, LLC**, Colo.
    - 100% int. in **Maryland Health and Wellness Center, Inc.**, Md.
    - 100% int. in **Meshow, LLC**, Md.
    - 100% int. in **Ohio Investors 2017, LLC**, Ohio
      - 100% int. in **GTI Ohio, LLC**, Ohio
    - 100% int. in **RISE Holdings, Inc.**, Mass.
    - 100% int. in **Southern CT Wellness & Healing, LLC**, Conn.
  - 100% int. in **TWD18, LLC**, Del.
  - 100% int. in **VCP IP Holdings, LLC**, Del.
  - 100% int. in **VCP Real Estate Holdings, LLC**, Del.
  - 100% int. in **Vision Management Services, LLC**, Del.

Note: The preceding list includes only the major related companies in which interests are held.

Financial Statistics

Periods ended:	12m Dec. 31/22[A]		12m Dec. 31/21[A]
	US$000s	%Chg	US$000s
Operating revenue	**1,017,375**	**+14**	**893,560**
Cost of goods sold	489,295		387,330
General & admin expense	193,290		198,586
Stock-based compensation	27,140		19,600
Operating expense	**709,725**	**+17**	**605,516**
Operating income	**307,650**	**+7**	**288,044**
Deprec., depl. & amort.	96,664		68,458
Finance income	4,070		1,432
Finance costs, gross	21,201		21,976
Investment income	(4,259)		1,799
Write-downs/write-offs	(89,922)[1]		(4,744)
Pre-tax income	**108,432**	**-47**	**204,975**
Income taxes	94,777		124,612
Net income	**13,655**	**-83**	**80,363**
Net inc. for equity hldrs	**11,978**	**-84**	**75,436**
Net inc. for non-cont. int.	**1,677**	**-66**	**4,927**
Cash & equivalent	177,682		230,420
Inventories	115,675		95,471
Accounts receivable	30,975		22,099
Current assets	351,351		364,230
Long-term investments	99,677		125,239
Fixed assets, net	557,873		409,074
Right-of-use assets	242,357		176,327
Intangibles, net	1,179,210		1,308,340
Total assets	**2,433,528**	**+2**	**2,385,851**
Accts. pay. & accr. liabs.	118,870		110,832
Current liabilities	146,571		204,379
Long-term debt, gross	275,668		239,934
Long-term debt, net	274,631		239,151
Long-term lease liabilities	249,281		182,539
Shareholders' equity	1,664,916		1,621,116
Non-controlling interest	516		(1,638)
Cash from oper. activs.	**158,564**	**+20**	**132,048**
Cash from fin. activs.	8,644		295,344
Cash from invest. activs.	(219,946)		(280,730)
Net cash position	**177,682**	**-23**	**230,420**
Capital expenditures	(179,500)		(187,850)
Capital disposals	869		109
	US$		US$
Earnings per share*	0.05		0.34
Cash flow per share*	0.67		0.59
	shs		shs
No. of shs. o/s*	236,013,375		234,124,512
Avg. no. of shs. o/s*	236,713,056		223,192,326
	%		%
Net profit margin	1.34		8.99
Return on equity	0.73		5.96
Return on assets	0.68		4.75
Foreign sales percent	100		100
No. of employees (FTEs)	3,763		3,730

* Common

[A] Reported in accordance with U.S. GAAP

[1] Includes US$44,392,000 goodwill impairment of Nevada consumer packaged goods operations, US$12,980,000 goodwill impairment of Nevada retail operations and US$31,131,000 impairment of tradename intangible assets.

Note: Shares and average shares outstanding include multiple and super voting shares converted into subordinate voting shares on a 100-for-1 basis.

Latest Results

Periods ended:	3m Mar. 31/23[A]		3m Mar. 31/22[A]
	US$000s	%Chg	US$000s
Operating revenue	248,536	+2	242,600
Net income	9,405	-68	29,686
Net inc. for equity hldrs.	9,139	-68	28,939
Net inc. for non-cont. int.	266		747
	US$		US$
Earnings per share*	0.04		0.12

* Common

[A] Reported in accordance with U.S. GAAP

Historical Summary

(as originally stated)

Fiscal Year	Oper. Rev.	Net Inc. Bef. Disc.	EPS*
	US$000s	US$000s	US$
2022[A]	1,017,375	13,655	0.05
2021[A]	893,560	80,363	0.34
2020[A]	556,573	19,078	0.07
2019[A]	216,433	(59,547)	(0.31)
2018[B1]	62,494	19,948	(0.05)

* Common

[A] Reported in accordance with U.S. GAAP

[B] Reported in accordance with IFRS

[1] Results reflect the June 12, 2018 reverse takeover acquisition of VCP23, LLC.

G.82 GreenBank Capital Inc.

Symbol - GBC **Exchange** - CSE **CUSIP** - 393576

Head Office - 5700-100 King St W, Toronto, ON, M5X 1C7 **Telephone** - (647) 931-9768 **Fax** - (647) 693-9413

Website - www.greenbankcapitalinc.com

Email - vilhjalmur@jvcapital.co.uk

Investor Relations - Vilhjálmur T. Vilhjálmsson 354-869-7296

Auditors - Littlejohn LLP C.A., London, Middx. United Kingdom

Transfer Agents - Reliable Stock Transfer Inc., Toronto, Ont.

Profile - (B.C. 2013) Operates as merchant bank specializing in making equity investments in and providing loans to small capitalization companies, and facilitating mergers, acquisitions and private equity transactions.

The company's investments include the following: **Staminier Limited**, a U.K.-based merchant banking company which acquires substantial interests in undervalued companies; and **We Deliver Local Limited** (operating as Beelivery), a U.K.-based rapid grocery delivery company; **Blockchain Evolution Inc.**, owners of the world's first identification-based blockchain, and developers of Xbook, a user-permissioned and revenue sharing social media platform; **Ubique Minerals Limited**, a mineral exploration company with interests in Newfoundland and Namibia; **Buchans Wileys Exploration Inc.**, **Gander Exploration Inc.**, **GBC Grand Exploration Inc.** and **TRU Precious Metals Corp.**, all mineral exploration companies with interests in Newfoundland; and **Kabaddi Games Inc.**, developers of a mobile application game based on the sport of kabaddi.

Recent Merger and Acquisition Activity

Status: completed **Announced:** Sept. 23, 2022

GreenBank Capital Inc. acquired an additional 29.5% interest in Staminier Limited, a U.K.-based a merchant banking company, pursuant to the partial exercise of a put option for issuance of 31,848,428 common shares valued at $7,962,107, bringing its interest in Staminier to 48.5%. GreenBank also agreed to extend the expiry date of the put option, under which it may acquire the remaining interest in Staminier, to Mar. 31, 2023.

Directors - Vilhjálmur T. Vilhjálmsson, chr. & CEO, Reykjavik, Iceland; Steve O'Carroll, COO, United Kingdom; Richard Beresford, United Kingdom; Sir Robert J. M. (Bob) Neill, United Kingdom; Peter D. Wanner, Georgetown, Ont.

Other Exec. Officers - Miles A. Nagamatsu, CFO

Capital Stock

	Authorized (shs.)	Outstanding (shs.)[1]	Par
Preference			
Series C	unlimited	nil	$0.33
Common	unlimited	117,771,001	n.p.v.

[1] At June 29, 2023

Major Shareholder - Widely held at June 20, 2022.

Price Range - GBC/CSE

Year	Volume	High	Low	Close
2022	9,144,895	$0.83	$0.11	$0.14
2021	22,936,527	$2.00	$0.25	$0.67
2020	1,680,801	$0.55	$0.20	$0.34
2018	1,427,385	$1.89	$0.10	$0.30

Recent Close: $0.06

Capital Stock Changes - In September 2022, 31,848,428 common shares were issued to acquire an additional 29.5% interest in Staminier Limited and 20,700,000 common shares were issued to acquire a £4,975,000 loan made to Staminier Limited.

During fiscal 2022, common shares were issued as follows: 100,000 for consulting services, 114,937 on exercise of options and 100,842 on deconsolidation of a subsidiary; 114,937 common shares were returned to treasury.

Wholly Owned Subsidiaries

GreenBank Financial Inc., Ont.

Subsidiaries

52.5% int. in **Blockchain Evolution Inc.**, Canada.
- 100% int. in **Xbook Network Inc.**, Canada.

59.5% int. in **Kabaddi Games Inc.**, Canada.

Investments

25.16% int. in **Buchans Wileys Exploration Inc.**, N.L.
5% int. in **Codikoat Limited**, Haverhill, Suffolk, United Kingdom.
25% int. in **Flex Capital ehf.**, Iceland.
47.47% int. in **GBC Grand Exploration Inc.**, N.L.
34.76% int. in **Gander Exploration Inc.**

0.69% int. in **St-Georges Eco-Mining Corp.**, Montréal, Qué. (see separate coverage)
48.5% int. in **Staminier Limited**, London, Middx., United Kingdom.
• 100% int. in **The Substantia Group Limited**, United Kingdom.
0.86% int. in **TRU Precious Metals Corp.**, Fredericton, N.B. (see Survey of Mines)
20.27% int. in **Ubique Minerals Limited**, Toronto, Ont. (see Survey of Mines)
5.62% int. in **We Deliver Local Limited**, Congleton, Cheshire, United Kingdom. Operating as Beelivery

Financial Statistics

Periods ended:	12m July 31/22A		12m July 31/21◻A
	$000s	%Chg	$000s
Operating revenue	**50**	**+285**	**13**
Exploration expense	121		nil
General & admin expense	1,029		1,547
Stock-based compensation	nil		770
Operating expense	**1,150**	**-50**	**2,317**
Operating income	**(1,100)**	**n.a.**	**(2,304)**
Finance costs, gross	296		49
Investment income	(63)		170
Write-downs/write-offs	(62)		nil
Pre-tax income	**378**	**n.a.**	**(3,234)**
Net income	**378**	**n.a.**	**(3,234)**
Net inc. for equity hldrs	**1,002**	**n.a.**	**(3,103)**
Net inc. for non-cont. int	**(624)**	**n.a.**	**(130)**
Cash & equivalent	192		1,116
Accounts receivable	1		1
Current assets	203		1,212
Long-term investments	7,629		4,520
Explor./devel. properties	nil		881
Total assets	**8,052**	**+22**	**6,613**
Accts. pay. & accr. liabs	301		298
Current liabilities	4,600		1,300
Long-term debt, gross	4,488		2,247
Long-term debt, net	440		1,759
Shareholders' equity	3,312		2,792
Non-controlling interest	(301)		761
Cash from oper. activs	**(1,085)**	**n.a.**	**(817)**
Cash from fin. activs	823		3,356
Cash from invest. activs	(663)		(1,467)
Net cash position	**192**	**-83**	**1,116**
Capital expenditures	(545)		(161)
	$		$
Earnings per share*	0.02		(0.06)
Cash flow per share*	(0.02)		(0.02)
	shs		shs
No. of shs. o/s*	60,568,979		59,968,137
Avg. no. of shs. o/s*	60,161,226		53,361,938
	%		%
Net profit margin	756.00		n.m.
Return on equity	32.83		(210.23)
Return on assets	9.19		(74.56)

* Common
◻ Restated
A Reported in accordance with IFRS

Latest Results

Periods ended:	3m Oct. 31/22A		3m Oct. 31/21◻A
	$000s	%Chg	$000s
Operating revenue	nil	n.a.	50
Net income	(7,337)	n.a.	(280)
Net inc. for equity hldrs	(7,329)	n.a.	(183)
Net inc. for non-cont. int	(8)		(97)
	$		$
Earnings per share*	(0.09)		(0.00)

* Common
◻ Restated
A Reported in accordance with IFRS

Historical Summary
(as originally stated)

Fiscal Year	Oper. Rev. $000s	Net Inc. Bef. Disc. $000s	EPS* $
2022A	50	378	0.02
2021A	13	(3,234)	(0.06)
2020A	nil	(1,513)	(0.04)
2019A	13	(1,179)	(0.04)
2018A	160	(2,466)	(0.09)

* Common
A Reported in accordance with IFRS

G.83 Greenbank Ventures Inc.

Symbol - GBNK.H **Exchange** - TSX-VEN (S) **CUSIP** - 393583
Head Office - 600-535 Howe St, Vancouver, BC, V6C 2Z4 **Telephone** - (604) 209-9800
Email - jen@jchansoncr.com
Investor Relations - John LaGourgue (604) 209-9800
Auditors - Dale Matheson Carr-Hilton LaBonte LLP C.A.
Bankers - The Toronto-Dominion Bank
Lawyers - Miller Thomson LLP, Vancouver, B.C.
Transfer Agents - Endeavor Trust Corporation, Vancouver, B.C.
Profile - (B.C. 1969) Holds nine undeveloped residential lots in Manitou Beach, Sask., overlooking Little Manitou Lake.

The company's long-term aim is to develop these properties. In addition, the company is also seeking other business opportunities in the real estate industry as well as in other industries.

Common suspended from TSX-VEN, May 7, 2021.

Predecessor Detail - Name changed from Leis Industries Limited, Aug. 25, 2020.

Directors - Andreas Schleich, CEO, North Vancouver, B.C.; Bryson Goodwin, Langley, B.C.; John LaGourgue, Surrey, B.C.

Other Exec. Officers - Natasha Sever, CFO & corp. sec.

Capital Stock

	Authorized (shs.)	Outstanding (shs.)[1]
Common	unlimited	8,667,595

[1] At May 1, 2023

Class A Preferred - Redeemable at $1.215 per share. Convertible into common shares on a 1-for-1 basis. Non-voting.
Class B Preferred - Non-voting.
Common - One vote per share.
Major Shareholder - Widely held at Dec. 3, 2021.

Price Range - GBNK.H/TSX-VEN (S)

Year	Volume	High	Low	Close
2018	135,350	$0.75	$0.23	$0.75

Wholly Owned Subsidiaries

Salt Resorts Inc., Sask. Formerly Tranquility Resort Inc.

Financial Statistics

Periods ended:	12m Dec. 31/21A		12m Dec. 31/20A
	$000s	%Chg	$000s
General & admin. expense	107		118
Operating expense	**107**	**-9**	**118**
Operating income	**(107)**	**n.a.**	**(118)**
Finance costs, gross	47		31
Write-downs/write-offs	nil		(25)
Pre-tax income	**(211)**	**n.a.**	**(189)**
Net income	**(211)**	**n.a.**	**(189)**
Cash & equivalent	37		13
Accounts receivable	12		8
Current assets	300		339
Properties	206		205
Total assets	**761**	**-3**	**788**
Accts. pay. & accr. liabs	130		93
Current liabilities	928		353
Long-term debt, gross	16		652
Long-term debt, net	nil		392
Shareholders' equity	(167)		44
Cash from oper. activs	**(79)**	**n.a.**	**(89)**
Cash from fin. activs	100		100
Cash from invest. activs	(1)		(199)
Net cash position	**37**	**+185**	**13**
Capital expenditures	(1)		(8)
	$		$
Earnings per share*	(0.02)		(0.02)
Cash flow per share*	(0.01)		(0.01)
	shs		shs
No. of shs. o/s*	8,651,595		8,651,595
Avg. no. of shs. o/s*	8,651,595		8,651,595
	%		%
Net profit margin	n.a.		n.a.
Return on equity	n.m.		(136.46)
Return on assets	(21.17)		(22.13)

* Common
A Reported in accordance with IFRS

Latest Results

Periods ended:	6m June 30/22A		6m June 30/21A
	$000s	%Chg	$000s
Net income	(7)	n.a.	(49)
	$		$
Earnings per share*	(0.00)		(0.01)

* Common
A Reported in accordance with IFRS

Historical Summary
(as originally stated)

Fiscal Year	Total Rev. $000s	Net Inc. Bef. Disc. $000s	EPS* $
2021A	nil	(211)	(0.02)
2020A	nil	(189)	(0.02)
2019A	nil	62	0.01
2018A	nil	(464)	(0.07)
2017A	nil	(360)	(0.06)

* Common
A Reported in accordance with IFRS

G.84 Greenbriar Capital Corp.

Symbol - GRB **Exchange** - TSX-VEN **CUSIP** - 39364R
Head Office - 632 Foster Ave, Coquitlam, BC, V3J 2L7 **Telephone** - (949) 903-5906 **Fax** - (604) 608-9572
Website - www.greenbriarcapitalcorp.ca
Email - westernwind@shaw.ca
Investor Relations - Jeffrey J. Ciachurski (949) 903-5906
Auditors - Davidson & Company LLP C.A., Vancouver, B.C.
Transfer Agents - Computershare Trust Company of Canada Inc., Vancouver, B.C.
Profile - (B.C. 2009) Develops renewable energy and sustainable real estate projects. Also holds exclusive Canadian rights for the distribution of smart glass energy products.

The company's projects include Sage Ranch, a 995-unit sustainable subdivision housing project under development in Tehachapi, Calif., where all houses will have solar roof panels; the Montalva solar project, a proposed 146-MW to 300-MW solar photovoltaic renewable generating facility located in the municipalities of Guanica and Lajas, Puerto Rico, which is pending approval; and up to 400 MW of solar farm projects in Alberta. **Captiva Verde Wellness Corp.** has an option to earn 50% net profit interest in Sage Ranch.

In addition, holds exclusive Canadian sales, distribution and marketing rights for smart glass energy products developed and built by Tel-Aviv, Israel-based **Gauzy Ltd.** The technology embedded into glass offers varying degrees of opacity for privacy or projection, or transparency for an open atmosphere. Smart glass can be installed in homes, office buildings, hospitals, apartments, universities, schools, hotels, trucks and automobiles.

During 2022, the company sold all 36,487,500 shares of **Captiva Verde Wellness Corp.** it held for $722,393.

Also during 2022, the company acquired water rights for the Sage Ranch project in Tehachapi, Calif., by way of debt settlement of $1,000,000 with an officer and director of the company in exchange for 925,926 units (1 common share & 1 warrant) of the company.

On July 6, 2022, the company engaged **Paul Morris Forward Living Realty** to sell to institutional real estate investors its fully entitled 995 home Sage Ranch entry level subdivision in California for US$139,000,000 net or US$3.71 per share fully diluted, with the company and its general contractor to manage and execute the construction oversight and permitting.

Recent Merger and Acquisition Activity

Status: pending **Announced:** June 29, 2022
Greenbriar Capital Corp. received an unsolicited offer to purchase its 995-unit Sage Ranch sustainable housing project in Tehachapi, Calif., from Phantom Developments Limited for US$62,000,000.

Directors - Daniel J. (Dan) Kunz, chr., Boise, Idaho; Jeffrey J. (Jeff) Ciachurski, CEO, Coquitlam, B.C.; Clifford M. (Cliff) Webb, pres., Glen Ivy, Calif.; J. Michael (Mike) Boyd, Tucson, Ariz.; William (Bill) Sutherland, Mississauga, Ont.

Other Exec. Officers - Anthony Balic, CFO & corp. sec.

Capital Stock

	Authorized (shs.)	Outstanding (shs.)[1]
Common	unlimited	34,073,355

[1] At May 30, 2023

Major Shareholder - Widely held at May 25, 2023.

Price Range - GRB/TSX-VEN

Year	Volume	High	Low	Close
2022	4,859,442	$1.59	$0.93	$1.30
2021	10,643,954	$3.06	$1.22	$1.42
2020	29,008,787	$4.63	$0.50	$1.60
2019	4,467,228	$1.31	$0.46	$0.61
2018	5,540,241	$1.57	$0.79	$0.85

Recent Close: $0.98

Capital Stock Changes - In May 2023, private placement of 360,000 units (1 common share & 1 warrant) at $1.25 per unit was completed, with warrants exercisable at $1.50 per share for five years.

In March 2022, private placement of 2,059,000 units (1 common share & 1 warrant) at $1.25 per unit was completed. In November 2022, private placement of 577,000 units (1 common share & 1 warrant) at $1.30 per unit was completed. Also during 2022, common shares were issued as follows: 925,926 on acquisition of water rights for the Sage Ranch project, 770,500 on exercise of options and 150,000 on exercise of warrants.

Wholly Owned Subsidiaries

AG Solar One, LLC, Vancouver, B.C.
• 100% int. in **PBJL Energy Corporation**, Puerto Rico.
Greenbriar Capital Holdco Inc., United States.
• 100% int. in **Greenbriar Capital (U.S.) LLC**, United States.
RealBlock Limited, Toronto, Ont.
2587344 Ontario Inc., Ont.

Financial Statistics

Periods ended:	12m Dec. 31/22[A]		12m Dec. 31/21[A]
	$000s	%Chg	$000s
General & admin expense	2,283		5,681
Stock-based compensation	954		990
Operating expense	**3,238**	**-51**	**6,671**
Operating income	**(3,238)**	**n.a.**	**(6,671)**
Finance costs, gross	34		56
Pre-tax income	**(2,763)**	**n.a.**	**(9,325)**
Net income	**(2,763)**	**n.a.**	**(9,325)**
Cash & equivalent	1,845		463
Current assets	1,918		1,819
Fixed assets, net	112,458		8,015
Total assets	**15,053**	**+44**	**10,436**
Bank indebtedness	718		648
Accts. pay. & accr. liabs	4,856		5,536
Current liabilities	5,574		6,184
Shareholders' equity	9,479		4,252
Cash from oper. activs	**(2,469)**	**n.a.**	**(2,041)**
Cash from fin. activs	4,162		3,604
Cash from invest. activs	(1,677)		(1,633)
Net cash position	**25**	**+178**	**9**
Capital expenditures	(2,399)		(1,575)
	$		$
Earnings per share*	(0.09)		(0.34)
Cash flow per share*	(0.08)		(0.07)
	shs		shs
No. of shs. o/s*	33,474,855		28,992,429
Avg. no. of shs. o/s*	31,316,532		27,470,371
	%		%
Net profit margin	n.a.		n.a.
Return on equity	(40.24)		(154.72)
Return on assets	(21.41)		(87.32)

* Common
[A] Reported in accordance with IFRS

Latest Results

Periods ended:	3m Mar. 31/23[A]		3m Mar. 31/22[A]
	$000s	%Chg	$000s
Net income	(585)	n.a.	(909)
	$		$
Earnings per share*	(0.02)		(0.03)

* Common
[A] Reported in accordance with IFRS

Historical Summary
(as originally stated)

Fiscal Year	Oper. Rev.	Net Inc. Bef. Disc.	EPS*
	$000s	$000s	$
2022[A]	nil	(2,763)	(0.09)
2021[A]	nil	(9,325)	(0.34)
2020[A]	nil	(3,145)	(0.14)
2019[A]	nil	3,231	0.16
2018[A]	nil	(3,804)	(0.21)

* Common
[A] Reported in accordance with IFRS

G.85 Greenbrook TMS Inc.

Symbol - GBNH **Exchange** - NASDAQ **CUSIP** - 393704
Head Office - 700-890 Yonge St, Toronto, ON, M4W 3P4 **Telephone** - (416) 322-9700 **Toll-free** - (855) 797-4867
Website - www.greenbrooktms.com
Email - eloubser@greenbrooktms.com
Investor Relations - Erns Loubser (855) 797-4867
Auditors - KPMG LLP C.A., Vaughan, Ont.
Transfer Agents - Computershare Trust Company of Canada Inc., Toronto, Ont.
Employees - 629 at Dec. 31, 2022
Profile - (Ont. 2018) Operates treatment centres in the U.S. offering Transcranial Magnetic Stimulation (TMS) therapy for the treatment of Major Depressive Disorder and other mental health disorders.

TMS is performed using a U.S. FDA-cleared medical device designed to deliver local electromagnetic stimulation to specific brain regions known to be directly associated with mood regulation. A course of treatment usually requires treatment sessions five times per week, conducted over a four to six-week period that can last from 19 to 45 minutes per session. During the three-month period ended Mar. 31, 2023, the company performed 92,533 TMS treatments compared with 59,067 during the same year earlier period. The company also offers Spravato® (esketamine nasal spray) at its 45 TMS centres to treat adults with treatment-resistant depression and to treat depressive symptoms in adults with Major Depressive Disorder and suicidal thoughts or actions.

At March 31, 2023, the company owned and operated 162 TMS centres in Massachusetts, Virginia, Pennsylvania, Maryland, Delaware, North Carolina, Missouri, Illinois, Ohio, Texas, Connecticut, Florida, South Carolina, Michigan, Alaska, Oregon, California, Iowa, New Jersey and Nevada.

On Mar. 6, 2023, the company announced a restructuring plan that includes the closure of 50 treatment centres over the next 45 days, that would leave the company with 133 treatment centres.

On Feb. 27, 2023, the company announced it would voluntarily delist from the Toronto Stock Exchange, effective Mar. 13, 2023. The company's shares would continue to trade the on NASDAQ.

In January 2023, the company entered into a commercial partnership with **Neuronetics, Inc.**, a medical technology company based in the U.S., which designs and develops products for people suffering from neurohealth conditions. Under the agreement, Neuronetics would supply Transcranial Magnetic Stimulation (TMS) devices to the company exclusively for six years. In addition, both parties would work to grow through co-branding and co-marketing programs, enhanced patient and clinician awareness, improved patient access to care and collaboration on product development and publications.

In August 2022, the company acquired a portion of the non-controlling interest in **TMS NeuroHealth Centers Rockville LLC** for US$500,000. As a result, the company held 100% interest in TMS NeuroHealth Centers Rockville.

Common delisted from TSX, Mar. 14, 2023.

Recent Merger and Acquisition Activity

Status: completed **Revised:** July 14, 2022
UPDATE: The transaction was completed for issuance of 11,634,660 common shares at US$1.35 per share. PREVIOUS: Greenbrook TMS Inc., through wholly owned TMS NeuroHealth Centers Inc., agreed to acquire West Palm Beach, Fla.-based Check Five LLC (dba Success TMS) for issuance of 11,867,923 common shares valued at US$27,300,000, of which US$20,500,000 would be payable on closing and US$6,800,000 would be held in an escrow account following determination of certain adjustments and indemnities. Success TMS operates 45 treatment centres in the U.S. offering Transcranial Magnetic Stimulation (TMS) therapy for the treatment of depression. Upon closing, Greenbrook's TMS centres would grow to 191 across the U.S. with new presence in additional states, including new management regions in Illinois, New Jersey, Nevada, Pennsylvania and Wisconsin. The transaction was expected to be completed during the third quarter of 2022.

Directors - Elias Vamvakas, chr., Toronto, Ont.; William P. (Bill) Leonard, pres. & CEO, Md.; Colleen Campbell†, Ont.; Brian P. Burke, Pa.; Sasha Cucuz, North York, Ont.; Dr. Adrienne L. Graves, N.C.; Frank Tworecke, Md.

Other Exec. Officers - Erns Loubser, CFO, treas. & corp. sec.; Dr. Geoffrey Grammer, CMO; Dr. Lindsay Israel, chief medical development officer; Latoya Blaylock, v-p, revenue cycle; Annie Farley, v-p, opers., West; Iris Krug, v-p, compliance & privacy officer; Nicole Lowry, v-p, sales & development; Bryce Neumann, v-p, opers., East; Egan Pratt, v-p, opers., business innovation; Brittany Schwemmer, v-p, HR
† Lead director

Capital Stock

	Authorized (shs.)	Outstanding (shs.)[1]
Preferred	unlimited	nil
Common	unlimited	40,800,180

[1] At May 5, 2023

Major Shareholder - Benjamin Klein held 21.4% interest, Greybrook Capital Inc. held 17.2% interest, Madryn Asset Management LP held 15.5% interest and Marlin Fund LP, Marlin Fund II LP and MSS GB SPV LP held 10.6% interest at May 5, 2023.

Price Range - GTMS/TSX (D)

Year	Volume	High	Low	Close
2022	2,282,677	$7.65	$1.66	$2.70
2021	2,759,621	$22.40	$5.37	$5.39
2020	1,763,777	$14.20	$5.00	$12.70
2019	1,693,640	$19.50	$7.50	$8.75
2018	863,717	$20.35	$13.20	$14.35

Consolidation: 1-for-5 cons. in Feb. 2021

Capital Stock Changes - In March 2023, private placement of 11,363,635 common shares was completed at US$0.55 per share.

On July 14, 2022, 11,634,660 common shares were issued pursuant to the acquisition of Check Five LLC (dba Success TMS).

Wholly Owned Subsidiaries

TMS NeuroHealth Centers Inc., Del.
- 100% int. in **Achieve TMS Central, LLC**, Iowa
- 100% int. in **Achieve TMS East, LLC**, Mass.
- 100% int. in **Check Five LLC**, West Palm Beach, Fla.

Note: The preceding list includes only the major related companies in which interests are held.

Financial Statistics

Periods ended:	12m Dec. 31/22[A]		12m Dec. 31/21[A]
	US$000s	%Chg	US$000s
Operating revenue	**69,104**	**+32**	**52,198**
Cost of sales	63,046		46,637
General & admin expense	26,237		20,667
Stock-based compensation	348		879
Other operating expense	660		862
Operating expense	**90,291**	**+31**	**69,046**
Operating income	**(21,187)**	**n.a.**	**(16,848)**
Deprec., depl. & amort	9,517		6,394
Finance income	12		15
Finance costs, gross	11,056		7,890
Pre-tax income	**(62,425)**	**n.a.**	**(24,860)**
Net income	**(62,425)**	**n.a.**	**(24,860)**
Net inc. for equity hldrs	**(61,726)**	**n.a.**	**(24,751)**
Net inc. for non-cont. int	**(698)**	**n.a.**	**(108)**
Cash & equivalent	1,624		10,700
Accounts receivable	13,898		10,997
Current assets	19,043		24,859
Fixed assets, net	3,720		1,925
Right-of-use assets	51,838		29,520
Intangibles, net	25,846		16,340
Total assets	**100,446**	**+38**	**72,644**
Bank indebtedness	94		85
Accts. pay. & accr. liabs	20,272		9,771
Current liabilities	37,147		18,526
Long-term debt, gross	52,404		13,567
Long-term debt, net	50,028		13,053
Long-term lease liabilities	41,802		24,476
Shareholders' equity	(28,343)		17,327
Non-controlling interest	(2,253)		(738)
Cash from oper. activs	**(13,211)**	**n.a.**	**(16,339)**
Cash from fin. activs	3,968		24,420
Cash from invest. activs	167		(15,138)
Net cash position	**1,624**	**-85**	**10,700**
Capital expenditures	(34)		(32)
	US$		US$
Earnings per share*	(2.66)		(1.60)
Cash flow per share*	(0.57)		(1.06)
	shs		shs
No. of shs. o/s*	29,436,545		17,801,885
Avg. no. of shs. o/s*	23,235,655		15,423,870
	%		%
Net profit margin	(90.33)		(47.63)
Return on equity	n.m.		(240.28)
Return on assets	(59.36)		(24.03)
Foreign sales percent	100		100
No. of employees (FTEs)	629		430

* Common
[A] Reported in accordance with IFRS

Latest Results

Periods ended:	3m Mar. 31/23[A]		3m Mar. 31/22[A]
	US$000s	%Chg	US$000s
Operating revenue	19,908	+52	13,065
Net income	(9,285)	n.a.	(8,005)
Net inc. for equity hldrs	(9,232)	n.a.	(7,838)
Net inc. for non-cont. int	(53)		(167)
	US$		US$
Earnings per share*	(0.30)		(0.44)

* Common
[A] Reported in accordance with IFRS

Historical Summary
(as originally stated)

Fiscal Year	Oper. Rev.	Net Inc. Bef. Disc.	EPS*
	US$000s	US$000s	US$
2022[A]	69,104	(62,425)	(2.66)
2021[A]	52,198	(24,860)	(1.60)
2020[A]	43,129	(30,403)	(2.32)
2019[A]	35,686	(15,852)	(1.48)
2018[A]	21,259	(4,709)	(0.60)

* Common
[A] Reported in accordance with IFRS
Note: Adjusted throughout for 1-for-5 cons. in Feb. 2021

G.86 GreenFirst Forest Products Inc.

Symbol - GFP **Exchange** - TSX **CUSIP** - 39526A
Head Office - 1000-401 The West Mall, Toronto, ON, M9C 5J5 **Telephone** - (416) 775-2821 **Fax** - (416) 621-3119
Website - greenfirst.ca
Email - alfred.colas@greenfirst.ca
Investor Relations - Alfred Colas (416) 775-2821
Auditors - KPMG LLP C.A., Toronto, Ont.
Bankers - Bank of Montreal, Vancouver, B.C.
Lawyers - McCullough O'Connor Irwin LLP, Vancouver, B.C.
Transfer Agents - Computershare Trust Company of Canada Inc., Vancouver, B.C.

FP500 Revenue Ranking - 473
Employees - 1,500 at Dec. 31, 2022
Profile - (Ont. 2022; orig. B.C., 1979) Manufactures and markets a wide range of forest products including spruce, pine or fir (SPF) lumber, wood chips and other by-products.
Operations are organized into two segments: Forest Products and Paper Products.
Forest Products segment manufactures and markets SPF lumber products for use in residential and commercial construction. By-products from production are sold to pulp-producers and the Paper Products segment. Operations consist of five sawmills mills in Kenora, Chapleau, Cochrane, Hearst and Kapuskasing, Ont., with a total annual production capacity of 660,000 mfbm of lumber.
Paper Products segment manufactures and markets paper grade products used to print newspapers, advertising material, food service bags and other publications. Operations consist of one newsprint mill in Kapuskasing, Ont., with annual production capacity of 205,000 tonnes per year.

Periods ended:	12m Dec. 31/22	12m Dec. 31/21
Lumber prod., mfbm	386,700	140,900
Lumber sales, mfbm	381,100	138,900
Newsprint prod., tonnes	113,817	37,381

Recent Merger and Acquisition Activity

Status: completed **Revised:** Mar. 14, 2023
UPDATE: The transaction was completed for $94,000,000, including $43,000,000 for specific working capital items. PREVIOUS: GreenFirst Forest Products Inc. agreed to sell its La Sarre and Béarn sawmills, with a combined annual capacity of 245,000 mfbm, and related Abitibi and Témiscamingue forestry operations, all in Quebec, to Chantiers Chibougamau Ltée for $90,000,000, including $40,000,000 for specific working capital items. GreenFirst's board of directors unanimously approved the transaction.
Status: completed **Revised:** Nov. 9, 2022
UPDATE: The transaction was completed. PREVIOUS: GreenFirst Forest Products Inc. agreed to sell 203,000 acres of private forest land, located in the boreal forest south of Kapuskasing, Ont., to Perimeter Forest Limited Partnership for $49,250,000.
Status: completed **Announced:** May 2, 2022
Interfor Corporation acquired a total of 28,684,433 common shares of GreenFirst Forest Products Inc. from Rayonier A.M. Canada G.P., which represents 16.2% of GreenFirst's issued and outstanding common shares, at a price of Cdn$1.94 per share for a total cash consideration of $56,000,000. GreenFirst manufactures and markets a wide range of forest products including spruce, pine or fir (SPF) lumber, wood chips and other by-products.
Predecessor Detail - Name changed from Itasca Capital Ltd., Jan. 13, 2021.
Directors - Paul C. Rivett, exec. chr. & interim CEO, Toronto, Ont.; Marty L. Proctor†, Calgary, Alta.; Barbara Anie, Toronto, Ont.; The Hon. Candice Bergen, Winnipeg, Man.; Rick Doman, Alta.; William G. Harvey, S.C.; Michael Mitchell, Colo.; Larry G. Swets Jr., Fla.; W. Sean Willy, Saskatoon, Sask.
Other Exec. Officers - Michel Lessard, pres.; Alfred Colas, CFO & corp. sec.; Ankit Kapoor, v-p, fin.
† Lead director

Capital Stock

	Authorized (shs.)	Outstanding (shs.)[1]
Preferred	100,000,000	nil
Common	unlimited	177,572,272

[1] At May 15, 2023

Major Shareholder - Senvest Management, LLC held 23.57% interest, Ballantyne Strong, Inc. & Fundamental Global Investors, LLC held 16.6% interest and Rayonier Advanced Materials Inc. held 16.15% interest at Apr. 6, 2023.

Price Range - GFP/TSX

Year	Volume	High	Low	Close
2022	31,574,041	$2.53	$1.34	$1.53
2021	25,009,035	$11.36	$1.30	$1.86
2020	2,267,696	$1.63	$0.38	$1.47
2019	1,658,854	$0.57	$0.22	$0.48
2018	2,585,509	$0.79	$0.16	$0.26

Recent Close: $1.13
Capital Stock Changes - There were no changes to capital stock during 2022.

Wholly Owned Subsidiaries

GreenFirst Forest Products (QC) Inc., Qué.
2776034 Ontario Inc., Ont.

Financial Statistics

Periods ended:	12m Dec. 31/22[A]		12m Dec. 31/21[oA]
	$000s	%Chg	$000s
Operating revenue	**492,109**	**+269**	**133,315**
Cost of sales	382,812		103,865
Salaries & benefits	10,546		1,601
General & admin expense	13,707		6,619
Stock-based compensation	995		249
Other operating expense	45,850		10,708
Operating expense	**453,910**	**+269**	**123,042**
Operating income	**38,199**	**+272**	**10,273**
Deprec., depl. & amort.	20,372		6,043
Finance income	661		22
Finance costs, gross	13,457		6,195
Pre-tax income	**(4,775)**	**n.a.**	**(12,054)**
Income taxes	(643)		(2,031)
Net inc. bef. disc. opers	**(4,132)**	**n.a.**	**(10,023)**
Income from disc. opers	3,222		1,861
Net income	**(910)**	**n.a.**	**(8,162)**
Cash & equivalent	25,353		36,173
Inventories	78,294		107,204
Accounts receivable	40,732		36,040
Current assets	224,702		182,770
Long-term investments	1,143		500
Fixed assets, net	116,058		182,317
Right-of-use assets	2,569		3,382
Intangibles, net	11,420		11,716
Total assets	**371,504**	**-11**	**417,394**
Accts. pay. & accr. liabs	51,952		27,481
Current liabilities	86,035		54,040
Long-term debt, gross	53,434		115,221
Long-term debt, net	45,934		108,882
Long-term lease liabilities	1,521		2,132
Shareholders' equity	224,462		229,159
Cash from oper. activs	**57,863**	**n.m.**	**3,935**
Cash from fin. activs	(83,748)		278,610
Cash from invest. activs	15,065		(251,654)
Net cash position	**25,353**	**-30**	**36,173**
Capital expenditures	(33,603)		(6,092)
Capital disposals	48,668		nil
	$		$
Earns. per sh. bef disc opers*	(0.02)		(0.13)
Earnings per share*	nil		(0.10)
Cash flow per share*	0.33		0.05
	shs		shs
No. of shs. o/s*	177,572,272		177,572,272
Avg. no. of shs. o/s*	177,572,272		78,721,554
	%		%
Net profit margin	(0.84)		(7.52)
Return on equity	(1.82)		(8.31)
Return on assets	1.91		(2.24)
Foreign sales percent	60		n.a.
No. of employees (FTEs)	1,500		1,500

* Common
[o] Restated
[A] Reported in accordance with IFRS

Latest Results

Periods ended:	3m Apr. 1/23[A]		3m Mar. 26/22[oA]
	$000s	%Chg	$000s
Operating revenue	99,117	-17	119,717
Net inc. bef. disc. opers	(20,200)	n.a.	21,293
Income from disc. opers	1,783		14,021
Net income	(18,417)	n.a.	35,314
	$		$
Earns. per sh. bef. disc. opers.*	(0.11)		0.12
Earnings per share*	(0.10)		0.20

* Common
[o] Restated
[A] Reported in accordance with IFRS

Historical Summary
(as originally stated)

Fiscal Year	Oper. Rev. $000s	Net Inc. Bef. Disc. $000s	EPS* $
2022[A]	492,109	(4,132)	(0.02)
2021[A]	190,479	(9,619)	(0.12)
2020[A]	nil	(2,250)	(0.11)
2019[A]	nil	47	0.00
2018[A]	nil	(6,252)	(0.29)

* Common
[A] Reported in accordance with IFRS

G.87 Greenlane Renewables Inc.

Symbol - GRN **Exchange** - TSX **CUSIP** - 395332
Head Office - 110-3605 Gilmore Way, Burnaby, BC, V5G 4X5
Telephone - (604) 493-2004
Website - www.greenlanerenewables.com
Email - monty.balderston@greenlanerenewables.com
Investor Relations - Monty R. Balderston (604) 493-2004
Auditors - PricewaterhouseCoopers LLP C.A., Vancouver, B.C.
Lawyers - McMillan LLP, Vancouver, B.C.
Transfer Agents - Olympia Trust Company, Vancouver, B.C.
Employees - 121 at Dec. 31, 2022
Profile - (B.C. 2018) Designs, develops, sells, installs and services biogas upgrading systems that produce clean, low-carbon and carbon-negative renewable natural gas (RNG) from organic waste sources including landfills, wastewater treatment plants, dairy farms and food waste, suitable for either injection into the natural gas grid or for direct use as vehicle fuel.
The company's upgrading systems, marketed under the Greenlane Biogas™ brand, remove impurities and carbon dioxide from raw biogas to create high purity biomethane, also known as renewable natural gas (RNG). Biogas, which is a mixture of approximately 60% methane, 40% carbon dioxide and trace impurities, is produced naturally from the anaerobic decomposition of organic matter. Sources of biogas include wastewater treatment plants, food waste, agricultural crops, livestock manure and landfills. RNG produced is suitable for either injection into the natural gas grid or for direct use as vehicle fuel.
The company offers and actively deploys three main biogas upgrading technologies: water wash, pressure swing adsorption and membrane separation. Systems can be designed using one, two or all three technologies. Water wash technology is the most popular global biogas upgrading method.
Also provides biogas desulfurization and air deodorization products through wholly owned **Airdep S.r.l.**
Manufacturing of upgrading equipment is outsourced to third party fabricators and sales are made primarily in North America and Europe. At March 31, 2023, the company had a sales backlog of $25,100,000 (Dec. 31, 2022 - $27,700,000).
Post installation, the company provides maintenance, support and aftercare service including 24/7 technical support and remote monitoring, as well as maintenance and spare parts.
Predecessor Detail - Name changed from Creation Capital Corp., June 3, 2019, pursuant to Qualifying Transaction reverse takeover acquisition of PT Biogas Holdings Limited.
Directors - Wade D. Nesmith, chr., Vancouver, B.C.; Brad Douville, exec. v-chr., Vancouver, B.C.; Ian Kane, pres. & CEO, Alta.; Elaine A. Wong†, Vancouver, B.C.; Candice Alderson, Vancouver, B.C.; David C. Blaiklock, North Vancouver, B.C.; David R. Demers, Vancouver, B.C.; Patricia A. Fortier, Ottawa, Ont.
Other Exec. Officers - Alex Chassels, COO; Monty R. Balderston, CFO; Sandra Keyton, chief HR officer; H. Maura Lendon, chief legal officer; Sanford Selman, sr. v-p, project fin.; Jim Bornholdt, v-p, purch.; Dale Goudie, v-p, products; Donald (Allen) MacKinnon, v-p, srvc.; Stephen D. Wortley, corp. sec.
† Lead director

Capital Stock

	Authorized (shs.)	Outstanding (shs.)[1]
Common	unlimited	153,013,239

[1] At May 11, 2023

Major Shareholder - Widely held at May 3, 2023.

Price Range - GRN/TSX

Year	Volume	High	Low	Close
2022	57,765,033	$1.32	$0.46	$0.49
2021	179,059,066	$2.96	$1.12	$1.24
2020	242,605,206	$2.75	$0.19	$2.31
2019	22,214,582	$0.44	$0.15	$0.42
2018	39,250	$0.26	$0.19	$0.26

Recent Close: $0.22
Capital Stock Changes - During 2022, common shares were issued as follows: 1,387,392 pursuant to the acquisition of Airdep S.r.l., 278,332 on exercise of options and 81,066 under restricted share unit plan.

Wholly Owned Subsidiaries

Greenlane Biogas Global Limited, B.C.
- 100% int. in **Greenlane Biogas Europe B.V.**, Netherlands.

Greenlane Biogas Italy S.r.l., Italy.
- 100% int. in **Airdep S.r.l.**, Vicenza, Italy.

Greenlane Biogas US Corp, N.C.
Greenlane Renewables Capital Inc., United States.
PT Biogas Holdings Limited, United Kingdom.
- 100% int. in **Greenlane Biogas Europe Limited**, United Kingdom.
- 100% int. in **Greenlane Biogas North America Limited**, Canada.
- 100% int. in **Greenlane Biogas UK Limited**, United Kingdom.
- 100% int. in **PT Biogas Technology Limited**, United Kingdom.

Financial Statistics

Periods ended:	12m Dec. 31/22[A]		12m Dec. 31/21[A]
	$000s	%Chg	$000s
Operating revenue	**71,241**	**+29**	**55,351**
Cost of goods sold	54,429		41,215
General & admin expense	22,349		14,738
Operating expense	**76,778**	**+37**	**55,953**
Operating income	**(5,537)**	**n.a.**	**(602)**
Deprec., depl. & amort.	2,332		1,571
Finance income	359		162
Finance costs, gross	109		87
Pre-tax income	**(5,489)**	**n.a.**	**(2,526)**
Income taxes	16		(76)
Net income	**(5,505)**	**n.a.**	**(2,450)**
Cash & equivalent	21,381		31,471
Inventories	1,129		785
Accounts receivable	13,027		16,096
Current assets	53,024		61,086
Fixed assets, net	1,732		688
Intangibles, net	26,431		16,901
Total assets	**83,387**	**+6**	**78,786**
Accts. pay. & accr. liabs	23,021		20,148
Current liabilities	25,781		21,938
Long-term lease liabilities	967		217
Shareholders' equity	53,483		56,481
Cash from oper. activs	**40**	**n.a.**	**(10,476)**
Cash from fin. activs	(231)		25,722
Cash from invest. activs	(9,912)		(217)
Net cash position	**21,381**	**-32**	**31,471**
Capital expenditures	(515)		(187)
	$		$
Earnings per share*	(0.04)		(0.02)
Cash flow per share*	0.00		(0.07)
	shs		shs
No. of shs. o/s*	152,040,781		150,293,991
Avg. no. of shs. o/s*	150,917,997		143,851,178
	%		%
Net profit margin	(7.73)		(4.43)
Return on equity	(10.01)		(5.95)
Return on assets	(6.65)		(3.88)
No. of employees (FTEs)	121		69

* Common
[A] Reported in accordance with IFRS

Latest Results

Periods ended:	3m Mar. 31/23[A]		3m Mar. 31/22[A]
	$000s	%Chg	$000s
Operating revenue	15,479	-5	16,273
Net income	(2,319)	n.a.	(2,151)
	$		$
Earnings per share*	(0.01)		(0.01)

* Common
[A] Reported in accordance with IFRS

Historical Summary
(as originally stated)

Fiscal Year	Oper. Rev.	Net Inc. Bef. Disc.	EPS*
	$000s	$000s	$
2022[A]	71,241	(5,505)	(0.04)
2021[A]	55,351	(2,450)	(0.02)
2020[A]	22,500	(2,471)	(0.03)
2019[A]	9,123	(5,053)	(0.16)
	£000s	£000s	£
2018[A1]	10,501	(1,462)	n.a.

* Common
[A] Reported in accordance with IFRS
[1] Results pertain to PT Biogas Holdings Limited as shown in the filing statement dated May 13, 2019.

G.88 GreenPower Motor Company Inc.

Symbol - GPV **Exchange** - TSX-VEN **CUSIP** - 39540E
Head Office - 240-209 Carrall St, Vancouver, BC, V6B 2J2 **Telephone** - (604) 563-4144
Website - greenpowermotor.com
Email - fraseratkinson@telus.net
Investor Relations - Fraser Atkinson (604) 220-8048
Auditors - BDO Canada LLP C.A., Vancouver, B.C.
Lawyers - Clark Wilson LLP, Vancouver, B.C.
Transfer Agents - Computershare Trust Company of Canada Inc., Vancouver, B.C.
Employees - 112 at Mar. 31, 2023
Profile - (B.C. 2007; orig. B.C., 2010) Designs, manufactures and distributes a full suite of all-electric high floor and low floor vehicles, including transit buses, school buses, shuttle buses, a double decker bus and cargo van.

Offers a range of electric powered buses deploying electric drive and battery technologies with a lightweight chassis and low or high floor body. Bus parts such as batteries, motors, brakes, axles, and dash and control systems are sourced from global suppliers. Products include EV250 (30 feet), EV350 (40 feet) and EV550 double decker (45 feet) transit buses, EV Star (25 feet) mini buses and BEAST (Battery Electric Automotive School Transportation) Type-D (40 feet) and Nano-BEAST Type A (25 feet) school buses product line.

During fiscal 2023, the company delivered 299 buses which include 226 EV Star CC's, 40 EV Star 22-foot cargo, 3 EV Star Cargo Plus, 19 EV Stars, 7 BEAST Type D school buses, 2 Nano BEAST Type A school buses and 2 EV 250's.

In July 2022, the company acquired California-based **Lion Truck Body Inc.** for total purchase price of US$240,000 and assumption of US$1,450,000 liabilities. Lion Truck installs a range of resilient state-of-the-art truck bodies for industries such as goods movement, construction, catering, landscaping, utility and service sectors.

In March 2022, the company launched the Nano-BEAST (Battery Electric Automotive School Transportation) Type A school bus, a 25-feet all-electric school bus that is constructed using a vehicle with a cutaway front section and has a range of up to 150 miles per charge.

Common reinstated on TSX-VEN, July 21, 2023.

Common suspended from TSX-VEN, July 7, 2023.

Predecessor Detail - Succeeded Oakmont Minerals Corp., Dec. 23, 2014, following reverse takeover acquisition of (old) GreenPower Motor Company Inc.; basis 1 new for 2 old shs.

Directors - Fraser Atkinson, chr. & CEO, Vancouver, B.C.; Brendan Riley, pres., Calif.; Mark S. Achtemichuk, Vancouver, B.C.; Malcolm F. Clay, West Vancouver, B.C.; Catherine (Cathy) McLay, Surrey, B.C.; G. David Richardson, Vancouver, B.C.

Other Exec. Officers - Michael Sieffert, CFO & corp. sec.; Mark Nestlen, v-p, bus. devel. & strategy; Michael Perez, v-p, school bus, contracts & grants; Claus Tritt, v-p, medium duty & comml. vehicle sales; Yanyan Zhang, v-p, program mgt.; Frank Zhang, contr.

Capital Stock

	Authorized (shs.)	Outstanding (shs.)[1]
Preferred	unlimited	nil
Common	unlimited	24,948,305

[1] At July 14, 2023

Major Shareholder - Fraser Atkinson held 11.7% interest and G. David Richardson held 11.6% interest at Feb. 17, 2023.

Price Range - GPV/TSX-VEN

Year	Volume	High	Low	Close
2022	6,784,369	$12.33	$2.27	$2.35
2021	8,837,107	$43.62	$9.95	$11.94
2020	16,478,542	$42.53	$1.16	$37.02
2019	1,331,825	$4.34	$1.58	$1.96
2018	1,940,662	$5.60	$2.17	$3.12

Consolidation: 1-for-7 cons. in Aug. 2020
Recent Close: $4.80

Capital Stock Changes - During fiscal 2023, common share were issued as follows: 1,565,268 under an at-the-market program and 3,322 on exercise of options.

During fiscal 2022, common share were issued as follows: 1,925,656 on exercise of warrants and 329,822 on exercise of options.

Wholly Owned Subsidiaries

Gerui New Energy Vehicle (Nanjing) Co., Ltd., People's Republic of China.
GreenPower Motor Company, Inc., United States.
- 100% int. in **EA Green-Power Private Ltd.**, India.
- 100% int. in **GreenPower Manufacturing WV Inc.**, W.Va.
- 100% int. in **Lion Truck Body Incorporated**, Nev.

0939181 B.C. Ltd., B.C.
- 100% int. in **San Joaquin Equipment Valley Leasing, Inc.**, Utah

0999314 B.C. Ltd., Canada.
- 100% int. in **Electric Vehicle Logistics Inc.**, Nev.
- 100% int. in **GP GreenPower Industries Inc.**, B.C.

Financial Statistics

Periods ended:	12m Mar. 31/23[A]		12m Mar. 31/22[A]
	US$000s	%Chg	US$000s
Operating revenue	**39,425**	**+132**	**17,012**
Cost of sales	32,446		13,360
Research & devel. expense	2,090		1,381
General & admin expense	13,485		10,239
Stock-based compensation	3,646		5,771
Operating expense	**51,667**	**+68**	**30,752**
Operating income	**(12,241)**	**n.a.**	**(13,740)**
Deprec., depl. & amort.	1,219		662
Finance income	270		225
Finance costs, gross	1,550		516
Write-downs/write-offs	(346)		(617)
Pre-tax income	**(15,044)**	**n.a.**	**(15,010)**
Net income	**(15,044)**	**n.a.**	**(15,010)**
Cash & equivalent	600		885
Inventories	41,609		32,255
Accounts receivable	10,273		2,917
Current assets	54,156		43,095
Fixed assets, net	2,605		3,443
Right-of-use assets	4,846		117
Total assets	**63,525**	**+28**	**49,607**
Bank indebtedness	6,612		5,766
Accts. pay. & accr. liabs	7,316		1,734
Current liabilities	26,500		11,514
Long-term debt, gross	610		nil
Long-term debt, net	609		nil
Long-term lease liabilities	4,571		nil
Shareholders' equity	27,662		34,385
Cash from oper. activs	**(14,758)**	**n.a.**	**(20,344)**
Cash from fin. activs	8,189		12,665
Cash from invest. activs	303		(536)
Net cash position	**600**	**-91**	**6,888**
Capital expenditures	(356)		(536)
	US$		US$
Earnings per share*	(0.64)		(0.69)
Cash flow per share*	(0.63)		(0.93)
	shs		shs
No. of shs. o/s*	24,716,628		23,148,038
Avg. no. of shs. o/s*	23,522,755		21,877,488
	%		%
Net profit margin	(38.16)		(88.23)
Return on equity	(48.49)		(42.56)
Return on assets	(23.86)		(32.49)
Foreign sales percent	100		93
No. of employees (FTEs)	112		69

* Common
[A] Reported in accordance with IFRS

Historical Summary
(as originally stated)

Fiscal Year	Oper. Rev.	Net Inc. Bef. Disc.	EPS*
	US$000s	US$000s	US$
2023[A]	39,425	(15,044)	(0.64)
2022[A]	17,012	(15,010)	(0.69)
2021[A]	11,648	(7,837)	(0.43)
2020[A]	13,393	(5,146)	(0.35)
2019[A]	6,047	(4,544)	(0.35)

* Common
[A] Reported in accordance with IFRS
Note: Adjusted throughout for 1-for-7 cons. in Aug. 2020

G.89 Greenrise Global Brands Inc.

Symbol - XCX **Exchange** - CSE **CUSIP** - 39540L
Head Office - Charlottenstrasse 59, Berlin, Germany, 10117 **Overseas Tel** - 49-30-209-45800 **Overseas Fax** - 49-30-209-45811
Website - greenriseglobal.com
Email - investor@greenriseglobal.com
Investor Relations - Dr. Stefan Feuerstein (236) 833-1602
Auditors - Dale Matheson Carr-Hilton LaBonte LLP C.A., Vancouver, B.C.
Bankers - Bank of Montreal, Montréal, Qué.
Lawyers - Sangra Moller LLP, Vancouver, B.C.
Transfer Agents - Computershare Trust Company of Canada Inc., Calgary, Alta.
Profile - (B.C. 2014; orig. Alta., 1997) Imports European Union-Good Manufacturing Practice (GMP) certified medical cannabis into Germany primarily from Europe and Canada. Also produces and sells cannabidiol (CBD) products.

Wholly owned **AMP Alternative Medical Products GmbH** (AMP Germany) sources, stores, transports, delivers and sells medical cannabis products to pharmaceutical wholesalers in Germany who supply pharmacies in the country permitted to dispense medical cannabis prescribed by German physicians. AMP Germany operates in accordance with German Narcotic Drug Act to ensure that medical cannabis products meet the EU-GMP standard.

Subsidiary **CannaCare Health GmbH** produces and sells cannabidiol (CBD) products, including tinctures, sprays and oils, and skincare products under the CANOBO brand.

In May 2022, the company acquired a 51% interest in Hamburg, Germany-based **CannaCare Health GmbH**, which produces and sells cannabidiol (CBD) products, including tinctures, sprays and oils, and skincare products under the CANOBO brand, for issuance of 5,000,000 common shares. The company has an exclusive option to acquire the remaining 49% in CannaCare for two years. Subsequently in November 2022, the company agreed to sell its 20% interest in CannaCare to a third party for €250,000. Upon completion, the company's interest in CannaCare would decrease to 31% from 51%.

Predecessor Detail - Name changed from AMP Alternative Medical Products Inc., Nov. 8, 2021.

Directors - Dr. Stefan Feuerstein, Berlin, Germany; Frank Otto, Hamburg, Germany; Oliver Schindler, Hamburg, Germany

Exec. Officers - Tom S. Kusumoto, interim CEO & interim CFO; Stefan Blodgett, v-p, corp. devel.

Capital Stock

	Authorized (shs.)	Outstanding (shs.)[1]
Preferred	unlimited	nil
Common	unlimited	47,236,039

[1] At Oct. 28, 2022

Major Shareholder - Tom S. Kusumoto held 12.23% interest at Oct. 28, 2022.

Price Range - XCX/CSE

Year	Volume	High	Low	Close
2022	1,812,970	$0.35	$0.10	$0.11
2021	5,412,069	$0.88	$0.24	$0.36
2020	5,511,772	$0.74	$0.24	$0.36
2019	8,194,766	$0.53	$0.11	$0.25
2018	1,021,508	$0.25	$0.07	$0.18

Recent Close: $0.03

Capital Stock Changes - In April 2022, private placement of 3,617,000 units (1 common share & 2 warrant) at Cdn$0.20 per unit was completed, with warrants exercisable at Cdn$0.35 and Cdn$0.50 per share for one year and two years, respectively.

Wholly Owned Subsidiaries

AMP Alternative Medical Products Canada Limited, Canada.
AMP Alternative Medical Products GmbH, Erfurt, Germany.
Greenrise GmbH, Germany.

Subsidiaries

51% int. in **CannaCare Health GmbH**, Hamburg, Germany.

Financial Statistics

Periods ended:	12m Dec. 31/21[A]		12m Dec. 31/20[A]
	€000s	%Chg	€000s
Operating revenue	**453**	**+331**	**105**
Cost of goods sold	410		105
Salaries & benefits	498		204
General & admin expense	1,635		1,455
Stock-based compensation	138		316
Operating expense	**2,681**	**+29**	**2,080**
Operating income	**(2,228)**	**n.a.**	**(1,975)**
Deprec., depl. & amort.	38		9
Finance costs, net	139		46
Write-downs/write-offs	(10)		(189)
Pre-tax income	**(3,640)**	**n.a.**	**(2,114)**
Net income	**(3,640)**	**n.a.**	**(2,114)**
Cash & equivalent	27		60
Inventories	48		nil
Accounts receivable	23		8
Current assets	99		309
Fixed assets, net	88		47
Right-of-use assets	66		17
Total assets	**253**	**-32**	**372**
Accts. pay. & accr. liabs	296		261
Current liabilities	383		267
Long-term debt, gross	1,842		1,065
Long-term debt, net	1,842		1,065
Long-term lease liabilities	32		12
Shareholders' equity	(2,004)		(973)
Cash from oper. activs	**(1,888)**	**n.a.**	**(1,831)**
Cash from fin. activs	1,918		1,629
Cash from invest. activs	(63)		45
Net cash position	**27**	**-55**	**60**
Capital expenditures	nil		(50)
	€		€
Earnings per share*	(0.12)		(0.08)
Cash flow per share*	(0.06)		(0.07)
	shs		shs
No. of shs. o/s*	36,919,039		27,160,611
Avg. no. of shs. o/s*	31,178,872		24,898,140
	%		%
Net profit margin	(803.53)		n.m.
Return on equity	n.m.		n.m.
Return on assets	n.m.		(467.84)

* Common
[A] Reported in accordance with IFRS

Latest Results

Periods ended:	6m June 30/22[A]		6m June 30/21[A]
	€000s	%Chg	€000s
Operating revenue	268	+13	237
Net income	(1,023)	n.a.	(1,123)
	€		€
Earnings per share*	(0.02)		(0.04)

* Common
[A] Reported in accordance with IFRS

Historical Summary
(as originally stated)

Fiscal Year	Oper. Rev.	Net Inc. Bef. Disc.	EPS*
	€000s	€000s	€
2021[A]	453	(3,640)	(0.12)
2020[A]	105	(2,114)	(0.08)
	$000s	$000s	$
2019[A]	nil	(3,980)	(0.25)
2018[A]	nil	(795)	(0.08)
2017[A]	nil	(388)	(0.04)

* Common
[A] Reported in accordance with IFRS

Note: Adjusted throughout for 3-for-1 split in Dec. 2018

G.90 GreenSpace Brands Inc.

Symbol - JTR.H **Exchange** - TSX-VEN (S) **CUSIP** - 39572A

Head Office - 106-2087 Dundas St E, Mississauga, ON, L4X 2V7 **Telephone** - (416) 934-5034 **Fax** - (416) 962-9558

Website - www.greenspacebrands.ca

Email - swarren@greenspacebrands.com

Investor Relations - Shawn R. Warren (416) 934-5034 ext. 210

Auditors - MNP LLP C.A., Mississauga, Ont.

Lawyers - Dentons Canada LLP, Toronto, Ont.

Transfer Agents - Computershare Trust Company of Canada Inc., Toronto, Ont.

Employees - 26 at Mar. 31, 2022

Profile - (Ont. 2013) Develops, markets and sells premium natural food products to North American consumers.

Product lines include Central Roast, an all-natural line of snack foods mainly consisting of raw and roasted nuts, seeds, popcorn and dried fruits; Love Child Organics, a line of organic food products for infants and toddlers; and Go Veggie®, a plant-based alternative cheese brand.

Products are sold online and in natural and mass retail grocery locations across Canada and the United States.

On Apr. 6, 2023, the company filed for protection under the Companies' Creditors Arrangement Act (CCAA). **PricewaterhouseCoopers Inc.** appointed monitor. Additionally the company has entered into an asset purchase agreement with **Pivot Financial I Limited Partnership**, its senior lender, under which the Love Child Organics™ business will be acquired. Unless there is a successful bid at the conclusion of the sale and investment solicitation process (SISP) that provides for a significantly higher value than the Pivot offer, any distribution to equity holders was unlikely.

Common suspended from TSX-VEN, Apr. 12, 2023.

Predecessor Detail - Name changed from Aumento Capital IV Corporation, Apr. 30, 2015, pursuant to the Qualifying Transaction reverse takeover acquisition of Life Choices Natural Food Corp.; basis 1 new for 2 old shs.

Directors - Paul K. Henderson, chr., Ont.; Glenn Fagan, Ont.; Michael G. LeClair, Toronto, Ont.; Tracy Tidy, Surrey, B.C.

Other Exec. Officers - Shawn R. Warren, pres. & CEO; Justin Guerin, CFO; Brittany Compton, pres., Love Child Organics

Capital Stock

	Authorized (shs.)	Outstanding (shs.)[1]
Common	unlimited	509,392,282

[1] At Dec. 31, 2022

Major Shareholder - PenderFund Capital Management Ltd. held 32.4% interest at Feb. 9, 2022.

Price Range - JTR.H/TSX-VEN (S)

Year	Volume	High	Low	Close
2022	72,289,837	$0.06	$0.01	$0.01
2021	107,797,138	$0.15	$0.05	$0.06
2020	55,110,511	$0.13	$0.03	$0.08
2019	41,630,700	$0.40	$0.06	$0.09
2018	21,961,644	$1.60	$0.30	$0.38

Recent Close: $0.01

Capital Stock Changes - In September 2021, bought deal private placement of 47,955,000 units (1 common share & ½ warrant) at 6¢ per unit was completed. Also during fiscal 2022, 16,362,316 common shares were issued for debt settlement.

Wholly Owned Subsidiaries

The Cold Press Corp., Toronto, Ont.
GSB Beverage Inc., Canada.
GSB Investment Corp., Ont.
- 100% int. in **Central Roast Inc.**, Toronto, Ont.

Galaxy Nutritional Foods Inc., North Kingstown, R.I.
Life Choices Natural Food Corp., Toronto, Ont.
- 100% int. in **The Everyday Fundraising Group**, Canada.
- 100% int. in **Grandview Farms Sales Limited**, Ont.
- 100% int. in **1706817 Ontario Limited**, Ont.
- 100% int. in **Roam Eggs Ltd.**, Ont.

Love Child (Brands) Inc., Whistler, B.C.
2047480 Ontario Inc., St. Jacobs, Ont.

Investments

Tend Botanicals Inc.

Financial Statistics

Periods ended:	12m Mar. 31/22[A]		12m Mar. 31/21[ᵒA]
	$000s	%Chg	$000s
Operating revenue	**14,479**	**-39**	**23,669**
Cost of goods sold	12,014		20,619
Salaries & benefits	3,489		5,068
General & admin expense	2,818		6,011
Stock-based compensation	265		171
Operating expense	**18,586**	**-42**	**31,869**
Operating income	**(4,107)**	**n.a.**	**(8,200)**
Deprec., depl. & amort.	428		1,078
Finance costs, gross	4,191		3,589
Write-downs/write-offs	(3,882)		(10,093)
Pre-tax income	**(10,228)**	**n.a.**	**(20,545)**
Net inc. bef. disc. opers	**(10,228)**	**n.a.**	**(20,545)**
Income from disc. opers	8		(234)
Net income	**(10,220)**	**n.a.**	**(20,779)**
Cash & equivalent	2,241		4,030
Inventories	3,488		4,489
Accounts receivable	2,091		2,921
Current assets	9,143		14,396
Fixed assets, net	51		44
Right-of-use assets	14		443
Intangibles, net	3,303		7,540
Total assets	**12,511**	**-44**	**22,423**
Accts. pay. & accr. liabs	2,597		6,344
Current liabilities	19,461		22,253
Long-term debt, gross	18,029		16,606
Long-term debt, net	1,174		1,007
Long-term lease liabilities	5		1,010
Shareholders' equity	(8,129)		(1,847)
Cash from oper. activs	**(3,843)**	**n.a.**	**(6,086)**
Cash from fin. activs	1,766		10,144
Cash from invest. activs	331		(1)
Net cash position	**2,241**	**-44**	**4,030**
Capital expenditures	(53)		(4)
Capital disposals	384		3
	$		$
Earnings per share*	(0.02)		(0.06)
Cash flow per share*	(0.01)		(0.02)
	shs		shs
No. of shs. o/s*	509,392,282		445,074,966
Avg. no. of shs. o/s*	467,883,445		347,596,221
	%		%
Net profit margin	(70.64)		(86.80)
Return on equity	n.m.		n.m.
Return on assets	(34.56)		(63.37)
No. of employees (FTEs)	26		43

* Common
ᵒ Restated
[A] Reported in accordance with IFRS

Latest Results

Periods ended:	9m Dec. 31/22[A]		9m Dec. 31/21[A]
	$000s	%Chg	$000s
Operating revenue	12,349	+8	11,479
Net inc. bef. disc. opers	(4,999)	n.a.	(4,965)
Income from disc. opers	(1)		11
Net income	(5,000)	n.a.	(4,954)
	$		$
Earnings per share*	(0.01)		n.a.

* Common
[A] Reported in accordance with IFRS

Historical Summary
(as originally stated)

Fiscal Year	Oper. Rev.	Net Inc. Bef. Disc.	EPS*
	$000s	$000s	$
2022[A]	14,479	(10,228)	(0.02)
2021[A]	23,691	(20,736)	(0.06)
2020[A]	41,071	(34,059)	(0.36)
2019[A]	67,441	(14,676)	(0.20)
2018[A]	56,305	(4,443)	(0.07)

* Common
[A] Reported in accordance with IFRS

G.91 Greenway Greenhouse Cannabis Corporation

Symbol - GWAY **Exchange** - CSE **CUSIP** - 39679F

Head Office - 1478 Seacliff Dr, Kingsville, ON, N9Y 2M2 **Telephone** - (519) 712-0311

Website - greenway.ca

Email - darrenp@greenway.ca
Investor Relations - Darren Peddle (519) 712-0311
Auditors - MNP LLP C.A., Ottawa, Ont.
Transfer Agents - TSX Trust Company, Toronto, Ont.
Profile - (Ont. 2018) Cultivates, propagates and distributes cannabis for the Canadian market.

Operates a 10,000-sq.-ft. indoor nursery in Kingsville, Ont.; and a cultivation facility in Leamington, Ont., with a 41,750-sq.-ft. greenhouse and a 15,000-sq.-ft. processing facility capable of producing 6,000 kg of cannabis biomass per year. Strains cultivated include Sun County Kush, Lemon Pound Cake, Blackberry Gelato #8 and Timbitz, which are supplied and sold at wholesale to other licensed cannabis operators.

Expansions were completed in November 2022 to increase the greenhouse space to 167,000 sq. ft. and the processing space to 22,000 sq. ft., bringing the production capacity to 24,000 kg per year. Subsequently in February 2023, the company received licence from Health Canada for the expansion of its licensed cultivation area in February 2023.

In January 2023, the company has received a standard processing licence from Health Canada which would complement to the companies B2B business model by allowing the company to provide value-added processing services, as well as allow the company to bring its own branded products to market.

On Dec. 1, 2022, common shares were listed on the OTCQB® Venture market under the stock symbol OTCQB.

Recent Merger and Acquisition Activity

Status: completed **Revised:** Jan. 19, 2023
UPDATE: The property was sold for $7,500,000. PREVIOUS: Greenway Greenhouse Cannabis Corporation agreed to market and sell its 10-acre hydroponic greenhouse in Leamington, Ont., which was used and leased by Sunrite Greenhouses Ltd.

Directors - Jamie D'Alimonte, co-founder, co-chr. & CEO, Leamington, Ont.; Carl Mastronardi, co-founder, co-chr. & pres., Leamington, Ont.; Darren Peddle, CFO, Kingsville, Ont.; Martin J. (Marty) Komsa, La Salle, Ont.; Dennis Staudt, Kingsville, Ont.
Other Exec. Officers - Jacob de Jong, CAO & corp. sec.

Capital Stock

	Authorized (shs.)	Outstanding (shs.)[1]
Common	unlimited	130,924,747

[1] At Mar. 31, 2023

Major Shareholder - Jamie D'Alimonte held 38.19% interest and Carl Mastronardi held 38.19% interest at Aug. 22, 2022.

Price Range - GWAY/CSE

Year	Volume	High	Low	Close
2022	5,745,229	$1.53	$0.30	$0.34
2021	5,339,002	$1.80	$0.44	$1.17

Recent Close: $0.20
Capital Stock Changes - There were no changes to capital stock during fiscal 2023.

In May 2021, private placement of 2,458,000 common shares was completed at 50¢ per share and 52,507,547 common shares were cancelled. In December 2021, private placement of 7,272,728 units (1 common share & 1 warrant) at $1.10 per unit was completed. Also during fiscal 2022, 2,020,000 common shares were issued on exercise of options.

Financial Statistics

Periods ended:	12m Mar. 31/23[A]		12m Mar. 31/22[A]
	$000s	%Chg	$000s
Operating revenue	**5,622**	**+183**	**1,984**
Cost of sales	3,672		754
Salaries & benefits	348		277
Research & devel. expense	nil		47
General & admin expense	1,517		1,113
Stock-based compensation	693		313
Operating expense	**6,230**	**+149**	**2,504**
Operating income	**(608)**	**n.a.**	**(520)**
Deprec., depl. & amort.	1,090		713
Finance costs, net	882		850
Write-downs/write-offs	nil		(898)
Pre-tax income	**(2,606)**	**n.a.**	**(2,923)**
Net income	**(2,606)**	**n.a.**	**(2,923)**
Cash & equivalent	3,642		7,480
Inventories	1,493		2,326
Accounts receivable	770		289
Current assets	6,371		10,988
Fixed assets, net	28,934		24,644
Total assets	**35,305**	**-1**	**35,632**
Accts. pay. & accr. liabs	6,401		2,097
Current liabilities	6,790		7,971
Long-term debt, gross	4,940		10,553
Long-term debt, net	4,900		4,900
Long-term lease liabilities	8,667		5,900
Shareholders' equity	14,947		16,860
Cash from oper. activs	**2,226**	**n.a.**	**(1,973)**
Cash from fin. activs	(6,493)		8,119
Cash from invest. activs	428		(2,122)
Net cash position	**3,642**	**-51**	**7,480**
Capital expenditures	(6,611)		(2,122)
Capital disposals	7,039		nil
	$		$
Earnings per share*	(0.02)		(0.02)
Cash flow per share*	0.02		(0.02)
	shs		shs
No. of shs. o/s*	130,924,747		130,924,747
Avg. no. of shs. o/s*	130,924,747		129,905,231
	%		%
Net profit margin	(46.35)		(147.33)
Return on equity	(16.39)		(21.55)
Return on assets	(7.35)		(9.62)

* Common
[A] Reported in accordance with IFRS

Historical Summary
(as originally stated)

Fiscal Year	Oper. Rev. $000s	Net Inc. Bef. Disc. $000s	EPS* $
2023[A]	5,622	(2,606)	(0.02)
2022[A]	1,984	(2,923)	(0.02)
2021[A]	nil	(1,232)	(0.01)
2020[A]	nil	(2,181)	(0.01)

* Common
[A] Reported in accordance with IFRS

G.92 Grey Wolf Animal Health Corp.

Symbol - WOLF **Exchange** - TSX-VEN **CUSIP** - 397885
Head Office - 201-65 Front St E, Toronto, ON, M5E 1B5 **Toll-free** - (855) 229-6522
Website - greywolfah.com
Email - investors@greywolfah.com
Investor Relations - Angela Cechetto (855) 229-6522
Auditors - PricewaterhouseCoopers LLP C.A., Oakville, Ont.
Transfer Agents - TSX Trust Company, Toronto, Ont.
Profile - (Ont. 2021) Sources, in-licenses, acquires and commercializes branded and generic pharmaceutical, nutraceutical and consumable products for use in veterinary clinics across Canada and operates a compounding pharmacy for veterinary and human customers.

The company operates business units: Animal Health; and Pharmacy.

The **Animal Health** business unit acquires the Canadian sales and marketing rights to late-stage development or commercial products, either through acquisition or long-term in-licensing or distribution agreements with animal health companies who do not have a presence in Canada. It then primarily focuses on selling, marketing, and distributing pharmaceutical, nutraceutical and consumable products to veterinary clinics across Canada using its integrated sales and marketing team to target clinics and pet owners.

Key branded and generic pharmaceutical products include Thryo-Tabs® (hypothyroidism for dogs); Ataject® (reversal of sedative and analgesic agents for dogs); Sedaject® (sedative and analgesic for cats and dogs) and Meloxicam (pain for dogs). Key nutraceutical products for cats and dogs: Entreo Aid+GI™ and Pro Care + GI™ (gastrointestinal upset); Composure™ Pro (behaviour) and Vertriflex® (joint supplements). Key consumable products are Medical Pet Shirt® (wound protection), advanced wound care portfolio and disposables (needles, syringes and catheters).

The company does not manufacture any of its products directly, but rather outsources this function to its licence and supply partners who provide the products.

The **Pharmacy** business unit, through wholly owned **Trutina Pharmacy Inc.**, carries on the business of compounding pharmaceuticals, primarily for horses including racehorses and equestrian, but also offers bioidentical hormone replacement therapy for women and men, including testosterone replacement therapy. Trutina receives prescriptions from veterinarians, physicians and patients specifying the exact dosage and format of specified ingredients, compounds the product at its facility and ships the compounded product directly to veterinarians who then dispense it to their patients or patients. Operates out of a 7,500-sq.-ft. facility in Ancaster, Ont.

Recent Merger and Acquisition Activity

Status: completed **Revised:** Nov. 15, 2022
UPDATE: The transaction was completed. PREVIOUS: Magen Ventures I Inc. entered into a letter of intent for the Qualifying Transaction reverse takeover acquisition of private Toronto, Ont.-based Grey Wolf Animal Health Inc., which develops, acquires and in-licenses companion animal health products that meet the underserved needs of veterinarians and pet owners across Canadian and around the world. Terms of the transaction were to be subsequently disclosed. Mar. 16, 2022 - The companies entered into a definitive agreement whereby Grey Wolf would amalgamate with a wholly owned subsidiary of Magen. It is expected that 25,900,000 post-consolidated common shares (following a 1-for-19.1667 consolidation) would be issued to Grey Wolf shareholders. On closing, Magen plans to change its name to Grey Wolf Animal Health Corp. July 29, 2022 - The consolidation ratio of the Magen shares was amended to 1-for-16.6667. Nov. 1, 2022 - Conditional TSX Venture Exchange approval was received.

Predecessor Detail - Name changed from Magen Ventures I Inc., Nov. 11, 2022, pursuant to the Qualifying Transaction reverse takeover acquisition of Grey Wolf Animal Health Inc.; basis 1 new for 16.6667 old shs.

Directors - Dr. Ian Sandler, chief veterinary medical officer, Toronto, Ont.; Jill T. Angevine, Calgary, Alta.; Shawn Aspden, Toronto, Ont.; Diane Bourassa, L'Assomption, Qué.; Robert (Rob) Harris, Milton, Ont.
Other Exec. Officers - Angela Cechetto, CEO & corp. sec.; Kevin Palmer, CFO; Murray Roach, chief comml. officer; Brandon Mair-Wren, v-p, opers.

Capital Stock

	Authorized (shs.)	Outstanding (shs.)[1]
Common	unlimited	31,032,222

[1] At Nov. 23, 2022

Major Shareholder - Bloom Burton & Co. Inc. held 11.6% interest and Dr. Ian Sandler held 10% interest at Nov. 23, 2022.

Price Range - WOLF/TSX-VEN

Year	Volume	High	Low	Close
2022	924,243	$2.33	$0.75	$0.78
2021	99,107	$3.17	$1.17	$1.58

Consolidation: 1-for-16.6667 cons. in Nov. 2022
Recent Close: $0.75
Capital Stock Changes - In November 2022, common shares were consolidated on a 1-for-16.6667 basis and 27,432,227 post-consolidated common shares were issued pursuant to the Qualifying Transaction reverse takeover acquisition of Grey Wolf Animal Health Inc.

Wholly Owned Subsidiaries

Grey Wolf Animal Health Inc., Toronto, Ont.
- 100% int. in **Trubalance Healthcare Inc.**, Ancaster, Ont.
- 100% int. in **2775506 Ontario Inc.**, Ont.
  - 100% int. in **Trutina Pharmacy Inc.**, Ancaster, Ont.

Financial Statistics

Periods ended:	12m Dec. 31/21[A1]		12m Dec. 31/20[A]
	$000s	%Chg	$000s
Operating revenue	**13,095**	**+70**	**7,682**
Cost of sales	5,946		3,540
General & admin expense	5,187		2,871
Stock-based compensation	181		160
Other operating expense	692		747
Operating expense	**13,025**	**+61**	**8,105**
Operating income	**70**	**n.a.**	**(423)**
Finance income	24		46
Finance costs, gross	1,655		277
Pre-tax income	**(1,891)**	**n.a.**	**(817)**
Income taxes	(922)		79
Net income	**(969)**	**n.a.**	**(896)**
Cash & equivalent	4,352		2,129
Inventories	2,869		1,466
Accounts receivable	1,125		999
Current assets	8,471		4,627
Fixed assets, net	1,352		12
Right-of-use assets	938		138
Intangibles, net	25,473		2,403
Total assets	**33,234**	**+363**	**7,179**
Accts. pay. & accr. liabs	2,221		1,218
Current liabilities	19,511		1,951
Long-term debt, gross	22,333		314
Long-term debt, net	10,028		284
Long-term lease liabilities	788		48
Shareholders' equity	4,076		2,822
Cash from oper. activs	**2,138**	**+259**	**596**
Cash from fin. activs	23,321		1,757
Cash from invest. activs	(23,238)		(600)
Net cash position	**4,352**	**+104**	**2,129**
Capital expenditures	(15)		nil
	$		$
Earnings per share*	n.a.		n.a.
	shs		shs
No. of shs. o/s	n.a.		n.a.
	%		%
Net profit margin	(7.40)		(11.66)
Return on equity	(28.10)		n.m.
Return on assets	(0.60)		n.a.

[A] Reported in accordance with IFRS

[1] Results for fiscal 2021 and prior periods pertain to Grey Wolf Animal Health Inc.

Note: Adjusted throughout for 1-for-16.6667 cons. in Nov. 2022

G.93 Grosvenor CPC I Inc.

Symbol - GRVA.P **Exchange** - TSX-VEN **CUSIP** - 39927B
Head Office - 1670-1 Place Ville Marie, Montréal, QC, H3B 2B6 **Telephone** - (514) 402-6360
Email - pmarleau@palos.ca
Investor Relations - Philippe Marleau (514) 402-6360
Auditors - MNP LLP C.A., Toronto, Ont.
Transfer Agents - TSX Trust Company, Toronto, Ont.
Profile - (Can. 2021) Capital Pool Company.
Directors - Philippe Marleau, CEO, CFO & corp. sec., Montréal, Qué.; Charles Marleau, Montréal, Qué.; Guillaume Poulin, Toronto, Ont.; Benjamin Yi, Grand Cayman, Cayman Islands

Capital Stock

	Authorized (shs.)	Outstanding (shs.)[1]
Common	unlimited	26,426,400

[1] At Dec. 12, 2022

Major Shareholder - Widely held at Oct. 3, 2022.

Price Range - GRVA.P/TSX-VEN

Year	Volume	High	Low	Close
2022	274,800	$0.13	$0.05	$0.05

Recent Close: $0.05

Capital Stock Changes - On Mar. 22, 2022, an initial public offering of 6,526,400 common shares was completed at 10¢ per share.

G.94 Grounded People Apparel Inc.

Symbol - SHOE **Exchange** - CSE **CUSIP** - 39943T
Head Office - 800-1199 Hastings St W, Vancouver, BC, V6C 2X6 **Telephone** - (236) 521-8784
Website - groundedpeople.ca
Email - gb@harmonycs.ca
Investor Relations - Geoffrey Balderson (236) 521-0626
Auditors - Crowe MacKay LLP C.A., Vancouver, B.C.
Transfer Agents - Endeavor Trust Corporation, Vancouver, B.C.
Profile - (B.C. 2020) Designs, develops and produces unisex canvas sneakers made from sustainable, ethically sourced and produced materials, and manufactured by fair trade workers.

The company's initial products, 100% vegan shoes, are manufactured by Brazil-based **Ahimsa Industria E Commercio De Calcados Ltda.**

Common listed on CSE, Oct. 5, 2022.

Predecessor Detail - Name changed from Grounded Clothing Inc., June 15, 2021.

Directors - Maximilian Justus, CEO, Vancouver, B.C.; Geoffrey (Geoff) Balderson, CFO & corp. sec., Vancouver, B.C.; Nima Bahrami, Vancouver, B.C.; Patrick C. T. (Pat) Morris, Vancouver, B.C.; Joel Shacker, Vancouver, B.C.

Capital Stock

	Authorized (shs.)	Outstanding (shs.)[1]
Common	unlimited	23,212,006

[1] At May 31, 2023

Major Shareholder - Widely held at Oct. 5, 2022.

Price Range - SHOE/CSE

Year	Volume	High	Low	Close
2022	80,677	$1.00	$0.15	$0.46

Recent Close: $0.80

Capital Stock Changes - In March 2022, private placement of 2,857,143 units (1 common share & 1 warrant) at 35¢ per unit was completed. In November 2022, private placement of 347,222 units (1 common share & 1 warrant) at 72¢ per unit was completed. In January 2023, private placement of 4,464,286 units (1 common share & 1 warrant) at 56¢ per unit was completed. Also during fiscal 2023, 76,686 common shares were issued for services.

Wholly Owned Subsidiaries

Grounded People Apparel (US) SPC, Wash.

Financial Statistics

Periods ended:	12m Feb. 28/23[A]		12m Feb. 28/22[A]
	$000s	%Chg	$000s
Operating revenue	**121**	**+572**	**18**
Cost of goods sold	298		5
Salaries & benefits	70		nil
General & admin expense	1,745		507
Stock-based compensation	109		379
Operating expense	**2,223**	**+149**	**892**
Operating income	**(2,101)**	**n.a.**	**(874)**
Write-downs/write-offs	(257)		nil
Pre-tax income	**(2,101)**	**n.a.**	**(874)**
Net income	**(2,101)**	**n.a.**	**(874)**
Cash & equivalent	1,153		21
Inventories	140		103
Accounts receivable	70		15
Current assets	2,149		276
Total assets	**2,149**	**+679**	**276**
Accts. pay. & accr. liabs	227		78
Current liabilities	227		78
Shareholders' equity	1,921		199
Cash from oper. activs	**(2,618)**	**n.a.**	**(682)**
Cash from fin. activs	3,750		511
Net cash position	**1,153**	**n.m.**	**21**
	$		$
Earnings per share*	(0.11)		(0.06)
Cash flow per share*	(0.14)		(0.05)
	shs		shs
No. of shs. o/s*	23,212,006		15,466,669
Avg. no. of shs. o/s*	18,974,244		14,499,726
	%		%
Net profit margin	n.m.		n.m.
Return on equity	(198.21)		(457.59)
Return on assets	(173.28)		(368.00)
Foreign sales percent	54		68

* Common

[A] Reported in accordance with IFRS

Latest Results

Periods ended:	3m May 31/23[A]		3m May 31/22[A]
	$000s	%Chg	$000s
Operating revenue	10	-80	49
Net income	(580)	n.a.	(443)
	$		$
Earnings per share*	(0.02)		(0.02)

* Common

[A] Reported in accordance with IFRS

Historical Summary
(as originally stated)

Fiscal Year	Oper. Rev.	Net Inc. Bef. Disc.	EPS*
	$000s	$000s	$
2023[A]	121	(2,101)	(0.11)
2022[A]	18	(874)	(0.06)
2021[A1]	nil	(60)	(0.01)

* Common

[A] Reported in accordance with IFRS

[1] 45 weeks ended Feb. 28, 2021.

G.95 Grown Rogue International Inc.

Symbol - GRIN **Exchange** - CSE **CUSIP** - 39986R
Head Office - 550 Airport Rd, Medford, OR, United States, 97504 **Telephone** - (458) 226-2100
Website - www.grownrogue.com
Email - jakeiotte@grownrogue.com
Investor Relations - Jakob Iotte (458) 226-2100
Auditors - Turner, Stone and Company LLP C.P.A., Dallas, Tex.
Transfer Agents - Capital Transfer Agency Inc., Toronto, Ont.
Employees - 181 at Oct. 31, 2022
Profile - (Ont. 2009 amalg.) Produces and distributes cannabis flower products in the United States.

Operates four cultivation facilities in Oregon: the 40,000-sq.-ft. outdoor Foothills (formerly Mira Vista) property; a 40,000-sq.-ft. outdoor property (Trail's End) in Jackson cty.; a 17,000-sq.-ft. indoor property (Rossanley) in Medford; a 30,000-sq.-ft. indoor property (Airport) near the Rossanley facility; and 40,000-sq.-ft. Ross Lane outdoor property. Total annual production capacity for the Oregon operations is between 13,000 and 18,000 lbs.

Subsidiary **Canopy Management, LLC** holds a 60% interest in **Golden Harvests, LLC**, owner of an 80,000-sq.-ft. indoor cultivation facility in Bay City, Mich.

In April 2022, the company acquired the 30,000-sq.-ft. indoor Airport cultivation facility in Medford, Ore., from **Acreage Holdings Inc.** for US$2,000,000. The company had assumed operation of the facility in February 2021 under a management services agreement. A related agreement to acquire a marijuana dispensary in Portland, Ore., from Acreage Holdings was terminated.

Predecessor Detail - Name changed from Novicius Corp., Nov. 1, 2018, pursuant to reverse takeover acquisition of Grown Rogue Unlimited, LLC.; basis 1 new for 1.4 old shs.

Directors - J. Obie Strickler, founder, pres. & CEO, Ore.; Ryan Kee, CFO, Wash.; Sean K. Conacher, Toronto, Ont.; Stephen M. Gledhill, Aurora, Ont.; Abhilash Patel, Calif.

Other Exec. Officers - Adam August, sr. v-p

Capital Stock

	Authorized (shs.)	Outstanding (shs.)[1]
Preferred	unlimited	nil
Common	unlimited	170,832,611

[1] At June 19, 2023

Major Shareholder - J. Obie Strickler held 20.02% interest and Bengal Catalyst Fund, LP held 14.26% interest at Jan. 29, 2023.

Price Range - GRIN/CSE

Year	Volume	High	Low	Close
2022	24,700,113	$0.15	$0.07	$0.15
2021	26,554,619	$0.35	$0.07	$0.12
2020	13,547,223	$0.18	$0.06	$0.12
2019	14,811,844	$0.48	$0.06	$0.10
2018	1,341,828	$0.60	$0.14	$0.37

Recent Close: $0.24

Capital Stock Changes - In December 2021, private placement of 13,166,400 common shares was completed at Cdn$0.125 per share. Also during fiscal 2022, 529,335 common shares were issued for services.

Wholly Owned Subsidiaries

Grown Rogue Unlimited, LLC, Jacksonville, Ore.
- 87% int. in **Canopy Management, LLC**, United States.
- 87% int. in **GR Michigan, LLC**, Mich.
- 100% int. in **GRIP, LLC**, Ore.
- 100% int. in **GRU Properties, LLC**, Ore.
- 60% int. in **Golden Harvests, LLC**, United Arab Emirates.
- 100% int. in **Grown Rogue Distribution, LLC**, Ore.
- 100% int. in **Grown Rogue Gardens, LLC**, Ore.
- 60% int. in **Idalia, LLC**, Ore.

Financial Statistics

Periods ended:	12m Oct. 31/22[A]		12m Oct. 31/21[A]
	US$000s	%Chg	US$000s
Operating revenue	**17,757**	**+89**	**9,379**
Cost of goods sold	9,634		3,278
Salaries & benefits	3,466		2,057
General & admin expense	2,386		1,926
Stock-based compensation	71		281
Operating expense	**15,557**	**+106**	**7,542**
Operating income	**2,200**	**+20**	**1,837**
Deprec., depl. & amort.	751		185
Finance costs, gross	894		1,148
Pre-tax income	**665**	**n.a.**	**(864)**
Income taxes	245		151
Net income	**420**	**n.a.**	**(1,015)**
Net inc. for equity hldrs	**447**	**n.a.**	**(2,410)**
Net inc. for non-cont. int.	**(28)**	**n.a.**	**1,396**
Cash & equivalent	1,582		1,114
Inventories	3,132		3,306
Accounts receivable	1,644		739
Current assets	7,910		6,706
Long-term investments	nil		1,360
Fixed assets, net	7,735		5,743
Intangibles, net	726		399
Total assets	**16,371**	**+15**	**14,208**
Accts. pay. & accr. liabs	1,822		1,767
Current liabilities	5,316		3,862
Long-term debt, gross	2,609		2,210
Long-term debt, net	839		1,366
Long-term lease liabilities	1,276		1,736
Shareholders' equity	6,933		5,087
Non-controlling interest	2,006		2,034
Cash from oper. activs	**2,004**	**n.a.**	**(238)**
Cash from fin. activs	(423)		3,862
Cash from invest. activs	(1,113)		(2,727)
Net cash position	**1,582**	**+42**	**1,114**
Capital expenditures	(1,111)		(2,047)
	US$		US$
Earnings per share*	0.00		(0.02)
Cash flow per share*	0.01		(0.00)
	shs		shs
No. of shs. o/s*	170,632,611		156,936,876
Avg. no. of shs. o/s*	169,193,812		135,231,802
	%		%
Net profit margin	2.37		(10.82)
Return on equity	7.45		n.m.
Return on assets	6.44		3.71
Foreign sales percent	100		100
No. of employees (FTEs)	181		110

* Common

[A] Reported in accordance with IFRS

Latest Results

Periods ended:	6m Apr. 30/23[A]		6m Apr. 30/22[A]
	US$000s	%Chg	US$000s
Operating revenue	10,535	+25	8,433
Net income	1,005	+235	300
Net inc. for equity hldrs	1,345	+119	613
Net inc. for non-cont. int.	(340)		(313)
	US$		US$
Earnings per share*	0.01		0.00

* Common

[A] Reported in accordance with IFRS

Historical Summary
(as originally stated)

Fiscal Year	Oper. Rev.	Net Inc. Bef. Disc.	EPS*
	US$000s	US$000s	US$
2022[A]	17,757	420	0.00
2021[A]	9,379	(1,015)	(0.02)
2020[A]	4,240	(2,356)	(0.03)
2019[A1]	3,925	(9,477)	(0.13)
	$000s	$000s	$
2018[A2]	nil	(516)	(0.14)

* Common

[A] Reported in accordance with IFRS

[1] Results reflect the Nov. 15, 2018, reverse takeover acquisition of Grown Rogue Unlimited, LLC.

[2] Results for fiscal 2018 and prior fiscal years pertain to Novicius Corp.

Note: Adjusted throughout for 1-for-1.4 cons. in Nov. 2018

G.96 Gstaad Capital Corp.

Symbol - GTD.H **Exchange** - TSX-VEN **CUSIP** - 362732

Head Office - 615-800 Pender St W, Vancouver, BC, V6C 2V6 **Telephone** - (604) 687-7767 **Fax** - (604) 688-9895

Email - plarkin@pro.net

Investor Relations - Paul A. Larkin (604) 687-7767

Auditors - Crowe MacKay LLP C.A., Vancouver, B.C.

Transfer Agents - Computershare Trust Company of Canada Inc., Vancouver, B.C.; Olympia Trust Company, Vancouver, B.C.

Profile - (B.C. 2010) Capital Pool Company.

Directors - Paul A. Larkin, pres., CEO & interim CFO, Vancouver, B.C.; Joseph R. (Joe) Martin, Vancouver, B.C.; Philip C. Pincus, Vancouver, B.C.

Other Exec. Officers - Erin L. Walmesley, corp. sec.

Capital Stock

	Authorized (shs.)	Outstanding (shs.)[1]
Common	unlimited	9,408,334

[1] At Nov. 29, 2022

Major Shareholder - Widely held at Mar. 9, 2021.

Price Range - GTD.H/TSX-VEN

Year	Volume	High	Low	Close
2021	359,000	$0.22	$0.13	$0.21
2020	98,500	$0.15	$0.07	$0.13
2019	72,000	$0.15	$0.11	$0.12
2018	21,500	$0.17	$0.12	$0.16

Capital Stock Changes - In September 2021, private placement of 5,000,000 common shares was completed at 10¢ per share. Also during fiscal 2022, 325,000 common shares were issued as finder's fee.

G.97 Guardian Capital Group Limited*

Symbol - GCG **Exchange** - TSX **CUSIP** - 401339

Head Office - Commerce Court West, 2700-199 Bay St, PO Box 201, Toronto, ON, M5L 1E8 **Telephone** - (416) 364-8341 **Toll-free** - (800) 253-9181 **Fax** - (416) 364-2067

Website - www.guardiancapital.com

Email - dyi@guardiancapital.com

Investor Relations - Donald Yi (416) 350-3136

Auditors - KPMG LLP C.A., Toronto, Ont.

Bankers - Bank of Montreal, Toronto, Ont.; Canadian Imperial Bank of Commerce, Toronto, Ont.

Transfer Agents - Computershare Trust Company of Canada Inc., Toronto, Ont.

FP500 Revenue Ranking - 653

Employees - 354 at Mar. 6, 2023

Profile - (Ont. 1962) Provides investment and wealth management products and services to institutional, retail and private clients in Canada and internationally. At Dec. 31, 2022, the company had assets under management of $49.6 billion and assets under administration and advisement of $3.7 billion.

Investment Management - In Canada, wholly owned **Guardian Capital LP** and **Guardian Smart Infrastructure Management Inc.** offer investment products and services to institutional clients, including government, university and corporate pension funds, insurance companies, foundations, endowments, charitable organizations, unions, labour associations and taxable corporations; provide portfolio management services to investment funds, third party wrap programs and affiliated entities under sub-advisory arrangements; and manage investment funds, including mutual funds and exchange-traded funds, for retail investors. In the United Kingdom, wholly owned **GuardCap Asset Management Limited** provides fundamental emerging markets and global equity investment management to institutional clients in the Americas, Europe, Asia and Australia. In the United States, operations are carried out through **Alta Capital Management, LLC** (70% owned), which provides primarily U.S. equity investment strategies to institutional investors and high net worth private clients; and **Agincourt Capital Management, LLC** (70% owned), which manages U.S. fixed-income portfolios for institutional clients. In addition, the company manages a diversified portfolio of direct Canadian real estate through wholly owned **Guardian Capital Real Estate Inc.**

Wealth Management - Operations are carried out through wholly owned **Guardian Capital Advisors LP**, which provides wealth management services to high net worth families, foundations and charities primarily in Canada; wholly owned **Guardian Partners Inc.**, which provides investment and related services in Canada as a private investment office serving ultra high net worth individuals and families and as an outsourced chief investment officer business focused on serving the board and management of foundations, endowments and select pension plans; **Rae & Lipskie Investment Counsel Inc.** (60% owned), which offers private wealth services to high net worth individuals, trusts, estates, foundations and corporations in Canada; **Modern Advisor Canada Inc.** (71% owned), a digital advisory operation which also serves as the technology platform for the company's digital strategy; and wholly owned **Alexandria Bancorp Limited**, a Caribbean-based international private bank which provides trust and corporate administration, investment management and banking services for international clients.

Corporate Activities & Investments - Consists of the management of the company's investment capital and provision of general corporate services. Investments include mutual or pooled funds and marketable equity securities, including a large investment in the **Bank of Montreal**. Corporate activities include general corporate, financial, human resources, legal, compliance and strategic planning and corporate development services provided to the other segments. At Dec. 31, 2022, the fair value of the investment portfolio was $660,413,000 (Dec. 31, 2021 - $751,885,000).

In March 2022, the company launched wholly owned **Guardian Smart Infrastructure Management Inc.**, a direct private infrastructure investment business focused on investing in opportunities and projects that apply proven, value-enhancing technologies to existing infrastructure and greenfield assets.

Recent Merger and Acquisition Activity

Status: completed **Revised:** Mar. 1, 2023

UPDATE: The transaction was completed. PREVIOUS: Guardian Capital Group Limited agreed to sell its life insurance distribution network and mutual fund and securities dealers to Desjardins Group for a sale price of $750,000,000. Desjardins is acquiring IDC Worldsource Insurance Network Inc. (82.2% owned by Guardian), one of the largest life insurance managing general agencies (MGA) in Canada; Worldsource Financial Management Inc. (WFM; 100% owned), a mutual fund dealer; and Worldsource Securities Inc. (WSI; 100% owned), a full-service investment dealer. IDC, WFM and WSI serve more than 5,000 independent advisors in the Canadian insurance and financial advice markets. Going forward, Guardian would focus on its core investment management business. Desjardins plans to operate the acquired companies as stand-alone entities. In addition to the proceeds expected to be received under the transaction, Guardian has a portfolio valued at $648,000,000 at Sept. 30, 2022.

Status: completed **Revised:** Sept. 1, 2022

UPDATE: The transaction was completed. PREVIOUS: Guardian Capital Group Limited agreed to acquire a 60% interest in Waterloo, Ont.-based Rae & Lipskie Investment Counsel Inc. (dba The RaeLipskie Partnership), a private wealth management firm with over $1.1 billion in assets under management, for $9,000,000, consisting of $7,200,000 on closing and $1,800,000 due two years from closing. The employees of The RaeLipskie Partnership would retain the remaining 40% ownership interest. The transaction was expected to close in the third quarter of 2022, subject to regulatory approvals and other customary closing conditions.

Directors - James S. Anas, chr., Burlington, Ont.; George Mavroudis, pres. & CEO, Toronto, Ont.; A. Michael Christodoulou, sr. v-p, strategic planning & devel., Toronto, Ont.; Petros N. Christodoulou, Athens, Greece; Marilyn De Mara, Coldwater, Ont.; Harold W. Hillier, Stouffville, Ont.; Edward T. McDermott, Unionville, Ont.; Barry J. Myers, Toronto, Ont.; Hans-Georg Rudloff, London, Middx., United Kingdom

Other Exec. Officers - Barry H. Gordon, man. dir. & head, Cdn. retail asset mgt.; Donald Yi, CFO; Robin P. Lacey, head, institutional asset mgt.; Paula Dunlop, exec. v-p, HR; C. Verner (Vern) Christensen, sr. v-p & corp. sec.; Matthew D. (Matt) Turner, sr. v-p & chief compliance officer; Ernest B. Dunphy, v-p & contr.; Eddy Fung, v-p, retail fin. & admin.; Rachel Hindson, v-p, legal; Angela Shim, v-p, corp. initiatives

Capital Stock

	Authorized (shs.)	Outstanding (shs.)[1]
Preferred	unlimited	nil
Class A	unlimited	23,369,673
Common	unlimited	2,743,379

[1] At Mar. 31, 2023

Preferred - Issuable in an unlimited number of series, the designation, rights, privileges, restrictions, conditions and other provisions of each series to be determined by the company. Non-voting.

Class A - Dividends and liquidation privileges on the same basis as common shares. Convertible into common shares on a 1-for-1 basis, under the following conditions: if in excess of 50% of the common shares is acquired by any person other than an insider of the company; and if holders of over 50% of the outstanding common shares agree to accept an offer to purchase common shares which is made to all common shareholders. Non-voting.

Common - Convertible into class A non-voting shares on a 1-for-1 basis. One vote per share.

Normal Course Issuer Bid - The company plans to make normal course purchases of up to 137,468 common shares representing 5% of the total outstanding. The bid commenced on Dec. 19, 2022, and expires on Dec. 18, 2023.

The company plans to make normal course purchases of up to 1,623,612 class A shares representing 10% of the public float. The bid commenced on Dec. 19, 2022, and expires on Dec. 18, 2023.

Major Shareholder - Christodoulou 2004 Family Trust held 49.59% interest and Rosemary Short held 21.85% interest at Mar. 31, 2023.

Price Range - GCG/TSX

Year	Volume	High	Low	Close
2022	122,539	$45.00	$25.00	$38.75
2021	206,661	$43.50	$26.00	$35.75
2020	153,731	$28.88	$15.26	$27.00
2019	111,726	$28.01	$22.00	$26.83
2018	100,583	$27.00	$20.40	$21.90

Recent Close: $42.00

Capital Stock Changes - During 2022, 707,000 class A shares were repurchased under a Normal Course Issuer Bid and 81,000 (net) class A shares were sold from treasury.

Dividends

GCG com Ra $1.36 pa Q est. Apr. 19, 2023[1]
Prev. Rate: $0.96 est. Apr. 19, 2022
Prev. Rate: $0.72 est. Apr. 19, 2021
Prev. Rate: $0.64 est. Apr. 17, 2020
GCG.A cl A N.V. Ra $1.36 pa Q est. Apr. 19, 2023[1]
Prev. Rate: $0.96 est. Apr. 19, 2022
Prev. Rate: $0.72 est. Apr. 19, 2021
Prev. Rate: $0.64 est. Apr. 17, 2020

[1] Divds. paid annually prior to July/13.

Long-Term Debt - At Dec. 31, 2022, the company had no long-term debt.

Wholly Owned Subsidiaries

Guardian Capital Enterprises Limited, Ont.
Guardian Capital Holdings International Limited, Cayman Islands.
- 100% int. in **ATC Corporate Services Inc.**, Barbados.

- 100% int. in **ATC Secretarial Services Inc.**, Barbados.
- 100% int. in **Alexandria Bancorp Limited**, Cayman Islands.
  - 100% int. in **Alexandria Global Investment Management Ltd.**, Cayman Islands.
  - 100% int. in **Blyth Nominees Limited**, Cayman Islands.
  - 100% int. in **Hyco Limited**, Cayman Islands.
  - 100% int. in **Value Director Services Ltd.**, Cayman Islands.
  - 100% int. in **Value Secretary Services Ltd.**, Cayman Islands.
- 100% int. in **Alexandria Trust Corporation**, Barbados.

Guardian Capital Holdings Ltd., Canada.

- 100% int. in **Guardian Capital Real Estate GP Inc.**, Ont.
  - 100% int. in **GCREF Holdings GP Inc.**, Ont.
- 100% int. in **Guardian Capital Real Estate Inc.**, Ont.
- 100% int. in **Guardian Ethical Management Inc.**, Ont.
- 100% int. in **Guardian Smart Infrastructure Management Inc.**, Toronto, Ont.

Guardian Capital Inc., Ont.

Guardian Capital LP, Toronto, Ont.

- 100% int. in **GuardCap Asset Management Limited**, London, Middx., United Kingdom.
- 100% int. in **Guardian Capital LLC**, Del.
  - 70% int. in **Agincourt Capital Management, LLC**, Richmond, Va.
  - 70% int. in **Alta Capital Management, LLC**, Salt Lake City, Utah.

Guardian Innovations Inc., Toronto, Ont.

- 71% int. in **Modern Advisor Canada Inc.**, Vancouver, B.C.

Guardian Partners Inc., Toronto, Ont. formerly BNY Mellon Wealth Management, Advisory Services, Inc.

- 100% int. in **Guardian Capital Advisors Inc.**, Ont.
- 100% int. in **Guardian Capital Advisors LP**, Ont.

Subsidiaries

60% int. in **Rae & Lipskie Investment Counsel Inc.**, Waterloo, Ont.

Note: The preceding list includes only the major related companies in which interests are held.

Financial Statistics

Periods ended:	12m Dec. 31/22^A		12m Dec. 31/21^{□A}
	$000s	%Chg	$000s
Total revenue	**200,996**	**+4**	**194,001**
Salaries & benefits	100,120		93,921
Stock-based compensation	3,597		2,602
Other operating expense	36,678		30,522
Operating expense	**140,395**	**+11**	**127,045**
Operating income	**60,601**	**-9**	**66,956**
Deprec. & amort.	12,127		10,875
Finance costs, gross	4,351		1,142
Pre-tax income	**(60,093)**	**n.a.**	**194,626**
Income taxes	(525)		25,672
Net inc bef disc ops, eqhldrs	(61,503)		166,147
Net inc bef disc ops, NCI	1,935		2,807
Net inc. bef. disc. opers	**(59,568)**	**n.a.**	**168,954**
Disc. opers., equity hldrs	18,425		18,092
Disc. opers., NCI	3,826		3,694
Income from disc. opers	22,251		21,786
Net income	**(37,317)**	**n.a.**	**190,740**
Net inc. for equity hldrs	**(43,078)**	**n.a.**	**184,239**
Net inc. for non-cont. int	**5,761**	**-11**	**6,501**
Cash & equivalent	54,894		77,081
Accounts receivable	48,398		77,570
Current assets	538,858		424,568
Long-term investments	660,413		751,885
Fixed assets, net	25,302		16,574
Intangibles	139,405		234,856
Total assets	**1,364,772**	**-4**	**1,428,675**
Bank indebtedness	131,566		114,873
Accts. pay. & accr. liabs	79,772		99,420
Current liabilities	509,473		482,875
Long-term lease liabilities	22,273		11,275
Shareholders' equity	767,864		838,520
Non-controlling interest	14,995		14,057
Cash from oper. activs	**81,228**	**-21**	**102,859**
Cash from fin. activs	(54,620)		1,877
Cash from invest. activs	(45,511)		(88,014)
Net cash position	**26,528**	**-41**	**44,887**
Capital expenditures	(651)		(734)
	$		$
Earns. per sh. bef disc opers*	(2.52)		6.63
Earnings per share*	(1.76)		7.35
Cash flow per share*	3.33		4.10
Cash divd. per share*	0.90		0.70
	shs		shs
No. of shs. o/s*	24,116,000		24,742,000
Avg. no. of shs. o/s*	24,426,000		25,068,000
	%		%
Net profit margin	(29.64)		87.09
Return on equity	(7.66)		21.60
Return on assets	(3.96)		13.16
Foreign sales percent	43		45
No. of employees (FTEs)	n.a.		662

* Class A & com.
□ Restated
A Reported in accordance with IFRS

Latest Results

Periods ended:	3m Mar. 31/23^A		3m Mar. 31/22^{□A}
	$000s	%Chg	$000s
Total revenue	54,493	+5	51,824
Net inc. bef. disc. opers	26,442	n.m.	224
Income from disc. opers	553,743		5,591
Net income	580,185	n.m.	5,815
Net inc. for equity hldrs	487,603	n.m.	4,262
Net inc. for non-cont. int	92,582		1,553
	$		$
Earns. per sh. bef. disc. opers.*	1.09		(0.01)
Earnings per share*	20.27		0.17

* Class A & com.
□ Restated
A Reported in accordance with IFRS

Historical Summary
(as originally stated)

Fiscal Year	Total Rev.	Net Inc. Bef. Disc.	EPS*
	$000s	$000s	$
2022^A	200,996	(59,568)	(2.52)
2021^A	285,087	190,740	7.35
2020^A	215,791	46,068	1.67
2019^A	186,102	126,460	4.77
2018^A	171,513	(13,607)	(0.63)

* Class A & com.
A Reported in accordance with IFRS

G.98 Gulf & Pacific Equities Corp.

Symbol - GUF **Exchange** - TSX-VEN **CUSIP** - 401915
Head Office - 800-1240 Bay St, Toronto, ON, M5R 2A7 **Telephone** - (416) 968-3337 **Fax** - (416) 968-3339
Website - www.gpequities.com
Email - acohen@gpequities.com
Investor Relations - Anthony J. Cohen (416) 968-3337
Auditors - MNP LLP C.A., Winnipeg, Man.
Bankers - The Bank of Nova Scotia
Lawyers - McKercher LLP, Saskatoon, Sask.
Transfer Agents - Computershare Trust Company of Canada Inc., Toronto, Ont.

Profile - (Alta. 1998) Acquires, manages and develops anchored shopping malls in rural centres in Western Canada.

Owns three shopping centre properties in Three Hills, St. Paul and Cold Lake, Alta., totaling 237,033 sq. ft. of gross leasable space. Also holds a vacant lot in Merritt, B.C., carried at nominal value.

Directors - Anthony J. Cohen, pres. & CEO, Toronto, Ont.; Greg K. W. Wong, CFO & corp. sec., Toronto, Ont.; Constantine D. (Dino) Buzunis, San Diego, Calif.; Dr. Ernest C. Cholakis, Winnipeg, Man.; Dean J. Dovolis, Minneapolis, Minn.

Other Exec. Officers - Paul F. Andersen, treas.

Capital Stock

	Authorized (shs.)	Outstanding (shs.)[1]
Preferred	unlimited	nil
Common	unlimited	21,290,685

[1] At Apr. 21, 2023

Major Shareholder - Anthony J. Cohen held 52.68% interest, Dwayne John Ross held 16.86% interest and Greg Steers held 13.03% interest at Apr. 21, 2023.

Price Range - GUF/TSX-VEN

Year	Volume	High	Low	Close
2022	426,289	$0.40	$0.25	$0.40
2021	2,524,386	$0.27	$0.16	$0.27
2020	265,500	$0.27	$0.17	$0.18
2019	278,000	$0.25	$0.19	$0.25
2018	596,562	$0.32	$0.19	$0.23

Recent Close: $0.55

Capital Stock Changes - There were no changes to capital stock from 2016 to 2022, inclusive.

Investments

Plato Gold Corp., Toronto, Ont. (see Survey of Mines)

Financial Statistics

Periods ended:	12m Dec. 31/22^A		12m Dec. 31/21^A
	$000s	%Chg	$000s
Total revenue	**4,216**	**+6**	**3,965**
Rental operating expense	1,909		1,629
Salaries & benefits	292		269
General & admin. expense	505		476
Stock-based compensation	nil		135
Operating expense	**2,706**	**+8**	**2,509**
Operating income	**1,510**	**+4**	**1,456**
Deprec. & amort.	20		20
Finance costs, gross	1,319		1,130
Pre-tax income	**1,809**	**-62**	**4,754**
Income taxes	236		364
Net income	**1,573**	**-64**	**4,390**
Cash & equivalent	185		178
Accounts receivable	500		275
Long-term investments	41		49
Income-producing props	47,830		43,500
Property interests, net	47,830		43,500
Right-of-use assets	2		21
Total assets	**48,616**	**+10**	**44,081**
Bank indebtedness	2,147		1,697
Accts. pay. & accr. liabs	2,825		2,377
Long-term debt, gross	21,161		20,970
Long-term lease liabilities	2		24
Shareholders' equity	20,822		19,249
Cash from oper. activs	**1,741**	**-9**	**1,917**
Cash from fin. activs	(1,185)		(1,736)
Cash from invest. activs	(2,918)		(151)
Net cash position	**185**	**+4**	**178**
	$		$
Earnings per share*	0.07		0.21
Cash flow per share*	0.08		0.09
	shs		shs
No. of shs. o/s*	21,290,685		21,290,685
Avg. no. of shs. o/s*	21,290,685		21,290,685
	%		%
Net profit margin	37.31		110.72
Return on equity	7.85		25.84
Return on assets	5.87		12.91

* Common
A Reported in accordance with IFRS

Latest Results

Periods ended:	3m Mar. 31/23^A		3m Mar. 31/22^A
	$000s	%Chg	$000s
Total revenue	975	+4	940
Net income	108	n.m.	3
	$		$
Earnings per share*	0.01		0.00

* Common
A Reported in accordance with IFRS

Historical Summary
(as originally stated)

Fiscal Year	Total Rev.	Net Inc. Bef. Disc.	EPS*
	$000s	$000s	$
2022^A	4,216	1,573	0.07
2021^A	3,965	4,390	0.21
2020^A	3,750	432	0.02
2019^A	3,838	(197)	(0.01)
2018^A	3,993	367	0.02

* Common
A Reported in accordance with IFRS

H

H.1 H2 Ventures 1 Inc.

Symbol - HO.P **Exchange** - TSX-VEN **CUSIP** - 44332Q
Head Office - 2695 Queenswood Dr, Victoria, BC, V8N 1X6 **Telephone** - (604) 760-7176
Email - edenhoff@shaw.ca
Investor Relations - Eric A. Denhoff (604) 760-7176
Auditors - Crowe MacKay LLP C.A., Vancouver, B.C.
Lawyers - Osler, Hoskin & Harcourt LLP, Vancouver, B.C.
Transfer Agents - Endeavor Trust Corporation, Vancouver, B.C.
Profile - (B.C. 2021) Capital Pool Company.
Directors - Eric A. Denhoff, pres., CEO & corp. sec., Victoria, B.C.; Ross Bailey, B.C.; Erin Campbell, Alta.; John Costigan, Vancouver, B.C.; Paul Kalil, Vancouver, B.C.; Chris Sacré, B.C.
Other Exec. Officers - Roy Belak, COO; David Schaffner, CFO; Warren Johnson, chief technical officer; David Pfeil, v-p, eng.

Capital Stock

	Authorized (shs.)	Outstanding (shs.)[1]
Common	unlimited	61,200,000

[1] At Feb. 9, 2022

Major Shareholder - Widely held at Feb. 9, 2022.

Price Range - HO.P/TSX-VEN

Year	Volume	High	Low	Close
2022............	2,535,865	$0.20	$0.06	$0.10

Recent Close: $0.07
Capital Stock Changes - On Feb. 9, 2022, an initial public offering of 50,000,000 common shares was completed at 10¢ per share.

H.2 H2O Innovation Inc.

Symbol - HEO **Exchange** - TSX **CUSIP** - 443300
Head Office - 340-330 rue Saint-Vallier E, Québec, QC, G1K 9C5 **Telephone** - (418) 688-0170 **Toll-free** - (888) 688-0170 **Fax** - (418) 688-9259
Website - www.h2oinnovation.com
Email - marc.blanchet@h2oinnovation.com
Investor Relations - Marc Blanchet (888) 688-0170
Auditors - Ernst & Young LLP C.A., Québec, Qué.
Bankers - National Bank of Canada
Lawyers - McCarthy Tétrault LLP, Québec, Qué.
Transfer Agents - TSX Trust Company, Montréal, Qué.
FP500 Revenue Ranking - 675
Employees - 1,000 at Sept. 30, 2022
Profile - (Can. 1995 amalg.) Designs, manufactures and commissions customized membrane water treatment systems, provides operation and maintenance services, and designs, manufactures and sells specialty products such as chemicals, consumables, couplings, fittings, cartridge filters and other components for multiple markets. Also designs and implements digital solutions for water treatment plants as well as offers maple equipment and products to maple syrup producers.

Operations are organized as follows:

Water Technologies and Services - Designs, manufactures and markets treatments solutions using membrane filtration technology (ultrafiltration, reverse osmosis and membrane bioreactor) for the production of drinking water and industrial process water, reclamation and reuse of water, desalination of seawater and treatment of wastewater. Proprietary treatment technologies include Bio-Brane and Bio-Wheel, FiberFlex, flexMBR and SILO. Also provides aftersales services, including sales of spare parts and technical services and maintenance; and digital solutions to facilitate the operation and maintenance of water and wastewater treatment systems such as the Intelogx software and SCADA (Supervisory and Data Acquisition) systems. Customers include municipal, industrial, energy and natural resources sectors.

Specialty Products - Offers a complete line of specialty chemicals, consumables and specialized products for the water treatment industry as well as maple equipment and products under the PWT, Genesys, Piedmont and H_2O Innovation Maple brand names. PWT manufactures and supplies specialty chemicals for membrane-based water treatment systems including membrane pretreatment chemicals, membrane cleaners, coagulants, flocculants and membrane preservatives. Genesys manufactures and distributes specialty reverse osmosis membrane chemicals, including antiscalants, flocculants, biocides and cleaning chemicals. Genesys also offers laboratory services, including feedwater and pretreatment tests, membrane autopsies and cleaning programs. Piedmont sells and provides a broad line of specialty products for various industrial and municipal applications in the water treatment industry, mainly the desalination market, such as couplings, fittings, cartridge filter housings, self-cleaning disc and screen filters, bag filters, cartridges and strainers. H_2O Innovation Maple offers equipment and products for the production of maple syrup such as evaporators, reverse osmosis separators, monitoring solutions, membranes, fittings, tubing, tanks and press filters. Specialty products are sold in over 75 countries primarily through a network of international distributors.

Operation and Maintenance Services - Operates, maintains and repairs water and wastewater utilities, including treatment systems, distribution equipment and associated assets for municipalities, municipal utility districts, industrial and mining customers. Operates over 600 utilities in two Canadian provinces and 13 U.S. states.

Production facilities are located in Ham-Nord, Que.; Champlin, Minn.; Vista, Calif.; Swanton, Vt.; and Cheshire, U.K.

At Sept. 30, 2022, the company's order backlog totaled $182,000,000 (Sept. 30, 2021 - $122,800,000).

Predecessor Detail - Name changed from H2O Innovation (2000) Inc., Jan. 21, 2009.
Directors - Lisa Henthorne, chr., Tucson, Ariz.; Richard A. Hoel, v-chr., Naples, Fla.; Frédéric Dugré, pres. & CEO, Québec, Qué.; Dr. Pierre Côté, Ancaster, Ont.; Leonard F. Graziano; Stéphane Guérin, Montréal, Qué.; Bertrand Lauzon, Mont-Tremblant, Qué.; Caroline Lemoine, Saint-Lambert, Qué.; Elisa M. Speranza, New Orleans, La.
Other Exec. Officers - Guillaume Clairet, COO; Marc Blanchet, CFO; Gregory L. Madden, chief strategy officer; Edith Allain, v-p, corp.& legal affairs & corp. sec.; Jean-Paul Bety, v-p, IT & bus. software solutions; William Douglass, v-p & man. dir., opers. & maint.; Rock Gaulin, v-p & man. dir., Maple; Denis Guibert, v-p & man. dir., water technologies & srvcs.; Jean-Philippe Pilote, v-p, fin.; Ties Venema, v-p & man. dir., specialty chemicals, components & consumables; Marie-Eve Audet, contr.

Capital Stock

	Authorized (shs.)	Outstanding (shs.)[1]
Preference	unlimited	nil
Common	unlimited	90,007,408

[1] At Dec. 31, 2022

Major Shareholder - Investissement Québec held 10% interest at Oct. 20, 2022.

Price Range - HEO/TSX

Year	Volume	High	Low	Close
2022............	16,576,162	$2.86	$1.75	$2.57
2021............	45,826,052	$3.70	$2.04	$2.61
2020............	26,029,957	$2.38	$0.54	$2.04
2019............	6,237,870	$1.31	$0.70	$0.99
2018............	4,758,778	$1.35	$0.75	$0.94

Recent Close: $2.79
Capital Stock Changes - During fiscal 2022, common shares were issued as follows; 3,762,471 on exercise of warrants and 1,107,733 on acquisition of JCO, Inc., and Environmental Consultants, L.L.C.

Wholly Owned Subsidiaries

H2O Innovation UK Holding Limited, United Kingdom.
- 100% int. in **Genesys International Limited**, Middlewich, Cheshire, United Kingdom.
- 0.01% int. in **Genesys Membrane Products Latinoamerica Limitada**, Santiago, Chile.
- 100% int. in **Genesys Membrane Products, S.L.U.**, Spain.
  - 99.99% int. in **Genesys Membrane Products Latinoamerica Limitada**, Santiago, Chile.

H2O Innovation USA Holding, Inc., Del.
- 100% int. in **H2O Innovation Operation & Maintenance, LLC**, Ga.
  - 100% int. in **Environmental Consultants, L.L.C.**, United States.
  - 100% int. in **JCO, Inc.**, United States.
- 100% int. in **H2O Innovation USA, Inc.**, Del.
  - 100% int. in **Professional Water Technologies, LLC**, Del.
- 100% int. in **Piedmont Pacific Corporation**, Oakland, Calif.

Piedmont Hong Kong Limited, Hong Kong, People's Republic of China.
Piedmont Pacific Inc., Canada.

Financial Statistics

Periods ended:	12m June 30/22[A]		12m June 30/21[A]
	$000s	%Chg	$000s
Operating revenue........................	**184,356**	**+28**	**144,324**
Cost of goods sold..........................	134,749		104,379
General & admin expense................	33,356		25,471
Operating expense........................	**168,105**	**+29**	**129,850**
Operating income.........................	**16,251**	**+12**	**14,474**
Deprec., depl. & amort....................	9,231		7,328
Finance income..............................	33		41
Finance costs, gross........................	2,392		2,376
Investment income..........................	nil		183
Write-downs/write-offs....................	(20)		(22)
Pre-tax income............................	**1,489**	**-69**	**4,822**
Income taxes..................................	(3,618)		1,703
Net income..................................	**5,107**	**+64**	**3,119**
Cash & equivalent...........................	7,382		15,409
Inventories.....................................	20,171		8,486
Accounts receivable........................	35,696		22,148
Current assets................................	80,058		56,485
Fixed assets, net.............................	15,632		5,657
Right-of-use assets.........................	16,012		10,094
Intangibles, net...............................	85,665		63,340
Total assets..................................	**205,663**	**+50**	**137,102**
Accts. pay. & accr. liabs..................	23,600		15,466
Current liabilities............................	43,444		28,538
Long-term debt, gross.....................	2,073		15,916
Long-term debt, net........................	510		12,941
Long-term lease liabilities................	15,027		9,318
Shareholders' equity.......................	96,428		79,395
Cash from oper. activs..................	**(6,250)**	**n.a.**	**7,284**
Cash from fin. activs.......................	30,769		2,930
Cash from invest. activs..................	(32,647)		(4,768)
Net cash position.........................	**7,382**	**-52**	**15,409**
Capital expenditures.......................	(9,658)		(1,186)
Capital disposals............................	nil		2,572
	$		$
Earnings per share*........................	0.06		0.04
Cash flow per share*......................	(0.07)		0.09
	shs		shs
No. of shs. o/s*...............................	90,007,408		85,137,204
Avg. no. of shs. o/s*........................	88,189,057		79,469,345
	%		%
Net profit margin............................	2.77		2.16
Return on equity.............................	5.81		4.21
Return on assets.............................	7.77		3.60
Foreign sales percent......................	88		87
No. of employees (FTEs)..................	1,000		725

* Common
[A] Reported in accordance with IFRS

Latest Results

Periods ended:	3m Sept. 30/22[A]		3m Sept. 30/21[A]
	$000s	%Chg	$000s
Operating revenue..........................	56,149	+46	38,384
Net income.....................................	9	-99	618
	$		$
Earnings per share*........................	0.00		0.01

* Common
[A] Reported in accordance with IFRS

Historical Summary
(as originally stated)

Fiscal Year	Oper. Rev.	Net Inc. Bef. Disc.	EPS*
	$000s	$000s	$
2022[A]..................	184,356	5,107	0.06
2021[A]..................	144,324	3,119	0.04
2020[A]..................	133,597	(4,227)	(0.06)
2019[A]..................	117,958	(2,180)	(0.04)
2018[A]..................	99,668	(3,449)	(0.09)

* Common
[A] Reported in accordance with IFRS

H.3 HAVN Life Sciences Inc.

Symbol - HAVN **Exchange** - CSE **CUSIP** - 419621
Head Office - 1480-885 Georgia St W, Vancouver, BC, V6C 3E8 **Telephone** - (604) 359-0060
Website - havnlife.com
Email - ir@havnlife.com
Investor Relations - Timothy Moore (604) 359-0060
Auditors - Davidson & Company LLP C.A., Vancouver, B.C.

Transfer Agents - Odyssey Trust Company, Vancouver, B.C.
Profile - (B.C. 2020) Researches and develops psychopharmacological and natural health care products, including the formulation of standardized psychoactive compounds derived from fungi.
Operates through two divisions:
HAVN Labs - Develops research protocols to cover the production of Psilocybe spp. mushrooms in sterile conditions, the extraction and purification of psilocybin, psilocin, baeocystin and other compounds found in the genus, and quality control and testing necessary for safety and formulation protocols with Psilocybe spp. and/or constituents. In partnership with **Hypha Wellness Jamaica Psilocybin**, a Jamaican-based food and psychoactive mushroom producer, the company has an operating mycology lab and production facility in Jamaica for the production of medical psilocybin. An application to Health Canada for a dealer's licence has been made.
HAVN Retail - Develops, formulates and sells a line of natural health supplements which addresses immunity support, cognitive support, stress prevention, energy support and brain injury. The product line uses plant-derived non-psychoactive compounds, with a focus on functional mushrooms. Products are sold under the HAVN brand through online channels and select retail locations in Canada. Production is conducted through contract manufacturing.
Common reinstated on CSE, Jan. 31, 2023.
Common suspended from CSE, Jan. 9, 2023.
Directors - Timothy (Tim) Moore, chr., CEO & interim CFO, Stouffville, Ont.; Dr. Ivan Casselman, chief psychedelics officer, Vancouver, B.C.; Alexzander Samuelsson, chief research officer, Vancouver, B.C.
Other Exec. Officers - Jenna Pozar, COO

Capital Stock

	Authorized (shs.)	Outstanding (shs.)[1]
Common	unlimited	14,738,611

[1] At Jan. 31, 2023

Major Shareholder - Widely held at Mar. 2, 2022.

Price Range - HAVN/CSE

Year	Volume	High	Low	Close
2022	8,622,682	$5.40	$0.06	$0.09
2021	2,703,068	$32.10	$4.50	$5.10
2020	1,704,688	$45.60	$15.00	$29.40

Consolidation: 1-for-30 cons. in Aug. 2022
Recent Close: $0.03
Capital Stock Changes - On Aug. 3, 2022, common shares were consolidated on a 1-for-30 basis.
In March 2022, private placement of 20,537,126 units (1 common share & 1 warrant) at $0.087 per unit was completed. Also during fiscal 2022, common shares were issued as follows: 18,601,315 pursuant to acquisition of intellectual property, 2,451,390 on exercise of warrants, 1,980,000 on exercise of restricted share rights, 900,000 for services, 508,320 on exercise of performance warrants and 191,400 on exercise of options.

Wholly Owned Subsidiaries

GCO Packaging and Manufacturing Ltd., B.C.
HAVN Research Inc., B.C.
1000053494 Ontario Inc., Ont.

Financial Statistics

Periods ended:	12m Apr. 30/22[A]		12m Apr. 30/21[◻A]
	$000s	%Chg	$000s
Operating revenue	**276**	**n.a.**	**nil**
Cost of goods sold	187		nil
Research & devel. expense	656		333
General & admin expense	6,882		16,277
Stock-based compensation	1,787		9,139
Operating expense	**9,511**	**-63**	**25,749**
Operating income	**(9,235)**	**n.a.**	**(25,749)**
Deprec., depl. & amort.	576		4,605
Finance income	30		nil
Finance costs, gross	64		17
Write-downs/write-offs	(11,793)		nil
Pre-tax income	**(22,444)**	**n.a.**	**(30,381)**
Net income	**(22,444)**	**n.a.**	**(30,381)**
Cash & equivalent	1,056		9,402
Inventories	1,149		nil
Accounts receivable	319		210
Current assets	2,745		10,610
Fixed assets, net	356		681
Intangibles, net	934		2,931
Total assets	**4,059**	**-71**	**14,240**
Accts. pay. & accr. liabs	529		584
Current liabilities	608		715
Long-term lease liabilities	310		325
Shareholders' equity	3,141		13,200
Cash from oper. activs	**(7,875)**	**n.a.**	**(10,422)**
Cash from fin. activs	1,560		18,603
Cash from invest. activs	(2,031)		(397)
Net cash position	**1,056**	**-89**	**9,402**
Capital expenditures	(103)		(33)
Capital disposals	28		nil
	$		$
Earnings per share*	(5.24)		(15.51)
Cash flow per share*	(1.84)		(5.32)
	shs		shs
No. of shs. o/s*	5,093,623		3,587,971
Avg. no. of shs. o/s*	4,278,817		1,958,950
	%		%
Net profit margin	n.m.		n.a.
Return on equity	(274.70)		n.m.
Return on assets	(244.60)		n.a.
No. of employees (FTEs)	n.a.		6

* Common
◻ Restated
[A] Reported in accordance with IFRS

Latest Results

Periods ended:	3m July 31/22[A]		3m July 31/21[A]
	$000s	%Chg	$000s
Operating revenue	68	+656	9
Net income	(3,903)	n.a.	(2,971)
	$		$
Earnings per share*	(0.90)		(0.90)

* Common
[A] Reported in accordance with IFRS
Note: Adjusted throughout for 1-for-30 cons. in Aug. 2022

H.4 H&R Real Estate Investment Trust*

Symbol - HR.UN **Exchange** - TSX **CUSIP** - 403925
Head Office - 500-3625 Dufferin St, Toronto, ON, M3K 1N4 **Telephone** - (416) 635-7520 **Toll-free** - (888) 635-7717
Website - www.hr-reit.com
Email - lfroom@hr-reit.com
Investor Relations - Larry Froom (416) 635-7520
Auditors - KPMG LLP C.A., Toronto, Ont.
Lawyers - Blake, Cassels & Graydon LLP, Toronto, Ont.
Transfer Agents - TSX Trust Company, Toronto, Ont.
FP500 Revenue Ranking - 370
Employees - 487 at Dec. 31, 2022
Profile - (Ont. 1996) Owns interests in residential, industrial, office and retail properties as well as development projects across Canada and the U.S.
The trust's focus is on residential and industrial properties and plans to sell its office and retail properties as market conditions permit. At Mar. 31, 2023, the trust owned and operated a portfolio of 399 properties, consisting of 24 residential, 73 industrial, 24 office and 278 retail properties totaling 28,706,000 sq. ft.
Geographic diversification at Mar. 31, 2023:

	Residential	Ind.	Office	Retail
Ontario	nil	36	14	30
Alberta	nil	17	1	1
Other Canada	nil	17	4	7
United States	24	3	5	240[1]
	24	73	24	278

[1] Includes 234 properties held by 33.7%-owned **ECHO Realty, L.P.**
Asset mix at Mar. 31, 2023:

	Area (sq. ft.)[1]
Residential[2]	7,498,000
Industrial	8,743,000
Office	6,757,000
Retail	5,708,000
	28,706,000

[1] Proportionate ownership interest.
[2] Consists of owned interest in 8,164 residential rental units.
At Dec. 31, 2022, the trust had interests in 30 properties under development (including 7 properties under development held through the trust's 33.7% interest in ECHO) in Canada and the U.S.
In July 2022, the trust acquired a 2.4-acre parcel of land in Dallas, Tex., for US$3,000,000. The land was expected to be developed into 250 residential rental units.
In June 2022, the trust sold its 50% interest in a 21,493-sq.-ft. industrial property in Calgary, Alta., for $3,500,000.
On Jan. 10, 2022, the trust exchanged all 13,344,071 exchangeable units of a subsidiary of **Primaris Real Estate Investment Trust** it held into 3,336,016 Primaris REIT units, series A. Subsequently, the trust sold all 3,336,016 Primaris REIT units, series A it held at $14.77 per unit for gross proceeds of $49,275,000.

Recent Merger and Acquisition Activity

Status: pending **Announced:** May 14, 2023
H&R Real Estate Investment Trust agreed to sell four Canadian retail properties for $68,000,000. The transaction was expected to close in July 2023.
Status: completed **Revised:** Apr. 20, 2023
UPDATE: The transaction was completed. PREVIOUS: H&R Real Estate Investment Trust agreed to sell the 27-storey, 973,611-sq.-ft. ONE60 Elgin office property located at 160 Elgin Street in Ottawa, Ont., for $277,000,000. The transaction was expected to be completed in April 2023.
Status: completed **Announced:** Jan. 31, 2023
H&R Real Estate Investment Trust sold its 50% interest in a 95,225-sq.-ft. office property in Calgary, Alta., and 50% interest in a 31,784-sq.-ft. industrial property in Sparwood, B.C., for a total of $19,000,000.
Status: completed **Announced:** Dec. 30, 2022
H&R Real Estate Investment Trust sold a 13,404-sq.-ft. automotive-tenanted retail property in McKinney, Tex., for US$5,000,000
Status: completed **Announced:** Dec. 19, 2022
H&R Real Estate Investment Trust acquired a 92,818-sq.-ft. office property in Dallas, Tex., for $49,000,000.
Status: completed **Announced:** Nov. 15, 2022
H&R Real Estate Investment Trust acquired a 2-acre parcel of land, held for future residential development, in Miami, Fla., for US$18,600,000.
Status: completed **Announced:** Oct. 24, 2022
H&R Real Estate Investment Trust sold a 123,000-sq.-ft. office property in Burlington, Ont., for $26,000,000.
Status: completed **Announced:** Oct. 14, 2022
H&R Real Estate Investment Trust acquired a 50% interest in 7-21, 23-31 Prince Andrew Place, a 73,997-sq.-ft. multi-tenanted industrial property in Toronto, Ont., for $10,500,000.
Status: completed **Announced:** Oct. 3, 2022
H&R Real Estate Investment Trust sold two automotive-tenanted retail properties, totaling 25,309 sq. ft., in Arizona for US$17,000,000.
Status: completed **Announced:** Sept. 1, 2022
H&R Real Estate Investment Trust acquired a 50% interest in a 4.2-acre parcel of land in Santa Ana, Calif., for US$26,300,000. The land was expected to be developed into two buildings with 325 and 319 residential rental units, respectively.
Status: completed **Revised:** Aug. 31, 2022
UPDATE: The transaction was completed. PREVIOUS: H&R Real Estate Investment Trust agreed to sell a 444,898-sq.-ft. office property in Toronto, Ont., for $120,700,000. H&R retained an option to repurchase the property for $159,500,000 in 2036 or earlier under certain circumstances.
Status: completed **Revised:** Aug. 31, 2022
UPDATE: The transaction was completed. PREVIOUS: H&R Real Estate Investment Trust agreed to sell its 50% in a 69,793-sq.-ft. office property and an 89,438-sq.-ft. retail property, both in Calgary, Alta., and a 129,181-sq.-ft. retail property in Kingston, Ont., for a total of $47,000,000.
Status: completed **Announced:** July 6, 2022
H&R Real Estate Investment Trust acquired a 5.8-acre parcel of land in Dallas, Tex., for US$14,700,000. The land was expected to be developed into 437 residential rental units.
Status: completed **Announced:** June 23, 2022
H&R Real Estate Investment Trust sold a 259,951-sq.-ft. residential property in San Antonio, Tex., consisting of 312 units, for US$69,300,000.
Status: completed **Announced:** June 23, 2022
H&R Real Estate Investment Trust acquired a 16.3-acre parcel of land in Orlando, Fla., for US$15,500,000. The land was expected to be developed into 371 residential rental units.
Status: completed **Announced:** June 10, 2022
H&R Real Estate Investment Trust sold seven automotive-tenanted retail properties, totaling 94,205 sq. ft., in Colorado (5), Auburn, Wash., and Gilbert, Ariz., for US$58,100,000.
Status: completed **Announced:** Apr. 11, 2022
H&R Real Estate Investment Trust acquired a 6.8-acre parcel of land in Clearwater, Fla., for US$17,100,000. The land was expected to be developed into 434 residential rental units.
Status: completed **Announced:** Mar. 1, 2022

H&R Real Estate Investment Trust sold its 33.3% non-managing interest in The Pearl, a 5-acre residential development project being developed into 383 residential rental units in Austin, Tex., for US$45,800,000.

Trustees - Thomas J. Hofstedter, exec. chr. & CEO, Toronto, Ont.; Donald E. (Don) Clow‡, Halifax, N.S.; Leonard M. Abramsky, Toronto, Ont.; Lindsay Brand, Toronto, Ont.; Jennifer A. Chasson, Toronto, Ont.; Mark M. Cowie, Toronto, Ont.; S. Stephen Gross, Toronto, Ont.; Brenna Haysom, Warwick, N.Y.; Juli Morrow, Toronto, Ont.; Marvin Rubner, Toronto, Ont.

Other Exec. Officers - Larry Froom, CFO; Cheryl Fried, exec. v-p, fin.; C. Robyn Kestenberg, exec. v-p, office & ind.; Matt Kingston, exec. v-p, devel. & const.; Blair Kundell, exec. v-p, opers.; Jason Birken, v-p, fin.; Schuyler Levine, v-p, tax

‡ Lead trustee

Capital Stock

	Authorized (shs.)	Outstanding (shs.)[1]
Trust Unit	unlimited	266,014,787
Exchangeable Unit	n.a.	17,974,186[2]
Special Voting Unit	13,013,698	13,013,698[3]

[1] At May 5, 2023

[2] Issued by various limited partnerships of the trust

[3] Held by holders of H&R REIT Management Services LP class B LP units

Options - At Dec. 31, 2022, options were outstanding to purchase 10,313,443 trust units at prices ranging from $13.86 to $16.84 per trust unit with a weighted average remaining life of 2.5 years.

Trust Unit - Entitled to monthly cash distributions. One vote per unit.

Exchangeable Unit - Includes class B limited participation LP units of H&R REIT Management Services LP held by the former external property manager and exchangeable units of H&R Portfolio Limited Partnership held by members of the Hofstedter or Rubinstein families. Entitled to cash distributions equal to those payable on trust units and exchangeable on a one-for-one basis for trust units. Non-voting. Puttable instruments classified as liabilities under IFRS.

Special Voting Unit - Issued to holders of class B limited participation LP units of H&R REIT Management Services LP. One vote per unit.

Normal Course Issuer Bid - The company plans to make normal course purchases of up to 26,028,249 trust units representing 10% of the public float. The bid commenced on Feb. 16, 2023, and expires on Feb. 15, 2024.

Major Shareholder - Widely held at Apr. 29, 2023.

Price Range - HR.UN/TSX

Year	Volume	High	Low	Close
2022	206,076,482	$16.33	$10.22	$12.11
2021	180,106,933	$17.27	$11.99	$16.25
2020	370,658,151	$21.88	$7.39	$13.29
2019	136,326,546	$23.66	$20.41	$21.10
2018	54,032,176	$21.62	$18.94	$20.65

HR.UN/TSX (D)

Year	Volume	High	Low	Close
2018	90,891,025	$21.50	$19.64	$20.26

Recent Close: $10.41

Capital Stock Changes - During 2022, trust units were issued as follows: 305,360 on conversion of exchangeable units and 13,119 on vesting of incentive units; 22,873,800 trust units were repurchased under a Normal Course Issuer Bid.

Dividends

HR.UN unit Var. Ra pa M

$0.05	Oct. 16/23	$0.05	Sept. 15/23
$0.05	Aug. 15/23	$0.05	July 14/23

Paid in 2023: $0.4958 + $0.05† 2022: $0.5055 + $0.10◆ + stk. + stk.◆**g** 2021: $0.69

† Extra ◆ Special **g** Capital Gain

Long-Term Debt - Outstanding at Dec. 31, 2022:

Term loans[1]	$750,000,000
Lines of credit	12,500,000
Mtges. payable[2]	1,613,361,000
Sr. debs.:	
3.42% ser.O due 2023	249,980,000
3.37% ser.N due 2024	349,548,000
4.07% ser.Q due 2025	398,892,000
2.91% ser.R due 2026	249,229,000
2.63% ser.S due 2027	299,019,000
	3,922,529,000

[1] Consist of $250,000,000 3.17% term loan due March 2024, $250,000,000 4.16% term loan due January 2026, $125,000,000 5.29% term loan due November 2024 and $125,000,000 5.19% term loan due November 2025.

[2] Bearing interest at a weighted average rate of 3.99%, and due between 2023 and 2032.

Minimum mortgage repayments were reported as follows:

2023	$187,826,000
2024	78,680,000
2025	145,351,000
2026	86,093 ,000
2027	447,267,000
Thereafter	676,434,000

Wholly Owned Subsidiaries

H&R MSLP GP Inc., Ont.
- 0.01% int. in **H&R REIT Management Services Limited Partnership**, Man.

H&R Ontario GP Trust, Ont.
- 0.01% int. in **H&R REIT U.S. Portfolio LP**, Ont.

H&R Portfolio LP Trust, Ont.
- 100% int. in **H&R Portfolio Beneficiary Inc.**, Ont.
  - 100% int. in **H&R Portfolio GP Trust**, Ont.
    - 0.01% int. in **H&R Portfolio Limited Partnership**, Man.
- 99.99% int. in **H&R Portfolio Limited Partnership**, Man.

Subsidiaries

99.99% int. in **H&R REIT Management Services Limited Partnership**, Man.

99.99% int. in **H&R REIT U.S. Portfolio LP**, Ont.
- 100% int. in **H&R REIT (U.S.) Holdings Inc.**, Del.

Investments

33.7% int. in **ECHO Realty, L.P.**, Pittsburgh, Pa.

Financial Statistics

Periods ended:	12m Dec. 31/22[A]		12m Dec. 31/21[A]
	$000s	%Chg	$000s
Total revenue	**834,640**	**-22**	**1,065,380**
Rental operating expense	299,691		403,798
General & admin. expense	22,121		27,936
Operating expense	**321,812**	**-25**	**431,734**
Operating income	**512,828**	**-19**	**633,646**
Investment income	47,139		125,649
Finance income	14,793		17,229
Finance costs, gross	220,262		236,878
Pre-tax income	**946,260**	**+57**	**603,446**
Income taxes	101,437		5,539
Net income	**844,823**	**+41**	**597,907**
Cash & equivalent	76,887		124,141
Accounts receivable	5,318		6,130
Long-term investments	1,229,458		1,238,798
Income-producing props	8,799,317		8,581,100
Properties under devel	880,778		481,432
Property interests, net	9,680,095		9,062,532
Total assets	**11,412,603**	**+9**	**10,501,141**
Accts. pay. & accr. liabs	181,527		204,724
Long-term debt, gross	3,922,529		3,894,906
Long-term lease liabilities	30,410		29,122
Shareholders' equity	5,487,287		4,773,833
Cash from oper. activs	**255,054**	**-44**	**452,107**
Cash from fin. activs	(528,262)		(1,886,639)
Cash from invest. activs	225,954		1,495,814
Net cash position	**76,887**	**-38**	**124,141**
Capital expenditures	(35,582)		(47,089)
Increase in property	(239,317)		(456,424)
Decrease in property	387,712		1,723,340
	$		$
Earnings per share*	n.a.		n.a.
Cash flow per share*	0.94		1.57
Funds from opers. per sh.*	1.17		1.53
Adj. funds from opers. per sh.*	0.99		1.21
Cash divd. per share*	0.49		0.69
Extra divd. - cash*	0.05		0.10
Extra stk. divd. - cash equiv.*	nil		0.63
Total divd. per share*	**0.54**		**1.42**
	shs		shs
No. of shs. o/s*	265,884,526		288,439,847
Avg. no. of shs. o/s*	272,671,167		287,659,788
	%		%
Net profit margin	101.22		56.12
Return on equity	16.47		11.03
Return on assets	9.51		6.98
Foreign sales percent	49		35
No. of employees (FTEs)	487		479

* Trust unit

[A] Reported in accordance with IFRS

Latest Results

Periods ended:	3m Mar. 31/23[A]		3m Mar. 31/22[A]
	$000s	%Chg	$000s
Total revenue	218,295	+8	201,702
Net income	94,802	-90	969,991
	$		$
Earnings per share*	n.a.		n.a.

[A] Reported in accordance with IFRS

Historical Summary
(as originally stated)

Fiscal Year	Total Rev.	Net Inc. Bef. Disc.	EPS*
	$000s	$000s	$
2022[A]	834,640	844,823	n.a.
2021[A]	1,065,380	597,907	n.a.
2020[A]	1,098,680	(624,559)	n.a.
2019[A]	1,149,450	340,289	n.a.
2018[A]	1,176,558	337,918	n.a.

* Trust unit

[A] Reported in accordance with IFRS

H.5 HIVE Digital Technologies Ltd.

Symbol - HIVE **Exchange** - TSX-VEN **CUSIP** - 433921

Head Office - 855-789 Pender St W, Vancouver, BC, V6C 1H2 **Telephone** - (604) 664-1078

Website - hivedigitaltechnologies.com

Email - darcy@hivedigitaltech.com

Investor Relations - Darcy Daubaras (604) 664-1078

Auditors - Davidson & Company LLP C.A., Vancouver, B.C.

Transfer Agents - Computershare Trust Company of Canada Inc., Vancouver, B.C.

FP500 Revenue Ranking - 594

Employees - 18 at June 29, 2023

Profile - (B.C. 1987) Owns and operates green energy-powered cryptocurrency mining facilities in Canada, Sweden and Iceland.

Cryptocurrency mining operations include Bitcoin mining at a leased facility in Lachute, Que.; Bitcoin mining at an owned facility in Grand Falls, N.B.; Ethereum and Bitcoin mining at three leased facilities in Boden, Robertsfors and Notviken, Sweden; a leased facility in Iceland mining Ethereum, Ethereum Classic and Bitcoin; and hosted equipment at **Borealis Data Park ehf**'s facility in Iceland for Bitcoin mining.

Also offers Nvidia Graphics Processing Units (GPU) which powers artificial intelligence technologies such as large language models and text-to-image models.

Predecessor Detail - Name changed from HIVE Blockchain Technologies Ltd., July 12, 2023.

Directors - Frank E. Holmes, exec. chr., San Antonio, Tex.; Susan B. McGee, Tex.; Marcus A. New, Port Moody, B.C.; Dave Perrill, Minn.

Other Exec. Officers - Aydin Kilic, pres. & CEO; Darcy Daubaras, CFO; Luke Rossy, v-p, opers.; Gabriel Ibghy, gen. counsel; Ian H. Mann, pres., HIVE Digital Data Ltd.; Johanna Thörnblad, pres., Sweden opers.

Capital Stock

	Authorized (shs.)	Outstanding (shs.)[1]
Preferred	unlimited	nil
Common	unlimited	85,500,511

[1] At July 31, 2023

Major Shareholder - Widely held at Nov. 10, 2022.

Price Range - HIVE/TSX-VEN

Year	Volume	High	Low	Close
2022	93,962,936	$17.50	$1.85	$1.95
2021	193,271,488	$36.25	$11.10	$16.55
2020	181,829,056	$15.75	$0.45	$11.95
2019	52,601,836	$4.10	$0.40	$0.48
2018	72,694,208	$18.50	$1.20	$1.33

Consolidation: 1-for-5 cons. in May 2022

Recent Close: $4.68

Capital Stock Changes - On May 24, 2022, common shares were consolidated on a 1-for-5 basis. During fiscal 2023, post-consolidated common shares were issued as follows: 1,306,476 under an at-the-market offering and 624,250 on vesting of restricted share units.

In April 2021, 5,000,000 common shares were issued pursuant to the acquisition of GPU Atlantic Inc. (renamed HIVE Atlantic Datacentres Ltd.). In January 2022, 19,170,500 units (1 common share & ½ warrant) were issued without further consideration on exchange of special warrants sold previously by bought deal private placement at $6.00 each. Also during fiscal 2022, common shares were issued as follows: 10,872,515 under an at-the-market program, 5,066,770 for investments, 1,934,120 on exercise of options and 1,454,000 on vesting of restricted share units.

Wholly Owned Subsidiaries

Bikupa Datacenter AB, Sweden.

Bikupa Datacenter 2 AB, Sweden.

HIVE Atlantic Datacentres Ltd., Grand Falls, N.B.

HIVE Digital Data Ltd., Bermuda.

HIVE Performance Computing Ltd., Bermuda.
- 100% int. in **HIVE Performance Cloud Inc.**, Qué.

Hive Blockchain Switzerland AG, Switzerland.
- 100% int. in **Hive Blockchain Iceland ehf.**, Iceland.

Liv Eiendom AS, Norway.

9376-9974 Quebec Inc., Qué.

Investments

DeFi Technologies Inc., Toronto, Ont. (see separate coverage)

Financial Statistics

Periods ended:	12m Mar. 31/23[A]		12m Mar. 31/22[α][A]
	US$000s	%Chg	US$000s
Operating revenue	**106,317**	**-50**	**211,184**
Cost of sales	55,719		47,251
General & admin expense	13,243		10,953
Stock-based compensation	8,378		6,753
Operating expense	**77,340**	**+19**	**64,957**
Operating income	**28,977**	**-80**	**146,227**
Deprec., depl. & amort.	81,730		67,022
Finance costs, gross	3,706		3,870
Write-downs/write-offs	(97,741)[1]		(13,330)[2]
Pre-tax income	**(236,133)**	**n.a.**	**82,038**
Income taxes	289		2,416
Net income	**(236,422)**	**n.a.**	**79,622**
Cash & equivalent	7,239		22,320
Inventories	65,899		170,000
Current assets	82,492		199,078
Fixed assets, net	87,228		177,543
Right-of-use assets	10,973		12,588
Intangibles, net	67		336
Total assets	**196,118**	**-57**	**452,274**
Bank indebtedness	7,139		9,375
Accts. pay. & accr. liabs	9,354		12,377
Current liabilities	21,893		26,155
Long-term debt, gross	17,807		21,291
Long-term debt, net	16,583		20,067
Long-term lease liabilities	8,138		10,485
Shareholders' equity	148,816		389,053
Cash from oper. activs	**44,781**	**-32**	**66,279**
Cash from fin. activs	(4,639)		110,775
Cash from invest. activs	(40,886)		(211,988)
Net cash position	**4,373**	**-18**	**5,319**
Capital expenditures	(4,075)		(198,342)
Capital disposals	192		2,979
	US$		US$
Earnings per share*	(2.85)		1.02
Cash flow per share*	0.54		0.85
	shs		shs
No. of shs. o/s*	84,172,711		82,241,988
Avg. no. of shs. o/s*	82,871,284		77,715,890
	%		%
Net profit margin	(222.37)		37.70
Return on equity	(87.91)		30.42
Return on assets	(71.78)		26.44
Foreign sales percent	100		100

* Common
[α] Restated
[A] Reported in accordance with IFRS
[1] Impairment for equipment of US$70,409,606 and US$27,331,287 for deposits.
[2] Impairment of US$13,154,585 to goodwill and US$175,443 to acquired intangible assets related to HIVE Atlantic Datacentres Ltd. (formerly GPU Atlantic Inc.).

Historical Summary
(as originally stated)

Fiscal Year	Oper. Rev.	Net Inc. Bef. Disc.	EPS*
	US$000s	US$000s	US$
2023[A]	106,317	(236,422)	(2.85)
2022[A]	211,184	79,622	1.02
2021[A]	67,694	42,540	0.61
2020[A]	29,220	(1,663)	(0.03)
2019[A]	31,824	(137,802)	(2.19)

* Common
[A] Reported in accordance with IFRS
Note: Adjusted throughout for 1-for-5 cons. in May 2022

H.6 HLS Therapeutics Inc.

Symbol - HLS **Exchange** - TSX **CUSIP** - 40390B
Head Office - 701-10 Carlson Crt, Etobicoke, ON, M9W 6L2 **Telephone** - (647) 495-9000 **Fax** - (416) 213-0045
Website - www.hlstherapeutics.com
Email - d.mason@hlstherapeutics.com
Investor Relations - Dave Mason (416) 247-9652
Auditors - Ernst & Young LLP C.A., Toronto, Ont.
Transfer Agents - Computershare Trust Company of Canada Inc., Toronto, Ont.
FP500 Revenue Ranking - 800
Employees - 96 at Mar. 15, 2023
Profile - (Ont. 2018) Acquires clinically differentiated pharmaceutical products in the central nervous system and cardiovascular therapeutic areas, primarily for commercialization in the North American market.

Lead product is Clozaril®, an atypical antipsychotic, for the Canadian and U.S. markets. In Canada, Clozaril® is indicated for the management of symptoms of treatment-resistant schizophrenia in adults over 18 years old. In the U.S., Clozaril® is indicated for the treatment of severely ill patients with schizophrenia who fail to respond adequately to standard drug treatment. Clozaril® is also indicated in the U.S. for reducing the risk of recurrent suicidal behaviour in patients with schizophrenia or schizoaffective disorder who are judged to be at chronic risk for re-experiencing suicidal behaviour, based on history and recent clinical state.

Also holds the Canadian rights for cardiovascular specialty drug Vascepa, which reduces the risk of cardiovascular events in statin-treated patients with elevated triglycerides. In addition, holds an exclusive agreement to develop and commercialize Perseris™, a novel long-acting injectable risperidone product for the treatment of schizophrenia, in Canada; a licensing agreement to commercialize and distribute cardiovascular disease drug candidate Trinomia in Canada; exclusive Canadian rights to CSAN® Pronto™, a point-of-care medical device designed to enhance and simplify the mandatory safety blood monitoring process for patients who are prescribed Clozaril®; exclusive Canadian rights to distribute the Mycare™ Insite, a point-of-care medical device intended to measure blood levels of patients prescribed common antipsychotic drugs as well as non-exclusive Canadian rights to distribute the full MyCare™ Psychiatry line of tests; and royalty rights to the EMBLEM S-ICD™ system, a subcutaneous implantable defibrillator for the treatment of life-threatening ventricular tachyarrhythmias; Obizur, a recombinant porcine factor VIII used for the treatment of acquired Hemophilia A; Eraxis, an echinocandin administered intravenously for the treatment of Candidemia and other forms of Candida infections; and Xenpozyme, a novel enzyme replacement therapy for acid sphingomyelinase deficiency.

In April 2022, the company entered into a letter of intent with pan-Canadian Pharmaceutical Alliance (pCPA) to which Vascepa, a cardiovascular specialty drug prescribed to statin-treated patients with high triglycerides to reduce the risk of cardiovascular events, would qualify for public market reimbursement in Canada. pCPA is a collaborative initiative between the federal, provincial, and territorial governments in Canada which negotiates drug prices and improves patient access to prescription drugs.

Directors - John Welborn, chr., Telluride, Colo.; Craig Millian, CEO, Mass.; Norma Beauchamp, Toronto, Ont.; Laura A. Brege, Portola Valley, Calif.; Dr. Kyle Dempsey, Mass.; John Hanna, Victoria, B.C.; Rodney G. Hill, Toronto, Ont.; Christian Roy, Beaconsfield, Qué.

Other Exec. Officers - Tim Hendrickson, CFO; Sanjiv Sharma, chief comml. officer; Ryan C. Lennox, sr. v-p, legal, HR & compliance & corp. sec.; Dr. Jason A. Gross, v-p, scientific affairs; Patricia Perry, v-p, HR; David A. Spence, v-p & contr.

Capital Stock

	Authorized (shs.)	Outstanding (shs.)[1]
Class A Preferred	12,976,527	nil[2]
Common	unlimited	32,245,954

[1] At Aug. 9, 2023
[2] Classified as debt.

Normal Course Issuer Bid - The company plans to make normal course purchases of up to 1,620,366 common shares representing 5% of the total outstanding. The bid commenced on Nov. 14, 2022, and expires on Nov. 13, 2023.

Major Shareholder - Polar Asset Management Partners Inc. held 19.81% interest, Stadium Capital Management, LLC held 18.44% interest, Athyrium Opportunities II Co-Invest 1 LP held 13.45% interest and Mawer Investment Management Limited held 10.01% interest at May 16, 2023.

Price Range - HLS/TSX

Year	Volume	High	Low	Close
2022	4,799,978	$16.44	$8.30	$9.83
2021	6,546,118	$21.76	$13.69	$15.00
2020	12,604,209	$25.68	$13.35	$18.00
2019	12,717,340	$25.92	$12.91	$25.50
2018	5,687,530	$16.75	$7.69	$14.65

Recent Close: $4.30

Capital Stock Changes - During 2022, common shares were issued as follows: 21,825 on exercise of options and 117,400 common shares were repurchased under a Normal Course Issuer Bid.

Dividends

HLS com omitted pa Q[1]
[1] Quarterly divd normally payable in Sept/23 has been omitted.

Wholly Owned Subsidiaries

HLS Therapeutics (USA Holdings), Inc., United States.
- 100% int. in **HLS Therapeutics (USA R&D), Inc.**, United States.
  - 100% int. in **HLS Therapeutics Royalty Sub LLC**, United States.

HLS Therapeutics (USA), Inc., Del.
Heritage Life Sciences (Barbados) Inc., Barbados.
- 100% int. in **Heritage R&D (Barbados) Ltd.**, Barbados.

Financial Statistics

Periods ended:	12m Dec. 31/22[A]		12m Dec. 31/21[A]
	US$000s	%Chg	US$000s
Operating revenue	**61,467**	**+2**	**60,009**
Cost of sales	4,981		3,972
General & admin expense	32,659		29,703
Stock-based compensation	2,922		2,354
Operating expense	**40,562**	**+13**	**36,029**
Operating income	**20,905**	**-13**	**23,980**
Deprec., depl. & amort.	34,402		30,264
Finance income	57		44
Finance costs, gross	5,097		5,399
Pre-tax income	**(23,722)**	**n.a.**	**(11,808)**
Income taxes	(124)		1,309
Net income	**(23,598)**	**n.a.**	**(13,117)**
Cash & equivalent	20,723		21,179
Inventories	8,902		8,925
Accounts receivable	10,999		11,511
Current assets	44,374		43,751
Fixed assets, net	1,127		1,569
Intangibles, net	195,018		229,181
Total assets	**241,652**	**-12**	**275,905**
Accts. pay. & accr. liabs	12,785		10,596
Current liabilities	31,190		27,672
Long-term debt, gross	96,335		96,134
Long-term debt, net	83,279		84,134
Long-term lease liabilities	482		826
Shareholders' equity	125,318		160,736
Cash from oper. activs	**16,942**	**+3**	**16,429**
Cash from fin. activs	(6,856)		(11,398)
Cash from invest. activs	(10,148)		(4,510)
Net cash position	**20,723**	**-2**	**21,179**
Capital expenditures	(45)		(47)
	US$		US$
Earnings per share*	(0.73)		(0.41)
Cash flow per share*	0.52		0.51
Cash divd. per share*	$0.20		$0.20
	shs		shs
No. of shs. o/s*	32,355,618		32,451,193
Avg. no. of shs. o/s*	32,432,851		32,184,076
	%		%
Net profit margin	(38.39)		(21.86)
Return on equity	(16.50)		(7.95)
Return on assets	(7.16)		(2.46)
Foreign sales percent	40		42
No. of employees (FTEs)	99		92

* Common
[A] Reported in accordance with IFRS

Latest Results

Periods ended:	3m Mar. 31/23[A]		3m Mar. 31/22[A]
	US$000s	%Chg	US$000s
Operating revenue	14,757	+1	14,556
Net income	(5,792)	n.a.	(3,616)
	US$		US$
Earnings per share*	(0.18)		(0.11)

* Common
[A] Reported in accordance with IFRS

Historical Summary
(as originally stated)

Fiscal Year	Oper. Rev.	Net Inc. Bef. Disc.	EPS*
	US$000s	US$000s	US$
2022[A]	61,467	(23,598)	(0.73)
2021[A]	60,009	(13,117)	(0.41)
2020[A]	56,109	(15,331)	(0.48)
2019[A]	54,160	(19,552)	(0.67)
2018[A1]	61,415	(24,806)	(0.92)

* Common
[A] Reported in accordance with IFRS
[1] Results reflect the Mar. 12, 2018, reverse takeover acquisition ot Automodular Corporation.

H.7 HPQ Silicon Inc.

Symbol - HPQ **Exchange** - TSX-VEN **CUSIP** - 40444L
Head Office - 306-3000 rue Omer-Lavallée, Montréal, QC, H1Y 3R8 **Telephone** - (514) 846-3271 **Toll-free** - (888) 666-3431 **Fax** - (514) 372-0066
Website - www.hpqsilicon.com
Email - bernard.tourillon@hpqsilicon.com
Investor Relations - Bernard J. Tourillon (888) 666-3431
Auditors - KPMG LLP C.A., Montréal, Qué.
Transfer Agents - Computershare Trust Company of Canada Inc., Montréal, Qué.
Profile - (Can. 1996) Developing technologies for the transformation of quartz into silicon materials primarily for use in lithium-ion batteries.

In partnership with **Pyrogenesis Canada Inc.**, the company is developing PUREVAP™ Quartz Reduction Reactor (QRR), which permits one-step transformation of quartz into high purity silicon; PUREVAP™ Nano Silicon Reactor (NSiR), a proprietary process that can use material produced by the QRR as feedstock to make a wide range of nano/micro spherical powders of different sizes and nanowires; and through wholly owned **HPQ Silica Polvere Inc.**, develops fumed silica reactor, a plasma-based process which allows a direct quartz-to-fumed-silica transformation, removing usage of hazardous chemicals in the making of fumed silica and eliminating hydrogen chloride gas associated with its manufacturing.

The company also has a partnership with **Novacium S.A.S.** for the development of a process to manufacture green hydrogen via electrolysis. In addition, the company is developing its own processes of making hydrogen via hydrolysis of nanosilicon materials made by its PUREVAP™ (NSiR).

In October 2022, the company and **EBH$_2$ Systems S.A.** terminated the memorandum of understanding announced in August 2021. Under the agreement, the company would haven been granted by EBH2 a perpetual world-wide licence to sell products where EBH2 Green Hydrogen Reactors (EBH2 GHR) are incorporated into any of the company's technologies. The companies would establish a new 50/50 joint venture Canadian corporation that would be responsible to market, sell and service EBH2 systems and products in North America. EBH2 is a Swiss company that has a proprietary electrolysis technology that can efficiently extract from virtually any water source including salt water

In September 2022, the company acquired from **PyroGenesis Canada Inc.** an intellectual property relating exclusively for carbon emission reduction in the production of silicon for $3,600,000.

In September 2022, the company entered into a memorandum of understanding with **Quebec Silica Resources Corp.** for the supply of quartz from Quebec Silica's Charlevoix Silica prospect in Quebec over a 1-year period. The quartz would be used for testing and developing the company's PUREVAP™ Quartz Reduction Reactor (QRR).

In August 2022, the company sold Roncevaux and Martinville properties in Quebec to **Quebec Silica Resources Corp.** for issuance of 3,000,000 units (1 common share & ½ warrant) at a deemed price of 10¢ per unit, with warrants exercisable at 15¢ per share for three years.

On July 15, 2022, completed a change of business from mining exploration to technology.

In May 2022, the ownership of the PUREVAP™ Quartz Reduction Reactor (QRR) pilot plant system was transferred from **PyroGenesis Canada Inc.** to the company.

Predecessor Detail - Name changed from HPQ-Silicon Resources Inc., July 4, 2022, pursuant to change of business from mining exploration to developing silicon and silica products.

Directors - Bernard J. Tourillon, chr., pres. & CEO, Montréal, Qué.; Patrick Levasseur, v-p & COO, Montréal, Qué.; Noëlle Drapeau, corp. sec., Qué.; Daryl J. Hodges, Toronto, Ont.; Richard Mimeau, Qué.; Robert Robitaille, Qué.; Dr. Peter H. Smith, Westmount, Qué.

Other Exec. Officers - François Rivard, v-p & CFO

Capital Stock

	Authorized (shs.)	Outstanding (shs.)[1]
Common	unlimited	360,478,770

[1] At May 30, 2023

Major Shareholder - Widely held at Apr. 28, 2023.

Price Range - HPQ/TSX-VEN

Year	Volume	High	Low	Close
2022	53,451,022	$0.62	$0.20	$0.25
2021	174,883,725	$1.68	$0.42	$0.46
2020	241,540,577	$1.17	$0.05	$1.10
2019	42,099,673	$0.12	$0.06	$0.08
2018	42,274,688	$0.14	$0.06	$0.06

Recent Close: $0.37

Capital Stock Changes - In May 2022, private placement of 6,800,000 units (1 common share & 1 warrant) at 53¢ per unit was completed. Also during 2022, common shares were issued as follows: 7,506,412 on exercise of warrants and 2,900,000 on exercise of options.

Wholly Owned Subsidiaries

HPQ Nano Silicon Powders Inc., Canada.

HPQ Silica Polvere Inc., Canada.

Investments

4.55% int. in **Beauce Gold Fields Inc.**, Montréal, Qué. (see Survey of Mines)

20% int. in **Novacium S.A.S.**, France.

PyroGenesis Canada Inc., Montréal, Qué. (see separate coverage)

Quebec Innovative Materials Corp., Vancouver, B.C. (see Survey of Mines)

Note: The preceding list includes only the major related companies in which interests are held.

Financial Statistics

Periods ended:	12m Dec. 31/22[A]		12m Dec. 31/21[A]
	$000s	%Chg	$000s
Salaries & benefits	756		3,176
Research & devel. expense	2,407		109
General & admin expense	1,073		1,110
Operating expense	**4,236**	**-4**	**4,396**
Operating income	**(4,236)**	**n.a.**	**(4,396)**
Deprec., depl. & amort.	2,179		234
Finance costs, net	741		574
Investment income	(35)		(54)
Write-downs/write-offs	(1,896)		nil
Pre-tax income	**(9,084)**	**n.a.**	**(6,331)**
Net income	**(9,084)**	**n.a.**	**(6,331)**
Net inc. for equity hldrs	**(9,207)**	**n.a.**	**(6,331)**
Net inc. for non-cont. int	**123**	**n.a.**	**nil**
Cash & equivalent	1,854		3,339
Accounts receivable	1,254		696
Current assets	5,512		4,411
Long-term investments	180		206
Fixed assets, net	3,839		5,087
Intangibles, net	11,867		9,856
Total assets	**21,612**	**-1**	**21,723**
Accts. pay. & accr. liabs	3,969		259
Current liabilities	4,435		601
Long-term debt, gross	927		1,024
Long-term debt, net	827		982
Long-term lease liabilities	17		n.a.
Shareholders' equity	14,394		18,332
Non-controlling interest	124		nil
Cash from oper. activs	**(4,879)**	**n.a.**	**(2,410)**
Cash from fin. activs	4,824		7,390
Cash from invest. activs	(1,491)		(4,196)
Net cash position	**1,144**	**-57**	**2,673**
Capital expenditures	(921)		(461)
	$		$
Earnings per share*	(0.03)		(0.02)
Cash flow per share*	(0.01)		(0.01)
	shs		shs
No. of shs. o/s*	351,998,770		334,792,358
Avg. no. of shs. o/s*	345,005,110		307,652,853
	%		%
Net profit margin	n.a.		n.a.
Return on equity	(56.27)		(41.08)
Return on assets	(41.92)		(32.15)

* Common

[A] Reported in accordance with IFRS

Latest Results

Periods ended:	3m Mar. 31/23[A]		3m Mar. 31/22[A]
	$000s	%Chg	$000s
Net income	(1,658)	n.a.	(745)
Net inc. for equity hldrs	(1,659)	n.a.	(745)
Net inc. for non-cont. int	1		nil
	$		$
Earnings per share*	(0.00)		(0.00)

* Common

[A] Reported in accordance with IFRS

Historical Summary
(as originally stated)

Fiscal Year	Oper. Rev.	Net Inc. Bef. Disc.	EPS*
	$000s	$000s	$
2022[A]	nil	(9,084)	(0.03)
2021[A]	nil	(6,331)	(0.02)
2020[A]	nil	(792)	(0.01)
2019[A]	nil	(1,384)	(0.01)
2018[A]	nil	(1,645)	(0.01)

* Common

[A] Reported in accordance with IFRS

H.8 HS GovTech Solutions Inc.

Symbol - HS **Exchange** - CSE **CUSIP** - 40453C

Head Office - 303-750 Pender St W, Vancouver, BC, V6C 2T7 **Telephone** - (778) 888-2019 **Toll-free** - (833) 565-0072

Website - hsgovtech.com

Email - dean.christie@hscloudsuite.com

Investor Relations - Dean Christie (833) 565-0072

Auditors - Hay & Watson C.A., Vancouver, B.C.

Lawyers - McMillan LLP, Vancouver, B.C.

Transfer Agents - Odyssey Trust Company, Vancouver, B.C.

Employees - 91 at Apr. 28, 2023

Profile - (B.C. 2015) Develops and markets Software-as-a-Service-based applications for data management, inspections, licensing, bill payment, complaint submission, revenue collection and communications for state, provincial and local governments in the United States and Canada.

Products include HSCloud, a fully-customizable cloud-based portal for managing applications, licences, permits, inspections and other compliance data; HSTouch, a mobile and tablet application available in iOS, Android and Windows versions which allows health inspectors to conduct paperless inspections without the need for an internet connection; HSTrace, a disease surveillance tools that allow public health agencies to track new cases in an outbreak, and provide an advanced suite of communication and tracking tools so they can stay in close touch with constituents that are sick; HSPay, an online and mobile payment platform for government revenue collection that provides easier methods of payment to private businesses; My Health Department (MyHD), an interactive dashboard for direct communication between government agencies, private industries and citizens, allowing users to apply for services, view and interact with inspection reports and permits, review the status of applications and streamline communication with the regulating agency; and GovCall, a teleconferencing and group communication platform tailored for specific government requirements.

Also has a legacy business, EnviroIntel EHS Manager, an Internet-based Windows client/server application that runs on desktop, laptop and tablet computers which allows users to access the system through a web browser to fill out forms, request information and view data, including real-time reports. The company has embarked on a program to migrate current EHS users to the HSCloud platform.

Predecessor Detail - Name changed from HealthSpace Data Systems Ltd., Apr. 27, 2022.

Directors - Ali Hakimzadeh, exec. chr., Vancouver, B.C.; Silas Garrison, CEO, Charlotte, N.C.; Alnesh P. Mohan, Vancouver, B.C.; Mark Redcliffe, B.C.

Other Exec. Officers - Dean Christie, CFO; Sheryl Dhillon, corp. sec.

Capital Stock

	Authorized (shs.)	Outstanding (shs.)[1]	Par
Common	unlimited	54,634,815	$2.00

[1] At May 29, 2023

Major Shareholder - Widely held at June 20, 2022.

Price Range - HS/CSE

Year	Volume	High	Low	Close
2022	12,431,933	$0.78	$0.27	$0.35
2021	16,858,790	$1.75	$0.69	$0.71
2020	24,930,319	$1.50	$0.24	$1.40
2019	5,569,273	$0.60	$0.24	$0.36
2018	23,993,364	$2.16	$0.20	$0.36

Consolidation: 1-for-8 cons. in Dec. 2020

Recent Close: $0.19

Capital Stock Changes - In March 2023, public offering of 5,613,800 units (1 common share & 1 warrant) at 37¢ per unit and private placement of 1,044,424 units (1 common share & 1 warrant) at 37¢ per unit were completed, both with warrants exercisable at 50¢ per share for three years.

In February 2022, public offering of 7,666,704 units (1 common share & ½ warrant) at 60¢ per unit, including 1,000,004 units on exercise of over-allotment option, and private placement of 1,131,349 units (1 common share & ½ warrant) at 60¢ per unit were completed. Also during 2022, common shares were issued as follows: 596,250 on vesting of restricted share units, 230,001 as finders' fees and 5,000 on exercise of options.

Wholly Owned Subsidiaries

HS GovTech USA Inc., Va.

Financial Statistics

Periods ended:	12m Dec. 31/22[A]		12m Dec. 31/21[A]
	US$000s	%Chg	US$000s
Operating revenue	**6,030**	**+6**	**5,678**
Cost of sales	1,545		1,579
Salaries & benefits	1,719		1,212
Research & devel. expense	56		60
General & admin expense	6,816		5,729
Stock-based compensation	452		1,600
Operating expense	**10,588**	**+4**	**10,180**
Operating income	**(4,558)**	**n.a.**	**(4,502)**
Deprec., depl. & amort.	537		373
Finance costs, gross	41		11
Pre-tax income	**(5,291)**	**n.a.**	**(4,990)**
Net income	**(5,291)**	**n.a.**	**(4,990)**
Cash & equivalent	907		915
Accounts receivable	1,297		975
Current assets	2,241		2,004
Fixed assets, net	160		249
Intangibles, net	5,237		4,080
Total assets	**8,239**	**+22**	**6,770**
Accts. pay. & accr. liabs	1,147		757
Current liabilities	3,554		1,986
Long-term debt, gross	1,447		24
Long-term debt, net	1,275		nil
Shareholders' equity	3,410		4,653
Cash from oper. activs	**(3,409)**	**n.a.**	**(3,145)**
Cash from fin. activs	5,327		1,072
Cash from invest. activs	(2,100)		(1,468)
Net cash position	**657**	**-28**	**915**
Capital expenditures	nil		(145)
	US$		US$
Earnings per share*	(0.12)		(0.14)
Cash flow per share*	(0.08)		(0.09)
	shs		shs
No. of shs. o/s*	46,441,815		36,812,511
Avg. no. of shs. o/s*	45,051,329		36,279,713
	%		%
Net profit margin	(87.74)		(87.88)
Return on equity	(131.24)		(87.42)
Return on assets	(69.96)		(64.65)
Foreign sales percent	90		89
No. of employees (FTEs)	93		88

* Common
[A] Reported in accordance with IFRS

Latest Results

Periods ended:	3m Mar. 31/23[A]		3m Mar. 31/22[A]
	US$000s	%Chg	US$000s
Operating revenue	1,888	+26	1,501
Net income	(1,023)	n.a.	(974)
	US$		US$
Earnings per share*	(0.02)		(0.02)

* Common
[A] Reported in accordance with IFRS

Historical Summary
(as originally stated)

Fiscal Year	Oper. Rev. US$000s	Net Inc. Bef. Disc. US$000s	EPS* US$
2022[A]	6,030	(5,291)	(0.12)
2021[A]	5,678	(4,990)	(0.14)
2020[A1]	1,657	(1,157)	(0.04)
2020[A]	2,648	(1,833)	(0.09)
2019[A]	2,586	(753)	(0.04)

* Common
[A] Reported in accordance with IFRS
[1] 5 months ended Dec. 31, 2020.
Note: Adjusted throughout for 1-for-8 cons. in Dec. 2020

H.9 HSBC Bank Canada

CUSIP - 40427H
Head Office - 300-885 Georgia St W, Vancouver, BC, V6C 3E9 **Telephone** - (604) 685-1000 **Toll-free** - (888) 310-4722 **Fax** - (604) 641-3098
Website - www.hsbc.ca
Email - investor_relations@hsbc.ca
Investor Relations - Investor Relations (604) 216-4524
Auditors - PricewaterhouseCoopers LLP C.A., Vancouver, B.C.
FP500 Revenue Ranking - 137
Profile - (Can. 1981) Provides personal and business banking and investment products and services across Canada.
The bank's ultimate parent company **HSBC Holdings plc** has four global lines of business that operate in Canada: **Commercial Banking**, which serves business customers with a full range of commercial financial solutions including working capital, term loans, payment services and international trade facilitation, mergers and acquisitions, and access to financial markets; **Wealth and Personal Banking**, which offers a full range of banking products and services including deposits and accounts, credit and lending, and financial advisory and investments to personal customers; **Global Banking**, which provides a comprehensive range of financial products and services to corporates, governments and institutions worldwide including transaction banking, financing, advisory, capital markets and risk management services; and **Markets and Securities Services**, which provides tailored financial services and products to government, corporate and institutional clients worldwide including sales and trading of fixed income securities, spot and derivative products, and financing solutions.

Recent Merger and Acquisition Activity

Status: pending **Announced:** Nov. 29, 2022
Royal Bank of Canada (RBC) agreed to acquire HSBC Holdings plc's Canadian banking business, HSBC Bank Canada, for $13.5 billion in cash. HSBC Bank Canada is a Canadian personal and commercial bank focused on globally connected clients. At Sept. 30, 2022, HSBC Bank Canada had $134 billion in assets, more than 130 branches, over 780,000 retail and commercial customers and 4,200 full-time equivalent employees. RBC would also acquire all of existing preferred shares and subordinated debt of HSBC Bank Canada held by HSBC Holdings plc at par value. The transaction was expected to close in late 2023.
Predecessor Detail - Name changed from Hongkong Bank of Canada, June 21, 1999.
Directors - Samuel Minzberg, chr., Montréal, Qué.; Linda Seymour, pres., CEO & grp. gen. mgr., Toronto, Ont.; Lorenzo (Larry) Tomei, exec. v-p & head, wealth & personal banking, Toronto, Ont.; Karen L. Gavan, Toronto, Ont.; Fiona Macfarlane, West Vancouver, B.C.; Robert G. McFarlane, Vancouver, B.C.; Andrea Nicholls, Qué.; Michael M. Roberts, New York, N.Y.; Mark S. Saunders, Toronto, Ont.
Other Exec. Officers - Caroline A. Tose, COO; Daniel (Dan) Hankinson, CFO; Lisa Dalton, chief of staff, office of the CEO; Sophia S. Tsui, chief risk officer; Alicia Evers, head, governance & corp. sec.; Kim Hallwood, head, corp. sustainability; Scott Lampard, exec. v-p, man. dir. & head, global banking; Georgia Stavridis, exec. v-p & chief compliance officer; Kim Toews, exec. v-p & head, HR; Alan Turner, exec. v-p & head, comml. banking; Anna Camilleri, sr. v-p & chief auditor; Kimberly Flood, sr. v-p & head, commun.; Lilac Bosma, gen. counsel

Capital Stock

	Authorized (shs.)	Outstanding (shs.)[1]
Class 1 Preferred	unlimited	
Series H		20,000,000
Series J		14,000,000
Series K		10,000,000
Class 2 Preferred	unlimited	nil
Common	unlimited	548,668,000

[1] At June 30, 2023

Class 1 Preferred - Issuable in series and non-voting. Includes non-viability contingency capital (NVCC) provisions, necessary for the shares to qualify as Tier 1 regulatory capital under Basel III. In the event that OSFI determines that a regulatory defined non-viability trigger event has occurred, NVCC provisions require the write off and cancellation of the shares against equity.
Series H - Entitled to non-cumulative dividends payable quarterly equal to the 90-day Government of Canada Treasury bill rate plus 2.94%. Redeemable on June 30, 2025, and on June 30 every five years thereafter at $25 per share, or at $25.50 per share in the case of redemptions on any other date. Convertible at the holder's option, on June 30, 2025, and on June 30 every five years thereafter, into fixed rate class 1 preferred shares series G on a share-for-share basis, subject to certain conditions.
Series J - Entitled to non-cumulative dividends payable quarterly equal to the 90-day Government of Canada Treasury bill rate plus 2.95%. Redeemable on Dec. 31, 2027, and on Dec. 31 every five years thereafter at $25 per share, or at $25.50 per share in the case of redemptions on any other date. Convertible at the holder's option, on Dec. 31, 2027, and on Dec. 31 every five years thereafter, into fixed rate class 1 preferred shares series I on a share-for-share basis, subject to certain conditions.
Series K - Entitled to non-cumulative annual dividends of $1.3625 per share payable quarterly to Sept. 30, 2024, and thereafter at a rate reset every five years equal to the five-year Government of Canada bond yield plus 4.011%. Redeemable on Sept. 30, 2024, and on September 30 every five years thereafter at $25 per share. Convertible at the holder's option, on Sept. 30, 2024, and on September 30 every five years thereafter, into floating rate class 1 preferred shares series L on a share-for-share basis, subject to certain conditions. The class 1 preferred shares series L would pay a quarterly dividend equal to the 90-day Government of Canada Treasury bill rate plus 4.011%.
Common - One vote per share.
Series I (old) - Were entitled to non-cumulative annual dividends of $1.15 per share payable quarterly. Converted into class 1 preferred shares series J on Dec. 31, 2022, on a share-for-share basis.
Major Shareholder - HSBC Holdings plc held 100% interest at Dec. 31, 2022.
Capital Stock Changes - During 2022, 14,000,000 class 1 preferred shares series I were converted into a like number of class 1 preferred shares series J.

Wholly Owned Subsidiaries

HSBC Finance Mortgages Inc., Toronto, Ont.
HSBC Global Asset Management (Canada) Limited, Vancouver, B.C.
HSBC Mortgage Corporation (Canada), Vancouver, B.C.
HSBC Private Investment Counsel (Canada) Inc., Toronto, Ont.
HSBC Securities (Canada) Inc., Toronto, Ont.
HSBC Trust Company (Canada), Vancouver, B.C.

Financial Statistics

Periods ended:	12m Dec. 31/22[A]		12m Dec. 31/21[A]
	$000s	%Chg	$000s
Interest income	**3,219,000**	**+78**	**1,813,000**
Interest expense	1,585,000		587,000
Net interest income	**1,634,000**	**+33**	**1,226,000**
Provision for loan losses	110,000		(45,000)
Other income	914,000		989,000
Salaries & pension benefits	607,000		604,000
Non-interest expense	1,358,000		1,308,000
Pre-tax income	**1,080,000**	**+13**	**952,000**
Income taxes	288,000		235,000
Net income	**792,000**	**+10**	**717,000**
Cash & equivalent	6,335,000		13,964,000
Securities	27,714,000		17,894,000
Net non-performing loans	276,000		215,000
Total loans	81,209,000		79,416,000
Fixed assets, net	332,000		263,000
Total assets	**128,302,000**	**+7**	**119,853,000**
Deposits	82,965,000		74,939,000
Other liabilities	38,408,000		37,027,000
Subordinated debt	1,011,000		1,011,000
Preferred share equity	1,100,000		1,100,000
Shareholders' equity	5,918,000		6,876,000
Cash from oper. activs	**(1,932,000)**	**n.a.**	**(1,631,000)**
Cash from fin. activs	(1,064,000)		(526,000)
Cash from invest. activs	(8,856,000)		4,637,000
Unfunded pension liability	65,000		98,000
	$		$
Earnings per share*	1.35		1.22
Cash flow per share*	(3.52)		(2.97)
Cash divd. per share*	nil		0.79
	shs		shs
No. of shs. o/s*	548,668,000		548,668,000
Avg. no. of shs. o/s*	548,668,000		548,668,000
	%		%
Basel III Common Equity Tier 1	11.60		14.00
Basel III Tier 1	14.10		16.80
Basel III Total	16.40		19.30
Net profit margin	31.08		32.37
Return on equity	13.99		11.63
Return on assets	0.64		0.60
No. of employees (FTEs)	n.a.		4,270

* Common
[A] Reported in accordance with IFRS

Latest Results

Periods ended:	6m June 30/23[A]		6m June 30/22[A]
	$000s	%Chg	$000s
Net interest income	894,000	+27	706,000
Net income	441,000	+23	359,000
	$		$
Earnings per share*	0.74		0.61

* Common
[A] Reported in accordance with IFRS

Historical Summary
(as originally stated)

Fiscal Year	Int. Inc. $000s	Net Inc. Bef. Disc. $000s	EPS* $
2022[A]	3,219,000	792,000	1.35
2021[A]	1,813,000	717,000	1.22
2020[A]	2,165,000	308,000	0.48
2019[A]	2,785,000	595,000	1.11
2018[A]	2,421,000	718,000	1.36

* Common
[A] Reported in accordance with IFRS

H.10 HTC Purenergy Inc.

Symbol - HTC **Exchange** - TSX-VEN **CUSIP** - 40432D
Head Office - 2-2305 Victoria Ave, Regina, SK, S4P 0S7 **Telephone** - (306) 352-6132 **Fax** - (306) 545-3262
Website - www.htcextraction.com
Email - jallison@htcenergy.com
Investor Relations - Jeffrey Allison (306) 525-5130
Auditors - PKF Antares Professional Corporation C.A., Calgary, Alta.
Bankers - Royal Bank of Canada, Regina, Sask.
Lawyers - McKercher LLP, Regina, Sask.; Borden Ladner Gervais LLP, Calgary, Alta.; McDougall Gauley LLP, Regina, Sask.
Transfer Agents - Odyssey Trust Company, Calgary, Alta.
Profile - (Alta. 1996) Processes industrial hemp for cannabinoid extraction, biofibre for bioplastics, biochar and cellulose, as well as hemp seeds, protein and hemp seed oil.
The company has a 27,000-sq.-ft. hemp biofibre processing and storage facility in Lajord, Sask., for the processing of biofibre into bioplastic pellets and biochar/hemp soil fertility pellets, as well as the storing and packaging of extraction-ready biomass. Hemp production and processing is carried out by wholly owned **KF Hemp Corp.**, which cultivates, processes, dries, stores and sells hemp and owns hemp

shredding, handling, drying, sizing and sorting equipment installed in its hemp processing facility in Lajord, Sask.

Common reinstated on TSX-VEN, May 24, 2023.

Common suspended from TSX-VEN, May 4, 2023.

Predecessor Detail - Name changed from HTC Hydrogen Technologies Corp., Feb. 21, 2008.

Directors - Wayne L. Bernakevitch†, chr., Regina, Sask.; Jeffrey (Jeff) Allison, pres., CEO & corp. sec., Calgary, Alta.; Garth Fredrickson, Regina, Sask.; Lionel P. Kambeitz, Regina, Sask.

Other Exec. Officers - Jacelyn Case, CFO

† Lead director

Capital Stock

	Authorized (shs.)	Outstanding (shs.)[1]
Preferred	unlimited	nil
Common	unlimited	206,983,741

[1] At Sept. 30, 2022

Major Shareholder - 102047601 Saskatchewan Ltd. held 17.44% interest at June 7, 2022.

Price Range - HTC/TSX-VEN

Year	Volume	High	Low	Close
2022	27,030,586	$0.04	$0.01	$0.01
2021	14,599,605	$0.13	$0.03	$0.03
2020	12,852,698	$0.30	$0.05	$0.12
2019	25,019,266	$1.24	$0.08	$0.20
2018	2,835,117	$0.19	$0.10	$0.11

Recent Close: $0.01

Dividends

HTC com N.S.R.

Listed May 24/23.

stk.[1] ◆ .... Aug. 10/22

Paid in 2023: n.a. 2022: stk.◆ 2021: n.a.

[1] Stk. divd. of 1 Delta CleanTech Inc com. sh. for ea. 17.25 shs. held.

◆ Special

Wholly Owned Subsidiaries

HTC Purification Corp.

KF Hemp Corp., Sask.
- 100% int. in **BlackRaven Gentics Corp.**
- 100% int. in **KF Farmacy Ltd.**

Subsidiaries

70% int. in **Oroverde Genetica Corp.**, Sask.

Investments

26% int. in **Delta CleanTech Inc.**, Regina, Sask. (see separate coverage)

11.23% int. in **Starling Brands Inc.**, Toronto, Ont.

Financial Statistics

Periods ended:	12m Dec. 31/21[A]		12m Dec. 31/20[◻A]
	$000s	%Chg	$000s
Operating revenue	**738**	**n.a.**	**nil**
Cost of sales	209		nil
Salaries & benefits	111		542
General & admin expense	544		621
Operating expense	**863**	**-26**	**1,163**
Operating income	**(125)**	**n.a.**	**(1,163)**
Deprec., depl. & amort	630		583
Finance income	3		139
Finance costs, gross	296		422
Investment income	(1,285)		nil
Write-downs/write-offs	(5,352)		(28,094)
Pre-tax income	**(8,315)**	**n.a.**	**(30,206)**
Income taxes	nil		(2,765)
Net inc. bef. disc. opers	**(8,315)**	**n.a.**	**(27,441)**
Income from disc. opers	3,692		(6,965)
Net income	**(4,624)**	**n.a.**	**(34,405)**
Net inc. for equity hldrs	**(4,414)**	**n.a.**	**(34,393)**
Net inc. for non-cont. int	**(209)**	**n.a.**	**(12)**
Cash & equivalent	1,452		293
Inventories	212		762
Accounts receivable	164		25
Current assets	1,842		2,454
Long-term investments	2,432		nil
Fixed assets, net	3,211		7,342
Right-of-use assets	92		349
Intangibles, net	nil		903
Total assets	**7,652**	**-31**	**11,135**
Accts. pay. & accr. liabs	732		1,028
Current liabilities	3,209		1,252
Long-term debt, gross	5,249		4,459
Long-term debt, net	5,249		4,459
Long-term lease liabilities	50		189
Shareholders' equity	(2,145)		4,305
Non-controlling interest	(225)		(16)
Cash from oper. activs	**(822)**	**n.a.**	**831**
Cash from fin. activs	701		(748)
Cash from invest. activs	37		(5,082)
Net cash position	**114**	**-42**	**198**
Capital expenditures, net	(63)		(3,864)
	$		$
Earns. per sh. bef disc opers*	(0.04)		(0.19)
Earnings per share*	(0.02)		(0.22)
Cash flow per share*	(0.00)		0.01
	shs		shs
No. of shs. o/s*	206,983,741		206,983,741
Avg. no. of shs. o/s*	206,983,741		159,088,563
	%		%
Net profit margin	n.m.		n.a.
Return on equity	n.m.		(183.36)
Return on assets	(85.37)		(93.51)

* Common

◻ Restated

[A] Reported in accordance with IFRS

Latest Results

Periods ended:	9m Sept. 30/22[A]		9m Sept. 30/21[◻A]
	$000s	%Chg	$000s
Operating revenue	258	-35	396
Net inc. bef. disc. opers	(1,482)	n.a.	(1,804)
Income from disc. opers	nil		2,223
Net income	(1,482)	n.a.	418
	$		$
Earns. per sh. bef. disc. opers.*	(0.01)		(0.01)
Earnings per share*	(0.01)		0.00

* Common

◻ Restated

[A] Reported in accordance with IFRS

Historical Summary
(as originally stated)

Fiscal Year	Oper. Rev.	Net Inc. Bef. Disc.	EPS*
	$000s	$000s	$
2021[A]	738	(8,315)	(0.04)
2020[A]	25	(31,014)	(0.22)
2019[A]	2,415	(5,518)	(0.08)
2018[A]	1,024	(3,857)	(0.08)
2017[A]	269	1,996	0.06

* Common

[A] Reported in accordance with IFRS

H.11 Haivision Systems Inc.

Symbol - HAI **Exchange** - TSX **CUSIP** - 40531F

Head Office - 500-2600 boul Alfred Nobel, Montréal, QC, H4S 0A9

Telephone - (514) 334-5445 **Toll-free** - (877) 224-5445

Website - www.haivision.com

Email - cfo@haivision.com

Investor Relations - Dan Rabinowitz (847) 362-6800

Auditors - Deloitte LLP C.A., Montréal, Qué.

Lawyers - Osler, Hoskin & Harcourt LLP, Montréal, Qué.

Transfer Agents - Computershare Trust Company of Canada Inc., Montréal, Qué.

FP500 Revenue Ranking - 737

Employees - 393 at Oct. 31, 2022

Profile - (Can. 2004) Provides end-to-end video streaming solutions, spanning the entire Internet Protocol (IP) video lifecycle of contribution, distribution and delivery of media, for enterprises and governments worldwide.

The company's products and services are offered for the video networking and streaming market, serving broadcasters, enterprises and governments around the world.

Products include **Makito X Series** video encoders and decoders for end-to-end transport of secure, high quality HD video; video transmitters and mobile encoders (**Haivision Pro**, **Haivision Air** and **Haivision Rack**); **Haivision StreamHub**, a video receiver and IP gateway that decodes and distributes live video streams coming from any Haivision/Aviwest mobile transmitter or third-party platform; **Haivision Kraken**, a real-time video transcoder for intelligence, surveillance and reconnaissance (ISR), situational awareness and field monitoring applications; **Haivision SRT** (Secure Reliable Transport), an open source video transport protocol that enables the secure transmission of real-time, low latency video over public Internet networks; **SRT Streaming Protocol**, an open-source video transport protocol that optimizes video streaming performance across unpredictable networks; **Haivision EMS**, a element management system for centrally managing and monitoring encoders and decoders; **Haivision Play Pro**, a free app for securely playing or streaming live SRT feeds from anywhere over the Internet; **Haivision Play**, a series of high performance video player applications for mobile devices, desktops, managed set-top boxes; **Haivision Media Platform**, a secure enterprise video and IPTV platform; and **Haivision Hub For Governmentt**, a video network service for live, low latency video streaming between government agencies and public.

Also offers Command 360, a software platform for situational awareness and real-time decision-making in mission-critical command and control environments.

The company is headquartered in Montreal, Que., with an office in Chicago, Ill., as well as research and development centres in Beaverton, Ore.; Austin, Tex.; Madrid, Spain; and Rendsburg, Germany. Also has additional sales offices in Atlanta, Ga.

Recent Merger and Acquisition Activity

Status: terminated **Revised:** Apr. 15, 2023

UPDATE: Haivision rejected the revised offer. PREVIOUS: Evertz Technologies Limited delivered an expression of interest letter to Haivision Systems Inc. outlining a proposal to acquire all of the issued and outstanding common shares of Haivision for $4.50 per share. Any formal, binding offer would be subject to completion of due diligence procedures by Evertz. Apr. 14, 2023 - Evertz submitted a revised offer of $4.75 per share. Mar. 23, 2023 - Haivision rejected the offer.

Status: completed **Announced:** Feb. 24, 2022

UPDATE: The transaction was completed. PREVIOUS: Haivision Systems Inc. agreed to acquire France-based AVIWEST S.A.S., which provides mobile IP-based video contribution systems as well as live video transmission over cellular networks, for €20,500,000.

Predecessor Detail - Name changed from Hajtek Vision Inc., June 14, 2004.

Directors - Miroslav (Mirko) Wicha, founder, chr., pres. & CEO, Montréal, Qué.; Neil Hindle†, Qué.; Harvey Bienenstock, Qué.; Sidney M. Horn, Outremont, Qué.; Maj.-Gen. (ret.) Lee K. Levy II, Okla.; Robin M. Rush, Tex.; Julie Tremblay, Montréal, Qué.

Other Exec. Officers - Jean-Marc Racine, chief product officer; Peter Maag, exec. v-p, strategic partnerships & chief strategic officer; Dan Rabinowitz, exec. v-p, opers., CFO & sec.; Leo Bull, sr. v-p, global accounts; Jean-Philippe Demers, sr. v-p, opers.; Ronan Poullaouec, sr. v-p, eng.; Paul Singh, sr. v-p, DevSecOps & quality eng.; Blake Wenzel, sr. v-p, products; Steve Brosseau, v-p, cust. success; Mariano Converti, v-p, eng., Cloud; Jill Ram, v-p, HR; Marcus Schioler, v-p, mktg.; Lawrence Wilk, v-p, fin.

† Lead director

Capital Stock

	Authorized (shs.)	Outstanding (shs.)[1]
Preferred	unlimited	nil
Common	unlimited	28,907,380

[1] At June 14, 2023

Major Shareholder - Miroslav (Mirko) Wicha held 12.8% interest and Dr. Thomas O. Hecht held 11.3% interest at Mar. 13, 2023.

Price Range - HAI/TSX

Year	Volume	High	Low	Close
2022	5,323,279	$7.17	$2.11	$3.20
2021	12,057,181	$17.50	$6.07	$6.96
2020	3,766,123	$12.84	$6.30	$10.40

Recent Close: $3.40

Capital Stock Changes - During fiscal 2021, common shares were issued as follows: 66,556 under restricted share unit plan and 4,166 under deferred share unit plan.

Wholly Owned Subsidiaries

AVIWEST S.A.S., France.

Haivision MCS, LLC, Atlanta, Ga.

Haivision Media Technologies S.L., Madrid, Spain.

Haivision Network Video GmbH, Germany.

Haivision Network Video Inc., Del.

Haivision US Holdings Inc., Del.

Financial Statistics

Periods ended:	12m Oct. 31/22^A		12m Oct. 31/21^A
	$000s	%Chg	$000s
Operating revenue	**125,697**	**+36**	**92,591**
Cost of sales	39,066		23,235
Research & devel. expense	29,347		18,617
General & admin expense	36,874		31,066
Stock-based compensation	2,696		16,831
Other operating expense	14,673		5,505
Operating expense	**122,656**	**+29**	**95,254**
Operating income	**3,041**	**n.a.**	**(2,663)**
Deprec., depl. & amort.	8,234		2,740
Finance income	17		76
Finance costs, gross	1,125		468
Write-downs/write-offs	nil		(84)
Pre-tax income	**(6,302)**	**n.a.**	**(5,880)**
Income taxes	(110)		2,903
Net income	**(6,192)**	**n.a.**	**(8,783)**
Cash & equivalent	5,773		26,838
Inventories	21,056		8,841
Accounts receivable	26,711		19,476
Current assets	61,665		60,380
Fixed assets, net	3,807		1,848
Right-of-use assets	8,948		7,926
Intangibles, net	68,100		47,612
Total assets	**148,596**	**+21**	**122,480**
Accts. pay. & accr. liabs.	17,841		12,504
Current liabilities	44,884		24,379
Long-term debt, gross	4,006		nil
Long-term debt, net	2,617		nil
Long-term lease liabilities	8,258		7,587
Shareholders' equity	90,251		88,921
Cash from oper. activs.	**(5,079)**	**n.a.**	**2,216**
Cash from fin. activs.	8,584		30,227
Cash from invest. activs.	(25,757)		(20,323)
Net cash position	**5,773**	**-78**	**26,838**
Capital expenditures	(783)		(777)
	$		$
Earnings per share*	(0.21)		(0.34)
Cash flow per share*	(0.18)		0.09
	shs		shs
No. of shs. o/s*	28,829,609		28,758,887
Avg. no. of shs. o/s*	28,854,663		25,783,477
	%		%
Net profit margin	(4.93)		(9.49)
Return on equity	(6.91)		(14.76)
Return on assets	(3.75)		(8.73)
Foreign sales percent	97		98
No. of employees (FTEs)	393		330

* Common

^A Reported in accordance with IFRS

Historical Summary
(as originally stated)

Fiscal Year	Oper. Rev.	Net Inc. Bef. Disc.	EPS*
	$000s	$000s	$
2022^A	125,697	(6,192)	(0.21)
2021^A	92,591	(8,783)	(0.34)
2020^A	83,112	5,797	n.a.
2019^A1	74,090	3,677	n.a.
2018^A1	67,480	2,577	n.a.

* Common

^A Reported in accordance with IFRS

[1] As shown in the prospectus dated Dec. 9, 2020.

H.12 Hakken Capital Corp.

Symbol - HAKK.P **Exchange** - TSX-VEN **CUSIP** - 405325

Head Office - 4626 Lockehaven Pl, North Vancouver, BC, V7G 2B8 **Telephone** - (604) 612-5450

Email - retrenaman@telus.net

Investor Relations - Robert E. Trenaman (604) 612-5450

Auditors - Manning Elliott LLP C.A., Vancouver, B.C.

Transfer Agents - TSX Trust Company, Vancouver, B.C.

Profile - (B.C. 2018) Capital Pool Company.

Recent Merger and Acquisition Activity

Status: pending **Announced:** June 28, 2022

Hakken Capital Corp. entered into a letter of intent for the Qualifying Transaction reverse takeover acquisition of private Charlottetown, P.E.I.-based Advanced Extraction Systems Inc. (AESI) for issuance of 32,000,000 Hakken common shares at a deemed price of 25¢ per share. An additional 24,000,000 Hakken common shares would be issued subject to certain milestones. AESI designs, engineers and fabricates CO2 extraction systems for the cannabis, hemp and botanical industries in North America. As part of the transaction, either Hakken or AESI would complete a financing for minimum proceeds of $1,125,000. Upon closing of the transaction, Hakken would change its name to Advanced Extraction Systems Inc.

Directors - David (Dave) Eto, pres. & CEO, New Westminster, B.C.; Barry D. McKnight, CFO & corp. sec., North Vancouver, B.C.; Douglas H. (Doug) Blakeway, Surrey, B.C.; Robert E. Trenaman, North Vancouver, B.C.

Capital Stock

	Authorized (shs.)	Outstanding (shs.)[1]
Common	unlimited	11,985,695

[1] At June 30, 2022

Major Shareholder - Widely held at Mar. 13, 2020.

Price Range - HAKK.P/TSX-VEN

Year	Volume	High	Low	Close
2022	150,500	$0.15	$0.10	$0.13
2021	152,600	$0.27	$0.15	$0.15
2020	89,500	$0.25	$0.09	$0.24

Recent Close: $0.09

Capital Stock Changes - During fiscal 2022, 385,695 common shares were issued on exercise of warrants.

H.13 Halmont Properties Corporation

Symbol - HMT **Exchange** - TSX-VEN **CUSIP** - 40637F

Head Office - 400-51 Yonge St, Toronto, ON, M5E 1J1 **Telephone** - (416) 956-5140 **Fax** - (416) 203-9931

Email - heather.fitzpatrick@brookfield.com

Investor Relations - Heather M. Fitzpatrick (647) 448-7147

Auditors - BDO Canada LLP C.A., Toronto, Ont.

Bankers - Bank of Montreal, Toronto, Ont.

Lawyers - Cohen LLP, Toronto, Ont.

Transfer Agents - TSX Trust Company, Toronto, Ont.

Profile - (Ont. 2009; orig. Yuk., 2000) Invests in commercial buildings, forest properties and securities of companies holding property, energy and infrastructure assets.

Owns four commercial real estate properties in Toronto, Ont.; $20,000,000 convertible preferred equity interest (yielding 4% annual dividend) in **Macer Forest Holdings Inc.**, which holds 45% investment in **Acadian Timber Corp.**, is convertible into a 7% equity interest in Acadian; 40% interest in **Haliburton Forest & Wildlife Reserve Ltd.**, which owns four sawmills as well as hardwood forest lands and a biochar production facility covering 100,000 acres near Haliburton, Ont.; and 60% interest in the Grandview Estates residential land development project in Huntsville, Ont., of which 30 units have been built and sold, and 227 units are in an advanced planning stage as of Mar. 31, 2023.

Also holds, directly and indirectly, investment interests in **Brookfield Corporation**, **Brookfield Asset Management Ltd.**, **Trisura Group Ltd.**, as well as other companies with real estate and related infrastructure interests.

During the first quarter of 2022, the company entered into a conditional sale contract and an option contract on two commercial buildings in Toronto, Ont., for an undisclosed amount.

Recent Merger and Acquisition Activity

Status: completed **Announced:** June 30, 2023

Halmont Properties Corporation sold a commercial property at 401 Yonge Street in Toronto, Ont., for $8,000,000.

Status: completed **Announced:** Mar. 31, 2022

Halmont Properties Corporation sold its 75% interest in the ground and second floor premises of a 47-storey residential complex at 224 King Street West in Toronto, Ont., for $7,800,000.

Predecessor Detail - Name changed from H.A.L. Concepts Ltd., Feb. 27, 2007.

Directors - David W. Kerr, chr., Toronto, Ont.; Heather M. Fitzpatrick, pres. & CEO, Toronto, Ont.; Claude A. Doughty, Huntsville, Ont.; Randal L. Froebelius, Toronto, Ont.; M. Diane Horton, Toronto, Ont.; Timothy R. Price, Toronto, Ont.

Other Exec. Officers - Ines N. Zaloshnja, CFO & contr.; Euan J. Darling, chief invest. officer; Anthony E. (Tony) Rubin, sec.-treas.

Capital Stock

	Authorized (shs.)	Outstanding (shs.)[1]
Preferred	unlimited	30,769,231
Class A Common	unlimited	83,940,000
Class B Common	unlimited	40,000,000

[1] At May 17, 2023

Preferred - Entitled to a 4% annual dividend. Mature on Dec. 31, 2028. Convertible into 30,769,230 class B common shares on or before Dec. 31, 2024. Non-voting.

Class A Common - One vote per share.

Class B Common - Non-voting.

Normal Course Issuer Bid - The company plans to make normal course purchases of up to 4,197,000 class A common representing 5% of the total outstanding. The bid commenced on Dec. 14, 2022, and expires on Dec. 13, 2023.

Major Shareholder - Brookfield Partners Foundation held 13.3% interest at May 17, 2023.

Price Range - HMT/TSX-VEN

Year	Volume	High	Low	Close
2022	97,119	$0.88	$0.53	$0.87
2021	386,661	$0.90	$0.61	$0.80
2020	1,430,764	$0.75	$0.57	$0.75
2019	4,651,713	$1.40	$0.56	$0.60
2018	97,400	$1.15	$0.56	$1.00

Recent Close: $0.88

Capital Stock Changes - There were no changes to capital stock during 2021 or 2022.

Financial Statistics

Periods ended:	12m Dec. 31/22^A		12m Dec. 31/21^A
	$000s	%Chg	$000s
Total revenue	**19,514**	**+45**	**13,492**
Cost of real estate sales	1,703		1,503
General & admin. expense	1,366		351
Operating expense	**3,069**	**+66**	**1,854**
Operating income	**16,445**	**+41**	**11,638**
Finance costs, gross	3,398		3,452
Pre-tax income	**13,047**	**+59**	**8,186**
Income taxes	2,377		934
Net income	**10,670**	**+47**	**7,252**
Net inc. for equity hldrs	**9,817**	**+47**	**6,699**
Net inc. for non-cont. int.	**853**	**+54**	**553**
Cash & equivalent	nil		87
Accounts receivable	72,095		81,095
Long-term investments	92,780		90,968
Income-producing props.	42,390		74,031
Properties for future devel.	16,767		19,640
Property interests, net	59,157		93,671
Total assets	**224,032**	**-16**	**265,821**
Accts. pay. & accr. liabs.	3,475		3,422
Long-term debt, gross	50,008		67,324
Preferred share equity	20,000		20,000
Shareholders' equity	107,663		99,581
Non-controlling interest	22,596		21,743
Cash from oper. activs.	**845**	**-57**	**1,986**
Cash from fin. activs.	(56,393)		35,973
Cash from invest. activs.	55,461		(37,936)
Net cash position	**nil**	**n.a.**	**87**
Capital disposals	37,966		nil
	$		$
Earnings per share*	0.07		0.05
Cash flow per share*	0.01		0.02
	shs		shs
No. of shs. o/s*	123,940,000		123,940,000
Avg. no. of shs. o/s*	123,940,000		123,940,000
	%		%
Net profit margin	54.68		53.75
Return on equity	11.74		7.72
Return on assets	5.49		4.24

* Cl.A com.

^A Reported in accordance with IFRS

Latest Results

Periods ended:	3m Mar. 31/23^A		3m Mar. 31/22^A
	$000s	%Chg	$000s
Total revenue	3,807	+27	2,993
Net income	2,333	+87	1,250
Net inc. for equity hldrs.	2,043	+88	1,086
Net inc. for non-cont. int.	290		164
	$		$
Earnings per share*	0.02		0.00

* Cl.A com.

^A Reported in accordance with IFRS

Historical Summary
(as originally stated)

Fiscal Year	Total Rev.	Net Inc. Bef. Disc.	EPS*
	$000s	$000s	$
2022^A	19,514	10,670	0.07
2021^A	13,492	7,252	0.05
2020^A	11,219	6,107	0.04
2019^A	13,474	7,073	0.06
2018^A	7,808	3,424	0.00

* Cl.A com.

^A Reported in accordance with IFRS

H.14 Halo Collective Inc.

CUSIP - 40638K

Head Office - Toronto-Dominion Centre, 400-77 King St W, Toronto, ON, M5K 0A1 **Telephone** - (416) 861-2694 **Fax** - (416) 861-8165

Website - www.haloco.com

Email - marshall@haloco.com

Investor Relations - Marshall Minor (416) 861-2694

Auditors - GreenGrowth C.P.A., Los Angeles, Calif.

Transfer Agents - Odyssey Trust Company, Vancouver, B.C.

Employees - 230 at Mar. 31, 2022

Profile - (Ont. 2005; orig. B.C., 1987) Cultivates, extracts, manufactures and distributes cannabis and cannabis products such as cannabis flowers, pre-rolls, vape carts, edibles and concentrates in Oregon and California, as well as develops cannabis software and technologies.

Has cultivation, processing, wholesaling, transportation and distribution operations in Oregon and California. Facilities are located in Medford and Evans Creek, Ore.; and Cathedral City, Ukiah and Lake cty., Calif. The facilities enable the company to produce branded and white label products across multiple product categories.

Cannabis products are sold principally in two dispensaries in Los Angeles, Calif. (2) under the brands Winberry Farms, Hush™, Mojave, Exhale, Flowershop* and retail brand Budega™.

Wholly owned **1285826 B.C. Ltd.** (dba H2C Beverages), manufactures flavoured waters and other plant-based beverages infused with cannabinoids and functional non-psychotropic mushroom extracts.

Wholly owned **1000116327 Ontario Ltd.** (dba Dissolve Medical), develops Cannabidiol (CBD) slits, a dissolvable strips with CBD, cannabinol (CBN) or cannabigerol (CBG) formulations which can be used for energy elixirs, herbal remedies and smokeless alternative option to medical and recreational users of CBD, CBN or CBG.

Wholly owned **Phytocann Holdings SA** manufactures and sells CBD oils, vapes, pollens, cosmetics, food and beverages under the brands Easy Weed and Ivory in Switzerland and France.

Wholly owned **Simply Sweet Gummy Ltd.** manufactures vegan, low-sugar and sugar-alcohol free candy with products including Blueberry Buzz, Peach Dream, Watermelon Adventure, Sour Cherry Blast and Strawberry Chill.

Wholly owned **Food Concepts LLC** cultivates, processes and wholesales cannabis from the 55,000-sq.-ft. Pistil Point facility in Portland, Ore.

Affiliate **Akanda Corp.** has medical cannabis cultivation, manufacturing and distribution operations in Lesotho and imports and sells medical cannabis-based products to the domestic market in the United Kingdom.

Also developing software assets including CannPOS, an application to manage customer flow in dispensaries; Cannalift, a delivery application; and CannaFeels, an application providing information and content on cannabis strains.

In September 2022, wholly owned **ANM Inc.** acquired the assets of **Decatur One LLC**, **Bradford Two LLC** and **Bradford Three LLC**, which include indoor and outdoor cultivation, manufacturing and distribution assets as well as an expanded library of genetics, for issuance of 47,224 common shares at a fair value of US$4,000,000.

In July 2022, the three operating KushBar retail cannabis stores in Camrose, Morinville and Medicine Hat, Alta., acquired from **High Tide Inc.** in July 2021, were returned to High Tide due to the company not meeting certain obligations under the agreement.

In June 2022, the company and **Red Light Holland Corp.** dissolved their 50/50 joint venture, **Red Light Oregon, Inc.**, which was formed in April 2021 to develop a commercialization strategy for psilocybin services in Oregon.

In April 2022, the company acquired **1000116327 Ontario Ltd.** (dba **Dissolve Medical**), which develops CBD slits, a precise, rapid, discreet and healthier option for cannabis consumption, consisting of strips with CBD, CBN or CBG formulations, for issuance of 5,000,000 common shares.

On Mar. 15, 2022, common shares of subsidiary **Akanda Corp.** commenced trading on The Nasdaq Capital Market. Akanda's initial public offering of 4,000,000 common shares at US$4.00 per share was completed on Mar. 17, 2022. On closing, the company held 12,674,957 Akanda common shares, representing a 43.8% interest.

Common delisted from NEO, Aug. 15, 2023.

Common suspended from NEO, June 19, 2023.

Recent Merger and Acquisition Activity

Status: terminated **Revised:** July 26, 2022

UPDATE: The transaction was terminated. PREVIOUS: Halo Collective Inc. agreed to acquire Villenueve, Switzerland-based Phytocann Holdings S.A. for issuance of common shares at a fair value of €12,200,000. Phytocann manufactures and sells CBD oils, vapes, pollens, cosmetics, food and beverages under the brands Easy Weed and Ivory in Switzerland and France.

Predecessor Detail - Name changed from Halo Labs Inc., Jan. 22, 2021.

Directors - Katharyn M. (Katie) Field, chr. & CEO, Los Angeles, Calif.; Avtar Dhaliwal, B.C.; Quinn Field-Dyte, Vancouver, B.C.; Cassidy McCord, Vancouver, B.C.; Alson Niu

Other Exec. Officers - Shailesh Bhushan, chief acctg. officer; Dustin Jessup, chief revenue officer; Sky Pinnick, chief mktg. officer; Joshua (Josh) Haddox, sr. v-p, opers.; Chad Kanner, sr. v-p, bus. devel.; Marshall Minor, sr. v-p, fin. & interim CFO

Capital Stock

	Authorized (shs.)	Outstanding (shs.)[1]
Restricted	unlimited	nil
Common	unlimited	150,210,195

[1] At Mar. 6, 2023

Major Shareholder - Widely held at Mar. 6, 2023.

Price Range - APE/TSX-VEN (D)

Year	Volume	High	Low	Close
2022	13,050,388	$177.00	$0.04	$0.05
2021	58,461	$2,100.00	$122.00	$123.00
2020	9,127	$3,300.00	$300.00	$500.00
2019	1,036	$8,100.00	$2,000.00	$2,800.00
2018	81	$4,500.00	$1,750.00	$2,800.00

Consolidation: 1-for-5 cons. in Oct. 2022; 1-for-20 cons. in June 2022; 1-for-100 cons. in Oct. 2021

Capital Stock Changes - In January and February 2023, 98,510,139 common shares were issued on conversion of debt.

On June 23, 2022, common shares were consolidated on a 1-for-20 basis. On Oct. 28, 2022, common shares were consolidated on a 1-for-5 basis. In November and December 2022, 24,651,361 post-consolidated common shares were issued on conversion of debt.

Wholly Owned Subsidiaries

ANM, Inc., Ore.
- 100% int. in **ANM Williams Farms LLC**, Ore.
- 100% int. in **Food Concepts LLC**, Ore.
- 100% int. in **HLO Ventures (NV), LLC**, Nev.
- 100% int. in **PSG Coastal Holdings LLC**, Calif.
  - 100% int. in **Coastal Harvest, LLC**, Calif.
  - 100% int. in **Crimson & Black LLC**, Nev.
  - 100% int. in **Industrial Court L13, LLC**, Calif.
  - 100% int. in **Industrial Court L9, LLC**, Calif.
  - 50% int. in **Lake County Natural Health LLC**, Calif.
  - 100% int. in **MFT11 LLC**, Nev.
    - 66.7% int. in **LKJ11 LLC**, Nev.
  - 100% int. in **Outer Galactic Chocolates LLC**, Calif.

Black & Crimson LLC, United States.
HLO Peripherals LLC, Nev.
Halo AccuDab Holdings Inc., B.C.
Halo Cannalift Delivery Inc., B.C.
Halo DispensaryTrack Software Inc., B.C.
Halo Labs (USA) holdings Inc., United States.
Halo Nasalbinoid Natural Devices Corp., B.C.
Halo Tek Inc.
Halo Winberry Holdings, LLC, Ore.
Mendo Distribution and Transportation LLC, Ukiah, Calif.
Nature's Best Resources LLC
1265292 B.C. Ltd., Canada. dba Cannafeels.
1275111 B.C. Ltd., B.C.
1285826 B.C. Ltd., B.C.
1307296 B.C. Ltd., B.C.
POI11 LLC, Nev.
Phytocann Holdings S.A., Switzerland.
SDF11 LLC
Simply Sweet Gummy Ltd., Vancouver, B.C.
Ukiah Ventures Inc., Ukiah, Calif.
ZXC11 LLC

Investments

43.8% int. in **Akanda Corp.**, New Romney, Kent, United Kingdom. (see separate coverage)
44% int. in **Bar X Farms, LLC**, Calif.
Elegance Brands, Inc., Beverly Hills, Calif.
44% int. in **Triangle Canna Corp.**, Calif.

Financial Statistics

Periods ended:	12m Dec. 31/21[A]		12m Dec. 31/20[A]
	US$000s	%Chg	US$000s
Operating revenue	**36,180**	**+67**	**21,641**
Cost of sales	31,728		17,373
Salaries & benefits	12,752		4,782
General & admin expense	25,290		15,934
Stock-based compensation	5,147		2,483
Other operating expense	193		nil
Operating expense	**75,110**	**+85**	**40,573**
Operating income	**(38,930)**	**n.a.**	**(18,932)**
Deprec., depl. & amort.	2,276		2,092
Finance costs, gross	3,946		2,657
Pre-tax income	**(96,852)**	**n.a.**	**(41,178)**
Income taxes	56		6
Net income	**(96,909)**	**n.a.**	**(41,183)**
Net inc. for equity hldrs	**(94,613)**	**n.a.**	**(41,183)**
Net inc. for non-cont. int	**(2,296)**	**n.a.**	**nil**
Cash & equivalent	1,712		2,758
Inventories	16,820		10,281
Accounts receivable	6,073		1,785
Current assets	35,716		28,694
Long-term investments	19,275		3,188
Fixed assets, net	17,513		16,231
Intangibles, net	29,132		39,641
Total assets	**104,797**	**+19**	**87,754**
Bank indebtedness	6,875		436
Accts. pay. & accr. liabs	10,624		8,312
Current liabilities	30,287		9,980
Long-term debt, gross	2,388		14,998
Long-term debt, net	2,388		14,998
Long-term lease liabilities	5,666		3,157
Equity portion of conv. debs	863		654
Shareholders' equity	66,456		59,620
Cash from oper. activs	**(35,230)**	**n.a.**	**(10,044)**
Cash from fin. activs	33,180		10,383
Cash from invest. activs	209		(2,727)
Net cash position	**1,839**	**-50**	**3,680**
Capital expenditures	(2,601)		(3,573)
	US$		US$
Earnings per share*	(455.00)		(700.00)
Cash flow per share*	(153.35)		(177.00)
	shs		shs
No. of shs. o/s*	330,255		141,378
Avg. no. of shs. o/s*	229,738		56,624
	%		%
Net profit margin	(267.85)		(190.31)
Return on equity	(150.09)		(98.16)
Return on assets	(96.56)		(59.39)
Foreign sales percent	100		100
No. of employees (FTEs)	276		278

* Common
[A] Reported in accordance with IFRS

Latest Results

Periods ended:	9m Sept. 30/22[A]		9m Sept. 30/21[A]
	US$000s	%Chg	US$000s
Operating revenue	19,973	-28	27,814
Net income	(31,035)	n.a.	(30,365)
Net inc. for equity hldrs	(30,366)	n.a.	(30,365)
Net inc. for non-cont. int	(670)		nil
	US$		US$
Earnings per share*	(13.30)		(150.00)

* Common
[A] Reported in accordance with IFRS

Historical Summary
(as originally stated)

Fiscal Year	Oper. Rev.	Net Inc. Bef. Disc.	EPS*
	US$000s	US$000s	US$
2021[A]	36,180	(96,909)	(422.00)
2020[A]	21,641	(41,184)	(700.00)
2019[A]	28,148	(27,617)	(1,400.00)
2018[A1]	10,898	(13,718)	(2,200.00)
	$000s	$000s	$
2018[A2]	nil	(1,281)	(1,400.00)

* Common
[A] Reported in accordance with IFRS
[1] Results reflect the Sept. 28, 2018, reverse takeover acquisition of ANM, Inc.
[2] Results for fiscal 2018 and prior fiscal years pertain to Apogee Opportunities Inc.

Note: Adjusted throughout for 1-for-5 cons. in Oct. 2022; 1-for-20 cons. in June 2022; 1-for-100 cons. in Oct. 2021

H.15 Hamilton Thorne Ltd.

Symbol - HTL **Exchange** - TSX-VEN **CUSIP** - 407891

Head Office - 100 Cummings Center, Suite 465E, Beverly, MA, United States, 01915 **Telephone** - (978) 921-2050 **Toll-free** - (800) 323-0503 **Fax** - (978) 921-0250

Website - www.hamiltonthorne.ltd

Email - ir@hamiltonthorne.ltd

Investor Relations - Francesco Fragasso (978) 921-2050

Auditors - MNP LLP C.A., Toronto, Ont.

Transfer Agents - Computershare Trust Company of Canada Inc., Toronto, Ont.

Profile - (Ont. 2007) Develops, manufactures and sells laboratory equipment, consumables and software, as well as provides services for the assisted reproductive technologies, research and cell biology markets.

Equipment

The company's proprietary instrument, equipment and software product lines include precision laser devices, imaging systems, incubators, laminar flow workstations, air purification systems, control rate freezers, lab monitoring systems, and micromanipulation systems. The Laser products attach to standard inverted microscopes and operate as micro-surgical devices, enabling a wide array of scientific applications and In Vitro Fertilization (IVF) procedures. The image analysis systems are designed to bring quality, efficiency and reliability to studies of reproductive cells in the human fertility, animal sciences and reproductive toxicology fields. The incubators, workstations and filtration products improve outcomes through controlling environmental factors such as temperature, airflow humidity and air quality. The micromanipulation system assists the embryologist in performing critical procedures in the IVF lab with a high level of precision and reliability. The control rate freezers preserve cells and tissue samples in the research and cell biology laboratories as well as the IVF clinic.

Consumables

Consumables are disposable products and accessories used in IVF procedures, and include the GM501 family of products, which provides the IVF laboratories with a comprehensive cell culture media solution for oocyte handling, sperm processing, embryo culture and cryopreservation. Also include the company's sperm preparation media, quality control products, dyes, stains and counting chambers which complements the company's computer assisted sperm analysis (CASA) products; line of glass micropipettes which complements the company's micromanipulator system; and quality control assays that are used in IVF laboratories for testing equipment and materials' toxicity to ensure the safest environment for successful embryo development.

Services

Services include equipment service contracts and maintenance programs; quality control testing services to manufacturers and users of medical devices, culture media and consumables used in IVF laboratories; and laboratory design and installation services.

Products and services are sold through direct sales force based in the U.S., Germany, France, Australia, Spain, Denmark and the U.K. and through distributors to more than 2,000 fertility clinics, hospitals, pharmaceutical companies, biotechnology companies, educational institutions and other commercial and academic research establishments in more than 75 countries.

Recent Merger and Acquisition Activity

Status: completed **Announced:** Dec. 1, 2022

Hamilton Thorne Ltd. acquired Barcelona, Spain-based Microptic, S.L., which develops artificial intelligence enabled computer assisted semen analysis (CASA) software, consumables and image analysis systems for the assisted reproductive technologies, for €9,900,000.

Predecessor Detail - Name changed from Calotto Capital Inc., Oct. 28, 2009, pursuant to Qualifyinig Transaction reverse takeover acquisition of Hamilton Thorne, Inc.; basis 1 new for 7.71226 old shs.

Directors - David Wolf, chr., pres. & CEO, Wayland, Mass.; Karen (Kari) Firestone, Boston, Mass.; Feng Han, Syosset, N.Y.; Bruno C. Maruzzo, Toronto, Ont.; Robert J. Potter, Chatham, Mass.; Marc H. Robinson, Toronto, Ont.; Dr. David B. Sable, New York, N.Y.; Daniel K. Thorne, London, Middx., United Kingdom

Other Exec. Officers - Francesco Fragasso, CFO; Brett Fulton, sr. v-p; Thomas Kenny, v-p, eng.

Capital Stock

	Authorized (shs.)	Outstanding (shs.)[1]
Common	unlimited	146,078,552

[1] At May 12, 2023

Major Shareholder - Daniel K. Thorne held 13.8% interest and FAX Capital Corp. held 12.1% interest at May 11, 2023.

Price Range - HTL/TSX-VEN

Year	Volume	High	Low	Close
2022	13,189,198	$2.15	$1.31	$1.63
2021	19,929,462	$2.20	$1.31	$2.06
2020	33,259,716	$1.50	$0.90	$1.40
2019	25,277,441	$1.25	$0.86	$1.04
2018	30,123,350	$1.28	$0.71	$0.90

Recent Close: $1.46

Capital Stock Changes - During 2022, common shares were issued as follows: 1,717,135 on exercise of options and 666,957 under restricted share unit plan.

Wholly Owned Subsidiaries

HTL Holding GmbH
- 100% int. in **Gynemed GmbH & Co. KG**, Germany.
- 100% int. in **Gynemed Verwaltungs GmbH**, Germany.

HTL Holdings Inc., Del.
- 100% int. in **Embryotech Laboratories, Inc.**, Mass.

Hamilton Thorne DK ApS, Denmark.
- 100% int. in **IVFTECH ApS**, Birkerod, Denmark.

Hamilton Thorne Holdings UK Limited, United Kingdom.
- 100% int. in **Planer Ltd.**, United Kingdom.
- 100% int. in **Tek-Event Pty Ltd.**, Australia.

Hamilton Thorne, Inc., Beverly, Mass.

Hamilton Thorne Spain S.L., Spain.
- 100% int. in **Automatic Diagnostic Systems S.L.U.**, Spain.
- 100% int. in **Microptic S.L.**, Barcelona, Spain.

Financial Statistics

Periods ended:	12m Dec. 31/22[A]		12m Dec. 31/21[A]
	US$000s	%Chg	US$000s
Operating revenue	**58,178**	**+11**	**52,353**
Cost of sales	29,098		26,142
Research & devel. expense	3,675		3,423
General & admin expense	19,367		15,714
Operating expense	**52,140**	**+15**	**45,279**
Operating income	**6,038**	**-15**	**7,074**
Deprec., depl. & amort.	3,746		3,258
Finance costs, net	434		364
Pre-tax income	**1,999**	**-53**	**4,259**
Income taxes	89		1,825
Net income	**1,911**	**-21**	**2,434**
Cash & equivalent	16,673		17,927
Inventories	12,274		9,526
Accounts receivable	7,037		5,193
Current assets	37,346		33,524
Fixed assets, net	2,560		1,678
Right-of-use assets	3,283		2,624
Intangibles, net	39,192		34,068
Total assets	**86,667**	**+15**	**75,063**
Accts. pay. & accr. liabs.	8,724		6,681
Current liabilities	13,596		10,466
Long-term debt, gross	14,410		6,492
Long-term debt, net	11,130		4,396
Long-term lease liabilities	2,638		2,112
Shareholders' equity	56,222		55,957
Cash from oper. activs.	**1,800**	**-68**	**5,605**
Cash from fin. activs.	7,222		(423)
Cash from invest. activs.	(10,275)		(9,084)
Net cash position	**16,673**	**-7**	**17,927**
Capital expenditures	(1,520)		(948)
Capital disposals	44		nil
	US$		US$
Earnings per share*	0.01		0.02
Cash flow per share*	0.01		0.04
	shs		shs
No. of shs. o/s*	144,929,952		142,545,860
Avg. no. of shs. o/s*	143,869,999		140,721,679
	%		%
Net profit margin	3.28		4.65
Return on equity	3.41		4.55
Return on assets	2.36		3.36

* Common
[A] Reported in accordance with IFRS

Latest Results

Periods ended:	3m Mar. 31/23[A]		3m Mar. 31/22[A]
	US$000s	%Chg	US$000s
Operating revenue	16,690	+19	14,052
Net income	77	-86	556
	US$		US$
Earnings per share*	0.00		0.00

* Common
[A] Reported in accordance with IFRS

Historical Summary
(as originally stated)

Fiscal Year	Oper. Rev. US$000s	Net Inc. Bef. Disc. US$000s	EPS* US$
2022[A]	58,178	1,911	0.01
2021[A]	52,353	2,434	0.02
2020[A]	39,778	971	0.01
2019[A]	35,358	793	0.01
2018[A]	29,214	2,960	0.03

* Common
[A] Reported in accordance with IFRS

H.16 Hammond Manufacturing Company Limited*

Symbol - HMM.A **Exchange** - TSX **CUSIP** - 40851T

Head Office - 394 Edinburgh Rd N, Guelph, ON, N1H 1E5 **Telephone** - (519) 822-2960 **Fax** - (519) 822-0715

Website - www.hammfg.com

Email - astirling@hammfg.com

Investor Relations - Alexander Stirling (519) 822-2960

Auditors - ATA Audits Pty Ltd. C.A., Norwood, S.A. Australia; KPMG LLP C.A., Waterloo, Ont.; Wise & Co. C.A., Godalming, Surrey United Kingdom

Bankers - HSBC Bank Canada

Lawyers - Borden Ladner Gervais LLP, Toronto, Ont.

Transfer Agents - Computershare Trust Company of Canada Inc., Toronto, Ont.

FP500 Revenue Ranking - 632

Employees - 988 at Dec. 31, 2022

Profile - (Ont. 1944, via letters patent) Manufactures electronic and electrical enclosures, outlet strips and electronic transformers for sale in North America and internationally directly to Original Equipment Manufacturers (OEMs) and through a global network of distributors and agents.

Products offered consist of metallic and non-metallic enclosures, racks, plastic and die-cast small cases, outlet strips, surge suppressors and electronic transformers. Electrical enclosures and racks are designed and manufactured at the company's plant in Guelph, Ont., which also offers full design and modification manufacturing capabilities for customer applications. Customers range from small, owner-operated businesses to divisions of large integrated companies and electrical OEMs.

Electronic products (plastic and metal small cases, racks, surge suppressors and transformers) are manufactured at the company's facilities in Waterloo and Guelph, Ont., Cheektowaga, N.Y., (plastic small cases) and the U.K., as well as through 40%-owned **RITEC Enclosures Inc.** in Taiwan. Products are sold on a worldwide basis through a network of agents and distributors. The company is also a reseller of products supplied by companies from Canada, the U.S., the U.K., the People's Republic of China, Germany, Portugal, Taiwan and other global sources.

The company operated 14 manufacturing and/or sales and distribution facilities, of which 11 are located in Canada, one in the U.S., one in the U.K. and one in Australia. Manufacturing and corporate services facilities total 804,000 sq. ft. of space, of which about 294,000 sq. ft. are leased.

Directors - Robert F. Hammond, chr. & CEO, Guelph, Ont.; Michael Fricker, East York, Ont.; Sheila Hammond, Guelph, Ont.; Sarah Hansen, Calgary, Alta.; Paul Quigley, Waterloo, Ont.; Edward (Ted) Sehl, Guelph, Ont.; Blaine Witt, Buffalo, N.Y.

Other Exec. Officers - Alexander Stirling, CFO & corp. sec.; Ross N. Hammond, asst. sec. & mgr., bus. devel.

Capital Stock

	Authorized (shs.)	Outstanding (shs.)[1]
Class A Subord. Vtg.	unlimited	8,556,000
Class B Common	unlimited	2,778,300
Class YA	unlimited	nil
Class YB	unlimited	nil

[1] At June 30, 2023

Class A Subordinate Voting - Share equally with respect to dividends on class B shares. One vote per share.

Class B Common - Annual dividends on class B shares may not exceed annual dividends on class A shares. Convertible into class A shares on a share-for-share basis. Four votes per share.

Class YA & YB - Entitled to non-cumulative discretionary dividends. No dividends shall be declared or paid on the Class YA shares unless the same dividend is simultaneously declared and paid on the Class YB shares.Redeemable, retractable. Non-voting.

Major Shareholder - Robert F. Hammond held 63.7% interest at Mar. 7, 2023.

Price Range - HMM.A/TSX

Year	Volume	High	Low	Close
2022	596,275	$4.62	$3.57	$4.12
2021	905,686	$4.15	$2.06	$3.64
2020	1,341,672	$2.14	$1.00	$2.13
2019	980,321	$2.15	$1.72	$1.90
2018	1,263,274	$2.87	$1.87	$1.95

Recent Close: $7.54

Capital Stock Changes - There were no changes to capital stock from 2008 to 2022, inclusive.

Dividends

HMM.A cl A S.V. N.S.R.

$0.03	Aug. 25/23	$0.03	Apr. 6/23
$0.03	Aug. 26/22	$0.03	Apr. 7/22

Paid in 2023: $0.06 2022: $0.06 2021: $0.04

Long-Term Debt - Outstanding at Dec. 31, 2022:

Demand term loans:	
4.1% due Dec. 2023	$5,837,000
4.43% due Oct. 2025	2,253,000
5.3% due Nov. 2025	1,769,000
4% due Dec. 2025	891,000
5.2% due Dec. 2026	1,296,000
Term loans:	
3.83% due Nov. 2028	4,880,000
6.5% due June 2029	4,027,000
Interest free term loan	1,245,000
	22,198,000
Less: Current portion	13,962,000
	8,236,000

Wholly Owned Subsidiaries

Hammond Electronics Limited, Basingstoke, Hants., United Kingdom.
- 100% int. in **Hammond Electronics Asia Limited**, People's Republic of China.
- 100% int. in **Hammond Electronics B.V.**, Netherlands.

Hammond Electronics Pty Ltd., Adelaide, S.A., Australia.

Hammond Manufacturing Company Inc., Cheektowaga, N.Y.
- 100% int. in **Hammond Holdings Inc.**, United States.
- 100% int. in **Paulding Electrical Products, Inc.**, United States.

Hammond Manufacturing (Quebec) Inc., Laval, Qué.

Investments

40% int. in **RITEC Enclosures Inc.**, Taipei, Republic of China.

Financial Statistics

Periods ended:	12m Dec. 31/22[A]		12m Dec. 31/21[□A]
	$000s	%Chg	$000s
Operating revenue	**225,922**	**+19**	**190,128**
Cost of sales	148,819		129,429
General & admin expense	50,084		42,151
Operating expense	**198,903**	**+16**	**171,580**
Operating income	**27,019**	**+46**	**18,548**
Deprec., depl. & amort.	7,562		6,790
Finance costs, net	3,208		1,495
Investment income	(199)		(117)
Pre-tax income	**16,035**	**+58**	**10,161**
Income taxes	4,032		2,459
Net income	**12,003**	**+56**	**7,702**
Cash & equivalent	942		4,069
Inventories	63,267		45,516
Accounts receivable	30,014		27,143
Current assets	96,082		78,527
Long-term investments	1,867		1,880
Fixed assets, net	57,286		41,141
Right-of-use assets	12,423		15,000
Intangibles, net	347		428
Total assets	**168,005**	**+23**	**136,976**
Bank indebtedness	14,446		995
Accts. pay. & accr. liabs	29,609		26,929
Current liabilities	63,417		45,741
Long-term debt, gross	22,198		20,676
Long-term debt, net	8,236		6,125
Long-term lease liabilities	9,163		10,905
Shareholders' equity	81,545		68,692
Cash from oper. activs	**4,824**	**-66**	**14,262**
Cash from fin. activs	11,091		(1,298)
Cash from invest. activs	(20,158)		(11,544)
Net cash position	**942**	**-77**	**4,069**
Capital expenditures	(20,169)		(11,445)
Capital disposals	60		21
	$		$
Earnings per share*	1.06		0.68
Cash flow per share*	0.43		1.26
Cash divd. per share*	0.06		0.04
	shs		shs
No. of shs. o/s*	11,334,300		11,334,300
Avg. no. of shs. o/s*	11,334,300		11,334,300
	%		%
Net profit margin	5.31		4.05
Return on equity	15.98		11.83
Return on assets	7.87		5.99
Foreign sales percent	64		61
No. of employees (FTEs)	988		935

* Class A & B
[□] Restated
[A] Reported in accordance with IFRS

Latest Results

Periods ended:	6m June 30/23[A]		6m July 1/22[A]
	$000s	%Chg	$000s
Operating revenue	123,909	+10	112,227
Net income	9,695	+115	4,500
	$		$
Earnings per share*	0.86		0.40

* Class A & B
[A] Reported in accordance with IFRS

Historical Summary
(as originally stated)

Fiscal Year	Oper. Rev. $000s	Net Inc. Bef. Disc. $000s	EPS* $
2022[A]	225,922	12,003	1.06
2021[A]	190,128	7,702	0.68
2020[A]	148,223	7,724	0.68
2019[A]	148,592	4,749	0.42
2018[A]	145,602	3,764	0.33

* Class A & B
[A] Reported in accordance with IFRS

H.17 Hammond Power Solutions Inc.

Symbol - HPS.A **Exchange** - TSX **CUSIP** - 408549
Head Office - 595 Southgate Dr, Guelph, ON, N1G 3W6 **Telephone** - (519) 822-2441 **Toll-free** - (888) 798-8882 **Fax** - (519) 822-9701
Website - www.hammondpowersolutions.com
Email - rvollering@hammondpowersolutions.com
Investor Relations - Richard C. Vollering (519) 822-2441
Auditors - KPMG LLP C.A., Waterloo, Ont.
Bankers - J.P. Morgan Chase Bank (Canada)
Lawyers - Borden Ladner Gervais LLP
Transfer Agents - Computershare Investor Services Inc.
FP500 Revenue Ranking - 444
Employees - 1,530 at Dec. 31, 2022

Profile - (Ont. 2000) Designs, manufactures and sells standard and custom-designed dry-type transformers, power quality products and related magnetics in electrical distribution networks through an extensive range of end-user applications.

Dry-type transformers and related products, which range in size from 12 to 34,000 volts, with sizing up to 35 MVA and 200 kV BIL, are designed and manufactured at plants in Guelph and Walkerton, Ont.; Granby, Que.; Monterrey, Mexico; Compton, Calif.; and Hyderabad, India. Power quality and induction heating products are manufactured in Walkerton, Ont., Guelph, Ont., and North Huntington, Pa. A warehouse facility is leased in Baraboo, Wisc., which functions as the U.S. head office as well as a warehousing and sales office. Also has two facilities in Mexico and four in India.

The company sells its products around the globe through distributors and direct to Original Equipment Manufacturer (OEM) and private label customers.

Products are used for original equipment manufacturers (OEMs), capital projects and the maintenance, repair and overhaul market (MROs).

Directors - William G. (Bill) Hammond, exec. chr., Guelph, Ont.; Adrian Thomas, CEO, Qué.; Grant C. Robinson†, Guelph, Ont.; Dahra Granovsky, Toronto, Ont.; Christopher R. (Chris) Huether, Guelph, Ont.; Fred M. Jaques, Toronto, Ont.; Anne Marie Turnbull, Oakville, Ont.; J. David M. Wood, London, Ont.

Other Exec. Officers - Richard C. Vollering, CFO & corp. sec.; Paul Gaynor, CIO; David Kinsella, chief comml. officer; Catherine McKeown, chief people officer; Bob Yusyp, chief opers. officer

† Lead director

Capital Stock

	Authorized (shs.)	Outstanding (shs.)[1]
Special	unlimited	nil
Cl.A Subord. Vtg.	unlimited	9,126,624
Cl.B Common	unlimited	2,778,300[2]

[1] At Apr. 3, 2023
[2] All held by Arathorn Investments Inc.

Special - Discretionary dividends. Redeemable, retractable and non-voting.

Class A Subordinate Voting - One vote per share.

Class B Common - Annual dividends on the class B common shares may not exceed the annual dividends on the class A subordinate voting shares. Convertible into class A subordinate voting shares on a one-for-one basis. Four votes per share.

Major Shareholder - William G. (Bill) Hammond held 59.62% interest at Mar. 27, 2023.

Price Range - HPS.A/TSX

Year	Volume	High	Low	Close
2022	2,285,885	$22.24	$10.75	$20.12
2021	2,509,975	$12.31	$8.30	$11.99
2020	1,947,831	$8.75	$4.28	$8.47
2019	892,758	$9.36	$5.75	$7.68
2018	1,080,128	$10.33	$5.35	$5.70

Recent Close: $54.81

Capital Stock Changes - During 2022, 45,000 class A subordinate voting shares were issued on exercise of options.

Dividends

HPS.A cl A S.V. Ra $0.50 pa Q est. Mar. 30, 2023[1]
Prev. Rate: $0.40 est. June 28, 2022
Prev. Rate: $0.34 est. Mar. 26, 2020
[1] Divds. paid semiannually prior to March/13.

Wholly Owned Subsidiaries

Continental Transformers S.r.l., Italy.
Corefficient S. de R.L. de C.V., Mexico.
Delta Transformers Inc., Granby, Qué.
Hammond Power Solutions, Inc., Baraboo, Wis.
Hammond Power Solutions Private Limited, India.
Hammond Power Solutions S.A. de C.V., Monterrey, N.L., Mexico.
Hammond Power Solutions S.p.A., Italy.
Mesta Electronics, Inc., Pa.
Montran S.A. de C.V., N.L., Mexico.

Subsidiaries

98% int. in **Hammond Power Solutions Latin America S.A. de C.V.**, N.L., Mexico.

Financial Statistics

Periods ended:	12m Dec. 31/22[A]		12m Dec. 31/21[A]
	$000s	%Chg	$000s
Operating revenue	**558,464**	**+47**	**380,202**
Cost of sales	384,030		271,583
General & admin expense	101,829		76,695
Stock-based compensation	2,183		1,210
Operating expense	**488,042**	**+40**	**349,488**
Operating income	**70,422**	**+129**	**30,714**
Deprec., depl. & amort.	10,981		7,563
Finance costs, gross	1,596		1,301
Investment income	4		61
Pre-tax income	**57,169**	**+169**	**21,250**
Income taxes	12,341		6,074
Net income	**44,828**	**+195**	**15,176**
Cash & equivalent	28,126		20,905
Inventories	106,353		62,467
Accounts receivable	86,701		72,004
Current assets	230,123		159,698
Long-term investments	3,121		16,573
Fixed assets, net	34,789		25,152
Right-of-use assets	6,953		5,808
Intangibles, net	19,674		22,719
Total assets	**72,550**	**-4**	**75,401**
Bank indebtedness	6,154		19,267
Accts. pay. & accr. liabs	92,301		75,760
Current liabilities	117,678		101,993
Long-term lease liabilities	7,005		6,361
Shareholders' equity	176,894		126,002
Cash from oper. activs	**37,013**	**+81**	**20,447**
Cash from fin. activs	(22,303)		(4,257)
Cash from invest. activs	(12,674)		(10,914)
Net cash position	**28,126**	**+35**	**20,905**
Capital expenditures	(8,646)		(5,051)
	$		$
Earnings per share*	3.79		1.29
Cash flow per share*	3.13		1.74
Cash divd. per share*	0.39		0.34
	shs		shs
No. of shs. o/s*	11,834,924		11,789,924
Avg. no. of shs. o/s*	11,833,674		11,778,674
	%		%
Net profit margin	8.03		3.99
Return on equity	29.60		12.65
Return on assets	62.29		22.28
Foreign sales percent	67		66
No. of employees (FTEs)	1,530		1,400

* Class A & B
[A] Reported in accordance with IFRS

Historical Summary
(as originally stated)

Fiscal Year	Oper. Rev. $000s	Net Inc. Bef. Disc. $000s	EPS* $
2022[A]	558,464	44,828	3.79
2021[A]	380,202	15,176	1.29
2020[A]	322,097	14,062	1.20
2019[A]	358,782	13,306	1.13
2018[A]	314,082	8,105	0.69

* Class A & B
[A] Reported in accordance with IFRS

H.18 Hampton Financial Corporation

Symbol - HFC **Exchange** - TSX-VEN **CUSIP** - 40915Q
Head Office - 1800-141 Adelaide St W, Toronto, ON, M5H 3L5 **Telephone** - (416) 862-8651 **Toll-free** - (877) 225-0229 **Fax** - (416) 862-8650
Website - www.hamptonsecurities.com
Email - pdeeb@hamptonsecurities.com
Investor Relations - Peter M. Deeb (416) 862-8651
Auditors - MNP LLP C.A., Burlington, Ont.
Lawyers - Torkin Manes LLP, Toronto, Ont.
Transfer Agents - Computershare Trust Company of Canada Inc., Toronto, Ont.

Profile - (Ont. 2014) Indirect wholly owned **Hampton Securities Limited** (HSL) offers wealth management and capital markets services.

HSL is a Canadian boutique investment dealer delivering wealth management and capital market services. HSL also engages in proprietary trading activities for its own account. At Aug. 31, 2022, HSL's private client group had $747,744,000 in assets under administration.

Predecessor Detail - Name changed from Dominion General Investment Corporation, July 29, 2016, pursuant to Qualifying Transaction reverse takeover acquisition of Hampton Equity Partners Limited.

Directors - Peter M. Deeb, exec. chr. & CEO, Toronto, Ont.; William E. (Bill) Thomson†, Toronto, Ont.; Michael D. Harris, East York, Ont.; Ralph E. Lean, Toronto, Ont.; Daniel Mathieson, Stratford, Ont.; John H. Sununu, Hampton Falls, N.H.

Other Exec. Officers - Olga Juravlev, acting CFO

† Lead director

Capital Stock

	Authorized (shs.)	Outstanding (shs.)[1]
Class A Preferred	unlimited	nil
Multiple Voting	unlimited	15,149,845
Subordinate Voting	unlimited	15,410,370

[1] At Jan. 30, 2023

Multiple Voting - Convertible into subordinate voting shares on a one-for-one basis. Twenty votes per share.

Subordinate Voting - One vote per share.

Class A Preferred (old) - Were entitled to fixed annual dividends of 80¢ per share payable quarterly. Redeemed on Sept. 30, 2022. Was classified as long-term debt.

Major Shareholder - Peter M. Deeb held 95.93% interest at Jan. 19, 2023.

Price Range - HFC/TSX-VEN

Year	Volume	High	Low	Close
2022	1,212,674	$0.73	$0.42	$0.72
2021	2,341,283	$0.60	$0.13	$0.50
2020	214,300	$0.20	$0.05	$0.14
2019	1,113,620	$0.30	$0.10	$0.12
2018	1,369,500	$0.47	$0.27	$0.30

Recent Close: $0.56

Capital Stock Changes - On Sept. 20, 2022, all 243,695 class A preferred shares were redeemed at $10 per share.

There were no changes to capital stock during fiscal 2022.

Dividends

HFC sub vtg S.V. Ra $0.02 pa Q
$0.02◆ Jan. 14/23 $0.02◆i Jan. 14/22
Paid in 2023: $0.02◆ 2022: $0.02◆i 2021: n.a.

pfd cl A cum. Ra $0.80 pa Q[1]
Delisted Oct 3/22.
$0.06f Sept. 30/22
[1] Redeemed Sept. 30, 2022 at $10 per sh.
◆ Special f Final Payment i Initial Payment

Wholly Owned Subsidiaries

Hampton Equity Partners Limited, Toronto, Ont.
- 100% int. in **Hampton Securities Incorporated**, Ont.
  - 100% int. in **Hampton Insurance Brokers Inc.**, Ont.
  - 100% int. in **Hampton Realty Partners Limited** Inactive.
  - 100% int. in **Hampton Securities (Asia) Limited** Inactive.
  - 100% int. in **Hampton Securities Corporation** Inactive.
  - 100% int. in **Hampton Securities Limited**, Ont.
  - 100% int. in **Hampton Securities (USA), Inc.** Inactive.

Financial Statistics

Periods ended:	12m Aug. 31/22[A]		12m Aug. 31/21[A]
	$000s	%Chg	$000s
Operating revenue	**15,478**	**+4**	**14,814**
General & admin expense	14,630		13,007
Stock-based compensation	11		297
Operating expense	**14,641**	**+10**	**13,304**
Operating income	**837**	**-45**	**1,510**
Deprec., depl. & amort.	152		152
Finance costs, gross	1,110		1,082
Investment income	1,711		1,017
Pre-tax income	**1,733**	**+34**	**1,293**
Net income	**1,733**	**+34**	**1,293**
Cash & equivalent	9,001		3,430
Accounts receivable	2,022		252
Current assets	12,091		12,851
Right-of-use assets	1,396		1,548
Total assets	**17,828**	**+2**	**17,519**
Bank indebtedness	3,254		2,020
Accts. pay. & accr. liabs	2,453		1,853
Current liabilities	10,139		11,924
Long-term debt, gross	8,877		5,443
Long-term debt, net	6,440		5,443
Long-term lease liabilities	1,675		1,805
Shareholders' equity	(426)		(1,653)
Cash from oper. activs	**4,053**	**n.a.**	**(788)**
Cash from fin. activs	1,705		693
Cash from invest. activs	(3,776)		2,057
Net cash position	**4,182**	**+89**	**2,207**
	$		$
Earnings per share*	0.06		0.04
Cash flow per share*	0.13		(0.03)
	shs		shs
No. of shs. o/s*	30,560,215		30,560,215
Avg. no. of shs. o/s*	30,560,215		30,958,845
	%		%
Net profit margin	11.20		8.73
Return on equity	n.m.		n.m.
Return on assets	16.09		16.66

* M.V. & S.V.
[A] Reported in accordance with IFRS

Latest Results

Periods ended:	3m Nov. 30/22[A]		3m Nov. 30/21[A]
	$000s	%Chg	$000s
Operating revenue	1,438	-73	5,387
Net income	(588)	n.a.	1,034
	$		$
Earnings per share*	(0.02)		0.03

* M.V. & S.V.
[A] Reported in accordance with IFRS

Historical Summary
(as originally stated)

Fiscal Year	Oper. Rev.	Net Inc. Bef. Disc.	EPS*
	$000s	$000s	$
2022[A]	15,478	1,733	0.06
2021[A]	14,814	1,293	0.04
2020[A]	8,209	(2,632)	(0.09)
2019[A]	10,766	(1,373)	(0.05)
2018[A]	12,097	(1,967)	(0.07)

* M.V. & S.V.
[A] Reported in accordance with IFRS

H.19 Hank Payments Corp.

Symbol - HANK **Exchange** - TSX-VEN **CUSIP** - 41043X

Head Office - 4100-66 Wellington St W, Toronto, ON, M5K 1B7 **Telephone** - (416) 706-2312 **Toll-free** - (833) 426-5729

Website - hankpayments.com

Email - jewart@hankpayments.com

Investor Relations - Jason G. Ewart (833) 426-5729

Auditors - McGovern Hurley LLP C.A., Toronto, Ont.

Lawyers - WeirFoulds LLP, Toronto, Ont.

Transfer Agents - Computershare Trust Company of Canada Inc., Toronto, Ont.

Profile - (Can. 2015) Offers a fintech software-as-a-service (SaaS) platform used solely by Americans to automatically manage their cash flow and align debits with credits.

Principal product is a loan and payment curation product, in which its technology debits cash when consumers have cash, stores it on a bank balance sheet (Federal Deposit Insurance Corporation (FDIC) approved and insured) and then remits the payment on the due dates to lenders/payees on behalf of consumers. Users pay a sign-up fee, a fee per debited payment (cash in) from their bank accounts and a fee for each incremental monthly payment made (cash out), using the platform. A monthly subscription or licensing fees are being introduced which would be based on the number of monthly transactions and other features subscribed by the user. Users are acquired through various channels including small-to-medium sized enterprises and larger enterprise businesses. The company has more than 42,000 active users.

In October 2022, continuation into Ontario from the Canada Business Corporation Act was proposed.

In March 2022, the company entered into a letter of intent to acquire a United States-based mortgage payment platform provider (target). The target has been curating mortgage payments in the Midwest through a network of more than 1,500 mortgage brokers, and the company has been processing payments for the target for more than a year. Terms of the transaction are expected to include issuance of US$624,000 of common shares at a price per share equal or greater than Cdn$0.15 per share or the company's stock price the day prior to closing, and issuance of 8% US$624,000 convertible notes due in four years.

Predecessor Detail - Name changed from Nobelium Tech Corp., Oct. 13, 2021, pursuant to the Qualifying Transaction reverse takeover acquisition of (old) Hank Payments Corp.; basis 1 new for 4 old shs.

Directors - Michael Hilmer, chr. & CEO, Toronto, Ont.; Jason G. Ewart, exec. v-p, capital markets, Cobourg, Ont.; Jennifer Fallon, Boston, Mass.; Timothy Farley, Ketchum, Idaho

Other Exec. Officers - Ashish Kapoor, CFO & corp. sec.; John Cerny, chief compliance officer; Matthew Mitchell, chief digital & mktg. officer; Megan Howell, sr. v-p, consumer engagement & automotive channels; Jim Bottrel, v-p, tech. & opers.; Patrick Ferguson, v-p, tech.

Capital Stock

	Authorized (shs.)	Outstanding (shs.)[1]
Common	unlimited	73,048,651

[1] At Oct. 14, 2022

Major Shareholder - Uptempo Inc. held 31.2% interest at Oct. 14, 2022.

Price Range - HANK/TSX-VEN

Year	Volume	High	Low	Close
2022	12,338,792	$0.30	$0.03	$0.04
2021	3,565,054	$1.34	$0.28	$0.28
2018	16,750	$0.36	$0.26	$0.34

Consolidation: 1-for-4 cons. in Oct. 2021

Recent Close: $0.06

Capital Stock Changes - Effective Oct. 13, 2021, common shares were consolidated on a 1-for-4 basis (effective on the TSX Venture Exchange on Oct. 20, 2021), 66,598,793 post-consolidated common shares ware issued pursuant to the Qualifying Transaction reverse takeover acquisition of (old) Hank Payments Corp. and 1,298,900 post-consolidated common shares were issued as finder's fee. Also during fiscal 2022, post-consolidated common shares were issued as follows: 766,583 under restricted share unit plan and 262,500 on exercise of options.

Wholly Owned Subsidiaries

Hank Payments Corp., Orlando, Fla.

Financial Statistics

Periods ended:	12m June 30/22[A]		12m June 30/21[◻A]
	$000s	%Chg	$000s
Operating revenue	**5,343**	**+22**	**4,369**
Cost of sales	591		669
Salaries & benefits	5,386		2,606
General & admin expense	5,077		1,992
Stock-based compensation	5,429		677
Operating expense	**16,483**	**+177**	**5,943**
Operating income	**(11,140)**	**n.a.**	**(1,574)**
Deprec., depl. & amort.	413		151
Finance costs, gross	42		162
Write-downs/write-offs	(255)		(170)
Pre-tax income	**(11,433)**	**n.a.**	**(2,055)**
Net income	**(11,433)**	**n.a.**	**(2,055)**
Cash & equivalent	803		311
Accounts receivable	1,027		1,119
Current assets	2,255		1,710
Intangibles, net	344		386
Total assets	**3,782**	**+54**	**2,449**
Accts. pay. & accr. liabs	2,819		1,111
Current liabilities	4,305		3,169
Long-term debt, gross	653		235
Long-term debt, net	634		nil
Shareholders' equity	(4,134)		(3,525)
Cash from oper. activs	**(1,439)**	**n.a.**	**(904)**
Cash from fin. activs	2,935		530
Cash from invest. activs	(854)		nil
Net cash position	**803**	**+158**	**311**
	$		$
Earnings per share*	(0.17)		(0.03)
Cash flow per share*	(0.02)		(0.01)
	shs		shs
No. of shs. o/s*	71,048,651		n.a.
Avg. no. of shs. o/s*	68,054,358		60,435,449
	%		%
Net profit margin	(213.98)		(47.04)
Return on equity	n.m.		n.m.
Return on assets	(365.67)		(89.12)
Foreign sales percent	100		100

* Common
◻ Restated
[A] Reported in accordance with IFRS

Historical Summary
(as originally stated)

Fiscal Year	Oper. Rev.	Net Inc. Bef. Disc.	EPS*
	$000s	$000s	$
2022[A]	5,343	(11,433)	(0.17)
	US$000s	US$000s	US$
2021[A]	3,407	(1,625)	(0.03)
2020[A1]	2,511	(1,626)	(0.03)
2019[A1]	2,185	(2,507)	(0.04)

* Common
[A] Reported in accordance with IFRS
[1] Results pertain to (old) Hank Payments Corp. (formerly The Card Collaborative International Corp.).

Note: Adjusted throughout for 1-for-4 cons. in Oct. 2021

H.20 Hansco Capital Corp.

Symbol - HCO.P **Exchange** - TSX-VEN **CUSIP** - 41130L

Head Office - 600-890 Pender St W, Vancouver, BC, V6C 1K4 **Telephone** - (604) 721-2650 **Fax** - (604) 357-1030

Email - aris@morfopoulos.com

Investor Relations - Aris Morfopoulos (604) 721-2650

Auditors - SHIM & Associates LLP C.A., Vancouver, B.C.

Lawyers - Beadle Raven LLP, Vancouver, B.C.

Transfer Agents - Computershare Trust Company of Canada Inc., Vancouver, B.C.

Profile - (B.C. 2019) Capital Pool Company.

In January 2023, the company terminated its July 2021 agreement to acquire **Aurex Energy Corp.**'s wholly owned **Desert Strike Resources (US) Inc.**, which holds 70% interest in Cook gold prospect in Humboldt cty., Nev., for issuance of 14,000,000 common shares at 15¢ per share, totaling $2,100,000. The acquisition would have constituted the company's Qualifying Transaction.

Directors - Robert J. Quinn, pres. & CEO, Kingwood, Tex.; Aris Morfopoulos, CFO & corp. sec., Vancouver, B.C.; Bob Hans, Surrey, B.C.; Raymond (Ray) Marks, Mission, B.C.

Capital Stock

	Authorized (shs.)	Outstanding (shs.)[1]
Common	unlimited	6,300,000

[1] At Dec. 31, 2022

Major Shareholder - Bob Hans held 44.17% interest at Feb. 1, 2022.

Price Range - HCO.P/TSX-VEN

Year	Volume	High	Low	Close
2021	143,950	$0.20	$0.16	$0.18
2020	497,300	$0.23	$0.13	$0.19

Recent Close: $0.04

H.21 Hapbee Technologies, Inc.

Symbol - HAPB **Exchange** - TSX-VEN **CUSIP** - 41136M
Head Office - c/o Baron Global Financial Canada Ltd., 2250-1055 Hastings St W, Vancouver, BC, V6E 2E9 **Telephone** - (604) 688-9588
Website - www.hapbee.com
Email - invest@hapbee.com
Investor Relations - Yona Shtern (604) 688-9588
Auditors - Olayinka Oyebola & Co. C.A., Lagos, Nigeria
Transfer Agents - Computershare Trust Company of Canada Inc.
Profile - (B.C. 2019) Develops and commercializes wearable wellness products that enhance the human experience through ultra-low radio frequency energy (uIRFE) technology.

Core product is Hapbee®, a wearable band that "plays" or delivers unique magnetic signals, which produce sensations. These sensations fall under categories including: happy, alert, boost, focus, relax, calm and sleepy. The product, which is available through Hapbee.com., can be controlled through the Hapbee App with both iOS and Android smartphones.

Also has exclusive global licences to adapt the uIRFE technology for other consumer products that are in development including Sleepee BedTopper, Sleepbee Mask and Hapbee Sleep & Relief Pillow.

Common reinstated on TSX-VEN, Dec. 19, 2022.

Common suspended from TSX-VEN, Dec. 6, 2022.

Predecessor Detail - Name changed from Elevation Technologies, Inc., May 7, 2020.

Directors - Yona Shtern, chr., pres. & CEO, Qué.; Robert (Rob) Dzisiak, Winnipeg, Man.; Michael Matysik, Wash.; Charles McNerney, Calif.; Chris Rivera, Wash.; Mark Timm, Ind.

Other Exec. Officers - Mitch Kujavsky, CFO; Eric Brassard, chief revenue officer; Yannick Desjardins, chief tech. officer; Dr. Brian Mogen, chief scientific officer; David Hoppenheim, v-p, cust. srvc. & fulfillment; Pat Murray, v-p, product devel.; Iggy Rodriguez, v-p, bus. devel. & partnerships; Ken Adessky, corp. sec.

Capital Stock

	Authorized (shs.)	Outstanding (shs.)[1]
Subordinate Vtg.	unlimited	74,418,850
Mulitiple Vtg.	unlimited	450,000

[1] At May 27, 2022

Subordinate Voting - One vote per share.

Multiple Voting - Convertible into subordinate voting shares on a 100-for-1 basis. 100 votes per share.

Major Shareholder - EMulate Therapeutics, Inc. held 30.07% interest and Scott Donnell held 18.04% interest at Aug. 5, 2021.

Price Range - HAPB/TSX-VEN

Year	Volume	High	Low	Close
2022	10,632,957	$0.33	$0.04	$0.05
2021	20,185,179	$1.30	$0.25	$0.30
2020	7,594,072	$0.87	$0.50	$0.67

Recent Close: $0.07

Capital Stock Changes - In January 2022, private placement of 5,307,894 units (1 subordinate voting share & 1 warrant) at Cdn$0.30 per unit was completed, with warrants exercisable at Cdn$0.50 per share for three years.

Wholly Owned Subsidiaries

Hapbee Technologies USA, Inc., Wash.
1253596 B.C. Ltd., B.C.

Financial Statistics

Periods ended:	12m Dec. 31/21[A]		12m Dec. 31/20[□A]
	US$000s	%Chg	US$000s
Operating revenue	**1,729**	**+161**	**662**
Cost of goods sold	1,249		517
Salaries & benefits	255		nil
Research & devel. expense	267		389
General & admin expense	5,800		2,462
Stock-based compensation	3,081		2,513
Operating expense	**10,651**	**+81**	**5,880**
Operating income	**(8,922)**	**n.a.**	**(5,218)**
Deprec., depl. & amort.	212		135
Finance costs, gross	nil		169
Pre-tax income	**(6,732)**	**n.a.**	**(10,336)**
Net income	**(6,732)**	**n.a.**	**(10,336)**
Cash & equivalent	3,630		3,415
Inventories	284		30
Accounts receivable	92		92
Current assets	4,006		3,765
Intangibles, net	2,283		2,475
Total assets	**6,289**	**+1**	**6,240**
Accts. pay. & accr. liabs	946		607
Current liabilities	1,578		795
Shareholders' equity	1,608		2,209
Cash from oper. activs	**(5,074)**	**n.a.**	**(2,121)**
Cash from fin. activs	5,264		5,167
Cash from invest. activs	(20)		(1,012)
Net cash position	**3,630**	**+6**	**3,415**
	US$		US$
Earnings per share*	(0.13)		(0.23)
Cash flow per share*	(0.10)		(0.05)
	shs		shs
No. of shs. o/s*	69,040,956		47,388,056
Avg. no. of shs. o/s*	50,722,011		45,356,219
	%		%
Net profit margin	(389.36)		n.m.
Return on equity	(352.74)		(441.43)
Return on assets	(107.46)		(214.63)

* Subord. Vtg.
□ Restated
[A] Reported in accordance with IFRS

Latest Results

Periods ended:	3m Mar. 31/22[A]		3m Mar. 31/21[A]
	US$000s	%Chg	US$000s
Operating revenue	360	+49	241
Net income	(2,250)	n.a.	(1,707)
	US$		US$
Earnings per share*	(0.05)		(0.04)

* Subord. Vtg.
[A] Reported in accordance with IFRS

Historical Summary
(as originally stated)

Fiscal Year	Oper. Rev.	Net Inc. Bef. Disc.	EPS*
	US$000s	US$000s	US$
2021[A]	1,729	(6,732)	(0.13)
2020[A]	662	(10,336)	(0.23)
2019[A]	nil	(402)	(0.01)

* Subord. Vtg.
[A] Reported in accordance with IFRS

H.22 Happy Belly Food Group Inc.

Symbol - HBFG **Exchange** - CSE **CUSIP** - 41138T
Head Office - 400-1681 Chestnut St, Vancouver, BC, V6J 4M6 **Toll-free** - (833) 375-2682 **Fax** - (604) 737-1140
Website - happybellyfg.com
Email - shawn@happybellyfg.com
Investor Relations - Shawn Moniz (833) 375-2682
Auditors - Buchanan Barry LLP C.A., Calgary, Alta.
Transfer Agents - Computershare Trust Company of Canada Inc., Vancouver, B.C.
Profile - (B.C. 2017; orig. Can., 2014) Acquires food brands and businesses focusing on quick service restaurants and consumer packaged goods sectors in North America.

Operates two segments: Quick Service Restaurant and Consumer Product Goods.

Quick Service Restaurant (QSR) - This segment includes 50% interest in **Heal Lifestyle Inc.**, which owns and operates Heal Wellness, a plant-based QSR offering a wide variety of smoothie bowls, smoothies, waffles, tea and coffee; Lettuce Love Café franchise, which specialize in gluten free and plant-based meals; and Yamchops, which engages in the preparation, distribution and retail sale of protein alternatives, prepared foods, meals and specialty food products through its plant-based butcher shop, marketplace and its QSR.

Consumer Product Goods - This segment includes Holy Crap, which manufactures and distributes a line of high-fibre, super-seed cereals and oatmeal; and LumberHeads, which manufactures and distributes plant-based kettle corn snacks that are peanut and nut free, gluten free, dairy free and allergen free.

Through 50% interest in a joint venture company, holds the franchising rights of PIRHO Fresh Greek Grill Restaurants, a gourmet bowls, wraps and pitas fast casual Greek restaurant.

On May 19, 2023, the company closed a franchise acquisition agreement that resulted in the formation of a joint venture company (JV) that would hold the franchising rights of PIRHO Fresh Greek Grill Restaurants, a gourmet bowls, wraps and pitas fast casual Greek restaurant founded by George Plagakis. The company would hold 50% interest in the JV in exchange for issuance of 1,666,666 common shares valued at $250,000, the remaining 50% would be owned by George Plagakis, who has contributed **PIRHO Grill Franchising Inc.** to the JV. PIRHO Grill Franchising operates all the franchisee activities such as collection of franchisee royalties and franchising fees, as well as global franchising rights, brand assets, intellectual property and brand trademarks. The company has the right to acquire the remaining 50% interest in the JV.

In April 2023, the company entered into a letter of intent to acquire 50% interest in Ontario-based KOA Natural Foods, a hand-crafted snack manufacturer, for $1,750,000 including issuance of $500,000 of common shares payable after closing of the transaction. The company is also providing KOA with a purchase order (PO) financing credit facility, as well as a capital investment into KOA upon closing in the form of new equipment for expanded facility needs. The company has the exclusive right to acquire the remaining 50% interest in KOA.

In December 2022, the company entered into a letter of intent to form a joint venture company (JV) that would operate Lady Glaze, a gourmet doughnut and dessert business based in Kitchener, Ont., with five existing locations in Ontario and a 3,000-sq.-ft. manufacturing facility. The company would earn 50% interest in the JV through an agreed earn-out consideration. The company would also provide a $250,000 line of credit to the JV. Lady Glaze would own the remaining 50% in exchange for providing the business operation, five locations, production facility and business assets of Lady Glaze to the JV. The company has the right to acquire the remaining 50% interest in the JV.

On Oct. 11, 2022, the company acquired all of the assets and property of **2563434 Ontario Inc.** (Lettuce Love), which operates the Lettuce Love Café franchise, specializing in gluten free and plant-based meals, in exchange for the assumption of $168,000 financial liabilities of Lettuce Love. The acquisition includes Lettuce Love location in Burlington, Ont.; the Oakville location has been removed from the acquisition.

In June 2022, the company, through 50%-owned **Heal Lifestyle Inc.**, opened another Heal Wellness restaurant in Toronto, Ont., that is co-branded with a YamChops quick service restaurant.

On May 9, 2022, 50%-owned **1000193142 Ontario Inc.** (JVCo) acquired private Ontario-based **Heal Lifestyle Inc.** for issuance of 200 JVCo common shares. In connection, the company subscribed for 200 JVCo common shares in exchange for 2,777,777 common shares of the company at 9¢ per share, and JVCo issued a $163,269 non-interest-bearing promissory note to the company, representing the debt and accrued interest of Heal Lifestyle as at closing. Heal Lifestyle operates three Heal Wellness plant-based quick service restaurants in southern Ontario. The remaining 50% interest in JVCo is owned by shareholders of Heal Lifestyle.

In April 2022, the company launched an oatmeal product line under the Holy Crap brand. The oat meal are 100% vegan, gluten free, high in fibre and Kosher certified, and are made with non-GMO (genetically modified organism) ingredients

Predecessor Detail - Name changed from Plant&Co. Brands Ltd., Sept. 1, 2022.

Directors - Alex Rechichi, chr., Ont.; Shawn Moniz, CEO & corp. sec., Toronto, Ont.; Sean Black, chief invest. officer; Kevin Cole, Ont.; Marco Contardi, Toronto, Ont.; Mark Rechichi, Ont.

Other Exec. Officers - Dean Callaway, CFO

Capital Stock

	Authorized (shs.)	Outstanding (shs.)[1]
Common	unlimited	107,207,198

[1] At Mar. 31, 2023

Major Shareholder - Widely held at Nov. 4, 2022.

Price Range - HBFG/CSE

Year	Volume	High	Low	Close
2022	33,650,474	$0.21	$0.07	$0.10
2021	108,781,990	$1.04	$0.16	$0.18
2020	22,191,247	$0.94	$0.15	$0.53
2019	7,693,949	$2.00	$0.05	$0.45
2018	7,487,075	$2.50	$0.59	$0.76

Consolidation: 1-for-10 cons. in July 2020; 4-for-1 split in Aug. 2019
Recent Close: $0.16

Capital Stock Changes - In May 2022, 2,777,777 common shares were issued pursuant to the acquisition of 200 common shares of 1000193142 Ontario Inc. Also during 2022, 272,000 common shares were issued on exercise of warrants.

Wholly Owned Subsidiaries

Holy Crap Foods Inc., B.C.
JBD Innovations Inc., Ont.
1000317391 Ontario Inc., Ont.
Plant & Company Brands Group Inc., B.C.
2574578 Ontario Inc., Ont.

Subsidiaries

51% int. in **1000061911 Ontario Inc.**, Ont.

Investments

50% int. in **Heal Lifestyle Inc.**, Ont.
50% int. in **1000193142 Ontario Inc.**, Ont.

Financial Statistics

Periods ended:	12m Dec. 31/22^A		12m Dec. 31/21^A
	$000s	%Chg	$000s
Operating revenue	**2,734**	**+119**	**1,249**
Cost of sales	1,528		597
Salaries & benefits	843		414
General & admin expense	1,834		4,478
Stock-based compensation	5		6,540
Operating expense	**4,210**	**-65**	**12,028**
Operating income	**(1,476)**	**n.a.**	**(10,779)**
Deprec., depl. & amort.	538		531
Finance costs, gross	267		47
Write-downs/write-offs	(495)		(15,316)
Pre-tax income	**(2,743)**	**n.a.**	**(26,577)**
Net income	**(2,743)**	**n.a.**	**(26,577)**
Cash & equivalent	1,102		936
Inventories	269		141
Accounts receivable	357		100
Current assets	1,849		1,328
Fixed assets, net	1,251		551
Intangibles, net	1,098		1,789
Total assets	**4,283**	**+17**	**3,668**
Accts. pay. & accr. liabs	515		246
Current liabilities	955		315
Long-term debt, gross	2,145		91
Long-term debt, net	1,947		91
Long-term lease liabilities	595		188
Equity portion of conv. debs	266		nil
Shareholders' equity	716		3,051
Non-controlling interest	70		24
Cash from oper. activs	**(1,618)**	**n.a.**	**(4,177)**
Cash from fin. activs	1,815		1,641
Cash from invest. activs	(31)		(665)
Net cash position	**1,102**	**+18**	**936**
Capital expenditures	(107)		(4)
Capital disposals	6		nil
	$		$
Earnings per share*	(0.03)		(0.27)
Cash flow per share*	(0.02)		(0.04)
	shs		shs
No. of shs. o/s*	107,207,198		104,157,421
Avg. no. of shs. o/s*	105,999,554		98,839,936
	%		%
Net profit margin	(100.33)		n.m.
Return on equity	(145.63)		(704.68)
Return on assets	(62.28)		(592.25)

* Common
^A Reported in accordance with IFRS

Latest Results

Periods ended:	3m Mar. 31/23^A		3m Mar. 31/22^A
	$000s	%Chg	$000s
Operating revenue	1,039	+220	325
Net income	(474)	n.a.	(415)
	$		$
Earnings per share*	(0.00)		(0.00)

* Common
^A Reported in accordance with IFRS

Historical Summary
(as originally stated)

Fiscal Year	Oper. Rev.	Net Inc. Bef. Disc.	EPS*
	$000s	$000s	$
2022^A	2,734	(2,743)	(0.03)
2021^A	1,249	(26,577)	(0.27)
2020^A	102	(4,380)	(0.11)
2019^A	87	(6,983)	(0.30)
2018^A	131	(4,738)	(0.30)

* Common
^A Reported in accordance with IFRS

Note: Adjusted throughout for 1-for-10 cons. in July 2020; 4-for-1 split in Aug. 2019

H.23 Harmony Acquisitions Corp.

Symbol - MONY.P **Exchange** - TSX-VEN **CUSIP** - 413181
Head Office - Five Bentall Centre, 2300-550 Burrard St, Vancouver, BC, V6C 2B5
Email - jklam@klamcolaw.com
Investor Relations - Jeffrey D. Klam (416) 317-7553
Auditors - Zeifmans LLP C.A., Toronto, Ont.
Lawyers - Caravel Law Professional Corporation, Toronto, Ont.
Transfer Agents - Odyssey Trust Company, Vancouver, B.C.
Profile - (B.C. 2021) Capital Pool Company.
Directors - Raymond D. Harari, CEO, Panama City, Panama; Mark Goldhar, CFO, Hubley, N.S.; Jeffrey D. Klam, corp. sec., Toronto, Ont.; Darren G. Collins, Alliston, Ont.; Jillian Monaghan, Panama City, Panama; Colin Moore, Vancouver, B.C.

Capital Stock

	Authorized (shs.)	Outstanding (shs.)[1]
Common	unlimited	6,201,301

[1] At Dec. 24, 2021

Major Shareholder - Widely held at Dec. 24, 2021.

Price Range - MONY.P/TSX-VEN

Year	Volume	High	Low	Close
2022	481,017	$0.12	$0.03	$0.03
2021	22,000	$0.12	$0.11	$0.12

Recent Close: $0.04

Capital Stock Changes - On Dec. 24, 2021, an initial public offering of 2,001,300 common shares was completed at 10¢ per share.

H.24 Harrys Manufacturing Inc.

Symbol - HARY **Exchange** - CSE **CUSIP** - 415865
Head Office - 1070-1055 Hastings St W, Vancouver, BC, V6E 2E9 **Telephone** - (604) 565-5100 **Fax** - (604) 909-2679
Website - www.harrysmfg.com
Email - ir@harrysmfg.com
Investor Relations - Corporate Communications (604) 565-5100
Auditors - Dale Matheson Carr-Hilton LaBonte LLP C.A., Vancouver, B.C.
Transfer Agents - Olympia Trust Company, Vancouver, B.C.
Profile - (B.C. 2007) Distributes value-priced tobacco cigarettes without additives to retailers in Canada.

Holds approved tobacco wholesale licences in British Columbia, Alberta, Saskatchewan, Manitoba, Ontario, and Newfoundland and Labrador. Operates under manufacturing, distribution and marketing agreements with **Altabac Inc.**, a cigarette manufacturer with operations in Ontario, and **Abenaki Enterprise**, a cigarette manufacturer with operations near Odanak, Que., whereby the company sources purchasers for tobacco products produced by the licensors in exchange for a portion of the revenues generated from sales. Has a 5,000-sq.-ft. distribution facility in Abbotsford, B.C.

Predecessor Detail - Name changed from Westridge Resources Inc., Oct. 4, 2018, pursuant to the acquisition of Harrys International Manufacturing Inc.
Directors - Ken Storey, v-p, sales & mktg., Kelowna, B.C.; Byron Striloff, corp. sec.
Other Exec. Officers - Nicolas (Nick) Brusatore, pres., CEO & interim CFO

Capital Stock

	Authorized (shs.)	Outstanding (shs.)[1]
Preferred	unlimited	nil
Common	unlimited	95,336,126

[1] At June 29, 2023

Major Shareholder - Widely held at Oct. 25, 2022.

Price Range - HARY/CSE

Year	Volume	High	Low	Close
2022	11,615,476	$0.12	$0.04	$0.06
2021	30,852,725	$0.20	$0.06	$0.08
2020	40,771,477	$0.32	$0.07	$0.14
2019	44,987,955	$0.24	$0.05	$0.19
2018	13,855,995	$0.79	$0.11	$0.12

Recent Close: $0.04

Capital Stock Changes - During fiscal 2022, common shares were issued as follows: 3,759,917 by private placement and 2,163,400 on conversion of debt.

Wholly Owned Subsidiaries

Harrys International Manufacturing Inc., Chilliwack, B.C.

Financial Statistics

Periods ended:	12m July 31/22^A		12m July 31/21^A
	$000s	%Chg	$000s
General & admin expense	667		582
Stock-based compensation	164		311
Operating expense	**831**	**-7**	**893**
Operating income	**(831)**	**n.a.**	**(893)**
Deprec., depl. & amort.	24		41
Finance costs, gross	109		66
Write-downs/write-offs	(240)		(200)
Pre-tax income	**(1,256)**	**n.a.**	**(1,200)**
Net income	**(1,256)**	**n.a.**	**(1,200)**
Cash & equivalent	9		364
Accounts receivable	8		9
Current assets	285		702
Fixed assets, net	4		105
Right-of-use assets	nil		238
Total assets	**289**	**-72**	**1,046**
Bank indebtedness	nil		186
Accts. pay. & accr. liabs	239		39
Current liabilities	397		289
Long-term debt, gross	105		164
Long-term debt, net	nil		164
Long-term lease liabilities	nil		253
Shareholders' equity	(107)		340
Cash from oper. activs	**(444)**	**n.a.**	**(884)**
Cash from fin. activs	289		1,211
Cash from invest. activs	(200)		(203)
Net cash position	**9**	**-98**	**364**
Capital expenditures	nil		(3)
	$		$
Earnings per share*	(0.01)		(0.01)
Cash flow per share*	(0.01)		(0.01)
	shs		shs
No. of shs. o/s*	90,770,007		84,846,690
Avg. no. of shs. o/s*	87,751,000		81,346,921
	%		%
Net profit margin	n.a.		n.a.
Return on equity	n.m.		(376.18)
Return on assets	(171.84)		(133.25)

* Common
^A Reported in accordance with IFRS

Latest Results

Periods ended:	3m Oct. 31/22^A		3m Oct. 31/21^A
	$000s	%Chg	$000s
Net income	(167)	n.a.	(202)
	$		$
Earnings per share*	(0.00)		(0.00)

* Common
^A Reported in accordance with IFRS

Historical Summary
(as originally stated)

Fiscal Year	Oper. Rev.	Net Inc. Bef. Disc.	EPS*
	$000s	$000s	$
2022^A	nil	(1,256)	(0.01)
2021^A	nil	(1,200)	(0.01)
2020^A	nil	(1,684)	(0.02)
2019^A	8	(14,073)	(0.19)
2018^A	nil	(665)	(0.02)

* Common
^A Reported in accordance with IFRS

H.25 The Hash Corporation

Symbol - REZN **Exchange** - CSE **CUSIP** - 41809C
Head Office - 801-1 Adelaide St E, Toronto, ON, M5C 2V9 **Telephone** - (647) 948-6966 **Toll-free** - (833) 420-7396
Website - thehashcorporation.com
Email - chris@hashco.ca
Investor Relations - Christopher Savoie (833) 420-7396
Auditors - Zeifmans LLP C.A., Toronto, Ont.
Transfer Agents - Capital Transfer Agency Inc., Toronto, Ont.
Profile - (Ont. 1967) Produces and sells cannabis-based hashish and other cannabis concentrates in Canada.

Products include Gold Seal Hash and Cold Tumbled Resin, as well as Fritz's HashCo Hash Rosin Gummies, a co-branded product with private Toronto-based **Fritz's Cannabis Company**.

The company does not have a Standard Processing License under the Cannabis Act. Instead, it holds a five-year collaboration agreement (effective Apr. 20, 2020) with private Toronto-based **Medz Cannabis Incorporated**, which provides the company with licensed processing space at Medz's licensed facility for the purposes of manufacturing, packing and selling products. The company will pay Medz a 3.5% royalty on all revenues generated from sale of the products produced in the Medz facility, and a 5% royalty on any tolling or service revenue earned by the company on certain service contracts.

Predecessor Detail - Name changed from Sententernet Phi Gamma Inc., July 8, 2019; basis 1 new for 20 old shs.

Directors - Christopher (Chris) Savoie, CEO, Toronto, Ont.; Donal V. Carroll, CFO & corp. sec., Etobicoke, Ont.; Tabitha Fritz, Toronto, Ont.; Thomas (Tom) Keevil, Toronto, Ont.; Binyomin Posen, Toronto, Ont.
Other Exec. Officers - Tyler Metford, COO

Capital Stock

	Authorized (shs.)	Outstanding (shs.)[1]
Common	unlimited	280,120,290

[1] At Aug. 29, 2022

Major Shareholder - Widely held at June 3, 2021.

Price Range - REZN/CSE

Year	Volume	High	Low	Close
2022	31,556,395	$0.02	$0.01	$0.01
2021	46,391,535	$0.10	$0.01	$0.02

Recent Close: $0.01

Financial Statistics

Periods ended:	12m Dec. 31/21[A]		12m Dec. 31/20[A]
	$000s	%Chg	$000s
Operating revenue	**892**	**n.a.**	**nil**
Cost of goods sold	618		nil
Salaries & benefits	880		546
General & admin expense	2,423		288
Stock-based compensation	1,497		1,168
Operating expense	**5,419**	**+171**	**2,002**
Operating income	**(4,527)**	**n.a.**	**(2,002)**
Deprec., depl. & amort.	106		19
Finance costs, gross	4		nil
Pre-tax income	**(4,637)**	**n.a.**	**(2,021)**
Net income	**(4,637)**	**n.a.**	**(2,021)**
Cash & equivalent	354		2,051
Accounts receivable	491		nil
Current assets	1,180		2,117
Fixed assets, net	188		104
Right-of-use assets	38		nil
Total assets	**1,406**	**-38**	**2,261**
Accts. pay. & accr. liabs.	193		225
Current liabilities	236		225
Long-term lease liabilities	6		nil
Shareholders' equity	1,164		2,036
Cash from oper. activs.	**(3,814)**	**n.a.**	**(904)**
Cash from fin. activs.	2,240		446
Cash from invest. activs.	(123)		(163)
Net cash position	**354**	**-83**	**2,051**
Capital expenditures	(164)		(122)
	$		$
Earnings per share*	(0.02)		(0.01)
Cash flow per share*	(0.01)		(0.00)
	shs		shs
No. of shs. o/s*	280,120,290		224,220,290
Avg. no. of shs. o/s*	260,617,139		190,399,252
	%		%
Net profit margin	(519.84)		n.a.
Return on equity	(289.81)		(90.24)
Return on assets	(252.69)		(81.56)

* Common
[A] Reported in accordance with IFRS

Latest Results

Periods ended:	6m June 30/22[A]		6m June 30/21[A]
	$000s	%Chg	$000s
Operating revenue	574	+524	92
Net income	(944)	n.a.	(3,305)
	$		$
Earnings per share*	(0.00)		(0.01)

* Common
[A] Reported in accordance with IFRS

Historical Summary
(as originally stated)

Fiscal Year	Oper. Rev. $000s	Net Inc. Bef. Disc. $000s	EPS* $
2021[A]	892	(4,637)	(0.02)
2020[A]	nil	(2,021)	(0.01)
2019[A]	nil	(2,041)	(0.03)
2018[A]	nil	(271)	(0.02)
2017[A]	nil	192	0.01

* Common
[A] Reported in accordance with IFRS
Note: Adjusted throughout for 1-for-20 cons. in July 2019

H.26 Haviland Enviro Corp.

Symbol - HEC.P **Exchange** - TSX-VEN **CUSIP** - 419612
Head Office - 600-890 Pender St W, Vancouver, BC, V6C 1J9
Email - acontardi@genericcapital.ca
Investor Relations - Albert Contardi (416) 361-2832
Auditors - McGovern Hurley LLP C.A., Toronto, Ont.
Transfer Agents - Odyssey Trust Company, Toronto, Ont.
Profile - (B.C. 2022) Capital Pool Company.

Common listed on TSX-VEN, Feb. 7, 2023.
Directors - Albert Contardi, CEO & CFO, Toronto, Ont.; Christopher O. (Chris) Irwin, Toronto, Ont.; David Johnston, Calgary, Alta.; David W. Snowden, Toronto, Ont.
Other Exec. Officers - Monique Charbonneau, corp. sec.

Capital Stock

	Authorized (shs.)	Outstanding (shs.)[1]
Common	unlimited	12,606,500

[1] At Feb. 7, 2023

Major Shareholder - Widely held at Feb. 7, 2023.
Recent Close: $0.13
Capital Stock Changes - On Feb. 7, 2023, an initial public offering of 5,206,500 common shares was completed at $0.10 per share.

H.27 Haw Capital 2 Corp.

Symbol - HAW.P **Exchange** - TSX-VEN **CUSIP** - 41966H
Head Office - 4500-855 2 St SW, Calgary, AB, T2P 4K7 **Telephone** - (403) 452-8002
Email - mewhaaa@gmail.com
Investor Relations - Marshall Mewha (403) 452-8002
Auditors - KPMG LLP C.A., Calgary, Alta.
Transfer Agents - Odyssey Trust Company, Vancouver, B.C.
Profile - (Alta. 2019) Capital Pool Company.

Recent Merger and Acquisition Activity

Status: terminated **Revised:** June 14, 2022
UPDATE: The transaction was terminated. PREVIOUS: Haw Capital 2 Corp. entered into a letter of intent for the Qualifying Transaction reverse takeover acquisition of private Alberta-based Songistry Inc. for the issuance of at least 33,151,282 post-consolidated common shares (following a 1-for-4.42 share consolidation) for deemed total consideration of $22,000,000. Songistry has developed MDIIO, a music asset/copyright management and licensing solution that leverages artificial intelligence for songwriters, artists, music publishers, record labels, music supervisors, filmmakers, and film and TV production companies. Closing was subject to Songistry completing an equity financing of between $4,000,000 and $5,500,000.
Directors - W. Scott McGregor, CEO, Calgary, Alta.; Marshall Mewha, CFO, Courtney, B.C.; John J. (Jay) Campbell, Calgary, Alta.; Robert McCue, Sin., Mexico
Other Exec. Officers - Suzanne Ferguson, corp. sec.

Capital Stock

	Authorized (shs.)	Outstanding (shs.)[1]
Common	unlimited	14,000,000

[1] At May 30, 2022

Major Shareholder - James McRoberts held 52.5% interest at May 25, 2022.

Price Range - HAW.P/TSX-VEN

Year	Volume	High	Low	Close
2022	45,000	$0.01	$0.01	$0.01
2021	164,000	$0.30	$0.16	$0.16

Recent Close: $0.01

H.28 Health Logic Interactive Inc.

Symbol - CHIP.H **Exchange** - TSX-VEN (S) **CUSIP** - 42227N
Head Office - 1400-350 7 Ave SW, Calgary, AB, T2P 3N9 **Telephone** - (403) 475-7779 **Toll-free** - (877) 456-4424
Email - info@healthlogicinteractive.com
Investor Relations - Harrison Ross (877) 456-4424
Auditors - CAN Partners LLP C.A., Markham, Ont.
Transfer Agents - Computershare Trust Company of Canada Inc., Calgary, Alta.
Profile - (B.C. 2007) Pursuing the acquisition of an artificial intelligence (AI) software company.
Previously was developing and commercializing consumer focused handheld point-of-care diagnostic devices that connect to patient's smartphones and digital continued care platforms that address areas of unmet needs, such as chronic disease management.
Common suspended from TSX-VEN, May 8, 2023.

Recent Merger and Acquisition Activity

Status: pending **Announced:** Aug. 9, 2023
Health Logic Interactive Inc. entered into a letter of intent to acquire Boston, Mass.-based ChipBrain, Inc., which developed an artificial intelligence (AI) software platform that allows sales professionals to gauge, analyze and react to real-time customer interactions over video calls, voice calls, and text messaging and emailing. Terms of the transaction were not disclosed.
Predecessor Detail - Name changed from Fanlogic Interactive Inc., Dec. 1, 2020; basis 1 new for 10 old shs.
Directors - Harrison Ross, interim CEO & interim CFO, Vancouver, B.C.; Graydon Bensler, Vancouver, B.C.; George Kovalyov, Richmond, B.C.; Rick Purdy, Edmonton, Alta.; Dr. George Shen, Edmonton, Alta.
Other Exec. Officers - Dr. Claudio Rigatto, CMO

Capital Stock

	Authorized (shs.)	Outstanding (shs.)[1]
Preferred	unlimited	nil
Common	unlimited	6,724,192

[1] At May 29, 2023

Major Shareholder - Braeden William S. Lichti held 13.62% interest and Peter A. Lacey held 10.04% interest at Nov. 16, 2021.

Price Range - CHIP.H/TSX-VEN (S)

Year	Volume	High	Low	Close
2022	755,860	$0.44	$0.02	$0.02
2021	759,083	$2.20	$0.24	$0.46
2019	393,300	$2.40	$0.40	$0.40
2018	661,472	$30.40	$0.80	$0.80

Consolidation: 1-for-4 cons. in Apr. 2022; 1-for-10 cons. in Jan. 2021
Recent Close: $0.05
Capital Stock Changes - On Apr. 18, 2022, common shares were consolidated on a 1-for-4 basis.

Wholly Owned Subsidiaries

Tank Resources USA Inc., United States. Inactive.

Financial Statistics

Periods ended:	12m Dec. 31/21[A]		12m Dec. 31/20[oA]
	$000s	%Chg	$000s
General & admin expense	1,742		369
Stock-based compensation	329		nil
Operating expense	**2,072**	**+462**	**369**
Operating income	**(2,072)**	**n.a.**	**(369)**
Finance costs, gross	13		32
Pre-tax income	**9,263**	**n.a.**	**(400)**
Net inc. bef. disc. opers.	**9,263**	**n.a.**	**(400)**
Income from disc. opers.	(1,822)		(35)
Net income	**7,441**	**n.a.**	**(435)**
Cash & equivalent	9		106
Accounts receivable	86		56
Current assets	102		162
Long-term investments	558		nil
Total assets	**660**	**+307**	**162**
Bank indebtedness	4		24
Accts. pay. & accr. liabs.	609		452
Current liabilities	675		626
Long-term debt, gross	nil		191
Long-term debt, net	nil		191
Shareholders' equity	(15)		(656)
Cash from oper. activs.	**(1,485)**	**n.a.**	**(244)**
Cash from fin. activs.	1,388		350
Net cash position	**9**	**-92**	**106**
	$		$
Earns. per sh. bef disc opers*	1.91		(0.22)
Earnings per share*	1.53		(0.24)
Cash flow per share*	(0.31)		(0.13)
	shs		shs
No. of shs. o/s*	6,724,192		1,849,351
Avg. no. of shs. o/s*	4,858,185		1,849,351
	%		%
Net profit margin	n.a.		n.a.
Return on equity	n.m.		n.m.
Return on assets	n.m.		(327.11)

* Common
[o] Restated
[A] Reported in accordance with IFRS

Latest Results

Periods ended:	9m Sept. 30/22[A]		9m Sept. 30/21[A]
	$000s	%Chg	$000s
Net inc. bef. disc. opers.	(236)	n.a.	(1,145)
Income from disc. opers.	nil		(1,225)
Net income	(236)	n.a.	(2,370)
	$		$
Earnings per share*	(0.04)		(0.27)

* Common
[A] Reported in accordance with IFRS

Historical Summary
(as originally stated)

Fiscal Year	Oper. Rev. $000s	Net Inc. Bef. Disc. $000s	EPS* $
2021[A]	nil	9,263	1.91
2020[A]	nil	(435)	(0.24)
2019[A]	nil	(68)	(0.04)
2018[A]	nil	(783)	(0.40)
2017[A]	40	(5,424)	(4.40)

* Common
[A] Reported in accordance with IFRS
Note: Adjusted throughout for 1-for-4 cons. in Apr. 2022; 1-for-10 cons. in Jan. 2021

H.29 Healthcare Special Opportunities Fund

Symbol - MDS.UN **Exchange** - TSX **CUSIP** - 42226J
Head Office - 205-10 Alcorn Ave, Toronto, ON, M4V 3A9 **Telephone** - (416) 362-4141 **Fax** - (416) 642-5054
Website - www.ldic.ca
Email - rkhakiani@ldic.ca
Investor Relations - Rahim Khakiani (416) 362-4141
Auditors - Ernst & Young LLP C.A., Toronto, Ont.

Lawyers - McMillan LLP, Toronto, Ont.
Transfer Agents - TSX Trust Company, Toronto, Ont.
Trustees - LDIC Inc., Toronto, Ont.
Investment Advisors - LDIC Inc., Toronto, Ont.
Managers - LDIC Inc., Toronto, Ont.
Profile - (Ont. 2015) Invests primarily in publicly traded issuers and private issuers that derive a significant portion of their revenue or earnings from medical and healthcare products and/or services.

The investments may include, but will not be limited to, issuers operating in the following healthcare industry sub-sectors: (i) healthcare services, financials and insurance; (ii) healthcare products and technology; (iii) healthcare facilities and real estate investment trusts; and (iv) retirement lifestyle, wellness and entertainment. The public portfolio will consist of securities of 20 to 30 large, mid and small capitalization publicly listed healthcare issuers based in developed markets. The fund may also invest up to 20% of the fund's total assets in private equity investments.

LDIC Inc., the fund's manager, receives a management fee at an annual rate of 1.25% of the net asset value of the fund, calculated daily and payable monthly in arrears, and a performance fee equal to 20% of the amount by which the cash proceeds at disposition of each private investment exceeds 106% of the threshold amount, which is 107% of the original book value of the investment.

The fund does not have a fixed termination date, but may be terminated at the discretion of the fund's manager.

Top 10 investments at Dec. 31, 2022 (as a percentage of net asset value):

Investments	Percentage
Cash	16.0%
Becton Dickinson and Co.	8.5%
Merck & Co Inc.	8.1%
Boston Scientific Corp.	7.9%
Abbott Laboratories	7.9%
UnitedHealth Group Inc.	6.8%
Stryker Corp.	5.8%
HCA Healthcare Inc.	5.4%
Danaher Corp.	5.0%
Arthritis Innovation Corp.	4.7%

Oper. Subsid./Mgt. Co. Directors - Michael B. Decter, chr., CEO, chief invest. officer & chief compliance officer, Toronto, Ont.; Ron E. Bailey, Winnipeg, Man.; Genevieve Roch-Decter, Toronto, Ont.; Graham W. S. Scott, Toronto, Ont.
Oper. Subsid./Mgt. Co. Officers - Rahim Khakiani, CFO

Capital Stock

	Authorized (shs.)	Outstanding (shs.)[1]
Class A Unit	unlimited	1,618,637
Class U Unit	unlimited	500

[1] At Dec. 31, 2022

Class A Unit - Cash distributions may be paid as determined by the manager based upon prevailing market conditions and the total return generated from the portfolio. Retractable in July of each year at a price equal to the net asset value (NAV) per class A unit, less any costs incurred to fund the retraction. Retractable in any other month at a price equal to the lesser of: (i) 95% of the weighted average trading price on the TSX for the 15 trading days immediately preceding the retraction date; and (ii) the closing price per unit. One vote per unit.

Class U Unit - Cash distributions may be paid as determined by the manager based upon prevailing market conditions and the total return generated from the portfolio. Retractable in July of each year at a price equal to the NAV per class U unit, less any costs incurred to fund the retraction. Retractable in any other month with class U unitholders receiving in U.S. dollars an amount equal to the U.S. dollar equivalent product of: (i) the monthly retraction price per class A unit; and (ii) a fraction, the numerator of which is the NAV per class U unit on the applicable monthly retraction date expressed in Canadian dollars at the determined U.S. dollar/Canadian dollar exchange rate and the denominator of which is the NAV per class A unit on the applicable monthly retraction date. Convertible into class A units on a weekly basis at a ratio based on the NAV per class U unit divided by the NAV per class A unit. One vote per unit.

Major Shareholder - Michael B. Decter held 17.9% interest at Mar. 31, 2023.

Price Range - MDS.UN/TSX

Year	Volume	High	Low	Close
2022	67,621	$13.25	$10.78	$11.50
2021	141,360	$15.80	$12.53	$12.92
2020	222,094	$13.74	$9.75	$13.70
2019	377,449	$12.51	$10.81	$12.50
2018	846,890	$12.50	$9.92	$10.85

Recent Close: $11.24
Capital Stock Changes - During 2022, 1,000,865 class A units and 100 class U units were retracted.

Dividends

MDS.UN cl A unit Var. Ra pa Q

$0.05933	July 14/23	$0.05992	Apr. 14/23
$0.05806	Dec. 30/22	$0.05949	Oct. 14/22

Paid in 2023: $0.11925 2022: $0.25163 2021: $0.26977

Financial Statistics

Periods ended:	12m Dec. 31/22[A]		12m Dec. 31/21[A]
	$000s	%Chg	$000s
Realized invest. gain (loss)	(880)		284
Unrealized invest. gain (loss)	(4,561)		1,265
Total revenue	**(4,686)**	**n.a.**	**2,011**
General & admin. expense	610		649
Other operating expense	55		73
Operating expense	**665**	**-8**	**721**
Operating income	**(5,351)**	**n.a.**	**1,290**
Pre-tax income	**(5,365)**	**n.a.**	**1,249**
Net income	**(5,365)**	**n.a.**	**1,249**
Cash & equivalent	3,106		3,333
Accounts receivable	36		55
Investments	22,405		32,876
Total assets	**22,405**	**-38**	**36,264**
Accts. pay. & accr. liabs.	2,999		74
Shareholders' equity	19,406		36,190
Cash from oper. activs.	**7,865**	**+111**	**3,719**
Cash from fin. activs.	(8,488)		(975)
Net cash position	**3,106**	**-7**	**3,333**
	$		$
Earnings per share*	(2.22)		0.48
Earnings per share**	(2.81)		(0.80)
Cash flow per share***	3.25		1.41
Net asset value per share*	11.98		13.81
Cash divd. per share*	0.25		0.27
	shs		shs
No. of shs. o/s***	1,619,137		2,620,102
Avg. no. of shs. o/s***	2,421,761		2,631,412
	%		%
Net profit margin	n.m.		62.11
Return on equity	(19.30)		3.46
Return on assets	(18.29)		3.46

* Cl.A Unit
** Cl.U Unit
*** Cl.A Unit & Cl.U Unit
[A] Reported in accordance with IFRS

Note: Net income reflects increase/decrease in net assets from operations.

Historical Summary
(as originally stated)

Fiscal Year	Total Rev.	Net Inc. Bef. Disc.	EPS*
	$000s	$000s	$
2022[A]	(4,686)	(5,365)	(2.22)
2021[A]	2,011	1,249	0.48
2020[A]	2,493	1,833	0.69
2019[A]	6,314	5,537	1.90
2018[A]	5,891	4,852	1.33

* Cl.A Unit
[A] Reported in accordance with IFRS

H.30 Helios Fairfax Partners Corporation

Symbol - HFPC.U **Exchange** - TSX **CUSIP** - 42328X
Head Office - 800-95 Wellington St W, Toronto, ON, M5J 2N7
Telephone - (416) 367-4941 **Fax** - (416) 367-4946
Website - www.heliosinvestment.com/helios-fairfax-partners
Email - investorrelations@heliosllp.com
Investor Relations - Julia Gray (647) 243-9882
Auditors - PricewaterhouseCoopers LLP C.A., Toronto, Ont.
Transfer Agents - Computershare Trust Company of Canada Inc., Toronto, Ont.
Employees - 14 at Dec. 31, 2022
Profile - (Can. 2016) Invests in public and private equity securities and debt instruments in Africa and African businesses or other businesses with customers, suppliers or business primarily conducted in, or dependent on, Africa. Also receives cash flows arising from management fees and carried interest earned by **Helios Investment Partners LLP** (Helios) in its separate asset management activities.

Holdings and investments consist of **NBA Africa, LLC**, a subsidiary of the National Basketball Association (NBA) which conducts the league's business in Africa including the Basketball Africa League (partnership between NBA and the International Basketball Federation); **Trone Investment Holdings Limited**, which holds an interest in a Moroccan medical technology distribution group, with operations in medical imaging and diagnostic equipment, and contrast pharmaceuticals for imaging; **Helios Investors IV, L.P.**, a private equity fund which invests in companies that operate primarily in Africa; **GroCapital Holdings Limited**, which owns a 4.8% interest in full-service South African commercial bank **Access Bank (South Africa) Limited** (formerly **GroBank Limited**); **Ascendant Learning Limited**, through subsidiary **Nova Pioneer Education Group**, offers preschool through secondary education through 13 campuses in South Africa and Kenya; **AFGRI Group Holdings (Pty) Ltd.**, which holds interests in agricultural and food-related companies that provide agricultural services, including grain management and storage, equipment, animal feed production and milling, financial services and retail; **Philafrica Foods (Pty) Ltd.**, which owns and operates maize and wheat mills and animal feed factories; **Event Horizon Entertainment Limited**, which creates and produces global events and travel experiences, with a focus on events that promote African culture; **Helios Digital Ventures LP**, a venture capital fund with a focus on investing in early-stage technology businesses across Africa; **Obashe Trust**, the sole limited partner of Helios Digital; **Helios Seven Rivers Fund Ltd.**, which invests in publicly traded financial instruments, including equities and credit, listed either on local African exchanges or non-African exchanges or traded OTC, in all cases, issued by entities that are domiciled in Africa or are expected to generate a significant share of the revenues or profits from African sources; and **Helios Sports and Entertainment Group Ltd.**, which holds a 25% interest in **Cooper Limited**, engaged in acquiring, owning, developing, investing in, and operating development sites for mixed-use sports, recreation and entertainment properties in the major urban centers in Africa.

Through wholly owned **HFA Topco, L.P.**, the company is also entitled to receive: (i) 25% of all carried interest amounts generated by any funds managed by Helios that commenced their investment period prior to July 10, 2020, including **Helios Investors II, L.P.** and **Helios Investors III, L.P.**; (ii) 50% of all carried interest amounts generated by any future funds managed by Helios, including Helios Investors IV, L.P.; and (iii) 100% of excess fees, defined as all management and other fees paid to Helios or any of its affiliates in connection with the management of any existing or future fund (including the management of the company and its subsidiaries) less expenses, administrative fees or other fees necessary for the operation of managing those funds.

HFA Topco acts as the portfolio advisor of the company, with Helios serving as the sub-advisor.

Recent Merger and Acquisition Activity

Status: pending **Announced:** July 28, 2023
Helios Fairfax Partners Corporation agreed to sell a portion of its investment in Mauritius-based Joseph Investment Holdings Limited for an undisclosed amount. The transaction covers of a portion of its interest in common shares and class A shares of Joseph Holdings, and a shareholder loan (tranche 1). In addition, Helios agreed to sell its remaining investment in Joseph Holdings, consisting of the remaining interest in common shares and class A shares of Joseph Holdings (tranche 2) for an undisclosed amount. The tranche 2 sale and purchase agreement was expected to close a year after the closing of tranche 1 sale and purchase agreement. Joseph Holdings owns an interest in AFGRI Group Holdings (Pty) Ltd., which holds interests in agricultural and food-related companies, and Philafrica Foods (Pty) Ltd., which owns and operates maize and wheat mills and animal feed factories.

Status: pending **Announced:** July 28, 2023
Helios Fairfax Partners Corporation agreed to sell its equity interest in Centurion, South Africa-based Philafrica Foods (Pty) Ltd. for an undisclosed amount. Philafrica owns and operates maize and wheat mills and animal feed factories in South Africa. The transaction was expected to close on or before the first anniversary of the closing of the tranche 1 sale and purchase agreement for a portion of Helios' investment in Joseph Investment Holdings Limited.

Predecessor Detail - Name changed from Fairfax Africa Holdings Corporation, Dec. 15, 2020.
Oper. Subsid./Mgt. Co. Directors - Ken Costa, chr., London, Middx., United Kingdom; Tope Lawani, co-CEO, London, Middx., United Kingdom; Babatunde Soyoye, co-CEO, London, Middx., United Kingdom; Christopher D. (Chris) Hodgson†, Markham, Ont.; Kofi Adjepong-Boateng, Accra, Ghana; Lt.-Gen. (ret.) Roméo Dallaire, Gatineau, Qué.; Quinn McLean, Toronto, Ont.; Sahar Nasr, Cairo, Egypt; Masai Ujiri, Toronto, Ont.
Oper. Subsid./Mgt. Co. Officers - Luciana Germinario, COO; Belinda Blades, CFO; Julia Gray, gen. counsel & corp. sec.
† Lead director

Capital Stock

	Authorized (shs.)	Outstanding (shs.)[1]
Preference	unlimited	
Multiple Voting	unlimited	55,452,865
Subordinate Voting	unlimited	52,876,843

[1] At June 30, 2023

Multiple Voting - Convertible into subordinate voting shares on a share-for-share basis, under certain circumstances. All held by Fairfax Financial Holdings Limited and HFP Investment Holdings S.A.R.L. Automatically convert into subordinate voting shares if transferred or held by another party. Fifty votes per share.
Subordinate Voting - One vote per share.
Normal Course Issuer Bid - The company plans to make normal course purchases of up to 2,643,017 subordinate voting shares representing 5% of the total outstanding. The bid commenced on June 23, 2023, and expires on June 22, 2024.
Major Shareholder - Fairfax Financial Holdings Limited held 53.3% interest and HFP Investment Holdings S.A.R.L. held 45.9% interest at June 30, 2023.

Price Range - HFPC.U/TSX

Year	Volume	High	Low	Close
2022	1,507,989	US$3.94	US$2.32	US$2.85
2021	2,094,176	US$5.50	US$2.90	US$3.37
2020	2,511,835	US$6.33	US$2.36	US$5.25
2019	6,040,428	US$9.88	US$5.70	US$5.91
2018	3,074,758	US$15.75	US$7.25	US$8.11

Recent Close: US$2.70
Capital Stock Changes - During 2022, 23,102 subordinate voting shares were issued under on vesting of restricted share units and

88,776 subordinate voting shares were repurchased under a Normal Course Issuer Bid.

Wholly Owned Subsidiaries

HFA Topco, L.P., Cayman Islands.
HFP Investments Limited, Mauritius.
HFP South Africa Investments (Pty) Ltd., South Africa.
HFP US Investments, Inc., United States.
- **NBA Africa, LLC**, United States.

Helios Sports and Entertainment Group Ltd., Guernsey.
- 100% int. in **Helios Sports and Entertainment Holdings Ltd.**, Guernsey.
  - 25% int. in **Copper Limited**, Guernsey.

Subsidiaries

56.3% int. in **Ascendant Learning Limited**, Mauritius.
93.7% int. in **Helios Seven Rivers Fund Ltd.**, Cayman Islands.
74.6% int. in **Joseph Investment Holdings Limited**, Mauritius.
- 62.73% int. in **AFGRI Holdings (Pty) Ltd.**, South Africa.
  - 100% int. in **AFGRI Group Holdings (Pty) Ltd.**, South Africa.
    - 73.2% int. in **AFGRI Agri Services (Pty) Limited**, South Africa.
    - 100% int. in **AFGRI International (Pty) Limited**, South Africa.
    - 60% int. in **Philafrica Foods (Pty) Ltd.**, Centurion, South Africa.

Investments

48.1% int. in **GroCapital Holdings Limited**, Centurion, South Africa.
- 4.8% int. in **Access Bank (South Africa) Limited**, South Africa.

14.1% int. in **Helios Investors IV, L.P.**, Cayman Islands.
26% int. in **Philafrica Foods (Pty) Ltd.**, Centurion, South Africa.
22% int. in **Trone Investment Holdings Limited**, London, Middx., United Kingdom.

Financial Statistics

Periods ended:	12m Dec. 31/22[A]		12m Dec. 31/21[A]
	US$000s	%Chg	US$000s
Realized invest. gain (loss)	28,736		(21,247)
Unrealized invest. gain (loss)	(51,925)		30,024
Total revenue	**(22,056)**	**n.a.**	**(3,277)**
Salaries & benefits	6,109		4,506
General & admin. expense	11,218		11,140
Operating expense	**17,327**	**+11**	**15,646**
Operating income	**(39,383)**	**n.a.**	**(18,923)**
Finance costs, gross	3,593		2,700
Pre-tax income	**(42,976)**	**n.a.**	**(27,696)**
Income taxes	7,801		(1,774)
Net income	**(50,777)**	**n.a.**	**(25,922)**
Cash & equivalent	125,241		76,284
Accounts receivable	405		2,978
Investments	523,120		607,106
Total assets	**652,612**	**-7**	**704,392**
Accts. pay. & accr. liabs.	218		136
Debt	99,226		98,632
Shareholders' equity	544,307		591,902
Cash from oper. activs.	**49,832**	**n.a.**	**(85,876)**
Cash from fin. activs.	(305)		97,413
Net cash position	**125,241**	**+64**	**76,284**
	US$		US$
Earnings per share*	(0.47)		(0.24)
Cash flow per share*	0.46		(0.79)
	shs		shs
No. of shs. o/s*	108,193,971		108,259,645
Avg. no. of shs. o/s*	108,193,971		109,071,609
	%		%
Net profit margin	n.m.		n.m.
Return on equity	(8.94)		(4.35)
Return on assets	(6.86)		(3.56)
Foreign sales percent	100		100
No. of employees (FTEs)	14		10

* Subord. Vtg.
[A] Reported in accordance with IFRS

Latest Results

Periods ended:	6m June 30/23[A]		6m June 30/22[A]
	US$000s	%Chg	US$000s
Total revenue	16,539	n.a.	(28,742)
Net income	11,026	n.a.	(39,350)
	US$		US$
Earnings per share*	0.10		(0.36)

* Subord. Vtg.
[A] Reported in accordance with IFRS

Historical Summary
(as originally stated)

Fiscal Year	Total Rev. US$000s	Net Inc. Bef. Disc. US$000s	EPS* US$
2022[A]	(22,056)	(50,777)	(0.47)
2021[A]	(3,277)	(25,922)	(0.24)
2020[A]	(173,033)	(206,646)	(3.31)
2019[A]	(46,242)	(61,199)	(1.01)
2018[A]	(42,108)	(60,580)	(1.06)

* Subord. Vtg.
[A] Reported in accordance with IFRS

H.31 Helix BioPharma Corp.

Symbol - HBP **Exchange** - TSX **CUSIP** - 422910
Head Office - 205-9120 Leslie St, Richmond Hill, ON, L4B 3J9 **Telephone** - (905) 841-2300 **Fax** - (905) 841-2244
Website - www.helixbiopharma.com
Email - cfo@helixbiopharma.com
Investor Relations - Hatem Kawar (416) 642-1807 ext. 304
Auditors - Clearhouse LLP C.A., Mississauga, Ont.
Lawyers - Osler, Hoskin & Harcourt LLP, Toronto, Ont.
Transfer Agents - Computershare Trust Company of Canada Inc., Toronto, Ont.
Employees - 7 at July 31, 2022
Profile - (Can. 1995 amalg.) Develops products for the treatment and prevention of cancer including lead drug candidate L-DOS47.

The company's proprietary DOS47 technology platform is designed to function by using a plant-derived compound called urease to act upon a natural substance in the body called urea in order to produce a potent cancer cell killing effect by increasing the pH of the microenvironment surrounding the cancerous cells, thus reversing the acidic extra-cellular conditions that are shown to be favourable for cancer cell survival. The company owns several patents in respect of the DOS47 technology and has licences with the National Research Council of Canada that cover the use of antibodies for L-DOS47, other DOS47 candidates and cellular therapy products. As at July 31, 2022, the company had rights to five U.S. patents and 64 foreign patents, as well as six pending U.S. patent applications and 42 pending foreign patent applications.

The DOS47 technology platform has produced drug product candidates L-DOS47, which is under two clinical studies for the treatment of non-small cell lung cancer (NSCLC) and pancreatic cancer; and V-DOS47, which is under preclinical development for the treatment of various cancers. Clinical studies for L-DOS47 includes a completed Phase I combination clinical study in the U.S. (LDOS001), and a Phase II combination study in Eastern Europe (LDOS003); as well as an ongoing Phase Ib/II clinical study in the U.S. for the treatment of pancreatic cancer (LDOS006). In addition, the company is pursuing Phase II clinical study for L-DOS47 in combination with therapies in Poland that may benefit from the pH-modulating effects of L-DOS47 on solid tumours that express CEACAM6.

The company is also developing a Chimeric Antigen Receptor T-Cell (CAR-T), a cell-based therapy that uses the patient's immune system to treat cancer. T cells are isolated and then transformed with specific CAR that recognize the cancer. The transformed T cells are infused back into the patient to effect the treatment. The company has selected to develop CEACAM6 and VEGFR2 specific CARs for solid tumour.

Research and development is conducted at a 4,155-sq.-ft. laboratory in Edmonton, Alta.

During fiscal 2022, the company's LDOS002 clinical trial, a Phase I/II monotherapy study concluded in Poland, did not proceed to Phase II and development of L-DOS47 as a monotherapy treatment of non-squamous non-small cell lung cancer was discontinued.

Predecessor Detail - Formed from International Helix Biotechnologies Inc. in Canada, July 31, 1995, on amalgamation with Intercon Pharma Inc.; basis 1 new for 2 old shs.

Directors - Jacek Antas, CEO, Poland; Malgorzata I. Luabe, Edmonton, Alta.; Christopher Maciejewski, Toronto, Ont.; Jerzy Wilczewski, Poland

Other Exec. Officers - Hatem Kawar, CFO; Dr. Frank G. Renshaw, CMO; Namrata Malhotra, corp. sec.

Capital Stock

	Authorized (shs.)	Outstanding (shs.)[1]
Preferred	10,000,000	nil
Common	unlimited	174,302,082

[1] At Oct. 31, 2022

Options - At July 31, 2022, options were outstanding to purchase 9,050,000 common shares at prices ranging from 35¢ to $1.30 per share with a weighted average remaining contractual life of 2.69 years.

Warrants - At July 31, 2022, warrants were outstanding to purchase 45,381,231 common shares at prices ranging from 70¢ to $2.24 per share with a weighted average remaining contractual life of 2 years.

Major Shareholder - CAIAC Fund Management AG held 18.5% interest and Jerzy Wilczewski held 13.77% interest at Dec. 14, 2021.

Price Range - HBP/TSX

Year	Volume	High	Low	Close
2022	5,731,080	$0.34	$0.16	$0.22
2021	5,979,199	$1.16	$0.25	$0.30
2020	5,571,214	$2.01	$0.25	$0.50
2019	4,353,135	$1.50	$0.24	$1.34
2018	2,702,398	$1.10	$0.34	$0.53

Recent Close: $0.21

Capital Stock Changes - In November 2022, private placement of 25,716,777 common shares was completed at 18¢ per share.

During fiscal 2022, common shares were issued as follows; 12,346,938 on exercise of warrants, 11,550,000 by private placement and 6,764,798 on conversion of notes.

Financial Statistics

Periods ended:	12m July 31/22[A]		12m July 31/21[A]
	$000s	%Chg	$000s
Research & devel. expense	4,260		5,709
General & admin expense	1,344		2,585
Stock-based compensation	424		664
Operating expense	**6,028**	**-33**	**8,958**
Operating income	**(6,028)**	**n.a.**	**(8,958)**
Deprec., depl. & amort.	12		173
Finance costs, net	524		443
Pre-tax income	**(6,563)**	**n.a.**	**(9,574)**
Net inc. bef. disc. opers	**(6,563)**	**n.a.**	**(9,574)**
Income from disc. opers	nil		1,536
Net income	**(6,563)**	**n.a.**	**(8,038)**
Cash & equivalent	3,252		3,565
Accounts receivable	279		353
Current assets	3,695		4,018
Fixed assets, net	35		47
Total assets	**3,730**	**-8**	**4,065**
Accts. pay. & accr. liabs	599		1,466
Current liabilities	3,411		3,874
Long-term debt, gross	2,468		3,612
Long-term debt, net	nil		1,584
Shareholders' equity	319		(1,393)
Cash from oper. activs	**(6,508)**	**n.a.**	**(9,304)**
Cash from fin. activs	6,205		6,562
Cash from invest. activs	nil		2,020
Net cash position	**3,252**	**-9**	**3,565**
	$		$
Earns. per sh. bef disc opers*	(0.04)		(0.07)
Earnings per share*	(0.04)		(0.06)
Cash flow per share*	(0.04)		(0.07)
	shs		shs
No. of shs. o/s*	171,794,753		141,133,017
Avg. no. of shs. o/s*	149,486,901		137,888,511
	%		%
Net profit margin	n.a.		n.a.
Return on equity	n.m.		n.m.
Return on assets	(168.39)		(213.44)
No. of employees (FTEs)	7		10

* Common
[A] Reported in accordance with IFRS

Historical Summary
(as originally stated)

Fiscal Year	Oper. Rev. $000s	Net Inc. Bef. Disc. $000s	EPS* $
2022[A]	nil	(6,563)	(0.04)
2021[A]	nil	(9,574)	(0.07)
2020[A]	nil	(8,561)	(0.07)
2019[A]	nil	(7,526)	(0.07)
2018[A]	nil	(8,625)	(0.09)

* Common
[A] Reported in accordance with IFRS

H.32 Hello Pal International Inc.

Symbol - HP **Exchange** - CSE (S) **CUSIP** - 423407
Head Office - 200-550 Denman St, Vancouver, BC, V6G 3H1 **Telephone** - (604) 683-0911 **Fax** - (604) 684-0642
Website - www.hellopal.com
Email - groehlig@shaw.ca
Investor Relations - Gunther Roehlig (604) 617-5421
Auditors - Mao & Ying LLP C.A., Vancouver, B.C.
Transfer Agents - Computershare Trust Company of Canada Inc., Vancouver, B.C.
Profile - (B.C. 1986; orig. Ont., 1985) Develops, markets and operates a proprietary suite of mobile applications that focus on international social interaction, language learning and live streaming. Also has cryptocurrency mining operations in People's Republic of China (PRC).

The company's Hello Pal platform enables users to find and easily interact with users from all over the world through a variety of means such as chat messaging, live streaming, and audio/video calling. The platform features include live streaming services, which enable users to broadcast themselves to other users and communicate real time through text messaging or joint audio sessions from selected users; gifts, payments and earnings, which enable users to give virtual gifts to other users that can be purchased using the platform's virtual currency which in turn can be redeemed for cash by the users who received the gifts; matching and chat abilities, which filters and matches users with other users, people or parties based on defined criteria such as language spoken, gender and nationality, then allows users to chat using text or audio messaging using built-in language tools such as translation services; and phrasebooks which is available in eight languages each with over 2,000 phrases whereby users can choose a phrase, listen to the recorded audio of the phrase, repeat the phrase and send their recording of the phrase to another user.

The software application consists of Hello Pal, Travel Pal, Language Pal apps, as well as live streaming service applications. The flagship Hello Pal app, which operates the company's core business of international livestreaming service, had 5,800,000 registered users from over 200 countries and regions, and 20,000 daily active users at May 31, 2021.

Through 51%-owned **Crypto Pal Technology Ltd.**, is engaged in cryptocurrency mining in PRC. A at July 30, 2021, Crypto Pal owned 12,500 mining rigs that are capable of mining Litecoin, Dogecoin, Bitcoin and Ethereum. The company plans to launch a Crypto Pal app to enhance livestreaming by permitting user access to mine and use cryptocurrency.

Common suspended from CSE, Sept. 7, 2022.

Predecessor Detail - Name changed from Neoteck Solutions Inc., May 9, 2016, pursuant to the acquisition of certain software assets of Hello Pal International, Inc.; basis 1 new for 1.5 old shs.

Directors - Kean Li (KL) Wong, founder, chr. & interim CEO, Hong Kong, Hong Kong, People's Republic of China; Gang (Adega) Zhou, pres., People's Republic of China; Gunther Roehlig, interim CFO, Salt Spring Island, B.C.; Jun (Vincent) Chai, sr. v-p, opers., People's Republic of China; James Y. Liang, Vancouver, B.C.

Other Exec. Officers - Jingsu (Jason) Huang, chief tech. officer

Capital Stock

	Authorized (shs.)	Outstanding (shs.)[1]
Common	unlimited	166,653,623

[1] At Jan. 27, 2022

Major Shareholder - Widely held at May 4, 2021.

Price Range - NEO.H/TSX-VEN (D)

Year	Volume	High	Low	Close
2022	21,446,557	$0.41	$0.07	$0.09
2021	144,080,317	$2.33	$0.21	$0.40
2020	46,763,648	$0.31	$0.05	$0.25
2019	8,030,573	$0.15	$0.03	$0.08
2018	14,555,594	$0.35	$0.07	$0.10

Recent Close: $0.09

Capital Stock Changes - On May 25, 2021, 1,800,000 units (1 common share & ½ warrant) were issued pursuant to the acquisition of 51% interest in Crypto Pal Technology Ltd., and 5,800,000 units (1 common share & ½ warrant) were issued without further consideration on exchange of subscription receipts issued previously at $1.25 each, with warrants exercisable at $2.00 per share for two years.

Wholly Owned Subsidiaries

Hangzhou Hello Pal River Technology Limited, People's Republic of China.

Hello Pal Asia Limited, Hong Kong, People's Republic of China.

Subsidiaries

51% int. in **Crypto Pal Technology Ltd.**

Latest Results

Periods ended:	9m Nov. 30/21[A]		9m Nov. 30/20[A]
	$000s	%Chg	$000s
Operating revenue	17,597	+101	8,740
Net income	(2,341)	n.a.	(1,592)
Net inc. for equity hldrs	(3,291)	n.a.	(1,592)
Net inc. for non-cont. int	950		nil
	$		$
Earnings per share*	(0.01)		(0.02)

* Common
[A] Reported in accordance with IFRS

H.33 Hemostemix Inc.

Symbol - HEM **Exchange** - TSX-VEN **CUSIP** - 423694
Head Office - 1150-707 7 Ave SW, Calgary, AB, T2P 3H6 **Telephone** - (403) 340-9207
Website - www.hemostemix.com
Email - tsmeenk@hemostemix.com
Investor Relations - Thomas A. Smeenk (403) 560-3373
Auditors - MNP LLP C.A., Toronto, Ont.
Transfer Agents - Computershare Trust Company of Canada Inc., Calgary, Alta.

Profile - (Alta. 2014 amalg.; orig. Alta., 2012) Develops, manufactures and commercializes blood-derived cell therapies to treat a variety of serious medical conditions including critical limb ischemia.

Lead product candidate is ACP-01, a potential treatment for ischemic diseases, cardiovascular diseases, peripheral arterial disease, angina pectoris, acute myocardial infraction and ischemic and dilated cardiomyopathy. The ACP-01 is under Phase II clinical trial for the treatment of critical limb ischemia, a severe blockage in the arteries of the lower extremities which markedly reduces blood flow. ACP-01 uses the patient's own cells to restore blood flow to ischemic limbs. Also developing NCP-01, a product that treats indications of amyotrophic lateral sclerosis, spinal cord injuries, Parkinson's disease and Alzheimer's disease through building new neuronal lineage cells in a patient; and BCP-01, a product that would potentially treat bone fractures, skeletal breaks and surgical procedures.

Holds 91 patents in several countries including the U.S., Canada, Thailand, Singapore, Mexico and in Europe for its technologies which include in-vitro techniques for use with stem cells, production from blood of cells neural lineage, regulating stem cells and automated cell therapy.

Predecessor Detail - Formed from Technical Ventures RX Corp. in Alberta, Nov. 10, 2014, following Qualifying Transaction reverse takeover of and amalgamation with TheraVite Inc. (deemed acquiror); basis 1 new for 5 old shs.

Directors - Thomas A. Smeenk, co-founder, pres. & CEO, Ont.; Peter A. Lacey, chr., Red Deer, Alta.; Dr. Ronnie Hershman, N.Y.; Loran Swanberg, Alta.

Other Exec. Officers - Christina Wu, interim CFO; Dr. Fraser C. Henderson Sr., CMO; Peter (Pete) Pavlin, v-p, opers.; Dr. Pierre Leimgruber, interim CMO

Capital Stock

	Authorized (shs.)	Outstanding (shs.)[1]
Preferred	unlimited	nil
Common	unlimited	81,089,626

[1] At May 29, 2023

Major Shareholder - Widely held at July 26, 2022.

Price Range - HEM/TSX-VEN

Year	Volume	High	Low	Close
2022	23,395,273	$0.42	$0.12	$0.18
2021	27,860,760	$0.72	$0.14	$0.16
2020	27,155,850	$0.80	$0.10	$0.70
2019	789,371	$2.20	$0.10	$0.20
2018	2,920,655	$2.80	$0.90	$1.60

Consolidation: 1-for-20 cons. in Dec. 2020
Recent Close: $0.12

Wholly Owned Subsidiaries

Kwalata Trading Ltd., Cyprus.

Financial Statistics

Periods ended:	12m Dec. 31/21[A]		12m Dec. 31/20[A]
	$000s	%Chg	$000s
Research & devel. expense	180		650
General & admin expense	6,113		4,492
Stock-based compensation	362		2,322
Operating expense	**6,655**	**-11**	**7,464**
Operating income	**(6,655)**	**n.a.**	**(7,464)**
Deprec., depl. & amort	1		2
Finance income	73		nil
Finance costs, gross	94		113
Pre-tax income	**(6,542)**	**n.a.**	**(7,768)**
Income taxes	(256)		nil
Net income	**(6,286)**	**n.a.**	**(7,768)**
Cash & equivalent	219		258
Current assets	562		2,321
Fixed assets, net	1		2
Total assets	**563**	**-76**	**2,323**
Bank indebtedness	nil		175
Accts. pay. & accr. liabs	4,365		3,247
Current liabilities	5,847		3,422
Long-term debt, gross	1,482		nil
Long-term debt, net	1,482		nil
Shareholders' equity	(5,284)		(1,099)
Cash from oper. activs	**(3,478)**	**n.a.**	**(5,975)**
Cash from fin. activs	3,268		6,209
Cash from invest. activs	171		nil
Net cash position	**219**	**-15**	**258**
	$		$
Earnings per share*	(0.11)		(0.24)
Cash flow per share*	(0.06)		(0.19)
	shs		shs
No. of shs. o/s*	59,150,862		55,535,652
Avg. no. of shs. o/s*	57,449,873		32,240,572
	%		%
Net profit margin	n.a.		n.a.
Return on equity	n.m.		n.m.
Return on assets	(429.36)		(630.82)

* Common
[A] Reported in accordance with IFRS

Latest Results

Periods ended:	3m Mar. 31/22[A]		3m Mar. 31/21[A]
	$000s	%Chg	$000s
Net income	(1,635)	n.a.	(684)
	$		$
Earnings per share*	(0.03)		(0.01)

* Common
[A] Reported in accordance with IFRS

Historical Summary
(as originally stated)

Fiscal Year	Oper. Rev.	Net Inc. Bef. Disc.	EPS*
	$000s	$000s	$
2021[A]	nil	(6,286)	(0.11)
2020[A]	nil	(7,768)	(0.24)
2019[A]	nil	(4,870)	(0.32)
2018[A]	nil	(6,181)	(0.40)
2017[A]	nil	(3,451)	(0.40)

* Common
[A] Reported in accordance with IFRS

Note: Adjusted throughout for 1-for-20 cons. in Dec. 2020

H.34 Hempsana Holdings Ltd.

Symbol - HMPS **Exchange** - CSE **CUSIP** - 423865
Head Office - 6060-3080 Yonge St, Toronto, ON, M4N 3N1 **Telephone** - (416) 844-7484 **Toll-free** - (888) 853-2434
Website - www.hempsana.ca
Email - randy@hempsana.ca
Investor Relations - Randy Ko (888) 853-2434
Auditors - Zeifmans LLP C.A., Toronto, Ont.
Transfer Agents - Computershare Trust Company of Canada Inc., Vancouver, B.C.

Profile - (B.C. 1980) Manufactures cannabis derivatives and produces cannabis extracts for use in products including vapeables, topical creams and infused consumables.

Operates an 8,000-sq.-ft. extraction facility in Goderich, Ont., where all product development and manufacturing, packaging and distribution activities are conducted.

Products include cannabidiol (CBD) crude oil, distillate and isolate. Services include wholesale distribution of the company's extracted cannabis oils and cannabis-infused products for licensed companies; Extraction-as-a-Service (EaaS), which provides full-service processing of biomass into crude or distillate for licensed producers and cultivators; Post-Processing-as-a-Service (PPaaS), which provides post-processing services, such as the conversion of full spectrum distillate to a tetrahydrocannabinol (THC)-free broad-spectrum distillate, for licensed companies and cultivators; Formulation-as-a-Service (FaaS), which provides turn-key formulation solutions for cannabis companies seeking developed products, and can provide formulations for vape cartridges, topicals and edibles; and white labelling, whereby the company works with cannabis companies to design, create and produce fully finished cannabis products that can be packaged and made ready for sale.

Predecessor Detail - Name changed from Stralak Resources Inc., June 25, 2021, pursuant to the reverse takeover acquisition of Hempsana Inc. and concurrent amalgamation of Hempsana with wholly owned 12954991 Canada Inc.

Directors - Randy Ko, pres. & CEO, Toronto, Ont.; Hyong-Gue (Michael) Bang, Toronto, Ont.; Shahzad Shad, Caledon, Ont.

Other Exec. Officers - David C. W. Chan, CFO & corp. sec.

Capital Stock

	Authorized (shs.)	Outstanding (shs.)[1]
Common	unlimited	24,129,323

[1] At June 6, 2023

Major Shareholder - Widely held at June 6, 2023.

Price Range - HMPS/CSE

Year	Volume	High	Low	Close
2022	814,862	$0.11	$0.03	$0.03
2021	2,296,644	$1.00	$0.07	$0.10

Recent Close: $0.02

Wholly Owned Subsidiaries

Hempsana Inc., Toronto, Ont.

Financial Statistics

Periods ended:	12m Dec. 31/21[A1]		12m Dec. 31/20[A2]
	$000s	%Chg	$000s
Operating revenue	**115**	**n.a.**	**nil**
Cost of sales	66		nil
Salaries & benefits	302		96
General & admin expense	3,570		1,063
Stock-based compensation	32		308
Other operating expense	67		18
Operating expense	**4,037**	**+172**	**1,485**
Operating income	**(3,922)**	**n.a.**	**(1,485)**
Deprec., depl. & amort.	206		151
Finance costs, gross	134		29
Pre-tax income	**(4,238)**	**n.a.**	**(1,654)**
Net income	**(4,238)**	**n.a.**	**(1,654)**
Cash & equivalent	46		81
Inventories	118		nil
Accounts receivable	25		nil
Current assets	493		384
Fixed assets, net	3,497		3,343
Intangibles, net	27		13
Total assets	**4,018**	**+7**	**3,740**
Accts. pay. & accr. liabs	893		1,355
Current liabilities	1,494		2,453
Long-term debt, gross	833		706
Long-term debt, net	298		555
Shareholders' equity	1,989		732
Cash from oper. activs	**(2,292)**	**n.a.**	**(347)**
Cash from fin. activs	2,514		627
Cash from invest. activs	(256)		(245)
Net cash position	**46**	**-43**	**81**
Capital expenditures	(228)		(245)
	$		$
Earnings per share*	(0.19)		(0.10)
Cash flow per share*	(0.10)		(0.02)
	shs		shs
No. of shs. o/s*	24,129,323		n.a.
Avg. no. of shs. o/s*	22,281,791		16,653,667
	%		%
Net profit margin	n.m.		n.a.
Return on equity	(311.50)		(158.35)
Return on assets	(105.80)		(45.59)

* Common

[A] Reported in accordance with IFRS

[1] Results reflect the July 12, 2021, reverse takeover acquisition of Hempsana Inc.

[2] Results pertain to Hempsana Inc.

Latest Results

Periods ended:	9m Sept. 30/22[A]		9m Sept. 30/21[A]
	$000s	%Chg	$000s
Operating revenue	881	n.m.	30
Net income	(1,265)	n.a.	(3,821)
	$		$
Earnings per share*	(0.05)		(0.18)

* Common

[A] Reported in accordance with IFRS

Historical Summary
(as originally stated)

Fiscal Year	Oper. Rev.	Net Inc. Bef. Disc.	EPS*
	$000s	$000s	$
2021[A]	115	(4,238)	(0.19)
2020[A1]	nil	(1,654)	(0.10)
2019[A1]	nil	(1,019)	(0.07)

* Common

[A] Reported in accordance with IFRS

[1] Results pertain to Hempsana Inc.

H.35 The Hempshire Group, Inc.

Symbol - HMPG **Exchange** - TSX-VEN **CUSIP** - 42386P
Head Office - 870 E Research Dr, Suite 2, Palm Springs, CA, United States, 92262 **Toll-free** - (855) 200-0420
Website - hempshiregroup.com
Email - bill@hempshiregroup.com
Investor Relations - William A. Hahn
Auditors - MNP LLP C.A., Calgary, Alta.
Transfer Agents - Odyssey Trust Company, Calgary, Alta.

Profile - (Alta. 2018) Produces and markets organic tobacco-free, cannabidiol (CBD) hemp cigarettes in the United States under the MOUNTAIN® Smokes brand.

Products are sold through the company's own e-commerce site MountainSmokes.com and distributed in Switzerland, South Africa and New Zealand. Plans to build out a business-to-business (B2B) sales channel through wholesale distributors and retailers in the United States and worldwide, with a particular focus on convenience stores, smoke shops and dispensaries.

The company's smokes are manufactured by a third-party service provider in California that provides manufacturing capacity of 1,500,000 smokes per day to the company.

Also offers white-label contract manufacturing services, including ingredient sourcing, blending, formulation and testing, package design and production and international distribution.

Recent Merger and Acquisition Activity

Status: completed **Revised:** June 24, 2022

UPDATE: The transaction was completed. PREVIOUS: Hoist Capital Corp. entered into an agreement for the Qualifying Transaction reverse takeover acquisition of private Palm Springs, Calif.-based The Hempshire Group, Inc. (THGI), a manufacturer of tobacco-free, hemp cigarettes, for issuance of 26,000,000 common shares at a deemed price of $0.10 per share. THGI plans to complete a private placement of up to 2,439,025 units at $2.05 per unit. June 14, 2022 - The companies entered into a definitive agreement. The exchange ratio was revised whereby Hoist would issue 20,000,000 common shares (preceding a 1-for-4 share consolidation) at a deemed price of $0.10 per pre-consolidated common share. The private placement was re-priced at $1.40 per unit.

Predecessor Detail - Name changed from Hoist Capital Corp., June 24, 2022, pursuant to the Qualifying Transaction reverse takeover acquisition of (old) The Hempshire Group, Inc.; basis 1 new for 4 old shs.

Directors - Jeff Ragovin, chr., East Hampton, N.Y.; Alex Shegelman, CEO; Samuel Isaac, Panama City, Panama; Jason Warnock

Other Exec. Officers - Tom Shuman, COO; William A. (Bill) Hahn, CFO; Eric Starr, chief mktg. officer; Sanjib (Sony) Gill, corp. sec.

Capital Stock

	Authorized (shs.)	Outstanding (shs.)[1]
Common	unlimited	79,583,914

[1] At May 1, 2023

Major Shareholder - Daniel Iannotte held 34.73% interest at Aug. 11, 2022.

Price Range - HMPG/TSX-VEN

Year	Volume	High	Low	Close
2022	1,030,900	$0.45	$0.07	$0.08
2021	20,000	$0.20	$0.10	$0.14
2020	492,375	$0.40	$0.06	$0.14
2019	79,500	$0.60	$0.14	$0.56
2018	17,625	$0.52	$0.40	$0.40

Consolidation: 1-for-4 cons. in Aug. 2022

Recent Close: $0.06

Capital Stock Changes - In June 2022, 76,783,914 post-consolidated common shares were issued pursuant to the Qualifying Transaction reverse takeover acquisition of (old) The Hempshire Group, Inc. On Aug. 11, 2022, common shares were consolidated on a 1-for-4 basis.

Wholly Owned Subsidiaries

The Hempshire Group, Inc., Calif.

Financial Statistics

Periods ended:	12m Dec. 31/21[A1]		12m Dec. 31/20[A]
	US$000s	%Chg	US$000s
Operating revenue	**286**	**-4**	**298**
Cost of sales	152		169
General & admin expense	1,322		285
Stock-based compensation	533		127
Operating expense	**2,007**	**+245**	**581**
Operating income	**(1,721)**	**n.a.**	**(283)**
Deprec., depl. & amort.	17		5
Finance income	2		nil
Finance costs, gross	76		18
Write-downs/write-offs	(203)		nil
Pre-tax income	**(2,163)**	**n.a.**	**(296)**
Net income	**(2,163)**	**n.a.**	**(296)**
Cash & equivalent	134		374
Inventories	192		135
Accounts receivable	7		nil
Current assets	340		374
Fixed assets, net	92		35
Right-of-use assets	29		nil
Total assets	**678**	**+66**	**409**
Accts. pay. & accr. liabs	287		69
Current liabilities	1,506		259
Long-term debt, gross	660		190
Long-term lease liabilities	8		nil
Shareholders' equity	(835)		150
Cash from oper. activs	**(960)**	**n.a.**	**(85)**
Cash from fin. activs	1,368		90
Cash from invest. activs	(280)		nil
Net cash position	**134**	**n.m.**	**7**
Capital expenditures	(64)		nil
	US$		US$
Earnings per share*	n.a.		n.a.
	shs		shs
No. of shs. o/s	n.a.		n.a.
	%		%
Net profit margin	(756.29)		(99.33)
Return on equity	n.m.		n.m.
Return on assets	(383.99)		n.a.
Foreign sales percent	100		100

[A] Reported in accordance with IFRS

[1] Results for 2021 and prior periods pertain to (old) Hempshire Group, Inc.

Note: Adjusted throughout for 1-for-4 cons. in Aug. 2022

H.36 Herbal Dispatch Inc.

Symbol - HERB **Exchange** - CSE **CUSIP** - 42704B
Head Office - 800-543 Granville St, Vancouver, BC, V6C 1X8
Telephone - (250) 419-7665 **Toll-free** - (833) 432-2420
Website - herbaldispatch.com
Email - philip@herbaldispatch.com
Investor Relations - Philip Campbell (250) 419-7665
Auditors - Kingston Ross Pasnak LLP C.A., Edmonton, Alta.
Transfer Agents - National Securities Administrators Ltd., Vancouver, B.C.

Profile - (B.C. 2018 amalg.) Owns and operates cannabis e-commerce platforms in Canada and the United States, including its flagship marketplace herbaldispatch.com.

Herbaldispatch.com operates as a member's only mail order dispensary for medical cannabis. Products available include dried flower, pre-rolls, oils and capsules, topical creams, concentrates, edibles and CBD products. Also has wholesale operations which includes recreational sales directly to private retail stores in British Columbia and plans to enter other provinces in the future. Offers licensed production services to select vendors/brands.

In November 2022, the company completed the sale of certain assets and licences at its Portland, Ore., processing facility for US$120,000.

In August 2022, the company acquired **1192515 B.C. Ltd.** for issuance of 140,000,000 common shares payable in instalments based on milestone structure linked to quarterly revenue targets. 1192515 owns and operates herbaldispatch.com, a cannabis e-commerce platform with age-verified, Canadian-resident cannabis consumers and has more than a 100,000 profiles, including over 60,000 active subscribers.

In August 2022, the company acquired **National Green Biomed Ltd.** (NG Biomed) by way of a three-cornered amalgamation of wholly owned **Rosebud Productions Inc.** and NG Biomed for $224,370 cash and issuance of 161,025,193 common shares. NG Biomed was a licensed producer of cannabis products for both recreational and medical use in Canada.

Predecessor Detail - Name changed from Luff Enterprises Ltd., Jan. 20, 2023.

Directors - Jeremy South, chr., West Vancouver, B.C.; Philip Campbell, CEO, Langley, B.C.; The Hon. Harbance Singh (Herb) Dhaliwal, Richmond, B.C.; Drew Malcolm, West Vancouver, B.C.

Other Exec. Officers - Jason Vandenberg, CFO; John Sweeney, chief opers. officer; Garett Senez, v-p, mktg.; Roderick W. (Rod) Kirkham, corp. sec.

Capital Stock

	Authorized (shs.)	Outstanding (shs.)[1]
Common	unlimited	733,547,725

[1] At Jan. 25, 2023

Major Shareholder - Widely held at Aug. 13, 2021.

Price Range - HERB/CSE

Year	Volume	High	Low	Close
2022	107,268,751	$0.03	$0.01	$0.01
2021	85,177,409	$0.06	$0.01	$0.02
2020	54,823,797	$0.07	$0.01	$0.02
2019	40,503,512	$0.25	$0.09	$0.10
2018	146,886,449	$0.98	$0.14	$0.19

Recent Close: $0.01

Capital Stock Changes - In August 2022, 161,025,193 common shares were issued pursuant to the acquisition of National Green Biomed Ltd.

Wholly Owned Subsidiaries

Agrima Botanicals Corp., Maple Ridge, B.C.
Agrima Scientific Corp., B.C.
Bloom Holdings Ltd., B.C.
National Green Biomed Ltd., B.C.
1192515 B.C. Ltd., B.C.
Pinecone Products Ltd., B.C.
Sweet Cannabis Inc., Ore.
- 100% int. in **Luff Enterprises LLC**, Ore. dba Sweet Cannabis

Westfork Holdings Inc., Ore.
Westfork Holdings NV Inc., Nev.
Wholesome Enterprise Corp.
Wholesome Holdings Inc.

Financial Statistics

Periods ended:	12m Dec. 31/21[A]		12m Dec. 31/20[A]
	$000s	%Chg	$000s
Operating revenue	**684**	**n.m.**	**20**
Cost of sales	445		4
General & admin expense	2,896		3,130
Stock-based compensation	311		30
Operating expense	**3,207**	**+1**	**3,163**
Operating income	**(2,523)**	**n.a.**	**(3,143)**
Deprec., depl. & amort.	665		955
Finance costs, gross	94		50
Write-downs/write-offs	(56)		(435)
Pre-tax income	**(2,381)**	**n.a.**	**(6,435)**
Income taxes	14		3
Net income	**(2,396)**	**n.a.**	**(6,438)**
Cash & equivalent	3,881		1,932
Inventories	345		143
Accounts receivable	360		679
Current assets	6,061		3,952
Fixed assets, net	nil		2,020
Right-of-use assets	105		139
Intangibles, net	35		30
Total assets	**7,251**	**-37**	**11,550**
Bank indebtedness	nil		2,000
Accts. pay. & accr. liabs	230		461
Current liabilities	341		2,602
Long-term debt, gross	427		427
Long-term debt, net	427		427
Long-term lease liabilities	nil		74
Shareholders' equity	6,483		8,446
Cash from oper. activs	**(2,959)**	**n.a.**	**(3,399)**
Cash from fin. activs	(1,414)		2,361
Cash from invest. activs	6,360		(861)
Net cash position	**3,881**	**+101**	**1,932**
Capital expenditures	(83)		(87)
Capital disposals	6,455		nil
	$		$
Earnings per share*	(0.01)		(0.02)
Cash flow per share*	(0.01)		(0.01)
	shs		shs
No. of shs. o/s*	431,539,032		390,083,032
Avg. no. of shs. o/s*	404,222,922		361,659,263
	%		%
Net profit margin	(350.29)		n.m.
Return on equity	(32.10)		(59.48)
Return on assets	(24.48)		(50.67)
Foreign sales percent	100		100

* Common
[A] Reported in accordance with IFRS

Latest Results

Periods ended:	6m June 30/22[A]		6m June 30/21[A]
	$000s	%Chg	$000s
Operating revenue	29	-90	280
Net income	(1,931)	n.a.	(2,241)
	$		$
Earnings per share*	(0.00)		(0.01)

* Common
[A] Reported in accordance with IFRS

Historical Summary
(as originally stated)

Fiscal Year	Oper. Rev.	Net Inc. Bef. Disc.	EPS*
	$000s	$000s	$
2021[A]	684	(2,396)	(0.01)
2020[A]	20	(6,438)	(0.02)
2019[A]	744	(22,396)	(0.07)
2018[A1,2]	1,568	(17,368)	(0.05)
2017[A3]	nil	(18)	(0.01)

* Common
[A] Reported in accordance with IFRS
[1] 7 months ended Dec. 31, 2018.
[2] Results reflect the Aug. 8, 2018, reverse takeover acquisition of (old) Ascent Industries Corp.
[3] Results for 2017 and prior periods pertain to Paget Minerals Corp.
Note: Adjusted throughout for 1-for-6 cons. in Aug. 2018

H.37 Heritage Cannabis Holdings Corp.

Symbol - CANN **Exchange** - CSE **CUSIP** - 42727B
Head Office - 600-77 Bloor St W, Toronto, ON, M5S 1M2 **Toll-free** - (888) 940-5925
Website - www.heritagecann.com
Email - kcastledine@heritagecann.com
Investor Relations - Kelly Castledine (647) 660-2560
Auditors - Welch LLP C.A., Ottawa, Ont.
Lawyers - Owens, Wright LLP, Toronto, Ont.
Transfer Agents - Computershare Trust Company of Canada Inc., Vancouver, B.C.

Profile - (Ont. 2019; orig. B.C., 2007) Produces cannabis products for the medical and recreational legal cannabis markets in Canada, the U.S. and internationally.

In Canada, the company operates primarily through wholly owned **Voyage Cannabis Corp.** and **CannaCure Corporation** which extract, formulate, manufacture and distribute medical and recreational cannabis products across Canada. Voyage owns and operates a 15,500-sq.-ft. facility in Falkland, B.C., located on 13 acres of land. CannaCure owns and operates a 122,000-sq.-ft. facility in Fort Erie, Ont., of which 24,260 sq. ft. is dedicated for cannabis activities. Products produced include dried flower, pre-rolls, concentrates, vapes, topicals, capsules and edibles under the brands Purefarma, Pura Vida, Really Awesome Dope (RAD), Premium 5, Thrifty, feelgood. and CB4. White label offerings are also provided to third parties.

In the United States, wholly owned **Opticann, Inc.** produces and sells cannabidiol (CBD) and cannabigerol (CBG) products made with the patented VESIsorb® drug delivery system. Main product offering is ArthroCBD, a softgel capsule brand, with additional medicinal hemp-based products under development. In addition, holds 30% interest in **EndoCanna Health, Inc.**, which offers a home-based DNA test kit using a saliva collection that provides a personalized report identifying how an individual's specific genetic makeup interacts with cannabinoids and terpenes. The report helps customers in cannabinoid formulation and dosing decisions.

In September 2022, the company acquired the remaining 25% interest in Vancouver, B.C.-based **Voyage Cannabis Corp.** from **Estek Ventures Corp.** for issuance of 2,000,000 common shares at 6¢ per share and $50,000 cash in exchange for the 500 class A voting common shares and 400,000 class G non-voting preferred shares of Voyage that Estek held. Voyage holds Health Canada cannabis licences.

In March 2022, the company sold its 18% interest in Vancouver, B.C.-based **Stanley Park Digital Ltd.** for $608,649 cash payable in two tranches, of which $444,489 was already received and the remaining $164,160 would be paid in six months after closing. Stanley provides technology consulting services focusing on all aspects of the blockchain technology.

Predecessor Detail - Name changed from Umbral Energy Corp., Jan. 10, 2018.

Directors - Clinton B. (Clint) Sharples, chr., Toronto, Ont.; David Schwede, pres. & CEO, Kelowna, B.C.; Céline Arsenault, Toronto, Ont.

Other Exec. Officers - Eoin Hegarty, COO; Jasmine Paige, interim CFO; Cory Larsen, chief comml. officer; Umar Syed, pres., U.S. & intl. medical products & corp. sec.

Capital Stock

	Authorized (shs.)	Outstanding (shs.)[1]
Common	unlimited	1,014,189,494

[1] At Apr. 16, 2023

Major Shareholder - Widely held at May 20, 2022.

Price Range - CANN/CSE

Year	Volume	High	Low	Close
2022	95,637,667	$0.08	$0.02	$0.03
2021	272,821,066	$0.22	$0.05	$0.07
2020	231,422,100	$0.32	$0.09	$0.14
2019	438,483,767	$0.72	$0.16	$0.25
2018	457,550,054	$0.84	$0.15	$0.17

Recent Close: $0.01

Capital Stock Changes - In November 2022, private placement of 79,030,611 common shares was completed at 5¢ per share with Obsidian Global Partners, LLC.

Wholly Owned Subsidiaries

Calyx Life Sciences Corp., B.C.
CannaCure Corporation, Fort Erie, Ont.
5450 Realty Inc., B.C.
Heritage Cannabis Exchange Corp., Ont.
- 100% int. in **Heritage (US) Colorado Corp.**, Del.
  - 100% int. in **Opticann, Inc.**, Colo.

Heritage US Holdings Corp., Del.
- 100% int. in **Heritage (US) Cali Corp.**, Calif.
  - 30% int. in **EndoCanna Health, Inc.**, Calif.
- 100% int. in **Heritage (US) Oregon Corp.**, Ore.

1005477 B.C. Ltd., Vancouver, B.C.
- 100% int. in **Voyage Cannabis Corp.**, Vancouver, B.C. Formerly PhyeinMed Inc.
  - 100% int. in **Mainstrain Market Ltd.**, Vancouver, B.C.

Premium 5 Ltd., Fort Saskatchewan, Alta.
Purefarma Solutions Inc., Kelowna, B.C.
333 Jarvis Realty Inc., Ont.

Investments

5% int. in **1186366 B.C. Ltd.**, B.C.

Financial Statistics

Periods ended:	12m Oct. 31/21[A]		12m Oct. 31/20[oA]
	$000s	%Chg	$000s
Operating revenue	**14,059**	**+70**	**8,256**
Cost of sales	13,241		3,037
Salaries & benefits	4,965		429
General & admin expense	7,592		4,931
Stock-based compensation	693		368
Operating expense	**26,491**	**+125**	**11,765**
Operating income	**(12,432)**	**n.a.**	**(3,509)**
Deprec., depl. & amort.	5,475		2,985
Finance income	122		278
Finance costs, gross	959		550
Investment income	(235)		(449)
Write-downs/write-offs	(36,851)		(5,670)
Pre-tax income	**(60,471)**	**n.a.**	**(9,851)**
Income taxes	(3,019)		(1,218)
Net income	**(57,452)**	**n.a.**	**(8,633)**
Net inc. for equity hldrs	**(57,507)**	**n.a.**	**(8,688)**
Net inc. for non-cont. int	**55**	**0**	**55**
Cash & equivalent	4,714		7,496
Inventories	16,124		5,225
Accounts receivable	4,773		1,064
Current assets	29,282		14,896
Long-term investments	3,080		3,562
Fixed assets, net	20,770		19,569
Intangibles, net	44,253		45,298
Total assets	**97,788**	**+17**	**83,432**
Accts. pay. & accr. liabs	7,785		2,436
Current liabilities	8,977		3,505
Long-term debt, gross	10,842		4,590
Long-term debt, net	10,836		4,070
Long-term lease liabilities	730		nil
Shareholders' equity	54,526		67,625
Non-controlling interest	695		640
Cash from oper. activs	**(20,126)**	**n.a.**	**(6,976)**
Cash from fin. activs	17,994		4,332
Cash from invest. activs	4,451		1,603
Net cash position	**3,764**	**+160**	**1,446**
Capital expenditures	(1,931)		(1,355)
Capital disposals	nil		2
	$		$
Earnings per share*	(0.08)		(0.02)
Cash flow per share*	(0.03)		(0.01)
	shs		shs
No. of shs. o/s*	786,128,570		496,136,722
Avg. no. of shs. o/s*	697,447,550		475,373,876
	%		%
Net profit margin	(408.65)		(104.57)
Return on equity	(94.16)		(12.37)
Return on assets	(62.40)		(9.27)
No. of employees (FTEs)	n.a.		57

* Common
[o] Restated
[A] Reported in accordance with IFRS

Latest Results

Periods ended:	9m July 31/22[A]		9m July 31/21[A]
	$000s	%Chg	$000s
Operating revenue	21,528	+129	9,410
Net income	2,848	n.a.	(14,774)
Net inc. for equity hldrs	2,152	n.a.	(15,314)
Net inc. for non-cont. int	696		540
	$		$
Earnings per share*	0.00		(0.02)

* Common
[A] Reported in accordance with IFRS

Historical Summary
(as originally stated)

Fiscal Year	Oper. Rev.	Net Inc. Bef. Disc.	EPS*
	$000s	$000s	$
2021[A]	14,059	(57,452)	(0.08)
2020[A]	8,256	(8,633)	(0.02)
2019[A]	3,564	(13,156)	(0.03)
2018[A]	nil	(6,671)	(0.04)
2017[A]	nil	22	0.00

* Common
[A] Reported in accordance with IFRS

H.38 Hero Innovation Group Inc.

Symbol - HRO **Exchange** - CSE **CUSIP** - 42771M
Head Office - 170-422 Richards St, Vancouver, BC, V6B 2Z4 **Toll-free** - (888) 820-1888
Website - www.heroinnovationgroup.com
Email - ir@heroinnovationgroup.com
Investor Relations - Mao Sun (800) 508-8813
Auditors - MSLL CPA LLP C.P.A., Vancouver, B.C.
Transfer Agents - Endeavor Trust Corporation, Vancouver, B.C.
Profile - (B.C. 2017) Provides financial products and services targeted for the unmet financial needs of kids, teens and their parents and international students studying in Canada.

Offers Hero Financials™, a full-service alternative-to-banking platform which includes digital wallet, data management, security and monitoring controls where kids and teens manage financial and spending decisions. Transfers are sent in real-time and funds can be used both in-store and online via contactless and chip payments wherever a prepaid Mastercard is accepted which could be used for purchases and savings without the limitations and restrictions imposed by traditional consumer banks.

The platform is paired with SideKick™, a prepaid Mastercard that equips kids with vital financial literacy skills which is also supported with a mobile application as well as a built-in budgeting tool, savings function, contactless payments, and security backed by third-party inscription also allowing guardians to send, monitor and control funds for their children. In addition, the product is designed specifically to aid international students studying in Canada with fair currency exchange rates and fast transactions whereby parents abroad could load money for immediate access.

In March 2022, the company terminated the proposed acquisition of Australia-based **NexPay Pty Ltd.**, a fintech company which provides payment processing services for the global education market, for issuance of 14,800,000 common shares at deemed price of 25¢ per share.

Predecessor Detail - Name changed from Euro Asia Pay Holdings Inc., June 1, 2022.
Directors - Morris Chen, chr., B.C.; Mao Sun, CEO, Richmond, B.C.; Wei Shao, Vancouver, B.C.; David Strebinger, Vancouver, B.C.; William Ying, B.C.
Other Exec. Officers - Luogang (Kevin) Chen, CFO; Markus Westerholz, chief tech. officer

Capital Stock

	Authorized (shs.)	Outstanding (shs.)[1]
Common	unlimited	73,709,435

[1] At Jan. 27, 2023

Major Shareholder - Morris Chen held 33.63% interest, Qiang W. Chen. held 25.25% interest and Perk Labs Inc. held 10.84% interest at Feb. 25, 2022.

Price Range - HRO/CSE

Year	Volume	High	Low	Close
2022	1,668,913	$0.36	$0.05	$0.10
2021	782,180	$0.37	$0.02	$0.37

Recent Close: $0.18
Capital Stock Changes - In January 2022, private placement of 2,301,128 units (1 common share & 1 warrant) at 25¢ per unit was completed. In addition, 3,016,196 units were issued for debt settlement.

Financial Statistics

Periods ended:	12m Sept. 30/22[A]		12m Sept. 30/21[oA]
	$000s	%Chg	$000s
Operating revenue	**110**	**+746**	**13**
Cost of sales	27		3
Research & devel. expense	1,413		279
General & admin expense	2,066		1,585
Stock-based compensation	223		389
Operating expense	**3,728**	**+65**	**2,256**
Operating income	**(3,618)**	**n.a.**	**(2,243)**
Deprec., depl. & amort.	4		6
Finance income	3		nil
Finance costs, gross	71		4
Pre-tax income	**(3,690)**	**n.a.**	**(2,199)**
Net income	**(3,690)**	**n.a.**	**(2,199)**
Cash & equivalent	428		613
Accounts receivable	42		26
Current assets	605		734
Fixed assets, net	nil		4
Total assets	**605**	**-18**	**739**
Accts. pay. & accr. liabs.	852		345
Current liabilities	2,806		784
Long-term debt, net	19		36
Shareholders' equity	(2,219)		(82)
Cash from oper. activs.	**(2,940)**	**n.a.**	**(1,539)**
Cash from fin. activs.	2,755		1,917
Cash from invest. activs.	nil		(2)
Net cash position	**399**	**-32**	**584**
Capital expenditures	nil		(5)
Capital disposals	nil		3
	$		$
Earnings per share*	(0.05)		(0.03)
Cash flow per share*	(0.04)		(0.02)
	shs		shs
No. of shs. o/s*	73,709,435		68,392,111
Avg. no. of shs. o/s*	72,281,770		64,870,353
	%		%
Net profit margin	n.m.		n.m.
Return on equity	n.m.		n.m.
Return on assets	(538.54)		(384.75)

* Common
[o] Restated
[A] Reported in accordance with IFRS

Historical Summary
(as originally stated)

Fiscal Year	Oper. Rev.	Net Inc. Bef. Disc.	EPS*
	$000s	$000s	$
2022[A]	110	(3,690)	(0.05)
2021[A]	13	(2,199)	(0.03)
2020[A]	nil	(1,998)	(0.03)
2019[A]	nil	(2,233)	(0.04)

* Common
[A] Reported in accordance with IFRS

H.39 Héroux-Devtek Inc.*

Symbol - HRX **Exchange** - TSX **CUSIP** - 42774L
Head Office - Tour O, Complexe Saint-Charles, 600-1111 rue Saint-Charles O, Longueuil, QC, J4K 5G4 **Telephone** - (450) 679-5450 **Fax** - (450) 679-3666
Website - www.herouxdevtek.com
Email - ir@herouxdevtek.com
Investor Relations - Stéphane Arsenault (450) 679-3330
Auditors - Ernst & Young LLP C.A., Montréal, Qué.
Lawyers - Fasken Martineau DuMoulin LLP, Montréal, Qué.; Hogan Lovells International LLP, London, Middx. United Kingdom; Lavery, de Billy LLP, Montréal, Qué.
Transfer Agents - Computershare Trust Company of Canada Inc., Montréal, Qué.
FP500 Revenue Ranking - 452
Employees - 1,806 at Mar. 31, 2023
Profile - (Que. 1942, via letters patent) Designs, develops, manufactures, repairs and overhauls landing gear, hydraulic and electromechanical flight control actuators, custom ball screws and fracture-critical components for the aerospace market, supplying both civil and defence sectors. Operations are carried out in Canada, the U.S., the U.K. and Spain.

Has 15 facilities located in Longueuil, Laval, Montreal and St-Hubert, Que.; Kitchener, Cambridge and Toronto, Ont.; Everett, Wash.; Springfield and Strongsville, Ohio; Livonia, Mich.; Runcorn and Nottingham, U.K.; and Madrid and Seville, Spain. Majority of the facilities are involved in the design, fabrication, assembly, and repair and overhaul of landing gear systems and components. The Toronto facility manufactures electronic enclosures, heat exchangers and cabinets; the Livonia facility designs and manufactures ball screws and electromechanical linear actuators system; and the Madrid facility designs, engineers, assembles and supports landing gear and actuation systems.

Primarily serves original equipment manufacturers (OEMs) and Tier 1 manufacturers. Customers include **The Boeing Company**, **Airbus S.E.**, **Lockheed Martin Corporation**, **Leonardo S.p.A.**, **Embraer S.A.**, **Saab AB**, **Dassault Aviation S.A.**, **Safran Landing Systems S.A.S.** and **Collins Aerospace**, as well as end users in the aftermarket where its largest customer is the U.S. Air Force.

During fiscal 2022, the company completed an $11,115,000 restructuring initiatives which resulted in a 15% reduction of its workforce, and the closure of its Montreal (Anjou) facility (formerly Alta Précision) in Quebec and APPH Wichita facility in Kansas.

Predecessor Detail - Name changed from Héroux Inc., Sept. 25, 2000.
Directors - Gilles Labbé, exec. chr., Outremont, Qué.; Martin Brassard, pres. & CEO, Longueuil, Qué.; Beverly Wyse†, Wash.; Nathalie Bourque, Montréal, Qué.; Ted Di Giorgio, Qué.; Didier Evrard, Paris, France; Louis Morin, Montréal, Qué.; James J. Morris, Palm Desert, Calif.; Brian A. Robbins, Aurora, Ont.; Annie Thabet, Ile-des-Soeurs, Qué.
Other Exec. Officers - Stéphane Arsenault, v-p & CFO; Anne-Marie Bertrand, v-p, eastern region; Dominique Dallaire, v-p & gen. mgr., central region; Guy Delisle, v-p, IT; Marc-Olivier Gagnon, v-p, eng. & product support; Patrick Gagnon, v-p & contr.; Jean Gravel, v-p, sales & programs; Hugo Lorrain, v-p, Spain; Daniel Normandin, v-p & gen. mgr., U.K. region; Stéphane Rainville, v-p, HR & envir.; Pedro Sallent, v-p, Spain; Jean-Philippe Sanche, v-p, legal affairs; Alexandre Verdon, v-p, bus. devel., M&A; François Renaud, corp. sec.
† Lead director

Capital Stock

	Authorized (shs.)	Outstanding (shs.)[1]
First Preferred	unlimited	nil
Second Preferred	unlimited	nil
Common	unlimited	34,005,873

[1] At Aug. 7, 2023

Options - At Mar. 31, 2023, options were outstanding to purchase 1,635,500 common shares at prices ranging from $9.83 to $17.45 per share with a weighted average years to maturity of 3.58 years.
Normal Course Issuer Bid - The company plans to make normal course purchases of up to 1,791,984 common shares representing 10% of the public float. The bid commenced on Aug. 10, 2023, and expires on Aug. 9, 2024.
Major Shareholder - Caisse de dépôt et placement du Québec held 14.1% interest, Fonds de solidarité des travailleurs du Québec (F.T.Q.) held 10.8% interest and Seymour Investment Management Ltd. held 10.6% interest at June 15, 2023.

Price Range - HRX/TSX

Year	Volume	High	Low	Close
2022	6,094,777	$18.59	$11.20	$13.15
2021	6,736,681	$19.65	$12.45	$18.00
2020	12,659,250	$21.64	$8.56	$14.10
2019	7,853,701	$20.30	$11.65	$19.10
2018	5,200,140	$16.75	$11.05	$12.93

Recent Close: $15.23
Capital Stock Changes - During fiscal 2023, 103,000 common shares were issued on exercise of options and 482,703 common shares were repurchased under a Normal Course Issuer Bid.

During fiscal 2022, 134,345 common shares were issued on exercise of options and 2,412,279 common shares were repurchased under a Normal Course Issuer Bid.

Long-Term Debt - Outstanding at Mar. 31, 2023:

Govt. loans[1]	89,032,000
Term loan[2]	75,000,000
Lease liabs.	15,946,000
Less: Def. fin. costs	2,070,000
	177,908,000
Less: Current portion	11,425,000
	166,483,000

[1] Bear interest at rates ranging from 0% to 6.6%.
[2] Bears interest at 5% at Mar. 31, 2023. Due September 2028.

Wholly Owned Subsidiaries

Devtek Aerospace Inc., Kitchener, Ont.
HDI Holdings (UK) Limited, United Kingdom.
- 100% int. in **APPH Limited**, United Kingdom.
- 100% int. in **Heroux-Devtek Spain S.L.**, Spain.
  - 100% int. in **Compañia Española de Sistemas Aeronauticos, S.A.**, Madrid, Spain.

Heroux Corp., Del.
- 100% int. in **Beaver Aerospace & Defense Inc.**, Livonia, Mich.
- 100% int. in **HDI Landing Gear USA Inc.**, Del.

Tékalia Aéronautik (2010) Inc., Montréal, Qué.
Note: The preceding list includes only the major related companies in which interests are held.

Financial Statistics

Periods ended:	12m Mar. 31/23^A		12m Mar. 31/22^A
	$000s	%Chg	$000s
Operating revenue	**543,622**	**+1**	**536,087**
Cost of sales	433,700		409,010
General & admin expense	48,556		44,028
Operating expense	**482,256**	**+6**	**453,038**
Operating income	**61,366**	**-26**	**83,049**
Deprec., depl. & amort.	36,387		35,982
Finance income	2,279		522
Finance costs, gross	9,854		4,792
Pre-tax income	**18,623**	**-54**	**40,488**
Income taxes	4,798		8,348
Net income	**13,825**	**-57**	**32,140**
Net inc. for equity hldrs	**13,825**	**-57**	**32,525**
Net inc. for non-cont. int.	**nil**	**n.a.**	**(385)**
Cash & equivalent	15,020		86,692
Inventories	262,995		200,342
Accounts receivable	126,721		105,389
Current assets	429,513		415,450
Fixed assets, net	205,490		208,838
Intangibles, net	166,038		155,520
Total assets	**821,337**	**+1**	**813,358**
Accts. pay. & accr. liabs.	131,019		114,508
Current liabilities	223,939		179,821
Long-term debt, gross	177,908		236,526
Long-term debt, net	166,483		225,691
Shareholders' equity	390,919		377,282
Cash from oper. activs.	**30,060**	**-52**	**63,166**
Cash from fin. activs.	(74,389)		(55,221)
Cash from invest. activs.	(28,292)		(16,131)
Net cash position	**15,020**	**-83**	**86,692**
Capital expenditures	(18,641)		(17,306)
Capital disposals	nil		2,881
Pension fund surplus	10,014		5,798
	$		$
Earnings per share*	0.40		0.91
Cash flow per share*	0.87		1.77
	shs		shs
No. of shs. o/s*	34,107,073		34,486,776
Avg. no. of shs. o/s*	34,384,106		35,748,639
	%		%
Net profit margin	2.54		6.00
Return on equity	3.60		8.47
Return on assets	2.59		4.31
Foreign sales percent	94		94
No. of employees (FTEs)	1,806		1,792

* Common
^A Reported in accordance with IFRS

Latest Results

Periods ended:	3m June 30/23^A		3m June 30/22^A
	$000s	%Chg	$000s
Operating revenue	140,697	+23	114,089
Net income	3,970	+311	965
	$		$
Earnings per share*	0.12		0.03

* Common
^A Reported in accordance with IFRS

Historical Summary
(as originally stated)

Fiscal Year	Oper. Rev.	Net Inc. Bef. Disc.	EPS*
	$000s	$000s	$
2023^A	543,622	13,825	0.40
2022^A	536,087	32,140	0.91
2021^A	570,685	19,813	0.55
2020^A	612,996	(50,658)	(1.38)
2019^A	483,877	26,194	0.73

* Common
^A Reported in accordance with IFRS

H.40 High Arctic Energy Services Inc.

Symbol - HWO **Exchange** - TSX **CUSIP** - 429644
Head Office - Calgary Place 1, 2350-330 5 Ave SW, Calgary, AB, T2P 0L4 **Telephone** - (403) 508-7836 **Toll-free** - (800) 668-7143 **Fax** - (403) 262-5176
Website - www.haes.ca
Email - mike.maguire@haes.ca
Investor Relations - Michael J. Maguire (403) 988-4702
Auditors - KPMG LLP C.A., Calgary, Alta.
Lawyers - DLA Piper (Canada) LLP, Calgary, Alta.
Transfer Agents - Odyssey Trust Company, Calgary, Alta.
Employees - 112 at Dec. 31, 2022
Profile - (Alta. 2007) Provides onshore drilling, well completion services and equipment rentals to the oil and gas industry in Papua New Guinea and provides nitrogen services and pressure control equipment rentals to exploration and production companies in western Canada.

Operations are carried out through two business segments: Drilling services and Ancillary services.

The **Drilling** segment consists of the company's drilling services in Papua New Guinea, where it operates two owned heli-portable rigs, 115 and 116, and one managed rig, 103.

The **Ancillary** segment consists of the company's oilfield rental equipment in Canada and Papua New Guinea as well as its Canadian Nitrogen and compliance services. At Dec. 31, 2022, the company had 12 cryogenic liquid nitrogen pumpers, used in applications such as fracturing, coil tubing clean out, purging pipelines, pressure testing vessels and in the completion of oil and gas wells; and five cryogenic liquid nitrogen bulkers, a trailer-mounted storage tanks used for transporting liquid nitrogen to well sites for use in pumping operations. The equipment rental services in Papua New Guinea include matting, cranes, forklifts, trucks, camps, pumps, generators, tanks, vehicles and lighting towers, while in Canada, services include high pressure blowout preventers, boilers, lighting towers, hydraulic catwalks and rig shacks. At Dec. 31, 2022, the company had 575 work site mats under contract in Papua New Guinea and an additional 4,605 on hand. The mats are suitable for drilling and mining activities, pipeline construction, plant construction and a base for camp facilities. Also owns one heli-portable hydraulic workover rig, 102, and one preserved heli-portable rig, 104, both in Papua New Guinea.

Recent Merger and Acquisition Activity

Status: completed **Revised:** July 28, 2022
UPDATE: The transaction was completed. PREVIOUS: High Arctic Energy Services Inc. agreed to sell its Canadian well servicing business to Precision Drilling Corporation for a purchase price of $38,200,000 including $10,200,000 payable at closing with the balance payable in January 2023. High Arctic expects to retain around $3,000,000 in closing working capital. High Arctic plans to focus on its existing business in Papua New Guinea. High Arctic's Canadian well servicing fleet marketed under the Concord Well Servicing brand consists of 51 marketable rigs and 29 inactive and out of service rigs, as well as oilfield rental equipment associated with well servicing including 17 modern hydraulic catwalks. The sale of this business together with the sale of the Canadian snubbing business to Team Snubbing Services Inc., would result in the elimination of High Arctic's Production Services segment. Post-closing, High Arctic would retain in Canada its Ancillary Services segment consisting of the nitrogen pumping business and a smaller rentals business focused on pressure control under the HAES Rental Services branding.

Status: completed **Revised:** July 28, 2022
UPDATE: The transaction was completed. PREVIOUS: High Arctic Energy Services Inc. agreed to sell its Canadian snubbing business to Team Snubbing Services Inc. for 420,000 Team common shares, representing 42% of the post-closing total outstanding Team shares, and a five-year convertible note receivable of $3,400,000. High Arctic's Canadian Snubbing fleet consists of seven marketable packages and 32 inactive and out of service snubbing units, under balance hoists and associated support equipment.

Directors - Michael R. Binnion, chr., Calgary, Alta.; Simon P. D. Batcup, Guelph, Ont.; The Hon. Joe Oliver, Toronto, Ont.; Douglas J. (Doug) Strong, Calgary, Alta.

Other Exec. Officers - Michael J. (Mike) Maguire, CEO; Stephen P (Steve) Lambert, COO; Lonn Bate, interim CFO

Capital Stock

	Authorized (shs.)	Outstanding (shs.)[1]
Preferred	unlimited	nil
Common	unlimited	48,673,568

[1] At Apr. 6, 2023

Normal Course Issuer Bid - The company plans to make normal course purchases of up to 750,000 common shares representing 1.5% of the total outstanding. The bid commenced on Dec. 15, 2022, and expires on Dec. 14, 2023.

Major Shareholder - FBC Holdings S.A.R.L. held 45% interest at Apr. 6, 2023.

Price Range - HWO/TSX

Year	Volume	High	Low	Close
2022	7,939,572	$1.95	$1.22	$1.55
2021	10,942,505	$2.00	$0.94	$1.49
2020	13,597,503	$2.30	$0.49	$1.16
2019	8,497,161	$4.05	$1.83	$2.31
2018	12,781,646	$4.39	$3.07	$3.17

Recent Close: $1.29

Capital Stock Changes - During 2022, 24,905 common shares were cancelled and 16,376 common shares were repurchased under a Normal Course Issuer Bid.

Dividends

HWO com Var. Ra pa M
$0.005 Sept. 14/23 $0.005 Aug. 14/23
$0.005 July 14/23 $0.005 June 14/23
Paid in 2023: $0.045 2022: $0.04 2021: $0.20◆

◆ Special

Wholly Owned Subsidiaries

HAES SD Holding Corp., Calgary, Alta.
- 49% int. in **Seh' Chene GP Inc.**, Calgary, Alta.
- 49% int. in **Seh' Chene Well Services Limited Partnership**, Calgary, Alta.
- 42% int. in **Team Snubbing Services Inc.**, Blackfalds, Alta.

High Arctic Energy Services Cyprus Limited, Nicosia, Cyprus.
- 100% int. in **High Arctic Energy Services Australia Pty Ltd.**, Qld., Australia.
- 100% int. in **High Arctic Energy Services PNG Limited**, Port Moresby, Papua New Guinea.
- 100% int. in **High Arctic Energy Services (Singapore) Pte. Ltd.**, Singapore.
- 100% int. in **PNG Industry Manpower Solutions Limited**, Port Moresby, Papua New Guinea.

Powerstroke Well Control Inc., Greeley, Colo.

Note: The preceding list includes only the major related companies in which interests are held.

Financial Statistics

Periods ended:	12m Dec. 31/22^A		12m Dec. 31/21^A
	$000s	%Chg	$000s
Operating revenue	**80,020**	**+5**	**76,442**
Cost of sales	68,103		61,226
General & admin expense	10,124		10,298
Stock-based compensation	784		709
Operating expense	**79,011**	**+9**	**72,233**
Operating income	**1,009**	**-76**	**4,209**
Deprec., depl. & amort.	17,698		23,639
Finance income	210		nil
Finance costs, gross	1,493		706
Investment income	1		nil
Write-downs/write-offs	(9,667)		nil
Pre-tax income	**(27,695)**	**n.a.**	**(19,916)**
Income taxes	8,888		(1,309)
Net income	**(36,583)**	**n.a.**	**(18,607)**
Cash & equivalent	19,559		12,037
Inventories	9,099		9,136
Accounts receivable	11,092		20,714
Current assets	69,278		45,132
Long-term investments	7,739		nil
Fixed assets, net	52,962		125,309
Right-of-use assets	1,374		5,268
Total assets	**133,957**	**-28**	**185,452**
Accts. pay. & accr. liabs.	8,671		13,367
Current liabilities	9,817		15,408
Long-term debt, gross	4,214		8,075
Long-term debt, net	4,028		7,779
Long-term lease liabilities	992		7,364
Shareholders' equity	115,231		148,851
Cash from oper. activs.	**7,863**	**n.a.**	**(1,797)**
Cash from fin. activs.	(6,737)		(13,389)
Cash from invest. activs.	6,652		(5,572)
Net cash position	**19,559**	**+62**	**12,037**
Capital expenditures	(4,073)		(7,242)
Capital disposals	11,401		1,196
	$		$
Earnings per share*	(0.75)		(0.38)
Cash flow per share*	0.16		(0.04)
Cash divd. per share*	0.05		nil
Extra divd. - cash*	nil		0.20
Total divd. per share*	**0.05**		**0.20**
	shs		shs
No. of shs. o/s*	48,691,864		48,733,145
Avg. no. of shs. o/s*	48,730,195		48,778,012
	%		%
Net profit margin	(45.72)		(24.34)
Return on equity	(27.71)		(11.41)
Return on assets	(21.67)		(8.98)
Foreign sales percent	49		19
No. of employees (FTEs)	112		479

* Common
^A Reported in accordance with IFRS

Historical Summary
(as originally stated)

Fiscal Year	Oper. Rev.	Net Inc. Bef. Disc.	EPS*
	$000s	$000s	$
2022^A	80,020	(36,583)	(0.75)
2021^A	76,442	(18,607)	(0.38)
2020^A	90,800	(25,900)	(0.52)
2019^A	185,500	(8,800)	(0.18)
2018^A	203,300	11,400	0.22

* Common
^A Reported in accordance with IFRS

H.41 High Liner Foods Incorporated*

Symbol - HLF **Exchange** - TSX **CUSIP** - 429695
Head Office - 100 Battery Point, PO Box 910, Lunenburg, NS, B0J 2C0 **Telephone** - (902) 634-8811 **Fax** - (902) 634-6228
Website - www.highlinerfoods.com
Email - investor@highlinerfoods.com
Investor Relations - Paul A. Jewer (902) 421-7100
Auditors - Ernst & Young LLP C.A., Halifax, N.S.
Bankers - Rabobank Canada; Canadian Imperial Bank of Commerce; Bank of Montreal; J.P. Morgan Chase Bank (Canada); Royal Bank of Canada, Halifax, N.S.
Lawyers - Stewart McKelvey LLP, Halifax, N.S.
Transfer Agents - TSX Trust Company, Halifax, N.S.
FP500 Revenue Ranking - 284
Employees - 1,174 at Dec. 31, 2022

Profile - (N.S. 1967 amalg.) Processes and markets prepared and packaged frozen seafood products across Canada and the U.S.

The Company processes and markets frozen seafood products and also supplies private-label, value-added, frozen seafood products to North American food retailers, foodservice and club store channels. Operations consist of the food retail division, which markets products throughout the U.S. and Canada under the High Liner, Fisher Boy, Mirabel, Sea Cuisine, and Catch of the Day brands, and are available in most grocery and club stores; and the food service division, which markets branded seafood that are usually eaten outside the home and includes sales to restaurants and institutional customers under the High Liner Culinary, Mirabel, Icelandic Seafood and FPI brands. Frozen seafood products include raw fillets and shellfish, cooked shellfish and value-added products such as sauced, glazed, breaded and battered seafood, along with seafood entrées. Products are sold both directly and through distributors to North American retail and club stores, and through foodservice distributors to hotels, cafeterias, restaurants and institutions (such as healthcare and educational organizations).

The company owns and operates three food processing plants in Lunenburg, N.S., Portsmouth, N.H., and Newport News, Va.

Operating Statistics

At Dec. 31, 2022	Capacity[1]	Utilization
Location	lb.	%
Lunenburg, N.S.	50,000,000	97
Portsmouth, N.H.	61,000,000	95
Newport News, Va.	61,000,000	96

[1] Based on production of finished pounds.

Predecessor Detail - Name changed from National Sea Products Limited, Dec. 31, 1998.

Directors - Robert L. Pace, chr., Halifax, N.S.; Rodney W. (Rod) Hepponstall, pres. & CEO, Portsmouth, N.H.; The Hon. Scott Brison, Montréal, Qué.; Joan K. Chow, Oak Park, Ill.; Robert P. (Rob) Dexter, Halifax, N.S.; Andrew J. Hennigar, N.S.; David J. Hennigar, Bedford, N.S.; Shelly L. Jamieson, Norwood, Ont.; M. Jolene Mahody, Halifax, N.S.; R. Andy Miller, St. John's, N.L.; Frank B. H. van Schaayk, Marion Bridge, N.S.

Other Exec. Officers - Anthony Rasetta, chief comml. officer; Paul A. Jewer, exec. v-p & CFO; Johanne McNally Myers, exec. v-p, HR; Timothy P. (Tim) Rorabeck, exec. v-p, corp. affairs, gen. counsel & corp. sec.; Magnus Baldursson, v-p, procurement opers.; Jen Bell, v-p, corp. commun.; Deepak Bhandari, v-p, finl. planning & analysis & strategy; Bill DiMento, v-p, sustainability & govt. affairs; Meggan Hodgson, v-p, quality assurance & food safety; Graeme Macdonald, v-p, mktg.; Dale Martin, v-p, procurement strategy; Tom Rupkey, v-p, North American foodservice sales; Michael (Mike) Sirois, v-p, product devel. & technical srvcs.; Ed Snook, v-p, opers.; Irene Stathakos, v-p, comml. centre of expertise; Kimberly Stephens, v-p, fin.; Tom Walker, v-p, IT & bus. transformation; Andy Tanner, treas.; Naomi Jewers, asst. corp. sec.

Capital Stock

	Authorized (shs.)	Outstanding (shs.)[1]	Par
Preference	5,999,994	nil	$25
Subord. Pfce.	1,025,542	nil	$1.00
Non-Vtg. Equity	unlimited	nil	n.p.v.
Common	unlimited	33,360,699	n.p.v.

[1] At Aug. 9, 2023

Options - At Dec. 31, 2022, options were outstanding to purchase 1,479,833 common shares at a weighted average exercise price of Cdn$10.19 per share with an average life of 1.64 to 1.99 years.

Normal Course Issuer Bid - The company plans to make normal course purchases of up to 200,000 common shares representing 0.6% of the total outstanding. The bid commenced on June 7, 2023, and expires on June 6, 2024.

Major Shareholder - Thornridge Holdings Limited held 34.8% interest at Mar. 21, 2023.

Price Range - HLF/TSX

Year	Volume	High	Low	Close
2022	5,116,400	$15.45	$10.77	$13.77
2021	6,229,143	$15.40	$10.50	$14.91
2020	11,501,366	$11.86	$5.19	$11.10
2019	19,565,095	$12.00	$6.57	$8.23
2018	23,376,672	$15.21	$6.19	$7.66

Recent Close: $12.18

Capital Stock Changes - During fiscal 2022, 13,040 common shares were issued on exercise of options and 163,468 common shares were repurchased under a Normal Course Issuer Bid.

Dividends

HLF com Ra $0.52 pa Q est. Dec. 15, 2022
Prev. Rate: $0.40 est. Dec. 15, 2021
Prev. Rate: $0.28 est. Dec. 15, 2020

Long-Term Debt - At Dec. 31, 2022, outstanding long-term debt totaled US$245,700,000 (US$7,500,000 current and net of US$4,972,000 deferred financing costs) and consisted entirely of a term loan bearing interest at Secured Overnight Financing Rate (SOFR) plus 3.75% (floor of 0.75%) and due October 2026.

Wholly Owned Subsidiaries

High Liner Foods (USA), Incorporated, Del.
- 100% int. in **ISF (USA), LLC**, Del.

Note: The preceding list includes only the major related companies in which interests are held.

Financial Statistics

Periods ended:	52w Dec. 31/22[A]		52w Jan. 1/22[A]
	US$000s	%Chg	US$000s
Operating revenue	**1,069,714**	**+22**	**875,405**
Cost of sales	832,478		667,713
General & admin expense	82,738		78,058
Other operating expense	55,173		46,162
Operating expense	**970,389**	**+23**	**791,933**
Operating income	**99,325**	**+19**	**83,472**
Deprec., depl. & amort.	23,578		23,081
Finance costs, gross	18,261		7,494
Write-downs/write-offs	(332)		(42)
Pre-tax income	**65,824**	**+34**	**49,082**
Income taxes	11,094		6,833
Net income	**54,730**	**+30**	**42,249**
Cash & equivalent	155		443
Inventories	472,311		308,183
Accounts receivable	96,531		87,122
Current assets	586,059		405,577
Fixed assets, net	120,036		115,852
Right-of-use assets	7,190		11,041
Intangibles, net	286,208		292,967
Total assets	**1,003,486**	**+21**	**826,469**
Bank indebtedness	127,554		4,388
Accts. pay. & accr. liabs	187,967		164,135
Current liabilities	336,351		187,035
Long-term debt, gross	245,700		250,619
Long-term debt, net	238,200		244,994
Long-term lease liabilities	2,813		6,851
Shareholders' equity	373,417		332,524
Cash from oper. activs	**(76,158)**	**n.a.**	**28,685**
Cash from fin. activs	100,137		(41,421)
Cash from invest. activs	(20,670)		(20,319)
Net cash position	**155**	**-65**	**443**
Capital expenditures	(20,670)		(20,319)
Unfunded pension liability	8,852		12,988
	US$		US$
Earnings per share*	1.62		1.25
Cash flow per share*	(2.26)		0.85
Cash divd. per share*	$0.43		$0.31
	shs		shs
No. of shs. o/s*	33,179,282		33,329,710
Avg. no. of shs. o/s*	33,737,340		33,865,092
	%		%
Net profit margin	5.12		4.83
Return on equity	15.51		13.55
Return on assets	7.64		6.08
Foreign sales percent	76		75
No. of employees (FTEs)	1,174		1,102

* Common
[A] Reported in accordance with IFRS

Latest Results

Periods ended:	26w July 1/23[A]		26w July 2/22[A]
	US$000s	%Chg	US$000s
Operating revenue	583,513	+6	548,187
Net income	19,775	-41	33,622
	US$		US$
Earnings per share*	0.59		0.99

* Common
[A] Reported in accordance with IFRS

Historical Summary
(as originally stated)

Fiscal Year	Oper. Rev.	Net Inc. Bef. Disc.	EPS*
	US$000s	US$000s	US$
2022[A]	1,069,714	54,730	1.62
2021[A]	875,405	42,249	1.25
2020[A1]	827,453	28,802	0.85
2019[A]	942,224	10,289	0.31
2018[A]	1,048,531	16,776	0.50

* Common
[A] Reported in accordance with IFRS
[1] 53 weeks ended Jan. 2, 2021.

H.42 High Mountain 2 Capital Corporation

Symbol - HMCC.P **Exchange** - TSX-VEN **CUSIP** - 42970W
Head Office - 1600-333 7 Ave SW, Calgary, AB, T2P 2Z1 **Telephone** - (403) 619-7118
Email - bkanters@telus.net
Investor Relations - William A. Kanters (403) 619-7118
Auditors - MNP LLP C.A., Calgary, Alta.
Transfer Agents - Odyssey Trust Company, Calgary, Alta.
Profile - (Alta. 2020) Capital Pool Company.

Recent Merger and Acquisition Activity

Status: pending **Announced:** Sept. 27, 2022
High Mountain 2 Capital Corporation entered into a letter of intent for the Qualifying Transaction reverse takeover acquisition of private British Columbia-based Interactive Health, Inc. (IHI), a digital technology development company, focused on the medical and health education sector, on a share-for-share basis, which would result in the issuance of 44,488,900 High Mountain post-consolidated common shares (following a 1-for-1.75 share consolidation). IHI develops and sells digitally enhanced, interactive, competency-based, learning tools for medical schools and healthcare learning centres to address the gap that exists between the theory and practice of medicine. IHI's first commercialized flagship product, CyberPatient 2.5, was a digital simulated hospital with 130 digitally enhanced simulated patients accessible by all students and educators at any time from anywhere. Upon completion, IHI would amalgamate with a wholly owned subsidiary of High Mountain, and High Mountain would change its name to Interactive Health International Inc. As a condition of the transaction, IHI must complete a private placement of a minimum of $2,200,000, in the form of subscription receipts at 35¢ per receipt.

Directors - William A. (Bill) Kanters, pres. & CEO, Calgary, Alta.; V. E. Dale Burstall, corp. sec., Calgary, Alta.; James W. Longshore, Nassau, Bahamas; Gordon Winter, Mississauga, Ont.

Other Exec. Officers - Ronald (Ron) Love, CFO

Capital Stock

	Authorized (shs.)	Outstanding (shs.)[1]
Common	unlimited	5,700,000

[1] At Nov. 28, 2022

Major Shareholder - William A. (Bill) Kanters held 10.53% interest at Nov. 5, 2020.

Price Range - HMCC.P/TSX-VEN

Year	Volume	High	Low	Close
2022	106,500	$0.28	$0.20	$0.21
2021	334,400	$0.40	$0.22	$0.30
2020	371,500	$0.35	$0.15	$0.27

Recent Close: $0.12

H.43 High Tide Inc.

Symbol - HITI **Exchange** - TSX-VEN **CUSIP** - 42981E
Head Office - Unit 112, 11127 15 St NE, Calgary, AB, T3K 2M4 **Telephone** - (403) 265-4207 **Toll-free** - (855) 747-6420 **Fax** - (403) 265-4244
Website - www.hightideinc.com
Email - vahan@hightideinc.com
Investor Relations - Vahan Ajamian (403) 703-4272
Auditors - Ernst & Young LLP C.A., Calgary, Alta.
Lawyers - Garfinkle Biderman LLP, Toronto, Ont.
Transfer Agents - Olympia Trust Company, Calgary, Alta.
FP500 Revenue Ranking - 531
Employees - 1,300 at Jan. 30, 2023

Profile - (Alta. 2018) Retails recreational cannabis and related products through retail stores in Alberta, Ontario, Saskatchewan, British Columbia and Manitoba, and through e-commerce platforms. Also manufactures and distributes consumption accessories and cannabis lifestyle products for wholesale customers internationally.

At Aug. 18, 2023, retail operations consisted of 155 cannabis stores in Alberta (77), Ontario (51), Saskatchewan (10), British Columbia (7) and Manitoba (10) under the Canna Cabana banner. The company's retail e-commerce platforms cater to consumers worldwide and include Grasscity, Smoke Cartel, DankStop and Daily High Club, which are focused on consumption accessories; and FABCBD, Blessed CBD and NewLeaf Naturals, which offer various hemp-derived CBD products.

Wholesale operations consist of the design, manufacture and distribution of consumption accessories and cannabis lifestyle products for wholesalers and retailers across the world through wholly owned **Valiant Distribution Canada Inc.** and **Valiant Distribution Inc.** Product offerings include proprietary brands, such as Atomik, Evolution, Puff Puff Pass, Vodka Glass and Cabana Cannabis Co., and licensed brands through partnerships with celebrities and entertainment companies.

In May 2023, the company acquired the remaining 20% interest in **Fab Nutrition, LLC** (dba FABCBD), an online retailer of CBD products, for issuance of 386,035 common shares valued at $748,000.

In May and August 2022, the company acquired three retail cannabis stores in Guelph, Scarborough and Toronto, Ont., from a winner of the Ontario cannabis lottery for $176,000 cash and settlement of a $3,463,000 notes receivable.

In July 2022, the company reacquired ownership of the three operating KushBar retail cannabis stores in Camrose, Morinville and Medicine Hat, Alta., which were sold to **Halo Collective Inc.** in July 2021, due to Halo not meeting certain obligations under the agreement.

In June 2022, the company acquired **Livonit Foods Inc.** (dba Bud Heaven), which operates two retail cannabis stores in Bracebridge, Ont., for $1,000,000 cash and issuance of 564,092 common shares valued at $1,800,000; and a retail cannabis store in Kensington, Alta., for $160,000 cash and settlement of a $523,000 notes receivable.

In April 2022, the company acquired **2080791 Alberta Ltd.** (dba Boreal Cannabis Company), which operates two retail cannabis stores in Slave Lake and St. Paul, Alta., for $200,000 cash and issuance of 443,301 common shares valued at $2,400,000; and three retail cannabis stores operating as Crossroads Cannabis in Stratford, Hanover and Markdale, Ont., for issuance of 378,079 common shares valued at $1,900,000. A fourth Crossroads Cannabis store in Woodstock, Ont., was acquired by the company in May 2022 for issuance of 138,656 common shares valued at $600,000.

Recent Merger and Acquisition Activity

Status: completed **Revised:** Dec. 29, 2022
UPDATE: The transaction was completed. High Tide issued 2,595,533 common shares. PREVIOUS: High Tide Inc. agreed to acquire 1171882 B.C. Ltd. (dba Jimmy's Cannabis Shop BC), resulting in High Tide

acquiring two of the five retail cannabis stores operated by Jimmy's Cannabis Shop BC in British Columbia for issuance of $5,300,000 of common shares. The stores are located in Cranbrook and Prince George.
Status: completed **Revised:** Sept. 1, 2022
UPDATE: The sale of the Ontario store was completed for $1,100,000, consisting of $300,000 cash and issuance of 364,185 common shares. PREVIOUS: Choom Holdings Inc. agreed to sell nine operating retail cannabis stores in British Columbia (2), Alberta (6) and Ontario (1) to High Tide Inc. for $5,100,000 to be satisfied by the issuance of High Tide common shares. The sale represents substantially all of Choom's operations. The transaction was the result of the sale and investment solicitation process permitted under Choom's previously announced proceedings under the Companies' Creditors Arrangement Act (Canada). Aug. 4, 2022 - The sale of the British Columbia and Alberta stores was completed for $4,200,000 satisfied through the issuance of 1,782,838 common shares. The sale of the Ontario operations was expected to close in September 2022.

Predecessor Detail - Name changed from High Tide Ventures Inc., Oct. 4, 2018.

Directors - Harkirat (Raj) Grover, founder, exec. chr., pres. & CEO, Calgary, Alta.; Andrea Elliott, Ont.; Nitin Kaushal, Richmond Hill, Ont.; Arthur H. Kwan, Calgary, Alta.; Chief Christian Sinclair, Opaskwayak, Man.

Other Exec. Officers - Aman Sood, COO; Sergio Patino, CFO; Omar Khan, chief commun. & public affairs officer; Andreas-Alexander (Andy) Palalas, chief revenue officer; Joy L. Avzar, v-p & legal counsel; Sandy Sharma, v-p, HR; Shimmy Posen, corp. sec.

Capital Stock

	Authorized (shs.)	Outstanding (shs.)[1]
Common	unlimited	75,086,823

[1] At Aug. 2, 2023

Major Shareholder - Widely held at May 26, 2023.

Price Range - HITI/TSX-VEN

Year	Volume	High	Low	Close
2022	18,210,221	$7.51	$1.75	$2.09
2021	49,022,121	$16.95	$3.75	$5.37
2020	10,062,251	$4.28	$1.28	$3.83
2019	5,358,968	$9.45	$2.40	$2.55
2018	337,959	$7.50	$4.50	$5.93

Consolidation: 1-for-15 cons. in May 2021
Recent Close: $1.69

Capital Stock Changes - In December 2022, 2,595,533 common shares were issued pursuant to acquisition of 1171882 B.C. Ltd. (dba Jimmy's Cannabis Shop BC). In May 2023, 386,035 common shares were issued pursuant to acquisition of the remaining 20% interest in Fab Nutrition, LLC (dba FABCBD).

In November 2021, 4,429,809 common shares were issued pursuant to acquisition of an 80% interest in NuLeaf Naturals, LLC. In July 2022, bought deal public offering of 4,956,960 units (1 common share & 1 warrant) at $2.32 per unit was completed. Also during fiscal 2022 common shares were issued as follows: 2,147,023 on acquisition of Choom retail stores, 1,758,167 under an at-the-market offering, 674,650 on acquisition of Bud Room Inc., 564,092 on acquisition of Livonit Foods Inc. (dba Bud Heaven), 530,423 on exercise of warrants, 516,735 on acquisition of Crossroads Cannabis retail stores, 500,000 as earn-out payment, 443,301 on acquisition of 2080791 Alberta Ltd. (dba Boreal Cannabis Company), 82,976 on vesting of restricted share units, 70,500 on exercise of options and 15,122 for fees; 28,553 common shares were cancelled.

Wholly Owned Subsidiaries

Canna Cabana Inc., Calgary, Alta.
HT Global Imports Inc., Alta.
Halo KushBar Retail Inc., Alta.
High Tide Inc. B.V., Amsterdam, Netherlands.
- 100% int. in **SJV B.V.**, Netherlands.
  - 95% int. in **SJV USA Inc.**, United States.
- 100% int. in **SJV2 B.V.**, Netherlands.

High Tide USA, Inc., Nev.
- 100% int. in **Boundless Earth, LLC**, Nev.
- 100% int. in **DHC Supply LLC**, Signal Hill, Calif.
- 100% int. in **DS Distribution Inc.**, Del. dba DankStop.com.
- 100% int. in **Fab Nutrition, LLC**, Milwaukee, Wis.
- 80% int. in **NuLeaf Naturals, LLC**, Denver, Colo.
- 100% int. in **Smoke Cartel, Inc.**, Savannah, Ga.
  - 5% int. in **SJV USA Inc.**, United States.
- 100% int. in **Valiant Distribution Inc.**, United States.

Meta Growth Corp., Toronto, Ont.
- 100% int. in **The Green Company Ltd.**, Calgary, Alta.
  - 100% int. in **New Leaf Cannabis Ltd.**, Alta.
- 100% int. in **META Western Canadian Holdings Ltd.**, Canada.
  - 100% int. in **META West Coast Ltd.**, B.C.
- 57% int. in **NAC Bio Inc.**, Vancouver, B.C.
- 49% int. in **NAC Northern Alberta GP Ltd.**, Alta.
- 49% int. in **NAC Northern Alberta Limited Partnership**, Alta.
- 100% int. in **NAC Southern Alberta Ltd.**, Alta.
- 100% int. in **NACM Management Ltd.**, Ont.
  - 51% int. in **National Access Cannabis Medical Inc.**, Ont.
- 100% int. in **National Access Canada Corporation**, Ottawa, Ont.
  - 100% int. in **2713865 Ontario Ltd.**, Ont.
- 100% int. in **National Access Cannabis GP Holdings Corp.**, Alta.
  - 51% int. in **NAC Northern Alberta GP Ltd.**, Alta.
- 100% int. in **National Access Cannabis LP Holdings Corp.**, Alta.
  - 51% int. in **NAC Northern Alberta Limited Partnership**, Alta.
- 100% int. in **National Access Cannabis Management Corp.**, Canada.
- 100% int. in **11604686 Canada Inc.**, Ont.
- 100% int. in **2208292 Alberta Ltd.**, Alta.

1171882 B.C. Ltd., B.C.
2049213 Ontario Inc., Ont.
2680495 Ontario Inc., Ont.
Valiant Distribution Canada Inc., Alta.

Subsidiaries

80% int. in **Enigmaa Ltd.**, United Kingdom.

Investments

50% int. in **Saturninus Partners GP**, Ont.

Financial Statistics

Periods ended:	12m Oct. 31/22[A]		12m Oct. 31/21[A]
	$000s	%Chg	$000s
Operating revenue	**356,852**	**+97**	**181,123**
Cost of sales	255,900		117,140
Salaries & benefits	44,055		27,595
General & admin expense	38,761		21,794
Stock-based compensation	8,080		4,879
Operating expense	**346,796**	**+102**	**171,408**
Operating income	**10,056**	**+4**	**9,715**
Deprec., depl. & amort.	30,169		23,565
Finance costs, gross	9,948		10,241
Write-downs/write-offs	(48,681)[1]		(2,733)
Pre-tax income	**(73,763)**	**n.a.**	**(35,767)**
Income taxes	(2,915)		(730)
Net income	**(70,848)**	**n.a.**	**(35,037)**
Net inc. for equity hldrs	**(71,756)**	**n.a.**	**(35,717)**
Net inc. for non-cont. int.	**908**	**+34**	**680**
Cash & equivalent	25,279		14,874
Inventories	23,414		17,042
Accounts receivable	8,200		7,175
Current assets	64,060		46,287
Fixed assets, net	31,483		24,756
Right-of-use assets	30,519		27,985
Intangibles, net	145,490		142,280
Total assets	**274,743**	**+12**	**246,215**
Accts. pay. & accr. liabs	23,034		16,532
Current liabilities	59,941		40,787
Long-term debt, gross	36,116		25,656
Long-term debt, net	17,027		19,110
Long-term lease liabilities	26,139		24,044
Equity portion of conv. debs	717		859
Shareholders' equity	156,350		147,209
Non-controlling interest	5,683		4,795
Cash from oper. activs	**4,495**	**n.a.**	**(2,825)**
Cash from fin. activs	15,167		37,808
Cash from invest. activs	(8,592)		(28,493)
Net cash position	**25,084**	**+79**	**14,014**
Capital expenditures	(7,759)		(10,563)
Capital disposals	nil		2,455
	$		$
Earnings per share*	(1.14)		(0.84)
Cash flow per share*	0.07		(0.07)
	shs		shs
No. of shs. o/s*	71,021,233		54,360,028
Avg. no. of shs. o/s*	62,775,446		42,431,689
	%		%
Net profit margin	(19.85)		(19.34)
Return on equity	(47.28)		(45.39)
Return on assets	(23.53)		(15.82)
Foreign sales percent	19		17

* Common
[A] Reported in accordance with IFRS
[1] Includes $45,077,000 goodwill impairment of e-commerce retail operations.

Latest Results

Periods ended:	6m Apr. 30/23[A]		6m Apr. 30/22[A]
	$000s	%Chg	$000s
Operating revenue	236,212	+54	153,249
Net income	(5,429)	n.a.	(15,629)
Net inc. for equity hldrs	(5,323)	n.a.	(16,250)
Net inc. for non-cont. int.	(106)		621
	$		$
Earnings per share*	(0.07)		(0.28)

* Common
[A] Reported in accordance with IFRS

Historical Summary
(as originally stated)

Fiscal Year	Oper. Rev.	Net Inc. Bef. Disc.	EPS*
	$000s	$000s	$
2022[A]	356,852	(70,848)	(1.14)
2021[A]	181,123	(35,037)	(0.84)
2020[A]	83,265	(6,354)	(0.45)
2019[A]	31,294	(26,292)	(1.95)
2018[A]	8,749	(4,533)	(0.60)

* Common
[A] Reported in accordance with IFRS

Note: Adjusted throughout for 1-for-15 cons. in May 2021

H.44 Highmark Interactive Inc.

Symbol - HMRK.H **Exchange -** TSX-VEN (S) **CUSIP -** 43111T
Head Office - 602-115 George St, Oakville, ON, L6J 0A2 **Telephone -** (647) 559-2838 **Toll-free -** (855) 969-5079 **Fax -** (647) 560-8646
Website - highmark.tech
Email - inder@highmark.tech
Investor Relations - Inderjit Saini (855) 969-5079
Auditors - MNP LLP C.A., Waterloo, Ont.
Transfer Agents - TSX Trust Company, Toronto, Ont.

Profile - (Ont. 2019) Develops medical software products focused on assessing human neurological and psychological function, and acquires and operates neurological and general rehabilitation clinics.

Operations are organized into two segments: **Digital Solutions**, and **Clinical Solutions**.

Digital Solutions - The company has developed a suite of software as a medical device (SAMD) products: EQ Active, which measures aspects of neurological function in a gamified format utilizing mobile devices; EQ Resilience 1.0, which measures cognitive neurological function using both mobile and desktop devices, and BrainFx, which measures cognitive neurological function using both mobile and desktop devices; EQ Vitality, which measures aspects of neurological function variables in a gamified format utilizing mobile devices,. Under development is EQ Resilience 2.0 and EQ Machine Learning Predictive Algorithm. Target customer markets include medical clinics, medical technology platform providers, universities, sports teams and workplaces.

Clinical Solutions - The company acquires and operates medical clinics focused on neurological and general rehabilitation. Rehabilitation services include sports medicine, neurology, physiatry, physical therapy, occupational therapy, kinesiology and chiropractic, speech and language pathology, psychology, neuropsychology and social work. Many of these services are provided virtually. Clinics include wholly owned **Highmark Health Mississauga Inc.**, which is focused on the diagnosis, management and treatment of concussion and post concussion syndrome, and wholly owned **Complex Injury Rehab Inc.**, which is focused on the assessment and treatment of clients who have experienced severe or catastrophic injuries.

Common suspended from TSX-VEN, May 8, 2023.

Predecessor Detail - Name changed from Stormcrow Holdings Corp., Nov. 5, 2021, following Qualifying Transaction reverse takeover acquisition of private Toronto, Ont.-based Highmark Innovations Inc.; basis 1 new for 6 old shs.

Directors - Dr. Sanjeev Sharma, chr. & CEO, Ont.; Sunil Sharma, v-p, corp. devel. & corp. sec., Mississauga, Ont.; Chris Schnarr†, Mississauga, Ont.; Brad Badeau, Toronto, Ont.; Dr. Harry R. Jacobson, Tenn.

Other Exec. Officers - Inderjit (Inder) Saini, CFO; Michael Affleck, v-p; Tracy Milner, v-p
† Lead director

Capital Stock

	Authorized (shs.)	Outstanding (shs.)[1]
Common	unlimited	40,032,810

[1] At Nov. 17, 2021

Major Shareholder - Dr. Sanjeev Sharma held 12.43% interest, Sunil Sharma held 11.03% interest and The Mazza/Long Family Trust held 10.86% interest at Nov. 17, 2021.

Price Range - HMRK.H/TSX-VEN (S)

Year	Volume	High	Low	Close
2022	5,693,822	$0.40	$0.04	$0.05
2021	614,470	$0.72	$0.19	$0.40
2020	389,983	$0.90	$0.48	$0.72

Consolidation: 1-for-6 cons. in Nov. 2021
Recent Close: $0.02

Wholly Owned Subsidiaries

Highmark Innovations Inc., Toronto, Ont.
- 100% int. in **BrainFx Inc.**, Ont.
  - 100% int. in **BrainFx USA Inc.**, United States.
- 100% int. in **Complex Injury Rehab Inc.**, Ont.
- 100% int. in **Higher Interactive (US), Inc.**, United States.
- 100% int. in **Highmark Health Corporation**, Canada.
  - 100% int. in **Highmark Health Mississauga Inc.**, Ont.

Financial Statistics

Periods ended:	12m Dec. 31/21[A]		12m Dec. 31/20[A1]
	$000s	%Chg	$000s
Operating revenue	**1,045**	**+42**	**736**
Cost of sales	749		327
General & admin expense	4,293		1,966
Stock-based compensation	400		397
Operating expense	**5,442**	**+102**	**2,690**
Operating income	**(4,397)**	**n.a.**	**(1,954)**
Deprec., depl. & amort.	176		12
Finance costs, gross	608		32
Pre-tax income	**(4,920)**	**n.a.**	**(1,675)**
Income taxes	(254)		nil
Net income	**(4,666)**	**n.a.**	**(1,675)**
Net inc. for equity hldrs	**(4,673)**	**n.a.**	**(1,662)**
Net inc. for non-cont. int.	**7**	**n.a.**	**(13)**
Cash & equivalent	3,396		913
Accounts receivable	929		129
Current assets	4,575		1,310
Fixed assets, net	19		17
Right-of-use assets	5		nil
Total assets	**10,003**	**+654**	**1,327**
Accts. pay. & accr. liabs	1,074		489
Current liabilities	1,688		935
Long-term debt, gross	3,967		471
Long-term debt, net	3,967		61
Equity portion of conv. debs	261		nil
Shareholders' equity	4,126		68
Non-controlling interest	nil		1
Cash from oper. activs	**(4,205)**	**n.a.**	**(1,307)**
Cash from fin. activs	9,288		2,037
Cash from invest. activs	(2,600)		nil
Net cash position	**3,396**	**+272**	**913**
	$		$
Earnings per share*	(0.17)		n.a.
	shs		shs
No. of shs. o/s*	40,032,810		n.a.
Avg. no. of shs. o/s*	26,781,432		n.a.
	%		%
Net profit margin	(446.51)		(227.58)
Return on equity	(222.84)		n.m.
Return on assets	(72.19)		(194.78)

* Common

[A] Reported in accordance with IFRS

[1] Results for 2020 and prior periods pertain to Highmark Group which consists of Highmark Innovations Inc. and Highmark Health Corporation.

Historical Summary
(as originally stated)

Fiscal Year	Oper. Rev.	Net Inc. Bef. Disc.	EPS*
	$000s	$000s	$
2021[A]	1,045	(4,666)	(0.17)
2020[A]	736	(1,675)	n.a.
2019[A]	744	(1,564)	n.a.

* Common

[A] Reported in accordance with IFRS

Note: Adjusted throughout for 1-for-6 cons. in Nov. 2021

H.45 Highwood Asset Management Ltd.

Symbol - HAM **Exchange** - TSX-VEN **CUSIP** - 43127Q
Head Office - 202-221 10 Ave SE, Calgary, AB, T2G 0V9 **Telephone** - (403) 719-0499 **Fax** - (587) 296-4916
Website - www.highwoodmgmt.com
Email - callchrome@highwoodmgmt.com
Investor Relations - Chris Allchorne (587) 393-0860
Auditors - RSM Alberta LLP C.A., Calgary, Alta.
Bankers - National Bank of Canada, Calgary, Alta.
Lawyers - DLA Piper (Canada) LLP, Calgary, Alta.
Transfer Agents - Odyssey Trust Company, Calgary, Alta.
Employees - 5 at May 2, 2022
Profile - (Alta. 2019 amalg.) Explores for, develops and produces oil and gas in Alberta, British Columbia and Saskatchewan, with a focus on oil. Also explores for and develops metallic minerals in Alberta and British Columbia; and owns and operates of midstream oil and gas infrastructure through its 100% working interest Wabasca River oil pipeline and 50% working interest in the Evi Terminal, both in Alberta.

Areas of interest include Wilson Creek, Brazeau, Ricinus and Harmattan in Alberta.

Also holds 50% working interest in a producing oil well, north of Swan Hills, Alta.; 55% average working interest in 53.4 sections of Doig lands in Fireweed, B.C.; and producing oil wells in the Tilston formation in Saskatchewan. Also owns Viking Kinsella lands in Alberta and an undeveloped lands in Ukalta, Alta., both lands have not been evaluated for oil and gas reserve as at Dec. 31, 2022. At Dec. 31, 2022, the company had 12 gross (10.1 net) producing oil wells and 22.25 gross (13.23 net) non-producing oil and gas wells. The company drilled no wells during 2022. Unproven properties totaled 33,953 gross (23,503 net) hectares at Dec. 31, 2022.

Also holds over 3,800,000 acres of industrial metal and mineral permits, with a focus on its Drumheller lithium-brine project and Ironstone iron-vanadium project. In addition, owns and operates the 210-km Wabasca River pipeline with a capacity to deliver 20,000 bbl per day of crude to the Plains Rainbow pipeline in northern Alberta; and Evi Terminal in Evi, Alta., which has a butane blending operation that generates revenues from the purchase and sale of butan, and has a heavy oil trucking facility which is not currently operation and is under assessment for reactivation.

During the third quarter of 2022, the company acquired an office space for $1,150,000.

In March 2022, the company sold a non-core property for $107,000. In addition, the company sold its 50% interest in 14-05 terminal to a private Canadian midstream company for $2,250,000, with the company remaining as the operator.

Periods ended:	12m Dec. 31/22	12m Dec. 31/21
Avg. oil prod., bbl/d	113	331
Avg. BOE prod., bbl/d	113	331
Avg. oil price, $/bbl	107.54	61.18
Oil reserves, net, mbbl	577	508
NGL reserves, net, mbbl	463	468
Gas reserves, net, mmcf	3,751	3,899
BOE reserves, net, mbbl	1,665	1,626

Recent Merger and Acquisition Activity

Status: completed **Revised:** Aug. 3, 2023
UPDATE: The transaction was completed. PREVIOUS: Highwood Asset Management Ltd. agreed to acquire Castlegate Energy Ltd., which explores for, develops and produces oil and gas in Alberta with a focus on light oil, for $36,700,000. The acquisition includes 1,400 BOE per day of production. The transaction was expected to close in the third quarter of 2023.

Status: completed **Revised:** Aug. 3, 2023
UPDATE: The transaction was completed. PREVIOUS: Highwood Asset Management Ltd. agreed to acquire Shale Petroleum Ltd., which explores for, develops and produces oil and gas in Alberta with a focus on natural gas, for a purchase price of $9,000,000 consisting of issuance of 1,277,030 common shares at $7.05 per share, subject to a working capital adjustment. The acquisition include 300 BOE per day of production. The transaction was expected to close in the third quarter of 2023.

Status: completed **Revised:** Aug. 3, 2023
UPDATE: The transaction was completed. PREVIOUS: Highwood Asset Management Ltd. agreed to acquire Boulder Energy Ltd., which explores for and develops oil and gas in Alberta with a focus on light oil, for consideration of $98,000,000, subject to working capital adjustment. Consideration was estimated to consist of $75,000,000 cash, $9,000,000 of common shares and a $14,00,000,000 unsecured subordinated promissory note. Boulder has production of 2,700 BOE per day. The transaction was expected to close in the third quarter of 2023.

Predecessor Detail - Name changed from Highwood Oil Company Ltd., July 19, 2021, pursuant to change of focus from oil and gas to asset management.

Directors - Joel A. MacLeod, exec. chr., Calgary, Alta.; Gregory A. (Greg) Macdonald, pres. & CEO, Okotoks, Alta.; David A. Gardner, Alta.; Stephen J. (Steve) Holyoake, Calgary, Alta.; Ryan Mooney, Calgary, Alta.; Garrett K. Ulmer, Calgary, Alta.

Other Exec. Officers - Chris Allchorne, CFO; Kelly McDonald, v-p, explor.; Trevor P. Wong-Chor, corp. sec.

Capital Stock

	Authorized (shs.)	Outstanding (shs.)[1]
Common	unlimited	15,114,323

[1] At Aug. 4, 2023

Major Shareholder - Joel A. MacLeod held 32% interest and HR Exploration & Energy Gmbh held 17% interest at Aug. 3, 2023.

Price Range - HAM/TSX-VEN

Year	Volume	High	Low	Close
2022	26,035	$12.50	$5.00	$11.25
2021	75,111	$19.00	$4.72	$12.50
2020	34,773	$23.25	$6.95	$7.00
2019	113,989	$30.10	$9.00	$16.75
2018	18,985	$14.84	$5.30	$9.01

Consolidation: 1-for-53 cons. in Jan. 2019
Recent Close: $5.40
Capital Stock Changes - In August 2023, 1,277,025 common shares were issued on acquisition of Shale Petroleum Ltd., and 5,833,333 units (1 common share & ½ warrant) were issued without further consideration on exchange of subscription receipts sold previously by bought deal public offering at $6.00 each.

During 2022, 23,334 common shares were issued under restricted share unit plan.

Wholly Owned Subsidiaries

Boulder Energy Ltd., Calgary, Alta.
Castlegate Energy Ltd., Calgary, Alta.
Cataract Creek Environmental Ltd., Alta.
Renewable EV Battery Cleantech Corp.
Shale Petroleum Ltd., Calgary, Alta.
2339364 Alberta Ltd., Alta.

Financial Statistics

Periods ended:	12m Dec. 31/22[A]		12m Dec. 31/21[A]
	$000s	%Chg	$000s
Operating revenue	**6,618**	**-13**	**7,593**
Cost of sales	2,140		4,970
Exploration expense	185		714
General & admin expense	2,775		3,028
Stock-based compensation	458		551
Operating expense	**5,558**	**-40**	**9,263**
Operating income	**1,060**	**n.a.**	**(1,670)**
Deprec., depl. & amort.	502		877
Finance costs, net	193		194
Write-downs/write-offs	nil		(46)
Pre-tax income	**2,957**	**n.a.**	**(2,789)**
Income taxes	711		(468)
Net income	**2,246**	**n.a.**	**(2,321)**
Cash & equivalent	6		nil
Accounts receivable	2,493		2,139
Current assets	2,820		2,570
Fixed assets, net	13,033		12,471
Right-of-use assets	19		86
Explor./devel. properties	951		738
Total assets	**16,841**	**+6**	**15,883**
Bank indebtedness	nil		1,075
Accts. pay. & accr. liabs	2,390		2,860
Current liabilities	2,409		4,131
Long-term lease liabilities	nil		17
Shareholders' equity	10,697		7,993
Cash from oper. activs	**722**	**n.a.**	**(2,157)**
Cash from fin. activs	(1,127)		(6,032)
Cash from invest. activs	535		2,390
Net cash position	**6**	**n.a.**	**(124)**
Capital expenditures	(2,045)		(273)
Capital disposals	2,473		1,978
	$		$
Earnings per share*	0.37		(0.39)
Cash flow per share*	0.12		(0.36)
	shs		shs
No. of shs. o/s*	6,037,298		6,013,965
Avg. no. of shs. o/s*	6,013,965		6,013,965
	%		%
Net profit margin	33.94		(30.57)
Return on equity	24.03		(26.14)
Return on assets	13.73		(5.69)

* Common

[A] Reported in accordance with IFRS

Latest Results

Periods ended:	3m Mar. 31/23[A]		3m Mar. 31/22[A]
	$000s	%Chg	$000s
Operating revenue	1,791	+11	1,618
Net income	(27)	n.a.	456
	$		$
Earnings per share*	(0.00)		0.07

* Common

[A] Reported in accordance with IFRS

Historical Summary
(as originally stated)

Fiscal Year	Oper. Rev.	Net Inc. Bef. Disc.	EPS*
	$000s	$000s	$
2022[A]	6,618	2,246	0.37
2021[A]	7,593	(2,321)	(0.39)
2020[A]	29,418	(9,284)	(1.54)
2019[A1]	25,910	(11,013)	(1.84)
2018[A2]	27,680	(1,810)	(16.96)

* Common

[A] Reported in accordance with IFRS

[1] Results reflect the Jan. 23, 2019, reverse takeover acquisition of (old) Highwood Oil Company Ltd.

[2] Results for 2018 and prior years pertain to (old) Highwood Oil Company Ltd.

Note: Adjusted throughout for 1-for-53 cons. in Jan. 2019

H.46 Hill Incorporated

Symbol - HILL **Exchange** - TSX-VEN **CUSIP** - 43147B
Head Office - 31-2410 Lucknow Dr, Mississauga, ON, L5S 1V1 **Toll-free** - (833) 346-2337
Website - hillincorporated.com
Email - craig@hillstreetbevco.com
Investor Relations - Craig Binkley (416) 543-4904
Auditors - MNP LLP C.A.
Transfer Agents - Computershare Trust Company of Canada Inc., Vancouver, B.C.
Profile - (Ont. 2018; orig. B.C., 2016) Holds a portfolio of bioscience-driven, technology-powered consumer solutions and licensing rights in the alcohol-free beverage and cannabis industries.

The company has two business lines: Hill Street Alcohol-Free Beverages; and Hill Avenue Cannabis.

Hill Street Alcohol-Free Beverages - This line of business represents the company's legacy consumer beverage marketing and distribution business. It includes Vin(Zero) alcohol-free wine in Canada, and on a smaller scale, in the United States and Australia. The products are sold in retail chain stores through Canadian distributors, exported outside of Canada through foreign distributors and offered direct to consumers online at www.hillstreetbeverages.com.

Hill Avenue Cannabis (HAC) - This line of business includes the company's rights to **Lexaria Bioscience Corp.**'s DehydraTECH™ biodelivery technology (for use with THC products) that is scientifically proven to consistently and rapidly deliver precise doses of bioactive substances like cannabinoids into the bloodstream, for unparalleled bioavailability and onset time. Also includes the rights to the DehydraTECH™ intellectual property portfolio which consists of 28 granted patents and approximately 50 patents pending worldwide. Licenses DehydraTECH™ technology to U.S. licensed cannabis producers. Key licensing partners include **DeHydr8 MI, LLC, Cannadips, For the Love of Charlie, NEO Alternatives, LLC** and **Evolution Edibles**. HAC also provides DehydraTECH™ enabled business-to-business solutions for both extractors or ingredient suppliers and consumer packaged goods manufacturers whose products are infused with cannabis or hemp extracts.

Has also applied for a licence to operate its Lucknow cannabis facility in Mississauga, Ont., to produce DehydraTECH™ cannabinoid powder.

In September 2022, the company withdrew its line of cannabis-infused grape-based sparkling beverages in Canada under the brand (V)ia Regal from the market. The product line was launched in May 2021.

Predecessor Detail - Name changed from Hill Street Beverage Company Inc., May 30, 2023; basis 1 new for 75 old shs.

Directors - Jack Fraser, chr., Toronto, Ont.; Craig Binkley, CEO, Los Angeles, Calif.; Kevin Ruddle, St. Catharines, Ont.; Lori A. Senecal, New York, N.Y.; Frank Vizcarra, San Diego, Calif.

Other Exec. Officers - Brian Bolshin, pres. & chief product officer; Matthew Jewell, CFO; Bruce Anderson, chief production officer; Pearl Chan, chief legal officer; Doug Taylor, chief comml. officer; Reuban Nadesan, v-p, strategy & corp. devel.; Bryan Brissette, contr.

Capital Stock

	Authorized (shs.)	Outstanding (shs.)[1]
Common	unlimited	3,244,405

[1] At May 30, 2023

Major Shareholder - HoldCo (St. Catharines) Ltd. held 26.22% interest at Mar. 20, 2023.

Price Range - HILL/TSX-VEN

Year	Volume	High	Low	Close
2022	374,215	$4.50	$1.50	$2.25
2021	509,717	$9.75	$3.00	$4.13
2020	516,189	$12.75	$3.00	$7.88
2019	610,753	$21.00	$3.00	$4.50
2018	755,884	$38.25	$11.63	$12.75

Consolidation: 1-for-75 cons. in May 2023

Recent Close: $0.90

Capital Stock Changes - On May 30, 2023, common shares were consolidated on a 1-for-75 basis.

During fiscal 2022, common shares were issued as follows: 11,764,706 pursuant to the acquisition of Lexaria Canpharm ULC rights and licence and 6,457,000 on exercise of warrants.

Wholly Owned Subsidiaries

Hill Avenue Cannabis Inc., Ont.
Hill Street Marketing Inc., Toronto, Ont.

Financial Statistics

Periods ended:	12m June 30/22[A]		12m June 30/21[◻A]
	$000s	%Chg	$000s
Operating revenue	**3,212**	**+46**	**2,195**
Cost of sales	1,675		1,071
Salaries & benefits	1,309		1,064
General & admin expense	1,784		1,978
Stock-based compensation	357		486
Operating expense	**5,125**	**+11**	**4,599**
Operating income	**(1,913)**	**n.a.**	**(2,404)**
Deprec., depl. & amort.	339		253
Finance costs, gross	231		291
Write-downs/write-offs	(116)		(18)
Pre-tax income	**(2,578)**	**n.a.**	**(3,086)**
Net income	**(2,578)**	**n.a.**	**(3,086)**
Cash & equivalent	1,153		2,722
Inventories	20		549
Accounts receivable	1,344		361
Current assets	2,701		3,804
Fixed assets, net	149		208
Intangibles, net	3,308		3,598
Total assets	**6,158**	**-19**	**7,609**
Accts. pay. & accr. liabs	988		705
Current liabilities	1,171		1,494
Long-term debt, gross	2,343		2,148
Long-term debt, net	2,176		2,126
Long-term lease liabilities	55		13
Shareholders' equity	2,756		3,977
Cash from oper. activs	**(1,749)**	**n.a.**	**(2,326)**
Cash from fin. activs	281		4,748
Cash from invest. activs	(100)		(400)
Net cash position	**1,153**	**-58**	**2,722**
Capital expenditures	(83)		(2)
	$		$
Earnings per share*	(0.75)		(1.50)
Cash flow per share*	(0.61)		(1.23)
	shs		shs
No. of shs. o/s*	2,972,539		2,729,583
Avg. no. of shs. o/s*	2,862,415		1,890,345
	%		%
Net profit margin	(80.26)		(140.59)
Return on equity	(76.58)		(148.29)
Return on assets	(34.10)		(58.07)

* Common
◻ Restated
[A] Reported in accordance with IFRS

Latest Results

Periods ended:	3m Sept. 30/22[A]		3m Sept. 30/21[A]
	$000s	%Chg	$000s
Operating revenue	354	-41	605
Net income	(666)	n.a.	(551)
	$		$
Earnings per share*	(0.23)		(0.20)

* Common
[A] Reported in accordance with IFRS

Historical Summary
(as originally stated)

Fiscal Year	Oper. Rev.	Net Inc. Bef. Disc.	EPS*
	$000s	$000s	$
2022[A]	3,212	(2,578)	(0.75)
2021[A]	2,195	(3,086)	(1.50)
2020[A]	1,731	(3,682)	(3.00)
2019[A1]	1,280	(5,944)	(5.25)
2018[A2]	671	(2,653)	n.a.

* Common
[A] Reported in accordance with IFRS
[1] Results reflect the July 25, 2018, Qualifying Transaction reverse takeover acquisition of Hill Street Marketing Inc.
[2] Results for fiscal 2018 and prior fiscal years pertain to Hill Street Marketing Inc.

Note: Adjusted throughout for 1-for-75 cons. in May 2023

H.47 Hillcrest Energy Technologies Ltd.

Symbol - HEAT **Exchange** - CSE **CUSIP** - 431502
Head Office - 1910-1030 Georgia St W, Vancouver, BC, V6E 2Y3 **Telephone** - (604) 609-0006 **Toll-free** - (855) 609-0006 **Fax** - (778) 379-0991
Website - www.hillcrestenergy.tech
Email - dcurrie@hillcrestenergy.tech
Investor Relations - Donald J. Currie (855) 609-0006
Auditors - De Visser Gray LLP C.A., Vancouver, B.C.
Lawyers - McMillan LLP, Vancouver, B.C.
Transfer Agents - Computershare Trust Company of Canada Inc., Vancouver, B.C.

Profile - (B.C. 2006) Developing clean energy and e-mobility technologies and intellectual property (IP) for electric and renewable energy systems systems including electric vehicles, motors and electric generators.

The company's proprietary inverter technology platform, Zero Voltage Switching (ZVS), which minimizes switching losses and increases efficiency, performance and reliability in electric systems such as electric vehicles (EV) and grid-connected energy systems. The ZVS platform is integrated into several products including an EV traction inverter, a simplified EV on-board charging solution, a grid-connected inverter and a multi-level inverter. In addition, technology portfolio includes the following:

Electric Machine Control Software

Wholly owned **Hillcrest Energy Technologies Royalty Holdings Ltd.** develops electric machine control software IP for electric motors, electric generators and other integrated power systems. Potential commercial applications include electrical generator controls that convert and deliver renewably generated electricity; precision control systems such as aeronautical applications and autonomous vehicles; traction control systems such as electric motors and powertrains; and control software enhancements that enable connectivity associated with emerging technologies such as blockchain and Internet of Things (IoT).

Systematec GmbH Collaboration

The company has a technology collaboration agreement with **Systematec GmbH**, a German power electronics engineering and electromechanical component design company, to leverage the company's electric machine control software and develop power electronics and electromechanical IP and technology for commercialization. All products and IP developed through this collaboration would be owned by the company. Potential commercial applications include automotive, aeronautics, renewable energy and consumer electronics.

Electric Machines

Subsidiary **ALSET Innovations Ltd. (Oropass Ltd.** 50%) has licensed rights to monetize certain U.S. patented technologies and related future innovations which could potentially provide energy efficiencies across current power and transportation infrastructure, including: potentially improved energy conversion efficiency in electric transformers; and less mechanical input power per watt of electric power generated for electric generators.

During 2022, wholly owned **2044573 Alberta Ltd.** and **Hillcrest Resources (Arizona) Ltd.** were dissolved.

In June 2022, the company ceased oil and gas operations at the West Hazel project in the West Canadian Sedimentary Basin in Saskatchewan. As a result, the company completed its exit from the fossil fuel business.

Periods ended:	12m Dec. 31/22	12m Dec. 31/21
Avg. oil prod., bbl/d	n.a.	51
Avg. oil price, $/bbl	n.a.	54

Predecessor Detail - Name changed from Hillcrest Petroleum Ltd., Apr. 9, 2021.

Directors - David P. Farrell, chr., Vancouver, B.C.; Donald J. (Don) Currie, CEO, Vancouver, B.C.; Kylie Dickson, North Vancouver, B.C.; Michael Krzus, Perth, W.A., Australia; Robert A. (Bob) Lambert, United Kingdom; Thomas G. (Tom) Milne, B.C.; Michael Moskowitz, Ont.

Other Exec. Officers - Jamie L. Hogue, COO & corp. sec.; Samuel C. K. (Sam) Yik, CFO; Ari Berger, chief tech. officer; James Bolen, chief commercialization officer

Capital Stock

	Authorized (shs.)	Outstanding (shs.)[1]
Preferred	unlimited	nil
Common	unlimited	61,322,932

[1] At June 8, 2023

Major Shareholder - Widely held at May 5, 2023.

Price Range - HEAT/CSE

Year	Volume	High	Low	Close
2022	11,290,928	$1.14	$0.57	$0.60
2021	59,405,184	$2.88	$0.36	$1.11
2020	52,220,280	$0.93	$0.06	$0.39
2019	2,553,192	$0.30	$0.12	$0.21
2018	5,900,043	$0.54	$0.15	$0.30

Consolidation: 1-for-6 cons. in June 2023

Recent Close: $0.60

Capital Stock Changes - In January 2023, private placement of 2,130,000 post-consolidated common shares was completed at 72¢ per share. In April and May 2023, private placement of 4,193,750 units (1 post-consolidated common share & 1 warrant) at 48¢ per unit was completed, with warrants exercisable at 90¢ per share for two years. On June 8, 2023, common shares were consolidated on a 1-for-6 basis.

During 2022, common shares were issued as follows: 6,671,000 on exercise of warrants, 3,962,500 under restricted share unit plan and 202,160 by private placement.

Wholly Owned Subsidiaries

ALSET Innovations Inc.
Hillcrest Energy Technologies Royalty Holdings Ltd.
Hillcrest Exploration Ltd.
102031850 Saskatchewan Ltd., Sask.

Financial Statistics

Periods ended:	12m Dec. 31/22[A]		12m Dec. 31/21[oA]
	$000s	%Chg	$000s
Research & devel. expense	1,434		625
General & admin expense	3,718		3,497
Stock-based compensation	1,151		6,748
Operating expense	**6,303**	**-42**	**10,870**
Operating income	**(6,303)**	**n.a.**	**(10,870)**
Deprec., depl. & amort.	241		56
Finance costs, gross	26		29
Pre-tax income	**(6,347)**	**n.a.**	**(10,973)**
Net inc. bef. disc. opers	**(6,347)**	**n.a.**	**(10,973)**
Income from disc. opers	(13)		(2,222)
Net income	**(6,360)**	**n.a.**	**(13,195)**
Cash & equivalent	456		3,685
Accounts receivable	17		44
Current assets	910		4,434
Fixed assets, net	622		605
Right-of-use assets	93		165
Intangibles, net	1,550		1,550
Total assets	**3,116**	**-53**	**6,631**
Accts. pay. & accr. liabs	312		641
Current liabilities	393		709
Long-term lease liabilities	30		111
Shareholders' equity	2,425		5,246
Cash from oper. activs	**(5,430)**	**n.a.**	**(4,447)**
Cash from fin. activs	2,255		10,021
Cash from invest. activs	(54)		(2,365)
Net cash position	**456**	**-88**	**3,685**
Capital expenditures	(186)		(617)
	$		$
Earnings per share*	(0.12)		(0.30)
Cash flow per share*	(0.10)		(0.10)
	shs		shs
No. of shs. o/s*	54,999,183		53,193,239
Avg. no. of shs. o/s*	54,143,600		45,170,928
	%		%
Net profit margin	n.a.		n.a.
Return on equity	(165.48)		n.m.
Return on assets	(129.70)		(259.34)

* Common
[o] Restated
[A] Reported in accordance with IFRS

Latest Results

Periods ended:	3m Mar. 31/23[A]		3m Mar. 31/22[oA]
	$000s	%Chg	$000s
Net inc. bef. disc. opers	(1,409)	n.a.	(1,103)
Income from disc. opers	(13)		6
Net income	(1,422)	n.a.	(1,097)
	$		$
Earnings per share*	(0.03)		(0.02)

* Common
[o] Restated
[A] Reported in accordance with IFRS

Historical Summary
(as originally stated)

Fiscal Year	Oper. Rev. $000s	Net Inc. Bef. Disc. $000s	EPS* $
2022[A]	nil	(6,347)	(0.12)
2021[A]	475	(13,195)	(0.30)
2020[A]	536	(2,247)	(0.12)
2019[A]	763	(1,202)	(0.06)
2018[A]	48	(1,867)	(0.12)

* Common
[A] Reported in accordance with IFRS
Note: Adjusted throughout for 1-for-6 cons. in June 2023

H.48 Hire Technologies Inc.

Symbol - HIRE **Exchange** - TSX-VEN (S) **CUSIP** - 43353R
Head Office - 635-333 Bay St, Toronto, ON, M5H 2R2 **Telephone** - (647) 872-6180 **Toll-free** - (888) 792-5320
Website - hire.company
Email - sdealy@hire.company
Investor Relations - Simon Dealy (647) 868-6961
Auditors - MNP LLP C.A., Ottawa, Ont.
Lawyers - LaBarge Weinstein LLP, Ottawa, Ont.; Watson Goepel LLP, Vancouver, B.C.
Transfer Agents - Computershare Trust Company of Canada Inc., Vancouver, B.C.
Profile - (B.C. 2018) Provides human resources services consisting of recurring contract staffing services, on-occurrence permanent placement services, and a Software-as-a-Service performance management tool.

Operates boutique executive search, staffing, office administration and consulting firms in southwestern Ontario that offer professional staffing services for industries including accounting, finance, information technology and human resources. The company provides cross-selling opportunities, access to proprietary operational tools, and a scalable, centralized back-office system to support growth. Also provides a web-based people management application, a simple and scalable tool designed around data analytics, meeting facilitation, immediate feedback and predictive insights, for managers requiring no upfront configuration and implementation steps. The product is available at pulsifyapp.com in trial and paid annual subscription versions.

Common suspended from TSX-VEN, May 8, 2023.

Predecessor Detail - Name changed from Bay Talent Group Inc., Apr. 21, 2020.

Directors - Simon Dealy, CEO, Boston, Mass.; Sean Cleary, Oakville, Ont.; Hamed Shahbazi, Vancouver, B.C.; Jonson Sun, Toronto, Ont.

Other Exec. Officers - Charlie Cooper, CFO

Capital Stock

	Authorized (shs.)	Outstanding (shs.)[1]
Common	unlimited	84,606,176

[1] At Aug. 8, 2022

Major Shareholder - Widely held at Aug. 8, 2022.

Price Range - HIRE/TSX-VEN (S)

Year	Volume	High	Low	Close
2022	20,784,473	$0.25	$0.02	$0.03
2021	18,682,022	$0.83	$0.21	$0.23
2020	18,030,972	$0.90	$0.13	$0.82
2019	375,375	$0.60	$0.20	$0.40

Recent Close: $0.01

Wholly Owned Subsidiaries

Bay Talent Group Inc., Toronto, Ont.
- 100% int. in **PTC Accounting and Finance Inc.**, Canada.
- 100% int. in **Provision IT Resources Ltd.**, Ont.

The Headhunters Recruitment, Inc., Alta.
- **New Wave Holdings Corp.**, Vancouver, B.C. (see Survey of Mines)

Leaders and Co., Consulting in Governance and Leadership Inc., Canada.
Taylor Ryan Inc., B.C.
2449983 Ontario Inc., Ont. dba Kavin Management & Recruiting.

Financial Statistics

Periods ended:	12m Dec. 31/21[A]		12m Dec. 31/20[A]
	$000s	%Chg	$000s
Operating revenue	**27,704**	**+143**	**11,398**
Cost of sales	15,523		7,959
Salaries & benefits	9,659		4,115
General & admin expense	4,654		2,572
Operating expense	**29,836**	**+104**	**14,645**
Operating income	**(2,132)**	**n.a.**	**(3,247)**
Deprec., depl. & amort.	909		279
Finance costs, gross	540		171
Write-downs/write-offs	(1,267)		(205)
Pre-tax income	**(5,047)**	**n.a.**	**(10,701)**
Income taxes	326		15
Net income	**(5,373)**	**n.a.**	**(10,716)**
Cash & equivalent	1,743		341
Accounts receivable	5,543		2,541
Current assets	7,730		3,205
Fixed assets, net	245		176
Right-of-use assets	193		235
Intangibles, net	15,995		8,855
Total assets	**24,164**	**+83**	**13,199**
Bank indebtedness	1,385		465
Accts. pay. & accr. liabs	7,264		2,233
Current liabilities	11,238		11,925
Long-term debt, gross	4,643		2,431
Long-term debt, net	2,961		142
Long-term lease liabilities	89		215
Shareholders' equity	4,020		(1,336)
Cash from oper. activs	**(2,209)**	**n.a.**	**(3,733)**
Cash from fin. activs	8,471		6,551
Cash from invest. activs	(4,860)		(4,782)
Net cash position	**1,743**	**+411**	**341**
Capital expenditures	(55)		nil
	$		$
Earnings per share*	(0.08)		(0.02)
Cash flow per share*	(0.03)		(0.08)
	shs		shs
No. of shs. o/s*	83,888,640		56,888,479
Avg. no. of shs. o/s*	68,293,875		48,591,463
	%		%
Net profit margin	(19.39)		(94.02)
Return on equity	n.m.		n.m.
Return on assets	(25.68)		(107.42)

* Common
[A] Reported in accordance with IFRS

Latest Results

Periods ended:	3m Mar. 31/22[A]		3m Mar. 31/21[A]
	$000s	%Chg	$000s
Operating revenue	9,109	+66	5,490
Net income	(1,471)	n.a.	2,247
	$		$
Earnings per share*	(0.02)		0.04

* Common
[A] Reported in accordance with IFRS

Historical Summary
(as originally stated)

Fiscal Year	Oper. Rev. $000s	Net Inc. Bef. Disc. $000s	EPS* $
2021[A]	27,704	(5,373)	(0.08)
2020[A]	11,398	(10,716)	(0.02)
2019[A]	11,962	(7,189)	(0.25)
2018[A1]	8,675	(1,693)	(0.09)
2017[A1,2]	392	(592)	(0.20)

* Common
[A] Reported in accordance with IFRS
[1] Results pertain to (old) Bay Talent Group Inc.
[2] 30 weeks ended Dec. 31, 2017.
Note: Adjusted throughout for 1-for-2 cons. in Dec. 2019

H.49 Hispania Resources Inc.

Symbol - ESPN **Exchange** - TSX-VEN **CUSIP** - 43359H
Head Office - 602-15 Toronto St, Toronto, ON, M5C 2E3 **Telephone** - (416) 457-0549
Website - meridaminerals.com
Email - norm@hispaniaresources.com
Investor Relations - Norman E. Brewster (416) 970-3223
Auditors - Dale Matheson Carr-Hilton LaBonte LLP C.A., Vancouver, B.C.
Transfer Agents - TSX Trust Company, Calgary, Alta.
Profile - (Ont. 2022; orig. Alta., 2018) Has mineral interests in Spain.

Holds Herrerias zinc-copper-lead prospect, 8,924 hectares, 80 km east-southeast of Badajoz; and Lumbrales tin-molybdenum property, 2,900 hectares, 150 km west of Salamanca, including formerly producing Mari Tere mine and two other artisanal tin prospects.

In April 2023, the company acquired Lumbrales tin-molybdenum property, which covers 2,900 hectares and includes formerly producing Mari Tere mine and two other artisanal tin prospects in the Stanniferous Iberian Belt in Spain, from **Sociedad DeInvestigación Y Explotación Minera De Castilla Y León, S.A.** for €250,000, which was paid during 2022.

During 2022, the company agreed to acquire Segoviana West property in Spain from **Sociedad DeInvestigación Y Explotación Minera De Castilla Y León, S.A.** for €300,000. The acquisition is subject to approval of Spanish mining authority and the transfer of the permit by the Spanish mining authority to the company. The company paid the purchase price as a refundable deposit which shall be returned if the mining authority does not grant the transfer of permit.

Recent Merger and Acquisition Activity

Status: completed **Revised:** Mar. 31, 2022
UPDATE: The transaction was completed. Winston issued a total of 51,010,159 common shares at a deemed price of 15¢ per share. PREVIOUS: Winston Capital Group Inc. entered into a letter of intent for the Qualifying Transaction reverse takeover acquisition of private Toronto, Ont.-based Merida Minerals Inc., which holds 90-sq.-km Puebla de la Reina zinc-copper-lead prospect in southwestern Spain, on a share-for-share basis, which would result in the issuance of 44,676,825 common shares at a deemed price of 10¢ per share. Upon completion, Merida would amalgamate with Winston's wholly owned 2797200 Ontario Inc., and Winston would change its name to Merida Minerals Inc. and continue its incorporation into Ontario from Alberta. Dec. 9, 2020 - A definitive agreement was entered into. Jan. 31, 2022 - Merida completed a private placement of 6,333,334 units (1 common share & ½ warrant) at 15¢ per unit, with warrants exercisable at 30¢ per share for two years.

Predecessor Detail - Name changed from Merida Minerals Holdings Inc., Dec. 14, 2022.

Directors - Norman E. Brewster, pres. & CEO, Norwood, Ont.; Rahim Allani, corp. sec., Toronto, Ont.; Eduardo Olarte, Spain

Other Exec. Officers - Kyle Appleby, CFO; Brian H. Newton, chief geologist

Capital Stock

	Authorized (shs.)	Outstanding (shs.)[1]
Preferred	unlimited	nil
Common	unlimited	58,510,159

[1] At May 30, 2023

Major Shareholder - Widely held at Oct. 14, 2022.

Price Range - ESPN/TSX-VEN

Year	Volume	High	Low	Close
2022	4,567,368	$0.18	$0.06	$0.11
2020	149,000	$0.35	$0.10	$0.10
2019	1,214,558	$0.55	$0.30	$0.55

Recent Close: $0.16

Capital Stock Changes - On Mar. 31, 2022, 51,010,159 common shares were issued pursuant to the Qualifying Transaction reverse takeover acquisition of (old) Merida Minerals Inc.

Wholly Owned Subsidiaries

La Joya Minerals S.L.U., Spain.
Merida Mining Corp., Canada.

Financial Statistics

Periods ended:	12m Dec. 31/22[A1]		6m Dec. 31/21[oA]
	$000s	%Chg	$000s
Exploration expense	31		7
General & admin expense	836		253
Operating expense	**867**	**n.a.**	**260**
Operating income	**(867)**	**n.a.**	**(260)**
Pre-tax income	**(1,516)**	**n.a.**	**(174)**
Net income	**(1,516)**	**n.a.**	**(174)**
Cash & equivalent	93		814
Current assets	93		814
Total assets	**1,051**	**+29**	**814**
Accts. pay. & accr. liabs	292		150
Long-term debt, gross	56		49
Long-term debt, net	nil		49
Shareholders' equity	(242)		197
Cash from oper. activs	**(229)**	**n.a.**	**(5)**
Cash from fin. activs	238		660
Cash from invest. activs	(724)		nil
Net cash position	**93**	**-89**	**814**
	$		$
Earnings per share*	(0.03)		(0.00)
Cash flow per share*	(0.00)		(0.00)
	shs		shs
No. of shs. o/s*	58,510,159		n.a.
Avg. no. of shs. o/s*	56,313,813		44,676,826
	%		%
Net profit margin	n.a.		...
Return on equity	n.m.		...
Return on assets	(248.93)		...

* Common
[o] Restated
[A] Reported in accordance with IFRS
[1] Results reflect the Mar. 31, 2022, reverse takeover acquisition of (old) Merida Minerals Inc.

Historical Summary
(as originally stated)

Fiscal Year	Oper. Rev.	Net Inc. Bef. Disc.	EPS*
	$000s	$000s	$
2022[A1]	nil	(1,516)	(0.03)
2021[A2]	nil	(1,305)	(0.03)
2020[A2]	nil	(1,035)	(0.02)

* Common
[A] Reported in accordance with IFRS
[1] Results reflect the Mar. 31, 2022, reverse takeover acquisition of (old) Merida Minerals Inc.
[2] Results pertain to (old) Merida Minerals Inc.

H.50 Home Capital Group Inc.*

Symbol - HCG **Exchange** - TSX **CUSIP** - 436913
Head Office - 2300-145 King St W, Toronto, ON, M5H 1J8 **Telephone** - (416) 360-4663 **Toll-free** - (877) 903-2133 **Fax** - (416) 363-7611
Website - www.homecapital.com
Email - jill.macrae@hometrust.ca
Investor Relations - Jill MacRae (877) 903-2133
Auditors - Ernst & Young LLP C.A., Toronto, Ont.
Bankers - Bank of Montreal; Royal Bank of Canada
Lawyers - Gowling WLG (Canada) LLP; Torys LLP
Transfer Agents - Computershare Trust Company of Canada Inc., Toronto, Ont.
FP500 Revenue Ranking - 342

Profile - (Ont. 1988; orig. Can., 1968) Through wholly owned **Home Trust Company**, a regulated financial institution, offers residential and non-residential commercial mortgage lending, securitization of mortgage products, consumer lending and credit card issuing services, and deposits.

Operations are carried out through three segments: mortgage lending, consumer lending and deposits.

Mortgage Lending - Consists of single-family residential lending, insured residential lending, residential commercial lending and non-residential commercial lending. The single-family residential portfolio includes the company's traditional or "Classic" mortgage loans. The traditional mortgages have loan-to-value ratios of 80% or less, serve selected segments of the Canadian financial services marketplace that are not the focus of the major financial institutions and are funded by the company's deposit products and financing activities. Insured residential lending consists of single-family Accelerator and multi-unit residential mortgages that are generally funded through **Canada Mortgage and Housing Corporation** sponsored mortgage-backed security and bond securitization programs. Residential commercial lending consists of insured and uninsured residential commercial mortgage loans that are secured by residential property. Non-residential commercial lending includes store and apartment mortgages and commercial mortgages.

Consumer Lending - Consists of credit card and line of credit lending and other consumer retail lending for durable household goods, such as water heaters and larger-ticket home improvement items. The company's Equityline VISA product, secured by residential property, represents more than 90% of the credit card portfolio. The company also offers cash-secured and unsecured credit card products. Consumer loans are supported by holdbacks or guarantees from the distributors of such items and/or collateral charges registered on title to real property. Credit card and consumer loans are funded by deposits.

Deposits - Home Trust offers deposits via brokers and financial planners and through its direct-to-consumer deposit brand Oaken Financial. Uninsured assets are largely funded by its deposit activities. Deposits are generally taken for fixed terms, varying from 30 days to five years, and carry fixed rates of interest over the full term of the deposit and variable rate savings accounts. The company is a member of the **Canada Deposit Insurance Corporation** (CDIC) and its retail deposit products are eligible for CDIC coverage, up to the applicable limits.

Home Trust also conducts business through wholly owned **Home Bank**, a Schedule I Bank offering deposit and mortgage products through a number of channels.

Loan Portfolio

As at Mar. 31, 2023	
Product Type	$000s
Single-family residential mtges	13,786,502
Securitized residential mtges	4,399,066
Residential commercial mtges	355,841
Non-residential comml. mtges	1,649,251
Credit cards & lines of credit	692,576
Other consumer retail loans	18,749
	20,901,985

On Aug. 15, 2022, the company announced that it had received an unsolicited, non-binding and conditional expression of interest from an arm's-length third party expressing an interest in acquiring all of the company's issued and outstanding common shares, which the board of directors reviewed and determined was not in the best interests of the company or its shareholders.

Recent Merger and Acquisition Activity

Status: pending **Revised:** Aug. 24, 2023
UPDATE: Regulatory approvals under the Bank Act (Canada) and Trust and Loan Companies Act (Canada) were received. Expected closing date was Aug/ 31, 2023. PREVIOUS: Smith Financial Corporation (SFC), a company controlled by Stephen Smith, agreed to acquire all outstanding common shares of Home Capital Group Inc. it does not already own for $44 per share. SFC owns 9.1% of the outstanding common shares of Home Capital. The agreement includes a go-shop period extending until Dec. 30, 2022, during which Home Capital is permitted to actively solicit, evaluate and enter into negotiations with third parties that express an interest in acquiring the company. If Home Capital terminates the agreement within five business days of expiry of the go-shop period, it must pay a $25,000,000 termination fee and a $50,000,000 termination fee is payable if Home Capital terminates more than five business days after expiry of go-shop period. A reverse termination fee of $60,000,000 is payable SFC under certain conditions. The transaction was expected to close in mid-2023. If the transaction closes on or after May 20, 2023, the purchase price would be increased by $0.00273973 per share. Feb. 9, 2023 - Court approval was received. Feb. 8, 2023 - Home Capital shareholders approved the transaction. Jan. 3, 2023 - The go-shop period expired, during which Home Capital did not receive an acquisition proposal. Apr. 17, 2023 - The Commissioner of Competition has issued a "no-action letter" in respect of the transaction. The issuance of the no-action letter satisfies the Competition Act closing condition of the transaction. The closing was expected to in mid-2023. If the transaction closes on or after May 20, 2023, the purchase price would be increased by an amount equal to $0.00273973 per share in cash per day up to and including the day prior to the closing.

Predecessor Detail - Name changed from Sonor Resources Corporation, Dec. 15, 1986.

Directors - Alan R. Hibben, chr., Yorks., United Kingdom; Yousry Bissada, pres. & CEO, Toronto, Ont.; Robert J. Blowes, Waterloo, Ont.; David C. Court, Toronto, Ont.; Betty K. DeVita, New York, N.Y.; Paul G. Haggis, Canmore, Alta.; Susan E. Hutchison, Toronto, Ont.; James H. Lisson, Toronto, Ont.; Joseph M. (Joe) Natale, Toronto, Ont.; Dr. Hossein Rahnama, Toronto, Ont.; Lisa L. Ritchie, Toronto, Ont.; Sharon H. Sallows, Toronto, Ont.; Edward J. (Ed) Waitzer, Toronto, Ont.

Other Exec. Officers - David J. F. Cluff, exec. v-p & chief risk officer; Victor DiRisio, exec. v-p & CIO; Mike Henry, exec. v-p, digital & strategy; Bradley W. (Brad) Kotush, exec. v-p & CFO; Brian Leland, exec. v-p, underwriting; Santokh Birk, sr. v-p, fin. & chief acctg. officer; Amy Bruyea, sr. v-p, HR; John Hong, sr. v-p, chief compliance officer & chief AML officer; Liane Kim, sr. v-p, internal audit; James Pelletier, sr. v-p, comml. real estate lending; Mark R. Hemingway, gen. counsel & corp. sec.; Joanna Grossman, asst. gen. counsel & asst. corp. sec.

Capital Stock

	Authorized (shs.)	Outstanding (shs.)[1]
Preferred	unlimited	nil
Common	unlimited	38,211,460

[1] At June 30, 2023

Options - At Dec. 31, 2022, options were outstanding to purchase 621,473 common shares at a weighted average exercise price of $23.28 per share with a weighted average remaining life of 1.7 years.

Major Shareholder - Widely held at Jan. 31, 2023.

Price Range - HCG/TSX

Year	Volume	High	Low	Close
2022	61,920,217	$43.02	$23.82	$42.58
2021	41,853,647	$46.92	$29.50	$39.07
2020	75,410,445	$34.79	$13.67	$29.70
2019	82,773,520	$35.49	$14.24	$32.96
2018	72,198,843	$18.63	$12.48	$14.40

Recent Close: $44.22

Capital Stock Changes - During 2022, 20,244 common shares were issued on exercise of options, 1,547,296 common shares were repurchased under a Substantial Issuer Bid, 3,562,293 common shares were repurchased under a Normal Course Issuer Bid and 11,310 common shares were returned to treasury.

Dividends

HCG com Var. Ra pa Q[1]

$0.15	Sept. 15/23	$0.15	June 15/23
$0.15	Mar. 15/23	$0.15	Dec. 15/22

Paid in 2023: $0.45 2022: $0.60 2021: n.a.

[1] Quarterly divd normally payable in June/17 has been omitted.

Long-Term Debt - At Dec. 31, 2022, the company had no long-term debt.

Wholly Owned Subsidiaries

Home Trust Company, Toronto, Ont.
- 100% int. in **Home Bank**, Toronto, Ont.

Financial Statistics

Periods ended:	12m Dec. 31/22[A]		12m Dec. 31/21[A]
	$000s	%Chg	$000s
Total revenue	**1,001,613**	**+19**	**844,821**
Salaries & benefits	107,060		105,039
General & admin. expense	148,250		134,345
Operating expense	**265,122**	**+7**	**248,832**
Operating income	**736,491**	**+24**	**595,989**
Finance costs, gross	510,071		295,476
Pre-tax income	**207,017**	**-38**	**334,172**
Income taxes	56,789		89,438
Net income	**150,228**	**-39**	**244,734**
Cash & equivalent	494,667		507,713
Investments	21,346,648		18,844,561
Fixed assets, net	7,116		8,932
Right-of-use assets	16,019		19,164
Intangibles, net	64,900		65,642
Total assets	**22,727,106**	**+13**	**20,146,954**
Bank indebtedness	nil		388,000
Accts. pay. & accr. liabs	75,388		116,307
Lease liabilities	20,759		23,701
Shareholders' equity	1,555,085		1,571,241
Cash from oper. activs	**183,236**	**-51**	**373,354**
Cash from fin. activs	(179,895)		(372,441)
Cash from invest. activs	(16,387)		(18,169)
Net cash position	**494,667**	**-3**	**507,713**
Capital expenditures	(1,012)		(1,116)
	$		$
Earnings per share*	3.68		4.84
Cash flow per share*	4.49		7.38
Cash divd. per share*	0.60		nil
	shs		shs
No. of shs. o/s*	37,885,649		42,986,304
Avg. no. of shs. o/s*	40,774,672		50,610,534
	%		%
Net profit margin	15.00		28.97
Return on equity	9.61		15.05
Return on assets	2.43		2.33

* Common
[A] Reported in accordance with IFRS

Latest Results

Periods ended:	6m June 30/23[A]		6m June 30/22[A]
	$000s	%Chg	$000s
Total revenue	718,588	+68	428,445
Net income	109,897	+28	85,969
	$		$
Earnings per share*	2.86		2.01

* Common
[A] Reported in accordance with IFRS

Historical Summary
(as originally stated)

Fiscal Year	Total Rev.	Net Inc. Bef. Disc.	EPS*
	$000s	$000s	$
2022[A]	1,001,613	150,228	3.68
2021[A]	844,821	244,734	4.84
2020[A]	948,646	175,690	3.35
2019[A]	933,963	135,986	2.29
2018[A]	830,399	132,603	1.66

* Common
[A] Reported in accordance with IFRS

H.51 Hopefield Ventures Two Inc.

Symbol - HVII.P **Exchange** - TSX-VEN **CUSIP** - 43954M
Head Office - 2200-885 Georgia St W, Vancouver, BC, V6C 3E8 **Telephone** - (604) 691-6100
Email - mark.binns1@gmail.com
Investor Relations - Mark Binns (604) 691-6100
Auditors - Hay & Watson C.A., Vancouver, B.C.
Lawyers - Cassels Brock & Blackwell LLP, Vancouver, B.C.
Transfer Agents - Computershare Trust Company of Canada Inc., Vancouver, B.C.
Profile - (B.C. 2022) Capital Pool Company.
Common listed on TSX-VEN, Jan. 9, 2023.
Directors - Mark Binns, CEO & corp. sec., North Vancouver, B.C.; Mitchell W. Demeter, Grand Cayman, Cayman Islands; Daniel (Dan) Reitzik, Vancouver, B.C.
Other Exec. Officers - Rob Binns, CFO

Capital Stock

	Authorized (shs.)	Outstanding (shs.)[1]
Common	unlimited	17,887,500

[1] At Jan. 9, 2023

Major Shareholder - Widely held at Jan. 9, 2023.
Recent Close: $0.09
Capital Stock Changes - On Jan. 9, 2023, an initial public offering of 2,500,000 common shares was completed at 10¢ per share.

H.52 Hoshi Resource Corp.

Symbol - HRC.P **Exchange** - TSX-VEN **CUSIP** - 441015
Head Office - 900-903 8 Ave SW, Calgary, AB, T2P 0P7 **Telephone** - (403) 617-9169
Email - hoshiresource@gmail.com
Investor Relations - John F. K. Aihoshi (403) 617-9169
Auditors - MNP LLP C.A., Calgary, Alta.
Transfer Agents - Odyssey Trust Company, Calgary, Alta.
Profile - (Alta. 2021) Capital Pool Company.
Directors - Kevin R. Baker, CEO, Calgary, Alta.; John F. K. Aihoshi, CFO & corp. sec., Calgary, Alta.; Al J. Kroontje, Calgary, Alta.; Alex Watson, Vancouver, B.C.

Capital Stock

	Authorized (shs.)	Outstanding (shs.)[1]
Common	unlimited	6,600,000

[1] At Feb. 8, 2022

Major Shareholder - Kevin R. Baker held 15.15% interest, Al J. Kroontje held 15.15% interest and Alex Watson held 15.15% interest at Feb. 8, 2022.

Price Range - HRC.P/TSX-VEN

Year	Volume	High	Low	Close
2022............	36,500	$0.15	$0.10	$0.15

Recent Close: $0.06
Capital Stock Changes - On Feb. 8, 2022, an initial public offering of 3,000,000 common shares was completed at 10¢ per share.

H.53 Humble & Fume Inc.

Symbol - HMBL **Exchange** - CSE **CUSIP** - 44502H
Head Office - 179G Degrassi St, Toronto, ON, M4M 2K8 **Telephone** - (778) 400-7894 **Toll-free** - (877) 438-4367
Website - corp.humbleandfume.com
Email - invest@humbleandfume.com
Investor Relations - Matthew Mackay (877) 438-4367
Auditors - MNP LLP C.A., Toronto, Ont.
Transfer Agents - Odyssey Trust Company
Profile - (Ont. 2007) Distributes cannabis and cannabis accessories in Canada and the U.S.
Operations are conducted through the following wholly owned subsidiaries:
B.O.B. Headquarters Inc. is a wholesale distributor of cannabis consumption devices for headshops, smoke shops and licensed cannabis stores across Canada, with an extensive portfolio of smoking accessory products including grinders, papers, pipes, vaporizers and cleaning products. Has a warehouse facility in Brandon, Man.
Windship Trading LLC is a distributor of cannabis consumption devices for headshops and smoke shops in the U.S., offering more than 8,000 products including grinders, papers, pipes, vaporizers and cleaning products. Has active operations in San Marcos, Tex.; Denver, Colo.; Las Vegas, Nev.; and Los Angeles, Calif.
Humble Cannabis Solutions Inc. is a North American cannabis sales agency, distributing both cannabis and cannabis accessories to more than 1,000 retail locations across Canada, as well as throughout California.
Brands offered include PAX, RYOT®, Pulsar, Grav, Canadian Lumber, Storz & Bickel, and Bic.
On Oct. 11, 2022, the company acquired **Barlow Printing, LLC**, a licensed California cannabis distributor, for $500,000.
On Apr. 16, 2022, the company acquired an 80% interest in **Cabo Connection**, a licensed California cannabis distributor, for $773,160 cash and issuance of 128,860 common shares. Subsequently, in the first quarter of fiscal 2023, the company's interest in Cabo decreased to 55%.
Predecessor Detail - Name changed from Canada Iron Inc., June 11, 2021, following reverse takeover acquisition of Canada Iron Inc. by Humble & Fume Inc.
Directors - Jakob Ripshtein, chr., CEO & CEO, Perennial Brands Inc., Toronto, Ont.; Robert Ritchot, pres., North American accessories, Brandon, Man.; Shawn Dym, Toronto, Ont.; Mark Hubler, North Oaks, Minn.; Matthew Shalhoub, Toronto, Ont.
Other Exec. Officers - Jared Yeager, COO; Matthew Mackay, CFO; Kimberley Thomas-Ritchot, contr.; Chris Candelario, pres., U.S. distrib.; Nathan Todd, CEO, U.S. opers.

Capital Stock

	Authorized (shs.)	Outstanding (shs.)[1]
Common	unlimited	124,161,329

[1] At Nov. 29, 2022

Major Shareholder - Matthew Shalhoub held 30.38% interest and Robert Ritchot held 18.73% interest at Oct. 19, 2022.

Price Range - HMBL/CSE

Year	Volume	High	Low	Close
2022............	6,300,153	$0.44	$0.01	$0.12
2021............	20,593,036	$0.83	$0.36	$0.43

Recent Close: $0.03
Capital Stock Changes - In November 2021, private placement of 18,795,471 common shares was completed at Cdn$0.53 per share for proceeds of US$8,000,000. Also during fiscal 2022, common shares were issued as follows: 650,279 on vesting of restricted share units, 471,698 as issuance cost and 202,500 on exercise of options; 117,370 common shares were returned to treasury.

Wholly Owned Subsidiaries

B.O.B. Headquarters Inc., Man.
Barlow Printing, LLC, Calif.
Fume Labs Inc., Ont.
Humble Cannabis Solutions Inc., Ont.
PWF Holdco Inc., Del.
- 100% int. in **Windship Trading, LLC**, Tex.

Subsidiaries

55% int. in **Cabo Connection**, Los Angeles, Calif.
55% int. in **HC Solutions Holdings Inc.**, Del.
55% int. in **HC Solutions of California LLC**, Del.

Financial Statistics

Periods ended:	12m June 30/22[A]		12m June 30/21[□A1]
	$000s	%Chg	$000s
Operating revenue........................	**66,150**	**-11**	**74,114**
Cost of sales....................................	53,484		60,453
Salaries & benefits..........................	13,233		11,444
General & admin expense...............	8,133		6,850
Stock-based compensation............	1,595		1,243
Other operating expense.................	1,214		920
Operating expense........................	**77,659**	**-3**	**79,667**
Operating income.........................	**(11,509)**	**n.a.**	**(5,553)**
Deprec., depl. & amort.....................	850		1,208
Finance income...............................	18		26
Finance costs, gross........................	254		4,499
Write-downs/write-offs....................	(3,180)		nil
Pre-tax income.............................	**(16,142)**	**n.a.**	**(13,037)**
Income taxes....................................	(52)		(38)
Net income....................................	**(16,090)**	**n.a.**	**(12,998)**
Cash & equivalent............................	6,305		9,655
Inventories.......................................	15,382		16,751
Accounts receivable........................	6,185		2,719
Current assets..................................	31,947		32,672
Fixed assets, net..............................	1,197		2,223
Right-of-use assets..........................	1,687		1,759
Intangibles, net................................	1,296		nil
Total assets....................................	**36,456**	**-1**	**36,654**
Accts. pay. & accr. liabs...................	8,031		5,250
Current liabilities..............................	8,211		5,873
Long-term lease liabilities................	1,745		1,474
Shareholders' equity........................	24,433		29,308
Non-controlling interest...................	2,068		nil
Cash from oper. activs..................	**(11,797)**	**n.a.**	**(5,711)**
Cash from fin. activs........................	11,140		8,452
Cash from invest. activs..................	(2,320)		87
Net cash position...........................	**6,305**	**-35**	**9,655**
Capital expenditures........................	(1,078)		(83)
	$		$
Earnings per share*.........................	(0.14)		(0.21)
Cash flow per share*........................	(0.10)		(0.10)
	shs		shs
No. of shs. o/s*................................	123,939,882		103,937,304
Avg. no. of shs. o/s*.........................	116,722,797		59,115,578
	%		%
Net profit margin..............................	(24.32)		(17.54)
Return on equity...............................	(59.88)		(84.17)
Return on assets..............................	(43.32)		(24.17)
Foreign sales percent......................	57		62

* Common
□ Restated
[A] Reported in accordance with IFRS
[1] Results prior to June 14, 2021, pertain to and reflect the reverse takeover acquisition of (old) Humble & Fume Inc.

Latest Results

Periods ended:	3m Sept. 30/22[A]		3m Sept. 30/21[A]
	$000s	%Chg	$000s
Operating revenue...........................	18,397	+2	18,052
Net income......................................	(4,729)	n.a.	(1,668)
	$		$
Earnings per share*.........................	(0.03)		(0.02)

* Common
[A] Reported in accordance with IFRS

Historical Summary
(as originally stated)

Fiscal Year	Oper. Rev.	Net Inc. Bef. Disc.	EPS*
	$000s	$000s	$
2022[A]...................	66,150	(16,090)	(0.14)
2021[A]...................	74,114	(12,998)	(0.20)
2020[A]...................	43,349	(15,693)	(0.26)
2019[A]...................	33,880	(5,072)	(0.15)

* Common
[A] Reported in accordance with IFRS

H.54 Hunter Technology Corp.

Symbol - HOC **Exchange** - TSX-VEN **CUSIP** - 445737
Head Office - 1800-510 Georgia St W, Vancouver, BC, V6B 0M3 **Telephone** - (604) 689-3355 **Toll-free** - (888) 977-0970
Website - huntertechnology.com
Email - ir@huntertechnology.com
Investor Relations - Dr. Konstantinos S. Ghertsos (778) 655-9202
Auditors - Dale Matheson Carr-Hilton LaBonte LLP C.A., Vancouver, B.C.
Bankers - The Bank of Nova Scotia, Calgary, Alta.
Lawyers - Lexas Law Group, Vancouver, B.C.
Transfer Agents - Computershare Trust Company of Canada Inc.
Profile - (B.C. 1980) Developing smart trading platforms for physical oil transactions under the brand name OilEx and OilExchange. Also seeking new business opportunities.
The OilEx trading platform facilitates the buying and selling of physical oil by independent producers to corporate consumers, traders and sovereign purchasers.
The OilExchange is an oil supply chain intelligence service which provides data collection, monitoring and analytics functions.
In December 2022, the company sold wholly owned **FinFabrik Limited** for a nominal cash consideration.
Predecessor Detail - Name changed from Hunter Oil Corp., Nov. 2, 2020, pursuant to change of business to focus on development of the Oilex trading platform.
Directors - Dr. Konstantinos S. (Kostas) Ghertsos, CEO & acting CFO, Zug, Switzerland; Alain E. Fernandez, Zug, Switzerland; Andrew Hromyk, Vancouver, B.C.

Capital Stock

	Authorized (shs.)	Outstanding (shs.)[1]
Preferred	25,000,000	nil
Common	unlimited	2,266,559

[1] At May 29, 2023

Major Shareholder - Dr. Konstantinos S. (Kostas) Ghertsos held 17.6% interest at Sept. 9, 2022.

Price Range - HOC/TSX-VEN

Year	Volume	High	Low	Close
2022............	652,767	$5.00	$0.23	$0.23
2021............	1,105,713	$35.40	$2.00	$2.50
2020............	102,237	$27.40	$1.74	$25.80
2019............	17,094	$4.00	$1.60	$2.73
2018............	80,008	$36.00	$1.87	$2.53

Consolidation: 1-for-2 cons. in Nov. 2022; 1-for-10 cons. in May 2022; 1.5-for-1 split in Nov. 2020
Recent Close: $0.19
Capital Stock Changes - On May 4, 2022, common shares were consolidated on a 1-for-10 basis. On Nov. 8, 2022, common shares were consolidated on a 1-for-2 basis.

Wholly Owned Subsidiaries

Digiledger Holdings AG, Switzerland.
Hunter Oil Management Corp., United States.
- 100% int. in **Hunter Oil Production Corp.**

Hunter Technology Holdings Ltd., United Kingdom.

Financial Statistics

Periods ended:	12m Dec. 31/22[A]		12m Dec. 31/21[A]
	US$000s	%Chg	US$000s
Salaries & benefits	nil		367
General & admin expense	374		557
Stock-based compensation	nil		465
Other operating expense	nil		906
Operating expense	**374**	**-84**	**2,295**
Operating income	**(374)**	**n.a.**	**(2,295)**
Deprec., depl. & amort.	nil		862
Finance costs, gross	32		nil
Write-downs/write-offs	nil		(9,139)
Pre-tax income	**(67)**	**n.a.**	**(12,226)**
Income taxes	nil		(756)
Net income	**(67)**	**n.a.**	**(11,470)**
Cash & equivalent	13		1
Accounts receivable	7		2
Current assets	25		8
Total assets	**52**	**+44**	**36**
Bank indebtedness	617		nil
Accts. pay. & accr. liabs	154		593
Current liabilities	771		692
Shareholders' equity	(719)		(657)
Cash from oper. activs	**(501)**	**n.a.**	**(1,751)**
Cash from fin. activs	535		99
Cash from invest. activs	(22)		(13)
Net cash position	**13**	**n.m.**	**1**
	US$		US$
Earnings per share*	(0.02)		(5.00)
Cash flow per share*	(0.22)		(0.77)
	shs		shs
No. of shs. o/s*	2,266,559		2,266,733
Avg. no. of shs. o/s*	2,266,559		2,266,733
	%		%
Net profit margin	n.a.		n.a.
Return on equity	n.m.		n.m.
Return on assets	(79.55)		(194.23)

* Common
[A] Reported in accordance with IFRS

Latest Results

Periods ended:	3m Mar. 31/23[A]		3m Mar. 31/22[A]
	US$000s	%Chg	US$000s
Net income	(81)	n.a.	87
	US$		US$
Earnings per share*	(0.04)		0.04

* Common
[A] Reported in accordance with IFRS

Historical Summary
(as originally stated)

Fiscal Year	Oper. Rev. US$000s	Net Inc. Bef. Disc. US$000s	EPS* US$
2022[A]	nil	(67)	(0.02)
2021[A]	nil	(11,470)	(5.00)
2020[A]	nil	(1,093)	(1.00)
2019[A]	nil	(544)	(0.53)
2018[A]	nil	(1,055)	(1.20)

* Common
[A] Reported in accordance with IFRS

Note: Adjusted throughout for 1-for-2 cons. in Nov. 2022; 1-for-10 cons. in May 2022; 1.5-for-1 split in Nov. 2020

H.55 Hut 8 Mining Corp.*

Symbol - HUT **Exchange** - TSX **CUSIP** - 44812T
Head Office - 500-24 Duncan St, Toronto, ON, M5V 2B8 **Telephone** - (647) 256-1992
Website - hut8.io
Email - sue@hut8.io
Investor Relations - Suzanne Ennis (416) 606-9212
Auditors - Raymond Chabot Grant Thornton LLP C.A., Montréal, Qué.
Transfer Agents - Computershare Trust Company of Canada Inc., Vancouver, B.C.
FP500 Revenue Ranking - 704
Employees - 98 at Dec. 31, 2022
Profile - (B.C. 2011) Mines and holds Bitcoin and provides cloud and colocation services.

Operations consist of the following:

Digital Asset Mining - Owns 93 mining containers, which are specialized freight data centres outfitted for Bitcoin mining, in Medicine Hat and Drumheller, Alta. The Drumheller facility consists of 37 mining containers operating at a maximum capacity of 42 MW; and the Medicine Hat facility consists of 56 mining containers operating at a maximum capacity of 67 MW. At Dec. 31, 2022, the company held 9,086 self-mined Bitcoin.

High Performance Computing - This business consists of five data centre facilities totaling 80,000 sq. ft., in Vaughan and Mississauga, Ont.; and Vancouver (2) and Kelowna, B.C., offering cloud and colocation services. Cloud services include Infrastructure-as-a-Service (IaaS) cloud computing, storage and disaster recovery cloud solutions and other offerings to customers across Canada. Data centre colocation services protect and connect customers' valuable information assets through managed hosting solutions that administer various aspects of customer's hardware, software or operating systems in public or privately accessible environment, as well as disaster recovery services, provided under custom contractual arrangements, which includes a back-up office facility that can be used in case of disaster.

On Feb. 9, 2023, the company received a notice of termination from **Validus Power Corp.** of the company's lease at the North Bay, Ont., facility. The company contends the notice of termination is without merit and reserves all rights in respect thereof, which it expects to address as part of the proceedings before the court. A counterclaim was received on Feb. 21, 2023, from Validus Power denying the allegations regarding its failure to meet contractual obligations under the power purchase agreement in which Validus would deliver new power of up to 100 MW on a physical off-take basis and develop a Bitcoin mining facility in North Bay. The company considers the counterclaim without merit and plans to prosecute the aforementioned matters.

In September 2022, the company discontinued Ethereum mining operations as a result of changing its consensus mechanism to proof-of-stake, an alternative method in validating cryptocurrency transactions.

In May 2022, the company acquired all of the mining equipments from the company's sole remaining hosting client, consisting of 960 MicroBT Whatsminer M31S+ machines for an undisclosed amount. As a result, the company adopted a 100% self-mining business model. The acquisition added fleet of mining equipments totaling 81 PH/s in incremental hashrate.

Recent Merger and Acquisition Activity

Status: pending **Revised:** Apr. 27, 2023
UPDATE: New Hut filed an amended registration statement whereby New Hut's expected installed self-mining capacity was increased to 7.02 EH/s. PREVIOUS: Hut 8 Mining Corp. and U.S. Data Mining Group, Inc. (USBTC) entered into a merger of equals transaction whereby shares of each company would be exchanged for shares of a new U.S. domiciled company named Hut 8 Corp. (New Hut). Shareholders of Hut 8 would receive 0.2 New Hut common shares for each Hut 8 common share held, which would effectively result in a consolidation of the Hut 8 shares on 1-for-5 basis. USBTC shareholders would receive 0.6716 New Hut common shares for each USBTC share held. On closing, existing Hut 8 shareholders and USBTC shareholders would each own 50% of the shares of New Hut and Hut 8 and USBTC would each be wholly owned subsidiaries of New Hut. The combined company would have 5.6 EH/s (exahashes per second) of installed self-mining capacity and 244 MW of total energy available at five sites with current self-mining operations: Medicine Hat, and Drumheller, Alta.; Niagara Falls, N.Y.; Granbury, and King Mountain, Tex. The 1.7 EH/s installed self-mining production at the King Mountain site is 50% owned by USBTC. New Hut would manage 220 MW of hosting infrastructure at its King Mountain site. The transaction was expected to close in the second quarter of 2023. Mar. 10, 2023 - Hut 8 received a no-action letter which confirms that Competition Bureau of Canada does not intend to challenge the merger before the Competition Tribunal under the provisions of Competition Act. Mar. 13, 2023 - The waiting period under the Hart-Scott-Rodino Antitrust Improvements Act of 1976 has expired.

Predecessor Detail - Name changed from Oriana Resources Corporation, Mar. 2, 2018, following Qualifying Transaction reverse takeover acquisition of (old) Hut 8 Mining Corp. and concurrent amalgamation of (old) Hut 8 with wholly owned 1149835 B.C. Ltd.; basis 1 new for 52.7777 old shs.

Directors - Bill Tai, chr., San Francisco, Calif.; Jaime Leverton, CEO, Toronto, Ont.; Joseph Flinn, Halifax, N.S.; K. Alexi Hefti, Dubai, United Arab Emirates; Carl J. (Rick) Rickertsen, Fla.

Other Exec. Officers - Shenif Visram, CFO; Aniss Amdiss, chief legal officer & corp. sec.; James Beer, sr. v-p, opers.; Erin Dermer, sr. v-p, commun. & culture; Suzanne (Sue) Ennis, v-p, corp. devel. & head, IR; Josh Rayner, v-p, sales

Capital Stock

	Authorized (shs.)	Outstanding (shs.)[1]
Common	unlimited	221,691,708

[1] At Aug. 8, 2023

Options - At Dec. 31, 2022, options were outstanding to purchase 480,000 common shares at the price of $5 per share with weighted average remaining life of 18 months.

Major Shareholder - Widely held at Aug. 8, 2023.

Price Range - HUT/TSX

Year	Volume	High	Low	Close
2022	657,143,885	$10.53	$1.08	$1.16
2021	604,500,262	$20.61	$3.71	$9.93
2020	116,147,487	$4.38	$0.51	$3.49
2019	22,692,484	$2.94	$0.76	$1.07
2018	16,940,779	$5.00	$1.06	$1.40

Recent Close: $3.07

Capital Stock Changes - During 2022, common shares were issued as follows: 49,646,368 under the at-the-market equity program, 1,197,499 on vesting of restricted share units, 76,296 on vesting of deferred share units, 3,333 on exercise of options and 863 on exercise of warrants.

Long-Term Debt - At Dec. 31, 2022, outstanding long term debt totaled $26,121,000 (none current and net of $1,000,000 deferred financing costs) and consisted entirely of 9.5% loan payable, repayable over three years.

Wholly Owned Subsidiaries

Hut 8 Asset Management Inc., Bridgetown, Barbados. Inactive.
Hut 8 High Performance Computing Inc., B.C.
Hut 8 Holdings Inc., Vancouver, B.C.

Financial Statistics

Periods ended:	12m Dec. 31/22[A]		12m Dec. 31/21[A]
	$000s	%Chg	$000s
Operating revenue	**150,682**	**-13**	**173,774**
Cost of sales	81,769		61,688
Salaries & benefits	7,756		4,046
General & admin expense	35,152		26,343
Stock-based compensation	6,913		9,875
Other operating expense	nil		(182)
Operating expense	**131,590**	**+29**	**101,770**
Operating income	**19,092**	**-73**	**72,004**
Deprec., depl. & amort.	94,528		23,288
Finance income	922		2,854
Finance costs, gross	7,592		1,355
Write-downs/write-offs	(113,876)		nil
Pre-tax income	**(233,220)**	**n.a.**	**(67,090)**
Income taxes	9,593		5,620
Net income	**(242,813)**	**n.a.**	**(72,710)**
Cash & equivalent	30,515		140,127
Accounts receivable	1,589		647
Current assets	245,623		468,079
Fixed assets, net	124,959		96,126
Intangibles, net	15,135		nil
Total assets	**412,937**	**-43**	**720,709**
Accts. pay. & accr. liabs	13,916		9,569
Current liabilities	30,133		26,064
Long-term debt, gross	26,121		40,694
Long-term debt, net	14,229		24,200
Long-term lease liabilities	16,973		nil
Shareholders' equity	351,390		565,967
Cash from oper. activs	**(105,034)**	**n.a.**	**(80,241)**
Cash from fin. activs	99,826		455,840
Cash from invest. activs	(103,608)		(235,067)
Net cash position	**30,515**	**-78**	**140,127**
Capital expenditures	(72,701)		(86,431)
	$		$
Earnings per share*	(1.29)		(0.54)
Cash flow per share*	(0.56)		(0.60)
	shs		shs
No. of shs. o/s*	220,547,442		169,590,061
Avg. no. of shs. o/s*	187,769,571		134,156,157
	%		%
Net profit margin	(161.14)		(41.84)
Return on equity	(52.94)		(21.34)
Return on assets	(41.44)		(16.45)
No. of employees (FTEs)	98		n.a.

* Common
[A] Reported in accordance with IFRS

Latest Results

Periods ended:	3m Mar. 31/23[A]		3m Mar. 31/22[A]
	$000s	%Chg	$000s
Operating revenue	19,021	-64	53,333
Net income	108,503	+95	55,708
	$		$
Earnings per share*	0.49		0.33

* Common
[A] Reported in accordance with IFRS

Historical Summary
(as originally stated)

Fiscal Year	Oper. Rev. $000s	Net Inc. Bef. Disc. $000s	EPS* $
2022[A]	150,682	(242,813)	(1.29)
2021[A]	173,774	(72,710)	(0.54)
2020[A]	40,710	19,040	0.20
2019[A]	81,990	2,131	0.02
2018[A1]	49,439	(136,766)	(2.43)

* Common
[A] Reported in accordance with IFRS
[1] Results reflect the Mar. 2, 2018, Qualifying Transaction reverse takeover acquisition of (old) Hut 8 Mining Corp.

H.56 Hydaway Ventures Corp.

Symbol - HIDE.P **Exchange** - TSX-VEN **CUSIP** - 44864E
Head Office - 204-998 Harbourside Dr, North Vancouver, BC, V7P 3T2 **Telephone** - (604) 689-7422
Email - rob@contactfinancial.com
Investor Relations - Robin Gamley (604) 689-7422
Auditors - Manning Elliott LLP C.A., Vancouver, B.C.
Transfer Agents - Endeavor Trust Corporation, Vancouver, B.C.
Profile - (B.C. 2021) Capital Pool Company.

Directors - Robin (Rob) Gamley, CEO, CFO & corp. sec., North Vancouver, B.C.; Gregory (Greg) Bronson, North Vancouver, B.C.; Michael (Mike) Leo, Vancouver, B.C.

Capital Stock

	Authorized (shs.)	Outstanding (shs.)[1]
Common	unlimited	4,500,001

[1] At Aug. 23, 2022

Major Shareholder - Robin (Rob) Gamley held 26.67% interest at Aug. 23, 2022.

Price Range - HIDE.P/TSX-VEN

Year	Volume	High	Low	Close
2022	475,463	$0.36	$0.15	$0.18

Recent Close: $0.13

Capital Stock Changes - On Aug. 23, 2022, an initial public offering of 2,500,000 common shares was completed at 10¢ per share.

H.57 Hydreight Technologies Inc.

Symbol - NURS **Exchange** - TSX-VEN **CUSIP** - 44877L
Head Office - 800-1500 Georgia St W, Vancouver, BC, V6G 2Z6
Email - shane@hydreight.com
Investor Relations - Shane Madden (702) 913-8419
Auditors - MNP LLP C.A., Waterloo, Ont.
Transfer Agents - TSX Trust Company, Vancouver, B.C.
Employees - 1 at Nov. 10, 2022

Profile - (B.C. 2018) Provides the Hydreight mobile application for patients to book at-home appointments with healthcare and wellness professionals, including doctors, naturopaths, pharmacists, nurses and emergency medical technicians, across the U.S.

The company's licenses, medical director offering and technology allow med-spas as well as the healthcare and wellness professionals to be able to offer their services, including IV drip, Botox®, COVID-19 testing, and other medical and medispa treatments, at a location of the customer's choice that is outside of hospitals and medical clinics, such as homes, offices and hotels.

Recent Merger and Acquisition Activity

Status: completed **Revised:** Nov. 28, 2022

UPDATE: The transaction was completed. PREVIOUS: Perihelion Capital Ltd. entered into a letter of intent for the Qualifying Transaction reverse takeover acquisition of Las Vegas, Nev.-based IV Hydreight Inc., a wholly owned subsidiary of Victory Square Technologies Inc. (VST). IV Hydreight provided a mobile application for booking at-home appointments with medical service providers across the U.S. Upon completion, Perihelion would consolidate its common shares on a 1-for-6.46805 basis. July 12, 2022 - A definitive agreement was entered into. As part of the transaction, Perihelion's wholly owned 1203500 B.C. Ltd. would amalgamate with VST's newly incorporated wholly owned 1362795 B.C. Ltd.; VST would transfer IV Hydreight to 1362795 B.C. Ltd. immediately prior to completion of the transaction for issuance of 27,896,825 common shares of 1362795 B.C. Ltd. Upon completion, Perihelion would issue a total of 28,511,479 post-consolidated common shares at a deemed price of 63¢ per share to indirectly acquire IV Hydreight through the acquisition of 1362795 B.C. Ltd. (representing the 27,896,825 shares issued to VST along with the 614,654 shares it had outstanding). Nov. 25, 2022 - Perihelion changed its name to Hydreight Technologies Inc. and completed the share consolidation. VST also completed the transfer of IV Hydreight to 1362795 B.C. Ltd.

Predecessor Detail - Name changed from Perihelion Capital Ltd., Nov. 25, 2022, pursuant to the Qualfying Transaction reverse takeover acquisition of IV Hydreight Inc., indirectly acquired through the acquisition of Victory Square Technologies Inc.'s newly incorporated wholly owned 1362795 B.C. Ltd. Victory Square was the former parent of IV Hydreight, which was transferred to 1362795 B.C. Ltd. immediately prior to completion of the transaction, with 1362795 B.C. Ltd. having concurrently amalgamated with Perihelion's wholly owned 1203500 B.C. Ltd. upon completion of the transaction; basis 1 new for 6.46805 old shs.

Directors - Shane Madden, CEO, Las Vegas, Nev.; Carey Dillen, Vancouver, B.C.; Gabriel (Gabi) Kabazo, Vancouver, B.C.; Dr. Joseph Palumbo, Ohio; Shafin D. Tejani, Vancouver, B.C.; Alexandros (Alexander) Tzilios, North Vancouver, B.C.

Other Exec. Officers - Joshua Sorin, CFO & corp. sec.

Capital Stock

	Authorized (shs.)	Outstanding (shs.)[1]
Common	unlimited	37,842,815

[1] At Dec. 1, 2022

Major Shareholder - Victory Square Technologies Inc. held 73.72% interest at Dec. 1, 2022.

Price Range - NURS/TSX-VEN

Year	Volume	High	Low	Close
2022	166,875	$0.71	$0.45	$0.50
2021	79,390	$1.94	$0.39	$0.71
2020	16,542	$0.71	$0.39	$0.52
2019	133,247	$2.59	$0.65	$0.65

Consolidation: 1-for-6.46805 cons. in Nov. 2022; 1-for-2 cons. in Aug. 2021

Recent Close: $0.33

Capital Stock Changes - In November 2022, common shares were consolidated on a 1-for-6.46805 basis (effective on the TSX Venture Exchange on Dec. 1, 2022), 28,511,479 post-consolidated common shares were issued pursuant to the Qualifying Transaction reverse takeover acquisition of IV Hydreight Inc. and 1,394,841 post-consolidated common shares were issued as finder's fee.

Wholly Owned Subsidiaries

1362795 B.C. Ltd., Vancouver, B.C.
- 100% int. in **IV Hydreight Inc.**, Las Vegas, Nev.
  - 100% int. in **Healthcare Prosoft, LLC**, Nev.

Financial Statistics

Periods ended:	12m Dec. 31/21[A1]		12m Dec. 31/20[A1]
	$000s	%Chg	$000s
Operating revenue	**1,199**	**+165**	**453**
Cost of sales	556		134
Salaries & benefits	279		166
Research & devel. expense	151		119
General & admin expense	731		265
Operating expense	**1,716**	**+151**	**684**
Operating income	**(517)**	**n.a.**	**(231)**
Pre-tax income	**(517)**	**n.a.**	**(231)**
Income taxes	11		nil
Net income	**(528)**	**n.a.**	**(231)**
Cash & equivalent	6		33
Current assets	46		41
Intangibles, net	383		nil
Total assets	**429**	**+946**	**41**
Accts. pay. & accr. liabs	405		18
Current liabilities	1,200		293
Shareholders' equity	(785)		(252)
Cash from oper. activs	**(148)**	**n.a.**	**21**
Cash from fin. activs	500		(1)
Cash from invest. activs	(378)		nil
Net cash position	**6**	**-82**	**33**
	$		$
Earnings per share*	n.a.		n.a.
	shs		shs
No. of shs. o/s	n.a.		n.a.
	%		%
Net profit margin	(44.04)		(50.99)
Return on equity	n.m.		n.m.
Return on assets	(224.68)		n.a.
Foreign sales percent	100		100

[A] Reported in accordance with IFRS
[1] Results pertain to IV Hydreight Inc.

Note: Adjusted throughout for 1-for-6.46805 cons. in Nov. 2022; 1-for-2 cons. in Aug. 2021

H.58 Hydro One Limited*

Symbol - H **Exchange** - TSX **CUSIP** - 448811
Head Office - South Tower, 800-483 Bay St, Toronto, ON, M5G 2P5
Telephone - (416) 345-5000 **Toll-free** - (877) 955-1155
Website - www.hydroone.com
Email - ojaved@hydroone.com
Investor Relations - Omar Javed (416) 345-5943
Auditors - KPMG LLP C.A., Toronto, Ont.
Lawyers - Osler, Hoskin & Harcourt LLP, Toronto, Ont.
Transfer Agents - Computershare Trust Company of Canada Inc., Toronto, Ont.
FP500 Revenue Ranking - 81
Employees - 6,503 at Dec. 31, 2022

Profile - (Ont. 2015) Provides electricity transmission and distribution services in Ontario.

The company's transmission and distribution businesses are operated primarily through wholly owned **Hydro One Networks Inc.** and are rate-regulated businesses that earn revenue mainly from charging transmission and distribution rates that must be approved by the **Ontario Energy Board**.

The transmission business owns and operates $19 billion of assets, consisting primarily of Hydro One Network's high-voltage transmission system which accounts for 92% of Ontario's transmission network. The system operates at 500 kV, 230 kV and 115 kV and transmits electricity to customers consisting of 35 local distribution companies including the company's own distribution business and 85 large industrial customers. Electricity is supplied by generators both within and outside Ontario, of which 135 in Ontario are connected directly to the transmission grid. The business also includes wholly owned **Hydro One Sault Ste. Marie L.P.** (formerly **Great Lakes Power Transmission L.P.**), the company's 66% interest in **B2M Limited Partnership**, a partnership with the Saugeen Ojibway Nation in respect of the Bruce-to-Milton transmission line, and the company's 55% interest in **Niagara Reinforcement Limited Partnership**, a limited partnership with Six Nations of the Grand River Development Corporation and the Mississaugas of the Credit First Nation which owns the Niagara transmission line. During 2022, 138 TWh of electricity was transmitted throughout Ontario. Also owns 309 transmission stations and 30,000-circuit-km of high-voltage lines whose major components include cables, conductors and wood or steel support structures.

The distribution business owns, operates and maintains $12 billion of assets, including 125,000-circuit-km of lower-voltage distribution lines and 1,000 distribution and regulating stations. The business also includes wholly owned **Hydro One Remote Communities Inc.**, which operates on a cost-recovery basis, and generates and distributes electricity to one grid-connected and 22 remote communities in northern Ontario; **Orillia Power Distribution Corporation**, which serves customers in the town of Orillia; and the distribution business and assets of **Peterborough Distribution Inc.**, which serves customers in Peterborough, Lakefield and Norwood. During 2022, 31 TWh of electricity was distributed.

Also has a telecommunications business, through wholly owned **Acronym Solutions Inc.** (formerly **Hydro One Telecom Inc.**), that provides support for the company's transmission and distribution businesses, and markets surplus fibre optic capacity to organizations with broadband network requirements. Acronym is a facilities-based carrier, providing broadband telecommunications services in Ontario with connections to Montreal, Que.; Buffalo, N.Y.; and Detroit, Mich. Broadband telecommunications and data management solutions offered include Internet and network connectivity, security, voice and collaboration, cloud services and managed IT solutions. Acronym's fibre network spans more than 8,700 km.

Periods ended:	12m Dec. 31/22	12m Dec. 31/21
Transmission lines, km	29,910	30,023
Distribution lines, km	125,013	124,825
Electric. dist., million KWh	30,803	29,966
Electric. customers	1,492,404	1,476,491

Directors - Timothy E. (Tim) Hodgson, chr., Toronto, Ont.; David Lebeter, pres. & CEO, Ont.; Cherie L. Brant, Ont.; David D. Hay, N.B.; Stacey Mowbray, Ont.; Mitch Panciuk, Ont.; Mark Podlasly, B.C.; Helga Reidel, Kingsville, Ont.; Melissa Sonberg, Montréal, Qué.; Brian T. Vaasjo, Edmonton, Alta.; Susan Wolburgh Jenah, Toronto, Ont.

Other Exec. Officers - Brad Bowness, CIO; Teri French, exec. v-p, opers. & cust. experience; Christopher (Chris) Lopez, exec. v-p & chief finl. & regulatory officer; Andrew Spencer, exec. v-p, capital portfolio delivery; Megan E. Telford, exec. v-p, strategy, energy transition, HR & safety; Omar Javed, v-p, IR; Cassidy McFarlane Colle, gen. counsel

Capital Stock

	Authorized (shs.)	Outstanding (shs.)[1]
Preferred	unlimited	
Series 1		nil
Series 2		nil
Common	unlimited	598,714,704

[1] At May 4, 2023

Preferred - Issuable in series. Non-voting.
Common - One vote per share.

Major Shareholder - Province of Ontario held 47% interest at Apr. 21, 2023.

Price Range - H/TSX

Year	Volume	High	Low	Close
2022	323,607,993	$38.27	$30.52	$36.27
2021	240,013,089	$33.00	$26.38	$32.91
2020	278,858,011	$30.43	$20.25	$28.65
2019	181,872,630	$26.20	$19.90	$25.08
2018	192,270,607	$22.45	$18.57	$20.25

Recent Close: $36.04

Capital Stock Changes - During 2022, common shares were issued as follows: 388,445 under a share grant plan and 108,710 under a long-term incentive plan.

Dividends

H com Ra $1.1856 pa Q est. June 30, 2023**
Prev. Rate: $1.1184 est. June 30, 2022
Prev. Rate: $1.0652 est. June 30, 2021
Prev. Rate: $1.0144 est. June 30, 2020
** Reinvestment Option

Long-Term Debt - Outstanding at Dec. 31, 2022:

Fixed-rate notes[1]	$13,270,000,000
6.6% sr. bonds due 2023	97,000,000
4.6% note pay. due 2023	36,000,000
7.35% debs. due 2030	400,000,000
Unamort. debt premiums	8,000,000
Less: Deferred debt issue costs	48,000,000
	13,763,000,000
Less: Current portion	733,000,000
	13,030,000,000

[1] Bear interest at rates ranging from 0.71% to 6.93% and due to 2064.

Note - In January 2023, offering of $300,000,000 of 3.93% medium-term notes due 2029; $450,000,000 of 4.16% medium-term notes due 2033; and $300,000,000 of 4.46% medium-term notes due 2053, was completed.

Wholly Owned Subsidiaries

Acronym Solutions Inc., Ont.
Hydro One Holdings Limited, Toronto, Ont.
Hydro One Inc., Toronto, Ont.
- 100% int. in **Hydro One Networks Inc.**, Toronto, Ont.
  - 100% int. in **Hydro One B2M Holdings Inc.**
    - 66% int. in **B2M Limited Partnership**, Ont.
  - 100% int. in **Hydro One Sault Ste. Marie L.P.**, Sault Ste. Marie, Ont.
  - 55% int. in **Niagara Reinforcement Limited Partnership**, Niagara Falls, Ont.
- 100% int. in **Hydro One Remote Communities Inc.**, Ont.
- 100% int. in **Orillia Power Distribution Corporation**, Orillia, Ont.

Note: The preceding list includes only the major related companies in which interests are held.

Financial Statistics

Periods ended:	12m Dec. 31/22[A]		12m Dec. 31/21[A]
	$000s	%Chg	$000s
Operating revenue	**7,780,000**	**+8**	**7,225,000**
General & admin expense	1,258,000		1,112,000
Other operating expense	3,724,000		3,579,000
Operating expense	**4,982,000**	**+6**	**4,691,000**
Operating income	**2,798,000**	**+10**	**2,534,000**
Deprec., depl. & amort.	831,000		815,000
Finance income	7,000		3,000
Finance costs, gross	493,000		464,000
Pre-tax income	**1,346,000**	**+17**	**1,151,000**
Income taxes	288,000		178,000
Net income	**1,058,000**	**+9**	**973,000**
Net inc. for equity hldrs	**1,050,000**	**+9**	**965,000**
Net inc. for non-cont. int.	**8,000**	**0**	**8,000**
Cash & equivalent	530,000		540,000
Inventories	25,000		22,000
Accounts receivable	767,000		699,000
Current assets	1,860,000		1,826,000
Long-term investments	35,000		22,000
Fixed assets, net	25,077,000		23,842,000
Right-of-use assets	56,000		57,000
Intangibles, net	981,000		943,000
Total assets	**31,457,000**	**+4**	**30,383,000**
Bank indebtedness	1,374,000		1,045,000
Accts. pay. & accr. liabs	295,000		255,000
Current liabilities	3,652,000		2,978,000
Long-term debt, gross	13,763,000		13,620,000
Long-term debt, net	13,030,000		13,017,000
Long-term lease liabilities	43,000		46,000
Shareholders' equity	11,306,000		10,888,000
Non-controlling interest	66,000		68,000
Cash from oper. activs	**2,260,000**	**+5**	**2,149,000**
Cash from fin. activs	(197,000)		(303,000)
Cash from invest. activs	(2,073,000)		(2,063,000)
Net cash position	**530,000**	**-2**	**540,000**
Capital expenditures	(1,966,000)		(1,928,000)
Unfunded pension liability	n.a.		713,000
Pension fund surplus	358,000		n.a.
	$		$
Earnings per share*	1.75		1.61
Cash flow per share*	3.78		3.59
Cash divd. per share*	1.11		1.05
	shs		shs
No. of shs. o/s*	598,714,704		598,217,549
Avg. no. of shs. o/s*	598,616,561		598,080,111
	%		%
Net profit margin	13.60		13.47
Return on equity	9.46		9.01
Return on assets	4.68		4.50
No. of employees (FTEs)	6,503		6,260

* Common
[A] Reported in accordance with U.S. GAAP

Latest Results

Periods ended:	3m Mar. 31/23[A]		3m Mar. 31/22[A]
	$000s	%Chg	$000s
Operating revenue	2,074,000	+1	2,047,000
Net income	284,000	-9	312,000
Net inc. for equity hldrs	282,000	-9	310,000
Net inc. for non-cont. int	2,000		2,000
	$		$
Earnings per share*	0.47		0.52

* Common
[A] Reported in accordance with U.S. GAAP

Historical Summary
(as originally stated)

Fiscal Year	Oper. Rev. $000s	Net Inc. Bef. Disc. $000s	EPS* $
2022[A]	7,780,000	1,058,000	1.75
2021[A]	7,225,000	973,000	1.61
2020[A]	7,290,000	1,796,000	2.96
2019[A]	6,480,000	802,000	1.30
2018[A]	6,150,000	(65,000)	(0.15)

* Common
[A] Reported in accordance with U.S. GAAP

H.59 Hydro-Québec

CUSIP - 448814
Head Office - Edifice Jean-Lesage, 75 boul René-Lévesque O, Montréal, QC, H2Z 1A4 **Telephone** - (514) 289-2211 ext. 2316
Website - www.hydroquebec.com
Email - archambault.philippe@hydroquebec.com
Investor Relations - Philippe Archambault (514) 816-2489
Auditors - Auditor General of Quebec, Québec, Qué.; Ernst & Young LLP C.A., Montréal, Qué.; KPMG LLP C.A., Montréal, Qué.
Bankers - National Bank of Canada
Transfer Agents - Computershare Trust Company of Canada Inc.
FP500 Revenue Ranking - 36
Employees - 18,808 at Dec. 31, 2022
Profile - (Qué. 1944) Generates, transmits and distributes most of the electricity consumed in Quebec, and is Canada's largest electricity producer.

Operates 62 hydroelectric generating stations with total installed capacity of 36,882 MW, 24 thermal generating stations with total installed capacity of 547 MW and two photovoltaic generating stations with total installed capacity of 10 MW. In addition, Hydro-Québec has access to almost all the output from Churchill Falls generating station (5,428 MW) under a contract with **Churchill Falls (Labrador) Corporation Limited** that will remain in effect until 2041. Also purchases all the output from 44 wind farms (3,932 MW) and 56 hydroelectric generating stations (708 MW), and almost all the output from 13 biomass and five biogas cogeneration plants (419 MW), operated by independent power producers. An additional 554 MW are available under long-term contracts with other suppliers.

The company's value chain consists of four main groups: developing strategies; planning and prioritizing; designing and building; and operating and marketing. These groups are supported and driven by six other cross-functional groups: digital technology; talent and culture; financial management; development sustainability, community relations and communications; corporate, legal, and regulatory and governance; and internal audit.

Periods ended:	12m Dec. 31/22	12m Dec. 31/21
Electric sales, GWh	216,194	211,419
Generating capacity, MW	37,438	37,248
Independent pwr. prod., MW	5,059	5,030
Transmission lines, km	34,678	34,775
Distribution lines, km	227,796	226,949
Electric. customers	4,508,906	4,457,198

Recent Merger and Acquisition Activity

Status: completed **Revised:** Feb. 10, 2023
UPDATE: The transaction was completed after all required regulatory approvals were obtained, including those from the Vermont Public Utility Commission and the Federal Energy Regulatory Commission. PREVIOUS: Hydro-Québec, through wholly owned HQI US Holding LLC, agreed to acquire Westborough, Mass.-based Great River Hydro, LLC, which owns and operates 13 hydropower generating stations on the Connecticut and Deerfield rivers in Vermont, New Hampshire and Massachusetts, from ArcLight Capital Partners, LLC for US$1.543 billion (Cdn$2.062 billion), including the assumption of US$750,000,000 of debt. The assets had a total installed capacity of 589 MW, 38 GWh of storage capacity and a long-term average annual output of 1.6 TWh, and supplied power to more than 213,000 New England homes each year.

Directors - Manon Brouilette, chr., Qué.; Michael J. Sabia, pres. & CEO, Montréal, Qué.; David Bahan, Qué.; Geneviève Bich, Westmount, Qué.; Geneviève Biron, Montréal, Qué.; Sarin Boivin-Picard, Montréal, Qué.; Geneviève Brouillette, Montréal, Qué.; Dr. Anne-Marie Croteau, Montréal, Qué.; Hanane Dagdougui, Montréal, Qué.; Marco Dodier, Qué.; Luc Doyon, Montréal, Qué.; Dominique Fagnoule, Montréal, Qué.; Hélène V. Gagnon, Montréal, Qué.; Marie-Josée Morency, Québec, Qué.; Claude Séguin, Westmount, Qué.; Paul Stinis, Montréal, Qué.; Claude Tessier, Laval, Qué.

Other Exec. Officers - Claudine Bouchard, exec. v-p, chief infrastructure & energy sys. officer & pres. & CEO, Société d'énergie de la Baie James; Pierre Gagnon, exec. v-p, corp., legal & regulatory affairs & chief governance officer; Jean-Hugues Lafleur, exec. v-p & CFO; Julie Boucher, v-p, sustainability, community rel. & commun.; Nathalie Dubois, v-p, talent & culture; Geneviève Fournier, v-p, mktg. & cust. experience; Bruno Marcil, v-p, internal audit; Jean-François Morin, v-p, digital tech.; Dave Rhéaume, v-p, integrated energy needs planning & risk mgt.; Régis Tellier, v-p, opers. & maint.; Mathieu Johnson, acting v-p, strategy & devel.

Capital Stock

	Authorized (shs.)	Outstanding (shs.)[1]	Par
Common	50,000,000	43,741,090	$100

[1] At Mar. 31, 2023

Major Shareholder - Province of Québec held 100% interest at Dec. 31, 2022.
Capital Stock Changes - There have been no capital stock changes in recent years.

Wholly Owned Subsidiaries

Groupe Financier HQ inc., Qué.
HQ Manicouagan inc., Qué.
- 60% int. in **Société en commandite Hydroélectrique Manicouagan**, Qué.

HQI Canada Holding Inc., Canada.
- 19.82% int. in **Innergex Renewable Energy Inc.**, Longueuil, Qué. (see separate coverage)

HQI US Holding LLC, United States.
- 100% int. in **Great River Hydro, LLC**, Westborough, Mass.
- 50% int. in **Innergex HQI USA LLC**, United States.

Hydro-Québec IndusTech inc., Montréal, Qué.
- 100% int. in **Services Hilo inc.**, Qué.
- 45% int. in **TM4 Inc.**, Boucherville, Qué.

Hydro-Québec International Inc., Qué.
Société d'énergie de la Baie James, Montréal, Qué.
Marketing d'énergie HQ inc., Montréal, Qué.
Société de transmission électrique de Cedars Rapids limitée, Qué.

Investments

34.2% int. in **Churchill Falls (Labrador) Corporation Limited**, St. John's, N.L.
- 50.4% int. in **Twin Falls Power Corporation Limited**, St. John's, N.L.

Note: The preceding list includes only the major related companies in which interests are held.

Financial Statistics

Periods ended:	12m Dec. 31/22[A]		12m Dec. 31/21[oA]
	$000s	%Chg	$000s
Operating revenue	**16,567,000**	**+14**	**14,526,000**
Operating expense	**6,678,000**	**+22**	**5,457,000**
Operating income	**9,889,000**	**+9**	**9,069,000**
Deprec., depl. & amort.	2,828,000		2,689,000
Finance costs, gross	2,161,000		2,181,000
Investment income	100,000		38,000
Pre-tax income	**5,787,000**	**+22**	**4,755,000**
Income taxes	1,230,000		1,191,000
Net income	**4,557,000**	**+28**	**3,564,000**
Cash & equivalent	3,788,000		1,678,000
Inventories	430,000		389,000
Accounts receivable	2,108,000		1,918,000
Current assets	8,080,000		5,310,000
Long-term investments	2,056,000		1,967,000
Fixed assets, net	69,856,000		68,255,000
Intangibles, net	1,224,000		1,165,000
Total assets	**89,374,000**	**+8**	**82,698,000**
Bank indebtedness	4,000		nil
Accts. pay. & accr. liabs	2,655,000		2,163,000
Current liabilities	8,377,000		9,372,000
Long-term debt, gross	51,541,000		49,698,000
Long-term debt, net	50,530,000		46,451,000
Shareholders' equity	26,877,000		23,260,000
Cash from oper. activs	**6,830,000**	**+34**	**5,091,000**
Cash from fin. activs	(492,000)		(647,000)
Cash from invest. activs	(5,881,000)		(4,598,000)
Net cash position	**1,773,000**	**+37**	**1,297,000**
Capital expenditures	(4,271,000)		(4,014,000)
Pension fund surplus	5,911,000		1,813,000
	$		$
Earnings per share*	n.a.		n.a.
	shs		shs
No. of shs. o/s*	43,741,090		43,741,090
Avg. no. of shs. o/s*	43,741,090		43,741,090
	%		%
Net profit margin	27.51		24.54
Return on equity	n.m.		n.m.
Return on assets	7.27		6.36
Foreign sales percent	11		8
No. of employees (FTEs)	18,808		18,163

[o] Restated
[A] Reported in accordance with U.S. GAAP

Note: Interest expense includes interest on debt securities less capitalized financial expenses.

Latest Results

Periods ended:	3m Mar. 31/23[A]		3m Mar. 31/22[A]
	$000s	%Chg	$000s
Operating revenue	5,484,000	+6	5,151,000
Net income	2,231,000	+8	2,062,000
	$		$
Earnings per share*	n.a.		n.a.

[A] Reported in accordance with U.S. GAAP

Historical Summary
(as originally stated)

Fiscal Year	Oper. Rev. $000s	Net Inc. Bef. Disc. $000s	EPS* $
2022[A]	16,567,000	4,557,000	n.a.
2021[A]	14,526,000	3,564,000	n.a.
2020[A]	13,594,000	2,303,000	n.a.
2019[A]	14,021,000	2,923,000	n.a.
2018[A]	14,370,000	3,192,000	n.a.

* Common
[A] Reported in accordance with U.S. GAAP

H.60 HydroGraph Clean Power Inc.

Symbol - HG **Exchange** - CSE **CUSIP** - 44888L
Head Office - 403-580 Hornby St, Vancouver, BC, V6C 3B6 **Telephone** - (778) 322-1891
Website - hydrograph.com
Email - kjirstin@hydrograph.com
Investor Relations - Kjirstin Breure (604) 220-3120
Auditors - MNP LLP C.A., Vancouver, B.C.
Transfer Agents - Endeavor Trust Corporation, Vancouver, B.C.
Profile - (B.C. 2017) Has developed a proprietary and patented detonation process to manufacture high-purity graphene, hydrogen and

other strategic materials in bulk, and to create customized graphene solutions for specific applications.

Has created two patented systems: Hyperion-A uses the patented detonation technology to produce synthetic graphene, in which the high-yield process converts acetylene and oxygen into 99.8% graphene powder; and Hyperion-E is a closed system that uses methane and oxygen to produce hydrogen and carbon monoxide.

The company has a commercial scale graphene production facility in Manhattan, Kan., which can house a series of modular production units with a total capacity of 60 metric tons per year. A large-scale hydrogen production facility in western Canada is also planned to be built in the longer term.

Directors - Stuart R. Jara, interim CEO & chr., N.J.; Kjirstin Breure, pres., Ont.; Paul Cox, Ill.; Dr. David Morris, Toronto, Ont.; David Williams, Surrey, United Kingdom

Other Exec. Officers - Robert (Bob) Wowk, CFO & corp. sec.; Dr. Ranjith Divigalpitiya, chief scientific officer; Mathew (Mat) Lee, chief acctg. officer; Stephen Corkill, v-p, opers.; Dr. Chris Sorensen, v-p, R&D, physics

Capital Stock

	Authorized (shs.)	Outstanding (shs.)[1]
Common	unlimited	174,775,224

[1] At Mar. 31, 2023

Major Shareholder - Widely held at May 6, 2023.

Price Range - HG/CSE

Year	Volume	High	Low	Close
2022	21,581,658	$0.39	$0.10	$0.15
2021	1,876,993	$0.69	$0.35	$0.40

Recent Close: $0.08

Capital Stock Changes - In April and May 2023, private placement of 20,087,666 units (1 common share & ½ warrant) at Cdn$0.12 per unit was completed, with warrants exercisable at Cdn$0.12 per share for two years.

In September 2022, private placement of 35,151,666 units (1 common share & ½ warrant) at 12¢ per unit was completed.

Wholly Owned Subsidiaries

Carbon-2D Graphene Corp., B.C.
Hydrograph Clean Power Ontario Inc., Ont.
HydroGraph USA Inc., Del.

Financial Statistics

Periods ended:	12m Sept. 30/22[A]		12m Sept. 30/21[A]
	US$000s	%Chg	US$000s
Operating revenue	**5**	**-38**	**8**
Cost of sales	3		nil
Research & devel. expense	177		236
General & admin expense	1,985		1,017
Stock-based compensation	536		292
Operating expense	**2,702**	**+74**	**1,553**
Operating income	**(2,697)**	**n.a.**	**(1,545)**
Deprec., depl. & amort.	190		24
Finance costs, gross	28		7
Pre-tax income	**(2,983)**	**n.a.**	**(1,509)**
Net income	**(2,983)**	**n.a.**	**(1,509)**
Cash & equivalent	2,801		277
Accounts receivable	nil		5
Current assets	3,472		5,461
Fixed assets, net	1,003		123
Right-of-use assets	286		345
Total assets	**7,939**	**-4**	**8,274**
Accts. pay. & accr. liabs	134		501
Current liabilities	209		5,703
Long-term lease liabilities	224		299
Shareholders' equity	7,486		2,253
Cash from oper. activs	**(3,580)**	**n.a.**	**(921)**
Cash from fin. activs	2,801		7,540
Cash from invest. activs	(1,844)		(1,302)
Net cash position	**2,801**	**-48**	**5,424**
Capital expenditures	(1,010)		(125)
	US$		US$
Earnings per share*	(0.03)		(0.02)
Cash flow per share*	(0.03)		(0.01)
	shs		shs
No. of shs. o/s*	154,687,558		93,515,892
Avg. no. of shs. o/s*	117,227,253		73,255,641
	%		%
Net profit margin	n.m.		n.m.
Return on equity	(61.26)		(91.15)
Return on assets	(36.45)		(31.61)

* Common
[A] Reported in accordance with IFRS

Latest Results

Periods ended:	6m Mar. 31/23[A]		6m Mar. 31/22[A]
	US$000s	%Chg	US$000s
Operating revenue	6	n.a.	nil
Net income	(2,495)	n.a.	(1,408)
	US$		US$
Earnings per share*	(0.02)		(0.01)

* Common
[A] Reported in accordance with IFRS

Historical Summary
(as originally stated)

Fiscal Year	Oper. Rev.	Net Inc. Bef. Disc.	EPS*
	US$000s	US$000s	US$
2022[A]	5	(2,983)	(0.03)
2021[A]	8	(1,509)	(0.02)
2020[A1]	nil	(140)	(0.00)

* Common
[A] Reported in accordance with IFRS
[1] As shown in the prospectus dated Nov. 17, 2021.

H.61 Hypercharge Networks Corp.

Symbol - HC **Exchange** - NEO **CUSIP** - 44916D
Head Office - Unit 208, 1075 1 St W, Vancouver, BC, V7P 3T4 **Toll-free** - (866) 764-5433
Website - hypercharge.com
Email - diana@greystonecorp.com
Investor Relations - Diana Mark (866) 764-5433
Auditors - Crowe MacKay LLP C.A., Vancouver, B.C.
Transfer Agents - Odyssey Trust Company, Vancouver, B.C.
Employees - 20 at June 29, 2023

Profile - (B.C. 2018) Provides smart electric vehicle (EV) charging equipment to multi-unit residential and commercial property owners and fleet operators in Canada and the U.S., and a network of public and private EV charging stations.

Equipment and services are offered primarily for medium and light duty commercial and personal vehicles.

Also provides a proprietary cloud-based platform that operates, maintains and manages the company's charging stations and handles associated charging data, back-end operations and payment processing, as well as provides EV drivers with station information such as location and availability. In addition, offers mobile applications compatible with iOS and Android operating systems for mobile devices to operate and utilize charging sessions and manage personal account details.

Products are produced by third-party manufacturers in the U.S., Italy and the People's Republic of China.

On Feb. 24, 2023 common shares were listed on the OTCQB Venture Market under the stock symbol HCNWF.

On Dec. 15, 2022 common shares were listed on the Frankfurt Stock Exchange under the stock symbol PB7.

In November 2022, the company changed its fiscal year end to March 31 from August 31.

On Apr. 22, 2022, the company acquired private British Columbia-based **Cosource Information Technology Services Inc.**, which provides a proprietary cloud-based service known as Plug and Charge for the electric vehicle charging ecosystem, for issuance of 3,800,000 common shares at a deemed price of 40¢ per share.

Common listed on NEO, Nov. 16, 2022.

Predecessor Detail - Name changed from Cliffwood Capital Corp., Mar. 10, 2021.

Directors - David Bibby, pres. & CEO, North Vancouver, B.C.; Liam Firus, B.C.; Vitaly Golomb, Calif.; W. Trent Kitsch, Kelowna, B.C.; Bronson Peever, B.C.; Shahab Samimi, B.C.

Other Exec. Officers - Navraj Dosanjh, CFO; Diana Mark, corp. sec.

Capital Stock

	Authorized (shs.)	Outstanding (shs.)[1]
Common	unlimited	68,106,252

[1] At June 29, 2023

Major Shareholder - Widely held at June 29, 2023.

Price Range - HC/NEO

Year	Volume	High	Low	Close
2022	146,500	$0.63	$0.48	$0.58

Recent Close: $0.62

Capital Stock Changes - In May 2023, private placement of 4,761,904 units (1 common share & ½ warrant) at $1.05 per unit was completed, with warrants exercisable at $1.35 per share for three years.

In November 2022, 10,000,000 common shares were issued without further consideration on exchange of subscription receipts sold previously by private placement at 60¢ each. Also during fiscal 2023, common shares were issued as follows: 200,000 on vesting of restricted share units, 154,725 on conversion of debt, 132,000 on vesting of performance share units, 100,000 on exercise of options, 41,666 for services and 14,896 on exercise of warrants.

In October 2021, private placement of 10,000,000 common shares was completed at 40¢ per share. On Nov. 1, 2021, 6,000,000 common shares were issued on acquisition of Spark Charging Solutions Inc. On Apr. 22, 2022, 3,800,000 common shares were issued on acquisition of Cosource Information Technology Services Inc. Also during fiscal 2022, common shares were issued as follows: 4,609,670 for services and 666,668 on vesting of performance share units.

Wholly Owned Subsidiaries

Cosource Information Technology Services Inc., B.C.
Hypercharge Networks Inc., Del.
Spark Charging Solutions Inc., Ont.
2836601 Ontario Ltd., Ont. Inactive.

Financial Statistics

Periods ended:	7m Mar. 31/23[A]		12m Aug. 31/22[A]
	$000s	%Chg	$000s
Operating revenue	**1,988**	**n.a.**	**484**
Cost of goods sold	1,543		316
Salaries & benefits	1,117		1,105
Research & devel. expense	38		nil
General & admin expense	2,548		2,566
Stock-based compensation	1,082		642
Operating expense	**6,328**	**n.a.**	**4,313**
Operating income	**(4,340)**	**n.a.**	**(3,829)**
Deprec., depl. & amort.	136		155
Finance costs, net	(3)		21
Write-downs/write-offs	nil		(2,128)
Pre-tax income	**(4,452)**	**n.a.**	**(9,641)**
Net income	**(4,452)**	**n.a.**	**(9,641)**
Cash & equivalent	2,686		1,119
Inventories	922		1,281
Accounts receivable	825		500
Current assets	5,851		8,950
Fixed assets, net	120		119
Right-of-use assets	400		234
Total assets	**6,405**	**n.a.**	**9,304**
Bank indebtedness	nil		98
Accts. pay. & accr. liabs	919		575
Current liabilities	1,554		1,248
Long-term lease liabilities	253		91
Shareholders' equity	4,504		7,964
Cash from oper. activs	**(3,746)**	**n.a.**	**(4,574)**
Cash from fin. activs	(380)		8,585
Cash from invest. activs	19		(240)
Net cash position	**2,686**	**n.a.**	**6,794**
Capital expenditures	(38)		(158)
Capital disposals	nil		55
	$		$
Earnings per share*	(0.07)		(0.21)
Cash flow per share*	(0.06)		(0.10)
	shs		shs
No. of shs. o/s*	61,916,325		51,273,038
Avg. no. of shs. o/s*	60,304,503		45,051,008
	%		%
Net profit margin	...		n.m.
Return on equity	...		(188.84)
Return on assets	...		(153.18)
No. of employees (FTEs)	16		n.a.

* Common
[A] Reported in accordance with IFRS

Historical Summary
(as originally stated)

Fiscal Year	Oper. Rev.	Net Inc. Bef. Disc.	EPS*
	$000s	$000s	$
2023[A1]	1,988	(4,452)	(0.07)
2022[A]	484	(9,641)	(0.21)
2021[A]	nil	(878)	(0.06)
2020[A]	nil	(53)	(0.01)

* Common
[A] Reported in accordance with IFRS
[1] 7 months ended Mar. 31, 2023.

I

I.1 I3 Interactive Inc.

Symbol - BETS **Exchange** - CSE (S) **CUSIP** - 45073W
Head Office - 810-789 Pender St W, Vancouver, BC, V6C 1H2
Website - i3company.com
Email - troy@i3company.com
Investor Relations - Troy J. Grant (902) 802-8847
Auditors - Zeifmans LLP C.A., Toronto, Ont.
Transfer Agents - TSX Trust Company, Vancouver, B.C.
Profile - (B.C. 2007) Developing online gaming product offerings, with a unique brand position and a blend of skill-based games and games of chance.

Product suite includes social gaming, fantasy sports, quiz games, poker, rummy, sports betting, as well as thrilling games of chance as part of its certifiably fair on-line casino.

The company has a strategic partnership with professional poker player and social media celebrity Dan Bilzerian. BlitzBet is the company's first global brand of online sports betting, casino and poker products and services. The company also launched its proprietary sportsbook and casino platform via BlitzBet.

Other service offerings include Blitzpools,which provides users with fantasy sports software combined with all the statistics needed in multiple sports such as Cricket, Football and Kabaddi, that is available for download in both the Google Play and iOS app store as well as on desktop; and Blitzpoker, one of the largest poker networks in the world which features a set of poker applications and is positioned to capitalize growth of online poker playing in India.

Has licensed from **Amelco UK Limited** a fully customizable technology platform that will enable the company to offer a full web and mobile sports betting platform, a casino platform in the United States and around the world, and an online social gaming product which does not involve the wagering of real money.

LineMovement.com, a sports content platform, was launched in July 2020.

Common suspended from CSE, Sept. 14, 2022.

Predecessor Detail - Name changed from Interactive Games Technologies Inc., May 18, 2021.

Directors - Troy J. Grant, interim CEO, Bedford, N.S.; Binyomin Posen, Toronto, Ont.; Brian Purdy, Ont.

Other Exec. Officers - James (Jim) Henning, CFO

Capital Stock

	Authorized (shs.)	Outstanding (shs.)[1]
Common	unlimited	222,753,428

[1] At Apr. 17, 2023

Major Shareholder - Dan Bilzerian held 10.28% interest at Apr. 27, 2021.

Price Range - FMR/TSX-VEN (D)

Year	Volume	High	Low	Close
2022	15,961,222	$0.16	$0.02	$0.02
2021	80,479,762	$0.91	$0.07	$0.15
2020	22,258,533	$1.01	$0.13	$0.21
2018	233,964	$5.50	$1.00	$1.15

Consolidation: 1-for-10 cons. in May 2020
Recent Close: $0.02

Wholly Owned Subsidiaries

Blitzbet Sports Holdings Ltd., Malta.
Deluxe Crown B.V., Curacao.
i3 India Holdings Corp.
Influencers Amalco 1 Ltd., B.C.
Influencers Amalco 2 Ltd., B.C.
Nigton Cloud Ltd., Curacao.
1248134 B.C. Ltd., Canada.
- 100% int. in **Redrush Online Pvt. Ltd.**, India.
  - 74% int. in **Esperanza Gaming Pvt. Ltd.**, India.
  - 35.94% int. in **LivePools Pvt. Ltd.**, Mumbai, India.

Subsidiaries

74% int. in **Esperanza Gaming Pvt. Ltd.**, India.

Investments

Moonshine Technology Private Limited, India. dba Baazi Games.

Latest Results

Periods ended:	9m Sept. 30/21[A]		9m Sept. 30/20[A]
	$000s	%Chg	$000s
Operating revenue	2,238	n.m.	94
Net income	(11,716)	n.a.	(28,154)
	$		$
Earnings per share*	(0.06)		(0.25)

* Common
[A] Reported in accordance with IFRS

I.2 IBC Advanced Alloys Corp.

Symbol - IB **Exchange** - TSX-VEN **CUSIP** - 44923T
Head Office - 401 Arvin Rd, Franklin, IN, United States, 46131 **Telephone** - (317) 738-2558 **Toll-free** - (800) 423-5612 **Fax** - (317) 738-2685
Website - www.ibcadvancedalloys.com
Email - jim.sims@ibcadvancedalloys.com
Investor Relations - Jim Sims (317) 738-2558
Auditors - Crowe MacKay LLP C.A., Vancouver, B.C.
Bankers - Bank of Montreal, Vancouver, B.C.
Lawyers - Blake, Cassels & Graydon LLP, Vancouver, B.C.
Transfer Agents - Computershare Trust Company of Canada Inc., Toronto, Ont.
Employees - 80 at Nov. 28, 2022
Profile - (B.C. 2002) Operates three plants in the United States which manufacture, heat-treat, machine and market beryllium-copper, beryllium-aluminum, copper-based master alloys and similar specialty alloy products including beryllium-aluminum castings.

Operations are organized into two divisions: Copper Alloys, which manufactures beryllium-copper and other specialty copper alloy products; and Engineered Materials, which produces beryllium-aluminum castings.

Copper Alloys

The copper alloys operation is based in Franklin, Ind., with casting, forging, heat treating and machining conducted at a 7,711-m^2 plant. The division offers alloys including oxygen-free high conductivity copper, berrylium-copper, aluminum-bronze alloys and chrome coppers, naval bronze, cupro nickels and other specialty alloys. Copper alloys in cast billet, slab or ingot are sourced from mills in North America, Europe and Asia and converted into industrial products serving the industrial welding, oil and gas, plastic mould, metal melting, marine defence, electronic and industrial equipment markets. Tooling components are provided to the North American automotive industry, European and North American consumer plastic tooling producers, the global oil and gas service industry, North American submarine and aircraft carrier producers and repair facilities including the U.S. Navy, and electronic and general equipment manufacturers.

Engineered Materials

The engineered materials operation is based at a 5,800-m^2 plant in Wilmington, Mass., and manufactures the proprietary Beralcast® family of beryllium-aluminum metal matrix composite used in commercial and military applications requiring complex, lightweight or high-stiffness parts. Beralcast® alloys serve as a higher performance or lower cost replacement materials for cast aluminum, magnesium, titanium, metal matrix composites, non-metallic composites and pure beryllium or powder metallurgy beryllium-aluminum. Applications include automotive braking and structural components and aerospace and satellite system components.

In addition, the company researches and develops scandium-containing aluminum alloys with **NioCorp Developments Ltd.**; and evaluates the potential use of beryllium oxide in enhanced nuclear fuels.

Predecessor Detail - Name changed from International Beryllium Corporation, Mar. 6, 2009.

Directors - Mark A. Smith, chr. & CEO, Centennial, Colo.; Simon J. Anderson, West Vancouver, B.C.; C. Geoffrey (Geoff) Hampson, Conn.; Mike Jarvis, Franklin, Ind.

Other Exec. Officers - Toni Wendel, CFO & corp. sec.; Ben Rampulla, chief tech. officer; Rajeev Jain, v-p, sales & eng.; Ken Shasteen, v-p, foundry opers.; Mark D. Doelling, pres., engineered materials div.; Mark Wolma, pres., IBC Copper Alloys

Capital Stock

	Authorized (shs.)	Outstanding (shs.)[1]	Par
Preferred	unlimited	nil	n.p.v.
Common	unlimited	87,630,783	n.p.v.

[1] At Nov. 28, 2022

Major Shareholder - Mark A. Smith held 17.8% interest at Oct. 25, 2022.

Price Range - IB/TSX-VEN

Year	Volume	High	Low	Close
2022	12,269,079	$0.31	$0.11	$0.13
2021	15,745,919	$0.32	$0.15	$0.19
2020	7,587,461	$0.26	$0.12	$0.17
2019	6,012,022	$0.31	$0.10	$0.21
2018	6,945,132	$0.38	$0.22	$0.27

Recent Close: $0.08

Capital Stock Changes - In December 2022, private placement of 11,269,444 units (1 common share & 1 warrant) at Cdn$0.108 per unit was completed, with warrants exercisable at Cdn$0.135 per share for two years.

During fiscal 2022, common shares were issued as follows: 3,998,300 on conversion of debentures, 1,659,118 to debenture holders, 600,000 for services and 75,000 on exercise of options.

Wholly Owned Subsidiaries

IBC US Holdings, Inc., Nev.
- 100% int. in **IBC Engineered Materials Corporation**, Del.
- 100% int. in **NF Industries, Inc.**, Ind.
  - 100% int. in **Freedom Alloys, Inc.**, Royersford, Pa.
  - 100% int. in **Nonferrous Products, Inc.**, Franklin, Ind.
    - 100% int. in **Specialloy Copper Alloys, LLC**, Mo.

Financial Statistics

Periods ended:	12m June 30/22[A]		12m June 30/21[A]
	US$000s	%Chg	US$000s
Operating revenue	**26,911**	**+23**	**21,809**
Cost of sales	20,018		16,537
Salaries & benefits	2,431		2,048
General & admin expense	2,344		1,969
Stock-based compensation	319		287
Operating expense	**25,112**	**+20**	**20,841**
Operating income	**1,799**	**+86**	**968**
Deprec., depl. & amort.	1,549		1,183
Finance costs, gross	1,566		1,270
Write-downs/write-offs	7		(38)
Pre-tax income	**(1,104)**	**n.a.**	**(1,508)**
Income taxes	28		13
Net income	**(1,132)**	**n.a.**	**(1,521)**
Cash & equivalent	478		2,359
Inventories	6,754		7,529
Accounts receivable	3,625		2,753
Current assets	11,139		12,916
Fixed assets, net	14,616		11,649
Total assets	**27,648**	**+10**	**25,178**
Bank indebtedness	3,733		3,470
Accts. pay. & accr. liabs	5,196		3,871
Current liabilities	17,915		12,939
Long-term debt, gross	4,407		4,121
Long-term debt, net	806		2,812
Long-term lease liabilities	2,050		2,762
Shareholders' equity	6,877		6,665
Cash from oper. activs	**1,052**	**-65**	**3,006**
Cash from fin. activs	1,011		1,251
Cash from invest. activs	(3,911)		(2,400)
Net cash position	**478**	**-80**	**2,359**
Capital expenditures	(4,061)		(2,403)
Capital disposals	150		3
	US$		US$
Earnings per share*	(0.01)		(0.02)
Cash flow per share*	0.01		0.05
	shs		shs
No. of shs. o/s*	84,757,459		78,425,041
Avg. no. of shs. o/s*	80,011,484		63,986,619
	%		%
Net profit margin	(4.21)		(6.97)
Return on equity	(16.72)		(24.45)
Return on assets	1.79		(1.08)
No. of employees (FTEs)	80		78

* Common
[A] Reported in accordance with IFRS

Latest Results

Periods ended:	3m Sept. 30/22[A]		3m Sept. 30/21[A]
	US$000s	%Chg	US$000s
Operating revenue	5,928	-16	7,090
Net income	(2,008)	n.a.	(581)
	US$		US$
Earnings per share*	(0.02)		(0.01)

* Common
[A] Reported in accordance with IFRS

Historical Summary
(as originally stated)

Fiscal Year	Oper. Rev.	Net Inc. Bef. Disc.	EPS*
	US$000s	US$000s	US$
2022[A]	26,911	(1,132)	(0.01)
2021[A]	21,809	(1,521)	(0.02)
2020[A]	21,148	(1,122)	(0.02)
2019[A]	18,668	(4,043)	(0.11)
2018[A]	19,399	(702)	(0.02)

* Common
[A] Reported in accordance with IFRS

I.3 IBEX Technologies Inc.

Symbol - IBT **Exchange** - TSX-VEN **CUSIP** - 448937
Head Office - 100-5485 rue Paré, Montréal, QC, H4P 1P7 **Telephone** - (514) 344-4004 **Fax** - (514) 344-8827
Website - www.ibex.ca
Email - pbaehr@ibexpharma.com
Investor Relations - Paul Baehr (514) 344-4004 ext. 143
Auditors - PricewaterhouseCoopers LLP C.A., Montréal, Qué.
Bankers - Royal Bank of Canada, Montréal, Qué.
Lawyers - Fasken Martineau DuMoulin LLP, Montréal, Qué.
Transfer Agents - Computershare Trust Company of Canada Inc., Toronto, Ont.
Profile - (Can. 1972) Manufactures and markets proprietary enzymes for in-vitro diagnostics and research, and arthritis diagnostic kits for osteoarthritis research.

The company produces Heparinase I, Heparinase II, Heparinase III, Chondroitinase AC and Chondroitinase B enzymes through a proprietary recombinant expression system which allows the economic production of high purity recombinant forms of these GAG lyases. These enzymes are sold directly to medical device manufacturers, quality control labs, low molecular weight heparin manufacturers and academic research institutions. Products are produced in Montreal, Que., and are sold primarily in the U.S. and Europe. Also provides lyophilization services for the making of components for disposable medical devices used in the hemostasis point-of-care market, and developing DiaMaze® (diamine oxidase), an enzyme targeted to persons suffering from histamine intolerance and will be marketed as a nutraceutical product.

In addition, the company also manufactures and sells arthritis diagnostic kits, which enable the study of both the synthesis and degradation of cartilage components. These kits are powerful tools in the study of osteo and rheumatoid arthritis. The kits are marketed for research use only to pharmaceutical companies, clinical research organizations and academic institutions in North America, Europe, Japan and the rest of the world.

Predecessor Detail - Name changed from Continental Pharma Cryosan Inc., Aug. 29, 1995.
Directors - Paul Baehr, chr., pres. & CEO, Montréal, Qué.; Robert J. DeLuccia†, White Plains, N.Y.; Christine Charette, Ont.; Dr. Bruce Connop, Ont.; Danilo Netto, Pierrefonds, Qué.; Dr. Joseph Zimmermann, Laval, Qué.
Other Exec. Officers - Belinda Franco, v-p, fin. & admin., CFO & corp. sec.; Mahendra Pallapothu, v-p, opers.
† Lead director

Capital Stock

	Authorized (shs.)	Outstanding (shs.)[1]
First Preferred	unlimited	nil
Second Preferred	unlimited	nil
Third Preferred	unlimited	nil
Common	unlimited	24,758,644

[1] At July 14, 2023

Normal Course Issuer Bid - The company plans to make normal course purchases of up to 1,500,000 common shares representing 9.9% of the public float. The bid commenced on Aug. 5, 2023, and expires on Aug. 4, 2024.
Major Shareholder - Neil S. Subin held 16.5% interest at Dec. 13, 2022.

Price Range - IBT/TSX-VEN

Year	Volume	High	Low	Close
2022	3,293,965	$0.80	$0.28	$0.80
2021	4,014,423	$0.60	$0.22	$0.51
2020	2,745,497	$0.31	$0.10	$0.25
2019	1,351,472	$0.20	$0.09	$0.14
2018	5,102,354	$0.31	$0.09	$0.16

Recent Close: $1.12
Capital Stock Changes - There were no changes to capital stock during fiscal 2022.

Wholly Owned Subsidiaries

Bio-Research Inc., Iowa
IBEX Pharmaceuticals Inc., Montréal, Qué.
Technologies IBEX R&D Inc., Qué.
IBEX Technologies Corporation, Del.

Financial Statistics

Periods ended:	12m July 31/22[A]		12m July 31/21[◻A]
	$000s	%Chg	$000s
Operating revenue	**7,892**	**+49**	**5,306**
Cost of sales	2,404		2,112
Research & devel. expense	342		141
General & admin expense	2,509		1,812
Operating expense	**5,255**	**+29**	**4,065**
Operating income	**2,638**	**+113**	**1,241**
Deprec., depl. & amort.	370		385
Finance income	48		7
Finance costs, gross	78		47
Pre-tax income	**2,387**	**+147**	**965**
Income taxes	712		204
Net income	**1,674**	**+120**	**762**
Cash & equivalent	7,641		4,434
Inventories	227		319
Accounts receivable	991		955
Current assets	9,026		5,829
Fixed assets, net	1,124		1,127
Right-of-use assets	1,547		1,216
Intangibles, net	nil		2
Total assets	**12,974**	**+29**	**10,092**
Accts. pay. & accr. liabs	1,575		941
Current liabilities	1,751		1,097
Long-term lease liabilities	1,449		1,092
Shareholders' equity	9,747		7,902
Cash from oper. activs	**3,581**	**+196**	**1,209**
Cash from fin. activs	(229)		(209)
Cash from invest. activs	(145)		(271)
Net cash position	**7,641**	**+72**	**4,434**
Capital expenditures	(145)		(271)
	$		$
Earnings per share*	0.07		0.03
Cash flow per share*	0.14		0.05
	shs		shs
No. of shs. o/s*	24,823,244		24,823,244
Avg. no. of shs. o/s*	24,823,244		24,823,244
	%		%
Net profit margin	21.21		14.36
Return on equity	18.97		10.15
Return on assets	15.41		8.55
Foreign sales percent	80		80

* Common
◻ Restated
[A] Reported in accordance with IFRS

Latest Results

Periods ended:	3m Oct. 31/22[A]		3m Oct. 31/21[A]
	$000s	%Chg	$000s
Operating revenue	1,752	-2	1,781
Net income	679	+2	665
	$		$
Earnings per share*	0.03		0.03

* Common
[A] Reported in accordance with IFRS

Historical Summary
(as originally stated)

Fiscal Year	Oper. Rev.	Net Inc. Bef. Disc.	EPS*
	$000s	$000s	$
2022[A]	7,892	1,674	0.07
2021[A]	5,306	762	0.03
2020[A]	5,210	966	0.04
2019[A]	4,308	(1,268)	(0.05)
2018[A]	4,730	(95)	(0.00)

* Common
[A] Reported in accordance with IFRS

I.4 IC Capitalight Corp.

Symbol - IC **Exchange** - CSE **CUSIP** - 45075C
Head Office - 7934 Government Rd, Burnaby, BC, V5A 2E2 **Toll-free** - (866) 653-9223
Website - www.capitalight.co
Email - brian@capitalight.co
Investor Relations - Brian Bosse (866) 653-9223
Auditors - MNP LLP C.A., Timmins, Ont.
Transfer Agents - TSX Trust Company, Vancouver, B.C.
Profile - (B.C. 2008) Invests in a portfolio of companies, securities and mineral properties and operates a proprietary subscription research business that publishes reports focused on the gold silver and critical metals sectors, Canadian preferred shares, bonds and economics.

Proprietary Research - Through wholly owned **Capitalight Research Inc.** (formerly **Murenbeeld & Co. Inc.**), operates a proprietary subscription-based research business with six brands: Murenbeeld Gold Monitor, Phases & Cycles, Critical Metals for a Sustainable World, Silver Monitor, Canadian Preferred Share Research, and Economic Monitor. Subscribers consist primarily of gold and silver mining companies and investment funds and wealth management companies.

Investments - At June 30, 2022, the company held 112,810 common shares of **Stone Investment Group Limited**, which provides wealth management services primarily through the management and distribution of mutual funds; and 409,333 common shares of **Prospector Metals Corp.**, which has mineral interests in Quebec, British Columbia, Ontario and Newfoundland.

Mineral Exploration - Also holds Blue Lake (formerly Retty Lake) copper-nickel-PGM property, 12,724 hectares, 60 km northeast of Schefferville, Que.

In July 2022, the company sold its **Stone Investment Group Limited** debenture investments for $3,335,200.

Predecessor Detail - Name changed from International Corona Capital Corp., Oct. 2, 2019, pursuant to the completion of a change of business transaction to an investment company through the acquisition of Murenbeeld & Co. Inc. and certain fixed income debentures of Stone Investment Group Limited.; basis 1 new for 2 old shs.
Directors - Brian Bosse, pres. & CEO, Toronto, Ont.; Marc Johnson, CFO & corp. sec., Toronto, Ont.; Elliot Beutel, Toronto, Ont.; Veronika Hirsch, Toronto, Ont.; Bryan E. Loree, Burnaby, B.C.; Douglas R. MacQuarrie, Whistler, B.C.
Other Exec. Officers - Adam Marchionni, v-p, corp. devel.

Capital Stock

	Authorized (shs.)	Outstanding (shs.)[1]
Preferred	unlimited	nil
Common	unlimited	90,419,146

[1] At June 30, 2022

Major Shareholder - Brian Bosse held 39.2% interest at May 18, 2022.

Price Range - IC/CSE

Year	Volume	High	Low	Close
2022	944,663	$0.09	$0.02	$0.03
2021	2,688,583	$0.10	$0.05	$0.09
2020	4,352,153	$0.10	$0.01	$0.08
2019	467,953	$0.07	$0.02	$0.04
2018	1,295,231	$0.16	$0.05	$0.07

Consolidation: 1-for-2 cons. in Oct. 2019
Recent Close: $0.05

Wholly Owned Subsidiaries

Capitalight Research Inc., Toronto, Ont. formerly Murenbeeld & Co. Inc.
- 100% int. in **Phases & Cycles Inc.**, Montréal, Qué.

Financial Statistics

Periods ended:	12m Dec. 31/21[A]		12m Dec. 31/20[◻A]
	$000s	%Chg	$000s
Operating revenue	**399**	**+34**	**297**
Salaries & benefits	257		257
Exploration expense	1		106
General & admin expense	848		572
Stock-based compensation	129		122
Operating expense	**1,234**	**+17**	**1,057**
Operating income	**(835)**	**n.a.**	**(760)**
Deprec., depl. & amort.	13		13
Finance costs, gross	48		21
Write-downs/write-offs	(248)		(8)
Pre-tax income	**166**	**n.a.**	**(612)**
Net income	**166**	**n.a.**	**(612)**
Cash & equivalent	423		76
Accounts receivable	11		13
Current assets	559		203
Long-term investments	2,868		1,842
Intangibles, net	nil		239
Total assets	**3,427**	**+50**	**2,285**
Bank indebtedness	282		nil
Accts. pay. & accr. liabs	624		453
Current liabilities	1,445		909
Long-term debt, gross	nil		40
Long-term debt, net	nil		40
Shareholders' equity	1,982		1,336
Cash from oper. activs	**(77)**	**n.a.**	**(384)**
Cash from fin. activs	315		40
Cash from invest. activs	109		(225)
Net cash position	**423**	**+457**	**76**
	$		$
Earnings per share*	0.00		(0.01)
Cash flow per share*	(0.00)		(0.00)
	shs		shs
No. of shs. o/s*	90,419,146		86,247,436
Avg. no. of shs. o/s*	89,317,142		85,198,252
	%		%
Net profit margin	41.60		(206.06)
Return on equity	10.01		(39.77)
Return on assets	7.49		(25.72)

* Common
◻ Restated
[A] Reported in accordance with IFRS

Latest Results

Periods ended:	6m June 30/22^A		6m June 30/21^A
	$000s	%Chg	$000s
Operating revenue	362	+77	205
Net income	(150)	n.a.	681
	$		$
Earnings per share*	(0.00)		0.01

* Common
^A Reported in accordance with IFRS

Historical Summary
(as originally stated)

Fiscal Year	Oper. Rev. $000s	Net Inc. Bef. Disc. $000s	EPS* $
2021^A	399	166	0.00
2020^A	297	(612)	(0.01)
2019^A	81	(849)	(0.02)
2018^A	nil	84	0.00
2017^A	nil	(592)	(0.02)

* Common
^A Reported in accordance with IFRS
Note: Adjusted throughout for 1-for-2 cons. in Oct. 2019

I.5 ICEsoft Technologies Canada Corp.

Symbol - ISFT **Exchange** - CSE **CUSIP** - 45090C
Head Office - 261-3553 31 St NW, Calgary, AB, T2L 2K7 **Telephone** - (403) 663-3322 **Fax** - (403) 663-3320
Website - www.icesoft.com
Email - brian.mckinney@icesoft.com
Investor Relations - Brian McKinney (403) 663-3322
Auditors - Baker Tilly WM LLP C.A., Vancouver, B.C.
Transfer Agents - Alliance Trust Company, Calgary, Alta.
Profile - (Can. 2010) Develops and licenses a software-as-a-service (SaaS)-based mass notification solution and application development tools to enterprise and government clients.

Voyent Alert! is a multi-purpose mass notification service that enables small to medium-sized communities, regional districts and enterprise clients to deliver context-enriched notifications during critical incidents as well as targeted day-to-day communications. Notifications can be received through mobile applications, SMS/text, email and voice as well as through social media channels.

Also has a legacy product ICEfaces, a feature-rich enterprise-grade UI framework for Java EE.

Predecessor Detail - Name changed from Stinton Exploration Ltd., Nov. 19, 2015, following reverse takeover acquisition of (old) ICEsoft Technologies Canada Corp.
Directors - Brian McKinney, pres. & CEO, Calgary, Alta.; Bruce W. Derrick, Tex.; Derrick Hunter, Alta.; Francis N. Shen, Toronto, Ont.
Other Exec. Officers - Caitlin Charron, CFO; Ken Fyten, v-p, product devel.

Capital Stock

	Authorized (shs.)	Outstanding (shs.)[1]
Common	unlimited	112,116,025

[1] At Nov. 24, 2021

Major Shareholder - Francis N. Shen held 23.2% interest, Bruce W. Derrick held 16.1% interest, Derrick Hunter held 14.2% interest, William Derrick held 12.7% interest and Brian McKinney held 11.7% interest at May 16, 2022.

Price Range - ISFT/CSE

Year	Volume	High	Low	Close
2022	581,266	$0.07	$0.03	$0.03
2021	3,438,887	$0.16	$0.04	$0.07
2020	5,500	$0.16	$0.10	$0.10
2019	3,500	$0.16	$0.07	$0.16

Recent Close: $0.01

Wholly Owned Subsidiaries
ICEsoft Technologies Holdings Ltd., Canada.
ICEsoft Technologies, Inc., Del.

Financial Statistics

Periods ended:	12m Dec. 31/21^A		12m Dec. 31/20^A
	$000s	%Chg	$000s
Operating revenue	**1,278**	**-1**	**1,287**
Cost of goods sold	327		n.a.
Research & devel. expense	1,088		1,015
General & admin expense	952		1,035
Stock-based compensation	nil		273
Operating expense	**2,367**	**+2**	**2,323**
Operating income	**(1,089)**	**n.a.**	**(1,036)**
Deprec., depl. & amort.	19		29
Finance costs, gross	25		84
Pre-tax income	**(1,089)**	**n.a.**	**(1,496)**
Net income	**(1,089)**	**n.a.**	**(1,496)**
Cash & equivalent	713		168
Accounts receivable	82		66
Current assets	829		255
Fixed assets, net	11		2
Right-of-use assets	nil		18
Total assets	**841**	**+207**	**274**
Accts. pay. & accr. liabs	959		800
Current liabilities	1,677		1,456
Long-term debt, gross	121		127
Long-term debt, net	26		22
Equity portion of conv. debs	6		6
Shareholders' equity	(914)		(1,282)
Cash from oper. activs	**(809)**	**n.a.**	**(1,003)**
Cash from fin. activs	1,398		1,136
Cash from invest. activs	(11)		(2)
Net cash position	**713**	**+324**	**168**
Capital expenditures	(11)		(2)
	$		$
Earnings per share*	(0.01)		(0.02)
Cash flow per share*	(0.01)		(0.01)
	shs		shs
No. of shs. o/s*	112,116,025		80,116,025
Avg. no. of shs. o/s*	90,110,547		73,771,196
	%		%
Net profit margin	(85.21)		(116.24)
Return on equity	n.m.		n.m.
Return on assets	(190.85)		(643.28)
No. of employees (FTEs)	n.a.		12

* Common
^A Reported in accordance with IFRS

Latest Results

Periods ended:	6m June 30/22^A		6m June 30/21^A
	$000s	%Chg	$000s
Operating revenue	700	+16	604
Net income	(594)	n.a.	(515)
	$		$
Earnings per share*	(0.01)		(0.01)

* Common
^A Reported in accordance with IFRS

Historical Summary
(as originally stated)

Fiscal Year	Oper. Rev. $000s	Net Inc. Bef. Disc. $000s	EPS* $
2021^A	1,278	(1,089)	(0.01)
2020^A	1,287	(1,496)	(0.02)
2019^A	1,415	(667)	(0.01)
2018^A	1,494	(416)	(0.01)
2017^A	1,754	(156)	(0.00)

* Common
^A Reported in accordance with IFRS

I.6 ICWHY Capital Ventures Inc.

Symbol - ICWY.P **Exchange** - TSX-VEN **CUSIP** - 45114Q
Head Office - 26-2365 Abbeyglen Way, Kamloops, BC, V1S 1Y3 **Telephone** - (778) 362-3037
Email - drcliff@telusplanet.net
Investor Relations - J. Randolph Clifford (778) 362-3037
Auditors - Saturna Group Chartered Accountants LLP C.A., Vancouver, B.C.
Lawyers - Vantage Law Corporation, Vancouver, B.C.
Transfer Agents - Computershare Trust Company of Canada Inc., Vancouver, B.C.
Profile - (B.C. 2021) Capital Pool Company.
Directors - J. Randolph (Randy) Clifford, pres., CEO, CFO & corp. sec., Kamloops, B.C.; Joshua J. (Josh) Gerstein, Toronto, Ont.; Jonathan Graham, Ont.; Kevin T. Patterson, White City, Sask.; Jimmy James (Jim) Sekora, Red Deer, Alta.

Capital Stock

	Authorized (shs.)	Outstanding (shs.)[1]
Common	unlimited	6,300,000

[1] At June 17, 2022

Major Shareholder - J. Randolph (Randy) Clifford held 15.87% interest and Jimmy James (Jim) Sekora held 11.11% interest at June 17, 2022.

Price Range - ICWY.P/TSX-VEN

Year	Volume	High	Low	Close
2022	10,000	$0.08	$0.08	$0.08

Capital Stock Changes - On June 17, 2022, an initial public offering of 2,500,000 common shares was completed at 10¢ per share.

I.7 IDG Holdings Inc.

Symbol - IDH.H **Exchange** - TSX-VEN **CUSIP** - 448948
Head Office - 25-4466 Saanich Rd W, Victoria, BC, V8Z 3E9 **Telephone** - (250) 384-0751 **Fax** - (250) 384-0771
Email - mlpferguson@shaw.ca
Investor Relations - Mark L. P. Ferguson (250) 384-0751
Auditors - KPMG LLP C.A., Victoria, B.C.
Transfer Agents - Computershare Trust Company of Canada Inc., Calgary, Alta.
Profile - (Alta. 1995) Pursuing acquisition of German-based cannabis retailer.
Directors - Mark L. P. Ferguson, CEO & interim CFO, Calgary, Alta.; Dr. Peter Born, Ottawa, Ont.; Richard Ko, Vancouver, B.C.

Capital Stock

	Authorized (shs.)	Outstanding (shs.)[1]
Preferred	unlimited	nil
Common	unlimited	13,839,500

[1] At Sept. 20, 2022

Major Shareholder - Xen Stefanopoulos held 48.3% interest at Oct. 9, 2020.

Price Range - IDH.H/TSX-VEN

Year	Volume	High	Low	Close
2021	216,530	$0.34	$0.05	$0.21
2020	67,800	$0.07	$0.05	$0.05
2019	62,005	$0.10	$0.05	$0.06
2018	64,615	$0.20	$0.07	$0.10

Capital Stock Changes - There were no changes to capital stock during fiscal 2022.

Financial Statistics

Periods ended:	12m June 30/22^A		12m June 30/21^A
	$000s	%Chg	$000s
General & admin expense	164		389
Other operating expense	nil		2
Operating expense	**164**	**-58**	**391**
Operating income	**(164)**	**n.a.**	**(391)**
Finance income	nil		2
Pre-tax income	**(164)**	**n.a.**	**(389)**
Net income	**(164)**	**n.a.**	**(389)**
Cash & equivalent	168		336
Current assets	168		336
Total assets	**168**	**-50**	**336**
Accts. pay. & accr. liabs	23		27
Current liabilities	23		27
Shareholders' equity	145		309
Cash from oper. activs	**(167)**	**n.a.**	**(377)**
Cash from fin. activs	nil		263
Net cash position	**168**	**-50**	**336**
	$		$
Earnings per share*	(0.01)		(0.04)
Cash flow per share*	(0.01)		(0.04)
	shs		shs
No. of shs. o/s*	13,839,500		13,839,500
Avg. no. of shs. o/s*	13,839,500		9,748,267
	%		%
Net profit margin	n.a.		n.a.
Return on equity	(72.25)		(104.57)
Return on assets	(65.08)		(98.98)

* Common
^A Reported in accordance with IFRS

Historical Summary
(as originally stated)

Fiscal Year	Oper. Rev. $000s	Net Inc. Bef. Disc. $000s	EPS* $
2022^A	nil	(164)	(0.01)
2021^A	nil	(389)	(0.04)
2020^A	nil	(38)	(0.01)
2019^A	nil	(39)	(0.01)
2018^A	nil	(41)	(0.01)

* Common
^A Reported in accordance with IFRS

I.8 IGEN Networks Corp.

Symbol - IGN **Exchange** - CSE (S) **CUSIP** - 45172B
Head Office - 28375 Rostrata Ave, Lake Elsinore, CA, United States, 92532 **Toll-free** - (855) 912-5378
Website - www.nimbotracking.com
Email - neilgchan@igennetworks.net
Investor Relations - Neil G. Chan (844) 332-5699
Auditors - GreenGrowth C.P.A., Los Angeles, Calif.

Transfer Agents - Signature Stock Transfer, Inc., Plano, Tex.

Employees - 10 at Dec. 31, 2022

Profile - (Nev. 2006) Develops and markets consumer automotive and commercial asset management solutions for the automotive, financial institutions, governments, fleet management and direct-to-consumer markets.

Principal business is the development and marketing of software services for the management and protection of commercial and consumer vehicle assets along with driving behaviour and profile of these assets. The software services are delivered from the Amazon Web Services Cloud infrastructure over wireless networks and accessed from any mobile or desktop devices. The company operates under brands: Nimbo Tracking, which focuses on real-time GPS tracking solutions for new and used car dealerships including lot inventory management, asset tracking and stolen vehicle recovery solutions; CU Trak, which focuses on tracking solutions for credit unions and other financial institutions; Medallion GPS Pro, which focuses on tracking solutions for medium-to-heavy duty commercial fleet owners; and FamilyShield, which focuses on tracking solutions for personal vehicle owners sold directly to consumers through Amazon.com.

Owns digital telematics signature (DTC) patent which serves as the basis for measuring driver behaviour.

Has a global distribution agreement with **Wireless Business Consultants**; a distribution and marketing agreement with **REMCOOP** for territory of Puerto Rico; a sales and marketing agreement with **Michigan Credit Union League Service Corporation** to promote CU Trak; a software licence and hardware supply agreement with **Positioning Universal Inc.**; and a partnership agreement with **Hyperion Partners LLC**, master agent for TMobile business.

Common suspended from CSE, June 8, 2023.

Directors - Robert Nealon, chr., Va.; Neil G. Chan, pres. & CEO, Victoria, B.C.; Abel I. Sierra, COO, Los Angeles, Calif.; Mark Wells, San Diego, Calif.

Capital Stock

	Authorized (shs.)	Outstanding (shs.)[1]	Par
Preferred	10,000,000	nil	US$0.0001
Series A Preferred	1,250,000	194,500	US$0.001
Series B Preferred	5,000,000	3,750,000	US$0.001
Common	2,900,000,000	2,034,481,764	US$0.001

[1] At Mar. 31, 2023

Series A Preferred - Entitled to 8% cumulative dividends payable upon conversion or redemption. Convertible after six months from date of issuance at 75% of common share's market price. Redeemable by the company for 270 days and mandatorily after 18 months from issuance date. Non-voting.

Series B Preferred - Not convertible into common shares of the company. Not entitled to received any dividends. If the holder ceases to be a board member, the company has the right to repurchase from the holder for a price of US$0.001 per share; if the holder proposes to transfer, the company has the right to repurchase for a price of US$0.001 per share within 90 days. 500 votes per share.

Common - One vote per share.

Major Shareholder - Widely held at Mar. 15, 2023.

Price Range - IGN/CSE (S)

Year	Volume	High	Low	Close
2022	42,926,844	$0.01	$0.01	$0.01
2021	252,520,300	$0.04	$0.01	$0.01
2020	111,155,138	$0.03	$0.01	$0.01
2019	3,254,105	$0.10	$0.02	$0.02
2018	5,060,692	$0.25	$0.04	$0.07

Recent Close: $0.01

Capital Stock Changes - During the first quarter of 2023, common shares were issued as follows: 88,156,667 on conversion of 79,125 series A preferred shares, 34,064,050 by private placement and 22,000,000 as share-based compensation. In May 2023, 83,333,333 common shares were issued for officers. In June 2023, 104,622,105 common shares were issued on conversion of 54,125 series A preferred shares.

During 2022, common shares were issued as follows: 264,726,807 on conversion of 430,375 series A preferred shares, 93,490,998 by private placement, 20,000,000 for officers, 19,560,705 on exercise of warrants, 12,500,000 for commitment fees and 3,113,005 for services.

Wholly Owned Subsidiaries

Nimbo Tracking LLC, Tex.

Financial Statistics

Periods ended:	12m Dec. 31/22[A]		12m Dec. 31/21[A]
	US$000s	%Chg	US$000s
Operating revenue	**318**	**+18**	**269**
Cost of sales	323		124
Salaries & benefits	339		284
General & admin expense	570		611
Stock-based compensation	36		2,590
Operating expense	**1,267**	**-65**	**3,609**
Operating income	**(949)**	**n.a.**	**(3,340)**
Deprec., depl. & amort.	23		5
Finance costs, gross	187		162
Pre-tax income	**(907)**	**n.a.**	**(3,428)**
Income taxes	1		1
Net income	**(908)**	**n.a.**	**(3,429)**
Cash & equivalent	nil		64
Inventories	30		71
Accounts receivable	22		39
Current assets	52		174
Right-of-use assets	53		76
Intangibles, net	506		506
Total assets	**616**	**-19**	**762**
Accts. pay. & accr. liabs	360		678
Current liabilities	1,186		1,084
Long-term debt, gross	794		356
Long-term debt, net	161		152
Long-term lease liabilities	27		55
Preferred share equity	142		89
Shareholders' equity	(978)		(694)
Cash from oper. activs	**(978)**	**n.a.**	**(963)**
Cash from fin. activs	914		1,001
Net cash position	**nil**	**n.a.**	**64**
	US$		US$
Earnings per share*	(0.00)		(0.00)
Cash flow per share*	(0.00)		(0.00)
	shs		shs
No. of shs. o/s*	1,890,261,047		1,476,869,532
Avg. no. of shs. o/s*	1,613,852,078		1,263,939,724
	%		%
Net profit margin	(285.53)		n.m.
Return on equity	n.m.		n.m.
Return on assets	(104.61)		(483.99)
No. of employees (FTEs)	10		10

* Common

[A] Reported in accordance with U.S. GAAP

Latest Results

Periods ended:	3m Mar. 31/23[A]		3m Mar. 31/22[A]
	US$000s	%Chg	US$000s
Operating revenue	47	+2	46
Net income	(117)	n.a.	(186)
	US$		US$
Earnings per share*	(0.00)		(0.00)

* Common

[A] Reported in accordance with U.S. GAAP

Historical Summary
(as originally stated)

Fiscal Year	Oper. Rev. US$000s	Net Inc. Bef. Disc. US$000s	EPS* US$
2022[A]	318	(908)	(0.00)
2021[A]	269	(3,429)	(0.00)
2020[A]	368	(2,639)	(0.00)
2019[A]	724	(479)	(0.01)
2018[A]	1,199	(1,153)	(0.02)

* Common

[A] Reported in accordance with U.S. GAAP

I.9 IGM Financial Inc.*

Symbol - IGM **Exchange -** TSX **CUSIP -** 449586

Head Office - One Canada Centre, 447 Portage Ave, Winnipeg, MB, R3B 3H5 **Telephone -** (204) 943-0361 **Fax -** (204) 947-1659

Website - www.igmfinancial.com

Email - investor.relations@igmfinancial.com

Investor Relations - Kyle Martens (204) 777-4888

Auditors - Deloitte LLP C.A., Winnipeg, Man.

Lawyers - Blake, Cassels & Graydon LLP, Toronto, Ont.

Transfer Agents - Computershare Trust Company of Canada Inc., Calgary, Alta.

FP500 Subsidiary Revenue Ranking - 25

Employees - 4,010 at Dec. 31, 2022

Profile - (Can. 1978) Provides financial planning, investment management and related services. Operations are carried out primarily through wholly owned **Investors Group Inc.** and **Mackenzie Financial Corporation** as well as subsidiary **Investment Planning Counsel Inc.**

The company's business is organized into three reporting segments: Wealth Management; Asset Management; and Strategic Investments and Other.

Wealth Management - Focused on providing financial planning and related services across Canada through wholly owned **Investors Group Inc.** and subsidiary **Investment Planning Counsel Inc.** Investors Group provides personalized financial advice and solutions to more than 1,000,000 clients through a network of 3,235 advisors under the IG Wealth Management brand. Investment Planning Counsel provides financial products, services and advice to 200,000 clients through a network of 653 independent financial advisors. IG Wealth Management clients receive comprehensive solutions including investment, retirement, tax and estate planning, brokerage, insurance, and mortgage and banking products and services. IG Wealth Management distributes, manages and administers investments including mutual funds, managed portfolios, model portfolios, segregated funds, separately managed accounts and other investment vehicles. Other investment solutions such as securities brokerage services and products are provided through wholly owned investment dealer **Investors Group Securities Inc.** Life, health, disability, critical illness, long-term care and group insurance products from various insurance companies are offered through wholly owned **I.G. Insurance Services Inc.** Mortgages are offered by IG Wealth Management and through Solutions Banking™, which is provided under a partnership with **National Bank of Canada**. Solutions Banking™ also offers bank accounts, loans and lines of credit, creditor insurance and credit cards. At Dec. 31, 2022, IG Wealth Management had $110.8 billion in assets under advisement (AUA), including $99.3 billion in assets under management (AUM); and Investment Planning Counsel had $29.5 billion in AUA, including $4.6 billion in AUM.

Asset Management - Operations are carried out through wholly owned **Mackenzie Financial Corporation** which provides investment management solutions to retail clients in Canada and institutional clients in North America, Europe and Asia under the Mackenzie Investments brand. Retail offerings include the management and distribution of mutual funds, exchange traded funds and alternative funds, and the provision of tax and estate planning, private wealth solutions, savings accounts, group plans and other related services. The retail distribution network consists of more than 30,000 third party financial advisors. In the institutional channel, investment management services are provided to pension plans, foundations and other institutions. Mackenzie also offers certain mutual funds and provides sub-advisory services to third party and related party investment programs offered by banks, insurance companies and other investment companies. At Dec. 31, 2022, Mackenzie had $186.6 billion in AUM, including $73.5 billion of assets related to sub-advisory to the Wealth Management segment.

Strategic Investments and Other - Consists of investments in **China Asset Management Co., Ltd.**, an asset management company in China; **Northleaf Capital Partners Ltd.**, a global private equity, private credit and infrastructure fund manager; **Wealthsimple Financial Corp.**, an online investment manager; **Portag3 Ventures Limited Partnership**, **Portag3 Ventures II Limited Partnership** and **Portage Ventures III Limited Partnership**, venture capital funds focused on the financial technology sector; **Great-West Lifeco Inc.**, a financial services holding company with interests in life and health insurance, retirement savings, investment management and reinsurance businesses; and **Rockefeller Capital Management L.P.**, a financial services advisory firm in the U.S., focused on the high-net-worth and ultra-high-net-worth segments.

During 2022, the company's ownership interest in **Investment Planning Counsel Inc.** decreased to 95.22% from 100%.

Recent Merger and Acquisition Activity

Status: completed **Announced:** Apr. 3, 2023

IGM Financial Inc. acquired a 20.5% interest in New York, N.Y.-based Rockefeller Capital Management L.P., an independent financial advisory firm, for US$622,000,000, which would be financed with short-term financing secured by IGM. Rockefeller provides family office, asset management and strategic advisory services to high-net-worth individuals and families, institutions and corporations.

Status: pending **Announced:** Apr. 3, 2023

The Canada Life Assurance Company, wholly owned by Great-West Lifeco Inc., agreed to acquire Investment Planning Counsel Inc. (IPC) for $575,000,000, which would be financed with cash on hand. IPC, 95.22%-owned by IGM Financial Inc. and 4.78%-owned by IPC Management, was a wealth dealer and investment company operating both MFDA and IIROC platforms with 650 advisors who manage $32 billion in assets under management (AUM). Upon completion, Canada Life would have more than 4,000 advisor relationships and more than $85 billion in AUM. The boards of directors of Great-West Lifeco and IGM unanimously approved the transaction, which was expected to be completed by the end of 2023, subject to regulatory approvals. Great-West Lifeco and IGM were both subsidiaries of Power Corporation of Canada.

Status: completed **Revised:** Jan. 12, 2023

UPDATE: The transaction was completed. PREVIOUS: Power Corporation of Canada agreed to sell its 13.9% interest in China Asset Management Co., Ltd. (ChinaAMC) to Mackenzie Financial Corporation, owned by IGM Financial Inc., for $1.15 billion. As a result, IGM's indirect interest in ChinaAMC would increase to 27.8%. To partially fund the transaction, IGM would sell $575,000,000 of Great-West Lifeco Inc. common shares to Power Corporation, representing a 1.6% interest. The sale of the Great-West Lifeco shares was conditional on the purchase of the ChinaAMC shares. The transaction expected to be completed in the first half of 2022.

Predecessor Detail - Name changed from Investors Group Inc., May 17, 2004.

Directors - R. Jeffrey Orr, chr., Montréal, Qué.; James P. O'Sullivan, pres. & CEO, Toronto, Ont.; Marc A. Bibeau, Baie-d'Urfé, Qué.; Marcel R. Coutu, Calgary, Alta.; André Desmarais, Westmount, Qué.; Paul Desmarais Jr., Westmount, Qué.; The Hon. Gary A. Doer, Winnipeg, Man.; Susan Doniz, Guelph, Ont.; Claude Généreux, Westmount, Qué.; Sharon L. Hodgson, Toronto, Ont.; Sharon MacLeod, Georgetown, Ont.;

Susan J. McArthur, Toronto, Ont.; Dr. John S. McCallum, Winnipeg, Man.; Gregory D. Tretiak, Westmount, Qué.; Elizabeth D. (Beth) Wilson, Toronto, Ont.

Other Exec. Officers - Cynthia Currie, exec. v-p & chief HR officer; Michael (Mike) Dibden, exec. v-p & COO; Rhonda Goldberg, exec. v-p & gen. counsel; Kelly Hepher, exec. v-p & chief risk officer; Douglas (Doug) Milne, exec. v-p & chief mktg. officer; Keith Potter, exec. v-p & CFO; Sonya Reiss, v-p & corp. sec.; Damon Murchison, pres. & CEO, Investors Group Inc.; Blaine Shewchuk, pres. & CEO, Investment Planning Counsel Inc.

Capital Stock

	Authorized (shs.)	Outstanding (shs.)[1]
First Preferred	unlimited	nil
Second Preferred	unlimited	nil
Common	unlimited	238,096,685
Class 1 Non-voting	unlimited	nil

[1] At July 31, 2023

First Preferred - Issuable in series and non-voting.

Second Preferred - Issuable in series and non-voting.

Common - One vote per share.

Class 1 Non-voting - Rank equally with common shares as to dividends and return of capital in the event of liquidation, dissolution or winding-up of the company. Non-voting.

Options - At Dec. 31, 2022, options were outstanding to purchase 11,725,342 common shares at prices ranging from $31.85 to $53.81 per share expiring on various dates to 2032.

Major Shareholder - Power Corporation of Canada held 62.2% interest at Feb. 17, 2023.

Price Range - IGM/TSX

Year	Volume	High	Low	Close
2022	88,077,722	$48.30	$33.45	$37.80
2021	80,815,037	$51.68	$33.43	$45.62
2020	85,292,942	$40.38	$20.96	$34.51
2019	51,003,520	$40.37	$30.59	$37.28
2018	64,554,243	$44.28	$29.84	$31.03

Recent Close: $37.85

Capital Stock Changes - During 2022, 879,019 common shares were issued on exercise of options and 2,890,000 common shares were repurchased under a Normal Course Issuer Bid.

Dividends

IGM com Ra $2.25 pa Q est. Jan. 30, 2015

Long-Term Debt - Outstanding at Dec. 31, 2022:

Debentures:	
3.44% due 2027	$400,000,000
6.65% due 2027	125,000,000
7.45% due 2031	150,000,000
7% due 2032	175,000,000
7.11% due 2033	150,000,000
6% due 2040	200,000,000
4.56% due 2047	200,000,000
4.115% due 2047	250,000,000
4.174% due 2048	200,000,000
4.206% due 2050	250,000,000
	2,100,000,000

Note - In May 2023, offering of $300,000,000 principal amount of 5.426% debentures due May 26, 2053, was completed.

Wholly Owned Subsidiaries

Investors Group Inc., Winnipeg, Man.
- 100% int. in **I.G. Insurance Services Inc.**, Man.
- 100% int. in **I.G. Investment Management, Ltd.**, Winnipeg, Man.
- 100% int. in **Investors Group Financial Services Inc.**, Canada.
- 100% int. in **Investors Group Securities Inc.**, Canada.
- 100% int. in **Investors Group Trust Co. Ltd.**, Canada.

Mackenzie Inc., Ont.
- 100% int. in **Mackenzie Financial Corporation**, Toronto, Ont.
  - 27.8% int. in **China Asset Management Co., Ltd.**, People's Republic of China.
  - 100% int. in **Mackenzie Investments Asia Limited**, Hong Kong, Hong Kong, People's Republic of China.
  - 100% int. in **Mackenzie Investments Corporation**, Boston, Mass.
  - 100% int. in **Mackenzie Investments Europe Limited**, Dublin, Ireland.
  - 56% int. in **Northleaf Capital Partners Ltd.**, Toronto, Ont. Owns 80% interest (Great-West Lifeco Inc. 20%) in entity that holds 70% economic interest (49.9% voting interest) in Northleaf.

Subsidiaries

95.22% int. in **Investment Planning Counsel Inc.**, Mississauga, Ont.
- 100% int. in **Counsel Portfolio Services Inc.**, Ont.
- 100% int. in **IPC Investment Corporation**, Ont.
- 100% int. in **IPC Securities Corporation**, Ont.

Investments

2.4% int. in **Great-West Lifeco Inc.**, Winnipeg, Man. (see separate coverage)
7.7% int. in **Portag3 Ventures II Limited Partnership**, Toronto, Ont.
18.5% int. in **Portag3 Ventures Limited Partnership**, Toronto, Ont.
4% int. in **Portage Ventures III Limited Partnership**, Toronto, Ont.
20.5% int. in **Rockefeller Capital Management L.P.**, New York, N.Y.
24% int. in **Wealthsimple Financial Corp.**, Toronto, Ont.

Financial Statistics

Periods ended:	12m Dec. 31/22[A]		12m Dec. 31/21[A]
	$000s	%Chg	$000s
Total revenue	**3,357,249**	**-3**	**3,447,995**
Other operating expense	2,016,544		1,966,591
Operating expense	**2,016,544**	**+3**	**1,966,591**
Operating income	**1,340,705**	**-9**	**1,481,404**
Deprec. & amort.	103,994		99,818
Finance costs, gross	113,768		113,936
Pre-tax income	**1,122,943**	**-11**	**1,267,650**
Income taxes	250,365		286,763
Net income	**872,578**	**-11**	**980,887**
Net inc. for equity hldrs	**867,244**	**-11**	**978,949**
Net inc. for non-cont. int	**5,334**	**+175**	**1,938**
Cash & equivalent	1,072,892		1,292,446
Accounts receivable	368,806		387,157
Investments	7,982,980		8,800,120
Fixed assets, net	326,288		315,964
Intangibles, net	4,165,815		4,158,770
Total assets	**18,873,176**	**+7**	**17,660,588**
Accts. pay. & accr. liabs	507,573		553,429
Debt	2,100,000		2,100,000
Lease liabilities	192,793		197,969
Shareholders' equity	6,196,413		6,449,828
Non-controlling interest	66,677		51,343
Cash from oper. activs	**737,670**	**-22**	**943,590**
Cash from fin. activs	(1,091,934)		(1,521,844)
Cash from invest. activs	134,710		1,099,115
Net cash position	**1,072,892**	**-17**	**1,292,446**
Capital expenditures, net	(37,672)		(10,643)
Unfunded pension liability	n.a.		21,624
Pension fund surplus	86,779		n.a.
	$		$
Earnings per share*	3.64		4.10
Cash flow per share*	3.09		3.95
Cash divd. per share*	2.25		2.25
	shs		shs
No. of shs. o/s*	237,668,062		239,679,043
Avg. no. of shs. o/s*	238,470,000		238,841,000
	%		%
Net profit margin	25.99		28.45
Return on equity	13.72		17.11
Return on assets	5.26		6.34
No. of employees (FTEs)	4,010		3,827

* Common
[A] Reported in accordance with IFRS

Latest Results

Periods ended:	6m June 30/23[A]		6m June 30/22[□A]
	$000s	%Chg	$000s
Total revenue	1,705,704	+12	1,516,811
Net inc. bef. disc. opers	516,411	+22	421,793
Income from disc. opers	4,918		6,703
Net income	521,329	+22	428,496
Net inc. for equity hldrs	519,539	+22	426,417
Net inc. for non-cont. int	1,790		2,079
	$		$
Earns. per sh. bef. disc. opers.*	2.16		1.75
Earnings per share*	2.18		1.78

* Common
[□] Restated
[A] Reported in accordance with IFRS

Historical Summary
(as originally stated)

Fiscal Year	Total Rev. $000s	Net Inc. Bef. Disc. $000s	EPS* $
2022[A]	3,357,249	872,578	3.64
2021[A]	3,447,995	980,887	4.10
2020[A]	3,017,982	764,606	3.21
2019[A]	3,232,606	748,947	3.12
2018[A]	3,249,071	776,168	3.19

* Common
[A] Reported in accordance with IFRS

I.10 IM Cannabis Corp.

Symbol - IMCC **Exchange** - CSE **CUSIP** - 44969Q
Head Office - Kibbutz Glil Yam, Tel Aviv, Israel, 4690500 **Overseas Tel** - 972-77-4442333 **Overseas Fax** - 972-77-4442331
Website - www.imcannabis.com
Email - oren@imcannabis.com
Investor Relations - Oren Shuster 972-77-3603504
Auditors - Kost Forer Gabbay & Kasierer C.A., Tel Aviv, Israel
Transfer Agents - Continental Stock Transfer & Trust Company, New York, N.Y.; Computershare Trust Company of Canada Inc., Vancouver, B.C.
Employees - 336 at Mar. 31, 2022

Profile - (B.C. 1980) Cultivates, processes, distributes and retails medical and recreational cannabis products in Israel, Germany and Canada.

In Israel, imports, distributes and sells medical cannabis products under the IMC and WAGNERS brands through operation of retail pharmacies, online retail platform and home delivery business, distribution centres and logistical hubs.

In Germany, subsidiary **Adjupharm GmbH** (90.02% owned) imports and distributes medical cannabis products under the IMC brand to pharmacies and distributors. Adjupharm operates an 8,000-sq.-ft. production and warehousing facility.

In Canada, owns and operates a 32,050-m^2 indoor cultivation and processing facility and a 1,400-m^2 processing facility in Kitchener, Ont. (TJAC); a 530-m^2 indoor cultivation and processing facility (Highland) in Antigonish. N.S.; and a 930-m^2 indoor cultivation facility (Sublime) in Laval, Que. Products include dried flower, pre-rolls, hash and kief which are sold to the Canadian recreational market as well as exported to the company's medical cannabis operations in Israel under the WAGNERS and Highland Grow brands.

In November 2022, the company announced it would exit the Canadian cannabis market. In connection wholly owned **Trichome Financial Corp.**, and certain of its wholly owned subsidiaries, including **Trichome JWC Acquisition Corp.**, **MYM Nutraceuticals Inc.**, **Trichome Retail Corp.**, **MYM International Brands Inc.**, and **Highland Grow Inc.** filed and obtained creditor protection under the Canadian Companies' Creditors Arrangement Act (CCAA).

In April 2022, the company announced the closure of affiliate **Focus Medical Herbs Ltd.**'s 300,000-sq.-ft. greenhouse facility in Moshav Sde Avraham, Israel. Focus has an exclusive commercial agreement with the company to distribute its production under the IMC brand. The company would focus on importing to Israel cannabis products from its Canadian facilities.

On Mar. 28, 2022, the company acquired a 51.3% interest in **Oranim Plus Pharm Ltd.** for $4,900,000, consisting of $4,200,000 cash and issuance of 251,001 common shares. Oranim Plus holds 99.5% of the rights in **Oranim Pharm Partnership**, a medical cannabis pharmacy in Jerusalem, Israel.

On Mar. 14, 2022, the company acquired a 51% interest in **Revoly Trading and Marketing Ltd.** (dba Vironna Pharm), a pharmacy located in Tira, Israel, licensed to dispense and sell medical cannabis, for $3,330,000, consisting of $1,950,000 cash and issuance of 485,362 common shares.

In addition, the company acquired **R.A. Yarok Pharm Ltd.**, a medical cannabis pharmacy in Netanya, Israel; and **Rosen High Way Ltd.**, operator of a trade and distribution centre in Netanya providing medical cannabis storage, distribution services and logistics solutions for cannabis companies and pharmacies in Israel. Total consideration was $4,600,000 cash. The transaction also included the acquisition of **High Way Shinua Ltd.**, an applicant for a medical cannabis transportation licence from the Israeli Medical Cannabis Agency. Closing of High Way Shinua acquisition remains pending.

Recent Merger and Acquisition Activity

Status: completed **Revised:** Mar. 14, 2022

UPDATE: The second closing was completed. PREVIOUS: IM Cannabis Corp. (IMC) agreed to acquire the Panaxia to the Home online pharmacy and trading centre IMC-GDP licence as well as certain distribution assets and an option to purchase a retail pharmacy licensed to dispense and sell medical cannabis to patients from Panaxia Labs Israel, Ltd., a manufacturer and distributor of medical cannabis-based pharmaceuticals in Israel and Europe. Panaxia to the Home offers medical cannabis products to patients across Israel through an online platform with home delivery services. Total consideration was $7,200,000, consisting of $2,900,000 cash and issuance of $4,300,000 of common shares to be paid/issued in instalments. The acquisition would close in two stages: upon the initial closing, all online-related activities and intellectual property, including the online sales platform, a CRM platform and use of a storage facility to support the operations of Panaxia to the Home, would be transferred to IMC; and upon the second closing, subject to approval of the Israeli Ministry of Health, the IMC-GDP licence for the distribution of medical cannabis would be transferred to IMC. June 1, 2021 - The first closing was completed.

Predecessor Detail - Name changed from Navasota Resources Inc., Oct. 4, 2019, pursuant to the reverse takeover acquisition of I.M.C. Holdings Ltd. and concurrent amalgamation of I.M.C. with wholly owned Navasota Acquisition Ltd.; basis 1 new for 2.83 old shs.

Directors - Marc Lustig, exec. chr., Vancouver, B.C.; Oren Shuster, CEO, Ra'anana, Israel; Moti Marcus; Brian Schinderle, Ill.; Einat Zakariya

Other Exec. Officers - Itay Vago, CFO; Yael Harrosh, chief legal & opers. officer

Capital Stock

	Authorized (shs.)	Outstanding (shs.)[1]
Common	unlimited	7,569,526

[1] At Nov. 17, 2022

Major Shareholder - Oren Shuster held 13.1% interest and Rafael Gabay held 11.6% interest at Mar. 31, 2022.

Price Range - IMCC/CSE

Year	Volume	High	Low	Close
2022	681,783	$42.60	$1.10	$1.30
2021	1,014,235	$144.00	$28.40	$42.20
2020	1,089,561	$140.00	$7.00	$100.40
2019	156,844	$30.00	$10.00	$13.60

Consolidation: 1-for-10 cons. in Nov. 2022; 1-for-4 cons. in Feb. 2021; 1-for-2.83 cons. in Oct. 2019

Recent Close: $0.96

Capital Stock Changes - On Nov. 17, 2022, common shares were consolidated on a 1-for-10 basis.

Wholly Owned Subsidiaries

I.M.C. Holdings Ltd., Israel.
- 90.02% int. in **Adjupharm GmbH**, Germany.
- 100% int. in **I.M.C. Farms Israel Ltd.**, Israel.
- 100% int. in **I.M.C. - International Medical Cannabis Portugal, Unipessoal, Lda.**, Portugal.
- 100% int. in **I.M.C. Pharma Ltd.**, Israel.
- 75% int. in **I.M.C Ventures Ltd.**
- 51.3% int. in **Oranim Plus Pharm Ltd.**, Israel.
  - 99.5% int. in **Oranim Pharm Partnership**, Israel.
- 100% int. in **R.A. Yarok Pharm Ltd.**, Israel.
- 51% int. in **Revoly Trading and Marketing Ltd.**, Israel.
- 100% int. in **Rosen High Way Ltd.**, Israel.
- **Xinteza API Ltd.**, Israel.

Trichome Financial Corp., Toronto, Ont.
- 100% int. in **MYM Nutraceuticals Inc.**, Vancouver, B.C.
  - 100% int. in **CannaCanada Inc.**, Qué.
  - 100% int. in **MYM International Brands Inc.**
    - 100% int. in **Highland Grow Inc.**, N.S.
- 100% int. in **Trichome Asset Funding Corp.**
- 100% int. in **Trichome Financial Cannabis GP Inc.**
- 100% int. in **Trichome Financial Cannabis Manager Inc.**, Ont.
- 100% int. in **Trichome JWC Acquisition Corp.**, Ont.
  - 100% int. in **SublimeCulture Inc.**, Qué.
- 100% int. in **Trichome Retail Corp.**

Note: The preceding list includes only the major related companies in which interests are held.

Financial Statistics

Periods ended:	12m Dec. 31/21[A]		12m Dec. 31/20[A]
	$000s	%Chg	$000s
Operating revenue	**54,300**	**+242**	**15,890**
Cost of sales	38,275		4,492
Research & devel. expense	n.a.		136
General & admin expense	40,939		15,195
Stock-based compensation	7,471		3,382
Operating expense	**86,685**	**+274**	**23,205**
Operating income	**(32,385)**	**n.a.**	**(7,315)**
Deprec., depl. & amort.	5,729		930
Finance income	22,024		277
Finance costs, gross	1,648		20,504
Write-downs/write-offs	(275)		nil
Pre-tax income	**(18,013)**	**n.a.**	**(28,472)**
Income taxes	505		262
Net income	**(18,518)**	**n.a.**	**(28,734)**
Net inc. for equity hldrs	**(17,763)**	**n.a.**	**(28,698)**
Net inc. for non-cont. int	**(755)**	**n.a.**	**(36)**
Cash & equivalent	17,032		8,885
Inventories	29,391		8,370
Accounts receivable	29,080		5,718
Current assets	84,311		27,143
Long-term investments	2,429		2,341
Fixed assets, net	30,268		5,532
Right-of-use assets	18,162		935
Intangibles, net	152,188		1,396
Total assets	**287,388**	**+654**	**38,116**
Bank indebtedness	9,502		nil
Accts. pay. & accr. liabs	34,132		6,102
Current liabilities	51,227		6,269
Long-term debt, gross	392		nil
Long-term debt, net	392		nil
Long-term lease liabilities	17,820		823
Shareholders' equity	201,236		11,097
Non-controlling interest	3,709		1,513
Cash from oper. activs	**(34,372)**	**n.a.**	**(7,919)**
Cash from fin. activs	48,731		6,740
Cash from invest. activs	(9,012)		(4,075)
Net cash position	**13,903**	**+56**	**8,885**
Capital expenditures	(4,578)		(2,617)
Unfunded pension liability	391		371
	$		$
Earnings per share*	(3.10)		(7.44)
Cash flow per share*	(5.93)		(2.05)
	shs		shs
No. of shs. o/s*	6,821,789		3,976,578
Avg. no. of shs. o/s*	5,796,300		3,856,500
	%		%
Net profit margin	(34.10)		(180.83)
Return on equity	(16.73)		n.m.
Return on assets	(10.34)		n.a.
Foreign sales percent	63		100
No. of employees (FTEs)	283		24

* Common
[A] Reported in accordance with IFRS

Latest Results

Periods ended:	3m Mar. 31/22[A]		3m Mar. 31/21[A]
	$000s	%Chg	$000s
Operating revenue	23,569	+169	8,767
Net income	(10,741)	n.a.	4,715
Net inc. for equity hldrs	(9,452)	n.a.	4,505
Net inc. for non-cont. int	(1,289)		210
	$		$
Earnings per share*	(1.40)		1.10

* Common
[A] Reported in accordance with IFRS

Historical Summary
(as originally stated)

Fiscal Year	Oper. Rev.	Net Inc. Bef. Disc.	EPS*
	$000s	$000s	$
2021[A]	54,300	(18,518)	(3.10)
2020[A]	15,890	(28,734)	(7.44)
2019[A1]	9,074	(7,419)	(2.28)
2019[A2]	nil	(123)	(1.13)
2018[A]	nil	(125)	(6.57)

* Common
[A] Reported in accordance with IFRS
[1] Results reflect the Oct. 11, 2019, reverse takeover acquistion of I.M.C. Holdings Ltd.
[2] Results for fiscal 2019 and prior fiscal years pertain to Navasota Resources Inc.

Note: Adjusted throughout for 1-for-10 cons. in Nov. 2022; 1-for-4 cons. in Feb. 2021; 1-for-2.83 cons. in Oct. 2019; 1-for-5 cons. in June 2018

I.11 IMAX Corporation

Symbol - IMAX **Exchange** - NYSE **CUSIP** - 45245E
Head Office - 2525 Speakman Dr, Mississauga, ON, L5K 1B1 **Telephone** - (905) 403-6500 **Fax** - (905) 403-6450 **Exec. Office** - 902 Broadway, 20th Flr, New York, NY, United States, 10010 **Telephone** - (212) 821-0100 **Fax** - (212) 371-1174
Website - www.imax.com
Email - jhorsley@imax.com
Investor Relations - Jennifer Horsley (212) 821-0154
Auditors - PricewaterhouseCoopers LLP C.A., Toronto, Ont.
Transfer Agents - Computershare Shareowner Services LLC, Ridgefield Park, N.J.; Computershare Trust Company of Canada Inc.
FP500 Revenue Ranking - 515
Employees - 779 at Dec. 31, 2022
Profile - (Can. 1994 amalg.) Provides digital remastering of films and other content into IMAX formats and designs, manufactures, sells and leases theatre systems for IMAX theatres owned and operated by commercial and institutional customers.

The company operates through three business segments: Content Solution; Technology Products & Services; and Others.

The **Content Solution** segment includes IMAX film remastering, a proprietary technology that digitally remasters films and other content into IMAX formats and enhances the image resolution of motion picture films while maintaining and enhancing the visual clarity and sound quality. The company receives a percentage of the box office receipts from a movie studio in exchange for converting the film and distributing it through the IMAX network. At Mar. 31, 2023, 16 IMAX film were released to the global IMAX theatre network compared to 13 films at Mar. 31, 2022.

Also includes the distribution of large-format documentary films, primarily to institutional theatres; IMAX Live™, which has 258 systems in the IMAX network configured with connectivity to deliver live and interactive events as at Mar. 31, 2023; provision of film and digital post-production services; and providing IMAX film and digital cameras to content creators under the IMAX certified camera program. At Dec. 31, 2022, the company had distribution rights with respect to 55 films, which cover subjects such as space, wildlife, music, sports, history and natural wonders.

The **Technology Products & Services** segment includes IMAX Theatre Systems, which are either sold or leased to exhibitor customers along with a licence for the use of the IMAX brand. The digital projection systems include a projector and a digital theatre control system; a digital audio system; a screen with a proprietary coating technology; and 3D glasses cleaning equipment. The company also provides extensive advice on theatre planning and design, and supervision of installation services as part of the arrangement to sell or lease the theatre systems. The theatre systems are offered under six configurations: flat screen and dome theatre systems, which are installed primarily in institutions such as museums and science centres; 3D GT and 3D SR theatre systems, which utilize a flat screen 3D system that produces realistic 3D images on an IMAX screen; Xenon theatre systems; and Laser theatre systems, which are designed for IMAX theatres in commercial multiplexes. At Mar. 31, 2023, there were 1,711 IMAX Theatre Systems operating in 87 countries and territories, including 1,631 commercial multiplexes, 12 commercial destinations and 68 institutional locations, compared with 1,690 IMAX Theatre Systems operating at Mar. 31, 2022.

Also include annual maintenance and extended warranty fee from theatre owners and operators for the provision of proactive and emergency maintenance services to every theatre in its network; and after-market sales of IMAX projection system parts and 3D glasses.

Others includes IMAX Enhanced, a new home entertainment licensing and certification program wherein consumer electronics manufacturers of 4K/8K televisions, projectors, A/V receivers, loudspeakers, subwoofers and soundbars must meet a carefully prescribed set of audio and video performance standards to be certified. At Mar. 31, 2023, more than 250 IMAX Enhanced titles have been released across five of the biggest streaming platforms worldwide including Disney+, Sony Bravia CORE, Tencent Video, iQiyi and Rakuten TV.

Also include revenues from wholly owned **SSIMWAVE Inc.**, which provides an artificial intelligence (AI)-driven video experience automation platform for media and entertainment companies that virtualizes and measures how humans perceive video and apply it in real-world environments; one owned and operated IMAX theatre in Sacramento, Calif.; commercial arrangement with one theatre resulting in profit sharing; management services to three other theatres; renting of 2D and 3D large-format film and digital cameras to third-party production companies; and advisory services to documentary and Hollywood filmmakers.

Recent Merger and Acquisition Activity

Status: completed **Announced:** Sept. 22, 2022
IMAX Corporation acquired private Waterloo, Ont.-based SSIMWAVE Inc., which provides an artificial intelligence (AI)-driven video experience automation platform for media and entertainment companies that virtualizes and measures how humans perceive video and apply it in real-world environments, for $18,500,000 cash and issuance of $2,500,000 of common shares. An additional earnout consideration of $4,000,000 would be paid subject to SSIMWAVE achieving certain operating performance and financial objectives.

Directors - Darren D. Throop, chr., Toronto, Ont.; Richard L. (Rich) Gelfond, CEO, New York, N.Y.; David W. Leebron†, Houston, Tex.; Gail Berman, Pacific Palisades, Calif.; Eric A. Demirian, Toronto, Ont.; Kevin G. Douglas, Larkspur, Calif.; Michael I. M. MacMillan, Toronto, Ont.; Steve Pamon, South Orange, N.J.; Dana Settle, Los Angeles, Calif.; Jennifer Wong, New York, N.Y.

Other Exec. Officers - Giovanni M. Dolci, chief sales officer; Michele Golden, chief people officer; Mark Jafar, global head, corp. commun.; Robert D. Lister, sr. exec. v-p & chief legal officer; Pablo Calamera, exec. v-p & chief tech. officer; Megan Colligan, exec. v-p & pres., IMAX Entertainment; Natasha Fernandes, exec. v-p & CFO; Vikram Arumilli, sr. v-p & gen. mgr., streaming & consumer tech.; Craig Dehmel, sr. v-p & exec. v-p & head of global distrib., IMAX Entertainment; Elizabeth Gitajn, sr. v-p, fin. & contr.; Jennifer Horsley, sr. v-p, IR; Denny Tu, sr. v-p & chief mktg. officer; Mark D. Welton, pres., IMAX Theatres; Daniel Manwaring, CEO, IMAX China Holding, Inc.; Kenneth Weissman, deputy gen. counsel & corp. sec.

† Lead director

Capital Stock

	Authorized (shs.)	Outstanding (shs.)[1]
Common	unlimited	54,620,083

[1] At June 30, 2023

Major Shareholder - Douglas family held 16.36% interest at Apr. 10, 2023.

Price Range - IMAX/NYSE

Year	Volume	High	Low	Close
2022	46,823,013	US$21.23	US$12.13	US$14.66
2021	53,811,858	US$25.05	US$13.61	US$17.84
2020	61,509,230	US$20.99	US$6.01	US$18.02
2019	25,926,759	US$25.74	US$18.50	US$20.43
2018	34,288,540	US$26.10	US$17.57	US$18.81

Capital Stock Changes - During 2022, common shares were issued as follows: 596,277 on vesting of restricted stock units and 160,547 pursuant to the acquisition of SSIMWAVE Inc; 5,261,852 common shares were repurchased and cancelled.

Wholly Owned Subsidiaries

Animal Orphans 3D Ltd., Ont.
Arizona Big Frame Theatres, LLC, Ariz.
4507592 Canada Ltd., Canada.
ILW Productions Inc., Del.
IMAX II U.S.A. Inc., Del.
IMAX AI Limited, Ireland.
IMAX (Barbados) Holding, Inc., Barbados.
IMAX Chicago Theatre LLC, Del.
IMAX Film Holding Co., Del.
IMAX GWG Inc., Del.
IMAX (Hong Kong) Holding, Limited, Hong Kong, People's Republic of China.
IMAX Indianapolis LLC, Ind.
IMAX International Sales Corporation, Canada.
IMAX Investment Management, LLC, Del.
IMAX Japan Inc., Japan.
IMAX Minnesota Holding Co., Del.
IMAX Music Ltd., Ont.
IMAX PV Development Inc., Del.
IMAX Post/DKP Inc., Del.
IMAX Providence General Partner Co., Del.
IMAX Providence Limited Partner Co., Del.
IMAX Rhode Island Limited Partnership, R.I.
IMAX (Rochester) Inc., Del.
IMAX Scribe Inc., Del.
IMAX Space Productions Ltd., Canada.
IMAX Spaceworks Ltd., Canada.
IMAX Theatre Holding (California I) Co., Del.
IMAX Theatre Holding (California II) Co., Del.
IMAX Theatre Holding Co., Del.
IMAX Theatre Holding (Nyack I) Co., Del.

IMAX Theatre Holding (Nyack II) Co., Del.
IMAX Theatre Holdings (OEI) Inc., Del.
IMAX Theatre Services Ltd., Ont.
IMAX Theatres International Limited, Ireland.
IMAX 3D TV Ventures, LLC, Del.
IMAX U.S.A. Inc., Del.
IMAX VR, LLC, Del.
Line Drive Films Inc., Del.
Madagascar Doc 3D Ltd., Canada.
Night Fog Productions Ltd., Canada.
9733248 Canada Ltd., Canada.
Nyack Theatre LLC, N.Y.
12582 Productions Inc., Del.
1329507 Ontario Inc., Ont.
Raining Arrows Productions Ltd., Canada.
Ridefilm Corporation, Del.
Ruth Quentin Films Ltd., Canada.
SSIMWAVE Inc., Waterloo, Ont.
SSIMWAVE USA Inc., Del.
Sacramento Theatre LLC, Del.
7096267 Canada Ltd., Canada.
7103077 Canada Ltd., Canada.
7109857 Canada Ltd., Canada.
7214316 Canada Ltd., Canada.
7550391 Canada Ltd., Canada.
7550405 Canada Ltd., Canada.
7742266 Canada Ltd., Canada.
7742274 Canada Ltd., Canada.
6822967 Canada Ltd., Canada.
Sonics Associates, Inc., Ala.
Starboard Theaters Ltd., Ont.
Strategic Sponsorship Corporation, Del.
Taurus-Littrow Productions Inc., Del.
3183 Films Ltd., Canada.
• 50% int. in **IMAX (Titanic) Inc.**, Del.
2328764 Ontario Ltd., Ont.
Walking Bones Pictures Ltd., Canada.

Subsidiaries

71.73% int. in **IMAX China Holding, Inc.**, Cayman Islands.
71.73% int. in **IMAX China (Hong Kong), Limited**, Hong Kong, People's Republic of China.
71.73% int. in **IMAX (Shanghai) Commerce and Trade Co., Ltd.**, People's Republic of China.
71.73% int. in **IMAX (Shanghai) Culture & Technology Co., Ltd.**, People's Republic of China.
71.73% int. in **IMAX (Shanghai) Digital Media Co., Ltd.**, People's Republic of China.
71.73% int. in **IMAX (Shanghai) Multimedia Technology Co., Ltd.**, People's Republic of China.
71.73% int. in **IMAX (Shanghai) Theatre Technology Services Co., Ltd.**, People's Republic of China.
88% int. in **IMAXSHIFT, LLC**, Del.
88% int. in **Plymouth 135-139, LLC**, Del.
53.81% int. in **Suzhou IMAX Fei Er Mu Project Investment Partnership Enterprise**, People's Republic of China.

Investments

15.63% int. in **Baseball Tour, LLC**, Del.
36.03% int. in **IMAX Documentary Films Capital, LLC**, Del.
35.87% int. in **IMAX Fei Er Mu (Shanghai) Investment Management Co., Ltd.**, People's Republic of China.
39.45% int. in **IMAX Fei Er Mu (Shanghai) Investment Partnership**, People's Republic of China.
35.87% int. in **IMAX Fei Er Mu YiKai (Shanghai) Equity Investment Management Partnership Enterprise**, People's Republic of China.
50% int. in **IMAX (Titanic) Inc.**, Del.
33.49% int. in **IMAX Virtual Reality Content Fund, LLC**, Del.
50% int. in **TCL-IMAX (Shanghai) Digital Technology Co. Ltd.**, People's Republic of China.
50% int. in **TCL-IMAX Entertainment Co., Limited**, Hong Kong, People's Republic of China.

Financial Statistics

Periods ended:	12m Dec. 31/22^A		12m Dec. 31/21^A
	US$000s	%Chg	US$000s
Operating revenue	**300,805**	**+18**	**254,883**
Cost of sales	91,462		67,782
Research & devel. expense	4,881		6,596
General & admin expense	111,758		92,609
Stock-based compensation	27,013		25,614
Operating expense	**235,114**	**+31**	**179,409**
Operating income	**65,691**	**-13**	**75,474**
Deprec., depl. & amort.	56,661		56,082
Finance income	1,428		2,218
Finance costs, gross	6,724		8,029
Write-downs/write-offs	(4,470)		nil
Pre-tax income	**(9,769)**	**n.a.**	**10,987**
Income taxes	10,108		20,564
Net income	**(19,877)**	**n.a.**	**(9,577)**
Net inc. for equity hldrs	**(22,800)**	**n.a.**	**(22,329)**
Net inc. for non-cont. int.	**2,923**	**-77**	**12,752**
Cash & equivalent	97,401		189,711
Inventories	31,534		26,924
Accounts receivable	136,142		110,050
Current assets	438,485		511,952
Long-term investments	2,035		2,087
Fixed assets, net	252,896		260,353
Intangibles, net	85,553		62,107
Total assets	**821,154**	**-7**	**883,247**
Bank indebtedness	36,111		2,472
Accts. pay. & accr. liabs.	25,237		15,943
Current liabilities	491,386		452,875
Long-term debt, gross	226,912		223,641
Long-term debt, net	226,912		223,641
Shareholders' equity	263,355		356,083
Non-controlling interest	65,691		73,531
Cash from oper. activs.	**17,321**	**+186**	**6,065**
Cash from fin. activs.	(58,514)		(132,720)
Cash from invest. activs.	(53,291)		(7)
Net cash position	**97,401**	**-49**	**189,711**
Capital expenditures	(8,424)		(3,590)
Unfunded pension liability	17,315		20,056
	US$		US$
Earnings per share*	(0.40)		(0.38)
Cash flow per share*	0.31		0.10
	shs		shs
No. of shs. o/s*	54,148,614		58,653,642
Avg. no. of shs. o/s*	56,674,000		59,126,000
	%		%
Net profit margin	(6.61)		(3.76)
Return on equity	(7.36)		(6.02)
Return on assets	(0.73)		(1.76)
Foreign sales percent	97		99
No. of employees (FTEs)	779		665

* Common
^A Reported in accordance with U.S. GAAP

Latest Results

Periods ended:	6m June 30/23^A		6m June 30/22^A
	US$000s	%Chg	US$000s
Operating revenue	184,925	+38	134,004
Net income	14,736	n.a.	(16,201)
Net inc. for equity hldrs	10,805	n.a.	(16,460)
Net inc. for non-cont. int.	3,931		259
	US$		US$
Earnings per share*	0.20		(0.28)

* Common
^A Reported in accordance with U.S. GAAP

Historical Summary
(as originally stated)

Fiscal Year	Oper. Rev.	Net Inc. Bef. Disc.	EPS*
	US$000s	US$000s	US$
2022^A	300,805	(19,877)	(0.40)
2021^A	254,883	(9,577)	(0.38)
2020^A	137,003	(157,486)	(2.43)
2019^A	395,664	58,571	0.76
2018^A	374,401	33,595	0.36

* Common
^A Reported in accordance with U.S. GAAP

I.12 INEO Tech Corp.

Symbol - INEO **Exchange** - TSX-VEN **CUSIP** - 45674Q
Head Office - 105-19130 24 Ave, Surrey, BC, V3Z 3S9 **Telephone** - (604) 283-2974
Website - www.ineosolutionsinc.com
Email - investor@ineosolutionsinc.com
Investor Relations - Pardeep Sangha (604) 572-6392
Auditors - Davidson & Company LLP C.A., Vancouver, B.C.
Transfer Agents - Computershare Trust Company of Canada Inc., Vancouver, B.C.

Employees - 25 at June 30, 2022
Profile - (B.C. 2008) Designs, manufactures, markets and deploys loss prevention systems for retailers that incorporate digital advertising and customer analytics data all in one unit.

The company's patented technology, INEO Media Network, is a loss-prevention, digital signage and data-capture kiosk that provides retail analytics and targeted advertising through its cloud-based Internet of things (IoT) and artificial intelligence (AI) technology. It consists of three pillars: AI-enabled Data, which captures customers that enter and exit the retail establishment; Analytics, paired with Data, assists retailers in their decision making processes by providing insights; and Advertising, which is displayed directly to consumers through its patented digital signage.

Lead product is INEO Welcoming Pedestal, a system which combines traditional retail security tag readers with digital advertising screens to target messages to shoppers as they enter and exit the retail establishment. Additional devices include: INEO Welcoming Pedestal DUO, a dual screen version of INEO Welcoming Pedestal; INEO Welcoming Player, for additional locations throughout a retailer; and INEO GATE, a loss prevention pedestal with fixed messaging such as corporate identification.

Predecessor Detail - Name changed from Metron Capital Corp., Jan. 27, 2020, following reverse takeover acquisition of INEO Solutions Inc.; basis 1 new for 1.6191 old shs.

Directors - Greg Watkin, chr., pres. & corp. sec., Surrey, B.C.; Kyle Hall, CEO, Vancouver, B.C.; David (Dave) Jaworski, Nashville, Tenn.; Steven E. Matyas, Toronto, Ont.; Eugene Syho, B.C.

Other Exec. Officers - Bernadette (Bernie) Ryle, CFO

Capital Stock

	Authorized (shs.)	Outstanding (shs.)[1]
Preferred	unlimited	nil
Common	unlimited	76,143,709

[1] At Jan. 11, 2023

Major Shareholder - Greg Watkin held 16.63% interest at Jan. 11, 2023.

Price Range - INEO/TSX-VEN

Year	Volume	High	Low	Close
2022	14,802,875	$0.32	$0.09	$0.12
2021	17,433,591	$0.59	$0.19	$0.29
2020	3,310,237	$0.43	$0.15	$0.43
2019	104,070	$0.11	$0.06	$0.08
2018	135,198	$0.13	$0.08	$0.10

Consolidation: 1-for-1.6191 cons. in Jan. 2020
Recent Close: $0.04

Capital Stock Changes - In November 2022, public offering of 12,025,000 units (1 common share & ½ warrant) at 12¢ per unit was completed, with warrants exercisable at 19¢ per share for three years.

During fiscal 2022, 44,370 common shares were issued on exercise of warrants.

Wholly Owned Subsidiaries

INEO Solutions Inc., Surrey, B.C.
• 100% int. in **FG Manufacturing Inc.**, Surrey, B.C.

Financial Statistics

Periods ended:	12m June 30/22^A		12m June 30/21^A
	$000s	%Chg	$000s
Operating revenue	**1,245**	**+67**	**745**
Cost of sales	741		455
Salaries & benefits	2,054		1,430
Research & devel. expense	115		91
General & admin expense	1,217		712
Stock-based compensation	222		246
Operating expense	**4,349**	**+48**	**2,934**
Operating income	**(3,104)**	**n.a.**	**(2,189)**
Deprec., depl. & amort.	159		111
Finance costs, gross	42		57
Write-downs/write-offs	(9)		(3)
Pre-tax income	**(3,293)**	**n.a.**	**(2,238)**
Net income	**(3,293)**	**n.a.**	**(2,238)**
Cash & equivalent	1,706		5,199
Inventories	155		99
Accounts receivable	205		109
Current assets	2,337		5,480
Fixed assets, net	781		562
Right-of-use assets	83		114
Intangibles, net	5		nil
Total assets	**3,206**	**-48**	**6,156**
Accts. pay. & accr. liabs	481		368
Current liabilities	794		561
Long-term debt, gross	280		156
Long-term lease liabilities	64		95
Shareholders' equity	2,348		5,404
Cash from oper. activs	**(3,078)**	**n.a.**	**(1,619)**
Cash from fin. activs	(25)		5,981
Cash from invest. activs	(390)		(415)
Net cash position	**1,706**	**-67**	**5,199**
Capital expenditures	(346)		(414)
	$		$
Earnings per share*	(0.05)		(0.05)
Cash flow per share*	(0.05)		(0.03)
	shs		shs
No. of shs. o/s*	60,190,138		60,145,768
Avg. no. of shs. o/s*	60,190,138		46,653,398
	%		%
Net profit margin	(264.50)		(300.40)
Return on equity	(84.96)		n.m.
Return on assets	(69.45)		n.a.
Foreign sales percent	60		28
No. of employees (FTEs)	25		25

* Common
^A Reported in accordance with IFRS

Latest Results

Periods ended:	3m Sept. 30/22^A		3m Sept. 30/21^A
	$000s	%Chg	$000s
Operating revenue	416	+74	239
Net income	(591)	n.a.	(731)
	$		$
Earnings per share*	(0.01)		(0.01)

* Common
^A Reported in accordance with IFRS

Historical Summary
(as originally stated)

Fiscal Year	Oper. Rev. $000s	Net Inc. Bef. Disc. $000s	EPS* $
2022^A	1,245	(3,293)	(0.05)
2021^A	745	(2,238)	(0.05)
2020^A1	527	(5,763)	(0.25)
2019^A2	nil	(316)	(0.03)
2018^A	nil	(451)	(0.03)

* Common
^A Reported in accordance with IFRS
[1] Results reflect the Jan. 27, 2020, reverse takeover acquisition of INEO Solutions Inc.
[2] Results for fiscal 2019 and prior fiscal years pertain to Metron Capital Corp.
Note: Adjusted throughout for 1-for-1.6191 cons. in Jan. 2020

I.13 The INX Digital Company, Inc.

Symbol - INXD **Exchange** - NEO **CUSIP** - 46187N
Head Office - 2900-550 Burrard St, Vancouver, BC, V6C 0A3 **Telephone** - (604) 631-3131
Website - www.inx.co
Email - douglas.borthwick@inx.co
Investor Relations - Douglas Borthwick (855) 657-2314
Auditors - Kost Forer Gabbay & Kasierer C.A., Tel Aviv, Israel
Transfer Agents - Odyssey Trust Company, Vancouver, B.C.
Profile - (B.C. 2018) Operates regulated trading platforms in the United States for digital securities and cryptocurrencies.

Offers professional traders and institutional investors trading platforms with established practices common in other regulated financial services markets, such as customary trading and settlement procedures, regulatory compliance, capital and liquidity reserves and operational transparency.

Operates two trading platforms: INX Digital, a trading platform for cryptocurrencies, such as Bitcoin and Ethereum; and INX Securities, a trading platform for digital securities, which are digital assets that constitute securities under applicable securities laws, such as the company's own INX Tokens and tokens of other issuers who chose to issue digital securities.

The company is qualified to operate as money transmitter in 29 U.S. states. Operates and is recognized as an Alternative Trading System by the United States Securities Exchange Commission. Initial revenue would be generated primarily from fees received in connection with activities on the platforms.

Recent Merger and Acquisition Activity

Status: pending **Announced:** Nov. 30, 2022
The INX Digital Company, Inc. submitted a non-binding letter of intent to purchase the assets of Voyager Digital Ltd., following Voyager's bankruptcy filing. INX is among other companies bidding for Voyager's assets.

Predecessor Detail - Name changed from Valdy Investments Ltd., Jan. 10, 2022, pursuant to the reverse takeover acquisition of INX Limited; basis 1 new for 2.72667 old shs.

Directors - David Weild, chr., Tenn.; Shy Datika, pres. & CEO, Israel; Demeta Kalogerou, Cyprus; Hilary Kramer, N.Y.; Thomas K. Lewis Jr., Utah; Alan Silbert, Md.; Nicholas Thadaney, Toronto, Ont.

Other Exec. Officers - Renata K. Szkoda, CFO; Itai Avneri, chief opers. officer; Jonathan Azeroual, chief blockchain officer; Douglas Borthwick, chief bus. officer; Paz Diamant, chief tech. officer; Maia Naor, chief product officer; Keren Avidar, gen. counsel; Alan Sibert, CEO, North America

Capital Stock

	Authorized (shs.)	Outstanding (shs.)[1]
Common	unlimited	204,136,150

[1] At Jan. 24, 2022

Major Shareholder - Shy Datika held 19.86% interest at Jan. 24, 2022.

Price Range - INXD/NEO

Year	Volume	High	Low	Close
2022	746,100	$1.41	$0.12	$0.15
2021	3,667	$0.21	$0.21	$0.21
2020	67,114	$0.35	$0.16	$0.18
2019	498,532	$0.55	$0.33	$0.38

Consolidation: 1-for-2.72667 cons. in Jan. 2022
Recent Close: $0.34

Wholly Owned Subsidiaries

INX Limited, Gibraltar.
- 100% int. in **I.L.S. Brokers Ltd.**, Israel.
- 100% int. in **ILSB UK Limited**, United Kingdom.
- 100% int. in **INX Digital, Inc.**, United States.
- 100% int. in **INX Securities, LLC**, Pa. formerly Openfinance Securities, LLC
- 100% int. in **INX Services, Inc.**, United States.
- 100% int. in **INX Solutions Limited**, Gibraltar.
- 100% int. in **Midgard Technologies Ltd.**, Israel.
- 100% int. in **Tokensoft Transfer Agent LLC**

I.14 IOU Financial Inc.

Symbol - IOU **Exchange** - TSX-VEN **CUSIP** - 44985J
Head Office - 1670-1 Place Ville-Marie, Montréal, QC, H3B 2B6 **Telephone** - (514) 789-0694 **Toll-free** - (866) 217-8564 **Fax** - (514) 789-0542
Website - www.ioufinancial.com
Email - dokeefe@ioufinancial.com
Investor Relations - Daniel O'Keefe (514) 789-0694 ext. 278
Auditors - KPMG LLP C.A., Montréal, Qué.
Transfer Agents - Computershare Trust Company of Canada Inc.
Employees - 84 at Mar. 31, 2023
Profile - (Que. 1977) Operates an Internet-based lending platform for small businesses in the U.S. and Canada.

Wholly owned **IOU Central Inc.** (IOU USA), based in Kennesaw, Ga., operates an Internet-based commercial lending business in the U.S., and wholly owned **IOU Financial Canada Inc.** is engaged in commercial lending business in Canada. Typical borrowers include grocery stores, pharmacies, liquor stores, contractors, wholesalers, light manufacturers, online retailers and retail stores. In addition, wholly owned **Zing Funding I, LLC** is engaged in commercial lending brokerage business where borrowers are sourced directly and referred either to a third-party lending platform or to IOU USA.

The company earns revenue from fees it charges to its borrowers, interest payments it receives on loans it has funded, gains on the sale of loans it has sold as well as servicing and other fees it charges institutional purchasers for servicing the loans. A referral fee is earned on loans that are referred to and funded by other third party lenders.

For the three-month period ended Mar. 31, 2023, loan originations totaled US$48,353,015 compared with US$59,564,614 for the three-month period ended Mar. 31, 2022. Loans under management at Mar. 31, 2023, was $198,621,882 compared with $140,621,791 at Mar. 31, 2022.

Recent Merger and Acquisition Activity

Status: pending **Announced:** July 24, 2023
North Mill Equipment Finance LLC (NMEF), an independent commercial equipment lender, has proposed an offer to acquire all of the issued and outstanding common shares of IOU Financial Inc. for $0.28 per share. If the rolling shareholders agree to forego their termination fee of $885,000, NMEF would increase the consideration by $0.0077 per share. Norwalk, Conn.-based NMEF is majority owned by affiliates of InterVest Capital Partners, Inc. (formerly Wafra Capital Partners, Inc.)

Status: pending **Announced:** July 14, 2023
9494-3677 Québec Inc., en entity formed by a group composed of funds managed by Neuberger Berman, Palos Capital and Fintech Ventures, agreed to acquire all of the common shares IOU Financial Inc., they do not already control for $0.22 per share in cash. Neuberger, Palos and FinTech control 48,621,313 IOU common shares, representing a 46.1% ownership interest, which they plan to exchange for shares of the purchaser. The transaction was expected to close in the third quarter of 2023.

Predecessor Detail - Name changed from MCO Capital Inc., Feb. 28, 2011, pursuant to reverse takeover acquisition of IOU Central Inc.; basis 1 new for 4 old shs.

Directors - Evan Price, chr., Saint-Laurent-Ile-d'Orléans, Qué.; Robert Gloer, pres. & CEO, Woodstock, Ga.; Philippe Marleau, Montréal, Qué.; Kathleen Miller, Fla.; Yves Roy, Montréal, Qué.; Lucas Timberlake, Ga.; Neil Wolfson, N.J.

Other Exec. Officers - Daniel (Danny) O'Keefe, CFO; Carl Brabander, exec. v-p, strategy; Dr. Jeffrey D. Turner, exec. v-p, risk mitigation; Madeline Wade, exec. v-p, opers.; Stewart Yeung, exec. v-p, fin.; Thomas Crevier, v-p, data analytics; Kimberley Haffey, v-p, sales; Lori Haygood, v-p, compliance; Rosey Painter, v-p, underwriting; Jason Stevens, v-p, loss mitigation; Rich Zapata, v-p, eng.

Capital Stock

	Authorized (shs.)	Outstanding (shs.)[1]
Common	unlimited	105,535,596

[1] At May 30, 2023

Major Shareholder - Neuberger Berman Group LLC held 14.84% interest and Lucas Timberlake held 12.88% interest at Apr. 24, 2023.

Price Range - IOU/TSX-VEN

Year	Volume	High	Low	Close
2022	5,006,255	$0.23	$0.14	$0.16
2021	7,727,878	$0.24	$0.10	$0.23
2020	3,834,531	$0.23	$0.05	$0.13
2019	8,420,102	$0.27	$0.16	$0.21
2018	11,857,818	$0.25	$0.10	$0.16

Recent Close: $0.22

Capital Stock Changes - During 2022, 345,000 common shares were issued on exercise of options.

Wholly Owned Subsidiaries

IOU Central Inc., Ga.
- 100% int. in **IOU Small Business Asset Fund II, LLC**, Del.
- 100% int. in **IOU Small Business Asset Fund, LLC**
- 100% int. in **ZING Funding I, LLC**, Del.

IOU Financial Canada Inc., Canada.

Financial Statistics

Periods ended:	12m Dec. 31/22^A		12m Dec. 31/21^A
	$000s	%Chg	$000s
Total revenue	**14,197**	**+58**	**8,999**
Salaries & benefits	9,836		6,853
General & admin. expense	7,878		3,432
Stock-based compensation	160		150
Other operating expense	nil		130
Operating expense	**17,874**	**+69**	**10,566**
Operating income	**(3,677)**	**n.a.**	**(1,566)**
Deprec. & amort.	351		459
Finance costs, gross	802		1,579
Pre-tax income	**157**	**-96**	**3,740**
Income taxes	118		18
Net income	**39**	**-99**	**3,722**
Cash & equivalent	4,154		7,359
Accounts receivable	15,542		12,711
Fixed assets, net	183		118
Right-of-use assets	80		214
Intangibles	1,698		764
Total assets	**25,809**	**-3**	**26,564**
Accts. pay. & accr. liabs	3,587		2,655
Long-term debt, gross	4,360		7,620
Long-term debt, net	4,360		7,620
Long-term lease liabilities	550		784
Shareholders' equity	17,312		15,506
Cash from oper. activs	**(176)**	**n.a.**	**1,805**
Cash from fin. activs	(3,721)		(3,607)
Cash from invest. activs	(53)		(775)
Net cash position	**4,154**	**-44**	**7,359**
Capital expenditures	(139)		(79)
	$		$
Earnings per share*	0.00		0.04
Cash flow per share*	(0.00)		0.02
	shs		shs
No. of shs. o/s*	105,335,596		104,990,596
Avg. no. of shs. o/s*	105,165,939		104,747,738
	%		%
Net profit margin	0.27		41.36
Return on equity	0.24		27.04
Return on assets	0.91		20.46
No. of employees (FTEs)	87		63

* Common
^A Reported in accordance with IFRS

Latest Results

Periods ended:	3m Mar. 31/23^A		3m Mar. 31/22^A
	$000s	%Chg	$000s
Total revenue	3,102	-2	3,154
Net income	(1,487)	n.a.	1,117
	$		$
Earnings per share*	(0.01)		0.01

* Common
^A Reported in accordance with IFRS

Historical Summary
(as originally stated)

Fiscal Year	Total Rev.	Net Inc. Bef. Disc.	EPS*
	$000s	$000s	$
2022^A	14,197	39	0.00
2021^A	8,999	3,722	0.04
2020^A	16,445	(2,819)	(0.03)
2019^A	23,322	1,523	0.02
2018^A	18,000	2,710	0.03

* Common
^A Reported in accordance with IFRS

i.15 iA Financial Corporation Inc.*

Symbol - IAG **Exchange** - TSX **CUSIP** - 45075E
Head Office - 1080 Grande Allée O, CP 1907 succ Terminus, Québec, QC, G1K 7M3 **Telephone** - (418) 750-5945 **Fax** - (418) 684-5000
Website - www.ia.ca
Email - marie-annick.bonneau@ia.ca
Investor Relations - Marie-Annick Bonneau (800) 463-6236
Auditors - Deloitte LLP C.A., Québec, Qué.
Transfer Agents - Computershare Trust Company of Canada Inc., Montréal, Qué.
FP500 Revenue Ranking - 75
Employees - 8,900 at Dec. 31, 2022
Profile - (Que. 2018) Provides life and health insurance products, savings and retirement plans, mutual funds, securities, mortgages, automobile and home insurance, and other financial products and services on both an individual and group basis across Canada and the U.S.

Operations are conducted through five business lines: Individual Insurance; Individual Wealth Management; Group Insurance; Group Savings and Retirement; and U.S. Operations.

Individual Insurance

The company offers life insurance (universal, participating, permanent and term), critical illness insurance, short and long-term disability insurance, mortgage insurance, accidental death and dismemberment (AD&D) insurance, creditor insurance and travel insurance.

Individual Wealth Management

The company provides retail savings and retirement products, including registered savings and disbursement plans and life and fixed-term annuities, segregated funds, mutual funds, securities, investment advice and private wealth management services. Operations include wholly owned **IA Clarington Investments Inc.** (fund management), **Investia Financial Services Inc.** (mutual fund brokerage), **iA Private Wealth Inc.** (securities brokerage), **Industrial Alliance Trust Inc.** (trust services) and **Industrial Alliance Investment Management Inc.** (investment management).

Group Insurance

Employee Plans - Products include a range of life and health insurance, AD&D insurance, dental care insurance, short and long-term disability insurance, critical illness and home care insurance. Also offers services and technology tools, including disability management, drug management and health and wellness programs, for plan administrators, plan members and benefits advisors.

Dealer Services - The company distributes creditor insurance products (life, disability, loss of employment and critical illness), car loan financing, and property and casualty products, which include extended warranties, replacement insurance, guaranteed asset protection and a full range of ancillary products.

Special Markets - This division specializes in certain niche group insurance markets that are underserved by traditional group insurance carriers. Products and services include AD&D insurance, critical illness insurance, term life insurance and other specialized insurance products to employers, professional associations and affinity groups, as well as travel medical and health insurance through distribution partners.

Group Savings & Retirement

Products offered consist of accumulation products, which include savings products, such as defined contribution or defined benefit plans, and institutional money management services; and disbursement products, which are insured annuities.

U.S. Operations

Individual Insurance - Products are offered through wholly owned **iA American Life Insurance Company** and four other subsidiaries based in Waco, Tex. Products offered include life insurance (universal, permanent and term), critical illness insurance, short-term disability insurance, accidental death, annuities and group life insurance.

Dealer Services - Through the company's iA American Warranty Group division, distributes casualty products which include extended warranties, guaranteed asset protection, a full range of ancillary vehicle protection products, as well as training and marketing services.

Through wholly owned **Industrial Alliance Auto and Home Insurance Inc.**, the company also markets automobile and home insurance products in Quebec.

At Dec. 31	2022	2021
	$millions	$millions
Assets under management:		
General fund	50,091	55,082
Segregated funds	37,334	39,577
Mutual funds	11,611	13,955
Other	3,670	2,862
	102,706	111,476
Assets under administration	97,717	109,687
	200,423	221,163

Recent Merger and Acquisition Activity

Status: completed **Announced:** June 1, 2023
iA Financial Corporation Inc. acquired Tampa, Fla.-based Continental-National, LLC, an agency specializing in the distribution of vehicle warranties through vehicle dealerships in the U.S., for $28,000,000 and a contingent consideration of up to $8,000,000.

Directors - Jacques Martin, chr., Larchmont, N.Y.; Denis Ricard, pres. & CEO, Pont-Rouge, Qué.; William F. (Bill) Chinery, Toronto, Ont.; Benoit Daignault, Hudson, Qué.; Nicolas Darveau-Garneau, Los Gatos, Calif.; Emma K. Griffin, Henley-on-Thames, Oxon., United Kingdom; Ginette Maillé, Montréal, Qué.; Monique Mercier, Montréal, Qué.; Danielle G. Morin, Longueuil, Qué.; Marc Poulin, Outremont, Qué.; Suzanne Rancourt, Verdun, Qué.; Ouma Sananikone, New York, N.Y.; Rebecca Schechter, Needham, Mass.; Ludwig W. Willisch, Old Greenwich, Conn.

Other Exec. Officers - Alain Bergeron, exec. v-p & chief invest. officer; Denis Berthiaume, exec. v-p, strategy & performance & co-head, acqs.; Stéphan Bourbonnais, exec. v-p, wealth mgt.; Stephanie Butt-Thibodeau, exec. v-p & chief talent & culture officer; Éric Jobin, exec. v-p, CFO & chief actuary; Renée Laflamme, exec. v-p, individual insce., savings & retirement; Pierre Miron, exec. v-p & chief growth officer, Cdn. opers.; Sean O'Brien, exec. v-p, grp. benefits & retirement solutions; Philippe Sarfati, exec. v-p & chief risk officer; Lilia Sham, exec. v-p, corp. strategy & devel.; Michael L. Stickney, exec. v-p, chief growth officer, U.S. opers. & co-head, acqs.; Alain Bergeron, sr. v-p, IT; Gwen M. Gareau, sr. v-p, dealer srvcs.; Manon Gauthier, sr. v-p, admin. individual insce., savings & retirement; Paul R. Grimes, sr. v-p, distrib. independent advisor network individual insce., savings & retirement; Alnoor R. Jiwani, sr. v-p, bus. devel. & fin. dealer srvcs.; Louis-Philippe Pouliot, sr. v-p, grp. benefits & retirement solutions; Pierre Vincent, sr. v-p, distrib. & products devel. individual insce., savings & retirement; Amélie Cantin, corp. sec.; Isabelle Blackburn, pres. & COO, Industrial Alliance Auto and Home Insurance Inc.; Louis H. DeConinck, pres., Investia Financial Services Inc.; Joe W. Dunlap, pres., iA American Life Insurance Company & pres., American-Amicable Life Insurance Company; Adam Elliott, pres. & CEO, IA Clarington Investments Inc. & pres., iA Private Wealth Inc.; Kristen Gruber, pres., iA American Warranty Group & pres., Dealers Assurance Company; Dominique Laberge, pres., Cabinet MRA inc.; Charles Parent, pres., iA Auto Finance Inc.; J. A. (Jim) Virtue, exec. chr. & CEO, PPI Management Inc.

Capital Stock

	Authorized (shs.)	Outstanding (shs.)[1]
Subsidiary Preferreds		
Class A Preferred	unlimited	
Series B		5,000,000
Series G		nil
Series I		nil
Limited Recourse		
Capital Notes	n.a.	
Series 2022-1		250,000
Common	unlimited	102,624,809

[1] At June 30, 2023

Note: Class A preferred shares were issued by wholly owned Industrial Alliance Insurance and Financial Services Inc.

Class A Preferred - Issuable in series and non-voting.

Series B - Entitled to non-cumulative preferential annual dividends in cash of $1.15 per share payable quarterly. Redeemable at $25 per share plus declared and unpaid dividends.

Limited Recourse Capital Notes (LRCN) - Notes with recourse limited to assets held in a consolidated trust. **Series 2022-1** - Bear interest at 6.611% per annum until June 30, 2027, and thereafter at an annual rate reset every five years equal to the five-year Government of Canada yield plus 4% until maturity on June 30, 2082. Trust assets consist of non-cumulative five-year reset class A preferred series A shares.

Common - One vote per share.

Options - At Dec. 31, 2022, options were outstanding to purchase 1,539,000 common shares at a weighted average exercise price of $59.30 per share with a weighted average remaining life of 6.05 years.

Class A Preferred Series G (old) - Were entitled to non-cumulative preferential annual dividends of $0.94425 per share payable quarterly. Redeemed on June 30, 2022, at $25 per share.

Class A Preferred Series I (old) - Were entitled to non-cumulative preferential annual dividends of $1.20 per share payable quarterly. Redeemed on Mar. 31, 2023, at $25 per share.

Normal Course Issuer Bid - The company plans to make normal course purchases of up to 5,265,045 common shares representing 5% of the total outstanding. The bid commenced on Nov. 14, 2022, and expires on Nov. 13, 2023.

Major Shareholder - Widely held at Mar. 14, 2023.

Price Range - IAG/TSX

Year	Volume	High	Low	Close
2022	59,510,193	$85.25	$58.70	$79.27
2021	54,712,227	$76.87	$53.95	$72.38
2020	83,219,239	$76.23	$30.38	$55.18
2019	59,109,660	$71.81	$42.79	$71.33
2018	56,070,643	$62.01	$41.32	$43.57

Recent Close: $83.17

Capital Stock Changes - On Mar. 31, 2023, all 6,000,000 class A preferred series I shares were redeemed at $25 per share.

On June 30, 2022, all 10,000,000 class A preferred series G shares were redeemed at $25 per share. In addition, 250,000 class A preferred series A shares were issued in conjunction with issuance of $250,000,000 of limited recourse capital notes series 2022-1 priced at $1,000 per note. Also during 2022, 324,600 common shares were issued on exercise of options and 3,109,402 common shares were repurchased under a Normal Course Issuer Bid.

Dividends

IAG com Ra $3.06 pa Q est. June 15, 2023**
Prev. Rate: $2.70 est. Sept. 15, 2022
Prev. Rate: $2.50 est. Dec. 15, 2021
Prev. Rate: $1.94 est. Mar. 16, 2020
$0.14◆ Dec. 15/21
Paid in 2023: $2.205 2022: $2.60 2021: $2.08 + $0.14◆

** Reinvestment Option ◆ Special

Long-Term Debt - Outstanding at Dec. 31, 2022:

3.3% subord. debs. due 2028[1]	$400,000,000
2.4% subord. debs. due 2030[2]	399,000,000
3.072% subord. debs. due 2031[3]	399,000,000
3.187% subord. debs. due 2032[4]	298,000,000
Fltg. rate notes due 2034[5]	4,000,000
	1,500,000,000

[1] Bear interest at 3.3%, payable semi-annually until Sept. 15, 2023, and thereafter at the three-month CDOR plus 2.14%, payable quarterly.
[2] Bear interest at 2.4%, payable semi-annually until Feb. 21, 2025, and thereafter at the three-month CDOR plus 0.71%, payable quarterly.
[3] Bear interest at 3.072%, payable semi-annually until Sept. 24, 2026, and thereafter at the three-month CDOR plus 1.31%, payable quarterly.
[4] Bear interest at 3.187%, payable semi-annually until Feb. 25, 2027, and thereafter at the three-month CDOR plus 0.91%, payable quarterly.
[5] Bear interest at the three-month LIBOR plus 4.25%, payable quarterly.

Note - In June 2023, offering of $400,000,000 principal amount of 5.685% fixed/floating unsecured subordinated debentures due June 20, 2033, was completed. The debentures bear interest at 5.685% until June 20, 2028, and thereafter at the daily compounded CORRA (Canadian Overnight Repo Rate Average) plus 1.96%.

Wholly Owned Subsidiaries

Industrial Alliance Insurance and Financial Services Inc., Québec, Qué.

- 100% int. in **American-Amicable Life Insurance Company of Texas**, Waco, Tex.
- 100% int. in **Dealers Alliance Corporation**, Addison, Tex.
- 100% int. in **Dealers Assurance Company**, Addison, Tex.
- 100% int. in **Ecoblock, Inc.**, Albuquerque, N.M.
- 100% int. in **First Automotive Service Corporation**, Albuquerque, N.M.
- 100% int. in **iA American Life Insurance Company**, Waco, Tex.
- 100% int. in **IA Clarington Investments Inc.**, Toronto, Ont.
- 100% int. in **IAS Parent Holdings, Inc.**, Austin, Tex.
- 100% int. in **iA American Warranty Corp.**, Albuquerque, N.M.
- 100% int. in **iA Auto Finance Inc.**, Oakville, Ont.
- 100% int. in **iA Private Wealth Inc.**, Montréal, Qué.
- 100% int. in **iA Private Wealth (USA) Inc.**, Toronto, Ont.
- 100% int. in **Industrial Alliance Auto and Home Insurance Inc.**, Québec, Qué.
- 100% int. in **Industrial Alliance Investment Management Inc.**, Québec, Qué.
- 100% int. in **Industrial Alliance Pacific General Insurance Corporation**, Québec, Qué.
- 100% int. in **Industrial Alliance Trust Inc.**, Québec, Qué.
- 100% int. in **Investia Financial Services Inc.**, Québec, Qué.
- 100% int. in **Lubrico Warranty Inc.**, London, Ont.
- 100% int. in **Michel Rhéaume et associés ltée**, Montréal, Qué.
- 100% int. in **National Warranties MRWV Limited**, Laval, Qué.
- 100% int. in **Occidental Life Insurance Company of North Carolina**, Waco, Tex.
- 100% int. in **PPI Management Inc.**, Toronto, Ont.
- 100% int. in **Pioneer American Insurance Company**, Waco, Tex.
- 100% int. in **Pioneer Security Life Insurance Company**, Waco, Tex.
- 100% int. in **Prysm General Insurance Inc.**, Québec, Qué.
- 100% int. in **SAL Marketing Inc.**, Vancouver, B.C.
- 70% int. in **Surexdirect.com Ltd.**, Magrath, Alta.
- 100% int. in **WGI Manufacturing Inc.**, Scarborough, Ont.
- 100% int. in **WGI Service Plan Division Inc.**, Vancouver, B.C.

Note: The preceding list includes only the major related companies in which interests are held.

Financial Statistics

Periods ended:	12m Dec. 31/22[A]		12m Dec. 31/21[A]
	$000s	%Chg	$000s
Net premiums earned	13,109,000		13,164,000
Net investment income	(6,600,000)		206,000
Total revenue	**8,595,000**	**-44**	**15,486,000**
Policy benefits & claims	6,991,000		6,991,000
Commissions	2,352,000		2,180,000
Salaries & benefits	910,000		861,000
General & admin. expense	907,000		739,000
Stock-based compensation	25,000		24,000
Premium taxes	154,000		141,000
Other operating expense	(4,017,000)		3,156,000
Operating expense	**331,000**	**-95**	**7,101,000**
Operating income	**1,273,000**	**-9**	**1,394,000**
Deprec. & amort.	220,000		199,000
Finance costs, gross	97,000		77,000
Pre-tax income	**956,000**	**-14**	**1,118,000**
Income taxes	156,000		259,000
Net income	**800,000**	**-7**	**859,000**
Net inc. for equity hldrs	**842,000**	**-1**	**852,000**
Net inc. for partic policyhldrs	**(42,000)**	**n.a.**	**7,000**
Cash & equivalent	1,358,000		1,546,000
Accounts receivable	1,162,000		1,183,000
Securities investments	31,320,000		36,799,000
Mortgages	2,831,000		2,922,000
Real estate	1,804,000		1,870,000
Total investments	38,627,000		44,105,000
Segregated fund assets	37,334,000		39,577,000
Total assets	**87,425,000**	**-8**	**94,659,000**
Accts. pay. & accr. liabs	1,569,000		1,669,000
Debt	1,500,000		1,450,000
Long-term lease liabilities	110,000		123,000
Policy liabilities & claims	30,970,000		37,117,000
Segregated fund liabilities	37,334,000		39,577,000
Partic. policyhldrs.' equity	6,000		48,000
Preferred share equity	525,000		525,000
Shareholders' equity	7,134,000		7,197,000
Cash from oper. activs	**613,000**	**+231**	**185,000**
Cash from fin. activs	(525,000)		(294,000)
Cash from invest. activs	(287,000)		(294,000)
Net cash position	**1,358,000**	**-12**	**1,546,000**
Capital expenditures, net	(287,000)		(248,000)
Pension fund surplus	148,000		69,000
	$		$
Earnings per share*	7.68		7.73
Cash flow per share*	5.78		1.73
Cash divd. per share*	2.60		2.08
Extra divd. - cash*	nil		0.14
Total divd. per share*	**2.60**		**2.22**
	shs		shs
No. of shs. o/s*	104,772,775		107,557,577
Avg. no. of shs. o/s*	106,000,000		107,000,000
	%		%
Net profit margin	9.31		5.55
Return on equity	12.30		13.15
Return on assets	0.97		1.01
Foreign sales percent	11		8
No. of employees (FTEs)	8,900		8,300

* Common
[A] Reported in accordance with IFRS

Latest Results

Periods ended:	6m June 30/23[A]		6m June 30/22[oA]
	$000s	%Chg	$000s
Total revenue	5,624,000	n.a.	(5,449,000)
Net income	477,000	+246	138,000
	$		$
Earnings per share*	4.49		1.18

* Common
[o] Restated
[A] Reported in accordance with IFRS

Historical Summary
(as originally stated)

Fiscal Year	Total Rev. $000s	Net Inc. Bef. Disc. $000s	EPS* $
2022[A]	8,595,000	800,000	7.68
2021[A]	15,486,000	859,000	7.73
2020[A]	17,639,000	632,000	5.71
2019[A]	15,265,000	699,000	6.43
2018[A1]	9,912,000	638,000	5.62

* Common
[A] Reported in accordance with IFRS
[1] Results for 2018 and prior years pertain to Industrial Alliance Insurance and Financial Services Inc.

I.16 iAnthus Capital Holdings, Inc.

Symbol - IAN **Exchange** - CSE **CUSIP** - 45074T
Head Office - 420 Lexington Ave, Suite 414, New York, NY, United States, 10170 **Telephone** - (646) 518-9411
Website - www.ianthus.com
Email - investors@ianthuscapital.com
Investor Relations - Jason Miller (646) 518-9418
Auditors - PKF O'Connor Davies, LLP C.P.A., New York, N.Y.
Lawyers - McMillan LLP, Vancouver, B.C.
Transfer Agents - Computershare Trust Company of Canada Inc., Vancouver, B.C.
FP500 Revenue Ranking - 645
Employees - 748 at Mar. 24, 2023

Profile - (B.C. 2013) Owns and operates licensed cannabis cultivation, processing and dispensary facilities throughout the U.S.

At June 30, 2023, the company owned and/or operated 35 dispensaries and 10 cultivation and/or processing facilities in Arizona, Colorado, Florida, Maryland, Massachusetts, Nevada, New Jersey and New York. The company's existing licences, interests and contractual arrangements permit the company to own and/or operate up to an additional 13 dispensary licences and/or dispensary facilities in five U.S. states, plus an uncapped number of dispensary licences in Florida, and up to 20 cultivation, manufacturing and/or processing facilities as well as the right to manufacture and distribute cannabis products in nine U.S. states.

Products developed and sold include the full spectrum of medical and adult-use cannabis, including flower and trim, pre-rolls, topicals, edibles, vape cartridges, concentrates, live resins, wax products, oils and tinctures. Brands owned by the company include GrowHealthy, Mayflower, Black Label and Melting Point Extracts (MPX). The company also manufactures and sells brands under white label and/or licensing agreements.

On Aug. 8, 2023, the company agreed to sell substantially all of the assets of wholly owned **GreenMart of Nevada NLV, LLC** (GMNV) for US$4,000,000. GMNV operates a 29,000-sq.-ft. cultivation and processing facility in North Las Vegas, Nev., and a dispensary in Las Vegas, Nev., as well as holds two conditional dispensary licences in Henderson and Reno, Nev.

On May 8, 2023, the company agreed to sell substantially all of the assets of wholly owned **iA CBD, LLC**, which owns and operates the company's assets associated with its cannabidiol (CBD) products branded as CBD For Life, to **C4L, LLC** for US$200,000. On the same date, C4L assumed operational and managerial control of the CBD business pursuant to a management agreement, which would remain in effect until closing of the sale or the termination of the sale agreement. As a result, the company deconsolidated its CBD operations.

On Feb. 6, 2023, the company agreed to sell its Vermont business conducted through wholly owned **Grassroots Vermont Management Services, LLC** (GVMS), sole owner of **FWR, Inc.** (dba Grassroots Vermont), which owns and operates a vertically integrated dispensary and cultivation/processing facility in Brandon, Vt., to **OG Farms, LLC** for US$200,000. Effective Mar. 8, 2023, pursuant to a management agreement, OG Farms assumed operational control of GVMS and FWR and would receive all related profits through the closing of the sale. As a result, the company deconsolidated its Vermont operations.

In August 2022, the company acquired **GreenMart of Maryland, LLC** and **Budding Rose, Inc.**, operators of dispensaries in Baltimore and Bethesda, Md., and **Rosebud Organics, Inc.**, a cannabis processor with a 4,000-sq.-ft. processing facility in Gaithersburg, Md. Terms were not disclosed.

On June 24, 2022, the company completed its recapitalization transaction, which was originally announced in July 2020, pursuant to a plan of arrangement under the British Columbia Business Corporations Act with holders of its 13% senior secured convertible debentures due May 2021 and holders of its 8% unsecured convertible debentures due March 2023.

Under the transaction, all 13% secured debentures and 8% unsecured debentures, consisting of US$97,500,000 and US$60,000,000 principal amount and US$38,500,000 and US$11,900,000 accrued interest, respectively, as well as the interim financing provided by the holders of the 13% secured debentures in the form of US$14,737,000 principal amount of 8% secured debentures due July 2025 were extinguished. Holders of 13% secured debentures (including interim financing) received 3,036,289,852 common shares of the company; US$99,700,000 principal amount of 8% senior secured debentures due June 2027; and US$5,000,000 principal amount of 8% unsecured debentures due June 2027. Holders of 8% unsecured debentures received 3,036,289,853 common shares of the company; and US$15,000,000 principal amount of 8% unsecured debentures due June 2027. Holders of the 13% secured debentures and 8% unsecured debentures each held 48.625% of the common shares upon completion of the transaction, with existing shareholders of the company retaining 2.75% ownership.

Directors - Michelle (Mich) Mathews-Spradlin, chr., Calif.; Richard (Richie) Proud, CEO; Scott Cohen, Calif.; Kenneth W. Gilbert, Conn.; John Paterson; Alexander Shoghi, Tex.

Other Exec. Officers - Philippe Faraut, CFO; Andrew R. Ryan, gen. counsel; Robert R. Galvin, interim COO

Capital Stock

	Authorized (shs.)	Outstanding (shs.)[1]
Preferred	unlimited	nil
Common	unlimited	6,459,843,879
Class A Common	unlimited	nil

[1] At Aug. 9, 2023

Major Shareholder - Gotham Green Partners, LLC held 39.94% interest, Oasis Investments II Master Fund Ltd. held 19.73% interest and Senvest Management, LLC held 16.5% interest at Mar. 24, 2023.

Price Range - IAN/CSE

Year	Volume	High	Low	Close
2022	10,160,660	$0.26	$0.04	$0.04
2021	84,688,909	$0.65	$0.12	$0.12
2020	130,405,561	$2.32	$0.07	$0.25
2019	144,363,958	$8.20	$1.49	$1.90
2018	81,016,343	$9.49	$2.45	$5.50

Recent Close: $0.02

Capital Stock Changes - On June 24, 2022, 6,072,579,705 common shares valued at US$455,443,000 were issued to secured lenders and all of the holders of unsecured debentures pursuant to a recapitalization transaction. Also during 2022, common shares were issued as follows: 219,596,000 on vesting of restricted share units and 408,000 on exercise of options; 61,013,000 common shares were cancelled.

Wholly Owned Subsidiaries

iAnthus Capital Management, LLC, Del.
- 100% int. in **GHHIA Management, Inc.**, Fla.
  - 100% int. in **McCrory's Sunny Hill Nursery, LLC**, Fla.
- 100% int. in **GTL Holdings, LLC**, N.J.
- 100% int. in **iA IT, LLC**, Ill.
  - 19% int. in **iA GP, LLC**, Ill.
  - 19% int. in **iA GPT, LLC**, Ill.
  - 18.8% int. in **Island Thyme, LLC**, Ill.
- 100% int. in **iAnthus Empire Holdings, LLC**, N.Y.
  - 100% int. in **Citiva Medical, LLC**, N.Y.
- 100% int. in **iAnthus Holdings Florida, LLC**, Fla.
  - 100% int. in **GrowHealthy Properties, LLC**, Fla.
- 100% int. in **iAnthus New Jersey, LLC**, N.J.
  - 100% int. in **MPX New Jersey, LLC**, N.J.
- 100% int. in **iAnthus Northern Nevada, LLC**, Nev.
- 100% int. in **Pakalolo, LLC**, Vt.
- 100% int. in **Pilgrim Rock Management, LLC**, Mass.
  - 100% int. in **Mayflower Medicinals, Inc.**, Mass.
- 100% int. in **Scarlet Globemallow, LLC**, Colo.
  - 100% int. in **Bergamot Properties, LLC**, Colo.

MPX Bioceutical ULC, Toronto, Ont.
- 100% int. in **CGX Life Sciences Inc.**, Nev.
  - 100% int. in **Ambary, LLC**, Ariz.
  - 100% int. in **Cannatech Medicinals, Inc**, Mass.
  - 100% int. in **Fall River Development Company, LLC**, Mass.
  - 100% int. in **GreenMart of Nevada NLV, LLC**, Nev.
  - 100% int. in **IMT, LLC**, Mass.
  - 100% int. in **iAnthus Arizona, LLC**, Ariz.
    - 100% int. in **ABACA, Inc.**, Ariz.
    - 100% int. in **The Healing Center Wellness Center LLC**, Ariz.
    - 100% int. in **Health for Life, Inc.**, Ariz.
    - 100% int. in **Soothing Options, Inc.**, Ariz.
  - 100% int. in **S8 Management LLC**, Ariz.
    - 100% int. in **Budding Rose, Inc.**, Md.
    - 100% int. in **GreenMart of Maryland, LLC**, Md.
    - 100% int. in **LMS Wellness, Benefit, LLC**, Md.
    - 100% int. in **Rosebud Organics, Inc.**, Md.
  - 100% int. in **S8 Rental Services, LLC**, Ariz.
- 100% int. in **MPX Luxembourg S.A.R.L.**, Luxembourg.

Financial Statistics

Periods ended:	12m Dec. 31/22[A]		12m Dec. 31/21[□A]
	US$000s	%Chg	US$000s
Operating revenue	**163,213**	**-20**	**203,018**
Cost of sales	88,781		93,490
Salaries & benefits	34,050		37,232
General & admin expense	61,311		51,101
Stock-based compensation	30,431		6,522
Operating expense	**214,573**	**+14**	**188,345**
Operating income	**(51,360)**	**n.a.**	**14,673**
Deprec., depl. & amort.	31,390		31,039
Finance income	86		517
Finance costs, gross	23,052		34,349
Write-downs/write-offs	(29,705)		(7,414)
Pre-tax income	**(438,700)**	**n.a.**	**(55,754)**
Income taxes	10,691		21,736
Net income	**(449,391)**	**n.a.**	**(77,490)**
Cash & equivalent	14,336		13,244
Inventories	29,800		28,692
Accounts receivable	3,999		3,595
Current assets	50,622		53,646
Long-term investments	232		568
Fixed assets, net	103,320		112,634
Right-of-use assets	28,399		30,429
Intangibles, net	117,047		139,062
Total assets	**303,467**	**-12**	**344,989**
Accts. pay. & accr. liabs	84,726		112,569
Current liabilities	92,566		285,308
Long-term debt, gross	147,312		193,380
Long-term debt, net	147,261		27,999
Long-term lease liabilities	28,836		27,814
Shareholders' equity	10,989		(23,639)
Cash from oper. activs	**(19,496)**	**n.a.**	**16,148**
Cash from fin. activs	22,064		10,238
Cash from invest. activs	(4,740)		(21,318)
Net cash position	**14,406**	**-13**	**16,578**
Capital expenditures	(6,939)		(19,440)
Capital disposals	2,399		275
	US$		US$
Earnings per share*	(0.13)		(0.45)
Cash flow per share*	(0.01)		0.09
	shs		shs
No. of shs. o/s*	6,403,289,000		171,718,192
Avg. no. of shs. o/s*	3,371,545,000		171,718,192
	%		%
Net profit margin	(275.34)		(38.17)
Return on equity	n.m.		n.m.
Return on assets	(130.97)		(8.46)
Foreign sales percent	100		100

* Common
□ Restated
[A] Reported in accordance with U.S. GAAP

Latest Results

Periods ended:	6m June 30/23[A]		6m June 30/22[A]
	US$000s	%Chg	US$000s
Operating revenue	75,468	-13	86,271
Net income	(38,744)	n.a.	(383,664)
	US$		US$
Earnings per share*	(0.01)		(1.03)

* Common
[A] Reported in accordance with U.S. GAAP

Historical Summary
(as originally stated)

Fiscal Year	Oper. Rev. US$000s	Net Inc. Bef. Disc. US$000s	EPS* US$
2022[A]	163,213	(449,391)	(0.13)
2021[A]	203,018	(76,248)	(0.44)
2020[A]	151,669	(309,849)	(1.81)
2019[B]	78,382	(301,254)	(1.90)
2018[B]	3,405	(62,028)	(0.97)

* Common
[A] Reported in accordance with U.S. GAAP
[B] Reported in accordance with IFRS

I.17 Icarus Capital Corp.

Symbol - ICRS.P **Exchange** - TSX-VEN **CUSIP** - 451062
Head Office - 2352 Marine Dr, Vancouver, BC, V7V 1K8 **Telephone** - (778) 866-9041
Email - garry@icaruscapital.ca
Investor Relations - Garry Yuill (778) 866-9041
Auditors - D & H Group LLP C.A., Vancouver, B.C.
Lawyers - Harder & Company
Transfer Agents - Computershare Trust Company of Canada Inc., Vancouver, B.C.
Profile - (B.C. 2021) Capital Pool Company.

Recent Merger and Acquisition Activity

Status: pending **Revised:** June 13, 2023
UPDATE: The closing date was extended to Sept. 15, 2023, from June 15, 2023. PREVIOUS: Icarus Capital Corp. entered into a letter of intent for the Qualifying Transaction reverse takeover acquisition of 1401935 Alberta Ltd. (dba Yuk Yuk's Comedy Club), which operates a Yuk Yuk's franchise comedy club in the Elbow River Casino in Calgary, Alta. In a concurrent transaction, a trademark licence agreement would be entered into between Icarus's newly formed 100% owned subsidiary (Icarus Media Inc.) and Yuk Yuk's Inc. and be granted the exclusive rights to use Yuk Yuk's trademarks worldwide. In addition, Icarus would acquire the right to exploit and host Yuk Yuk's branded shows. Yuk Yuk Inc. was in the business of licensing its trademarks to franchise comedy clubs across Canada. Mar. 23, 2023 - A definitive agreement was entered into. Consideration would be $324,750, consisting of a $200,000 bank loan, $100,000 in vendor financing and the issuance of 225,000 Icarus common shares at a deemed value of 11¢ per share.

Directors - Garry Yuill, pres. & CEO, Richmond, B.C.; Kenneth Wall, CFO & corp. sec., Burnaby, B.C.; Thomas N. Bell, Surrey, B.C.; Howard A. Blank, Vancouver, B.C.; Greg Mulvey, Cambridge, Ont.

Capital Stock

	Authorized (shs.)	Outstanding (shs.)[1]
Common	unlimited	4,000,000

[1] At Nov. 9, 2022

Major Shareholder - Garry Yuill held 35% interest at Mar. 14, 2022.

Price Range - ICRS.P/TSX-VEN

Year	Volume	High	Low	Close
2022	143,300	$0.15	$0.10	$0.11

Capital Stock Changes - On Mar. 14, 2022, an initial public offering of 2,000,000 common shares was completed at 10¢ per share.

I.18 Identillect Technologies Corp.

Symbol - ID **Exchange** - TSX-VEN **CUSIP** - 45168X
Head Office - 1600-609 Granville St, Vancouver, BC, V7Y 1C3 **Telephone** - (778) 331-8505 **Toll-free** - (888) 781-4080
Website - www.identillect.com
Email - todd.sexton@identillect.com
Investor Relations - Todd Sexton (949) 468-7878
Auditors - Charlton & Company C.A., Vancouver, B.C.
Transfer Agents - Computershare Trust Company of Canada Inc., Vancouver, B.C.
Profile - (B.C. 2014; orig. Can., 1985) Develops and markets email security software to protect critical information against cyber security attacks.

The Delivery Trust® email encryption solution is a blockchain-based software that ensures the safety of messages while in transit for organizations of all sizes and individuals such as medical professionals, insurance companies, accountants, lawyers, real estate agents and educators. The software also empowers senders to maintain control of their messages by restricting recipients' printing/forwarding/viewing privileges, audit log, read receipt as well as securing all replies from recipients, without any requirement for them to register. The software integrates multi-factor authentication (MFA) for account login as well as recipient verification. MFA combines two or more independent credentials including what the user knows (password), what the user possesses (token) or what the user is like (biometric verification). The goal of MFA is to create a layered defense and make it more difficult for an unauthorized person to access a target such as a physical location, computing device, network or database. If one factor is compromised or broken, the attacker still has at least one more barrier to breach before successfully breaking into the target. In addition, the software offers a Smart Scan technology that prevents the possibility of sensitive information being sent out inadvertently, prohibiting emails from being delivered which contain certain keywords within the subject, body or an attachment of an email that may be deemed sensitive or at risk of a security breach.

The product is sold to consumers on a monthly subscription basis and is accessible on many platforms such as Outlook, Office 365, and Office 365 for Apple, Outlook.com, Hotmail.com, Gmail.com, Web Mail and Mobile applications, through direct sales and reseller partnerships.

Predecessor Detail - Name changed from Quentin Ventures Ltd., May 19, 2016, following reverse takeover acquisition of (old) Identillect Technologies Corp.

Directors - Jeff Durno, chr., Vancouver, B.C.; Todd Sexton, pres. & CEO, San Diego, Calif.; Grant P. Block, Vancouver, B.C.

Other Exec. Officers - Robert (Rob) Chisholm, CFO & corp. sec.; Dr. Einar Mykletun, chief tech. officer; Mike Rogan, v-p, sales

Capital Stock

	Authorized (shs.)	Outstanding (shs.)[1]
Preferred	unlimited	nil
Common	unlimited	213,882,630

[1] At May 31, 2022

Major Shareholder - Widely held at May 31, 2022.

Price Range - ID/TSX-VEN

Year	Volume	High	Low	Close
2022	25,432,718	$0.03	$0.01	$0.01
2021	275,636,223	$0.07	$0.01	$0.02
2020	101,173,111	$0.03	$0.01	$0.02
2019	23,198,035	$0.09	$0.01	$0.01
2018	69,970,191	$0.35	$0.06	$0.07

Recent Close: $0.01

Capital Stock Changes - In February 2022, private placement of 66,666,666 common shares was completed at Cdn$0.015 per share.

Wholly Owned Subsidiaries

Identillect Technologies, Inc., Nev.

Financial Statistics

Periods ended:	12m Dec. 31/21[A]		12m Dec. 31/20[A]
	US$000s	%Chg	US$000s
Operating revenue	**612**	**+11**	**551**
Cost of sales	24		32
Salaries & benefits	500		633
General & admin expense	228		251
Stock-based compensation	372		1
Other operating expense	108		88
Operating expense	**1,232**	**+23**	**1,005**
Operating income	**(620)**	**n.a.**	**(454)**
Deprec., depl. & amort.	11		60
Finance costs, gross	82		67
Write-downs/write-offs	nil		(5)
Pre-tax income	**(681)**	**n.a.**	**(499)**
Net income	**(681)**	**n.a.**	**(499)**
Cash & equivalent	42		25
Accounts receivable	nil		9
Current assets	123		109
Fixed assets, net	7		2
Total assets	**130**	**+17**	**111**
Bank indebtedness	791		481
Accts. pay. & accr. liabs	699		684
Current liabilities	2,064		1,735
Long-term debt, gross	285		265
Long-term lease liabilities	5		24
Equity portion of conv. debs	9		9
Shareholders' equity	(1,933)		(1,624)
Cash from oper. activs	**(220)**	**n.a.**	**(320)**
Cash from fin. activs	238		340
Cash from invest. activs	(1)		(1)
Net cash position	**42**	**+68**	**25**
	US$		US$
Earnings per share*	(0.00)		(0.00)
Cash flow per share*	(0.00)		(0.00)
	shs		shs
No. of shs. o/s*	147,215,961		147,215,961
Avg. no. of shs. o/s*	147,215,961		138,336,180
	%		%
Net profit margin	(111.27)		(90.56)
Return on equity	n.m.		n.m.
Return on assets	(497.10)		(282.35)

* Common
[A] Reported in accordance with IFRS

Latest Results

Periods ended:	3m Mar. 31/22[A]		3m Mar. 31/21[A]
	US$000s	%Chg	US$000s
Operating revenue	158	+4	152
Net income	(109)	n.a.	(413)
	US$		US$
Earnings per share*	(0.00)		(0.00)

* Common
[A] Reported in accordance with IFRS

Historical Summary
(as originally stated)

Fiscal Year	Oper. Rev.	Net Inc. Bef. Disc.	EPS*
	US$000s	US$000s	US$
2021[A]	612	(681)	(0.00)
2020[A]	551	(499)	(0.00)
2019[A]	539	(766)	(0.01)
2018[A]	1,085	(1,419)	(0.01)
2017[A]	911	(1,979)	(0.03)

* Common
[A] Reported in accordance with IFRS

I.19 iFabric Corp.

Symbol - IFA **Exchange** - TSX **CUSIP** - 45172X
Head Office - Unit 1, 525 Denison St, Markham, ON, L3R 1B8 **Telephone** - (905) 752-0566 **Fax** - (905) 752-0567
Website - www.ifabriccorp.com
Email - hilton.price@rogers.com
Investor Relations - Hilton Price (647) 465-6161
Auditors - BDO Canada LLP C.A., Toronto, Ont.
Lawyers - McLeod Law LLP, Calgary, Alta.
Transfer Agents - Computershare Trust Company of Canada Inc., Calgary, Alta.
Profile - (Alta. 2007) Designs, manufactures and distributes women's intimate apparel and accessories. Also develops and supplies products and treatments suitable for textiles, plastics, liquids and hard surfaces.

Operations are organized into two divisions: Intimate Apparel and Intelligent Fabrics.

Intimate Apparel - Designs and distributes internationally branded intimate apparel and accessories and a range of specialty bras including the company's patented reversible bra, bandeaux bra and breast lift product. Products are marketed under its own trademarked brand the Natural® by Coconut Grove Intimates, Maidenform®, Verzus ALL® and Wick'em® brands, or under private label arrangements with retailers. Manufacturing is outsourced to major mills in the People's Republic of China (PRC). Head office, warehousing and product distribution centre for the Canadian and European markets is located in Markham, Ont., and contract warehouse facilities are located in Houston, Tex. Customer base includes major retailers, online distributors as well as specialty boutiques primarily in the U.K., the U.S. and Canada.

Intelligent Fabrics - Provides textile technologies and treatments including Protx2® and Protx2® AV, which are anti-microbial and anti-viral formulations; Enguard®, an insect repellant technology; Dreamskin®, a skin polymer; UVtx, an ultraviolet light blocker; FreshTx, an odour-absorbing technology; RepelTX, a durable water repellant; Omega+, for joint and muscle recovery; TempTx, a thermal regulator; Apollo, a body odour neutralizer; BioTX, metal free anti-stink solution; RepelTX Eco Plus, fluorine-free durable water repellant; DryTx, a moisture-wicking technology; DriFORCE, a fabric interior moisture-wicker; and imPRINT, a logo exposing moisture-wicker. Also designs and manufactures finished performance apparel which integrate one or more chemical enhancements. This division operates through wholly owned **Intelligent Fabric Technologies (North America) Inc.** and has supply centres in the PRC and Taiwan for the Asian market; a contract warehouse in Houston, Tex., for the U.S. market; warehouse in Markham, Ont., for the Canadian market; and technical support specialists in Asia. While the performance apparel design is handled by a design team in Markham, Ont., the production is outsourced to factories in Asia. Development, testing and improvement of the chemical formulations is mainly handled by a technical team in Asia.

Predecessor Detail - Name changed from Leezamax Capital Corp., Sept. 13, 2011, pursuant to Qualifying Transaction reverse takeover acquisition of Coconut Grove Textiles Inc.

Directors - Dr. Mark A. Cochran, chr., Baltimore, Md.; Hylton Karon, pres. & CEO, Toronto, Ont.; Hilton Price, CFO & corp. sec., Thornhill, Ont.; Giancarlo Beevis, pres. & CEO, Intelligent Fabric Technologies (North America) Inc., East Gwillimbury, Ont.; Cameron L. Groome, Ont.; Rich Macary, N.Y.

Capital Stock

	Authorized (shs.)	Outstanding (shs.)[1]
First Preferred	unlimited	nil
Second Preferred	unlimited	nil
Common	unlimited	30,299,467

[1] At Feb. 23, 2023

Major Shareholder - Hylton Karon held 62.84% interest at Feb. 23, 2023.

Price Range - IFA/TSX

Year	Volume	High	Low	Close
2022	2,713,016	$3.60	$0.54	$0.77
2021	1,809,906	$5.80	$2.30	$2.55
2020	2,630,464	$7.87	$0.82	$3.90
2019	414,423	$1.56	$0.52	$0.92
2018	1,428,605	$3.65	$1.17	$1.45

Recent Close: $1.26

Capital Stock Changes - During fiscal 2022, 200,000 common shares were issued on exercise of options.

Wholly Owned Subsidiaries

Coconut Grove Textiles Inc., Markham, Ont.
- 100% int. in **CG Intimates Inc.**, Del.
- 100% int. in **Coconut Grove Pads Inc.**, Ont.
- 100% int. in **Intelligent Fabric Technologies (North America) Inc.**, Ont.
  - 100% int. in **Intelligent Fabric Technologies Inc.**, N.Y.
- 75% int. in **2074160 Ontario Inc.**, Ont.

Protx (Shanghai) Trading Co., Ltd., Republic of China.

Financial Statistics

Periods ended:	12m Sept. 30/22[A]		12m Sept. 30/21[A]
	$000s	%Chg	$000s
Operating revenue	**19,743**	**0**	**19,764**
Cost of sales	12,717		12,003
General & admin expense	6,441		5,065
Stock-based compensation	473		22
Operating expense	**19,631**	**+15**	**17,090**
Operating income	**112**	**-96**	**2,674**
Deprec., depl. & amort.	104		90
Finance costs, gross	50		53
Pre-tax income	**(207)**	**n.a.**	**3,042**
Income taxes	245		667
Net income	**(452)**	**n.a.**	**2,375**
Net inc. for equity hldrs	**(455)**	**n.a.**	**2,370**
Net inc. for non-cont. int	**3**	**-40**	**5**
Cash & equivalent	945		8,902
Inventories	9,353		3,015
Accounts receivable	7,017		6,453
Current assets	22,694		23,195
Fixed assets, net	3,110		2,942
Right-of-use assets	53		54
Intangibles, net	55		55
Total assets	**27,369**	**-1**	**27,630**
Accts. pay. & accr. liabs	2,520		2,941
Current liabilities	3,989		4,801
Long-term debt, gross	1,139		1,215
Long-term lease liabilities	33		21
Shareholders' equity	22,753		22,267
Non-controlling interest	13		10
Cash from oper. activs	**(8,212)**	**n.a.**	**(2,222)**
Cash from fin. activs	42		10,459
Cash from invest. activs	(243)		(253)
Net cash position	**945**	**-89**	**8,902**
Capital expenditures	(243)		(253)
	$		$
Earnings per share*	(0.02)		0.08
Cash flow per share*	(0.28)		(0.08)
	shs		shs
No. of shs. o/s*	29,824,467		29,624,467
Avg. no. of shs. o/s*	29,689,399		28,136,650
	%		%
Net profit margin	(2.29)		12.02
Return on equity	(2.02)		15.00
Return on assets	(1.25)		10.71
Foreign sales percent	71		71

* Common
[A] Reported in accordance with IFRS

Latest Results

Periods ended:	3m Dec. 31/22[A]		3m Dec. 31/21[A]
	$000s	%Chg	$000s
Operating revenue	4,916	-2	4,994
Net income	132	-24	173
Net inc. for equity hldrs	135	-20	168
Net inc. for non-cont. int	(3)		5
	$		$
Earnings per share*	0.00		0.01

* Common
[A] Reported in accordance with IFRS

Historical Summary
(as originally stated)

Fiscal Year	Oper. Rev.	Net Inc. Bef. Disc.	EPS*
	$000s	$000s	$
2022[A]	19,743	(452)	(0.01)
2021[A]	19,764	2,375	0.08
2020[A]	11,522	(625)	(0.02)
2019[A]	10,435	(1,297)	(0.05)
2018[A]	15,121	927	0.04

* Common
[A] Reported in accordance with IFRS

I.20 Ikigai Capital Corp.

Symbol - IKC.P **Exchange** - TSX-VEN **CUSIP** - 45174R
Head Office - c/o Pacific Paragon Capital Group Ltd., 905-1030 Georgia St W, Vancouver, BC, V6E 2Y3 **Telephone** - (604) 689-2646 **Fax** - (604) 689-1289
Email - office@pacificparagon.com
Investor Relations - Harry Chew (604) 689-2646
Auditors - Saturna Group Chartered Accountants LLP C.A., Vancouver, B.C.
Transfer Agents - National Securities Administrators Ltd., Vancouver, B.C.
Profile - (B.C. 2021) Capital Pool Company.

Recent Merger and Acquisition Activity

Status: pending **Announced:** Sept. 14, 2022

Ikigai Capital Corp. agreed to the Qualifying Transaction reverse takeover acquisition of U.K.-based Eternal Bioworks Corp. on a share-for-share basis, which would result in the issuance of 165,523,575 Ikigai common shares. Eternal Bioworks was developing synthetic biology projects, particularly the use of fungi for several applications including food ingredients, construction materials and space applications. Upon completion, Ikigai would change its name to Eternal Bioworks Inc. and continue its incorporation into Ontario from British Columbia.

Directors - Harry Chew, pres., CEO & CFO, Vancouver, B.C.; Sonny Chew, Vancouver, B.C.; Trent S. Hunter, Calgary, Alta.; Dr. Terrance G. Owen, Abbotsford, B.C.

Other Exec. Officers - Courtney Chew, corp. sec.

Capital Stock

	Authorized (shs.)	Outstanding (shs.)[1]
Common	unlimited	9,100,000

[1] At Nov. 10, 2022

Major Shareholder - Harry Chew held 11% interest at Feb. 14, 2022.

Capital Stock Changes - On Feb. 14, 2022, an initial public offering of 3,000,000 common shares was completed at 10¢ per share.

I.21 illumin Holdings Inc.*

Symbol - ILLM **Exchange** - TSX **CUSIP** - 45232V

Head Office - 1200-70 University Ave, Toronto, ON, M5J 2M4 **Telephone** - (416) 218-9888 **Fax** - (866) 623-6822

Website - illumin.com

Email - bpedram@virtusadvisory.com

Investor Relations - Babak Pedram (416) 644-5081

Auditors - PricewaterhouseCoopers LLP C.A., Toronto, Ont.

Bankers - Silicon Valley Bank; The Toronto-Dominion Bank

Lawyers - Stikeman Elliott LLP, Toronto, Ont.

Transfer Agents - TSX Trust Company, Toronto, Ont.

FP500 Revenue Ranking - 739

Employees - 240 at Dec. 31, 2022

Profile - (Can. 2011) Provides targeted digital media service offerings which enable advertisers to connect with their audiences across online display, video, social and mobile campaigns.

The company's programmatic marketing platform allows advertisers to manage their purchasing of online display advertising in real-time using programmatic ad-buying, a method of buying online display advertising in which ad spots (called impressions) are released in an auction that occurs in milliseconds. The platform is powered by the company's proprietary machine learning technology that uses a voluminous amount of unstructured and semi-structured data to intelligently connect digital advertisers with the right consumers, in the right places, at the right times and for the right price. Key features of platform include audience targeting; tracking results; retargeting; and weather targeting. Offers illumin™, a journey advertising automation platform that offers planning, buying media and omnichannel intelligence from a single platform, allowing advertisers to map their consumer journey playbooks across devices and communication channels in real-time using programmatic technology. Journey advertising is a method of marketing where in advertisers target specific audiences at each phase of the marketing funnel.

The company is headquartered in Toronto, Ont., with regional offices in New York and Spain, and sales offices throughout the U.S., Canada and Latin America.

Predecessor Detail - Name changed from AcuityAds Holdings Inc., June 14, 2023.

Directors - Sheldon M. Pollack, chr., Toronto, Ont.; Tal Hayek, CEO, Toronto, Ont.; Roger Dent, Toronto, Ont.; Paul Khawaja, Ont.; Igal Mayer, Toronto, Ont.; Michele Tobin, Calif.; Yishay Waxman, Toronto, Ont.

Other Exec. Officers - Neil Phasey, COO; Elliot Muchnik, CFO; Nadeem Ahmed, chief revenue officer; Seraj Bharwani, chief strategy officer; Oren Hisherik, chief IT officer; Rachel Kapcan, chief product officer; Kristen Oliver, chief empowerment officer; Joel (Joe) Ontman, chief bus. devel. officer; Dr. Nathan Mekuz, v-p, AI; Tony Vlismas, v-p, mktg.

Capital Stock

	Authorized (shs.)	Outstanding (shs.)[1]
Preferred	unlimited	nil
Common	unlimited	56,185,631

[1] At Aug. 9, 2023

Options - At Dec. 31, 2022, options were outstanding to purchase 727,803 common shares at prices ranging from $0.96 to $2.09 per share with weighted average remaining contractual life ranging from 0.67 to 2.67 years.

Major Shareholder - Widely held at July 25, 2023.

Price Range - ILLM/TSX

Year	Volume	High	Low	Close
2022	69,737,113	$4.92	$1.86	$2.09
2021	156,378,336	$33.08	$3.77	$4.76
2020	124,849,102	$22.44	$0.72	$14.29
2019	39,202,563	$1.94	$1.07	$1.37
2018	15,817,970	$1.69	$0.59	$1.15

Recent Close: $2.51

Capital Stock Changes - During 2022, common shares were issued as follows: 347,527 on exercise of restricted share units, 247,866 on exercise of options and 183,505 on exercise of deferred share units; 4,703,780 common shares were repurchased under a Normal Course Issuer Bid.

Long-Term Debt - Outstanding at Dec. 31, 2022:

Terms loans[1]	$3,790,572
International loans[2]	431,774
	4,222,346
Less: Current portion	4,031,324
	191,022

[1] Consists of borrowings under a US$7,750,000 secured term loan bearing interest to the greater of prime plus 0.6% or 3.85%. Matures on Apr. 1, 2024.

[2] Consists of various government and bank loans and lines of credit of ADman Interactive S.L.

Wholly Owned Subsidiaries

AcuityAds Inc., Toronto, Ont.
- 100% int. in **AcuityAds US Inc.**, N.Y.
  - 100% int. in **140 Proof, Inc.**, San Francisco, Calif.
    - 100% int. in **Visible Measures Corp.**, Canada.
- 100% int. in **ADman Interactive S.L.**, Madrid, Spain.
  - 100% int. in **Adman Media Brasil Ltda.**, Brazil.
  - 100% int. in **Adman Media Columbia, S.A.S.**, Colombia.
  - 100% int. in **Adman Media Mexico S. de R.L. de C.V.**, Mexico.
  - 100% int. in **Adman Media S.A.S.**, Argentina.

Financial Statistics

Periods ended:	12m Dec. 31/22[A]		12m Dec. 31/21[oA]
	$000s	%Chg	$000s
Operating revenue	**121,038**	**-1**	**122,026**
Cost of goods sold	60,251		58,461
Research & devel. expense	16,805		12,680
General & admin expense	38,796		31,112
Stock-based compensation	5,851		4,132
Operating expense	**121,703**	**+14**	**106,385**
Operating income	**(665)**	**n.a.**	**15,641**
Deprec., depl. & amort.	4,853		5,057
Finance costs, gross	544		1,053
Pre-tax income	**209**	**-98**	**12,904**
Income taxes	962		1,151
Net income	**(753)**	**n.a.**	**11,753**
Cash & equivalent	85,941		102,209
Accounts receivable	33,792		30,973
Current assets	123,734		136,460
Fixed assets, net	7,117		5,370
Intangibles, net	10,099		7,914
Total assets	**141,647**	**-5**	**149,826**
Accts. pay. & accr. liabs	26,546		24,853
Current liabilities	33,502		30,768
Long-term debt, gross	4,223		6,799
Long-term debt, net	191		3,853
Long-term lease liabilities	3,768		2,149
Shareholders' equity	103,126		113,056
Cash from oper. activs	**1,782**	**-91**	**19,694**
Cash from fin. activs	(19,355)		58,135
Cash from invest. activs	(3,828)		(1,653)
Net cash position	**85,941**	**-16**	**102,209**
Capital expenditures	(91)		(394)
	$		$
Earnings per share*	(0.01)		0.20
Cash flow per share*	0.03		0.34
	shs		shs
No. of shs. o/s*	56,808,921		60,733,803
Avg. no. of shs. o/s*	59,065,118		57,624,420
	%		%
Net profit margin	(0.62)		9.63
Return on equity	(0.70)		16.20
Return on assets	(1.86)		11.44
Foreign sales percent	86		86
No. of employees (FTEs)	240		189

* Common
[o] Restated
[A] Reported in accordance with IFRS

Latest Results

Periods ended:	6m June 30/23[A]		6m June 30/22[oA]
	$000s	%Chg	$000s
Operating revenue	59,685	+15	52,081
Net income	(9,170)	n.a.	(3,089)
	$		$
Earnings per share*	(0.16)		(0.05)

* Common
[o] Restated
[A] Reported in accordance with IFRS

Historical Summary
(as originally stated)

Fiscal Year	Oper. Rev.	Net Inc. Bef. Disc.	EPS*
	$000s	$000s	$
2022[A]	121,038	(753)	(0.01)
2021[A]	122,026	10,556	0.18
2020[A]	104,894	3,691	0.07
2019[A]	119,134	(5,607)	(0.12)
2018[A]	70,236	(11,278)	(0.29)

* Common
[A] Reported in accordance with IFRS

I.22 Imaflex Inc.

Symbol - IFX **Exchange** - TSX-VEN **CUSIP** - 452435

Head Office - 5710 rue Notre-Dame O, Montréal, QC, H4C 1V2 **Telephone** - (514) 935-5710 **Toll-free** - (877) 935-5710 **Fax** - (514) 935-0264

Website - www.imaflex.com

Email - johnr@imaflex.com

Investor Relations - John Ripplinger (514) 935-5710 ext. 157

Auditors - Raymond Chabot Grant Thornton LLP C.A., Montréal, Qué.

Lawyers - Lavery, de Billy LLP, Montréal, Qué.

Transfer Agents - Computershare Trust Company of Canada Inc.

FP500 Revenue Ranking - 756

Employees - 237 at Dec. 31, 2022

Profile - (Can. 1996) Develops, manufactures and sells polyethylene (plastic) film and bags for the flexible packaging market and various mulch films for the agriculture market.

The company's flexible packaging products are primarily used to protect and preserve and consist primarily of polyethylene (plastic) films and bags, including garbage bags, as well as metalized films. Agriculture products consist of both non-metalized and metalized films, including common mulch, compostable and fumigant barrier films, as well as innovative crop protection films, that add pest/weed control and/or accelerated growth benefits.

Products include Shine N' Ripe (insect repellent fumigation films that are metalized and UV-reflective, with additional insect and disease control for mulched fruit and vegetable production), Shine N' Ripe XL (fights insect infestation and promotes growth through solar reflection), Can-Shine (insect repellent mulches that are metalized and UV-reflective films for conventional and organic fruit and vegetable production for additional insect and disease control), Can-Grow (used for weed control, increased and earlier harvest, higher quality produce and water retention), Can-Block (barrier films for pre-plant soil fumigation), Can-Eco (compostable mulch films for add-on insect repellency, growth acceleration yield boost as well as barrier film for bio fumigants) and ADVASEAL® HSM (crop protection film that releases herbicides for control of broadleaves and sedges).

Manufacturing facilities and a warehouse totaling 270,000 sq. ft. are located in Victoriaville and Montreal, Que., and Thomasville, N.C.

Predecessor Detail - Name changed from Cyclonic Investments Corporation, Feb. 11, 1999, following reverse takeover acquisition of (old) Imaflex Inc.

Directors - Joseph (Joe) Abbandonato, exec. chr., pres. & CEO, Sainte-Adèle, Qué.; Tony Abbandonato, v-p, mfg. & corp. sec., Montréal, Qué.; Michel Baril, Verdun, Qué.; Consolato Gattuso, Qué.; Roberto Longo, Qué.; Philip Nolan, Outremont, Qué.; Lorne Steinberg, Qué.

Other Exec. Officers - Dr. Ralf Dujardin, v-p, mktg. & innovation; Gerald R. (Gerry) Phelps, v-p, opers.; John Ripplinger, v-p, corp. affairs & interim CFO

Capital Stock

	Authorized (shs.)	Outstanding (shs.)[1]
Common	unlimited	51,838,637
Class B	unlimited	nil

[1] At May 12, 2023

Major Shareholder - Joseph (Joe) Abbandonato held 28.15% interest at May 12, 2023.

Price Range - IFX/TSX-VEN

Year	Volume	High	Low	Close
2022	2,052,253	$1.53	$1.01	$1.53
2021	4,417,196	$1.60	$0.98	$1.21
2020	3,726,106	$1.20	$0.36	$1.04
2019	2,968,120	$0.80	$0.47	$0.65
2018	4,059,000	$1.15	$0.70	$0.71

Recent Close: $1.02

Capital Stock Changes - During 2022, 100,000 common shares were issued on exercise of options.

Wholly Owned Subsidiaries

Imaflex USA, Inc., N.C.

Financial Statistics

Periods ended:	12m Dec. 31/22^A		12m Dec. 31/21^A
	$000s	%Chg	$000s
Operating revenue	**111,534**	**+4**	**107,477**
Cost of sales	89,596		86,474
General & admin expense	7,763		6,731
Operating expense	**97,359**	**+4**	**93,205**
Operating income	**14,175**	**-1**	**14,272**
Deprec., depl. & amort.	4,949		4,683
Finance costs, gross	449		411
Pre-tax income	**11,040**	**+13**	**9,798**
Income taxes	1,914		1,433
Net income	**9,125**	**+9**	**8,365**
Cash & equivalent	7,527		8,465
Inventories	12,188		14,920
Accounts receivable	12,079		15,073
Current assets	32,029		38,662
Fixed assets, net	37,757		24,507
Intangibles, net	2,209		1,822
Total assets	**71,995**	**+11**	**64,992**
Bank indebtedness	2,360		2,498
Accts. pay. & accr. liabs	6,607		8,286
Current liabilities	11,761		14,299
Long-term debt, gross	5,669		7,075
Long-term debt, net	2,979		4,230
Shareholders' equity	55,146		45,074
Cash from oper. activs	**17,275**	**+115**	**8,046**
Cash from fin. activs	(3,615)		(304)
Cash from invest. activs	(14,602)		(2,468)
Net cash position	**7,527**	**-11**	**8,465**
Capital expenditures	(14,602)		(2,468)
	$		$
Earnings per share*	0.18		0.17
Cash flow per share*	0.33		0.16
	shs		shs
No. of shs. o/s*	51,738,637		51,638,637
Avg. no. of shs. o/s*	51,700,418		50,659,253
	%		%
Net profit margin	8.18		7.78
Return on equity	18.21		20.64
Return on assets	13.86		14.64
Foreign sales percent	56		65
No. of employees (FTEs)	237		232

* Class A
^A Reported in accordance with IFRS

Historical Summary
(as originally stated)

Fiscal Year	Oper. Rev. $000s	Net Inc. Bef. Disc. $000s	EPS* $
2022^A	111,534	9,125	0.18
2021^A	107,477	8,365	0.17
2020^A	86,682	6,349	0.13
2019^A	81,071	1,536	0.03
2018^A	86,332	3,550	0.07

* Class A
^A Reported in accordance with IFRS

I.23 Imagin Medical Inc.

Symbol - IME **Exchange** - CSE **CUSIP** - 45250L
Head Office - 600-890 Pender St W, Vancouver, BC, V6C 1J9 **Toll-free** - (833) 246-2446 **Fax** - (604) 687-1327
Website - www.imaginmedical.com
Email - jvacha@imaginmedical.com
Investor Relations - John Vacha (833) 246-2446
Auditors - De Visser Gray LLP C.A., Vancouver, B.C.
Lawyers - McMillan LLP, Vancouver, B.C.
Transfer Agents - Computershare Trust Company of Canada Inc., Vancouver, B.C.

Profile - (B.C. 1986) Develops and commercializes medical devices for detection and treatment of urologic cancers such as bladder and prostate cancer through minimally invasive surgery.

Wholly owned **BSS Life Science Inc.** (BSS) holds an exclusive licence from **Lawrence Livermore National Security, LLC** (LLNS) to commercialize the technology invented by Dr. Stavros Demos. The technology is related to exclusive spectroscopic imaging for cancer and other medical applications and is adaptable to all endoscopes that are currently on the market. BSS is planning to commercialize its proprietary i/Blue™ Imaging System, an external device that attaches to an endoscope to emit both blue and white light to be used in combination with imaging agents to cause the cancerous cells to fluoresce within an hour or less, initially in application to bladder cancer. Once the i/Blue™ Imaging System is commercially available for urological indications, the company would focus on expanding the product platform from bladder cancer to laparoscopic (abdominal), colorectal, thoracic and other medical procedures.

Wholly owned **IME Acquisition Sub LLC** develops enCAGE Coil™ Precision Ablation System, a disposable focal therapy precision ablation device for prostate cancer which delivers bipolar radiofrequency energy through a distinctive coil electrode during minimally invasive office-based procedure and allows the surgeon to pre-set precise ablation margins to target only the cancerous tissue.

In August 2022, wholly owned **IME Acquisition LLC** acquired enCAGE Coil™ Precision Ablation System from **TROD Medical NV** for US$2,500,000. enCAGE Coil™ is a disposable focal therapy precision ablation device used in the treatment of prostate cancer.

Predecessor Detail - Name changed from Expedition Mining Inc., Feb. 4, 2016, following reverse takeover acquisition of BSS Life Science Inc.

Directors - Dr. Kevin Slawin, chr., Fla.; Jim Hutchens, pres. & CEO, Wellesley, Mass.; Chris Bleck, Mass.; Kenneth (Ken) Daignault, Mass.; Kayvon Namvar, Wash.

Other Exec. Officers - John Vacha, CFO & corp. sec.

Capital Stock

	Authorized (shs.)	Outstanding (shs.)[1]
Common	unlimited	10,830,116

[1] At Dec. 22, 2022

Major Shareholder - Widely held at Nov. 21, 2022.

Price Range - IME/CSE

Year	Volume	High	Low	Close
2022	1,189,441	$0.56	$0.12	$0.25
2021	5,482,168	$1.44	$0.35	$0.48
2020	6,134,933	$1.90	$0.30	$0.40
2019	3,019,033	$2.70	$0.90	$1.10
2018	13,701,823	$8.80	$1.80	$2.10

Consolidation: 1-for-20 cons. in Oct. 2020
Recent Close: $0.13

Capital Stock Changes - During fiscal 2022, common shares were issued as follows: 793,110 on conversion of debt, 750,000 pursuant to the acquisition of enCage Coil™ Precision Ablation System and 27,377 by private placement.

Wholly Owned Subsidiaries

BSS Life Sciences Inc., Vancouver, B.C.
Expedition Mining USA Inc. Inactive
IME Acquistion Sub LLC, Wilmington, Del.

Financial Statistics

Periods ended:	12m Sept. 30/22^A		12m Sept. 30/21^A
	$000s	%Chg	$000s
General & admin expense	3,406		3,754
Stock-based compensation	96		91
Operating expense	**3,502**	**-9**	**3,844**
Operating income	**(3,502)**	**n.a.**	**(3,844)**
Deprec., depl. & amort.	47		29
Finance costs, gross	n.a.		7,562
Finance costs, net	(1,034)		n.a.
Pre-tax income	**(2,492)**	**n.a.**	**(11,473)**
Net income	**(2,492)**	**n.a.**	**(11,473)**
Cash & equivalent	40		266
Accounts receivable	145		386
Current assets	186		651
Intangibles, net	1,165		123
Total assets	**1,351**	**+74**	**775**
Accts. pay. & accr. liabs	1,230		594
Current liabilities	14,686		12,315
Long-term debt, gross	13,123		11,721
Shareholders' equity	(13,335)		(11,541)
Cash from oper. activs	**(2,627)**	**n.a.**	**(4,094)**
Cash from fin. activs	3,183		4,339
Cash from invest. activs	(781)		(7)
Net cash position	**40**	**-85**	**266**
	$		$
Earnings per share*	(0.25)		(1.27)
Cash flow per share*	(0.26)		(0.45)
	shs		shs
No. of shs. o/s*	10,830,116		9,259,629
Avg. no. of shs. o/s*	9,998,469		9,049,948
	%		%
Net profit margin	n.a.		n.a.
Return on equity	n.m.		n.m.
Return on assets	(234.43)		(786.92)

* Common
^A Reported in accordance with IFRS

Historical Summary
(as originally stated)

Fiscal Year	Oper. Rev. $000s	Net Inc. Bef. Disc. $000s	EPS* $
2022^A	nil	(2,492)	(0.25)
2021^A	nil	(11,473)	(1.27)
2020^A	nil	(4,377)	(0.53)
2019^A	nil	(4,457)	(0.60)
2018^A	nil	(7,958)	(1.40)

* Common
^A Reported in accordance with IFRS

Note: Adjusted throughout for 1-for-20 cons. in Oct. 2020

I.24 ImagineAR Inc.

Symbol - IP **Exchange** - CSE **CUSIP** - 45250P
Head Office - 250-750 Pender St W, Vancouver, BC, V6C 2T7
Telephone - (604) 558-4300
Website - www.imaginear.com
Email - info@imaginear.com
Investor Relations - Alen Paul Silverrstieen (818) 850-2490
Auditors - Baker Tilly WM LLP C.A., Vancouver, B.C.
Lawyers - Boughton Law Corporation, Vancouver, B.C.
Transfer Agents - Computershare Trust Company of Canada Inc., Vancouver, B.C.

Profile - (Can. 2019; orig. B.C., 2011) Provides cloud-based augmented reality (AR) platform products with ImagineAR™ that can integrate into mobile app as a software development kit (SDK) or as a white label mobile app.

Products offered under the Imagine AR™ brand include ImagineAR™, which allows users to visualize the AR content once it is activated through ImagineAR Client Web Dashboard and can also deliver AR rewards, sweepstakes and create AR scavenger hunts; ImagineAR™ SDK/API, which allows companies to integrate the ImagineAR™ platform with their existing mobile application available through an annual licence agreement or revenue sharing with the company; ImagineAR White-Label Mobile App, a full function mobile app for both IOS and Android providing unlimited AR visual and GPS activations, scavenger hunts, reward cards and sweepstakes; and ImagineAR™ Cloud, a centralized content management system where the content is securely stored and managed.

The company also provides professional content services such as gaming content, including scavenger hunts, score boards and sweepstakes; and custom content, including 3D modelling, video animation and brand logo imaging.

Has been granted patents by US Patent and Trademark Office for its systems and methods for creating and delivering augmented reality content, and for capture and use of local elements in gameplay.

Predecessor Detail - Name changed from Imagination Park Technologies Inc., Apr. 16, 2020.

Directors - Alen Paul Silverrstieen, chr., pres. & CEO, Pa.; Tristram R. (Tris) Coffin, Montréal, Qué.; Gurdip (Gary) Panaich, Ont.; Mike Tunnicliffe, N.Y.

Other Exec. Officers - Leon Ho, interim CFO

Capital Stock

	Authorized (shs.)	Outstanding (shs.)[1]
Common	unlimited	203,645,782

[1] At Jan. 27, 2023

Major Shareholder - Widely held at Mar. 25, 2022.

Price Range - IP/CSE

Year	Volume	High	Low	Close
2022	59,448,126	$0.12	$0.03	$0.03
2021	400,873,611	$0.66	$0.09	$0.11
2020	534,588,940	$0.44	$0.02	$0.16
2019	95,298,908	$0.14	$0.02	$0.03
2018	50,513,559	$1.08	$0.07	$0.09

Recent Close: $0.02

Capital Stock Changes - During fiscal 2022, common shares were issued as follows: 200,000 on exercise of warrants and 125,000 for services.

Wholly Owned Subsidiaries

FameDays Inc., United States.
Imagine AR Inc., Del.

Subsidiaries

66.67% int. in **3 Seconds Holdings Inc.**, Canada.

Financial Statistics

Periods ended:	12m Aug. 31/22^A		12m Aug. 31/21^A
	$000s	%Chg	$000s
Operating revenue	**61**	**-83**	**354**
Cost of goods sold	135		81
Salaries & benefits	123		107
General & admin expense	3,709		3,728
Stock-based compensation	229		2,459
Operating expense	**4,196**	**-34**	**6,375**
Operating income	**(4,135)**	**n.a.**	**(6,022)**
Deprec., depl. & amort.	21		22
Finance costs, gross	1		4
Write-downs/write-offs	(40)		nil
Pre-tax income	**(4,067)**	**n.a.**	**(6,105)**
Net income	**(4,067)**	**n.a.**	**(6,105)**
Cash & equivalent	481		4,205
Accounts receivable	27		67
Current assets	619		4,316
Right-of-use assets	9		8
Intangibles, net	15		nil
Total assets	**643**	**-85**	**4,329**
Accts. pay. & accr. liabs	520		402
Current liabilities	562		440
Shareholders' equity	41		3,849
Cash from oper. activs	**(3,707)**	**n.a.**	**(3,364)**
Cash from fin. activs	20		2,921
Cash from invest. activs	(37)		(11)
Net cash position	**481**	**-89**	**4,205**
	$		$
Earnings per share*	(0.02)		(0.03)
Cash flow per share*	(0.02)		(0.02)
	shs		shs
No. of shs. o/s*	203,645,782		203,320,782
Avg. no. of shs. o/s*	203,546,946		195,110,006
	%		%
Net profit margin	n.m.		n.m.
Return on equity	(209.10)		(153.12)
Return on assets	(163.56)		(133.21)

* Common
^A Reported in accordance with IFRS

Latest Results

Periods ended:	3m Nov. 30/22^A		3m Nov. 30/21^A
	$000s	%Chg	$000s
Operating revenue	33	-72	119
Net income	(572)	n.a.	(988)
	$		$
Earnings per share*	(0.00)		(0.00)

* Common
^A Reported in accordance with IFRS

Historical Summary
(as originally stated)

Fiscal Year	Oper. Rev.	Net Inc. Bef. Disc.	EPS*
	$000s	$000s	$
2022^A	61	(4,067)	(0.02)
2021^A	354	(6,105)	(0.03)
2020^A	54	(9,394)	(0.07)
2019^A	135	(2,361)	(0.02)
2018^A	417	(3,104)	(0.05)

* Common
^A Reported in accordance with IFRS

I.25 Imaging Dynamics Company Ltd.

Symbol - IDL **Exchange** - TSX-VEN **CUSIP** - 451920
Head Office - 3510 29 St NE, Calgary, AB, T1Y 7E5 **Telephone** - (403) 251-9939 **Toll-free** - (866) 975-6737 **Fax** - (403) 251-1771
Website - www.imagingdynamics.com/en/
Email - nyan@imagingdynamics.com
Investor Relations - Xiaoyi Yan (866) 975-6737
Auditors - Kenway Mack Slusarchuk Stewart LLP C.A., Calgary, Alta.
Bankers - Connect First Credit Union Ltd., Calgary, Alta.; HSBC Bank Canada, Calgary, Alta.
Lawyers - Gowling WLG (Canada) LLP, Calgary, Alta.
Transfer Agents - Computershare Trust Company of Canada Inc., Calgary, Alta.
Profile - (Alta. 1995) Develops, manufactures and markets digital radiography (DR) technology for the medical imagery market on a worldwide basis.

The company's technology produces diagnostic quality radiographic images digitally, which replaces film-based diagnostic imaging and provides cost-effective solutions for medical facilities of all sizes, in thousands of installations in 42 countries. Products include DR Series (1600Plus X- series and Veterinary DR System), which are imaging detectors that can capture images from various patient positions in different radiography environments; Detector Series (CCD technology, VetnovaXion DR Series, Aquarius 8600), which are flat panel detectors; and proprietary software including Sirius© veterinary image processing software and Magellan© medical image processing software, which both connect directly with the DR systems.

Products are sold throughout North and South America, Europe, Asia, the Middle East and Pacific regions through dealers, distributors and original equipment manufacturer (OEM) partners.

The company is headquartered in Concord, Ont., with offices in Beijing, Guangzhou and Shanghai, People's Republic of China.

Predecessor Detail - Name changed from Imaging Dynamics Corporation, Nov. 2, 2001; basis 1 new for 5 old shs.

Directors - Rong Li; Dr. Paul Lin, Toronto, Ont.; Tim Seung, Toronto, Ont.; Shu Shang; Yan Yong

Other Exec. Officers - Yong Yan, CEO; Xiaoyi (Neil) Yan, CFO; Xin (Andy) Cheng, corp. sec.

Capital Stock

	Authorized (shs.)	Outstanding (shs.)[1]
Preferred	unlimited	nil
Common	unlimited	10,334,550

[1] At Aug. 26, 2022

Major Shareholder - Shuai Wang held 51.52% interest at Aug. 11, 2021.

Price Range - IDL/TSX-VEN

Year	Volume	High	Low	Close
2022	32,505	$1.33	$0.16	$0.17
2021	149,963	$2.40	$0.09	$0.15
2020	113,265	$2.80	$0.20	$1.00
2019	33,756	$1.00	$0.20	$0.20
2018	76,616	$3.00	$0.10	$0.80

Consolidation: 1-for-20 cons. in Nov. 2021
Recent Close: $0.11

Wholly Owned Subsidiaries

IDC Europe Inc.
IDC USA Inc., Del.
1370509 Alberta Inc., Alta.

Financial Statistics

Periods ended:	12m Dec. 31/21^A		12m Dec. 31/20^A
	$000s	%Chg	$000s
Operating revenue	**253**	**-24**	**334**
Cost of sales	131		104
General & admin expense	670		811
Operating expense	**801**	**-12**	**915**
Operating income	**(548)**	**n.a.**	**(581)**
Deprec., depl. & amort.	63		191
Finance income	nil		273
Finance costs, gross	97		53
Write-downs/write-offs	(2)		(118)
Pre-tax income	**(694)**	**n.a.**	**(563)**
Net income	**(694)**	**n.a.**	**(563)**
Cash & equivalent	48		118
Inventories	23		95
Accounts receivable	5		6
Current assets	107		245
Fixed assets, net	305		304
Total assets	**412**	**-25**	**549**
Bank indebtedness	1,523		955
Accts. pay. & accr. liabs	707		642
Current liabilities	2,341		1,730
Long-term debt, gross	26		22
Long-term debt, net	26		22
Long-term lease liabilities	220		277
Shareholders' equity	(2,174)		(1,480)
Cash from oper. activs	**(497)**	**n.a.**	**(521)**
Cash from fin. activs	491		584
Cash from invest. activs	(64)		(2)
Net cash position	**48**	**-59**	**118**
Capital expenditures	(64)		(2)
	$		$
Earnings per share*	(0.07)		(0.05)
Cash flow per share*	(0.05)		(0.05)
	shs		shs
No. of shs. o/s*	10,334,550		10,334,550
Avg. no. of shs. o/s*	10,334,550		10,334,550
	%		%
Net profit margin	(274.31)		(168.56)
Return on equity	n.m.		n.m.
Return on assets	(124.25)		(75.39)

* Common
^A Reported in accordance with IFRS

Latest Results

Periods ended:	6m June 30/22^A		6m June 30/21^A
	$000s	%Chg	$000s
Operating revenue	98	-55	218
Net income	(446)	n.a.	(129)
	$		$
Earnings per share*	(0.04)		(0.01)

* Common
^A Reported in accordance with IFRS

Historical Summary
(as originally stated)

Fiscal Year	Oper. Rev.	Net Inc. Bef. Disc.	EPS*
	$000s	$000s	$
2021^A	253	(694)	(0.07)
2020^A	334	(563)	(0.05)
2019^A	680	(3,898)	(0.60)
2018^A	749	(4,971)	(1.60)
2017^A	875	(4,023)	(1.40)

* Common
^A Reported in accordance with IFRS
Note: Adjusted throughout for 1-for-20 cons. in Nov. 2021

I.26 iMining Technologies Inc.

Symbol - IMIN **Exchange** - TSX-VEN (S) **CUSIP** - 45251C
Head Office - 750-580 Hornby St, Box 113, Vancouver, BC, V6C 3B6 **Telephone** - (604) 602-4935 **Toll-free** - (866) 602-4935 **Fax** - (604) 602-4936
Website - www.imining.com
Email - eeadie@imining.com
Investor Relations - Evan Eadie (866) 602-4935
Auditors - Baker Tilly WM LLP C.A., Vancouver, B.C.
Transfer Agents - TSX Trust Company, Vancouver, B.C.
Profile - (B.C. 2007) Provides technology for Proof-of-Stake (PoS) infrastructure on Ethereum, Cardano and Solano blockchains and invests in crypto and blockchain assets linked to decentralized finance and non-fungible tokens. Also operates a Bitcoin ATM network and is developing a digital asset exchange platform.

Through wholly owned **CanETH Staking Services Inc.**, offers a staking solution for Ethereum 2.0 (ETH 2.0), which provides clients the ability to participate in the ETH 2.0 Proof-of-Stake (PoS) movement. PoS is a consensus mechanism that is used to validate cryptocurrency transactions. Unlike Proof-of-Work (PoW) where miners are required to solve a cryptographic puzzle to validate transactions, PoS requires validators to stake tokens. Validators earn new coins in return for validating a new block and if the block is later found out to be invalid, validators lose some of the coins staked in.

The company has employed Ether 2.0 PoS validators, which directly earn Ethereum (ETH) token rewards and also provides the platform for customers to stake their ETH and Cardano tokens.Has also enabled the exchange and staking of Solano tokens. Customers are charged a staking fee which is paid as a percentage of cryptocurrency rewards earned by the customer.

Also offers a fractional staking pool product which enables more retail investors to partake in ETH 2.0 staking. Participants can join the pool with a minimum of 1 ETH and may earn a return of their investment in the form of staking rewards.

Wholly owned **BitBit Financial Inc.** is a FINTRAC-licensed Bitcoin ATM network operator, and is developing a digital asset exchange trading platform.

On May 4, 2022, wholly owned **Metaverse Advisory Group Inc.** sold two parcels of digital land in the decentraland metaverse, represented by non-fungible tokens (NFTs), to **Sniper Resources Ltd.** for issuance of 26,250,000 common shares at a deemed price of 2¢ per share.

Common suspended from TSX-VEN, Dec. 2, 2022.

Predecessor Detail - Name changed from iMining Blockchain and Cryptocurrency Inc., Aug. 3, 2021.

Directors - Khurram Shroff, chr., pres. & CEO, North York, Ont.; Saleem Moosa, CFO, Brampton, Ont.; Carlton Griffith; Tanya Lutzke, Surrey, B.C.

Capital Stock

	Authorized (shs.)	Outstanding (shs.)[1]
Common	unlimited	33,245,422

[1] At Aug. 12, 2022

Major Shareholder - Widely held at Oct. 5, 2021.

Price Range - IMIN/TSX-VEN (S)

Year	Volume	High	Low	Close
2022	11,464,552	$0.48	$0.06	$0.09
2021	50,011,272	$2.52	$0.32	$0.42
2020	5,108,731	$0.30	$0.06	$0.20
2019	6,417,784	$0.59	$0.09	$0.12
2018	1,983,829	$0.90	$0.08	$0.12

Consolidation: 1-for-3 cons. in Aug. 2022
Recent Close: $0.09

Capital Stock Changes - On Aug. 12, 2022, common shares were consolidated on a 1-for-3 basis. In September 2022, private placement of 11,764,705 units (1 post-consolidated common share & 1 warrant) at $0.085 per unit was completed, with warrants exercisable at 21¢ per share for two years.

On July 12, 2021, 10,000,000 common shares were issued pursuant to the acquisition of BitBit Financial Inc. On Aug. 23, 2021, 2,500,000 common shares were issued pursuant to the acquisition of three Ether 2.0 validators.

Wholly Owned Subsidiaries

BitBit Financial Inc., Brampton, Ont.
CanETH Staking Services Inc., Ont.
Metaverse Advisory Group Inc., Canada.
• **Metaville Labs Inc.**, Vancouver, B.C.

Financial Statistics

Periods ended:	12m May 31/21[A]		12m May 31/20[A]
	$000s	%Chg	$000s
General & admin expense	968		147
Stock-based compensation	2,555		nil
Operating expense	**3,523**	**n.m.**	**147**
Operating income	**(3,523)**	**n.a.**	**(147)**
Deprec., depl. & amort.	31		3
Finance costs, net	1		1
Write-downs/write-offs	nil		(610)
Pre-tax income	**(3,555)**	**n.a.**	**(862)**
Net income	**(3,555)**	**n.a.**	**(862)**
Cash & equivalent	1,485		1
Accounts receivable	52		13
Current assets	1,608		15
Fixed assets, net	406		1
Intangibles, net	14,454		nil
Total assets	**16,468**	**n.m.**	**16**
Accts. pay. & accr. liabs	252		269
Current liabilities	252		269
Shareholders' equity	16,215		(253)
Cash from oper. activs	**(1,094)**	**n.a.**	**(70)**
Cash from fin. activs	2,579		nil
Cash from invest. activs	nil		(98)
Net cash position	**1,485**	**n.m.**	**1**
	$		$
Earnings per share*	(0.15)		(0.09)
Cash flow per share*	(0.07)		(0.01)
	shs		shs
No. of shs. o/s*	28,145,422		9,695,422
Avg. no. of shs. o/s*	15,109,524		9,695,422
	%		%
Net profit margin	n.a.		n.a.
Return on equity	n.m.		n.m.
Return on assets	(43.13)		(209.73)

* Common
[A] Reported in accordance with IFRS

Latest Results

Periods ended:	6m Nov. 30/21[A]		6m Nov. 30/20[A]
	$000s	%Chg	$000s
Operating revenue	693	n.a.	nil
Net income	(254)	n.a.	(89)
	$		$
Earnings per share*	(0.01)		(0.01)

* Common
[A] Reported in accordance with IFRS

Historical Summary
(as originally stated)

Fiscal Year	Oper. Rev. $000s	Net Inc. Bef. Disc. $000s	EPS* $
2021[A]	nil	(3,555)	(0.15)
2020[A]	nil	(862)	(0.09)
2019[A]	304	(3,985)	(0.42)
2018[A]	29	193	0.03
2017[A]	nil	(354)	(0.09)

* Common
[A] Reported in accordance with IFRS
Note: Adjusted throughout for 1-for-3 cons. in Aug. 2022

I.27 ImmunoPrecise Antibodies Ltd.

Symbol - IPA **Exchange** - NASDAQ **CUSIP** - 45257F
Head Office - 3204-4464 Markham St, Victoria, BC, V8Z 7X8 **Telephone** - (250) 483-0308 **Toll-free** - (800) 620-4187 **Fax** - (250) 483-0309
Website - www.ipatherapeutics.com
Email - investors@ipatherapeutics.com
Investor Relations - Brad McConn (250) 483-0308
Auditors - Grant Thornton LLP C.P.A., Minneapolis, Minn.
Transfer Agents - Computershare Trust Company of Canada Inc., Vancouver, B.C.
Employees - 102 at Apr. 30, 2023
Profile - (B.C. 2016; orig. Alta., 1986 amalg.) Discovers, develops, optimizes, engineers and manufactures therapeutic antibodies against a broad range of target classes and diseases.

Antibodies are naturally occurring proteins capable of binding to specific target molecules, or antigens, which are used in research assays, diagnostics, purification, biologics and therapeutics.

Services include proprietary B cell sorting, screening and sequencing; custom immune and naive phage display production and screening; expertise with transgenic animals and multi-species antibody discovery; bi-specific, tri-specific, VHH and VNAR (shark) antibody manufacturing; DNA cloning, protein and antibody downstream processing, purification in gram scale levels, characterization and validation; antibody characterization on label-free biosensors, antibody engineering; transient and stable cell line generation; antibody optimization and humanization; hybridoma production with multiplexed, high-throughput screening and clone-picking; cryopreservation; and custom antigen modeling, design and manufacturing. Wholly owned **ImmunoPrecise Antibodies (Canada) Ltd.** and **ImmunoPrecise Antibodies (Europe) B.V.** have been designated as approved contract research organizations for the world's leading, transgenic animal platform producing human antibodies, and exercised an advantage in optimizing services for various transgenic animal vendors. In addition, through wholly owned **BioStrand B.V.**, offers LENSai™, an integrated intelligence platform which connects the biosphere's fundamental pillars into one framework (sequence, structure and function), and powered by HYFTs™ technology, which are Universal Fingerprint™ patterns found across the entire biosphere that function as encapsulated tokens carrying information such as scientific papers and medical records, to provide context and meaning.

Also has collaboration agreements with **LiteVax B.V.** to analyze the immunogenicity, safety and potency of the company's COVID-19 vaccine candidate, when formulated with LiteVax's adjuvant; **Twist Bioscience Corporation** for high-quality synthetic DNA using silicon platform for creation of novel, therapeutic molecules; and **ChemPartner Biologics Co. Ltd.** for manufacturing and supply of PolyTope® (TATX-03), a rationally designed four monoclonal antibody cocktail developed for use in human clinical trial for the potential prevention and treatment of infection with current and future variants of SARS-CoV-2.

In addition, holds licence to use Octet HTX biosensor for increased speed and sample throughput when characterizing large panels of therapeutic antibody candidates; and OmniAb® platform to access the generation of diverse mono- and bispecific, fully human antibodies, and the only platform comprised of the three species rats, mice, and chickens.

The company operates laboratory facilities in Fargo, N.D., Victoria, B.C., and Utrecht and Oss, the Netherlands.

In March 2023, the company, through wholly owned **Talem Therapeutics LLC**, has entered into a research collaboration and exclusive option licence agreement with **Astellas Pharma Inc.** to discover and develop antibodies against tumour microenvironment targets. Astellas would have the exclusive option to license any development candidates generated as a part of the collaboration.

In March 2023, the company, through wholly owned **Talem Therapeutics LLC**, has entered into a collaboration agreement with **Libera Bio S.L.** to develop novel antibodies targeting intracellular proteins for cancer therapy.

In November 2022, the company, through wholly owned **BioStrand B.V.**, entered into a research collaboration and licence agreement with **BriaCell Therapeutics Corp.** to design, discover and develop anti-cancer antibodies. Upon successful antibody discovery, BioStrand would receive US$500,000 and would be eligible to receive future success-based development milestones.

Common delisted from TSX-VEN, Nov. 28, 2022.

Recent Merger and Acquisition Activity

Status: completed **Announced:** Apr. 13, 2022
ImmunoPrecise Antibodies Ltd. acquired BioStrand B.V., BioKey B.V., and BioClue B.V., a group of Belgian biotech companies and pioneers in the field of bioinformatics and biotechnology, for €3,734,500 cash, issuance of 4,077,774 common shares valued at €21,300,000, and deferred payments of €500,000 payable in 90 days subsequent to closing and €500,000 over a three-year period.

Predecessor Detail - Name changed from Tanqueray Exploration Ltd., Dec. 29, 2016, following acquisition of (old) ImmunoPrecise Antibodies Ltd.

Directors - Dr. James Kuo, chr., La Jolla, Calif.; Dr. Jennifer Bath, pres. & CEO, Minn.; Dr. Robert D. Burke, Victoria, B.C.; Lisa Helbling, N.D.; Greg Smith, Vancouver, B.C.

Other Exec. Officers - Brad McConn, CFO; Dr. Ilse Roodink, chief scientific officer; Dr. Barry Duplantis, v-p, client rel.; Kari Graber, v-p, comml. srvcs.; Dawn Wattie, corp. sec.

Capital Stock

	Authorized (shs.)	Outstanding (shs.)[1]
Common	unlimited	25,050,260

[1] At July 10, 2023

Major Shareholder - Widely held at July 10, 2023.

Price Range - IPA/TSX-VEN (D)

Year	Volume	High	Low	Close
2022	4,398,476	$8.44	$4.52	$6.50
2021	14,321,117	$23.89	$6.39	$6.89
2020	16,856,103	$26.25	$2.55	$19.44
2019	3,462,616	$4.25	$2.23	$2.85
2018	5,623,844	$6.60	$1.65	$3.55

Consolidation: 1-for-5 cons. in Nov. 2020

Capital Stock Changes - During fiscal 2023, common shares were issued as follows: 309,877 on conversion of debentures and 263,537 on exercise of options.

During fiscal 2022, common shares were issued as follows: 4,077,774 pursuant to the acquisition of BioStrand B.V., 925,076 on exercise of warrants, 188,000 on exercise of options, 75,292 on conversion of debentures and 41,488 as deferred payment on acquisition of ImmunoPrecise Antibodies (Europe) B.V. (formerly ModiQuest Research B.V.).

Wholly Owned Subsidiaries

ImmunoPrecise Antibodies (Canada) Ltd.
ImmunoPrecise Antibodies (N.D.) Ltd., United States.
ImmunoPrecise Antibodies (Quebec), Ltd., Qué.
ImmunoPrecise Antibodies (USA) Ltd.
- 100% int. in **ImmunoPrecise Antibodies (MA) LLC**, United States.
- 100% int. in **Talem Therapeutics LLC**, United States.

ImmunoPrecise Netherlands B.V., Netherlands.
- 80% int. in **BioClue B.V.**, Belgium.
- 80% int. in **BioKey B.V.**, Belgium.
- 75.01% int. in **BioStrand B.V.**, Belgium.
- 100% int. in **Idea Family B.V.**, Belgium.
  - 20% int. in **BioClue B.V.**, Belgium.
  - 20% int. in **BioKey B.V.**, Belgium.
  - 24.99% int. in **BioStrand B.V.**, Belgium.
- 100% int. in **ImmunoPrecise Antibodies (Europe) B.V.**, Netherlands.

9438-9244 Quebec, Inc., Qué.

Financial Statistics

Periods ended:	12m Apr. 30/23[A]		12m Apr. 30/22[◻A]
	$000s	%Chg	$000s
Operating revenue	**20,665**	**+7**	**19,364**
Cost of sales	9,102		8,381
Research & devel. expense	12,280		7,663
General & admin expense	14,792		13,216
Stock-based compensation	1,943		3,083
Operating expense	**38,117**	**+30**	**29,260**
Operating income	**(17,452)**	**n.a.**	**(9,896)**
Deprec., depl. & amort.	6,685		3,769
Finance income	270		279
Finance costs, gross	30		85
Write-downs/write-offs	(6,685)		(167)
Pre-tax income	**(27,752)**	**n.a.**	**(15,848)**
Income taxes	(1,192)		861
Net income	**(26,560)**	**n.a.**	**(16,709)**
Cash & equivalent	8,280		29,965
Inventories	2,060		1,615
Accounts receivable	3,247		2,503
Current assets	16,792		37,470
Long-term investments	115		142
Fixed assets, net	10,392		3,559
Intangibles, net	50,096		51,935
Total assets	**77,813**	**-17**	**93,647**
Accts. pay. & accr. liabs	3,386		4,768
Current liabilities	5,920		9,292
Long-term debt, gross	nil		1,312
Long-term lease liabilities	6,151		468
Equity portion of conv. debs	nil		103
Shareholders' equity	57,803		75,285
Cash from oper. activs	**(19,833)**	**n.a.**	**(9,921)**
Cash from fin. activs	(621)		2,883
Cash from invest. activs	(1,967)		(5,208)
Net cash position	**8,366**	**-72**	**30,047**
Capital expenditures	(1,495)		(1,066)
	$		$
Earnings per share*	(1.07)		(0.85)
Cash flow per share*	(0.80)		(0.50)
	shs		shs
No. of shs. o/s*	25,050,260		24,476,846
Avg. no. of shs. o/s*	24,897,185		19,688,487
	%		%
Net profit margin	(128.53)		(86.29)
Return on equity	(39.91)		(25.28)
Return on assets	(30.98)		(20.70)
Foreign sales percent	97		97
No. of employees (FTEs)	102		85

* Cl.A Common
[◻] Restated
[A] Reported in accordance with IFRS

Historical Summary
(as originally stated)

Fiscal Year	Oper. Rev. $000s	Net Inc. Bef. Disc. $000s	EPS* $
2023[A]	20,665	(26,560)	(1.07)
2022[A]	19,364	(16,709)	(0.85)
2021[A]	17,912	(7,340)	(0.45)
2020[A]	14,058	(4,947)	(0.35)
2019[A]	10,926	(7,617)	(0.60)

* Cl.A Common
[A] Reported in accordance with IFRS
Note: Adjusted throughout for 1-for-5 cons. in Nov. 2020

I.28 Immutable Holdings Inc.

Symbol - HOLD **Exchange** - NEO **CUSIP** - 45258G
Head Office - Scotia Plaza, 5800-40 King St W, Toronto, ON, M5H 3S1
Website - www.immutableholdings.com
Email - jordan@immutableholdings.com
Investor Relations - Jordan Fried (234) 248-2646
Auditors - Richter LLP C.A.
Transfer Agents - Odyssey Trust Company, Vancouver, B.C.
Employees - 30 at Mar. 31, 2023
Profile - (B.C. 2017) Operates as a full-service blockchain holding company that builds businesses in the blockchain space.

Has multiple subsidiary digital assets businesses:

Wholly owned **1800Bitcoin.com LLC** plans to offer exposure and educational products to the mass market and to sell bitcoin directly to consumers in the United States over the phone and Internet; 1-800-Bitcoin was expected to launch in late 2021,

Subsidiary **NFT.com LLC** is developing a profile-based network of creators and collectors who can display non-fungible tokens (NFI) that they already own. NFTs represent ownership in unique, one-of-a-kind assets . A secondary market would also be made available for users to buy and sell their NFTs using either cryptocurrency or fiat currency, as the regulatory environment allows. NFT.com was expected to launch in the fourth of 2021.

Wholly owned **Immutable Asset Management LLC** plans to focus on Hedera Hashgraph HBAR as its first assets.

Wholly owned **HBAR Labs, LLC** owns and operates HBAR.com, a community portal which is expected to drive awareness,adoption, and access to the Hedera Hashgraph network and its native platform token HBAR.

Wholly owned **Immutable Advisory LLC** is an advisory and consulting arm focused on the blockchain and cryptocurrency space and was expected to launch in 2022.

Wholly owned **CBDC.com Inc.** plans to offer consulting and advisory services to countries in their research and development of a central bank digital currency.

Predecessor Detail - Name changed from Bexar Ventures Inc., Sept. 24, 2021, pursuant to the reverse takeover acquisition of (old) Immutable Holdings Inc.; basis 1 new for 12.4346 old shs.

Directors - Jordan Fried, chr. & CEO, Dorado, Puerto Rico; Alberto Franco, Golden Beach, Fla.; Jeffrey Long, Alexandria, Va.; Rajiv (Roger) Rai, Toronto, Ont.; Happy Walters, San Juan, Puerto Rico

Other Exec. Officers - David Namdar, pres.; Melyssa Charlton, interim CFO; Don Thibeau, chief product officer; Kyle Armour, v-p, tactical opers.; Jacob Avidar, v-p, eng.; Shane Marzola, v-p, bus. devel. & partnerships

Capital Stock

	Authorized (shs.)	Outstanding (shs.)[1]
Mulltiple Voting	unlimited	69,536
Subordinate Voting	unlimited	28,555,383

[1] At Mar. 31, 2023

Multiple Voting - Convertible into subordinate voting shares on a 1,000-for-1 basis. 1,000 votes per share.

Subordinate Voting - One vote per share.

Major Shareholder - Jordan Fried held 60.05% interest at Dec. 31, 2022.

Price Range - HOLD/NEO

Year	Volume	High	Low	Close
2022	838,900	$3.25	$0.19	$0.24
2021	626,965	$5.30	$0.62	$2.28
2020	2,794	$0.37	$0.19	$0.19
2019	820	$0.44	$0.37	$0.37
2018	13,302	$2.49	$0.25	$1.37

Consolidation: 1-for-12.4346 cons. in Sept. 2021

Recent Close: $0.10

Wholly Owned Subsidiaries

CBDC.com Inc., Puerto Rico.
HBAR Labs LLC, Puerto Rico.
Immutable Advisory LLC, Puerto Rico.
Immutable Asset Management LLC, Puerto Rico.
1800Bitcoin.com LLC, Puerto Rico.

Subsidiaries

51% int. in **NFT.com LLC**, Puerto Rico.

I.29 Impact Acquisitions Corp.

Symbol - IMPC.P **Exchange** - TSX-VEN **CUSIP** - 45258Y

Head Office - 409-221 Esplanade W, North Vancouver, BC, V7M 3J3 **Telephone** - (604) 833-6820

Email - gkabazo@gmail.com

Investor Relations - Gabriel Kabazo (604) 833-6820

Auditors - Dale Matheson Carr-Hilton LaBonte LLP C.A., Vancouver, B.C.

Lawyers - MacDonald Tuskey Corporate & Securities Lawyers, North Vancouver, B.C.

Transfer Agents - Odyssey Trust Company, Vancouver, B.C.

Profile - (B.C. 2019) Capital Pool Company.

Directors - Itamar David, pres., CEO & corp. sec., Vancouver, B.C.; Gilad Bebzuck, Burnaby, B.C.; Meghan Brown, Vancouver, B.C.; Andrew M. Gertler, Westmount, Qué.

Other Exec. Officers - Gabriel (Gabi) Kabazo, CFO

Capital Stock

	Authorized (shs.)	Outstanding (shs.)[1]
Common	unlimited	5,800,000

[1] At Mar. 9, 2022

Major Shareholder - Itamar David held 27.59% interest at Mar. 9, 2022.

Price Range - IMPC.P/TSX-VEN

Year	Volume	High	Low	Close
2022	368,500	$0.14	$0.12	$0.12

Recent Close: $0.12

Capital Stock Changes - On Mar. 9, 2022, an initial public offering of 3,000,000 common shares was completed at 10¢ per share.

I.30 Imperial Equities Inc.

Symbol - IEI **Exchange** - TSX-VEN **CUSIP** - 452737

Head Office - Scotia Place, 2151-10060 Jasper Ave, Edmonton, AB, T5J 3R8 **Telephone** - (780) 424-7227 **Fax** - (780) 425-6379

Website - www.imperialequities.com

Email - sine@imperialequities.com

Investor Relations - Sine Chadi (780) 424-7227

Auditors - Kingston Ross Pasnak LLP C.A., Edmonton, Alta.

Bankers - Royal Bank of Canada, Edmonton, Alta.; Canadian Western Bank, Edmonton, Alta.; HSBC Bank Canada, Edmonton, Alta.; Canadian Imperial Bank of Commerce, Edmonton, Alta.

Lawyers - Bennett Jones LLP, Edmonton, Alta.

Transfer Agents - Computershare Trust Company of Canada Inc., Calgary, Alta.

Profile - (Alta. 1996) Acquires, develops and leases commercial and industrial real estate in Alberta and British Columbia.

At Sept. 30, 2022, the company owned 42 properties, including 10 properties held for future development, totaling 1,084,003 sq. ft. of gross leasable area (GLA).

Alberta

Alberta:	GLA Sq. Ft.
Edmonton	786,227[1]
Red Deer	78,196
Fort McMurray	51,424
Leduc	41,630
Vegreville	33,295
Hanna	28,891
Nisku	37,200
Fort Saskatchewan	6,000
	1,062,863
Fort St. John, B.C.	21,140

[1] Includes space available for lease.

In March 2022, the company acquired two contiguous properties in Edmonton, Alta., for total consideration of $2,250,000. The acquired properties consist of a 0.72-acre parcel of land with a 5,847-sq.-ft. industrial building; and a 0.91-acre vacant parcel of land. Subsequently in August 2022, the company sold the 0.72-acre parcel of land for $1,675,000.

Directors - Sine Chadi, founder, chr., pres., CEO & corp. sec., Edmonton, Alta.; Kevin L. Lynch, corp. counsel, Edmonton, Alta.; Diane Buchanan, Edmonton, Alta.; Susan L. Green, Edmonton, Alta.; David (Dave) Majeski, Edmonton, Alta.

Other Exec. Officers - Meghan DeRoo McConnan, interim CFO

Capital Stock

	Authorized (shs.)	Outstanding (shs.)[1]
Common	unlimited	9,451,242

[1] At Aug. 16, 2023

Major Shareholder - Sine Chadi held 46.35% interest, Jamel H. Chadi Professional Corporation held 20.48% interest and Diane Buchanan held 12.9% interest at Feb. 9, 2023.

Price Range - IEI/TSX-VEN

Year	Volume	High	Low	Close
2022	2,068,518	$5.00	$4.04	$4.70
2021	3,482,762	$5.14	$3.43	$4.88
2020	995,307	$4.85	$3.00	$3.45
2019	719,700	$4.45	$3.49	$4.06
2018	252,400	$4.69	$4.05	$4.05

Recent Close: $4.72

Capital Stock Changes - There were no changes to capital stock during fiscal 2022.

Dividends

IEI com N.S.R.

$0.02	Aug. 3/23	$0.02	May 3/23
$0.02	Jan. 31/23	$0.02	Oct. 31/22

Paid in 2023: $0.06 2022: $0.075 2021: $0.06

Wholly Owned Subsidiaries

Imperial Eight Limited, Alta.
Imperial Equities Properties Ltd., Alta.
Imperial Five Limited, Alta.
Imperial Four Limited, Alta.
Imperial One Limited, Alta.
Imperial Seven Limited, Alta.
Imperial Six Limited, Alta.
Imperial Three Limited, Alta.
Imperial Two Limited, Alta.

Financial Statistics

Periods ended:	12m Sept. 30/22[A]		12m Sept. 30/21[oA]
	$000s	%Chg	$000s
Total revenue	**19,067**	**+5**	**18,110**
Rental operating expense	5,608		4,971
General & admin. expense	1,477		1,582
Operating expense	**7,085**	**+8**	**6,553**
Operating income	**11,982**	**+4**	**11,557**
Deprec. & amort.	150		150
Finance income	15		18
Finance costs, gross	4,392		4,439
Pre-tax income	**9,804**	**+15**	**8,527**
Income taxes	1,950		1,685
Net income	**7,854**	**+15**	**6,842**
Cash & equivalent	233		196
Accounts receivable	435		280
Current assets	1,627		3,881
Income-producing props.	235,674		232,421
Properties under devel.	5,520		121
Properties for future devel.	12,402		12,402
Property interests, net	253,596		244,944
Right-of-use assets	513		663
Total assets	**257,176**	**+3**	**249,488**
Bank indebtedness	18,883		20,360
Accts. pay. & accr. liabs.	3,754		1,701
Current liabilities	45,649		52,930
Long-term debt, gross	108,042		108,510
Long-term debt, net	89,073		82,294
Long-term lease liabilities	409		565
Shareholders' equity	105,871		98,679
Cash from oper. activs.	**11,210**	**+7**	**10,446**
Cash from fin. activs.	(8,158)		(2,376)
Cash from invest. activs.	(3,015)		(7,997)
Net cash position	**233**	**+19**	**196**
Increase in property	(7,899)		(13,648)
Decrease in property	203		nil
	$		$
Earnings per share*	0.83		0.72
Cash flow per share*	1.19		1.11
Cash divd. per share*	0.07		0.05
	shs		shs
No. of shs. o/s*	9,451,242		9,451,242
Avg. no. of shs. o/s*	9,451,242		9,452,628
	%		%
Net profit margin	41.19		37.78
Return on equity	7.68		7.17
Return on assets	4.49		4.28

* Common
[o] Restated
[A] Reported in accordance with IFRS

Historical Summary
(as originally stated)

Fiscal Year	Total Rev.	Net Inc. Bef. Disc.	EPS*
	$000s	$000s	$
2022[A]	19,067	7,854	0.83
2021[A]	18,110	6,842	0.72
2020[A]	16,076	1,416	0.15
2019[A]	16,598	6,420	0.67
2018[A]	15,243	2,343	0.24

* Common
[A] Reported in accordance with IFRS

I.31 Imperial Ginseng Products Ltd.

Symbol - IGP **Exchange** - TSX-VEN **CUSIP** - 452924

Head Office - Four Bentall Centre, 732-1055 Dunsmuir St, PO Box 49256, Vancouver, BC, V7X 1L2 **Telephone** - (604) 689-8863 **Fax** - (604) 428-8470

Website - www.imperialginseng.com

Email - info@imperialginseng.com

Investor Relations - Stephen P. McCoach (604) 689-8863

Auditors - Grant Thornton LLP C.A., Vancouver, B.C.

Bankers - Royal Bank of Canada, Vancouver, B.C.

Lawyers - Borden Ladner Gervais LLP, Vancouver, B.C.

Transfer Agents - Computershare Trust Company of Canada Inc., Vancouver, B.C.

Profile - (B.C. 1989) Cultivates ginseng in Ontario for marketing, through a distributor, primarily in the People's Republic of China and southeast Asia.

During fiscal 2022, 104 acres of ginseng were harvested to produce 374,000 lbs. of ginseng compared with 169 acres to produce 479,000 lbs of ginseng in fiscal 2021. The average selling price per pound decreased to $10 during fiscal 2022 from $11 in fiscal 2021.

The final harvest of the remaining 45 acres of ginseng was expected to be completed in the fall of 2022, After the final harvest, the company would liquidate and wind up its ginseng operations by June 2023.

In October 2022, the company entered into an agreement to sell its property in Milldale, Ont., for $2,600,000. The transaction was expected to be completed in April 2023.

Predecessor Detail - Name changed from Canadian Imperial Ginseng Products Ltd., Dec. 4, 1995.

Directors - Stephen P. McCoach, chr., CEO & corp. sec., Vancouver, B.C.; Maurice Levesque, exec. v-p, Edmonton, Alta.; Cam Hui, Vancouver, B.C.

Other Exec. Officers - Amelia Yeo, CFO; Mike Peever, pres., Canadian Imperial Ginseng Ontario Ltd.

Capital Stock

	Authorized (shs.)	Outstanding (shs.)[1]	Par
Convert. Pfce.	unlimited	nil	n.p.v.
Common	unlimited	7,652,547	n.p.v.

[1] At Oct. 25, 2022

Major Shareholder - Stephen P. McCoach held 31.53% interest and Maurice Levesque held 17.42% interest at Oct. 25, 2022.

Price Range - IGP/TSX-VEN

Year	Volume	High	Low	Close
2022	460,183	$1.22	$0.72	$1.22
2021	1,405,028	$1.49	$0.28	$0.95
2020	652,127	$0.55	$0.23	$0.26
2019	255,641	$1.40	$0.42	$0.46
2018	585,640	$2.00	$1.25	$1.30

Recent Close: $1.60

Capital Stock Changes - There were no changes to capital stock during fiscal 2022.

Wholly Owned Subsidiaries

Canadian Imperial Ginseng Ontario Ltd., Ont.

Knightswood Holdings Ltd., Canada.

Financial Statistics

Periods ended:	12m June 30/22[A]		12m June 30/21[A]
	$000s	%Chg	$000s
Operating revenue	**3,444**	**-52**	**7,196**
Cost of sales	3,549		6,830
Salaries & benefits	1,676		1,081
General & admin expense	125		117
Stock-based compensation	nil		62
Operating expense	**5,350**	**-34**	**8,090**
Operating income	**(1,906)**	**n.a.**	**(894)**
Deprec., depl. & amort.	165		249
Finance income	25		8
Finance costs, gross	44		128
Write-downs/write-offs	(95)		nil
Pre-tax income	**2,983**	**n.a.**	**(5,712)**
Income taxes	665		(1,230)
Net income	**2,318**	**n.a.**	**(4,482)**
Cash & equivalent	10,613		4,219
Inventories	1,203		1,289
Accounts receivable	56		59
Current assets	12,685		7,423
Long-term investments	nil		167
Fixed assets, net	3,336		4,467
Right-of-use assets	14		128
Total assets	**16,339**	**+26**	**12,950**
Accts. pay. & accr. liabs	656		507
Current liabilities	1,404		738
Long-term lease liabilities	nil		15
Shareholders' equity	14,339		12,013
Cash from oper. activs	**5,853**	**+127**	**2,576**
Cash from fin. activs	(44)		(2,297)
Cash from invest. activs	586		1,799
Net cash position	**10,613**	**+152**	**4,219**
Capital expenditures	(13)		(18)
Capital disposals	422		1,326
	$		$
Earnings per share*	0.31		(0.61)
Cash flow per share*	0.79		0.35
	shs		shs
No. of shs. o/s*	7,391,747		7,391,747
Avg. no. of shs. o/s*	7,391,747		7,335,657
	%		%
Net profit margin	67.31		(62.28)
Return on equity	17.59		(31.53)
Return on assets	16.06		(26.03)

* Common

[A] Reported in accordance with IFRS

Historical Summary
(as originally stated)

Fiscal Year	Oper. Rev.	Net Inc. Bef. Disc.	EPS*
	$000s	$000s	$
2022[A]	3,444	2,318	0.31
2021[A]	7,196	(4,482)	(0.61)
2020[A]	5,788	(7,354)	(1.00)
2019[A]	7,813	(4,953)	(0.68)
2018[A]	4,506	4,730	0.66

* Common

[A] Reported in accordance with IFRS

I.32 Imperial Oil Limited*

Symbol - IMO **Exchange** - TSX **CUSIP** - 453038

Head Office - 505 Quarry Park Blvd SE, Calgary, AB, T2C 5N1 **Telephone** - (587) 476-4743 **Fax** - (587) 476-1166

Website - www.imperialoil.ca

Email - investor.relations@esso.ca

Investor Relations - Ian R. Laing (800) 567-3776

Auditors - PricewaterhouseCoopers LLP C.A., Calgary, Alta.

Transfer Agents - TSX Trust Company, Toronto, Ont.

FP500 Revenue Ranking - 6

Employees - 5,300 at Dec. 31, 2022

Profile - (Can. 1880, via Dominion charter) Explores for, produces, transports and markets crude oil and natural gas; manufactures, transports and sells petroleum products; and manufactures and markets petrochemicals across Canada.

Operations are conducted in three main segments: Upstream, Downstream and Chemical.

Upstream

Operations include the exploration for and production of crude oil, natural gas, synthetic crude oil and bitumen.

Owns the Cold Lake in-situ oil sands operations located near Cold Lake and Bonnyville in northeastern Alberta which include five plants (Leming, Maskwa, Mahihkan, Mahkeses and Nabiye). Production at Cold Lake was 144,000 gross (106,000 net) bbl of bitumen per day during 2022. The Cold Lake expansion project is a proposed in-situ solvent-assisted steam-assisted gravity drainage (SA-SAGD) project in the Grand Rapids formation, estimated to produce 50,000 bbl per day.

Holds 70.96% interest (**Exxon Mobil Corporation** 29.04%) in the Kearl oil sands mining project, 70 km north of Fort McMurray, Alta. The company's share of production at Kearl was 172,000 gross (157,000 net) bbl of bitumen per day during 2022.

Holds 25% interest (**Suncor Energy Inc.** 58.74%, **Sinopec Oil Sands Partnership** 9.03%, **CNOOC Oil Sands Canada** 7.23%) in the Syncrude oil sands mining and upgrading joint venture located near Fort McMurray, Alta. The company's share of production at Syncrude was 77,000 gross (63,000 net) bbl of synthetic crude oil per day during 2022.

Additional oils sands interests include Aspen in-situ development project, 45 km northeast of Fort McMurray, Alta.; and other oil sands leases in the Athabasca region of northern Alberta, including Clarke Creek, Corner, Clyden and Chard.

Conventional and unconventional oil and natural gas interests are also held in British Columbia and Alberta, Arctic Islands, Beaufort Sea, Mackenzie Delta, the Northwest Territories and offshore Atlantic.

Downstream

Operations include the transportation and refining of crude oil, blending of refined products, and the distribution and marketing of these products. The company owns and operates three refineries located in Strathcona, Alta., and Sarnia and Nanticoke, Ont., which produce primarily gasoline, heating oil, diesel, jet fuel, fuel oil and asphalt. Petroleum products are transported and distributed through a network of terminals, pipelines, tankers, rail and road transport. The company owns and operates fuel terminals across Canada and natural gas liquids and products pipelines in Alberta, Manitoba and Ontario; and holds interests in two products pipeline companies as well as the Edmonton Rail Terminal, located next to the Strathcona refinery, which has capacity to ship up to 210,000 bbl per day.

Petroleum products are marketed throughout Canada under the Mobil and Esso brands to retail, industrial and wholesale customers. Fuel is supplied to Mobil and Esso-branded retail service stations owned and operated by independent third parties. At Dec. 31, 2022, there were about 2,400 branded retail sites served by the company. In addition, the company's industrial and wholesale businesses provide petroleum products to large industrial and transportation customers, independent marketers, resellers and other refiners, as well as the agriculture, residential heating and commercial markets.

Chemical

Operations consist of the manufacturing and marketing of benzene, aromatic and aliphatic solvents, plasticizer intermediates and polyethylene resin as well as marketing of refinery grade propylene, with petrochemical and polyethylene manufacturing operations located in Sarnia, Ont., adjacent to the company's refinery.

Sales Volumes of Net Petroleum Products

Year ended Dec. 31	2022	2021
Gasolines[1]	229,000	224,000
Heating, diesel & jet fuels[1]	176,000	160,000
Heavy fuel oils[1]	23,000	27,000
Lube oils & other[1]	47,000	45,000
	475,000	456,000

[1] Bbl per day.

Sales Volumes of Petrochemicals

Year ended Dec. 31	2022	2021
Polymers & basic chemicals[1]	635,000	599,000
Intermediates[1]	207,000	232,000
	842,000	831,000

[1] Tonnes.

Refinery Utilization

Year ended Dec. 31	2022	2021
Refinery throughput[1]	418,000	379,000
Refinery capacity[1]	433,000	428,000
Utilization rate	98%	89%

[1] Bbl per day.

At Dec. 31, 2022, the company had 4,277 gross (4,264 net) producing oil wells, 2,419 gross (774 net) producing gas wells, 420 non-producing oil wells and 6 gross (2 net) non-producing gas wells. During 2022, 31 development wells were drilled, representing 24 oil wells, 3 stratigraphic wells and 4 service wells. Developed and undeveloped land holdings totaled 3,641,000 gross (1,412,000 net) acres at Dec. 31, 2022.

In January 2023, the company approved a $720,000,000 investment to construct a renewable diesel complex at its Strathcona refinery near Edmonton, Alta., which was expected to produce more than 1 billion litres per year of renewable diesel primarily from locally sourced feedstock. A significant portion of the renewable diesel would be supplied to the Province of British Columbia. Production was expected to start in 2025, subject to regulatory approvals.

Periods ended:	12m Dec. 31/22	12m Dec. 31/21
Avg. oil prod., bbl/d	334,000	363,000
Avg. NGL prod., bbl/d	1,000	1,000
Avg. gas prod., mcf/d	83,000	115,000
Avg. BOE prod., bbl/d	349,000	383,000
Avg. oil price, $/bbl	97.45	59.84
Avg. NGL price, $/bbl	64.92	35.87
Avg. gas price, $/mcf	5.69	3.83
Oil reserves, net, mbbl[1]	3,295,000	3,761,000
Gas reserves, net, mmcf	22,000	250,000
BOE reserves, net, mbbl	3,299,000	3,803,000

[1] Include NGL reserves.

Recent Merger and Acquisition Activity

Status: completed **Revised:** Aug. 31, 2022

UPDATE: The transaction was completed. PREVIOUS: Imperial Oil Limited and ExxonMobil Canada Ltd. agreed to sell jointly owned XTO Energy Canada ULC to Whitecap Resources Inc. for total cash consideration of $1.9 billion, of which Imperial's share was $940,000,000. Assets include 567,000 net acres in the Montney shale, 72,000 net acres in the Duvernay shale and additional acreage in other areas of Alberta, with net production of about 140,000 mcf of natural gas per day and about 9,000 bbl of crude, condensate and natural gas liquids per day. ExxonMobil Canada was owned by Exxon Mobil Corporation. The transaction was expected to close before the end of the third quarter 2022.

Directors - Bradley W. (Brad) Corson, chr., pres. & CEO, Calgary, Alta.; David W. Cornhill, Calgary, Alta.; Matthew R. Crocker, Spring, Tex.; Sharon R. Driscoll, Vancouver, B.C.; John N. Floren, Oakville, Ont.; Gary J. Goldberg, Castle Pines, Colo.; Miranda C. Hubbs, Toronto, Ont.

Other Exec. Officers - Sherri L. Evers, sr. v-p, comml. devel. & product solutions; Daniel E. (Dan) Lyons, sr. v-p, fin. & admin. & contr.; Simon P. Younger, sr. v-p, upstream; Kristi L. Desjardins, v-p, HR; Ian R. Laing, v-p, gen. counsel & corp. sec.; Kitty Lee, treas.; Bruce A. Jolly, asst. contr.

Capital Stock

	Authorized (shs.)	Outstanding (shs.)[1]
Common	1,100,000,000	584,152,718

[1] At June 15, 2023

Normal Course Issuer Bid - The company plans to make normal course purchases of up to 29,207,635 common shares representing 5% of the total outstanding. The bid commenced on June 29, 2023, and expires on June 28, 2024.

Major Shareholder - Exxon Mobil Corporation held 69.6% interest at Feb. 8, 2023.

Price Range - IMO/TSX

Year	Volume	High	Low	Close
2022	369,547,531	$79.83	$46.30	$65.95
2021	361,102,473	$45.94	$24.01	$45.62
2020	396,119,506	$35.80	$10.27	$24.16
2019	218,841,715	$40.59	$31.51	$34.35
2018	269,661,063	$44.91	$33.43	$34.59

Recent Close: $75.03

Capital Stock Changes - In June 2022, 32,467,532 common shares were repurchased under a Substantial Issuer Bid. In December 2022, 20,689,655 common shares were repurchased under a Substantial Issuer Bid. Also during 2022, 40,769,959 common shares were repurchased under a Normal Course Issuer Bid.

Dividends

IMO com Ra $2.00 pa Q est. July 1, 2023**
Prev. Rate: $1.76 est. Jan. 1, 2023
Prev. Rate: $1.36 est. Apr. 1, 2022
Prev. Rate: $1.08 est. July 1, 2021
Prev. Rate: $0.88 est. July 1, 2019
** Reinvestment Option

Long-Term Debt - At Dec. 31, 2022, outstanding long-term debt totaled $4.055 billion ($22,000,000 current) and consisted of $3.447 billion in borrowings under a $7.75 billion variable rate loan due June 30, 2025, and $608,000,000 of finance lease obligations.

Wholly Owned Subsidiaries

Canada Imperial Oil Limited, Calgary, Alta.

Imperial Oil Resources Limited, Calgary, Alta.

Investments

25% int. in **Syncrude Canada Ltd.**, Fort McMurray, Alta.

Note: The preceding list includes only the major related companies in which interests are held.

Financial Statistics

Periods ended:	12m Dec. 31/22^A		12m Dec. 31/21^A
	$000s	%Chg	$000s
Operating revenue	**59,413,000**	**+58**	**37,508,000**
Cost of goods sold	7,404,000		6,316,000
Exploration expense	5,000		32,000
General & admin expense	882,000		784,000
Other operating expense	39,938,000		25,144,000
Operating expense	**48,229,000**	**+49**	**32,276,000**
Operating income	**11,184,000**	**+114**	**5,232,000**
Deprec., depl. & amort.	1,897,000		1,977,000
Finance costs, gross	60,000		54,000
Investment income	99,000		33,000
Pre-tax income	**9,484,000**	**+189**	**3,283,000**
Income taxes	2,144,000		804,000
Net income	**7,340,000**	**+196**	**2,479,000**
Cash & equivalent	3,749,000		2,153,000
Inventories	2,268,000		1,791,000
Accounts receivable	4,719,000		3,869,000
Current assets	10,736,000		7,813,000
Long-term investments	893,000		757,000
Fixed assets, net	30,506,000		31,240,000
Right-of-use assets	245,000		245,000
Intangibles, net	166,000		166,000
Total assets	**43,524,000**	**+7**	**40,782,000**
Bank indebtedness	100,000		100,000
Accts. pay. & accr. liabs	6,094,000		5,082,000
Current liabilities	8,898,000		5,554,000
Long-term debt, gross	4,055,000		5,076,000
Long-term debt, net	4,033,000		5,054,000
Long-term lease liabilities	151,000		147,000
Shareholders' equity	22,413,000		21,735,000
Cash from oper. activs	**10,482,000**	**+91**	**5,476,000**
Cash from fin. activs	(8,268,000)		(3,082,000)
Cash from invest. activs	(618,000)		(1,012,000)
Net cash position	**3,749,000**	**+74**	**2,153,000**
Capital expenditures	(1,526,000)		(1,108,000)
Capital disposals	904,000		81,000
Unfunded pension liability	n.a.		410,000
Pension fund surplus	167,000		n.a.
	$		$
Earnings per share*	11.47		3.48
Cash flow per share*	16.37		7.70
Cash divd. per share*	1.46		1.03
	shs		shs
No. of shs. o/s*	584,152,718		678,079,864
Avg. no. of shs. o/s*	640,200,000		711,600,000
	%		%
Net profit margin	12.35		6.61
Return on equity	33.25		11.49
Return on assets	17.52		6.39
Foreign sales percent	21		19
No. of employees (FTEs)	5,300		5,400

* Common

^A Reported in accordance with U.S. GAAP

Latest Results

Periods ended:	6m June 30/23^A		6m June 30/22^A
	$000s	%Chg	$000s
Operating revenue	23,821,000	-20	29,942,000
Net income	1,923,000	-46	3,582,000
	$		$
Earnings per share*	3.29		5.37

* Common

^A Reported in accordance with U.S. GAAP

Historical Summary
(as originally stated)

Fiscal Year	Oper. Rev.	Net Inc. Bef. Disc.	EPS*
	$000s	$000s	$
2022^A	59,413,000	7,340,000	11.47
2021^A	37,508,000	2,479,000	3.48
2020^A	22,284,000	(1,857,000)	(2.53)
2019^A	34,002,000	2,200,000	2.88
2018^A	34,964,000	2,314,000	2.87

* Common

^A Reported in accordance with U.S. GAAP

I.33 Inceptus Capital Ltd.

Symbol - ICI.P **Exchange** - TSX-VEN (S) **CUSIP** - 45332T

Head Office - 220-3580 Moncton St, Richmond, BC, V7E 3A4 **Telephone** - (604) 370-3796 **Fax** - (866) 591-6416

Email - peterchen@proterragroup.ca

Investor Relations - Yung Tan Chen (604) 370-3796

Auditors - Davidson & Company LLP C.A., Vancouver, B.C.

Transfer Agents - Computershare Trust Company of Canada Inc., Vancouver, B.C.

Profile - (B.C. 2017) Capital Pool Company.

Common suspended from TSX-VEN, Nov. 15, 2019.

Directors - Yung Tan (Peter) Chen, pres. & CEO, Richmond, B.C.; Yu Chung (Tony) Chan, Richmond, B.C.; Kuei Hai (Jason) Lan, Richmond, B.C.; Christopher T. Twells, Richmond, B.C.

Other Exec. Officers - Wing Kin (Eric) Lam, CFO & corp. sec.

Capital Stock

	Authorized (shs.)	Outstanding (shs.)[1]
Class A Common	unlimited	4,747,500
Class B Common	unlimited	nil
Class C Common	unlimited	nil
Class D Common	unlimited	nil

[1] At Nov. 29, 2022

Major Shareholder - Yung Tan (Peter) Chen held 17.7% interest and Kuei Hai (Jason) Lan held 17.7% interest at July 15, 2022.

Price Range - ICI.P/TSX-VEN (S)

Year	Volume	High	Low	Close
2018	680,600	$0.33	$0.15	$0.21

Capital Stock Changes - There were no changes to capital stock from fiscal 2019 to fiscal 2022, inclusive.

Wholly Owned Subsidiaries

1262595 B.C. Ltd., B.C. Inactive.

I.34 Income Financial Trust

Symbol - INC.UN **Exchange** - TSX **CUSIP** - 453299

Head Office - c/o Quadravest Capital Management Inc., 2510-200 Front St W, PO Box 51, Toronto, ON, M5V 3K2 **Telephone** - (416) 304-4440 **Toll-free** - (877) 478-2372

Website - www.quadravest.com

Email - info@quadravest.com

Investor Relations - Shari Payne (877) 478-2372

Auditors - PricewaterhouseCoopers LLP C.A., Toronto, Ont.

Lawyers - Blake, Cassels & Graydon LLP, Toronto, Ont.

Transfer Agents - Computershare Trust Company of Canada Inc., Toronto, Ont.

Trustees - RBC Investor Services Trust, Toronto, Ont.

Investment Managers - Quadravest Capital Management Inc., Toronto, Ont.

Managers - Quadravest Capital Management Inc., Toronto, Ont.

Profile - (Ont. 1999) Invests in North American financial services companies whose shares are included in the S&P TSX Capped Financials Index, the S&P Financials Index or the S&P MidCap Financials Index.

To generate additional returns above the dividend and interest income earned on the portfolio and to reduce risk, the trust may, from time to time, write covered call options in respect of all or part of the securities in the portfolio.

The trust will terminate on Jan. 1, 2024, or earlier at the discretion of the manager if the trust units are delisted by the TSX or if the net asset value of the trust declines to less than $5,000,000, and at such time all outstanding trust units will be redeemed. The termination date may be extended beyond Jan. 1, 2024, for a further five years and thereafter for additional successive periods of five years as determined by the manager.

The investment manager receives a management fee at an annual rate equal to 0.65% of the net asset value of the trust calculated and payable monthly in arrears. In addition, the manager receives an administration fee at an annual rate equal to 0.1% of the net asset value of the trust calculated and payable monthly in arrears, as well a service fee payable to dealers at a rate of 0.25% per annum.

Top 10 holdings at Mar. 31, 2023 (as a percentage of net assets):

Holdings	Percentage
Goldman Sachs Group Inc.	8.3%
Royal Bank of Canada	5.2%
Sun Life Financial Inc.	4.8%
Guardian Capital Group Ltd.	4.2%
TMX Group Inc.	4.1%
National Bank of Canada	3.7%
The Toronto-Dominion Bank	3.5%
American Express Company	3.4%
Morgan Stanley	3.4%
Bank of America Corporation	3.0%

Oper. Subsid./Mgt. Co. Directors - S. Wayne Finch, chr., pres. & CEO, Caledon, Ont.; Laura L. Johnson, corp. sec., Oakville, Ont.; Peter F. Cruickshank, Oakville, Ont.; Michael W. Sharp, Toronto, Ont.; John D. Steep, Stratford, Ont.

Other Exec. Officers - Silvia Gomes, CFO

Capital Stock

	Authorized (shs.)	Outstanding (shs.)[1]
Trust Unit	unlimited	3,309,270

[1] At Mar. 24, 2023

Trust Unit - Entitled to monthly cash distributions targeted to be 10% per annum based on the weighted average trading price over the last three trading days of the preceding month. Retractable on the last day of February of each year at a price equal to the net asset value per unit less any retraction costs, or on the last day of any other month at a price equal to the net asset value per unit less a 2% discount and less any retraction costs. All outstanding trust units will be redeemed on Jan. 1, 2024, at the net asset value per trust unit. One vote per trust unit.

Price Range - INC.UN/TSX

Year	Volume	High	Low	Close
2022	1,227,155	$15.88	$10.94	$11.60
2021	1,081,429	$19.30	$7.75	$15.07
2020	1,260,257	$9.34	$3.50	$7.76
2019	594,534	$12.50	$8.96	$9.08
2018	1,116,480	$19.19	$9.10	$9.99

Recent Close: $8.60

Capital Stock Changes - During 2022, 720,100 trust units were issued under an at-the-market equity program.

Dividends

INC.UN tr unit red. Var. Ra pa M

$0.08133	Sept. 8/23	$0.08425	Aug. 10/23
$0.08433	July 10/23	$0.093	June 9/23

Paid in 2023: $0.8255 2022: $1.34234 2021: $1.27868

Financial Statistics

Periods ended:	12m Dec. 31/22^A		12m Dec. 31/21^A
	$000s	%Chg	$000s
Realized invest. gain (loss)	363		431
Unrealized invest. gain (loss)	(2,148)		566
Total revenue	**(1,028)**	**n.a.**	**4,449**
General & admin. expense	297		281
Other operating expense	153		123
Operating expense	**450**	**+11**	**404**
Operating income	**(1,478)**	**n.a.**	**4,045**
Pre-tax income	**(1,479)**	**n.a.**	**4,045**
Net income	**(1,479)**	**n.a.**	**4,045**
Cash & equivalent	3,310		1,939
Accounts receivable	57		51
Investments	21,360		18,744
Total assets	**24,727**	**+19**	**20,734**
Accts. pay. & accr. liabs	48		62
Shareholders' equity	24,357		20,348
Cash from oper. activs	**(4,158)**	**n.a.**	**194**
Cash from fin. activs	5,479		839
Net cash position	**3,310**	**+71**	**1,939**
	$		$
Earnings per share*	(0.50)		1.75
Cash flow per share*	(1.39)		0.08
Net asset value per share*	7.53		8.09
Cash divd. per share*	1.31		1.34
	shs		shs
No. of shs. o/s*	3,235,070		2,514,970
Avg. no. of shs. o/s*	2,985,537		2,308,878
	%		%
Net profit margin	n.m.		90.92
Return on equity	(6.62)		22.48
Return on assets	(6.51)		22.10

* Trust unit

^A Reported in accordance with IFRS

Note: Net income reflects increase/decrease in net assets resulting from operations.

Historical Summary
(as originally stated)

Fiscal Year	Total Rev.	Net Inc. Bef. Disc.	EPS*
	$000s	$000s	$
2022^A	(1,028)	(1,479)	(0.50)
2021^A	4,449	4,045	1.75
2020^A	(1,051)	(1,416)	(0.62)
2019^A	4,094	3,696	1.59
2018^A	(3,285)	(3,742)	(1.61)

* Trust unit

^A Reported in accordance with IFRS

I.35 Indigenous Bloom Hemp Corp.

Symbol - IBH **Exchange** - CSE **CUSIP** - 45569M

Head Office - 2220 Horizon Dr, Kelowna, BC, V1Z 3L4 **Telephone** - (250) 763-4660

Website - indigenousbloom.com

Email - info@indigenousbloom.com

Investor Relations - Lorne Mark Roseborough (250) 763-4660

Auditors - BF Borgers CPA PC C.P.A., Lakewood, Colo.

Transfer Agents - Computershare Trust Company of Canada Inc., Vancouver, B.C.

Profile - (B.C. 2014) Operates a large-scale industrial hemp farm in southern Manitoba on 200 acres of zoned farmland.

Sells pre-processed hemp biomass to customers and partners who process the biomass into hemp extracts. In addition, plans to develop or acquire the rights to additional hemp products such as health supplements, nutritional products, food stuffs and beauty products for general consumer end-use.

During 2022, the company produced 1,400 kg of kief.

Predecessor Detail - Name changed from Veritas Pharma Inc., Sept. 24, 2021, pursuant to the reverse takeover acquisition of (old) Indigenous Bloom Hemp Corporation and concurrent amalgamation of (old) Indigenous Bloom with wholly owned 12302161 Canada Inc.; basis 1 new for 2 old shs.

Directors - Lorne Mark Roseborough, chr., CEO & acting CFO, Kelowna, B.C.; Howard Ash, Fla.; Sharon Blady, Man.

Capital Stock

	Authorized (shs.)	Outstanding (shs.)[1]
Common	unlimited	71,135,969

[1] At Dec. 5, 2022

Major Shareholder - Michael Matvieshen held 16.4% interest and Lorne Mark Roseborough held 10.05% interest at June 1, 2022.

Price Range - IBH/CSE

Year	Volume	High	Low	Close
2022	8,300,230	$0.18	$0.01	$0.03
2021	507,969	$0.48	$0.07	$0.08
2020	492,470	$0.46	$0.13	$0.30
2019	978,229	$2.60	$0.26	$0.29
2018	3,956,651	$19.40	$1.70	$2.00

Consolidation: 1-for-2 cons. in Sept. 2021; 1-for-10 cons. in Feb. 2019

Recent Close: $0.02

Capital Stock Changes - On Sept. 1, 2021, common shares were consolidated on a 1-for-2 basis. On Sept. 24, 2021, 62,221,972 post-consolidated common shares were issued pursuant to the reverse takeover acquisition of (old) Indigenous Bloom Hemp Corporation.

Wholly Owned Subsidiaries

Cannevert Therapeutics Ltd., Vancouver, B.C.
Indigenous Bloom Hemp Corporation, Kelowna, B.C.
12302161 Canada Inc., Canada.
Sechelt Organic Marijuana Corp., B.C.
Veritas Hemp Corp.

Financial Statistics

Periods ended:	12m May 31/22[A1]		12m May 31/21[A2]
	$000s	%Chg	$000s
General & admin expense	529		271
Operating expense	**529**	**+95**	**271**
Operating income	**(529)**	**n.a.**	**(271)**
Deprec., depl. & amort.	109		117
Finance costs, gross	8		12
Write-downs/write-offs	(17)		nil
Pre-tax income	**(2,290)**	**n.a.**	**(400)**
Net income	**(2,290)**	**n.a.**	**(400)**
Cash & equivalent	66		26
Inventories	242		nil
Current assets	310		135
Fixed assets, net	424		415
Right-of-use assets	26		134
Total assets	**760**	**+11**	**685**
Accts. pay. & accr. liabs.	933		244
Current liabilities	2,763		1,065
Long-term debt, gross	688		153
Long-term debt, net	13		26
Long-term lease liabilities	nil		92
Shareholders' equity	(2,449)		(498)
Cash from oper. activs.	**(295)**	**n.a.**	**(375)**
Cash from fin. activs.	335		401
Net cash position	**66**	**+154**	**26**
	$		$
Earnings per share*	(0.04)		(0.02)
Cash flow per share*	(0.00)		(0.04)
	shs		shs
No. of shs. o/s*	71,135,969		n.a.
Avg. no. of shs. o/s*	68,303,027		19,178,086
	%		%
Net profit margin	n.a.		n.a.
Return on equity	n.m.		n.m.
Return on assets	(315.85)		(113.12)

* Common
[A] Reported in accordance with IFRS
[1] Results reflect the Sept. 24, 2021, reverse takeover acquisition of Indigenous Bloom Hemp Corporation.
[2] Results pertain to (old) Indigenous Bloom Hemp Corporation.

Latest Results

Periods ended:	3m Aug. 31/22[A]		3m Aug. 31/21[oA]
	$000s	%Chg	$000s
Net income	(109)	n.a.	6,029
	$		$
Earnings per share*	(0.00)		n.a.

* Common
[o] Restated
[A] Reported in accordance with IFRS

Historical Summary
(as originally stated)

Fiscal Year	Oper. Rev.	Net Inc. Bef. Disc.	EPS*
	$000s	$000s	$
2022[A]	nil	(2,290)	(0.04)
2021[A]	nil	(400)	(0.02)
2021[A1]	nil	(602)	(0.07)
2020[A]	nil	(1,782)	(0.28)
2019[A]	nil	(11,899)	(2.64)

* Common
[A] Reported in accordance with IFRS
[1] Results for fiscal 2021 and prior fiscal years pertain to Veritas Pharma Inc.

Note: Adjusted throughout for 1-for-2 cons. in Sept. 2021

I.36 Indigo Books & Music Inc.*

Symbol - IDG **Exchange** - TSX **CUSIP** - 45567S
Head Office - 400-620 King St W, Toronto, ON, M5V 1M6 **Telephone** - (416) 364-4499 **Fax** - (416) 364-0355
Website - www.chapters.indigo.ca
Email - kgregory@indigo.ca
Investor Relations - Kate Gregory (416) 364-4499 ext. 6659
Auditors - Ernst & Young LLP C.A., Toronto, Ont.
Lawyers - Torys LLP, Toronto, Ont.
Transfer Agents - TSX Trust Company, Toronto, Ont.
FP500 Revenue Ranking - 333
Employees - 5,000 at Apr. 1, 2023

Profile - (Ont. 2001 amalg.) Operates book superstores and small format bookstores across Canada and in Short Hills, N.J., offering an assortment of books, gifts, baby, kids, wellness and lifestyle products.

Superstores - At July 7, 2023, the company operated 87 superstores under the names Chapters and Indigo, including one store in Short Hills, N.J. All superstores are leased and have an average selling area of 24,000 sq. ft. These superstores offer an extensive on-hand book selection, as well as general merchandise such as home, fashion, paper, wellness, toys and electronics products. Select superstores feature concept shops such as !ndigoKids, which offers kids' toys, books, lifestyle products and decor, and IndigoBaby, which offers an assortment of essential products for expectant and new parents.

Small Format Stores - At July 7, 2023, the company operated 84 small format stores under the names Coles and Indigospirit. These stores are located in retail shopping centres, street-front retail areas and central business districts, and have an average selling area of 2,800 sq. ft. Small format stores offer popular books, paper products and a limited section of general merchandise, toys and baby products.

Digital Platforms - Operates www.indigo.ca and indigo mobile app, an online platform and mobile application which offers more than 12,000,000 book titles in paperback, e-books and audio books as well as electronics, gifts, fashion, kids, baby, wellness and home merchandise; and www.thoughtfull.co, an online gifting platform which offers giftable experiences, services and subscriptions.

During fiscal 2023, the company opened one superstore, and closed two superstores and one small format store.

During fiscal 2022, the company closed four small format stores.

Predecessor Detail - Formed from Chapters Inc. in Ontario, Aug. 16, 2001, on amalgamation with Indigo Books & Music Inc.

Directors - Peter Ruis, CEO, Toronto, Ont.; Jonathan H. Deitcher, Montréal, Qué.; Markus Dohle, N.Y.; Wendy F. Evans, Toronto, Ont.; Andrea Johnson, Calif.; Donald W. (Don) Lewtas, Toronto, Ont.; Gerald W. (Gerry) Schwartz, Toronto, Ont.; Joel Silver, Calif.

Other Exec. Officers - Andrea Limbardi, pres.; Gildave (Gil) Dennis, COO; Daniel Marcotte, chief info. security officer & interim chief tech. & info. officer; Katharine Poulter, chief comml. officer; R. Craig Loudon, exec. v-p, supply chain & CFO

Capital Stock

	Authorized (shs.)	Outstanding (shs.)[1]
Common	unlimited	27,597,253

[1] At Aug. 10, 2023

Options - At Apr. 1, 2023, options were outstanding to purchase 3,191,750 common shares at a weighted average exercise price of $4.12 per share with a weighted average remaining contractual life of 2.9 years.

Major Shareholder - Gerald W. (Gerry) Schwartz held 56.26% interest at July 10, 2023.

Price Range - IDG/TSX

Year	Volume	High	Low	Close
2022	6,294,985	$4.75	$1.80	$1.95
2021	6,591,309	$5.25	$2.81	$3.83
2020	14,694,832	$4.31	$0.82	$3.26
2019	2,965,514	$11.28	$3.90	$4.35
2018	2,455,191	$20.25	$10.57	$11.28

Recent Close: $1.34

Capital Stock Changes - During fiscal 2023, 3,000 common shares were issued on exercise of options.

During fiscal 2022, 75,750 common shares were issued on exercise of options.

Long-Term Debt - At Apr. 1, 2023, the company had no long-term debt.

Wholly Owned Subsidiaries

Indigo Cultural Department Store Inc., Del.
Indigo Design Studio, Inc., Del.
YYZ Holdings Inc., Del.

Financial Statistics

Periods ended:	12m Apr. 1/23[A]		52w Apr. 2/22[A]
	$000s	%Chg	$000s
Operating revenue	**1,057,740**	**0**	**1,062,250**
Cost of sales	641,529		619,212
General & admin expense	374,220		349,091
Stock-based compensation	846		864
Operating expense	**1,016,595**	**+5**	**969,167**
Operating income	**41,145**	**-56**	**93,083**
Deprec., depl. & amort.	66,984		64,036
Finance costs, net	24,143		23,694
Investment income	nil		(32)
Write-downs/write-offs	nil		(2,027)
Pre-tax income	**(49,751)**	**n.a.**	**3,265**
Income taxes	(185)		nil
Net income	**(49,566)**	**n.a.**	**3,265**
Cash & equivalent	64,009		83,624
Inventories	244,063		273,849
Accounts receivable	14,069		12,941
Current assets	332,028		390,013
Long-term investments	nil		97
Fixed assets, net	52,464		64,319
Right-of-use assets	318,302		333,767
Intangibles, net	35,287		21,171
Total assets	**738,081**	**-9**	**809,367**
Accts. pay. & accr. liabs.	169,860		178,138
Current liabilities	327,916		331,693
Long-term lease liabilities	428,284		448,084
Shareholders' equity	(19,977)		27,820
Cash from oper. activs.	**77,803**	**-4**	**81,281**
Cash from fin. activs.	(71,797)		(66,079)
Cash from invest. activs.	(25,645)		(13,539)
Net cash position	**65,113**	**-25**	**86,469**
Capital expenditures	(3,343)		(3,248)
	$		$
Earnings per share*	(1.78)		0.12
Cash flow per share*	2.80		2.93
	shs		shs
No. of shs. o/s*	27,352,711		27,349,711
Avg. no. of shs. o/s*	27,814,444		27,771,387
	%		%
Net profit margin	(4.69)		0.31
Return on equity	n.m.		12.96
Return on assets	(6.41)		0.41
No. of employees (FTEs)	5,000		5,000

* Common
[A] Reported in accordance with IFRS

Latest Results

Periods ended:	13w July 1/23[A]		13w July 2/22[A]
	$000s	%Chg	$000s
Operating revenue	179,171	-12	204,556
Net income	(28,508)	n.a.	(25,407)
	$		$
Earnings per share*	(1.02)		(0.91)

* Common
[A] Reported in accordance with IFRS

Historical Summary
(as originally stated)

Fiscal Year	Oper. Rev.	Net Inc. Bef. Disc.	EPS*
	$000s	$000s	$
2023[A]	1,057,740	(49,566)	(1.78)
2022[A]	1,062,250	3,265	0.12
2021[A1]	904,738	(57,867)	(2.09)
2020[A]	957,722	(184,998)	(6.72)
2019[A]	1,046,824	(36,798)	(1.35)

* Common
[A] Reported in accordance with IFRS
[1] 53 weeks ended Apr. 3, 2021.

I.37 Indiva Limited

Symbol - NDVA **Exchange** - TSX-VEN **CUSIP** - 45580J
Head Office - 710-333 Preston St, Ottawa, ON, K1S 5N4 **Telephone** - (613) 883-8541 **Toll-free** - (888) 649-6686
Website - www.indiva.com
Email - ir@indiva.com
Investor Relations - Anthony Simone (416) 881-5154
Auditors - Ernst & Young LLP C.A., Toronto, Ont.
Transfer Agents - Computershare Trust Company of Canada Inc., Vancouver, B.C.

Profile - (Ont. 2017; orig. B.C., 1979) Produces and sells medical and recreational cannabis and cannabis-based products under a licence from Health Canada.

Wholly owned **Indiva Inc.** holds a licence to cultivate, process and sell dried cannabis, oil, fresh cannabis, plants, seeds, edibles, topicals, extracts and cannabis-based products under the Cannabis Act from a 40,000-sq.-ft. production and processing facility in London, Ont.

Products include pre-rolls, dry flowers, extracts, edibles and capsules, which are sold under the INDIVA™, Indiva Life and Artisan Batch brands; and cannabis-infused chocolates, which are sold under the Bhang® brand. In addition, the company has licences to manufacture and distribute cannabis-infused Jewels™ fruit-based chews, Wana™ sour gummies and soft chews, Grön gummies and chocolates and Dime Industries™ vape products in Canada. Also provides production and manufacturing services to peer entities.

On May 30, 2023, the company and **Canopy Growth Corporation** entered into a licence assignment and assumption agreement providing Canopy exclusive rights and interests to manufacture, distribute and sell the company's Wana™ branded products in Canada. The company would also manufacture Wana™ for Canopy in Canada. As consideration for the company entering into the agreements, the company completed a private placement of common shares on June 16, 2023, with Canopy subscribing for 37,230,000 common shares for an aggregate purchase price of $2,155,617 at a price per share of $0.0579. Upon closing of the private placement, Canopy held control over 19.99% of the common shares of the company.

Predecessor Detail - Name changed from Rainmaker Resources Ltd., Dec. 11, 2017, following reverse takeover acquisition of and amalgamation of INDIVA Corporation with a wholly owned subsidiary; basis 1 new for 10.878 old shs.

Directors - Carmine (Niel) Marotta, pres. & CEO, Ottawa, Ont.; Rachel Goldman, Montréal, Qué.; Andre Lafleche, Long Sault, Ont.; John Marotta, Toronto, Ont.; H. Hamish Sutherland, Toronto, Ont.; L. Russell Wilson, Calgary, Alta.; James Yersh, Waterloo, Ont.

Other Exec. Officers - Rob Carse, COO; Jennifer Welsh, CFO & corp. sec.; Melissa Kurek, v-p, opers.; Leslie Tomlenovich, v-p, quality assurance & regulatory

Capital Stock

	Authorized (shs.)	Outstanding (shs.)[1]
Preference	unlimited	nil
Common	unlimited	149,014,983

[1] At May 30, 2023

Major Shareholder - Canopy Growth Corporation held 19.99% interest at June 16, 2023.

Price Range - NDVA/TSX-VEN

Year	Volume	High	Low	Close
2022	17,869,697	$0.39	$0.11	$0.11
2021	73,830,565	$0.74	$0.25	$0.36
2020	38,812,965	$0.48	$0.19	$0.28
2019	46,294,793	$0.64	$0.16	$0.25
2018	71,381,867	$1.33	$0.32	$0.39

Recent Close: $0.03

Capital Stock Changes - In June 2023, private placement of 37,230,000 common shares was completed at $0.0579 per share with Canopy Growth Corporation.

During 2022, common shares were issued as follows: 978,388 for debt settlement, 134,626 on vesting of restricted units and 33,821 for convertible debenture interest payment.

Wholly Owned Subsidiaries

Indiva Amalco Ltd., Ont.
- 100% int. in **Indiva Inc.**, Ont.
- 100% int. in **Vieva Canada Limited**, Ont.

2639177 Ontario Inc., Ont.

Financial Statistics

Periods ended:	12m Dec. 31/22[A]		12m Dec. 31/21[□A]
	$000s	%Chg	$000s
Operating revenue	**34,403**	**+7**	**32,204**
Cost of goods sold	26,250		25,354
Research & devel. expense	1,016		417
General & admin expense	12,235		11,015
Stock-based compensation	586		474
Operating expense	**40,087**	**+8**	**37,260**
Operating income	**(5,685)**	**n.a.**	**(5,056)**
Deprec., depl. & amort.	410		485
Finance income	36		5
Finance costs, gross	4,718		3,024
Write-downs/write-offs	(205)		(27)
Pre-tax income	**(11,050)**	**n.a.**	**(15,484)**
Income taxes	(118)		(267)
Net income	**(10,932)**	**n.a.**	**(15,217)**
Cash & equivalent	2,786		2,480
Inventories	4,138		4,138
Accounts receivable	4,134		5,870
Current assets	11,682		15,514
Fixed assets, net	22,541		22,396
Intangibles, net	1,659		1,866
Total assets	**37,849**	**-11**	**42,441**
Accts. pay. & accr. liabs	12,654		7,878
Current liabilities	13,373		8,891
Long-term debt, gross	21,446		20,927
Long-term debt, net	21,196		20,226
Long-term lease liabilities	401		564
Shareholders' equity	2,149		12,029
Cash from oper. activs	**1,550**	**n.a.**	**(17,843)**
Cash from fin. activs	(215)		21,800
Cash from invest. activs	(1,029)		(1,791)
Net cash position	**2,786**	**+12**	**2,480**
Capital expenditures	(1,068)		(1,796)
Capital disposals	3		nil
	$		$
Earnings per share*	(0.08)		(0.11)
Cash flow per share*	0.01		(0.13)
	shs		shs
No. of shs. o/s*	147,297,037		146,150,202
Avg. no. of shs. o/s*	134,906,609		134,477,941
	%		%
Net profit margin	(31.78)		(47.25)
Return on equity	(150.99)		(130.90)
Return on assets	(15.60)		(30.01)

* Common
[□] Restated
[A] Reported in accordance with IFRS

Note: Cost of sales is net of fair value adjustment on sale of inventory and unrealized gain (loss) in fair value of biological assets.

Latest Results

Periods ended:	3m Mar. 31/23[A]		3m Mar. 31/22[□A]
	$000s	%Chg	$000s
Operating revenue	9,412	+6	8,879
Net income	(2,252)	n.a.	(3,074)
	$		$
Earnings per share*	(0.02)		(0.02)

* Common
[□] Restated
[A] Reported in accordance with IFRS

Historical Summary
(as originally stated)

Fiscal Year	Oper. Rev. $000s	Net Inc. Bef. Disc. $000s	EPS* $
2022[A]	34,403	(10,932)	(0.08)
2021[A]	32,470	(15,009)	(0.11)
2020[A]	14,651	(15,423)	(0.16)
2019[A]	924	(11,398)	(0.14)
2018[A]	58	(8,527)	(0.11)

* Common
[A] Reported in accordance with IFRS

I.38 infinitii ai inc.

Symbol - IAI **Exchange** - CSE **CUSIP** - 45675H
Head Office - 488-1090 Georgia St W, Vancouver, BC, V6E 3V7 **Telephone** - (778) 379-0275
Website - www.infinitii.ai
Email - nathan@infinitii.ai
Investor Relations - Nathan Rudyk (778) 200-2093
Auditors - Baker Tilly WM LLP C.A., Vancouver, B.C.
Lawyers - Clark Wilson LLP, Vancouver, B.C.
Transfer Agents - Computershare Trust Company of Canada Inc., Vancouver, B.C.

Profile - (B.C. 2014) Develops software that performs real-time analysis, checks flow monitoring status, sets alarms through a single interface, accepts all types of data from any source and offers predictive and prescriptive analytics to industrial and Smart City infrastructure applications that rely on time-series data.

The company's infinitii dataworks platform is the umbrella for its technology. It ensures Smart City and Smart Industry infrastructure facilities keep water, raw materials and energy resources flowing while meeting compliance goals for clean water, air and soil. Operations are organized into two business segments: Smart City water infrastructure; and Smart Industry infrastructure.

The **Smart City water infrastructure** product portfolio includes infinitii flowworks; infinitii flowworks+ infinitii flowworks pro; infinitii face; infinitii face pro; infinitii auto i&i; infinitii api connect; infinitii api pro; infinitii cso predict; and infinitii flood risk forecast (in Beta).

The **Smart Industry infrastructure** product portfolio includes infinitii real time monitoring; infinitii advanced calculation engine; infinitii auto qa/qc (in Beta); and infinitii api pro.

The company also has complementary operations in Vancouver, B.C., which provide software application development and hardware research and development; in Seattle, Wash., for the U.S. sales team support; and in Gdansk, Poland, which provides data science development and expertise.

Predecessor Detail - Name changed from Carl Data Solutions Inc., Oct. 7, 2022.

Directors - Jean-Charles Phaneuf, CEO, Beaconsfield, Qué.; Chris Johnston, B.C.; Kevin Ma, Vancouver, B.C.; Vikas Ranjan, Toronto, Ont.; Rick Sanderson, B.C.

Other Exec. Officers - D. Gregory (Greg) Johnston, pres.; Cale Thomas, CFO; Piotr Stepinski, chief tech. officer; David Daniels, v-p, envirl. monitoring as a srvc. (EMaaS) sales; David Fromont, v-p, tech. & bus. solutions; Kevin Marsh, v-p, bus. devel.; Mike McDonald, v-p, eng.; Alastair Brownlow, contr.

Capital Stock

	Authorized (shs.)	Outstanding (shs.)[1]
Common	unlimited	126,424,783

[1] At Oct. 28, 2022

Major Shareholder - Sheldon Inwentash held 11.8% interest at Oct. 20, 2022.

Price Range - IAI/CSE

Year	Volume	High	Low	Close
2022	25,476,430	$0.12	$0.03	$0.04
2021	88,151,114	$0.48	$0.05	$0.06
2020	15,735,850	$0.22	$0.07	$0.10
2019	35,501,253	$0.26	$0.06	$0.19
2018	33,458,619	$0.36	$0.06	$0.07

Recent Close: $0.07

Capital Stock Changes - There were no changes to capital stock during fiscal 2022.

Wholly Owned Subsidiaries

Astra Smart Systems Inc., B.C.
Carl Data Solutions PL, Poland.
Extend to Social Media Inc., Vancouver, B.C.
i4C Innovation Inc., Trail, B.C.
infinitii ai corporation, Seattle, Wash.

Financial Statistics

Periods ended:	12m June 30/22^A		12m June 30/21^A
	$000s	%Chg	$000s
Operating revenue	**1,618**	**-39**	**2,631**
Salaries & benefits	1,378		1,005
General & admin expense	2,010		2,974
Stock-based compensation	237		785
Operating expense	**3,625**	**-24**	**4,764**
Operating income	**(2,007)**	**n.a.**	**(2,133)**
Deprec., depl. & amort.	206		540
Finance costs, gross	85		251
Write-downs/write-offs	(194)		(47)
Pre-tax income	**(2,458)**	**n.a.**	**(4,625)**
Net income	**(2,458)**	**n.a.**	**(4,625)**
Cash & equivalent	1,193		2,903
Accounts receivable	401		705
Current assets	1,606		3,667
Fixed assets, net	3		321
Intangibles, net	119		199
Total assets	**1,728**	**-59**	**4,187**
Accts. pay. & accr. liabs	339		808
Current liabilities	924		1,143
Long-term debt, gross	258		199
Equity portion of conv. debs	70		70
Shareholders' equity	584		2,781
Cash from oper. activs	**(1,585)**	**n.a.**	**(1,113)**
Cash from fin. activs	(143)		3,926
Net cash position	**1,193**	**-59**	**2,903**
	$		$
Earnings per share*	(0.02)		(0.05)
Cash flow per share*	(0.01)		(0.01)
	shs		shs
No. of shs. o/s*	126,424,783		126,424,783
Avg. no. of shs. o/s*	126,424,783		93,914,693
	%		%
Net profit margin	(151.92)		(175.79)
Return on equity	(146.09)		n.m.
Return on assets	(80.24)		(124.19)
Foreign sales percent	56		17

* Common

^A Reported in accordance with IFRS

Historical Summary
(as originally stated)

Fiscal Year	Oper. Rev.	Net Inc. Bef. Disc.	EPS*
	$000s	$000s	$
2022^A	1,618	(2,458)	(0.02)
2021^A	2,631	(4,625)	(0.05)
2020^A	2,534	(3,358)	(0.04)
2019^A	1,650	(3,369)	(0.04)
2018^A	1,259	(4,709)	(0.08)

* Common

^A Reported in accordance with IFRS

I.39 Information Services Corporation

Symbol - ISV **Exchange** - TSX **CUSIP** - 45676A
Head Office - 300-10 Research Dr, Regina, SK, S4S 7J7 **Telephone** - (306) 787-8179 **Toll-free** - (866) 275-4721 **Fax** - (306) 798-6839
Website - company.isc.ca
Email - jonathan.hackshaw@isc.ca
Investor Relations - Jonathan Hackshaw (855) 341-8363
Auditors - Deloitte LLP C.A., Regina, Sask.
Transfer Agents - TSX Trust Company, Calgary, Alta.
FP500 Revenue Ranking - 668
Employees - 550 at Dec. 31, 2022
Profile - (Sask. 2000) Provides registry and information management services for public data and records.

Operations are carried out through three segments: Registry Operations; Services; and Technology Solutions.

The **Registry Operations** segment delivers registry and information services on behalf of governments and private sectors organizations. The company holds the exclusive right from the Province of Saskatchewan to manage and operate land titles registry, land survey, personal property registry and corporate registry systems as well as the Common Business Identifier and Business Registration Saskatchewan programs until May 30, 2033. The Saskatchewan Land Registry includes Land Titles Registry, which issues titles to land and registers transactions affecting titles; Land Surveys Directory, which registers land survey plans and creates a representation of Saskatchewan land parcels in the cadastral parcel mapping system; and Geomatics, which manages geographic data related to the cadastral parcel mapping system that is integrated with Land Titles Registry and Land Surveys Directory. The Saskatchewan Personal Property Registry is a notice-based public registry where individuals, corporations, lenders and others can register and search security interests and certain other interests in personal property other than land, buildings and other property affixed to land. The Saskatchewan Corporate Registry is a province-wide system for registering and maintaining records of business corporations, non-profit corporations, co-operatives, sole proprietorships, partnerships and business names. The Common Business Identifier program allows for the use of the Canada Revenue Agency Business Number as the common business identifier for business entities that interact with participating public sector programs in Saskatchewan; and the Business Registration Saskatchewan program is a single online point of access that enables new businesses to integrate with other government agencies. In addition, provides property tax assessment services through wholly owned **Reamined Systems Inc.** to more than 440 municipalities in Ontario facilitating the management of property tax rates and distribution.

The **Services** segment consists of operations of wholly owned **ESC Corporate Services Ltd.**, which delivers solutions to support the registration, due diligence and lending practices of mainly legal and financial sector clients across Canada through three divisions, Corporate Solutions, Regulatory Solutions and Recovery Solutions. Corporate Solutions provides incorporation services to legal professionals or the general public, including nationwide business name registration and renewals and security/corporate filings and registrations; and corporate supplies, including customized corporate minute books, seals, stamps and corporate legal packages, for businesses and corporations. Regulatory Solutions supports the credit/banking and legal processes of customers by providing know-your-customer (KYC) and due diligence services, which involve due diligence activities of verifying and authenticating an individual's or business's data for compliance purposes, and public record search services for corporate profiles, business name, NUANS, PPSA, security, real estate, and birth, death and marriage certificate; and collateral management services, which include Personal Property Security Act (PPSA) or Registre des Droits Personnels et Réels Mobiliers (RDPRM) search and registrations, fixture filings, garage/repair liens and U.S. Uniform Commercial Code (UCC) search and filings. Recovery Solutions offers a fully managed service across Canada and the U.S. for identification, retrieval and disposal of movable assets, such as automobiles, boats, aircraft and other forms of portable physical assets used as collateral security for primarily consumer-focused credit transactions; and accounts receivable management, which includes recovery services related to past due accounts in both a first party capacity representing the company's customers, and a third-party collections capacity.

The **Technology Solutions** segment provides the development, delivery and support of registry and regulatory technology solutions. Through wholly owned **Enterprise Registry Solutions Ltd.**, offers RegSys, a complete registry software solution which provides a readily transferable technology platform capable of serving wide rage of registry needs such as submission, enforcement and enquiry processing.

In December 2022, wholly owned **ISC Atlantic Services Inc.** acquired all outstanding shares of **Regulis S.A.**, for $600,000 (€400,000) cash and additional payments of up to €1,600,000 upon achievement of certain criteria. Regulis holds a contract under the Luxembourg Rail Protocol of the Cape Town Convention which provides it the exclusive right and obligation to develop, deliver and operate the International Registry for Railway Rolling Stock (Registry) for a period of ten years from the date the Registry goes live as defined in the Luxembourg Rail Protocol.

Recent Merger and Acquisition Activity

Status: completed **Announced:** June 1, 2022
Information Services Corporation acquired private Toronto, Ont.-based Reamined Systems Inc. for $45,900,000. Reamined provides property tax management infrastructure and services in Ontario.

Directors - Joel D. Teal, chr., Saskatoon, Sask.; Douglas A. (Doug) Emsley, v-chr., Regina, Sask.; Amber Biemans, Humboldt, Sask.; Roger Brandvold, Calgary, Alta.; Anthony R. (Tony) Guglielmin, Vancouver, B.C.; Iraj Pourian, Vancouver, B.C.; Laurie Powers, Kelowna, B.C.; James N. (Jim) Roche, Ottawa, Ont.; Heather D. Ross, Toronto, Ont.; Dion E. Tchorzewski, Regina, Sask.

Other Exec. Officers - Shawn B. Peters, pres. & CEO; Robert (Bob) Antochow, CFO; Kenneth W. Budzak, exec. v-p, registry opers.; Loren Cisyk, exec. v-p, tech. solutions; Kathy E. Hillman-Weir, exec. v-p, chief corp. officer, gen. counsel & corp. sec.; Laurel Garven, v-p, corp. devel. & bus. strategy; Catherine McLean, v-p, people & culture; Clare Colledge, pres., ESC Corporate Services Ltd.

Capital Stock

	Authorized (shs.)	Outstanding (shs.)[1]
Preferred	unlimited	nil
Class A Limited Vtg.	unlimited	17,701,498
Class B Golden	1	1

[1] At Apr. 6, 2023

Class A Limited Voting - One vote per share.

Class B Golden - Held by the Government of Saskatchewan. Non-voting except to veto a transfer of the company's registered office outside of Saskatchewan, all or part of its head office operations or all or any part of functions constituting the company's head office functions outside of the province or the sale, lease or exchange of all or substantially all of the company's property, any proposal to apply for continuance in a jurisdiction outside of Saskatchewan and any proposal to amend the company's articles or as otherwise provided by law.

Major Shareholder - Crown Investments Corporation of Saskatchewan held 30.6% interest, CI Investments Inc. held 13.9% interest and QV Investors Inc. held 12.5% interest at Apr. 6, 2023.

Price Range - ISV/TSX

Year	Volume	High	Low	Close
2022	2,064,094	$27.40	$19.12	$24.17
2021	2,167,977	$33.87	$19.68	$25.29
2020	2,523,392	$20.79	$12.02	$19.91
2019	2,076,348	$18.10	$15.26	$15.36
2018	1,571,134	$18.50	$14.36	$15.30

Recent Close: $23.75

Capital Stock Changes - During 2022, 201,498 class A limited voting shares were issued on exercise of options.

Dividends

ISV cl A Ra $0.92 pa Q est. Jan. 15, 2022
Prev. Rate: $0.80 est. Oct. 15, 2013

Wholly Owned Subsidiaries

Enterprise Registry Solutions Ltd., Dublin, Ireland.
ISC Atlantic Services Inc., Canada.
- 100% int. in **Regulis S.A.**, Luxembourg.

ISC Enterprises Inc., Canada.
- 100% int. in **ESC Corporate Services Ltd.**, Toronto, Ont.
  - 100% int. in **Credit Bureau of Stratford (1970) Limited**
  - 100% int. in **Credit Risk Management Canada Ltd.**

ISC Operations Inc., Ont.
- 100% int. in **Reamined Systems Inc.**, Toronto, Ont.

ISC Saskatchewan Inc., Sask.

Financial Statistics

Periods ended:	12m Dec. 31/22^A		12m Dec. 31/21^A
	$000s	%Chg	$000s
Operating revenue	**189,895**	**+12**	**169,379**
Cost of goods sold	49,215		40,359
Salaries & benefits	54,267		48,757
General & admin expense	22,244		18,338
Other operating expense	3,239		1,393
Operating expense	**128,965**	**+18**	**108,847**
Operating income	**60,930**	**+1**	**60,532**
Deprec., depl. & amort.	14,735		13,778
Finance income	463		140
Finance costs, gross	3,640		2,813
Pre-tax income	**43,018**	**-2**	**44,081**
Income taxes	12,249		12,003
Net income	**30,769**	**-4**	**32,078**
Cash & equivalent	34,479		40,140
Accounts receivable	14,933		12,771
Current assets	57,216		56,447
Fixed assets, net	1,813		1,351
Right-of-use assets	7,553		7,861
Intangibles, net	190,233		138,201
Total assets	**283,454**	**+22**	**232,498**
Accts. pay. & accr. liabs	25,358		18,364
Current liabilities	39,626		36,905
Long-term debt, gross	66,047		40,975
Long-term debt, net	66,047		40,975
Long-term lease liabilities	6,508		7,186
Shareholders' equity	155,588		137,705
Cash from oper. activs	**43,536**	**-29**	**61,212**
Cash from fin. activs	6,247		(54,274)
Cash from invest. activs	(55,619)		(366)
Net cash position	**34,479**	**-14**	**40,104**
Capital expenditures	(574)		(10)
Capital disposals	4		2
	$		$
Earnings per share*	1.75		1.83
Cash flow per share*	2.47		3.50
Cash divd. per share*	0.92		0.83
	shs		shs
No. of shs. o/s*	17,701,498		17,500,000
Avg. no. of shs. o/s*	17,598,864		17,500,000
	%		%
Net profit margin	16.20		18.94
Return on equity	20.98		24.70
Return on assets	12.94		14.37
Foreign sales percent	3		5
No. of employees (FTEs)	550		400

* Class A

^A Reported in accordance with IFRS

Historical Summary
(as originally stated)

Fiscal Year	Oper. Rev.	Net Inc. Bef. Disc.	EPS*
	$000s	$000s	$
2022^A	189,895	30,769	1.75
2021^A	169,379	32,078	1.83
2020^A	136,723	20,883	1.19
2019^A	132,968	19,400	1.11
2018^A	119,131	18,671	1.07

* Class A

^A Reported in accordance with IFRS

I.40 InMed Pharmaceuticals Inc.

Symbol - INM **Exchange** - NASDAQ **CUSIP** - 457637
Head Office - 310-815 Hastings St W, Vancouver, BC, V6C 1B4 **Telephone** - (604) 669-7207 **Fax** - (778) 945-6800
Website - www.inmedpharma.com
Email - cclancy@inmedpharma.com
Investor Relations - Colin Clancy (604) 416-0999
Auditors - Marcum LLP C.P.A.
Lawyers - Farris LLP, Vancouver, B.C.
Transfer Agents - Computershare Trust Company of Canada Inc., Vancouver, B.C.
Employees - 13 at Sept. 1, 2022

Profile - (B.C. 1981) Researches, develops and manufactures rare cannabinoids and cannabinoid analogs for treatment of diseases with high unmet medical needs.

Operations are carried out into two segments: InMed and BayMedica.

The **InMed** segment researches and develops cannabinoid-based pharmaceuticals products. The company had developed IntegraSyn™, its own flexible, integrated manufacturing system to efficiently produce bioidentical, pharmaceutical-grade cannabinoids. Its initial two drug candidate under development are INM-755 (which commenced phase II clinical trials in September 2021), a cannabinol (CBN) topical skin cream for rare genetic skin disease epidermolysis bullosa, and INM-088 (eye drop) for the treatment of glaucoma.

The **BayMedica** segment is conducted through wholly owned **BayMedica, LLC,** which manufactures and commercializes rare cannabinoids for consumer applications and cannabinoid-derived new chemical entities for pharmaceutical applications. Products include Prodiol® cannabichromene (CBC), cannabicitran (CBT), cannabidivarin (CBDV) and delta 9-dominant tetrahydrocannabivarin (d9-THCV), which can be used as a raw ingredient for a variety of consumer health and wellness products applications including cosmetics, nutraceuticals, supplements and animal health.

Predecessor Detail - Name changed from Cannabis Technologies Inc., Oct. 6, 2014.

Directors - Eric A. Adams, pres. & CEO, B.C.; Bryan Baldasare, Ohio; Janet P. Grove, Vancouver, B.C.; Andrew Hull, Ill.; Nicole Lemerond, N.Y.

Other Exec. Officers - Michael Woudenberg, COO; Jonathan Tegge, interim CFO; Alexandra D. J. (Alex) Mancini, sr. v-p, clinical & regulatory affairs; Dr. Philip Barr, v-p, discovery; Colin Clancy, v-p, IR & corp. commun.; Jerry Griffin, v-p, sales & mktg.; Dr. Eric C. Hsu, v-p, pre-clinical R&D; Dr. Jim Kealey, v-p, synthetic biology; Sarah Li, v-p, acctg. & contr.; Dr. Charles (Chuck) Marlowe, v-p, chemistry; Dr. Chris Meiering, v-p, comml. opers.

Capital Stock

	Authorized (shs.)	Outstanding (shs.)[1]
Preferred	unlimited	nil
Common	unlimited	908,761

[1] At Sept. 23, 2022

Major Shareholder - Widely held at Oct. 28, 2021.

Price Range - INM/NASDAQ

Year	Volume	High	Low	Close
2022............	10,009,928	US$35.50	US$1.23	US$2.02
2021............	929,912	US$160.00	US$31.50	US$32.75

IN/TSX (D)

Year	Volume	High	Low	Close
2021............	104,024	$205.00	$83.75	$104.75
2020............	112,981	$354.75	$94.00	$103.75
2019............	58,231	$660.00	$177.38	$193.88
2018............	292,606	$1,996.50	$247.50	$280.50

Consolidation: 1-for-25 cons. in Sept. 2022

Capital Stock Changes - On Sept. 7, 2022, common shares were consolidated on a 1-for-25 basis. Also In September 2022, private placement of 691,245 post-consolidated common shares or pre-funded warrants was completed at US$8.68 per share.

In July 2021, private placement of 890,000 common shares was completed at US$2.973 per share. In June 2022, direct offering of 1,625,050 common shares was completed at US$0.858 per share. Also during fiscal 2022, common shares were issued as follows: 3,146,327 on exercise of pre-funded warrants, 2,050,000 pursuant to the acquisition of BayMedica Inc., 268,975 under an at-the-market equity offering, 157,325 on exercise of warrants and 78,300 for services.

Wholly Owned Subsidiaries

BayMedica, LLC, San Francisco, Calif.
Biogen Sciences Inc. Inactive.
InMed Pharmaceuticals Ltd., Del.
Sweetnam Consulting Inc., Toronto, Ont. Inactive.

Financial Statistics

Periods ended:	12m June 30/22[A]		12m June 30/21[A]
	US$000s	%Chg	US$000s
Research & devel. expense.............	7,004		5,134
General & admin expense...............	6,448		4,074
Stock-based compensation............	698		610
Operating expense........................	**14,150**	**+44**	**9,817**
Operating income.......................	**(14,150)**	**n.a.**	**(9,817)**
Deprec., depl. & amort....................	186		121
Finance income................................	96		16
Finance costs, gross........................	nil		360
Write-downs/write-offs....................	(3,473)		nil
Pre-tax income...........................	**(18,600)**	**n.a.**	**(10,203)**
Net income..................................	**(18,600)**	**n.a.**	**(10,203)**
Cash & equivalent............................	6,222		7,410
Inventories.......................................	2,491		nil
Accounts receivable.........................	88		12
Current assets..................................	9,598		8,378
Fixed assets, net..............................	904		327
Intangibles, net................................	2,109		1,062
Total assets..................................	**12,788**	**+31**	**9,781**
Accts. pay. & accr. liabs..................	2,415		2,135
Current liabilities............................	3,320		2,215
Long-term lease liabilities...............	389		189
Shareholders' equity........................	9,079		7,377
Cash from oper. activs..................	**(15,584)**	**n.a.**	**(9,791)**
Cash from fin. activs........................	15,070		10,855
Cash from invest. activs..................	(673)		(2)
Net cash position..........................	**6,177**	**-16**	**7,363**
Capital expenditures........................	(39)		(2)
	US$		US$
Earnings per share*.........................	(33.17)		(38.00)
Cash flow per share*.......................	(27.79)		(36.43)
	shs		shs
No. of shs. o/s*...............................	650,667		322,028
Avg. no. of shs. o/s*........................	560,829		268,793
	%		%
Net profit margin.............................	n.a.		n.a.
Return on equity..............................	(226.06)		(156.19)
Return on assets..............................	(164.83)		(112.94)
No. of employees (FTEs).................	n.a.		12

* Common
[A] Reported in accordance with U.S. GAAP

Historical Summary
(as originally stated)

Fiscal Year	Oper. Rev.	Net Inc. Bef. Disc.	EPS*
	US$000s	US$000s	US$
2022[A]....................	nil	(18,600)	(33.16)
2021[A]....................	nil	(10,203)	(38.00)
	$000s	$000s	$
2020[B]....................	nil	(11,857)	(57.75)
2019[B]....................	nil	(13,255)	(66.00)
2018[B]....................	nil	(8,521)	(49.50)

* Common
[A] Reported in accordance with U.S. GAAP
[B] Reported in accordance with IFRS

Note: Adjusted throughout for 1-for-25 cons. in Sept. 2022; 1-for-33 cons. in July 2020

I.41 Innergex Renewable Energy Inc.*

Symbol - INE **Exchange** - TSX **CUSIP** - 45790B

Head Office - 1000-1225 rue Saint-Charles O, Longueuil, QC, J4K 0B9 **Telephone** - (450) 928-2550 **Fax** - (450) 928-2544

Website - www.innergex.com

Email - investorrelations@innergex.com

Investor Relations - Jean Trudel (450) 928-2550 ext. 1252

Auditors - KPMG LLP C.A., Montréal, Qué.

Lawyers - McCarthy Tétrault LLP, Montréal, Qué.

Transfer Agents - Computershare Trust Company of Canada Inc., Montréal, Qué.

FP500 Revenue Ranking - 365

Employees - 538 at Dec. 31, 2022

Profile - (Can. 2002) Develops, acquires, owns and operates renewable power-generating and energy storage facilities with a focus on hydroelectric, wind and solar facilities in Quebec, Ontario, British Columbia, the U.S., France and Chile.

The company has interests (at May 9, 2023) in 87 operating facilities with a total net installed capacity of 3,696 MW and an energy storage capacity of 159 MWh, consisting of 40 hydroelectric facilities, 35 wind farms, 11 solar farms and a stand-alone battery energy storage facility in Canada, the U.S., France and Chile. Also has interests in 12 projects under development, five of which are under construction, with a total net installed capacity of 709 MW and an energy storage capacity of 605 MWh; and 78 prospective projects at different stages of development with an aggregate gross capacity of 8,883 MW.

Hydroelectric - Holds interests in 40 run-of-river hydroelectric facilities in Quebec (9), Ontario (3), British Columbia (21), Idaho (1), New York (2) and Chile (4) with a total net installed capacity of 919 MW.

Wind - Holds interests in 35 wind farms in France (16), Quebec (7), British Columbia (1), Texas (2), Idaho (6) and Chile (3) with a total net installed capacity of 2,084 MW.

Solar - Holds interests in 11 solar farms in Ontario (4), Michigan (1), Indiana (1), Texas (1), Ohio (1) and Chile (3) with a total net installed capacity of 693 MW. One of the solar farms in Chile has a storage capacity of 150 MWh.

Storage - Owns the 9-MW/9-MWh Tonnerre battery storage facility in France.

Projects under construction are the 7.5-MW Innavik hydroelectric facility (50% interest) in Quebec; the 329.8-MW Boswell Springs wind project in Wyoming; the 30-MW/120-MWh Hale Kuawehi solar and battery storage project in Hawaii; and the 50-MW/250-MWh Salvador and 35-MW/175-MWh San Andrés battery storage projects in Chile. Other development projects consist of the 109-MW Frontera (75% interest) and 3-MW Rucacura hydroelectric facilities in Chile; the 9-MW Lazenay (25% interest), 29.4-MW Auxy Bois Régnier and 13.5-MW Montjean 2 wind projects in France; the 200-MW Palomino solar project in Ohio; and the 15-MW/60-MWh Paeahu solar and battery storage project in Hawaii.

In April 2023, the company sold the proposed 20-MW/80-MWh Kahana solar and battery storage project in Hawaii for a nominal amount.

In March 2023, the company and **Mi'gmawei Mawiomi Business Corporation** (MMBC) announced that their 102-MW Mesgi'g Ugju's'n 2 wind project was selected in Hydro-Québec's request for proposals. The project, which will be located in the MRC d'Avignon, is an extension to the existing 15-MW Mesgi'g Ugju's'n wind facility, and a result of a 50/50 partnership between the company and the three Mi'gmaq communities in Quebec (Gesgapegiag, Gespeg and Listuguj) represented by MMBC. Its commissioning is scheduled in 2026.

On July 22, 2022, the company commissioned the 9-MW/9-MWh Tonnerre battery storage project in Joux-la-Ville, France, the company's first stand-alone battery facility.

On Mar. 4, 2022, the company sold its 50% interest in the 204-MW Shannon wind facility in Texas for a nominal amount.

Periods ended:	12m Dec. 31/22	12m Dec. 31/21
Generating capacity, MW..............	3,634	3,101
Electric gen., GWh.........................	10,254	9,055

Recent Merger and Acquisition Activity

Status: completed **Revised:** Mar. 9, 2023
UPDATE: The transaction was completed. PREVIOUS: Innergex Renewable Energy Inc. agreed to acquire three operating solar facilities totaling 60 MW in Sault Ste. Marie, Ont., from Fengate Asset Management, a unit of Fengate Capital Management Ltd., for a purchase price of $50,200,000 as well as the assumption of $169,500,000 of debt.

Status: completed **Announced:** Dec. 14, 2022
Innergex Renewable Energy Inc. acquired all class A shares of Mountain Air Alternatives LLC, which has a portfolio of six wind farms totaling 138 MW in Idaho, from its tax equity partner, an affiliate of MetLife Investment Management, for US$47,500,000 (Cdn$64,400,000). These shares represented the remaining 37.75% interest in Mountain Air not already owned by Innergex. MetLife Investment Management is owned by MetLife, Inc.

Status: completed **Revised:** Oct. 4, 2022
UPDATE: The transaction was completed. PREVIOUS: Innergex Renewable Energy Inc. agreed to acquire the remaining 30.45% interest in Innergex Europe (2015) Limited Partnership held by Régime de rentes du Mouvement Desjardins for $96,400,000. Innergex Europe has a wind portfolio of 16 assets in France.

Status: completed **Revised:** June 9, 2022
UPDATE: The transaction was completed for US$685,600,000. PREVIOUS: Innergex Renewable Energy Inc. agreed to acquire Aela Generación S.A. and Aela Energía S.p.A. (collectively Aela), which owns a 332-MW portfolio of three newly-built operating wind farms in Chile, for a purchase price of US$686,000,000, including the assumption of US$386,000,000 of debt, subject to closing adjustments. The portfolio includes the 170-MW Sarco wind farm, the 129-MW Aurora wind farm and the 33-MW Cuel wind farm. The transaction was expected to close in the second quarter 2022.

Directors - Daniel L. Lafrance, chr., Kirkland, Qué.; Michel Letellier, pres. & CEO, Saint-Lambert, Qué.; Pierre G. Brodeur, Mont-Royal, Qué.; Radha D. Curpen, Vancouver, B.C.; Nathalie Francisci, Montréal, Qué.; Richard Gagnon, Laval, Qué.; Monique Mercier, Montréal, Qué.; Ouma Sananikone, New York, N.Y.; Louis Veci, Laval, Qué.

Other Exec. Officers - Jean Trudel, CFO; Yves Baribeault, chief legal officer & corp. sec.; Alexandra Boislard-Pépin, chief HR officer; Pascale Tremblay, chief assets officer; Renaud de Batz de Trenquelléon, sr. v-p, Latin America; Patrick Beaudoin, v-p, asset optimization & procurement; Alex Couture, v-p, devel. Canada; Jacques Desrochers, v-p, info. & opers. tech.; Colleen Giroux-Schmidt, v-p, corp. rel.; Robert Guillemette, v-p, technical srvcs.; Guillaume Jumel, v-p & man. dir., France; Matthew (Matt) Kennedy, v-p, envir.; David Little, v-p & man. dir., U.S.A.; Nikolaos (Niko) Nikolaidis, v-p, invests. & financing; Jamie Pino, v-p & man. dir., Chile; Julie Turgeon, v-p, const.

Capital Stock

	Authorized (shs.)	Outstanding (shs.)[1]
Preferred	unlimited	
Series A		3,400,000
Series C		2,000,000
Common	unlimited	204,216,044

[1] At May 8, 2023

Preferred - Issuable in series and non-voting.

Series A - Entitled to fixed cumulative preferential annual dividends of $0.811 per share payable quarterly to Jan. 15, 2026, and thereafter at a rate reset every five years equal to the five-year Government of

Canada bond yield plus 2.79%. Redeemable on Jan. 15, 2026, and on January 15 every five years thereafter at $25 per share. Convertible at the holder's option on Jan. 15, 2026, and on January 15 every five years thereafter, into floating rate series B preferred shares on a share-for-share basis, subject to certain conditions. The series B shares would pay a quarterly dividend equal to the 90-day Canadian Treasury bill rate plus 2.79%.

Series C - Entitled to fixed cumulative preferential annual dividends of $1.4375 per share payable quarterly. Redeemable at $25 per share.

Common - One vote per share.

Options - At Dec. 31, 2022, options were outstanding to purchase 284,769 common shares at a weighted average exercise price of $16.75 per share with a weighted average contractual life of five years.

Major Shareholder - Hydro-Québec held 19.82% interest at Mar. 31, 2023.

Price Range - INE/TSX

Year	Volume	High	Low	Close
2022	112,844,681	$20.46	$14.23	$16.20
2021	170,291,415	$32.48	$17.57	$18.60
2020	115,425,188	$27.63	$13.97	$27.37
2019	67,817,970	$17.38	$12.50	$16.86
2018	54,595,022	$14.53	$11.66	$12.54

Recent Close: $12.98

Capital Stock Changes - In February 2022, bought deal public offering of 9,718,650 common shares, including 1,267,650 common shares on exercise of over-allotment option, and concurrent private placement of 2,100,000 common shares with Hydro-Québec all at $17.75 per share were completed. Also during 2022, 73,865 common shares were issued under the dividend reinvestment plan, 253,681 common shares were repurchased under a Normal Course Issuer Bid and 50,996 (net) common shares were repurchased and held in trust.

Dividends

INE com Ra $0.72 pa Q est. July 15, 2020
Prev. Rate: $0.70 est. Apr. 15, 2019
INE.PR.A pfd ser A cum. red. exch. Adj. Ra $0.811 pa Q est. Apr. 15, 2021
INE.PR.C pfd ser C cum. red. Ra $1.4375 pa Q

Long-Term Debt - Outstanding at Dec. 31, 2022:

Revolv. term credit facility[1]	$718,232,000
5.13% subord. unsec. term loan due 2023	150,000,000
4.75% conv. debs. due 2025[2]	144,650,000
4.65% conv. debs. due 2026[3]	138,028,000
Tax equity financing:	
Solar segment[4]	44,064,000
Wind segment[5]	399,083,000
Project-level debt:	
6.28% green bonds due 2036	887,572,000
Hydroelectric segment[6]	1,661,290,000
Wind segment[7]	1,219,997,000
Solar segment[8]	319,597,000
Other debt[9]	155,000,000
Less: Deferred financing costs	78,303,000
	5,759,210,000
Less: Current portion	374,397,000
	5,384,813,000

[1] Bears interest at prime rate, bankers' acceptance rates, base rate, SOFR or EURIBOR plus a spread. Due 2027.
[2] Convertible into common shares at $20 per share.
[3] Convertible into common shares at $22.90 per share.
[4] Bears interest at rates ranging from 5.15% to 8%. Due from 2023 to 2028.
[5] Bears interest at rates ranging from 6.8% to 7.5%. Due from 2029 to 2031.
[6] Bears interest at rates ranging from 4.07% to 15.5%. Due from 2023 to 2064.
[7] Bears interest at rates ranging from 1.15% to 6.44%. Due from 2024 to 2039.
[8] Bears interest at rates ranging from 2.7% to 8.73%. Due from 2023 to 2032.
[9] Bears interest at rates ranging from 5.01% to 5.1%. Due from 2028 to 2031.

Note - In February 2023, the company refinanced its subordinated unsecured term loan due 2023 with non-revolving term credit facilities consisting of $75,000,000 bearing interest at 6.25% and $75,000,000 bearing interest at bankers' acceptance rates plus 1.85%, both due 2025.

Wholly Owned Subsidiaries

Aela Generación S.A., Chile.
- 100% int. in **Aela Energía S.p.A.**, Chile.

Alterra Power Corp., Vancouver, B.C.
- 100% int. in **Alterra Renewable Holdings Corp.**, B.C.
  - 25.5% int. in **Dokie General Partnership**, B.C.
    - 100% int. in **Dokie Wind Energy Inc.**, B.C.
  - 50.99% int. in **Jimmie Creek GP Inc.**, B.C.
    - 100% int. in **Jimmie Creek Limited Partnership**, B.C.
  - 40% int. in **Toba Montrose General Partnership**, B.C.
    - 100% int. in **Toba Montrose Hydro Inc.**, B.C.

Ashlu Creek Investments Limited Partnership, B.C.
Big Silver Creek Power LP, B.C.
Brown Miller Power LP, B.C.
Creek Power Inc., B.C.
- 100% int. in **Boulder Creek Power LP**, B.C.
- 100% int. in **Fitzsimmons Creek Hydro LP**, B.C.
- 100% int. in **Upper Lillooet River Power LP**, B.C.

Foard City Holdings LLC, Tex.
- 100% int. in **Foard City Wind, LLC**, Del.

Glen Miller Power, LP, Ont.
Griffin Trail Wind, LLC, Del.
Hillcrest Solar I, LLC, Del.
Hydro-Windsor, LP, Qué.
Innergex Cartier Energy LP, Qué.
Innergex Europe (2015) Limited Partnership, Longueuil, Qué.
- 100% int. in **Energie Antoigné**, France.
- 100% int. in **Energie des Cholletz**, France.
- 100% int. in **Energie des Vallottes**, France.
- 100% int. in **Energie du Porcien**, France.
- 100% int. in **Energie Eoles Beaumont S.A.S.**, France.
- 100% int. in **Energies du Plateau Central S.A.S.**, France.
- 100% int. in **Energies du Plateau Central 2 S.A.S.**, France.
- 100% int. in **Energies du Rechet S.A.S.**, France.
- 100% int. in **Eole de Plan Fleury S.A.S.**, France.
- 100% int. in **Eoles Yonne S.A.S.**, France.
- 100% int. in **Eoliennes de Longueval**, France.
- 100% int. in **Montjean Energies**, France.
- 100% int. in **Les Renardières S.A.S.**, France.
- 100% int. in **Société d'Exploitation du Parc Eolien du Bois d'Anchat**, France.
- 100% int. in **Theil-Rabier Energies**, France.

Innergex Inc., Qué.
- 49% int. in **Begetekong Power Corporation**, Ont.
  - 100% int. in **Umbata Falls LP**, Ont.
- 50% int. in **Kwoiek Creek Resources GP Inc.**, B.C.
  - 100% int. in **Kwoiek Creek Resources LP**, B.C.
- 50% int. in **Mesgi'g Ugju's'n (MU) Wind Farm Inc.**, Qué.
  - 100% int. in **Mesgi'g Ugju's'n (MU) Wind Farm, LP**, Qué.
- 50% int. in **Parc éolien communautaire Viger-Denonville Inc.**, Qué.
  - 100% int. in **Parc éolien communautaire Viger-Denonville, S.E.C.**, Qué.

Innergex Montmagny, LP, Qué.
Innergex 1.0 General Partnership, Qué.
Innergex Renewable Energy Chile S.p.A., Chile.
- 100% int. in **Duqueco S.p.A.**, Chile.
- 69.47% int. in **Energia Coyanco S.A.**, Chile.
- 55% int. in **Pampa Elvira Solar S.p.A.**, Chile.

Innergex USA, Inc., United States.
- 100% int. in **Horseshoe Bend Hydroelectric Company**, Idaho

Magpie Limited Partnership, Qué. Holds 70% of voting rights.
Mountain Air Alternatives LLC, United States.
- 100% int. in **Mountain Air Wind, LLC**, United States.

Northwest Stave River Hydro LP, B.C.
PV Salvador S.A., Chile.
Phoebe Energy Project, LLC, Del.
Rutherford Creek Power LP, B.C.
San Andrés S.p.A., Chile.
Spartan Holdings, LLC, Mich.
- 100% int. in **Spartan PV 1, LLC**, Del.

Stardale Solar LP, Ont.
Trent-Severn Power, LP, Ont.
Tretheway Creek Power LP, B.C.

Subsidiaries

80% int. in **Cayoose Creek Power Inc.**, B.C.
50.01% int. in **Cloudworks Holdings Inc.**, B.C.
- 100% int. in **Harrison Hydro Inc.**, B.C.
  - 100% int. in **Harrison Hydro Limited Partnership**, B.C.
    - 100% int. in **Harrison Hydro Project Inc.**, B.C.
      - 100% int. in **Douglas Creek Project LP**, B.C.
      - 100% int. in **Fire Creek Project LP**, B.C.
      - 100% int. in **Lamont Creek Project LP**, B.C.
      - 100% int. in **Stokke Creek Project LP**, B.C.
      - 100% int. in **Tipella Creek Project LP**, B.C.
      - 100% int. in **Upper Stave Project LP**, B.C.

50.01% int. in **Innergex Sainte-Marguerite, S.E.C.**, Qué.
90% int. in **Muko Holdings, LLC**, Del.
- 100% int. in **Kokomo Solar I, LLC**, Del.

Investments

49% int. in **Cayoose Creek Power LP**, B.C.
50% int. in **Innergex HQI USA LLC**, United States.
- 100% int. in **Curtis/Palmer Hydroelectric Company LP**, N.Y.

Note: The preceding list includes only the major related companies in which interests are held.

Financial Statistics

Periods ended:	12m Dec. 31/22[A]		12m Dec. 31/21[oA]
	$000s	%Chg	$000s
Operating revenue	**870,494**	**+16**	**747,208**
Research & devel. expense	24,740		27,367
General & admin expense	53,071		45,098
Other operating expense	207,768		149,106
Operating expense	**285,579**	**+29**	**221,571**
Operating income	**584,915**	**+11**	**525,637**
Deprec., depl. & amort.	336,053		255,640
Finance income	5,190		1,071
Finance costs, gross	319,865		252,888
Investment income	14,382		(189,889)
Write-downs/write-offs	(47,868)		(36,986)
Pre-tax income	**(97,692)**	**n.a.**	**(211,634)**
Income taxes	(6,577)		(26,240)
Net inc bef disc ops, eqhldrs	(81,619)		(191,805)
Net inc bef disc ops, NCI	(9,496)		6,411
Net income	**(91,115)**	**n.a.**	**(185,394)**
Net inc. for equity hldrs	**(81,619)**	**n.a.**	**(191,805)**
Net inc. for non-cont. int	**(9,496)**	**n.a.**	**6,411**
Cash & equivalent	162,971		166,266
Accounts receivable	174,108		113,395
Current assets	527,159		388,677
Long-term investments	151,583		133,398
Fixed assets, net	6,212,371		5,513,392
Intangibles, net	1,408,636		1,104,852
Total assets	**8,602,427**	**+16**	**7,396,068**
Accts. pay. & accr. liabs	186,868		115,925
Current liabilities	650,824		733,527
Long-term debt, gross	5,759,210		4,924,435
Long-term debt, net	5,384,813		4,411,239
Long-term lease liabilities	260,333		152,972
Preferred share equity	131,069		131,069
Equity portion of conv. debs	2,819		2,819
Shareholders' equity	1,316,195		1,093,112
Non-controlling interest	170,232		267,568
Cash from oper. activs	**430,243**	**+62**	**265,498**
Cash from fin. activs	197,536		414,077
Cash from invest. activs	(635,766)		(667,054)
Net cash position	**162,971**	**-2**	**166,266**
Capital expenditures, net	(119,189)		(250,621)
	$		$
Earnings per share*	(0.43)		(1.09)
Cash flow per share*	2.13		1.47
Cash divd. per share*	0.72		0.72
	shs		shs
No. of shs. o/s*	203,540,576		191,952,738
Avg. no. of shs. o/s*	201,835,956		180,856,774
	%		%
Net profit margin	(10.47)		(24.81)
Return on equity	(8.13)		(21.46)
Return on assets	2.59		0.50
Foreign sales percent	51		42
No. of employees (FTEs)	538		488

* Common
[o] Restated
[A] Reported in accordance with IFRS

Latest Results

Periods ended:	3m Mar. 31/23[A]		3m Mar. 31/22[A]
	$000s	%Chg	$000s
Operating revenue	197,399	+5	188,723
Net income	(13,036)	n.a.	(34,930)
Net inc. for equity hldrs	(14,336)	n.a.	(34,402)
Net inc. for non-cont. int	1,300		(528)
	$		$
Earnings per share*	(0.08)		(0.18)

* Common
[A] Reported in accordance with IFRS

Historical Summary
(as originally stated)

Fiscal Year	Oper. Rev.	Net Inc. Bef. Disc.	EPS*
	$000s	$000s	$
2022[A]	870,494	(91,115)	(0.43)
2021[A]	747,208	(185,394)	(1.09)
2020[A]	613,207	(29,111)	(0.23)
2019[A]	557,042	(53,026)	(0.40)
2018[A]	576,616	25,718	0.21

* Common
[A] Reported in accordance with IFRS

I.42 InnoCan Pharma Corporation

Symbol - INNO **Exchange** - CSE **CUSIP** - 45783P
Head Office - 10 Hamenofim St, Herzliya, Israel, 4672561 **Overseas Tel** - 972-54-301-2842
Website - www.innocanpharma.com

Email - irisb@innocanpharma.com
Investor Relations - Iris Bincovich 972-54-301-2842
Auditors - BDO Ziv Haft C.P.A., Tel Aviv, Israel
Lawyers - Burnet, Duckworth & Palmer LLP, Calgary, Alta.
Transfer Agents - Odyssey Trust Company, Calgary, Alta.
Profile - (Can. 2018) Develops several drug delivery platforms, combining cannabinoids, especially cannabidiol (CBD), with other pharmaceutical ingredients as well as the development and sale of CBD-intergrated pharmaceuticals and topical products.

Operates in four segments relating to the incorporation of CBD in the formulation of pharmaceutical products: (i) the research and development of the treatment of COVID-19 (and other viruses causing lung inflammation, such as Severe Acute Respiratory Syndrome (SARS) and Middle East Respiratory Syndrome (MERS) as well as other central nervous system diseases such as epilepsy and Alzheimer's disease by using CBD loaded exosomes; (ii) the research and development of the use of CBD loaded liposomes to provide pain relief and treat epilepsy and other central nervous system disorders and other indications; (iii) the commercialization and sale of branded CBD integrated pharmaceutical and topical treatment products for relief of psoriasis symptoms as well as the treatment of muscle pain and rheumatic pain; and (iv) third party research, development and licensing services. The company's operations and research and development activities are based in Israel.

At Dec. 31, 2022, the company had 14 families of patent applications that target various skin conditions including cannabinoid pain-relieving topical compositions; antipruritic treatments; hemorrhoid treatment; psoriasis treatment; vaginal moisturizer and lubricant treatment; diabetes symptoms; and hair loss prevention treatment. Brands include SHIR™, which includes CBD-integrated derma cosmetic products such as facial cream, eye serum, facial oil, sleeping mask, recovery body lotion and face glow oil; Relief & Go™, which includes muscle relaxant and pain relief cream, roll-on and spray; and SYNONY™, which is a premium cosmetic line of products containing a tailored blend of highly concentrated ingredients formulated with hemp. The company has agreements for the production and distribution of its branded products with Portugal-based **Fancystage - Unipessola Lda.** (in the European market); **Biogenesis Inc.** (in the U.S.); **Active Therapeutics Ltd.** (in the U.K. and Ireland); **Ayurcann Inc.** (in Canada); **iAmHealth Distribution UG** (in Germany); **Polyflame Europe** (in France); **Health Investment Group S.A.** (in Poland); and **Cloud 9 Switzerland LLC** (in Italy and Switzerland). Has research and license agreement with Hebrew University of Jerusalem (Yissum) for the CBD loaded liposomes technology (LPT). Also licenses and commercializes strategy work with respect to cannabinoid therapy in the veterinary field.

Directors - Iris Bincovich, founder, pres. & CEO, Israel; Ron Mayron, founder & exec. chr., Israel; Eyal Flom, corp. sec., Israel; Peter D. Bloch, Toronto, Ont.; Ralph C. L. Bossino, Gibraltar; Joshua A. Lintern, Ont.

Other Exec. Officers - Nir Avram, founder & chief tech. officer; Yoram Drucker, founder & exec. v-p, bus. devel.; Roni Kamhi, COO; Nelson Halpern, CFO

Capital Stock

	Authorized (shs.)	Outstanding (shs.)[1]
First Preferred	unlimited	nil
Second Preferred	unlimited	nil
Common	unlimited	251,806,374
Non-Voting	unlimited	nil

[1] At May 30, 2023

Major Shareholder - Tamar Innovest Limited held 10.88% interest at May 25, 2023.

Price Range - INNO/CSE

Year	Volume	High	Low	Close
2022	12,922,542	$0.85	$0.20	$0.22
2021	66,161,804	$1.65	$0.30	$0.80
2020	59,120,660	$0.36	$0.05	$0.34
2019	924,895	$0.40	$0.14	$0.16

Recent Close: $0.42

Capital Stock Changes - In August 2023, private placement of 8,409,735 units (1 common share, ½ class A warrant & ½ class B warrant) at Cdn$0.23 per unit was completed, with class A and class B warrants exercisable at Cdn$0.29 per share for three years and Cdn$0.40 per share for five years, respectively.

During 2022, common shares were issued as follows: 1,152,026 on exercise of options and 79,940 on exercise of warrants.

Wholly Owned Subsidiaries

InnoCan Pharma Ltd., Israel.
- 60% int. in **B.I. Sky Global Ltd.**, Israel.
- 100% int. in **Innocan Pharma UK Ltd.**, United Kingdom.
- 100% int. in **Synony US LLC**, United States.

Financial Statistics

Periods ended:	12m Dec. 31/22[A]		12m Dec. 31/21[A]
	US$000s	%Chg	US$000s
Operating revenue	**2,559**	**n.m.**	**196**
Cost of sales	452		75
Salaries & benefits	1,277		1,314
Research & devel. expense	1,103		1,107
General & admin expense	4,991		2,973
Stock-based compensation	967		2,164
Operating expense	**8,790**	**+15**	**7,633**
Operating income	**(6,231)**	**n.a.**	**(7,437)**
Deprec., depl. & amort.	35		43
Finance costs, gross	417		2,611
Pre-tax income	**(3,889)**	**n.a.**	**(10,091)**
Net income	**(3,889)**	**n.a.**	**(10,091)**
Net inc. for equity hldrs	**(3,764)**	**n.a.**	**(10,047)**
Net inc. for non-cont. int	**(125)**	**n.a.**	**(44)**
Cash & equivalent	4,947		11,048
Inventories	1,131		510
Accounts receivable	15		nil
Current assets	6,878		12,521
Fixed assets, net	58		39
Right-of-use assets	40		15
Total assets	**6,976**	**-45**	**12,575**
Accts. pay. & accr. liabs	413		485
Current liabilities	731		3,564
Shareholders' equity	6,225		9,011
Cash from oper. activs	**(6,067)**	**n.a.**	**(6,629)**
Cash from fin. activs	125		15,303
Cash from invest. activs	(31)		(48)
Net cash position	**4,947**	**-55**	**11,048**
	US$		US$
Earnings per share*	(0.02)		(0.05)
Cash flow per share*	(0.02)		(0.03)
	shs		shs
No. of shs. o/s*	249,728,111		248,496,145
Avg. no. of shs. o/s*	248,953,220		224,541,780
	%		%
Net profit margin	(151.97)		n.m.
Return on equity	(49.41)		n.m.
Return on assets	(35.52)		(88.47)

* Common
[A] Reported in accordance with IFRS

Latest Results

Periods ended:	3m Mar. 31/23[A]		3m Mar. 31/22[A]
	US$000s	%Chg	US$000s
Operating revenue	1,560	+500	260
Net income	(1,228)	n.a.	(729)
Net inc. for equity hldrs	(1,270)	n.a.	(651)
Net inc. for non-cont. int	42		(78)
	US$		US$
Earnings per share*	(0.00)		(0.00)

* Common
[A] Reported in accordance with IFRS

Historical Summary
(as originally stated)

Fiscal Year	Oper. Rev.	Net Inc. Bef. Disc.	EPS*
	US$000s	US$000s	US$
2022[A]	2,559	(3,889)	(0.02)
2021[A]	196	(10,091)	(0.05)
2020[A]	8	(9,953)	(0.06)
2019[A]	nil	(3,335)	(0.03)
2018[A]	nil	(1,192)	n.a.

* Common
[A] Reported in accordance with IFRS

I.43 Innovotech Inc.

Symbol - IOT **Exchange** - TSX-VEN **CUSIP** - 45772U
Head Office - L131-2011 94 St, Edmonton, AB, T6N 1H1 **Telephone** - (780) 448-0585 **Toll-free** - (888) 670-5445 **Fax** - (780) 424-0941
Website - www.innovotech.ca
Email - james.timourian@innovotech.ca
Investor Relations - Dr. James Timourian (780) 448-0585 ext. 221
Auditors - D & H Group LLP C.A., Vancouver, B.C.
Bankers - Canadian Imperial Bank of Commerce, Edmonton, Alta.
Lawyers - Parlee McLaws LLP, Edmonton, Alta.
Transfer Agents - Computershare Trust Company of Canada Inc., Calgary, Alta.
Profile - (Alta. 2001) Provides contract research services, including testing and qualifying medical devices for their susceptibility to the formation of microbial biofilms; and develops, manufactures and sells products that addresses the medical, agricultural and industrial problems caused by microbial biofilms.

Has two main businesses: contract research, and the production and sale of MBEC Assay® Kit.

The contract research business offers biofilm expertise through a contract research program to external clients such as medical device manufacturers developing products or seeking regulatory approval, oil and gas industries interested in solving pipeline corrosion problems and food manufacturers monitoring the safety of their products and procedures.

The company's core biofilm technology is the MBEC Assay® Kit, a high-throughput screening system used to determine the efficacy of antimicrobials against biofilms of a variety of microorganisms. The company's intellectual property includes a family of silver periodate antimicrobial compounds (InnovoSIL™) for medical applications, and a right to acquire a linked molecule to be tested for effective subdermal antioxidant delivery. Other products under development include Agress® and AgreGuard™, environmentally friendly seed treatments and plant sprays designed to protect crops against both bacterial and fungal infections; and BESTplus Assay™ (Biofilm Eradication Surface Testing), an in-vitro platform which is used for testing coated catheters, tubes and stents that are used in blood stream, peritoneal, spinal or urinary applications.

Also seeking investment opportunities in other consumer-focused biotech products and businesses.

Directors - Dr. James Timourian, chr. & corp. sec., Edmonton, Alta.; Dr. Craig Milne, CEO, Edmonton, Alta.; Alan C. Savage, CFO, West Vancouver, B.C.; Dr. Karen Farkas, Sherwood Park, Alta.; Bernard Grobbelaar, Edmonton, Alta.; David S. Tam, Edmonton, Alta.; Dr. Gerard Tertzakian, Edmonton, Alta.; Julie Wright, Calif.

Other Exec. Officers - Dr. Tyler Boone, COO; Dr. Patricia Nadworny, chief scientific officer

Capital Stock

	Authorized (shs.)	Outstanding (shs.)[1]
Common	unlimited	38,909,612

[1] At May 24, 2022

Major Shareholder - Alan C. Savage held 34.5% interest at Sept. 7, 2021.

Price Range - IOT/TSX-VEN

Year	Volume	High	Low	Close
2022	1,762,953	$0.23	$0.14	$0.14
2021	4,388,029	$0.25	$0.12	$0.19
2020	5,793,189	$0.30	$0.06	$0.20
2019	6,703,957	$0.12	$0.04	$0.12
2018	4,716,379	$0.17	$0.04	$0.06

Recent Close: $0.10

Financial Statistics

Periods ended:	12m Dec. 31/21[A]		12m Dec. 31/20[A]
	$000s	%Chg	$000s
Operating revenue	**1,482**	**+24**	**1,193**
Cost of sales	363		327
Research & devel. expense	35		48
General & admin expense	699		681
Stock-based compensation	46		62
Operating expense	**1,143**	**+2**	**1,117**
Operating income	**339**	**+346**	**76**
Deprec., depl. & amort.	71		18
Finance income	18		10
Finance costs, gross	4		3
Pre-tax income	**367**	**+246**	**106**
Net income	**367**	**+246**	**106**
Cash & equivalent	422		530
Inventories	60		39
Accounts receivable	369		144
Current assets	994		753
Fixed assets, net	229		70
Total assets	**1,433**	**+74**	**822**
Accts. pay. & accr. liabs	105		112
Current liabilities	219		157
Long-term debt, gross	nil		20
Long-term debt, net	nil		20
Long-term lease liabilities	37		nil
Shareholders' equity	1,177		645
Cash from oper. activs	**25**	**-86**	**175**
Cash from fin. activs	(73)		306
Cash from invest. activs	(60)		(38)
Net cash position	**422**	**-20**	**530**
Capital expenditures	(60)		(38)
	$		$
Earnings per share*	0.01		0.00
Cash flow per share*	0.00		0.00
	shs		shs
No. of shs. o/s*	38,909,612		38,284,612
Avg. no. of shs. o/s*	38,818,859		38,284,612
	%		%
Net profit margin	24.76		8.89
Return on equity	40.29		28.53
Return on assets	32.90		19.87
Foreign sales percent	96		97

* Common
[A] Reported in accordance with IFRS

Latest Results

Periods ended:	3m Mar. 31/22^A		3m Mar. 31/21^A
	$000s	%Chg	$000s
Operating revenue	277	-10	309
Net income	(32)	n.a.	22
	$		$
Earnings per share*	(0.00)		0.00

* Common
^A Reported in accordance with IFRS

Historical Summary
(as originally stated)

Fiscal Year	Oper. Rev.	Net Inc. Bef. Disc.	EPS*
	$000s	$000s	$
2021^A	1,482	367	0.01
2020^A	1,193	106	0.00
2019^A	986	(49)	(0.00)
2018^A	827	(128)	(0.00)
2017^A	990	753	0.02

* Common
^A Reported in accordance with IFRS

I.44 Inovalis Real Estate Investment Trust

Symbol - INO.UN **Exchange** - TSX **CUSIP** - 45780E
Head Office - 1100-151 Yonge St, Toronto, ON, M5C 2W7 **Telephone** - (647) 775-8431
Website - www.inovalisreit.com
Email - khalil.hankach@inovalis.com
Investor Relations - Khalil Hankach 33-1-5643-3313
Auditors - Ernst & Young Audit C.A., Paris, France
Lawyers - Goodmans LLP, Toronto, Ont.
Transfer Agents - TSX Trust Company, Toronto, Ont.
Managers - Inovalis S.A., Paris, France
Profile - (Ont. 2013) Invests in office properties in France, Germany and Spain.

The trust holds a leasehold interest in 13 office properties in France (6), Germany (6) and Spain totaling 1,540,218 sq. ft. of gross leasable area. The manager of the trust and its properties is **Inovalis S.A.**, a French-based real estate investment manager with $7 billion of assets under management. Inovalis S.A. has granted the trust the first right to acquire properties it manages or owns.

Recent Merger and Acquisition Activity

Status: completed **Revised:** Dec. 23, 2022
UPDATE: The transaction was completed. PREVIOUS: Inovalis Real Estate Investment Trust agreed to sell its 95,900-sq.-ft. office property in Courbevoie, France, for €27,200,000 (Cdn$42,310,000). The transaction was expected to be completed in 2021. Mar. 31, 2022 - An extension to the commitment to sell was agreed on with the buyers for a sale by Dec. 31, 2022.

Status: completed **Announced:** Mar. 31, 2022
Inovalis Real Estate Investment Trust acquired Delgado property, a 119,922-sq.-ft. office building, in the Alcobenda area of Madrid, Spain, for €31,200,000 (Cdn$43,100,000), including acquisition costs, with was financed through a five-year mortgage.

Status: completed **Announced:** Mar. 28, 2022
Inovalis Real Estate Investment Trust acquired the GAIA property, a 119,499-sq.-ft. office building near Paris, France, for €40,900,000 (Cdn$56,700,000), including €3,700,000 (Cdn$5,200,000) acquisition costs and rental guarantee. The acquisition was financed by a five-year mortgage loan.

Trustees - Jean-Daniel Cohen, chr., Luxembourg; Michael Bonneveld, Elora, Ont.; Marc Manasterski, Lebanon; Laetitia Pacaud, Toronto, Ont.; Robert Waxman, Toronto, Ont.
Other Exec. Officers - Stéphane J. Amine, pres. & CEO; Khalil Hankach, interim CFO, chief invest. officer & corp. sec.

Capital Stock

	Authorized (shs.)	Outstanding (shs.)[1]
Trust Unit	unlimited	32,781,062[2]
Special Voting Unit	unlimited	938,036

[1] At Mar. 31, 2023
[2] At May 12, 2023.

Trust Unit - The trust will endeavour to make initial monthly cash distributions equal to approximately 93% of adjusted funds from operations. One vote per trust unit.
Special Voting Unit - Issued to holders of common shares, interest bearing notes and non-interest bearing notes of subsidiary CanCorpEurope S.A. Each special voting unit entitles the holder to a number of votes at unitholder meetings equal to the number of trust units into which the common shares and notes are exchangeable.
Normal Course Issuer Bid - The company plans to make normal course purchases of up to 3,047,058 trust units representing 10% of the public float. The bid commenced on May 25, 2023, and expires on May 24, 2024.
Major Shareholder - Widely held at Mar. 15, 2023.

Price Range - INO.UN/TSX

Year	Volume	High	Low	Close
2022	32,211,262	$10.43	$3.32	$3.77
2021	15,821,148	$10.26	$8.83	$9.61
2020	19,205,433	$11.10	$3.39	$8.93
2019	11,696,605	$11.26	$9.31	$10.66
2018	6,494,146	$10.60	$9.12	$9.45

Recent Close: $3.35
Capital Stock Changes - During 2022, 190,890 common shares were issued under distribution reinvestment plan.

Dividends

INO.UN unit Ra $0.4125 pa M est. Oct. 17, 2022**
Prev. Rate: $0.825 est. June 17, 2013
$0.307◆ July 15/21
Paid in 2023: $0.309375 2022: $0.721875 2021: $0.825 + $0.307◆
** Reinvestment Option ◆ Special

Wholly Owned Subsidiaries

Metropolitan LLC, United States.

Subsidiaries

89.18% int. in **CanCorp Europe S.A.**, Luxembourg.
- 100% int. in **Arcueil SI General Partner S.A.R.L.**, Luxembourg.
- 100% int. in **Arcueil S.C.S.**, Luxembourg.
- 100% int. in **Cancorp Cologne 2 S.A.R.L.**, Germany.
- 50% int. in **CanCorp Duisburg S.A.R.L.**, Germany.
- 94.9% int. in **Cancorp Trio 1**, Germany.
- 94.9% int. in **Cancorp Trio 3**, Germany.
- 94.9% int. in **Cancorp Trio 2**, Germany.
- 100% int. in **Cancorp Vegacinco SLU**, Spain.
- 100% int. in **CanCorpCologne S.A.R.L.**, Luxembourg.
- 100% int. in **INOPCI1**, France.
  - 100% int. in **Baldi S.C.I.**, France.
  - 50% int. in **Delizy S.C.I.**, France.
  - 99.99% int. in **Gaia Nanterre S.C.I.**, France.
  - 99% int. in **Metropolitain S.C.I.**, France.
  - 99.9% int. in **SCI Lenine Arcueil**, France.
  - 100% int. in **Sablière S.C.I.**, France.
  - 100% int. in **Véronèse S.C.I.**, France.
- 50% int. in **TFI Cancorp Isenburg S.A.R.L. ("Neu Isenberg")**, Germany.
- 50% int. in **TFI Cancorp Kosching S.A.R.L**, Luxembourg, Luxembourg.
- 50% int. in **TFI CanCorp Stuttgart S.A.R.L.**, Luxembourg.
- 100% int. in **Walpur Four S.A.S**, Luxembourg.

Financial Statistics

Periods ended:	12m Dec. 31/22^A		12m Dec. 31/21^A1
	$000s	%Chg	$000s
Total revenue	**30,902**	**-10**	**34,168**
Rental operating expense	9,415		9,585
General & admin. expense	6,974		8,392
Other operating expense	95		682
Operating expense	**16,484**	**-12**	**18,659**
Operating income	**14,418**	**-7**	**15,509**
Investment income	(3,585)		(2,316)
Finance income	6,705		3,702
Finance costs, gross	5,766		7,492
Pre-tax income	**(39,757)**	**n.a.**	**30,889**
Income taxes	(2,780)		590
Net income	**(36,977)**	**n.a.**	**30,299**
Net inc. for equity hldrs	**(36,854)**	**n.a.**	**30,333**
Net inc. for non-cont. int	**(123)**	**n.a.**	**(34)**
Cash & equivalent	45,176		76,627
Accounts receivable	8,227		9,368
Current assets	62,419		90,323
Long-term investments	55,693		64,327
Income-producing props	437,422		427,631
Property interests, net	437,422		427,631
Total assets	**561,107**	**-4**	**587,245**
Accts. pay. & accr. liabs	18,960		11,248
Current liabilities	70,104		54,897
Long-term debt, gross	138,084		102,081
Long-term debt, net	96,499		48,996
Long-term lease liabilities	102,121		106,351
Shareholders' equity	286,979		344,786
Non-controlling interest	1,198		1,299
Cash from oper. activs	**21,427**	**n.a.**	**(7,915)**
Cash from fin. activs	9,704		(97,541)
Cash from invest. activs	(60,471)		106,614
Net cash position	**45,176**	**-41**	**76,627**
Increase in property	(1,955)		(958)
Decrease in property	39,386		103,173
	$		$
Earnings per share*	(1.13)		0.94
Cash flow per share*	0.66		(0.24)
Funds from opers. per sh.*	0.51		0.47
Adj. funds from opers. per sh.*	0.52		0.42
Cash divd. per share*	0.69		0.83
Extra divd. - cash*	nil		0.31
Total divd. per share*	**0.69**		**1.13**
	shs		shs
No. of shs. o/s*	32,778,699		32,587,809
Avg. no. of shs. o/s*	32,672,428		32,428,247
	%		%
Net profit margin	(119.66)		88.68
Return on equity	(11.67)		8.43
Return on assets	(5.51)		5.79
Foreign sales percent	100		100

* Trust Unit
^A Reported in accordance with IFRS
[1] Amended.

Latest Results

Periods ended:	3m Mar. 31/23^A		3m Mar. 31/22^A
	$000s	%Chg	$000s
Total revenue	8,806	+37	6,448
Net income	1,618	-24	2,136
Net inc. for equity hldrs	1,622	-23	2,094
Net inc. for non-cont. int	(4)		42
	$		$
Earnings per share*	0.05		0.06

* Trust Unit
^A Reported in accordance with IFRS

Historical Summary
(as originally stated)

Fiscal Year	Total Rev.	Net Inc. Bef. Disc.	EPS*
	$000s	$000s	$
2022^A	30,902	(36,977)	(1.13)
2021^A	34,168	30,299	0.94
2020^A	35,708	18,213	0.62
2019^A	33,490	36,531	1.51
2018^A	32,682	22,296	0.97

* Trust Unit
^A Reported in accordance with IFRS

I.45 Inspire Semiconductor Holdings Inc.

Symbol - INSP **Exchange** - TSX-VEN **CUSIP** - 39483L
Head Office - 11305 Four Points Dr, Unit 2-250, Austin, TX, United States, 78726 **Telephone** - (415) 225-5952
Website - inspiresemi.com
Email - jkennedy@inspiresemi.com
Investor Relations - John B. Kennedy (415) 225-5952

Auditors - Davidson & Company LLP C.A., Vancouver, B.C.
Transfer Agents - Odyssey Trust Company
Employees - 12 at July 31, 2022
Profile - (B.C. 2021) Developing accelerator chips for high performance computing (HPC), artificial intelligence (AI) and blockchain applications.

The company is developing the Thunderbird Accelerated Computing Solution, which is based on an array of thousands of custom-designed 64-bit RISC-V central processing unit (CPU) cores, tightly integrated with memory and a proprietary high-speed mesh network fabric that removes crucial bottlenecks and is compatible with an established software ecosystem. Thunderbird was expected to enter commercial production in the second half of 2023.

The HPC applications include engineering, scientific, genomics/life sciences, climate modeling, energy, financial services, digital twins, and many other applications broadly called simulation. The AI applications include fraud prevention, disease mapping, smart assistants, manufacturing robots, predictive analytics, recommendation engines, autonomous vehicles and personalized learning. The blockchain applications include cryptocurrency mining, smart contracts, finance/insurance and supply chain management.

The company conducts its own research and development from operations in Austin, Tex., and manufacturing is outsourced to third parties.

Recent Merger and Acquisition Activity

Status: completed **Revised:** Sept. 20, 2022
UPDATE: The transaction was completed. PREVIOUS: Greenfield Acquisition Corp. entered into a non-binding letter of intent with Inspire Semiconductor, Inc. to complete a business combination intended to constitute Greenfield's Qualifying Transaction. Austin, Tex.-based Inspire is a chip design company that develops solutions for blockchain, high performance computing, artificial intelligence and other computer-intensive applications. May 12, 2022 - Greenfield and Inspire entered into a definitive agreement whereby Inspire would merge with Greenfield Subco Inc., a wholly owned Delaware subsidiary of Greenfield, Inspire shareholders would receive 158,141,787 common shares of Greenfield at a deemed price of 11¢ per share, and Greenfield would change its name to Inspire Semiconductor Holdings Inc.

Predecessor Detail - Name changed from Greenfield Acquisition Corp., Sept. 20, 2022, following Qualifying Transaction three-cornered amalgamation with Inspire Semiconductor, Inc. constituting a reverse takeover acquisition by Inspire.

Directors - James J. Hickman, exec. chr., Puerto Rico; William R. (Ron) Van Dell, CEO, Whitefish, Mont.; Alexander Gray, pres. & chief tech. officer, Austin, Tex.; Mitchell Jacobson, Austin, Tex.; Jeff R. Schneider, Nashville, Tenn.; Muneeb Yusuf, Toronto, Ont.

Other Exec. Officers - Thomas Fedorko, COO; John B. Kennedy, CFO; Douglas (Doug) Norton, chief mktg. officer; James (Jim) O'Connor, v-p, eng.; Andrew T. Hunter, corp. sec.

Capital Stock

	Authorized (shs.)	Outstanding (shs.)[1]
Subord. Vtg.	unlimited	51,006,913
Proportinate Vtg.	unlimited	1,293,085

[1] At Sept. 22, 2022

Proportionate Voting - Convertible into subordinate voting shares on a 100-for-1 basis. 100 votes per share.

Subordinate Voting - One vote per share.

Major Shareholder - Alexander Gray held 26.75% interest at Sept. 20, 2022.

Price Range - INSP/TSX-VEN

Year	Volume	High	Low	Close
2022............	1,226,549	$0.70	$0.15	$0.17
2021............	35,000	$0.12	$0.11	$0.11

Recent Close: $0.07

Capital Stock Changes - Pursuant to the Qualifying Transaction reverse takeover acquisition of Inspire Semiconductor, Inc. (ISI) on Sept. 20, 2022, common shares were redesignated as subordinate voting shares and a new class of proportionate voting shares was created and 31,006,913 subordinate voting shares and 1,293,085 proportionate voting shares were issued to ISI shareholders.

Wholly Owned Subsidiaries

Inspire Semiconductor, Inc., Austin, Tex.

Financial Statistics

Periods ended:	12m Dec. 31/21[A1]		37w Dec. 31/20[A2]
	US$000s	%Chg	US$000s
Salaries & benefits..........................	901		300
Research & devel. expense.............	1,908		1,019
General & admin expense...............	319		220
Stock-based compensation............	312		484
Operating expense.......................	**3,440**	**n.a.**	**2,023**
Operating income........................	**(3,440)**	**n.a.**	**(2,023)**
Deprec., depl. & amort....................	468		52
Finance costs, gross.......................	336		249
Pre-tax income............................	**(4,917)**	**n.a.**	**(2,253)**
Net income..................................	**(4,917)**	**n.a.**	**(2,253)**
Cash & equivalent..........................	4,535		101
Current assets................................	4,576		129
Fixed assets, net.............................	67		147
Intangibles, net...............................	876		990
Total assets.................................	**5,519**	**+336**	**1,266**
Accts. pay. & accr. liabs.................	745		1,162
Current liabilities...........................	829		2,063
Long-term debt, gross......................	nil		904
Long-term debt, net.........................	nil		904
Long-term lease liabilities...............	nil		68
Preferred share equity....................	11,063		nil
Shareholders' equity.......................	4,690		(1,769)
Cash from oper. activs..................	**(3,520)**	**n.a.**	**(358)**
Cash from fin. activs.......................	8,228		1,460
Cash from invest. activs..................	(274)		(1,000)
Net cash position.........................	**4,535**	**n.m.**	**101**
Capital expenditures.......................	nil		(10)
	US$		US$
Earnings per share*........................	(0.41)		(0.19)
Cash flow per share*.......................	(0.30)		(0.03)
	shs		shs
No. of shs. o/s................................	n.a.		n.a.
Avg. no. of shs. o/s*........................	11,875,100		11,875,100
	%		%
Net profit margin............................	n.a.		...
Return on equity.............................	n.m.		...
Return on assets............................	(135.03)		...

* Subord. Vtg.
[A] Reported in accordance with IFRS
[1] Results reflect the Sept. 20, 2022, Qualifying Transaction reverse takeover acquisition of Insipre Semiconductor, Inc.
[2] Results pertain to Inspire Semiconductor, Inc.

I.46 InsuraGuest Technologies Inc.

Symbol - ISGI **Exchange -** TSX-VEN **CUSIP -** 457800
Head Office - 1140-625 Howe St, Vancouver, BC, V6C 2T6 **Telephone -** (604) 685-4745 **Fax -** (604) 685-9182
Website - www.insuraguest.com
Email - loganbanderson@outlook.com
Investor Relations - Logan B. Anderson (604) 685-4745
Auditors - MNP LLP C.A., Vancouver, B.C.
Transfer Agents - Endeavor Trust Corporation, Vancouver, B.C.
Profile - (B.C. 2010) Develops and markets software-as-a-service-based insurtech (insurance and technology) platform that delivers digitally embedded, opt-in and subscription-based digital insurance packages for the vacation rental, hotels, sports and ticketed events sectors.

Solutions consist of Vacation Rental Insurance for owners and guests, and Hospitality Insurance for hotels and guests, which both include no-fault accidental medical protection for guests, vacation rental/hotel property and contents protection, and vacation rental/hotel theft protection; Medical Injury Insurance for sports and activities, which includes no-fault accidental medical protection for all participants with option to upgrade for additional coverage; and Travel Insurance, which includes coverages for trip cancellation and interruptions caused by weather, natural disaster, strike, illness, traffic accident and job reasons, coverages for losses caused by accident, sickness, evacuation and pre-existing medical conditions, and coverages for losses caused by baggage delay, loss and theft.

Also provides a fully automated agency/broker software program that allows agents and brokers to sign up instantly online, enabling them to become channels to sell the company's products to their own customers.

Predecessor Detail - Name changed from Manado Gold Corp., Jan. 23, 2020, pursuant to the reverse takeover acquisition of InsuraGuest Inc.; basis 1 new for 2 old shs.

Directors - Douglas K. Anderson, chr. & CEO, Salt Lake City, Utah; Logan B. Anderson, CFO, North Vancouver, B.C.; Christopher J. Panos, v-p, sales & mktg., Salt Lake City, Utah; David K. (Dave) Ryan, v-p, corp. commun. & corp. sec., Langley, B.C.; Charles J. Cayias, pres., InsuraGuest Agency, Salt Lake City, Utah; Sean C. O'Neill, Vernon, B.C.; R. Hall Risk, Vancouver, B.C.

Other Exec. Officers - Reed Wright, pres.; James C. Kilduff, chief insurance officer; Tony Sansone, v-p, fin. & chief opers. officer; Alexander Walker, corp. counsel

Capital Stock

	Authorized (shs.)	Outstanding (shs.)[1]
Preferred	unlimited	nil
Common	unlimited	59,304,675

[1] At Nov. 28, 2022

Major Shareholder - Douglas K. Anderson held 15.92% interest at May 24, 2022.

Price Range - ISGI/TSX-VEN

Year	Volume	High	Low	Close
2022............	8,167,773	$0.27	$0.05	$0.06
2021............	26,655,675	$0.45	$0.17	$0.20
2020............	8,172,592	$0.40	$0.10	$0.23
2019............	29,000	$0.10	$0.09	$0.09
2018............	2,854,980	$0.30	$0.07	$0.07

Consolidation: 1-for-2 cons. in Feb. 2020
Recent Close: $0.03

Capital Stock Changes - During fiscal 2022, common shares were issued as follows: 5,799,731 on exercise of warrants and 700,000 on exercise of options.

Wholly Owned Subsidiaries

ISG Acquisition Corp., Nev.
- 100% int. in **InsuraGuest Inc.**, Salt Lake City, Utah.

ISG Sports, LLC, Nev.
InsuraGuest Insurance Agency, LLC, United States.
InsuraGuest Risk Purchasing Group, LLC, United States.
Insure The People, LLC, United States.
MDO Mining Corp., B.C. Inactive.

Financial Statistics

Periods ended:	12m June 30/22[A]		12m June 30/21[oA]
	US$000s	%Chg	US$000s
Operating revenue.......................	**345**	**+252**	**98**
Cost of sales..................................	96		22
General & admin expense...............	1,492		1,136
Stock-based compensation............	142		435
Operating expense.......................	**1,730**	**+9**	**1,593**
Operating income........................	**(1,385)**	**n.a.**	**(1,495)**
Deprec., depl. & amort....................	25		22
Pre-tax income............................	**(1,410)**	**n.a.**	**(1,506)**
Net income..................................	**(1,410)**	**n.a.**	**(1,506)**
Cash & equivalent..........................	603		870
Accounts receivable.......................	48		32
Current assets................................	664		1,019
Intangibles, net...............................	56		81
Total assets.................................	**720**	**-37**	**1,136**
Accts. pay. & accr. liabs.................	195		149
Current liabilities...........................	266		205
Shareholders' equity.......................	454		931
Cash from oper. activs..................	**(1,094)**	**n.a.**	**(1,804)**
Cash from fin. activs.......................	832		2,235
Cash from invest. activs..................	nil		11
Net cash position.........................	**568**	**-35**	**870**
Capital disposals............................	nil		11
	US$		US$
Earnings per share*........................	(0.02)		(0.04)
Cash flow per share*.......................	(0.02)		(0.04)
	shs		shs
No. of shs. o/s*..............................	59,304,675		52,804,944
Avg. no. of shs. o/s*........................	58,521,783		42,421,546
	%		%
Net profit margin............................	(408.70)		n.m.
Return on equity.............................	(203.61)		n.m.
Return on assets............................	(151.94)		n.a.

* Common
[o] Restated
[A] Reported in accordance with IFRS

Latest Results

Periods ended:	3m Sept. 30/22[A]		3m Sept. 30/21[oA]
	US$000s	%Chg	US$000s
Operating revenue..........................	81	+98	41
Net income.....................................	(181)	n.a.	(574)
	US$		US$
Earnings per share*........................	(0.00)		(0.01)

* Common
[o] Restated
[A] Reported in accordance with IFRS

Historical Summary
(as originally stated)

Fiscal Year	Oper. Rev.	Net Inc. Bef. Disc.	EPS*
	US$000s	US$000s	US$
2022[A]	345	(1,410)	(0.02)
2021[A]	156	(1,506)	(0.04)
2020[A1]	49	(4,070)	(0.15)
	$000s	$000s	$
2019[A2]	nil	(469)	(0.06)
2018[A]	nil	(349)	(0.06)

* Common
[A] Reported in accordance with IFRS
[1] Results reflect the Feb. 26, 2020, reverse takeover acquisition of InsuraGuest Inc.
[2] Results for fiscal 2019 and prior fiscal years pertain to Manado Gold Corp.
Note: Adjusted throughout for 1-for-2 cons. in Feb. 2020

I.47 Intact Financial Corporation*

Symbol - IFC **Exchange** - TSX **CUSIP** - 45823T
Head Office - 1500-700 University Ave, Toronto, ON, M5G 0A1 **Telephone** - (416) 341-1464 **Toll-free** - (877) 341-1464 **Fax** - (416) 941-5320
Website - www.intactfc.com
Email - maida.sit@intact.net
Investor Relations - Maida Sit (416) 341-1464 ext. 45153
Auditors - Ernst & Young LLP C.A., Toronto, Ont.
Transfer Agents - Computershare Trust Company of Canada Inc., Toronto, Ont.
FP500 Revenue Ranking - 25
Employees - 28,500 at Dec. 31, 2022
Profile - (Can. 1982) Underwrites and distributes property and casualty (P&C) insurance and specialty insurance solutions in Canada, the U.S., the U.K., Ireland and Europe.

Canada

Offers automobile, home and commercial insurance products to individuals and businesses across Canada which are distributed through a wide network of brokers, including wholly owned **Brokerlink Inc.**, directly to consumers by telephone or online, affinity groups and a managing general agent (MGA) platform. Brands include Intact Insurance, RSA, belairdirect (direct-to-consumer brand), Johnson Insurance (affinity insurance brand), Intact Prestige, and MGAs Intact Public Entities and Coast Underwriters.

Personal Automobile - Provides coverage to customers for their vehicles including accident benefits, third party property and physical damage. Coverage is also available for motor homes, recreational vehicles, motorcycles, snowmobiles and all terrain vehicles.

Personal Property - Offers customers protection for their homes and contents from fire, theft, vandalism, water damage and other damages as well as personal liability coverage. Property coverage is also provided to tenants, condominium owners, non-owner-occupied residences and seasonal residences. Also provides travel insurance.

Commercial Insurance (including specialty lines) - These insurance products are marketed mainly to businesses and consist of commercial property insurance, which covers the physical assets of a business; liability coverages, which include commercial general liability, product liability, professional liability as well as cyber coverage; and commercial vehicle insurance, which covers commercial automobiles, fleets, garage operations, light trucks, public vehicles and the specific needs of the sharing economy.

Canadian operations also include wholly owned **On Side Restoration Services Ltd.**, which provides repair and restoration services to damaged residential, commercial and government properties.

U.K. and International

Provides personal, commercial and specialty insurance solutions to individuals and businesses across the U.K., Ireland and Europe, as well as internationally through the company's global network. Personal insurance products are provided to customers in the U.K. and Ireland for their home, motor, pet and other insurance needs. Commercial lines include a broad range of general insurance, specialty lines and risk management solutions for businesses and other organizations in the U.K., Ireland, France, Belgium, Spain and the Netherlands. Products are distributed through a network of affinity partners and brokers or directly to consumers under various brands including RSA and direct-to-consumer brands MORE THAN and 123.ie.

U.S.

Provides specialty insurance products and services primarily to small- and medium-sized businesses under the Intact Insurance Specialty Solutions brand in the U.S. Solutions target industries including accident and health, technology, ocean and inland marine, builder's risk, entertainment, financial services and financial institutions, as well as product/customer groups such as specialty property, surety, tuition reimbursement, management liability, cyber and environmental. Solutions are distributed through independent agencies, regional and national brokers, wholesalers and managing general agencies.

Corporate and Other

Consists of investment management, treasury and capital management, corporate reinsurance and other corporate activities.

Investment Management - The company's investment portfolio is mostly managed by wholly owned **Intact Investment Management Inc.** (IIM). IIM also provides investment management services to majority of the company's employee pension plans and certain third parties. At Dec. 31, 2022, investments totaled $35.6 billion.

On Feb. 27, 2023, the company announced that the respective trustees of its two major U.K. defined benefit pension plans (Royal Insurance Group pension scheme and Sal pension scheme) had entered into an agreement with **Pension Insurance Corporation plc** (PIC), a specialist insurer of defined benefit pension schemes, for a bulk purchase of annuity buy-in insurance contracts with respect to £6.5 billion of pension plan liabilities of wholly owned **Royal & Sun Alliance Insurance Limited** and **RSA Insurance Group Limited** (collectively, RSA UK). The buy-ins fully insured the defined benefit liabilities of RSA UK to PIC. The transaction transferred substantially all remaining economic and demographic risks associated with the pension schemes and eliminated the company's obligation to contribute £75,000,000 per year to the schemes and released £150,000,000 of capital. The company would facilitate this transaction through an upfront contribution to the two pension schemes of £500,000,000 and by transferring the schemes' assets to PIC.

On Jan. 1, 2023, wholly owned **Ascentus Insurance Ltd.** was amalgamated into wholly owned **Intact Insurance Company**.

On Sept. 20, 2022, wholly owned **Regent Bidco Limited** was liquidated.

Recent Merger and Acquisition Activity

Status: completed **Revised:** Aug. 1, 2022
UPDATE: The transaction was completed for US$186,000,000. PREVIOUS: Intact Financial Corporation, through Intact Insurance Group USA LLC (dba Intact Insurance Specialty Solutions), agreed to acquire specialty managing general agent Highland Insurance Solutions, LLC, the U.S. construction division of Tokio Marine Highland (TMH), from Tokio Marine Kiln (TMK). Terms were not disclosed. TMK is owned by Tokio Marine Holdings, Inc. The transaction was expected to close in the second half of 2022.

Status: completed **Revised:** July 7, 2022
UPDATE: The transaction was completed for $175,000,000. PREVIOUS: RSA Insurance Group Ltd., wholly owned by Intact Financial Corporation, agreed to sell its 50% interest in Royal & Sun Alliance Insurance (Middle East) B.S.C. (RSA Middle East) to National Life & General Insurance Company, majority owned by Oman International Development and Investment Co. SAOG (OMINVEST). Terms were not disclosed. RSA Middle East, a joint venture of RSA Insurance Group Ltd., with majority shareholding, and regional shareholders in the Middle East, is a provider of property and casualty insurance with operations in Bahrain, U.A.E., Oman and the Kingdom of Saudi Arabia. It operates as local publicly listed companies in Oman, under Al Ahlia Insurance Company, and in Saudi Arabia, under Al Alamiya For Cooperative Insurance Company. The transaction was expected to close by Sept. 30, 2022.

Status: completed **Revised:** May 2, 2022
UPDATE: The transaction was completed. PREVIOUS: Intact Financial Corporation and Tryg A/S, through jointly owned Scandi JV Co 2 A/S, agreed to sell Codan Forsikring A/S's Danish business to Copenhagen, Denmark-based Alm. Brand A/S for DKr12.6 billion (Cdn$2.52 billion). Intact would receive 50% of the proceeds. The jointly owned Danish operations were acquired as part of Intact and Tryg's acquisition of RSA Insurance Group plc. The transaction was expected to close in the first half of 2022 following the transfer by Intact and Tryg of the Danish business of Codan Forsikring into a Danish legal entity incorporated for such purpose.

Predecessor Detail - Name changed from ING Canada Inc., May 13, 2009.

Directors - William L. (Bill) Young, chr., Lexington, Mass.; Charles J. G. Brindamour, CEO, Toronto, Ont.; Emmanuel Clarke, Horgen, Switzerland; Janet De Silva, Toronto, Ont.; Michael Katchen, Toronto, Ont.; Stephani E. Kingsmill, Toronto, Ont.; Jane E. Kinney, Toronto, Ont.; Robert G. Leary, North Palm Beach, Fla.; Sylvie Paquette, Québec, Qué.; Dr. Stuart J. Russell, Berkeley, Calif.; Dr. Indira V. Samarasekera, Vancouver, B.C.; Frederick Singer, Great Falls, Va.; Carolyn A. Wilkins, Ottawa, Ont.

Other Exec. Officers - Patrick Barbeau, exec. v-p & COO; Frédéric Cotnoir, exec. v-p, chief legal officer & corp. sec.; Anne Fortin, exec. v-p, direct distrib. & chief mktg. & commun. officer; Darren Godfrey, exec. v-p, global specialty lines; Louis Marcotte, exec. v-p & CFO; Benoit Morissette, exec. v-p & chief risk & actuarial officer; Werner Muehlemann, exec. v-p & man. dir., Intact Investment Management Inc.; Carla Smith, exec. v-p & chief HR, strategy & climate officer; Maude Choquette, sr. v-p & grp. chief internal auditor; Louis Gagnon, CEO, Canada; T. Michael (Mike) Miller, CEO, global specialty lines; Ken Norgrove, CEO, RSA U.K. & intl.; Robin Richardson, deputy sr. v-p & grp. chief compliance officer

Capital Stock

	Authorized (shs.)	Outstanding (shs.)[1]
Class A Preferred	unlimited	
Series 1		10,000,000
Series 3		10,000,000
Series 5		6,000,000
Series 6		6,000,000
Series 7		10,000,000
Series 9		6,000,000
Series 11		6,000,000
Limited Recourse Capital Notes		n.a
Series 1		300,000
Common	unlimited	175,256,968

[1] At Aug. 2, 2023

Class A Preferred - Issuable in series. Non-voting except for specific situations.

Series 1 - Entitled to fixed non-cumulative preferential annual dividends of $1.21025 per share payable quarterly to Dec. 31, 2027, and thereafter at a rate reset every five years equal to the five-year Government of Canada yield plus 1.72%. Redeemable on Dec. 31, 2027, and on December 31 every five years thereafter at $25 per share plus accrued dividends. Convertible at the holder's option, on Dec. 31, 2027, and on December 31 every five years thereafter, into floating rate class A preferred series 2 shares on a share-for-share basis, subject to certain conditions. The series 2 shares would pay a quarterly dividend equal to the 90-day Canadian Treasury bill rate plus 1.72%.

Series 3 - Entitled to fixed non-cumulative preferential annual dividends of $0.86425 per share payable quarterly to Sept. 30, 2026, and thereafter at a rate reset every five years equal to the five-year Government of Canada yield plus 2.66%. Redeemable on Sept. 30, 2026, and on September 30 every five years thereafter at $25 per share plus accrued dividends. Convertible at the holder's option, on Sept. 30, 2026, and on September 30 every five years thereafter, into floating rate class A preferred series 4 shares on a share-for-share basis, subject to certain conditions. The series 4 shares would pay a quarterly dividend equal to the 90-day Canadian Treasury bill rate plus 2.66%.

Series 5 - Entitled to fixed non-cumulative preferential annual dividends of $1.30 per share payable quarterly. Redeemable at $26 per share and declining by 25¢ per share on June 30 annually to June 30, 2026, and at $25 per share thereafter.

Series 6 - Entitled to fixed non-cumulative preferential annual dividends of $1.325 per share payable quarterly. Redeemable at $26 per share and declining by 25¢ per share on September 30 annually to Sept. 30, 2026, and at $25 per share thereafter.

Series 7 - Entitled to fixed non-cumulative preferential annual dividends of $1.503 per share payable quarterly to June 30, 2028, and thereafter at a rate reset every five years equal to the five-year Government of Canada yield plus 2.55%. Redeemable on June 30, 2028, and on June 30 every five years thereafter at $25 per share plus accrued dividends. Convertible at the holder's option, on June 30, 2028, and on June 30 every five years thereafter, into floating rate class A preferred series 8 shares on a share-for-share basis, subject to certain conditions. The series 8 shares would pay a quarterly dividend equal to the 90-day Canadian Treasury bill rate plus 2.55%.

Series 9 - Entitled to fixed non-cumulative preferential annual dividends of $1.35 per share payable quarterly. Redeemable at $26 per share on or after Mar. 31, 2025, and declining by 25¢ per share annually to Mar. 31, 2029, and at $25 per share thereafter.

Series 11 - Entitled to fixed non-cumulative preferential annual dividends of $1.3125 per share payable quarterly. Redeemable at $26 per share on or after Mar. 31, 2027, and declining by 25¢ per share annually to Mar. 31, 2031, and at $25 per share thereafter.

Limited Recourse Capital Notes (LRCN) - Notes with recourse limited to assets held in a consolidated trust. **Series 1** - Bear interest at 7.338% per annum until June 30, 2028, and thereafter at an annual rate reset every five years equal to the five-year Government of Canada yield plus 3.95% until maturity on June 30, 2083. Trust assets consist of non-cumulative five-year reset class A series 12 preferred shares.

Common - One vote per share.

Normal Course Issuer Bid - The company plans to make normal course purchases of up to 5,257,709 common shares representing 3% of the total outstanding. The bid commenced on Feb. 17, 2023, and expires on Feb. 16, 2024.

Major Shareholder - Caisse de dépôt et placement du Québec held 10.2% interest at Mar. 15, 2023.

Price Range - IFC/TSX

Year	Volume	High	Low	Close
2022	95,883,811	$209.57	$159.89	$194.91
2021	67,892,949	$178.28	$140.50	$164.42
2020	88,078,150	$157.74	$104.81	$150.72
2019	65,605,643	$140.96	$96.37	$140.42
2018	57,219,148	$109.17	$91.65	$99.19

Recent Close: $194.68

Capital Stock Changes - In March 2023, 300,000 class A series 12 preferred shares were issued in conjunction with issuance of $300,000,000 of limited recourse capital notes series 1 priced at $1,000 per note.

In March 2022, bought deal public offering of 6,000,000 class A series 11 preferred shares was completed at $25 per share. Also during 2022, 824,990 common shares were repurchased under a Normal Course Issuer Bid.

Dividends

IFC com Ra $4.40 pa Q est. Mar. 31, 2023
Prev. Rate: $4.00 est. Mar. 31, 2022
Prev. Rate: $3.64 est. Dec. 31, 2021
Prev. Rate: $3.32 est. Mar. 31, 2020
IFC.PR.A pfd A ser 1 red. exch. Adj. Ra $1.21025 pa Q est. Mar. 31, 2023
IFC.PR.C pfd A ser 3 red. exch. Adj. Ra $0.86425 pa Q est. Dec. 31, 2021
IFC.PR.E pfd A ser 5 red. Ra $1.30 pa Q
IFC.PR.F pfd A ser 6 red. Ra $1.325 pa Q
IFC.PR.G pfd A ser 7 red. exch. Adj. Ra $1.503 pa Q est. Sept. 30, 2023
IFC.PR.I pfd A ser 9 red. Ra $1.35 pa Q
IFC.PR.K pfd A ser 11 red. Ra $1.3125 pa Q
Listed Mar 15/22.
$0.3848i............... June 30/22
pfd A ser 4 red. exch. Fltg. Ra pa Q
Delisted Oct 1/21.
$0.174485............ Sept. 30/21 $0.170345........ June 30/21
$0.170693............ Mar. 31/21
Paid in 2023: n.a. 2022: n.a. 2021: $0.515523

i Initial Payment

Long-Term Debt - Outstanding at Dec. 31, 2022:

Credit facility due 2027	$2,000,000
4.13% hybrid notes due 2081[1]	247,000,000
Commercial paper	135,000,000
Other debt	7,000,000
Guaranteed subordinated debt:	
8.95% US$ bonds due 2029	17,000,000
5.13% GBP notes due 2045	285,000,000
Medium-term notes:	
1.21% due 2024	374,000,000
3.69% due 2025	299,000,000
3.77% due 2026	249,000,000
2.85% due 2027	424,000,000
2.18% due 2028	373,000,000
1.93% due 2030	299,000,000
5.46% due 2032	669,000,000
6.4% due 2039	248,000,000
5.16% due 2042	249,000,000
2.95% due 2050	298,000,000
3.77% due 2053	248,000,000
6.2% due 2061	99,000,000
	4,522,000,000

[1] Bear interest at a fixed annual rate of 4.13% until Mar. 31, 2026, and thereafter at a rate reset every five years until maturity on Mar. 31, 2081, at a fixed interest rate per annum equal to the Government of Canada yield plus 3.196%. The notes automatically convert into class A series 10 preferred shares upon certain bankruptcy or insolvency related events.

Wholly Owned Subsidiaries

8658471 Canada Inc., Canada.
- 100% int. in **Belair Insurance Company Inc.**, Qué.
- 100% int. in **Intact Insurance Company**, Toronto, Ont.
- 100% int. in **Jevco Insurance Company**, Montréal, Qué.
- 100% int. in **The Nordic Insurance Company of Canada**, Toronto, Ont.
- 100% int. in **Novex Insurance Company**, Toronto, Ont.
- 100% int. in **Trafalgar Insurance Company of Canada**, Toronto, Ont.

866295 Alberta Ltd., Alta.
- 100% int. in **Brokerlink Inc.**, Calgary, Alta.
- 100% int. in **Intact Public Entities Inc.**, Princeton, Ont.

IB Reinsurance Inc., Barbados.
Intact International Ventures S.A.R.L., Luxembourg.
Intact Investment Management Inc., Canada.
Intact Ventures Inc., Canada.
- 100% int. in **Intact Insurance Group USA Holdings Inc.**, Plymouth, Minn.
  - 100% int. in **Intact U.S. Holdings Inc.**, Del.
    - 100% int. in **Atlantic Specialty Insurance Company**, Plymouth, Minn.
      - 100% int. in **The Guarantee Company of North America USA**, Southfield, Mich.
      - 100% int. in **Homeland Insurance Company of Delaware**, Del.
      - 100% int. in **Homeland Insurance Company of New York**, N.Y.
      - 100% int. in **OBI America Insurance Company**, Plymouth, Minn.
      - 100% int. in **OBI National Insurance Company**, Plymouth, Minn.

Johnson Inc., St. John's, N.L.
On Side Developments Ltd., Vancouver, B.C.
- 100% int. in **On Side Restoration Services Ltd.**, Vancouver, B.C.

12747031 Canada Inc., Canada.
- 100% int. in **Canadian Northern Shield Insurance Company**, Toronto, Ont.
- 100% int. in **Québec Assurance Company**, Canada.
- 100% int. in **Royal & Sun Alliance Insurance Company of Canada**, Toronto, Ont.
- 100% int. in **Unifund Assurance Company**, St. John's, N.L.
- 100% int. in **Western Assurance Company**, Toronto, Ont.

Royal & Sun Alliance Insurance Limited, United Kingdom.
- 100% int. in **RSA Insurance Ireland DAC**, Ireland.
- 100% int. in **RSA Luxembourg S.A.**, Luxembourg.
- 100% int. in **Royal & Sun Alliance Reinsurance Limited**, Ireland.

Note: The preceding list includes only the major related companies in which interests are held.

Financial Statistics

Periods ended:	12m Dec. 31/22[A]		12m Dec. 31/21[oA]
	$000s	%Chg	$000s
Net premiums earned	19,792,000		16,238,000
Net investment income	943,000		723,000
Total revenue	**21,289,000**	**+18**	**17,971,000**
Policy benefits & claims	11,022,000		8,967,000
Other operating expense	6,569,000		5,645,000
Operating expense	**6,569,000**	**+16**	**5,645,000**
Operating income	**3,698,000**	**+10**	**3,359,000**
Finance costs, gross	177,000		153,000
Pre-tax income	**2,942,000**	**+15**	**2,568,000**
Income taxes	522,000		480,000
Net income	**2,420,000**	**+16**	**2,088,000**
Net inc. for equity hldrs	**2,424,000**	**+17**	**2,067,000**
Net inc. for non-cont. int	**(4,000)**	**n.a.**	**21,000**
Cash & equivalent	1,010,000		2,276,000
Accounts receivable	9,007,000		8,809,000
Securities investments	33,114,000		32,840,000
Real estate	476,000		634,000
Total investments	35,836,000		35,446,000
Total assets	**64,959,000**	**-2**	**66,349,000**
Accts. pay. & accr. liabs	4,143,000		3,991,000
Claims provisions	25,144,000		25,116,000
Debt	4,522,000		5,229,000
Long-term lease liabilities	622,000		638,000
Preferred share equity	1,322,000		1,175,000
Shareholders' equity	15,400,000		15,674,000
Non-controlling interest	285,000		1,109,000
Cash from oper. activs	**3,665,000**	**+16**	**3,146,000**
Cash from fin. activs	(2,207,000)		4,189,000
Cash from invest. activs	(2,746,000)		(5,972,000)
Net cash position	**1,010,000**	**-56**	**2,276,000**
Capital expenditures, net	(411,000)		(327,000)
Pension fund surplus	495,000		802,000
	$		$
Earnings per share*	13.46		12.40
Cash flow per share*	20.87		19.37
Cash divd. per share*	4.00		3.40
	shs		shs
No. of shs. o/s*	175,256,968		176,081,958
Avg. no. of shs. o/s*	175,600,000		162,400,000
	%		%
Net profit margin	11.37		11.62
Return on equity	16.54		17.58
Return on assets	3.91		4.36
Foreign sales percent	31		26
No. of employees (FTEs)	28,500		26,000

* Common
[o] Restated
[A] Reported in accordance with IFRS

Latest Results

Periods ended:	6m June 30/23[A]		6m June 30/22[oA]
	$000s	%Chg	$000s
Total revenue	13,578,000	-3	13,932,000
Net income	637,000	-63	1,722,000
Net inc. for equity hldrs	629,000	-64	1,733,000
Net inc. for non-cont. int	8,000		(11,000)
	$		$
Earnings per share*	3.36		9.68

* Common
[o] Restated
[A] Reported in accordance with IFRS

Historical Summary
(as originally stated)

Fiscal Year	Total Rev.	Net Inc. Bef. Disc.	EPS*
	$000s	$000s	$
2022[A]	21,289,000	2,420,000	13.46
2021[A]	17,971,000	2,088,000	12.40
2020[A]	12,537,000	1,082,000	7.20
2019[A]	11,403,000	754,000	5.08
2018[A]	10,624,000	707,000	4.79

* Common
[A] Reported in accordance with IFRS

I.48 IntelGenx Technologies Corp.

Symbol - IGX **Exchange** - TSX **CUSIP** - 45822R
Head Office - 6420 rue Abrams, Saint-Laurent, QC, H4S 1Y2
Telephone - (514) 331-7440 **Fax** - (514) 331-0436
Website - www.intelgenx.com
Email - stephen@intelgenx.com
Investor Relations - Stephen Kilmer (514) 331-7440 ext. 232
Auditors - Richter LLP C.A., Montréal, Qué.
Lawyers - McCarthy Tétrault LLP, Montréal, Qué.
Transfer Agents - Philadelphia Stock Transfer, Inc., Ardmore, Pa.

Profile - (Del. 2003) Develops and manufactures oral pharmaceutical films as well as cannabis and psychedelics oral films.

Oral drug delivery solutions are based on three proprietary platform technologies: VersaFilm™, an oral film technology which allows for the instant delivery of pharmaceuticals to the oral cavity; VetaFilm™, a technology platform for veterinary applications which achieve rapid adhesion to the oral mucosa of the animal, formulated with appealing flavours to pets; and DISINTEQ™, which allows for a slower release of drug into the oral cavity thereby avoiding saturation of the oral mucosal membranes and increasing mucosal absorption.

Partners are usually granted exclusive rights to market and sell products in exchange for potential upfront and milestone payments, together with a share of partner's net profits or a royalty on net sales. The company retains manufacturing rights for its film products

Most advanced products include RIZAPORT® VersaFilm™ for the treatment of acute migraines; cannabis-infused VersaFilm®; and Tadalafil oral film, a bioequivalent of Cialis for erectile dysfunction. Early stage products include Montelukast VersaFilm® for patients with mild to moderate Alzheimer's disease and dementia and Loxapine film for treatment of anxiety and aggression in patients with schizophrenia or bipolar 1 disorder. The company's pharmaceutical film manufacturing facility, which supports lab-scale to pilot and commercial-scale production, is in Saint-Laurent, Que.

Also offers comprehensive pharmaceuticals services include research and development, clinical monitoring, regulatory support, tech transfer and manufacturing scale-up, and commercial manufacturing.

Directors - Dr. Horst G. Zerbe, chr., Hudson, Qué.; Clemens Mayr, Montréal, Qué.; Bernd J. Melchers; Mark H. Nawacki, Montréal, Qué.; Dr. Srinivas (Srini) Rao, Encinitas, Calif.; Frank Stegert, Berlin, Germany; Dr. Monika Trzcinska, Boston, Mass.

Other Exec. Officers - Dwight Gorham, CEO; André Godin, pres. & CFO; Tommy Kenny, sr. v-p & gen. counsel; Dr. David Kideckel, sr. v-p & head, corp. devel. & strategic alliances; Karen Kalayajian, v-p, fin. & contr.; Rodolphe Obeid, v-p, opers.; Nadine Paiement, v-p, R&D; Ingrid Zerbe, corp. sec.

Capital Stock

	Authorized (shs.)	Outstanding (shs.)[1]	Par
Preferred	20,000,000	nil	US$0.00001
Common	450,000,000	174,646,197	US$0.00001

[1] At Mar. 29, 2023

Major Shareholder - ATAI Life Sciences AG held 34.19% interest at Mar. 28, 2023.

Price Range - IGX/TSX

Year	Volume	High	Low	Close
2022	6,988,396	$0.53	$0.15	$0.25
2021	14,904,411	$0.85	$0.28	$0.46
2020	21,202,244	$0.80	$0.16	$0.29
2019	6,563,833	$1.06	$0.50	$0.62
2018	15,276,586	$2.36	$0.62	$0.72

Recent Close: $0.21

Capital Stock Changes - During 2022, common shares were issued as follows: 19,501,223 on conversion of debentures and 573,684 for convertible debenture interest payment.

Wholly Owned Subsidiaries

IntelGenx Corp., Canada.

Note: The preceding list includes only the major related companies in which interests are held.

Financial Statistics

Periods ended:	12m Dec. 31/22[A]		12m Dec. 31/21[A]
	US$000s	%Chg	US$000s
Operating revenue	**950**	**-38**	**1,535**
Research & devel. expense	3,031		2,717
General & admin expense	6,555		6,009
Operating expense	**9,586**	**+10**	**8,726**
Operating income	**(8,636)**	**n.a.**	**(7,191)**
Deprec., depl. & amort.	777		791
Finance income	4		152
Finance costs, gross	1,281		1,488
Pre-tax income	**(10,690)**	**n.a.**	**(9,318)**
Income taxes	nil		(6)
Net income	**(10,690)**	**n.a.**	**(9,312)**
Cash & equivalent	2,527		9,949
Inventories	62		62
Accounts receivable	709		680
Current assets	3,788		11,437
Fixed assets, net	4,425		5,213
Right-of-use assets	732		1,003
Total assets	**9,190**	**-49**	**17,905**
Accts. pay. & accr. liabs.	2,102		2,299
Current liabilities	2,374		7,020
Long-term debt, gross	9,772		10,456
Long-term debt, net	9,772		6,209
Long-term lease liabilities	467		726
Shareholders' equity	(3,423)		3,871
Cash from oper. activs.	**(9,516)**	**n.a.**	**(7,173)**
Cash from fin. activs.	2,965		15,492
Cash from invest. activs.	3,509		(5,074)
Net cash position	**1,210**	**-69**	**3,945**
Capital expenditures	(271)		(108)
	US$		US$
Earnings per share*	(0.07)		(0.07)
Cash flow per share*	(0.06)		(0.05)
	shs		shs
No. of shs. o/s*	174,646,196		154,571,289
Avg. no. of shs. o/s*	164,746,054		137,003,313
	%		%
Net profit margin	n.m.		(606.64)
Return on equity	n.m.		n.m.
Return on assets	(69.45)		(53.92)
Foreign sales percent	89		83

* Common
[A] Reported in accordance with U.S. GAAP

Latest Results

Periods ended:	3m Mar. 31/23[A]		3m Mar. 31/22[A]
	US$000s	%Chg	US$000s
Operating revenue	162	-32	237
Net income	(2,924)	n.a.	(2,686)
	US$		US$
Earnings per share*	(0.02)		(0.02)

* Common
[A] Reported in accordance with U.S. GAAP

Historical Summary
(as originally stated)

Fiscal Year	Oper. Rev. US$000s	Net Inc. Bef. Disc. US$000s	EPS* US$
2022[A]	950	(10,690)	(0.07)
2021[A]	1,535	(9,312)	(0.07)
2020[A]	1,544	(7,044)	(0.07)
2019[A]	742	(10,660)	(0.11)
2018[A]	1,824	(10,108)	(0.14)

* Common
[A] Reported in accordance with U.S. GAAP

I.49 Intellabridge Technology Corporation

Symbol - KASH **Exchange** - CSE (S) **CUSIP** - 45790Y
Head Office - c/o Varshney Capital Corp., Royal Centre, 2050-1055 Georgia St W, Vancouver, BC, V6E 3P3 **Telephone** - (604) 684-2181 **Toll-free** - (855) 684-2181 **Fax** - (604) 682-4768
Website - www.kash.io
Email - john@intellabridge.com
Investor Relations - John Eagleton (604) 684-2181
Auditors - EBT Chartered Accountants LLP C.A.
Transfer Agents - Capital Transfer Agency Inc., Toronto, Ont.
Profile - (B.C. 1986) Operates as a fintech blockchain company offering decentralized (DeFi) banking services.

Develops Kash, a decentralized financial peer-to-peer blockchain banking application with financial services similar to traditional banks but running on stablecoin blockchain financial rails as an alternative to legacy fiat financial rails. Kash features DeFi interest-bearing savings accounts, stablecoin checking, fiat-crypto on-ramps, synthetic stock, exchange-traded fund and commodity investing, and other DeFi banking services. Kash was officially launched in October 2021.

Other products are ChargaCard (application is inactive), a payment processing platform that allows individuals to pay their bills in instalments and for service sector businesses to get paid on time and in full; and BitDropGo (project on hold), a gaming app which allows users to play augmented reality games and collect digital asset rewards, and allows businesses to promote their brands in an engaging and immersive gaming environment.

Common suspended from CSE, May 9, 2022.
Predecessor Detail - Name changed from Cryptanite Blockchain Technologies Corp., Oct. 24, 2019.
Directors - John Eagleton, co-founder, chr. & CEO, Boulder, Colo.; Maria Eagleton, COO, CFO & corp. sec., Kyiv, Ukraine; Terri Clouse, Nashville, Tenn.; Lee Fan, San Francisco, Calif.
Other Exec. Officers - Keith A. Turner, pres.

Capital Stock

	Authorized (shs.)	Outstanding (shs.)[1]
Common	unlimited	72,567,476

[1] At Sept. 30, 2022

Major Shareholder - John Eagleton held 17% interest and Maria Nosikova held 15% interest at July 13, 2022.

Price Range - WEST.H/TSX-VEN (D)

Year	Volume	High	Low	Close
2022	9,190,109	$0.88	$0.36	$0.38
2021	111,465,120	$1.95	$0.09	$0.73
2020	48,897,924	$0.20	$0.01	$0.16
2019	19,639,016	$0.09	$0.01	$0.01
2018	17,361,534	$0.84	$0.03	$0.04

Wholly Owned Subsidiaries

ChargaCard, Inc., Boulder, Colo.
Intellabridge LLC, Ukraine.

Financial Statistics

Periods ended:	12m Dec. 31/21[A]		12m Dec. 31/20[A]
	US$000s	%Chg	US$000s
Operating revenue	**nil**	**n.a.**	**83**
Cost of sales	nil		49
Salaries & benefits	207		196
General & admin expense	1,237		131
Stock-based compensation	nil		4
Operating expense	**1,445**	**+280**	**380**
Operating income	**(1,445)**	**n.a.**	**(297)**
Deprec., depl. & amort.	1		16
Finance income	13		4
Finance costs, gross	9		8
Write-downs/write-offs	nil		(59)
Pre-tax income	**(1,042)**	**n.a.**	**(356)**
Net income	**(1,042)**	**n.a.**	**(356)**
Cash & equivalent	5,080		7
Accounts receivable	19		9
Current assets	8,557		332
Fixed assets, net	nil		1
Total assets	**8,557**	**n.m.**	**333**
Accts. pay. & accr. liabs.	82		169
Current liabilities	141		524
Shareholders' equity	8,416		(191)
Cash from oper. activs.	**(1,972)**	**n.a.**	**(113)**
Cash from fin. activs.	8,223		98
Cash from invest. activs.	(1,212)		nil
Net cash position	**5,080**	**n.m.**	**7**
	US$		US$
Earnings per share*	(0.02)		(0.01)
Cash flow per share*	(0.03)		(0.00)
	shs		shs
No. of shs. o/s*	72,507,476		56,471,844
Avg. no. of shs. o/s*	66,345,424		56,471,844
	%		%
Net profit margin	n.a.		(428.92)
Return on equity	n.m.		n.m.
Return on assets	(23.24)		(84.16)
No. of employees (FTEs)	n.a.		18

* Common
[A] Reported in accordance with IFRS

Latest Results

Periods ended:	9m Sept. 30/22[A]		9m Sept. 30/21[A]
	US$000s	%Chg	US$000s
Net income	(4,462)	n.a.	(2,101)
	US$		US$
Earnings per share*	(0.06)		(0.03)

* Common
[A] Reported in accordance with IFRS

Historical Summary
(as originally stated)

Fiscal Year	Oper. Rev. US$000s	Net Inc. Bef. Disc. US$000s	EPS* US$
2021[A]	nil	(1,042)	(0.02)
2020[A]	83	(356)	(0.01)
2019[A]	648	(734)	(0.01)
2018[A1]	6	(6,773)	(0.18)
2017[A]	nil	(233)	n.a.

* Common
[A] Reported in accordance with IFRS
[1] Amended. Results reflect the Mar. 7, 2018, reverse takeover acquisition of ChargaCard, Inc.

I.50 IntelliPharmaCeutics International Inc.

Symbol - IPCI **Exchange** - TSX **CUSIP** - 458173
Head Office - 30 Worcester Rd, Toronto, ON, M9W 5X2 **Telephone** - (416) 798-3001 **Fax** - (416) 798-3007
Website - www.intellipharmaceutics.com
Email - aodidi@intellipharmaceutics.com
Investor Relations - Dr. Amina Odidi (416) 798-3001
Auditors - MNP LLP C.A., Toronto, Ont.
Transfer Agents - American Stock Transfer & Trust Company, LLC, New York, N.Y.; Computershare Shareowner Services LLC, Jersey City, N.J.; TSX Trust Company, Toronto, Ont.
Employees - 11 at Nov. 30, 2022
Profile - (Can. 2009 amalg.) Researches, develops and manufactures novel or generic controlled-release and targeted-release oral solid dosage pharmaceutical products.

Through its HYPERMATRIX™ drug delivery technology, the company develops controlled release (once-a-day) versions of existing branded immediate release drugs and generic versions of existing controlled release drugs covered by patents about to expire or already expired. The company has products in various stages of development in therapeutic areas that include neurology, cardiovascular, gastrointestinal tract, diabetes and pain.

Lead product is a generic version of hyperactivity disorder drug Focalin XR® (Dexmethylphenidate ER, being commercialized in partnership with Par Pharmaceutical, Inc.), which has received U.S. FDA approval for eight different strengths. Other lead product candidates include generic versions of anti-depressant Effexor XR® (Venlafaxine ER); stomach ulcers drug Protonix® (Pantoprazole DR); type 2 diabetes drug Glucophage® XR (Metphormin ER); schizophrenia, bipolar disorder and major depressive order treatment Seroquel XR® (Quetiapine ER); heart failure and hypertension drug Coreg CR® (Carvdilol ER); anti-convulsant drug for epilepsy Lamictal® XR™ (Lamotrigine ER); epilepsy drug for partial onset seizures Keppra XR® (Levetiracetam ER); anti-depressant Pristiq® (Desvenlafaxine ER); anti-anginal medication Ranexa® (Ranolazine ER); management of neurophatic pain Lyrica® (Pregabalin ER); and Roxicodone® (Oxycodone IR, IPCI006) and OxyContin® (Oxycodone CR) for pain relief.

Non-generic products under development include Oxycodone ER (Aximris™, formerly Rexista™), a drug intended to treat moderate-to-severe pain and designed to overcome abuses associated with oxycodone and other opioid analgesics; and Regabatin™ XR, a controlled release version of pregabalin (Lyrica®) indicated for the management of neuropathic pain. Both Oxycodone ER and Regabatin™ XR are novel product candidates for which the company is pursuing a New Drug Application with the U.S. FDA.

The company also has the nPODDDS™ (Point of Divergence Drug Delivery System), a technology which is intended to provide drugs with significant barrier to tampering when subjected to various forms of physical and chemical manipulation commonly used by abusers and it is designed to prevent dose dumping when co-administered with alcohol. The nPODDDS™ technology supports the company's Oxycodone ER. In addition, the company has the PODRAS™ (Paradoxical OverDose Resistance Activating System) delivery technology, which is designed to prevent overdose when more pills than prescribed are swallowed intact. An alternate Oxycodone ER product candidate is currently being developed in which the PODRAS™ technology is incorporated. The company's Oxycodone IR (IPCI006) tablets, a generic version of Roxicodone®, incorporates both the nPODDDS™ and PODRAS™ technologies.

The company also holds a Cannabis Drug Licence from Health Canada and plans to develop pharmaceutical cannabidiol-based products.

Operations are conducted from a 65,000-sq.-ft. research laboratory and manufacturing scale-up facility in Toronto, Ont.

In August 2022, the company entered into a licence and supply agreement with **TaroPharmaceuticals Inc.**, whereby the company granted Taro an exclusive licence to market, sell and distribute Desvenlafaxine ER tablets in the 50 mg and 100 mg strengths which are approved for sale in the Canadian market by the Pharmaceutical Drugs Directory (PDD) of Health Canada.

Directors - Dr. Isa Odidi, chr., CEO & co-chief scientist, Toronto, Ont.; Dr. Amina Odidi, pres., COO, CFO & co-chief scientist, Toronto, Ont.; Dr. Norman M. Betts, Fredericton, N.B.; The Hon. Shawn Graham, Fredericton, N.B.; Bahadur Madhani, Toronto, Ont.
Other Exec. Officers - Christian Akyempon, v-p, comml. & bus. devel.; Dr. Patrick N. Yat, v-p, chemistry & analytical srvs.

Capital Stock

	Authorized (shs.)	Outstanding (shs.)[1]
Preference	unlimited	nil
Common	unlimited	33,092,665

[1] At June 13, 2023

Major Shareholder - Widely held at June 13, 2023.

Price Range - IPCI/TSX

Year	Volume	High	Low	Close
2022............	3,046,758	$0.28	$0.09	$0.10
2021............	7,479,269	$0.60	$0.11	$0.17
2020............	17,019,426	$1.26	$0.08	$0.19
2019............	20,778,682	$1.09	$0.12	$1.08
2018............	2,118,454	$12.90	$0.27	$0.32

Recent Close: $0.11

Capital Stock Changes - There were no changes to capital stock during fiscal 2022.

Wholly Owned Subsidiaries

IntelliPharmaCeutics Ltd., Del.
- 35.7% int. in **IntelliPharmaCeutics Corp.**, N.S.

Vasogen, Corp., Del.

Subsidiaries

64.3% int. in **IntelliPharmaCeutics Corp.**, N.S.

Financial Statistics

Periods ended:	12m Nov. 30/22[A]		12m Nov. 30/21[A]
	US$000s	%Chg	US$000s
Operating revenue	**66**	**n.a.**	**nil**
Research & devel. expense	2,149		2,662
General & admin expense	561		1,238
Stock-based compensation	nil		12
Operating expense	**2,710**	**-31**	**3,912**
Operating income	**(2,644)**	**n.a.**	**(3,912)**
Deprec., depl. & amort.	206		262
Finance costs, gross	292		549
Write-downs/write-offs	nil		(515)
Pre-tax income	**(2,887)**	**n.a.**	**(5,259)**
Income taxes	5		(114)
Net income	**(2,892)**	**n.a.**	**(5,145)**
Cash & equivalent	84		772
Accounts receivable	1		nil
Current assets	493		1,102
Fixed assets, net	788		994
Right-of-use assets	151		nil
Total assets	**1,432**	**-32**	**2,096**
Accts. pay. & accr. liabs	6,586		6,052
Current liabilities	12,009		10,252
Long-term debt, gross	1,800		1,751
Long-term lease liabilities	165		nil
Shareholders' equity	(10,577)		(8,155)
Cash from oper. activs	**(1,388)**	**n.a.**	**(2,461)**
Cash from fin. activs	200		3,031
Cash from invest. activs	500		nil
Net cash position	**84**	**-89**	**772**
	US$		US$
Earnings per share*	(0.09)		(0.17)
Cash flow per share*	(0.04)		(0.08)
	shs		shs
No. of shs. o/s*	33,092,665		33,092,665
Avg. no. of shs. o/s*	33,092,665		29,430,014
	%		%
Net profit margin	n.m.		n.a.
Return on equity	n.m.		n.m.
Return on assets	(147.36)		(168.08)
No. of employees (FTEs)	11		11

* Common
[A] Reported in accordance with U.S. GAAP

Latest Results

Periods ended:	3m Feb. 28/23[A]		3m Feb. 28/22[A]
	US$000s	%Chg	US$000s
Operating revenue	326	+293	83
Net income	(356)	n.a.	(881)
	US$		US$
Earnings per share*	(0.01)		(0.03)

* Common
[A] Reported in accordance with U.S. GAAP

Historical Summary
(as originally stated)

Fiscal Year	Oper. Rev. US$000s	Net Inc. Bef. Disc. US$000s	EPS* US$
2022[A]	66	(2,892)	(0.09)
2021[A]	nil	(5,145)	(0.17)
2020[A]	1,402	(3,391)	(0.14)
2019[A]	3,481	(8,085)	(0.37)
2018[A]	1,713	(13,747)	(2.89)

* Common
[A] Reported in accordance with U.S. GAAP

I.51 Inter-Rock Minerals Inc.

Symbol - IRO **Exchange** - TSX-VEN **CUSIP** - 458354
Head Office - 500-2 Toronto St, Toronto, ON, M5C 2B6 **Telephone** - (416) 367-3003 **Fax** - (416) 367-3638
Website - www.interrockminerals.com
Email - mcrombie@interrockminerals.com
Investor Relations - Dr. Michael B. Crombie (416) 367-3003
Auditors - RSM Canada LLP C.A., Toronto, Ont.
Lawyers - Norton Rose Fulbright Canada LLP, Toronto, Ont.
Transfer Agents - TSX Trust Company, Toronto, Ont.
FP500 Revenue Ranking - 754

Profile - (Ont. 2017; orig. Ont., 1952) Produces, markets and distributes premium dairy feed nutritional supplements and dolomite minerals for the dairy and beef cattle feed industries primarily in the U.S. Also has gold interests in Nevada.

Wholly owned **MIN-AD Inc.** quarries, processes and markets specialty dolomite from its dolomite quarry and processing plant in Winnemucca, Nev., serving the dairy and beef feed industries. Wholly owned **Papillon Agricultural Company Inc.** develops, produces and markets specialty nutritional products, including proteins and rumen probiotics that are produced under toll agreements to dairy consultants, feed suppliers and dairy producers. Papillon also distributes MIN-AD's products and a clostridia control product, which defends dairy cows against the bacteria that can reduce their feed consumption and lower milk production.

Wholly owned **Secret Pass Gold Inc.** holds two claim groups in northern Nevada consisting of the Sentinel gold property, 22 claims covering 440 acres, and Varyville gold property, 8 claims.

Predecessor Detail - Name changed from Inter-Rock Gold Inc., Feb. 3, 1999.

Directors - David R. Crombie, chr. & corp. sec., Portugal; Dr. Michael B. Crombie, pres. & CEO, Toronto, Ont.; Keith M. Belingheri, v-p, opers., Nev.; Scott M. Kelly, Toronto, Ont.; Frank van de Water, Toronto, Ont.

Other Exec. Officers - Robert Crombie, CFO; David Briggs, pres., Papillon Agricultural Company Inc.

Capital Stock

	Authorized (shs.)	Outstanding (shs.)[1]
Series A Preferred	n.a.	17,136,980[2]
Common	unlimited	22,277,811

[1] At Aug. 16, 2023
[2] Classified as debt.

Series A Preferred - Redeemable and retractable on demand at US$0.20 per share and convertible into one common share. Liability component totaling US$3,417,000 has been classified as part of long-term debt. One vote per share.

Common - One vote per share.

Normal Course Issuer Bid - The company plans to make normal course purchases of up to 1,000,000 common shares representing 4.5% of the total outstanding. The bid commenced on Jan. 16, 2023, and expires on Jan. 15, 2024.

Major Shareholder - The Cromwell Trust held 69.05% interest at Apr. 25, 2023.

Price Range - IRO/TSX-VEN

Year	Volume	High	Low	Close
2022............	419,659	$0.80	$0.48	$0.60
2021............	897,181	$0.51	$0.37	$0.49
2020............	2,314,028	$0.45	$0.16	$0.37
2019............	1,479,411	$0.35	$0.19	$0.23
2018............	1,752,171	$0.59	$0.20	$0.28

Recent Close: $0.70

Capital Stock Changes - There were no changes to capital stock during 2022.

Wholly Owned Subsidiaries

Secret Pass Gold Inc., United States.
- 100% int. in **MIN-AD Inc.**, Winnemucca, Nev.
  - 100% int. in **Papillon Agricultural LLC**, United States.
    - 100% int. in **Papillon Agricultural Company Inc.**, Easton, Md.

Financial Statistics

Periods ended:	12m Dec. 31/22[A]		12m Dec. 31/21[A]
	US$000s	%Chg	US$000s
Operating revenue	**87,225**	**+36**	**64,177**
Cost of sales	76,548		55,888
General & admin expense	6,823		5,392
Operating expense	**83,371**	**+36**	**61,280**
Operating income	**3,854**	**+33**	**2,897**
Deprec., depl. & amort.	935		860
Finance costs, gross	270		277
Pre-tax income	**2,649**	**+27**	**2,078**
Income taxes	2,130		505
Net inc. bef. disc. opers	**519**	**-67**	**1,573**
Income from disc. opers	50		(272)
Net income	**569**	**-56**	**1,301**
Cash & equivalent	3,048		2,266
Inventories	2,590		1,624
Accounts receivable	9,292		5,161
Current assets	15,640		16,756
Fixed assets, net	2,917		2,354
Intangibles, net	2,854		3,176
Total assets	**21,411**	**-5**	**22,548**
Accts. pay. & accr. liabs	7,364		4,345
Current liabilities	7,946		9,828
Long-term debt, gross	3,697		5,013
Long-term debt, net	3,417		3,697
Long-term lease liabilities	676		422
Shareholders' equity	9,144		8,575
Cash from oper. activs	**22**	**-99**	**2,966**
Cash from fin. activs	1,348		(781)
Cash from invest. activs	(588)		(1,991)
Net cash position	**3,048**	**+35**	**2,266**
Capital expenditures	(588)		(328)
	US$		US$
Earns. per sh. bef disc opers*	0.02		0.07
Earnings per share*	0.03		0.06
Cash flow per share*	0.00		0.13
	shs		shs
No. of shs. o/s*	22,303,311		22,303,311
Avg. no. of shs. o/s*	22,303,311		22,305,560
	%		%
Net profit margin	0.60		2.45
Return on equity	5.86		19.85
Return on assets	2.60		8.11

* Common
[A] Reported in accordance with IFRS

Historical Summary
(as originally stated)

Fiscal Year	Oper. Rev. US$000s	Net Inc. Bef. Disc. US$000s	EPS* US$
2022[A]	87,225	519	0.02
2021[A]	64,177	1,573	0.07
2020[A]	55,548	1,778	0.08
2019[A]	44,664	1,633	0.07
2018[A]	47,266	999	0.04

* Common
[A] Reported in accordance with IFRS

I.52 Interfield Global Software Inc.

Symbol - IFSS **Exchange** - NEO **CUSIP** - 458989
Head Office - 1560-200 Burrard St, Vancouver, BC, V6C 3L6 **Telephone** - (778) 628-8916
Website - interfieldsolutions.com
Email - info@interfieldsolutions.com
Investor Relations - Harold R. Hemmerich 971-50-558-8349
Auditors - MNP LLP C.A.
Transfer Agents - Computershare Trust Company of Canada Inc., Vancouver, B.C.

Profile - (B.C. 2005) Provides data management and marketplace software for industrial companies worldwide.

Primary products are ToolSuite, a cloud-based data collection and management platform that digitizes industrial processes and provides real-time auditable data; and Equipment Hound, an e-commerce industrial equipment marketplace that connects buyers and suppliers in oil and gas, mining, construction, automotive, renewables, maritime and other sectors globally. ToolSuite users are charged a monthly service fee in addition to any applicable development fee for customized modules. Revenue generated from Equipment Hound includes membership fees, advertising revenue, sales commissions and fees for add-on services such as logistics and third-party verification.

Common delisted from TSX-VEN, Feb. 14, 2023.
Common listed on NEO, Feb. 14, 2023.

Recent Merger and Acquisition Activity

Status: completed **Revised:** Feb. 15, 2023
UPDATE: The transaction was completed. PREVIOUS: Highbury Projects Inc. entered into a non-binding letter of intent for the reverse takeover acquisition of private Dubai, U.A.E.-based Interfield Solutions Ltd. Interfield has developed a Software-as-a-Service (SaaS) data management platform for the industrial sector as well as a business-to-business online marketplace for buying and selling

industrial equipment. Aug. 25, 2022 - A definitive agreement was entered into. Highbury would issue 250,000,000 post-split common shares (following a 3.44-for-1 share split), representing a deemed price of $76.95 per Interfield share for a total consideration of $87,500,000. Following the share split on closing, Highbury would then complete a 1-for-2.86 share consolidation and change its name to Interfield Solutions (Holdings) Ltd. Feb. 10, 2023 - Interfield completed a private placement of 40,876 subscription receipts at US$49 per receipt was completed for gross proceeds of US$2,002,924. Shares of the resulting issuer would be listed on the NEO Exchange Inc.

Predecessor Detail - Name changed from IFS Global Software Inc., May 1, 2023.

Directors - Harold R. (Hal) Hemmerich, chr. & CEO, Dubai, United Arab Emirates; Steele Hemmerich, pres., Dubai, United Arab Emirates; Crae M. Garrett, man. dir., Calgary, Alta.; Edward C. (Ed) Farrauto, Vancouver, B.C.; Jeffrey Parsons, Montréal, Qué.; Mark Sarssam, Dubai, United Arab Emirates; Sophia Shane, Vancouver, B.C.

Other Exec. Officers - Dain Hemmerich, COO; Danny W. K. Lee, CFO & corp. sec.; Saagar Laxman, chief tech. officer

Capital Stock

	Authorized (shs.)	Outstanding (shs.)[1]
Common	unlimited	104,874,730

[1] At Aug. 10, 2023

Major Shareholder - Steele Hemmerich held 31.28% interest and Dain Hemmerich held 27.59% interest at May 8, 2023.

Price Range - HPI/TSX-VEN (D)

Year	Volume	High	Low	Close
2022	30,069	$0.29	$0.25	$0.29
2021	95,622	$0.25	$0.17	$0.25
2020	37,527	$0.25	$0.18	$0.19
2019	214,699	$0.25	$0.14	$0.25
2018	163,159	$0.29	$0.17	$0.18

Consolidation: 1-for-2.86 cons. in Feb. 2023; 3.44-for-1 split in Feb. 2023

Recent Close: $0.41

Capital Stock Changes - In February 2023, common shares were split on a 3.44-for-1 basis followed by a share consolidation on a 1-for-2.86 basis and 87,515,908 common shares were issued pursuant to the reverse takeover acquisition of Interfield Solutions Ltd. In addition, 4,375,000 common shares were issued as finders' fees. In July 2023, private placement of up to 6,666,667 units (1 common share & 1 warrant) at 30¢ per unit was announced, with warrants exercisable at 40¢ per share.

There were no changes to capital stock during 2021 or 2022.

Wholly Owned Subsidiaries

Interfield Solutions Ltd., Dubai, United Arab Emirates.
- 100% int. in **Interfield Software Solutions LLC**, Dubai, United Arab Emirates.

Financial Statistics

Periods ended:	12m Dec. 31/22[A1]		12m Dec. 31/21[A]
	$000s	%Chg	$000s
General & admin expense	65		66
Operating expense	**65**	**-2**	**66**
Operating income	**(65)**	**n.a.**	**(66)**
Finance costs, gross	6		nil
Write-downs/write-offs	(52)		(45)
Pre-tax income	**(123)**	**n.a.**	**(111)**
Net income	**(123)**	**n.a.**	**(111)**
Cash & equivalent	8		15
Accounts receivable	3		3
Current assets	12		18
Total assets	**12**	**-33**	**18**
Bank indebtedness	97		nil
Accts. pay. & accr. liabs	27		17
Current liabilities	125		17
Shareholders' equity	(113)		1
Cash from oper. activs	**(55)**	**n.a.**	**(65)**
Cash from fin. activs	100		nil
Cash from invest. activs	(52)		(45)
Net cash position	**8**	**-47**	**15**
Capital expenditures	(52)		(45)
	$		$
Earnings per share*	(0.02)		(0.01)
Cash flow per share*	(0.01)		(0.01)
	shs		shs
No. of shs. o/s*	4,371,366		12,489,044
Avg. no. of shs. o/s*	4,371,366		12,489,044
	%		%
Net profit margin	n.a.		n.a.
Return on equity	n.m.		(196.46)
Return on assets	(780.00)		(151.02)

* Common

[A] Reported in accordance with IFRS

[1] Results for 2022 and prior periods pertain to Highbury Projects Inc.

Latest Results

Periods ended:	6m June 30/23[A]		6m June 30/22[oA]
	US$000s	%Chg	US$000s
Operating revenue	34	+55	22
Net income	(15,373)	n.a.	(350)
	US$		US$
Earnings per share*	(0.19)		(7.00)

* Common

[o] Restated

[A] Reported in accordance with IFRS

Historical Summary
(as originally stated)

Fiscal Year	Oper. Rev.	Net Inc. Bef. Disc.	EPS*
	$000s	$000s	$
2022[A]	nil	(123)	(0.02)
2021[A]	nil	(111)	(0.01)
2020[A]	nil	(114)	(0.01)
2019[A]	nil	(111)	(0.01)
2018[A]	nil	(106)	(0.01)

* Common

[A] Reported in accordance with IFRS

Note: Adjusted throughout for 1-for-2.86 cons. in Feb. 2023; 3.44-for-1 split in Feb. 2023

I.53 Interfor Corporation*

Symbol - IFP **Exchange** - TSX **CUSIP** - 45868C

Head Office - Metrotower II, 1600-4720 Kingsway, Burnaby, BC, V5H 4N2 **Telephone** - (604) 689-6800 **Fax** - (604) 688-0313

Website - www.interfor.com

Email - richard.pozzebon@interfor.com

Investor Relations - Richard Pozzebon (604) 422-3400

Auditors - KPMG LLP C.A., Vancouver, B.C.

Lawyers - McCarthy Tétrault LLP, Vancouver, B.C.

Transfer Agents - Computershare Trust Company of Canada Inc., Vancouver, B.C.

FP500 Revenue Ranking - 122

Employees - 5,408 at Dec. 31, 2022

Profile - (B.C. 1979 amalg.) Harvests timber, and manufactures and markets lumber products, logs and wood chips, with sawmilling operations across Canada and the United States.

Operations include 12 sawmills in Canada located in British Columbia, Ontario, Quebec and New Brunswick, an I-joist plant in Sault Ste. Marie, Ont., a value-added manufacturing plant in Quebec and a woodlands management division in Miramichi, N.B., as well as 17 sawmills in the United States located in Washington, Oregon, Georgia, South Carolina, Arkansas, Mississippi, Alabama and Louisiana, and a value-added remanufacturing plant in Sumas, Wash.

In Canada, timber supplies are sourced from a combination of logs harvested from the company's own timber tenures, long-term trade and supply agreements, and log purchases on the open market. Forest and tree farm licences held for its British Columbia facilities allows for an annual cut of 3,416,000 m^3. Sustainable forest, forest resource, supply and crown timber licences, and crown timber sub-licences held for its facilities in Eastern Canada (Ontario, Quebec and New Brunswick) allows for an annual cut of 4,691,000 m^3. The I-joist plant in Sault Ste. Marie purchases hi-grade Black Spruce machine stress rated lumber from internal and external sources, and oriented strand board from a variety of regional producers.

In the northwest region of the United States, timber supplies are sourced from a broad distribution of forest land ownership (forest industrial lands, small private landowners, and state and federal lands). In the southern United States, timber supplies are sourced primarily from privately held timberlands with only minor volumes coming from publicly owned timberlands. Private timberland ownership includes non-industrial private owners, timber real estate investment trusts and various institutional investors such as pension funds, who are typically represented by a timberland investment management organization.

Periods ended:	12m Dec. 31/22	12m Dec. 31/21
Lumber prod., mfbm[1]	3,792,000	2,891,000
Lumber sales, mfbm	3,928,000	2,852,000
Avg. lumber price, $/mfbm[2]	992	1,026
Log prod., m³	2,042,000	1,765,000
Log purchases, m³	1,070,000	1,399,000
Log sales, m³	719,000	728,000

[1] Includes B.C. Coast lumber custom-cut at third party facilities under the direction of Interfor management.

[2] Gross sales before duties.

Recent Merger and Acquisition Activity

Status: completed **Revised:** Nov. 30, 2022

UPDATE: The transaction was completed. PREVIOUS: Interfor Corporation agreed to acquire the entities that consist of Chaleur Forest Products from an affiliate of the Kilmer Group for a purchase price of Cdn$325,000,000, including Cdn$31,000,000 of net working capital. Chaleur owns two sawmills in Belledune and Bathurst, N.B., with a combined annual lumber production capacity of 350 mmfbm, and operates a woodlands management division based out of Miramichi that manages 30% of the total Crown forest in New Brunswick. In addition, Interfor would assume Chaleur's countervailing (CV) and anti-dumping (AD) duty deposits at closing, for consideration equal to 55% of the total deposits on an after-tax basis. As at Aug. 31, 2022, Chaleur had paid cumulative CV and AD duties of US$82,000,000. The transaction was expected to close in the fourth quarter of 2022.

Status: completed **Revised:** May 13, 2022

UPDATE: The transaction was completed. PREVIOUS: Interfor Corporation agreed to sell its Acorn specialty sawmill near Vancouver, B.C., to an affiliate of San Industries Ltd., a privately held British Columbia-based forest products company, for $25,200,000. The mill is on a 30-acre leased site on the Fraser River in Delta, B.C., and specializes in producing lumber squares for the traditional Japanese home market. The transaction was expected to close in the second quarter of 2022.

Status: completed **Announced:** May 2, 2022

Interfor Corporation acquired a total of 28,684,433 common shares of GreenFirst Forest Products Inc. from Rayonier A.M. Canada G.P., which represents 16.2% of GreenFirst's issued and outstanding common shares, at a price of Cdn$1.94 per share for a total cash consideration of $56,000,000. GreenFirst manufactures and markets a wide range of forest products including spruce, pine or fir (SPF) lumber, wood chips and other by-products.

Predecessor Detail - Name changed from International Forest Products Limited, May 6, 2014.

Directors - E. Lawrence Sauder, chr., Vancouver, B.C.; Ian M. Fillinger, pres. & CEO, Kamloops, B.C.; Nicolle Butcher, Toronto, Ont.; Christopher R. Griffin, Chicago, Ill.; Rhonda D. Hunter, Ark.; J. Eddie McMillan, Pensacola, Fla.; Thomas V. (Tom) Milroy, Toronto, Ont.; Gillian L. Platt, Kelowna, B.C.; Curtis M. Stevens, Portland, Ore.; Thomas (Tom) Temple, Wash.; Douglas W. G. (Doug) Whitehead, West Vancouver, B.C.

Other Exec. Officers - Andrew Horahan, exec. v-p, Cdn. opers.; Bruce Luxmoore, exec. v-p, U.S. opers.; Richard (Rick) Pozzebon, exec. v-p & CFO; J. Barton (Bart) Bender, sr. v-p, sales & mktg.; Timothy (Tim) Hartnett, sr. v-p, HR; Éric Larouche, sr. v-p, eastern opers.; Xenia Kritsos, gen. counsel & corp. sec.

Capital Stock

	Authorized (shs.)	Outstanding (shs.)[1]
Preference	5,000,000	nil
Common	150,000,000	51,444,803

[1] At Aug. 3, 2023

Share Appreciation Rights (SARs) - At Dec. 31, 2022, SARs were outstanding to purchase 42,428 common shares at a weighted average strike price of $15.68 per share with a weighted average remaining unit life ranging from 0.2 to 1.2 years.

Options - At Dec. 31, 2022, options were outstanding to purchase 555,811 common shares at a weighted average exercise price of $20.18 per share with a weighted average remaining unit life ranging from 5 to 8.9 years.

Normal Course Issuer Bid - The company plans to make normal course purchases of up to 5,105,002 common shares representing 10% of the public float. The bid commenced on Nov. 11, 2022, and expires on Nov. 10, 2023.

Major Shareholder - Widely held at Mar. 8, 2023.

Price Range - IFP/TSX

Year	Volume	High	Low	Close
2022	88,409,728	$44.56	$19.75	$21.00
2021	116,417,547	$40.66	$21.53	$40.51
2020	96,495,850	$24.36	$4.75	$23.77
2019	75,674,596	$18.42	$10.91	$14.67
2018	98,721,970	$27.27	$13.26	$14.42

Recent Close: $21.97

Capital Stock Changes - In September 2022, 3,355,704 common shares were repurchased under a Substantial Issuer Bid. Also during 2022, 28,123 common shares were issued on exercise of options and 6,041,701 common shares were repurchased under a Normal Course Issuer Bid.

Dividends

IFP com S.V. N.S.R.
$2.00◆r............... June 28/21
Paid in 2023: n.a. 2022: n.a. 2021: $2.00◆r

◆ Special r Return of Capital

Long-Term Debt - Outstanding at Dec. 31, 2022:

Sr. secured notes:	
Revolv. term line due 2026	$135,440,000
4.33% ser.A due 2023[1]	2,009,000
4.02% ser.B due 2023[2]	5,327,000
4.17% ser.C due 2026[3]	135,440,000
4.95% ser.D due 2029[4]	61,693,000
4.82% ser.E due 2029[5]	51,738,000
3.34% ser.F due 2030[6]	67,720,000
3.25% ser.G due 2030[6]	67,720,000
7.06% ser. H due to 2033[7]	270,880,000
	797,967,000
Less: Current portion	7,336,000
	790,631,000

[1] US$1,483,334.

[2] US$3,933,334.

[3] US$100,000,000.

[4] US$45,550,000.

[5] US$38,200,000.

[6] US$50,000,000.

[7] US$200,000,000.

Minimum long-term debt repayments were reported as follows:

2023	$7,336,000
2024	45,146,000
2025	45,146,000
2026	180,588,000
2027	37,809,000
Thereafter	481,942,000

Wholly Owned Subsidiaries

Chaleur Forest Products GP Inc., N.B.
Chaleur Forest Products Inc., N.B.
Chaleur Forest Products Limited Partnership, Man.
EACOM Timber Corporation, Montréal, Qué.
Interfor Cedarprime Inc., Wash.
Interfor East Ltd., B.C.
Interfor Japan Ltd., Japan.
Interfor Sales & Marketing Ltd., B.C.
Interfor U.S. Inc., Wash.
Interfor U.S. Timber Inc., Wash.
Interfor U.S. Holdings Inc., Wash.

Note: The preceding list includes only the major related companies in which interests are held.

Financial Statistics

Periods ended:	12m Dec. 31/22[A]		12m Dec. 31/21[A]
	$000s	%Chg	$000s
Operating revenue	**4,584,045**	**+39**	**3,289,146**
Cost of sales	3,382,127		1,948,239
General & admin expense	67,174		52,421
Stock-based compensation	(8,431)		31,682
Other operating expense	84,912		42,101
Operating expense	**3,525,782**	**+70**	**2,074,443**
Operating income	**1,058,263**	**-13**	**1,214,703**
Deprec., depl. & amort	194,632		126,573
Finance income	10,449		4,366
Finance costs, gross	26,094		22,196
Write-downs/write-offs	(3,176)		(5,637)
Pre-tax income	**814,883**	**-25**	**1,089,090**
Income taxes	216,644		270,079
Net income	**598,239**	**-27**	**819,011**
Cash & equivalent	77,606		538,561
Inventories	396,908		250,481
Accounts receivable	174,053		147,764
Current assets	778,581		965,707
Long-term investments	43,887		nil
Fixed assets, net	1,917,690		1,200,991
Right-of-use assets	33,998		33,547
Intangibles, net	590,405		344,405
Total assets	**3,619,833**	**+39**	**2,603,510**
Bank indebtedness	nil		2,202
Accts. pay. & accr. liabs	285,604		218,825
Current liabilities	325,997		321,642
Long-term debt, gross	797,967		373,473
Long-term debt, net	790,631		366,605
Long-term lease liabilities	20,456		26,850
Shareholders' equity	2,027,038		1,635,973
Cash from oper. activs	**732,357**	**-30**	**1,052,381**
Cash from fin. activs	31,059		(316,249)
Cash from invest. activs	(1,243,688)		(656,493)
Net cash position	**77,606**	**-86**	**538,561**
Capital expenditures	(1,216,894)		(716,708)
Capital disposals	32,068		59,501
Pension fund surplus	18,445		8,338
	$		$
Earnings per share*	10.89		12.88
Cash flow per share*	13.34		16.55
Extra divd. - cash*	nil		2.00
	shs		shs
No. of shs. o/s*	51,434,895		60,804,177
Avg. no. of shs. o/s*	54,916,230		63,593,452
	%		%
Net profit margin	13.05		24.90
Return on equity	32.66		60.30
Return on assets	19.84		37.59
Foreign sales percent	82		89
No. of employees (FTEs)	5,408		3,488

* Common
[A] Reported in accordance with IFRS

Latest Results

Periods ended:	6m June 30/23[A]		6m June 30/22[A]
	$000s	%Chg	$000s
Operating revenue	1,701,700	-38	2,738,087
Net income	(55,400)	n.a.	666,913
	$		$
Earnings per share*	(1.08)		11.68

* Common
[A] Reported in accordance with IFRS

Historical Summary
(as originally stated)

Fiscal Year	Oper. Rev.	Net Inc. Bef. Disc.	EPS*
	$000s	$000s	$
2022[A]	4,584,045	598,239	10.89
2021[A]	3,289,146	819,011	12.88
2020[A]	2,183,609	280,296	4.18
2019[A]	1,875,821	(103,785)	(1.54)
2018[A]	2,186,567	111,678	1.60

* Common
[A] Reported in accordance with IFRS

I.54 Intermap Technologies Corporation*

Symbol - IMP **Exchange** - TSX **CUSIP** - 458977
Head Office - 8310 South Valley Hwy, Suite 240, Englewood, CO, United States, 80112-5809 **Telephone** - (303) 708-0955 **Exec. Office** - 8310 South Valley Hwy, Suite 240, Englewood, CO, United States, 80112-5809 **Telephone** - (303) 708-0955 **Toll-free** - (877) 837-7246 **Fax** - (303) 708-0952
Website - www.intermap.com
Email - cfo@intermap.com
Investor Relations - Jennifer Bakken (303) 708-0955
Auditors - KPMG LLP C.A., Ottawa, Ont.
Transfer Agents - Odyssey Trust Company
Employees - 69 at Dec. 31, 2022
Profile - (Alta. 1997 amalg.) Creates geospatial solutions and analytics for applications in location-based information, risk assessment, geographic information systems, engineering, utilities, global positioning systems maps, oil and gas, renewable energy, hydrology, environmental planning, land management, wireless communications, transportation, outdoor advertising and 3D visualization.

Has three product categories: (i) geospatial data acquisition and collection, which are project-based, typically with sovereign clients, and each project is tailored to the specific needs of the client; (ii) value-added data production and licensing, in which a worldwide database of location-based information created and updated by the company are licensed to a broad group of customers; and (iii) software solutions and services, which bundles the company's proprietary data collection, processing infrastructure and archive library.

Products and services include NEXTMap®, which is a high-resolution database that contains a fusion of proprietary multi-frequency radar imagery and data, including unique Interferometric Synthetic Aperture Radar (IFSAR)-derived data, proprietary data models, and purchased third-party data, collected from multiple commodity sensor technologies; InsitePro®, which is an insurance underwriting software that calculates location-specific risk to create accurate and dependable risk assessments for natural catastrophe risk; Aquarius software and solutions, which involve the provision of flood risk data, models and software for the insurance industry in Czech and three other countries, and has a continuing relationship with the national insurance association; and NEXTView™, which in partnership with **Lufthansa Systems GmbH & Co. KG**, offers a configurable data solution that delivers terrain and obstacle awareness to improve airborne safety and efficiency to various aviation markets; and NEXTMap One™, which offers precision, 3D geospatial data at 1-m resolution anywhere in the world. Also offers additional mapping and image products including custom contours, terrain-derived hydrology and coastline datasets, slop and aspect maps, hillshade images, contours, clutter and land cover.

Customers include government agencies such as United States federal agencies, National Geospatial Intelligence Agency and United States Geological Survey; and geospatial data market including automakers, telecommunications companies, software providers and engineering firms. Distributions are held through direct sales, channel partners, value-added partners, original equipment manufacturers or through the company's Internet-based store. Distributions are held through direct sales, channel partners, value-added partners, original equipment manufacturers or through the company's Internet-based store.

The company is headquartered in Englewood, Colo., and has offices in Calgary, Alta.; Jakarta, Indonesia; and Prague, Czech Republic.

Predecessor Detail - Name changed from Intermap Technologies Ltd., June 10, 1999; basis 1 new for 12.5 old shs.

Directors - Patrick A. Blott, exec. chr. & CEO, N.Y.; Philippe Frappier, Toronto, Ont.; John (Jack) Hild, Md.; Jordan N. Tongalson, N.Y.

Other Exec. Officers - Jack Schneider, COO; Ralph Hope, chief tech. officer; Dr. Carolyn Johnston, chief scientist; Jennifer Bakken, exec. v-p, fin. & CFO; Ivan Maddox, exec. v-p, comml. solutions; Bob Antoniazzi, v-p, professional srvcs.

Capital Stock

	Authorized (shs.)	Outstanding (shs.)[1]
Class A Partic. Pref.	unlimited	nil
Class A Common	unlimited	38,503,710

[1] At Aug. 14, 2023

Options - At Dec. 31, 2022, options were outstanding to purchase 801,943 class A common shares at a weighted average exercise price of Cdn$0.72 per share with a weighted average remaining contractual life of 4.20 years.

Warrants - At Dec. 31, 2022, warrants were outstanding to purchase 3,840,467 class A common shares at prices ranging from US$0.42 to US$0.88 per share expiring to December 2024.

Major Shareholder - Patrick A. Blott held 16.4% interest at May 25, 2023.

Price Range - IMP/TSX

Year	Volume	High	Low	Close
2022	3,874,890	$0.84	$0.36	$0.56
2021	5,930,941	$1.47	$0.57	$0.74
2020	5,771,318	$1.25	$0.14	$0.74
2019	2,943,790	$0.39	$0.12	$0.22
2018	3,855,711	$0.63	$0.13	$0.14

Recent Close: $0.60

Capital Stock Changes - In February and March 2022, private placement of 4,008,288 class A common shares was completed at Cdn$0.51 per share. In November 2022, private placement of 3,020,000 units (1 class A common share & 1 warrant) at Cdn$0.40 per unit was completed. Also during 2022, 1,250,000 class A common shares common shares were issued by private placement.

Long-Term Debt - Outstanding at Dec. 31, 2022:

Project financing	US$177,000
Bank loans[1]	108,000
Government loans[2]	483,000
	768,000
Less: Current portion	145,000
	623,000

[1] CKr2,500,000 (US$110,000). Bearing interest at 10.71%.
[2] Consist of a US$333,000 non-interest bearing loan due 2026; and a US$150,000 loan bearing interest at 3.75% due 2050.

Wholly Owned Subsidiaries

Intermap Technologies Inc., Englewood, Colo.
- 100% int. in **Intermap Federal Services, Inc.**, Va.
- 100% int. in **Intermap Insurance Solutions, Inc.**, Del.

Intermap Technologies s.r.o., Prague, Czech Republic.
PT ExsaMap Asia, Indonesia.

Financial Statistics

Periods ended:	12m Dec. 31/22[A]		12m Dec. 31/21[A]
	US$000s	%Chg	US$000s
Operating revenue	**6,795**	**+17**	**5,799**
Salaries & benefits	6,230		5,457
Stock-based compensation	366		146
Other operating expense	3,629		3,677
Operating expense	**10,225**	**+10**	**9,280**
Operating income	**(3,430)**	**n.a.**	**(3,481)**
Deprec., depl. & amort	1,775		1,762
Finance income	6		3
Finance costs, gross	57		61
Pre-tax income	**(5,287)**	**n.a.**	**(3,338)**
Income taxes	(4)		18
Net income	**(5,283)**	**n.a.**	**(3,356)**
Cash & equivalent	843		188
Accounts receivable	1,290		914
Current assets	2,523		2,253
Long-term investments	1,011		1,062
Fixed assets, net	1,387		2,480
Right-of-use assets	343		497
Intangibles, net	1,016		1,117
Total assets	**6,335**	**-15**	**7,448**
Accts. pay. & accr. liabs	3,633		3,656
Current liabilities	6,954		5,641
Long-term debt, gross	768		674
Long-term debt, net	623		665
Long-term lease liabilities	177		290
Shareholders' equity	(1,419)		852
Cash from oper. activs	**(1,509)**	**n.a.**	**(2,493)**
Cash from fin. activs	2,409		2,269
Cash from invest. activs	(243)		(1,385)
Net cash position	**843**	**+348**	**188**
Capital expenditures	(32)		(1,124)
Capital disposals	nil		6
	US$		US$
Earnings per share*	(0.16)		(0.12)
Cash flow per share*	(0.05)		(0.09)
	shs		shs
No. of shs. o/s*	37,693,710		29,415,422
Avg. no. of shs. o/s*	33,378,811		27,039,139
	%		%
Net profit margin	(77.75)		(57.87)
Return on equity	n.m.		(287.08)
Return on assets	(75.83)		(43.66)
Foreign sales percent	100		100
No. of employees (FTEs)	69		72

* Cl.A com.
[A] Reported in accordance with IFRS

Latest Results

Periods ended:	6m June 30/23[A]		6m June 30/22[A]
	US$000s	%Chg	US$000s
Operating revenue	3,538	-21	4,469
Net income	(1,864)	n.a.	(1,903)
	US$		US$
Earnings per share*	(0.05)		(0.06)

* Cl.A com.
[A] Reported in accordance with IFRS

Historical Summary
(as originally stated)

Fiscal Year	Oper. Rev.	Net Inc. Bef. Disc.	EPS*
	US$000s	US$000s	US$
2022[A]	6,795	(5,283)	(0.16)
2021[A]	5,799	(3,356)	(0.12)
2020[A]	4,720	26,532	1.35
2019[A]	10,052	(4,813)	(0.28)
2018[A]	15,820	(2,818)	(0.17)

* Cl.A com.
[A] Reported in accordance with IFRS

I.55 International Clean Power Dividend Fund

Symbol - CLP.UN **Exchange** - TSX **CUSIP** - 459275
Head Office - c/o Middlefield Limited, 1 First Canadian Place, 5800-100 King St W, PO Box 192, Toronto, ON, M5X 1A6 **Telephone** - (416) 362-0714 **Toll-free** - (888) 890-1868 **Fax** - (416) 362-7925
Website - www.middlefield.com/icpdf.htm
Email - sroberts@middlefield.com
Investor Relations - Sarah Roberts (416) 847-5355
Auditors - Deloitte LLP C.A., Toronto, Ont.
Lawyers - Fasken Martineau DuMoulin LLP
Transfer Agents - TSX Trust Company
Trustees - Middlefield Limited, Calgary, Alta.
Investment Advisors - Middlefield Capital Corporation, Toronto, Ont.
Managers - Middlefield Limited, Calgary, Alta.
Profile - (Alta. 2021) Invests in primarily dividend paying securities of international issuers focused on, involved in, or that derive a significant portion of their revenue from renewable power and related sectors.

The fund's investment advisor integrates Environmental, Social and Governance (ESG) considerations to complement fundamental analysis in selecting companies it believes have sustainable competitive advantages.

The fund does not have a fixed termination date, but may be terminated by the manager without the approval of unitholders.

The manager is entitled to a management fee at an annual rate of 1.25% of net asset value, calculated and payable monthly.

Top 10 holdings at Mar. 31, 2023 (as a percentage of net asset value):

Holdings	Percentage
SSE plc	5.3%
AltaGas Ltd.	5.2%
TransAlta Corporation	5.0%
RWE AG	5.0%
Drax Group plc	4.9%
NextEra Energy plc	4.8%
The AES Corporation	4.7%
Atlantica Sustainable Infrastructure	4.6%
Boralex Inc.	4.3%
Energias de Portugal, S.A.	4.3%

Oper. Subsid./Mgt. Co. Directors - Jeremy T. Brasseur, exec. chr., Toronto, Ont.; Dean Orrico, pres. & CEO, Vaughan, Ont.; Craig Rogers, COO & chief compliance officer, Toronto, Ont.

Capital Stock

	Authorized (shs.)	Outstanding (shs.)[1]
Fund Unit	unlimited	18,965,634

[1] At Mar. 15, 2023

Fund Unit - Entitled to initial monthly cash distributions targeted to be $0.04167 per unit (to yield 5% per annum based on an issue price of $10 per unit). Retractable in March of each year for an amount equal to the net asset value per unit, less any costs to fund the retraction. Retractable in any other month at a price per unit equal to the lesser of: (i) 94% of the weighted average trading price on TSX during the 15 trading days immediately preceding the monthly retraction date; and (ii) the closing market price, less retraction costs. One vote per unit.

Normal Course Issuer Bid - The company plans to make normal course purchases of up to 1,876,923 fund units representing 10% of the public float. The bid commenced on Mar. 29, 2023, and expires on Mar. 28, 2024.

Major Shareholder - Widely held at Mar. 10, 2023.

Price Range - CLP.UN/TSX

Year	Volume	High	Low	Close
2022	4,904,392	$8.90	$6.58	$7.60
2021	6,225,803	$9.99	$8.50	$8.96

Recent Close: $6.62

Capital Stock Changes - During 2022, fund units were issued as follows: 179,500 for cash and 9,934 were released from treasury; 507,800 fund units were repurchased under a Normal Course Issuer Bid and 43,900 fund units were repurchased in the market in accordance with the declaration of trust.

Dividends

CLP.UN unit Ra $0.50004 pa M est. June 15, 2021**[1]
Listed Mar 18/21.
$0.04167i............ June 15/21
[1] Dividend reinvestment plan implemented eff. March 18, 2021.
** Reinvestment Option i Initial Payment

Financial Statistics

Periods ended:	12m Dec. 31/22[A]		41w Dec. 31/21[A]
	$000s	%Chg	$000s
Realized invest. gain (loss)	(1,045)		(9,745)
Unrealized invest. gain (loss)	(13,760)		9,481
Total revenue	**(11,204)**	**n.a.**	**2,355**
General & admin. expense	2,544		2,525
Other operating expense	285		437
Operating expense	**2,829**	**n.a.**	**2,962**
Operating income	**(14,033)**	**n.a.**	**(607)**
Finance costs, gross	615		291
Pre-tax income	**(14,647)**	**n.a.**	**(897)**
Income taxes	312		352
Net income	**(14,960)**	**n.a.**	**(1,249)**
Cash & equivalent	10,713		15,453
Accounts receivable	251		198
Investments	150,026		212,921
Total assets	**166,901**	**-27**	**228,599**
Accts. pay. & accr. liabs.	277		560
Debt	10,000		50,000
Shareholders' equity	149,939		177,227
Cash from oper. activs.	**48,186**	**n.a.**	**(213,039)**
Cash from fin. activs.	(52,955)		228,970
Net cash position	**10,713**	**-31**	**15,453**
	$		$
Earnings per share*	(0.77)		(0.06)
Cash flow per share*	2.49		(10.75)
Net asset value per share*	7.87		9.12
Cash divd. per share*	0.50		0.33
	shs		shs
No. of shs. o/s*	19,060,634		19,422,900
Avg. no. of shs. o/s*	19,321,430		19,825,135
	%		%
Net profit margin	n.m.		...
Return on equity	(9.15)		...
Return on assets	(7.25)		...

* Fund Unit
[A] Reported in accordance with IFRS

I.56 International Parkside Products Inc.

Symbol - IPD **Exchange** - TSX-VEN **CUSIP** - 459953
Head Office - 304-788 Beatty St, Vancouver, BC, V6B 2M1 **Telephone** - (604) 681-6472 **Fax** - (604) 681-6194
Website - www.internationalparksideproducts.com
Email - info@lenspen.com
Investor Relations - K. Murray Keating (877) 608-0868
Auditors - Davidson & Company LLP C.A., Vancouver, B.C.
Lawyers - Vector Corporate Finance Lawyers, Vancouver, B.C.
Transfer Agents - Computershare Trust Company of Canada Inc., Vancouver, B.C.
Profile - (B.C. 1983) Manufactures and distributes optical, screen and eyeglass cleaning products using patented carbon black technology and light carbon formula for international distribution.

Wholly owned **Parkside Optical Inc.** manufactures and sells to wholesale distributors the following optical lens cleaning devices and kits: LensPen, PEEPS, DigiKlear, Mini-Pro, Mini-Pro II, MicroPro, Smartphone camera cleaner, Laptop Pro, ScreenKlean, FilterKlear, DSLR Pro Kit, SensorKlear, SensorKlear Loupe Kit, SmartKlear, HunterPro Kits, Outdoor Pro Kits, FogKlear, Photo Pro Kits, Hurricane blower and Microfiber cloth.

Products are sold through a network of 80 distributors in over 85 countries.

Predecessor Detail - Name changed from Parkside Ventures Inc., Feb. 3, 1995; basis 1 new for 3 old shs.

Directors - K. Murray Keating, pres. & CEO, Surrey, B.C.; Ryan Keating, v-p, sales, Delta, B.C.; Arka Chorbajian, Vancouver, B.C.; Peter Henricsson, Vancouver, B.C.

Other Exec. Officers - Mindy Sirsiris, CFO & corp. sec.; Julia Behrendt, v-p, European sales

Capital Stock

	Authorized (shs.)	Outstanding (shs.)[1]
Common	unlimited	16,508,054
Class B Preferred	n.a.	91,111[2]

[1] At Dec. 16, 2022
[2] Securities of wholly owned Parkside Optical Inc.

Common - One vote per share.

Class B Preferred - Securities of wholly owned Parkside Optical Inc. Entitled to cash dividends of 6.5% per share per annum, payable quarterly, based on the weighted average of funds invested during the quarter. Convertible into common shares at the holder's option on a 1-for-1 basis. Non-voting. At July 31, 2022, accrued dividends payable totaled $13,300.

Major Shareholder - K. Murray Keating held 25.42% interest and Peter Henricsson held 14.2% interest at Oct. 28, 2022.

Price Range - IPD/TSX-VEN

Year	Volume	High	Low	Close
2022	485,586	$0.09	$0.04	$0.04
2021	1,104,880	$0.10	$0.07	$0.08
2020	259,513	$0.09	$0.06	$0.09
2019	713,918	$0.15	$0.06	$0.07
2018	893,681	$0.18	$0.11	$0.11

Recent Close: $0.07

Capital Stock Changes - There were no changes to capital stock from fiscal 2020 to fiscal 2022, inclusive.

Wholly Owned Subsidiaries

EIC - Energy Interface Corporation, B.C.
Parkside Optical Inc., B.C.

Financial Statistics

Periods ended:	12m July 31/22[A]		12m July 31/21[A]
	$000s	%Chg	$000s
Operating revenue	**3,690**	**+1**	**3,663**
Cost of goods sold	2,387		2,513
Salaries & benefits	672		579
General & admin expense	598		552
Operating expense	**3,657**	**0**	**3,644**
Operating income	**33**	**+74**	**19**
Deprec., depl. & amort.	108		107
Finance costs, gross	24		37
Pre-tax income	**(76)**	**n.a.**	**(111)**
Income taxes	(13)		(157)
Net income	**(63)**	**n.a.**	**46**
Cash & equivalent	260		323
Inventories	92		96
Accounts receivable	607		442
Current assets	966		984
Fixed assets, net	238		286
Right-of-use assets	156		24
Intangibles, net	64		69
Total assets	**1,423**	**+4**	**1,363**
Bank indebtedness	75		150
Accts. pay. & accr. liabs.	404		225
Current liabilities	520		515
Long-term lease liabilities	131		nil
Preferred share equity	41		41
Shareholders' equity	702		766
Cash from oper. activs.	**72**	**-48**	**139**
Cash from fin. activs.	(124)		(179)
Net cash position	**260**	**-20**	**323**
	$		$
Earnings per share*	(0.01)		0.01
Cash flow per share*	0.00		0.01
	shs		shs
No. of shs. o/s*	16,508,054		16,508,054
Avg. no. of shs. o/s*	16,508,054		16,508,054
	%		%
Net profit margin	(1.71)		1.26
Return on equity	(9.09)		6.13
Return on assets	(3.09)		1.86

* Common
[A] Reported in accordance with IFRS

Latest Results

Periods ended:	3m Oct. 31/22[A]		3m Oct. 31/21[A]
	$000s	%Chg	$000s
Operating revenue	1,354	-3	1,389
Net income	27	-74	102
	$		$
Earnings per share*	0.01		0.01

* Common
[A] Reported in accordance with IFRS

Historical Summary
(as originally stated)

Fiscal Year	Oper. Rev.	Net Inc. Bef. Disc.	EPS*
	$000s	$000s	$
2022[A]	3,690	(63)	(0.01)
2021[A]	3,663	46	0.01
2020[A]	3,644	(19)	(0.00)
2019[A]	4,825	(161)	(0.01)
2018[A]	6,863	182	0.01

* Common
[A] Reported in accordance with IFRS

I.57 International Zeolite Corp.

Symbol - IZ **Exchange** - TSX-VEN **CUSIP** - 460582
Head Office - 900-1021 Hastings St W, Vancouver, BC, V6E 0C3 **Telephone** - (604) 684-3301 **Fax** - (604) 684-3451
Website - www.internationalzeolite.com
Email - ray@internationalzeolite.com
Investor Relations - L. Raymon Paquette (604) 684-3301

Auditors - Clearhouse LLP C.A., Mississauga, Ont.
Transfer Agents - TSX Trust Company, Calgary, Alta.

Profile - (B.C. 2016; orig. Alta., 1987) Has zeolite interests in British Columbia, and markets and distributes zeolite products to the retail, industrial and commercial sectors.

In British Columbia, holds 92.97% interest (**Progressive Planet Solutions Inc.** 7.03%) in Bromley Creek zeolite prospect, 1,135 hectares, 9 km southwest of Princeton, with measured resources of 240,900 tonnes with average cation exchange capacity of 101.7 at August 2018; and 97.5% interest (Progressive Planet 2.5%) in Sun Group zeolite prospect, 949 hectares, Similkameen mining district, with Progressive Planet holding option to earn an additional 42.97% and 47.5% interest in Bromley Creek and Sun Group, respectively.

Through wholly owned **Earth Innovations Inc.**, markets and distributes zeolite products, including EcoTraction™ and EcoTraction™ Pro, which provide an alternative and environment-friendly ice and snow traction; and Smell Grabber, which naturally eliminates unpleasant odours from garbage and compost bins, smelly mildew, diaper pails, cat litters, cages for small animals, outhouses and temporary toilets, carpet stench and others.

Also develops and commercializes NEREA®, a proprietary technology that embeds nutrients directly into zeolite which produces higher yields of crops by 20 to 30%, a higher quality of product, uses less water by 30% and has lower plant infection by fungus, viruses and microorganisms. In addition, the company distributes zeolite products of Progressive Planet including Barn Sense, a solution for moisture, ammonia and odour management in livestock operations; The Green Patch, a soil conditioner which helps retain moisture and nutrients while improving aeration; and Z-Lite feed, a formula for use in animal feed as a natural anti-caking agent or flowing agent.

Predecessor Detail - Name changed from Canadian Zeolite Corp., Mar. 6, 2018.

Directors - L. Raymon (Ray) Paquette, CEO, Vancouver, B.C.; Mark Pearlman, pres. & COO; Stephen Coates, Toronto, Ont.; David J. C. (Dave) Kepkay, Vancouver, B.C.; Ronald (Ron) Schneider, B.C.

Other Exec. Officers - Hatem Kawar, CFO; Andrew Corradini, chief comml. officer; Ken Malone, chief revenue officer; Dr. Gerardo Rodriguez-Fuentes, chief science officer; Catherine Beckett, corp. sec.

Capital Stock

	Authorized (shs.)	Outstanding (shs.)[1]
Preferred	unlimited	nil
Common	unlimited	41,276,962

[1] At Oct. 26, 2022

Major Shareholder - L. Raymon (Ray) Paquette held 15.3% interest at Feb. 28, 2022.

Price Range - IZ/TSX-VEN

Year	Volume	High	Low	Close
2022	8,968,703	$0.25	$0.10	$0.15
2021	21,775,330	$0.33	$0.08	$0.25
2020	16,715,662	$0.11	$0.02	$0.08
2019	20,217,960	$0.16	$0.05	$0.05
2018	20,254,409	$0.47	$0.05	$0.11

Recent Close: $0.09

Capital Stock Changes - During fiscal 2022, common shares were issued as follows: 2,287,500 by private placement and 620,000 on exercise of options.

Wholly Owned Subsidiaries

Canadian Zeolite Corp.
Canmin Mexico S.A.
Earth Innovations Inc., Canada.

Financial Statistics

Periods ended:	12m June 30/22[A]		12m June 30/21[A]
	$000s	%Chg	$000s
Operating revenue	**674**	**+32**	**511**
Cost of goods sold	338		248
General & admin expense	912		665
Stock-based compensation	149		247
Operating expense	**1,400**	**+21**	**1,160**
Operating income	**(726)**	**n.a.**	**(649)**
Finance costs, net	104		104
Pre-tax income	**(830)**	**n.a.**	**(754)**
Net income	**(830)**	**n.a.**	**(754)**
Cash & equivalent	284		70
Inventories	128		140
Accounts receivable	22		2
Current assets	438		214
Intangibles, net	743		743
Explor./devel. properties	281		284
Total assets	**1,484**	**+17**	**1,263**
Accts. pay. & accr. liabs	829		455
Current liabilities	1,295		455
Long-term debt, gross	1,127		1,067
Long-term debt, net	661		1,067
Shareholders' equity	(492)		(279)
Cash from oper. activs	**(250)**	**n.a.**	**(65)**
Cash from fin. activs	461		100
Cash from invest. activs	2		(1)
Net cash position	**284**	**+306**	**70**
Capital expenditures	(10)		(8)
	$		$
Earnings per share*	(0.02)		(0.02)
Cash flow per share*	(0.01)		(0.00)
	shs		shs
No. of shs. o/s*	41,276,962		38,369,462
Avg. no. of shs. o/s*	40,070,142		36,858,476
	%		%
Net profit margin	(123.15)		(147.55)
Return on equity	n.m.		n.m.
Return on assets	(60.43)		(58.72)

* Common
[A] Reported in accordance with IFRS

Historical Summary
(as originally stated)

Fiscal Year	Oper. Rev.	Net Inc. Bef. Disc.	EPS*
	$000s	$000s	$
2022[A]	674	(830)	(0.02)
2021[A]	511	(754)	(0.02)
2020[A]	635	(263)	(0.01)
2019[A]	697	(916)	(0.02)
2018[A]	397	(1,337)	(0.04)

* Common
[A] Reported in accordance with IFRS

I.58 InterRent Real Estate Investment Trust

Symbol - IIP.UN **Exchange** - TSX **CUSIP** - 46071W
Head Office - 207-485 Bank St, Ottawa, ON, K2P 1Z2 **Telephone** - (613) 569-5699 **Fax** - (613) 569-5698
Website - www.interrentreit.com
Email - sandy.rose@interrentreit.com
Investor Relations - Sandy Rose (888) 696-5698
Auditors - RSM Canada LLP C.A., Toronto, Ont.
Lawyers - Gowling WLG (Canada) LLP, Toronto, Ont.
Transfer Agents - TSX Trust Company, Toronto, Ont.
FP500 Revenue Ranking - 643
Employees - 448 at Dec. 31, 2022

Profile - (Ont. 2006) Acquires, manages and rents income producing multi-residential properties in Ontario, Quebec and British Columbia.

Portfolio at Mar. 31, 2023:

Region	Suites
Greater Toronto & Hamilton Area	4,748
National Capital Region	3,013
Other Ontario	2,003
Greater Montreal Area	3,210
Greater Vancouver Area	866
	13,840

In September 2022, the trust acquired an additional 2.5% interest in a development property in Ottawa, Ont. for $2,431,000. At closing, the trust interest in the property increased to 16.67% from 14.17%.

Recent Merger and Acquisition Activity

Status: completed **Announced:** Mar. 27, 2023
InterRent Real Estate Investment Trust acquired a 605-suite apartment community, consisting of two high-rise towers at 18 and 22 storeys each, in Brampton, Ont., for $185,500,000, consisting of cash and an assumption of a $100,000,000 existing mortgage.

Status: completed **Announced:** June 30, 2022
InterRent Real Estate Investment Trust acquired a 50% interest in a 254-suite multi-residential property in Brossard, Que., for $59,025,000.

Trustees - Mike McGahan, exec. chr., Ottawa, Ont.; Bradley (Brad) Cutsey, pres. & CEO, Mississauga, Ont.; Paul Amirault‡, Ottawa, Ont.; Jean-Louis Bellemare, Ottawa, Ont.; Judy Hendriks, Ottawa, Ont.; W. John Jussup, Ottawa, Ont.; Ronald A. (Ron) Leslie, Ottawa, Ont.; Meghann O'Hara-Fraser, Toronto, Ont.; Cheryl Pangborn, Ottawa, Ont.

Oper. Subsid./Mgt. Co. Officers - Dave Nevins, COO; Curt Millar, CFO; Will Chan, CIO; Catherine Hébert, chief talent officer; Asad Hanif, v-p, acqs.; Craig Stewart, v-p, fin.; Chris Willoughby, v-p, mktg.
‡ Lead trustee

Capital Stock

	Authorized (shs.)	Outstanding (shs.)[1]
Trust Unit	unlimited	144,066,050
Special Voting Unit	unlimited	3,410,766
Class B LP Unit	unlimited	3,410,766[2 3]

[1] At Aug. 2, 2023
[2] Classified as debt.
[3] Securities of InterRent Holdings Limited Partnership.

Trust Unit - The trust will endeavour to make monthly cash distributions. Retractable at a price equal to the lesser of: (i) 90% of the market price of the units on the principal market on which the trust units are traded during the 10-trading-day period immediately preceding the retraction date; and (ii) 100% of the closing market price of the trust units on the principal market on which the units traded on the unit retraction date. One vote per trust unit.

Special Voting Unit - Issued to holders of class B limited partnership units of InterRent Holdings Limited Partnership. Each special voting unit entitles the holder to a number of votes at unitholder meetings equal to the number of trust units into which the class B limited partnership units are exchangeable.

Class B Limited Partnership Unit - Entitled to distributions paid by wholly owned InterRent Holdings Limited Partnership equal to those provided to trust units. Exchangeable into trust units on a 1-for-1 basis. Classified as long-term debt under IFRS.

Normal Course Issuer Bid - The company plans to make normal course purchases of up to 13,582,032 trust units representing 10% of the public float. The bid commenced on May 23, 2023, and expires on May 22, 2024.

Major Shareholder - Widely held at May 9, 2023.

Price Range - IIP.UN/TSX

Year	Volume	High	Low	Close
2022	94,459,927	$17.19	$10.79	$12.80
2021	73,955,040	$18.64	$12.96	$17.31
2020	122,101,748	$19.05	$10.39	$13.69
2019	73,916,903	$16.61	$12.06	$15.64
2018	74,600,986	$13.54	$8.77	$13.05

Recent Close: $12.21

Capital Stock Changes - During 2022, trust units were issued as follows: 1,422,730 under distribution reinvestment plan, 217,913 under the deferred unit plan and 68,387 on exercise of options.

Dividends

IIP.UN tr unit Ra $0.36 pa M est. Dec. 15, 2022**
Prev. Rate: $0.342 est. Dec. 15, 2021
Prev. Rate: $0.3255 est. Dec. 15, 2020
** Reinvestment Option

Wholly Owned Subsidiaries

InterRent Trust, Toronto, Ont.
- 100% int. in **InterRent Holdings General Partner Limited**, Toronto, Ont.
- 100% int. in **InterRent Holdings Limited Partnership**, Toronto, Ont.
  - 100% int. in **InterRent Holdings Manager Limited Partnership**, Ont.
  - 100% int. in **InterRent No. 1 Limited Partnership**, Toronto, Ont.
  - 100% int. in **InterRent No. 2 Limited Partnership**, Toronto, Ont.
  - 100% int. in **InterRent No. 3 Limited Partnership**, Toronto, Ont.
  - 100% int. in **InterRent No. 4 Limited Partnership**, Toronto, Ont.
  - 100% int. in **InterRent No. 5 Limited Partnership**, Toronto, Ont.
  - 100% int. in **InterRent No. 8 Limited Partnership**, Ont.
  - 100% int. in **InterRent No. 9 Limited Partnership**, Ont.
  - 100% int. in **InterRent No. 10 Limited Partnership**, Ont.
  - 100% int. in **InterRent No. 11 Limited Partnership**, Ont.
  - 100% int. in **InterRent No. 12 Limited Partnership**, Ont.
  - 100% int. in **InterRent No. 7 Limited Partnership**, Ont.
  - 100% int. in **InterRent No. 7A Limited Partnership**, Ont.
  - 100% int. in **InterRent No. 6 Limited Partnership**, Toronto, Ont.
  - 100% int. in **Park Place Equities 2000 Limited Partnership**, Toronto, Ont.
  - 100% int. in **Silvercreek Parkway Guelph Limited Partnership No. 2**, Guelph, Ont.
  - 100% int. in **Silvercreek Parkway Guelph Limited Partnership**, Guelph, Ont.

Investments

25% int. in **Fairview Limited Partnership**, Ont.
40% int. in **TIP Albert Limited Partnership**, Ottawa, Ont.

Financial Statistics

Periods ended:	12m Dec. 31/22[A]		12m Dec. 31/21[A]
	$000s	%Chg	$000s
Total revenue	**216,400**	**+17**	**185,148**
Rental operating expense	33,906		29,945
General & admin. expense	33,642		27,996
Property taxes	23,851		21,857
Operating expense	**91,399**	**+15**	**79,798**
Operating income	**125,001**	**+19**	**105,350**
Investment income	37		39
Deprec. & amort.	1,257		908
Finance income	480		386
Finance costs, gross	49,724		33,765
Pre-tax income	**103,959**	**-72**	**369,686**
Net income	**103,959**	**-72**	**369,686**
Cash & equivalent	4,267		2,064
Accounts receivable	9,095		5,738
Long-term investments	32,040		30,399
Fixed assets	8,653		6,479
Income-producing props.	4,152,141		3,998,193
Properties under devel.	100,903		64,400
Property interests, net	4,248,707		4,065,923
Right-of-use assets	783		551
Total assets	**4,315,593**	**+5**	**4,118,699**
Accts. pay. & accr. liabs.	38,587		32,626
Long-term debt, gross	1,698,107		1,571,112
Shareholders' equity	2,497,376		2,420,003
Cash from oper. activs.	**91,181**	**-5**	**96,020**
Cash from fin. activs.	108,570		460,122
Cash from invest. activs.	(197,548)		(605,720)
Net cash position	**4,267**	**+107**	**2,064**
Capital expenditures	(123,745)		(90,149)
Increase in property	(74,393)		(517,851)
	$		$
Earnings per share*	n.a.		n.a.
Cash flow per share*	0.64		0.69
Funds from opers. per sh.*	0.53		0.51
Adj. funds from opers. per sh.*	0.47		0.46
Cash divd. per share*	0.35		0.33
Total divd. per share*	**0.35**		**0.33**
	shs		shs
No. of shs. o/s*	141,888,874		140,179,844
	%		%
Net profit margin	48.04		199.67
Return on equity	4.23		16.47
Return on assets	3.64		11.00
No. of employees (FTEs)	448		435

* Trust unit

[A] Reported in accordance with IFRS

Latest Results

Periods ended:	3m Mar. 31/23[A]		3m Mar. 31/22[A]
	$000s	%Chg	$000s
Total revenue	57,709	+11	51,863
Net income	82,761	-13	94,632
	$		$
Earnings per share*	n.a.		n.a.

[A] Reported in accordance with IFRS

Historical Summary
(as originally stated)

Fiscal Year	Total Rev. $000s	Net Inc. Bef. Disc. $000s	EPS* $
2022[A]	216,400	103,959	n.a.
2021[A]	185,148	369,686	n.a.
2020[A]	159,955	150,648	n.a.
2019[A]	145,302	384,889	n.a.
2018[A]	127,286	168,297	n.a.

* Trust unit

[A] Reported in accordance with IFRS

I.59 Intertidal Capital Corp.

Symbol - TIDE.P **Exchange** - TSX-VEN **CUSIP** - 461136
Head Office - 270-1820 Fir St, Vancouver, BC, V6J 3B1 **Telephone** - (604) 306-7027
Email - hughrogersinc@gmail.com
Investor Relations - Hugh A. D. Rogers (888) 718-7474
Auditors - De Visser Gray LLP C.A., Vancouver, B.C.
Lawyers - S. Paul Simpson Law Corporation, Vancouver, B.C.
Transfer Agents - Odyssey Trust Company, Vancouver, B.C.
Profile - (B.C. 2018) Capital Pool Company.

In October 2022, the company's proposed Qualifying Transaction reverse takeover acquisition of **Sendero Resources Corp.** was terminated. Sendero holds Penas Negras copper prospect in Argentina.

Directors - Hugh A. D. Rogers, CEO, Vancouver, B.C.; Giuseppe (Pino) Perone, corp. sec., Vancouver, B.C.; Chris Beltgens, North Vancouver, B.C.; Dain Currie, George Town, Cayman Islands; Alexander (Alex) Langer, North Vancouver, B.C.

Other Exec. Officers - Christopher Ross, CFO

Capital Stock

	Authorized (shs.)	Outstanding (shs.)[1]
Common	unlimited	5,600,000

[1] At Mar. 18, 2022

Major Shareholder - Dain Currie held 17.86% interest, Alexander (Alex) Langer held 17.86% interest and Hugh A. D. Rogers held 17.86% interest at Mar. 18, 2022.

Price Range - TIDE.P/TSX-VEN

Year	Volume	High	Low	Close
2022	65,585	$0.28	$0.10	$0.15

Recent Close: $0.05

Capital Stock Changes - On Mar. 18, 2022, an initial public offering of 2,000,000 common shares was completed at 10¢ per share.

I.60 Intouch Insight Ltd.

Symbol - INX **Exchange** - TSX-VEN **CUSIP** - 46118C
Head Office - 400 March Rd, Ottawa, ON, K2K 3H4 **Telephone** - (613) 270-7900 **Toll-free** - (800) 263-2980 **Fax** - (800) 238-6861
Website - www.intouchinsight.com
Email - csmith@intouchinsight.com
Investor Relations - Cathy Smith (800) 263-2980
Auditors - BDO Canada LLP C.A., Montréal, Qué.
Bankers - The Toronto-Dominion Bank, Ottawa, Ont.
Lawyers - Fasken Martineau DuMoulin LLP
Transfer Agents - Computershare Trust Company of Canada Inc., Toronto, Ont.
Profile - (Can. 2002; orig. Alta., 1996) Offers customer experience management products and services that help clients please their customers, strengthen brand reputation and improve financial performance.

The company has developed software platforms that provide for the rapid development of data collection programs including lead capture, customer satisfaction surveys, and mobile forms, checklist and audits. Also uses its technology to enable its own data collection services including mystery shopping, third party audit and customer experience programs.

Software platforms include LiaCX®, which helps clients collect and centralize data from multiple customer touch points, gives them actionable, real-time insights, and provides them with the tools to continuously improve customer experience; IntouchIntelligence™, which allows data sources from any of the Intouch software or services to be aggregated and reported from a single location; IntouchCheck™, which allows business to create unlimited mobile forms and checklists to easily collect and aggregate data from all locations; and IntouchSurvey™, which allows businesses to perform web-based surveys to collect feedback and view results using real-time dashboards.

In June 2023, the company signed a non-binding letter of intent to acquire an undisclosed customer experience measurement company based in North America (target) for US$1,500,000 cash upon closing, a US$500,000 promissory note payable over three years with interest and additional contingency payments expected to be approximately US$400,000 per year based on performance for four years post-closing. The undisclosed target company has approximately US$5,000,000 in annual revenues. The transaction is expected to close on Sept. 1, 2023.

Predecessor Detail - Name changed from In-Touch Survey Systems Ltd., July 15, 2016.

Directors - Eric Beutel, chr., Toronto, Ont.; Cameron Watt, pres. & CEO, Ont.; Jennifer Batley, Ont.; Lee Bennett, Ont.; Michael J. Gaffney, N.S.; W. David Oliver, Toronto, Ont.; Rainer N. Paduch, Ottawa, Ont.

Other Exec. Officers - Cathy Smith, CFO & corp. sec.; David Newby, v-p, HR & cust. experience; Luke Waite, v-p, engineering

Capital Stock

	Authorized (shs.)	Outstanding (shs.)[1]
Preferred	unlimited	nil
Common	unlimited	25,515,594

[1] At May 11, 2023

Major Shareholder - Eric Beutel held 11.6% interest at May 11, 2023.

Price Range - INX/TSX-VEN

Year	Volume	High	Low	Close
2022	2,387,591	$0.88	$0.41	$0.58
2021	3,099,244	$0.94	$0.56	$0.71
2020	6,817,276	$0.84	$0.20	$0.75
2019	4,972,718	$0.60	$0.22	$0.43
2018	4,378,444	$0.70	$0.34	$0.37

Recent Close: $0.38

Capital Stock Changes - During 2022, 408,141 common shares were issued on exercise of options.

Wholly Owned Subsidiaries

Intouch Insight Corp., United States.
Intouch Insight Inc., Ottawa, Ont.
Mystery Researchers, LLC, Atlanta, Ga.

Financial Statistics

Periods ended:	12m Dec. 31/22[A]		12m Dec. 31/21[A]
	$000s	%Chg	$000s
Operating revenue	**23,487**	**+47**	**16,017**
Cost of sales	11,279		7,084
Research & devel. expense	2,090		1,887
General & admin expense	7,988		5,866
Operating expense	**21,357**	**+44**	**14,837**
Operating income	**2,130**	**+81**	**1,180**
Deprec., depl. & amort.	1,044		1,048
Finance costs, gross	191		120
Write-downs/write-offs	(181)		(1)
Pre-tax income	**532**	**n.a.**	**(277)**
Income taxes	(78)		39
Net income	**610**	**n.a.**	**(315)**
Cash & equivalent	860		740
Accounts receivable	4,416		3,446
Current assets	5,696		4,492
Fixed assets, net	991		1,536
Intangibles, net	3,630		4,154
Total assets	**10,500**	**+3**	**10,182**
Bank indebtedness	1,140		840
Accts. pay. & accr. liabs.	832		909
Current liabilities	3,586		3,511
Long-term lease liabilities	383		563
Shareholders' equity	6,531		5,638
Cash from oper. activs.	**985**	**-13**	**1,131**
Cash from fin. activs.	(756)		77
Cash from invest. activs.	(109)		(2,334)
Net cash position	**860**	**+16**	**740**
Capital expenditures	(109)		(187)
Capital disposals	nil		3
	$		$
Earnings per share*	0.02		(0.01)
Cash flow per share*	0.04		0.05
	shs		shs
No. of shs. o/s*	25,515,594		25,107,453
Avg. no. of shs. o/s*	25,340,978		23,405,549
	%		%
Net profit margin	2.60		(1.97)
Return on equity	10.03		(6.19)
Return on assets	8.02		(2.06)
Foreign sales percent	76		71

* Common

[A] Reported in accordance with IFRS

Latest Results

Periods ended:	3m Mar. 31/23[A]		3m Mar. 31/22[A]
	$000s	%Chg	$000s
Operating revenue	5,097	-3	5,244
Net income	(185)	n.a.	(266)
	$		$
Earnings per share*	(0.01)		(0.01)

* Common

[A] Reported in accordance with IFRS

Historical Summary
(as originally stated)

Fiscal Year	Oper. Rev. $000s	Net Inc. Bef. Disc. $000s	EPS* $
2022[A]	23,487	610	0.02
2021[A]	16,017	(315)	(0.01)
2020[A]	12,795	(7)	(0.00)
2019[A]	19,255	116	0.01
2018[A]	14,888	(2,802)	(0.13)

* Common

[A] Reported in accordance with IFRS

I.61 Inventronics Limited

Symbol - IVX **Exchange** - TSX-VEN **CUSIP** - 461208
Head Office - 1420 Van Horne Ave E, Brandon, MB, R7A 7B6 **Telephone** - (204) 728-2001 **Toll-free** - (888) 235-7862 **Fax** - (204) 726-0807
Website - www.inventronics.com
Email - dstearne@inventronics.com
Investor Relations - Dan J. Stearne (204) 717-0487
Auditors - MNP LLP C.A., Brandon, Man.
Bankers - Bank of Scotland plc; Royal Bank of Canada
Lawyers - Burnet, Duckworth & Palmer LLP, Calgary, Alta.
Transfer Agents - Computershare Trust Company of Canada Inc., Calgary, Alta.
Profile - (Alta. 2000; orig. Man., 1970) Designs, manufactures and markets protective enclosures for the telecommunication networks, cable television networks, electric power distribution networks and oil and gas installations in North America.

Products include pedestals, cabinets, traffic control enclosures, urban refuse and recycling bins and other enclosure series that are utilized in both outdoor and indoor applications to house and protect passive and/or active electrical and electronic components. Products are sold directly to utilities, original equipment manufacturers and/or through distributors.

Directors - Dan J. Stearne, pres. & CEO, Cobble Hill, B.C.; Robert P. (Rob) Brookwell, CFO, Calgary, Alta.; Tracy L. Dobson, v-p, opers., Brandon, Man.; Daniel C. Y. (Dan) O'Greysik, v-p, sales & mktg., Brandon, Man.; Michael J. Martin, Alta.; Nicole L. Maruzzo, Toronto, Ont.

Capital Stock

	Authorized (shs.)	Outstanding (shs.)[1]
Common	unlimited	4,871,145

[1] At Mar. 31, 2023

Major Shareholder - Tracy L. Dobson held 18% interest, Daniel C. Y. (Dan) O'Greysik held 18% interest, Dan J. Stearne held 18% interest and W. Garth Wilson held 18% interest at Sept. 27, 2022.

Price Range - IVX/TSX-VEN

Year	Volume	High	Low	Close
2022	718,829	$4.59	$1.45	$3.50
2021	1,149,898	$2.98	$0.25	$2.40
2020	1,065,776	$0.34	$0.10	$0.25
2019	382,601	$0.30	$0.06	$0.22
2018	219,800	$0.26	$0.06	$0.06

Recent Close: $2.60

Capital Stock Changes - During 2022, 33,000 common shares were issued on exercise of options.

Dividends

IVX com Ra $0.12

$0.12◆	June 7/23	$0.35◆	Nov. 4/22
$0.20◆	Nov. 3/21		

Paid in 2023: $0.12◆ 2022: $0.35◆ 2021: $0.20◆

◆ Special

Financial Statistics

Periods ended:	12m Dec. 31/22[A]		12m Dec. 31/21[oA]
	$000s	%Chg	$000s
Operating revenue	**14,245**	**+43**	**9,985**
Cost of sales	10,125		7,689
General & admin expense	944		633
Operating expense	**11,069**	**+33**	**8,322**
Operating income	**3,176**	**+91**	**1,663**
Deprec., depl. & amort.	134		138
Finance costs, gross	114		156
Pre-tax income	**2,928**	**+114**	**1,369**
Income taxes	835		(521)
Net income	**2,093**	**+11**	**1,890**
Cash & equivalent	379		216
Inventories	1,856		1,324
Accounts receivable	1,264		852
Current assets	3,536		2,419
Fixed assets, net	2,491		2,298
Total assets	**6,027**	**+15**	**5,228**
Accts. pay. & accr. liabs	774		840
Current liabilities	1,142		892
Long-term debt, gross	2,047		2,101
Long-term debt, net	1,989		2,049
Shareholders' equity	2,892		2,287
Cash from oper. activs	**2,295**	**+71**	**1,340**
Cash from fin. activs	(1,805)		(1,129)
Cash from invest. activs	(327)		(126)
Net cash position	**379**	**+75**	**216**
Capital expenditures	(327)		(126)
	$		$
Earnings per share*	0.43		0.41
Cash flow per share*	0.48		0.29
Extra divd. - cash*	0.35		0.20
	shs		shs
No. of shs. o/s*	4,838,145		4,805,145
Avg. no. of shs. o/s*	4,817,565		4,614,486
	%		%
Net profit margin	14.69		18.93
Return on equity	80.83		105.12
Return on assets	38.64		46.94

* Common
[o] Restated
[A] Reported in accordance with IFRS

Latest Results

Periods ended:	3m Mar. 31/23[A]		3m Mar. 31/22[oA]
	$000s	%Chg	$000s
Operating revenue	3,335	-12	3,787
Net income	325	-35	501
	$		$
Earnings per share*	0.07		0.10

* Common
[o] Restated
[A] Reported in accordance with IFRS

Historical Summary
(as originally stated)

Fiscal Year	Oper. Rev.	Net Inc. Bef. Disc.	EPS*
	$000s	$000s	$
2022[A]	14,245	2,093	0.43
2021[A]	9,843	1,890	0.41
2020[A]	5,640	684	0.16
2019[A]	5,656	195	0.04
2018[A]	4,616	16	0.00

* Common
[A] Reported in accordance with IFRS

I.62 Invesque Inc.

Symbol - IVQ **Exchange** - TSX **CUSIP** - 46136U

Head Office - 3400-333 Bay St, Toronto, ON, M5H 2S7 **Toll-free** - (855) 885-7702

Website - www.invesque.com

Email - swhite@invesque.com

Investor Relations - Scott White (317) 643-6648

Auditors - KPMG LLP C.A., Toronto, Ont.

Lawyers - Goodmans LLP, Toronto, Ont.

Transfer Agents - Computershare Trust Company of Canada Inc., Toronto, Ont.

FP500 Revenue Ranking - 602

Employees - 1,517 at Dec. 31, 2022

Profile - (B.C. 2016; orig. Ont., 2007) Primarily owns land and buildings that are leased on a long-term triple-net lease basis to operators of seniors housing and care facilities in 16 U.S. states and Canada which offer primarily skilled nursing and assisted living services, including post-acute transitional rehabilitation, and long-term care, including dementia and memory care. Also owns a management company that provides management services to over 30 seniors housing properties.

At Mar. 15, 2023, the company owned or held majority interest in a portfolio of 76 properties in the U.S. consisting of 56 assisted living and memory care facilities, 13 skilled nursing facilities, four transitional care properties and three medical office buildings. Includes 36 independent living, assisted living, and memory care properties that wholly owned **Commonwealth Senior Living, LLC** (CSL) manages the day-to-day operations of, eight of which are owned by third parties, primarily in Virginia. In Ontario, owns an interest in four seniors housing and care facilities.

Properties in the U.S. are located in Missouri, Illinois (11), Pennsylvania (8), Indiana (3), Texas (8), Arkansas (2), Florida, Maryland (3), Georgia (2), Virginia (23), New Jersey (2), Louisiana, South Carolina (3), Tennessee, Wisconsin, Michigan and New York (5).

In March 2022, the company sold a vacant property in Port Royal, S.C., for US$3,500,000.

Recent Merger and Acquisition Activity

Status: pending **Revised:** June 1, 2023
UPDATE: The sale of seven facilities was completed. The sale of the eighth was expected to be completed within 30 days. PREVIOUS: Invesque Inc. agreed to sell eight skilled nursing facilities in Illinois, for US$125,000,000. The transaction was expected to close before the end of the second quarter of 2023.

Status: pending **Announced:** Jan. 20, 2023
Invesque Inc. agreed to sell MetroWest Medical Center, a 25,394-sq.-ft. medical office building, in Orlando, Fla., for US$6,400,000. The transaction was expected to close before the end of the second quarter of 2023.

Status: completed **Revised:** Nov. 28, 2022
UPDATE: The transaction was completed. PREVIOUS: Invesque Inc. agreed to sell Brantford Medical Centre, a 44,811-sq.-ft. medical office building in Brantford, Ont., for US$5,800,000. The transaction was expected to close in November 2023.

Status: completed **Announced:** Aug. 30, 2022
Invesque Inc. sold two skilled nursing facilities with a total of 148 beds in Nebraska for US$25,000,000. The properties were sold to the existing tenant and operator, Hillcrest Health Services.

Status: completed **Announced:** July 28, 2022
Invesque Inc. sold nine medical office buildings in Canada to private Kelowna, B.C.-based Appelt Properties Inc. for Cdn$94,300,000.

Status: completed **Announced:** July 26, 2022
Invesque Inc. sold the University Boulevard medical office building in Orlando, Fla., for US$9,850,000.

Status: completed **Announced:** June 15, 2022
Invesque Inc. sold two 55+ communities in Wheatfield, N.Y., which operate as age restricted apartment complexes, for US$10,000,000.

Status: completed **Announced:** Apr. 1, 2022
Invesque Inc. sold two seniors housing properties with a total of 99 units in New York for US$19,200,000.

Status: completed **Announced:** Apr. 1, 2022
Invesque Inc. sold four nursing care facilities with a total of 339 beds in Texas for US$52,000,000. The properties sold was part of Invesque's Jaguarundi Ventures, LP joint venture with Magnetar Capital, of which Invesque owns approximately 66% ownership interest.

Status: completed **Announced:** Mar. 1, 2022
Invesque Inc. sold five non-core seniors housing properties in Harrisburg, Pa., for US$5,500,000.

Predecessor Detail - Name changed from Mainstreet Health Investments Inc., Jan. 8, 2018.

Directors - Scott White, chr. & CEO, Westfield, N.J.; Adlai Chester, exec. v-p, invest. & CFO, Carmel, Ind.; Michael Faber†, Washington, D.C.; Brad Benbow, Traverse City, Mich.; Shaun Hawkins, Zionsville, Ind.; Randy Maultsby, New York, N.Y.; Gail Steinel, N.J.

Other Exec. Officers - Vineet Bedi, chief strategy officer; Quinn Haselhorst, sr. v-p, fin.; Bryan E. Hickman, sr. v-p, invest.; Mark Lyons, sr. v-p & contr.; Dennis Dechow, v-p, asset mgt. svcs.; Matt Monson, v-p, acq. & bus. devel.; Kari Onweller, v-p, partner rel. & portfolio mgt.
† Lead director

Capital Stock

	Authorized (shs.)	Outstanding (shs.)[1]
Class A Preferred	unlimited	nil
Series 1		2,802,009
Series 2		3,172,086
Series 3		1,586,042
Series 4		1,538,461
Non-Voting	unlimited	nil
Common	unlimited	56,232,594

[1] At Aug. 14, 2023

Note: Certain funds managed by Magnetar Financial LLC hold all class A series 1, 2, 3 and 4 preferred shares.

Preferred - Issuable in series and non-voting. Convertible into common shares on a one-for-one basis based on the liquidation preference and conversion price of US$9.75 per share, subject to an accretion of 5.65% per annum, compounded quarterly. **Series 1**, **2** and **3** - Redeemable at US$9.75 per share. **Series 4** - Redeemable at US$9.75 per share plus a 4% premium, which is reduced by 1% annually to Aug. 27, 2023, and at US$9.75 per share thereafter.

Common - One vote per share.

Normal Course Issuer Bid - The company plans to make normal course purchases of up to 2,806,947 common shares representing 5% of the total outstanding. The bid commenced on Dec. 22, 2022, and expires on Dec. 21, 2023.

Major Shareholder - Tiptree Operating Company, LLC held 30.16% interest and Magnetar Financial, LLC held 25.86% interest at May 9, 2023.

Price Range - IVQ/TSX

Year	Volume	High	Low	Close
2022	3,396,664	$2.76	$1.13	$1.23
2021	5,202,944	$4.57	$1.61	$2.60
2020	5,233,677	$9.37	$1.92	$2.27
2019	1,351,491	$9.86	$7.97	$8.78

IVQ.U/TSX

Year	Volume	High	Low	Close
2019	6,888,289	US$8.00	US$5.94	US$6.73
2018	7,430,510	US$9.53	US$6.20	US$7.13

Recent Close: $0.85

Capital Stock Changes - During 2022, common shares were issued as follows: 251,097 on vesting of deferred shares, 186,359 on settlement of equity settled deferred shares and 25,000 on conversion of debentures; 587,400 common shares were repurchased under a Normal Course Issuer Bid.

Wholly Owned Subsidiaries

Invesque International Holdings Inc., B.C.
- 100% int. in **Invesque US Holdings, Inc.**, Del.
  - 100% int. in **Foxhound Holdings, LLC**, Del.
  - 100% int. in **Foxhound Manco Holdings, LLC**, Del.
    - 100% int. in **Commonwealth Senior Living, LLC**, United States.
  - 100% int. in **Invesque Holdings, LP**, Del.
    - 100% int. in **Care Investment Trust LLC**, New York, N.Y.

MHI Canada Holdings Inc., B.C.
- 100% int. in **Mohawk Medical Properties Real Estate Investment Trust**, Toronto, Ont.

Note: The preceding list includes only the major related companies in which interests are held.

Financial Statistics

Periods ended:	12m Dec. 31/22[A]		12m Dec. 31/21[DA]
	US$000s	%Chg	US$000s
Total revenue	**194,699**	**+1**	**193,328**
Rental operating expense	36,087		35,825
Salaries & benefits	79,253		72,174
General & admin. expense	7,587		7,462
Property taxes	12,093		14,539
Operating expense	**135,020**	**+4**	**130,000**
Operating income	**59,679**	**-6**	**63,328**
Investment income	6,395		(14,906)
Deprec. & amort.	16,516		22,152
Finance income	1,539		1,468
Finance costs, gross	43,948		47,922
Write-downs/write-offs	(20,974)		(3,435)
Pre-tax income	**(43,137)**	**n.a.**	**(6,523)**
Income taxes	(1,127)		nil
Net inc. bef. disc. opers	**(42,010)**	**n.a.**	**(6,523)**
Income from disc. opers	(6,800)		(5,712)
Net income	**(48,810)**	**n.a.**	**(12,235)**
Cash & equivalent	27,579		19,369
Accounts receivable	6,311		5,593
Current assets	81,764		76,549
Long-term investments	49,077		50,440
Fixed assets	497,251		517,360
Income-producing props	538,591		716,344
Property interests, net	538,591		716,344
Right-of-use assets	941		1,470
Total assets	**1,097,340**	**-16**	**1,301,011**
Accts. pay. & accr. liabs	13,085		17,356
Current liabilities	483,134		91,058
Long-term debt, gross	823,363		959,985
Long-term debt, net	379,071		904,636
Long-term lease liabilities	1,612		1,470
Preferred share equity	85,389		85,389
Equity portion of conv. debs	5,243		6,370
Shareholders' equity	231,647		288,306
Cash from oper. activs	**11,912**	**-37**	**18,974**
Cash from fin. activs	(141,187)		(152,926)
Cash from invest. activs	137,485		119,188
Net cash position	**27,579**	**+42**	**19,369**
Capital expenditures	(6,516)		(7,575)
Capital disposals	118,414		3,247
Increase in property	(14,511)		nil
Decrease in property	22,081		113,104
	US$		US$
Earns. per sh. bef disc opers*	(0.74)		(0.12)
Earnings per share*	(0.86)		(0.22)
Cash flow per share*	0.21		0.34
Funds from opers. per sh.*	0.42		0.47
Adj. funds from opers. per sh.*	0.39		0.44
	shs		shs
No. of shs. o/s*	56,111,348		56,236,292
Avg. no. of shs. o/s*	56,634,772		56,312,407
	%		%
Net profit margin	(21.58)		(3.37)
Return on equity	(24.20)		(3.18)
Return on assets	0.07		2.96
Foreign sales percent	98		98
No. of employees (FTEs)	1,517		1,323

* Common
[D] Restated
[A] Reported in accordance with IFRS

Historical Summary
(as originally stated)

Fiscal Year	Total Rev.	Net Inc. Bef. Disc.	EPS*
	US$000s	US$000s	US$
2022[A]	194,699	(42,010)	(0.74)
2021[A]	206,333	(12,235)	(0.22)
2020[A]	213,637	(184,004)	(3.30)
2019[A]	144,689	(5,359)	(0.10)
2018[A]	112,379	(12,275)	(0.24)

* Common
[A] Reported in accordance with IFRS

I.63 Iocaste Ventures Inc.

Symbol - ICY.P **Exchange** - TSX-VEN **CUSIP** - 46188C
Head Office - 200-305 10 Ave SE, Calgary, AB, T2G 0W2 **Telephone** - (403) 860-0675
Email - michaelperkinsmj@gmail.com
Investor Relations - Michael J. Perkins (403) 860-0675
Auditors - MNP LLP C.A., Toronto, Ont.
Transfer Agents - Odyssey Trust Company, Calgary, Alta.
Profile - (B.C. 2021) Capital Pool Company.

Recent Merger and Acquisition Activity

Status: pending **Announced:** May 31, 2023
Iocaste Ventures Inc. entered into a letter of intent for the Qualifying Transaction reverse takeover acquisition of Simulacra Corporation, a holding company that owns three subsidiaries involved in adult entertainment, AI-driven robotics and medical simulation. Its flagship company Abyss Creations LLC manufactures Realdoll, a high end love doll. Terms were to be entered into and a definitive agreement signed. Simulacra plans to raise minimum proceeds of $2,500,000 via a private placement of subscription receipts.

Directors - Lorne M. Sugarman, pres., CEO, CFO & corp. sec., Toronto, Ont.; Andrew G. Kiguel, Toronto, Ont.; Michael J. Perkins, Calgary, Alta.

Capital Stock

	Authorized (shs.)	Outstanding (shs.)[1]
Common	unlimited	11,205,260

[1] At Jan. 20, 2023

Major Shareholder - Navjeet S. (Bob) Dhillon held 18.18% interest, Andrew G. Kiguel held 18.18% interest and Lorne M. Sugarman held 18.18% interest at Nov. 10, 2021.

Price Range - ICY.P/TSX-VEN

Year	Volume	High	Low	Close
2022	385,667	$0.70	$0.12	$0.19
2021	12,300	$0.20	$0.14	$0.14

Recent Close: $0.06

Capital Stock Changes - On Nov. 10, 2021, an initial public offering of 3,000,000 common shares was completed at 10¢ per share. Also during fiscal 2022, 205,260 common shares were issued on exercise of options.

I.64 Ionic Brands Corp.

Symbol - IONC **Exchange** - CSE (S) **CUSIP** - 462202
Head Office - 1142 Broadway, Suite 300, Tacoma, WA, United States, 98402 **Telephone** - (253) 248-7920
Website - www.ionicbrands.com
Email - dave.croom@ionicbrands.com
Investor Relations - David Croom (253) 248-7927
Lawyers - McMillan LLP, Vancouver, B.C.
Transfer Agents - Odyssey Trust Company, Vancouver, B.C.
Profile - (B.C. 2013; orig. Ont., 2012) Manufactures, brands and distributes cannabis concentrate, flower and consumables in the United States.

Operations are located in Washington and Oregon. The company's products include vapes, concentrates, flower and consumables which are offered under the IONIC, Dabulous, Zoots and Wicked brands as well as the Cowlitz brand portfolio (Dab Dudes, Cowlitz Gold and Hi Guys). The company primarily relies on licensed cannabis processors and producers in offering its products by providing the related services and assets. Solutions provided include leasing of processing and transportation equipment; operating and marketing support; licensing of intellectual property; and procurement and supply of devices, packaging and labeling. The third parties license the company's proprietary formulations, devices, packaging and equipment to manufacture and sell consumer products for the recreational and medicinal markets. In addition, the company owns certain assets related to the Cowlitz business in Washington, including the property lease for a manufacturing and production facility in Tacoma, Wash. In Oregon, the company owns a 6,000-sq.-ft. manufacturing facility in Estacada, Ore.

Common suspended from CSE, Aug. 8, 2022.

Recent Merger and Acquisition Activity

Status: pending **Announced:** Apr. 20, 2022
YourWay Cannabis Brands Inc. agreed to acquire Ionic Brands Corp. on the basis of 0.0525 YourWay common share for each Ionic Brands held, including all Ionic Brands' Shares issuable on conversion of Ionic Brands' issued and outstanding preferred shares.

Predecessor Detail - Name changed from Zara Resources Inc., Mar. 22, 2019, following reverse takeover acquisition of Blacklist Holdings Inc.; basis 1 new for 35.9389 old shs.

Directors - John P. Gorst, chr. & CEO, Tacoma, Wash.; Bryen J. Salas, pres., Tacoma, Wash.; Christian D. Vara, COO, Wash.; Christian D. Struzan, chief brand officer, Wash.; Austin T. Gorst, v-p, Wash.

Other Exec. Officers - David (Dave) Croom, CFO; Dr. Zachary W. Bell, chief science officer; Joanne Salas, CAO

Capital Stock

	Authorized (shs.)	Outstanding (shs.)[1]
Preferred	unlimited	
Series A		nil
Series B		nil
Series C		nil
Series D		59,104,012
Series E		90,376,072
Common	unlimited	350,035,491[2]

[1] At Sept. 30, 2021
[2] At Oct. 11, 2022.

Preferred Series A, B and C - Entitled to cumulative preferential dividends at a rate of 5% per annum, payable in common shares based upon the prevailing market price of the common shares. Convertible into such number of common shares equal to the quotient of the paid-up capital of the preferred shares divided by the market price of the common shares on the date of conversion. Non-voting.

Preferred Series D - Entitled to a cumulative preferential dividend at a rate of 12% per annum, payable in series D preferred shares, or 10% per annum, payable in cash. Convertible into common shares on 1-for-1 basis. Redeemable after May 16, 2022, at Cdn$0.30 per share plus accrued and unpaid dividends. One vote per share.

Preferred Series E - Entitled to a cumulative preferential dividend at a rate of 13% per annum, until Mar. 5, 2023, payable in cash or common shares. Convertible into common shares on 1-for-1 basis. Automatically converted into common shares on Mar. 5, 2025. Non-voting.

Common - One vote per share.

Major Shareholder - Widely held at Jan. 27, 2021.

Price Range - IONC/CSE (S)

Year	Volume	High	Low	Close
2022	157,970,322	$0.03	$0.01	$0.01
2021	91,482,820	$0.46	$0.02	$0.03
2020	14,304,947	$0.24	$0.03	$0.15
2019	19,333,292	$5.40	$0.12	$0.12
2018	6,697	$51.75	$15.09	$15.09

Consolidation: 1-for-6 cons. in Feb. 2021; 1-for-35.9389 cons. in Apr. 2019

Wholly Owned Subsidiaries

Blacklist Brands CA Inc., Calif.
Blacklist Finco Inc., Canada.
Blacklist Holdings OR Inc., Ore.
Natural Extractions, Inc., Wash. dba Zoots.
Valley Capital Corp., B.C.

Latest Results

Periods ended:	9m Sept. 30/21[A]		9m Sept. 30/20[A]
	US$000s	%Chg	US$000s
Operating revenue	19,729	+170	7,311
Net income	(8,047)	n.a.	(2,107)
	US$		US$
Earnings per share*	(0.08)		(0.07)

* Common
[A] Reported in accordance with IFRS

I.65 Irwin Naturals Inc.

Symbol - IWIN **Exchange** - CSE **CUSIP** - 46414Q
Head Office - 5310 Beethoven St, Los Angeles, CA, United States, 90066 **Telephone** - (310) 433-3009
Website - irwinnaturals.com
Email - investors@irwinnaturals.com
Investor Relations - Cassandra Bassanetti-Drumm (310) 306-3636
Auditors - Armanino LLP C.P.A., Woodland Hills, Calif.
Bankers - The Toronto-Dominion Bank
Transfer Agents - Odyssey Trust Company
FP500 Revenue Ranking - 736
Profile - (B.C. 1987) Develops and distributes vitamins and other health supplements, including cannabidiol (CBD) products, through more than 100,000 retailers across North America; licenses its brands and formulas to manufacturers and distributors of cannabis products; and operates a network of mental health clinics in the U.S. that offer ketamine-assisted psychedelic treatments.

Wholly owned **Irwin Naturals, a Nevada Corporation** develops vitamins and other health supplements and distributes these products primarily in the U.S. and Canada through mass-market retailers and health food stores. It developed a streamlined production process where it formulates products in-house based on available science and research on vitamins, minerals and botanicals; and contract manufacturers to produce and package the products. More than 300 products are offered in the dietary supplement, CBD ingestible, CBD topical and CBD pet categories. Products are sold through major retailers including Wal-Mart, CVS and Walgreens, Whole Foods, Vitamin Shoppe and Sprouts as well as independent health food specialty retailers. Brands include Irwin Naturals, a line of more than 130 soft-gel supplements which target weight management, sexual health, mood, brain health and more; Irwin Naturals CBD, a broad range of CBD ingestible and topical products; Applied Nutrition, which includes products such as Green Tea Fat Burner, Libido-Max, 14-Day Acai Berry Cleanse and Liquid Collagen; Nature's Secret, a line of digestive care and cleansing products; and floCHI for Pets.

Wholly owned **Irwin Naturals Cannabis, Inc.** participates in the adult-use cannabis market through agreements with third parties that are licensed to manufacture and distribute products containing tetrahydrocannabinol (THC). The third parties license the Irwin Naturals THC brand and produce and distribute in their respective jurisdictions Irwin Naturals' formulas such as Power to Sleep, augmented with THC. The company has licensing agreements with cannabis manufacturers in California, Colorado, Michigan, Ohio, New Mexico and Canada.

Wholly owned **Irwin Naturals Emergence, Inc.** operates a network of 10 mental health clinics in Florida, Vermont, New Hampshire, Iowa and Georgia that offer ketamine-assisted psychedelic treatments for disorders such as depression and anxiety. The company intends to expand treatment options at its clinics by offering a broad portfolio of next-generation therapies including ketamine, stellate ganglion block, transcranial magnetic stimulation and holotropic breathwork, as well as group therapy integration.

In September 2022, the company agreed to acquire **Happier You, LLC**, which operates a ketamine clinic in central Ohio. Terms of the transaction were not disclosed.

In August 2022, the company acquired two ketamine clinics in Atlanta and Woodstock, Ga., operating under the name Invictus Clinic, from **Invictus Clinics, LLC**; and the assets of **Hobie Fuerstman DO PLC** (dba Preventive Medicine), operator of a ketamine clinic in Colchester, Vt. Terms of the transactions were not disclosed.

On May 20, 2022, the company acquired **KHC Capital Group, LLC**, operator of five ketamine treatment clinics in Florida with a partnership contract with an affiliate clinic in Mexico. Consideration was issuance of 10,660 proportionate voting shares and 667 subordinate voting shares valued at US$2,699,000.

On Mar. 14, 2022, the company acquired **Midwest Ketafusion LLC**, operator of a ketamine clinic in Iowa City, Iowa, for issuance of 7,500 proportionate voting shares valued at US$2,248,000.

Sub vtg reinstated on CSE, June 1, 2023.

Sub vtg suspended from CSE, May 9, 2023.

Predecessor Detail - Name changed from Datinvest International Ltd., Aug. 12, 2021, pursuant to the reverse takeover acquisition of Irwin Naturals and GVB Biopharma; basis 1 new for 8.316 old shs.

Directors - Klee Irwin, chr. & CEO, Los Angeles, Calif.; Marc-David Bismuth, Los Angeles, Calif.; Rod Knight, Asheville, N.C.

Other Exec. Officers - Sean Sands, CFO & corp. sec.

Capital Stock

	Authorized (shs.)	Outstanding (shs.)[1]
Multiple Vtg.	unlimited	18,240
Proportionate Vtg.	unlimited	18,160
Subordinate Vtg.	unlimited	1,200,668
Cl.B Non-vtg.	n.a.	320,000,000[2]

[1] At June 30, 2022

[2] Securities of wholly owned Irwin Naturals, a Nevada Corporation

Multiple Voting - All held by Klee Irwin. Convertible into subordinate voting shares on a 1-for-1 basis. 15,000 votes per share.

Proportionate Voting - 100 votes per share.

Subordinate Voting - One vote per share.

Class B Non-voting - Issued by wholly owned Irwin Naturals, a Nevada Corporation. Convertible into subordinate voting shares on a 1-for-1 basis.

Normal Course Issuer Bid - The company plans to make normal course purchases of up to 75,466 subordinate voting shares representing 5% of the total outstanding. The bid commenced on Sept. 26, 2022, and expires on Sept. 26, 2023.

Major Shareholder - Klee Irwin held 98.91% interest at June 3, 2022.

Price Range - IWIN/CSE

Year	Volume	High	Low	Close
2022	309,282	$4.47	$1.50	$3.54
2021	32,838	$4.75	$2.00	$3.99

DAI.H/TSX-VEN (D)

Year	Volume	High	Low	Close
2020	211,153	$1.33	$0.42	$1.33
2019	34,992	$2.37	$0.71	$0.75
2018	6,114	$9.98	$2.91	$4.99

Consolidation: 1-for-8.316 cons. in Aug. 2021

Recent Close: $1.30

Wholly Owned Subsidiaries

DAI US Holdco Inc., Nev.

- 100% int. in **Irwin Naturals, a Nevada Corporation**, Los Angeles, Calif.
  - 100% int. in **5310 Holdings, LLC**, Los Angeles, Calif.
- 100% int. in **Irwin Naturals Cannabis Inc.**
- 100% int. in **Irwin Naturals Emergence, Inc.**
  - 100% int. in **Ketamine Health Centers, LLC**, Miami, Fla.
    - 100% int. in **KHC Capital Group, LLC**
    - 100% int. in **Ketamine Health Centers of Bonita Springs, LLC**
    - 100% int. in **Ketamine Health Centers of Orlando, LLC**
    - 100% int. in **Ketamine Health Centers of West Palm Beach, LLC**
    - 100% int. in **Ketamine Health Centers of Weston, LLC**
    - 100% int. in **Ketamine Management, LLC**
    - 100% int. in **Midwest Ketafusion LLC**

Financial Statistics

Periods ended:	12m Dec. 31/21[A]		12m Dec. 31/20[A1]
	US$000s	%Chg	US$000s
Operating revenue	**100,342**	**+12**	**89,377**
Cost of sales	55,648		52,876
General & admin expense	32,718		27,468
Operating expense	**88,366**	**+10**	**80,344**
Operating income	**11,976**	**+33**	**9,033**
Deprec., depl. & amort.	1,406		1,428
Finance income	nil		10
Finance costs, gross	131		312
Pre-tax income	**7,928**	**+8**	**7,356**
Income taxes	(2,186)		116
Net income	**10,114**	**+40**	**7,240**
Net inc. for equity hldrs	**8,615**	**+19**	**7,240**
Net inc. for non-cont. int	**1,499**	**n.a.**	**nil**
Cash & equivalent	625		442
Inventories	18,652		14,577
Accounts receivable	16,394		17,214
Current assets	37,141		33,889
Fixed assets, net	190		262
Right-of-use assets	3,722		2,047
Intangibles, net	87		87
Total assets	**47,219**	**+30**	**36,421**
Accts. pay. & accr. liabs	13,310		11,616
Current liabilities	21,668		20,837
Long-term debt, gross	6,178		7,500
Long-term lease liabilities	2,434		812
Shareholders' equity	23,116		14,772
Cash from oper. activs	**10,955**	**+33**	**8,218**
Cash from fin. activs	(10,709)		(8,066)
Cash from invest. activs	(52)		(81)
Net cash position	**625**	**+41**	**442**
Capital expenditures	(51)		(134)
Capital disposals	nil		53
	US$		US$
Earnings per share*	8.43		n.a.
Cash flow per share*	9.13		n.a.
	shs		shs
No. of shs. o/s*	1,200,001		n.a.
Avg. no. of shs. o/s*	1,200,001		n.a.
	%		%
Net profit margin	10.08		8.10
Return on equity	45.48		98.79
Return on assets	24.58		42.85

* Common

[A] Reported in accordance with IFRS

[1] Results pertain to Irwin Naturals, a Nevada Corporation

Latest Results

Periods ended:	6m June 30/22[A]		6m June 30/21[A]
	US$000s	%Chg	US$000s
Operating revenue	44,403	-12	50,728
Net income	1,692	-75	6,692
Net inc. for equity hldrs	1,341	-80	6,692
Net inc. for non-cont. int	351		nil
	US$		US$
Earnings per share*	1.41		n.a.

* Common

[A] Reported in accordance with IFRS

Historical Summary
(as originally stated)

Fiscal Year	Oper. Rev.	Net Inc. Bef. Disc.	EPS*
	US$000s	US$000s	US$
2021[A]	100,342	10,114	8.43
2020[A]	89,377	7,240	n.a.
	$000s	$000s	$
2019[A1]	nil	(105)	(0.02)
2018[A]	nil	(352)	(0.18)
2017[A]	nil	(125)	(0.06)

* Common

[A] Reported in accordance with IFRS

[1] Results for 2019 and prior periods pertain to Datinvest International Ltd.

Note: Results for 2019 and prior periods pertain to Datinvest International Ltd.

I.66 iSign Media Solutions Inc.

Symbol - ISD **Exchange** - TSX-VEN **CUSIP** - 46432X

Head Office - Unit 3, 45A Wilmot St W, Richmond Hill, ON, L4B 2P2

Telephone - (905) 780-6200 **Fax** - (866) 859-0142

Website - www.isignmedia.com

Email - bob@isignmedia.com

Investor Relations - Robert W. H. MacBean (905) 780-6200

Auditors - McGovern Hurley LLP C.A., Toronto, Ont.

Bankers - Royal Bank of Canada, Toronto, Ont.

Lawyers - Beard Winter LLP, Toronto, Ont.

Transfer Agents - TSX Trust Company, Toronto, Ont.

Profile - (Ont. 2007) Provides interactive mobile proximity marketing and public security alert technologies for advertisers, manufacturers, retailers and advertising agencies.

Products include Passive Historical Contact Tracing (PHACT), a smart space analytics platform which utilizes publicly available anonymous interactions between mobile devices to accurately determine occupancy levels and movements of individuals without violating any privacy issues. The PHACT platform is housed in hardware units including Hybrid Analytics Location Observation (HALO), a software platform and listening device that provides a suite of functions specifically designed to maximize safety and security within a managed environment such as schools, hospitals, shopping plazas and concert venues; and Hybrid Analytics Location Observation with object recognition (HALOfx), which includes all features of HALO, augmented with the addition of object recognition modules for true security and area management. Also holds exclusive rights from **SIMBL Business Enablement Inc.** to sell InHome Care, an artificial intelligence powered appliance for personal health and wellness designed to work with existing and bespoke health sensors to create a virtual twin of an individual, aggregating health information, providing reminders and beneficial suggestions and making recommendations for improved health and well being.

Partners include Hi-Tek Media, City of Richmond Hill, Mtrex Network Solutions, Baylor University, Mobile Hwy Advertising Media Network , Verizon, IBM, Unacast, Omni Veil Network, US Federal Contractor Registration (USFCR) and Canadian Association of Defence and Security Industries (CADSI).

Predecessor Detail - Name changed from Corbal Capital Corp., Dec. 2, 2009, pursuant to Qualifying Transaction reverse takeover acquisition of iSign Media Corporation.

Directors - David M. Beck, chr., Toronto, Ont.; Remko Noteboom, interim CEO; Robert W. H. (Bob) MacBean, CFO, Burlington, Ont.; Brian Rohaly, Toronto, Ont.; Gregory Wade, Toronto, Ont.

Other Exec. Officers - Mark Janke, chief tech. officer; Rod Milne, contr.

Capital Stock

	Authorized (shs.)	Outstanding (shs.)[1]
Common	unlimited	226,597,786

[1] At Sept. 28, 2022

Major Shareholder - Josip (Joe) Kozar held 19.47% interest at Dec. 15, 2021.

Price Range - ISD/TSX-VEN

Year	Volume	High	Low	Close
2022	22,522,124	$0.07	$0.01	$0.01
2021	59,454,313	$0.17	$0.04	$0.05
2020	42,490,585	$0.09	$0.03	$0.07
2019	18,876,294	$0.08	$0.05	$0.06
2018	18,290,190	$0.14	$0.05	$0.08

Recent Close: $0.01

Capital Stock Changes - In August 2022, private placement of 11,500,000 units (1 common share & 1 warrant) at $0.05 per unit was announced, with warrants exercisable at $0.125 per share for two years.

During fiscal 2022, common shares were issued as follows: 24,650,200 by private placement, 27,031,213 for debt settlement and 19,490,000 pursuant licensing agreement with SIMBL Business Enablement Inc.

Wholly Owned Subsidiaries

iSIGN Media Network Corp., Ont.

iSign Media Corporation, B.C.

Pinpoint Commerce Inc., Ont.

Financial Statistics

Periods ended:	12m Apr. 30/22^A		12m Apr. 30/21^A
	$000s	%Chg	$000s
Operating revenue	**nil**	**n.a.**	**1**
Cost of sales	18		17
Salaries & benefits	93		59
Research & devel. expense	243		91
General & admin expense	1,169		699
Stock-based compensation	15		66
Operating expense	**1,537**	**+65**	**931**
Operating income	**(1,537)**	**n.a.**	**(930)**
Deprec., depl. & amort.	50		26
Finance costs, gross	642		341
Pre-tax income	**(2,249)**	**n.a.**	**(1,174)**
Income taxes	(106)		nil
Net income	**(2,143)**	**n.a.**	**(1,174)**
Cash & equivalent	46		3
Inventories	9		9
Current assets	101		78
Fixed assets, net	19		4
Right-of-use assets	64		106
Intangibles, net	997		46
Total assets	**1,181**	**+405**	**234**
Bank indebtedness	nil		657
Accts. pay. & accr. liabs	653		1,278
Current liabilities	1,023		4,317
Long-term debt, gross	2,506		2,011
Long-term debt, net	2,481		nil
Equity portion of conv. debs.	222		162
Shareholders' equity	(2,803)		(4,505)
Cash from oper. activs	**(1,064)**	**n.a.**	**(400)**
Cash from fin. activs	1,139		397
Cash from invest. activs	(19)		nil
Net cash position	**46**	**n.a.**	**(9)**
	$		$
Earnings per share*	(0.01)		(0.01)
Cash flow per share*	(0.01)		(0.00)
	shs		shs
No. of shs. o/s*	226,597,786		155,426,373
Avg. no. of shs. o/s*	180,313,720		147,960,853
	%		%
Net profit margin	n.a.		n.m.
Return on equity	n.m.		n.m.
Return on assets	(216.43)		(462.78)

* Common

^A Reported in accordance with IFRS

Latest Results

Periods ended:	3m July 31/22^A		3m July 31/21^A
	$000s	%Chg	$000s
Net income	(316)	n.a.	(358)
	$		$
Earnings per share*	(0.00)		(0.00)

* Common

^A Reported in accordance with IFRS

Historical Summary
(as originally stated)

Fiscal Year	Oper. Rev. $000s	Net Inc. Bef. Disc. $000s	EPS* $
2022^A	nil	(2,143)	(0.01)
2021^A	1	(1,174)	(0.01)
2020^A	28	(1,193)	(0.01)
2019^A	26	(1,383)	(0.01)
2018^A	19	(1,236)	(0.01)

* Common

^A Reported in accordance with IFRS

I.67 Isracann Biosciences Inc.

Symbol - IPOT **Exchange** - CSE (S) **CUSIP** - 46501D
Head Office - 1600-595 Burrard St, Vancouver, BC, V7X 1L3
Telephone - (604) 343-8661 **Toll-free** - (855) 205-0226
Website - www.isracann.com
Email - info@isracann.com
Investor Relations - Ajay Singh Kaila (604) 343-2724
Auditors - MNP LLP C.A., Toronto, Ont.
Transfer Agents - Computershare Trust Company of Canada Inc., Vancouver, B.C.

Profile - (B.C. 2018; orig. Alta., 2010) Developing cannabis cultivation and distribution operations in Israel for sale of medical cannabis in domestic and European markets.

Developing a 232,900-sq.-ft. facility in Nir, Israel through 73.93%-owned **Cannisra Crops Ltd.** (CCL), a joint venture with a farming company that holds breeding and cultivation licences from the Israeli Ministry of Health. Phase I of the development includes build out of two greenhouses totaling 115,000 sq. ft. and Phase II involves the build out of two additional greenhouses totaling 115,000 sq. ft. The facility would be capable of producing 23,500 kg of cannabis annually for medical cannabis cultivation. The company is in the process of transferring the cannabis licence rights held by the farming company to CCL.

In addition, 50%-owned **Cannation Ltd.** holds preliminary cannabis nursery and cultivation licences for 5,000-m^2 and 10,000-m^2 growing facilities in the HaSharon region in Israel. The facilities houses 165,000 sq. ft. of greenhouse canopy on a 2,000,000-sq.-ft. land, with a combined projected annual yield of 12,600 kg of dried cannabis. Facilities include 54,000 sq. ft. greenhouse and expanded post harvest facility (to be able to service the total 165,000 sq. ft. of proposed commercial greenhouse facilities), which was completed in August 2021.

On Apr. 12, 2022, the company acquired **Praesidio Health Inc.**, a private Canadian medical research company that develops and validates natural health medicine (NHM) using an evidence-based process, for issuance of $4,000,000 of common shares, of which 12,210,008 common shares with a deemed value of $1,000,000 were issued upon completion, and shares with a deemed value of $500,000 will be issued every six months thereafter until the third anniversary of completion.

Common suspended from CSE, Apr. 6, 2023.

Predecessor Detail - Name changed from Atlas Blockchain Group Inc., Oct. 7, 2019, pursuant to the acquisition of private (old) Isracann Biosciences Inc., a low-cost industrial-scale cannabis producer.; basis 1 new for 3 old shs.

Directors - Yana Popova, CFO & corp. sec., Vancouver, B.C.; Desmond M. (Des) Balakrishnan, Vancouver, B.C.; Sean Bromley, Vancouver, B.C.; Dr. George Vrabec, B.C.

Other Exec. Officers - Ajay Singh Kaila, interim CEO; Matthew (Matt) Chatterton, chief science officer; Bob Mehr, v-p, natural health product devel.; Stephen Parker, v-p, bus. devel.

Capital Stock

	Authorized (shs.)	Outstanding (shs.)[1]
Preferred	unlimited	nil
Common	unlimited	176,729,944

[1] At Feb. 23, 2023

Major Shareholder - Widely held at Feb. 23, 2023.

Price Range - IPOT/CSE (S)

Year	Volume	High	Low	Close
2022	17,256,752	$0.16	$0.01	$0.01
2021	37,172,739	$0.40	$0.04	$0.05
2020	88,654,065	$0.52	$0.15	$0.25
2019	58,007,603	$0.68	$0.25	$0.48
2018	8,505,044	$4.11	$0.32	$0.38

Consolidation: 1-for-3 cons. in Oct. 2019
Recent Close: $0.02

Capital Stock Changes - On Apr. 12, 2022, 12,210,008 common shares were issued pursuant to the acquisition of Praesidio Health Inc.

Wholly Owned Subsidiaries

Isracann Holdings Inc., B.C.
- 100% int. in **Isracann Biosciences Capital Ltd.**, Israel.
  - 100% int. in **Isracann Administrative Services Ltd.**, Israel.
  - 100% int. in **Isracann Agritech Ltd.**, Israel.
  - 100% int. in **Isracann Development Ltd.**, Israel.

Isracann Operations Ltd., Israel.
- 50% int. in **Cannation Ltd.**, Israel.

Praesidio Health Inc., Canada.

Subsidiaries

99.9% int. in **Cannisra Holdings Ltd.**, Israel.
- 74% int. in **Cannisra Crops Ltd.**, Israel.

Financial Statistics

Periods ended:	12m May 31/21^A		12m May 31/20^A
	$000s	%Chg	$000s
General & admin expense	4,154		10,552
Stock-based compensation	739		1,178
Operating expense	**4,893**	**-58**	**11,729**
Operating income	**(4,893)**	**n.a.**	**(11,729)**
Deprec., depl. & amort.	41		45
Finance income	76		140
Finance costs, gross	139		nil
Write-downs/write-offs	(20,621)		(12,060)
Pre-tax income	**(25,092)**	**n.a.**	**(23,988)**
Income taxes	31		(69)
Net inc. bef. disc. opers	**(25,123)**	**n.a.**	**(23,919)**
Income from disc. opers	(32)		(283)
Net income	**(25,155)**	**n.a.**	**(24,202)**
Net inc. for equity hldrs	**(25,155)**	**n.a.**	**(24,198)**
Net inc. for non-cont. int	**nil**	**n.a.**	**(3)**
Cash & equivalent	1,958		3,891
Accounts receivable	208		243
Current assets	2,251		5,478
Long-term investments	254		269
Fixed assets, net	89		117
Intangibles, net	nil		20,619
Total assets	**4,400**	**-84**	**28,274**
Accts. pay. & accr. liabs	465		751
Current liabilities	465		1,718
Shareholders' equity	3,938		26,559
Non-controlling interest	(3)		(3)
Cash from oper. activs	**(4,230)**	**n.a.**	**(10,400)**
Cash from fin. activs	2,165		12,757
Cash from invest. activs	134		(2,633)
Net cash position	**1,958**	**-50**	**3,891**
	$		$
Earnings per share*	(0.18)		(0.26)
Cash flow per share*	(0.03)		(0.11)
	shs		shs
No. of shs. o/s*	146,080,110		134,194,547
Avg. no. of shs. o/s*	138,402,684		92,758,275
	%		%
Net profit margin	n.a.		n.a.
Return on equity	(164.76)		(114.18)
Return on assets	(152.93)		(107.15)

* Common

^A Reported in accordance with IFRS

Latest Results

Periods ended:	3m Aug. 31/21^A		3m Aug. 31/20^oA
	$000s	%Chg	$000s
Net inc. bef. disc. opers	(469)	n.a.	(218)
Income from disc. opers	nil		(32)
Net income	(469)	n.a.	(250)
	$		$
Earnings per share*	(0.00)		(0.00)

* Common

^o Restated

^A Reported in accordance with IFRS

Historical Summary
(as originally stated)

Fiscal Year	Oper. Rev. $000s	Net Inc. Bef. Disc. $000s	EPS* $
2021^A	nil	(25,123)	(0.18)
2020^A	nil	(23,919)	(0.26)
2019^A	1,766	(9,904)	(0.27)
2018^A	1,106	(7,475)	(0.33)
2017^A	322	(668)	(0.12)

* Common

^A Reported in accordance with IFRS

Note: Adjusted throughout for 1-for-3 cons. in Oct. 2019

I.68 Itafos Inc.

Symbol - IFOS **Exchange** - TSX-VEN **CUSIP** - 465270
Head Office - 3500 South DuPont Hwy, Kent County, Dover, DE, United States, 19901
Website - www.itafos.com
Email - matthew.o'neill@itafos.com
Investor Relations - Matthew O'Neill (713) 242-8446
Auditors - PricewaterhouseCoopers LLP C.A., Toronto, Ont.
Bankers - HSBC Bank Canada
Lawyers - Cassels Brock & Blackwell LLP, Toronto, Ont.
Transfer Agents - TSX Trust Company, Toronto, Ont.
Employees - 417 at Dec. 31, 2022

Profile - (Del. 2021; orig. Alta., 1999) Owns the Conda phosphate operations in Idaho and 98.4% interest in the Arraias single super phosphate operations in Brazil. Also holds other phosphate projects in Brazil, West Africa and Peru.

Holds the Conda phosphate operations (CPO), 1,693 hectares, Conda, Idaho, which includes phosphate production facilities and adjacent phosphate mineral rights. CPO produces 550,000 tonnes per year of mono-ammonium phosphate (MAP), MAP with micronutrients (MAP+), super phosphoric acid (SPA), merchant grade phosphoric acid (MGA) and specialty products including ammonium polyphosphate (APP) serving the North American fertilizer market. It also produces 27,000 tonnes per year of hydrofluorosilicic acid (HFSA). At July 2019, proven and probable reserves were 13,100,000 tons grading 26.6% phosphate, sufficient for mine life up to mid-2026. The company has begun capital activities associated with the HuskY1 1/North Dry Ridge mine development which would extend Conda's resource life through 2037, with mineral resources expected from 2026 onward.

Holds 98.4% interest in Arraias single super phosphate (SSP) business, 105,421 hectares, 7 km northeast of Campos Belos, Brazil, consisting of a phosphate mine and mill, beneficiation plant, a sulphuric acid plant, an SSP acidulation plant and a granulation plant, with production capacity of 500,000 tonnes of SSP, SSP with micronutrients (SSP+) and premium PK compounds per year. The facility also sell excess sulphuric acid as a by-product of the SSP production process, at 40,000 tonnes per year. At March 2013, proven and probable reserves were 64,811,000 tonnes grading 5.07% phosphate, sufficient for a 25-year mine life. Commercial production was achieved on July 3, 2018, and was idled on Nov. 21, 2019. The company completed the recommissioning of the sulfuric acid plant at Arraias and commenced sulfuric acid production and sales during first quarter of 2022.

Also in Brazil, holds 99.4% interest in Santana phosphate project, 233,070 hectares, 200 km from Santana do Araguaia (Pará state) and Vila Rica (Mato Grosso state). A prefeasibility study completed in January 2012 forecast production of 500,000 tonnes of SSP per year from an open-pit operation over a 32-year mine life. Total capital costs were estimated at US$427,000,000. At October 2013, proven and probable reserves were 45,481,000 tonnes grading 12.86% phosphate. Also holds Araxá phosphate-rare-niobium earth-niobium project, 226 hectares, 5 km south of Araxá. At January 2013, measured and indicated resource was 6,340,000 tonnes grading 5.01% total rare earth oxide.

In West Africa, holds Farim phosphate project, 30,625 hectares, 5 km west of Farim, Guinea-Bissau. An updated feasibility study completed in May 2023 proposed an open-pit mine with an average annual production of 1,750,000 tonnes of phosphate over a 25-year mine life. Initial capital costs were estimated at US$308,270,000. Proven reserves were 43,800,000 tonnes grading 30% phosphate.

In Peru, holds Mantaro phosphate prospect, 12,800 hectares, 250 km east of Lima, with measured and indicated resources of 39,500,000 tonnes grading 10% phosphate. Mantaro is currently in the process of being wound down.

Sales

Year ended Dec. 31	2022	2021
	tonnes	tonnes
Conda		
MAP	349,589	287,652
MAP+	34,631	61,635
SPA	131,999	129,257
MGA	783	576
APP	22,493	30,199
HFSA	2,852	nil
Arraias		
Sulfuric acid	89,607	nil

In March 2023, the company commenced a strategic alternatives review process to explore and evaluate various strategic alternatives that may be available to the company to enhance shareholder value which may include, among other things, the sale of the company, merger, recapitalization or continued execution of the company's long-term business plan.

During 2022, the company completed the wind down process of its Paris Hills phosphate project in Idaho.

Predecessor Detail - Name changed from Itafos, July 1, 2021, pursuant to change of jurisdication from Cayman Islands to Delaware.

Directors - Anthony (Tony) Cina, chr., Woodbridge, Ont.; G. David Delaney, CEO, Ill.; Ricardo De Armas, Minn.; Stephen Shapiro, Ont.; Isaiah Toback, N.Y.; Elena Viyella de Paliza, Dominican Republic; Ronald A. Wilkinson, Bragg Creek, Alta.

Other Exec. Officers - Matthew O'Neill, CFO; David Brush, chief strategy officer; Dr. Wynand van Dyk, v-p, eng., R&D & devel.; Timothy Vedder, v-p, opers. & gen. mgr., Conda; M. Lee Reeves, gen. counsel & corp. sec.

Capital Stock

	Authorized (shs.)	Outstanding (shs.)[1]
Preferred	unlimited	nil
Common	5,000,000,000	190,608,358

[1] At Aug. 9, 2023

Major Shareholder - Rory O'Neill held 65.1% interest at June 7, 2023.

Price Range - IFOS/TSX-VEN

Year	Volume	High	Low	Close
2022	23,210,648	$3.94	$1.10	$1.43
2021	6,569,008	$1.90	$0.24	$1.49
2020	939,294	$0.66	$0.21	$0.25
2019	5,065,913	$1.63	$0.45	$0.65
2018	3,038,529	$2.90	$0.91	$1.00

Recent Close: $1.41

Capital Stock Changes - During 2022, 2,054,621 common shares were issued under restricted share unit plan.

Wholly Owned Subsidiaries

Itafos Brazil Holdings, Cayman Islands.
- 0.01% int. in **Itafos International Holdings Cooperatie U.A.**, Netherlands.

Itafos Guinea-Bissaue Holdings, Cayman Islands.
- 100% int. in **Itafos Farim Holdings**, Cayman Islands.
  - 100% int. in **GB Minerals AG**, Switzerland.
    - 100% int. in **Itafos Farim, S.A.R.L.**, Guinea-Bissau.

Itafos Ltd., Cayman Islands.
- 0.01% int. in **Itafos I LP**, Cayman Islands.
- 0.01% int. in **Itafos II LP**, Cayman Islands.

Itafos Services LLC, Del.

Itafos US Holdings Inc., Del.
- 100% int. in **Itafos Conda Holdings LLC**, Del.
  - 100% int. in **Itafos Conda LLC**, Del.
  - 100% int. in **Itafos Conda Services LLC**, Del.

Subsidiaries

99.99% int. in **Itafos I LP**, Cayman Islands.
- 20.58% int. in **Stonegate Agricom Ltd.**, Toronto, Ont.

99.99% int. in **Itafos II LP**, Cayman Islands.
- 14.59% int. in **Stonegate Agricom Ltd.**, Toronto, Ont.
  - 100% int. in **Mantaro (BVI) Ltd.**, British Virgin Islands.
    - 99.95% int. in **Mantaro Peru S.A.C.**, Peru.

99.99% int. in **Itafos International Holdings Cooperatie U.A.**, Netherlands.
- 99.99% int. in **Araxia Mineraciao e Metalurgia S.A.**, Brazil.
- 100% int. in **Itafos Arraias Holdings B.V.**, Netherlands.
  - 100% int. in **Araxia Mineraciao e Metalurgia S.A.**, Brazil.
  - 59.04% int. in **Itafos Arraias Mineração e Fertilizantes S.A.**, Brazil.
  - 99.99% int. in **Itafos Brazil Trading Company Ltda.**, Brazil.
  - 0.01% int. in **Itafos Santana Mineração e Fertilizantes S.A.**, Brazil.
- 8.24% int. in **Itafos Arraias Mineração e Fertilizantes S.A.**, Brazil.
- 100% int. in **Itafos Brazil Holdings I B.V.**, Netherlands.
  - 33.33% int. in **Itafos Fundo de Investimento em Participações Multiestratégia (FIP)**, Brazil.
    - 31.09% int. in **Itafos Arraias Mineração e Fertilizantes S.A.**, Brazil.
- 100% int. in **Itafos Brazil Holdings II B.V.**, Netherlands.
  - 33.33% int. in **Itafos Fundo de Investimento em Participações Multiestratégia (FIP)**, Brazil.
    - 17.79% int. in **Itafos Santana Mineração e Fertilizantes S.A.**, Brazil.
- 100% int. in **Itafos Brazil Holdings III B.V.**, Netherlands.
  - 33.33% int. in **Itafos Fundo de Investimento em Participações Multiestratégia (FIP)**, Brazil.
    - 100% int. in **Itafos Desenvolvimento S.A.**, Brazil.
- 0.01% int. in **Itafos Brazil Trading Company Ltda.**, Brazil.
- 81.52% int. in **Itafos Santana Mineração e Fertilizantes S.A.**, Brazil.

64.83% int. in **Stonegate Agricom Ltd.**, Toronto, Ont.
- 0.05% int. in **Mantaro Peru S.A.C.**, Peru.

Financial Statistics

Periods ended:	12m Dec. 31/22[A]		12m Dec. 31/21[A]
	US$000s	%Chg	US$000s
Operating revenue	**593,288**	**+44**	**413,247**
Cost of goods sold	344,706		250,528
Salaries & benefits	13,935		12,368
General & admin expense	10,708		9,401
Stock-based compensation	4,850		4,127
Operating expense	**374,199**	**+35**	**276,424**
Operating income	**219,089**	**+60**	**136,823**
Deprec., depl. & amort.	33,705		25,844
Finance income	190		5
Finance costs, gross	46,114		37,249
Pre-tax income	**146,854**	**+100**	**73,545**
Income taxes	32,154		22,106
Net income	**114,700**	**+123**	**51,439**
Net inc. for equity hldrs	**115,096**	**+126**	**51,028**
Net inc. for non-cont. int.	**(396)**	**n.a.**	**411**
Cash & equivalent	42,811		31,565
Inventories	122,335		112,704
Accounts receivable	22,892		39,688
Current assets	198,401		195,130
Fixed assets, net	294,040		313,073
Explor./devel. properties	116,736		120,746
Total assets	**614,009**	**-3**	**633,853**
Accts. pay. & accr. liabs	60,838		61,469
Current liabilities	97,077		121,836
Long-term debt, gross	128,124		239,848
Long-term debt, net	98,907		187,010
Long-term lease liabilities	12,806		11,700
Shareholders' equity	252,349		133,440
Non-controlling interest	769		1,165
Cash from oper. activs	**208,369**	**+120**	**94,499**
Cash from fin. activs	(158,324)		(38,433)
Cash from invest. activs	(39,003)		(34,076)
Net cash position	**42,811**	**+36**	**31,565**
Capital expenditures	(39,003)		(34,076)
	US$		US$
Earnings per share*	0.61		0.28
Cash flow per share*	1.11		0.51
	shs		shs
No. of shs. o/s*	188,869,463		186,814,842
Avg. no. of shs. o/s*	188,265,419		186,413,304
	%		%
Net profit margin	19.33		12.45
Return on equity	59.67		47.44
Return on assets	24.16		13.95
No. of employees (FTEs)	417		377

* Common
[A] Reported in accordance with IFRS

Latest Results

Periods ended:	6m June 30/23[A]		6m June 30/22[A]
	US$000s	%Chg	US$000s
Operating revenue	235,699	-23	304,858
Net income	48,637	-37	77,290
	US$		US$
Earnings per share*	0.26		0.41

* Common
[A] Reported in accordance with IFRS

Historical Summary
(as originally stated)

Fiscal Year	Oper. Rev.	Net Inc. Bef. Disc.	EPS*
	US$000s	US$000s	US$
2022[A]	593,288	114,700	0.61
2021[A]	413,247	51,439	0.28
2020[A]	260,185	(62,306)	(0.34)
2019[A]	339,430	(144,171)	(1.02)
2018[A]	302,182	(113,487)	(0.82)

* Common
[A] Reported in accordance with IFRS

I.69 Ivrnet Inc.

Symbol - IVI **Exchange** - TSX-VEN **CUSIP** - 465891
Head Office - PO Box 47078 Creekside, Calgary, AB, T2P 0B9 **Telephone** - (403) 538-0400 **Toll-free** - (800) 351-7227 **Fax** - (403) 444-5088
Website - www.ivrnet.com
Email - investors@ivrnet.com
Investor Relations - Andrew Watts (800) 351-7227
Auditors - Kenway Mack Slusarchuk Stewart LLP C.A., Calgary, Alta.
Bankers - Royal Bank of Canada, Calgary, Alta.
Lawyers - Lindsey MacCarthy LLP
Transfer Agents - Olympia Trust Company
Employees - 14 at Dec. 1, 2022
Profile - (Alta. 2003; orig. Alta., 1999) Develops, hosts, sells and supports value added business automation software.

The company's applications facilitate automated interaction such as personalized communication between people, mass communication for disseminating information to thousands of people concurrently and personalized communication between people and automated systems. The applications are accessible via voice, phone, fax, email, texting or over the Internet.

Ivrnet Central is a consolidated software suite that provides an online platform offering communication, community management and payment modules for organizations to reduce overhead, increase efficiency and enhance customer engagement. Communication modules enable organizations to engage with stakeholders, clients and staff through multiple channels and technologies. Community management modules enable organizations to manage community stakeholders such as residents, members or customers. Payment module includes Telepay, an online payment portal providing organizations with cost effective over-the-phone, Payment Card Industry Data Security Standard (PCI DSS) compliant payment solutions which give customers secure touchless payment choice resulting in quicker payments, reduced receivables and enhanced customer experience.

Revenue is derived from the sale of software licences and from providing software-related services including training, installation, consulting and maintenance; contract development, which includes website and software development for communications, which include telephone, fax, toll-free, audio conference and invoicing services; user engagement, which includes texting and text advertising services; business process, which includes website, server, community management and registration system hosting; financial technology, which includes Payment Card Industry (PCI) services and merchant fees; and custom applications, which include Safe Team, 311, merchandising, call monitoring, call marketing tracking, reporting and outbound calling applications.

Recent Merger and Acquisition Activity

Status: pending **Revised:** Nov. 24, 2022

UPDATE: The transaction was still pending, and remained subject to certain conditions, including TSX Venture Exchange approval. PREVIOUS: Ivrnet Inc. entered into a definitive agreement for a reverse takeover acquisition of Flexity Systems Ltd. by way of a three-cornered amalgamation of Flexity and wholly owned 1333749 B.C. Ltd. Ivrnet would issue common shares to Flexity shareholders on a 1-for-77.803251 post-consolidated basis. Concurrent with closing, Ivrnet would consolidate its shares on a 1-for-20 basis, change its name to Flexity Enterprise Inc. and complete a private placement of up to 12,105,262 subscription receipts at $0.9567 per subscription receipt, including an over-allotment option of 1,578,946 . In addition, all outstanding preferred shares, convertible debentures and options of Flexity would be exchanged for preferred shares, convertible debentures and options of Ivrnet on the same terms and conditions as the original security. Mar. 29, 2022 - The transaction was approved by Flexity shareholders. Ivrnet would issue 3,750,000 post-consolidated common share to Flexity shareholders on a 75.4989184-for-1 basis; 6,267 preferred shares convertible to 8,352,613 post-consolidated Ivrnet shares at a deemed price of $1,000 per share; 33,019,956 options in exchange for the issued and outstanding common share option of Flexity; and 6,562 convertible debenture convertible into 8,749,775 post-consolidated Ivrnet shares. In addition, Flexity, instead of Ivrnet, would complete a private placement of up to 12,105,262 subscription receipts at 95¢ per receipt. Underwriters were granted an over-allotment option of up to an additional 1,578,948 shares.

Predecessor Detail - Name changed from Entreplex Technology Corporation, Oct. 6, 2000.

Directors - Andrew Watts, pres. & CEO, Calgary, Alta.; Robert (Rob) Barlow, Uxbridge, Ont.; David L. (Dave) King, North Vancouver, B.C.; David L. (Dave) Snell, Calgary, Alta.

Other Exec. Officers - William Harper, CFO; Jim Jeffries, v-p, opers.

Capital Stock

	Authorized (shs.)	Outstanding (shs.)[1]
Preferred	unlimited	nil
Common	unlimited	99,311,181

[1] At Nov. 24, 2022

Major Shareholder - David L. (Dave) Snell held 21.87% interest at Aug. 26, 2022.

Price Range - IVI/TSX-VEN

Year	Volume	High	Low	Close
2021	127,214,542	$0.17	$0.03	$0.05
2020	25,159,666	$0.06	$0.01	$0.06
2019	8,719,729	$0.03	$0.01	$0.02
2018	14,539,517	$0.06	$0.02	$0.04

Wholly Owned Subsidiaries

1333749 B.C. Ltd., Canada.

Financial Statistics

Periods ended:	12m Dec. 31/21[A]		12m Dec. 31/20[oA]
	$000s	%Chg	$000s
Operating revenue	**3,049**	**-2**	**3,117**
Cost of sales	930		1,065
Salaries & benefits	682		1,023
General & admin expense	1,091		590
Stock-based compensation	231		nil
Operating expense	**2,934**	**+10**	**2,678**
Operating income	**115**	**-74**	**439**
Deprec., depl. & amort.	424		572
Finance costs, gross	691		724
Write-downs/write-offs	(148)		(100)
Pre-tax income	**(1,147)**	**n.a.**	**(1,055)**
Net income	**(1,147)**	**n.a.**	**(1,055)**
Cash & equivalent	215		201
Accounts receivable	405		509
Current assets	636		722
Fixed assets, net	30		133
Right-of-use assets	nil		158
Intangibles, net	268		633
Total assets	**934**	**-43**	**1,645**
Accts. pay. & accr. liabs	1,194		1,307
Current liabilities	4,520		4,556
Long-term debt, gross	3,528		3,453
Long-term debt, net	40		40
Long-term lease liabilities	121		121
Shareholders' equity	(3,906)		(3,322)
Cash from oper. activs	**(163)**	**n.a.**	**(865)**
Cash from fin. activs	177		1,030
Cash from invest. activs	nil		(4)
Net cash position	**215**	**+7**	**201**
Capital expenditures	nil		(4)
	$		$
Earnings per share*	(0.01)		(0.01)
Cash flow per share*	(0.00)		(0.01)
	shs		shs
No. of shs. o/s*	99,311,181		90,581,391
Avg. no. of shs. o/s*	96,228,767		90,243,646
	%		%
Net profit margin	(37.62)		(33.85)
Return on equity	n.m.		n.m.
Return on assets	(35.36)		(17.94)

* Common

[o] Restated

[A] Reported in accordance with IFRS

Latest Results

Periods ended:	9m Sept. 30/22[A]		9m Sept. 30/21[A]
	$000s	%Chg	$000s
Operating revenue	2,195	-3	2,254
Net income	(819)	n.a.	(1,199)
	$		$
Earnings per share*	(0.01)		(0.01)

* Common

[A] Reported in accordance with IFRS

Historical Summary
(as originally stated)

Fiscal Year	Oper. Rev.	Net Inc. Bef. Disc.	EPS*
	$000s	$000s	$
2021[A]	3,049	(1,147)	(0.01)
2020[A]	3,117	(1,055)	(0.01)
2019[A]	2,929	(2,270)	(0.03)
2018[A]	3,051	(621)	(0.01)
2017[A]	3,522	(425)	(0.01)

* Common

[A] Reported in accordance with IFRS

I.70 Izotropic Corporation

Symbol - IZO **Exchange** - CSE **CUSIP** - 46604F

Head Office - 424, 800-15355 24 Ave, Surrey, BC, V4A 2H9 **Toll-free** - (833) 496-2677

Website - www.izocorp.com

Email - bthast@izocorp.com

Investor Relations - Robert L. Thast (833) 496-2677

Auditors - Dale Matheson Carr-Hilton LaBonte LLP C.A., Vancouver, B.C.

Lawyers - Clark Wilson LLP, Vancouver, B.C.

Transfer Agents - Odyssey Trust Company, Vancouver, B.C.; The Canadian Depository for Securities Limited

Profile - (Can. 2016) Commercializing the IzoView 3D breast computed tomography (CT) imaging platform for early diagnosis of breast cancer.

The IZOview platform produces high resolution breast images in 3D and is ideal for imaging patients with dense breast tissue. The equipment acquires approximately 500 images in a single 10 second breast CT scan without painful breast compression and provides radiologists with fully 3D viewing of the scanned breast.

The company holds an exclusive worldwide licence from the University of California, Davis to commercialize the technology. The licence also includes intellectual property, trade secrets, patents and patent-pending applications that are the foundation of the company's breast CT imaging platform.

In August 2022, the company has relocated IzoView platform and associated components, and completed the transition of all major medical device engineering and product development operations to its in-house facility in Sacramento, Calif.

Directors - Dr. John Boone, founder, Calif.; Robert L. (Bob) Thast, chr. & interim CEO, Surrey, B.C.; Ralph Proceviat, interim CFO, Vancouver, B.C.; Ali Sodagar, Vancouver, B.C.; Alexander Tokman

Other Exec. Officers - Dr. Younes Achkire, COO; Jaclyn Thast, corp. sec.

Capital Stock

	Authorized (shs.)	Outstanding (shs.)[1]
Common	unlimited	49,103,954

[1] At Aug. 26, 2022

Major Shareholder - Widely held at Sept. 1, 2021.

Price Range - IZO/CSE

Year	Volume	High	Low	Close
2022	9,112,082	$0.95	$0.29	$0.70
2021	28,359,165	$1.56	$0.66	$0.94
2020	49,934,424	$1.52	$0.12	$1.22
2019	1,799,900	$0.45	$0.22	$0.22
2018	432,950	$0.50	$0.26	$0.28

Recent Close: $0.23

Capital Stock Changes - During fiscal 2022, common shares were issued as follows: 2,078,881 on exercise of warrants, 450,000 on vesting of restricted share units, 181,495 for services and 125,000 on exercise of options.

Wholly Owned Subsidiaries

Izotropic Imaging Corp., Nev.

Financial Statistics

Periods ended:	12m Apr. 30/22[A]		12m Apr. 30/21[A]
	$000s	%Chg	$000s
Research & devel. expense	3,412		793
General & admin expense	2,146		1,927
Stock-based compensation	1,070		2,255
Operating expense	**6,628**	**+33**	**4,974**
Operating income	**(6,628)**	**n.a.**	**(4,974)**
Deprec., depl. & amort.	7		2
Finance costs, gross	20		nil
Pre-tax income	**(6,655)**	**n.a.**	**(4,976)**
Net income	**(6,655)**	**n.a.**	**(4,976)**
Cash & equivalent	1,857		4,064
Accounts receivable	41		44
Current assets	2,250		4,685
Fixed assets, net	19		2
Total assets	**2,269**	**-52**	**4,687**
Accts. pay. & accr. liabs	615		169
Current liabilities	2,644		169
Long-term debt, gross	2,028		nil
Shareholders' equity	(375)		4,517
Cash from oper. activs	**(4,764)**	**n.a.**	**(3,081)**
Cash from fin. activs	2,581		6,532
Cash from invest. activs	(24)		nil
Net cash position	**1,857**	**-54**	**4,064**
Capital expenditures	(24)		nil
	$		$
Earnings per share*	(0.15)		(0.14)
Cash flow per share*	(0.11)		(0.09)
	shs		shs
No. of shs. o/s*	44,841,454		42,006,078
Avg. no. of shs. o/s*	43,101,242		35,304,860
	%		%
Net profit margin	n.a.		n.a.
Return on equity	n.m.		(190.51)
Return on assets	(190.77)		(182.14)

* Common

[A] Reported in accordance with IFRS

Historical Summary
(as originally stated)

Fiscal Year	Oper. Rev.	Net Inc. Bef. Disc.	EPS*
	$000s	$000s	$
2022[A]	nil	(6,655)	(0.15)
2021[A]	nil	(4,976)	(0.14)
2020[A]	nil	(1,156)	(0.05)
2019[A]	nil	(399)	(0.02)
2018[A]	nil	(730)	(0.05)

* Common

[A] Reported in accordance with IFRS

J

J.1 J4 Ventures Inc.

Symbol - JJJJ.P **Exchange** - TSX-VEN **CUSIP** - 47746L
Head Office - 503-905 Pender St W, Vancouver, BC, V6C 1L6 **Telephone** - (604) 722-9842
Email - jeremy@nicofinancepartners.com
Investor Relations - Jeremy Poirier (604) 722-9842
Auditors - Davidson & Company LLP C.A., Vancouver, B.C.
Transfer Agents - Odyssey Trust Company, Vancouver, B.C.
Profile - (B.C. 2021) Capital Pool Company.
Directors - Jeremy Poirier, CEO, North Vancouver, B.C.; R. Timothy (Tim) Henneberry, Mill Bay, B.C.; Jordan Witham-Carroll, Kamloops, B.C.
Other Exec. Officers - Joel Leonard, CFO

Capital Stock

	Authorized (shs.)	Outstanding (shs.)[1]
Common	unlimited	8,550,000

[1] At June 20, 2022

Major Shareholder - Jeremy Poirier held 17.54% interest at Aug. 20, 2021.

Price Range - JJJJ.P/TSX-VEN

Year	Volume	High	Low	Close
2022	201,300	$0.18	$0.06	$0.06
2021	108,000	$0.17	$0.13	$0.14

Recent Close: $0.06

Capital Stock Changes - On Aug. 20, 2021, an initial public offering of 2,000,000 common shares was completed at 10¢ per share.

J.2 JFT Strategies Fund

Symbol - JFS.UN **Exchange** - TSX **CUSIP** - 466135
Head Office - 200-15 York St, Toronto, ON, M5J 0A3 **Telephone** - (416) 642-1289 **Toll-free** - (877) 642-1289 **Fax** - (416) 365-0501
Website - www.cifinancial.com
Email - moxby@ci.com
Investor Relations - Murrax Oxby (416) 681-3254
Auditors - Ernst & Young LLP C.A., Toronto, Ont.
Lawyers - Blake, Cassels & Graydon LLP, Toronto, Ont.
Transfer Agents - Computershare Trust Company of Canada Inc., Toronto, Ont.
Trustees - CI Investments Inc., Toronto, Ont.
Managers - CI Investments Inc., Toronto, Ont.
Portfolio Managers - Timelo Investment Management Inc., Aurora, Ont.
Profile - (Ont. 2012) Invests in an actively managed portfolio consisting of long and short positions in any one or a combination of equities, debt securities or other securities.

The portfolio may include, at any time, equities, warrants, options on equities, government treasury instruments, corporate bonds (including non-investment grade bonds), convertible bonds, exchange-traded funds (ETFs) and similar securities, such as American Depository Receipts (ADRs). The fund may also have exposure to commodities through ETFs. The fund does not have a fixed termination date but may be terminated by the manager upon the approval of the unitholders.

Portfolio allocation at July 31, 2023 (as a percentage of total investment portfolio):

Sector	Percentage
Cash & cash equivalents	60.28%
Fixed income	17.73%
Energy	11.25%
Basic materials	7.64%
Financial services	5.29%
Consumer goods	4.94%
Industrial goods	1.80%
Real estate	1.28%
Healthcare	0.79%
Other	(11)%

Oper. Subsid./Mgt. Co. Directors - Darie P. Urbanky, pres. & COO, Toronto, Ont.; Yvette Zhang, CFO, Toronto, Ont.; Elsa Li, sr. v-p & gen. counsel, Toronto, Ont.
Oper. Subsid./Mgt. Co. Officers - William Chinkiwsky, chief compliance officer

Capital Stock

	Authorized (shs.)	Outstanding (shs.)[1]
Class A Unit	unlimited	2,985,325
Class F Unit	unlimited	4,304,681
Private Placement Unit	unlimited	285,093

[1] At Aug. 25, 2023

Class A Unit - Retractable in January of each year at a price equal to the net asset value (NAV) per unit less associated costs. Retractable monthly at a price equal to the lesser of: (i) 95% of the weighted average price of the units on the TSX during the 10 trading days preceding the retraction date; and (ii) the closing price per unit. Convertible into class F units by delivering a notice and surrendering such class A units at least 10 business days prior to the conversion date. One vote per unit.

Class F Unit - Retractable in January of each year at a price equal to NAV per unit less associated costs. Retractable monthly at a price equal to the product of: (i) class A monthly redemption amount, and (ii) a fraction, the numerator of which is the most recently calculated NAV per class F unit and the denominator of which is the most recently calculated NAV per class A unit. Convertible into class A units in any month on the second last business day of such month by delivering a notice and surrendering such class F units at least 10 business days prior to the conversion date. One vote per unit.

Private Placement Unit - Retractable in January of each year at a price equal to NAV per unit less associated costs. Retractable monthly at a price equal to the product of: (i) class A monthly redemption amount, and (ii) a fraction, the numerator of which is the most recently calculated NAV per private placement unit and the denominator of which is the most recently calculated NAV per class A unit. Convertible into class A units in any month on the second last business day of such month by delivering a notice and surrendering such private placement units at least 10 business days prior to the conversion date. Non-voting.

Major Shareholder - Widely held at Mar. 24, 2023.

Price Range - JFS.UN/TSX

Year	Volume	High	Low	Close
2022	670,211	$24.06	$20.28	$23.16
2021	916,489	$24.00	$18.91	$21.08
2020	2,445,397	$19.99	$11.28	$19.39
2019	2,378,476	$14.99	$13.71	$14.12
2018	2,585,076	$14.33	$13.44	$13.87

Recent Close: $23.87

Capital Stock Changes - During 2022, 243,993 class F units were converted into 260,229 class A units, 505,279 class A units were converted into 473,292 class F units and 257,962 class F units and 237,313 class A units were retracted.

Dividends

JFS.UN unit Ra $0.25
stk.[1]◆g .... Jan. 13/23 stk.[2]◆ .... Jan. 14/22
Paid in 2023: stk.◆g 2022: stk.◆ 2021: n.a.

[1] Distributions will be automatically reinvested and the units will be consolidated immediately after distribution. Equiv to $2.0671.
[2] Equiv to $1.966989.
◆ Special **g** Capital Gain

Financial Statistics

Periods ended:	12m Dec. 31/22[A]		12m Dec. 31/21[oA]
	$000s	%Chg	$000s
Realized invest. gain (loss)	23,055		47,435
Unrealized invest. gain (loss)	(6,674)		(9,788)
Total revenue	**21,369**	**-46**	**39,489**
General & admin. expense	8,098		13,184
Operating expense	**8,098**	**-39**	**13,184**
Operating income	**13,271**	**-50**	**26,305**
Finance costs, gross	66		89
Pre-tax income	**13,175**	**-50**	**26,207**
Net income	**13,175**	**-50**	**26,207**
Cash & equivalent	502		nil
Accounts receivable	991		365
Investments	222,680		190,903
Total assets	**249,598**	**-17**	**299,115**
Bank indebtedness	nil		6,590
Accts. pay. & accr. liabs	1,349		6,759
Shareholders' equity	186,351		184,278
Cash from oper. activs	**18,084**	**+43**	**12,623**
Cash from fin. activs	(11,058)		(16,935)
Net cash position	**502**	**n.a.**	**(6,590)**
	$		$
Earnings per share*	1.49		2.96
Earnings per share**	1.75		3.21
Cash flow per share***	2.47		1.61
Net asset value per share*	23.15		21.62
Extra stk. divd. - cash equiv.*	2.07		1.97
	shs		shs
No. of shs. o/s***	7,271,696		7,782,722
Avg. no. of shs. o/s***	7,335,396		7,855,953
	%		%
Net profit margin	61.65		66.37
Return on equity	7.11		14.59
Return on assets	4.83		8.88

* Class A unit
** Class F unit
*** Class A unit & Class F unit
[o] Restated
[A] Reported in accordance with IFRS

Historical Summary
(as originally stated)

Fiscal Year	Total Rev.	Net Inc. Bef. Disc.	EPS*
	$000s	$000s	$
2022[A]	21,369	13,175	1.49
2021[A]	39,489	26,207	2.96
2020[A]	51,105	37,266	3.58
2019[A]	15,792	7,475	0.55
2018[A]	9,965	956	0.03

* Class A unit
[A] Reported in accordance with IFRS

J.3 JM Capital II Corp.

Symbol - JCI.H **Exchange** - TSX-VEN **CUSIP** - 46622N
Head Office - 900-135 Yorkville Ave, Toronto, ON, M5R 0C7 **Telephone** - (416) 972-9993 **Fax** - (416) 972-6208
Email - lena@jjrcapital.com
Investor Relations - Elena Masters (416) 972-9993
Auditors - RSM Canada LLP C.A., Toronto, Ont.
Lawyers - Fogler, Rubinoff LLP, Toronto, Ont.
Transfer Agents - TSX Trust Company, Toronto, Ont.
Profile - (Ont. 2012) Capital Pool Company.

In September 2022, the company terminated the proposed Qualifying Transaction reverse takeover acquisition of private British Columbia-based **1135809 B.C. Ltd.**, which holds the Screech mineral exploration project in British Columbia. The transaction was originally entered into in February 2018.

Directors - Jay W. Freeman, pres. & CEO, Toronto, Ont.; Elena (Lena) Masters, CFO & corp. sec., Toronto, Ont.; Robert (Rob) Barlow, Uxbridge, Ont.

Capital Stock

	Authorized (shs.)	Outstanding (shs.)[1]
Common	unlimited	4,600,000

[1] At May 31, 2022

Price Range - JCI.H/TSX-VEN

Year	Volume	High	Low	Close
2022	89,632	$0.11	$0.03	$0.03

Recent Close: $0.01

J.4 JVR Ventures Inc.

Symbol - JVR.P **Exchange** - TSX-VEN **CUSIP** - 46654Y
Head Office - 2500-700 Georgia St W, Vancouver, BC, V7Y 1B3 **Telephone** - (604) 908-4495
Email - jvr.cpc@gmail.com
Investor Relations - Kristen Reinertson (604) 908-4495
Auditors - SHIM & Associates LLP C.A., Vancouver, B.C.
Transfer Agents - Odyssey Trust Company, Vancouver, B.C.
Profile - (B.C. 2021) Capital Pool Company.
Directors - Kristen Reinertson, pres., CEO, CFO & corp. sec., Vancouver, B.C.; Jessica Van Den Akker, Vancouver, B.C.; Joanna Vastardis, B.C.

Capital Stock

	Authorized (shs.)	Outstanding (shs.)[1]
Preferred	unlimited	nil
Common	unlimited	6,000,000

[1] At May 2, 2023

Major Shareholder - Jessica Van Den Akker held 16.67% interest at Feb. 12, 2023.

Price Range - JVR.P/TSX-VEN

Year	Volume	High	Low	Close
2022	87,501	$0.10	$0.06	$0.06

Recent Close: $0.11

Capital Stock Changes - On May 12, 2022, an initial public offering of 4,000,000 common shares was completed at 10¢ per share.

J.5 Jabbo Capital Corp.

Symbol - JAB.P **Exchange** - TSX-VEN **CUSIP** - 466312
Head Office - 1703-595 Burrard St, Vancouver, BC, V7X 1J1 **Telephone** - (604) 488-5427 **Fax** - (604) 681-4692
Email - bayley@earlston.ca
Investor Relations - Brian E. Bayley (604) 681-4692
Auditors - Davidson & Company LLP C.A., Vancouver, B.C.
Transfer Agents - Computershare Trust Company of Canada Inc., Vancouver, B.C.
Profile - (B.C. 2020) Capital Pool Company.

Recent Merger and Acquisition Activity

Status: terminated **Revised:** May 11, 2022

UPDATE: The transaction was terminated. PREVIOUS: Jabbo Capital Corp. entered into a letter of intent for the Qualifying Transaction reverse takeover acquisition of private BPG Metals Corp., which holds Luanga PGE-gold-nickel project in Pará state, Brazil, for issuance of post-consolidated common shares on a to-be-determined basis (following a 1-for-2 share consolidation). Upon completion, Jabbo would change its name to BPG Metals Corp.

Directors - Brian E. Bayley, pres., CEO, CFO & corp. counsel, North Vancouver, B.C.; John Downes, Port Moody, B.C.; Sandra Lee, Vancouver, B.C.

Capital Stock

	Authorized (shs.)	Outstanding (shs.)[1]
Common	unlimited	3,360,000

[1] At Feb. 22, 2022

Major Shareholder - Ionic Securities Ltd. held 43.48% interest and Brian E. Bayley held 11.59% interest at Apr. 5, 2021.

Price Range - JAB.P/TSX-VEN

Year	Volume	High	Low	Close
2022	5,500	$0.38	$0.30	$0.30
2021	307,200	$0.50	$0.30	$0.35
2020	55,200	$0.40	$0.30	$0.35

Recent Close: $0.31

J.6 Jack Nathan Medical Corp.

Symbol - JNH **Exchange** - TSX-VEN **CUSIP** - 466377
Head Office - Suite 491, 6-6150 Hwy 7, Woodbridge, ON, L4H 0R6 **Telephone** - (416) 274-2160
Website - www.jacknathanhealth.com
Email - spence.walker@jacknathanhealth.com
Investor Relations - Spence Walker (416) 274-2160
Auditors - MNP LLP C.A., Toronto, Ont.
Lawyers - Ellison Law Professional Corporation, Toronto, Ont.
Transfer Agents - TSX Trust Company, Toronto, Ont.

Profile - (Ont. 2017) Develops medical clinics located in Walmart stores in Canada and Mexico under the Jack Nathan Health brand.

At June 26, 2023, the company had 75 clinics in Walmart locations in British Columbia, Alberta, Saskatchewan, Manitoba, Ontario and Quebec, 26 of which were owned and operated by the company, as well as 131 corporate-owned and operated clinics in Mexico including four clinics inside Walmart's distribution centres to service Walmart associates.

Services provided by the company's clinics include family care, walk-in and urgent care services, telemedicine, specialist health care services, travel medicine, allied health services and dental under JNH medical clinics; platelet rich plasma treatment, skin rejuvenation, laser hair removal, hair restoration, belkyra, facials, chemical peels and injectables under the JNH Medspa clinics; and physiotherapy, chiropractic services, massage therapy, chiropody, orthotics, custom bracing, compression hosiery and acupuncture under the JNH Rehab clinics.

Primary source of revenue results from the operation of medical clinics and usage-based licence fees in exchange for the right to use the Jack Nathan Health brand and licensed premises.

Predecessor Detail - Name changed from Woodbridge Ventures Inc., Sept. 29, 2020, pursuant to Qualifying Transaction reverse takeover acquisition of Jack Nathan Medical Inc.; basis 1 new for 3 old shs.

Directors - Michael (Mike) Marchelletta, exec. v-chr., Woodbridge, Ont.; Dr. Glenn Copeland, pres., CEO & CMO, Ont.; Anthony DeCristofaro, Toronto, Ont.; Blake D. Lyon, Toronto, Ont.; Mark Redinger, Ont.

Other Exec. Officers - Marcy Herriman, COO; Spence Walker, interim CFO; Serge Cinelli, chief tech. officer

Capital Stock

	Authorized (shs.)	Outstanding (shs.)[1]
Common	unlimited	85,452,751

[1] At June 26, 2023

Major Shareholder - Michael (Mike) Marchelletta held 24.83% interest and George Barakat held 14.51% interest at June 16, 2023.

Price Range - JNH/TSX-VEN

Year	Volume	High	Low	Close
2022	17,114,369	$0.28	$0.08	$0.10
2021	24,235,420	$1.07	$0.16	$0.18
2020	30,553,007	$2.72	$0.48	$1.01
2019	41,666	$0.45	$0.24	$0.32

Consolidation: 1-for-3 cons. in Oct. 2020
Recent Close: $0.09

Capital Stock Changes - During fiscal 2023, common shares were issued as follows: 850,000 pursuant to the acquisition of five Bridger clinics and 69,612 pursuant to the acquisition of Comox Valley medical clinic.

Wholly Owned Subsidiaries

Jack Nathan Functional Health Inc.
1883853 Ontario Ltd., Canada. dba Redeem MedSpas.
Redeem Cosmetic & Surgical Inc., Canada.
Vivify Wellness Inc.
Writi Inc., Burlington, Ont.

Subsidiaries

99.9% int. in **JNH Mexico**
95% int. in **JNH Shanghai** Inactive.

Financial Statistics

Periods ended:	12m Jan. 31/23[A]		12m Jan. 31/22[A]
	$000s	%Chg	$000s
Operating revenue	**15,488**	**+61**	**9,639**
Salaries & benefits	1,826		1,765
General & admin expense	17,022		12,397
Stock-based compensation	1,127		2,500
Operating expense	**19,975**	**+20**	**16,662**
Operating income	**(4,487)**	**n.a.**	**(7,023)**
Deprec., depl. & amort.	1,070		516
Finance income	12		35
Finance costs, gross	410		182
Write-downs/write-offs	(1,403)		(929)
Pre-tax income	**(6,989)**	**n.a.**	**(8,233)**
Income taxes	(86)		(218)
Net income	**(6,903)**	**n.a.**	**(8,016)**
Net inc. for equity hldrs	**(6,903)**	**n.a.**	**(7,808)**
Net inc. for non-cont. int.	**nil**	**n.a.**	**(208)**
Cash & equivalent	1,462		1,064
Accounts receivable	839		842
Current assets	2,514		2,240
Fixed assets, net	1,797		1,764
Right-of-use assets	758		845
Intangibles, net	1,293		3,190
Total assets	**6,451**	**-21**	**8,139**
Accts. pay. & accr. liabs	3,165		1,817
Current liabilities	5,612		2,696
Long-term debt, gross	3,791		307
Long-term debt, net	1,666		107
Long-term lease liabilities	437		544
Shareholders' equity	(1,868)		4,083
Cash from oper. activs	**(2,005)**	**n.a.**	**(4,341)**
Cash from fin. activs	5,277		(164)
Cash from invest. activs	(2,686)		(2,140)
Net cash position	**1,462**	**+37**	**1,064**
Capital expenditures	(2,586)		(951)
	$		$
Earnings per share*	(0.08)		(0.10)
Cash flow per share*	(0.02)		(0.05)
	shs		shs
No. of shs. o/s*	84,329,547		83,409,935
Avg. no. of shs. o/s*	84,298,351		82,229,879
	%		%
Net profit margin	(44.57)		(83.16)
Return on equity	n.m.		(123.78)
Return on assets	(89.08)		(83.43)
Foreign sales percent	23		26

* Common
[A] Reported in accordance with IFRS

Latest Results

Periods ended:	3m Apr. 30/23[A]		3m Apr. 30/22[A]
	$000s	%Chg	$000s
Operating revenue	4,227	+9	3,893
Net income	(790)	n.a.	(1,267)
	$		$
Earnings per share*	(0.01)		(0.02)

* Common
[A] Reported in accordance with IFRS

Historical Summary
(as originally stated)

Fiscal Year	Oper. Rev.	Net Inc. Bef. Disc.	EPS*
	$000s	$000s	$
2023[A]	15,488	(6,903)	(0.08)
2022[A]	9,639	(8,016)	(0.10)
2021[A1]	3,852	(9,914)	(0.19)
2020[A]	3,617	(1,356)	n.a.
2019[A]	2,925	2,107	n.a.

* Common
[A] Reported in accordance with IFRS
[1] Results prior to Oct. 1, 2020, pertain to and reflect the Qualifying Transaction reverse takeover acquisition of Jack Nathan Medical Inc.

Note: Adjusted throughout for 1-for-3 cons. in Oct. 2020

J.7 Jackpot Digital Inc.

Symbol - JJ **Exchange** - TSX-VEN **CUSIP** - 466391
Head Office - 303-570 Granville St, Vancouver, BC, V6C 3P1 **Telephone** - (604) 681-0204 **Toll-free** - (888) 605-8227 **Fax** - (604) 681-9428
Website - www.jackpotdigital.com
Email - investors@jackpotdigital.com
Investor Relations - Mathieu McDonald (604) 681-0204 ext. 6105
Auditors - Smythe LLP C.A., Vancouver, B.C.
Transfer Agents - Computershare Trust Company of Canada Inc., Vancouver, B.C.
Employees - 17 at May 2, 2022

Profile - (B.C. 1980) Manufactures and leases electronic table games for the cruise ship and onshore regulated casino industries.

The company specializes in multiplayer gaming products with a focus on poker and casino games, which are complemented by a suite of backend tools for operators to efficiently control and optimize their gaming business. Its flagship product, Jackpot Blitz®, is a dealerless electronic table game (ETG) with an 84-inch, 4k touchscreen, which offers digital casino games including poker, blackjack and baccarat. The ETGs operate on land-based casinos mostly in Canada and the U.S., as well as several major cruise lines including Carnival Cruise Lines, Princess, Virgin Voyages and Costa Cruise Lines. The company earns a percentage of table gross gaming revenues or a mutually agreed-upon fixed monthly fee. In addition, the company plans to enter the Asian casino market.

In January 2023, the company entered into an agreement with an undisclosed gaming equipment manufacturer to outsource the production and delivery of Jackpot Blitz® to casinos worldwide. The agreement is expected to reduce the manufacturing costs of the electronic table games.

Predecessor Detail - Name changed from Las Vegas From Home.com Entertainment Inc., June 18, 2015.

Directors - Jacob H. (Jake) Kalpakian, chr., pres. & CEO, Vancouver, B.C.; Neil Spellman, CFO, Carlsbad, Calif.; Alan Artunian, Los Angeles, Calif.; Gregory T. McFarlane, Wash.

Other Exec. Officers - Angelo Palmisano, chief strategy officer; Maria Arenas, corp. sec.; Mathieu McDonald, mgr., IR

Capital Stock

	Authorized (shs.)	Outstanding (shs.)[1]
Preferred	unlimited	nil
Common	unlimited	131,959,302

[1] At May 30, 2023

Major Shareholder - AlphaNorth Partners Fund Inc., AlphaNorth Asset Management Inc. & Value Preservation Fund PCC Ltd. collectively held 13.4% interest at Oct. 21, 2022.

Price Range - JJ/TSX-VEN

Year	Volume	High	Low	Close
2022	18,383,163	$0.16	$0.04	$0.08
2021	16,974,137	$0.41	$0.13	$0.13
2020	10,007,312	$0.35	$0.05	$0.20
2019	2,440,670	$2.10	$0.25	$0.30
2018	1,513,697	$7.00	$1.55	$1.85

Consolidation: 1-for-10 cons. in May 2020
Recent Close: $0.07

Capital Stock Changes - In March and April 2022, private placement of 21,498,554 units (1 common share & 1 warrant) at 9¢ per unit was completed. In September and October 2022, private placement of 25,600,032 units (1 common share & 1 warrant) at 5¢ per unit was completed.

Dividends

JJ com N.S.R.
stk.[1] .... Nov. 4/21
Paid in 2023: n.a. 2022: n.a. 2021: stk.

[1] Stk. divd. of 1 Yo Eleven Gaming Inc com. sh. for ea. 5 shs. held.

Wholly Owned Subsidiaries

Jackpot Digital (NV), Inc., Nev.
Touche Capital Inc., B.C.

Investments

5.17% int. in **37 Capital Inc.**, Vancouver, B.C. (see Survey of Mines)

Financial Statistics

Periods ended:	12m Dec. 31/22[A]		12m Dec. 31/21[A]
	$000s	%Chg	$000s
Operating revenue	**1,431**	**+241**	**420**
Cost of sales	138		36
Salaries & benefits	1,718		1,715
General & admin expense	1,886		929
Stock-based compensation	267		764
Operating expense	**4,009**	**+16**	**3,444**
Operating income	**(2,578)**	**n.a.**	**(3,024)**
Deprec., depl. & amort.	907		659
Finance income	1		191
Finance costs, gross	1,091		1,103
Investment income	(11)		(136)
Write-downs/write-offs	(131)		(225)
Pre-tax income	**(5,123)**	**n.a.**	**(6,555)**
Net income	**(5,123)**	**n.a.**	**(6,555)**
Cash & equivalent	101		253
Accounts receivable	326		220
Current assets	600		567
Long-term investments	9		102
Fixed assets, net	2,764		2,936
Right-of-use assets	276		624
Intangibles, net	156		88
Total assets	**3,844**	**-12**	**4,390**
Bank indebtedness	7		7
Accts. pay. & accr. liabs	1,533		1,212
Current liabilities	11,236		5,458
Long-term debt, gross	5,186		4,994
Long-term debt, net	nil		4,274
Equity portion of conv. debs	13		20
Shareholders' equity	(8,155)		(6,419)
Cash from oper. activs	**(1,900)**	**n.a.**	**(2,878)**
Cash from fin. activs	2,325		3,246
Cash from invest. activs	(578)		(554)
Net cash position	**101**	**-60**	**253**
Capital expenditures	(608)		(516)
Capital disposals	30		nil
	$		$
Earnings per share*	(0.05)		(0.09)
Cash flow per share*	(0.02)		(0.04)
	shs		shs
No. of shs. o/s*	131,959,302		84,860,716
Avg. no. of shs. o/s*	108,254,779		70,695,482
	%		%
Net profit margin	(358.00)		n.m.
Return on equity	n.m.		n.m.
Return on assets	(97.94)		(145.93)

* Common
[A] Reported in accordance with IFRS

Latest Results

Periods ended:	3m Mar. 31/23[A]		3m Mar. 31/22[A]
	$000s	%Chg	$000s
Operating revenue	590	+119	270
Net income	(223)	n.a.	(1,150)
	$		$
Earnings per share*	(0.00)		(0.01)

* Common
[A] Reported in accordance with IFRS

Historical Summary
(as originally stated)

Fiscal Year	Oper. Rev.	Net Inc. Bef. Disc.	EPS*
	$000s	$000s	$
2022[A]	1,431	(5,123)	(0.05)
2021[A]	420	(6,555)	(0.09)
2020[A]	603	(3,830)	(0.24)
2019[A]	2,141	(1,671)	(0.20)
2018[A]	2,075	(3,574)	(0.80)

* Common
[A] Reported in accordance with IFRS
Note: Adjusted throughout for 1-for-10 cons. in May 2020

J.8 Jade Power Trust

Symbol - JPWR.H **Exchange** - TSX-VEN **CUSIP** - 469887
Head Office - Brookfield Place, 1800-181 Bay St, Toronto, ON, M5J 2T9 **Telephone** - (647) 987-7663 **Fax** - (416) 863-1515
Website - www.jadepower.com
Email - bsoares@jadepower.com
Investor Relations - Betty Soares (416) 803-6760
Auditors - BDO Canada LLP C.A., Toronto, Ont.
Transfer Agents - TSX Trust Company, Toronto, Ont.
Administrators - Jade Power Administrator Inc., Toronto, Ont.
Profile - (Ont. 2014) No operations.

Previously owned and operated two run-of-river hydroelectric power plants, two wind projects and two photovoltaic solar power plants in Romania.

Periods ended:	12m Dec. 31/21	12m Dec. 31/20
Electric gen., GWh	153,044	159

Recent Merger and Acquisition Activity

Status: completed **Revised:** Nov. 22, 2022
UPDATE: The transaction was completed. The net cash payment paid by the purchaser to Jade at the closing was €66,000,000 (Cdn$90,930,000). Units of Jade are to be moved to NEX board of TSX Venture Exchange. The initial distribution would be $3.24 per unit. PREVIOUS: Jade Power Trust agreed to sell all of its renewable energy operating assets to Enery Power Holding GmbH, an Austrian-based renewable energy company with operations throughout the Czech Republic, Slovakia and Bulgaria, for a purchase price of €71,000,000 payable in cash. Jade plans to distribute the net proceeds to unitholders in two or more special distributions. A total of Cdn$75,600,000 (Cdn$3.40 per unit) was expected to be distributed, with an initial distribution of Cdn$67,300,000 (Cdn$3.03 per unit) . Jade would also seek unitholder approval to delist its trust units from the TSX Venture Exchange. Sept. 26, 2022 - The amount of initial distribution was now expected to be Cdn$3.16 per unit. Oct. 20, 2022 - Jade unitholders approved the proposed sale.

Predecessor Detail - Name changed from Blockchain Power Trust, Oct. 4, 2019.

Oper. Subsid./Mgt. Co. Directors - David Barclay, CEO, Fla.; John M. H. Huxley, Toronto, Ont.

Oper. Subsid./Mgt. Co. Officers - Betty Soares, CFO

Capital Stock

	Authorized (shs.)	Outstanding (shs.)[1]
Trust Unit	unlimited	22,252,912

[1] At Sept. 19, 2022

Major Shareholder - RG Renovatio Group Limited held 23.59% interest and MMCAP International Inc. held 18.47% interest at Sept. 19, 2022.

Price Range - JPWR.H/TSX-VEN

Year	Volume	High	Low	Close
2022	4,302,899	$3.79	$0.02	$0.04
2021	1,984,193	$2.48	$1.00	$2.40
2020	1,347,570	$2.50	$0.80	$1.50
2019	2,879,240	$2.05	$0.55	$1.70
2018	5,728,845	$7.50	$0.80	$1.05

Consolidation: 1-for-10 cons. in Sept. 2021
Recent Close: $0.04

Dividends

JPWR.H tr unit Var. Ra pa Q
1-for-10 cons eff. Sept. 23, 2021
$3.24◆ Dec. 12/22
Paid in 2023: n.a. 2022: $3.24◆ 2021: n.a.
◆ Special

Wholly Owned Subsidiaries

East Wind Farm S.R.L., Romania.
Jade Power Holdings Inc., Ont.
- 100% int. in **Holrom Renewable Energy S.R.L.**, Romania.
- 0.01% int. in **SC Corabia Solar S.A.**, Romania.
- 0.01% int. in **SC Power L.I.V.E One S.A.**, Romania.
- 5% int. in **Transeastern Hidroelectrica Del Ucea SPV I S.R.L.**, Romania.
- 100% int. in **Transeastern Power B.V.**, Netherlands.
  - 100% int. in **Rott Energy S.A.**, Romania.
  - 99.99% int. in **SC Corabia Solar S.A.**, Romania.
  - 99.99% int. in **SC Power L.I.V.E One S.A.**, Romania.
  - 95% int. in **Transeastern Hidroelectrica Del Ucea SPV I S.R.L.**, Romania.
    - 99% int. in **Zagra Hidro S.A.**, Romania.
  - 1% int. in **Zagra Hidro S.A.**, Romania.

Jade Power Holdings 3 Inc., Canada.
Jade Power Holdings 2 Inc., Canada.
Mediterranean Resources Ltd., Vancouver, B.C.
Transeastern Power Coöperatief U.A., Netherlands.
Transeastern Power Services Limited, Romania.
Transeastern Rott Energy SPV III S.R.L., Romania.

Financial Statistics

Periods ended:	12m Dec. 31/21[A]		12m Dec. 31/20[A]
	$000s	%Chg	$000s
Operating revenue	**18,651**	**0**	**18,720**
Cost of sales	5,829		5,864
General & admin expense	3,182		2,779
Operating expense	**9,010**	**+4**	**8,643**
Operating income	**9,641**	**-4**	**10,077**
Deprec., depl. & amort.	3,715		3,858
Finance costs, gross	1,122		1,948
Pre-tax income	**5,004**	**+32**	**3,779**
Income taxes	1,327		122
Net inc. bef. disc. opers	**3,677**	**+1**	**3,657**
Income from disc. opers	nil		(667)
Net income	**3,677**	**+23**	**2,990**
Cash & equivalent	8,114		2,918
Accounts receivable	3,387		7,573
Current assets	16,475		15,432
Fixed assets, net	43,401		52,007
Intangibles, net	193		276
Total assets	**69,516**	**-15**	**81,315**
Accts. pay. & accr. liabs	4,978		5,813
Current liabilities	7,755		13,621
Long-term debt, gross	nil		1,647
Long-term lease liabilities	12,216		16,289
Shareholders' equity	44,665		46,916
Cash from oper. activs	**16,279**	**+90**	**8,586**
Cash from fin. activs	(9,621)		(7,966)
Cash from invest. activs	(96)		(56)
Net cash position	**8,114**	**+178**	**2,918**
Capital expenditures	(96)		(56)
	$		$
Earns. per sh. bef disc opers*	0.16		0.20
Earnings per share*	0.16		0.10
Cash flow per share*	0.71		0.37
	shs		shs
No. of shs. o/s*	22,581,612		23,121,626
Avg. no. of shs. o/s*	23,043,358		23,131,766
	%		%
Net profit margin	19.71		19.54
Return on equity	8.03		8.11
Return on assets	5.97		6.93
Foreign sales percent	100		100

* Trust Unit
[A] Reported in accordance with IFRS

Latest Results

Periods ended:	3m Mar. 31/22[A]		3m Mar. 31/21[A]
	$000s	%Chg	$000s
Operating revenue	3,024	+68	1,803
Net income	2,162	+24	1,748
	$		$
Earnings per share*	0.10		0.10

* Trust Unit
[A] Reported in accordance with IFRS

Historical Summary
(as originally stated)

Fiscal Year	Oper. Rev.	Net Inc. Bef. Disc.	EPS*
	$000s	$000s	$
2021[A]	18,651	3,677	0.16
2020[A]	18,720	3,657	0.20
2019[A]	17,678	4,159	0.20
2018[A]	17,337	5,605	0.30
2017[A]	12,311	(34,612)	(7.10)

* Trust Unit
[A] Reported in accordance with IFRS
Note: Adjusted throughout for 1-for-10 cons. in Sept. 2021

J.9 Jamieson Wellness Inc.

Symbol - JWEL **Exchange** - TSX **CUSIP** - 470748
Head Office - 2200-1 Adelaide St E, Toronto, ON, M5C 2V9 **Telephone** - (416) 960-0052 **Toll-free** - (833) 223-2666
Website - www.jamiesonvitamins.com
Email - csnowden@jamiesonlabs.com
Investor Relations - Christopher Snowden (833) 223-2666
Auditors - Ernst & Young LLP C.A., Toronto, Ont.
Lawyers - McCarthy Tétrault LLP, Toronto, Ont.
Transfer Agents - Computershare Trust Company of Canada Inc., Toronto, Ont.
FP500 Revenue Ranking - 449
Employees - 1,226 at Dec. 31, 2022
Profile - (Ont. 2017; orig. B.C., 2014) Manufactures, distributes and markets vitamins, minerals and supplements, sports nutrition products and certain over-the-counter remedies under the Jamieson, youtheory, Smart Solutions, Progressive, Precision and Iron Vegan brands.

Products include vitamins A, B, B Complex C, D, E and K; multivitamin compounds formulated specifically for different genders, ages and life stages; nutritional supplements including CoQ10, omega oils, digestive health products, beauty products and natural sleep aids; minerals including magnesium, potassium, calcium and iron; herbal products with a broad range of ingredients including echinacea, ginseng, cranberry and turmeric; sports nutrition and protein products including protein, testosterone, and fat-burning and performance supporting products for athletes and bodybuilders; cough and cold products to help reduce cold and influenza symptoms; and joint care products to help prevent and manage joint pain. Products are offered in a variety of delivery formats including tablets, caplets, capsules, gummies, drink mixes, chewable tablets and powders.

Manufacturing and distribution facilities are located in Windsor and Scarborough, Ont. Manufacturing and warehousing facilities for youtheory products are located in Irvine, Calif. Products are distributed through food, drug, mass, club, health food store, specialty and online retail channels across Canada and in more than 50 international markets under international distribution arrangements. In addition, contract manufacturing services are offered to select blue-chip consumer health companies and retailers worldwide.

Recent Merger and Acquisition Activity

Status: completed **Revised:** May 16, 2023
UPDATE: The transaction was completed. PREVIOUS: Jamieson Wellness Inc. agreed to sell a 33.3% interest in its Chinese operations to DCP Capital, an international private equity firm, in exchange for a capital contribution of US$35,000,000 by DCP. DCP also agreed to subscribe for US$75,000,000 of preferred shares of Jamieson which will be retractable by DCP between the second and fifth anniversary of their purchase. DCP will also subscribe for warrants to purchase 2,527,121 Jamieson common shares at Cdn$40.19 per share between the second and fifth anniversary of the issue date. The transaction was expected to close during the second quarter of 2023.

Status: completed **Revised:** May 4, 2023
UPDATE: The transaction was completed for a price of about $26,000,000. PREVIOUS: Jamieson Wellness Inc. agreed to acquire the tangible and intangible assets from its Chinese distribution partner, allowing it to directly operate its sales, marketing and distribution activities in the People's Republic of China. Terms were not disclosed. The transaction was expected to close on Apr. 1, 2023.

Status: completed **Revised:** July 19, 2022
UPDATE: The transaction was completed. PREVIOUS: Jamieson Wellness Inc. agreed to acquire Nutrawise Health & Beauty Corporation, a manufacturer and marketer of premium supplements under the youtheory brand in the United States and other international markets, for US$210,000,000 (Cdn$265,000,000) on closing, including US$25,000,000 in common shares, plus potential additional consideration contingent on achieving pre-determined growth targets post-closing. The transaction was expected to close during the third quarter of 2022.

Directors - Timothy H. (Tim) Penner, chr., Toronto, Ont.; Michael (Mike) Pilato, pres. & CEO, Toronto, Ont.; Heather Allen, Windsor, Berks., United Kingdom; Dr. Louis J. Aronne, Greenwich, Conn.; Tania M. Clarke, Pierrefonds, Qué.; Catherine Potechin, Mississauga, Ont.; François Vimard, Ont.; Mei Ye, Shanghai, Shanghai, People's Republic of China

Other Exec. Officers - Christopher (Chris) Snowden, CFO & corp. sec.; John Doherty, chief science & innovation officer; Regan Stewart, chief opers. & people officer; Don Bird, exec. v-p, USA & global strategic partners; Joel Scales, exec. v-p, Jamieson worldwide, global strategy & e-commerce; Eric Bentz, sr. v-p, global mktg. & man. dir., China; Paul Galbraith, sr. v-p & man. dir.; Tara Martin, sr. v-p & gen. counsel; Robert Chan, v-p, fin.

Capital Stock

	Authorized (shs.)	Outstanding (shs.)[1]
Preferred	unlimited	nil
Common	unlimited	41,888,995

[1] At Mar. 31, 2023

Major Shareholder - Mackenzie Financial Corporation held 10% interest at Mar. 23, 2023.

Price Range - JWEL/TSX

Year	Volume	High	Low	Close
2022	15,353,339	$40.30	$31.62	$35.09
2021	19,458,377	$41.74	$32.70	$40.14
2020	25,122,082	$46.01	$23.42	$36.13
2019	15,387,124	$26.48	$17.38	$25.75
2018	13,283,522	$27.88	$17.15	$21.33

Recent Close: $26.15

Capital Stock Changes - During 2022, common shares were issued as follows: 926,612 pursuant to the acquisition of businesses, 342,655 on exercise of options and 17,996 under employee stock purchase plan.

Dividends

JWEL com Ra $0.76 pa Q est. Sept. 15, 2023
Prev. Rate: $0.68 est. Sept. 15, 2022
Prev. Rate: $0.60 est. Sept. 15, 2021
Prev. Rate: $0.50 est. Sept. 15, 2020

Wholly Owned Subsidiaries

Jamieson Laboratories Ltd., Toronto, Ont.
- 100% int. in **Body Plus Nutritional Products Inc.**, Ont.
- 100% int. in **International Nutrient Technologies Ltd.**, Ont.
- 100% int. in **Jamieson Health Products Australia Pty Ltd.**, N.S.W., Australia.
- 100% int. in **Jamieson Health Products (Cayman Islands) Limited**, Cayman Islands.
- 100% int. in **Jamieson Health Products (Hong Kong) Limited**
- 100% int. in **Jamieson Health Products (Hong Kong) Trading Limited**, People's Republic of China.
- 100% int. in **Jamieson Health Products Netherlands B.V.**, Netherlands.
- 100% int. in **Jamieson Health Products (Shanghai) Co. Ltd.**, Shanghai, Shanghai, People's Republic of China.
- 100% int. in **Jamieson Health Products U.K. Ltd.**, United Kingdom.
- 100% int. in **Jamieson Health Products USA Ltd.**, Del.
  - 100% int. in **Nutrawise Health & Beauty Corporation**, Irvine, Calif.
- 100% int. in **Nutrawise Japan GK**, Japan.
- 100% int. in **Nutrawise UK Ltd.**, United Kingdom.

Financial Statistics

Periods ended:	12m Dec. 31/22[A]		12m Dec. 31/21[A]
	$000s	%Chg	$000s
Operating revenue	**547,369**	**+21**	**451,032**
Cost of sales	331,783		274,317
General & admin expense	110,239		80,739
Stock-based compensation	4,910		5,672
Operating expense	**446,932**	**+24**	**360,728**
Operating income	**100,437**	**+11**	**90,304**
Deprec., depl. & amort.	17,248		14,274
Finance costs, gross	12,417		5,657
Pre-tax income	**70,503**	**0**	**70,465**
Income taxes	17,695		18,383
Net income	**52,808**	**+1**	**52,082**
Cash & equivalent	26,240		6,775
Inventories	154,488		119,006
Accounts receivable	160,798		104,186
Current assets	352,404		237,145
Fixed assets, net	83,894		74,334
Right-of-use assets	27,815		22,643
Intangibles, net	640,121		315,651
Total assets	**1,107,263**	**+70**	**652,475**
Accts. pay. & accr. liabs	142,566		74,533
Current liabilities	154,805		83,622
Long-term debt, gross	400,000		149,125
Long-term debt, net	400,000		149,125
Long-term lease liabilities	25,238		20,872
Shareholders' equity	431,591		342,021
Cash from oper. activs	**50,589**	**+14**	**44,405**
Cash from fin. activs	225,406		(16,512)
Cash from invest. activs	(256,530)		(22,284)
Net cash position	**26,240**	**+287**	**6,775**
Capital expenditures	(13,933)		(21,498)
	$		$
Earnings per share*	1.29		1.30
Cash flow per share*	1.23		1.11
Cash divd. per share*	0.64		0.55
	shs		shs
No. of shs. o/s*	41,694,203		40,406,940
Avg. no. of shs. o/s*	40,998,065		40,150,724
	%		%
Net profit margin	9.65		11.55
Return on equity	13.65		16.42
Return on assets	7.06		8.92
Foreign sales percent	31		25
No. of employees (FTEs)	1,226		1,000

* Common
[A] Reported in accordance with IFRS

Latest Results

Periods ended:	3m Mar. 31/23[A]		3m Mar. 31/22[A]
	$000s	%Chg	$000s
Operating revenue	136,725	+32	103,675
Net income	7,065	-27	9,741
	$		$
Earnings per share*	0.17		0.24

* Common
[A] Reported in accordance with IFRS

Historical Summary
(as originally stated)

Fiscal Year	Oper. Rev.	Net Inc. Bef. Disc.	EPS*
	$000s	$000s	$
2022[A]	547,369	52,808	1.29
2021[A]	451,032	52,082	1.30
2020[A]	403,661	41,598	1.05
2019[A]	344,980	31,657	0.82
2018[A]	319,776	26,673	0.70

* Common
[A] Reported in accordance with IFRS

J.10 Jasper Commerce Inc.

Symbol - JPIM **Exchange** - TSX-VEN **CUSIP** - 47157P
Head Office - 900-200 Wellington St W, Toronto, ON, M5V 3C7
Toll-free - (844) 752-7737
Website - www.jasperpim.com
Email - ghurlow@meteorcapital.ca
Investor Relations - Gerald S. Hurlow (844) 752-7737
Auditors - MNP LLP C.A., Toronto, Ont.
Transfer Agents - Odyssey Trust Company, Calgary, Alta.

Profile - (B.C. 2021) Offers a software-as-a-service (SaaS) Product Information Management (PIM) solution empowering e-commerce retailers, wholesalers or distributors to manage and merchandise their products from a single source.

The PIM solution is integrated with e-commerce platforms, including three primary discovery/distribution channels, specifically Shopify, Square and BigCommerce, with a customer base of 1,000,000, 2,000,000 and 60,000 merchants, respectively.

The PIM solution enables merchants to schedule promotional pricing in advance, enrich product data with complex imagery, videos and marketing content, manage complex attribution, and setup product relationships between multiple products in order to upsell or cross-sell their goods and services, all through one web-based dashboard. It also supports the batch management of product information, including multiple languages, currencies and inventory/warehouse locations.

The company earns revenue on a subscription basis, whereby customers signup for a month-to-month, annual term or multi-year contract, agreeing to pay the company for the usage of the PIM platform.

In January 2023, the company terminated the agreement to acquire **Cartika Internet Solutions Provider Inc.**, a full-service information technology infrastructure provider specializing in managed cloud and Infrastructure-as-a-Service support for mid-market businesses, for $300,000 cash, $200,000 notes payable and issuance of $1,050,000 common shares as well as contingent consideration of up to $2,000,000.

Predecessor Detail - Name changed from SaaSquatch Capital Corp., Feb. 16, 2022, pursuant to the Qualifying Transaction reverse takeover acquisition of Jasper Interactive Studios Inc. and concurrent amalgamation of Jasper with wholly owned 2869943 Ontario Inc.; basis 1 new for 2 old shs.

Directors - Gerald S. (Gerry) Hurlow, chr. & interim CEO, Toronto, Ont.; Jon C. Marsella, chief growth officer, Toronto, Ont.; Silas Garrison, Charlotte, N.C.; Jeffrey D. Klam, Toronto, Ont.; Maged Saad, Mississauga, Ont.

Other Exec. Officers - Sean Coutts, pres., COO & chief tech. officer; Ken Gutierrez, interim CFO; Michael E. Durance, exec. v-p, strategy

Capital Stock

	Authorized (shs.)	Outstanding (shs.)[1]
Common	unlimited	58,079,619

[1] At Dec. 22, 2022

Major Shareholder - Patricia Marsella held 12.01% interest and Jon C. Marsella held 11.59% interest at Dec. 22, 2022.

Price Range - JPIM/TSX-VEN

Year	Volume	High	Low	Close
2022	14,173,799	$0.45	$0.02	$0.02

Recent Close: $0.02

Capital Stock Changes - On Aug. 11, 2021, an initial public offering of 1,000,000 post-consolidated common shares was completed at 10¢ per share. On Feb. 16, 2022, common shares were consolidated on a 1-for-2 basis (effective on the TSX Venture Exchange on Feb. 24, 2022), 50,138,835 post-consolidated common shares were issued pursuant to the Qualifying Transaction reverse takeover acquisition of Jasper Interactive Studios Inc. and 1,440,784 post-consolidated common shares were issued as finder's fee.

Wholly Owned Subsidiaries

Jasper Interactive Studios Inc., Toronto, Ont.

Financial Statistics

Periods ended:	12m July 31/22[A1]		12m July 31/21[A2]
	$000s	%Chg	$000s
Operating revenue	**1,679**	**+23**	**1,369**
Research & devel. expense	1,011		819
General & admin expense	5,126		1,364
Stock-based compensation	441		58
Operating expense	**6,578**	**+194**	**2,241**
Operating income	**(4,899)**	**n.a.**	**(872)**
Deprec., depl. & amort.	22		10
Finance costs, gross	2,957		760
Pre-tax income	**(7,886)**	**n.a.**	**(1,657)**
Net income	**(7,886)**	**n.a.**	**(1,657)**
Cash & equivalent	2,316		1,289
Accounts receivable	227		128
Current assets	3,171		1,900
Fixed assets, net	78		15
Total assets	**3,250**	**+68**	**1,932**
Accts. pay. & accr. liabs	778		532
Current liabilities	1,013		1,104
Long-term debt, gross	313		4,160
Long-term debt, net	180		3,760
Shareholders' equity	2,008		(2,974)
Cash from oper. activs	**(4,573)**	**n.a.**	**(954)**
Cash from fin. activs	4,693		2,122
Cash from invest. activs	906		(6)
Net cash position	**2,316**	**+80**	**1,289**
Capital expenditures	(85)		(6)
	$		$
Earnings per share*	(0.19)		n.a.
Cash flow per share*	(0.11)		n.a.
	shs		shs
No. of shs. o/s*	58,079,619		n.a.
Avg. no. of shs. o/s*	41,172,599		n.a.
	%		%
Net profit margin	(469.68)		(121.04)
Return on equity	n.m.		n.m.
Return on assets	(190.24)		n.a.
Foreign sales percent	82		69

* Common
[A] Reported in accordance with IFRS
[1] Results reflect the Feb. 16, 2022, Qualifying Transaction reverse takeover acquisition of Jasper Interactive Studios Inc.
[2] Results pertain to Jasper Interactive Studios Inc.

Latest Results

Periods ended:	3m Oct. 31/22[A]		3m Oct. 31/21[A]
	$000s	%Chg	$000s
Operating revenue	380	-16	452
Net income	(1,312)	n.a.	(992)
	$		$
Earnings per share*	(0.02)		n.a.

* Common
[A] Reported in accordance with IFRS
Note: Adjusted throughout for 1-for-2 cons. in Feb. 2022

J.11 Jemtec Inc.

Symbol - JTC **Exchange** - TSX-VEN **CUSIP** - 475901
Head Office - 200-38 Fell Ave, North Vancouver, BC, V7P 3S2 **Telephone** - (604) 929-4559 **Toll-free** - (877) 929-4559 **Fax** - (604) 929-4198
Website - www.jemtec.ca
Email - info@jemtec.ca
Investor Relations - Eric Caton (877) 929-4559
Auditors - Crowe MacKay LLP C.A., Vancouver, B.C.
Lawyers - Sui & Company, Vancouver, B.C.
Transfer Agents - Computershare Trust Company of Canada Inc., Vancouver, B.C.
Profile - (Ont. 1987; orig. Can., 1987) Provides integrated technology systems for offender monitoring in Canadian federal and provincial correctional departments. Also offers monitoring and security services through a public-private partnership.
Offender location detection and verification technologies include offender reporting via telephone contact, offender reporting kiosks with integrated database, global positioning systems (GPS) active and passive tracking, voice verification, electronic monitoring house arrest systems, remote alcohol in-home monitoring and private monitoring services.
In Canada, the company is the distributor of monitoring and tracking solutions supplied by **BI Incorporated**, **Satellite Tracking of People LLC**, **SuperCom Inc.**, **Sierra Wireless, Inc.** and **Attenti Electronic Monitoring, Ltd.**
Predecessor Detail - Name changed from Justice Electronic Monitoring Systems Inc., Apr. 28, 1994; basis 1 new for 10 old shs.
Directors - Jeremy N. Kendall, chr., Toronto, Ont.; Eric Caton, pres. & CEO, North Vancouver, B.C.; Leslie N. Markow, corp. sec., Toronto, Ont.; Gordon R. Baker, Toronto, Ont.
Other Exec. Officers - Loui Mellios, CFO

Capital Stock

	Authorized (shs.)	Outstanding (shs.)[1]
First Preference	unlimited	nil
Second Preference		
Series A	25,000	nil
Common	unlimited	2,794,679

[1] At Dec. 16, 2022
Major Shareholder - Eric Caton held 21.07% interest and Paul E. Crossett held 20.24% interest at Dec. 16, 2022.

Price Range - JTC/TSX-VEN

Year	Volume	High	Low	Close
2022	271,417	$2.24	$1.01	$1.09
2021	343,184	$2.20	$1.70	$2.09
2020	552,792	$2.15	$1.10	$1.99
2019	958,218	$2.74	$1.00	$1.51
2018	193,320	$1.25	$0.64	$1.25

Recent Close: $0.99
Capital Stock Changes - There were no changes to capital stock during fiscal 2022.

Dividends

JTC com N.S.R.
$0.25◆ Feb. 10/21
Paid in 2023: n.a. 2022: n.a. 2021: $0.25◆
◆ Special

Financial Statistics

Periods ended:	12m July 31/22[A]		12m July 31/21[A]
	$000s	%Chg	$000s
Operating revenue	**2,804**	**+9**	**2,564**
Salaries & benefits	295		339
General & admin expense	1,621		1,516
Stock-based compensation	64		nil
Operating expense	**1,980**	**+7**	**1,855**
Operating income	**824**	**+16**	**708**
Deprec., depl. & amort.	34		29
Finance income	6		3
Finance costs, gross	1		1
Pre-tax income	**781**	**+15**	**677**
Income taxes	230		115
Net income	**551**	**-2**	**562**
Cash & equivalent	2,167		1,663
Accounts receivable	318		364
Current assets	2,536		2,051
Fixed assets, net	32		34
Total assets	**2,608**	**+22**	**2,136**
Accts. pay. & accr. liabs	164		275
Current liabilities	174		312
Long-term lease liabilities	nil		4
Shareholders' equity	2,435		1,820
Cash from oper. activs	**567**	**+120**	**258**
Cash from fin. activs	(30)		(688)
Cash from invest. activs	(32)		(1)
Net cash position	**2,167**	**+30**	**1,663**
Capital expenditures	(32)		(1)
	$		$
Earnings per share*	0.20		0.20
Cash flow per share*	0.20		0.09
Extra divd. - cash*	nil		0.25
	shs		shs
No. of shs. o/s*	2,794,679		2,794,679
Avg. no. of shs. o/s*	2,794,679		2,766,104
	%		%
Net profit margin	19.65		21.92
Return on equity	25.90		30.08
Return on assets	23.26		25.17

* Common
[A] Reported in accordance with IFRS

Latest Results

Periods ended:	3m Oct. 31/22[A]		3m Oct. 31/21[A]
	$000s	%Chg	$000s
Operating revenue	374	-51	767
Net income	(17)	n.a.	214
	$		$
Earnings per share*	(0.01)		0.08

* Common
[A] Reported in accordance with IFRS

Historical Summary
(as originally stated)

Fiscal Year	Oper. Rev.	Net Inc. Bef. Disc.	EPS*
	$000s	$000s	$
2022[A]	2,804	551	0.20
2021[A]	2,564	562	0.20
2020[A]	2,349	409	0.15
2019[A]	2,311	490	0.19
2018[A]	1,840	235	0.09

* Common
[A] Reported in accordance with IFRS

J.12 Jericho Energy Ventures Inc.

Symbol - JEV **Exchange** - TSX-VEN **CUSIP** - 476339
Head Office - 2100-1055 Georgia St W, PO Box 11110 Stn Royal Centre, Vancouver, BC, V6E 3P3 **Telephone** - (604) 343-4534 **Toll-free** - (800) 750-3520
Website - jerichoenergyventures.com
Email - adam@jerichoenergyventures.com
Investor Relations - Adam Rabiner (800) 750-3520
Auditors - Manning Elliott LLP C.A., Vancouver, B.C.
Lawyers - Clark Wilson LLP, Vancouver, B.C.; MacDonald Tuskey Corporate & Securities Lawyers, Vancouver, B.C.
Transfer Agents - Computershare Trust Company of Canada Inc., Vancouver, B.C.
Profile - (B.C. 2010) Explores for, develops and produces oil and gas in Oklahoma. Also invests in hydrogen technologies, energy storage, carbon capture and new energy systems.
In Oklahoma, holds 50% working interest in 55,000 acres in Alfalfa, Pottawatomie, Seminole, Creek, Payne and Lincol ctys. Also holds interest in 14,000 acres in Blaine and Major ctys.
At Dec. 31, 2021, the company had 208 gross (83 net) oil and gas wells.
Also provides low-carbon solutions related to the hydrogen value chain through its product cleanH2steam DCC™, a hydrogen-based boiler system which burns pure hydrogen in a vacuum chamber to create high-temperature heat and steam with zero emissions through a closed-loop process.

Periods ended:	12m Dec. 31/21	12m Dec. 31/20
Avg. oil prod., bbl/d	125	127
Avg. NGL prod., bbl/d	37	45
Avg. gas prod., mcf/d	213	254
Avg. oil price, US$/bbl	61.03	34.59
Avg. NGL price, US$/bbl	25.51	8.91
Avg. gas price, US$/mcf	3.21	1.18
Oil reserves, net, mbbl	1,767	1,719
NGL reserves, net, mbbl	401	528
Gas reserves, net, mmcf	2,358	2,568

Predecessor Detail - Name changed from Jericho Oil Corporation, Mar. 3, 2021.
Directors - Brian Williamson, CEO & pres., Pa.; Nicholas W. Baxter, Aberdeen., United Kingdom; Carolyn Hauger, Ohio; Markus Seyweld, London, Middx., United Kingdom; Allen Wilson, United Kingdom
Other Exec. Officers - Ben Holman, CFO & corp. sec.

Capital Stock

	Authorized (shs.)	Outstanding (shs.)[1]
Common & Variable Vtg.	unlimited	225,503,169

[1] At June 29, 2022
Variable Voting - Held by U.S. residents only. Automatically convert into common shares on a one-for-one basis if become owned or controlled by a non-U.S. resident, One vote per share except that: (i) holders shall not have an entitlement to vote at a class meeting or series meeting of which only holders of another particular class or series of shares of the company shall have the right to vote; and (ii) if the number of votes that may be exercised, in connection with the election or removal of directors, in respect of all issued and outstanding variable voting shares exceeds 49.9% of the total number of votes that may be exercised, in connection with the election or removal of directors, in respect of all issued and outstanding common and variable voting shares, the vote attached to each variable voting share would decrease automatically and pro rata and without further act or formality to equal the maximum permitted vote per variable voting share. The number of variable voting shares as a class cannot carry more than 49.9% of the total number of votes, in connection with the election or removal of directors, attached to all issued and outstanding common and variable voting shares.
Common - Held by non-U.S. residents only. Automatically convert into variable voting shares on a one-for-one basis if become owned or controlled by a U.S. resident. One vote per share.
Major Shareholder - Michael L. Graves held 16.48% interest and Andrew J. McKenna held 10.81% interest at May 20, 2022.

Price Range - JEV/TSX-VEN

Year	Volume	High	Low	Close
2022	7,706,315	$0.84	$0.31	$0.36
2021	21,277,243	$1.22	$0.23	$0.61
2020	3,719,057	$0.29	$0.08	$0.23
2019	3,634,629	$0.50	$0.17	$0.22
2018	12,966,250	$1.38	$0.41	$0.42

Recent Close: $0.25
Capital Stock Changes - On June 27, 2022, a new class of shares, variable voting shares, was created and all common shares held by U.S. residents were converted into variable voting shares on a one-for-one basis.

Wholly Owned Subsidiaries

JEV USA Inc., Del.
- 100% int. in **JEV KS, LLC**, Del.
  - 100% int. in **Hydrogen Technologies LLC**, Del.
  - 50% int. in **Lurgan Oil LLC**, United States.
  - 26.5% int. in **RSTACK Walnut, LLC**, United States.
- 100% int. in **JEV OK, LLC**, Del.
  - 31% int. in **Cherry Rancher LLC**
  - 50% int. in **Eagle Road Oil, LLC**, United States.
  - 50% int. in **Jericho Buckmanville Oil LLC**, United States.
- 100% int. in **JEV Ventures, LLC**, Del.

Financial Statistics

Periods ended:	12m Dec. 31/21[A]		12m Dec. 31/20[A]
	$000s	%Chg	$000s
Operating revenue	**60**	**+7**	**56**
Cost of sales	40		88
Salaries & benefits	564		n.a.
General & admin expense	4,100		1,702
Stock-based compensation	1,282		982
Operating expense	**5,985**	**+116**	**2,772**
Operating income	**(5,925)**	**n.a.**	**(2,716)**
Deprec., depl. & amort.	510		24
Finance costs, gross	50		36
Investment income	560		(16,742)
Write-downs/write-offs	(392)		(403)
Pre-tax income	**(6,298)**	**n.a.**	**(20,128)**
Net income	**(6,298)**	**n.a.**	**(20,128)**
Cash & equivalent	6,189		3,543
Accounts receivable	31		3
Current assets	6,272		3,559
Long-term investments	16,193		15,899
Intangibles, net	3,639		nil
Explor./devel. properties	222		192
Total assets	**28,296**	**+44**	**19,656**
Accts. pay. & accr. liabs.	1,097		404
Current liabilities	19,097		404
Long-term debt, gross	4,992		64
Long-term debt, net	4,992		64
Shareholders' equity	22,198		19,112
Cash from oper. activs.	**(4,169)**	**n.a.**	**(1,996)**
Cash from fin. activs.	10,478		4,823
Cash from invest. activs.	(3,338)		(829)
Net cash position	**6,189**	**+75**	**3,543**
Capital expenditures	(52)		nil
Capital disposals	54		24
	$		$
Earnings per share*	(0.03)		(0.13)
Cash flow per share*	(0.02)		(0.01)
	shs		shs
No. of shs. o/s*	222,406,869		178,608,142
Avg. no. of shs. o/s*	209,201,449		156,476,994
	%		%
Net profit margin	n.m.		n.m.
Return on equity	(30.49)		(76.62)
Return on assets	(26.06)		(74.75)
No. of employees (FTEs)	26		25

* Com. & var. vtg.
[A] Reported in accordance with IFRS

Latest Results

Periods ended:	3m Mar. 31/22[A]		3m Mar. 31/21[A]
	$000s	%Chg	$000s
Operating revenue	11	-50	22
Net income	(3,238)	n.a.	(2,076)
	$		$
Earnings per share*	(0.01)		(0.01)

* Com. & var. vtg.
[A] Reported in accordance with IFRS

Historical Summary
(as originally stated)

Fiscal Year	Oper. Rev.	Net Inc. Bef. Disc.	EPS*
	$000s	$000s	$
2021[A]	60	(6,298)	(0.03)
2020[A]	56	(20,128)	(0.13)
2019[A]	238	(8,530)	(0.07)
2018[A]	409	(4,064)	(0.03)
2017[A]	391	(6,015)	(0.07)

* Com. & var. vtg.
[A] Reported in accordance with IFRS

J.13 Jesmond Capital Ltd.

Symbol - JES.P **Exchange** - TSX-VEN **CUSIP** - 476870
Head Office - 1250-639 5 Ave SW, Calgary, AB, T2P 0M9 **Telephone** - (403) 298-1049 **Fax** - (403) 695-3478
Email - gordon.chmilar@gowlingwlg.com
Investor Relations - Gordon Chmilar (403) 589-2468
Auditors - Kenway Mack Slusarchuk Stewart LLP C.A., Calgary, Alta.
Lawyers - TingleMerrett LLP, Calgary, Alta.
Transfer Agents - Alliance Trust Company, Calgary, Alta.
Profile - (Alta. 2020) Capital Pool Company.

Recent Merger and Acquisition Activity

Status: pending **Revised:** Feb. 13, 2023
UPDATE: Jesmond plans to complete a private placement of 12,000,000 subscription receipts $0.25 per receipts for gross proceeds of $3,000,000. PREVIOUS: .Jesmond Capital Ltd. entered into a letter of intent for the qualifying Transaction reverse takeover acquisition of Quattro Energy Limited, which has an agreement to acquire oil and gas interests offshore United Kingdom. Jesmond would issue 22,357,669 common shares to Quattro shareholders.

Directors - Stuart M. Olley, CEO, Calgary, Alta.; Gordon Chmilar, CFO & corp. sec., Calgary, Alta.; Rupert Williams, Godalming, Surrey, United Kingdom; Jeremy Woodgate, London, Middx., United Kingdom

Capital Stock

	Authorized (shs.)	Outstanding (shs.)[1]
Common	unlimited	9,440,100

[1] At Jan. 19, 2023

Major Shareholder - Rupert Williams held 15.89% interest and Stuart M. Olley held 10.59% interest at Feb. 19, 2021.

Price Range - JES.P/TSX-VEN

Year	Volume	High	Low	Close
2022	159,003	$0.12	$0.06	$0.06
2021	431,800	$0.23	$0.10	$0.11

Recent Close: $0.06

J.14 Jewett-Cameron Trading Company Ltd.

Symbol - JCTCF **Exchange** - NASDAQ **CUSIP** - 47733C
Head Office - 32275 N.W. Hillcrest, PO Box 1010, North Plains, OR, United States, 97133 **Telephone** - (503) 647-0110 **Toll-free** - (800) 547-5877 **Fax** - (503) 647-2272
Website - www.jewettcameron.com
Email - chads@jewettcameron.com
Investor Relations - Chad M. Summers (800) 547-5877
Auditors - Davidson & Company LLP C.A., Vancouver, B.C.
Transfer Agents - Computershare Trust Company of Canada Inc., Vancouver, B.C.
Employees - 75 at Aug. 31, 2022
Profile - (B.C. 1987) Wholesales wood products; manufactures and distributes specialty metal products; and processes and distributes industrial wood products, primarily treated plywood, as well as agricultural seeds.

Wholly owned **Jewett-Cameron Company** (JCC) operates from a 5.6-acre owned facility in North Plains, Ore., which includes an office, a warehouse and a paved yard. JCC wholesales, and manufactures and distributes of products that include an array of pet enclosures, kennels, and pet welfare and comfort products, proprietary gate support systems, perimeter fencing, greenhouses, and fencing in-fill products made of wood, metal and composites. JCC products are marketed under the Luck Dog for pet products; Adjust-A-Gate™, Fit-Right®, Perimeter Patrol®, INFINITY Euro Fence and Lifetime Post™ brands for gates and fencing; and Early Start, Spring Gardner™, Greenline® and Weatherguard brands for greenhouses. JCC uses contract manufacturers to make all products. Primary customers are home centers, eCommerce partners, on-line direct consumers as well as other retailers.

Wholly owned **Greenwood Products, Inc.** operates from the same facility as JCC and distributes industrial wood and other specialty industrial building products. A major product category is treated plywood that is sold primarily to the transportation industry, including the municipal and mass transit transportation sectors. Inventory is maintained at non-owned warehouse and wood treating facilities throughout the U.S. and is primarily shipped to customers on a just-in-time basis.

Wholly owned **Jewett-Cameron Seed Company** processes and distributes agricultural seed and operates out of a 12-acre owned facility near North Plains, Ore. Most of this segment's sales come from selling seed to distributors with a lesser amount of sales derived from cleaning seed.

Directors - Charles E. Hopewell, chr., Hillsboro, Ore.; Chad M. Summers, pres. & CEO, West Linn, Ore.; Geoffrey (Geoff) Guilfoy, Portland, Ore.; Mike Henningsen, Wash.; Sarah Johnson, Portland, Ore.; Chris Karlin, Portland, Ore.; Michael C. Nasser, Portland, Ore.; Michelle Walker, Ore.

Other Exec. Officers - Mitch Van Domelen, CFO & corp. sec.

Capital Stock

	Authorized (shs.)	Outstanding (shs.)[1]
Preferred	10,000,000	nil
Common	21,567,564	3,498,899

[1] At Jan. 11, 2023

Major Shareholder - Oregon Community Foundation held 30.5% interest at Jan. 11, 2023.

Price Range - JCTCF/NASDAQ

Year	Volume	High	Low	Close
2022	292,351	US$8.84	US$4.85	US$5.77
2021	231,989	US$13.59	US$8.25	US$8.42
2020	243,281	US$11.36	US$5.01	US$8.75
2019	466,965	US$9.31	US$6.38	US$7.71
2018	484,190	US$10.00	US$6.68	US$7.11

Capital Stock Changes - During fiscal 2022, 6,181 common shares were issued under the restricted share plan.

Wholly Owned Subsidiaries

JC USA Inc., Portland, Ore.
- 100% int. in **Greenwood Products, Inc.**, Ore.
- 100% int. in **Jewett-Cameron Company**, Ore.
- 100% int. in **Jewett-Cameron Seed Company**, Ore.

Financial Statistics

Periods ended:	12m Aug. 31/22[A]		12m Aug. 31/21[A]
	US$000s	%Chg	US$000s
Operating revenue	**62,902**	**+9**	**57,502**
Cost of sales	49,109		43,355
Salaries & benefits	7,496		6,958
General & admin expense	4,008		3,205
Operating expense	**60,613**	**+13**	**53,518**
Operating income	**2,289**	**-43**	**3,984**
Deprec., depl. & amort.	320		244
Finance costs, gross	163		3
Pre-tax income	**1,581**	**-64**	**4,424**
Income taxes	417		969
Net income	**1,164**	**-66**	**3,455**
Cash & equivalent	484		1,184
Inventories	20,632		14,391
Accounts receivable	7,192		7,087
Current assets	29,630		25,221
Fixed assets, net	4,828		3,887
Intangibles, net	33		31
Total assets	**34,517**	**+18**	**29,138**
Bank indebtedness	7,000		3,000
Accts. pay. & accr. liabs.	3,422		3,148
Current liabilities	10,422		6,148
Shareholders' equity	24,095		22,874
Cash from oper. activs.	**(3,440)**	**n.a.**	**(4,423)**
Cash from fin. activs.	4,000		3,000
Cash from invest. activs.	(1,259)		(1,193)
Net cash position	**484**	**-59**	**1,184**
Capital expenditures	(1,256)		(1,163)
	US$		US$
Earnings per share*	0.33		0.99
Cash flow per share*	(0.98)		(1.27)
	shs		shs
No. of shs. o/s*	3,495,342		3,489,161
Avg. no. of shs. o/s*	3,493,807		3,486,537
	%		%
Net profit margin	1.85		6.01
Return on equity	4.96		16.37
Return on assets	4.03		13.19
Foreign sales percent	98		97
No. of employees (FTEs)	75		74

* Common
[A] Reported in accordance with U.S. GAAP

Latest Results

Periods ended:	3m Nov. 30/22[A]		3m Nov. 30/21[A]
	US$000s	%Chg	US$000s
Operating revenue	12,578	-3	12,918
Net income	(74)	n.a.	(391)
	US$		US$
Earnings per share*	(0.02)		(0.11)

* Common
[A] Reported in accordance with U.S. GAAP

Historical Summary
(as originally stated)

Fiscal Year	Oper. Rev.	Net Inc. Bef. Disc.	EPS*
	US$000s	US$000s	US$
2022[A]	62,902	1,164	0.33
2021[A]	57,502	3,455	0.99
2020[A]	44,945	2,785	0.77
2019[A]	45,446	2,100	0.50
2018[A]	53,923	2,921	0.66

* Common
[A] Reported in accordance with U.S. GAAP

J.15 Jolt Health Inc.

Symbol - JOLT **Exchange** - CSE **CUSIP** - 479861
Head Office - Marine Building, 1780-355 Burrard St, Vancouver, BC, V6C 2G8 **Telephone** - (604) 343-2977 **Toll-free** - (844) 906-2189
Website - jolt-health.com
Email - geraldtritt@me.com
Investor Relations - Gerald Tritt (778) 717-3489
Auditors - Baker Tilly WM LLP C.A., Vancouver, B.C.
Lawyers - Dentons Canada LLP, Vancouver, B.C.
Transfer Agents - Odyssey Trust Company, Vancouver, B.C.
Profile - (B.C. 2021; orig. Alta., 1994) Holds exclusive rights/licences to produce, market, package, sell and distribute pharmaceutical and therapeutic products throughout North America and Europe, with a focus on the global sexual wellness and enhancement market.

Wholly owned **212774 Alberta Ltd.** holds a royalty and product licence agreement with **Callitas Health Inc.** providing 212774 the right to use

Callitas' technology to produce, market and sell Callitas' products, including cannabidiol (CBD) oral strips (Auralief), CBD biphasic candies, arousal gel (Bloom), and other related technologies and products, in North America and Europe for a 10-year period.

In addition, the company plans to focus on pharmaceutical and biotechnology ventures including drug delivery technology such as transdermal patches that can reduce side effects, transforming patient outcomes with established, approved medicines allowing for streamlined market entry with long-term intellectual property protections.

In December 2022, the company sold wholly owned **MicroDoz Therapy Inc.** for $100,000 through notes payable in twelve months. MicroDoz facilitates research into the efficacy of psilocybin assisted treatment of cannabis use disorder. MicroDoz, which facilitates research into the efficacy of psilocybin assisted treatment of cannabis use disorder, was acquired in May 2022 by the company for issuance of 10,000,000 common shares at 5¢ per share at closing.

In October 2022, the company acquired **Doc Hygiene Pharmaceuticals Inc.** for a total consideration of US$300,000 including issuance of US$150,000 convertible promissory note and assumption of US$150,000 indebtedness of Doc Hygiene. Doc Hygiene which has a hygiene product line and brand for hygiene and sanitizing needs and an e-commerce platform for its products.

In October 2022, the company signed a letter of intent to acquire **Naltrexone Therapeutics Inc.** for issuance of $2,000,000 in common shares. Naltrexone Therapeutics holds intellectual property for transdermal delivery of opioid antagonist drug Naltrexone.

In September 2022, the company invested US$592,000 in **Starton Therapeutics Inc.** in exchange for 145,161 common shares at US$3.10 per share. New jersey-based Starton is focused on transforming standard of care therapies in oncology.

Predecessor Detail - Name changed from Love Pharma Inc., May 26, 2023.

Directors - Gerald Tritt, CEO; Douglas J. (Doug) Taylor, Vancouver, B.C.; Mark T. Tommasi, North Vancouver, B.C.

Other Exec. Officers - Joshua Maurice, COO; Tatiana Kovaleva, CFO

Capital Stock

	Authorized (shs.)	Outstanding (shs.)[1]
Preferred	unlimited	nil
Common	unlimited	50,422,762

[1] At May 26, 2023

Major Shareholder - Widely held at May 30, 2022.

Price Range - JOLT/CSE

Year	Volume	High	Low	Close
2022	8,304,572	$0.40	$0.05	$0.05
2021	1,107,719	$1.50	$0.35	$0.35
2020	160,012	$0.60	$0.10	$0.60
2019	47,940	$0.50	$0.20	$0.20
2018	2,538,490	$2.30	$0.30	$0.40

Consolidation: 1-for-10 cons. in Mar. 2023; 1-for-2 cons. in Sept. 2021

Recent Close: $0.02

Capital Stock Changes - On Mar. 2, 2023, common shares were consolidated on a 1-for-10 basis

In April and May 2022, private placement of 18,925,000 units (1 common share & 1 warrant) at 2¢ per unit was completed, with warrants exercisable at 5¢ per share for two years. In June 2022, private placement of 123,707,769 units (1 common share & 1 warrant) at $0.011 per unit was completed, with warrants exercisable at 5¢ per share for two years. In August and September 2022, private placement of 36,675,000 units (1 common share & 1 warrant) at $0.014 per unit was completed, with warrants exercisable at 5¢ per share for two years.

Wholly Owned Subsidiaries

Kick Pharmaceuticals Inc., Vancouver, B.C.
- 100% int. in **LSB Life Sciences Biotech Inc.** Inactive.
- 100% int. in **Life Pharmaceuticals Company Inc.** Inactive.
- 100% int. in **Nabilone Pharma Inc.** Inactive.
- 100% int. in **212774 Alberta Ltd.**, Alta.

1288339 B.C. Ltd., B.C.

Financial Statistics

Periods ended:	12m Dec. 31/21[A1]		12m Dec. 31/20[A2]
	$000s	%Chg	$000s
General & admin expense	1,607		162
Stock-based compensation	552		nil
Operating expense	**2,159**	**n.m.**	**162**
Operating income	**(2,159)**	**n.a.**	**(162)**
Deprec., depl. & amort.	34		nil
Finance costs, gross	10		7
Write-downs/write-offs	1,234		nil
Pre-tax income	**(9,521)**	**n.a.**	**(158)**
Net income	**(9,521)**	**n.a.**	**(158)**
Cash & equivalent	335		531
Current assets	626		537
Long-term investments	681		nil
Intangibles, net	510		239
Total assets	**1,817**	**+134**	**777**
Bank indebtedness	224		213
Accts. pay. & accr. liabs	259		136
Current liabilities	606		349
Shareholders' equity	1,211		428
Cash from oper. activs	**(1,410)**	**n.a.**	**(54)**
Cash from fin. activs	1,384		792
Cash from invest. activs	(169)		(200)
Net cash position	**335**	**-37**	**531**
	$		$
Earnings per share*	(0.44)		(0.13)
Cash flow per share*	(0.07)		(0.04)
	shs		shs
No. of shs. o/s*	31,491,985		7,830,000
Avg. no. of shs. o/s*	21,452,452		1,232,196
	%		%
Net profit margin	n.a.		n.a.
Return on equity	(1,161.81)		(31.89)
Return on assets	(733.31)		(20.54)

* Common

[A] Reported in accordance with IFRS

[1] Results reflect the Sept. 21, 2021, reverse takeover acquisition of Kick Pharmaceuticals Inc.

[2] Results pertain to Kick Pharmaceuticals Inc.

Latest Results

Periods ended:	9m Sept. 30/22[A]		9m Sept. 30/21[A]
	$000s	%Chg	$000s
Net income	(1,418)	n.a.	(6,702)
	$		$
Earnings per share*	(0.04)		(0.37)

* Common

[A] Reported in accordance with IFRS

Historical Summary
(as originally stated)

Fiscal Year	Oper. Rev.	Net Inc. Bef. Disc.	EPS*
	$000s	$000s	$
2021[A]	nil	(9,521)	(0.44)
2020[A]	nil	(158)	(0.13)
2020[A1]	nil	(325)	(0.04)
2019[A]	nil	(121)	(0.02)
2018[A]	nil	(387)	(0.06)

* Common

[A] Reported in accordance with IFRS

[1] Results for fiscal 2020 and prior fiscal years pertain to Glenbriar Technologies Inc.

Note: Adjusted throughout for 1-for-10 cons. in Mar. 2023; 1-for-2 cons. in Sept. 2021

J.16 Jones Soda Co.

Symbol - JSDA **Exchange** - CSE **CUSIP** - 48023P

Head Office - 4786 1 Ave S, Suite 103, Seattle, WA, United States, 98134 **Telephone** - (206) 624-3357 **Toll-free** - (800) 656-6050 **Fax** - (206) 624-6857

Website - www.jonessoda.com

Email - joec@jonessoda.com

Investor Relations - Joe Culp (800) 656-6050

Auditors - Armanino LLP C.P.A., Bellevue, Wash.

Transfer Agents - Odyssey Trust Company, Vancouver, B.C.

Employees - 29 at Mar. 27, 2023

Profile - (Wash. 2000; orig. B.C., 1986) Develops, produces, markets and distributes premium craft beverages under the brands Jones® Soda and Lemoncocco®, as well as soda dispenser, cups and sodas under the Fountain brand. Also develops, produces and sells a variety of cannabis products under the Mary Jones brand.

Product manufacturing is outsourced to third-party bottlers and independent contract manufacturers located in Ontario, Illinois, Washington and Pennsylvania.

The company's products are sold in grocery stores, convenience and gas stores, on fountain in restaurants, up and down the street in independent accounts such as delicatessens, sandwich shops and burger restaurants, as well as through our national accounts with several large retailers.

Products are primarily across North America through its network of independent distributors and directly to its national and regional retail accounts. Mary Jones products are only sold in California although the company intends to expand into other states that have legalized the recreational use of cannabis. During 2022, sales in the U.S. represented 80% of total sales, with 19% in Canada and the remaining 1% internationally.

Recent Merger and Acquisition Activity

Status: terminated **Revised:** June 7, 2022

UPDATE: The transaction was terminated. PREVIOUS: Simply Better Brands Corp. (SBBC) agreed to acquire Jones Soda Co. for US$0.75 per share payable in SBBC common shares. In addition, SBBC would assume all outstanding debt of Jones and exchange any dilutive securities of Jones for materially similar securities of SBBC based on an implied ratio of 0.20548 SBBC common shares for each Jones share held, with the aggregate value being of the transaction being approximately US$98,902,257. Upon completion, SBBC planned to change its name to Jones Soda or something similar.

Predecessor Detail - Name changed from Urban Juice and Soda Company Ltd., Aug. 3, 2000.

Directors - Paul Norman, chr., Miami, Fla.; Chad Bronstein, Oak Brook, Ill.; Gregg Reichman; Clive Sirkin, Chicago, Ill.

Other Exec. Officers - David Knight, pres. & CEO; Eric Chastain, COO, corp. sec. & pres., Jones Beverage division; Joe Culp, interim CFO & contr.; Bohb Blair, chief mktg. officer; Dan Buchanan, v-p, sales

Capital Stock

	Authorized (shs.)	Outstanding (shs.)[1]
Common	100,000,000	100,698,135

[1] At May 5, 2023

Major Shareholder - SOL Verano Blocker I LLC held 25.3% interest at Mar. 28, 2022.

Price Range - JSDA/CSE

Year	Volume	High	Low	Close
2022	4,190,042	$1.02	$0.18	$0.31

Recent Close: $0.24

Capital Stock Changes - On Feb. 15, 2022, 20,000,048 common shares were issued pursuant to the acquisition of Pinestar Gold Inc. and 4,025,035 common shares were issued on conversion of US$2,000,000 debenture. Also during 2022, common shares were issued as follows: 6,447,111 on conversion of debentures and 1,950,000 as share-based compensation.

Wholly Owned Subsidiaries

Jones Soda (Canada) Inc., B.C.
Jones Soda Cannabis Inc.
Jones Soda Co. (USA) Inc., Wash.
Mary Jones California, LLC, Calif.
Mary Jones Michigan, LLC
Pinestar Gold Inc., Vancouver, B.C. Inactive.

Financial Statistics

Periods ended:	12m Dec. 31/22^A		12m Dec. 31/21^oA
	US$000s	%Chg	US$000s
Operating revenue	**19,085**	**+29**	**14,792**
Cost of goods sold	13,942		10,394
General & admin expense	9,462		5,974
Stock-based compensation	1,364		144
Operating expense	**24,768**	**+50**	**16,512**
Operating income	**(5,683)**	**n.a.**	**(1,720)**
Deprec., depl. & amort.	414		166
Finance income	6		4
Finance costs, gross	377		225
Write-downs/write-offs	4		(21)
Pre-tax income	**(6,404)**	**n.a.**	**(1,784)**
Income taxes	nil		27
Net income	**(6,404)**	**n.a.**	**(1,811)**
Cash & equivalent	7,971		4,667
Inventories	2,621		1,923
Accounts receivable	3,170		2,662
Current assets	14,975		10,513
Fixed assets, net	127		238
Right-of-use assets	nil		365
Total assets	**15,102**	**+35**	**11,149**
Accts. pay. & accr. liabs	2,713		2,783
Current liabilities	3,335		4,488
Long-term debt, gross	nil		2,463
Long-term debt, net	nil		1,778
Long-term lease liabilities	nil		266
Shareholders' equity	11,767		4,617
Cash from oper. activs	**(5,957)**	**n.a.**	**(3,431)**
Cash from fin. activs	9,214		3,515
Cash from invest. activs	100		(31)
Net cash position	**7,971**	**+71**	**4,667**
Capital expenditures	(29)		(35)
Capital disposals	98		4
	US$		US$
Earnings per share*	(0.07)		(0.03)
Cash flow per share*	(0.06)		(0.04)
	shs		shs
No. of shs. o/s*	100,263,135		67,840,941
Avg. no. of shs. o/s*	94,177,863		65,542,609
	%		%
Net profit margin	(33.56)		(12.24)
Return on equity	(78.17)		(40.26)
Return on assets	(47.55)		(15.67)
Foreign sales percent	81		78

* Common
^o Restated
^A Reported in accordance with U.S. GAAP

Latest Results

Periods ended:	3m Mar. 31/23^A		3m Mar. 31/22^A
	US$000s	%Chg	US$000s
Operating revenue	3,870	-14	4,523
Net income	(1,363)	n.a.	(1,664)
	US$		US$
Earnings per share*	(0.01)		(0.02)

* Common
^A Reported in accordance with U.S. GAAP

Historical Summary
(as originally stated)

Fiscal Year	Oper. Rev.	Net Inc. Bef. Disc.	EPS*
	US$000s	US$000s	US$
2022^A	19,085	(6,404)	(0.07)
2021^A	14,792	(1,811)	(0.03)
2020^A	11,895	(2,997)	(0.05)
2019^A	11,508	(2,778)	(0.05)

* Common
^A Reported in accordance with U.S. GAAP

J.17 Jushi Holdings Inc.

Symbol - JUSH **Exchange** - CSE **CUSIP** - 48213Y
Head Office - 301 Yamato Rd, Suite 3250, Boca Raton, FL, United States, 33431 **Telephone** - (561) 617-9100
Website - www.jushico.com
Email - investors@jushico.com
Investor Relations - Lisa Forman (617) 767-4419
Auditors - Macias Gini & O'Connell LLP C.P.A., San Jose, Calif.
Transfer Agents - Odyssey Trust Company, Vancouver, B.C.
FP500 Revenue Ranking - 526
Employees - 1,486 at Dec. 31, 2022
Profile - (B.C. 2007) Has cannabis operations in the U.S., including retail, distribution, cultivation and processing, for the medical and adult-use markets.

Owns or manages cannabis operations and/or holds licences in the adult-use and/or medicinal cannabis marketplace in Pennsylvania, Illinois, Virginia, Massachusetts, California, Nevada and Ohio. Retail operations consist of 35 cannabis dispensaries (at August 2023) in Pennsylvania (16), Illinois (4), Virginia (6), Massachusetts (2), California (2), Nevada (4) and Ohio operating under the Beyond Hello brand, except for the locations in Massachusetts which operate under the Nature's Remedy brand and certain locations in Nevada operating under the NuLeaf brand. Cultivation and production operations include facilities in Scranton, Pa.; Manassas, Va.; Lakeville, Mass.; North Las Vegas, Sparks and Reno, Nev.; and Columbus and Toledo, Ohio, which produce all cannabis product categories under the proprietary brands The Bank, The Lab, Tasteology, Sèchè and Nira + Medicinals.

During 2022, the company discontinued its cannabidiol (CBD) retail operations, which conducted online sales throughout U.S. of a line of physician-formulated hemp-derived CBD products under the Nira brand.

In September 2022, the company acquired the remaining 22% interest in a retail licence holder in Grover Beach, Calif., for an undisclosed amount.

In April 2022, the company acquired **NuLeaf, Inc.**, a Nevada-based vertically-integrated operator, for US$45,000,000, consisting of US$15,750,000 cash, a US$15,750,000 promissory note and issuance of 4,662,384 class B subordinate voting shares at US$2.87 per share. NuLeaf operates two dispensaries in Las Vegas and Lake Tahoe; a 27,000-sq.-ft. cultivation facility in Sparks; and a 13,000-sq.-ft. processing facility in Reno. NuLeaf also owns a dispensary under development located directly on Las Vegas Boulevard.

In March 2022, the company acquired a dispensary operating under the name The Apothecarium in Las Vegas, Nev., for US$6,000,000 cash, a US$10,000,000 promissory note and issuance of 527,704 class B subordinate voting shares at US$3.79 per share.

Predecessor Detail - Name changed from Tanzania Minerals Corp., June 5, 2019, pursuant to reverse takeover acquisition of Jushi Inc.; basis 1 new for 22.7571 old shs.

Directors - James A. (Jim) Cacioppo, chr. & CEO, Fla.; Benjamin Cross, Conn.; Marina Hahn, N.Y.; Stephen (Steve) Monroe, N.Y.; Billy Wafford, Tex.

Other Exec. Officers - L. Jonathan (Jon) Barack, pres.; Michelle O. Mosier, CFO & chief acctg. officer; Tobi Lebowitz, chief legal officer & corp. sec.; Andreas (Dre) Neumann, chief creative dir.; Shaunna Patrick, chief comml. dir.; Nicole Upshaw, chief retail & people officer; Trenton (Trent) Woloveck, chief strategy dir.; Ryan Cook, exec. v-p, opers.; Matt Leeth, exec. v-p, legal affairs

Capital Stock

	Authorized (shs.)	Outstanding (shs.)[1]
Preferred	unlimited	nil
Class B Subord. Vtg.	unlimited	196,631,598
Class A Super Vtg.	unlimited	nil
Class C Multiple Vtg.	unlimited	nil

[1] At Aug. 7, 2023

Major Shareholder - Denis Arsenault held 12.4% interest at Apr. 21, 2023.

Price Range - JUSH/CSE

Year	Volume	High	Low	Close
2022	52,723,783	$6.05	$0.93	$1.02
2021	77,407,574	$11.59	$4.01	$4.10
2020	39,183,666	$8.00	$1.00	$7.49
2019	3,460,448	$3.40	$1.38	$1.72
2018	87,066	$27.31	$2.62	$3.53

Consolidation: 1-for-22.7571 cons. in June 2019
Recent Close: $0.48
Capital Stock Changes - In January 2022, private placement of 3,717,392 class B subordinate voting shares was completed at US$3.68 per share. Also during 2022, class B subordinate voting shares were issued as follows: 4,662,384 pursuant to the acquisition of NuLeaf, Inc., 3,176,601 on exercise of warrants, 910,000 on conversion of debt, 888,880 as contingent consideration, 527,704 pursuant to the acquisition of The Apothecarium dispensary, 121,976 on exercise of options and 114,416 for services; 140,340 class B subordinate voting shares were cancelled.

Wholly Owned Subsidiaries

Jushi Inc., Boca Raton, Fla.
- 100% int. in **Agape Total Health Care Inc.**, Pa.
- 100% int. in **Bear Flag Assets, LLC**, Calif.
  - 100% int. in **GSG SBCA, Inc.**, Calif.
- 100% int. in **Beyond Hello CA, LLC**, Calif.
- 100% int. in **Beyond Hello IL Holdings, LLC**, Ill.
  - 100% int. in **Beyond Hello IL, LLC**, Ill.
- 100% int. in **Franklin Bioscience - Penn LLC**, Pa.
  - 100% int. in **Franklin Bioscience - NE, LLC**, Pa.
  - 100% int. in **Franklin Bioscience - SE, LLC**, Pa.
  - 100% int. in **Franklin Bioscience - SW, LLC**, Pa.
- 100% int. in **JMGT, LLC**, Fla.
- 100% int. in **JREH, LLC**, Del.
  - 100% int. in **JREHCA, LLC**, Calif.
  - 100% int. in **JREHIL, LLC**, Ill.
  - 100% int. in **JREHNV, LLC**, Nev.
  - 100% int. in **JREHOH, LLC**, Ohio
  - 100% int. in **JREHPA, LLC**, Pa.
  - 100% int. in **JREHVA, LLC**, Va.
- 100% int. in **Jushi GB Holdings, LLC**, Calif.
  - 78% int. in **Milkman, LLC**, Calif.
- 100% int. in **Jushi IP, LLC**, Del.
- 100% int. in **Jushi MA, Inc.**, Mass.
- 100% int. in **Jushi OH, LLC**, Ohio
  - 100% int. in **Campbell Hill Ventures, LLC**, Ohio
  - 100% int. in **Franklin Bioscience OH, LLC**, Ohio
  - 100% int. in **OhiGrow, LLC**, Ohio
- 100% int. in **Jushi PS Holdings, LLC**, Calif.
  - 100% int. in **Organic Solutions of the Desert, LLC**, Calif.
- 100% int. in **Jushi VA, LLC**, Va.
  - 100% int. in **Dalitso, LLC**, Alexandria, Va.
- 100% int. in **Mojave Suncup Holdings, LLC**, Nev.
  - 100% int. in **Jushi NV CLV, Inc.**, Nev.
  - 100% int. in **Jushi NV, Inc.**, Nev.
  - 100% int. in **Production Excellence, LLC**, Nev.
    - 100% int. in **Franklin Bioscience NV, LLC**, Nev.
  - 100% int. in **SF-D, INC**, Nev.
- 100% int. in **Northeast Venture Holdings, LLC**, Pa.
  - 100% int. in **Pennsylvania Dispensary Solutions, LLC**, Pa.
- 100% int. in **PASPV Holdings, LLC**, Pa.
  - 100% int. in **Pennsylvania Medical Solutions, LLC**, Pa.
- 100% int. in **Sound Wellness Holdings, Inc.**, Del.
- 100% int. in **Valiant Enterprises, LLC**, Mass.

Subsidiaries

51% int. in **Jushi Europe S.A.**, Switzerland.
- 100% int. in **JPTREH Lda.**, Portugal.

Note: The preceding list includes only the major related companies in which interests are held.

Financial Statistics

Periods ended:	12m Dec. 31/22^A		12m Dec. 31/21^oA
	US$000s	%Chg	US$000s
Operating revenue	**284,284**	**+36**	**209,292**
Cost of goods sold	175,038		123,292
Salaries & benefits	71,237		58,228
General & admin expense	49,132		34,276
Stock-based compensation	23,073		14,506
Operating expense	**318,480**	**+38**	**230,302**
Operating income	**(34,196)**	**n.a.**	**(21,010)**
Deprec., depl. & amort.	26,492		8,411
Finance income	142		243
Finance costs, gross	45,733		30,853
Write-downs/write-offs	(159,645)[1]		(6,344)
Pre-tax income	**(193,876)**	**n.a.**	**47,104**
Income taxes	8,448		29,625
Net income	**(202,324)**	**n.a.**	**17,479**
Net inc. for equity hldrs	**(202,324)**	**n.a.**	**20,251**
Net inc. for non-cont. int	**nil**	**n.a.**	**(2,772)**
Cash & equivalent	26,196		94,962
Inventories	35,089		43,319
Accounts receivable	4,809		3,200
Current assets	70,051		154,356
Long-term investments	977		1,500
Fixed assets, net	177,755		137,280
Right-of-use assets	130,265		111,296
Intangibles, net	138,321		238,294
Total assets	**529,341**	**-19**	**652,049**
Accts. pay. & accr. liabs	59,722		54,339
Current liabilities	107,628		83,926
Long-term debt, gross	189,262		125,979
Long-term debt, net	180,558		119,798
Long-term lease liabilities	117,922		103,460
Shareholders' equity	47,278		182,370
Non-controlling interest	(1,387)		(1,387)
Cash from oper. activs	**(21,416)**	**n.a.**	**(14,304)**
Cash from fin. activs	33,983		137,663
Cash from invest. activs	(80,859)		(113,455)
Net cash position	**27,146**	**-72**	**95,487**
Capital expenditures	(56,881)		(75,296)
	US$		US$
Earnings per share*	(1.06)		0.12
Cash flow per share*	(0.11)		(0.08)
	shs		shs
No. of shs. o/s*	196,686,372		182,707,359
Avg. no. of shs. o/s*	190,021,550		170,292,035
	%		%
Net profit margin	(71.17)		8.35
Return on equity	(174.60)		n.m.
Return on assets	(25.61)		5.72
Foreign sales percent	100		100
No. of employees (FTEs)	1,486		1,200

* Subord. Vtg.
^o Restated
^A Reported in accordance with U.S. GAAP
[1] Includes impairments of US$39,643,000 and US$111,515,000 on goodwill and certain intangible assets, respectively, in California, Massachusetts, Nevada, Ohio and Pennsylvania.

Latest Results

Periods ended:	6m June 30/23[A]		6m June 30/22[A]
	US$000s	%Chg	US$000s
Operating revenue	136,298	+1	134,645
Net income	(26,476)	n.a.	(7,691)
	US$		US$
Earnings per share*	(0.14)		(0.04)

* Subord. Vtg.
[A] Reported in accordance with U.S. GAAP

Historical Summary
(as originally stated)

Fiscal Year	Oper. Rev.	Net Inc. Bef. Disc.	EPS*
	US$000s	US$000s	US$
2022[A]	284,284	(202,324)	(1.06)
2021[B]	209,292	21,364	0.15
2020[B]	80,772	(211,866)	(2.11)
2019[B1]	10,229	(30,771)	(0.37)
	$000s	$000s	$
2019[B2]	nil	(129)	(0.46)

* Subord. Vtg.
[A] Reported in accordance with U.S. GAAP
[B] Reported in accordance with IFRS
[1] Results reflect the June 6, 2019, reverse takeover acquisition of Jushi Inc.
[2] Results for fiscal 2019 and prior fiscal years pertain to Tanzania Minerals Corp.
Note: Adjusted throughout for 1-for-22.75711 cons. in June 2019

J.18 Just Kitchen Holdings Corp.

Symbol - JK **Exchange** - TSX-VEN **CUSIP** - 48214J
Head Office - 1430-800 Pender St W, Vancouver, BC, V6C 2V6 **Toll-free** - (855) 578-5246
Website - investors.justkitchen.com
Email - jason@justkitchen.com
Investor Relations - Hsin-How Chen (855) 578-5248
Auditors - KPMG LLP C.A., Vancouver, B.C.
Transfer Agents - Odyssey Trust Company, Vancouver, B.C.

Profile - (B.C. 2019) Produces meals and beverages for online delivery in East and Southeast Asia that are prepared at food manufacturing centres (ghost kitchens) instead of restaurants. Also operates an online grocery delivery business in Taiwan.

Operates ghost kitchens, which are kitchens that are used to provide meals for online delivery only and act as the production centres for meals ordered through delivery apps. The company uses a hub-and-spoke operating model, wherein advanced food preparation takes place at larger hub kitchens and final meal preparation takes place at smaller spoke kitchens located in areas with higher population densities. Orders are generated through its proprietary mobile app, as well as on third-party ordering and delivery platforms such as Uber Eats and Foodpanda. The company's ghost kitchens offer a portfolio of in-house and licensed menus and brands. In-house brands include Hot Ones, Just Chicken, K Bao, Bodyfit, BIT Beef Noodle, Boba Mania, LuWei Lab, Thai High, Go Lean, Blue Avocado, Unadon Japanese Eel Rice & Curry Rice, SiChuan Beef Noodle, Burgers & Dogs, Old Brew Noodle Soup, Craftsman's Soul-Made Ramen, Cali Vibe Bento and Wow Pal. At May 30, 2023, the company had 25 ghost kitchens located in Taiwan, Hong Kong, the Philippines, Malaysia and Thailand. Also has communal virtual food courts in Taiwan called Co-Op: The Future Food Hall.

The company also operates JustMarket, an online grocery delivery platform that sells basic grocery items that can be ordered on its own or as an addition to JustKitchen food orders.

In December 2022, the company launched Co-Op: The Future Food Hall, which are communal virtual food courts in Taiwan wherein consumers pick-up food items and sit in the communal dining area. A location opened in November 2022 in the Neihu Science Park, and a second location opened at the Hotel Episode in the HsinZhu Science Park.

In September 2022, the company expanded into Thailand. GrabKitchen would provide the physical kitchen on a Kitchen-as-a-Service basis for the company's in-house delivery-only brands including Master Don, K.Bao and Bodyfit.

In June 2022, the Company announced the opening of its first two ghost kitchens in Malaysia located in Petaling Jaya and Bukit Bintang, which would utilize GrabFood, Foodpanda and Shopee Food as delivery service partners.

In June 2022, the company entered into a royalty-based virtual kitchen services agreement with New Delhi, India-based **Cloud Retail Solutions Private Limited** (dba Kitchens Centre) to make the company's portfolio of food brands available for delivery in India. Pursuant to the agreement, Kitchens Centre would perform all services related to order intake and fulfillment including food preparation, packaging and coordination of order pick-ups by third-party delivery service providers. The company would receive a percentage of net receipts on all orders and has agreed to provide access to its manuals and portals, training to Kitchens Centre's personnel, complete inspections and execute a mutually agreed upon a marketing strategy, among other terms.

Recent Merger and Acquisition Activity

Status: pending **Announced:** May 23, 2023
JF Investment Co., Ltd., which is jointly owned by Jason Hsin-How Chen, Freddie Hsi-Liang Liu, Jerry TaiHan Chiu and Sheng Min Su, agreed to acquire all of Vancouver, B.C.-based Just Kitchen Holdings Corp.'s common shares, other than the 14,440,001 Just Kitchen common shares already owned by them, for 9¢ per share. In connection, all of the continuing assets of Just Kitchen would be transferred to JustKitchen Co. Ltd. (JK Taiwan), Just Kitchen's wholly owned subsidiary in Taiwan. Just Kitchen shareholders can elect not to receive the cash consideration and instead hold an equivalent number of JK Taiwan shares, such that the shareholder would have the same equity interest in JK Taiwan as they had with Just Kitchen immediately prior to closing of the transaction. Evans & Evans, Inc. has provided an opinion to the effect that, as of May 19, 2023, the consideration to be received by Just Kitchen shareholders is fair, from a financial point of view, to such holders, subject to the respective limitations, qualifications, assumptions and other matters set forth in such opinion.

Directors - Kai Huang, chr., Los Gatos, Calif.; Hsin-How (Jason) Chen, pres. & CEO, Taipei, Republic of China; Darryl S. Cardey, Vancouver, B.C.; Darren P. Devine, West Vancouver, B.C.; Hsi-Liang (Freddie) Liu, Taipei, Republic of China; Edward Wright, Vancouver, B.C.; Kent Wu, Taipei, Republic of China

Other Exec. Officers - Adam R. Kniec, CFO & corp. sec.; Ken Chang, chief tech. officer; Mark Lin, CIO; Yang Liu, chief strategy officer; John Yu, chief mktg. officer; Michael Liu, exec. v-p, opers.

Capital Stock

	Authorized (shs.)	Outstanding (shs.)[1]
Common	unlimited	100,471,387

[1] At May 30, 2023

Major Shareholder - Widely held at Jan. 18, 2022.

Price Range - JK/TSX-VEN

Year	Volume	High	Low	Close
2022	16,713,653	$1.33	$0.09	$0.10
2021	23,046,597	$2.02	$0.88	$1.22

Recent Close: $0.08

Capital Stock Changes - In March 2023, private placement of 17,840,000 common shares was completed at 10¢.

During fiscal 2022, 37,500 common shares were issued on exercise of options.

Wholly Owned Subsidiaries

Just Kitchen Malaysia Sdn. Bhd., Malaysia.
Just Kitchen Thailand
Just Kitchen (USA) Inc., United States.
JustKitchen Co. Ltd., Taipei, Republic of China.
- 100% int. in **StarKitchen Co. Ltd.**, Republic of China.

JustKitchen Concepts Pte. Ltd., Singapore.
JustKitchen Hong Kong Corp. Limited, Hong Kong, People's Republic of China.
JustKitchen Philippines Inc., Philippines.

Subsidiaries

51% int. in **JustKitchen TDG. Inc.**, Philippines.

Financial Statistics

Periods ended:	12m Sept. 30/22[A]		12m Sept. 30/21[A]
	$000s	%Chg	$000s
Operating revenue	**18,969**	**+59**	**11,926**
Cost of sales	12,837		8,073
Salaries & benefits	9,320		4,606
Research & devel. expense	54		108
General & admin expense	9,240		7,101
Stock-based compensation	2,156		2,370
Operating expense	**33,607**	**+51**	**22,258**
Operating income	**(14,638)**	**n.a.**	**(10,332)**
Deprec., depl. & amort.	2,197		964
Finance income	110		27
Finance costs, gross	128		102
Investment income	(117)		nil
Pre-tax income	**(17,517)**	**n.a.**	**(11,238)**
Net income	**(17,517)**	**n.a.**	**(11,238)**
Cash & equivalent	2,765		20,797
Inventories	591		854
Accounts receivable	603		515
Current assets	5,671		22,635
Long-term investments	599		nil
Fixed assets, net	3,106		2,026
Right-of-use assets	3,139		2,809
Intangibles, net	153		241
Total assets	**13,132**	**-53**	**27,938**
Accts. pay. & accr. liabs	2,846		3,257
Current liabilities	4,206		4,374
Long-term debt, gross	92		230
Long-term lease liabilities	2,178		1,979
Shareholders' equity	6,743		21,585
Cash from oper. activs	**(13,638)**	**n.a.**	**(7,301)**
Cash from fin. activs	(13,638)		29,668
Cash from invest. activs	(2,581)		(2,016)
Net cash position	**2,765**	**-87**	**20,797**
Capital expenditures	(1,853)		(1,775)
	$		$
Earnings per share*	(0.23)		(0.21)
Cash flow per share*	(0.18)		(0.14)
	shs		shs
No. of shs. o/s*	75,181,387		75,143,887
Avg. no. of shs. o/s*	75,166,490		53,711,134
	%		%
Net profit margin	(92.35)		(94.23)
Return on equity	(123.67)		(104.03)
Return on assets	(84.68)		(71.46)
Foreign sales percent	100		100

* Common
[A] Reported in accordance with IFRS

Latest Results

Periods ended:	6m Mar. 31/23[A]		6m Mar. 31/22[A]
	$000s	%Chg	$000s
Operating revenue	6,777	-26	9,206
Net income	(5,929)	n.a.	(9,014)
	$		$
Earnings per share*	(0.08)		(0.12)

* Common
[A] Reported in accordance with IFRS

Historical Summary
(as originally stated)

Fiscal Year	Oper. Rev.	Net Inc. Bef. Disc.	EPS*
	$000s	$000s	$
2022[A]	18,969	(17,517)	(0.23)
2021[A]	11,926	(11,238)	(0.21)
2020[A1]	1,834	(2,521)	(0.11)

* Common
[A] Reported in accordance with IFRS
[1] 44 weeks ended Sept. 30, 2020.

J.19 Justera Health Ltd.

Symbol - VTAL **Exchange** - CSE **CUSIP** - 482139
Head Office - 2802-2300 Yonge St, Toronto, ON, M4P 1E4 **Telephone** - (416) 901-5611
Website - www.justerahealth.com
Email - investors@datametrex.com
Investor Relations - Priya Atwal (416) 901-5611 ext. 204
Auditors - SHIM & Associates LLP C.A., Vancouver, B.C.
Transfer Agents - Computershare Trust Company of Canada Inc., Toronto, Ont.

Profile - (Ont. 1945) Provides health and medical solutions in Canada, including personal home care, nursing, on-call urgent medical care, intravenous (IV) vitamin therapy, natural health supplements, and health screening services such as COVID-19 testing and breast cancer screening.

Wholly owned **Concierge Medical Consultants Inc.** provides medical concierge services, including personal home care, nursing care upon request, on-call urgent medical care and event medical services, as well as intravenous (IV) vitamin therapy services, from its locations in Vancouver, B.C., and Toronto, Ont.

Wholly owned **Naturevan Nutrition Ltd.** sells natural health supplement products online and through distribution agents. Products include Cissus Plus, Probiotics Premium, Albumin Max, Phytogen Plus, Lutein Super Vision and Milk Thistle Liver Care.

Wholly owned **ScreenPro Security Ltd.** provides turnkey on-site COVID-19 testing solutions to businesses and government organizations in Canada through its ScreenPro testing platform. Indirect wholly owned **GoStop Inc.** provides COVID-19 digital passport services.

Wholly owned **Add Biomedical Inc.** is a biomedical screening company with a focus on breast cancer detection. Its primary product is an at-home rapid test kit.

On May 13, 2022, the company acquired private British Columbia-based **Naturevan Nutrition Ltd.**, for $2,200,000, consisting of $650,000 cash and issuance of 25,833,333 units (1 common share & 1 warrant) at 6¢ per unit, with warrants exercisable at 7¢ per share for two years. NatureVan sold natural health supplement products online and through distribution agents.

Recent Merger and Acquisition Activity

Status: completed **Revised:** Mar. 18, 2022

UPDATE: The transaction was completed for revised consideration of $3,300,000, consisting of issuance of 33,000,000 units (1 common share & 1 warrant) at 10¢ per unit, with warrants exercisable at 15¢ per share for two years. PREVIOUS: ScreenPro Security Inc. agreed to acquire private British Columbia-based Add Biomedical Inc., a biomedical screening company with an initial focus on breast cancer detection, for $5,000,000, which would consist of the issuance of ScreenPro units (1 common share & 1 warrant) at 15¢ per unit, with warrants exercisable at 20¢ per share for two years. Add Biomedical's primary product is an at-home rapid test kit, and it also plans to expand into veterinary diagnostics.

Predecessor Detail - Name changed from ScreenPro Security Inc., May 17, 2023.

Directors - Dr. Jibron Sharif, CMO & pres., Concierge Medical Services Inc., Vancouver, B.C.; Youngcho Lee, Vancouver, B.C.; Charles Schade, Toronto, Ont.

Other Exec. Officers - Edward Park, CEO; Paul Haber, CFO

Capital Stock

	Authorized (shs.)	Outstanding (shs.)[1]
Common	unlimited	118,772,247

[1] At May 5, 2023

Major Shareholder - Widely held at July 11, 2022.

Price Range - VTAL/CSE

Year	Volume	High	Low	Close
2022	99,294,144	$0.45	$0.02	$0.03
2021	80,138,816	$10.00	$0.15	$0.20

Consolidation: 1-for-10 cons. in Feb. 2022

Recent Close: $0.03

Capital Stock Changes - On Feb. 24, 2022, common shares were consolidated on a 1-for-10 basis. On Mar. 18, 2022, 33,000,000 units (1 post-consolidated common share & 1 warrant) at 10¢ per unit were issued pursuant to the acquisition of Add Biomedical Inc., with warrants exercisable at 15¢ per share for two years. On May 13, 2022, 25,833,333 units (1 post-consolidated common share & 1 warrant) at 6¢ per unit were issued pursuant to the acquisition of Naturevan Nutrition Ltd., with warrants exercisable at 7¢ per share for two years.

Wholly Owned Subsidiaries

Add Biomedical Inc., B.C.
Concierge Medical Consultants Inc., Vancouver, B.C.
Naturevan Nutrition Ltd., Canada.
ScreenPro Security Ltd., Vancouver, B.C.
- 100% int. in **GoStop Inc.**, B.C.

Financial Statistics

Periods ended:	13m Dec. 31/21[A1]		30w Nov. 30/20[A]
	$000s	%Chg	$000s
Operating revenue	**21,225**	**n.a.**	**582**
Cost of sales	18,529		479
Salaries & benefits	1,009		55
General & admin expense	3,530		451
Stock-based compensation	nil		549
Operating expense	**23,068**	**n.a.**	**1,533**
Operating income	**(1,843)**	**n.a.**	**(952)**
Deprec., depl. & amort.	1,996		46
Finance costs, gross	13		nil
Write-downs/write-offs	nil		(43)
Pre-tax income	**(10,157)**	**n.a.**	**(1,040)**
Net income	**(10,156)**	**n.a.**	**(1,040)**
Cash & equivalent	208		446
Inventories	2,288		661
Accounts receivable	55		60
Current assets	2,776		1,275
Fixed assets, net	886		427
Total assets	**4,887**	**+187**	**1,702**
Accts. pay. & accr. liabs	3,920		808
Current liabilities	3,969		808
Long-term lease liabilities	72		nil
Shareholders' equity	846		894
Cash from oper. activs	**(501)**	**n.a.**	**(736)**
Cash from fin. activs	942		1,361
Cash from invest. activs	(679)		(179)
Net cash position	**208**	**-53**	**446**
Capital expenditures	(797)		(139)
	$		$
Earnings per share*	(0.31)		n.a.
Cash flow per share*	(0.15)		(0.21)
	shs		shs
No. of shs. o/s*	41,638,916		n.a.
Avg. no. of shs. o/s*	32,674,560		n.a.
	%		%
Net profit margin	(47.85)		...
Return on equity	(1,167.36)		...
Return on assets	(307.88)		...

* Common
[A] Reported in accordance with IFRS
[1] Results prior to Mar. 5, 2021, pertain to and reflect the reverse takeover acquisition of ScreenPro Security Ltd.

Latest Results

Periods ended:	6m June 30/22[A]		7m June 30/21[A]
	$000s	%Chg	$000s
Operating revenue	8,320	-33	12,378
Net income	(2,869)	n.a.	(4,413)
	$		$
Earnings per share*	(0.04)		(0.17)

* Common
[A] Reported in accordance with IFRS
Note: Adjusted throughout for 1-for-10 cons. in Feb. 2022

J.20 Juva Life Inc.

Symbol - JUVA **Exchange** - CSE **CUSIP** - 48222R

Head Office - 8 N. San Pedro Rd, Suite 200, San Jose, CA, United States, 95110 **Toll-free** - (833) 333-5882

Website - www.juvalife.com

Email - mat@juvalife.com

Investor Relations - Mathew Lee (833) 333-5882

Auditors - BF Borgers CPA PC C.P.A., Lakewood, Colo.

Transfer Agents - VStock Transfer. LLC, Woodmere, N.Y.

Profile - (B.C. 2019) Acquires, owns and operates cannabis businesses in California.

Operations consist of five divisions: Juva Cultivation, which cultivates and distributes cannabis to medical and recreational users via licensed cannabis retailers; Juva Research, which researches and develops "precision cannabis" products to deliver the right medicine to the right patient at the right time; Juva Manufacturing, which creates Juva branded and white-label products for other recreational and medical-related cannabis companies; Juva Distribution, which focuses on distribution of branded products and products from other licensed cannabis companies; and Juva Retail, which consists of a network of cannabis facilities and a planned non-storefront retail delivery businesses, and strategic storefront brick and mortar cannabis retail stores.

Owns a 30,000-sq.-ft. cultivation, manufacturing, retail sales and wholesale distribution facility in Stockton, Calif. Also has a leased property in Redwood, Calif., where the company is in the process of building out its facilities and obtaining the necessary state and local authorizations to operate.

During the second quarter of 2022, the company acquired its previously leased property in Stockton, Calif., for an undisclosed amount.

Directors - Douglas (Doug) Chloupek, pres. & CEO, Morgan Hill, Calif.; Kari Gothie, v-p, fin., San Francisco, Calif.; Dr. Rakesh Patel, Los Altos, Calif.

Other Exec. Officers - Neil Ruditsky, COO; Mathew (Mat) Lee, CFO, treas. & corp. sec.; Sanjeev Gangwar, v-p, chemistry; Daniel Hughes, v-p, opers.; Thomas Leschak, v-p, cultivation

Capital Stock

	Authorized (shs.)	Outstanding (shs.)[1]
Common	unlimited	164,070,767

[1] At May 26, 2023

Major Shareholder - Douglas (Doug) Chloupek held 21.9% interest at May 20, 2022.

Price Range - JUVA/CSE

Year	Volume	High	Low	Close
2022	5,299,542	$0.44	$0.09	$0.09
2021	77,460,332	$2.29	$0.23	$0.23
2020	10,104,676	$1.23	$0.76	$1.23

Recent Close: $0.06

Capital Stock Changes - During 2022, 54,544 common shares were issued on vesting of restricted share units.

Wholly Owned Subsidiaries

Juva RWC, Inc., Calif.
Juva Retail RWC, Inc., Calif.
Juva Stockton, Inc., Calif.
1177988 B.C. Ltd., B.C.
Precision Apothecary, Inc., Calif.
San Juan, LLC, Calif.

Financial Statistics

Periods ended:	12m Dec. 31/22[A]		12m Dec. 31/21[A]
	US$000s	%Chg	US$000s
Operating revenue	**5,764**	**+49**	**3,868**
Cost of goods sold	5,230		2,871
Salaries & benefits	3,377		2,860
Research & devel. expense	498		329
General & admin expense	2,965		5,490
Stock-based compensation	1,875		1,996
Operating expense	**13,945**	**+3**	**13,546**
Operating income	**(8,181)**	**n.a.**	**(9,678)**
Deprec., depl. & amort.	821		672
Finance costs, gross	1,897		691
Write-downs/write-offs	(18)		nil
Pre-tax income	**(10,396)**	**n.a.**	**(11,307)**
Income taxes	87		52
Net income	**(10,483)**	**n.a.**	**(11,358)**
Cash & equivalent	641		2,681
Inventories	357		321
Accounts receivable	222		128
Current assets	3,046		4,249
Fixed assets, net	16,937		12,552
Right-of-use assets	88		3,717
Total assets	**20,375**	**-2**	**20,687**
Accts. pay. & accr. liabs	2,441		1,882
Current liabilities	2,733		2,375
Long-term debt, gross	7,897		nil
Long-term debt, net	7,897		nil
Long-term lease liabilities	nil		3,977
Shareholders' equity	9,744		14,334
Cash from oper. activs	**(7,335)**	**n.a.**	**(8,791)**
Cash from fin. activs	10,506		10,578
Cash from invest. activs	(5,303)		(1,289)
Net cash position	**641**	**-76**	**2,681**
Capital expenditures	(5,327)		(1,959)
	US$		US$
Earnings per share*	(0.06)		(0.07)
Cash flow per share*	(0.04)		(0.06)
	shs		shs
No. of shs. o/s*	164,070,767		164,016,223
Avg. no. of shs. o/s*	164,029,373		157,725,352
	%		%
Net profit margin	(181.87)		(293.64)
Return on equity	(87.08)		(107.98)
Return on assets	(41.74)		(58.79)

* Common
[A] Reported in accordance with IFRS

Latest Results

Periods ended:	3m Mar. 31/23[A]		3m Mar. 31/22[A]
	US$000s	%Chg	US$000s
Operating revenue	1,725	+49	1,157
Net income	(1,467)	n.a.	(3,066)
	US$		US$
Earnings per share*	(0.01)		(0.02)

* Common
[A] Reported in accordance with IFRS

Historical Summary
(as originally stated)

Fiscal Year	Oper. Rev. US$000s	Net Inc. Bef. Disc. US$000s	EPS* US$
2022[A]	5,764	(10,483)	(0.06)
2021[A]	3,868	(11,358)	(0.07)
2020[A]	967	(16,237)	(0.13)
2019[A]	nil	(8,981)	(0.11)
2018[A1]	nil	(3,369)	(0.07)

* Common
[A] Reported in accordance with IFRS
[1] 26 weeks ended Dec. 31, 2018.

K

K.1 K-Bro Linen Inc.

Symbol - KBL **Exchange** - TSX **CUSIP** - 48243M
Head Office - 14903 137 Ave NW, Edmonton, AB, T5V 1R9 **Telephone** - (780) 453-5218 **Fax** - (780) 455-6676
Website - www.k-brolinen.com
Email - kristie.plaquin@k-brolinen.com
Investor Relations - Kristie L. Plaquin (866) 232-0222
Auditors - PricewaterhouseCoopers LLP C.A., Edmonton, Alta.
Bankers - The Toronto-Dominion Bank, Edmonton, Alta.
Lawyers - Stikeman Elliott LLP, Toronto, Ont.
Transfer Agents - TSX Trust Company, Calgary, Alta.
FP500 Revenue Ranking - 578
Employees - 2,550 at Mar. 15, 2022
Profile - (Alta. 2010) Provides laundry and linen services to healthcare institutions, hotels and other commercial operations across Canada and to the hospitality, healthcare, manufacturing and pharmaceutical sectors in Scotland and the North East of England.

In Canada, operates under the banners K-Bro Linen Systems, Buanderie HMR and Les Buanderies Dextraze, offering services including processing, management and distribution of linens, including sheets, blankets, towels, surgical gowns and drapes, and other linen. Owns and operates nine laundry and linen processing facilities in ten cities including Vancouver and Victoria, B.C., Calgary and Edmonton, Alta., Toronto, Ont., Regina, Prince Albert and Saskatoon, Sask., and Montreal and Quebec, Que., and two distribution centres in Saskatchewan.

In the U.K., wholly owned **Fishers Topco Ltd.** provides linen rental, workwear hire and cleanroom garment services in Scotland and the North East of England through five sites in Cupar, Perth, Newcastle, Livingston and Coatbridge.

Recent Merger and Acquisition Activity

Status: completed **Announced:** Mar. 2, 2023
K-Bro Linen Inc. acquired private Buanderie Para-Net Inc., which provides laundry and linen services for the healthcare and hospitality markets in Quebec City, Que., for $11,500,000, which was satisfied by K-Bro drawing down on its revolving credit facility.

Predecessor Detail - Succeeded K-Bro Linen Income Fund, Jan. 1, 2011, pursuant to plan of arrangement whereby K-Bro Linen Inc. was formed to facilitate the conversion of the fund into a corporation and the fund was subsequently dissolved.

Directors - Dr. Michael B. (Mike) Percy, chr., Edmonton, Alta.; Linda J. McCurdy, pres. & CEO, Toronto, Ont.; Matthew B. (Matt) Hills, Boston, Mass.; Steven E. Matyas, Toronto, Ont.; Elise Rees, Vancouver, B.C.

Other Exec. Officers - Kristie L. Plaquin, CFO; Sean P. Curtis, sr. v-p & COO

Capital Stock

	Authorized (shs.)	Outstanding (shs.)[1]
Preferred	n.a.	nil
Common	unlimited	10,766,685

[1] At Aug. 8, 2023

Normal Course Issuer Bid - The company plans to make normal course purchases of up to 881,481 common shares representing 10% of the public float. The bid commenced on May 18, 2023, and expires on May 17, 2024.

Major Shareholder - Polar Asset Management Partners Inc. held 12.9% interest at Apr. 21, 2023.

Price Range - KBL/TSX

Year	Volume	High	Low	Close
2022	2,887,913	$35.99	$26.53	$27.30
2021	4,080,819	$47.22	$33.36	$34.20
2020	6,501,529	$46.44	$23.73	$38.97
2019	1,579,270	$43.16	$32.74	$42.05
2018	3,870,339	$41.71	$32.00	$33.44

Recent Close: $33.75

Capital Stock Changes - During 2022, 55,362 common shares were issued under long-term incentive plan and 1,950 common shares were forfeited under long-term incentive plan.

Dividends

KBL com Ra $1.20 pa M est. June 13, 2014

Wholly Owned Subsidiaries

K-Bro Linen Systems Inc., Edmonton, Alta.
- 100% int. in **K-Bro Acquisition UK Inc.**, Canada.
  - 100% int. in **FTL Guernsey Ltd.**, Guernsey.
  - 100% int. in **FTL UK Acquisition Company Ltd.**, United Kingdom.
    - 100% int. in **Fishers Topco Ltd.**, United Kingdom.
      - 100% int. in **Fishers Services Limited**, United Kingdom.
        - 100% int. in **Deeside Cleaners Ltd.**, United Kingdom.
- 100% int. in **K-Bro Linen Limited**, Alta.
  - 0.01% int. in **KBL Limited Partnership**, Man.
- 99.99% int. in **KBL Limited Partnership**, Man.

Note: The preceding list includes only the major related companies in which interests are held.

Financial Statistics

Periods ended:	12m Dec. 31/22[A]		12m Dec. 31/21[A]
	$000s	%Chg	$000s
Operating revenue	**276,623**	**+23**	**223,992**
Cost of sales	118,307		80,009
Salaries & benefits	110,957		84,840
General & admin expense	11,014		9,452
Operating expense	**240,278**	**+33**	**181,201**
Operating income	**36,345**	**-15**	**42,791**
Deprec., depl. & amort.	26,068		26,862
Finance costs, gross	4,980		3,449
Pre-tax income	**5,444**	**-56**	**12,480**
Income taxes	1,538		3,788
Net income	**3,906**	**-55**	**8,692**
Cash & equivalent	2,636		1,110
Accounts receivable	37,761		36,847
Current assets	80,779		73,772
Fixed assets, net	203,185		213,526
Intangibles, net	41,796		45,221
Total assets	**325,760**	**-2**	**332,519**
Accts. pay. & accr. liabs	32,505		30,114
Current liabilities	43,474		43,501
Long-term debt, gross	45,166		37,973
Long-term debt, net	45,166		37,973
Long-term lease liabilities	44,042		47,733
Shareholders' equity	176,542		186,401
Cash from oper. activs	**26,130**	**-18**	**31,875**
Cash from fin. activs	(13,107)		(22,694)
Cash from invest. activs	(11,425)		(10,492)
Net cash position	**2,636**	**+137**	**1,110**
Capital expenditures	(11,370)		(10,132)
Capital disposals	33		nil
	$		$
Earnings per share*	0.37		0.82
Cash flow per share*	2.45		3.00
Cash divd. per share*	1.20		1.20
	shs		shs
No. of shs. o/s*	10,773,190		10,719,778
Avg. no. of shs. o/s*	10,657,742		10,608,539
	%		%
Net profit margin	1.41		3.88
Return on equity	2.15		4.62
Return on assets	2.27		3.38
Foreign sales percent	23		18

* Common
[A] Reported in accordance with IFRS

Historical Summary
(as originally stated)

Fiscal Year	Oper. Rev.	Net Inc. Bef. Disc.	EPS*
	$000s	$000s	$
2022[A]	276,623	3,906	0.37
2021[A]	223,992	8,692	0.82
2020[A]	196,591	3,782	0.36
2019[A]	252,410	10,906	1.04
2018[A]	239,534	6,169	0.59

* Common
[A] Reported in accordance with IFRS

K.2 KDA Group Inc.

Symbol - KDA **Exchange** - TSX-VEN **CUSIP** - 48669F
Head Office - 300-1351 rue Notre-Dame E, Thetford Mines, QC, G6G 0G5 **Telephone** - (418) 755-0821 **Toll-free** - (877) 221-4445 **Fax** - (418) 755-0822
Website - groupekda.ca
Email - info@groupekda.ca
Investor Relations - Marc Lemieux (514) 622-7370
Auditors - Mazars, LLP C.A.
Lawyers - Thibeault Joyal, Montréal, Qué.
Transfer Agents - Computershare Trust Company of Canada Inc., Montréal, Qué.
Profile - (Que. 2008) Provides a range of solutions and services to pharmacies and pharmaceutical companies, as well as technological platform for the health industry.

The company's products and services are KRx e-prescribing platform for dentists, Adherize+ medication adherence digital platform for pharmacies and pharmaceutical companies; and L'Apothicaire (Apothecary) and L'Assistant (Wizard) digital solutions to optimize pharmaceutical treatment.

In December 2022, the company acquired **Covapharm Inc.**, which owns and operates the L'Apothicaire and L'Assistant digital solutions to optimize pharmaceutical treatment, for $200,000 payable in two years and issuance of 1,825,000 class A common shares.

Recent Merger and Acquisition Activity

Status: completed **Revised:** June 28, 2023
UPDATE: The transaction was completed. PREVIOUS: KDA Group Inc. agreed to sell wholly owned Agence L.I.V. Inc. to 9486,4410 Quebec Inc., a subsidiary of U.S.-based Clinical Education Alliance, LLC, for $13,500,000. Agence L.I.V. creates medical education content and supports logistical organization of scientific meetings and exchanges related to the environment of medical education.

Status: completed **Revised:** May 1, 2023
KDA Group Inc. agreed to sell its pharmacist and pharmacy technical assistant placement agency business for $10,200,000. 9483-0296 Québec Inc. (9483) would acquire all of the assets held by AlliancePharma Opérations Inc., a wholly owned subsidiary of KDA, necessary to operate the pharmacy placement agency business for $8,100,000, of which $6,900,000 was payable on closing and balance of $1,200,000 through issuance of 9483 preferred shares. Halsa Health Group Inc. agreed to acquire wholly owned Élitis Pharma Inc. and Logistique Pharma Inc.,which operates the placement business, for a purchase price of $2,100,000. The closing was expected to be held on or before Apr. 14, 2023

Predecessor Detail - Name changed from AlliancePharma Inc., Feb. 1, 2017.

Directors - Marc Lemieux, chr., pres. & CEO, Adstock, Qué.; Isabelle Bégin, exec. v-p, pharmacy srvcs. div., Québec, Qué.; Patrick Fernet, Dorval, Qué.; Michael W. (Mike) Kinley, Halifax, N.S.

Other Exec. Officers - Jean-Pierre Robert, COO; Luc Olivier, CFO; Dr. Giuseppe D'Aprano, chief scientific officer; Annie Mercier, contr.

Capital Stock

	Authorized (shs.)	Outstanding (shs.)[1]
Preferred Series A	unlimited	nil
Preferred Series B	unlimited	
Series B-1		nil[2]
Series B-2		nil[2]
Series B-3		1,461,000
Class A Common	unlimited	149,965,947

[1] At May 10, 2023
[2] Classified as debt.

Preferred Series B-3 - Not entitled to dividends. Bear interest at 9% interest annually. All held by private equity firm Persistence Capital Partners. Mature on Dec. 31, 2023. One vote per share.

Class A Common - One vote per share.

Preferred Series B-1 and B-2 (old) - Exchanged for series B-3 shares in May 2023.

Major Shareholder - Tenshi Life Sciences Pte. Limited held 13.21% interest and Marc Lemieux held 11.12% interest at May 10, 2023.

Price Range - KDA/TSX-VEN

Year	Volume	High	Low	Close
2022	11,527,241	$0.15	$0.06	$0.10
2021	12,548,845	$0.22	$0.10	$0.11
2020	11,363,521	$0.28	$0.06	$0.16
2019	8,789,316	$0.40	$0.09	$0.29
2018	3,684,081	$0.39	$0.06	$0.15

Recent Close: $0.07

Capital Stock Changes - In May 2023, all 4,000,000 series B-1 preferred shares and all 2,886,819 series B-2 preferred shares were exchanged for 1,461,000 series B-3 preferred shares.

During fiscal 2022, class A common shares were issued as follows: 500,000 under restricted share unit plan and 100,000 on exercise of options.

Wholly Owned Subsidiaries

Covapharm Inc.
KDA Technologique Inc.

Financial Statistics

Periods ended:	12m July 31/22[A]		12m July 31/21[oA]
	$000s	%Chg	$000s
Operating revenue	**28,824**	**+18**	**24,369**
Cost of sales	20,763		17,169
General & admin expense	5,652		4,194
Stock-based compensation	284		881
Operating expense	**26,699**	**+20**	**22,244**
Operating income	**2,125**	**0**	**2,125**
Deprec., depl. & amort.	625		480
Finance costs, net	5,935		(1,501)
Write-downs/write-offs	(281)		(201)
Pre-tax income	**(4,646)**	**n.a.**	**342**
Income taxes	(84)		(543)
Net inc. bef. disc. opers	**(4,562)**	**n.a.**	**885**
Income from disc. opers	nil		(324)
Net income	**(4,562)**	**n.a.**	**562**
Cash & equivalent	2,737		1,717
Inventories	nil		55
Accounts receivable	5,045		3,726
Current assets	7,882		5,845
Fixed assets, net	99		120
Right-of-use assets	1,803		224
Intangibles, net	16,474		14,110
Total assets	**20,785**	**-6**	**22,198**
Bank indebtedness	nil		980
Accts. pay. & accr. liabs	4,223		3,135
Current liabilities	22,441		7,765
Long-term debt, gross	20,684		11,719
Long-term debt, net	4,591		9,971
Long-term lease liabilities	1,564		213
Shareholders' equity	(203)		3,913
Cash from oper. activs	**1,417**	**-52**	**2,943**
Cash from fin. activs	2,284		93
Cash from invest. activs	(2,681)		(3,102)
Net cash position	**2,737**	**+59**	**1,717**
Capital expenditures	(45)		(48)
	$		$
Earns. per sh. bef disc opers*	(0.03)		0.01
Earnings per share*	(0.03)		0.00
Cash flow per share*	0.01		0.02
	shs		shs
No. of shs. o/s*	148,140,947		147,540,947
Avg. no. of shs. o/s*	148,016,289		126,394,358
	%		%
Net profit margin	(15.83)		3.63
Return on equity	n.m.		n.m.
Return on assets	(21.23)		4.20

* Cl.A Common
o Restated
A Reported in accordance with IFRS

Latest Results

Periods ended:	6m Jan. 31/23[A]		6m Jan. 31/22[A]
	$000s	%Chg	$000s
Operating revenue	15,119	+24	12,221
Net income	(73)	n.a.	(2,901)
	$		$
Earnings per share*	(0.00)		(0.02)

* Cl.A Common
A Reported in accordance with IFRS

Historical Summary
(as originally stated)

Fiscal Year	Oper. Rev. $000s	Net Inc. Bef. Disc. $000s	EPS* $
2022[A]	28,824	(4,562)	(0.03)
2021[A]	24,359	885	0.01
2020[A]	22,892	(4,557)	(0.04)
2019[A]	23,094	(8,322)	(0.11)
2018[A]	26,084	(5,295)	(0.12)

* Cl.A Common
A Reported in accordance with IFRS

K.3 KMT-Hansa Corp.

Symbol - KMC.H **Exchange** - TSX-VEN **CUSIP** - G5300R
Head Office - The Law Building, Suite 100, The Valley, Anguilla, AI-2640 **Telephone** - (264) 497-3800 **Fax** - (264) 497-3801
Website - kmthansacorp.com
Email - vieira@kmthansacorp.com
Investor Relations - Jacinto Vieira (416) 417-4588
Auditors - Buckley Dodds C.P.A., Vancouver, B.C.
Bankers - Scotiabank Anguilla Limited
Lawyers - Gerald R. Tuskey, Personal Law Corporation, Vancouver, B.C.
Transfer Agents - TSX Trust Company, Vancouver, B.C.
Profile - (Anguilla 1996; orig. Can., 1978) Seeking new business opportunities.

Previously built blockchain-based applications for clients and had developed its own proprietary blockchain network named Cresco Coin.

In October 2022, the company terminated its acquisition of 125 acres of land within the China-Malaysia Qinzhou Industrial Park. The transaction included 82 acres from **Guangxi Hemp Biotech Co. Ltd.** for issuance of 1,067,000,000 common shares at a deemed price of Cdn$0.11 per share; and 43 acres from **Tou Kit Ming Sing Investment Ltd.** for issuance of 756,364,000 common shares at a deemed price of Cdn$0.11 per share. The Guangxi property had been zoned for research, development and extraction of industrial hemp as well as manufacturing of consumer products containing cannabidiol (CBD) and cannabigerol (CBG); the Tou Kit property had been zoned for industrial and office use, including the operation of a data centre.

Recent Merger and Acquisition Activity

Status: terminated **Revised:** Oct. 28, 2022
UPDATE: The transaction was terminated. PREVIOUS: KMT-Hansa Corp. entered into a letter of intent to acquire 50% interest in Seychelles-based QXCENTURY Ventures Ltd. (QXCV) for issuance of 60,367,045 common shares at a deemed price of Cdn$0.11 per share. QXCV, through its wholly owned Guangxi Hemp Biotech Co. Ltd., is focused on technology and certification in growing and cultivation of industrial hemp and other herbs in various locations in the People's Republic of China.

Status: terminated **Revised:** Oct. 28, 2022
UPDATE: The transaction was terminated. PREVIOUS: The KMT-Hansa Corp. entered into a letter of intent to acquire HDD Investment Holdings Corp.'s Lumuwan Forest Farm party (property) for 6,779,405,190 common shares at Cdn$0.11 per share. The property is an 8,237 acre-forest land zoned for agricultural and commercial use in Danzhou city, People's Republic of China.

Predecessor Detail - Name changed from Hansa.net Global Commerce, Inc., Sept. 27, 2013.

Directors - Jacinto (Jay) Vieira, pres. & CEO, Richmond Hill, Ont.; Yongbiao (Winfield) Ding, Toronto, Ont.; Robert (Bob) Duffield, Cheltenham, Gloucs., United Kingdom; Louis Guiraud, Spain; Don Wu, Toronto, Ont.

Other Exec. Officers - Ankit Gosain, CFO & corp. sec.

Capital Stock

	Authorized (shs.)	Outstanding (shs.)[1]
Common	unlimited	35,169,714

1 At Nov. 29, 2022

Major Shareholder - Logic Nominees Ltd. held 38.68% interest at Sept. 16, 2022.

Price Range - KMC.H/TSX-VEN

Year	Volume	High	Low	Close
2022	28,000	$0.04	$0.04	$0.04
2019	273,000	$0.11	$0.05	$0.11
2018	860,966	$0.16	$0.03	$0.04

Recent Close: $0.04

Capital Stock Changes - There were no changes to capital stock during fiscal 2021 or fiscal 2022.

Wholly Owned Subsidiaries

Coetus Global Inc., Markham, Ont.

Financial Statistics

Periods ended:	12m June 30/22[A]		12m June 30/21[A]
	US$000s	%Chg	US$000s
General & admin expense	154		165
Operating expense	**154**	**-7**	**165**
Operating income	**(154)**	**n.a.**	**(165)**
Pre-tax income	**157**	**n.a.**	**(165)**
Net income	**157**	**n.a.**	**(165)**
Bank indebtedness	80		82
Accts. pay. & accr. liabs	773		939
Current liabilities	853		1,021
Shareholders' equity	(853)		(1,021)
Cash from oper. activs	**10**	**+900**	**1**
	US$		US$
Earnings per share*	0.01		(0.01)
Cash flow per share*	0.00		nil
	shs		shs
No. of shs. o/s*	35,169,714		35,169,714
Avg. no. of shs. o/s*	35,169,714		35,169,714
	%		%
Net profit margin	n.a.		n.a.
Return on equity	n.m.		n.m.
Return on assets	n.m.		n.m.

* Common
A Reported in accordance with IFRS

Latest Results

Periods ended:	3m Sept. 30/22[A]		3m Sept. 30/21[A]
	US$000s	%Chg	US$000s
Net income	(15)	n.a.	(39)
	US$		US$
Earnings per share*	(0.01)		(0.01)

* Common
A Reported in accordance with IFRS

Historical Summary
(as originally stated)

Fiscal Year	Oper. Rev. US$000s	Net Inc. Bef. Disc. US$000s	EPS* US$
2022[A]	nil	157	0.01
2021[A]	nil	(165)	(0.01)
2020[A]	nil	(753)	(0.02)
2019[A]	nil	(97)	(0.00)
2018[A]	nil	(130)	(0.00)

* Common
A Reported in accordance with IFRS

K.4 KP Tissue Inc.

Symbol - KPT **Exchange** - TSX **CUSIP** - 48265Y
Head Office - 500-2 Prologis Blvd, Mississauga, ON, L5W 0G8 **Telephone** - (905) 812-6936 **Fax** - (905) 812-6910
Website - www.kptissueinc.com
Email - francois.paroyan@krugerproducts.ca
Investor Relations - François Paroyan (905) 812-6962
Auditors - PricewaterhouseCoopers LLP C.A., Mississauga, Ont.
Lawyers - McCarthy Tétrault LLP, Toronto, Ont.
Transfer Agents - TSX Trust Company, Toronto, Ont.
Profile - (Ont. 2012) Holds 13.5% interest (at May 11, 2023) in **Kruger Products Inc.** (KPI), which produces, distributes, markets and sells disposable tissue products including bathroom tissue, facial tissue, paper towels and napkins for both the consumer and the away-from-home markets in North America. **Kruger Inc.** holds the other 86.5% interest in KPI.

KPI's brands include Bonterra™, Cashmere®, Embassy®, Esteem®, Purex®, Scotties®, SpongeTowels®, White Cloud®, White Swan®, Metro®, Satinelle®, Soft & Pure® and Chalet®.

KPI's Canadian manufacturing facilities, consisting of four tissue plants in Crabtree, Sherbrooke, Lennoxville and Laurier, Que., and one plant in New Westminster, B.C., have a combined annual tissue production capacity of 350,000 tonnes. KPI's U.S. manufacturing facility is located in Memphis, Tenn., consisting of one conventional light dry crepe paper machine with an aggregate annual capacity of 30,000 tonnes and one adjacent 55,000-tonne through-air-dried (TAD) tissue machine. KPI also operates three paper converting plants in Richelieu, Que., and Trenton and Scarborough, Ont.

KPI's consumer products are sold to the Canadian and U.S. retail grocery industry, either directly or through wholesalers, and to a number of other retail distribution groups including drug stores, variety stores, mass merchandisers and wholesale clubs. Away-from-home products are sold directly to commercial customers, general or specialized distributors and wholesalers, and to building services contractors.

Pursuant to a corporate reorganization effective Jan. 1, 2023, **Kruger Products L.P.** (KPLP) sold and assigned to its wholly owned subsidiary, **Kruger Products Inc.** (KPI), and KPI purchased and assumed from KPLP, in exchange for common shares, all of the properties, operations, assets and liabilities of KPLP; KPLP was subsequently dissolved.

In November 2022, the company announced that old production assets including a light dry crepe paper machine and six converting lines would be shut down at its plant in Memphis, Tenn. in early January 2023. High quality facial tissue and premium Through Air Dry products would continue to be produced at the plant. As a result of the discontinued operations, the Memphis plant would have an annual production capacity of 85,000 tonnes of tissue products.

In June 2022, affiliate **Kruger Products Inc.** announced its plan for a capital investment of $351,500,000 for an expansion project to build a new tissue plant on a site adjacent to the Sherbrooke plant in Quebec by 2024. The project includes the construction of a double-wide tissue machine featuring light dry crepe technology, as well as the installation of two additional converting lines, one in the existing Sherbrooke plant and the other in the new plant, which would bring an overall annual production to more than 130,000 tonnes of tissue products.

Directors - François Vimard, chr., Ont.; Louise M. Denys Wendling, Qué.; James Hardy, Ont.; John Ashforth (Jay) Wright, Ont.

Other Exec. Officers - Dino J. Bianco, CEO; Mark Holbrook, CFO; Susan Irving, chief mktg. officer; Mina Fior, sr. v-p, HR; Gordon Goss, sr. v-p & gen. mgr., consumer bus., USA & Mexico; Michel Manseau, sr. v-p & gen. mgr., consumer bus., Canada; Robert (Rob) Martin, sr. v-p, opers.; John O'Hara, sr. v-p & gen. mgr., away-for-home bus.; Michael (Mike) Yang, sr. v-p, tech. & supply chain; François Paroyan, gen. counsel & corp. sec.

Capital Stock

	Authorized (shs.)	Outstanding (shs.)[1]
Common	unlimited	9,953,658

1 At May 11, 2023

Major Shareholder - Caisse de dépôt et placement du Québec held 19.1% interest at May 10, 2023.

Price Range - KPT/TSX

Year	Volume	High	Low	Close
2022	2,865,713	$12.51	$10.04	$10.14
2021	5,655,846	$11.36	$10.00	$10.41
2020	4,647,202	$14.00	$8.00	$10.77
2019	2,657,790	$10.10	$7.73	$9.65
2018	4,415,337	$14.09	$6.58	$8.07

Recent Close: $10.10

Capital Stock Changes - During 2022, 50,557 common shares were issued under dividend reinvestment plan.

Dividends

KPT com Ra $0.72 pa Q est. July 15, 2013**[1]

[1] Dividend reinvestment plan implemented eff. December 13, 2012.

** Reinvestment Option

Investments

13.5% int. in **Kruger Products Inc.**, Mississauga, Ont.
- 100% int. in **8528365 Canada Inc.**, Canada.
- 100% int. in **Kruger Products AFH G.P. Inc.**, Canada.
  - 0.99% int. in **Kruger Products AFH L.P.**, Ont.
- 99.01% int. in **Kruger Products AFH L.P.**, Ont.
- 100% int. in **Kruger Products Real Estate Holdings Inc.**
- 100% int. in **Kruger Products SB Inc.**, Canada.
- 100% int. in **Kruger Products (USA) Inc.**, Del.
- 100% int. in **TAD1 Canco I Inc.**, Canada.
  - 100% int. in **TAD 1 GP ULC**, Del.
    - 0.01% int. in **TAD1 US LP**, Del.
  - 99.99% int. in **TAD1 US LP**, Del.
    - 100% int. in **TAD1 Canco II Inc.**, Canada.
      - 100% int. in **K.T.G. US Holdco Inc.**, Del.
      - 100% int. in **K.T.G. (USA) Inc.**, Del.
        - 100% int. in **Community Benefit Partners LLC**, Del.
- 100% int. in **TAD2 GP ULC**, Alta.
  - 0.01% int. in **TAD2 US LP**, Del.
- 99.99% int. in **TAD2 US LP**, Del.
  - 100% int. in **Kruger Products Sherbrooke Inc.**, Canada.
    - 50% int. in **Kruger Sherbrooke Water Treatment Inc.**, Canada.
- 100% int. in **West Tree Farms Limited**, B.C.
- 100% int. in **Westminister Paper Company Limited**, B.C.

Financial Statistics

Periods ended:	12m Dec. 31/22[A]		12m Dec. 31/21[A]
	$000s	%Chg	$000s
Total revenue	**(13,299)**	**n.a.**	**800**
Operating income	**(13,299)**	**n.a.**	**800**
Pre-tax income	**(12,547)**	**n.a.**	**1,121**
Income taxes	(2,298)		(118)
Net income	**(10,249)**	**n.a.**	**1,239**
Accounts receivable	1,790		1,781
Current assets	2,370		1,989
Long-term investments	79,338		78,727
Total assets	**81,708**	**+1**	**80,716**
Current liabilities	1,960		4,041
Shareholders' equity	74,030		75,869
Cash from fin. activs	(6,617)		(5,560)
Cash from invest. activs	6,617		5,560
	$		$
Earnings per share*	(1.03)		0.13
Cash divd. per share*	0.72		0.72
	shs		shs
No. of shs. o/s*	9,945,976		9,895,419
Avg. no. of shs. o/s*	9,936,187		9,835,582
	%		%
Net profit margin	n.m.		154.88
Return on equity	(13.67)		1.74
Return on assets	(12.62)		1.63

* Common

[A] Reported in accordance with IFRS

Latest Results

Periods ended:	3m Mar. 31/23[A]		3m Mar. 31/22[A]
	$000s	%Chg	$000s
Total revenue	(7,059)	n.a.	(1,108)
Net income	(10,678)	n.a.	978
	$		$
Earnings per share*	(1.07)		0.10

* Common

[A] Reported in accordance with IFRS

Historical Summary
(as originally stated)

Fiscal Year	Total Rev.	Net Inc. Bef. Disc.	EPS*
	$000s	$000s	$
2022[A]	(13,299)	(10,249)	(1.03)
2021[A]	800	1,239	0.13
2020[A]	(1,428)	(1,953)	(0.20)
2019[A]	(5,375)	(6,528)	(0.68)
2018[A]	1,390	(173)	(0.02)

* Common

[A] Reported in accordance with IFRS

K.5 KWESST Micro Systems Inc.

Symbol - KWE **Exchange** - TSX-VEN **CUSIP** - 501506
Head Office - Unit 1, 155 Terence Mathews Cres, Ottawa, ON, K2M 2A8 **Telephone** - (613) 319-3674
Website - www.kwesst.com
Email - archambault@kwesst.com
Investor Relations - Steven J. Archambault (613) 319-0537
Auditors - KPMG LLP C.A., Ottawa, Ont.
Transfer Agents - TSX Trust Company
Employees - 17 at Sept. 30, 2022

Profile - (B.C. 2017) Develops and commercializes next-generation technology solutions that deliver a tactical advantage for military, public safety agencies and personal defense markets in Canada, the U.S., in countries that are members of the North Atlantic Treaty Organization (NATO), as well as in Australia and New Zealand.

Focuses on three niche market segments which include non-lethal products for consumer and professional markets, digitization products for real-time situational awareness targeting and counter-threat products for protection against lasers, electronic detection and hostile drones.

Non-lethal Products

PARA OPS™ - A munitions technology system that consists of firing platforms, a cartridge casing that generate spin to a projectile, soft and frangible projectiles, different payloads for various application and velocities and muzzle energy that are far below the lethal threshold.

ARWEN™ - A product line of non-lethal devices including launchers and cartridges designed for riot control and tactical teams.

Digitization Products

Micro Integrated Sensor Software Technology (MISST) - An integration of miniaturized sensors, optics, ballistics and software that enable real-time networked situational awareness for soldiers and their weapons systems, smart management of ordnance systems and solutions for countering drone attacks and countermeasures against weaponized lasers.

Android Tactical Assault Kit (ATAK) - A U.S.government-owned situational awareness, command and control management application that is hosted on android end user devices.

TASCS Networked Observation and Reconnaissance System (TASCS NORS) - A technology consisting of a sensor package mounted to a soldier's weapon and a display. TASCS NORS allows the sniper and spotter's station to be accurately located on the battlefield and its cameras allow viewing through sniper's sight or spotter's scope on the display device and share target information and imagery between the sniper, spotter and to all TASCS equipped systems in the user's communication network.

TASCS Integrated Fire Modules System (TASCS IFM) - A device that equips existing systems with a sensor pack which also locates the weapon on the battlefield, as well as provides a bearing line indicating the direction the weapon is pointed. When connected to a display, and combined with the company's ballistic algorithm, users are able to engage target using a map location only, without any requirement to see the target. When networked across the TASCS system, targeting information can be received from and on any source of the network.

Critical Incident Management System (CIMS) - A cloud-based application that addresses critical incidents by integrating emergency operations, incident command post, incident commanders and all responders including mobile or dismounted to provide stakeholders with fushion and sharing of crucial real-time position, imagery and time-sensitive emergency services data and information for effective and coordinated delivery of emergency services including rescue, fire suppression, emergency medical care, law enforcement and other forms of hazard control and mitigation.

Counter-threat Products

Phantom™ - An electromagnetic transmitter capable of mimicking the electromagnetic footprint of a small tactical military unit.

Battlefield Laser Defense System (BLDS) - A system which provides increasing level of detection and target emitter location resolution, consisting of three models including Individual (B1), Squad or Outpost (B2) and Vehicular mounted (B3).

Products under development include Shot Counter, a device fitted inside a pistol grip that tracks the number of rounds fired and the type of ammunition fired. Information is gathered by near-field communication devices; GhostNet™, a counterdrone system; and Loitering Munition, an autonomous, military grade suicide or kamikaze drone with built-in warhead that can hover in a n area for extended periods to search for targets, then attack selectively once a desired target is located.

Also holds exclusive rights to manufacture, operate and use **AerialX Drone Solutions**'s drone which acts as a projectile intercept aerial threats using kinetic force for Counter Unmanned Aerial Systems market, for the U.S. Department of Defense and Canada's Department of National Defense.

On Dec. 7, 2022, common shares were listed on Nasdaq Capital Market under the symbol KWE.

On Mar. 29, 2022, common shares were listed on Frankfurt Stock exchange under the symbol 62U.

Common listed on NASDAQ, Dec. 7, 2022.

Predecessor Detail - Name changed from Foremost Ventures Corp., Sept. 22, 2020, following Qualifying Transaction reverse takeover acquisition of KWESST Inc. by way of a three-cornered amalgamation.; basis 1 new for 4.67 old shs.

Directors - David E. Luxton, exec. chr., Merrickville, Ont.; Jeffrey D. MacLeod, pres. & CEO, Ont.; Paul Fortin, Ashton, Ont.; Paul Mangano, Kennebunkport, Me.; John McCoach, Vancouver, B.C.

Other Exec. Officers - Sean Homuth, CFO & chief compliance officer; Rick Bowes, v-p, opers.

Capital Stock

	Authorized (shs.)	Outstanding (shs.)[1]
Common	unlimited	4,073,106

[1] At Mar. 31, 2023

Major Shareholder - Widely held at Jan. 27, 2023.

Price Range - KWE/TSX-VEN

Year	Volume	High	Low	Close
2022	310,198	$91.00	$3.01	$3.43
2021	533,165	$187.60	$53.90	$86.80
2020	108,989	$106.40	$34.30	$92.40
2019	203	$44.13	$35.96	$35.96
2018	838	$75.19	$40.86	$44.13

Consolidation: 1-for-70 cons. in Oct. 2022; 1-for-4.67 cons. in Sept. 2020

Recent Close: $2.50

Capital Stock Changes - On Oct. 28, 2022, common shares were consolidated on a 1-for-70 basis. In December 2022, public offering of 3,226,392 post-consolidated units (1 common share & 1 warrant) at US$4.13 per unit was completed, with warrants exercisable at US$5.00 per share for five years.

In July 2022, private placement of 22,857 post-consolidated units (1 common share & ½ warrant) at $15.05 per unit was completed. Also during fiscal 2022, post-consolidated common shares were issued as follows: 19,000 on exercise of warrants, 18,525 as bonus shares, 8,349 on vesting of restricted/performance share units, 4,840 pursuant to the 2021 acquisition of Police Ordnance Company Inc. and 143 for debt settlement.

Wholly Owned Subsidiaries

KWESST Inc., Kanata, Ont.
KWESST Public Safety Systems Canada Inc., Ont.
KWESST U.S. Holdings Inc., Del.
- 100% int. in **KWESST Defense Systems U.S. Inc.**, Del.
- 100% int. in **KWESST Public Safety Systems U.S. Inc.**, Del.

2720178 Ontario Inc., Ont.
- 100% int. in **Police Ordnance Company Inc.**, Ont.

Financial Statistics

Periods ended:	12m Sept. 30/22[A]		12m Sept. 30/21[A]
	$000s	%Chg	$000s
Operating revenue	**722**	**-43**	**1,276**
Cost of sales	537		799
Research & devel. expense	1,689		1,825
General & admin expense	6,301		5,250
Stock-based compensation	1,960		2,462
Operating expense	**10,486**	**+1**	**10,337**
Operating income	**(9,765)**	**n.a.**	**(9,061)**
Deprec., depl. & amort	326		141
Finance income	6		8
Finance costs, gross	512		116
Pre-tax income	**(10,570)**	**n.a.**	**(9,315)**
Income taxes	(49)		nil
Net income	**(10,520)**	**n.a.**	**(9,315)**
Cash & equivalent	171		2,688
Accounts receivable	172		699
Current assets	1,516		4,056
Fixed assets, net	832		904
Right-of-use assets	208		266
Intangibles, net	4,743		3,471
Total assets	**7,323**	**-16**	**8,718**
Accts. pay. & accr. liabs	4,459		1,127
Current liabilities	6,926		1,159
Long-term debt, gross	2,279		53
Long-term debt, net	79		53
Long-term lease liabilities	206		276
Shareholders' equity	(1,003)		6,124
Cash from oper. activs	**(4,257)**	**n.a.**	**(6,255)**
Cash from fin. activs	2,853		6,943
Cash from invest. activs	(1,114)		(1,073)
Net cash position	**171**	**-94**	**2,688**
Capital expenditures	(187)		(810)
	$		$
Earnings per share*	(14.41)		(14.70)
Cash flow per share*	(5.83)		(9.88)
	shs		shs
No. of shs. o/s*	773,225		699,509
Avg. no. of shs. o/s*	730,302		632,722
	%		%
Net profit margin	n.m.		(730.02)
Return on equity	n.m.		(186.67)
Return on assets	(124.81)		(129.34)
Foreign sales percent	54		97
No. of employees (FTEs)	17		17

* Common

[A] Reported in accordance with IFRS

Latest Results

Periods ended:	3m Dec. 31/22[A]		3m Dec. 31/21[A]
	$000s	%Chg	$000s
Operating revenue	317	n.m.	17
Net income	(2,208)	n.a.	(3,243)
	$		$
Earnings per share*	(1.37)		(4.90)

* Common

[A] Reported in accordance with IFRS

Historical Summary
(as originally stated)

Fiscal Year	Oper. Rev.	Net Inc. Bef. Disc.	EPS*
	$000s	$000s	$
2022[A]	722	(10,520)	(14.41)
2021[A]	1,276	(9,315)	(14.70)
2020[A1,2]	862	(3,565)	(8.40)
2019[A3]	509	(1,297)	n.a.
2018[A]	103	(858)	n.a.

* Common
[A] Reported in accordance with IFRS
[1] 9 months ended Sept. 30, 2020.
[2] Results reflect the Sept. 17, 2020, reverse takeover acquisition of KWESST Inc.
[3] Results pertain to KWESST Inc.

Note: Adjusted throughout for 1-for-70 cons. in Oct. 2022; 1-for-4.67 cons. in Sept. 2020

K.6 Kadestone Capital Corp.

Symbol - KDSX **Exchange** - TSX-VEN **CUSIP** - 482846
Head Office - Three Bentall Centre, 2600-595 Burrard St, PO Box 49314, Vancouver, BC, V7X 1L3 **Telephone** - (604) 671-8142
Website - www.kadestone.com
Email - dnegus@kadestone.com
Investor Relations - David Negus
Auditors - KPMG LLP C.A., Vancouver, B.C.
Transfer Agents - Computershare Trust Company of Canada Inc., Vancouver, B.C.

Profile - (B.C. 2019) Acquires, develops and manages residential and commercial properties, as well as procures and sells building materials within major urban centres and emerging markets in Canada, with an initial focus on the Metro Vancouver markets.

Holds 80% interest in two development properties in Squamish and Chilliwack, all in British Columbia. The properties in Squamish and Chilliwack would be used for future light industrial and commercial development.

Has entered into agreements to establish strategic alliances with **Attollo Management Inc.**, **Denciti Development Corporation** and **Yigeda HoldingsLtd.**, whereby the company has access to opportunities to acquire commercial property identified by the strategic partners for investment and/or development on terms to be negotiated between the company and the applicable partner and to assist in identifying and evaluating real estate opportunities for investment and/or development by the company.

During 2022, the company sold wholly owned **1230609 B.C. Ltd.**, which holds a 51% interest in the Marine Drive commercial real estate property with 6,463 sq. ft. of gross leasable area in West Vancouver, B.C., to **0995793 B.C. Ltd.** for $1,943,949, consisting of $1,848,117 cash and $95,832 non-cash settlement of net loss payable.

Directors - Brent Billey, founder, pres. & CEO, West Vancouver, B.C.; Dr. Anthony F. (Tony) Holler, chr., Penticton, B.C.; Norman (Norm) Mayr, Port Moody, B.C.; David Negrin, West Vancouver, B.C.; Jacqueline M. Tucker, Calgary, Alta.
Other Exec. Officers - David Negus, CFO & corp. sec.

Capital Stock

	Authorized (shs.)	Outstanding (shs.)[1]
Common	unlimited	46,928,247

[1] At May 29, 2023

Major Shareholder - Travis Chen held 31.73% interest and Brent Billey held 16.54% interest at May 17, 2023.

Price Range - KDSX/TSX-VEN

Year	Volume	High	Low	Close
2022	1,209,371	$2.00	$0.92	$1.30
2021	425,361	$2.00	$1.12	$1.75
2020	45,306	$2.00	$1.50	$1.50

Recent Close: $1.04

Capital Stock Changes - During 2022, 404,885 common shares were issued on exercise of options.

Wholly Owned Subsidiaries

Kadestone (Kyle Road) Property Ltd.
Kadestone Building Materials Ltd.
Kadestone Properties Squamish Ltd.
- 80% int. in **Denciti Squamish Limited Partnership**, Canada.

Kadestone Property (Lickman Road) Ltd.
- 80% int. in **Denciti Chilliwack Limited Partnership**, Canada.

Financial Statistics

Periods ended:	12m Dec. 31/22[A]		12m Dec. 31/21[A]
	$000s	%Chg	$000s
Total revenue	**(126)**	**n.a.**	**211**
Rental operating expense	nil		202
Cost of real estate sales	nil		51
Salaries & benefits	1,520		593
General & admin. expense	1,246		816
Stock-based compensation	1,368		1,026
Operating expense	**4,134**	**+54**	**2,688**
Operating income	**(4,260)**	**n.a.**	**(2,477)**
Investment income	101		15
Finance income	198		40
Finance costs, gross	1,088		592
Pre-tax income	**(4,558)**	**n.a.**	**(2,885)**
Net income	**(4,558)**	**n.a.**	**(2,885)**
Cash & equivalent	8,886		5,017
Accounts receivable	27		122
Current assets	9,961		6,186
Long-term investments	17,643		15,495
Property interests, net	nil		1,454
Total assets	**27,604**	**+19**	**23,134**
Accts. pay. & accr. liabs	965		362
Current liabilities	965		362
Long-term debt, gross	15,422		8,689
Long-term debt, net	15,422		8,689
Equity portion of conv. debs	396		396
Shareholders' equity	11,218		14,083
Cash from oper. activs	**(2,349)**	**n.a.**	**(1,383)**
Cash from fin. activs	6,418		3,880
Cash from invest. activs	(200)		(6,282)
Net cash position	**7,873**	**+57**	**5,017**
Increase in property	nil		(665)
Decrease in property	1,848		9,863
	$		$
Earnings per share*	(0.10)		(0.06)
Cash flow per share*	(0.05)		(0.03)
	shs		shs
No. of shs. o/s*	46,928,247		46,523,362
Avg. no. of shs. o/s*	46,608,741		46,514,526
	%		%
Net profit margin	n.m.		n.m.
Return on equity	(36.03)		(19.48)
Return on assets	(13.68)		(10.47)

* Common
[A] Reported in accordance with IFRS

Latest Results

Periods ended:	3m Mar. 31/23[A]		3m Mar. 31/22[A]
	$000s	%Chg	$000s
Total revenue	nil	n.a.	13
Net income	(750)	n.a.	(1,030)
	$		$
Earnings per share*	(0.02)		(0.02)

* Common
[A] Reported in accordance with IFRS

Historical Summary
(as originally stated)

Fiscal Year	Total Rev.	Net Inc. Bef. Disc.	EPS*
	$000s	$000s	$
2022[A]	(126)	(4,558)	(0.10)
2021[A]	211	(2,885)	(0.06)
2020[A]	14	(2,536)	(0.08)
2019[A1]	nil	(496)	n.a.

* Common
[A] Reported in accordance with IFRS
[1] 26 weeks ended Dec. 31, 2019.

K.7 Kalma Capital Corp.

Symbol - KALM.P **Exchange** - TSX-VEN **CUSIP** - 48344K
Head Office - 480-1500 Georgia St W, Vancouver, BC, V6G 2Z6 **Telephone** - (604) 684-4535
Email - legal@smalleylawcorp.com
Investor Relations - David W. Smalley (604) 684-4535
Auditors - Davidson & Company LLP C.A., Vancouver, B.C.
Transfer Agents - Odyssey Trust Company, Vancouver, B.C.
Profile - (B.C. 2021) Capital Pool Company.

Common listed on TSX-VEN, June 23, 2023.

Directors - Luc Pelchat, pres. & CEO, Nay., Mexico; Peter J. Hawley, Gatineau, Qué.; Jacob H. (Jake) Kalpakian, Vancouver, B.C.; Normand Latourelle, Outremont, Qué.
Other Exec. Officers - Pui Hong (Eric) Tsung, CFO; David W. Smalley, corp. sec.

Capital Stock

	Authorized (shs.)	Outstanding (shs.)[1]
Common	unlimited	7,000,200

[1] At June 23, 2023

Major Shareholder - Luc Pelchat held 28.57% interest at June 23, 2023.

Recent Close: $0.08

Capital Stock Changes - On June 23, 2023, an initial public offering of 3,000,000 common shares was completed at 10¢ per share.

K.8 Kalon Acquisition Corp.

Symbol - KAC.P **Exchange** - TSX-VEN **CUSIP** - 48345H
Head Office - 2200-885 Georgia St W, Vancouver, BC, V6C 3E8
Email - pshaerf@amausa.com
Investor Relations - Peter S. Shaerf (212) 682-2480
Auditors - MNP LLP C.A., Toronto, Ont.
Lawyers - Cassels Brock & Blackwell LLP
Transfer Agents - TSX Trust Company, Vancouver, B.C.
Profile - (B.C. 2019) Capital Pool Company.
Directors - Peter S. Shaerf, chr., N.Y.; Mudit Paliwal, CEO & corp. sec., Denmark; Robert Perri, Greece
Other Exec. Officers - Andrew Benjamin, CFO & chief comml. officer

Capital Stock

	Authorized (shs.)	Outstanding (shs.)[1]
Common	unlimited	10,780,000

[1] At Oct. 31, 2022

Major Shareholder - Mudit Paliwal held 55.66% interest at May 31, 2022.

Price Range - KAC.P/TSX-VEN

Year	Volume	High	Low	Close
2022	78,470	$0.17	$0.12	$0.12
2021	270,000	$0.18	$0.15	$0.16
2020	307,000	$0.20	$0.15	$0.15

Recent Close: $0.02

Capital Stock Changes - There were no changes to capital stock during fiscal 2021 or fiscal 2022.

K.9 Kane Biotech Inc.

Symbol - KNE **Exchange** - TSX-VEN **CUSIP** - 483809
Head Office - 290-100 Innovation Dr, Winnipeg, MB, R3T 6G2 **Telephone** - (204) 453-1301 **Fax** - (204) 818-0374
Website - www.kanebiotech.com
Email - rdupuis@kanebiotech.com
Investor Relations - Ray Dupuis (204) 298-2200
Auditors - MNP LLP C.A., Winnipeg, Man.
Lawyers - MLT Aikins LLP, Winnipeg, Man.
Transfer Agents - TSX Trust Company, Calgary, Alta.

Profile - (Can. 2003 amalg.) Develops and markets technologies and products that prevent and remove microbial biofilms.

Biofilms are a major cause of a number of human and animal health problems including tooth decay, wound infections, chronic inflammatory skin disorders and wounds, recurrent urinary tract infections, medical device-associated and hospital acquired infections and foodborne bacterial outbreaks.

Products include StrixNB™, bluestem™ and Vetradent™ oral care technology for inhibiting dental plaque formation and minimizing gingivitis and periodontal disease with application in the pet oral care market; DispersinB® technology for inhibiting and dispersing microbial biofilms with applications in wound care, in the form of a topical spray (for atopic dermatitis-associated infections for veterinary use), a skin cream and a shampoo (for human use); Aledex® technology for the prevention of catheter associated infections and dental plaque and oral bacteria associated with periodontal disease; Silkstem™, an anti-itch shampoo with anti-biofilm formulation for dogs and cats; DermaKB™, prescription products that treat minor health ailments caused by biofilms including scalp detoxifier, shampoo and shampoo bars; and KBI Antibacterial Disinfectant, a hard surface disinfectant approved by Health Canada for household domestic, hospital and industrial use.

Also under early stage development is coactiv+™ as an antimicrobial surgical hydrogel used in surgical/accute wounds, an antimicrobial wound rinse used in accute and chronic wounds, and an antimicrobial wound spray used in acute, chronic wounds and first and second degree burns; and DispersinB™, as a hydrogel for prosthetic joint infections.

In May 2023, the company received 510(k) clearance of its coactiv+™ antimicrobial wound gel from the U.S. FDA for the management of ulcers (including diabetic foot and leg ulcers and pressure ulcers), first and second degree burns, partial & full thickness wounds, large surface area wounds and surgical incisions for adult populations.

In April 2023, the company entered into a licensing agreement with **Skout's Honor Pet Supply Company** for its patented coactiv+™ technology in pet oral care applications. Skout's Honor has been granted a ten-year license for the non-exclusive use of coactiv+™ under their own brand in North America while the company's subsidiary **STEM Animal Health Inc.** would continue to commercialize its bluestem™ line of pet oral care products. STEM would receive a US$500,000 licensing fee from Skout's Honor to be paid over the course of the agreement as well as an ongoing royalty on all sales of products that use the coactiv+™.

In April 2022, subsidiary **Stem Animal Health Inc.** received the Veterinarian Oral Health Council (VOHC) efficacy certification for its pet oral care water additive which would activate approximately $1,300,000 in milestone payments and minimum royalty payments pursuant to its licensing and royalty agreements.

Predecessor Detail - Formed from Vinson Biotech Inc., Oct. 1, 2003, following the Sept. 24, 2003, non-arm's length Major Transaction reverse takeover acquisition of and subsequent amalgamation with Kane Biotech Inc.

Directors - R. Phillip Renaud, chr., Milan, Italy; Marc Edwards, pres. & CEO, Bromont, Qué.; Georges E. Morin, Westmount, Qué.

Other Exec. Officers - Ray Dupuis, CFO; Dr. Gregory Schultz, chief scientific officer; Lori Christofalos, v-p, quality & compliance; Dr. Nanda Yakandawala, v-p, R&D

Capital Stock

	Authorized (shs.)	Outstanding (shs.)[1]
Class A Common	unlimited	nil
Common	unlimited	124,846,869
Preferred	unlimited	nil

[1] At May 24, 2023

Major Shareholder - R. Phillip Renaud held 21.94% interest at Apr. 18, 2023.

Price Range - KNE/TSX-VEN

Year	Volume	High	Low	Close
2022	13,083,185	$0.17	$0.08	$0.09
2021	17,612,757	$0.24	$0.11	$0.16
2020	16,877,568	$0.26	$0.09	$0.14
2019	10,263,443	$0.15	$0.07	$0.14
2018	9,610,713	$0.11	$0.06	$0.09

Recent Close: $0.08

Capital Stock Changes - In May 2022, private placement of 10,000,000 common shares was completed at 10¢ per share. Also during 2022, 16,667 common shares were issued under restricted share unit plan.

Subsidiaries

66.66% int. in **STEM Animal Health Inc.**, Winnipeg, Man.

Financial Statistics

Periods ended:	12m Dec. 31/22[A]		12m Dec. 31/21[A]
	$000s	%Chg	$000s
Operating revenue	**2,668**	**+66**	**1,608**
Cost of sales	1,255		1,039
Research & devel. expense	977		1,262
General & admin expense	3,527		3,936
Operating expense	**5,759**	**-8**	**6,237**
Operating income	**(3,091)**	**n.a.**	**(4,629)**
Deprec., depl. & amort.	263		188
Finance costs, net	460		(34)
Write-downs/write-offs	(10)		(66)
Pre-tax income	**(3,824)**	**n.a.**	**(4,850)**
Net income	**(3,824)**	**n.a.**	**(4,850)**
Cash & equivalent	1,105		1,153
Inventories	763		519
Accounts receivable	582		596
Current assets	3,097		2,880
Fixed assets, net	1,252		1,436
Intangibles, net	826		829
Total assets	**5,620**	**-8**	**6,134**
Bank indebtedness	4,000		2,379
Accts. pay. & accr. liabs	1,848		2,058
Current liabilities	6,342		4,721
Long-term debt, gross	1,769		1,116
Long-term debt, net	1,595		1,116
Long-term lease liabilities	983		1,088
Shareholders' equity	(4,138)		(1,567)
Cash from oper. activs	**(3,043)**	**n.a.**	**(2,289)**
Cash from fin. activs	3,103		2,808
Cash from invest. activs	(108)		(374)
Net cash position	**1,105**	**-4**	**1,153**
Capital expenditures	(13)		(187)
	$		$
Earnings per share*	(0.03)		(0.04)
Cash flow per share*	(0.03)		(0.02)
	shs		shs
No. of shs. o/s*	124,830,202		114,813,535
Avg. no. of shs. o/s*	120,702,074		112,600,420
	%		%
Net profit margin	(143.33)		(301.62)
Return on equity	n.m.		n.m.
Return on assets	(65.07)		(86.84)

* Common

[A] Reported in accordance with IFRS

Latest Results

Periods ended:	3m Mar. 31/23[A]		3m Mar. 31/22[A]
	$000s	%Chg	$000s
Operating revenue	678	+20	565
Net income	(1,245)	n.a.	(1,152)
	$		$
Earnings per share*	(0.01)		(0.01)

* Common

[A] Reported in accordance with IFRS

Historical Summary
(as originally stated)

Fiscal Year	Oper. Rev.	Net Inc. Bef. Disc.	EPS*
	$000s	$000s	$
2022[A]	2,668	(3,824)	(0.03)
2021[A]	1,608	(4,850)	(0.04)
2020[A]	1,342	(3,846)	(0.03)
2019[A]	1,694	(960)	(0.01)
2018[A]	506	(3,261)	(0.04)

* Common

[A] Reported in accordance with IFRS

K.10 Katipult Technology Corp.

Symbol - FUND **Exchange** - TSX-VEN **CUSIP** - 48600A
Head Office - 1600-144 4 Ave SW, Calgary, AB, T2P 3N4
Website - www.katipult.com
Email - gbreese@katipult.com
Investor Relations - Gord Breese (604) 760-4000
Auditors - Ernst & Young LLP C.A., Calgary, Alta.
Transfer Agents - TSX Trust Company

Profile - (Alta. 2019; orig. B.C., 2016) Offers a cloud-based software infrastructure that allows firms to design, set up and operate an investment platform for powering the exchange of capital in equity and debt markets.

The company's private placements platform, DealFlow, functions as the operating system for investment capital. The platform includes features and functionality that enables firms to offer debt and real-estate financing, as well as securities on a prospectus-exempt basis to various types of investors. It automates many components of investor and investment management including components of financial transactions, investment marketing and dividend payouts, as well as managing regulatory requirements in a variety of geographic jurisdictions. Also offers DealFlow: DataHub, which extracts large volumes of data and customers will no longer need to manually input or update the data that will populate the subscription documents. Under development is DealFlow Marketing, which would provide **Raymond James** an automated, multi-staged distribution capability to disseminate pertinent deal information, monitor investor interest and secure investor commitments in a fully integrated, compliant and auditable workflow.

In addition, includes modules for various user types, including but not limited to investors, issuers, administrators and auditors. The administrators are selected by clients from their staff and are provided a content management system which allows them the ability to manipulate content on the platform. Customers pay one-time charges from activities which include the provision of regulatory consulting, marketing, and the customization services of the platform; fees for qualifying services and/or transactions processed through the platform; and a monthly subscription fee for provision of software updates, new features and technical support.

Directors - Pheak Meas, co-founder, chief product officer & head, UX & design, Calgary, Alta.; Brock Murray, co-founder & head, global devel., Bangkok, Thailand; Brian N. Craig, chr., Calgary, Alta.; Gord Breese, pres. & CEO, Vancouver, B.C.; George W. Reznik, Vancouver, B.C.

Other Exec. Officers - Karim Teja, CFO; Ben Cadieux, chief tech. officer; James Church, v-p, product; Barry Holder, v-p, mktg.; Julia Sabyan, v-p, cust. success; Stephen Smith, v-p, sales; William Van Horne, corp. sec.

Capital Stock

	Authorized (shs.)	Outstanding (shs.)[1]
Common	unlimited	71,523,066

[1] At May 23, 2023

Major Shareholder - Pheak Meas held 25.5% interest and Brock Murray held 25.5% interest at Aug. 4, 2022.

Price Range - FUND/TSX-VEN

Year	Volume	High	Low	Close
2022	2,751,133	$0.17	$0.04	$0.08
2021	3,221,981	$0.39	$0.12	$0.13
2020	3,651,258	$0.39	$0.17	$0.25
2019	4,858,389	$0.51	$0.15	$0.17
2018	21,606,883	$1.72	$0.34	$0.39

Recent Close: $0.11

Capital Stock Changes - There were no changes to capital stock during 2022.

Financial Statistics

Periods ended:	12m Dec. 31/22[A]		12m Dec. 31/21[A]
	$000s	%Chg	$000s
Operating revenue	**1,864**	**+9**	**1,713**
Cost of sales	401		356
Research & devel. expense	1,047		972
General & admin expense	1,813		2,114
Operating expense	**3,261**	**-5**	**3,442**
Operating income	**(1,397)**	**n.a.**	**(1,729)**
Deprec., depl. & amort.	17		30
Finance income	10		6
Finance costs, gross	678		544
Write-downs/write-offs	(10)		10
Pre-tax income	**(1,608)**	**n.a.**	**(2,270)**
Net income	**(1,608)**	**n.a.**	**(2,270)**
Cash & equivalent	1,370		2,503
Accounts receivable	321		33
Current assets	1,693		2,549
Fixed assets, net	nil		2
Right-of-use assets	nil		16
Total assets	**1,693**	**-34**	**2,567**
Accts. pay. & accr. liabs	285		373
Current liabilities	949		753
Long-term debt, gross	4,229		3,686
Long-term debt, net	4,186		3,686
Equity portion of conv. debs	1,292		1,292
Shareholders' equity	(3,442)		(1,872)
Cash from oper. activs	**(1,083)**	**n.a.**	**(1,466)**
Cash from fin. activs	(22)		3,102
Net cash position	**1,370**	**-45**	**2,503**
	$		$
Earnings per share*	(0.02)		(0.03)
Cash flow per share*	(0.02)		(0.02)
	shs		shs
No. of shs. o/s*	71,523,066		71,523,066
Avg. no. of shs. o/s*	71,523,066		70,852,569
	%		%
Net profit margin	(86.27)		(132.52)
Return on equity	n.m.		n.m.
Return on assets	(43.66)		(97.73)

* Common

[A] Reported in accordance with IFRS

Latest Results

Periods ended:	3m Mar. 31/23[A]		3m Mar. 31/22[A]
	$000s	%Chg	$000s
Operating revenue	485	+7	455
Net income	(799)	n.a.	(710)
	$		$
Earnings per share*	(0.01)		(0.01)

* Common

[A] Reported in accordance with IFRS

Historical Summary
(as originally stated)

Fiscal Year	Oper. Rev.	Net Inc. Bef. Disc.	EPS*
	$000s	$000s	$
2022[A]	1,864	(1,608)	(0.02)
2021[A]	1,713	(2,270)	(0.03)
2020[A]	1,319	(1,877)	(0.03)
2019[A]	1,616	(306)	(0.00)
2018[A]	1,225	(2,073)	(0.03)

* Common

[A] Reported in accordance with IFRS

K.11 The Keg Royalties Income Fund

Symbol - KEG.UN **Exchange** - TSX **CUSIP** - 487522
Head Office - 10100 Shellbridge Way, Richmond, BC, V6X 2W7
Telephone - (604) 821-6416 **Fax** - (604) 276-2681
Website - www.kegincomefund.com
Email - nick.dean@kegrestaurants.com
Investor Relations - Nicholas Dean (416) 695-2400
Auditors - KPMG LLP C.A., Vancouver, B.C.
Transfer Agents - Computershare Trust Company of Canada Inc., Toronto, Ont.
Administrators - The Keg Rights Limited Partnership, Richmond, B.C.

Profile - (Ont. 2002) Owns trademarks, trade names, operating procedures and systems, and other intellectual property used by **Keg Restaurants Ltd.** in the operation of Keg steakhouse restaurants and bars.

Wholly owned **The Keg Rights Limited Partnership** has granted **Keg Restaurants Ltd.** (KRL) an exclusive 99-year licence to use the Keg rights in consideration for a royalty, payable by KRL to the partnership, equal to 4% of the gross sales from Keg restaurants included in the royalty pool. The fund also earns interest income on a $57,000,000 7.5% note due from KRL and due May 31, 2042.

KRL operates and franchises casual dining steakhouse restaurants in Canada and franchises in select markets in the U.S. through its wholly owned subsidiaries.

At Mar. 31, 2023, there were 105 Keg restaurants, of which 97 were in Canada and 8 in the U.S.

Trustees - Christopher C. (Kip) Woodward, chr. & corp. sec., Vancouver, B.C.; Tim Kerr, Vancouver, B.C.

Oper. Subsid./Mgt. Co. Officers - Nicholas (Nick) Dean, pres.; Neil Maclean, exec. v-p & CFO

Capital Stock

	Authorized (shs.)	Outstanding (shs.)[1]
Fund Unit	unlimited	11,353,500
Class A Exch. Unit	n.a.	905,944[2]
Class B Exch. Unit	n.a.	176,700[2]
Class D Exch. Unit	n.a.	4,367,667[2]
Class C Partnership Unit	n.a.	5,700,000[2]

[1] At Mar. 31, 2023

[2] Classified as debt.

Note: Class A, B and D exchangeable units are securities of The Keg Rights Limited Partnership.

Fund Unit - The fund intends to make monthly distributions of amounts determined by the trustees. Redeemable at the lesser of: (i) 90% of the current market price of a unit immediately prior to the date on which the units were surrendered for redemption; (ii) an amount equal to: (a) the closing price of the units on the principal stock exchange on which the units are listed if there was a trade on the unit redemption date and the exchange provides a closing price; (b) an amount equal to the average of the highest and lowest prices of the units if there was a trade on the unit redemption date and the stock exchange provides only the highest and lowest prices of the units traded on a particular date; or (c) the average of the last bid and ask prices of the units on the stock exchange if there was no trading on the unit redemption date. One vote per fund unit.

Class C Partnership Unit - Entitled to a preferential monthly distribution of $0.0625 per unit as long as the note receivable from Keg Restaurants Ltd. (KRL) is outstanding. KRL has the right to transfer the class C units to The Keg Holdings Trust (KHT) in consideration for the assumption by KHT of an amount of the note receivable from KRL equal to $10.00 per class C unit transferred.

Exchangeable Partnership Unit - The class A, class B and class D exchangeable partnership units of The Keg Rights Limited Partnership are entitled to vote in all votes of fund unitholders as if they were holders of the number of fund units they would receive if they were exchanged into fund units as of the record date of such votes, and are treated in all respects as fund unitholders for the purpose of any such votes.

Class A Exchangeable Partnership Unit - Entitled to a preferential proportionate distribution equal to the distribution on the class C limited partnership units, multiplied by the number of class A units divided by the number of limited partnership units outstanding. In addition, the class A units receive a residual distribution proportionately with the class B units, class D units, limited partnership units and general partnership units relative to the aggregate number of each class outstanding (or in the case of the class B units and class D units, the number outstanding multiplied by the class B and class D current distribution entitlement, respectively). Class A units are exchangeable for fund units on a one-for-one basis.

Class B Exchangeable Partnership Unit - Entitled to a preferential proportionate distribution and a residual distribution based on the incremental royalty paid to the partnership from new Keg restaurants. The distribution entitlements of the class B units are adjusted annually on January 1. Class B units held by Keg Restaurants Ltd. are exchangeable for fund units on a one-for-one basis.

Class D Exchangeable Partnership Unit - Entitled to a preferential proportionate distribution and a residual distribution based on the incremental royalty paid to the partnership from new Keg restaurants. The distribution entitlements of the class D units are adjusted annually on January 1. Class D units held by Keg Restaurants Ltd. are exchangeable for fund units on a one-for-one basis.

Major Shareholder - Recipe Unlimited Corporation held 33.92% interest at Jan. 1, 2023.

Price Range - KEG.UN/TSX

Year	Volume	High	Low	Close
2022	4,197,384	$17.00	$13.65	$15.97
2021	3,543,897	$16.71	$11.94	$14.63
2020	7,584,217	$15.95	$5.75	$12.16
2019	3,312,928	$17.81	$15.21	$15.27
2018	3,199,376	$20.04	$15.01	$16.09

Recent Close: $14.79

Capital Stock Changes - There were no changes to capital stock from 2012 to 2022, inclusive.

Dividends

KEG.UN unit Ra $1.1352 pa M est. Oct. 29, 2021
Prev. Rate: $0.84 est. July 30, 2021
Prev. Rate: $0.42 est. Feb. 26, 2021
Prev. Rate: $0.60 est. Oct. 30, 2020

Wholly Owned Subsidiaries

The Keg Holdings Trust, Richmond, B.C.
- 100% int. in **The Keg Rights Limited Partnership**, Richmond, B.C.

Subsidiaries

90% int. in **The Keg GP Ltd.**, Richmond, B.C.

Financial Statistics

Periods ended:	12m Dec. 31/22[A]		12m Dec. 31/21[A]
	$000s	%Chg	$000s
Total revenue	**31,361**	**+46**	**21,449**
General & admin. expense	474		440
Operating expense	**474**	**+8**	**440**
Operating income	**30,887**	**+47**	**21,009**
Finance costs, gross	13,495		9,749
Pre-tax income	**9,998**	**n.a.**	**(2,327)**
Income taxes	4,695		3,039
Net income	**5,303**	**n.a.**	**(5,366)**
Cash & equivalent	3,287		2,371
Accounts receivable	3,140		2,583
Current assets	6,845		5,367
Long-term investments	57,000		57,000
Intangibles	196,958		191,974
Total assets	**260,803**	**+3**	**254,341**
Accts. pay. & accr. liabs	290		233
Current liabilities	4,667		3,072
Long-term debt, gross	158,015		145,620
Long-term debt, net	158,015		145,620
Shareholders' equity	95,473		103,058
Cash from oper. activs	**26,624**	**+59**	**16,713**
Cash from fin. activs	(25,708)		(17,351)
Net cash position	**3,287**	**+39**	**2,371**
	$		$
Earnings per share*	0.47		(0.47)
Cash flow per share*	2.35		1.47
Cash divd. per share*	1.04		0.76
	shs		shs
No. of shs. o/s*	11,353,500		11,353,500
Avg. no. of shs. o/s*	11,353,500		11,353,500
	%		%
Net profit margin	16.91		(25.02)
Return on equity	5.34		(4.87)
Return on assets	4.84		6.77

* Fund unit
[A] Reported in accordance with IFRS

Latest Results

Periods ended:	3m Mar. 31/23[A]		3m Mar. 31/22[A]
	$000s	%Chg	$000s
Total revenue	8,759	+30	6,722
Net income	5,128	n.a.	(8,176)
	$		$
Earnings per share*	0.45		(0.72)

* Fund unit
[A] Reported in accordance with IFRS

Historical Summary
(as originally stated)

Fiscal Year	Total Rev.	Net Inc. Bef. Disc.	EPS*
	$000s	$000s	$
2022[A]	31,361	5,303	0.47
2021[A]	21,449	(5,366)	(0.47)
2020[A]	18,168	22,256	1.96
2019[A]	29,694	16,999	1.50
2018[A]	29,658	29,217	2.57

* Fund unit
[A] Reported in accordance with IFRS

K.12 Kelly Ventures Ltd.

Symbol - KKL.P **Exchange** - TSX-VEN **CUSIP** - 48815M

Head Office - 615-800 Pender St W, Vancouver, BC, V6C 2V6 **Telephone** - (604) 687-7767 **Fax** - (604) 688-9895

Email - plarkin@pro.net

Investor Relations - Paul A. Larkin (604) 728-4080

Auditors - Crowe MacKay LLP C.A., Vancouver, B.C.

Lawyers - Owen Bird Law Corporation, Vancouver, B.C.

Transfer Agents - Computershare Trust Company of Canada Inc., Vancouver, B.C.

Profile - (B.C. 2016) Capital Pool Company.

Recent Merger and Acquisition Activity

Status: terminated **Revised:** May 10, 2023

UPDATE: The transaction was terminated. PREVIOUS: Kelly Ventures Ltd. entered into a letter of intent for the Qualifying Transaction reverse takeover acquisition of private Ebers Tech Inc., which holds a portfolio of patents and development methods for producing cocrystals, on the basis of 20 Kelly post-consolidated common shares (following a 1-for-4 share consolidation) for each Ebers share held, which would result in the issuance of 52,878,440 Kelly post-consolidated common shares at a deemed price of $1.00 per share. Cocrystallisation enables the development of drugs with superior physicochemical properties of the active pharmaceutical ingredients (API) while holding the properties of the drug molecule itself constant.

Directors - Paul A. Larkin, CEO, CFO & corp. sec., Vancouver, B.C.; Erin L. Walmesley, Furry Creek, B.C.; Jonathan Younie, Vancouver, B.C.

Capital Stock

	Authorized (shs.)	Outstanding (shs.)[1]
Common	unlimited	4,191,150

[1] At July 5, 2023

Major Shareholder - Paul A. Larkin held 28.63% interest and Jonathan Younie held 14.31% interest at July 5, 2023.

Price Range - KKL.P/TSX-VEN

Year	Volume	High	Low	Close
2020	59,000	$0.20	$0.12	$0.17
2019	440,844	$0.19	$0.10	$0.10
2018	70,000	$0.15	$0.15	$0.15

Recent Close: $0.19

Capital Stock Changes - There were no changes to capital stock during 2021 or 2022.

K.13 Kelso Technologies Inc.

Symbol - KLS **Exchange** - TSX **CUSIP** - 48826D

Head Office - 13966 18B Ave, South Surrey, BC, V4A 8J1 **Telephone** - (250) 764-3618

Website - www.kelsotech.com

Email - lee@kelsotech.com

Investor Relations - Richard Lee (866) 535-7685

Auditors - Smythe LLP C.A., Vancouver, B.C.

Bankers - Bank of Montreal, Vancouver, B.C.

Lawyers - Clark Wilson LLP, Vancouver, B.C.

Transfer Agents - Computershare Trust Company, N.A., Denver, Colo.; Computershare Trust Company of Canada Inc., Vancouver, B.C.

Employees - 38 at Dec. 31, 2022

Profile - (B.C. 1987) Develops, manufactures and distributes transportation components for the rail, trucking and rugged vehicle markets in the U.S. and Canada.

Key products consist of proprietary valves (pressure relief valves, vacuum relief valves, top ball valves and bottom outlet valves) and one-bolt manway for rail tank cars. Other products for the rail sector include emergency response kits for hazmat first responders, rail wheel cleaning units, check valves, tank gauges, laboratory test equipment, pressure cars and pressure differential car components, as well as no-spill fuel loading systems. Products provided for truck tankers include pressure/vacuum valves and one-bolt manway. Primary customers include rail tank car manufacturers and retrofit/repair businesses.

Also, the company is developing a suite of driver assistance software and transportation equipment for the motor vehicles market. This includes the flagship Road-To-No-Road™ suspension system, which is targeted for commercial wilderness operations in rugged terrains. The system is designed to ensure stable and balanced vehicle manoeuvres, whether automated or manual, in complex and dynamic environments. It enables performance in challenging scenarios such as ledge climbs, ledge drops, extreme obstacles, severe side-slope challenges, as well as the production of ordinance trailers, non-penetrable body panels, and custom tires.

Operations include a 44,000-sq.-ft. production facility and a 6,000-sq.-ft. engineering facility, both in Bonham, Tex., for rail equipment products; and a 3,500-sq.-ft. research and development facility in Kelowna B.C., for wilderness transportation equipment.

Predecessor Detail - Name changed from Kelso Resources Ltd., July 21, 1994.

Directors - James R. (Rik) Bond, pres. & CEO, Kelowna, B.C.; Anthony J. (Tony) Andrukaitis, exec. v-p, bus. devel. & COO, Tex.; Frank C. Busch, Calgary, Alta.; E. Paul Cass, B.C.; Jesse V. Crews, Calif.; Laura B. Roach, Tex.

Other Exec. Officers - Richard (Rick) Lee, CFO; Amanda Smith, v-p, opers.; Kathy Love, corp. sec.; Patrick Hankey, contr.; Chris Stewart, pres., KIQ X Industries Inc.

Capital Stock

	Authorized (shs.)	Outstanding (shs.)[1]
Class A Preference	unlimited	
Series 1	5,000,000	nil
Common	unlimited	54,320,086

[1] At Apr. 19, 2023

Major Shareholder - Widely held at Apr. 19, 2023.

Price Range - KLS/TSX

Year	Volume	High	Low	Close
2022	2,149,075	$0.72	$0.28	$0.42
2021	16,302,102	$1.85	$0.54	$0.56
2020	5,404,542	$1.32	$0.55	$0.71
2019	7,229,852	$2.19	$0.55	$0.93
2018	8,094,708	$1.25	$0.46	$0.58

Recent Close: $0.33

Capital Stock Changes - There were no changes to capital stock during 2022.

Wholly Owned Subsidiaries

KIQ X Industries Inc., B.C.
KIQ Industries Inc., Nev.
KXI Wildertec Industries Inc., B.C.
Kel-Flo Industries Inc., Nev.
Kelso Technologies (USA) Inc., Nev.

Financial Statistics

Periods ended:	12m Dec. 31/22[A]		12m Dec. 31/21[A]
	US$000s	%Chg	US$000s
Operating revenue	**10,931**	**+47**	**7,426**
Cost of goods sold	5,904		4,098
Research & devel. expense	543		686
General & admin expense	4,440		4,062
Stock-based compensation	163		134
Operating expense	**11,050**	**+23**	**8,980**
Operating income	**(119)**	**n.a.**	**(1,554)**
Deprec., depl. & amort.	1,044		1,573
Write-downs/write-offs	(260)		(119)
Pre-tax income	**(1,189)**	**n.a.**	**(2,586)**
Income taxes	166		173
Net income	**(1,355)**	**n.a.**	**(2,759)**
Cash & equivalent	2,712		3,377
Inventories	4,144		5,535
Accounts receivable	1,382		807
Current assets	8,331		9,881
Fixed assets, net	3,277		3,246
Intangibles, net	471		474
Total assets	**12,147**	**-12**	**13,729**
Accts. pay. & accr. liabs	1,184		1,119
Current liabilities	1,331		1,210
Long-term lease liabilities	35		196
Shareholders' equity	10,782		12,055
Cash from oper. activs	**314**	**n.a.**	**(1,823)**
Cash from fin. activs	(136)		4,540
Cash from invest. activs	(875)		(401)
Net cash position	**2,412**	**-29**	**3,377**
Capital expenditures	(754)		(131)
Capital disposals	27		28
	US$		US$
Earnings per share*	(0.02)		(0.05)
Cash flow per share*	0.01		(0.03)
	shs		shs
No. of shs. o/s*	54,320,086		54,320,086
Avg. no. of shs. o/s*	54,320,086		53,082,689
	%		%
Net profit margin	(12.40)		(37.15)
Return on equity	(11.87)		(23.97)
Return on assets	(10.47)		(21.43)
No. of employees (FTEs)	38		45

* Common
[A] Reported in accordance with IFRS

Latest Results

Periods ended:	3m Mar. 31/23[A]		3m Mar. 31/22[A]
	US$000s	%Chg	US$000s
Operating revenue	2,460	-17	2,964
Net income	787	n.a.	(54)
	US$		US$
Earnings per share*	0.01		(0.00)

* Common
[A] Reported in accordance with IFRS

Historical Summary
(as originally stated)

Fiscal Year	Oper. Rev. US$000s	Net Inc. Bef. Disc. US$000s	EPS* US$
2022[A]	10,931	(1,355)	(0.02)
2021[A]	7,426	(2,759)	(0.05)
2020[A]	11,149	(1,308)	(0.03)
2019[A]	20,551	3,334	0.07
2018[A]	12,717	194	0.00

* Common
[A] Reported in accordance with IFRS

K.14 Keon Capital Inc.

Symbol - KEON.H **Exchange** - TSX-VEN **CUSIP** - 491895
Head Office - 1800-510 Georgia St W, Vancouver, BC, V6B 0M3 **Telephone** - (604) 288-2553
Email - lmontaine@gmail.com
Investor Relations - Luke Montaine (604) 760-8755
Auditors - Davidson & Company LLP C.A., Vancouver, B.C.
Lawyers - Norton Rose Fulbright Canada LLP, Vancouver, B.C.
Transfer Agents - Endeavor Trust Corporation, Vancouver, B.C.
Profile - (B.C. 2008) Seeking new opportunities.
Predecessor Detail - Name changed from Prospero Silver Corp., Mar. 19, 2021.
Directors - William Murray, chr., Richmond, B.C.; Nader Vatanchi, CEO, Vancouver, B.C.; Luke Montaine, CFO & corp. sec., Vancouver, B.C.; Nicholas (Nick) Houghton, Vancouver, B.C.; Ashish (Ash) Misquith
Other Exec. Officers - Ralph Rushton, exec. v-p, bus. devel.

Capital Stock

	Authorized (shs.)	Outstanding (shs.)[1]
Common	unlimited	4,983,466

[1] At May 29, 2023

Major Shareholder - William D. (Bill) McCartney held 15.66% interest and William Murray held 14.93% interest at May 26, 2022.

Price Range - KEON.H/TSX-VEN

Year	Volume	High	Low	Close
2022	192,066	$0.50	$0.24	$0.24
2021	456,768	$1.35	$0.30	$0.40
2020	849,420	$1.47	$0.30	$0.57
2019	342,417	$3.30	$0.75	$0.90
2018	337,039	$4.50	$1.50	$1.80

Consolidation: 1-for-3 cons. in Feb. 2021; 1-for-10 cons. in July 2020
Recent Close: $0.22
Capital Stock Changes - In June 2022, private placement of 2,000,000 common shares was completed at 25¢ per share. Also during 2022, 1,067,738 common shares were issued in settlement of debt.

Financial Statistics

Periods ended:	12m Dec. 31/22[A]		12m Dec. 31/21[A]
	$000s	%Chg	$000s
General & admin expense	225		112
Operating expense	**225**	**+101**	**112**
Operating income	**(225)**	**n.a.**	**(112)**
Finance costs, gross	2		5
Pre-tax income	**(293)**	**n.a.**	**(117)**
Net income	**(293)**	**n.a.**	**(117)**
Cash & equivalent	157		1
Accounts receivable	10		1
Current assets	198		2
Total assets	**198**	**n.m.**	**2**
Bank indebtedness	nil		65
Accts. pay. & accr. liabs	36		298
Current liabilities	36		364
Shareholders' equity	162		(361)
Cash from oper. activs	**(273)**	**n.a.**	**(59)**
Cash from fin. activs	428		50
Net cash position	**157**	**n.m.**	**1**
	$		$
Earnings per share*	(0.08)		(0.06)
Cash flow per share*	(0.08)		(0.03)
	shs		shs
No. of shs. o/s*	4,983,466		1,915,728
Avg. no. of shs. o/s*	3,497,670		1,915,728
	%		%
Net profit margin	n.a.		n.a.
Return on equity	n.m.		n.m.
Return on assets	(291.00)		n.m.

* Common
[A] Reported in accordance with IFRS

Historical Summary
(as originally stated)

Fiscal Year	Oper. Rev. $000s	Net Inc. Bef. Disc. $000s	EPS* $
2022[A]	nil	(293)	(0.08)
2021[A]	nil	(117)	(0.06)
2020[A]	nil	(324)	(0.17)
2019[A]	nil	(4,081)	(2.13)
2018[A]	nil	(2,096)	(1.38)

* Common
[A] Reported in accordance with IFRS

Note: Adjusted throughout for 1-for-3 cons. in Feb. 2021; 1-for-10 cons. in July 2020

K.15 Keyera Corp.*

Symbol - KEY **Exchange** - TSX **CUSIP** - 493271
Head Office - The Ampersand, West Tower, 200-144 4 Ave SW, Calgary, AB, T2P 3N4 **Telephone** - (403) 205-8300 **Toll-free** - (888) 699-4853 **Fax** - (403) 205-8318
Website - www.keyera.com
Email - ir@keyera.com
Investor Relations - Dan Cuthbertson (888) 699-4853
Auditors - Deloitte LLP C.A., Calgary, Alta.
Bankers - The Toronto-Dominion Bank, Calgary, Alta.; Royal Bank of Canada, Calgary, Alta.
Lawyers - Norton Rose Fulbright Canada LLP, Calgary, Alta.
Transfer Agents - Odyssey Trust Company, Calgary, Alta.
FP500 Revenue Ranking - 92
Employees - 1,098 at Dec. 31, 2022
Profile - (Alta. 2011, amalg.) Operates a natural gas liquids energy infrastructure business primarily in western Canada providing a range of integrated gathering, processing, fractionation, storage, transportation and marketing services.

Operations are carried out through three business segments: Gathering and Processing; Liquids Infrastructure; and Marketing.

The **Gathering and Processing** segment consists of 12 active gas plants, of which nine are operated by the company, with the majority of the gross processing capacity located in the western side of the Western Canadian Sedimentary Basin (WCSB). Active gas plants include Brazeau River (94% interest), Strachan (100%), Nordegg River (89%), Pembina North (100%), Edson (22%), Simonette (100%), Rimbey (99%), Cynthia (94%), Alder Flats (70%), Zeta Creek (60%), Wapiti (100%) and Pipestone (99.9%). Interests are held in over 4,400 km of raw gas gathering pipelines that deliver raw gas to the gas plants for processing. Also holds interests in five inactive gas plants including Minnehik Buck Lake (80%), West Pembina (83%), Bigoray (100%), Brazeau North (100%) and Ricinus (71%).

The **Liquids Infrastructure** segment provides processing, fractionation, storage, transportation, liquids blending and terminalling services for NGL and crude oil, and produces iso-octane compound. Facilities are primarily located in, or connected to, the Edmonton/Fort Saskatchewan area of Alberta. Assets include the Fort Saskatchewan facilities (98% interest), including NGL fractionation, de-ethanizer, underground storage caverns, limited surface storage tanks and multiple by-directional pipelines connecting to the Edmonton Terminal; the Keyera Butane system (100%) which transports butane between Fort Saskatchewan and Edmonton; the Dow Fort Saskatchewan facilities, including a de-ethanizer (10%) and fractionator (18%); the Rimbey gas plant (99%), including NGL fractionation, other liquids processing, rail and truck terminal facilities and ethane extraction; the Edmonton Terminal (100%), including rail and truck facilities for NGL, and a rail loading facility capable of loading iso-octane, connecting to the Fort Saskatchewan facilities, and is also pipeline connected to the Alberta Diluent Terminal and Alberta EnviroFuels facility; the Rimbey Pipeline (100%), connecting the Rimbey gas plant and other facilities to the Edmonton Terminal; the Keylink Pipeline (100%), which connects and gathers NGL from multiple gas plants of the company to the Rimbey gas plant for fractionation into specification products; the Fort Saskatchewan Condensate System Pipelines (100%), connecting the company's Fort Saskatchewan Pipeline system with **Brookfield Infrastructure Partners L.P.**'s Polaris pipeline, the company's Edmonton Terminal to **Enbridge Inc.**'s Southern Lights pipeline and direct connections to **Pembina Pipeline Corporation**'s Cochin pipeline, Enbridge's CRW pool, Pembina Pipeline's Canadian Diluent Hub and north west Sturgeon Refinery, **TC Energy Corporation** and **PetroChina Canada Ltd.**'s South Grand Rapids pipeline, and Brookfield's Access and Cold Lake Diluent pipelines; the Norlite Pipeline (30%) serving the Fort Hills oil sands project; the Alberta Diluent Terminal facilities (100%), including truck, rail and storage facilities; the North Condensate Connector (100%), connecting Fort Saskatchewan to Redwater, Alta.; the Alberta Crude Terminal (100%), including truck and rail facilities; the Josephburg Terminal (100%), including rail and truck terminal facilities; the South Cheecham Terminal (50%), including storage, truck and rail loading and offloading facilities; the Alberta EnviroFuels iso-octane manufacturing and storage facility (100%) located immediately south of the Edmonton Terminal; the Base Line Terminal (50%), including 12 tanks; the Oklahoma Liquids Terminal (100%), a logistics and liquids blending facility in Tulsa, Okla.; and the Wildhorse terminal (90%), a crude oil storage and blending terminal in Cushing, Okla. Also developing Key Access Pipeline System (KAPS, 50%), an NGL and condensate gathering system that would transport Montney and Duvernay production in northwestern Alberta to Fort Saskatchewan, Alta., and was expected to be operational in the second quarter of 2023. In addition, the company has exclusive right for the use of a butane-on-demand blending and distribution system at **Kinder Morgan Canada Limited**'s Galena Park Products Terminal in Texas for 25 years to December 2045.

The **Marketing** segment markets a range of products associated with the company's facilities, including natural gas liquid, crude oil and iso-octane. During 2022, the company marketed an average of 179,100 bbl per day of natural gas liquids and iso-octane compared to 167,200 bbl per day in 2021.

Operating Statistics

Year ended Dec. 31	2022	2021
Natural Gas Processing:		
Gross capacity, mmcf/day	3,393	3,373
Avg. gross throughput, mmcf/day	1,572	1,460
Utilization rate, %	46	43
NGL Storage:		
Net capacity, bbl	23,616,500	20,748,500

In March 2022, the company signed a memorandum of agreement with **Shell Canada Limited** to collaborate on potential low-carbon projects in Alberta. This collaboration would leverage existing assets, adjacent lands, and strong leadership to support industry's journey to a lower-carbon future and attract new investment opportunities to the region.

Recent Merger and Acquisition Activity

Status: completed **Revised:** Feb. 13, 2023
UPDATE: The transaction was completed. PREVIOUS: Keyera Corp. agreed to acquire an additional 21% working interest in the Keyera Fort Saskatchewan complex from Plains Midstream Canada ULC, increasing its ownership interest to 98%, for total cash consideration of $365,000,000. The transaction was expected to close in the first quarter of 2023.

Predecessor Detail - Succeeded Keyera Facilities Income Fund, Jan. 1, 2011, pursuant to plan of arrangement whereby Keyera Corp. was formed to facilitate the conversion of the fund into a corporation and the fund was subsequently dissolved.
Directors - James V. (Jim) Bertram, chr., Calgary, Alta.; C. Dean Setoguchi, pres. & CEO, Calgary, Alta.; Douglas J. (Doug) Haughey†, Calgary, Alta.; Isabelle Brassard, Montréal, Qué.; Michael Crothers, Calgary, Alta.; J. Blair Goertzen, Red Deer, Alta.; Gianna M. Manes, S.C.; Michael J. Norris, Toronto, Ont.; Thomas O'Connor, Denver, Colo.; Charlene A. Ripley, Vancouver, B.C.; Janet P. Woodruff, West Vancouver, B.C.
Other Exec. Officers - Jarrod Beztilny, sr. v-p, opers. & eng.; Desiree Crawford, sr. v-p, safety, people & tech.; Eileen Marikar, sr. v-p & CFO; K. James (Jamie) Urquhart, sr. v-p & chief comml. officer; Marty Buller,

v-p, bus. devel.; Kelly Hill, v-p, IT; John Hunszinger, v-p, opers., liquids infrastructure; Jason Johnson, v-p, eng.; Jennifer Laing, v-p, bus. devel.; Darren Rousch, v-p, mktg. & U.S. opers.; Monica Santander, v-p, opers., gathering & processing; Bradley (Brad) Slessor, v-p, KAPS & oilsands bus. devel. & new ventures

† Lead director

Capital Stock

	Authorized (shs.)	Outstanding (shs.)[1]
First Preferred	unlimited	nil
Second Preferred	unlimited	nil
Common	unlimited	229,153,373

[1] At Mar. 31, 2023

Major Shareholder - Widely held at Mar. 22, 2023.

Price Range - KEY/TSX

Year	Volume	High	Low	Close
2022	246,190,227	$35.48	$26.34	$29.59
2021	214,745,960	$35.75	$22.41	$28.53
2020	310,103,194	$36.56	$10.04	$22.62
2019	150,918,506	$35.84	$25.26	$34.02
2018	136,245,989	$38.91	$24.05	$25.81

Recent Close: $33.40

Capital Stock Changes - In December 2022, bought deal public offering of 8,130,500 common shares was completed at $28.30 per share, including 1,060,500 common shares on exercise of over-allotment option.

Dividends

KEY com Ra $2.00 pa Q est. Sept. 29, 2023
Prev. Rate: $1.92 est. Sept. 16, 2019

Long-Term Debt - Outstanding debt at Dec. 31, 2022:

Credit facility due 2024	$40,000,000
Cdn$ sr. notes[1]	3,222,000,000
US$ sr. notes[2]	450,666,000
Less: Issuance costs	19,921,000
	3,692,745,000
Less: Current portion	30,000,000
	3,662,745,000

[1] Consists of $30,000,000 of 3.5% senior notes due 2023; $17,000,000 of 4.91% senior notes due 2024; $100,000,000 of 4.92% senior notes due 2025; $20,000,000 of 5.05% senior notes due 2025; $30,000,000 of 4.15% senior notes due 2026; $200,000,000 of 3.96% senior notes due 2026; $400,000,000 of 3.68% senior notes due 2027; $400,000,000 of 3.93% senior notes due 2028; $100,000,000 of 5.09% senior notes due 2028; $100,000,000 of 4.11% senior notes due 2028; $75,000,000 of 5.34% senior notes due 2029; $400,000,000 of 3.96% senior notes due 2030; $400,000,000 of 5.02% senior notes due 2032; $600,000,000 of 6.88% senior notes due 2079; and $350,000,000 of 5.95% senior notes due 2081.

[2] Consists of $173,229,000 (US$128,000,000) of 4.19% senior notes due 2024; $189,469,000 (US$140,000,000) of 4.75% senior notes due 2025; and $87,968,000 (US$65,000,000) of 4.95% senior notes due 2028.

Wholly Owned Subsidiaries

Alberta Diluent Terminal Ltd., Alta.
Alberta Envirofuels Inc., Alta.
Keyera Energy Inc., Del.
Keyera Energy Ltd., Alta.
- 2.54% int. in **Keyera Partnership**, Alta.

Keyera RP Ltd., Alta.
Keyera Rimbey Ltd., Alta.
- 100% int. in **Rimbey Pipeline Limited Partnership**, Man.

Subsidiaries

97.46% int. in **Keyera Partnership**, Alta.

Note: The preceding list includes only the major related companies in which interests are held.

Financial Statistics

Periods ended:	12m Dec. 31/22[A]		12m Dec. 31/21[A]
	$000s	%Chg	$000s
Operating revenue	**7,060,223**	**+42**	**4,984,906**
General & admin expense	82,843		80,697
Other operating expense	5,884,442		3,939,606
Operating expense	**5,967,285**	**+48**	**4,020,303**
Operating income	**1,092,938**	**+13**	**964,603**
Deprec., depl. & amort.	258,264		257,638
Finance costs, gross	165,351		169,309
Write-downs/write-offs	(180,277)		(115,771)
Pre-tax income	**433,200**	**+2**	**426,261**
Income taxes	104,906		102,055
Net income	**328,294**	**+1**	**324,206**
Cash & equivalent	nil		15,940
Inventories	300,883		280,736
Accounts receivable	708,781		750,420
Current assets	1,108,132		1,099,128
Fixed assets, net	6,992,196		6,582,276
Right-of-use assets	238,685		226,757
Intangibles, net	91,706		104,108
Total assets	**8,568,188**	**+5**	**8,130,306**
Bank indebtedness	1,803		nil
Accts. pay. & accr. liabs.	778,862		680,348
Current liabilities	999,999		912,959
Long-term debt, gross	3,692,745		3,514,485
Long-term debt, net	3,662,745		3,454,485
Long-term lease liabilities	181,170		151,745
Shareholders' equity	2,818,716		2,657,634
Cash from oper. activs.	**925,327**	**+58**	**583,839**
Cash from fin. activs.	(100,650)		(173,854)
Cash from invest. activs.	(843,921)		(397,124)
Net cash position	**(1,803)**	**n.a.**	**15,940**
Capital expenditures	(895,929)		(516,633)
Capital disposals	39,815		18,191
	$		$
Earnings per share*	1.48		1.47
Cash flow per share*	4.18		2.64
Cash divd. per share*	1.92		1.92
	shs		shs
No. of shs. o/s*	229,153,373		221,022,873
Avg. no. of shs. o/s*	221,290,000		221,022,873
	%		%
Net profit margin	4.65		6.50
Return on equity	11.99		11.97
Return on assets	5.43		5.77
Foreign sales percent	19		22
No. of employees (FTEs)	1,098		1,005

* Common
[A] Reported in accordance with IFRS

Latest Results

Periods ended:	3m Mar. 31/23[A]		3m Mar. 31/22[A]
	$000s	%Chg	$000s
Operating revenue	1,789,503	+6	1,690,220
Net income	137,789	+21	113,794
	$		$
Earnings per share*	0.60		0.51

* Common
[A] Reported in accordance with IFRS

Historical Summary
(as originally stated)

Fiscal Year	Oper. Rev.	Net Inc. Bef. Disc.	EPS*
	$000s	$000s	$
2022[A]	7,060,223	328,294	1.48
2021[A]	4,984,906	324,206	1.47
2020[A]	3,012,510	62,030	0.28
2019[A]	3,616,922	443,609	2.07
2018[A]	4,465,211	394,224	1.90

* Common
[A] Reported in accordance with IFRS

K.16 Khiron Life Sciences Corp.

Symbol - KHRN **Exchange** - TSX-VEN (S) **CUSIP** - 49374L
Head Office - 2300-500 Burrard St, Vancouver, BC, V6C 2B5 **Telephone** - (604) 683-6498
Website - www.khiron.ca
Email - cnaprawa@khiron.ca
Investor Relations - Christopher Naprawa (416) 705-1144
Auditors - BDO Canada LLP C.A., Vancouver, B.C.
Transfer Agents - TSX Trust Company, Toronto, Ont.

Profile - (B.C. 2012) Holds a licence in Colombia to cultivate, produce, distribute and export tetrahydrocannabinol (THC) and cannabidiol (CBD) medical cannabis for the domestic and international markets. Also develops and markets cannabis-based products in Colombia, the U.K., Germany, Peru and Mexico; and operates a network of clinics in Colombia, Peru, the U.K. and Brazil; and facilitates a digital medical cannabis education platform.

Operations are organized into two segments: Medical Cannabis Products and Health Services.

The **Medical Cannabis Products** segment includes producing, developing and commercializing medical cannabis products and services primarily in Colombia, the U.K., Germany, Peru and Mexico.

The company owns 80,000 sq. ft. greenhouse and 14,000 sq. ft. harvest facilities near Ibagué, Colombia, which holds all licences and certification to manufacture high, low and dominant THC and CBD medical cannabis as well as to manufacture the psychoactive whole plant extract for both export and domestic purposes. Products are sold across Colombia through retailers, clinics and pharmacies. The sale of low-THC medical cannabis commenced in March 2020 and high-THC medical cannabis in May 2020.

In addition, products are being exported in Peru including Alixen™ CBD-rich products through wholly owned **Khiron Peru S.A.**'s import and commercialization license as well as manufacturing and distribution agreements; in Germany, the U.K. and Europe through wholly owned **Pharmadrug Production GmbH**'s manufacture and commercialization licenses; and in Mexico including medical cannabis extracts through wholly owned **Khiron Colombia S.A.S.**'s cultivation, production, domestic distribution and international export licenses.

In Uruguay, wholly owned **NettaGrowth International Inc.** holds a licence to distribute medical cannabis with THC from Colombia to Brazil.

The **Health Services** segment includes the health centres and satellite clinics operating under the ILANS™ and Zerenia™ brands, which offer health, medical and surgical services for neurological, psychiatric, urological and orthopaedic diseases, in Colombia, Peru, the U.K. and Brazil in alignment with insurance company partners. Teleconsultation, home delivery services, physician education and training, and web or app-based telehealth application DoctorZerenia.com are also included in the segment.

The company also offers medical education in medical cannabis through Khiron Academy, which is a cloud-based e-learning platform designed to familiarize health professionals with specific regulatory considerations, and to educate them on medical cannabis clinical evidence and research, safety and drug interactions, and practical recommendations to best meet patient needs for conditions that include chronic pain, mental health, cancer and refractory epilepsy. It is accessible in Colombia, Peru, Mexico, Deutschland and the U.K.

In August 2022, the company acquired **Pharmadrug Production GmbH** from **Pharmadrug Inc.** for issuance of 5,968,750 common shares at a deemed price of 16¢ per share and issuance of $974,137 promissory note. Pharmadrug Production imports and distributes medical cannabis to pharmacies in Germany and the rest of the European Union, as markets become legalized.

Common suspended from TSX-VEN, May 8, 2023.

Predecessor Detail - Name changed from Adent Capital Corp., Mar. 5, 2018, pursuant to Qualifying Transaction reverse takeover acquisition of (old) Khiron Life Sciences Corp.; basis 1 new for 8 old shs.

Directors - Alvaro Torres, co-founder & CEO, Bogota, Colombia; Christopher (Chris) Naprawa, chr., Toronto, Ont.; Dr. Juan Carlos Echeverry, Bethesda, Md.; Vicente Fox, Gto., Mexico; Alvaro Yañez, Bogota, Colombia

Other Exec. Officers - Michael O'Connor, CFO; Andres Galofre, chief comml. officer; Juan D. Alvarez, v-p, corp. affairs; Manuel Buendia, v-p, opers.; Rodrigo Duran, v-p, Pharma; Matthew C. (Matt) Murphy, v-p, compliance; Dr. Paulo Vega, v-p, medical; Livia Maduri, gen. counsel & corp. sec.; Franziska Katterbach, pres., Khiron Europe

Capital Stock

	Authorized (shs.)	Outstanding (shs.)[1]
Common	unlimited	232,409,396

[1] At Apr. 12, 2023

Major Shareholder - Widely held at May 17, 2022.

Price Range - KHRN/TSX-VEN (S)

Year	Volume	High	Low	Close
2022	50,148,656	$0.28	$0.05	$0.06
2021	111,298,275	$0.76	$0.17	$0.21
2020	109,635,447	$1.20	$0.30	$0.38
2019	205,988,808	$4.35	$0.79	$1.06
2018	85,724,810	$2.07	$0.87	$1.53

Recent Close: $0.04

Capital Stock Changes - In April 2023, bought deal public offering of 13,800,000 units (1 common share & 1 warrant), including 1,800,000 units on exercise of over-allotment, at 5¢ per unit was completed, with warrants exercisable at 8¢ per share for two years.

In June 2022, bought deal public offering of 30,705,000 units (1 common share & 1 warrant), including 4,005,000 units on exercise of over-allotment, at 15¢ per unit was completed, with warrants exercisable at 20¢ per share for two years.

Wholly Owned Subsidiaries

Khiron Brasil Farmaceutica Ltda., Brazil.
- 100% int. in **Zerenia Clinic Servicos Medicos Ltda.**, Brazil.

Khiron Chile S.p.A., Chile.
Khiron Europe GmbH, Germany.
Khiron Life Sciences Corp., Toronto, Ont.
- 100% int. in **Khiron Colombia S.A.S.**, Colombia.
  - 22% int. in **ILANS S.A.S.**, Bogota, Colombia.
  - 99% int. in **Khiron Peru S.A.**, Peru.
  - 99% int. in **Kuida Life Mexico S.A. de C.V.**, Mexico.
  - 100% int. in **NAS I.P.S.**, Colombia.
    - 1% int. in **Khiron Peru S.A.**, Peru.
    - 1% int. in **Kuida Life Mexico S.A. de C.V.**, Mexico.

Khiron Life Sciences Spain S.L., Spain.
Khiron Life Sciences UK Limited, United Kingdom.

Khiron Life Sciences USA Inc., Del.
NettaGrowth International Inc., Uruguay.
- 100% int. in **K Life Sciences Uruguay S.A.**, Uruguay.
- 100% int. in **Prosel S.A.**, Uruguay.

Pharmadrug Production GmbH, Germany.
Zerenia Clinics Limited, United Kingdom.

Subsidiaries

78% int. in **ILANS S.A.S.**, Bogota, Colombia.

Note: The preceding list includes only the major related companies in which interests are held.

Financial Statistics

Periods ended:	12m Dec. 31/21[A]		12m Dec. 31/20[□A]
	$000s	%Chg	$000s
Operating revenue	**12,795**	**+60**	**8,017**
Cost of sales	9,180		11,574
Salaries & benefits	8,776		11,806
Research & devel. expense	1,216		1,526
General & admin expense	13,130		10,887
Stock-based compensation	2,322		5,716
Operating expense	**34,624**	**-17**	**41,509**
Operating income	**(21,829)**	**n.a.**	**(33,492)**
Deprec., depl. & amort.	1,115		1,167
Finance costs, gross	445		468
Write-downs/write-offs	(14,966)		nil
Pre-tax income	**(33,594)**	**n.a.**	**(23,950)**
Income taxes	(465)		89
Net income	**(33,129)**	**n.a.**	**(24,039)**
Cash & equivalent	8,923		21,649
Inventories	9,454		8,337
Accounts receivable	2,880		4,583
Current assets	23,774		36,415
Fixed assets, net	13,557		17,518
Intangibles, net	4,943		19,246
Total assets	**42,274**	**-42**	**73,179**
Accts. pay. & accr. liabs.	4,308		6,264
Current liabilities	8,944		7,342
Long-term debt, gross	2,540		2,790
Long-term debt, net	914		1,712
Shareholders' equity	33,329		63,229
Cash from oper. activs.	**(20,400)**	**n.a.**	**(24,532)**
Cash from fin. activs.	10,895		12,172
Cash from invest. activs.	(2,086)		24,867
Net cash position	**8,923**	**-59**	**21,649**
Capital expenditures	(1,744)		(2,693)
	$		$
Earnings per share*	(0.20)		(0.20)
Cash flow per share*	(0.12)		(0.20)
	shs		shs
No. of shs. o/s*	179,262,068		150,717,068
Avg. no. of shs. o/s*	164,517,000		120,293,691
	%		%
Net profit margin	(258.92)		(299.85)
Return on equity	(68.62)		(36.08)
Return on assets	(56.63)		(30.39)
Foreign sales percent	100		100
No. of employees (FTEs)	334		327

* Common
[□] Restated
[A] Reported in accordance with IFRS

Latest Results

Periods ended:	9m Sept. 30/22[A]		9m Sept. 30/21[A]
	$000s	%Chg	$000s
Operating revenue	12,501	+36	9,159
Net income	(11,159)	n.a.	(13,628)
	$		$
Earnings per share*	(0.06)		(0.09)

* Common
[A] Reported in accordance with IFRS

Historical Summary
(as originally stated)

Fiscal Year	Oper. Rev.	Net Inc. Bef. Disc.	EPS*
	$000s	$000s	$
2021[A]	12,795	(33,129)	(0.20)
2020[A]	8,017	(24,039)	(0.20)
2019[A]	9,582	(36,378)	(0.36)
2018[A1]	892	(19,807)	(0.41)
2017[A2]	nil	(3,779)	n.a.

* Common
[A] Reported in accordance with IFRS
[1] Results prior to May 16, 2018, pertain to and reflect the Qualifying Transaction reverse takeover acquisition of (old) Khiron Life Sciences Corp.
[2] 45 weeks ended Dec. 31, 2017.

Note: Adjusted throughout for 1-for-8 cons. in May 2018

K.17 Kiaro Holdings Corp.

Symbol - KO **Exchange** - TSX-VEN (S) **CUSIP** - 49374K
Head Office - 300-110 Cordova St E, Vancouver, BC, V6A 1K9 **Telephone** - (604) 687-6575 **Toll-free** - (888) 623-2420
Website - www.kiaro.com
Email - investors@kiaro.com
Investor Relations - David M. Jenkins (888) 623-2420
Auditors -
Transfer Agents - Odyssey Trust Company, Vancouver, B.C.

Profile - (B.C. 2017) Operates cannabis retail stores in British Columbia, Saskatchewan and Ontario.

Has 16 operational retail stores across British Columbia (6), Saskatchewan (2) and Ontario (8). Also operates e-commerce platforms which sell vaporizers and accessories across Canada, the U.S. and Australia.

On Nov. 30, 2022, the company sold Warman, Sask.-based wholly owned **National Cannabis Distribution Inc.** (NCD) to **1371511 B.C. Ltd.** for $500,000 cash plus an up to $1,000,000 earnout payment. NCD is a business-to-business wholesaler that acquires finished goods from licensed producers and sells to 92 licensed retail cannabis operators in the Saskatchewan including the company's own Saskatchewan retail cannabis stores.

On Sept. 12, 2022, the company sold all of the assets of the business used in connection with the operation of two cannabis retail stores in La Ronge and Saskatoon, Sask., for $823,595.

On Apr. 29, 2022, the company closed Cozy Cannabis retail store in Ontario.

Common suspended from TSX-VEN, June 7, 2023.

Predecessor Detail - Name changed from DC Acquisition Corp., Oct. 20, 2020, pursuant to Qualifying Transaction reverse takeover acquisition of Kiaro Brands Inc., and concurrent amalgamation of Kiaro Brands with wholly owned 1251542 B.C. Ltd.; basis 1 new for 1.71429 old shs.

Directors - David M. (Dave) Jenkins, interim CEO & interim CFO, Langley, B.C.

Capital Stock

	Authorized (shs.)	Outstanding (shs.)[1]
Common	unlimited	36,734,495

[1] At Feb. 23, 2023

Major Shareholder - Aegis Brands Inc. held 17.99% interest and Daniel E. Petrov held 14.8% interest at Feb. 23, 2023.

Price Range - KO/TSX-VEN (S)

Year	Volume	High	Low	Close
2022	7,353,232	$0.80	$0.01	$0.02
2021	7,529,256	$1.95	$0.65	$0.75
2020	1,279,778	$1.80	$0.60	$0.70
2019	11,841	$1.80	$1.37	$1.80
2018	123,821	$2.57	$1.46	$1.46

Consolidation: 1-for-10 cons. in Sept. 2022; 1-for-1.71429 cons. in Oct. 2020

Recent Close: $0.01

Capital Stock Changes - On Sept. 29, 2022, common shares were consolidated on a 1-for-10 basis. In October 2022, private placement of 10,000,000 units (1 post-consolidated common share & 1 warrant) at 5¢ per unit was completed, with warrants exercisable at 5¢ per share for two years.

Wholly Owned Subsidiaries

Kiaro Brands Inc., B.C.
- 100% int. in **Kiaro Retail BC Ltd.**, B.C.
- 100% int. in **National Cannabis Distribution Inc.**
- 100% int. in **2209917 Alberta Ltd.**, Alta.

2687921 Ontario Inc., Ont.
2734524 Ontario Inc., Canada. dba Hemisphere Cannabis Co.

Financial Statistics

Periods ended:	12m Jan. 31/22[A]		12m Jan. 31/21[A1]
	$000s	%Chg	$000s
Operating revenue	**26,903**	**+58**	**17,072**
Cost of sales	19,205		11,958
Salaries & benefits	5,915		3,740
General & admin expense	3,287		2,081
Stock-based compensation	644		1,136
Operating expense	**29,051**	**+54**	**18,915**
Operating income	**(2,148)**	**n.a.**	**(1,843)**
Deprec., depl. & amort.	2,384		1,867
Finance income	164		182
Finance costs, gross	924		1,598
Write-downs/write-offs	(4,084)		(19)
Pre-tax income	**(9,732)**	**n.a.**	**(9,337)**
Income taxes	(541)		nil
Net income	**(9,191)**	**n.a.**	**(9,337)**
Cash & equivalent	2,352		1,305
Inventories	2,772		1,744
Accounts receivable	298		142
Current assets	5,998		3,530
Fixed assets, net	4,616		1,598
Right-of-use assets	7,654		3,618
Intangibles, net	2,250		609
Total assets	**20,694**	**+114**	**9,665**
Accts. pay. & accr. liabs.	2,954		1,325
Current liabilities	4,870		2,421
Long-term debt, gross	3,478		741
Long-term debt, net	858		120
Long-term lease liabilities	5,092		1,587
Shareholders' equity	7,683		4,829
Cash from oper. activs.	**(1,116)**	**n.a.**	**(1,415)**
Cash from fin. activs.	4,849		(503)
Cash from invest. activs.	(2,686)		1,804
Net cash position	**2,352**	**+80**	**1,305**
Capital expenditures	(1,031)		(636)
	$		$
Earnings per share*	(0.40)		(0.80)
Cash flow per share*	(0.05)		(0.13)
	shs		shs
No. of shs. o/s*	26,816,055		17,356,568
Avg. no. of shs. o/s*	21,763,600		11,294,201
	%		%
Net profit margin	(34.16)		(54.69)
Return on equity	(146.91)		(317.59)
Return on assets	(54.80)		(65.43)

* Common
[A] Reported in accordance with IFRS
[1] Results prior to Oct. 13, 2020, pertain to and reflect the Qualifying Transaction reverse takeover acquisition of Kiaro Brands Inc.

Latest Results

Periods ended:	9m Oct. 31/22[A]		9m Oct. 31/21[□A]
	$000s	%Chg	$000s
Operating revenue	19,206	+49	12,893
Net inc. bef. disc. opers.	(10,699)	n.a.	(3,399)
Income from disc. opers.	910		276
Net income	(9,789)	n.a.	(3,123)
	$		$
Earns. per sh. bef. disc. opers.*	(0.40)		(0.16)
Earnings per share*	(0.40)		(0.15)

* Common
[□] Restated
[A] Reported in accordance with IFRS

Historical Summary
(as originally stated)

Fiscal Year	Oper. Rev.	Net Inc. Bef. Disc.	EPS*
	$000s	$000s	$
2022[A]	26,903	(9,191)	(0.40)
2021[A]	17,072	(9,337)	(0.80)
2020[A1]	5,172	(12,503)	n.a.
2018[A]	nil	(2,522)	n.a.

* Common
[A] Reported in accordance with IFRS
[1] 13 months ended Jan. 31, 2020.

Note: Adjusted throughout for 1-for-10 cons. in Sept. 2022; 1-for-1.7142857 cons. in Oct. 2020

K.18 Kidoz Inc.

Symbol - KIDZ **Exchange** - TSX-VEN **CUSIP** - 493947
Head Office - 220-1685 4 Ave W, Vancouver, BC, V6J 1L8 **Toll-free** - (888) 374-2163 **Fax** - (604) 694-0301
Website - www.kidoz.net
Email - henry@kidoz.net
Investor Relations - Henry W. Bromley (888) 374-2163
Auditors - Davidson & Company LLP C.A., Vancouver, B.C.
Bankers - Canadian Imperial Bank of Commerce, Vancouver, B.C.

Lawyers - MacDonald Tuskey Corporate & Securities Lawyers, North Vancouver, B.C.

Transfer Agents - Computershare Trust Company of Canada Inc.

Employees - 42 at Dec. 31, 2022

Profile - (Can. 2023; orig. Anguilla, 2004) Develops and owns a mobile content discovery and recommendation platform for kids, teens and families.

Owns KIDOZ Safe Advertising Network which is powered by KIDOZ Publisher software development kit (SDK) and Kidoz Connect Programmatic solution that app developers install into their apps before releasing them into the app stores. The advertising network enables content producers to monetize their apps and videos with safe, relevant and fun ads, and helps the world's largest brands safely reach and engage with kids. The proprietary advertising system is compliant with COPPA (Children's Online Privacy Protection Act), GDPR (General Data Protection Regulation) and other regulations adopted to protect children in the digital world.

Also owns Prado, a mobile advertising platform that can access hundreds of thousands famous apps and reach over a billion monthly active users without compromising kids safety for advertisements; KIDOZ Kid Mode operating system that is installed on millions of original equipment manufacturer (OEM) tablets worldwide; and Rooplay which offers game content safe for children, engaging children to learn technology, solve puzzles, paint pictures, practice language, learn math and other educational games. Rooplay has interactive games featuring Garfield, Mr. Bean, Mr. Men, Moomin and hundreds more kid-focused learning games.

In addition, has other mobile products that are free-to-play mobile games live in the Apple, Google and Amazon App Stores. Revenues are generated through in-application purchases within the games; on smartphones and tablet devices, such as Apple's iPhone and iPad; and mobile devices utilizing Google's Android operating system.

In March 2023, subsidiary **Shoal Games (UK) Plc** was discontinued.

On Jan. 1, 2023, the company continued from the jurisdiction of Anguilla to Canada.

During 2022, wholly owned **Coral Reef Marketing Inc.** merged with wholly owned **Kidoz Inc.**

Predecessor Detail - Name changed from Shoal Games Ltd., Apr. 9, 2019.

Directors - Tryon M. (Tarrnie) Williams Sr., chr., Vancouver, B.C.; Jason M. Williams, CEO, London, Middx., United Kingdom; Eldad Ben Tora, pres. & gen. mgr., Europe, Middle East & Africa, Netanya, Israel; Fiona Curtis, Little Harbour, Anguilla; Moshe David, Israel; Claes Kalborg, Saltsjobaden, Sweden

Other Exec. Officers - Henry W. Bromley, CFO; T. H. (Tarrnie) Williams, v-p, product

Capital Stock

	Authorized (shs.)	Outstanding (shs.)[1]
Common	unlimited	131,304,499

[1] At Apr. 19, 2023

Normal Course Issuer Bid - The company plans to make normal course purchases of up to 6,579,074 common shares representing 5% of the total outstanding. The bid commenced on Sept. 15, 2022, and expires on Sept. 14, 2023.

Major Shareholder - Pendinas Ltd. held 21.2% interest and Tryon M. (Tarrnie) Williams Sr. held 12.98% interest at Apr. 19, 2023.

Price Range - KIDZ/TSX-VEN

Year	Volume	High	Low	Close
2022	2,626,549	$0.60	$0.25	$0.35
2021	5,484,515	$1.25	$0.45	$0.59
2020	1,239,239	$0.56	$0.13	$0.50
2019	565,667	$0.61	$0.21	$0.26
2018	350,492	$0.67	$0.34	$0.52

Recent Close: $0.25

Capital Stock Changes - During 2022, 156,510 common shares were issued for services and 233,500 common shares were repurchased under Normal Course Issuer Bid.

Wholly Owned Subsidiaries

Kidoz Ltd., Israel.
Rooplay Media Kenya Limited, Kenya.
Rooplay Media Ltd., B.C.
Shoal Media (Canada) Inc., Vancouver, B.C.
Shoal Media Inc., Anguilla.
Shoal Media (UK) Ltd., United Kingdom.

Note: The preceding list includes only the major related companies in which interests are held.

Financial Statistics

Periods ended:	12m Dec. 31/22[A]		12m Dec. 31/21[oA]
	US$000s	%Chg	US$000s
Operating revenue	**15,097**	**+21**	**12,485**
Cost of sales	9,973		7,152
Salaries & benefits	752		694
Research & devel. expense	2,497		1,679
General & admin expense	1,810		1,254
Stock-based compensation	696		660
Other operating expense	161		403
Operating expense	**15,889**	**+34**	**11,842**
Operating income	**(792)**	**n.a.**	**643**
Deprec., depl. & amort.	586		606
Pre-tax income	**(1,498)**	**n.a.**	**26**
Income taxes	(150)		217
Net income	**(1,347)**	**n.a.**	**(190)**
Cash & equivalent	2,364		2,079
Accounts receivable	7,400		6,628
Current assets	9,835		8,812
Fixed assets, net	34		21
Right-of-use assets	37		65
Intangibles, net	4,449		4,996
Total assets	**14,387**	**+3**	**13,926**
Accts. pay. & accr. liabs	5,531		4,166
Current liabilities	5,688		4,275
Long-term debt, gross	44		47
Long-term debt, net	nil		47
Long-term lease liabilities	7		42
Shareholders' equity	8,692		9,351
Cash from oper. activs	**434**	**-49**	**852**
Cash from fin. activs	(122)		1
Cash from invest. activs	(27)		nil
Net cash position	**2,364**	**+14**	**2,079**
Capital expenditures	(23)		(8)
	US$		US$
Earnings per share*	(0.01)		(0.00)
Cash flow per share*	0.00		0.01
	shs		shs
No. of shs. o/s*	131,347,999		131,340,989
Avg. no. of shs. o/s*	131,481,983		131,340,989
	%		%
Net profit margin	(8.92)		(1.52)
Return on equity	(14.93)		(2.11)
Return on assets	(9.52)		(1.53)
No. of employees (FTEs)	42		14

* Common
[o] Restated
[A] Reported in accordance with U.S. GAAP

Latest Results

Periods ended:	3m Mar. 31/23[A]		3m Mar. 31/22[oA]
	US$000s	%Chg	US$000s
Operating revenue	1,674	-27	2,287
Net income	(1,067)	n.a.	(731)
	US$		US$
Earnings per share*	(0.01)		(0.01)

* Common
[o] Restated
[A] Reported in accordance with U.S. GAAP

Historical Summary
(as originally stated)

Fiscal Year	Oper. Rev.	Net Inc. Bef. Disc.	EPS*
	US$000s	US$000s	US$
2022[A]	15,097	(1,347)	(0.01)
2021[A]	12,475	(190)	(0.00)
2020[A]	7,148	104	0.00
2019[A]	4,517	(14,654)	(0.12)
2018[A]	107	(2,593)	(0.04)

* Common
[A] Reported in accordance with U.S. GAAP

K.19 Killam Apartment Real Estate Investment Trust

Symbol - KMP.UN **Exchange** - TSX **CUSIP** - 49410M

Head Office - 100-3700 Kempt Rd, Halifax, NS, B3K 4X8 **Telephone** - (902) 453-9000 **Toll-free** - (866) 453-8900 **Fax** - (902) 455-4525

Website - www.killamreit.com

Email - chawksworth@killamreit.com

Investor Relations - Claire Hawksworth (902) 442-5322

Auditors - Ernst & Young LLP C.A., Halifax, N.S.

Lawyers - Stewart McKelvey LLP, Halifax, N.S.; Bennett Jones LLP, Calgary, Alta.

Transfer Agents - Computershare Trust Company of Canada Inc., Montréal, Qué.

FP500 Revenue Ranking - 548

Employees - 750 at Dec. 31, 2022

Profile - (Ont. 2015) Acquires, manages and develops primarily multi-family residential apartment buildings and manufactured home communities in Atlantic Canada, Ontario, Alberta and British Columbia.

At Dec. 31, 2022, the trust's residential property portfolio consisted of 231 apartment properties, totaling 19,527 units, and 5,975 manufactured home sites located within 40 manufactured home communities in Nova Scotia, New Brunswick, Ontario, Newfoundland & Labrador, Prince Edward Island, Alberta and British Columbia.

Apartment Portfolio

	Props.	Units
Nova Scotia	69	5,986
New Brunswick	77	5,073
Ontario	29	3,954
Newfoundland & Labrador	15	1,103
Prince Edward Island	26	1,249
Alberta	10	1,646
British Columbia	5	516
	231	19,527

The average monthly rent in the company's apartment portfolio was $1,289 at Dec. 31, 2022.

Manufactured Home Communities Portfolio

	Number	Sites
Nova Scotia	18	2,850
Ontario	17	2,284
New Brunswick	3	671
Newfoundland & Labrador	2	170
	40	5,975

Manufactured home communities, also known as land lease communities or trailer parks, are residential developments designed for manufactured homes purchased by the tenant and placed on improved sites rented from the trust. The trust, as owner of the community, owns the underlying land and infrastructure supporting the community, and is responsible for enforcing the community guidelines and maintenance standards.

In addition, the trust owns commercial properties in Halifax, N.S. (5), Charlottetown, P.E.I. (1), Waterloo, Ont. (2) and Dieppe, N.B. (1), totaling 946,372 sq. ft., and ancillary commercial space, totaling 181,117 sq. ft., in various residential properties across its portfolio.

On July 4, 2022, the trust acquired a 99-site manufactured home community park in Amherst, N.S., for $2,500,000.

In March 2022, the trust acquired a 5,000-sq.-ft. commercial property along with 0.75 acres of land located adjacent to its Northfield Gardens apartment complex in Waterloo, Ont., for $3,850,000.

Recent Merger and Acquisition Activity

Status: completed **Announced:** Apr. 24, 2023
Killam Apartment Real Estate Investment Trust sold a 108-unit apartment building in Halifax, N.S., for $33,000,000.

Status: completed **Announced:** Mar. 17, 2023
Killam Apartment Real Estate Investment Trust sold a 43-unit apartment building located at 266 Bronson Avenue in Ottawa, Ont., for $9,800,000.

Status: completed **Revised:** May 18, 2022
UPDATE: The transaction was completed. PREVIOUS: Killam Apartment Real Estate Investment Trust agreed to acquire two apartment properties, The Shores and The Residences, in Courtenay, B.C., for $55,600,000. The Shores consists of two, four-storey buildings with 94 units, and The Residences consists of one, four-storey building with 56 units.

Status: completed **Announced:** Apr. 29, 2022
Killam Apartment Real Estate Investment Trust acquired a 12-storey, 84-unit apartment building (671 Woolwich Street) and an adjacent development land (665 Woolwich Street) in Guelph, Ont., for $25,000,000. 665 Woolwich has been zoned for potential 10 storeys and 100 to 150-unit development.

Status: completed **Announced:** Apr. 6, 2022
Killam Apartment Real Estate Investment Trust acquired 1358 Hollis Street, a 27-unit apartment building in Halifax, N.S., for $6,200,000.

Status: completed **Announced:** Mar. 31, 2022
Killam Apartment Real Estate Investment Trust acquired Craigflower House, a 49-unit apartment building in Victoria, B.C., for $14,000,000.

Status: completed **Announced:** Mar. 7, 2022
Killam Apartment Real Estate Investment Trust acquired 510-516 Quiet Place, a four-building, 24-unit apartment property located on 1.2 acres of land in Waterloo, Ont., for $7,900,000. The property has future development potential, with zoning for about 300 units.

Predecessor Detail - Succeeded Killam Properties Inc., Jan. 1, 2016, pursuant to plan of arrangement whereby Killam Apartment Real Estate Investment Trust was formed to facilitate the conversion of the corporation into a trust.

Trustees - Robert G. Kay, chr., Moncton, N.B.; Philip D. Fraser, pres. & CEO, Halifax, N.S.; Robert G. Richardson, exec. v-p, Halifax, N.S.; Aldéa M. Landry, Moncton, N.B.; James C. Lawley, Halifax, N.S.; Karine L. MacIndoe, Toronto, Ont.; Laurie M. MacKeigan, Halifax, N.S.; A. Douglas (Doug) McGregor, Toronto, Ont.; Shant Poladian, Toronto, Ont.; Andrée Savoie, Dieppe, N.B.; Manfred J. Walt, Toronto, Ont.

Other Exec. Officers - Dale Noseworthy, CFO; Ruth Buckle, sr. v-p, prop. mgt.; Erin Cleveland, sr. v-p, fin.; Michael McLean, sr. v-p, devel.; Carrie Curtis, v-p, Ont. & Alta.; Jeremy Jackson, v-p, mktg. & govt. rel.; Brian Jessop, v-p, opers.; Colleen McCarville, v-p, HR; Ronald M. (Ron) Barron, corp. sec.

Capital Stock

	Authorized (shs.)	Outstanding (shs.)[1]
Trust Unit	unlimited	117,444,108
Special Voting Unit	unlimited	3,898,020
Class B LP Unit	n.a.	3,898,020[2 3]

[1] At June 8, 2023

[2] Classified as debt.

[3] Securities of Killam Apartment Limited Partnership.

Trust Unit - The trust will endeavour to make monthly cash distributions. Retractable at a price equal to the lesser of: (i) 90% of the market price of the units on the principal market on which the trust units are traded during the 10 trading days immediately preceding the retraction date; and (ii) 100% of the closing market price of the trust units on the principal market on which the units traded on the unit retraction date. One vote per trust unit.

Special Voting Unit - Issued to holders of class B limited partnership units of subsidiary Killam Apartment Limited Partnership. Each special voting unit entitles the holder to a number of votes at unitholder meetings equal to the number of trust units into which the class B limited partnership units are exchangeable.

Class B Limited Partnership Unit - Entitled to distributions equal to those provided to trust units. Directly exchangeable into trust units on a 1-for-1 basis at any time by holder. Classified as long-term debt under IFRS.

Normal Course Issuer Bid - The company plans to make normal course purchases of up to 3,000,000 trust units representing 2.6% of the total outstanding. The bid commenced on June 22, 2023, and expires on June 21, 2024.

Major Shareholder - Widely held at Mar. 22, 2023.

Price Range - KMP.UN/TSX

Year	Volume	High	Low	Close
2022	58,845,676	$24.15	$14.62	$16.21
2021	50,184,133	$23.62	$16.85	$23.59
2020	85,611,306	$23.37	$13.90	$17.11
2019	75,562,602	$21.21	$15.34	$18.94
2018	48,887,443	$17.02	$12.59	$15.94

Recent Close: $17.88

Capital Stock Changes - In February 2022, bought deal public offering 4,715,000 trust units was completed at $20.80 per unit, including 615,000 trust units on exercise of over-allotment option. Also during 2022, trust units were issued as follows: 1,360,631 under distribution reinvestment plan, 106,250 on exchange of exchangeable units and 61,205 on redemption of restricted trust units.

Dividends

KMP.UN unit Ra $0.69996 pa M est. Oct. 15, 2021**[1]

Prev. Rate: $0.68004 est. Apr. 15, 2020

[1] Killam Properties Inc. com prior to Jan. 7, 2016.

** Reinvestment Option

Wholly Owned Subsidiaries

Killam Apartment General Partner Ltd., Ont.

Killam Apartment Limited Partnership, Ont.

- 100% int. in **Killam Apartment Subsidiary II Limited Partnership**, Ont.
- 100% int. in **Killam Apartment Subsidiary Limited Partnership**, Ont.
  - 100% int. in **Killam Investments Inc.**, Halifax, N.S.
  - 100% int. in **Killam Investments (P.E.I.) Inc.**, P.E.I.
  - 100% int. in **Killam Properties Apartments Trust**, Halifax, N.S.
  - 100% int. in **Killam Properties M.H.C. Trust**, Halifax, N.S.
- 100% int. in **Killam Properties Inc.**, Canada.
- 100% int. in **Killam Properties SGP Ltd.**, Ont.

Financial Statistics

Periods ended:	12m Dec. 31/22[A]		12m Dec. 31/21[oA]
	$000s	%Chg	$000s
Total revenue	**330,644**	**+13**	**291,976**
Rental operating expense	82,414		72,165
General & admin. expense	17,153		15,988
Property taxes	39,521		35,517
Operating expense	**139,088**	**+12**	**123,670**
Operating income	**191,556**	**+14**	**168,306**
Deprec. & amort.	573		573
Finance costs, gross	61,499		51,521
Pre-tax income	**141,345**	**-57**	**327,920**
Income taxes	18,813		42,393
Net income	**122,532**	**-57**	**285,527**
Net inc. for equity hldrs	**122,516**	**-57**	**285,514**
Net inc. for non-cont. int	**16**	**+23**	**13**
Cash & equivalent	9,150		6,484
Inventories	4,597		212
Accounts receivable	9,580		7,768
Current assets	34,532		25,324
Fixed assets	17,238		16,721
Income-producing props	4,637,792		4,284,030
Properties under devel	135,196		201,319
Properties for future devel	39,813		55,528
Property interests, net	4,820,680		4,548,808
Total assets	**4,859,530**	**+6**	**4,578,507**
Accts. pay. & accr. liabs	48,254		56,982
Current liabilities	624,033		451,182
Long-term debt, gross	2,258,615		2,149,121
Long-term debt, net	1,702,522		1,772,852
Long-term lease liabilities	9,627		9,604
Shareholders' equity	2,273,169		2,111,469
Non-controlling interest	162		142
Cash from oper. activs	**125,331**	**-11**	**140,542**
Cash from fin. activs	154,383		355,191
Cash from invest. activs	(277,048)		(496,860)
Net cash position	**9,150**	**+41**	**6,484**
Capital expenditures	(93,920)		(76,812)
Increase in property	(183,415)		(416,030)
	$		$
Earnings per share*	n.a.		n.a.
Cash flow per share*	1.09		1.31
Funds from opers. per sh.*	1.11		1.07
Adj. funds from opers. per sh.*	0.93		0.90
Cash divd. per share*	0.70		0.69
Total divd. per share*	**0.70**		**0.69**
	shs		shs
No. of shs. o/s*	116,800,552		110,557,466
Avg. no. of shs. o/s*	115,517,000		107,435,000
	%		%
Net profit margin	37.06		97.79
Return on equity	5.59		14.72
Return on assets	3.73		7.91
No. of employees (FTEs)	750		689

* Trust Unit

[o] Restated

[A] Reported in accordance with IFRS

Historical Summary
(as originally stated)

Fiscal Year	Total Rev.	Net Inc. Bef. Disc.	EPS*
	$000s	$000s	$
2022[A]	330,644	122,532	n.a.
2021[A]	291,976	285,527	n.a.
2020[A]	262,331	146,040	n.a.
2019[A]	247,808	283,525	n.a.
2018[A]	216,924	175,171	n.a.

* Trust Unit

[A] Reported in accordance with IFRS

K.20 Kinaxis Inc.*

Symbol - KXS **Exchange** - TSX **CUSIP** - 49448Q

Head Office - 3199 Palladium Dr, Ottawa, ON, K2T 0N9 **Telephone** - (613) 592-5780 **Toll-free** - (877) 546-2947 **Fax** - (613) 592-0584

Website - www.kinaxis.com

Email - rwadsworth@kinaxis.com

Investor Relations - Rick Wadsworth (613) 907-7613

Auditors - KPMG LLP C.A., Ottawa, Ont.

Lawyers - Dentons Canada LLP, Toronto, Ont.

Transfer Agents - TSX Trust Company, Toronto, Ont.

FP500 Revenue Ranking - 478

Employees - 1,536 at Dec. 31, 2022

Profile - (Can. 2013 amalg.; orig. Can., 1984) Provides supply chain management (SCM) subscription software on a Software-as-a-Service (SaaS), fixed term (on-premise) and hybrid basis to large multinational companies in high technology and electronics manufacturing, aerospace and defence, industrial products, life sciences and pharmaceuticals, automotive, consumer products and retail sectors.

RapidResponse® is a single cloud-based product which provides supply chain planning algorithms and analytic capabilities that create the foundation for managing multiple, instantaneously synchronized SCM processes. RapidResponse® applications include sales and operations planning; demand planning; supply planning; inventory management; command and control centre; and live lens insights. The company also offers Planning One®, which combines the essential capabilities of a control tower, including end-to-end visibility, root cause analysis and KPI-driven dashboards, with the instant and continuous synchronization of concurrent planning across demand, supply, inventory and operational planning to enable companies of any size to go from spreadsheets to advanced planning in weeks.

Customer agreements are typically between three to five years, and are generally recurring in nature. Revenue is derived from product subscriptions of SaaS application, on-premise subscription licences and hybrid subscriptions of software products (where customers has an option to take the hosted software on-premise), provision of professional services including business transformation, implementation and continuous leaning, as well as from maintenance and support services provided to customers with legacy perpetual licences to its software products.

The company has offices in Ottawa and Toronto, Ont.; Chicago, Ill.; Irving, Tex.; Tokyo, Japan; Hong Kong, People's Republic of China; Amsterdam, Netherlands; Seoul, South Korea; London, U.K.; Singapore; Mexico; Romania; Paris, France; Munich, Germany; Dublin, Ireland; and Chennai, India. Cloud solutions are hosted in secure data centres in the U.S., Canada, the Netherlands and Japan.

Recent Merger and Acquisition Activity

Status: completed **Announced:** Aug. 15, 2022

Kinaxis Inc. acquired Rotterdam, Netherlands-based MP Objects B.V. (MPO) for US$33,828,000 cash and contingent consideration of 86,335 common shares. MPO has developed a unified cloud-based supply chain Software-as-a-Service (SaaS) platform for multi party orchestration of orders, inventory and transport. The MPO platform includes software for control tower, supply chain visibility, digital order management, transportation management, network inventory management, returns management, spare parts management and supply management.

Directors - John (Ian) Giffen, chr., Toronto, Ont.; John Sicard, pres. & CEO, Ottawa, Ont.; Robert G. (Bob) Courteau, Toronto, Ont.; Gillian H. (Jill) Denham, Toronto, Ont.; Angel L. Mendez, Rancho Santa Fe, Calif.; Pamela Passman, Washington, D.C.; Elizabeth (Betsy) Rafeal, La Quinta, Calif.; Kelly J. Thomas, Birmingham, Mich.

Other Exec. Officers - Megan Paterson, COO; Blaine Fitzgerald, CFO; Andrew Bell, chief product officer; Margaret Franco, chief mktg. officer; Jamie Hollingworth, chief legal officer & corp. sec.; Michael Mauger, chief cust. success officer; Amber Pate, chief HR officer; Dr. Anne G. Robinson, chief strategy officer; David Kelly, exec. v-p, professional srvcs.; Gelu Ticala, exec. v-p, eng.; Paul Z. Carreiro, pres., global field opers.; Martin Verwijmeren, pres., MP Objects B.V.

Capital Stock

	Authorized (shs.)	Outstanding (shs.)[1]
Common	unlimited	28,413,395

[1] At Aug. 9, 2023

Options - At Dec. 31, 2022, options were outstanding to purchase 1,720,326 common shares at prices ranging from US$1.00 to US$180 per share with a weighted average remaining contractual life of 2.67 years.

Major Shareholder - Widely held at Apr. 28, 2023.

Price Range - KXS/TSX

Year	Volume	High	Low	Close
2022	15,770,779	$179.98	$119.48	$151.91
2021	21,661,624	$229.98	$124.05	$177.33
2020	29,419,586	$224.98	$86.53	$180.34
2019	22,155,505	$109.00	$62.76	$100.02
2018	19,327,789	$100.68	$60.01	$65.90

Recent Close: $165.54

Capital Stock Changes - During 2022, common shares were issued as follows: 492,631 on exercise of options, 93,388 on vesting of restricted share units and 3,776 on vesting of performance share units.

Long-Term Debt - At Dec. 31, 2022, the company had no long-term debt.

Wholly Owned Subsidiaries

Kinaxis Corp., Del.

Kinaxis Europe B.V., Netherlands.

- 100% int. in **Kinaxis UK Limited**, United Kingdom.

Kinaxis India Private Limited, India.

Kinaxis Japan KK, Japan.

MP Objects B.V., Rotterdam, Netherlands.

Financial Statistics

Periods ended:	12m Dec. 31/22^A		12m Dec. 31/21^oA
	US$000s	%Chg	US$000s
Operating revenue	**366,889**	**+46**	**250,726**
Cost of sales	113,916		73,765
Research & devel. expense	66,507		48,043
General & admin expense	107,247		82,247
Stock-based compensation	26,238		24,343
Operating expense	**313,908**	**+37**	**228,398**
Operating income	**52,981**	**+137**	**22,328**
Deprec., depl. & amort.	25,060		20,409
Finance costs, net	(1,240)		264
Pre-tax income	**31,486**	**n.m.**	**1,097**
Income taxes	11,406		2,262
Net income	**20,080**	**n.a.**	**(1,165)**
Cash & equivalent	225,823		233,388
Accounts receivable	155,827		89,030
Current assets	397,140		331,137
Fixed assets, net	51,852		52,093
Right-of-use assets	53,537		53,578
Intangibles, net	101,585		50,766
Total assets	**648,273**	**+25**	**520,269**
Accts. pay. & accr. liabs	37,427		36,883
Current liabilities	190,007		145,809
Long-term lease liabilities	49,977		53,233
Shareholders' equity	401,428		321,218
Cash from oper. activs	**24,518**	**-51**	**50,138**
Cash from fin. activs	26,840		5,851
Cash from invest. activs	(74,987)		(34,633)
Net cash position	**175,347**	**-14**	**203,220**
Capital expenditures	(18,249)		(33,833)
	US$		US$
Earnings per share*	0.73		(0.04)
Cash flow per share*	0.89		1.84
	shs		shs
No. of shs. o/s*	28,052,629		27,462,834
Avg. no. of shs. o/s*	27,667,100		27,248,193
	%		%
Net profit margin	5.47		(0.46)
Return on equity	5.56		(0.39)
Return on assets	3.44		(0.25)
Foreign sales percent	97		97
No. of employees (FTEs)	1,536		152

* Common
^o Restated
^A Reported in accordance with IFRS

Latest Results

Periods ended:	6m June 30/23^A		6m June 30/22^A
	US$000s	%Chg	US$000s
Operating revenue	206,902	+16	178,908
Net income	(1,351)	n.a.	9,890
	US$		US$
Earnings per share*	(0.05)		0.36

* Common
^A Reported in accordance with IFRS

Historical Summary
(as originally stated)

Fiscal Year	Oper. Rev. US$000s	Net Inc. Bef. Disc. US$000s	EPS* US$
2022^A	366,889	20,080	0.73
2021^A	250,726	(1,165)	(0.04)
2020^A	224,189	13,730	0.51
2019^A	191,549	23,331	0.89
2018^A	150,727	14,408	0.56

* Common
^A Reported in accordance with IFRS

K.21 Kings Entertainment Group Inc.

Symbol - JKPT **Exchange** - CSE **CUSIP** - 49601P
Head Office - 1500-1055 Georgia St W, Vancouver, BC, V6E 4N7
Telephone - (604) 961-0296
Website - kingsentertainment.games
Email - klee@k2capital.ca
Investor Relations - Kelvin Lee (604) 416-4099
Auditors - Reliant CPA PC C.P.A.
Transfer Agents - Olympia Trust Company, Vancouver, B.C.
Profile - (B.C. 2020) Provides online lottery, casino and sportsbook gambling services.

Wholly owned **Legacy Eight Curacao N.V.** operates an online platform which allows users to wager on various regulated, government-operated lotteries, scratchcards and casino games worldwide. Global lottery brands include LottoKings and WinTrillions.

Wholly owned **Azteca Messenger Services S.A. de C.V.** provides banking, payment processing and relationship management services support for Legacy Eight's Latin American business.

Wholly owned **Phoenix Digital Services Ltd.** provides operational and management support for Legacy Eight's operations.

Recent Merger and Acquisition Activity

Status: terminated **Revised:** Apr. 3, 2023
UPDATE: The transaction was terminated. PREVIOUS: Kings Entertainment Group Inc. agreed to the reverse takeover acquisition of private Toronto, Ont.-based Sports Venture Holdings Inc. (SVH), which operates the Bet99 brand, an online sport and casino betting website, on the basis of 1.5536 Kings Entertainment post-consolidated common shares for each SVH share held, which would result in the issuance of 25,900,000 Kings Entertainment post-consolidated common shares (following a 1-for-20 share consolidation). Upon completion, SVH would amalgamate with a wholly owned subsidiary of Kings Entertainment, and Kings Entertainment would change its name to Interactive Entertainment Group Inc. The boards of directors of both companies unanimously approved the transaction. Sept. 26, 2022 - Conditional approval of the Canadian Securities Exchange (CSE) was received. Oct. 25, 2022 - Kings Entertainment's shareholders voted in favour of the transaction.

Predecessor Detail - Name changed from 1242455 B.C. Ltd., July 28, 2021.

Directors - Robin (Rob) Godfrey, chr., Toronto, Ont.; Steve Budin, CEO, Miami, Fla.; Kelvin Lee, CFO & corp. sec., Vancouver, B.C.; Jakub Babelek; Hanna Chaban; Laryssa Hetmanczuk, Toronto, Ont.; Joseph Krutel, Miami, Fla.

Other Exec. Officers - Damian Godwin, COO; James Dominique, chief mktg. officer

Capital Stock

	Authorized (shs.)	Outstanding (shs.)[1]
Common	unlimited	68,463,500

[1] At Sept. 30, 2022

Major Shareholder - Adam Arviv held 24.53% interest at Sept. 23, 2022.

Price Range - JKPT/CSE

Year	Volume	High	Low	Close
2022	5,101,573	$0.51	$0.17	$0.19

Recent Close: $0.08

Capital Stock Changes - In January 2022, 17,789,000 common shares were issued without further consideration on exchange of subscription receipts sold previously by private placement at Cdn$0.50 each.

Wholly Owned Subsidiaries

Legacy Eight Curacao N.V., Curacao.
- 1% int. in **Azteca Messenger Services S.A. de C.V.**, Mexico City, D.F., Mexico.
- 100% int. in **Bulleg Eight Limited**, Cyprus.
- 100% int. in **Legacy Eight Malta Ltd.**, Malta.

Phoenix Digital Services Ltd., London, Middx., United Kingdom.
- 100% int. in **Litermi S.A.**, Uruguay.

Subsidiaries

99% int. in **Azteca Messenger Services S.A. de C.V.**, Mexico City, D.F., Mexico.

Financial Statistics

Periods ended:	12m Dec. 31/21^A1		12m Dec. 31/20^A2
	US$000s	%Chg	US$000s
Operating revenue	**5,841**	**-5**	**6,158**
Cost of sales	2,610		2,584
Salaries & benefits	1,505		1,312
General & admin expense	1,638		1,013
Operating expense	**5,753**	**+17**	**4,909**
Operating income	**88**	**-93**	**1,249**
Deprec., depl. & amort.	7		49
Finance costs, gross	88		60
Write-downs/write-offs	(9)		(54)
Pre-tax income	**(8,874)**	**n.a.**	**473**
Income taxes	143		87
Net income	**(9,017)**	**n.a.**	**386**
Cash & equivalent	7,225		425
Accounts receivable	805		938
Current assets	9,270		1,582
Fixed assets, net	3		3
Right-of-use assets	nil		7
Total assets	**9,387**	**+486**	**1,602**
Accts. pay. & accr. liabs	2,564		831
Current liabilities	2,913		1,201
Shareholders' equity	6,474		401
Cash from oper. activs	**217**	**n.a.**	**(619)**
Cash from fin. activs	6,967		(57)
Net cash position	**7,225**	**n.m.**	**425**
	US$		US$
Earnings per share*	n.a.		n.a.
	shs		shs
No. of shs. o/s*	50,674,500		n.a.
	%		%
Net profit margin	(154.37)		6.27
Return on equity	(262.31)		n.m.
Return on assets	(162.48)		23.10
No. of employees (FTEs)	38		38

^A Reported in accordance with IFRS
[1] Results reflect the Dec. 30, 2021, reverse takeover acquisition of the LottoKings Group.
[2] Results pertain to the LottoKings Group.

Latest Results

Periods ended:	9m Sept. 30/22^A		9m Sept. 30/21^A
	US$000s	%Chg	US$000s
Operating revenue	3,243	-28	4,531
Net income	(4,627)	n.a.	338
	US$		US$
Earnings per share*	n.a.		n.a.

^A Reported in accordance with IFRS

Historical Summary
(as originally stated)

Fiscal Year	Oper. Rev. US$000s	Net Inc. Bef. Disc. US$000s	EPS* US$
2021^A	5,841	(9,017)	n.a.
2020^A1	6,158	386	n.a.
2019^A1	8,431	1,821	n.a.

* Common
^A Reported in accordance with IFRS
[1] Results pertain to the LottoKings Group.

K.22 Kintavar Exploration Inc.

Symbol - KTR **Exchange** - TSX-VEN **CUSIP** - 49720T
Head Office - 75 boul de Mortagne, Boucherville, QC, J4B 6Y4
Telephone - (450) 641-5119
Website - www.kintavar.com
Email - kmugerman@kintavar.com
Investor Relations - Kiril Mugerman (450) 641-5119 ext. 5653
Auditors - MNP LLP C.A., Montréal, Qué.
Lawyers - McMillan LLP, Montréal, Qué.
Transfer Agents - Computershare Trust Company of Canada Inc., Montréal, Qué.
Profile - (Que. 2017 amalg.; orig. Que., 2014 amalg.) Has mineral interests in Quebec. Also operates a hunting and fishing and outdoor outfitter in the Hautes-Laurentides region of Quebec.

Holds Mitchi copper-silver prospect, 29,883 hectares, 100 km north of Mont-Laurier; Anik gold prospect, 5,375 hectares, 40 km southeast of Chapais, up to 80% optioned to **IAMGOLD Corporation**, requiring exploration expenditures of $4,000,000 by May 2025 to earn an initial 75% interest; Wabash copper-silver-cobalt prospect, 8,932 hectares, 15 km east of Parent; Baie Johan Beetz (BJB) copper-silver-gold prospect, 1,628 hectares, Havre-Saint-Pierre area, 100% optioned to **Brunswick Exploration Inc.**, requiring payment of $1,020,000 and exploration expenditures of $2,000,000 by April 2026; Rivière à l'aigle gold prospect, 6,269 hectares, 55 km south of Chapais; New Mosher gold prospect, 670 hectares, 45 km south of Chibougamau, up to 85% optioned to **Gitennes Exploration Inc.**; Cousineau copper-silver-tungsten prospect, 1,229 hectares, 30 km north of Sainte-Anne-du-Lac; and Genex prospect.

Owns and operates Pourvoirie Fer à Cheval, which covers 238 km^2 of exclusive territory located north of Mont-Laurier, offering hunting, fishing, snowmobile, all terrain vehicle (ATV) and accommodation services.

Predecessor Detail - Formed from Black Springs Capital Corp. in Quebec, Mar. 24, 2017, following Qualifying Transaction amalgamation with Groupe Ressources Geomines Inc.; basis 1 new for 2 old shs.

Directors - Mark A. Billings, chr., Montréal, Qué.; Kiril Mugerman, pres. & CEO, Montréal, Qué.; Maxime Lemieux, corp. sec., Montréal, Qué.; Geneviéve Ayotte, Qué.; David A. Charles, Qué.; Richard R. Faucher, Montréal, Qué.; Guy Le Bel, Qué.

Other Exec. Officers - Mathieu Bourdeau, CFO; Alain Cayer, v-p, explor.

Capital Stock

	Authorized (shs.)	Outstanding (shs.)[1]
Common	unlimited	128,557,128

[1] At May 19, 2023

Major Shareholder - GeoMegA Resources Inc. held 13.11% interest at May 12, 2023.

Price Range - KTR/TSX-VEN

Year	Volume	High	Low	Close
2022	15,732,915	$0.20	$0.04	$0.05
2021	24,704,501	$0.24	$0.09	$0.19
2020	22,368,816	$0.15	$0.05	$0.14
2019	13,070,736	$0.28	$0.10	$0.15
2018	29,566,141	$0.65	$0.11	$0.25

Recent Close: $0.04

Investments

Gitennes Exploration Inc., Vancouver, B.C. (see Survey of Mines)
Northern Superior Resources Inc., Toronto, Ont. (see Survey of Mines)

Financial Statistics

Periods ended:	12m Dec. 31/21[A]		12m Dec. 31/20[oA]
	$000s	%Chg	$000s
Operating revenue	**2,415**	**+92**	**1,259**
Cost of sales	934		399
Salaries & benefits	1,612		1,091
Exploration expense	823		334
General & admin expense	707		623
Stock-based compensation	149		205
Operating expense	**4,225**	**+59**	**2,652**
Operating income	**(1,810)**	**n.a.**	**(1,393)**
Deprec., depl. & amort.	299		216
Finance income	16		44
Finance costs, gross	76		95
Write-downs/write-offs	(4)		(23)
Pre-tax income	**(2,027)**	**n.a.**	**(1,645)**
Income taxes	(289)		(142)
Net income	**(1,739)**	**n.a.**	**(1,503)**
Cash & equivalent	4,242		3,822
Inventories	62		28
Accounts receivable	933		694
Current assets	5,390		4,663
Fixed assets, net	4,359		2,788
Explor./devel. properties	2,505		2,570
Total assets	**12,255**	**+22**	**10,021**
Bank indebtedness	nil		7
Accts. pay. & accr. liabs	583		239
Current liabilities	1,408		562
Long-term debt, gross	1,066		1,162
Long-term debt, net	985		1,068
Shareholders' equity	9,805		8,348
Cash from oper. activs	**(1,145)**	**n.a.**	**(1,579)**
Cash from fin. activs	2,880		1,357
Cash from invest. activs	(2,226)		(242)
Net cash position	**3,153**	**-13**	**3,643**
Capital expenditures	(1,456)		(175)
Capital disposals	5		9
	$		$
Earnings per share*	(0.02)		(0.02)
Cash flow per share*	(0.01)		(0.02)
	shs		shs
No. of shs. o/s*	122,908,378		105,929,134
Avg. no. of shs. o/s*	108,246,234		92,004,232
	%		%
Net profit margin	(72.01)		(119.38)
Return on equity	(19.16)		(17.81)
Return on assets	(15.03)		(13.84)

* Common
[o] Restated
[A] Reported in accordance with IFRS

Latest Results

Periods ended:	3m Mar. 31/22[A]		3m Mar. 31/21[A]
	$000s	%Chg	$000s
Operating revenue	1,052	+231	318
Net income	(278)	n.a.	(300)
	$		$
Earnings per share*	(0.00)		(0.00)

* Common
[A] Reported in accordance with IFRS

Historical Summary
(as originally stated)

Fiscal Year	Oper. Rev.	Net Inc. Bef. Disc.	EPS*
	$000s	$000s	$
2021[A]	2,415	(1,739)	(0.02)
2020[A]	1,259	(1,503)	(0.02)
2019[A]	341	(3,546)	(0.04)
2018[A]	nil	(4,657)	(0.07)
2017[A1]	nil	(2,431)	(0.06)

* Common
[A] Reported in accordance with IFRS
[1] Results reflect the Mar. 24, 2017, reverse takeover acquisition of Groupe Ressources Géomines Inc.

K.23 Kits Eyecare Ltd.

Symbol - KITS **Exchange** - TSX **CUSIP** - 49804N
Head Office - 1020-510 Seymour St, Vancouver, BC, V6B 3J5
Toll-free - (888) 416-3461
Website - www.kits.ca
Email - sabrina@kits.com
Investor Relations - Sabrina Liak (604) 235-5550
Auditors - MNP LLP C.A., Vancouver, B.C.
Transfer Agents - Computershare Trust Company of Canada Inc., Vancouver, B.C.
FP500 Revenue Ranking - 784
Employees - 115 at Dec. 31, 2022

Profile - (B.C. 2018) Sells and manufactures contact lenses and eyeglasses through e-commerce sites and a flagship retail store in Vancouver, B.C.

The company sells prescription eyewear, sunglasses and contact lenses to customers primarily in Canada and the U.S. Frames and contact lenses are offered under the Kits brand and brands of leading eyewear, including Gucci, Oakley, Prive Revaux, Ray-Ban and Tom Ford, and contact lens manufacturers, including Alcon, Bausch & Lomb, CooperVision and Johnson & Johnson. Owns a fully automated optical lab for glasses in Vancouver, B.C., which can produce a finished pair of glasses in as little as 10 minutes.

Directors - Roger V. Hardy, chr. & CEO, Vancouver, B.C.; Sabrina Liak, pres., CFO & corp. sec., B.C.; Edward (Ted) Goldthorpe†, New York, N.Y.; Nicholas S. (Nick) Bozikis, B.C.; Anne Kavanagh, N.Y.; Peter Lee, Wash.

Other Exec. Officers - Joseph Thompson, COO; Arshil Abdulla, chief tech. officer; Stefan Harvalias, chief mktg. officer; Rob Long, CIO
† Lead director

Capital Stock

	Authorized (shs.)	Outstanding (shs.)[1]
Preferred	unlimited	nil
Common	unlimited	31,383,216

[1] At Aug. 8, 2023

Major Shareholder - Arshil Abdulla, Fayaz Abdulla and Shaneef Mitha collectively held 34.1% interest, Roger V. Hardy held 32.1% interest and Sabrina Liak held 12.3% interest at Apr. 26, 2023.

Price Range - KITS/TSX

Year	Volume	High	Low	Close
2022	3,314,241	$3.05	$1.97	$2.68
2021	12,686,860	$10.20	$2.39	$2.90

Recent Close: $5.00

Capital Stock Changes - During 2022, 160,072 common shares were issued on vesting of restricted share units.

Wholly Owned Subsidiaries

Kits.com Technologies Inc., Richmond, B.C.

Financial Statistics

Periods ended:	12m Dec. 31/22[A]		12m Dec. 31/21[oA]
	$000s	%Chg	$000s
Operating revenue	**91,639**	**+11**	**82,403**
Cost of sales	62,392		61,512
General & admin expense	21,063		24,805
Other operating expense	12,582		11,467
Operating expense	**21,063**	**-78**	**97,784**
Operating income	**70,576**	**n.a.**	**(15,381)**
Deprec., depl. & amort.	2,298		2,377
Finance costs, net	1,524		1,798
Pre-tax income	**(5,876)**	**n.a.**	**(18,843)**
Income taxes	(1,324)		(4,226)
Net income	**(4,552)**	**n.a.**	**(14,617)**
Cash & equivalent	18,790		20,505
Inventories	16,414		13,485
Accounts receivable	897		440
Current assets	36,998		35,711
Fixed assets, net	2,828		3,423
Right-of-use assets	7,209		7,511
Intangibles, net	41,708		40,747
Total assets	**93,865**	**+3**	**90,944**
Accts. pay. & accr. liabs	16,809		10,298
Current liabilities	24,440		16,822
Long-term debt, gross	13,141		16,086
Long-term debt, net	10,042		13,035
Long-term lease liabilities	5,674		6,302
Shareholders' equity	53,709		54,785
Cash from oper. activs	**4,677**	**n.a.**	**(19,461)**
Cash from fin. activs	(5,128)		41,478
Cash from invest. activs	(258)		(3,633)
Net cash position	**18,790**	**-8**	**20,505**
Capital expenditures	(258)		(3,633)
	$		$
Earnings per share*	(0.15)		(0.49)
Cash flow per share*	0.15		(0.65)
	shs		shs
No. of shs. o/s*	31,316,452		31,156,380
Avg. no. of shs. o/s*	31,274,298		30,125,772
	%		%
Net profit margin	(4.97)		(17.74)
Return on equity	(8.39)		n.m.
Return on assets	(4.93)		(20.08)
Foreign sales percent	69		73
No. of employees (FTEs)	115		95

* Common
[o] Restated
[A] Reported in accordance with IFRS

Historical Summary
(as originally stated)

Fiscal Year	Oper. Rev.	Net Inc. Bef. Disc.	EPS*
	$000s	$000s	$
2022[A]	91,639	(4,552)	(0.15)
2021[A]	82,403	(14,617)	(0.49)
2020[A1]	75,217	(6,583)	(0.72)
2019[A1]	36,897	53	0.01

* Common
[A] Reported in accordance with IFRS
[1] Shares and per share figures adjusted to reflect 2.3-for-1 share split effective Dec. 14, 2020.

K.24 Kiwetinohk Energy Corp.

Symbol - KEC **Exchange** - TSX **CUSIP** - 49836K
Head Office - 1700-250 2 St SW, Calgary, AB, T2P 0C1 **Telephone** - (587) 392-4396 **Fax** - (587) 392-4425
Website - kiwetinohk.com
Email - jbrogowski@kiwetinohk.com
Investor Relations - Jakub Brogowski (587) 999-3905
Auditors - Deloitte LLP C.A., Calgary, Alta.
Transfer Agents - Computershare Trust Company of Canada Inc.
FP500 Revenue Ranking - 396
Employees - 78 at Dec. 31, 2022

Profile - (Can. 2021; orig. Alta., 2018) Explores for, develops and produces oil and gas, with a focus on gas, as well as developing solar and gas-fired power projects, all in Alberta.

Upstream operations are primarily focused in the Fox Creek region of northwestern Alberta, and has land and smaller operations in the Thorhild Radway and west central Alberta regions.

At Dec. 31, 2022, the company had 211 gross (198.6 net) producing gas wells, 18 gross (12 net) producing oil wells, 225 gross (113.3 net) non-producing gas wells and 83 gross (44.7 net) non-producing oil wells; and undeveloped and developed land holdings totaled 219,263 and 118,829 net acres, respectively. During 2022, 12 development gas wells were drilled.

Developing seven solar and gas-fired power projects, consisting of the 400-MW Homestead (Solar 1) project near Claresholm; the 350-MW Granum (Solar 2) project; the 170-MW Phoenix (Solar 3) project near Red Deer; the 101-MW Opal gas-fired (firm renewable 1) project located immediately south of Fox Creek, with a carbon capture pilot; the

124-MW Little Flipi gas-fired (firm renewable 2) project; and two natural gas combined cycle projects totaling 1,000 MW.

Also investigating power generation and/or hydrogen production in the Chicago, Ill., area where the company currently ships 120,000 mcf per day of natural gas; hydrogen production in Alberta; manufacturing of ammonia; and providing its product and services to other co-located business.

Periods ended:	12m Dec. 31/22	12m Dec. 31/21
Avg. oil prod., bbl/d	6,197[1]	486
Avg. NGL prod., bbl/d	2,012	3,824
Avg. gas prod., mcf/d	57,859	32,942
Avg. BOE prod., bbl/d	17,852	9,801
Avg. light oil price, $/bbl	n.a.	82.46
Avg. heavy oil price, $/bbl	n.a.	59.22
Avg. oil price, US$/bbl	115.82[1]	n.a.
Avg. NGL price, $/bbl	74.06	52.6
Avg. gas price, $/mcf	8.69	5.29
Avg. BOE price, $/bbl	76.72	51.06
Oil reserves, net, mbbl	1,187	1,642
NGL reserves, net, mbbl	12,002	11,612
Gas reserves, net, mmcf	648,932	517,469

[1] Includes condensate.

Recent Merger and Acquisition Activity

Status: completed **Revised:** Sept. 15, 2022

UPDATE: The transaction was completed for $58,300,000. PREVIOUS: Kiwetinohk Energy Corp. agreed to acquire an additional 28.5% working interest in Montney assets in the Placid area of Alberta for $61,400,000. The acquisition includes 1,200 boe per day of current Montney production and increases the Kiwetinohk's Placid area natural gas processing and condensate handing capacity to 100 mmcf per day and 5,000 bbl per day, respectively. The transaction was expected to close on Sept. 15, 2022.

Status: completed **Announced:** May 18, 2022

Kiwetinohk Energy Corp. acquired an early stage 150-300 MW solar development project (Solar 3) in Alberta for $9,000,000 cash, of which $2,500,000 was paid on closing with the remaining balances contingent on certain milestones.

Predecessor Detail - Name changed from Kiwetinohk Resources Corp., Sept. 22, 2021, following the acquisition of the remaining 50% interest in Distinction Energy Corp.

Directors - Kevin J. Brown, chr., Calgary, Alta.; Patrick B. (Pat) Carlson, CEO, Calgary, Alta.; Judith J. Athaide, Calgary, Alta.; Colin Bergman, Calgary, Alta.; Leland P. Corbett, Calgary, Alta.; Kaush Rakhit, Calgary, Alta.; Beth Reimer-Heck, Calgary, Alta.; Steven W. (Steve) Sinclair, Calgary, Alta.; John K. Whelen, Calgary, Alta.

Other Exec. Officers - J. Michael (Mike) Backus, COO, upstream; Jakub Brogowski, CFO; Janet E. Annesley, chief sustainability officer; Sue Kuethe, exec. v-p, land & community inclusion; Michael A. (Mike) Hantzsch, sr. v-p, midstream & market devel.; Lisa Wong, sr. v-p, bus. sys.; Tim Alberts, v-p, prod.; Frank Angyal, v-p, drilling; Mike Carlson, v-p, completions; Shelley Leggitt, v-p, geoscience; Chris Lina, v-p, projects; Lyle Strom, v-p, petroleum mktg.; Kevin Nielsen, contr.

Capital Stock

	Authorized (shs.)	Outstanding (shs.)[1]
Preferred	unlimited	nil
Common	unlimited	44,097,217

[1] At May 2, 2023

Normal Course Issuer Bid - The company plans to make normal course purchases of up to 2,209,159 common shares representing 5% of the total outstanding. The bid commenced on Dec. 22, 2022, and expires on Dec. 21, 2023.

Major Shareholder - ARC Financial Corp. held 62.3% interest and Luminus Energy IE DAC held 11.8% interest at Mar. 27, 2023.

Price Range - KEC/TSX

Year	Volume	High	Low	Close
2022	6,116,081	$18.92	$11.09	$14.57

Recent Close: $12.82

Capital Stock Changes - During 2022, 508,598 common shares were issued on exercise of options and 6,471 common shares were repurchased under a Normal Course Issuer Bid.

Wholly Owned Subsidiaries

Kiwetinohk Marketing US Corp., Del.

Financial Statistics

Periods ended:	12m Dec. 31/22[A]		12m Dec. 31/21[A]
	$000s	%Chg	$000s
Operating revenue	**724,296**	**+161**	**277,659**
Cost of sales	63,204		29,272
Exploration expense	8,255		56,238
General & admin expense	239,984		120,362
Stock-based compensation	11,270		14,472
Other operating expense	34,628		18,193
Operating expense	**357,341**	**+50**	**238,537**
Operating income	**366,955**	**+838**	**39,122**
Deprec., depl. & amort.	83,214		30,203
Finance costs, gross	9,493		4,585
Investment income	nil		19,618
Pre-tax income	**167,318**	**n.a.**	**(32,126)**
Income taxes	(23,671)		(9,811)
Net income	**190,989**	**n.a.**	**(22,315)**
Net inc. for equity hldrs	**190,989**	**n.a.**	**(41,511)**
Net inc. for non-cont. int	**nil**	**n.a.**	**19,196**
Cash & equivalent	nil		2,343
Inventories	7		nil
Accounts receivable	79,847		43,179
Current assets	96,062		47,557
Fixed assets, net	790,746		534,707
Explor./devel. properties	nil		29,604
Total assets	**932,650**	**+52**	**614,337**
Accts. pay. & accr. liabs	77,048		54,397
Current liabilities	110,300		92,316
Long-term debt, gross	119,199		32,868
Long-term debt, net	119,199		32,868
Long-term lease liabilities	11,162		nil
Shareholders' equity	600,619		397,434
Cash from oper. activs	**242,850**	**+578**	**35,820**
Cash from fin. activs	85,502		177,437
Cash from invest. activs	(330,152)		(265,390)
Net cash position	**nil**	**n.a.**	**2,343**
Capital expenditures	(255,962)		(48,431)
Capital disposals	4,358		nil
	$		$
Earnings per share*	4.34		(0.70)
Cash flow per share*	5.51		1.13
	shs		shs
No. of shs. o/s*	44,176,710		43,674,583
Avg. no. of shs. o/s*	44,046,000		31,689,000
	%		%
Net profit margin	26.37		(8.04)
Return on equity	38.27		(14.73)
Return on assets	26.09		(4.86)
No. of employees (FTEs)	78		67

* Common

[A] Reported in accordance with IFRS

Latest Results

Periods ended:	3m Mar. 31/23[A]		3m Mar. 31/22[A]
	$000s	%Chg	$000s
Operating revenue	127,201	-4	132,425
Net income	70,557	n.a.	(24,552)
	$		$
Earnings per share*	1.22		(0.56)

* Common

[A] Reported in accordance with IFRS

Historical Summary
(as originally stated)

Fiscal Year	Oper. Rev.	Net Inc. Bef. Disc.	EPS*
	$000s	$000s	$
2022[A]	724,296	190,989	4.34
2021[A]	277,659	(22,315)	(0.70)
2020[A]	9,154	(4,869)	(0.04)

* Common

[A] Reported in accordance with IFRS

K.25 Klimat X Developments Inc.

Symbol - KLX **Exchange** - TSX-VEN **CUSIP** - 49863L

Head Office - 390-1050 Homer St, Vancouver, BC, V6C 2W9 **Telephone** - (778) 373-3736

Website - www.klimatx.com

Email - james.tansey@klimatx.com

Investor Relations - Dr. James Tansey (604) 562-4546

Auditors - BDO Canada LLP C.A., Calgary, Alta.

Transfer Agents - Odyssey Trust Company, Vancouver, B.C.

Profile - (B.C. 2018; orig. B.C., 1963) Developing validated and verified carbon credits from afforestation and reforestation of degraded land areas in Sierra Leone, Guyana, Suriname and Mexico, for sale into international voluntary carbon markets.

The company plans to acquire, develop, own and operate a portfolio of agroforestry and carbon assets.

Holds rights in Sierra Leone to a minimum of 51% of the carbon credits to be generated by **Rewilding Maforki Ltd.** from its planned project being developed on 60,000 hectares of land within the Maforki Chiefdom.

Holds 74% interest in **Pomeroon Trading (Holdings) Ltd.**, which has coconut farms in Guyana and plans to develop a coconut water processing facility powered with renewable energy that was expected to generate carbon offset credits.

Holds exclusive rights to develop forest and mangrove carbon credit projects covering 100,000 hectares within the State of Yucatan, Mexico, alongside the Government of the State of Yucatan. Has the right to 5% of the net value of the carbon credits successfully sold.

On Apr. 25, 2023, the company signed an agreement with the government of Suriname to develop mangrove carbon credit and agroforestry projects; it would conduct fieldwork to establish project size and feasibility.

On June 29, 2022, the company completed a change of business transaction which included the following: acquisition of 74% interest in **Pomeroon Trading (Holdings) Ltd.**, which carries on the business of sustainable agriculture, including the rehabilitation of coconut estates, for $981,300 cash and issuance of 9,917,575 common shares valued at $1,399,298; assignment from **Rewilding Maforki Ltd.** of 51% of the carbon credits and timber revenues from its Maforki project in Sierra Leone for issuance of 7,500,000 common shares valued at $1,050,000; and an assignment from **Compania Mexicana de Captacion de Carbono** of all its rights and interests to develop and market carbon credits under its existing contract with the Government of the State of Yucatan, Mexico, for $50,000.

Predecessor Detail - Name changed from Earl Resources Limited, June 29, 2022, pursuant to a change of business to carbon credits.

Directors - Dr. James Tansey, CEO, Vancouver, B.C.; Neil Passmore, dir., corp. devel., London, Middx., United Kingdom; Abayomi Akinjide, London, Middx., United Kingdom; Celia Francis, London, Middx., United Kingdom

Other Exec. Officers - Matthew (Matt) Roma, CFO & corp. sec.; Kevin Godlington, dir., opers.

Capital Stock

	Authorized (shs.)	Outstanding (shs.)[1]
Common	unlimited	86,222,661

[1] At May 29, 2023

Major Shareholder - Dr. James Tansey held 11.58% interest, Neil Passmore held 10.65% interest and Kevin Godlington held 10.19% interest at Apr. 6, 2023.

Price Range - KLX/TSX-VEN

Year	Volume	High	Low	Close
2022	6,447,233	$0.25	$0.10	$0.16
2021	1,276,758	$0.55	$0.34	$0.45
2020	2,385,406	$0.40	$0.09	$0.37
2019	52,583	$0.15	$0.12	$0.15
2018	313,082	$0.53	$0.12	$0.12

Recent Close: $0.14

Capital Stock Changes - Pursuant to the change of business transaction completed on June 29, 2022, common shares were issued as follows: 9,915,625 on acquisition of 65% interest in Pomeroon Trading (Holdings) Ltd., 7,500,000 related to assignment of carbon credits on Maforki project in Sierra Leone and 7,250,000 for Yucatan carbon credits contract. Concurrently, common shares were issued as follows: 21,705,127 without further consideration on exchange of subscription receipts sold previously by private placement at 45¢ each, 807,588 in settlement of accounts payable and 553,921 as finders' fees.

Subsidiaries

74% int. in **Pomeroon Trading (Holdings) Limited**, Cayman Islands.
- 100% int. in **Pomeroon Suriname N.V.**, Suriname.
- 100% int. in **Pomeroon Trading Inc.**, Guyana.

Financial Statistics

Periods ended:	12m Dec. 31/22[A]		12m Dec. 31/21[A]
	$000s	%Chg	$000s
Operating revenue	**69**	**n.a.**	**nil**
Cost of sales	173		nil
General & admin expense	3,437		547
Stock-based compensation	1,221		1,522
Operating expense	**4,658**	**+125**	**2,069**
Operating income	**(4,589)**	**n.a.**	**(2,069)**
Deprec., depl. & amort.	61		nil
Finance costs, gross	135		nil
Pre-tax income	**(4,873)**	**n.a.**	**(2,069)**
Net income	**(4,873)**	**n.a.**	**(2,069)**
Net inc. for equity hldrs	**(4,750)**	**n.a.**	**(2,069)**
Net inc. for non-cont. int.	**(123)**	**n.a.**	**nil**
Cash & equivalent	2,319		165
Accounts receivable	75		nil
Current assets	2,667		166
Fixed assets, net	381		nil
Right-of-use assets	4,728		nil
Total assets	**11,907**	**n.m.**	**166**
Accts. pay. & accr. liabs	787		287
Current liabilities	918		335
Long-term debt, gross	297		nil
Long-term debt, net	297		nil
Long-term lease liabilities	1,428		nil
Shareholders' equity	8,553		(170)
Non-controlling interest	710		nil
Cash from oper. activs	**(4,037)**	**n.a.**	**(353)**
Cash from fin. activs	9,469		nil
Cash from invest. activs	(3,278)		165
Net cash position	**2,319**	**n.m.**	**165**
	$		$
Earnings per share*	(0.08)		(0.05)
Cash flow per share*	(0.06)		(0.01)
	shs		shs
No. of shs. o/s*	86,222,661		38,490,400
Avg. no. of shs. o/s*	63,099,902		38,490,400
	%		%
Net profit margin	n.m.		n.a.
Return on equity	n.m.		n.m.
Return on assets	(78.49)		(604.97)

* Common
[A] Reported in accordance with IFRS

Latest Results

Periods ended:	3m Mar. 31/23[A]		3m Mar. 31/22[A]
	$000s	%Chg	$000s
Operating revenue	46	n.a.	nil
Net income	(887)	n.a.	(326)
Net inc. for equity hldrs.	(819)	n.a.	(326)
Net inc. for non-cont. int.	(68)		nil
	$		$
Earnings per share*	(0.01)		(0.01)

* Common
[A] Reported in accordance with IFRS

Historical Summary
(as originally stated)

Fiscal Year	Oper. Rev.	Net Inc. Bef. Disc.	EPS*
	$000s	$000s	$
2022[A]	69	(4,873)	(0.08)
2021[A]	nil	(2,069)	(0.05)
2020[A]	nil	(75)	(0.00)
2019[A]	nil	(93)	(0.00)
2018[A]	nil	(132)	(0.00)

* Common
[A] Reported in accordance with IFRS

K.26 kneat.com, inc.

Symbol - KSI **Exchange** - TSX **CUSIP** - 498824
Head Office - Hawthorn House, Plassey Business Campus, Castletroy, Limerick, Ireland, V94 5F68 **Overseas Tel** - 353-61-203826
Website - www.kneat.com
Email - katie.keita@kneat.com
Investor Relations - Katie Keita (902) 706-9074
Auditors - KPMG LLP C.A., Montréal, Qué.
Transfer Agents - Computershare Trust Company of Canada Inc., Montréal, Qué.
Employees - 261 at Dec. 31, 2022
Profile - (Can. 2013) Designs, develops and supplies software for data and document management within regulated environments.

The company's product is Kneat Gx, a configurable, commercial off-the-shelf application focused on validation lifecycle management and testing within the life sciences industry, such as biotechnology, pharmaceutical and medical device manufacturing. Within the platform, users can author, review, approve, execute testing online, manage any exceptions and post approve final deliverables. Complete and comprehensively documented validation of processes, products, equipment and software is a significant and costly regulatory requirement in the life sciences industry. The Kneat Gx application provides a compliant digital solution that enables life science companies to become efficient and compliant with an automated process that has traditionally been manual, inefficient and paper-based.

Predecessor Detail - Name changed from Fortune Bay Corp., July 5, 2016.

Directors - Ian Ainsworth, chr., Toronto, Ont.; Edmund (Eddie) Ryan, pres. & CEO, Cork, Ireland; Kevin Fitzgerald, chief product officer, Ireland; Nutan Behki, Ottawa, Ont.; Wade K. Dawe, Halifax, N.S.; Carol A. Leaman, Kitchener, Ont.

Other Exec. Officers - Hugh Kavanagh, CFO; Brian Ahearne, CIO; Keith Holmes, chief tech. officer; Fiona McCarthy, chief people & culture officer; Jacob H. Michelsen, sr. v-p, global sales

Capital Stock

	Authorized (shs.)	Outstanding (shs.)[1]
Common	unlimited	77,692,911

[1] At May 9, 2023

Major Shareholder - BEEK Investments Limited held 17.4% interest at Apr. 18, 2023.

Price Range - KSI/TSX

Year	Volume	High	Low	Close
2022	7,063,834	$3.91	$2.16	$2.67
2021	10,071,001	$4.85	$2.32	$3.96
2020	14,380,604	$3.19	$1.05	$2.82
2019	9,173,195	$2.75	$0.93	$2.74
2018	3,691,192	$1.61	$0.68	$0.98

Recent Close: $3.09

Capital Stock Changes - During 2022, common shares were issued as follows: 258,964 on vesting of deferred share units, 219,566 on exercise of warrants and 206,305 on exercise of options.

Wholly Owned Subsidiaries

Kneat Solutions Limited, Ireland.
- 100% int. in **Kneat Solutions Inc.**, Norristown, Pa.

Financial Statistics

Periods ended:	12m Dec. 31/22[A]		12m Dec. 31/21[A]
	$000s	%Chg	$000s
Operating revenue	**23,749**	**+53**	**15,501**
Cost of sales	9,095		6,180
Research & devel. expense	10,992		8,326
General & admin expense	7,741		2,945
Operating expense	**16,835**	**-4**	**17,451**
Operating income	**6,914**	**n.a.**	**(1,950)**
Deprec., depl. & amort.	5,696		4,404
Finance income	3		6
Finance costs, gross	229		285
Pre-tax income	**(9,132)**	**n.a.**	**(9,838)**
Income taxes	17		21
Net income	**(9,148)**	**n.a.**	**(9,859)**
Cash & equivalent	12,282		21,563
Accounts receivable	8,915		6,079
Current assets	22,129		28,143
Fixed assets, net	7,807		8,480
Intangibles, net	19,365		13,443
Total assets	**50,406**	**-2**	**51,281**
Accts. pay. & accr. liabs	5,768		3,385
Current liabilities	16,974		10,192
Long-term debt, gross	nil		113
Long-term lease liabilities	6,503		6,864
Shareholders' equity	25,980		34,187
Cash from oper. activs	**2,994**	**+30**	**2,308**
Cash from fin. activs	(384)		21,200
Cash from invest. activs	(11,912)		(10,043)
Net cash position	**12,282**	**-43**	**21,563**
Capital expenditures	(332)		(646)
	$		$
Earnings per share*	(0.12)		(0.13)
Cash flow per share*	0.04		0.03
	shs		shs
No. of shs. o/s*	77,662,911		76,978,076
Avg. no. of shs. o/s*	77,444,009		74,114,534
	%		%
Net profit margin	(38.52)		(63.60)
Return on equity	(30.41)		(36.92)
Return on assets	(17.54)		(22.50)
No. of employees (FTEs)	261		165

* Common
[A] Reported in accordance with IFRS

Latest Results

Periods ended:	3m Mar. 31/23[A]		3m Mar. 31/22[A]
	$000s	%Chg	$000s
Operating revenue	7,965	+53	5,200
Net income	(2,474)	n.a.	(3,426)
	$		$
Earnings per share*	(0.03)		(0.04)

* Common
[A] Reported in accordance with IFRS

Historical Summary
(as originally stated)

Fiscal Year	Oper. Rev.	Net Inc. Bef. Disc.	EPS*
	$000s	$000s	$
2022[A]	23,749	(9,148)	(0.12)
2021[A]	15,501	(9,859)	(0.13)
2020[A]	7,422	(5,691)	(0.09)
2019[A]	3,950	(6,197)	(0.11)
2018[A]	1,307	(4,609)	(0.09)

* Common
[A] Reported in accordance with IFRS

K.27 Knight Therapeutics Inc.

Symbol - GUD **Exchange** - TSX **CUSIP** - 499053
Head Office - 1055-3400 boul de Maisonneuve O, Montréal, QC, H3Z 3B8 **Telephone** - (514) 484-4483 **Fax** - (514) 481-4116
Website - knighttx.com
Email - ssakhia@gud-knight.com
Investor Relations - Samira Sakhia (514) 678-8930
Auditors - Ernst & Young LLP C.A., Montréal, Qué.
Lawyers - Davies Ward Phillips & Vineberg LLP, Montréal, Qué.
Transfer Agents - Computershare Trust Company of Canada Inc.
FP500 Revenue Ranking - 571
Employees - 698 at Mar. 28, 2023
Profile - (Can. 2013) Acquires, licenses, markets and distributes innovative prescription and over-the-counter pharmaceutical products, consumer health products and medical devices.

Also acquires specialty pharmaceutical businesses in select international markets, develops specialty therapeutics that are in late stage development and finances other life sciences companies in Canada and internationally.

Prescription pharmaceutical product portfolio includes Nerlynx®, tafasitamab (sold as Monjuvi® in the U.S. and Minjuvi® in Europe), pemigatinib (Pemazyre®), Akynzeo®, Aloxi®, fostamatinib, Trelstar®, Vidaza®, Abraxane®, Halaven®, Lenvima®, Ladevina®, Zyvalix®, Karfib®, Leprid®, Rembre®, Palbocil®, Ambisome®, Cresemba®, Impavido®, Dolufevir®, Exelon®, Ibsrela™, Salofalk®, Ursofalk®, Imvexxy™, Bijuva™, Fibridoner®, Toliscrin® DPI, Toliscrin® 1-2, and Tobradosa Haler®, Advaxis family, Antibe family, 60P family and Triumvira family.

Consumer health product which include Neuragen®, Synergy family and Crescita family of products. Medical device portfolio includes Profound family.

Directors - Jonathan R. Goodman, founder & exec. chr., Montréal, Qué.; Samira Sakhia, pres. & CEO, Montréal, Qué.; James C. Gale†, New York, N.Y.; Robert N. Lande, New York, N.Y.; Janice Murray, Beaconsfield, Qué.; Nicolás Sujoy, Buenos Aires, Argentina; Michael J. Tremblay, Ont.

Other Exec. Officers - Arvind Utchanah, CFO; Amal Khouri, chief bus. officer; Leopoldo Bosano, v-p, mfg. & opers.; Susan Emblem, v-p, HR; Jeff Martens, v-p, comml.; Monica Percario, v-p, scientific affairs; Stephani Saverio, v-p, bus. devel.

† Lead director

Capital Stock

	Authorized (shs.)	Outstanding (shs.)[1]
Common	unlimited	107,177,220

[1] At June 30, 2023

Normal Course Issuer Bid - The company plans to make normal course purchases of up to 5,999,524 common shares representing 10% of the public float. The bid commenced on July 14, 2023, and expires on July 13, 2024.

Major Shareholder - Jonathan R. Goodman held 20.2% interest at Mar. 22, 2023.

Price Range - GUD/TSX

Year	Volume	High	Low	Close
2022	40,575,561	$6.20	$5.03	$5.18
2021	82,534,044	$5.86	$4.88	$5.30
2020	91,417,937	$8.12	$4.73	$5.35
2019	75,614,640	$8.88	$7.10	$7.58
2018	35,483,336	$8.81	$7.38	$7.69

Recent Close: $4.58

Capital Stock Changes - During 2022, 71,939 common shares were issued under share purchase plan and 5,649,189 common shares were repurchased under a Normal Course Issuer Bid.

Wholly Owned Subsidiaries

Abir Therapeutics Ltd., Israel.
Biotoscana Investments S.A., Luxembourg.
- 100% int. in **Biotoscana Colveh 4 S.A.S**, Colombia.
- 100% int. in **Biotoscana Colveh 1 S.A.S**, Colombia.
- 100% int. in **Biotoscana Colveh 3 S.A.S**, Colombia.
- 100% int. in **Biotoscana Colveh 2 S.A.S**, Colombia.
- 100% int. in **Biotoscana Ecuador S.A.**, Ecuador.
- 100% int. in **Biotoscana Farma de Perú S.A.C.**, Peru.
- 100% int. in **Biotoscana Farma S.A.**, Argentina.
- 100% int. in **Biotoscana Farma S.A.**, Colombia.
- 100% int. in **Biotoscana Uruguay S.A.**, Uruguay.
- 100% int. in **GBT - Grupo Biotoscana S.A.**, Uruguay.
- 100% int. in **Grupo Biotoscana Costa Rica S.R.L.**, Costa Rica.
- 100% int. in **Grupo Biotoscana de Especialidad S.A. de C.V.**, Mexico.
- 100% int. in **Grupo Biotoscana Panamá S.A.**, Panama.
- 100% int. in **Grupo Biotoscana S.L.U.**, Spain.
- 100% int. in **LKM Laboratories Ecuador S.A.**, Ecuador.
- 100% int. in **Laboratoria LKM Chile S.p.A.**, Chile.

- 100% int. in **Laboratorio Biotoscana Farma Ltda.**, Chile.
- 100% int. in **Laboratorio LKM Bolivia S.A.**, Bolivia.
- 100% int. in **Laboratorio LKM Paraguay S.A.**, Paraguay.
- 100% int. in **Laboratorio LKM S.A.**, Argentina.
- 100% int. in **Latin American Pharma Company ETVE S.L.U.**, Spain.
- 100% int. in **United Medical Distribution Ltda.**, Brazil.
- 100% int. in **United Medical Ltda.**, Brazil.

Knight Therapeutics Europe S.A., Luxembourg.
Knight Therapeutics International S.A., Uruguay.
Knight Therapeutics (USA) Inc., Del.
11718991 Canada Inc., Canada.

Note: The preceding list includes only the major related companies in which interests are held.

Financial Statistics

Periods ended:	12m Dec. 31/22[A]		12m Dec. 31/21[A]
	$000s	%Chg	$000s
Operating revenue	**293,563**	**+21**	**243,478**
Cost of sales	144,623		121,327
Research & devel. expense	14,755		12,692
General & admin expense	88,624		74,376
Operating expense	**248,002**	**+19**	**208,395**
Operating income	**45,561**	**+30**	**35,083**
Deprec., depl. & amort.	62,621		47,915
Finance income	10,632		7,382
Finance costs, gross	6,600		3,618
Pre-tax income	**(43,960)**	**n.a.**	**6,690**
Income taxes	(14,068)		(8,985)
Net income	**(29,892)**	**n.a.**	**15,675**
Cash & equivalent	157,505		149,502
Inventories	92,489		72,397
Accounts receivable	107,820		60,444
Current assets	395,619		304,969
Long-term investments	147,573		156,464
Fixed assets, net	16,806		25,265
Right-of-use assets	5,827		4,671
Intangibles, net	421,054		425,702
Total assets	**1,054,836**	**+6**	**991,891**
Accts. pay. & accr. liabs	106,061		65,309
Current liabilities	141,321		105,302
Long-term debt, gross	70,072		35,927
Long-term debt, net	52,398		9,265
Long-term lease liabilities	5,050		3,417
Shareholders' equity	825,857		842,018
Cash from oper. activs	**40,481**	**-9**	**44,618**
Cash from fin. activs	1,762		(78,310)
Cash from invest. activs	(63,079)		(105,279)
Net cash position	**71,679**	**-17**	**85,963**
Capital expenditures	(2,885)		(3,832)
	$		$
Earnings per share*	(0.26)		0.13
Cash flow per share*	0.35		0.36
	shs		shs
No. of shs. o/s*	112,205,939		117,783,189
Avg. no. of shs. o/s*	114,890,252		124,480,259
	%		%
Net profit margin	(10.18)		6.44
Return on equity	(3.58)		1.81
Return on assets	(2.48)		2.38
Foreign sales percent	96		97

* Common
[A] Reported in accordance with IFRS

Historical Summary
(as originally stated)

Fiscal Year	Oper. Rev.	Net Inc. Bef. Disc.	EPS*
	$000s	$000s	$
2022[A]	293,563	(29,892)	(0.26)
2021[A]	243,478	15,675	0.13
2020[A]	199,519	31,760	0.32
2019[A]	47,461	18,033	0.10
2018[A]	12,500	24,079	0.17

* Common
[A] Reported in accordance with IFRS

K.28 Koios Beverage Corp.

Symbol - FIT **Exchange** - CSE **CUSIP** - 500271
Head Office - 810-789 Pender St W, Vancouver, BC, V6C 1H2 **Toll-free** - (844) 255-6467
Website - www.koiosbeveragecorp.com
Email - chris@koiosbeveragecorp.com
Investor Relations - Christopher Miller (604) 283-1722
Auditors - Dale Matheson Carr-Hilton LaBonte LLP C.A., Vancouver, B.C.
Lawyers - K MacInnes Law Group, Vancouver, B.C.
Transfer Agents - TSX Trust Company, Vancouver, B.C.
Profile - (B.C. 2012 amalg.) Develops, manufactures, packages, markets and distributes branded nutritional supplements and organic beverages.

Focuses on producing nutritional beverage drinks which use a proprietary blend of nootropics, which are supplements or other substances that improve cognitive functions, and natural organic compounds to enhance focus, concentration, mental capacity, memory retention, alertness, brain capacity and create all day mental clarity without using harmful chemicals or stimulants. Ingredients specifically target brain function by increasing blood flow, oxygen levels and neural connections in the brain. Products include nootropic supplement powder, nootropic beverages, Fit Sodas™, specialty ground coffee and supplement stick packs. Products are distributed on a network of more than 4,400 retail locations across the U.S., including UNFI, Europa Sports, McLane, Muscle Foods USA, KeHe and Wishing-U-Well under KOIOS™ and Fit Soda™ brands.

In addition, 50%-owned **Bevcreation LLC** operates a commercial-scale beverage canning facility in Denver, Colo., which packages the company's products as well as undertakes contract production work for other functional beverage brands.

On Apr. 25, 2022, the company acquired private **Retox Beverage Corp.**, which produces soft beverages, sodas and seltzers, for issuance of 15,000,000 units (1 common share & 1 warrant) at a deemed price of 10¢ per unit, with warrants exercisable at $0.175 per share for one year.

Common reinstated on CSE, Jan. 17, 2023.

Common suspended from CSE, Dec. 23, 2022.

Predecessor Detail - Name changed from Super Nova Petroleum Corp., Apr. 13, 2018, following reverse takeover acquisition of Koios, LLC.

Directors - Christopher (Chris) Miller, CEO & interim CFO, Denver, Colo.; Sherron Lewis, pres., opers., Colo.; Erik LeVang, Ark.; Josh Luman, Colo.

Capital Stock

	Authorized (shs.)	Outstanding (shs.)[1]
Common	unlimited	79,747,942

[1] At Jan. 30, 2023

Major Shareholder - Widely held at June 2, 2022.

Price Range - FIT/CSE

Year	Volume	High	Low	Close
2022	105,510,796	$0.75	$0.02	$0.03
2021	9,021,688	$1.90	$0.11	$0.20
2020	5,717,178	$2.35	$0.40	$0.50
2019	11,381,465	$9.40	$1.30	$1.35
2018	9,840,904	$10.50	$1.70	$3.00

Consolidation: 1-for-10 cons. in Oct. 2021
Recent Close: $0.04

Capital Stock Changes - In October 2022, private placement of 2,000,000 units (1 common share & 1 warrant) at 5¢ per unit was completed, with warrants exercisable at $0.075 per share for five years. In addition, 11,500,000 common shares were issued for debt settlement. In April 2023, private placement of 33,451,619 units (1 common share & 1 warrant) at 5¢ per unit was arranged, with warrants exercisable at 5¢ per share for five years.

On Oct. 18, 2021, common shares were consolidated on a 1-for-10 basis. In February 2022, private placement of 27,443,000 units (1 post-consolidated common share & 1 warrant) at Cdn$0.10 per unit was completed. On Apr. 25, 2022, 15,000,000 units (1 post-consolidated common share & 1 warrant) were issued pursuant to the acquisition of Retox Beverage Corp. Also during fiscal 2022, post-consolidated common shares were issued as follows: 6,598,823 on conversion of debenture, 5,350,000 on exercise of warrants, 3,000,000 for services and 172,662 for debt settlement.

Wholly Owned Subsidiaries

Cannavated Beverage Co., B.C.
Cannavated Beverage Corp., Nev.
Koios, Inc., United States.
Retox beverage Inc., Canada.

Investments

50% int. in **BevCreation LLC**, Colo.

Financial Statistics

Periods ended:	12m May 31/22[A]		12m May 31/21[A]
	US$000s	%Chg	US$000s
Operating revenue	**1,201**	**+87**	**641**
Cost of goods sold	1,160		793
General & admin expense	2,558		1,462
Stock-based compensation	16,253		344
Operating expense	**19,971**	**+668**	**2,599**
Operating income	**(18,770)**	**n.a.**	**(1,958)**
Deprec., depl. & amort.	56		42
Finance costs, gross	244		71
Investment income	41		(4)
Pre-tax income	**(21,160)**	**n.a.**	**(2,081)**
Net income	**(21,160)**	**n.a.**	**(2,081)**
Cash & equivalent	1,313		1,029
Inventories	543		167
Accounts receivable	156		59
Current assets	2,293		1,355
Long-term investments	86		45
Fixed assets, net	90		157
Total assets	**2,505**	**+61**	**1,557**
Bank indebtedness	94		16
Accts. pay. & accr. liabs	1,199		495
Current liabilities	1,573		1,282
Long-term debt, gross	3		519
Shareholders' equity	915		207
Cash from oper. activs	**(2,439)**	**n.a.**	**(1,381)**
Cash from fin. activs	2,654		1,364
Cash from invest. activs	nil		(59)
Net cash position	**1,313**	**+28**	**1,029**
Capital expenditures	nil		(9)
	US$		US$
Earnings per share*	(1.00)		(0.30)
Cash flow per share*	(0.12)		(0.17)
	shs		shs
No. of shs. o/s*	66,247,942		8,683,468
Avg. no. of shs. o/s*	20,960,561		8,072,628
	%		%
Net profit margin	n.m.		(324.65)
Return on equity	(3,771.84)		(518.95)
Return on assets	n.m.		(134.67)

* Common
[A] Reported in accordance with IFRS

Latest Results

Periods ended:	6m Nov. 30/22[A]		6m Nov. 30/21[A]
	US$000s	%Chg	US$000s
Operating revenue	517	+12	462
Net income	(4,700)	n.a.	(939)
	US$		US$
Earnings per share*	(0.07)		(0.01)

* Common
[A] Reported in accordance with IFRS

Historical Summary
(as originally stated)

Fiscal Year	Oper. Rev.	Net Inc. Bef. Disc.	EPS*
	US$000s	US$000s	US$
2022[A]	1,201	(21,160)	(1.00)
2021[A]	641	(2,081)	(0.30)
2020[A]	872	(2,999)	(0.40)
2019[A]	242	(3,126)	(1.60)
2018[A1]	nil	(4,017)	(1.60)

* Common
[A] Reported in accordance with IFRS
[1] Results reflect the Apr.13, 2018, reverse takeover of Koios, Inc.
Note: Adjusted throughout for 1-for-10 cons. in Oct. 2021

K.29 Komo Plant Based Foods Inc.

Symbol - YUM **Exchange** - CSE **CUSIP** - 50046B
Head Office - 1605 5 Ave W, Vancouver, BC, V6J 1N5 **Toll-free** - (866) 969-0882
Website - komocomfortfoods.com
Email - will@komoeats.com
Investor Relations - William White (866) 969-0882
Auditors - Saturna Group Chartered Accountants LLP C.A., Vancouver, B.C.
Transfer Agents - Endeavor Trust Corporation, Vancouver, B.C.
Profile - (B.C. 2010) Develops, manufactures, markets and sells a variety of plant-based frozen and fresh meals.

Frozen plant-based products include ready-to-bake lasagnas, shepherd's pies and chickenless pot pies, and a line of meal starters consisting of bolognese sauces and taco fillings. Products are sold through the company's and third party e-commerce platforms, wholesale distribution network and brick-and-mortar retailer channels in Canada and the U.S. The products are available in 790 retail locations including Loblaws, Safeway, IGA, Metro, Thrifty Foods, Whole Foods Market, Foodland, Fresh St. Market, Choices, Stong's Market, Country

Grocer, Nestors, Nature's Fare Market, Foodland, Aisle24, Goodness Me!, Nature's Emporium, Ambrosia, Highland Farms, La Boite à Grains, Pasquier and Fairway Market.

Also offers Komo Eats, which sells freshly made, ready-to-eat plant-based meals, including mac and cheese bowls, vegan wraps and desserts, in Vancouver, B.C., through food delivery apps.

Predecessor Detail - Name changed from Fasttask Technologies Inc., June 1, 2021, pursuant to the reverse takeover acquisition of Komo Plant Based Comfort Foods Inc. (Komo Comfort) and concurrent amalgamation of Komo Comfort and wholly owned 1285877 B.C. Ltd.

Directors - William White, pres. & CEO, West Vancouver, B.C.; Daniel Kang, Calif.; Angelo Rajassoria, Port Coquitlam, B.C.

Other Exec. Officers - Yucai (Rick) Huang, CFO; Melissa Vettoretti, corp. sec.; Jeffrey Ma, pres. & CEO, Komo Plant Based Comfort Foods Inc.

Capital Stock

	Authorized (shs.)	Outstanding (shs.)[1]
Common	unlimited	9,707,102

[1] At Jan. 30, 2023

Major Shareholder - Widely held at June 3, 2021.

Price Range - YUM/CSE

Year	Volume	High	Low	Close
2022	2,890,876	$1.75	$0.25	$0.30
2021	9,411,779	$4.00	$0.75	$1.60
2020	586,751	$9.50	$0.50	$1.00
2019	205,557	$12.50	$4.00	$5.00

Consolidation: 1-for-10 cons. in Jan. 2023; 1-for-5 cons. in Dec. 2020

Recent Close: $0.06

Capital Stock Changes - On Jan. 30, 2023, common shares were consolidated on a 1-for-10 basis.

In February 2022, private placement of 7,008,625 units (1 common share & 1 warrant) at 14¢ per unit was completed. Also during fiscal 2022, common shares were issued as follows: 2,402,375 on exercise of warrants, 800,000 by private placement, 707,458 for debt settlement, 423,820 on conversion of debentures and 290,000 on exercise of options.

Wholly Owned Subsidiaries

FastTask Inc., Canada.
Komo Plant Based Comfort Foods Inc., Vancouver, B.C.
10758914 Canada Inc., Canada.

Financial Statistics

Periods ended:	12m July 31/22[A]		12m July 31/21[A1]
	$000s	%Chg	$000s
Operating revenue	**650**	**+932**	**63**
Cost of goods sold	430		35
Salaries & benefits	639		199
Research & devel. expense	61		43
General & admin expense	2,739		1,465
Stock-based compensation	914		441
Operating expense	**4,783**	**+119**	**2,184**
Operating income	**(4,133)**	**n.a.**	**(2,121)**
Deprec., depl. & amort.	16		9
Finance costs, gross	281		15
Write-downs/write-offs	nil		(29)
Pre-tax income	**(4,603)**	**n.a.**	**(6,457)**
Net inc. bef. disc. opers	**(4,603)**	**n.a.**	**(6,457)**
Income from disc. opers	nil		(15)
Net income	**(4,603)**	**n.a.**	**(6,472)**
Cash & equivalent	224		343
Inventories	92		18
Accounts receivable	260		174
Current assets	700		686
Fixed assets, net	26		19
Intangibles, net	34		34
Total assets	**761**	**+3**	**739**
Accts. pay. & accr. liabs	352		253
Current liabilities	786		401
Long-term debt, gross	nil		227
Long-term debt, net	1,243		97
Shareholders' equity	(1,269)		241
Cash from oper. activs	**(2,870)**	**n.a.**	**(1,827)**
Cash from fin. activs	2,778		1,351
Cash from invest. activs	(27)		783
Net cash position	**224**	**-35**	**342**
Capital expenditures	(27)		(15)
	$		$
Earnings per share*	(0.50)		(0.80)
Cash flow per share*	(0.31)		(0.23)
	shs		shs
No. of shs. o/s*	9,707,094		8,543,866
Avg. no. of shs. o/s*	9,193,016		7,818,308
	%		%
Net profit margin	(708.15)		n.m.
Return on equity	n.m.		n.m.
Return on assets	n.a.		n.m.

* Common
[A] Reported in accordance with IFRS
[1] Results reflect the June 7, 2021, reverse takeover acquisition of Komo Plant Based Comfort Foods Inc.

Latest Results

Periods ended:	3m Oct. 31/22[A]		3m Oct. 31/21[A]
	$000s	%Chg	$000s
Operating revenue	178	+89	94
Net income	(244)	n.a.	(1,778)
	$		$
Earnings per share*	(0.03)		(0.20)

* Common
[A] Reported in accordance with IFRS

Historical Summary
(as originally stated)

Fiscal Year	Oper. Rev.	Net Inc. Bef. Disc.	EPS*
	$000s	$000s	$
2022[A]	650	(4,603)	(0.50)
2021[A]	63	(6,457)	(0.80)
2020[A1]	19	(6,516)	(3.70)
2019[A]	18	(4,663)	(3.64)
2018[A]	1	(1,755)	(2.99)

* Common
[A] Reported in accordance with IFRS
[1] Results for 2020 and prior years pertain to Fasttask Technologies Inc.

Note: Adjusted throughout for 1-for-10 cons. in Jan. 2023; 1-for-5 cons. in Dec. 2020

K.30 Kontrol Technologies Corp.

Symbol - KNR **Exchange** - NEO **CUSIP** - 50050C
Head Office - 201-11 Cidermill Ave, Vaughan, ON, L4K 4B6 **Telephone** - (905) 766-0400 **Toll-free** - (844) 566-8123
Website - kontrolcorp.com
Email - paul@kontrolcorp.com
Investor Relations - Paul Ghezzi (844) 566-8123
Auditors - MNP LLP C.A., Burlington, Ont.
Lawyers - Purdy Law Professional Corporation, Toronto, Ont.
Transfer Agents - Computershare Trust Company of Canada Inc., Toronto, Ont.
Employees - 350 at Dec. 31, 2022

Profile - (Ont. 2021; orig. B.C., 2006) Provides green technology solutions and services in the areas of energy management, emission compliance and air quality to commercial, industrial and multi-residential buildings and facilities in the U.S. and Canada.

Products and services include the following:

Energy Management - Provides software solutions to analyze the management of heating, ventilation and cooling (HVAC) systems, design and engineering of improvements and/or retrofits, and ongoing mission critical services. Solutions include SmartMax Gateway, SmartSite® software for building HVAC control and optimization and SmartSuite® hardware and software for in-suite energy management. Also provides detailed energy efficiency analysis, energy audits, management of facility system solutions, electrical and mechanical design, energy conservation studies, monitoring operation and service of essential heating, cooling ventilation and utility systems, installations of complex HVAC and business automation systems.

Emission Compliance - Provides environmental and engineering services including stack emission testing, continuous emission testing, power generation, due diligence, odour assessment and analytics, compliance and other engineering services. Also provides emission monitoring solutions and services. Also offers Kontrol Carbon, a solution which supports commercial and industrial customers in the areas of green house gas (GHG) emission monitoring, management, and carbon credit monetization.

Air Quality - Offers BioCloud™, a non-medical device for the real-time detection of airborne viruses and pathogens with the use of detection chamber which uses both a viral collider and a chemical process to trap virus particles for identification.

Also developing BioWater, an extension of the BioCloud™ technology, for early viral detection in water systems.

In February 2023, the company's wholly owned **Global HVAC & Automation Inc.** filed for voluntary bankruptcy and ceased its operations.

In February 2023, the company entered into an exclusive negotiation with a European manufacturer of emission technology to establish a joint venture, which would distribute continuous emission technology across North America. The manufacturer operates globally with more than 30 years of history. Final documentation is expected to be completed in the first quarter of 2023 or early second quarter of 2023.

In October 2022, the company entered into a letter of intent to acquire Alta.-based building service and solutions company (target) for $3,500,000 cash and issuance of $500,000 in common shares. The undisclosed target company provides services in mechanical materials, heating and building retrofits for municipalities, property managers, developers and real estate investments trusts.

Predecessor Detail - Name changed from Kontrol Energy Corp., Jan. 25, 2021.

Directors - Paul Ghezzi, CEO, Vaughan, Ont.; Claudio Del Vasto, CFO, Ont.; Ernest W. (Ernie) Belyea, Ont.; Andrew Bowerbank, Ont.; Zhengquan (Philip) Chen, Toronto, Ont.; Joanna Osawe, Ont.; Joseph Ragusa, Ont.

Capital Stock

	Authorized (shs.)	Outstanding (shs.)[1]
Common	unlimited	55,203,659

[1] At Mar. 31, 2023

Major Shareholder - Paul Ghezzi held 10.6% interest at Mar. 31, 2023.

Price Range - KNR/NEO

Year	Volume	High	Low	Close
2022	1,479,900	$2.38	$0.35	$0.38
2021	29,286,850	$6.11	$0.82	$2.05
2020	58,878,540	$6.64	$0.22	$3.00
2019	7,717,679	$0.94	$0.45	$0.62
2018	4,414,161	$1.58	$0.46	$0.66

Recent Close: $0.27

Capital Stock Changes - In February 2023, private placement of 7,695,840 units (1 common share & 1 warrant) at 65¢ per unit was completed, with warrants exercisable at 81¢ per share for five years.

During 2022, common shares were issued as follows: 925,000 on conversion of debentures, 172,000 on exercise of options, 130,116 as share-based compensation, 130,000 under an at-the-market offering, 122,452 on exercise of warrants and 2,000 to debenture holders; 22,000 common shares were repurchased under a Normal Course Issued Bid.

Wholly Owned Subsidiaries

CEM Specialties Inc., London, Ont.
Efficiency Engineering Inc., Cambridge, Ont.
Kontrol BioCloud Inc., Ont.
Kontrol Energy Group Inc., Toronto, Ont.
New Found Air HVAC Services Inc., Stouffville, Ont.
Ortech Consulting Inc., Mississauga, Ont.

Financial Statistics

Periods ended:	12m Dec. 31/22[A]		12m Dec. 31/21[A]
	$000s	%Chg	$000s
Operating revenue	**89,392**	**+55**	**57,664**
Cost of sales	79,680		41,826
Salaries & benefits	14,405		8,224
General & admin expense	4,313		3,692
Stock-based compensation	493		1,409
Operating expense	**98,891**	**+79**	**55,151**
Operating income	**(9,499)**	**n.a.**	**2,513**
Deprec., depl. & amort.	1,871		1,328
Finance costs, gross	2,500		1,883
Write-downs/write-offs	(28,784)[1]		(154)
Pre-tax income	**(47,190)**	**n.a.**	**1,784**
Income taxes	(2,653)		759
Net income	**(44,537)**	**n.a.**	**1,026**
Cash & equivalent	1,981		3,263
Inventories	674		755
Accounts receivable	4,208		22,991
Current assets	7,421		34,631
Fixed assets, net	897		666
Right-of-use assets	1,171		877
Intangibles, net	13,927		20,557
Total assets	**23,416**	**-61**	**60,698**
Accts. pay. & accr. liabs	23,602		18,120
Current liabilities	42,304		30,949
Long-term debt, gross	15,479		5,979
Long-term debt, net	123		617
Long-term lease liabilities	692		499
Equity portion of conv. debs	2		7
Shareholders' equity	(23,871)		19,528
Cash from oper. activs	**(9,224)**	**n.a.**	**4,684**
Cash from fin. activs	8,471		4,684
Cash from invest. activs	(529)		(7,110)
Net cash position	**1,981**	**-39**	**3,263**
Capital expenditures	(387)		(175)
	$		$
Earnings per share*	(0.92)		0.02
Cash flow per share*	(0.19)		0.10
	shs		shs
No. of shs. o/s*	49,342,685		47,883,117
Avg. no. of shs. o/s*	48,601,483		45,002,226
	%		%
Net profit margin	(49.82)		1.78
Return on equity	n.m.		7.66
Return on assets	(100.29)		5.09
Foreign sales percent	2		4
No. of employees (FTEs)	350		350

* Common
[A] Reported in accordance with IFRS
[1] Pertains to the expected credit losses over the non-collection of accounts receivable related to the process of ceasing operations of wholly owned Global HVAC & Automation Inc.

Latest Results

Periods ended:	3m Mar. 31/23^A		3m Mar. 31/22^{□A}
	$000s	%Chg	$000s
Operating revenue	4,461	+36	3,282
Net inc. bef. disc. opers	(469)	n.a.	(1,059)
Income from disc. opers	(105)		2,700
Net income	(574)	n.a.	1,642
	$		$
Earnings per share*	(0.01)		(0.02)

* Common
□ Restated
A Reported in accordance with IFRS

Historical Summary
(as originally stated)

Fiscal Year	Oper. Rev. $000s	Net Inc. Bef. Disc. $000s	EPS* $
2022^A	89,392	(44,537)	(0.92)
2021^A	57,664	1,026	0.02
2020^A	12,350	(1,905)	(0.06)
2019^A	14,559	(2,690)	(0.09)
2018^A	10,727	(2,226)	(0.08)

* Common
A Reported in accordance with IFRS

K.31 Kovo Healthtech Corporation

Symbol - KOVO **Exchange** - TSX-VEN **CUSIP** - 50073R
Head Office - 1600-925 Georgia St W, Vancouver, BC, V6C 3L2
Toll-free - (866) 558-6777
Website - www.kovo.co
Email - investors@kovo.co
Investor Relations - Greg Noble (866) 539-0874
Auditors - SRCO Professional Corporation C.A., Richmond Hill, Ont.
Transfer Agents - Computershare Trust Company of Canada Inc.
Profile - (B.C. 2020) Provides software products and services primarily in revenue cycle management (RCM) and electronic health records to more than 1,700 United States healthcare providers.

The company acquires and grows U.S.-based RCM and other software businesses. Has four revenue streams consisting of recurring revenue from RCM businesses; licensing revenue from inpatient systems; Software-as-a-Service revenue for ambulatory and eHealth software; and revenue from associated services for the company's products including electronic claim process, eligibility for reimbursement verifications, and electronic remittance advice.

Directors - Dr. Peter Bak, exec. chr., Toronto, Ont.; Greg Noble, CEO, Evergreen, Colo.; Harp Gahunia, Toronto, Ont.

Other Exec. Officers - Inderjit (Inder) Saini, CFO & corp. sec.; Jonathan Marshall, chief mktg. officer; Jeana K. Noble, chief compliance officer; Mark Detz, sr. v-p, fin.

Capital Stock

	Authorized (shs.)	Outstanding (shs.)[1]
Common	unlimited	39,781,406

1 At Nov. 25, 2022

Major Shareholder - Jeana K. Noble held 34% interest and Dr. Peter Bak held 16% interest at June 30, 2022.

Price Range - KOVO/TSX-VEN

Year	Volume	High	Low	Close
2022	2,505,370	$0.39	$0.07	$0.12
2021	3,832,491	$1.15	$0.32	$0.39

Recent Close: $0.12

Wholly Owned Subsidiaries

Kovo Acquisitions LLC
Kovo Human Capital LLC, United States.
MedWorxs Inc., Evergreen, Colo.
- 100% int. in **NOC5280 LLC**, Colo.
- 100% int. in **RPM Billing LLC**, Nev.

Financial Statistics

Periods ended:	12m Dec. 31/21^A		12m Dec. 31/20^{□A}
	US$000s	%Chg	US$000s
Operating revenue	**5,904**	**+96**	**3,019**
Salaries & benefits	4,420		2,554
General & admin expense	1,980		892
Stock-based compensation	147		167
Operating expense	**6,547**	**+81**	**3,613**
Operating income	**(643)**	**n.a.**	**(594)**
Deprec., depl. & amort	589		445
Finance costs, gross	542		338
Pre-tax income	**(2,700)**	**n.a.**	**(1,199)**
Net income	**(2,700)**	**n.a.**	**(1,199)**
Cash & equivalent	711		153
Accounts receivable	155		73
Current assets	1,198		448
Right-of-use assets	604		132
Intangibles, net	5,342		2,604
Total assets	**7,334**	**+130**	**3,184**
Accts. pay. & accr. liabs	993		538
Current liabilities	3,469		1,675
Long-term debt, gross	4,271		2,332
Long-term debt, net	3,006		1,594
Long-term lease liabilities	366		95
Shareholders' equity	(170)		(614)
Cash from oper. activs	**(1,000)**	**n.a.**	**(461)**
Cash from fin. activs	2,954		579
Cash from invest. activs	(1,396)		(38)
Net cash position	**711**	**+365**	**153**
	US$		US$
Earnings per share*	(0.08)		(0.05)
Cash flow per share*	(0.03)		(0.02)
	shs		shs
No. of shs. o/s*	36,154,184		n.a.
Avg. no. of shs. o/s*	32,637,284		26,602,799
	%		%
Net profit margin	(45.73)		(39.72)
Return on equity	n.m.		n.m.
Return on assets	(41.03)		(48.47)

* Common
□ Restated
A Reported in accordance with IFRS

Latest Results

Periods ended:	6m June 30/22^A		6m June 30/21^A
	US$000s	%Chg	US$000s
Operating revenue	5,446	+211	1,751
Net income	(549)	n.a.	(892)
	US$		US$
Earnings per share*	(0.01)		(0.03)

* Common
A Reported in accordance with IFRS

Historical Summary
(as originally stated)

Fiscal Year	Oper. Rev. US$000s	Net Inc. Bef. Disc. US$000s	EPS* US$
2021^A	5,904	(2,700)	(0.08)
2020^{A1}	3,019	(1,199)	(0.05)
2019^A	1,769	9	0.00

* Common
A Reported in accordance with IFRS
1 Results for 2020 and prior periods pertain to MedWorxs Inc.

K.32 Kraken Robotics Inc.

Symbol - PNG **Exchange** - TSX-VEN **CUSIP** - 50077N
Head Office - 189 Glencoe Dr, Mount Pearl, NL, A1N 4P6 **Telephone** - (709) 757-5757 **Fax** - (709) 575-5858
Website - www.krakenrobotics.com
Email - jmackay@krakenrobotics.com
Investor Relations - Joseph MacKay (416) 303-0605
Auditors - KPMG LLP C.A., Toronto, Ont.
Lawyers - Gowling WLG (Canada) LLP, Toronto, Ont.
Transfer Agents - Computershare Trust Company of Canada Inc., Vancouver, B.C.
Employees - 211 at Dec. 31, 2022
Profile - (Can. 2015; orig. B.C., 2008) Designs, manufactures and sells subsea sensors, batteries and underwater robotics equipment used in military and commercial applications. Also offers high-resolution 3D acoustic imaging solutions for the sub-seabed.

Operations are organized into two operating segments: Products; and Services.

The **Products** segment involves the design, manufacture and sale of underwater sonar and laser scanner sensor equipment, underwater vehicle platforms and subsea power equipment. Products include AquaPix® INSAS, an Interferometric Synthetic Aperture Sonar; AquaPix® MINSAS, a Miniature Interferometric Synthetic Aperture Sonar; SeaVision®, an underwater laser imaging system; KATFISH™, an intelligent towed synthetic aperture sonar (SAS) system for manned or unmanned surface vessel for real-time 3D seabed mapping; Tentacle Winch®, which uses an integrated motion reference unit and intelligent control algorithms to measure both the surface vessel and vehicle motions to perform safe and effective deployment and recovery operations in harsh environments; and SeaScout®, an autonomous launch and recovery system (ALARS) which works with KATFISH™ to enable full unmanned launch and recovery operations; and SeaPower™ batteries, which are deep sea pressure-tolerant batteries.

The **Services** segment consists of services provided by Robotics-as-a-Service (RaaS) portfolio of equipment including the Sub-Bottom Imager™, Acoustic Corer™, KATFISH™, and SeaVision®.

Predecessor Detail - Name changed from Kraken Sonar Inc., Sept. 22, 2017.

Directors - Greg Reid, pres. & CEO, Toronto, Ont.; V-Adm. Michael J. Connor, Groton, Conn.; M. Shaun McEwan, Carp, Ont.; Bernard Mills, Ottawa, Ont.; Larry Puddister, N.L.

Other Exec. Officers - Joseph (Joe) MacKay, CFO & corp. sec.; Moya Cahill, exec. v-p, srvcs.; David Shea, exec. v-p, products & chief tech. officer

Capital Stock

	Authorized (shs.)	Outstanding (shs.)[1]
Common	unlimited	206,051,735

1 At May 29, 2023

Major Shareholder - Ocean Infinity Limited held 10.33% interest at May 9, 2023.

Price Range - PNG/TSX-VEN

Year	Volume	High	Low	Close
2022	28,331,750	$0.65	$0.27	$0.57
2021	68,959,138	$1.16	$0.34	$0.38
2020	57,395,287	$0.83	$0.28	$0.57
2019	52,455,710	$0.92	$0.38	$0.60
2018	51,569,562	$0.58	$0.15	$0.37

Recent Close: $0.45

Capital Stock Changes - In May 2023, share consolidation of between 1-for-2 and 1-for-7 was proposed.

During 2022, common shares were issued as follows: 326,250 on exercise of options and 5,000 on exercise of warrants.

Wholly Owned Subsidiaries

Kraken Robotics Systems Inc., N.L.
- 100% int. in **Kraken Power GmbH**, Germany.
- 100% int. in **Kraken Robotics Denmark ApS**, Denmark.
- 100% int. in **Kraken Robotics US Inc.**, Del.
- 100% int. in **Kraken Robotik GmbH**, Germany.
- 100% int. in **Ocean Discovery Inc.**, Canada.
- 100% int. in **13 Robotics Ltda.**, Brazil. operating as Kraken Robotics Brasil Ltda.

PGH Capital Inc., St. John's, N.L.
- 100% int. in **Kraken Robotics Services Ltd.**, N.L.
- 100% int. in **Kraken Robotics Services UK Limited**, N.L.

Financial Statistics

Periods ended:	12m Dec. 31/22^A		12m Dec. 31/21^A
	$000s	%Chg	$000s
Operating revenue	**40,908**	**+60**	**25,629**
Cost of sales	23,871		14,310
Research & devel. expense	1,262		2,310
General & admin expense	12,364		8,271
Stock-based compensation	797		433
Operating expense	**38,294**	**+51**	**25,324**
Operating income	**2,614**	**+757**	**305**
Deprec., depl. & amort.	4,781		2,914
Finance costs, gross	3,261		1,657
Pre-tax income	**(5,302)**	**n.a.**	**(3,643)**
Income taxes	(1,059)		(106)
Net income	**(4,243)**	**n.a.**	**(3,537)**
Cash & equivalent	8,265		6,754
Inventories	11,367		14,977
Accounts receivable	12,221		6,095
Current assets	37,827		31,724
Fixed assets, net	19,303		18,679
Intangibles, net	13,230		14,774
Total assets	**71,365**	**+9**	**65,465**
Bank indebtedness	6,366		4,943
Accts. pay. & accr. liabs.	11,220		10,667
Current liabilities	39,862		25,360
Long-term debt, gross	6,024		5,745
Long-term debt, net	938		5,514
Long-term lease liabilities	3,022		3,586
Shareholders' equity	23,655		27,602
Cash from oper. activs.	**5,237**	**n.a.**	**(11,006)**
Cash from fin. activs.	(41)		11,923
Cash from invest. activs.	(3,366)		(7,244)
Net cash position	**8,265**	**+22**	**6,754**
Capital expenditures	(5,144)		(5,498)
	$		$
Earnings per share*	(0.02)		(0.02)
Cash flow per share*	0.03		(0.06)
	shs		shs
No. of shs. o/s*	201,524,235		201,192,985
Avg. no. of shs. o/s*	201,214,585		182,459,224
	%		%
Net profit margin	(10.37)		(13.80)
Return on equity	(16.56)		(16.22)
Return on assets	(2.39)		(3.85)
Foreign sales percent	97		95
No. of employees (FTEs)	211		225

* Common
^A Reported in accordance with IFRS

Latest Results

Periods ended:	3m Mar. 31/23^A		3m Mar. 31/22^A
	$000s	%Chg	$000s
Operating revenue	7,578	+37	5,512
Net income	(1,336)	n.a.	(2,559)
	$		$
Earnings per share*	(0.01)		(0.01)

* Common
^A Reported in accordance with IFRS

Historical Summary
(as originally stated)

Fiscal Year	Oper. Rev.	Net Inc. Bef. Disc.	EPS*
	$000s	$000s	$
2022^A	40,908	(4,243)	(0.02)
2021^A	25,629	(3,537)	(0.02)
2020^A	12,275	(5,535)	(0.04)
2019^A	15,146	(3,003)	(0.02)
2018^A	6,708	(2,852)	(0.03)

* Common
^A Reported in accordance with IFRS

K.33 Kua Investments Inc.

Symbol - KUAI.P **Exchange** - TSX-VEN **CUSIP** - 50117A
Head Office - 909-510 Burrard St, Vancouver, BC, V6C 3A8 **Telephone** - (604) 895-7267
Email - derek.lew@growthworks.ca
Investor Relations - Derek Lew (604) 895-7267
Auditors - Dale Matheson Carr-Hilton LaBonte LLP C.A., Vancouver, B.C.
Lawyers - Richards Buell Sutton LLP, Vancouver, B.C.
Transfer Agents - Endeavor Trust Corporation, Vancouver, B.C.
Profile - (B.C. 2021) Capital Pool Company.
Directors - Derek Lew, CEO, Vancouver, B.C.; Olivia Edwards, B.C.; David Goldsmith, B.C.; Mark Rutledge, Vancouver, B.C.; Mark T. Tommasi, North Vancouver, B.C.
Other Exec. Officers - Mark Leung, CFO & corp. sec.

Capital Stock

	Authorized (shs.)	Outstanding (shs.)[1]
Common	unlimited	6,250,001

[1] At Mar. 31, 2022

Major Shareholder - Widely held at Mar. 31, 2022.

Price Range - KUAI.P/TSX-VEN

Year	Volume	High	Low	Close
2022	237,000	$0.20	$0.11	$0.15

Recent Close: $0.10
Capital Stock Changes - On Mar. 31, 2022, an initial public offering of 2,225,500 common shares was completed at 10¢ per share.

K.34 Kure Technologies, Inc.

Symbol - KUR.H **Exchange** - TSX-VEN **CUSIP** - 501282
Head Office - 2-120 Spinnaker Way, Concord, ON, L4K 2P6 **Telephone** - (416) 361-3121
Website - kuretechnologies.com
Email - irinfo@kuretechnologies.com
Investor Relations - Igor Keselman (905) 660-8100
Auditors - Dale Matheson Carr-Hilton LaBonte LLP C.A., Vancouver, B.C.
Lawyers - DeWitt Sedun, Vancouver, B.C.
Transfer Agents - TSX Trust Company, Toronto, Ont.
Profile - (Ont. 1998 amalg.) Seeking new business opportunities primarily in the connected intelligent device sector.
Common reinstated on TSX-VEN, May 11, 2023.
Common suspended from TSX-VEN, Jan. 9, 2023.
Predecessor Detail - Name changed from Unique Broadband Systems, Inc., Mar. 20, 2017; basis 1 new for 10 old shs.
Directors - Alex Dolgonos, chr. & interim CEO, Toronto, Ont.; Igor Keselman, interim CFO, Toronto, Ont.; Nicholas T. (Nick) Macos, Toronto, Ont.

Capital Stock

	Authorized (shs.)	Outstanding (shs.)[1]
Common	unlimited	15,097,800
Class A	unlimited	nil

[1] At Dec. 29, 2021

Major Shareholder - Alex Dolgonos held 34.52% interest and Blair L. Naughty held 12.25% interest at July 26, 2021.

Price Range - KUR.H/TSX-VEN

Year	Volume	High	Low	Close
2022	1,093,162	$0.28	$0.06	$0.11
2021	5,716,740	$0.47	$0.03	$0.18
2020	965,899	$0.12	$0.01	$0.09
2019	3,354,268	$0.13	$0.02	$0.03
2018	520,137	$0.14	$0.06	$0.07

Recent Close: $0.13

Wholly Owned Subsidiaries

UBS Wireless Services Inc., Ont.

Financial Statistics

Periods ended:	12m Aug. 31/21^A		12m Aug. 31/20^A
	$000s	%Chg	$000s
Salaries & benefits	265		63
General & admin expense	120		129
Operating expense	**385**	**+101**	**192**
Operating income	**(385)**	**n.a.**	**(192)**
Finance costs, gross	18		12
Write-downs/write-offs	nil		68
Pre-tax income	**(656)**	**n.a.**	**(136)**
Net income	**(656)**	**n.a.**	**(136)**
Cash & equivalent	117		14
Accounts receivable	nil		4
Current assets	131		33
Total assets	**131**	**+274**	**35**
Bank indebtedness	185		114
Accts. pay. & accr. liabs.	814		531
Current liabilities	1,290		645
Long-term debt, gross	107		nil
Long-term debt, net	107		nil
Shareholders' equity	(1,266)		(610)
Cash from oper. activs.	**(89)**	**n.a.**	**(14)**
Cash from fin. activs.	192		26
Net cash position	**117**	**+736**	**14**
	$		$
Earnings per share*	(0.04)		(0.01)
Cash flow per share*	(0.01)		(0.00)
	shs		shs
No. of shs. o/s*	15,097,800		15,097,800
Avg. no. of shs. o/s*	15,097,800		15,097,800
	%		%
Net profit margin	n.a.		n.a.
Return on equity	n.m.		n.m.
Return on assets	(768.67)		(125.25)

* Common
^A Reported in accordance with IFRS

Latest Results

Periods ended:	3m Nov. 30/21^A		3m Nov. 30/20^A
	$000s	%Chg	$000s
Net income	10	n.a.	(37)
	$		$
Earnings per share*	0.00		(0.00)

* Common
^A Reported in accordance with IFRS

Historical Summary
(as originally stated)

Fiscal Year	Oper. Rev.	Net Inc. Bef. Disc.	EPS*
	$000s	$000s	$
2021^A	nil	(656)	(0.04)
2020^A	nil	(136)	(0.01)
2019^A	nil	(664)	(0.04)
2018^A	nil	(858)	(0.06)
2017^A	nil	(1,313)	(0.09)

* Common
^A Reported in accordance with IFRS

K.35 KuuHubb Inc.

Symbol - KUU **Exchange** - TSX-VEN **CUSIP** - 501498
Head Office - 1417-25 Adelaide St E, Toronto, ON, M5C 3A1 **Telephone** - (416) 366-2221 **Toll-free** - (800) 714-7938 **Fax** - (416) 366-7722
Website - www.kuuhubb.com
Email - bill@kuuhubb.com
Investor Relations - Bill Mitoulas (416) 479-9547
Auditors - MS Partners LLP C.A., Toronto, Ont.
Transfer Agents - TSX Trust Company, Toronto, Ont.
Profile - (Can. 2004; orig. Ont., 1990) Designs and develops free-to-play mobile video games and online applications targeting the female audience.
Focused on developing and distributing mobile online games and lifestyle applications and content for distribution on mobile platforms such as iOS and Android. Principal products include Recolor, a digital colouring book mobile app; Recolor By Numbers, an art-based number colouring game; My Hospital, a medical simulation mobile game; and Tiles &Tales, a story driven match 3 puzzles where player's choices affect the plot. Other lifestyle applications include Incolour, Dance Talent (formerly Dancing Diaries), Neybers and Match Royale.
Operations are based in Helsinki, Finland.
Predecessor Detail - Name changed from Delrand Resources Limited, June 16, 2017, pursuant to acquisition of KuuHubb Oy.
Directors - Jouni Keränen, chr. & acting CEO, Helsinki, Finland; Christian Kolster, exec. v-p & corp. sec., Espoo, Finland; Elmer I. Kim, Toronto, Ont.; André Lüdi, Switzerland
Other Exec. Officers - Charles Sung, CFO

Capital Stock

	Authorized (shs.)	Outstanding (shs.)[1]
Common	unlimited	64,458,043

[1] At Nov. 29, 2022

Major Shareholder - Joki Capital OU held 17.9% interest at Mar. 23, 2022.

Price Range - KUU/TSX-VEN

Year	Volume	High	Low	Close
2022	2,896,828	$0.09	$0.02	$0.02
2021	10,047,098	$0.18	$0.03	$0.03
2020	16,961,115	$0.62	$0.08	$0.08
2019	9,917,243	$0.71	$0.28	$0.62
2018	11,589,989	$1.70	$0.25	$0.31

Recent Close: $0.02
Capital Stock Changes - In May 2023, private placement of up to 20,000,000 common shares was announced at 5¢ per share.
There were no changes to capital stock during fiscal 2022.

Wholly Owned Subsidiaries

Kuuhubb AG, Switzerland.
KuuHubb Oy, Finland.
- 100% int. in **Kemojo KuuHubb Studios Inc.**, B.C.
- 100% int. in **Neybers AB**, Sweden.
- 100% int. in **Recolor India Pvt. Ltd.**, India.
- 100% int. in **Recolor Oy**, Helsinki, Finland.

Financial Statistics

Periods ended:	12m June 30/22[A]		12m June 30/21[A]
	US$000s	%Chg	US$000s
Operating revenue	**3,831**	**-28**	**5,295**
Cost of sales	1,105		2,190
General & admin expense	5,115		5,903
Stock-based compensation	130		452
Operating expense	**6,349**	**-26**	**8,544**
Operating income	**(2,518)**	**n.a.**	**(3,249)**
Deprec., depl. & amort.	21		31
Finance costs, gross	1,126		1,579
Pre-tax income	**4,197**	**n.a.**	**(5,013)**
Net income	**4,197**	**n.a.**	**(5,013)**
Cash & equivalent	225		24
Accounts receivable	228		479
Current assets	654		1,035
Fixed assets, net	57		85
Total assets	**711**	**-36**	**1,119**
Accts. pay. & accr. liabs	2,408		2,442
Current liabilities	7,878		10,149
Long-term debt, gross	5,565		11,159
Long-term debt, net	1,547		4,303
Shareholders' equity	(8,714)		(13,529)
Cash from oper. activs	**(1,806)**	**n.a.**	**(1,453)**
Cash from fin. activs	1,584		1,036
Cash from invest. activs	nil		(5)
Net cash position	**225**	**+838**	**24**
Capital expenditures	nil		(5)
	US$		US$
Earnings per share*	0.06		(0.08)
Cash flow per share*	(0.03)		(0.02)
	shs		shs
No. of shs. o/s*	66,658,043		66,658,043
Avg. no. of shs. o/s*	66,658,043		59,658,876
	%		%
Net profit margin	109.55		(94.67)
Return on equity	n.m.		n.m.
Return on assets	581.75		(201.11)

* Common
[A] Reported in accordance with IFRS

Latest Results

Periods ended:	3m Sept. 30/22[A]		3m Sept. 30/21[A]
	US$000s	%Chg	US$000s
Operating revenue	884	-12	1,002
Net income	(606)	n.a.	(972)
	US$		US$
Earnings per share*	(0.01)		(0.02)

* Common
[A] Reported in accordance with IFRS

Historical Summary
(as originally stated)

Fiscal Year	Oper. Rev. US$000s	Net Inc. Bef. Disc. US$000s	EPS* US$
2022[A]	3,831	4,197	0.06
2021[A]	5,295	(5,013)	(0.08)
2020[A]	1,008	(6,393)	(0.12)
2019[A]	12,362	(15,153)	(0.27)
2018[A]	20,795	(16,610)	(0.34)

* Common
[A] Reported in accordance with IFRS

L

L.1 LDB Capital Corp.

Symbol - LDB.P **Exchange** - TSX-VEN **CUSIP** - 50203W
Head Office - 2250-1055 Hastings St W, Vancouver, BC, V6E 2E9 **Telephone** - (778) 331-2080
Email - david.eaton@barongroupintl.com
Investor Relations - David A. Eaton (778) 331-2080
Auditors - De Visser Gray LLP C.A., Vancouver, B.C.
Transfer Agents - Odyssey Trust Company, Vancouver, B.C.
Profile - (B.C. 2021) Capital Pool Company.
Directors - David A. Eaton, CEO, CFO & corp. sec., Vancouver, B.C.; Luke A. Norman, Vancouver, B.C.; Richard S. Silas, Vancouver, B.C.

Capital Stock

	Authorized (shs.)	Outstanding (shs.)[1]
Common	unlimited	4,100,002

[1] At July 25, 2023

Major Shareholder - David A. Eaton held 17.07% interest, Luke A. Norman held 17.07% interest and Richard S. Silas held 17.07% interest at July 5, 2023.

Price Range - LDB.P/TSX-VEN

Year	Volume	High	Low	Close
2022............	142,500	$0.25	$0.16	$0.19

Recent Close: $0.18
Capital Stock Changes - On Mar. 22, 2022, an initial public offering of 2,000,000 common shares was completed at 10¢ per share.

L.2 LQWD Technologies Corp.

Symbol - LQWD **Exchange** - TSX-VEN **CUSIP** - 502154
Head Office - 1710-1050 Pender St W, Vancouver, BC, V6E 3S7 **Telephone** - (604) 682-6496 **Toll-free** - (800) 811-2322 **Fax** - (604) 682-1174
Website - www.lqwdfintech.com
Email - ashley@lqwdfintech.com
Investor Relations - Ashley Garnot (604) 669-0912
Auditors - Kingston Ross Pasnak LLP C.A., Edmonton, Alta.
Lawyers - Blake, Cassels & Graydon LLP
Transfer Agents - Computershare Trust Company of Canada Inc., Vancouver, B.C.
Employees - 9 at June 28, 2022
Profile - (B.C. 2004; orig. Yuk., 1999) Operates as a financial technology company that develops payment network infrastructure and solutions on top of the Lightning Network, a scalable Layer 2 solution built on top of the Bitcoin blockchain. Also stakes Bitcoin on the Lightning Network.

The Bitcoin Lightning Network is a Layer 2 solution made up of a network of nodes connected via payment channels. It is built on top of the Bitcoin blockchain and enables instantaneous, low fee transactions. The company is developing a Lightning Network Software-as-a-Service platform that enables the set-up payment channels as a service.

Also stakes Bitcoin on the Lightning Network that help facilitate the exchange of digital assets, generating fees per transaction.

On May 20, 2022, operation of coincurve.com was temporarily halted in order to focus on developing the Lightning Network and platform.

Predecessor Detail - Name changed from LQwD FinTech Corp., July 28, 2023.
Directors - Shone Anstey, chr. & CEO, Richmond, B.C.; Giuseppe (Pino) Perone, corp. sec., Vancouver, B.C.; Kim Evans, North Vancouver, B.C.; Ashley Garnot, North Vancouver, B.C.; Alex P. Guidi, Vancouver, B.C.
Other Exec. Officers - Barry MacNeil, CFO; Aziz Pulatov, chief tech. officer; Alexandra Moxin, v-p, product; Stephanie Yoneda, contr.

Capital Stock

	Authorized (shs.)	Outstanding (shs.)[1]
Common	unlimited	11,603,026

[1] At July 28, 2023

Major Shareholder - Widely held at July 27, 2022.

Price Range - LQWD/TSX-VEN

Year	Volume	High	Low	Close
2022............	3,482,954	$4.30	$0.40	$0.53
2021............	2,534,926	$16.50	$3.25	$4.10
2020............	275,350	$3.50	$1.15	$3.50
2019............	275,188	$8.25	$1.05	$1.75
2018............	109,234	$3.75	$1.75	$3.75

Consolidation: 1-for-10 cons. in Nov. 2022; 2-for-1 split in Aug. 2019
Recent Close: $0.44
Capital Stock Changes - On Nov. 14, 2022, common shares were consolidated on a 1-for-10 basis.

Wholly Owned Subsidiaries

LQwD Financial Corp., Vancouver, B.C.
Skyrun Technology Corp., Vancouver, B.C.
0980862 B.C. Ltd., Canada.
0997680 B.C. Ltd., Canada.
- 100% int. in **Coronado Resources USA LLC**, Mont.

0997684 B.C. Ltd., Canada.

Financial Statistics

Periods ended:	12m Feb. 28/22[A]		12m Feb. 28/21[A]
	$000s	%Chg	$000s
Operating revenue........................	**70**	**-44**	**126**
Salaries & benefits..........................	428		88
Research & devel. expense.............	580		39
General & admin expense...............	1,523		555
Stock-based compensation............	1,451		72
Operating expense........................	**3,982**	**+428**	**754**
Operating income..........................	**(3,912)**	**n.a.**	**(628)**
Deprec., depl. & amort....................	856		180
Finance income................................	2		2
Finance costs, gross........................	5		4
Pre-tax income.............................	**(22,960)**	**n.a.**	**(813)**
Net income....................................	**(22,960)**	**n.a.**	**(813)**
Cash & equivalent...........................	9,167		2,224
Accounts receivable........................	40		62
Current assets.................................	9,254		2,340
Fixed assets, net.............................	178		3
Intangibles, net...............................	8,488		561
Total assets...................................	**17,986**	**+511**	**2,943**
Accts. pay. & accr. liabs...................	401		93
Current liabilities.............................	453		93
Long-term lease liabilities...............	77		nil
Shareholders' equity.......................	17,456		2,851
Cash from oper. activs..................	**(3,159)**	**n.a.**	**(516)**
Cash from fin. activs........................	11,163		1,759
Cash from invest. activs..................	(8,969)		(391)
Net cash position..........................	**871**	**-53**	**1,837**
Capital expenditures........................	(58)		nil
	$		$
Earnings per share*.........................	(3.30)		(0.30)
Cash flow per share*.......................	(0.45)		(0.19)
	shs		shs
No. of shs. o/s*................................	9,762,781		3,068,319
Avg. no. of shs. o/s*.........................	6,996,125		2,728,984
	%		%
Net profit margin.............................	n.m.		(645.24)
Return on equity..............................	(226.13)		(36.08)
Return on assets..............................	(219.36)		(34.60)

* Common
[A] Reported in accordance with IFRS

Latest Results

Periods ended:	9m Nov. 30/22[A]		9m Nov. 30/21[A]
	$000s	%Chg	$000s
Operating revenue...........................	5	-92	62
Net income......................................	(7,794)	n.a.	(3,588)
	$		$
Earnings per share*.........................	(0.80)		(0.60)

* Common
[A] Reported in accordance with IFRS

Historical Summary
(as originally stated)

Fiscal Year	Oper. Rev.	Net Inc. Bef. Disc.	EPS*
	$000s	$000s	$
2022[A]....................	70	(22,960)	(3.30)
2021[A]....................	126	(813)	(0.30)
2020[A]....................	53	(1,356)	(0.80)
2019[A]....................	nil	(714)	(0.55)
2018[A]....................	nil	(91)	(0.07)

* Common
[A] Reported in accordance with IFRS

Note: Adjusted throughout for 1-for-10 cons. in Nov. 2022; 2-for-1 split in Aug. 2019; 2-for-1 split in Aug. 2018

L.3 LSL Pharma Group Inc.

Symbol - LSL **Exchange** - TSX-VEN **CUSIP** - 50190N
Head Office - 1800-540 rue d'Avaugour, Boucherville, QC, J4B 0G6 **Telephone** - (514) 664-7700
Website - www.laboratoirelsl.com
Email - info@laboratoirelsl.com
Investor Relations - Sylvain Richer (514) 644-7700
Auditors - KPMG LLP C.A., Montréal, Qué.
Transfer Agents - TSX Trust Company
Profile - (Can. 2010) Develops, manufactures and distributes dietary supplements and vitamins and sterile injectable and ophthalmic products as a contract manufacturer.

Dietary supplements, such as electrolyte powder, calcium and, iron, and vitamins are manufactured primarily in tablet, capsule and powder form. The company has the capacity to perform the entire manufacturing process: mixing, tablet or capsule manufacturing, coating, bottling and labeling. These products are manufactured at an 8,000-sq.-ft. facility La Pocatière, Qué.

Wholly owned **Steri-Med Pharma Inc.** produces ophthalmic ointments, eye drops, injectable solutions and sterile disinfectants, for the pharmaceutical and veterinary markets. Lead products are Erythromycin and Sterisporin ophthalmic ointments. These products are manufactured in 22,000 sq. ft. of manufacturing space at a plant near Saint-Hyacinthe, Que,

Class A reinstated on TSX-VEN, Mar. 1, 2023.

Recent Merger and Acquisition Activity

Status: completed **Revised:** Feb. 22, 2023
UPDATE: The transaction was completed for issuance of 68,089,000 common shares at a deemed price of $0.70 per share. PREVIOUS: Îledor Exploration Corporation entered into a letter of intent for change of business reverse takeover acquisition of LSL Laboratory Inc., which develops, manufactures and distributes sterile ophthalmic and injectable pharmaceutical products as well as natural health products. On closing, the company plans to change its name to LSL Pharma Group Corporation.

Predecessor Detail - Name changed from Îledor Exploration Corporation, Feb. 17, 2023, pursuant to the reverse takeover acquisition of LSL Laboratory Inc.; basis 1 new for 25 old shs.
Directors - François Roberge, chr., pres. & CEO, Boucherville, Qué.; Sylvain Aird, Montréal, Qué.; Frank J. Dellafera, N.Y.; Pierre B. Lafrenière, Montréal, Qué.; Alain Larochelle, Saint-Michel-de-Bellechasse, Qué.; Luc Mainville, Montréal, Qué.
Other Exec. Officers - Sylvain Richer, CFO; Marc Boudreault, v-p, commun.; Mélanie St-Pierre, contr.

Capital Stock

	Authorized (shs.)	Outstanding (shs.)[1]
Common	unlimited	82,226,435

[1] At Feb. 28, 2023

Major Shareholder - François Roberge held 29.69% interest at Feb. 28, 2023.
Recent Close: $0.49
Capital Stock Changes - On Feb. 22, 2023, 68,089,000 post-consolidated common shares were issued pursuant to the reverse takeover acquisition of LSL Laboratory Inc. In addition, 1,575,000 post-consolidated common shares as finder's fee and private placement of 11,736,566 post-consolidated units (1 common share & ½ warrant) at $0.70 per unit was completed, with warrants exercisable at $1.00 per share for 18 months. On Mar. 1, 2023, common shares were consolidated on a 1-for-25 basis.

Wholly Owned Subsidiaries

LSL Laboratory Inc., La Pocatière, Qué.
- 100% int. in **Steri-Med Pharma Inc.**, Qué.

Financial Statistics

Periods ended:	12m July 31/22[A1]		12m July 31/21[A]
	$000s	%Chg	$000s
General & admin expense...............	71		88
Operating expense........................	**71**	**-19**	**88**
Operating income..........................	**(71)**	**n.a.**	**(88)**
Finance costs, gross........................	3		3
Pre-tax income.............................	**(74)**	**n.a.**	**(91)**
Net income....................................	**(74)**	**n.a.**	**(91)**
Current assets.................................	25		17
Total assets...................................	**25**	**+47**	**17**
Accts. pay. & accr. liabs...................	172		94
Current liabilities.............................	285		203
Shareholders' equity.......................	(260)		(186)
Cash from oper. activs..................	**(3)**	**n.a.**	**(75)**
Cash from fin. activs........................	4		65
	$		$
Earnings per share*.........................	(0.09)		(0.11)
Cash flow per share*.......................	(0.00)		(0.09)
	shs		shs
No. of shs. o/s*................................	825,869		825,869
Avg. no. of shs. o/s*.........................	825,869		825,869
	%		%
Net profit margin.............................	n.a.		n.a.
Return on equity..............................	n.m.		n.m.
Return on assets..............................	(338.10)		(15.00)

* Common
[A] Reported in accordance with IFRS
[1] Results for fiscal 2022 and prior periods pertain to Îledor Exploration Corporation.

Note: Adjusted throughout for 1-for-25 cons. in Mar. 2023

L.4 LXRandCo, Inc.

Symbol - LXR **Exchange** - TSX **CUSIP** - 550789
Head Office - 7399 boul Saint-Laurent, Montréal, QC, H2R 1W7 **Telephone** - (514) 564-9993
Website - www.lxrco.com
Email - nadine.e@lxrco.com
Investor Relations - Nadine Eap (514) 564-9993 ext. 037
Auditors - PricewaterhouseCoopers LLP C.A., Montréal, Qué.
Transfer Agents - TSX Trust Company, Toronto, Ont.
Employees - 42 at Mar. 31, 2023
Profile - (Ont. 2015) Retails authenticated branded pre-owned luxury handbags and personal accessories across North America by selling directly through its own website at www.lxrco.com and indirectly through the e-commerce and other platforms of its key retail channel partners as well as some stores within department stores in Canada.
Sells vintage luxury handbags and other personal accessories from designer brands including Hermès, Chanel, Louis Vuitton, Gucci and Prada. Vintage products are carried through its e-commerce website www.lxrco.com, as well as ecommerce platforms of channel partners and a network of 8 LXRandCo branded stores in Canada.
Merchandise is sourced and purchased from third party channels in Asia and North America and, to a lesser extent, from individual consumers.
Operations include office in Montreal, Que., which serves as headquarters and for warehousing and distribution support services in Canada; office in Tokyo, Japan; and a warehouse facility in Plattsburgh, N.Y.
Predecessor Detail - Name changed from Gibraltar Growth Corporation, June 9, 2017, following reverse takeover acquisition of LXR Produits de Luxe Internationale Inc.
Directors - Valerie C. Sorbie, chr., Toronto, Ont.; Camillo O. (Cam) di Prata, Toronto, Ont.; Eric Graveline, Las Vegas, Nev.; Joseph (Joe) Mimran, Toronto, Ont.; Javier San Juan, Madrid, Spain; Nicolas Topiol, Hallandale Beach, Fla.
Other Exec. Officers - Nadine Eap, co-CEO & CFO; Laura Swan, co-CEO; Aurore Colliaux, chief digital officer; Joslyn Paredes, chief strategy & opers. officer; Francois Larrivee, v-p, fin.; Damien Verhagen, v-p, bus. devel.

Capital Stock

	Authorized (shs.)	Outstanding (shs.)[1]
Cl.A Restricted Vtg.	unlimited	nil
Class B	unlimited	91,425,499[2]

[1] At May 11, 2023
[2] Excludes 1,357,656 forfeited founder's shares.

Major Shareholder - Camillo O. (Cam) di Prata held 26.93% interest at May 2, 2023.

Price Range - LXR/TSX

Year	Volume	High	Low	Close
2022	22,203,506	$0.14	$0.09	$0.11
2021	29,650,829	$0.25	$0.10	$0.14
2020	6,776,456	$0.52	$0.12	$0.25
2019	8,787,787	$0.64	$0.14	$0.21
2018	5,308,678	$5.80	$0.17	$0.24

Recent Close: $0.08
Capital Stock Changes - During 2022, 1,357,656 class B shares were cancelled.

Wholly Owned Subsidiaries

LXR Produits de Luxe International Inc., Montréal, Qué.
- 100% int. in **Groupe Global LXR Inc.**, Canada.
  - 100% int. in **LXR&CO**, Nev.
- 100% int. in **LXR Canada Inc.**, Canada.
- 100% int. in **LXR Luxe Inc.**, Nev.

Financial Statistics

Periods ended:	12m Dec. 31/22[A]		12m Dec. 31/21[A]
	$000s	%Chg	$000s
Operating revenue	**20,007**	**+11**	**18,031**
Cost of sales	12,369		11,741
Salaries & benefits	4,099		3,496
General & admin expense	5,089		3,961
Stock-based compensation	521		749
Operating expense	**22,078**	**+11**	**19,947**
Operating income	**(2,070)**	**n.a.**	**(1,916)**
Deprec., depl. & amort.	325		320
Finance costs, gross	590		543
Write-downs/write-offs	58		30
Pre-tax income	**(1,624)**	**n.a.**	**(2,889)**
Income taxes	23		9
Net income	**(1,647)**	**n.a.**	**(2,898)**
Cash & equivalent	2,586		3,696
Inventories	4,255		4,608
Accounts receivable	2,607		3,262
Current assets	9,970		12,361
Fixed assets, net	639		830
Intangibles, net	3		16
Total assets	**10,613**	**-20**	**13,208**
Accts. pay. & accr. liabs	5,000		4,510
Current liabilities	10,919		5,309
Long-term debt, gross	5,252		5,999
Long-term debt, net	nil		5,699
Shareholders' equity	(2,558)		289
Cash from oper. activs	**(10)**	**n.a.**	**(3,553)**
Cash from fin. activs	(1,023)		36
Cash from invest. activs	(17)		(43)
Net cash position	**2,587**	**-30**	**3,696**
Capital expenditures	(17)		(44)
Capital disposals	nil		1
	$		$
Earnings per share*	(0.02)		(0.03)
Cash flow per share*	(0.00)		(0.04)
	shs		shs
No. of shs. o/s*	91,425,499		92,783,155
Avg. no. of shs. o/s*	92,020,636		92,783,155
	%		%
Net profit margin	(8.23)		(16.07)
Return on equity	n.m.		(170.87)
Return on assets	(8.80)		(17.37)
Foreign sales percent	69		65
No. of employees (FTEs)	42		44

* Cl.B
[A] Reported in accordance with IFRS

Latest Results

Periods ended:	3m Mar. 31/23[A]		3m Mar. 31/22[A]
	$000s	%Chg	$000s
Operating revenue	3,715	-14	4,296
Net income	(337)	n.a.	(924)
	$		$
Earnings per share*	(0.00)		(0.01)

* Cl.B
[A] Reported in accordance with IFRS

Historical Summary
(as originally stated)

Fiscal Year	Oper. Rev. $000s	Net Inc. Bef. Disc. $000s	EPS* $
2022[A]	20,007	(1,647)	(0.02)
2021[A]	18,031	(2,898)	(0.03)
2020[A]	13,777	(7,711)	(0.24)
2019[A]	40,069	(10,035)	(0.43)
2018[A]	39,019	(19,628)	(1.40)

* Cl.B
[A] Reported in accordance with IFRS

L.5 Lanebury Growth Capital Ltd.

Symbol - LLL **Exchange** - CSE **CUSIP** - 515504
Head Office - 401-750 Pender St W, Vancouver, BC, V6C 2T7 **Telephone** - (604) 428-7050 **Fax** - (604) 428-7052
Email - srempel@aroconsulting.ca
Investor Relations - Sheri Rempel (604) 484-7122
Auditors - Dale Matheson Carr-Hilton LaBonte LLP C.A., Vancouver, B.C.
Transfer Agents - Odyssey Trust Company, Vancouver, B.C.
Profile - (B.C. 2011) Invests in Internet and mobile technology companies.
At Sept. 30, 2022, the company held a total investment with a fair value of $4,130,398. Investments include **Finhaven Technology Inc.**, which provides connection between issuers and accredited investors using safe, secure distributed ledger technology (blockchain) and digital securities; **Katabatic Power Corp.**, a wind development company, carried at nominal value; **Mobio Technologies Inc.**, which launches, acquires and integrates early-stage, high-growth technology companies; **Plank Ventures Ltd.**, which invests in technology start-up companies; **Premium Sound Inc.**, which provides high-end headphones and accessories; and **Fission Internet Software Services for Open Networks Inc.**
Directors - Lance Tracey, CEO, North Vancouver, B.C.; Sheri Rempel, CFO & corp. sec., Vancouver, B.C.; Timothy Grzyb, B.C.; Gary Schroeder, B.C.

Capital Stock

	Authorized (shs.)	Outstanding (shs.)[1]	Par
Preferred	unlimited	nil	$100
Common	unlimited	10,320,803	

[1] At Nov. 25, 2022

Major Shareholder - Lance Tracey held 84.44% interest at May 31, 2022.

Price Range - LLL/CSE

Year	Volume	High	Low	Close
2022	64,013	$0.39	$0.16	$0.16
2021	381,336	$0.40	$0.13	$0.30
2020	425,249	$0.25	$0.05	$0.11
2019	95,927	$0.20	$0.05	$0.06
2018	169,835	$0.69	$0.16	$0.16

Recent Close: $0.15
Capital Stock Changes - There were no changes to capital stock from fiscal 2019 to fiscal 2022, inclusive.

Investments

Finhaven Technology Inc., Vancouver, B.C.
Fission Internet Software Services for Open Networks Inc.
Katabatic Power Corp., Richmond, B.C.
Mobio Technologies Inc., Vancouver, B.C. (see separate coverage)
Plank Ventures Ltd., Vancouver, B.C. (see separate coverage)
Premium Sound Inc.

Financial Statistics

Periods ended:	12m June 30/22[A]		12m June 30/21[A]
	$000s	%Chg	$000s
General & admin expense	113		85
Operating expense	**113**	**+33**	**85**
Operating income	**(113)**	**n.a.**	**(85)**
Finance income	250		213
Finance costs, gross	124		73
Investment income	(62)		(341)
Pre-tax income	**38**	**n.a.**	**(88)**
Net income	**38**	**n.a.**	**(88)**
Cash & equivalent	28		607
Current assets	28		607
Long-term investments	3,497		2,796
Total assets	**5,040**	**+8**	**4,648**
Bank indebtedness	792		526
Accts. pay. & accr. liabs	41		32
Current liabilities	833		558
Equity portion of conv. debs	124		44
Shareholders' equity	4,207		4,090
Cash from oper. activs	**(104)**	**n.a.**	**(60)**
Cash from fin. activs	200		527
Cash from invest. activs	(675)		(852)
Net cash position	**28**	**-95**	**607**
	$		$
Earnings per share*	0.00		(0.01)
Cash flow per share*	(0.01)		(0.01)
	shs		shs
No. of shs. o/s*	10,320,803		10,320,803
Avg. no. of shs. o/s*	10,320,803		10,320,803
	%		%
Net profit margin	n.a.		n.a.
Return on equity	0.92		(2.14)
Return on assets	3.34		(0.34)

* Common
[A] Reported in accordance with IFRS

Latest Results

Periods ended:	3m Sept. 30/22[A]		3m Sept. 30/21[A]
	$000s	%Chg	$000s
Net income	88	n.a.	(479)
	$		$
Earnings per share*	0.01		(0.05)

* Common
[A] Reported in accordance with IFRS

Historical Summary
(as originally stated)

Fiscal Year	Oper. Rev. $000s	Net Inc. Bef. Disc. $000s	EPS* $
2022[A]	nil	38	0.00
2021[A]	nil	(88)	(0.01)
2020[A]	nil	(132)	(0.01)
2019[A]	nil	(402)	(0.04)
2018[A]	nil	(408)	(0.17)

* Common
[A] Reported in accordance with IFRS

L.6 Lanesborough Real Estate Investment Trust

Symbol - LRT.UN **Exchange** - TSX-VEN **CUSIP** - 515555
Head Office - c/o Shelter Canadian Properties Limited, 2600-7 Evergreen Pl, Winnipeg, MB, R3L 2T3 **Telephone** - (204) 475-9090 **Fax** - (204) 452-5505
Website - www.lreit.com
Email - gromagnoli@lreit.com
Investor Relations - Gino Romagnoli (204) 475-9090 ext. 2208
Auditors - MNP LLP C.A., Winnipeg, Man.
Lawyers - MLT Aikins LLP, Winnipeg, Man.
Transfer Agents - TSX Trust Company, Calgary, Alta.
Profile - (Man. 2002) Owns multi-family residential properties primarily in Fort McMurray, Alta.

Residential portfolio at Mar. 31, 2023:

Location	Properties	Suites
Fort McMurray, Alta.	10	673
Other	2	149
	12	822

Also owns a 93-suite seniors' housing complex in Moose Jaw, Sask., which it plans to sell and is classified as discontinued operations.

Shelter Canadian Properties Limited is the administrator of the trust and property manager of the trust's portfolio.

Recent Merger and Acquisition Activity

Status: completed **Revised:** Mar. 3, 2023
UPDATE: The transaction was completed. PREVIOUS: Lanesborough Real Estate Investment Trust agreed to sell three properties in Fort McMurray (2) and Edson, Alta., to 7254751 Manitoba Ltd. for $43,010,000, plus closing adjustments of $128,744. The consideration would be payable through: the assumption of $22,891,289 of mortgages; the assumption of an accrued forbearance fee of $169,500 on one of the properties; the reduction of $20,002,955 owing under the line of credit from a sister company of 7254751 Manitoba to the REIT; and deposits paid of $75,000.

Status: completed **Announced:** Mar. 15, 2022
Lanesborough Real Estate Investment Trust sold Woodland Park, a 102-suite property in Alberta for $13,200,000

Trustees - Arni C. Thorsteinson, v-chr., Winnipeg, Man.; Charles K. (Chuck) Loewen‡, Winnipeg, Man.; Earl S. Coleman, Winnipeg, Man.
Other Exec. Officers - Gino Romagnoli, CEO; Gary W. Benjaminson, CFO & corp. sec.
‡ Lead trustee

Capital Stock

	Authorized (shs.)	Outstanding (shs.)[1]
Trust Unit	unlimited	680,473,620
Class B LP Unit	unlimited	nil

[1] At May 25, 2023

Trust Unit - The trust will endeavour to make quarterly cash distributions equal to, on an annual basis, about 90% of the trust's distributable income. One vote per trust unit.
Class B Limited Partnership Unit - Entitled to distributions equal to those paid to trust units. Transferable and exchangeable at the option of the holder for trust units on a 1-for-1 basis. Non-voting.
Major Shareholder - Widely held at May 25, 2023.

Price Range - LRT.UN/TSX-VEN

Year	Volume	High	Low	Close
2022	30,078,241	$0.03	$0.01	$0.01
2021	9,284,852	$0.07	$0.01	$0.02
2020	7,668,424	$0.03	$0.01	$0.01
2019	2,979,967	$0.02	$0.01	$0.01
2018	5,261,110	$0.03	$0.01	$0.01

Recent Close: $0.01
Capital Stock Changes - On Feb. 24, 2022, 659,916,300 trust units were issued at a deemed price of 5¢ per share on exchange of $24,810,000 principal amount of 5% series G subordinated debentures due June 30, 2022.

Wholly Owned Subsidiaries

LREIT Holdings 32 Corporation

Financial Statistics

Periods ended:	12m Dec. 31/22[A]		12m Dec. 31/21[A]
	$000s	%Chg	$000s
Total revenue	**17,911**	**-4**	**18,566**
Rental operating expense	13,079		12,833
Operating expense	**13,079**	**+2**	**12,833**
Operating income	**4,832**	**-16**	**5,733**
Finance costs, gross	11,390		12,251
Pre-tax income	**26,221**	**n.a.**	**(15,985)**
Net inc. bef. disc. opers	**26,221**	**n.a.**	**(15,985)**
Income from disc. opers	(2,325)		(3,346)
Net income	**23,896**	**n.a.**	**(19,331)**
Cash & equivalent	822		1,975
Accounts receivable	123		270
Current assets	51,173		20,698
Income-producing props	75,887		102,336
Property interests, net	75,887		102,336
Total assets	**128,468**	**0**	**128,858**
Accts. pay. & accr. liabs	6,953		4,402
Current liabilities	213,351		287,343
Long-term debt, gross	241,974		305,257
Long-term debt, net	62,653		26,146
Shareholders' equity	(147,536)		(184,631)
Cash from oper. activs	**(3,098)**	**n.a.**	**815**
Cash from fin. activs	(8,343)		2,879
Cash from invest. activs	10,289		(2,503)
Net cash position	**822**	**-58**	**1,975**
Change in property, net	(2,390)		(2,180)
	$		$
Earns. per sh. bef disc opers*	0.05		(0.76)
Earnings per share*	0.04		(0.91)
Cash flow per share*	(0.01)		0.04
Funds from opers. per sh.*	(0.02)		(0.37)
Adj. funds from opers. per sh.*	(0.02)		(0.47)
	shs		shs
No. of shs. o/s*	680,473,620		20,557,320
Avg. no. of shs. o/s*	582,842,167		20,557,320
	%		%
Net profit margin	146.40		(86.10)
Return on equity	n.m.		n.m.
Return on assets	29.23		(2.80)

* Trust unit
[A] Reported in accordance with IFRS

Latest Results

Periods ended:	3m Mar. 31/23[A]		3m Mar. 31/22[□A]
	$000s	%Chg	$000s
Total revenue	3,503	-26	4,725
Net inc. bef. disc. opers	1,744	-90	16,712
Income from disc. opers	(589)		(493)
Net income	1,155	-93	16,219
	$		$
Earns. per sh. bef. disc. opers.*	0.00		0.06
Earnings per share*	0.00		0.06

* Trust unit
[□] Restated
[A] Reported in accordance with IFRS

Historical Summary
(as originally stated)

Fiscal Year	Total Rev.	Net Inc. Bef. Disc.	EPS*
	$000s	$000s	$
2022[A]	17,911	26,221	0.04
2021[A]	18,566	(15,985)	(0.76)
2020[A]	17,721	(44,610)	(2.11)
2019[A]	16,745	(29,407)	(1.39)
2018[A]	17,270	(45,817)	(2.17)

* Trust unit
[A] Reported in accordance with IFRS

L.7 Lassonde Industries Inc.*

Symbol - LAS.A **Exchange** - TSX **CUSIP** - 517907
Head Office - 755 rue Principale, Rougemont, QC, J0L 1M0 **Telephone** - (450) 469-4926 **Toll-free** - (866) 552-7643 **Fax** - (450) 469-1366
Website - www.lassonde.com
Email - info@lassonde.com
Investor Relations - Éric Gemme (450) 469-4926 ext. 10782
Auditors - Deloitte LLP C.A., Montréal, Qué.
Lawyers - Dentons Canada LLP, Montréal, Qué.; BCF LLP, Montréal, Qué.; Blake, Cassels & Graydon LLP, Montréal, Qué.
Transfer Agents - TSX Trust Company, Montréal, Qué.
FP500 Revenue Ranking - 210
Employees - 2,700 at July 1, 2023
Profile - (Can. 1981) Develops, produces and markets private label and national brand products including ready-to-drink beverages, fruit-based snacks, frozen juice concentrates, and specialty food products such as cranberry sauce, pasta sauce, soups and fondue broths and sauces to customers in North America. Also imports and markets selected wines from several countries of origin and produces apple cider and cider-based drinks.

Operations are organized into two market segments: **Retail**, including sales to food retailers and wholesalers such as supermarket chains, independent grocers, superstores, warehouse clubs, major pharmaceutical chains and online sales; and **Food Service**, which includes sales to restaurants, hotels, hospitals, schools and wholesalers. The company has 16 plants in Canada and the U.S.

The company's national brand products are sold in various packages under company-owned trademarks including Antico, Apple & Eve, Arte Nova, Bombay, Canton, Double Vie, Dublin's Pub, Fairlee, Fruité, Grown Right, Kiju, Mont-Rouge, Oasis, Old Orchard, Old South, Orange Maison, Rougemont, Simple Drop and Sun-Rype. Products are also sold under commercial brands to which the company has user rights such as Allen's, Arizona, Del Monte and Graves. Also manufactures private label products for retailers and wholesalers in North America.

Directors - Pierre-Paul Lassonde, chr., Rougemont, Qué.; Nathalie Lassonde, v-chr. & CEO, Rougemont, Qué.; Chantal Bélanger, Blainville, Qué.; Denis Boudreault, Montréal, Qué.; Paul Bouthillier, Montréal, Qué.; Luc Doyon, Montréal, Qué.; Pierre Lessard, Qué.; Nathalie Pilon, Dorval, Qué.; Michel Simard, Qué.
Other Exec. Officers - Vincent R. (Vince) Timpano, pres. & COO; Éric Gemme, CFO; Caroline Lemoine, chief legal officer & corp. sec.; Mathieu Simard, chief HR officer; Pierre Turner, sr. v-p, innovation, quality, sustainability; Sylvain Morissette, v-p, commun.; Yves Toupin, v-p, treasury; Claire Bara, pres., A. Lassonde Inc.; Lesli Bradley, pres., snack div.; Amanda Burns, pres., private label, Lassonde Pappas and Company, Inc.; Vito Monopoli, pres., Lassonde Specialties Inc.

Capital Stock

	Authorized (shs.)	Outstanding (shs.)[1]
First Preferred	unlimited	nil
Second Preferred	unlimited	nil
Class A Subordi. Vtg.	unlimited	3,069,000
Class B Multiple Vtg.	unlimited	3,752,620

[1] At July 1, 2023

Class A Subordinate & Class B Multiple Voting - Rank equal to each other with respect to payment of dividends and distribution of capital. Class B shares are entitled to 10 votes per share and are convertible on a share-for-share basis at any time at the holder's option into class A shares. Class A shares are entitled to one vote per share and are convertible share-for-share into class B shares under certain circumstances involving a change of control of the company.
Major Shareholder - Pierre-Paul Lassonde held 92.51% interest at Mar. 13, 2023.

Price Range - LAS.A/TSX

Year	Volume	High	Low	Close
2022	672,765	$158.79	$99.16	$111.28
2021	782,047	$199.00	$140.00	$157.34
2020	687,839	$179.09	$100.10	$173.03
2019	729,904	$213.52	$153.10	$155.47
2018	646,798	$297.84	$184.40	$199.22

Recent Close: $139.98
Capital Stock Changes - During 2022, 111,400 class A subordinate voting shares were repurchased under a Normal Course Issuer Bid.

Dividends

LAS.A cl A S.V. Ra $2.00 pa Q est. June 15, 2023
Prev. Rate: $2.80 est. June 15, 2022
Prev. Rate: $3.52 est. June 15, 2021
Prev. Rate: $2.60 est. June 15, 2020

Long-Term Debt - Outstanding at Dec. 31, 2022:

U.S. revolv. credit facility[1]	$92,099,000
Term credit facility[2]	8,930,000
Canadian revolv. credit facility[3]	113,352,000
Lease liabs	35,014,000
	249,395,000
Less: Current portion	100,821,000
	148,574,000

[1] Bears interest at base rate plus 0.25% to 1% and/or at LIBOR plus 1.25% to 2%, and due on May 2023.
[2] Bears interest at rates 3.21% and 5.81%, and due on January 2024 and April 2026.
[3] Bears interest at Canadian or U.S. prime rate plus up to 1% for open-end borrowings, and/or CDOR or LIBOR plus 1.15% to 2.25%, and due on April 2027.

Minimum long-term debt repayments, excluding lease liabilities, were reported as follows:

2023	$96,227,000
2024	2,050,000
2025	2,100,000
2026	660,000
2027	113,352,000

Note - In January 2023, the company's U.S. revolving credit facility capacity was increased to $160,000,000 from $100,000,000 and the maturity date was extended to December 2025 from May 2023.

Wholly Owned Subsidiaries

A. Lassonde Inc., Rougemont, Qué.
Lassonde Specialties Inc., Qué.
Lassonde (U.S.A.) Inc., Canada.
- 90% int. in **Pappas Lassonde Holdings, Inc.**, United States.
  - 100% int. in **Lassonde Pappas and Company, Inc.**, N.J.

Subsidiaries

90% int. in **Apple & Eve, LLC**, Del.
90% int. in **Old Orchard Brands Real Estate Holdings, LLC**, United States.

Investments

19.2% int. in **Diamond Estates Wines & Spirits Inc.**, Niagara-on-the-Lake, Ont. (see separate coverage)

Note: The preceding list includes only the major related companies in which interests are held.

Financial Statistics

Periods ended:	12m Dec. 31/22[A]		12m Dec. 31/21[A]
	$000s	%Chg	$000s
Operating revenue	**2,150,975**	**+14**	**1,892,862**
Cost of sales	1,598,981		1,343,452
General & admin expense	411,133		371,589
Operating expense	**2,010,114**	**+17**	**1,715,041**
Operating income	**140,861**	**-21**	**177,821**
Deprec., depl. & amort.	59,513		59,505
Finance costs, gross	10,390		11,124
Investment income	(914)		(764)
Pre-tax income	**70,602**	**-33**	**106,014**
Income taxes	17,268		27,562
Net income	**53,334**	**-32**	**78,452**
Net inc. for equity hldrs	**53,938**	**-30**	**77,511**
Net inc. for non-cont. int	**(604)**	**n.a.**	**941**
Cash & equivalent	2,678		305
Inventories	414,043		309,748
Accounts receivable	173,654		154,369
Current assets	638,763		489,749
Long-term investments	7,439		8,353
Fixed assets, net	399,969		384,389
Intangibles, net	526,556		512,354
Total assets	**1,604,715**	**+13**	**1,419,595**
Bank indebtedness	4,388		5,028
Accts. pay. & accr. liabs	307,037		269,115
Current liabilities	418,551		370,338
Long-term debt, gross	249,395		175,432
Long-term debt, net	148,574		91,045
Shareholders' equity	877,166		808,415
Non-controlling interest	60,401		57,092
Cash from oper. activs	**23,999**	**-74**	**93,732**
Cash from fin. activs	27,650		(64,881)
Cash from invest. activs	(48,047)		(40,401)
Net cash position	**(1,710)**	**n.a.**	**(4,723)**
Capital expenditures	(41,244)		(31,770)
Capital disposals	79		43
Pension fund surplus	30,612		22,717
	$		$
Earnings per share*	7.85		11.18
Cash flow per share*	3.49		13.52
Cash divd. per share*	2.98		3.29
	shs		shs
No. of shs. o/s*	6,821,620		6,933,020
Avg. no. of shs. o/s*	6,875,000		6,933,020
	%		%
Net profit margin	2.48		4.14
Return on equity	6.40		10.01
Return on assets	4.05		6.19
Foreign sales percent	55		54
No. of employees (FTEs)	2,700		2,700

* Class A & B
[A] Reported in accordance with IFRS

Latest Results

Periods ended:	6m July 1/23[A]		6m July 2/22[A]
	$000s	%Chg	$000s
Operating revenue	1,126,746	+8	1,038,591
Net income	43,390	+50	29,021
Net inc. for equity hldrs	42,199	+46	28,968
Net inc. for non-cont. int	1,191		53
	$		$
Earnings per share*	6.19		4.19

* Class A & B
[A] Reported in accordance with IFRS

Historical Summary
(as originally stated)

Fiscal Year	Oper. Rev.	Net Inc. Bef. Disc.	EPS*
	$000s	$000s	$
2022[A]	2,150,975	53,334	7.85
2021[A]	1,892,862	78,452	11.18
2020[A]	1,980,925	101,874	14.11
2019[A]	1,678,301	74,944	10.37
2018[A]	1,593,996	68,015	9.50

* Class A & B
[A] Reported in accordance with IFRS

L.8 Laurentian Bank of Canada*

Symbol - LB **Exchange** - TSX **CUSIP** - 51925D
Head Office - 600-1360 boul Rene-Levesque O, Montréal, QC, H3G 0E5 **Telephone** - (514) 284-4500 **Toll-free** - (800) 252-1846 **Fax** - (514) 284-3396
Website - lbcfg.ca
Email - andrew.chornenky@lbcfg.ca
Investor Relations - Andrew Chomenky (416) 846-4845
Auditors - Ernst & Young LLP C.A., Montréal, Qué.
Lawyers - Osler, Hoskin & Harcourt LLP, Montréal, Qué.
Transfer Agents - Computershare Trust Company of Canada Inc., Montréal, Qué.
FP500 Revenue Ranking - 238
Employees - 3,126 at Oct. 31, 2022

Profile - (Can. 1871) A Schedule I Canadian chartered bank providing a broad range of advice-based financial solutions and services to personal, commercial and institutional customers across Canada and the United States. Operations include a network of branches and automated banking machines (ABMs) based in Quebec, a network of advisors and brokers across Canada, digital banking for all Canadian clients as well as a presence in select U.S. markets.

Personal Banking - Provides day-to-day banking, financing, protection and investment advice, products and services to retail clients in Quebec, served through a network of 58 branches and 145 automated banking machines (ABMs), and across Canada through an advisors and brokers channel targeting independent financial intermediaries and a digital direct-to-consumer platform, LBCDirect, including online, mobile and telephone services. Products and services include bank accounts, transactional packages, term deposits, mutual funds, credit cards, unsecured credit, residential real estate secured financing and creditor protection. Also offers a variety of wealth management and financial planning services through its Private Banking team. Through wholly owned **B2B Bank**, a Schedule I Canadian bank, offers financial advisors and brokers as well as their customers with a suite of banking products and services including loans, mortgages, savings and investment accounts.

Commercial Banking - Serves commercial clients, including small and medium-sized businesses (SMEs), large-scale enterprises and real estate developers, across Canada and in certain regions and markets in the U.S. Operations specialize in the areas of real estate financing, including project financing of residential and commercial properties as well as land financing; equipment and inventory financing; commercial SME financing; and syndication, which offers financing solutions for working capital, fixed assets, mergers and acquisitions, and real estate construction projects as well as includes participation in loan syndicates with other Canadian banks.

Capital Markets - Operations are conducted primarily through wholly owned **Laurentian Bank Securities Inc.**, which offers a range of products and services to institutional and retail customers. The institutional segment consists of fixed income and foreign exchange solutions, including fixed income sales and trading, securitized products, foreign exchange sales and trading, government finance, debt capital markets, and economics and strategy; institutional equity and capital markets, consisting of equity sales and trading, equity research, investment banking and advisory services, and government and corporate underwriting; and institutional and dealer services. Retail customers are provided with full-service retail brokerage including investment and wealth management services; financial planning and insurance; portfolio management; discount brokerage; and corporate support/corresponding business services, including middle and back office operations and support.

Predecessor Detail - Name changed from The Montreal City and District Savings Bank, Sept. 28, 1987.

Directors - Michael P. (Mike) Mueller, chr., Guelph, Ont.; Rania Llewellyn, pres. & CEO, Toronto, Ont.; Sonia A. Baxendale, Toronto, Ont.; Andrea Bolger, Toronto, Ont.; Michael T. Boychuk, Baie-d'Urfé, Qué.; Laurent Desmangles, New York, N.Y.; Suzanne Gouin, Montréal, Qué.; David L. (Dave) Mowat, Vancouver, B.C.; Michelle R. Savoy, Toronto, Ont.; Susan Wolburgh Jenah, Toronto, Ont.; Nicholas (Nick) Zelenczuk, Toronto, Ont.

Other Exec. Officers - Bindu Cudjoe, chief legal officer & corp. sec.; Karine Abgrall-Teslyk, exec. v-p & head, personal banking; Sébastien Bélair, exec. v-p & chief HR officer; Yves Denommé, exec. v-p, opers.; Yvan Deschamps, exec. v-p & CFO; Kelsey Gunderson, exec. v-p, capital markets & pres. & CEO, Laurentian Bank Securities Inc.; William Mason, exec. v-p & chief risk officer; Eric Provost, exec. v-p, head, comml. banking & pres., Que. market; Beel Yaqub, exec. v-p & chief IT officer

Capital Stock

	Authorized (shs.)	Outstanding (shs.)[1]
Class A Preferred	unlimited	
Series 13		5,000,000
Limited Recourse Capital Notes	n.a.	[2]
Series 1		125,000
Common	unlimited	43,479,161

[1] At May 25, 2023
[2] Number of shares represent the number of notes issued.

Class A Preferred - Issuable in series. All series rank on a parity with each other with respect to the payment of dividends and the distribution of assets in the event of liquidation, dissolution, etc. Voting rights would be set by the directors for each series. Subject to the provisions of the Bank Act, the bank may not, without approval of the class A preferred shareholders, create any other class of shares ranking equal with or prior to the class A preferred shares. In addition, approval of the holders of class A preferred shares as a class is required if dividends are in arrears on any outstanding series of class A preferred shares for the creation or issuance of additional shares or any other shares ranking prior to or on parity with the class A preferred shares.

The provisions of the class A preferred shares as a class may be amended or any other authorization be given only by the affirmative vote of at least two-thirds of the votes cast at a meeting scheduled at which a quorum of the outstanding class A preferred shares is represented. At any such meeting, each class A preferred shareholder would be entitled to have one vote for each class A preferred share held.

Class A Preferred Series 13 - Entitled to non-cumulative preferential annual dividends of $1.03075 payable quarterly to June 15, 2024, and thereafter at a rate reset every five years equal to the five-year Government of Canada bond yield plus 2.55%. Redeemable on June 15, 2024, and on June 15 every five years thereafter at $25 per share plus declared and unpaid dividends. Convertible at the holder's option, on June 15, 2024, and on June 15 every five years thereafter, into non-cumulative floating rate preferred series 14 shares on a share-for-share basis, subject to certain conditions. The series 14 shares would pay a quarterly dividend equal to the 90-day Canadian Treasury bill rate plus 2.55%. Convertible into common shares upon occurrence of certain trigger events related to financial viability. The contingent conversion formula is 1.0 multiplied by $25 plus declared and unpaid dividends divided by the greater of (i) a floor price of $5.00; and (ii) current market price of the common shares.

Limited Recourse Capital Notes, Series 1 - Notes with recourse limited to assets held by a third party trustee in a trust. Bear interest at 5.3% per annum until June 15, 2026, and thereafter at an annual rate reset every five years equal to the five-year Government of Canada bond yield plus 4.334% until maturity on June 15, 2081. Trust assets consist of non-cumulative five-year reset class A preferred series 17 shares.

Common - One vote per share.

Options - At Oct. 31, 2022, options were outstanding to purchase 1,154,275 common shares at a weighted average exercise price of $38.18 per share with a weighted average remaining contractual life of 7.9 years.

Class A Preferred Series 15 (old) - Were entitled to non-cumulative preferential annual dividends of $1.4625 payable quarterly to June 15, 2021. Redeemed on June 15, 2021, at $25 per share.

Major Shareholder - Widely held at June 1, 2023.

Price Range - LB/TSX

Year	Volume	High	Low	Close
2022	50,573,784	$45.29	$28.23	$32.30
2021	50,644,636	$45.13	$30.85	$40.17
2020	77,848,388	$44.90	$25.74	$31.20
2019	61,016,627	$46.99	$37.70	$44.43
2018	74,719,967	$56.88	$36.21	$38.07

Recent Close: $38.58

Capital Stock Changes - During fiscal 2022, common shares were issued as follows: 106,666 under dividend reinvestment and share purchase plan and 42,266 on exercise of options; 401,200 common shares were repurchased under a Normal Course Issuer Bid.

Dividends

LB com Ra $1.88 pa Q est. Aug. 1, 2023**
Prev. Rate: $1.84 est. Feb. 1, 2023
Prev. Rate: $1.80 est. Aug. 1, 2022
Prev. Rate: $1.76 est. Feb. 1, 2022
Prev. Rate: $1.60 est. Aug. 1, 2020
LB.PR.H pfd A ser 13 red. exch. Adj. Ra $1.03075 pa Q est. Sept. 15, 2019**
pfd A ser 15 red. exch. Adj. Ra $1.4625 pa Q est. June 15, 2016**[1]
$0.365625**f** June 15/21
[1] Redeemed June 15, 2021 at $25 per sh.
** Reinvestment Option **f** Final Payment

Long-Term Debt - At Oct. 31, 2022, outstanding debt totaled $336,553,000 (net of $1,668,000 of unamortized issuance costs) and consisted entirely of notes due June 15, 2032, bearing interest at 5.095% per annum until June 15, 2027, and thereafter at the three-month CDOR plus 2.42% per annum until maturity.

Wholly Owned Subsidiaries

B2B Bank, Toronto, Ont. Book value of voting shares owned by the bank at Oct. 31, 2022, totaled $622,389,000.
LBC Capital Inc., Burlington, Ont. Book value of voting shares owned by the bank at Oct. 31, 2022, totaled $2,863,751,000.
- 100% int. in **NCF Commercial Finance Holdings Inc.**, Alpharetta, Ga.
  - 100% int. in **Northpoint Commercial Finance LLC**, Alpharetta, Ga.

LBC Financial Services Inc., Montréal, Qué. Book value of voting shares owned by the bank at Oct. 31, 2022, totaled $405,229,000.
LBC Investment Management Inc., Montréal, Qué. Book value of voting shares owned by the bank at Oct. 31, 2022, totaled $429,115,000.
- 100% int. in **V.R. Holding Insurance Company Ltd.**, St. James, Barbados.
  - 100% int. in **Venture Reinsurance Company Ltd.**, St. James, Barbados.

LBC Tech Inc., Toronto, Ont. Book value of voting shares owned by the bank at Oct. 31, 2022, totaled $1,574,000.
LBC Trust, Montréal, Qué. Book value of voting shares owned by the bank at Oct. 31, 2022, totaled $84,400,000.
Laurentian Bank Securities Inc., Montréal, Qué. Book value of voting shares owned by the bank at Oct. 31, 2022, totaled $220,976,000.

Laurentian Trust of Canada Inc., Montréal, Qué. Book value of voting shares owned by the bank at Oct. 31, 2022, totaled $108,421,000.
NCF International Holding Kft, Budapest, Hungary. Book value of voting shares owned by the bank at Oct. 31, 2022, totaled $66,564,000.
Note: The preceding list includes only the major related companies in which interests are held.

Financial Statistics

Periods ended:	12m Oct. 31/22[A]		12m Oct. 31/21[□A]
	$000s	%Chg	$000s
Interest income	**1,474,358**	**+18**	**1,253,315**
Interest expense	741,022		560,974
Net interest income	**733,336**	**+6**	**692,341**
Provision for loan losses	56,878		49,500
Other income	300,899		310,116
Salaries & pension benefits	386,157		370,400
Non-interest expense	701,661		880,362
Pre-tax income	**275,696**	**+280**	**72,595**
Income taxes	49,113		15,526
Net income	**226,583**	**+297**	**57,069**
Cash & equivalent	1,890,923		667,123
Securities	6,184,461		6,499,193
Net non-performing loans	105,385		163,918
Total loans	41,115,337		36,213,988
Fixed assets, net	121,227		100,576
Total assets	**50,716,758**	**+13**	**45,077,024**
Deposits	27,131,806		22,988,229
Other liabilities	20,467,296		19,098,143
Subordinated debt	336,553		349,782
Preferred share equity	244,403		245,683
Shareholders' equity	2,781,103		2,640,870
Cash from oper. activs	**896,888**	**+858**	**93,661**
Cash from fin. activs	(140,707)		(73,758)
Cash from invest. activs	(759,033)		(16,615)
Pension fund surplus	38,254		24,307
	$		$
Earnings per share*	4.96		1.03
Cash flow per share*	20.70		2.16
Cash divd. per share*	1.78		1.60
	shs		shs
No. of shs. o/s*	43,334,388		43,586,656
Avg. no. of shs. o/s*	43,329,000		43,407,000
	%		%
Basel III Common Equity Tier 1	9.10		10.20
Basel III Tier 1	10.10		11.40
Basel III Total	12.10		13.60
Net profit margin	21.91		5.69
Return on equity	8.71		1.88
Return on assets	0.47		0.13
Foreign sales percent	15		9
No. of employees (FTEs)	3,126		2,871

* Common
□ Restated
A Reported in accordance with IFRS

Latest Results

Periods ended:	6m Apr. 30/23[A]		6m Apr. 30/22[A]
	$000s	%Chg	$000s
Net interest income	371,301	+3	361,008
Net income	101,201	-12	115,067
	$		$
Earnings per share*	2.20		2.52

* Common
A Reported in accordance with IFRS

Historical Summary
(as originally stated)

Fiscal Year	Int. Inc.	Net Inc. Bef. Disc.	EPS*
	$000s	$000s	$
2022[A]	1,474,358	226,583	4.96
2021[A]	1,253,315	57,069	1.03
2020[A]	1,422,253	114,085	2.37
2019[A]	1,556,382	172,710	3.78
2018[A]	1,490,783	224,646	5.10

* Common
A Reported in accordance with IFRS

L.9 LeanLife Health Inc.

Symbol - LLP **Exchange** - CSE (S) **CUSIP** - 521855
Head Office - 380-580 Hornby St, Vancouver, BC, V6C 3P6 **Telephone** - (778) 373-8589 **Toll-free** - (888) 521-0872 **Fax** - (604) 608-5442
Website - www.leanlifehealth.com
Email - slis@leanlifehealth.com
Investor Relations - Stanislaw Lis (604) 764-0518
Auditors - Charlton & Company C.A., Vancouver, B.C.
Transfer Agents - Endeavor Trust Corporation, Vancouver, B.C.
Profile - (B.C. 2014) Develops proprietary plant-based food products and energy drink.

Offers omega-3 products which are derived from high quality flaxseed oil and food grade reagents. The products are formulated as liquids, emulsions or powders and could be used as food additives to boost nutritional quality of processed foods. Also holds distribution rights for Iron Energy, a retail energy drink made from ingredients like taurine, ginseng, inositol and vitamins. In addition, the company is building relationships with global food manufacturers in Canada, the United States, Mexico, the People's Republic of China, Japan, Australia and Poland.

Common suspended from CSE, Aug. 8, 2022.
Predecessor Detail - Name changed from LeenLife Pharma International Inc., Jan. 15, 2018.
Directors - Stanislaw (Stan) Lis, chr., Vancouver, B.C.; Robert Hall; Dr. Marcin Lukaszewicz, Wroclaw, Poland; Glen C. Macdonald, Vancouver, B.C.
Other Exec. Officers - Anis Barakat, CEO; Gavin Mah, COO; Daniel Cruz, CFO; Monita Faris, corp. sec.; Raymond Lin, contr.

Capital Stock

	Authorized (shs.)	Outstanding (shs.)[1]
Common	unlimited	207,106,077

[1] At Aug. 22, 2023

Price Range - LLP/CSE (S)

Year	Volume	High	Low	Close
2022	40,293,077	$0.05	$0.01	$0.02
2021	118,790,550	$0.17	$0.03	$0.03
2020	103,490,494	$0.13	$0.03	$0.12
2019	61,996,056	$0.11	$0.03	$0.06
2018	34,284,378	$0.45	$0.04	$0.05

Capital Stock Changes - In January 2022, private placement of 7,300,000 units (1 common share & ½ warrant) at 5¢ per unit was completed, with warrants exercisable at $0.075 per share for two years. In March 2022, 17,478,774 common shares were issued at 7¢ per share for debt settlement.

Wholly Owned Subsidiaries

Leanlife America, Inc., Nev.

Financial Statistics

Periods ended:	12m Mar. 31/21[A]		12m Mar. 31/20[□A]
	$000s	%Chg	$000s
General & admin expense	3,003		2,418
Stock-based compensation	631		199
Operating expense	**3,634**	**+39**	**2,617**
Operating income	**(3,634)**	**n.a.**	**(2,617)**
Deprec., depl. & amort.	2		6
Finance costs, gross	6		31
Write-downs/write-offs	nil		(27)
Pre-tax income	**(3,671)**	**n.a.**	**(2,952)**
Net income	**(3,671)**	**n.a.**	**(2,952)**
Cash & equivalent	263		nil
Inventories	178		nil
Accounts receivable	107		46
Current assets	1,137		46
Fixed assets, net	150		4
Total assets	**1,287**	**n.m.**	**50**
Accts. pay. & accr. liabs	457		875
Current liabilities	1,057		1,253
Shareholders' equity	230		(1,203)
Cash from oper. activs	**(1,214)**	**n.a.**	**(307)**
Cash from fin. activs	1,625		151
Cash from invest. activs	(148)		129
Capital expenditures	(148)		(16)
	$		$
Earnings per share*	(0.02)		(0.03)
Cash flow per share*	(0.01)		(0.00)
	shs		shs
No. of shs. o/s*	195,356,077		121,706,618
Avg. no. of shs. o/s*	158,097,070		102,794,743
	%		%
Net profit margin	n.a.		n.a.
Return on equity	n.m.		n.m.
Return on assets	(548.24)		(730.25)

* Common
□ Restated
A Reported in accordance with IFRS

Latest Results

Periods ended:	6m Sept. 30/21[A]		6m Sept. 30/20[□A]
	$000s	%Chg	$000s
Net income	(1,436)	n.a.	(730)
	$		$
Earnings per share*	(0.01)		(0.01)

* Common
□ Restated
A Reported in accordance with IFRS

Historical Summary
(as originally stated)

Fiscal Year	Oper. Rev.	Net Inc. Bef. Disc.	EPS*
	$000s	$000s	$
2021[A]	nil	(3,671)	(0.02)
2020[A]	nil	(2,952)	(0.03)
2019[A]	nil	(2,721)	(0.04)
2018[A]	nil	(2,361)	(0.06)
2017[A]	nil	(982)	(0.03)

* Common
A Reported in accordance with IFRS

L.10 Leef Brands Inc.

Symbol - LEEF **Exchange** - CSE **CUSIP** - 52426X
Head Office - 810-789 Pender St W, Vancouver, BC, V6C 1H2 **Telephone** - (604) 687-2038 **Fax** - (604) 687-3141
Website - leefbrands.com
Email - ir@leefca.com
Investor Relations - Kevin Wilson (778) 999-4226
Auditors - Macias Gini & O'Connell LLP C.P.A., Los Angeles, Calif.
Transfer Agents - National Securities Administrators Ltd., Vancouver, B.C.
Profile - (B.C. 2011) Operates as a vertically integrated cannabis company in California.

The company operates as a cannabis extraction and manufacturing company and provides bulk concentrate to cannabis brands in California. Operations include a 12,000-sq.-ft. extraction and manufacturing facility with significant throughput and distillate extraction capability. Core manufacturing competencies include ethanol extraction, hydrocarbon extraction and solventless extraction. Brands include Real Deal Resin, Ganga Gold, Heady and LEEF.

In September 2022, the company agreed to acquire **The Leaf at 73740 LLC**, a premium California retailer. Terms were not disclosed.

In May 2022, the company agreed to acquire **DNA Organics, Inc.** (dba Lifted Organics), a premium California-based cultivator and manufacturer, for a purchase price payable in common shares. The purchase would consist of 1.0x multiple of revenue for the period beginning Sept. 30, 2022, to Sept. 30, 2023, less the estimated revenue value of the current inventory on hand calculated at the time of close and less any estimated revenue value of produced between the time of close until Sept. 30, 2022.

Recent Merger and Acquisition Activity

Status: completed **Revised:** Apr. 20, 2022
UPDATE: The transaction was completed for issuance of 758,274,035 common shares. PREVIOUS: Icanic Brands Company Inc. agreed to acquire La Jolla, Calif.-based LEEF Holdings, Inc., which extracts and produces cannabis products in California, for the higher of US$120,000,000 or two times the trailing 12-months (TTM) revenue of LEEF for the period ended Sept. 30, 2021, which would be satisfied through the issuance of common shares. A performance earn-out payment would also be paid through the issuance of common shares in relation to the TTM revenue following certain periods upon completion of the transaction. Jan. 25, 2022 -The companies entered into a definitive agreement.

Predecessor Detail - Name changed from Icanic Brands Company Inc., Dec. 7, 2022.
Directors - Mark Smith, exec. chr., Edwards, Colo.; Micah Anderson, CEO; Emily Heitman, chief revenue officer, Calif.; Christopher P. (Chris) Cherry, Vancouver, B.C.; Andrew J. Glashow, R.I.
Other Exec. Officers - Kevin Wilson, CFO; Dr. Clive R. Spray, chief scientific & opers. officer

Capital Stock

	Authorized (shs.)	Outstanding (shs.)[1]
Preferred	unlimited	nil
Common	unlimited	1,019,258,205

[1] At Dec. 7, 2022

Major Shareholder - Alex Patel held 20.02% interest at May 12, 2022.

Price Range - LEEF/CSE

Year	Volume	High	Low	Close
2022	15,433,406	$0.28	$0.05	$0.06
2021	69,112,154	$0.82	$0.18	$0.21
2020	69,714,309	$0.77	$0.06	$0.56
2019	36,222,081	$0.56	$0.14	$0.22
2018	60,670,561	$2.02	$0.31	$0.34

Recent Close: $0.02
Capital Stock Changes - In April 2022, 758,274,035 common shares were issued pursuant to the reverse takeover acquisition of LEEF Holdings, Inc.

Wholly Owned Subsidiaries

De Krown Enterprises LLC, Calif.
GanjaGold Inc., Oakland, Calif.
LEEF Holdings, Inc., La Jolla, Calif.
1127466 B.C. Ltd., B.C.
- 100% int. in **X-Spray Industries Inc.**, Del.

1200665 B.C. Ltd., B.C.
- 100% int. in **Sullivan Park Capital LLC**, Nev.
- 100% int. in **V6E Holdings LLC**, Nev.

Latest Results

Periods ended:	9m Sept. 30/22[A]
	US$000s
Operating revenue	22,481
Net income	(6,907)
Net inc. for equity hldrs	(6,077)
Net inc. for non-cont. int	(830)
	US$
Earnings per share*	(0.01)

* Common
[A] Reported in accordance with IFRS

L.11 Left Field Capital Corp.

Symbol - LFC.P **Exchange** - TSX-VEN **CUSIP** - 524945
Head Office - 1703-595 Burrard St, Vancouver, BC, V7X 1J1 **Telephone** - (604) 488-5427
Email - lee@earlston.ca
Investor Relations - Brian E. Bayley (604) 488-5427
Auditors - Davidson & Company LLP C.A., Vancouver, B.C.
Transfer Agents - Odyssey Trust Company, Vancouver, B.C.
Profile - (B.C. 2022) Capital Pool Company.
Directors - Brian E. Bayley, pres., CEO, CFO & corp. sec., North Vancouver, B.C.; John Downes, Port Moody, B.C.; Scott A. McLean, Vancouver, B.C.

Capital Stock

	Authorized (shs.)	Outstanding (shs.)[1]
Common	unlimited	3,550,000

[1] At June 14, 2023

Major Shareholder - Iconic Securities Ltd. held 42.25% interest and Brian E. Bayley held 11.27% interest at June 14, 2023.

Price Range - LFC.P/TSX-VEN

Year	Volume	High	Low	Close
2022	20,000	$0.30	$0.25	$0.30

Recent Close: $0.20
Capital Stock Changes - On July 21, 2022, an initial public offering of 1,450,000 common shares was completed at 15¢ per share.

L.12 Legend Power Systems Inc.

Symbol - LPS **Exchange** - TSX-VEN **CUSIP** - 524937
Head Office - 1480 Frances St, Vancouver, BC, V5L 1Y9 **Telephone** - (604) 420-1500 **Toll-free** - (866) 772-8797 **Fax** - (604) 420-1533
Website - www.legendpower.com
Email - rbuchamer@legendpower.com
Investor Relations - Randall G. Buchamer (604) 671-9522
Auditors - MNP LLP C.A., Vancouver, B.C.
Lawyers - Owen Bird Law Corporation, Vancouver, B.C.
Transfer Agents - Computershare Trust Company of Canada Inc., Vancouver, B.C.
Profile - (B.C. 1987) Provides an intelligent energy management platform that analyzes and improves building energy challenges, significantly impacting asset management and corporate performance.
The company offers a single-solution energy management platform to enable owners or operators of light industrial and commercial buildings to both diagnose and then overcome the building level impacts of electric grid volatility which results in a less than optimal power supply, ensuring consistent power availability and reducing electricity bills and maintenance costs through SmartGATE Insights™ service and SmartGATE™ platform.
SmartGATE Insights™ is a metering and monitoring gateway that measures the high impact attributes of electricity and then applies an array of industry standard calculations to determine what effects they are having on a building. Findings are summarized and communicated to building owners via a Power Impact Report, with an easy-to-understand scorecard of relative building health, an assessment of the hidden financial and human costs, and finally a custom solution based on the company's turnkey technologies.
SmartGATE™ platform uses patented technology to correct the power issues uncovered by SmartGATE Insights. Has a small footprint and is uniquely suitable for a large array of commercial as well as light industrial applications.
Customers include the big box retailers, office buildings, social/co-op housing, condominiums, K-12 schools, cannabis, universities/colleges, prisons, industrial facilities, hotels/motels, government, rental apartments, grocery stores and mixed use-sectors. The company has agreements with distribution partners to resell SmartGATE and SmartGATE Insights.
Predecessor Detail - Name changed from Texas Gas & Oil Inc., July 3, 2008, following reverse takeover acquisition of Legend Power Systems Inc.
Directors - Cosimo (Cos) La Porta, chr., B.C.; Randall G. (Randy) Buchamer, pres. & CEO, North Vancouver, B.C.; Michael J. Atkinson, Vancouver, B.C.; David D. (Dave) Guebert, Calgary, Alta.; Jonathan Lansky, B.C.
Other Exec. Officers - Paul Moffat, COO; Florence Tan, CFO & corp. sec.; Mike Cioce, v-p, sales & mktg.; Mark Petersen, v-p, eng.

Capital Stock

	Authorized (shs.)	Outstanding (shs.)[1]
Common	unlimited	117,568,971

[1] At Dec. 22, 2022

Major Shareholder - Widely held at Aug. 4, 2022.

Price Range - LPS/TSX-VEN

Year	Volume	High	Low	Close
2022	14,837,322	$0.39	$0.14	$0.31
2021	31,672,364	$0.96	$0.32	$0.36
2020	12,328,255	$0.55	$0.16	$0.50
2019	12,891,892	$0.50	$0.14	$0.19
2018	15,729,361	$1.19	$0.31	$0.32

Recent Close: $0.18
Capital Stock Changes - During fiscal 2022, 26,668 common shares were issued on exercise of options.

Wholly Owned Subsidiaries

0809882 B.C. Ltd., B.C. Inactive.
- 100% int. in **LPSI (Barbados) Limited**, Barbados. Inactive.
- 100% int. in **Legend Power Systems Corp.**, Del.

Financial Statistics

Periods ended:	12m Sept. 30/22[A]		12m Sept. 30/21[A]
	$000s	%Chg	$000s
Operating revenue	**2,118**	**-22**	**2,714**
Cost of sales	1,914		2,143
Salaries & benefits	3,362		2,195
Research & devel. expense	486		535
General & admin expense	901		929
Stock-based compensation	513		755
Operating expense	**7,176**	**+9**	**6,557**
Operating income	**(5,058)**	**n.a.**	**(3,843)**
Deprec., depl. & amort	188		166
Finance costs, gross	17		20
Write-downs/write-offs	nil		(8)
Pre-tax income	**(5,346)**	**n.a.**	**(3,838)**
Net income	**(5,346)**	**n.a.**	**(3,838)**
Cash & equivalent	3,086		9,287
Inventories	1,590		1,274
Accounts receivable	716		562
Current assets	5,927		11,321
Fixed assets, net	120		144
Right-of-use assets	207		314
Intangibles, net	50		18
Total assets	**6,304**	**-47**	**11,797**
Accts. pay. & accr. liabs	558		990
Current liabilities	784		1,174
Long-term lease liabilities	64		192
Shareholders' equity	5,351		10,088
Cash from oper. activs	**(6,073)**	**n.a.**	**(2,565)**
Cash from fin. activs	(161)		9,562
Cash from invest. activs	(63)		(28)
Net cash position	**3,086**	**-67**	**9,287**
Capital expenditures	(11)		(12)
Capital disposals	nil		2
	$		$
Earnings per share*	(0.04)		(0.04)
Cash flow per share*	(0.05)		(0.02)
	shs		shs
No. of shs. o/s*	117,568,971		117,542,303
Avg. no. of shs. o/s*	117,558,304		107,256,318
	%		%
Net profit margin	(252.41)		(141.41)
Return on equity	(69.25)		(56.85)
Return on assets	(58.88)		(45.94)
Foreign sales percent	1		4

* Common
[A] Reported in accordance with IFRS

Historical Summary
(as originally stated)

Fiscal Year	Oper. Rev.	Net Inc. Bef. Disc.	EPS*
	$000s	$000s	$
2022[A]	2,118	(5,346)	(0.04)
2021[A]	2,714	(3,838)	(0.04)
2020[A]	2,028	(4,784)	(0.05)
2019[A]	2,335	(6,093)	(0.06)
2018[A]	6,595	(2,559)	(0.03)

* Common
[A] Reported in accordance with IFRS

L.13 Legible Inc.

Symbol - READ **Exchange** - CSE **CUSIP** - 52475E
Head Office - 2230 Ontario St, Vancouver, BC, V5T 2X2 **Telephone** - (672) 514-2665
Website - legible.com
Email - invest@legible.com
Investor Relations - Deborah Harford (672) 514-2665
Auditors - KPMG LLP C.A., Vancouver, B.C.
Transfer Agents - Olympia Trust Company
Profile - (Alta. 1996) Operates Legible, a browser-based and mobile-first digital reading and publishing platform.
The Legible platform allows readers to access a large catalogue of eBooks quickly, easily and affordably. The platform offers a catalogue of millions of eBooks for sale, rental, subscription and sponsored reading to online readers, as well as a proprietary AI-based curation tool called LibrarianAI. The company's business model contemplates five different revenue streams including eBook sales, monthly recurring subscription fees, ad revenue, digital rentals and comprehensive data and analytics.
The company also offers a global B2B eBook conversion and production service called Legible Publishing.
Predecessor Detail - Name changed from Twenty20 Investments Inc., Nov. 26, 2021, pursuant to the reverse takeover acquisition of Legible Media Inc.
Directors - Kaleeg Hainsworth, pres. & CEO, B.C.; Shannon Kaustinen; David Van Seters, B.C.
Other Exec. Officers - Edward J. (Ed) Duda, CFO; Angela Doll, chief opers. officer & chief publishing officer; Deborah Harford, exec. v-p, strategic partnerships

Capital Stock

	Authorized (shs.)	Outstanding (shs.)[1]
Common	unlimited	126,943,209

[1] At Aug. 8, 2023

Major Shareholder - Kaleeg Hainsworth held 27.07% interest at Dec. 1, 2021.

Price Range - READ/CSE

Year	Volume	High	Low	Close
2022	20,860,596	$0.64	$0.08	$0.10
2021	3,532,586	$1.40	$0.47	$0.50

Recent Close: $0.13
Capital Stock Changes - In June and July 2023, private placement of 15,237,585 units (1 common share & 1 warrant) at 9¢ per unit was completed, with warrants exercisable at 12¢ per share for one year.
In November 2022, private placement of 6,945,656 units (1 common share & 1 warrant) at 10¢ per unit was completed. Also during 2022, common shares were issued as follows: 4,451,130 as pre-paid interest on debentures, 2,200,000 on conversion of debentures and 1,230,000 on exercise of warrants.

Wholly Owned Subsidiaries

Legible Media Inc., Vancouver, B.C.

Financial Statistics

Periods ended:	12m Dec. 31/22[A]		12m Dec. 31/21[A1]
	$000s	%Chg	$000s
Operating revenue	**21**	**n.m.**	**1**
Cost of sales	11		1
Salaries & benefits	3,411		3,331
General & admin expense	2,501		3,240
Stock-based compensation	491		1,329
Operating expense	**6,414**	**-19**	**7,901**
Operating income	**(6,393)**	**n.a.**	**(7,900)**
Deprec., depl. & amort	563		364
Finance costs, gross	434		nil
Write-downs/write-offs	(1,710)		nil
Pre-tax income	**(8,966)**	**n.a.**	**(12,911)**
Income taxes	(184)		nil
Net income	**(8,782)**	**n.a.**	**(12,911)**
Cash & equivalent	150		833
Accounts receivable	58		111
Current assets	319		1,217
Fixed assets, net	12		103
Intangibles, net	nil		2,213
Total assets	**331**	**-91**	**3,533**
Bank indebtedness	651		nil
Accts. pay. & accr. liabs	2,045		719
Current liabilities	2,724		869
Long-term debt, gross	1,267		nil
Long-term debt, net	1,267		nil
Equity portion of conv. debs	481		nil
Shareholders' equity	(3,660)		2,664
Cash from oper. activs	**(3,842)**	**n.a.**	**(6,354)**
Cash from fin. activs	3,143		8,304
Cash from invest. activs	17		(1,264)
Net cash position	**150**	**-82**	**833**
Capital expenditures	(23)		(126)
Capital disposals	40		nil
	$		$
Earnings per share*	(0.13)		(0.26)
Cash flow per share*	(0.06)		(0.13)
	shs		shs
No. of shs. o/s*	77,774,786		62,948,000
Avg. no. of shs. o/s*	67,041,676		49,095,325
	%		%
Net profit margin	n.m.		n.m.
Return on equity	n.m.		(576.64)
Return on assets	(432.55)		(460.12)

* Common
[A] Reported in accordance with IFRS
[1] Results reflect the Nov. 26, 2021, reverse takeover acquisition of Legible Media Inc.

Latest Results

Periods ended:	3m Mar. 31/23[A]		3m Mar. 31/22[A]
	$000s	%Chg	$000s
Operating revenue	11	n.a.	nil
Net income	(1,217)	n.a.	(2,749)
	$		$
Earnings per share*	(0.01)		(0.05)

* Common
[A] Reported in accordance with IFRS

Historical Summary
(as originally stated)

Fiscal Year	Oper. Rev. $000s	Net Inc. Bef. Disc. $000s	EPS* $
2022[A]	21	(8,782)	(0.13)
2021[A]	1	(12,911)	(0.26)
2020[A1,2]	nil	(874)	(0.03)

* Common
[A] Reported in accordance with IFRS
[1] 49 weeks ended Dec. 31, 2020.
[2] Results pertain to Legible Media Inc.

L.14 Lendified Holdings Inc.

Symbol - LHI.H **Exchange** - TSX-VEN (S) **CUSIP** - 526024
Head Office - 811-365 Bay St, Toronto, ON, M5H 2V1 **Toll-free** - (844) 451-3594
Website - www.lendified.com
Email - eoghan.bergin@lendified.com
Investor Relations - Eoghan Bergin (844) 451-3594
Auditors - McGovern Hurley LLP C.A., Toronto, Ont.
Transfer Agents - Computershare Trust Company of Canada Inc., Montréal, Qué.
Profile - (Can. 2018) No operations.

On Dec. 15, 2022, certain secured creditors of wholly owned **Lendified PrivCo Holding Corporation**, **Lendified Inc.** and **WPCFP SPV Inc.** will be appointing a receiver over all of the assets of the subsidiaries, consisting mostly of loan portfolios, and initiating proceedings under the Bankruptcy and Insolvency Act (Canada) and the Personal Property Security Act (Ontario) to seize the subsidiaries' assets comprising the security under the loan agreements with such secured creditors in the amount of $6,631,120 in which the subsidiaries are unable to pay.

On Jan. 18, 2023, the secured assets that were seized by the secured creditors under the Personal Property Security (Ontario) were sold for $1,470,704. The subsidiaries remain indebted to the secured creditors in the amount of $5,042,000. The sale of assets also included certain intellectual property. As a result of the sale of the assets, the company no longer has an operating business.

Common suspended from TSX-VEN, May 8, 2023.

Predecessor Detail - Name changed from Hampton Bay Capital Inc., Apr. 28, 2020, pursuant to Qualifying Transaction reverse takeover acquisition of (old) Lendified Holdings Inc.; basis 1 new for 1.88 old shs.

Directors - Chris Tambakis, chr., Toronto, Ont.; Eoghan Bergin, CEO, Ont.; Perry N. Dellelce, Toronto, Ont.

Other Exec. Officers - Pratik Bhandari, CFO & corp. sec.

Capital Stock

	Authorized (shs.)	Outstanding (shs.)[1]
Common	unlimited	446,199,349

[1] At May 27, 2022

Major Shareholder - Alfonso, Melina and Maria Cristina Rizzuto collectively held 28.47% interest at Nov. 1, 2021.

Price Range - LHI.H/TSX-VEN (S)

Year	Volume	High	Low	Close
2022	19,837,219	$0.03	$0.01	$0.01
2021	21,156,831	$0.13	$0.02	$0.02
2020	8,954,072	$0.25	$0.01	$0.03
2019	480,010	$0.23	$0.10	$0.11

Consolidation: 1-for-1.88 cons. in May 2020
Recent Close: $0.01

Wholly Owned Subsidiaries

Lendified I.N. Funding Inc.
Lendified PrivCo Holding Corporation, Ont.
- 100% int. in **Lendified Inc.**, Toronto, Ont.
  - 100% int. in **Castle Return Inc.**, Toronto, Ont.
  - 100% int. in **First Return Inc.**, Toronto, Ont.
  - 100% int. in **WPCFP SPV Inc.**

Vault Circle Inc.

Financial Statistics

Periods ended:	12m Dec. 31/21[A]		12m Dec. 31/20[A1]
	$000s	%Chg	$000s
Operating revenue	**1,726**	**-67**	**5,227**
Salaries & benefits	999		1,601
Research & devel. expense	145		442
General & admin expense	819		2,163
Other operating expense	(642)		9,867
Operating expense	**1,322**	**-91**	**14,073**
Operating income	**404**	**n.a.**	**(8,846)**
Deprec., depl. & amort.	9		56
Finance costs, gross	1,360		3,308
Write-downs/write-offs	nil		(103)
Pre-tax income	**612**	**n.a.**	**(11,089)**
Net inc. bef. disc. opers	**612**	**n.a.**	**(11,089)**
Income from disc. opers	nil		(1,002)
Net income	**612**	**n.a.**	**(12,092)**
Cash & equivalent	1,168		548
Accounts receivable	1,812		4,753
Current assets	3,713		7,117
Long-term investments	329		472
Fixed assets, net	nil		4
Intangibles, net	nil		5
Total assets	**4,042**	**-47**	**7,625**
Accts. pay. & accr. liabs	3,419		5,144
Current liabilities	9,766		24,285
Long-term debt, gross	7,336		19,373
Long-term debt, net	1,119		365
Shareholders' equity	(6,843)		(17,195)
Cash from oper. activs	**198**	**n.a.**	**(7,280)**
Cash from fin. activs	423		4,105
Cash from invest. activs	nil		767
Net cash position	**1,168**	**+113**	**548**
	$		$
Earns. per sh. bef disc opers*	0.00		(0.11)
Earnings per share*	0.00		(0.12)
Cash flow per share*	0.00		(0.04)
	shs		shs
No. of shs. o/s*	446,199,349		190,292,639
Avg. no. of shs. o/s*	296,114,146		100,366,073
	%		%
Net profit margin	35.46		(212.15)
Return on equity	n.m.		n.m.
Return on assets	33.80		(47.25)

* Common
[A] Reported in accordance with IFRS
[1] Results prior to Apr. 30, 2020, pertain to and reflect the Qualifying Transaction reverse takeover acquisition of (old) Lendifield Holdings Inc.

Latest Results

Periods ended:	3m Mar. 31/22[A]		3m Mar. 31/21[A]
	$000s	%Chg	$000s
Operating revenue	265	-55	593
Net income	(392)	n.a.	(539)
	$		$
Earnings per share*	(0.00)		(0.00)

* Common
[A] Reported in accordance with IFRS

Historical Summary
(as originally stated)

Fiscal Year	Oper. Rev. $000s	Net Inc. Bef. Disc. $000s	EPS* $
2021[A]	1,726	612	0.00
2020[A]	5,227	(11,089)	(0.11)
2019[A]	7,059	(14,899)	n.a.
2018[A]	4,097	(9,717)	n.a.

* Common
[A] Reported in accordance with IFRS
Note: Adjusted throughout for 1-for-1.88 cons. in May 2020

L.15 LeoNovus Inc.

Symbol - LTV **Exchange** - TSX-VEN **CUSIP** - 526681
Head Office - 125-2611 Queensview Dr, Ottawa, ON, K2B 8K2
Telephone - (613) 319-5117 **Toll-free** - (866) 299-0815
Website - www.leonovus.com
Email - mgaffney@leonovus.com
Investor Relations - Michael J. Gaffney (613) 319-5117
Auditors - Kenway Mack Slusarchuk Stewart LLP C.A., Canmore, Alta.
Transfer Agents - TSX Trust Company, Toronto, Ont.
Profile - (Ont. 2008) Provides a suite of secure data management software products that focus on applying data-centric, rather than infrastructure-centric, security and compliance controls.

Solutions include Vault, a software-based multi-cloud data controller solution that enables efficient, secure and cost-effective use of on-premises, private and public cloud storage; Data Discovery Tool, a software-based solution which allows customers to visualize their file storage profile and create reports that include the number of files and the amount of storage they consume according to file type and the date they were last accessed to address exponential data growth by tiering out infrequently accessed data; Smart Filer, which seamlessly and automatically migrates infrequently accessed data from file servers to secondary or cloud storage, freeing capacity while ensuring that data remains accessible throughout the migration process; Data View Gateways, a solution that controls repository internal or external data sharing wherein only authenticated and authorized users gain access and then all interactions are fully tracked and logged; Smart Secure Data Lake, a multi-sourced context-rich repository for advanced analytics which is the entry point of the organization's data pipeline that secures and enhances the quality of the data from its origin; Consolidata, a multi-sourced data collation and aggregation for near real-time insights which unifies data that enable users to have one stop sourcing for real-time tracking or reporting, diagnostic, analytic, and process information; and Torozo (formerly XVault), a Software-as-a-Service (SaaS) data sharing, transfer and storage platform that encrypts, shreds and distributes files across a range of cloud storage providers, ensuring security by making files unreadable in transit.

Predecessor Detail - Name changed from Work Horse Capital & Strategic Acquisitions Ltd., Feb. 17, 2011.

Directors - Michael J. Gaffney, chr. & CEO, N.S.; Daniel (Dan) Willis, chief tech. officer, Smiths Falls, Ont.; Denis Archambault, Ottawa, Ont.

Other Exec. Officers - Christopher (Chris) Carmichael, CFO; Eric Lee, v-p, bus. devel., U.S.A.; Sean O'Hagan, v-p, eng.

Capital Stock

	Authorized (shs.)	Outstanding (shs.)[1]
Preferred	unlimited	nil
Common	unlimited	20,900,996

[1] At May 1, 2023

Major Shareholder - Widely held at Apr. 28, 2022.

Price Range - LTV/TSX-VEN

Year	Volume	High	Low	Close
2022	7,896,410	$0.28	$0.04	$0.04
2021	12,376,034	$1.95	$0.13	$0.19
2020	5,938,685	$1.50	$0.30	$0.42
2019	2,346,696	$6.00	$0.30	$0.60
2018	7,330,959	$11.55	$3.90	$4.35

Consolidation: 1-for-30 cons. in Oct. 2020
Recent Close: $0.02

Wholly Owned Subsidiaries

LeoNovus USA, Inc., Palo Alto, Calif.

Financial Statistics

Periods ended:	12m Dec. 31/21[A]		12m Dec. 31/20[◻A]
	$000s	%Chg	$000s
Operating revenue	**78**	**-76**	**327**
Salaries & benefits	569		738
Research & devel. expense	179		131
General & admin expense	1,410		933
Stock-based compensation	157		34
Operating expense	**2,315**	**+26**	**1,836**
Operating income	**(2,237)**	**n.a.**	**(1,509)**
Deprec., depl. & amort.	187		182
Finance costs, gross	116		199
Pre-tax income	**(2,581)**	**n.a.**	**(1,802)**
Net income	**(2,581)**	**n.a.**	**(1,802)**
Cash & equivalent	1,247		834
Accounts receivable	86		182
Current assets	1,349		1,528
Fixed assets, net	1,419		1,606
Total assets	**2,768**	**-12**	**3,134**
Bank indebtedness	nil		296
Accts. pay. & accr. liabs	404		548
Current liabilities	606		1,510
Long-term lease liabilities	741		826
Shareholders' equity	1,421		798
Cash from oper. activs	**(2,052)**	**n.a.**	**(1,192)**
Cash from fin. activs	2,407		1,259
Cash from invest. activs	nil		50
Net cash position	**1,247**	**+50**	**834**
	$		$
Earnings per share*	(0.14)		(0.19)
Cash flow per share*	(0.11)		(0.12)
	shs		shs
No. of shs. o/s*	20,900,996		14,757,424
Avg. no. of shs. o/s*	18,780,201		9,560,995
	%		%
Net profit margin	n.m.		(551.07)
Return on equity	(232.63)		(197.00)
Return on assets	(83.53)		(54.13)

* Common
◻ Restated
[A] Reported in accordance with IFRS

Latest Results

Periods ended:	9m Sept. 30/22^A		9m Sept. 30/21^A
	$000s	%Chg	$000s
Operating revenue	5	-94	78
Net income	(1,577)	n.a.	(1,970)
	$		$
Earnings per share*	(0.08)		(0.11)

* Common
A Reported in accordance with IFRS

Historical Summary
(as originally stated)

Fiscal Year	Oper. Rev.	Net Inc. Bef. Disc.	EPS*
	$000s	$000s	$
2021^A	78	(2,581)	(0.14)
2020^A	327	(1,802)	(0.19)
	US$000s	US$000s	US$
2019^A	24	(5,193)	(0.60)
2018^A	14	(4,924)	(0.60)
2017^A	14	(2,725)	(0.30)

* Common
A Reported in accordance with IFRS
Note: Adjusted throughout for 1-for-30 cons. in Oct. 2020

L.16 Leon's Furniture Limited*

Symbol - LNF **Exchange** - TSX **CUSIP** - 526682
Head Office - 45 Gordon Mackay Rd, Toronto, ON, M9N 3X3 **Telephone** - (416) 243-7880 **Fax** - (416) 243-7890
Website - www.leons.ca
Email - investors@leons.ca
Investor Relations - Constantine Pefanis (416) 243-4074
Auditors - Ernst & Young LLP C.A., Toronto, Ont.
Transfer Agents - TSX Trust Company, Toronto, Ont.
FP500 Revenue Ranking - 187
Employees - 8,244 at Dec. 31, 2022
Profile - (Ont. 1969) Retails household furniture, mattresses, appliances and home electronics through 202 corporate stores and 101 franchised outlets across Canada under the banners Leon's, The Brick (includes the Midnorthern Appliance banner), Appliance Canada, Brick Outlet and The Brick Mattress Store.

Retail

Owns and operates 53 retail furniture stores under the banner Leon's Furniture and 117 stores operating under the banner The Brick which offer branded and private label household furniture, home electronics, home office products, appliances and mattresses. Also operates six The Brick Outlet stores, which feature the Brick lineup as well as special buys, last chance discontinued, one-of-a-kind and clearance products; and 21 The Brick Mattress stores, which carry product lines not typically carried at The Brick locations and feature mid- to high-end national brands and exclusive specialty products. Under the banner Appliance Canada, operates five showrooms which sell higher end appliances, electronics and mattresses. The company also has 35 Leon's Furniture and 66 The Brick franchise stores.

Commercial

Under the banners The Brick, Appliance Canada and Brick's Midnorthern Appliance, supplies home appliances to builders, developers, renovators, property management companies, hotel and extended care industries, landlords, insurance companies and government sectors. Also owns commercial real estate leased to third parties.

Other Services

eCommerce Division - Offers products online, including certain products that are not carried by the stores, through the leons.ca, thebrick.com, furniture.ca, midnorthern.com, transglobalservice.com and appliancecanada.com websites.

Trans Global Services - Provides household furniture, electronics and mechanical repair services to customers and performs work in respect of warranties for products sourced without manufacturer warranties, for products sold with extended warranties and for products sent to the repair services division by manufacturers who need to repair a product under their manufacturer's warranty. Also provides repair services to third parties.

Credit Insurance Services - Offers its customers insurance on their purchase card balances, which provides coverage for a variety of circumstances.

Extended Warranty Programs - Through wholly owned **King & State Limited**, offers warranties on appliances, electronics and furniture to provide coverage that extends beyond the manufacturer's warranty period by up to five years.

Foreign Operations - Through wholly owned **First Oceans Trading Corporation**, **First Oceans Hong Kong Limited** and **First Oceans Shanghai Limited**, holds foreign assets or operations in the People's Republic of China, Malaysia, Taiwan and Vietnam. These operations relate to the company's import program for sourcing products from Asia for resale in Canada through its retail operations.

On May 4, 2023, the company announced plans to create a real estate investment trust (REIT) which it plans to vend in a significant portion of its 5,200,000 sq. ft. of real estate. The company was exploring various strategic alternatives for the REIT transaction which could involve an initial public offering of the REIT or a shareholder approved spin out of the REIT to the company's shareholders. The company plans to maintain a majority ongoing ownership interest in the REIT. Timing of the transaction would be subject to prevailing market conditions and receipt of required regulatory approvals including approval to list the units on the Toronto Stock Exchange.

In November 2022, the company announced a 50/50 joint venture with Toronto, Ont.-based agency **Little Rocket Inc.** to offer commercial solutions that bridge e-commerce with bricks and mortar for North American clients. Little Rocket specializes in e-commerce implementation and product development, and is a noted Shopify® Plus partner.

In October 2022, the company announced plans to develop a new 500,000-sq.-ft. distribution centre and head office for The Brick in Edmonton, Alta. The new facility, which was slated to open in 2024, would replace the existing 365,000-sq.-ft. facility in Edmonton. The facility is a 50/50 joint venture with **Qualico Properties**.

Directors - Mark J. Leon, chr., Toronto, Ont.; Terrence T. (Terry) Leon, v-chr., Toronto, Ont.; Frank Gagliano, Toronto, Ont.; Alan J. Lenczner, Toronto, Ont.; Edward F. Leon, King City, Ont.; Joseph M. Leon II, Mississauga, Ont.; Mary Ann Leon, Toronto, Ont.; The Hon. Lisa Raitt, Ont.

Other Exec. Officers - Michael J. (Mike) Walsh, pres. & CEO; Constantine (Costa) Pefanis, CFO; Moe Assaf, v-p, finl. srvcs.; John A. Cooney, v-p, legal & corp. sec.; Victor Diab, v-p, fin.; Luke Leon, v-p, opers. & corp. strategy; David B. (Dave) Freeman, pres., Brick div.; Lewis Leon, pres., Leon's furniture div.

Capital Stock

	Authorized (shs.)	Outstanding (shs.)[1]
Non-voting	unlimited	[2]
Series 2012	306,500	54,532
Series 2013	1,485,000	279,887
Series 2014	740,000	171,464
Series 2015	880,000	260,121
Common	unlimited	67,880,867

[1] At Mar. 31, 2023
[2] Classified as debt.

Normal Course Issuer Bid - The company plans to make normal course purchases of up to 3,341,165 common shares representing 5% of the total outstanding. The bid commenced on Sept. 15, 2022, and expires on Sept. 14, 2023.

Major Shareholder - Leon family held 69.5% interest at May 3, 2023.

Price Range - LNF/TSX

Year	Volume	High	Low	Close
2022	7,852,986	$25.41	$14.61	$17.19
2021	4,168,454	$26.78	$19.67	$24.85
2020	4,181,320	$21.68	$10.25	$20.63
2019	4,397,085	$17.29	$14.01	$16.67
2018	2,290,330	$19.50	$14.70	$15.03

Recent Close: $18.55

Capital Stock Changes - In January 2022, 7,999,993 common shares were repurchased under a Substantial Issuer Bid. During 2022, common shares were issued as follows: 4,295 on conversion of a like number of non-voting series 2009 shares, 14,756 on conversion of a like number of non-voting series 2012 shares, 22,118 on conversion of a like number of non-voting series 2013 shares, 3,804 on conversion of a like number of non-voting series 2014 shares, 6,483 on conversion of a like number of non-voting series 2015 shares and 903,013 under a management share purchase plan. In addition, 1,594,300 were repurchased under an automatic share purchase plan and 299,200 common shares were repurchased under a Normal Course Issuer Bid.

Dividends

LNF com Ra $0.64 pa Q est. Jan. 7, 2021
Prev. Rate: $0.56 est. Oct. 8, 2020
$1.25◆ Oct. 8/21 $0.30◆ Jan. 7/21
Paid in 2023: $0.64 2022: $0.64 2021: $0.64 + $1.55◆
◆ Special

Long-Term Debt - Outstanding at Dec. 31, 2022:

Sr. credit facility due May 2024[1]	$234,375,000
Non-voting shares	7,000
	234,382,000
Less: Current portion	7,500,000
	226,882,000

[1] Bears interest at Canadian prime, LIBOR and banker's acceptance rates plus an applicable standby fee on undrawn amounts.

Non-voting Series 2012/2013/2014/2015 - Issuable in series. Purchased by employees using non-interest bearing loans advanced by the company, which are repayable through the application of any dividends on these shares, with any balance repayable on the date the shares are converted to common shares. Employee share purchase loans have been netted against the redeemable share liability based upon their terms. Each Series 2012 are convertible at the option of the holder into common shares on a 1-for-1 basis at any time after the fifth anniversary date of issue, while Series 2013, 2014 and 2015 are convertible at the option of the holder into common shares on a 1-for-1 basis at any time after the third anniversary date of issue. Series 2012 are redeemable at the option of the holder or the company at any time after the fifth anniversary date of issue and prior to the tenth anniversary of such issue at the original issue price, while Series 2013, 2014 and 2015 are redeemable at the option of the holder or the company at any time after the third anniversary date of issue and prior to the tenth anniversary of the issue at the original price.

Wholly Owned Subsidiaries

Ablan Insurance Corporation, Barbados.
The Brick Ltd., Edmonton, Alta.
- 100% int. in **The Brick GP Ltd.**, Canada.
- 100% int. in **The Brick Warehouse LP**, Man.
  - 100% int. in **United Furniture GP Ltd.**, Canada.
  - 100% int. in **United Furniture Warehouse LP**, Man.
    - 100% int. in **First Oceans Trading Corporation**, Alta.
      - 100% int. in **First Oceans Hong Kong Limited**, Hong Kong, Hong Kong, People's Republic of China.
        - 100% int. in **First Oceans Shanghai Limited**, People's Republic of China.
    - 100% int. in **Trans Global Warranty Corp.**, Canada.
      - 100% int. in **Trans Global Insurance Company**, Alta.
      - 100% int. in **Trans Global Life Insurance Company**, Alta.

King & State Limited, Barbados.
Leon Holdings (1967) Limited, Ont.
Murlee Holdings Limited, Ont.

Financial Statistics

Periods ended:	12m Dec. 31/22^A		12m Dec. 31/21^A
	$000s	%Chg	$000s
Operating revenue	**2,517,659**	**0**	**2,512,670**
Cost of goods sold	1,408,226		1,404,446
Salaries & benefits	425,579		420,068
General & admin expense	319,147		287,011
Operating expense	**2,152,952**	**+2**	**2,111,525**
Operating income	**364,707**	**-9**	**401,145**
Deprec., depl. & amort.	109,967		112,012
Finance income	4,486		5,767
Finance costs, gross	26,015		20,752
Pre-tax income	**236,221**	**-15**	**276,379**
Income taxes	56,792		69,221
Net income	**179,429**	**-13**	**207,158**
Cash & equivalent	226,369		490,416
Inventories	410,612		395,646
Accounts receivable	180,482		160,093
Current assets	851,912		1,075,289
Long-term investments	14,470		14,850
Fixed assets, net	608,465		657,809
Intangibles, net	659,861		660,293
Total assets	**2,193,643**	**-11**	**2,453,133**
Accts. pay. & accr. liabs	249,846		543,737
Current liabilities	610,235		1,199,744
Long-term debt, gross	234,382		90,013
Long-term debt, net	226,882		13
Long-term lease liabilities	248,466		291,334
Shareholders' equity	928,885		791,193
Cash from oper. activs	**14,297**	**-95**	**313,753**
Cash from fin. activs	(244,605)		(316,462)
Cash from invest. activs	(36,703)		16,212
Net cash position	**115,127**	**-70**	**382,138**
Capital expenditures	(26,798)		(14,896)
Capital disposals	322		1,138
	$		$
Earnings per share*	2.66		2.67
Cash flow per share*	0.21		4.04
Cash divd. per share*	0.64		0.64
Extra divd. - cash*	nil		1.25
Total divd. per share*	**0.64**		**1.89**
	shs		shs
No. of shs. o/s*	67,861,289		76,800,313
Avg. no. of shs. o/s*	67,512,284		77,623,382
	%		%
Net profit margin	7.13		8.24
Return on equity	20.86		22.93
Return on assets	8.57		9.14
No. of employees (FTEs)	8,244		8,434

* Common
A Reported in accordance with IFRS

Latest Results

Periods ended:	3m Mar. 31/23^A		3m Mar. 31/22^A
	$000s	%Chg	$000s
Operating revenue	513,013	-6	547,220
Net income	12,917	-48	24,758
	$		$
Earnings per share*	0.19		0.37

* Common
A Reported in accordance with IFRS

Historical Summary
(as originally stated)

Fiscal Year	Oper. Rev.	Net Inc. Bef. Disc.	EPS*
	$000s	$000s	$
2022[A]	2,517,659	179,429	2.66
2021[A]	2,512,670	207,158	2.67
2020[A]	2,220,180	163,250	2.05
2019[A]	2,283,411	106,929	1.38
2018[A]	2,241,437	111,030	1.45

* Common
[A] Reported in accordance with IFRS

L.17 Leveljump Healthcare Corp.

Symbol - JUMP **Exchange** - TSX-VEN **CUSIP** - 52731E
Head Office - 304-85 Scarsdale Rd, Toronto, ON, M3B 2R2 **Toll-free** - (877) 772-6965 **Fax** - (416) 900-0957
Website - www.leveljumphealthcare.com
Email - mitch@leveljumphealthcare.com
Investor Relations - Mitchell Geisler (877) 722-6965
Auditors - Clearhouse LLP C.A., Mississauga, Ont.
Transfer Agents - Odyssey Trust Company, Vancouver, B.C.
Employees - 5 at June 20, 2022
Profile - (Can. 2019) Provides remote radiology (teleradiology) services to smaller and rural hospitals, as well as imaging centres in Canada using licensed IT platforms and hosted servers.

Teleradiology is the process of providing remote off site reading of radiology scans such as Computed Tomography (CT), Magnetic Resonance Imaging (MRI), Ultrasound and X-ray. Hospital staff scan their emergency room patients, then page the company's radiologist on call, who can then remotely view the images via secured server, diagnose the patient and provide a report back to the hospital. The target market is primarily hospitals' emergency room care.

The company plans to expand by acquiring independent healthcare facilities focused on diagnostic imaging as well as marketing its services in other provinces.

Affiliate **Shaw Lens Inc.** (34.6% owned) holds a U.S. patent protected lens technology that can solve aniseikonia, a condition for people who wear glasses that causes each eye to perceive the size of objects differently.

In November 2022, the company acquired an existing Independent Health Facility (IHF) licence to operate a diagnostic imaging centre for $1,400,000, consisting of $500,000 cash, $700,000 6.66% term loan and issuance of 2,000,000 common shares at a deemed price of 10¢ per share.

In July 2022, the company terminated the agreement to acquire additional 10.44% interest in private Mississauga, Ont.-based **Real Time Medical Inc.** Previously, the company acquired 16.9% interest in Real Time in December 2021, for issuance of 2,494,576 units (3 common shares & 1 warrant) at 66¢ per unit and 392,875 units (3 common shares & 1 warrant) at 50¢ per unit, as well as 8.31% interest in February 2022, for issuance of 1,420,961 (5 common shares & 1 warrant) at 65¢ per unit. As a result, the company held 25.21% interest in Real Time. Real Time provides teleradiology services and develops diagnostic workload balancing, workflow orchestration, peer learning and diagnostic operations software.

In April 2022, the company acquired an additional 10.8% interest in private Ontario-based **Shaw Vision Inc.** and **Shaw Lens Inc.** for $104,000. Previously, the company acquired 23.8% interest in Shaw Vision and Shaw Lens for $129,500, issuance of 350,000 common shares at 28¢ per share and 350,000 warrants. Shaw Vision and Shaw Lens holds a U.S. patent-protected lens technology that can solve a condition for people who wear glasses, known as aniseikonia. As a result, the company held 34.6% interest in Shaw Vision and Shaw Lens.

Recent Merger and Acquisition Activity

Status: pending **Announced:** Nov. 21, 2022
Leveljump Healthcare Corp. agreed to acquire four diagnostic imaging clinics in Calgary, Alta., for $5,880,000 including $100,000 deposit, $4,950,000 cash, issuance of 830,000 common shares at $0.10 per share and issuance of 830,000 class A series 1 preferred shares at $0.90 per share. The clinics offer medical imaging including X-ray, ultrasound, fluoroscopy and bone mineral density scans.

Status: terminated **Revised:** July 19, 2022
UPDATE: The transaction was terminated. PREVIOUS: Leveljump Healthcare Corp. agreed to acquire private midwest U.S.-based Telehospital Corp. for US$7,130,000 including US$100,000 paid upon the signing of definitive agreements, US$4,900,000 cash payable on closing, issuance of US$500,000 5% note and issuance of 4,000,000 common shares at Cdn$0.20 per share. In addition, a US$1,000,000 bonus payment on the achievement of certain gross revenue targets. Telehospital provides remote medical care, particularly for rural and underserved communities. Telehospital has created its own examination cart and peripherals that can be easily utilized by onsite staff to provide real time data to remote hospitalists and subspecialists for ER or hospital patients.

Predecessor Detail - Name changed from Good2Go2 Corp., Dec. 4, 2020, following Qualifying Transaction three-cornered amalgamation with private Canadian Teleradiology Services, Inc.; basis 1 new for 1.8 old shs.

Directors - Mitchell (Mitch) Geisler, chr. & CEO, Toronto, Ont.; Robert (Rob) Landau, CFO & corp. sec., Toronto, Ont.; Jackie Glazer, Ont.; Richard Jagodnik, Sainte-Anne-de-Bellevue, Qué.; Gary Prihar, Surrey, B.C.

Capital Stock

	Authorized (shs.)	Outstanding (shs.)[1]
Common	unlimited	85,043,229

[1] At Nov. 29, 2022

Major Shareholder - Robert (Rob) Landau held 15.31% interest and Mitchell (Mitch) Geisler held 14.78% interest at Sept. 6, 2022.

Price Range - JUMP/TSX-VEN

Year	Volume	High	Low	Close
2022	13,723,141	$0.18	$0.04	$0.08
2021	28,718,281	$0.63	$0.10	$0.11
2020	1,919,782	$0.47	$0.18	$0.41

Recent Close: $0.06

Capital Stock Changes - In February and March 2022, private placement of 10,168,559 units (1 common share & 1 warrant) at 15¢ per unit was completed, with warrants exercisable at 20¢ per share for 22 months. In June 2022, private placement of 5,846,668 units (1 common share & 1 warrant) at 15¢ per unit was completed, with warrants exercisable at 20¢ per share for 21 months. In October 2022, private placement of up to 10,000,000 units (1 common share & 1 class A preferred share, series 1) at $1.00 per unit was announced.

Wholly Owned Subsidiaries

Canadian Teleradiology Services, Inc., North York, Ont.
- 100% int. in **Belleville X-ray & Ultrasound Ltd.**
- 100% int. in **Kente X-ray and Ultrasound Ltd.**

Leveljump Technologies Inc., Ont.

Investments

25.6% int. in **Real Time Medical Inc.**, Ont.
34.6% int. in **Shaw Lens Inc.**, Toronto, Ont.
34.6% int. in **Shaw Vision Inc.**, Toronto, Ont.

Financial Statistics

Periods ended:	12m Dec. 31/21[A]		12m Dec. 31/20[ōA]
	$000s	%Chg	$000s
Operating revenue	**6,719**	**+23**	**5,456**
Cost of sales	5,367		4,414
Salaries & benefits	1,444		513
General & admin expense	1,327		457
Stock-based compensation	744		68
Other operating expense	nil		2,121
Operating expense	**8,883**	**+17**	**7,573**
Operating income	**(2,164)**	**n.a.**	**(2,117)**
Deprec., depl. & amort.	34		33
Finance costs, gross	38		81
Pre-tax income	**(2,229)**	**n.a.**	**(11,563)**
Net income	**(2,229)**	**n.a.**	**(11,563)**
Cash & equivalent	2,086		906
Accounts receivable	728		562
Current assets	3,950		1,917
Long-term investments	105		nil
Fixed assets, net	25		nil
Right-of-use assets	18		51
Total assets	**4,098**	**+108**	**1,967**
Accts. pay. & accr. liabs.	1,872		1,347
Current liabilities	1,898		1,431
Long-term debt, gross	nil		60
Long-term debt, net	nil		60
Long-term lease liabilities	nil		27
Shareholders' equity	1,977		327
Cash from oper. activs.	**(1,766)**	**n.a.**	**(2,985)**
Cash from fin. activs.	1,642		3,544
Cash from invest. activs.	(25)		348
Net cash position	**756**	**-17**	**906**
	$		$
Earnings per share*	(0.05)		(4.36)
Cash flow per share*	(0.04)		(1.12)
	shs		shs
No. of shs. o/s*	59,923,197		40,364,400
Avg. no. of shs. o/s*	47,700,351		2,654,247
	%		%
Net profit margin	(33.17)		(211.93)
Return on equity	(193.49)		n.m.
Return on assets	(72.25)		(859.43)

* Common
[ō] Restated
[A] Reported in accordance with IFRS

Latest Results

Periods ended:	9m Sept. 30/22[A]		9m Sept. 30/21[A]
	$000s	%Chg	$000s
Operating revenue	6,612	+34	4,925
Net income	(737)	n.a.	(1,705)
	$		$
Earnings per share*	(0.01)		(0.04)

* Common
[A] Reported in accordance with IFRS

Historical Summary
(as originally stated)

Fiscal Year	Oper. Rev.	Net Inc. Bef. Disc.	EPS*
	$000s	$000s	$
2021[A]	6,719	(2,229)	(0.05)
2020[A1]	5,456	(11,563)	(4.36)
2019[A2]	5,373	106	n.a.
2018[A]	4,260	(107)	n.a.

* Common
[A] Reported in accordance with IFRS
[1] Results reflect the Dec. 7, 2020, reverse takeover acquisition of Canadian Teleradiology Services, Inc.
[2] Results for 2019 and 2018 pertain to Canadian Teleradiology Services, Inc.
Note: Adjusted throughout for 1-for-1.8 cons. in Dec. 2020

L.18 Levitee Labs Inc.

Symbol - LVT **Exchange** - CSE (S) **CUSIP** - 527424
Head Office - 215-800 Pender St W, Vancouver, BC, V6C 1J8 **Telephone** - (250) 465-8640 **Toll-free** - (800) 465-8640
Website - www.leviteelabs.com
Email - ir@leviteelabs.com
Investor Relations - David Bentil (250) 465-8640
Auditors - RSM Alberta LLP C.A., Edmonton, Alta.
Transfer Agents - Odyssey Trust Company
Profile - (B.C. 2019) Operates addiction and pain management clinics and pharmacies, as well as a telemedicine platform; also develops and sells high potency mushroom extract nutraceuticals, and supplies and equipment for mushroom cultivation.

The company operates five addiction and pain management clinics; and three pharmacies specialized in filling prescriptions for patients with substance abuse disorders, mental health conditions and chronic pain, all in Alberta.

Wholly owned **BlockMD Ltd.** operates a telemedicine platform used by addiction patients to access doctors and order prescriptions in Alberta.

The company has two product divisions: Monk-E, which produces a retail line of mushroom-based nutraceutical supplements with a core focus on mushroom extracts; and Sporeo Supply, which produces supplies for mushroom cultivation, specifically, sterilized spawn and substrates which are necessary for mushroom cultivation at various scales.

Monk-E offers two mushroom blends, Mind Blend and Body Blend, designed to enhance general health and well-being. Products are sold in Canada and the U.S. through Amazon.com and other distribution channels. Sporeo branded mushroom spawn and mushroom substrate are produced at the company's manufacturing facility in Port Coquitlam, B.C. Sporeo products are sold through e-commerce channels and through a distribution agreement with **My Green Planet Wholesale Ltd.**

Wholly owned **Earth Circle Organics Chain Inc.** sells supplements and superfood products primarily in the U.S.through its e-commerce platform. Products include Ayurvedics, nuts, seeds, berries, coconut oil, premium Himalayan pink salt, chlorella powder, fulvic acid and Nori seaweed.

Common suspended from CSE, Feb. 7, 2023.

Predecessor Detail - Name changed from Fibonacci Capital Corp., Nov. 30, 2020.

Directors - David Bentil, CEO; Kelly Abbott, COO, New Westminster, B.C.; David M. (Dave) Jenkins, interim CFO, Langley, B.C.; Mackenzie (Ken) Osborne, head, M&A, Vancouver, B.C.; Amin Lahijani, Vancouver, B.C.

Other Exec. Officers - Dr. Fady Hannah-Shmouni, chief medical & scientific officer & pres., Levitee clinics & pharmacies

Capital Stock

	Authorized (shs.)	Outstanding (shs.)[1]
Common	unlimited	90,930,444

[1] At Aug. 29, 2022

Major Shareholder - Widely held at July 21, 2021.

Price Range - LVT/CSE (S)

Year	Volume	High	Low	Close
2022	41,087,510	$0.33	$0.01	$0.01
2021	23,158,888	$0.65	$0.28	$0.32

Recent Close: $0.01

Capital Stock Changes - In February 2022, private placement of 7,500,000 units (1 common share & 1 warrant) at 20¢ per unit was completed, with warrants exercisable at 40¢ per share.

Wholly Owned Subsidiaries

BlockMD Ltd., Alta.
Earth Circle Organics Chain Inc., Las Vegas, Nev.
Levitee Labs Holdings Inc., B.C.
- 15% int. in **BODIE Phytoceuticals Ltd.**, B.C.
- 100% int. in **Levitee Alternative Medicines Inc.**
- 100% int. in **Levitee Clinics Inc.**
- 100% int. in **Levitee Digital Health Inc.**
- 100% int. in **Levitee Nutraceuticals Inc.**
- 100% int. in **Levitee Pharmacies Inc.**
- 100% int. in **Levitee Real Estate Inc.**
- 100% int. in **Sporeo Grow Supply Corp.**

2017162 Alberta Ltd., Alta.
2143327 Alberta Ltd., Alta.
2144209 Alberta Ltd., Alta.

Financial Statistics

Periods ended:	12m Sept. 30/21[A]		12m Sept. 30/20[A]
	$000s	%Chg	$000s
Operating revenue	**1,721**	**n.a.**	**nil**
Cost of sales	1,034		nil
Salaries & benefits	1,689		nil
General & admin expense	4,104		431
Stock-based compensation	5,542		nil
Operating expense	**12,369**	**n.m.**	**431**
Operating income	**(10,648)**	**n.a.**	**(431)**
Deprec., depl. & amort.	269		nil
Finance income	34		nil
Finance costs, gross	46		nil
Investment income	276		(16)
Write-downs/write-offs	(748)		nil
Pre-tax income	**(11,374)**	**n.a.**	**(442)**
Income taxes	29		nil
Net income	**(11,403)**	**n.a.**	**(442)**
Cash & equivalent	752		120
Inventories	1,186		nil
Accounts receivable	530		nil
Current assets	2,788		157
Fixed assets, net	859		nil
Right-of-use assets	775		nil
Intangibles, net	7,716		nil
Total assets	**12,965**	**n.m.**	**157**
Bank indebtedness	313		nil
Accts. pay. & accr. liabs.	1,344		3
Current liabilities	3,120		3
Long-term lease liabilities	575		nil
Shareholders' equity	8,662		154
Cash from oper. activs.	**(4,630)**	**n.a.**	**(159)**
Cash from fin. activs.	11,364		nil
Cash from invest. activs.	(6,071)		(96)
Net cash position	**705**	**n.m.**	**43**
Capital expenditures	(725)		nil
	$		$
Earnings per share*	(0.27)		(0.10)
Cash flow per share*	(0.11)		(0.04)
	shs		shs
No. of shs. o/s*	61,425,584		5,855,561
Avg. no. of shs. o/s*	41,474,193		4,543,996
	%		%
Net profit margin	(662.58)		n.a.
Return on equity	(258.69)		(178.23)
Return on assets	(173.10)		(171.98)

* Common

[A] Reported in accordance with IFRS

Latest Results

Periods ended:	9m June 30/22[A]		9m June 30/21[A]
	$000s	%Chg	$000s
Operating revenue	6,074	n.a.	nil
Net income	(5,890)	n.a.	(6,137)
	$		$
Earnings per share*	(0.08)		(0.23)

* Common

[A] Reported in accordance with IFRS

Historical Summary
(as originally stated)

Fiscal Year	Oper. Rev. $000s	Net Inc. Bef. Disc. $000s	EPS* $
2021[A]	1,721	(11,403)	(0.27)
2020[A]	nil	(442)	(0.10)
2019[A1]	nil	(310)	(0.13)

* Common

[A] Reported in accordance with IFRS

[1] 35 weeks ended Sept. 30, 2019.

L.19 LexaGene Holdings Inc.

Symbol - LXG.H **Exchange** - TSX-VEN (S) **CUSIP** - 52886L

Head Office - 500 Cummings Center, Suite 4550, Beverly, MA, United States, 01915 **Toll-free** - (800) 215-1824

Website - www.lexagene.com

Email - jregan@lexagene.com

Investor Relations - Dr. John F. Regan (800) 215-1824

Auditors - RSM US LLP C.P.A., Boston, Mass.

Lawyers - McMillan LLP, Vancouver, B.C.

Transfer Agents - Computershare Trust Company of Canada Inc., Vancouver, B.C.

Employees - 33 at July 28, 2022

Profile - (B.C. 2007) Ceased operations.

On Feb. 24, 2023, the company ceased operations, and together with wholly owned **LexaGene, Inc.** and indirect wholly owned **Bionomics Diagnostics, Inc.**, filed for Chapter 7 bankruptcy in the U.S. The filing will result in federal appointment of a bankruptcy trustee to liquidate the company's assets and distribute any proceeds. The company does not intend to undertake any proceedings under the Companies' Creditors Arrangement Act (CCAA) or other similar proceedings in Canada. The company also does not intend to seek a voluntary delisting from the TSX Venture Exchange.

Common suspended from TSX-VEN, Feb. 28, 2023.

Predecessor Detail - Name changed from Wolfeye Resource Corp., Oct. 12, 2016, following reverse takeover acquisition of Bionomics Diagnostics Inc.

Directors - Dr. John F. (Jack) Regan, chr. & CEO, Mass.; Joseph Caruso, Boston, Mass.; Stephen J. Mastrocola, Mass.; Thomas R. (Tom) Slezak, San Francisco, Calif.; Dr. Jane Sykes, Calif.

Other Exec. Officers - Steven (Steve) Armstrong, COO; Jeffrey Mitchell, CFO, corp. sec. & treas.; Dr. Nathan Walsh, v-p, applications - bioinformatics

Capital Stock

	Authorized (shs.)	Outstanding (shs.)[1]
Common	unlimited	138,730,373

[1] At Aug. 31, 2022

Major Shareholder - Meridian Veterinary Capital LLC held 13.41% interest at Feb. 18, 2022.

Price Range - LXG.H/TSX-VEN (S)

Year	Volume	High	Low	Close
2022	13,194,258	$0.40	$0.07	$0.16
2021	49,726,333	$1.54	$0.26	$0.28
2020	55,440,273	$1.28	$0.43	$0.90
2019	18,148,449	$0.93	$0.45	$0.88
2018	15,980,801	$1.50	$0.50	$0.69

Recent Close: $0.11

Wholly Owned Subsidiaries

Bionomics Diagnostics Inc., Vancouver, B.C.
- 100% int. in **LexaGene, Inc.**, Mass.

Financial Statistics

Periods ended:	12m Feb. 28/22[A]		12m Feb. 28/21[◘A]
	US$000s	%Chg	US$000s
Operating revenue	**75**	**+29**	**58**
Cost of sales	543		160
Salaries & benefits	5,271		4,710
Research & devel. expense	1,766		2,142
General & admin expense	1,615		1,287
Stock-based compensation	1,285		1,453
Operating expense	**10,480**	**+7**	**9,752**
Operating income	**(10,405)**	**n.a.**	**(9,694)**
Deprec., depl. & amort.	496		475
Finance costs, gross	68		83
Pre-tax income	**(10,958)**	**n.a.**	**(10,243)**
Net income	**(10,958)**	**n.a.**	**(10,243)**
Cash & equivalent	4,723		9,624
Inventories	1,396		1,066
Accounts receivable	14		44
Current assets	6,573		11,119
Fixed assets, net	369		515
Right-of-use assets	1,162		1,483
Intangibles, net	48		62
Total assets	**8,201**	**-38**	**13,179**
Accts. pay. & accr. liabs.	571		717
Current liabilities	897		1,058
Long-term lease liabilities	838		1,141
Shareholders' equity	6,466		10,979
Cash from oper. activs.	**(9,658)**	**n.a.**	**(9,055)**
Cash from fin. activs.	4,608		15,486
Cash from invest. activs.	(18)		(68)
Net cash position	**4,723**	**-51**	**9,624**
Capital expenditures	(18)		(68)
	US$		US$
Earnings per share*	(0.09)		(0.10)
Cash flow per share*	(0.08)		(0.09)
	shs		shs
No. of shs. o/s*	138,106,860		118,566,834
Avg. no. of shs. o/s*	119,976,237		103,619,326
	%		%
Net profit margin	n.m.		n.m.
Return on equity	(126.32)		(138.10)
Return on assets	(101.79)		(106.01)
No. of employees (FTEs)	n.a.		34

* Common

[◘] Restated

[A] Reported in accordance with U.S. GAAP

Latest Results

Periods ended:	6m Aug. 31/22[A]		6m Aug. 31/21[◘A]
	US$000s	%Chg	US$000s
Operating revenue	76	+85	41
Net income	(4,213)	n.a.	(5,637)
	US$		US$
Earnings per share*	(0.03)		(0.05)

* Common

[◘] Restated

[A] Reported in accordance with U.S. GAAP

Historical Summary
(as originally stated)

Fiscal Year	Oper. Rev. US$000s	Net Inc. Bef. Disc. US$000s	EPS* US$
2022[A]	75	(10,958)	(0.09)
2021[B]	58	(9,891)	(0.10)
2020[B]	nil	(7,499)	(0.10)
2019[B]	nil	(8,321)	(0.13)
2018[B]	nil	(4,005)	(0.08)

* Common

[A] Reported in accordance with U.S. GAAP

[B] Reported in accordance with IFRS

L.20 Lexston Life Sciences Corp.

Symbol - LEXT **Exchange** - CSE **CUSIP** - 52978A

Head Office - 929 Mainland St, Vancouver, BC, V6B 1S3 **Telephone** - (604) 928-8913 **Fax** - (604) 628-0129

Website - lexston.ca

Email - info@lexston.ca

Investor Relations - Jagdip S. Bal (604) 928-8913

Auditors - WDM Chartered Accountants C.A., Vancouver, B.C.

Bankers - Coast Capital Savings Federal Credit Union, Surrey, B.C.

Lawyers - Linas Antanavicius, Barrister & Solicitor, Vancouver, B.C.

Transfer Agents - Odyssey Trust Company, Vancouver, B.C.

Profile - (B.C. 2020) Holds cannabis testing and research services businesses.

Wholly owned **Egret Bioscience Ltd.** and **Zenalytics Laboratories Ltd.** operated two lab testing facilities in Kelowna, B.C., including a 1,250-sq.-ft. licensed facility that provided analytical testing of cannabis, pathogens and toxins. These operations were suspended effective June 15, 2022. The company was evaluating whether to restart operations with a significant change to operations or close indefinitely. Also holds a licence under Section 56 the Controlled Drugs and Substances Act of Canada which enables the company to expand its focus on the detection and quantification of psychedelic molecules in the lab and point-of-care.

Predecessor Detail - Name changed from Lexston Capital Corp., Jan. 18, 2021, pursuant to the reverse takeover acquisition of Egret Bioscience Ltd.

Directors - Jagdip S. (Jag) Bal, pres. & CEO, Surrey, B.C.; Jatinder J. Manhas, CFO & corp. sec., Surrey, B.C.; Clinton B. (Clint) Sharples, Toronto, Ont.; Richard G. Walker Jr.

Capital Stock

	Authorized (shs.)	Outstanding (shs.)[1]
Common	unlimited	30,309,167

[1] At Apr. 20, 2023

Major Shareholder - Widely held at July 11, 2022.

Price Range - LEXT/CSE

Year	Volume	High	Low	Close
2022	6,176,864	$1.00	$0.04	$0.05
2021	1,993,529	$1.95	$0.43	$0.85

Consolidation: 1-for-5 cons. in May 2022

Recent Close: $0.08

Capital Stock Changes - In July 2022, private placement of 18,562,440 units (1 common share & 1 warrant) at 5¢ per unit was completed, with warrants exercisable at $0.075 per share for five years.

On May 26, 2022, common shares were consolidated on a 1-for-5 basis. Also during fiscal 2022, post-consolidated common shares were issued as follows: 978,333 on exercise of warrants, 540,000 on exercise of options and 234,742 pursuant to acquisition of Zenalytic Laboratories Ltd.

Wholly Owned Subsidiaries

Egret Bioscience Ltd., West Kelowna, B.C.
Zenalytic Laboratories Ltd., Kelowna, B.C.

Investments

Psy Integrated Health Inc., Vancouver, B.C.

Financial Statistics

Periods ended:	12m May 31/22[A]		11m May 31/21[A1]
	$000s	%Chg	$000s
Operating revenue	**361**	**+142**	**149**
Cost of sales	120		89
Salaries & benefits	456		287
Research & devel. expense	125		43
General & admin expense	784		188
Stock-based compensation	707		21
Operating expense	**2,193**	**+249**	**629**
Operating income	**(1,832)**	**n.a.**	**(480)**
Deprec., depl. & amort.	32		11
Write-downs/write-offs	(424)		(33)
Pre-tax income	**(2,320)**	**n.a.**	**(876)**
Net income	**(2,320)**	**n.a.**	**(876)**
Cash & equivalent	590		949
Accounts receivable	38		37
Current assets	815		989
Long-term investments	29		nil
Fixed assets, net	108		114
Total assets	**953**	**-14**	**1,103**
Accts. pay. & accr. liabs	79		35
Current liabilities	79		39
Shareholders' equity	874		1,064
Cash from oper. activs	**(1,401)**	**n.a.**	**(483)**
Cash from fin. activs	1,153		620
Cash from invest. activs	(110)		812
Net cash position	**590**	**-38**	**949**
Capital expenditures	nil		(125)
	$		$
Earnings per share*	(0.21)		(0.15)
Cash flow per share*	(0.13)		(0.10)
	shs		shs
No. of shs. o/s*	11,746,727		9,993,652
Avg. no. of shs. o/s*	11,162,186		5,063,070
	%		%
Net profit margin	(642.66)		(587.92)
Return on equity	(239.42)		n.m.
Return on assets	(225.68)		n.a.

* Common

[A] Reported in accordance with IFRS

[1] Results reflect the Feb. 4, 2021, reverse takeover acquisition of Egret Bioscience Ltd.

Latest Results

Periods ended:	3m Aug. 31/22[A]		3m Aug. 31/21[A]
	$000s	%Chg	$000s
Operating revenue	nil	n.a.	144
Net income	(289)	n.a.	(521)
	$		$
Earnings per share*	(0.01)		(0.05)

* Common

[A] Reported in accordance with IFRS

Note: Adjusted throughout for 1-for-5 cons. in May 2022

L.21 Li-Metal Corp.

Symbol - LIM **Exchange** - CSE **CUSIP** - 50203F
Head Office - 90 Riviera Dr, Markham, ON, L3R 5M1 **Telephone** - (647) 795-1653
Website - li-metal.com
Email - ir@li-metal.com
Investor Relations - Salisha Ilyas (647) 494-4887
Auditors - Grant Thornton LLP C.A., Toronto, Ont.
Transfer Agents - TSX Trust Company, Toronto, Ont.
Profile - (Ont. 2008) Develops patent-pending processes for producing low-cost metallic anodes for next generation batteries without using lithium foil.

Two distinct battery anode products are being developed: copper substrate lithium anodes and aluminum substrate lithium anodes. The next generation of batteries, which include solid-state, lithium-air and lithium sulphur batteries, are primarily targeted for electric vehicles, electric aircraft, handheld devices and many other applications. Additional growth potential markets include pharmaceuticals, aerospace alloys, specialty chemicals and primary lithium metal batteries.

The company has a facility in Markham, Ont., which includes offices, process development space suitable for pilot scale operation of the company's lithium metal production process, and an advanced anode materials research laboratory; and a pilot scale lithium anode production facility in Rochester, N.Y., used to produce lithium anode samples for customers for product sampling and qualification.

Predecessor Detail - Name changed from Eurotin Inc., Oct. 25, 2021, pursuant to the reverse takeover acquisition of 2555663 Ontario Limited (dba Li-Metal) and concurrent amalgamation of Li-Metal with wholly owned 2848302 Ontario Inc. (and continued as Li-Metal North America Inc.); basis 1 new for 124.722 old shs.

Directors - Mark Wellings, chr., Toronto, Ont.; Maciej Jastrzebski, chief tech. officer, Toronto, Ont.; Colin Farrell, Hong Kong, People's Republic of China; Timothy G. (Tim) Johnston, Toronto, Ont.; Ernie Ortiz, Fla.; Anthony Tse, Hong Kong, Hong Kong, People's Republic of China

Other Exec. Officers - Dr. Srini Godavarthy, CEO; Keshav Kochhar, COO; Richard P. Halka, CFO; Dr. Jonathan Goodman, chief scientist; Nelson Moleiro, v-p, capital projects & govt. rel.

Capital Stock

	Authorized (shs.)	Outstanding (shs.)[1]
Common	unlimited	154,953,828

[1] At Feb. 28, 2023

Major Shareholder - Widely held at Dec. 23, 2021.

Price Range - LIM/CSE

Year	Volume	High	Low	Close
2022	3,903,682	$2.70	$0.25	$0.28
2021	9,444,548	$3.75	$0.47	$2.60
2020	232,161	$1.25	$0.16	$0.62
2019	204,556	$3.12	$0.16	$0.31
2018	139,625	$3.90	$0.16	$0.94

Split: 4-for-1 split in Feb. 2022; 1-for-124.722 cons. in Oct. 2021
Recent Close: $0.30
Capital Stock Changes - On Oct. 25, 2021, common shares were consolidated on a 1-for-124.721682 basis and 104,097,688 post-consolidated/post-split common shares were issued pursuant to the reverse takeover acquisition of 2555663 Ontario Limited (dba Li-Metal). On Feb. 1, 2022, common shares were split on a 4-for-1 basis. Also during fiscal 2022, post-split common shares were issued as follows: 42,000,000 on exercise of warrants and 1,122,836 on exercise of options.

Wholly Owned Subsidiaries

Li-Metal US Inc., Toronto, Ont.

Financial Statistics

Periods ended:	15m Mar. 31/22[A1]		12m Mar. 31/21[A2]
	$000s	%Chg	$000s
Salaries & benefits	1,296		169
Research & devel. expense	2,151		...
General & admin expense	6,752		189
Stock-based compensation	4,654		nil
Operating expense	**14,854**	**n.a.**	**358**
Operating income	**(14,854)**	**n.a.**	**(358)**
Deprec., depl. & amort.	611		nil
Finance income	41		2
Finance costs, gross	275		nil
Pre-tax income	**(18,735)**	**n.a.**	**(359)**
Net income	**(18,735)**	**n.a.**	**(359)**
Cash & equivalent	23,162		4
Accounts receivable	nil		10
Current assets	23,856		14
Fixed assets, net	2,618		nil
Right-of-use assets	1,230		n.a.
Total assets	**27,703**	**n.m.**	**14**
Accts. pay. & accr. liabs	447		1,711
Current liabilities	865		1,711
Long-term lease liabilities	903		n.a.
Shareholders' equity	25,917		(1,697)
Cash from oper. activs	**(9,719)**	**n.a.**	**(315)**
Cash from fin. activs	32,807		316
Cash from invest. activs	(2,974)		4
Net cash position	**23,162**	**n.m.**	**4**
Capital expenditures	(2,749)		nil
	$		$
Earnings per share*	(0.21)		(0.11)
Cash flow per share*	(0.11)		(0.09)
	shs		shs
No. of shs. o/s*	154,953,828		3,423,345
Avg. no. of shs. o/s*	87,297,163		3,423,345
	%		%
Net profit margin	...		n.a.
Return on equity	...		n.m.
Return on assets	...		n.m.

* Common

[A] Reported in accordance with IFRS

[1] Results reflect the Oct. 25, 2021, reverse takeover acquisition of 2555663 Ontario Limited.

[2] Results for fiscal 2021 and prior fiscal years pertain to Eurotin Inc.

Historical Summary
(as originally stated)

Fiscal Year	Oper. Rev.	Net Inc. Bef. Disc.	EPS*
	$000s	$000s	$
2022[A1]	nil	(18,735)	(0.21)
2021[A]	nil	(359)	(0.11)
2020[A]	nil	(1,254)	(0.31)
2019[A]	nil	(344)	(0.09)
2018[A]	nil	(2,814)	(1.25)

* Common

[A] Reported in accordance with IFRS

[1] 15 months ended Mar. 31, 2022.

Note: Adjusted throughout for 4-for-1 split in Feb. 2022; 1-for-124.721682 cons. in Oct. 2021

L.22 Liberty Defense Holdings, Ltd.

Symbol - SCAN **Exchange** - TSX-VEN **CUSIP** - 53044R
Head Office - 187 Ballardvale St, Suite 110, Wilmington, MA, United States, 01887 **Toll-free** - (888) 617-7226
Website - libertydefense.com
Email - jay@libertydefense.com
Investor Relations - Jay Adelaar (833) 923-3334
Auditors - Davidson & Company LLP C.A., Vancouver, B.C.
Transfer Agents - Computershare Trust Company of Canada Inc., Vancouver, B.C.
Employees - 27 at Oct. 11, 2022
Profile - (B.C. 2020; orig. Ont., 2012) Provides security solutions for concealed weapon detection in high volume foot traffic areas and locations requiring enhanced security such as airports, stadiums, schools and more.

Products integrated with artificial intelligence include HEXWAVE™, is a walk-through security detection system which detects metal and non-metal concealed weapons underclothing and hand-held baggage in real-time using 3D imaging; and AVIATION, which scans passengers at the airport for concealed weapons without the need for shoe removal using advanced imaging technology millimetre-wave body scanner.

Also developed a portable, handheld smokeless gunpowder detection device, which it plans to sell to law enforcement agencies and critical infrastructure providers including schools, sporting venues, hotels, places of worship and private business markets globally.

Predecessor Detail - Name changed from Gulfstream Acquisition 1 Corp., Apr. 4, 2019, pursuant to the Qualifying Transaction reverse takeover acquisition of Liberty Defense Holdings, Inc. and concurrent amalgamation of Liberty with wholly owned 2675553 Ontario Limited (and continued as LDH GS Amalco Corp.).; basis 1 new for 2.5 old shs.

Directors - Daryl Rebeck, chr., Vancouver, B.C.; William (Bill) Frain, CEO, Mass.; Arjun Grewal, Ont.; Linda L. Jacksta, S.C.

Other Exec. Officers - Michael Lanzaro, pres. & chief tech. officer; Omar Garcia Abrego, CFO & corp. sec.; Jay Adelaar, sr. v-p, capital markets; Jeffrey Gordon, v-p, eng.

Capital Stock

	Authorized (shs.)	Outstanding (shs.)[1]
Preference	unlimited	nil
Common	unlimited	125,575,467

[1] At May 24, 2023

Major Shareholder - Widely held at Oct. 25, 2022.

Price Range - SCAN/TSX-VEN

Year	Volume	High	Low	Close
2022	20,854,300	$0.55	$0.18	$0.22
2021	22,966,576	$0.84	$0.34	$0.40
2020	367,077	$1.02	$0.28	$0.31
2019	3,683,653	$6.01	$0.99	$1.18
2018	5,967	$1.78	$0.78	$1.71

Consolidation: 1-for-6.2 cons. in Mar. 2021; 1-for-2.5 cons. in Apr. 2019
Recent Close: $0.21
Capital Stock Changes - From April to June 2023, private placement of 10,261,061 units (1 common share & ½ warrant) at Cdn$0.20 per unit was completed, with warrants exercisable at Cdn$0.30 per share for two years.

In March 2022, private placement of 26,136,345 units (1 common share & ½ warrant) at Cdn$0.33 per unit was completed. In October 2022, public offering of 18,691,700 units (1 common share & ½ warrant) at Cdn$0.275 per unit was completed. Also during 2022, common shares were issued follows: 6,579,750 on vesting of performance share units, 1,141,666 by private placement, 246,600 on exercise of warrants and 50,000 on vesting of restricted share units.

Wholly Owned Subsidiaries

DrawDown Detection Inc., North Vancouver, B.C.
- 100% int. in **DrawDown Technologies Inc.**, United States.

LDH GS Amalco Corp., Vancouver, B.C.
- 100% int. in **Liberty Defense Technologies, Inc.**, Mass.

Financial Statistics

Periods ended:	12m Dec. 31/22[A]		12m Dec. 31/21[A1]
	US$000s	%Chg	US$000s
Salaries & benefits	5,871		3,722
Research & devel. expense	1,549		1,251
General & admin expense	1,644		4,277
Stock-based compensation	1,987		2,903
Operating expense	**11,051**	**-9**	**12,153**
Operating income	**(11,051)**	**n.a.**	**(12,153)**
Deprec., depl. & amort.	1,124		164
Finance income	nil		55
Finance costs, gross	56		90
Pre-tax income	**(12,159)**	**n.a.**	**(12,390)**
Net income	**(12,159)**	**n.a.**	**(12,390)**
Cash & equivalent	677		1,342
Inventories	486		nil
Accounts receivable	55		49
Current assets	1,495		1,567
Fixed assets, net	1,002		769
Intangibles, net	3,730		4,135
Total assets	**6,234**	**-4**	**6,500**
Bank indebtedness	29		28
Accts. pay. & accr. liabs	1,476		757
Current liabilities	1,629		892
Long-term lease liabilities	514		640
Shareholders' equity	4,091		4,943
Cash from oper. activs	**(8,856)**	**n.a.**	**(7,207)**
Cash from fin. activs	9,302		9,268
Cash from invest. activs	(925)		(572)
Net cash position	**677**	**-50**	**1,342**
Capital expenditures	(770)		(94)
	US$		US$
Earnings per share*	(0.13)		(0.25)
Cash flow per share*	(0.10)		(0.15)
	shs		shs
No. of shs. o/s*	116,839,406		63,993,345
Avg. no. of shs. o/s*	91,659,543		49,242,082
	%		%
Net profit margin	n.a.		n.a.
Return on equity	n.m.		n.m.
Return on assets	n.a.		(354.31)

* Common

[A] Reported in accordance with IFRS

[1] Results reflect the Mar. 18, 2021, reverse takeover acquisition of DrawDown Detection Inc.

Latest Results

Periods ended:	3m Mar. 31/23[A]		3m Mar. 31/22[A]
	US$000s	%Chg	US$000s
Net income	(2,123)	n.a.	(2,501)
	US$		US$
Earnings per share*	(0.02)		(0.04)

* Common

[A] Reported in accordance with IFRS

Historical Summary
(as originally stated)

Fiscal Year	Oper. Rev.	Net Inc. Bef. Disc.	EPS*
	US$000s	US$000s	US$
2022[A]	nil	(12,159)	(0.13)
2021[A]	nil	(12,390)	(0.25)
2020[A]	nil	(2,553)	(0.25)
2019[A1]	nil	(11,587)	(1.12)
2018[A2]	nil	(2,778)	(0.64)

* Common

[A] Reported in accordance with IFRS

[1] Results prior to Apr. 4, 2019, pertain to and reflect the Qualifying Transaction reverse takeover acquisition of Liberty Defense Holdings, Inc.

[2] 8 months ended Dec. 31, 2018.

Note: Adjusted throughout for 1-for-6.2 cons. in Mar. 2021; 1-for-2.5 cons. in Apr. 2019

L.23 Life & Banc Split Corp.

Symbol - LBS **Exchange** - TSX **CUSIP** - 53184C
Head Office - c/o Brompton Group Limited, Bay Wellington Tower, Brookfield Place, 2930-181 Bay St, PO Box 793, Toronto, ON, M5J 2T3 **Telephone** - (416) 642-9061 **Toll-free** - (866) 642-6001 **Fax** - (416) 642-6001
Website - www.bromptongroup.com
Email - wong@bromptongroup.com
Investor Relations - Ann P. Wong (416) 642-6000
Auditors - PricewaterhouseCoopers LLP C.A., Toronto, Ont.
Transfer Agents - TSX Trust Company, Toronto, Ont.
Managers - Brompton Funds Limited, Toronto, Ont.
Portfolio Managers - Brompton Funds Limited, Toronto, Ont.

Profile - (Ont. 2006) Invests in a portfolio of the common shares of the six major Canadian banks and the four largest Canadian life insurance companies by market capitalization.

The portfolio consists of common shares of **Bank of Montreal**, **Canadian Imperial Bank of Commerce**, **National Bank of Canada**, **Royal Bank of Canada**, **The Bank of Nova Scotia**, **The Toronto-Dominion Bank**, **Great-West Lifeco Inc.**, **iA Financial Group**, **Manulife Financial Corporation** and **Sun Life Financial Inc.** The portfolio is rebalanced on an equally weighted basis, at least annually, to adjust for changes in the market values of investments, and to reflect the impact of a merger or acquisition affecting one or more of the portfolio constituents.

To generate additional income, the company may write covered call or put options in respect of common shares held in the portfolio. The company will terminate on Oct. 30, 2028, unless extended.

The manager receives a management fee at an annual rate equal to 0.60% of the net asset value calculated and payable monthly in arrears.

In April 2023, the maturity date of the company's preferred and class A shares was extended for an additional five years, to Oct. 30, 2028.

Directors - Mark A. Caranci, pres. & CEO, Toronto, Ont.; Ann P. Wong, CFO & chief compliance officer, Toronto, Ont.; Christopher S. L. Hoffmann, Toronto, Ont.; Raymond R. Pether, Toronto, Ont.

Exec. Officers - Laura Lau, chief invest. officer; Kathryn A. H. Banner, sr. v-p & corp. sec.; Michael D. Clare, sr. v-p & sr. portfolio mgr.; Christopher Cullen, sr. v-p; Manith (Manny) Phanvongsa, sr. v-p; Michelle L. Tiraborelli, sr. v-p

Capital Stock

	Authorized (shs.)	Outstanding (shs.)[1]
Preferred	unlimited	37,661,005[2]
Class A	unlimited	37,661,005
Class J	unlimited	100[2]

[1] At Jan. 25, 2023

[2] Classified as debt.

Preferred - Entitled to fixed cumulative preferential quarterly distributions of $0.13625 per share (to yield 5.45% per annum on the original issue price of $10). Retractable in November of each year at a price per unit equal to the net asset value (NAV) per unit (one class A share and one preferred share), less any costs associated with the retraction. Retractable in any other month at a price per share equal to 96% of the lesser of: (i) the NAV per unit less the cost to the company to purchase a class A share for cancellation; and (ii) $10. All outstanding preferred shares will be redeemed on Oct. 30, 2028, at a price per share equal to the lesser of: (i) $10 plus any accrued and unpaid distributions; and (ii) the NAV per share. Rank in priority to class A shares and class J shares with respect to payment of distributions and repayment of capital on the dissolution, liquidation or winding-up of company. Non-voting.

Class A - Entitled to monthly non-cumulative cash distributions targeted to be 10¢ per share (to yield 8% per annum on the original issue price). No distributions will be paid if the distributions payable on the preferred shares are in arrears or in respect of a cash distribution, after payment of the distribution, the NAV per unit (1 class A share and 1 preferred share) would be less than $15. In addition, no distributions in excess of 10¢ per month would be paid on the class A shares if, after payment of the distribution, the NAV per unit would be less than $25 unless the company has to make such distributions to fully recover refundable taxes. Retractable in November of each year along with an equal number of preferred shares at a price per share equal to the NAV per unit (one class A share and one preferred share), less any costs associated with the retraction, including commissions. Retractable in any other month at a price per share equal to 96% of the difference between: (i) the NAV per unit on the retraction date; and (ii) the cost to the company to purchase a preferred share for cancellation. All outstanding class A shares will be redeemed on Oct. 30, 2028, at a price per share equal to the greater of: (i) the NAV per unit minus $10 and any accrued and unpaid distributions on a preferred share; and (ii) nil. Rank subsequent to preferred shares but in priority to class J shares with respect to payment of distributions and repayment of capital on the dissolution, liquidation or winding-up of company. Non-voting.

Class J - Not entitled to receive dividends. Redeemable and retractable at any time at $1.00 per share. Rank subsequent to preferred shares and class A shares with respect to distributions on dissolution, liquidation or winding-up of company. One vote per share.

Major Shareholder - Life & Banc Split Trust held 100% interest at Mar. 23, 2023.

Price Range - LBS/TSX

Year	Volume	High	Low	Close
2022	19,322,379	$11.76	$7.00	$8.64
2021	18,330,582	$10.35	$6.89	$10.09
2020	20,091,428	$8.55	$2.90	$7.20
2019	13,846,786	$8.95	$6.24	$7.97
2018	13,698,518	$10.44	$4.93	$6.68

Recent Close: $8.30

Capital Stock Changes - In January 2023, public offering of 2,900,922 preferred shares and 2,319,200 class A shares was completed at $9.85 and $9.00 per share, respectively.

In April 2022, public offering of 3,059,700 preferred shares and 3,059,700 class A shares was completed at $10.05 and $10.70 per share, respectively. In July 2022, public offering of 2,319,200 preferred shares and 2,319,200 class A shares was completed at $10 and $8.65 per share, respectively.

Dividends

LBS cl A N.V. Var. Ra pa M**[1]

$0.10	Sept. 15/23	$0.10	Aug. 15/23
$0.10	July 17/23	$0.10	June 14/23

Paid in 2023: $0.90 2022: $1.20 2021: $1.20

LBS.PR.A pfd cum. red. ret. Ra $0.545 pa Q

[1] Monthly divd normally payable in Apr/20 has been omitted.

** Reinvestment Option

Financial Statistics

Periods ended:	12m Dec. 31/22[A]		12m Dec. 31/21[A]
	$000s	%Chg	$000s
Realized invest. gain (loss)	17,306		9,227
Unrealized invest. gain (loss)	(84,296)		129,238
Total revenue	**(40,232)**	**n.a.**	**161,405**
General & admin. expense	4,500		4,228
Operating expense	**4,500**	**+6**	**4,228**
Operating income	**(44,732)**	**n.a.**	**157,177**
Finance costs, gross	19,592		17,018
Pre-tax income	**(64,344)**	**n.a.**	**140,157**
Net income	**(64,344)**	**n.a.**	**140,157**
Cash & equivalent	604,713		602,144
Accounts receivable	1,467		1,908
Investments	603,713		602,144
Total assets	**608,193**	**0**	**606,522**
Accts. pay. & accr. liabs	14		72
Debt	351,951		298,162
Shareholders' equity	247,273		300,959
Cash from oper. activs	**(64,413)**	**n.a.**	**(16,896)**
Cash from fin. activs	64,952		17,341
Net cash position	**2,984**	**+22**	**2,445**
	$		$
Earnings per share*	(1.95)		4.73
Cash flow per share*	(1.95)		(0.57)
Net asset value per share*	7.03		10.09
Cash divd. per share*	1.20		1.20
	shs		shs
No. of shs. o/s*	35,195,121		29,816,221
Avg. no. of shs. o/s*	33,019,115		29,644,144
	%		%
Net profit margin	n.m.		86.84
Return on equity	(23.47)		59.01
Return on assets	(7.37)		29.79

* Class A

[A] Reported in accordance with IFRS

Note: Net income reflects increase/decrease in net assets from operations.

Historical Summary
(as originally stated)

Fiscal Year	Total Rev.	Net Inc. Bef. Disc.	EPS*
	$000s	$000s	$
2022[A]	(40,232)	(64,344)	(1.95)
2021[A]	161,405	140,157	4.73
2020[A]	(10,994)	(28,880)	(1.06)
2019[A]	104,977	85,461	3.17
2018[A]	(56,181)	(74,361)	(3.16)

* Class A

[A] Reported in accordance with IFRS

L.24 Lifeist Wellness Inc.

Symbol - LFST **Exchange** - TSX-VEN **CUSIP** - 53228D
Head Office - 2500-666 Burrard St, Vancouver, BC, V6C 2X8 **Toll-free** - (877) 660-2365
Website - lifeist.com
Email - ir@lifeist.com
Investor Relations - Meni Morim (877) 660-2365
Auditors - Baker Tilly WM LLP C.A., Toronto, Ont.
Lawyers - Ricketts, Harris LLP
Transfer Agents - Computershare Trust Company of Canada Inc., Vancouver, B.C.

Profile - (B.C. 2005) Sells and distributes cannabis products, accessories and wellness products on its e-commerce websites and through supply agreements with provincial government cannabis control boards and retailing bodies, as well as operates cannabis processing and extraction facilities. Also develops and commercializes therapies for cellular health and recovery.

Operations are conducted through the following segments:

The **CannMart** segment sells and distributes cannabis and cannabis-derived products under its Roilty and Zest Cannabis brand names to recreational cannabis consumers in Canada through supply agreements with provincial agencies and cannabis retailers across Canada. CannMart operates a 4,000-sq.-ft. processing facility in Etobicoke, Ont., for processing and distribution of in-house and licensed branded cannabis and cannabis-derived products. Wholly owned **CannMart Labs Inc.** operates a purpose-built 6,000-sq.-ft. facility in Etobicoke, Ont., for the extraction of BHO (butane hash oil). CannMart has also applied for a licence to store and distribute controlled substances such as psilocybin, psilocin, ketamine, LSD, DMT and MDMA.

The **Mikra Cellular Sciences** segment develops and commercializes therapies for cellular health including CELLF™, a novel cellular therapeutic compound targeting systemic fatigue, and RESCUE™, a naturally derived and fast-acting digestive aid.

The **Australian Vaporizers** segment sells and distributes vaporizers, related parts and accessories, grinders and aromatherapy herbs and essential oils in Australia through its e-commerce site.

On July 21, 2023, the company acquired **1000501971 Ontario Inc.** (operating as Zest Cannabis, an established cannabis brand in Canada) from **13735346 Canada Inc.** and **1000496959 Ontario Ltd.** for $3,411,708, paid by issuance of 68,234,158 common shares at 5¢ per share.

In January 2023, wholly owned **Mikra Cellular Sciences Inc.** announced plans to expand into the health food and snacks product category with the production and distribution of nutritional bars in the second half of 2023. Mikra also signed a distribution agreement with **GNC Holdings, LLC** to make GNC the exclusive distribution partner for CELLF and its future derivates in the United States.

Recent Merger and Acquisition Activity

Status: completed **Announced:** May 25, 2022
Lifeist Wellness Inc. sold Sweden-based Findify AB to Maropost Inc. for US$4,450,000 cash. Findify develops an e-commerce SaaS (Software-as-a-Service) application that provides personalized search, recommendations and advanced data analytics using artificial intelligence algorithms to deliver a personalized e-commerce experience.

Predecessor Detail - Name changed from Namaste Technologies Inc., Sept. 8, 2021.

Directors - Branden Spikes, chr., Calif.; Meni Morim, CEO, Ont.; Laurens Feenstra, Göteborg, Sweden

Other Exec. Officers - Faraaz Jamal, COO; Slava Klems, CFO

Capital Stock

	Authorized (shs.)	Outstanding (shs.)[1]
Common	unlimited	445,644,312

[1] At Feb. 28, 2023

Major Shareholder - Widely held at Nov. 7, 2022.

Price Range - LFST/TSX-VEN

Year	Volume	High	Low	Close
2022	56,994,438	$0.15	$0.04	$0.06
2021	272,660,032	$0.45	$0.08	$0.08
2020	239,261,287	$0.71	$0.19	$0.20
2019	595,694,475	$1.67	$0.26	$0.31
2018	1,082,769,553	$3.95	$0.75	$0.80

Recent Close: $0.02

Capital Stock Changes - On July 21, 2023, 68,234,158 common shares were issued pursuant to the acquisition of 1000501971 Ontario Inc.

During fiscal 2022, common shares were issued as follows: 24,878,244 pursuant to the acquisition of the remaining 49% interest in CannMart Labs Inc., 3,164,121 by private placement and 4,348,237 as share-based compensation.

Wholly Owned Subsidiaries

Australian Vaporizers Pty Ltd., Australia.
CannMart Inc., Toronto, Ont.
CannMart Labs Inc., Mississauga, Ont.
CannMart Marketplace Inc., Ont.
Lifeist Worldwide Inc., Canada.
- 100% int. in **CannMart MD Inc.**, Canada.
- 100% int. in **Lifeist Bahamas Inc.**, Bahamas.

Mikra Cellular Sciences Inc.
1000501971 Ontario Ltd., Ont.

Investments

Atlas Biotechnologies Inc., Edmonton, Alta.
49% int. in **Choklat Inc.**, Calgary, Alta.
Inolife R&D Inc.
Kief Cannabis Company Ltd.
Lovelabs.com Inc.
PeakBirch Commerce Inc., Vancouver, B.C. (see separate coverage)
YPB Group Ltd.

Financial Statistics

Periods ended:	12m Nov. 30/22[A]		12m Nov. 30/21[◻A]
	$000s	%Chg	$000s
Operating revenue	**22,069**	**+4**	**21,146**
Cost of goods sold	17,351		19,174
Salaries & benefits	7,540		10,246
Research & devel. expense	130		631
General & admin expense	9,015		10,022
Stock-based compensation	756		1,264
Operating expense	**34,792**	**-16**	**41,337**
Operating income	**(12,723)**	**n.a.**	**(20,191)**
Deprec., depl. & amort.	1,474		1,720
Finance costs, net	131		773
Write-downs/write-offs	(3,423)		(1,851)
Pre-tax income	**(18,920)**	**n.a.**	**(22,068)**
Income taxes	(224)		163
Net inc. bef. disc. opers	**(18,696)**	**n.a.**	**(22,231)**
Income from disc. opers	3,260		(1,570)
Net income	**(15,435)**	**n.a.**	**(23,801)**
Cash & equivalent	3,802		12,739
Inventories	4,537		5,370
Accounts receivable	5,806		4,370
Current assets	15,059		27,596
Long-term investments	76		363
Fixed assets, net	3,096		3,717
Intangibles, net	2,085		5,837
Total assets	**20,669**	**-46**	**37,957**
Accts. pay. & accr. liabs	6,194		8,480
Current liabilities	7,121		11,219
Long-term lease liabilities	184		364
Shareholders' equity	13,365		26,063
Cash from oper. activs	**(15,347)**	**n.a.**	**(18,277)**
Cash from fin. activs	(252)		21,016
Cash from invest. activs	6,689		(230)
Net cash position	**3,802**	**-70**	**12,739**
Capital expenditures	(693)		(366)
Capital disposals	nil		131
	$		$
Earns. per sh. bef disc opers*	(0.04)		(0.06)
Earnings per share*	(0.03)		(0.06)
Cash flow per share*	(0.04)		(0.05)
	shs		shs
No. of shs. o/s*	437,041,518		404,650,916
Avg. no. of shs. o/s*	416,362,028		390,076,063
	%		%
Net profit margin	(84.72)		(105.13)
Return on equity	(94.84)		(80.38)
Return on assets	(63.78)		(57.60)
Foreign sales percent	28		42

* Common
[◻] Restated
[A] Reported in accordance with IFRS

Latest Results

Periods ended:	3m Feb. 28/23[A]		3m Feb. 28/22[◻A]
	$000s	%Chg	$000s
Operating revenue	5,909	+22	4,862
Net inc. bef. disc. opers	(3,304)	n.a.	(4,059)
Income from disc. opers	nil		(512)
Net income	(3,304)	n.a.	(4,571)
	$		$
Earns. per sh. bef. disc. opers.*	(0.01)		(0.01)
Earnings per share*	(0.01)		(0.01)

* Common
[◻] Restated
[A] Reported in accordance with IFRS

Historical Summary
(as originally stated)

Fiscal Year	Oper. Rev. $000s	Net Inc. Bef. Disc. $000s	EPS* $
2022[A]	22,069	(18,696)	(0.04)
2021[A]	22,820	(23,801)	(0.06)
2020[A]	25,104	(26,429)	(0.08)
2019[A]	16,340	(63,230)	(0.20)
2018[A1]	23,795	(41,617)	(0.16)

* Common
[A] Reported in accordance with IFRS
[1] 15 months ended Nov. 30, 2018.

L.25 LifeSpeak Inc.

Symbol - LSPK **Exchange** - TSX **CUSIP** - 53228G
Head Office - 301-49 Wellington St E, Toronto, ON, M5E 1C9
Telephone - (416) 687-6695
Website - lifespeak.com
Email - mikemckenna@lifespeak.com
Investor Relations - Michael McKenna (416) 687-6695
Auditors - MNP LLP C.A., Toronto, Ont.
Lawyers - Fasken Martineau DuMoulin LLP, Toronto, Ont.
Transfer Agents - TSX Trust Company, Toronto, Ont.
Employees - 148 at Mar. 31, 2023

Profile - (Can. 2004) Provides a software-as-a-service (SaaS)-based digital mental, physical and total well-being educational resource platform for mid- and enterprise-sized organizations.

Provides organizations with a range of proprietary digital educational resources, available online and on mobile applications, focused on four segments: mental health and total wellbeing, which is offered under the LifeSpeak brand and includes videos, podcasts and articles on a wide range of topics, from depression to stress management to financial health; physical wellbeing, which includes on-demand workout library and automated and live sessions offered under the Wellbeats and LIFT session brands; caregiver support, which is offered under the Torchlight brand and includes caregiving content, one-on-one advising and concierge services; and substance use disorders, which is offered under the ALAViDA brand and features self-guided resources, medication-assisted therapy, assessments, personalized treatment plans. Care coordination and reporting. Solutions are marketed as individual products or as fully integrated suite of tools through direct sales channels, referral partners and to embedded solution clients, wherein the company's platform is integrated into the clients own products or provided as an add-on service.

Serves 990 diverse clients globally (at Mar. 31, 2023), including Fortune 500 companies, government agencies, insurance providers and other health technology firms.

Directors - Michael Held, founder, pres. & CEO, Toronto, Ont.; Nolan J. Bederman, exec. chr., Toronto, Ont.; Mario Di Pietro†, Toronto, Ont.; Sanjiv Samant, Toronto, Ont.; Dr. Kevin P. D. Smith, Toronto, Ont.; Caroline Starner Dadras, Laguna Beach, Calif.; Rajesh Uttamchandani, Toronto, Ont.

Other Exec. Officers - Jason Campana, COO; Michael (Mike) McKenna, CFO & corp. sec.; Doug Berkowitz, CAO; Aimee Gindin, chief mktg. officer; Adam Goldberg, chief strategy officer; Anna Mittag, chief product officer; Raffi Tchakmakjian, chief revenue officer; Jill Ross, sr. v-p, fin.
† Lead director

Capital Stock

	Authorized (shs.)	Outstanding (shs.)[1]
Preferred	unlimited	nil
Common	unlimited	50,913,507

[1] At May 15, 2023

Major Shareholder - Michael Held held 19.2% interest and Round 13 Growth, L.P. held 10.4% interest at May 8, 2023.

Price Range - LSPK/TSX

Year	Volume	High	Low	Close
2022	18,671,979	$8.25	$0.71	$0.95
2021	7,465,378	$9.90	$5.82	$6.35

Recent Close: $0.62

Capital Stock Changes - In March 2022, private placement of 2,953,020 common shares was completed at $7.45 per share. Also during 2022, 70,935 common shares were issued on release from escrow and 266,800 common shares were repurchased under a Normal Course Issuer Bid.

Wholly Owned Subsidiaries

ALAViDA Health Ltd., Toronto, Ont.
LIFT Digital Inc., Montréal, Qué.
LifeSpeak (USA) Inc., United States.
- 100% int. in **EnCompass Education Solutions, Inc.**, Burlington, Mass.
- 100% int. in **Wellbeats, Inc.**, St. Louis Park, Minn.

Financial Statistics

Periods ended:	12m Dec. 31/22[A]		12m Dec. 31/21[□A]
	$000s	%Chg	$000s
Operating revenue	**47,370**	**+104**	**23,267**
Cost of sales	2,501		1,207
Salaries & benefits	26,718		8,892
General & admin expense	15,317		9,615
Stock-based compensation	8,844		8,919
Operating expense	**53,380**	**+86**	**28,632**
Operating income	**(6,010)**	**n.a.**	**(5,365)**
Deprec., depl. & amort.	14,992		1,069
Finance income	43		63
Finance costs, gross	8,807		845
Write-downs/write-offs	(26,503)[1]		nil
Pre-tax income	**(51,348)**	**n.a.**	**(27,243)**
Income taxes	(3,434)		(918)
Net income	**(47,914)**	**n.a.**	**(26,325)**
Cash & equivalent	6,531		31,858
Accounts receivable	7,239		6,904
Current assets	17,069		41,830
Fixed assets, net	491		16
Right-of-use assets	882		239
Intangibles, net	132,659		46,770
Total assets	**152,432**	**+70**	**89,739**
Accts. pay. & accr. liabs	5,247		4,578
Current liabilities	42,366		17,405
Long-term debt, gross	88,668		15,485
Long-term debt, net	65,210		12,702
Long-term lease liabilities	604		67
Shareholders' equity	37,174		54,283
Cash from oper. activs	**(7,612)**	**n.a.**	**(10,640)**
Cash from fin. activs	83,468		79,392
Cash from invest. activs	(101,372)		(37,024)
Net cash position	**6,530**	**-80**	**31,858**
Capital expenditures	(227)		nil
	$		$
Earnings per share*	(0.95)		(0.76)
Cash flow per share*	(0.15)		(0.31)
	shs		shs
No. of shs. o/s*	50,911,297		48,083,207
Avg. no. of shs. o/s*	50,410,872		34,578,555
	%		%
Net profit margin	(101.15)		(113.14)
Return on equity	(104.78)		n.m.
Return on assets	(32.51)		(53.47)
Foreign sales percent	58		7
No. of employees (FTEs)	158		101

* Common
□ Restated
[A] Reported in accordance with IFRS
[1] Pertains to impairment of goodwill.

Latest Results

Periods ended:	3m Mar. 31/23[A]		3m Mar. 31/22[A]
	$000s	%Chg	$000s
Operating revenue	13,396	+54	8,710
Net income	(354)	n.a.	(16,354)
	$		$
Earnings per share*	(0.01)		(0.33)

* Common
[A] Reported in accordance with IFRS

Historical Summary
(as originally stated)

Fiscal Year	Oper. Rev.	Net Inc. Bef. Disc.	EPS*
	$000s	$000s	$
2022[A]	47,370	(47,914)	(0.95)
2021[A]	23,267	(26,325)	(0.76)
2020[A1]	10,084	98	0.00
2019[A1]	7,430	(594)	(0.01)
2018[A1]	6,700	533	0.01

* Common
[A] Reported in accordance with IFRS
[1] As shown in the prospectus dated June 28, 2021.

L.26 Lightspeed Commerce Inc.*

Symbol - LSPD **Exchange** - TSX **CUSIP** - 53229C
Head Office - 300-700 rue Saint-Antoine E, Montréal, QC, H2Y 1A6 **Telephone** - (514) 907-1801 **Toll-free** - (888) 951-4172 **Fax** - (514) 221-4499
Website - www.lightspeedhq.com
Email - investorrelations@lightspeedhq.com
Investor Relations - Gus Papageorgiou (514) 907-1801
Auditors - PricewaterhouseCoopers LLP C.A., Montréal, Qué.
Lawyers - Stikeman Elliott LLP, Montréal, Qué.
Transfer Agents - American Stock Transfer & Trust Company, LLC, New York, N.Y.; TSX Trust Company, Montréal, Qué.
FP500 Revenue Ranking - 408
Employees - 3,000 at Mar. 31, 2023
Profile - (Can. 2005) Offers a cloud-based omnichannel commerce platform for small and medium-sized businesses in more than 100 countries.

The company's platform provides its customers with all-in-one solutions that enable them to sell across multiple channels (in store, online, social and marketplaces), manage operations, engage with consumers, accept payments, leverage actionable insights from transactions, connect to suppliers and grow their business. Functionalities of the platform include point of sale (POS), e-commerce, payment processing, inventory management, employee management, product and menu management, delivery and order management, bookings and membership management, multi-location connectivity, customer management, loyalty, analytics and reporting, and financial solutions. Primary customers are retailers, hospitality businesses and golf course operators.

During fiscal 2023, the company's platform processed gross transaction volume of US$87.1 billion compared with US$74 billion for fiscal 2022.

On Jan. 17, 2023, the company announced a reorganization that included the reduction of about 300 roles representing about 10% of the company's headcount-related operating expenditures, with half of the cost reduction coming from management. A restructuring charge of US$25,549,000 was incurred during the fourth quarter of fiscal 2023.

Predecessor Detail - Name changed from Lightspeed POS Inc., Aug. 10, 2021.

Directors - Dax Dasilva, founder & exec. chr., Westmount, Qué.; Jean-Paul (JP) Chauvet, CEO, Outremont, Qué.; Patrick Pichette†, London, Middx., United Kingdom; Nathalie Gaveau, London, Middx., United Kingdom; Paul McFeeters, Ont.; Dale Murray, United Kingdom; Rob Williams, Edmonds, Wash.

Other Exec. Officers - Jean-David (JD) Saint-Martin, pres.; Asha Bakshani, CFO; Daniel (Dan) Micak, chief legal officer & corp. sec.; Shirvani Mudaly, chief people officer; Kady Srinivasan, chief mktg. officer; Ryan Tabone, chief product & tech. officer; Cameron Walker, chief of staff
† Lead director

Capital Stock

	Authorized (shs.)	Outstanding (shs.)[1]
Preferred	unlimited	nil
Subordinate Voting	unlimited	152,185,121

[1] At Aug. 1, 2023

Options - At Mar. 31, 2023, options were outstanding to purchase 10,060,296 subordinate voting shares at prices ranging from US$2.17 to US$93.45 per share with a weighted average remaining contractual life of 5.19 years.

Major Shareholder - Caisse de dépôt et placement du Québec held 15.99% interest and Fidelity Management & Research Company held 11.16% interest at June 26, 2023.

Price Range - LSPD/TSX

Year	Volume	High	Low	Close
2022	358,971,791	$52.73	$17.27	$19.35
2021	197,652,796	$165.87	$49.00	$51.08
2020	186,034,013	$90.76	$10.50	$89.84
2019	56,878,334	$49.70	$18.05	$36.07

Recent Close: $20.16

Capital Stock Changes - During fiscal 2023, subordinate voting shares were issued as follows: 2,224,787 on exercise of options and vesting of share awards and 284,206 as acquisition-related compensation.

In April 2021, 2,692,277 subordinate voting shares were issued pursuant to the acquisition of Vend Limited. In July 2021, 2,143,393 subordinate voting shares were issued pursuant to the acquisition of NuORDER, Inc. In August 2021, public offering of 8,855,000 subordinate voting shares was completed at US$93 per share, including 1,155,000 subordinate voting shares on exercise of over-allotment option. In October 2021, 4,471,586 subordinate voting shares were issued pursuant to the acquisition of Ecwid, Inc. Also during fiscal 2022, subordinate voting shares were issued as follows: 1,332,218 on exercise of options and vesting of share awards and 638,323 as acquisition-related compensation.

Long-Term Debt - At Mar. 31, 2023, the company had no long-term debt.

Wholly Owned Subsidiaries

Ecwid, Inc., Encinitas, Calif.
Kounta Holdings Pty Ltd., Australia.
Lightspeed Commerce USA Inc., New York, N.Y.
Lightspeed Netherlands B.V., Netherlands.
Lightspeed NuORDER Inc., Del.
Lightspeed Payments USA Inc., Del.
Upserve, Inc., Providence, R.I.
Vend Limited, Auckland, New Zealand.

Note: The preceding list includes only the major related companies in which interests are held.

Financial Statistics

Periods ended:	12m Mar. 31/23[A]		12m Mar. 31/22[A]
	US$000s	%Chg	US$000s
Operating revenue	**730,506**	**+33**	**548,372**
Cost of sales	398,545		277,199
Research & devel. expense	140,442		121,150
General & admin expense	356,310		311,912
Operating expense	**895,297**	**+26**	**710,261**
Operating income	**(164,791)**	**n.a.**	**(161,889)**
Deprec., depl. & amort.	115,261		104,548
Finance income	26,866		5,855
Finance costs, gross	2,054		2,867
Write-downs/write-offs	(748,712)[1]		nil
Pre-tax income	**(1,074,228)**	**n.a.**	**(315,354)**
Income taxes	(4,219)		(26,921)
Net income	**(1,070,009)**	**n.a.**	**(288,433)**
Cash & equivalent	800,154		953,654
Inventories	12,839		7,540
Accounts receivable	84,334		45,766
Current assets	934,332		1,042,495
Long-term investments	1,519		nil
Fixed assets, net	19,491		16,456
Right-of-use assets	20,973		25,539
Intangibles, net	1,662,095		2,513,936
Total assets	**2,668,732**	**-26**	**3,619,980**
Accts. pay. & accr. liabs	68,827		78,307
Current liabilities	150,457		157,852
Long-term debt, gross	nil		29,841
Long-term debt, net	nil		29,841
Long-term lease liabilities	18,574		23,037
Shareholders' equity	2,497,449		3,399,289
Cash from oper. activs	**(125,284)**	**n.a.**	**(87,218)**
Cash from fin. activs	(35,411)		798,057
Cash from invest. activs	8,817		(563,931)
Net cash position	**800,154**	**-16**	**953,654**
Capital expenditures	(9,227)		(10,653)
	US$		US$
Earnings per share*	(7.11)		(2.04)
Cash flow per share*	(0.83)		(0.62)
	shs		shs
No. of shs. o/s*	151,170,305		148,661,312
Avg. no. of shs. o/s*	150,404,130		141,580,917
	%		%
Net profit margin	(146.48)		(52.60)
Return on equity	(36.29)		(10.82)
Return on assets	(33.96)		(9.98)
Foreign sales percent	94		94
No. of employees (FTEs)	3,000		3,000

* Subord. Vtg.
[A] Reported in accordance with IFRS
[1] Pertains to goodwill impairment.

Latest Results

Periods ended:	3m June 30/23[A]		3m June 30/22[A]
	US$000s	%Chg	US$000s
Operating revenue	209,086	+20	173,882
Net income	(48,703)	n.a.	(100,796)
	US$		US$
Earnings per share*	(0.32)		(0.68)

* Subord. Vtg.
[A] Reported in accordance with IFRS

Historical Summary
(as originally stated)

Fiscal Year	Oper. Rev.	Net Inc. Bef. Disc.	EPS*
	US$000s	US$000s	US$
2023[A]	730,506	(1,070,009)	(7.11)
2022[A]	548,372	(288,433)	(2.04)
2021[A]	221,728	(124,278)	(1.18)
2020[A]	120,637	(53,531)	(0.62)
2019[A]	77,451	(183,525)	(5.53)

* Subord. Vtg.
[A] Reported in accordance with IFRS

L.27 The Limestone Boat Company Limited

Symbol - BOAT **Exchange** - TSX-VEN **CUSIP** - 53263G
Head Office - 65A Hurontario St, Collingwood, ON, L9Y 2L7 **Toll-free** - (800) 720-2395
Website - limestoneboats.com
Email - bill@limestoneboats.com
Investor Relations - Bill Mitoulas (800) 720-2395
Auditors - MNP LLP C.A., Toronto, Ont.
Transfer Agents - TSX Trust Company, Toronto, Ont.
Profile - (Ont. 2018) Manufactures recreational and commercial power boats under the Limestone®, Aquasport and Seventeen Fifty-Two brands.

Models under the Limestone® brand (L-200CC, L-200R, L-270DC and L-290DC) range in size from 20 ft. to 29 ft., and include runabouts, centre and dual consoles with classic day boat arrangements. Models under the Aquasport brand (2100, 2300, 2500, 3000, 244 Bay and 230 Pro) range in size from 21 ft. to 30 ft., and include centre consoles and bay boats. Boats are sold through a dealer network in Canada and the United States. In partnership with L-200R, **Marine Technologies, Inc.** is developing a line of electric boats under the Seventeen Fifty-Two brand. Its first protype is the 21-ft. 2.1 Center Console EV. Manufacturing operations were expected to recommence in the first quarter of calendar 2024 with initial shipments of the L-270DC model expected to follow in fiscal 2025.

In February 2023, the company announced plans to build Limestone boats in New Brunswick, including the L-200CC, L-200R, L-270DC and L-290DC models. Recommencement of production in New Brunswick was targeted for the first quarter of 2024.

In January 2023, wholly owned U.S subsidiaries **Ebbtide Holdings, LLC** (dba TN Composites) and **Limestone US Inc.** filed for relief under Chapter 7 of the Bankruptcy Code in Tennessee. The business operations of these subsidiaries ceased immediately and the trustee immediately took charge of the assets and was expected to liquidate the assets. As a result, the company would no longer be producing boats at the White Bluff, Tenn., facility and plans to pursue manufacturing opportunities in Canada.

During 2022, Boca Bay model lineup were rebranded and were included in the Aquasport line.

Predecessor Detail - Name changed from LL One Inc., Mar. 2, 2021, pursuant to the Qualifying Transaction revere takeover acquisition of The Limestone Boat Company Inc. (LBCI) and concurrent amalgamation of LBCI with wholly owned 2790889 Ontario Inc.

Directors - Telfer Hanson, chr., Burlington, Ont.; Scott Hanson, CEO, Ont.; Bryan Pearson†, Toronto, Ont.; Alan D. Gaines, Nev.; David Grandin, N.H.; Charles A. V. Pennock, Toronto, Ont.

Other Exec. Officers - Ryan Lupton, interim CFO; Taylor Hanson, v-p, product mgt.

† Lead director

Capital Stock

	Authorized (shs.)	Outstanding (shs.)[1]
Common	unlimited	119,665,940

[1] At Aug. 29, 2022

Major Shareholder - Scott Hanson held 12.74% interest and Telfer Hanson held 11.35% interest at June 1, 2022.

Price Range - BOAT/TSX-VEN

Year	Volume	High	Low	Close
2022	19,147,716	$0.23	$0.01	$0.01
2021	18,169,866	$0.43	$0.18	$0.20
2020	839,997	$0.26	$0.07	$0.13
2019	5,162,345	$1.13	$0.15	$0.25

Recent Close: $0.01

Wholly Owned Subsidiaries

Ebbtide Holdings, LLC, Tenn.

The Limestone Boat Company Inc., Canada.

- 100% int. in **Limestone US, Inc.**, United States.

Financial Statistics

Periods ended:	12m Dec. 31/21[A1]		50w Dec. 31/20[A2]
	$000s	%Chg	$000s
Operating revenue	**6,554**	**n.a.**	**nil**
Cost of goods sold	8,097		nil
Salaries & benefits	2,393		571
Research & devel. expense	144		nil
General & admin expense	7,457		809
Stock-based compensation	427		212
Operating expense	**18,517**	**n.m.**	**1,592**
Operating income	**(11,963)**	**n.a.**	**(1,592)**
Finance costs, gross	1,782		6
Pre-tax income	**(13,437)**	**n.a.**	**(1,619)**
Income taxes	(521)		nil
Net income	**(12,916)**	**n.a.**	**(1,619)**
Cash & equivalent	nil		130
Inventories	2,364		nil
Accounts receivable	715		118
Current assets	3,580		424
Fixed assets, net	3,788		799
Right-of-use assets	5,729		nil
Intangibles, net	4,405		nil
Total assets	**18,319**	**n.m.**	**1,223**
Bank indebtedness	104		nil
Accts. pay. & accr. liabs	3,990		780
Current liabilities	4,447		1,005
Long-term debt, gross	10,855		nil
Long-term debt, net	10,730		nil
Long-term lease liabilities	1,966		nil
Shareholders' equity	820		219
Cash from oper. activs	**(11,216)**	**n.a.**	**(682)**
Cash from fin. activs	16,506		1,552
Cash from invest. activs	(5,543)		(713)
Net cash position	**(104)**	**n.a.**	**130**
Capital expenditures	(2,157)		(713)
	$		$
Earnings per share*	(0.13)		(0.03)
Cash flow per share*	(0.11)		(0.01)
	shs		shs
No. of shs. o/s*	118,450,940		n.a.
Avg. no. of shs. o/s*	99,442,049		50,000,000
	%		%
Net profit margin	(197.07)		n.a.
Return on equity	(2,486.24)		n.m.
Return on assets	(114.66)		n.a.

* Common

[A] Reported in accordance with IFRS

[1] Results reflect the Mar. 2, 2021, reverse takeover acquisition of The Limestone Boat Company Inc.

[2] Results pertain to The Limestone Boar Company Inc.

Latest Results

Periods ended:	6m June 30/22[A]		6m June 30/21[A]
	$000s	%Chg	$000s
Operating revenue	8,131	+538	1,275
Net income	(4,312)	n.a.	(5,535)
	$		$
Earnings per share*	(0.04)		(0.06)

* Common

[A] Reported in accordance with IFRS

L.28 Liminal BioSciences Inc.

Symbol - LMNL **Exchange** - NASDAQ **CUSIP** - 53272L

Head Office - 300-440 boul Armand-Frappier, Laval, QC, H7V 4B4 **Telephone** - (450) 781-0115 **Fax** - (450) 781-4477

Website - www.liminalbiosciences.com

Email - s.inamdar@liminalbiosciences.com

Investor Relations - Shrinal Inamdar (450) 781-0115

Auditors - PricewaterhouseCoopers LLP C.A., Montréal, Qué.

Lawyers - Borden Ladner Gervais LLP, Montréal, Qué.

Transfer Agents - Computershare Trust Company of Canada Inc., Toronto, Ont.

Employees - 43 at Dec. 31, 2022

Profile - (Can. 1994) Researches and develops distinctive novel small molecule therapeutics for inflammatory, fibrotic and metabolic diseases using its drug discovery platform and data-driven approach.

Has three development antagonist programs: LMNL6511, is an oral, selective antagonist of GPR84 designed to treat metabolic diseases, inflammation and/or fibrosis in several different therapeutic categories; OXER1, an oral potent human eosinophil chemoattractants used to treat type 2 inflammation-driven diseases, including respiratory diseases and gastro-intestinal diseases; and GPR40 agonist, a potential therapeutic treatment for type 2 diabetes. Phase 1 clinical trial for LMNL6511 is expected to commence in the second half of 2023 while OXER1 antagonists and GPR40 agonists are both at the preclinical stage.

In February 2023, the company sold a dormant manufacturing facility in Belleville, Ont. The facility had a carrying value of $3,958,000 at Dec. 31, 2022. Terms were not disclosed.

In December 2022, the company sold the Labrosse facility in Pointe-Claire, Que., for $3,175,000 cash. The Labrosse facility was formerly part of the plasma-derived therapeutics segment that was completely divested in October 2021. The segment was devoted to leverage the company's experience in bioseparation technologies used to isolate and purify biopharmaceuticals from human plasma.

On Aug. 8, 2022, the company acquired the remaining interest in **Pathogen Removal Diagnostic Technologies Inc.** (PRDT) for US$30,000. PRDT owns certain prion reduction technology and is the licensee of certain prion reduction technology. At Dec. 31, 2021, the company held 77% interest in PRDT.

In July 2022, the company decided to discontinue the development of lead small molecule product candidate, fezagepras, following the results of its Phase 1a single ascending dose (SAD) clinical trial, which indicated that fezagepras was significantly inferior compared to Sodium Phenylbutyrate as a nitrogen scavenger. Previously, the company also announced that it would not be progressing the development of fezagepras for the treatment of idiopathic pulmonary fibrosis (IPF) nor hypertriglyceridemia.

Recent Merger and Acquisition Activity

Status: pending **Revised:** July 12, 2023

UPDATE: Structured Alpha and Liminal entered into a definitive agreement whereby Structured would acquire all shares of Liminal its does not already own for US$8.50 per share. The transaction was expected to close no later than Sept. 30, 2023. PREVIOUS: Structured Alpha LP submitted a proposal to acquire the remaining 35.97% interest in Liminal BioSciences Inc., representing the remaining 1,116,634 common shares not already held, for US$7.50 cash per share. Eugene Siklos, a board of director of Liminal, was deemed to have sole voting and investment power of the securities held by Structured Alpha.

Predecessor Detail - Name changed from ProMetic Life Sciences Inc., Oct. 3, 2019.

Directors - Alek Krstajic, chr., Toronto, Ont.; Dr. Gary J. Bridger, interim chief scientific officer, Wash.; Prof. Simon G. Best†, Edinburgh, Midlothian, United Kingdom; Neil A. Klompas, B.C.; Eugene Siklos, Ont.; Timothy S. Wach, Ont.

Other Exec. Officers - Bruce Pritchard, CEO; Patrick Sartore, pres.; N. Nicole Rusaw, CFO; Marie Iskra, gen. counsel & corp. sec.

† Lead director

Capital Stock

	Authorized (shs.)	Outstanding (shs.)[1]
Preferred	unlimited	nil
Common	unlimited	3,104,222

[1] At May 3, 2023

Major Shareholder - Eugene Siklos held 64% interest at Apr. 14, 2023.

Price Range - LMNL/NASDAQ

Year	Volume	High	Low	Close
2022	153,657	US$11.60	US$3.23	US$3.30
2021	2,647,224	US$69.50	US$8.97	US$10.90
2020	1,244,873	US$314.50	US$35.10	US$42.00

LMNL/TSX (D)

Year	Volume	High	Low	Close
2020	208,794	$324.80	$75.00	$228.40
2019	222,180	$4,400.00	$70.30	$109.60
2018	30,919	$18,000.00	$2,550.00	$2,550.00

Consolidation: 1-for-10 cons. in Feb. 2023

Capital Stock Changes - On Feb. 1, 2023, common shares were consolidated on a 1-for-10 basis.

There were no changes to capital stock during 2022.

Wholly Owned Subsidiaries

Fairhaven Pharmaceuticals Inc., Vancouver, B.C.

Liminal R&D BioSciences Inc., Laval, Qué.

- 100% int. in **Liminal BioSciences Holdings Limited**, United Kingdom.
  - 100% int. in **Liminal BioSciences Limited**, United Kingdom.

Pathogen Removal and Diagnostic Technologies Inc., Washington, D.C.

Prometic Biotherapeutics B.V., Amsterdam, Netherlands.

Prometic Biotherapeutics Ltd., United Kingdom.

Prometic Pharma SMT B.V., Netherlands.

Telesta Therapeutics Inc., Saint-Laurent-Ile-d'Orléans, Qué.

Subsidiaries

73% int. in **NantPro BioSciences, LLC**, Wilmington, Del.

Financial Statistics

Periods ended:	12m Dec. 31/22[A]		12m Dec. 31/21[A]
	$000s	%Chg	$000s
Operating revenue	**401**	**-38**	**643**
Research & devel. expense	15,298		18,347
General & admin expense	16,746		27,584
Operating expense	**32,044**	**-30**	**45,931**
Operating income	**(31,643)**	**n.a.**	**(45,288)**
Deprec., depl. & amort.	1,120		4,344
Finance costs, net	1,078		6,330
Write-downs/write-offs	nil		(341)
Pre-tax income	**(29,441)**	**n.a.**	**(44,945)**
Income taxes	(525)		118
Net inc bef disc ops, eqhldrs	(29,038)		(44,394)
Net inc bef disc ops, NCI	122		(669)
Net inc. bef. disc. opers	**(28,916)**	**n.a.**	**(45,063)**
Disc. opers., equity hldrs	29,538		57,276
Income from disc. opers	29,538		57,276
Net income	**622**	**-95**	**12,213**
Net inc. for equity hldrs	**500**	**-96**	**12,882**
Net inc. for non-cont. int	**122**	**n.a.**	**(669)**
Cash & equivalent	37,144		108,490
Accounts receivable	1,177		1,068
Current assets	41,318		114,629
Fixed assets, net	4,344		5,483
Right-of-use assets	1,146		1,609
Intangibles, net	3,240		3,516
Total assets	**50,459**	**-60**	**126,053**
Accts. pay. & accr. liabs	5,968		7,343
Current liabilities	10,103		18,494
Long-term debt, gross	nil		38,311
Long-term debt, net	nil		38,311
Long-term lease liabilities	752		15,277
Shareholders' equity	36,208		42,637
Non-controlling interest	nil		(8,756)
Cash from oper. activs	**(31,820)**	**n.a.**	**(99,603)**
Cash from fin. activs	(45,446)		(8,424)
Cash from invest. activs	3,819		170,692
Net cash position	**37,144**	**-66**	**108,490**
Capital expenditures	(13)		(293)
Capital disposals	3		52
	$		$
Earns. per sh. bef disc opers*	(9.36)		(14.70)
Earnings per share*	0.16		4.30
Cash flow per share*	(10.25)		(33.02)
	shs		shs
No. of shs. o/s*	3,104,256		3,104,256
Avg. no. of shs. o/s*	3,104,300		3,016,400
	%		%
Net profit margin	n.m.		n.m.
Return on equity	(73.66)		(135.07)
Return on assets	(32.76)		(36.96)
Foreign sales percent	99		88
No. of employees (FTEs)	43		48

* Common
[A] Reported in accordance with IFRS

Latest Results

Periods ended:	3m Mar. 31/23[A]		3m Mar. 31/22[◻A]
	$000s	%Chg	$000s
Operating revenue	136	n.a.	nil
Net inc. bef. disc. opers	(7,581)	n.a.	(11,188)
Income from disc. opers	149		24
Net income	(7,432)	n.a.	(11,164)
Net inc. for equity hldrs	(7,432)	n.a.	(10,705)
Net inc. for non-cont. int	nil		(459)
	$		$
Earns. per sh. bef. disc. opers.*	(2.44)		(3.46)
Earnings per share*	(2.44)		(3.45)

* Common
[◻] Restated
[A] Reported in accordance with IFRS

Historical Summary
(as originally stated)

Fiscal Year	Oper. Rev.	Net Inc. Bef. Disc.	EPS*
	$000s	$000s	$
2022[A]	401	(28,916)	(9.36)
2021[A]	643	(45,063)	(14.70)
2020[A]	3,317	(122,137)	(49.60)
2019[A]	4,904	(234,224)	(145.20)
2018[A]	47,374	(237,896)	(2,700.00)

* Common
[A] Reported in accordance with IFRS

Note: Adjusted throughout for 1-for-10 cons. in Feb. 2023; 1-for-1,000 cons. in July 2019

L.29 Linamar Corporation*

Symbol - LNR **Exchange** - TSX **CUSIP** - 53278L
Head Office - 287 Speedvale Ave W, Guelph, ON, N1H 1C5 **Telephone** - (519) 836-7550 **Fax** - (519) 824-8479
Website - www.linamar.com
Email - andrea.bowman@linamar.com
Investor Relations - Andrea Bowman (519) 836-7550
Auditors - PricewaterhouseCoopers LLP C.A., Kitchener, Ont.
Transfer Agents - Computershare Trust Company of Canada Inc., Toronto, Ont.
FP500 Revenue Ranking - 80
Employees - 27,905 at Dec. 31, 2022
Profile - (Ont. 1966) Designs, develops and manufactures precision machined components, modules and assembly for original equipment manufacturers (OEMs) and Tier 1 customers; and designs and manufactures aerial work platforms, telehandlers and agricultural equipment.

Operations are organized into two segments: Mobility and Industrial.

Mobility

This segment designs, develops and manufactures precision metallic components, modules and systems for powertrain, driveline, and body and chassis systems for the electrified and traditionally powered highway vehicle markets. Operations consist of 56 manufacturing facilities, six research and development (R&D) centres and 10 sales offices in 12 countries in North America, Europe and Asia. This segment includes the machining and assembly, metal forming, light metal casting and forging operating groups.

Manufactured precision-machined components and assemblies are used in high-efficiency transmissions, engines and driveline systems, as well as body/structural and chassis systems. Transmission products include gears, transmission cases, shafts, shafts and shell assemblies, clutch modules and clutch subcomponents, valve bodies, pumps, planetary gear assemblies and housings/covers. In the driveline systems segment, core product areas are power transfer units, rear drive units and engineered gears. Primary engine components manufactured are cylinder blocks and assemblies, cylinder heads and complete head assemblies, camshaft assemblies, connecting rods, flywheels, fuel rails and fuel body/pump.

The company's McClaren Engineering group provides design, development and testing services for the Mobility segment. The company has also formed eLIN Product Solutions group that would focus on leveraging electrification opportunities, both for the Mobility and Industrial segments.

In addition, Linamar MedTech group offers manufacturing services for medical devices and precision medical components, including the manufacture and assembly of complex medical devices and components. Targeted products include surgical, respiratory, and imaging devices, as well as precision components for devices, orthopaedics and prostheses.

Industrial

This segment consists of the Skyjack business and the agricultural business, which includes the MacDon and Salford units. Operations consist of 10 manufacturing facilities, seven research and design centres and 18 sales offices in 11 countries in North and South America, Europe, Australia and Asia. Skyjack designs and manufactures aerial work platforms including scissor lifts, vertical mast lifts, boom lifts and telehandlers. MacDon specializes in harvesting equipment such as combine draper headers, self-propelled windrowers, pick-up headers and hay products. Salford supplies the agriculture market with farm tillage and crop nutrition application equipment.

In May 2023, the company announced a definitive commercialization agreement with **Exro Technologies Inc.** following the continued successful testing and validation by the company of the co-developed integrated electric axle (eAxle) utilizing Exro's Coil Driver™ traction inverter. The agreement is set for an initial five-year term to build a demonstration vehicle containing the eAxle product to be utilized as a joint marketing asset for the medium duty commercial vehicle market. The agreement contemplates the start of series production by the fourth quarter of 2024 and includes annual commercial volume targets that build to 25,000 units per annum by 2027. The company is granted exclusivity to Exro's Coil Driver™ product for use in medium duty Class 3-6 electric beam axle applications.

On May 19, 2022, the company announced the creation of Linamar MedTech, a new medical manufacturing group which would focus on leveraging its expert capabilities in precision manufacturing to pursue opportunities in the medical device and precision medical component markets. Potential targeted products include surgical, respiratory, and imaging devices and precision components for devices, orthopaedics and prosthesis.

Recent Merger and Acquisition Activity

Status: completed **Revised:** Aug. 3, 2023
UPDATE: The transaction was completed. PREVIOUS: Linamar Corporation agreed to acquire three electric vehicle battery enclosure factories via the acquisition of Dura-Shiloh's battery enclosures business for US$325,000,000. The factories are in Alabama, Czechia and North Macedonia. Dura-Shiloh is a portfolio company of private equity firm MiddleGround Capital LLC. The transaction was expected to close during the third quarter of 2023.

Status: completed **Revised:** June 3, 2022
UPDATE: The transaction was completed. PREVIOUS: Linamar Corporation agreed to acquire Ontario-based Salford Group, Inc., which manufactures tillage and precision application equipment for agricultural industry, with facilities in Iowa, Georgia, Ontario and Manitoba, for $260,000,000. The transaction was expected to close in the second quarter of 2022.

Status: completed **Revised:** Apr. 1, 2022
UPDATE: The transaction was completed. PREVIOUS: Linamar Corporation entered into an agreement with GF Casting Solution (GF), a division of Georg Fischer AG, to acquire GF's 50% interest in GF Linamar LLC (GFL), a 50/50 joint venture between Linamar and GF, for $$121,300,000. The joint venture was formed to provide integrated casting and machine solutions to automotive, industrial, and commercial customers. The transaction was expected to close in the first week of April 2022.

Predecessor Detail - Name changed from Linamar Machine Limited, Nov. 26, 1992.

Directors - Linda S. Hasenfratz, exec. chr. & CEO, Guelph, Ont.; James (Jim) Jarrell, pres. & COO, Guelph, Ont.; Mark Stoddart, exec. v-p, sales & mktg. & chief tech. officer, Guelph, Ont.; Lisa Forwell, Oakville, Ont.; Dennis Grimm, Kitchener, Ont.; Terry J. Reidel, Kitchener, Ont.

Other Exec. Officers - Dale Schneider, CFO; Salvatore (Sam) Cocca, grp. pres., Europe; Sean Congdon, grp. pres., North America; Wenzhang (Henry) Huang, grp. pres., Linamar Machining & Assembly, Asia Pacific; Ken McDougall, grp. pres., Skyjack Inc.; Roger Fulton, exec. v-p, HR, gen. counsel & corp. sec.

Capital Stock

	Authorized (shs.)	Outstanding (shs.)[1]
Special	unlimited	nil
Common	unlimited	61,528,157

[1] At Aug. 9, 2023

Options - At Dec. 31, 2022, options were outstanding to purchase 1,150,000 common shares at a weighted average exercise price of $61.20 per share with a weighted average remaining life of 6.1 years.

Major Shareholder - Linda S. Hasenfratz held 32.9% interest at Mar. 8, 2023.

Price Range - LNR/TSX

Year	Volume	High	Low	Close
2022	41,477,022	$81.25	$45.46	$61.30
2021	35,196,690	$91.98	$63.44	$74.93
2020	46,877,655	$71.09	$24.57	$67.42
2019	47,242,846	$53.64	$35.33	$49.13
2018	69,650,216	$76.86	$43.03	$45.30

Recent Close: $69.22

Capital Stock Changes - During 2022, 50,000 common shares were issued on exercise of options and 3,972,540 common shares were repurchased under a Normal Course Issuer Bid.

Dividends

LNR com Ra $0.88 pa Q est. Apr. 18, 2023
Prev. Rate: $0.80 est. Dec. 3, 2021
Prev. Rate: $0.64 est. Apr. 15, 2021
Prev. Rate: $0.48 est. Dec. 4, 2020

Long-Term Debt - Outstanding at Dec. 31, 2022:

Credit facilities[1]	$694,940,000
Sr. unsecured notes[2]	461,782,000
Non-int. bearing govt. loans	72,126,000
Lease liabs	79,526,000
	1,308,374,000
Less: Current portion	26,733,000
	1,281,641,000

[1] Represents amounts drawn on $1.175 billion revolving credit facility due November 2026.
[2] Bears rate at 1.37% and due on January 2031.

Wholly Owned Subsidiaries

GF Linamar LLC, N.C.
Industrias de Linamar S.A. de C.V., Germany.
Linamar Agriculture Inc., Man.
Linamar Antriebstechnik GmbH, Crimmitschau, Germany.
Linamar Automotive Systems NL, Inc., United States.
Linamar Automotive Systems (Wuxi) Co., Ltd., People's Republic of China.
Linamar (Barbados) Holdings Inc., Barbados.
Linamar (China) Investment Co., Ltd., People's Republic of China.
Linamar Forging Holding GmbH, Germany.
Linamar Forgings Carolina Inc., N.C.
Linamar GmbH, Germany.
Linamar Holding Nevada Inc., Nev.
Linamar Holdings de Mexico S.A. de C.V., Ramos Arizpe, Coah., Mexico.
Linamar Holdings Inc., Ont.
Linamar Hungary Zrt., Hungary.
Linamar Light Metals-MR, LLC, N.C.
Linamar Light Metals Ruse EOOD, Germany.
Linamar Light Metals S.A., France.
Linamar Motorkomponenten GmbH, Germany.
Linamar North Carolina, Inc., N.C.
Linamar Plettenberg GmbH, Germany.
Linamar Powertrain GmbH, Germany.
Linergy Manufacturing Inc., Ont.
MacDon Industries Ltd., Winnipeg, Man.
McLaren Performance Technologies, Inc.
Salford Group, Inc., Salford, Ont.
Skyjack Inc., Guelph, Ont.
Skyjack UK Limited, United Kingdom.

Note: The preceding list includes only the major related companies in which interests are held.

Financial Statistics

Periods ended:	12m Dec. 31/22[A]		12m Dec. 31/21[A]
	$000s	%Chg	$000s
Operating revenue	**7,917,911**	**+21**	**6,536,574**
Cost of sales	6,504,807		5,153,339
General & admin expense	408,498		346,478
Operating expense	**6,913,305**	**+26**	**5,499,817**
Operating income	**1,004,606**	**-3**	**1,036,757**
Deprec., depl. & amort.	440,972		448,754
Finance income	18,916		21,505
Finance costs, gross	44,573		32,227
Investment income	(6,086)		(28,345)
Pre-tax income	**563,088**	**0**	**562,166**
Income taxes	136,894		141,608
Net income	**426,194**	**+1**	**420,558**
Cash & equivalent	860,515		928,428
Inventories	1,509,302		1,066,456
Accounts receivable	1,160,509		870,551
Current assets	3,693,286		2,982,193
Long-term investments	18,185		14,375
Fixed assets, net	2,793,091		2,415,916
Intangibles, net	1,851,837		1,659,764
Total assets	**8,576,391**	**+16**	**7,390,390**
Accts. pay. & accr. liabs.	2,011,694		1,603,466
Current liabilities	2,156,425		1,745,120
Long-term debt, gross	1,308,374		791,545
Long-term debt, net	1,281,641		770,490
Shareholders' equity	4,811,711		4,598,796
Cash from oper. activs.	**468,131**	**-48**	**908,764**
Cash from fin. activs.	156,388		(572,079)
Cash from invest. activs.	(715,742)		(267,319)
Net cash position	**860,515**	**-7**	**928,428**
Capital expenditures	(410,650)		(243,058)
Capital disposals	36,170		6,883
	$		$
Earnings per share*	6.67		6.43
Cash flow per share*	7.33		13.88
Cash divd. per share*	0.80		0.68
	shs		shs
No. of shs. o/s*	61,528,157		65,450,697
Avg. no. of shs. o/s*	63,877,686		65,450,697
	%		%
Net profit margin	5.38		6.43
Return on equity	9.06		9.40
Return on assets	5.76		5.95
Foreign sales percent	48		50
No. of employees (FTEs)	27,905		25,613

* Common
[A] Reported in accordance with IFRS

Latest Results

Periods ended:	6m June 30/23[A]		6m June 30/22[A]
	$000s	%Chg	$000s
Operating revenue	4,845,496	+29	3,759,729
Net income	251,988	+26	200,760
	$		$
Earnings per share*	4.10		3.08

* Common
[A] Reported in accordance with IFRS

Historical Summary
(as originally stated)

Fiscal Year	Oper. Rev.	Net Inc. Bef. Disc.	EPS*
	$000s	$000s	$
2022[A]	7,917,911	426,194	6.67
2021[A]	6,536,574	420,558	6.43
2020[A]	5,815,573	279,133	4.27
2019[A]	7,416,624	430,441	6.59
2018[A]	7,620,582	591,481	9.05

* Common
[A] Reported in accordance with IFRS

L.30 Lincoln Ventures Ltd.

Symbol - LX.H **Exchange** - TSX-VEN **CUSIP** - 53500R
Head Office - 650-669 Howe St, Vancouver, BC, V6C 0B4 **Telephone** - (778) 725-1487 **Fax** - (604) 428-1124
Email - eau@jproust.ca
Investor Relations - Eileen Au (778) 725-1487
Auditors - MNP LLP C.A., Vancouver, B.C.
Lawyers - Fasken Martineau DuMoulin LLP, Vancouver, B.C.
Transfer Agents - Olympia Trust Company
Profile - (Alta. 2002) Seeking new business opportunities.

Previously developed, produced, manufactured and commercialized advanced composite materials for industrial and structural applications.

Predecessor Detail - Name changed from TekModo Industries Inc., July 13, 2018; basis 1 new for 10 old shs.

Directors - John G. Proust, pres., Vancouver, B.C.; Vincent (Vince) Boon, CFO, B.C.; Murray G. Flanigan, B.C.

Other Exec. Officers - Eileen Au, corp. sec.

Capital Stock

	Authorized (shs.)	Outstanding (shs.)[1]
Preferred	unlimited	nil
Exchangeable	unlimited	287,265[2]
Common	unlimited	24,016,810[3]

[1] At Mar. 31, 2022
[2] Exchangeable non-voting common shares of TekModo Holdings Inc.
[3] At May 8, 2022.

Exchangeable - Issued by TekModoHoldings Inc. to former owners of TekModo group of companies. Exchangeable for common shares of the company, subject to a release schedule over time. Non-voting.

Common - One vote per share.

Major Shareholder - Jacob (Jake) Vogel held 36.69% interest and John G. Proust held 19.62% interest at Aug. 3, 2021.

Price Range - LX.H/TSX-VEN

Year	Volume	High	Low	Close
2022	463,601	$0.18	$0.05	$0.05
2021	352,534	$0.20	$0.11	$0.14
2020	1,322,843	$0.14	$0.06	$0.13
2019	1,322,885	$0.15	$0.10	$0.12
2018	1,050,909	$0.85	$0.08	$0.10

Recent Close: $0.05

Capital Stock Changes - In June 2022, private placement of 1,250,000 units (1 common share & 1 warrant) at 8¢ per unit was completed, with warrants exercisable at $0.105 per share for one year. In addition, 1,793,794 units (1 common share & 1 warrant) were issued for debt settlement, with warrants exercisable at $0.105 per share for one year; and 1,875,000 common shares were issued for services.

Wholly Owned Subsidiaries

CarbonOne Holding Corp., B.C.
EcoCarbon Technologies Canada Inc., Canada.
Palo Duro Operating (US), Inc., Tex. inactive
TekModo Holdings Inc., United States.

Financial Statistics

Periods ended:	12m Dec. 31/21[A]		12m Dec. 31/20[A]
	$000s	%Chg	$000s
General & admin expense	153		301
Stock-based compensation	nil		23
Operating expense	**153**	**-53**	**324**
Operating income	**(153)**	**n.a.**	**(324)**
Pre-tax income	**(153)**	**n.a.**	**(324)**
Net income	**(153)**	**n.a.**	**(324)**
Cash & equivalent	11		83
Accounts receivable	1		14
Current assets	13		97
Total assets	**13**	**-87**	**97**
Accts. pay. & accr. liabs.	353		284
Current liabilities	353		284
Shareholders' equity	(340)		(187)
Cash from oper. activs.	**(71)**	**n.a.**	**(173)**
Cash from fin. activs.	nil		48
Net cash position	**11**	**-87**	**83**
	$		$
Earnings per share*	(0.01)		(0.01)
Cash flow per share*	(0.00)		(0.01)
	shs		shs
No. of shs. o/s*	24,016,810		24,016,810
Avg. no. of shs. o/s*	24,070,735		24,070,735
	%		%
Net profit margin	n.a.		n.a.
Return on equity	n.m.		n.m.
Return on assets	(278.18)		(207.03)

* Common
[A] Reported in accordance with IFRS

Latest Results

Periods ended:	3m Mar. 31/22[A]		3m Mar. 31/21[A]
	$000s	%Chg	$000s
Net income	(61)	n.a.	(28)
	$		$
Earnings per share*	(0.00)		(0.00)

* Common
[A] Reported in accordance with IFRS

Historical Summary
(as originally stated)

Fiscal Year	Oper. Rev.	Net Inc. Bef. Disc.	EPS*
	$000s	$000s	$
2021[A]	nil	(153)	(0.01)
2020[A]	nil	(324)	(0.01)
2019[A]	nil	(556)	(0.03)
2018[A]	nil	(805)	(0.28)
2017[A]	4,843	(13,355)	(6.30)

* Common
[A] Reported in accordance with IFRS

Note: Adjusted throughout for 1-for-10 cons. in July 2018

L.31 The Lion Electric Company

Symbol - LEV **Exchange** - TSX **CUSIP** - 536221
Head Office - 921 ch de la Rivière-du-Nord, Saint-Jérôme, QC, J7Y 5G2 **Telephone** - (450) 432-5466 **Toll-free** - (855) 546-6706
Website - thelionelectric.com
Email - isabelle.adjahi@thelionelectric.com
Investor Relations - Isabelle Adjahi (855) 546-6706
Auditors - Raymond Chabot Grant Thornton LLP C.A., Montréal, Qué.
Transfer Agents - American Stock Transfer & Trust Company, LLC, New York, N.Y.; TSX Trust Company, Montréal, Qué.
Employees - 1,400 at May 8, 2023
Profile - (Que. 2008) Creates, designs and manufactures all-electric class 5 to class 8 commercial urban trucks and all-electric buses and minibuses for the school, paratransit and mass transit markets.

Commercialized medium and heavy-duty electric vehicles (EVs) consist of Lion6 (class 6 truck), Lion8 (class 8 truck) and LionC (type C school bus). Development pipeline includes Lion5 (class 5 truck), Lion8 Tractor truck, LionA (type A school bus) and LionD (type D school bus), which are all targeted to be commercialized in 2023, as well as LionM minibus. The company designs, builds and assembles many of its vehicles' components, including chassis, battery packs, truck cabins and bus bodies. For certain specialized trucks, such as all-electric ambulances, bucket trucks, utility trucks and refuse collection trucks, the company has partnerships and other contractual relationships with suppliers and upfitters to offer clients with various vehicle configurations, upfit equipment options and applications. EVs developed are specifically designed to address the needs of the sub 250-mile (400-km) mid-range urban market, and are sold through direct-to-consumer channels.

The company also offers various services as a complement to its product line-up, including LionEnergy, the company's division that assists clients with selecting, purchasing, project managing and deploying charging infrastructure ahead of vehicle delivery and which generates revenues through project management and consulting services as well as the resale of charging stations from charging infrastructure manufacturers; LionCapital Solutions, which offers financing alternatives for the company's vehicles and related charging infrastructure; LionGrant, which assists clients in identifying and applying for grant and subsidy funding opportunities from various governmental bodies; and LionBeat, an EV telematics software solution offered as an aftermarket support for the company's vehicles.

At May 8, 2023, vehicle order book was 2,565 EVs, consisting of 295 trucks and 2,270 buses, representing a total order value of US$625,000,000. In addition, LionEnergy had an order book of 347 charging stations, representing a total order value of US$6,000,000.

Facilities consist of the headquarters and manufacturing facility in Saint-Jérôme, Que., totaling 200,000 sq. ft., with the facility having an annual production capacity of up to 2,500 vehicles; a 900,000-sq.-ft. manufacturing facility in Joliet, Ill., with an annual production capacity of up to 20,000 vehicles; and the Lion Campus at the YMX International Aerocity of Mirabel, Que., consisting of an innovation centre and a 175,000-sq.-ft. battery manufacturing plant, with an annual battery production capacity of 5 GWh. Production from the Joliet facility and the battery manufacturing plant were achieved in late 2022, with ramp up continuing through 2023. By the end of 2023, the Joliet and battery facilities were expected to reach production capacity of 2,500 buses and 1.7 GWh, respectively, on an annual basis. Construction of the innovation centre is ongoing. In addition, R&D activities are conducted from three centres in Saint-Jérôme, Mirabel and Montreal, Que.

The company has 12 experience centres which allow prospective customers, policymakers and other transportation industry stakeholders to familiarize themselves with the company's EVs, learn about their specifications and advantages, obtain sales support and meet sales representatives, discuss grant and subsidy assistance, obtain charging infrastructure assistance, receive vehicle training, maintenance support and have existing vehicles serviced. Locations are in Saint-Jérôme and Terrebonne, Que., Moncton, N.B., Richmond, B.C., Auburn, Wash., Los Angeles and Sacramento, Calif., Jacksonville, Fla., Shakopee, Minn., Richmond, Va., Milton, Vt., and Denver, Colo.

Recent Merger and Acquisition Activity

Status: completed **Announced:** Feb. 2, 2023
BTB Real Estate Investment Trust acquired The Lion Electric Company's newly constructed battery manufacturing building located near Mirabel airport in Mirabel, Que., for a purchase price of Cdn$28,000,000, excluding fees and adjustments. The 176,819-sq.-ft. battery factory for motorized electric transport, such as trucks and buses, was leased back by Lion Electric. The transaction excluded the innovation centre building, which remained the property of Lion Electric.

Directors - Marc Bedard, founder & CEO, Qué.; Pierre Larochelle, chr., Montréal, Qué.; Michel Ringuet†, Qué.; Latasha Akoma, Fla.; Sheila C. Bair, Md.; Dane L. Parker, Tex.; Ann L. Payne, Fla.; Pierre-Olivier Perras, Westmount, Qué.; Lorenzo Roccia, Milan, Italy; Pierre Wilkie, Qué.

Other Exec. Officers - Yannick Poulin, COO; François Beaulieu, CIO; Nathalie Giroux, chief people officer; Dominique Perron, chief legal officer & corp. sec.; Brian S. Piern, chief comml. officer; Nicolas Brunet, exec. v-p & CFO; Nate A. Baguio, sr. v-p, comml. devel., USA; Richard Coulombe, sr. v-p, strategic initiatives; Jud Kenney, sr. v-p, procurement & supply chain; Rocco Mezzatesta, sr. v-p, product devel. & vehicle eng. & chief tech. officer; Isabelle Adjahi, v-p, IR & sustainable devel.; Dominik Beckman, v-p, mktg. & commun.; Patrick Gervais, v-p, truck & comml. devel., Canada; Philippe LeBlanc, v-p, R&D & eng.; Benoît Morin, v-p, bus sales, Canada; Marc-André Pagé, v-p, comml. opers.; Vince Spadafora, v-p, finl. reporting
† Lead director

Capital Stock

	Authorized (shs.)	Outstanding (shs.)[1]
Preferred	unlimited	nil
Common	unlimited	224,639,505

[1] At June 30, 2023

Major Shareholder - Power Corporation of Canada held 34.3% interest and Marc Bedard held 11.84% interest at June 30, 2023.

Price Range - LEV/TSX

Year	Volume	High	Low	Close
2022	100,896,534	$12.95	$2.50	$3.04
2021	53,495,169	$28.39	$11.31	$12.50

Recent Close: $2.77

Capital Stock Changes - In January 2023, 2,952,755 units (1 common share & 1 warrant) were issued on exercise of over-allotment option pursuant to the public offering completed in December 2022. Warrants are exercisable at US$2.80 per share for five years.

In December 2022, public offering of 19,685,040 units (1 common share & 1 warrant) at US$2.54 per unit was completed. Also during 2022, common shares were issued as follows: 8,346,789 under an at-the-market equity program, 45,121 on exercise of options and 300 on exercise of warrants.

Wholly Owned Subsidiaries

Lion Electric Holding USA Inc., Del.
- 100% int. in **The Lion Electric Co. USA Inc.**, Del.
- 100% int. in **Lion Electric Manufacturing USA Inc.**, Del.
- 100% int. in **Northern Genesis Acquisition Corp.**, Kansas City, Mo.

Note: The preceding list includes only the major related companies in which interests are held.

Financial Statistics

Periods ended:	12m Dec. 31/22[A]		12m Dec. 31/21[oA]
	US$000s	%Chg	US$000s
Operating revenue	**139,914**	**+142**	**57,710**
Cost of sales	147,383		55,820
General & admin expense	61,803		102,727
Operating expense	**209,186**	**+32**	**158,547**
Operating income	**(69,272)**	**n.a.**	**(100,837)**
Deprec., depl. & amort.	11,492		5,260
Finance costs, gross	955		8,332
Pre-tax income	**17,776**	**n.a.**	**(43,325)**
Net income	**17,776**	**n.a.**	**(43,325)**
Cash & equivalent	88,267		241,702
Inventories	167,192		115,979
Accounts receivable	62,972		37,899
Current assets	323,498		400,227
Fixed assets, net	160,756		32,668
Right-of-use assets	60,508		60,902
Intangibles, net	151,364		81,900
Total assets	**710,411**	**+20**	**590,604**
Accts. pay. & accr. liabs	75,222		39,930
Current liabilities	81,092		58,116
Long-term debt, gross	110,673		13,078
Long-term debt, net	110,649		62
Long-term lease liabilities	58,310		57,518
Shareholders' equity	437,117		368,682
Cash from oper. activs	**(119,553)**	**n.a.**	**(130,969)**
Cash from fin. activs	172,802		434,697
Cash from invest. activs	(204,607)		(62,599)
Net cash position	**88,267**	**-63**	**241,702**
Capital expenditures	(129,574)		(19,825)
Capital disposals	24		nil
	US$		US$
Earnings per share*	0.09		(0.27)
Cash flow per share*	(0.62)		(0.81)
	shs		shs
No. of shs. o/s*	218,079,962		190,002,712
Avg. no. of shs. o/s*	193,113,983		162,245,092
	%		%
Net profit margin	12.70		(75.07)
Return on equity	4.41		n.m.
Return on assets	2.88		(9.75)
Foreign sales percent	13		35
No. of employees (FTEs)	1,400		985

* Common
[o] Restated
[A] Reported in accordance with IFRS

Latest Results

Periods ended:	3m Mar. 31/23[A]		3m Mar. 31/22[A]
	US$000s	%Chg	US$000s
Operating revenue	54,703	+142	22,647
Net income	(15,583)	n.a.	2,102
	US$		US$
Earnings per share*	(0.07)		0.01

* Common
[A] Reported in accordance with IFRS

Historical Summary
(as originally stated)

Fiscal Year	Oper. Rev.	Net Inc. Bef. Disc.	EPS*
	US$000s	US$000s	US$
2022[A]	139,914	17,776	0.09
2021[A]	57,710	(43,325)	(0.27)
2020[A1]	23,423	(97,352)	(0.88)
2019[A1]	30,862	(3,071)	(0.03)
2018[A1]	16,621	(5,358)	(0.05)

* Common
[A] Reported in accordance with IFRS
[1] Shares and per share figures adjusted to reflect 4.1289-for-1 split for former Lion shareholders effective upon completion of the business combination with Northern Genesis Acquisition Corp. on May 6, 2021.

L.32 Lions Bay Capital Inc.

Symbol - LBI **Exchange** - TSX-VEN **CUSIP** - 536263
Head Office - 795 Glenferrie Rd, Suite 6, Hawthorn, VIC, Australia, 3122 **Overseas Tel** - 61-3-9236-2800
Website - www.lionsbaycapital.com
Email - jbyrne@lionsbaycapital.com
Investor Relations - John J. Byrne 61-3-9236-2800
Auditors - Davidson & Company LLP C.A., Vancouver, B.C.
Transfer Agents - Computershare Trust Company of Canada Inc., Toronto, Ont.

Profile - (B.C. 2010) Invests in securities of publicly traded companies in the resource, energy and resource-related technology sectors in Australia and Canada. Also has mineral interest in Australia.

Investment portfolio consisting of public companies includes **Kalina Power Limited**, which offers power generation services; **Fidelity Minerals Corp.**, which has mineral interests in Peru; **Parkway Corporate Limited** (formerly **Parkway Minerals NL**), an Australian-based fertilizer minerals company; **South Harz Potash Ltd.** (formerly **Davenport Resources Ltd.**), which owns German potash projects; **Elementos Limited**, a global tin company; **Meryllion Resources Corp.**, which owns Australian properties; **Arctic Star Exploration Corp.**, which has diamond interests in the Northwest Territories, Nunavut and Finland; and **Heavy Rare Earths Limited**, an Australian-based rare earth exploration company

In Australia, holds option from **Savic Pty Ltd.** to earn 50% interest in 920-sq.-km rare earth property, requiring exploration expenditures of A$5,000,000 over three years to January 2025; and option to earn up to 90% interest in a portfolio of claims in Queensland.

Directors - John J. Byrne, exec. chr., pres. & CEO, Melbourne, Vic., Australia; Anthony Balic, CFO, Burnaby, B.C.; J. Ross MacLachlan, Vancouver, B.C.

Capital Stock

	Authorized (shs.)	Outstanding (shs.)[1]
Preferred	unlimited	nil
Common	unlimited	142,105,852

[1] At Sept. 28, 2022

Major Shareholder - John J. Byrne held 55% interest at Feb. 7, 2022.

Price Range - LBI/TSX-VEN

Year	Volume	High	Low	Close
2022	7,476,163	$0.10	$0.02	$0.03
2021	10,962,605	$0.13	$0.06	$0.11
2020	22,048,327	$0.14	$0.01	$0.10
2019	3,933,500	$0.10	$0.03	$0.04
2018	3,814,991	$0.14	$0.04	$0.04

Recent Close: $0.03

Capital Stock Changes - During fiscal 2022, 7,048,889 common shares were issued by private placement.

Wholly Owned Subsidiaries

Pan Andean Capital Pty Ltd., Melbourne, Vic., Australia.

Subsidiaries

80% int. in **Epic Minerals Pty Ltd.**, Australia.

Investments

0.16% int. in **Arctic Star Exploration Corp.**, Vancouver, B.C. (see Survey of Mines)
2.52% int. in **Elementos Limited**, Australia.
48.79% int. in **Fidelity Minerals Corp.**, Vancouver, B.C. (see Survey of Mines)
Heavy Rare Earths Limited, Australia.
3.25% int. in **Kalina Power Ltd.**
2.33% int. in **Meryllion Resources Corp.**
7.55% int. in **Parkway Corporate Limited**, Australia.
1.07% int. in **South Harz Potash Ltd.**

Financial Statistics

Periods ended:	12m May 31/22[A]		12m May 31/21[A]
	$000s	%Chg	$000s
Realized invest. gain (loss)	3,518		1,024
Unrealized invest. gain (loss)	(1,701)		6,747
Total revenue	**1,410**	**-83**	**8,259**
General & admin. expense	812		636
Stock-based compensation	97		nil
Operating expense	**910**	**+43**	**636**
Operating income	**500**	**-93**	**7,623**
Finance costs, gross	368		104
Pre-tax income	**(4)**	**n.a.**	**7,381**
Income taxes	94		1,247
Net income	**(98)**	**n.a.**	**6,134**
Cash & equivalent	11,478		11,639
Current assets	13,212		12,876
Explor./devel. properties	480		nil
Total assets	**13,692**	**+6**	**12,876**
Accts. pay. & accr. liabs	155		74
Current liabilities	962		717
Long-term debt, gross	529		514
Shareholders' equity	11,662		11,013
Cash from oper. activs	**40**	**n.a.**	**(1,548)**
Cash from fin. activs	295		1,722
Net cash position	**554**	**+204**	**182**
	$		$
Earnings per share*	(0.00)		0.05
Cash flow per share*	0.00		(0.01)
	shs		shs
No. of shs. o/s*	142,105,852		135,056,963
Avg. no. of shs. o/s*	140,058,777		116,242,403
	%		%
Net profit margin	(6.95)		74.27
Return on equity	(0.86)		92.02
Return on assets	67.13		74.88

* Common
[A] Reported in accordance with IFRS

Historical Summary
(as originally stated)

Fiscal Year	Total Rev.	Net Inc. Bef. Disc.	EPS*
	$000s	$000s	$
2022[A]	1,410	(98)	(0.00)
2021[A]	8,259	6,134	0.05
2020[A]	(482)	(432)	(0.00)
2019[A]	(2,225)	(3,642)	(0.04)
2018[A1]	2,461	772	0.02

* Common
[A] Reported in accordance with IFRS
[1] Results reflect the Nov. 14, 2017, Qualifying Transaction reverse takeover acquisition of Pan Andean Capital Pty Ltd.

L.33 Lions Gate Entertainment Corp.

Symbol - LGF.A **Exchange** - NYSE **CUSIP** - 535919
Head Office - 2000-250 Howe St, Vancouver, BC, V6C 3R8 **Telephone** - (604) 648-6559 **Fax** - (604) 683-5214 **Exec. Office** - 2700 Colorado Ave, Suite 200, Santa Monica, CA, United States, 90404 **Telephone** - (310) 449-9200 **Toll-free** - (877) 848-3866 **Fax** - (310) 255-3870
Website - investors.lionsgate.com
Email - nshah@lionsgate.com
Investor Relations - Nilay Shah (877) 848-3866
Auditors - Ernst & Young LLP C.P.A., Los Angeles, Calif.
Bankers - JPMorgan Chase & Co., Chicago, Ill.
Transfer Agents - Computershare Trust Company of Canada Inc., Toronto, Ont.
FP500 Revenue Ranking - 126
Employees - 1,448 at May 20, 2022

Profile - (B.C. 1997 amalg.) Develops, produces and distributes feature films and television programming and operates a subscription platform for worldwide audiences. Other businesses include location-based entertainment, interactive games and premium pay television networks.

Operations are organized into three segments: Motion Picture; Television Production; and Media Networks.

Motion Picture consists of the development, production, acquisition, distribution and licensing of feature films worldwide. In-house film production and distribution businesses include Lionsgate, Summit Entertainment and Good Universe. Films developed and produced in-house, co-developed and co-produced, and acquired or licensed from third parties are distributed around the world through theatrical releases, home entertainment and television markets. The company distributes films directly to movie theatres in the U.S., the U.K. and Ireland, through a sub-distributor in Canada and through licensed third party distributors internationally. The home entertainment distribution operation consists of packaged media, which involves the marketing, promotion, sale and/or lease of physical discs to wholesalers and retailers; and digital media, which includes distribution through pay-per-view and video-on-demand platforms, electronic sell-through and digital rental. Television distribution includes the licensing of films to the linear pay, basic cable and free television markets. In addition, this segment includes the licensing, development and production of live shows and experiences, location-based entertainment destinations such as theme parks and attractions, games, physical and digital merchandise; music management, including sales and licensing of music from the company's films; and licensing of films at non-theatrical venues, including educational and institutional facilities, U.S. military bases, hospitals, hotels, prisons and all forms of common carrier transportation such airlines and ships.

Television Production includes the development, production, syndication and distribution of scripted and unscripted series, television movies, mini-series and non-fiction programming to broadcast television networks, pay and basic cable networks, digital platforms and syndicators of first-run programming worldwide. Television productions are also sold and distributed on home entertainment (packaged media and via digital delivery). Operations also include the licensing of television programs to other ancillary markets; sales and licensing of music from the television broadcast of the company's productions; and 51% interest in **3 Arts Entertainment, LLC**, a talent management and television/film production company.

Media Networks consists of the Starz business, which produces and distributes original series and movies worldwide across subscription television platforms. In the U.S., Starz consists of the STARZ, STARZ ENCORE and MOVIEPLEX banners of 17 premium pay television channels and associated on-demand and online viewing platforms, including the STARZ application. Starz is sold through over-the-top (OTT) platforms, multichannel video programming distributors including cable operators, satellite television providers and telecommunication companies, and other online and digital platforms. Outside the U.S., Starz is available in over 50 countries under the LIONSGATE+ banner in Europe, Latin America and Australia, under the STARZ banner in Canada, under the Lionsgate Play banner in South and Southeast Asia, and through STARZPLAY Arabia in the Middle East and North Africa. Services are provided through OTT providers, Internet protocol television (IPTV) providers, PayTV companies, the LIONSGATE+ application, and cable and satellite providers in Canada only as a linear service. At Sept. 30, 2022, STARZ, LIONSGATE+ and STARZPLAY Arabia had 21,000,000, 14,800,000 and 2,000,000 subscribers, respectively.

On Nov. 3, 2022, the company announced a decision to exit its LIONSGATE+ streaming business in seven international territories (France, Germany, Italy, Spain, Benelux, the Nordics and Japan).

In September 2022, the company announced a potential spin-out or other transaction involving its studio business, consisting of the Motion Picture and Television Production segments. This replaced the company's previous plan announced in November 2021 to explore a spin-out and other alternatives for its Media Networks segment (Starz).

On Sept. 29, 2022, the company rebranded its premium international streaming business, STARZPLAY, into LIONSGATE+ in 35 countries in Europe, Latin America and Asia-Pacific. The U.S. and Canadian markets retained the STARZ brand, along with the STARZPLAY Arabia brand in the Middle East and North Africa and the Lionsgate Play brand in South and Southeast Asia.

Directors - Dr. Mark H. Rachesky, chr., New York, N.Y.; Michael R. Burns, v-chr., Los Angeles, Calif.; Jon Feltheimer, CEO, Los Angeles, Calif.; Mignon L. Clyburn, Washington, D.C.; Gordon (Gordy) Crawford, La Cañada Flintridge, Calif.; Emily Fine, New York, N.Y.; Michael T. (Mike) Fries, Denver, Colo.; Amb. Susan R. McCaw, North Palm Beach, Fla.; Yvette Ostolaza, Dallas, Tex.; Daryl D. Simm, Naples, Fla.; Hardwick Simmons, Mass.; Harry E. Sloan, Los Angeles, Calif.

Other Exec. Officers - Brian Goldsmith, COO; James W. (Jimmy) Barge, CFO; Corii D. Berg, exec. v-p & gen. counsel; Nilay Shah, exec. v-p & head, IR; Peter D. Wilkes, exec. v-p, corp. commun.

Capital Stock

	Authorized (shs.)	Outstanding (shs.)[1]
Class A Vtg.	500,000,000	83,394,680
Class B Non-Vtg.	500,000,000	145,326,897

[1] At Oct. 31, 2022

Class A Voting - One vote per share.

Class B Non-Voting - Non-voting.

Major Shareholder - Dr. Mark H. Rachesky held 23.2% interest at July 22, 2022.

Price Range - LGF.A/NYSE

Year	Volume	High	Low	Close
2022	56,705,850	US$18.84	US$5.46	US$5.71
2021	66,302,134	US$21.41	US$11.06	US$16.64
2020	80,497,473	US$11.53	US$4.18	US$11.37
2019	69,604,666	US$19.00	US$7.66	US$10.66
2018	58,097,405	US$36.47	US$13.64	US$16.10

Capital Stock Changes - During fiscal 2022, 300,000 class A voting common shares were issued as share-based compensation; and class B non-voting common shares were issued as follows: 3,500,000 as share-based compensation and 300,000 on exercise of options.

Wholly Owned Subsidiaries

Artisan Entertainment Inc., Santa Monica, Calif.
Artisan Home Entertainment Inc., Santa Monica, Calif.
BMP Funding LLC, Santa Monica, Calif.
Debmar-Mercury LLC, Calif.
Debmar Studios, Inc., Santa Monica, Calif.
Entertainment Capital Holdings International S.A.R.L., Luxembourg.
Entertainment Capital Lux S.A.R.L., Luxembourg.
Film Holdings Co. Inc., Santa Monica, Calif.
For Our Kids Entertainment, LLC, Santa Monica, Calif.
Good Universe Media, LLC, Santa Monica, Calif.
IPF Library Holdings LLC, Del.
IPF Library LLC, Del.
IPF Receivables LLC, Del.
LG Capital Holdings Inc., Del.
LG Receivables Funding, LLC, Del.
LG Rights Holdings, LLC, Del.
LG TCM LLC, Del.
LGAC International LLC, Del.
LGAC 1, LLC, Del.
LGAC 3, LLC, Del.
LGTV Development (UK) Limited, United Kingdom.
Lions Gate X Productions Corp., Toronto, Ont.
Lions Gate X Productions, LLC, Del.
Lions Gate Capital Holdings, LLC, Del.
Lions Gate China UK Limited, United Kingdom.
Lions Gate Entertainment (Hong Kong) Limited, Hong Kong, People's Republic of China.
Lions Gate Entertainment Inc., Del.
Lions Gate Films Inc., Del.
Lions Gate Home Entertainment UK Limited, United Kingdom.
Lions Gate India S.a.r.l., Luxembourg.
Lions Gate International Media Limited, United Kingdom.
Lions Gate International Motion Pictures S.A.R.L., Luxembourg.
Lions Gate International Slate Investment S.A.R.L., Luxembourg.
Lions Gate International (UK) Film Development Limited, United Kingdom.
Lions Gate International (UK) Limited, United Kingdom.
Lions Gate International (UK) TV Development Limited, United Kingdom.
Lions Gate Media Canada GP Inc., B.C.
Lions Gate Media Canada Limited Partnership, B.C.
Lions Gate Media Ltd., United Kingdom.
Lions Gate Pictures UK Limited, United Kingdom.
Lions Gate Television Inc., Del.
Lions Gate True North Corp., Del.
Lions Gate True North Media, LLC, Del.
Lions Gate UK Limited, United Kingdom.
Lions Gate X-US Productions, LLC, Del.
Mandate Films, LLC, Del.
Mandate Pictures, LLC, Beverly Hills, Calif.
Starz Entertainment, LLC, Calif.
Starz Entity Holding Company, LLC, Del.
Starz Independent, LLC, Del.
Starz LLC, Calif.
StarzPlay Canada, LP, Vancouver, B.C.
StarzPlay Direct UK Limited, United Kingdom.
StarzPlay Direct US, LLC, Del.
StarzPlay Management US, LLC, Del.
StarzPlay UK, Limited, United Kingdom.
StarzPlay US, LLC, Del.
Summit Distribution, LLC, Santa Monica, Calif.
Summit Entertainment, LLC, Calif.
True North Media, LLC, Beverly Hills, Calif.

Subsidiaries

62.5% int. in **Pilgrim Media Group, LLC**, Los Angeles, Calif.
51% int. in **3 Arts Entertainment, LLC**, Beverly Hills, Calif.

Investments

50% int. in **Pantelion, LLC**, Santa Monica, Calif.
43% int. in **Roadside Attractions, LLC**, Los Angeles, Calif.

Note: The preceding list includes only the major related companies in which interests are held.

Financial Statistics

Periods ended:	12m Mar. 31/22[A]		12m Mar. 31/21[A]
	US$000s	%Chg	US$000s
Operating revenue	**3,604,300**	**+10**	**3,271,500**
Cost of sales	495,300		534,100
General & admin expense	1,237,600		1,122,400
Stock-based compensation	100,000		89,000
Operating expense	**1,832,900**	**+5**	**1,745,500**
Operating income	**1,771,400**	**+16**	**1,526,000**
Deprec., depl. & amort.	1,745,600		1,378,300
Finance income	30,800		5,800
Finance costs, gross	176,000		181,500
Investment income	(3,000)		(6,100)
Pre-tax income	**(177,000)**	**n.a.**	**(17,400)**
Income taxes	28,400		17,100
Net income	**(205,400)**	**n.a.**	**(34,500)**
Net inc. for equity hldrs	**(188,200)**	**n.a.**	**(18,900)**
Net inc. for non-cont. int.	**(17,200)**	**n.a.**	**(15,600)**
Cash & equivalent	371,200		528,700
Inventories	14,100		14,300
Accounts receivable	442,200		383,700
Current assets	1,058,100		1,186,700
Long-term investments	3,069,600		2,254,600
Fixed assets, net	81,200		91,100
Right-of-use assets	170,700		127,000
Intangibles, net	4,204,700		4,339,600
Total assets	**8,991,200**	**+8**	**8,306,200**
Accts. pay. & accr. liabs	544,400		504,000
Current liabilities	2,403,100		1,692,900
Long-term debt, gross	2,424,900		2,630,900
Long-term debt, net	2,202,100		2,542,900
Long-term lease liabilities	159,300		119,900
Shareholders' equity	2,681,600		2,793,000
Non-controlling interest	1,800		1,600
Cash from oper. activs	**(660,900)**	**n.a.**	**(500)**
Cash from fin. activs	599,400		237,900
Cash from invest. activs	(80,500)		(31,100)
Net cash position	**384,600**	**-27**	**528,700**
Capital expenditures	(33,100)		(35,000)
	US$		US$
Earnings per share*	(0.84)		(0.09)
Cash flow per share*	(2.95)		(0.00)
	shs		shs
No. of shs. o/s*	225,300,000		221,200,000
Avg. no. of shs. o/s*	224,100,000		220,500,000
	%		%
Net profit margin	(5.70)		(1.05)
Return on equity	(6.88)		(0.69)
Return on assets	(0.01)		4.00
Foreign sales percent	98		99

* Cl.A
[A] Reported in accordance with U.S. GAAP

Latest Results

Periods ended:	6m Sept. 30/22[A]		6m Sept. 30/21[A]
	US$000s	%Chg	US$000s
Operating revenue	1,769,100	-1	1,789,000
Net income	(1,936,000)	n.a.	(48,500)
Net inc. for equity hldrs	(1,930,100)	n.a.	(37,900)
Net inc. for non-cont. int	(5,900)		(10,600)
	US$		US$
Earnings per share*	(8.51)		(0.17)

* Cl.A
[A] Reported in accordance with U.S. GAAP

Historical Summary
(as originally stated)

Fiscal Year	Oper. Rev.	Net Inc. Bef. Disc.	EPS*
	US$000s	US$000s	US$
2022[A]	3,604,300	(205,400)	(0.84)
2021[A]	3,271,500	(34,500)	(0.09)
2020[A]	3,890,000	(206,400)	(0.86)
2019[A]	3,680,500	(299,600)	(1.33)
2018[A]	4,129,100	468,100	2.27

* Cl.A
[A] Reported in accordance with U.S. GAAP

L.34 Liquid Avatar Technologies Inc.

Symbol - LQID **Exchange** - CSE (S) **CUSIP** - 53633C
Head Office - 500-7030 Woodbine Ave, Markham, ON, L3R 6G2 **Telephone** - (647) 725-7742
Website - www.liquidavatartechnologies.com
Email - ir@liquidavatar.com
Investor Relations - David M. Lucatch (647) 725-7742 ext. 701
Auditors - RSM Canada LLP C.A., Toronto, Ont.
Transfer Agents - Odyssey Trust Company, Toronto, Ont.
Profile - (B.C. 2014) Operates as a fintech company in Canada and the U.S., with a focus on verification, management and monetization

of Self Sovereign Identity, empowering users to control and benefit from the use of their online identity.

Operations are carried out through three business lines: Digital Identity, Digital Items Agency and Mixed Reality.

Digital Identity - Offers a suite of financial and related services through the Liquid Avatar platform, which consists of the Liquid Avatar mobile app and the Liquid Avatar Verifiable Credentials Ecosystem (LAVCE). LAVCE is a biometrically based and blockchain-powered digital identity validation and verification ecosystem that empowers users to create high-quality digital icons representing their online personas referred to as "Liquid Avatars", which allow users to manage and control their digital identity, their verifiable access and identity credentials, and to use these Liquid Avatars to share public and permission-based private data. The company is also developing other programs which support the Liquid Avatar mobile app, including LQID Card, an approved prepaid card program that allows customers to hold a digital payment method, without needing a credit card account, and provides cashback and other loyalty incentives; and KABN KASH, a cashback and reward platform that has over 600 online merchants. The company's key intellectual property in its business is licensed from **KABN (Gibraltar) Limited** for an annual renewal fee of US$250,000. The initial licence fee was US$1,000,000.

Digital Items Agency - Through wholly owned **Oasis Digital Studios Limited**, provides management, digital marketing and creative services, and works with producers of digital items such as games, enhanced Non-Fungible Tokens (NFTs), avatars and related digital credentials on behalf of artists and Intellectual Property (IP) holders.

Mixed Reality - Through 50%-owned **Aftermath Islands Metaverse Limited**, offers a virtual world that provides online users with theme-based first-person, Augmented Reality (AR), Extended Reality (XR) and Virtual Reality (VR) experiences, quests, games and integrated e-commerce activities, creating a virtual world supported by users and brands.

Common suspended from CSE, May 8, 2023.

Predecessor Detail - Name changed from KABN Systems NA Holdings Corp., Mar. 3, 2021.

Directors - David M. Lucatch, co-founder, chr., pres. & CEO, Vaughan, Ont.; Ralph J. (RJ) Reiser III, chief bus. devel. officer, Houston, Tex.; Andra Enescu, Etobicoke, Ont.; Steven Hollerbach, Tex.; J. Patrick (Jeff) Mesina, Toronto, Ont.

Other Exec. Officers - Craig McCannell, CFO; Lynn Cumiskey, chief compliance officer; Michael Konikoff, chief revenue officer

Capital Stock

	Authorized (shs.)	Outstanding (shs.)[1]
Preferred	unlimited	nil
Common	unlimited	162,292,473

[1] At Nov. 28, 2022

Major Shareholder - Widely held at May 10, 2022.

Price Range - LQID/CSE (S)

Year	Volume	High	Low	Close
2022	119,123,119	$0.21	$0.02	$0.02
2021	247,807,901	$0.55	$0.06	$0.20
2020	58,736,763	$0.45	$0.05	$0.33
2019	737,591	$1.10	$0.15	$0.20
2018	1,511,480	$2.00	$0.40	$0.65

Consolidation: 1-for-10 cons. in June 2020

Recent Close: $0.02

Capital Stock Changes - In July and August 2022, private placement of 20,614,000 units (1 common share & 1 warrant) at 5¢ per unit was completed, with warrants exercisable at 10¢ per share for 36 months.

Wholly Owned Subsidiaries

Liquid Avatar Operations Inc., Canada.

Oasis Digital Studios Limited

- 50% int. in **Aftermath Islands Metaverse Limited**, St. Michael, Barbados.

Financial Statistics

Periods ended:	12m Dec. 31/21[A]		12m Dec. 31/20[A1]
	$000s	%Chg	$000s
Operating revenue	**16**	**n.a.**	**nil**
General & admin expense	8,676		3,724
Stock-based compensation	2,351		672
Operating expense	**11,027**	**+151**	**4,396**
Operating income	**(11,011)**	**n.a.**	**(4,396)**
Deprec., depl. & amort	281		269
Finance costs, gross	28		18
Pre-tax income	**(11,364)**	**n.a.**	**(5,639)**
Net income	**(11,364)**	**n.a.**	**(5,639)**
Cash & equivalent	646		2,589
Accounts receivable	713		nil
Current assets	2,108		3,138
Fixed assets, net	24		18
Intangibles, net	639		908
Total assets	**2,956**	**-28**	**4,121**
Accts. pay. & accr. liabs	844		516
Current liabilities	2,531		691
Shareholders' equity	424		3,429
Cash from oper. activs	**(8,057)**	**n.a.**	**(2,727)**
Cash from fin. activs	6,255		5,332
Cash from invest. activs	(141)		(16)
Net cash position	**646**	**-75**	**2,589**
Capital expenditures	(18)		(19)
	$		$
Earnings per share*	(0.10)		(0.10)
Cash flow per share*	(0.07)		(0.05)
	shs		shs
No. of shs. o/s*	141,178,473		96,216,472
Avg. no. of shs. o/s*	115,944,720		58,342,249
	%		%
Net profit margin	n.m.		n.a.
Return on equity	n.m.		n.m.
Return on assets	n.a.		(271.94)

* Common

[A] Reported in accordance with IFRS

[1] Results reflect the June 4, 2020, reverse takeover acquisition of KABN Systems North America Inc.

Latest Results

Periods ended:	9m Sept. 30/22[A]		9m Sept. 30/21[A]
	$000s	%Chg	$000s
Operating revenue	2	-88	16
Net income	(7,203)	n.a.	(7,895)
	$		$
Earnings per share*	(0.05)		(0.07)

* Common

[A] Reported in accordance with IFRS

Historical Summary
(as originally stated)

Fiscal Year	Oper. Rev. $000s	Net Inc. Bef. Disc. $000s	EPS* $
2021[A]	16	(11,364)	(0.10)
2020[A]	nil	(5,639)	(0.10)
2019[A1]	nil	(242)	(0.04)
2018[A]	nil	(879)	(0.20)
2017[A]	nil	(2,774)	(0.70)

* Common

[A] Reported in accordance with IFRS

[1] Results for 2019 and prior years pertain to Torino Power Solutions Inc.

Note: Adjusted throughout for 1-for-10 cons. in June 2020

L.35 Liquid Meta Capital Holdings Ltd.

Symbol - LIQD **Exchange** - NEO **CUSIP** - 53635T

Head Office - 66 Hendel Dr, Thornhill, ON, L4J 9H7 **Telephone** - (647) 203-9190

Website - liquidmeta.io

Email - jon@liquidmeta.io

Investor Relations - Jonathan Wiesblatt (647) 203-9190

Auditors - RSM Canada LLP C.A., Toronto, Ont.

Transfer Agents - Odyssey Trust Company, Toronto, Ont.

Employees - 8 at Aug. 29, 2022

Profile - (B.C. 2021 amalg.) Engages in the staking of digital assets and develops tools in the decentralized finance (DeFi) sector.

Stakes digital assets across multiple block-chain based protocols through liquidity pools that facilitate the exchange of digital assets and generate service fees per transaction. Also developing blockchain-based protocols, platforms and applications that facilitate the growth of DeFi through proof-of-stake network consensus, along with other growing areas including non-fungible tokens, gaming, and governance and node-operations.

Predecessor Detail - Formed from 1287413 B.C. Ltd. in British Columbia, Dec. 17, 2021, pursuant to the reverse takeover acquisition of and amalgamation with (old) Liquid Meta Capital Holdings Ltd. (deemed acquiror); basis 1 new com. sh. for 5.5146 1287413 B.C. com. shs. and 2.5858 new com. shs. for 1 (old) Liquid Meta com. sh.

Directors - Jonathan (Jon) Wiesblatt, pres. & CEO, Thornhill, Ont.; Nicolas del Pino, Fla.; Michael Ostfield; M. David Prussky, Toronto, Ont.

Other Exec. Officers - Sendy Shorser, CFO & corp. sec.; Daniel Opperman, chief technical officer; Christel Sasse, chief product officer

Capital Stock

	Authorized (shs.)	Outstanding (shs.)[1]
Common	unlimited	53,837,246

[1] At Feb. 28, 2023

Major Shareholder - Nico Nolledo held 27.72% interest at Oct. 25, 2022.

Price Range - LIQD/NEO

Year	Volume	High	Low	Close
2022	744,500	$0.99	$0.10	$0.17
2021	9,000	$1.25	$0.90	$0.99

Recent Close: $0.05

Capital Stock Changes - Pursuant to the reverse takeover acquisition of and amalgamation with (old) Liquid Meta Capital Holdings Ltd. completed on Dec. 17, 2021, 802,511 common shares were issued to the shareholders of 1287413 B.C. Ltd. (1 new for 5.5146 old basis) and 52,825,329 common shares were issued to the shareholders of (old) Liquid Meta (2.5858 new for 1 old basis), including 20,350,000 issued without further consideration on exchange of subscription receipts sold previously by private placement at US$1.00 each and 125,999 issued as finder's fees. Also during fiscal 2022, 209,406 common shares were issued on exercise of warrants.

Financial Statistics

Periods ended:	12m May 31/22[A1]		12m May 31/21[A]
	US$000s	%Chg	US$000s
Operating revenue	**4,747**	**n.m.**	**34**
Cost of sales	71		nil
General & admin expense	2,882		92
Stock-based compensation	4,359		109
Operating expense	**7,312**	**n.m.**	**201**
Operating income	**(2,565)**	**n.a.**	**(167)**
Deprec., depl. & amort	1		nil
Pre-tax income	**(7,075)**	**n.a.**	**(166)**
Net income	**(7,075)**	**n.a.**	**(166)**
Cash & equivalent	20,496		2,177
Inventories	13		7
Accounts receivable	2		nil
Current assets	21,976		2,193
Fixed assets, net	3		3
Total assets	**21,979**	**+901**	**2,196**
Accts. pay. & accr. liabs	447		112
Current liabilities	47		112
Shareholders' equity	21,532		2,084
Cash from oper. activs	**(23,119)**	**n.a.**	**39**
Cash from fin. activs	21,362		2,140
Cash from invest. activs	(1)		(3)
Net cash position	**418**	**-81**	**2,177**
Capital expenditures	(1)		(3)
	US$		US$
Earnings per share*	(0.17)		(0.02)
Cash flow per share*	(0.56)		0.01
	shs		shs
No. of shs. o/s*	53,837,246		n.a.
Avg. no. of shs. o/s*	40,955,004		n.a.
	%		%
Net profit margin	(149.04)		(488.24)
Return on equity	(59.92)		n.m.
Return on assets	(58.53)		n.a.

* Common

[A] Reported in accordance with IFRS

[1] Results prior to Dec. 12, 2021, pertain to and reflect the reverse takeover acquisition of (old) Liquid Meta Capital Holdings Ltd.

Latest Results

Periods ended:	6m Nov. 30/22[A]		6m Nov. 30/21[oA]
	US$000s	%Chg	US$000s
Operating revenue	(312)	n.a.	676
Net income	(6,468)	n.a.	(197)
	US$		US$
Earnings per share*	(0.12)		n.a.

* Common

[o] Restated

[A] Reported in accordance with IFRS

L.36 Lite Access Technologies Inc.

Symbol - LTE **Exchange** - TSX-VEN **CUSIP** - 536736

Head Office - 20108 Logan Ave, Langley, BC, V3A 4L6 **Telephone** - (604) 247-4704 **Toll-free** - (800) 252-0893

Website - www.liteaccess.com

Email - rob@contactfinancial.com

Investor Relations - Rob Gamley (604) 689-7422

Auditors - SHIM & Associates LLP C.A., Vancouver, B.C.

Transfer Agents - Computershare Trust Company of Canada Inc., Vancouver, B.C.

Profile - (B.C. 2014) Develops and provides a suite of micro-duct and air-blown fibre technologies to builders of fibre optic telecommunications networks throughout Canada, the United Kingdom, South America, Africa, Australia and Asia.

The company's broadband and fibre optic solutions and installation technology extend the network provider's ability to deliver broadband connectivity directly to end-users, such as homes, government and educational institutions, and emergency response facilities.

During fiscal 2022, the company liquidated wholly owned **10483737 Limited**.

In June 2022, the company sold wholly owned **AMEC Cutting & Coring Limited** back to its former owner for forgiveness of $322,438 business acquisition payable and $193,245 contingent consideration payable. Additionally, the company will provide AMEC with $80,000 of additional working capital and forgive intercompany indebtedness of $180,000.

Recent Merger and Acquisition Activity

Status: pending **Announced:** May 3, 2023

Lite Access Technologies Inc. entered into a letter of intent to acquire private 1097195 B.C. Ltd. for $6,000,000 cash and issuance of 85,392,538 common shares. 1097195 B.C.'s wholly owned Ironman Directional Drilling Ltd. provides 24/7 horizontal directional drilling services for homeowners, businesses and industrial clients throughout western Canada. Underground infrastructure installations offered by Ironman include telecom, electrical, water and sewer, oil and gas, geothermal and irrigation.

Directors - Michael A. Plotnikoff, interim CEO, Surrey, B.C.; Mike Irmen, B.C.; Alexander (Alex) McAulay, Vancouver, B.C.; Mark T. Tommasi, North Vancouver, B.C.; R. David Toyoda, Vancouver, B.C.

Other Exec. Officers - Linda Han, interim CFO; Michael Priest, chief comml. officer; Scott Grant, v-p, sales; Bob Moody, v-p, opers.

Capital Stock

	Authorized (shs.)	Outstanding (shs.)[1]
Preferred	unlimited	nil
Common	unlimited	85,892,538

[1] At Feb. 28, 2023

Major Shareholder - Widely held at Oct. 12, 2022.

Price Range - LTE/TSX-VEN

Year	Volume	High	Low	Close
2022	20,425,703	$0.17	$0.05	$0.06
2021	101,216,710	$0.42	$0.11	$0.12
2020	63,665,233	$1.00	$0.12	$0.14
2019	19,186,369	$0.56	$0.10	$0.34
2018	16,404,339	$1.50	$0.32	$0.39

Recent Close: $0.10

Capital Stock Changes - In November 2022, private placement of 11,040,000 common shares was completed at 5¢ per share.

In March 2022, private placement of 8,355,000 units (1 common share & 1 warrant) at 10¢ per unit was completed. Also during fiscal 2022, 2,265,440 common shares were issued for debt settlement.

Wholly Owned Subsidiaries

Lite Access Technologies (Canada) Inc., Canada.

Lite Access Technologies (USA) Inc., United States.

Financial Statistics

Periods ended:	12m Sept. 30/22[A]		12m Sept. 30/21[oA]
	$000s	%Chg	$000s
Operating revenue	**5,777**	**+8**	**5,355**
Cost of sales	5,298		4,384
Salaries & benefits	1,632		1,970
General & admin expense	1,139		823
Stock-based compensation	37		535
Operating expense	**8,106**	**+5**	**7,712**
Operating income	**(2,329)**	**n.a.**	**(2,357)**
Deprec., depl. & amort.	192		444
Finance income	2		4
Finance costs, gross	19		27
Write-downs/write-offs	(86)		32
Pre-tax income	**(2,593)**	**n.a.**	**(2,768)**
Net inc. bef. disc. opers	**(2,593)**	**n.a.**	**(2,768)**
Income from disc. opers	(268)		4,916
Net income	**(2,861)**	**n.a.**	**2,147**
Cash & equivalent	239		628
Inventories	96		373
Accounts receivable	2,372		1,519
Current assets	2,749		3,852
Fixed assets, net	861		2,696
Total assets	**3,610**	**-45**	**6,548**
Bank indebtedness	310		419
Accts. pay. & accr. liabs	782		2,049
Current liabilities	2,870		3,413
Long-term debt, gross	85		139
Long-term debt, net	80		89
Long-term lease liabilities	61		381
Shareholders' equity	598		2,472
Cash from oper. activs	**(2,155)**	**n.a.**	**(1,685)**
Cash from fin. activs	938		1,019
Cash from invest. activs	(40)		108
Net cash position	**239**	**-62**	**628**
Capital expenditures	(67)		nil
Capital disposals	27		108
	$		$
Earns. per sh. bef disc opers*	(0.04)		(0.04)
Earnings per share*	(0.04)		0.03
Cash flow per share*	(0.03)		(0.03)
	shs		shs
No. of shs. o/s*	74,852,538		64,232,098
Avg. no. of shs. o/s*	68,831,480		61,970,349
	%		%
Net profit margin	(44.88)		(51.69)
Return on equity	(168.93)		n.m.
Return on assets	(50.68)		(30.13)
Foreign sales percent	nil		1

* Common

[o] Restated

[A] Reported in accordance with IFRS

Historical Summary
(as originally stated)

Fiscal Year	Oper. Rev.	Net Inc. Bef. Disc.	EPS*
	$000s	$000s	$
2022[A]	5,777	(2,593)	(0.04)
2021[A]	7,188	(2,877)	(0.05)
2020[A]	18,867	(17,438)	(0.36)
2019[A]	12,195	(5,262)	(0.12)
2018[A]	9,699	(10,380)	(0.24)

* Common

[A] Reported in accordance with IFRS

L.37 Little Fish Acquisition I Corp.

Symbol - LILL.P **Exchange** - TSX-VEN **CUSIP** - 537226

Head Office - 230-997 Seymour St, Office 9, Vancouver, BC, V6B 3M1 **Telephone** - (604) 339-0339

Email - simonchengnow@gmail.com

Investor Relations - Yee Sing Cheng (604) 339-0339

Auditors - SHIM & Associates LLP C.A., Vancouver, B.C.

Lawyers - Oziel Law, Toronto, Ont.

Transfer Agents - Odyssey Trust Company, Vancouver, B.C.

Profile - (B.C. 2021) Capital Pool Company.

Directors - Yee Sing (Simon) Cheng, CEO, CFO & corp. sec., Calgary, Alta.; Julie Hajduk, Vancouver, B.C.; Konstantin Lichtenwald, Vancouver, B.C.; Steven Pearce, Singapore, Singapore

Capital Stock

	Authorized (shs.)	Outstanding (shs.)[1]
Common	unlimited	4,292,000

[1] At Apr. 30, 2022

Major Shareholder - Konstantin Lichtenwald held 16.31% interest and Steven Pearce held 16.31% interest at Oct. 6, 2021.

Price Range - LILL.P/TSX-VEN

Year	Volume	High	Low	Close
2022	148,622	$0.15	$0.07	$0.07
2021	45,400	$0.23	$0.11	$0.11

Recent Close: $0.05

Capital Stock Changes - On Oct. 6, 2021, an initial public offering of 2,192,000 common shares was completed at 10¢ per share.

L.38 Lobe Sciences Ltd.

Symbol - LOBE **Exchange** - CSE **CUSIP** - 53946V

Head Office - 1400-1199 Hastings St W, Vancouver, BC, V6E 3T5 **Telephone** - (604) 834-9499

Website - www.lobesciences.com

Email - info@lobesciences.com

Investor Relations - Brian Zasitko (604) 834-9499

Auditors - Davidson & Company LLP C.A., Vancouver, B.C.

Transfer Agents - Olympia Trust Company, Calgary, Alta.

Profile - (B.C. 2010) Develops and commercializes therapeutics and devices using psychedelic and other naturally occurring compounds for the treatment of neuropsychiatric disorders.

Developing psychedelic-based proprietary compounds for the treatment of severe forms of anxiety such as post-traumatic stress disorder, cluster headaches and an undisclosed paediatric orphan disease associated with severe anxiety.

Programs under development consist of L-130 salt form and L-131 prodrug which are stable psilocin analogue compounds for multiple indications. In addition, the company collaborates with clinical research organizations including the first-in-man study and research of up to 22 subjects which are focused on safety and pharmacokinetics with **Sancilio & Company, LLC**; and investigation of steady state bioavailability of L-130 (Phase Ib), performing multiple ascending dose and Phase II studies on sub-hallucinogenic dose of levels of L-130 in Australia with **iNGENu Pty Ltd.** Moreover, pre-clinical studies of L-131 are planned for the first quarter of 2023 which would encompass the safety, pharmacokinetics and the kinetics of conversion of the prodrug to psilocin in rodent models.

Also holds 50% interest in **Krysalix VX Corp.**, which is developing psychedelic/virtual experience pod, the Krysalis™ pod, a headset-free, virtual experience that uses multi-sensory stimulation to create an application that can offer treatment options for cognitive, psychological, motor and functional impairments across a wide range of clinical health conditions.

In April 2022, the company entered into a voluntary lock-up agreement with **Ionic Brands Corp.** and **Yourway Cannabis Brands Inc.** to convert 36,707,180 Ionic series E non-voting preferred shares to 57,229,991 Ionic common shares, which would be converted to approximately 3,000,000 Yourway common shares at an exchange ratio of 0.0525 Yourway common shares for each Ionic common share.

Predecessor Detail - Name changed from GreenStar Biosciences Corp., Nov. 16, 2020.

Directors - Philip J. Young, CEO & corp. sec., Boca Raton, Fla.; Michael Petter, Mill Valley, Calif.; Baxter F. Phillips III

Other Exec. Officers - Brian Zasitko, CFO; Maghsoud Dariani, chief science officer

Capital Stock

	Authorized (shs.)	Outstanding (shs.)[1]
Preferred	unlimited	nil
Common	unlimited	76,970,172

[1] At Jan. 27, 2023

Major Shareholder - Widely held at Jan. 25, 2022.

Price Range - LOBE/CSE

Year	Volume	High	Low	Close
2022	11,187,421	$0.29	$0.03	$0.04
2021	22,386,934	$1.62	$0.15	$0.18
2020	29,803,984	$1.41	$0.12	$0.81
2019	6,527,515	$1.80	$0.48	$0.51
2018	2,166	$1.32	$0.84	$0.84

Consolidation: 1-for-6 cons. in June 2022; 1-for-2 cons. in June 2019

Recent Close: $0.02

Capital Stock Changes - In September 2022, private placement of 28,262,800 units (1 common share & 1 warrant) at 5¢ per unit was completed, with warrants exercisable at 5¢ per share for two years.

On June 10, 2022, common shares were consolidated on a 1-for-6 basis. During fiscal 2022, post-consolidated common shares were issued as follows: 694,445, on exercise of options, 187,501 on vesting of restricted share units and 166,667 for services.

Wholly Owned Subsidiaries

Eleusian Biosciences Corp., Toronto, Ont.

Lobe Sciences Australia Pty Ltd., Australia.

Investments

50% int. in **Krysalix VX Corp.**

Financial Statistics

Periods ended:	12m Aug. 31/22[A]		12m Aug. 31/21[oA]
	$000s	%Chg	$000s
Research & devel. expense	418		1,372
General & admin expense	3,074		4,082
Stock-based compensation	621		922
Operating expense	**4,113**	**-35**	**6,376**
Operating income	**(4,113)**	**n.a.**	**(6,376)**
Deprec., depl. & amort.	10		nil
Investment income	1,915		1,471
Write-downs/write-offs	72		(7,345)
Pre-tax income	**(12,253)**	**n.a.**	**(23,844)**
Income taxes	nil		(1,024)
Net inc. bef. disc. opers	**(12,253)**	**n.a.**	**(22,821)**
Income from disc. opers	nil		13,162
Net income	**(12,253)**	**n.a.**	**(9,658)**
Cash & equivalent	908		7,426
Accounts receivable	18		196
Current assets	1,036		9,669
Long-term investments	682		2,324
Intangibles, net	30		40
Total assets	**1,748**	**-86**	**12,098**
Accts. pay. & accr. liabs	1,302		805
Current liabilities	1,302		805
Shareholders' equity	446		11,293
Cash from oper. activs	**(2,731)**	**n.a.**	**(5,037)**
Cash from fin. activs	753		4,918
Cash from invest. activs	1,743		1,067
Net cash position	**908**	**-20**	**1,142**
	$		$
Earnings per share*	(0.32)		(0.70)
Cash flow per share*	(0.07)		(0.15)
	shs		shs
No. of shs. o/s*	38,487,648		37,439,035
Avg. no. of shs. o/s*	37,861,638		32,493,654
	%		%
Net profit margin	n.a.		n.a.
Return on equity	(208.76)		(195.33)
Return on assets	(176.99)		(182.07)

* Common
[o] Restated
[A] Reported in accordance with IFRS

Latest Results

Periods ended:	3m Nov. 30/22[A]		3m Nov. 30/21[A]
	$000s	%Chg	$000s
Net income	(2,017)	n.a.	(4,575)
	$		$
Earnings per share*	(0.03)		(0.12)

* Common
[A] Reported in accordance with IFRS

Historical Summary
(as originally stated)

Fiscal Year	Oper. Rev.	Net Inc. Bef. Disc.	EPS*
	$000s	$000s	$
2022[A]	nil	(12,253)	(0.32)
2021[A]	nil	(22,821)	(0.70)
2020[A]	885	(3,436)	(0.30)
2019[A1]	774	(754)	(0.06)
2018[A2]	nil	(148)	(0.24)

* Common
[A] Reported in accordance with IFRS
[1] Results reflect the May 30, 2019, reverse takeover acquisition of GreenStar Biosciences Inc.
[2] Results for fiscal 2018 and prior fiscal years pertain to Bethpage Capital Corp.

Note: Adjusted throughout for 1-for-6 cons. in June 2022; 1-for-2 cons. in June 2019

L.39 Loblaw Companies Limited*

Symbol - L **Exchange** - TSX **CUSIP** - 539481
Head Office - 1 President's Choice Cir, Brampton, ON, L6Y 5S5 **Telephone** - (905) 459-2500 **Toll-free** - (888) 495-5111 **Fax** - (905) 861-2206
Website - www.loblaw.ca
Email - roy.macdonald@loblaw.ca
Investor Relations - Roy MacDonald (800) 296-2332
Auditors - PricewaterhouseCoopers LLP C.A.
Lawyers - Borden Ladner Gervais LLP, Toronto, Ont.
Transfer Agents - Computershare Trust Company of Canada Inc., Toronto, Ont.
FP500 Subsidiary Revenue Ranking - 1
Employees - 221,000 at Dec. 31, 2022
Profile - (Can. 1956) Provides grocery, pharmacy and healthcare services, health and beauty products, apparel, general merchandise, financial services, and wireless mobile products and services across Canada.

The company's operations are organized into two segments: Retail and Financial Services.

Retail

At Dec. 31, 2022, the company operated 547 corporate stores, 551 franchised stores, 1,346 associate-owned stores and 298 healthcare clinics across Canada.

Full-service or market banners consist of Loblaws (45), Provigo (58), Provigo Le Marché (13), Valu-Mart (31), Independent (150), City Market (9), Zehrs (42), Atlantic Superstore (52), Dominion (11), T&T Supermarket (31) and Fortinos (23). Discount banners consist of Maxi (127), Extra Foods (7), No Frills (271) and Real Canadian Superstore (120). Wholesale and apparel banners consist of Cash & Carry (5), Club Entrepôt (4), Presto (6), Real Canadian Wholesale Club (41) and Joe Fresh (2).

Wholly owned **Shoppers Drug Mart Corporation** provides pharmacy, health and beauty products and services through full-service drug stores primarily under the banner Shoppers Drug Mart (Pharmaprix in Quebec). Most of the stores are owned and operated by associates. An associate is a pharmacist-owner of a corporation that is licensed to operate a retail drug store at a specific location using the company's trademarks. At Dec. 31, 2022, associate-owned stores consists of 1,310 standalone retail drug stores operating under the Shoppers Drug Mart and Pharmaprix names, and 36 medical clinic pharmacies operating as Shoppers Simply Pharmacy.

Shoppers Drug Mart also owns and operates 43 Wellwise by Shoppers stores which provide a wide range of home-care, medical and mobility products and services; six health clinic providing primary care services under the name The Health Clinic by Shoppers; one standalone Beauty Boutique by Shoppers Drug Mart site offering luxury beauty products; and 298 Lifemark healthcare clinics. In addition, also owns **Shoppers Drug Mart Specialty Health Network Inc.**, a provider of specialty drug distribution, pharmacy and comprehensive patient support services; **MediSystem Technologies Inc.**, a provider of pharmaceutical products and services to long-term care facilities; and **QHR Corporation**, a provider of electronic medical records technology for physicians and other health care providers. Also operates Health Solutions by Shoppers™ program which provides wellness solutions to employers; and PC Health, an application which provides access to healthcare resources and support.

The total size of the company's corporate stores, franchised stores and associate-owned Shoppers Drug Mart stores was 36,100,000 sq. ft., 17,200,000 sq. ft. and 18,900,000 sq. ft., respectively. The company owned 6% of the real estate on which its corporate stores are located, 4% of the real estate on which its franchised stores are located, as well as various properties under development or held for future development. The majority of Shoppers Drug Mart stores are leased on a long-term basis from a diverse group of lessors.

The company also markets control brand products in the food, health and beauty, and general merchandise categories under brand names including President's Choice, no name, PC Organics, PC Blue Menu, PC Black Label Collection, Life at Home, T&T, Farmers Market, Everyday Essentials, Quo Beauty and Life Brand.

Financial Services

Wholly owned **President's Choice Bank** provides financial products and services under the President's Choice Financial brand, including PC Mastercard® and PC Money Account, which enables customers to save or send money, to spend money in person or online and to earn PC Optimum points under the company's PC Optimum loyalty program. Also offers guaranteed investment certificates, and automobile and home insurance through insurance entities. In addition, offers gift cards, and prepaid mobile products and services under The Mobile Shop™ brand.

In March 2023, wholly owned **Shoppers Drug Mart Corporation** announced plans to move away from medical cannabis distribution by transitioning its Medical Cannabis by Shoppers business to **Avicanna Inc.** Medical Cannabis by Shoppers was first launched in Ontario in January 2019, providing patients access to medical cannabis products from more than 30 licensed cannabis brands.

In June 2022, the company announced its intention to build a 1,200,000-sq.-ft. automated, multi-temperature distribution facility located at the corner of Highway 404 and Green Lane East in Ontario. The company expects to bring the distribution facility into its operations in the first quarter of 2024.

Recent Merger and Acquisition Activity

Status: completed **Announced:** Jan. 31, 2023
Choice Properties Real Estate Investment Trust acquired three retail properties, totaling 354,671 sq. ft., in Vernon, B.C., and Calgary (2), Alta., from Loblaw Companies Limited for a total of $99,149,000. Loblaw leased back the two Calgary properties.

Status: completed **Announced:** June 17, 2022
Choice Properties Real Estate Investment Trust acquired a 98,125-sq.-ft. retail property in Halifax, N.S., from Loblaw Companies Limited for $15,228,000, including $2,034,000 of assumed debt. The property was leased back by Loblaw.

Status: completed **Revised:** May 9, 2022
UPDATE: The transaction was completed. PREVIOUS: Loblaw Companies Limited agreed to acquire private Calgary, Alta.-based LifeMark Health Limited Partnership, which provides physiotherapy, massage therapy, occupational therapy, chiropractic, mental health and other rehabilitation services, for $845,000,000. LifeMark had more than 300 clinics across Canada. The transaction was subject to regulatory approvals and other customary closing conditions, and was expected to be completed in the second quarter of 2022.

Status: completed **Announced:** Mar. 1, 2022
Choice Properties Real Estate Investment Trust acquired a parcel of industrial development land in Ottawa, Ont., from Loblaw Companies Limited for $27,218,000.

Directors - Galen G. Weston, chr. & pres., Toronto, Ont.; William A. (Billy) Downe†, Winnetka, Ill.; Scott B. Bonham, Atherton, Calif.; Shelley Broader, Naples, Fla.; Christie J. B. (Chris) Clark, Toronto, Ont.; Daniel Debow, Toronto, Ont.; Janice R. Fukakusa, Toronto, Ont.; M. Marianne Harris, Toronto, Ont.; Kevin Holt, Quincy, Mass.; Claudia Kotchka, Los Angeles, Calif.; Sarah E. Raiss, Calgary, Alta.; Cornell C. V. Wright, Toronto, Ont.

Other Exec. Officers - Robert Sawyer, COO; Richard Dufresne, CFO; Robert (Rob) Wiebe, CAO; Nicholas (Nick) Henn, exec. v-p, chief legal officer & corp. sec.; Dr. David Markwell, exec. v-p & chief tech. & analytics officer; Mark Wilson, exec. v-p & chief HR officer; Kevin Groh, sr. v-p, corp. affairs & commun.; Mary MacIsaac, sr. v-p, mktg.; Lauren Steinberg, sr. v-p, Loblaw Digital; Roy MacDonald, v-p, IR; Barry K. Columb, pres., President's Choice Financial; Ian Freedman, pres., Joe Fresh; Frank Gambioli, pres., discount div.; Greg Ramier, pres., market div.

† Lead director

Capital Stock

	Authorized (shs.)	Outstanding (shs.)[1]
First Preferred	1,000,000	nil
Second Preferred	unlimited	
Series B		9,000,000
Common	unlimited	316,369,658

[1] At June 30, 2023

Second Preferred Series B - Entitled to non-cumulative annual dividend of $1.325 per share payable quarterly. Redeemable at $26 per share, and declining by 25¢ per share annually to June 30, 2024, and at $25 per share thereafter. Non-voting.

Common - One vote per share.

Options - At Dec. 31, 2022, options were outstanding to purchase 5,782,615 common shares at a weighted average exercise price of $71.07 per share with a weighted average remaining contractual life of up to 6.1 years.

Normal Course Issuer Bid - The company plans to make normal course purchases of up to 16,055,686 common shares representing 5% of the total outstanding. The bid commenced on May 5, 2023, and expires on May 4, 2024.

Major Shareholder - George Weston Limited held 52.6% interest at Mar. 13, 2023.

Price Range - L/TSX

Year	Volume	High	Low	Close
2022	131,931,835	$126.29	$90.46	$119.72
2021	139,589,905	$105.15	$60.86	$103.64
2020	179,509,175	$77.00	$59.01	$62.81
2019	135,060,835	$76.31	$60.37	$67.00
2018	140,602,277	$69.94	$51.90	$61.11

Recent Close: $116.55

Capital Stock Changes - During fiscal 2022, 1,487,377 common shares were issued on exercise of options, 10,952,138 common shares were repurchased under a Normal Course Issuer Bid and 626,783 (net) common shares were purchased and held in trust.

Dividends

L com Ra $1.784 pa Q est. July 1, 2023**[1]
Prev. Rate: $1.62 est. July 1, 2022
Prev. Rate: $1.46 est. Oct. 1, 2021
Prev. Rate: $1.34 est. Dec. 30, 2020
L.PR.B pfd 2nd ser B cum. red. Ra $1.325 pa Q
[1] Dividend reinvestment plan implemented eff. July/09.
** Reinvestment Option

Long-Term Debt - Outstanding at Dec. 31, 2022:

3.92% notes due 2024	$400,000,000
6.65% notes due 2027	100,000,000
6.45% notes due 2028	200,000,000
4.49% notes due 2028	400,000,000
6.5% notes due 2029	175,000,000
2.28% notes due 2030	350,000,000
11.4% notes due 2031	181,000,000
5.01% notes due 2032	400,000,000
6.85% notes due 2032	200,000,000
6.54% notes due 2033	200,000,000
8.75% notes due 2033	200,000,000
6.05% notes due 2034	200,000,000
6.15% notes due 2035	200,000,000
5.9% notes due 2036	300,000,000
6.45% notes due 2039	200,000,000
7% notes due 2040	150,000,000
5.86% notes due 2043	55,000,000
5.34% notes due 2052	400,000,000
Guarant. invest. certificates[1]	1,567,000,000
Indep. securitization trusts[2]	1,350,000,000
Indep. funding trusts[3]	574,000,000
Less: Trans. costs & other	19,000,000
	7,783,000,000
Less: Current portion	727,000,000
	7,056,000,000

[1] Bear interest at 0.40% to 5.36%. Due 2023 to 2027.
[2] Consist of term notes which bear interest at 1.34% to 6.83% and collateralized by wholly owned President's Choice Bank's credit card receivables. Due 2023 to 2027.
[3] Borrowings of independent funding trusts from a revolving credit facility.

Minimum long-term debt repayments were reported as follows:

2023	$727,000,000
2024	1,091,000,000
2025	1,138,000,000
2026	494,000,000
2027	541,000,000
Thereafter	3,811,000,000

Wholly Owned Subsidiaries

Loblaws Inc., Ont.
- 100% int. in **T&T Supermarket Inc.**, Richmond, B.C.

President's Choice Bank, Toronto, Ont.
Provigo Distribution Inc., Montréal, Qué.
Shoppers Drug Mart Corporation, Toronto, Ont.
- 100% int. in **LifeMark Health Limited Partnership**, Calgary, Alta.
- 100% int. in **Medisystem Technologies Inc.**, North York, Ont.
- 100% int. in **Pharmaprix Inc.**, Ont.
- 100% int. in **Sanis Health Inc.**
- 100% int. in **Shoppers Drug Mart Inc.**, Canada.
  - 100% int. in **QHR Corporation**, Kelowna, B.C.
- 100% int. in **Shoppers Drug Mart Specialty Health Network Inc.**, Ont.

Note: The preceding list includes only the major related companies in which interests are held.

Financial Statistics

Periods ended:	52w Dec. 31/22[A]		52w Jan. 1/22[A]
	$000s	%Chg	$000s
Operating revenue	**56,504,000**	**+6**	**53,170,000**
Cost of goods sold	38,528,000		36,436,000
General & admin expense	11,805,000		11,079,000
Operating expense	**50,333,000**	**+6**	**47,515,000**
Operating income	**6,171,000**	**+9**	**5,655,000**
Deprec., depl. & amort.	2,795,000		2,664,000
Finance income	33,000		196,000
Finance costs, gross	716,000		691,000
Write-downs/write-offs	(34,000)		(54,000)
Pre-tax income	**2,659,000**	**+9**	**2,442,000**
Income taxes	665,000		466,000
Net inc bef disc ops, eqhldrs	1,921,000		1,875,000
Net inc bef disc ops, NCI	73,000		101,000
Net income	**1,994,000**	**+1**	**1,976,000**
Net inc. for equity hldrs	**1,921,000**	**+2**	**1,875,000**
Net inc. for non-cont. int.	**73,000**	**-28**	**101,000**
Cash & equivalent	1,934,000		2,440,000
Inventories	5,855,000		5,166,000
Accounts receivable	5,153,000		4,390,000
Current assets	13,376,000		12,637,000
Long-term investments	147,000		184,000
Fixed assets, net	5,696,000		5,447,000
Right-of-use assets	7,409,000		7,175,000
Intangibles, net	10,828,000		10,351,000
Total assets	**38,147,000**	**+4**	**36,614,000**
Bank indebtedness	708,000		502,000
Accts. pay. & accr. liabs	6,218,000		5,433,000
Current liabilities	10,098,000		9,196,000
Long-term debt, gross	7,783,000		7,213,000
Long-term debt, net	7,056,000		6,211,000
Long-term lease liabilities	7,714,000		7,542,000
Preferred share equity	221,000		221,000
Shareholders' equity	11,299,000		11,573,000
Non-controlling interest	157,000		164,000
Cash from oper. activs	**4,755,000**	**-1**	**4,827,000**
Cash from fin. activs	(2,751,000)		(3,249,000)
Cash from invest. activs	(2,368,000)		(1,271,000)
Net cash position	**1,608,000**	**-19**	**1,976,000**
Capital expenditures	(1,152,000)		(803,000)
Capital disposals	164,000		80,000
Pension fund surplus	193,000		320,000
	$		$
Earnings per share*	5.82		5.49
Cash flow per share*	14.49		14.23
Cash divd. per share*	1.58		1.40
	shs		shs
No. of shs. o/s*	322,840,330		332,931,874
Avg. no. of shs. o/s*	328,068,749		339,097,833
	%		%
Net profit margin	3.53		3.72
Return on equity	17.02		16.85
Return on assets	6.77		7.00
No. of employees (FTEs)	221,000		215,000

* Common
[A] Reported in accordance with IFRS

Latest Results

Periods ended:	24w June 17/23[A]		24w June 18/22[A]
	$000s	%Chg	$000s
Operating revenue	26,733,000	+6	25,109,000
Net income	978,000	+9	901,000
Net inc. for equity hldrs	932,000	+12	830,000
Net inc. for non-cont. int.	46,000		71,000
	$		$
Earnings per share*	2.89		2.48

* Common
[A] Reported in accordance with IFRS

Historical Summary
(as originally stated)

Fiscal Year	Oper. Rev.	Net Inc. Bef. Disc.	EPS*
	$000s	$000s	$
2022[A]	56,504,000	1,994,000	5.82
2021[A]	53,170,000	1,976,000	5.49
2020[A1]	52,714,000	1,192,000	3.08
2019[A]	48,037,000	1,131,000	2.93
2018[A]	46,693,000	753,000	1.88

* Common
[A] Reported in accordance with IFRS
[1] 53 weeks ended Jan. 2, 2021.

L.40 Logica Ventures Corp.

Symbol - LOG.P **Exchange** - TSX-VEN (S) **CUSIP** - 54140G
Head Office - 800-365 Bay St, Toronto, ON, M5H 2V1 **Telephone** - (416) 367-4484
Email - munaf@logicaventures.com
Investor Relations - Munaf Ali (416) 831-3598
Auditors - McGovern Hurley LLP C.A., Toronto, Ont.
Transfer Agents - Computershare Trust Company of Canada Inc., Toronto, Ont.
Profile - (Ont. 2019) Capital Pool Company.
Common suspended from TSX-VEN, Apr. 21, 2021.

Recent Merger and Acquisition Activity

Status: terminated **Revised:** Mar. 15, 2023
UPDATE: The transaction was terminated. PREVIOUS: Logica Ventures Corp. entered into a letter of intent for the Qualifying Transaction reverse takeover acquisition of private Toronto, Ont.-based Alpha Gold North Inc. (AGN), which holds the 500-hectare Mine Brook gold prospect in Newfoundland, on a share-for-share basis. Upon completion, AGN would amalgamate with a wholly owned subsidiary of Logica.

Directors - Munaf Ali, chr., Dubai, United Arab Emirates; Clayton Fisher, CEO, Vancouver, B.C.; Przemek Cerazy, CFO & corp. sec.; Anthony Viele, Woodbridge, Ont.

Capital Stock

	Authorized (shs.)	Outstanding (shs.)[1]
Common	unlimited	6,740,000

[1] At Apr. 11, 2022

Major Shareholder - Munaf Ali held 19.9% interest and Robert H. Kidd held 19.9% interest at Mar. 11, 2022.

Price Range - LOG.P/TSX-VEN (S)

Year	Volume	High	Low	Close
2021	391,000	$0.11	$0.08	$0.10
2020	898,500	$0.20	$0.08	$0.10
2019	316,200	$0.13	$0.10	$0.13

L.41 Logistec Corporation*

Symbol - LGT.B **Exchange** - TSX **CUSIP** - 541411
Head Office - 1400-600 rue de la Gauchetiere O, Montréal, QC, H3B 4L2 **Telephone** - (514) 844-9381 **Toll-free** - (888) 844-9381 **Fax** - (514) 844-9650
Website - www.logistec.com
Email - cdelisle@logistec.com
Investor Relations - Carl Delisle (888) 844-9381
Auditors - KPMG LLP C.A., Montréal, Qué.
Bankers - Harris N.A., Chicago, Ill.; Canadian Imperial Bank of Commerce; Bank of America Corporation; Bank of Montreal, Montréal, Qué.; The Toronto-Dominion Bank, Montréal, Qué.; The Bank of Nova Scotia, Montréal, Qué.; HSBC Bank Canada, Montréal, Qué.
Transfer Agents - Computershare Trust Company of Canada Inc., Montréal, Qué.
FP500 Revenue Ranking - 361
Employees - 3,426 at Dec. 31, 2022
Profile - (Que. 1952, via letters patent) Provides specialized marine services and environmental services to the marine, industrial, municipal and other governmental customers. Services include cargo handling, terminal operations, marine transportation services, marine agency services, contaminated site remediation and water main rehabilitation.

Operations are carried out through two segments: Marine Services and Environmental Services.

Marine Services operations, carried out through wholly owned **Logistec Stevedoring Inc.** and its subsidiaries and joint ventures, consist of specialized cargo handling services for all types of dry cargo including bulk, break-bulk, container cargo handling and other specialized services in 60 ports and 90 terminals in eastern North America and the U.S. Gulf Coast. Cargo handling services include loading and unloading ships as well as loading and unloading of cargo to/from truck and/or rail in the company's various facilities. Other related services provided include warehousing, container stuffing and destuffing and distribution. Terminal operations provide the shippers with the facilities for short-term or long-term warehousing, pending movement of goods from piers and sheds. Marine transportation services are offered and geared primarily to the Arctic coastal trade through subsidiary **Transport Nanuk Inc.** and its subsidiaries and joint ventures. Marine agency services are offered to foreign shipowners and operators serving the Canadian market through wholly owned **Logistec Marine Agencies Inc.** and its subsidiaries.

Environmental Services are provided to industries, governments and municipalities through wholly owned **Sanexen Environmental Services Inc.** and subsidiary **FER-PAL Construction Ltd.** Services, provided principally in Canada, include renewal of underground water mains, site remediation, dredging and dewatering soils, contaminated soils and materials management, risk assessment and manufacturing of fluid transportation products. The renewal services are carried out directly and through licensees.

Recent Merger and Acquisition Activity

Status: completed **Revised:** Apr. 3, 2023
UPDATE: The transaction was completed. PREVIOUS: Logistec Corporation agreed to acquire the Canadian and U.S. terminal business of Fednav Limited, including Federal Marine Terminals, Inc. and the logistics division, Fednav Direct (collectively FMT), for US$105,000,000, which would be financed via an increased revolving credit facility. The FMT business provides stevedoring, handling and warehousing services for bulk, containerized, project cargo and general cargo, as well as offers value-added on-carriage services, inventory management and 24/7 inland cargo transportation in Canada and the U.S. During 2022, FMT generated revenue of US$89,800,000 (Cdn$116,800,000). The acquisition would add 11 terminals to Logistec's network, which would bring its total to 90 terminals in 60 ports across North America.

Status: completed **Announced:** July 29, 2022
Logistec Corporation acquired an additional 16.3% interest in FER-PAL Construction Ltd. from non-controlling interest shareholders for $19,100,000, thereby increasing Logistec's ownership to 67.33% from 51.03%. FER-PAL provides water main rehabilitation solutions utilizing trenchless technology.

Predecessor Detail - Name changed from Quebec Terminals Ltd., Apr. 3, 1969.

Directors - J. Mark Rodger, chr., Toronto, Ont.; Madeleine M. Paquin, pres. & CEO, Montréal, Qué.; Suzanne Paquin, v-p, Montréal, Qué.; Michael J. Dodson, Pa.; Lukas Loeffler, Ga.; Nicole Paquin, Montréal, Qué.; Jane Skoblo, Toronto, Ont.; Dany St-Pierre, Chicago, Ill.; Luc Villeneuve, Qué.

Other Exec. Officers - Carl Delisle, CFO, treas. & asst. sec.; Martin Ponce, CIO; Trip Bailey, v-p, U.S. opers.; Michel Brisebois, v-p, HR; George Di Sante, v-p, bulk market devel.; Alain Pilotte, v-p, strategic initiatives; Frank Robertson, v-p, opers.; Marie-Chantal Savoy, v-p, strategy & commun.; Ingrid Stefancic, v-p, corp. & legal srvcs. & corp. sec.; Dany Trudel, v-p & contr.; Jean-Francois Bolduc, pres., LOGISTEC Environmental Services Inc. & SANEXEN Environmental Services Inc.; Rodney Corrigan, pres., LOGISTEC Stevedoring Inc.; Benoit (Ben) Côté, pres., Sanexen Water Inc.

Capital Stock

	Authorized (shs.)	Outstanding (shs.)[1]
Preferred	unlimited	nil
Cl.A Common	unlimited	7,361,022
Cl.B Subord. Vtg.	unlimited	5,455,591

[1] At Aug. 1, 2023

Preferred - Non-voting and issuable in series.
Class A Common - Convertible, at the holder's option, into class B subordinate voting shares on a one-for-one basis. 30 votes per share.
Class B Subordinate Voting - Entitled to 110% of any dividend declared on each class A common share. One vote per share.
Major Shareholder - Paquin family held 76.9% interest and Caisse de dépôt et placement du Québec held 13.7% interest at Mar. 14, 2023.

Price Range - LGT.B/TSX

Year	Volume	High	Low	Close
2022	355,422	$46.97	$35.00	$41.47
2021	482,974	$47.07	$35.00	$44.00
2020	406,496	$39.85	$23.28	$35.16
2019	480,952	$46.00	$36.55	$40.00
2018	404,483	$57.00	$40.61	$43.27

Recent Close: $67.00

Capital Stock Changes - During 2022, 19,450 class B subordinate voting shares were issued under the employee stock purchase plan and 16,000 class A common shares were converted into a like number of class B subordinate voting shares; 262,895 class B subordinate voting shares were repurchased under a Normal Course Issuer Bid.

Dividends

LGT.A cl A M.V. Ra $0.47128 pa Q est. Oct. 7, 2022
Prev. Rate: $0.39272 est. Oct. 8, 2021
Prev. Rate: $0.374 est. Oct. 11, 2019
LGT.B cl B S.V. Ra $0.51836 pa Q est. Oct. 7, 2022
Prev. Rate: $0.43196 est. Oct. 8, 2021
Prev. Rate: $0.4114 est. Oct. 11, 2019

Long-Term Debt - Outstanding at Dec. 31, 2022:

Government loan due 2023	$300,000
Revolv. credit facility due 2025[1]	186,709,000
Unsecured loans due 2027[2]	47,401,000
Term credit facility[3]	625,000
	235,035,000
Less: Current portion	10,925,000
	224,110,000

[1] Bears interest at prime and/or bankers' acceptance rates and LIBOR.
[2] Consist of two loans bearing interest at 4.5%.
[3] Bears interest at prime plus 0.25% to 0.75%.

Wholly Owned Subsidiaries

Gestion Castaloop Inc., Canada.
Logistec Environmental Services Inc., Qué.
- 67.33% int. in **FER-PAL Construction Ltd.**, Toronto, Ont.
  - 100% int. in **Fer-Pal Construction USA, LLC**, Mich.
- 100% int. in **Sanexen Environmental Services Inc.**, Montréal, Qué.
  - 100% int. in **American Process Group**, Edmonton, Alta.
  - 49% int. in **Avataani Environmental Services Inc.**, Canada.
  - 100% int. in **Niedner Inc.**, Coaticook, Qué.
  - 50% int. in **9260-0873 Québec Inc.**, Qué.
  - 49% int. in **Qikiqtaaluk Environmental Inc.**
  - 100% int. in **Sanexen Water, Inc.**, Del.

Logistec Marine Services Inc., Canada.
- 100% int. in **Logistec Marine Agencies Inc.**, Canada.
  - 100% int. in **Ramsey Greig & Co. Ltd.**, Québec, Qué.
  - 100% int. in **Sorel Maritime Agencies Inc.**, Qué.
- 100% int. in **Logistec Stevedoring Inc.**, Montréal, Qué.
  - 50% int. in **Flexiport Mobile Docking Structures Inc.**, Canada.
  - 100% int. in **Logistec Stevedoring (New Brunswick) Inc.**, N.B.
  - 100% int. in **Logistec Stevedoring (Nova Scotia) Inc.**, N.S.
  - 100% int. in **Logistec Stevedoring (Ontario) Inc.**, Ont.
  - 100% int. in **Logistec Stevedoring U.S.A. Inc.**, Del.
    - 100% int. in **GSM Maritime Holdings, LLC**, Del.
      - 100% int. in **GSM Intermediate Holdings, Inc.**, Del.
        - 100% int. in **Gulf Stream Marine, Inc.**, Tex.
    - 100% int. in **Logistec USA Inc.**, Del.
      - 100% int. in **BalTerm, LLP**, Baltimore, Md.
        - 100% int. in **Tartan Terminals, Inc.**, Md.
      - 100% int. in **CrossGlobe Transport, Ltd.**, Newport News, Va.
      - 60% int. in **Logistec Everglades LLC**, Del.
      - 100% int. in **Logistec Gulf Coast, LLC**, Del.
    - 100% int. in **Pate Stevedore Company, Inc.**, Pensacola, Fla.
  - 50% int. in **Moorings (Trois-Rivières) Ltd.**, Qué.
  - 100% int. in **MtlLINK Multimodal Solutions Inc.**, Canada.
  - 50% int. in **Quebec Maritime Services Inc.**, Canada.
  - 50% int. in **Quebec Mooring Inc.**, Qué.
  - 100% int. in **SETL Real Estate Management Inc.**, Qué.
  - 25% int. in **St. Lawrence Mooring Inc.**, Qué.
  - 100% int. in **Les Terminaux Rideau Bulk Terminals Inc.**, Qué.
  - 50% int. in **Termont Terminal Inc.**, Qué.
    - 25% int. in **Termont Montréal Inc.**, Qué.
- 50% int. in **Transport Nanuk Inc.**, Montréal, Qué.
  - 25% int. in **NEAS Group Inc.**
    - 100% int. in **NEAS Inc.**
      - 100% int. in **Northern Bear Shipping B.V.**, Netherlands.
      - 100% int. in **Northern Fox Shipping B.V.**, Netherlands.
      - 100% int. in **Northern Hare Shipping B.V.**, Netherlands.
      - 100% int. in **Northern Loon Shipping B.V.**, Netherlands.
      - 100% int. in **Northern Wolf Shipping B.V.**, Netherlands.
      - 40% int. in **Nunavik Eastern Arctic Shipping Inc.**
      - 40% int. in **Nunavut Eastern Arctic Shipping Inc.**, Iqaluit, Nun.
  - 100% int. in **Transport Aujaq Inc.**, Canada.
  - 100% int. in **Transport Inukshuk Inc.**, Canada.
  - 100% int. in **Transport Mitiq Inc.**, Canada.
  - 100% int. in **Transport Nunalik Inc.**
  - 100% int. in **Transport Qamutik Inc.**, Canada.
  - 100% int. in **Transport Sinaaq Inc.**, Canada.
  - 100% int. in **Transport Umialarik Inc.**, Canada.

Financial Statistics

Periods ended:	12m Dec. 31/22[A]		12m Dec. 31/21[A]
	$000s	%Chg	$000s
Operating revenue	**897,565**	**+21**	**743,703**
Salaries & benefits	421,751		357,981
Other operating expense	347,310		270,647
Operating expense	**776,768**	**+23**	**633,978**
Operating income	**120,797**	**+10**	**109,725**
Deprec., depl. & amort.	56,196		49,100
Finance income	613		541
Finance costs, gross	15,429		11,103
Investment income	18,760		10,084
Pre-tax income	**64,806**	**+16**	**56,095**
Income taxes	10,804		10,471
Net income	**54,002**	**+18**	**45,624**
Net inc. for equity hldrs	**53,543**	**+18**	**45,364**
Net inc. for non-cont. int	**459**	**+77**	**260**
Cash & equivalent	36,043		37,530
Inventories	20,000		16,830
Accounts receivable	198,247		183,322
Current assets	289,203		263,233
Long-term investments	46,140		46,311
Fixed assets, net	234,602		207,321
Right-of-use assets	167,274		135,049
Intangibles, net	224,237		223,749
Total assets	**983,672**	**+9**	**898,971**
Bank indebtedness	nil		8,600
Accts. pay. & accr. liabs	126,330		126,255
Current liabilities	175,382		181,427
Long-term debt, gross	235,035		195,354
Long-term debt, net	224,110		191,927
Long-term lease liabilities	157,500		125,249
Shareholders' equity	359,487		314,561
Non-controlling interest	1,604		1,048
Cash from oper. activs	**98,678**	**+24**	**79,586**
Cash from fin. activs	(42,418)		3,595
Cash from invest. activs	(61,367)		(92,858)
Net cash position	**36,043**	**-4**	**37,530**
Capital expenditures	(52,146)		(44,306)
Capital disposals	2,434		699
Unfunded pension liability	12,335		16,097
	$		$
Earnings per share*	4.15		3.49
Cash flow per share*	7.65		6.12
Cash divd. per share*	0.48		0.42
Cash divd. per share**	0.41		0.38
	shs		shs
No. of shs. o/s*	12,816,613		13,060,058
Avg. no. of shs. o/s*	12,897,633		13,013,011
	%		%
Net profit margin	6.02		6.13
Return on equity	15.89		14.74
Return on assets	7.10		6.44
Foreign sales percent	49		46
No. of employees (FTEs)	3,426		3,200

* Class A & B
** Class A
[A] Reported in accordance with IFRS

Latest Results

Periods ended:	6m June 24/23[A]		6m June 25/22[A]
	$000s	%Chg	$000s
Operating revenue	403,847	+12	360,414
Net income	(5,666)	n.a.	7,252
Net inc. for equity hldrs	(5,828)	n.a.	7,006
Net inc. for non-cont. int	162		246
	$		$
Earnings per share*	(0.44)		0.52
Earnings per share**	(0.48)		0.57

* Class A & B
** Class A
[A] Reported in accordance with IFRS

Historical Summary
(as originally stated)

Fiscal Year	Oper. Rev.	Net Inc. Bef. Disc.	EPS*
	$000s	$000s	$
2022[A]	897,565	54,002	4.15
2021[A]	743,703	45,624	3.49
2020[A]	604,701	32,788	2.53
2019[A]	639,942	26,437	2.05
2018[A]	584,878	17,994	1.43

* Class A & B
[A] Reported in accordance with IFRS

L.42 Lomiko Metals Inc.

Symbol - LMR **Exchange** - TSX-VEN **CUSIP** - 54163Q
Head Office - 439-7184 120 St, Surrey, BC, V3W 0M6 **Telephone** - (778) 228-1170 **Fax** - (604) 583-1932
Website - www.lomiko.com
Email - apaulgill@lomiko.com
Investor Relations - A. Paul Gill (604) 729-5312
Auditors - Dale Matheson Carr-Hilton LaBonte LLP C.A., Vancouver, B.C.
Bankers - Royal Bank of Canada
Lawyers - Shelley McDonald Paralegal, Surrey, B.C.
Transfer Agents - Olympia Trust Company, Vancouver, B.C.
Profile - (B.C. 1987) Holds mineral interest in Quebec. Also invests primarily in the green energy and technology sectors.

Holds La Loutre graphite prospect, 4,528 hectares, 117 km northwest of Montreal, Que. A preliminary economic assessment released in July 2021 proposed an open-pit operation with an average annual production of 97,400 tonnes graphite over a 14.7-year mine life. Initial capital costs were estimated at $236,140,000. At May 2021, indicated resource was 23,165,000 tonnes grading 4.51% graphite. Also holds option from **Critical Elements Lithium Corporation** to earn up to 70% interest in Bourier lithium-copper-zinc-gold-silver prospect, 10,252 hectares, James Bay area, requiring exploration expenditures of $1,300,000 by December 2023 for an initial 49% interest; and six other graphite properties totaling 14,255 hectares.

Wholly owned **Lomiko Technologies Inc.** holds investments in **Graphene ESD Corp.**, which develops energy storage devices based on graphene platelets; **Smart Home Devices Ltd.**, which develops energy saving, connected building automation and security products; and **Promethieus Technologies Inc.**, which invests in and funds start-up companies with a focus on electric vehicle infrastructure, clean energy, Internet of Things (IoT) and blockchain industries.

In July 2019, the company agreed to sell wholly owned **Lomiko Technologies Inc.** to **Promethieus Technologies Inc.** (PTI) for $1,236,625. Lomiko Technologies holds investment interests in various companies. The company holds a 20% interest in PIT, which would be exchanged for 20% interest in **Promethieus Ventures N.V.**, a newly formed entity that intends to list on the **Dutch Caribbean Securities Exchange N.V.** In December 2022, the transaction was not completed after the approval of the extension of the closing date to Nov. 30, 2022 by the shareholders. The company will review alternatives to the previously proposed transaction.

Predecessor Detail - Name changed from Lomiko Resources Inc., Oct. 3, 2008; basis 4 new for 1 old sh.
Directors - A. Paul Gill, exec. chr., Surrey, B.C.; Belinda E. Labatte, CEO, Toronto, Ont.; Dominique Dionne, Qué.; Eric Levy, Montréal, Qué.; Lee A. Lewis, Ont.; Sagiv Shiv, New York, N.Y.
Other Exec. Officers - Gordana Slepcev, COO; Vincent (Vince) Osbourne, CFO & corp. sec.; Jacqueline Michael, contr.

Capital Stock

	Authorized (shs.)	Outstanding (shs.)[1]
Common	unlimited	346,573,313

[1] At Jan. 23, 2023

Major Shareholder - Widely held at Nov. 1, 2022.

Price Range - LMR/TSX-VEN

Year	Volume	High	Low	Close
2022	73,030,009	$0.11	$0.03	$0.03
2021	157,488,181	$0.28	$0.06	$0.10
2020	75,215,491	$0.07	$0.02	$0.06
2019	38,901,922	$0.09	$0.02	$0.03
2018	30,764,233	$0.31	$0.04	$0.04

Recent Close: $0.02

Capital Stock Changes - In December 2022, private placement of 18,625,000 flow-through units (1 common share & 1 warrant) at 4¢ per unit and 40,520,497 units (1 common share & 1 warrant) at 3¢ per unit was completed, with warrants exercisable at 6¢ per share for two years and 5¢ per share for five years, respectively.

During fiscal 2022, common shares were issued as follows: 47,156,270 by private placement, 1,400,000 on exercise of options and 920,000 on exercise of warrants.

Wholly Owned Subsidiaries

The Conac Company Inc.
Conac Software (USA) Inc.
Lomiko Metals USA LLC, Colo.
Lomiko Technologies Inc., Surrey, B.C.
- 40% int. in **Graphene ESD Corp.**, Del.
- 20% int. in **Promethieus Technologies Inc.**, B.C.
- 18.25% int. in **Smart Home Devices Ltd.**, B.C.

Financial Statistics

Periods ended:	12m July 31/22^A		12m July 31/21^A
	$000s	%Chg	$000s
Salaries & benefits	425		n.a.
General & admin expense	2,084		1,401
Stock-based compensation	1,357		502
Operating expense	**3,866**	**+103**	**1,903**
Operating income	**(3,866)**	**n.a.**	**(1,903)**
Finance costs, gross	nil		4
Write-downs/write-offs	(153)		nil
Pre-tax income	**(3,401)**	**n.a.**	**(1,736)**
Net income	**(3,401)**	**n.a.**	**(1,736)**
Cash & equivalent	3,768		5,040
Current assets	3,877		5,247
Explor./devel. properties	9,350		6,023
Total assets	**13,684**	**+19**	**11,528**
Accts. pay. & accr. liabs	812		173
Current liabilities	1,179		501
Shareholders' equity	12,506		11,027
Cash from oper. activs	**(2,377)**	**n.a.**	**(1,853)**
Cash from fin. activs	4,179		8,696
Cash from invest. activs	(3,074)		(1,822)
Net cash position	**3,768**	**-25**	**5,040**
Capital expenditures	(2,722)		(1,717)
	$		$
Earnings per share*	(0.01)		(0.01)
Cash flow per share*	(0.01)		(0.01)
	shs		shs
No. of shs. o/s*	287,427,816		237,951,546
Avg. no. of shs. o/s*	260,692,480		169,762,145
	%		%
Net profit margin	n.a.		n.a.
Return on equity	(28.90)		(24.13)
Return on assets	(26.98)		(22.58)

* Common
^A Reported in accordance with IFRS

Historical Summary
(as originally stated)

Fiscal Year	Oper. Rev.	Net Inc. Bef. Disc.	EPS*
	$000s	$000s	$
2022^A	nil	(3,401)	(0.01)
2021^A	nil	(1,736)	(0.01)
2020^A	nil	(1,186)	(0.01)
2019^A	nil	(1,766)	(0.03)
2018^A	nil	(5,526)	(0.16)

* Common
^A Reported in accordance with IFRS

L.43 Looking Glass Labs Ltd.

Symbol - NFTX **Exchange** - NEO **CUSIP** - 54342Q
Head Office - 810-789 Pender St W, Vancouver, BC, V6C 1H2 **Telephone** - (604) 687-2038 **Toll-free** - (833) 545-6389 **Fax** - (604) 687-3141
Website - www.lgl.io
Email - info@lgl.io
Investor Relations - Dorian Banks (833) 545-6389
Auditors - WDM Chartered Accountants C.A., Vancouver, B.C.
Transfer Agents - Endeavor Trust Corporation, Vancouver, B.C.
Profile - (B.C. 2015) Designs, develops and sells exclusive non-fungible tokens (NFTs) using 3D principles suitable for personal and commercial application in extended reality (XR) environments.

Creates and issues NFT collections and provides a full range of support services to brands, artists and communities, including the House of Kibaa® digital studio which provides utilities and platform tools that enable users to showcase their individual style and NFT collections within a proprietary metaverse. Through royalty streams, earns a share of value each time NFTs change hands within certain ecosystems.

Effective Nov. 14, 2022, common shares began trading on the AQSE Growth Market in London, U.K. under the symbol NFTX.

In September 2022, the company acquired **Web 3.0 Holdings Corp.**, a Web3 infrastructure development company, for issuance of 13,827,250 common shares.

Predecessor Detail - Name changed from BluKnight Aquafarms Inc., Oct. 8, 2021, following the acquisition of HOK Technologies Inc. (dba House of Kibaa).

Directors - Kevin Cornish, Calgary, Alta.; James (Jim) Henning, Vancouver, B.C.; Lucas Stemshorn-Russell, Victoria, B.C.

Other Exec. Officers - Dorian Banks, CEO; Francis Rowe, CFO & corp. sec.; Neil Stevenson-Moore, chief product officer

Capital Stock

	Authorized (shs.)	Outstanding (shs.)[1]
Preferred	unlimited	nil
Common	unlimited	141,587,668

[1] At Mar. 17, 2023

Major Shareholder - Jason Nguyen held 16.63% interest at Feb. 3, 2022.

Price Range - NFTX/NEO

Year	Volume	High	Low	Close
2022	18,527,000	$0.93	$0.07	$0.07

Recent Close: $0.02

Capital Stock Changes - On Sept. 7, 2022, 13,827,250 common shares were issued pursuant to the acquisition of Web 3.0 Holdings Corp.

In September 2021, private placement of 11,600,000 common shares was completed at 10¢ per share. On Sept. 30, 2021, 45,000,000 common shares were issued pursuant to the acquisition of HOK Technologies Inc. In November 2021, private placement of 5,000,000 units (1 common share & 1 warrant) at 50¢ per unit was completed. Also during fiscal 2022, common shares were issued as follows: 9,500,000 by private placement, 4,475,000 under restricted share unit plan, 2,592,205 for earn out payment, 2,395,950 as finders' fees, 500,000 on exercise of warrants, 200,000 for debt settlement and 99,999 on exercise of options.

Wholly Owned Subsidiaries

GenZeroes Productions Inc., B.C.
HOK Technologies (BVI) Inc., British Virgin Islands. Inactive
HOK Technologies Inc., Richmond, B.C. dba House of Kibaa.
HOK Vietnam Company Limited, Ho Chi Minh City, Vietnam.
Web 3.0 Holdings Inc., Canada.

Financial Statistics

Periods ended:	12m July 31/22^A		12m July 31/21^A
	$000s	%Chg	$000s
Operating revenue	**7,005**	**n.a.**	**nil**
Cost of sales	723		nil
Salaries & benefits	855		nil
General & admin expense	7,782		53
Stock-based compensation	5,970		nil
Operating expense	**15,330**	**n.m.**	**53**
Operating income	**(8,325)**	**n.a.**	**(53)**
Deprec., depl. & amort	238		nil
Finance costs, gross	27		nil
Write-downs/write-offs	(3,193)		nil
Pre-tax income	**(11,907)**	**n.a.**	**(53)**
Net income	**(11,907)**	**n.a.**	**(53)**
Cash & equivalent	462		2
Accounts receivable	215		nil
Current assets	985		2
Fixed assets, net	61		nil
Right-of-use assets	397		nil
Intangibles, net	5,773		nil
Total assets	**7,601**	**n.m.**	**2**
Bank indebtedness	40		105
Accts. pay. & accr. liabs	908		45
Current liabilities	1,126		150
Long-term lease liabilities	244		nil
Shareholders' equity	3,626		(147)
Cash from oper. activs	**(646)**	**n.a.**	**(12)**
Cash from fin. activs	3,860		nil
Cash from invest. activs	(2,886)		nil
Net cash position	**308**	**n.m.**	**2**
Capital expenditures	(506)		nil
Capital disposals	93		nil
	$		$
Earnings per share*	(0.12)		(0.00)
Cash flow per share*	(0.01)		(0.00)
	shs		shs
No. of shs. o/s*	115,908,755		34,545,601
Avg. no. of shs. o/s*	98,240,652		35,738,697
	%		%
Net profit margin	(169.98)		n.a.
Return on equity	n.m.		n.m.
Return on assets	(312.51)		(623.53)

* Common
^A Reported in accordance with IFRS

Latest Results

Periods ended:	3m Oct. 31/22^A		3m Oct. 31/21^A
	$000s	%Chg	$000s
Operating revenue	137	-98	6,497
Net income	(2,348)	n.a.	5,771
	$		$
Earnings per share*	(0.02)		0.10

* Common
^A Reported in accordance with IFRS

Historical Summary
(as originally stated)

Fiscal Year	Oper. Rev.	Net Inc. Bef. Disc.	EPS*
	$000s	$000s	$
2022^A	7,005	(11,907)	(0.12)
2021^A	nil	(53)	(0.00)
2020^A	nil	(60)	(0.00)

* Common
^A Reported in accordance with IFRS

L.44 Loop Energy Inc.

Symbol - LPEN **Exchange** - TSX **CUSIP** - 54352E
Head Office - 2880 Production Way, Burnaby, BC, V5A 4T6 **Telephone** - (604) 222-3400 **Toll-free** - (855) 222-1534 **Fax** - (604) 222-4365
Website - www.loopenergy.com
Email - paul.cataford@loopenergy.com
Investor Relations - Paul G. Cataford (604) 222-3400
Auditors - KPMG LLP C.A., Vancouver, B.C.
Lawyers - Fasken Martineau DuMoulin LLP, Vancouver, B.C.
Transfer Agents - Computershare Trust Company of Canada Inc., Vancouver, B.C.
Employees - 134 at Dec. 31, 2022
Profile - (B.C. 2012) Designs, manufactures and supplies hydrogen fuel cell systems targeted for the electrification of commercial vehicles.

Fuel cell products feature the company's proprietary eFlow™ technology which uses trapezoid bipolar plates with narrowing channels, rather than a typical rectangular shaped channel, allowing better control of the flows of hydrogen, oxygen and coolant in the fuel stack to ensure uniform current and power density across the entire active area and increasing gas velocity throughout the plate to enhance performance and water management. Products available and in development include: the S300 with target power range of 15kW to 30kW; the T505/T600 with a range of 25kW to 60kW; the S1200 with a range of 60kW to 120kW; and the T2500, expected to be launched in 2025 or later, with units ranging from 120kW to 240kW. Core applications of the company's products include buses, trucks, logistic and delivery vans, material handling equipment, tractors, port stackers and transport machinery.

Development, manufacturing, assembly and testing of fuel cells are conducted at manufacturing facilities in Burnaby, B.C. (14,000 sq. ft.) and Shanghai, People's Republic of China (PRC; 35,000 sq. ft.). Also operates a service centre in Essex, U.K.; and, through **InPower-Loop Energy Technology (Beijing) Co., Ltd.** (26.9% owned, **Beijing In-Power Renewable Energy Co., Ltd.** 73.1%), a 35,000-sq.-ft. manufacturing facility in Langfang, PRC.

Directors - Kent P. Thexton, chr., Toronto, Ont.; Benjamin (Ben) Nyland, pres. & CEO, West Vancouver, B.C.; Paul G. Cataford, interim CFO & corp. sec., Calgary, Alta.; Christopher C. Clulow, Columbus, Ind.; Sophia J. Langlois, Calgary, Alta.; Brad Miller, Vancouver, B.C.; Dr. Andreas Truckenbrodt, Squamish, B.C.

Other Exec. Officers - Dr. Daryl Musselman, COO; Dr. Sean MacKinnon, chief scientist; George L. Rubin, chief comml. officer; Kirk Livingston, v-p, Asia Pacific region; Quan Hu, pres., Loop Energy Shanghai

Capital Stock

	Authorized (shs.)	Outstanding (shs.)[1]
Common	unlimited	34,312,571

[1] At May 12, 2023

Major Shareholder - Cummins Inc. held 20.2% interest at May 12, 2023.

Price Range - LPEN/TSX

Year	Volume	High	Low	Close
2022	5,616,068	$4.49	$0.85	$1.05
2021	7,281,477	$17.44	$3.54	$4.45

Recent Close: $0.55

Capital Stock Changes - During 2022, common shares were issued as follows: 611,667 on exercise of options and 11,667 on vesting of restricted share units; 266,857 common shares were cancelled.

Wholly Owned Subsidiaries

1123640 B.C. Ltd., B.C.
1299502 B.C. Ltd., B.C.
- 100% int. in **Loop Energy Technologies (Shanghai) Co., Ltd.**, People's Republic of China.

Investments

26.9% int. in **InPower-Loop Energy Technology (Beijing) Co., Ltd.**, Beijing, Beijing, People's Republic of China.

Financial Statistics

Periods ended:	12m Dec. 31/22[A]		12m Dec. 31/21[A]
	$000s	%Chg	$000s
Operating revenue	**3,328**	**+134**	**1,424**
Cost of sales	11,417		5,881
Salaries & benefits	16,693		10,441
Research & devel. expense	3,206		267
General & admin expense	6,440		6,096
Stock-based compensation	1,729		2,284
Operating expense	**39,485**	**+58**	**24,968**
Operating income	**(36,157)**	**n.a.**	**(23,544)**
Deprec., depl. & amort.	1,710		1,157
Finance income	735		227
Finance costs, gross	394		318
Investment income	nil		(275)
Pre-tax income	**(37,487)**	**n.a.**	**(25,020)**
Net income	**(37,487)**	**n.a.**	**(25,020)**
Cash & equivalent	24,524		67,030
Inventories	4,288		1,280
Accounts receivable	3,842		2,066
Current assets	34,655		78,356
Fixed assets, net	20,344		5,260
Total assets	**55,238**	**-34**	**84,093**
Accts. pay. & accr. liabs	3,939		2,846
Current liabilities	6,926		6,327
Long-term debt, gross	4,103		394
Long-term debt, net	3,928		219
Long-term lease liabilities	2,764		1,350
Shareholders' equity	39,510		75,155
Cash from oper. activs	**(33,177)**	**n.a.**	**(20,341)**
Cash from fin. activs	5,222		90,832
Cash from invest. activs	(14,962)		(6,662)
Net cash position	**24,524**	**-63**	**67,030**
Capital expenditures	(14,970)		(6,662)
Capital disposals	8		nil
	$		$
Earnings per share*	(1.11)		(0.80)
Cash flow per share*	(0.98)		(0.65)
	shs		shs
No. of shs. o/s*	34,005,791		33,649,314
Avg. no. of shs. o/s*	33,782,374		31,216,445
	%		%
Net profit margin	n.m.		n.m.
Return on equity	(65.39)		(82.27)
Return on assets	(53.24)		(52.37)
No. of employees (FTEs)	134		79

* Common
[A] Reported in accordance with IFRS

Latest Results

Periods ended:	3m Mar. 31/23[A]		3m Mar. 31/22[A]
	$000s	%Chg	$000s
Operating revenue	903	+407	178
Net income	(7,283)	n.a.	(8,047)
	$		$
Earnings per share*	(0.21)		(0.24)

* Common
[A] Reported in accordance with IFRS

Historical Summary
(as originally stated)

Fiscal Year	Oper. Rev.	Net Inc. Bef. Disc.	EPS*
	$000s	$000s	$
2022[A]	3,328	(37,487)	(1.11)
2021[A]	1,424	(25,020)	(0.80)
2020[A1]	546	(8,921)	(0.50)
2019[A1]	468	(4,289)	(0.25)
2018[A1]	nil	(4,439)	(0.27)

* Common
[A] Reported in accordance with IFRS
[1] Shares and per share figures adjusted to reflect 1-for-3 share consolidation effective Feb. 25, 2021 (concurrent with the company's initial public offering).

L.45 Lords & Company Worldwide Holdings Inc.

Symbol - LRDS **Exchange** - CSE (S) **CUSIP** - 54404Q
Head Office - 300-1055 Hastings St W, Vancouver, BC, V6E 2E9 **Telephone** - (604) 609-6171
Website - lordsholdings.com
Email - chris@lordsholdings.com
Investor Relations - Christopher Farnworth (604) 609-6171
Auditors - Crowe MacKay LLP C.A., Vancouver, B.C.
Transfer Agents - Olympia Trust Company, Calgary, Alta.
Profile - (B.C. 2012) Operates an e-commerce platform which offers dietary supplements and natural health and wellness products in Canada and the United States.

Also owns a 45% interest in **1293953 B.C. Ltd.** (**Rock Creek Farms Ltd.** 51%) which cultivates, sells and processes industrial hemp from its 100-acre outdoor facility in Rock Creek, B.C.

In February 2023, the company acquired **PNW Apparel Inc.**, the parent company of **Lords of Gastown Motorcycle Company Inc.**, for issuance of 22,000,000 common shares at a deemed price of $0.05 per share. Lords of Gastown is a cannabis and motorcycle lifestyle brand and apparel.

Common suspended from CSE, June 2, 2023.

Predecessor Detail - Name changed from Pac Roots Cannabis Corp., Nov. 19, 2021.

Directors - Christopher (Chris) Farnworth, pres., CEO, interim CFO & interim corp. sec., London, Middx., United Kingdom; Matthew McGill, v-p, strategy, Langley, B.C.; Chadwick (Chad) Clelland, Surrey, B.C.

Capital Stock

	Authorized (shs.)	Outstanding (shs.)[1]
Common	unlimited	28,880,990

[1] At Oct. 27, 2022

Major Shareholder - Widely held at Dec. 13, 2021.

Price Range - LRDS/CSE (S)

Year	Volume	High	Low	Close
2022	3,002,168	$0.70	$0.03	$0.03
2021	547,662	$2.40	$0.55	$0.70
2020	467,250	$7.20	$1.10	$1.60
2018	128,729	$9.00	$2.50	$4.50

Consolidation: 1-for-10 cons. in Feb. 2022
Recent Close: $0.02

Capital Stock Changes - On Feb. 4, 2022, common shares were consolidated on a 1-for-10 basis. From February to June 2022, private placement of 2,236,181 units (1 post-consolidated common share & 1 warrant) at $0.11 per unit and 16,570,154 units (1 post-consolidated common share & 1 warrant) at $0.083 per unit was completed, with warrants exercisable at $0.20 per share for two years.

Wholly Owned Subsidiaries

Lords of Grasstown Holdings Ltd., B.C.
1157630 B.C. Ltd., Vancouver, B.C.
- 100% int. in **Go Green B.C. Medicinal Marijuana Ltd.**, Lake Country, B.C.

Investments

49% int. in **1293953 B.C. Ltd.**, Canada.

Financial Statistics

Periods ended:	12m Nov. 30/21[A]		15m Nov. 30/20[A1]
	$000s	%Chg	$000s
General & admin expense	1,003		679
Stock-based compensation	575		554
Operating expense	**1,578**	**n.a.**	**1,233**
Operating income	**(1,578)**	**n.a.**	**(1,233)**
Deprec., depl. & amort.	115		122
Finance income	nil		1
Finance costs, gross	211		114
Write-downs/write-offs	(2,707)		(4,232)
Pre-tax income	**(3,257)**	**n.a.**	**(8,857)**
Net income	**(3,257)**	**n.a.**	**(8,857)**
Cash & equivalent	5		28
Accounts receivable	45		112
Current assets	70		359
Fixed assets, net	nil		1,019
Right-of-use assets	nil		146
Total assets	**72**	**-96**	**1,862**
Bank indebtedness	nil		40
Accts. pay. & accr. liabs	849		827
Current liabilities	1,079		1,496
Long-term lease liabilities	nil		34
Shareholders' equity	(1,007)		(570)
Cash from oper. activs	**(856)**	**n.a.**	**(896)**
Cash from fin. activs	1,135		1,399
Cash from invest. activs	(303)		(485)
Net cash position	**5**	**-82**	**28**
Capital expenditures	nil		(46)
	$		$
Earnings per share*	(0.39)		(2.40)
Cash flow per share*	(0.10)		(0.25)
	shs		shs
No. of shs. o/s*	8,702,792		7,107,964
Avg. no. of shs. o/s*	8,350,844		3,633,274
	%		%
Net profit margin	n.a.		...
Return on equity	n.m.		...
Return on assets	(314.99)		...

* Common
[A] Reported in accordance with IFRS
[1] Results reflect the Apr. 28, 2020, reverse takeover acquisition of 1157630 B.C. Ltd.

Latest Results

Periods ended:	9m Aug. 31/22[A]		9m Aug. 31/21[A]
	$000s	%Chg	$000s
Operating revenue	1,981	n.a.	nil
Net income	(790)	n.a.	(1,579)
	$		$
Earnings per share*	(0.05)		(0.20)

* Common
[A] Reported in accordance with IFRS

Historical Summary
(as originally stated)

Fiscal Year	Oper. Rev.	Net Inc. Bef. Disc.	EPS*
	$000s	$000s	$
2021[A]	nil	(3,257)	(0.39)
2020[A1]	nil	(8,857)	(2.40)
2019[A2]	nil	(506)	(0.46)
2018[A]	nil	118	0.22
2017[A]	nil	(3,622)	(12.00)

* Common
[A] Reported in accordance with IFRS
[1] 15 months ended Nov. 30, 2020.
[2] Results for fiscal 2019 and prior fiscal years pertain to Mountain Lake Minerals Inc.

Note: Adjusted throughout for 1-for-10 cons. in Feb. 2022; 1-for-10 cons. in July 2018

L.46 Lorne Park Capital Partners Inc.

Symbol - LPC **Exchange** - TSX-VEN **CUSIP** - 544178
Head Office - 1295 Cornwall Rd, Unit A3, Oakville, ON, L6J 7T5 **Telephone** - (905) 337-2227 **Toll-free** - (866) 469-7990 **Fax** - (905) 337-3552
Website - www.lpcp.ca
Email - bob.sewell@lpcp.ca
Investor Relations - Robert Sewell (905) 337-2227
Auditors - MNP LLP C.A., Toronto, Ont.
Transfer Agents - Computershare Trust Company of Canada Inc., Toronto, Ont.
Profile - (Ont. 2013 amalg.; orig. Alta., 2011) Provides discretionary investment management services primarily to affluent Canadian investors, estates, trusts, endowments and foundations.

Through wholly owned **Bellwether Investment Management Inc.** (BIM), provides investment management services that focus on a North American dividend growth strategy. Also offers a suite of investment solutions which include Canadian, U.S., and global equity and fixed income strategies. In addition, has pooled funds that enable the implementation of the North American strategy in smaller client accounts.

BIM divisions include archerETF Portfolio Management, which offers global tactical solutions for affluent families utilizing Exchange Traded Funds (ETFs); Index Wealth Management, which provides solutions for high net worth individuals, foundations, non-profit corporations, estates and trusts, maximizing the benefits of ETFs often combined with equity options; Adaptive ETF, which offers tailored investment solutions for individuals and organizations; and Crestridge Asset Management, which provides discretionary investment management services for affluent families, non-profit organizations, trusts, estates and foundations utilizing equities, fixed income investments as well as ETFs.

Assets under management at Mar. 31, 2023, totaled $2.77 billion.

On May 31, 2022, the company made cash contributions of $1,360,000 to **Infinite Wealth LP**. Infinite had $80,000,000 in assets under management, all of which was managed by the company.

On May 2, 2022, the company made cash contributions of $1,570,000 and $782,413 to **Fife Bay Financial LP** and **Scugog Financial LP**, respectively. Fife Bay and Scugog had $120,000,000 and $90,000,000 in assets under management, respectively, all of which were managed by the company.

Recent Merger and Acquisition Activity

Status: completed **Announced:** Jan. 3, 2023
Lorne Park Capital Partners Inc. acquired an 80% interest in Texas-based Promus Asset Management, LLC, an investment advisor that holds US$430,000,000 in assets under management, for US$4,489,382.

Status: terminated **Revised:** Mar. 31, 2022
UPDATE: The agreement was not finalized. Any efforts to conclude the transaction have been deferred to a later date. PREVIOUS: Lorne Park Capital Partners Inc. agreed to acquire private Ontario-based W.H. Shutt and Associates Inc., which had $145,000,000 in assets under management, all of which was managed by Lorne Park, for $5,850,000. The transaction was expected to close on or about Feb. 14, 2022.

Predecessor Detail - Formed from Big Five Capital Corp. in Ontario, Oct. 25, 2013, pursuant to Qualifying Transaction amalgamation with Bellwether Asset Management Inc. (deemed acquiror); basis 1 new for 2 old shs.

Directors - Christopher J. (Chris) Dingle, chr., Toronto, Ont.; Robert Sewell, pres. & CEO, Mississauga, Ont.; David S. Brown, Toronto, Ont.; Stephen (Steve) Meehan, Mississauga, Ont.; Peter B. Patchet, Ont.; James Williams, Mississauga, Ont.

Other Exec. Officers - Carlo Pannella, CFO

Capital Stock

	Authorized (shs.)	Outstanding (shs.)[1]
Preferred	unlimited	nil
Common	unlimited	53,885,080

[1] At May 19, 2023

Major Shareholder - Robert Sewell held 26.8% interest and Stephen (Steve) Meehan held 22.7% interest at May 19, 2023.

Price Range - LPC/TSX-VEN

Year	Volume	High	Low	Close
2022	992,479	$1.50	$0.76	$1.35
2021	373,570	$0.85	$0.61	$0.85
2020	300,150	$0.70	$0.28	$0.61
2019	741,440	$0.70	$0.40	$0.55
2018	1,081,625	$0.50	$0.30	$0.45

Recent Close: $1.15

Capital Stock Changes - During 2022, common shares were issued as follows: 1,347,016 on exercise of options, 415,000 by private placement and 144,091 from treasury pursuant to employee share savings plan.

Dividends

LPC com Ra $0.028 pa Q est. Apr. 28, 2023
Prev. Rate: $0.024 est. July 29, 2022
Prev. Rate: $0.02 est. Apr. 27, 2021
$0.005i................ Apr. 27/21
i Initial Payment

Wholly Owned Subsidiaries

Bellwether Estate and Insurance Services Inc., Ont.
Bellwether Investment Management Inc., Oakville, Ont.
Bellwether Investment Management USA, Inc., United States.
• 80% int. in **Promus Asset Management, LLC**, Tex.

Financial Statistics

Periods ended:	12m Dec. 31/22[A]		12m Dec. 31/21[oA]
	$000s	%Chg	$000s
Operating revenue	**26,550**	**+6**	**25,151**
Salaries & benefits	17,374		15,709
General & admin expense	3,110		4,144
Stock-based compensation	296		180
Operating expense	**20,780**	**+4**	**20,033**
Operating income	**5,770**	**+13**	**5,118**
Deprec., depl. & amort.	2,764		2,214
Finance income	32		3
Finance costs, gross	645		585
Pre-tax income	**2,288**	**+3**	**2,226**
Income taxes	1,286		995
Net income	**1,002**	**-19**	**1,231**
Net inc. for equity hldrs	**2,336**	**+6**	**2,211**
Net inc. for non-cont. int.	**(1,334)**	**n.a.**	**(980)**
Cash & equivalent	2,261		4,521
Accounts receivable	2,535		4,897
Current assets	5,120		9,504
Fixed assets, net	142		157
Right-of-use assets	636		660
Intangibles, net	35,808		21,694
Total assets	**41,787**	**+30**	**32,087**
Accts. pay. & accr. liabs	4,477		5,846
Current liabilities	4,682		8,037
Long-term debt, gross	6,962		6,208
Long-term debt, net	6,962		4,153
Long-term lease liabilities	482		545
Shareholders' equity	10,592		9,161
Non-controlling interest	15,871		10,191
Cash from oper. activs	**5,370**	**+18**	**4,568**
Cash from fin. activs	168		(1,364)
Cash from invest. activs	(6,408)		(2,086)
Net cash position	**2,206**	**-28**	**3,076**
Capital expenditures	(18)		(131)
Capital disposals	nil		626
	$		$
Earnings per share*	0.04		0.04
Cash flow per share*	0.10		0.09
Cash divd. per share*	0.02		0.02
	shs		shs
No. of shs. o/s*	53,790,887		51,884,780
Avg. no. of shs. o/s*	53,254,912		51,764,789
	%		%
Net profit margin	3.77		4.89
Return on equity	23.65		26.62
Return on assets	3.48		5.49

* Common
[o] Restated
[A] Reported in accordance with IFRS

Latest Results

Periods ended:	3m Mar. 31/23[A]		3m Mar. 31/22[A]
	$000s	%Chg	$000s
Operating revenue	7,219	+9	6,644
Net income	34	-85	233
Net inc. for equity hldrs	369	-27	507
Net inc. for non-cont. int.	(336)		(274)
	$		$
Earnings per share*	0.01		0.01

* Common
[A] Reported in accordance with IFRS

Historical Summary
(as originally stated)

Fiscal Year	Oper. Rev. $000s	Net Inc. Bef. Disc. $000s	EPS* $
2022[A]	26,550	1,002	0.04
2021[A]	25,151	1,231	0.04
2020[A]	18,722	110	0.01
2019[A]	16,650	991	0.02
2018[A]	9,745	(60)	(0.00)

* Common
[A] Reported in accordance with IFRS

L.47 Lotus Ventures Inc.

Symbol - J **Exchange** - CSE **CUSIP** - 54571Q
Head Office - 1010-1030 Georgia St W, Vancouver, BC, V6E 2Y3 **Telephone** - (604) 644-9844 **Fax** - (604) 602-0670
Website - www.lotuscannabis.ca
Email - dalemcclanaghan@gmail.com
Investor Relations - Dale McClanaghan (604) 644-9844
Auditors - De Visser Gray LLP C.A., Vancouver, B.C.
Transfer Agents - Computershare Trust Company of Canada Inc., Vancouver, B.C.

Profile - (B.C. 2014 amalg.) Cultivates, processes and sells cannabis under licences from Health Canada.

Owns a 22,500-sq.-ft. indoor facility located on 23 acres of land in Armstrong, B.C., designed to produce 2,000 kg of cannabis flowers per year. A 30,000-sq.-ft. facility expansion is underway which is expected to produce an additional 5,000 kg of cannabis flowers per year. Cannabis products are marketed under the Lotus Cannabis Co. brand for wholesale and distribution to licensed wholesale partners across Canada.

Predecessor Detail - Formed from Strachan Resources Ltd. in British Columbia, Nov. 27, 2014, following Qualifying Transaction acquisition of and amalgamation with (old) Lotus Ventures Inc. (deemed acquiror).

Directors - Albert Duwyn, chr.; Dale McClanaghan, pres. & CEO, Vancouver, B.C.; Carl Correia, COO, Vernon, B.C.; Maurice Creagh, B.C.; Simon Davie, B.C.

Other Exec. Officers - Gavin Dew, CFO

Capital Stock

	Authorized (shs.)	Outstanding (shs.)[1]
Common	unlimited	89,969,799

[1] At July 11, 2022

Major Shareholder - Widely held at Jan. 10, 2021.

Price Range - J/CSE

Year	Volume	High	Low	Close
2022	15,178,537	$0.12	$0.04	$0.05
2021	15,045,009	$0.20	$0.09	$0.11
2020	23,696,114	$0.20	$0.06	$0.18
2019	28,401,618	$0.47	$0.10	$0.15
2018	53,865,802	$1.00	$0.16	$0.22

Recent Close: $0.04

Financial Statistics

Periods ended:	12m Aug. 31/21[A]		12m Aug. 31/20[A]
	$000s	%Chg	$000s
Operating revenue	**5,481**	**+18**	**4,630**
Cost of sales	2,707		918
General & admin expense	1,594		1,238
Stock-based compensation	183		162
Operating expense	**4,484**	**+93**	**2,318**
Operating income	**997**	**-57**	**2,312**
Deprec., depl. & amort.	710		739
Finance costs, gross	46		79
Pre-tax income	**241**	**-84**	**1,494**
Net income	**241**	**-84**	**1,494**
Cash & equivalent	580		283
Inventories	1,149		1,362
Accounts receivable	211		527
Current assets	3,372		2,968
Fixed assets, net	13,536		13,940
Total assets	**16,908**	**0**	**16,908**
Bank indebtedness	320		729
Accts. pay. & accr. liabs	363		813
Current liabilities	1,125		1,993
Shareholders' equity	15,782		14,915
Cash from oper. activs	**909**	**+343**	**205**
Cash from fin. activs	(5)		621
Cash from invest. activs	(607)		(654)
Net cash position	**580**	**+105**	**283**
Capital expenditures	(607)		(654)
	$		$
Earnings per share*	0.00		0.02
Cash flow per share*	0.01		0.00
	shs		shs
No. of shs. o/s*	89,969,799		85,049,799
Avg. no. of shs. o/s*	89,740,648		84,959,225
	%		%
Net profit margin	4.40		32.27
Return on equity	1.57		10.68
Return on assets	1.70		9.68

* Common
[A] Reported in accordance with IFRS

Latest Results

Periods ended:	3m Nov. 30/21[A]		3m Nov. 30/20[A]
	$000s	%Chg	$000s
Operating revenue	411	-70	1,376
Net income	65	n.a.	(340)
	$		$
Earnings per share*	0.00		(0.00)

* Common
[A] Reported in accordance with IFRS

Historical Summary
(as originally stated)

Fiscal Year	Oper. Rev. $000s	Net Inc. Bef. Disc. $000s	EPS* $
2021[A]	5,481	241	0.00
2020[A]	4,630	1,494	0.02
2019[A]	nil	(2,912)	(0.04)
2018[A]	nil	(2,501)	(0.05)
2017[A]	nil	(724)	(0.02)

* Common
[A] Reported in accordance with IFRS

L.48 Lowell Farms Inc.

Symbol - LOWL **Exchange** - CSE **CUSIP** - 547572
Head Office - 19 Quail Run Cir, Suite B, Salinas, CA, United States, 93907
Website - lowellfarms.com
Email - ir@lowellfarms.com
Investor Relations - Mark Ainsworth (831) 998-8214
Auditors - GreenGrowth C.P.A., Los Angeles, Calif.
Transfer Agents - Odyssey Trust Company, Calgary, Alta.
Employees - 123 at Mar. 27, 2023

Profile - (B.C. 2019; orig. Ont., 2005) Cultivates, extracts, manufactures and distributes cannabis products in California.

Operations include a 225,000-sq.-ft. greenhouse cultivation facility and a 40,000-sq.-ft. processing facility, both in Monterey cty., Calif.; a 15,000-sq.-ft. manufacturing and laboratory facility and a 20,000-sq.-ft. distribution and packaging facility, both in Salinas, Calif.; and a 10,000-sq.-ft. distribution facility in Los Angeles, Calif. Products produced include flower, vape pens, oils, extracts, chocolate edibles, mints, gummies, tinctures, topicals and pre-rolls under owned and third-party brands. Owned brands include Lowell Herb Co., Lowell Smokes, Cypress Reserve, Flavor Extracts, Kaizen, House Weed, Moon, Altai, Humble Flower, Original Pot and CannaStripe. The Lowell Herb Co. and Lowell Smokes brands have been licensed to cannabis operators in Illinois, Massachusetts, Colorado and New Mexico. In addition, provides third-party extraction processing services to cultivators as well as bulk sales of flower, biomass and concentrates to licensed manufacturers and distributors in California.

Predecessor Detail - Name changed from Indus Holdings, Inc., Mar. 5, 2021.

Directors - Ann Lawrence, chr.; Mark Ainsworth, CEO, San Mateo, Calif.; William (Bill) Anton, Henderson, Nev.; Summer Frein, Calif.; Jeffrey Monat, Fair Haven, N.J.; Brian Shure, D.C.

Other Exec. Officers - Jenny Montenegro, COO; Bryan Dunmire, chief product officer; Tessa O'Dowd, sr. v-p, fin. & interim CFO

Capital Stock

	Authorized (shs.)	Outstanding (shs.)[1]
Subord. Vtg.	unlimited	112,761,904
Super Vtg.	unlimited	202,590
Class B	unlimited	9,008,271[2]

[1] At Mar. 30, 2023

[2] Issued by wholly owned Indus Holding Company.

Subordinate Voting - One vote per share.

Super Voting - Not entitled to dividends. Redeemable by the company under certain circumstances. 1,000 votes per share.

Class B - Convertible into subordinate voting shares on a one-for-one basis. Non-voting.

Major Shareholder - Robert Weakley held 64.24% interest and Gregory Heyman held 12.51% interest at Mar. 27, 2023.

Price Range - LOWL/CSE

Year	Volume	High	Low	Close
2022	6,911,393	$0.64	$0.10	$0.14
2021	29,827,428	$2.73	$0.38	$0.40
2020	20,464,240	$2.33	$0.24	$1.45
2019	6,935,728	$15.95	$0.51	$1.08
2018	16,279	$19.41	$2.43	$2.43

Consolidation: 1-for-485.3 cons. in Apr. 2019

Recent Close: $0.05

Wholly Owned Subsidiaries

Indus Holding Company, Salinas, Calif.
- 100% int. in **Cypress Holding Company, LLC**, Del.
- 100% int. in **Cypress Manufacturing Company**, Calif.
- 100% int. in **Indus LF LLC**, Calif.
- 100% int. in **Lowell SR LLC**, Calif.
  - 100% int. in **20800 Spence Road LLC**, Calif.
- 100% int. in **Wellness Innovation Group Incorporated**, Calif.

Financial Statistics

Periods ended:	12m Dec. 31/22‡A		12m Dec. 31/21A
	US$000s	%Chg	US$000s
Operating revenue	**43,535**	**-19**	**53,723**
Cost of goods sold	...		48,910
Salaries & benefits	...		6,234
General & admin expense	...		14,520
Stock-based compensation	...		1,355
Operating expense	**...**	**n.a.**	**71,019**
Operating income	**...**	**n.a.**	**(17,296)**
Deprec., depl. & amort.	...		4,236
Finance costs, gross	6,363		4,492
Write-downs/write-offs	...		(357)
Pre-tax income	**(24,373)**	**n.a.**	**(24,464)**
Income taxes	191		213
Net income	**(24,564)**	**n.a.**	**(24,677)**
Cash & equivalent	...		7,887
Inventories	...		13,343
Accounts receivable	...		8,222
Current assets	...		31,428
Fixed assets, net	...		64,779
Intangibles, net	...		40,756
Total assets	**118,823**	**-14**	**137,379**
Accts. pay. & accr. liabs	...		3,752
Current liabilities	...		10,123
Long-term debt, gross	30,396		23,118
Long-term debt, net	8,716		22,897
Long-term lease liabilities	...		34,052
Shareholders' equity	48,117		70,307
Cash from oper. activs	**(6,444)**	**n.a.**	**(26,048)**
Cash from fin. activs	3,845		15,955
Cash from invest. activs	(4,190)		(7,771)
Net cash position	**1,098**	**-86**	**7,887**
Capital expenditures	...		(3,593)
Capital disposals	...		1,978
	US$		US$
Earnings per share*	(0.22)		(0.27)
Cash flow per share*	(0.06)		(0.29)
	shs		shs
No. of shs. o/s*	121,973,000		112,009,000
Avg. no. of shs. o/s*	113,183,000		90,746,000
	%		%
Net profit margin	(56.42)		(45.93)
Return on equity	(41.48)		(42.39)
Return on assets	(14.17)		(16.13)
Foreign sales percent	100		100

* Subord. Vtg.

‡ Preliminary

A Reported in accordance with U.S. GAAP

Historical Summary
(as originally stated)

Fiscal Year	Oper. Rev.	Net Inc. Bef. Disc.	EPS*
	US$000s	US$000s	US$
2022‡A	43,535	(24,564)	(0.22)
2021A	53,723	(24,677)	(0.27)
2020B	42,618	(7,616)	(0.22)
2019B1	37,045	(50,752)	(1.62)
	$000s	$000s	$
2018B2	nil	(519)	(4.85)

* Subord. Vtg.

‡ Preliminary

A Reported in accordance with U.S. GAAP

B Reported in accordance with IFRS

[1] Results reflect the Apr. 29, 2019, reverse takeover acquisition of Indus Holding Company.

[2] Results for 2018 and prior years pertain to Mezzotin Minerals Inc.

Note: Adjusted throughout for 1-for-485.3 cons. in Apr. 2019

L.49 Lucara Diamond Corp.

Symbol - LUC **Exchange** - TSX **CUSIP** - 54928Q

Head Office - 502-1250 Homer St, Vancouver, BC, V6B 2Y5 **Telephone** - (604) 674-0272

Website - www.lucaradiamond.com

Email - hannah.reynish@lucaradiamond.com

Investor Relations - Hannah Reynish (604) 674-0272

Auditors - PricewaterhouseCoopers LLP C.A., Vancouver, B.C.

Bankers - The Bank of Nova Scotia, Vancouver, B.C.

Lawyers - Blake, Cassels & Graydon LLP, Vancouver, B.C.

Transfer Agents - Computershare Trust Company of Canada Inc., Vancouver, B.C.

FP500 Revenue Ranking - 612

Employees - 601 at Dec. 31, 2022

Profile - (B.C. 2004; orig. Colo., 1981) Holds the producing Karowe diamond mine in Botswana. Also owns Clara Diamond Solutions, a digital platform using blockchain technology for the sale of rough diamonds directly between diamond producers and manufacturers.

The Karowe open-pit diamond mine (formerly AK6), 15 km^2, Orapa district, commenced commercial production in July 2012 and provides an average annual of 2,600,000 tonnes kimberlite feed to the mill. During 2022, 327,028 carats of diamonds were sold at an average price of US$506 per carat compared to 380,493 carats of diamonds sold at an average price of US$536 during 2021. A feasibility study released in November 2019 proposed the development of an underground mine at Karowe where construction commenced in mid-2020 and ore from underground mining would seamlessly integrate into current operations providing mill feed with a ramp up to 2,700,000 tonnes per annum to the processing plant by 2026. Pre-production costs for the underground project were estimated at US$547,000,000. The combined open-pit and underground operation would result in life-of-mine production of 7,800,000 carats out to 2040. Effective Dec. 31, 2022, probable reserves were 53,100,000 tonnes grading 13.1 carats per hundred tonnes.

Wholly owned **Clara Diamond Solutions Limited Partnership** owns Clara, a digital platform using cloud and blockchain technologies for the sale of rough diamonds. The platform matches rough diamond production to specific polished manufacturing demand on a stone by stone basis and allows buyers to source rough diamonds tailored to specific polished diamond demand.

Predecessor Detail - Name changed from Bannockburn Resources Limited, Aug. 14, 2007; basis 5 new for 1 old sh.

Directors - Catherine E. McLeod-Seltzer, co-founder, West Vancouver, B.C.; Paul K. Conibear, chr., West Vancouver, B.C.; William Lamb, pres. & CEO, West Vancouver, B.C.; David Dicaire, B.C.; Marie Inkster, Ont.; Adam I. Lundin, Vancouver, B.C.; Peter J. O'Callaghan, B.C.

Other Exec. Officers - Zara E. Boldt, CFO & corp. sec.; Dr. John Armstrong, v-p, technical srvcs.

Capital Stock

	Authorized (shs.)	Outstanding (shs.)[1]
Common	unlimited	454,578,873

[1] At Mar. 31, 2023

Major Shareholder - Estate of Adolf H. Lundin held 24.48% interest and Letko, Brosseau & Associates Inc. held 12.46% interest at Mar. 15, 2023.

Price Range - LUC/TSX

Year	Volume	High	Low	Close
2022	32,442,996	$0.74	$0.47	$0.50
2021	44,949,563	$1.00	$0.50	$0.59
2020	60,673,891	$0.90	$0.40	$0.52
2019	78,351,085	$1.87	$0.78	$0.85
2018	98,874,662	$2.91	$1.38	$1.48

Recent Close: $0.44

Capital Stock Changes - During 2022, 531,942 common shares were issued on vesting of share units.

Wholly Owned Subsidiaries

African Diamonds Limited, United Kingdom.
- 40% int. in **Debwat Exploration (Pty) Ltd.**, Botswana.
- 40% int. in **Lucara Botswana (Pty) Ltd.**, Botswana.
- 100% int. in **Wati Ventures (Pty) Ltd.**, Botswana.

Clara Diamond Solutions GP Inc., Vancouver, B.C.
- 0.1% int. in **Clara Diamond Solutions Limited Partnership**, Vancouver, B.C.

Lucara Diamond Holdings (I) Inc., Mauritius.
- 100% int. in **Boteti Diamond Holdings Inc.**, Mauritius.
  - 60% int. in **Debwat Exploration (Pty) Ltd.**, Botswana.
  - 60% int. in **Lucara Botswana (Pty) Ltd.**, Botswana.
- 100% int. in **Mothae Diamond Holdings Inc.**, Mauritius.

Lucara Management Services Ltd., United Kingdom.

Subsidiaries

99.9% int. in **Clara Diamond Solutions Limited Partnership**, Vancouver, B.C.

Financial Statistics

Periods ended:	12m Dec. 31/22A		12m Dec. 31/21A
	US$000s	%Chg	US$000s
Operating revenue	**188,833**	**-8**	**205,207**
Cost of goods sold	79,266		80,348
Salaries & benefits	7,849		7,696
General & admin expense	11,723		11,390
Stock-based compensation	1,977		1,852
Operating expense	**100,815**	**0**	**101,286**
Operating income	**88,018**	**-15**	**103,921**
Deprec., depl. & amort.	25,411		51,165
Finance costs, gross	3,690		3,704
Pre-tax income	**64,812**	**+43**	**45,393**
Income taxes	24,378		21,566
Net income	**40,434**	**+70**	**23,827**
Cash & equivalent	26,418		27,011
Inventories	38,372		36,522
Accounts receivable	33,102		38,779
Current assets	100,339		102,312
Long-term investments	661		2,256
Fixed assets, net	332,369		244,899
Intangibles, net	18,224		20,724
Total assets	**495,839**	**+20**	**411,955**
Bank indebtedness	15,338		23,000
Accts. pay. & accr. liabs	29,689		26,285
Current liabilities	59,857		51,805
Long-term debt, gross	62,151		23,730
Long-term debt, net	62,151		23,730
Long-term lease liabilities	2,313		975
Shareholders' equity	270,061		248,972
Cash from oper. activs	**96,233**	**+15**	**83,390**
Cash from fin. activs	29,139		36,795
Cash from invest. activs	(125,421)		(97,541)
Net cash position	**26,418**	**-2**	**27,011**
Capital expenditures	(125,331)		(97,503)
	US$		US$
Earnings per share*	0.09		0.06
Cash flow per share*	0.21		0.20
	shs		shs
No. of shs. o/s*	453,566,923		453,034,981
Avg. no. of shs. o/s*	453,479,480		422,894,218
	%		%
Net profit margin	21.41		11.61
Return on equity	15.58		10.42
Return on assets	9.42		6.91
No. of employees (FTEs)	601		573

* Common

A Reported in accordance with IFRS

Historical Summary
(as originally stated)

Fiscal Year	Oper. Rev.	Net Inc. Bef. Disc.	EPS*
	US$000s	US$000s	US$
2022A	188,833	40,434	0.09
2021A	205,207	23,827	0.06
2020A	111,752	(26,278)	(0.07)
2019A	173,347	12,714	0.03
2018A	158,572	11,652	0.03

* Common

A Reported in accordance with IFRS

L.50 lululemon athletica inc.

Symbol - LULU **Exchange** - NASDAQ **CUSIP** - 550021

Head Office - 400-1818 Cornwall Ave, Vancouver, BC, V6J 1C7 **Telephone** - (604) 732-6124 **Fax** - (604) 874-6124

Website - www.lululemon.com

Email - htubin@lululemon.com

Investor Relations - Howard Tubin (604) 732-6124

Auditors - PricewaterhouseCoopers LLP C.A., Vancouver, B.C.

Lawyers - McCarthy Tétrault LLP

Transfer Agents - Computershare Trust Company, Inc., Denver, Colo.

FP500 Revenue Ranking - 56

Employees - 34,000 at Jan. 29, 2023

Profile - (Del. 2005) Designs and retails athletic apparel and accessories under the lululemon brand in Canada, the United States, Asia-Pacific and Europe.

Offers apparel for women and men including pants, shorts, tops and jackets designed for healthy lifestyle including athletic activities such as yoga, running and training. Also offers apparel designed for casual wear and being on the move and other fitness-related products including bags, hats, yoga mats and equipment, and water bottles. In addition, offers lululemon Studio (formerly MIRROR), which consists of in-home fitness equipment with an interactive workout platform that allows guests to subscribe for live and on-demand classes.

Products are primarily sold through corporate-owned stores and direct to consumer channels through www.lululemon.com e-commerce website and mobile apps. At Apr. 30, 2023, the company operated 662 corporate-owned stores in Canada (69), the United States (357), Australia (32), the United Kingdom (20), New Zealand (8), the People's Republic of China (117), Singapore (7), Malaysia (2), South Korea (16), Japan (7), Ireland (4), Germany (9), Switzerland (1), France (4), the Netherlands (1), Spain (3), Sweden (2) and Norway (1). Other sales channels include outlets and warehouse sales; seasonal stores; wholesale accounts including premium yoga studios, health club and fitness centres; and licence and supply arrangements. At Apr. 30, 2023, 26 retail locations in Mexico (12), the United Arab Emirates (7), Qatar (3) and Kuwait (1) were operated by third parties under licence.

Manufacturing is contracted to about 40 third parties in Southeast Asia, South Asia and China. Distribution is conducted through facilities in Delta, B.C., 155,000 sq. ft.; Toronto, Ont., 250,000 sq. ft.; Sumner, Wash., 150,000 sq. ft.; and Columbus, Ohio, 310,000 sq. ft.

During the 52-week period ended Jan. 29, 2023, the company opened 81 net new corporate-owned stores, including 31 stores in the People's Republic of China, nine in the rest of Asia Pacific, 32 in North America and nine in Europe, including its first location in Spain.

Directors - Martha A. M. (Marti) Morfitt, chr., Fla.; Calvin McDonald, CEO, Ont.; David M. Mussafer†; Michael Casey, Seattle, Wash.; Isabel Ge Mahe; Kourtney Gibson, Atlanta, Ga.; Kathryn Henry; Alison Loehnis, London, Middx., United Kingdom; Jon McNeill; Glenn K. Murphy, Toronto, Ont.; Emily White

Other Exec. Officers - Meghan Frank, CFO; Sun (Michelle) Choe, chief product officer; Ted Dagnese, chief supply chain officer; Nicole (Nikki) Neuburger, chief brand officer; Julie Averill, exec. v-p & chief tech. officer; André Maestrini, exec. v-p, intl.; Susan Gelinas, sr. v-p, people & culture; Shannon Higginson, sr. v-p, chief compliance officer & gen. counsel; Dr. Tom Waller, sr. v-p, advanced innovation & chief science officer; Alex Grieve, v-p & contr.; Howard Tubin, v-p, IR; Celeste Burgoyne, pres., Americas & global guest innovation

† Lead director

Capital Stock

	Authorized (shs.)	Outstanding (shs.)[1]	Par
Preferred	5,000,000	nil	US$0.01
Common	400,000,000	121,949,471	US$0.005
Special Voting	60,000,000	5,115,961	US$0.000005
Exchangeable	60,000,000	5,115,961[2]	n.p.v.

[1] At May 26, 2023

[2] Securities of wholly owned Lulu Canadian Holding, Inc.

Common - One vote per share.

Special Voting - Not entitled to dividends or any consideration in the event of liquidation, dissolution or winding-up of the company. Attached to exchangeable shares of wholly owned Lulu Canadian Holding, Inc. entitling exchangeable shareholders to vote together with common shares. One vote per share.

Exchangeable - Entitled to dividend and liquidation rights equivalent to common shares. Convertible at any time by the holder into common shares on a 1-for-1 basis plus cash payment for accrued and unpaid dividends. Convertible at any time by the company on the earliest of: (i) July 26, 2047; (ii) the date on which fewer than 4,200,000 exchangeable shares are outstanding; or (iii) in the event of certain events such as a change in control. Non-voting.

Major Shareholder - FMR LLC held 14.4% interest at Apr. 1, 2023.

Price Range - LULU/NASDAQ

Year	Volume	High	Low	Close
2022	130,344,045	US$410.70	US$252.01	US$320.38
2021	103,458,244	US$485.66	US$269.52	US$391.45
2020	154,080,966	US$399.87	US$128.93	US$348.03
2019	161,378,294	US$235.10	US$118.30	US$231.67
2018	172,911,045	US$164.79	US$74.90	US$121.61

Capital Stock Changes - During the 52-week period ended Jan. 29, 2023, 87,000 common shares were issued on exchange of a like number of exchangeable shares, 322,000 common shares were issued upon settlement of stock-based compensation, 105,000 common shares were withheld related to net share settlement of performance-based restricted stock units and 1,396,000 common shares were repurchased.

Wholly Owned Subsidiaries

Curiouser Products Inc., New York, N.Y. dba MIRROR
Lincoln Park LLC, Delaware, Ont.
lululemon athletica australia holdings Pty Ltd., Australia.
• 100% int. in **lululemon athletica australia Pty Ltd.**, Australia. Formerly New Harbour Yoga Pty Ltd.
lululemon athletica CH GmbH, Switzerland.
lululemon athletica DK ApS, Denmark.
lululemon athletica DE GmbH, Germany.
lululemon athletica FR S.A.R.L., France.
lululemon athletica Ireland Limited, Ireland.
lululemon athletica JP GK, Japan.
lululemon athletica Korea Ltd., South Korea.
lululemon athletica Malaysia Sdn. Bhd.
lululemon athletica NL B.V., Netherlands.
lululemon athletica new zealand limited, New Zealand.
lululemon athletica Norway AS, Norway.
lululemon athletica SG Pte. Ltd., Singapore.
lululemon athletica Trading (Shanghai) Ltd., Republic of China.
lululemon athletica TW Ltd., Republic of China.
lululemon athletica UK Ltd., United Kingdom.
Lululemon Callco ULC, Alta.
• 100% int. in **Lulu Canadian Holding, Inc.**, B.C.
  • 100% int. in **Curiouser Products Canada Inc.**, B.C. dba Mirror
  • 100% int. in **lululemon athletica canada inc.**, B.C.
Lululemon Hong Kong Limited, Hong Kong, People's Republic of China.
lululemon India (Services) Private Limited, India.
lululemon LU Holdings S.A.R.L., Luxembourg.
Lululemon Macau Limited, Macau, People's Republic of China.
lululemon Sweden AB, Sweden.
lululemon usa inc., United States.

Financial Statistics

Periods ended:	52w Jan. 29/23[A]		52w Jan. 30/22[A]
	US$000s	%Chg	US$000s
Operating revenue	**8,110,518**	**+30**	**6,256,617**
Cost of goods sold	3,257,395		2,502,068
General & admin expense	2,479,573		2,146,812
Operating expense	**5,736,968**	**+23**	**4,648,880**
Operating income	**2,373,550**	**+48**	**1,607,737**
Deprec., depl. & amort.	291,791		224,206
Write-downs/write-offs	(407,913)[1]		nil
Pre-tax income	**1,332,571**	**0**	**1,333,869**
Income taxes	477,771		358,547
Net income	**854,800**	**-12**	**975,322**
Cash & equivalent	1,154,867		1,259,871
Inventories	1,447,367		966,481
Accounts receivable	132,906		77,001
Current assets	3,159,453		2,614,853
Fixed assets, net	1,269,614		927,710
Right-of-use assets	969,419		803,543
Intangibles, net	24,375		458,179
Total assets	**5,607,038**	**+13**	**4,942,478**
Accts. pay. & accr. liabs	571,955		620,528
Current liabilities	1,492,198		1,405,334
Long-term lease liabilities	862,362		692,056
Shareholders' equity	3,148,799		2,740,046
Cash from oper. activs	**966,463**	**-30**	**1,389,108**
Cash from fin. activs	(467,487)		(844,987)
Cash from invest. activs	(569,937)		(427,891)
Net cash position	**1,154,867**	**-8**	**1,259,871**
Capital expenditures	(638,657)		(394,502)
	US$		US$
Earnings per share*	6.70		7.52
Cash flow per share*	7.57		10.70
	shs		shs
No. of shs. o/s*	127,321,000		128,500,000
Avg. no. of shs. o/s*	127,666,000		129,768,000
	%		%
Net profit margin	10.54		15.59
Return on equity	29.03		36.81
Return on assets	16.21		21.37
Foreign sales percent	86		85
No. of employees (FTEs)	34,000		29,000

* Com. & exch.

[A] Reported in accordance with U.S. GAAP

[1] Includes US$362,492,000 goodwill impairment charge related to lululemon Studio business (formerly MIRROR).

Latest Results

Periods ended:	13w Apr. 30/23[A]		13w May 1/22[A]
	US$000s	%Chg	US$000s
Operating revenue	200,792	-88	1,613,463
Net income	290,405	+53	189,998
	US$		US$
Earnings per share*	2.28		1.48

* Com. & exch.

[A] Reported in accordance with U.S. GAAP

Historical Summary
(as originally stated)

Fiscal Year	Oper. Rev.	Net Inc. Bef. Disc.	EPS*
	US$000s	US$000s	US$
2023[A]	8,110,518	854,800	6.70
2022[A]	6,256,617	975,322	7.52
2021[A]	4,401,879	588,913	4.52
2020[A]	3,979,296	645,596	4.95
2019[A1]	3,288,319	483,801	3.63

* Com. & exch.

[A] Reported in accordance with U.S. GAAP

[1] 53 weeks ended Feb. 3, 2019.

L.51 Lumiera Health Inc.

Symbol - NHP **Exchange** - TSX-VEN (S) **CUSIP** - 550254

Head Office - 2700-1000 rue Sherbrooke O, Montréal, QC, H3A 3G4 **Telephone** - (514) 987-5025 **Toll-free** - (866) 722-2442 **Fax** - (514) 987-1213

Website - www.lumiera.ca

Email - infolumiera@gmail.com

Investor Relations - Andre Rancourt (514) 500-0059

Auditors - Richter LLP C.A.

Lawyers - Brouillette & Partners, Montréal, Qué.

Transfer Agents - Computershare Trust Company of Canada Inc.

Profile - (Can. 2013) Develops and commercializes evidence-based botanical products to help manage a wide range of therapeutic needs, sleeping disorder and pain for the consumer healthcare industry.

Products include Holizen, a herbal tonics and supplements product line that covers a wide range of therapeutic needs including cardiovascular, health, energy and immunity, stress relief, bones, joints and muscle mobility; Bazzzics™, a line of natural sleeping-aids derived from the company's patented ingredient CALPXT96, that act in synergy to procure a natural and effective solution to sleep disorders caused by anxiety and stress; and Awaye™, an over-the counter pain relief cream for the treatment of pain caused by knee osteoarthritis. Products are sold through direct-to-consumer platforms including Holizen.com and Awaye.ca; other e-commerce platforms including Well.ca, Amazon.ca and Amazon.com; and distribution agreements with national distributors as well as major key accounts and independent natural health stores.

Also has more than 66 Natural Product Numbers (NPNs) registered with Health Canada in its product portfolio and intends to leverage theses assets through new product launches and licensing deals in various channels and market segments.

Common suspended from TSX-VEN, Apr. 13, 2023.

Predecessor Detail - Name changed from Mondias Natural Products Inc., Nov. 5, 2020, following acquisition of Lumiera Health Innovation Inc.

Directors - Kevin Cole, chr., Ont.; Louis E. Doyle, acting CFO, Kirkland, Qué.; Marie Bélanger, Qué.; Jacqueline Khayat, Laval, Qué.

Other Exec. Officers - Jamil Samsatly, chief scientific officer; Derek Lindsay, v-p, corp. devel.; Gilles Seguin, corp. sec.

Capital Stock

	Authorized (shs.)	Outstanding (shs.)[1]
Common	unlimited	169,965,217

[1] At Nov. 30, 2022

Major Shareholder - Robert Brouillette held 17.2% interest and André Rancourt held 10.1% interest at Apr. 14, 2022.

Price Range - NHP/TSX-VEN (S)

Year	Volume	High	Low	Close
2022	62,943,601	$0.03	$0.01	$0.01
2021	62,774,131	$0.12	$0.02	$0.02
2020	10,088,010	$0.17	$0.04	$0.04
2019	15,417,932	$0.43	$0.09	$0.15
2018	2,364,453	$0.32	$0.16	$0.17

Recent Close: $0.01

Wholly Owned Subsidiaries

Holizen Laboratory Inc., Longueuil, Qué.
Lumiera Health Innovation Inc.

Financial Statistics

Periods ended:	12m Nov. 30/21[A]		12m Nov. 30/20[A]
	$000s	%Chg	$000s
Operating revenue	**538**	**+7**	**504**
Cost of goods sold	270		217
Cost of sales	274		80
Salaries & benefits	855		436
General & admin expense	860		774
Stock-based compensation	88		99
Operating expense	**2,348**	**+46**	**1,606**
Operating income	**(1,810)**	**n.a.**	**(1,102)**
Deprec., depl. & amort.	84		16
Finance costs, gross	n.a.		810
Finance costs, net	(378)		n.a.
Pre-tax income	**(1,203)**	**n.a.**	**(1,929)**
Net income	**(1,203)**	**n.a.**	**(1,929)**
Cash & equivalent	701		1,761
Inventories	247		187
Accounts receivable	67		107
Current assets	1,017		2,066
Fixed assets, net	4		6
Intangibles, net	1,110		1,192
Total assets	**2,132**	**-35**	**3,265**
Accts. pay. & accr. liabs	202		628
Current liabilities	420		2,575
Long-term debt, gross	1,117		773
Long-term debt, net	1,117		773
Shareholders' equity	594		(82)
Cash from oper. activs	**(2,520)**	**n.a.**	**(684)**
Cash from fin. activs	1,147		807
Cash from invest. activs	313		1,546
Net cash position	**701**	**-60**	**1,761**
Capital expenditures, net	2		(7)
	$		$
Earnings per share*	(0.01)		(0.03)
Cash flow per share*	(0.02)		(0.01)
	shs		shs
No. of shs. o/s*	169,965,217		98,798,549
Avg. no. of shs. o/s*	122,167,042		66,457,814
	%		%
Net profit margin	(223.61)		(382.74)
Return on equity	n.m.		n.m.
Return on assets	(44.58)		(59.58)

* Common

[A] Reported in accordance with IFRS

Latest Results

Periods ended:	6m May 31/22[A]		6m May 31/21[A]
	$000s	%Chg	$000s
Operating revenue	316	+29	245
Net income	(955)	n.a.	(667)
	$		$
Earnings per share*	(0.01)		(0.01)

* Common

[A] Reported in accordance with IFRS

Historical Summary
(as originally stated)

Fiscal Year	Oper. Rev. $000s	Net Inc. Bef. Disc. $000s	EPS* $
2021[A]	538	(1,203)	(0.01)
2020[A]	504	(1,929)	(0.03)
2019[A]	495	(1,712)	(0.03)
2018[A1]	537	(1,474)	(0.04)
2017[A2]	141	(241)	(0.01)

* Common

[A] Reported in accordance with IFRS

[1] Results reflect the Nov. 14, 2018, Qualifying Transaction reverse takeover acquisition of Mondias Natural Products Inc.

[2] Results pertain to (old) Mondias Natural Products Inc.

Note: Adjusted throughout for 1-for-1.5 cons. in Nov. 2018

L.52 Lumine Group Inc.

Symbol - LMN **Exchange** - TSX-VEN **CUSIP** - 55027C
Head Office - 100-5060 Spectrum Way, Mississauga, ON, L4W 5N5 **Telephone** - (647) 469-8295 **Fax** - (905) 238-8408
Website - www.luminegroup.com
Email - david.nyland@luminegroup.com
Investor Relations - David Nyland (647) 469-8295
Auditors - KPMG LLP C.A., Toronto, Ont.
Transfer Agents - Computershare Trust Company of Canada Inc.
Employees - 2,300 at Dec. 31, 2022
Profile - (Ont. 2022) Acquires, manages and builds vertical market software (VMS) businesses in the communications and media industry.

The Communications Operating Groups

The two communications operating groups include 23 independently managed software business units globally which supply software and services primarily in the following communications sub-vertical markets: cable, fixed-line, fixed-wireless and fibre Internet service providers (ISPs), mobile operators, fixed line consumer operators, fixed line business-to-business operators, mobile virtual network operators (MVNOs), mobile tower operators, and mobile financial service operators. Solution areas include: data and financial clearing, network roaming, interconnect, service orchestration, service management, enterprise IoT enablement, consumer and enterprise billing and revenue management, subscription billing, billing mediation, device intelligence and device management, MVNO billing and real-time charging, content delivery networks, mobile tower asset management, network optimization and monetization, digital asset management, multi-media contact center management, revenue assurance and fraud management, mobile financial services, fibre network provisioning and assurance, customer insight and engagement, and mobile security. Companies include Titanium, Wiztivi, Tomia, Incognito Software Systems, MDS Global, Ubersmith, WDS Mobile, Lifecycle Software, Velocix, NetEngage, Tarantula, Flash Networks, TransMedia Dynamics, VAS-X, Collab, Neural Technologies, Telepin, Netadmin Systems, Sicap, Advantage 360, Kansys, Aleyant, Avance Metering and Symbrio.

The Media Operating Group

Through WideOrbit business supplies software and services primarily in the television, radio, cable/networks, regional sports, new media (digital) and international markets. Core solution areas include a full enterprise resource planning system to manage advertising sales and operations from air to invoice and for any media type or sales channel. This includes advertising sales and operations from scheduling content to advertising order entry, optimization, and advertising scheduling, as well as invoicing and payments. This is managed for any media type and direct or indirect sales channels. This includes advertising sales and commercial operations, inventory management, order management, ad placement and optimization, business analytics, billing and accounts receivable.

On Feb. 22, 2023, the company acquired **Lumine Group (Holdings) Inc.**, a global portfolio of communications and media software companies and wholly owned by **Constellation Software Inc.** (CSI), for issuance of 63,582,712 subordinate voting shares and 55,233,745 preferred shares. Immediately following the acquisition, the company amalgamated with Lumine Group (Holdings), with the resulting entity being the company. In December 2022, Lumine Group (Holdings) entered into an agreement to acquire **WideOrbit Inc.** for a purchase price of $490,000,000. This acquisition was completed on Feb. 22, 2023, and WideOrbit became a wholly owned subsidiary of the company. WideOrbit is a software business that primarily operates in the advertising market for cable networks, local television stations and radio stations. On Feb. 23, 2023, CSI distributed to its shareholders, as a dividend-in-kind, 63,582,706 subordinate voting shares of the company it received on the basis of 3.0003833 subordinate voting shares of the company for each CSI common share held.

Sub vtg listed on TSX-VEN, Mar. 24, 2023.

Recent Merger and Acquisition Activity

Status: completed **Revised:** Mar. 8, 2023
UPDATE: The transaction was completed for cash consideration of $31,400,000 on closing plus cash holdbacks of $14,400,000 and contingent consideration with an estimated acquisition date fair value of $4,100,000 for total consideration of $49,900,000. The cash holdbacks are payable over a two-year period and are adjusted, as necessary, for such items as working capital or net tangible asset assessments. PREVIOUS: Lumine Group Inc. agreed to acquire Titanium Software Holdings Inc., a software company catering to the communications and media market. Terms were not disclosed.

Directors - Mark R. Miller, chr., Oakville, Ont.; David Nyland, CEO, Ont.; Brian Beattie, CFO, Toronto, Ont.; Paul Cowling, Toronto, Ont.; Lucie Laplante, Ont.; Eric Mathewson, San Francisco, Calif.; Robin Van Poelje, Netherlands

Capital Stock

	Authorized (shs.)	Outstanding (shs.)[1]
Preferred	unlimited	63,582,712
Special	unlimited	10,178,504
Subordinate Vtg.	unlimited	63,671,176
Super Vtg	1	1[2]

[1] At Mar. 24, 2023

[2] Held by Constellation Software Inc.

Preferred - Entitled to fixed preferential cumulative annual dividends of 5%. Convertible into subordinate voting shares on a 2.4302106-for-1 basis. Redeemable by holder for an amount of cash equal to the initial equity value of the preferred shares. Non-voting.

Special Shares - Entitled to fixed preferential cumulative annual dividends of 5%. Convertible into subordinate voting shares on a 3.4302106-for-1 basis. Redeemable by holder for an amount of cash equal to the initial equity value of the special shares. One vote per share.

Subordinate Voting - Entitled to dividends. Non-convertible. One vote per share.

Super Voting - Entitled to dividends. Convertible, at any time by Constellation Software Inc., into one subordinate voting share. Entitled to that number of votes that equals 50.1% of the aggregate number of votes attached to all of the outstanding super voting shares and subordinate voting shares at such time.

Major Shareholder - Constellation Software Inc. held 50.1% interest at Mar. 24, 2023.

Recent Close: $22.44

Capital Stock Changes - On Feb. 22, 2023, 63,582,712 subordinate voting shares and 55,233,745 preferred shares were issued pursuant to acquisition of Lumine Group (Holdings) Inc., a wholly owned subsidiary of Constellation Software Inc., and 10,204,294 special shares were issued pursuant to acquisition of WideOrbit Inc. A further 8,348,967 preferred shares were also issued to a wholly owned subsidiary of Constellation.

Wholly Owned Subsidiaries

A Metering AB, Sweden.
Advantage 360 Software, LLC, Calif.
Aleyant Spain S.L., Spain.
Aleyant Systems LLC, Ill.
Flash Networks B.V., Netherlands.
Flash Networks Inc., United States.
Flash Networks Ltd., Israel.
Flash Networks Singapore Pte. Ltd., Singapore.
Incognito Interactive Limited, Ireland.
Incognito Software Systems Inc., Vancouver, B.C.
Incognito USA Inc., United States.
Kansys Inc., Kan.
Kansys International Limited, United Kingdom.
Lifecycle Software Ltd., United Kingdom.
Lumine Group UK Holdco Ltd., United Kingdom.
Lumine Group US Holdco Inc., United States.
Lumine HoldCo EU A/S, Denmark.
Lumine Holdings Group (Israel) Ltd., Israel.
MACH Clearing Solutions India Pvt. Ltd., India.
MDS CEM Holdings Limited, United Kingdom.
MDS Global Ltd., United Kingdom.
Mobixell Networks (Europe) Ltd., United Kingdom.
Mobixell Networks (Israel) Ltd., Israel.
Morse Holding, Inc., United States.
Morse Intermediate Holdings, Inc.
NT8 Integrated Solutions (Malaysia) Sdn. Bhd., Malaysia.
Netadmin System I Sverige AB, Sweden.
Netadmin Systems i Sverige AB, Sweden.
Netengage Ltd., United Kingdom.
Neural Technologies GmbH, Germany.
Neural Technologies Incorporated, Kan.
Neural Technologies Limited, United Kingdom.
Neural Technologies (S) Pte. Ltd., Singapore.
Oy Wiztivi Gaming Ltd., Finland.
PT. Neural Technologies Integrated Solutions, Indonesia.
SICAP Schweiz AG, Switzerland.
Sicap France S.A.S., France.
StarHome B.V., Netherlands.
Starhome Ltd., Israel.
Starhome Mach GmbH, Switzerland.
Starhome Mach S.A.R.L., Luxembourg.
Starhome S.A.R.L., Luxembourg.
Symbrio AB, Sweden.
Tarantula Asia Pacific Pte. Ltd., Singapore.
Tarantula Global Holdings Pte. Ltd., Singapore.
Tarantula.net India Pvt. Ltd., India.
Tarantula.net Limited, United Kingdom.
Telarix Inc., United States.
Telarix Intermediate Holdings, Inc., United States.
Telarix Italy S.r.l., Italy.
Telarix (M) Sdn. Bhd., Malaysia.
Telarix Singapore Pte. Ltd., Singapore.
Telepin Software Systems Inc., Ont.
Tomia Ltd., United Kingdom.
TransMedia Dynamics (Asia) Sdd. Bhd., Malaysia.
TransMedia Dynamics Inc., United States.
TransMedia Dynamics Limited, United Kingdom.
TransMedia Holdings Limited, United Kingdom.
Ubersmith Inc., United States.
Unipier Mobile Ltd., Israel.
Vas-X Australia Pty Ltd., Australia.
Vas-X (Pty) Ltd., South Africa.
Velocix Solutions India LLP, India.
Velocix Solutions Limited, Cambridge, Cambs., United Kingdom.
Velocix Solutions Portugal Unipessoal Lda., Portugal.
Velocix Solutions USA Inc., United States.
WDS Mobile Limited, United Kingdom.
Wiztivi S.A.S., France.

Subsidiaries

99.99% int. in **Neural Technologies (Hong Kong) Ltd.**, Hong Kong, People's Republic of China.
99.99% int. in **Sicap India Pvt. Ltd.**, India.

Financial Statistics

Periods ended:	12m Dec. 31/22[A1]		12m Dec. 31/21[A]
	US$000s	%Chg	US$000s
Operating revenue	**255,745**	**+12**	**228,355**
Salaries & benefits	134,316		120,092
General & admin expense	31,452		18,473
Other operating expense	11,734		20,828
Operating expense	**177,502**	**+11**	**159,393**
Operating income	**78,243**	**+13**	**68,962**
Deprec., depl. & amort.	37,139		30,682
Finance costs, gross	581		153
Pre-tax income	**35,878**	**-4**	**37,536**
Income taxes	8,476		10,070
Net income	**27,402**	**0**	**27,466**
Cash & equivalent	67,085		27,110
Accounts receivable	63,677		45,109
Current assets	163,754		207,772
Fixed assets, net	3,138		2,517
Right-of-use assets	5,349		4,503
Intangibles, net	216,797		103,249
Total assets	**400,461**	**+22**	**328,406**
Accts. pay. & accr. liabs	63,879		51,169
Current liabilities	117,445		126,218
Long-term debt, gross	19,113		nil
Long-term debt, net	18,138		nil
Long-term lease liabilities	4,719		2,250
Shareholders' equity	153,780		173,149
Cash from oper. activs	**34,625**	**-60**	**86,027**
Cash from fin. activs	120,800		(79,635)
Cash from invest. activs	(115,343)		(14,179)
Net cash position	**67,085**	**+147**	**27,110**
Capital expenditures	(7,883)		(700)
	US$		US$
Earnings per share*	0.11		n.a.
	shs		shs
No. of shs. o/s	n.a.		n.a.
	%		%
Net profit margin	10.71		12.03
Return on equity	16.76		n.m.
Return on assets	7.64		n.a.
No. of employees (FTEs)	2,300		n.a.

* Sub. Vtg.

[A] Reported in accordance with IFRS

[1] Results for 2022 and 2021 pertain to Lumine Group (Holdings) Inc.

L.53 Luxxfolio Holdings Inc.

Symbol - LUXX **Exchange** - CSE **CUSIP** - 55069Q

Head Office - 417-1080 Mainland St, Vancouver, BC, V6B 2T4 **Telephone** - (604) 398-3837 **Toll-free** - (888) 928-8883

Website - www.luxxfolio.com

Email - dlinden@luxxfolio.com

Investor Relations - Dean Linden (888) 928-8883

Auditors - Kenway Mack Slusarchuk Stewart LLP C.A., Calgary, Alta.

Transfer Agents - Computershare Trust Company of Canada Inc., Vancouver, B.C.

Profile - (B.C. 2017) Operates an industrial scale cryptocurrency mining facility in the United States; and develops a platform which enables third parties to authenticate, secure and track their digital-based assets, contracts and documents or physical assets (uniquely identified assets or UIAs) via a highly secure verifiable ledger, and monetize or securitize these assets on the blockchain ecosystem.

Operations are carried out through three business segments: Asset Integrity; Asset Management; and Data Centre and Custodian.

The **Asset Integrity** segment has developed a platform which provides users a secure and reliable place to authenticate and track their UIAs, and provide the ability to monetize or securitize these assets. The physical asset platform enables users to register physical goods, such as industrial assets, collectibles, memorabilia, vintage automobiles and artwork, that would be authenticated in person. A verification tag would be secured to the item, which would have a unique static quick response (QR) code. The QR code would be scanned using the application and would be recorded to the company's private blockchain. The physical asset would then be added to the user's Personal Luxxfolio as a secured asset. Registering the physical goods and having the asset stored by an approved and professionally managed custodian such as a data centre, allows the user to create a non-fungible token that may be traded on a marketplace.

The **Asset Management** segment generates revenues from UIAs through block rewards and transaction fees by mining primarily Bitcoin. The company also earns a margin from staking, lending, UIA securitizations and financial engineering utilizing Bitcoin, Ethereum, stable coins and other cryptocurrency assets.

The **Data Centre and Custodian** segment works with third party data centres and custodians to maintain the integrity of company-owned UIAs. Wholly owned **WestBlock Capital Inc.**, which operates a 15-MW cryptocurrency mining and hosting facility in Shiprock, N.M., acts as a custodian and operator for the company-owned and third party cryptocurrency miners.

Predecessor Detail - Name changed from AX1 Capital Corp., Mar. 26, 2019, pursuant to the reverse takeover acquisition of Luxxfolio Network Inc.

Directors - Geoffrey McCord, CFO & interim CEO, Ont.

Other Exec. Officers - Dean Linden, co-founder & chief commun. strategist

Capital Stock

	Authorized (shs.)	Outstanding (shs.)[1]
Common	unlimited	86,717,944

[1] At Feb. 28, 2023

Major Shareholder - Widely held at Mar. 31, 2023.

Price Range - LUXX/CSE

Year	Volume	High	Low	Close
2022	66,932,561	$0.52	$0.01	$0.01
2021	74,190,723	$1.21	$0.17	$0.48
2020	5,695,618	$0.59	$0.01	$0.48
2019	1,695,987	$0.20	$0.01	$0.03

Recent Close: $0.02

Capital Stock Changes - In December 2021, bought deal public offering of 13,600,000 units (1 common share & ½ warrant) at Cdn$0.70 per unit was completed, including 600,000 units on exercise of over-allotment option, with warrants exercisable at Cdn$1.00 per share for two years. Net proceeds would be used working capital requirements and for the development, sustaining capital and maintenance of the company's Bitcoin mining operation. In June 2022, private placement of 12,500,000 units (1 common share & 1 warrant) at Cdn$0.16 per unit was completed, with warrants exercisable at Cdn$0.21 per share for two years.

Wholly Owned Subsidiaries

Luxxfolio Network Inc., B.C.

WestBlock Capital Inc., Calgary, Alta.

- 100% int. in **WestBlock Hosting Arizona Inc.**
  - 100% int. in **WestBlock, LLC**
- 100% int. in **WestBlock Hosting Inc.**

Financial Statistics

Periods ended:	12m Aug. 31/21[A]		12m Aug. 31/20[oA]
	US$000s	%Chg	US$000s
Operating revenue	**607**	**n.a.**	**nil**
Salaries & benefits	45		nil
Research & devel. expense	(30)[1]		8
General & admin expense	1,027		68
Stock-based compensation	899		nil
Operating expense	**1,941**	**n.m.**	**77**
Operating income	**(1,334)**	**n.a.**	**(77)**
Deprec., depl. & amort.	144		nil
Finance costs, gross	350		nil
Pre-tax income	**(1,828)**	**n.a.**	**(101)**
Net income	**(1,828)**	**n.a.**	**(101)**
Cash & equivalent	314		95
Accounts receivable	64		nil
Current assets	1,908		98
Fixed assets, net	3,229		nil
Intangibles, net	4,622		nil
Total assets	**18,528**	**n.m.**	**98**
Accts. pay. & accr. liabs	542		22
Current liabilities	4,757		22
Long-term debt, gross	8,958		nil
Long-term debt, net	4,742		nil
Shareholders' equity	9,029		76
Cash from oper. activs	**(1,207)**	**n.a.**	**(110)**
Cash from fin. activs	12,091		123
Cash from invest. activs	(10,666)		nil
Net cash position	**314**	**+231**	**95**
Capital expenditures	(10,805)		nil
	US$		US$
Earnings per share*	(0.06)		(0.01)
Cash flow per share*	(0.04)		(0.01)
	shs		shs
No. of shs. o/s*	49,415,475		17,647,415
Avg. no. of shs. o/s*	30,345,126		17,099,420
	%		%
Net profit margin	(301.15)		n.a.
Return on equity	(40.37)		n.m.
Return on assets	(15.96)		(96.15)
Foreign sales percent	100		n.a.

* Common

[o] Restated

[A] Reported in accordance with IFRS

[1] Includes research expense recovery of $43,352 through the Scientific Research and Experimental Development (SR&ED) program.

Latest Results

Periods ended:	3m Nov. 30/21[A]		3m Nov. 30/20[oA]
	US$000s	%Chg	US$000s
Operating revenue	3,525	n.a.	nil
Net income	951	n.a.	(10)
	US$		US$
Earnings per share*	0.02		(0.00)

* Common

[o] Restated

[A] Reported in accordance with IFRS

Historical Summary
(as originally stated)

Fiscal Year	Oper. Rev.	Net Inc. Bef. Disc.	EPS*
	US$000s	US$000s	US$
2021[A]	607	(1,828)	(0.06)
	$000s	$000s	$
2020[A]	nil	(136)	(0.01)
2019[A1]	nil	(1,038)	(0.08)
2018[A2,3]	nil	(1,100)	(0.31)

* Common

[A] Reported in accordance with IFRS

[1] Results reflect the Apr. 11, 2019, reverse takeover acquisition of Luxxfolio Network Inc.

[2] 39 weeks ended Aug. 31, 2018.

[3] Results pertain to Luxxfolio Network Inc.

L.54 Lynx Global Digital Finance Corporation

Symbol - LYNX **Exchange** - CSE (S) **CUSIP** - 55183P

Head Office - 303-595 Howe St, Vancouver, BC, V6C 2T5 **Telephone** - (604) 559-8893 **Toll-free** - (888) 273-1332

Website - lynxglobal.io

Email - mpenner@lynxglobal.io

Investor Relations - Michael Penner (604) 396-9974

Lawyers - W.L. Macdonald Law Corporation, Vancouver, B.C.

Transfer Agents - National Securities Administrators Ltd., Vancouver, B.C.

Profile - (B.C. 2016) Developing Lynx digital payment platform which supports multiple payment types primarily in Southeast Asia and Ocenia.

The Lynx platform has a full suite of payment solutions including virtual assets licences which allows for cryptocurrency and non-fungible token exchange and custody; business licences for domestic, cross-border and international money transfer; card issuing; full e-commerce marketplace payment and business management suite; and processing of merchant credit card payments.

The company's legacy revenue-generating product is BloomKit™, a cloud-based solution that can link any online industry sector to consumers by way of its marketplace solution.

Common suspended from CSE, May 10, 2022.

Predecessor Detail - Name changed from CannaOne Technologies Inc., Apr. 19, 2021.

Directors - Solomon Riby-Williams, co-founder, Vancouver, B.C.; Michael Penner, pres., CEO & chr.; Christopher P. (Chris) Cherry, CFO & corp. sec., Vancouver, B.C.; Christoper Share Aldaba, B.C.; Dr. Georg Hochwimmer, Munich, Germany

Other Exec. Officers - Scott Williamson, co-founder & v-p, technical opers.; John Schaub, chief product officer

Capital Stock

	Authorized (shs.)	Outstanding (shs.)[1]
Common	unlimited	115,652,943

[1] At Aug. 23, 2023

Major Shareholder - Raymond A. Babst held 13.71% interest at May 7, 2021.

Price Range - LYNX/CSE (S)

Year	Volume	High	Low	Close
2022	20,192,097	$0.29	$0.05	$0.06
2021	44,582,532	$1.55	$0.11	$0.27
2020	2,744,352	$0.35	$0.04	$0.10
2019	14,854,665	$1.84	$0.23	$0.24
2018	255,999	$1.07	$0.55	$1.07

Wholly Owned Subsidiaries

Ausphil Technologies Inc., Philippines.

- 52.15% int. in **Binangonan Rural Bank**, Philippines.

Subsidiaries

51% int. in **Arkin technologies Pty Ltd.**, Australia.

51% int. in **Direct Agent 5 Inc.**, Makati City, Philippines.

51% int. in **Payright Pte. Ltd.**, Singapore.

51% int. in **Vasu International Payments Solutions Inc.**, Philippines.

Investments

21.62% int. in **StyloPay Limited**, London, Middx., United Kingdom.

M

M.1 M Split Corp.

Symbol - XMF.A **Exchange** - TSX **CUSIP** - 55376A
Head Office - c/o Quadravest Capital Management Inc., 2510-200 Front St W, PO Box 51, Toronto, ON, M5V 3K2 **Telephone** - (416) 304-4440 **Toll-free** - (877) 478-2372
Website - www.quadravest.com
Email - info@quadravest.com
Investor Relations - Shari Payne (877) 478-2372
Auditors - PricewaterhouseCoopers LLP C.A., Toronto, Ont.
Lawyers - Blake, Cassels & Graydon LLP, Toronto, Ont.
Transfer Agents - Computershare Trust Company of Canada Inc., Toronto, Ont.
Investment Managers - Quadravest Capital Management Inc., Toronto, Ont.
Managers - Quadravest Capital Management Inc., Toronto, Ont.
Profile - (Ont. 2007) Holds common shares of **Manulife Financial Corporation** in order to provide a stable yield and downside protection for preferred shareholders and to enable capital shareholders to participate in any capital appreciation of Manulife's common shares and to benefit from any increases in the dividends paid by Manulife on its common shares.

At Nov. 30, 2022, the company held 544,900 common shares of **Manulife Financial Corporation** with a market value of $13,202,927. To supplement the dividends earned on the investment portfolio and to reduce risk, the company may from time to time write covered call options in respect of all or a part of the common shares of Manulife it holds.

The company terminates on Dec. 1, 2024, or earlier if the class I preferred shares, class II (2014) preferred shares or capital (2014) shares are delisted by the TSX or if the net asset value of the company declines to less than $5,000,000. At such time all outstanding class I preferred shares, class II (2014) preferred shares and capital (2014) shares will be redeemed. The termination date may be extended beyond Dec. 1, 2024, for a further five years and thereafter for additional successive periods of five years as determined by the board of directors.

The investment manager receives a management fee at an annual rate equal to 0.45% of the net asset value of the company calculated and payable monthly in arrears. In addition, the manager receives an administration fee at an annual rate equal to 0.1% of the net asset value of the company calculated and payable monthly in arrears, as well a service fee payable to dealers on the capital (2014) shares at a rate of 0.5% per annum.

Directors - S. Wayne Finch, chr., pres. & CEO, Caledon, Ont.; Laura L. Johnson, corp. sec., Oakville, Ont.; Peter F. Cruickshank, Oakville, Ont.; Michael W. Sharp, Toronto, Ont.; John D. Steep, Stratford, Ont.
Other Exec. Officers - Silvia Gomes, CFO

Capital Stock

	Authorized (shs.)	Outstanding (shs.)[1]
Class I Preferred	unlimited	2,275,889[2]
Class II (2014) Preferred	unlimited	2,275,889[2]
Class B	1,000	1,000[2]
Capital (2014)	unlimited	2,275,889

[1] At Feb. 23, 2023
[2] Classified as debt.

Class I Preferred - Entitled to receive fixed cumulative preferential monthly dividends of $0.03125 per share (to yield 7.50% per annum on the $5.00 issue price). Redeemable on Dec. 1, 2024, for $5.00. Retractable on the last business day of each month at the lesser of (i) $5.00, and (ii) 97% of the net asset value (NAV) per unit (one class I preferred share, one class II (2014) preferred share and one capital (2014) share) less the cost to the company of the purchase of a class II (2014) preferred share and a capital (2014) share in the market for cancellation. Shareholders who concurrently retract a class I preferred share, a class II (2014) preferred share and a capital (2014) share in October of each year will receive an amount equal to the NAV per unit. Rank in priority to the capital (2014) shares, the class II (2014) preferred shares and the class B shares with respect to the payment of dividends and the repayment of capital upon dissolution, liquidation or winding-up of the company.
Class II (2014) Preferred - Entitled to receive fixed cumulative preferential monthly dividends of $0.03125 per share (to yield 7.50% per annum on the $5.00 notional issue price if and when the NAV per unit exceeds $10). Redeemable on Dec. 1, 2024, for the original issue price of $5.00. Retractable on the last business day of each month at the lesser of (i) $5.00, and (ii) 97% of the NAV per unit less the cost to the company of the purchase of a class I preferred share and a capital (2014) share in the market for cancellation. Shareholders who concurrently retract a class I preferred share, a class II (2014) preferred share and a capital (2014) share in October of each year will receive an amount equal to the NAV per unit. Rank subsequent to the class I preferred shares and in priority to the class B shares and the capital (2014) shares with respect to the payment of dividends and the repayment of capital upon dissolution, liquidation or winding-up of the company.
Class B - Not entitled to receive dividends. Retractable at $1.00 per share and have a liquidation entitlement of $1.00 per share. Rank subsequent to the class I preferred shares and the class II (2014) preferred shares and prior to the capital (2014) shares with respect to repayment of capital on the dissolution, liquidation or winding-up of the company. One vote per share.
Capital (2014) - Dividends on the capital shares may be reinstated only if and when the NAV per unit exceeds $15, and the dividend rate would be set by the board of directors at its discretion. No dividend payments will be made on the capital (2014) shares unless all dividends on the class I preferred shares and, if applicable, class II (2014) preferred shares have been declared and paid. Retractable on the last business day of each month at a price equal to 97% of the NAV per unit less the cost to the company of the purchase of a class I preferred share and a class II (2014) preferred share in the market for cancellation. Shareholders who concurrently retract a class I preferred share, a class II (2014) preferred share and a capital (2014) share in October of each year will receive an amount equal to the NAV per unit. Entitled to receive upon final redemption the balance, if any, of the value of the company remaining after paying the class I and class II (2014) preferred share repayment amounts and the nominal issue price of the class B shares to the holders thereof. Rank subordinate to the class I preferred shares, the class II (2014) preferred shares and the class B shares with respect to the payment of dividends and the repayment of capital upon dissolution, liquidation or winding-up of the company.
Major Shareholder - M Split Corp. Holding Trust held 100% interest at Feb. 23, 2023.

Price Range - XMF.A/TSX

Year	Volume	High	Low	Close
2022............	105,378	$0.28	$0.15	$0.15
2021............	432,372	$0.50	$0.19	$0.21
2020............	602,198	$0.49	$0.11	$0.49
2019............	564,270	$0.47	$0.14	$0.15
2018............	628,462	$0.86	$0.17	$0.17

Consolidation: 0.72292-for-1 cons. in Dec. 2019
Recent Close: $0.18
Capital Stock Changes - There were no changes to capital stock during fiscal 2021 or fiscal 2022.

Dividends

XMF.PR.B pfd I cum. ret. Ra $0.375 pa M

Financial Statistics

Periods ended:	12m Nov. 30/22[A]		12m Nov. 30/21[A]
	$000s	%Chg	$000s
Realized invest. gain (loss)..............	40		(276)
Unrealized invest. gain (loss)...........	556		453
Total revenue..............................	**1,361**	**+52**	**895**
General & admin. expense..............	183		185
Other operating expense.................	90		112
Operating expense........................	**273**	**-8**	**297**
Operating income.........................	**1,088**	**+82**	**598**
Finance costs, gross........................	1,087		598
Net income..................................	**nil**	**n.a.**	**nil**
Cash & equivalent............................	1,131		218
Accounts receivable.........................	180		198
Investments......................................	13,303		13,711
Total assets..................................	**14,513**	**+3**	**14,127**
Accts. pay. & accr. liabs..................	31		31
Debt..	14,242		14,008
Cash from oper. activs..................	**1,766**	**+77**	**999**
Cash from fin. activs........................	(853)		(853)
Net cash position..........................	**1,131**	**+419**	**218**
	$		$
Earnings per share*.........................	nil		nil
Cash flow per share*........................	0.78		0.44
	shs		shs
No. of shs. o/s*...............................	2,275,889		2,275,889
Avg. no. of shs. o/s*........................	2,275,889		2,275,889
	%		%
Net profit margin.............................	n.a.		n.a.
Return on equity..............................	n.m.		n.m.
Return on assets..............................	n.m.		n.m.

* Capital
[A] Reported in accordance with IFRS

Note: Net income reflects increase/decrease in net assets from operations.

Historical Summary
(as originally stated)

Fiscal Year	Total Rev.	Net Inc. Bef. Disc.	EPS*
	$000s	$000s	$
2022[A]..................	1,361	nil	nil
2021[A]..................	895	nil	nil
2020[A]..................	(2,527)	nil	nil
2019[A]..................	4,339	nil	nil
2018[A]..................	(3,874)	nil	nil

* Capital
[A] Reported in accordance with IFRS
Note: Adjusted throughout for 0.72292-for-1 cons. in Dec. 2019

M.2 M3 Capital Corp.

Symbol - MCT.P **Exchange** - TSX-VEN **CUSIP** - 55378U
Head Office - 800-333 7 Ave SW, Calgary, AB, T2P 2Z1 **Telephone** - (587) 225-2865
Email - jchow@tehchiagroup.com
Investor Relations - Jimmy Chow (587) 225-2865
Auditors - De Visser Gray LLP C.A., Vancouver, B.C.
Transfer Agents - Computershare Trust Company of Canada Inc., Calgary, Alta.
Profile - (Alta. 2021) Capital Pool Company.
Common listed on TSX-VEN, Dec. 12, 2022.
Directors - Morris Chia, CEO, Winnipeg, Man.; Jimmy Chow, CFO & corp. sec., Calgary, Alta.; V. E. Dale Burstall, Calgary, Alta.; Armin W. Martens, Winnipeg, Man.

Capital Stock

	Authorized (shs.)	Outstanding (shs.)[1]
Common	unlimited	15,620,200

[1] At Dec. 12, 2022

Major Shareholder - Widely held at Dec. 12, 2022.
Recent Close: $0.10
Capital Stock Changes - On Dec. 12, 2022, an initial public offering of 10,000,000 common shares was completed at 10¢ per share.

M.3 MAV Beauty Brands Inc.

Symbol - MAV **Exchange** - TSX **CUSIP** - 57767U
Head Office - 810-100 New Park Pl, Vaughan, ON, L4K 0H9 **Telephone** - (416) 347-8954 **Toll-free** - (888) 295-8856
Website - mavbeautybrands.com
Email - ir@mavbeautybrands.com
Investor Relations - Craig Armitage (416) 347-8954
Auditors - Ernst & Young LLP C.A., Toronto, Ont.
Transfer Agents - TSX Trust Company, Toronto, Ont.
FP500 Revenue Ranking - 745
Employees - 73 at Dec. 31, 2022
Profile - (B.C. 2016) Manages and markets hair care, body care and beauty products under the brands Marc Anthony True Professional, Renpure, Cake Beauty and The Mane Choice.

Products include hair care, body care and beauty products such as shampoo, conditioner, hair styling products, treatments, body wash, and body and hand lotion across multiple collections, and are sold in more than 25 countries around the world, through major retailers. Products are primarily sold in North America through food, drug and mass (FDM), club, dollar, off-price, specialty and online channels, and internationally through partnerships with leading distributors. The company uses multiple third-party suppliers and manufacturers based in North America and Asia to source and manufacture all of its products.

Marc Anthony True Professional is a brand that offers professional quality hair care products to consumers. Renpure is a personal care brand that offers plant-based or plant-derived, naturally-inspired hair and body care products. Cake Beauty is a luxe lifestyle beauty brand that offers hair, body, bath and skin care products that contain natural, cruelty-free and vegan ingredients. The Mane Choice is a hair care brand that serves the wavy to textured hair care market.

Directors - Chris Elshaw, chr., N.Y.; Jeffrey Barber, Mass.; Kathy Mayor, Fla.; Stephen A. (Steve) Smith, Toronto, Ont.
Other Exec. Officers - Serge Jureidini, pres. & CEO; Laurel MacKay-Lee, CFO

Capital Stock

	Authorized (shs.)	Outstanding (shs.)[1]
Preferred	unlimited	nil
Proportionate Vtg.	unlimited	3,178
Common	unlimited	36,853,401
Exchangeable Unit		2,463,963[2]

[1] At May 9, 2023
[2] Securities of subsidiary MAV Midco Holdings, LLC

Proportionate Voting - Convertible into common shares on a 1,000-for-1 basis. Entitled to 1,000 times the amount paid or distributed per common share with respect to dividends or liquidation, etc. 1,000 votes per share.
Common - Convertible into proportionate voting shares on a 1-for-1,000 basis. One vote per share.
Class B Exchangeable Unit - Issued by subsidiary MAV Midco Holdings, LLC. Exchangeable into common shares of the company on a 1-for-1 basis, subject to certain terms and conditions. Restrictions expire at the rate of 20% per quarter.
Major Shareholder - TA Associates Management, L.P. held 31.8% interest and Marc Anthony Venere held 26% interest at Apr. 27, 2023.

Price Range - MAV/TSX

Year	Volume	High	Low	Close
2022............	4,913,632	$1.30	$0.34	$0.45
2021............	5,711,602	$7.34	$1.16	$1.17
2020............	4,492,789	$5.60	$1.78	$4.90
2019............	20,002,203	$10.74	$2.25	$4.05
2018............	6,397,845	$14.15	$9.50	$10.68

Recent Close: $0.09

Capital Stock Changes - During 2022, 88,732 common shares were issued for cash.

Wholly Owned Subsidiaries

Marc Anthony Cosmetics Ltd., B.C.
- 100% int. in **Marc Anthony Cosmetics USA, Inc.**, Del.
  - 94.9% int. in **MAV Midco Holdings, LLC**, Del.
    - 100% int. in **The Mane Choice Hair Solution, LLC**, United States.
    - 100% int. in **Renpure, LLC**, Del.
    - 5.1% int. in **TMC Newco, LLC**, Del.

Financial Statistics

Periods ended:	12m Dec. 31/22[A]		12m Dec. 31/21[A]
	US$000s	%Chg	US$000s
Operating revenue	**90,692**	**-15**	**107,156**
Cost of sales	52,201		63,179
General & admin expense	26,199		27,302
Stock-based compensation	1,559		810
Operating expense	**26,199**	**-71**	**91,291**
Operating income	**64,493**	**+307**	**15,865**
Deprec., depl. & amort.	4,381		4,385
Finance costs, gross	7,804		6,566
Pre-tax income	**(147,927)**	**n.a.**	**(121,657)**
Income taxes	7,912		(24,021)
Net income	**(155,839)**	**n.a.**	**(97,636)**
Cash & equivalent	10,483		11,982
Inventories	31,573		33,703
Accounts receivable	14,586		18,316
Current assets	58,776		66,980
Fixed assets, net	2,218		2,876
Right-of-use assets	2,145		2,456
Intangibles, net	61,024		209,691
Total assets	**125,234**	**-57**	**294,460**
Accts. pay. & accr. liabs	11,408		13,794
Current liabilities	18,089		21,350
Long-term debt, gross	124,640		132,321
Long-term debt, net	118,215		125,896
Long-term lease liabilities	2,204		2,704
Shareholders' equity	(13,274)		139,543
Cash from oper. activs	**8,090**	**+26**	**6,406**
Cash from fin. activs	(8,490)		(10,352)
Cash from invest. activs	(1,099)		(3,146)
Net cash position	**10,483**	**-13**	**11,982**
Capital expenditures	(187)		(568)
	US$		US$
Earnings per share*	(4.24)		(2.66)
Cash flow per share*	0.22		0.17
	shs		shs
No. of shs. o/s*	36,853,401		36,764,669
Avg. no. of shs. o/s*	36,765,641		36,764,669
	%		%
Net profit margin	(171.83)		(91.12)
Return on equity	n.m.		(52.07)
Return on assets	(70.35)		(25.63)
No. of employees (FTEs)	73		83

* Common
[A] Reported in accordance with IFRS

Latest Results

Periods ended:	3m Mar. 31/23[A]		3m Mar. 31/22[A]
	US$000s	%Chg	US$000s
Operating revenue	19,255	-9	21,137
Net income	(3,869)	n.a.	(632)
	US$		US$
Earnings per share*	(0.10)		(0.02)

* Common
[A] Reported in accordance with IFRS

Historical Summary
(as originally stated)

Fiscal Year	Oper. Rev.	Net Inc. Bef. Disc.	EPS*
	US$000s	US$000s	US$
2022[A]	90,692	(155,839)	(4.24)
2021[A]	107,156	(97,636)	(2.66)
2020[A]	116,543	6,506	0.18
2019[A]	108,496	4,072	0.11
2018[A]	94,039	(10,402)	(0.43)

* Common
[A] Reported in accordance with IFRS

M.4 MCAN Mortgage Corporation*

Symbol - MKP **Exchange** - TSX **CUSIP** - 579176
Head Office - 600-200 King St W, Toronto, ON, M5H 3T4 **Telephone** - (416) 572-4880 **Toll-free** - (855) 213-6226 **Fax** - (416) 598-4142
Website - mcanfinancial.com
Email - spinto@mcanfinancial.com
Investor Relations - Sylvia Pinto (855) 213-6226
Auditors - Ernst & Young LLP C.A., Toronto, Ont.
Bankers - Bank of Montreal, Toronto, Ont.
Lawyers - Goodmans LLP, Toronto, Ont.
Transfer Agents - Computershare Trust Company of Canada Inc., Toronto, Ont.
FP500 Revenue Ranking - 692
Employees - 128 at Dec. 31, 2022

Profile - (Can. 1991, via Federal Loan Companies Act) Operates as a loan company under the Trust and Loan Companies Act (Canada) and as a mortgage investment company under the Income Tax Act (Canada).

The company has three lines of business: MCAN Home, MCAN Capital and MCAN Wealth. These businesses include mortgage lending including residential, residential construction, non-residential construction and commercial loans, as well as investing in securities, loans and real estate investments.

MCAN Home - Wholly owned **MCAN Home Mortgage Corporation** (formerly **XMC Mortgage Corporation**) originates insured and uninsured residential mortgages through an exclusive mortgage broker network across Canada.

MCAN Capital - Provides construction loans (residential and non-residential) and commercial loans, which include multi family residential loans and other commercial loans such as term mortgages secured by retail and industrial buildings and higher yielding mortgage loans, as well as invests in real estate investment trusts (REITs) and private real estate development and mortgage funds focused on lending to and developing Canadian communities. Also includes 13.65% equity investment in **MCAP Commercial Limited Partnership**, Canada's largest independent mortgage finance company (majority owned by Caisse de dépôt et placement du Québec).

MCAN Wealth - Offers investors Canada Deposit Insurance Corporation (CDIC) insured term deposits sourced through a broker distribution network across Canada consisting of third party deposit agents and financial advisors.

Breakdown of corporate mortgage portfolio:

At Dec. 31:	2022	2021
Product Type	$000s	$000s
Residential - uninsured	865,220	832,492
Residential - insured	144,569	196,595
Construction	825,126	684,298
Commercial - multi family	98,238	74,696
Commercial - other	6,341	18,065
	1,939,494	1,806,146

Geographic distribution of corporate mortgage portfolio at Dec. 31, 2022:

Region	Percentage
Ontario	57.6%
British Columbia	29.4%
Alberta	11%
Quebec	1.2%
Atlantic Canada	0.3%
Other	0.5%
	100%

At Dec. 31, 2022, the company's securitization mortgage portfolio totaled $1.751 billion ($1.584 billion at Dec. 31, 2021).

During 2022, the company invested in **Crown Realty V Limited Partnership**, which integrates environmental, social and governance (ESG) initiatives to acquire, lease, manage and reposition commercial real estate properties across Ontario, representing a 7.7% partnership interest; **TAS Impact Development LP 4**, which acquires residential, mixed-use development and repositioning properties with a focus on developing and repositioning assets that drive ESG impacts, representing a 17.6% partnership interest; **Broccolini Limited Partnership No. 8**, which manages real estate development funds primarily focused on ground up development of industrial, residential and mixed-use properties across Canada, representing a 5.7% partnership interest; **Harbour Equity JV Development Fund VI**, which provides equity capital to real estate developers for ground up development of residential and mixed-use properties across Canada, representing a 12.1% partnership interest; and **Fiera Real Estate Development Fund IV, LP**, which develops and redevelops multi-residential, industrial, office and retail properties in Canada, representing a 7.1% partnership interest.

Effective Apr. 1, 2022, the company commenced doing business as MCAN Financial Group and wholly owned **XMC Mortgage Corporation** changed its name to **MCAN Home Mortgage Corporation**.

Predecessor Detail - Name changed from MCAP Inc., Sept. 15, 2006.

Directors - Derek G. Sutherland, chr. & interim CEO, Toronto, Ont.; John E. Coke†, Toronto, Ont.; Bonnie Agostinho, Burlington, Ont.; Brian W. Chu, Toronto, Ont.; Glenn Doré, Montréal, Qué.; Philip C. Gillin, Toronto, Ont.; Gordon J. Herridge, Peachland, B.C.; Gaelen J. Morphet, Toronto, Ont.

Other Exec. Officers - Carl Brown, sr. v-p, invests. & corp. devel.; Avish Buck, sr. v-p, COO & pres., MCAN Home Mortgage Corporation; Floriana G. Cipollone, sr. v-p & CFO; Aaron Corr, v-p & chief risk officer; Paul Gill, v-p, IT; Michael E. (Mike) Jensen, v-p & chief compliance officer; Nazeera Khan, v-p & chief audit officer; Michelle Liotta, v-p, HR; Sylvia Pinto, v-p, corp. sec. & governance officer; Alysha Rahim, v-p, fin.; Peter Ryan, v-p & contr.; Justin A. Silva, v-p & treas.
† Lead director

Capital Stock

	Authorized (shs.)	Outstanding (shs.)[1]
Common	unlimited	34,804,642

[1] At May 8, 2023

Major Shareholder - KingSett Capital Inc. held 12.85% interest at Aug. 1, 2023.

Price Range - MKP/TSX

Year	Volume	High	Low	Close
2022	7,796,243	$19.49	$14.00	$15.00
2021	6,164,288	$19.31	$15.41	$17.23
2020	4,246,968	$17.25	$10.36	$15.77
2019	3,974,750	$17.53	$13.31	$17.10
2018	5,123,242	$19.46	$12.21	$13.32

Recent Close: $16.19

Capital Stock Changes - In December 2022, 2,450,407 common shares were issued at $14 per share pursuant to a rights offering. Also during 2022, common shares were issued as follows: 1,522,308 as stock dividend, 458,781 under dividend reinvestment plan, 236,600 under an at-the-market program and 16,669 under executive share purchase plan.

Dividends

MKP com Ra $1.52 pa Q est. Sept. 29, 2023**
Prev. Rate: $1.44 est. Mar. 31, 2022
Prev. Rate: $1.36 est. Mar. 30, 2020
stk.[1]◆ Mar. 31/22 stk.[2]◆ Mar. 31/21
Paid in 2023: $1.46 2022: $1.42 + stk.◆ + rt. 2021: $1.36 + stk.◆ + rt.

[1] Equiv to $0.97.
[2] Equiv to $0.85.
** Reinvestment Option ◆ Special

Long-Term Debt - At Dec. 31, 2022, the company had no long-term debt.

Wholly Owned Subsidiaries

MCAN Home Mortgage Corporation, Toronto, Ont.

Investments

13.65% int. in **MCAP Commercial Limited Partnership**, Toronto, Ont.

Note: The preceding list includes only the major related companies in which interests are held.

Financial Statistics

Periods ended:	12m Dec. 31/22[A]		12m Dec. 31/21[A]
	$000s	%Chg	$000s
Realized invest. gain (loss)	(1,786)		3,845
Unrealized invest. gain (loss)	(10,288)		10,918
Total revenue	**165,483**	**+8**	**152,870**
Salaries & benefits	19,607		18,364
General & admin. expense	9,030		9,083
Operating expense	**28,637**	**+4**	**27,447**
Operating income	**136,846**	**+9**	**125,423**
Provision for loan losses	(1,069)		460
Finance costs, gross	72,428		52,333
Pre-tax income	**55,066**	**-14**	**63,965**
Income taxes	(288)		(397)
Net income	**55,354**	**-14**	**64,362**
Cash & equivalent	131,953		184,962
Accounts receivable	50		19
Investments	3,896,469		3,553,660
Fixed assets, net	601		628
Properties	435		435
Right-of-use assets	1,453		1,759
Intangibles, net	373		346
Total assets	**4,078,676**	**+7**	**3,808,070**
Bank indebtedness	6,532		57,340
Accts. pay. & accr. liabs	9,078		8,637
Lease liabilities	2,070		2,426
Shareholders' equity	489,310		433,258
Cash from oper. activs	**28,267**	**n.a.**	**(113,571)**
Cash from fin. activs	(90,391)		129,216
Cash from invest. activs	18,065		17,695
Net cash position	**78,210**	**-36**	**122,269**
Capital expenditures	(282)		(161)
	$		$
Earnings per share*	1.77		2.40
Cash flow per share*	0.90		(4.24)
Cash divd. per share*	1.44		1.36
Extra stk. divd. - cash equiv.*	0.97		0.85
Total divd. per share*	**2.41**		**2.21**
	shs		shs
No. of shs. o/s*	34,305,704		29,620,939
Avg. no. of shs. o/s*	31,262,000		26,766,000
	%		%
Net profit margin	33.45		42.10
Return on equity	12.00		16.51
Return on assets	3.25		3.58
No. of employees (FTEs)	128		128

* Common
[A] Reported in accordance with IFRS

Latest Results

Periods ended:	3m Mar. 31/23[A]		3m Mar. 31/22[A]
	$000s	%Chg	$000s
Total revenue	58,965	+57	37,466
Net income	23,277	+50	15,479
	$		$
Earnings per share*	0.67		0.52

* Common
[A] Reported in accordance with IFRS

Historical Summary
(as originally stated)

Fiscal Year	Total Rev.	Net Inc. Bef. Disc.	EPS*
	$000s	$000s	$
2022[A]	165,483	55,354	1.77
2021[A]	152,870	64,362	2.40
2020[A]	121,775	42,893	1.75
2019[A]	120,162	48,294	2.01
2018[A]	103,215	36,293	1.54

* Common
[A] Reported in accordance with IFRS

M.5 MCI Onehealth Technologies Inc.

Symbol - DRDR **Exchange** - TSX **CUSIP** - 58118M
Head Office - 300-4881 Yonge St, Toronto, ON, M2N 5X3 **Telephone** - (416) 440-4040
Website - www.mcionehealth.com
Email - scott@mcionehealth.com
Investor Relations - G. Scott Nirenberski (416) 581-8850
Auditors - BDO Canada LLP C.A., Burlington, Ont.
Transfer Agents - Computershare Trust Company of Canada Inc., Toronto, Ont.
Employees - 400 at Sept. 30, 2022
Profile - (Can. 2020; orig. Ont., 2012) Operates medical clinics in Ontario providing healthcare and healthcare related services to patients and employees of corporate customers as well as offering telehealth/virtual care services and digital health and data-driven technologies.

Has 19 medical clinics in Ontario offering in-person, telehealth and virtual care with comprehensive medical and occupational health services. The company serves over 1,000,000 patients and 500 corporate customers, through over 300 physicians and nurses, 400 employees and other third-party healthcare contractors.

Technologies include MCI Connect, a web-based virtual care platform offering telemedicine services, including online consultation and follow-up, online booking and access to electronic medical records; Khure Health, an artificial intelligence (AI)-enabled clinical intelligence platform that allows physicians to rapidly identify and assess patients with rare disease and facilitate more personalized treatment; brightOS, a data analytics platform that enables clinicians and data scientists to visualize and derive insights from de-identified clinical data; and Onehealth Assistant, an AI-powered, data-driven chat application for patient symptom checking and triage that would be integrated into the company's other platforms.

The company also offers executive concierge medicine, technology-enabled rare disease screening, clinical research and pulmonary function testing services.

On July 19, 2023, the company agreed to sell 11 of its 14 primary care medical clinics in southern Ontario to **WELL Health Technologies Corp.** for a purchase price of $1,500,000. The sale was expected to close on or around Oct. 1, 2023. The acquisition brings more than 130 physicians to WELL, adding to over 3,000 providers in WELL's patient services business units across North America. These clinics are expected to generate annual revenue of more than $21,000,000. The company plans to focus on AI-powered healthcare technology and clinical research. The company would complete a 10% convertible debenture financing of between $7,500,000 and $10,000,000, with WELL participating for a minimum of $2,500,000. The companies would also enter into a strategic alliance agreement designed to offer WELL clinics and providers technology from the company. WELL would also be granted an option to acquire up to 30,800,000 class A subordinate voting shares and class B multiple voting shares of the company over time, representing a total voting interest of 81.5%. The exercise of the option is conditional on the achievement by the company of a number of performance milestones.

On June 1, 2023, the company sold wholly owned **MCI Medical Clinics (Alberta) Inc.**, owner and operator of five multidisciplinary primary care clinics in Calgary, Alta., to **WELL Health Technologies Corp.** for $2,000,000.

Directors - Dr. Alexander (Alex) Dobranowski, co-founder & CEO, Toronto, Ont.; Dr. George Christodoulou, exec. co-chr., Toronto, Ont.; Dr. Sven Grail, exec. co-chr., Toronto, Ont.; J. R. Kingsley Ward†, Toronto, Ont.; Bashar Al-Rehany, Mississauga, Ont.; Dr. Robert Francis, Toronto, Ont.; Anthony (Tony) Lacavera, Toronto, Ont.

Other Exec. Officers - G. Scott Nirenberski, CFO & corp. sec.; Saleema Khimji, chief innovation officer; Madeline Walker, pres., MCI Medical

† Lead director

Capital Stock

	Authorized (shs.)	Outstanding (shs.)[1]
Preferred	unlimited	nil
Cl.A Subord. Vtg.	unlimited	53,869,773
Cl.B Multiple Vtg.	unlimited	36,000,000

[1] At May 15, 2023

Class A Subordinate Voting - One vote per share.
Class B Multiple Voting - Nine votes per share. Have no other rights or entitlements.
Major Shareholder - Dr. George Christodoulou held 42.89% interest and Dr. Sven Grail held 41.22% interest at Mar. 31, 2022.

Price Range - DRDR/TSX

Year	Volume	High	Low	Close
2022	1,194,132	$1.60	$0.43	$0.60
2021	9,645,564	$4.93	$1.01	$1.25

Recent Close: $0.39

Wholly Owned Subsidiaries

MCI Medical Clinics Inc., Ont.
- 100% int. in **Khure Health Inc.**, Toronto, Ont.
- 80% int. in **MCI Polyclinic Group Inc.**, Canada.
  - 100% int. in **Canadian Phase Onward Inc.**, Toronto, Ont.
  - 100% int. in **Executive Medical Concierge Canada (2021) Ltd.**, Toronto, Ont.
  - 100% int. in **North York Pulmonary Function Center Inc.**, Toronto, Ont.
  - 100% int. in **The Quit Clinic Inc.**, Toronto, Ont.
- 80% int. in **MCI Prime Urgent Care Clinic Inc.**, Mississauga, Ont.
- 100% int. in **Onehealth Technologies Inc.**, Toronto, Ont.

Investments

Acorn Biolabs, Inc., Toronto, Ont.
ORO Health, Inc., Montréal, Qué.
ReGen Scientific Inc., Toronto, Ont.

Financial Statistics

Periods ended:	12m Dec. 31/21[A]		12m Dec. 31/20[A]
	$000s	%Chg	$000s
Operating revenue	**47,817**	**+24**	**38,573**
Cost of sales	32,806		25,649
Salaries & benefits	12,461		5,828
Research & devel. expense	155		nil
General & admin expense	8,842		6,626
Stock-based compensation	6,111		nil
Operating expense	**60,375**	**+58**	**38,103**
Operating income	**(12,558)**	**n.a.**	**470**
Deprec., depl. & amort.	3,882		2,955
Finance income	109		64
Finance costs, gross	593		607
Pre-tax income	**(16,288)**	**n.a.**	**(1,339)**
Income taxes	(747)		(312)
Net income	**(15,541)**	**n.a.**	**(1,027)**
Net inc. for equity hldrs	**(15,670)**	**n.a.**	**(1,029)**
Net inc. for non-cont. int	**129**	**n.m.**	**2**
Cash & equivalent	7,142		894
Accounts receivable	6,328		3,637
Current assets	16,511		5,778
Long-term investments	4,538		nil
Fixed assets, net	13,931		13,572
Intangibles, net	22,523		640
Total assets	**60,890**	**+172**	**22,358**
Accts. pay. & accr. liabs	9,350		6,872
Current liabilities	14,493		10,743
Long-term lease liabilities	11,261		11,298
Shareholders' equity	29,494		114
Non-controlling interest	1,720		123
Cash from oper. activs	**(7,098)**	**n.a.**	**4,222**
Cash from fin. activs	21,990		(4,222)
Cash from invest. activs	(8,644)		(234)
Net cash position	**7,142**	**+699**	**894**
Capital expenditures	(833)		(85)
	$		$
Earnings per share*	(0.33)		(0.03)
Cash flow per share*	(0.15)		0.11
	shs		shs
No. of shs. o/s*	50,075,202		40,000,000
Avg. no. of shs. o/s*	47,998,837		38,332,737
	%		%
Net profit margin	(32.50)		(2.66)
Return on equity	(105.85)		(91.26)
Return on assets	(35.98)		(2.49)

* Cl.A subord. vtg.
[A] Reported in accordance with IFRS

Latest Results

Periods ended:	9m Sept. 30/22[A]		9m Sept. 30/21[A]
	$000s	%Chg	$000s
Operating revenue	39,421	+16	33,881
Net income	(17,545)	n.a.	(10,730)
Net inc. for equity hldrs	(17,535)	n.a.	(10,709)
Net inc. for non-cont. int	(10)		(21)
	$		$
Earnings per share*	(0.35)		(0.23)

* Cl.A subord. vtg.
[A] Reported in accordance with IFRS

Historical Summary
(as originally stated)

Fiscal Year	Oper. Rev.	Net Inc. Bef. Disc.	EPS*
	$000s	$000s	$
2021[A]	47,817	(15,541)	(0.33)
2020[A]	38,573	(1,027)	(0.03)
2019[A]	46,291	(121)	n.a.
2018[A]	45,060	(242)	n.a.

* Cl.A subord. vtg.
[A] Reported in accordance with IFRS

M.6 MCX Technologies Corporation

Symbol - MCX **Exchange** - TSX-VEN **CUSIP** - 582576
Head Office - 176 South Capital Blvd, Boise, ID, United States, 83702 **Telephone** - (216) 264-0055 **Toll-free** - (866) 526-2655
Website - www.mcxtechnologies.io
Email - cr@mcxtechnologies.io
Investor Relations - Christopher Rowlison (208) 863-6243
Auditors - MaloneBailey, LLP C.P.A., Houston, Tex.
Lawyers - Conrad C. Lysiak, Spokane, Wash.; Davis Wright Tremaine LLP, Seattle, Wash.; McMillan LLP, Vancouver, B.C.
Transfer Agents - Computershare Trust Company of Canada Inc., Vancouver, B.C.; Computershare Trust Company, N.A., Canton, Mass.
Profile - (Calif. 2001) Developing Web 3.0 technologies to create a protocol that is able to connect the metaverse to the physical world. Also delivers digital transformation services to customer-centric organizations through integrated marketing, data science, analytics, commerce and machine learning.

Web 3.0 refers to the next version of the Internet which would focus on decentralization and user ownership. The company focused on developing platforms that: (i) create revenue at every loyalty transaction level between digital and physical interactions; (ii) monetize digital engagement and assets as users interact in both worlds; and (iii) build how users control how data is monetized inside and outside of the metaverse.

Through wholly owned **The Collective Experience, LLC,** provides digital transformation services including brand strategy, data science, pricing science, customer experience management consulting and implementation in support of these strategies. This is the company's sole source of revenue. The company would no longer be signing new client engagements within this segment as of April 2022, as the company was not pursuing this segment to focus on Web 3.0 technologies.

In March 2022, the company sold a vacant land for US$86,530.

Predecessor Detail - Name changed from McorpCX, Inc., Sept. 30, 2020.

Directors - Gregg R. Budoi, chr. & interim CFO, Shaker Heights, Ohio; Christopher Rowlison, CEO, Shaker Heights, Ohio; Shone Anstey, Richmond, B.C.; Susan Olson

Other Exec. Officers - Matthew Kruchko, pres.; Lynn Davison, COO

Capital Stock

	Authorized (shs.)	Outstanding (shs.)[1]
Common	500,000,000	20,426,158

[1] At Aug. 25, 2022

Major Shareholder - Michael Hinshaw held 25.46% interest, Eva Lundin held 14.2% interest and Alex P. Guidi held 13.52% interest at Apr. 14, 2022.

Price Range - MCX/TSX-VEN

Year	Volume	High	Low	Close
2022	603,023	$0.20	$0.03	$0.03
2021	1,496,948	$0.75	$0.08	$0.17
2020	457,200	$0.14	$0.03	$0.08
2019	922,423	$0.15	$0.07	$0.09
2018	949,672	$0.50	$0.10	$0.12

Recent Close: $0.02

Capital Stock Changes - In February 2022, private placement of up to 25,000,000 common shares at US$0.10 per share was announced.

Wholly Owned Subsidiaries

The Collective Experience, LLC, Del.

Financial Statistics

Periods ended:	12m Dec. 31/21[A]		12m Dec. 31/20[A]
	US$000s	%Chg	US$000s
Operating revenue	**752**	**n.m.**	**48**
Cost of goods sold	380		45
Salaries & benefits	39		81
General & admin expense	692		347
Operating expense	**1,112**	**+135**	**474**
Operating income	**(360)**	**n.a.**	**(426)**
Deprec., depl. & amort.	nil		2
Pre-tax income	**(361)**	**n.a.**	**(429)**
Net inc. bef. disc. opers	**(361)**	**n.a.**	**(429)**
Income from disc. opers	nil		384
Net income	**(361)**	**n.a.**	**(45)**
Cash & equivalent	51		298
Accounts receivable	171		nil
Current assets	222		298
Fixed assets, net	85		85
Total assets	**793**	**-30**	**1,125**
Accts. pay. & accr. liabs	164		52
Current liabilities	173		183
Shareholders' equity	620		942
Cash from oper. activs	**(488)**	**n.a.**	**(425)**
Cash from fin. activs	nil		411
Cash from invest. activs	241		(277)
Net cash position	**51**	**-83**	**298**
	US$		US$
Earnings per share*	(0.02)		(0.00)
Cash flow per share*	(0.02)		(0.02)
	shs		shs
No. of shs. o/s*	20,426,158		20,426,158
Avg. no. of shs. o/s*	20,426,158		20,426,158
	%		%
Net profit margin	(48.01)		(893.75)
Return on equity	(46.22)		(46.01)
Return on assets	(37.64)		(36.62)

* Common
[A] Reported in accordance with U.S. GAAP

Latest Results

Periods ended:	6m June 30/22[A]		6m June 30/21[A]
	US$000s	%Chg	US$000s
Operating revenue	93	-70	309
Net income	(312)	n.a.	(109)
	US$		US$
Earnings per share*	(0.02)		(0.01)

* Common
[A] Reported in accordance with U.S. GAAP

Historical Summary
(as originally stated)

Fiscal Year	Oper. Rev.	Net Inc. Bef. Disc.	EPS*
	US$000s	US$000s	US$
2021[A]	752	(361)	(0.02)
2020[A]	48	(429)	(0.02)
2019[A]	3,240	(761)	(0.04)
2018[A]	3,987	(411)	(0.02)
2017[A]	2,514	(411)	(0.02)

* Common
[A] Reported in accordance with U.S. GAAP

M.7 MDA Ltd.*

Symbol - MDA **Exchange** - TSX **CUSIP** - 55292X
Head Office - 9445 Airport Rd, Brampton, ON, L6S 4J3 **Telephone** - (905) 790-4544 **Fax** - (905) 790-4400
Website - www.mda.space
Email - shereen.zahawi@mda.space
Investor Relations - Shereen Zahawi (647) 401-3230
Auditors - KPMG LLP C.A., Vancouver, B.C.
Lawyers - Goodmans LLP
Transfer Agents - TSX Trust Company, Toronto, Ont.
FP500 Revenue Ranking - 422
Profile - (Ont. 2020) Provides advanced space technologies and solutions, serving almost all sectors of the global space market, including robotics, satellite systems and earth observation offerings.

Operations are divided into three business areas: Geointellegence; Robotics and Space Operations; and Satellite Systems.

Geointellegence

Provides end-to-end solutions and services related to Earth observation and intelligence systems, using satellite-generated imagery and data to deliver critical and value-added insights for a wide range of use cases including in the areas of national security, climate change monitoring and maritime surveillance. The Earth observation business includes the collection, processing and dissemination of Earth imagery data from space. Owns and operates worldwide commercial data distribution for the RADARSAT-2 satellite, consisting of 90 billion km^2 of Earth imagery data, and also distributes high resolution optical imagery, satellite-based AIS (automatic identification system) data and radio-frequency data from many other third party missions. The company is also developing CHORUS, a next-generation radar satellite constellation that would provide data continuity for RADSAT-2. Imagery solutions provide customers with timely, accurate and mission-critical information about the changing planet and support a wide variety of uses and sectors, including defense and intelligence, energy and natural resources, industrials, agriculture and forestry, public authorities, services (ex. finance, insurance, news and media) and weather. Also provides defence information solutions, including command and control systems and airborne surveillance solutions. One of the key programs include Canadian Surface Combatant, which was designed integrating electronic warfare suite system for the Royal Canadian Navy warships. In addition, the company also provides advanced aeronautical navigation information solutions for increase safety and efficiency of aircraft landings and departures as well as operates a long endurance unmanned aerial vehicle surveillance service that provides real-time, multi-sensor intelligence to support critical operations.

Robotics and Space Operations

Enables humanity's exploration of space by providing autonomous robotics and vision sensors that operate in space and on the surfaces of the Moon and Mars. Includes technologies for exploration mobility, space manipulation, control and autonomy, perception, robotic interfaces, vision and sensor systems, and on-orbit servicing. Provided robotics on more than 100 space shuttle missions and sensors, which supported 49 space shuttle and ISS missions. Holds patent portfolio for 3D imaging, robotics, on-orbit servicing, and autonomous guidance and navigation of planetary rovers. Products include electro-optic and LiDAR (light detection and ranging) sensors, robotic interfaces, robotic arms, tooling, robotic ground stations and operations services, vision and targeting systems, guidance/navigation/control subsystems and planetary rover locomotion subsystems. Principal customers are Canadian, U.S. and international government agencies, as well as commercial customers in multiple markets.

Satellite Systems

Provides sub-systems and spacecraft to enable space-based technology, solutions and services including next generation communication technologies designed to deliver space-based broadband Internet and direct satellite-to-device connectivity from non geostationary orbit (NGSO), which includes low Earth orbit (LEO) and medium Earth orbit (MEO) satellite constellations as well as solutions that span across the full communication frequency spectrum. Developing a range of digital payload components (ex. channelizer, on-board processor and active antennas) to address industry transition from analog satellites to digital satellites. Supplies satellite systems and sub-systems used in LEO, MEO and geosynchronous orbit (GEO) satellites for commercial and government customers worldwide, including antenna, electronics and payload.

Geointelligence facilities contain satellite mission centres for EO and space observation. Robotics facilities contain space robotics manufacturing, integration and test facilities with simulation capabilities to design, rehearse and troubleshoot on-orbit robotics motion and dynamics, as well as contain a wide range of sensor and autonomous control laboratories, and robotics simulation and virtual reality environments. The Satellite Systems facility in Quebec contains compact and near field ranges for satellite testing, as well as contains a wide range of thermal, environmental, Platform Independent Model, and vibration test facilities and fourth generation manufacturing environment employing robotic assembly to produce high volume NGSO satellite systems. At Mar 31, 2023, the company has integrated into more than 350 satellite missions.

At Mar. 31, 2023, the company had a backlog of $1.232 billion compared with $1.517 billion at Mar. 31, 2022.

Predecessor Detail - Name changed from Neptune Acquisition Holdings Inc., Mar. 19, 2021.

Directors - John C. Risley, chr., Chester, N.S.; Michael (Mike) Greenley, CEO, Ont.; Alison Alfers, Colo.; Yaprak Baltacioglu, Ottawa, Ont.; Darren Farber, Md.; Brendan J. Paddick, Freeport City, Bahamas; Jill D. Smith, Mass.; Louis O. Vachon, Montréal, Qué.

Other Exec. Officers - Anita Bernie, man. dir., U.K.; Vito Culmone, CFO; Cameron Ower, chief tech. officer; Margaret Bailey, v-p, HR; Martin Herman, v-p, legal, gen. counsel & corp. sec.; Holly Johnson, v-p, robotics & space opers.; Amy MacLeod, v-p, corp. commun.; Ian McLeod, v-p, corp. devel.; Pat Nihill, v-p, strategy; Luigi Pozzebon, v-p, satellite sys.; Daniel Smith, v-p, IT; Dr. Minda Suchan, v-p, geointelligence

Capital Stock

	Authorized (shs.)	Outstanding (shs.)[1]
Common	unlimited	119,102,054

[1] At May 11, 2023

Options - At Dec. 31, 2022, options were outstanding to purchase 8,881,616 common shares at a weighted average exercise price of $11.23 per share with a weighted average life of 8 years.

Major Shareholder - Senvest Management, LLC held 11.9% interest at Mar. 31, 2023.

Price Range - MDA/TSX

Year	Volume	High	Low	Close
2022	32,951,186	$11.62	$5.59	$6.40
2021	13,568,128	$18.88	$8.76	$9.50

Recent Close: $10.05

Capital Stock Changes - During 2022, 322,605 common shares were issued as stock-based compensation.

Long-Term Debt - At Dec. 31, 2022, outstanding long-term debt totaled $243,600,000 (none current) and consisted entirely of senior revolving credit facility bearing interest at banker's prime rate or alternate base rate Canada plus an applicable margin of 0.45% to 1.75% or CDOR or LIBOR plus an applicable margin of 1.45% to 2.75%, due May 2027.

Wholly Owned Subsidiaries

Neptune Operations Ltd., B.C.
- 100% int. in **MDA Geospatial Services Inc.**, Canada.
- 100% int. in **MDA Space and Robotics Limited**, United Kingdom.
- 100% int. in **MDA Systems Inc.**, Del.
- 100% int. in **MDA Systems Ltd.**, Canada.
- 100% int. in **MacDonald, Dettwiler and Associates Corporation**, Canada.
- 100% int. in **MacDonald, Dettwiler and Associates Inc.**, Ont.

Note: The preceding list includes only the major related companies in which interests are held.

Financial Statistics

Periods ended:	12m Dec. 31/22[A]		12m Dec. 31/21[oA]
	$000s	%Chg	$000s
Operating revenue	**641,200**	**+34**	**476,900**
Cost of sales	65,400		19,400
Salaries & benefits	323,700		266,200
Research & devel. expense	32,800		21,100
General & admin expense	60,000		58,300
Stock-based compensation	8,500		13,500
Operating expense	**490,400**	**+30**	**378,500**
Operating income	**150,800**	**+53**	**98,400**
Deprec., depl. & amort.	76,200		79,800
Finance costs, gross	34,200		32,200
Pre-tax income	**34,200**	**+203**	**11,300**
Income taxes	7,900		8,400
Net income	**26,300**	**+807**	**2,900**
Cash & equivalent	39,300		83,600
Inventories	7,500		8,000
Accounts receivable	276,500		176,300
Current assets	378,200		293,800
Fixed assets, net	235,100		109,900
Right-of-use assets	7,100		14,800
Intangibles, net	972,300		991,100
Total assets	**1,750,800**	**+14**	**1,534,600**
Accts. pay. & accr. liabs	124,300		71,300
Current liabilities	318,600		225,900
Long-term debt, gross	243,600		144,700
Long-term debt, net	243,600		144,700
Long-term lease liabilities	1,600		7,800
Shareholders' equity	1,000,600		961,700
Cash from oper. activs	**57,000**	**-21**	**72,100**
Cash from fin. activs	78,800		30,600
Cash from invest. activs	(180,100)		(98,800)
Net cash position	**39,300**	**-53**	**83,600**
Capital expenditures	(137,800)		(52,500)
	$		$
Earnings per share*	0.22		0.03
Cash flow per share*	0.48		0.66
	shs		shs
No. of shs. o/s*	119,014,233		118,691,628
Avg. no. of shs. o/s*	119,011,468		109,301,909
	%		%
Net profit margin	4.10		0.61
Return on equity	2.68		0.41
Return on assets	3.20		0.75
Foreign sales percent	53		48
No. of employees (FTEs)	n.a.		2,400

* Common
[o] Restated
[A] Reported in accordance with IFRS

Latest Results

Periods ended:	3m Mar. 31/23[A]		3m Mar. 31/22[A]
	$000s	%Chg	$000s
Operating revenue	201,900	+57	128,400
Net income	16,100	+92	8,400
	$		$
Earnings per share*	0.14		0.07

* Common
[A] Reported in accordance with IFRS

Historical Summary
(as originally stated)

Fiscal Year	Oper. Rev.	Net Inc. Bef. Disc.	EPS*
	$000s	$000s	$
2022[A]	641,200	26,300	0.22
2021[A]	476,900	2,900	0.03
2020[A1,2]	295,600	(17,300)	(0.21)

* Common
[A] Reported in accordance with IFRS
[1] 38 weeks ended Dec. 31, 2020.
[2] As shown in the prospectus dated Apr. 1, 2021. Shares and per share figures adjusted to reflect 1-for-6 share consolidation effective March 2021. Results from Apr. 8, 2020, reflecting the date of indirect acquisition by wholly owned Nepture Operations Ltd. of Maxar Technologies ULC and carrying on of Maxar's Canadian and U.K. businesses.

M.8 MDK Acquisition Inc.

Symbol - MDK.P **Exchange** - TSX-VEN **CUSIP** - 55285V
Head Office - 3369 Huntleigh Crt, North Vancouver, BC, V7H 1C9 **Telephone** - (604) 562-3181
Email - dking@earlystage.ca
Investor Relations - David L. King (604) 562-3181
Auditors - Dale Matheson Carr-Hilton LaBonte LLP C.A., Vancouver, B.C.
Lawyers - DuMoulin Black LLP, Vancouver, B.C.
Transfer Agents - Endeavor Trust Corporation, Vancouver, B.C.
Profile - (B.C. 2022) Capital Pool Company.
Common listed on TSX-VEN, June 28, 2023.
Directors - David L. (Dave) King, CEO & corp. sec., North Vancouver, B.C.; Hani Zabaneh, CFO, North Vancouver, B.C.; Robert (Rob) Barlow, Uxbridge, Ont.; John Burdiga, Calgary, Alta.; Justin Isaacs, Coquitlam, B.C.

Capital Stock

	Authorized (shs.)	Outstanding (shs.)[1]
Common	unlimited	6,210,000

[1] At June 28, 2023

Major Shareholder - ESJT Holdings Ltd. held 11.27% interest and David L. (Dave) King held 11.27% interest at June 28, 2023.
Recent Close: $0.13
Capital Stock Changes - On June 28, 2023, an initial public offering of 2,000,000 common shares was completed at 10¢ per share.

M.9 MEG Energy Corp.*

Symbol - MEG **Exchange** - TSX **CUSIP** - 552704
Head Office - 2100-600 3 Ave SW, Calgary, AB, T2P 0G5 **Telephone** - (403) 770-0446 **Fax** - (403) 264-1711
Website - www.megenergy.com
Email - lyle.yuzdepski@megenergy.com
Investor Relations - Lyle S. Yuzdepski (587) 293-6045
Auditors - PricewaterhouseCoopers LLP C.A., Calgary, Alta.
Lawyers - Burnet, Duckworth & Palmer LLP, Calgary, Alta.
Transfer Agents - Computershare Trust Company of Canada Inc., Toronto, Ont.
FP500 Revenue Ranking - 100
Employees - 429 at Dec. 31, 2022
Profile - (Alta. 1999) Focuses on sustainable in situ oil sands development and production in the southern Athabasca oil sands region of Alberta and is developing enhanced oil recovery projects that utilize steam-assisted gravity drainage (SAGD) extraction methods.

Holds the Christina Lake project, 80 sq. miles, with estimated to support an average of 210,000 bbl per day of sustained bitumen production. Phases 1, 2 and 2B at Christina Lake have a combined bitumen production capacity of 110,000 bbl per day. Phase 3 contemplates a multi-phased development totaling an additional 150,000 bbl per day, which would bring Christina Lake to full production capacity (before accounting for anticipated production increases associated with the production enhancement program). Also holds nearby Surmont project, 32 sq. miles; and 181-sq.-mile May River project, including May River and Thornbury oil sands leases; and 170 sq. miles of additional properties including Duncan, East Kirby and West Kirby oil sands leases.

Phase 2 and Phase 2B at Christina Lake each include an 85-MW cogeneration facility, which produces 42% of the steam for current SAGD operations. The Christina Lake facilities utilize the steam and electricity produced, with surplus power sold into the Alberta power pool.

Power Sales

Year ended Dec. 31	2022	2021
Power sold, $000	144,000	87,000
Power price, $/MWh	162.33	90.10

At Dec. 31, 2022, the company had 328 producing bitumen production wells, 75 non-producing bitumen production wells and 92 gross (83 net) non-producing gas wells. During 2022, 15 stratigraphic test wells, 20 SAGD wells, 10 observation wells and 6 infill wells were drilled. Undeveloped land holdings totaled 235,025 acres at Dec. 31, 2022.

Periods ended:	12m Dec. 31/22	12m Dec. 31/21
Avg. oil prod., bbl/d	95,338	93,733
Avg. oil price, $/bbl[1]	91.95	62.47
Oil reserves, net, mbbl	1,448,400	1,502,700

[1] Before transportation and royalties.

Directors - Ian D. Bruce, chr., Calgary, Alta.; Derek W. Evans, pres. & CEO, Calgary, Alta.; Gary A. Bosgoed, Alta.; Robert B. (Bob) Hodgins, Calgary, Alta.; Kim Lynch Proctor, Calgary, Alta.; Susan M. MacKenzie, Calgary, Alta.; Jeffrey J. McCaig, Calgary, Alta.; James D. (Jim) McFarland, Calgary, Alta.; Diana J. McQueen, Drayton Valley, Alta.
Other Exec. Officers - Darlene M. Gates, COO; Ryan M. Kubik, CFO; David M. Granger, sr. v-p, HR; Lyle S. Yuzdepski, sr. v-p, legal, gen. counsel & corp. sec.; Tom Gear, v-p, opers.

Capital Stock

	Authorized (shs.)	Outstanding (shs.)[1]
Preferred	unlimited	nil
Common	unlimited	285,400,000

[1] At July 27, 2023

Options - At Dec. 31, 2022, options were outstanding to purchase 294,000 common shares at prices ranging from $4.57 to $9.63 per share with a weighted average remaining life of 3.16 years.
Normal Course Issuer Bid - The company plans to make normal course purchases of up to 28,596,214 common shares representing 10% of the public float. The bid commenced on Mar. 10, 2023, and expires on Mar. 9, 2024.
Major Shareholder - Widely held at Mar. 15, 2023.

Price Range - MEG/TSX

Year	Volume	High	Low	Close
2022	699,120,200	$24.47	$11.99	$18.85
2021	575,979,552	$12.34	$4.22	$11.70
2020	929,363,134	$8.07	$1.13	$4.45
2019	638,690,354	$8.62	$4.06	$7.39
2018	535,973,979	$11.70	$4.28	$7.71

Recent Close: $23.15
Capital Stock Changes - During 2022, common shares were issued as follows: 2,867,000 upon vesting and release of restricted and performance share units, 2,003,000 on exercise of options and 20,654,000 common shares were repurchased under a Normal Course Issuer Bid.
Long-Term Debt - Outstanding at Dec. 31, 2022:

7.125% sr. unsecured notes[1]	$785,000,000
5.875% sr. unsecured notes[2]	812,000,000
Less: Unamort. def. debt issue costs	16,000,000
	1,581,000,000
Less: Current portion	3,000,000
	1,578,000,000

[1] US$1.2 billion. Due Feb. 1, 2027.
[2] US$600,000,000. Due Feb. 2, 2029.

Wholly Owned Subsidiaries

MEG Energy (U.S.) Inc., Del.

Financial Statistics

Periods ended:	12m Dec. 31/22[A]		12m Dec. 31/21[A]
	$000s	%Chg	$000s
Operating revenue	**6,118,000**	**+42**	**4,321,000**
Cost of goods sold	3,941,000		2,885,000
General & admin expense	61,000		56,000
Stock-based compensation	36,000		26,000
Operating expense	**4,038,000**	**+36**	**2,967,000**
Operating income	**2,080,000**	**+54**	**1,354,000**
Deprec., depl. & amort	507,000		450,000
Finance income	4,000		2,000
Finance costs, gross	221,000		269,000
Pre-tax income	**1,222,000**	**+234**	**366,000**
Income taxes	320,000		83,000
Net income	**902,000**	**+219**	**283,000**
Cash & equivalent	192,000		361,000
Inventories	185,000		157,000
Accounts receivable	473,000		479,000
Current assets	943,000		1,050,000
Fixed assets, net	5,763,000		5,878,000
Intangibles, net	4,000		5,000
Explor./devel. properties	126,000		126,000
Total assets	**7,033,000**	**-7**	**7,593,000**
Accts. pay. & accr. liabs	617,000		580,000
Current liabilities	654,000		899,000
Long-term debt, gross	1,581,000		2,762,000
Long-term debt, net	1,578,000		2,477,000
Long-term lease liabilities	227,000		244,000
Shareholders' equity	4,383,000		3,808,000
Cash from oper. activs	**1,888,000**	**+174**	**690,000**
Cash from fin. activs	(1,727,000)		(165,000)
Cash from invest. activs	(354,000)		(281,000)
Net cash position	**192,000**	**-47**	**361,000**
Capital expenditures	(376,000)		(331,000)
Capital disposals	6,000		44,000
	$		$
Earnings per share*	2.97		0.92
Cash flow per share*	6.21		2.25
	shs		shs
No. of shs. o/s*	291,081,000		306,865,000
Avg. no. of shs. o/s*	304,000,000		306,000,000
	%		%
Net profit margin	14.74		6.55
Return on equity	22.02		7.74
Return on assets	14.56		6.63
Foreign sales percent	76		57
No. of employees (FTEs)	429		411

* Common
[A] Reported in accordance with IFRS

Latest Results

Periods ended:	6m June 30/23[A]		6m June 30/22[A]
	$000s	%Chg	$000s
Operating revenue	2,771,000	-11	3,102,000
Net income	217,000	-63	587,000
	$		$
Earnings per share*	0.75		1.90

* Common
[A] Reported in accordance with IFRS

Historical Summary
(as originally stated)

Fiscal Year	Oper. Rev.	Net Inc. Bef. Disc.	EPS*
	$000s	$000s	$
2022[A]	6,118,000	902,000	2.97
2021[A]	4,321,000	283,000	0.92
2020[A]	2,292,000	(357,000)	(1.18)
2019[A]	3,931,000	(62,000)	(0.21)
2018[A]	2,732,704	(119,197)	(0.40)

* Common
[A] Reported in accordance with IFRS

M.10 METRO Inc.*

Symbol - MRU **Exchange** - TSX **CUSIP** - 59162N
Head Office - 11011 boul Maurice-Duplessis, Montréal, QC, H1C 1V6 **Telephone** - (514) 643-1000 **Toll-free** - (800) 361-4681 **Fax** - (514) 643-1030
Website - www.corpo.metro.ca
Email - srivet@metro.ca
Investor Relations - Simon Rivet (514) 643-1000
Auditors - Ernst & Young LLP C.A., Montréal, Qué.
Bankers - MUFG Bank, Ltd., Canada Branch; HSBC Bank Canada; Canadian Imperial Bank of Commerce; BNP Paribas; Royal Bank of Canada; Caisse centrale Desjardins; The Toronto-Dominion Bank; Bank of Montreal; National Bank of Canada
Transfer Agents - TSX Trust Company
FP500 Revenue Ranking - 28
Employees - 29,645 at Sept. 24, 2022
Profile - (Que. 1982 amalg.) Operates and services a network of 975 food stores in Quebec and Ontario under several banners including Metro, Metro Plus, Super C, Food Basics, Adonis, Marché Richelieu, Marché Ami, Les 5 Saisons and Première Moisson; and 645 drugstores in Quebec, Ontario and New Brunswick primarily under the Jean Coutu, Brunet, Metro Pharmacy and Food Basics Pharmacy banners.

As a retailer, franchisor and distributor, operates under different grocery banners primarily within the conventional supermarket and discount segments. Supermarkets operate under the banners Metro, Metro Plus (Quebec only) and Adonis in Quebec and Ontario. Discount stores operate under the Super C banner in Quebec and the Food Basics banner in Ontario. In Quebec, also operates neighbourhood stores under the banners Marché Richelieu and Marché Ami, and acts as a distributor for independent neighbourhood grocery stores. In addition, operates artisanal bakeries under the Première Moisson banner in Quebec and Ontario, and a gourmet food emporium under the Les 5 Saisons banner in Quebec. Stores are either owned by the company, by franchisees or by affiliate retailers under franchise or affiliation agreements.

Pharmacy operations include franchised drugstores owned by independent pharmacists operating under the PJC Jean Coutu and PJC Santé banners in Quebec, Ontario and New Brunswick, under the PJC Santé Beauté banner in Quebec and New Brunswick, and under the Brunet, Brunet Plus, Brunet Clinique and Clini Plus banners in Quebec; and company-owned drugstores under the Metro Pharmacy and Food Basics Pharmacy banners which are located within grocery stores in Ontario. In addition, wholly owned **Pro-Doc Ltée**, a generic drug manufacturer, supplies the company, drug wholesalers and pharmacists in Quebec.

Servicing majority of the company's food retail network, the company owns four warehouses for the procurement and storage of grocery products, general merchandise, non-perishable goods and certain dairy products; nine warehouses for the procurement and storage of meat, frozen foods, fruits and vegetables as well as for the supply of neighbourhood grocery stores; a facility for the production of ready-to-eat meals, salads and dips; two distribution centres specializing in Mediterranean and Middle Eastern products; and two food preparation plants for bakery, pastry and deli products. For its pharmacy operations, the company operates two distribution centres in Varennes, Que., which serve company-owned and franchised drugstores.

At Sept. 24, 2022, the company's network consisted of 975 corporate, franchised or affiliated food stores in Quebec (698) and Ontario (277) under the banners Metro (207), Metro Plus (119), Adonis (15), Super C (99), Food Basics (142), Marché Richelieu (53), Marché Ami (314), Première Moisson (24) and Les 5 Saisons (2); and 645 corporate or franchised drugstores in Quebec (532), Ontario (85) and New Brunswick (28) under the banners PJC Jean Coutu (352), PJC Santé (42), PJC Santé Beauté (29), Brunet (70), Brunet Plus (49), Brunet Clinique (21), Clini Plus (6), Metro Pharmacy (46) and Food Basics Pharmacy (30).

On May 25, 2023, the company officially launched its Moi rewards program, an evolution of the metro&moi program launched in 2010. Moi is offered in Quebec in the Metro, Super C, Jean Coutu, Brunet and Première Moisson banners, as well as in Jean Coutu pharmacies in Ontario and New Brunswick. Jean Coutu withdrew from the AIR MILES loyalty program to join Moi. **Royal Bank of Canada** became a partner in Moi and began offering a co-branded moi-RBC credit card to earn bonus points on in-store purchases as well as earn points on purchases at other retailers.

During fiscal 2022, the company opened five new stores, renovated 17 stores and relocated one store. In addition, the company opened four new pharmacies.
Predecessor Detail - Name changed from Métro-Richelieu Inc., Jan. 25, 2000.
Directors - Pierre Boivin, chr., Montréal, Qué.; Eric R. La Flèche, pres. & CEO, Mount Royal, Qué.; Lori-Ann Beausoleil, Toronto, Ont.; Maryse Bertrand, Westmount, Qué.; François J. Coutu, Montréal, Qué.; Michel Coutu, Montréal, Qué.; Stephanie L. Coyles, Toronto, Ont.; Russell

Goodman, Mont-Tremblant, Qué.; Marc Guay, Oakville, Ont.; Christian W. E. Haub, Munich, Germany; Christine A. Magee, Toronto, Ont.; Brian McManus, Beaconsfield, Qué.

Other Exec. Officers - Carmen Fortino, exec. v-p, natl. supply chain & procurement; Marc Giroux, exec. v-p & COO, food; François Thibault, exec. v-p, CFO & treas.; Serge Boulanger, sr. v-p, natl. procurement & corp. brands; Yves Vézina, natl. v-p, logistics & distrib.; Martin Allaire, v-p, real estate & eng.; Marie-Claude Bacon, v-p, public affairs & commun.; Christina Bédard, v-p, eCommerce & digital strategy; Sam Bernier, v-p, technological infrastructure; Geneviève Bich, v-p, HR; Dan Gabbard, v-p, supply chain; Karin Jonsson, v-p & contr.; Frédéric Legault, v-p & CIO; Simon Rivet, v-p, gen. counsel & corp. sec.; Alain Tadros, v-p, mktg.; Jean-Michel Coutu, pres., Jean Coutu Group (PJC) Inc.

Capital Stock

	Authorized (shs.)	Outstanding (shs.)[1]
Preferred	unlimited	nil
Common	unlimited	232,759,000

[1] At Mar. 11, 2023

Options - At Sept. 24, 2022, options were outstanding to purchase 2,092,000 common shares at prices ranging from $40.23 to $62.82 per share with a weighted average remaining life of 47.2 months.

Normal Course Issuer Bid - The company plans to make normal course purchases of up to 7,000,000 common shares representing 3% of the total outstanding. The bid commenced on Nov. 25, 2022, and expires on Nov. 24, 2023.

Major Shareholder - Fidelity Management & Research Company held 17.71% interest at Dec. 2, 2022.

Price Range - MRU/TSX

Year	Volume	High	Low	Close
2022	111,487,569	$78.90	$62.86	$74.97
2021	124,659,976	$68.34	$52.63	$67.32
2020	170,706,350	$66.25	$49.03	$56.80
2019	127,325,124	$59.03	$46.04	$53.59
2018	135,056,018	$48.09	$38.32	$47.34

Recent Close: $69.90

Capital Stock Changes - During fiscal 2022, 538,000 common shares were issued on exercise of options and 107,000 common shares were released from treasury. In addition, 7,000,000 common shares were repurchased under a Normal Course Issuer Bid.

Dividends

MRU com Ra $1.21 pa Q est. Mar. 6, 2023
Prev. Rate: $1.10 est. Mar. 7, 2022
Prev. Rate: $1.00 est. Mar. 8, 2021
Prev. Rate: $0.90 est. Mar. 10, 2020

Long-Term Debt - Outstanding at Sept. 24, 2022:

Revolv. credit facility[1]	$20,900,000
Loans[2]	49,200,000
1.92% Ser.J notes due 2024	285,100,000
3.39% Ser.G notes due 2027	450,000,000
5.97% Ser.B notes due 2035	400,000,000
5.03% Ser.D notes due 2044	300,000,000
4.27% Ser.H notes due 2047	450,000,000
3.41% Ser.I notes due 2050	400,000,000
Less: Deferred financing costs	12,500,000
	2,342,700,000
Less: Current portion	18,200,000
	2,324,500,000

[1] Bearing interest at rates that fluctuate with changes in bankers' acceptance rates and due 2026.

[2] Bearing interest at an average rate of 3.43% and due on various dates through 2060.

Minimum long-term debt repayments were reported as follows:

Fiscal 2023	$18,200,000
Fiscal 2024	22,800,000
Fiscal 2025	301,500,000
Fiscal 2026	1,400,000
Fiscal 2027	900,000
Thereafter	2,025,300,000

Note - In February 2023, private placement of $300,000,000 principal amount of 4.657% series K senior unsecured notes due Feb. 7, 2033, was completed.

Wholly Owned Subsidiaries

The Jean Coutu Group (PJC) Inc., Varennes, Qué.
- 46.5% int. in **Le Groupe Médicus Inc.**, Montréal, Qué.
- 100% int. in **Pro-Doc Ltée**, Laval, Qué.
- 100% int. in **RX Information Centre Ltd.**, Canada.

Metro Brands G.P., Qué.

Metro Ontario Inc., Etobicoke, Ont.
- 100% int. in **Metro Ontario Pharmacies Limited**, Canada.
- 100% int. in **Metro Ontario Real Estate Limited**, Canada.

Metro Richelieu Inc., Canada.
- 100% int. in **Cuisine Centrale Prêt-à-Manger Inc.**, Canada.
- 100% int. in **Groupe Adonis Inc.**, Montréal, Qué.
- 100% int. in **Groupe Phoenicia Inc.**, Montréal, Qué.
- 100% int. in **Groupe Première Moisson Inc.**, Qué.
- 100% int. in **McMahon Distributeur pharmaceutique inc.**, Pointe-aux-Trembles, Qué.
- 100% int. in **Metro Québec Immobilier Inc.**, Montréal, Qué.
- 100% int. in **Metro Québec Real Estate Inc.**, Canada.

Financial Statistics

Periods ended:	52w Sept. 24/22[A]		52w Sept. 25/21[oA]
	$000s	%Chg	$000s
Operating revenue	**18,888,900**	**+3**	**18,283,000**
Cost of sales	15,105,600		14,628,200
Other operating expense	1,964,000		1,929,700
Operating expense	**17,069,600**	**+3**	**16,557,900**
Operating income	**1,819,300**	**+5**	**1,725,100**
Deprec., depl. & amort.	503,300		478,300
Finance income	17,200		14,300
Finance costs, gross	134,800		147,800
Write-downs/write-offs	(70,100)		n.a.
Pre-tax income	**1,153,600**	**+3**	**1,120,700**
Income taxes	304,100		295,000
Net income	**849,500**	**+3**	**825,700**
Net inc. for equity hldrs	**846,100**	**+3**	**823,000**
Net inc. for non-cont. int.	**3,400**	**+26**	**2,700**
Cash & equivalent	13,400		445,800
Inventories	1,331,100		1,169,000
Accounts receivable	775,100		772,000
Current assets	2,183,300		2,466,800
Long-term investments	23,900		43,700
Fixed assets, net	3,457,700		3,129,800
Right-of-use assets	995,100		1,064,700
Intangibles, net	6,040,200		6,155,900
Total assets	**13,401,300**	**-1**	**13,592,100**
Bank indebtedness	100		100
Accts. pay. & accr. liabs	1,575,300		1,546,500
Current liabilities	1,952,500		2,198,200
Long-term debt, gross	2,342,700		2,636,700
Long-term debt, net	2,324,500		2,318,200
Long-term lease liabilities	1,502,700		1,657,500
Shareholders' equity	6,604,500		6,399,900
Non-controlling interest	13,900		12,900
Cash from oper. activs	**1,461,400**	**-8**	**1,583,300**
Cash from fin. activs	(1,416,000)		(1,107,400)
Cash from invest. activs	(477,800)		(471,600)
Net cash position	**13,400**	**-97**	**445,800**
Capital expenditures	(522,900)		(520,000)
Capital disposals	47,500		22,400
Pension fund surplus	160,400		133,600
	$		$
Earnings per share*	3.53		3.34
Cash flow per share*	6.09		6.43
Cash divd. per share*	1.08		0.98
	shs		shs
No. of shs. o/s*	236,594,000		242,949,000
Avg. no. of shs. o/s*	239,900,000		246,200,000
	%		%
Net profit margin	4.50		4.52
Return on equity	13.01		13.12
Return on assets	7.03		6.92
No. of employees (FTEs)	29,645		29,525

* Common
[o] Restated
[A] Reported in accordance with IFRS

Latest Results

Periods ended:	24w Mar. 11/23[A]		24w Mar. 12/22[A]
	$000s	%Chg	$000s
Operating revenue	9,225,400	+7	8,590,800
Net income	449,900	+11	405,800
Net inc. for equity hldrs	448,200	+11	404,100
Net inc. for non-cont. int.	1,700		1,700
	$		$
Earnings per share*	1.91		1.68

* Common
[A] Reported in accordance with IFRS

Historical Summary
(as originally stated)

Fiscal Year	Oper. Rev.	Net Inc. Bef. Disc.	EPS*
	$000s	$000s	$
2022[A]	18,888,900	849,500	3.53
2021[A]	18,283,000	825,700	3.34
2020[A]	17,997,500	796,400	3.15
2019[A]	16,767,500	714,400	2.79
2018[A]	14,383,400	1,718,500	7.20

* Common
[A] Reported in accordance with IFRS

M.11 MINT Income Fund

Symbol - MID.UN **Exchange** - TSX **CUSIP** - 60446Q

Head Office - c/o Middlefield Limited, 1 First Canadian Place, 5800-100 King St W, PO Box 192, Toronto, ON, M5X 1A6 **Telephone** - (416) 362-0714 **Toll-free** - (888) 890-1868 **Fax** - (416) 362-7925

Website - www.middlefield.com

Email - sroberts@middlefield.com

Investor Relations - Sarah Roberts (416) 847-5355

Auditors - Deloitte LLP C.A., Toronto, Ont.

Bankers - The Toronto-Dominion Bank; The Bank of Nova Scotia; Royal Bank of Canada; Canadian Imperial Bank of Commerce; Bank of Montreal

Lawyers - McCarthy Tétrault LLP; Fasken Martineau DuMoulin LLP; DLA Piper (Canada) LLP; Bennett Jones LLP

Transfer Agents - TSX Trust Company

Trustees - Middlefield Limited, Calgary, Alta.

Managers - Middlefield Limited, Calgary, Alta.

Portfolio Advisors - Middlefield Capital Corporation, Toronto, Ont.

Profile - (Ont. 1997) Invests primarily in a diversified portfolio consisting of dividend paying, equity income securities and non-paying securities with capital appreciation potential.

The fund limits investment in the securities of any one issuer to not more than 10% of the total assets. To generate additional returns, the fund may, from time to time, write covered call options in respect of all or part of the common shares in the portfolio.

Top 10 holdings at Mar. 31, 2023 (as a percentage of net asset value):

Holdings	Percentage
Canadian Apartment Properties REIT	4.5%
Middlefield Healthcare Dividend ETF	4.5%
Westshore Terminals Ltd.	4.4%
TransAlta Corporation	4.3%
Blackstone Core+ Real Estate LP	4.3%
Bombardier Inc.	4.1%
Middlefield Health & Wellness ETF	4.1%
Headwater Exploration Inc.	4.1%
AltaGas Ltd.	3.8%
Tourmaline Oil Corp.	3.8%

Predecessor Detail - Name changed from Middlefield High Income Trust, Aug. 26, 2002.

Oper. Subsid./Mgt. Co. Directors - Jeremy T. Brasseur, exec. chr., Toronto, Ont.; Dean Orrico, pres. & CEO, Vaughan, Ont.; Craig Rogers, COO & chief compliance officer, Toronto, Ont.

Capital Stock

	Authorized (shs.)	Outstanding (shs.)[1]
Trust Unit	unlimited	12,284,463
Class A Unit	unlimited	nil

[1] At May 12, 2023

Trust Unit - Entitled to monthly cash distributions of 4¢ per unit. Retractable in November of each year for an amount equal to the net asset value per trust unit, less any costs to fund the retraction. Retractable in any other month for an amount equal to the lesser of: (i) 94% of the weighted average trading price of the shares on TSX during the 15 trading days preceding the retraction date; and (ii) the closing market price per trust unit on the monthly retraction date. One vote per trust unit.

Normal Course Issuer Bid - The company plans to make normal course purchases of up to 1,226,409 trust units representing 10% of the public float. The bid commenced on May 25, 2023, and expires on May 24, 2024.

Major Shareholder - Widely held at Mar. 10, 2023.

Price Range - MID.UN/TSX

Year	Volume	High	Low	Close
2022	3,325,745	$7.33	$6.30	$7.09
2021	3,704,137	$6.95	$5.20	$6.61
2020	3,559,741	$6.51	$4.15	$5.28
2019	6,794,467	$6.79	$5.61	$6.19
2018	7,293,158	$7.28	$5.61	$5.76

Recent Close: $6.94

Capital Stock Changes - During 2022, trust units were issued as follows: 1,229,700 for cash and 2,990 were released from treasury; 1,967,303 trust units were retracted, 73,400 trust units were repurchased under a Normal course Issuer Bid and 500 trust units were repurchased in the market in accordance with the declaration of trust.

Dividends

MID.UN tr unit Ra $0.48 pa M est. Feb. 12, 2016**
** Reinvestment Option

Financial Statistics

Periods ended:	12m Dec. 31/22[A]		12m Dec. 31/21[A]
	$000s	%Chg	$000s
Realized invest. gain (loss)	15,366		10,979
Unrealized invest. gain (loss)	(9,096)		12,789
Total revenue	**9,740**	**-63**	**26,562**
General & admin. expense	1,406		1,127
Other operating expense	275		148
Operating expense	**1,681**	**+32**	**1,276**
Operating income	**8,059**	**-68**	**25,286**
Finance costs, gross	149		136
Pre-tax income	**7,910**	**-69**	**25,151**
Income taxes	55		61
Net income	**7,856**	**-69**	**25,090**
Cash & equivalent	81,004		3,088
Accounts receivable	369		301
Investments	81,004		95,075
Total assets	**89,063**	**-10**	**98,494**
Accts. pay. & accr. liabs	193		149
Debt	5,000		9,750
Shareholders' equity	83,383		88,077
Cash from oper. activs	**22,054**	**+404**	**4,378**
Cash from fin. activs	(17,450)		(3,871)
Net cash position	**7,690**	**+149**	**3,088**
	$		$
Earnings per share*	0.59		1.80
Cash flow per share*	1.65		0.31
Net asset value per share*	6.92		6.85
Cash divd. per share*	0.44		0.48
	shs		shs
No. of shs. o/s*	12,052,748		12,861,261
Avg. no. of shs. o/s*	13,330,427		13,968,143
	%		%
Net profit margin	80.66		94.46
Return on equity	9.16		30.51
Return on assets	8.53		28.72

* Trust unit

[A] Reported in accordance with IFRS

Note: Net income reflects increase /decrease in net assets from operations.

Historical Summary
(as originally stated)

Fiscal Year	Total Rev.	Net Inc. Bef. Disc.	EPS*
	$000s	$000s	$
2022[A]	9,740	7,856	0.59
2021[A]	26,562	25,090	1.80
2020[A]	(6,270)	(8,113)	(0.53)
2019[A]	21,148	18,363	0.94
2018[A]	(10,384)	(14,271)	(0.63)

* Trust unit

[A] Reported in accordance with IFRS

M.12 MPX International Corporation

Symbol - MPXI **Exchange** - CSE **CUSIP** - 55344L
Head Office - 701-5255 Yonge St, Toronto, ON, M2N 6P4 **Telephone** - (416) 840-3725 **Fax** - (877) 595-1828
Website - www.mpxinternationalcorp.com
Email - scott@mpxinternationalcorp.com
Investor Relations - W. Scott Boyes (416) 840-4703
Auditors - Grant Thornton LLP C.A., Toronto, Ont.
Transfer Agents - TSX Trust Company, Toronto, Ont.

Profile - (Ont. 2018) Cultivates, manufactures and markets cannabis products which include cannabinoids as their primary active ingredient.

In Canada, wholly owned **Canveda Inc.** owns and operates a 12,000-sq.-ft. cultivation, processing and distribution facility in Peterborough, Ont., which produces, sells and exports cannabis products, including topicals, extracts and edibles under the Salus BioPharma medical brand, the Strain Rec recreational brand. Products also include Kingsway brand of pre-rolls, Daize brand of full spectrum vapes and Pennies brand of soft gels. Wholly owned **Salus BioPharma Corporation** develops pharmaceutical-grade cannabinoid medicinal products, medicinal preparations and medicinal accessories. The products are targeted at patients that suffer from a variety of conditions such as PTSD, chronic pain, cancer, epilepsy, Parkinson's, Alzheimer's, anorexia and HIV/AIDS. Wholly owned **Spartan Wellness Corporation** and **MCLN Inc.** operate Spartan Network and Medical Cannabis Learning Network, an integrated platform which includes a private online network educational platform providing information about the use of medical cannabis, a telemedicine platform for patients to obtain advice and cannabis prescriptions from medical practitioners, and a sales platform for cannabis licence holders through the fulfillment of medical cannabis prescriptions.

In Switzerland, wholly owned **HolyWorld, S.A.** (dba HolyWeed) owns and operates a production laboratory and developing a manufacturing facility, both located in Geneva, Switzerland. Products include CBD muscle balm, candles, teas, oils, vape cartridges and vape starter packs which are marketed under the HolyWeed brand. Products are sold through its HolyWeed retail store in Geneva, the HolyWeed e-commerce store and the e-commerce platform CBDetc, which offers multiple brands of CBD products for customers across Europe. HolyWorld also sells white label CBD distillate and other derivatives to brands in the U.K., European Union (EU) and Switzerland.

In Malta, subsidiary **MPXI Malta Operations Ltd.** (80% owned) owns a facility in Birkirkara, Malta, which has a licence to produce and export medical cannabis flower products from Malta into European markets and elsewhere.

In South Africa, subsidiary **First Growth Holdings (Pty) Ltd.** (80% owned) is constructing a 53,000-sq.-ft. greenhouse cultivation facility in the Stellenbosch region in Western Cape. Full development of the facility would result in up to 646,000 sq. ft. of greenhouse cultivation and extraction and processing laboratory.

In Southeast Asia, subsidiary **Salus International Management Ltd.** (50% owned; SIM) provides management services, including design, planning, financing, training and ongoing operational support, to cannabis initiatives, partnerships and joint ventures in the region. SIM is providing services to **Salus Bioceutical (Thailand) Co. Ltd.** (25% owned by SIM) for the development of an 800-m^2 cultivation, processing and distribution facility in Chiang Mai province, Thailand.

On July 25, 2022, the company and certain of its Canadian and foreign subsidiaries obtained an order from the Ontario Superior Court of Justice providing protection from their creditors pursuant to the Companies' Creditors Arrangement Act (CCAA). **KSV Restructuring Inc.** was appointed as monitor.

During the second quarter of fiscal 2022, the company shut down the operations of wholly owned **MPX Australia Pty Ltd.** Previously, MPX Australia planned to import and distribute medical cannabis in Australia.

Directors - W. Scott Boyes, chr., pres. & CEO, Toronto, Ont.; Jeremy D. Blumer, CFO, Oakville, Ont.; Jeremy S. Budd, exec. v-p, gen. counsel & corp. sec., Toronto, Ont.; Timothy E. Childs, Sliema, Malta; Alastair Crawford, Malta; Robert Petch, Cranbrook, Kent, United Kingdom

Other Exec. Officers - Michael Arnkvarn, COO, Canada; Dr. Amer Cheema, v-p, cultivation; Jonathan Chu, v-p, fin. & acctg.

Capital Stock

	Authorized (shs.)	Outstanding (shs.)[1]
Common	unlimited	144,322,554

[1] At June 3, 2022

Major Shareholder - Widely held at June 3, 2022.

Price Range - MPXI/CSE

Year	Volume	High	Low	Close
2022	14,013,296	$0.08	$0.01	$0.01
2021	16,643,777	$0.32	$0.03	$0.03
2020	12,408,354	$0.45	$0.07	$0.07
2019	33,068,090	$1.23	$0.31	$0.33

Recent Close: $0.01

Wholly Owned Subsidiaries

Biocannabis Products Ltd., Ont.
Canveda Inc., Peterborough, Ont. formerly 8423695 Canada Inc.
The CinG-X Corporation, Ont.
HolyWorld, S.A., Switzerland.
- 100% int. in **MPXI Labs S.A.**, Nyon, Switzerland.

MCLN Inc., Ont. formerly 2702148 Ontario Inc.
MPXI Malta Holding Limited, Malta.
- 100% int. in **MPXI SA Pty Ltd.**, South Africa.
  - 80% int. in **First Growth Holdings (Pty) Ltd.**, South Africa.

Salus BioPharma Corporation, Peterborough, Ont.
Spartan Wellness Corporation, Toronto, Ont.

Subsidiaries

80% int. in **MPXI Malta Operations Ltd.**, Malta.
- 100% int. in **MPXI Malta Property Ltd.**, Malta.
  - 100% int. in **Alphafarma Operations Ltd.**, Malta.

Investments

50% int. in **Salus International Management Ltd.**, Ont.
- 25% int. in **Salus Bioceutical (Thailand) Co. Ltd.**, Thailand.

Financial Statistics

Periods ended:	12m Sept. 30/21[A]		12m Sept. 30/20[A]
	$000s	%Chg	$000s
Operating revenue	**7,211**	**+127**	**3,171**
Cost of sales	2,677		(1,462)[1]
Salaries & benefits	4,946		5,108
General & admin expense	7,043		10,698
Stock-based compensation	1,036		84
Operating expense	**15,702**	**+9**	**14,427**
Operating income	**(8,491)**	**n.a.**	**(11,256)**
Deprec., depl. & amort.	6,072		4,777
Finance income	nil		14
Finance costs, gross	4,323		885
Investment income	nil		(33)
Write-downs/write-offs	(7,563)[2]		(24,667)[3]
Pre-tax income	**(26,403)**	**n.a.**	**(41,732)**
Income taxes	232		(687)
Net income	**(26,635)**	**n.a.**	**(41,045)**
Net inc. for equity hldrs	**(25,604)**	**n.a.**	**(40,731)**
Net inc. for non-cont. int	**(1,031)**	**n.a.**	**(314)**
Cash & equivalent	6,197		1,309
Inventories	3,012		4,385
Accounts receivable	1,903		1,380
Current assets	12,845		7,642
Fixed assets, net	12,972		8,558
Right-of-use assets	3,753		3,679
Intangibles, net	20,647		31,990
Total assets	**50,670**	**-3**	**52,370**
Bank indebtedness	961		876
Accts. pay. & accr. liabs	7,297		6,206
Current liabilities	14,758		8,409
Long-term debt, gross	12,375		4,795
Long-term debt, net	7,474		4,795
Long-term lease liabilities	4,061		4,047
Shareholders' equity	17,477		33,957
Non-controlling interest	5,368		63
Cash from oper. activs	**(8,126)**	**n.a.**	**(12,176)**
Cash from fin. activs	18,302		1,175
Cash from invest. activs	(5,220)		(4,092)
Net cash position	**6,197**	**+373**	**1,309**
Capital expenditures	(5,260)		(4,243)
Unfunded pension liability	161		323
	$		$
Earnings per share*	(0.18)		(0.29)
Cash flow per share*	(0.06)		(0.09)
	shs		shs
No. of shs. o/s*	143,861,129		141,670,225
Avg. no. of shs. o/s*	143,017,086		140,063,088
	%		%
Net profit margin	(369.37)		n.m.
Return on equity	(99.56)		(78.78)
Return on assets	(43.23)		(62.00)
Foreign sales percent	30		25

* Common

[A] Reported in accordance with IFRS

[1] Net of unrealized gain from changes in fair value of biological assets of $2,032,120.

[2] Includes $4,904,204 Spartan goodwill impairment and $1,169,129 MPX Australia medicinal cannabis licence impairment.

[3] Includes $14,122,604 HolyWeed goodwill impairment and $9,972,399 inventory write-down.

Latest Results

Periods ended:	6m Mar. 31/22[A]		6m Mar. 31/21[A]
	$000s	%Chg	$000s
Operating revenue	3,577	-13	4,096
Net income	(12,569)	n.a.	(10,848)
Net inc. for equity hldrs	(10,154)	n.a.	(10,739)
Net inc. for non-cont. int	(2,415)		(109)
	$		$
Earnings per share*	(0.07)		(0.08)

* Common

[A] Reported in accordance with IFRS

Historical Summary
(as originally stated)

Fiscal Year	Oper. Rev.	Net Inc. Bef. Disc.	EPS*
	$000s	$000s	$
2021[A]	7,211	(26,635)	(0.18)
2020[A]	3,171	(41,045)	(0.29)
2019[A1]	1,592	(9,378)	(0.13)
2018[A]	64	(2,105)	n.a.
2018[A2]	9	(773)	n.a.

* Common
[A] Reported in accordance with IFRS
[1] Results reflect the Feb. 5, 2019, plan of arrangement with iAnthus Capital Holdings Inc.
[2] Results were prepared on a carve-out basis primarily derived from MPX Bioceutical Corporation's wholly owned non-U.S. subsidiaries.

M.13 MTL Cannabis Corp.

Symbol - MTLC **Exchange** - CSE **CUSIP** - 553926
Head Office - 1773 Bayly St, Pickering, ON, L1W 2Y7 **Telephone** - (844) 414-2911 **Toll-free** - (844) 696-3349 **Fax** - (844) 414-2866
Website - mtlcannabis.ca
Email - spearce@mtlcannabis.ca
Investor Relations - Steven Pearce (844) 696-3349
Auditors - MNP LLP C.A., Montréal, Qué.
Lawyers - Bennett Jones LLP, Toronto, Ont.
Transfer Agents - Computershare Trust Company of Canada Inc., Toronto, Ont.
Profile - (Can. 1995; orig. B.C., 1982) Holds licences to produce, cultivate and sell medical and recreational cannabis in Canada, operates clinics providing specialized cannabis therapy services, and offers software that tracks, proves and optimizes the efficacy of medical marijuana. Also operates cannabis dispensaries in Alberta, New Brunswick, Saskatchewan and Ontario.

Owns and operates a 57,000-sq.-ft. production facility in Pointe Claire, Que., with room to expand to 130,000 sq. ft. in the existing two buildings and possible expansion to over 300,000 sq. ft.; a 22,000-sq.-ft. production facility in Pickering, Ont.; a 64,000-sq.-ft. indoor production facility in Louiseville, Que.; an adjacent 450,000 sq. ft. of land that could accommodate the construction of facilities which would provide additional production capacity of 50,000 kg of cannabis; and cannabis dispensaries in Alberta, New Brunswick, Saskatchewan and Ontario. Holds licences to cultivate, produce and sells dried cannabis flower, strains, kush, cannabis oil, marijuana seeds, recreational cannabis, raisins, concentrates, vape pens, topicals and edible products under the Cannabis Act.

Products are sold under the MTL Cannabis, LowKey by MTL, R'Belle, Abba™, Fleurs de Chez Nous™, Vandoos™, H-series™, ICM Terre™, ICM Fogo™ and ICM Air™ brands. Also holds licences to sell **InPlanta Biotechnology Inc.**'s VetStar Day™ and VetStar Night™ strains; **Rubicon Organics Inc.** and **Pure Extracts Technologies Corp.**'s line of concentrate products; **Groupe Fuga Inc.**'s Tropicanna cookies; and **Santa Cruz Medicinals Limited**'s cannabidiol (CBD)-infused health care products.

In addition, wholly owned **672800 N.B. Inc.**, (dba **Canada House Clinics Inc.**) owns and operates medicinal cannabis clinics across Canada that provides services to assist its patients in selecting a licensed producer, identify appropriate strains, and consult and support patients regarding the use of medical cannabis inclusive of issuing a medical document (authorization to purchase medical cannabis); wholly owned **Margaree Health Group Inc.**, which operates medical cannabis clinic in Nova Scotia dedicated to veterans; and wholly owned **690050 N.B. Inc.**, (dba Knalysis Technologies) offers the Knalysis Wellness Tracker Application, a cloud-based software for patients, clinics, dispensaries and growers that provides data information needed to determine what medical marijuana products and strains to take, prescribe, stock and grow. The application has the capacity to quantify the effectiveness of cannabis products in treating the symptoms of patients by keeping track of their treatments, moods and general physical condition throughout the day.

Recent Merger and Acquisition Activity

Status: completed **Revised:** July 28, 2023
UPDATE: The second tranche of the transaction was completed. Canada House acquired the remaining 75.01% interest in MTL for issuance of 70,713,556 common shares. All 93,492,896 common shares issued to acquire MTL were issued at a deemed price of $1.05 per share. PREVIOUS: Canada House Wellness Group Inc. agreed to the reverse takeover acquisition of Montréal Cannabis Médical Inc. (MTL) on a share-for-share basis. The purchase price would include performance-based cash earnout payment of $5,000,000, conditional upon MTL Cannabis achieving certain agreed upon milestones. MTL holds licence to cultivate and produce medical cannabis and cannabis products under Cannabis Act at its 57,000-sq.-ft. licensed facility with room to expand to 130,000 sq. ft. in the existing two buildings and possible expansion to more than 300,000 sq. ft. in Pointe Claire, Que. Prior to closing, Canada House would consolidate its common shares on a 1-for-30 basis and all $6,500,000 of convertible debenture into common shares. The acquisition was expected to close in the fourth quarter of calendar 2021. Aug. 30, 2022 - The first tranche of the transaction was completed. Canada House acquired 24.99% interest in MTL for issuance of 22,779,340 post-consolidated common shares (following 1-for-30 share consolidation effective Aug. 23, 2022).

Predecessor Detail - Name changed from Canada House Cannabis Group Inc., July 28, 2023, pursuant to the reverse takeover acquisition of Montréal Cannabis Médical Inc.

Directors - Dennis Moir, chr., Toronto, Ont.; Richard Clément, chief cultivation officer, Montréal, Qué.; Erik Bertacchini, pres., IsoCanMed Inc., Louiseville, Qué.; Tarek Ahmed, Calgary, Alta.; Yves Metten, Hudson, Qué.

Other Exec. Officers - Michael Perron, CEO; Michel Clément, COO; Peili Miao, CFO; Alex Kroon, exec. v-p, pres., Canada House Clinics Inc. & pres., Abba Medix Corp.; Steven Pearce, v-p, legal & corp. sec.

Capital Stock

	Authorized (shs.)	Outstanding (shs.)[1]
Common	unlimited	116,997,561

[1] At July 28, 2023

Major Shareholder - Michel Clément held 36.96% interest and Richard Clément held 36.96% interest at July 28, 2023.

Price Range - MTLC/CSE

Year	Volume	High	Low	Close
2021	2,701,016	$1.80	$0.60	$1.05
2020	2,281,162	$1.35	$0.60	$0.60
2019	3,305,819	$5.70	$0.45	$0.90
2018	10,052,750	$25.50	$3.75	$5.10

Consolidation: 1-for-30 cons. in Aug. 2022
Recent Close: $0.50
Capital Stock Changes - On July 28, 2023, 70,713,556 common shares were issued pursuant to the acquisition of the remaining 75.01% interest in Montréal Cannabis Médical Inc.

On Aug. 23, 2022, common shares were consolidated on a 1-for-30 basis. On Aug. 30, 2022, 22,779,340 post-consolidated common shares were issued pursuant to the acquisition of a 24.99% interest in Montréal Cannabis Médical Inc.

There were no changes to capital stock during fiscal 2022.

Wholly Owned Subsidiaries

Abba Medix Corp., Pickering, Ont.
IsoCanMed Inc., Louiseville, Qué.
The Longevity Project Corp., London, Ont.
Montréal Cannabis Médical Inc., Qué.
672800 N.B. Inc., Oromocto, N.B. dba Canada House Clinics Inc.
• 100% int. in **Margaree Health Group Inc.**, N.S.
690050 N.B. Inc., Fredericton, N.B. dba Knalysis Technologies.
2104071 Alberta Inc., Edmonton, Alta.

Financial Statistics

Periods ended:	15m July 31/22[A1]		12m Apr. 30/21[A]
	$000s	%Chg	$000s
Operating revenue	**26,666**	**n.a.**	**10,560**
Cost of sales	15,270		5,336
Salaries & benefits	6,960		6,221
General & admin expense	5,084		2,538
Stock-based compensation	467		461
Operating expense	**27,781**	**n.a.**	**14,556**
Operating income	**(1,115)**	**n.a.**	**(3,996)**
Deprec., depl. & amort.	2,081		1,371
Finance costs, net	4,502		2,736
Write-downs/write-offs	(4,228)		(2,266)
Pre-tax income	**(11,061)**	**n.a.**	**(11,297)**
Income taxes	32		68
Net income	**(11,093)**	**n.a.**	**(11,365)**
Cash & equivalent	450		1,835
Inventories	3,601		5,018
Accounts receivable	3,058		1,945
Current assets	7,727		9,873
Fixed assets, net	12,954		14,587
Right-of-use assets	2,182		2,413
Intangibles, net	11,186		10,119
Total assets	**34,049**	**n.a.**	**36,992**
Accts. pay. & accr. liabs.	11,574		8,345
Current liabilities	17,044		12,139
Long-term debt, gross	20,000		15,440
Long-term debt, net	16,667		14,173
Long-term lease liabilities	1,910		1,952
Equity portion of conv. debs.	2,174		2,174
Shareholders' equity	(3,753)		6,873
Cash from oper. activs.	**(1,525)**	**n.a.**	**(3,355)**
Cash from fin. activs.	2,298		4,087
Cash from invest. activs.	(2,158)		(664)
Net cash position	**450**	**n.a.**	**1,835**
Capital expenditures	(2,431)		(794)
	$		$
Earnings per share*	(0.49)		(0.60)
Cash flow per share*	(0.07)		(0.16)
	shs		shs
No. of shs. o/s*	22,781,787		22,781,787
Avg. no. of shs. o/s*	22,781,787		21,707,921
	%		%
Net profit margin	...		(107.62)
Return on equity	...		(190.26)
Return on assets	...		(44.20)

* Common
[A] Reported in accordance with IFRS
[1] Results for fiscal 2022 and prior fiscal years pertain to Canada House Cannabis Group Inc.

Latest Results

Periods ended:	9m Apr. 30/23[A]		9m Apr. 30/22[◻A]
	$000s	%Chg	$000s
Operating revenue	23,145	+38	16,779
Net income	1,452	n.a.	(7,222)
	$		$
Earnings per share*	0.03		(0.32)

* Common
◻ Restated
[A] Reported in accordance with IFRS

Historical Summary
(as originally stated)

Fiscal Year	Oper. Rev.	Net Inc. Bef. Disc.	EPS*
	$000s	$000s	$
2022[A1,2]	26,666	(11,093)	(0.49)
2021[A]	10,560	(11,365)	(0.60)
2020[A]	5,310	(9,520)	(0.90)
2019[A]	4,875	(11,415)	(1.80)
2018[A]	3,289	(12,917)	(2.70)

* Common
[A] Reported in accordance with IFRS
[1] 15 months ended July 31, 2022.
[2] Results for fiscal 2022 and prior fiscal years pertain to Canada House Cannabis Group Inc.
Note: Adjusted throughout for 1-for-30 cons. in Aug. 2022

M.14 MTY Food Group Inc.*

Symbol - MTY **Exchange** - TSX **CUSIP** - 55378N
Head Office - 8210 aut Transcanadienne, Saint-Laurent, QC, H4S 1M5 **Telephone** - (514) 336-8885 **Toll-free** - (866) 891-6633 **Fax** - (514) 336-9222
Website - www.mtygroup.com
Email - eric@mtygroup.com
Investor Relations - Eric Lefebvre (514) 336-8885
Auditors - PricewaterhouseCoopers LLP C.A., Montréal, Qué.
Lawyers - Fasken Martineau DuMoulin LLP, Montréal, Qué.
Transfer Agents - Computershare Trust Company of Canada Inc., Montréal, Qué.
FP500 Revenue Ranking - 400
Employees - 7,062 at Nov. 30, 2022
Profile - (B.C. 1986) Franchises and operates more than 85 banners of quick service, fast casual and casual dining restaurants throughout Canada, the U.S. and other international locations.

The company's multi-concept model enables positioning across a broad range of demographic, economic and geographic sectors. Operations mainly consist of franchising in the quick service restaurant (QSR) industry.

Banners include Allô Mon Coco®, America's Taco Shop®, Bâton Rouge, Baja Fresh Mexican Grill®, Ben & Florentine, Bakers Square®, Barrio Queen™, Built Custom Burgers, Big Smoke Burger®, Café Dépôt®, Blimpie®, Casa Grecque®, Country Style®, Champps®, Cultures®, Cold Stone Creamery®, Dagwoods Sandwiches & Salads®, Craft Republic, Extreme Pita®, Famous Dave's®, Giorgio Ristorante®, Fox & Hound, Jugo Juice®, Frullati Café & Bakery®, Kim Chi Korean Delight®, Grabbagreen®, Koryo Korean Barbeque®, Granite City, Koya Japan®, Great Steak®, Küto Comptoir à Tartares®, Jhonnie's New York Pizzeria, La Crémière®, Kahala Coffee Traders®, La Diperie, Madisons®, La Salsa Fresh Mexican Grill®, Manchu Wok®, Mikes®, Maui Wowi Hawaiian Coffees & Smoothies®, MMMuffins®, Mr. Souvlaki®, NrGize Lifestyle Café™, Mr. Sub®, Ms. Vanellis®, Pinkberry®, Mucho Burrito®, Planet Smoothie®, Muffin Plus®, Ranch One®, O'Burger®, Real Urban BBQ™, Papa Murphy's®, Rocky Mountain Chocolate Factory®, Pizza Delight®, Rollerz™, Scores®, Samurai Sam's®, Sauce Pizza and Wine, SensAsian®, Surf City Squeeze®, South Street Burger®, SweetFrog®, Steak Frites St-Paul®, Taco Time®, Sukiyaki®, Tahoe Joe's®, SushiGo®, Tasti D-Lite™, Sushi-Man®, Sushi Shop®, The Counter®, Taco Time®, The Works Gourmet Burger Bistro®, TCBY®, Van Houtte®, Thaï Express®/Pad Thaï®, Village Inn®, Thaïzone®, The Coop Wicked Chicken®, Tiki Mining®, Timothy's World Coffee®, Tosto Quickfire Pizza Pasta®, Turtle Jack's®, Tutti Frutti®, Valentine®, Vie & Nam®, Villa Madina®, Wasabi Grill & Noodle®, Wetzel's Pretzels and Yuzu®.

At May 31, 2023, the company had 7,124 locations in operation, of which 6,900 were franchised or under operator agreements, 224 were corporate-owned. Locations include food courts and shopping malls, street front, as well as non-traditional formats within airports, hospitals, campuses, petroleum retailers, convenience stores, groceries, cinemas, amusement parks, food-trucks or carts, and other venues or retailers shared sites. Revenues from franchise locations are generated from royalty fees, initial franchise fees, master licence fees, renewal fees, sales of turnkey projects, sale of goods and equipment, rent, sign rental, supplier contributions, gift card program fees and breakage, bookkeeping accounting fees, and transfer fees and other fees. Revenues are also earned from promotional funds, sales of corporate owned locations, as well as from its distribution centres in St-Hyacinthe, Delson and Laval, Que., and food processing plants in Levis and Laval, Que.

Also operates three distribution centres and two food processing plants, all in Quebec.

Restaurant breakdown at May 31, 2023:

Geographic	% of locations
Canada	35%
United States	58%
International	7%
Type	
QSR	80%
Fast casual	10%
Casual dining	10%
Location	
Shopping mall & food court	16%
Street front	63%
Non-traditional format	21%

During fiscal 2022, the company's network closed 507 locations, of which 207 were in Canada, 239 in the U.S. and 61 internationally. Of the locations closed in 2022, 48% were located on street front, 23% in food courts and 29% in other non-traditional formats.

Recent Merger and Acquisition Activity

Status: completed **Announced:** Dec. 15, 2022
MTY Food Group Inc. acquired the assets of Sauce Pizza and Wine for Cdn$14,789,000 (US$10,842,000), including a holdback on acquisition of Cdn$1,142,000 (US$837,000). Sauce Pizza and Wine operates fast casual restaurants in Arizona, and has 13 corporate-owned restaurants in operation at the closing of the transaction.

Status: completed **Revised:** Dec. 8, 2022
UPDATE: The transaction was completed. PREVIOUS: MTY Food Group Inc. agreed to acquire Pasadena, Calif.-based Wetzel's Pretzels, LLC, which franchises and operates the Wetzel's Pretzels bakery chain primarily in the U.S., as well as in Canada and Panama, from CenterOak Partners LLC for US$207,000,000 (Cdn$282,000,000). Wetzel's Pretzels had a network of more than 350 locations, 90% of which were franchised.

Status: completed **Revised:** Sept. 28, 2022
UPDATE: The transaction was completed for total consideration of US$207,100,000. PREVIOUS: MTY Food Group Inc. agreed to acquire BBQ Holdings, Inc. for US$17.25 cash per share, representing a transaction value of US$200,000,000, including net debt. BBQ Holdings, a Minnetonka, Minn.-based company listed on the NASDAQ, was a franchisor and operator of casual and fast casual dining restaurants across 37 states in the U.S., Canada, and the United Arab Emirates under multiple banners including Famous Dave's, Village Inn, Barrio Queen and Granite City. At Aug. 8, 2022, BBQ Holdings operated more than 200 franchised and 100 corporate-owned restaurants. Upon completion, MTY would have 7,000 locations, including more than 3,900 in the U.S. Sept. 26, 2022 - A total of 9,724,637 BBQ Holdings shares were tendered to the offer, representing a 91.94% interest.

Predecessor Detail - Name changed from iNsu Innovations Group Inc., July 8, 2003.

Directors - Stanley Ma, chr. & pres., Saint-Laurent, Qué.; Eric Lefebvre, CEO, Laval, Qué.; Claude St-Pierre, corp. sec., Laval, Qué.; Murat Armutlu, Saint-Laurent, Qué.; Victor Mandel, Nev.; Dickie Orr, B.C.; Suzan Zalter, Qué.

Other Exec. Officers - Marie-Line Beauchamp, COO, casual dining; Marc Benzacar, COO, fast casual div.; Jason Brading, COO, quick srvc. restaurants; Nik Rupp, COO, Papa Murphy's div.; Jeff Smit, COO, U.S. opers.; Renée St-Onge, CFO; Jenny Moody, chief legal officer; Albert Hank, co-COO, BBQ Holdings Inc.; Adam Lehr, co-COO, BBQ Holdings Inc.

Capital Stock

	Authorized (shs.)	Outstanding (shs.)[1]
Common	unlimited	24,413,461

[1] At July 10, 2023

Options - At Nov. 30 2022, options were outstanding to purchase 440,000 common shares at weighted average exercise price of $50.97 per share with weighted average remaining contractual life of 5.3 years.

Normal Course Issuer Bid - The company plans to make normal course purchases of up to 1,220,673 common shares representing 5% of the total outstanding. The bid commenced on July 3, 2023, and expires on July 2, 2024.

Major Shareholder - Stanley Ma held 16.41% interest at Mar. 20, 2023.

Price Range - MTY/TSX

Year	Volume	High	Low	Close
2022	11,582,068	$63.96	$45.20	$57.07
2021	20,445,965	$72.10	$47.15	$63.28
2020	60,247,692	$62.82	$14.23	$57.95
2019	16,691,147	$71.86	$51.61	$55.49
2018	16,657,485	$73.19	$44.97	$60.64

Recent Close: $64.80

Capital Stock Changes - During fiscal 2022, 256,400 common shares were repurchased under a Normal Course Issuer Bid.

Dividends

MTY com Ra $1.00 pa Q est. Feb. 15, 2023[1]

[1] First divd. since Feb/20.

Long-Term Debt - Outstanding at Nov. 30, 2022:

Minority put options[1]	$1,853,000
Contract cancellation fees[2]	142,000
Contingent consid. on acquis.[3]	3,626,000
Credit facility[4]	550,055,000
Repurchase oblig. in a J.V.[5]	7,867,000
Less: Credit facility fin. costs	2,584,000
	560,959,000
Less: Current portion	9,530,000
	551,429,000

[1] Due on demand.
[2] Non-interest-bearing contract cancellation fees and holdbacks on acquisitions.
[3] Due December 2022.
[4] Funds drawn in Canadian or in U.S. dollars at company's discretion. Matures Oct. 28, 2025.
[5] Due to December 2024.

Wholly Owned Subsidiaries

BBQ Holdings, Inc., Minnetonka, Minn.
BF Acquisition Holdings, LLC, Del.
Built Franchise Systems, LLC, Culver City, Calif.
CB Franchise Systems, LLC, Culver City, Calif.
Kahala Brands Inc., Tenn.
MTY Franchising Inc., Canada.
MTY Franchising USA, Inc., United States.
Papa Murphy's Holdings, Inc., Vancouver, Wash.

Subsidiaries

65% int. in **9974644 Canada Inc.**
70% int. in **11554891 Canada Inc.**, Canada.
Note: The preceding list includes only the major related companies in which interests are held.

Financial Statistics

Periods ended:	12m Nov. 30/22[A]		12m Nov. 30/21[□A]
	$000s	%Chg	$000s
Operating revenue	**716,522**	**+30**	**551,903**
Cost of sales	198,150		145,865
Salaries & benefits	135,512		97,481
General & admin expense	200,778		139,226
Operating expense	**534,440**	**+40**	**382,572**
Operating income	**182,082**	**+8**	**169,331**
Deprec., depl. & amort.	51,021		44,616
Finance income	10,463		11,751
Finance costs, gross	25,848		23,959
Investment income	nil		(709)
Write-downs/write-offs	(14,885)		(7,453)
Pre-tax income	**96,170**	**-14**	**112,072**
Income taxes	20,991		26,129
Net income	**75,179**	**-13**	**85,943**
Net inc. for equity hldrs	**74,817**	**-13**	**85,639**
Net inc. for non-cont. int	**362**	**+19**	**304**
Cash & equivalent	59,479		61,231
Inventories	18,517		10,707
Accounts receivable	78,099		57,459
Current assets	264,656		233,468
Long-term investments	nil		25,911
Fixed assets, net	90,878		17,526
Right-of-use assets	159,706		59,937
Intangibles, net	1,544,819		1,248,664
Total assets	**2,325,303**	**+22**	**1,904,594**
Accts. pay. & accr. liabs	154,988		119,462
Current liabilities	435,492		358,488
Long-term debt, gross	560,959		360,728
Long-term debt, net	551,429		347,612
Long-term lease liabilities	400,377		371,575
Shareholders' equity	723,408		647,639
Non-controlling interest	1,218		1,259
Cash from oper. activs	**142,797**	**+3**	**139,299**
Cash from fin. activs	105,296		(129,582)
Cash from invest. activs	(258,420)		7,071
Net cash position	**59,479**	**-3**	**61,231**
Capital expenditures	(8,670)		(6,439)
Capital disposals	1,131		6,465
	$		$
Earnings per share*	3.06		3.47
Cash flow per share*	5.84		5.64
Cash divd. per share*	0.84		0.37
	shs		shs
No. of shs. o/s*	24,413,461		24,669,861
Avg. no. of shs. o/s*	24,439,892		24,704,866
	%		%
Net profit margin	10.49		15.57
Return on equity	10.91		13.93
Return on assets	4.51		5.32
Foreign sales percent	48		49
No. of employees (FTEs)	7,062		1,978

* Common
[□] Restated
[A] Reported in accordance with IFRS

Latest Results

Periods ended:	6m May 31/23[A]		6m May 31/22[A]
	$000s	%Chg	$000s
Operating revenue	591,222	+95	303,012
Net income	48,950	+8	45,388
Net inc. for equity hldrs	48,746	+8	45,256
Net inc. for non-cont. int	204		132
	$		$
Earnings per share*	2.00		1.85

* Common
[A] Reported in accordance with IFRS

Historical Summary

(as originally stated)

Fiscal Year	Oper. Rev.	Net Inc. Bef. Disc.	EPS*
	$000s	$000s	$
2022[A]	716,522	75,179	3.06
2021[A]	551,903	85,943	3.47
2020[A]	511,117	(36,895)	(1.50)
2019[A]	550,942	77,736	3.09
2018[A]	353,303	98,991	4.07

* Common
[A] Reported in accordance with IFRS

M.15 MX Gold Corp.

Symbol - MXL.H **Exchange** - TSX-VEN **CUSIP** - 62848A
Head Office - 1300 Redonda St, Winnipeg, MB, R2C 3T7 **Telephone** - (204) 697-7640
Website - www.mxgoldcorp.com
Email - dano@mxgoldcorp.com
Investor Relations - Dan Omeniuk (204) 697-7640
Auditors - Manning Elliott LLP C.A., Vancouver, B.C.
Lawyers - Clark Wilson LLP, Vancouver, B.C.
Transfer Agents - Computershare Trust Company of Canada Inc., Vancouver, B.C.
Profile - (B.C. 1999) Seeking new business opportunities.
Predecessor Detail - Name changed from Discovery Ventures Inc., June 6, 2016.
Directors - Dan Omeniuk, chr., CEO & CFO, Man.; Robert Jeffery, B.C.; Connor Macaulay, Man.; Lorne Mark Roseborough, Kelowna, B.C.

Capital Stock

	Authorized (shs.)	Outstanding (shs.)[1]
Common	unlimited	14,272,362

[1] At Apr. 28, 2022

Major Shareholder - Widely held at Nov. 25, 2021.

Price Range - MXL.H/TSX-VEN

Year	Volume	High	Low	Close
2022	1,023,291	$0.15	$0.04	$0.04
2021	2,621,110	$0.22	$0.06	$0.08
2020	7,876,971	$0.40	$0.08	$0.14
2018	996,195	$3.00	$1.60	$2.20

Consolidation: 1-for-20 cons. in May 2020
Recent Close: $0.05

Investments

Metallica Metals Corp., Vancouver, B.C. (see Survey of Mines)

Financial Statistics

Periods ended:	12m Dec. 31/21[A]		12m Dec. 31/20[A]
	$000s	%Chg	$000s
General & admin expense	218		286
Operating expense	**218**	**-24**	**286**
Operating income	**(218)**	**n.a.**	**(286)**
Finance costs, gross	1		1
Pre-tax income	**121**	**n.a.**	**(288)**
Net income	**121**	**n.a.**	**(288)**
Cash & equivalent	262		20
Current assets	274		73
Total assets	**274**	**+275**	**73**
Accts. pay. & accr. liabs	418		680
Current liabilities	1,776		1,696
Shareholders' equity	(1,502)		(1,623)
Cash from oper. activs	**(333)**	**n.a.**	**(31)**
Cash from invest. activs	425		39
Net cash position	**112**	**+460**	**20**
	$		$
Earnings per share*	0.02		(0.02)
Cash flow per share*	(0.02)		(0.00)
	shs		shs
No. of shs. o/s*	14,272,362		14,272,362
Avg. no. of shs. o/s*	14,272,362		14,272,362
	%		%
Net profit margin	n.a.		n.a.
Return on equity	n.m.		n.m.
Return on assets	70.32		(329.89)

* Common
[A] Reported in accordance with IFRS

Latest Results

Periods ended:	3m Mar. 31/22[A]		3m Mar. 31/21[A]
	$000s	%Chg	$000s
Net income	(150)	n.a.	(35)
	$		$
Earnings per share*	(0.01)		(0.00)

* Common
[A] Reported in accordance with IFRS

Historical Summary
(as originally stated)

Fiscal Year	Oper. Rev.	Net Inc. Bef. Disc.	EPS*
	$000s	$000s	$
2021[A]	nil	121	0.02
2020[A]	nil	(288)	(0.02)
2019[A]	nil	(1,062)	(0.07)
2018[A]	321	(15,613)	(1.20)
2017[A]	nil	(10,428)	(1.00)

* Common
[A] Reported in accordance with IFRS
Note: Adjusted throughout for 1-for-20 cons. in May 2020

M.16 MYND Life Sciences Inc.

Symbol - MYND **Exchange** - CSE **CUSIP** - 62857B
Head Office - 733 Finns Rd, Kelowna, BC, V1X 5B7 **Telephone** - (780) 965-0123
Website - myndsciences.com
Email - lyleo@myndsciences.com
Investor Relations - Dr. Lyle Oberg (780) 965-0122
Auditors - MNP LLP C.A., Vancouver, B.C.
Transfer Agents - Odyssey Trust Company, Vancouver, B.C.
Profile - (B.C. 2020 amalg.) Developing psychedelics for the treatment of neuropsychiatric disorders.

Developing MYND-604 for the treatment of major depressive disorder and MYND-778 for the treatment of sepsis. Both are oral dosage products in the evaluation stage, and the company intends to seek approval to proceed directly into a Phase 2 clinical trial based on existing pre-clinical and clinical data for the active pharmaceutical ingredients in both. Also holds intellectual property for the use of psychedelics to treat Dementia. In addition, the company has a license to manufacture and distribute **Eyam Vaccines and Immunotherapeutics Ltd.**'s Central Nervous system vaccines.

The company, through wholly owned **MYND Diagnostics Inc.**, is developing a monoclonal antibody biomarker diagnostic test to measure the levels of the human mycogene acting as a diagnostic and monitoring tool for depression and other inflammatory conditions.

In June 2022, the company terminated the agreement to acquire **Tidal Care Inc.** (dba Tidal Psychedelics), an integrated psilocybin company with access to a $10,000,000 leasehold facility purpose built for cannabis and mycelium cultivation, for an undisclosed amount.

Predecessor Detail - Formed from Winter Soldier Capital Corp. in British Columbia, Nov. 26, 2020, pursuant to the reverse takeover acquisition of and amalgamation with (old) MYND Life Sciences Inc. (deemed acquiror); basis 1 new com. sh. for 1 com. sh. of both Winter Soldier and (old) MYND.

Directors - Dr. Wilfred Jefferies, co-founder, chr. & chief scientific officer, B.C.; Dr. Lyle Oberg, co-founder & CEO, B.C.; John J. (Jay) Campbell, Calgary, Alta.; Scott L. Nicoll, Surrey, B.C.; Roslyn Ritchie-Derrien, B.C.

Other Exec. Officers - Lih-Ming Tam, interim CFO & contr.; Dr. Iryna Saranchova, chief clinical officer

Capital Stock

	Authorized (shs.)	Outstanding (shs.)[1]
Preferred	unlimited	nil
Common	unlimited	46,817,182

[1] At July 31, 2022

Major Shareholder - Dr. Wilfred Jefferies held 22.5% interest at Nov. 15, 2021.

Price Range - MYND/CSE

Year	Volume	High	Low	Close
2022	4,875,829	$0.29	$0.03	$0.04
2021	2,360,367	$2.50	$0.18	$0.27

Recent Close: $0.02
Capital Stock Changes - In June 2022, a private placement of up to $3,500,000 common shares was announced.

Wholly Owned Subsidiaries

MYND Diagnostics Inc.
Pacific Myco Bioscience Ltd., Kelowna, B.C.

Financial Statistics

Periods ended:	12m Oct. 31/21[A]		12m Oct. 31/20[A]
	$000s	%Chg	$000s
Salaries & benefits	499		50
Research & devel. expense	1,079		nil
General & admin expense	1,465		7
Stock-based compensation	1,163		nil
Operating expense	**4,206**	**n.m.**	**57**
Operating income	**(4,206)**	**n.a.**	**(57)**
Deprec., depl. & amort.	86		nil
Finance costs, gross	135		nil
Write-downs/write-offs	(109)		nil
Pre-tax income	**(4,536)**	**n.a.**	**(56)**
Income taxes	(168)		nil
Net income	**(4,367)**	**n.a.**	**(56)**
Cash & equivalent	1,900		nil
Accounts receivable	98		nil
Current assets	2,042		nil
Fixed assets, net	33		nil
Right-of-use assets	295		nil
Total assets	**2,670**	**n.a.**	**nil**
Accts. pay. & accr. liabs	285		54
Current liabilities	355		54
Long-term debt, gross	2,002		nil
Long-term debt, net	2,002		nil
Long-term lease liabilities	251		nil
Equity portion of conv. debs	132		nil
Shareholders' equity	68		(54)
Cash from oper. activs	**(2,982)**	**n.a.**	**(3)**
Cash from fin. activs	2,752		3
Cash from invest. activs	2,130		nil
Net cash position	**1,900**	**n.a.**	**nil**
Capital expenditures	(44)		nil
	$		$
Earnings per share*	(0.10)		(0.00)
Cash flow per share*	(0.07)		(0.00)
	shs		shs
No. of shs. o/s*	45,933,382		n.a.
Avg. no. of shs. o/s*	44,957,177		28,227,186
	%		%
Net profit margin	n.a.		n.a.
Return on equity	n.m.		n.m.
Return on assets	n.m.		n.a.

* Common
[A] Reported in accordance with IFRS

Latest Results

Periods ended:	9m July 31/22[A]		9m July 31/21[A]
	$000s	%Chg	$000s
Net income	(3,014)	n.a.	(778)
	$		$
Earnings per share*	(0.06)		(0.06)

* Common
[A] Reported in accordance with IFRS

M.17 Mackenzie Master Limited Partnership

Symbol - MKZ.UN **Exchange** - TSX **CUSIP** - 554905
Head Office - 180 Queen St W, Toronto, ON, M5V 3K1 **Telephone** - (416) 922-5322 **Toll-free** - (800) 387-0614 **Fax** - (416) 922-5660
Website - www.mackenzieinvestments.com
Email - court.elliott@mackenzieinvestments.com
Investor Relations - Court Elliott (800) 387-0614
Auditors - KPMG LLP C.A., Toronto, Ont.
Transfer Agents - Mackenzie Financial Corporation, Toronto, Ont.
Profile - (Ont. 1995) Arranges for the distribution of securities of mutual funds sponsored by **MacKenzie Financial Corporation**, sold under redemption charge basis, to earn distribution fees to finance the selling commissions paid to registered dealers.

MMLP GP Inc. (formerly **Mackenzie Financial Services Inc.**) is the general partner of the partnership. The partnership also invests excess cash in units of **Mackenzie Canadian Money Market Fund**. The partnership will be terminated on Dec. 31, 2094.

Oper. Subsid./Mgt. Co. Directors - Luke Gould, CEO, Winnipeg, Man.; Terry Rountes, CFO, Woodbridge, Ont.; Matt Grant, corp. sec., Toronto, Ont.

Capital Stock

	Authorized (shs.)	Outstanding (shs.)[1]
L.P. Unit	unlimited	6,264,511

[1] At Dec. 31, 2022

Major Shareholder - Widely held at Mar. 30, 2023.

Price Range - MKZ.UN/TSX

Year	Volume	High	Low	Close
2022	1,000,124	$0.82	$0.59	$0.59
2021	1,482,219	$0.95	$0.70	$0.82
2020	1,337,498	$1.02	$0.69	$0.83
2019	1,224,929	$1.10	$0.91	$0.98
2018	1,478,873	$1.10	$0.90	$0.94

Recent Close: $0.41
Capital Stock Changes - There were no changes to limited partnership units from 2000 to 2022, inclusive.

Dividends

MKZ.UN ltd ptnrshp unit Ra $0.085 pa A est. Jan. 20, 2023
Prev. Rate: $0.095 est. Jan. 21, 2022
Prev. Rate: $0.086 est. Jan. 22, 2021

Financial Statistics

Periods ended:	12m Dec. 31/22[A]		12m Dec. 31/21[A]
	$000s	%Chg	$000s
Total revenue	**844**	**-11**	**944**
Operating expense	**104**	**-5**	**110**
Operating income	**740**	**-11**	**834**
Pre-tax income	**725**	**-11**	**818**
Income taxes	192		217
Net income	**533**	**-11**	**601**
Cash & equivalent	730		796
Accounts receivable	58		77
Total assets	**788**	**-10**	**873**
Accts. pay. & accr. liabs	62		55
Shareholders' equity	533		601
Cash from oper. activs	**535**	**-10**	**592**
Cash from fin. activs	(601)		(597)
Net cash position	**730**	**-8**	**796**
	$		$
Earnings per share*	0.09		0.10
Cash flow per share*	0.09		0.09
Net asset value per share*	0.09		0.10
Cash divd. per share*	0.09		0.10
	shs		shs
No. of shs. o/s*	6,264,511		6,264,511
Avg. no. of shs. o/s*	6,264,511		6,264,511
	%		%
Net profit margin	63.15		63.67
Return on equity	94.00		100.33
Return on assets	64.18		68.72

* L.P. unit
[A] Reported in accordance with IFRS

Historical Summary
(as originally stated)

Fiscal Year	Total Rev.	Net Inc. Bef. Disc.	EPS*
	$000s	$000s	$
2022[A]	844	533	0.09
2021[A]	944	601	0.10
2020[A]	930	597	0.10
2019[A]	1,130	746	0.12
2018[A]	1,225	809	0.13

* L.P. unit
[A] Reported in accordance with IFRS

M.18 Madison Pacific Properties Inc.

Symbol - MPC **Exchange** - TSX **CUSIP** - 557903
Head Office - 389 6 Ave W, Vancouver, BC, V5Y 1L1 **Telephone** - (604) 732-6540 **Fax** - (604) 732-6550
Website - www.madisonpacific.ca
Email - byip@madisonpacific.ca
Investor Relations - Bernice Yip (604) 732-6540
Auditors - PricewaterhouseCoopers LLP C.A., Vancouver, B.C.
Transfer Agents - Computershare Trust Company of Canada Inc., Vancouver, B.C.
Employees - 10 at Nov. 22, 2022
Profile - (Can. 1990; orig. N.S., 1963) Owns, develops and manages office, industrial, commercial and multi-family rental properties in British Columbia, Alberta and Ontario.

Property portfolio at Jan. 12, 2023:

	Industrial[1]	Retail[1]	Office[1]
British Columbia	1,344,637	132,474	116,689
Alberta	269,036	nil	nil
Ontario	63,030	nil	nil
	1,676,703	132,474	116,689

[1] Net leasable area (sq. ft.). Excluding properties under development and the company's 50% interest in a 54-unit multi-family residential apartment in Vancouver, B.C.

Development properties include a 50% interest in **Silverdale Hills Limited Partnership** which owns 1,397 acres of under development residential lands in Mission, B.C., where construction commenced development of 162 townhomes and 65 single family lots on the site in June 2020.

In September and December 2022, 50%-owned **Silverdale Hills Limited Partnership** acquired approximately 20 acres of residential development land in Mission, B.C., for $18,060,000 including closing costs and taxes.

Recent Merger and Acquisition Activity

Status: completed **Announced:** Aug. 31, 2022
Madison Pacific Properties Inc. acquired a 20,040-sq.-ft. industrial property in Vancouver, B.C., for $18,049,000, and a highway-commercial property with a 5,484-sq.-ft. building and a 31,363-sq.-ft. site area in Chilliwack, B.C., for $3,939,000.

Directors - John DeLucchi, chr., pres. & CEO, B.C.; Peter J. Bonner, West Vancouver, B.C.; Michael W. Delesalle, Coquitlam, B.C.; Mark E. Elliott, B.C.; Samuel (Sam) Grippo, B.C.; Jonathan H. B. Rees, Vancouver, B.C.

Other Exec. Officers - Bernice Yip, CFO & corp. sec.; Rob Hackett, v-p, prop. mgt.; Nathan Worbets, v-p, devel.

Capital Stock

	Authorized (shs.)	Outstanding (shs.)[1]
Class A Preferred	unlimited	nil
Class B Common	unlimited	7,355,420
Class C Common	unlimited	52,107,135

[1] At Jan. 12, 2023

Class A Preferred - Non-voting.

Class B Common - One vote per share.

Class C Common - Non-voting and closely held.

Major Shareholder - Madison Venture Corporation held 49% interest, Delcor Holdings Ltd. held 12.4% interest and Vanac Development Corp. held 10.7% interest at Jan. 9, 2023.

Price Range - MPC/TSX

Year	Volume	High	Low	Close
2022	150,525	$7.51	$6.30	$6.98
2021	253,500	$7.74	$3.78	$6.99
2020	157,563	$4.14	$3.10	$4.14
2019	206,988	$4.00	$3.20	$3.62
2018	364,733	$4.68	$3.30	$3.78

Recent Close: $6.26

Capital Stock Changes - During fiscal 2022, 99,928 class B common shares and 792,046 class C common shares were issued on acquisition of an investment property.

Dividends

MPC cl B Ra $0.105 pa S est. Aug. 29, 2007
$0.34◆ May 4/21
Paid in 2023: $0.105 2022: $0.105 2021: $0.105 + $0.34◆

MPC.C cl C N.V. Ra $0.105 pa S est. Feb. 28, 2008
$0.34◆ May 4/21
Paid in 2023: $0.105 2022: $0.105 2021: $0.105 + $0.34◆

◆ Special

Wholly Owned Subsidiaries

MP Western Properties Inc., Vancouver, B.C.
- 100% int. in **1073774 Properties Inc.**, B.C.

Madison Silverdale Developments Corp., B.C.
- 50% int. in **Silverdale Hills Limited Partnership**, B.C.
  - 100% int. in **Polygon Archer Green Homes Limited Partnership**
  - 100% int. in **Silverdale Nelson Street South Limited Partnership**

3530639 Canada Inc., Vancouver, B.C. Formerly The Spectra Group of Great Restaurants Inc.

Subsidiaries

99.8% int. in **Metro Vancouver Properties Corp.**, Vancouver, B.C.
- 100% int. in **801325 B.C. Ltd.**
- 100% int. in **MPW Properties Partnership**
- 75% int. in **MT Management Inc.**
- 60.9% int. in **MT Properties Limited Partnership**
- 100% int. in **Madison Developments 2800 Barnet Ltd.**, B.C.
  - 50% int. in **2798 Barnet Development Limited Partnership**, B.C.

Investments

33.85% int. in **Grant Street Properties Inc.**, B.C.
50% int. in **1100935 B.C. Ltd.**, B.C.

Financial Statistics

Periods ended:	12m Aug. 31/22[A]		12m Aug. 31/21[A]
	$000s	%Chg	$000s
Total revenue	**37,390**	**+14**	**32,791**
Rental operating expense	3,991		3,316
Salaries & benefits	1,736		1,895
General & admin. expense	2,393		1,923
Property taxes	7,196		6,088
Operating expense	**15,316**	**+16**	**13,222**
Operating income	**22,074**	**+13**	**19,569**
Investment income	14,819		3,668
Finance income	662		463
Finance costs, gross	3,460		7,860
Pre-tax income	**78,195**	**+26**	**61,871**
Income taxes	12,798		8,305
Net income	**65,397**	**+22**	**53,566**
Net inc. for equity hldrs	**63,301**	**+26**	**50,288**
Net inc. for non-cont. int	**2,096**	**-36**	**3,278**
Cash & equivalent	41,959		42,254
Accounts receivable	351		243
Current assets	45,954		46,364
Long-term investments	94,219		70,829
Property interests, net	678,783		605,096
Total assets	**842,149**	**+14**	**741,339**
Accts. pay. & accr. liabs	2,441		2,960
Current liabilities	99,807		66,881
Long-term debt, gross	310,456		280,047
Long-term debt, net	222,952		226,132
Shareholders' equity	450,313		388,012
Non-controlling interest	12,800		11,139
Cash from oper. activs	**10,886**	**+14**	**9,551**
Cash from fin. activs	20,962		(15,960)
Cash from invest. activs	(32,143)		(22,787)
Net cash position	**41,959**	**-1**	**42,254**
Increase in property	23,618		17,415
	$		$
Earnings per share*	1.07		0.86
Cash flow per share*	0.18		0.16
Cash divd. per share*	0.11		0.11
Extra divd. - cash*	nil		0.34
Total divd. per share*	**0.11**		**0.45**
	shs		shs
No. of shs. o/s*	59,462,555		58,570,581
Avg. no. of shs. o/s*	59,391,685		58,570,581
	%		%
Net profit margin	174.91		163.36
Return on equity	15.10		13.36
Return on assets	8.63		8.39

* Cl.B & C com.
[A] Reported in accordance with IFRS

Latest Results

Periods ended:	3m Nov. 30/22[A]		3m Nov. 30/21[A]
	$000s	%Chg	$000s
Total revenue	9,631	+7	8,978
Net income	6,623	-29	9,311
Net inc. for equity hldrs	6,422	-27	8,746
Net inc. for non-cont. int	201		565
	$		$
Earnings per share*	0.11		0.15

* Cl.B & C com.
[A] Reported in accordance with IFRS

Historical Summary
(as originally stated)

Fiscal Year	Total Rev.	Net Inc. Bef. Disc.	EPS*
	$000s	$000s	$
2022[A]	37,390	65,397	1.07
2021[A]	32,791	53,566	0.86
2020[A]	31,077	30,112	0.51
2019[A]	31,117	36,238	0.59
2018[A]	31,228	43,997	0.72

* Cl.B & C com.
[A] Reported in accordance with IFRS

M.19 Magellan Aerospace Corporation*

Symbol - MAL **Exchange** - TSX **CUSIP** - 558912
Head Office - 3160 Derry Rd E, Mississauga, ON, L4T 1A9 **Telephone** - (905) 677-1889 **Fax** - (905) 677-5658
Website - www.magellan.aero
Email - elena.milantoni@magellan.aero
Investor Relations - Elena M. Milantoni (905) 677-1889
Auditors - BDO Canada LLP C.A., Toronto, Ont.
Lawyers - Burnet, Duckworth & Palmer LLP, Calgary, Alta.
Transfer Agents - Computershare Trust Company of Canada Inc., Toronto, Ont.
FP500 Revenue Ranking - 386
Employees - 3,500 at Dec. 31, 2022

Profile - (Ont. 1996) Engineers, manufactures, repairs and overhauls aeroengine and aerostructure components and assemblies, and other advanced aerospace products for the commercial aerospace, defence and space markets in Canada, Europe and the U.S.

Activities are grouped into one segment, Aerospace, which includes the design, development, manufacture, repair and overhaul, and sale of systems and components for defence and civil aviation.

The **Aerospace** segment offers aerostructure and aeroengine products to the commercial sector, which includes large commercial jet, business jet, regional aircraft and helicopter markets, and the defence sector for major military aircrafts. Aerostructure products are supplied to international customers by producing components using conventional and high-speed automated machining centres. Aeroengine products include complex cast, fabricated and machined gas turbine engine components, both static and rotating, and integrated nacelle components, flow paths and engine exhaust systems.

Other products include Wire Strike Protection System (WSPS)™, a helicopter safety measure, rockets, space mission solutions, sand castings, oriented gas turbine driven power generation solutions and other supporting materials.

Also supplies systems and design engineering to develop and sell proprietary space and rocket motor systems to a global customer base. In addition, also provides repair and overhaul services for jet engines and nacelle components.

Manufacturing facilities are located in Canada (4), the U.S. (6), Europe (7) and India (2).

In March 2023, the company secured a contract with the Government of Canada to design, build and operate the Redwing microsatellite. Redwing would perform space object tracking, observe space objects and provide near real-time tasking. The satellite would be developed at the company's facility in Winnipeg, Man. and launched in 2026. The contract was valued at $15,800,000.

In November 2022, the company was awarded a multi-year contact to provide machined titanium components of the F-35 aircraft to **Lockheed Martin Corporation**.

In October 2022, the company was awarded a multi-year contract to support the production of CH-53K® low rate initial production configuration helicopter to **Sikorsky Aircraft Corporation**.

In May 2022, the company announced a contract with **RocketFrac Services Ltd.** to develop a fracturing technology that uses solid rocket propellant. RocketFrac is an energy service company which uses fracturing technology to extract tight reservoirs without water.

Predecessor Detail - Name changed from Fleet Aerospace Corporation, Oct. 22, 1996; basis 1 new for 5 old shs.

Directors - N. Murray Edwards, chr., Switzerland; Phillip C. (Phil) Underwood, pres. & CEO, Mississauga, Ont.; Beth M. Budd Bandler, Ont.; Larry G. J. Moeller, Calgary, Alta.; Steven (Steve) Somerville, Oshawa, Ont.; James Patrick (JP) Veitch, Calgary, Alta.

Other Exec. Officers - Elena M. Milantoni, CFO & corp. sec.; Jason Addis, v-p, India opers.; Don Boitson, v-p, North American opers.; Jonathan Goodwin, v-p, European opers.; Michael Gribe, v-p, HR; Haydn R. Martin, v-p, bus. devel., mktg. & contracts; Ian Roberts, v-p, IT; Dr. Karen S. Yoshiki-Gravelsins, v-p, corp. stewardship & operational excellence

Capital Stock

	Authorized (shs.)	Outstanding (shs.)[1]
Preference	unlimited	nil
Common	unlimited	57,359,516

[1] At Aug. 4, 2023

Normal Course Issuer Bid - The company plans to make normal course purchases of up to 2,868,106 common shares representing 5% of the total outstanding. The bid commenced on May 27, 2023, and expires on May 26, 2024.

Major Shareholder - N. Murray Edwards held 75% interest at Mar. 17, 2023.

Price Range - MAL/TSX

Year	Volume	High	Low	Close
2022	3,411,990	$10.20	$6.60	$10.00
2021	4,328,218	$11.73	$8.80	$9.96
2020	12,358,995	$14.61	$4.80	$8.77
2019	3,345,404	$19.00	$13.65	$14.06
2018	4,683,012	$21.49	$13.20	$14.98

Recent Close: $7.26

Capital Stock Changes - During 2022, 282,972 common shares were repurchased under a Normal Course Issuer Bid.

Dividends

MAL com Ra $0.10 pa Q est. Dec. 30, 2022
Prev. Rate: $0.20 est. Sept. 29, 2022
Prev. Rate: $0.32 est. June 30, 2022
Prev. Rate: $0.42 est. Dec. 31, 2019

Long-Term Debt - At Dec. 31, 2022, outstanding long-term debt totaled $5,465,000 ($4,831,000 current) and consisted of $2,695,000 bank loans bearing interest at SOFR plus 3% due October 2023; and $2,770,000 government loans bearing interest at 2.875% due April 2024.

Note - In June 2023, the company extended the maturity of its $75,000,000 facility agreement from June 30, 2023, to June 30, 2025. The facility bears interest at banker's acceptance rate or adjusted SOFR rates plus 1.00%.

Wholly Owned Subsidiaries

Magellan Aerospace Limited, Mississauga, Ont.
- 100% int. in **Magellan Aerospace USA, Inc.**, Middleton, Mass.
  - 100% int. in **Magellan Aerospace Glendale, Inc.**, Ariz.
  - 100% int. in **Magellan Aerospace Haverhill, Inc.**, Delaware, Ont.
  - 100% int. in **Magellan Aerospace Middletown, Inc.**, Ohio

- 100% int. in **Magellan Aerospace New York, Inc.**, New York, N.Y.
- 100% int. in **Magellan Aerospace Processing, Long Island, Inc.**, Del.

Magellan Aerospace (UK) Limited, Bristol, Gloucs., United Kingdom.

Subsidiaries

75% int. in **Magellan Aerospace Tumkur Private Limited**, India.

Note: The preceding list includes only the major related companies in which interests are held.

Financial Statistics

Periods ended:	12m Dec. 31/22[A]		12m Dec. 31/21[A]
	$000s	%Chg	$000s
Operating revenue	**764,580**	**+11**	**688,358**
Salaries & benefits	25,764		25,262
General & admin expense	20,021		16,286
Other operating expense	684,304		591,147
Operating expense	**730,089**	**+15**	**632,695**
Operating income	**34,491**	**-38**	**55,663**
Deprec., depl. & amort.	47,405		51,892
Finance costs, gross	2,838		2,895
Write-downs/write-offs	(2,483)		nil
Pre-tax income	**(18,604)**	**n.a.**	**1,869**
Income taxes	3,088		2,846
Net income	**(21,692)**	**n.a.**	**(977)**
Cash & equivalent	40,940		32,482
Inventories	226,359		208,577
Accounts receivable	169,562		164,234
Current assets	512,284		481,294
Long-term investments	1,621		1,659
Fixed assets, net	384,084		396,845
Right-of-use assets	30,825		34,389
Intangibles, net	63,604		69,564
Total assets	**1,010,894**	**+1**	**1,003,818**
Accts. pay. & accr. liabs	132,940		103,377
Current liabilities	181,559		133,648
Long-term debt, gross	5,465		7,307
Long-term debt, net	634		2,755
Long-term lease liabilities	27,761		30,644
Shareholders' equity	728,353		762,447
Non-controlling interest	3,377		3,377
Cash from oper. activs	**58,540**	**+367**	**12,526**
Cash from fin. activs	(26,274)		(73,009)
Cash from invest. activs	(23,856)		(20,804)
Net cash position	**40,940**	**+26**	**32,482**
Capital expenditures	(23,494)		(17,675)
Capital disposals	607		1,509
	$		$
Earnings per share*	(0.38)		(0.02)
Cash flow per share*	1.02		0.22
Cash divd. per share*	0.26		0.42
	shs		shs
No. of shs. o/s*	57,446,134		57,729,106
Avg. no. of shs. o/s*	57,637,104		57,729,106
	%		%
Net profit margin	(2.84)		(0.14)
Return on equity	(2.91)		(0.13)
Return on assets	(1.82)		(0.24)
Foreign sales percent	57		54
No. of employees (FTEs)	3,500		3,400

* Common

[A] Reported in accordance with IFRS

Latest Results

Periods ended:	6m June 30/23[A]		6m June 30/22[A]
	$000s	%Chg	$000s
Operating revenue	443,027	+16	380,371
Net income	5,839	n.a.	(1,485)
	$		$
Earnings per share*	0.10		(0.03)

* Common

[A] Reported in accordance with IFRS

Historical Summary
(as originally stated)

Fiscal Year	Oper. Rev.	Net Inc. Bef. Disc.	EPS*
	$000s	$000s	$
2022[A]	764,580	(21,692)	(0.38)
2021[A]	688,358	(977)	(0.02)
2020[A]	744,414	3,313	0.06
2019[A]	1,016,219	67,381	1.16
2018[A]	966,753	89,120	1.53

* Common

[A] Reported in accordance with IFRS

M.20 Magna International Inc.*

Symbol - MG **Exchange** - TSX **CUSIP** - 559222

Head Office - 337 Magna Dr, Aurora, ON, L4G 7K1 **Telephone** - (905) 726-2462 **Fax** - (905) 726-7164

Website - www.magna.com

Email - louis.tonelli@magna.com

Investor Relations - Louis B. Tonelli (905) 726-7035

Auditors - Deloitte LLP C.A., Toronto, Ont.

Lawyers - Sidley Austin LLP, New York, N.Y.; Osler, Hoskin & Harcourt LLP, Toronto, Ont.

Transfer Agents - Computershare Trust Company, N.A., Canton, Mass.; Computershare Trust Company of Canada Inc., Toronto, Ont.

FP500 Revenue Ranking - 10

Employees - 168,000 at Dec. 31, 2022

Profile - (Ont. 1961) Designs, develops and manufactures automotive systems, assemblies, modules and components, and engineers and assembles complete vehicles for original equipment manufacturers (OEMs) of cars and light trucks. Also has electronic and software capabilities integrated to its products.

The company has 351 manufacturing facilities and 103 product development, engineering and sales centres in 30 countries with operations reported on four global, product-oriented segments: **Body Exteriors and Structures**, which includes the body and chassis, exteriors, roof and fuel systems operations; **Power and Vision**, which includes powertrain, electronics, mirrors and lighting and mechatronics operations; **Seating Systems**, which consists of complete seating systems, seat structures, mechanism and hardware solutions and foam and trim products; and **Complete Vehicles**, which consists of contract manufacturing, fuel systems and complete vehicle engineering operations.

Light Vehicle Production Volume

Year ended Dec. 31	2022	2021
	000s	000s
North America	14,277	13,145
Europe	15,608	15,958
China	26,856	24,502

In August 2023, the company sold all its investments in Russia for a total of US$15,000,000.

In October 2022, the company entered into a joint venture agreement with **Guangdong Huatie-Tongda Express Train Systems Inc.** to supply seating solutions to certain automakers on their new energy vehicles. The joint venture would be located in Qingdao, People's Republic of China.

In September 2022, the company invested US$25,000,000 in **Yulu Bikes Pvt. Ltd.**, a Bangalore, India-based electrified shared mobility provider. As part of the transaction, the company and Yulu established a battery swapping entity, **Magna Yuma**, to support electrification of mobility and required infrastructure. Yulu contributed certain assets and intellectual property for a 49% interest in Magna Yuma and the company contributed US$52,000,000 cash for a 51% interest in Magna Yuma.

In April 2022, **LG Magna e-Powertrain**, a joint venture (JV) between **LG Electronics** (LG) and the company, broke ground on its new plant in Ramos Arizpe, Mexico. The new 260,000-sq.-ft. plant, which is scheduled for completion in 2023, would produce inverters, motors, and on-board chargers to support **General Motors**' electric vehicle (EV) production.

Also in April 2022, the company opened a new 22,000-m^2 facility in Kechnec, Slovakia to produce advanced cameras and electronics for inverters for two European automakers.

Recent Merger and Acquisition Activity

Status: completed **Announced:** June 30, 2023

Magna International Inc. sold two buildings as a result of restructuring activities for US$10,000,000.

Status: completed **Revised:** June 1, 2023

UPDATE: The transaction was completed. The business would be combined with Magna's existing ADAS business and integrated into Magna's electronics operating unit. PREVIOUS: Magna International Inc. agreed to acquire Veoneer, Inc.'s Active Safety business from New York, N.Y.-based investment firm SSW Partners, LP for US$1.525 billion. Veoneer's Active Safety systems provide early warnings to alert drivers to prevent accidents by using features such as autonomous emergency braking, forward collision warning and blind spot detection. The acquisition was expected to add to Magna's sensor and full systems capabilities, including radar, camera and driver monitoring, and add 2,200 engineers, including 1,800 for systems, software and sensor development. Veoneer Active Safety sales were projected to be US$1.1 billion in 2022 and increase to US$1.9 billion in 2024. Veoneer was acquired by SSW on Apr. 1, 2022. The transaction was expected to be completed near the middle of 2023, subject to regulatory approvals and other customary closing conditions.

Status: completed **Revised:** Mar. 31, 2023

UPDATE: The transaction was completed. PREVIOUS: Magna International Inc. agreed to sell a European Power and Vision operation which includes powertrain, electronics, mirrors and lighting and mechatronics operations for an undisclosed amount. Magna is obligated to provide the buyer with up to $42,000,000 of funding.

Predecessor Detail - Name changed from Magna Electronics Corporation Limited, Jan. 2, 1973.

Directors - Robert F. (Rob) MacLellan, chr., Toronto, Ont.; Seetarama S. (Swamy) Kotagiri, CEO, Mich.; Peter G. Bowie, Toronto, Ont.; Mary S. Chan, N.J.; The Hon. V. Peter Harder, Manotick, Ont.; Jan R. Hauser, Mass.; Jay K. Kunkel, Tokyo, Japan; Mary Lou Maher, Toronto, Ont.; William A. Ruh, N.S.W., Australia; Dr. Indira V. Samarasekera, Vancouver, B.C.; Matthew Tsien, Wash.; Dr. Thomas Weber, Germany; Lisa S. Westlake, Fla.

Other Exec. Officers - Vincent J. (Vince) Galifi, pres.; Joanne N. Horibe, chief compliance officer; Bruce R. Cluney, exec. v-p & chief legal officer; Matteo Del Sorbo, exec. v-p, Magna new mobility; Uwe Geissinger, exec. v-p, operational efficiency; Anton Mayer, exec. v-p & chief tech. officer; Patrick W. D. McCann, exec. v-p & CFO; Aaron D. McCarthy, exec. v-p & chief HR officer; Boris Shulkin, exec. v-p & chief digital info. officer; Tom J. (Tommy) Skudutis, exec. v-p & COO; Eric J. Wilds, exec. v-p & chief sales & mktg. officer; Bassem A. Shakeel, v-p & corp. sec.; Guenther F. Apfalter, pres., Magna Europe & Asia & pres., Magna Steyr GmbH; John H. Farrell, pres., Cosma, exteriors & seating; Tom J. Rucker, pres., MPT, MML, electronics & complete vehicles

Capital Stock

	Authorized (shs.)	Outstanding (shs.)[1]
Preference	99,760,000	nil
Common	unlimited	286,309,052

[1] At Aug. 3, 2023

Normal Course Issuer Bid - The company plans to make normal course purchases of up to 28,445,000 common shares representing 10% of the public float. The bid commenced on Nov. 15, 2022, and expires on Nov. 14, 2023.

Major Shareholder - Widely held at Mar. 24, 2023.

Price Range - MG/TSX

Year	Volume	High	Low	Close
2022	218,958,982	$112.62	$63.55	$76.06
2021	183,964,075	$126.00	$87.42	$102.35
2020	254,326,967	$96.11	$33.22	$90.11
2019	213,470,348	$76.11	$57.34	$71.20
2018	274,524,802	$87.13	$58.74	$61.97

Recent Close: $76.93

Capital Stock Changes - During 2022, common shares were issued as follows: 500,000 on release of restricted stock and stock units and 200,000 on exercise of options; 12,600,000 common shares were repurchased under a Normal Course Issuer Bid and 200,000 common shares were cancelled.

Dividends

MG com Ra US$1.84 pa Q est. Mar. 10, 2023**
Prev. Rate: US$1.80 est. Mar. 11, 2022
Prev. Rate: US$1.72 est. Mar. 19, 2021
Prev. Rate: US$1.60 est. Mar. 20, 2020
** Reinvestment Option

Long-Term Debt - Outstanding at Dec. 31, 2022:

Bank term debt[1]	US$114,000,000
Government loans[2]	8,000,000
1.9% sr. notes due 2023[3]	588,000,000
3.625% sr. notes due 2024[4]	749,000,000
4.15% sr. notes due 2025[5]	647,000,000
1.5% sr. notes due 2027[6]	640,000,000
2.45% sr. notes due 2030[4]	744,000,000
Other	11,000,000
	3,501,000,000
Less: Current portion	654,000,000
	2,847,000,000

[1] Bears a weighted average interest rate of 3.98% (2021 - 4.86%). Denominated primarily in Chinese renminbi, Brazilian real, the euro and Indian rupee.

[2] Bears a weighted average interest rate of 0.12% (2021 - 0.13%). Denominated primarily in the euro, Canadian dollar and Brazilian real.

[3] €550,000,000.

[4] US$750,000,000.

[5] US$650,000,000.

[6] €600,000,000.

Minimum long-term debt repayments were reported as follows:

2023	US$655,000,000
2024	762,000,000
2025	694,000,000
2026	3,000,000
2027	643,000,000
Thereafter	756,000,000

Note - In March 2023, private placement of Cdn$350,000,000 principal amount of 4.95% senior notes due Jan. 31, 2031; US$300,000,000 principal amount of 5.98% series 1 senior notes due Mar. 21, 2026; US$500,000,000 principal amount of 5.5% series 2 senior notes due Mar. 21, 2033; and €550,000,000 principal amount of 4.375% senior notes due Mar. 17 2032, were completed.

Wholly Owned Subsidiaries

Magna Exteriors Inc., Ont.

Magna Internacional de Mexico, S.A. de C.V., Mexico.

Magna International (Hong Kong) Limited, Hong Kong, Hong Kong, People's Republic of China.

Magna Powertrain de Mexico, S.A. de C.V., Mexico.

Magna Powertrain Inc., Ont.

Magna Seating Inc., Ont.
1305290 Ontario Inc., Ont.
- 100% int. in **Magna International Investments S.A.**, Luxembourg.
  - 100% int. in **Magna International Automotive Holding GmbH**, Austria.
    - 100% int. in **Magna Automotive Europe GmbH**, Austria.
      - 100% int. in **Magna Automotive Holding GmbH**, Austria.
        - 100% int. in **Magna Metalforming GmbH**, Austria.
          - 100% int. in **Magna Steyr GmbH & Co. KG**, Austria.
            - 100% int. in **Magna Powertrain GmbH & Co. KG**, Austria.
          - 100% int. in **Magna Steyr Fahrzeugtechnik AG & Co. KG**, Austria.
            - 100% int. in **Engineering Center Steyr GmbH**, Austria.
              - 100% int. in **Magna Powertrain GmbH**, Austria.
    - 100% int. in **Magna Automotive Holding (Germany) GmbH**, Germany.
      - 100% int. in **Magna PT Holding GmbH**, Germany.

175 Holdings ULC, Alta.
- 100% int. in **Magna US Holding, Inc.**, Del.
  - 100% int. in **Cosma International of America, Inc.**, Mich.
  - 100% int. in **Intier Automotive of America, Inc.**, Del.
    - 100% int. in **Intier Automotive of America Holdings, Inc.**, Del.
      - 100% int. in **Magna Seating of America, Inc.**, Del.
  - 100% int. in **Magna Exteriors Holdings, Inc.**, Del.
    - 100% int. in **Magna Exteriors of America, Inc.**, Del.
  - 100% int. in **Magna Mirrors of America, Inc.**, Mich.

Note: The preceding list includes only the major related companies in which interests are held.

Financial Statistics

Periods ended:	12m Dec. 31/22[A]		12m Dec. 31/21[A]
	US$000s	%Chg	US$000s
Operating revenue	**37,840,000**	**+4**	**36,242,000**
Cost of goods sold	33,188,000		31,097,000
General & admin expense	1,660,000		1,717,000
Operating expense	**34,848,000**	**+6**	**32,814,000**
Operating income	**2,992,000**	**-13**	**3,428,000**
Deprec., depl. & amort.	1,419,000		1,512,000
Finance income	45,000		44,000
Finance costs, gross	126,000		122,000
Investment income	89,000		148,000
Write-downs/write-offs	(376,000)		nil
Pre-tax income	**878,000**	**-55**	**1,948,000**
Income taxes	237,000		395,000
Net income	**641,000**	**-59**	**1,553,000**
Net inc. for equity hldrs	**592,000**	**-61**	**1,514,000**
Net inc. for non-cont. int	**49,000**	**+26**	**39,000**
Cash & equivalent	1,234,000		2,948,000
Inventories	4,180,000		3,969,000
Accounts receivable	6,791,000		6,307,000
Current assets	12,525,000		13,502,000
Long-term investments	1,429,000		1,593,000
Fixed assets, net	8,173,000		8,293,000
Right-of-use assets	1,595,000		1,700,000
Intangibles, net	2,483,000		2,615,000
Total assets	**27,789,000**	**-4**	**29,086,000**
Bank indebtedness	8,000		nil
Accts. pay. & accr. liabs	6,999,000		6,465,000
Current liabilities	10,998,000		10,401,000
Long-term debt, gross	3,501,000		3,993,000
Long-term debt, net	2,847,000		3,538,000
Long-term lease liabilities	1,288,000		1,406,000
Shareholders' equity	10,935,000		11,836,000
Non-controlling interest	400,000		389,000
Cash from oper. activs	**2,095,000**	**-29**	**2,940,000**
Cash from fin. activs	(1,733,000)		(1,106,000)
Cash from invest. activs	(2,038,000)		(2,283,000)
Net cash position	**1,234,000**	**-58**	**2,948,000**
Capital expenditures	(1,681,000)		(1,372,000)
Capital disposals	130,000		40,000
Unfunded pension liability	107,000		157,000
	US$		US$
Earnings per share*	2.04		5.04
Cash flow per share*	7.21		9.78
Cash divd. per share*	1.80		1.72
	shs		shs
No. of shs. o/s*	285,931,816		297,871,976
Avg. no. of shs. o/s*	290,400,000		300,600,000
	%		%
Net profit margin	1.69		4.29
Return on equity	5.20		13.05
Return on assets	2.58		5.72
Foreign sales percent	87		88
No. of employees (FTEs)	168,000		158,000

* Common
[A] Reported in accordance with U.S. GAAP

Latest Results

Periods ended:	6m June 30/23[A]		6m June 30/22[A]
	US$000s	%Chg	US$000s
Operating revenue	21,655,000	+14	19,004,000
Net income	571,000	+144	234,000
Net inc. for equity hldrs	548,000	+163	208,000
Net inc. for non-cont. int	23,000		26,000
	US$		US$
Earnings per share*	1.92		0.71

* Common
[A] Reported in accordance with U.S. GAAP

Historical Summary
(as originally stated)

Fiscal Year	Oper. Rev.	Net Inc. Bef. Disc.	EPS*
	US$000s	US$000s	US$
2022[A]	37,840,000	641,000	2.04
2021[A]	36,242,000	1,553,000	5.04
2020[A]	32,647,000	677,000	2.52
2019[A]	39,431,000	1,632,000	5.61
2018[A]	40,827,000	2,332,000	6.65

* Common
[A] Reported in accordance with U.S. GAAP

M.21 Magnetic North Acquisition Corp.

Symbol - MNC **Exchange** - TSX-VEN (S) **CUSIP** - 55948L
Head Office - 1000-250 5 St SW, Calgary, AB, T2P 0C1 **Telephone** - (403) 470-4355 **Fax** - (403) 271-1769
Website - www.magneticnac.com
Email - stephen@magneticnac.com
Investor Relations - Stephen McCormick (403) 619-6898
Auditors - PKF Antares Professional Corporation C.A., Calgary, Alta.
Lawyers - DLA Piper (Canada) LLP
Transfer Agents - TSX Trust Company
Profile - (Can. 2008; orig. Alta., 1997) Operates as a merchant bank providing capital, management and board representation to small to mid-capitalization private companies.

Industries of focus for investments include clean power technology, consumer products, oilfield services and technology inclusive of software and hardware.

Portfolio of investments include 50% interest in **CXTL Recycling Canada Corp.**, which converts plastics and other hydrocarbons into upgraded fuel and feedstocks; 32% interest in **Previcare Inc.**, a healthcare company focused on the research, development, sales and marketing of hand sanitizer and hard surface disinfectant products; 40% interest in **Power Symmetry Inc.**, which develops solid state energy storage solutions to power producers and users; and less than 1% interest in **Ignite Alliance Corp.**, which provides strategic portfolio management, agile, enterprise content management and automation software and consultancy services.

Through wholly owned subsidiary **Bluenose Quartz Ltd.**, owns and operates White Rock industrial minerals (quartz, kaolin and mica) mine, 1,650 hectares, 45 km north of Shelburne, N.S. Operations have been suspended at the mine since January 2009.

Common suspended from TSX-VEN, July 4, 2023.

Predecessor Detail - Name changed from Black Bull Resources Inc., Sept. 16, 2019, pursuant to change of business from resource company to investment company.

Directors - Ian G. Wild, chr., Calgary, Alta.; Kevin Spall, co-CEO, Toronto, Ont.; Andrew E. Osis, pres. & co-CEO, Calgary, Alta.; Jeff Davison, Calgary, Alta.; Trent Larson, Calgary, Alta.

Other Exec. Officers - Lance McIntosh, CFO; Stephen McCormick, v-p, capital markets

Capital Stock

	Authorized (shs.)	Outstanding (shs.)[1]
Series A Preferred	unlimited	1,750,825
Common	unlimited	59,097,178

[1] At June 27, 2022

Series A Preferred - Redeemable by the company after Mar. 31, 2026. Non-voting.
Common - One vote per share.
Major Shareholder - Andrew E. Osis held 29% interest and Kevin Spall held 29% interest at Sept. 23, 2020.

Price Range - MNC/TSX-VEN (S)

Year	Volume	High	Low	Close
2022	1,419,244	$0.22	$0.02	$0.03
2021	2,545,979	$0.74	$0.16	$0.19
2020	5,627,518	$1.03	$0.08	$0.76
2019	913,251	$0.26	$0.08	$0.20

Recent Close: $0.03

Wholly Owned Subsidiaries

Bluenose Quartz Ltd., N.S.

Investments

50% int. in **CXTL Recycling Canada Corp.**, Canada.
Ignite Alliance Corp., Calgary, Alta.
40% int. in **Power Symmetry Inc.**, Toronto, Ont.
32% int. in **Previcare, Inc.**, Brighton, Ont.

Financial Statistics

Periods ended:	12m Dec. 31/21[A]		15m Dec. 31/20[◊A]
	$000s	%Chg	$000s
Exploration expense	12		(51)
General & admin expense	1,082		1,623
Stock-based compensation	1,107		3,713
Operating expense	**2,201**	**n.a.**	**5,285**
Operating income	**(2,201)**	**n.a.**	**(5,285)**
Deprec., depl. & amort.	2		1
Finance income	4		79
Finance costs, gross	1		7
Pre-tax income	**(3,109)**	**n.a.**	**(15,658)**
Net income	**(3,109)**	**n.a.**	**(15,658)**
Cash & equivalent	27		76
Accounts receivable	18		133
Current assets	671		244
Long-term investments	4,259		5,170
Fixed assets, net	3		5
Total assets	**5,242**	**-8**	**5,723**
Bank indebtedness	177		177
Accts. pay. & accr. liabs	924		417
Current liabilities	1,101		594
Shareholders' equity	(13,086)		(11,106)
Cash from oper. activs	**(470)**	**n.a.**	**(1,756)**
Cash from fin. activs	1,022		4,310
Cash from invest. activs	(579)		(3,957)
Net cash position	**nil**	**n.a.**	**26**
Capital expenditures	nil		(5)
	$		$
Earnings per share*	(0.05)		(0.27)
Cash flow per share*	(0.01)		(0.03)
	shs		shs
No. of shs. o/s*	59,097,178		59,051,105
Avg. no. of shs. o/s*	59,086,652		59,051,105
	%		%
Net profit margin	n.a.		...
Return on equity	n.m.		...
Return on assets	(43.26)		...

* Common
[◊] Restated
[A] Reported in accordance with IFRS

Latest Results

Periods ended:	3m Mar. 31/22[A]		3m Mar. 31/21[◊A]
	$000s	%Chg	$000s
Net income	(357)	n.a.	(365)
	$		$
Earnings per share*	(0.01)		(0.01)

* Common
[◊] Restated
[A] Reported in accordance with IFRS

Historical Summary
(as originally stated)

Fiscal Year	Oper. Rev.	Net Inc. Bef. Disc.	EPS*
	$000s	$000s	$
2021[A]	nil	(3,109)	(0.05)
2020[A1]	nil	(13,980)	(0.24)
2019[A]	nil	(1,468)	(0.16)
2018[A]	nil	(115)	(0.03)
2017[A]	nil	(176)	(0.05)

* Common
[A] Reported in accordance with IFRS
[1] 15 months ended Dec. 31, 2020.

M.22 Mainstreet Equity Corp.

Symbol - MEQ **Exchange** - TSX **CUSIP** - 560915
Head Office - 100-305 10 Ave SE, Calgary, AB, T2G 0W2 **Telephone** - (403) 215-6060 **Toll-free** - (866) 480-6246 **Fax** - (403) 266-8867
Website - www.mainst.biz
Email - tcui@mainst.biz
Investor Relations - Na Cui (866) 480-6246
Auditors - PricewaterhouseCoopers LLP C.A., Calgary, Alta.
Bankers - The Toronto-Dominion Bank, Calgary, Alta.
Lawyers - Borden Ladner Gervais LLP, Calgary, Alta.; WBA Law LLP, Calgary, Alta.
Transfer Agents - Computershare Trust Company of Canada Inc., Calgary, Alta.
FP500 Revenue Ranking - 678
Employees - 497 at Dec. 9, 2022
Profile - (Alta. 1997) Acquires and manages mid-market multi-family residential real estate properties in British Columbia, Alberta, Saskatchewan and Manitoba.

At Sept. 30, 2022, the company's property portfolio consisted of 421 buildings, totaling 15,895 units, including townhouses, garden-style apartments, mid-rise and high-rise apartments and freestanding commercial houses.

Location	Props.	Units
Lower Mainland, B.C.[1]	30	2,944
B.C., excluding Lower Mainland[2]	9	480
Calgary, Alta.[3]	101	3,537
Edmonton, Alta.[4]	157	5,496
Saskatoon, Sask.	59	2,333
Regina, Sask.	62	991
Winnipeg, Man.	3	114
	421	15,895

[1] Includes Abbotsford, Chilliwack, New Westminster and Surrey.
[2] Includes Courtenay, Kamloops, Penticton, Prince George and Vernon.
[3] Includes Lethbridge, Cochrane and Airdrie.
[4] Includes Fort Saskatchewan.

Subsequent to fiscal 2022, the company acquired 548 residential units in Alberta and Manitoba for total consideration of $57,600,000.

During fiscal 2022, the company acquired 412 units in Edmonton, Alta., 174 units in British Columbia, 148 units in Calgary, Alta., 53 units in Regina, Sask., 27 units in Winnipeg, Man., and a unit in Saskatoon, Sask., for total consideration of $90,573,000.

Directors - Navjeet S. (Bob) Dhillon, founder, pres. & CEO, Calgary, Alta.; Joseph B. (Joe) Amantea, corp. sec. & treas., Calgary, Alta.; Ron B. Anderson, Vancouver, B.C.; Karanveer V. Dhillon, San Francisco, Calif.; Richard (Rich) Grimaldi, Westport, Conn.; John Irwin, London, Ont.

Other Exec. Officers - Na (Trina) Cui, CFO; Sheena J. Keslick, v-p, opers.

Capital Stock

	Authorized (shs.)	Outstanding (shs.)[1]
Preferred	unlimited	nil
Common	unlimited	9,318,818

[1] At May 19, 2023

Normal Course Issuer Bid - The company plans to make normal course purchases of up to 474,499 common shares representing 10% of the public float. The bid commenced on June 3, 2023, and expires on June 2, 2024.

Major Shareholder - Navjeet S. (Bob) Dhillon held 46.3% interest at Feb. 8, 2023.

Price Range - MEQ/TSX

Year	Volume	High	Low	Close
2022	552,863	$154.36	$104.00	$118.00
2021	301,455	$126.74	$74.43	$120.19
2020	905,352	$96.25	$41.75	$79.07
2019	452,906	$80.00	$40.45	$79.00
2018	425,469	$48.97	$39.01	$41.61

Recent Close: $133.19

Capital Stock Changes - During fiscal 2022, 18,500 common shares were repurchased under a Normal Course Issuer Bid.

Wholly Owned Subsidiaries

MEQ Asset Management Corp.

Financial Statistics

Periods ended:	12m Sept. 30/22[A]		12m Sept. 30/21[A]
	$000s	%Chg	$000s
Total revenue	**180,573**	**+13**	**159,925**
Rental operating expense	54,320		46,525
General & admin. expense	14,937		12,240
Property taxes	16,588		15,552
Operating expense	**85,845**	**+16**	**74,317**
Operating income	**94,728**	**+11**	**85,608**
Deprec. & amort.	919		905
Finance income	776		426
Finance costs, gross	42,475		38,343
Pre-tax income	**143,166**	**-45**	**258,902**
Income taxes	22,630		33,368
Net income	**120,536**	**-47**	**225,534**
Cash & equivalent	44,560		19,224
Inventories	1,859		1,899
Accounts receivable	1,547		1,195
Current assets	67,210		50,457
Fixed assets	12,582		11,467
Income-producing props	2,817,905		2,616,154
Property interests, net	2,825,251		2,622,919
Intangibles, net	1,031		1,193
Total assets	**2,893,492**	**+8**	**2,674,569**
Accts. pay. & accr. liabs	8,328		7,491
Current liabilities	128,111		96,569
Long-term debt, gross	1,433,453		1,357,177
Long-term debt, net	1,321,072		1,274,762
Shareholders' equity	1,210,750		1,092,309
Cash from oper. activs	**52,683**	**+48**	**35,609**
Cash from fin. activs	74,886		185,547
Cash from invest. activs	(102,233)		(240,404)
Net cash position	**44,560**	**+132**	**19,224**
Capital expenditures	(566)		(702)
Capital disposals	14,164		1,240
Increase in property	(115,425)		(218,586)
	$		$
Earnings per share*	12.90		24.13
Cash flow per share*	5.64		3.81
Funds from opers. per sh.*	5.65		5.08
	shs		shs
No. of shs. o/s*	9,326,718		9,345,218
Avg. no. of shs. o/s*	9,341,683		9,345,350
	%		%
Net profit margin	66.75		141.02
Return on equity	10.47		23.02
Return on assets	5.61		10.54
No. of employees (FTEs)	487		449

* Common
[A] Reported in accordance with IFRS

Latest Results

Periods ended:	3m Dec. 31/22[A]		3m Dec. 31/21[A]
	$000s	%Chg	$000s
Total revenue	48,862	+13	43,250
Net income	15,002	+21	12,404
	$		$
Earnings per share*	1.61		1.33

* Common
[A] Reported in accordance with IFRS

Historical Summary
(as originally stated)

Fiscal Year	Total Rev.	Net Inc. Bef. Disc.	EPS*
	$000s	$000s	$
2022[A]	180,573	120,536	12.90
2021[A]	159,925	225,534	24.13
2020[A]	149,770	68,550	7.32
2019[A]	137,613	58,685	6.41
2018[A]	115,665	72,723	8.23

* Common
[A] Reported in accordance with IFRS

M.23 Major Drilling Group International Inc.*

Symbol - MDI **Exchange** - TSX **CUSIP** - 560909
Head Office - 100-111 St. George St, Moncton, NB, E1C 1T7 **Telephone** - (506) 857-8636 **Toll-free** - (866) 264-3986 **Fax** - (506) 857-9211
Website - www.majordrilling.com
Email - ian.ross@majordrilling.com
Investor Relations - Ian Ross (506) 857-8636
Auditors - Deloitte LLP C.A., Moncton, N.B.
Transfer Agents - TSX Trust Company, Toronto, Ont.
FP500 Revenue Ranking - 418
Employees - 3,462 at Apr. 30, 2023
Profile - (Can. 1994 amalg.) Provides drilling and a variety of mine services to customers worldwide with varied exploration drilling requirements.

The company offers all types of drilling services including surface and underground coring, directional, reverse circulation, sonic, geotechnical, environmental, water-well, coal-bed methane, shallow gas, underground percussive/longhole drilling, surface drill and blast, and a variety of mine services.

Drilling contracts are usually based on standard industry terms and priced on the basis of an assessment of the terrain, size of core, depth of hole, and drilling equipment mobilization and demobilization costs.

Field operations and offices are located in Canada, the U.S., Mexico, South America, Asia, Africa and Australia.

Drill rigs per geographic location at Apr. 30, 2023:

Location	No. of drill rigs
Canada & the U.S.	285
South & Central America	198
Australasia & Africa	117

Periods ended:	12m Apr. 30/23	12m Apr. 30/22
No. of drill rigs	600	603

Directors - Kimberly A. (Kim) Keating, chr., Portugal Cove-St. Philips, N.L.; Denis Larocque, pres. & CEO, Dieppe, N.B.; Caroline Donally, Houston, Tex.; Louis-Pierre Gignac, Brossard, Qué.; Robert L. (Rob) Krcmarov, Toronto, Ont.; Juliana L. (Julie) Lam, Toronto, Ont.; Janice G. Rennie, Edmonton, Alta.; Sybil E. Veenman, Toronto, Ont.; Jo Mark Zurel, St. John's, N.L.

Other Exec. Officers - Ian Ross, CFO; John Ross (JR) Davies, v-p, opers., Australasia & Africa; Ben Graham, v-p, HR & safety; Marc Landry, v-p, tech. & logistics; Ashley Martin, v-p, opers., Latin America; Andrew McLaughlin, v-p, legal affairs, gen. counsel & corp. sec.; Kevin Slemko, v-p, opers., U.S.; Barry Zerbin, v-p, opers., Cdn.

Capital Stock

	Authorized (shs.)	Outstanding (shs.)[1]
Common	unlimited	82,958,679

[1] At Aug. 9, 2023

Options - At Apr. 30, 2023, options were outstanding to purchase 950,925 common shares at prices ranging from $3.60 to $10.50 per share with a weighted average remaining life of 3.36 to 3.56 years.

Normal Course Issuer Bid - The company plans to make normal course purchases of up to 4,150,251 common shares representing 5% of the total outstanding. The bid commenced on Mar. 27, 2023, and expires on Mar. 26, 2024.

Major Shareholder - Fidelity Investments Inc. held 10.51% interest at July 13, 2023.

Price Range - MDI/TSX

Year	Volume	High	Low	Close
2022	36,327,970	$12.86	$7.25	$10.52
2021	54,891,307	$11.34	$6.41	$8.26
2020	54,120,249	$8.38	$2.26	$7.69
2019	26,139,258	$6.78	$3.89	$5.67
2018	17,342,235	$7.89	$4.17	$4.60

Recent Close: $7.99

Capital Stock Changes - During fiscal 2023, 321,675 common shares were issued on exercise of options.

During fiscal 2022, common shares were issued as follows: 1,318,101 pursuant to the acquisition of McKay Drilling Pty Limited and 732,600 on exercise of options.

Long-Term Debt - At Apr. 30, 2023, outstanding long-term debt totaled $19,972,000 (none current and net of $28,000 fair value variance from an interest rate swap) and consisted entirely of revolving term loan bearing interest at prime rate plus 0.5% or bankers' acceptance rate plus 2% for Canadian dollar draws, and SOFR plus 2% for U.S. dollar draws, maturing in September 2027.

Wholly Owned Subsidiaries

Forage Major Kennebec Drilling Ltd., Thetford Mines, Qué.
- 100% int. in **Maine Diamond Drilling Inc.**, Me.
  - 100% int. in **Major Drilling America, Inc.**, United States.
- 50% int. in **Major Energia S.A.**, Argentina.

MD Colombia S.A., Colombia.
MD Guyana Inc., Guyana.
MDGI Philippines, Inc., Philippines.
Major Drilling Chile S.A., Chile.
Major Drilling do Brasil Ltda., Brazil.
Major Drilling Group Australasia Pty Ltd., Australia.
- 100% int. in **Major Drilling Pty Ltd.**, Australia.
  - 100% int. in **McKay Drilling Pty Limited**, Perth, W.A., Australia.
  - 100% int. in **PT Major Drilling Indonesia**, Indonesia.

Major Drilling International Inc., Barbados.
- 100% int. in **MDM Leasing and Drilling Services Inc.**, Mauritius.
  - 100% int. in **Major Drilling Mozambique S.A.**, Mozambique.
- 100% int. in **Major Drilling Botswana (Pty) Ltd.**, Botswana.
- 100% int. in **Major Drilling Burkina Faso S.A.**, Burkina Faso.
- 100% int. in **Major Drilling de Mexico, S.A. de C.V.**, Mexico.
- 100% int. in **Major Drilling International Suriname**, Suriname.
- 100% int. in **Major Drilling Namibia (Pty) Ltd.**, Namibia.
- 75% int. in **Major Drilling South Africa (Pty) Limited**, South Africa.
- 100% int. in **Major Perforaciones, S.A.**, Argentina.

Major Drilling Kazakhstan LLP, Kazakhstan.
Major Drilling Mongolia XXK, Mongolia.
Major Drilling (NI) Limited, Ireland.
Major Guyane S.A.S., French Guiana.
Major Procurement Inc., Canada.
Norex Drilling Limited, Timmins, Ont.

Investments

50% int. in **Major Energia S.A.**, Argentina.

Financial Statistics

Periods ended:	12m Apr. 30/23^A		12m Apr. 30/22^A
	$000s	%Chg	$000s
Operating revenue	**735,742**	**+13**	**650,415**
Cost of sales	515,190		470,064
General & admin expense	61,130		53,641
Stock-based compensation	508		369
Operating expense	**576,828**	**+10**	**524,074**
Operating income	**158,914**	**+26**	**126,341**
Deprec., depl. & amort.	47,478		43,981
Finance costs, gross	n.a.		1,629
Finance costs, net	(832)		n.a.
Pre-tax income	**97,572**	**+42**	**68,484**
Income taxes	22,650		15,025
Net income	**74,922**	**+40**	**53,459**
Cash & equivalent	94,432		71,260
Inventories	115,128		96,782
Accounts receivable	137,633		142,621
Current assets	360,525		321,660
Fixed assets, net	220,722		203,675
Intangibles, net	25,994		27,394
Total assets	**611,685**	**+10**	**557,080**
Accts. pay. & accr. liabs	102,144		102,596
Current liabilities	114,573		117,739
Long-term debt, gross	19,972		50,000
Long-term debt, net	19,972		50,000
Long-term lease liabilities	3,965		3,885
Shareholders' equity	452,577		359,758
Cash from oper. activs	**113,186**	**+19**	**94,873**
Cash from fin. activs	(29,608)		38,254
Cash from invest. activs	(63,978)		(85,845)
Net cash position	**94,432**	**+33**	**71,260**
Capital expenditures	(58,690)		(49,939)
Capital disposals	3,501		2,144
	$		$
Earnings per share*	0.90		0.65
Cash flow per share*	1.37		1.15
	shs		shs
No. of shs. o/s*	83,028,129		82,706,454
Avg. no. of shs. o/s*	82,876,000		82,255,000
	%		%
Net profit margin	10.18		8.22
Return on equity	18.45		16.71
Return on assets	12.82		11.58
Foreign sales percent	77		71
No. of employees (FTEs)	3,462		3,825

* Common
^A Reported in accordance with IFRS

Historical Summary
(as originally stated)

Fiscal Year	Oper. Rev.	Net Inc. Bef. Disc.	EPS*
	$000s	$000s	$
2023^A	735,742	74,922	0.90
2022^A	650,415	53,459	0.65
2021^A	432,076	10,034	0.12
2020^A	409,144	(70,962)	(0.88)
2019^A	384,822	(18,084)	(0.23)

* Common
^A Reported in accordance with IFRS

M.24 Mandala Capital Inc.

Symbol - MAN.P **Exchange** - TSX-VEN **CUSIP** - 56256W
Head Office - Royal Centre, 1500-1055 Georgia St W, PO Box 11117, Vancouver, BC, V6E 4N7
Email - patrick.sapphire@principlecp.com
Investor Relations - Patrick Sapphire (647) 530-1117
Auditors - PKF Antares Professional Corporation C.A., Calgary, Alta.
Lawyers - McMillan LLP
Transfer Agents - Odyssey Trust Company, Vancouver, B.C.
Profile - (B.C. 2021) Capital Pool Company.
Common listed on TSX-VEN, Feb. 8, 2023.
Directors - Patrick Sapphire, CEO, Toronto, Ont.; Jon Sharun, CFO, West Vancouver, B.C.; Wendy T. Chan, Vancouver, B.C.; Zheng (Harry) Tian; Michael J. Williams, West Vancouver, B.C.
Other Exec. Officers - Dr. John-Mark G. Staude, v-p, corp. devel.; Rajeev (Raj) Dewan, corp. sec.

Capital Stock

	Authorized (shs.)	Outstanding (shs.)[1]
Common	unlimited	9,110,000

[1] At May 28, 2023
Major Shareholder - Widely held at Feb. 8, 2023.
Recent Close: $0.10
Capital Stock Changes - On Feb. 8, 2023, an initial public offering of 5,150,000 common shares was completed at 10¢ per share.

M.25 Mandeville Ventures Inc.

Symbol - MAND.P **Exchange** - TSX-VEN **CUSIP** - 562657
Head Office - 314-1568 Merivale Rd, Ottawa, ON, K2G 5Y7 **Telephone** - (613) 612-6060
Email - deanhanisch@hotmail.com
Investor Relations - Dean Hanisch (613) 612-6060
Auditors - Stern & Lovrics LLP C.A., Toronto, Ont.
Transfer Agents - Marrelli Transfer Services Corp., Toronto, Ont.
Profile - (Ont. 2021) Capital Pool Company.

Recent Merger and Acquisition Activity

Status: pending **Announced:** June 14, 2023
Mandeville Ventures Inc. entered into an agreement for the Qualifying Transaction reverse takeover acquisition of Sumer Resources Inc., which has copper prospects in Botswana and Namibia. The parties are to enter into a definitive agreement in on or before Sept. 1, 2023. It is expected that Mandeville would change its name to Sumer Resources Corp., consolidate its common shares on a 1-for-10 basis and continue from Ontario to British Columbia.
Directors - Dean Hanisch, pres., CEO, CFO & corp. sec., Ottawa, Ont.; Robin B. Dow, West Vancouver, B.C.; Raj (Rick) Kumar, Ottawa, Ont.; John Kutkevicius, Toronto, Ont.
Other Exec. Officers - Jason York, v-p

Capital Stock

	Authorized (shs.)	Outstanding (shs.)[1]
Common	unlimited	26,549,000

[1] At Apr. 21, 2022
Major Shareholder - Widely held at Apr. 21, 2022.

Price Range - MAND.P/TSX-VEN

Year	Volume	High	Low	Close
2022	2,099,351	$0.25	$0.04	$0.05

Recent Close: $0.08
Capital Stock Changes - On Apr. 21, 2022, an initial public offering of 6,549,000 common shares was completed at 10¢ per share.

M.26 Manganese X Energy Corp.

Symbol - MN **Exchange** - TSX-VEN **CUSIP** - 562678
Head Office - 145 rue Graveline, Saint-Laurent, QC, H4T 1R3 **Telephone** - (514) 802-1814 **Toll-free** - (877) 234-0692
Website - www.manganesexenergycorp.com
Email - martin@kepman.com
Investor Relations - Martin Kepman (877) 234-0692
Auditors - Wasserman Ramsay C.A., Markham, Ont.
Lawyers - Garfinkle Biderman LLP, Toronto, Ont.
Transfer Agents - Capital Transfer Agency Inc., Toronto, Ont.
Profile - (B.C. 2007) Has mineral interests in New Brunswick and Quebec. Also developing technology in the air purification sector.
In New Brunswick, holds Battery Hill manganese property, 1,407 hectares, 6 km west-northwest of Woodstock, with measured and indicated resource of 35,140,000 tonnes grading 6.39% manganese and 10.64% iron at May 12, 2022. A preliminary economic assessment released in June 2022 contemplated an open-pit mining with an average annual production of 68,000 tonnes of high- purity manganese sulfate over a 40-year mine production life and seven years of stockpile reclaim feed. Capital costs were estimated at $350,000,000.
In Quebec, holds 40% interest in Peter Lake copper-nickel-cobalt prospect, 2,568 hectares, Mont-Laurier terrane, with option to acquire the remaining 60% interest.
Through wholly owned **Disruptive Battery Corp.** (DBC), the company is accelerating a manganese thesis relating to fuel cells and stored energy, with the goal of advancing manganese as a viable mineral for greener power production and penetrating the electric vehicle market. In addition, DBC owns a U.S. patent for a system and method for air quality disinfection, sterilization and deodorization. The technology under development is designed to circulate air disinfection agents via a building's HVAC distribution system. DBC also owns 50% interest in **Pure Biotic Air Corp.**, a joint venture with **PureBiotic Air Inc.** formed to provide an air purification process that incorporates the company's patented HVAC distribution system and PureBiotic's PureBiotics Air Mist Solutions, which are proprietary biological solutions for the purification of air and surfaces. DBC intends to work in partnership with universities, chemical labs and global HVAC companies and experts in the field of environmental science.
Predecessor Detail - Name changed from Sunset Cove Mining Inc., Dec. 2, 2016.
Directors - Roger F. Dahn, chr., N.B.; Martin Kepman, pres. & CEO, Knowlton, Qué.; James A. (Jay) Richardson, CFO, Toronto, Ont.; Dr. Luisa Moreno, Ont.; Robert Tjandra, Toronto, Ont.
Other Exec. Officers - Perry MacKinnon, v-p, explor.; Janet Francis, corp. sec.

Capital Stock

	Authorized (shs.)	Outstanding (shs.)[1]
Common	unlimited	135,763,865

[1] At Apr. 10, 2023
Major Shareholder - Widely held at Apr. 10, 2023.

Price Range - MN/TSX-VEN

Year	Volume	High	Low	Close
2022	28,769,188	$0.58	$0.17	$0.18
2021	151,441,912	$1.04	$0.22	$0.30
2020	107,300,202	$1.11	$0.06	$0.28
2019	11,723,464	$0.18	$0.06	$0.07
2018	25,770,214	$0.28	$0.09	$0.13

Recent Close: $0.09
Capital Stock Changes - During fiscal 2022, 307,500 common shares were issued on exercise of warrants.

Dividends

MN com N.S.R.
stk.[1] Aug. 27/21
Paid in 2023: n.a. 2022: n.a. 2021: stk.
[1] Stk. divd. of 1 Graphano Energy Ltd com. sh. for ea. 8 shs. held. Equiv to $0.00625.

Wholly Owned Subsidiaries

Disruptive Battery Corp., Canada.

Investments

Mountain Spring Oil and Gas Limited, Calgary, Alta.

Financial Statistics

Periods ended:	12m Mar. 31/22^A		12m Mar. 31/21^A
	$000s	%Chg	$000s
Research & devel. expense	74		67
Exploration expense	813		799
General & admin expense	664		1,607
Stock-based compensation	2,417		1,613
Other operating expense	285		316
Operating expense	**4,253**	**-3**	**4,401**
Operating income	**(4,253)**	**n.a.**	**(4,401)**
Deprec., depl. & amort.	15		15
Pre-tax income	**(4,274)**	**n.a.**	**(4,881)**
Net income	**(4,274)**	**n.a.**	**(4,881)**
Cash & equivalent	3,511		5,562
Current assets	3,935		5,846
Intangibles, net	120		135
Total assets	**4,055**	**-32**	**5,981**
Accts. pay. & accr. liabs	128		244
Current liabilities	128		244
Shareholders' equity	3,926		5,738
Cash from oper. activs	**(2,097)**	**n.a.**	**(2,912)**
Cash from fin. activs	46		7,898
Cash from invest. activs	nil		42
Net cash position	**3,511**	**-37**	**5,562**
	$		$
Earnings per share*	(0.03)		(0.05)
Cash flow per share*	(0.02)		(0.03)
	shs		shs
No. of shs. o/s*	124,557,907		124,250,407
Avg. no. of shs. o/s*	124,514,219		92,428,998
	%		%
Net profit margin	n.a.		n.a.
Return on equity	(88.45)		(146.05)
Return on assets	(85.17)		(138.37)

* Common
^A Reported in accordance with IFRS

Historical Summary
(as originally stated)

Fiscal Year	Oper. Rev.	Net Inc. Bef. Disc.	EPS*
	$000s	$000s	$
2022^A	nil	(4,274)	(0.03)
2021^A	nil	(4,881)	(0.05)
2020^A	nil	(923)	(0.01)
2019^A	nil	(1,205)	(0.02)
2018^A	nil	(1,339)	(0.03)

* Common
^A Reported in accordance with IFRS

M.27 ManifestSeven Holdings Corporation

Symbol - MSVN **Exchange** - CSE (S) **CUSIP** - 563259
Head Office - 111 Pacifica, Suite 100, Irvine, CA, United States, 92618 **Toll-free** - (833) 654-2462
Website - manifest7.com
Email - ir@manifest7.com
Investor Relations - Sturges Karban
Auditors - Dale Matheson Carr-Hilton LaBonte LLP C.A., Vancouver, B.C.
Transfer Agents - Odyssey Trust Company, Vancouver, B.C.
Profile - (B.C. 2007) Operates ancillary e-commerce platforms and subscription services, including Rolling Paper Deport, Hippie Butler and Puff Pack.
Has a proprietary subscription-based e-commerce platform, myjane.com, through which consumers can directly buy cannabis products. Also sells ancillary products, including accessories, consumables and hemp-based cannabidiol (CBD) products directly to end-consumers throughout the U.S. and internationally utilizing proprietary and third-party e-commerce platforms supported by a centralized fulfillment hub in Arizona.
Class A suspended from CSE, Apr. 6, 2022.
Predecessor Detail - Name changed from P&P Ventures Inc., Sept. 4, 2020, following reverse takeover acquisition of MJIC, Inc. (dba ManifestSeven) by way of a three-cornered amalgamation; basis 1 new for 1.33333 old shs.
Directors - Scott Wessler, chr., Calif.; Sturges Karban, CEO, Calif.; Gaelan Bloomfield, Calif.; Kristin Fox, Ill.; Charles Parker, Tex.; Urban Smedeby, Calif.
Other Exec. Officers - Jordan Gerber, CFO; Dmitry Gordeychev, CIO

Capital Stock

	Authorized (shs.)	Outstanding (shs.)[1]
Cl.A Subord. Vtg.	unlimited	187,172,142
Cl.B Subord. Non-vtg.	unlimited	3,690,393
Cl.C Proportionate Vtg.	unlimited	1,042,339

[1] At Jan. 27, 2023

Class A Subordinate Voting - One vote per share.

Class B Subordinate Non-voting - Not entitled to dividends. Convertible, at the holder's option, into subordinate voting shares on a one-for-one basis. Non-voting.

Class C Proportionate Voting - Entitled to dividends. Convertible, at the holder's option, into subordinate voting shares on a 10-for-1 basis. 10 votes per share.

Major Shareholder - Widely held at Apr. 12, 2021.

Price Range - PPV.H/TSX-VEN (D)

Year	Volume	High	Low	Close
2022	12,693,000	$0.05	$0.01	$0.02
2021	24,991,937	$0.56	$0.02	$0.04
2020	3,341,009	$0.60	$0.28	$0.35
2019	19,787	$0.14	$0.13	$0.14
2018	8,156	$0.16	$0.07	$0.10

Consolidation: 1-for-1.33333 cons. in Sept. 2020

Capital Stock Changes - In March 2022, private placement of 25,823,494 units (1 class A subordinate voting share & ½ warrant) at 7¢ per unit was completed, with warrants exercisable at 25¢ per share for 18 months.

Wholly Owned Subsidiaries

CM Smoke Supply, LLC, Ariz.
CannaFundr, LLC, Calif.
M7 Media, LLC, Del.
ManifestSeven, Inc., Commerce, Calif.
- 100% int. in **M7 IP Inc.**, Calif.
- 100% int. in **M7 Infrastructure Inc.**, Calif.
  - 100% int. in **M7 Properties II LLC**, Calif.
    - 10% int. in **FortGreen LLC**, Calif.
  - 100% int. in **M7 Properties III LLC**, Calif.
    - 15% int. in **FortOrange LLC**, Calif.
  - 100% int. in **M7 Properties LLC**, Calif.
    - 25% int. in **FortNorth LLC**, Calif.
- 100% int. in **M7 Management Inc.**, Calif.
  - 100% int. in **DG Construction Solutions LLC**, Calif.
  - 100% int. in **M7 Fleet Inc.**, Calif.
  - 100% int. in **Plutus Professional Services LLC**, Calif.
- 100% int. in **M7 Regulated Inc.**, Calif.
  - 100% int. in **Brisbane Distribution Solutions, LLC**, Calif.
  - 80% int. in **Davis People's Harvest**, Calif.
  - 80% int. in **Healthy Healing Holistic Options Inc.**, Calif.
  - 100% int. in **Long Beach Distribution Solutions, LLC**, Calif. The company does not own the equity of this entity. However, the equity owner is an executive of the company and it has been deemed that the company effectively controls this entity, and as such has consolidated it in the financial statements.
  - 100% int. in **M Delivers Inc.**, Calif.
  - 100% int. in **NorCal Delivery Solutions, LLC**, Calif. The company does not own the equity of this entity. However, the equity owner is an executive of the company and it has been deemed that the company effectively controls this entity, and as such has consolidated it in the financial statements.
  - 100% int. in **NorCal Distribution Solutions, LLC**, Calif. The company does not own the equity of this entity. However, the equity owner is an executive of the company and it has been deemed that the company effectively controls this entity, and as such has consolidated it in the financial statements.
  - 100% int. in **Peninsula Delivery Solutions, LLC**, Calif.
  - 100% int. in **Peninsula Distribution Solutions, LLC**, Calif.
- 100% int. in **M7 Solutions, LLC**, Calif.
  - 100% int. in **CFO Worldwide, LLC**, Ill.
- 100% int. in **M7 Unregulated, Inc.**, Calif.
  - 100% int. in **CM Sales LLC**, Ariz.
  - 100% int. in **Dargos Ventures, LLC**, Ariz.
  - 100% int. in **Empathy Hemp Co. LLC**, Calif.
  - 100% int. in **MyJane, LLC**, Calif.
  - 100% int. in **Puff Pack LLC**, Calif.
  - 100% int. in **Rolling Paper Depot, LLC**, Ariz.
  - 100% int. in **White Coat Hemp Co. LLC**, Ariz.
- 100% int. in **Panther Micro Opportunity Fund I, LLC**, Del.

Obelus Professional Services, LLC, Calif.
San Diego Delivery Solutions, LLC, Calif.
West Coast Retail Solutions, Inc., Calif.

Subsidiaries

51% int. in **Monterey Retail Solutions, LLC**, Calif.

Investments

33% int. in **GTI SPV, LLC**, Calif.

M.28 Manitex Capital Inc.

Symbol - MNX **Exchange** - TSX-VEN **CUSIP** - 56342H
Head Office - 16667 boul Hymus, Kirkland, QC, H9H 4R9 **Telephone** - (514) 693-8844 **Fax** - (514) 694-0443
Email - steve@manitexcapital.com
Investor Relations - Steven Saviuk (514) 694-0150
Auditors - MNP LLP C.A., Montréal, Qué.
Transfer Agents - Computershare Investor Services Inc.

Profile - (Can. 1998; orig. Ont., 1986) Invests in emerging and established companies in diversified sectors including life sciences, cleantech and sustainable products and technologies.

Investments include **Valeo Pharma Inc.** (27.7% owned), which acquires (either through acquisitions, in-licensing or similar arrangements) innovative, patent protected, pharmaceutical products in specific therapeutic areas for the Canadian market, as well as selected drugs; **Ortho Regenerative Technologies Inc.** (19.2% owned), which develops novel therapeutic tissue repaid technologies to improve the success rate of orthopaedic musculoskeletal surgeries; **Ocean Trout Canada Inc.** (12% owned), which produces premium steelhead products for seafood consumers in the North American market place; **Central America Nickel Inc.** (3% owned), which processes and purifies energy metals; and **NuGen Medical Devices Inc.**, which develops and commercializes needle-free injection systems.

Predecessor Detail - Name changed from Manitex Minerals Inc., June 16, 1992; basis 1 new for 6 old shs.

Directors - Steven (Steve) Saviuk, chr., pres. & CEO, Beaconsfield, Qué.; Helen Saviuk, CFO, Pincourt, Qué.; Marc Bélair, Qué.; Natasha Saviuk, Montréal, Qué.; Michael Tinmouth, Beaconsfield, Qué.

Other Exec. Officers - Guy-Paul Allard, v-p, legal affairs & corp. sec.

Capital Stock

	Authorized (shs.)	Outstanding (shs.)[1]
Preferred	unlimited	
Series A	2,000,000	nil
Common	unlimited	12,561,276

[1] At Oct. 31, 2021

Major Shareholder - Simcor Canada Holdings Inc. held 47.9% interest at Feb. 25, 2021.

Price Range - MNX/TSX-VEN

Year	Volume	High	Low	Close
2022	87,281	$0.75	$0.50	$0.60
2021	218,020	$1.30	$0.71	$0.72
2020	900,260	$1.01	$0.15	$1.01
2019	594,962	$0.39	$0.14	$0.14
2018	1,346,700	$0.43	$0.15	$0.17

Recent Close: $0.49

Wholly Owned Subsidiaries

MedbrAin Inc., Canada. Inactive.
VPI Pharma International Inc. Inactive.

Subsidiaries

60% int. in **ANRis Pharmaceuticals Inc.**
75% int. in **Hywood Pharmachem Inc.** Inactive.

Investments

3% int. in **Central America Nickel Inc.**
11% int. in **ChitogenX Inc.**, Kirkland, Qué. (see separate coverage)
NuGen Medical Devices Inc., Toronto, Ont.
12% int. in **Ocean Trout Canada Inc.**, St. Stephen, N.B.
29% int. in **Valeo Pharma Inc.**, Kirkland, Qué. (see separate coverage)

Financial Statistics

Periods ended:	12m Oct. 31/21[A]		12m Oct. 31/20[A]
	$000s	%Chg	$000s
General & admin expense	441		627
Stock-based compensation	6		32
Operating expense	**447**	**-32**	**659**
Operating income	**(447)**	**n.a.**	**(659)**
Finance income	168		161
Finance costs, gross	nil		7
Investment income	(2,640)		(223)
Pre-tax income	**(4,722)**	**n.a.**	**4,371**
Income taxes	(773)		633
Net inc. bef. disc. opers	**(3,949)**	**n.a.**	**3,738**
Income from disc. opers	nil		149
Net income	**(3,949)**	**n.a.**	**3,887**
Cash & equivalent	5,282		6,422
Accounts receivable	421		1,464
Current assets	5,711		10,042
Long-term investments	8,488		10,541
Fixed assets, net	8		8
Total assets	**11,246**	**-47**	**21,208**
Accts. pay. & accr. liabs	804		367
Current liabilities	804		367
Shareholders' equity	16,052		19,970
Non-controlling interest	(295)		(295)
Cash from oper. activs	**(215)**	**n.a.**	**(364)**
Cash from fin. activs	nil		(448)
Cash from invest. activs	652		644
Net cash position	**768**	**+131**	**332**
	$		$
Earns. per sh. bef disc opers*	(0.31)		0.30
Earnings per share*	(0.31)		0.31
Cash flow per share*	(0.02)		(0.03)
	shs		shs
No. of shs. o/s*	12,561,276		12,561,276
Avg. no. of shs. o/s*	12,561,276		12,561,276
	%		%
Net profit margin	n.a.		n.a.
Return on equity	(21.93)		20.73
Return on assets	(24.34)		19.48

* Common
[A] Reported in accordance with IFRS

Historical Summary
(as originally stated)

Fiscal Year	Oper. Rev. $000s	Net Inc. Bef. Disc. $000s	EPS* $
2021[A]	nil	(3,949)	(0.31)
2020[A]	nil	3,738	0.30
2019[A]	nil	(1,130)	(0.09)
2018[A]	4,382	(3,458)	(0.28)
2017[A]	1,277	(2,319)	(0.19)

* Common
[A] Reported in accordance with IFRS

M.29 The Manitoba Hydro-Electric Board

CUSIP - 563452
Head Office - 360 Portage Ave, Winnipeg, MB, R3C 0G8 **Telephone** - (204) 480-5900 **Toll-free** - (888) 624-9376
Website - www.hydro.mb.ca
Email - spowell@hydro.mb.ca
Investor Relations - Scott Powell (204) 360-4417
Auditors - KPMG LLP C.A., Winnipeg, Man.
FP500 Revenue Ranking - 168
Employees - 4,962 at Mar. 31, 2022

Profile - (Man. 1949) Generates, transmits and distributes electricity and conducts natural gas distribution activities in Manitoba.

Electric facilities include 16 hydroelectric generating stations primarily on the Nelson (6), Winnipeg (6), Saskatchewan (1), Burntwood (1) and Laurie (2) rivers; a thermal generating station at Brandon; and four small remote diesel generating stations at Brochet, Lac Brochet, Sharnattawa and Tadoule Lake. Power is also purchased from two independent wind farms at St. Leon and St. Joseph, Man. Excess electricity is sold to electric utilities and marketers in the midwestern U.S., Alberta, Saskatchewan and Ontario.

Wholly owned **Centra Gas Manitoba Inc.** conducts natural gas distribution activities, serving customers in Winnipeg, Brandon and other centres throughout southern Manitoba. Natural gas is purchased from producers in Alberta and transported to Manitoba through the TransCanada Pipeline network. Gas deliveries during fiscal 2022 were 2.111 billion m^3 compared with 2.059 billion m^3 in fiscal 2021. At Mar. 31, 2022, the company had 293,256 gas customers.

Periods ended:	12m Mar. 31/22	12m Mar. 31/21
Electric sales, GWh	28,778	32,609
Generating capacity, MW	5,860	5,608
Transmission lines, km	14,728	11,045
Distribution lines, km	75,530	75,320
Electric. customers	608,554	600,991

Directors - Edward S. Kennedy, chr., Winnipeg, Man.; Beth Bell, v-chr., Winnipeg, Man.; David G. (Dave) Brown, Winnipeg, Man.; James (Jim) Downey, Winnipeg, Man.; Ron Evans, Winnipeg, Man.; Melanie

McKague, Winnipeg, Man.; Gordon O. Pollard, Winnipeg, Man.; Harold E. Reid, Brandon, Man.; Brent VanKoughnet, Carman, Man.; Valerie Wowryk, St. Andrews, Man.

Exec. Officers - Jagdish K. (Jay) Grewal, pres. & CEO; Jeffrey W. (Jeff) Betker, v-p, external, indigenous rel. & commun.; Alex Chiang, v-p, cust. solutions & experience; Ian D. Fish, v-p, digital & tech.; Jamie Hanly, v-p, HR, safety, health & envir.; Shane Mailey, v-p, opers.; Aurel Tess, v-p & CFO; Hal Turner, v-p, asset planning & delivery

Major Shareholder - Province of Manitoba held 100% interest at Mar. 31, 2022.

Wholly Owned Subsidiaries

Centra Gas Manitoba Inc., Winnipeg, Man.
Manitoba Hydro International Ltd., Winnipeg, Man.
Manitoba Hydro Utility Services Ltd., Winnipeg, Man.
Minell Pipelines Ltd., Man.
6690271 Manitoba Ltd., Man.
Teshmont LP Holdings Ltd., Man.
- 40% int. in **Teshmont Consultants Limited Partnership**, Man.

Subsidiaries

82.5% int. in **Keeyask Hydropower Limited Partnership**, Man.
67% int. in **Wuskwatim Power Limited Partnership**, Man.

Financial Statistics

Periods ended:	12m Mar. 31/22^A		12m Mar. 31/21^◻A
	$000s	%Chg	$000s
Operating revenue	**3,040,000**	**+8**	**2,821,000**
Cost of goods sold	405,000		277,000
Salaries & benefits	469,000		453,000
General & admin expense	282,000		235,000
Other operating expense	674,000		479,000
Operating expense	**1,830,000**	**+27**	**1,444,000**
Operating income	**1,210,000**	**-12**	**1,377,000**
Deprec., depl. & amort.	608,000		529,000
Finance income	24,000		24,000
Finance costs, gross	1,068,000		846,000
Pre-tax income	**(259,000)**	**n.a.**	**117,000**
Net income	**(259,000)**	**n.a.**	**117,000**
Net inc. for equity hldrs	**(248,000)**	**n.a.**	**119,000**
Net inc. for non-cont. int	**(11,000)**	**n.a.**	**(2,000)**
Cash & equivalent	1,078,000		1,135,000
Inventories	106,000		118,000
Accounts receivable	376,000		326,000
Current assets	1,721,000		1,747,000
Fixed assets, net	26,376,000		26,023,000
Intangibles, net	1,130,000		1,167,000
Total assets	**31,138,000**	**+1**	**30,715,000**
Bank indebtedness	50,000		nil
Accts. pay. & accr. liabs	482,000		453,000
Current liabilities	1,935,000		1,872,000
Long-term debt, gross	24,758,000		24,186,000
Long-term debt, net	23,617,000		23,065,000
Shareholders' equity	2,629,000		2,700,000
Non-controlling interest	325,000		323,000
Cash from oper. activs	**164,000**	**-34**	**248,000**
Cash from fin. activs	599,000		1,067,000
Cash from invest. activs	(822,000)		(1,099,000)
Net cash position	**1,083,000**	**-5**	**1,142,000**
Capital expenditures	(805,000)		(1,073,000)
Unfunded pension liability	600,000		737,000
	$		$
Earnings per share*	n.a.		n.a.
	shs		shs
No. of shs. o/s	n.a.		n.a.
	%		%
Net profit margin	(8.52)		4.15
Return on equity	(9.31)		4.67
Return on assets	2.62		3.21
Foreign sales percent	16		19
No. of employees (FTEs)	4,962		4,954

◻ Restated
A Reported in accordance with IFRS

Historical Summary
(as originally stated)

Fiscal Year	Oper. Rev.	Net Inc. Bef. Disc.	EPS*
	$000s	$000s	$
2022^A	3,040,000	(259,000)	n.a.
2021^A	2,821,000	117,000	n.a.
2020^A	2,629,000	99,000	n.a.
2019^A	2,576,000	118,000	n.a.
2018^A	2,330,000	29,000	n.a.

* Common
A Reported in accordance with IFRS

M.30 Manulife Financial Corporation*

Symbol - MFC **Exchange** - TSX **CUSIP** - 56501R

Head Office - 200 Bloor St E, Toronto, ON, M4W 1E5 **Telephone** - (416) 926-3000 **Toll-free** - (888) 626-8543 **Fax** - (416) 926-5454

Website - www.manulife.com

Email - hung_ko@manulife.com

Investor Relations - Hung Ko (416) 806-9921

Auditors - Ernst & Young LLP C.A., Toronto, Ont.

Lawyers - Torys LLP, Toronto, Ont.

Transfer Agents - Rizal Commercial Banking Corporation, Makati City, Philippines; Tricor Investor Services Limited, Hong Kong, Hong Kong People's Republic of China; American Stock Transfer & Trust Company, LLC, New York, N.Y.; TSX Trust Company, Montréal, Qué.

FP500 Revenue Ranking - 33

Employees - 40,000 at Dec. 31, 2022

Profile - (Can. 1999, via Insurance Companies Act) Provides insurance, retirement, investment and asset management products and services to individual, group and institutional customers mainly in Asia, Canada and the U.S. Also offers reinsurance services, primarily property and casualty. Operates as Manulife across Canada, Asia and Europe, and primarily as John Hancock in the U.S.

The company's business is organized into four operating segments: Asia; Canada; U.S.; and Global Wealth and Asset Management.

Asia - Provides insurance products and insurance-based wealth accumulation products in Hong Kong, Macau, Japan, mainland China, Singapore, Vietnam, Indonesia, the Philippines, Malaysia, Cambodia and Myanmar. Products and services are offered to individuals and corporate customers through a multi-channel distribution network, which includes more than 116,000 contracted agents, more than 100 bank partnerships, independent agents, financial advisors and brokers. Bank partnerships include 10 exclusive partnerships which give access to more than 35,000,000 bank customers, including regional partnerships with **DBS Bank Ltd.** in Singapore, Hong Kong, mainland China and Indonesia and **Vietnam Joint Stock Commercial Bank for Industry and Trade** (dba VietinBank) in Vietnam.

Canada - Offers a wide range of insurance products, insurance-based wealth accumulation products and banking solutions through a diversified multi-channel distribution network. Financial protection solutions include retail and group insurance products. Retail insurance products include life, health, disability and specialty products, such as mortgage creditor and travel insurance, which are offered to individuals, families and business owners through advisors, sponsor groups and associations as well as direct-to-customer channels. Group insurance products, which include group life, health and disability insurance, are offered to about 26,000 Canadian businesses and organizations. Banking solutions include savings and chequing accounts, guaranteed investment certificates, lines of credit, investment loans, mortgages and other specialized lending programs provided through wholly owned **Manulife Bank of Canada**. The Canadian segment also has an in-force variable annuity business.

United States - Operating under the brand name John Hancock, provides life insurance products and insurance-based wealth accumulation products distributed through licensed financial advisors and direct-to-consumer channels. Insurance products offered are designed to provide estate, business and income protection solutions for high net worth, emerging affluent and middle markets. This segment also administers in-force long-term care insurance as well as in-force annuity policies, including fixed deferred, variable deferred and payout products.

Global Wealth and Asset Management (Global WAM) - Operating as Manulife Investment Management, serves individual, retirement and institutional clients in 19 markets through three business lines: retirement, retail and institutional asset management. The retirement business provides financial guidance, advice, investment solutions and recordkeeping services to plan participants and rollover individuals in North America and Asia. This business focuses on providing group retirement solutions in Canada through defined contribution plans as well as to group plan members when they retire or leave their plan; employer sponsored retirement plans and personal retirement accounts in the U.S.; and retirement offerings to employers and individuals in select Asian markets, including Mandatory Provident Fund schemes and administration in Hong Kong and various retirement solutions in Indonesia and Malaysia. The retail business distributes investment products, including mutual funds and exchange-traded funds, through proprietary advice channels in Canada and Asia as well as through intermediaries and banks in North America, Europe and Asia, and offers investment strategies worldwide through affiliated and select unaffiliated asset managers. In Canada, the retail business provides personal advice to individual clients and investment management, private banking and wealth and estate solutions to high net worth clients. In addition, wealth management services are provided for insurance-based wealth accumulation products distributed by the other segments and through proprietary advice channels. The institutional asset management business provides comprehensive asset management solutions to pension plans, foundations, endowments, financial institutions and other institutional investors worldwide.

The company also has a property and casualty reinsurance business and run-off reinsurance operations, which include variable annuities and accident and health.

Assets Under Management and Administration

At Dec. 31	2022	2021
	$millions	$millions
Asia[1]	149,493	154,712
Canada[1]	146,128	161,996
U.S.[1]	219,493	244,450
Global WAM[2]	779,912	855,927
Corp. & Other[1]	19,540	8,703
	1,314,566	1,425,788

[1] Pertains to assets under management (AUM).
[2] Consists of $609.7 billion of AUM and $170.2 billion of assets under administration (Dec. 31, 2021 - $668.3 billion and $187.6 billion, respectively). Excludes $229.5 billion of AUM managed for the other segments (Dec. 31, 2021 - $246.8 billion).

On Feb. 1, 2022, the company, through wholly owned **John Hancock Life Insurance Company (U.S.A.)** (JHUSA), closed a transaction to reinsure over 75% of its legacy U.S. variable annuity (VA) block to **Corporate Solutions Life Insurance Company**, wholly owned by **Venerable Holdings, Inc.** The U.S. VA block consisted primarily of about 143,000 policies with guaranteed minimum withdrawal benefits (GMWB) rider and about 20,000 with a guarantee minimum death benefits (GMDB) rider, as well as Cdn$2.3 billion of IFRS reserves at Sept. 30, 2021. These policies were written outside of New York state, between 2003 and 2012. On Oct. 3, 2022, the company, through wholly owned **John Hancock Life Insurance Company of New York** (JHNY), completed another reinsurance transaction with Venerable to reinsure a block of legacy New York VA policies, which involved the 80% quota share reinsurance of US$1.6 billion of account value as of Aug. 31, 2022, and consisted primarily of policies with GMWB riders, issued between 2003 and 2012, as well as a small block of policies with only GMDB riders. JHUSA and JHNY would continue to administer the policies.

Recent Merger and Acquisition Activity

Status: completed **Announced:** Nov. 30, 2022
Manulife Financial Corporation acquired the remaining 51% interest in Manulife TEDA Fund Management Co., Ltd. from its joint venture partner, a Chinese state-owned company, for Cdn$334,000,000. Manulife TEDA markets and manages public mutual funds in China, and had Cdn$11.8 billion (Cn¥62.8 billion) of assets under management as of September 2022.

Status: completed **Revised:** Sept. 23, 2022
UPDATE: The transaction was completed. PREVIOUS: Capital Power Corporation and Manulife Investment Management (MIM), the global wealth and asset management segment of Manulife Financial Corporation, agreed to acquire MCV Holding Company LLC from OMERS Infrastructure Management Inc. and co-investors for a total of US$894,000,000, including the assumption of US$521,000,000 of project level debt. MCV, through wholly owned Midland Cogeneration Venture Limited Partnership, owns and operates a 1,633-MW natural gas combined-cycle cogeneration facility in Midland, Mich. Under a 50/50 joint venture, Capital Power and MIM would each contribute US$186,000,000 subject to working capital and other closing adjustments. Capital Power would finance the transaction using cash on hand and existing credit facilities. Capital Power would be responsible for operations and maintenance and asset management in exchange for an annual management fee. The transaction was expected to close in the third quarter of 2022, subject to regulatory approvals and other customary closing conditions.

Directors - Donald R. (Don) Lindsay, chr., Vancouver, B.C.; Rocco (Roy) Gori, pres. & CEO, Toronto, Ont.; Nicole S. Arnaboldi, Greenwich, Conn.; Guy L. T. Bainbridge, Edinburgh, Midlothian, United Kingdom; Susan F. (Sue) Dabarno, Bracebridge, Ont.; Julie E. Dickson, Ottawa, Ont.; Tsun-yan Hsieh, Singapore, Singapore; Vanessa Kanu, Ottawa, Ont.; C. James (Jim) Prieur, Chicago, Ill.; Andrea S. Rosen, Toronto, Ont.; May Tan, Hong Kong, Hong Kong, People's Republic of China; Leagh E. Turner, Toronto, Ont.

Other Exec. Officers - Colin L. Simpson, CFO; Steven A. (Steve) Finch, chief actuary; Scott S. Hartz, chief invest. officer; Rahim Hirji, chief auditor; Rahul M. Joshi, chief opers. officer; Pamela O. Kimmet, chief HR officer; Karen A. Leggett, chief mktg. officer; Halina K. von dem Hagen, chief risk officer; Shamus E. Weiland, CIO; Marc Costantini, global head, inforce mgt.; Antonella Deo, sr. v-p, global head, governance & corp. legal affairs & corp. sec.; James D. Gallagher, gen. counsel; Naveed Irshad, pres. & CEO, Manulife Canada; Paul R. Lorentz, pres. & CEO, global wealth & asset mgt.; Brooks Tingle, pres. & CEO, John Hancock Insurance Company; Philip J. Witherington, pres. & CEO, Manulife Asia

Capital Stock

	Authorized (shs.)	Outstanding (shs.)[1]
Class A Preferred	unlimited	
Series 2		14,000,000
Series 3		12,000,000
Class 1 Preferred	unlimited	
Series 3		6,537,903
Series 4		1,462,097
Series 9		10,000,000
Series 11		8,000,000
Series 13		8,000,000
Series 15		8,000,000
Series 17		14,000,000
Series 19		10,000,000
Series 25		10,000,000
Class B Preferred	unlimited	nil
Limited Recourse Capital Notes	n.a.	
Series 1		2,000,000
Series 2		1,200,000
Series 3		1,000,000
Common	unlimited	1,828,737,429

[1] At July 31, 2023

Class A Preferred - Issuable in series and non-voting.

Series 2 - Entitled to non-cumulative preferential annual dividends of $1.1625 per share payable quarterly. With regulatory approval, redeemable at par.

Series 3 - Entitled to non-cumulative preferential annual dividends of $1.125 per share payable quarterly. With regulatory approval, redeemable at par.

Class 1 Preferred - Issuable in series and non-voting. Rank pari passu with class A preferred shares and senior to class B preferred shares.

Series 3 - Entitled to non-cumulative preferential annual dividends of $0.587 per share payable quarterly to June 19, 2026, and thereafter at a rate reset every five years equal to the five-year Government of Canada bond yield plus 1.41%. Redeemable on June 19, 2026, and on June 19 every five years thereafter at $25 per share plus declared and unpaid dividends. Convertible at the holder's option, on June 19, 2026, and on June 19 every five years thereafter, into floating rate class 1 preferred series 4 shares on a share-for-share basis, subject to certain conditions.

Series 4 - Entitled to non-cumulative preferential dividends payable quarterly equal to the 90-day Canadian Treasury bill rate plus 1.41%. Redeemable on June 19, 2026, and on June 19 every five years thereafter at $25 per share, or at $25.50 per share in the case of redemptions on any other date, plus declared and unpaid dividends in each case. Convertible at the holder's option, on June 19, 2026, and on June 19 every five years thereafter, into fixed rate class 1 preferred series 3 shares on a share-for-share basis, subject to certain conditions.

Series 9 - Entitled to non-cumulative preferential annual dividends of $1.4945 per share payable quarterly to Sept. 19, 2027, and thereafter at a rate reset every five years equal to the five-year Government of Canada bond yield plus 2.86%. Redeemable on Sept. 19, 2027, and on September 19 every five years thereafter at $25 per share plus declared and unpaid dividends. Convertible at the holder's option, on Sept. 19, 2027, and on September 19 every five years thereafter, into floating rate class 1 preferred series 10 shares on a share-for-share basis, subject to certain conditions. The class 1 preferred series 10 shares would pay a quarterly dividend equal to the 90-day Canadian Treasury bill rate plus 2.86%.

Series 11 - Entitled to non-cumulative preferential annual dividends of $1.5397 per share payable quarterly to Mar. 19, 2028, and thereafter at a rate reset every five years equal to the five-year Government of Canada bond yield plus 2.61%. Redeemable on Mar. 19, 2028, and on March 19 every five years thereafter at $25 per share plus declared and unpaid dividends. Convertible at the holder's option, on Mar. 19, 2028, and on March 19 every five years thereafter, into floating rate class 1 preferred series 12 shares on a share-for-share basis, subject to certain conditions. The class 1 preferred series 12 shares would pay a quarterly dividend equal to the 90-day Canadian Treasury bill rate plus 2.61%.

Series 13 - Entitled to non-cumulative preferential annual dividends of $1.1035 per share payable quarterly to Sept. 19, 2023, and thereafter at a rate reset every five years equal to the five-year Government of Canada bond yield plus 2.22%. Redeemable on Sept. 19, 2023, and on September 19 every five years thereafter at $25 per share plus declared and unpaid dividends. Convertible at the holder's option, on Sept. 19, 2023, and on September 19 every five years thereafter, into floating rate class 1 preferred series 14 shares on a share-for-share basis, subject to certain conditions. The class 1 preferred series 14 shares would pay a quarterly dividend equal to the 90-day Canadian Treasury bill rate plus 2.22%.

Series 15 - Entitled to non-cumulative preferential annual dividends of $0.9465 per share payable quarterly to June 19, 2024, and thereafter at a rate reset every five years equal to the five-year Government of Canada bond yield plus 2.16%. Redeemable on June 19, 2024, and on June 19 every five years thereafter at $25 per share plus declared and unpaid dividends. Convertible at the holder's option, on June 19, 2024, and on June 19 every five years thereafter, into floating rate class 1 preferred series 16 shares on a share-for-share basis, subject to certain conditions. The class 1 preferred series 16 shares would pay a quarterly dividend equal to the 90-day Canadian Treasury bill rate plus 2.16%.

Series 17 - Entitled to non-cumulative preferential annual dividends of $0.95 per share payable quarterly to Dec. 19, 2024, and thereafter at a rate reset every five years equal to the five-year Government of Canada bond yield plus 2.36%. Redeemable on Dec. 19, 2024, and on December 19 every five years thereafter at $25 per share plus declared and unpaid dividends. Convertible at the holder's option, on Dec. 19, 2024, and on December 19 every five years thereafter, into floating rate class 1 preferred series 18 shares on a share-for-share basis, subject to certain conditions. The class 1 preferred series 18 shares would pay a quarterly dividend equal to the 90-day Canadian Treasury bill rate plus 2.36%

Series 19 - Entitled to non-cumulative preferential annual dividends of $0.9188 per share payable quarterly to Mar. 19, 2025, and thereafter at a rate reset every five years equal to the five-year Government of Canada bond yield plus 2.3%. Redeemable on Mar. 19, 2025, and on March 19 every five years thereafter at $25 per share plus declared and unpaid dividends. Convertible at the holder's option, on Mar. 19, 2025, and on March 19 every five years thereafter, into floating rate class 1 preferred series 20 shares on a share-for-share basis, subject to certain conditions. The class 1 preferred series 20 shares would pay a quarterly dividend equal to the 90-day Canadian Treasury bill rate plus 2.3%.

Series 25 - Entitled to non-cumulative preferential annual dividends of $1.4855 per share payable quarterly to June 19, 2028, and thereafter at a rate reset every five years equal to the five-year Government of Canada bond yield plus 2.55%. Redeemable on June 19, 2028, and on June 19 every five years thereafter at $25 per share plus declared and unpaid dividends. Convertible at the holder's option, on June 19, 2028, and on June 19 every five years thereafter, into floating rate class 1 preferred series 26 shares on a share-for-share basis, subject to certain conditions. The class 1 preferred series 26 shares would pay a quarterly dividend equal to the 90-day Canadian Treasury bill rate plus 2.55%.

Class B Preferred - Issuable in series and non-voting.

Limited Recourse Capital Notes (LRCN) - Notes with recourse limited to assets held in a consolidated trust. **Series 1** - Bear interest at 3.375% per annum until June 18, 2026, and thereafter at an annual rate reset every five years equal to the five-year Government of Canada bond yield plus 2.839% until maturity on June 19, 2081. Trust assets consist of non-cumulative five-year reset class 1 preferred series 27 shares. **Series 2** - Bear interest at 4.1% per annum until Mar. 18, 2027, and thereafter at an annual rate reset every five years equal to the five-year Government of Canada bond yield plus 2.704% until maturity on Mar. 19, 2082. Trust assets consist of non-cumulative five-year reset class 1 preferred series 28 shares. **Series 3** - Bear interest at 7.117% per annum until June 18, 2027, and thereafter at an annual rate reset every five years equal to the five-year Government of Canada bond yield plus 3.95% until maturity on June 19, 2082. Trust assets consist of non-cumulative five-year reset class 1 preferred series 29 shares.

Common - One vote per share.

Options - At Dec. 31, 2022, options were outstanding to purchase 20,000,000 common shares at a weighted average exercise price of $22.42 per share with a weighted average contractual remaining life of 4.56 years.

Class A Preferred Series 7 (old) - Were entitled to non-cumulative preferential annual dividends of $1.078 per share payable quarterly to Mar. 19, 2022. Redeemed on Mar. 19, 2022, at $25 per share.

Class A Preferred Series 23 (old) - Were entitled to non-cumulative preferential annual dividends of $1.2125 per share payable quarterly to Mar. 19, 2022. Redeemed on Mar. 19, 2022, at $25 per share.

Normal Course Issuer Bid - The company plans to make normal course purchases of up to 55,700,000 common shares representing 3% of the total outstanding. The bid commenced on Feb. 23, 2023, and expires on Feb. 22, 2024.

Major Shareholder - Widely held at Mar. 15, 2023.

Price Range - MFC/TSX

Year	Volume	High	Low	Close
2022	2,049,303,718	$28.09	$20.81	$24.15
2021	1,791,927,286	$27.68	$22.33	$24.11
2020	1,894,705,969	$27.78	$12.58	$22.65
2019	1,228,832,696	$26.54	$18.94	$26.36
2018	993,899,082	$27.77	$18.33	$19.37

Recent Close: $24.33

Capital Stock Changes - In March 2022, all 10,000,000 class 1 preferred series 7 shares and 19,000,000 class 1 preferred series 23 shares were redeemed at $25 per share. In June 2022, 1,000,000 class 1 preferred series 29 shares were issued in conjunction with issuance of $1,000,000,000 of limited recourse capital notes series 3 priced at $1,000 per note. Also during 2022, 1,000,000 common shares were issued on exercise of options and deferred share units and 79,000,000 common shares were repurchased under a Normal Course Issuer Bid.

Dividends

MFC com Ra $1.46 pa Q est. Mar. 20, 2023**
Prev. Rate: $1.32 est. Dec. 20, 2021
Prev. Rate: $1.12 est. Mar. 19, 2020
MFC.PR.B pfd A ser 2 red. exch. Ra $1.1625 pa Q
MFC.PR.C pfd A ser 3 red. exch. Ra $1.125 pa Q
MFC.PR.F pfd 1 ser 3 red. exch. Adj. Ra $0.587 pa Q est. Sept. 19, 2021
MFC.PR.I pfd 1 ser 9 red. exch. Adj. Ra $1.4945 pa Q est. Dec. 19, 2022
MFC.PR.J pfd 1 ser 11 red. exch. Adj. Ra $1.53975 pa Q est. June 19, 2023
MFC.PR.K pfd 1 ser 13 red. exch. Adj. Ra $1.1035 pa Q est. Dec. 19, 2018
MFC.PR.L pfd 1 ser 15 red. exch. Adj. Ra $0.9465 pa Q est. Sept. 19, 2019
MFC.PR.M pfd 1 ser 17 red. exch. Adj. Ra $0.95 pa Q est. Mar. 19, 2020
MFC.PR.N pfd 1 ser 19 red. exch. Adj. Ra $0.91875 pa Q est. June 19, 2020
MFC.PR.P pfd 1 ser 4 red. exch. Fltg. Ra pa Q
$0.369828 Sept. 19/23 $0.376823 June 19/23
$0.34089 Mar. 19/23 $0.273873 Dec. 19/22
Paid in 2023: $1.087541 2022: $0.681434 2021: $0.381363
MFC.PR.Q pfd 1 ser 25 red. exch. Adj. Ra $1.4855 pa Q est. Sept. 19, 2023
pfd 1 ser 5 red. exch. Adj. Ra $0.97275 pa Q est. Mar. 19, 2017[1]
$0.243188**f** Dec. 19/21
pfd 1 ser 7 red. exch. Adj. Ra $1.078 pa Q est. June 19, 2017[2]
$0.2695**f** Mar. 19/22
pfd 1 ser 21 red. exch. Adj. Ra $1.40 pa Q est. June 19, 2016[3]
$0.35**f** June 19/21
pfd 1 ser 23 red. exch. Adj. Ra $1.2125 pa Q est. Mar. 19, 2017[2]
$0.303125**f** Mar. 19/22

[1] Redeemed Dec. 19, 2021 at $25 per sh.
[2] Redeemed March 18, 2022 at $25 per sh.
[3] Redeemed June 19, 2021 at $25 per sh.
** Reinvestment Option **f** Final Payment

Long-Term Debt - Outstanding at Dec. 31, 2022:

Senior notes:	
4.15% due 2026[1]	$1,351,000,000
3.527% due 2026[2]	365,000,000
2.484% due 2027[3]	674,000,000
2.396% due 2027[4]	270,000,000
3.703% due 2032[5]	1,011,000,000
5.375% due 2046[5]	1,004,000,000
3.05% due 2060[6]	1,559,000,000
Capital instruments:	
7.375% surplus notes due 2024[7]	615,000,000
3.317% subord. debs. due 2028[8]	600,000,000
3.049% subord. debs. due 2029[9]	749,000,000
3% subord. notes due 2029[10]	504,000,000
2.237% subord. debs. due 2030[11]	998,000,000
4.061% subord. notes due 2032[12]	1,013,000,000
2.818% subord. debs. due 2035[13]	996,000,000
Fltg. rate subord. notes due 2036[14]	647,000,000
	12,356,000,000

[1] US$1 billion.
[2] US$270,000,000.
[3] US$500,000,000.
[4] US$200,000,000.
[5] US$750,000,000.
[6] US$1.155 billion.
[7] US$450,000,000.
[8] Bear interest at 3.317% to May 9, 2023, and thereafter at the three-month CDOR plus 0.78%.
[9] Bear interest at 3.049% to Aug. 20, 2024, and thereafter at the three-month CDOR plus 1.05%.
[10] S$500,000,000. Bear interest at 3% to Nov. 20, 2024, and thereafter at the five-year Singapore Dollar Swap Rate plus 0.832%.
[11] Bear interest at 2.237% to May 12, 2025, and thereafter at the three-month CDOR plus 1.49%.
[12] US$750,000,000. Bear interest at 4.061% to Feb. 23, 2027, and thereafter at the five-year U.S. Dollar Mid-Swap Rate plus 1.647%.
[13] Bear interest at 2.818% to May 13, 2030, and thereafter at the three-month CDOR plus 1.82%.
[14] Bear interest at the 90-day bankers' acceptance rate plus 0.72%.

Note - In March 2023, offering of $1.2 billion principal amount of 5.409% fixed/floating subordinated debentures due Mar. 10, 2033, was completed. The debentures bear interest at 5.409% to Mar. 10, 2028, and thereafter at the daily compounded CORRA plus 1.85%. In May 2023, all outstanding $600,000,000 principal amount of 3.317% fixed/floating subordinated debentures due May 9, 2028, were redeemed.

Wholly Owned Subsidiaries

The Manufacturers Life Insurance Company, Toronto, Ont.
- 100% int. in **Berkshire Insurance Services Inc.**, Toronto, Ont.
  - 100% int. in **JH Investments (Delaware), LLC**, Boston, Mass.
- 100% int. in **EIS Services (Bermuda) Limited**, Hamilton, Bermuda.
- 100% int. in **First North American Insurance Company**, Toronto, Ont.
- 100% int. in **Manulife Assurance Company of Canada**, Toronto, Ont.
- 100% int. in **Manulife Bank of Canada**, Waterloo, Ont.
- 100% int. in **Manulife Holdings (Alberta) Limited**, Calgary, Alta.
  - 100% int. in **John Hancock Financial Corporation**, Boston, Mass.
    - 100% int. in **The Manufacturers Investment Corporation**, Boston, Mass.
      - 100% int. in **John Hancock Insurance Agency, Inc.**, Boston, Mass.
      - 100% int. in **John Hancock Life Insurance Company (U.S.A.)**, Boston, Mass.
        - 100% int. in **John Hancock Distributors, LLC**, Boston, Mass.
        - 100% int. in **John Hancock Life & Health Insurance Company**, Boston, Mass.

            - 100% int. in **John Hancock Life Insurance Company of New York**, New York, N.Y.
            - 100% int. in **John Hancock Subsidiaries LLC**, Boston, Mass.
                - 100% int. in **John Hancock Financial Network, Inc.**, Boston, Mass.
                - 100% int. in **John Hancock Investment Management LLC**, Boston, Mass.
                    - 100% int. in **John Hancock Investment Management Distributors LLC**, Boston, Mass.
                - 100% int. in **Manulife Investment Management Timberland and Agriculture Inc.**, Boston, Mass.
                - 100% int. in **Manulife Investment Management (US) LLC**, Boston, Mass.
            - 100% int. in **John Hancock Variable Trust Advisers LLC**, Boston, Mass.
        - 100% int. in **John Hancock Reassurance Company Ltd.**, Boston, Mass.
        - 100% int. in **Manulife Reinsurance Limited**, Hamilton, Bermuda.
            - 100% int. in **Manulife Reinsurance (Bermuda) Limited**, Hamilton, Bermuda.
- 100% int. in **Manulife Holdings (Bermuda) Limited**, Hamilton, Bermuda.
    - 100% int. in **Manufacturers P&C Limited**, St. Michael, Barbados.
    - 100% int. in **Manulife Financial Asia Limited**, Hong Kong, Hong Kong, People's Republic of China.
        - 100% int. in **The Manufacturers Life Insurance Co. (Phils.), Inc.**, Makati City, Philippines.
            - 60% int. in **Manulife Chinabank Life Assurance Corporation**, Makati City, Philippines.
        - 100% int. in **Manufacturers Life Reinsurance Limited**, St. Michael, Barbados.
        - 100% int. in **Manulife (Cambodia) plc**, Phnom Penh, Cambodia.
        - 61.6% int. in **Manulife Holdings Bhd.**, Kuala Lumpur, Malaysia.
            - 100% int. in **Manulife Insurance Bhd.**, Kuala Lumpur, Malaysia.
            - 100% int. in **Manulife Investment Management (Malaysia) Bhd.**, Kuala Lumpur, Malaysia.
        - 100% int. in **Manulife International Holdings Limited**, Hong Kong, Hong Kong, People's Republic of China.
            - 100% int. in **Manulife (International) Limited**, Hong Kong, Hong Kong, People's Republic of China.
                - 51% int. in **Manulife-Sinochem Life Insurance Co. Ltd.**, Shanghai, Shanghai, People's Republic of China.
            - 100% int. in **Manulife Investment Management International Holdings Limited**, Hong Kong, Hong Kong, People's Republic of China.
                - 100% int. in **Manulife Investment Management (Hong Kong) Limited**, Hong Kong, Hong Kong, People's Republic of China.
                    - 100% int. in **Manulife Investment Management (Taiwan) Co., Ltd.**, Taipei, Republic of China.
        - 100% int. in **Manulife Investment Management (Singapore) Pte. Ltd.**, Singapore.
        - 100% int. in **Manulife Life Insurance Company**, Tokyo, Japan.
            - 100% int. in **Manulife Investment Management (Japan) Limited**, Tokyo, Japan.
        - 100% int. in **Manulife Myanmar Life Insurance Company Limited**, Yangon, Myanmar.
        - 100% int. in **Manulife (Singapore) Pte. Ltd.**, Singapore.
        - 100% int. in **Manulife TEDA Fund Management Co., Ltd.**, Beijing, Beijing, People's Republic of China.
        - 100% int. in **Manulife (Vietnam) Limited**, Ho Chi Minh City, Vietnam.
            - 100% int. in **Manulife Investment Fund Management (Vietnam) Company Ltd.**, Ho Chi Minh City, Vietnam.
        - 100% int. in **PT Asuransi Jiwa Manulife Indonesia**, Jakarta, Indonesia.
            - 100% int. in **PT Manulife Aset Manajemen Indonesia**, Jakarta, Indonesia.
- 100% int. in **Manulife Investment Management (Europe) Limited**, London, Middx., United Kingdom.
- 100% int. in **Manulife Investment Management Holdings (Canada) Inc.**, Toronto, Ont.
    - 100% int. in **Manulife Investment Management Limited**, Toronto, Ont.
- 100% int. in **Manulife Investment Management (North America) Limited**, Toronto, Ont.
- 100% int. in **Manulife Securities Incorporated**, Oakville, Ont.
- 100% int. in **Manulife Securities Investment Services, Inc.**, Oakville, Ont.

Note: The preceding list includes only the major related companies in which interests are held.

Financial Statistics

Periods ended:	12m Dec. 31/22^A		12m Dec. 31/21^A
	$000s	%Chg	$000s
Net premiums earned	37,853,000		39,065,000
Net investment income	(29,870,000)		11,624,000
Total revenue	**17,147,000**	**-72**	**61,821,000**
Policy benefits & claims	(9,299,000)		35,822,000
Commissions	6,260,000		6,638,000
General & admin. expense	7,782,000		7,828,000
Premium taxes	444,000		417,000
Other operating expense	1,863,000		1,980,000
Operating expense	**16,349,000**	**-3**	**16,863,000**
Operating income	**10,097,000**	**+11**	**9,136,000**
Finance costs, gross	1,350,000		1,011,000
Pre-tax income	**8,747,000**	**+8**	**8,125,000**
Income taxes	1,565,000		1,213,000
Net income	**7,182,000**	**+4**	**6,912,000**
Net inc. for equity hldrs	**7,294,000**	**+3**	**7,105,000**
Net inc. for non-cont. int	**(1,000)**	**n.a.**	**255,000**
Net inc. for partic policyhldrs	**(111,000)**	**n.a.**	**(448,000)**
Cash & equivalent	19,153,000		22,594,000
Accounts receivable	1,448,000		1,294,000
Securities investments	227,423,000		252,206,000
Mortgages	54,638,000		52,014,000
Real estate	11,394,000		11,421,000
Total investments	392,970,000		402,692,000
Segregated fund assets	348,562,000		399,788,000
Total assets	**848,941,000**	**-7**	**917,643,000**
Debt	12,356,000		11,862,000
Policy liabilities & claims	374,653,000		395,392,000
Segregated fund liabilities	348,562,000		399,788,000
Partic. policyhldrs.' equity	(1,346,000)		(1,233,000)
Preferred share equity	6,660,000		6,381,000
Shareholders' equity	56,061,000		58,408,000
Non-controlling interest	1,664,000		1,694,000
Cash from oper. activs	**17,735,000**	**-23**	**23,155,000**
Cash from fin. activs	(3,005,000)		(2,047,000)
Cash from invest. activs	(18,610,000)		(24,442,000)
Net cash position	**18,635,000**	**-15**	**21,930,000**
Unfunded pension liability	72,000		50,000
	$		$
Earnings per share*	3.68		3.55
Cash flow per share*	9.29		11.92
Cash divd. per share*	1.32		1.17
	shs		shs
No. of shs. o/s*	1,865,000,000		1,943,000,000
Avg. no. of shs. o/s*	1,910,000,000		1,942,000,000
	%		%
Net profit margin	41.88		11.18
Return on equity	13.87		13.71
Return on assets	0.94		0.86
Foreign sales percent	72		78
No. of employees (FTEs)	40,000		38,000

* Common
^A Reported in accordance with IFRS

Latest Results

Periods ended:	6m June 30/23^A		6m June 30/22^{oA}
	$000s	%Chg	$000s
Total revenue	24,697,000	+127	10,856,000
Net income	2,581,000	n.a.	(3,326,000)
Net inc. for equity hldrs	2,431,000	n.a.	(3,339,000)
Net inc. for non-cont. int	80,000		54,000
Net inc. for partic policyhldrs	70,000		(41,000)
	$		$
Earnings per share*	1.23		(1.79)

* Common
^o Restated
^A Reported in accordance with IFRS

Historical Summary
(as originally stated)

Fiscal Year	Total Rev. $000s	Net Inc. Bef. Disc. $000s	EPS* $
2022^A	17,147,000	7,182,000	3.68
2021^A	61,821,000	6,912,000	3.55
2020^A	78,908,000	5,576,000	2.94
2019^A	79,570,000	5,502,000	2.77
2018^A	38,972,000	4,887,000	2.34

* Common
^A Reported in accordance with IFRS

M.31 Many Bright Ideas Technologies Inc.

Symbol - MBI.H **Exchange** - TSX-VEN **CUSIP** - 565085
Head Office - 598 East Kent Ave S, Vancouver, BC, V5X 4V6 **Telephone** - (604) 732-7332 **Fax** - (604) 732-4801
Website - www.medbiogene.com
Email - iainw@medbiogene.com
Investor Relations - Dr. Iain Weir-Jones (800) 641-3593
Auditors - De Visser Gray LLP C.A., Vancouver, B.C.
Lawyers - Farris LLP, Vancouver, B.C.
Transfer Agents - Computershare Trust Company of Canada Inc., Vancouver, B.C.
Profile - (B.C. 2006 amalg.) Seeking new business opportunities in the technology sector.
Predecessor Detail - Name changed from Med BioGene Inc., June 15, 2022.
Directors - Dr. Iain Weir-Jones, chr. & CEO, B.C.; David Diebolt, B.C.; Shumsheer Sidhu, B.C.; Toby Weir-Jones, Va.
Other Exec. Officers - Ibrahim Ghobrial, CFO & corp. sec.

Capital Stock

	Authorized (shs.)	Outstanding (shs.)[1]
Preferred	unlimited	
Common	unlimited	17,257,838

[1] At June 15, 2022

Major Shareholder - Dr. Iain Weir-Jones held 35.22% interest at Mar. 30, 2022.

Price Range - MBI.H/TSX-VEN

Year	Volume	High	Low	Close
2022	1,136,994	$0.07	$0.02	$0.03
2021	3,694,677	$0.23	$0.06	$0.07
2020	1,928,791	$0.13	$0.02	$0.06
2019	2,674,452	$0.07	$0.02	$0.03
2018	1,865,775	$0.24	$0.03	$0.03

Recent Close: $0.02

Capital Stock Changes - In February 2022, 2,000,000 common shares were issued for debt settlement.

Wholly Owned Subsidiaries

DTX Acquisition Company Inc., Alta.

Financial Statistics

Periods ended:	12m Dec. 31/21^A		12m Dec. 31/20^A
	US$000s	%Chg	US$000s
General & admin expense	60		55
Operating expense	**60**	**+9**	**55**
Operating income	**(60)**	**n.a.**	**(55)**
Pre-tax income	**(60)**	**n.a.**	**(55)**
Net income	**(60)**	**n.a.**	**(55)**
Cash & equivalent	9		79
Accounts receivable	nil		1
Current assets	11		82
Total assets	**11**	**-87**	**82**
Accts. pay. & accr. liabs	33		43
Current liabilities	92		178
Shareholders' equity	(81)		(96)
Cash from oper. activs	**(145)**	**n.a.**	**73**
Cash from fin. activs	75		nil
Net cash position	**9**	**-89**	**79**
	US$		US$
Earnings per share*	(0.00)		(0.00)
Cash flow per share*	(0.01)		0.01
	shs		shs
No. of shs. o/s*	15,257,838		13,257,838
Avg. no. of shs. o/s*	15,219,482		13,257,838
	%		%
Net profit margin	n.a.		n.a.
Return on equity	n.m.		n.m.
Return on assets	(129.03)		(115.79)

* Common
^A Reported in accordance with IFRS

Latest Results

Periods ended:	3m Mar. 31/22^A		3m Mar. 31/21^A
	US$000s	%Chg	US$000s
Net income	(13)	n.a.	(21)
	US$		US$
Earnings per share*	(0.00)		(0.00)

* Common
^A Reported in accordance with IFRS

Historical Summary
(as originally stated)

Fiscal Year	Oper. Rev. US$000s	Net Inc. Bef. Disc. US$000s	EPS* US$
2021^A	nil	(60)	(0.00)
2020^A	nil	(55)	(0.00)
2019^A	nil	(63)	(0.01)
2018^A	nil	(55)	(0.01)
2017^A	nil	(339)	(0.04)

* Common
^A Reported in accordance with IFRS

M.32 Mapath Capital Corp.

Symbol - MPTH.H **Exchange** - TSX-VEN **CUSIP** - 56509K
Head Office - 654-999 Canada Pl, Vancouver, BC, V6C 3E1 **Telephone** - (778) 588-6643

Email - marcus.new@investx.com
Investor Relations - Marcus A. New (778) 588-6643
Auditors - Dale Matheson Carr-Hilton LaBonte LLP C.A., Vancouver, B.C.
Transfer Agents - Computershare Trust Company of Canada Inc., Vancouver, B.C.
Profile - (Colo. 1994) Seeking new business opportunities.
In December 2022, name change to **Mapath Capital Corp.** and continuation of incorporation into British Columbia from Colorado were approved.
Predecessor Detail - Name changed from Invictus Financial Inc., Dec. 22, 2022.
Directors - Marcus A. New, pres. & CEO, Port Moody, B.C.; Paul Chow, Vancouver, B.C.; Theofilos (Theo) Sanidas, North Vancouver, B.C.
Other Exec. Officers - Chris McClymont, CFO & corp. sec.

Capital Stock

	Authorized (shs.)	Outstanding (shs.)[1]
Series A Convertible Preferred	5,000,000	nil
Common	75,000,000	26,124,503

[1] At Dec. 22, 2022

Major Shareholder - Marcus A. New held 76.56% interest at Nov. 8, 2021.

Price Range - MPTH.H/TSX-VEN

Year	Volume	High	Low	Close
2022	89,760	$0.06	$0.04	$0.05
2021	44,182	$0.07	$0.04	$0.05
2020	221,449	$0.08	$0.03	$0.07
2019	62,347	$0.12	$0.03	$0.03
2018	436,389	$0.20	$0.07	$0.07

Recent Close: $0.03

Financial Statistics

Periods ended:	12m Dec. 31/21[A]		12m Dec. 31/20[A]
	US$000s	%Chg	US$000s
General & admin expense	70		81
Operating expense	**70**	**-14**	**81**
Operating income	**(70)**	**n.a.**	**(81)**
Finance costs, net	(1)		(3)
Pre-tax income	**(70)**	**n.a.**	**180**
Net income	**(70)**	**n.a.**	**180**
Cash & equivalent	199		198
Current assets	199		199
Total assets	**199**	**0**	**199**
Accts. pay. & accr. liabs	15		8
Current liabilities	409		339
Shareholders' equity	(210)		(140)
Cash from oper. activs	**1**	**n.a.**	**(180)**
Net cash position	**199**	**+1**	**198**
	US$		US$
Earnings per share*	(0.00)		0.01
Cash flow per share*	nil		(0.01)
	shs		shs
No. of shs. o/s*	26,124,503		26,124,503
Avg. no. of shs. o/s*	26,124,503		26,124,503
	%		%
Net profit margin	n.a.		n.a.
Return on equity	n.m.		n.m.
Return on assets	(35.18)		62.39

* Common
[A] Reported in accordance with IFRS

Latest Results

Periods ended:	3m Mar. 31/22[A]		3m Mar. 31/21[A]
	US$000s	%Chg	US$000s
Net income	(10)	n.a.	(16)
	US$		US$
Earnings per share*	(0.00)		(0.00)

* Common
[A] Reported in accordance with IFRS

Historical Summary
(as originally stated)

Fiscal Year	Oper. Rev. US$000s	Net Inc. Bef. Disc. US$000s	EPS* US$
2021[A]	nil	(70)	(0.00)
2020[A]	nil	180	0.01
2019[A]	nil	(77)	(0.00)
2018[A]	nil	(147)	(0.01)
2017[A]	nil	(141)	(0.06)

* Common
[A] Reported in accordance with IFRS

Note: Adjusted throughout for 1-for-2 cons. in June 2018

M.33 Maple Leaf Foods Inc.*

Symbol - MFI **Exchange** - TSX **CUSIP** - 564905
Head Office - 6985 Financial Dr, Mississauga, ON, L5N 0A1 **Telephone** - (905) 285-5000 **Toll-free** - (800) 268-3708 **Fax** - (905) 285-6000
Website - www.mapleleaffoods.com
Email - investor.relations@mapleleaf.com
Investor Relations - Michael R. Rawle (800) 268-3708
Auditors - KPMG LLP C.A., Toronto, Ont.
Lawyers - Osler, Hoskin & Harcourt LLP, Toronto, Ont.
Transfer Agents - Computershare Trust Company of Canada Inc., Toronto, Ont.
FP500 Revenue Ranking - 118
Employees - 13,500 at Mar. 8, 2023
Profile - (Can. 1927) Processes and produces meat protein and plant protein products for customers worldwide.

The **Meat Protein** products consist of prepared meats, ready-to-cook and ready-to-serve meals, snacks kits, value-added fresh pork and poultry products. The value-added products include bacon, hams, wieners, meat snacks, delicatessen products, processed chicken products such as fully cooked chicken breasts and wings, processed turkey products, specialty sausages, a complete line of cooked meats, sliced meats, cooked sausage products, lunch kits and canned meats. Products are primarily sold in Canada, the U.S. and Asia under the Maple Leaf®, Maple Leaf Prime®, Maple Leaf Natural Selections®, Schneiders®, Schneiders® Country Naturals®, Mina®, Greenfield Natural Meat Co.®, Viau®, Sila®, Fantimo & Mondello®, Swift Premium®, Hygrade®, Mitchell's Gourmet™, Larsen® and Shopsy's®.

The **Plant Protein** products consist of refrigerated plant protein products, premium grain-based protein and vegan cheese products including plant-based sausages, weiners, bacon, grounds, burgers, deli meat, chicken products, loaves and roasts, along with tempeh, plant-based cheeses and frozen appetizers. Products are primarily sold in Canada and the U.S. under the Lightlife®, Field Roast™ and Chao™ brands.

Principal customers include major grocery chains, independent grocery outlets, large discount stores, retail and wholesale buying groups, food service restaurants and distributors, institutional buyers, other food processors and e-commerce platforms. The company also operates an international export business through a network of offices located in Canada, Korea, Japan, Philippines and the People's Republic of China.

The company's hog production operations have 200 production locations in Manitoba, Saskatchewan and Alberta, with 66,700 sows under management at Dec. 31, 2022. Also owns five feed mills in Manitoba which produce more than 600,000 tonnes of animal feed annually primarily used to feed the company's hogs.

In April 2023, the company agreed to sell its land and building related to a closed poultry facility in St. Mary's, Ont. Terms were not yet disclosed.

In September 2022, the company completed the construction of 660,000-sq.-ft. poultry facility in London, Ont., with strategic investment totaling $772,000,000. Production from three of the company's plants in St. Marys, Toronto and Brampton, Ont., was consolidated into the new facility.

Recent Merger and Acquisition Activity

Status: completed **Revised:** June 30, 2022
UPDATE: The transaction was completed. PREVIOUS: Maple Leaf Foods Inc. agreed to acquire four pig farms in central Saskatchewan, including two sow barns and two nursery barns with potential to supply 140,000 pigs, from a group of companies operating as Polar Pork. Maple Leaf would invest up to $27,000,000 in the barns over time, inclusive of acquisition costs and capital investments. The transaction was expected to close in June 2022.

Directors - Michael H. McCain, exec. chr., Toronto, Ont.; Curtis E. Frank, co-pres., CEO & COO, Carlisle, Ont.; Thomas P. (Tom) Hayes†, Boston, Mass.; William E. (Bill) Aziz, Oakville, Ont.; Ronald G. (Ron) Close, Toronto, Ont.; Dr. Katherine N. (Kay) Lemon, Holliston, Mass.; Andrew G. Macdonald, Toronto, Ont.; Linda P. Mantia, Toronto, Ont.; Jonathan W. F. McCain, Toronto, Ont.; Beth Newlands Campbell, Cape Elizabeth, Me.

Other Exec. Officers - Casey Richards, co-pres. & chief growth officer; Geert Verellen, CFO; Dr. Randall D. Huffman, chief food safety & sustainability officer; Andreas Liris, chief IT officer; Iain W. Stewart, chief supply chain officer; Bentley A. (Ben) Brooks, sr. v-p & gen. mgr., poultry; Stéphane Dubreuil, sr. v-p, strategy & corp. devel.; Jumoke Fagbemi, sr. v-p, people; Suzanne G. Hathaway, sr. v-p, gen. counsel, commun. & corp. sec.; Joshua H. (Josh) Kuehnbaum, sr. v-p, foodservice & intl.; Lynda J. Kuhn, sr. v-p, global govt. & industry rel.; Robert S. Lorimer, sr. v-p, retail sales; Patrick Lutfy, sr. v-p, mktg.; Stephen L. Elmer, v-p & contr.; René R. McLean, v-p, bus. fin.; Michael R. Rawle, v-p, IR & treasury; Jonathan Sawatzky, v-p, Maple Leaf Agri-Farms; Adam J. Grogan, pres., alternative proteins & pres., Greenleaf Foods, SPC; Dennis Organ, pres., pork complex; Michelle Garraway, asst. sec.
† Lead director

Capital Stock

	Authorized (shs.)	Outstanding (shs.)[1]
Preference	unlimited	nil
Non-Vtg. Common	unlimited	nil
Common	unlimited	122,118,414

[1] At July 28, 2023

Preference - Issuable in series and non-voting.
Non-voting Common - Has rights identical to common shares except no voting rights as specified in the Canada Business Corporations Act. Convertible at any time into common shares on a one-for-one basis. Entitled to vote separately as a class on any amendment to the company's articles if the class of shares would be affected by such amendment in a manner which is different than common shares.
Common - One vote per share.
Options - At Dec. 31, 2022, options were outstanding to purchase 6,099,680 common shares at a weighted average exercise price of $26.82 per share with a weighted average remaining term of 3.6 years.
Normal Course Issuer Bid - The company plans to make normal course purchases of up to 7,200,000 common shares representing 10% of the public float. The bid commenced on May 25, 2023, and expires on May 24, 2024.
Major Shareholder - Michael H. McCain held 39.93% interest at Mar. 15, 2023.

Price Range - MFI/TSX

Year	Volume	High	Low	Close
2022	61,611,773	$32.60	$18.85	$24.45
2021	81,775,016	$31.77	$23.56	$29.26
2020	79,312,489	$30.77	$17.04	$28.22
2019	70,444,066	$35.82	$21.87	$25.88
2018	57,400,522	$36.08	$26.05	$27.33

Recent Close: $29.13

Capital Stock Changes - During 2022, common shares were issued as follows: 254,000 under stock-based compensation plans and 330,000 on exercise of options; 2,504,000 common shares were repurchased under a Normal Course Issuer Bid and 271,000 common shares held in treasury were cancelled.

Dividends

MFI com Ra $0.84 pa Q est. Mar. 31, 2023
Prev. Rate: $0.80 est. Mar. 31, 2022
Prev. Rate: $0.72 est. Mar. 31, 2021
Prev. Rate: $0.64 est. Mar. 31, 2020

Long-Term Debt - Outstanding at Dec. 31, 2022:

Revolv. credit facility due Apr. 30, 2024[1]	$999,523,000
Term facility due Apr. 30, 2023[1]	350,000,000
Term facility due Apr. 30, 2024[2]	358,664,000
Government loans due to 2032	7,027,000
Less: Deferred fin. charges	4,800,000
	1,710,414,000
Less: Current portion	921,000
	1,709,493,000

[1] Bears interest at banker's acceptance and prime rates.
[2] Bears interest at SOFR.

Minimum long-term debt repayments were reported as follows:

2023	$1,153,000
2024	1,167,000
2025	796,000
2026	350,796,000
Thereafter	1,362,369,000

Note - In June 2023, credit facility facility was amended by adding an additional $400,000,000 of unsecured committed term credit tranche maturing on June 2024.

Wholly Owned Subsidiaries

Greenleaf Foods, SPC, Chicago, Ill.
Note: The preceding list includes only the major related companies in which interests are held.

Financial Statistics

Periods ended:	12m Dec. 31/22^A		12m Dec. 31/21^A
	$000s	%Chg	$000s
Operating revenue	**4,739,063**	**+5**	**4,521,082**
Cost of goods sold	4,080,988		3,661,152
General & admin expense	431,715		467,067
Operating expense	**4,512,703**	**+9**	**4,128,219**
Operating income	**226,360**	**-42**	**392,863**
Deprec., depl. & amort.	233,937		200,855
Finance costs, gross	56,041		22,870
Write-downs/write-offs	(190,911)[1]		n.a.
Pre-tax income	**(298,968)**	**n.a.**	**149,706**
Income taxes	12,925		46,883
Net inc bef disc ops, eqhldrs	(311,893)		102,823
Net income	**(311,893)**	**n.a.**	**102,823**
Cash & equivalent	91,076		162,031
Inventories	485,979		409,677
Accounts receivable	167,611		167,082
Current assets	1,045,758		937,111
Long-term investments	23,712		22,326
Fixed assets, net	2,303,424		2,189,165
Right-of-use assets	159,199		161,662
Intangibles, net	837,914		1,023,991
Total assets	**4,439,436**	**+1**	**4,385,806**
Accts. pay. & accr. liabs	485,114		526,189
Current liabilities	633,940		668,700
Long-term debt, gross	1,710,414		1,252,249
Long-term debt, net	1,709,493		1,247,073
Long-term lease liabilities	144,569		144,391
Shareholders' equity	1,660,588		2,035,926
Cash from oper. activs	**49,318**	**-84**	**304,791**
Cash from fin. activs	256,742		379,896
Cash from invest. activs	(377,015)		(623,484)
Net cash position	**91,076**	**-44**	**162,031**
Capital expenditures	(355,734)		(580,349)
Capital disposals	607		1,499
Unfunded pension liability	15,801		49,384
	$		$
Earnings per share*	(2.52)		0.83
Cash flow per share*	0.40		2.47
Cash divd. per share*	0.80		0.72
	shs		shs
No. of shs. o/s*	122,548,872		124,722,678
Avg. no. of shs. o/s*	123,600,000		123,500,000
	%		%
Net profit margin	(6.58)		2.27
Return on equity	(16.87)		5.18
Return on assets	(5.74)		2.87
Foreign sales percent	25		26
No. of employees (FTEs)	14,000		13,500

* Common
^A Reported in accordance with IFRS
[1] Consists entirely of impairment of all goodwill that was allocated to the Plant Protein group due to changes in macro-economic conditions.

Latest Results

Periods ended:	6m June 30/23^A		6m June 30/22^A
	$000s	%Chg	$000s
Operating revenue	2,444,553	+5	2,321,686
Net income	(111,382)	n.a.	(40,925)
	$		$
Earnings per share*	(0.92)		(0.33)

* Common
^A Reported in accordance with IFRS

Historical Summary
(as originally stated)

Fiscal Year	Oper. Rev. $000s	Net Inc. Bef. Disc. $000s	EPS* $
2022^A	4,739,063	(311,893)	(2.52)
2021^A	4,521,082	102,823	0.83
2020^A	4,303,722	113,277	0.92
2019^A	3,941,545	74,628	0.60
2018^A	3,495,519	101,348	0.81

* Common
^A Reported in accordance with IFRS

M.34 Maple Leaf Green World Inc.

Symbol - MGW **Exchange** - NEO **CUSIP** - 565297
Head Office - 20-3515 27 St NE, Calgary, AB, T1Y 5E4 **Telephone** - (403) 235-2641
Website - www.mlgreenworld.com
Email - rlai@mlgreenworld.com
Investor Relations - Raymond Siu Cheong Lai (403) 235-2641
Auditors - Paul J. Rozek Professional Corporation C.A., Calgary, Alta.
Transfer Agents - Odyssey Trust Company, Calgary, Alta.
Profile - (B.C. 2005 amalg.) Engages in hemp-related activities in California.

Through wholly owned **Golden State Green World LLC** (GSGW), owns 20 acres of agricultural land in Riverside, Calif., and leases an additional four acres in Fallbrook, Calif., with an agreement in place to purchase the property. GSGW has launched two brands, ReNao Wellness, for cannabigerol (CBG), cannabidiol (CBD) and cannabinol (CBN) health and wellness products, and Phoenix Crave, which markets CBG cigarettes, pre-rolls and vapes.

Predecessor Detail - Name changed from Maple Leaf Reforestation Inc., Oct. 5, 2012.

Directors - Raymond Siu Cheong Lai, chr., pres. & CEO, Calgary, Alta.; Terence Lam, CFO & corp. sec., Calgary, Alta.; Wentong (Winston) Gao, v-p, fin. & PR; Andrew Wang; Thomas West

Other Exec. Officers - Jeffrey Stein, COO

Capital Stock

	Authorized (shs.)	Outstanding (shs.)[1]
Preferred	unlimited	nil
Common	unlimited	33,142,394

[1] At May 27, 2022

Major Shareholder - Widely held at May 27, 2021.

Price Range - MGW/NEO

Year	Volume	High	Low	Close
2022	11,599,348	$0.14	$0.04	$0.06
2021	4,478,952	$0.60	$0.07	$0.12
2020	231,916	$0.87	$0.27	$0.36
2019	252,750	$1.89	$0.21	$0.30
2018	21,675,350	$12.36	$0.75	$0.84

Consolidation: 1-for-6 cons. in Oct. 2021
Recent Close: $0.03

Wholly Owned Subsidiaries

Golden State Green World LLC, Calif.
SSGW LLC, Nev.
- 100% int. in **BioNeva Innovations of Henderson, LLC**, Nev.

Financial Statistics

Periods ended:	12m Dec. 31/21^A		12m Dec. 31/20^oA
	$000s	%Chg	$000s
Salaries & benefits	201		177
General & admin expense	666		500
Other operating expense	570		(893)
Operating expense	**1,437**	**n.a.**	**(216)**
Operating income	**(1,437)**	**n.a.**	**216**
Deprec., depl. & amort.	57		91
Finance costs, gross	290		757
Write-downs/write-offs	(976)		(10,579)
Pre-tax income	**(2,539)**	**n.a.**	**(10,728)**
Net income	**(2,539)**	**n.a.**	**(10,728)**
Cash & equivalent	nil		48
Accounts receivable	17		18
Current assets	17		1,314
Fixed assets, net	383		419
Right-of-use assets	nil		103
Total assets	**400**	**-78**	**1,852**
Accts. pay. & accr. liabs	6,784		6,642
Current liabilities	8,848		7,738
Long-term debt, gross	1,875		1,020
Long-term lease liabilities	nil		83
Shareholders' equity	(8,508)		(6,030)
Cash from oper. activs	**(641)**	**n.a.**	**(52)**
Cash from fin. activs	592		(981)
Cash from invest. activs	nil		871
Net cash position	**nil**	**n.a.**	**48**
Capital expenditures	nil		(269)
	$		$
Earnings per share*	(0.09)		(0.40)
Cash flow per share*	(0.02)		(0.03)
	shs		shs
No. of shs. o/s*	27,477,394		26,892,566
Avg. no. of shs. o/s*	27,153,736		26,892,566
	%		%
Net profit margin	n.a.		n.a.
Return on equity	n.m.		n.m.
Return on assets	(199.73)		(142.25)
No. of employees (FTEs)	...		1

* Common
^o Restated
^A Reported in accordance with IFRS

Latest Results

Periods ended:	3m Mar. 31/22^A		3m Mar. 31/21^A
	$000s	%Chg	$000s
Net income	(266)	n.a.	(659)
	$		$
Earnings per share*	(0.01)		(0.02)

* Common
^A Reported in accordance with IFRS

Historical Summary
(as originally stated)

Fiscal Year	Oper. Rev. $000s	Net Inc. Bef. Disc. $000s	EPS* $
2021^A	nil	(2,539)	(0.09)
2020^A	nil	(10,728)	(0.40)
2019^A	nil	(2,750)	(0.06)
2018^A	nil	(11,282)	(0.42)
2017^A	212	(1,806)	(0.06)

* Common
^A Reported in accordance with IFRS
Note: Adjusted throughout for 1-for-6 cons. in Oct. 2021

M.35 Maple Peak Investments Inc.

Symbol - MAP **Exchange** - TSX-VEN **CUSIP** - 56531K
Head Office - 170-6751 Graybar Rd, Richmond, BC, B6W 1H3 **Telephone** - (604) 999-8253
Email - thurmanso@shaw.ca
Investor Relations - Tat Hong So (604) 488-5219
Auditors - MNP LLP C.A., Vancouver, B.C.
Lawyers - TRL Law Corporation, Vancouver, B.C.
Transfer Agents - Computershare Trust Company of Canada Inc., Vancouver, B.C.
Profile - (B.C. 2013) Invests in companies involved in casinos, gaming and game of chance, leisure and entertainment, and resort projects.

Holds an investment in **Melco International Development Ltd.**, an investment holding company listed on **The Stock Exchange of Hong Kong Limited** (SHEK), which develops, owns and operates integrated resort facilities in Asia and Europe.

During fiscal 2022, the company sold its investment in and **Loto Interactive Ltd.** for proceeds of $41,460.

Directors - Lawrence Yau Lung Ho, chr., Hong Kong, Hong Kong, People's Republic of China; Dennis Chi-Wai Tam, CEO, Hong Kong, Hong Kong, People's Republic of China; Samuel Yuen-Wai Tsang, CFO & corp. sec., Hong Kong, Hong Kong, People's Republic of China; Ravinder (Robert) Kang, Vancouver, B.C.; Tat Hong (Thurman) So, Richmond, B.C.

Capital Stock

	Authorized (shs.)	Outstanding (shs.)[1]
Common	unlimited	59,000,000

[1] At July 12, 2022

Major Shareholder - Lawrence Yau Lung Ho held 50.85% interest, Dennis Chi-Wai Tam held 11.19% interest and Samuel Yuen-Wai Tsang held 11.19% interest at Oct. 15, 2020.

Price Range - MAP/TSX-VEN

Year	Volume	High	Low	Close
2022	193,502	$0.04	$0.01	$0.01
2021	545,510	$0.16	$0.03	$0.03
2020	331,000	$0.08	$0.02	$0.04
2019	182,500	$0.15	$0.02	$0.02
2018	97,500	$0.35	$0.10	$0.10

Recent Close: $0.02

Investments

Melco International Development Limited

Financial Statistics

Periods ended:	12m Apr. 30/22^A		12m Apr. 30/21^A
	$000s	%Chg	$000s
Salaries & benefits	nil		605
General & admin expense	329		345
Operating expense	**329**	**-65**	**950**
Operating income	**(329)**	**n.a.**	**(950)**
Finance costs, gross	1		1
Investment income	nil		8
Pre-tax income	**(324)**	**n.a.**	**(930)**
Income taxes	181		23
Net income	**(505)**	**n.a.**	**(953)**
Cash & equivalent	1,702		2,150
Accounts receivable	2		nil
Current assets	1,708		2,154
Long-term investments	1,615		3,881
Total assets	**3,323**	**-45**	**6,035**
Accts. pay. & accr. liabs	98		262
Current liabilities	98		262
Shareholders' equity	3,225		5,773
Cash from oper. activs	**(489)**	**n.a.**	**(747)**
Cash from invest. activs	42		nil
Net cash position	**1,702**	**-21**	**2,150**
	$		$
Earnings per share*	(0.01)		(0.02)
Cash flow per share*	(0.01)		(0.01)
	shs		shs
No. of shs. o/s*	59,000,000		59,000,000
Avg. no. of shs. o/s*	59,000,000		59,000,000
	%		%
Net profit margin	n.a.		n.a.
Return on equity	(11.22)		(15.07)
Return on assets	(10.76)		(14.65)

* Common
^A Reported in accordance with IFRS

Historical Summary
(as originally stated)

Fiscal Year	Oper. Rev. $000s	Net Inc. Bef. Disc. $000s	EPS* $
2022[A]	nil	(505)	(0.01)
2021[A]	nil	(953)	(0.02)
2020[A]	nil	(1,043)	(0.02)
2019[A]	nil	(907)	(0.02)
2018[A]	nil	(707)	(0.01)

* Common
[A] Reported in accordance with IFRS

M.36 Marble Financial Inc.

Symbol - MRBL **Exchange** - CSE **CUSIP** - 566055
Head Office - 404-999 Canada Pl, Vancouver, BC, V6C 3E2 **Telephone** - (604) 336-0185 **Toll-free** - (855) 661-2390
Website - www.mymarble.ca
Email - ir@marblefinancial.ca
Investor Relations - Michele N. Marrandino (855) 661-2390
Auditors - Hay & Watson C.A., Vancouver, B.C.
Lawyers - Vantage Law Corporation, Vancouver, B.C.
Transfer Agents - Odyssey Trust Company, Vancouver, B.C.
Profile - (Can. 2016; orig. B.C., 2015) Operates a consumer lending business, providing proprietary fintech solutions for Canadians to rebuild their credit. Also offers banking verification solutions to the financial services industry, and online lead generation technology for businesses.

Has developed MyMarble, a Software-as-a-Service (SaaS)-based personal finance, credit wellness and financial literacy platform which allows customers to access the company's products, including Score-Up, Marble Learn, Fast-Track loans and Marble Boost, under one easy-to-use platform. MyMarble provides solutions including budgeting, cash flow analysis, trends and insights with up-to-date and live financial recommendations that enable the customers to analyze areas of financial improvement based on their financial profile; credit insights, recommendations and simulators through Score-Up; access to industry expert course programs designed to improve financial literacy through Marble Learn; a consumer proposal exit loan solution through Fast-Track; access to **Jenson Graf Risk Management Inc.**'s The Secured Future Credit Plan product, which is a savings and credit-rebuilding tool; and a consumer loan repayment program through Marble Boost. The platform also includes an affiliate portal that allows third party lenders, debt restructuring service providers and other financial service companies to refer their customers to the company and monitor their progress.

Also developing Credit-Meds, an interactive software diagnostic tool, which identifies preferred options for cash management (budgeting and personal finances), debt management and credit rebuilding while balancing a customer's current situation and long-term goals.

Wholly owned **Inverite Verification Inc.** operates a cloud-based SaaS platform that offers bank verification, ID verification, expense categorization and risk scoring products to the financial services industry for income verification, credit decisioning, fraud reduction and know-your-client/anti-money laundering purposes.

Wholly owned **Accumulate.ai Software Ltd.** operates a cloud-based SaaS platform that utilizes AI-based lead generation technology to accumulate customers for clients; and assists in secured vehicle financing through Drive Away.

In June 2023, the company entered into a memorandum of understanding with **Grit Financial Inc.** wherein the company's artificial intelligence (AI)-driven technology would be integrated into Grit's mobile application and offered to its customers in the U.S. in exchange for a $10,000,000 credit facility. The platform would be re-named as Grit Score-Up™. In addition, Grit would also have the option to be the exclusive provider of Inverite platform in the U.S., and in return, the company would have the option to be the exclusive provider of GRIT debt/charge card and earned wage access (EWA) in Canada. Grit offers financial services, including financial wellness tools, budgeting, banking-as-a-service (BaaS) and EWA in the U.S.

On Oct. 18, 2022, wholly owned **Accumulate.ai Software Ltd.** acquired the Autocarz technology assets of **eBunch Data & Development Ltd.** for $125,000 cash and earn-out consideration of up to $425,000 in common shares. The Autocarz technology assets consist of eBunch's inventory management system and online lead generation technology for auto dealerships and related assets.

Predecessor Detail - Name changed from MLI Marble Lending Inc., Nov. 8, 2019.

Directors - Michele N. (Mike) Marrandino, exec. chr., Vancouver, B.C.; Karim Nanji, CEO, B.C.; Farhan Abbas, Ont.; Jason W. Scharfe, Vancouver, B.C.

Other Exec. Officers - Jim Chan, COO & chief tech. officer; Rose Zanic, CFO; Toby Lim, corp. sec.; Bo (Bennett) Liu, contr.

Capital Stock

	Authorized (shs.)	Outstanding (shs.)[1]
Common	unlimited	172,043,918

[1] At June 2, 2023

Major Shareholder - Bradley N. (Brad) Scharfe held 13.05% interest and Michele N. (Mike) Marrandino held 10.08% interest at Nov. 28, 2022.

Price Range - MRBL/CSE

Year	Volume	High	Low	Close
2022	8,345,915	$0.15	$0.05	$0.08
2021	36,366,437	$0.44	$0.11	$0.13
2020	11,006,245	$0.23	$0.12	$0.21
2019	8,809,103	$0.33	$0.16	$0.22

Recent Close: $0.07

Capital Stock Changes - In April and May 2023, 44,298,850 common shares were issued for settlement of $4,069,415 of debt.

In November and December 2022, private placement of 20,952,437 units (1 common share & ½ warrant) at 7¢ per unit was completed. Also during 2022, common shares were issued as follows: 4,883,988 on exercise of warrants, 1,577,000 pursuant to the acquisition of Inverite Verification Inc., 800,000 under restricted share unit plan and 75,040 as finder's fees.

Wholly Owned Subsidiaries

Accumulate.ai Software Ltd., Canada.
Credit Meds Corp., Ont.
Inverite Verification Inc., Burnaby, B.C.
1301771 B.C. Ltd., B.C.
Score-Up Inc., Ont.
TPF The Phoenix Fund Inc., B.C.
TPFM The Phoenix Fund Management Ltd., B.C.

Financial Statistics

Periods ended:	12m Dec. 31/22[A]		12m Dec. 31/21[A]
	$000s	%Chg	$000s
Total revenue	**1,091**	**-20**	**1,360**
Salaries & benefits	1,954		1,666
General & admin. expense	2,346		3,074
Stock-based compensation	288		482
Operating expense	**4,588**	**-12**	**5,222**
Operating income	**(3,497)**	**n.a.**	**(3,862)**
Deprec. & amort.	227		234
Finance costs, gross	757		747
Write-downs/write-offs	(793)		(221)
Pre-tax income	**(5,358)**	**n.a.**	**(5,056)**
Income taxes	(66)		nil
Net income	**(5,292)**	**n.a.**	**(5,056)**
Cash & equivalent	44		1,107
Accounts receivable	115		157
Investments	352		773
Fixed assets, net	22		30
Intangibles, net	2,728		3,320
Total assets	**3,536**	**-41**	**6,031**
Accts. pay. & accr. liabs	1,364		813
Debt	6,295		6,477
Lease liabilities	nil		125
Equity portion of conv. debs	71		115
Shareholders' equity	(5,643)		(2,964)
Cash from oper. activs	**(2,508)**	**n.a.**	**(2,888)**
Cash from fin. activs	1,577		4,162
Cash from invest. activs	(131)		(1,493)
Net cash position	**44**	**-96**	**1,107**
Capital expenditures	(6)		(52)
	$		$
Earnings per share*	(0.05)		(0.06)
Cash flow per share*	(0.03)		(0.04)
	shs		shs
No. of shs. o/s*	121,508,618		93,220,153
Avg. no. of shs. o/s*	99,264,731		77,718,956
	%		%
Net profit margin	(485.06)		(371.76)
Return on equity	n.m.		n.m.
Return on assets	(95.00)		(81.28)
No. of employees (FTEs)	...		13

* Common
[A] Reported in accordance with IFRS

Latest Results

Periods ended:	3m Mar. 31/23[A]		3m Mar. 31/22[A]
	$000s	%Chg	$000s
Total revenue	325	+7	304
Net income	(956)	n.a.	(1,197)
	$		$
Earnings per share*	(0.01)		(0.01)

* Common
[A] Reported in accordance with IFRS

Historical Summary
(as originally stated)

Fiscal Year	Total Rev. $000s	Net Inc. Bef. Disc. $000s	EPS* $
2022[A]	1,091	(5,292)	(0.05)
2021[A]	1,360	(5,056)	(0.06)
2020[A]	878	(3,551)	(0.06)
2019[A]	572	(3,152)	(0.06)
2018[A]	783	(1,215)	(0.03)

* Common
[A] Reported in accordance with IFRS

M.37 MariMed Inc.

Symbol - MRMD **Exchange** - CSE **CUSIP** - 56782V
Head Office - 10 Oceana Way, Norwood, MA, United States, 02062 **Telephone** - (781) 277-0007
Website - marimedinc.com
Email - svillare@marimedinc.com
Investor Relations - Susan M. Villare (617) 795-5140
Auditors - M&K CPAS, PLLC C.P.A., Houston, Tex.
Lawyers - Fogler, Rubinoff LLP, Toronto, Ont.
Transfer Agents - Odyssey Trust Company, Calgary, Alta.; Olde Monmouth Stock Transfer Co., Inc., Atlantic Highlands, N.J.
Employees - 592 at Dec. 31, 2022
Profile - (Del. 2011) Has medicinal and recreational cannabis cultivation, production and dispensing operations in the U.S., as well as licenses proprietary brands of cannabis and hemp-infused products.

The company has operations in six U.S. states (Massachusetts, Illinois, Maryland, Delaware, Illinois and Ohio) consisting of six cultivation, production and processing facilities with more than 500,000 sq. ft. of cultivation space and nine retail dispensaries under the Panacea Wellness™ and Thrive™ banners serving both the medical and adult-use markets.

Products include cannabis flower, vapes, concentrates and edibles under the brands Nature's Heritage™, Betty's Eddies™, Bubby's Baked, Vibations: High + Energy, Kalm Fusion and K Fusion™, InHouse™ and Mari Melts™.

In March 2023, the company acquired the operating assets of **Ermont Inc.**, a cannabis dispensary in Quincy, Mass., for US$3,000,000 cash, issuance of 6,580,390 common shares and a US$7,000,000 6% promissory note due 2029.

In December 2022, the company acquired a dispensary licence held by **Green House Naturals, LLC** for a dispensary in Beverly, Mass., for US$100,000 cash, issuance of 2,000,000 common shares and a US$5,000,000 promissory note due 2026.

In September 2022, the company agreed to acquire **Robust Missouri Process and Manufacturing 1, LLC**, a Missouri wholesale and cultivator, for US$700,000. The closing was expected to occur in 2023.

In August 2022, the company agreed to acquire **Allgreens Dispensary, LLC**, an operator of a dispensary in Illinois, for US$2,250,000. The transaction was expected to close during 2023.

In May 2022, the company acquired **Green Growth Group, Inc.**, an operator of a dispensary in Mt. Vernon, Ill., for $US1,900,000 cash and issuance of 2,343,750 common shares.

In April 2022, the company acquired **Kind Therapeutics U.S.A., LLC**, an operator of a dispensary in Hagerstown, Md., for US$13,500,000 cash and a US$6,500,000 6% promissory note due 2026. The company had been providing services to Kind for the operation of the dispensary.

Predecessor Detail - Name changed from Worlds Online Inc., May 11, 2017.

Directors - Edward Gildea, chr.; Jon R. Levine, pres. & CEO; David Allen; Dr. Eva Selhub; Kathleen Tucker

Other Exec. Officers - Timothy Shaw, COO; Susan M. Villare, CFO & treas.; Ryan Crandall, chief revenue officer; Howard Schacter, chief commun. officer; Jay O'Malley, v-p, mktg. & R&D; Matt Truppo, v-p, retail sales

Capital Stock

	Authorized (shs.)	Outstanding (shs.)[1]	Par
Series B Preferred	4,908,333	4,908,333	US$0.001
Series C Preferred	6,216,216	6,216,216	US$0.001
Common	700,000,000	362,190,245[2]	US$0.001

[1] At Mar. 1, 2023
[2] At May 4, 2023.

Series B Preferred - Entitled to dividends. Convertible, at the holder's option, into common shares at a conversion price of US$3.00 per share. Entitled to the number of votes equal to the number of common shares into which series B preferred shares are convertible.

Series C Preferred - Entitled to dividends on an as-converted basis. Convertible, at the holder's option, into 5 common shares. Have a liquidation preference equal to US$3.70 per share, plus declared but unpaid dividends. Non-voting.

Common - One vote per share.

Major Shareholder - Jon R. Levine held 12.79% interest at Apr. 10, 2023.

Price Range - MRMD/CSE

Year	Volume	High	Low	Close
2022	207,619	$1.00	$0.35	$0.35

Recent Close: $0.41

Capital Stock Changes - In March 2023, 6,580,390 common shares were issued pursuant to acquisition of the operating assets of Ermont Inc.

During 2022, common shares were issued as follows: 2,343,750 pursuant to the acquisition of Green Growth Group Inc., 2,000,000 pursuant to the acquisition of Greenhouse Naturals LLC, 1,142,858 on conversion of promissory notes, 422,535 on acquisition of property and equipment, 402,203 for stock grants, 375,000 for services, 317,298 on exercise of warrants, 218,345 for royalty payment and 255,000 on exercise of options; 32,609 common shares were returned and cancelled.

Wholly Owned Subsidiaries

ARL Healthcare Inc., New Bedford, Mass.
Green Growth Group, Inc.
KPG Anna LLC, Ill.
KPG of Harrisburg LLC, Ill.
Kind Therapeutics USA LLC, Md.

MMMO LLC, Mo.
MariMed Advisors Inc., Del.
- 100% int. in **Hartwell Realty Holdings LLC**, Mass.
- 100% int. in **iRollie LLC**, United States.
- 100% int. in **Mari Holdings IL LLC**, Ill.
- 99.7% int. in **Mari Holdings MD LLC**, Md.
- 100% int. in **Mari Holdings NJ LLC**, N.J.
- 100% int. in **Mari Holdings NV LLC**, Nev.
- 70% int. in **Mari Metropolis LLC**, Ill.
- 100% int. in **Mari Mfg LLC**, N.J.
- 100% int. in **Mari Mt. Vernon LLC**, Ill.
- 100% int. in **MariMed OH LLC**, Ohio
- 94.3% int. in **Mia Development LLC**, Del.

MariMed Hemp Inc., Del.
- 100% int. in **MediTaurus LLC**, United States.

Investments

WM Technology, Inc.

Financial Statistics

Periods ended:	12m Dec. 31/22[A]		12m Dec. 31/21[A1]
	US$000s	%Chg	US$000s
Operating revenue	**134,010**	**+10**	**121,464**
Cost of sales	70,053		55,201
Salaries & benefits	14,404		8,351
General & admin expense	19,757		26,398
Operating expense	**104,214**	**+16**	**89,950**
Operating income	**29,796**	**-5**	**31,514**
Deprec., depl. & amort.	4,714		2,788
Finance income	959		108
Finance costs, gross	1,693		2,356
Write-downs/write-offs	(3,752)		(1,862)
Pre-tax income	**19,508**	**-18**	**23,816**
Income taxes	5,894		16,192
Net income	**13,614**	**+79**	**7,624**
Net inc. for equity hldrs	**13,468**	**+86**	**7,225**
Net inc. for non-cont. int	**146**	**-63**	**399**
Cash & equivalent	9,860		29,934
Inventories	19,477		9,768
Accounts receivable	4,157		1,666
Current assets	44,146		44,613
Fixed assets, net	71,641		62,150
Right-of-use assets	5,644		5,127
Intangibles, net	22,280		2,230
Total assets	**152,202**	**+24**	**123,205**
Accts. pay. & accr. liabs	9,717		8,248
Current liabilities	26,490		27,223
Long-term debt, gross	29,717		18,672
Long-term debt, net	25,943		17,262
Long-term lease liabilities	4,634		4,596
Preferred share equity	37,725		37,725
Shareholders' equity	(83,924)		(97,392)
Non-controlling interest	(1,511)		(1,563)
Cash from oper. activs	**7,311**	**-80**	**35,855**
Cash from fin. activs	(1,013)		7,453
Cash from invest. activs	(26,244)		(16,624)
Net cash position	**9,737**	**-67**	**29,683**
Capital expenditures	(12,140)		(17,874)
	US$		US$
Earnings per share*	0.04		0.02
Cash flow per share*	0.02		0.11
	shs		shs
No. of shs. o/s*	341,474,728		334,030,348
Avg. no. of shs. o/s*	337,697,000		326,466,794
	%		%
Net profit margin	10.16		6.28
Return on equity	n.m.		n.m.
Return on assets	10.74		8.39
Foreign sales percent	100		100
No. of employees (FTEs)	592		n.a.

* Common
[A] Reported in accordance with U.S. GAAP
[1] As shown in the prospectus dated June 29, 2022.

Latest Results

Periods ended:	3m Mar. 31/23[A]		3m Mar. 31/22[A]
	US$000s	%Chg	US$000s
Operating revenue	34,380	+10	31,282
Net income	(664)	n.a.	4,241
Net inc. for equity hldrs	(645)	n.a.	4,188
Net inc. for non-cont. int	(19)		53
	US$		US$
Earnings per share*	(0.00)		0.01

* Common
[A] Reported in accordance with U.S. GAAP

Historical Summary
(as originally stated)

Fiscal Year	Oper. Rev. US$000s	Net Inc. Bef. Disc. US$000s	EPS* US$
2022[A]	134,010	13,614	0.04
2021[A1]	121,464	7,624	0.02
2020[A1]	50,895	2,429	0.01

* Common
[A] Reported in accordance with U.S. GAAP
[1] As shown in the prospectus dated June 29, 2022.

M.38 Maritime Launch Services Inc.

Symbol - MAXQ **Exchange** - NEO **CUSIP** - 57033N
Head Office - 303-1883 Upper Water St, Halifax, NS, B3J 1S9
Telephone - (902) 403-0441
Website - www.maritimelaunch.com
Email - sarah.mclean@maritimelaunch.com
Investor Relations - Sarah McLean (902) 402-6947
Auditors - MNP LLP C.A.
Transfer Agents - TSX Trust Company, Toronto, Ont.
Employees - 6 at May 11, 2023
Profile - (Ont. 2008 amalg.; orig. Que., 1956) Developing Spaceport Nova Scotia, a commercial spaceport that launches satellites to both polar and sun-synchronous orbit.

The development of Spaceport Nova Scotia will allow the company's Cyclone-4M lift vehicle and other prospective launch vehicles to place their satellites into low-Earth orbit, building to a launch tempo of eight launches per year. Spaceport Nova Scotia will be the first commercial orbital launch complex in Canada.

The launch complex, which is under construction since September 2022, is located within a leased 334-acre parcel of land near the rural communities of Canso, Little Dover and Hazel Hill in Nova Scotia and will consist of three areas: a vertical launch pad, a launch vehicle processing site and a control centre. The company plans to complete a first small vehicle launch demonstration in the first phase, in the third quarter of 2023.

In May 2023, the company entered into a multi-mission agreement with a leading international space logistics and transportation company to launch Orbital Transfer Vehicles (OTVs) from the company's Spaceport Nova Scotia. Pursuant to the agreement, the company is committed to provide medium-class launch vehicle capacity on multiple missions on a rideshare and dedicated payload basis from 2025 onwards.

In January 2023, the company agreed to launch up to five of **Spaceflight Inc.**'s Sherpa™ Orbital Transfer Vehicles (OTVs) from the company's Spaceport Nova Scotia. The OTVs would launch beginning in 2025, aboard the company's Cyclone-4M lift vehicle.

In September 2022, the company entered into a letter of intent and memorandum of understanding with **Skyrora Ltd.** to launch the Skyrora XL vehicle from the company's Spaceport Nova Scotia. Skyrora would supply launch vehicles for the company's satellite clients, as well as host their own satellite clients under a lease agreement. Skyrora XL is a three-stage, small class launch vehicle intended to place payloads into sun-synchronous and polar orbit.

In May 2022, the company entered into a letter of intent with **Reaction Dynamics** (RDX) to conduct launches from the company's Spaceport Nova Scotia. A first suborbital launch, planned for 2023, would use RDX's small class launch vehicle, Aurora, and its advanced hybrid technology. RDX would provide the vehicle and support equipment to the Spaceport, and the company would provide launch services and facility support infrastructure.

Recent Merger and Acquisition Activity

Status: completed **Revised:** Apr. 1, 2022
UPDATE: The transaction was completed. Jaguar issued a total of 390,544,092 common shares. PREVIOUS: Jaguar Financial Corporation entered into a letter of intent for the reverse takeover acquisition of private Halifax, N.S.-based Maritime Launch Services Ltd. (MLS), which was developing Spaceport Nova Scotia, a commercial spaceport that launches satellites to both polar and sun-synchronous orbit, on the basis of 4.5 Jaguar common shares for each MLS share held. Upon completion, MLS would amalgamate with Jaguar's wholly owned 4374344 Nova Scotia Limited to form Maritime Launch Services (Nova Scotia) Ltd., and Jaguar would change its name to Maritime Launch Services Inc. MLS' Cyclone-4M lift vehicle was a low-Earth orbit-oriented rocket launcher.

Status: terminated **Revised:** Mar. 30, 2022
UPDATE: Ceres did not anticipate entering into a definitive agreement with MLS and was exploring other potential targets for a Qualifying Transaction. PREVIOUS: Ceres Acquisition Corp. entered into a letter of intent for the Qualifying Acquisition of private Halifax, N.S.-based Maritime Launch Services Ltd. (MLS), which was developing Spaceport Nova Scotia, a commercial spaceport that launches satellites to both polar and sun-synchronous orbit. Consideration would be the issuance of Ceres common shares. MLS' Cyclone-4M lift vehicle was a low-Earth orbit-oriented rocket launcher.

Predecessor Detail - Name changed from Jaguar Financial Corporation, Apr. 1, 2022, pursuant to the reverse takeover acquisition of Maritime Launch Services Ltd. and concurrent amalgamation of Maritime Launch with wholly owned 4374344 Nova Scotia Limited (and continued as Maritime Launch Services (Nova Scotia) Ltd.).

Directors - Sasha Jacob, chr., Toronto, Ont.; Stephen Matier, pres. & CEO, Halifax, N.S.; Sylvain Laporte, Gatineau, Qué.; L. Rita Theil, Toronto, Ont.

Other Exec. Officers - Martin J. Doane, COO & corp. sec.; Keith B. Abriel, CFO; Sarah McLean, v-p, commun. & corp. affairs; Robert Feierbach, pres., Maritime Launch USA Inc.

Capital Stock

	Authorized (shs.)	Outstanding (shs.)[1]
Common	unlimited	410,484,741

[1] At May 11, 2023

Major Shareholder - Sasha Jacob held 28.67% interest and Stephen Matier held 21.23% interest at Oct. 25, 2022.

Price Range - MAXQ/NEO

Year	Volume	High	Low	Close
2022	609,500	$0.25	$0.09	$0.10
2021	7,002,070	$0.60	$0.04	$0.05
2020	10,265,049	$0.80	$0.01	$0.23
2019	2,050,848	$0.06	$0.02	$0.02
2018	3,869,720	$0.35	$0.04	$0.04

Recent Close: $0.16

Capital Stock Changes - On Apr. 1, 2022, 390,544,092 common shares were issued pursuant to the reverse takeover acquisition of Maritime Launch Services Ltd.

Wholly Owned Subsidiaries

Maritime Launch Services (Nova Scotia) Ltd., Halifax, N.S.
- 100% int. in **Martime Launch USA Inc.**, Del.

Financial Statistics

Periods ended:	12m Dec. 31/22[A1]		12m Dec. 31/21[◻A]
	$000s	%Chg	$000s
Salaries & benefits	1,567		446
Research & devel. expense	nil		72
General & admin expense	2,705		1,586
Stock-based compensation	1,407		115
Operating expense	**5,680**	**+156**	**2,219**
Operating income	**(5,680)**	**n.a.**	**(2,219)**
Deprec., depl. & amort.	34		11
Finance costs, gross	382		508
Pre-tax income	**(7,451)**	**n.a.**	**(4,317)**
Net income	**(7,451)**	**n.a.**	**(4,317)**
Cash & equivalent	2,971		3,989
Current assets	3,363		8,242
Fixed assets, net	8,057		3,161
Right-of-use assets	211		93
Total assets	**11,630**	**-2**	**11,871**
Accts. pay. & accr. liabs	1,081		806
Current liabilities	8,505		13,737
Long-term debt, gross	7,392		7,308
Long-term lease liabilities	174		93
Shareholders' equity	2,951		(1,959)
Cash from oper. activs	**(4,345)**	**n.a.**	**(1,983)**
Cash from fin. activs	2,543		12,671
Cash from invest. activs	784		(6,798)
Net cash position	**2,871**	**-26**	**3,889**
Capital expenditures	(3,226)		(2,756)
	$		$
Earnings per share*	(0.02)		(0.06)
Cash flow per share*	(0.01)		(0.03)
	shs		shs
No. of shs. o/s*	403,460,590		n.a.
Avg. no. of shs. o/s*	389,875,866		n.a.
	%		%
Net profit margin	n.a.		n.a.
Return on equity	n.m.		n.m.
Return on assets	(120.55)		(63.90)

* Common
◻ Restated
[A] Reported in accordance with IFRS
[1] Results reflect Apr. 1, 2022, reverse takeover acquisition of Maritime Launch Services Ltd.

Latest Results

Periods ended:	3m Mar. 31/23[A]		3m Mar. 31/22[◻A]
	$000s	%Chg	$000s
Net income	(1,135)	n.a.	(265)
	$		$
Earnings per share*	(0.00)		(0.00)

* Common
◻ Restated
[A] Reported in accordance with IFRS

Historical Summary
(as originally stated)

Fiscal Year	Oper. Rev.	Net Inc. Bef. Disc.	EPS*
	$000s	$000s	$
2022[A]	nil	(7,451)	(0.02)
2021[A1]	nil	(205)	(0.02)
2020[A2]	20	(590)	(0.05)
2019[A]	(33)	(243)	(0.02)
2018[A]	(137)	(403)	(0.04)

* Common
[A] Reported in accordance with IFRS
[1] Results for 2021 and prior years pertain to Jaguar Financial Corporation.
[2] Amended.

M.39 Marret High Yield Strategies Fund

Symbol - MHY.UN **Exchange** - CSE **CUSIP** - 571624
Head Office - c/o Marret Asset Management Inc., 200-15 York St, Toronto, ON, M5J 0A3 **Telephone** - (416) 214-5800
Website - www.marret.com
Email - kcooney@marret.com
Investor Relations - Kathleen Cooney (416) 214-5800
Auditors - PricewaterhouseCoopers LLP C.A., Toronto, Ont.
Transfer Agents - Computershare Trust Company of Canada Inc., Toronto, Ont.
Trustees - TSX Trust Company, Toronto, Ont.
Managers - Marret Asset Management Inc., Toronto, Ont.
Portfolio Advisors - Marret Asset Management Inc., Toronto, Ont.
Profile - (Ont. 2009) Undergoing termination.

The fund's primary investment is illiquid equity and debt securities of **Cline Mining Inc.**, a private Canadian mining company undergoing restructuring. At Dec. 31, 2021, the fair value of the fund's investment was $13,283,585. The fund would continue until such time as the Cline investment is sold and the remaining net assets are distributed to unitholders.

Oper. Subsid./Mgt. Co. Directors - Edward D. (Ted) Kelterborn, Toronto, Ont.; Darie P. Urbanky, Toronto, Ont.
Oper. Subsid./Mgt. Co. Officers - Kathleen Cooney, COO & chief compliance officer; Amit Muni, CFO; Adrian Prenc, v-p; Adam Tuer, v-p

Capital Stock

	Authorized (shs.)	Outstanding (shs.)[1]
Fund Unit	unlimited	36,729,002

[1] At Dec. 31, 2021

Major Shareholder - Widely held at Feb. 28, 2022.

Price Range - MHY.UN/CSE

Year	Volume	High	Low	Close
2022	7,477,038	$0.30	$0.09	$0.09
2021	1,754,499	$0.44	$0.08	$0.26
2020	2,072,341	$0.15	$0.04	$0.10
2019	3,545,411	$0.20	$0.04	$0.14
2018	6,847,123	$0.17	$0.01	$0.05

Recent Close: $0.03

Financial Statistics

Periods ended:	12m Dec. 31/21[A]		12m Dec. 31/20[A]
	$000s	%Chg	$000s
Unrealized invest. gain (loss)	1,980		nil
Total revenue	**1,996**	**n.m.**	**4**
General & admin. expense	146		47
Operating expense	**146**	**+211**	**47**
Operating income	**1,850**	**n.a.**	**(43)**
Pre-tax income	**1,850**	**n.a.**	**(43)**
Net income	**1,850**	**n.a.**	**(43)**
Cash & equivalent	128		265
Investments	13,284		16,682
Total assets	**13,503**	**-20**	**16,947**
Shareholders' equity	13,491		16,840
Cash from oper. activs	**5,063**	**n.m.**	**193**
Cash from fin. activs	(5,199)		nil
Net cash position	**128**	**-52**	**265**
	$		$
Earnings per share*	0.05		(0.00)
Cash flow per share*	0.14		0.01
Net asset value per share*	0.37		0.46
Capital gains divd.*	0.14		nil
	shs		shs
No. of shs. o/s*	36,729,002		36,729,002
Avg. no. of shs. o/s*	36,729,002		36,729,002
	%		%
Net profit margin	92.69		n.m.
Return on equity	12.20		(0.26)
Return on assets	12.15		(0.25)

* Fund unit
[A] Reported in accordance with IFRS

Historical Summary
(as originally stated)

Fiscal Year	Total Rev.	Net Inc. Bef. Disc.	EPS*
	$000s	$000s	$
2021[A]	1,996	1,850	0.05
2020[A]	4	(43)	(0.00)
2019[A]	(9,653)	(9,720)	(0.26)
2018[A]	10	(79)	(0.00)
2017[A]	72	(27)	(0.00)

* Fund unit
[A] Reported in accordance with IFRS

M.40 Marret Multi-Strategy Income Fund

Symbol - MMF.UN **Exchange** - CSE **CUSIP** - 57162P
Head Office - c/o Marret Asset Management Inc., 200-15 York St, Toronto, ON, M5J 0A3 **Telephone** - (416) 214-5800
Website - www.marret.com
Email - kcooney@marret.com
Investor Relations - Kathleen Cooney (416) 214-5800
Auditors - PricewaterhouseCoopers LLP C.A., Toronto, Ont.
Transfer Agents - Computershare Trust Company of Canada Inc., Toronto, Ont.
Trustees - TSX Trust Company, Toronto, Ont.
Managers - Marret Asset Management Inc., Toronto, Ont.
Portfolio Advisors - Marret Asset Management Inc., Toronto, Ont.
Profile - (Ont. 2011) Undergoing termination.

The fund's sole investment is illiquid equity and debt securities of **Cline Mining Corporation**, a private Canadian company undergoing restructuring. At Dec. 31, 2021, the fair value of the fund's investment in Cline was $957,303. The fund would continue until such time as the Cline investment is sold and the remaining net assets are distributed to unitholders.

Directors - Edward D. (Ted) Kelterborn, Toronto, Ont.; Darie P. Urbanky, Toronto, Ont.
Other Exec. Officers - Kathleen Cooney, COO & chief compliance officer; Amit Muni, CFO; Adrian Prenc, v-p

Capital Stock

	Authorized (shs.)	Outstanding (shs.)[1]
Class A Unit	unlimited	3,301,850
Class F Unit	unlimited	285,992

[1] At Dec. 31, 2021

Class A & F Unit - Retraction privileges were suspended in December 2014. Class F units are convertible into class A units on a monthly basis at a ratio based on the NAV per class F unit divided by the NAV per class A unit. The only differences between the class A units and the class F units are the agents' fees paid on issuance of units and the service fee component of the management fees payable in respect of the units of each class. One vote per unit.

Major Shareholder - Widely held at Feb. 28, 2022.

Price Range - MMF.UN/CSE

Year	Volume	High	Low	Close
2022	311,935	$0.10	$0.01	$0.01
2021	186,939	$0.19	$0.02	$0.10
2020	396,760	$0.08	$0.01	$0.02
2019	306,578	$0.09	$0.02	$0.06
2018	260,667	$0.11	$0.02	$0.02

Recent Close: $0.01

Financial Statistics

Periods ended:	12m Dec. 31/21[A]		12m Dec. 31/20[A]
	$000s	%Chg	$000s
Realized invest. gain (loss)	nil		1
Unrealized invest. gain (loss)	143		nil
Total revenue	**153**	**n.m.**	**1**
General & admin. expense	87		51
Operating expense	**87**	**+71**	**51**
Operating income	**66**	**n.a.**	**(50)**
Pre-tax income	**66**	**n.a.**	**(50)**
Net income	**66**	**n.a.**	**(50)**
Cash & equivalent	6		6
Accounts receivable	10		nil
Investments	957		1,202
Total assets	**973**	**-19**	**1,208**
Shareholders' equity	780		837
Cash from oper. activs	**123**	**n.m.**	**1**
Cash from fin. activs	(123)		nil
Net cash position	**6**	**0**	**6**
	$		$
Earnings per share*	0.02		(0.01)
Earnings per share**	0.01		(0.02)
Cash flow per share***	0.03		nil
Net asset value per share*	0.22		0.23
Capital gains divd.*	0.03		nil
	shs		shs
No. of shs. o/s***	3,587,842		3,587,842
Avg. no. of shs. o/s***	3,587,842		3,587,842
	%		%
Net profit margin	43.14		n.m.
Return on equity	8.16		(5.80)
Return on assets	6.05		(4.14)

* Cl.A unit
** Cl.F unit
*** Cl.A unit & Cl.F unit
[A] Reported in accordance with IFRS

Historical Summary
(as originally stated)

Fiscal Year	Total Rev.	Net Inc. Bef. Disc.	EPS*
	$000s	$000s	$
2021[A]	153	66	0.02
2020[A]	1	(50)	(0.01)
2019[A]	(696)	(758)	(0.21)
2018[A]	1	(74)	(0.02)
2017[A]	5	(98)	(0.03)

* Cl.A unit
[A] Reported in accordance with IFRS

M.41 Martello Technologies Group Inc.

Symbol - MTLO **Exchange** - TSX-VEN **CUSIP** - 573074
Head Office - 110-390 March Rd, Ottawa, ON, K2K 0G7 **Telephone** - (613) 271-5989
Website - www.martellotech.com
Email - tking@martellotech.com
Investor Relations - Tracy King (613) 410-7636
Auditors - Welch LLP C.A., Ottawa, Ont.
Lawyers - Tupper Jonsson & Yeadon, Vancouver, B.C.
Transfer Agents - Computershare Trust Company of Canada Inc., Vancouver, B.C.
Employees - 76 at Mar. 31, 2023
Profile - (Can. 2018; orig. B.C., 1981) Develops software that monitors, analyzes, reports and optimizes the user's experience of enterprise cloud communications and productivity services with a focus on Microsoft 365, Microsoft Teams and Mitel unified communications.

Products include Vantage DX™, a single platform modern workplace optimization suite which monitors and manages the Microsoft 365 and Microsoft Teams user experience from end-to-end by correlating network performance data with synthetic and real user monitoring information to provide an actionable insight to resolve performance problems which are impacting the user's experience of the service and for better call, meeting and workflow experiences; and Mitel Performance Analytics, which manages the performance of **Mitel Networks Corporation**'s unified communications solutions.

Product portfolio includes subscription-based offerings and software license sales, including the provision of licenses and maintenance and support for certain legacy software products. Products are sold directly to enterprises, via value-added resellers and global system integrators.

Predecessor Detail - Name changed from Newcastle Energy Corp., Sept. 12, 2018, following reverse takeover acquisition of private Kanata, Ont.-based Martello Technologies Inc. via a three-cornered amalgamation whereby Martello amalgamated with a wholly owned subsidiary of Newcastle.

Directors - Dr. Terence H. (Terry) Matthews, chr., Ottawa, Ont.; John Proctor, pres. & CEO, Ottawa, Ont.; Colley Clarke, Waterloo, Ont.; Michael (Mike) Galvin, Beds., United Kingdom; Antoine Leboyer, Geneva, Switzerland; Donald W. (Don) Smith, Ottawa, Ont.

Other Exec. Officers - Jim Clark, CFO; Doug Bellinger, chief tech. officer; Sussane (Sue) Bond, sr. v-p, sales & partnerships; Rob Doucette, v-p, product mgt.; Tracy King, v-p, mktg.; Olivier Raynaut, v-p, client delivery; Christa Plumley, corp. sec.

Capital Stock

	Authorized (shs.)	Outstanding (shs.)[1]
Common	unlimited	478,707,430

[1] At Aug. 18, 2023

Major Shareholder - Wesley Clover International Corporation held 44.97% interest at Aug. 18, 2023.

Price Range - MTLO/TSX-VEN

Year	Volume	High	Low	Close
2022	57,009,705	$0.08	$0.02	$0.03
2021	94,356,626	$0.26	$0.07	$0.08
2020	127,085,662	$0.34	$0.14	$0.21
2019	266,161,397	$1.00	$0.18	$0.30
2018	146,649,021	$1.67	$0.16	$0.27

Recent Close: $0.02

Capital Stock Changes - From April to June 2023, private placement of 36,000,000 common shares was completed at 5¢ per share.

In January 2023, private placement of 54,000,000 common shares was completed at 5¢ per share. In March 2023, private placement of 12,000,000 common shares was completed at 5¢ per share.

During fiscal 2022, common shares were issued as follows: 24,110,472 by private placement and 200,000 on exercise of options.

Wholly Owned Subsidiaries

GSX Participations S.A., Geneva, Switzerland.
- 100% int. in **GSX Groupware Solutions Inc.**, Mass.
- 100% int. in **Sàrl GSX Groupware Solutions**, France.

Martello Technologies Corporation, Ont.
- 100% int. in **Martello Technologies Incorporated**, Del.
- 100% int. in **NetVitesse S.A.S.**, France.
- 100% int. in **Savision B.V.**, Amsterdam, Netherlands.

Financial Statistics

Periods ended:	12m Mar. 31/23[A]		12m Mar. 31/22[A]
	$000s	%Chg	$000s
Operating revenue	**16,099**	**-8**	**17,540**
Cost of sales	1,854		1,632
Research & devel. expense	5,564		6,507
General & admin expense	10,917		12,429
Stock-based compensation	210		424
Operating expense	**18,545**	**-12**	**20,992**
Operating income	**(2,446)**	**n.a.**	**(3,452)**
Deprec., depl. & amort.	1,906		2,310
Finance income	29		5
Finance costs, gross	2,631		2,267
Write-downs/write-offs	(19,164)[1]		nil
Pre-tax income	**(25,328)**	**n.a.**	**(8,227)**
Income taxes	(138)		(8)
Net income	**(25,190)**	**n.a.**	**(8,219)**
Cash & equivalent	2,219		5,023
Inventories	42		45
Accounts receivable	4,397		4,231
Current assets	9,438		11,168
Long-term investments	304		304
Fixed assets, net	111		180
Right-of-use assets	752		1,119
Intangibles, net	9,550		29,165
Total assets	**20,154**	**-52**	**41,935**
Accts. pay. & accr. liabs	2,986		3,113
Current liabilities	17,682		8,901
Long-term debt, gross	9,846		10,174
Long-term debt, net	1,091		9,904
Long-term lease liabilities	610		917
Shareholders' equity	(1,268)		19,676
Cash from oper. activs	**(4,848)**	**n.a.**	**(4,652)**
Cash from fin. activs	2,024		1,231
Cash from invest. activs	60		(14)
Net cash position	**2,118**	**-56**	**4,853**
Capital expenditures	(10)		(14)
	$		$
Earnings per share*	(0.07)		(0.03)
Cash flow per share*	(0.01)		(0.02)
	shs		shs
No. of shs. o/s*	392,707,430		326,707,430
Avg. no. of shs. o/s*	337,077,759		308,682,325
	%		%
Net profit margin	(156.47)		(46.86)
Return on equity	n.m.		(35.49)
Return on assets	(72.71)		(13.00)
Foreign sales percent	69		66
No. of employees (FTEs)	76		97

* Common

[A] Reported in accordance with IFRS

[1] Includes impairment of goodwill amounting to $18,935,053.

Historical Summary
(as originally stated)

Fiscal Year	Oper. Rev.	Net Inc. Bef. Disc.	EPS*
	$000s	$000s	$
2023[A]	16,099	(25,190)	(0.07)
2022[A]	17,540	(8,219)	(0.03)
2021[A]	16,831	(6,051)	(0.02)
2020[A]	13,123	(8,184)	(0.04)
2019[A1]	10,360	(5,412)	(0.03)

* Common

[A] Reported in accordance with IFRS

[1] Results reflect the Aug. 15, 2018, reverse takeover acquisition of Martello Technologies Inc.

M.42 Martinrea International Inc.*

Symbol - MRE **Exchange** - TSX **CUSIP** - 573459

Head Office - 3210 Langstaff Rd, Vaughan, ON, L4K 5B2 **Telephone** - (416) 749-0314 **Fax** - (289) 982-3001

Website - www.martinrea.com

Email - neil.forster@martinrea.com

Investor Relations - Neil Forster (289) 982-3020

Auditors - KPMG LLP C.A., Toronto, Ont.

Lawyers - Wildeboer Dellelce LLP, Toronto, Ont.

Transfer Agents - Computershare Trust Company of Canada Inc., Toronto, Ont.

FP500 Revenue Ranking - 117

Employees - 18,400 at Dec. 31, 2022

Profile - (Ont. 1998 amalg.) Designs, develops and manufactures lightweight structures and propulsion systems primarily for the automotive sector from 58 locations in Canada, the U.S., Mexico, Brazil, Germany, Spain, Slovakia, South Africa, Japan and the People's Republic of China (PRC).

The company focuses on original equipment manufacturers (OEMs) as a Tier 1 assemblies, systems and parts supplier in the automotive sector and provides products for transit, vehicles and industrial applications.

Products are manufactured for use in fuel systems, propulsion, power steering and brakes, heating, ventilating and air conditioning (HVAC) systems, exhaust systems, body and chassis, and modules. Services provided and manufacturing activities include research and development, engineering, prototyping, testing, material technologies development, fluid management, steel metal forming, hydroforming, stamping and hot stamping, laser cutting, permanent mould casting, sand casting, high pressure die casting, aluminum rolling, machining, tooling and die making, assembly and program management.

Operations are carried out from owned and leased facilities in Brampton, Vaughan, Etobicoke, St. Mary's, Tillsonburg, Dresden and Ridgetown, Ont.; Manchester, Jonesville, North Adams and Auburn Hills, Mich.; Corydon and North Vernon, Ind.; Shelbyville and Hopkinsville, Ky.; Springfield, Tenn.; Riverside, Mo.; Tupelo and Canton, Miss.; Tuscaloosa, Ala.; Hermosillo, Saltillo, Silao, Queretaro, Ramos Arizpe, Arteaga and San Luis Potosi, Mexico; Monte Mor, Brazil; Hofheim, Nuttlar, Bergneustadt and Meschede, Germany; Madrid, Spain; Svaty Jur, Slovakia; Tokyo, Japan; Shanghai, Yuyao, Beijing and Shenyang, PRC; and Brits, South Africa.

Key customers are **Stellantis N.V.**, **Ford Motor Company**, **General Motors Corporation** and **Nissan Motor Company**. Also has North American product mandates from other OEMs, including **Lucid**, **Volkswagen**, **BMW**, **Daimler Trucks**, **Mercedes Benz Automotive**, **American Honda Motor Co., Inc.**, **Tesla** and **Toyota**. Non-automobile customers include **John Deere & Company**, **Caterpillar Inc.** and **Thermo King Corporation.**

During 2022, the company acquired the assets of Montreal, Que.-based **Effenco Development Inc.**, which designs, manufactures and markets technologies for the electrification and connectivity of heavy-duty vocational trucks. Terms were not disclosed.

Recent Merger and Acquisition Activity

Status: completed **Announced:** Mar. 24, 2023

Martinrea International Inc. sold its 50% interest in VoltaXplore Inc., its joint venture with NanoXplore Inc., to NanoXplore Inc. for $10,000,000 satisfied through the issuance of 3,420,406 NanoXplore common shares for $2.92 per share. On closing, Martinrea's equity interest in NanoXplore increased to 22.7% from 21.1%. VoltaXplore was formed to develop and produce electric vehicle batteries enhanced with graphene.

Predecessor Detail - Name changed from Royal Laser Tech Corporation, June 27, 2002.

Directors - Robert P. E. (Rob) Wildeboer, exec. chr., Burlington, Ont.; Pat D'Eramo, pres. & CEO, Caryville, Tenn.; Fred Olson†, Rochester, Mich.; Terrence A. (Terry) Lyons, Vancouver, B.C.; Maureen Midgley, St. Louis, Mo.; Sandra Pupatello, Windsor, Ont.; David (Dave) Schoch, Williamsburg, Va.; Dr. Molly S. Shoichet, Toronto, Ont.; Edward J. (Ed) Waitzer, Toronto, Ont.

Other Exec. Officers - Fred Di Tosto, CFO; Ganesh Iyer, chief tech. officer; Hany Morsy, chief internal auditor; Alfredo Alonso, exec. v-p, fluid bus. unit & propulsion systems comml. grp.; Peter J. Cirulis, exec. v-p, aluminum bus. unit & lightweight structures comml. grp.; Megan Hunter, exec. v-p, procurement & supply chain opers.; Bruce Johnson, exec. v-p, Martinrea Innovation Developments Inc.; Armando Pagliari, exec. v-p, HR; Larry Paine, exec. v-p, metallics bus. unit; Mike Leal, v-p, corp. lean mfg.; Kerri Pope, gen. counsel & corp. sec.

† Lead director

Capital Stock

	Authorized (shs.)	Outstanding (shs.)[1]
Common	unlimited	79,592,540

[1] At Aug. 9, 2023

Options - At Dec. 31, 2022, options were outstanding to purchase 2,435,000 common shares at prices ranging from $10.00 to $16.99 per share expiring to 2030.

Normal Course Issuer Bid - The company plans to make normal course purchases of up to 5,000,000 common shares representing 7% of the public float. The bid commenced on Apr. 4, 2023, and expires on Apr. 3, 2024.

Major Shareholder - TMRE Investors, LLC held 13.43% interest at May 2, 2023.

Price Range - MRE/TSX

Year	Volume	High	Low	Close
2022	87,245,647	$12.54	$7.43	$11.26
2021	77,826,625	$16.27	$9.59	$11.50
2020	65,044,682	$15.80	$5.64	$14.86
2019	54,310,128	$14.75	$9.33	$14.31
2018	58,249,578	$17.50	$9.45	$10.86

Recent Close: $13.21

Capital Stock Changes - During 2022, 20,000 common shares were issued on exercise of options.

Dividends

MRE com Ra $0.20 pa Q est. Apr. 15, 2020
Prev. Rate: $0.18 est. July 15, 2018

Long-Term Debt - Outstanding at Dec. 31, 2022:

Banking facility due 2025[1]	$1,022,169,000
Equip. loans due to 2028[2]	48,199,000
	1,070,368,000
Less: Current portion	16,198,000
	1,054,170,000

[1] Consists of loans denominated in Canadian dollars bearing interest at bankers' acceptance rate plus 2.25%, and loans denominated in U.S. dollars bearing interest at LIBOR plus 2.25%.

[2] Consist of loans denominated in Canadian dollars and Euro, bearing interest at fixed rates between 0% and 5.22%.

Minimum long-term debt principal repayments were reported as follows:

2023	$17,220,000
2024	13,976,000
2025	1,036,050,000
2026	5,223,000
Thereafter	288,000

Note - In June 2023, the banking facility was amended whereby the interest rate benchmark of the U.S. revolving credit line was changed from LIBOR to SOFR.

Wholly Owned Subsidiaries

Martinrea Automotive Inc., Ont.
- 100% int. in **2008788 Ontario Ltd.**, Ont.

Martinrea Automotive Japan Inc., Japan.

Martinrea Automotive Systems Canada Ltd., Ont.

Martinrea China Holdings Inc., Ont.
- 100% int. in **Martinrea Automotive Parts (Shanghai) Co. Ltd.**, Shanghai, People's Republic of China.

Martinrea Honsel Holdings B.V., Netherlands.
- 100% int. in **Martinrea Holdings Germany GmbH**, Germany.
  - 100% int. in **Martinrea Bergneustadt GmbH**, Germany.
    - 100% int. in **Martinrea Automotive Technology (Beijing) Co. Ltd.**, People's Republic of China.
    - 100% int. in **Martinrea Southern African Division (Pty) Ltd.**, South Africa.
      - 100% int. in **Martinrea Stamping Plant Properties (Pty) Ltd.**, South Africa.
- 100% int. in **Martinrea Honsel Aluminum Parts (Holdings) Co. Ltd.**, People's Republic of China.
  - 100% int. in **Martinrea Honsel Aluminum Parts (Yuyao) Co. Ltd.**, People's Republic of China.
  - 100% int. in **Martinrea Shenyang Automotive Components Co. Ltd.**, People's Republic of China.
- 100% int. in **Martinrea Honsel Germany Developments GmbH**, Germany.
- 100% int. in **Martinrea Honsel Germany GmbH**, Germany.
- 100% int. in **Martinrea Honsel Mexico S.A. de C.V.**, Mexico.
- 100% int. in **Martinrea Honsel Spain S.L.U.**, Spain.

Martinrea Innovation Developments Inc., Ont.

Martinrea Internacional de Mexico, S.A. de C.V., Mexico.

Martinrea International US Holdings Inc., Del.
- 100% int. in **Martinrea International US Inc.**, Del.

Martinrea Metal Holdings (USA), Inc., Del.
- 100% int. in **Martinrea Holdings (USA), Inc.**, Del.
  - 100% int. in **Martinrea of America, Inc.**, Del.
    - 100% int. in **Martinrea Industries, Inc.**, Del.
      - 100% int. in **Icon Metal Forming, LLC**, Mich.
      - 100% int. in **Martinrea Riverside LLC**, Del.
- 100% int. in **Martinrea Metals of America, Inc.**, Del.
  - 100% int. in **Martinrea Metal Industries Inc.**, Del.
    - 100% int. in **Martinrea Automotive Structures (USA) Inc.**, Mich.
    - 100% int. in **Martinrea Automotive Systems (USA) LLC**, Mich.
    - 100% int. in **Martinrea Heavy Stampings Inc.**, Del.
    - 100% int. in **Martinrea Hopkinsville LLC**, Mich.

- 100% int. in **Martinrea Jonesville LLC**, Mich.
- 100% int. in **Martinrea Tuscaloosa, Inc.**, Ala.

Martinrea Metallic Canada Inc., Ont.
Martinrea Pilot Acquisition, Inc., Ont.
- 100% int. in **2146826 Ontario Limited**, Ont.
  - 100% int. in **Industrias Martinrea de Mexico, S.A. de C.V.**, Mexico.
  - 100% int. in **Martinrea Automotive Structures S. de R.L. de C.V.**, Mexico.
  - 100% int. in **Martinrea Developments de Mexico, S.A. de C.V.**, Mexico.

Martinrea Slovakia Fluid Systems s.r.o., Slovakia.
MiNDCAN Inc., Ont.
14156048 Canada Inc., Canada.
Royal Automotive Group Ltd., Ont.
2244760 Ontario Inc., Ont.
- 100% int. in **Martinrea Honsel Brasil Fundição e Comércio de Peças em Alumínio Ltda**, Brazil.

Investments

22.7% int. in **NanoXplore Inc.**, Montréal, Qué. (see separate coverage)
Note: The preceding list includes only the major related companies in which interests are held.

Financial Statistics

Periods ended:	12m Dec. 31/22[A]		12m Dec. 31/21[oA]
	$000s	%Chg	$000s
Operating revenue	**4,757,588**	**+26**	**3,783,953**
Cost of sales	3,939,565		3,218,203
Research & devel. expense	36,918		32,622
General & admin expense	276,146		228,346
Operating expense	**4,252,629**	**+22**	**3,479,171**
Operating income	**504,959**	**+66**	**304,782**
Deprec., depl. & amort.	274,707		235,434
Finance costs, gross	42,710		19,532
Investment income	(1,024)		3,876
Write-downs/write-offs	(4,494)		nil
Pre-tax income	**174,045**	**+268**	**47,261**
Income taxes	41,207		11,381
Net income	**132,838**	**+270**	**35,880**
Cash & equivalent	161,655		153,291
Inventories	665,316		590,784
Accounts receivable	789,931		634,184
Current assets	1,659,593		1,420,760
Long-term investments	55,858		55,215
Fixed assets, net	1,948,773		1,727,914
Right-of-use assets	254,065		222,934
Intangibles, net	45,916		47,809
Total assets	**4,143,119**	**+14**	**3,621,351**
Accts. pay. & accr. liabs.	1,315,380		1,110,350
Current liabilities	1,422,365		1,188,072
Long-term debt, gross	1,070,368		1,010,990
Long-term debt, net	1,054,170		990,817
Long-term lease liabilities	229,455		200,455
Shareholders' equity	1,376,905		1,169,775
Cash from oper. activs.	**437,779**	**+143**	**180,032**
Cash from fin. activs.	(41,722)		129,928
Cash from invest. activs.	(381,269)		(305,855)
Net cash position	**161,655**	**+5**	**153,291**
Capital expenditures	(376,439)		(290,230)
Capital disposals	3,364		944
Unfunded pension liability	246		11,840
	$		$
Earnings per share*	1.65		0.45
Cash flow per share*	5.45		2.24
Cash divd. per share*	0.20		0.20
	shs		shs
No. of shs. o/s*	80,387,095		80,367,095
Avg. no. of shs. o/s*	80,378,469		80,337,393
	%		%
Net profit margin	2.79		0.95
Return on equity	10.43		3.06
Return on assets	4.27		1.45
Foreign sales percent	84		84
No. of employees (FTEs)	18,400		16,400

* Common
[o] Restated
[A] Reported in accordance with IFRS

Latest Results

Periods ended:	6m June 30/23[A]		6m June 30/22[A]
	$000s	%Chg	$000s
Operating revenue	2,664,944	+17	2,268,913
Net income	98,071	+94	50,679
	$		$
Earnings per share*	1.22		0.63

* Common
[A] Reported in accordance with IFRS

Historical Summary
(as originally stated)

Fiscal Year	Oper. Rev. $000s	Net Inc. Bef. Disc. $000s	EPS* $
2022[A]	4,757,588	132,838	1.65
2021[A]	3,783,953	35,880	0.45
2020[A]	3,375,286	(27,317)	(0.34)
2019[A]	3,863,659	181,221	2.20
2018[A]	3,662,900	185,883	2.15

* Common
[A] Reported in accordance with IFRS

M.43 Marvel Biosciences Corp.

Symbol - MRVL **Exchange** - TSX-VEN **CUSIP** - 57384M
Head Office - 420-505 8 Ave SW, Calgary, AB, T2P 1G2 **Telephone** - (403) 770-2469
Website - marvelbiotechnology.com
Email - bpedram@virtusadvisory.com
Investor Relations - Babak Pedram (416) 644-5081
Auditors - MNP LLP C.A., Calgary, Alta.
Transfer Agents - Odyssey Trust Company, Vancouver, B.C.
Profile - (B.C. 2018) Focuses on the discovery and the development of pharmaceutical products for the treatment of neurological diseases, cancer and non-alcoholic steatohepatitis liver fibrosis.

Identifies assets or compounds or new chemical entities that have come off patent protection for a certain and already approved disease indication and develops synthetic chemical derivatives to significantly enhance certain compounds that results in a new, novel and patentable asset for a new disease indication. The result is that there is significantly less cost and time to develop the company's assets compared to traditional biotechnology companies.

Has developed a number of new patented and patentable chemical entities, using synthetic chemical derivatives of known, off-patent drugs, that inhibit the A2a adenosine receptor with application to neurological diseases (depression and anxiety, Alzheimer's and ADHD) and application to the non-neurological disease of non-alcoholic steatohepatitis liver fibrosis.

Lead compound under pre-clinical investigational new drug studies is MB-204, a synthetically derivative of A2a adenosine receptor, also known as KW6002 (Nourianz), for neurological diseases. Also identified a series of related compounds that appear to be potent, fast acting, water soluble and orally available small tryptamine derivatives of psychedelics that have anti-depressive activity but no overt hallucinatory activity in pilot studies.

Predecessor Detail - Name changed from Alphanco Venture Corp., July 12, 2021, pursuant to the Qualifying Transaction reverse takeover acquisition of Marvel Biotechnology Inc., and concurrent amalgamation of (old) Marvel with wholly owned 2306696 Alberta Ltd.

Directors - J. Roderick (Rod) Matheson, chr. & CEO, Calgary, Alta.; Dr. Mark Williams, pres. & chief science officer, Winnipeg, Man.; Neil A. Johnson, Toronto, Ont.; Babak Pedram, Toronto, Ont.; S. Randall (Randy) Smallbone, Burlington, Ont.

Other Exec. Officers - Harpreet (Harry) Nijjar, CFO; Jacqueline (Jackie) Groot, corp. sec.

Capital Stock

	Authorized (shs.)	Outstanding (shs.)[1]
Common	unlimited	39,786,231

[1] At Jan. 23, 2023

Major Shareholder - J. Roderick (Rod) Matheson held 15.01% interest and Dr. Mark Williams held 12.57% interest at Jan. 23, 2023.

Price Range - MRVL/TSX-VEN

Year	Volume	High	Low	Close
2022	3,006,498	$0.27	$0.08	$0.13
2021	3,849,478	$0.39	$0.18	$0.27
2020	15,000	$0.20	$0.17	$0.20
2019	290,250	$0.20	$0.17	$0.17

Recent Close: $0.08

Capital Stock Changes - In August 2022, private placement of 2,700,000 units (1 common share & 1 warrant) at 10¢ per unit was completed, with warrants exercisable at 15¢ per share for one year.

In July 2022, private placement of 4,500,000 units (1 common share & 1 warrant) at 10¢ per unit was completed.

Wholly Owned Subsidiaries

Marvel Biotechnology Inc., Calgary, Alta.

Financial Statistics

Periods ended:	12m July 31/22[A]		12m July 31/21[A1]
	$000s	%Chg	$000s
General & admin expense	1,171		2,548
Other operating expense	1,377		613
Operating expense	**2,548**	**-19**	**3,161**
Operating income	**(2,548)**	**n.a.**	**(3,161)**
Finance costs, gross	2		2
Pre-tax income	**(2,554)**	**n.a.**	**(3,039)**
Net income	**(2,554)**	**n.a.**	**(3,039)**
Cash & equivalent	593		2,393
Current assets	914		2,468
Total assets	**914**	**-63**	**2,468**
Accts. pay. & accr. liabs.	718		112
Current liabilities	718		112
Shareholders' equity	196		2,356
Cash from oper. activs.	**(2,194)**	**n.a.**	**(1,371)**
Cash from fin. activs.	394		3,157
Cash from invest. activs.	nil		382
Net cash position	**593**	**-75**	**2,393**
	$		$
Earnings per share*	(0.08)		(0.17)
Cash flow per share*	(0.07)		(0.08)
	shs		shs
No. of shs. o/s*	37,086,231		32,586,231
Avg. no. of shs. o/s*	32,758,834		17,697,166
	%		%
Net profit margin	n.a.		n.a.
Return on equity	(200.16)		(245.58)
Return on assets	(150.92)		(219.75)

* Common
[A] Reported in accordance with IFRS
[1] Results reflect the July 8, 2021, Qualifying Transaction reverse takeover acquisition of Marvel Biotechnology Inc.

Latest Results

Periods ended:	3m Oct. 31/22[A]		3m Oct. 31/21[A]
	$000s	%Chg	$000s
Net income	(296)	n.a.	(510)
	$		$
Earnings per share*	(0.01)		(0.02)

* Common
[A] Reported in accordance with IFRS

Historical Summary
(as originally stated)

Fiscal Year	Oper. Rev. $000s	Net Inc. Bef. Disc. $000s	EPS* $
2022[A]	nil	(2,554)	(0.08)
2021[A]	nil	(3,039)	(0.17)
2020[A1]	nil	(956)	(0.13)

* Common
[A] Reported in accordance with IFRS
[1] Results pertain to Marvel Biotechnology Inc.

M.44 Marwest Apartment Real Estate Investment Trust

Symbol - MAR.UN **Exchange** - TSX-VEN **CUSIP** - 57386R
Head Office - 500-220 Portage Ave, Winnipeg, MB, R3C 0A5 **Telephone** - (204) 947-1200
Website - marwestreit.com
Email - wcm@marwest.ca
Investor Relations - William Martens (204) 947-1200
Auditors - KPMG LLP C.A., Winnipeg, Man.
Transfer Agents - TSX Trust Company, Calgary, Alta.
Profile - (Man. 2020) Acquires and owns multi-family residential properties in western Canada.

At Oct. 31, 2022, the trust owned four multi-family rental properties, totaling 516 units, in Winnipeg, Man. **Marwest Asset Management Inc.**, a unit of the **Marwest Group of Companies**, is the asset and property manager of the trust.

Recent Merger and Acquisition Activity

Status: completed **Announced:** Oct. 31, 2022
Marwest Apartment Real Estate Investment Trust acquired a newly constructed 153-unit apartment building (View Pointe) in Winnipeg, Man., for $42,000,000.

Trustees - Luke Cain, chr., Winnipeg, Man.; William Martens, CEO, Winnipeg, Man.; James (Jim) Green, Winnipeg, Man.; Cornelius Martens, Winnipeg, Man.; Jason Pellaers, Winnipeg, Man.

Other Exec. Officers - Jennifer Nazimek, CFO & corp. sec.; Armin W. Martens, exec. v-p

Capital Stock

	Authorized (shs.)	Outstanding (shs.)[1]
Class A Trust Unit	unlimited	8,667,564
Special Vtg. Unit	unlimited	10,841,274
Class B LP Unit		10,841,274

[1] At June 30, 2022

Class A Trust Unit - One vote per unit.

Special Voting Unit - Issued to holders of class B limited partnership units of Marwest Apartment REIT L.P. Each special voting unit entitles the holder to a number of votes at unitholder meetings equal to the number of trust units into which the class B limited partnership units are exchangeable.

Class B Limited Partnership Unit - Entitled to distributions equal to those provided to class A trust units. Directly exchangeable into class A trust units on a 1-for-1 basis at any time by holder. Classified as liabilities under IFRS.

Major Shareholder - Widely held at May 13, 2022.

Price Range - MAR.UN/TSX-VEN

Year	Volume	High	Low	Close
2022	1,358,047	$1.05	$0.55	$1.00
2021	1,324,567	$1.30	$0.75	$0.84
2020	30,414	$0.75	$0.60	$0.75

Recent Close: $0.60

Dividends

MAR.UN unit Ra $0.0153 pa M est. Sept. 15, 2023
Prev. Rate: $0.015 est. Jan. 17, 2022
$0.00125i............ Jan. 17/22
i Initial Payment

Wholly Owned Subsidiaries

Marwest Apartment REIT L.P
- 100% int. in **Marwest Apartments I G.P. Ltd.**, Man.
- 100% int. in **Marwest Apartments I L.P.**, Man.
- 100% int. in **Marwest Apartments VII G.P. Ltd.**, Man.
- 100% int. in **Marwest Apartments VII L.P.**, Man.
- 100% int. in **Marwest (Element) Apartments G.P. Inc.**, Man.
- 100% int. in **Marwest (Element) Apartments L.P.**, Man.

Financial Statistics

Periods ended:	12m Dec. 31/21[A]		26w Dec. 31/20[A]
	$000s	%Chg	$000s
Total revenue	**3,340**	**n.a.**	**nil**
Rental operating expense	950		nil
General & admin. expense	439		102
Property taxes	367		nil
Operating expense	**1,756**	**n.a.**	**102**
Operating income	**1,584**	**n.a.**	**(102)**
Finance costs, gross	783		nil
Pre-tax income	**9,215**	**n.a.**	**(102)**
Net income	**9,215**	**n.a.**	**(102)**
Cash & equivalent	4,218		472
Accounts receivable	12		nil
Current assets	4,338		472
Property interests, net	87,082		nil
Total assets	**91,420**	**n.m.**	**472**
Accts. pay. & accr. liabs	396		15
Long-term debt, gross	65,546		nil
Long-term debt, net	63,900		nil
Shareholders' equity	15,893		457
Cash from oper. activs	**690**	**n.a.**	**(87)**
Cash from fin. activs	2,971		559
Cash from invest. activs	83		nil
Net cash position	**4,218**	**+794**	**472**
Capital expenditures	(97)		nil
Increase in property	203		nil
	$		$
Earnings per share*	n.a.		n.a.
Cash flow per share*	0.08		(0.01)
Funds from opers. per sh.*	0.07		n.a.
Adj. funds from opers. per sh.*	0.06		n.a.
Cash divd. per share*	0.00		nil
Total divd. per share*	**0.00**		**nil**
	shs		shs
No. of shs. o/s*	8,831,564		1,800,000
Avg. no. of shs. o/s*	12,090,883		n.a.
	%		%
Net profit margin	275.90		...
Return on equity	112.72		...
Return on assets	21.76		...

* Cl.A Trust Unit
[A] Reported in accordance with IFRS

Latest Results

Periods ended:	6m June 30/22[A]		6m June 30/21[A]
	$000s	%Chg	$000s
Total revenue	3,238	+316	779
Net income	5,027	n.a.	(511)
	$		$
Earnings per share*	n.a.		n.a.

[A] Reported in accordance with IFRS

M.45 Mary Agrotechnologies Inc.

Symbol - MARY **Exchange** - CSE **CUSIP** - 573865
Head Office - Unit 4, 115 Apple Creek Blvd, Markham, ON, L3R 6C9
Toll-free - (844) 504-5234
Website - www.mary.ag
Email - frank@mary.ag
Investor Relations - Chuhan Qin (844) 504-5234
Auditors - Mao & Ying LLP C.A., Vancouver, B.C.
Transfer Agents - Odyssey Trust Company, Vancouver, B.C.

Profile - (Ont. 2017) Manufactures and sells growing devices for the cultivation of cannabis indoors or in small areas.

The flagship consumer product is Mary Model Z, an at-home grow box used specifically to grow cannabis, in which an artificially controlled environment is created using a Wi-Fi connected growing system that is automated by cloud-based artificial intelligence, with built-in air conditioning, filtering system to control odour and mould, multi-directional lighting, pre-made nutrient pack and a smartphone app that can monitor and control the unit from anywhere. The company does not provide any cannabis plants for cultivation. The product is currently available in Canada and legal jurisdictions in the United States.

Also plans to build commercial indoor vertical farms. In connection, subsidiary **Yunnan Moquan Agrotechnologies Ltd.** (75% owned) has secured a license to grow industrial hemp (valid until Apr. 23, 2022) over a maximum area of 66 hectares, as well as secured conditional approval to process industrial hemp, in Yunnan province, People's Republic of China (PRC). In addition, Yunnan Moquan has a partnership with **CBDer Biotechnology**, a company based in Yunnan province, to grow indoor industrial hemp using CBDer's greenhouses in PRC and outside of PRC. The company also has a partnership with **Changzhi Yufeng Agricultural Technology Development Co. Ltd.**, which owns and operates vertical farms in PRC, to collaborate on a pilot project of 700 m^2 (7,535 sq. ft.) with the company's proprietary automation technology, including its proprietary vertical farming hardware and AI-driven automation software.

Directors - Chuhan (Frank) Qin, CEO, Richmond Hill, Ont.; Larry Lisser, Denver, Colo.; Ying Xu, Burnaby, B.C.; Joanne F. Q. Yan, Vancouver, B.C.; Buck Young, Barrie, Ont.

Other Exec. Officers - David Byer, COO; Xin Ran (Irene) Mai, CFO & corp. sec.

Capital Stock

	Authorized (shs.)	Outstanding (shs.)[1]
Common	unlimited	43,127,924

[1] At Feb. 22, 2022

Major Shareholder - Chuhan (Frank) Qin held 45.13% interest and Peng Han held 11.13% interest at Feb. 15, 2022.

Price Range - MARY/CSE

Year	Volume	High	Low	Close
2022	306,470	$0.50	$0.10	$0.14
2021	343,095	$1.20	$0.30	$0.30

Recent Close: $0.03

Wholly Owned Subsidiaries

Mary Agrotechnologies Hong Kong Limited, Hong Kong, Hong Kong, People's Republic of China.

Subsidiaries

75% int. in **Yunnan Moquan Agrotechnologies Ltd.**, People's Republic of China.

Financial Statistics

Periods ended:	12m Sept. 30/21[A]		12m Sept. 30/20[oA]
	$000s	%Chg	$000s
Operating revenue	**77**	**-9**	**85**
Cost of sales	148		84
Salaries & benefits	663		426
Research & devel. expense	116		625
General & admin expense	468		398
Stock-based compensation	402		125
Operating expense	**1,797**	**+8**	**1,658**
Operating income	**(1,720)**	**n.a.**	**(1,573)**
Deprec., depl. & amort.	75		39
Finance income	1		1
Finance costs, gross	11		7
Pre-tax income	**(1,549)**	**n.a.**	**(1,416)**
Net income	**(1,549)**	**n.a.**	**(1,416)**
Cash & equivalent	1,744		145
Inventories	270		71
Accounts receivable	57		34
Current assets	2,176		256
Fixed assets, net	254		299
Total assets	**2,430**	**+337**	**556**
Accts. pay. & accr. liabs	218		86
Current liabilities	314		271
Long-term debt, gross	60		40
Long-term debt, net	60		40
Long-term lease liabilities	48		106
Shareholders' equity	2,008		139
Cash from oper. activs	**(1,345)**	**n.a.**	**(1,023)**
Cash from fin. activs	2,974		955
Cash from invest. activs	(29)		(48)
Net cash position	**1,744**	**n.m.**	**145**
Capital expenditures	(29)		(48)
	$		$
Earnings per share*	(0.04)		(0.05)
Cash flow per share*	(0.03)		(0.03)
	shs		shs
No. of shs. o/s*	43,127,924		36,256,457
Avg. no. of shs. o/s*	40,747,405		30,310,047
	%		%
Net profit margin	n.m.		n.m.
Return on equity	(144.29)		n.m.
Return on assets	(103.01)		(299.47)

* Common
[o] Restated
[A] Reported in accordance with IFRS

Latest Results

Periods ended:	3m Dec. 31/21[A]		3m Dec. 31/20[A]
	$000s	%Chg	$000s
Operating revenue	55	+104	27
Net income	(552)	n.a.	(437)
	$		$
Earnings per share*	(0.01)		(0.01)

* Common
[A] Reported in accordance with IFRS

Historical Summary
(as originally stated)

Fiscal Year	Oper. Rev. $000s	Net Inc. Bef. Disc. $000s	EPS* $
2021[A]	77	(1,549)	(0.04)
2020[A]	85	(1,416)	(0.05)
2019[A]	nil	(667)	(0.03)

* Common
[A] Reported in accordance with IFRS

M.46 Mason Graphite Inc.

Symbol - LLG **Exchange** - TSX-VEN **CUSIP** - 57520W
Head Office - 600-3030 boul Le Carrefour, Laval, QC, H7T 2P5
Telephone - (514) 289-3580
Website - www.masongraphite.com
Email - info@masongraphite.com
Investor Relations - Pascale Choquet (514) 289-3580
Auditors - PricewaterhouseCoopers LLP C.A., Montréal, Qué.
Transfer Agents - TSX Trust Company, Toronto, Ont.

Profile - (Ont. 2011) Has graphite project in Quebec and is developing value-added products from graphite concentrates.

In Quebec, holds Lac Guéret graphite project, 11,630 hectares, 285 km north of Baie-Comeau, 51% optioned to **Nouveau Monde Graphite Inc.**, requiring exploration expenditures of $10,000,000 over two years to July 2024 and completion of an updated feasibility study with 250,000-tonne-per-annum production scale. An updated feasibility study completed in December 2018 proposed an open-pit operation with an average annual production of 51,900 tonnes of graphite concentrate over a 25-year mine life. Initial capital costs were estimated at $258,200,000. Proven and probable reserves were 4,741,000 tonnes grading 27.77% graphitic carbon.

Also developing coated spherical purified graphite, a material used to manufacture the anodes of lithium-ion batteries used for electric vehicles, mobile phones and other portable devices as well as stationary storage of energy.

Affiliate **Black Swan Graphene Inc.** is developing graphene products aimed at several industrial sectors including concrete, polymers and lithium-ion batteries.

On Oct. 26, 2022, the company completed a change of business from a mining company to an investment company in which the company would focus on seeking investment opportunities, including the joint venture in which the company would retain a 49% interest in Lac Guéret graphite project in Quebec upon **Nouveau Monde Graphite Inc.** exercising its option to earn a 51% interest.

Recent Merger and Acquisition Activity

Status: completed **Revised:** Aug. 2, 2022

UPDATE: The transaction was completed. PREVIOUS: Dragonfly Capital Corp. enter into a letter of intent for the Qualifying Transaction reverse takeover acquisition of private Toronto, Ont.-based Black Swan Graphite Inc., a graphene processing technology company that recently acquired strategic assets related to the patented Graphene Technology from Thomas Swan & Co. Limited. Terms and structure of the transaction were to be negotiated. Black Swan planned to complete a concurrent financing for gross proceeds of $5,000,000. Principal Black Swan shareholders were Mason Graphite Inc. (56.03% interest), Thomas Swan & Co. and Fahad Al-Tamimi, chair and second largest shareholder of Mason Graphite. Jan. 17, 2022 - A definitive agreement was entered into. Dragonfly would acquire Black Swan for issuance of 210,229,434 common shares at a deemed price of 15¢ per share. Mar. 14, 2022 - Dragonfly completed a private placement of 46,669,665 subscription receipts at 15¢ per receipt for gross proceeds of $7,000,500. Apr. 21, 2022 - The closing date was extended to June 17, 2022, and the exchange ratio was modified whereby Black Swan shareholders would receive 15.2 Dragonfly common shares for each share held, which would result in the issuance of 210,230,349 Dragonfly common shares. July 22, 2022 - Conditional TSX Venture Exchange approval was received.

Predecessor Detail - Name changed from POCML 1 Inc., Oct. 11, 2012, pursuant to Qualifying Transaction reverse takeover acquisition of Mason Graphite Corp.

Directors - Fahad S. Al-Tamimi, chr., Riyadh, Saudi Arabia; Peter Damouni, pres. & CEO, London, Middx., United Kingdom; Tayfun Eldem†, Montréal, Qué.; Adree DeLazzer; Navjit (Nav) Dhaliwal, Vancouver, B.C.; Roy McDowall, Chambly, Qué.; François Perron, Toronto, Ont.

Other Exec. Officers - Jean L'Heureux, COO; Carmelo (Carm) Marrelli, CFO; Pascale Choquet, interim CFO & dir., fin. & admin.; Paul Hardy, v-p, corp. devel.; Deena Siblock, corp. sec.

† Lead director

Capital Stock

	Authorized (shs.)	Outstanding (shs.)[1]
Common	unlimited	141,292,585

[1] At May 29, 2023

Major Shareholder - Investissement Québec held 12.49% interest at June 17, 2022.

Price Range - LLG/TSX-VEN

Year	Volume	High	Low	Close
2022	16,487,210	$0.74	$0.13	$0.16
2021	46,722,671	$1.19	$0.40	$0.69
2020	45,685,736	$0.57	$0.12	$0.48
2019	32,410,161	$0.63	$0.19	$0.20
2018	30,970,556	$2.80	$0.44	$0.55

Recent Close: $0.23

Capital Stock Changes - In July 2022, private placement of 5,000,000 common shares was completed at 50¢ per share.

There were no changes to capital stock during fiscal 2022.

Investments

41.49% int. in **Black Swan Graphene Inc.**, Toronto, Ont. (see separate coverage)

Financial Statistics

Periods ended:	12m June 30/22[A]		12m June 30/21[A]
	$000s	%Chg	$000s
Salaries & benefits	1,329		858
Research & devel. expense	8		8
General & admin expense	1,852		2,836
Stock-based compensation	811		1,178
Other operating expense	210		1,797
Operating expense	**4,519**	**-32**	**6,678**
Operating income	**(4,519)**	**n.a.**	**(6,678)**
Deprec., depl. & amort	23		31
Pre-tax income	**(4,466)**	**n.a.**	**(6,545)**
Net inc. bef. disc. opers	**(4,466)**	**n.a.**	**(6,545)**
Income from disc. opers	(2,918)		nil
Net income	**(7,384)**	**n.a.**	**(6,545)**
Net inc. for equity hldrs	**(6,100)**	**n.a.**	**(6,545)**
Net inc. for non-cont. int	**(1,284)**	**n.a.**	**nil**
Cash & equivalent	7,317		20,126
Current assets	20,747		20,360
Fixed assets, net	5,696		5,719
Total assets	**26,443**	**0**	**26,510**
Accts. pay. & accr. liabs	178		1,619
Current liabilities	277		1,619
Shareholders' equity	20,475		24,892
Cash from oper. activs	**(5,123)**	**n.a.**	**(4,908)**
Cash from fin. activs	2,980		30
Cash from invest. activs	(6,541)		(1,634)
Net cash position	**7,317**	**-64**	**20,126**
Capital expenditures	(1,333)		(1,371)
	$		$
Earns. per sh. bef disc opers*	(0.04)		(0.05)
Earnings per share*	(0.05)		(0.05)
Cash flow per share*	n.a.		(0.04)
	shs		shs
No. of shs. o/s*	136,292,585		136,292,585
Avg. no. of shs. o/s*	136,227,585		136,252,818
	%		%
Net profit margin	n.a.		n.a.
Return on equity	(14.03)		(23.75)
Return on assets	(16.87)		(21.91)

* Common

[A] Reported in accordance with IFRS

Historical Summary
(as originally stated)

Fiscal Year	Oper. Rev.	Net Inc. Bef. Disc.	EPS*
	$000s	$000s	$
2022[A]	nil	(4,466)	(0.04)
2021[A]	nil	(6,545)	(0.05)
2020[A]	nil	26,454	0.19
2019[A]	(50)	840	0.01
2018[A]	(50)	(1,116)	(0.01)

* Common

[A] Reported in accordance with IFRS

M.47 Masonite International Corporation

Symbol - DOOR **Exchange** - NYSE **CUSIP** - 575385

Head Office - 2771 Rutherford Rd, Concord, ON, L4K 2N6 **Toll-free** - (800) 895-2723

Website - www.masonite.com

Email - mdevlin@masonite.com

Investor Relations - Marcus Devlin (800) 895-2723

Auditors - Ernst & Young LLP C.P.A., Tampa, Fla.

Transfer Agents - American Stock Transfer & Trust Company, LLC, New York, N.Y.

FP500 Revenue Ranking - 145

Employees - 10,000 at Jan. 1, 2023

Profile - (B.C. 2011 amalg.) Designs, manufactures and distributes interior and exterior doors for the new construction, repair, renovation and remodelling of the residential and non-residential building construction markets.

Manufactured products consist of a broad line of interior doors; door components for internal use and for sale to other door manufacturers; and exterior residential steel, fibreglass and wood doors and entry systems. Products are marketed and sold to remodelling contractors, builders, homeowners, retailers, dealers, lumberyards, commercial and general contractors, and architects through wholesale and retail distribution channels. The company's brands include Masonite®, Marshfield-Algoma™, Premdor®, Mohawk®, Door-Stop International™, Harring Doors™, Masonite Architectural™, Solidor®, Residor®, Nicedor®, Graham-Maiman™, USA Wood Door™, Louisiana Millwork, Florida Made Door, Baillargeon™, BWI™ and National Hickman™.

The company operates 59 manufacturing and distribution facilities in the U.S., Canada, Mexico, Chile, the U.K., Ireland and Malaysia. During the 52-week ended Jan. 1, 2023, the company sold 31,000,000 doors to 6,500 customers globally.

During the fourth quarter of fiscal 2022, the company liquidated wholly owned **Premdor Kapi Sanayi Ve Ticaret, A.S.** in Turkey.

In June 2022, the company opened an exterior door manufacturing facility in Stoke-on-Trent, U.K. The facility combines the previous Solidor® production and storage sites into one manufacturing hub.

Recent Merger and Acquisition Activity

Status: completed **Revised:** Jan. 3, 2023

UPDATE: The transaction was completed. PREVIOUS: Masonite International Corporation agreed to acquire Delaware-based EPI Holdings, Inc. (dba Endura Products) for US$375,000,000. EPI manufactures high-performance door frames and door system components, including engineered frames, self-adjusting sill systems, weather sealing, multi-point locks and installation accessories for residential applications in the U.S. The transaction was expected to be completed in the fourth quarter of fiscal 2022.

Predecessor Detail - Name changed from Premdor Inc., Jan. 2, 2002.

Directors - Robert J. Byrne, chr., Winter Park, Fla.; Howard C. Heckes, pres. & CEO, Tampa, Fla.; Jody L. Bilney, Louisville, Ky.; Peter R. Dachowski, Berwyn, Pa.; Jonathan F. Foster, New York, N.Y.; Daphne E. Jones, Miami Beach, Fla.; Barry (A.) Ruffalo, Chattanooga, Tenn.; Francis M. (Fran) Scricco, Boston, Mass.; Jay Steinfeld, Bellaire, Tex.

Other Exec. Officers - Russell T. Tiejema, exec. v-p & CFO; Alex Legall, sr. v-p & bus. leader, architectural; Robert A. Paxton, sr. v-p, HR; James (Jim) Pelletier, sr. v-p, gen. counsel & corp. sec.; Vicky Philemon, sr. v-p & gen. mgr., Europe; Jennifer Renaud, sr. v-p & chief mktg. officer; Dan Shirk, sr. v-p & CIO; Cory Sorice, sr. v-p & chief innovation officer; Randal A. (Randy) White, sr. v-p, global opers. & supply chain; Richard Leland, v-p, fin. & treas.; Katie Shellabarger, v-p & chief acctg. officer; Chris Ball, pres., global residential

Capital Stock

	Authorized (shs.)	Outstanding (shs.)[1]
Common	unlimited	22,003,429
Special	unlimited	nil

[1] At Aug. 7, 2023

Major Shareholder - The Vanguard Group, Inc. held 10.3% interest at Mar. 20, 2023.

Price Range - DOOR/NYSE

Year	Volume	High	Low	Close
2022	12,558,737	US$119.28	US$65.71	US$80.61
2021	11,423,817	US$132.22	US$92.81	US$117.95
2020	15,146,476	US$109.71	US$34.88	US$98.34
2019	11,861,299	US$74.43	US$44.33	US$72.21
2018	13,280,186	US$75.05	US$43.90	US$44.83

Capital Stock Changes - During fiscal 2022, common shares were issued as follows: 194,500 as share-based awards and 16,567 under employee stock purchase plan; 1,679,919 common shares were repurchased under a share repurchase program.

Wholly Owned Subsidiaries

Crown Door Corp., Ont.
Dominance Industries Inc., Okla.
Door-Stop International Limited, Notts., United Kingdom.
EPI Holdings, Inc., Del.
Eger Properties Co., Calif.
Endura Products, LLC, N.C.
Evergreen Finance LP, Del.
Inversiones Premdor S.A., Costa Rica.
Liora Enterprises Limited, Cyprus.
Masonite Chile Holdings S.A., Chile.
Masonite Chile S.A., Chile.
Masonite Components, Ireland.
Masonite Corporation, Del.
Masonite Costa Rica S.A., Costa Rica.
Masonite Distribution, LLC, Del.
Masonite Doors Private Ltd., India.
Masonite Europe Limited, United Kingdom.
Masonite Europe, Ireland.
Masonite Ireland, Ireland.
Masonite Luxembourg S.A., Luxembourg.
Masonite Mexico S.A. de C.V., Mexico.
Masonite PL Sp. z.o.o., Poland.
Masonite (Shanghai) Trading Company Limited, Shanghai, Shanghai, People's Republic of China.
1388199 B.C. Unlimited Liability Company, B.C.
Premdor Crosby Limited, United Kingdom.
Premdor Karmiel Holdings B.V., Netherlands.
Premdor Ltd., Israel.
Premdor U.K. Holdings Limited, United Kingdom.
SC Premdor Ukraine, Ukraine.
Sacopan, Inc., Qué.
Shop Masonite LLC, Fla.
Sierra Lumber, Inc., Fla.
Steelwood LLC, Del.
Technoforest Del Norte S.A., Costa Rica.
VanAir Design, Inc., B.C.
0993477 B.C. Unlimited Liability Company, B.C.

Investments

Magna Foremost Sdn. Bhd., Kuala Lumpur, Malaysia.

Note: The preceding list includes only the major related companies in which interests are held.

Financial Statistics

Periods ended:	52w Jan. 1/23[A]		52w Jan. 2/22[A]
	US$000s	%Chg	US$000s
Operating revenue	**2,891,687**	**+11**	**2,596,920**
Cost of goods sold	2,146,624		1,914,500
General & admin expense	327,487		287,089
Operating expense	**2,474,111**	**+12**	**2,201,589**
Operating income	**417,576**	**+6**	**395,331**
Deprec., depl. & amort.	88,295		91,982
Finance costs, net	41,331		59,706
Write-downs/write-offs	nil		(69,900)
Pre-tax income	**290,197**	**+102**	**143,966**
Income taxes	71,753		44,772
Net income	**218,444**	**+120**	**99,194**
Net inc. for equity hldrs	**214,233**	**+127**	**94,501**
Net inc. for non-cont. int.	**4,211**	**-10**	**4,693**
Cash & equivalent	296,922		381,395
Inventories	406,828		347,476
Accounts receivable	375,918		343,414
Current assets	1,163,640		1,134,126
Long-term investments	16,111		14,994
Fixed assets, net	652,329		626,797
Right-of-use assets	160,695		176,445
Intangibles, net	205,924		227,589
Total assets	**2,248,178**	**0**	**2,246,618**
Accts. pay. & accr. liabs	310,200		350,537
Current liabilities	348,933		384,639
Long-term debt, gross	866,116		865,721
Long-term debt, net	866,116		865,721
Long-term lease liabilities	151,242		165,670
Shareholders' equity	732,119		688,239
Non-controlling interest	10,663		11,539
Cash from oper. activs	**189,197**	**+21**	**156,457**
Cash from fin. activs	(157,398)		(63,737)
Cash from invest. activs	(111,098)		(76,142)
Net cash position	**308,921**	**-21**	**391,505**
Capital expenditures	(114,307)		(86,670)
Capital disposals	6,413		6,027
Unfunded pension liability	1,989		n.a.
Pension fund surplus	n.a.		387
	US$		US$
Earnings per share*	9.51		3.91
Cash flow per share*	8.40		6.47
	shs		shs
No. of shs. o/s*	22,155,035		23,623,887
Avg. no. of shs. o/s*	22,532,722		24,176,846
	%		%
Net profit margin	7.55		3.82
Return on equity	30.17		13.76
Return on assets	9.72		4.52
Foreign sales percent	86		86
No. of employees (FTEs)	10,000		10,300

* Common
[A] Reported in accordance with U.S. GAAP

Latest Results

Periods ended:	6m July 2/23[A]		6m July 3/22[A]
	US$000s	%Chg	US$000s
Operating revenue	1,467,868	-1	1,488,091
Net income	88,389	-31	128,095
Net inc. for equity hldrs	86,736	-31	126,097
Net inc. for non-cont. int	1,653		1,998
	US$		US$
Earnings per share*	3.92		5.53

* Common
[A] Reported in accordance with U.S. GAAP

Historical Summary
(as originally stated)

Fiscal Year	Oper. Rev.	Net Inc. Bef. Disc.	EPS*
	US$000s	US$000s	US$
2022[A]	2,891,687	218,444	9.51
2021[A]	2,596,920	99,194	3.91
2020[A1]	2,257,075	73,689	2.81
2019[A]	2,176,683	49,039	1.77

* Common
[A] Reported in accordance with U.S. GAAP
[1] 53 weeks ended Jan. 3, 2021.

M.48 Matachewan Consolidated Mines, Limited

Symbol - MCM.A **Exchange** - TSX-VEN **CUSIP** - 576471
Head Office - 1910-130 Adelaide St W, Toronto, ON, M5H 3P5
Telephone - (416) 364-2173 **Fax** - (416) 364-0193
Email - ed.dumond@mcc3group.com
Investor Relations - Edward G. Dumond (416) 814-3155
Auditors - MNP LLP C.A., Toronto, Ont.
Transfer Agents - Computershare Trust Company of Canada Inc., Toronto, Ont.

Profile - (Ont. 1933) Invests in petroleum interests and holds mineral prospect in Ontario. Also invests in natural resource companies.

In Ontario, holds 50% interest (**Osisko Mining Inc.** 50%) in formerly producing Hislop gold property consisting of 8 mining leases in Hislop and Guibord twps., near Matheson; and royalty interest in Matachewan property, 24 claims.

At Mar. 31, 2023, the company's position in marketable securities and investment in other companies had a combined fair value of $7,915,313.

Predecessor Detail - Name changed from Matachewan Canadian Gold, Ltd., July 10, 1932.

Directors - Richard D. (Bo) McCloskey, chr., pres. & CEO, Toronto, Ont.; Edward G. (Ed) Dumond, CFO & corp. sec., Newmarket, Ont.; Douglas (Doug) Bolton, Toronto, Ont.; Richard B. German, Toronto, Ont.; Michael T. Zurowski, Toronto, Ont.

Capital Stock

	Authorized (shs.)	Outstanding (shs.)[1]
Common	unlimited	12,445,025

[1] At May 8, 2023

Major Shareholder - Richard D. (Bo) McCloskey held 51.05% interest at May 8, 2023.

Price Range - MCM.A/TSX-VEN

Year	Volume	High	Low	Close
2022	236,629	$0.33	$0.17	$0.24
2021	883,969	$0.27	$0.16	$0.23
2020	463,587	$0.19	$0.10	$0.16
2019	539,483	$0.25	$0.11	$0.12
2018	402,434	$0.30	$0.15	$0.15

Recent Close: $0.21

Capital Stock Changes - There were no capital stock changes from 1998 to 2022, inclusive.

Financial Statistics

Periods ended:	12m Dec. 31/22[A]		12m Dec. 31/21[A]
	$000s	%Chg	$000s
Realized invest. gain (loss)	1,908		(15)
Unrealized invest. gain (loss)	(5,475)		1,693
Total revenue	**1,681**	**-10**	**1,874**
General & admin. expense	264		229
Stock-based compensation	224		nil
Operating expense	**488**	**+113**	**229**
Operating income	**1,193**	**-27**	**1,645**
Deprec. & amort.	14		15
Pre-tax income	**(729)**	**n.a.**	**1,614**
Income taxes	(136)		175
Net income	**(593)**	**n.a.**	**1,439**
Cash & equivalent	6,224		5,880
Accounts receivable	8		58
Current assets	6,233		5,974
Long-term investments	1,124		1,594
Right-of-use assets	74		5
Total assets	**7,506**	**-2**	**7,653**
Bank indebtedness	1,032		837
Accts. pay. & accr. liabs	69		60
Current liabilities	1,292		904
Long-term lease liabilities	46		nil
Shareholders' equity	6,168		6,537
Cash from oper. activs	**149**	**+684**	**19**
Cash from fin. activs	176		69
Cash from invest. activs	(103)		(164)
Net cash position	**394**	**+129**	**172**
	$		$
Earnings per share*	(0.05)		0.12
Cash flow per share*	0.01		0.00
	shs		shs
No. of shs. o/s*	12,445,025		12,445,025
Avg. no. of shs. o/s*	12,445,025		12,445,025
	%		%
Net profit margin	(35.28)		76.79
Return on equity	(9.33)		24.74
Return on assets	(7.82)		21.17

* Common
[A] Reported in accordance with IFRS

Latest Results

Periods ended:	3m Mar. 31/23[A]		3m Mar. 31/22[A]
	$000s	%Chg	$000s
Total revenue	539	+233	162
Net income	458	+285	119
	$		$
Earnings per share*	0.04		0.01

* Common
[A] Reported in accordance with IFRS

Historical Summary
(as originally stated)

Fiscal Year	Total Rev.	Net Inc. Bef. Disc.	EPS*
	$000s	$000s	$
2022[A]	1,681	(593)	(0.05)
2021[A]	1,874	1,439	0.12
2020[A]	1,635	1,389	0.11
2019[A]	1,193	852	0.07
2018[A]	(368)	(709)	(0.06)

* Common
[A] Reported in accordance with IFRS

M.49 Maven Brands Inc.

Symbol - MJ **Exchange** - CSE **CUSIP** - 57768L
Head Office - 32-100 Kalamalka Lake Rd, Vernon, BC, V1T 9G1
Telephone - (250) 260-0676 **Fax** - (250) 545-3239
Website - mavenbrands.ca
Email - darcy@mavenbrands.ca
Investor Relations - Darcy E. Bomford (250) 260-0676
Auditors - Davidson & Company LLP C.A., Vancouver, B.C.
Transfer Agents - National Securities Administrators Ltd., Vancouver, B.C.

Profile - (B.C. 2014) Holds licences from Health Canada to cultivate, process and sell medical cannabis from a 19,500-sq.-ft. facility in Lumby, B.C.

The company has subdivided a section of its 40-acre property in Lumby, B.C., and listed the resultant six lots for sale. The lots are zoned industrial and for cannabis use.

On Jan. 2, 2022, the company laid off all staff in an effort to conserve cash while awaiting the sale of its subdivision lots. Between December 2021 and July 2022, the company accepted offers to sell three of its lots for a total of $1,115,000.

Predecessor Detail - Name changed from True Leaf Brands Inc., Oct. 29, 2021.

Directors - Darcy E. Bomford, founder, interim CEO & corp. sec., Vernon, B.C.; The Hon. Michael F. (Mike) Harcourt, chr., Vancouver, B.C.; Jennifer Pace, CFO, B.C.

Capital Stock

	Authorized (shs.)	Outstanding (shs.)[1]
Preferred	unlimited	nil
Common	unlimited	35,040,866

[1] At July 29, 2022

Major Shareholder - Widely held at Jan. 31, 2022.

Price Range - MJ/CSE

Year	Volume	High	Low	Close
2022	1,932,728	$0.18	$0.02	$0.02
2021	11,253,660	$0.89	$0.13	$0.14
2020	5,052,807	$2.03	$0.14	$0.52
2019	3,235,687	$5.76	$0.95	$1.17
2018	6,662,316	$17.10	$2.93	$4.23

Consolidation: 1-for-9 cons. in Dec. 2020

Recent Close: $0.03

Capital Stock Changes - During fiscal 2022, common shares were issued as follows: 1,346,442 for cash, 150,003 for bonus payments and 91,346 for debt settlement.

Wholly Owned Subsidiaries

True Leaf Investments Corp., Vancouver, B.C. Inactive.
- 100% int. in **Lind Asset Management XV-II LLC** Inactive.
- 100% int. in **Maven Cannabis Inc.**, Vancouver, B.C.
- 100% int. in **1279166 B.C. Ltd.**, B.C. Inactive.
- 100% int. in **True Leaf USA LLC** Inactive.

Financial Statistics

Periods ended:	12m Mar. 31/22^A		12m Mar. 31/21^A
	$000s	%Chg	$000s
Salaries & benefits	373		628
General & admin expense	1,264		1,724
Stock-based compensation	289		577
Operating expense	**1,926**	**-36**	**2,989**
Operating income	**(1,926)**	**n.a.**	**(2,989)**
Deprec., depl. & amort.	134		118
Finance costs, gross	579		4,663
Pre-tax income	**(2,402)**	**n.a.**	**(7,463)**
Income taxes	63		nil
Net inc. bef. disc. opers	**(2,465)**	**n.a.**	**(7,463)**
Income from disc. opers	nil		1,240
Net income	**(2,465)**	**n.a.**	**(6,223)**
Cash & equivalent	188		481
Accounts receivable	20		176
Current assets	628		1,051
Fixed assets, net	4,391		4,489
Intangibles, net	50		63
Total assets	**5,070**	**-10**	**5,603**
Accts. pay. & accr. liabs	427		506
Current liabilities	6,590		5,206
Long-term debt, gross	6,100		4,700
Shareholders' equity	(1,520)		396
Cash from oper. activs	**(1,766)**	**n.a.**	**(7,753)**
Cash from fin. activs	1,636		8,099
Cash from invest. activs	(163)		(81)
Net cash position	**188**	**-61**	**481**
Capital expenditures	(160)		(123)
	$		$
Earns. per sh. bef disc opers*	(0.07)		(0.51)
Earnings per share*	(0.07)		(0.44)
Cash flow per share*	(0.05)		(0.45)
	shs		shs
No. of shs. o/s*	35,040,366		33,453,014
Avg. no. of shs. o/s*	34,051,138		17,053,455
	%		%
Net profit margin	n.a.		n.a.
Return on equity	n.m.		n.m.
Return on assets	(35.06)		(49.31)

* Common
^A Reported in accordance with IFRS

Historical Summary
(as originally stated)

Fiscal Year	Oper. Rev.	Net Inc. Bef. Disc.	EPS*
	$000s	$000s	$
2022^A	nil	(2,465)	(0.07)
2021^A	nil	(7,463)	(0.51)
2020^A	nil	(13,135)	(0.90)
2019^A	2,311	(5,509)	(0.54)
2018^A	1,401	(3,968)	(0.45)

* Common
^A Reported in accordance with IFRS
Note: Adjusted throughout for 1-for-9 cons. in Dec. 2020

M.50 Maxim Power Corp.

Symbol - MXG **Exchange** - TSX **CUSIP** - 57773Y
Head Office - 1800-715 5 Ave SW, Calgary, AB, T2P 2X6 **Telephone** - (403) 263-3021 **Fax** - (403) 263-9125
Website - www.maximpowercorp.com
Email - investors@maximpowercorp.com
Investor Relations - Kyle Mitton (403) 263-3021
Auditors - KPMG LLP C.A., Calgary, Alta.
Bankers - Bank of Montreal
Lawyers - Bennett Jones LLP, Calgary, Alta.
Transfer Agents - Computershare Trust Company of Canada Inc., Calgary, Alta.
FP500 Revenue Ranking - 722
Employees - 42 at Dec. 31, 2022
Profile - (Alta. 2010 amalg.) Acquires, develops, owns and operates power generation facilities as well as holds coal projects in Alberta.

Owns and operates the 204-MW Milner 2 (M2) natural-gas fired power plant located at the company's HR Milner site near Grande Cache, Alta. Electricity generation operations at the HR Milner site are expected to resume by the third quarter of 2023. Other projects in various stages of development include the combined cycle gas turbine expansion which would increase total generation capacity of M2 to 300-MW and would repower 96-MW of the 150-MW HR Milner coal and natural gas-fired generation facility at the Milner site; and the 200-MW Buffalo Atlee wind generation project near Brooks, Alta.

Also holds 4,877-hectare Mine 14 and 1,792-hectare Mine 16S coal projects located north of Grande Cache. Proven and probable reserves at Mine 14 were 18,950,000 tonnes at March 2013. The Mine 14 project was 100% optioned to a third party.

During 2022, wholly owned **Forked River II, LLC** was dissolved.

In September 2022, a non-injury fire damaged the air inlet filter house of the Milner 2 (M2) operating facility, which caused operations to halt. The company expects that electricity generation at the HR Milner site will remain offline until the third quarter of 2023.

In April 2022, the company sold a parcel of land in Forked River, Man., for US$3,000,000.

Periods ended:	12m Dec. 31/22	12m Dec. 31/21
Electric gen., GWh	1,065	1,450

Predecessor Detail - Name changed from Jupiter Power International Inc., Feb. 19, 2001, following reverse takeover acquisition of Maxim Energy Group Ltd.
Directors - M. Bruce Chernoff, chr. & CEO, Calgary, Alta.; W. Brett Wilson†, v-chr., Calgary, Alta.; Wiley D. Auch, Calgary, Alta.; Michael R. (Mike) Mayder, Calgary, Alta.; Bradley J. (Brad) Wall, Swift Current, Sask.; Andrea Whyte, Calgary, Alta.
Other Exec. Officers - Robert (Bob) Emmott, pres. & COO; Kevin Dyck, v-p, fin. & contr.; Kyle Mitton, v-p, corp. devel. & CFO; Rob Watson, v-p, opers.; Kim Karran, corp. sec. & sr. HR advisor
† Lead director

Capital Stock

	Authorized (shs.)	Outstanding (shs.)[1]
Class A Preferred	unlimited	nil
Class B Preferred	unlimited	nil
Common	unlimited	50,499,307

[1] At Aug. 27, 2023

Major Shareholder - M. Bruce Chernoff held 35.45% interest and W. Brett Wilson held 35.25% interest at Apr. 17, 2023.

Price Range - MXG/TSX

Year	Volume	High	Low	Close
2022	3,782,832	$4.83	$3.04	$3.40
2021	5,277,290	$4.24	$2.12	$3.97
2020	5,342,983	$2.40	$1.03	$2.23
2019	4,052,179	$2.20	$1.44	$1.82
2018	8,778,278	$2.75	$1.79	$2.17

Recent Close: $4.95
Capital Stock Changes - During 2022, 436,143 common shares were issued on exercise of options and 363,505 common shares were repurchased under a Normal Course Issuer Bid.

Wholly Owned Subsidiaries

Deerland Power Inc., Alta.
• 1% int. in **Deerland Power Limited Partnership**, Alta.
Milner Power II Inc., Alta.
Milner Power II Limited Partnership, Alta.
Milner Power Inc., Alta.
Milner Power Limited Partnership, Alta.
Summit Coal Inc., Alta.
Summit Coal Limited Partnership, Alta.

Subsidiaries

99% int. in **Deerland Power Limited Partnership**, Alta.

Financial Statistics

Periods ended:	12m Dec. 31/22^A		12m Dec. 31/21^oA
	$000s	%Chg	$000s
Operating revenue	**141,263**	**-9**	**156,014**
Cost of goods sold	76,945		67,627
Salaries & benefits	8,514		7,552
Operating expense	**85,459**	**+14**	**75,179**
Operating income	**55,804**	**-31**	**80,835**
Deprec., depl. & amort.	10,551		7,968
Finance income	1,265		140
Finance costs, gross	7,489		5,495
Write-downs/write-offs	(7,861)		(5,347)
Pre-tax income	**52,595**	**-46**	**98,147**
Income taxes	10,318		19,638
Net income	**42,277**	**-46**	**78,509**
Cash & equivalent	51,378		13,550
Accounts receivable	15,109		20,766
Current assets	70,616		35,866
Fixed assets, net	296,548		260,590
Total assets	**382,109**	**+22**	**312,437**
Accts. pay. & accr. liabs	9,991		19,216
Current liabilities	16,253		19,669
Long-term debt, gross	82,673		53,650
Long-term debt, net	81,204		53,650
Long-term lease liabilities	140		203
Shareholders' equity	268,654		227,182
Cash from oper. activs	**76,413**	**-27**	**105,216**
Cash from fin. activs	19,276		(1,859)
Cash from invest. activs	(57,790)		(85,314)
Net cash position	**51,378**	**+279**	**13,550**
Capital expenditures	(81,089)		(88,577)
	$		$
Earnings per share*	0.84		...
Cash flow per share*	1.53		2.10
	shs		shs
No. of shs. o/s*	50,167,850		50,095,212
Avg. no. of shs. o/s*	50,099,365		50,056,116
	%		%
Net profit margin	29.93		50.32
Return on equity	17.05		41.86
Return on assets	13.91		30.05
No. of employees (FTEs)	42		34

* Common
^o Restated
^A Reported in accordance with IFRS

Historical Summary
(as originally stated)

Fiscal Year	Oper. Rev.	Net Inc. Bef. Disc.	EPS*
	$000s	$000s	$
2022^A	141,263	42,277	0.84
2021^A	156,014	78,509	1.57
2020^A	46,726	9,260	0.19
2019^A	28,335	(5,850)	(0.11)
2018^A	19,744	4,377	0.08

* Common
^A Reported in accordance with IFRS

M.51 Mayfair Acquisition Corporation

Symbol - MFA.P **Exchange** - TSX-VEN **CUSIP** - 57807J
Head Office - 600-777 Hornby St, Vancouver, BC, V6Z 1S4 **Telephone** - (416) 519-6886
Email - cw@seabulkers.com
Investor Relations - Charles B. Walensky (612) 928-5421
Auditors - Davidson & Company LLP C.A., Vancouver, B.C.
Lawyers - CC Corporate Counsel Professional Corporation, Vaughan, Ont.
Transfer Agents - Capital Transfer Agency Inc., Toronto, Ont.
Profile - (B.C. 2021) Capital Pool Company.
Directors - Charles B. Walensky, CEO, Minn.; Arthur L. Regan, pres. & sec.-treas., N.J.; Bart Kelleher, Conn.; Peter S. Shaerf, N.Y.
Other Exec. Officers - Robert D. B. (Rob) Suttie, CFO

Capital Stock

	Authorized (shs.)	Outstanding (shs.)[1]
Common	unlimited	8,136,668

[1] At May 30, 2022

Major Shareholder - Widely held at Apr. 5, 2022.

Price Range - MFA.P/TSX-VEN

Year	Volume	High	Low	Close
2022	140,960	$0.25	$0.15	$0.15

Recent Close: $0.15
Capital Stock Changes - On Apr. 5, 2022, an initial public offering of 4,000,000 common shares was completed at 10¢ per share.

M.52 McCoy Global Inc.*

Symbol - MCB **Exchange** - TSX **CUSIP** - 57980Q
Head Office - 201-9910 39 Ave NW, Edmonton, AB, T6E 5H8 **Telephone** - (780) 453-8451 **Fax** - (780) 453-8756
Website - www.mccoyglobal.com

Email - jrakievich@mccoyglobal.com
Investor Relations - James W. Rakievich (780) 453-8707
Auditors - PricewaterhouseCoopers LLP C.A., Edmonton, Alta.
Bankers - The Bank of Nova Scotia, Edmonton, Alta.
Lawyers - DLA Piper (Canada) LLP, Calgary, Alta.
Transfer Agents - Computershare Trust Company of Canada Inc., Toronto, Ont.
Employees - 114 at Dec. 31, 2022
Profile - (Alta. 1996) Provides equipment and technologies designed to support tubular running operations, enhance wellbore integrity and assist with collecting critical data for the global energy industry.

Manufactures and distributes drilling equipment and data collection technologies used in rugged applications for the global energy industry as well as in construction, marine and aerospace. Equipment product offerings include hydraulic power tongs used to make-up and break-out casing, tubing and drill-pipe, for both land and offshore rig applications; casing running tools; tubular running technologies; mud handling equipment; torque-turn monitoring and control software system; wireless data subs; bucking units used for assembling couplings to casing in tubular manufacturing plants, make/break machines used for assembling or breaking out downhole tool assemblies and testing tubular connections; diesel and electric hydraulic power units; roughnecks; load monitoring systems; portable aircraft digital scales; and winch control systems.

Aftermarket products and services include replacement parts for equipment product offerings; dies and inserts for a wide variety of tubular make-up and handling equipment; repair, maintenance, training and calibration of capital equipment and similar competitor products; rental of technologies; remote support service for tubular running service; applied calibration machine learning technology for tubular make-up equipment servicing requirements; and gauging services.

Has offices in Canada, the U.S. and the U.A.E., and operates internationally in more than 50 countries through a combination of direct sales and key distributors.

Recent Merger and Acquisition Activity

Status: completed **Announced:** Dec. 22, 2022
McCoy Global Inc. completed the sale and leaseback of its Cedar Park, Tex., production and service facility for proceeds of Cdn$9,000,000 (US$6,700,000).

Predecessor Detail - Name changed from McCoy Corporation, July 10, 2014.

Directors - Terry D. Freeman, chr., Edmonton, Alta.; James W. (Jim) Rakievich, pres. & CEO, Edmonton, Alta.; Michael (Mike) Buker, Houston, Tex.; Katherine L. (Kathy) Demuth, Edmonton, Alta.; Alexander (Alex) Ryzhikov, Montréal, Qué.; William (John) Walker, Houston, Tex.

Other Exec. Officers - Bing Deng, v-p, mktg. & tech.; Lindsay McGill, v-p & CFO

Capital Stock

	Authorized (shs.)	Outstanding (shs.)[1]
Preferred	unlimited	nil
Common	unlimited	28,578,589

[1] At Aug. 15, 2023

Options - At Dec. 31, 2022, options were outstanding to purchase 1,555,000 common shares at a weighted average exercise price of $1.52 per share with a weighted average remaining contractual life of 5.09 years.

Normal Course Issuer Bid - The company plans to make normal course purchases of up to 1,605,053 common shares representing 10% of the public float. The bid commenced on Aug. 22, 2023, and expires on Aug. 21, 2024.

Major Shareholder - Cannell Capital LLC held 16.27% interest, Ewing Morris & Co. Investment Partners Ltd. held 13.09% interest, Burgundy Asset Management Ltd. held 10.94% interest and Fidelity Management & Research Company held 10.81% interest at Apr. 4, 2023.

Price Range - MCB/TSX

Year	Volume	High	Low	Close
2022	4,354,341	$1.26	$0.66	$0.95
2021	3,999,299	$0.90	$0.46	$0.66
2020	2,279,787	$0.67	$0.32	$0.48
2019	11,278,071	$1.27	$0.41	$0.60
2018	2,175,776	$1.60	$0.93	$1.00

Recent Close: $1.42

Capital Stock Changes - During 2022, common shares were issued as follows: 172,500 under restricted share plan and 20,000 on exercise of options; 25,700 common shares were repurchased under a Normal Course Issuer Bid.

Dividends

MCB com N.S.R. [1]

$0.01 Oct. 15/23 $0.01[2] July 15/23

Paid in 2023: $0.02 2022: n.a. 2021: n.a.

[1] Quarterly divd normally payable in Oct/15 has been omitted.
[2] First divd. since June/11.

Long-Term Debt - At Dec. 31, 2022, outstanding long-term debt totaled $4,517,000 ($2,265,000 current) and consisted entirely of a senior secured term loan bearing interest at U.S. prime plus 4.95% and due in 2024.

Wholly Owned Subsidiaries

McCoy Global Canada Corp., Edmonton, Alta.
McCoy Global FZE, United Arab Emirates.
McCoy Global USA, Inc., Lafayette, La.

Financial Statistics

Periods ended:	12m Dec. 31/22[A]		12m Dec. 31/21[A]
	$000s	%Chg	$000s
Operating revenue	**52,428**	**+60**	**32,796**
Cost of sales	33,908		20,943
Research & devel. expense	2,960		1,994
General & admin expense	7,509		6,192
Stock-based compensation	566		592
Operating expense	**44,943**	**+51**	**29,721**
Operating income	**7,485**	**+143**	**3,075**
Deprec., depl. & amort.	2,997		2,959
Finance income	17		17
Finance costs, gross	788		860
Pre-tax income	**7,789**	**+91**	**4,078**
Income taxes	(974)		nil
Net income	**8,763**	**+115**	**4,078**
Cash & equivalent	21,469		11,139
Inventories	22,029		15,518
Accounts receivable	12,976		6,030
Current assets	58,459		34,445
Fixed assets, net	7,335		10,117
Intangibles, net	10,878		10,537
Total assets	**77,793**	**+41**	**55,138**
Accts. pay. & accr. liabs.	10,862		4,897
Current liabilities	19,399		8,387
Long-term debt, gross	4,517		4,194
Long-term debt, net	2,252		3,690
Long-term lease liabilities	4,428		3,051
Shareholders' equity	51,714		40,010
Cash from oper. activs.	**2,871**	**+97**	**1,459**
Cash from fin. activs.	(308)		1,398
Cash from invest. activs.	6,912		(3,715)
Net cash position	**21,469**	**+93**	**11,139**
Capital expenditures	(1,116)		(1,905)
Capital disposals	8,810		241
	$		$
Earnings per share*	0.31		0.15
Cash flow per share*	0.10		0.05
	shs		shs
No. of shs. o/s*	28,391,789		28,224,989
Avg. no. of shs. o/s*	28,324,835		28,013,427
	%		%
Net profit margin	16.71		12.43
Return on equity	19.11		10.80
Return on assets	14.52		9.16
Foreign sales percent	99		97
No. of employees (FTEs)	114		100

* Common
[A] Reported in accordance with IFRS

Latest Results

Periods ended:	6m June 30/23[A]		6m June 30/22[A]
	$000s	%Chg	$000s
Operating revenue	33,112	+52	21,754
Net income	1,955	+60	1,225
	$		$
Earnings per share*	0.07		0.04

* Common
[A] Reported in accordance with IFRS

Historical Summary
(as originally stated)

Fiscal Year	Oper. Rev.	Net Inc. Bef. Disc.	EPS*
	$000s	$000s	$
2022[A]	52,428	8,763	0.31
2021[A]	32,796	4,078	0.15
2020[A]	38,674	(2,175)	(0.08)
2019[A]	53,392	233	0.01
2018[A]	49,076	(3,791)	(0.14)

* Common
[A] Reported in accordance with IFRS

M.53 mCloud Technologies Corp.

Symbol - MCLD **Exchange** - TSX-VEN (S) **CUSIP** - 582270
Head Office - 550-510 Burrard St, Vancouver, BC, V6C 3A8 **Toll-free** - (866) 420-1781
Website - www.mcloudcorp.com
Email - ir@mcloudcorp.com
Investor Relations - Russel H. McMeekin (604) 669-9973
Auditors - KPMG LLP C.A., Vancouver, B.C.
Transfer Agents - TSX Trust Company, Toronto, Ont.
Employees - 140 at Sept. 30, 2022
Profile - (B.C. 2010) Provides AssetCare™ solutions for asset management by leveraging Internet of Things (IoT), cloud computing and artificial intelligence to unlock untapped potential of energy-intensive assets such as heating, ventilation and air conditioning (HVAC) units, refrigerators, control systems, heat exchangers, compressors and wind turbines.

Provides AssetCare™ for buildings, which includes AI and analytics to automate and remotely manage commercial buildings, driving improvements in energy efficiency, occupant health and safety through indoor air quality optimization, food safety and inventory protection; AssetCare™ for workers, which includes cloud software connected to third party hands-free, head-mounted smart glasses combined with AR capabilities to help workers in the field stay connected to experts remotely, facilitate repairs, and provide workers with an AI-powered digital assistant; AssetCare™ for energy, which includes inspection of wind turbine blades using AI-powered computer vision and the deployment of analytics to maximize wind farm energy production yield and availability; AssetCare™ for industry, which includes process assets and control endpoint monitoring, equipment health, and asset inventory management capabilities, driving lower cost of operation for field assets and access to the 3D digital twins, enabling remote management of Change operations across distributed teams; and AssetCare™ for health, which includes HIPAA-compliant remote health monitoring and connectivity to caregivers using mobile apps and wireless sensors that enable 24/7 care without the need for in-person visits, including at elder care facilities, age-in-place situations and medical clinics.

AssetCare™ is delivered to customers through commercial multi-year subscription contracts and deployed to customers through a cloud-based interface accessible on desktops, mobile devices and hands-free digital eyewear. The company has a customer base of more than 100 enterprise customers globally including brands such as **Aramco**, **Mercedes-Benz**, **Toshiba**, **Bank of America/Jones Lang LaSalle**, **Duke Energy**, **Cenovus**, **AltaGas**, **SoftBank**, **TELUS**, **General Dynamics**, **Idemitsu** and **Lockheed Martin**.

On July 29, 2022, the company lost its control over **AGNITY Global, Inc.** following the acquisition of AGNITY by a third party. The company obtained control over AGNITY in January 2019, by acquiring **Flow Capital Corp.**'s royalty agreement with AGNITY which gave the company the right to nominate a majority of the members of its Operations Committee. AGNITY offers LTE/4G/5G mobile IoT (Internet of things) applications.

Common suspended from TSX-VEN, June 5, 2023.

Predecessor Detail - Name changed from Universal mCloud Corp., Nov. 6, 2019.

Directors - Costantino (Tino) Lanza, co-founder & chief growth & rev. officer, Westlake Village, Calif.; Russel H. (Russ) McMeekin, co-founder, pres. & CEO, Calgary, Alta.; Michael W. (Mike) Allman, chr., Rancho Santa Fe, Calif.; Dina Alnahdy, Saudi Arabia; Elizabeth J. (Betsy) MacLean, Phoenix, Ariz.; Ian Russell, Toronto, Ont.

Other Exec. Officers - James (Jim) Christian, chief product & tech. officer; Dr. Barry Po, exec. v-p & chief mktg. officer; Chantal T. M. Schutz, exec. v-p & CFO; Dave Weinerth, exec. v-p & pres., AssetCare solutions; Ibrahim Al-Hindawi, pres., mCloud MENA; Vincent Higgins, pres., North America; Nitin Kapoor, pres., mCloud UK & EMEA; Yan Zhao, pres., Greater China

Capital Stock

	Authorized (shs.)	Outstanding (shs.)[1]
Common	unlimited	16,229,036
pfd ser A	2,300,000	420,000[2]

[1] At Nov. 28, 2022
[2] At Dec. 28, 2022.

Major Shareholder - Widely held at Nov. 18, 2022.

Price Range - MCLD/TSX-VEN (S)

Year	Volume	High	Low	Close
2022	2,350,320	$6.34	$1.10	$1.31
2021	5,548,944	$9.75	$3.15	$6.19
2020	4,028,962	$19.50	$4.71	$5.55
2019	1,744,473	$15.30	$8.40	$14.85
2018	863,019	$18.90	$8.55	$8.70

Consolidation: 1-for-3 cons. in Nov. 2021; 1-for-10 cons. in Dec. 2019

Recent Close: $0.76

Capital Stock Changes - In November 2022, private placement of 15,789,474 common shares at US$1.14 per share was announced. In December 2022, public offering of 420,000 units (1 preferred series A shares & 25 warrants) at Cdn$25 per unit was completed, with warrants exercisable at Cdn$4.75 per share for 47 months.

Wholly Owned Subsidiaries

mCloud Corp. (HK), Hong Kong, Hong Kong, People's Republic of China. Inactive.
- 100% int. in **mCloud (Beijing) Corp.** Inactive
- 100% int. in **mCloud (Wuhan) Corp.** Inactive

mCloud Technologies Australia Holdings Pty Ltd., Australia.
- 100% int. in **mCloud Technologies Australia Pty Ltd.**, Australia.
  - 100% int. in **Kanepi Group Pty Ltd.**, Perth, W.A., Australia.
    - 100% int. in **Kanepi Services Pty. Ltd.**, Australia.
    - 100% int. in **mCloud Technologies Singapore, Inc.**, Singapore.

mCloud Technologies (Canada) Holdings, Inc., Alta. Inactive
- 100% int. in **mCloud Technologies Services Inc.**

mCloud Technologies (USA) Inc., San Francisco, Calif.
- 100% int. in **CSA & EBO, spol. s.r.o.**, Slovakia.
- 100% int. in **CSA Systems s.r.o.**, Slovakia.
- 100% int. in **Construction Systems Associates, Inc.**, United States.
- 100% int. in **Field Diagnostic Services, Inc.**, Del.
- 100% int. in **mCloud Technologies (Canada) Inc.**, B.C.

NGRAIN (Canada) Corporation, Canada.
- 100% int. in **NGRAIN (U.S.) Corporation**, United States.

Financial Statistics

Periods ended:	12m Dec. 31/21[A]		12m Dec. 31/20[oA]
	$000s	%Chg	$000s
Operating revenue	**25,597**	**-5**	**26,928**
Cost of sales	9,684		10,282
Salaries & benefits	21,692		20,885
Research & devel. expense	3,179		1,078
General & admin expense	19,002		16,165
Stock-based compensation	1,868		1,454
Operating expense	**55,424**	**+11**	**49,864**
Operating income	**(29,827)**	**n.a.**	**(22,936)**
Deprec., depl. & amort.	8,925		6,778
Finance costs, gross	8,619		6,034
Pre-tax income	**(46,364)**	**n.a.**	**(35,825)**
Income taxes	(1,665)		(964)
Net income	**(44,699)**	**n.a.**	**(34,861)**
Net inc. for equity hldrs	**(44,763)**	**n.a.**	**(36,448)**
Net inc. for non-cont. int	**63**	**-96**	**1,587**
Cash & equivalent	4,588		1,111
Accounts receivable	14,567		12,313
Current assets	21,907		15,195
Fixed assets, net	649		506
Right-of-use assets	916		3,661
Intangibles, net	47,668		54,854
Total assets	**72,106**	**-7**	**77,319**
Bank indebtedness	3,460		977
Accts. pay. & accr. liabs	12,421		12,924
Current liabilities	64,016		28,248
Long-term debt, gross	35,511		38,924
Long-term debt, net	878		29,489
Long-term lease liabilities	635		3,110
Shareholders' equity	1,791		9,165
Non-controlling interest	2,495		2,293
Cash from oper. activs	**(28,330)**	**n.a.**	**(24,856)**
Cash from fin. activs	32,927		31,857
Cash from invest. activs	(1,064)		(6,395)
Net cash position	**4,588**	**+313**	**1,111**
Capital expenditures	(625)		(128)
	$		$
Earnings per share*	(3.76)		(5.01)
Cash flow per share*	(2.38)		(3.42)
	shs		shs
No. of shs. o/s*	16,138,069		9,168,434
Avg. no. of shs. o/s*	11,898,183		7,272,464
	%		%
Net profit margin	(174.63)		(129.46)
Return on equity	(951.07)		(545.67)
Return on assets	(48.71)		(42.27)
Foreign sales percent	58		49

* Common
[o] Restated
[A] Reported in accordance with IFRS

Latest Results

Periods ended:	9m Sept. 30/22[A]		9m Sept. 30/21[oA]
	$000s	%Chg	$000s
Operating revenue	9,605	-55	21,426
Net income	(31,607)	n.a.	(34,368)
Net inc. for equity hldrs	(26,364)	n.a.	(34,667)
Net inc. for non-cont. int	(5,243)		299
	$		$
Earnings per share*	(1.63)		(3.15)

* Common
[o] Restated
[A] Reported in accordance with IFRS

Historical Summary
(as originally stated)

Fiscal Year	Oper. Rev.	Net Inc. Bef. Disc.	EPS*
	$000s	$000s	$
2021[A]	25,597	(44,699)	(3.76)
2020[A]	26,928	(34,861)	(5.07)
2019[A]	18,340	(28,710)	(7.50)
2018[A]	1,794	(12,188)	(5.40)
2017[A1]	840	(6,210)	(6.60)

* Common
[A] Reported in accordance with IFRS
[1] Results reflect the Oct. 13, 2017, reverse takeover acquisition of mCloud Corp.

Note: Adjusted throughout for 1-for-3 cons. in Nov. 2021; 1-for-10 cons. in Dec. 2019

M.54 mdf commerce inc.*

Symbol - MDF **Exchange** - TSX **CUSIP** - 55283M
Head Office - East Tower, 255-1111 rue Saint-Charles O, Longueuil, QC, J4K 5G4 **Telephone** - (450) 449-0102 **Toll-free** - (877) 677-9088 **Fax** - (450) 449-8725
Website - www.mdfcommerce.com
Email - deborah.dumoulin@mdfcommerce.com
Investor Relations - Deborah Dumoulin (450) 449-0102 ext. 2134
Auditors - Deloitte LLP C.A., Montréal, Qué.
Bankers - The Bank of Nova Scotia, Montréal, Qué.
Transfer Agents - Computershare Trust Company of Canada Inc., Montréal, Qué.
FP500 Revenue Ranking - 764
Employees - 669 at Mar. 31, 2023
Profile - (Can. 1996) Develops and operates software-as-a-service (SaaS) commerce platforms.

Offerings consist of eProcurement (formerly strategic sourcing) which focuses on procurement and tendering solutions for buyers and suppliers and includes MERX (public and private sector tenders in Canada), BidNet, BidNet Direct and GovernmentBids (government bids and contracts in the U.S.), Construction BidBoard (construction bids in California and adjacent states), ASC (contract, document, form and configure, price and quote lifecycle management), Vendor Registry (procurement solutions for U.S. local agencies and schools) and Periscope (eProcurement solution for state, provinces and local government agencies and suppliers in the U.S. and Canada); ecommerce which provides end-to-end omnichannel solutions for businesses of all sizes through Orckestra and k-eCommerce; and emarketplaces which provide transactional platforms in various industries and include Carrus Technologies (automotive aftermarket), The Broker Forum (electronic components), Power Source OnLine (computer equipment and telecommunications), Polygon (gems and jewellery), Jobboom (employment and talent acquisition) and Réseau Contact (online dating).

The company conducts business from its offices in Longueuil, Que.; Ottawa (2), Ont.; Latham, N.Y.; Austin, Tex.; American Fork, Utah; Shenzhen, People's Republic of China; and Northville, Mich.

Recent Merger and Acquisition Activity

Status: completed **Announced:** Oct. 5, 2022
mdf commerce inc. sold wholly owned subsidiary InterTrade Systems Inc. to SPS Commerce, Inc., for US$48,500,000 in cash. The InterTrade solution provides business-to-business (B2B) integration solutions to better manage the Supply Chain Collaboration between trading partners and was part of mdf commerce's Unified Commerce platform.

Predecessor Detail - Name changed from Mediagrif Interactive Technologies Inc., Sept. 23, 2020.
Directors - Pierre Chadi, chr., Montréal, Qué.; Luc Filiatreault, pres. & CEO, Saint-Bruno-de-Montarville, Qué.; Mary-Ann Bell, Montréal, Qué.; Brian Nelson, Stamford, Conn.; Martial Vincent
Other Exec. Officers - Deborah Dumoulin, CFO; Julie Bélanger, v-p, HR; Julie T. Bélanger, v-p, org. performance; Patrick Boisvert, v-p, IT; Julie Pilon, v-p, emarketplaces; Nicolas Vanasse, v-p, chief legal officer & corp. sec.; Pascal Cardinal, pres., ecommerce; Mark Eigenbauer, pres., eprocurement

Capital Stock

	Authorized (shs.)	Outstanding (shs.)[1]
Preferred	unlimited	nil
Common	unlimited	43,970,943

[1] At Aug. 8, 2023

Options - At Mar. 31, 2023, options were outstanding to purchase 978,000 common shares at prices ranging from $5.81 to $15.15 per share with a weighted average contractual life of 4.69 years.
Major Shareholder - Fonds de solidarité des travailleurs du Québec (F.T.Q.) held 13.59% interest, Investissement Québec held 12.21% interest and Long Path Partners LP held 12.12% interest at Aug. 8, 2023.

Price Range - MDF/TSX

Year	Volume	High	Low	Close
2022	19,433,785	$5.80	$1.51	$3.60
2021	19,822,582	$16.90	$4.40	$5.64
2020	13,561,281	$14.22	$2.22	$12.28
2019	3,237,508	$11.00	$5.20	$6.91
2018	2,552,462	$12.91	$9.03	$9.56

Recent Close: $3.16
Capital Stock Changes - There were no changes to capital stock during fiscal 2023.

In August 2021, 15,057,389 common shares were issued without further consideration on exchange of subscription receipts sold previously by bought deal public offering (8,480,000) and private placement with Fonds de solidarité FTQ and Investissement Québec (6,577,389) at $8.00 each and 509,438 common shares were issued pursuant to the acquisition of Periscope Intermediate Corp.

Long-Term Debt - Outstanding at Mar. 31, 2023:

Revolv. credit facility due 2024[1]	$7,375,000
Less: Deferred financing fees	425,000
	6,950,000
Less: Current portion	nil
	6,950,000

[1] As at Mar. 31, 2023, bears interest at bankers' acceptance rate plus 3.25% for borrowings denominated in Canadian dollars.

Wholly Owned Subsidiaries

ASC Networks Inc., Canada.
The Broker Forum Inc., Longueuil, Qué.
- 100% int. in **Mediagrif Information Consulting (Shenzhen) Co. Ltd.**, People's Republic of China.

Carrus Technologies Inc., Longueuil, Qué.
4222661 Canada Inc., Canada.
Jobboom Inc., Longueuil, Qué.
kCentric Technologies Inc., Laval, Qué.
MERX Networks Inc., Longueuil, Qué.
Orckestra Technologies Inc., Canada.
- 100% int. in **Orckestra A/S**, Denmark.

Réseau Contact Inc., Longueuil, Qué.
TIM USA Inc., Del.
- 100% int. in **ASC Networks U.S.A. Inc.**, Del.
- 100% int. in **Construction BidBoard Inc.**, San Diego, Calif.
- 100% int. in **International Data Base Corporation**, Albany, N.Y.
- 100% int. in **kCentric USA Inc.**, Northville, Mich.
- 100% int. in **Market Velocity, Inc.**, Duluth, Ga.
- 100% int. in **Periscope Intermediate Corp.**, Austin, Tex.
  - 100% int. in **Nebraska Procurement, LLC**, Neb.
  - 100% int. in **Periscope Holdings, Inc.**, Del.
  - 100% int. in **RFP Depot, LLC**, Utah
- 100% int. in **PolyGroup, Ltd.**, Del.
- 100% int. in **Power Source On-Line Inc.**, Calif.

Financial Statistics

Periods ended:	12m Mar. 31/23[A]		12m Mar. 31/22[oA]
	$000s	%Chg	$000s
Operating revenue	**128,295**	**+19**	**108,259**
Cost of sales	55,056		46,911
Research & devel. expense	32,973		25,880
General & admin expense	43,186		46,671
Operating expense	**131,215**	**+10**	**119,462**
Operating income	**(2,920)**	**n.a.**	**(11,203)**
Deprec., depl. & amort.	18,822		14,337
Finance income	183		517
Finance costs, gross	2,392		1,822
Write-downs/write-offs	(85,604)		nil
Pre-tax income	**(85,424)**	**n.a.**	**(26,854)**
Income taxes	(419)		(2,916)
Net income	**(85,005)**	**n.a.**	**(23,938)**
Cash & equivalent	3,998		5,985
Accounts receivable	16,360		10,391
Current assets	48,593		64,120
Fixed assets, net	1,252		2,258
Right-of-use assets	4,766		8,917
Intangibles, net	259,883		374,174
Total assets	**331,996**	**-28**	**463,307**
Accts. pay. & accr. liabs	23,569		41,737
Current liabilities	61,040		74,636
Long-term debt, gross	6,950		49,762
Long-term debt, net	6,950		48,262
Long-term lease liabilities	2,442		7,739
Shareholders' equity	251,269		318,941
Cash from oper. activs	**(27,131)**	**n.a.**	**263**
Cash from fin. activs	(49,759)		148,636
Cash from invest. activs	57,321		(233,293)
Net cash position	**8,812**	**-67**	**26,529**
Capital expenditures	(228)		(547)
Capital disposals	61,870		nil
	$		$
Earnings per share*	(1.93)		(0.64)
Cash flow per share*	(0.62)		0.01
	shs		shs
No. of shs. o/s*	43,970,943		43,970,943
Avg. no. of shs. o/s*	43,970,943		37,367,735
	%		%
Net profit margin	(66.26)		(22.11)
Return on equity	(29.82)		(8.81)
Return on assets	(20.74)		(6.03)
Foreign sales percent	64		60
No. of employees (FTEs)	669		800

* Common
[o] Restated
[A] Reported in accordance with IFRS

Historical Summary
(as originally stated)

Fiscal Year	Oper. Rev.	Net Inc. Bef. Disc.	EPS*
	$000s	$000s	$
2023[A]	128,295	(85,005)	(1.93)
2022[A]	108,259	(23,938)	(0.64)
2021[A]	84,719	(7,591)	(0.38)
2020[A]	75,428	(5,752)	(0.39)
2019[A]	83,082	(25,641)	(1.73)

* Common
[A] Reported in accordance with IFRS

M.55 Medcolcanna Organics Inc.

Symbol - MCCN **Exchange** - CSE (S) **CUSIP** - 58406X
Head Office - Carrera 49b #93-62, Bogota, Colombia, 111211 **Overseas Tel** - 57-310-258-9163
Email - peter.yates@enernext.ca
Investor Relations - Peter W. Yates (403) 971-9104
Auditors - MNP LLP C.A., Toronto, Ont.
Transfer Agents - TSX Trust Company
Profile - (B.C. 2019; orig. Alta., 2010) Holds licences to grow, cultivate, manufacture, sell and distribute medicinal cannabis products in Colombia for domestic use and international export. Also provides extraction services and distributes cannabis vaping products.

Holds license to high- and low-tetrahydrocannabinol (THC) cultivation licence to grow and cultivate both psychoactive and non-psychoactive cannabis plants, and manufacture and produce medical cannabis for domestic consumption, seeds for cultivation, storage and disposal, as well as for international export. Products include cannabis isolates, oil, flower and biomass, and tinctures.

Holds 19 acres of cultivation facility in Cota, Colombia, including four acres for commercial production, one acre for breeding, one acre for research and development and agronomical evaluation, and five acres for outdoor cultivation. The economic benefits on three acres of Cota cultivation facility are owned by **Dona Blanca Limited**. Also has 17 acres of cultivation facilities in Neiva, Colombia.

In addition, wholly owned **Extralia Labs S.A.S.** operates as an extraction contract manufacturing company for the company, Dona Blanca and third party companies using Bio-Herbolysis™, a patent pending process for the extraction and preservation of cannabis from newly harvested or dried material, through its two facilities located in Bogota and Neiva, Colombia, which have capacity to process up to 800 tons of dried cannabis per year; wholly owned **MCCN S.A.** produces, develops, and distributes cannabis vaping and other cannabis related consumer products in Europe under Cannav™ brand; and subsidiary **Medicina Nueva S.A.S.** (50.01% owned) has leased a laboratory in Colombia to develop specific formulations of THC and cannabidiol (CBD) compounds for patients, available by prescription only.

Common suspended from CSE, July 11, 2022.

Predecessor Detail - Name changed from Integrated Energy Storage Corp., May 17, 2019, pursuaunt to reverse takeover acquisition of Medcolcanna (BVI) Inc.

Directors - Robert J. Metcalfe, chr., Toronto, Ont.; Felipe de la Vega, pres. & CEO, Bogota, Colombia; Christopher D. (Chris) Reid, CFO, Bogota, Colombia

Other Exec. Officers - Nicolas Rodriguez, COO; Peter W. Yates, corp. sec.

Capital Stock

	Authorized (shs.)	Outstanding (shs.)[1]
Preferred	unlimited	nil
Common	unlimited	169,738,595

[1] At Sept. 26, 2022

Major Shareholder - Thomas Yang held 29.46% interest at Sept. 26, 2022.

Price Range - MCCN/TSX-VEN (D)

Year	Volume	High	Low	Close
2022	1,546,063	$0.08	$0.01	$0.01
2021	1,236,500	$0.15	$0.03	$0.05
2020	10,301,152	$0.15	$0.04	$0.06
2019	12,718,104	$0.36	$0.07	$0.11

Capital Stock Changes - In March 2022, private placement of 50,000,000 units (1 common share & ½ warrant) at 5¢ per unit was completed, with warrants exercisable at 10¢ per share for two years.

Wholly Owned Subsidiaries

Innovative CBD Products B.V., Netherlands.
MCCN S.A., Switzerland.
Medcolcanna (BVI) Inc., Tortola, British Virgin Islands.
- 100% int. in **Medcolcanna S.A.S.**, Colombia.
  - 100% int. in **Extralia Labs S.A.S.**, Colombia.
  - 50.01% int. in **Medicina Nueva S.A.S.**, Colombia.

M.56 Medexus Pharmaceuticals Inc.

Symbol - MDP **Exchange** - TSX **CUSIP** - 58410Q
Head Office - Unit 1, 35 Nixon Rd, Bolton, ON, L7E 1K1 **Telephone** - (905) 676-0003 **Fax** - (905) 676-9171
Website - medexus.com
Email - ken.dentremont@medexus.com
Investor Relations - Ken d'Entremont (905) 676-0800
Auditors - PricewaterhouseCoopers LLP C.A., Montréal, Qué.
Transfer Agents - Computershare Trust Company of Canada Inc., Montréal, Qué.
FP500 Revenue Ranking - 777
Employees - 98 at Mar. 31, 2023
Profile - (Can. 2013 amalg.) Acquires, distributes, sells and licenses prescription medicines and other pharmaceutical products in the areas of autoimmune disease, hematology, specialty oncology, rheumatology, allergy, dermatology and pediatrics in Canada and the U.S.

Products include Rupall™ (rupatadine), an antihistamine for the relief of the symptoms associated with seasonal allergic rhinitis, perennial allergic rhinitis and chronic spontaneous urticaria; Metoject®, an injectable rheumatoid arthritis and psoriasis treatment; Gleolan®, an imaging agent that makes high-grade gliomas (malignant, rapidly progressive brain tumours) fluoresce under blue light, assisting neurosurgeons to better visualize these gliomas for more complete removal; Treosulfan (Trecondyv® in Canada), a medication used as a conditioning treatment to clear the bone marrow and make room for the transplanted bone marrow cells, which can then produce healthy blood cells; Relaxa®, a treatment of occasional constipation; Cuvposa™, a treatment to reduce chronic severe drooling in patients with neurologic conditions associated with drooling problem; Pediapharm Naproxen Suspension™, a treatment for juvenile rheumatoid arthritis; Otixal™, a treatment of acute otitis media with tympanostomy tubes; Triamcinolone Hexacetinide (Trispan®) for juvenile idiopathic arthritis treatment; NYDA®, a treatment for head lice; Oralvisc® for osteoarthritis; Tricovel® for short-term hair loss; Calcia® for calcium supplement; and Terbinafine Hydrochloride nail lacquer (Topical Terbinafine in Canada), for fungal nail infections treatment.

In the U.S., wholly owned **Medexus Pharma, Inc.** develops and commercializes treatments for autoimmune diseases and oncology. Medexus Pharma markets rheumatoid arthritis, psoriasis and juvenile idiopathic arthritis treatment Rasuvo®, a single-dose auto-injector containing a prescription medicine, methotrexate. In addition, wholly owned **Aptevo BioTherapeutics LLC** owns the worldwide rights to the commercial hematology asset, IXINITY®, an intravenous recombinant factor IX therapeutic for use in patients 12 years old and above with Hemophilia B, which is a hereditary bleeding disorder characterized by a deficiency of clotting factor IX in the blood that is necessary to control bleeding under Phase IV clinical trial.

Products distributed originate from transactions whereby the company either acquires intellectual property rights through licensing agreements (in-licensing) that enables the company to register the products with Health Canada in order to commercialize them, or through acquisitions. The company does not produce, manufacture or develop products. The company also commercializes certain non-prescription drugs and medical devices.

In March 2022, wholly owned **Medexus Pharma, Inc.** acquired the exclusive right to commercialize Gleolan in the U.S. from **NX Development Corp.** (NXDC) for an undisclosed amount. Under the agreement, Medexus would commercialize Gleolan in the U.S. and would pay NXDC annual royalty payments and periodic low- to mid-single-digit-million dollar milestone payments.

Predecessor Detail - Name changed from Pediapharm Inc., Dec. 19, 2018; basis 1 new for 15 old shs.

Directors - Michael P. (Mike) Mueller, chr., Guelph, Ont.; Ken d'Entremont, CEO, Mississauga, Ont.; Dr. Harmony P. Garges, N.C.; Benoit Gravel, Laval, Qué.; Adele M. Gulfo, N.J.; Stephen Nelson, Toronto, Ont.; Menassie Taddese, N.J.

Other Exec. Officers - Marcel Konrad, CFO; Michael D. Adelman, gen. mgr., U.S. opers.; Richard Labelle, gen. mgr., Cdn. opers.; Ian C. Wildgoose Brown, gen. counsel & corp. sec.

Capital Stock

	Authorized (shs.)	Outstanding (shs.)[1]
Preferred	unlimited	nil
Common	unlimited	20,413,504

[1] At Aug. 8, 2023

Major Shareholder - Widely held at Aug. 9, 2023.

Price Range - MDP/TSX

Year	Volume	High	Low	Close
2022	7,240,385	$3.45	$0.88	$2.08
2021	14,255,828	$9.75	$2.40	$2.55
2020	2,397,623	$7.00	$1.42	$6.85
2019	2,026,913	$5.08	$3.50	$3.94
2018	1,592,686	$7.35	$3.75	$4.80

Recent Close: $3.19

Capital Stock Changes - During fiscal 2023, 228,952 common shares were issued under restricted share unit plan.

During fiscal 2022, common shares were issued as follows: 398,875 under restricted share unit plan and 387,081 on conversion of debentures.

Wholly Owned Subsidiaries

MI Acquisitions, Inc.
- 100% int. in **Medexus Pharma, Inc.**, United States.
  - 100% int. in **Aptevo BioTherapeutics LLC**, Del.

Financial Statistics

Periods ended:	12m Mar. 31/23[A]		12m Mar. 31/22[A]
	US$000s	%Chg	US$000s
Operating revenue	**108,096**	**+41**	**76,701**
Cost of sales	42,330		33,027
Research & devel. expense	2,943		5,873
General & admin expense	46,939		41,818
Stock-based compensation	1,579		2,300
Operating expense	**93,791**	**+13**	**83,018**
Operating income	**14,305**	**n.a.**	**(6,317)**
Deprec., depl. & amort.	6,081		6,145
Finance costs, gross	13,499		9,767
Write-downs/write-offs	nil		(1,750)
Pre-tax income	**(5,041)**	**n.a.**	**(3,820)**
Income taxes	(6,262)		(941)
Net income	**1,221**	**n.a.**	**(2,879)**
Cash & equivalent	13,069		10,018
Inventories	22,848		21,351
Accounts receivable	22,381		14,407
Current assets	72,969		49,111
Fixed assets, net	899		1,221
Intangibles, net	80,655		87,251
Total assets	**161,329**	**+16**	**139,225**
Accts. pay. & accr. liabs	33,415		29,174
Current liabilities	83,496		48,108
Long-term debt, gross	42,786		57,573
Long-term debt, net	27,377		42,527
Shareholders' equity	22,448		17,792
Cash from oper. activs	**(1,444)**	**n.a.**	**(1,180)**
Cash from fin. activs	6,405		663
Cash from invest. activs	(1,721)		(8,196)
Net cash position	**13,069**	**+30**	**10,018**
Capital expenditures	(61)		(97)
	US$		US$
Earnings per share*	0.06		(0.15)
Cash flow per share*	(0.07)		(0.06)
	shs		shs
No. of shs. o/s*	20,181,490		19,952,538
Avg. no. of shs. o/s*	19,976,167		19,454,155
	%		%
Net profit margin	1.13		(3.75)
Return on equity	6.07		(16.08)
Return on assets	(1.36)		3.12
Foreign sales percent	73		68
No. of employees (FTEs)	98		100

* Common
[A] Reported in accordance with IFRS

Historical Summary
(as originally stated)

Fiscal Year	Oper. Rev.	Net Inc. Bef. Disc.	EPS*
	US$000s	US$000s	US$
2023[A]	108,096	1,221	0.06
2022[A]	76,701	(2,879)	(0.15)
2021[A]	79,660	(28,264)	(1.86)
	$000s	$000s	$
2020[A]	74,359	(6,236)	(0.43)
2019[A]	33,864	(6,522)	(0.66)

* Common
[A] Reported in accordance with IFRS

M.57 MediaValet Inc.

Symbol - MVP **Exchange** - TSX **CUSIP** - 58450L
Head Office - 500-990 Homer St, Vancouver, BC, V6B 2W7 **Telephone** - (604) 688-2321 **Toll-free** - (877) 688-2321 **Fax** - (604) 605-0051
Website - www.mediavalet.com
Email - rob.chase@mediavalet.com
Investor Relations - Robert Chase (604) 512-1554
Auditors - Baker Tilly WM LLP C.A., Vancouver, B.C.
Lawyers - McMillan LLP, Vancouver, B.C.
Transfer Agents - TSX Trust Company, Toronto, Ont.
Employees - 98 at Dec. 31, 2022
Profile - (Alta. 1993) Develops and markets MediaValet®, a cloud-based enterprise software for digital asset management and creative operations of organizations across all sectors including agencies, government, healthcare, higher education, manufacturing, nonprofit, real estate and construction and technology.

MediaValet® is a software-as-a-service (SaaS) digital asset management system that allows digital assets, such as videos, photos, graphics, animations, audio files, documents, and other brand assets and marketing materials, to be aggregated into one central media library on the cloud and accessed at anytime and anywhere. The software is built exclusively on Microsoft's platform-as-a-service cloud offering, Microsoft Azure Service Fabric, and is available across 61 Microsoft data centre regions in 140 countries. The company also offers integrations into Slack, Adobe Creative Suite, Microsoft Office 365, WorkFront, Wrike, Drupal, WordPress and other third party applications.

Predecessor Detail - Name changed from VRX WorldWide Inc., Oct. 2, 2014, following sale of its photography services business VRX Studios.

Directors - Andrew Shen, chr.; Robert (Rob) Chase, pres. & CEO, Vancouver, B.C.; Robert W. (Bob) Garnett, Richmond, B.C.; Geordie Henderson, Vancouver, B.C.; Thomas Kenny, San Clemente, Calif.; Jake Sorofman, N.C.; John Tobia, Ont.

Other Exec. Officers - David (Dave) Miller, CFO; Jean Lozano, chief tech. officer; Beth Kszan, v-p, mktg.; Eric Simmons, v-p, sales

Capital Stock

	Authorized (shs.)	Outstanding (shs.)[1]
First Preferred	unlimited	nil
Second Preferred	unlimited	nil
Third Preferred	unlimited	nil
Fourth Preferred	unlimited	nil
Common	unlimited	43,490,436

[1] At Aug. 15, 2023

Major Shareholder - Francis N. Shen held 22.08% interest at May 5, 2023.

Price Range - MVP/TSX

Year	Volume	High	Low	Close
2022	12,598,669	$2.22	$1.04	$1.11
2021	10,743,550	$3.24	$1.61	$2.00
2020	14,133,091	$2.94	$0.76	$2.78
2019	4,282,146	$1.50	$0.30	$1.19
2018	3,326,862	$1.50	$0.30	$0.45

Consolidation: 1-for-15 cons. in Sept. 2019

Recent Close: $1.25

Capital Stock Changes - In January 2023, private placement of 2,692,315 units (1 common share & 1 warrant) at $1.30 per unit was completed, with warrants exercisable at $1.50 per share for three years.

During 2022, common shares were issued as follows: 2,287,162 on exercise of warrants and 99,611 on exercise of options.

Financial Statistics

Periods ended:	12m Dec. 31/22[A]		12m Dec. 31/21[A]
	$000s	%Chg	$000s
Operating revenue	**12,841**	**+37**	**9,341**
Cost of sales	1,914		1,309
Salaries & benefits	12,901		9,876
Research & devel. expense	2,594		2,241
General & admin expense	5,114		4,261
Stock-based compensation	1,044		757
Operating expense	**23,567**	**+28**	**18,443**
Operating income	**(10,726)**	**n.a.**	**(9,102)**
Deprec., depl. & amort.	393		326
Finance income	23		68
Finance costs, gross	102		148
Pre-tax income	**(11,095)**	**n.a.**	**(9,499)**
Net income	**(11,095)**	**n.a.**	**(9,499)**
Cash & equivalent	217		6,677
Accounts receivable	4,721		3,421
Current assets	5,701		11,113
Fixed assets, net	320		281
Right-of-use assets	477		700
Total assets	**7,711**	**-39**	**12,744**
Bank indebtedness	501		nil
Accts. pay. & accr. liabs	2,886		1,962
Current liabilities	13,043		10,381
Long-term debt, gross	nil		1,000
Long-term lease liabilities	308		547
Equity portion of conv. debs	nil		483
Shareholders' equity	(6,226)		1,664
Cash from oper. activs	**(7,715)**	**n.a.**	**(7,470)**
Cash from fin. activs	1,428		163
Cash from invest. activs	(187)		(252)
Net cash position	**217**	**-97**	**6,677**
Capital expenditures	(194)		(246)
	$		$
Earnings per share*	(0.28)		(0.25)
Cash flow per share*	(0.20)		(0.20)
	shs		shs
No. of shs. o/s*	40,775,122		38,388,349
Avg. no. of shs. o/s*	39,487,582		38,214,918
	%		%
Net profit margin	(86.40)		(101.69)
Return on equity	n.m.		(162.45)
Return on assets	(107.48)		(57.88)
Foreign sales percent	87		85
No. of employees (FTEs)	98		102

* Common

[A] Reported in accordance with IFRS

Historical Summary
(as originally stated)

Fiscal Year	Oper. Rev. $000s	Net Inc. Bef. Disc. $000s	EPS* $
2022[A]	12,841	(11,095)	(0.28)
2021[A]	9,341	(9,499)	(0.25)
2020[A]	7,472	(3,891)	(0.12)
2019[A]	5,161	(3,592)	(0.20)
2018[A]	2,923	(4,234)	(0.30)

* Common

[A] Reported in accordance with IFRS

Note: Adjusted throughout for 1-for-15 cons. in Sept. 2019

M.58 Medical Facilities Corporation

Symbol - DR **Exchange** - TSX **CUSIP** - 58457V

Head Office - 701-4576 Yonge St, Toronto, ON, M2N 6N4 **Telephone** - (416) 848-7380 **Toll-free** - (877) 402-7162 **Fax** - (416) 925-6083

Website - www.medicalfacilitiescorp.ca

Email - investors@medicalfc.com

Investor Relations - David N. T. Watson (800) 385-5451

Auditors - Grant Thornton LLP C.P.A., Miami, Fla.

Transfer Agents - Computershare Trust Company of Canada Inc., Toronto, Ont.

FP500 Revenue Ranking - 450

Employees - 1,593 at Dec. 31, 2022

Profile - (B.C. 2005; orig. Ont., 2004) Owns indirect majority interest in four specialty surgical hospitals in South Dakota (2), Oklahoma and Arkansas, and six ambulatory surgery centres in California, Michigan, Missouri, Nebraska, Ohio and Pennsylvania at Mar. 31, 2023.

The specialty hospitals perform scheduled surgical, imaging and diagnostic procedures, including primary and urgent care and derive revenue from fees charged for the use of their facilities. Hospitals include Arkansas Surgical Hospital in North Little Rock, Ark., which performs joint replacements; Oklahoma Spine Hospital; and The South Dakota MFC Hospitals located in Rapid City and Sioux Falls, S.D. Collectively, the MFC Hospitals have 46 operating rooms, 125 overnight stay rooms, six procedure rooms, 475 physicians with medical staff privileges and a clinical staff of 1,089.

The six ambulatory surgical centres specialize in outpatient surgical and diagnostic procedures, with patient stays for less than 24 hours. Collectively, the ambulatory surgical centres have 15 operating rooms, eight procedure rooms, 131 physicians with medical staff privileges and a clinical staff of 86.

In December 2022, subsidiary **Mountain Plains Real Estate Holdings, LLC** was wound up.

In December 2022, the company sold its remaining 31.7% interest in Unity Medical and Surgical Hospital for US$606,000.

On Sept. 13, 2022, the company announced plans to suspend acquisitions, divest its non-core assets, pursue overhead cost reductions, and evaluate and implement strategies to return capital to its shareholders, including the commencement of a Substantial Issuer Bid.

On Mar. 11, 2022, the company sold its 0.4% non-controlling interest in **Black Hills Surgical Physicians, LLC** for US$336,000.

Directors - Michael V. Gisser, chr., Seattle, Wash.; Jason P. Redman, interim pres. & interim CEO, Stouffville, Ont.; Yanick Blanchard, Outremont, Qué.; Erin S. Enright, Austin, Tex.; Dr. Reza Shahim, Little Rock, Ark.; Adina G. Storch, N.Y.

Other Exec. Officers - John F. Schario, COO; David N. T. Watson, CFO; James D. Rolfe, chief devel. officer

Capital Stock

	Authorized (shs.)	Outstanding (shs.)[1]
Common	unlimited	25,498,062

[1] At Mar. 31, 2023

Normal Course Issuer Bid - The company plans to make normal course purchases of up to 2,615,186 common shares representing 10% of the public float. The bid commenced on Dec. 1, 2022, and expires on Nov. 30, 2023.

Major Shareholder - Widely held at Mar. 27, 2023.

Price Range - DR/TSX

Year	Volume	High	Low	Close
2022	17,801,105	$12.25	$7.39	$8.04
2021	17,783,753	$10.17	$6.51	$9.35
2020	29,180,377	$7.62	$2.25	$7.04
2019	47,943,666	$17.64	$4.31	$4.80
2018	38,378,033	$16.24	$12.99	$15.04

Recent Close: $9.11

Capital Stock Changes - During 2022, 3,053,097 common shares were repurchased under a Substantial Issuer Bid and 1,827,200 were repurchased under a Normal Course Issuer Bid.

Dividends

DR com Ra $0.322 pa Q est. Jan. 15, 2022
Prev. Rate: $0.28 est. Apr. 15, 2020

Wholly Owned Subsidiaries

Medical Facilities America, Inc., Del.

- 100% int. in **Medical Facilities America Holdco 1 LLC**, Wilmington, Del.
  - 100% int. in **Medical Facilities America Holdco 2 LLC**, Wilmington, Del.
    - 100% int. in **Medical Facilities (USA) Holdings, Inc.**, Del.
      - 51% int. in **Arkansas Surgical Hospital, L.L.C**, Little Rock, Ark.
      - 54.2% int. in **Black Hills Surgical Hospital, LLP**, Rapid City, S.D.
      - 90% int. in **MFC Nueterra Holding Company, LLC**, United States.
      - 64% int. in **Oklahoma Spine Hospital, LLC**, Oklahoma City, Okla.
      - 51% int. in **Sioux Falls Surgical Hospital, LLP**, Sioux Falls, S.D.
      - 51% int. in **The Surgery Center of Newport Coast, LLC**, Newport Beach, Calif.

Note: The preceding list includes only the major related companies in which interests are held.

Financial Statistics

Periods ended:	12m Dec. 31/22[A]		12m Dec. 31/21[oA]
	US$000s	%Chg	US$000s
Operating revenue	**414,389**	**+1**	**411,732**
Cost of sales	143,925		130,027
Salaries & benefits	127,352		119,901
General & admin expense	70,861		57,385
Stock-based compensation	n.a.		292
Operating expense	**342,138**	**+11**	**307,605**
Operating income	**72,251**	**-31**	**104,127**
Deprec., depl. & amort.	20,763		26,769
Finance income	319		76
Finance costs, gross	13,412		14,847
Investment income	(574)		(125)
Write-downs/write-offs	(16,549)		nil
Pre-tax income	**17,503**	**-66**	**50,889**
Income taxes	5,208		4,396
Net income	**12,295**	**-74**	**46,493**
Net inc. for equity hldrs	**(4,405)**	**n.a.**	**15,500**
Net inc. for non-cont. int	**16,700**	**-46**	**30,993**
Cash & equivalent	34,926		61,044
Inventories	9,227		10,649
Accounts receivable	64,040		61,444
Current assets	119,329		148,894
Fixed assets, net	74,155		77,203
Right-of-use assets	50,564		55,550
Intangibles, net	133,723		150,432
Total assets	**377,791**	**-15**	**446,966**
Accts. pay. & accr. liabs	48,613		48,879
Current liabilities	86,819		87,996
Long-term debt, gross	85,593		79,570
Long-term debt, net	75,864		74,275
Long-term lease liabilities	47,178		51,843
Shareholders' equity	79,134		127,552
Non-controlling interest	35,558		45,598
Cash from oper. activs	**57,013**	**-25**	**75,642**
Cash from fin. activs	(77,353)		(72,058)
Cash from invest. activs	(5,775)		(8,688)
Net cash position	**34,926**	**-43**	**61,044**
Capital expenditures	(6,718)		(8,421)
	US$		US$
Earnings per share*	(0.15)		0.50
Cash flow per share*	1.94		2.43
Cash divd. per share*	$0.32		$0.29
	shs		shs
No. of shs. o/s*	25,915,962		30,796,259
Avg. no. of shs. o/s*	29,366,985		31,126,780
	%		%
Net profit margin	2.97		11.29
Return on equity	(4.13)		12.15
Return on assets	5.27		13.29
Foreign sales percent	100		100
No. of employees (FTEs)	1,593		1,589

* Common

[o] Restated

[A] Reported in accordance with IFRS

Latest Results

Periods ended:	3m Mar. 31/23[A]		3m Mar. 31/22[A]
	US$000s	%Chg	US$000s
Operating revenue	109,250	+6	102,598
Net income	9,666	n.a.	(1,115)
Net inc. for equity hldrs	4,411	n.a.	(7,861)
Net inc. for non-cont. int	5,255		6,746
	US$		US$
Earnings per share*	0.17		(0.26)

* Common

[A] Reported in accordance with IFRS

Historical Summary
(as originally stated)

Fiscal Year	Oper. Rev. US$000s	Net Inc. Bef. Disc. US$000s	EPS* US$
2022[A]	414,389	12,295	(0.15)
2021[A]	411,732	46,493	0.50
2020[A]	389,862	37,422	0.31
2019[A]	398,103	59,677	1.21
2018[A]	431,602	51,549	0.68

* Common

[A] Reported in accordance with IFRS

M.59 Medicenna Therapeutics Corp.

Symbol - MDNA **Exchange** - TSX **CUSIP** - 58490H

Head Office - 700-2 Bloor St W, Toronto, ON, M4W 3E2 **Telephone** - (416) 648-5555 **Fax** - (416) 572-7501

Website - www.medicenna.com

Email - ddavan@medicenna.com

Investor Relations - Delphine Davan (514) 968-1046

Auditors - PricewaterhouseCoopers LLP C.A., Oakville, Ont.
Lawyers - McCarthy Tétrault LLP, Québec, Qué.
Transfer Agents - TSX Trust Company, Calgary, Alta.
Employees - 16 at Mar. 31, 2023
Profile - (Alta. 2015) Develops immunotherapies based on engineered interleukins (Superkines, Empowered Superkines and BiSKITs™), which are immune-system modulators, for the treatment of cancer, inflammation and immune-mediated diseases.

Superkines are novel, highly selective versions of three major interleukin families, IL-2, IL-4 and IL-13, that have been engineered in order to precisely activate or inhibit relevant signalling pathways or immune cells. Superkines can be developed either on their own as short or long-acting therapeutics or fused with cell-killing proteins to expand their functionality and transform them into Empowered Superkines that precisely deliver potent toxins to cancer cells without harming adjacent healthy cells. Superkines can also be fused with various proteins, antibodies and other Superkines in order to incorporate two synergistic therapeutic activities into one molecule referred to as Bi-Functional SuperKine ImmunoTherapies (BiSKITs).

The company's lead clinical product is Bizaxofusp (formerly MDNA55), an Empowered Superkine developed for the treatment of recurrent glioblastoma (rGBM), the most common and uniformly fatal form of brain cancer. MDNA55 has received Orphan Drug (FDA, EMA) and Fast Track (FDA) designations. Phase IIb clinical trial has been completed, with Phase III clinical trial being pursued. Second lead candidate is MDNA11, a long-acting IL-2 Superkine that activates cancer-killing immune cells instead of immuno-suppressive cells. It is being developed as a therapeutic for solid tumours under phase I/II clinical study.

Pre-clinical Superkine candidates include IL-2 antagonists (MDNA109 and MDNA209), dual IL-4/IL-13 antagonists (MDNA413) and IL-13 Superkine (MDNA132 and MDNA213). Under the BiSKITs platform, the company is evaluating MDNA19-MDNA413 to target immunologically cold tumours and MDNA223, an IL-2 Superkine fused to a checkpoint inhibitor to activate cancer killing immune cells via IL-2 receptor while simultaneously preventing their exhaustion through the validated method of blocking PD-1 signaling.

In March 2022, wholly owned **Medicenna Therapeutics UK Limited** was dissolved.

Predecessor Detail - Name changed from A2 Acquisition Corp., Mar. 3, 2017, following reverse takeover acquisition of Medicenna Therapeutics Inc.; basis 1 new for 14 old shs.

Directors - Dr. Fahar Merchant, chr., pres. & CEO, Toronto, Ont.; Rosemina Merchant, chief devel. officer, Toronto, Ont.; Albert G. Beraldo†, Toronto, Ont.; Karen Dawes, Palm Beach Gardens, Fla.; Dr. John (Jack) Geltosky, Portland, Ore.; Dr. Chandrakant J. (Chandra) Panchal, Pierrefonds, Qué.; Dr. John H. Sampson, N.C.

Other Exec. Officers - Brent Meadows, chief bus. officer; Delphine Davan, v-p, IR & corp. commun.; Dr. Evelyn Pau, v-p, external collaborations; Eamonn Peters, v-p, fin.; Dr. Minh To, v-p, oncology research; Dr. Martin Bexon, acting CMO

† Lead director

Capital Stock

	Authorized (shs.)	Outstanding (shs.)[1]
Preferred	unlimited	nil
Common	unlimited	69,637,469

[1] At Mar. 31, 2023

Major Shareholder - Dr. Fahar Merchant held 14.34% interest and Rosemina Merchant held 14.21% interest at Aug. 2, 2022.

Price Range - MDNA/TSX

Year	Volume	High	Low	Close
2022	11,125,591	$2.49	$0.54	$0.64
2021	20,071,780	$6.15	$1.90	$2.10
2020	23,669,733	$7.25	$2.15	$5.95
2019	13,615,091	$3.87	$0.64	$3.40
2018	2,274,202	$3.05	$0.68	$0.70

Recent Close: $0.51

Capital Stock Changes - In August 2022, public offering of 13,333,334 units (1 common share & ½ warrant) at US$1.50 per unit was completed. Also during fiscal 2023, 656,656 common shares were issued under an at-the-market program.

During fiscal 2022, common shares were issued as follows: 1,748,600 under an at-the-market program, 266,290 on exercise of warrants and 84,880 on exercise of options.

Wholly Owned Subsidiaries

Medicenna Therapeutics Inc., Toronto, Ont.
- 100% int. in **Medicenna Australia Pty Ltd.**, Adelaide, S.A., Australia.
- 100% int. in **Medicenna Biopharma Inc.**, Del.
- 100% int. in **Medicenna Biopharma Inc.**, B.C.

Financial Statistics

Periods ended:	12m Mar. 31/23[A]		12m Mar. 31/22[A]
	$000s	%Chg	$000s
Salaries & benefits	3,209		3,722
Research & devel. expense	6,533		11,490
General & admin expense	5,185		5,808
Stock-based compensation	1,371		1,416
Operating expense	**16,298**	**-27**	**22,436**
Operating income	**(16,298)**	**n.a.**	**(22,436)**
Deprec., depl. & amort.	5		37
Finance income	914		69
Pre-tax income	**(10,048)**	**n.a.**	**(22,577)**
Net income	**(10,048)**	**n.a.**	**(22,577)**
Cash & equivalent	33,596		20,535
Accounts receivable	855		1,308
Current assets	36,385		23,391
Intangibles, net	61		65
Total assets	**36,446**	**+55**	**23,456**
Accts. pay. & accr. liabs	3,800		2,621
Current liabilities	3,800		2,621
Shareholders' equity	29,486		20,835
Cash from oper. activs	**(12,657)**	**n.a.**	**(23,584)**
Cash from fin. activs	24,760		3,878
Cash from invest. activs	nil		10,050
Net cash position	**33,596**	**+64**	**20,535**
	$		$
Earnings per share*	(0.16)		(0.42)
Cash flow per share*	(0.20)		(0.43)
	shs		shs
No. of shs. o/s*	69,637,469		55,647,479
Avg. no. of shs. o/s*	64,736,493		54,286,671
	%		%
Net profit margin	n.a.		n.a.
Return on equity	(39.94)		(76.56)
Return on assets	(33.55)		(68.72)
No. of employees (FTEs)	16		18

* Common
[A] Reported in accordance with IFRS

Historical Summary
(as originally stated)

Fiscal Year	Oper. Rev.	Net Inc. Bef. Disc.	EPS*
	$000s	$000s	$
2023[A]	nil	(10,048)	(0.16)
2022[A]	nil	(22,577)	(0.42)
2021[A]	nil	(17,289)	(0.35)
2020[A]	nil	(8,277)	(0.26)
2019[A]	nil	(4,708)	(0.18)

* Common
[A] Reported in accordance with IFRS

M.60 Medicine Man Technologies, Inc.

Symbol - SHWZ **Exchange -** NEO **CUSIP -** 58468U
Head Office - 4880 Havana St, Suite 201, Denver, CO, United States, 80239 **Telephone -** (303) 371-0387 **Fax -** (303) 371-0598
Website - ir.schwazze.com
Email - dan@schwazze.com
Investor Relations - Dan Pabon (303) 371-0387
Auditors - BF Borgers CPA PC C.P.A., Lakewood, Colo.
Transfer Agents - Globex Transfer, LLC, Deltona, Fla.
Employees - 389 at Mar. 25, 2022
Profile - (Nev. 2014) Grows, cultivates, markets and distributes medical and recreational cannabis and cannabis products in Colorado and New Mexico.

Operations are organized into three segments: Retail; Wholesale; and Other.

Retail - At Jan. 1, 2023, owned and operated 41 retail cannabis dispensaries, consisting of 25 locations in Colorado primarily under the Star Buds and Emerald Fields banners and 16 locations in New Mexico under the R. Greenleaf banner. These dispensaries sell various cannabis products including loose flower, concentrates, edibles, pre-rolls, topicals and other associated cannabis products.

Wholesale - Consists of manufacturing, cultivation and wholesale businesses through seven cultivation facilities in Colorado and New Mexico, totaling 111,000 sq. ft. of indoor space, 3 acres of outdoor grow and 60,000 sq. ft. of hoop houses; and two extraction and manufacturing facilities in Pueblo, Colo. (7,000 sq. ft.) and Albuquerque, N.M. (6,000 sq. ft.). The facilities produce products under the brands Purplebee's, Autograph, Grow Forth Gardens, EDW, Level 10 and N-Fuzed.

Other - Manufactures and distributes through wholesale and retail channels plant nutrients as well as the Three A Light™ grow guide for the cannabis industry; operates a retail location in Aurora, Colo., under the The Big Tomato banner, which supplies hydroponics and indoor gardening supplies in the metro Denver area, including indoor gardening products, grow boxes, grow lights, hydroponic systems, ballasts, bulbs, nutrients and additives; and offers private consulting services, seminars on various cannabis topics, facility design and management services, and new state licensing application support.

In December 2022, the company acquired two cannabis dispensaries in Denver and Aurora, Colo., from **Lightshade Labs LLC** for US$2,750,000.

In July 2022, the company acquired a non-controlling interest in Colorado-based **Mission Holdings US, Inc.**, which offers various products and brands including cannabis-infused gummies and flower for medical and recreational sale in Colorado and California. Terms were not disclosed.

In May 2022, the company acquired substantially all of the assets of **Urban Health & Wellness, Inc.** (dba Urban Dispensary), which operates a cannabis dispensary as well as a 7,200-sq.-ft. indoor cannabis cultivation facility in Denver, Colo., for US$3,200,000, consisting of US$1,317,5000 cash and issuance of 1,670,230 common shares, of which 219,847 common shares were held back.

Directors - Justin Dye, chr.; Nirup Krishnamurthy, CEO; Jonathan Berger†; Jeffery A. (Jeff) Cozad; Jeff Garwood; Dr. Paul J. Montalbano; Pratap Mukharji; Marc Rubin; Bradley Stewart

Other Exec. Officers - Forrest Hoffmaster, CFO; Dan Pabon, chief govt. affairs officer, gen. counsel & corp. sec.; David (Dave) Kaufman, exec. v-p, integrated supply chain; Todd Williams, exec. v-p, M&A & real estate; Laura Beane, v-p, integration & project mgt. office; Dan Bonach, v-p, HR; Jeremy Bullock, v-p, comml. sales; Ed Eissenstat, v-p, IT & CIO; Sachin Kolgaonkar, v-p, SRO & data analytics; Eric McQueen, v-p, finl. planning & analysis; Julie Suntrup, v-p, corp. mktg. & brands; Ken Diehl, pres., New Mexico div.; Collin Lodge, pres., Colorado div.; Jim Parco, pres., Schwazze Biosciences; Steve Pear, pres., wholesale div.

† Lead director

Capital Stock

	Authorized (shs.)	Outstanding (shs.)[1]	Par
Preferred	10,000,000		US$0.001
Series A	110,000	86,050	
Common	250,000,000	54,741,506[2]	US$0.001

[1] At Oct. 31, 2022
[2] Net of 886,459 common shares held in treasury.

Series A Preferred - Entitled to cumulative annual dividends of 8%. Convertible, at the holder's option, into common shares by dividing the preference amount (equal to an initial US$1,000 and subject to increase) by US$1.20 per share under certain circumstances. Entitled to cast the number of votes equal to the number of whole common shares into which the series A preferred shares held would convert into as of the record date.

Common - One vote per share.

Major Shareholder - Justin Dye held 26.79% interest, Jeffery A. (Jeff) Cozad held 18.08% interest and Marc Rubin held 18% interest at Oct. 5, 2022.

Price Range - SHWZ/NEO

Year	Volume	High	Low	Close
2022	20,100	$2.85	$1.21	$1.97

Recent Close: $0.90

Capital Stock Changes - On Feb. 9, 2022, 7,116,564 common shares were issued pursuant to the acquisition of MCG, LLC. On May 31, 2022, 1,670,230 common shares were issued pursuant to the acquisition of Urban Health & Wellness, Inc.

Wholly Owned Subsidiaries

Double Brow, LLC, Colo.
Elemental Kitchen and Laboratories, LLC, N.M.
Emerald Fields Merger Sub, LLC, Colo.
Flower Mountain Holdings, LLC, Colo.
MIH Manager, LLC, Colo.
Medicine Man Consulting Inc., Colo.
Mesa Organics II Ltd., Colo.
Mesa Organics III Ltd., Colo.
Mesa Organics IV Ltd., Colo.
Mission Holding, LLC, Colo.
Nuevo Elemental Holding, LLC, N.M.
Nuevo Holdings LLC, N.M.
PBS HoldCo LLC, Colo.
SBUD LLC, Colo.
SCG Holding, LLC, Colo.
Schwazze Biosciences, LLC, Colo.
Schwazze Colorado LLC, Colo.
Schwazze IP Holdco, LLC, Colo.
Schwazze New Mexico, LLC, N.M.
Two J's LLC, Colo. dba The Big Tomato.

Financial Statistics

Periods ended:	12m Dec. 31/21^A		12m Dec. 31/20^A
	US$000s	%Chg	US$000s
Operating revenue	**108,420**	**+352**	**24,001**
Cost of goods sold	59,067		17,226
Salaries & benefits	11,943		8,378
General & admin expense	13,386		12,592
Stock-based compensation	5,038		8,231
Operating expense	**89,434**	**+93**	**46,427**
Operating income	**18,986**	**n.a.**	**(22,426)**
Deprec., depl. & amort.	8,577		477
Finance costs, net	7,014		41
Pre-tax income	**18,915**	**n.a.**	**(20,316)**
Income taxes	4,396		(899)
Net income	**14,519**	**n.a.**	**(19,417)**
Cash & equivalent	106,400		1,231
Inventories	11,122		2,619
Accounts receivable	3,867		1,351
Current assets	123,912		5,997
Long-term investments	494		277
Fixed assets, net	10,253		2,585
Right-of-use assets	8,512		2,579
Intangibles, net	140,899		56,129
Total assets	**285,031**	**+303**	**70,683**
Bank indebtedness	134		5,000
Accts. pay. & accr. liabs.	2,586		3,557
Current liabilities	45,263		12,360
Long-term debt, gross	97,482		13,902
Long-term debt, net	97,482		13,902
Long-term lease liabilities	8,715		2,646
Shareholders' equity	133,570		41,775
Cash from oper. activs.	**57,334**	**n.a.**	**(9,800)**
Cash from fin. activs.	128,998		31,902
Cash from invest. activs.	(81,164)		(33,219)
Net cash position	**106,400**	**n.m.**	**1,231**
Capital expenditures	(5,638)		(768)
	US$		US$
Earnings per share*	0.17		(0.47)
Cash flow per share*	1.32		(0.24)
	shs		shs
No. of shs. o/s*	44,967,270		42,169,041
Avg. no. of shs. o/s*	43,339,092		41,217,026
	%		%
Net profit margin	13.39		(80.90)
Return on equity	8.18		(56.99)
Return on assets	8.16		(37.74)
Foreign sales percent	100		100

* Common
^A Reported in accordance with U.S. GAAP

Latest Results

Periods ended:	9m Sept. 30/22^A		9m Sept. 30/21^A
	US$000s	%Chg	US$000s
Operating revenue	119,232	+46	81,904
Net income	8,872	+425	1,689
	US$		US$
Earnings per share*	0.07		0.04

* Common
^A Reported in accordance with U.S. GAAP

Historical Summary
(as originally stated)

Fiscal Year	Oper. Rev.	Net Inc. Bef. Disc.	EPS*
	US$000s	US$000s	US$
2021^A	108,420	14,519	0.17
2020^A	24,001	(19,417)	(0.47)
2019^A	12,401	(16,976)	(0.50)

* Common
^A Reported in accordance with U.S. GAAP

M.61 Medicure Inc.

Symbol - MPH **Exchange** - TSX-VEN **CUSIP** - 58469E
Head Office - 2-1250 Waverley St, Winnipeg, MB, R3T 6C6 **Telephone** - (204) 487-7412 **Toll-free** - (888) 435-2220 **Fax** - (204) 488-9823
Website - www.medicure.com
Email - ir@medicure.com
Investor Relations - Dr. Albert D. Friesen (888) 435-2220 ext. 228
Auditors - Ernst & Young LLP C.A., Winnipeg, Man.
Bankers - The Toronto-Dominion Bank
Lawyers - McMillan LLP, Toronto, Ont.; MLT Aikins LLP, Winnipeg, Man.
Transfer Agents - Computershare Trust Company of Canada Inc., Toronto, Ont.
Employees - 48 at Dec. 31, 2022
Profile - (Can. 2000; orig. Alta., 1999 amalg.) Researches, clinically develops and commercializes human therapeutics, with a focus on cardiovascular products.

Primary products include AGGRASTAT® (tirofiban hydrochloride), an injectable glycoprotein (GP) IIb/IIIa inhibitor for the treatment of non-ST elevation acute coronary syndrome including unstable angina, which is characterized by chest pain when one is at rest, and non-Q-wave myocardial infarction; ZYPITAMAG™ (pitavastatin magnesium), an oral drug for the treatment of primary hyperlipidemia or mixed dyslipidemia; and Sodium Nitroprusside Injection (SNP), which is used for the immediate reduction of blood pressure for adults and paediatric patients in hypersensitive crisis. The products are distributed in the U.S. and its territories by wholly owned **Medicure Pharma, Inc.** and **Marley Drug, Inc.**, which operates an e-commerce and mail order pharmaceutical business.

The company's research and development program, which is conducted by wholly owned **Medicure International, Inc.**, is focused on developing and implementing a new regulatory, brand and life cycle management strategy for AGGRASTAT® and developing new cardiovascular generic and reformulation products. Products under development include two cardiovascular generic drugs; and TARDOXAL™ and pyridoxal 5 phosphate (P5P/MC-1), both treatment for tardive dyskinesia, a movement disorder resulting from long-term treatment with antipsychotic drugs, as well as other neurological disorders. The company is focused on development of P5P for the treatment of seizures associated with pyridox(am)ine 5'-phosphate oxidase deficiency and the advancement of TARDOXAL™ has been put on hold.

In October 2022, wholly owned **Apigen Investments Limited** was wound up.

Predecessor Detail - Formed from Lariat Capital Inc. in Alberta, Dec. 22, 1999, on Qualifying Transaction amalgamation with Medicure Inc. constituting a reverse takeover by Medicure.

Directors - Dr. Albert D. Friesen, chr. & CEO, Winnipeg, Man.; Brent Fawkes, Winnipeg, Man.; James Kinley, Winnipeg, Man.; Dr. Arnold Naimark, Winnipeg, Man.; Peter Quick, Mill Neck, N.Y.

Other Exec. Officers - Dr. Neil Owens, pres. & COO; Haaris Uddin, CFO & corp. sec.; Dr. Reuben Saba, v-p, clinical & medical affairs

Capital Stock

	Authorized (shs.)	Outstanding (shs.)[1]
Preferred	unlimited	nil
Common	unlimited	10,436,313

[1] At May 26, 2023

Major Shareholder - Dr. Albert D. Friesen held 25.98% interest and MM Asset Management Inc. held 23.51% interest at Apr. 10, 2023.

Price Range - MPH/TSX-VEN

Year	Volume	High	Low	Close
2022	831,403	$1.50	$0.80	$1.01
2021	1,271,789	$2.01	$0.91	$0.92
2020	3,046,907	$4.40	$0.70	$1.19
2019	1,926,128	$6.90	$3.00	$4.40
2018	3,665,065	$7.97	$5.56	$6.15

Recent Close: $1.30

Capital Stock Changes - There were no changes to capital stock during 2021 or 2022.

Wholly Owned Subsidiaries

Medicure International, Inc., St. James, Barbados.
Medicure Pharma Europe Limited, Dublin, Ireland.
Medicure Pharma, Inc., Somerset, N.J.
- 100% int. in **Marley Drug, Inc.**, Winston-Salem, N.C.

Medicure U.S.A. Inc., Wilmington, Del.

Note: The preceding list includes only the major related companies in which interests are held.

Financial Statistics

Periods ended:	12m Dec. 31/22^A		12m Dec. 31/21^A
	$000s	%Chg	$000s
Operating revenue	**23,065**	**+6**	**21,744**
Cost of goods sold	6,416		7,378
Salaries & benefits	4,969		4,513
Research & devel. expense	2,278		1,547
General & admin expense	6,105		7,132
Stock-based compensation	47		135
Operating expense	**19,815**	**-4**	**20,705**
Operating income	**3,250**	**+213**	**1,039**
Deprec., depl. & amort.	2,057		3,132
Finance income	10		78
Finance costs, gross	3		67
Pre-tax income	**1,385**	**n.a.**	**(759)**
Income taxes	20		(32)
Net income	**1,365**	**n.a.**	**(727)**
Cash & equivalent	4,857		3,694
Inventories	3,221		3,329
Accounts receivable	5,635		4,659
Current assets	14,847		12,554
Fixed assets, net	1,187		1,611
Intangibles, net	13,801		14,186
Total assets	**29,898**	**+5**	**28,408**
Accts. pay. & accr. liabs.	7,128		6,668
Current liabilities	8,390		8,512
Long-term lease liabilities	503		789
Shareholders' equity	21,005		18,411
Cash from oper. activs.	**1,828**	**-54**	**3,989**
Cash from fin. activs.	(355)		(316)
Cash from invest. activs.	(310)		(2,694)
Net cash position	**4,857**	**+31**	**3,694**
Capital expenditures	(14)		(377)
	$		$
Earnings per share*	0.13		(0.07)
Cash flow per share*	0.18		0.39
	shs		shs
No. of shs. o/s*	10,251,313		10,251,313
Avg. no. of shs. o/s*	10,251,313		10,251,313
	%		%
Net profit margin	5.92		(3.34)
Return on equity	6.93		(3.87)
Return on assets	4.69		(2.12)
Foreign sales percent	100		100
No. of employees (FTEs)	48		45

* Common
^A Reported in accordance with IFRS

Latest Results

Periods ended:	3m Mar. 31/23^A		3m Mar. 31/22^A
	$000s	%Chg	$000s
Operating revenue	5,628	-2	5,716
Net income	290	-40	482
	$		$
Earnings per share*	0.03		0.05

* Common
^A Reported in accordance with IFRS

Historical Summary
(as originally stated)

Fiscal Year	Oper. Rev.	Net Inc. Bef. Disc.	EPS*
	$000s	$000s	$
2022^A	23,065	1,365	0.13
2021^A	21,744	(727)	(0.07)
2020^A	11,610	(6,845)	(0.64)
2019^A	20,173	(19,786)	(1.32)
2018^A	29,109	3,926	0.25

* Common
^A Reported in accordance with IFRS

M.62 MediPharm Labs Corp.

Symbol - LABS **Exchange** - TSX **CUSIP** - 58504D
Head Office - 151 John St, Barrie, ON, L4N 2L1 **Telephone** - (705) 719-7425 **Toll-free** - (888) 719-7425
Website - www.medipharmlabs.com
Email - kstrachan@medipahrmlabs.com
Investor Relations - Keith Strachan (416) 913-7425 ext. 1525
Auditors - MNP LLP C.A.
Transfer Agents - TSX Trust Company, Toronto, Ont.
Employees - 130 at Dec. 31, 2022
Profile - (Ont. 2017) Formulates, develops, processes, packages and distributes cannabis concentrates, active pharmaceutical ingredients (API) and advanced derivative products to Canadian and international markets. Produces and sells medical and recreational cannabis and cannabis products for the Canadian and international markets, with a focus on Germany and Australia, and operates medical cannabis clinics in Canada.

Specializes in the development and manufacture of cannabis concentrates, active pharmaceutical ingredients (API) and formulated products for pharmaceutical, consumer packaged goods (CPG), licensed producers and direct to consumer brands. Solutions provided include bulk wholesale of concentrate, distillate or isolate-based products, product development and formulation, white label manufacturing and end-to-end contract manufacturing as well as cannabis flower sourcing, processing and distribution. The company is able to provide tailored product formats and solutions in various product categories, including formulated cannabis oil bottles, topicals, gels disposable vaporizer pens, vaporizer cartridges, soft chews, dried flower and pre-roll products, for the medical, wellness and adult-use segments. Finished formulated products are sold both under the MediPharm family of brands (white label) and customer brands through private label and contract manufacturing arrangements. Dried flower and pre-roll products are marketed under the Shelter Cannabis brand. Operates a 70,000-sq.-ft. manufacturing facility in Barrie, Ont., which is licensed to manufacture and sell flower alternative format medical products.

Through VIVO division produces and sells cannabis and cannabis-derived products for the medical and recreational markets in Canada and international jurisdictions. Ethanol extraction, product formulation and European union good manufacturing practices (EU-GMP) related processes include the 29,000-sq.-ft. indoor Vanluven facility and 86,000-sq.-ft. seasonal airhouse Kimmetts facility, both in Napanee, Ont., and a 47,000-sq.-ft. facility in Hope, B.C. for indoor cannabis cultivation, packaging and solventless extraction and concentrate production. In Canada, medical cannabis is sold directly to patients through the cannafarms.ca online platform, while adult-use cannabis is sold through partnerships with third party cannabis retailers and supply agreements with provincial agents. Internationally, the company imports, supplies and distributes medical cannabis in Germany and Australia. Products are offered under the Canna Farms™, Beacon Medical™, Fireside™ and Lumina™ brands.

VIVO operates three medical cannabis clinics under the Harvest Medicine™ name in Calgary and St. Albert, Alta., and Cole Harbour, N.S. Also provides services to patients across Canada through the telemedicine platform, HMED Connect.

In March 2022, the company acquired the intellectual property portfolio of Shelter Cannabis, including cannabis dried flower and pre-roll brands and products (Wildlife and Craft), trademarks, marketing assets and provincial listings, in exchange for future cash consideration based on sales. The acquisition expanded the company's portfolio to include dried flower and pre-rolls.

Recent Merger and Acquisition Activity

Status: completed **Revised:** Apr. 3, 2023

UPDATE: The transaction was completed. PREVIOUS: MediPharm Labs Corp. agreed to acquire VIVO Cannabis Inc. on the basis of between 0.211 and 0.4267 common shares of MediPharm for each VIVO common share held, subject to adjustment. The exchange ratio is based on interim working capital of VIVO at closing, taking in to account any funds advanced by MediPharm to VIVO up to a maximum of $3,750,000, by way of a promissory note. The transaction was expected to close during the first half of 2023. Mar. 21, 2023 -VIVO shareholders approved the transaction.

Status: completed **Revised:** Oct. 6, 2022

UPDATE: The transaction was completed. PREVIOUS: MediPharm Labs Corp. agreed to sell wholly owned MediPharm Labs Australia Pty Ltd., a manufacturer and supplier of medical cannabis products for the Australian and international markets, to OneLife Botanicals Pty Ltd. for a minimum value of A$6,900,000 (Cdn$6,200,000). The transaction included MediPharm's 10,000-sq.-ft. facility in Wonthaggi, Australia, specialized licensing, operational knowledge, and Australian and New Zealand customers served from that facility. All international contracts outside of Australia and New Zealand would remain with MediPharm.

Predecessor Detail - Name changed from POCML 4 Inc., Oct. 4, 2018, following Qualifying Transaction reverse takeover acquistion of MediPharm Labs Inc. completed by way of an amalgamation of MediPharm Labs and a wholly owned subsidiary of POCML 4; basis 1 new for 2 old shs.

Directors - Chris Taves, chr., Mississauga, Ont.; David A. Pidduck, CEO, Ont.; Dr. Michael (Mike) Bumby, Toronto, Ont.; Chris Halyk, Oakville, Ont.; Miriam McDonald, Sudbury, Ont.; Shelley Potts, Oro-Medonte, Ont.

Other Exec. Officers - Keith Strachan, pres.; Greg Hunter, CFO; Geoff Marr, exec. v-p & gen. counsel

Capital Stock

	Authorized (shs.)	Outstanding (shs.)[1]
Common	unlimited	397,474,222

[1] At Aug. 13, 2023

Major Shareholder - Widely held at May 3, 2023.

Price Range - LABS/TSX

Year	Volume	High	Low	Close
2022	121,304,196	$0.23	$0.06	$0.07
2021	301,090,247	$1.00	$0.17	$0.19
2020	194,601,273	$4.44	$0.49	$0.53
2019	243,368,344	$7.39	$1.60	$3.86
2018	19,863,043	$3.55	$0.53	$1.74

Recent Close: $0.08

Capital Stock Changes - In April 2023, 107,930,964 common shares were issued pursuant to the acquisition of VIVO Cannabis Inc.

During 2022, 8,627,715 common shares were issued on vesting of restricted share units.

Wholly Owned Subsidiaries

MediPharm Labs Inc., Barrie, Ont.
- 100% int. in **MPL International Holdings Inc.**, Canada. Inactive.
- 100% int. in **MPL Manufacturing Inc.**, Ont. Inactive.
- 100% int. in **MPL Property Holdings Inc.**, Ont.
- 100% int. in **2612785 Ontario Inc.**, Ont. Inactive.

VIVO Cannabis Inc., Napanee, Ont.
- 100% int. in **2649924 Ontario Inc.**, Ont.
  - 100% int. in **ABcann Medicinals Inc.**, Napanee, Ont.
  - 100% int. in **Beacon Medical Australia Pty. Ltd.**, Australia.
  - 100% int. in **Beacon Medical Germany GmbH**, Germany.
  - 100% int. in **Canna Farms Limited**, Hope, B.C.
  - 100% int. in **Green Earth Realty Inc.**, Ont.
  - 100% int. in **Harvest Medicine Inc.**, Calgary, Alta.
  - 100% int. in **Patients' Choice Botanicals Inc.**, Napanee, Ont.
  - 100% int. in **Universal Botanicals Inc.**, Ont.

Financial Statistics

Periods ended:	12m Dec. 31/22[A]		12m Dec. 31/21[A]
	$000s	%Chg	$000s
Operating revenue	**22,117**	**+2**	**21,711**
Cost of sales	21,997		32,738
Research & devel. expense	1,002		1,355
General & admin expense	21,885		20,631
Stock-based compensation	2,872		2,402
Operating expense	**47,756**	**-16**	**57,126**
Operating income	**(25,639)**	**n.a.**	**(35,415)**
Deprec., depl. & amort.	2,872		5,633
Finance income	479		225
Finance costs, gross	31		10,506
Write-downs/write-offs	(134)		(11,036)
Pre-tax income	**(29,989)**	**n.a.**	**(54,688)**
Income taxes	(6)		113
Net income	**(29,983)**	**n.a.**	**(54,801)**
Cash & equivalent	24,145		34,110
Inventories	7,776		10,976
Accounts receivable	12,876		16,918
Current assets	47,345		65,547
Fixed assets, net	18,111		25,894
Intangibles, net	39		44
Total assets	**65,495**	**-29**	**92,361**
Accts. pay. & accr. liabs	7,121		6,213
Current liabilities	9,456		8,877
Long-term debt, gross	632		216
Long-term debt, net	34		103
Shareholders' equity	56,005		83,146
Cash from oper. activs	**(16,069)**	**n.a.**	**(13,213)**
Cash from fin. activs	796		27,804
Cash from invest. activs	5,158		35
Net cash position	**24,145**	**-29**	**34,110**
Capital expenditures	(863)		(783)
Capital disposals	6,014		818
	$		$
Earnings per share*	(0.11)		(0.22)
Cash flow per share*	(0.06)		(0.05)
	shs		shs
No. of shs. o/s*	282,164,905		273,537,190
Avg. no. of shs. o/s*	276,861,109		249,906,804
	%		%
Net profit margin	(135.57)		(252.41)
Return on equity	(43.09)		(67.84)
Return on assets	(37.95)		(42.05)
Foreign sales percent	34		44
No. of employees (FTEs)	130		190

* Common

[A] Reported in accordance with IFRS

Historical Summary
(as originally stated)

Fiscal Year	Oper. Rev.	Net Inc. Bef. Disc.	EPS*
	$000s	$000s	$
2022[A]	22,117	(29,983)	(0.11)
2021[A]	21,711	(54,801)	(0.22)
2020[A]	36,012	(67,110)	(0.48)
2019[A]	129,252	1,131	0.01
2018[A1]	10,198	(8,466)	(0.12)

* Common

[A] Reported in accordance with IFRS

[1] Results reflect the Oct. 1, 2018, Qualifying Transaction reverse takeover acquisition of MediPharm Labs Inc.

M.63 Medivolve Inc.

Symbol - MEDV **Exchange** - NEO **CUSIP** - 58503M

Head Office - 198 Davenport Rd, Toronto, ON, M5R 1J2 **Telephone** - (416) 861-5888 **Fax** - (416) 861-8165

Email - info@medivolve.ca

Investor Relations - David Preiner (612) 876-1621

Auditors - McGovern Hurley LLP C.A., Toronto, Ont.

Lawyers - Maitland & Company, Vancouver, B.C.

Transfer Agents - TSX Trust Company, Vancouver, B.C.

Employees - 40 at Mar. 31, 2023

Profile - (Can. 2009; orig. B.C., 2005) Developing a telehealth platform, which provides virtual consultation, diagnosis and treatment services in partnership with qualified health practitioners. In addition, owns an electronic health records app, and owns and operates a pharmacy in California.

The telehealth platform is designed to enable physicians to analyze numerous biomarkers, symptoms, conditions, risk factors and demographics to help them choose the most effective medication for each patient. The telehealth services would be provided through virtual and in-person meetings, whereby patients will have virtual meetings with medical professionals through a web-based and/or mobile application to be followed by in-person visits at the company's testing sites to collect samples. In addition, the company is also exploring opportunities in remote patient monitoring by leveraging the telehealth platform and offering remote patient monitoring devices to patients to use at home. These devices will enable patients to check important health metrics such as blood sugar, blood pressure and weight.

Wholly owned **Collection Sites, LLC** owns a cloud-based electronic health records app, which streamlines clinical operations and backend administration such as electronic health records management, connectivity and coordinated-care solutions, revenue cycle management, training and electronic claims administration services.

Wholly owned **Medivolve Pharmacy Inc.** operates a retail pharmacy in San Juan Capistrano, Calif., which provides mail-order services related to COVID-19, antibiotics, dermatology, family medicine, immunology, neurology, pain management, paediatrics, preventive medicine and psychiatry.

Wholly owned **Medivolve Management Services, LLC**, a management services organization, will coordinate physician/patient interactions, provide medical billing and practice management services, and facilitate access to diagnostic testing and pharmacy services.

In June 2023, a name change to **Medidoc Inc.** was approved.

In May 2023, the company closed its remaining mobile COVID-19 testing locations in order to focus its resources on the telehealth platform rollout.

Subsequent to Dec. 31, 2022, the company closed 11 COVID-19 testing locations in California and Florida.

During 2022, the company closed six COVID-19 testing locations located outside of California.

Predecessor Detail - Name changed from QuestCap Inc., Dec. 29, 2020.

Directors - Wen Ye, exec. chr., Ont.; Daniyal Baizak, Ont.; Dr. Beverly Richardson, B.C.

Other Exec. Officers - David Preiner, CEO; Indivar Pathak, COO, collection sites; Peter Michel, CFO; Neil Said, gen. counsel; Aaron Atin, corp. sec.

Capital Stock

	Authorized (shs.)	Outstanding (shs.)[1]
Preferred	unlimited	nil
Common	unlimited	27,019,248

[1] At May 19, 2023

Major Shareholder - Widely held at May 19, 2023.

Price Range - MEDV/NEO

Year	Volume	High	Low	Close
2022	3,575,700	$1.50	$0.12	$0.14
2021	4,270,582	$10.80	$0.60	$1.20
2020	13,333,193	$15.00	$0.75	$6.00
2019	625,648	$2.63	$0.68	$2.18
2018	791,085	$3.15	$1.43	$2.33

Consolidation: 1-for-15 cons. in Dec. 2022

Recent Close: $0.05

Capital Stock Changes - In January 2023, private placement of up to 26,666,667 common shares was announced at 15¢ per share.

On Dec. 8, 2022, common shares were consolidated on a 1-for-15 basis. Also during 2022, 3,333 post-consolidated common shares were issued on exercise of warrants.

Wholly Owned Subsidiaries

Collection Sites, LLC, Las Vegas, Nev.
Medivolve Management Services, LLC, Puerto Rico.
Medivolve Pharmacy Inc., Calif. dba Marbella Pharmacy
Noble Bioscience Corp., Ont.
Optimum Care Pharmacy Inc., Calif.

Investments

10% int. in **Amino Therapeutics Inc.**, Cambridge, Mass.
30% int. in **Glenco Medical Corp**, Ont.
40% int. in **Latin-Canada Pharma Inc.**, B.C.
- 70% int. in **Sanaty IPS S.A.S.**, Colombia.

13.2% int. in **Marvel Diagnostics Inc.**
Sulliden Mining Capital Inc., Toronto, Ont. (see Survey of Mines)

Financial Statistics

Periods ended:	12m Dec. 31/22^A		12m Dec. 31/21^oA
	$000s	%Chg	$000s
Operating revenue	**37,175**	**-57**	**86,825**
Cost of sales	22,790		50,256
General & admin expense	22,838		14,162
Other operating expense	2,514		3,873
Operating expense	**48,142**	**-30**	**68,291**
Operating income	**(10,967)**	**n.a.**	**18,534**
Deprec., depl. & amort.	1,546		4,823
Finance costs, net	238		425
Write-downs/write-offs	(9,799)		(10,302)
Pre-tax income	**(22,878)**	**n.a.**	**(154)**
Income taxes	(4,512)		6,456
Net income	**(18,365)**	**n.a.**	**(6,611)**
Cash & equivalent	4,274		117
Inventories	343		389
Accounts receivable	11,708		55,315
Current assets	16,848		55,857
Long-term investments	nil		488
Fixed assets, net	398		595
Right-of-use assets	136		nil
Intangibles, net	1,437		2,355
Total assets	**18,818**	**-68**	**59,295**
Bank indebtedness	96		850
Accts. pay. & accr. liabs	12,414		33,199
Current liabilities	17,680		40,521
Long-term debt, gross	1,088		965
Long-term debt, net	nil		965
Equity portion of conv. debs	255		255
Shareholders' equity	326		17,809
Cash from oper. activs	**6,044**	**n.a.**	**(8,322)**
Cash from fin. activs	(1,885)		8,210
Cash from invest. activs	nil		(626)
Net cash position	**4,272**	**n.m.**	**112**
Capital expenditures	nil		(43)
	$		$
Earnings per share*	(0.68)		(0.34)
Cash flow per share*	0.22		(0.43)
	shs		shs
No. of shs. o/s*	27,019,257		27,015,924
Avg. no. of shs. o/s*	27,016,105		19,323,713
	%		%
Net profit margin	(49.40)		(7.61)
Return on equity	(202.54)		n.m.
Return on assets	(47.02)		(16.86)
Foreign sales percent	100		100

* Common
^o Restated
^A Reported in accordance with IFRS

Latest Results

Periods ended:	3m Mar. 31/23^A		3m Mar. 31/22^A
	$000s	%Chg	$000s
Operating revenue	1,433	-91	16,694
Net income	(2,912)	n.a.	(1,437)
	$		$
Earnings per share*	(0.11)		(0.05)

* Common
^A Reported in accordance with IFRS

Historical Summary
(as originally stated)

Fiscal Year	Oper. Rev.	Net Inc. Bef. Disc.	EPS*
	$000s	$000s	$
2022^A	37,175	(18,365)	(0.68)
2021^A	86,825	(6,611)	(0.34)
2020^A	10,583	(37,672)	(5.70)
2019^A	(152)	(2,718)	(1.20)
2018^A	nil	(712)	(0.30)

* Common
^A Reported in accordance with IFRS
Note: Adjusted throughout for 1-for-15 cons. in Dec. 2022

M.64 MedMen Enterprises Inc.

Symbol - MMEN **Exchange** - CSE **CUSIP** - 58507M
Head Office - 10115 Jefferson Blvd, Culver City, CA, United States, 90232 **Toll-free** - (855) 292-8399
Website - investors.medmen.com
Email - investors@medmen.com
Investor Relations - Amit Pandey (855) 292-8399
Auditors - Marcum LLP C.P.A.
Transfer Agents - Odyssey Trust Company, Vancouver, B.C.
FP500 Revenue Ranking - 682
Employees - 510 at June 25, 2022
Profile - (B.C. 1987) Operates retail cannabis stores in the U.S., with 24 stores in operation in California (13), New York (4), Nevada (3), Illinois (2), Massachusetts and Arizona. Also has cultivation and manufacturing operations in Nevada, California, New York and Arizona.

Products are sold under the MedMen Red, Moss and LuxLyte brands, including cannabis dry flower, vape pens, oils, extracts, edibles, pre-rolls, tinctures, lotion, topical pain spray, ground flower and capsules. Also manages two permitted dispensaries in Venice and Los Angeles, Calif., through a long-term management contract.

Operations include four cultivation and production facilities in Mustang, Nev. (45,000 sq. ft.), Desert Hot Springs, Calif. (45,000 sq. ft.), Utica, N.Y. (25,641 sq. ft.), and Mesa, Ariz. (20,000 sq. ft.).

On Mar. 11, 2022, the company completed the closure of its distribution facility in Los Angeles, Calif., to reduce overhead costs.

Recent Merger and Acquisition Activity

Status: completed **Revised:** Aug. 22, 2022
UPDATE: The transaction was completed for US$67,000,000, consisting of US$63,000,000 and assumption of US$4,000,000 liabilities. PREVIOUS: MedMen Enterprises Inc. agreed to sell substantially all of its Florida-based assets, including its license, dispensaries, inventory and cultivation operations, and assumption of certain liabilities, to Green Sentry Holdings, LLC of Fort Lauderdale, Fla. for US$83,000,000. In connection with the sale, MedMen will license the trade name "MedMen" to Green Sentry for use in Florida for two years.

Status: terminated **Revised:** Aug. 15, 2022
UPDATE: The transaction was terminated. PREVIOUS: Ascend Wellness Holdings, Inc. (AWH) agreed to invest US$73,000,000 in MedMen NY, Inc. (MMNY), which operates a cultivation and manufacturing facility in Utica, N.Y., and has four operational medical cannabis dispensaries in the state. MMNY is owned by MedMen Enterprises Inc. Under terms of the agreement, MMNY would assume US$73,000,000 of MedMen's secured debt, AWH would invest US$35,000,000 in cash in MMNY and a subsidiary of AWH would issue a senior secured promissory note in favour of MMNY's senior secured lender in the principal amount of US$28,000,000. Following its investment, AWH would hold a controlling interest in MMNY equal to approximately 86.7% of the equity in MMNY. Jan. 3, 2022 - MedMen announced the termination of the agreement. Jan. 13, 2022 - AWH filed a lawsuit with the Supreme Court of the State of New York, New York County - Commercial Division, claiming the agreement was improperly terminated and seeking specific performance of agreement. May 11, 2022 - AWH agreed to purchase 100% interest in MedMen's New York state operations for US$88,000,000, consisting of US$15,000,000 cash and assumption of US$73,000,000 of debt. The agreement resolves the litigation between MedMen and AWH concerning the transaction.

Predecessor Detail - Name changed from Ladera Ventures Corp., May 28, 2018, following reverse takeover acquisition of MM Enterprises USA, LLC; basis 1 new for 9.2623 old shs.

Directors - Michael Serruya, chr., Toronto, Ont.; Ellen B. Deutsch, CEO; Melvin Elias, Calif.; David Hsu, Wash.; Edward (Ed) Record, Tex.; Cameron Smith, Tex.

Other Exec. Officers - Amit Pandey, CFO; Roger Blanchard, chief stores officer; Karen Torres, chief product officer; Kimble Cannon, sr. v-p, capital markets & legal affairs

Capital Stock

	Authorized (shs.)	Outstanding (shs.)[1]	Par
Preferred	unlimited	nil	
Class A Super Vtg.	unlimited	nil	
Class B Subord. Vtg.	unlimited	1,308,619,247	
MM Can USA Class B Redeem.	1,000,000	90,975,185[2]	US$0.001
MM Enterprises USA Common	n.a.	725,016[3]	

[1] At Jan. 30, 2023
[2] Securities of MM Can USA, Inc.
[3] Securities of MM Enterprises USA, LLC

Preferred - Issuable in series.
Class A Super Voting - 1,000 votes per share. Not entitled to dividends.
Class B Subordinate Voting - One vote per share.
MM Can USA Class B Redeemable - Redeemable or exchangeable for an equivalent number of class B subordinate voting shares of the company. Non-voting.
MM Enterprises USA Common - Redeemable or exchangeable for an equivalent number of class B subordinate voting shares of the company. Non-voting.
Major Shareholder - Widely held at Aug. 31, 2022.

Price Range - MMEN/CSE

Year	Volume	High	Low	Close
2022	212,729,066	$0.24	$0.02	$0.02
2021	487,315,557	$1.83	$0.17	$0.21
2020	313,762,552	$0.84	$0.14	$0.17
2019	225,255,043	$5.06	$0.48	$0.70
2018	208,839,489	$9.88	$0.93	$3.85

Recent Close: $0.03

Capital Stock Changes - In August 2021, 395,833,307 units (1 class B subordinate voting share & 1 warrant) at US$0.24 per unit were issued under a subscription agreement. Also during fiscal 2022, class B subordinate voting shares were issued as follows: 45,874,448 in settlement of accounts payable and accrued liabilities, 43,331,119 in settlement of debt and accrued interest, 30,146,495 on redemption of a like number of class B common shares of MM Can USA, Inc., 16,014,665 on conversion of debt, 10,421,300 on vesting of restricted stock units, 10,416,666 as backstop commitment fee, 8,807,605 on exercise of warrants, 8,021,593 for financing fees, 4,216,844 for compensation and 1,473,534 on exercise of options.

Wholly Owned Subsidiaries

Convergence Management Services, Ltd., Vancouver, B.C.
LCR SLP, LLC, Del.
MM Can USA, Inc., Culver City, Calif.
- 100% int. in **MM Enterprises USA, LLC**, Culver City, Calif.
  - 100% int. in **Desert Hot Springs Green Horizon, Inc.**, Calif.
  - 100% int. in **Farmacy Collective**, Los Angeles, Calif.
  - 100% int. in **MME AZ Group, LLC**, Mesa, Ariz.
    - 100% int. in **EBA Holdings, Inc.**, Ariz.
  - 100% int. in **MME CYON Retail, Inc.**, Los Angeles, Calif.
    - 100% int. in **BH Fund II Group, LLC**, Los Angeles, Calif.
  - 100% int. in **MME Florida, LLC**, Eustis, Fla.
  - 100% int. in **MME IL Group LLC**, Oak Park, Ill.
    - 100% int. in **Future Transactions Holdings LLC**, Oak Park, Ill.
  - 100% int. in **MME Morton Grove Retail, LLC**, Ill.
  - 100% int. in **MME 1001 North Retail, LLC**, Chicago, Ill.
  - 100% int. in **MME Sorrento Valley, LLC**, San Diego, Calif.
    - 100% int. in **Sure Felt, LLC**, San Diego, Calif.
  - 60% int. in **MME Sutter Retail, LLC**, San Francisco, Calif.
  - 60% int. in **MME Union Retail, LLC**, San Francisco, Calif.
  - 100% int. in **MME VMS, LLC**, San Jose, Calif.
    - 100% int. in **Viktoriya's Medical Supplies, LLC**, San Jose, Calif.
  - 100% int. in **MMNV2 Holdings I, LLC**, Nev.
  - 100% int. in **MMOF Downtown Collective, LLC**, Los Angeles, Calif.
    - 100% int. in **Advanced Patients' Collective**, Los Angeles, Calif.
      - 100% int. in **DT Fund II Group, LLC**, Calif.
  - 100% int. in **MMOF Fremont, LLC**, Las Vegas, Nev.
    - 100% int. in **MMOF Fremont Retail, Inc.**, Las Vegas, Nev.
  - 100% int. in **MMOF SM, LLC**, Santa Monica, Calif.
    - 100% int. in **MMOF Santa Monica, Inc.**, Santa Monica, Calif.
  - 100% int. in **MMOF San Diego Retail, Inc.**, San Diego, Calif.
    - 100% int. in **San Diego Retail Group II, LLC**, San Diego, Calif.
  - 100% int. in **MMOF Vegas, LLC**, Las Vegas, Nev.
    - 100% int. in **MMOF Vegas Retail, Inc.**, Las Vegas, Nev.
  - 100% int. in **MMOF Vegas 2, LLC**, Las Vegas, Nev.
    - 100% int. in **MMOF Vegas Retail 2, Inc.**, Las Vegas, Nev.
  - 100% int. in **MMOF Venice, LLC**, Venice, Calif.
    - 100% int. in **The Compassion Network, LLC**, Venice, Calif.
  - 100% int. in **Manlin I, LLC**, Los Angeles, Calif.
  - 100% int. in **MattnJeremy, Inc.**, Long Beach, Calif.
  - 90% int. in **MedMen Boston, LLC**, Boston, Mass.
  - 90% int. in **MedMen Newton Retail, LLC**, Newton, Mass.
  - 100% int. in **Project Compassion Venture, LLC**, N.Y.
    - 100% int. in **Project Compassion Capital, LLC**, N.Y.
      - 100% int. in **Project Compassion NY, LLC**, N.Y.
        - 100% int. in **MedMen NY, Inc.**, Utica, N.Y.
  - 100% int. in **Rochambeau, Inc.**, Emeryville, Calif.
  - 100% int. in **The Source Santa Ana**, Orange County, Calif.
    - 100% int. in **SA Fund Group RT, LLC**, Orange County, Calif.

Financial Statistics

Periods ended:	52w June 25/22[A]		52w June 26/21[□A]
	US$000s	%Chg	US$000s
Operating revenue	**140,812**	**+6**	**132,247**
Cost of goods sold	69,494		69,348
General & admin expense	106,675		105,838
Stock-based compensation	5,255		4,345
Operating expense	**181,424**	**+1**	**179,531**
Operating income	**(40,612)**	**n.a.**	**(47,284)**
Deprec., depl. & amort.	25,648		28,478
Finance income	92		649
Finance costs, gross	32,798		68,891
Write-downs/write-offs	(101,799)[1]		(2,363)
Pre-tax income	**(175,451)**	**n.a.**	**(122,496)**
Income taxes	(9,896)		1,834
Net inc bef disc ops, eqhldrs	(149,848)		(90,878)
Net inc bef disc ops, NCI	(15,707)		(33,452)
Net inc. bef. disc. opers	**(165,555)**	**n.a.**	**(124,330)**
Disc. opers., equity hldrs	(45,339)		(33,268)
Income from disc. opers	(45,339)		(33,268)
Net income	**(210,894)**	**n.a.**	**(157,598)**
Net inc. for equity hldrs	**(195,187)**	**n.a.**	**(124,146)**
Net inc. for non-cont. int	**(15,707)**	**n.a.**	**(33,452)**
Cash & equivalent	13,534		14,612
Inventories	10,011		16,014
Accounts receivable	1,151		917
Current assets	161,496		175,842
Fixed assets, net	64,108		107,059
Right-of-use assets	47,649		61,801
Intangibles, net	45,556		116,339
Total assets	**323,224**	**-32**	**472,464**
Accts. pay. & accr. liabs	38,906		45,265
Current liabilities	326,417		346,659
Long-term debt, gross	333,997		380,089
Long-term debt, net	232,932		276,387
Long-term lease liabilities	44,092		62,136
Shareholders' equity	151,808		191,760
Non-controlling interest	(470,321)		(445,394)
Cash from oper. activs	**(62,529)**	**n.a.**	**(59,420)**
Cash from fin. activs	72,895		50,746
Cash from invest. activs	(10,875)		10,940
Net cash position	**10,796**	**-7**	**11,575**
Capital expenditures	(9,040)		(2,688)
	US$		US$
Earns. per sh. bef disc opers*	(0.13)		(0.18)
Earnings per share*	(0.17)		(0.24)
Cash flow per share*	(0.05)		(0.11)
	shs		shs
No. of shs. o/s*	1,301,423,950		726,866,374
Avg. no. of shs. o/s*	1,153,538,255		530,980,011
	%		%
Net profit margin	(117.57)		(94.01)
Return on equity	(87.23)		(51.69)
Return on assets	(33.83)		(10.40)
Foreign sales percent	100		100
No. of employees (FTEs)	510		875

* Common

[□] Restated

[A] Reported in accordance with U.S. GAAP

[1] Includes impairment costs of US$32,309,044 on properties in California and Nevada, US$35,531,877 on intangible assets in California and Nevada, US$23,090,408 on California group goodwill and US$3,964,559 on certain operating lease right-of-use assets in California.

Latest Results

Periods ended:	26w Dec. 24/22[A]		26w Dec. 25/21[□A]
	US$000s	%Chg	US$000s
Operating revenue	59,598	-18	72,253
Net inc. bef. disc. opers	(39,427)	n.a.	(54,381)
Income from disc. opers	26,132		(26,587)
Net income	(13,294)	n.a.	(80,968)
Net inc. for equity hldrs	(12,047)	n.a.	(74,357)
Net inc. for non-cont. int	(1,247)		(6,611)
	US$		US$
Earns. per sh. bef. disc. opers.*	(0.03)		(0.05)
Earnings per share*	(0.02)		(0.07)

* Common

[□] Restated

[A] Reported in accordance with U.S. GAAP

Historical Summary

(as originally stated)

Fiscal Year	Oper. Rev. US$000s	Net Inc. Bef. Disc. US$000s	EPS* US$
2022[A]	140,812	(165,555)	(0.13)
2021[A]	145,066	(145,445)	(0.22)
2020[A]	157,113	(475,749)	(0.73)
2019[B]	129,963	(277,047)	(0.75)
2018[B1]	39,783	(112,265)	(2.77)

* Common

[A] Reported in accordance with U.S. GAAP

[B] Reported in accordance with IFRS

[1] Results reflect the May 28, 2018, reverse takeover acquisition of MM Enterprises USA, LLC.

M.65 MedMira Inc.

Symbol - MIR **Exchange** - TSX-VEN **CUSIP** - 58501R

Head Office - 1-155 Chain Lake Dr, Halifax, NS, B3S 1B3 **Telephone** - (902) 450-1588 **Toll-free** - (877) 633-6372 **Fax** - (902) 450-1580

Website - www.medmira.com

Email - m.meile@medmira.com

Investor Relations - Markus M. Meile (877) 633-6372

Auditors - Arsenault Best Cameron Ellis C.A., Charlottetown, P.E.I.

Lawyers - Stewart McKelvey LLP, Halifax, N.S.

Transfer Agents - Computershare Trust Company of Canada Inc., Halifax, N.S.

Profile - (Alta. 1999) Develops and produces rapid test kits for detection of diseases through its Rapid Vertical Flow Technology™ platform.

The company's line of rapid tests are used to detect HIV 1/2, syphilis, hepatitis B/C, SARS-CoV-2 and Helicobacter pylori. Products are marketed and sold under the Reveal®, REVEALCOVID-19®, Multiplo® and Miriad® brands through a worldwide network of medical distributors and partners to customers in the healthcare industry, including laboratories, hospitals, point-of-care facilities, governments, aid organizations and public health agencies. The company has received regulatory approvals in Canada, the U.S., China and the European Union for its patented Rapid Vertical Flow Technology™.

During the first quarter of fiscal 2023, the company has received the CE mark for its VYRATM COVID-19 antigen test and launched the product with its strategically positioned distribution partners in Europe.

Directors - Thomas Bergmann, chr., Basel, Switzerland; Hermes Chan, pres. & CEO, Halifax, N.S.; Steven (Steve) Cummings, Halifax, N.S.; Jianhe Mao, St. Gallen, Switzerland; Pascale Nini

Other Exec. Officers - Markus M. Meile, CFO

Capital Stock

	Authorized (shs.)	Outstanding (shs.)[1]
Preferred Series A	unlimited	5,000,000
Common	unlimited	658,364,320

[1] At Dec. 31, 2022

Preferred Series A - Redeemable at $0.001 per share. Convertible into common shares on a 1-for-1 basis upon achievement of certain milestones. Non-voting.

Common - One vote per share.

Major Shareholder - MedMira Holding AG held 70.5% interest at Dec. 31, 2022.

Price Range - MIR/TSX-VEN

Year	Volume	High	Low	Close
2022	32,225,822	$0.28	$0.05	$0.08
2021	160,480,030	$0.52	$0.11	$0.20
2020	451,066,922	$0.89	$0.01	$0.25
2019	20,963,467	$0.04	$0.01	$0.01
2018	13,694,493	$0.03	$0.01	$0.01

Recent Close: $0.09

Capital Stock Changes - During fiscal 2022, common shares were issued as follows: 24,582,317 for debt settlement and 11,487,527 by private placement.

Wholly Owned Subsidiaries

Maple BioSciences Inc., Toronto, Ont.

MedMira International AG, Switzerland.

MedMira Laboratories Inc., Ont.

MedMira (US) Inc., United States.

Precious Life Saving Products Inc., Canada.

Financial Statistics

Periods ended:	12m July 31/22[A]		12m July 31/21[A]
	$000s	%Chg	$000s
Operating revenue	**952**	**-56**	**2,144**
Cost of sales	648		423
Research & devel. expense	191		359
General & admin expense	537		327
Other operating expense	817		1,012
Operating expense	**2,193**	**+3**	**2,121**
Operating income	**(1,241)**	**n.a.**	**23**
Deprec., depl. & amort.	212		208
Finance costs, gross	562		653
Pre-tax income	**(1,832)**	**n.a.**	**(676)**
Net income	**(1,832)**	**n.a.**	**(676)**
Cash & equivalent	33		nil
Inventories	202		236
Accounts receivable	1,250		1,251
Current assets	1,658		1,576
Fixed assets, net	2,171		2,314
Total assets	**3,830**	**-2**	**3,890**
Bank indebtedness	nil		10
Accts. pay. & accr. liabs	2,750		2,700
Current liabilities	14,138		17,415
Long-term debt, gross	6,140		9,222
Long-term debt, net	40		40
Long-term lease liabilities	2,008		2,159
Preferred share equity	3		3
Shareholders' equity	(12,356)		(15,724)
Cash from oper. activs	**(1,884)**	**n.a.**	**(505)**
Cash from fin. activs	1,987		139
Cash from invest. activs	(70)		(37)
Net cash position	**33**	**n.a.**	**nil**
Capital expenditures	(70)		(37)
	$		$
Earnings per share*	(0.00)		(0.00)
Cash flow per share*	(0.00)		(0.00)
	shs		shs
No. of shs. o/s*	697,445,660		661,375,816
Avg. no. of shs. o/s*	680,646,006		658,327,299
	%		%
Net profit margin	(192.44)		(31.53)
Return on equity	n.m.		n.m.
Return on assets	(32.90)		(0.63)
Foreign sales percent	98		99

* Common

[A] Reported in accordance with IFRS

Latest Results

Periods ended:	3m Oct. 31/22[A]		3m Oct. 31/21[A]
	$000s	%Chg	$000s
Operating revenue	121	-40	202
Net income	(632)	n.a.	(489)
	$		$
Earnings per share*	(0.00)		(0.00)

* Common

[A] Reported in accordance with IFRS

Historical Summary

(as originally stated)

Fiscal Year	Oper. Rev. $000s	Net Inc. Bef. Disc. $000s	EPS* $
2022[A]	952	(1,832)	(0.00)
2021[A]	2,144	(676)	(0.00)
2020[A]	919	(2,045)	(0.00)
2019[A]	527	(2,106)	(0.00)
2018[A]	589	(2,509)	(0.00)

* Common

[A] Reported in accordance with IFRS

M.66 Mednow Inc.

Symbol - MNOW **Exchange** - TSX-VEN **CUSIP** - 58503L

Head Office - 4484 Main St, Vancouver, BC, V3V 5R5 **Telephone** - (604) 876-6410 **Toll-free** - (855) 633-6691

Website - investors.mednow.ca

Email - ir@mednow.ca

Investor Relations - Benjamin Ferdinand (855) 686-6300

Auditors - SRCO Professional Corporation C.A., Richmond Hill, Ont.

Transfer Agents - Endeavor Trust Corporation, Vancouver, B.C.

Profile - (B.C. 2018) Has developed web and mobile application to facilitate the sale and distribution of prescription medications, and the delivery of virtual care and telemedicine services.

Through its web application, the company provides customers with a convenient and secure way to fill, order, receive and manage their prescriptions without going to a physical brick-and-mortar pharmacy.

Owns and operates five retail brick-and-mortar pharmacies in British Columbia and Ontario operating under Mednow Pharmacy (3), Infusicare and London Pharmacare brands. In addition, has entered into a franchise agreement with **Pharmacie Raji Al-Kurdi Inc.** (franchisee) to operate retail brick-and-mortar pharmacies in Quebec. Also provides doctor services, including telemedicine and virtual care, as well as doctor home visits for patients in Ontario who are unable to leave their homes.

In addition, Holds a licence to use the TruDiagnostic™ technology and TruDiagnostic™ platform for the development, importation, use, marketing, sale and distribution of the TruDiagnostic™ Epigenetic Testing Kits in Canada.

In May 2023, the company shut down **Liver Care Canada Inc.**, which provided services and treatments for liver disease patients; and **London Pharmacare Inc.**, which provided specialty pharmacy services and expertise, both in Ontario.

On May 2, 2023, the company announced a change in business model from owning the pharmacies in all its provinces, to operating and funding only pharmacies in Ontario and British Columbia. In the rest of the country, the company moved to a partner pharmacy and franchising model.

On Mar. 31, 2022, the company acquired Ontario-based **Mednow East Inc.**, which operates an online pharmacy delivering prescriptions in Ontario, for $65,578 cash and the conversion of $1,374,422 Mednow East debt to the company into a non-interest bearing on-demand convertible promissory note.

Directors - Amir Ali Reyhany-Bozorg, chr., pres. & CEO, Richmond Hill, Ont.; Fellipe Campusano, treas. & corp. sec., London, Ont.; Kia Besharat, Nassau, Bahamas; Malidi Sliams, Vancouver, B.C.

Other Exec. Officers - Benjamin Ferdinand, CFO; Dave Marantz, chief revenue officer; Anthony Perlman, sr. v-p, benefits strategy

Capital Stock

	Authorized (shs.)	Outstanding (shs.)[1]
Class A Common	unlimited	25,864,377
Class B Common	unlimited	nil
Class C Common	unlimited	nil

[1] At May 30, 2023

Major Shareholder - Amir Ali Reyhany-Bozorg held 29.31% interest and Fellipe Campusano held 23.48% interest at May 3, 2022.

Price Range - MNOW/TSX-VEN

Year	Volume	High	Low	Close
2022	5,139,147	$1.35	$0.18	$0.28
2021	6,383,043	$5.56	$0.88	$1.10

Recent Close: $0.31

Capital Stock Changes - In May 2023, public offering of 1,945,415 units (1 class A common share & 1 warrant) and private placement of 2,166,667 units at 27¢ per unit were completed, with warrants exercisable at 41¢ per share for five years.

There were no changes to capital stock during fiscal 2022.

Wholly Owned Subsidiaries

Infusicare Canada Inc., London, Ont.
Mednow Clinic Services Inc.
Mednow East Inc., Ont.
Mednow Medical Inc., Canada.
Mednow Ontario Ltd., Ont.
Mednow Operations Inc., Canada.
Mednow Pharmacy AB Ltd., Alta.
Mednow Pharmacy Inc., B.C.
Mednow Pharmacy MB Ltd., Man.
Mednow Pharmacy NS Ltd., N.S.
Mednow Pharmacy Services Inc.
Mednow Technology Inc.
10111132 Manitoba Ltd., Man. dba Mednow MB.
2716725 Ontario Inc., Ont. dba Medvisit.

Subsidiaries

70% int. in **Mednow Virtual Care Ltd.**

Note: The preceding list includes only the major related companies in which interests are held.

Financial Statistics

Periods ended:	12m July 31/22[A]		12m July 31/21[A]
	$000s	%Chg	$000s
Operating revenue	**16,639**	**n.m.**	**414**
Salaries & benefits	10,874		2,320
General & admin expense	8,712		3,517
Stock-based compensation	3,079		3,374
Operating expense	**22,665**	**+146**	**9,211**
Operating income	**(6,026)**	**n.a.**	**(8,797)**
Deprec., depl. & amort.	1,760		201
Finance income	158		50
Finance costs, gross	189		1
Investment income	(147)		(5)
Write-downs/write-offs	(177)		nil
Pre-tax income	**(30,072)**	**n.a.**	**(8,954)**
Income taxes	(516)		nil
Net income	**(29,556)**	**n.a.**	**(8,954)**
Net inc. for equity hldrs	**(29,483)**	**n.a.**	**(8,954)**
Net inc. for non-cont. int.	**(73)**	**n.a.**	**nil**
Cash & equivalent	4,971		28,759
Inventories	972		nil
Accounts receivable	1,709		nil
Current assets	8,486		31,683
Long-term investments	nil		495
Fixed assets, net	2,362		1,081
Right-of-use assets	3,954		382
Intangibles, net	2,900		530
Total assets	**18,132**	**-47**	**34,171**
Bank indebtedness	2,674		nil
Accts. pay. & accr. liabs	3,903		1,293
Current liabilities	8,555		1,370
Long-term debt, gross	30		nil
Long-term debt, net	30		nil
Long-term lease liabilities	3,119		314
Shareholders' equity	6,082		32,487
Non-controlling interest	(73)		nil
Cash from oper. activs	**(16,087)**	**n.a.**	**(5,588)**
Cash from fin. activs	339		32,676
Cash from invest. activs	(8,041)		(3,584)
Net cash position	**4,971**	**-83**	**28,759**
Capital expenditures	(1,594)		(655)
	$		$
Earnings per share*	(1.37)		(0.49)
Cash flow per share*	(0.75)		(0.30)
	shs		shs
No. of shs. o/s*	21,568,359		21,568,359
Avg. no. of shs. o/s*	21,568,359		18,402,826
	%		%
Net profit margin	(177.63)		n.m.
Return on equity	(152.88)		(47.28)
Return on assets	(112.31)		(45.09)

* Cl.A Common
[A] Reported in accordance with IFRS

Historical Summary
(as originally stated)

Fiscal Year	Oper. Rev.	Net Inc. Bef. Disc.	EPS*
	$000s	$000s	$
2022[A]	16,639	(29,556)	(1.37)
2021[A]	414	(8,954)	(0.49)
2020[A]	nil	(470)	(0.06)
2019[A]	nil	(12)	(0.00)

* Cl.A Common
[A] Reported in accordance with IFRS

M.67 MedX Health Corp.

Symbol - MDX **Exchange** - TSX-VEN **CUSIP** - 585090
Head Office - Unit 1, 1495 Bonhill Rd, Mississauga, ON, L5T 1M2 **Telephone** - (905) 670-4428 **Toll-free** - (888) 363-3112 **Fax** - (905) 670-4749
Website - medxhealth.com
Email - bill@medxhealth.com
Investor Relations - Bill Mitoulas (888) 363-3112
Auditors - Kreston GTA LLP C.A., Markham, Ont.
Lawyers - Fogler, Rubinoff LLP, Toronto, Ont.
Transfer Agents - TSX Trust Company, Toronto, Ont.

Profile - (Ont. 1999) Develops, manufactures and distributes SIAscopy™-based phototherapy devices which are used to scan skin for suspicious moles or lesions.

The company's main product line is SIAscopy™, a medical device technology that utilizes light and its remittance to view up to 2 mm beneath suspicious moles and lesions in a pain free, non-invasive manner, with the company's software then creating real-time images for physicians and dermatologists to evaluate all types of moles or lesions within seconds. Also includes DermSecure™ telemedicine platform which enables the web-based operation of its SIAscopy™ scanning technology and allows the company to deploy its technology in networks of third-party locations for remote assessment. Its other product line is phototherapeutic medical devices, which use light energy in lower-level laser and LED to provide effective treatment offering rapid, drug-free and non-invasive healing in the rehabilitation market for treating pain, tissue damage, swelling and inflammation including SIAscopy™ technology embedded with SIAMETRICS®, SIMSYS® and MoleMate®.

SIAscopy™ and therapeutic light products are manufactured at its ISO 13485 certified manufacturing and testing facility in Mississuaga, Ont. All products have been cleared by the U.S. FDA and Health Canada and CE Marked for sale in Europe with equivalent approval in Brazil, Australia, Turkey and a number of other jurisdictions totalling 35 countries. In addition, the company offers its teledermatology assessment and screening technology services across Canada.

Directors - Kenneth (Ken) McKay, chr., Toronto, Ont.; David J. Hennigar, v-chr., Bedford, N.S.; Stephen Lockyer, CEO; Edmund (Ed) Ho, Toronto, Ont.

Other Exec. Officers - Louie Canitano, COO; Christopher H. Freeman, acting CFO & corp. sec.; Tarek El Hoss, v-p, market devel. & sales; Mike Druhan, pres., dermatological srvcs. & products

Capital Stock

	Authorized (shs.)	Outstanding (shs.)[1]
Common	unlimited	183,799,459

[1] At May 30, 2023

Major Shareholder - Widely held at May 19, 2023.

Price Range - MDX/TSX-VEN

Year	Volume	High	Low	Close
2022	25,071,052	$0.09	$0.02	$0.04
2021	56,332,003	$0.26	$0.07	$0.08
2020	42,653,253	$0.16	$0.07	$0.12
2019	29,492,253	$0.18	$0.09	$0.13
2018	70,126,681	$0.33	$0.11	$0.14

Recent Close: $0.07

Capital Stock Changes - During 2022, 100,000 common shares were issued on exercise of warrants.

Wholly Owned Subsidiaries

LaserPath Therapeutics Inc. Inactive.
MedX Electronics Inc., Ont. Inactive.

Financial Statistics

Periods ended:	12m Dec. 31/22[A]		12m Dec. 31/21[oA]
	$000s	%Chg	$000s
Operating revenue	**512**	**-9**	**563**
Cost of sales	253		272
Research & devel. expense	682		995
General & admin expense	3,009		3,528
Stock-based compensation	332		228
Operating expense	**4,276**	**-15**	**5,023**
Operating income	**(3,764)**	**n.a.**	**(4,460)**
Deprec., depl. & amort.	103		102
Finance costs, net	1,269		778
Pre-tax income	**(5,134)**	**n.a.**	**(5,324)**
Net income	**(5,134)**	**n.a.**	**(5,324)**
Cash & equivalent	142		107
Inventories	377		371
Accounts receivable	8		10
Current assets	543		541
Fixed assets, net	138		190
Total assets	**681**	**-7**	**731**
Bank indebtedness	1,060		150
Accts. pay. & accr. liabs	2,752		1,765
Current liabilities	6,885		1,969
Long-term debt, gross	3,938		2,431
Long-term debt, net	877		2,392
Equity portion of conv. debs	3,466		2,149
Shareholders' equity	(7,081)		(3,630)
Cash from oper. activs	**(2,801)**	**n.a.**	**(4,517)**
Cash from fin. activs	2,837		4,602
Cash from invest. activs	nil		(16)
Net cash position	**142**	**+33**	**107**
Capital expenditures	nil		(16)
	$		$
Earnings per share*	(0.03)		(0.03)
Cash flow per share*	(0.02)		(0.03)
	shs		shs
No. of shs. o/s*	183,799,459		183,699,459
Avg. no. of shs. o/s*	183,742,473		180,184,680
	%		%
Net profit margin	n.m.		(945.65)
Return on equity	n.m.		n.m.
Return on assets	(727.20)		(726.83)
Foreign sales percent	62		56

* Common
[o] Restated
[A] Reported in accordance with IFRS

Latest Results

Periods ended:	3m Mar. 31/23[A]		3m Mar. 31/22[A]
	$000s	%Chg	$000s
Operating revenue	49	-23	64
Net income	(1,230)	n.a.	(1,225)
	$		$
Earnings per share*	(0.01)		(0.01)

* Common
[A] Reported in accordance with IFRS

Historical Summary
(as originally stated)

Fiscal Year	Oper. Rev. $000s	Net Inc. Bef. Disc. $000s	EPS* $
2022[A]	512	(5,134)	(0.03)
2021[A]	563	(5,324)	(0.03)
2020[A]	530	(3,199)	(0.02)
2019[A]	860	(3,276)	(0.02)
2018[A]	1,087	(4,187)	(0.03)

* Common
[A] Reported in accordance with IFRS

M.68 Meed Growth Corp.

Symbol - MEED.P **Exchange** - TSX-VEN **CUSIP** - 585103
Head Office - 250 Bay St, Victoria, BC, V9A 3K5 **Toll-free** - (833) 676-0762
Website - meedgrowth.com
Email - mgustavson@meedgrowth.com
Investor Relations - Matthew Gustavson (833) 676-0762
Auditors - KPMG LLP C.A., Victoria, B.C.
Transfer Agents - Computershare Trust Company of Canada Inc., Vancouver, B.C.
Profile - (B.C. 2021) Capital Pool Company.
Directors - John C. Simmons, CEO, Victoria, B.C.; Matthew Gustavson, CFO & corp. sec., Victoria, B.C.; Dave Stevenson, Victoria, B.C.; Geoff Wilcox, Victoria, B.C.

Capital Stock

	Authorized (shs.)	Outstanding (shs.)[1]
Common	unlimited	13,500,000

[1] At Mar. 31, 2022

Major Shareholder - John C. Simmons held 17.78% interest, Jim Meekison and Carolyn Keystone collectively held 10.37% interest, Dave Stevenson held 10.37% interest and Geoff Wilcox held 10.37% interest at June 30, 2021.

Price Range - MEED.P/TSX-VEN

Year	Volume	High	Low	Close
2022	171,000	$0.30	$0.07	$0.08
2021	45,000	$0.24	$0.19	$0.24

Recent Close: $0.05

M.69 Mega View Digital Entertainment Corp.

Symbol - MVD.H **Exchange** - TSX-VEN **CUSIP** - 58517E
Head Office - 50 Melham Crt, Toronto, ON, M1B 2E5 **Telephone** - (647) 478-8468 **Fax** - (905) 731-4615
Email - philip.chong@knpgroup.ca
Investor Relations - Philip Chong (416) 298-8516 ext. 222
Auditors - RSM Canada LLP C.A., Toronto, Ont.
Transfer Agents - TSX Trust Company, Toronto, Ont.
Profile - (Ont. 2007) Seeking new business opportunities.
Predecessor Detail - Name changed from Middle Kingdom Paradiso Corp., July 20, 2009, following Qualifying Transaction reverse takeover acquisition of Mega View Management Services Inc.
Directors - Philip Chong, chr., pres. & CEO, Toronto, Ont.; Michael Lam, CFO, Markham, Ont.; Paul Chan, Toronto, Ont.; Michael A. Dehn, Erin, Ont.; Franz K. Kozich-Koschitzky, Austria

Capital Stock

	Authorized (shs.)	Outstanding (shs.)[1]
Common	unlimited	9,008,877

[1] At May 30, 2022

Major Shareholder - Philip Chong held 52.35% interest, Erika Chong held 17.6% interest and Robert Ng held 16.66% interest at Apr. 5, 2021.

Price Range - MVD.H/TSX-VEN

Year	Volume	High	Low	Close
2022	14,500	$0.03	$0.03	$0.03
2021	6,980	$0.06	$0.05	$0.06
2020	13,100	$0.06	$0.06	$0.06
2019	24,000	$0.05	$0.05	$0.05
2018	8,000	$0.04	$0.04	$0.04

Recent Close: $0.02

Wholly Owned Subsidiaries

Mega View Investment Services (Shanghai) Co. Ltd., People's Republic of China. Inactive.
Mega View Management Services Inc., British Virgin Islands. Inactive.

Financial Statistics

Periods ended:	12m Dec. 31/21[A]		12m Dec. 31/20[oA]
	$000s	%Chg	$000s
General & admin expense	24		26
Operating expense	**24**	**-8**	**26**
Operating income	**(24)**	**n.a.**	**(26)**
Pre-tax income	**(24)**	**n.a.**	**(26)**
Net income	**(24)**	**n.a.**	**(26)**
Cash & equivalent	7		7
Current assets	8		7
Total assets	**8**	**+14**	**7**
Accts. pay. & accr. liabs	12		12
Current liabilities	98		73
Shareholders' equity	(90)		(66)
Cash from oper. activs	**(25)**	**n.a.**	**(33)**
Cash from fin. activs	25		20
Net cash position	**7**	**0**	**7**
	$		$
Earnings per share*	(0.00)		(0.00)
Cash flow per share*	(0.00)		(0.00)
	shs		shs
No. of shs. o/s*	9,008,877		9,008,877
Avg. no. of shs. o/s*	9,008,877		9,008,877
	%		%
Net profit margin	n.a.		n.a.
Return on equity	n.m.		n.m.
Return on assets	(320.00)		(192.59)

* Common
[o] Restated
[A] Reported in accordance with IFRS

Latest Results

Periods ended:	3m Mar. 31/22[A]		3m Mar. 31/21[A]
	$000s	%Chg	$000s
Net income	(3)	n.a.	(4)
	$		$
Earnings per share*	(0.00)		(0.00)

* Common
[A] Reported in accordance with IFRS

Historical Summary
(as originally stated)

Fiscal Year	Oper. Rev. $000s	Net Inc. Bef. Disc. $000s	EPS* $
2021[A]	nil	(24)	(0.00)
2020[A]	nil	(26)	(0.00)
2019[A]	nil	(57)	(0.01)
2018[A]	nil	(59)	(0.01)
2017[A]	nil	(77)	(0.01)

* Common
[A] Reported in accordance with IFRS

M.70 Melcor Developments Ltd.*

Symbol - MRD **Exchange** - TSX **CUSIP** - 585467
Head Office - 900-10310 Jasper Ave, Edmonton, AB, T5J 1Y8 **Telephone** - (780) 423-6931 **Toll-free** - (855) 673-6931 **Fax** - (780) 426-1796
Website - www.melcor.ca
Email - ir@melcor.ca
Investor Relations - Nicole Forsythe (855) 673-6937
Auditors - PricewaterhouseCoopers LLP C.A., Edmonton, Alta.
Lawyers - Bryan & Company LLP
Transfer Agents - Odyssey Trust Company
FP500 Revenue Ranking - 617
Employees - 123 at Dec. 31, 2022
Profile - (Alta. 1968, via memorandum of association) Acquires, plans and develops land to be sold as residential and commercial lots in Alberta, Saskatchewan, British Columbia, Arizona and Colorado. Also owns and manages mixed-use residential communities, business and industrial parks, office buildings, retail commercial centres and golf courses.
Community Development - This division carries out the acquisition, planning, development and marketing of urban communities and large-scale commercial and industrial centres. Developments are located in the regions of northern, southern and central Alberta; British Columbia; Saskatchewan; and the U.S. The majority of residential lots and parcels are sold to selected homebuilders that purchase sites through agreements for sale.
Undeveloped land holdings at Dec. 31, 2022:

Location	Acres
Alberta	7,334
British Columbia	517
Saskatchewan	583
Colorado	1,083
Arizona	248
Texas	92
	9,857

Property Development - This division acquires prime serviced commercial sites from the community development division to develop and lease high-quality retail, office, industrial and multi-family residential revenue-producing properties that deliver appreciation gains and long-term returns. Once completed and substantially leased, these properties are transferred to the investment property division, with a mandate to hold and manage the assets. At Dec. 31, 2022, active property development sites totaled 1,735,670 sq. ft., and future development sites totaled 1,888,000 sq. ft. An additional 2,520,740 sq. ft. of future development potential remains in the active project sites.
Investment Property - This division acquires and owns high-quality residential, office, retail and industrial properties, which are held as long-term investments. Holdings include 1,458,010 sq. ft. gross leasable area of commercial properties in Canada and the U.S., consisting of industrial, retail and office properties; four residential properties, totaling 476 units, in Edmonton, Calgary, and St. Albert, Alta., and Scottsdale, Ariz.; 11 parking lots in Edmonton, Lethbridge, St. Albert and Fort McMurray, Alta., Regina, Sask., and Kelowna, B.C.; and three development sites in Edmonton, Alta. Subsidiary **Melcor Real Estate Investment Trust** owns a portfolio of 38 income-producing properties in western Canada, totaling 3,146,006 sq. ft. gross leasable area.
Recreation Property - This division owns and manages three 18-hole golf courses, The Links at Spruce Grove in Spruce Grove, Alta., Lewis Estates Golf Course in Edmonton, Alta. (60% owned) and Black Mountain Golf Club in Kelowna, B.C. The company also holds a 50% interest in the Jagare Ridge Golf Club in Edmonton, Alta.
During the first quarter of 2023, the company acquired a 40-acre of parcel of land in Leduc, Alta., for $2,400,00 cash. In addition, the company sold three residential units in Arizona for $1,229,000 cash.
During 2022, the company acquired two parcels of land, totaling 13.01 acres, in Buckeye, Ariz., for $4,247,000. In addition, the company sold 117 residential units in Phoenix, Ariz., for total consideration of $35,000,000.
Predecessor Detail - Name changed from Melton Real Estate Ltd., June 11, 1976.
Directors - Timothy C. (Tim) Melton, exec. chr. & CEO, Edmonton, Alta.; Catherine M. (Cathy) Roozen†, Edmonton, Alta.; Douglas O. (Doug) Goss, Edmonton, Alta.; Andrew J. (Andy) Melton, Calgary, Alta.; Kathleen M. Melton, Calgary, Alta.; Bruce Pennock, Edmonton, Alta.; Janet M. Riopel, Edmonton, Alta.; Ralph B. Young, Edmonton, Alta.
Other Exec. Officers - Naomi M. Stefura, COO, CFO & corp. sec.; Randy Ferguson, sr. v-p, invest. properties; Susan (Sue) Keating, v-p, community devel. Edmonton; Leah Margiotta, v-p, prop. devel.; Graeme Melton, v-p, community devel. Calgary & USA; Sinead O'Meara, v-p, fin.; Guy Pelletier, v-p, Red Deer region
† Lead director

Capital Stock

	Authorized (shs.)	Outstanding (shs.)[1]
First Pref.	unlimited	nil
Common	unlimited	31,248,628

[1] At May 29, 2023

Options - At Dec. 31, 2022, options were outstanding to purchase 223,000 common shares at prices ranging from $12.42 to $13.01 per share and expiring to Dec. 11, 2024.
Normal Course Issuer Bid - The company plans to make normal course purchases of up to 1,562,431 common shares representing 5% of the total outstanding. The bid commenced on June 7, 2023, and expires on June 6, 2024.
Major Shareholder - Melton Holdings Ltd. held 50.2% interest at Mar. 31, 2023.

Price Range - MRD/TSX

Year	Volume	High	Low	Close
2022	3,358,845	$17.84	$9.76	$10.65
2021	2,218,518	$15.34	$8.72	$14.24
2020	2,642,405	$13.45	$5.58	$9.42
2019	1,058,544	$14.00	$11.44	$13.32
2018	1,323,253	$15.95	$12.01	$12.29

Recent Close: $11.96
Capital Stock Changes - During 2022, 65,275 common shares were issued on exercise of options and 1,777,662 common shares were repurchased under a Normal Course Issuer Bid.

Dividends

MRD com Ra $0.64 pa Q est. Mar. 31, 2023
Prev. Rate: $0.60 est. Sept. 30, 2022
Prev. Rate: $0.56 est. June 30, 2022
Prev. Rate: $0.48 est. Sept. 30, 2021
Prev. Rate: $0.40 est. Mar. 31, 2021
Prev. Rate: $0.32 est. June 30, 2020

Long-Term Debt - Outstanding at Dec. 31, 2022:

Revolv. credit facilities[1]	$96,839,000
Melcor REIT facility	31,634,000
Debt on land inventory[2]	5,717,000
Melcor REIT conv. debs.[3]	44,468,000
Project specific financing[4]	22,597,000
Mtges.[5]	539,110,000
	740,365,000

[1] Consist of borrowings under a $196,350,000 loan facility due 2023, bearing interest at prime plus 0.75% to 1.25% or banker's acceptance plus 3% stamping fee.
[2] Consists of agreements bearing interest at rates ranging from 4% to 4.25% and due to 2023.
[3] Bear interest at 5.1%, due Dec. 31, 2024, and convertible into Melcor REIT units at $8.90 per unit.

[4] Consists of $13,234,000 debt on land, bearing interest at rates ranging from 7.83% to 8.42% and due on demand; and $9,363,000 debt on investment properties under development, bearing interest at 6.95%.

[5] Bearing interest at rates ranging from 2.62%% to 8.05% and due to 2028.

Minimum debt repayments on investment properties for the next five years were reported as follows:

2023	$91,523,000
2024	60,312,000
2025	57,396,000
2026	80,217,000
2027	32,132,000
Thereafter	220,431,000

Wholly Owned Subsidiaries

Melcor Developments Arizona, Inc., Ariz.
Melcor Homes Ltd.
Melcor Lakeside Inc., Alta.
Stanley Investments Inc., Edmonton, Alta.

Subsidiaries

55.4% int. in **Melcor Real Estate Investment Trust**, Edmonton, Alta. (see separate coverage)

Note: The preceding list includes only the major related companies in which interests are held.

Financial Statistics

Periods ended:	12m Dec. 31/22[A]		12m Dec. 31/21[A]
	$000s	%Chg	$000s
Total revenue	**241,747**	**-23**	**315,628**
Salaries & benefits	11,721		11,808
General & admin. expense	10,115		8,613
Stock-based compensation	841		1,132
Other operating expense	122,479		174,550
Operating expense	**145,156**	**-26**	**196,103**
Operating income	**96,591**	**-19**	**119,525**
Deprec. & amort.	1,350		1,334
Finance income	1,614		572
Finance costs, gross	16,169		27,868
Pre-tax income	**112,418**	**+42**	**78,890**
Income taxes	23,064		22,579
Net income	**89,354**	**+59**	**56,311**
Cash & equivalent	80,465		59,920
Accounts receivable	109,719		137,836
Income-producing props	1,093,350		1,105,264
Properties under devel.	252,433		201,020
Properties for future devel.	384,681		387,598
Property interests, net	1,886,522		1,857,498
Total assets	**2,167,050**	**+3**	**2,113,927**
Accts. pay. & accr. liabs	53,213		50,476
Long-term debt, gross	740,365		716,913
Shareholders' equity	1,178,336		1,116,469
Cash from oper. activs	**18,351**	**-75**	**72,822**
Cash from fin. activs	(17,259)		(24,556)
Cash from invest. activs	18,330		(17,678)
Net cash position	**80,465**	**+34**	**59,920**
Capital expenditures	(735)		(1,218)
Capital disposals	74		283
Increase in property	(16,007)		(24,168)
Decrease in property	34,998		7,425
	$		$
Earnings per share*	2.75		1.70
Cash flow per share*	0.57		2.20
Funds from opers. per sh.*	1.88		2.46
Cash divd. per share*	0.58		0.44
Total divd. per share*	**0.58**		**0.44**
	shs		shs
No. of shs. o/s*	31,248,628		32,961,015
Avg. no. of shs. o/s*	32,452,749		33,038,543
	%		%
Net profit margin	36.96		17.84
Return on equity	7.79		5.13
Return on assets	4.77		3.70
Foreign sales percent	7		22
No. of employees (FTEs)	123		124

* Common
[A] Reported in accordance with IFRS

Latest Results

Periods ended:	3m Mar. 31/23[A]		3m Mar. 31/22[A]
	$000s	%Chg	$000s
Total revenue	36,077	-32	53,306
Net income	2,153	-13	2,470
	$		$
Earnings per share*	0.07		0.08

* Common
[A] Reported in accordance with IFRS

Historical Summary
(as originally stated)

Fiscal Year	Total Rev.	Net Inc. Bef. Disc.	EPS*
	$000s	$000s	$
2022[A]	241,747	89,354	2.75
2021[A]	315,628	56,311	1.70
2020[A]	226,818	11,464	0.34
2019[A]	207,971	37,741	1.13
2018[A]	267,434	64,273	1.92

* Common
[A] Reported in accordance with IFRS

M.71 Melcor Real Estate Investment Trust

Symbol - MR.UN **Exchange** - TSX **CUSIP** - 58546R
Head Office - 900-10310 Jasper Ave, Edmonton, AB, T5J 1Y8 **Telephone** - (780) 423-6931 **Toll-free** - (855) 673-6931
Website - www.melcorreit.ca
Email - nstefura@melcor.ca
Investor Relations - Naomi M. Stefura (855) 673-6931
Auditors - PricewaterhouseCoopers LLP C.A., Edmonton, Alta.
Lawyers - Bryan & Company LLP, Edmonton, Alta.
Transfer Agents - Odyssey Trust Company
Managers - Melcor Developments Ltd., Edmonton, Alta.
Profile - (Alta. 2013) Owns and acquires office, retail and industrial properties in western Canada.

At Mar. 31, 2023, the trust owned 38 properties in Edmonton (20), Calgary (7), Red Deer (1), Lethbridge (3) and Grande Prairie (1), Alta., Regina (5), Sask., and Kelowna (1), B.C., totaling 3,146,006 sq. ft., including 50% interest in a 308-unit manufactured home land lease community in Calgary. **Melcor Developments Ltd.** is the trust's manager.

Geographic diversification of property portfolio at Mar. 31, 2023:

Region	GLA[1]	% of GLA
Northern Alberta	1,959,315	62%
Southern Alberta	889,283	28%
Saskatchewan & B.C.	297,408	10%
	3,146,006	100%

[1] Gross leasable area (sq. ft.).

Breakdown by property type at Mar. 31, 2023:

Type	Props.	GLA	% of GLA
Office	20	1,541,429	49.0%
Retail	14	1,396,486	44.4%
Industrial	3	208,091	6.6%
Other[1]	1	n.a.	n.a.
	38	3,146,006	100%

[1] Land lease community.

Recent Merger and Acquisition Activity

Status: completed **Announced:** Feb. 2, 2023
Melcor Real Estate Investment Trust sold the Kelowna Business Centre, a 71,600-sq. ft. office building in Kelowna, B.C., for $19,500,000, excluding closing costs.

Trustees - Ralph B. Young, chr., Edmonton, Alta.; Andrew J. (Andy) Melton, CEO, Calgary, Alta.; Naomi M. Stefura, CFO & corp. sec., Edmonton, Alta.; Laurence M. (Larry) Pollock‡, Edmonton, Alta.; Carolyn J. Graham, Edmonton, Alta.; Richard Kirby, Edmonton, Alta.; Bernadette (Bernie) Kollman, Edmonton, Alta.
‡ Lead trustee

Capital Stock

	Authorized (shs.)	Outstanding (shs.)[1]
Trust Unit	unlimited	12,963,169
Special Voting Unit	unlimited	16,125,147
Class B LP Unit	unlimited	16,125,147[2]
Class C LP Unit	unlimited	10,785,613[2]

[1] At Mar. 31, 2023
[2] Classified as debt.

Note: Limited partnership units are securities of indirect subsidiary Melcor REIT Limited Partnership.

Trust Unit - One vote per unit.

Special Voting Unit - Issued to holders of class B limited partnership units of subsidiary Melcor REIT Limited Partnership. Each special voting unit entitles the holder to a number of votes at unitholder meetings equal to the number of trust units into which the class B limited partnership units are exchangeable.

Class B Limited Partnership Unit - Entitled to distributions equal to those provided to trust units. Directly exchangeable into trust units on a 1-for-1 basis at any time by holder. All held by Melcor Developments Ltd. Classified as financial liabilities under IFRS.

Class C Limited Partnership Unit - Entitled to distributions in an amount sufficient to permit Melcor Developments to satisfy required principal and interest payments on retained debt. Rank in priority to class B limited partnership units with respect to payment of distributions. All held by Melcor Developments. Classified as financial liabilities under IFRS.

Major Shareholder - Melcor Developments Ltd. held 55.4% interest at May 10, 2023.

Price Range - MR.UN/TSX

Year	Volume	High	Low	Close
2022	2,145,483	$7.69	$5.00	$5.53
2021	3,033,286	$7.31	$4.65	$6.79
2020	4,557,754	$8.35	$2.61	$4.83
2019	2,751,267	$8.22	$7.31	$8.12
2018	2,920,526	$8.69	$6.76	$7.46

Recent Close: $4.80

Capital Stock Changes - During 2022, 3,824 trust units were repurchased under a Normal Course Issuer Bid.

Dividends

MR.UN unit Ra $0.48 pa M est. Sept. 15, 2021
Prev. Rate: $0.42 est. Feb. 16, 2021
Prev. Rate: $0.36 est. May 15, 2020

Wholly Owned Subsidiaries

Melcor REIT GP Inc., Edmonton, Alta.
- 44.6% int. in **Melcor REIT Limited Partnership**, Edmonton, Alta.

Financial Statistics

Periods ended:	12m Dec. 31/22[A]		12m Dec. 31/21[A]
	$000s	%Chg	$000s
Total revenue	**74,105**	**0**	**74,094**
Rental operating expense	31,060		30,340
General & admin. expense	3,358		2,953
Operating expense	**34,418**	**+3**	**33,293**
Operating income	**39,687**	**-3**	**40,801**
Finance income	31		30
Finance costs, gross	18,431		28,391
Pre-tax income	**29,610**	**n.a.**	**(16,287)**
Net income	**29,610**	**n.a.**	**(16,287)**
Cash & equivalent	3,304		7,255
Accounts receivable	2,079		1,996
Current assets	26,839		11,222
Income-producing props	672,010		699,142
Property interests, net	672,010		699,142
Total assets	**730,769**	**-1**	**735,668**
Bank indebtedness	31,634		nil
Accts. pay. & accr. liabs	2,216		1,566
Current liabilities	127,682		85,073
Long-term debt, gross	494,665		551,117
Long-term debt, net	411,669		477,579
Shareholders' equity	189,197		165,834
Cash from oper. activs	**11,936**	**-20**	**14,881**
Cash from fin. activs	(11,435)		(9,048)
Cash from invest. activs	(4,452)		(2,322)
Net cash position	**3,304**	**-54**	**7,255**
Capital expenditures	(3,452)		(2,322)
	$		$
Earnings per share*	2.28		(1.25)
Cash flow per share*	0.92		1.15
Funds from opers. per sh.*	0.85		0.92
Adj. funds from opers. per sh.*	0.59		0.69
Cash divd. per share*	0.48		0.45
Total divd. per share*	**0.48**		**0.45**
	shs		shs
No. of shs. o/s*	12,963,169		12,966,993
Avg. no. of shs. o/s*	12,963,955		12,989,119
	%		%
Net profit margin	39.96		(21.98)
Return on equity	16.68		(9.20)
Return on assets	6.55		1.66

* Trus unit
[A] Reported in accordance with IFRS

Latest Results

Periods ended:	3m Mar. 31/23[A]		3m Mar. 31/22[A]
	$000s	%Chg	$000s
Total revenue	18,990	0	18,965
Net income	3,656	n.a.	(6,538)
	$		$
Earnings per share*	0.28		(0.50)

* Trus unit
[A] Reported in accordance with IFRS

Historical Summary
(as originally stated)

Fiscal Year	Total Rev.	Net Inc. Bef. Disc.	EPS*
	$000s	$000s	$
2022[A]	74,105	29,610	2.28
2021[A]	74,094	(16,287)	(1.25)
2020[A]	74,572	5,763	0.44
2019[A]	71,159	(488)	(0.04)
2018[A]	70,173	17,610	1.34

* Trus unit
[A] Reported in accordance with IFRS

M.72 Memex Inc.

Symbol - OEE **Exchange** - TSX-VEN **CUSIP** - 58600T
Head Office - Unit 200, 880 Laurentian Dr, Burlington, ON, L7N 3V6 **Telephone** - (905) 635-3040 **Toll-free** - (866) 573-3895 **Fax** - (905) 631-9640
Website - www.memexoee.com
Email - investor.relations@memexoee.com
Investor Relations - Edward A. Crymble (866) 573-3895
Auditors - McGovern Hurley LLP C.A., Toronto, Ont.
Lawyers - Lindsey MacCarthy LLP, Calgary, Alta.

Transfer Agents - Computershare Trust Company of Canada Inc.
Profile - (Alta. 2013 amalg.; orig. Alta., 2011) Develops, sells and manufactures MERLIN, a hardware and software solution that provides real-time manufacturing analytics from the shop-floor to top-floor.

Software products include MERLIN Tempus™, which measures and analyzes manufacturing time; MERLIN Tempus Enterprise Edition (EE), which extends the capabilities of MERLIN Tempus™ with full Overall Equipment Effectiveness (OEE), a dynamic job scheduler and connectivity to Enterprise Resource Planning (ERP) systems; MERLIN Financial Overall Equipment Effectiveness (FOEE) calculates the average profit throughput rate using the data collected by MERLIN Tempus EE, which then used to calculate the Contribution of Constraint hour (CCh); MERLIN Continuous Improvement (CI) fast-track services, a nine-step roadmap to faster productivity improvement; MERLIN Operator Portal, a Windows-based Human Machine Interface (HMI) that provides operators with a live window into what information is being collected from the machines, in real-time; MERLIN ERP connector, a bi-synchronous import and export of work orders; and AX2245 scangun bar code scanner.

Hardware products include MERLIN MTC-One, which incorporate sensor-based process-driven data; MERLIN AX760-MTC, a fully configurable MTConnect hardware adapter; and MERLIN software adapter for Siemens Sinumerik 840D.

Customers include manufacturing and aerospace sectors worldwide.
Predecessor Detail - Name changed from Astrix Networks Inc., July 22, 2015.
Directors - David R. McPhail, pres. & CEO, Norval, Ont.; Edward A. Crymble, CFO & corp. sec., Brantford, Ont.; Joseph (Joe) Brennan, Calgary, Alta.; Michael Christiansen, Las Vegas, Nev.; Scott Kaplanis, Toronto, Ont.
Other Exec. Officers - Rick Mosca, COO & interim chief tech. officer; John R. Rattray, sr. v-p, bus. devel. & mktg.

Capital Stock

	Authorized (shs.)	Outstanding (shs.)[1]
Preferred	unlimited	nil
Common	unlimited	137,622,995

[1] At Jan. 31, 2023

Major Shareholder - David R. McPhail held 12.47% interest at Jan. 31, 2023.

Price Range - OEE/TSX-VEN

Year	Volume	High	Low	Close
2022	20,056,388	$0.03	$0.01	$0.01
2021	92,483,663	$0.04	$0.01	$0.03
2020	44,809,392	$0.05	$0.01	$0.02
2019	53,933,759	$0.07	$0.02	$0.04
2018	45,531,694	$0.18	$0.02	$0.02

Recent Close: $0.01
Capital Stock Changes - There were no changes to capital stock during fiscal 2022.

Wholly Owned Subsidiaries
Astrix Networks America Inc., Del.
Memex Automation Inc., Burlington, Ont.

Financial Statistics

Periods ended:	12m Sept. 30/22[A]		12m Sept. 30/21[A]
	$000s	%Chg	$000s
Operating revenue	**2,141**	**-30**	**3,040**
Cost of sales	496		555
Salaries & benefits	1,205		1,398
General & admin expense	669		501
Stock-based compensation	65		5
Operating expense	**2,435**	**-1**	**2,459**
Operating income	**(294)**	**n.a.**	**581**
Deprec., depl. & amort	122		126
Finance costs, gross	44		249
Pre-tax income	**(437)**	**n.a.**	**166**
Net income	**(437)**	**n.a.**	**166**
Cash & equivalent	290		709
Inventories	160		142
Accounts receivable	107		250
Current assets	586		1,139
Fixed assets, net	41		54
Right-of-use assets	186		254
Intangibles, net	81		121
Total assets	**894**	**-43**	**1,569**
Accts. pay. & accr. liabs	200		169
Current liabilities	1,519		1,305
Long-term debt, gross	898		735
Long-term debt, net	519		543
Long-term lease liabilities	164		248
Shareholders' equity	(1,308)		(936)
Cash from oper. activs	**(132)**	**n.a.**	**431**
Cash from fin. activs	(286)		(267)
Cash from invest. activs	nil		(4)
Net cash position	**290**	**-59**	**709**
Capital expenditures	nil		(4)
	$		$
Earnings per share*	(0.00)		0.00
Cash flow per share*	(0.00)		0.00
	shs		shs
No. of shs. o/s*	137,622,995		137,622,995
Avg. no. of shs. o/s*	137,622,995		136,737,830
	%		%
Net profit margin	(20.41)		5.46
Return on equity	n.m.		n.m.
Return on assets	(31.91)		25.45
Foreign sales percent	91		87

* Common
[A] Reported in accordance with IFRS

Latest Results

Periods ended:	3m Dec. 31/22[A]		3m Dec. 31/21[A]
	$000s	%Chg	$000s
Operating revenue	557	+11	502
Net income	(19)	n.a.	(178)
	$		$
Earnings per share*	(0.00)		(0.00)

* Common
[A] Reported in accordance with IFRS

Historical Summary
(as originally stated)

Fiscal Year	Oper. Rev.	Net Inc. Bef. Disc.	EPS*
	$000s	$000s	$
2022[A]	2,141	(437)	(0.00)
2021[A]	3,040	166	0.00
2020[A]	2,252	(749)	(0.01)
2019[A]	3,251	(1,072)	(0.01)
2018[A]	2,853	(2,254)	(0.02)

* Common
[A] Reported in accordance with IFRS

M.73 Mene Inc.

Symbol - MENE **Exchange** - TSX-VEN **CUSIP** - 58680T
Head Office - 307-334 Adelaide St W, Toronto, ON, M5V 1R4 **Telephone** - (647) 494-0296 **Fax** - (647) 499-4435
Website - www.mene.com
Email - ir@mene.com
Investor Relations - Gavin Johnson (289) 748-3702
Auditors - McGovern Hurley LLP C.A., Toronto, Ont.
Transfer Agents - Computershare Trust Company of Canada Inc., Vancouver, B.C.
Profile - (Ont. 2018; orig. B.C., 1980) Designs, manufactures and markets gold and platinum jewelry through an e-commerce site under the Mene brand.

The company's collection of pure 24 karat gold and platinum jewelry includes charms, chains, bands, earrings, pendants, rings, bracelets, medallions and gifts. Jewelry is sold by the gold and platinum weight value on the date of sale plus a transparent design and manufacturing premium, which ranges from 20% to 43% of the daily precious metal value. The company offers a lifetime Buyback Guarantee to buy back or exchange any authentic Mene jewelry at the prevailing precious metal value minus a 10% fee on the spot price of the precious metal weight on the date of authenticity. The company has sold jewelry to customers in the U.S., Canada and over 60 countries through mene.com.

The company has manufacturing and fulfillment centres in the United States; a technology and customer support office in Toronto, Ont.; and a design and marketing office in Paris, France. All physical gold and platinum used in the crafting of jewelry is provided by **GoldMoney Inc.** at a price of 0.5% over the spot price.

On Oct. 26, 2022, the company acquired a manufacturing facility in the United States for $678,309 cash and issuance of 1,206,583 class B subordinate voting shares at $0.44 per share. The acquisition included all the equipment and rights used in connection with the operation of the facility.
Predecessor Detail - Name changed from Amador Gold Corp., Oct. 30, 2018, pursuant to reverse takeover acquisition of (old) Mene Inc.
Directors - Roy Sebag, co-founder, chr., pres. & CEO, Oxford, Oxon., United Kingdom; Sunjoo Moon, chief creative officer, Beverly Hills, Calif.; Joshua D. (Josh) Crumb, Huntsville, Ont.; Andres Finkielsztain, Buenos Aires, Argentina
Other Exec. Officers - Diana Widmaier-Picasso, co-founder & chief artistic officer; Gavin Johnson, CFO; Karen Li, v-p, opers. & logistics; Anja Rubik, dir., content creative

Capital Stock

	Authorized (shs.)	Outstanding (shs.)[1]
Class A Superior Vtg.	unlimited	110,342,154
Class B Subord. Vtg.	unlimited	149,388,759

[1] At May 30, 2023

Class A Superior Voting - Convertible into class B shares on a 1-for-1 basis. 20 votes per share.
Class B Subordinate Voting - One vote per share.
Major Shareholder - Roy Sebag held 70.3% interest, GoldMoney Inc. held 13.7% interest and Diana Widmaier-Picasso held 10.69% interest at May 27, 2022.

Price Range - MENE/TSX-VEN

Year	Volume	High	Low	Close
2022	2,123,350	$0.80	$0.39	$0.50
2021	5,809,630	$1.03	$0.50	$0.80
2020	12,548,546	$0.85	$0.24	$0.67
2019	23,635,006	$0.88	$0.37	$0.55
2018	15,963,753	$1.10	$0.54	$0.60

Recent Close: $0.41
Capital Stock Changes - On Oct. 26, 2022, 1,206,583 class B subordinate voting shares were issued pursuant to the acquisition of a manufacturing facility in the United States. Also during 2022, class B subordinate voting shares were issued as follows: 125,000 on exercise of warrants and 65,476 on vesting of restricted share units.

Wholly Owned Subsidiaries
Mene, Inc., Del.

Financial Statistics

Periods ended:	12m Dec. 31/22[A]		12m Dec. 31/21[A]
	$000s	%Chg	$000s
Operating revenue	**26,912**	**+1**	**26,773**
Cost of sales	20,268		20,251
Research & devel. expense	523		634
General & admin expense	5,905		5,329
Stock-based compensation	132		69
Other operating expense	219		nil
Operating expense	**27,047**	**+3**	**26,284**
Operating income	**(135)**	**n.a.**	**489**
Deprec., depl. & amort.	179		171
Finance income	160		28
Finance costs, gross	333		378
Pre-tax income	**(1,281)**	**n.a.**	**(216)**
Income taxes	182		(183)
Net income	**(1,463)**	**n.a.**	**(33)**
Cash & equivalent	12,966		8,645
Inventories	14,899		18,535
Accounts receivable	72		44
Current assets	28,543		27,698
Fixed assets, net	946		486
Right-of-use assets	874		nil
Intangibles, net	1,351		1,510
Total assets	**31,714**	**+7**	**29,694**
Accts. pay. & accr. liabs	1,232		1,091
Current liabilities	13,507		12,073
Long-term lease liabilities	738		nil
Shareholders' equity	17,469		17,621
Cash from oper. activs	**4,700**	**n.a.**	**(1,017)**
Cash from fin. activs	14		(4,685)
Cash from invest. activs	(11,508)		3,967
Net cash position	**1,057**	**-86**	**7,486**
Capital expenditures	(730)		(36)
Capital disposals	nil		2
	$		$
Earnings per share*	(0.01)		(0.00)
Cash flow per share*	0.02		(0.00)
	shs		shs
No. of shs. o/s*	258,333,854		258,333,854
Avg. no. of shs. o/s*	258,631,693		253,938,678
	%		%
Net profit margin	(5.44)		(0.12)
Return on equity	(8.34)		(0.23)
Return on assets	(3.53)		0.08

* Common
[A] Reported in accordance with IFRS

Latest Results

Periods ended:	3m Mar. 31/23[A]		3m Mar. 31/22[A]
	$000s	%Chg	$000s
Operating revenue	7,152	-3	7,346
Net income	(634)	n.a.	(264)
	$		$
Earnings per share*	(0.00)		(0.00)

* Common
[A] Reported in accordance with IFRS

Historical Summary
(as originally stated)

Fiscal Year	Oper. Rev. $000s	Net Inc. Bef. Disc. $000s	EPS* $
2022[A]	26,912	(1,463)	(0.01)
2021[A]	26,773	(33)	(0.00)
2020[A]	21,130	(3,345)	(0.01)
2019[A]	13,062	(6,765)	(0.03)
2018[A1]	7,928	(6,967)	(0.03)

* Common
[A] Reported in accordance with IFRS
[1] Results reflect the Oct. 31, 2018, reverse takeover acquisition of (old) Mene Inc.

M.74 Meraki Acquisition One, Inc.

Symbol - MRKI.P **Exchange** - TSX-VEN **CUSIP** - 587330
Head Office - 1000-595 Howe St, Vancouver, BC, V6C 2T5 **Telephone** - (516) 299-9092
Email - joel@merakiacquisition.com
Investor Relations - Joel Arberman (516) 299-9092
Auditors - RSM Alberta LLP C.A., Calgary, Alta.
Lawyers - Oziel Law, Toronto, Ont.
Transfer Agents - Odyssey Trust Company, Vancouver, B.C.
Profile - (B.C. 2021) Capital Pool Company.

Recent Merger and Acquisition Activity

Status: pending **Revised:** Nov. 21, 2022
UPDATE: The companies entered into a definitive agreement. Shares of Vaultex would be exchanged for shares of Meraki on a one-for-one basis based on Vaultex having a deemed price of Cdn$0.25 per share in exchange for one Meraki common share having a deemed price of $0.25 per share. A total of 100,000,000 Vaultex shares were expected to be outstanding on closing, excluding shares to be issued under a concurrent financing and on conversion of a convertible debenture. The resulting issuer was expected to change its name to Vaultex Group Inc. PREVIOUS: Meraki Acquisition One, Inc. entered into a letter of intent for the Qualifying Transaction reverse takeover acquisition of Vaultex Pte. Ltd., an allocated gold and commodity trading platform based and regulatory compliant in Singapore. Terms were to be entered into. As part the transaction, Meraki would continue from the jurisdiction of British Columbia to the Cayman Islands or another offshore jurisdiction.

Directors - Joel Arberman, CEO & CFO, Fla.; Sunil Cherian, Calif.; Mary-Frances Coleman, Ariz.; Benjamin McMillan, Fla.; Sokhie S. Puar, Vancouver, B.C.
Other Exec. Officers - Michael Rennie, corp. sec.

Capital Stock

	Authorized (shs.)	Outstanding (shs.)[1]
Common	unlimited	4,400,000

[1] At Feb. 14, 2022

Major Shareholder - Joel Arberman held 34.09% interest at Feb. 14, 2022.

Price Range - MRKI.P/TSX-VEN

Year	Volume	High	Low	Close
2022	60,500	$0.20	$0.14	$0.20

Capital Stock Changes - On Feb. 14, 2022, an initial public offering of 2,000,000 common shares was completed at 10¢ per share.

M.75 Metalore Resources Limited

Symbol - MET **Exchange** - TSX-VEN **CUSIP** - 591307
Head Office - PO Box 422, Simcoe, ON, N3Y 4L5 **Telephone** - (519) 428-2464 **Fax** - (519) 428-2466
Website - www.metaloreresources.ca
Email - armen.chilian@gmail.com
Investor Relations - Armen A. Chilian (519) 428-2464
Auditors - Scarrow & Donald LLP C.A., Winnipeg, Man.
Bankers - Royal Bank of Canada
Transfer Agents - Computershare Trust Company of Canada Inc., Toronto, Ont.
Profile - (Ont. 1943) Explores for, develops and produces natural gas in southwestern Ontario and has mineral interests in northwestern Ontario.

Owns and/or controls 40,000 acres of natural gas leases in Charlotteville, Walsingham and Houghton twps. in Norfolk cty., Ont., including 80 producing natural gas wells. Distributes gas to 100 commercial and residential customers under a cooperative agreement with **Enbridge Gas Inc.**

Mineral property holdings include 1% NSR royalty on 18 claims in the Brookbank and Beardmore area, and 21% to 26% participating interest in over 600 mining claims in Sandra, Irwin, Walters, Leduc and LeGault twps., the majority of which are subject to a working option agreement with **Greenstone Gold Mines GP Inc.** and **Centerra Gold Inc.**, all northwestern Ontario.

Periods ended:	12m Mar. 31/22	12m Mar. 31/21
Avg. gas prod., mcf/d	359	486
Gas reserves, net, mmcf	5,313	4,422

Predecessor Detail - Name changed from New Metalore Mining Company Limited, Oct. 22, 1976.
Directors - John C. McVicar†, chr., Brantford, Ont.; Armen A. Chilian, pres., CEO & corp. sec., London, Ont.; Donald W Bryson, CFO, Simcoe, Ont.; Timothy J. Cronkwright, Simcoe, Ont.; Bruce A. Davis, Grand Rapids, Minn.
† Lead director

Capital Stock

	Authorized (shs.)	Outstanding (shs.)[1]
Common	4,000,000	1,775,035

[1] At Sept. 1, 2022

Major Shareholder - Agrita Chilian held 32.7% interest and Carl Chilian held 26.4% interest at Sept. 1, 2022.

Price Range - MET/TSX-VEN

Year	Volume	High	Low	Close
2022	71,179	$3.00	$2.20	$2.42
2021	60,145	$3.50	$2.15	$2.24
2020	68,649	$3.65	$1.00	$2.71
2019	30,103	$2.60	$0.89	$1.95
2018	40,663	$3.00	$1.40	$1.63

Recent Close: $2.65
Capital Stock Changes - There were no changes in capital stock from fiscal 2004 to fiscal 2022, inclusive.

Financial Statistics

Periods ended:	12m Mar. 31/22[A]		12m Mar. 31/21[A]
	$000s	%Chg	$000s
Operating revenue	**762**	**+24**	**613**
Cost of goods sold	365		357
Exploration expense	53		80
General & admin expense	124		162
Operating expense	**542**	**-10**	**599**
Operating income	**220**	**n.m.**	**14**
Deprec., depl. & amort.	117		316
Finance income	28		58
Finance costs, gross	31		5
Write-downs/write-offs	2,278		(3,255)
Pre-tax income	**2,378**	**+242**	**696**
Income taxes	629		38
Net income	**1,749**	**+166**	**657**
Cash & equivalent	4,663		4,644
Inventories	28		21
Accounts receivable	105		62
Current assets	4,838		4,767
Fixed assets, net	6,700		4,385
Total assets	**11,538**	**+26**	**9,152**
Accts. pay. & accr. liabs	68		104
Current liabilities	78		104
Shareholders' equity	9,014		7,259
Cash from oper. activs	**160**	**-95**	**3,108**
Cash from invest. activs	705		(128)
Net cash position	**1,426**	**-60**	**3,564**
Capital expenditures	(147)		(101)
	$		$
Earnings per share*	0.99		0.37
Cash flow per share*	0.09		1.75
	shs		shs
No. of shs. o/s*	1,775,035		1,775,035
Avg. no. of shs. o/s*	1,775,035		1,775,035
	%		%
Net profit margin	229.53		107.18
Return on equity	21.50		9.40
Return on assets	17.13		7.89

* Common
[A] Reported in accordance with IFRS

Latest Results

Periods ended:	3m June 30/22[A]		3m June 30/21[A]
	$000s	%Chg	$000s
Operating revenue	248	+73	143
Net income	82	n.a.	(96)
	$		$
Earnings per share*	0.05		(0.05)

* Common
[A] Reported in accordance with IFRS

Historical Summary
(as originally stated)

Fiscal Year	Oper. Rev. $000s	Net Inc. Bef. Disc. $000s	EPS* $
2022[A]	762	1,749	0.99
2021[A]	613	657	0.37
2020[A]	577	(619)	(0.35)
2019[A]	726	396	0.22
2018[A]	701	267	0.15

* Common
[A] Reported in accordance with IFRS

M.76 Metamaterial Exchangeco Inc.

Symbol - MMAX **Exchange** - CSE **CUSIP** - 59134L
Head Office - 1 Research Dr, Dartmouth, NS, B2Y 4M9 **Telephone** - (902) 482-5729 **Fax** - (902) 466-6889
Email - george.palikaras@metamaterial.com
Investor Relations - George Palikaras (902) 428-5729
Transfer Agents - American Stock Transfer & Trust Company, LLC, New York, N.Y.
Profile - (Ont. 2020) Wholly owned subsidiary of **Meta Materials Inc.**, which designs and manufactures advanced materials and performance functional films which are engineered at the nanoscale to control light and electromagnetic waves. Materials are developed for the a variety of applications in the automotive, aerospace, consumer electronics and medical industries.

The company does not prepare separate financial statements due to exemption from the continuous disclosure requirements under the Securities Act. One of the conditions of the exemption is that the company is required to file with the Canadian securities commissions all documents filed by U.S. parent company **Meta Materials Inc.**, with the U.S. Securities Exchange Commission.

Predecessor Detail - Name changed from 2798832 Ontario Inc., Feb. 3, 2021.
Directors - John A. Brda, CEO, Mo.; Roger Wurtele, CFO, Tex.; Eric M. Leslie, Calgary, Alta.

Capital Stock

	Authorized (shs.)	Outstanding (shs.)[1]
Exchangeable	unlimited	99,665,362

[1] At June 29, 2021

Exchangeable - Entitled to receive dividends equivalent to dividends declared by parent company Meta Materials Inc. on its common shares. Exchangeable at any time at the holder's option for common shares of Meta Material Inc., on a one-for-one basis. Redeemable by the company at any time on or after June 28, 2028. Retractable by holder at any time. One vote per share.

Common - One vote per share.

Major Shareholder - Meta Materials Inc. held 100% interest at June 29, 2021.

Price Range - MMAX/CSE

Year	Volume	High	Low	Close
2022	3,242,066	$3.65	$0.76	$1.34
2021	3,837,508	$15.90	$3.00	$3.23

Recent Close: $0.26

Wholly Owned Subsidiaries

Metamaterial Inc., Dartmouth, N.S.
- 100% int. in **Medical Wireless Sensing Limited**, United Kingdom.
- 100% int. in **Metamaterial Technologies Canada Inc.**, Dartmouth, N.S.
  - 100% int. in **Lamda Guard Inc.**, Canada. dormant.
  - 100% int. in **Lamda Lux Inc.**, Canada. dormant.
  - 100% int. in **Lamda Solar Inc.**, Canada. dormant.
- 100% int. in **Metamaterial Technologies USA, Inc.**, United States.

M.77 MetaWorks Platforms, Inc.

Symbol - MWRK **Exchange -** CSE **CUSIP -** 23131W

Head Office - 3250 Oakland Hills Crt, Fairfield, CA, United States, 94534 **Telephone -** (424) 570-9446

Website - metaworksplatforms.io

Email - scott@metaworksplatforms.io

Investor Relations - Scott Gallagher (424) 570-9446

Auditors -

Transfer Agents - Computershare Trust Company of Canada Inc., Vancouver, B.C.

Employees - 2 at Mar. 24, 2022

Profile - (Nev. 2010) Provides a turnkey set of services for companies to develop and integrate Web 3.0/Metaverse technologies, Non-Fungible Tokens (NFTs), blockchain and cryptocurrency technologies into their business operations.

Services include strategic planning, project planning, structure development and administration, business plan modelling, technology development support, whitepaper preparation, due diligence reporting, governance planning and management, and movie distribution. These services are provided by a combination of the company's management, **Business Instincts Group Inc.**, and other external consultants.

Platforms offered include MusicFX, an NFT platform that uses blockchain technology for fans and artists to connect through digital innovations and engagement; Motoclub, a platform dedicated for the creation and sale of collectible NFTs based on premier automotive vehicles and memorabilia: VUELE™, a premier platform for collecting, watching and trading exclusive, limited edition feature-length film; BitRail, which allows e-commerce providers to operate regulatory compliant cryptocurrencies for payments; FreedomCoin, which is designed for inexpensive, instant and secure payments and money transfers; KodakOne (Ryde), which allows professionals in the photo industry to easily monitor and monetize unlicensed image use worldwide; WAX and Topps, which allows users to trade Garbage Pail Kids Series 1 NFTs worldwide; and a security token reporting system developed in partnership with the Canadian Stock Exchange (CSE) and **Odyssey Trust Company** which associates a unique security token with each issuer on the CSE that opts into the platform.

The company generates revenue from NFT sales, consulting services and movie distribution, and may also accept tokens, coins or equity in payment for its services.

Predecessor Detail - Name changed from CurrencyWorks Inc., Aug. 24, 2022.

Directors - Cameron Chell, chr., Bowen Island, B.C.; James P. (Jimmy) Geiskopf†, Fairfield, Calif.; Edmund C. Moy, Arlington, Va.; Shelly Murphy

Other Exec. Officers - Scott Gallagher, pres.; Swapan Kakumanu, CFO, contr. & sec.-treas.; Michael (Mike) Arbach, v-p, tech.

† Lead director

Capital Stock

	Authorized (shs.)	Outstanding (shs.)[1]	Par
Common	400,000,000	78,145,066	US$0.001

[1] At Nov. 10, 2022

Major Shareholder - Widely held at Apr. 20, 2022.

Price Range - MWRK/CSE

Year	Volume	High	Low	Close
2022	5,546,445	$0.40	$0.01	$0.04
2021	55,541,674	$4.63	$0.26	$0.34
2020	24,177,515	$0.70	$0.04	$0.54
2019	8,927,879	$0.55	$0.07	$0.08
2018	418,640	$0.65	$0.35	$0.50

Recent Close: $0.08

Wholly Owned Subsidiaries

CurrencyWorks USA Inc., Nev.

Subsidiaries

51% int. in **EnderbyWorks, LLC**, Del.
80% int. in **Motoclub LLC**, Del.

Investments

6.31% int. in **VON Republic Holdings Inc.**, Bowen Island, B.C.

Financial Statistics

Periods ended:	12m Dec. 31/21[A]		12m Dec. 31/20[A]
	US$000s	%Chg	US$000s
Operating revenue	**472**	**+148**	**190**
General & admin expense	10,433		795
Operating expense	**10,433**	**n.m.**	**795**
Operating income	**(9,961)**	**n.a.**	**(605)**
Deprec., depl. & amort.	75		nil
Finance income	212		315
Finance costs, gross	65		151
Pre-tax income	**(23,661)**	**n.a.**	**(4,056)**
Net income	**(23,661)**	**n.a.**	**(4,056)**
Net inc. for equity hldrs	**(22,749)**	**n.a.**	**(4,013)**
Net inc. for non-cont. int	**(912)**	**n.a.**	**(43)**
Cash & equivalent	567		33
Accounts receivable	nil		90
Current assets	655		142
Long-term investments	481		nil
Intangibles, net	2,925		nil
Total assets	**5,336**	**n.m.**	**142**
Accts. pay. & accr. liabs	1,250		280
Current liabilities	1,250		1,799
Long-term debt, gross	nil		1,026
Long-term debt, net	nil		102
Shareholders' equity	4,506		(5,393)
Non-controlling interest	(895)		(333)
Cash from oper. activs	**(4,763)**	**n.a.**	**(338)**
Cash from fin. activs	9,547		370
Cash from invest. activs	(4,250)		nil
Net cash position	**567**	**n.m.**	**33**
	US$		US$
Earnings per share*	(0.37)		(0.13)
Cash flow per share*	(0.08)		(0.01)
	shs		shs
No. of shs. o/s*	73,359,430		35,426,033
Avg. no. of shs. o/s*	61,125,454		29,922,263
	%		%
Net profit margin	n.m.		n.m.
Return on equity	n.m.		n.m.
Return on assets	(861.48)		n.m.

* Common
[A] Reported in accordance with U.S. GAAP

Latest Results

Periods ended:	9m Sept. 30/22[A]		9m Sept. 30/21[A]
	US$000s	%Chg	US$000s
Operating revenue	1,564	+469	275
Net income	(2,997)	n.a.	(21,606)
Net inc. for equity hldrs	(3,112)	n.a.	(20,976)
Net inc. for non-cont. int	115		(630)
	US$		US$
Earnings per share*	(0.04)		(0.36)

* Common
[A] Reported in accordance with U.S. GAAP

Historical Summary
(as originally stated)

Fiscal Year	Oper. Rev. US$000s	Net Inc. Bef. Disc. US$000s	EPS* US$
2021[A]	472	(23,661)	(0.37)
2020[A]	190	(4,056)	(0.13)
2019[A]	250	(4,888)	(0.20)
2018[A]	nil	(4,020)	(0.24)
2017[A]	500	(467)	(0.07)

* Common
[A] Reported in accordance with U.S. GAAP

M.78 Methanex Corporation*

Symbol - MX **Exchange -** TSX **CUSIP -** 59151K

Head Office - Waterfront Centre, 1800-200 Burrard St, Vancouver, BC, V6C 3M1 **Telephone -** (604) 661-2600 **Toll-free -** (800) 661-8851 **Fax -** (604) 661-2676

Website - www.methanex.com

Email - sherriott@methanex.com

Investor Relations - Sarah Herriott (800) 661-8551

Auditors - KPMG LLP C.A., Vancouver, B.C.

Bankers - Royal Bank of Canada, Vancouver, B.C.

Lawyers - Paul, Weiss, Rifkind, Wharton & Garrison LLP, New York, N.Y.; McCarthy Tétrault LLP, Vancouver, B.C.

Transfer Agents - American Stock Transfer & Trust Company, LLC, New York, N.Y.; TSX Trust Company, Toronto, Ont.

FP500 Revenue Ranking - 106

Employees - 1,410 at Dec. 31, 2022

Profile - (Can. 1992; orig. Alta., 1968) Produces and markets methanol, a clear liquid commodity chemical predominantly produced from natural gas and coal, and also purchases methanol produced by others under offtake contracts and on the spot market.

Methanol is used primarily to produce formaldehyde, acetic acid and a variety of other chemicals that form the basis of a wide variety of industrial and consumer products including wood adhesives for plywood, particleboard, oriented strand board, medium-density fibreboard, paper, paints, plastics, resins, solvents, pharmaceuticals, textiles, coatings, films, fibres, paint removers, explosives, herbicides, pesticides and poultry feed additives. Energy-related applications of methanol include methanol-to-olefins, the basic building blocks used to make many plastics; methyl tertiary butyl ether, a gasoline component; dimethyl ether, which can be blended with liquefied petroleum gas for use in household cooking and heating; fuel applications, including vehicle fuel, marine fuel and as a fuel for industrial boilers and kilns; and biodiesel.

Methanol production facilities are located in New Zealand, consisting of the two Motunui plants and the Waitara Valley facility; in Louisiana, U.S. (Geismar 1 and 2); the Titan plant and the 63.1%-owned Atlas plant (with **British Petroleum plc** holding the remaining 36.9% interest), both in Trinidad; a 50%-owned facility in Damietta, Egypt; in Medicine Hat, Alta.; and in Punta Arenas, Chile (Chile I and Chile IV).

The methanol produced is pumped from coastal plants via pipeline to the adjacent deepwater ports for shipping. Storage and terminal facilities, which are leased or owned, are located in the United States, Canada, Europe, Latin America and Asia. Deliveries of methanol are made using barges, rails, trucks and pipelines. At Dec. 31, 2022, the company owned or managed a fleet of 30 ocean-going vessels to ship the methanol.

Methanol is sold on a worldwide basis through an extensive marketing and distribution system, with marketing offices located in North America (Vancouver, B.C.; and Dallas, Tex.), Europe (Brussels), Asia Pacific (Hong Kong, Shanghai and Beijing, People's Republic of China; Tokyo, Japan; and Seoul, South Korea), South America (Santiago, Chile) and the Middle East (Dubai, U.A.E.).

Methanol Operations

Year ended Dec. 31	2022 000s	2021 000s	Capacity 000s
Production (tonnes):			
Chile (2)	888	807	1,700
Trinidad[1]	981	1,161	1,960
New Zealand (3)	1,230	1,348	2,200
Egypt[2]	385	581	630
Medicine Hat	593	628	640
Louisiana (2)	2,041	1,989	2,200
Total production	6,118	6,514	9,330
Sales volume (tonnes):			
Methanex-produced	6,141	6,207	
Purchased methanol	3,688	3,750	
Commission sales	945	1,227	
Total sales volume	10,774	11,184	
Avg. real. price, US$/tonne	397	393	

[1] Includes wholly owned Titan facility and 63.1%-owned Atlas facility.
[2] 50%-owned.

Predecessor Detail - Name changed from Ocelot Industries Ltd., Mar. 23, 1992.

Directors - Douglas J. (Doug) Arnell, chr., West Vancouver, B.C.; Richard W. (Rich) Sumner, pres. & CEO, North Vancouver, B.C.; James V. (Jim) Bertram, Calgary, Alta.; Paul Dobson, Naples, Fla.; Dr. Maureen E. Howe, Vancouver, B.C.; Robert J. Kostelnik, Fulshear, Tex.; Leslie A. O'Donoghue, Calgary, Alta.; Kevin Rodgers, London, Middx., United Kingdom; Margaret Walker, Austin, Tex.; Benita M. Warmbold, Toronto, Ont.; Xiaoping Yang, Henderson, Nev.

Other Exec. Officers - Mark Allard, sr. v-p, low carbon solutions; Bradley W. (Brad) Boyd, sr. v-p, corp. resources; Karine Delbarre, sr. v-p, global mktg. & logistics; Kevin Maloney, sr. v-p, corp. devel.; Gustavo Parra, sr. v-p, mfg.; Kevin Price, sr. v-p, gen. counsel & corp. sec.; Dean Richardson, sr. v-p, fin. & CFO

Capital Stock

	Authorized (shs.)	Outstanding (shs.)[1]
Preferred	25,000,000	nil
Common	unlimited	67,377,492

[1] At July 25, 2023

Options - At Dec. 31, 2022, options were outstanding to purchase 102,531 common shares at a weighted average exercise price of US$43.96 per share with a weighted average remaining contractual life of 2.25 years.

Normal Course Issuer Bid - The company plans to make normal course purchases of up to 3,506,405 common shares representing 5% of the total outstanding. The bid commenced on Sept. 26, 2022, and expires on Sept. 25, 2023.

Major Shareholder - M&G Investment Management Limited held 20.3% interest at Mar. 9, 2023.

Price Range - MX/TSX

Year	Volume	High	Low	Close
2022	53,746,064	$71.63	$39.00	$51.26
2021	61,874,055	$65.22	$37.85	$50.04
2020	114,023,460	$61.25	$13.24	$58.49
2019	75,550,441	$83.99	$40.11	$50.15
2018	78,388,533	$107.07	$62.48	$65.66

Recent Close: $56.10

Capital Stock Changes - During 2022, 16,800 common shares were issued on exercise of options and 5,551,751 common shares were repurchased under a Normal Course Issuer Bid.

Dividends

MX com Ra US$0.74 pa Q est. June 30, 2023
Prev. Rate: US$0.70 est. Sept. 30, 2022
Prev. Rate: US$0.50 est. Sept. 30, 2021
Prev. Rate: US$0.15 est. June 30, 2020

Long-Term Debt - Outstanding at Dec. 31, 2022:

4.25% notes due Dec. 2024	US$298,836,000
5.125% notes due Oct. 2027	693,649,000
5.25% notes due Dec. 2029	695,283,000
5.65% notes due Dec. 2044	295,606,000
Other limited recourse debt:[1]	
5.58% recourse debt due June 2031	61,978,000
5.35% recourse debt due Sept. 2033	70,312,000
5.08% recourse debt due Sept. 2036	35,849,000
	2,151,513,000
Less: Current portion	15,133,000
	2,136,380,000

[1] Relating to financing for certain ocean going vessels.

Minimum principal repayments of long-term debt for the next five years were as follows:

2023	US$15,067,000
2024	312,580,000
2025	13,660,000
2026	13,796,000
2027	715,173,000
Thereafter	1,100,599,000

Wholly Owned Subsidiaries

Methanex Asia Pacific Limited, Hong Kong, Hong Kong, People's Republic of China.
Methanex Chile S.p.A, Chile.
Methanex Europe N.V., Belgium.
Methanex Louisiana LLC, Del.
Methanex Methanol Company, LLC, Del.
Methanex New Zealand Limited, New Zealand.
Methanex Services (Shanghai) Co., Ltd., Republic of China.
Methanex Trinidad (Titan) Unlimited, Trinidad and Tobago.
Methanex U.S.A. LLC, Del.

Subsidiaries

63.1% int. in **Atlas Methanol Company Unlimited**, Trinidad and Tobago.
60% int. in **Waterfront Shipping Company Limited**, Vancouver, B.C.

Investments

50% int. in **Egyptian Methanex Methanol Company S.A.E.**, Egypt.

Financial Statistics

Periods ended:	12m Dec. 31/22[A]		12m Dec. 31/21[oA]
	US$000s	%Chg	US$000s
Operating revenue	**4,311,188**	**-2**	**4,414,559**
Cost of sales	2,789,921		2,739,817
Salaries & benefits	203,614		212,009
Stock-based compensation	15,398		(1,160)
Other operating expense	437,168		388,844
Operating expense	**3,446,101**	**+3**	**3,339,510**
Operating income	**865,087**	**-20**	**1,075,049**
Deprec., depl. & amort.	372,420		363,084
Finance costs, gross	130,752		144,406
Investment income	76,938		97,743
Pre-tax income	**582,147**	**-13**	**666,338**
Income taxes	119,859		110,427
Net income	**462,288**	**-17**	**555,911**
Net inc. for equity hldrs	**353,830**	**-27**	**482,358**
Net inc. for non-cont. int	**108,458**	**+47**	**73,553**
Cash & equivalent	857,747		932,069
Inventories	439,771		459,556
Accounts receivable	485,939		539,412
Current assets	1,876,374		1,988,797
Long-term investments	202,703		221,939
Fixed assets, net	4,155,283		3,686,149
Total assets	**6,631,480**	**+9**	**6,089,620**
Accts. pay. & accr. liabs	789,200		835,951
Current liabilities	942,617		963,218
Long-term debt, gross	2,151,513		2,158,192
Long-term debt, net	2,136,380		2,146,417
Long-term lease liabilities	761,427		618,800
Shareholders' equity	2,112,013		1,683,576
Non-controlling interest	317,444		271,155
Cash from oper. activs	**987,349**	**-1**	**994,369**
Cash from fin. activs	(508,534)		(643,093)
Cash from invest. activs	(553,137)		(253,048)
Net cash position	**857,747**	**-8**	**932,069**
Capital expenditures	(577,381)		(245,437)
Unfunded pension liability	15,329		15,600
	US$		US$
Earnings per share*	4.95		6.34
Cash flow per share*	13.82		13.08
Cash divd. per share*	0.62		0.33
	shs		shs
No. of shs. o/s*	69,239,136		74,774,087
Avg. no. of shs. o/s*	71,422,360		76,039,118
	%		%
Net profit margin	10.72		12.59
Return on equity	18.64		34.06
Return on assets	8.90		11.48
Foreign sales percent	96		96
No. of employees (FTEs)	1,410		1,300

* Common
[o] Restated
[A] Reported in accordance with IFRS

Latest Results

Periods ended:	6m June 30/23[A]		6m June 30/22[A]
	US$000s	%Chg	US$000s
Operating revenue	1,977,784	-14	2,313,040
Net income	180,931	-34	275,905
Net inc. for equity hldrs	116,460	-52	243,600
Net inc. for non-cont. int	64,471		32,305
	US$		US$
Earnings per share*	1.71		3.34

* Common
[A] Reported in accordance with IFRS

Historical Summary
(as originally stated)

Fiscal Year	Oper. Rev.	Net Inc. Bef. Disc.	EPS*
	US$000s	US$000s	US$
2022[A]	4,311,188	462,288	4.95
2021[A]	4,414,559	555,911	6.34
2020[A]	2,649,963	(125,327)	(2.06)
2019[A]	3,283,514	116,366	1.15
2018[A]	3,931,847	657,984	7.07

* Common
[A] Reported in accordance with IFRS

M.79 Michichi Capital Corp.

Symbol - MCCP.P **Exchange** - TSX-VEN **CUSIP** - 594110
Head Office - 1242-12 Royal Vista Way NW, Calgary, AB, T3R 0N2 **Telephone** - (403) 934-0258 **Fax** - (403) 475-2227
Email - mcdougaldelson@gmail.com
Investor Relations - Elson J. McDougald (403) 998-7595
Auditors - KPMG LLP C.A., Calgary, Alta.
Lawyers - Borden Ladner Gervais LLP, Calgary, Alta.
Transfer Agents - Computershare Trust Company of Canada Inc., Calgary, Alta.
Profile - (B.C. 2021) Capital Pool Company.

Recent Merger and Acquisition Activity

Status: terminated **Revised:** Jan. 13, 2023

UPDATE: The transaction was terminated. PREVIOUS: Michichi Capital Corp. entered into a letter of intent for the Qualifying Transaction reverse takeover acquisition of private Calgary, Alta.-based PsiloTec Health Solutions Inc. (dba Zylorion Health) on a share-for-share basis, resulting in the issuance of 28,509,000 Michichi common shares at $0.50 per share. PsiloTec is focused on the genomic sequencing, organic cultivation, drug research, development and commercialization of psychedelic-based compounds coupled with therapeutic treatment programs targeting a continuum of mental health conditions.

Directors - Elson J. McDougald, pres., CEO, CFO & corp. sec., Drumheller, Alta.; Jeffrey J. McCaig, Calgary, Alta.; Brent Moen, Calgary, Alta.

Capital Stock

	Authorized (shs.)	Outstanding (shs.)[1]
Preferred	unlimited	nil
Common	unlimited	2,100,000

[1] At May 25, 2023

Major Shareholder - Widely held at July 15, 2021.

Capital Stock Changes - There were no changes to capital stock during 2022.

M.80 Microbix Biosystems Inc.

Symbol - MBX **Exchange** - TSX **CUSIP** - 59501P
Head Office - 265 Watline Ave, Mississauga, ON, L4Z 1P3 **Telephone** - (905) 361-8910 **Toll-free** - (800) 794-6694 **Fax** - (905) 361-8911
Website - www.microbix.com
Email - jim.currie@microbix.com
Investor Relations - James S. Currie (800) 794-6694
Auditors - Ernst & Young LLP C.A., Toronto, Ont.
Bankers - The Toronto-Dominion Bank
Transfer Agents - TSX Trust Company, Toronto, Ont.
Profile - (Ont. 1990 amalg.) Develops and manufactures biological materials and technology solutions including antigens, quality assessment products and viral transport medium for the global diagnostics industry.

Primary products include antigens, which are purified and inactivated bacteria and viruses used in the immunoassay format of tests to assess exposure to or immunity from those pathogens; Quality Assessment Products (QAPs™), which consist of samples of pure intact and inactivated pathogen samples and negative mock samples used to establish whether or not an immunoassay or molecular test is being performed properly; and DxTM™, a viral transport medium which supports Canadian RT-PCR testing and stabilizes the nucleic acids and antigens in patient specimen until such time that they can be tested using laboratory-based instruments. The antigens and QAPs™are sold to more than 100 customers worldwide, primarily to multinational diagnostics and laboratory accreditation organizations and DxTM™ are sold to procurement representatives in Ontario.

Also develops Urokinase (Kinlytic®), a clot-busting protein for acute massive pulmonary embolism, deep vein thrombosis, stroke, heart attack and catheter clearance. In addition, the company holds the LumiSort™ technology, a cell-sorting platform for sorting of particles to be used to enrich cell populations of interest such as sexing semen for the livestock industry.

Owns and operates an antigens manufacturing facility which has a pathogen and toxin licence from the Public Health Agency of Canada in Mississauga, Ont.

Predecessor Detail - Formed from Autocrown Corporation Limited in Ontario, Oct. 1, 1990, on amalgamation with Microbix Biosystems Inc.

Directors - Martin Marino, chr., Ont.; Cameron L. Groome, pres. & CEO, Ont.; Joseph D. (Joe) Renner†, N.J.; Dr. Peter M. Blecher, Ont.; Dr. Mark A. Cochran, Baltimore, Md.; Vaughn C. Embro-Pantalony, Toronto, Ont.; Jennifer Stewart, Kanata, Ont.

Other Exec. Officers - Dr. Kenneth (Ken) Hughes, COO; James S. (Jim) Currie, CFO; Phillip (Phil) Casselli, sr. v-p, sales, mktg. & bus. devel.; Dr. Mark Luscher, sr. v-p, scientific affairs; Christopher B Lobb, gen. counsel & corp. sec.
† Lead director

Capital Stock

	Authorized (shs.)	Outstanding (shs.)[1]
Preferred	unlimited	nil
Common	unlimited	137,303,874

[1] At June 30, 2023

Normal Course Issuer Bid - The company plans to make normal course purchases of up to 6,949,568 common shares representing 5% of the total outstanding. The bid commenced on Oct. 3, 2022, and expires on Oct. 2, 2023.

Major Shareholder - Widely held at Feb. 13, 2023.

Price Range - MBX/TSX

Year	Volume	High	Low	Close
2022	13,022,257	$0.84	$0.38	$0.41
2021	37,283,314	$0.87	$0.40	$0.83
2020	47,292,364	$0.50	$0.17	$0.43
2019	21,964,537	$0.39	$0.20	$0.25
2018	12,749,677	$0.34	$0.16	$0.24

Recent Close: $0.33

Capital Stock Changes - During fiscal 2022, common shares were issued as follows: 7,480,293 on exercise of warrants, 2,960,000 on exercise of options and 2,173,913 on conversion of debentures.

Wholly Owned Subsidiaries

Crucible Biotechnologies Limited, Canada.

Financial Statistics

Periods ended:	12m Sept. 30/22^A		12m Sept. 30/21^A
	$000s	%Chg	$000s
Operating revenue	**19,076**	**+3**	**18,593**
Cost of goods sold	2,267		3,162
Salaries & benefits	9,306		7,023
Research & devel. expense	(15)		(58)
General & admin expense	3,430		2,546
Stock-based compensation	442		261
Operating expense	**15,430**	**+19**	**12,934**
Operating income	**3,646**	**-36**	**5,659**
Deprec., depl. & amort.	1,036		822
Finance income	82		nil
Finance costs, gross	827		1,603
Pre-tax income	**1,866**	**-42**	**3,233**
Net income	**1,866**	**-42**	**3,233**
Cash & equivalent	1,348		9,986
Inventories	5,285		4,408
Accounts receivable	3,058		4,175
Current assets	22,408		19,094
Fixed assets, net	8,906		8,083
Intangibles, net	1,498		1,652
Total assets	**33,145**	**+15**	**28,829**
Accts. pay. & accr. liabs	nil		1,795
Current liabilities	2,651		5,194
Long-term debt, gross	4,821		6,537
Long-term debt, net	4,710		4,090
Long-term lease liabilities	846		988
Equity portion of conv. debs	2,273		2,904
Shareholders' equity	24,939		18,556
Cash from oper. activs	**3,465**	**+64**	**2,107**
Cash from fin. activs	2,062		8,409
Cash from invest. activs	(2,026)		(622)
Net cash position	**13,488**	**+35**	**9,986**
Capital expenditures	(2,026)		(1,243)
	$		$
Earnings per share*	0.01		0.03
Cash flow per share*	0.03		0.02
	shs		shs
No. of shs. o/s*	138,991,373		126,377,167
Avg. no. of shs. o/s*	135,376,255		114,845,425
	%		%
Net profit margin	9.78		17.39
Return on equity	8.58		25.68
Return on assets	8.69		21.77

* Common
^A Reported in accordance with IFRS

Historical Summary
(as originally stated)

Fiscal Year	Oper. Rev.	Net Inc. Bef. Disc.	EPS*
	$000s	$000s	$
2022^A	19,076	1,866	0.01
2021^A	18,593	3,233	0.03
2020^A	10,525	(6,228)	(0.06)
2019^A	13,412	32	0.00
2018^A	12,511	(8,622)	(0.09)

* Common
^A Reported in accordance with IFRS

M.81 Micromem Technologies Inc.

Symbol - MRM **Exchange -** CSE **CUSIP -** 59509P
Head Office - 602-121 Richmond St W, Toronto, ON, M5H 2K1 **Telephone -** (416) 364-6513 **Toll-free -** (877) 388-8930 **Fax -** (416) 360-4034
Website - www.micromeminc.com
Email - jfuda@micromeminc.com
Investor Relations - Joseph Fuda (877) 388-8930
Auditors - MNP LLP C.A., Toronto, Ont.
Transfer Agents - TSX Trust Company, Toronto, Ont.
Profile - (Ont. 1985) Developing sensor-based technologies for large multinational companies in the oil and gas, utilities, automotive, healthcare, government, information technology and manufacturing industries.

The company's magnetic sensor technology combines the use of the company's proprietary microelectromechanical systems (MEMS) and nanoelectromechanical systems (NEMS).

Magnetic sensor technology products include the AROMA-TRACER produced fluid tracer analyzer, which provide real time sub part per billion detection of common tracer agents in oil-field produced fluid and other complex sampling environments; power transformer oil degradation sensor, a wireless sensor system that measures partial discharges within electrical transformers; MEMS sensor system, which are designed for detecting wear contaminants in lubricating fluids; integrated oil pan plug analysis system, which simultaneously provides accurate measurements of oil level, as well as particulate analysis of any contaminants in the oil pan; structural integrity sensors systems for monitoring and detecting micro-fractures in cement, corrosion of pipes and potential power line sag-induced failures; and nanoparticle detection solutions, which include nanoscale fracking sensors and magnetic nanoparticle detection solutions. Also developing an energy storage system which would lower costs compared to building new power generating plants.

Predecessor Detail - Name changed from AvantiCorp International Inc., Jan. 14, 1999.
Directors - Joseph Fuda, pres. & CEO, Ont.; Alex Dey, Toronto, Ont.; Oliver Nepomuceno, Lugano, Switzerland
Other Exec. Officers - Dan P. Amadori, CFO

Capital Stock

	Authorized (shs.)	Outstanding (shs.)[1]
Preference	2,000,000	nil
Common	unlimited	498,209,037

[1] At Apr. 30, 2023

Major Shareholder - Widely held at July 23, 2020.

Price Range - MRM/CSE

Year	Volume	High	Low	Close
2022	20,037,461	$0.10	$0.04	$0.05
2021	48,519,734	$0.26	$0.06	$0.07
2020	27,481,076	$0.17	$0.02	$0.08
2019	27,363,677	$0.16	$0.02	$0.04
2018	15,028,849	$0.40	$0.03	$0.04

Recent Close: $0.12

Capital Stock Changes - In March 2023, private placement of 5,100,000 common shares was completed at Cdn$0.05 per share. In April 2023, private placement of 2,939,500 common shares was completed at Cdn$0.12 per share.

During fiscal 2022, common shares were issued as follows: 26,443,820 on conversion of debentures, 5,012,450 by private placement and 413,674 for debt settlement.

Wholly Owned Subsidiaries

Memtech International Inc., Bahamas. Inactive.
• 100% int. in **Memtech International (U.S.A.) Inc.**, Del. Inactive.
Micromem Applied Sensors Technology Inc., Del. Inactive.
Micromem Holdings (Barbados) Inc., Barbados. Inactive.
Pageant Technologies Inc., Barbados. Inactive.
• 100% int. in **Pageant Technologies (U.S.A.) Inc.**, Utah Inactive.
7070179 Canada Inc., Ont.

Financial Statistics

Periods ended:	12m Oct. 31/22^A		12m Oct. 31/21^A
	US$000s	%Chg	US$000s
Salaries & benefits	467		184
General & admin expense	425		421
Stock-based compensation	41		360
Operating expense	**933**	**-3**	**965**
Operating income	**(933)**	**n.a.**	**(965)**
Deprec., depl. & amort.	30		36
Finance costs, gross	1,499		212
Pre-tax income	**(2,287)**	**n.a.**	**(1,013)**
Net income	**(2,287)**	**n.a.**	**(1,013)**
Cash & equivalent	33		171
Current assets	51		195
Fixed assets, net	48		26
Intangibles, net	nil		4
Total assets	**100**	**-56**	**225**
Accts. pay. & accr. liabs	326		384
Current liabilities	4,774		3,648
Long-term debt, gross	3,836		2,501
Long-term debt, net	44		48
Long-term lease liabilities	29		nil
Equity portion of conv. debs	793		14
Shareholders' equity	(4,748)		(3,471)
Cash from oper. activs	**(997)**	**n.a.**	**(763)**
Cash from fin. activs	859		748
Cash from invest. activs	nil		(5)
Net cash position	**33**	**-81**	**171**
Capital expenditures	nil		(5)
	US$		US$
Earnings per share*	(0.01)		(0.00)
Cash flow per share*	(0.00)		(0.00)
	shs		shs
No. of shs. o/s*	467,607,678		435,737,734
Avg. no. of shs. o/s*	451,177,796		422,613,046
	%		%
Net profit margin	n.a.		n.a.
Return on equity	n.m.		n.m.
Return on assets	(484.92)		(318.49)

* Common
^A Reported in accordance with IFRS

Latest Results

Periods ended:	6m Apr. 30/23^A		6m Apr. 30/22^A
	US$000s	%Chg	US$000s
Net income	(4,112)	n.a.	(1,285)
	US$		US$
Earnings per share*	(0.01)		(0.00)

* Common
^A Reported in accordance with IFRS

Historical Summary
(as originally stated)

Fiscal Year	Oper. Rev.	Net Inc. Bef. Disc.	EPS*
	US$000s	US$000s	US$
2022^A	nil	(2,287)	(0.01)
2021^A	nil	(1,013)	(0.00)
2020^A	nil	(1,245)	(0.00)
2019^A	nil	(2,833)	(0.01)
2018^A	nil	(2,362)	(0.01)

* Common
^A Reported in accordance with IFRS

M.82 Midasco Capital Corp.

Symbol - MGC.H **Exchange -** TSX-VEN **CUSIP -** 595919
Head Office - 228-1122 Mainland St, Vancouver, BC, V6B 5L1 **Telephone -** (604) 503-0986 **Fax -** (604) 503-0833
Email - wcp@mininggroup.com
Investor Relations - William C. Pettigrew (604) 503-0986
Auditors - Dale Matheson Carr-Hilton LaBonte LLP C.A., Vancouver, B.C.
Lawyers - Alianza W.J. S.A., Bogota, Colombia; Anfield Sujir Kennedy & Durno LLP, Vancouver, B.C.
Transfer Agents - Computershare Trust Company of Canada Inc., Vancouver, B.C.
Profile - (B.C. 2008; orig. Ont., 1991) Seeking new business opportunities.
Predecessor Detail - Name changed from Midasco Gold Corp., July 17, 2001.
Directors - William C. Pettigrew, pres. & CEO, Vancouver, B.C.; Ryan E. Cheung, CFO & corp. sec., Vancouver, B.C.; Colin Brownlee; Burton Egger

Capital Stock

	Authorized (shs.)	Outstanding (shs.)[1]
Preferred	unlimited	nil
Common	unlimited	16,468,360

[1] At Apr. 5, 2022

Major Shareholder - Burton Egger held 23.62% interest and William C. Pettigrew held 16.12% interest at Aug. 23, 2021.

Price Range - MGC.H/TSX-VEN

Year	Volume	High	Low	Close
2022	99,400	$0.16	$0.08	$0.08
2021	726,121	$0.15	$0.08	$0.12
2020	387,545	$0.09	$0.07	$0.09
2019	217,112	$0.15	$0.08	$0.08
2018	639,900	$0.15	$0.07	$0.09

Recent Close: $0.08

Financial Statistics

Periods ended:	12m Dec. 31/21^A		12m Dec. 31/20^A
	$000s	%Chg	$000s
General & admin expense	57		92
Operating expense	**57**	**-38**	**92**
Operating income	**(57)**	**n.a.**	**(92)**
Finance costs, gross	17		nil
Pre-tax income	**(74)**	**n.a.**	**(92)**
Net income	**(74)**	**n.a.**	**(92)**
Cash & equivalent	183		21
Current assets	185		21
Total assets	**185**	**+781**	**21**
Accts. pay. & accr. liabs	5		33
Current liabilities	5		186
Shareholders' equity	179		(165)
Cash from oper. activs	**(70)**	**n.a.**	**(42)**
Cash from fin. activs	232		nil
Net cash position	**183**	**+771**	**21**
	$		$
Earnings per share*	(0.01)		(0.01)
Cash flow per share*	(0.01)		(0.00)
	shs		shs
No. of shs. o/s*	16,468,360		12,273,360
Avg. no. of shs. o/s*	13,478,497		12,273,360
	%		%
Net profit margin	n.a.		n.a.
Return on equity	n.m.		n.m.
Return on assets	(55.34)		(213.95)

* Common
^A Reported in accordance with IFRS

Historical Summary
(as originally stated)

Fiscal Year	Oper. Rev.	Net Inc. Bef. Disc.	EPS*
	$000s	$000s	$
2021[A]	nil	(74)	(0.01)
2020[A]	nil	(92)	(0.01)
2019[A]	nil	(76)	(0.01)
2018[A]	nil	(99)	(0.01)
2017[A]	nil	(81)	(0.01)

* Common
[A] Reported in accordance with IFRS

M.83 Middlefield Global Real Asset Fund

Symbol - RA.UN **Exchange** - TSX **CUSIP** - 596334
Head Office - c/o Middlefield Limited, 1 First Canadian Place, 5800-100 King St W, PO Box 192, Toronto, ON, M5X 1A6 **Telephone** - (416) 362-0714 **Toll-free** - (888) 890-1868 **Fax** - (416) 362-7925
Website - www.middlefield.com
Email - sroberts@middlefield.com
Investor Relations - Sarah Roberts (416) 847-5355
Auditors - Deloitte LLP C.A., Toronto, Ont.
Bankers - The Toronto-Dominion Bank; The Bank of Nova Scotia; Royal Bank of Canada; Canadian Imperial Bank of Commerce; Bank of Montreal
Lawyers - McCarthy Tétrault LLP; Fasken Martineau DuMoulin LLP; DLA Piper (Canada) LLP; Bennett Jones LLP
Transfer Agents - Middlefield Capital Corporation, Toronto, Ont.
Trustees - Middlefield Limited, Calgary, Alta.
Investment Advisors - Middlefield Capital Corporation, Toronto, Ont.
Managers - Middlefield Limited, Calgary, Alta.
Profile - (Alta. 2019) Invests primarily in dividend paying securities of global issuers focused on, involved in or that derive a significant portion of their revenue from physical real estate or infrastructure assets.

At least 80% of the fund's assets will be invested in an actively managed, diversified, global portfolio consisting primarily of dividend paying securities of publicly listed real asset issuers. These are issuers whose operations are related to data transmission and storage, transportation and networks, industrial properties and logistics, infrastructure services and healthcare facilities. Up to 20% of the fund's assets will be invested in the securities of private, unlisted real asset issuers.

Top 10 holdings at Mar. 31, 2023 (as a percentage of net asset value):

Holding	Percentage
Blackstone Core+ Real Estate LP	26.8%
Linde plc	4.5%
Boralex Inc.	4.3%
Tourmaline Oil Corp.	4.0%
Granite REIT	3.9%
Canadian Apartment Properties REIT	3.9%
TransAlta Corporation	3.9%
Broadwalk REIT	3.9%
Minto Apartment REIT	3.8%
Westshore Terminals Ltd.	3.8%

Oper. Subsid./Mgt. Co. Directors - Jeremy T. Brasseur, exec. chr., Toronto, Ont.; Dean Orrico, pres. & CEO, Vaughan, Ont.; Craig Rogers, COO & chief compliance officer, Toronto, Ont.

Capital Stock

	Authorized (shs.)	Outstanding (shs.)[1]
Fund Unit	unlimited	4,653,929

[1] At Dec. 31, 2022

Fund Unit - Entitled to a monthly cash distribution of $0.04167 per unit (to yield 5% per annum based on an issue price of $10 per unit). Retractable in November of each year for an amount equal to the net asset value per unit, less any costs to fund the retraction. Retractable at any other time for a price per unit equal to the lesser of: (i) 94% of the weighted average trading price on TSX during the 15 trading days immediately preceding the retraction date; and (ii) the closing market price. One vote per fund unit.
Normal Course Issuer Bid - The company plans to make normal course purchases of up to 639,662 fund units representing 10% of the public float. The bid commenced on Dec. 13, 2022, and expires on Dec. 12, 2023.
Major Shareholder - Widely held at Mar. 10, 2023.

Price Range - RA.UN/TSX

Year	Volume	High	Low	Close
2022	1,878,831	$9.60	$7.76	$8.34
2021	3,224,863	$9.96	$8.47	$9.60
2020	4,074,144	$9.94	$6.49	$9.33
2019	530,719	$10.02	$9.80	$9.90

Recent Close: $7.65
Capital Stock Changes - During 2022, fund units were issued as follows: 158,400 for cash and 128 were released from treasury; 1,742,697 fund units were retracted, 196,100 fund units were repurchased under a Normal Course Issuer Bid and 22,500 fund units were repurchased in the market in accordance with the declaration of trust.

Dividends

RA.UN unit Ra $0.50 pa M est. Apr. 15, 2020**
** Reinvestment Option

Financial Statistics

Periods ended:	12m Dec. 31/22[A]		12m Dec. 31/21[A]
	$000s	%Chg	$000s
Realized invest. gain (loss)	662		6,339
Unrealized invest. gain (loss)	(6,650)		346
Total revenue	**(4,169)**	**n.a.**	**8,682**
General & admin. expense	1,250		1,492
Other operating expense	69		57
Operating expense	**1,319**	**-15**	**1,549**
Operating income	**(5,488)**	**n.a.**	**7,133**
Finance costs, gross	200		166
Pre-tax income	**(5,689)**	**n.a.**	**6,967**
Income taxes	77		178
Net income	**(5,766)**	**n.a.**	**6,789**
Cash & equivalent	1,287		9,586
Accounts receivable	91		54
Investments	41,209		67,720
Total assets	**42,594**	**-45**	**77,372**
Accts. pay. & accr. liabs.	157		107
Debt	3,000		13,000
Shareholders' equity	39,242		63,996
Cash from oper. activs	**20,940**	**-43**	**36,558**
Cash from fin. activs	(29,258)		(33,971)
Net cash position	**1,287**	**-87**	**9,586**
	$		$
Earnings per share*	(0.90)		0.73
Cash flow per share*	3.28		3.92
Net asset value per share*	8.43		9.91
Cash divd. per share*	0.50		0.50
	shs		shs
No. of shs. o/s*	4,653,929		6,456,698
Avg. no. of shs. o/s*	6,392,333		9,331,506
	%		%
Net profit margin	n.m.		78.20
Return on equity	(11.17)		8.55
Return on assets	(9.27)		7.63

* Fund Unit
[A] Reported in accordance with IFRS

Note: Net income reflects increase /decrease in net assets from operations.

Historical Summary
(as originally stated)

Fiscal Year	Total Rev.	Net Inc. Bef. Disc.	EPS*
	$000s	$000s	$
2022[A]	(4,169)	(5,766)	(0.90)
2021[A]	8,682	6,789	0.73
2020[A]	8,768	6,452	0.63
2019[A]	250	(252)	(0.02)

* Fund Unit
[A] Reported in accordance with IFRS

M.84 Midwest Energy Emissions Corp.

Symbol - MEEC **Exchange** - TSX-VEN **CUSIP** - 59833H
Head Office - 1810 Jester Dr, Corsicana, TX, United States, 75109-9593 **Telephone** - (614) 505-6115 **Fax** - (614) 505-7377
Website - www.me2cenvironmental.com
Email - shyatt@me2cenvironmental.com
Investor Relations - Stacey Hyatt (614) 505-6115 ext. 1001
Auditors - Marcum LLP C.P.A., Saddle Brook, N.J.
Lawyers - McInnes Cooper
Transfer Agents - TSX Trust Company, Toronto, Ont.; Transfer Online, Inc., Portland, Ore.
Employees - 11 at Dec. 31, 2022
Profile - (Del. 2007; orig. Utah, 1983) Develops and delivers mercury emissions removal technologies to power plants in North America, Europe and Asia.

Mercury capture solutions are provided using a two-part Sorbent Enhancement Additive (SEA®) process, which consists of a front-end sorbent injected directly into the boiler in minimal amounts combined with a back-end sorbent injection solution to ensure maximum mercury capture, and is specifically tailored and formulated to each customer's coal-fired units.

Also developing new technologies to improve the capture rate and environmental concerns of processing rare earth elements.

Common listed on TSX-VEN, July 10, 2023.

Directors - Christopher Greenberg, chr., S.D.; Richard MacPherson, pres., CEO & corp. sec., St. James, Barbados; Troy J. Grant, Bedford, N.S.; David M. Kaye, N.J.
Other Exec. Officers - Gregory R. (Greg) Powell, CFO; John Pavlish, sr. v-p & chief tech. officer; James Trettel, v-p, opers.

Capital Stock

	Authorized (shs.)	Outstanding (shs.)[1]	Par
Preferred	2,000,000	nil	US$0.001
Common	150,000,000	94,267,296	US$0.001

[1] At July 10, 2023

Major Shareholder - Richard MacPherson held 12.5% interest and Alterna Core Capital Assets Fund II, L.P. held 12.4% interest at July 10, 2023.
Recent Close: $0.35
Capital Stock Changes - During 2022, common shares were issued as follows: 3,250,000 for compensation, 500,000 for consulting services and 221,845 on exercise of options.

Wholly Owned Subsidiaries

MES, Inc., N.D.

Financial Statistics

Periods ended:	12m Dec. 31/22[A]		12m Dec. 31/21[A]
	US$000s	%Chg	US$000s
Operating revenue	**21,620**	**+66**	**13,012**
Cost of sales	14,599		7,939
General & admin expense	4,891		4,287
Stock-based compensation	672		968
Operating expense	**20,161**	**+53**	**13,194**
Operating income	**1,459**	**n.a.**	**(182)**
Deprec., depl. & amort.	555		679
Finance costs, gross	1,570		2,818
Pre-tax income	**(1,563)**	**n.a.**	**(3,610)**
Income taxes	18		23
Net income	**(1,581)**	**n.a.**	**(3,633)**
Cash & equivalent	1,504		1,388
Inventories	991		1,075
Accounts receivable	2,778		1,015
Current assets	5,540		3,791
Fixed assets, net	1,829		1,830
Right-of-use assets	52		390
Intangibles, net	1,910		2,114
Total assets	**9,340**	**+15**	**8,135**
Accts. pay. & accr. liabs.	2,947		2,268
Current liabilities	3,325		15,483
Long-term debt, gross	9,938		12,540
Long-term debt, net	9,894		55
Shareholders' equity	(7,417)		(10,239)
Cash from oper. activs	**71**	**-66**	**206**
Cash from fin. activs	56		602
Cash from invest. activs	(11)		(11)
Net cash position	**1,504**	**+8**	**1,388**
Capital expenditures	(11)		(11)
	US$		US$
Earnings per share*	(0.02)		(0.04)
Cash flow per share*	0.00		0.00
	shs		shs
No. of shs. o/s*	93,087,796		89,115,951
Avg. no. of shs. o/s*	90,025,209		84,666,319
	%		%
Net profit margin	(7.31)		(27.92)
Return on equity	n.m.		n.m.
Return on assets	0.08		n.a.
No. of employees (FTEs)	11		n.a.

* Common
[A] Reported in accordance with U.S. GAAP

Latest Results

Periods ended:	3m Mar. 31/23[A]		3m Mar. 31/22[A]
	US$000s	%Chg	US$000s
Operating revenue	3,013	-10	3,342
Net income	(1,447)	n.a.	(1,148)
	US$		US$
Earnings per share*	(0.02)		(0.01)

* Common
[A] Reported in accordance with U.S. GAAP

M.85 Mijem Newcomm Tech Inc.

Symbol - MJEM **Exchange** - CSE **CUSIP** - 59863N
Head Office - 50 Carroll St, Toronto, ON, M4M 3G3 **Telephone** - (416) 915-4747
Website - investor.mijem.com
Email - investorrelations@mijem.com
Investor Relations - Stephen Coates (647) 291-4673
Auditors - Clearhouse LLP C.A., Mississauga, Ont.
Transfer Agents - Odyssey Trust Company, Toronto, Ont.
Profile - (Can. 2017) Offers Mijem, a mobile application designed for students to connect with other students and to efficiently buy, sell and trade goods and services on and off campus.

The Mijem app primarily targets post-secondary students in the U.S. and Canada, including their Generation Z (Gen Z) peers. At Apr. 30, 2023, the app had 167 cumulative downloads. Items posted for sale at Mijem include textbooks, jewelry, sporting goods, clothing, electronics, furniture, and concert tickets. Users can also post events, search for roommates or rideshares, and offer services such as tutoring to other students. Additional features of Mijem include allowing users to join local communities based on users' college or university campuses, an in-app payment system and a loyalty program where users earn 1 point for every $1.00 transacted. Points can be redeemed for Bitcoin SV cryptocurrency. The platform also offers in-app paid advertising and sponsorships for brands and advertisers targeting the Gen Z and college demographic, and through a partnership with Ticketmaster, the app also runs live event promotions, allowing users to purchase tickets for local events.

Predecessor Detail - Name changed from Great Oak Enterprises Ltd., Dec. 23, 2021, pursuant to the reverse takeover acquisition of Mijem Inc. and concurrent amalgamation of Great Oak with wholly owned 2845964 Ontario Inc.

Directors - Phuong Dinh, chr., Kitchener, Ont.; Stephen Coates, interim CEO, Toronto, Ont.; Laurie Freudenberg, Toronto, Ont.; A. Alexandru (Alex) Pekurar, Toronto, Ont.

Other Exec. Officers - Jordan Domey, interim CFO; Michael E. Durance, v-p, strategy; Robert Gorrie, v-p, devel.

Capital Stock

	Authorized (shs.)	Outstanding (shs.)[1]
Common	unlimited	27,787,636
Class A	unlimited	nil
Class B	unlimited	nil
Class C	unlimited	nil

[1] At Apr. 30, 2023

Common - One vote per share.

Class A, B & C - Automatically convertible into common shares in May 2022, September 2022 and January 2023, respectively. One vote per share.

Major Shareholder - Phuong Dinh held 12.75% interest at Dec. 20, 2022.

Price Range - MJEM/CSE

Year	Volume	High	Low	Close
2022	5,468,811	$0.25	$0.01	$0.01

Recent Close: $0.01

Capital Stock Changes - On Jan. 6, 2022, 11,486,552 common shares, 4,619,820 class A common shares, 4,619,820 class B common shares and 4,619,820 class C common shares were issued pursuant to the reverse takeover acquisition of Mijem Inc., including 9,946,630 common shares issued on exchange of subscription receipts sold previously by private placement at 25¢ each, and 412,438 common shares, 732,487 class A common shares, 732,487 class B common shares and 732,487 class C common shares issued on conversion of promissory note. In May 2022, all 4,619,820 class A common shares were converted into a like number of common shares.

Wholly Owned Subsidiaries

Mijem Inc., Toronto, Ont.

Financial Statistics

Periods ended:	12m July 31/22[A1]		12m July 31/21[A2]
	$000s	%Chg	$000s
Operating revenue	**7**	**0**	**7**
Salaries & benefits	294		148
Research & devel. expense	311		30
General & admin expense	1,854		279
Stock-based compensation	306		82
Operating expense	**2,765**	**+413**	**539**
Operating income	**(2,758)**	**n.a.**	**(531)**
Deprec., depl. & amort.	5		7
Finance income	3		nil
Finance costs, gross	64		68
Pre-tax income	**(2,776)**	**n.a.**	**(492)**
Net income	**(2,776)**	**n.a.**	**(492)**
Cash & equivalent	463		363
Current assets	637		2,813
Fixed assets, net	1		3
Intangibles, net	44		50
Total assets	**682**	**-76**	**2,866**
Accts. pay. & accr. liabs	163		257
Current liabilities	163		2,710
Long-term debt, gross	nil		749
Long-term debt, net	nil		687
Shareholders' equity	519		(682)
Cash from oper. activs	**(1,941)**	**n.a.**	**(456)**
Cash from fin. activs	2,041		712
Cash from invest. activs	(33)		41
Net cash position	**430**	**+18**	**363**
Capital expenditures	nil		(2)
	$		$
Earnings per share*	(0.13)		(0.02)
Cash flow per share*	(0.09)		(0.02)
	shs		shs
No. of shs. o/s*	27,787,636		n.a.
Avg. no. of shs. o/s*	21,232,662		29,922,417
	%		%
Net profit margin	n.m.		n.m.
Return on equity	n.m.		n.m.
Return on assets	(152.87)		(27.75)

* Common

[A] Reported in accordance with IFRS

[1] Results reflect the Jan. 6, 2022, reverse takeover acquisition of Mijem Inc.

[2] Results pertain to Mijem Inc.

Latest Results

Periods ended:	9m Apr. 30/23[A]		9m Apr. 30/22[A]
	$000s	%Chg	$000s
Operating revenue	nil	n.a.	6
Net income	(727)	n.a.	(2,210)
	$		$
Earnings per share*	(0.03)		(0.12)

* Common

[A] Reported in accordance with IFRS

Historical Summary
(as originally stated)

Fiscal Year	Oper. Rev.	Net Inc. Bef. Disc.	EPS*
	$000s	$000s	$
2022[A]	7	(2,776)	(0.13)
2021[A1]	7	(492)	(0.02)
2020[A1]	nil	(361)	(0.01)

* Common

[A] Reported in accordance with IFRS

[1] Results pertain to Mijem Inc.

M.86 Milestone Pharmaceuticals Inc.

Symbol - MIST **Exchange -** NASDAQ **CUSIP -** 59935V

Head Office - 420-1111 boul Dr. Frederik-Phillips, Montréal, QC, H4M 2X6 **Telephone -** (514) 336-0444

Website - www.milestonepharma.com

Email - joliveto@milestonepharma.com

Investor Relations - Joseph Oliveto (514) 336-0444

Auditors - PricewaterhouseCoopers LLP C.A., Montréal, Qué.

Transfer Agents - Computershare Trust Company of Canada Inc., Montréal, Qué.

Employees - 39 at Dec. 31, 2022

Profile - (Que. 2017; orig. Can., 2003) Develops and commercializes etripamil for the treatment of cardiovascular indications.

Etripamil is a novel, potent and short-acting calcium channel blocker that the company designed and is developing as a rapid-onset nasal spray to be administered by the patient to terminate episodes of paroxysmal supraventricular tachycardia (PSVT), a rapid heart condition, as they occur. Etripamil is also being developed for atrial fibrillation, rapid ventricular rate and other cardiovascular indications.

Undergoing Phase 3 clinical trial in Canada and the U.S. for the treatment of PSVT and a Phase 2 proof-of-concept clinical trial to evaluate the potential effectiveness of etripaml nasal spray to reduce ventricular rate in atrial fibrillation.

In October 2022, the company reported that the Phase 3 RAPID clinical trial of etripamil, the company's lead investigational product, in patients with paroxysmal supraventricular tachycardia met its primary endpoint, with 64.3% of patients self-administering etripamil converting to sinus rhythm within 30 minutes compared to 31.2% on placebo.

Recent Merger and Acquisition Activity

Status: pending **Announced:** Mar. 27, 2023

Milestone Pharmaceuticals Inc. entered into an agreement with RTW Investments, LP whereby RTW would pay US$75,000,000 to the company, subject to U.S. FDA approval of etripamil, in return for tiered rate, cash royalty payments based on aggregate net sales of etripamil within the United States. The royalty payments would be equal to (i) 7% of annual net sales up to US$500,000,000; (ii) 4% of annual net sales greater than US$500,000,000 and less than or equal to US$800,000,000; and (iii) 1% of annual net sales greater than US$800,000,000.

Directors - Robert Wills, chr., N.J.; Joseph Oliveto, pres. & CEO, N.C.; Seth H. Z. Fischer, N.J.; Lisa Giles, S.C.; Debra K. Liebert, Calif.; Dr. Richard C. Pasternak, N.Y.; Michael Tomsicek, Mass.

Other Exec. Officers - Jeff Nelson, COO; Dr. David Bharucha, CMO; Lorenz Muller, chief comml. officer; Amit Hasija, exec. v-p, corp. devel. & CFO; Guy Rousseau, sr. v-p, regulatory affairs & quality mgt.; Debbie K. Everidge, v-p, IT; Roshan Girglani, v-p, mktg.; Anita Holz, v-p, medical affairs; John Jackimiec, v-p, market access; Harish Pimplaskar, v-p, chemistry, mfg. & controls; Kimberly Sheehan, v-p, HR; Cameron Szakacs, v-p, drug devel.

Capital Stock

	Authorized (shs.)	Outstanding (shs.)[1]
Common	unlimited	33,369,447

[1] At Apr. 21, 2023

Major Shareholder - Widely held at Mar. 31, 2023.

Price Range - MIST/NASDAQ

Year	Volume	High	Low	Close
2022	13,730,013	US$9.80	US$3.39	US$3.96
2021	3,771,298	US$9.00	US$5.09	US$6.55
2020	101,404,598	US$23.20	US$1.69	US$6.70
2019	1,216,655	US$27.73	US$15.09	US$16.01

Capital Stock Changes - During 2022, common shares were issued as follows: 3,809,523 on exercise of warrants, 361,236 under an at-the-market offering and 217,684 on exercise of options.

Wholly Owned Subsidiaries

Milestone Pharmaceuticals USA, Inc., Del.

Financial Statistics

Periods ended:	12m Dec. 31/22[A]		12m Dec. 31/21[A]
	US$000s	%Chg	US$000s
Operating revenue	**5,000**	**-67**	**15,000**
Cost of sales	7,759		5,781
Research & devel. expense	36,257		35,532
General & admin expense	11,489		9,388
Stock-based compensation	9,048		7,279
Operating expense	**64,553**	**+11**	**57,980**
Operating income	**(59,553)**	**n.a.**	**(42,980)**
Deprec., depl. & amort.	89		93
Finance costs, net	(1,254)		(220)
Pre-tax income	**(58,388)**	**n.a.**	**(42,853)**
Net income	**(58,388)**	**n.a.**	**(42,853)**
Cash & equivalent	64,585		114,141
Accounts receivable	1,213		483
Current assets	71,803		118,923
Fixed assets, net	257		215
Right-of-use assets	2,423		711
Total assets	**74,483**	**-38**	**119,849**
Accts. pay. & accr. liabs	5,644		6,551
Current liabilities	6,139		6,775
Long-term lease liabilities	1,996		474
Shareholders' equity	66,348		112,600
Cash from oper. activs	**(52,469)**	**n.a.**	**(33,224)**
Cash from fin. activs	3,088		5,055
Cash from invest. activs	(57,124)		70,000
Net cash position	**7,636**	**-93**	**114,141**
Capital expenditures	(272)		nil
	US$		US$
Earnings per share*	(1.38)		(1.02)
Cash flow per share*	(1.24)		(1.13)
	shs		shs
No. of shs. o/s*	34,286,002		29,897,559
Avg. no. of shs. o/s*	42,450,316		41,833,861
	%		%
Net profit margin	n.m.		(285.69)
Return on equity	(65.26)		(33.52)
Return on assets	(60.09)		(31.76)
No. of employees (FTEs)	39		29

* Common

[A] Reported in accordance with U.S. GAAP

Latest Results

Periods ended:	3m Mar. 31/23[A]		3m Mar. 31/22[A]
	US$000s	%Chg	US$000s
Operating revenue	1,000	n.a.	nil
Net income	(14,950)	n.a.	(14,007)
	US$		US$
Earnings per share*	(0.35)		(0.33)

* Common

[A] Reported in accordance with U.S. GAAP

Historical Summary
(as originally stated)

Fiscal Year	Oper. Rev.	Net Inc. Bef. Disc.	EPS*
	US$000s	US$000s	US$
2022[A]	5,000	(58,388)	(1.38)
2021[A]	15,000	(42,853)	(1.02)
2020[A]	nil	(49,967)	(1.70)
2019[A]	nil	(55,229)	(3.50)
2018[A1]	nil	(23,185)	n.a.

* Common

[A] Reported in accordance with U.S. GAAP

[1] As shown in the prospectus dated May 2, 2019.

M.87 MiMedia Holdings Inc.

Symbol - MIM **Exchange -** TSX-VEN **CUSIP -** 60250B

Head Office - c/o WeWork, 85 Broad St, New York, NY, United States, 10004 **Telephone -** (347) 687-4403

Website - www.mimedia.com

Email - chris@mimedia.com

Investor Relations - Christopher Giordano (888) 502-9398

Auditors - McGovern Hurley LLP C.A., Toronto, Ont.

Transfer Agents - Odyssey Trust Company

Profile - (B.C. 2018) Offers MiMedia, a consumer cloud platform for securely storing and accessing digital content (photos, videos, music, document files) across multiple devices.

The MiMedia platform enables all types of personal media to be secured in the cloud and accessed seamlessly across all devices (smartphones, tablets, laptops/desktops and web) and on all operating systems (Android, iOS, MAC, PC) at any time. The company partners with telecommunications companies and smartphone original equipment manufacturers, with a focus on Latin America, Southeast Asia and Africa. In these partnerships, it private-labels the platform for partners, helps lead the operations of the back-end network and drives the revenue generation strategy with multiple recurring and high-margin revenue streams that the company can turn-on as early as the first day of deployment. In exchange for revenue share and access to the platform, partners would lead the marketing efforts and deliver access to large user bases while assuming most, if not all, of the back-end or infrastructure costs required to support the platform. The company may either share in the revenue generated with its partners or charge a licence fee per user of its software.

Recent Merger and Acquisition Activity

Status: completed **Revised:** Mar. 15, 2022
UPDATE: The transaction was completed. A total of 19,108,896 subordinate voting shares and 8,887,372 multiple voting shares were issued at a deemed price of $0.25 and $1.25 per share, respectively. MiMedia amalgamated with Elk Media Inc., wholly owned by EECC. PREVIOUS: Efficacious Elk Capital Corp. (EECC) entered into a letter of intent for the Qualifying Transaction reverse takeover acquisition of New York, N.Y.-based MiMedia Inc., which has developed a consumer cloud platform that enable all types of personal media to be secured on the cloud and accessed seamlessly across all device at any time. Its platform is deployed through partnerships with smartphone device manufacturers and telecom carriers. A total of 40,506,329 common shares would be issued at a deemed price of Cdn$0.25 per share to MiMedia shareholders. MiMedia plans to raise a minimum of US$3,000,000 via a private placement of subscription receipts. Nov. 16, 2021 - An agreement was announced whereby MiMedia would merge with a newly Delaware incorporated subsidiary of EECC, Elk Media Inc. and EECC would change its name to MiMedia Holdings Inc. Prior to closing, EECC common shares would be consolidated on a 1-for-0.52083 basis and redesignated as subordinate voting shares and a new class of multiple voting shares created. A total of 16,586,000 subordinate voting shares are to be issued on exchange of MiMedia subscription receipts and 7,983,068 multiple voting shares would be issued to MiMedia shareholders in exchange for about 39,915,343 MiMedia shares held. MiMedia completed a private placement of 16,586,000 subscription receipts at Cdn$0.25 per receipt.

Predecessor Detail - Name changed from Efficacious Elk Capital Corp., Mar. 15, 2022, pursuant to the Qualifying Transaction reverse takeover acquisition of MiMedia Inc.; basis 0.52083 new for 1 old sh.

Directors - Christopher (Chris) Giordano, pres. & CEO, Brooklyn, N.Y.; David W. Smalley, corp. sec., B.C.; Cole Brodman, Wash.; John D. MacPhail, North Vancouver, B.C.; Seth Solomons, N.Y.

Other Exec. Officers - Philip Ellard, CFO; Joao Allende, v-p, bus. devel.

Capital Stock

	Authorized (shs.)	Outstanding (shs.)[1]
Subordinate Vtg.	unlimited	31,861,674
Multiple Vtg.	unlimited	7,847,296

[1] At Sept. 30, 2022

Subordinate Voting - One vote per share.

Multiple Voting - Convertible into subordinate voting shares on a 5-for-1 basis. Five votes per share.

Major Shareholder - Jeffrey A. Keswin held 28.75% interest at Mar. 22, 2022.

Price Range - MIM/TSX-VEN

Year	Volume	High	Low	Close
2022	13,504,082	$0.39	$0.18	$0.30
2020	107,290	$0.15	$0.02	$0.10
2019	31,249	$0.20	$0.19	$0.19
2018	1,041	$0.38	$0.38	$0.38

Consolidation: 0.52083-for-1 cons. in Mar. 2022

Recent Close: $0.45

Capital Stock Changes - Pursuant to the Qualifying Transaction reverse takeover acquisition of MiMedia Inc., completed on Mar. 15, 2022, capital stock changes were as follows: common shares were consolidated on a 1-for-0.52083 basis, common shares were reclassified as subordinate voting shares, a new class of multiple voting shares was created and 19,108,896 post-consolidated subordinate voting shares and 8,887,372 multiple voting shares were issued to MiMedia shareholders. Concurrently, private placement of 4,376,000 units (1 post-consolidated subordinate voting share & ½ warrant) at $0.25 per unit was completed, with warrants exercisable at $0.32 per share for two years.

Wholly Owned Subsidiaries

MiMedia Inc., Brooklyn, N.Y.

M.88 Minaean SP Construction Corp.

Symbol - MSP **Exchange** - TSX-VEN **CUSIP** - 60250V

Head Office - 2050-1055 Georgia St W, PO Box 11121, Vancouver, BC, V6C 3P3 **Telephone** - (604) 684-2181 **Toll-free** - (855) 684-2181 **Fax** - (604) 682-4768

Website - www.minaean.com

Email - info@minaean.com

Investor Relations - Capt. Mervyn J. Pinto (604) 684-2181

Auditors - Davidson & Company LLP C.A., Vancouver, B.C.

Lawyers - Borden Ladner Gervais LLP, Vancouver, B.C.

Transfer Agents - Computershare Trust Company of Canada Inc., Vancouver, B.C.

Profile - (B.C. 2015; orig. Alta., 1998) Develops, produces and markets inexpensive, easily assembled and environmentally friendly building framing systems.

The company's building framing systems utilize the Light Gauge Steel (LGS) technology, a cold formed galvanized steel that comes in a coil form and is used to produce a range of uniform shapes and products.

The Modular Quik-Build™ framing system uses generic steel framing methods for structures that are composed of several individual modules, with insulation, cladding, electrical wiring, plumbing, drainage and assembly done primarily in factories. The modules are then shipped to site and installed with minimal onsite work. End users include retail, housing, schools, health centres, army barracks, field buildings, vacation homes and resort housing. The Vesta Quik-Build™ framing system is designed for the rapid distribution of housing construction kits to developing nations in need homes or poor populace and uses cold-rolled galvanized corrugated steel sheets as wall panels, roof tresses and roof-sheeting panels installed on a concrete foundation. The Artisan Quik-Build™ framing system uses an engineered floor and steel framed wall system to construct a high-quality building. It is also a combination of novel modular, load-bearing roll-formed LGS studs for framing in commercial and residential construction.

Also provides contracting services including consulting on large scale construction projects, engineering, procurement, construction and design-build capabilities in the residential, commercial, industrial, healthcare and hospitality sectors.

Predecessor Detail - Name changed from Minaean International Corp., Aug. 28, 2015; basis 1 new for 2 old shs.

Directors - Capt. Mervyn J. Pinto, chr., pres., CEO & corp. sec., Surrey, B.C.; Hari B. Varshney, CFO, Vancouver, B.C.; Subramanya Iyer Kuppuswamy, Mumbai, India; Mohan Dass Saini, Dubai, United Arab Emirates; Fali Vajifdar, Dubai, United Arab Emirates

Capital Stock

	Authorized (shs.)	Outstanding (shs.)[1]
Common	unlimited	60,718,215

[1] At Aug. 26, 2022

Major Shareholder - Shapoorji Pallonji International FZC held 43.36% interest at June 2, 2022.

Price Range - MSP/TSX-VEN

Year	Volume	High	Low	Close
2022	5,672,684	$0.20	$0.04	$0.07
2021	52,265,035	$0.46	$0.04	$0.13
2020	6,233,679	$0.08	$0.03	$0.04
2019	3,601,989	$0.10	$0.03	$0.05
2018	2,455,405	$0.28	$0.07	$0.14

Recent Close: $0.05

Capital Stock Changes - During fiscal 2022, 608,333 common shares were issued on exercise of options.

Wholly Owned Subsidiaries

Minaean Building Solutions Inc., India.
• 100% int. in **Minaean Habitat (India) Pvt. Limited**, Mumbai, India.
Minaean (Ghana) Limited, Ghana.

Financial Statistics

Periods ended:	12m Mar. 31/22[A]		12m Mar. 31/21[A]
	$000s	%Chg	$000s
Operating revenue	**300**	**0**	**300**
Salaries & benefits	128		54
General & admin expense	174		161
Stock-based compensation	nil		79
Operating expense	**302**	**+2**	**295**
Operating income	**(2)**	**n.a.**	**5**
Finance income	32		14
Finance costs, gross	17		13
Write-downs/write-offs	(953)		(288)
Pre-tax income	**(940)**	**n.a.**	**(282)**
Net income	**(940)**	**n.a.**	**(282)**
Cash & equivalent	82		107
Accounts receivable	13		11
Current assets	118		141
Fixed assets, net	1		1
Total assets	**657**	**-51**	**1,333**
Accts. pay. & accr. liabs	259		265
Current liabilities	583		421
Long-term debt, gross	37		34
Long-term debt, net	37		34
Shareholders' equity	36		878
Cash from oper. activs	**(115)**	**n.a.**	**(182)**
Cash from fin. activs	91		252
Net cash position	**64**	**-27**	**88**
	$		$
Earnings per share*	(0.02)		(0.00)
Cash flow per share*	(0.00)		(0.00)
	shs		shs
No. of shs. o/s*	60,178,216		59,569,883
Avg. no. of shs. o/s*	59,942,394		58,246,113
	%		%
Net profit margin	(313.33)		(94.00)
Return on equity	(205.69)		(32.21)
Return on assets	(92.76)		(19.93)

* Common
[A] Reported in accordance with IFRS

Latest Results

Periods ended:	3m June 30/22[A]		3m June 30/21[A]
	$000s	%Chg	$000s
Net income	(90)	n.a.	(69)
	$		$
Earnings per share*	(0.00)		(0.00)

* Common
[A] Reported in accordance with IFRS

Historical Summary
(as originally stated)

Fiscal Year	Oper. Rev.	Net Inc. Bef. Disc.	EPS*
	$000s	$000s	$
2022[A]	300	(940)	(0.02)
2021[A]	300	(282)	(0.00)
2020[A]	350	13	0.00
2019[A]	352	(145)	(0.00)
2018[A]	815	145	0.00

* Common
[A] Reported in accordance with IFRS

M.89 Minco Capital Corp.

Symbol - MMM **Exchange** - TSX-VEN **CUSIP** - 602532

Head Office - 2060-1055 Georgia St W, PO Box 11176, Vancouver, BC, V6E 3R5 **Telephone** - (604) 688-8002 **Toll-free** - (888) 288-8288 **Fax** - (604) 688-8030

Website - www.mincocapitalcorp.com

Email - rlin@mincomining.ca

Investor Relations - Renee Lin (604) 688-8002

Auditors - Smythe LLP C.A., Vancouver, B.C.

Lawyers - Sangra Moller LLP, Vancouver, B.C.; Salley Bowes Harwardt Law Corp., Vancouver, B.C.

Transfer Agents - Computershare Trust Company of Canada Inc., Vancouver, B.C.

Profile - (B.C. 1982) Invests primarily in publicly traded and privately held companies.

Investments include common shares, preferred shares, warrants, royalties, convertible debentures, bridge loans and other investment vehicles.

At Mar. 31, 2023, total fair value of investments was $6,053,956 and included equities in public resource companies such as **Minco Silver Corporation, Amerigo Resources Ltd., Asante Gold Corp., Western Alaska Minerals Corp., Neo Performance Materials Inc., Global X Lithium & Battery ETF, Vaneck Vectors ETF, Cobalt Blue Holding Ltd., Sherritt International Corporation** and **Teck Resources Limited**; and an equity interest in private Peruvian-based **El Olivar Imperial S.A.C.**

Predecessor Detail - Name changed from Minco Gold Corporation, Feb. 27, 2019.

Directors - Dr. Ken Z. Cai, chr., acting pres. & CEO, Beijing, People's Republic of China; Malcolm F. Clay, West Vancouver, B.C.; Dr. Michael D. Doggett, Vancouver, B.C.

Other Exec. Officers - Renee Lin, CFO & corp. sec.

Capital Stock

	Authorized (shs.)	Outstanding (shs.)[1]
Common	100,000,000	44,479,881

[1] At May 19, 2023

Normal Course Issuer Bid - The company plans to make normal course purchases of up to 3,410,425 common shares representing 10% of the public float. The bid commenced on Apr. 1, 2023, and expires on Mar. 31, 2024.

Major Shareholder - Widely held at May 4, 2023.

Price Range - MMM/TSX-VEN

Year	Volume	High	Low	Close
2022	6,221,693	$0.09	$0.04	$0.05
2021	7,068,444	$0.11	$0.06	$0.07
2020	8,479,547	$0.12	$0.04	$0.07
2019	5,011,736	$0.14	$0.07	$0.12
2018	3,512,541	$0.19	$0.07	$0.07

Recent Close: $0.07

Capital Stock Changes - During 2022, 1,978,000 common shares were repurchased under a Normal Course Issuer Bid and 5,000 common shares were returned to treasury.

Financial Statistics

Periods ended:	12m Dec. 31/22^A		12m Dec. 31/21^A
	$000s	%Chg	$000s
Realized invest. gain (loss)	390		110
Unrealized invest. gain (loss)	(2,642)		(1,250)
Total revenue	**(2,193)**	**n.a.**	**(1,109)**
Salaries & benefits	95		109
General & admin. expense	229		282
Stock-based compensation	nil		67
Operating expense	**324**	**-29**	**458**
Operating income	**(2,517)**	**n.a.**	**(1,567)**
Deprec. & amort.	44		38
Finance costs, gross	18		5
Pre-tax income	**(2,572)**	**n.a.**	**(1,624)**
Net income	**(2,572)**	**n.a.**	**(1,624)**
Cash & equivalent	902		408
Accounts receivable	5		7
Current assets	6,953		9,696
Fixed assets, net	3		12
Right-of-use assets	191		39
Total assets	**7,160**	**-27**	**9,759**
Accts. pay. & accr. liabs	46		96
Current liabilities	79		138
Long-term lease liabilities	180		13
Shareholders' equity	6,902		9,609
Cash from oper. activs	**672**	**n.a.**	**(1,970)**
Cash from fin. activs	(178)		(143)
Cash from invest. activs	nil		(1)
Net cash position	**882**	**+127**	**388**
Capital expenditures	nil		(1)
	$		$
Earnings per share*	(0.06)		(0.03)
Cash flow per share*	0.01		(0.04)
	shs		shs
No. of shs. o/s*	44,788,881		46,771,881
Avg. no. of shs. o/s*	45,718,141		47,683,525
	%		%
Net profit margin	n.m.		n.m.
Return on equity	(31.15)		(15.56)
Return on assets	(30.19)		(15.30)

* Common
^A Reported in accordance with IFRS

Latest Results

Periods ended:	3m Mar. 31/23^A		3m Mar. 31/22^A
	$000s	%Chg	$000s
Total revenue	29	-88	241
Net income	(69)	n.a.	140
	$		$
Earnings per share*	(0.00)		0.00

* Common
^A Reported in accordance with IFRS

Historical Summary
(as originally stated)

Fiscal Year	Total Rev.	Net Inc. Bef. Disc.	EPS*
	$000s	$000s	$
2022^A	(2,193)	(2,572)	(0.06)
2021^A	(1,109)	(1,624)	(0.03)
2020^A	(1,228)	(1,965)	(0.04)
2019^A	2,501	1,682	0.03
2018^A	(5,400)	(6,399)	(0.13)

* Common
^A Reported in accordance with IFRS

M.90 Mind Cure Health Inc.

Symbol - MCUR **Exchange** - CSE **CUSIP** - 60254M
Head Office - 170-422 Richards St, Vancouver, BC, V6B 2Z4 **Toll-free** - (888) 593-8995
Website - mindcure.com
Email - investors@mindcure.com
Investor Relations - Philip Tapley (888) 593-8995
Auditors - Davidson & Company LLP C.A., Vancouver, B.C.
Bankers - Bank of Montreal
Lawyers - Farris LLP, Vancouver, B.C.
Transfer Agents - Computershare Trust Company of Canada Inc., Vancouver, B.C.
Profile - (B.C. 2020) Pursuing acquisition of oil and gas company.

During fiscal 2022, the company initiated a wind-down of operations and placed the company and its assets under limited care and maintenance which resulted in a halting of all non-committed expenditures related to research, development and marketing of its iSTRYM product, the company's psychedelic digital therapeutics platform; synthetic ibogaine program; and the Desire project, a clinical research program focused on the treatment of female hypoactive sexual desire disorder (HSDD) using MDMA-assited psychotherapy, and a company-wide workforce reduction.

Recent Merger and Acquisition Activity

Status: pending **Revised:** May 5, 2023
UPDATE: Mind Cure and LNG entered an agreement. Mind Cure would consolidate its common shares on a 1-for-1 basis and shares of the resulting issuer would be listed on the TSX Venture Exchange and continue from the jurisdiction of British Columbia to Ontario. LNG has arranged a private placement of subscription receipts for gross proceeds of at least $25,000,000. PREVIOUS: Mind Cure Health Inc. entered into a letter of intent for the revere takeover acquisition of LNG Energy Group Inc. Terms were to be entered into. The transaction would include a number of conditions including a 1-for-2.4 share consolidation by Mind Cure and a name change to LNG Energy Group Inc. and completion of private placements, including subscription receipts for proceeds of at least US$15,000,000 and no greater than US$30,000,000, and debt financings of between US$65,000,000 and US$85,000,000 and a listing of resulting issuer shares on Canadian Securities Exchange. The transaction was expected to close in the first quarter of 2023.

Directors - Philip Tapley, chr. & interim CEO, Surrey, B.C.; Robert C. (Rob) Hill, West Vancouver, B.C.; Jason Pamer, Vancouver, B.C.
Other Exec. Officers - Tarik Lebbadi, COO; Michael A. Wolfe, CFO; Geoff Belair, chief tech. officer; Dr. Claire Purvis, chief product officer; Dr. Doron Sagman, CMO

Capital Stock

	Authorized (shs.)	Outstanding (shs.)[1]
Preferred	unlimited	nil
Common	unlimited	93,906,327

[1] At May 5, 2023

Major Shareholder - Widely held at Oct. 21, 2022.

Price Range - MCUR/CSE

Year	Volume	High	Low	Close
2022	31,584,418	$0.23	$0.04	$0.08
2021	83,190,899	$0.80	$0.18	$0.20
2020	28,221,820	$1.09	$0.32	$0.73

Recent Close: $0.08

Capital Stock Changes - During fiscal 2022, common shares were issued as follows: 149,220 for services, 55,325 on exercise of options and 40,185 on exercise of warrants.

Wholly Owned Subsidiaries

Mind Cure Health (US) Inc., Nev.

Financial Statistics

Periods ended:	12m May 31/22^A		12m May 31/21^A
	$000s	%Chg	$000s
Research & devel. expense	48		50
General & admin expense	9,441		8,097
Stock-based compensation	562		2,316
Operating expense	**10,051**	**-4**	**10,464**
Operating income	**(10,051)**	**n.a.**	**(10,464)**
Deprec., depl. & amort.	10		nil
Finance income	94		33
Finance costs, gross	7		4
Write-downs/write-offs	(2,541)		(171)
Pre-tax income	**(14,141)**	**n.a.**	**(10,173)**
Net income	**(14,141)**	**n.a.**	**(10,173)**
Cash & equivalent	8,711		18,281
Inventories	nil		186
Accounts receivable	95		86
Current assets	8,990		19,013
Long-term investments	nil		1,238
Fixed assets, net	1		2
Intangibles, net	nil		549
Total assets	**8,991**	**-58**	**21,301**
Accts. pay. & accr. liabs	1,889		697
Current liabilities	1,889		697
Shareholders' equity	7,102		20,604
Cash from oper. activs	**(9,209)**	**n.a.**	**(8,290)**
Cash from fin. activs	21		27,233
Cash from invest. activs	(383)		(1,272)
Net cash position	**8,711**	**-52**	**18,281**
Capital expenditures	(37)		(2)
	$		$
Earnings per share*	(0.15)		(0.18)
Cash flow per share*	(0.10)		(0.14)
	shs		shs
No. of shs. o/s*	93,906,327		93,661,597
Avg. no. of shs. o/s*	93,854,522		57,312,612
	%		%
Net profit margin	n.a.		n.a.
Return on equity	(102.08)		n.m.
Return on assets	(93.32)		n.a.
No. of employees (FTEs)	n.a.		14

* Common
^A Reported in accordance with IFRS

Latest Results

Periods ended:	3m Aug. 31/22^A		3m Aug. 31/21^A
	$000s	%Chg	$000s
Net income	(408)	n.a.	(2,841)
	$		$
Earnings per share*	(0.00)		(0.03)

* Common
^A Reported in accordance with IFRS

M.91 Mind Medicine (MindMed) Inc.

Symbol - MMED **Exchange** - NEO **CUSIP** - 60255C
Head Office - One World Trade Center, Suite 8500, New York, NY, United States, 10007 **Telephone** - (203) 648-5275
Website - www.mindmed.co
Email - cliao@mindmed.co
Investor Relations - Carrie F. Liao (212) 220-6633
Auditors - KPMG LLP C.A.
Lawyers - Cooley LLP; Osler, Hoskin & Harcourt LLP
Transfer Agents - Computershare Trust Company of Canada Inc.
Employees - 48 at Dec. 31, 2022
Profile - (B.C. 2010) Developing pharmaceutical and digital medicine products to treat brain health disorders.

Drug candidates being developed include pharmaceutically optimized drug products derived from the psychedelic and empathogen drug classes. These drugs, with and without acute perceptual effects, target neurotransmitter pathways that play key roles in brain health disorders. Development pipeline includes MM-120 [Lysergide (LSD) D-tartrate], a form of LSD to treat generalized anxiety disorder (GAD) as well as adult attention deficit hyperactivity disorder (ADHD) and chronic pain; MM-402 (R(-)-MDMA), a synthetic R-enantiomer of methylenedioxy-methylamphetamine (MDMA) for the treatment of core symptoms of autism spectrum disorder; and MM-110 [zolunicant HCl or 18-methoxycoronaridine (18-MC)], a derivative of ibogaine to treat opioid withdrawal.

Digital medicine products consist of a suite of regulated and unregulated products for use by clinicians and patients to diagnose, prevent, manage or treat brain health disorders, or to facilitate the use of certain pharmaceutical products. These digital therapeutics may include software-as-a-medical device (SaMD), such wearables and machine learning, and be applied during different clinical periods (pre-treatment, during treatment and post-treatment sessions).

The company has also entered into partnerships for research and development including with University Hospital Basel's (UHB) Liechti Lab in Switzerland for LSD, psilocybin, MDMA, mescaline, dimethyltryptamine (DMT) and other psychedelic compounds; and **MindShift Compounds AG** in Switzerland to develop next-generation psychedelic and empathogenic substances. The company and UHB Liechti Lab are also collaborating on the development of a personalized medicine technology to optimize the dosing of MDMA, LSD and other psychedelics based on a patient's characteristics including age, sex, pharmacogenetics, personality traits, states of mood, metabolic markers and therapeutic drug monitoring.

Predecessor Detail - Name changed from Broadway Gold Mining Ltd., Feb. 27, 2020, pursuant to the reverse takeover acquisition of private Reno, Nev.-based Mind Medicine, Inc.; basis 1 new for 8 old shs.

Directors - Carol A. Vallone, chr., Manchester, Mass.; Andreas Krebs, v-chr., Germany; Robert Barrow, CEO, Madison, Wis.; Dr. Suzanne Bruhn, N.H.; Dr. Roger Crystal, Santa Monica, Calif.; David Gryska, N.C.
Other Exec. Officers - Dr. Miriam (Miri) Halperin Wenli, pres.; Schond L. Greenway, CFO; Dr. Daniel R. Karlin, CMO; Carrie F. Liao, chief acctg. officer; François Lilienthal, chief comml. officer; Mark R. Sullivan, chief legal officer & corp. sec.; Carole Abel, v-p, programs & portfolio office; Maxim Jacobs, v-p, IR & corp. commun.; Dr. Peter Mack, v-p, pharmaceutical devel.; Dr. Robert (Rob) Silva, v-p & head, devel.; Bridget Walton, v-p, global regulatory affairs

Capital Stock

	Authorized (shs.)	Outstanding (shs.)[1]	Par
Common	unlimited	38,595,310	US$0.001

[1] At Apr. 25, 2023

Major Shareholder - Widely held at Apr. 1, 2023.

Price Range - MMED/NEO

Year	Volume	High	Low	Close
2022	1,249,680	$28.65	$2.91	$2.99
2021	2,797,480	$107.85	$25.80	$25.95
2020	6,948,200	$97.05	$3.98	$58.20
2019	46,879	$16.80	$7.20	$9.00
2018	99,836	$61.20	$7.20	$8.40

Consolidation: 1-for-15 cons. in Aug. 2022; 1-for-8 cons. in Mar. 2020
Recent Close: $5.18

Capital Stock Changes - During the first quarter of 2022, all remaining 4,521 multiple voting shares were converted into 452,060 subordinate voting shares. On July 4, 2022, subordinate voting shares were redesignated as common shares. On Aug. 29, 2022, common shares were consolidated on a 1-for-15 basis. In September 2022, public offering of 7,058,823 post-consolidated common shares was completed at US$4.25 per share. Also during 2022, post-consolidated common shares were issued as follows: 2,311,652 under an at-the-market program, 367,950 on vesting of restricted share units, 76,021 on exercise of warrants and 38,275 on exercise of options.

Wholly Owned Subsidiaries

HealthMode, Inc., San Francisco, Calif.
Mind Medicine, Inc., Reno, Nev.
• 100% int. in **MindMed Pty Ltd.**, Australia.
MindMed Discover GmbH, Zug, Switzerland.

Financial Statistics

Periods ended:	12m Dec. 31/22[A]		12m Dec. 31/21[A]
	US$000s	%Chg	US$000s
Research & devel. expense	27,372		24,999
General & admin expense	22,052		23,523
Stock-based compensation	13,707		42,716
Operating expense	**63,131**	**-31**	**91,238**
Operating income	**(63,131)**	**n.a.**	**(91,238)**
Deprec., depl. & amort.	3,200		2,616
Finance costs, net	(1,495)		359
Pre-tax income	**(56,796)**	**n.a.**	**(94,193)**
Income taxes	nil		(1,157)
Net income	**(56,796)**	**n.a.**	**(93,036)**
Cash & equivalent	142,142		133,539
Current assets	146,055		137,215
Intangibles, net	23,607		26,787
Total assets	**169,993**	**+4**	**164,002**
Accts. pay. & accr. liabs.	7,988		10,408
Current liabilities	17,892		10,408
Shareholders' equity	150,917		151,664
Cash from oper. activs.	**(50,139)**	**n.a.**	**(45,824)**
Cash from fin. activs.	59,051		98,824
Cash from invest. activs.	nil		(297)
Net cash position	**142,142**	**+6**	**133,539**
	US$		US$
Earnings per share*	(1.84)		(3.45)
Cash flow per share*	(1.62)		(1.67)
	shs		shs
No. of shs. o/s*	37,979,136		28,126,417[1]
Avg. no. of shs. o/s*	30,857,463		27,377,082
	%		%
Net profit margin	n.a.		n.a.
Return on equity	(37.54)		n.m.
Return on assets	(34.01)		n.a.
No. of employees (FTEs)	48		n.a.

* Common
[A] Reported in accordance with U.S. GAAP
[1] Includes multiple voting shares converted into subordinate voting shares on a 100-for-1 basis.

Latest Results

Periods ended:	3m Mar. 31/23[A]		3m Mar. 31/22[A]
	US$000s	%Chg	US$000s
Net income	(24,815)	n.a.	(18,451)
	US$		US$
Earnings per share*	(0.65)		(0.60)

* Common
[A] Reported in accordance with U.S. GAAP

Historical Summary
(as originally stated)

Fiscal Year	Oper. Rev.	Net Inc. Bef. Disc.	EPS*
	US$000s	US$000s	US$
2022[A]	nil	(56,796)	(1.84)
2021[A]	nil	(93,036)	(3.45)
2020[B1]	nil	(35,339)	(1.50)
	$000s	$000s	$
2019[B2]	nil	(1,479)	(3.60)
2018[B]	nil	(1,096)	(3.60)

* Common
[A] Reported in accordance with U.S. GAAP
[B] Reported in accordance with IFRS
[1] Results reflect the Feb. 27, 2020, reverse takeover acquisition of Mind Medicine, Inc.
[2] Results for fiscal 2019 and prior periods pertain to Broadway Gold Mining Ltd.
Note: Adjusted throughout for 1-for-15 cons. in Aug. 2022; 1-for-8 cons. in Mar. 2020

M.92 MindBio Therapeutics Corp.

Symbol - MBIO **Exchange** - CSE **CUSIP** - 60256C
Head Office - Level 4, 9197 William St, Melbourne, VIC, Australia, 3000 **Overseas Tel** - 61-4-3314-0886
Website - www.mindbiotherapeutics.com
Email - justin@mindbiotherapeutics.com
Investor Relations - Justin A. Hanka 61-4-3314-0886
Auditors - MNP LLP C.A., Toronto, Ont.
Transfer Agents - Odyssey Trust Company, Toronto, Ont.
Profile - (B.C. 2021) Researches microdosing of psychedelic medicines to treat a range of medical conditions such as depression, anxiety, post-traumatic stress disorder (PTSD), panic disorder, chronic pain and opiate addictions.

Microdosing involves the repeated administration of small sub-hallucinogenic doses of psychedelic medicines, such as lysergic acid diethylamide (LSD) or psilocybin-containing mushrooms, which are believed to have significant impact on improvements in mood, creativity, happiness and energy. The company has developed a multi-disciplinary platform for developing treatments, is involved in psychedelic medicine development, has completed Phase 1 clinical trials microdosing LSD, has a Phase 2 clinical trial in development microdosing LSD in patients with major depressive disorder and a Phase 2 clinical trial in development microdosing LSD in late stage cancer patients suffering from depression and end of life distress.

Also operates a digital technology and research business with a core focus on establishing and executing research protocols through formal clinical trials that are facilitated via digital therapeutic platforms. In addition, the company is developing a safe medication delivery device which has anti-tampering characteristics and can limit dosage amount and frequency to a strict treatment regimen. The device would support medication adherence and integrate with wearables and other technologies that can report drug adherence and biometric data back to clinicians.

On May 1, 2023, **Blackhawk Growth Corp.** completed a plan of arrangement whereby Australia-based wholly owned **MindBio Therapeutics Pty Ltd.** and **Digital Mind Technology Pty Ltd.** were transferred to the company (formerly named **1286409 B.C. Ltd.**) and shares of the company were spun-out to Blackhawk shareholders on a one-for-one basis.

Common listed on CSE, May 5, 2023.

Directors - Gavin Upiter, chr., Melbourne, Vic., Australia; Justin A. Hanka, CEO, Vic., Australia; Dr. Zena Burgess, Melbourne, Vic., Australia
Other Exec. Officers - John Dinan, CFO & corp. sec.

Capital Stock

	Authorized (shs.)	Outstanding (shs.)[1]
Common	unlimited	133,047,305

[1] At May 5, 2023

Major Shareholder - Widely held at May 5, 2023.
Recent Close: $0.04

Wholly Owned Subsidiaries

Digital Mind Technology Pty Ltd., Australia.
MindBio Therapeutics Pty Ltd., Australia.
• 98% int. in **MindBio Therapeutics Pty Ltd.**, New Zealand.

M.93 Mindset Pharma Inc.

Symbol - MSET **Exchange** - CSE **CUSIP** - 60268M
Head Office - 401-217 Queen St W, Toronto, ON, M5V 0R2 **Telephone** - (647) 938-5266
Website - www.mindsetpharma.com
Email - jlanthier@mindsetpharma.com
Investor Relations - James Lanthier (416) 409-1091
Auditors - MNP LLP C.A., Toronto, Ont.
Lawyers - Irwin Lowy LLP, Toronto, Ont.
Transfer Agents - Computershare Trust Company of Canada Inc., Vancouver, B.C.
Profile - (B.C. 2020; orig. Alta., 2011) Develops psychedelic medicines for the treatment of neuropsychiatric and neurological indications with unmet needs.

The company conducts research and development using a proprietary platform for discovering and developing novel and patentable next-generation psychedelic drug candidates for the treatment of neurological and psychiatric disorders. Its initial focus was on psilocybin-inspired new chemical entities (NCEs) but has been expanded to include dimethyltryptamine (DMT)-inspired NCEs. Has developed four families of novel, next-generation psychedelics. Its lead Family 1 candidate is MSP-1014. The company has a co-development agreement with the McQuade Center for Strategic Research and Development, an affiliate of **Otsuka Pharmaceuticals Co., Ltd.**, for its short-duration compounds.

In September 2022, the company agreed to acquire an exclusive licence for an extensive targeted class of tryptamine-based molecules to **Cybin Inc.** for a licence fee of US$500,000, plus additional payments totaling up to US$9,500,000 payable by cash and common shares upon achievement of certain clinical development milestones.

Predecessor Detail - Name changed from North Sur Resources Inc., Sept. 8, 2020, pursuant to the reverse takeover acquisition of (old) Mindset Pharma Inc.

Directors - Richard J. Patricio, chr., Toronto, Ont.; Joseph Araujo, chief scientific officer, Grimsby, Ont.; Ken Belotskiy, Tel Aviv, Israel; James C. Passin, Ill.; Philip (Phil) Williams, Toronto, Ont.
Other Exec. Officers - James Lanthier, CEO; Arvin Ramos, CFO; Dr. Abdelmalik (Malik) Slassi, sr. v-p, innovation; Jason Atkinson, v-p, corp. devel.; Christopher O. (Chris) Irwin, corp. sec.

Capital Stock

	Authorized (shs.)	Outstanding (shs.)[1]
Common	unlimited	101,298,924

[1] At May 30, 2023

Major Shareholder - Widely held at Jan. 16, 2023.

Price Range - MSET/CSE

Year	Volume	High	Low	Close
2022	17,908,852	$0.98	$0.28	$0.32
2021	64,719,369	$1.55	$0.33	$0.85
2020	782,003	$2.20	$0.85	$0.94

Recent Close: $0.70
Capital Stock Changes - During fiscal 2022, common shares were issued as follows: 7,260,575 on exercise of warrants, 2,257,367 for services and 505,389 on conversion of debentures.

Wholly Owned Subsidiaries

Mindset Pharma Limited, Ont.

Financial Statistics

Periods ended:	12m June 30/22[A]		12m June 30/21[A]
	$000s	%Chg	$000s
Operating revenue	**3,906**	**n.a.**	**nil**
Research & devel. expense	7,394		2,222
General & admin expense	5,306		2,485
Stock-based compensation	5,016		2,002
Operating expense	**17,716**	**+164**	**6,709**
Operating income	**(13,810)**	**n.a.**	**(6,709)**
Pre-tax income	**(16,610)**	**n.a.**	**(11,653)**
Net income	**(16,610)**	**n.a.**	**(11,653)**
Cash & equivalent	8,715		6,580
Current assets	9,612		9,884
Right-of-use assets	156		200
Total assets	**9,768**	**-3**	**10,084**
Accts. pay. & accr. liabs.	740		387
Current liabilities	8,149		893
Long-term debt, gross	nil		471
Long-term lease liabilities	132		172
Shareholders' equity	1,487		9,020
Cash from oper. activs.	**386**	**n.a.**	**(8,367)**
Cash from fin. activs.	1,749		13,369
Cash from invest. activs.	nil		1,038
Net cash position	**8,715**	**+32**	**6,580**
	$		$
Earnings per share*	(0.18)		(0.20)
Cash flow per share*	0.00		(0.15)
	shs		shs
No. of shs. o/s*	94,619,280		84,595,949
Avg. no. of shs. o/s*	90,061,087		57,658,870
	%		%
Net profit margin	(425.24)		n.a.
Return on equity	(316.17)		(245.61)
Return on assets	(167.34)		(218.94)

* Common
[A] Reported in accordance with IFRS

Latest Results

Periods ended:	9m Mar. 31/23[A]		9m Mar. 31/22[A]
	$000s	%Chg	$000s
Operating revenue	6,109	n.a.	nil
Net income	(5,552)	n.a.	(16,052)
	$		$
Earnings per share*	(0.06)		(0.18)

* Common
[A] Reported in accordance with IFRS

Historical Summary
(as originally stated)

Fiscal Year	Oper. Rev.	Net Inc. Bef. Disc.	EPS*
	$000s	$000s	$
2022[A]	3,906	(16,610)	(0.18)
2021[A]	nil	(11,653)	(0.20)
2020[A1,2]	nil	(482)	(0.03)
2019[A3]	nil	(33)	(0.00)
2018[A]	nil	(14)	(0.00)

* Common
[A] Reported in accordance with IFRS
[1] 38 weeks ended June 30, 2020.
[2] Results pertain to (old) Mindset Pharma Inc.
[3] Results for 2019 and prior years pertain to North Sur Resources Inc.

M.94 MineHub Technologies Inc.

Symbol - MHUB **Exchange** - TSX-VEN **CUSIP** - 60273M
Head Office - 717-1030 Georgia St W, Vancouver, BC, V6E 2Y3 **Telephone** - (604) 628-5623
Website - minehub.com
Email - arnoud@minehub.com
Investor Relations - Arnoud Star Busmann (604) 628-5623
Auditors - Dale Matheson Carr-Hilton LaBonte LLP C.A., Vancouver, B.C.
Lawyers - Miller Thomson LLP, Vancouver, B.C.
Transfer Agents - Odyssey Trust Company, Vancouver, B.C.
Profile - (B.C. 2018) Develops and operates a blockchain technology platform for digital trade for the global mining and metals supply chain.

The platform uses blockchain technology to enable users to track, authenticate, share and centralize sensitive documents and information. Services parties involved in physical commodities transactions and has applications in trade finance, metal concentrates and ESG (environmental, social and governance) transactions.

The company is developing the platform alongside **International Business Machines Corporation** (IBM) and other various vendors.

Also develops a Software-as-a-Service (SaaS) platform providing seamless order processing, real-time shipment tracking, inventory management and reporting for the commodities ecosystem.

In March 2023, the company acquired certain operational assets, intellectual property, contracts and accounts receivable of **Waybridge Technologies Inc.** for issuance of 8,176,634 common shares. Waybridge develops a Software-as-a-Service (SaaS) platform provides seamless order processing, real-time shipment tracking, inventory management and reporting for the commodities ecosystem.

Directors - Vince Sorace, founder & exec. chr., Vancouver, B.C.; Alison Graham; Guy Halford-Thompson, Vancouver, B.C.; Joseph Nakhla, Port Moody, B.C.; Arnoud Star Busmann, Netherlands

Other Exec. Officers - Andrea Aranguren, pres., COO & CEO; Gavin Cooper, CFO & corp. sec.; Mariana Southern, v-p, product

Capital Stock

	Authorized (shs.)	Outstanding (shs.)[1]
Common	unlimited	94,865,128

[1] At June 27, 2023

Major Shareholder - Widely held at May 19, 2023.

Price Range - MHUB/TSX-VEN

Year	Volume	High	Low	Close
2022............	7,672,863	$1.15	$0.17	$0.44
2021............	4,893,815	$1.90	$0.85	$0.97

Recent Close: $0.40

Capital Stock Changes - In March 2023, 8,176,634 common shares were issued pursuant to the acquisition CMDTY UK Ltd. In April 2023, private placement of 4,075,000 units (1 common share & ½ warrant) at 25¢ per unit was completed, with warrants exercisable at 40¢ per share for two years. In June 2023, private placement of 5,000,000 units (1 common share & ½ warrant) at 20¢ per unit was completed, with warrants exercisable at 40¢ per share for two years.

In April 2022, private placement of 3,500,000 units (1 common share & ½ warrant) at 90¢ per share was completed. In November 2022, private placement of 12,600,000 common shares was completed at 20¢ per share. Also during fiscal 2023, common shares were issued as follows: 810,000 on conversion of debt and 100,000 on exercise of warrants.

Wholly Owned Subsidiaries

CMDTY UK Ltd.
MineHub Technologies Netherlands B.V., Netherlands.
MineHub Technologies Singapore Pte Ltd.
Minehub (USA) Inc., Nev.
Yitong Digital Trade (Shanghai) Network Technology Development Co. Ltd.

Financial Statistics

Periods ended:	12m Jan. 31/23[A]		12m Jan. 31/22[A]
	$000s	%Chg	$000s
Operating revenue........................	**187**	**n.a.**	**nil**
Salaries & benefits..........................	949		484
Research & devel. expense.............	1,737		3,639
General & admin expense...............	5,132		3,839
Stock-based compensation............	622		904
Operating expense........................	**8,441**	**-5**	**8,866**
Operating income.........................	**(8,254)**	**n.a.**	**(8,866)**
Finance costs, gross........................	267		749
Pre-tax income.............................	**(8,530)**	**n.a.**	**(9,648)**
Net income....................................	**(8,530)**	**n.a.**	**(9,648)**
Cash & equivalent............................	1,153		2,941
Accounts receivable.........................	281		191
Current assets..................................	1,581		3,815
Total assets...................................	**1,581**	**-59**	**3,815**
Accts. pay. & accr. liabs..................	634		659
Current liabilities............................	1,632		1,904
Long-term debt, gross......................	842		1,246
Equity portion of conv. debs............	88		104
Shareholders' equity........................	(50)		1,911
Cash from oper. activs..................	**(7,258)**	**n.a.**	**(8,588)**
Cash from fin. activs........................	5,470		11,073
Net cash position..........................	**1,153**	**-61**	**2,941**
	$		$
Earnings per share*.........................	(0.13)		(0.18)
Cash flow per share*.......................	(0.11)		(0.16)
	shs		shs
No. of shs. o/s*................................	77,613,493		60,603,493
Avg. no. of shs. o/s*.........................	66,761,958		53,461,536
	%		%
Net profit margin..............................	n.m.		n.a.
Return on equity...............................	n.m.		n.m.
Return on assets...............................	(306.26)		(381.93)

* Common
[A] Reported in accordance with IFRS

Latest Results

Periods ended:	3m Apr. 30/23[A]		3m Apr. 30/22[A]
	$000s	%Chg	$000s
Operating revenue...........................	342	n.a.	nil
Net income......................................	(2,310)	n.a.	(2,560)
	$		$
Earnings per share*.........................	(0.03)		(0.04)

* Common
[A] Reported in accordance with IFRS

Historical Summary
(as originally stated)

Fiscal Year	Oper. Rev.	Net Inc. Bef. Disc.	EPS*
	$000s	$000s	$
2023[A]....................	187	(8,530)	(0.13)
2022[A]....................	nil	(9,648)	(0.18)
2021[A]....................	67	(3,246)	(0.08)
2020[A]....................	nil	(4,046)	(0.13)

* Common
[A] Reported in accordance with IFRS

M.95 MiniLuxe Holding Corp.

Symbol - MNLX **Exchange** - TSX-VEN **CUSIP** - 60365X
Head Office - One Faneuil Hall Sq, 7th Flr, Boston, MA, United States, 02109 **Telephone** - (617) 684-2731
Website - www.miniluxe.com
Email - zkrislock@miniluxe.com
Investor Relations - Zoe Krislock (617) 684-2731
Auditors - RSM US LLP C.P.A., Boston, Mass.
Lawyers - Owens, Wright LLP, Toronto, Ont.
Transfer Agents - Computershare Trust Company of Canada Inc., Toronto, Ont.

Profile - (Ont. 2021) Operates nail and beauty studios, and sells nail care and beauty products online and in-studio.

Provides nail care services, hand and foot therapies, waxing and tweezing services, and brow and lash tinting at its studio fleet as well as via digitally-enabled partner channels such as mobile kiosks. At Apr. 2, 2023, the company had 21 studio locations in Massachusetts, Rhode Island, California, Texas and New York.

Products sold include a branded line of polishes, hand and body treatments, and other self-care products, primarily via e-commerce. Branded products are also used throughout the fleet of studios.

In May 2023, the company opened a studio location in the downtown area of Tampa Bay, Fla.

In August 2022, the company acquired all of the assets of **Paintbox LLC**, a New York-based high-design nail studio service provider, for issuance of 1,744,298 class A subordinate voting shares at US$1.031 per share.

Predecessor Detail - Name changed from Rise Capital Corp., Dec. 1, 2021, pursuant to the Qualifying Transaction reverse takeover acquisition of Boston, Mass.-based MiniLuxe, Inc.; basis 1 new for 4 old shs.

Directors - Anthony K. (Tony) Tjan, chr., Milton, Mass.; Zoe Krislock, CEO, Orlando, Fla.; Stefanie Jay, San Francisco, Calif.; Mats Lederhausen, Chicago, Ill.; Vernon Lobo, Toronto, Ont.

Other Exec. Officers - Brian Moran, CFO & treas.; Christine M. Chang, chief of bus. devel. & partnerships; Aditi Gupta, chief growth officer; Elizabeth Lorber, chief comml. officer & corp. sec.; Allie Burak, contr.

Capital Stock

	Authorized (shs.)	Outstanding (shs.)[1]
Cl.A Subordinate Vtg.	unlimited	56,047,450
Cl.B Proportionate Vtg.	unlimited	91,064

[1] At Apr. 2, 2023

Class A Subordinate Voting - One vote per share.

Class B Proportionate Voting - Each convertible into 1,000 class A subordinate voting shares. 1,000 votes per share.

Normal Course Issuer Bid - The company plans to make normal course purchases of up to 2,800,000 class A subordinate voting shares representing 5% of the total outstanding. The bid commenced on Sept. 20, 2022, and expires on Sept. 19, 2023.

Major Shareholder - Cue Ball Capital, LP held 44.32% interest at Nov. 7, 2022.

Price Range - MNLX/TSX-VEN

Year	Volume	High	Low	Close
2022............	981,825	$1.55	$0.30	$0.36
2021............	251,375	$1.80	$1.08	$1.46

Recent Close: $0.30

Capital Stock Changes - On Aug. 16, 2022, 1,067,961 class A subordinate voting shares were issued pursuant to the acquisition of all of the assets of Paintbox LLC. Also during 2022, 43,790 class A subordinate voting shares were issued on exercise of options and 30,000 class A subordinate voting shares were repurchased under a Normal Course Issuer Bid.

Wholly Owned Subsidiaries

MiniLuxe, Inc., Boston, Mass.

Financial Statistics

Periods ended:	12m Jan. 1/23[A]		12m Dec. 26/21[A1]
	US$000s	%Chg	US$000s
Operating revenue........................	**21,470**	**+29**	**16,682**
Cost of sales....................................	12,096		8,517
Salaries & benefits..........................	7,481		6,369
General & admin expense...............	8,283		6,117
Stock-based compensation............	168		216
Other operating expense.................	32		232
Operating expense........................	**28,060**	**+31**	**21,451**
Operating income.........................	**(6,590)**	**n.a.**	**(4,769)**
Deprec., depl. & amort.....................	3,106		3,018
Finance income................................	nil		10
Finance costs, gross........................	1,381		2,894
Pre-tax income.............................	**(11,613)**	**n.a.**	**(54,373)**
Income taxes....................................	65		61
Net income....................................	**(11,677)**	**n.a.**	**(54,434)**
Cash & equivalent............................	8,343		19,120
Inventories.......................................	1,703		1,686
Current assets..................................	10,719		21,219
Long-term investments....................	50		50
Fixed assets, net..............................	6,257		6,827
Right-of-use assets.........................	4,527		4,633
Intangibles, net.................................	894		497
Total assets...................................	**23,753**	**-29**	**33,496**
Accts. pay. & accr. liabs..................	2,638		3,575
Current liabilities............................	6,558		6,335
Long-term debt, gross......................	2,470		2,460
Long-term debt, net..........................	2,470		2,460
Long-term lease liabilities................	5,318		5,507
Shareholders' equity........................	8,777		19,194
Cash from oper. activs..................	**(8,362)**	**n.a.**	**(3,769)**
Cash from fin. activs........................	(1,692)		21,299
Cash from invest. activs..................	(723)		(1,276)
Net cash position..........................	**8,343**	**-56**	**19,120**
Capital expenditures........................	(310)		(729)
	US$		US$
Earnings per share*.........................	(0.08)		(1.40)
Cash flow per share*.......................	(0.15)		(0.12)
	shs		shs
No. of shs. o/s*................................	56,054,077		54,972,326
Avg. no. of shs. o/s*.........................	55,380,678		30,536,265
	%		%
Net profit margin..............................	(54.39)		(326.30)
Return on equity...............................	(83.49)		n.m.
Return on assets...............................	(35.94)		(192.78)
Foreign sales percent......................	100		100

* Cl.A Subord. Vtg.
[A] Reported in accordance with IFRS
[1] Results reflect the Dec. 1, 2021, Qualifying Transaction reverse takeover acquisition of MiniLuxe, Inc.

Latest Results

Periods ended:	3m Apr. 2/23[A]		3m Mar. 27/22[A]
	US$000s	%Chg	US$000s
Operating revenue...........................	5,218	+18	4,407
Net income......................................	(191)	n.a.	(2,710)
	US$		US$
Earnings per share*.........................	(0.00)		(0.02)

* Cl.A Subord. Vtg.
[A] Reported in accordance with IFRS

Historical Summary
(as originally stated)

Fiscal Year	Oper. Rev.	Net Inc. Bef. Disc.	EPS*
	US$000s	US$000s	US$
2022[A]....................	21,470	(11,677)	(0.08)
2021[A]....................	16,682	(54,434)	(1.40)
2020[A1]..................	10,610	5,971	0.69
2019[A1]..................	22,324	(27,915)	(37.39)

* Cl.A Subord. Vtg.
[A] Reported in accordance with IFRS
[1] Results pertain to MiniLuxe, Inc.

Note: Adjusted throughout for 1-for-4 cons. in Dec. 2021

M.96 The Mint Corporation

Symbol - MIT **Exchange** - TSX-VEN (S) **CUSIP** - 60447G
Head Office - 1700-333 Bay St, Toronto, ON, M5H 2R2 **Telephone** - (647) 352-0666
Website - www.themintcorp.com
Email - info@themintcorp.com
Investor Relations - Viswanathan Karamadam (416) 729-1363
Auditors - PKF Antares Professional Corporation C.A., Calgary, Alta.
Lawyers - Beard Winter LLP, Toronto, Ont.
Transfer Agents - Computershare Trust Company of Canada Inc., Toronto, Ont.

Profile - (Alta. 1997) Provides financial services supported through prepaid and payroll cards linked to the Mint mobile application in the United Arab Emirates (U.A.E.).

Operations are carried out through its subsidiaries and affiliates in the U.A.E.:

Subsidiary **Mint Middle East, LLC** (MME) is a payroll card services provider facilitating an automated and secure payroll system to employers in the U.A.E. in accordance with the Wages Protection System legislation. MME also manages the issuance, administration, customer support, payment processing, set-up, sponsorship and regulated reporting of the cards and related activities to government authorities.

Affiliate **Mint Gateway For Electronic Payment Services LLC** is in the process of building and acquiring the software platform and related infrastructure to carry on the new third party payment processing operations being contemplated by the company.

Affiliate **Mint Electronic Payment Services LLC** operates the business assets acquired from ePAY, a division of **Global Business Systems for Multimedia**, a U.A.E. company operating in the point of sale terminals, mobile airtime top-up and merchant network solutions business. At Nov. 28, 2022, Mint Electronic was inactive.

Affiliate **Hafed Holdings LLC** provides microloans to its customer base. At Nov. 28, 2022, Hafed was inactive.

On Jan. 16, 2020, subsidiaries **Mint Middle East, LLC** and **Mint Gateway for Electronic Payment Services LLC** (collectively Mint UAE) agreed to sell its direct payroll disbursement service business through its payroll card portfolio in the U.A.E. to **Edenred Prepaid Cards Management Services LLC**, a payroll disbursement and card provider in the U.A.E., for an initial payment of $29,500,000 (received on Jan. 26, 2020), as well as a performance-based maximum additional cash payment of up to $7,100,000 based on the success of the migration of the card portfolio. Mint UAE would remain focused on payment card processing and prepaid card products. Final approval from the TSX Venture Exchange for the disposition of the payroll disbursement service business was received May 13, 2020. Migration of the card portfolio was completed in the first half of 2021. At Nov. 28, 2022, the transition of existing Mint UAE customers to Edenred was proceeding.

In April 2022, the company completed the debt settlement agreement with **Mobile Telecommunications Group LLC** (MTG) and **Global Business Services for Multimedia** (collectively creditors), subsidiary **Mint Middle East LLC** (MME) and affiliate **Mint Gateway for Electronic Payment Services LLC** (MGEPS) whereby the company would settle Cdn$20,000,000 outstanding series A debentures and Cdn$7,000,000 of aggregate debt through payment of US$10,000,000 to the creditors. In addition, MME and MGEPS would settle Cdn$42,000,000 of debt owed to the company through payment of US$11,000,000; and Cdn$6,500,000 of debt owed to MTG by MGEPS would be cancelled.

Common suspended from TSX-VEN, May 8, 2023.

Predecessor Detail - Name changed from Mint Technology Corp., Aug. 12, 2013; basis 1 new for 10 old shs.

Directors - Viswanathan (Vishy) Karamadam, chr., pres. & CEO, Mississauga, Ont.; Firas Al Fraih, Dubai, United Arab Emirates; Randy Koroll, Etobicoke, Ont.; Vikas Ranjan, Toronto, Ont.

Other Exec. Officers - Yongbiao (Winfield) Ding, CFO

Capital Stock

	Authorized (shs.)	Outstanding (shs.)[1]
Preferred	unlimited	nil
Common	unlimited	235,876,725

[1] At Nov. 28, 2022

Major Shareholder - Firas Al Fraih held 59.69% interest at Aug. 23, 2021.

Price Range - MIT/TSX-VEN (S)

Year	Volume	High	Low	Close
2022	10,764,652	$0.12	$0.03	$0.07
2021	19,627,301	$0.13	$0.04	$0.09
2020	18,614,829	$0.06	$0.02	$0.04
2019	20,225,185	$0.17	$0.02	$0.03
2018	52,250,029	$0.48	$0.11	$0.16

Recent Close: $0.06

Capital Stock Changes - In January 2022, 16,000,000 common shares were issued on exchange of subscription receipts issued previously to series A debenture holders.

Wholly Owned Subsidiaries

Mint Block Corp. Inactive.

Mint Capital, LLC, Dubai, United Arab Emirates.

- 49% int. in **Mint Gateway For Electronic Payment Services LLC**, United Arab Emirates.
  - 10% int. in **Hafed Holding LLC** Inactive.

2417624 Ontario Inc., Ont. Inactive.

Subsidiaries

51% int. in **Mint Middle East, LLC**, Dubai, United Arab Emirates.

- 49% int. in **Mint Electronic Payment Services LLC**, United Arab Emirates. Inactive.

Financial Statistics

Periods ended:	12m Dec. 31/21[A]		12m Dec. 31/20[A]
	$000s	%Chg	$000s
General & admin expense	456		653
Stock-based compensation	nil		9
Operating expense	**456**	**-31**	**663**
Operating income	**(456)**	**n.a.**	**(663)**
Finance costs, net	4,779		4,222
Investment income	(200)		2,665
Pre-tax income	**(5,035)**	**n.a.**	**(1,380)**
Net income	**(5,035)**	**n.a.**	**(1,380)**
Cash & equivalent	20		22
Current assets	48		76
Long-term investments	2,465		2,665
Total assets	**2,514**	**-8**	**2,741**
Accts. pay. & accr. liabs	104		107
Current liabilities	31,031		8,810
Long-term debt, gross	24,291		19,708
Long-term debt, net	nil		17,413
Shareholders' equity	(28,517)		(23,482)
Cash from oper. activs	**(1)**	**n.a.**	**(27)**
Cash from fin. activs	nil		45
Net cash position	**20**	**-9**	**22**
	$		$
Earnings per share*	(0.02)		(0.01)
Cash flow per share*	nil		(0.00)
	shs		shs
No. of shs. o/s*	219,876,725		219,876,725
Avg. no. of shs. o/s*	219,876,725		199,689,000
	%		%
Net profit margin	n.a.		n.a.
Return on equity	n.m.		n.m.
Return on assets	(191.63)		(96.47)

* Common

[A] Reported in accordance with IFRS

Latest Results

Periods ended:	9m Sept. 30/22[A]		9m Sept. 30/21[A]
	$000s	%Chg	$000s
Net income	30,804	n.a.	(5,007)
	$		$
Earnings per share*	0.13		(0.02)

* Common

[A] Reported in accordance with IFRS

Historical Summary
(as originally stated)

Fiscal Year	Oper. Rev.	Net Inc. Bef. Disc.	EPS*
	$000s	$000s	$
2021[A]	nil	(5,035)	(0.02)
2020[A]	nil	(1,380)	(0.01)
2019[A]	nil	(5,246)	(0.03)
2018[A]	nil	37,265	0.20
2017[A]	nil	(9,794)	(0.07)

* Common

[A] Reported in accordance with IFRS

M.97 Minto Apartment Real Estate Investment Trust

Symbol - MI.UN **Exchange** - TSX **CUSIP** - 60448E

Head Office - 200-180 Kent St, Ottawa, ON, K1P 0B6 **Telephone** - (613) 230-7051

Website - www.mintoapartmentreit.com

Email - jmoss@mintoapartmentreit.com

Investor Relations - John Moss (613) 782-5737

Auditors - KPMG LLP C.A., Toronto, Ont.

Lawyers - Goodmans LLP, Toronto, Ont.

Transfer Agents - TSX Trust Company, Toronto, Ont.

FP500 Revenue Ranking - 714

Employees - 278 at Dec. 31, 2022

Profile - (Ont. 2018) Owns, develops and operates income-producing multi-residential properties in urban markets in Canada.

The trust's property portfolio at Mar. 31, 2023:

Region	Props.	Suites
Ottawa	14	3,095
Toronto	7	2,484
Edmonton	2	190
Calgary	4	665
Montreal	4	1,793
	31	8,227

Recent Merger and Acquisition Activity

Status: completed **Announced:** Mar. 7, 2023

Minto Apartment Real Estate Investment Trust sold Hi-Level Place, a 64-suite multi-residential property in Edmonton, Alta., for $9,920,000.

Status: completed **Revised:** May 6, 2022

UPDATE: The transaction was completed. PREVIOUS: Minto Apartment Real Estate Investment Trust agreed to acquire 220 4th Avenue SW, a 252-suite multi-residential property in Calgary, Alta., for $86,500,000. Payment would include $24,300,000 cash and assumption of $62,200,000 debt. The transaction was expected to close by May 6, 2022.

Status: completed **Revised:** Apr. 22, 2022

UPDATE: The transaction was completed. PREVIOUS: Minto Apartment Real Estate Investment Trust agreed to acquire 28.35% interest in 39 Niagara Street, a 501-suite multi-residential property in Toronto, Ont., for $114,500,000. Payment would includes $2,600,000 cash, assumption of $46,200,000 debt and issuance of 2,985,956 class B limited partner units at $22 per unit, exchangeable into Mintro trust units on a one-for-one basis. The transaction was expected to close by Apr. 22, 2022.

Trustees - Roger Greenberg, chr., Ottawa, Ont.; Jonathan Li, pres. & CEO, Toronto, Ont.; Allan S. Kimberley‡, Toronto, Ont.; Heather C. Kirk, Toronto, Ont.; Jo-Ann Lempert, Montréal, Qué.; Jacqueline C. (Jackie) Moss, Toronto, Ont.; Michael Waters, Ottawa, Ont.

Other Exec. Officers - Edward (Eddie) Fu, CFO; R. Glen MacMullin, chief invest. officer; Paul Baron, sr. v-p, opers.; Ben Mullen, sr. v-p, asset mgt.; Martin Tovey, sr. v-p, invests.; Stephen Marshall, v-p, opers.; John Moss, gen. counsel & corp. sec.

‡ Lead trustee

Capital Stock

	Authorized (shs.)	Outstanding (shs.)[1]
Trust Unit	unlimited	39,887,612
Special Vtg. Unit	unlimited	25,755,029
Class A LP Unit	unlimited	n.a
Class B LP Unit	unlimited	25,755,029[2]
Class C LP Unit	unlimited	22,978,700[2]

[1] At Mar. 31, 2023

[2] Classified as debt.

Note: Class A, B and C limited partnership units are securities of Minto Apartment Limited Partnership.

Trust Unit - The trust will endeavour to make monthly cash distributions. Retractable at a price equal to the lesser of: (i) 90% of the market price of the units on the principal market on which the trust units are traded during the 10 trading days immediately preceding the retraction date; and (ii) 100% of the closing market price on the unit retraction date. One vote per trust unit.

Special Voting Unit - Issued to holders of class B limited partnership units of subsidiary Minto Apartment Limited Partnership. Each special voting unit entitles the holder to a number of votes at unitholder meetings equal to the number of trust units into which the class B limited partnership units are exchangeable.

Class A Limited Partnership Unit - Held by the trust.

Class B Limited Partnership Unit - Entitled to distributions equal to those provided to trust units. Directly exchangeable into trust units on a 1-for-1 basis at any time by holder. All held by Minto Properties Inc. Classified as debt under IFRS.

Class C Limited Partnership Unit - Entitled to distributions in an amount sufficient to permit Minto Properties to satisfy required principal and interest payments on retained debt. Rank in priority to trust units, class A LP units and class B LP units with respect to payment of distributions. All held by Minto Properties. Classified as debt under IFRS.

Major Shareholder - Minto Properties Inc. held 40.6% interest at Mar. 15, 2023.

Price Range - MI.UN/TSX

Year	Volume	High	Low	Close
2022	38,943,367	$23.41	$12.41	$14.05
2021	25,725,886	$25.41	$18.37	$21.89
2020	42,122,424	$28.31	$15.58	$20.37
2019	22,146,404	$24.03	$17.82	$23.15
2018	9,753,622	$19.79	$15.45	$18.50

Recent Close: $13.21

Capital Stock Changes - During 2022, 182,227 trust units were repurchased under a Normal Course Issuer Bid.

Dividends

MI.UN tr unit Ra $0.48996 pa M est. Dec. 15, 2022

Prev. Rate: $0.475 est. Dec. 15, 2021

Prev. Rate: $0.455 est. Sept. 15, 2020

Wholly Owned Subsidiaries

Minto Apartment GP Inc., Ont.

Minto Apartment Limited Partnership, Ont.

Financial Statistics

Periods ended:	12m Dec. 31/22^A		12m Dec. 31/21^A
	$000s	%Chg	$000s
Total revenue	**143,790**	**+16**	**123,547**
Rental operating expense	40,878		33,978
General & admin. expense	9,303		7,602
Property taxes	15,116		13,322
Operating expense	**65,297**	**+19**	**54,902**
Operating income	**78,493**	**+14**	**68,645**
Finance income	4,818		3,129
Finance costs, gross	44,590		35,310
Pre-tax income	**225,400**	**+139**	**94,161**
Net income	**225,400**	**+139**	**94,161**
Cash & equivalent	5,323		2,851
Accounts receivable	3,287		2,088
Current assets	42,422		38,909
Income-producing props	2,553,283		2,325,343
Properties for future devel.	57,811		35,222
Property interests, net	2,611,094		2,360,565
Total assets	**2,734,812**	**+12**	**2,440,714**
Accts. pay. & accr. liabs	23,168		18,038
Current liabilities	331,531		182,642
Long-term debt, gross	1,473,422		1,390,358
Long-term debt, net	1,183,980		1,243,514
Shareholders' equity	1,213,537		1,010,001
Cash from oper. activs	**82,499**	**+14**	**72,119**
Cash from fin. activs	45,659		81,238
Cash from invest. activs	(125,686)		(153,113)
Net cash position	**5,323**	**+87**	**2,851**
Increase in property	(95,514)		(134,918)
	$		$
Earnings per share*	n.a.		n.a.
Cash flow per share*	2.07		1.80
Funds from opers. per sh.*	0.84		0.81
Adj. funds from opers. per sh.*	0.73		0.71
Cash divd. per share*	0.48		0.46
Total divd. per share*	**0.48**		**0.46**
	shs		shs
No. of shs. o/s*	39,887,612		40,069,839
	%		%
Net profit margin	156.76		76.21
Return on equity	20.27		10.12
Return on assets	10.43		5.58
No. of employees (FTEs)	278		246

* Trust Unit
^A Reported in accordance with IFRS

Latest Results

Periods ended:	3m Mar. 31/23^A		3m Mar. 31/22^A
	$000s	%Chg	$000s
Total revenue	38,403	+18	32,526
Net income	(24,227)	n.a.	34,640
	$		$
Earnings per share*	n.a.		n.a.

^A Reported in accordance with IFRS

Historical Summary
(as originally stated)

Fiscal Year	Total Rev.	Net Inc. Bef. Disc.	EPS*
	$000s	$000s	$
2022^A	143,790	225,400	n.a.
2021^A	123,547	94,161	n.a.
2020^A	124,929	179,638	n.a.
2019^A	104,438	19,966	n.a.
2018^A1	42,475	49,390	n.a.

* Trust Unit
^A Reported in accordance with IFRS
[1] 36 weeks ended Dec. 31, 2018.

M.98 Mission Ready Solutions Inc.

Symbol - MRS.H **Exchange** - TSX-VEN (S) **CUSIP** - 60511F
Head Office - 400-1681 Chestnut St, Vancouver, BC, V6J 4M6 **Toll-free** - (877) 479-7778
Website - www.mrscorp.com
Email - info@mrscorp.com
Investor Relations - Terry Nixon (877) 479-7778 ext. 5
Auditors - Fruci & Associates II, PLLC C.P.A., Spokane, Wash.
Transfer Agents - Endeavor Trust Corporation, Vancouver, B.C.
Profile - (B.C. 2009) Manufactures and distributes personal protective solutions including fire, military, emergency and law enforcement products to the global defence, security and first-responder markets.

Through wholly owned **Unifire, Inc.**, distributes fire, military, emergency and law enforcement products through its technology infrastructure used to provide procurement solutions to program managers, military and federal contracting offices, base supply centers and other government supply agencies.

Wholly owned **Protect the Force Inc.** develops and markets products in the area of wearable technologies synthesizing advanced textiles with electronics and computation for personal protection and safety. Products include Flex9Armor and Tactical Shield Cover.

Wholly owned **PTF Manufacturing Inc.** manufactures a full range of products dedicated to the tactical and defense industry including tactical outerwear, canine armor, bomb suits/blankets, riot control protection, carriers, textiles with integrated electronics and ballistic panels.

Wholly owned **No Contact, LLC** (dba PTF Innovations) researches new and advanced technology to meet the needs of the global defense, security and personal protection markets.

Customers include the U.S. Department of Defense, law enforcement and private security. The company is headquartered and has offices in Vancouver, B.C., and Spokane, Wash.; and has a manufacturing facility in Jacksboro, Tenn.

Common suspended from TSX-VEN, July 21, 2023.

Predecessor Detail - Name changed from Mission Ready Services Inc., June 5, 2018.

Capital Stock

	Authorized (shs.)	Outstanding (shs.)[1]
Preferred	unlimited	nil
Common	unlimited	215,550,000

[1] At May 1, 2023

Major Shareholder - Widely held at Mar. 3, 2023.

Price Range - MRS.H/TSX-VEN (S)

Year	Volume	High	Low	Close
2022	39,202,385	$0.47	$0.07	$0.09
2021	211,569,401	$1.00	$0.16	$0.27
2020	151,031,098	$0.29	$0.04	$0.20
2019	103,423,160	$0.32	$0.08	$0.08
2018	81,918,283	$0.38	$0.19	$0.22

Recent Close: $0.04

Capital Stock Changes - During 2022, common shares were issued as follows: 10,957,875 by private placement, 3,595,856 for debt settlement and 1,019,000 on exercise of options.

Wholly Owned Subsidiaries

Mission Ready Holdings Ltd., Vancouver, B.C.
- 100% int. in **10-20 Services Inc.**, Lakewood, Wash.
- 100% int. in **Protect The Force Inc.**, Alpharetta, Ga.
  - 100% int. in **No Contact, LLC**, Natick, Mass.

Mission Ready Holdings U.S.A. Inc., United States.
PTF Manufacturing Inc., Tenn.
Unifire, Inc., Spokane, Wash.

Financial Statistics

Periods ended:	12m Dec. 31/22^A		12m Dec. 31/21^A
	$000s	%Chg	$000s
Operating revenue	**5,522**	**-94**	**91,986**
Cost of goods sold	4,593		83,892
Salaries & benefits	3,102		3,241
Research & devel. expense	2		83
General & admin expense	2,041		2,307
Stock-based compensation	605		3,178
Operating expense	**10,343**	**-89**	**92,700**
Operating income	**(4,821)**	**n.a.**	**(714)**
Deprec., depl. & amort.	562		300
Finance costs, gross	653		376
Write-downs/write-offs	(18,085)[1]		(11)
Pre-tax income	**(22,502)**	**n.a.**	**(744)**
Net income	**(22,502)**	**n.a.**	**(744)**
Cash & equivalent	357		7,897
Inventories	241		463
Accounts receivable	763		2,654
Current assets	1,568		11,998
Fixed assets, net	192		207
Intangibles, net	934		18,926
Total assets	**2,694**	**-91**	**31,131**
Accts. pay. & accr. liabs	1,688		1,640
Current liabilities	9,420		4,796
Long-term debt, gross	9,704		18,159
Long-term debt, net	2,244		15,147
Shareholders' equity	(8,970)		11,189
Cash from oper. activs	**(1,930)**	**n.a.**	**(1,211)**
Cash from fin. activs	(5,891)		7,256
Cash from invest. activs	(15)		(2)
Net cash position	**357**	**-95**	**7,897**
Capital expenditures	(15)		(8)
Capital disposals	nil		6
	$		$
Earnings per share*	(0.11)		(0.00)
Cash flow per share*	(0.01)		(0.01)
	shs		shs
No. of shs. o/s*	213,976,875		198,404,144
Avg. no. of shs. o/s*	203,047,826		196,112,721
	%		%
Net profit margin	(407.50)		(0.81)
Return on equity	n.m.		(8.29)
Return on assets	(129.19)		(1.13)

* Common
^A Reported in accordance with IFRS
[1] Includes impairment on goodwill and intangible assets totaling $17,809,224.

Historical Summary
(as originally stated)

Fiscal Year	Oper. Rev.	Net Inc. Bef. Disc.	EPS*
	$000s	$000s	$
2022^A	5,522	(22,502)	(0.11)
2021^A	91,986	(744)	(0.00)
2020^A	105,070	(1,341)	(0.01)
2019^A	21,193	(7,438)	(0.05)
2018^A	3,082	(4,865)	(0.04)

* Common
^A Reported in accordance with IFRS

M.99 Miza III Ventures Inc.

Symbol - MIZA.P **Exchange** - TSX-VEN **CUSIP** - 60700R
Head Office - 1510-789 Pender St W, Vancouver, BC, V6H 1H2 **Telephone** - (604) 728-7715
Email - azimdhalla@icloud.com
Investor Relations - Azim Dhalla (604) 728-7715
Auditors - Dale Matheson Carr-Hilton LaBonte LLP C.A., Vancouver, B.C.
Transfer Agents - Endeavor Trust Corporation, Vancouver, B.C.
Profile - (B.C. 2021) Capital Pool Company.
Directors - Azim Dhalla, pres., CEO, CFO & corp. sec., Vancouver, B.C.; Nizar Y. Bharmal, Burnaby, B.C.; Jason D'Silva, Calgary, Alta.

Capital Stock

	Authorized (shs.)	Outstanding (shs.)[1]
Common	unlimited	18,000,000

[1] At May 31, 2023

Major Shareholder - Azim Dhalla held 11.11% interest at July 15, 2022.

Price Range - MIZA.P/TSX-VEN

Year	Volume	High	Low	Close
2022	53,000	$0.26	$0.13	$0.14
2021	273,600	$0.26	$0.13	$0.26

Recent Close: $0.13

Capital Stock Changes - There were no changes to capital stock during fiscal 2023.

M.100 Mobilum Technologies Inc.

Symbol - MBLM **Exchange** - CSE **CUSIP** - 60743X
Head Office - 700-838 Hastings St W, Vancouver, BC, V6C 0A6 **Telephone** - (604) 314-5675 **Toll-free** - (833) 205-6945
Website - mobilum.com
Email - kpladson@mobilum.com
Investor Relations - Kelly Pladson (604) 726-6749
Auditors - BF Borgers CPA PC C.P.A., Lakewood, Colo.
Lawyers - Cassels Brock & Blackwell LLP, Vancouver, B.C.
Transfer Agents - Odyssey Trust Company, Vancouver, B.C.
Profile - (B.C. 2010) Provides payment processing technology solutions for exchanges, wallets and cryptocurrency businesses.

Provides digital services which makes digital assets and cryptocurrencies accessible through traditional finance and payment infrastructure and digital asset management technologies. Products include Mobilum, the company's umbrella brand which offers plug and play fiat-to-crypto gateway and payment processing on-ramp and off-ramp technology solution for exchanges, wallets, brokers, liquidity providers, cryptocurrency businesses, non-fungible token (NFT) marketplaces, protocols, decentralized applications and decentralized autonomous organizations, metaverse and play-to-earn games, and traditional finance institutions.

Predecessor Detail - Name changed from TechX Technologies Inc., July 20, 2021.

Directors - Wojceich Kaszycki, chr., Warsaw, Poland; Robert Niziol, N.J.; Jung Ho (Thomas) Park

Other Exec. Officers - Dr. John Henderson, interim CEO, COO & interim CFO; Piotr Majka, chief trading officer; Kelly Pladson, corp. sec.

Capital Stock

	Authorized (shs.)	Outstanding (shs.)[1]
Preferred	unlimited	nil
Common	unlimited	160,878,138

[1] At July 4, 2023

Major Shareholder - Blockcorp Sociedad Anonima held 15.2% interest and Wojceich Kaszycki held 13.7% interest at Sept. 13, 2022.

Price Range - MBLM/CSE

Year	Volume	High	Low	Close
2022	26,146,894	$0.30	$0.02	$0.02
2021	82,769,663	$1.68	$0.09	$0.29
2020	9,399,615	$0.19	$0.04	$0.09
2019	13,688,120	$0.73	$0.16	$0.18
2018	3,292,530	$0.83	$0.29	$0.49

Consolidation: 1-for-2.5 cons. in Feb. 2021
Recent Close: $0.02

Wholly Owned Subsidiaries

AXS Innovations Inc.
Mobilum OU, Canada.
- 100% int. in **Mobilum Pay Sp.zo.o**, Warsaw, Poland.

Mobilum OU, Tallinn, Estonia.
Mobilum Technologies USA Inc., Wyo.
Mobilum Technology UAB, Lithuania.
TechX Labs Inc., B.C.

Financial Statistics

Periods ended:	12m Feb. 28/22[A]		12m Feb. 28/21[A]
	US$000s	%Chg	US$000s
Operating revenue	**1,085**	**n.m.**	**3**
General & admin expense	4,082		1,556
Stock-based compensation	3,931		1,382
Operating expense	**8,013**	**+173**	**2,938**
Operating income	**(6,928)**	**n.a.**	**(2,935)**
Deprec., depl. & amort.	2		186
Finance costs, gross	19		33
Write-downs/write-offs	(23,022)		(1,845)
Pre-tax income	**(31,672)**	**n.a.**	**(4,841)**
Net inc. bef. disc. opers	**(31,672)**	**n.a.**	**(4,841)**
Income from disc. opers	(124)		nil
Net income	**(31,796)**	**n.a.**	**(4,841)**
Net inc. for equity hldrs	**(31,796)**	**n.a.**	**(4,828)**
Net inc. for non-cont. int	**nil**	**n.a.**	**(13)**
Cash & equivalent	4,529		418
Accounts receivable	107		113
Current assets	5,868		762
Long-term investments	nil		196
Fixed assets, net	2		nil
Right-of-use assets	32		nil
Intangibles, net	7,437		nil
Total assets	**13,339**	**n.m.**	**958**
Bank indebtedness	nil		360
Accts. pay. & accr. liabs	2,486		691
Current liabilities	3,108		1,090
Long-term debt, gross	28		33
Long-term debt, net	28		33
Long-term lease liabilities	8		14
Shareholders' equity	10,195		(1,067)
Non-controlling interest	nil		887
Cash from oper. activs	**(1,692)**	**n.a.**	**(1,086)**
Cash from fin. activs	7,106		1,096
Cash from invest. activs	48		(196)
Net cash position	**4,529**	**+983**	**418**
	US$		US$
Earnings per share*	(0.23)		(0.07)
Cash flow per share*	(0.01)		(0.02)
	shs		shs
No. of shs. o/s*	158,197,920		83,218,711
Avg. no. of shs. o/s*	139,870,402		69,681,837
	%		%
Net profit margin	n.m.		n.m.
Return on equity	n.m.		n.m.
Return on assets	(442.79)		(441.71)

* Common
[A] Reported in accordance with IFRS

Latest Results

Periods ended:	6m Aug. 31/22[A]		6m Aug. 31/21[A]
	US$000s	%Chg	US$000s
Operating revenue	933	n.m.	47
Net inc. bef. disc. opers	(2,764)	n.a.	(5,004)
Income from disc. opers	nil		18
Net income	(2,764)	n.a.	(4,986)
	US$		US$
Earnings per share*	(0.02)		(0.04)

* Common
[A] Reported in accordance with IFRS

Historical Summary
(as originally stated)

Fiscal Year	Oper. Rev.	Net Inc. Bef. Disc.	EPS*
	US$000s	US$000s	US$
2022[A]	1,085	(31,672)	(0.23)
2021[A]	3	(4,841)	(0.07)
2020[A]	176	(9,462)	(0.13)
2019[A1,2]	218	(10,772)	(0.22)

* Common
[A] Reported in accordance with IFRS
[1] 15 months ended Feb. 28, 2019.
[2] Results reflect the acquisition of blockchain assets from Blockcorp Sociedad Anonima and concurrent acquisition of AXS Innovations Inc.
Note: Adjusted throughout for 1-for-2.5 cons. in Feb. 2021

M.101 Mobio Technologies Inc.

Symbol - MBO **Exchange** - TSX-VEN **CUSIP** - 60743K
Head Office - 401-750 Pender St W, Vancouver, BC, V6C 2T7 **Telephone** - (604) 428-7050
Website - www.mobio.net
Email - laurie@mobio.net
Investor Relations - Laurie Baggio (604) 837-4360
Auditors - Dale Matheson Carr-Hilton LaBonte LLP C.A., Vancouver, B.C.
Lawyers - Cassels Brock & Blackwell LLP, Vancouver, B.C.
Transfer Agents - Computershare Trust Company of Canada Inc., Vancouver, B.C.
Profile - (Alta. 1998) Operates a social promotions platform which helps marketers to promote their brands to potential customers through contests and sweepstakes.

Wholly owned **Strutta.com Media Inc.** operates Strutta, a social promotions platform which allows brands to run contests and sweepstakes across multiple web channels.

In May 2022, agreement to acquire **Elite Window Cleaning Inc.** for $2,110,000 was terminated. Elite offers professional window cleaning services from high-rise towers to residential homes in Canada.

Recent Merger and Acquisition Activity

Status: pending **Announced:** Mar. 14, 2022
Mobio Technologies Inc. agreed to a reverse takeover acquisition of Vancouver, B.C.-based Tracksuit Movers Inc. for $12,000,000. Tracksuit provides moving services including local, furniture, seniors, commercial, office and premium long distance moving as well as provides packing services and boxes in Canada and the U.S. Concurrently, Mobio would also complete a $3,000,000 to $4,000,000 private placement financing.

Predecessor Detail - Name changed from LX Ventures Inc., July 7, 2014.

Directors - Laurie Baggio, CEO, Victoria, B.C.; Brian S. R. O'Neill, Vancouver, B.C.; Melanie Pump, Vancouver, B.C.

Other Exec. Officers - Ray Walia, COO; Vladislav Pasko, CFO; Patrick Audley, chief tech. officer

Capital Stock

	Authorized (shs.)	Outstanding (shs.)[1]
Preferred	unlimited	nil
Common	unlimited	42,583,260

[1] At June 6, 2023

Major Shareholder - Lance Tracey held 40% interest and Laurie Baggio held 13.15% interest at Nov. 29, 2022.

Price Range - MBO/TSX-VEN

Year	Volume	High	Low	Close
2022	174,437	$0.15	$0.09	$0.10
2021	576,932	$0.19	$0.08	$0.10
2020	1,430,665	$0.18	$0.07	$0.08
2019	1,787,520	$0.14	$0.05	$0.07
2018	2,822,962	$0.41	$0.07	$0.08

Capital Stock Changes - There were no changes to capital stock during fiscal 2022.

In August 2022, private placement of 4,285,714 common shares was completed at 7¢ per share.

Wholly Owned Subsidiaries

Strutta.com Media Inc., Canada.

Financial Statistics

Periods ended:	12m July 31/22[A]		12m July 31/21[oA]
	$000s	%Chg	$000s
Operating revenue	**8**	**-43**	**14**
Salaries & benefits	75		181
General & admin expense	133		92
Operating expense	**208**	**-24**	**273**
Operating income	**(200)**	**n.a.**	**(259)**
Finance costs, gross	50		38
Pre-tax income	**(218)**	**n.a.**	**(1,465)**
Net income	**(218)**	**n.a.**	**(1,465)**
Cash & equivalent	15		18
Accounts receivable	6		42
Current assets	40		73
Total assets	**40**	**-45**	**73**
Accts. pay. & accr. liabs	171		162
Current liabilities	721		542
Long-term debt, gross	580		405
Long-term debt, net	30		25
Equity portion of conv. debs	73		73
Shareholders' equity	(711)		(493)
Cash from oper. activs	**(160)**	**n.a.**	**(295)**
Cash from fin. activs	125		15
Cash from invest. activs	32		(366)
Net cash position	**15**	**-17**	**18**
	$		$
Earnings per share*	(0.01)		(0.04)
Cash flow per share*	(0.00)		(0.01)
	shs		shs
No. of shs. o/s*	38,297,546		38,297,546
Avg. no. of shs. o/s*	38,297,546		38,297,546
	%		%
Net profit margin	n.m.		n.m.
Return on equity	n.m.		n.m.
Return on assets	(297.35)		(39.93)

* Common
[o] Restated
[A] Reported in accordance with IFRS

Latest Results

Periods ended:	3m Oct. 31/22[A]		3m Oct. 31/21[A]
	$000s	%Chg	$000s
Operating revenue	nil	n.a.	3
Net income	(64)	n.a.	(49)
	$		$
Earnings per share*	(0.00)		(0.00)

* Common
[A] Reported in accordance with IFRS

Historical Summary
(as originally stated)

Fiscal Year	Oper. Rev.	Net Inc. Bef. Disc.	EPS*
	$000s	$000s	$
2022[A]	8	(218)	(0.01)
2021[A]	7	(1,465)	(0.04)
2020[A]	5	(244)	(0.01)
2019[A]	46	(836)	(0.02)
2018[A]	71	(952)	(0.06)

* Common
[A] Reported in accordance with IFRS

M.102 Mobi724 Global Solutions Inc.

Symbol - MOS **Exchange** - TSX-VEN (S) **CUSIP** - 60705U
Head Office - 500-1275 av des Canadiens-de-Montreal, Montréal, QC, H3B 0G4 **Telephone** - (514) 394-5200 **Toll-free** - (855) 521-1221 **Fax** - (514) 419-6686
Website - www.mobi724.com
Email - marcel.vienneau@mobi724.com
Investor Relations - Marcel Vienneau (855) 521-1221
Auditors - MNP LLP C.A., Montréal, Qué.
Lawyers - AG Avocat Conseil Inc., Westmount, Qué.
Transfer Agents - Computershare Trust Company of Canada Inc., Toronto, Ont.
Profile - (Alta. 2005) Provides Smart Transaction Processing platform which offers card-linked solutions in a white label format; and Artificial Intelligence (AI) for predictive analysis of the card-linked campaigns for merchants and banks.

The Card-Linked solutions enables enrolled cardholders to make payment transactions and receive cash backs or points based on rules and features offers and programs including Pay with Points, Points 4 Value, Cash-back, Points for Travel, Pay with Instalments Notification, Points Bank, Digital Marketing and Transaction Eraser. The Artificial Intelligence solutions provides predictive analysis which can be used to identify, understand and predict the cardholder's behaviour and purchase patterns as well as enhance the merchant's or bank's card-linked campaigns.

Common suspended from TSX-VEN, June 30, 2023.

Recent Merger and Acquisition Activity

Status: pending **Revised:** July 5, 2022
UPDATE: The transaction was still pending. PREVIOUS: Mobi724 Global Solutions Inc. agreed to acquire Argentina-based Avenida Compras S.A. for US$4,000,000 consisting of US$3,500,000 cash and issuance of US$500,000 common shares subject to a minimum per share price of US$0.05 per share. Avenida Compras operates a white label marketplace and e-commerce website which sells home, clothing and electronic devices in Latin America. Earn-out consideration of up to US$6,000,000 would be payable based on Avenida's financial performance.

Predecessor Detail - Name changed from Hybrid Paytech World Inc., Feb. 13, 2015.

Directors - Allan Rosenhek, chr., Nev.; Marcel Vienneau, pres., CEO & interim chief sales officer, Qué.; Jacques Côté, CFO, Beaconsfield, Qué.; David A. Robinson, Toronto, Ont.; Alejandro Rodriguez, Mexico City, D.F., Mexico

Other Exec. Officers - Johnny Hawa, COO; David L. Beauchemin, chief tech. officer; Armando Calvo, chief revenue officer

Capital Stock

	Authorized (shs.)	Outstanding (shs.)[1]
Preferred	unlimited	nil
Common	unlimited	285,588,031

[1] At Sept. 30, 2022

Major Shareholder - Widely held at Aug. 8, 2022.

Price Range - MOS/TSX-VEN (S)

Year	Volume	High	Low	Close
2022	48,950,752	$0.05	$0.01	$0.01
2021	50,084,312	$0.10	$0.02	$0.03
2020	41,934,175	$0.06	$0.02	$0.05
2019	31,263,694	$0.09	$0.03	$0.04
2018	56,462,322	$0.29	$0.05	$0.08

Recent Close: $0.01

Capital Stock Changes - In August 2022, private placement of 20,000,000 units (1 common share & 1 warrant) at $0.025 per unit was completed, with warrants exercisable at $0.05 per share for five years.

Wholly Owned Subsidiaries

First Equity Strategy LLC, Del.
Mobi724 Smart Transactions Inc., Canada.
Mobi724 Smart Transactions México, S.A. de C.V., Mexico.
Mobi724 Solutions S.R.L., Argentina.

Financial Statistics

Periods ended:	12m Dec. 31/21[A]		12m Dec. 31/20[oA]
	$000s	%Chg	$000s
Operating revenue	**2,949**	**+163**	**1,120**
Research & devel. expense	1,206		1,617
General & admin expense	2,949		2,195
Stock-based compensation	190		143
Operating expense	**4,345**	**+10**	**3,955**
Operating income	**(1,396)**	**n.a.**	**(2,835)**
Deprec., depl. & amort.	25		270
Finance costs, net	1,374		445
Pre-tax income	**(4,961)**	**n.a.**	**(3,493)**
Income taxes	nil		(63)
Net income	**(4,961)**	**n.a.**	**(3,430)**
Cash & equivalent	880		385
Accounts receivable	405		296
Current assets	1,303		721
Fixed assets, net	25		35
Total assets	**1,382**	**+83**	**756**
Accts. pay. & accr. liabs	966		1,028
Current liabilities	9,366		2,606
Long-term debt, gross	8,406		5,336
Long-term debt, net	546		4,258
Equity portion of conv. debs	40		156
Shareholders' equity	(8,567)		(6,107)
Cash from oper. activs	**(3,653)**	**n.a.**	**(1,383)**
Cash from fin. activs	4,985		716
Cash from invest. activs	(8)		(27)
Net cash position	**880**	**+129**	**385**
Capital expenditures	(8)		(27)
	$		$
Earnings per share*	(0.02)		(0.02)
Cash flow per share*	(0.01)		(0.01)
	shs		shs
No. of shs. o/s*	265,588,031		218,678,031
Avg. no. of shs. o/s*	254,269,976		218,678,031
	%		%
Net profit margin	(168.23)		(306.25)
Return on equity	n.m.		n.m.
Return on assets	(464.08)		(200.64)

* Common
[o] Restated
[A] Reported in accordance with IFRS

Latest Results

Periods ended:	9m Sept. 30/22[A]		9m Sept. 30/21[A]
	$000s	%Chg	$000s
Operating revenue	367	-42	633
Net income	(4,261)	n.a.	(2,857)
	$		$
Earnings per share*	(0.02)		(0.01)

* Common
[A] Reported in accordance with IFRS

Historical Summary
(as originally stated)

Fiscal Year	Oper. Rev.	Net Inc. Bef. Disc.	EPS*
	$000s	$000s	$
2021[A]	2,949	(4,961)	(0.02)
2020[A]	1,120	(3,430)	(0.02)
2019[A]	1,064	(5,720)	(0.02)
2018[A]	2,571	(7,276)	(0.04)
2017[A]	2,874	(10,767)	(0.07)

* Common
[A] Reported in accordance with IFRS

M.103 Modern Plant Based Foods Inc.

Symbol - MEAT **Exchange** - CSE **CUSIP** - 607677
Head Office - 2500-700 Georgia St W, Vancouver, BC, V7Y 1B3 **Telephone** - (604) 395-0974
Website - modernfoods.ca
Email - investors@modernfoods.ca
Investor Relations - Yuying Liang (604) 657-9010
Auditors - Dale Matheson Carr-Hilton LaBonte LLP C.A., Vancouver, B.C.
Transfer Agents - Computershare Trust Company of Canada Inc., Toronto, Ont.

Profile - (B.C. 2017; orig. B.C., 1987) Develops and sells a range of plant-based food products and services including meat alternatives, homemade style soups, vegan cheeses, sauces and candies.

Brands include Modern Meat, which offers plant-based meat alternatives including frozen crab cakes, burger, mini burger, crumble, meatballs and gyoza; KitsKitchen, which offers plant-based, wheat-free soups and plant-based cheeses; and Snacks from the Sun, which offers plant-based popped crisps. Products are available at select restaurants and retailers across Canada.

Has a plant-based seafood division that focuses on research and development, production, and manufacturing of plant-based seafood alternatives. In addition, the company is seeking acquisitions of luxury brands in the vegan food space.

In March 2023, the company signed a letter of intent to acquire private British Columbia-based **1396974 B.C. Ltd** (dba Northern Pacific Kaviar), which develops vegan caviar using a blend of seaweed, flavourings and chia seeds, for issuance of 4,000,000 common shares.

In January 2023, the company closed the Hornby Street location of its Modern Health and Wellness Bar retail store in Vancouver, B.C.

In September 2022, the company acquired Vancouver, B.C.-based **Sausage-less Food Company Inc.**, which produces plant-based products including Sausage-less Roll, Sausage-less Links and Sausage-less Longanisa, for issuance of 8,571,429 common shares.

During fiscal 2022, the company halted production at its Vancouver, B.C., manufacturing facility and changed the facility into a rentable kitchen named Modern Commissary. In addition, the company closed its Modern Health and Wellness Bar retail store on West Broadway in Vancouver and terminated sales in the United States of its plant-based snacks under the brands Snacks from the Sun and Sunsations.

In June 2022, the company launched Modern Commissary, a facility which offers kitchen space and resources to prepare meals and ghost kitchen businesses. In addition, it accommodates variety of food products and has a storage required for frozen, cooler and dry goods. Also in June 2022, the company sold the rights and recipes for its Modern breakfast sausage for $1,000,000.

In March 2022, the company acquired private Vancouver, B.C.-based **Vegables Food Inc.**, which produces plant-based lunch kits, for issuance of 10,769,229 common shares.

Predecessor Detail - Name changed from Modern Meat Inc., Mar. 1, 2021.

Directors - Yuying Liang, CFO, Vancouver, B.C.; Mohsen Rahimi, head, Modern Wellness Bars div., B.C.; Robert W. C. Becher, Caledon, Ont.; Aryan Beytoei

Other Exec. Officers - Avtar Dhaliwal, CEO

Capital Stock

	Authorized (shs.)	Outstanding (shs.)[1]
Preferred	unlimited	nil
Common	unlimited	66,810,087

[1] At Feb. 28, 2023

Major Shareholder - Widely held at Oct. 29, 2021.

Price Range - MEAT/CSE

Year	Volume	High	Low	Close
2022	26,568,284	$1.05	$0.09	$0.09
2021	17,102,665	$4.49	$0.46	$0.50
2020	25,550,770	$5.12	$0.87	$4.00
2018	454,812	$0.35	$0.12	$0.15

Split: 2-for-1 split in June 2020
Recent Close: $0.13

Capital Stock Changes - In September 2022, 8,571,429 common shares were issued pursuant to the acquisition of Sausage-less Food Company Inc.

In September 2021, private placement of 924,370 units (1 common share & 1 warrant) at $1.19 per unit was completed. In March 2022, 10,769,229 common shares were issued pursuant to the acquisition of Vegables Food Inc. In July 2022, private placement of 2,040,816 units (1 common share & 1 warrant) at 49¢ per unit was completed. Also during fiscal 2022, common shares were issued as follows: 861,538 as finders' fees, 810,406 on exercise of warrants, 618,811 for debt settlement and 334,448 as bonus shares.

Wholly Owned Subsidiaries

Kitskitchen Health Foods Inc., Canada.
MWB Franchise Ltd., Canada.
Modern Foods, Inc., Del.
- 100% int. in **Modern Foods JDW, LLC**, Del.

Modern Meals and Supplement Inc., Canada.
Modern Seafood Inc.
1257189 B.C. Ltd., B.C.
Sausage-less Food Company Inc., Vancouver, B.C.
Star Minerals Group U.S. LLC, United States.
Vegables Food Inc., Vancouver, B.C.

Subsidiaries

99.14% int. in **Modern Meat Holdings Inc.**, Vancouver, B.C.

Financial Statistics

Periods ended:	12m Aug. 31/22[A]		12m Aug. 31/21[A]
	$000s	%Chg	$000s
Operating revenue	**1,650**	**-27**	**2,267**
Cost of sales	1,627		1,880
Salaries & benefits	314		517
Research & devel. expense	85		311
General & admin expense	3,879		3,549
Stock-based compensation	6,960		429
Operating expense	**12,865**	**+92**	**6,687**
Operating income	**(11,215)**	**n.a.**	**(4,420)**
Deprec., depl. & amort.	235		302
Finance costs, gross	47		46
Write-downs/write-offs	(1,065)		(1,381)
Pre-tax income	**(11,604)**	**n.a.**	**(6,212)**
Income taxes	(22)		(23)
Net income	**(11,582)**	**n.a.**	**(6,188)**
Net inc. for equity hldrs	**(11,586)**	**n.a.**	**(6,179)**
Net inc. for non-cont. int	**4**	**n.a.**	**(9)**
Cash & equivalent	217		647
Inventories	132		551
Accounts receivable	192		223
Current assets	675		1,547
Fixed assets, net	45		241
Right-of-use assets	110		347
Intangibles, net	405		1,348
Total assets	**1,236**	**-65**	**3,483**
Bank indebtedness	nil		150
Accts. pay. & accr. liabs	928		1,078
Current liabilities	1,048		1,398
Long-term lease liabilities	49		211
Shareholders' equity	109		1,827
Non-controlling interest	(7)		(11)
Cash from oper. activs	**(1,975)**	**n.a.**	**(4,068)**
Cash from fin. activs	1,557		2,662
Cash from invest. activs	(5)		(733)
Net cash position	**217**	**-66**	**647**
Capital expenditures	nil		(141)
Capital disposals	18		nil
	$		$
Earnings per share*	(0.28)		(0.21)
Cash flow per share*	(0.05)		(0.14)
	shs		shs
No. of shs. o/s*	49,681,922		33,322,304
Avg. no. of shs. o/s*	40,922,883		29,754,510
	%		%
Net profit margin	(701.94)		(272.96)
Return on equity	(1,196.90)		n.m.
Return on assets	(488.88)		n.a.

* Common
[A] Reported in accordance with IFRS

Latest Results

Periods ended:	6m Feb. 28/23[A]		6m Feb. 28/22[A]
	$000s	%Chg	$000s
Operating revenue	502	-57	1,157
Net income	(3,347)	n.a.	(3,264)
Net inc. for equity hldrs	(3,346)	n.a.	(3,261)
Net inc. for non-cont. int	(1)		(3)
	$		$
Earnings per share*	(0.06)		(0.09)

* Common
[A] Reported in accordance with IFRS

Historical Summary
(as originally stated)

Fiscal Year	Oper. Rev.	Net Inc. Bef. Disc.	EPS*
	$000s	$000s	$
2022[A]	1,650	(11,582)	(0.28)
2021[A]	2,267	(6,188)	(0.21)
2020[A1]	82	(5,162)	(0.20)
2019[A2]	nil	(122)	(0.01)
2018[A]	nil	(698)	(0.09)

* Common
[A] Reported in accordance with IFRS
[1] Results reflect the June 26, 2020 reverese takeover acquisition of Modern Meat Holdings Inc.
[2] Results for fiscal 2019 and prior fiscal years pertain to Navis Resources Corp.
Note: Adjusted throughout for 2-for-1 split in June 2020

M.104 Mogo Inc.

Symbol - MOGO **Exchange** - TSX **CUSIP** - 60800C
Head Office - 2100-401 Georgia St W, Vancouver, BC, V6B 5A1 **Telephone** - (604) 659-4380 **Fax** - (604) 733-4944
Website - investors.mogo.ca
Email - craiga@mogo.ca
Investor Relations - Craig Armitage (416) 347-8954

Auditors - KPMG LLP C.A., Vancouver, B.C.
Lawyers - Stikeman Elliott LLP, Vancouver, B.C.
Transfer Agents - Computershare Trust Company of Canada Inc., Vancouver, B.C.
Employees - 255 at Dec. 31, 2022
Profile - (B.C. 2019; orig. Can., 1972) Offers various financial applications and products, helping users with wealth building, digital payments and obtaining loans.

Software and applications include MogoTrade, which allows users to invest in and trade stocks on the NASDAQ, TSX, TSX Venture Exchange and NYSE, among others, without any commission or foreign transaction fees; Moka, which allows users to save and invest with no prior investment knowledge by rounding up everyday purchases and investing the spare change into a fully managed investment portfolio; and Carta, a platform that provides infrastructure to help fintech and payments businesses build and manage their payment systems, offering support for prepaid, debit and credit card issuer processing.

Also developed MogoApp which provides free monthly credit score monitoring; MogoProtect, a free identity fraud protection product; MogoCard, a digital spending account that works with the reloadable prepaid VISA Platinum debit card MogoCard; MogoMoney, an online lending platform which offers fixed-rate line of credit and instalment loans; and MogoMortgage, an online mortgage brokerage platform for mortgage application and tracking. The company plans to discontinue the MogoApp as part of its goal to simplify into one application and eliminate unprofitable or subscale business segments.

Also has an investment portfolio managed through Mogo Ventures, which includes 34% interest in **Coinsquare Ltd.**, which operates digital asset trading platforms; investments in leading and emerging Web 3.0 platforms including **Gemini Trust Co. LLC**, **NFT Trader** and **Tetra Trust Company**; and investments in gaming companies including **Enthusiast Gaming Holdings Inc.** and **Eleven Holdings Corp.** Mogo Ventures also manages the company's portfolio of legacy investments including Hootsuite, Blue Ant Media and Alida. Mogo Ventures focuses on monetizing these investments.

In December 2022, the company retired MogoCrypto, the company's platform for buying and selling bitcoin. In addition, the company sold its digital assets consisting of investments in Bitcoin and Ethereum for $600,000.

During the fourth quarter of 2022, sales operation of the Moka application in France was wound down.

In March 2022, the company formed Mogo Ventures to manage its existing investment portfolio which is valued at $124,000,000. The portfolio includes 39% interest in **Coinsquare Ltd.**; investments in leading and emerging Web 3.0 platforms including **Gemini Trust Co. LLC**, **NFT Trader** and **Tetra Trust Company**; investments in gaming companies including **Enthusiast Gaming Holdings Inc.** and **Eleven Holdings Corp.**; and investments in Bitcoin and Ethereum.

Recent Merger and Acquisition Activity

Status: completed **Revised:** July 10, 2023
UPDATE: The transaction was completed. PREVIOUS: WonderFi Technologies Inc. agreed to acquire private Coinsquare Ltd. and public CoinSmart Financial Inc., both Toronto, Ont.-based companies operating cryptocurrency trading platforms, for issuance of 269,727,080 and 119,181,733 common shares, respectively. The combined company would have transacted more than $17 billion since 2017 and have more than $600,000,000 in assets under custody, with a registered user base in excess of 1,650,000 Canadians. Upon completion, WonderFi, Coinsquare and CoinSmart shareholders would hold a 38%, 43% and 19% interest, respectively, in the combined company. Mogo Inc., which held a 34% interest in Coinsquare, would become the largest shareholder of the combined company with a 14% interest.

Predecessor Detail - Name changed from Difference Capital Financial Inc., June 20, 2019, pursuant to acquisition of Mogo Finance Technology Inc.

Directors - David (Dave) Feller, chr. & CEO, B.C.; Gregory Feller, pres. & CFO, New York, N.Y.; Kristin McAlister, Calif.; Christopher Payne, Ont.; Kees C. Van Winters, Toronto, Ont.; Michael A. Wekerle, Caledon, Ont.

Capital Stock

	Authorized (shs.)	Outstanding (shs.)[1]
Preferred	unlimited	nil
Common	unlimited	24,900,000

[1] At Aug. 21, 2023

Normal Course Issuer Bid - The company plans to make normal course purchases of up to 2,183,000 common shares representing 10% of the public float. The bid commenced on Mar. 22, 2023, and expires on Mar. 21, 2024.

Major Shareholder - Widely held at May 19, 2023.

Price Range - MOGO/TSX

Year	Volume	High	Low	Close
2022	18,789,380	$13.80	$1.74	$2.25
2021	32,728,374	$46.02	$11.79	$12.93
2020	11,172,967	$15.90	$2.37	$14.52
2019	1,936,337	$15.75	$8.40	$10.05
2018	222,773	$11.85	$6.00	$9.90

Consolidation: 1-for-3 cons. in Aug. 2023
Recent Close: $2.38
Capital Stock Changes - On Aug. 14, 2023, common shares were consolidated on a 1-for-3 basis.

During 2022, common shares were issued as follows: 47,000 on exercise of options and 40,000 on vesting of restricted share units; 1,803,000 common shares were cancelled.

Wholly Owned Subsidiaries

Carta Solutions Holding Corporation, Oakville, Ont.
- 100% int. in **Carta Americas Inc.**, United States.
- 100% int. in **Carta Financial Services Ltd.**, United Kingdom.
- 100% int. in **Carta Solutions Processing Services Corp.**, Morocco.
- 100% int. in **Carta Solutions Processing Services (Cyprus) Ltd.**
- 100% int. in **Carta Solutions Singapore Pte. Ltd.**, Singapore.
- 100% int. in **Carta Worldwide Inc.**

Mogo Asset Management Inc., Montréal, Qué.
Mogo Finance Technology Inc., Vancouver, B.C.
- 100% int. in **Hornby Leasing Inc.**
- 100% int. in **Hornby Loan Brokers (Ottawa) Inc.**
- 100% int. in **Mogo Blockchain Technology Inc.**, Canada.
- 100% int. in **Mogo Financial (Alberta) Inc.**, Alta.
- 100% int. in **Mogo Financial (B.C.) Inc.**, B.C.
- 100% int. in **Mogo Financial Inc.**, Man.
- 100% int. in **Mogo Financial (Ontario) Inc.**, Ont.
- 100% int. in **Mogo Mortgage Technology Inc.**, B.C.
- 100% int. in **Mogo Technology Inc.**, Del.
- 100% int. in **Mogo Wallet Inc.**, B.C.
- 100% int. in **MogoTrade Inc.**, Montréal, Qué.
- 100% int. in **Thurlow Capital (Alberta) Inc.**
- 100% int. in **Thurlow Capital (B.C.) Inc.**
- 100% int. in **Thurlow Capital (Manitoba) Inc.**
- 100% int. in **Thurlow Capital (Ontario) Inc.**
- 100% int. in **Thurlow Capital (Ottawa) Inc.**
- 100% int. in **Thurlow Management Inc.**, B.C.

Moka Financial Technologies Europe, France.
Moka Financial Technologies Inc., Montréal, Qué.
NumberJacks Services Inc.
Tactex Advisors Inc., United States.

Investments

14% int. in **WonderFi Technologies Inc.**, Vancouver, B.C. (see separate coverage)

Financial Statistics

Periods ended:	12m Dec. 31/22[A]		12m Dec. 31/21[◻A]
	$000s	%Chg	$000s
Total revenue	**68,949**	**+20**	**57,519**
Salaries & benefits	28,628		26,509
Stock-based compensation	8,712		10,838
Other operating expense	29,839		30,643
Operating expense	**67,179**	**-2**	**68,835**
Operating income	**1,770**	**n.a.**	**(11,316)**
Deprec. & amort.	12,636		12,736
Provision for loan losses	14,730		7,540
Finance costs, gross	8,000		9,202
Write-downs/write-offs	(90,021)[1]		nil
Pre-tax income	**(166,014)**	**n.a.**	**(33,441)**
Income taxes	(336)		(232)
Net income	**(165,678)**	**n.a.**	**(33,209)**
Cash & equivalent	29,268		67,762
Accounts receivable	2,347		2,112
Investments	37,509		121,909
Fixed assets, net	1,101		1,186
Right-of-use assets	2,622		3,430
Intangibles, net	80,184		122,416
Total assets	**221,494**	**-44**	**393,867**
Accts. pay. & accr. liabs	20,982		20,783
Debt	84,446		84,777
Lease liabilities	3,280		3,948
Shareholders' equity	110,886		269,777
Cash from oper. activs	**(27,009)**	**n.a.**	**(31,090)**
Cash from fin. activs	(3,079)		125,864
Cash from invest. activs	(9,149)		(39,594)
Net cash position	**29,268**	**-57**	**67,762**
Capital expenditures	(455)		(464)
	$		$
Earnings per share*	(6.51)		(1.59)
Cash flow per share*	(1.06)		(1.41)
	shs		shs
No. of shs. o/s*	24,891,241		25,362,076
Avg. no. of shs. o/s*	25,442,000		21,001,667
	%		%
Net profit margin	(240.29)		(57.74)
Return on equity	(87.05)		(24.15)
Return on assets	(51.25)		(9.66)
Foreign sales percent	10		n.a.
No. of employees (FTEs)	255		344

* Common
◻ Restated
[A] Reported in accordance with IFRS
[1] Consists of $58,263,000 impairment of investment in Coinsquare Ltd. and $31,758,000 impairment of goodwill.

Latest Results

Periods ended:	3m Mar. 31/23[A]		3m Mar. 31/22[A]
	$000s	%Chg	$000s
Total revenue	15,877	-8	17,255
Net income	(6,884)	n.a.	(18,870)
	$		$
Earnings per share*	(0.27)		(0.75)

* Common
[A] Reported in accordance with IFRS

Historical Summary
(as originally stated)

Fiscal Year	Total Rev.	Net Inc. Bef. Disc.	EPS*
	$000s	$000s	$
2022[A]	68,949	(165,678)	(6.51)
2021[A]	57,519	(33,209)	(1.59)
2020[A]	44,245	(13,445)	(1.41)
2019[A1]	59,805	(10,825)	(1.26)
2018[A2]	2,173	(3,216)	(1.65)

* Common
[A] Reported in accordance with IFRS
[1] Results reflect the June 21, 2019, reverse takeover acquisition of Mogo Finance Technology Inc.
[2] Results for 2018 and prior years pertain to Difference Capital Financial Inc.

Note: Adjusted throughout for 1-for-3 cons. in Aug. 2023

M.105 Mojave Brands Inc.

Symbol - MOJO **Exchange** - CSE **CUSIP** - 608384
Head Office - 2050-1055 Georgia St W, PO Box 11121, Royal Centre, Vancouver, BC, V6E 3P3 **Telephone** - (604) 684-2181
Website - www.mojavejane.com
Email - info@mojavejane.com
Investor Relations - Peeyush K. Varshney (604) 684-2181
Auditors - Dale Matheson Carr-Hilton LaBonte LLP C.A., Vancouver, B.C.
Transfer Agents - Computershare Trust Company of Canada Inc.
Profile - (B.C. 2010) Seeking new business opportunities.
Predecessor Detail - Name changed from Mojave Jane Brands Inc., Mar. 30, 2021; basis 1 new for 25 old shs.
Directors - Capt. Mervyn J. Pinto, pres., CEO & CFO, Surrey, B.C.; Campbell (Cam) Birge, corp. sec., Victoria, B.C.; Peeyush K. Varshney, Vancouver, B.C.

Capital Stock

	Authorized (shs.)	Outstanding (shs.)[1]
Common	unlimited	10,242,428

[1] At Jan. 28, 2023

Major Shareholder - Widely held at Nov. 15, 2022.

Price Range - MOJO/CSE

Year	Volume	High	Low	Close
2022	731,069	$0.16	$0.04	$0.05
2021	5,843,502	$1.63	$0.12	$0.16
2020	1,519,602	$0.75	$0.13	$0.13
2019	2,457,854	$11.38	$0.38	$0.50
2018	3,617,712	$37.00	$4.25	$6.00

Consolidation: 1-for-25 cons. in Apr. 2021
Recent Close: $0.06
Capital Stock Changes - There were no changes to capital stock during fiscal 2022.

Financial Statistics

Periods ended:	12m Aug. 31/22[A]		12m Aug. 31/21[A]
	$000s	%Chg	$000s
General & admin expense	181		349
Operating expense	**181**	**-48**	**349**
Operating income	**(181)**	**n.a.**	**(349)**
Finance income	6		19
Write-downs/write-offs	191		211
Pre-tax income	**34**	**n.a.**	**(118)**
Net inc. bef. disc. opers	**34**	**n.a.**	**(118)**
Income from disc. opers	33		(70)
Net income	**67**	**n.a.**	**(189)**
Cash & equivalent	881		915
Current assets	884		945
Total assets	**884**	**-6**	**945**
Bank indebtedness	nil		9
Accts. pay. & accr. liabs	140		150
Current liabilities	140		268
Long-term debt, gross	40		40
Long-term debt, net	40		40
Shareholders' equity	704		637
Cash from oper. activs	**(25)**	**n.a.**	**(337)**
Cash from fin. activs	(9)		699
Cash from invest. activs	nil		496
Net cash position	**881**	**-4**	**915**
	$		$
Earns. per sh. bef disc opers*	0.00		(0.02)
Earnings per share*	0.01		(0.03)
Cash flow per share*	(0.00)		(0.06)
	shs		shs
No. of shs. o/s*	10,242,428		10,242,428
Avg. no. of shs. o/s*	10,242,428		5,287,432
	%		%
Net profit margin	n.a.		n.a.
Return on equity	5.07		(29.35)
Return on assets	3.72		(14.69)

* Common
[A] Reported in accordance with IFRS

Latest Results

Periods ended:	3m Nov. 30/22[A]		3m Nov. 30/21[A]
	$000s	%Chg	$000s
Net income	(16)	n.a.	(38)
	$		$
Earnings per share*	(0.00)		(0.00)

* Common
[A] Reported in accordance with IFRS

Historical Summary
(as originally stated)

Fiscal Year	Oper. Rev.	Net Inc. Bef. Disc.	EPS*
	$000s	$000s	$
2022[A]	nil	34	0.00
2021[A]	nil	(118)	(0.02)
2020[A]	nil	(3,056)	(0.75)
2019[A]	205	(22,465)	(6.00)
2018[A]	52	(9,164)	(4.50)

* Common
[A] Reported in accordance with IFRS
Note: Adjusted throughout for 1-for-25 cons. in Apr. 2021

M.106 Molecule Holdings Inc.

Symbol - MLCL **Exchange** - CSE **CUSIP** - 60855E
Head Office - 591 Reynolds Rd, Lansdowne, ON, K0E 1L0 **Toll-free** - (888) 665-2853
Website - molecule.ca
Email - andre@molecule.ca
Investor Relations - André D. Audet (888) 665-2853 ext. 101
Auditors - McGovern Hurley LLP C.A., Toronto, Ont.
Transfer Agents - Computershare Trust Company of Canada Inc., Montréal, Qué.
Profile - (Can. 2004; orig. Alta., 1996) Manufactures and packages cannabis-infused beverages under its own house brands as well as for craft beverage producers

Holds a cannabis processing licence under the Cannabis Act and operates from a 200,000-sq.-ft. facility in Lansdowne, Ont. Products are sold under PHRESH, KLON, Canajo and Embody brands.

In September 2022, the company entered into a letter of intent to acquire **Canna-Day Development Inc.**, which develops cannabis-based beverages, for issuance of 15,000,000 common shares at a deemed price of 5¢ per share.

Predecessor Detail - Name changed from Everton Resources Inc., Sept. 15, 2020, pursuant to reverse takeover acquisition of private Lansdowne, Ont.-based Molecule Inc. on a post-consolidation share-for-share basis; basis 1 new for 10 old shs.

Directors - André D. Audet, chr., Ottawa, Ont.; David Reingold, pres. & CEO, Toronto, Ont.; Dr. Philip (Phil) Waddington, COO, Chelsea, Qué.; Amy Proulx, Ont.; Lindsay Weatherdon, Burlington, Ont.

Other Exec. Officers - Jeffrey (Jeff) Stoss, CFO

Capital Stock

	Authorized (shs.)	Outstanding (shs.)[1]
Preferred	9,313,447	9,313,447
Common	unlimited	97,781,903

[1] At Sept. 28, 2022

Preferred - Created immediately prior to completion of the Sept. 16, 2020, reverse takeover acquisition of Molecule Inc., issued on a one-for-one post-consolidated common share basis. Provides shareholders the right to receive, on a pro rata basis, up to a maximum of $500,000, in the event that any of the company's remaining mining royalties are triggered and generate revenue within five years of issuance. The preferred shares do not otherwise have any rights or recourses. Valued at nil on balance sheet.
Common - One vote per share.
Major Shareholder - Widely held at Mar. 24, 2022.

Price Range - MLCL/CSE

Year	Volume	High	Low	Close
2022	30,348,828	$0.12	$0.02	$0.03
2021	77,607,438	$0.17	$0.05	$0.06
2020	35,645,771	$0.20	$0.07	$0.10
2019	776,179	$0.35	$0.20	$0.25
2018	5,708,445	$0.60	$0.20	$0.30

Consolidation: 1-for-10 cons. in Sept. 2020
Recent Close: $0.01
Capital Stock Changes - In September 2022, private placement of up to 75,000,000 units (1 common share & ½ warrant) at 5¢ per unit was announced, with warrants exercisable at 10¢ per share for two years.

Wholly Owned Subsidiaries

Dominican Metals Inc., Tortola, British Virgin Islands.
- 100% int. in **Everton Minera Dominicana S.R.L.**, Santo Domingo, Dominican Republic. Inactive.

Everton Dominicana (2014) Inc., Ont. Inactive.
Hays Lake Gold Inc., Ottawa, Ont. Inactive.
Linear Gold Caribe, S.A., Panama. Inactive.
Molecule Inc., Lansdowne, Ont.
- 100% int. in **Burrard Bay Capital Corp.**, Ont.

Pan Caribbean Metals Inc., Tortola, British Virgin Islands.

Financial Statistics

Periods ended:	12m Oct. 31/21[A]		12m Oct. 31/20[A1]
	$000s	%Chg	$000s
Operating revenue	**455**	**n.a.**	**nil**
Cost of goods sold	881		nil
Salaries & benefits	403		320
General & admin expense	1,299		1,167
Stock-based compensation	990		393
Operating expense	**3,573**	**+90**	**1,880**
Operating income	**(3,118)**	**n.a.**	**(1,880)**
Deprec., depl. & amort	203		48
Finance income	nil		8
Finance costs, gross	661		44
Write-downs/write-offs	(74)		nil
Pre-tax income	**(4,227)**	**n.a.**	**(3,327)**
Net income	**(4,227)**	**n.a.**	**(3,327)**
Cash & equivalent	1,203		1,142
Inventories	640		145
Accounts receivable	391		nil
Current assets	2,707		1,527
Fixed assets, net	3,248		3,920
Total assets	**5,956**	**+9**	**5,447**
Accts. pay. & accr. liabs	817		1,094
Current liabilities	4,355		1,137
Long-term debt, gross	4,305		698
Long-term debt, net	817		698
Long-term lease liabilities	85		135
Shareholders' equity	638		3,437
Cash from oper. activs	**(2,869)**	**n.a.**	**(926)**
Cash from fin. activs	3,003		806
Cash from invest. activs	167		(1,265)
Net cash position	**1,203**	**+33**	**903**
Capital expenditures	(77)		(1,898)
Capital disposals	77		nil
	$		$
Earnings per share*	(0.05)		(0.04)
Cash flow per share*	(0.03)		(0.01)
	shs		shs
No. of shs. o/s*	95,379,326		86,235,740
Avg. no. of shs. o/s*	91,855,662		75,710,587
	%		%
Net profit margin	(929.01)		n.a.
Return on equity	n.m.		(168.80)
Return on assets	n.a.		(102.19)

* Common
[A] Reported in accordance with IFRS
[1] Results reflect the Sept. 16, 2020, reverse takeover acquisition of Molecule Inc.

Latest Results

Periods ended:	9m July 31/22[A]		9m July 31/21[A]
	$000s	%Chg	$000s
Operating revenue	1,462	+353	323
Net income	(3,091)	n.a.	(3,450)
	$		$
Earnings per share*	(0.03)		(0.04)

* Common
[A] Reported in accordance with IFRS

Historical Summary
(as originally stated)

Fiscal Year	Oper. Rev.	Net Inc. Bef. Disc.	EPS*
	$000s	$000s	$
2021[A]	455	(4,227)	(0.05)
2020[A]	nil	(3,327)	(0.04)
2019[A1]	nil	(2,920)	(0.31)
2018[A]	nil	(346)	(0.04)
2017[A]	nil	(10,709)	(1.20)

* Common
[A] Reported in accordance with IFRS
[1] Results for fiscal 2019 and prior fiscal years pertain to Everton Resources Inc.
Note: Adjusted throughout for 1-for-10 cons. in Sept. 2020

M.107 Molson Coors Canada Inc.

Symbol - TPX.B **Exchange** - TSX **CUSIP** - 608711
Head Office - 33 Carlingview Dr, Toronto, ON, M9W 5E4 **Telephone** - (416) 679-1786 **Toll-free** - (800) 665-7661 **Fax** - (416) 679-0630
Website - www.molsoncoors.com
Email - david.knaff@molsoncoors.com
Investor Relations - David Knaff (414) 759-3746
Auditors - PricewaterhouseCoopers
Transfer Agents - Computershare Trust Company, Inc.
Profile - (Can. 1997) Wholly owned subsidiary of **Molson Coors Beverage Company**, which conducts brewing operations in the U.S. through wholly owned **MillerCoors LLC**; in Canada through indirectly wholly owned **Molson Coors Canada**; in Bulgaria, Croatia, Czech Republic, Hungary, Montenegro, the Republic of Ireland, Romania, Serbia, the United Kingdom and other European countries through wholly owned **Molson Coors Europe**; and in various other countries through **Molson Coors International**.

Has two reporting segments which include the Americas, operating in the U.S., Canada and various countries in Caribbean, Latin and South America; and EMEA&APAC, operating in Bulgaria, Croatia, the Czech Republic, Hungary, Montenegro, the Republic of Ireland, Romania, Serbia, the U.K., various other European countries, and certain countries within the Middle East, Africa and Asia Pacific.

Brands include Aspall Cider, Blue Moon, Coors Original, Hop Valley, Leinenkugel's, Miller Genuine Draft, Molson Ultra, Sharp's, Staropramen, Vizzy Hard Seltzer, Bergenbier, Borsodi, Carling, Coors Banquet, Coors Light, Jelen, Kamenitza, Miller Lite, Molson Canadian, Molson Dry, Molson Export, Niksicko, Ozujsko, Branik, Icehouse, Keystone, Miller High Life, Milwaukee's Best and Steel Reserve.

The company does not prepare separate financial statements due to an exemption from the continuous disclosure requirements under the Securities Act (Ontario). Similar exemption orders were obtained from each of the other Canadian securities commissions. One of the conditions of these exemption orders is that the company is required to file with Canadian securities commissions all documents filed by parent company Molson Coors Beverage Company with the U.S. Securities Exchange Commission.

Capital Stock

	Authorized (shs.)	Outstanding (shs.)[1]
Cl. A Exchangeable	unlimited	2,717,367
Cl. B Exchangeable	unlimited	10,983,834
Common	n.a.	n.a

[1] At Feb. 14, 2023

Class A Exchangeable - Provide substantially the same economic and voting rights as class A common share of Molson Coors Beverage, with such voting rights exercised through special class A voting stock of Molson Coors Beverage of which there is one share outstanding. Each exchangeable share may, at the option of the holder, be exchanged for one share of Molson Coors Beverage class A common stock; retractable at any time at the holders' option for a price to be satisfied by delivery of one class A common share of Molson Coors Beverage for each share, together with a cash amount equal to the full amount of all unpaid dividends thereon. All class A exchangeable shares will be redeemed in February 2045.

Class B Exchangeable - Provide substantially the same economic and voting rights as class B common share of Molson Coors Beverage, with such voting rights exercised through special class B voting stock of Molson Coors Beverage of which there is one share outstanding. Each exchangeable share may, at the option of the holder, be exchanged for one share of Molson Coors Beverage class B common stock; retractable at any time at the holders' option for a price to be satisfied by delivery of one class B common share of Molson Coors Beverage for each share, together with a cash amount equal to the full amount of all unpaid dividends thereon. All class B exchangeable shares will be redeemed in February 2045.

Common - One vote per share. All held by Molson Coors Beverage.

Major Shareholder - Molson Coors Beverage Company held 100% interest at Feb. 14, 2023.

Price Range - TPX.B/TSX

Year	Volume	High	Low	Close
2022............	253,413	$78.05	$59.32	$70.00
2021............	562,960	$73.97	$53.00	$58.80
2020............	1,515,751	$82.50	$43.38	$57.65
2019............	886,861	$90.09	$67.11	$71.97
2018............	1,001,183	$118.99	$74.25	$78.77

Recent Close: $87.49

Capital Stock Changes - During 2022, 100,000 class B exchangeable shares were exchanged for 100,000 class B common shares of Molson Coors Beverage Company.

Dividends

TPX.A cl A exch N.S.R. [1]

US$0.53............... Sept. 15/23 US$0.55........... June 15/23
$0.552967........... Mar. 15/23 $0.50............... Dec. 15/22
Paid in 2023: $0.552967 + US$1.08 2022: $1.95 2021: $0.84

TPX.B cl B exch N.S.R. [2]

US$0.53............... Sept. 15/23 US$0.55........... June 15/23
$0.552967........... Mar. 17/23 $0.50............... Dec. 15/22
Paid in 2023: $0.552967 + US$1.08 2022: $1.95 2021: $0.84

[1] Quarterly divd normally payable in June/20 has been omitted. Pays Cdn$ equiv of rate paid on Molson Coors Brewing Company Cl A sh.

[2] Quarterly divd normally payable in June/20 has been omitted. Pays Cdn$ equiv of rate paid on Molson Coors Brewing Company Cl B sh.

Wholly Owned Subsidiaries

Molson ULC, Montréal, Qué.
- 100% int. in **Molson Canada (2005)**, Ont.
- 100% int. in **Molson Coors Canada**, Toronto, Ont.
- 100% int. in **3230600 Nova Scotia Company**, N.S.

Note: The preceding list includes only the major related companies in which interests are held.

M.108 Monaghan Capital Fund Ltd.

Symbol - EIRE.P **Exchange** - TSX-VEN **CUSIP** - 609002
Head Office - 2600-1066 Hastings St W, Vancouver, BC, V6E 3X1 **Telephone** - (416) 602-4415
Email - drew@drewgreen.ca
Investor Relations - Drew Green (416) 602-4415
Auditors - Baker Tilly HMA LLP C.A., Winnipeg, Man.
Transfer Agents - TSX Trust Company, Toronto, Ont.
Profile - (B.C. 2021) Capital Pool Company.

Recent Merger and Acquisition Activity

Status: pending **Announced:** Mar. 13, 2023
Gravitas III Capital Corp. entered into a letter of intent for the Qualifying Transaction reverse takeover acquisition of Matador Gold Technologies Inc., which operates a mobile application that allows users to buy and sell gold from their smartphone. The transaction was expected to be completed by way of a three-cornered amalgamation of Matador and a wholly -owned subsidiary of Gravitas. Each Matador share would be exchange for one post-consolidated common shares of Gravitas (following a 1-for-2.46 share consolidation).

Predecessor Detail - Name changed from Gravitas III Capital Corp., July 12, 2023.

Directors - Drew Green, chr., CEO & CFO, Vancouver, B.C.; Ted Hastings, Waterloo, Ont.; Maruf Raza, Toronto, Ont.

Other Exec. Officers - Mahdi Shams, corp. sec.

Capital Stock

	Authorized (shs.)	Outstanding (shs.)[1]
Common	unlimited	12,288,000

[1] At July 12, 2023

Major Shareholder - Widely held at Aug. 8, 2022.

Price Range - EIRE.P/TSX-VEN

Year	Volume	High	Low	Close
2022............	96,000	$0.22	$0.11	$0.11

Recent Close: $0.06

Capital Stock Changes - On Aug. 8, 2022, an initial public offering of 2,288,000 common shares was completed at 20¢ per share.

M.109 Monarch West Ventures Inc.

Symbol - MONA.P **Exchange** - TSX-VEN **CUSIP** - 609187
Head Office - 1208 Rosewood Cres, Vancouver, BC, V7P 1H4 **Telephone** - (604) 889-4790
Email - kendra@vancouvercorporate.ca
Investor Relations - Kendra Low (604) 889-4790
Auditors - MNP LLP C.A., Vancouver, B.C.
Transfer Agents - National Securities Administrators Ltd., Vancouver, B.C.
Profile - (B.C. 2021) Capital Pool Company.
Directors - Mark Orsmond, CEO, North Vancouver, B.C.; Brian Levinkind, Richmond, B.C.; Catherine (Zhilan) Luo, B.C.
Other Exec. Officers - Kyle Haddow, CFO; Kendra Low, corp. sec.

Capital Stock

	Authorized (shs.)	Outstanding (shs.)[1]
Common	unlimited	26,000,000

[1] At May 27, 2022

Major Shareholder - Widely held at Nov. 23, 2021.

Price Range - MONA.P/TSX-VEN

Year	Volume	High	Low	Close
2022............	538,500	$0.13	$0.06	$0.06
2021............	180,510	$0.29	$0.13	$0.13

Recent Close: $0.05

M.110 Mongolia Growth Group Ltd.

Symbol - YAK **Exchange** - TSX-VEN **CUSIP** - 60936L
Head Office - 1 First Canadian Place, 5600-100 King St W, Toronto, ON, M5X 1C9 **Telephone** - (289) 848-2035 **Toll-free** - (877) 644-1186 **Fax** - (866) 468-9119
Website - www.mongoliagrowthgroup.com
Email - gwalkden@mongoliagrowthgroup.com
Investor Relations - Genevieve Walkden (289) 848-2035
Auditors - Davidson & Company LLP C.A., Vancouver, B.C.
Lawyers - Farris LLP, Vancouver, B.C.; Borden Ladner Gervais LLP, Calgary, Alta.
Transfer Agents - Computershare Trust Company of Canada Inc., Toronto, Ont.
Profile - (Alta. 2007) Owns commercial and residential investment property assets in Ulaanbaatar, Mongolia. Also offers a data analytics service that tracks various event-driven strategies.

Properties are managed by wholly owned **Big Sky Capital LLC** and its subsidiaries and include those held for rental revenue, capital appreciation, and/or redevelopment.

The property portfolio at Mar. 31, 2023:

Type	Props.
Office...	2
Retail...	1
Land & redevelopment...............................	2
	5

Also provides KEDM, a data analytics service which helps investors to monitor and track corporate events, catalysts and situations to generate returns.

During 2022, the company sold five investment properties for $919,621.

During the first quarter of 2022, the company sold two investment properties for $376,215.

Predecessor Detail - Name changed from Summus Capital Corp., Feb. 4, 2011; basis 1 new for 2 old shs.

Directors - Harris Kupperman, exec. chr., pres. & CEO, United States; Nick Cousyn, United States; Jim Dwyer, Ulaanbaatar, Mongolia; Bradley D. (Brad) Farquhar, Regina, Sask.; Robert J. (Rob) Scott, Vancouver, B.C.

Other Exec. Officers - Genevieve Walkden, CFO & corp. sec.

Capital Stock

	Authorized (shs.)	Outstanding (shs.)[1]
Preferred	unlimited	nil
Common	unlimited	27,307,799

[1] At May 23, 2023

Normal Course Issuer Bid - The company plans to make normal course purchases of up to 1,900,000 common shares representing 6.9% of the total outstanding. The bid commenced on Mar. 27, 2023, and expires on Mar. 26, 2024.

Major Shareholder - Harris Kupperman held 24.5% interest at July 29, 2022.

Price Range - YAK/TSX-VEN

Year	Volume	High	Low	Close
2022............	4,365,303	$2.07	$1.28	$1.45
2021............	10,265,219	$1.81	$0.30	$1.46
2020............	4,918,831	$0.39	$0.14	$0.30
2019............	2,802,424	$0.40	$0.18	$0.21
2018............	3,753,141	$0.42	$0.20	$0.29

Recent Close: $1.24

Capital Stock Changes - During 2022, 68,000 common shares were repurchased under a Normal Course Issuer Bid.

Wholly Owned Subsidiaries

Lemontree PR LLC, Puerto Rico.
MGG US Inc., Del.
Mongolia (Barbados) Corp., St. Michael, Barbados.
- 100% int. in **Big Sky Capital LLC**, Ulaanbaatar, Mongolia.
  - 100% int. in **Biggie Industries LLC**, Ulaanbaatar, Mongolia.
  - 100% int. in **Carrollton LLC**, Ulaanbaatar, Mongolia.
  - 100% int. in **Crescent City LLC**, Ulaanbaatar, Mongolia.
  - 100% int. in **Oceanus LLC**, Ulaanbaatar, Mongolia. Inactive.
  - 100% int. in **Zulu LLC**, Ulaanbaatar, Mongolia.
- 100% int. in **MGG Properties LLC**, Ulaanbaatar, Mongolia.

Financial Statistics

Periods ended:	12m Dec. 31/22[A]		12m Dec. 31/21[oA]
	$000s	%Chg	$000s
Total revenue..............................	**3,927**	**+121**	**1,777**
Salaries & benefits..........................	1,252		888
General & admin. expense..............	1,446		1,642
Operating expense........................	**2,698**	**+7**	**2,529**
Operating income........................	**1,229**	**n.a.**	**(752)**
Deprec. & amort..............................	104		72
Finance income................................	7		nil
Write-downs/write-offs....................	128		54
Pre-tax income..............................	**10,628**	**-34**	**16,082**
Income taxes....................................	2,689		533
Net income.....................................	**7,938**	**-49**	**15,549**
Cash & equivalent............................	51,289		40,199
Accounts receivable.........................	15		30
Current assets..................................	51,617		40,809
Fixed assets......................................	2,804		2,220
Income-producing props..................	10,087		11,886
Property interests, net.....................	12,940		14,218
Total assets....................................	**64,558**	**+17**	**55,027**
Accts. pay. & accr. liabs..................	659		913
Current liabilities..............................	15,462		13,839
Long-term debt, gross.....................	60		60
Shareholders' equity........................	46,124		40,177
Cash from oper. activs...................	**(1,127)**	**n.a.**	**8,981**
Cash from fin. activs........................	(457)		(2,141)
Cash from invest. activs..................	(1,321)		(5,768)
Net cash position...........................	**2,051**	**-14**	**2,396**
Capital expenditures, net................	(712)		(942)
Change in property, net...................	920		2,125
	$		$
Earnings per share*.........................	0.29		0.53
Cash flow per share*.......................	(0.04)		0.31
	shs		shs
No. of shs. o/s*................................	27,710,499		27,778,499
Avg. no. of shs. o/s*.........................	27,761,956		29,309,116
	%		%
Net profit margin..............................	202.14		875.01
Return on equity...............................	18.40		46.40
Return on assets..............................	13.28		37.47
Foreign sales percent......................	100		100

* Common
[o] Restated
[A] Reported in accordance with IFRS

Latest Results

Periods ended:	3m Mar. 31/23[A]		3m Mar. 31/22[A]
	$000s	%Chg	$000s
Total revenue..................................	1,132	+35	840
Net income.......................................	(1,261)	n.a.	6,281
	$		$
Earnings per share*.........................	(0.05)		0.23

* Common
[A] Reported in accordance with IFRS

Historical Summary
(as originally stated)

Fiscal Year	Total Rev.	Net Inc. Bef. Disc.	EPS*
	$000s	$000s	$
2022[A]...................	3,927	7,938	0.29
2021[A]...................	1,777	15,549	0.53
2020[A]...................	931	3,728	0.12
2019[A]...................	1,141	(3,250)	(0.10)
2018[A]...................	1,472	1,557	0.05

* Common
[A] Reported in accordance with IFRS

M.111 Montfort Capital Corp.

Symbol - MONT **Exchange** - TSX-VEN **CUSIP** - 61288M
Head Office - Bay Wellington Tower, 2920-181 Bay St, Toronto, ON, M5J 2T3 **Telephone** - (604) 644-1926 **Toll-free** - (778) 782-7758
Website - montfortcapital.com
Email - ir@montfortcapital.com
Investor Relations - Andrew Abouchar (604) 398-8839
Auditors - PricewaterhouseCoopers LLP C.A., Vancouver, B.C.
Lawyers - MLT Aikins LLP, Vancouver, B.C.
Transfer Agents - Computershare Trust Company of Canada Inc., Vancouver, B.C.
Profile - (B.C. 2007) Provides revenue-based financing, loans, residential mortgages and policy-backed lending solutions to Software-as-a-Service (SaaS) and hardware-enabled businesses, small to mid-sized Canadian enterprises, and high net worth individuals and entrepreneurs across Canada and the U.S.

Operations are organized into four divisions: Technology Lending; Asset-backed Lending; Residential Mortgage Lending; and Insurance Lending.

Technology Lending - This division provides two types of financing: Interest-Only Loan, which is usually for durations of two to three years; and Amortized Loan, which is for three to six years, both in exchange for monthly payments in the form of a royalty based on the investee's gross revenue. Provides capital to SaaS businesses with recurring revenue between $2,000,000 to $20,000,000.

Asset-backed Lending - This division includes Pivot Financial, an asset manager that deploys funds on behalf of institutions, retail investors, high net worth individuals, its management team and shareholders. It provides loans of $500,000 to $10,000,000 with terms of six to 18 months to small to mid-sized Canadian enterprises with revenue of $1,000,000 to $100,000,000. Structures include revolving accounts receivable factoring, purchase order financing, revolving ABL governed by working capital borrowing bases, senior term loans (interest only or amortizing) and subordinate term loans (interest only or amortizing).

Residential Mortgage Lending - This division includes Brightpath, which uses investor loans to administer first and second mortgages secured by residential properties. Brightpath is a registered Mortgage Brokerage and Mortgage Administrator. At Aug. 23, 2023, this segment included a portfolio of more than 600 mortgages secured by residential property primarily in Ontario, and typically have a maturity of one year.

Insurance Lending - This division provides insurance policy-backed lending solutions to high net worth individuals and entrepreneurs across Canada. It also offers wholesale financing and advisory services for capital and estate planning, tax, insurance and investment solutions.

In June 2023, the company entered into an agreement with **ArenaInvestors, LP**, a US based institutional investment manager, to form a joint venture with initial capacity to provide up to $100,000,000 of funding. The purpose of the joint venture is to provide growth capital to entrepreneurs in the technology sector.

On Apr. 1, 2023, wholly owned **10260835 Canada Corp., 14637208 Canada Inc.** (formerly **Albright Holdings Inc.**), **9975756 Canada Inc.**, **14637542 Canada Inc.** (formerly **2754681Ontario Inc.**) were amalgamated into wholly owned **Brightpath Capital Corporation**.

Recent Merger and Acquisition Activity

Status: completed **Revised:** Oct. 3, 2022

UPDATE: The transaction was completed. PREVIOUS: TIMIA Capital Corporation greed to acquire 78% interest in Langhaus Financial Partners Inc., a Canadian-based provider of insurance policy-backed lending solutions to high net worth individuals and entrepreneurs across Canada, for $9,330,000 consisting of $7,020,000 in cash plus contingent consideration of up to $2,340,000 upon achievement of certain milestones. The transaction was expected to close on or before June 30, 2022.

Status: completed **Revised:** Aug. 16, 2022

UPDATE: The transaction was completed. PREVIOUS: Timia Capital Corp. entered into a letter of intent to acquire private Waterloo, Ont.-based Brightpath Capital Corp. and Brightpath Residential Mortgage LP I (collectively Brightpath), which provide residential mortgages focused on Ontario and British Columbia, for $30,500,000, consisting of the issuance of 31,250,000 common shares at a deemed value of 40¢ per share and 18,000,000 series A preferred shares at a deemed value of $1.00 per share.

Predecessor Detail - Name changed from Timia Capital Corp., June 15, 2022.

Directors - Howard J. Atkinson, chr., Toronto, Ont.; Andrew Abouchar, interim CEO, Waterloo, Ont.; Blake Albright, chief capital officer, Kitchener, Ont.; Kenneth (Ken) Thomson, chief strategic officer, Toronto, Ont.; David R. Demers, Vancouver, B.C.; Paul L. Geyer, Vancouver, B.C.; Janice Y. (Jan) Lederman, Winnipeg, Man.; Thealzel Lee, Vancouver, B.C.; Roberto E. (Robert) Napoli, Vancouver, B.C.

Other Exec. Officers - Brooke Jutzi, CFO; Dan Flaro, pres., Pivot Financial Inc.; Monique Morden, pres., TIMIA Capital Corporation

Capital Stock

	Authorized (shs.)	Outstanding (shs.)[1]
Series A Preferred	unlimited	28,485,994
Common	unlimited	92,370,956

[1] At Aug. 23, 2023

Series A Preferred - Entitled to non-cumulative preferential cash dividends, if, as and when declared, at an annual rate of $0.08 per share payable quarterly. Retractable by the company at any time on or after Nov. 27, 2023, for cash or common shares. All shares are to be retracted on Nov. 27, 2025. Convertible into common shares on a one-for-one basis. Non-voting.

Common - One vote per share.

Normal Course Issuer Bid - The company plans to make normal course purchases of up to 4,575,286 common shares representing 5% of the total outstanding. The bid commenced on Nov. 3, 2022, and expires on Nov. 3, 2023.

Major Shareholder - Blake Albright held 19.1% interest and Kenneth (Ken) Thomson held 18.8% interest at Apr. 6, 2023.

Price Range - MONT/TSX-VEN

Year	Volume	High	Low	Close
2022	5,804,187	$0.60	$0.33	$0.46
2021	9,335,077	$0.50	$0.17	$0.40
2020	3,866,409	$0.24	$0.14	$0.20
2019	8,446,611	$0.27	$0.17	$0.19
2018	6,369,221	$0.21	$0.11	$0.20

Recent Close: $0.16

Capital Stock Changes - In January 2022, private placement of 6,253,571 units (1 common share & ½ warrant) at 35¢ per unit was completed. In August 2022, 31,250,000 common shares and 18,000,000 series A preferred shares were issued pursuant to the acquisition of Brightpath Capital Corp. and Brightpath Residential Mortgage LP I. Also during 2022, common shares were issued as follows: 892,096 on exercise of options and 298,326 on exercise of warrants; 103,500 common shares were repurchased under a Normal Course Issuer Bid.

Dividends

MONT.PR.A pfd A Ra $0.08 pa Q

$0.0211i.............. Mar. 31/21

i Initial Payment

Wholly Owned Subsidiaries

Brightpath Capital Corp., Waterloo, Ont.

Brightpath Residential Mortgage LP I, Canada.

Brightpath Servicing Corporation, Canada.

Pivot Financial I Limited Partnership, Canada.

Pivot Financial Services Inc.

TIMIA Capital II General Partner Inc., Canada.

TIMIA Capital III General Partner Inc., Canada.

TIMIA Capital GP Inc.

TIMIA Capital Holdings Limited Partnership, Canada.

TIMIA SPIV I Inc., Canada.

2862454 Ontario Inc., Canada.

Subsidiaries

78% int. in **Langhaus Financial Corporation**, Canada.

78% int. in **Langhaus Financial Partners Inc.**, Canada.

78% int. in **Langhaus Insurance Finance GP Corporation**, Canada.

78% int. in **Langhaus Insurance Finance GP II Corporation**, Canada.

78% int. in **Langhaus Insurance Finance GP III Corporation**, Canada.

78% int. in **Langhaus Insurance Finance Limited Partnership II**, Canada.

78% int. in **Langhaus Insurance Finance Limited Partnership III**, Canada.

78% int. in **Langhaus Insurance Finance Limited Partnership**, Canada.

78% int. in **Langhaus Speciality Finance Corporation**, Canada.

Financial Statistics

Periods ended:	12m Dec. 31/22[A]		13m Dec. 31/21[A]
	$000s	%Chg	$000s
Total revenue	**31,266**	**+221**	**9,728**
General & admin. expense	9,638		3,687
Stock-based compensation	607		150
Operating expense	**10,245**	**+167**	**3,837**
Operating income	**21,022**	**+257**	**5,891**
Deprec. & amort.	1,323		99
Finance costs, gross	15,285		2,716
Pre-tax income	**3,936**	**+61**	**2,444**
Income taxes	4		2
Net income	**3,932**	**+61**	**2,442**
Net inc. for equity hldrs	**591**	**n.a.**	**(760)**
Net inc. for non-cont. int	**3,341**	**+4**	**3,202**
Cash & equivalent	7,008		9,315
Accounts receivable	6,091		688
Current assets	385,742		81,078
Long-term investments	3,674		1,334
Right-of-use assets	125		203
Intangibles	61,714		6,539
Total assets	**462,469**	**+270**	**125,080**
Bank indebtedness	nil		4,485
Accts. pay. & accr. liabs	nil		5,676
Current liabilities	311,817		79,238
Long-term debt, gross	nil		1,225
Long-term debt, net	nil		1,206
Preferred share equity	39,848		9,560
Equity portion of conv. debs	44		68
Shareholders' equity	59,864		13,127
Cash from oper. activs	**(49,329)**	**n.a.**	**(5,531)**
Cash from fin. activs	47,022		2,226
Cash from invest. activs	(2,225)		176
Net cash position	**7,008**	**-25**	**9,315**
	$		$
Earnings per share*	0.01		(0.03)
Cash flow per share*	(0.69)		(0.12)
	shs		shs
No. of shs. o/s*	91,631,956		53,041,463
Avg. no. of shs. o/s*	71,632,269		47,910,437
	%		%
Net profit margin	12.58		25.10
Return on equity	5.01		(23.23)
Return on assets	6.54		6.17

* Common

[A] Reported in accordance with IFRS

Latest Results

Periods ended:	6m June 30/23[A]		6m June 30/22[A]
	$000s	%Chg	$000s
Total revenue	26,353	+178	9,479
Net income	(3,027)	n.a.	2,254
Net inc. for equity hldrs	(2,980)	n.a.	727
Net inc. for non-cont. int	(48)		1,527
	$		$
Earnings per share*	(0.04)		0.01

* Common

[A] Reported in accordance with IFRS

Historical Summary
(as originally stated)

Fiscal Year	Total Rev.	Net Inc. Bef. Disc.	EPS*
	$000s	$000s	$
2022[A]	31,266	3,932	0.01
2021[A1]	9,728	2,442	(0.03)
2020[A]	6,088	1,901	(0.01)
2019[A]	3,288	(1,088)	(0.03)
2018[A]	3,321	19	0.00

* Common

[A] Reported in accordance with IFRS

[1] 13 months ended Dec. 31, 2021.

M.112 Moon River Capital Ltd.

Symbol - MOO.P **Exchange** - TSX-VEN **CUSIP** - 615450

Head Office - 401-217 Queen St W, Toronto, ON, M5V 0R2 **Telephone** - (416) 567-2440

Email - jlevy@genmining.com

Investor Relations - Jamie B. Levy (416) 567-2440

Auditors - Wasserman Ramsay C.A., Markham, Ont.

Lawyers - Irwin Lowy LLP, Toronto, Ont.

Transfer Agents - TSX Trust Company, Toronto, Ont.

Profile - (Ont. 2019) Capital Pool Company.

Directors - Jamie B. Levy, CEO, CFO & treas., Toronto, Ont.; Kerry J. Knoll, corp. sec., B.C.; Ian J. McDonald, Toronto, Ont.

Capital Stock

	Authorized (shs.)	Outstanding (shs.)[1]
Common	unlimited	11,660,000
Special	unlimited	nil

[1] At May 19, 2023

Major Shareholder - Kerry J. Knoll held 17.54% interest, Jamie B. Levy held 17.54% interest and Ian J. McDonald held 17.54% interest at Jan. 28, 2022.

Price Range - MOO.P/TSX-VEN

Year	Volume	High	Low	Close
2022	155,500	$0.55	$0.23	$0.24
2021	50,000	$0.40	$0.27	$0.27
2020	129,000	$0.30	$0.15	$0.30

Recent Close: $0.25

Capital Stock Changes - During 2022, 260,000 common shares were issued on exercise of options.

M.113 Moovly Media Inc.

Symbol - MVY **Exchange** - TSX-VEN **CUSIP** - 61634Q

Head Office - 1558 Hastings St W, Vancouver, BC, V6G 3J4 **Telephone** - (604) 639-4452 **Fax** - (604) 639-4451

Website - www.moovly.com

Email - bgrunewald@moovly.com

Investor Relations - Brendon Grunewald (604) 639-4452

Auditors - Davidson & Company LLP C.A., Vancouver, B.C.

Lawyers - TingleMerrett LLP, Calgary, Alta.

Transfer Agents - Odyssey Trust Company, Vancouver, B.C.

Profile - (B.C. 2006) Provides a cloud-based digital media and content creation platform.

Moovly platforms include Moovly Studios, a second-generation video editor based on HTML 5 which features unlimited access to royalty-free media objects such as stock videos, motion graphics, photos, illustrations, music and sound loops; and Moovly Video Automators and Application Programming Interface, which enable semi and fully automated creation of videos. Also offers a mobile app available for iOS and Android devices to display videos and presentations, capture images, sound or video clips, and create videos using pre-formatted clips and templates. The mobile app also acts as an input device for the Moovly platforms. The platform is integrated into different platforms and services including YouTube, Vimeo, Wordpress, Bynder digital asset management system and cloud storages such as OneDrive, DropBox, GDrive and Transistor. Clients include consumers, students, educational institutions and companies of all sizes.

Predecessor Detail - Name changed from Pantheon Ventures Ltd., June 15, 2016, pursuant to reverse takeover acquisition of Moovly N.V.; basis 1 new for 1.5 old shs.

Directors - Brendon Grunewald, co-founder, pres. & CEO, Brussels, Belgium; Geert Coppens, chief tech. officer, Belgium; Michelle Gahagan, Vancouver, B.C.; Robert Meister, North Vancouver, B.C.; James (Jamie) Newall, London, Middx., United Kingdom

Other Exec. Officers - Kelsey Chin, CFO & corp. sec.

Capital Stock

	Authorized (shs.)	Outstanding (shs.)[1]
Common	unlimited	172,362,707

[1] At Jan. 27, 2023

Major Shareholder - Widely held at Nov. 18, 2021.

Price Range - MVY/TSX-VEN

Year	Volume	High	Low	Close
2022	23,536,709	$0.19	$0.05	$0.11
2021	119,840,403	$1.02	$0.11	$0.11
2020	14,042,695	$0.12	$0.01	$0.11
2019	11,569,162	$0.10	$0.04	$0.05
2018	37,877,852	$0.15	$0.07	$0.08

Recent Close: $0.05

Capital Stock Changes - During fiscal 2022, 1,000,000 common shares were issued on exercise on stock options.

Wholly Owned Subsidiaries

Moovly N.V., Ghent, Belgium.

Financial Statistics

Periods ended:	12m Sept. 30/22[A]		12m Sept. 30/21[A]
	$000s	%Chg	$000s
Operating revenue	**1,401**	**-13**	**1,605**
Salaries & benefits	729		573
General & admin expense	1,954		3,030
Stock-based compensation	237		644
Operating expense	**2,920**	**-31**	**4,247**
Operating income	**(1,519)**	**n.a.**	**(2,642)**
Deprec., depl. & amort.	361		415
Finance costs, gross	179		285
Pre-tax income	**(2,062)**	**n.a.**	**(3,354)**
Net income	**(2,062)**	**n.a.**	**(3,354)**
Cash & equivalent	151		1,795
Accounts receivable	93		184
Current assets	279		1,994
Fixed assets, net	12		10
Intangibles, net	532		482
Total assets	**822**	**-67**	**2,486**
Bank indebtedness	2,641		1,970
Accts. pay. & accr. liabs	1,597		1,709
Current liabilities	4,659		4,278
Long-term debt, gross	299		688
Long-term debt, net	299		688
Shareholders' equity	(4,136)		(2,480)
Cash from oper. activs	**(1,439)**	**n.a.**	**(2,211)**
Cash from fin. activs	278		4,312
Cash from invest. activs	(443)		(389)
Net cash position	**151**	**-92**	**1,795**
Capital expenditures	(9)		(15)
	$		$
Earnings per share*	(0.01)		(0.02)
Cash flow per share*	(0.01)		(0.02)
	shs		shs
No. of shs. o/s*	162,087,707		161,087,707
Avg. no. of shs. o/s*	161,880,721		147,190,332
	%		%
Net profit margin	(147.18)		(208.97)
Return on equity	n.m.		n.m.
Return on assets	(113.85)		(190.62)
Foreign sales percent	100		100

* Common

[A] Reported in accordance with IFRS

Historical Summary
(as originally stated)

Fiscal Year	Oper. Rev.	Net Inc. Bef. Disc.	EPS*
	$000s	$000s	$
2022[A]	1,401	(2,062)	(0.01)
2021[A]	1,605	(3,354)	(0.02)
2020[A]	1,470	(1,713)	(0.01)
2019[A]	1,220	(1,808)	(0.01)
2018[A]	893	(3,843)	(0.03)

* Common

[A] Reported in accordance with IFRS

M.114 Morguard Corporation*

Symbol - MRC **Exchange** - TSX **CUSIP** - 617577

Head Office - 1000-55 City Centre Dr, Mississauga, ON, L5B 1M3 **Telephone** - (905) 281-3800 **Toll-free** - (800) 928-6255 **Fax** - (905) 281-5890

Website - www.morguard.com

Email - pmiatello@morguard.com

Investor Relations - Paul Miatello (905) 281-5943

Auditors - Ernst & Young LLP C.A., Toronto, Ont.

Bankers - The Toronto-Dominion Bank; Royal Bank of Canada

Transfer Agents - Computershare Trust Company of Canada Inc., Toronto, Ont.

FP500 Revenue Ranking - 316

Profile - (Can. 2008 amalg.) Acquires, owns, develops, manages and leases multi-suite residential, commercial and hotel income producing properties across Canada and in the U.S., and provides real estate advisory and management services to Canadian institutional and private investors.

Real Estate

The company and its subsidiaries, including **Morguard North American Residential Real Estate Investment Trust** (Morguard Residential REIT) and **Morguard Real Estate Investment Trust** (Morguard REIT), own a portfolio of 178 multi-suite residential, retail, office, industrial and hotel properties located across Canada and the U.S.

The trust's real estate assets at June 30, 2023:

	Props.	GLA[1]	Suites/rooms
Residential	55	n.a.	17,566
Retail	37	8,228,000	n.a.
Office	49	7,835,000	n.a.
Industrial	20	1,079,000	n.a.
Hotel	17	n.a.	2,907
	178	17,142,000	20,473

[1] Owned gross leasable area (sq. ft.)

The Canadian multi-suite residential portfolio consists of 24 properties consisting of high-rise, mid-rise and low-rise buildings primarily located in the Greater Toronto Area. The U.S. multi-suite residential portfolio consists of 31 properties consisting of high-rise, mid-rise, and low-rise garden-style communities located in California, Texas, Louisiana, Illinois, Georgia, Florida, North Carolina, Virginia and Maryland.

The retail portfolio includes enclosed full-scale, regional shopping centres and neighbourhood and community shopping centres anchored by food retailers and discount department stores, consisting of 25 properties in Canada and 12 properties in Florida, Louisiana and Maryland.

The office portfolio includes a mix of single-tenant buildings and multi-tenant properties primarily in the Greater Toronto Area and downtown Ottawa, Ont.; Calgary, Alta.; and Vancouver, B.C.

The industrial portfolio consists of properties in Ontario, Quebec and British Columbia.

The hotel portfolio consists of 13 branded and four unbranded hotel properties in British Columbia, Ontario and Nova Scotia. Branded hotels include Hilton, Marriott and Holiday Inn.

Subsidiary Morguard Residential REIT owns interests in 16 Canadian and 27 U.S. multi-suite residential properties, totaling 13,089 units, in Ontario, Alberta, Colorado, Illinois, Florida, Georgia, Louisiana, North Carolina, Virginia, Maryland and Texas.

Subsidiary Morguard REIT owns a portfolio of 46 retail, office and industrial properties in British Columbia, Alberta, Saskatchewan, Manitoba, Ontario and Quebec.

Advisory and Management Services

Wholly owned **Morguard Investments Limited** (MIL) provides real estate portfolio and asset and property management services to major institutional clients and private investors including the company and Morguard REIT. Through 60%-owned **Lincluden Investment Management Limited**, offers a range of global investment products across equity, fixed-income and balanced portfolios to institutional and private investors. On behalf of third parties, the company manages $7.8 billion of assets as at June 30, 2023.

During the first quarter of 2023, the company sold three industrial properties, totaling 19,875 sq. ft., for $1,549,000.

In September 2022, the company sold Days Hotel and Suites in Lloydminster, Alta., for $2,000,000.

In July 2022, the company sold Saskatoon Inn in Saskatoon, Sask., for $4,250,000.

In June 2022, the company sold Keewatin Square, a 37,500-sq.-ft. office property in Regina, Sask., for $2,900,000.

Recent Merger and Acquisition Activity

Status: completed **Announced:** Jan. 5, 2023
Morguard North American Residential Real Estate Investment Trust acquired the remaining 50% interest in The Fenestra at Rockville Town Square, an apartment complex consisting of three buildings and 492 suites in Rockville, Md., from Morguard Corporation for US$71,500,000, including assumption of US$34,000,000 of mortgages.

Status: completed **Announced:** Dec. 23, 2022
Morguard Corporation sold Fort McMurray portfolio in Fort McMurray, Alta., for $18,815,000.

Status: completed **Announced:** Dec. 22, 2022
Morguard Corporation acquired a 50% interest in a 109,208-sq.-ft. class A office building (215 Slater Street) in downtown Ottawa, Ont., for $28,813,000.

Status: completed **Announced:** Sept. 26, 2022
Morguard Corporation acquired Rockville Town Square, a 186,712-sq.-ft. retail property in Rockville, Md., for US$33,313,000.

Status: completed **Announced:** Aug. 31, 2022
Morguard Corporation sold Temple Garden and Mineral Spa in Moose Jaw, Sask., for $23,354,000.

Status: completed **Revised:** Aug. 22, 2022
UPDATE: The transaction was completed. PREVIOUS: Morguard Corporation agreed to acquire a 163,580-sq.-ft. class A office building in Kanata, Ont., which was the headquarters of Kinaxis Inc., for $65,886,000.

Status: completed **Announced:** May 31, 2022
Morguard Corporation sold Hilton Garden Inn in Edmonton, Alta., for $12,450,000.

Status: completed **Announced:** May 19, 2022
Morguard Corporation sold Wingate by Wyndham Regina in Regina, Sask., for $6,473,000.

Status: completed **Announced:** May 19, 2022
Morguard Corporation sold Holiday Inn Winnipeg South in Winnipeg, Man., for $12,450,000.

Status: completed **Announced:** Apr. 14, 2022
Morguard Corporation sold its 70% interest in Acclaim Hotel Calgary Airport in Calgary, Alta., for $8,680,000.

Status: completed **Announced:** Mar. 31, 2022
Morguard Corporation sold two hotels (Days Inn and Suites Sibley and Days Inn and Suites North) totaling 184 rooms in Thunder Bay, Ont., for $18,100,000.

Predecessor Detail - Name changed from Acktion Corporation, Aug. 2, 2002.

Directors - K. Rai Sahi, chr. & CEO, Mississauga, Ont.; Angela Sahi, exec. v-p, residential, office & ind., Mississauga, Ont.; Bruce K. Robertson†, Toronto, Ont.; William J. Braithwaite, Toronto, Ont.; Chris J. Cahill, McLean, Va.; L. Peter Sharpe, Toronto, Ont.; Stephen R. Taylor, Oakville, Ont.

Other Exec. Officers - Beverley G. Flynn, sr. v-p, gen. counsel & corp. sec.; Paul Miatello, sr. v-p & CFO; Brian Athey, v-p, devel.; Robert McFarlane, v-p, internal audit; Christopher A. Newman, v-p, fin.

† Lead director

Capital Stock

	Authorized (shs.)	Outstanding (shs.)[1]
Preference	unlimited	nil
Common	unlimited	10,813,224

[1] At Aug. 2, 2023

Normal Course Issuer Bid - The company plans to make normal course purchases of up to 554,788 common shares representing 5% of the total outstanding. The bid commenced on Sept. 22, 2022, and expires on Sept. 21, 2023.

Major Shareholder - K. Rai Sahi held 60.71% interest at Mar. 14, 2023.

Price Range - MRC/TSX

Year	Volume	High	Low	Close
2022	853,319	$138.10	$104.00	$112.46
2021	1,740,560	$158.01	$102.99	$136.46
2020	1,254,128	$212.99	$95.05	$115.45
2019	348,341	$219.48	$171.50	$201.00
2018	916,004	$190.00	$161.00	$176.01

Recent Close: $102.80

Capital Stock Changes - During 2022, 79,000 common shares were repurchased under a Normal Course Issuer Bid.

Dividends

MRC com Ra $0.60 pa Q est. Dec. 31, 2008**

** Reinvestment Option

Long-Term Debt - Outstanding at Dec. 31, 2022:

Mtges.[1]	$4,642,151,000
Morguard Residential REIT conv. debs.[2]	80,126,000
Morguard REIT conv. debs.[3]	91,968,000
4.402% ser. G debs. due 2023	175,000,000
4.715% ser. E debs. due 2024	225,000,000
4.204% ser. F debs. due 2024	225,000,000
Less: Unamort. costs	857,000
	5,438,388,000
Less: Current Portion	1,020,970,000
	4,417,418,000

[1] Bear interest at rates ranging from 2.03% to 7.73% and due 2023 to 2058.

[2] Bear interest at 4.5% and due Mar. 31, 2023. Convertible into Morguard Residential REIT trust units at $20.20 per unit.

[3] Bear interest at 5.25% and due Dec. 31, 2026. Convertible into Morguard REIT trust units at $7.80 per unit.

Minimum debt repayments for the mortgages were reported as follows:

2023	$769,771,000
2024	769,625,000
2025	567,791,000
2026	452,750,000
2027	489,367,000
Thereafter	1,614,510,000

Wholly Owned Subsidiaries

Morguard Investments Limited, Ont.
- 60% int. in **Lincluden Investment Management Ltd.**, Oakville, Ont.

Revenue Properties (America), Inc., Kenner, La.
- 100% int. in **Morguard Management Company Inc.**, United States.

Temple Hotels Inc., Mississauga, Ont.

Subsidiaries

64.9% int. in **Morguard Real Estate Investment Trust**, Mississauga, Ont. (see separate coverage)

Investments

45.2% int. in **Morguard North American Residential Real Estate Investment Trust**, Mississauga, Ont. (see separate coverage)

Note: The preceding list includes only the major related companies in which interests are held.

Financial Statistics

Periods ended:	12m Dec. 31/22[A]		12m Dec. 31/21[oA]
	$000s	%Chg	$000s
Total revenue	**1,136,675**	**+9**	**1,044,844**
Rental operating expense	349,821		295,771
General & admin. expense	77,613		80,201
Property taxes	129,142		136,992
Other operating expense	63,086		55,845
Operating expense	**619,662**	**+9**	**568,809**
Operating income	**517,013**	**+9**	**476,035**
Investment income	1,207		24,017
Deprec. & amort.	26,514		32,499
Finance costs, gross	229,335		220,312
Write-downs/write-offs	nil		(45,289)
Pre-tax income	**135,460**	**-67**	**408,102**
Income taxes	23,208		151,481
Net income	**112,252**	**-56**	**256,621**
Net inc. for equity hldrs	**122,771**	**-51**	**249,760**
Net inc. for non-cont. int	**(10,519)**	**n.a.**	**6,861**
Cash & equivalent	111,808		173,656
Accounts receivable	80,159		63,971
Current assets	339,126		290,979
Long-term investments	224,537		257,791
Fixed assets	33,271		44,762
Income-producing props	10,418,017		10,139,816
Properties under devel	21,604		12,360
Properties for future devel	111,453		92,699
Property interests, net	10,906,809		10,720,892
Right-of-use assets	1,070		1,247
Intangibles, net	45,592		50,740
Total assets	**11,705,252**	**+2**	**11,492,543**
Bank indebtedness	189,306		8,039
Accts. pay. & accr. liabs	208,406		189,987
Current liabilities	1,455,561		1,104,449
Long-term debt, gross	5,438,388		5,623,117
Long-term debt, net	4,417,418		4,767,016
Long-term lease liabilities	170,934		166,531
Shareholders' equity	3,865,254		3,632,176
Non-controlling interest	520,217		541,571
Cash from oper. activs	**252,854**	**-5**	**265,443**
Cash from fin. activs	(234,489)		(106,631)
Cash from invest. activs	(84,509)		(125,617)
Net cash position	**111,808**	**-36**	**173,656**
Capital expenditures	(1,664)		(677)
Increase in property	(430,633)		(178,109)
Decrease in property	354,065		40,708
Pension fund surplus	69,572		75,912
	$		$
Earnings per share*	11.08		22.50
Cash flow per share*	22.82		23.91
Funds from opers. per sh.*	19.10		16.93
Cash divd. per share*	0.60		0.60
Total divd. per share*	**0.60**		**0.60**
	shs		shs
No. of shs. o/s*	11,022,000		11,101,000
Avg. no. of shs. o/s*	11,079,000		11,101,000
	%		%
Net profit margin	9.88		24.56
Return on equity	3.28		7.13
Return on assets	2.61		3.51
Foreign sales percent	29		27

* Common

[o] Restated

[A] Reported in accordance with IFRS

Latest Results

Periods ended:	6m June 30/23[A]		6m June 30/22[A]
	$000s	%Chg	$000s
Total revenue	598,799	+9	547,706
Net income	64,518	-87	479,802
Net inc. for equity hldrs	55,128	-87	438,977
Net inc. for non-cont. int	9,390		40,825
	$		$
Earnings per share*	5.01		39.55

* Common

[A] Reported in accordance with IFRS

Historical Summary
(as originally stated)

Fiscal Year	Total Rev. $000s	Net Inc. Bef. Disc. $000s	EPS* $
2022[A]	1,136,675	112,252	11.08
2021[A]	1,044,844	256,621	22.50
2020[A]	1,044,189	(250,050)	(8.83)
2019[A]	1,192,973	188,796	16.57
2018[A]	1,157,878	344,058	27.96

* Common

[A] Reported in accordance with IFRS

M.115 Morguard North American Residential Real Estate Investment Trust

Symbol - MRG.UN **Exchange** - TSX **CUSIP** - 61761E

Head Office - c/o Morguard Corporation, 1000-55 City Centre Dr, Mississauga, ON, L5B 1M3 **Telephone** - (905) 281-3800 **Toll-free** - (800) 928-6255 **Fax** - (905) 281-5890

Website - www.morguard.com

Email - bflynn@morguard.com

Investor Relations - Beverley G. Flynn (800) 928-6255

Auditors - Ernst & Young LLP C.A., Toronto, Ont.

Bankers - The Toronto-Dominion Bank, Toronto, Ont.; Royal Bank of Canada, Toronto, Ont.

Transfer Agents - Computershare Trust Company of Canada Inc., Toronto, Ont.

FP500 Revenue Ranking - 577

Profile - (Ont. 2012) Holds 43 multi-suite residential properties, consisting of buildings in Ontario, Alberta and the United States, totaling 13,089 suites and 239,500 sq. ft. of commercial area.

Property portfolio at Mar. 31, 2023:

Region	Props.	Suites
Canada:		
Toronto	6	1,997
Mississauga	7	2,219
Kitchener	1	472
Ottawa	1	370
Edmonton	1	277
	16	5,335
U.S.:		
Colorado	2	454
Texas	3	1,021
Louisiana	2	249
Illinois	4	1,795
Georgia	2	522
Florida	9	2,253
North Carolina	2	864
Virginia	1	104
Maryland	2	492
	27	7,754

Morguard (Canada) GP Limited and **Morguard Management Company Inc.**, wholly owned by **Morguard Corporation**, administer and operate the trust's Canadian and the U.S. properties, respectively.

Recent Merger and Acquisition Activity

Status: completed **Announced:** Mar. 29, 2023
Morguard North American Residential Real Estate Investment Trust acquired Xavier Apartments, an 18-storey class A mixed-use residential building, consisting of 240 suites, in downtown Chicago, Ill., for US$81,000,000, which was funded with net proceeds from a prior property disposition and cash on hand.

Status: completed **Announced:** Jan. 5, 2023
Morguard North American Residential Real Estate Investment Trust acquired the remaining 50% interest in The Fenestra at Rockville Town Square, an apartment complex consisting of three buildings and 492 suites in Rockville, Md., from Morguard Corporation for US$71,500,000, including assumption of US$34,000,000 of mortgages.

Status: completed **Revised:** Oct. 1, 2022
UPDATE: The transaction was completed. PREVIOUS: Morguard North American Residential Real Estate Investment Trust agreed to sell Blue Isle Apartment Homes, a two-storey residential garden community consisting of 340 suites in 23 buildings in Coconut Creek, Fla., for US$92,000,000.

Status: completed **Announced:** Sept. 27, 2022
Morguard North American Residential Real Estate Investment Trust acquired the retail portion of Rockville Town Square in Rockville, Md., consisting of 183,000 sq. ft. of retail, dining, and municipal and financial services, for US$33,000,000. Rockville Town Square was connected to the REIT's Fenestra Apartments, which was acquired on a 50/50 basis with Morguard Corporation in 2017.

Status: completed **Revised:** Aug. 24, 2022
UPDATE: The transaction was completed for US$25,247,000. PREVIOUS: Morguard North American Residential Real Estate Investment Trust entered into a conditional agreement to sell Greenbrier Estates, a low-rise apartment complex consisting of 18 buildings and 144 suites in Slidell, La., for US$24,280,000.

Status: completed **Revised:** Aug. 8, 2022
UPDATE: The transaction was completed. PREVIOUS: Morguard North American Residential Real Estate Investment Trust agreed to acquire Echelon Chicago, a class A, 39-storey luxury residential complex with 350 suites in Chicago, Ill., for US$133,000,000.

Status: completed **Revised:** June 6, 2022
UPDATE: The transaction was completed for US$74,152,000. PREVIOUS: Morguard North American Residential Real Estate Investment Trust entered into a conditional agreement to sell Briarhill Apartments, a low-rise apartment complex consisting of 14 buildings and 292 suites in Atlanta, Ga., for US$75,500,000.

Trustees - K. Rai Sahi, chr. & CEO, Mississauga, Ont.; Avtar T. Bains‡, Vancouver, B.C.; Dino Chiesa, Toronto, Ont.; Mel Leiderman, Toronto, Ont.; Frank M. Munsters, Toronto, Ont.; Bruce K. Robertson, Toronto, Ont.; William O. Wallace, Toronto, Ont.

Oper. Subsid./Mgt. Co. Officers - Christopher A. Newman, CFO; Beverley G. Flynn, sr. v-p, gen. counsel & corp. sec.; Paul Miatello, sr. v-p; Angela Sahi, sr. v-p; Brian Athey, v-p; John Talano, v-p, opers., U.S.

‡ Lead trustee

Capital Stock

	Authorized (shs.)	Outstanding (shs.)[1]
Trust Unit	unlimited	38,380,023
Special Voting Unit	unlimited	17,223,090
Class A LP Unit		8,270,000
Class B LP Unit		17,223,090[2]

[1] At July 25, 2023

[2] Classified as debt.

Trust Unit - The trust will endeavour to make monthly cash distributions. One vote per trust unit.

Special Voting Unit - Issued to holders of class B limited partnership units of affiliate Morguard NAR Canada Limited Partnership. Each special voting unit entitles the holder to a number of votes at unitholder meetings equal to the number of trust units into which the class B limited partnership units are exchangeable.

Class A Limited Partnership Unit - Issued by Morguard NAR Canada Limited Partnership. Entitled to distributions equal to those provided to trust units. Non-voting.

Class B Limited Partnership Unit - Entitled to distributions equal to those provided to trust units. Exchangeable for trust units on a 1-for-1 basis at any time by holder. All held by Morguard Corporation. Classified as long-term debt under IFRS.

Normal Course Issuer Bid - The company plans to make normal course purchases of up to 1,474,371 trust units representing 10% of the public float. The bid commenced on Jan. 10, 2023, and expires on Jan. 9, 2024.

Major Shareholder - Morguard Corporation held 45.2% interest at June 30, 2023.

Price Range - MRG.UN/TSX

Year	Volume	High	Low	Close
2022	9,634,466	$20.52	$14.50	$16.20
2021	10,599,167	$19.50	$14.65	$17.71
2020	18,426,736	$20.98	$10.73	$15.95
2019	14,544,599	$20.73	$16.29	$18.49
2018	6,919,000	$18.50	$13.17	$17.15

Recent Close: $15.89

Capital Stock Changes - During 2022, 47,528 trust units were issued under dividend reinvestment plan.

Dividends

MRG.UN unit Ra $0.72 pa M est. Dec. 15, 2022**
Prev. Rate: $0.6996 est. Dec. 16, 2019
** Reinvestment Option

Wholly Owned Subsidiaries

Morguard NAR GP Limited, Ont.
Morguard NAR (U.S.) Holdings LLC, Del.

Subsidiaries

69.4% int. in **Morguard NAR Canada Limited Partnership**, Ont.

Financial Statistics

Periods ended:	12m Dec. 31/22[A]		12m Dec. 31/21[A]
	$000s	%Chg	$000s
Total revenue	**278,491**	**+13**	**245,566**
Rental operating expense	127,276		116,071
Operating expense	**127,276**	**+10**	**116,071**
Operating income	**151,215**	**+17**	**129,495**
Investment income	(3,822)		(2,691)
Finance costs, gross	63,681		65,719
Pre-tax income	**309,900**	**0**	**310,492**
Income taxes	70,337		65,518
Net income	**239,563**	**-2**	**244,974**
Net inc. for equity hldrs	**219,282**	**-9**	**242,088**
Net inc. for non-cont. int	**20,281**	**+603**	**2,886**
Cash & equivalent	14,636		26,562
Accounts receivable	11,402		7,188
Current assets	202,102		120,753
Long-term investments	105,462		96,376
Income-producing props	3,626,853		3,256,158
Property interests, net	3,626,853		3,256,158
Total assets	**3,934,417**	**+13**	**3,473,287**
Accts. pay. & accr. liabs	53,719		47,713
Current liabilities	273,664		144,690
Long-term debt, gross	1,746,314		1,679,895
Long-term debt, net	1,526,369		1,582,918
Long-term lease liabilities	16,235		9,065
Shareholders' equity	1,753,475		1,484,738
Non-controlling interest	101,914		76,647
Cash from oper. activs	**75,173**	**+18**	**63,696**
Cash from fin. activs	(78,880)		(33,053)
Cash from invest. activs	(11,058)		(31,300)
Net cash position	**14,636**	**-45**	**26,562**
Increase in property	(261,915)		(30,012)
Decrease in property	250,857		nil
	$		$
Earnings per share*	n.a.		n.a.
Cash flow per share*	1.92		1.63
Funds from opers. per sh.*	1.47		1.15
Cash divd. per share*	0.70		0.70
Total divd. per share*	**0.70**		**0.70**
	shs		shs
No. of shs. o/s*	39,111,793		39,064,265
	%		%
Net profit margin	86.02		99.76
Return on equity	13.54		17.58
Return on assets	7.80		9.05
Foreign sales percent	64		62

* Trust Unit
[A] Reported in accordance with IFRS

Latest Results

Periods ended:	3m Mar. 31/23[A]		3m Mar. 31/22[A]
	$000s	%Chg	$000s
Total revenue	79,648	+22	65,257
Net income	34,249	-80	171,142
Net inc. for equity hldrs	29,495	-82	162,430
Net inc. for non-cont. int	4,754		8,712
	$		$
Earnings per share*	n.a.		n.a.

[A] Reported in accordance with IFRS

Historical Summary
(as originally stated)

Fiscal Year	Total Rev.	Net Inc. Bef. Disc.	EPS*
	$000s	$000s	$
2022[A]	278,491	239,563	n.a.
2021[A]	245,566	244,974	n.a.
2020[A]	248,683	166,805	n.a.
2019[A]	245,596	80,128	n.a.
2018[A]	241,368	174,710	n.a.

* Trust Unit
[A] Reported in accordance with IFRS

M.116 Morguard Real Estate Investment Trust*

Symbol - MRT.UN **Exchange** - TSX **CUSIP** - 617914
Head Office - c/o Morguard Corporation, 1000-55 City Centre Dr, Mississauga, ON, L5B 1M3 **Telephone** - (905) 281-3800 **Toll-free** - (800) 928-6255 **Fax** - (905) 281-5890
Website - www.morguard.com
Email - atamlin@morguard.com
Investor Relations - Andrew Tamlin (800) 928-6255
Auditors - Ernst & Young LLP C.A., Toronto, Ont.
Bankers - The Toronto-Dominion Bank; Bank of Montreal
Lawyers - Stikeman Elliott LLP, Toronto, Ont.
Transfer Agents - Computershare Trust Company of Canada Inc., Toronto, Ont.
Employees - 8 at Dec. 31, 2022
Profile - (Ont. 1997) Owns a portfolio of income-producing retail, office and industrial properties located across Canada. At June 30, 2023, the trust owned a portfolio of 46 properties totaling 8,168,000 sq. ft. of gross leasable area in British Columbia, Alberta, Saskatchewan, Manitoba, Ontario and Quebec.

Morguard Investments Limited, a company controlled by the trust's major unitholder **Morguard Corporation**, manages most of the trust's real estate portfolio under a property management agreement.

Retail - This segment includes enclosed, full-scale regional shopping centres that are dominant in their respective markets, and community strip centres anchored by food retailers, discount department stores and banks.

Office - This segment is focused on well-located, high quality office buildings in major urban centres across Canada. Office properties include single-tenant buildings under long-term lease to government and large national tenants and multi-tenant properties.

Industrial - This segment includes operations relating to industrial and mixed-use properties. Industrial properties consist of distribution facilities, warehouse buildings and properties used for light manufacturing located in industrial parks and areas in and around major cities in Canada.

The trust's property portfolio at June 30, 2023:

Province	Props.	Area[1]
British Columbia	5	1,015,000
Alberta	14	1,995,000
Saskatchewan	1	499,000
Manitoba	3	659,000
Ontario	20	3,333,000
Quebec	1	448,000
	44	7,949,000

[1] Gross leasable area (sq. ft.).

Type	Props.	Area[1]
Retail	18	4,411,000
Office	22	3,245,000
Industrial	4	293,000
	44	7,949,000

[1] Gross leasable area (sq. ft.).

At June 30, 2023, the trust held one retail property for development with 67,000 sq. ft. of gross leasable area; and an equity accounted-investment of one office property in Alberta with 152,000 sq. ft. of gross leasable area.

Trustees - K. Rai Sahi, chr., pres. & CEO, Mississauga, Ont.; Bart S. Munn‡, Toronto, Ont.; Timothy J. (Tim) Murphy, Toronto, Ont.; Donald W. Turple, Vancouver, B.C.; Timothy J. (Tim) Walker, Lefroy, Ont.

Other Exec. Officers - Andrew Tamlin, CFO; Beverley G. Flynn, sr. v-p, gen. counsel & corp. sec.; Paul Miatello, sr. v-p; Angela Sahi, sr. v-p
‡ Lead trustee

Capital Stock

	Authorized (shs.)	Outstanding (shs.)[1]
Trust Unit	unlimited	64,251,391

[1] At June 30, 2023

Normal Course Issuer Bid - The company plans to make normal course purchases of up to 3,211,342 trust units representing 5% of the total outstanding. The bid commenced on Feb. 9, 2023, and expires on Feb. 8, 2024.

Major Shareholder - Morguard Corporation held 64.9% interest at June 30, 2023.

Price Range - MRT.UN/TSX

Year	Volume	High	Low	Close
2022	11,598,233	$5.92	$4.95	$5.30
2021	16,636,802	$7.34	$4.85	$5.42
2020	32,393,512	$12.74	$4.14	$5.39
2019	7,556,593	$12.55	$11.03	$11.79
2018	7,963,658	$14.21	$10.45	$11.40

Recent Close: $5.58

Capital Stock Changes - During 2022, 65,757 trust units were issued under distribution reinvestment plan.

Dividends

MRT.UN tr unit Ra $0.24 pa M est. Mar. 15, 2021**
Prev. Rate: $0.48 est. June 15, 2020
$0.015◆ .... Jan. 14/22 stk.[1]◆g .... Dec. 31/21
Paid in 2023: $0.16 2022: $0.24 + $0.015◆ 2021: $0.26 + stk.◆g

[1] Immediately following the distribution, the outstanding units will be consolidated. Equiv to $0.10.
** Reinvestment Option ◆ Special **g** Capital Gain

Long-Term Debt - Outstanding at Dec. 31, 2022:

Mtges.[1]	$1,051,502,000
5.25% conv. debs.[2]	149,835,000
	1,201,337,000
Less: Current portion	311,999,000
	889,338,000

[1] Bearing interest at a weighted average contractual interest rate of 3.6%.
[2] Convertible into trust units at $7.80 per unit and due Dec. 31, 2026. Equity component totaling $6,879,000 was included in unitholder's equity.

Minimum mortgage repayments were reported as follows:

2023	$312,773,000
2024	301,303,000
2025	131,071,000
2026	65,357,000
2027	51,334,000
Thereafter	191,863,000

Financial Statistics

Periods ended:	12m Dec. 31/22[A]		12m Dec. 31/21[A]
	$000s	%Chg	$000s
Total revenue	**242,629**	**0**	**241,440**
Rental operating expense	111,982		109,837
General & admin. expense	3,741		3,845
Other operating expense	8,330		8,290
Operating expense	**124,053**	**+2**	**121,972**
Operating income	**118,576**	**-1**	**119,468**
Investment income	(3,022)		(1,078)
Deprec. & amort.	83		83
Finance costs, gross	53,523		53,281
Write-downs/write-offs	(118)		(1,184)
Pre-tax income	**(86,097)**	**n.a.**	**4,885**
Net income	**(86,097)**	**n.a.**	**4,885**
Cash & equivalent	9,712		11,270
Accounts receivable	15,736		12,269
Current assets	26,648		23,904
Long-term investments	11,658		18,578
Income-producing props	2,260,657		2,395,750
Properties under devel.	25,948		15,401
Properties for future devel.	51,200		40,150
Property interests, net	2,337,805		2,451,301
Right-of-use assets	76		159
Total assets	**2,376,187**	**-5**	**2,493,942**
Bank indebtedness	55,622		7,526
Accts. pay. & accr. liabs	46,457		38,887
Current liabilities	414,245		252,149
Long-term debt, gross	1,201,337		1,273,565
Long-term debt, net	889,338		1,067,997
Long-term lease liabilities	16,384		16,550
Equity portion of conv. debs	6,879		6,879
Shareholders' equity	1,050,828		1,151,988
Cash from oper. activs	**73,968**	**-8**	**80,187**
Cash from fin. activs	(43,108)		(74,618)
Cash from invest. activs	(32,418)		(2,946)
Net cash position	**9,712**	**-14**	**11,270**
Increase in property	(32,418)		(17,446)
Decrease in property	nil		14,500
	$		$
Earnings per share*	(1.34)		0.08
Cash flow per share*	1.15		1.25
Funds from opers. per sh.*	1.04		1.07
Adj. funds from opers. per sh.*	0.67		0.80
Cash divd. per share*	0.24		0.26
Extra divd. - cash*	nil		0.02
Extra stk. divd. - cash equiv.*	nil		0.10
Total divd. per share*	**0.24**		**0.38**
	shs		shs
No. of shs. o/s*	64,226,854		64,161,097
Avg. no. of shs. o/s*	64,187,000		64,141,000
	%		%
Net profit margin	(35.49)		2.02
Return on equity	(7.82)		0.42
Return on assets	(1.34)		2.30
No. of employees (FTEs)	8		8

* Trust unit
[A] Reported in accordance with IFRS

Latest Results

Periods ended:	6m June 30/23[A]		6m June 30/22[A]
	$000s	%Chg	$000s
Total revenue	126,707	+4	121,838
Net income	(6,985)	n.a.	67,558
	$		$
Earnings per share*	(0.11)		1.05

* Trust unit
[A] Reported in accordance with IFRS

Historical Summary
(as originally stated)

Fiscal Year	Total Rev.	Net Inc. Bef. Disc.	EPS*
	$000s	$000s	$
2022[A]	242,629	(86,097)	(1.34)
2021[A]	241,440	4,885	0.08
2020[A]	253,764	(357,419)	(5.75)
2019[A]	273,074	14,840	0.24
2018[A]	276,473	73,015	1.20

* Trust unit
[A] Reported in accordance with IFRS

M.117 Moss Genomics Inc.

Symbol - MOSS **Exchange** - CSE **CUSIP** - 61965T
Head Office - 907-1030 Georgia St W, Vancouver, BC, V6E 2Y3 **Toll-free** - (858) 531-6100
Website - www.mossgenomics.com
Email - karl@mossgenomics.com
Investor Relations - Karl Cahill (604) 629-5974
Auditors - Davidson & Company LLP C.A., Vancouver, B.C.

Transfer Agents - Odyssey Trust Company, Vancouver, B.C.
Profile - (B.C. 2018) Uses DNA and gut microbiome sequencing data along with artificial intelligence (AI) to analyze an individual's gut biology and provide personalized health, anti-aging and wellness offerings.
Provides genomic, microbiome and epigenome testing services in which consumers provide a saliva sample (genomic testing) and fecal sample (microbiome testing). A DNA analysis and a gut health or gut and mental health report containing personalized and actionable wellness recommendations is then provided based on the results. Products include a line of personalized prebiotic and probiotic formulations. An initial offering of six different probiotics solutions are expected to launch commercially in the first half of 2023 in the U.S. and in the second half of 2023 in Canada.
Additional customized health reports are being developed for: pain, including shoulder and neck pain, inflammation, and joint, chronic and back pain; skin, including eczema, acne, psoriasis and varicose veins; female, including female fertility, sexual dysfunction and urinary tract infection; overall health, including asthma, blood pressure, gum disease and kidney stones; and weight/diet, including underactive/overactive thyroid, cholesterol and blood sugar.
Additional products being developed include a healing balm, sports cream and pure cannabidiol (CBD) drops.
Operations are conducted in San Diego, Calif.
Common listed on CSE, Jan. 19, 2023.
Predecessor Detail - Name changed from Nou Camp Capital Corp., June 18, 2021.
Directors - Karl Cahill, CEO, San Diego, Calif.; Nitin Kaushal, Richmond Hill, Ont.; Dr. Min Seob Lee, San Diego, Calif.; Mark T. Tommasi, North Vancouver, B.C.
Other Exec. Officers - Michelle K. Lee, pres., interim CFO & corp. sec.

Capital Stock

	Authorized (shs.)	Outstanding (shs.)[1]
Common	unlimited	44,527,000

[1] At Jan. 19, 2023

Major Shareholder - Lucas Cahill held 11.23% interest at Jan. 19, 2023.
Recent Close: $0.08
Capital Stock Changes - During fiscal 2022, common shares were issued as follows: 11,277,000 pursuant to the acquisition of Standard Acquisition Corp., 10,000,000 by private placement, 5,000,000 on acquisition of equipment and 4,550,000 on exercise of warrants.

Wholly Owned Subsidiaries

Moss Genomics Holdings Inc., Vancouver, B.C.
- 100% int. in **Moss Genomics (US) Inc.**, Carson City, Nev.

Financial Statistics

Periods ended:	12m June 30/22[A]		12m June 30/21[A]
	$000s	%Chg	$000s
General & admin expense	617		108
Operating expense	**617**	**+471**	**108**
Operating income	**(617)**	**n.a.**	**(108)**
Deprec., depl. & amort.	38		nil
Pre-tax income	**(655)**	**n.a.**	**(108)**
Net income	**(655)**	**n.a.**	**(108)**
Cash & equivalent	688		1
Current assets	689		109
Fixed assets, net	112		nil
Total assets	**802**	**+636**	**109**
Bank indebtedness	nil		4
Accts. pay. & accr. liabs	140		117
Current liabilities	140		120
Shareholders' equity	661		(12)
Cash from oper. activs	**(568)**	**n.a.**	**(2)**
Cash from fin. activs	1,260		2
Cash from invest. activs	(5)		nil
Net cash position	**688**	**n.m.**	**1**
Capital expenditures	(51)		nil
	$		$
Earnings per share*	(0.02)		(0.01)
Cash flow per share*	(0.02)		(0.00)
	shs		shs
No. of shs. o/s*	44,077,000		13,250,000
Avg. no. of shs. o/s*	32,880,069		9,019,232
	%		%
Net profit margin	n.a.		n.a.
Return on equity	n.m.		n.m.
Return on assets	(143.80)		n.a.

* Common
[A] Reported in accordance with IFRS

M.118 Mount Logan Capital Inc.

Symbol - MLC **Exchange** - NEO **CUSIP** - 621886
Head Office - 800-365 Bay St, Toronto, ON, M5H 2V1
Website - www.mountlogancapital.ca
Email - jason.roos@mountlogancapital.ca
Investor Relations - Jason T. Roos (212) 891-5046
Auditors - Deloitte LLP C.P.A., New York, N.Y.
Bankers - Canadian Imperial Bank of Commerce
Lawyers - Wildeboer Dellelce LLP, Toronto, Ont.
Transfer Agents - Odyssey Trust Company, Toronto, Ont.
Employees - 9 at Dec. 31, 2022
Profile - (Ont. 2008 amalg.) Invests primarily in public and private debt securities in North America. Also provides insurance and reinsurance of long-term care policies and annuity products.
Actively sources, evaluates, underwrites, monitors and primarily invests in loans, debt securities and other credit-oriented instruments that present attractive risk-adjusted returns and present low risk of principal impairment through the credit cycle, and minority equity stakes in funds and companies. The company generates interest income, dividend income and management fees from managing its own on-balance sheet investments, as well as managing third party capital and other fund products.
The company operates its insurance business through wholly owned **Ability Insurance Company** which is an insurer and reinsurer of long-term care policies and annuity products. Long-term care insurance policies reimburse policyholders a daily amount (up to a pre-selected limit), upon meeting certain requirements, for services to assist with daily living assisted living facilities as they age. Annuities are a contract with an insurer where individuals agree to pay a certain amount of money, either in a lump sum or through installments, which entitles them to receive a series of payments at a future date. Ability is no longer insuring new long-term care risk and would continue to expand and diversify its business including through the reinsurance of annuity products which commenced in the second quarter of 2022.
Provides investment advisory services to **Logan Ridge Finance Corporation** and manages assets across two collateralized loan obligations through wholly owned **Mount Logan Management LLC**. Also holds 24.99% interest in **Sierra Crest Investment Management LLC** (SCIM), which manages **Portman Ridge Finance Corporation** and **Alternative Credit Income Fund** (formerly **Resource Credit Income Fund**), as well as a minority interest in **Crown Private Credit Partners Inc.**, which manages **Crown Capital Partner Funding L.P.**
Investment portfolio at Mar. 31, 2023:

Security Type	Fair Value US$000s
Debt securities	749,023
Mortgage loans	130,887
Investments in associates	13,066
Equity securities	10,621
Other invested assets	29,188
Total	932,785

In July 2023, the company acquired all of the membership interests of **Ovation Partners, LP**, a Texas-based specialty finance focused asset manager, and certain assets from the Ovation advisor, for issuance of 3,186,398 common shares at a deemed price of Cdn$2.8314 per share and assumption of US$1,800,000 line of credit. Pursuant to the agreement, wholly owned **Mount Logan Management, LLC** would become the investment adviser to the Ovation platform, which is focused on investments in commercial lending, real estate lending, consumer finance and litigation finance.
Predecessor Detail - Name changed from Marret Resource Corp., Oct. 19, 2018, following completion of a plan of arrangement whereby the company changed its investment strategy from a focus on natural resource lending to a broader lending-oriented credit platform.
Directors - Edward (Ted) Goldthorpe, chr. & CEO, New York, N.Y.; Sabrina Liak†, B.C.; David Allen, Tex.; Perry N. Dellelce, Toronto, Ont.; Buckley Ratchford, N.Y.; Rudolph Reinfrank, Calif.; Stephen Usher, Calif.
Other Exec. Officers - Matthias Ederer, co-pres.; Henry Wang, co-pres.; Jason T. Roos, CFO & corp. sec.; David Held, chief compliance officer
† Lead director

Capital Stock

	Authorized (shs.)	Outstanding (shs.)[1]
Preference	unlimited	nil
Common	unlimited	22,547,337

[1] At June 30, 2023

Major Shareholder - EJF Capital LLC and Neal J. Wilson held 11.27% interest at May 18, 2023.

Price Range - MLC/NEO

Year	Volume	High	Low	Close
2022	17,100	$4.04	$2.80	$3.00
2021	43,900	$4.21	$2.70	$4.00
2020	13,700	$3.40	$2.70	$2.90
2019	2,625	$4.08	$3.52	$3.84
2018	702,583	$6.96	$2.88	$3.68

Consolidation: 1-for-8 cons. in Dec. 2019
Recent Close: $2.55
Capital Stock Changes - There were no changes to capital stock during 2022.

Dividends

MLC com N.S.R.

$0.02	Aug. 31/23	$0.02	May 31/23
$0.02	Dec. 21/22	$0.02	June 24/22

Paid in 2023: $0.04 2022: $0.06 2021: $0.08

Wholly Owned Subsidiaries

Great Lakes Senior MLC I LLC, Del.
Lind Bridge GP Inc., Ont.
Lind Bridge LP, Cayman Islands.
- 100% int. in **Ability Insurance Company**, Omaha, Neb.
  - 100% int. in **Cornhusker Feeder LLC**, Del.
    - 100% int. in **Cornhusker Funding 1A LLC**, Del.
    - 100% int. in **Cornhusker Funding 1B LLC**, Del.
    - 100% int. in **Cornhusker Funding 1C LLC**, Del.

MLC US Holdings LLC, Del.
- 100% int. in **MLCSC Holdings Finance LLC**, Del.
  - 100% int. in **MLCSC Holdings LLC**, Del.
    - 24.99% int. in **Sierra Crest Investment Management LLC**, United States.
- 100% int. in **Mount Logan Management, LLC**, Del.

Financial Statistics

Periods ended:	12m Dec. 31/22[A]		12m Dec. 31/21[A]
	US$000s	%Chg	US$000s
Realized invest. gain (loss)	(3,873)		38
Unrealized invest. gain (loss)	(102,986)		(1,184)
Total revenue	**31,060**	**+168**	**11,579**
General & admin. expense	26,748		10,239
Operating expense	**26,748**	**+161**	**10,239**
Operating income	**4,312**	**+222**	**1,340**
Deprec. & amort.	559		787
Finance costs, gross	3,677		2,863
Pre-tax income	**18,636**	**-40**	**30,874**
Income taxes	430		2,144
Net income	**18,206**	**-37**	**28,730**
Cash & equivalent	1,525		14,433
Long-term investments	915,232		916,379
Intangibles	60,505		57,519
Total assets	**1,348,872**	**-3**	**1,393,311**
Accts. pay. & accr. liabs	29,676		10,337
Long-term debt, gross	55,422		44,958
Shareholders' equity	102,144		85,306
Cash from oper. activs	**118,795**	**n.a.**	**(56,467)**
Cash from fin. activs	8,741		(11,949)
Cash from invest. activs	(106,098)		88,659
Net cash position	**65,951**	**+49**	**44,301**
	US$		US$
Earnings per share*	0.82		1.55
Cash flow per share*	5.35		(3.04)
Net asset value per share*	4.60		3.84
Cash divd. per share*	$0.06		$0.08
	shs		shs
No. of shs. o/s*	22,190,195		22,190,195
Avg. no. of shs. o/s*	22,190,195		18,581,531
	%		%
Net profit margin	58.62		248.12
Return on equity	19.42		44.72
Return on assets	1.59		4.23
No. of employees (FTEs)	9		11

* Common
[A] Reported in accordance with IFRS

Latest Results

Periods ended:	6m June 30/23[A]		6m June 30/22[□A]
	US$000s	%Chg	US$000s
Total revenue	24,775	n.a.	(31,201)
Net income	(30,107)	n.a.	29,015
	US$		US$
Earnings per share*	(1.36)		1.31

* Common
[□] Restated
[A] Reported in accordance with IFRS

Historical Summary
(as originally stated)

Fiscal Year	Total Rev.	Net Inc. Bef. Disc.	EPS*
	US$000s	US$000s	US$
2022[A]	31,060	18,206	0.82
2021[A]	11,579	28,730	1.55
2020[A]	3,499	(2,805)	(0.24)
2019[A]	2,804	228	0.02
	$000s	$000s	$
2018[A]	1,973	(204)	(0.08)

* Common
[A] Reported in accordance with IFRS
Note: Adjusted throughout for 1-for-8 cons. in Dec. 2019

M.119 Mountain Valley MD Holdings Inc.

Symbol - MVMD **Exchange** - CSE **CUSIP** - 62430M
Head Office - 4-260 Edgeley Blvd, Concord, ON, L4K 3Y4 **Telephone** - (647) 725-9755
Website - www.mountainvalleymd.com
Email - dennis@mountainvalleymd.com
Investor Relations - Dennis Hancock (647) 725-9755
Auditors - PricewaterhouseCoopers LLP C.A., Vancouver, B.C.
Transfer Agents - Odyssey Trust Company, Vancouver, B.C.
Profile - (B.C. 2005) Develops and commercializing delivery, solubility and adjuvant technologies for pharmaceutical, vaccine and nutraceutical applications.
The company's technologies consist of the patented Quicksome oral drug formulation and delivery technologies; the patented Quicksol

solubility formulation technology; and the patent-pending porous aluminum nanostructure (PANA) adjuvant.

The Quicksome desiccation technology utilizes advanced liposomes and other stabilizing molecules in a two-step encapsulation and desiccation process to formulate normally un-bioavailable active ingredients into highly effective product formats that are consumed orally. This technology enables the company to develop products formulations that can deliver vaccines, drugs and nutraceuticals into the body faster, with greater impact, efficiency and accuracy.

The Quicksol technology utilizes an advanced solubilization technique to create injectable and liquid formulations. The technology has been applied to macrocyclic lactone drugs, ivermectin and selamectin, to produce water solubilized formulations, Ivectosol and Selactosol, respectively.

Together with the application of the Quicksome technology, Ivectosol is under various studies for COVID-19 in injectable format and as an oral sublingual tablet; as an injectable treatment of various parasites in husbandry animals; and for certain cancers, such as breast cancer, metastatic melanoma and Lewis lung carcinoma, through intratumoral injection and intravenous infusion. Selactosol is being evaluated in treating mycobacterium-based infections such as tuberculosis. Quicksome and Quicksol are also being formulated and tested for cannabinoid products, insulin and nutraceuticals.

PANA is a dose sparing adjuvant used in vaccines. Adjuvants are added to a vaccine to boost the immune response to produce more antibodies and longer-lasting immunity, thus minimizing the dose of antigen needed. PANA is being evaluated for vaccines against various infectious diseases, including polio.

Also holds right to resell Agrarius products, an organic product owned by **Agrarius Corp.** designed to be applied to agricultural crops to naturally increase yields, reduce fertilizer usage and increase resilience to pests and climate change.

Predecessor Detail - Name changed from Meadow Bay Gold Corporation, Feb. 21, 2020; basis 1 new for 8 old shs.

Directors - Dennis Hancock, chr., pres. & CEO, Ont.; Paul Lockhard, Ont.; Kevin Puloski, Ont.; Nancy Richardson, Ont.

Other Exec. Officers - Aaron Triplett, CFO & corp. sec.; Antonina Szaszkiewicz, legal counsel

Capital Stock

	Authorized (shs.)	Outstanding (shs.)[1]
Common	unlimited	329,653,424
Class B	50,056,229	50,056,229

[1] At Aug. 25, 2022

Common - One vote per share.

Class B - Non-voting.

Major Shareholder - Widely held at Aug. 25, 2022.

Price Range - MVMD/CSE

Year	Volume	High	Low	Close
2022	132,953,481	$0.30	$0.03	$0.04
2021	525,868,356	$2.29	$0.10	$0.10
2020	241,523,092	$0.72	$0.04	$0.45
2019	393,674	$0.44	$0.20	$0.28
2018	2,807,919	$2.88	$0.24	$0.24

Consolidation: 1-for-8 cons. in Mar. 2020

Recent Close: $0.04

Capital Stock Changes - During fiscal 2022, common shares were issued as follows: 885,000 on exercise of warrants, 600,000 on exercise of options and 258,958 for services.

Wholly Owned Subsidiaries

Mountain Valley MD Inc., Ont.
- 100% int. in **Colverde MD S.A.S.**, Colombia.
- 100% int. in **MVMD (Colombia) Inc.**, Ont.
- **Sixth Wave Innovations Inc.**, Bedford, N.S. (see separate coverage)

Investments

Circadian Wellness Corp., Ont.
Mexican Gold Mining Corp., Vancouver, B.C. (see Survey of Mines)
Nevada King Gold Corp., Vancouver, B.C. (see Survey of Mines)
Palisades Goldcorp Ltd., Vancouver, B.C. (see separate coverage)
Radio Fuels Energy Corp., Toronto, Ont. (see Survey of Mines)

Financial Statistics

Periods ended:	12m Mar. 31/22[A]		12m Mar. 31/21[oA]
	$000s	%Chg	$000s
Operating revenue	**110**	**n.a.**	**nil**
Cost of sales	40		n.a.
Research & devel. expense	2,209		1,362
General & admin expense	3,537		2,530
Stock-based compensation	3,615		840
Operating expense	**9,361**	**+98**	**4,732**
Operating income	**(9,251)**	**n.a.**	**(4,732)**
Deprec., depl. & amort.	451		430
Finance income	52		9
Finance costs, gross	nil		20
Investment income	336		(125)
Write-downs/write-offs	nil		(498)
Pre-tax income	**(9,709)**	**n.a.**	**(8,143)**
Net income	**(9,709)**	**n.a.**	**(8,143)**
Cash & equivalent	14,221		19,510
Current assets	15,071		21,077
Long-term investments	5,454		5,473
Fixed assets, net	227		289
Intangibles, net	4,518		4,769
Total assets	**25,270**	**-20**	**31,608**
Accts. pay. & accr. liabs.	238		776
Current liabilities	416		1,066
Long-term lease liabilities	6		44
Shareholders' equity	24,848		30,498
Cash from oper. activs.	**(5,587)**	**n.a.**	**(3,860)**
Cash from fin. activs.	395		21,777
Cash from invest. activs.	(98)		(149)
Net cash position	**14,221**	**-27**	**19,510**
Capital expenditures	nil		(333)
	$		$
Earnings per share*	(0.03)		(0.03)
Cash flow per share*	(0.02)		(0.01)
	shs		shs
No. of shs. o/s*	329,581,549		327,837,591
Avg. no. of shs. o/s*	329,236,773		263,510,981
	%		%
Net profit margin	n.m.		n.a.
Return on equity	(35.08)		n.m.
Return on assets	(34.14)		n.a.

* Common
[o] Restated
[A] Reported in accordance with IFRS

Latest Results

Periods ended:	3m June 30/22[A]		3m June 30/21[A]
	$000s	%Chg	$000s
Net income	(1,852)	n.a.	(2,128)
	$		$
Earnings per share*	(0.01)		(0.01)

* Common
[A] Reported in accordance with IFRS

Historical Summary
(as originally stated)

Fiscal Year	Oper. Rev.	Net Inc. Bef. Disc.	EPS*
	$000s	$000s	$
2022[A]	110	(9,709)	(0.03)
2021[A]	nil	(8,143)	(0.03)
2020[A1]	nil	(18,845)	(0.09)
2019[A2]	nil	(22,846)	(3.68)
2018[A]	nil	(962)	(0.24)

* Common
[A] Reported in accordance with IFRS
[1] Results reflect the Feb. 24, 2020, reverse takeover acquisition of Mountain Valley MD Inc.
[2] Results for fiscal 2019 and prior fiscal years pertain to Meadow Bay Gold Corporation.

Note: Adjusted throughout for 1-for-8 cons. in Mar. 2020

M.120 Mullen Group Ltd.*

Symbol - MTL **Exchange** - TSX **CUSIP** - 625284

Head Office - 121A-31 Southridge Dr, Okotoks, AB, T1S 2N3 **Telephone** - (403) 995-5200 **Toll-free** - (866) 995-7711 **Fax** - (403) 995-5296

Website - www.mullen-group.com

Email - sclark@mullen-group.com

Investor Relations - P. Stephen Clark (403) 995-5200

Auditors - PricewaterhouseCoopers LLP C.A., Calgary, Alta.

Bankers - Royal Bank of Canada, Calgary, Alta.

Lawyers - Dentons Canada LLP, Calgary, Alta.; Burnet, Duckworth & Palmer LLP, Calgary, Alta.

Transfer Agents - Computershare Trust Company of Canada Inc., Toronto, Ont.

FP500 Revenue Ranking - 221

Employees - 7,102 at Mar. 17, 2023

Profile - (Alta. 2009) Provides less-than-truckload, truckload, warehousing, logistics, transload, oversized, third party logistics and specialized hauling transportation services across North America, as well as specialized services including water management, fluid hauling and environmental reclamation to the energy, mining, forestry and construction industries in western Canada.

Operations are carried out through four business segments: Less-Than-Truckload; Logistics and Warehousing; Specialized and Industrial Services; and U.S. and International Logistics. The segments consist of 38 operating entities, each operating as a separate business, utilizing their own equipment and the services and equipment of owner-operators and dedicated subcontractors. At Dec. 31, 2022, the operating entities owned or leased 3,124 power units, had access to an additional 1,114 power units under contract with owner-operators or subcontractors, and owned or leased 9,004 trailers. In addition, the operating entities owned a fleet of truck-mounted drilling units, consisting of 30 hydraulic single rigs, 9 auger rigs and one dual rotary rig, 171 pieces of earthmoving equipment, 791 light duty vehicles and 652 skid and trailer mounted dri-prime diesel pumps, 713 submersible pumps, 148 portable diesel generators, 68 sediment control tanks, 19 fusion machines, 70 portable engineered barges, three portable dredges and 859 intermodal containers.

Less-Than-Truckload

Consists of 11 operating entities that offer final or last mile delivery of general freight consisting of smaller shipments, packages and parcels. Operations are carried out through indirect wholly owned **APPS Cartage Inc.**, **APPS Cargo Terminals Inc.**, **Argus Carriers Ltd.**, **West Direct Express Ltd.**, **Gardewine Group Limited Partnership**, **Grimshaw Trucking L.P.**, **Hi-Way 9 Express Ltd.**, **Jay's Transportation Group Ltd.**, **Number 8 Freight Ltd.**, **Pacific Coast Express Limited** and **1297683 Alberta Ltd.** (dba Willy's Trucking Service).

Logistics and Warehousing

Consists of 11 operating entities that provide trucking, warehousing and logistics services including full truckload, specialized transportation, fulfillment centres that handle e-commerce transactions and transload facilities for intermodal and bulk shipments. Operations are carried out through indirect wholly owned **Bandstra Transportation Systems Ltd.**, **Caneda Transport Ltd.**, **Cascade Carriers L.P.**, **DWS Logistics Inc.**, **International Warehousing & Distribution Inc.**, **Kleysen Group Ltd.**, **Mullen Trucking Corp.**, **Payne Transportation Ltd.**, **RDK Transportation Co. Inc.**, **Tenold Transportation Ltd.** and **Tri Point Intermodal Services Inc.**

Specialized and Industrial Services

Consists of 16 operating entities that provide specialized equipment and services to the natural resources, energy, infrastructure and construction sectors. Operations are carried out through indirect wholly owned **Babine Truck & Equipment Ltd.**, **Butler Ridge Energy Services (2011) Ltd.**, **Canadian Dewatering L.P.**, **Cascade Energy Services L.P.**, **Cordova Oilfield Services Ltd.**, **E-Can Oilfield Services L.P.**, **Envolve Energy Services Corp.**, **Formula Powell L.P.**, **Heavy Crude Hauling L.P.**, **Mullen Oilfield Services L.P.**, **OK Drilling Services L.P.**, **Premay Equipment L.P.**, **Premay Pipeline Hauling L.P.**, **Smook Contractors Ltd.**, **Spearing Service L.P.** and **TREO Drilling Services L.P.**

U.S. and International Logistics

Consists of operations of wholly owned **HAUListic LLC**, which provides logistics services through a combination of professional representatives and a network of independently owned and managed station agents, to more than 2,700 customers in the U.S. and Mexico, utilizing more than 6,000 certified sub-contractor carriers. HAUListic also owns SilverExpress, an integrated transportation management platform that provides real time information to customers and carriers, offering price and capacity discovery along with tracking and tracing capabilities.

On Mar. 1, 2023, the company acquired the remaining 68% interest in Hudson's Hope, B.C.-based **Butler Ridge Energy Services (2011) Ltd.** for $3,100,000, consisting of $2,000,000 cash and issuance of 57,180 common shares. Butler Ridge offers a comprehensive package of fluid management services to the energy sector in the Peace River region of British Columbia.

On Jan. 1, 2023, wholly owned **24/7 The Storehouse (2015) Ltd.** was integrated into the operations of wholly owned **APPS Cargo Terminals Inc.**

Recent Merger and Acquisition Activity

Status: completed **Announced:** May 1, 2023
Mullen Group Ltd. acquired Bonnyville, Alta.-based B. & R. Eckel's Transport Ltd. (B&R), a provider of freight and shipping services, including less-than-truckload, full deck and truckload, dry bulk trucking and hotshot service, as well as oilfield services such as transporting over dimensional and heavy-haul equipment in western Canada. B&R has a network of 16 facilities and operates a fleet of 400 power units and more than 950 trailers that generate annualized revenue of $85,000,000. Terms of the transaction were not disclosed.

Status: completed **Announced:** Dec. 15, 2022
Mullen Group Ltd. sold a real property that included an operating terminal and associated lands totaling 4.5 acres in Surrey, B.C., for $32,600,000.

Status: completed **Announced:** Dec. 12, 2022
Mullen Group Ltd. sold non-core hydrovac assets to Environmental 360 Solutions, Inc. for $16,500,000. The assets include the hydrovac assets and business operating out of Sherwood Park, Alta., under the former operating entity Canadian Hydrovac Ltd. and the hydrovac assets and business operating out of Hardisty, Alta., under the former operating entity Recon Utility Search L.P.

Status: completed **Announced:** Nov. 1, 2022
Mullen Group Ltd. acquired the remaining 66% interest in private Fort St. John, B.C.-based Cordova Oilfield Services Ltd. for $8,100,000,

consisting of $4,200,000 cash and issuance of 284,078 Mullen common shares. Cordova provides transportation, storage and inventory of oilfield fluids and oil country tubular goods in the Peace River region of British Columbia.

Status: completed **Announced:** May 1, 2022

Mullen Group Ltd. acquired private Edmonton, Alta.-based 1297683 Alberta Ltd. (dba Willy's Trucking Service) for $18,900,000 cash. Willy's Trucking Service provides regional less-than-truckload, general freight and logistic services across northern Alberta and northeastern British Columbia.

Directors - Murray K. Mullen, chr., pres. & CEO, Calgary, Alta.; Sonia Tibbatts†, Calgary, Alta.; Benoît Durand, Montréal-Ouest, Qué.; Stephen H. Lockwood, Calgary, Alta.; Christine E. (Chris) McGinley, Calgary, Alta.; David E. Mullen, Calgary, Alta.; Jamil Murji, Coquitlam, B.C.; Richard F. (Rick) Whitley, Calgary, Alta.

Other Exec. Officers - Carson P. Urlacher, CFO & contr.; Richard J. Maloney, sr. v-p; Lee Hellyer, v-p, opers.; Joanna K. Scott, v-p, corp. srvcs., gen. counsel & corp. sec.

† Lead director

Capital Stock

	Authorized (shs.)	Outstanding (shs.)[1]
Preferred	unlimited	nil
Common	unlimited	88,740,372

[1] At June 30, 2023

Options - At Dec. 31, 2022, options were outstanding to purchase 3,755,000 common shares at prices ranging from $10.15 to $28.07 per share (weighted average price of $16.47 per share) with a weighted average remaining contractual life of 5.33 years.

Normal Course Issuer Bid - The company plans to make normal course purchases of up to 8,644,508 common shares representing 10% of the public float. The bid commenced on Mar. 10, 2023, and expires on Mar. 9, 2024.

Major Shareholder - Widely held at Mar. 17, 2023.

Price Range - MTL/TSX

Year	Volume	High	Low	Close
2022	77,890,242	$15.98	$10.83	$14.55
2021	70,275,183	$14.48	$9.80	$11.63
2020	101,129,143	$11.84	$3.85	$10.90
2019	72,920,543	$13.00	$7.30	$9.27
2018	30,779,748	$16.93	$11.39	$12.21

Recent Close: $14.50

Capital Stock Changes - During 2022, 284,078 common shares were issued pursuant to the acquisition of Cordova Oilfield Services Ltd. and 1,863,251 common shares were repurchased under a Normal Course Issuer Bid.

Dividends

MTL com Ra $0.72 pa M est. June 15, 2022
Prev. Rate: $0.60 est. Feb. 15, 2022
Prev. Rate: $0.48 est. Aug. 16, 2021

Long-Term Debt - Outstanding at Dec. 31, 2022:

Notes payable due to 2026[1]	Cdn$481,810,000
5.75% conv. debs. due Nov. 2026[2]	115,806,000
	597,616,000
Less: Current portion	213,000
	597,403,000

[1] Consist of US$117,000,000 principal amount of 3.84% series G notes, Cdn$30,000,000 principal amount of 3.88% series I notes and Cdn$58,000,000 principal amount of 3.95% series K notes, all due Oct. 22, 2024; and US$112,000,000 principal amount of 3.94% series H notes, Cdn$3,000,000 principal amount of 4% series J notes and Cdn$80,000,000 principal amount of 4.07% series L notes, all due Oct. 22, 2026.

[2] Convertible into common shares at $14 per share. Equity component totaling $9,116,000 was classified as part of shareholders' equity.

Wholly Owned Subsidiaries

MT Investments Inc., Okotoks, Alta.
- 100% int. in **APPS Cargo Terminals Inc.**, Canada.
- 100% int. in **APPS Cartage Inc.**, Ont.
- 100% int. in **Argus Carriers Ltd.**, Burnaby, B.C.
- 100% int. in **Babine Truck & Equipment Ltd.**, Prince George, B.C.
- 100% int. in **Bandstra Transportation Systems Ltd.**, Smithers, B.C.
- 100% int. in **Butler Ridge Energy Services (2011) Ltd.**, Hudson's Hope, B.C.
- 100% int. in **Canadian Dewatering L.P.**, Edmonton, Alta.
- 100% int. in **Caneda Transport Inc.**, Calgary, Alta.
- 100% int. in **Cascade Carriers L.P.**, Calgary, Alta.
- 100% int. in **Cascade Energy Services L.P.**, Fort St. John, B.C.
- 100% int. in **Cordova Oilfield Services Ltd.**, Fort St. John, B.C.
- 100% int. in **DWS Logistics Inc.**, Mississauga, Ont.
- 100% int. in **E-Can Oilfield Services L.P.**, Elk Point, Alta.
- 100% int. in **Envolve Energy Services Corp.**, Grande Prairie, Alta.
- 100% int. in **Formula Powell L.P.**, Grande Prairie, Alta.
- 100% int. in **Gardewine Group Limited Partnership**, Winnipeg, Man.
- 100% int. in **Grimshaw Trucking L.P.**, Edmonton, Alta.
- 100% int. in **Heavy Crude Hauling L.P.**, Lloydminster, Alta.
- 100% int. in **Hi-Way 9 Express Ltd.**, Drumheller, Alta.
- 100% int. in **International Warehousing & Distribution Inc.**, Mississauga, Ont.
- 100% int. in **Jay's Transportation Group Ltd.**, Regina, Sask.
- 100% int. in **Kleysen Group Ltd.**, Alta.
- 100% int. in **MGL Holding Co. Ltd.**, Okotoks, Alta.
- 100% int. in **Mullen Oilfield Services L.P.**, Calgary, Alta.
- 100% int. in **Mullen Trucking Corp.**, Alta.
- 100% int. in **Number 8 Freight Ltd.**, B.C.
- 100% int. in **OK Drilling Services L.P.**, Red Deer, Alta.
- 100% int. in **1297683 Alberta Ltd.**, Edmonton, Alta. dba Willy's Trucking Service
- 100% int. in **Pacific Coast Express Limited**, Alta.
- 100% int. in **Payne Transportation Ltd.**, Alta.
- 100% int. in **Premay Equipment L.P.**, Edmonton, Alta.
- 100% int. in **Premay Pipeline Hauling L.P.**, Edmonton, Alta.
- 100% int. in **RDK Transportation Co. Inc.**, Saskatoon, Sask.
- 100% int. in **Smook Contractors Ltd.**, Thompson, Man.
- 100% int. in **Spearing Service L.P.**, Alta.
- 100% int. in **TREO Drilling Services L.P.**, Calgary, Alta.
- 100% int. in **Tenold Transportation Ltd.**, Alta.
- 100% int. in **Tri Point Intermodal Services Inc.**, Mississauga, Ont.
- 100% int. in **West Direct Express Ltd.**, Calgary, Alta.

MTL U.S. Corp., Wilmington, Del.
- 100% int. in **HAUListic LLC**, Naperville, Ill.

Investments

Kriska Transportation Group Limited, Prescott, Ont.
Thrive Management Group Ltd., Staten Island, N.Y.

Financial Statistics

Periods ended:	12m Dec. 31/22[A]		12m Dec. 31/21[A]
	$000s	%Chg	$000s
Operating revenue	**1,999,453**	**+35**	**1,477,434**
Other operating expense	1,669,564		1,241,056
Operating expense	**1,669,564**	**+35**	**1,241,056**
Operating income	**329,889**	**+40**	**236,378**
Deprec., depl. & amort.	112,513		113,964
Finance income	395		422
Finance costs, gross	35,462		30,827
Investment income	8,550		1,657
Pre-tax income	**210,881**	**+120**	**95,995**
Income taxes	52,262		23,559
Net income	**158,619**	**+119**	**72,436**
Cash & equivalent	8,757		nil
Inventories	42,035		35,121
Accounts receivable	284,899		248,868
Current assets	360,324		309,109
Long-term investments	45,570		38,518
Fixed assets, net	981,624		985,971
Right-of-use assets	87,756		78,032
Intangibles, net	465,619		457,881
Total assets	**1,996,131**	**+4**	**1,921,996**
Bank indebtedness	22,800		89,045
Accts. pay. & accr. liabs	151,023		144,198
Current liabilities	219,991		258,306
Long-term debt, gross	597,616		575,017
Long-term debt, net	597,403		574,963
Long-term lease liabilities	70,871		63,363
Equity portion of conv. debs	9,116		9,116
Shareholders' equity	973,397		888,664
Cash from oper. activs	**262,970**	**+33**	**197,967**
Cash from fin. activs	(215,137)		(46,285)
Cash from invest. activs	(36,993)		(255,594)
Net cash position	**8,757**	**n.a.**	**nil**
Capital expenditures	(81,410)		(68,204)
Capital disposals	48,604		20,746
	$		$
Earnings per share*	1.70		0.75
Cash flow per share*	2.82		2.06
Cash divd. per share*	0.68		0.48
	shs		shs
No. of shs. o/s*	92,953,005		94,532,178
Avg. no. of shs. o/s*	93,351,897		96,068,715
	%		%
Net profit margin	7.93		4.90
Return on equity	17.04		8.12
Return on assets	9.46		5.26
Foreign sales percent	11		8
No. of employees (FTEs)	7,107		7,202

* Common
[A] Reported in accordance with IFRS

Latest Results

Periods ended:	6m June 30/23[A]		6m June 30/22[A]
	$000s	%Chg	$000s
Operating revenue	992,108	+7	928,437
Net income	68,212	+16	59,054
	$		$
Earnings per share*	0.75		0.63

* Common
[A] Reported in accordance with IFRS

Historical Summary
(as originally stated)

Fiscal Year	Oper. Rev.	Net Inc. Bef. Disc.	EPS*
	$000s	$000s	$
2022[A]	1,999,453	158,619	1.70
2021[A]	1,477,434	72,436	0.75
2020[A]	1,164,331	63,979	0.64
2019[A]	1,278,502	72,241	0.69
2018[A]	1,260,798	(43,787)	(0.42)

* Common
[A] Reported in accordance with IFRS

M.121 Must Capital Inc.

Symbol - MUST.H **Exchange** - TSX-VEN **CUSIP** - 62818R
Head Office - 218-20 Great Cuff Dr, Vaughan, ON, L4K 0K7
Email - mike@pacwest.ca
Investor Relations - Michele N. Marrandino (604) 722-5225
Auditors - Dale Matheson Carr-Hilton LaBonte LLP C.A., Vancouver, B.C.
Lawyers - WeirFoulds LLP, Toronto, Ont.
Transfer Agents - TSX Trust Company, Toronto, Ont.
Profile - (Ont. 2010) Seeking new business opportunities.
Predecessor Detail - Name changed from Intrinsic4D Inc., Jan. 29, 2019; basis 1 new for 25 old shs.
Directors - Michael Feola, chr., Montréal, Qué.; Michele N. (Mike) Marrandino, pres. & CEO, Vancouver, B.C.; Vikas Ranjan, Toronto, Ont.; Bradley N. (Brad) Scharfe, Vancouver, B.C.
Other Exec. Officers - Cale Thomas, CFO & corp. sec.

Capital Stock

	Authorized (shs.)	Outstanding (shs.)[1]
Common	unlimited	27,564,812

[1] At Aug. 19, 2022

Major Shareholder - Jason D. Meretsky held 11.52% interest, Vikas Ranjan held 10.77% interest and Bradley N. (Brad) Scharfe held 10.77% interest at June 12, 2019.

Price Range - MUST.H/TSX-VEN

Year	Volume	High	Low	Close
2022	339,541	$0.09	$0.04	$0.07
2021	531,145	$0.15	$0.08	$0.09
2020	775,958	$0.09	$0.07	$0.09
2019	715,676	$0.25	$0.06	$0.11
2018	314,401	$1.63	$0.13	$0.25

Consolidation: 1-for-25 cons. in Jan. 2019
Recent Close: $0.07

Financial Statistics

Periods ended:	12m Dec. 31/21[A]		12m Dec. 31/20[A]
	$000s	%Chg	$000s
General & admin expense	162		89
Operating expense	**162**	**+82**	**89**
Operating income	**(162)**	**n.a.**	**(89)**
Pre-tax income	**(162)**	**n.a.**	**(85)**
Net income	**(162)**	**n.a.**	**(85)**
Cash & equivalent	518		15
Current assets	518		20
Total assets	**518**	**n.m.**	**20**
Accts. pay. & accr. liabs	6		79
Current liabilities	6		79
Shareholders' equity	511		(58)
Cash from oper. activs	**(229)**	**n.a.**	**(55)**
Cash from fin. activs	731		nil
Net cash position	**518**	**n.m.**	**15**
	$		$
Earnings per share*	(0.01)		(0.00)
Cash flow per share*	(0.01)		(0.00)
	shs		shs
No. of shs. o/s*	27,564,812		20,064,812
Avg. no. of shs. o/s*	25,407,278		20,064,812
	%		%
Net profit margin	n.a.		n.a.
Return on equity	n.m.		n.m.
Return on assets	(60.22)		(182.80)

* Common
[A] Reported in accordance with IFRS

Latest Results

Periods ended:	6m June 30/22[A]		6m June 30/21[A]
	$000s	%Chg	$000s
Net income	(50)	n.a.	(119)
	$		$
Earnings per share*	(0.00)		(0.01)

* Common
[A] Reported in accordance with IFRS

Historical Summary
(as originally stated)

Fiscal Year	Oper. Rev.	Net Inc. Bef. Disc.	EPS*
	$000s	$000s	$
2021A	nil	(162)	(0.01)
2020A	nil	(85)	(0.00)
2019A	nil	(333)	(0.03)
2018A	nil	(587)	(0.17)
	US$000s	US$000s	US$
2017A	nil	(1,131)	(0.50)

* Common
A Reported in accordance with IFRS
Note: Adjusted throughout for 1-for-25 cons. in Jan. 2019

M.122 MustGrow Biologics Corp.

Symbol - MGRO **Exchange** - TSX-VEN **CUSIP** - 62822A
Head Office - 1005-201 1 Ave S, Saskatoon, SK, S7K 1J5 **Telephone** - (306) 668-2652 **Fax** - (306) 651-1931
Website - www.mustgrow.ca
Email - cgiasson@sasktel.net
Investor Relations - Corey J. Giasson (306) 668-2652
Auditors - Ernst & Young LLP C.A., Saskatoon, Sask.
Transfer Agents - Computershare Trust Company of Canada Inc., Vancouver, B.C.
Profile - (Sask. 2018; orig. B.C., 2014) Develops and commercializes mustard-derived crop protection products and technologies for control of soil-borne diseases and pests.
Products use AITC (allyl isothiocyanate) and thiocyanate, which are non-synthetic compounds that form part of the mustard (Brassica) plant's defence mechanism against disease, pests and weeds. These natural compounds and molecules are extracted from the mustard seed and are formulated in a dry and liquid form for use as a commercial biopesticide, biofumigant and bioherbicide. The company owns issued patents and patent applications covering the extraction, formulation and use of these natural compounds. The company previously commercialized a technology that used AITC from mustard seed as a biopesticide that is in granule format. The product is approved for use across a number of U.S. states and approved by Health Canada as a biopesticide for high value crops such as fruit and vegetables. The company is seeking regulatory approval for a more concentrated, liquid formula appropriate for use in typical chemical application systems such as drip lines, sprayers and shank under the brand TerraMG™.
The company is also developing an organic mustard-based soil amendment and biofertility technology under the brand Terasante™ which contain nutritious plant proteins and carbohydrates that feed soil microbes to improve beneficial microbial activity and ensure long-term sustainable soil health.
During 2022, the company's biofungicide product under the brand CannaPM™ was discontinued. CannaPM™ is a powdery mildew biofungicide that contains Streptomyces lydicus WYEC 108, a beneficial bacteria and natural enemy of fungal pathogens.
On Mar. 31, 2022, wholly owned **MustGrow Biologics Columbia S.A.S.** was wound up.
Common delisted from CSE, Nov. 14, 2022.
Common listed on TSX-VEN, Nov. 11, 2022.
Directors - Bradley R. (Brad) Munro, chr., Saskatoon, Sask.; Corey J. Giasson, pres. & CEO, Saskatoon, Sask.; Colin Bletsky, COO, Saskatoon, Sask.; David Borecky, San Francisco, Calif.; Thomas (Tom) Flow, Kelowna, B.C.; Matt Kowalski, Spring, Tex.; Laura Westby, Minn.
Other Exec. Officers - Todd L. Lahti, CFO & corp. sec.

Capital Stock

	Authorized (shs.)	Outstanding (shs.)[1]
Common	unlimited	49,677,755

[1] At Mar. 31, 2023
Major Shareholder - Widely held at May 23, 2023.

Price Range - MGRO/TSX-VEN

Year	Volume	High	Low	Close
2022	10,007,120	$4.25	$2.36	$3.54
2021	24,020,046	$5.60	$1.26	$3.99
2020	28,822,036	$1.29	$0.25	$1.25
2019	6,111,968	$0.70	$0.25	$0.52

Recent Close: $1.60
Capital Stock Changes - During 2022 common shares were issued as follows: 1,850,000 on exercise of warrants and 25,000 on exercise of options.

Financial Statistics

Periods ended:	12m Dec. 31/22A		12m Dec. 31/21oA
	$000s	%Chg	$000s
Operating revenue	**6**	**-54**	**13**
Research & devel. expense	476		458
General & admin expense	3,521		2,296
Stock-based compensation	1,695		271
Operating expense	**5,692**	**+88**	**3,025**
Operating income	**(5,686)**	**n.a.**	**(3,012)**
Finance income	104		3
Finance costs, gross	10		53
Pre-tax income	**(5,566)**	**n.a.**	**(3,064)**
Net income	**(5,566)**	**n.a.**	**(3,064)**
Cash & equivalent	7,016		9,620
Current assets	7,134		9,702
Total assets	**7,134**	**-26**	**9,702**
Accts. pay. & accr. liabs.	222		496
Current liabilities	1,540		863
Long-term debt, gross	759		749
Long-term debt, net	355		382
Shareholders' equity	5,239		8,457
Cash from oper. activs.	**(3,258)**	**n.a.**	**(2,412)**
Cash from fin. activs.	654		8,719
Net cash position	**7,016**	**-27**	**9,620**
	$		$
Earnings per share*	(0.11)		(0.07)
Cash flow per share*	(0.07)		(0.06)
	shs		shs
No. of shs. o/s*	49,659,237		47,784,237
Avg. no. of shs. o/s*	49,010,264		43,736,196
	%		%
Net profit margin	n.m.		n.m.
Return on equity	(81.28)		(56.84)
Return on assets	(66.00)		(46.06)

* Common
o Restated
A Reported in accordance with IFRS

Latest Results

Periods ended:	3m Mar. 31/23A		3m Mar. 31/22A
	$000s	%Chg	$000s
Operating revenue	nil	n.a.	1
Net income	(1,046)	n.a.	(1,010)
	$		$
Earnings per share*	(0.02)		(0.02)

* Common
A Reported in accordance with IFRS

Historical Summary
(as originally stated)

Fiscal Year	Oper. Rev.	Net Inc. Bef. Disc.	EPS*
	$000s	$000s	$
2022A	6	(5,566)	(0.11)
2021A	13	(3,064)	(0.07)
2020A	nil	(3,310)	(0.09)
2019A	nil	(1,518)	(0.06)
2018A	2	(1,893)	(0.09)

* Common
A Reported in accordance with IFRS

M.123 Mydecine Innovations Group Inc.

Symbol - MYCO **Exchange** - NEO **CUSIP** - 62849F
Head Office - 810-789 Pender St W, Vancouver, BC, V6C 1H2 **Telephone** - (250) 488-6728 **Toll-free** - (888) 871-3936
Website - mydecine.com
Email - jbartch@mydecineinc.com
Investor Relations - D. Joshua Bartch (888) 871-3936
Auditors - BF Borgers CPA PC C.P.A., Lakewood, Colo.
Lawyers - Miller Thomson LLP, Toronto, Ont.
Transfer Agents - National Securities Administrators Ltd., Vancouver, B.C.
Profile - (B.C. 2013) Develops psychedelic therapies and a telehealth platform for mental health problems and wellbeing.
Drug Development - Researches and develops novel drug candidates based on psychedelic compounds, primarily psilocybin, for the treatment of mental health disorders. Lead candidates include MYCO-001, a pure psilocybin under various Phase II clinical trials for post traumatic stress disorder (PTSD) and smoking addiction; MYCO-002 (pre-clinical), a reduced harm entactogenic compound for PTSD and anxiety; MYCO-003 (pre-clinical), a psilocybin-based formula with reduced anxiety serotonin releasing agent for PTSD and anxiety; and MYCO-004 (pre-clinical), a patch delivered tryptamine compound for substance use disorder and smoking cessation.
The company has partnered with Applied Pharmaceutical Innovation (API) to cultivate, extract, conduct research and development, import and export psilocybin and other tryptamines at API's pharmaceutical manufacturing facility in Alberta. The company also operates a mycology lab in Denver, Colo., focused on developing proprietary technology for the company's drug candidates and genetic research for cultivation of rare medicinal mushrooms.
Digital Health Platform - Operates the Mindleap mobile application which provides services for mental health and wellbeing such as psychedelic integration services, including psychedelic aftercare and wellness services.
In September 2022, the company entered into a letter of intent to sell wholly owned **Mindleap Health Inc.**, which operates the Mindleap mobile application which provides services for mental health and wellbeing, to **PanGenomic Health Inc.** for issuance of 20,000,000 units (1 class A common share & 1 warrant) at 20¢ per unit, with warrants exercisable at 30¢ per share for two years.

Recent Merger and Acquisition Activity

Status: completed **Revised:** Dec. 12, 2022
UPDATE: The transaction was completed. PREVIOUS: PanGenomic Health Inc. agreed to acquire Mydecine Innovations Group, Inc.'s wholly owned Mindleap Health Inc., a telehealth platform for psychedelic integration available on the iOS and Android mobile stores, for $3,600,000 payable by the issuance of units (1 class common share & 1 warrant) at $0.20, with warrants exercisable at $0.30 per share for two years. Upon Closing, Mydecine was expected to hold 19.4% of the issued and outstanding common shares of PanGenomic.
Predecessor Detail - Name changed from NewLeaf Brands Inc., June 5, 2020.
Directors - D. Joshua Bartch, chr., pres. & CEO; Robert (Rob) Roscow, chief science officer, Colo.
Other Exec. Officers - Damon Michaels, COO; John C. Ross, CFO & corp. sec.; Dr. Rakesh Jetly, CMO; Michel Rudolphie, pres., European opers.

Capital Stock

	Authorized (shs.)	Outstanding (shs.)[1]
Common	unlimited	24,942,320

[1] At May 15, 2023
Major Shareholder - Widely held at June 3, 2022.

Price Range - MYCO/NEO

Year	Volume	High	Low	Close
2022	817,650	$14.50	$0.42	$0.50
2021	2,981,484	$32.50	$6.50	$6.75
2020	5,827,285	$57.50	$2.00	$21.25
2019	226,615	$157.50	$6.50	$6.75
2018	426,303	$832.50	$101.25	$135.00

Consolidation: 1-for-50 cons. in Apr. 2022; 1-for-45 cons. in Apr. 2019
Recent Close: $0.18
Capital Stock Changes - On Apr. 21, 2022, common shares were consolidated on a 1-for-50 basis.

Wholly Owned Subsidiaries

Mindleap Health Inc., Vancouver, B.C.
Mydecine Group, B.C. dba Mydecine Group.
NeuroPharm Inc., Toronto, Ont.

M.124 MyndTec Inc.

Symbol - MYTC **Exchange** - CSE **CUSIP** - 62858B
Head Office - 122-1900 Minnesota Crt, Mississauga, ON, L5N 3C9 **Telephone** - (905) 363-0564 **Toll-free** - (888) 363-0581 **Fax** - (877) 796-4624
Website - www.myndtec.com
Email - craig.leon@myndtec.com
Investor Relations - Craig Leon (416) 569-0430
Auditors - MNP LLP C.A., Mississauga, Ont.
Transfer Agents - Marrelli Trust Company Limited, Vancouver, B.C.
Profile - (Ont. 2008) Developing and commercializing non-invasive neurological and nervous system electrical stimulation therapeutics for the treatment of neurological diseases and injury.
The company's first product, MyndMove, is a proprietary non-invasive functional electrical stimulation based intervention. The device is an U.S. FDA and Heath Canada approved product that restores voluntary movement to stroke and spinal cord injury patients. MyndMove applies advanced principles of neuroplasticity and functional electrical stimulation to assist patients with paralysis of the arm and hand to make lasting gains in the recovery of natural, voluntary movement. MyndMove's first indications are for paralysis caused by stroke and spinal cord injury. In Canada and the United States, the company loans on a service fee basis and sells MyndMove directly to clinics and institutions. Has also developed a variation of the device, called MyndSearch, that has been modified for research purposes.
Directors - Dr. Milos R. Popovic, co-founder, Ont.; Craig Leon, CEO, Toronto, Ont.; Dr. Harvey Griggs, Ont.; William J. (Bill) Jackson, Hamilton, Ont.; Richard Widgren, Mich.
Other Exec. Officers - Scott W. Franklin, CFO & corp. sec.; Ronald Kurtz, v-p, eng.

Capital Stock

	Authorized (shs.)	Outstanding (shs.)[1]
Common	unlimited	22,601,432

[1] At May 11, 2023
Major Shareholder - Life Beyond Barriers, LLC held 22.6% interest, Dr. Harvey Griggs held 20.7% interest and Milos And Kathrin Inc. held 10.7% interest at May 11, 2023.

Price Range - MYTC/CSE

Year	Volume	High	Low	Close
2022	2,000	$0.95	$0.90	$0.90

Recent Close: $0.70

N

N.1 NAVCO Pharmaceuticals Inc.

Symbol - NAV **Exchange** - TSX-VEN **CUSIP** - 63942R
Head Office - 600-1090 Georgia St W, Vancouver, BC, V6E 3V7 **Telephone** - (604) 861-8980
Investor Relations - Geoffrey Lee (604) 861-8980
Auditors - Dale Matheson Carr-Hilton LaBonte LLP C.A., Vancouver, B.C.
Transfer Agents - Computershare Trust Company of Canada Inc., Vancouver, B.C.
Profile - (B.C. 2018) Manufactures and researches nanotechnology products and materials using computerized nano-meter algorithms to protect against viruses, bacteria and infectious diseases. These products have applications in the medical, textile, chemical and additive industries.

The company's products are tailored to defend against microorganisms such as viruses, bacteria, fungi and genetic manipulation tools such as clustered regularly interspaced short palindromic repeats. The product line consists of NAVCO Nano Silver, which is for surfaces, clothes, doorknobs and even skin; NAVCO Hand Cream, an alcohol-free hand sanitizing cream; NAVCO Sanitizer, a non-alcohol hand sanitizer; and NAVCO Spray, a aerosol spray which can be used on walkways, hallways, countertops and many other surfaces to protect against micrqrganisms. The company plans to distribute and sell the products through distributors, to consumers through social media channels, to retailers for sale to their customers, and directly to the general public.

Recent Merger and Acquisition Activity

Status: completed **Revised:** Apr. 13, 2023
UPDATE: The transaction was completed. PREVIOUS: BMGB Capital Corp. entered into a letter of intent for the Qualifying Transaction reverse takeover acquisition of private Burlington, Ont.-based NAVCO Pharmaceuticals Limited for issuance of up to 14,500,000 BMHB common shares at a deemed price of 30¢ per share. NAVCO manufactures and researches nano-technology products and materials using Computerized Nano-meter Algorithms (CAN). Oct. 28, 2020 - The transaction was amended whereby BMGB would acquire NAVCO through the issuance of 21,340,000 BMGB common shares at a deemed price of 25¢ per share. Jan. 18, 2021 - The parties entered into a share exchange agreement.

Predecessor Detail - Name changed from BMGB Capital Corp., pursuant to the Qualifying Transaction reverse takeover acquisition of NAVCO Pharmaceuticals Limited.
Directors - Geoffrey (Geoff) Lee, CEO, Vancouver, B.C.; Marek Jasinski, COO, Burlington, Ont.; Thomas Jusdanis, corp. sec., Hamilton, Ont.; Peter Espig, Vancouver, B.C.; Dr. Akbar Khan, Scarborough, Ont.
Other Exec. Officers - Christopher R. (Chris) Cooper, CFO

Capital Stock

	Authorized (shs.)	Outstanding (shs.)[1]
Common	unlimited	40,350,441

[1] At Apr. 18, 2023

Major Shareholder - Marek Jasinski held 14.22% interest at Apr. 18, 2023.

Price Range - NAV/TSX-VEN

Year	Volume	High	Low	Close
2020	34,000	$0.15	$0.10	$0.10
2019	3,000	$0.17	$0.17	$0.17
2018	87,000	$0.20	$0.15	$0.16

Recent Close: $0.03
Capital Stock Changes - In April 2023, 21,340,000 common shares were issued pursuant to the Qualifying Transaction reverse takeover acquisition of NAVCO Pharmaceuticals Limited and private placement of 14,070,441 units (1 common share & 1 warrant) at 15¢ per unit was completed, with warrants exercisable at 25¢ per share for two years.

There were no changes to capital stock of BMGB Capital Corp. during fiscal 2022.

Wholly Owned Subsidiaries

NAVCO Pharmaceuticals Limited, Burlington, Ont.

N.2 NEO Battery Materials Ltd.

Symbol - NBM **Exchange** - TSX-VEN **CUSIP** - 62908A
Head Office - 700-838 Hastings St W, Vancouver, BC, V6C 0A6 **Telephone** - (604) 681-2626 **Fax** - (604) 646-8088
Website - www.neobatterymaterials.com
Email - shuh@neobatterymaterials.com
Investor Relations - Sung Bum Huh (604) 697-2408
Auditors - De Visser Gray LLP C.A., Vancouver, B.C.
Lawyers - McMillan LLP, Vancouver, B.C.
Transfer Agents - Computershare Trust Company of Canada Inc., Vancouver, B.C.
Profile - (Ont. 2023; orig. B.C., 2006) Develops silicon materials for lithium-ion batteries in electric vehicles, and operates in Canada and South Korea.

The company, together with Yonsei University, has developed a nanotechnology process to produce silicon anode materials for electric vehicles' lithium-ion batteries. The company launched its product named NBMSiDE™, which is manufactured based on the use of nanocoating technology for increasing energy density and life span of LiBs in electric vehicles, consumer electronics and energy storage applications.

The company is building a 107,000-sq.-ft. commercial plant in South Korea for mass production of NBMSiDE™. The plant would be capable of supplying silicon anodes to up to 160,000 electric vehicles. The company is engaged in business development and relationship building initiatives to also market the company's core silicon anode materials in the United States.

In March 2023, the company continued into Ontario from British Columbia.

On Nov. 30, 2022, Golden silicon prospect in British Columbia and Chanape and Pucacorral copper-gold-silver prospects in Peru were abandoned and related costs written off.

In November 2022, the company completed a change of business from a mining issuer to a technology issuer with a focus on developing electric vehicle lithium-ion battery materials.

Predecessor Detail - Name changed from Pan Andean Minerals Ltd., Mar. 8, 2021.
Directors - Sung Bum (Spencer) Huh, pres. & CEO, Toronto, Ont.; Dr. Jong Hyeok Park, chief science officer; Christopher (Chris) Chung, sr. v-p, fin., Vancouver, B.C.; Sung Rock Hwang, sr. v-p & COO; Roberto (Rob) Fia, Toronto, Ont.; John M. Kowalchuk, Vancouver, B.C.; Larry M. Okada, Burnaby, B.C.
Other Exec. Officers - Nancy Zhao, CFO; Dr. S. G. Kim, chief tech. officer; Dr. Basudev Swain, chief science officer; Dong Wha Cho, v-p, corp. fin., Korean market; Ryan T. Kim, v-p, corp. devel.; Gunmin Park, v-p, corp. strategies; Jacqueline A. Collins, corp. sec.

Capital Stock

	Authorized (shs.)	Outstanding (shs.)[1]
Preferred	unlimited	nil
Common	unlimited	101,170,646

[1] At June 26, 2023

Major Shareholder - Widely held at Jan. 20, 2023.

Price Range - NBM/TSX-VEN

Year	Volume	High	Low	Close
2022	46,235,272	$0.55	$0.12	$0.22
2021	208,386,196	$1.31	$0.08	$0.39
2020	1,239,500	$0.10	$0.08	$0.09
2019	15,361,963	$0.10	$0.03	$0.09
2018	13,790,471	$0.13	$0.03	$0.04

Recent Close: $0.35
Capital Stock Changes - During fiscal 2023, common shares were issued as follows: 1,878,333 on exercise of options and 1,399,999 on exercise of warrants.

Wholly Owned Subsidiaries

Circum Pacific Holdings Ltd., B.C.
- 100% int. in **Cima de Oro S.A.C.**, Peru.
- 100% int. in **Minera Chanape S.A.C.**, Peru.

NEO Battery Materials America LLC, Del.
Neo Battery Materials America Ltd., United States.

Subsidiaries

60% int. in **Neo Battery Materials Korea Co., Ltd.**, South Korea.

Investments

Pembridge Resources plc, United Kingdom.

Financial Statistics

Periods ended:	12m Feb. 28/23[A]	%Chg	12m Feb. 28/22[□A]
	$000s	%Chg	$000s
Salaries & benefits	490		46
Research & devel. expense	305		133
Exploration expense	nil		13
General & admin expense	1,062		1,138
Stock-based compensation	nil		683
Operating expense	**1,856**	**-8**	**2,012**
Operating income	**(1,856)**	**n.a.**	**(2,012)**
Deprec., depl. & amort.	113		74
Finance income	1		nil
Finance costs, gross	2		81
Write-downs/write-offs	(1)		nil
Pre-tax income	**(1,915)**	**n.a.**	**(2,065)**
Net income	**(1,915)**	**n.a.**	**(2,065)**
Net inc. for equity hldrs	**(1,610)**	**n.a.**	**(2,065)**
Net inc. for non-cont. int	**(306)**	**n.a.**	**nil**
Cash & equivalent	1,629		1,256
Accounts receivable	23		21
Current assets	1,752		1,439
Fixed assets, net	554		181
Right-of-use assets	nil		10
Intangibles, net	55		49
Explor./devel. properties	nil		1
Total assets	**3,128**	**+81**	**1,724**
Accts. pay. & accr. liabs	179		166
Current liabilities	179		178
Shareholders' equity	1,891		1,546
Non-controlling interest	1,058		nil
Cash from oper. activs	**(1,766)**	**n.a.**	**(1,480)**
Cash from fin. activs	3,306		2,297
Cash from invest. activs	(1,162)		(195)
Net cash position	**1,626**	**+30**	**1,248**
Capital expenditures	(480)		(177)
	$		$
Earnings per share*	(0.02)		(0.02)
Cash flow per share*	(0.02)		(0.02)
	shs		shs
No. of shs. o/s*	100,803,979		97,525,647
Avg. no. of shs. o/s*	98,324,449		87,949,916
	%		%
Net profit margin	n.a.		n.a.
Return on equity	(95.01)		n.m.
Return on assets	(79.66)		(160.65)

* Common
□ Restated
[A] Reported in accordance with IFRS

Historical Summary
(as originally stated)

Fiscal Year	Oper. Rev.	Net Inc. Bef. Disc.	EPS*
	$000s	$000s	$
2023[A]	nil	(1,915)	(0.02)
2022[A]	nil	(2,079)	(0.02)
2021[A]	nil	(1,657)	(0.02)
2020[A]	nil	(1,089)	(0.02)
2019[A]	nil	(3,813)	(0.08)

* Common
[A] Reported in accordance with IFRS

N.3 NFI Group Inc.*

Symbol - NFI **Exchange** - TSX **CUSIP** - 62910L
Head Office - 711 Kernaghan Ave, Winnipeg, MB, R2C 3T4 **Telephone** - (204) 224-1251 **Fax** - (204) 224-4214
Website - www.nfigroup.com
Email - stephen.king@nfigroup.com
Investor Relations - Stephen King (204) 224-6382
Auditors - Deloitte LLP C.A., Winnipeg, Man.
Lawyers - Torys LLP, Toronto, Ont.
Transfer Agents - Computershare Trust Company of Canada Inc., Toronto, Ont.
FP500 Revenue Ranking - 180
Employees - 7,700 at Jan. 1, 2023
Profile - (Ont. 2005) Provides scalable smart mobility solutions including zero-emission electric mobility buses and coaches, charging infrastructure installation, telematics technology, and aftermarket full parts and services for public and private customers worldwide.

Manufactures zero-emission buses, heavy-duty transit buses, single and double-deck buses, medium-duty buses, low-floor cutaway buses and motor coaches, and provides aftermarket parts and services for public and private customers worldwide.

Provides mass transportation solutions under several brands: New Flyer® (heavy-duty transit buses), Alexander Dennis Limited (single and double-deck buses), Plaxton (motor coaches), ARBOC® (low-floor cutaway and medium-duty buses), MCI® (motor coaches) and NFI Parts™ (bus and coach parts, support and service). The company's vehicles incorporate the widest range of drive systems available ranging from clean diesel, natural gas, diesel-electric hybrid, trolley-electric, battery-electric and fuel cell electric.

Major facilities are located in Anniston, Ala., Crookston, Minn., Jamestown, N.Y., St. Cloud, Minn., Winnipeg, Man., Arnprior, Ont., Blackwood, N.J., Dallas Tex., Des Plaines, Ill., Montreal, Que., Renton, Wash., and San Francisco, Calif. for the New Flyer® brand; Anston, Falkirk, Franborough, Harlow, Larbert, Skelmersdale and Scarborough, U.K., Dublin, Ireland, Ballymena, Northern Ireland, Ciudad de Mexico, Mexico, Berlin, Germany, Kowloon, Hong Kong, The People's Republic of China (PRC), Auckland, New Zealand, and Singapore, for the Alexander Dennis Limited brand; Middlebury, Ind., for the ARBOC® brand; Crookston, Minn., Dallas, Tex., Pembina, N.D., Winnipeg, Man., Blackwood, N.J., Des Plaines, Ill., Montreal, Que., Arnprior, Ont., Renton, Wash., and San Francisco, Calif. for the MCI® brand; Fresno, Calif., Winnipeg, Man., Brampton, Ont., Delaware, Ohio, East Brunswick, N.J. and Louisville, Ky., for the NFI Parts™ brand. Manufacturing facilities for heavy-duty and medium-duty transit bus and motor coach in North America are ISO 9001 certified. Manufacturing facilities for heavy-duty transit bus are also ISO 14001 and ISO 45001 certified. Also has build partner facilities in Zhuhai, PRC, and Tauranga, New Zealand.

At Jan. 1, 2023, the company's total backlog, which includes buses and coaches to be manufactured in 2022 and future years, was 9,186 equivalent units (8,448 at Jan. 2, 2022), including US$2.515 billion in firm orders and US$3.123 billion in options.

In January 2023, the company finalized agreements with **Manitoba Development Corporation**, a financial services organization, for a US$37,000,000 debt facility and with **Export Development Canada** (EDC), an export credit agency, for US$50,000,000 debt facility and surety and performance bonding requirements for new contracts for up to US$100,000,000. The debt facilities both have one-year terms with options to extend for up to an aditional 24 months and the EDC bonding support facility has a one-year term for each new contract. Interest payments under these facilities are based on base rate plus applicable margin.

In November 2022, the company introduced the first Enviro400FCEV, a next-generation zero-emission hydrogen double deck bus.

In September 2022, the company introduced D45 Commuter Rapid Transit (CRT) CHARGE™, a zero-emission and battery-electric variant of the D45 CRT series public transit coach.

In September 2022, the company introduced its next generation, zero-emission hydrogen fuel cell-electric Xcelsior Charge FC™ heavy-duty transit bus.

In May 2022, the company announced that it would integrate its Delaware parts distribution facility into its existing NFI Parts™ footprint during the third quarter of 2022. In addition, the company would close the Motor Coach Industries (MCI) coach manufacturing facility in Pembina, N.D., expected to be completed in 2025.

Predecessor Detail - Name changed from New Flyer Industries Inc., May 18, 2018.

Directors - Wendy W. T. Kei, chr., Toronto, Ont.; Colin Robertson, v-chr., Edinburgh, Midlothian, United Kingdom; Paul Soubry, pres. & CEO, Winnipeg, Man.; Phyllis Cochran, Bluffton, S.C.; Paulo Cezar da Silva Nunes, Porto Alegre, Brazil; Larry Edwards, Tulsa, Okla.; Adam Gray, Greenwich, Conn.; Krystyna T. (Kyrs) Hoeg, Toronto, Ont.; Jannet Walker-Ford, Jacksonville, Fla.; Katherine S. Winter, Palatine, Ill.

Other Exec. Officers - Janice Harper, exec. v-p, people & culture; Colin Pewarchuk, exec. v-p, gen. counsel & corp. sec.; Pipasu H. Soni, exec. v-p & CFO; David White, exec. v-p, supply mgt.; Paul Davies, pres. & man. dir., Alexander Dennis Limited; Brian Dewsnup, pres., NFI parts & ARBOC; Chris Stoddart, pres., North American bus & coach

Capital Stock

	Authorized (shs.)	Outstanding (shs.)[1]
Common	unlimited	77,176,763

[1] At May 26, 2023

Options - At Jan. 1, 2023, options were outstanding to purchase 1,910,057 common shares at a weighted average exercise price of Cdn$27.41 per share expiring to Apr. 3, 2030.

Major Shareholder - Turtle Creek Asset Management Inc. held 13.4% interest and Coliseum Capital Management, LLC held 12.4% interest at May 26, 2023.

Price Range - NFI/TSX

Year	Volume	High	Low	Close
2022	80,489,638	$20.90	$8.34	$9.52
2021	81,925,718	$32.74	$18.41	$20.26
2020	89,643,062	$33.94	$9.12	$24.09
2019	78,510,939	$39.33	$24.89	$26.65
2018	57,051,531	$61.25	$31.88	$34.04

Recent Close: $12.20

Capital Stock Changes - In May 2023, private placement of 21,656,624 common shares at US$6.1567 per share to Coliseum Capital Management, LLC for gross proceeds of US$133,000,000 was arranged. Net proceeds would be used to repay outstanding indebtedness under existing credit facilities and for working capital and general corporate purposes. On June 6, 2023, bought deal public offering of 15,102,950 subscription receipts at Cdn$8.25 per receipt was completed, each entitling the holder to receive 1 common share, without payment of additional consideration or further action, upon satisfaction of certain escrow release conditions, including that the other elements of the company's previously announced comprehensive refinancing plan close concurrently.

During fiscal 2022, 24,269 common shares were issued on exercise of restricted share units.

Dividends

NFI com omitted [1]

$0.0531	Oct. 17/22	$0.0531	July 15/22
$0.0531	Apr. 15/22	$0.2125	Jan. 17/22

Paid in 2023: n.a. 2022: $0.3718 2021: $0.85

[1] Monthly divd normalyy paid in Jan/23 has been omitted.

Long-Term Debt - Outstanding at Jan. 1, 2023:

Revolv. credit facilities[1]	US$896,626,000
5% conv. debs.[2]	216,512,000
	1,113,138,000
Less: Current portion	17,901,000
	1,095,237,000

[1] Borrowings under a US$1 billion facility due Aug. 2, 2024, bearing interest at LIBOR or U.S. base rate for loans denominated in U.S. dollars and Canadian prime or bankers' acceptance rate for loans denominated in Canadian dollars, plus an applicable margin; and a £40,000,000 U.K. facility bearing interest at LIBOR plus applicable margin and due June 30, 2023.

[2] Cdn$338,000,000. Convertible into common shares at Cdn$33.15 per share and due Jan. 15, 2027.

Note - In May 2023, amendments to the company's existing credit facilities were proposed including: the US$1 billion revolving North American facility would convert to a US$400,000,000 first lien term loan and a US$361,000,000 first lien revolving credit facility and the maturity date extended from Aug. 2, 2024 to Apr. 30, 2026. The £40,00,000 revolving U.K. facility would convert to a £16,000,000 term loan and a £15,000,000 revolving credit facility and the maturity date extended from June 30, 2023, to Apr. 30, 2026.

Wholly Owned Subsidiaries

Alexander Dennis (Canada) Inc., Canada.

NFI Holdings Canada Inc., Canada.

- 100% int. in **Carfair Composites Inc.**, Canada.

NFI International Limited, United Kingdom.

- 100% int. in **Alexander Dennis Limited**, Larbert, Stirling., United Kingdom.

New Flyer Holdings, Inc., Del.

- 100% int. in **ARBOC Specialty Vehicles, LLC**, Middlebury, Ind.
- 100% int. in **The Aftermarket Parts Company, LLC**, Del.
- 100% int. in **Alexander Dennis Incorporated**, Del.
- 100% int. in **Carfair Composites USA, Inc. (Delaware)**, Del.
- 100% int. in **KMG Fabrication, Inc.**, Del.
- 100% int. in **MCI Sales and Services Inc.**, Del.
- 100% int. in **MCIL Holdings, Ltd.**, Canada.
  - 100% int. in **Motor Coach Industries Limited**, Winnipeg, Man.
- 100% int. in **Motor Coach Industries, Inc.**, Del.
- 100% int. in **New Flyer Industries Canada ULC**, Alta.
- 100% int. in **New Flyer of America Inc.**, N.D.

Note: The preceding list includes only the major related companies in which interests are held.

Financial Statistics

Periods ended:	52w Jan. 1/23[A]	%Chg	53w Jan. 2/22[A]
	US$000s	%Chg	US$000s
Operating revenue	**2,053,933**	**-12**	**2,343,794**
Cost of sales	1,916,308		2,011,045
General & admin expense	238,702		203,431
Stock-based compensation	1,346		1,738
Operating expense	**2,156,356**	**-3**	**2,216,214**
Operating income	**(102,423)**	**n.a.**	**127,580**
Deprec., depl. & amort.	88,495		97,154
Finance costs, gross	36,734		39,036
Write-downs/write-offs	(103,900)[1]		nil
Pre-tax income	**(325,184)**	**n.a.**	**(4,928)**
Income taxes	(47,421)		9,556
Net income	**(277,763)**	**n.a.**	**(14,484)**
Cash & equivalent	49,987		77,318
Inventories	732,096		567,698
Accounts receivable	366,224		396,535
Current assets	1,207,097		1,070,938
Fixed assets, net	195,783		221,338
Right-of-use assets	107,631		121,761
Intangibles, net	986,421		1,144,963
Total assets	**2,589,270**	**0**	**2,599,620**
Accts. pay. & accr. liabs	455,368		458,864
Current liabilities	643,357		604,627
Long-term debt, gross	1,113,139		812,179
Long-term debt, net	1,095,238		812,179
Long-term lease liabilities	114,044		120,414
Shareholders' equity	577,151		871,772
Cash from oper. activs	**(241,850)**	**n.a.**	**115,230**
Cash from fin. activs	238,279		(59,992)
Cash from invest. activs	(24,531)		(30,792)
Net cash position	**49,987**	**-35**	**77,318**
Capital expenditures	(21,371)		(33,514)
Capital disposals	1,687		6,182
Unfunded pension liability	n.a.		7,095
Pension fund surplus	11,820		n.a.
	US$		US$
Earnings per share*	(3.60)		(0.21)
Cash flow per share*	(3.14)		1.65
Cash divd. per share*	$0.16		$1.06
	shs		shs
No. of shs. o/s*	77,155,016		77,130,747
Avg. no. of shs. o/s*	77,144,445		70,039,835
	%		%
Net profit margin	(13.52)		(0.62)
Return on equity	(38.34)		(1.94)
Return on assets	(9.50)		3.74
No. of employees (FTEs)	7,700		7,500

* Common

[A] Reported in accordance with IFRS

[1] Pertains to impairment loss on goodwill

Latest Results

Periods ended:	13w Apr. 2/23[A]	%Chg	13w Apr. 3/22[oA]
	US$000s	%Chg	US$000s
Operating revenue	524,411	+14	459,330
Net income	(45,964)	n.a.	(27,795)
	US$		US$
Earnings per share*	(0.60)		(0.36)

* Common

[o] Restated

[A] Reported in accordance with IFRS

Historical Summary
(as originally stated)

Fiscal Year	Oper. Rev.	Net Inc. Bef. Disc.	EPS*
	US$000s	US$000s	US$
2022[A]	2,053,933	(277,763)	(3.60)
2021[A1]	2,343,794	(14,484)	(0.21)
2020[A]	2,419,175	(157,736)	(2.52)
2019[A]	2,893,436	57,698	0.93

* Common

[A] Reported in accordance with IFRS

[1] 53 weeks ended Jan. 2, 2022.

N.4 NFT Technologies Inc.

Symbol - NFT **Exchange** - NEO **CUSIP** - 65345K

Head Office - 202-1965 4 Ave W, Vancouver, BC, V6J 1M8 **Telephone** - (604) 800-5838

Website - www.nfttech.com

Email - wayne@nfttech.com

Investor Relations - Wayne Lloyd (604) 800-5838

Auditors - Kingston Ross Pasnak LLP C.A., Edmonton, Alta.

Transfer Agents - Odyssey Trust Company, Vancouver, B.C.

Employees - 8 at May 12, 2022

Profile - (B.C. 2016) Develops and invests in new technologies that enhance non-fungible tokens (NFTs) across the digital asset, cryptocurrency and blockchain technology sector.

Has three main business lines: the technology business line is focused on emerging technologies and creating new intellectual property in the NFT space; the investing business line is focused on the acquisition and trade of NFTs, including creating and maintaining a curated portfolio of collectible NFTs, investing in companies whose focus is on developing technology and launching NFTs, and the generation and sale of tokens in connection with play to earn blockchain games and associated gaming guilds; and the consulting business line is focused on assisting clients with the launch and marketing of their own brand of NFT.

On Feb. 24, 2023, the company acquired Australia-based **Run it Wild Pty Ltd.**, a multi-disciplinary Web3 development company, for $50,000 cash and issuance of 10,000,000 common shares at a deemed price of $0.055 per share.

Directors - Wayne Lloyd, exec. chr., interim CEO & corp. sec., Vancouver, B.C.; Kelly Allin, Ont.; Jeremy L. Gardner, Fla.; Curt Marvis, Los Angeles, Calif.

Other Exec. Officers - Mark Leung, CFO

Capital Stock

	Authorized (shs.)	Outstanding (shs.)[1]
Preferred	unlimited	nil
Common	unlimited	105,318,659

[1] At May 16, 2023

Major Shareholder - Widely held at May 12, 2022.

Price Range - NFT/NEO

Year	Volume	High	Low	Close
2022	1,332,500	$0.62	$0.07	$0.09

Recent Close: $0.03

Capital Stock Changes - On Feb. 24, 2023, 10,000,000 common shares were issued pursuant to the acquisition of Run it Wild Pty Ltd.

Wholly Owned Subsidiaries

Run it Wild Pty Ltd., Australia.

Investments

3% int. in **Fantasy Revolution, S.A.**, Lisbon, Portugal.
2% int. in **Rev3al Technologies LLC**, Del.
2% int. in **2821840 Ontario Inc.**, Ont.

Financial Statistics

Periods ended:	12m Dec. 31/21[A]
	$000s
Salaries & benefits	539
Research & devel. expense	2,144
General & admin expense	1,716
Stock-based compensation	850
Operating expense	**5,249**
Operating income	**(5,249)**
Deprec., depl. & amort.	2
Pre-tax income	**(6,016)**
Net income	**(6,016)**
Cash & equivalent	3,918
Current assets	4,463
Long-term investments	247
Fixed assets, net	23
Total assets	**4,733**
Accts. pay. & accr. liabs	215
Current liabilities	246
Shareholders' equity	4,488
Cash from oper. activs	**(4,019)**
Cash from fin. activs	8,612
Cash from invest. activs	(676)
Net cash position	**3,918**
Capital expenditures	(25)
	$
Earnings per share*	(0.18)
Cash flow per share*	(0.12)
	shs
No. of shs. o/s*	73,791,241
Avg. no. of shs. o/s*	34,276,403
	%
Net profit margin	n.a.
Return on equity	n.m.
Return on assets	n.a.

* Common
[A] Reported in accordance with IFRS

N.5 NL2 Capital Inc.

Symbol - NLII.P **Exchange** - TSX-VEN **CUSIP** - 629170
Head Office - 1300-1969 Upper Water St, Halifax, NS, B3J 3R7 **Telephone** - (902) 401-9480
Email - cdobbin@precipicecapital.com
Investor Relations - Christopher Dobbin (902) 401-9480
Auditors - KPMG LLP C.A., Halifax, N.S.
Lawyers - McInnes Cooper
Transfer Agents - Computershare Trust Company of Canada Inc., Montréal, Qué.
Profile - (Can. 2022) Capital Pool Company.
Common listed on TSX-VEN, Mar. 28, 2023.

Directors - Christopher (Chris) Dobbin, pres., CEO, CFO & corp. sec., Halifax, N.S.; Dana M. Hatfield, Halifax, N.S.; R. Wayne Myles, N.B.; Michael A. (Mike) O'Keefe, Halifax, N.S.

Capital Stock

	Authorized (shs.)	Outstanding (shs.)[1]
Common	unlimited	18,974,500

[1] At Mar. 28, 2023

Major Shareholder - Christopher (Chris) Dobbin held 13.18% interest, Wayne Fulcher held 13.18% interest, Nicklas Coleman held 10.54% interest, Todd McDonald held 10.54% interest and R. Wayne Myles held 10.54% interest at Mar. 28, 2023.

Recent Close: $0.10

Capital Stock Changes - On Mar. 28, 2023, an initial public offering of 5,274,500 common shares was completed at 10¢ per share.

N.6 NTG Clarity Networks Inc.

Symbol - NCI **Exchange** - TSX-VEN **CUSIP** - 62940V
Head Office - 202-2820 14 Ave, Markham, ON, L3R 0S9 **Telephone** - (905) 305-1325 **Toll-free** - (800) 838-7894 **Fax** - (905) 752-0469
Website - www.ntgclarity.com
Email - klewis@ntgclarity.com
Investor Relations - Kristine Lewis (800) 838-7894
Auditors - NVS Chartered Accountants Professional Corporation C.A., Markham, Ont.
Bankers - Bank of Montreal, Montréal, Qué.
Lawyers - Borden Ladner Gervais LLP, Calgary, Alta.
Transfer Agents - Computershare Trust Company of Canada Inc., Toronto, Ont.

Profile - (Alta. 2000) Provides telecommunications engineering, information technology (IT), networking and related software solutions in Canada and internationally.

Provides network, telecom, IT and infrastructure solutions to medium and large network service providers through more than 500 network professionals. Also has developed niche software products directed at telecom service providers and utilities as well as provide professional services network and managed services. The company also provides products and technical resources to assist financial and government sector customers with projects that include digital transformation.

Solutions include NTGapps digital toolbox, StageEM, workflow management, network inventory management, Partner Relationship Management (PRM), NTS asset management, NTS trouble ticket management, NTS utility billing, Mi-World, VoWifi Capability, NTS Telco In a Box, Last Mile Delivery, End-to-End business solutions and Internet of Things solutions. Services include solution development, system integration, testing-as-a-services (TaaS), outsourcing, consulting, training, smart cities/building, digital transformation and data migration.

The company is headquartered in Markham, Ont., and has offices in Cairo, Egypt; the U.S.; Riyadh, Saudi Arabia; and Oman.

Predecessor Detail - Name changed from Clarity Telecom Networking Inc., Mar. 16, 2001.

Directors - Ashraf Zaghloul, chr. & CEO, Thornhill, Ont.; Kristine Lewis, pres. & CFO, Thornhill, Ont.; Syed Zeeshan Hasnain; Mohamed Saleem Siddiqi

Other Exec. Officers - Gamal Metwally, exec. v-p; Ashraf Fayed, sr. v-p, KSA; Mohamed Fouad, v-p, opers.; Alaa Ibrahim, v-p, software devel.; Adel Zaghloul, chr. & CEO, NTG Egypt Advanced Software & Network Technology Group

Capital Stock

	Authorized (shs.)	Outstanding (shs.)[1]
First Preferred	unlimited	nil
Second Preferred	unlimited	nil
Common	unlimited	147,972,355

[1] At May 23, 2023

Major Shareholder - Ashraf Zaghloul held 13.98% interest, Kristine Lewis held 12.32% interest and 2729252 Ontario Inc. held 10.14% interest at May 23, 2023.

Price Range - NCI/TSX-VEN

Year	Volume	High	Low	Close
2022	35,774,689	$0.06	$0.03	$0.03
2021	221,240,503	$0.16	$0.02	$0.05
2020	50,581,236	$0.05	$0.01	$0.03
2019	26,956,949	$0.06	$0.01	$0.01
2018	18,179,784	$0.16	$0.03	$0.03

Recent Close: $0.04

Capital Stock Changes - In May 2023, a 1-for-5 share consolidation was proposed.

During 2022, 500,000 common shares were issued on exercise of options.

Wholly Owned Subsidiaries

NTG Clarity Networks U.S. Inc., Del.

Subsidiaries

95% int. in **NTG Egypt Advanced Software & Network Technology Group**, Egypt.

Financial Statistics

Periods ended:	12m Dec. 31/22[A]		12m Dec. 31/21[A]
	$000s	%Chg	$000s
Operating revenue	**17,652**	**+48**	**11,896**
Cost of sales	1,234		365
Salaries & benefits	12,761		7,670
General & admin expense	1,108		970
Stock-based compensation	328		810
Operating expense	**15,431**	**+57**	**9,816**
Operating income	**2,221**	**+7**	**2,080**
Deprec., depl. & amort.	438		244
Finance costs, gross	322		206
Write-downs/write-offs	nil		(22)
Pre-tax income	**(1,248)**	**n.a.**	**1,370**
Net income	**(1,248)**	**n.a.**	**1,370**
Cash & equivalent	725		159
Accounts receivable	3,881		3,747
Current assets	4,711		4,026
Fixed assets, net	222		183
Right-of-use assets	30		100
Intangibles, net	3,206		2,181
Total assets	**8,168**	**+26**	**6,491**
Bank indebtedness	1,091		1,048
Accts. pay. & accr. liabs	6,985		6,540
Current liabilities	8,269		7,783
Long-term debt, gross	6,829		6,708
Long-term debt, net	6,676		6,587
Long-term lease liabilities	nil		39
Shareholders' equity	6,777		(7,919)
Cash from oper. activs	**2,493**	**+38**	**1,802**
Cash from fin. activs	(497)		(239)
Cash from invest. activs	(1,431)		(1,548)
Net cash position	**725**	**+356**	**159**
Capital expenditures	(128)		(97)
	$		$
Earnings per share*	(0.01)		0.01
Cash flow per share*	0.02		0.01
	shs		shs
No. of shs. o/s*	147,972,355		147,472,355
Avg. no. of shs. o/s*	147,972,355		147,472,355
	%		%
Net profit margin	(7.07)		11.52
Return on equity	n.m.		n.m.
Return on assets	(12.63)		32.62

* Common
[A] Reported in accordance with IFRS

Latest Results

Periods ended:	3m Mar. 31/23[A]		3m Mar. 31/22[A]
	$000s	%Chg	$000s
Operating revenue	6,127	+42	4,321
Net income	1,088	+757	127
	$		$
Earnings per share*	0.00		0.00

* Common
[A] Reported in accordance with IFRS

Historical Summary
(as originally stated)

Fiscal Year	Oper. Rev.	Net Inc. Bef. Disc.	EPS*
	$000s	$000s	$
2022[A]	17,652	(1,248)	(0.01)
2021[A]	11,896	1,370	0.01
2020[A]	7,907	(1,632)	(0.01)
2019[A]	8,626	(8,812)	(0.16)
2018[A]	11,706	(353)	(0.01)

* Common
[A] Reported in accordance with IFRS

N.7 NXT Energy Solutions Inc.

Symbol - SFD **Exchange** - TSX **CUSIP** - 62948Q
Head Office - 302-3320 17 Ave SW, Calgary, AB, T3E 0B4 **Telephone** - (403) 264-7020 **Fax** - (403) 264-6442
Website - www.nxtenergy.com
Email - nxt_info@nxtenergy.com
Investor Relations - Eugene Woychyshyn (403) 206-0805
Auditors - MNP LLP C.A., Calgary, Alta.
Bankers - Royal Bank of Canada, Calgary, Alta.
Lawyers - Norton Rose Fulbright Canada LLP, Caracas, Venezuela
Transfer Agents - Computershare Trust Company of Canada Inc., Calgary, Alta.
Employees - 10 at Dec. 31, 2022

Profile - (Alta. 2003; orig. Nev., 1994) Provides airborne detection technology enabling clients to focus their exploration decisions concerning land commitments, data acquisition expenditures and prospect prioritization on areas with the greatest potential.

The company's proprietary airborne Stress Field Detection (SFD®) survey system provides a survey method that can be used both onshore and offshore to remotely identify traps and reservoirs with hydrocarbon and geothermal exploration potential. SFD® is environmentally friendly and unaffected by ground security issues or difficult terrain.

Predecessor Detail - Name changed from Energy Exploration Technologies Inc., Sept. 22, 2008.

Directors - Bruce G. Wilcox, interim CEO, New York, N.Y.; Thomas E. (Tom) Valentine, corp. sec., Calgary, Alta.; Charles V. Selby†, Calgary, Alta.; Theodore Patsellis, Greece; Gerry Sheehan, Ireland; John Tilson, Montecito, Calif.

Other Exec. Officers - Eugene Woychyshyn, v-p, fin. & CFO

† Lead director

Capital Stock

	Authorized (shs.)	Outstanding (shs.)[1]
Preferred	unlimited	
Common	unlimited	77,653,870

[1] At May 15, 2023

Major Shareholder - George Liszicasz held 23.55% interest and Ben Shani held 10.57% interest at Apr. 29, 2022.

Price Range - SFD/TSX

Year	Volume	High	Low	Close
2022	3,308,333	$0.81	$0.16	$0.21
2021	3,448,763	$0.79	$0.36	$0.61
2020	5,010,711	$1.00	$0.20	$0.79
2019	2,754,508	$0.87	$0.31	$0.54
2018	2,899,391	$1.34	$0.22	$0.37

Recent Close: $0.18

Capital Stock Changes - In January 2023, private placement of 8,510,000 common shares was completed at $0.195 per share.

During 2022, common shares were issued as follows: 2,149,180 pursuant to a rights offering, 1,148,282 by private placement, 212,304 under the restricted stock unit plan and 188,633 under the employee share purchase plan.

Wholly Owned Subsidiaries

Cascade Petroleum Inc., Alta. Inactive.
NXT Aero USA, Inc., Nev. Inactive.
NXT Energy Services (SFD) Inc., Canada. Inactive.
NXT Energy USA, Inc., Nev. Inactive.
PetroCaza Exploration Inc., Alta. Inactive.

Financial Statistics

Periods ended:	12m Dec. 31/22[A]		12m Dec. 31/21[A]
	$000s	%Chg	$000s
Operating revenue	**nil**	**n.a.**	**3,134**
Cost of sales	1,178		1,224
General & admin expense	3,521		2,902
Stock-based compensation	215		288
Operating expense	**4,915**	**+11**	**4,414**
Operating income	**(4,915)**	**n.a.**	**(1,280)**
Deprec., depl. & amort.	1,769		1,776
Finance costs, net	36		38
Pre-tax income	**(6,733)**	**n.a.**	**(3,124)**
Net income	**(6,733)**	**n.a.**	**(3,124)**
Cash & equivalent	263		2,808
Accounts receivable	57		842
Current assets	357		3,915
Fixed assets, net	544		625
Right-of-use assets	1,259		1,943
Intangibles, net	13,169		14,867
Total assets	**15,575**	**-28**	**21,584**
Accts. pay. & accr. liabs	1,276		501
Current liabilities	2,038		1,098
Long-term debt, gross	935		1,000
Long-term debt, net	824		935
Long-term lease liabilities	596		1,370
Shareholders' equity	12,093		18,159
Cash from oper. activs	**(2,934)**	**n.a.**	**(1,033)**
Cash from fin. activs	389		875
Cash from invest. activs	550		(274)
Net cash position	**263**	**-88**	**2,258**
	$		$
Earnings per share*	(0.10)		(0.05)
Cash flow per share*	(0.04)		(0.02)
	shs		shs
No. of shs. o/s*	68,949,109		65,250,710
Avg. no. of shs. o/s*	65,602,875		64,658,380
	%		%
Net profit margin	n.a.		(99.68)
Return on equity	(44.51)		(16.06)
Return on assets	(36.24)		(13.70)
No. of employees (FTEs)	10		10

* Common
[A] Reported in accordance with U.S. GAAP

Latest Results

Periods ended:	3m Mar. 31/23[A]		3m Mar. 31/22[A]
	$000s	%Chg	$000s
Net income	(1,615)	n.a.	(1,841)
	$		$
Earnings per share*	(0.02)		(0.03)

* Common
[A] Reported in accordance with U.S. GAAP

Historical Summary
(as originally stated)

Fiscal Year	Oper. Rev.	Net Inc. Bef. Disc.	EPS*
	$000s	$000s	$
2022[A]	nil	(6,733)	(0.10)
2021[A]	3,134	(3,124)	(0.05)
2020[A]	137	(6,000)	(0.09)
2019[A]	11,976	3,773	0.06
2018[A]	nil	(6,969)	(0.11)

* Common
[A] Reported in accordance with U.S. GAAP

N.8 Nabati Foods Global Inc.

Symbol - MEAL **Exchange** - CSE **CUSIP** - 62955C
Head Office - 1570-505 Burrard St, Vancouver, BC, V7X 1M5 **Telephone** - (604) 416-4099
Email - ir@nabatifoods.com
Investor Relations - Daniel Thomas (780) 800-6624
Auditors - Paul J. Rozek Professional Corporation C.A., Calgary, Alta.
Transfer Agents - Olympia Trust Company, Vancouver, B.C.
Profile - (B.C. 2020) No operations.

Previously designed, developed, manufactured, sold and distributed plant-based foods in Canada and the U.S.

In July 2022, the company ceased operations due to failure to raise capital. Its leased manufacturing facility in Edmonton, Alta., was seized by the landlord.

Common reinstated on CSE, Sept. 29, 2022.

Predecessor Detail - Name changed from 1279006 B.C. Ltd., Mar. 11, 2021, pursuant to the reverse takeover acquisition of Nabati Foods Inc.

Directors - Daniel Thomas, CEO; Aryan Beytoei, CFO; David Bentil

Capital Stock

	Authorized (shs.)	Outstanding (shs.)[1]
Common	unlimited	48,425,711

[1] At Apr. 29, 2023

Major Shareholder - Ahmad Yehya held 20.47% interest and Magdy Yehya held 15.27% interest at Oct. 4, 2021.

Price Range - MEAL/CSE

Year	Volume	High	Low	Close
2022	16,898,024	$0.49	$0.01	$0.01
2021	15,427,205	$1.37	$0.35	$0.45

Recent Close: $0.01

Wholly Owned Subsidiaries

Nabati Foods Inc., Edmonton, Alta.
- 100% int. in **Nabati Foods Inc.**, Seattle, Wash.
- 100% int. in **Nabati Foods UK Ltd.**, United Kingdom.

Financial Statistics

Periods ended:	12m Dec. 31/21[A1]		12m Dec. 31/20[A2]
	$000s	%Chg	$000s
Operating revenue	**818**	**+71**	**479**
Cost of sales	4,428		312
Salaries & benefits	560		203
General & admin expense	4,315		458
Stock-based compensation	2,968		nil
Operating expense	**12,271**	**n.m.**	**973**
Operating income	**(11,453)**	**n.a.**	**(494)**
Deprec., depl. & amort.	53		68
Finance costs, gross	121		50
Write-downs/write-offs	(82)		(50)
Pre-tax income	**(21,830)**	**n.a.**	**(535)**
Net income	**(21,830)**	**n.a.**	**(535)**
Cash & equivalent	25		15
Inventories	246		103
Accounts receivable	433		169
Current assets	703		287
Fixed assets, net	nil		107
Right-of-use assets	nil		128
Total assets	**714**	**+33**	**537**
Accts. pay. & accr. liabs	1,867		172
Long-term debt, gross	25		560
Long-term debt, net	nil		528
Long-term lease liabilities	1,200		72
Shareholders' equity	(3,109)		(1,837)
Cash from oper. activs	**(6,362)**	**n.a.**	**(609)**
Cash from fin. activs	7,808		672
Cash from invest. activs	(1,436)		(56)
Net cash position	**25**	**+67**	**15**
Capital expenditures	(1,293)		(41)
	$		$
Earnings per share*	(0.67)		n.a.
Cash flow per share*	(0.20)		n.a.
	shs		shs
No. of shs. o/s*	45,859,233		n.a.
Avg. no. of shs. o/s*	32,631,484		n.a.
	%		%
Net profit margin	n.m.		(111.69)
Return on equity	n.m.		n.m.
Return on assets	n.m.		(129.33)

* Common
[A] Reported in accordance with IFRS
[1] Results reflect the March 11, 2021, reverse takeover acquisition of Nabati Foods Inc.
[2] Results for 2020 and prior periods pertain to Nabati Foods Inc.

Latest Results

Periods ended:	6m June 30/22[A]		6m June 30/21[A]
	$000s	%Chg	$000s
Operating revenue	279	-17	335
Net income	(2,340)	n.a.	(10,187)
	$		$
Earnings per share*	(0.05)		(0.31)

* Common
[A] Reported in accordance with IFRS

Historical Summary
(as originally stated)

Fiscal Year	Oper. Rev.	Net Inc. Bef. Disc.	EPS*
	$000s	$000s	$
2021[A]	818	(21,830)	(0.67)
2020[A]	479	(535)	n.a.
2019[A]	298	(273)	n.a.

* Common
[A] Reported in accordance with IFRS

N.9 Nalcor Energy

CUSIP - 123456
Head Office - Hydro Place, 500 Columbus Dr, PO Box 12800, St. John's, NL, A1B 0C9 **Telephone** - (709) 737-1440 **Fax** - (709) 737-1816
Website - www.nalcorenergy.com
Email - deannefisher@nalcorenergy.com
Investor Relations - Deanne Fisher (709) 733-5299
Auditors - Deloitte LLP C.A., St. John's, N.L.
FP500 Revenue Ranking - 337
Profile - (N.L. 2007) Newfoundland and Labrador's energy company, whose business includes the development, generation, transmission and sale of electricity including energy trading; and development, production and sale of oil and gas.

Operates through the following business segments:

Hydro Regulated - This segment's activities encompass sales of electricity to customers within the province that are regulated by the Newfoundland and Labrador Board of Commissioners of Public Utilities (PUB).

Muskrat Falls - This segment includes the operation of the 824-MW hydroelectric generating facility in Labrador on the Lower Churchill River.

LCP Transmission - This segment includes the construction of the Labrador-Island Link (LIL) and operation of the Labrador Transmission Assets (LTA), which consist of transmission lines connecting the Muskrat Falls and Churchill Falls generating stations and certain portions of the transmission system in Labrador to the Island.

Churchill Falls - This segment owns and operates a 5,428-MW hydroelectric generating facility (65.8% owned), which sells electricity to **Hydro-Québec** and **Newfoundland and Labrador Hydro** (NL Hydro).

Energy Trading - This segment includes energy trading and commercial activities related to maximizing the value of the province's surplus power and transmission interconnections with external electricity markets.

Other Electric - This segment includes revenues and expenditures associated with the delivery of the Nova Scotia Block of energy to **Emera Inc.**; expenditures associated with the Maritime Link (which is owned and managed by Emera, but consolidated by the company); NL Hydro's sales of electricity to mining operations in Labrador West; and revenues and costs recovered from Hydro-Québec associated with the operation of the Menihek generating station.

Oil and Gas - This segment includes the company's share in the development, production, transportation and processing of oil and gas from the Hebron, White Rose and Hibernia South Extension (HSE) fields.

Corporate - This segment includes shared services functions along with community and business development.

On Nov. 1, 2022, subsidiary **Churchill Falls (Labrador) Corporation Limited** (65.8% owned) acquired the remaining 49.6% interest in **Twin Falls Power Corporation Limited** from **Iron Ore Company of Canada** (IOC) for a nominal amount and provided an indemnity to IOC for any contingent environmental liabilities associated with Twin Falls. As a result, Churchill Falls held a 100% interest in Twin Falls.

The partners of the West White Rose project announced its restart on May 31, 2022, with first oil from the platform anticipated in 2026. Major construction activities were suspended at the project in 2020, after which a full review of the scope, schedule and cost of the project was conducted.

Oil & Gas Oper. Stats.

Periods ended:	12m Dec. 31/22	12m Dec. 31/21
Avg. BOE prod., bbl/d	n.a.	10,420
Oil reserves, net, mbbl	29,751	32,173

Utilities Oper. Stats.

Periods ended:	12m Dec. 31/22	12m Dec. 31/21
Electric sales, GWh	n.a.	41,063
Generating capacity, MW	n.a.	8,034
Electric gen., GWh	n.a.	39,564
Transmission lines, km	n.a.	5,059

Directors - Albert Williams, chr., N.L.; Jennifer Williams, pres. & interim CEO, St. John's, N.L.; Geoffrey S. (Geoff) Goodyear, N.L.; John M. Green, St. John's, N.L.; John J. (Jack) Hillyard, N.L.; Mark MacLeod, N.L.; Debbie Molloy, N.W.T.; David J. Oake, St. John's, N.L.; Derek Purchase, Ont.; Dr. Edna Turpin, St. John's, N.L.

Other Exec. Officers - Robert Collett, v-p, hydro eng. & NLSO; Gail Collins, v-p, people & corp. affairs; Scott Crosbie, v-p, hydro opers.; Gerard Dunphy, v-p, Churchill Falls & Muskrat Falls; Kevin Fagan, v-p, regulatory & stakeholder rel.; Lisa A. Hutchens, v-p & CFO; Michael Ladha, v-p, chief legal officer & corp. sec.; Walter Parsons, v-p, transmission interconnections & bus. devel.; Meredith D. Baker, asst. sec.

Capital Stock

	Authorized (shs.)	Outstanding (shs.)[1]
Common	unlimited	122,500,000

[1] At June 30, 2023

Major Shareholder - Province of Newfoundland and Labrador held 100% interest at June 30, 2023.

Capital Stock Changes - There were no changes to capital stock from 2009 to 2022, inclusive.

Wholly Owned Subsidiaries

Gull Island Power Company Limited, St. John's, N.L. Inactive.
Labrador-Island Link General Partner Corporation, N.L.
- 100% int. in **Labrador-Island Link Limited Partnership**, N.L.

Labrador-Island Link General Partner (2021) Corporation, N.L.
- 100% int. in **LIL (2021) Limited Partnership**, N.L.

Labrador-Island Link Holding Corporation, N.L.
Labrador-Island Link Holding (2021) Corporation, N.L.
Labrador-Island Link Operating Corporation, N.L.
Labrador Transmission Corporation, N.L.
Lower Churchill Management Corporation, N.L.
Muskrat Falls Corporation, N.L.
Nalcor Energy Marketing Corporation, N.L.
Nalcor Energy - Oil and Gas Inc., N.L.
Newfoundland and Labrador Hydro, St. John's, N.L.
- 65.8% int. in **Churchill Falls (Labrador) Corporation Limited**, St. John's, N.L.
  - 100% int. in **Twin Falls Power Corporation Limited**, St. John's, N.L.
- 51% int. in **Lower Churchill Development Corporation**, N.L. Inactive.

Financial Statistics

Periods ended:	12m Dec. 31/22[A]		12m Dec. 31/21[oA]
	$000s	%Chg	$000s
Operating revenue	**1,359,000**	**+34**	**1,013,000**
Cost of sales	299,000		233,000
Salaries & benefits	143,000		140,000
General & admin expense	144,000		114,000
Operating expense	**586,000**	**+20**	**487,000**
Operating income	**773,000**	**+47**	**526,000**
Deprec., depl. & amort.	224,000		202,000
Finance income	41,000		9,000
Finance costs, gross	292,000		154,000
Investment income	26,000		18,000
Pre-tax income	**580,000**	**+706**	**72,000**
Net income	**580,000**	**+706**	**72,000**
Cash & equivalent	627,000		415,000
Inventories	132,000		115,000
Accounts receivable	187,000		177,000
Current assets	2,283,000		1,544,000
Long-term investments	241,000		nil
Fixed assets, net	17,921,000		17,739,000
Intangibles, net	35,000		38,000
Total assets	**21,291,000**	**+8**	**19,774,000**
Bank indebtedness	131,000		55,000
Accts. pay. & accr. liabs	301,000		384,000
Current liabilities	719,000		581,000
Long-term debt, gross	10,790,000		9,860,000
Long-term debt, net	10,721,000		9,792,000
Shareholders' equity	7,150,000		6,508,000
Cash from oper. activs	**348,000**	**+241**	**102,000**
Cash from fin. activs	548,000		314,000
Cash from invest. activs	(737,000)		(338,000)
Net cash position	**566,000**	**+39**	**407,000**
Capital expenditures	(271,000)		(452,000)
Capital disposals	nil		40,000
	$		$
Earnings per share*	n.a.		n.a.
	shs		shs
No. of shs. o/s*	122,500,000		122,500,000
Avg. no. of shs. o/s*	122,500,000		122,500,000
	%		%
Net profit margin	42.68		7.11
Return on equity	8.49		1.14
Return on assets	4.25		1.16
No. of employees (FTEs)	n.a.		1,499

[o] Restated
[A] Reported in accordance with IFRS

Historical Summary
(as originally stated)

Fiscal Year	Oper. Rev.	Net Inc. Bef. Disc.	EPS*
	$000s	$000s	$
2022[A]	1,359,000	580,000	n.a.
2021[A]	1,013,000	72,000	n.a.
2020[A]	930,000	(90,000)	n.a.
2019[A]	1,038,000	127,000	n.a.
2018[A]	1,018,000	182,000	n.a.

* Common
[A] Reported in accordance with IFRS

N.10 NameSilo Technologies Corp.

Symbol - URL **Exchange** - CSE **CUSIP** - 62987T

Head Office - 1052-409 Granville St, Vancouver, BC, V6C 1T2 **Telephone** - (604) 644-0072 **Fax** - (604) 688-4712

Website - www.namesilo.com

Email - paul@brisio.com

Investor Relations - Paul Andreola (604) 644-0072

Auditors - Mao & Ying LLP C.A., Vancouver, B.C.

Lawyers - Northwest Law Group, Vancouver, B.C.

Transfer Agents - Computershare Trust Company of Canada Inc.

Profile - (B.C. 2014; orig. Alta., 1993) Provides domain name registration services and management services for the buying and selling of domain names. Also invests in the securities of public and private companies in a wide variety of industries excluding the resource and resource service sectors.

Subsidiary **NameSilo, LLC** provides domain name registration services and operates a domain marketplace which processes aftermarket or secondary domain name sales. It has over 4,670,000 active domains under management from 160 countries. NameSilo offers customers the ability to search for and register available domain names with the relevant registry, shared website hosting, email accounts, secure socket layer (SSL), logo maker, new domain search, NameSilo blog, NameLot brokerage service, SEO strategy working and search engine optimization.

At Mar. 31, 2023, the company's investment portfolio had a fair value of $4,448,028 compared with $5,804,849 at Dec. 31, 2022.

Predecessor Detail - Name changed from Brisio Innovations Inc., Dec. 3, 2018.

Directors - Paul Andreola, pres. & CEO, Vancouver, B.C.; Colin Bowkett, West Vancouver, B.C.; Paul Kozak, Ont.; Kristaps Ronka, Toronto, Ont.

Other Exec. Officers - Natasha Tsai, CFO & corp. sec.

Capital Stock

	Authorized (shs.)	Outstanding (shs.)[1]
Preferred	unlimited	nil
Common	unlimited	91,585,648

[1] At May 30, 2023

Major Shareholder - Widely held at Mar. 14, 2023.

Price Range - URL/CSE

Year	Volume	High	Low	Close
2022	18,534,914	$0.22	$0.13	$0.17
2021	35,042,436	$0.27	$0.16	$0.16
2020	31,116,324	$0.55	$0.17	$0.25
2019	20,251,656	$0.54	$0.33	$0.50
2018	21,807,239	$0.48	$0.28	$0.35

Recent Close: $0.17

Capital Stock Changes - During fiscal 2022, 1,061,000 common shares were repurchased under a Normal Course Issuer Bid.

Wholly Owned Subsidiaries

Netco Argentina S.A., Argentina.
1155064 B.C. Ltd., B.C.

Subsidiaries

81.5% int. in **NameSilo, LLC**, Phoenix, Ariz.
- 100% int. in **NamePal.com, LLC**, United States.

Financial Statistics

Periods ended:	12m Dec. 31/22[A]		12m Dec. 31/21[A]
	$000s	%Chg	$000s
Total revenue	**45,004**	**+24**	**36,427**
Salaries & benefits	202		191
General & admin. expense	4,713		4,167
Stock-based compensation	231		333
Other operating expense	36,987		29,570
Operating expense	**42,133**	**+23**	**34,262**
Operating income	**2,871**	**+33**	**2,165**
Deprec. & amort.	1,135		1,090
Finance costs, gross	686		549
Pre-tax income	**(1,234)**	**n.a.**	**(8,277)**
Income taxes	880		588
Net income	**(2,114)**	**n.a.**	**(8,865)**
Net inc. for equity hldrs	**(2,002)**	**n.a.**	**(8,795)**
Net inc. for non-cont. int	**(112)**	**n.a.**	**(70)**
Cash & equivalent	1,203		1,417
Accounts receivable	66		152
Current assets	24,471		22,588
Long-term investments	5,805		4,947
Fixed assets, net	77		82
Intangibles	10,925		11,322
Total assets	**43,344**	**+6**	**41,064**
Accts. pay. & accr. liabs	6,481		3,482
Current liabilities	32,212		27,324
Long-term debt, gross	3,469		3,249
Long-term debt, net	3,469		3,249
Equity portion of conv. debs	566		566
Shareholders' equity	4,319		6,286
Non-controlling interest	418		931
Cash from oper. activs	**1,754**	**-16**	**2,081**
Cash from fin. activs	(863)		(2,777)
Cash from invest. activs	(638)		(243)
Net cash position	**1,203**	**-15**	**1,417**
Capital expenditures	nil		(83)
	$		$
Earnings per share*	(0.02)		(0.10)
Cash flow per share*	0.02		0.02
	shs		shs
No. of shs. o/s*	91,585,648		92,646,648
Avg. no. of shs. o/s*	92,556,536		92,646,648
	%		%
Net profit margin	(4.70)		(24.34)
Return on equity	(37.76)		(85.55)
Return on assets	(2.22)		(19.35)

* Common
[A] Reported in accordance with IFRS

Latest Results

Periods ended:	3m Mar. 31/23[A]		3m Mar. 31/22[A]
	$000s	%Chg	$000s
Total revenue	11,909	+11	10,760
Net income	(1,817)	n.a.	331
Net inc. for equity hldrs	(1,857)	n.a.	150
Net inc. for non-cont. int	40		181
	$		$
Earnings per share*	(0.02)		0.00

* Common
[A] Reported in accordance with IFRS

Historical Summary
(as originally stated)

Fiscal Year	Total Rev. $000s	Net Inc. Bef. Disc. $000s	EPS* $
2022A	45,004	(2,114)	(0.02)
2021A	36,427	(8,865)	(0.10)
2020A	31,051	6,480	0.09
2019A	27,166	(4,041)	(0.07)
2018A	9,869	(6,953)	(0.14)

* Common
A Reported in accordance with IFRS

N.11 NamSys Inc.

Symbol - CTZ **Exchange** - TSX-VEN **CUSIP** - 630000
Head Office - 274-150 King St W, Toronto, ON, M5H 1J9 **Telephone** - (905) 857-9500
Website - www.namsys.com
Email - kbsparks@namsys.com
Investor Relations - K. Barry Sparks (416) 369-6081
Auditors - McGovern Hurley LLP C.A., Toronto, Ont.
Bankers - Royal Bank of Canada; The Bank of Nova Scotia
Lawyers - Gowling WLG (Canada) LLP, Toronto, Ont.
Transfer Agents - TSX Trust Company, Toronto, Ont.
Profile - (Ont. 1999; orig. Alta., 1997) Develops and markets cloud-based currency management and processing software products for banking and merchant industries primarily in North America.

Products include Cirreon, a cloud-based software to help banks and armored carriers manage networks of smart safes, with the ability to provide the client's customers with daily credit platform, collect detailed information about all transaction types to see who interacts with the safe, and manage and configure software and firmware centrally; and Currency Controller®, a cash vault system which handles all aspects of the logistics and management in cash processing centres.

Predecessor Detail - Name changed from CencoTech Inc., Nov. 1, 2016.

Directors - K. Barry Sparks, exec. chr., Toronto, Ont.; Jason B. Siemens, pres. & CEO, Ont.; Leslie T. Gord, corp. sec., Toronto, Ont.; Gabriel Bouchard-Phillips, Westmount, Qué.; G. James Johnson, St. Petersburg, Fla.; H. Joe Prodan, Redwood City, Calif.; Nicole A. Sparks, Waltham, Mass.; E. Christopher Stait-Gardner, Vaughan, Ont.

Other Exec. Officers - Christine Gray, COO; Christopher J. Adams, CFO

Capital Stock

	Authorized (shs.)	Outstanding (shs.)[1]
Preferred	unlimited	nil
Common	unlimited	27,286,332

[1] At Mar. 28, 2023

Major Shareholder - K. Barry Sparks held 33.2% interest and Topline Capital Management LLC held 19.99% interest at Mar. 29, 2023.

Price Range - CTZ/TSX-VEN

Year	Volume	High	Low	Close
2022	1,474,894	$0.90	$0.57	$0.69
2021	3,558,566	$1.19	$0.70	$0.70
2020	5,342,069	$1.20	$0.65	$0.94
2019	5,757,152	$0.89	$0.54	$0.87
2018	3,436,008	$0.71	$0.46	$0.55

Recent Close: $0.85

Capital Stock Changes - There were no changes to capital stock from fiscal 2012 to fiscal 2022, inclusive.

Financial Statistics

Periods ended:	12m Oct. 31/22A		12m Oct. 31/21A
	$000s	%Chg	$000s
Operating revenue	**5,395**	**+8**	**4,975**
Cost of sales	889		862
Salaries & benefits	2,076		1,626
General & admin expense	652		562
Operating expense	**3,616**	**+19**	**3,050**
Operating income	**1,779**	**-8**	**1,925**
Deprec., depl. & amort.	23		75
Finance income	6		17
Finance costs, gross	nil		2
Write-downs/write-offs	(3)		(20)
Pre-tax income	**1,899**	**+10**	**1,725**
Income taxes	504		459
Net income	**1,394**	**+10**	**1,267**
Cash & equivalent	5,508		4,561
Accounts receivable	1,039		605
Current assets	6,662		5,364
Fixed assets, net	33		36
Right-of-use assets	nil		11
Total assets	**6,706**	**+23**	**5,462**
Accts. pay. & accr. liabs.	433		426
Current liabilities	659		810
Shareholders' equity	6,047		4,652
Cash from oper. activs.	**962**	**n.a.**	**(1,612)**
Cash from fin. activs.	(11)		(68)
Cash from invest. activs.	1,207		2,695
Net cash position	**4,708**	**+85**	**2,550**
Capital expenditures	(9)		(12)
	$		$
Earnings per share*	0.05		0.05
Cash flow per share*	0.04		(0.06)
	shs		shs
No. of shs. o/s*	27,286,332		27,286,332
Avg. no. of shs. o/s*	27,286,332		27,286,332
	%		%
Net profit margin	25.84		25.47
Return on equity	26.06		31.53
Return on assets	22.91		18.79
Foreign sales percent	96		96

* Common
A Reported in accordance with IFRS

Latest Results

Periods ended:	3m Jan. 31/23A		3m Jan. 31/22A
	$000s	%Chg	$000s
Operating revenue	1,497	+18	1,273
Net income	379	+30	291
	$		$
Earnings per share*	0.01		0.01

* Common
A Reported in accordance with IFRS

Historical Summary
(as originally stated)

Fiscal Year	Oper. Rev. $000s	Net Inc. Bef. Disc. $000s	EPS* $
2022A	5,395	1,394	0.05
2021A	4,975	1,267	0.05
2020A	4,746	(1,091)	(0.04)
2019A	4,119	1,299	0.05
2018A	3,242	1,148	0.04

* Common
A Reported in accordance with IFRS

N.12 Nanalysis Scientific Corp.

Symbol - NSCI **Exchange** - TSX-VEN **CUSIP** - 63000Y
Head Office - Bay 1, 4600 5 St NE, Calgary, AB, T2E 7C3 **Telephone** - (403) 769-9499 **Fax** - (403) 775-6683
Website - www.nanalysis.com
Email - sean.krakiwsky@nanalysis.com
Investor Relations - Sean Krakiwsky (587) 899-0513
Auditors - Ernst & Young LLP C.A., Calgary, Alta.
Transfer Agents - Odyssey Trust Company, Toronto, Ont.
Employees - 374 at Dec. 31, 2022
Profile - (B.C. 2017) Develops, manufactures and sells nuclear magnetic resonance (NMR) spectrometers and related products for security, pharmaceutical, biotech, nutraceutical, chemical, food, materials, education, life science and medical applications.

Provides patent-protected magnetic resonance (MR) technology to facilitate simple and rapid unknown chemical identification, quantification and diagnostics in a number of end markets including pharmaceutical, biotechnology, chemical, security, food, oil and gas, and educational industries. Also designs and builds electronic components for precision analytical instruments including medical and industrial magnetic resonance imaging (MRI), as well as both compact and full-sized nuclear magnetic resonance (NMR) devices.

Products include 100 and 60 MHz Benchtop NMR Spectrometers, high-field QUAD NMR Console, high-field Gecho customizable MNR console and Cameleon 4 MRI Console. Software portfolio includes NMRGui, SPINit,and NMRFx. Technology under development include Permanent magnet Based MRI, Robust Industrial Detector and Full High-Field NMR Systems. Also offers accessories for Benchtop NMR including AUTOsample-60 and NMReady-Flow.

Product development and manufacturing is carried out at the company's Calgary, Alta., leased facility and Strasbourg, France.

Through wholly owned **K'Prime Technologies Inc.**, sells, leases and services third-party chemical laboratory and analytical instruments, as well as offers various security solutions including maintenance of complex and large-scale security systems, and maintenance and installation of items such as metal detectors, scanning devices, airport security and general commercial security.

On Mar. 8, 2022, the company acquired a 43% interest in **QUAD Systems AG**, a Zurich-based Nuclear Magnetic Resonance (NMR) company focused on high-field NMR for pharmaceutical and other vertical markets, for issuance of 260,000 common shares. The company has an option to acquire the remaining 57% interest in QUAD until July 1, 2023.

Predecessor Detail - Name changed from Canvass Ventures Ltd., June 4, 2019, pursuant to Qualifying Transaction reverse takeover acquisition of Nanalysis Corp.; basis 1 new for 4 old shs.

Directors - Martin A. Burian, chr., Vancouver, B.C.; Sean Krakiwsky, pres. & CEO, Calgary, Alta.; Kham Lin, man. dir., Calgary, Alta.; Guido Cloetens, Belgium; Werner Gartner, Calgary, Alta.; Dr. René Lenggenhager, Switzerland; Dr. Michal Okoniewski, Calgary, Alta.

Other Exec. Officers - Randall McRae, CFO & contr.; Julien Muller, chief tech. officer

Capital Stock

	Authorized (shs.)	Outstanding (shs.)[1]
Common	unlimited	101,405,304

[1] At May 31, 2023

Major Shareholder - Widely held at May 31, 2023.

Price Range - NSCI/TSX-VEN

Year	Volume	High	Low	Close
2022	19,569,556	$1.45	$0.63	$0.73
2021	26,662,685	$1.76	$0.42	$1.45
2020	17,905,598	$0.79	$0.38	$0.48
2019	6,965,935	$0.64	$0.35	$0.48
2018	436,336	$0.90	$0.36	$0.40

Consolidation: 1-for-4 cons. in June 2019

Recent Close: $0.45

Capital Stock Changes - In April and May 2023, private placement of 6,881,167 units (1 common share & 1 warrant) at 60¢ per unit was completed, with warrants exercisable at 80¢ per share for one year.

In January 2022, 2,760,000 common shares were issued pursuant to the acquisition of K'(Prime) Technologies Inc. In February 2022, public offering of 11,212,500 common shares, including 1,462,500 on exercise of over-allotment option, and concurrent private placement of 2,628,137 common shares all at $1.10 per share were completed. Also during 2022, common shares were issued as follows: 496,695 on exercise of options, 164,944 for debt settlement and 20,000 on vesting of restricted share units.

Wholly Owned Subsidiaries

K'(Prime) Technologies Inc., Calgary, Alta.
- 100% int. in **KPrime Group USA**, Nev.
  - 100% int. in **KPrime Technologies**, Nev.

Nanalysis Corp., Calgary, Alta.
- 100% int. in **Nanalysis GmbH**, Germany.

One Moon Scientific, Inc., New York, N.Y.
RS2D S.A.S., Strasbourg, France.

Investments

43% int. in **QUAD Systems AG**, Zurich, Switzerland.
43% int. in **Quad Systems Ltd.**, United Kingdom.

Financial Statistics

Periods ended:	12m Dec. 31/22A		12m Dec. 31/21A
	$000s	%Chg	$000s
Operating revenue	**24,821**	**+55**	**16,043**
Cost of goods sold	8,220		5,046
Cost of sales	1,307		nil
Salaries & benefits	11,359		4,917
Research & devel. expense	1,089		nil
General & admin expense	6,558		4,104
Stock-based compensation	1,556		591
Operating expense	**30,089**	**+105**	**14,658**
Operating income	**(5,268)**	**n.a.**	**1,385**
Deprec., depl. & amort.	4,642		2,576
Finance costs, net	76		(2)
Write-downs/write-offs	(145)		nil
Pre-tax income	**(10,399)**	**n.a.**	**(1,772)**
Income taxes	(484)		nil
Net income	**(9,915)**	**n.a.**	**(1,772)**
Net inc. for equity hldrs	**(9,101)**	**n.a.**	**(1,772)**
Net inc. for non-cont. int	**(814)**	**n.a.**	**nil**
Cash & equivalent	3,525		10,405
Inventories	7,387		3,679
Accounts receivable	6,085		4,972
Current assets	21,955		20,762
Fixed assets, net	3,138		1,268
Right-of-use assets	3,286		1,271
Intangibles, net	39,710		14,492
Total assets	**69,902**	**+85**	**37,793**
Accts. pay. & accr. liabs	5,759		4,441
Current liabilities	13,506		8,646
Long-term debt, gross	4,900		4,681
Long-term debt, net	3,786		2,751
Shareholders' equity	47,572		23,961
Cash from oper. activs	**(8,355)**	**n.a.**	**(1,199)**
Cash from fin. activs	13,206		11,793
Cash from invest. activs	(11,731)		(3,347)
Net cash position	**3,525**	**-66**	**10,405**
Capital expenditures	(2,127)		(595)
Capital disposals	82		3
	$		$
Earnings per share*	(0.10)		(0.03)
Cash flow per share*	(0.09)		(0.02)
	shs		shs
No. of shs. o/s*	94,448,000		77,166,000
Avg. no. of shs. o/s*	92,476,000		70,402,000
	%		%
Net profit margin	(39.95)		(11.05)
Return on equity	(25.45)		(9.25)
Return on assets	(18.41)		(5.74)
Foreign sales percent	77		94
No. of employees (FTEs)	374		107

* Common
A Reported in accordance with IFRS

Latest Results

Periods ended:	3m Mar. 31/23A		3m Mar. 31/22A
	$000s	%Chg	$000s
Operating revenue	4,674	-16	5,554
Net income	(4,320)	n.a.	(1,492)
Net inc. for equity hldrs	(3,955)	n.a.	(1,450)
Net inc. for non-cont. int	(365)		(42)
	$		$
Earnings per share*	(0.04)		(0.02)

* Common
A Reported in accordance with IFRS

Historical Summary
(as originally stated)

Fiscal Year	Oper. Rev.	Net Inc. Bef. Disc.	EPS*
	$000s	$000s	$
2022A	24,821	(9,915)	(0.10)
2021A	16,043	(1,772)	(0.03)
2020A	7,874	(3,678)	(0.06)
2019A1	8,364	(1,660)	(0.03)
2018A2	8,381	73	n.a.

* Common
A Reported in accordance with IFRS
1 Results reflect the June 4, 2019, Qualifying Transaction reverse takeover acquisition of Nanalysis Corp.
2 Results for 2018 and prior year pertains to Nanalysis Corp.
Note: Adjusted throughout for 1-for-4 cons. in June 2019

N.13 Nano One Materials Corp.

Symbol - NANO **Exchange** - TSX **CUSIP** - 63010A
Head Office - Unit 101B, 8575 Government St, Burnaby, BC, V3N 4V1
Telephone - (604) 420-2041 **Fax** - (604) 608-9009
Website - www.nanoone.ca
Email - pam.kinsman@nanoone.ca
Investor Relations - Pamela Kinsman (604) 420-2041
Auditors - Davidson & Company LLP C.A., Vancouver, B.C.
Transfer Agents - Computershare Trust Company of Canada Inc., Vancouver, B.C.
Employees - 118 at Mar. 29, 2023
Profile - (B.C. 2004; orig. Alta., 1987) Develops environmentally sustainable and low-cost manufacturing technology for the production of cathode and active materials (CAM) for lithium-ion battery applications in electric vehicles, energy storage systems and consumer electronics.

The company's One-Pot Process, a patented technology that uses a lithium feedstock in the form of carbonate to reduce total cost and carbon footprint of feedstock needs per kilogram of CAM, eliminates the need to convert metal to sulphate, thereby removing downstream sulphate waste equivalent to nearly two times of CAM product volume and reduces water consumption, greenhouse gas emissions and added process costs. The One-Pot Process combines all input components including lithium, metals, additives and coatings in a single reaction to produce a precursor that, when dried and fired, forms quickly into a single nanocrystal cathode material simultaneously with its protective coating. The company has built a pilot plant for demonstration of high volume production and optimization of its technology as well as partnered with automotive equipment manufacturers and cathode manufacturers. Also, it is converting its Lithium Iron Phosphate (LFP) production facility in Candiac, Que. to its One-Pot process and is expected to commence production in the third quarter of 2023.

Also developing M2CAM® (metals to cathode active material), a patent pending technology which reduces cost, waste and carbon footprint in the lithium-ion battery supply chain by using class one metals instead of sulphates; and Coated Nanocrystal Cathode, which contains individually coated nanocrystals formed in one step and resists fracture that boosts durability and performance.

Cathode formulations under development include Lithium Iron Phosphate (LFP), Lithium Nickel Manganese Oxide (LNMO or High Voltage Spinel HVS) and Lithium Nickel Manganese Cobalt Oxide (NMC).

Has 27 patents granted in Canada, the People's Republic of China, Japan, Korea, Taiwan and the U.S., and more than 55 pending patent applications in various jurisdictions.

Recent Merger and Acquisition Activity

Status: completed **Revised:** Nov. 1, 2022
UPDATE: The transaction was completed. PREVIOUS: Nano One Materials Corp. agreed to acquire private Candiac, Que.-based Johnson Matthey Battery Materials Ltd. (JMBM), which owns a 2,400-tonne-per-annum capacity lithium iron phosphate (LFP) production facility, for $10,500,000. JMBM supplies LFP cathode material to the lithium-ion battery sector for both automotive and non-automotive applications for a select group of customers, globally.

Predecessor Detail - Name changed from Dundarave Resources Inc., Mar. 5, 2015, following reverse takeover acquisition of Perfect Lithium Corp.; basis 1 new for 2 old shs.

Directors - Dan Blondal, co-founder & CEO, Vancouver, B.C.; Paul F. Matysek, exec. chr., Vancouver, B.C.; Gordon M. (Gord) Kukec†, Vancouver, B.C.; Lyle Brown, Vancouver, B.C.; Dr. Joseph Guy, Hendersonville, N.C.; Carla Matheson, Victoria, B.C.; Lisa Skakun, Vancouver, B.C.

Other Exec. Officers - Alexander (Alex) Holmes, COO; Daniel (Dan) Martino, CFO; Dr. Stephen Campbell, chief tech. officer; Denis Geoffroy, chief commercialization officer; Kelli Forster, sr. v-p, people & culture; Adam Johnson, sr. v-p, external affairs; Pamela Kinsman, corp. sec. & dir., sustainability & corp. affairs
† Lead director

Capital Stock

	Authorized (shs.)	Outstanding (shs.)1
Common	unlimited	104,434,440

1 At Aug. 9, 2023

Major Shareholder - Widely held at May 30, 2023.

Price Range - NANO/TSX

Year	Volume	High	Low	Close
2022	34,485,754	$4.05	$1.30	$2.44
2021	45,140,830	$6.33	$2.91	$3.04
2020	67,736,777	$6.50	$0.75	$6.09
2019	10,652,919	$1.69	$1.07	$1.16
2018	34,254,925	$2.64	$0.94	$1.24

Recent Close: $2.56

Capital Stock Changes - In June 2022, private placement of 4,643,148 common shares was completed at $2.70 per share. Also during 2022, common shares were issued as follows: 200,375 on exercise of options, 141,993 on exercise of warrants and 2,876 under restricted share unit plan.

Wholly Owned Subsidiaries

Nano One Materials Québec Inc., Qué.
- 100% int. in **Nano One Materials Candiac Inc.**, Candiac, Qué.

Financial Statistics

Periods ended:	12m Dec. 31/22A		12m Dec. 31/21A
	$000s	%Chg	$000s
Salaries & benefits	7,919		1,823
Research & devel. expense	3,253		2,133
General & admin expense	2,076		2,298
Stock-based compensation	1,746		4,386
Operating expense	**14,994**	**+41**	**10,640**
Operating income	**(14,994)**	**n.a.**	**(10,640)**
Deprec., depl. & amort.	1,051		677
Finance income	924		199
Finance costs, gross	67		75
Write-downs/write-offs	nil		(131)
Pre-tax income	**(15,821)**	**n.a.**	**(11,323)**
Net income	**(15,821)**	**n.a.**	**(11,323)**
Cash & equivalent	39,445		52,652
Inventories	317		nil
Accounts receivable	1,486		411
Current assets	42,628		53,349
Fixed assets, net	13,041		1,824
Intangibles, net	31		26
Total assets	**56,076**	**+1**	**55,358**
Accts. pay. & accr. liabs	1,853		784
Current liabilities	2,040		947
Long-term lease liabilities	587		656
Shareholders' equity	53,449		53,755
Cash from oper. activs	**(9,361)**	**n.a.**	**(7,019)**
Cash from fin. activs	12,955		31,604
Cash from invest. activs	(16,801)		317
Net cash position	**39,445**	**-25**	**52,652**
Capital expenditures	(1,233)		(764)
	$		$
Earnings per share*	(0.16)		(0.12)
Cash flow per share*	(0.10)		(0.07)
	shs		shs
No. of shs. o/s*	100,516,495		95,528,103
Avg. no. of shs. o/s*	98,185,028		93,876,156
	%		%
Net profit margin	n.a.		n.a.
Return on equity	(29.52)		(27.40)
Return on assets	(28.28)		(26.06)
No. of employees (FTEs)	119		46

* Common
A Reported in accordance with IFRS

Latest Results

Periods ended:	6m June 30/23A		6m June 30/22A
	$000s	%Chg	$000s
Net income	(15,764)	n.a.	(8,728)
	$		$
Earnings per share*	(0.15)		(0.09)

* Common
A Reported in accordance with IFRS

Historical Summary
(as originally stated)

Fiscal Year	Oper. Rev.	Net Inc. Bef. Disc.	EPS*
	$000s	$000s	$
2022A	nil	(15,821)	(0.16)
2021A	nil	(11,323)	(0.12)
2020A	nil	(5,212)	(0.07)
2019A	nil	(3,781)	(0.06)
2018A	nil	(4,998)	(0.08)

* Common
A Reported in accordance with IFRS

N.14 NanoSphere Health Sciences Inc.

Symbol - NSHS **Exchange** - CSE **CUSIP** - 63010P
Head Office - 488-1090 Georgia St W, Vancouver, BC, V6E 3V7
Telephone - (604) 351-3351 **Toll-free** - (888) 781-1067
Email - maiverson@telus.net
Investor Relations - Michael A. Iverson (604) 351-3351
Auditors - Davidson & Company LLP C.A., Vancouver, B.C.
Lawyers - Fasken Martineau DuMoulin LLP, Vancouver, B.C.
Transfer Agents - TSX Trust Company, Vancouver, B.C.
Profile - (B.C. 2007; orig. Alta., 2005) Developing the NanoSphere Delivery System™, a platform using nanotechnology in the biodelivery of supplements, nutraceuticals and over-the-counter medications for the cannabis, pharmaceutical and animal health industries.

The company's primary product is the transdermal Evolve Formula NanoSerum™, which utilizes the NanoSphere Delivery System™ to transport tetrahydrocannabinol (THC) or CBD directly to the bloodstream to ease inflammation, anxiety, pain, sleep and mood. Also developing an intra-oral and intra-nasal cannabis product, which utilizes the NanoSphere Delivery System™.

Predecessor Detail - Name changed from Corazon Gold Corp., Dec. 4, 2017, following reverse takeover acquisition of NanoSphere Health Sciences LLC.

Directors - Michael A. (Mike) Iverson, chr. & interim CFO, Langley, B.C.; Toby Lim, CEO, North Vancouver, B.C.; Stephanie Hopper, Colo.

Capital Stock

	Authorized (shs.)	Outstanding (shs.)[1]
Preferred	unlimited	nil
Common	unlimited	10,275,205

[1] At Aug. 2, 2022

Major Shareholder - Widely held at Oct. 19, 2021.

Price Range - NSHS/CSE

Year	Volume	High	Low	Close
2022	924,272	$0.26	$0.02	$0.03
2021	1,288,444	$1.00	$0.20	$0.27
2020	659,404	$1.60	$0.20	$0.30
2019	1,476,300	$10.20	$0.80	$1.20
2018	1,275,579	$23.20	$4.00	$4.60

Consolidation: 1-for-20 cons. in July 2021
Recent Close: $0.02

Wholly Owned Subsidiaries

NanoSphere Cannabis International Inc.
NanoSphere Health Sciences LLC, Denver, Colo.

Financial Statistics

Periods ended:	12m Dec. 31/21[A]		12m Dec. 31/20[A]
	US$000s	%Chg	US$000s
Salaries & benefits	150		225
Research & devel. expense	60		nil
General & admin expense	154		239
Stock-based compensation	23		89
Operating expense	**386**	**-30**	**553**
Operating income	**(386)**	**n.a.**	**(553)**
Deprec., depl. & amort.	nil		14
Write-downs/write-offs	nil		(31)
Pre-tax income	**(356)**	**n.a.**	**(591)**
Net income	**(356)**	**n.a.**	**(591)**
Cash & equivalent	131		13
Accounts receivable	2		3
Current assets	133		16
Long-term investments	nil		40
Total assets	**133**	**+142**	**55**
Accts. pay. & accr. liabs	1,208		1,435
Current liabilities	1,208		1,509
Shareholders' equity	(1,075)		(1,454)
Cash from oper. activs	**(65)**	**n.a.**	**(47)**
Cash from fin. activs	182		34
Net cash position	**131**	**+908**	**13**
	US$		US$
Earnings per share*	(0.05)		(0.11)
Cash flow per share*	(0.01)		(0.01)
	shs		shs
No. of shs. o/s*	10,275,205		5,417,753
Avg. no. of shs. o/s*	6,815,100		5,417,753
	%		%
Net profit margin	n.a.		n.a.
Return on equity	n.m.		n.m.
Return on assets	(378.72)		(303.86)

* Common
[A] Reported in accordance with IFRS

Latest Results

Periods ended:	6m June 30/22[A]		6m June 30/21[A]
	US$000s	%Chg	US$000s
Net income	(153)	n.a.	(194)
	US$		US$
Earnings per share*	(0.02)		(0.04)

* Common
[A] Reported in accordance with IFRS

Historical Summary
(as originally stated)

Fiscal Year	Oper. Rev.	Net Inc. Bef. Disc.	EPS*
	US$000s	US$000s	US$
2021[A]	nil	(356)	(0.05)
2020[A]	nil	(591)	(0.11)
2019[A]	218	(3,469)	(0.60)
2018[A]	38	(4,515)	(1.00)
2017[A1]	nil	(9,910)	(18.00)

* Common
[A] Reported in accordance with IFRS
[1] Results reflect the Nov. 17, 2017, reverse takeover acquisition of Nanosphere Health Sciences LLC.

Note: Adjusted throughout for 1-for-20 cons. in July 2021

N.15 NanoXplore Inc.

Symbol - GRA **Exchange** - TSX **CUSIP** - 63010G
Head Office - 4500 boul Thimens, Montréal, QC, H4R 2P2 **Telephone** - (514) 935-1377 **Fax** - (514) 935-1344
Website - nanoxplore.ca
Email - martin.gagne@nanoxplore.ca
Investor Relations - Martin Gagné (438) 476-1342
Auditors - PricewaterhouseCoopers LLP C.A., Québec, Qué.
Lawyers - Lavery, de Billy LLP
Transfer Agents - TSX Trust Company, Toronto, Ont.
FP500 Revenue Ranking - 781
Employees - 450 at June 30, 2022

Profile - (Can. 2012; orig. Alta., 1995) Manufactures and supplies graphene powder for use in industrial markets, designs and produces standard and custom graphene-enhanced plastics and composite products for a wide variety of customers in transportation, packaging (non food-contact), building, construction, industrial and energy storage materials sectors.

Has developed a proprietary graphene production platform to produce and supply high quality graphene powder and graphene value-added products. Graphene has capabilities for energy storage, thermal conductivity, electrical conductivity, barrier properties, lubricity and the ability to impart physical property improvements when incorporated into plastics, composites, or other matrices. Products include Graphene powder, which is marketed under the GrapheneBlack™ brand; standard and custom thermoplastic and thermosets products enhanced with GrapheneBlack™; and graphene-enhanced molded plastic and composite products including precision plastic injection parts and large composite products.

Products are being used for interiors, composite body panels, energy storage for vehicles, packaging, piping, roofing, producing concrete and insulation materials, agricultural products, passenger and commercial vehicles, medical, electro-mechanical, watch-making, wind turbine, fuel and brake lines, corrosion resistance, anti-viral and anti-dirt properties.

In addition, wholly owned **VoltaXplore Inc.** is constructing a demonstration facility to develop and produce electric vehicle (EV) batteries enhanced with graphene to service the electric transportation and grid storage market.

Mason Graphite Inc. is the supplier of graphite to the company and is also a sales, marketing and distribution agent and Mason Graphite has licensed the company's thinned graphite production technology which has applications in alkaline batteries, conductive polymers and thermal diffusers.

In August 2022, the company acquired a portion of Michigan-based **XG Sciences Inc.**'s assets, including mechanical milling platform, research and development laboratory, and pending patents and trademark, for US$3,000,000.

Recent Merger and Acquisition Activity

Status: completed **Announced:** Mar. 24, 2023
Martinrea International Inc. sold its 50% interest in VoltaXplore Inc., its joint venture with NanoXplore Inc., to NanoXplore Inc. for $10,000,000 satisfied through the issuance of 3,420,406 NanoXplore common shares for $2.92 per share. On closing, Martinrea's equity interest in NanoXplore increased to 22.7% from 21.1%. VoltaXplore was formed to develop and produce electric vehicle batteries enhanced with graphene.

Predecessor Detail - Name changed from Graniz Mondal Inc., Aug. 23, 2017, pursuant to the reverse takeover acquisition of Group NanoXplore Inc.; basis 1 new for 15 old shs.

Directors - Robert P. E. (Rob) Wildeboer, v-chr., Burlington, Ont.; Dr. Soroush Nazarpour, pres. & CEO, Montréal, Qué.; Benoît Gascon†, Montréal, Qué.; Dr. Cameron Harris, Toronto, Ont.; Denis Labrecque, Trois-Rivières, Qué.; Catherine Loubier, Moorpark, Calif.; Arinder S. Mahal, Toronto, Ont.; Joseph G. (Joe) Peter

Other Exec. Officers - Rocco Marinaccio, COO; Pedro Azevedo, CFO
† Lead director

Capital Stock

	Authorized (shs.)	Outstanding (shs.)[1]
First Preferred	unlimited	nil
Second Preferred	unlimited	nil
Common	unlimited	165,575,525

[1] At Nov. 11, 2022

Major Shareholder - Martinrea International Inc. held 22.7% interest at June 30, 2023.

Price Range - GRA/TSX

Year	Volume	High	Low	Close
2022	37,311,198	$6.53	$2.05	$2.60
2021	37,416,536	$9.03	$2.99	$6.53
2020	15,817,769	$4.86	$0.90	$4.19
2019	4,513,584	$1.55	$1.12	$1.36
2018	4,955,431	$2.30	$1.03	$1.45

Recent Close: $2.58

Capital Stock Changes - In February 2022, bought deal private placement of 6,522,000 common shares was completed at $4.60 per share. Also during fiscal 2022, 771,466 common shares were issued on exercise of options.

Wholly Owned Subsidiaries

Canuck Compounders Inc., Cambridge, Ont.
NanoXplore Holdings USA, Inc., Del.
- 100% int. in **NanoXplore USA, Inc.**, Del.

NanoXplore Switzerland Holding S.A., Switzerland.
- 100% int. in **CEBO Injections S.A.**, Switzerland.

Sigma Industries Inc., Saint-Éphrem-de-Beauce, Qué.
- 100% int. in **Faroex Ltd.**, Gimli, Man.
- 100% int. in **René Composites Materials Ltd.**, Saint-Éphrem-de-Beauce, Qué.
  - 100% int. in **RMC Advanced Technologies Inc.**, Tenn.
    - 100% int. in **RMC USA Inc.**, Ohio
- 100% int. in **Sigma US Industries Inc.**, Del.

VoltaXplore Inc., Dollard-des-Ormeaux, Qué.

Financial Statistics

Periods ended:	12m June 30/22[A]		12m June 30/21[A]
	$000s	%Chg	$000s
Operating revenue	**92,334**	**+39**	**66,655**
Cost of sales	89,256		59,026
Research & devel. expense	3,579		3,550
General & admin expense	16,399		14,047
Stock-based compensation	699		673
Operating expense	**109,933**	**+42**	**77,296**
Operating income	**(17,599)**	**n.a.**	**(10,641)**
Deprec., depl. & amort.	7,376		6,206
Finance income	458		234
Finance costs, gross	1,220		1,884
Investment income	(744)		(53)
Pre-tax income	**(16,517)**	**n.a.**	**(12,831)**
Income taxes	(976)		(1,023)
Net income	**(15,541)**	**n.a.**	**(11,808)**
Cash & equivalent	51,232		50,525
Inventories	17,508		11,036
Accounts receivable	21,078		12,733
Current assets	90,951		77,335
Long-term investments	4,239		3,983
Fixed assets, net	54,329		54,934
Right-of-use assets	8,381		4,885
Intangibles, net	9,176		3,815
Total assets	**167,258**	**+15**	**145,302**
Bank indebtedness	4,649		1,343
Accts. pay. & accr. liabs	17,030		15,229
Current liabilities	27,875		24,471
Long-term debt, gross	9,451		11,652
Long-term debt, net	6,282		8,155
Shareholders' equity	117,531		102,987
Cash from oper. activs	**(20,115)**	**n.a.**	**(6,135)**
Cash from fin. activs	26,547		38,087
Cash from invest. activs	(5,740)		(15,145)
Net cash position	**51,232**	**+1**	**50,525**
Capital expenditures	(3,298)		(8,817)
Capital disposals	8,325		101
Unfunded pension liability	297		811
	$		$
Earnings per share*	(0.10)		(0.08)
Cash flow per share*	(0.13)		(0.04)
	shs		shs
No. of shs. o/s*	165,223,525		157,930,059
Avg. no. of shs. o/s*	160,559,612		148,056,067
	%		%
Net profit margin	(16.83)		(17.72)
Return on equity	(14.09)		(14.40)
Return on assets	(9.21)		(7.78)
Foreign sales percent	71		55
No. of employees (FTEs)	450		376

* Common
[A] Reported in accordance with IFRS

Latest Results

Periods ended:	3m Sept. 30/22[A]		3m Sept. 30/21[A]
	$000s	%Chg	$000s
Operating revenue	27,147	+52	17,830
Net income	(5,924)	n.a.	(4,731)
	$		$
Earnings per share*	(0.04)		(0.03)

* Common
[A] Reported in accordance with IFRS

Historical Summary
(as originally stated)

Fiscal Year	Oper. Rev.	Net Inc. Bef. Disc.	EPS*
	$000s	$000s	$
2022[A]	92,334	(15,541)	(0.10)
2021[A]	66,655	(11,808)	(0.08)
2020[A]	62,202	(8,273)	(0.07)
2019[A]	68,700	(10,603)	(0.11)
2018[A1]	7,856	(6,124)	(0.08)

* Common
[A] Reported in accordance with IFRS
[1] Results reflect the Aug. 29, 2017, reverse takeover acquisition of Group NanoXplore Inc.

N.16 Nass Valley Gateway Ltd.

Symbol - NVG **Exchange** - CSE (S) **CUSIP** - 631520
Head Office - 170-422 Richards St, Vancouver, BC, V6B 2Z4 **Telephone** - (604) 617-6794 **Toll-free** - (800) 839-4499
Website - www.nassvalleygateway.com
Email - michael.s@nassvalleygateway.com
Investor Relations - Michael Semler (604) 617-6794
Auditors - Manning Elliott LLP C.A., Vancouver, B.C.
Transfer Agents - Computershare Trust Company of Canada Inc., Vancouver, B.C.

Profile - (B.C. 2005) Develops and sells organic, non-GMO hemp-based cannabidiol (CBD) products for human and pet consumption.

Develops and sells hemp-based CBD products with zero tetrahydrocannabinol (THC) sold under the Nass Valley Gardens brand through retail, wholesale, direct sales, and digital sales channels. Products include CBD gummies, oil, coffee, skincare, bath bombs, hair care, essential oils, relief rubs, delta 8 distillates, soft gel capsules, smokables as well as treats and tinctures for pets.

In addition, the company has an agreement with **Dynamic Blending Specialists** (DBS), a contract manufacturer of zero-THC CBD cosmetic and dermatological products located in Vineyard, Utah, whereby DBS would provide the company with zero-THC CBD products.

Common suspended from CSE, July 14, 2023.

Directors - Michael Semler, CEO, West Palm Beach, Fla.; Armand Assante, N.Y.; Troy Dooly; Jeanine B. Getz, Greenwich, Conn.; Michael Racaniello; Jeff Rogers

Other Exec. Officers - Jakob Hershey, COO; Gregory Vax, CFO

Capital Stock

	Authorized (shs.)	Outstanding (shs.)[1]
Common	unlimited	312,832,777

[1] At Aug. 29, 2022

Major Shareholder - Global 1 Solutions LLC and NBI LLC, collevtively held 32.47% interest at Mar. 29, 2021.

Price Range - NVG/CSE (S)

Year	Volume	High	Low	Close
2022	3,200,273	$0.14	$0.03	$0.05
2021	14,382,593	$0.79	$0.09	$0.09
2020	3,739,470	$0.28	$0.01	$0.20
2019	2,431,206	$0.31	$0.02	$0.06

Recent Close: $0.02

Wholly Owned Subsidiaries

Advanced Bioceutical Limited, N.J.
Nass Valley Gardens Inc.
Pro-Thotics Technology, Inc., N.Y.

Financial Statistics

Periods ended:	12m Dec. 31/21[A]		12m Dec. 31/20[A]
	$000s	%Chg	$000s
Operating revenue	**56**	**+250**	**16**
Cost of sales	26		8
General & admin expense	4,131		2,587
Stock-based compensation	nil		7
Operating expense	**4,157**	**+60**	**2,602**
Operating income	**(4,101)**	**n.a.**	**(2,586)**
Finance costs, gross	17		11
Write-downs/write-offs	(175)		(289)
Pre-tax income	**(4,294)**	**n.a.**	**(2,895)**
Net inc. bef. disc. opers	**(4,294)**	**n.a.**	**(2,895)**
Income from disc. opers	(120)		(267)
Net income	**(4,414)**	**n.a.**	**(3,162)**
Cash & equivalent	57		827
Inventories	128		23
Accounts receivable	5		5
Current assets	1,169		1,380
Total assets	**1,169**	**-15**	**1,380**
Accts. pay. & accr. liabs	96		87
Current liabilities	13,616		9,411
Shareholders' equity	(12,447)		(8,030)
Cash from oper. activs	**(4,843)**	**n.a.**	**(2,692)**
Cash from fin. activs	4,081		3,589
Net cash position	**57**	**-93**	**827**
	$		$
Earns. per sh. bef disc opers*	(0.01)		(0.01)
Earnings per share*	(0.01)		(0.01)
Cash flow per share*	(0.02)		(0.01)
	shs		shs
No. of shs. o/s*	312,832,777		312,832,777
Avg. no. of shs. o/s*	312,832,777		312,832,777
	%		%
Net profit margin	n.m.		n.m.
Return on equity	n.m.		n.m.
Return on assets	(335.58)		n.a.

* Common
[A] Reported in accordance with IFRS

Latest Results

Periods ended:	6m June 30/22[A]		6m June 30/21[A]
	$000s	%Chg	$000s
Operating revenue	10	-47	19
Net inc. bef. disc. opers	(646)	n.a.	(3,523)
Income from disc. opers	(61)		(59)
Net income	(707)	n.a.	(3,583)
	$		$
Earns. per sh. bef. disc. opers.*	(0.00)		(0.01)
Earnings per share*	(0.00)		(0.01)

* Common
[A] Reported in accordance with IFRS

Historical Summary
(as originally stated)

Fiscal Year	Oper. Rev.	Net Inc. Bef. Disc.	EPS*
	$000s	$000s	$
2021[A]	56	(4,294)	(0.01)
2020[A]	16	(2,895)	(0.01)
2019[A1]	nil	(2,158)	(0.01)
2018[A2]	nil	(174)	(0.01)
2017[A]	nil	(112)	(0.00)

* Common
[A] Reported in accordance with IFRS
[1] Results reflect the Mar. 9, 2019, reverse takeover acquisition of Advanced Bioceutical Limited.
[2] Results for 2018 and prior years pertain to (old) Nass Valley Gateway Ltd.

N.17 National Bank of Canada*

Symbol - NA **Exchange** - TSX **CUSIP** - 633067
Head Office - National Bank Tower, 400-600 rue de la Gauchetière O, Montréal, QC, H3B 4L2 **Telephone** - (514) 394-5000
Website - www.nbc.ca
Email - investorrelations@nbc.ca
Investor Relations - Linda Boulanger (866) 517-5455
Auditors - Deloitte LLP C.A., Montréal, Qué.
Lawyers - McCarthy Tétrault LLP, Montréal, Qué.
Transfer Agents - Computershare Trust Company of Canada Inc., Montréal, Qué.
FP500 Revenue Ranking - 44
Employees - 29,509 at Oct. 31, 2022

Profile - (Can. 1979) A Schedule I Canadian chartered bank providing banking and investment solutions, securities brokerage, insurance, wealth management, corporate and investment banking, and mutual fund and pension fund management to 2,700,000 retail, commercial, corporate and institutional clients.

Personal & Commercial Banking - This segment offers everyday transaction solutions, mortgage and consumer loans, credit cards, insurance, payment solutions and savings and investment solutions to close to 2,600,000 individuals and over 145,000 businesses across Canada through 378 branches, 939 automated banking machines, and telephone and Internet banking. Personal banking offers individuals and small business clients financial products and services including everyday transaction solutions, mortgage loans and home equity lines of credit, consumer loans, payment solutions, savings and investment solutions as well as a range of insurance products. Commercial banking serves small and medium-sized businesses and large corporations across Canada. Services include credit, deposit and investment solutions, international trade, foreign exchange, payroll, cash management, insurance, electronic transactions and complementary services.

Wealth Management - This segment consists of wealth management services including trust and estate planning, financial and succession planning, portfolio management, administrative and trade execution, custodial and brokerage, insurance and annuity, banking solutions and complementary services. All its investment solutions, products and specialized services are provided through 835 investment advisors at 86 service outlets across Canada. At Oct. 31, 2022, assets under administration and management totaled $728.511 billion compared to $768.716 billion at Oct. 31, 2021.

Financial Markets - This segment consists of corporate and investment banking services including loan origination and syndication as well as debt and equity underwriting for project financing, merger and acquisition transactions and corporate financing solutions to large and mid-sized corporations in the public sector and institutions across Canada. The segment also include solutions covering fixed income securities, currencies, equities, commodities as well as providing liquidity, research and counterparty services to institutional investors in the United States and internationally. In addition, the bank engages in trading activities with large European-based institutions in local equity and equity-linked securities. More than 900 professionals serve client needs through offices in North America, Europe, the U.K., and Asia.

U.S. Specialty Finance and International - The segment includes the operations of wholly owned **Credigy Ltd.**, a specialty finance corporation located in Atlanta, Ga., with an expertise in investment and management of performing and non-performing debt portfolios, operating exclusively outside Canada; and wholly owned **Advanced Bank of Asia Limited** (ABA Bank), a major financial institution offering financial products and services to individuals and businesses through its 81 branches, 962 automated teller machines and other self-service machines, and advanced online banking and mobile banking platforms in Cambodia.

In addition, through subsidiary **Flinks Technology Inc.** (86% owned), the bank provides services to a wide North American fintech ecosystem and offers attractive data technology solutions including loan underwriting, money transfer, wealth and personal finance planning and investment.

Recent Merger and Acquisition Activity

Status: pending **Announced:** Aug. 1, 2023
National Bank of Canada agreed to acquire the commercial loan portfolio of Silicon Valley Bank's Canadian branch. Terms were not disclosed. The bank would acquire a portfolio in the technology, life science and global fund banking sectors and consists of $ 1 billion in loan commitments of which around $325,000,000 are outstanding. The assets would be integrated into National Bank's Technology and Innovation Banking Group.

Directors - Robert Paré, chr., Westmount, Qué.; Laurent Ferreira, pres. & CEO, Westmount, Qué.; Maryse Bertrand, Westmount, Qué.; Pierre J. Blouin, Montréal, Qué.; Pierre Boivin, Montréal, Qué.; Yvon Charest, Québec, Qué.; Patricia Curadeau-Grou, Montréal, Qué.; Annick Guérard, Montréal, Qué.; Karen A. Kinsley, Ottawa, Ont.; B. Lynn Loewen, Westmount, Qué.; Rebecca McKillican, Oakville, Ont.; Pierre Pomerleau, Montréal, Qué.; Emmanuele A. (Lino) Saputo Jr., Montréal, Qué.; Macky Tall, Indialantic, Fla.

Other Exec. Officers - Stéphane Achard, exec. v-p & head, ABA Bank; Lucie Blanchet, exec. v-p, personal banking & client experience; William Bonnell, exec. v-p, risk mgt. & chief risk officer; Eric Bujold, exec. v-p; Michael Denham, exec. v-p & head, comml. banking & private banking; Etienne Dubuc, exec. v-p & head, finl. markets; Marie Chantal Gingras, exec. v-p, fin. & CFO; Denis Girouard, exec. v-p; Brigitte Hébert, exec. v-p, employee experience; Julie Lévesque, exec. v-p, tech. & opers.; Ghislain Parent, exec. v-p, intl.; Martin Verschuere, exec. v-p, man. dir., head, currencies & equities & co-head, structured products; Dominic Paradis, sr. v-p, legal affairs & corp. sec.; Jonathan Durocher, pres., NBF Wealth Management

Capital Stock

	Authorized (shs.)	Outstanding (shs.)[1]
First Preferred	unlimited	
Series 30		14,000,000
Series 32		12,000,000
Series 38		16,000,000
Series 40		12,000,000
Series 42		12,000,000
Second Preferred	15,000,000	nil
Limited Recourse Capital Notes	n.a.	
Series 1		500,000
Series 2		500,000
Series 3		500,000
Common	unlimited	337,869,397

[1] At May 26, 2023

First Preferred - Issuable for a maximum aggregate consideration of $5 billion. Issuable in series at the discretion of directors. Non-voting.

Pursuant to the Bank Act, the bank will not, without approval of the holders of the first preferred shares, create or issue any other class of shares ranking in priority to or pari passu with the first preferred shares. In addition, approval of the holders of first preferred shares as a class is required if dividends are in arrears on any outstanding series of first preferred shares for the creation or issuance of additional series of first preferred shares.

Series 30 - Entitled to non-cumulative annual dividends of $1.0063 payable quarterly to May 15, 2024, and thereafter at a rate reset every five years equal to the five-year Government of Canada yield plus 2.4%. Redeemable on May 15, 2024, and on May 15 every five years thereafter at $25 per share plus declared and unpaid dividends. Convertible at the holder's option, on May 15, 2024, and on May 15 every five years thereafter, into non-cumulative floating rate preferred series 31 shares on a share-for-share basis, subject to certain conditions. The series 31 shares would pay a quarterly dividend equal to the 90-day Canadian Treasury bill rate plus 2.4%. Convertible into common shares upon occurrence of certain trigger events related to financial viability. The contingent conversion formula is 1.0 multiplied by $25 plus declared and unpaid dividends divided by the greater of (i) a floor price of $5.00; and (ii) current market price of the common shares.

Series 32 - Entitled to non-cumulative annual dividends of $0.9598 payable quarterly to Feb. 15, 2025, and thereafter at a rate reset every five years equal to the five-year Government of Canada yield plus 2.25%. Redeemable on Feb. 15, 2025, and on February 15 every five years thereafter at $25 per share plus declared and unpaid dividends. Convertible at the holder's option, on Feb. 15, 2025, and on February 15 every five years thereafter, into non-cumulative floating rate preferred series 33 shares on a share-for-share basis, subject to certain conditions. The series 33 shares would pay a quarterly dividend equal to the 90-day Canadian Treasury bill rate plus 2.25%. Convertible into common shares upon occurrence of certain trigger events related to financial viability. The contingent conversion formula is 1.0 multiplied by $25 plus declared and unpaid dividends divided by the greater of (i) a floor price of $5.00; and (ii) current market price of the common shares.

Series 38 - Entitled to non-cumulative annual dividends of $1.75675 payable quarterly to Nov. 15, 2027, and thereafter at a rate reset every five years equal to the five-year Government of Canada yield plus 3.43%. Redeemable on Nov. 15, 2027, and on November 15 every five years thereafter at $25 per share plus declared and unpaid dividends. Convertible at the holder's option, on Nov. 15, 2027, and on November 15 every five years thereafter, into non-cumulative floating rate preferred series 39 shares on a share-for-share basis, subject to certain conditions. The series 39 shares would pay a quarterly dividend equal to the 90-day Canadian Treasury bill rate plus 3.43%. Convertible into common shares upon occurrence of certain trigger events related to financial viability. The contingent conversion formula is 1.0 multiplied by $25 plus declared and unpaid dividends divided by the greater of (i) a floor price of $5.00; and (ii) current market price of the common shares.

Series 40 - Entitled to non-cumulative annual dividends of $1.15 payable quarterly to May 15, 2023, and thereafter at a rate reset every five years equal to the five-year Government of Canada yield plus 2.58%. Redeemable on May 15, 2023, and on May 15 every five years thereafter at $25 per share plus declared and unpaid dividends. Convertible at the holder's option, on May 15, 2023, and on May 15 every five years thereafter, into non-cumulative floating rate preferred series 41 shares on a share-for-share basis, subject to certain conditions. The series 41 shares would pay a quarterly dividend equal to the 90-day Canadian

Treasury bill rate plus 2.58%. Convertible into common shares upon occurrence of certain trigger events related to financial viability. The contingent conversion formula is 1.0 multiplied by $25 plus declared and unpaid dividends divided by the greater of (i) a floor price of $5.00; and (ii) current market price of the common shares.

Series 42 - Entitled to non-cumulative annual dividends of $1.2375 payable quarterly to Nov. 15, 2023, and thereafter at a rate reset every five years equal to the five-year Government of Canada yield plus 2.77%. Redeemable on Nov. 15, 2023, and on November 15 every five years thereafter at $25 per share plus declared and unpaid dividends. Convertible at the holder's option, on Nov. 15, 2023, and on November 15 every five years thereafter, into non-cumulative floating rate preferred series 43 shares on a share-for-share basis, subject to certain conditions. The series 43 shares would pay a quarterly dividend equal to the 90-day Canadian Treasury bill rate plus 2.77%. Convertible into common shares upon occurrence of certain trigger events related to financial viability. The contingent conversion formula is 1.0 multiplied by $25 plus declared and unpaid dividends divided by the greater of (i) a floor price of $5.00; and (ii) current market price of the common shares.

Second Preferred - Issuable for a maximum aggregate consideration of $300,000,000. Non-voting.

Limited Recourse Capital Notes (LRCNs) - Notes with recourse limited to assets held by an independent trustee in a consolidated limited recourse trust. **LRCN - Series 1** - Bear interest at 4.3% per annum until Nov. 15, 2025, exclusively and, thereafter, at an annual rate reset every five years equal to the yield on five-year Government of Canada bonds plus 3.943% until maturity on Nov. 15, 2080. Trust assets consist of non-cumulative five-year reset first preferred series 44 shares. **LRCN - Series 2** - Bear interest at 4.05% per annum until Aug. 15, 2026, exclusively and, thereafter, at an annual rate reset every five years equal to the yield on five-year Government of Canada bonds plus 3.045% until maturity on Aug. 15, 2081. Trust assets consist of non-cumulative five-year reset first preferred series 45 shares. **LRCN - Series 3** - Bear interest at 7.5% per annum until Nov. 16, 2027, exclusively and, thereafter, at an annual rate reset every five years equal to the yield on five-year Government of Canada bonds plus 4.281% until maturity on Nov. 16, 2082. Trust assets consist of non-cumulative five-year reset first preferred series 46 shares.

Common - One vote per share.

Options - At Oct. 31, 2022, options were outstanding to purchase 11,861,749 common shares at prices ranging from $38.36 to $96.35 per share and expiring to December 2031.

First Preferred Series 34 (old) - Were entitled to non-cumulative annual dividends of $1.40 payable quarterly to May 15, 2021. Redeemed on May 17, 2021, at $25 per share plus declared and unpaid dividends.

First Preferred Series 36 (old) - Were entitled to non-cumulative annual dividends of $1.35 payable quarterly to Aug. 15, 2021. Redeemed on Aug. 16, 2021, at $25 per share plus declared and unpaid dividends.

Normal Course Issuer Bid - The company plans to make normal course purchases of up to 7,000,000 common shares representing 2.1% of the total outstanding. The bid commenced on Dec. 12, 2022, and expires on Dec. 11, 2023.

Major Shareholder - Widely held at Mar. 9, 2023.

Price Range - NA/TSX

Year	Volume	High	Low	Close
2022	389,417,319	$104.83	$82.16	$91.23
2021	378,066,817	$106.10	$70.81	$96.44
2020	420,079,907	$75.01	$38.67	$71.64
2019	290,030,465	$73.22	$55.44	$72.08
2018	242,523,608	$65.95	$54.37	$56.05

Recent Close: $98.16

Capital Stock Changes - In September 2022, 500,000 first preferred series 46 shares were issued in conjunction with the issuance of $500,000,000 of limited recourse capital notes series 3 priced at $1,000 per note. Also during fiscal 2022, 1,193,663 common shares were issued on exercise of options, 2,500,000 common shares were repurchased under a Normal Course Issuer Bid, 18,295 common shares were repurchased for trading and 5,527 common shares were repurchased for other purposes.

Dividends

NA com Ra $4.08 pa Q est. Aug. 1, 2023**
Prev. Rate: $3.88 est. Feb. 1, 2023
Prev. Rate: $3.68 est. Aug. 1, 2022
Prev. Rate: $3.48 est. Feb. 1, 2022
Prev. Rate: $2.84 est. Feb. 1, 2020
NA.PR.S pfd 1st ser 30 red. exch. Adj. Ra $1.00625 pa Q est. Aug. 15, 2019
NA.PR.W pfd 1st ser 32 red. exch. Adj. Ra $0.95975 pa Q est. May 15, 2020
NA.PR.C pfd 1st ser 38 red. exch. Adj. Ra $1.75675 pa Q est. Feb. 15, 2023
NA.PR.E pfd 1st ser 40 red. exch. Adj. Ra $1.4545 pa Q est. Aug. 15, 2023
NA.PR.G pfd 1st ser 42 red. exch. Adj. Ra $1.2375 pa Q est. Nov. 15, 2018
pfd 1st ser 34 red. exch. Adj. Ra $1.40 pa Q est. May 15, 2016[1]
$0.35**f** May 15/21
pfd 1st ser 36 red. exch. Adj. Ra $1.35 pa Q est. Nov. 15, 2016[2]
$0.3375**f** Aug. 15/21
[1] Redeemed May 15, 2021 at $25 per sh.
[2] Redeemed Aug. 16, 2021 at $25 per sh.
** Reinvestment Option **f** Final Payment

Long-Term Debt - Outstanding at Oct. 31, 2022:

Medium-term notes due 2028[1]	$750,000,000
Medium-term notes due 2032[2]	750,000,000
Fair value hedge adj.	2,000,000
Unamort. issuance costs	(3,000,000)
	1,499,000,0000

[1] Bearing interest at 3.183% until Feb. 1, 2023, and thereafter at a floating rate equal to the three-month CDOR plus 0.72%.

[2] Bearing interest at 5.426% until Aug. 16, 2027, and thereafter at a floating rate equal to the Canadian Overnight Repo Rate Average (CORRA) compounded daily plus 2.32%.

Note - In February 2023, all $750,000,000 principal amount of 3.183% medium-term notes due 2028 were redeemed.

Wholly Owned Subsidiaries

ATA IT Ltd., Bangkok, Thailand. Carrying value of voting shares owned by the bank at Oct. 31, 2022, totaled $3,000,000.

Advanced Bank of Asia Limited, Cambodia. Carrying value of voting shares owned by the bank at Oct. 31, 2022, totaled $621,000,000.

NBC Financial Markets Asia Limited, Hong Kong, Hong Kong, People's Republic of China. Carrying value of voting shares owned by the bank at Oct. 31, 2022, totaled $5,000,000.

NatBC Holding Corporation, Hollywood, Fla. Carrying value of voting shares owned by the bank at Oct. 31, 2022, totaled $31,000,000.
- 100% int. in **Natbank, National Association**, Hollywood, Fla.

Natcan Global Holdings Ltd., Sliema, Malta. Carrying value of voting shares owned by the bank at Oct. 31, 2022, totaled $22,000,000.
- 100% int. in **NBC Global Finance Limited**, Dublin, Ireland.

National Bank Acquisition Holding Inc., Montréal, Qué. Carrying value of voting shares owned by the bank at Oct. 31, 2022, totaled $1,785,000,000.
- 100% int. in **Natcan Trust Company**, Montréal, Qué. Carrying value of voting shares owned by the bank at Oct. 31, 2022, totaled $238,000,000.
- 100% int. in **National Bank Financial Inc.**, Montréal, Qué.
  - 100% int. in **NBF International Holdings Inc.**, Montréal, Qué.
    - 100% int. in **National Bank of Canada Financial Group Inc.**, New York, N.Y.
      - 100% int. in **Credigy Ltd.**, Norcross, Ga.
      - 100% int. in **National Bank of Canada Financial Inc.**
- 100% int. in **National Bank Investments Inc.**, Montréal, Qué. Carrying value of voting shares owned by the bank at Oct. 31, 2022, totaled $441,000,000.
- 100% int. in **National Bank Life Insurance Company**, Montréal, Qué.

National Bank Realty Inc., Montréal, Qué. Carrying value of voting shares owned by the bank at Oct. 31, 2022, totaled $80,000,000.

National Bank Trust Inc., Montréal, Qué. Carrying value of voting shares owned by the bank at Oct. 31, 2022, totaled $195,000,000.

Subsidiaries

86% int. in **Flinks Technology Inc.**, Montréal, Qué. Carrying value of voting shares owned by the bank at Oct. 31, 2022, totaled $144,000,000.

Investments

2.5% int. in **TMX Group Limited**, Toronto, Ont. (see separate coverage)

Note: The preceding list includes only the major related companies in which interests are held.

Financial Statistics

Periods ended:	12m Oct. 31/22[A]		12m Oct. 31/21[□A]
	$000s	%Chg	$000s
Interest income	**9,545,000**	**+37**	**6,987,000**
Interest expense	4,274,000		2,204,000
Net interest income	**5,271,000**	**+10**	**4,783,000**
Provision for loan losses	145,000		2,000
Other income	4,381,000		4,144,000
Salaries & pension benefits	3,284,000		3,027,000
Non-interest expense	5,230,000		4,903,000
Pre-tax income	**4,277,000**	**+6**	**4,022,000**
Income taxes	894,000		882,000
Net income	**3,383,000**	**+8**	**3,140,000**
Net inc. for equity hldrs	**3,384,000**	**+8**	**3,140,000**
Net inc. for non-cont. int	**(1,000)**	**n.a.**	**nil**
Cash & equivalent	31,870,000		33,879,000
Securities	109,719,000		106,304,000
Net non-performing loans	479,000		283,000
Total loans	226,689,000		183,369,000
Fixed assets, net	1,397,000		1,216,000
Total assets	**403,740,000**	**+14**	**355,621,000**
Deposits	266,394,000		240,938,000
Other liabilities	114,101,000		95,233,000
Subordinated debt	1,499,000		768,000
Preferred share equity	3,150,000		2,650,000
Shareholders' equity	21,744,000		18,679,000
Non-controlling interest	2,000		3,000
Cash from oper. activs	**(1,922,000)**	**n.a.**	**6,038,000**
Cash from fin. activs	(381,000)		(1,739,000)
Cash from invest. activs	(1,456,000)		1,467,000
Pension fund surplus	498,000		691,000
	$		$
Earnings per share*	9.72		8.95
Cash flow per share*	(5.70)		17.91
Cash divd. per share*	3.58		2.84
	shs		shs
No. of shs. o/s*	336,582,124		337,912,283
Avg. no. of shs. o/s*	337,099,000		337,212,000
	%		%
Basel III Common Equity Tier 1	12.70		12.40
Basel III Tier 1	15.40		15.00
Basel III Total	16.90		15.90
Net profit margin	35.05		35.17
Return on equity	18.83		20.48
Return on assets	0.89		0.91
Foreign sales percent	16		15
No. of employees (FTEs)	29,509		26,920

* Common
[□] Restated
[A] Reported in accordance with IFRS

Latest Results

Periods ended:	6m Apr. 30/23[A]		6m Apr. 30/22[□A]
	$000s	%Chg	$000s
Net interest income	1,981,000	-25	2,645,000
Net income	1,728,000	-5	1,819,000
Net inc. for equity hldrs	1,729,000	-5	1,820,000
Net inc. for non-cont. int	(1,000)		(1,000)
	$		$
Earnings per share*	4.92		5.24

* Common
[□] Restated
[A] Reported in accordance with IFRS

Historical Summary
(as originally stated)

Fiscal Year	Int. Inc.	Net Inc. Bef. Disc.	EPS*
	$000s	$000s	$
2022[A]	9,545,000	3,383,000	9.72
2021[A]	6,987,000	3,177,000	9.06
2020[A]	7,578,000	2,083,000	5.73
2019[A]	8,174,000	2,322,000	6.39
2018[A]	6,935,000	2,232,000	6.01

* Common
[A] Reported in accordance with IFRS

N.18 Naturally Splendid Enterprises Ltd.

Symbol - NSP **Exchange** - TSX-VEN (S) **CUSIP** - 63902L
Head Office - 108-19100 Airport Way, Pitt Meadows, BC, V3Y 0E2
Telephone - (604) 465-0548 **Toll-free** - (888) 692-0902 **Fax** - (604) 465-1128
Website - www.naturallysplendid.com
Email - info@naturallysplendid.com
Investor Relations - Craig J. Goodwin (604) 570-0902
Auditors - Buckley Dodds C.P.A., Vancouver, B.C.
Transfer Agents - Computershare Trust Company of Canada Inc., Vancouver, B.C.

Profile - (B.C. 2010) Develops, manufactures, markets and distributes plant-based meat-alternative products under the Plantein™ brand in Canada.

The company was granted by Australian-based **Flexitarian Foods Pty. Ltd.** to exclusively manufacture and distribute Plantein™ products in Canada. Plantein™ consists of a line of meat-alternatives, primarily appetizers and entrees, including beef, chicken, pork, fish and shellfish, which are sold through retail, food service and e-commerce sites. The company also intends to provide contract manufacturing and private label services of plant-based products.

The company has a former manufacturing facility in Pitt Meadows, B.C., which is being repurposed for packaging and distribution. The company plans to move manufacturing operations to a new location in Ontario.

In November 2022, the company announced the discontinuation of its existing product lines as well as the contract manufacturing of private label bars and bites. The products included Elevate Me™ protein bars; Woods Wild™ mushroom bars; NATERA, which included sports bars, bites and supplements (NATERA™ Sport) as well as hemp foods (NATERA™ Hemp Foods); CHII™ line of hemp foods; Pawsitive FX™ health and wellness products for canines; and Timer's Nutrition™ hemp-based nutritional products for the equestrian market.

In August 2022, the company announced the termination of its joint venture, **Plasm Pharmaceutical Inc.**, with **Biologic Publishing Inc.** Plasm was formed to pursue the commercialization of Cavaltinib™ for multiple indications, including COVID-19. The company was acquiring a 16% interest in Plasm.

In April 2022, the company entered into an agreement with **Flexitarian Foods Pty. Ltd.** for the exclusive use of Flexitarian's Plantein™ brand in Canada for an initial 10 years and a renewable term for another 10 years.

Common suspended from TSX-VEN, July 18, 2023.

Predecessor Detail - Name changed from Race Capital Corp., Feb. 28, 2013, pursuant to Qualifying Transaction reverse takeover acquisition of Naturally Splendid Enterprises Ltd.

Directors - Bryan Carson, co-founder, v-p, opers. & interim CFO, Burnaby, B.C.; Craig J. Goodwin, co-founder, pres. & CEO, Burnaby, B.C.; Larry Gilmour, B.C.

Other Exec. Officers - Kris Tarr, v-p, e-commerce; Ranbir (Reena) Sall, contr.

Capital Stock

	Authorized (shs.)	Outstanding (shs.)[1]
Preferred	unlimited	nil
Common	unlimited	22,041,631

[1] At Nov. 29, 2022

Major Shareholder - Widely held at July 27, 2022.

Price Range - NSP/TSX-VEN (S)

Year	Volume	High	Low	Close
2022	4,635,336	$0.75	$0.04	$0.04
2021	10,462,668	$1.50	$0.30	$0.38
2020	12,310,287	$2.10	$0.38	$0.83
2019	2,913,987	$2.63	$0.90	$1.05
2018	10,118,655	$7.80	$1.65	$1.88

Consolidation: 1-for-15 cons. in Sept. 2022

Recent Close: $0.02

Capital Stock Changes - In January 2022, private placement of 2,446,458 units (1 post-consolidated common share & 1 warrant) at 45¢ per unit was completed, with warrants exercisable at 75¢ per share for two years. On Sept. 22, 2022, common shares were consolidated on a 1-for-15 basis.

Wholly Owned Subsidiaries

Naturally Splendid Extracts Ltd., Canada.
Naturally Splendid Foods Ltd., Canada.
Naturally Splendid U.S.A. Ltd., United States.
PROsnack Natural Foods Inc., Vancouver, B.C.

Financial Statistics

Periods ended:	12m Dec. 31/21[A]		12m Dec. 31/20[A]
	$000s	%Chg	$000s
Operating revenue	**764**	**-52**	**1,576**
Cost of sales	682		1,460
Research & devel. expense	12		nil
General & admin expense	2,253		3,241
Stock-based compensation	nil		376
Operating expense	**2,947**	**-42**	**5,077**
Operating income	**(2,183)**	**n.a.**	**(3,501)**
Deprec., depl. & amort.	566		643
Finance costs, gross	306		290
Write-downs/write-offs	(200)		(259)
Pre-tax income	**(3,142)**	**n.a.**	**(4,660)**
Net income	**(3,142)**	**n.a.**	**(4,660)**
Cash & equivalent	1,388		202
Inventories	701		873
Accounts receivable	50		351
Current assets	2,288		1,499
Fixed assets, net	1,893		2,433
Intangibles, net	27		56
Total assets	**4,274**	**+5**	**4,053**
Bank indebtedness	293		255
Accts. pay. & accr. liabs	3,952		3,261
Current liabilities	4,746		3,943
Long-term lease liabilities	830		1,058
Shareholders' equity	(1,302)		(948)
Cash from oper. activs	**(1,213)**	**n.a.**	**(1,756)**
Cash from fin. activs	2,392		1,888
Cash from invest. activs	8		(44)
Net cash position	**1,388**	**+587**	**202**
Capital expenditures	nil		(124)
Capital disposals	8		85
	$		$
Earnings per share*	(0.15)		(0.45)
Cash flow per share*	(0.08)		(0.15)
	shs		shs
No. of shs. o/s*	19,551,728		13,611,134
Avg. no. of shs. o/s*	14,561,289		11,419,989
	%		%
Net profit margin	(411.26)		(295.69)
Return on equity	n.m.		n.m.
Return on assets	(68.12)		(90.53)

* Common
[A] Reported in accordance with IFRS

Latest Results

Periods ended:	9m Sept. 30/22[A]		9m Sept. 30/21[A]
	$000s	%Chg	$000s
Operating revenue	250	-60	620
Net income	(2,218)	n.a.	(2,487)
	$		$
Earnings per share*	(0.10)		(0.15)

* Common
[A] Reported in accordance with IFRS

Historical Summary
(as originally stated)

Fiscal Year	Oper. Rev.	Net Inc. Bef. Disc.	EPS*
	$000s	$000s	$
2021[A]	764	(3,142)	(0.15)
2020[A]	1,576	(4,660)	(0.45)
2019[A]	3,038	(7,030)	(0.90)
2018[A]	2,074	(6,683)	(1.05)
2017[A]	1,773	(4,817)	(0.90)

* Common
[A] Reported in accordance with IFRS

Note: Adjusted throughout for 1-for-15 cons. in Sept. 2022

N.19 Navigator Acquisition Corp.

Symbol - NAQ.P **Exchange** - TSX-VEN **CUSIP** - 63941A
Head Office - 970-1050 Pender St W, Vancouver, BC, V6E 3S7
Website - www.navigatoracquisition.com
Email - kshostak@navigatorprincipalinvestors.com
Investor Relations - Kyle Shostak (212) 909-5870
Auditors - Davidson & Company LLP C.A., Vancouver, B.C.
Lawyers - Miller Thomson LLP, Vancouver, B.C.
Transfer Agents - TSX Trust Company, Vancouver, B.C.
Profile - (B.C. 2018) Capital Pool Company.

Recent Merger and Acquisition Activity

Status: pending **Revised:** Mar. 31, 2023

UPDATE: The parties entered into a definitive agreement. PREVIOUS: Navigator Acquisition Corp. entered into a letter of intent for the Qualifying Transaction reverse takeover acquisition of Santa Monica, Calif.-based MGID Group Holdings Limited, which operates a native advertising platform that connects and intertwines global audiences through verifiable publishers with highly engaged traffic, for issuance of 194,695,000 common shares. MGID offers a variety of ad formats including native, display and video.

Status: terminated **Revised:** July 10, 2022

UPDATE: The transaction was terminated. PREVIOUS: Navigator Acquisition Corp. entered into a letter of intent for the Qualifying Transaction reverse takeover acquisition of Russia-based Arifmetika MCC LCC, a microlending company that provides cash loans for individuals, for issuance of 224,927,143 common shares at a deemed price of 36¢ per share. Dec. 24, 2021 - A definitive agreement was entered into.

Directors - Kyle Shostak, pres. & CEO, N.J.; Alex Lyamport, CFO, Sunny Isles, Fla.; C. Geoffrey (Geoff) Hampson, corp. sec., Conn.; Brent Janis, B.C.; Basil Karatzas, New York, N.Y.

Capital Stock

	Authorized (shs.)	Outstanding (shs.)[1]
Common	unlimited	16,937,920

[1] At May 30, 2023

Major Shareholder - Kyle Shostak held 17.72% interest at Nov. 4, 2022.

Price Range - NAQ.P/TSX-VEN

Year	Volume	High	Low	Close
2020	373,500	$0.11	$0.03	$0.05
2019	656,950	$0.39	$0.06	$0.10
2018	705,240	$0.20	$0.11	$0.12

Capital Stock Changes - There were no changes to capital stock during 2021 or 2022.

N.20 nDatalyze Corp.

Symbol - NDAT **Exchange** - CSE **CUSIP** - 63948H
Head Office - 1150-707 7 Ave SW, Calgary, AB, T2P 3H6 **Telephone** - (403) 689-3901
Website - ndatalyze.com
Email - jimd@ndatalyze.com
Investor Relations - James M. Durward (403) 689-3901
Auditors - Kenway Mack Slusarchuk Stewart LLP C.A., Calgary, Alta.
Lawyers - Heighington Law Firm, Calgary, Alta.
Transfer Agents - TSX Trust Company, Calgary, Alta.
Profile - (Alta. 2018) Develops mental health platforms that use machine learning to predict probabilities of mental health conditions and potential mental health benefits of entheogenic compounds. Also manufactures and sells essential oil and carbon dioxide (CO_2) extraction equipment.

Mental health platforms include YMI (why-am-I) and MLdelic (formerly SHAMAN-AI). YMI is an application that uses a proprietary reference database and machine-learning to predict probabilities of personal mental health conditions. The reference database contains more than 1,200 biometric records that includes associated electroencephalogram (EEG) data. MLdelic is a mobile health platform that also uses the reference database and applies machine learning to predict potential benefits associated with the use of entheogenic compounds within the mental health sector.

Extractor products include small-scale CO_2 extractors (Disruptor 21, and 3 oz. and 6 oz. extractors); large-scale CO_2 extractors with a capacity of 5 liters to 500 liters; and alcohol-based extractor with a capacity of approximately 3 liters (Essential).

In October 2022, a resolution to pause, suspend, sell or otherwise dispose of the extractor operations over the next 36 months was proposed.

Predecessor Detail - Name changed from MedXtractor Corp., Oct. 22, 2021.

Directors - James M. Durward, founder, pres., CEO & corp. sec., Calgary, Alta.; Gordon N. Crawford, Calgary, Alta.; Dusan Kuzma, Calgary, Alta.; G. Steven Price, Calgary, Alta.

Other Exec. Officers - Dwayne A. Vinck, CFO

Capital Stock

	Authorized (shs.)	Outstanding (shs.)[1]
Common	unlimited	38,712,425

[1] At Oct. 19, 2022

Major Shareholder - James M. Durward held 25.83% interest at Oct. 21, 2022.

Price Range - NDAT/CSE

Year	Volume	High	Low	Close
2022	3,638,753	$0.36	$0.16	$0.20
2021	15,747,411	$0.33	$0.12	$0.17
2020	5,355,452	$0.30	$0.04	$0.18
2019	400,800	$0.08	$0.04	$0.08

Recent Close: $0.08

Wholly Owned Subsidiaries

2273670 Alberta Ltd., Alta.

Financial Statistics

Periods ended:	12m Feb. 28/22[A]		12m Feb. 28/21[A]
	$000s	%Chg	$000s
Operating revenue	**425**	**-36**	**663**
Cost of sales	195		286
Research & devel. expense	832		23
General & admin expense	523		345
Stock-based compensation	49		695
Operating expense	**1,598**	**+18**	**1,349**
Operating income	**(1,173)**	**n.a.**	**(686)**
Deprec., depl. & amort.	2		1
Finance income	7		2
Finance costs, gross	5		9
Pre-tax income	**(1,173)**	**n.a.**	**(699)**
Net income	**(1,173)**	**n.a.**	**(699)**
Cash & equivalent	1,595		781
Inventories	67		68
Accounts receivable	18		nil
Current assets	1,691		865
Fixed assets, net	2		2
Intangibles, net	18		6
Total assets	**1,711**	**+96**	**873**
Accts. pay. & accr. liabs	81		72
Current liabilities	81		72
Shareholders' equity	1,629		801
Cash from oper. activs	**(1,125)**	**n.a.**	**21**
Cash from fin. activs	1,953		168
Cash from invest. activs	(14)		(2)
Net cash position	**1,595**	**+104**	**781**
Capital expenditures	(1)		nil
	$		$
Earnings per share*	(0.03)		(0.03)
Cash flow per share*	(0.03)		0.00
	shs		shs
No. of shs. o/s*	37,921,425		27,846,425
Avg. no. of shs. o/s*	36,586,836		25,810,329
	%		%
Net profit margin	(276.00)		(105.43)
Return on equity	(96.54)		(97.22)
Return on assets	(90.40)		(89.20)
Foreign sales percent	62		58

* Common

[A] Reported in accordance with IFRS

Latest Results

Periods ended:	6m Aug. 31/22[A]		6m Aug. 31/21[A]
	$000s	%Chg	$000s
Operating revenue	97	-62	257
Net income	(511)	n.a.	(165)
	$		$
Earnings per share*	(0.01)		(0.00)

* Common

[A] Reported in accordance with IFRS

Historical Summary
(as originally stated)

Fiscal Year	Oper. Rev.	Net Inc. Bef. Disc.	EPS*
	$000s	$000s	$
2022[A]	425	(1,173)	(0.03)
2021[A]	663	(699)	(0.03)
2020[A]	531	(37)	(0.00)
2019[A1]	162	(257)	(0.01)

* Common

[A] Reported in accordance with IFRS

[1] 57 weeks ended Feb. 28, 2019.

N.21 Neighbourly Pharmacy Inc.

Symbol - NBLY **Exchange** - TSX **CUSIP** - 64016L
Head Office - Unit 400, 190 Attwell Dr, Toronto, ON, M9W 6H8 **Telephone** - (416) 309-9102
Website - neighbourlypharmacy.ca
Email - investorrelations@nbly.ca
Investor Relations - Billy Wong (416) 309-9102
Auditors - Ernst & Young LLP C.A., Toronto, Ont.
Lawyers - Skadden, Arps, Slate, Meagher & Flom LLP, Toronto, Ont.; Stikeman Elliott LLP, Toronto, Ont.
Transfer Agents - Computershare Trust Company of Canada Inc., Toronto, Ont.
FP500 Revenue Ranking - 501
Employees - 3,648 at Mar. 25, 2023
Profile - (Can. 2015) Owns and operates retail pharmacies across Canada.

Owns and operates 291 retail pharmacies (at July 31, 2023) across two primary formats: Community Pharmacies, with a target size of 3,000 to 6,000 sq. ft., and located in communities with populations of less than 100,000; and Clinic Pharmacies, with a target size of less than 2,000 sq. ft., and located near or within clinics or hospitals. The company's locations on average generate 70% to 80% of their revenue from prescription medications and 20% to 30% from front shop sales. Retail pharmacies are operated under banners including IDA/Guardian, Pharmachoice, Pharmasave, Remedy's RX and Drug Trading.

In June 2023, the company acquired seven retail pharmacies, five in Saskatchewan and two in British Columbia. Terms were not disclosed.

In May 2023, the company agreed to acquire three retail pharmacies in Ontario. Terms were not disclosed.

In August 2022, the company acquired a retail pharmacy in Manitoba. Terms of the transaction were not disclosed.

In June 2022, the company acquired two retail pharmacies in Alberta. Terms were not disclosed.

In April 2022, the company acquired a retail pharmacy in Manitoba. Terms were not disclosed.

Recent Merger and Acquisition Activity

Status: completed **Announced:** Mar. 20, 2023
Neighbourly Pharmacy Inc. completed the sale and leaseback of 18 real estate properties which had been acquired as part of the Rubicon Pharmacies acquisition for net proceeds of $12,000,000.

Status: completed **Revised:** Dec. 16, 2022
UPDATE: The acquisition of the two pharmacies in British Columbia was completed. PREVIOUS: Neighbourly Pharmacy Inc. agreed to acquire six community pharmacies in New Brunswick and Nova Scotia and two pharmacies in British Columbia for a total of $15,500,000, which would be funded from cash on hand and drawings on a credit facility. The B.C. pharmacies, Cloverdale Pharmacy Ltd. and Steveston Health Centre Ltd., located in Surrey and Richmond, B.C., respectively, would be purchased from CloudMD Software & Services Inc. for $3,800,000. Nov. 7, 2022 - The acquisition of the six pharmacies in Atlantic Canada was completed.

Status: completed **Revised:** June 27, 2022
UPDATE: The transaction was completed. PREVIOUS: Neighbourly Pharmacy Inc. agreed to acquire an entity that owns and operates, directly or indirectly through its subsidiaries, a network of retail independent pharmacies known as Rubicon Pharmacies for total cash consideration of $435,000,000, subject to adjustments. Rubicon Pharmacies owns and operates 100 pharmacy locations in western Canada, including 60 in Saskatchewan. All of the Rubicon Pharmacies locations are subject to rights of first refusal (ROFRs) in favour of certain third parties. If one or more ROFRs are exercised by a third party before the closing, the transaction closing would still occur but the pharmacies affected by the exercised ROFR(s) would be excluded from the transaction. The purchase would be financed in part with proceeds from a minimum $250,000,000 equity issuance of subscription receipts, of which $120,000,000 would be purchased on a private placement basis by Neighbourly's major shareholder, Persistence Capital Partners. The transaction was expected to close during the second quarter of 2022. June 7, 2022 - As part of an agreement with the Competition Bureau, Neighbourly agreed to sell two pharmacy locations in Saskatchewan.

Predecessor Detail - Name changed from Rx Drug Mart Inc., Apr. 30, 2021.

Directors - Stuart M. Elman, chr., Westmount, Qué.; Skip Bourdo, CEO, Ill.; Josh Blair, Vancouver, B.C.; Lisa Greatrix, Ont.; Dean C. McCann, Toronto, Ont.; Robert O'Meara, Ill.; Valerie C. Sorbie, Toronto, Ont.

Other Exec. Officers - Billy Wong, CFO; Steve Losty, v-p, corp. devel.; Alicia Matthews-Kent, v-p, pharmacy; Jari Villanen, v-p, natl. opers.; Roy J. Wieschkowski, v-p, HR; Zev Zelman, corp. sec.

Capital Stock

	Authorized (shs.)	Outstanding (shs.)[1]
Preferred	unlimited	nil
Common	unlimited	44,695,464

[1] At July 10, 2023

Major Shareholder - Persistence Capital Partners LP held 50.2% interest at June 14, 2023.

Price Range - NBLY/TSX

Year	Volume	High	Low	Close
2022	10,679,375	$40.07	$19.00	$23.39
2021	5,613,048	$39.99	$20.50	$39.94

Recent Close: $16.00

Capital Stock Changes - In June 2022, 9,947,500 common shares were issued without further consideration on exchange of subscription receipts sold previously by bought deal public offering and private placement at $28.95 each. Also during fiscal 2023, common shares were issued as follows: 318,089 on exercise of options and 93,685 under restricted share unit plan; 228,902 common shares were cancelled under a settlement agreement.

On May 25, 2021, an initial public offering of 10,295,000 common shares and concurrent private placement of 1,058,823 shares all at $17 per share were completed. In October 2021, bought deal public offering of 977,000 common shares was completed at $30.75 per share. Also during fiscal 2022, common shares were issued as follows: 56,464 on exercise of options and 430 under restricted share unit plan.

Dividends

NBLY com Ra $0.18 pa Q est. Oct. 12, 2021
Listed May 25/21.
Prev. Rate: $0.052 est. Sept. 7, 2021
$0.013**i**................ Sept. 7/21
i Initial Payment

Wholly Owned Subsidiaries

AB-MB Holding LP, Man.
Amenity Holdings Inc., Sask.
Apex Pharmacy Ltd., Alta.
Neighbourly Pharmacy Operations Inc., Canada.
- 100% int. in **Lovell Drugs Limited**, Ont.
- 100% int. in **9206809 Canada Inc.**, Canada.
  - 100% int. in **Forewest Holdings Inc.**, Langley, B.C.
- 100% int. in **RxDM Ontario Inc.**, Ont.

102028500 Saskatchewan Ltd., Sask.
1105855 B.C. Ltd., B.C.
1239251 B.C. Ltd., B.C.
2003945 Albeta Ltd., Alta.

Note: The preceding list includes only the major related companies in which interests are held.

Financial Statistics

Periods ended:	52w Mar. 25/23[A]		52w Mar. 26/22[A]
	$000s	%Chg	$000s
Operating revenue	**749,149**	**+75**	**427,509**
Cost of sales	456,420		269,037
Salaries & benefits	164,684		88,313
General & admin expense	48,856		24,268
Stock-based compensation	4,845		4,783
Operating expense	**674,805**	**+75**	**386,401**
Operating income	**74,344**	**+81**	**41,108**
Deprec., depl. & amort.	59,837		25,354
Finance income	8,740		10,385
Finance costs, gross	23,446		10,389
Write-downs/write-offs	(723)		(324)
Pre-tax income	**(19,362)**	**n.a.**	**(78,439)**
Income taxes	(4,563)		(6,044)
Net income	**(14,799)**	**n.a.**	**(72,395)**
Net inc. for equity hldrs	**(15,499)**	**n.a.**	**(73,356)**
Net inc. for non-cont. int	**700**	**-27**	**961**
Cash & equivalent	22,889		40,410
Inventories	94,227		55,721
Accounts receivable	38,236		24,616
Current assets	161,399		122,756
Fixed assets, net	27,986		12,366
Right-of-use assets	80,207		47,163
Intangibles, net	809,530		373,065
Total assets	**1,102,001**	**+94**	**569,265**
Bank indebtedness	62		62
Accts. pay. & accr. liabs	105,697		61,226
Current liabilities	132,317		78,493
Long-term debt, gross	228,987		86,156
Long-term debt, net	225,237		83,656
Long-term lease liabilities	64,637		37,177
Shareholders' equity	610,415		340,939
Non-controlling interest	5,073		7,683
Cash from oper. activs	**49,748**	**+350**	**11,050**
Cash from fin. activs	388,885		89,897
Cash from invest. activs	(456,154)		(106,451)
Net cash position	**22,889**	**-43**	**40,410**
Capital expenditures	(8,544)		(2,973)
Capital disposals	14,270		nil
	$		$
Earnings per share*	(0.37)		(2.57)
Cash flow per share*	1.12		0.39
Cash divd. per share*	0.18		0.15
	shs		shs
No. of shs. o/s*	44,607,271		34,476,899
Avg. no. of shs. o/s*	41,809,575		28,510,994
	%		%
Net profit margin	(1.98)		(16.93)
Return on equity	(3.26)		n.m.
Return on assets	0.37		(12.44)
No. of employees (FTEs)	3,648		2,036

* Common

† Unaudited

[A] Reported in accordance with IFRS

Latest Results

Periods ended:	12w June 17/23[A]		12w June 18/22[A]
	$000s	%Chg	$000s
Operating revenue	196,842	+72	114,376
Net income	(12,005)	n.a.	(743)
Net inc. for equity hldrs	(12,113)	n.a.	(999)
Net inc. for non-cont. int	108		256
	$		$
Earnings per share*	(0.27)		(0.03)

* Common

[A] Reported in accordance with IFRS

Historical Summary
(as originally stated)

Fiscal Year	Oper. Rev. $000s	Net Inc. Bef. Disc. $000s	EPS* $
2023†A	749,149	(14,799)	(0.37)
2022A	427,509	(72,395)	(2.57)
2021A	306,494	(90,517)	(19.88)
2020A1	186,627	(23,344)	(5.08)
2019A1	150,126	(22,759)	(4.96)

* Common
† Unaudited
A Reported in accordance with IFRS
[1] As shown in the prospectus dated May 17, 2021.

N.22 Neo Performance Materials Inc.

Symbol - NEO **Exchange** - TSX **CUSIP** - 64046G
Head Office - 1740-121 King St W, Toronto, ON, M5H 3T9 **Telephone** - (416) 367-8588
Website - www.neomaterials.com
Email - a.mahdavi@neomaterials.com
Investor Relations - Ali Mahdavi (416) 962-3300
Auditors - KPMG LLP C.A., Toronto, Ont.
Transfer Agents - Computershare Trust Company of Canada Inc., Toronto, Ont.
FP500 Revenue Ranking - 371
Employees - 1,758 at Dec. 31, 2022
Profile - (Ont. 2017) Manufactures advanced industrial materials such as magnetic powders and magnets, specialty chemicals, metals and alloys used for micro motors, traction motors, auto catalysts, water emission-controls, healthcare, aerospace, clean energy technologies, smartphones and tablets, fibre optics, hard disk drive and others. Also holds mineral interests in southwest Greenland.

Operates through three business segments: Magnequench; Chemicals and Oxides; and Rare Metals.

The **Magnequench** segment produces bonded neodymium-iron-boron powders and bonded permanent magnets. The company's magnetic powders were used in bonded and hot deformed fully dense neodymium-iron-boron magnets. These powders are formed through technology related to the development, processing and manufacturing of magnetic powders. A proprietary process is used to manufacture powders using a blend various inputs. These powders are used in the production of bonded permanent magnets that are components in automotive motors, micro motors, traction motors, sensors, computer and office equipment, home appliances, heating and cooling circulation pumps, consumer electronics and other applications requiring high levels of magnetic strength, improved performance and reduced size and weight. Also produces bonded magnets made from various Magnequench powder grades, which results in a slight reduction of the magnetic strength of the material, but allows it to be formed into a variety of shapes without further processing. Production facilities are located in Tianjin and Chuzhou, People's Republic of China (PRC); and Korat, Thailand.

The **Chemicals and Oxides** segment manufactures and distributes a broad range of advanced industrial materials, which are able to meet the specifications from manufacturers that need custom engineered materials. Applications of these products include, automotive catalysts, wastewater treatment, medical, petroleum refinement, chemical catalysis, advanced electronics and other end market applications, including the production of cerium, lanthanum, neodymium and praseodymium oxides and salts. Production facilities are located in Zibo and Jiangyin, PRC; and Sillamäe, Estonia.

The **Rare Metals** segment sources, reclaims, produces, refines and markets high value metals and their compounds. These products include both high temperature metals (tantalum, niobium, hafnium and rhenium) and electronic metals (gallium and indium). Applications from products made in this segment primarily include superalloys for jet engines, medical imaging, wireless technologies and LED lighting. Other applications include their use in flat panel displays, solar, steel additives, batteries and electronics applications. Production facilities are located in Sillamäe, Estonia; Sagard, Germany; Peterborough, Ont.; and Quapaw, Okla.

In addition, the company holds Sarfartoq rare earth project and Nukittooq niobium-tantalum project, both in Greenland. The company is headquartered in Toronto, Ont., with additional corporate offices in Greenwood, Colo.; Singapore; and Beijing, PRC.

In April 2023, the company acquired Sarfartoq rare earth project and Nukittooq niobium-tantalum project, both in Greenland, from **Hudson Resources Inc.** for US$3,500,000.

In October 2022, **OPPS NPM S.A.R.L.**, a fund managed by **Oaktree Capital Management, L.P.**, sold 8,974,127 common shares of the company it held (representing a 22.1% interest) to **Hastings Technology Metals Limited** of Perth, Australia for Cdn$15 per share totaling $134,611,905. As a result, Oaktree's interest in the company decreased to 2.2%. Hastings has rare earth interests in Australia.

Recent Merger and Acquisition Activity

Status: completed **Revised:** Apr. 19, 2023
UPDATE: The transaction was completed. PREVIOUS: Neo Performance Materials Inc. agreed to acquire 90% interest in England, U.K.-based SG Technologies Group Limited, which manufactures rare-earth-based and other high-performance magnets for industrial and commercial markets including electric vehicles, electronics and clean energy in Europe, for US$13,400,000.

Directors - Claire M. C. Kennedy, chr., Toronto, Ont.; Rahim Suleman, pres. & CEO, Toronto, Ont.; Eric Noyrez†, France; G. Gail Edwards, Toronto, Ont.; Edgar Lee, Medina, Wash.; Yadin Rozov, Armonk, N.Y.

Other Exec. Officers - Kevin D. Morris, chief strategy officer; Jonathan Baksh, exec. v-p & CFO; Jeffrey R. (Jeff) Hogan, exec. v-p, chemicals & oxides bus. segment; Gregory K. Kroll, exec. v-p, Magnequench bus. segment; Ali Mahdavi, sr. v-p, corp. devel. & capital markets; Frank Timmerman, sr. v-p, rare metals bus. segment
† Lead director

Capital Stock

	Authorized (shs.)	Outstanding (shs.)[1]
Preferred	unlimited	nil
Common	unlimited	45,196,921

[1] At June 5, 2023

Normal Course Issuer Bid - The company plans to make normal course purchases of up to 3,585,011 common shares representing 10% of the public float. The bid commenced on June 19, 2023, and expires on June 18, 2024.

Major Shareholder - Hastings Technology Metals Limited held 19.86% interest and Mawer Investment Management Limited held 11.4% interest at Apr. 26, 2023.

Price Range - NEO/TSX

Year	Volume	High	Low	Close
2022	28,619,274	$20.35	$8.31	$9.60
2021	23,780,897	$22.85	$13.50	$20.28
2020	3,218,994	$14.19	$5.55	$13.78
2019	13,437,057	$17.01	$9.70	$12.35
2018	6,674,811	$18.65	$11.40	$15.40

Recent Close: $8.71

Capital Stock Changes - In September 2022, bought deal public offering of 4,506,734 common shares was completed at Cdn$15 per share. Also during 2022, 21,285 common shares were issued as stock-based compensation.

Dividends

NEO com Ra $0.40 pa Q est. June 28, 2019

Wholly Owned Subsidiaries

Magnequench Magnetics (Chu Zhou) Co., Ltd., People's Republic of China.
Magnet Ventures Europe OU, Estonia.
Magnet Ventures Pte. Ltd., Singapore.
NPM C&O Euope OU, Estonia.
Neo Cayman Holdings Ltd., Cayman Islands.
- 100% int. in **Magnequench Limited**, Barbados.
  - 20% int. in **GQD Special Material (Thailand) Co., Ltd.**, Thailand.
  - 100% int. in **Magnequench International Trading (Tianjin) Co., Ltd.**, People's Republic of China.
  - 100% int. in **Magnequench (Korat) Co., Ltd.**, Thailand.
  - 100% int. in **Zibo Jia Xin Magnetic Materials Limited**, Shandong, People's Republic of China.
- 100% int. in **Magnequench, LLC**, Wilmington, Del.
  - 25% int. in **Gan Zhou Ke Li Rare Earth New Material**, Jiangsu, People's Republic of China.
  - 100% int. in **Magnequench International, LLC**, Wilmington, Del.
    - 98.9% int. in **Xin Bao Investment Limited**, Hong Kong, Hong Kong, People's Republic of China.
      - 100% int. in **Magnequench (Tianjin) Company Limited**, People's Republic of China.
    - 33% int. in **Toda Magnequench Magnetic Material (Tianjin) Co., Ltd.**, People's Republic of China.
  - 100% int. in **Magnequench Neo Powders Pte. Ltd.**, Singapore.
    - 100% int. in **NPM Silmet OÜ**, Estonia.
  - 100% int. in **NPM Holdings (US), Inc.**, Del.
    - 100% int. in **Neo Chemicals & Oxides, LLC**, Del.
    - 100% int. in **Neo Magnequench Distribution, LLC**, Del.
    - 80% int. in **Neo Rare Metals (Oklahoma), LLC**, Del.
    - 100% int. in **Neo Rare Metals (Utah), LLC**, Utah
- 100% int. in **Neo Chemicals & Oxides (Europe) Ltd.**, United Kingdom.
  - 100% int. in **Magnequench Japan, Inc.**, Japan.
  - 100% int. in **NMT Holdings GmbH**, Tübingen, Germany.
    - 50% int. in **Buss & Buss Spezialmetalle GmbH**, Sagard, Germany.
    - 100% int. in **Magnequench GmbH**, Tübingen, Germany.
  - 100% int. in **Neo Performance Materials Korea Inc.**, Seoul, South Korea.
  - 100% int. in **Neo Performance Materials ULC**, B.C.
    - 100% int. in **Neo Japan, Inc.**, Japan.
    - 80% int. in **Neo Rare Metals (Korea) Inc.**, South Korea.
    - 1.1% int. in **Xin Bao Investment Limited**, Hong Kong, Hong Kong, People's Republic of China.
- 100% int. in **Neo International Corp.**, Bridgetown, Barbados.
  - 95% int. in **Jiangyin Jiahua Advanced Material Resources Co., Ltd.**, Jiangyin, Jiangsu, People's Republic of China.
  - 100% int. in **Neo Performance Materials (Singapore) Pte. Ltd.**, Singapore, Singapore.
    - 100% int. in **Neo Performance Materials (Beijing) Co., Ltd.**, Beijing, Beijing, People's Republic of China.
  - 98% int. in **Zibo Jiahua Advanced Material Resources Co., Ltd.**, Zibo, Shandong, People's Republic of China.
- 100% int. in **Neo US Holdings, Inc.**, Del.

Neo North Star Holdings, LLC, United States.
Neo Water Treatment LLC, United States.

Subsidiaries

98% int. in **Neo Jia Hua Advanced Materials (Zibo) Co., Ltd**, People's Republic of China.
66.67% int. in **Neo North Star Resources Inc.**, Del.
90% int. in **SG Technologies Group Limited**, United Kingdom.
59.6% int. in **Zibo Shijia Trading Co., Ltd.**, People's Republic of China.

Financial Statistics

Periods ended:	12m Dec. 31/22A	%Chg	12m Dec. 31/21A
	US$000s	%Chg	US$000s
Operating revenue	**640,298**	**+19**	**539,251**
Cost of sales	481,524		380,548
Research & devel. expense	20,810		19,859
General & admin expense	58,915		58,445
Stock-based compensation	2,483		4,526
Operating expense	**563,732**	**+22**	**463,378**
Operating income	**76,566**	**+1**	**75,873**
Deprec., depl. & amort.	16,719		15,865
Finance costs, net	15,259		3,943
Write-downs/write-offs	(1,233)		(121)
Pre-tax income	**41,428**	**-1**	**41,806**
Income taxes	17,793		9,580
After-tax income (expense)	2,783		3,817
Net income	**26,418**	**-27**	**36,043**
Net inc. for equity hldrs	**25,947**	**-26**	**35,177**
Net inc. for non-cont. int	**471**	**-46**	**866**
Cash & equivalent	147,491		89,037
Inventories	212,702		200,954
Accounts receivable	81,409		65,209
Current assets	466,415		377,361
Long-term investments	16,363		13,759
Fixed assets, net	75,767		73,378
Intangibles, net	109,026		120,043
Total assets	**676,460**	**+14**	**594,082**
Bank indebtedness	17,288		6,502
Accts. pay. & accr. liabs	69,093		94,201
Current liabilities	128,642		131,070
Long-term debt, gross	30,632		nil
Long-term debt, net	29,885		nil
Long-term lease liabilities	813		1,388
Shareholders' equity	474,450		427,625
Non-controlling interest	3,193		2,891
Cash from oper. activs	**3,696**	**n.a.**	**(2,162)**
Cash from fin. activs	74,793		26,201
Cash from invest. activs	(17,431)		(7,006)
Net cash position	**147,491**	**+66**	**89,037**
Capital expenditures	(17,354)		(9,159)
Capital disposals	nil		426
Unfunded pension liability	407		1,109
	US$		US$
Earnings per share*	0.62		0.92
Cash flow per share*	0.09		(0.06)
Cash divd. per share*	$0.40		$0.40
	shs		shs
No. of shs. o/s*	45,196,921		40,668,902
Avg. no. of shs. o/s*	41,992,938		38,140,110
	%		%
Net profit margin	4.13		6.68
Return on equity	5.75		8.91
Return on assets	4.16		6.67
No. of employees (FTEs)	1,758		1,844

* Common
A Reported in accordance with IFRS

Latest Results

Periods ended:	3m Mar. 31/23A	%Chg	3m Mar. 31/22A
	US$000s	%Chg	US$000s
Operating revenue	135,530	-18	166,282
Net income	(10,700)	n.a.	22,701
Net inc. for equity hldrs	(10,454)	n.a.	22,350
Net inc. for non-cont. int	(246)		351
	US$		US$
Earnings per share*	(0.23)		0.55

* Common
A Reported in accordance with IFRS

Historical Summary
(as originally stated)

Fiscal Year	Oper. Rev. US$000s	Net Inc. Bef. Disc. US$000s	EPS* US$
2022A	640,298	26,418	0.62
2021A	539,251	36,043	0.92
2020A	346,692	(60,089)	(1.54)
2019A	407,464	23,075	0.59
2018A	454,195	41,139	1.02

* Common
A Reported in accordance with IFRS

N.23 Nepra Foods Inc.

Symbol - NPRA **Exchange** - CSE **CUSIP** - 64067L
Head Office - 7025 S. Revere Pky, Unit 100, Centennial, CO, United States, 80112 **Telephone** - (720) 729-8500
Website - neprafoods.com
Email - david.wood@neprafoods.com
Investor Relations - David Wood (844) 566-1917

Auditors - Dale Matheson Carr-Hilton LaBonte LLP C.A., Vancouver, B.C.
Lawyers - McMillan LLP
Transfer Agents - Olympia Trust Company, Calgary, Alta.
Profile - (B.C. 2020) Manufactures and packages plant-based, allergen-free and gluten-free foods and ingredients which are sold to commercial food manufacturers and directly to consumers across North America.

At June 30, 2022, the company's plant-based product lines consisted of 18 gluten-free and allergen-free specialty ingredients, blends and mixes; seven meat alternatives; eight dairy alternatives; 12 baked goods, snacks and spreads; and five ready-to-eat meals. Specialty ingredients, which are typically sold business-to-business, include blends of modified tapioca starch, low- and high-fibre content cassava flour, hemp heart oil and flour, and psyllium powder. Meat alternatives include THP™ (textured hemp protein) which also comes in various flavours including beef, chicken and pork. Dairy alternatives ranges from milk to cheese, yogurt, dressing, dips and sour cream. Ready-to-eat meals include PROPASTA™, a line of plant-based frozen pasta meals that are high in plant proteins, low in carbohydrates and high in fibre. Products sold directly to consumers are also available on its e-commerce platform, www.neprafoods.com.

The company also provides private label product development and ingredients consulting services, and has already formulated various products for food manufacturers including gluten-free pretzels, shelf-stable allergen-free bread and hemp-based cookies.

Headquarters and main manufacturing facility is located in Centennial, Colo.

Directors - David Wood, chr., pres., interim CEO, COO & interim corp. sec., Denver, Colo.; Chadwick White, CEO, Denver, Colo.; David Breda, Denver, Colo.; Joel Leonard, Vancouver, B.C.; Marc Olmsted, Denver, Colo.
Other Exec. Officers - Kate Cash, v-p, consumer-packaged goods sales; Eric Kriegisch, v-p, ingredient sales

Capital Stock

	Authorized (shs.)	Outstanding (shs.)[1]
Subordinate Vtg.	unlimited	46,783,876
Proportionate Vtg.	unlimited	273,468

[1] At Aug. 29, 2022

Subordinate Voting - One vote per share.
Proportionate Voting - Each convertible into 100 subordinate voting shares. 100 votes per share.
Major Shareholder - David Wood held 14.61% interest and Chadwick White held 10.9% interest at May 19, 2022.

Price Range - NPRA/CSE

Year	Volume	High	Low	Close
2022	21,424,189	$0.75	$0.05	$0.08
2021	11,717,899	$0.93	$0.63	$0.68

Recent Close: $0.06
Capital Stock Changes - In March 2022, public offering of 10,000,000 units (1 subordinate voting share & 1 warrant) at 45¢ per unit was completed, with warrants exercisable at 70¢ per share for three years.

Wholly Owned Subsidiaries

Nepra Foods, Ltd., Centennial, Colo.
- 100% int. in **Gluten Free Baking Solutions, LLC**, Centennial, Colo.
- 100% int. in **Total Blending Solutions, Ltd.**, Centennial, Colo.

Financial Statistics

Periods ended:	12m Dec. 31/21[A1]		12m Dec. 31/20[□A]
	$000s	%Chg	$000s
Operating revenue	**6,052**	**+112**	**2,855**
Cost of sales	5,267		2,290
Salaries & benefits	1,803		414
Research & devel. expense	156		41
General & admin expense	3,611		185
Stock-based compensation	719		429
Operating expense	**11,555**	**+244**	**3,358**
Operating income	**(5,503)**	**n.a.**	**(503)**
Deprec., depl. & amort.	286		29
Finance costs, gross	403		43
Write-downs/write-offs	(17)		(2)
Pre-tax income	**(6,680)**	**n.a.**	**(542)**
Net income	**(6,680)**	**n.a.**	**(542)**
Cash & equivalent	1,464		493
Inventories	1,816		535
Accounts receivable	590		143
Current assets	4,908		1,278
Fixed assets, net	448		64
Right-of-use assets	2,300		23
Intangibles, net	21		nil
Total assets	**7,918**	**+423**	**1,513**
Bank indebtedness	32		1,049
Accts. pay. & accr. liabs	1,216		526
Current liabilities	1,670		1,603
Long-term debt, gross	403		212
Long-term debt, net	388		197
Long-term lease liabilities	2,444		13
Shareholders' equity	3,415		(300)
Cash from oper. activs	**(6,616)**	**n.a.**	**(422)**
Cash from fin. activs	8,279		1,072
Cash from invest. activs	(544)		(174)
Net cash position	**1,534**	**+211**	**493**
Capital expenditures	(391)		(18)
	$		$
Earnings per share*	(0.35)		n.a.
Cash flow per share*	(0.34)		n.a.
	shs		shs
No. of shs. o/s*	36,828,412		n.a.
Avg. no. of shs. o/s*	19,225,623		n.a.
	%		%
Net profit margin	(110.38)		(18.98)
Return on equity	n.m.		n.m.
Return on assets	(133.11)		(53.66)

* Subord. Vtg.
□ Restated
[A] Reported in accordance with IFRS
[1] Results reflect the Apr. 15, 2021, reverse takeover acquisition of Nepra Foods, Ltd.

Latest Results

Periods ended:	6m June 30/22[A]		6m June 30/21[A]
	$000s	%Chg	$000s
Operating revenue	3,312	+4	3,190
Net income	(3,854)	n.a.	(1,543)
	$		$
Earnings per share*	(0.09)		(0.14)

* Subord. Vtg.
[A] Reported in accordance with IFRS

Historical Summary
(as originally stated)

Fiscal Year	Oper. Rev.	Net Inc. Bef. Disc.	EPS*
	$000s	$000s	$
2021[A]	6,052	(6,680)	(0.35)
2020[A1]	2,855	(542)	n.a.
2019[A1]	1,640	(217)	n.a.

* Subord. Vtg.
[A] Reported in accordance with IFRS
[1] Results pertain to Nepra Foods, Ltd.

N.24 Neptune Digital Assets Corp.

Symbol - NDA **Exchange** - TSX-VEN **CUSIP** - 64073L
Head Office - 2700-1133 Melville St, Vancouver, BC, V6E 4E5
Telephone - (604) 319-6955 **Toll-free** - (800) 545-0941
Website - neptunedigitalassets.com
Email - info@neptunedigitalassets.com
Investor Relations - Cale J. Moodie (604) 319-6955
Auditors - RSM Canada LLP C.A., Toronto, Ont.
Lawyers - DLA Piper (Canada) LLP, Vancouver, B.C.
Transfer Agents - TSX Trust Company, Toronto, Ont.
Profile - (B.C. 2018 amalg.) Engages in bitcoin mining, proof-of-stake mining, operating blockchain nodes, decentralized finance (DeFi) and associated blockchain technologies. Also invests and manages a portfolio of cryptocurrency assets.

Has bitcoin mining operations in Alberta and Delaware with a total capacity of 75 petahash per second.

Portfolio includes interest in cryptocurrencies and associated blockchain related technologies including ATOM, Fantom, Bitcoin, Dash, Ethereum, Litecoin, Stellar, Neo, OMG Network, Qtum, The Graph, MEMO and Ocean.

Holds investments in **Space Exploration Technologies Corp.** ,an American spacecraft manufacturer, space launch provider, and satellite communications provider; and **Rapture Labs Inc.**, a private Canadian company focused on Web3 innovation and gaming.

Common reinstated on TSX-VEN, Apr. 5, 2023.
Common suspended from TSX-VEN, Jan. 6, 2023.
Predecessor Detail - Name changed from Neptune Dash Technologies Corp., Dec. 17, 2020.
Directors - Cale J. Moodie, chr., pres. & CEO, Vancouver, B.C.; Kalle Radage, COO & corp. sec., B.C.; Carmen To, CFO, B.C.; Mitchell W. Demeter, Grand Cayman, Cayman Islands; Dario Meli, Vancouver, B.C.

Capital Stock

	Authorized (shs.)	Outstanding (shs.)[1]
Common	unlimited	125,534,811

[1] At July 31, 2023

Major Shareholder - Widely held at July 24, 2023.

Price Range - NDA/TSX-VEN

Year	Volume	High	Low	Close
2022	29,877,571	$0.58	$0.14	$0.14
2021	321,374,568	$2.22	$0.18	$0.58
2020	110,304,660	$0.46	$0.06	$0.37
2019	110,320,209	$0.23	$0.04	$0.09
2018	87,459,042	$0.85	$0.03	$0.06

Recent Close: $0.23
Capital Stock Changes - There were no changes to capital stock during fiscal 2022.

Wholly Owned Subsidiaries

Neptune Digital USA Corp., Del.
Neptune Stake Technologies Corp.

Investments

Rapture Labs Inc., Canada.
41.45% int. in **Space Exploration Technologies Corp.**, United States.

Financial Statistics

Periods ended:	12m Aug. 31/22[A]		12m Aug. 31/21[□A]
	$000s	%Chg	$000s
Operating revenue	**4,957**	**+728**	**599**
Cost of sales	484		n.a.
General & admin expense	2,306		1,602
Stock-based compensation	184		5,590
Operating expense	**2,975**	**-59**	**7,192**
Operating income	**1,982**	**n.a.**	**(6,593)**
Deprec., depl. & amort.	976		178
Finance income	2,448		1,467
Write-downs/write-offs	(8,923)		nil
Pre-tax income	**(21,072)**	**n.a.**	**(593)**
Net income	**(21,072)**	**n.a.**	**(593)**
Cash & equivalent	8,710		3,482
Accounts receivable	322		214
Current assets	26,637		45,775
Fixed assets, net	4,878		2,797
Intangibles, net	4,105		6,103
Total assets	**36,042**	**-34**	**54,676**
Accts. pay. & accr. liabs	891		769
Current liabilities	891		769
Shareholders' equity	35,152		53,907
Cash from oper. activs	**(461)**	**n.a.**	**(1,012)**
Cash from fin. activs	nil		38,536
Cash from invest. activs	5,061		(37,487)
Net cash position	**4,755**	**n.m.**	**155**
Capital expenditures	(4,082)		nil
	$		$
Earnings per share*	(0.17)		(0.01)
Cash flow per share*	(0.00)		(0.01)
	shs		shs
No. of shs. o/s*	124,909,811		124,909,811
Avg. no. of shs. o/s*	124,909,811		102,493,569
	%		%
Net profit margin	(425.10)		(99.00)
Return on equity	(47.32)		(2.06)
Return on assets	(46.46)		(2.03)

* Common
□ Restated
[A] Reported in accordance with IFRS

Latest Results

Periods ended:	9m May 31/23[A]		9m May 31/22[¤A]
	$000s	%Chg	$000s
Operating revenue	2,271	-52	4,698
Net income	(335)	n.a.	4,061
	$		$
Earnings per share*	(0.00)		0.03

* Common
¤ Restated
A Reported in accordance with IFRS

Historical Summary
(as originally stated)

Fiscal Year	Oper. Rev.	Net Inc. Bef. Disc.	EPS*
	$000s	$000s	$
2022[A]	4,957	(21,072)	(0.17)
2021[A]	599	(2,035)	(0.02)
2020[A]	149	163	0.01
2019[A]	202	(4,361)	(0.05)
2018[A1,2]	423	(22,077)	(0.33)

* Common
A Reported in accordance with IFRS
1 10 months ended Aug. 31, 2018.
2 Results reflect the Jan. 17, 2018, reverse takeover acquisition of Neptune Dash Nodes Corp.

N.25 Neptune Wellness Solutions Inc.

Symbol - NEPT **Exchange** - NASDAQ **CUSIP** - 64079L
Head Office - 100-545 prom du Centropolis, Laval, QC, H7T 0A3 **Telephone** - (450) 687-2262 **Toll-free** - (888) 664-9166 **Fax** - (450) 687-2272
Website - www.neptunewellness.com
Email - m.brown@neptunecorp.com
Investor Relations - Morry Brown (888) 664-9166
Auditors - KPMG LLP C.A., Montréal, Qué.
Transfer Agents - Computershare Trust Company, N.A., Golden, Colo.; Computershare Trust Company of Canada Inc., Montréal, Qué.
Employees - 155 at June 30, 2022
Profile - (Que. 1998) Provides health and wellness products and solutions across the nutraceuticals, beauty and personal care, and organic foods and beverages markets.
Nutraceuticals - Provides specialty ingredients and turnkey product services, including custom formulation, development, packaging and distribution, for business customers primarily in Canada and the U.S. Specialty ingredients offered include MaxSimil, a patented fish oil used as a carrier oil that enhances the absorption of fat-soluble and nutritional ingredients; natural grade and concentrated fish/marine oils; seed oils from camellia, chia seed, hemp seed, flaxseed, evening primrose, olive, coconut and various other sources; and a range of vitamins and supplements such as prebiotics, probiotics and fibre. Products are provided as raw material or transformed into finished products under customers' brands in different delivery forms, such as softgels, capsules, liquids, powders, sprays and pumps, which may include proprietary specialty ingredients.
Beauty and Personal Care - Develops and sells plant-based supplements under the brand Forest Remedies, which consists of a line of multi-omega supplements sold through retailers and directly to consumers online.
Organic Foods and Beverages - Subsidiary **Sprout Foods, Inc.** (50.1% owned) manufactures and distributes organic meals and snacks for babies, toddlers and kids of all ages under the brands Sprout, Nosh! and NurturMe. Products are sold in the U.S. and Canada through retail stores and online channels.
Also owns a 50,000-sq.-ft. cannabis manufacturing facility in Sherbrooke, Que., which includes a laboratory for full testing and research and development. Products include oils, capsules, hashish, dried flower, pre-roll and vapes which are marketed under the brands Mood Ring and PanHash in British Columbia, Ontario, Quebec and Alberta. Cannabis operations are held for sale.
The company changed its reporting currency to the U.S. dollar from the Canadian dollar, effective Mar. 31, 2022.

Recent Merger and Acquisition Activity

Status: pending **Announced:** Oct. 17, 2022
Neptune Wellness Solutions Inc. agreed to dispose of its cannabis business to cannabis company PurCann Pharma Inc. for $5,150,000 cash in order to become a pure consumers packaged goods (CPG) company. The assets includes the cannabis manufacturing plant in Sherbrooke, Que., the Mood Ring and PanHash brands, and related assets. PurCann Pharma is a subsidiary of Quebec-based Groupe SiliCycle, which extracts and purifies active ingredients from natural biomass. The transaction was expected to close on or before Nov. 15, 2022.
Predecessor Detail - Name changed from Neptune Technologies & Bioressources inc., Sept. 21, 2018.
Directors - Julie Phillips, chr., Ga.; Michael Cammarata, pres. & CEO, Jupiter, Fla.; Joseph Buaron, Ont.; Michael A. de Geus, Va.; Dr. Ronald Denis, Montréal, Qué.; Philip Sanford, Ga.
Other Exec. Officers - Lisa Gainsborg, interim CFO; John S. Wirt, exec. v-p, legal & bus. affairs, chief legal officer & gen. counsel; Morry Brown, v-p, IR; Christopher Piazza, deputy gen. counsel, corp.; Sarah Tynan, CEO, Sprout Organics; Christopher J. C. Waldon, deputy gen. counsel, litigation

Capital Stock

	Authorized (shs.)	Outstanding (shs.)[1]
Preferred	unlimited	
Series A		nil
Common	unlimited	11,198,357

1 At Oct. 12, 2022
Major Shareholder - Widely held at July 28, 2022.

Price Range - NEPT/TSX (D)

Year	Volume	High	Low	Close
2022	1,430,365	$24.15	$1.27	$1.97
2021	2,006,626	$159.25	$15.75	$17.50
2020	1,862,966	$168.00	$47.25	$69.30
2019	1,992,049	$301.00	$113.75	$125.30
2018	2,211,139	$232.40	$99.40	$121.10

Consolidation: 1-for-35 cons. in June 2022
Capital Stock Changes - On June 13, 2022, common shares were consolidated on a 1-for-35 basis. Also in June 2022, direct offering of 1,300,000 post-consolidated common shares was completed at US$2.57 per share. In October 2022, direct offering of 3,208,557 post-consolidated common shares was completed at US$1.87 per share.
In March 2022, direct offering of 18,500,000 common shares was completed at US$0.32 per share. Also during fiscal 2022, common shares were issued as follows: 6,500,000 on exercise of warrants and 3,783,016 under restricted share unit plan.

Wholly Owned Subsidiaries

Biodroga Nutraceuticals Inc., Qué.
Neptune Holdings USA, Inc., Del.
- 100% int. in **Neptune Care, Inc.**, Del.
- 100% int. in **Neptune Forest, Inc.**, Del.
- 100% int. in **Neptune Growth Ventures, Inc.**, Del.
  - 50.1% int. in **Sprout Foods, Inc.**, Montvale, N.J.
- 100% int. in **Neptune Health & Wellness Innovation, Inc.**, Del.
- 100% int. in **SugarLeaf Labs, Inc.**, Del.

Neptune Wellness Brands Canada, Inc., Qué.
9354-7537 Quebec Inc., Qué.
9418-1252 Quebec Inc., Qué.

Financial Statistics

Periods ended:	12m Mar. 31/22[A]		12m Mar. 31/21[¤A]
	US$000s	%Chg	US$000s
Operating revenue	**48,797**	**+38**	**35,400**
Cost of sales	53,849		59,430
Research & devel. expense	880		1,922
General & admin expense	56,942		48,106
Operating expense	**111,671**	**+2**	**109,458**
Operating income	**(62,874)**	**n.a.**	**(74,058)**
Deprec., depl. & amort.	6,080		19,062
Finance income	7		826
Finance costs, gross	2,144		1,787
Write-downs/write-offs	(19,581)[1]		(37,753)[2]
Pre-tax income	**(84,425)**	**n.a.**	**(127,742)**
Income taxes	nil		(3,478)
Net income	**(84,425)**	**n.a.**	**(124,264)**
Net inc. for equity hldrs	**(74,972)**	**n.a.**	**(123,170)**
Net inc. for non-cont. int	**(9,453)**	**n.a.**	**(1,094)**
Cash & equivalent	8,746		59,856
Inventories	17,059		17,317
Accounts receivable	7,600		8,667
Current assets	37,388		89,528
Long-term investments	nil		150
Fixed assets, net	21,448		37,346
Right-of-use assets	2,295		2,899
Intangibles, net	43,823		51,410
Total assets	**104,955**	**-44**	**186,948**
Accts. pay. & accr. liabs	22,701		19,882
Current liabilities	30,317		34,809
Long-term debt, gross	11,648		11,313
Long-term debt, net	11,648		11,313
Long-term lease liabilities	2,063		2,887
Shareholders' equity	48,116		115,368
Non-controlling interest	12,722		22,178
Cash from oper. activs	**(54,346)**	**n.a.**	**(56,645)**
Cash from fin. activs	5,952		115,001
Cash from invest. activs	(2,327)		(10,122)
Net cash position	**8,726**	**-85**	**59,837**
Capital expenditures	(1,939)		(6,618)
Capital disposals	nil		15
	US$		US$
Earnings per share*	(15.54)		(35.55)
Cash flow per share*	(11.27)		(16.35)
	shs		shs
No. of shs. o/s*	5,554,456		4,732,084
Avg. no. of shs. o/s*	4,824,336		3,465,058
	%		%
Net profit margin	(173.01)		(351.03)
Return on equity	(91.17)		(112.78)
Return on assets	(56.39)		(80.20)
Foreign sales percent	74		62
No. of employees (FTEs)	161		127

* Common
¤ Restated
A Reported in accordance with U.S. GAAP
1 Includes impairment of US$13,785,640 of property, plant and equipment (PP&E) related to the Canadian cannabis assets, US$979,942 of PP&E of the SugarLeaf unit, as well as goodwill and trademark impairment of US$3,288,847 and US$1,527,000, respectively, of subsidiary Sprout Foods, Inc.
2 Includes impairment of goodwill, PP&E and right-of-use asset of US$26,898,016, US$1,533,766 and US$107,650, respectively, related to the SugarLeaf unit, and PP&E impairment of US$9,213,926 related to the cannabis processing business.

Latest Results

Periods ended:	3m June 30/22[A]		3m June 30/21[A]
	US$000s	%Chg	US$000s
Operating revenue	16,272	+61	10,079
Net income	(6,504)	n.a.	(18,856)
Net inc. for equity hldrs	(4,284)	n.a.	(16,908)
Net inc. for non-cont. int	(2,220)		(1,948)
	US$		US$
Earnings per share*	(0.72)		(3.56)

* Common
A Reported in accordance with U.S. GAAP

Historical Summary
(as originally stated)

Fiscal Year	Oper. Rev.	Net Inc. Bef. Disc.	EPS*
	US$000s	US$000s	US$
2022[A]	48,797	(84,425)	(15.54)
	$000s	$000s	$
2021[B]	46,810	(168,594)	(48.24)
2020[B]	29,578	(60,863)	(23.68)
2019[B]	24,442	(23,192)	(10.21)
2018[B]	27,646	9,339	7.80

* Common
[A] Reported in accordance with U.S. GAAP
[B] Reported in accordance with IFRS
Note: Adjusted throughout for 1-for-35 cons. in June 2022

N.26 Nerds On Site Inc.

Symbol - NERD **Exchange** - CSE **CUSIP** - 64082A
Head Office - Unit 120-121, 4026 Meadowbrook Dr, London, ON, N6L 1C7 **Telephone** - (519) 639-4382 **Toll-free** - (877) 775-3024
Website - www.nerdsonsite.com
Email - charlie@nerdsonsite.com
Investor Relations - Charles Regan (877) 778-2335
Auditors - MNP LLP C.A., Toronto, Ont.
Transfer Agents - TSX Trust Company, Calgary, Alta.
Profile - (Ont. 1997) Provides mobile managed information technology (IT) and cybersecurity services to small and medium-sized enterprises in Canada and the U.S., under the Nerds on Site brand.
Operates a network of technically proficient and specially trained independent IT consultants to help clients on site by providing effective, consistent and customized IT solutions. Services provided include computer set up and repair, network security services, network installation, website design and development, and support and tailored software services.
Also operates a network of sub-contractors that services an average of 12,000 customers per year in Canada. These are consultants that are independent contractors and each consultant is responsible for their own costs relating to client origination and development. A consultant retains 37% to 50% of revenues from each client contract, with the balance of the revenue being provided to the company. Revenues are derived primarily from service fees charged for consulting services performed by the consultants under written service contracts with customers, and sale of off-the-shelf software, hardware and related support.
Directors - Charles (Charlie) Regan, CEO, Ont.; John Harbarenko, pres., Ont.; David Redekop, v-p, chief tech. officer & corp. sec., Ont.; Kevin Ernst, N.J.; Nicole Holden, Va.; Eugene Konaryev, Ont.
Other Exec. Officers - Rakesh Malhotra, CFO

Capital Stock

	Authorized (shs.)	Outstanding (shs.)[1]
Class B Preferred	1,000,000	1,000,000[2]
Subordinate Vtg.	unlimited	89,411,115

[1] At Oct. 28, 2022
[2] Classified as debt.
Class B Preferred - Non-participating and not entitled to receive dividends. On wind-up of the company, are not entitled to receive out of the assets and property of the company. Ten votes per share.
Subordinate Voting - One vote per share.
Major Shareholder - Charles (Charlie) Regan held 31.09% interest, David Redekop held 11.26% interest and John Harbarenko held 10.39% interest at June 6, 2022.

Price Range - NERD/CSE

Year	Volume	High	Low	Close
2022	6,744,249	$0.11	$0.05	$0.08
2021	55,803,825	$0.42	$0.04	$0.08
2020	26,869,078	$0.10	$0.03	$0.04
2019	34,122,999	$0.30	$0.05	$0.06
2018	2,520,978	$0.37	$0.16	$0.19

Recent Close: $0.07
Capital Stock Changes - There were no changes to capital stock during fiscal 2022.

Wholly Owned Subsidiaries
Nerds on Site USA Inc., United States.

Financial Statistics

Periods ended:	12m May 31/22[A]		12m May 31/21[□A]
	$000s	%Chg	$000s
Operating revenue	**9,630**	**-5**	**10,121**
Cost of sales	7,095		7,494
Salaries & benefits	325		388
Research & devel. expense	344		366
General & admin expense	2,572		2,922
Operating expense	**10,336**	**-7**	**11,170**
Operating income	**(706)**	**n.a.**	**(1,049)**
Deprec., depl. & amort.	106		146
Finance income	154		142
Finance costs, gross	275		270
Write-downs/write-offs	nil		(65)
Pre-tax income	**(933)**	**n.a.**	**(1,388)**
Net income	**(933)**	**n.a.**	**(1,388)**
Cash & equivalent	279		390
Inventories	141		70
Accounts receivable	180		132
Current assets	1,038		1,080
Fixed assets, net	122		176
Right-of-use assets	152		177
Total assets	**1,676**	**-28**	**2,336**
Bank indebtedness	250		127
Accts. pay. & accr. liabs	857		749
Current liabilities	1,569		1,360
Long-term debt, gross	84		90
Long-term debt, net	57		64
Long-term lease liabilities	149		168
Shareholders' equity	(189)		744
Cash from oper. activs	**(826)**	**n.a.**	**(290)**
Cash from fin. activs	741		373
Cash from invest. activs	(27)		(9)
Net cash position	**279**	**-29**	**391**
Capital expenditures	(27)		(9)
	$		$
Earnings per share*	(0.01)		(0.02)
Cash flow per share*	(0.01)		(0.00)
	shs		shs
No. of shs. o/s*	89,411,115		89,411,115
Avg. no. of shs. o/s*	89,411,115		86,402,581
	%		%
Net profit margin	(9.69)		(13.71)
Return on equity	n.m.		(139.50)
Return on assets	(32.80)		(43.22)
Foreign sales percent	5		5

* Subord. Vtg.
□ Restated
[A] Reported in accordance with IFRS

Latest Results

Periods ended:	3m Aug. 31/22[A]		3m Aug. 31/21[A]
	$000s	%Chg	$000s
Operating revenue	2,547	-1	2,569
Net income	(169)	n.a.	(215)
	$		$
Earnings per share*	(0.00)		(0.00)

* Subord. Vtg.
[A] Reported in accordance with IFRS

Historical Summary
(as originally stated)

Fiscal Year	Oper. Rev.	Net Inc. Bef. Disc.	EPS*
	$000s	$000s	$
2022[A]	9,630	(933)	(0.01)
2021[A]	10,121	(1,388)	(0.02)
2020[A]	10,143	(2,035)	(0.02)
2019[A]	8,906	(3,423)	(0.05)
2018[A]	8,440	(1,518)	(0.03)

* Subord. Vtg.
[A] Reported in accordance with IFRS

N.27 NervGen Pharma Corp.

Symbol - NGEN **Exchange** - TSX-VEN **CUSIP** - 64082X
Head Office - 480-2955 Virtual Way, Vancouver, BC, V5M 4X6 **Telephone** - (604) 722-5361 **Fax** - (604) 681-4692
Website - www.nervgen.com
Email - htracey@nervgen.com
Investor Relations - Huitt Tracey (604) 537-2094
Auditors - KPMG LLP C.A., Vancouver, B.C.
Transfer Agents - Computershare Trust Company of Canada Inc., Vancouver, B.C.
Employees - 10 at Dec. 31, 2022
Profile - (B.C. 2017) Developing pharmaceutical products for the treatment of nervous system damage due to injuries or diseases.
The company's core technology, licensed from Case Western Reserve University of Cleveland, Ohio, targets protein tyrosine phosphatase sigma (PTP sigma), a neural receptor that impedes nerve regeneration or repair. Inhibition of the PTP sigma receptor has been shown to promote regeneration of damaged nerves and improvement of nerve function in animal models for various indications. Lead drug candidate is NVG-291, a PTP sigma inhibitor being developed for the treatment of nervous system trauma (such as acute and chronic spinal cord injuries, and traumatic brain injury) and diseases (such as multiple sclerosis, stroke, amyotrophic lateral sclerosis, frontotemporal dementia and Parkinson's disease). NVG-291 was granted an orphan designation in Europe for SPI.
Directors - Dr. Harold M. Punnett, co-founder, B.C.; William J. (Bill) Radvak, co-founder & exec. chr., Vancouver, B.C.; Michael Kelly, pres. & CEO, Pa.; Brian E. Bayley, North Vancouver, B.C.; Glenn A. Ives, Vancouver, B.C.; Dr. Randall E. Kaye, N.Y.; Krista McKerracher, Fla.; Dr. Adam Rogers, Boston, Mass.; Craig Thompson, Calif.
Other Exec. Officers - William J. (Bill) Adams, CFO & corp. sec.; Daniel Mikol, CMO; Nana Collett, v-p, program mgt.; Dr. Matvey Lukashev, v-p, research & preclinical devel.

Capital Stock

	Authorized (shs.)	Outstanding (shs.)[1]
Common	unlimited	59,211,172

[1] At May 14, 2023
Major Shareholder - PFP Biosciences Holdings LLC held 16.9% interest at Apr. 3, 2023.

Price Range - NGEN/TSX-VEN

Year	Volume	High	Low	Close
2022	8,524,717	$2.82	$1.50	$1.60
2021	11,237,290	$3.33	$1.26	$2.73
2020	6,737,265	$3.25	$0.80	$2.23
2019	3,516,091	$2.25	$1.22	$1.96

Recent Close: $1.89
Capital Stock Changes - In July 2022, private placement of 10,150,000 units (1 common share & ½ warrant) at US$1.50 per unit was completed. Also during 2022, common shares were issued as follows: 1,739,492 on exercise of warrants, 500,000 as finders' fees and 200,000 on exercise of options.

Wholly Owned Subsidiaries
NervGen Australia Pty Ltd.
NervGen US Inc., United States.

Financial Statistics

Periods ended:	12m Dec. 31/22[A]		12m Dec. 31/21[A]
	$000s	%Chg	$000s
Salaries & benefits	3,621		2,317
Research & devel. expense	13,452		4,768
General & admin expense	3,062		1,668
Stock-based compensation	2,775		4,016
Operating expense	**22,910**	**+79**	**12,769**
Operating income	**(22,910)**	**n.a.**	**(12,769)**
Deprec., depl. & amort.	115		43
Finance income	201		29
Finance costs, gross	515		nil
Pre-tax income	**(20,722)**	**n.a.**	**(12,727)**
Net income	**(20,722)**	**n.a.**	**(12,727)**
Cash & equivalent	22,452		16,929
Accounts receivable	27		64
Current assets	23,149		17,420
Fixed assets, net	295		2,691
Intangibles, net	431		473
Total assets	**23,875**	**+33**	**17,896**
Accts. pay. & accr. liabs	2,894		804
Current liabilities	3,398		1,078
Shareholders' equity	13,461		16,818
Cash from oper. activs	**(17,784)**	**n.a.**	**(8,269)**
Cash from fin. activs	22,641		19,613
Cash from invest. activs	(21)		(45)
Net cash position	**22,452**	**+33**	**16,929**
Capital expenditures	(21)		(3)
	$		$
Earnings per share*	(0.39)		(0.32)
Cash flow per share*	(0.34)		(0.21)
	shs		shs
No. of shs. o/s*	58,779,076		46,189,584
Avg. no. of shs. o/s*	52,649,035		39,289,224
	%		%
Net profit margin	n.a.		n.a.
Return on equity	(136.87)		(111.94)
Return on assets	(96.75)		(103.59)
No. of employees (FTEs)	10		10

* Common
[A] Reported in accordance with IFRS

Latest Results

Periods ended:	3m Mar. 31/23[A]		3m Mar. 31/22[A]
	$000s	%Chg	$000s
Net income	(4,709)	n.a.	(4,968)
	$		$
Earnings per share*	(0.08)		(0.11)

* Common
[A] Reported in accordance with IFRS

Historical Summary
(as originally stated)

Fiscal Year	Oper. Rev. $000s	Net Inc. Bef. Disc. $000s	EPS* $
2022[A]	nil	(20,722)	(0.39)
2021[A]	nil	(12,727)	(0.32)
2020[A]	nil	(11,186)	(0.35)
2019[A]	nil	(9,766)	(0.38)
2018[A]	nil	(1,358)	(0.17)

* Common
[A] Reported in accordance with IFRS

N.28 NetCents Technology Inc.

Symbol - NC **Exchange** - CSE (S) **CUSIP** - 64112G
Head Office - 350-375 Water St, Vancouver, BC, V6B 5C6 **Telephone** - (604) 633-9967
Website - www.net-cents.com
Email - investor@net-cents.com
Investor Relations - Clayton Moore (604) 633-9967
Auditors - PKF Antares Professional Corporation C.A., Calgary, Alta.
Transfer Agents - TSX Trust Company, Toronto, Ont.
Profile - (B.C. 2014) Offers electronic payment processing software that enables merchants to securely receive payments from customers who want to pay for goods and services using different cryptocurrencies. Also operates a cryptocurrency exchange for its proprietary cryptocurrency, NetCents Coin.

The company offers an entire cryptocurrency ecosystem to merchants, partners and users by providing full payment integration, instant settlements and security while giving users access to over 40,000,000 merchants worldwide, servicing over 55 countries and 33 fiat currencies. Supported cryptocurrencies include Bitcoin, Ether, Bitcoin Cash, XRP, Verge, Zen, Tron and NEM.

The company's own payment token, NetCents Coin, is an independent and decentralized asset-backed digital currency that allows users to make fast and secure transactions. NetCents Coin operates as a "stablecoin", which means that it is stable, transactional-based currency that provides merchants and users with the ability to transact using cryptocurrency without the highly volatile swings in pricing that is commonly experienced by other cryptocurrencies.

Common suspended from CSE, May 7, 2021.

Directors - Clayton Moore, founder & CEO, Vancouver, B.C.; Jennifer (Jenn) Lowther, pres., B.C.; Frank Amaro; Jason Dukowski

Other Exec. Officers - Gaurav Mohan, chief revenue officer; Nilang Vyas, chief technical officer; Marcie Verdin, exec. v-p, card & solutions devel.; Pat Albright, sr. v-p, strategic devel.; Marcus Laun, v-p, corp. fin.

Capital Stock

	Authorized (shs.)	Outstanding (shs.)[1]
Class B Preferred	unlimited	nil
Common	unlimited	110,281,173

[1] At Dec. 5, 2022

Major Shareholder - Clayton Moore held 15.57% interest at Nov. 10, 2020.

Price Range - NC/CSE (S)

Year	Volume	High	Low	Close
2021	29,358,435	$1.75	$0.64	$0.69
2020	79,739,820	$2.75	$0.22	$1.26
2019	11,941,095	$1.45	$0.21	$0.24
2018	32,888,320	$3.99	$0.71	$0.72

Wholly Owned Subsidiaries

NetCents International Ltd., United Kingdom.
Netcents Systems Ltd., Alta.

N.29 NetraMark Holdings Inc.

Symbol - AIAI **Exchange** - CSE **CUSIP** - 64119M
Head Office - 101-1655 Dupont St, Toronto, ON, M6P 3T1 **Telephone** - (416) 859-8838
Website - netramark.com
Email - swapan@netramark.com
Investor Relations - Swapan Kakumanu (416) 859-8838
Auditors - MNP LLP C.A., Toronto, Ont.
Lawyers - Fasken Martineau DuMoulin LLP, Toronto, Ont.
Transfer Agents - Odyssey Trust Company, Vancouver, B.C.
Profile - (B.C. 2021; orig. Ont., 2019) Develops artificial intelligence (AI)/machine learning (ML) solutions targeted at the pharmaceutical industry.

Technology solutions uses a novel topology-based algorithm that has the ability to parse patient data sets into subsets of people that are strongly related according to several variables simultaneously. Also increasing new drug/device development, accelerate clinical trials, mitigate placebo response and how disorders are treated through an enhanced disease taxonomy.

Through wholly owned **NetraMark Corp.**, offers AI solutions for pharmaceutical and biotechnology companies. Products include NetraAI, NetraMark's core platform, Netra Shatter, Netra Health Atlas and Netra Placebo which apply various ML methods to process, organize and derive insights from complex data. Applications of NetraMark's solutions include preventing clinical trial failure through precise patient stratification; re-igniting failed clinical trials; identifying new indications for existing drugs; and determining new molecular combinations for drug creation.

Predecessor Detail - Name changed from Nurosene Health Inc., Feb. 1, 2023.

Directors - Kevin R. Taylor, chr., Fort Lauderdale, Fla.; Dr. Joseph Geraci, chief scientific officer, Toronto, Ont.; Gino L. DeMichele, Calgary, Alta.; Sheetal Jaitly, Toronto, Ont.; Andrew Parks, Toronto, Ont.

Other Exec. Officers - George Achilleos, pres. & CEO; Swapan Kakumanu, CFO; Dr. Douglas J. (D.J.) Cook, CMO; Daniel (Dan) Gallucci, chief performance officer; Dr. Luca Pani, chief innovation & regulatory officer; Jaime Hackett, v-p, mktg.; Joseph Loren, v-p, eng.; Josh Spiegel, pres., NetraMark Corp.

Capital Stock

	Authorized (shs.)	Outstanding (shs.)[1]
Common	unlimited	50,524,520

[1] At May 18, 2023

Major Shareholder - Widely held at Feb. 16, 2023.

Price Range - AIAI/CSE

Year	Volume	High	Low	Close
2022	7,620,360	$1.06	$0.15	$0.17
2021	12,975,029	$3.17	$0.88	$1.10

Recent Close: $0.26

Capital Stock Changes - In October 2021, 6,148,325 common shares were issued pursuant to the acquisition of NetraMark Corp. Also during fiscal 2022, common shares were issued as follows: 1,487,500 by private placement, 933,924 for services, 133,602 on exercise of warrants, 25,000 on vesting of restricted share units and 21,140 on exercise of options.

Wholly Owned Subsidiaries

NetraMark Corp., Toronto, Ont.

Financial Statistics

Periods ended:	12m Sept. 30/22[A]		12m Sept. 30/21[0A]
	$000s	%Chg	$000s
Operating revenue	**113**	**n.a.**	**nil**
Salaries & benefits	1,539		97
General & admin expense	4,662		3,740
Stock-based compensation	1,247		1,209
Other operating expense	nil		38
Operating expense	**7,448**	**+46**	**5,084**
Operating income	**(7,335)**	**n.a.**	**(5,084)**
Deprec., depl. & amort.	597		nil
Write-downs/write-offs	(5,763)[1]		nil
Pre-tax income	**(13,696)**	**n.a.**	**(5,084)**
Income taxes	(248)		nil
Net income	**(13,448)**	**n.a.**	**(5,084)**
Cash & equivalent	15,092		6,326
Accounts receivable	8		nil
Current assets	277		6,820
Intangibles, net	8,921		1,582
Total assets	**9,198**	**+9**	**8,403**
Accts. pay. & accr. liabs.	1,064		459
Current liabilities	1,087		459
Shareholders' equity	8,111		7,944
Cash from oper. activs.	**(4,778)**	**n.a.**	**(2,604)**
Cash from fin. activs.	692		8,669
Cash from invest. activs.	2,189		1,622
Net cash position	**10**	**-100**	**6,286**
	$		$
Earnings per share*	(0.33)		(0.20)
Cash flow per share*	(0.12)		(0.10)
	shs		shs
No. of shs. o/s*	42,521,102		33,771,611
Avg. no. of shs. o/s*	40,545,673		25,763,227
	%		%
Net profit margin	n.m.		n.a.
Return on equity	(167.52)		(104.06)
Return on assets	(152.81)		(98.02)

* Common
[0] Restated
[A] Reported in accordance with IFRS
[1] Pertains to impairment of goodwill and intangible assets.

Latest Results

Periods ended:	6m Mar. 31/23[A]		6m Mar. 31/22[A]
	$000s	%Chg	$000s
Operating revenue	89	+19	75
Net income	(3,517)	n.a.	(5,378)
	$		$
Earnings per share*	(0.08)		(0.14)

* Common
[A] Reported in accordance with IFRS

Historical Summary
(as originally stated)

Fiscal Year	Oper. Rev. $000s	Net Inc. Bef. Disc. $000s	EPS* $
2022[A]	113	(13,448)	(0.33)
2021[A]	nil	(5,084)	(0.20)
2020[A1]	nil	(292)	(0.06)

* Common
[A] Reported in accordance with IFRS
[1] As shown in the prospectus dated May 20, 2021.

N.30 Network Media Group Inc.

Symbol - NTE **Exchange** - TSX-VEN **CUSIP** - 64128U
Head Office - 207-1525 8 Ave W, Vancouver, BC, V6J 1T5 **Telephone** - (604) 739-8825 **Fax** - (604) 909-2895
Website - www.networkmediagroup.ca
Email - trevor@networkentertainment.ca
Investor Relations - Trevor Treweeke (778) 870-5028
Auditors - Baker Tilly WM LLP C.A., Vancouver, B.C.
Bankers - Royal Bank of Canada
Lawyers - McMillan LLP, Vancouver, B.C.
Transfer Agents - Computershare Trust Company of Canada Inc., Vancouver, B.C.
Profile - (B.C. 2010) Develops, produces, markets and distributes factual/non-scripted television series, documentaries, biographies, docudramas, theatrical documentary films, online programming, and specialty sports and entertainment productions. Also developing Non-Fungible Tokens (NFT) to create, distribute and monetize digital collectibles.

The company builds its production slate in two primary forms including documentary films and docu-series, which are distributed throughout the world on theatrical networks, television networks, streaming services and on any device including mobile, tablet and desktop. Distribution platforms include ABC, AHC, AMC, Applet TV+, Discovery, ESPN, ESPN Classic, CBC, CMT, CTV, HBO Canada, History Channel, National Geographic, Paramount Network, Peacock, EPIX, Spike, Sundance, TMN, TSN and YouTube. Revenue is generated through licensing to television networks, over-the-top (OTT) media services (streamers), distributors and syndicators; ancillary distribution including DVD/digital distribution, plus online/video-on-demand (VOD) sales; and third party service work.

Also developing NFTs by partnering with top creators from film, music, art, fashion and sports to create Web 3.0 experiences and limited edition collections for customers to buy, collect and trade digital collectibles.

Predecessor Detail - Name changed from Andele Capital Corporation, Jan. 3, 2012, pursuant to Qualifying Transaction reverse takeover acquisition of Network Entertainment Inc.

Directors - Ali Pejman, chr., B.C.; Derik A. Murray, CEO, B.C.; Paul Gertz, COO & corp. sec., North Vancouver, B.C.; Timothy (Tim) Gamble, Vancouver, B.C.; Dr. Greg Zeschuk, Alta.

Other Exec. Officers - Curtis White, pres.; Darren Battersby, CFO; Kent Wingerak, sr. v-p, bus. affairs; Brian Gersh, pres., Network Entertainment USA; Tom Lombardi, pres., NFT Studios

Capital Stock

	Authorized (shs.)	Outstanding (shs.)[1]
Common	unlimited	89,123,537

[1] At July 31, 2023

Major Shareholder - Widely held at Nov. 1, 2022.

Price Range - NTE/TSX-VEN

Year	Volume	High	Low	Close
2022	10,711,373	$0.26	$0.04	$0.06
2021	46,777,580	$0.46	$0.11	$0.20
2020	29,956,269	$0.24	$0.13	$0.18
2019	21,440,273	$0.21	$0.11	$0.19
2018	31,746,598	$0.24	$0.08	$0.13

Recent Close: $0.04

Capital Stock Changes - There were no changes to capital stock during fiscal 2022.

Wholly Owned Subsidiaries

Network Entertainment Inc., B.C.
- 100% int. in **Network Entertainment Corp.**, Canada.
- 100% int. in **Network Entertainment Services Corp.**, Delaware, Ont.
- 100% int. in **Network Films Eighteen Inc.**, B.C.
- 100% int. in **Network Films Nineteen Inc.**, B.C.
- 100% int. in **Network Films Twenty Inc.**, B.C.
- 100% int. in **Network Films Twenty-One Inc.**, B.C.
- 100% int. in **Network Films Twenty-Two Inc.**, B.C.
- 100% int. in **Network NFT Studios Inc.**, B.C.
- 100% int. in **Network Pictures Twenty-Four Inc.**, B.C.
- 100% int. in **Network Pictures Twenty Inc.**, B.C.
- 100% int. in **Network Pictures Twenty-One Inc.**, B.C.
- 100% int. in **Network Pictures Twenty-Two Inc.**, B.C.

Note: The preceding list includes only the major related companies in which interests are held.

Financial Statistics

Periods ended:	12m Nov. 30/22[A]		12m Nov. 30/21[A]
	$000s	%Chg	$000s
Operating revenue	**12,434**	**+252**	**3,534**
Cost of goods sold	1,485		1,425
Salaries & benefits	1,368		921
General & admin expense	755		503
Stock-based compensation	531		491
Operating expense	**4,139**	**+24**	**3,339**
Operating income	**8,295**	**n.m.**	**195**
Deprec., depl. & amort.	7,393		3,286
Finance income	5		1
Finance costs, gross	205		154
Write-downs/write-offs	(87)		(360)
Pre-tax income	**602**	**n.a.**	**(2,579)**
Income taxes	5		(83)
Net income	**597**	**n.a.**	**(2,496)**
Cash & equivalent	708		2,789
Accounts receivable	1,126		292
Current assets	6,300		4,747
Long-term investments	11,714		11,021
Fixed assets, net	223		223
Right-of-use assets	154		454
Intangibles, net	400		nil
Total assets	**20,559**	**+11**	**18,536**
Bank indebtedness	185		290
Accts. pay. & accr. liabs	4,884		2,076
Current liabilities	9,024		7,753
Long-term debt, gross	1,095		nil
Long-term debt, net	795		1,177
Long-term lease liabilities	6		151
Shareholders' equity	10,583		9,455
Cash from oper. activs	**5,324**	**-10**	**5,888**
Cash from fin. activs	1,718		2,228
Cash from invest. activs	(9,032)		(6,186)
Net cash position	**708**	**-75**	**2,789**
Capital expenditures	(41)		(109)
	$		$
Earnings per share*	0.01		(0.03)
Cash flow per share*	0.06		0.08
	shs		shs
No. of shs. o/s*	89,123,537		89,123,537
Avg. no. of shs. o/s*	89,123,537		75,658,909
	%		%
Net profit margin	4.80		(70.63)
Return on equity	5.96		(26.74)
Return on assets	4.09		(14.38)

* Common

[A] Reported in accordance with IFRS

Latest Results

Periods ended:	6m May 31/23[A]		6m May 31/22[oA]
	$000s	%Chg	$000s
Operating revenue	3,094	+221	963
Net income	(1,407)	n.a.	(1,813)
	$		$
Earnings per share*	(0.02)		(0.02)

* Common

[o] Restated

[A] Reported in accordance with IFRS

Historical Summary
(as originally stated)

Fiscal Year	Oper. Rev.	Net Inc. Bef. Disc.	EPS*
	$000s	$000s	$
2022[A]	12,434	597	0.01
2021[A]	3,534	(2,496)	(0.03)
2020[A]	9,924	1,516	0.02
2019[A]	16,279	4,030	0.06
2018[A]	2,685	(525)	(0.01)

* Common

[A] Reported in accordance with IFRS

N.31 NeuPath Health Inc.

Symbol - NPTH **Exchange** - TSX-VEN **CUSIP** - 64133P
Head Office - Unit 9, 6400 Millcreek Dr, Mississauga, ON, L5N 3E7
Telephone - (905) 858-1368 **Toll-free** - (800) 265-3429
Website - www.neupath.com
Email - jzygouras@neupath.com
Investor Relations - Jeff Zygouras (905) 858-1368
Auditors - Ernst & Young LLP C.A., Toronto, Ont.
Transfer Agents - TSX Trust Company, Toronto, Ont.
Employees - 152 at Dec. 31, 2022

Profile - (Ont. 2019) Operates an interdisciplinary network of medical clinics in Ontario and Alberta. Also provides workplace health services and independent medical assessments across Canada.

Has 14 medical clinics in Ontario (12) and Alberta (2) as well as a minority equity interest in two physiotherapy and sport medicine clinics in Alberta which provide comprehensive assessments and rehabilitation services to clients with chronic pain, musculoskeletal/back injuries, sports-related injuries and concussions. Clinics are operated under the banners InMedic and NeuPath Centre for Pain & Spine in Ontario and HealthPointe in Alberta. Clinical operations are supported by the company's KumoCare telemedicine and home care virtual platform.

Also provides workplace health services and independent medical assessments to employers and disability insurers through a national network of health care providers. In addition, provides physician staffing for provincial and federal correctional institutions and hospital health departments as well as contract research services to pharmaceutical companies.

Predecessor Detail - Name changed from Klinik Health Ventures Corp., June 25, 2020, pursuant to Qualifying Transaction reverse takeover acquisition of 2576560 Ontario Inc. (dba NeuPath Health); basis 1 new for 5 old shs.

Directors - Daniel N. (Dan) Chicoine, chr., Port Sydney, Ont.; Joseph (Joe) Walewicz, CEO, Westmount, Qué.; Jolyon Burton, Toronto, Ont.; Sasha Cucuz, North York, Ont.; Daniel (Dan) Legault, Toronto, Ont.

Other Exec. Officers - Jeff Zygouras, CFO & corp. sec.; Denise Hill, v-p, western Canada; Bjorn Thies, v-p, people & culture

Capital Stock

	Authorized (shs.)	Outstanding (shs.)[1]
Preferred	unlimited	nil
Common	unlimited	54,597,892

[1] At Apr. 25, 2023

Major Shareholder - Bloom Burton Investment Group Inc. held 13.74% interest and Claret Asset Management Corporation held 11.07% interest at Apr. 25, 2023.

Price Range - NPTH/TSX-VEN

Year	Volume	High	Low	Close
2022	10,591,929	$0.60	$0.12	$0.18
2021	20,014,543	$0.87	$0.40	$0.50
2020	12,980,082	$1.43	$0.65	$0.77
2019	31,000	$1.10	$0.90	$0.90

Consolidation: 1-for-5 cons. in July 2020

Recent Close: $0.15

Capital Stock Changes - During 2022, common shares were issued as follows: 2,890,000 on exercise of warrants and 843,000 on vesting of restricted share units.

Wholly Owned Subsidiaries

Aidly Inc., Ont.

5033421 Ontario Inc., Toronto, Ont.

- 100% int. in **CompreMed Canada Inc.**, Mississauga, Ont.
- 100% int. in **Renaissance Asset Management (London) Inc.**, Ont.
  - 100% int. in **InMedic Corporation**, Ont.
  - 100% int. in **2276321 Ontario Inc.**, London, Ont.
- 100% int. in **Viable Healthworks Canada Corp.**, B.C.
  - 100% int. in **AIM Health Group Corp.**, Ont.
    - 100% int. in **Accident Injury Management Clinic (Hamilton-Rosedale) Inc.**
  - 100% int. in **Viable Clinical Research Corp.**, Ont.

HealthPointe Medical Centres Ltd., Edmonton, Alta.

- 50% int. in **HealthPointe@CAO Services Ltd.**, Alta.

Financial Statistics

Periods ended:	12m Dec. 31/22[A]		12m Dec. 31/21[A]
	$000s	%Chg	$000s
Operating revenue	**62,653**	**+3**	**60,856**
Cost of sales	47,162		45,870
Salaries & benefits	9,146		8,713
General & admin expense	4,838		4,887
Stock-based compensation	98		142
Operating expense	**61,244**	**+3**	**59,612**
Operating income	**1,409**	**+13**	**1,244**
Deprec., depl. & amort.	2,665		3,085
Finance income	22		34
Finance costs, gross	832		876
Write-downs/write-offs	(1,938)		nil
Pre-tax income	**(4,081)**	**n.a.**	**(3,247)**
Income taxes	194		(17)
Net income	**(4,275)**	**n.a.**	**(3,230)**
Net inc. for equity hldrs	**(4,144)**	**n.a.**	**(3,230)**
Net inc. for non-cont. int	**(131)**	**n.a.**	**nil**
Cash & equivalent	1,517		5,903
Inventories	281		215
Accounts receivable	8,894		8,474
Current assets	11,081		15,365
Fixed assets, net	5,054		4,574
Right-of-use assets	6,487		7,025
Intangibles, net	21,721		23,771
Total assets	**45,086**	**-12**	**51,342**
Accts. pay. & accr. liabs	8,800		8,284
Current liabilities	13,870		13,708
Long-term debt, gross	3,092		4,728
Long-term debt, net	nil		1,287
Long-term lease liabilities	5,856		6,628
Shareholders' equity	21,784		25,830
Non-controlling interest	(131)		nil
Cash from oper. activs	**738**	**-62**	**1,919**
Cash from fin. activs	(3,452)		(3,367)
Cash from invest. activs	(1,672)		(3,499)
Net cash position	**1,517**	**-74**	**5,903**
Capital expenditures, net	(1,232)		(411)
	$		$
Earnings per share*	(0.09)		(0.07)
Cash flow per share*	0.02		0.04
	shs		shs
No. of shs. o/s*	50,292,892		46,560,341
Avg. no. of shs. o/s*	48,477,000		45,135,000
	%		%
Net profit margin	(6.82)		(5.31)
Return on equity	(17.41)		(12.09)
Return on assets	(7.06)		(4.84)
No. of employees (FTEs)	152		165

* Common

[A] Reported in accordance with IFRS

Latest Results

Periods ended:	3m Mar. 31/23[A]		3m Mar. 31/22[A]
	$000s	%Chg	$000s
Operating revenue	16,061	+4	15,411
Net income	(225)	n.a.	(910)
Net inc. for equity hldrs	(192)	n.a.	(907)
Net inc. for non-cont. int	(33)		(3)
	$		$
Earnings per share*	(0.00)		(0.02)

* Common

[A] Reported in accordance with IFRS

Historical Summary
(as originally stated)

Fiscal Year	Oper. Rev.	Net Inc. Bef. Disc.	EPS*
	$000s	$000s	$
2022[A]	62,653	(4,275)	(0.09)
2021[A]	60,856	(3,230)	(0.07)
2020[A1]	47,639	(5,058)	(0.21)
2019[A]	49,638	(5,310)	n.a.
2018[A]	40,164	(5,319)	n.a.

* Common

[A] Reported in accordance with IFRS

[1] Results prior to June 25, 2020, pertain to and reflect the Qualifying Transaction reverse takeover acquisition of 2576560 Ontario Inc. (dba NeuPath Health).

Note: Adjusted throughout for 1-for-5 cons. in July 2020

N.32 NeutriSci International Inc.

Symbol - NU **Exchange** - TSX-VEN **CUSIP** - 64129Y
Head Office - 1600-609 Granville St, Vancouver, BC, V7Y 1C3
Toll-free - (855) 777-0660
Website - www.neutrisci.com
Email - grehman@neutrisci.com
Investor Relations - Glen Rehman (403) 264-6320

Auditors - Davidson & Company LLP C.A., Vancouver, B.C.
Lawyers - Anfield Sujir Kennedy & Durno LLP, Vancouver, B.C.
Transfer Agents - Computershare Trust Company of Canada Inc., Vancouver, B.C.
Profile - (B.C. 2014; orig. B.C., 2000) Develops and markets science-based nutraceutical products.

Products utilize pTeroPure® pterostilbene, a form of all-trans pterostilbene, found naturally in blueberries, and is manufactured by **ChromaDex Corp.** in the U.S. Its first product is neuenergy®, an innovative energy tab designed to deliver enhanced focus and mental clarity with no sugar, no calories and no crash that is associated with typical energy products. It is based on a molecular combination of pTeroPure® pterostilbene and a low dose of caffeine, called PurEnergy® (also manufactured by ChromaDex). Neuenergy® is available at major convenience stores, groceries, pharmacies and other retail outlets across Canada, the U.S. and Europe and online distribution such as Amazon.com. Also available online in Canada, the U.S. and Europe via the company's e-commerce websites www.getneuenergy.com and www.getneuenergy.de. The company granted rights to market and distribute neuenergy™ to **ANB Canada Inc.** in Canada (through Shopper's Drug Mart, Walmart and Costco retailers); **TH International Consulting GmbH** in Europe; **B-Well Medical Supplies (Pty) Ltd.** in South Africa; and **Canada Grand Enterprises Inc.** in the People's Republic of China, Hong Kong, Macau and Taiwan.

The company, together with **Pacwest Manufacturing Group Inc.**, develops various new product lines which include cannabidiol (CBD) beverages and Delta 8 (D8), a psychoactive cannabinoid found in the cannabis plant. Also, in partnership with **Naturally Splendid USA Ltd.**, develops CBD/HempOmega® fortified sublingual tablet and HempOmega® fortified sublingual tablet, which are being marketed by Naturally Splendid's partner distribution network in South Korea, Japan and Australia. The company granted rights to market and distribute sub-lingual CBD tablet to **LaSanta Botanicals Ltd.** in Mexico and Central and South America; and rights to distribute and sell a broad-spectrum hemp product line of quick melting sub-lingual CBD tablet to **Tabletz LLC** in Japan under Tabletz brand.

Through wholly owned **Ambarii Trade Corporation**, produces and commercializes a line of healthy, sugar-free, edible cannabinoid tablets combining the company's proprietary pterostilbene tablet formula and **Lexaria Biosciences Corp.**'s patented technologies. In addition, the company, together with **Nutritional High International Inc.**, was producing a chewable, sublingual tetrahydrocannabinol (THC) product for sale and distribution in California, at Nutritional High's FLI NorCal facility in Sacramento, Calif., using the company's patent pending Cryolisation™ technology. Cryolisation process is used to prepare oral dosage forms comprising cannabinoid and stilbenoid compounds which improve the dissolution rate and bioavailability of cannabinoid compound. Cannabis-infused chewable tablets include Kushtabs™, Dablets™ and Zenstix™ and are being distributed by **Cryopharm Corporation**, which holds manufacturing and distribution rights in Nevada, California, Washington and Oklahoma.

Predecessor Detail - Name changed from Disani Capital Corp., Nov. 26, 2014, following reverse takeover acquisition of (old) NeutriSci International Inc.; basis 1 new for 3 old shs.

Directors - Jeff Durno, chr., Vancouver, B.C.; Glen Rehman, pres. & CEO, Calgary, Alta.; Anthony Hugens, Edmonton, Alta.; Dana Montenegro, Puerto Rico

Other Exec. Officers - Robert (Rob) Chisholm, CFO & corp. sec.; Gerd Zobel, sr. v-p, product devel. & cust. experience; Chris Neufeld, v-p, opers.

Capital Stock

	Authorized (shs.)	Outstanding (shs.)[1]
Preferred	unlimited	nil
Common	unlimited	166,124,267

[1] At Nov. 29, 2022

Major Shareholder - Widely held at June 2, 2022.

Price Range - NU/TSX-VEN

Year	Volume	High	Low	Close
2022	15,728,536	$0.10	$0.02	$0.02
2021	62,695,814	$0.35	$0.05	$0.06
2020	67,338,132	$0.16	$0.02	$0.13
2019	37,683,020	$0.12	$0.02	$0.03
2018	185,636,133	$0.35	$0.07	$0.08

Recent Close: $0.01

Capital Stock Changes - In November 2022, private placement of 12,500,000 units (1 common share & 1 warrant) at 2¢ per unit was announced, with warrants exercisable at 5¢ per share for two years.

Wholly Owned Subsidiaries

Ambarii Trade Corporation
NeutriSci International Corp., Alta.

Financial Statistics

Periods ended:	12m Dec. 31/21[A]		12m Dec. 31/20[A]
	$000s	%Chg	$000s
Operating revenue	**81**	**+8**	**75**
Cost of sales	101		80
Salaries & benefits	225		241
General & admin expense	594		1,329
Stock-based compensation	503		332
Operating expense	**1,423**	**-28**	**1,982**
Operating income	**(1,342)**	**n.a.**	**(1,907)**
Deprec., depl. & amort.	45		27
Finance costs, gross	1		1
Write-downs/write-offs	(90)		nil
Pre-tax income	**(1,572)**	**n.a.**	**(1,953)**
Net income	**(1,572)**	**n.a.**	**(1,953)**
Cash & equivalent	31		7
Inventories	495		273
Current assets	650		314
Fixed assets, net	170		215
Total assets	**820**	**+55**	**528**
Accts. pay. & accr. liabs	570		582
Current liabilities	807		619
Long-term debt, gross	60		nil
Long-term debt, net	60		nil
Shareholders' equity	(48)		(90)
Cash from oper. activs	**(1,041)**	**n.a.**	**(1,521)**
Cash from fin. activs	1,172		1,639
Cash from invest. activs	(107)		(110)
Net cash position	**31**	**+343**	**7**
Capital expenditures	(107)		(110)
	$		$
Earnings per share*	(0.01)		(0.01)
Cash flow per share*	(0.01)		(0.01)
	shs		shs
No. of shs. o/s*	166,124,267		149,996,934
Avg. no. of shs. o/s*	158,585,032		143,378,391
	%		%
Net profit margin	n.m.		n.m.
Return on equity	n.m.		n.m.
Return on assets	(233.09)		(377.93)
Foreign sales percent	93		80

* Common
[A] Reported in accordance with IFRS

Latest Results

Periods ended:	9m Sept. 30/22[A]		9m Sept. 30/21[A]
	$000s	%Chg	$000s
Operating revenue	407	+640	55
Net income	(553)	n.a.	(1,209)
	$		$
Earnings per share*	(0.00)		(0.01)

* Common
[A] Reported in accordance with IFRS

Historical Summary
(as originally stated)

Fiscal Year	Oper. Rev.	Net Inc. Bef. Disc.	EPS*
	$000s	$000s	$
2021[A]	81	(1,572)	(0.01)
2020[A]	75	(1,953)	(0.01)
2019[A]	97	(1,613)	(0.01)
2018[A]	83	(2,383)	(0.02)
2017[A]	151	(2,122)	(0.03)

* Common
[A] Reported in accordance with IFRS

N.33 Nevis Brands Inc.

Symbol - NEVI **Exchange** - CSE **CUSIP** - 64155A
Head Office - Fluke Hall, 4000 Mason Rd, Suite 304, Seattle, WA, United States, 98195-2141 **Telephone** - (206) 221-3443
Website - www.nevisbrands.com
Email - john@nevisbrands.com
Investor Relations - John Kueber (425) 380-2151
Auditors - Smythe LLP C.A., Vancouver, B.C.
Lawyers - McMillan LLP
Transfer Agents - Computershare Trust Company of Canada Inc., Vancouver, B.C.
Profile - (B.C. 2011) Licenses partners the exclusive right to manufacture and distribute THC (tetrahydrocannabinol)-infused beverages to U.S. retailers under the Major™ brand.

The company has negotiated licence and manufacturing agreements with multiple business partners in five different U.S. states (Washington, Oregon, Arizona, Colorado and Ohio) and provides bottles, labels and flavours to these manufacturing partners who are responsible for the actual production and distribution of the products. **SoRSE Technology Corporation** independently provides its emulsion technology, which produces a water-soluble solution of THC distillate that is added to the beverages, to the licensed producers. In return for licensing the trademarks and formulas, each manufacturing partner pays a royalty or licensing fee to the company. Royalties range from 10% to 20% of gross sales by the drink manufacturers.

Other trademarks include Happy Apple™, Pearl™, Utopia™, Atomic Apple, Vertus, Velvet Swing™ and Velvet Kiss.

In July 2023, the company completed an agreement with **SoRSE Technology Corporation** to acquire from SoRSE the assets consisting of the THC Essentials business for US$1,125,000.

Common listed on CSE, July 6, 2023.

Common delisted from TSX-VEN, May 24, 2023.

Predecessor Detail - Name changed from Pascal Biosciences Inc., June 12, 2023; basis 1 new for 5 old shs.

Directors - John K. Bell, chr., Cambridge, Ont.; John Kueber, CEO, Seattle, Wash.; Vahan Ajamian, Toronto, Ont.; Dr. Patrick W. Gray, Seattle, Wash.

Other Exec. Officers - Harold (Hardy) Forzley, CFO & corp. sec.

Capital Stock

	Authorized (shs.)	Outstanding (shs.)[1]
Common	unlimited	38,140,325

[1] At July 6, 2023

Major Shareholder - Widely held at July 5, 2023.

Price Range - PAS/TSX-VEN (D)

Year	Volume	High	Low	Close
2022	1,494,992	$0.50	$0.08	$0.08
2021	2,915,178	$0.73	$0.30	$0.35
2020	3,584,884	$2.25	$0.33	$0.63
2019	1,790,437	$1.55	$0.35	$0.53
2018	39,459,108	$4.40	$0.90	$1.13

Consolidation: 1-for-5 cons. in June 2023
Recent Close: $0.11

Capital Stock Changes - On June 12, 2023, common shares were consolidated on a 1-for-5 basis. On June 30, 2023, 3,775,000 post-consolidated common shares were issued on acquisition of the assets of THC Essentials, 1,246,372 post-consolidated common shares were issued for debt settlement and private placement of 15,195,000 post-consolidated units (1 post-consolidated common share & 1 warrant) at 10¢ per unit was completed, with warrants exercisable at 20¢ per share for one year. An additional 4,805,000 units were issued on July 6, 2023.

During fiscal 2022, 500,000 common shares were issued in lieu of salaries.

Wholly Owned Subsidiaries

bioMmune Advanced Technologies Inc., Vancouver, B.C.
Nevis Brands U.S. Inc., Seattle, Wash.

Financial Statistics

Periods ended:	12m Nov. 30/22[A1]		12m Nov. 30/21[A]
	$000s	%Chg	$000s
Salaries & benefits	233		292
Research & devel. expense	(49)		58
General & admin expense	187		465
Stock-based compensation	47		200
Operating expense	**418**	**-59**	**1,015**
Operating income	**(418)**	**n.a.**	**(1,015)**
Deprec., depl. & amort.	8		16
Finance costs, gross	4		6
Write-downs/write-offs	(129)		51
Pre-tax income	**(480)**	**n.a.**	**(1,089)**
Net income	**(480)**	**n.a.**	**(1,089)**
Cash & equivalent	8		nil
Accounts receivable	7		142
Current assets	19		145
Fixed assets, net	nil		10
Total assets	**19**	**-88**	**155**
Bank indebtedness	nil		8
Accts. pay. & accr. liabs	627		589
Current liabilities	225		646
Shareholders' equity	(944)		(492)
Cash from oper. activs	**(148)**	**n.a.**	**(615)**
Cash from fin. activs	155		624
Cash from invest. activs	9		nil
Net cash position	**8**	**n.a.**	**(8)**
Capital disposals	9		nil
	$		$
Earnings per share*	(0.05)		(0.10)
Cash flow per share*	(0.01)		(0.05)
	shs		shs
No. of shs. o/s*	13,118,954		13,018,954
Avg. no. of shs. o/s*	13,109,365		12,696,872
	%		%
Net profit margin	n.a.		n.a.
Return on equity	n.m.		n.m.
Return on assets	(547.13)		(784.78)
No. of employees (FTEs)	...		6

* Common
[A] Reported in accordance with IFRS
[1] Results for fiscal 2022 and prior periods pertain Pascal Biosciences Inc.

Latest Results

Periods ended:	3m Feb. 28/23^A		3m Feb. 28/22^A
	$000s	%Chg	$000s
Net income	(133)	n.a.	(137)
	$		$
Earnings per share*	(0.01)		(0.01)

* Common
^A Reported in accordance with IFRS

Historical Summary
(as originally stated)

Fiscal Year	Oper. Rev. $000s	Net Inc. Bef. Disc. $000s	EPS* $
2022^A	nil	(480)	(0.05)
2021^A	nil	(1,089)	(0.10)
2020^A	nil	(1,238)	(0.10)
2019^A	nil	(3,412)	(0.30)
2018^A	nil	(3,245)	(0.35)

* Common
^A Reported in accordance with IFRS
Note: Adjusted throughout for 1-for-5 cons. in June 2023

N.34 New Brunswick Power Corporation

CUSIP - 642798
Head Office - 515 King St, PO Box 2000 Stn A, Fredericton, NB, E3B 4X1 **Telephone** - (506) 458-4444 **Toll-free** - (800) 663-6272 **Fax** - (506) 458-4000
Website - www.nbpower.com
Email - jmcneil@nbpower.com
Investor Relations - Janice McNeil (800) 663-6272
Auditors - KPMG LLP C.A., Fredericton, N.B.
FP500 Revenue Ranking - 204
Employees - 2,603 at Mar. 31, 2022
Profile - (N.B. 2013) Generates, transmits and distributes electricity throughout New Brunswick.

Electricity is generated at 13 hydro, coal, oil and diesel-powered stations with an installed net capacity totaling 3,130 MW, consisting of 1,716 MW of thermal, 889 MW of hydro and 525 MW of combustion turbine capacity, as well as a 660-MW nuclear reactor at Point Lepreau, and delivered via power lines, substations and terminals to 420,129 customers (at Mar. 31, 2022) both directly in New Brunswick as well as exported, through wholly owned **New Brunswick Energy Marketing Corporation**, to Quebec, Nova Scotia, Prince Edward Island and New England.

An additional installed generating capacity of 607 MW, including 512 MW of renewables, is provided by third parties through power purchase agreements.

Periods ended:	12m Mar. 31/22	12m Mar. 31/21
Electric sales, GWh	19,449	17,289
Generating capacity, MW	3,790	3,790
Electric gen., GWh	20,372	18,214
Transmission lines, km	6,870	6,875
Distribution lines, km	21,562	21,434
Electric. customers	420,129	412,784

Predecessor Detail - Succeeded New Brunswick Power Holding Corporation, Oct. 1, 2013, following reorganization into a single crown corporation.
Directors - Andrew J. (Andy) MacGillivray, chr., N.B.; Lori Clark, pres. & CEO, N.B.; Anne E. Bertrand, Fredericton, N.B.; Alain Bossé, N.B.; Chantal Cormier, N.B.; Paul D. McCoy, Chicago, Ill.; Scott Northard, Minn.; Michelyne Paulin, N.B.; Mark E. Reddemann, Richland, Wash.; Nancy Whipp, N.B.
Other Exec. Officers - Jean Marc Landry, chief cust. officer; James M. Petrie, chief legal officer; Darren Murphy, sr. v-p, corp. srvcs. & CFO; Suzanne Desrosiers, v-p, HR; Brett Plummer, v-p, nuclear & chief nuclear officer
Major Shareholder - Province of New Brunswick held 100% interest at Mar. 31, 2022.

Wholly Owned Subsidiaries
New Brunswick Energy Marketing Corporation, Fredericton, N.B.

Financial Statistics

Periods ended:	12m Mar. 31/22^A		12m Mar. 31/21^A
	$000s	%Chg	$000s
Operating revenue	**2,198,000**	**+20**	**1,834,000**
Salaries & benefits	321,000		307,000
Operating expense	**1,569,000**	**+16**	**1,357,000**
Operating income	**629,000**	**+32**	**477,000**
Deprec., depl. & amort	344,000		321,000
Finance costs, gross	248,000		235,000
Investment income	59,000		91,000
Write-downs/write-offs	(2,000)		(2,000)
Pre-tax income	**80,000**	**n.a.**	**(4,000)**
Net income	**80,000**	**n.a.**	**(4,000)**
Cash & equivalent	52,000		3,000
Inventories	276,000		222,000
Accounts receivable	395,000		272,000
Current assets	932,000		522,000
Fixed assets, net	4,645,000		4,741,000
Intangibles, net	59,000		56,000
Total assets	**7,935,000**	**+7**	**7,434,000**
Bank indebtedness	859,000		608,000
Accts. pay. & accr. liabs	376,000		320,000
Current liabilities	1,498,000		1,385,000
Long-term debt, gross	4,631,000		4,734,000
Long-term debt, net	4,406,000		4,334,000
Long-term lease liabilities	33,000		25,000
Shareholders' equity	716,000		317,000
Cash from oper. activs	**321,000**	**+10**	**291,000**
Cash from fin. activs	65,000		28,000
Cash from invest. activs	(337,000)		(319,000)
Net cash position	**52,000**	**n.m.**	**3,000**
Capital expenditures, net	(334,000)		(316,000)
	$		$
Earnings per share*	n.a.		n.a.
	shs		shs
No. of shs. o/s	n.a.		n.a.
	%		%
Net profit margin	3.64		(0.22)
Return on equity	15.49		(1.32)
Return on assets	4.27		3.09
No. of employees (FTEs)	2,603		2,576

^A Reported in accordance with IFRS

Historical Summary
(as originally stated)

Fiscal Year	Oper. Rev. $000s	Net Inc. Bef. Disc. $000s	EPS* $
2022^A	2,198,000	80,000	n.a.
2021^A	1,834,000	(4,000)	n.a.
2020^A	1,924,000	(16,000)	n.a.
2019^A	1,796,000	20,000	n.a.
2018^A	1,754,000	23,000	n.a.

* Common
^A Reported in accordance with IFRS

N.35 New Commerce Split Fund

Symbol - YCM **Exchange** - TSX **CUSIP** - 200701
Head Office - c/o Quadravest Capital Management Inc., 2510-200 Front St W, PO Box 51, Toronto, ON, M5V 3K2 **Telephone** - (416) 304-4440 **Toll-free** - (877) 478-2372
Website - www.quadravest.com
Email - info@quadravest.com
Investor Relations - Shari Payne (877) 478-2372
Auditors - PricewaterhouseCoopers LLP C.A., Toronto, Ont.
Lawyers - Blake, Cassels & Graydon LLP, Toronto, Ont.
Transfer Agents - Computershare Trust Company of Canada Inc., Toronto, Ont.
Investment Managers - Quadravest Capital Management Inc., Toronto, Ont.
Managers - Quadravest Capital Management Inc., Toronto, Ont.
Profile - (Ont. 2010) Holds common shares of **Canadian Imperial Bank of Commerce** in order to provide a stable yield and downside protection for preferred shareholders and enable capital shareholders to participate in any capital appreciation of the bank's common shares and to benefit from any increases in the dividends paid by the bank on its common shares.

At Nov. 30, 2022, the fund held 164,452 common shares of **Canadian Imperial Bank of Commerce** with a fair value of $10,654,845. To supplement the dividends earned on the investment portfolio and to reduce risk, the fund may from time to time write covered call options in respect of all or a part of the common shares of the bank it holds.

The company terminates on Dec. 1, 2024, or earlier if the class I preferred shares, class II preferred shares or capital shares are delisted by the TSX or if the net asset value of the company declines to less than $5,000,000. At such time all outstanding class I preferred shares, class II preferred shares and capital shares will be redeemed. The termination date may be extended beyond Dec. 1, 2024, for a further five years and thereafter for additional successive periods of five years as determined by the board of directors.

The investment manager receives a management fee at an annual rate equal to 0.45% of the net asset value of the company calculated and payable monthly in arrears. In addition, the manager receives an administration fee at an annual rate equal to 0.1% of the net asset value of the company calculated and payable monthly in arrears, as well as service fee payable to dealers on the capital shares at a rate of 0.5% per annum.
Directors - S. Wayne Finch, chr., pres. & CEO, Caledon, Ont.; Laura L. Johnson, corp. sec., Oakville, Ont.; Peter F. Cruickshank, Oakville, Ont.; Michael W. Sharp, Toronto, Ont.; John D. Steep, Stratford, Ont.
Other Exec. Officers - Silvia Gomes, CFO

Capital Stock

	Authorized (shs.)	Outstanding (shs.)[1]
Class I Preferred	unlimited	896,532[2]
Class II Preferred	unlimited	896,532[2]
Class B	1,000	1,000[2]
Capital	unlimited	896,532

[1] At Feb. 23, 2023
[2] Classified as debt.

Class I Preferred - Entitled to receive fixed cumulative preferential monthly dividends of $0.025 per share (to yield 6% per annum on the notional issue price of $5.00). Retractable at any time at a price per share equal to the lesser of: (i) $5.00; and (ii) 97% of the net asset value (NAV) per unit (one class I preferred share, one class II preferred share and one capital share) less the cost to the company of purchasing one class II preferred share and one capital share in the market for cancellation. Shareholders who concurrently retract a class I preferred share, a class II preferred share and a capital share in October of each year are entitled to receive an amount equal to the NAV per unit. All outstanding class I preferred shares will be redeemed on Dec. 1, 2024, at $5.00 per share. Rank subsequent to class B shares and prior to class II preferred and capital shares with respect to the payment of dividends and the repayment of capital. Non-voting.
Class II Preferred - Entitled to receive fixed cumulative preferential monthly dividends of $0.03125 per share (to yield 7.50% per annum on the notional issue price of $5.00) if and when the NAV per unit exceeds $10. Retractable at any time at a price per share equal to the lesser of: (i) $5.00; and (ii) 97% of the NAV per unit less the cost to the company of purchasing one class I preferred share and one capital share in the market for cancellation. Shareholders who concurrently retract a class I preferred share, a class II preferred share and a capital share in October of each year are entitled to receive an amount equal to the NAV per unit. All outstanding class II preferred shares will be redeemed on Dec. 1, 2024, at $5.00 per share. Rank subsequent to the class I preferred and in priority to capital shares with respect to the payment of dividends and subsequent to class I preferred and in priority to class B and capital shares with the repayment of capital. Non-voting.
Class B - Not entitled to receive dividends. Retractable at $1.00 per share and have a liquidation entitlement of $1.00 per share. Rank subsequent to the class I preferred shares and the class II preferred shares and prior to the capital shares with respect to repayment of capital on the dissolution, liquidation or winding-up of the company. One vote per share.
Capital - Dividends on the capital shares may be reinstated only if and when the fund NAV per unit exceeds $15, and the dividend rate would be set by the board of directors at its discretion. A special year-end non-cash dividend is permitted even if, after payment of such a dividend, the NAV is less than $15. No dividend payments will be made on the capital shares unless all dividends on the class I preferred shares and, if applicable, class II preferred shares have been declared and paid. Retractable on the last business day of each month at a price equal to 97% of the NAV per unit less the cost to the company of the purchase of a class I preferred share and a class II preferred share in the market for cancellation. Shareholders who concurrently retract a class I preferred share, a class II preferred share and a capital share in October of each year will receive an amount equal to the fund's NAV per unit. Entitled to receive upon final redemption the balance, if any, of the value of the fund remaining after paying the class I and class II preferred share repayment amounts and the nominal issue price of the class B shares to the holders thereof. Rank subsequent to the class I preferred, class II preferred and class B shares with respect to the payment of dividends and the repayment of capital. Non-voting.
Major Shareholder - Commerce Split Corp. Holding Trust held 100% interest at Feb. 23, 2023.

Price Range - YCM/TSX

Year	Volume	High	Low	Close
2022	282,188	$6.25	$1.48	$1.59
2021	426,075	$5.45	$1.60	$5.12
2020	207,498	$2.80	$0.30	$1.80
2019	144,306	$2.59	$0.69	$1.53
2018	84,242	$3.97	$1.49	$1.49

Consolidation: 0.578956-for-1 cons. in Dec. 2019
Recent Close: $0.86
Capital Stock Changes - There were no changes to capital stock during fiscal 2021 or fiscal 2022.

Dividends

YCM cap sh N.V. N.S.R. [1]

$0.05	Apr. 8/22	$0.05	Mar. 10/22
$0.05	Feb. 10/22	$0.05	Dec. 10/21

Paid in 2023: n.a. 2022: $0.15 2021: $0.25**i**

YCM.PR.A pfd I ret. Ra $0.30 pa M
YCM.PR.B pfd II ret. Var. Ra pa M[2]

$0.03125	Sept. 8/23	$0.03125	Aug. 10/23
$0.03125	July 10/23	$0.03125	June 9/23

Paid in 2023: $0.28125 2022: $0.375 2021: $0.375

[1] Divd normally payable in Aug/21 has been omitted.
[2] Monthly divd normally payable in Feb/16 has been omitted.
i Initial Payment

Financial Statistics

Periods ended:	12m Nov. 30/22[A]		12m Nov. 30/21[A]
	$000s	%Chg	$000s
Realized invest. gain (loss)	291		9
Unrealized invest. gain (loss)	(1,494)		2,810
Total revenue	**(632)**	**n.a.**	**3,347**
General & admin. expense	171		170
Other operating expense	81		74
Operating expense	**252**	**+4**	**243**
Operating income	**(884)**	**n.a.**	**3,104**
Finance costs, gross	605		605
Pre-tax income	**(1,490)**	**n.a.**	**2,499**
Net income	**(1,490)**	**n.a.**	**2,499**
Cash & equivalent	754		195
Investments	10,655		12,767
Total assets	**11,410**	**-12**	**12,963**
Accts. pay. & accr. liabs	29		35
Debt	8,965		8,965
Shareholders' equity	2,234		3,858
Cash from oper. activs	**1,344**	**+140**	**560**
Cash from fin. activs	(784)		(784)
Net cash position	**754**	**+287**	**195**
	$		$
Earnings per share*	(1.66)		2.79
Cash flow per share*	1.50		0.62
Net asset value per share*	2.49		4.30
Cash divd. per share*	0.15		0.25
	shs		shs
No. of shs. o/s*	896,532		896,532
Avg. no. of shs. o/s*	896,532		896,532
	%		%
Net profit margin	n.m.		74.66
Return on equity	(48.92)		91.84
Return on assets	(7.26)		26.27

* Capital
[A] Reported in accordance with IFRS

Note: Net income reflects increase/decrease in net assets from operations.

Historical Summary
(as originally stated)

Fiscal Year	Total Rev.	Net Inc. Bef. Disc.	EPS*
	$000s	$000s	$
2022[A]	(632)	(1,490)	(1.66)
2021[A]	3,347	2,499	2.79
2020[A]	49	(717)	(0.80)
2019[A]	1,492	124	0.14
2018[A]	(313)	(1,715)	(1.80)

* Capital
[A] Reported in accordance with IFRS

Note: Adjusted throughout for 0.578956-for-1 cons. in Dec. 2019

N.36 New Frontier Ventures Inc.

Symbol - VFI.X **Exchange** - CSE **CUSIP** - 64440E
Head Office - 702-200 Consumers Rd, Toronto, ON, M2J 4R4 **Telephone** - (647) 252-1674
Email - vikas@gravitasfinancial.com
Investor Relations - Vikas Ranjan (647) 352-2666
Auditors - McGovern Hurley LLP C.A., Toronto, Ont.
Lawyers - Dentons Canada LLP, Toronto, Ont.
Transfer Agents - Computershare Trust Company of Canada Inc., Toronto, Ont.
Profile - (Can. 1996) Seeking new business opportunities.

The company previously provided capital market services, portfolio management, merchant banking, corporate services and investor exposure services and held equity, debt and convertible debt investments in early-stage public and private companies.

Predecessor Detail - Name changed from Gravitas Financial Inc., Oct. 4, 2022; basis 1 new for 25 old shs.

Directors - Viswanathan (Vishy) Karamadam, co-founder & exec. v-p, Mississauga, Ont.; Vikas Ranjan, co-founder, pres. & CEO, Toronto, Ont.; Yongbiao (Winfield) Ding, interim CFO, Toronto, Ont.; Lawrence Xing, Ont.

Capital Stock

	Authorized (shs.)	Outstanding (shs.)[1]
Common	unlimited	2,904,082

[1] At Oct. 4, 2022

Major Shareholder - David Carbonaro held 24.71% interest, Yuhua International Capital Corporation held 18% interest, Viswanathan (Vishy) Karamadam held 14.05% interest and Vikas Ranjan held 14.05% interest at Mar. 9, 2021.

Price Range - VFI.X/CSE

Year	Volume	High	Low	Close
2022	166,941	$0.50	$0.06	$0.07
2021	464,155	$1.38	$0.38	$0.38
2020	256,021	$2.75	$0.13	$0.50
2019	222,231	$1.25	$0.13	$0.13
2018	235,125	$3.13	$0.25	$0.63

Consolidation: 1-for-25 cons. in Oct. 2022
Recent Close: $0.08
Capital Stock Changes - On Oct. 4, 2022, common shares were consolidated on a 1-for-25 basis.

Wholly Owned Subsidiaries

Capital Ideas Media Inc., Canada.
Global Compliance Network Inc., Canada.
Gravitas Financial Services Holdings Inc., Canada.
Gravitas Global GP Inc., Canada.
Gravitas Select Flow-Through GP Inc., Canada.
Gravitas Siraj Holdco Inc., Canada.
SearchGold Guinée S.A.R.L., Guinea. Inactive.
Siraj Ontario Corporation, Canada.

Subsidiaries

55% int. in **Revenue.com US Corporation**, United States.

Financial Statistics

Periods ended:	12m Dec. 31/21[A]		12m Dec. 31/20[A]
	$000s	%Chg	$000s
Operating revenue	**31**	**-78**	**141**
Cost of sales	21		604
Salaries & benefits	138		471
General & admin expense	78		281
Operating expense	**237**	**-83**	**1,357**
Operating income	**(206)**	**n.a.**	**(1,216)**
Finance income	nil		42
Finance costs, gross	7		13
Pre-tax income	**(213)**	**n.a.**	**83,877**
Income taxes	nil		(268)
Net income	**(213)**	**n.a.**	**84,145**
Cash & equivalent	11		99
Accounts receivable	17		14
Current assets	29		114
Total assets	**29**	**-75**	**114**
Accts. pay. & accr. liabs	266		145
Current liabilities	266		145
Long-term debt, gross	28		21
Long-term debt, net	28		21
Shareholders' equity	(265)		(52)
Cash from oper. activs	**(108)**	**n.a.**	**(1,082)**
Cash from fin. activs	20		(1,149)
Cash from invest. activs	nil		320
Net cash position	**11**	**-89**	**99**
	$		$
Earnings per share*	(0.07)		29.00
Cash flow per share*	(0.04)		(0.37)
	shs		shs
No. of shs. o/s*	2,904,052		2,904,052
Avg. no. of shs. o/s*	2,904,052		2,904,052
	%		%
Net profit margin	(687.10)		n.m.
Return on equity	n.m.		n.m.
Return on assets	(288.11)		n.m.

* Common
[A] Reported in accordance with IFRS

Latest Results

Periods ended:	3m Mar. 31/22[A]		3m Mar. 31/21[A]
	$000s	%Chg	$000s
Operating revenue	nil	n.a.	7
Net income	(40)	n.a.	(46)
	$		$
Earnings per share*	(0.02)		(0.02)

* Common
[A] Reported in accordance with IFRS

Historical Summary
(as originally stated)

Fiscal Year	Oper. Rev.	Net Inc. Bef. Disc.	EPS*
	$000s	$000s	$
2021[A]	31	(213)	(0.07)
2020[A]	141	84,145	29.00
2019[A]	1,171	(16,715)	(5.75)
2018[A]	10,239	13,859	4.75
2017[A]	11,637	(30,914)	(10.75)

* Common
[A] Reported in accordance with IFRS

Note: Adjusted throughout for 1-for-25 cons. in Oct. 2022

N.37 New Leaf Ventures Inc.

Symbol - NLV **Exchange** - CSE **CUSIP** - 64639M
Head Office - 1910-1030 Georgia St W, Vancouver, BC, V6E 2Y3 **Telephone** - (778) 930-1321
Website - newleafventuresinc.com
Email - investors@newleafventuresinc.com
Investor Relations - Investor Relations (604) 862-2793
Auditors - Smythe LLP C.A.
Lawyers - Cassels Brock & Blackwell LLP, Vancouver, B.C.
Transfer Agents - Odyssey Trust Company, Vancouver, B.C.
Profile - (B.C. 2018) Provides licenses, consulting services, real property, intellectual property and equipment for lease, and ancillary services to **New Leaf Enterprises, Inc.** (NLE), a Seattle, Wash.-based licensed cannabis processor focused on processing, packaging and distributing cannabis and cannabis related products.

Owns a 30,000-sq.-ft. processing facility in Seattle, Wash., which it leases to NLE. The facility includes warehousing facilities, a lab and a commercial kitchen, where NLE can process cannabis flower and trim, vape products, oils, wax, pre-rolls, capsules, and other edibles and oils. NLE's products, all of which are licensed from the company and are produced and distributed from the company's facility, include dàmà Premium dried flower; dàmà Budlets; dàmà Pre-roll, a pre-rolled cannabis cigarette; dàmà Infused Pre-roll, a cannabis cigarette infused with cannabis distillate; dàmà Oil, an ethanol-extracted concentrate; dàmà Vape; dàmà Capsules; dàmà Hemp & CBD, which features herbal blend tinctures, soft gels and topicals; dàmà Select, a high end greenhouse flower; Weed Flower; Astara, a tetrahydrocannabinol and cannabidiol infused beverage; Tasty Tokes, a super potent infused pre-roll made with 90% pure distillate and kief; Green State, a line of quality sourced biomass; Spaceballs, which are 10 mg chewy candies; and Goodies, an infused edible with easy microdose control.

In October 2022, the company entered into a letter of intent to acquire British Columbia-based **High Profile Holdings Corp.**, a retail-focused cannabis company, for an undisclosed amount.

In June 2022, the company sold its cultivation infrastructure and equipment to a third-party for US$266,797. The company also relinquished its master lease on the cultivation facility in Seattle, Wash.

Directors - Dean Medwid, CEO; Jay Garnett, chief strategy officer, B.C.; Ryan Arthur, corp. sec., B.C.

Other Exec. Officers - Terence Lee, CFO

Capital Stock

	Authorized (shs.)	Outstanding (shs.)[1]
Preferred	unlimited	nil
Common	unlimited	12,554,019

[1] At Nov. 29, 2022

Major Shareholder - Robert (Dax) Colwell held 10.08% interest and Boris Gorodnitsky held 10.08% interest at Sept. 19, 2022.

Price Range - NLV/CSE

Year	Volume	High	Low	Close
2022	1,386,214	$0.95	$0.10	$0.10
2021	8,468,170	$3.90	$0.48	$0.48
2020	1,943,705	$3.10	$1.08	$1.28

Consolidation: 1-for-5 cons. in Sept. 2022
Recent Close: $0.10
Capital Stock Changes - On Sept. 12, 2022, common shares were consolidated on a 1-for-5 basis. In December 2022, private placement of 15,000,000 units (1 post-consolidated common share & 1 warrant) at 10¢ per unit was announced, with warrants exercisable at 20¢ per share for two years.

Wholly Owned Subsidiaries

New Leaf USA Inc., Seattle, Wash.
- 100% int. in **New Leaf Equipment LLC**, Seattle, Wash.
- 100% int. in **New Leaf Hemp Company LLC**, Seattle, Wash.
- 100% int. in **New Leaf IP LLC**, Seattle, Wash.
- 100% int. in **New Leaf Real Estate LLC**, Seattle, Wash.
- 100% int. in **New Leaf Services LLC**, Seattle, Wash.

Financial Statistics

Periods ended:	12m Dec. 31/21^A		12m Dec. 31/20^A
	$000s	%Chg	$000s
Operating revenue	**2,472**	**+21**	**2,051**
Salaries & benefits	1,760		2,079
Research & devel. expense	nil		80
General & admin expense	4,748		1,968
Stock-based compensation	526		104
Operating expense	**7,034**	**+66**	**4,231**
Operating income	**(4,562)**	**n.a.**	**(2,180)**
Deprec., depl. & amort.	193		442
Finance income	372		257
Finance costs, gross	452		401
Write-downs/write-offs	nil		(48)
Pre-tax income	**(3,962)**	**n.a.**	**(6,600)**
Net income	**(3,962)**	**n.a.**	**(6,600)**
Cash & equivalent	59		137
Accounts receivable	43		80
Current assets	2,358		2,618
Fixed assets, net	871		844
Total assets	**5,955**	**-8**	**6,487**
Accts. pay. & accr. liabs	739		651
Current liabilities	1,928		3,895
Long-term lease liabilities	2,720		3,031
Shareholders' equity	1,307		(439)
Cash from oper. activs	**(2,706)**	**n.a.**	**(2,616)**
Cash from fin. activs	3,399		3,115
Cash from invest. activs	(742)		(489)
Net cash position	**59**	**-57**	**137**
Capital expenditures	(223)		(129)
	$		$
Earnings per share*	(0.40)		(1.20)
Cash flow per share*	(0.27)		(0.47)
	shs		shs
No. of shs. o/s*	11,617,517		7,819,433
Avg. no. of shs. o/s*	10,004,159		5,583,562
	%		%
Net profit margin	(160.28)		(321.79)
Return on equity	n.m.		n.m.
Return on assets	(56.42)		(185.65)

* Common
^A Reported in accordance with IFRS

Latest Results

Periods ended:	9m Sept. 30/22^A		9m Sept. 30/21^A
	$000s	%Chg	$000s
Operating revenue	1,743	-6	1,851
Net income	463	n.a.	(3,437)
	$		$
Earnings per share*	0.05		(0.35)

* Common
^A Reported in accordance with IFRS

Historical Summary
(as originally stated)

Fiscal Year	Oper. Rev. $000s	Net Inc. Bef. Disc. $000s	EPS* $
2021^A	2,472	(3,962)	(0.40)
2020^A	2,051	(6,600)	(1.20)
2019^A	nil	(1,171)	(0.55)

* Common
^A Reported in accordance with IFRS
Note: Adjusted throughout for 1-for-5 cons. in Sept. 2022

N.38 New Media Capital 2.0 Inc.

Symbol - NEME.P **Exchange** - TSX-VEN **CUSIP** - 647039
Head Office - 8634-53 Ave, Edmonton, AB, T6E 5G2 **Telephone** - (780) 425-9460 **Fax** - (780) 425-9463
Email - jputters@visionstate.com
Investor Relations - John A. Putters (587) 985-2601
Auditors - Kenway Mack Slusarchuk Stewart LLP C.A., Calgary, Alta.
Lawyers - Parlee McLaws LLP, Edmonton, Alta.
Transfer Agents - TSX Trust Company, Toronto, Ont.
Profile - (Alta. 2021) Capital Pool Company.

Recent Merger and Acquisition Activity

Status: terminated **Revised:** Mar. 31, 2023
UPDATE: The transaction was terminated. PREVIOUS: New Media Capital 2.0 Inc. entered into a non-binding letter of intent for the Qualifying Transaction reverse takeover acquisition of Brisbane, Australia-based Hypersonix Launch Systems Ltd. for issuance of 39,333,333 post-consolidated common shares (following a 1-for-6 share consolidation) at a deemed price of $1.20 per share. Hypersonix engineers, designs and builds hydrogen-powered scramjet engines and hypersonic vehicles, including a hypersonic drone technology demonstrator and a small satellite launch platform for delivering satellites into low earth orbit, for the aviation, space and defence sectors. In connection with the transaction, New Media would change its name to Hypersonix Launch Systems Inc. Mar. 1, 2022 - A definitive agreement was entered into.

Directors - John A. Putters, CEO, Sherwood Park, Alta.; Randa Kachkar, CFO, Edmonton, Alta.; Catherine D. (Cathy) Hume, Toronto, Ont.; Timothy J. (Tim) Latimer, Edmonton, Alta.
Other Exec. Officers - David S. Tam, corp. sec.

Capital Stock

	Authorized (shs.)	Outstanding (shs.)[1]
Preferred	unlimited	nil
Common	unlimited	7,800,000

[1] At July 31, 2023

Major Shareholder - Randa Kachkar held 10.26% interest at Dec. 21, 2021.

Capital Stock Changes - There were no changes to capital stock during fiscal 2023.

On Dec. 21, 2021, an initial public offering of 5,000,000 common shares was completed at 10¢ per share.

N.39 Newtopia Inc.

Symbol - NEWU **Exchange** - TSX-VEN **CUSIP** - 653226
Head Office - 500-33 Bloor St E, Toronto, ON, M4W 3H1 **Telephone** - (416) 223-0212 **Toll-free** - (888) 639-8181
Website - www.newtopia.com
Email - jruby@newtopia.com
Investor Relations - Jeffrey Ruby (888) 639-8181
Auditors - MNP LLP C.A., Toronto, Ont.
Transfer Agents - TSX Trust Company, Toronto, Ont.
Profile - (Ont. 2008) Develops personalized health habits focused on preventing chronic diseases, including type 2 diabetes, obesity, heart disease, musculoskeletal issues, anxiety and depression, which is provided to insurers and employers through a proprietary virtual habit change platform.

Delivers disease prevention solutions technology by leveraging precision health tools through genetic analysis, social and behavioural evaluations to help individuals prevent, reverse and slow the progression of chronic disease and reduce costs for employers and insurers. The platform focuses on virtual programs which are personalized based on a participant's personality, lifestyle and genetics for sustainable habit change to maintain health, avoid or reduce the likelihood of developing metabolic disease, diabetes, mental health challenges, hypertension, weight management and musculoskeletal disorders with real-time online human coaching. Data is collected through customized set of smart digital tools to track progress, including a wearable activity tracker and digital scale, as well as a library of online content outlining the steps necessary to achieve goals such as losing weight, lowering cholesterol, managing diabetes and improving mental well-being. Revenues consist of welcome kit sales, which usually occur in bulk at the outset of a new customer contract or in phases, monthly subscription fees and outcome milestone fees.

Directors - Jeffrey (Jeff) Ruby, founder & CEO, Toronto, Ont.; Karen Basian, chr., Ont.; Carleen Hawn, San Francisco, Calif.; Michael Palmer, Boston, Mass.; Roger Poirier, Toronto, Ont.
Other Exec. Officers - Collin Swenson, CFO; Lara Dodo, chief growth & oper. officer; Peter Seider, chief info., privacy & security officer; Bill Van Wyck, chief tech. officer & head, product; Leonard Fensterheim, sr. v-p, outcomes, analytics & reporting; Robert (Rob) Halpern, sr. v-p, mktg.; Mark Jackson, sr. v-p, comml.; Edmond Lem, sr. v-p, fin.; Natasha Vani, v-p, program devel. & opers.

Capital Stock

	Authorized (shs.)	Outstanding (shs.)[1]
Class A Preferred	unlimited	nil
Common	unlimited	148,920,776

[1] At May 30, 2023

Major Shareholder - Rural India Supporting Trust held 15.5% interest, Jeffrey (Jeff) Ruby held 10.4% interest and Dennis Bennie held 10.3% interest at Aug. 15, 2022.

Price Range - NEWU/TSX-VEN

Year	Volume	High	Low	Close
2022	15,744,600	$0.40	$0.02	$0.10
2021	25,511,523	$0.81	$0.31	$0.40
2020	30,537,222	$1.33	$0.47	$0.79

Recent Close: $0.08

Capital Stock Changes - In April 2022, private placement of 17,500,000 units (1 common share & ½ warrant) at 20¢ per unit was completed. Also during 2022, 8,999,990 common shares were issued by private placement.

Financial Statistics

Periods ended:	12m Dec. 31/22^A		12m Dec. 31/21^A
	$000s	%Chg	$000s
Operating revenue	**11,166**	**+7**	**10,456**
Cost of sales	5,140		5,384
General & admin expense	11,756		10,963
Stock-based compensation	493		1,071
Operating expense	**17,389**	**0**	**17,419**
Operating income	**(6,223)**	**n.a.**	**(6,963)**
Deprec., depl. & amort.	216		251
Finance costs, gross	982		468
Write-downs/write-offs	(200)		nil
Pre-tax income	**(7,700)**	**n.a.**	**(7,650)**
Net income	**(7,700)**	**n.a.**	**(7,650)**
Cash & equivalent	346		812
Inventories	326		131
Accounts receivable	1,558		1,382
Current assets	2,701		2,818
Fixed assets, net	8		66
Right-of-use assets	nil		370
Intangibles, net	3,235		2,252
Total assets	**5,945**	**+8**	**5,506**
Bank indebtedness	4,824		2,331
Accts. pay. & accr. liabs	2,584		1,965
Current liabilities	10,410		4,801
Long-term debt, gross	3,478		2,182
Long-term debt, net	1,069		2,182
Long-term lease liabilities	nil		367
Shareholders' equity	(5,534)		(1,844)
Cash from oper. activs	**(5,915)**	**n.a.**	**(5,949)**
Cash from fin. activs	6,439		4,234
Cash from invest. activs	(989)		(2,147)
Net cash position	**346**	**-57**	**812**
Capital expenditures	(4)		(3)
	$		$
Earnings per share*	(0.07)		(0.08)
Cash flow per share*	(0.05)		(0.06)
	shs		shs
No. of shs. o/s*	126,992,776		100,492,786
Avg. no. of shs. o/s*	112,736,347		100,350,455
	%		%
Net profit margin	(68.96)		(73.16)
Return on equity	n.m.		n.m.
Return on assets	(117.33)		(107.18)

* Common
^A Reported in accordance with IFRS

Latest Results

Periods ended:	3m Mar. 31/23^A		3m Mar. 31/22^A
	$000s	%Chg	$000s
Operating revenue	2,649	-8	2,867
Net income	(1,373)	n.a.	(1,628)
	$		$
Earnings per share*	(0.01)		(0.02)

* Common
^A Reported in accordance with IFRS

Historical Summary
(as originally stated)

Fiscal Year	Oper. Rev. $000s	Net Inc. Bef. Disc. $000s	EPS* $
2022^A	11,166	(7,700)	(0.07)
2021^A	10,456	(7,650)	(0.08)
2020^A	11,416	(7,732)	(0.12)
2019^A	6,109	(10,141)	(0.65)
2018^A	3,074	(6,389)	(0.41)

* Common
^A Reported in accordance with IFRS

N.40 Nexe Innovations Inc.

Symbol - NEXE **Exchange** - TSX-VEN **CUSIP** - 65344W
Head Office - 109-19353 22 Ave, Surrey, BC, V3Z 3S6 **Telephone** - (604) 359-4725
Website - nexeinnovations.com
Email - invest@nexeinnovations.com
Investor Relations - Kam Mangat (604) 359-4725
Auditors - MNP LLP C.A., Vancouver, B.C.
Transfer Agents - TSX Trust Company, Vancouver, B.C.
Profile - (B.C. 2019) Designs, manufactures and commercializes fully compostable (plant-based) single-serve pods for Keurig® and Nespresso® beverage systems.

The company's proprietary and fully compostable capsules, NEXE pods, are manufactured at its 20,000-sq.-ft. research, development and manufacturing facility in Surrey, B.C. A 54,000-sq.-ft. manufacturing facility is being developed in Windsor, Ont., with operations expected to commence by the end of 2022. The company produces coffee and non-coffee-based products under its brands XOMA Superfoods, which consist of coffee and superfood ingredient pods compatible with Keurig® machines, and NEXE Coffee, a line of coffee pods compatible with Keurig® and Nespresso® machines. Products are available through the company's online stores and third party e-commerce platforms in Canada and the U.S, as well as select retail stores in Canada. Also provides private label and co-manufacturing services to brands and consumer packaged goods (CPG) businesses.

Plans to expand by providing various compostable solutions for consumer products such as various beverages including coffee, tea and other food items.

Predecessor Detail - Name changed from Whatcom Capital Corp., Dec. 18, 2020, pursuant to the Qualifying Transaction reverse takeover acquisition of (old) NEXE Innovations Inc.; basis 1 new for 2.5 old shs.

Directors - Darren Footz, chr. & CEO, Surrey, B.C.; Ashvani (Ash) Guglani, pres. & acting CFO, Vancouver, B.C.; Graham Gilley†, North Vancouver, B.C.; Haytham H. Hodaly, New Westminster, B.C.; Killian Ruby, B.C.

Other Exec. Officers - Kam Mangat, v-p, IR & corp. strategy; Christopher (Chris) Murray, v-p, sales & mktg.

† Lead director

Capital Stock

	Authorized (shs.)	Outstanding (shs.)[1]
Common	unlimited	97,293,297

[1] At Oct. 31, 2022

Major Shareholder - Darren Footz held 11.49% interest at Mar. 25, 2022.

Price Range - NEXE/TSX-VEN

Year	Volume	High	Low	Close
2022	16,107,832	$0.71	$0.22	$0.27
2021	99,875,600	$5.90	$0.56	$0.63
2020	7,231,298	$2.20	$0.38	$2.06

Recent Close: $0.39

Capital Stock Changes - During fiscal 2022, common shares were issued as follows: 169,609 on exercise of warrants, 34,300 on exercise of options and 25,000 for services.

Wholly Owned Subsidiaries

G-Pak Holdings Inc., B.C.
NEXE Technology Corp., B.C.
Xoma Operations Inc., B.C.

Financial Statistics

Periods ended:	12m May 31/22[A]		12m May 31/21[A1]
	$000s	%Chg	$000s
Operating revenue	**27**	**n.a.**	**nil**
Cost of goods sold	56		nil
Salaries & benefits	1,715		719
Research & devel. expense	336		667
General & admin expense	4,487		8,075
Stock-based compensation	627		2,376
Operating expense	**7,221**	**-39**	**11,837**
Operating income	**(7,194)**	**n.a.**	**(11,837)**
Deprec., depl. & amort.	673		253
Finance income	157		13
Finance costs, gross	309		290
Write-downs/write-offs	(251)		(2,121)
Pre-tax income	**(8,340)**	**n.a.**	**(17,094)**
Net inc. bef. disc. opers	**(8,340)**	**n.a.**	**(17,094)**
Income from disc. opers	nil		(85)
Net income	**(8,340)**	**n.a.**	**(17,179)**
Cash & equivalent	28,462		50,527
Inventories	930		322
Accounts receivable	1,338		603
Current assets	34,740		53,370
Fixed assets, net	11,585		3,442
Right-of-use assets	514		651
Intangibles, net	79		79
Total assets	**49,170**	**-15**	**57,676**
Bank indebtedness	nil		805
Accts. pay. & accr. liabs	1,574		1,517
Current liabilities	3,011		3,868
Long-term debt, gross	1,245		1,456
Long-term debt, net	985		956
Long-term lease liabilities	381		515
Shareholders' equity	44,792		52,337
Cash from oper. activs	**(9,993)**	**n.a.**	**(10,445)**
Cash from fin. activs	(1,199)		58,674
Cash from invest. activs	(23,828)		(1,014)
Net cash position	**15,507**	**-69**	**50,527**
Capital expenditures	(8,755)		(1,615)
	$		$
Earnings per share*	(0.09)		(0.37)
Cash flow per share*	(0.10)		(0.22)
	shs		shs
No. of shs. o/s*	96,857,583		96,628,674
Avg. no. of shs. o/s*	96,783,076		46,496,414
	%		%
Net profit margin	n.m.		n.a.
Return on equity	(17.17)		(71.64)
Return on assets	(15.03)		(50.68)

* Common
[A] Reported in accordance with IFRS
[1] Results reflect the Dec. 15, 2020, Qualifying Transaction reverse takeover acquisition of (old) NEXE Innovations Inc.

Latest Results

Periods ended:	3m Aug. 31/22[A]		3m Aug. 31/21[A]
	$000s	%Chg	$000s
Operating revenue	27	n.a.	nil
Net income	(1,950)	n.a.	(2,017)
	$		$
Earnings per share*	(0.02)		(0.02)

* Common
[A] Reported in accordance with IFRS

Historical Summary
(as originally stated)

Fiscal Year	Oper. Rev.	Net Inc. Bef. Disc.	EPS*
	$000s	$000s	$
2022[A]	27	(8,340)	(0.09)
2021[A]	nil	(17,094)	(0.37)
2020[A1]	nil	(1,854)	n.a.
2019[A]	nil	(1,158)	n.a.

* Common
[A] Reported in accordance with IFRS
[1] Results for fiscal 2020 and prior periods pertain to (old) NEXE Innovations Inc.

Note: Adjusted throughout for 1-for-2.5 cons. in Dec. 2020

N.41 NexgenRx Inc.

Symbol - NXG **Exchange** - TSX-VEN **CUSIP** - 65337X
Head Office - 905-191 The West Mall, Toronto, ON, M9C 5L6 **Telephone** - (416) 695-3393 **Toll-free** - (866) 424-0257 **Fax** - (647) 722-3056
Website - www.nexgenrx.com
Email - rloucks@nexgenrx.com
Investor Relations - Ronald C. Loucks (416) 695-3393 ext. 801
Auditors - Grant Thornton LLP C.A., Mississauga, Ont.
Bankers - Royal Bank of Canada, Mississauga, Ont.
Lawyers - TingleMerrett LLP, Calgary, Alta.
Transfer Agents - TSX Trust Company, Toronto, Ont.

Profile - (Ont. 2003) Provides administration and health benefit claims adjudication services to various organizations who manage health benefit plans on behalf of a number of plan sponsors (employers and associations) and occasionally directly to large Canadian plan sponsors who wish to provide an administrative services only (ASO) health benefit plan to their plan members.

Benefit claims include drug, dental, extended health and health care spending account claims which are offered through the company's NexSys® adjudication platform. Revenue consists of fees per health benefit claim transaction adjudicated, in addition to a per member administration fee.

Other products and services offered include NexAdmin®, a web-based administration platform which offers eligibility, enrolment and billing functionality that enable sponsors to take complete control of benefit plan administration; NexPension, a pension administration solution designed to help sponsors record and tabulate contributions for their membership group in a multi-employer environment; NexPSPAssist service which helps Patient Support Programs (PSP) to optimize their deliverables to their manufacturer clients; and NexMobile which provides members with instant access to personal benefit and claims information.

Directors - Thomas F. Corcoran, chr., Toronto, Ont.; Ronald C. (Ron) Loucks, pres. & CEO, Mississauga, Ont.; David Bennett, Waterloo, Ont.; Charles M. Burns, Maple, Ont.; Randy McGlynn, Waterloo, Qué.

Other Exec. Officers - Kelly Ehler, CFO; Andrew Munroe, sr. v-p, pharma and payor partners; Jason Robinson, sr. v-p, admin.; Mark Payne, v-p, IT; Paul A. Bolger, corp. sec.

Capital Stock

	Authorized (shs.)	Outstanding (shs.)[1]
Preferred	unlimited	
Series 1	unlimited	6,600,000
Common	unlimited	70,335,883

[1] At Apr. 10, 2023

Preferred series 1 - Entitled to 8% cumulative preferential dividends payable annually. Non-voting.

Common - One vote per share.

Major Shareholder - Paul E. Crossett held 19.99% interest and Ronald C. (Ron) Loucks held 10.43% interest at Apr. 10, 2023.

Price Range - NXG/TSX-VEN

Year	Volume	High	Low	Close
2022	5,138,046	$0.46	$0.24	$0.27
2021	5,199,712	$0.60	$0.23	$0.40
2020	3,821,842	$0.26	$0.14	$0.24
2019	2,346,789	$0.33	$0.15	$0.20
2018	3,222,544	$0.30	$0.20	$0.26

Recent Close: $0.28

Capital Stock Changes - There were no changes to capital stock during 2022.

Dividends

NXG com N.S.R.
$0.005 June 30/23 $0.005 Oct. 10/22
$0.005i Feb. 4/22
Paid in 2023: $0.005 2022: $0.01**i** 2021: n.a.

i Initial Payment

Wholly Owned Subsidiaries

Canadian Benefit Administrators Ltd.
My Benetech Inc.

Financial Statistics

Periods ended:	12m Dec. 31/22[A]		12m Dec. 31/21[A]
	$000s	%Chg	$000s
Operating revenue	**12,781**	**+8**	**11,841**
Cost of sales	2,598		2,028
General & admin expense	8,428		6,176
Stock-based compensation	62		104
Operating expense	**11,088**	**+33**	**8,307**
Operating income	**1,693**	**-52**	**3,534**
Deprec., depl. & amort.	1,406		1,335
Finance costs, gross	153		189
Pre-tax income	**134**	**-93**	**2,010**
Income taxes	157		(2,008)
Net income	**(22)**	**n.a.**	**4,018**
Cash & equivalent	1,767		2,317
Accounts receivable	410		479
Current assets	18,004		20,831
Fixed assets, net	835		504
Intangibles, net	5,339		6,357
Total assets	**25,747**	**-13**	**29,436**
Accts. pay. & accr. liabs	922		1,414
Current liabilities	16,506		19,551
Long-term lease liabilities	390		172
Preferred share equity	1,650		1,650
Shareholders' equity	8,851		9,713
Cash from oper. activs	**1,066**	**-72**	**3,824**
Cash from fin. activs	(1,110)		(940)
Cash from invest. activs	(507)		(1,370)
Net cash position	**1,767**	**-24**	**2,317**
Capital expenditures	(389)		(127)
	$		$
Earnings per share*	(0.00)		0.06
Cash flow per share*	0.02		0.05
Cash divd. per share*	0.01		nil
	shs		shs
No. of shs. o/s*	70,335,883		70,335,883
Avg. no. of shs. o/s*	70,335,883		70,335,883
	%		%
Net profit margin	(0.17)		33.93
Return on equity	(2.88)		64.06
Return on assets	(0.17)		16.08

* Common
[A] Reported in accordance with IFRS

Latest Results

Periods ended:	3m Mar. 31/23[A]		3m Mar. 31/22[A]
	$000s	%Chg	$000s
Operating revenue	3,459	+9	3,174
Net income	195	-48	378
	$		$
Earnings per share*	0.00		0.00

* Common
[A] Reported in accordance with IFRS

Historical Summary
(as originally stated)

Fiscal Year	Oper. Rev.	Net Inc. Bef. Disc.	EPS*
	$000s	$000s	$
2022[A]	12,781	(22)	(0.00)
2021[A]	11,841	4,018	0.06
2020[A]	11,041	2,116	0.03
2019[A]	9,540	(208)	(0.00)
2018[A]	7,169	(697)	(0.01)

* Common
[A] Reported in accordance with IFRS

N.42 NexLiving Communities Inc.

Symbol - NXLV **Exchange** - TSX-VEN **CUSIP** - 65344P
Head Office - 1805-45 Alderney Dr, Dartmouth, NS, B2Y 2N6 **Telephone** - (902) 441-2654
Website - nexliving.ca
Email - sstathonikos@nexliving.ca
Investor Relations - Stavro Stathonikos (416) 876-6617
Auditors - PricewaterhouseCoopers LLP C.A., Halifax, N.S.
Lawyers - McInnes Cooper, Halifax, N.S.; Cox & Palmer LLP, Halifax, N.S.; Jessome Law, Halifax, N.S.
Transfer Agents - Computershare Trust Company of Canada Inc.

Profile - (Can. 2011) Acquires, owns, operates and manages low and mid-rise multi-unit residential properties in Canada focused upon residents aged 55 years and up.

Has multi-unit residential properties in Moncton and Saint John, N.B.; and Oshawa, Lindsay and Strathoy, Ont., totaling 1,166 units.

Recent Merger and Acquisition Activity

Status: completed **Revised:** Feb. 28, 2023

UPDATE: The transaction was completed for $39,600,000, consisting of issuance of 37,500,000 common shares valued at a deemed price of 20¢ per share, $1,400,000 cash, $30,700,000 in mortgage debt and $1,000,000 bridge loan with the remaining balance in cash. PREVIOUS: NexLiving Communities Inc. agreed to acquire Northpoint Management Inc., which owns two newly built adjacent multi-family buildings totaling 150 units in Moncton, N.B., from Sheaco Holdings Inc. for $39,600,000.
Status: completed **Announced:** Dec. 16, 2022
NexLiving Communities Inc. acquired two apartment properties totaling 149 suites in Saint John, N.B. for $34,300,000. The acquisition includes an adjacent parcel of land that is approved for a future development project of up to 85 units.
Status: completed **Revised:** Dec. 5, 2022
UPDATE: NexLiving agreed to directly acquire the owner of 2251 Mountain Road and 2261 Mountain Road. PREVIOUS: NexLiving Communities Inc. agreed to acquire ten apartment properties in Moncton and Riverview, N.B., totaling 370 units, for $72,600,000, which would be partially funded with proceeds from a proposed public offering and private placement. The portfolio includes a 75-unit five-storey building located at 2251 Mountain Road; a property at 2261 Mountain Road which is in the construction stage; a 64-unit four-storey building located at 1009 Cleveland Avenue; and seven buildings totaling 156 units located at Cleveland and Whitepine. Dec. 22, 2021 - The acquisition of the seven buildings totaling 156 units located at Cleveland and Whitepine in Moncton, N.B. was completed for $21,300,000. Apr. 5, 2022 - The acquisition of the 64-unit four-storey building located at 1009 Cleveland Avenue in Riverview, N.B., was completed for $11,700,000.
Status: completed **Announced:** Aug. 10, 2022
NexLiving Communities Inc. acquired a three-storey, 40-suite building in Strathroy, Ont., for $9,400,000, which was financed with cash on hand and $7,900,000 of new short-term debt.
Status: completed **Announced:** Apr. 18, 2022
NexLiving Communities Inc. acquired a six-storey, 58-suite building in Lindsay, Ont., for $13,400,000, which was financed with cash on hand and $10,100,000 of new short-term debt.

Predecessor Detail - Name changed from ViveRe Communities Inc., June 1, 2021.

Directors - T. Richard (Rick) Turner, chr., West Vancouver, B.C.; Michael T. (Mike) Anaka, exec. v-chr., Dartmouth, N.S.; William (Bill) Hennessey, N.B.; Drew Koivu, Ont.; Andrea Morwick, Ont.; David Pappin, N.S.; Dr. Brian Ramjattan, N.L.

Other Exec. Officers - Stavro Stathonikos, pres. & CEO; Glenn A. Holmes, CFO & corp. sec.

Capital Stock

	Authorized (shs.)	Outstanding (shs.)[1]
Preferred	unlimited	nil
Common	unlimited	16,539,132

[1] At Aug. 3, 2023

Normal Course Issuer Bid - The company plans to make normal course purchases of up to 26,000,000 common shares representing 9.8% of the public float. The bid commenced on May 30, 2023, and expires on May 30, 2024.

Major Shareholder - Sheaco Holdings Inc. held 11.34% interest at May 25, 2023.

Price Range - NXLV/TSX-VEN

Year	Volume	High	Low	Close
2022	960,844	$4.40	$2.50	$3.00
2021	698,753	$4.70	$3.20	$4.60
2020	384,094	$7.00	$2.60	$3.90
2019	105,359	$4.90	$1.50	$4.60
2018	14,314	$5.00	$1.40	$1.90

Consolidation: 1-for-20 cons. in Aug. 2023
Recent Close: $2.05

Capital Stock Changes - In February 2023, 1,875,000 post-consolidated common shares were issued on acquisition of Northpoint Management Inc. On Aug. 3, 2023, common shares were consolidated on a 1-for-20 basis.

In January 2022, private placement of 6,000,000 common shares was completed at 20¢ per share. Also during 2022, common shares were issued as follows: 4,012,500 on exercise of warrants and 1,720,666 under deferred share unit plan.

Dividends

NXLV com Ra $0.04 pa Q est. Mar. 21, 2021
1-for-20 cons eff. Aug. 3, 2023
$0.0005**i** .... Mar. 21/21
i Initial Payment

Wholly Owned Subsidiaries

Emma and Albert Development Inc., Ont.
4196762 Nova Scotia Limited, Canada.
10664316 Canada Inc., Canada.
720083 NB Inc., N.B.
725298 N.B. Inc., Canada.
694476 NB Inc., N.B.
3329586 Nova Scotia Limited, N.S.
3335170 Nova Scotia Limited, N.S.
3335171 Nova Scotia Limited, N.S.
3339594 Nova Scotia Limited, N.S.
3342102 Nova Scotia Limited, N.S.
Village View #4 GP Inc., Canada.
Village View No. 4 Limited Partnership, Saint John, N.B.
Village View No. 3 Limited Partnership, N.B.
Village View No. 2 Limited Partnership, N.B.
- 100% int. in **11295594 Canada Inc.**, Canada.
- 100% int. in **11295608 Canada Inc.**, Canada.

Financial Statistics

Periods ended:	12m Dec. 31/22^A		12m Dec. 31/21^A
	$000s	%Chg	$000s
Total revenue	**11,865**	**+58**	**7,526**
Rental operating expense	5,194		3,275
Operating expense	**7,017**	**+46**	**4,810**
Operating income	**4,848**	**+78**	**2,716**
Non-operating overhead	1,823		1,535
Finance costs, gross	3,383		3,250
Pre-tax income	**8,113**	**-14**	**9,404**
Income taxes	600		nil
Net income	**7,513**	**-20**	**9,404**
Cash & equivalent	814		17,696
Accounts receivable	587		90
Current assets	2,644		18,597
Income-producing props	203,071		125,162
Property interests, net	203,071		125,162
Total assets	**205,715**	**+43**	**143,759**
Accts. pay. & accr. liabs	1,280		708
Current liabilities	35,311		21,255
Long-term debt, gross	133,938		82,248
Long-term debt, net	99,907		61,702
Equity portion of conv. debs	nil		1,043
Shareholders' equity	69,897		60,802
Cash from oper. activs	**2,281**	**+236**	**678**
Cash from fin. activs	18,728		38,520
Cash from invest. activs	(37,891)		(23,947)
Net cash position	**814**	**-95**	**17,696**
Increase in property	(37,891)		(24,457)
Decrease in property	nil		510
	$		$
Earnings per share*	0.60		1.20
Cash flow per share*	0.16		0.09
Cash divd. per share*	0.04		0.04
	shs		shs
No. of shs. o/s*	14,664,132		14,077,474
Avg. no. of shs. o/s*	14,687,148		7,808,157
	%		%
Net profit margin	63.32		124.95
Return on equity	11.50		23.38
Return on assets	6.09		11.18

* Common
^A Reported in accordance with IFRS

Latest Results

Periods ended:	3m Mar. 31/23^A		3m Mar. 31/22^A
	$000s	%Chg	$000s
Total revenue	4,205	+65	2,553
Net income	2,645	+124	1,179
	$		$
Earnings per share*	0.18		0.08

* Common
^A Reported in accordance with IFRS

Historical Summary
(as originally stated)

Fiscal Year	Total Rev.	Net Inc. Bef. Disc.	EPS*
	$000s	$000s	$
2022^A	11,865	7,513	0.60
2021^A	7,526	9,404	1.20
2020^A	3,626	(2,200)	(0.60)
2019^A	1,090	(1,406)	(0.80)
2018^A	157	(692)	(1.00)

* Common
^A Reported in accordance with IFRS
Note: Adjusted throughout for 1-for-20 cons. in Aug. 2023

N.43 NexOptic Technology Corp.

Symbol - NXO **Exchange** - TSX-VEN **CUSIP** - 65341P
Head Office - 1500-409 Granville St, Vancouver, BC, V6C 1T2 **Telephone** - (604) 669-7330 **Toll-free** - (844) 669-7330 **Fax** - (604) 662-3231
Website - www.nexoptic.com
Email - joel.sutherland@nexoptic.com
Investor Relations - Joel Sutherland (604) 669-7330 ext. 2
Auditors - Smythe LLP C.A., Vancouver, B.C.
Transfer Agents - Computershare Trust Company of Canada Inc., Toronto, Ont.

Profile - (B.C. 2007) Develops technologies relating to imagery and light concentration for lens and image capture systems.

The company's patent pending technology, All Light Intelligent Imaging Solutions (ALIIS™), delivers superior light performance by learning a camera profile and optimally enhancing images and videos, pixel by pixel its quality and resolution in a fraction of a second using edge processing. The result is superior resolution and sharpness, dramatic reductions to image noise and motion blur, noticeable enhancements to long-range image stabilization by enabling faster shutter speeds, and significantly reduced file and bandwidth requirements for storage or streaming applications. ALIIS™ also improves downstream applications such as computational imaging, facial recognition and object detection. Also owns patent pending NexCompress™, a video compression enhancement solution offering significant bandwidth and storage savings for video storage and streaming applications.

In addition, the company was developing DoubleTake™, a shock and water-resistant, and lightweight binocular engineered with extra-low dispersion optical glass and no plastic lens components. DoubleTake™ was still on hold in order for the company to apply full resources and attention to ALIIS™'s growth and commercialization.

Predecessor Detail - Name changed from Elissa Resources Ltd., Feb. 17, 2016.

Directors - Dr. Richard J. (Rich) Geruson, chr., Los Gatos, Calif.; Paul T. McKenzie, pres. & CEO, Vancouver, B.C.; Arch Meredith, Woodside, Calif.; Stephen Petranek, Leesburg, Va.

Other Exec. Officers - Chulhyun (Wayne) Cho, CFO; Kevin Gordon, v-p, AI technologies; Izhar Matzkevich, v-p, bus. devel.; Shauna L. Hartman, legal counsel & corp. sec.; Daewon Baek, pres., NexOptic Asia

Capital Stock

	Authorized (shs.)	Outstanding (shs.)[1]
Common	unlimited	195,217,675

[1] At May 29, 2023

Major Shareholder - Widely held at Dec. 6, 2022.

Price Range - NXO/TSX-VEN

Year	Volume	High	Low	Close
2022	38,392,673	$0.53	$0.07	$0.08
2021	105,292,681	$1.07	$0.18	$0.49
2020	76,189,521	$1.53	$0.17	$0.46
2019	42,370,761	$0.78	$0.29	$0.40
2018	32,026,358	$1.48	$0.48	$0.65

Recent Close: $0.03

Capital Stock Changes - In November 2022, private placement of 39,564,053 units (1 common share & 1 warrant) at $0.05625 per unit was completed. Also during 2022, 1,500,000 common shares were issued on exercise of restricted share units.

Wholly Owned Subsidiaries

NexOptic Asia Ltd., South Korea.
Red Hill Energy (US), Inc., Nev.
Spectrum Optix Inc., Calgary, Alta.

Financial Statistics

Periods ended:	12m Dec. 31/22^A		12m Dec. 31/21^A
	$000s	%Chg	$000s
Salaries & benefits	681		695
Research & devel. expense	289		201
General & admin expense	1,320		1,416
Stock-based compensation	1,385		1,090
Other operating expense	117		131
Operating expense	**3,793**	**+7**	**3,533**
Operating income	**(3,793)**	**n.a.**	**(3,533)**
Finance costs, gross	6		6
Pre-tax income	**(3,882)**	**n.a.**	**(3,317)**
Net income	**(3,882)**	**n.a.**	**(3,317)**
Cash & equivalent	762		337
Accounts receivable	45		25
Current assets	1,009		418
Total assets	**1,009**	**+141**	**418**
Accts. pay. & accr. liabs	1,920		1,004
Current liabilities	1,920		1,004
Long-term debt, gross	60		54
Long-term debt, net	nil		54
Shareholders' equity	(988)		(640)
Cash from oper. activs	**(1,729)**	**n.a.**	**(2,064)**
Cash from fin. activs	2,154		66
Net cash position	**762**	**+126**	**337**
	$		$
Earnings per share*	(0.03)		(0.02)
Cash flow per share*	(0.01)		(0.01)
	shs		shs
No. of shs. o/s*	188,495,203		147,431,150
Avg. no. of shs. o/s*	153,473,503		147,335,725
	%		%
Net profit margin	n.a.		n.a.
Return on equity	n.m.		n.m.
Return on assets	(543.24)		(231.05)

* Common
^A Reported in accordance with IFRS

Latest Results

Periods ended:	3m Mar. 31/23^A		3m Mar. 31/22^A
	$000s	%Chg	$000s
Net income	(858)	n.a.	(1,081)
	$		$
Earnings per share*	(0.01)		(0.01)

* Common
^A Reported in accordance with IFRS

Historical Summary
(as originally stated)

Fiscal Year	Oper. Rev. $000s	Net Inc. Bef. Disc. $000s	EPS* $
2022[A]	nil	(3,882)	(0.03)
2021[A]	nil	(3,317)	(0.02)
2020[A]	nil	(5,806)	(0.04)
2019[A]	nil	(57,335)	(0.43)
2018[A]	nil	(12,287)	(0.10)

* Common
[A] Reported in accordance with IFRS

N.44 NexPoint Hospitality Trust

Symbol - NHT.U **Exchange** - TSX-VEN **CUSIP** - 65344N
Head Office - 3400-333 Bay St, Toronto, ON, M5H 2S7
Website - nht.nexpoint.com
Email - bmitts@nexpoint.com
Investor Relations - Brian Mitts (972) 419-2556
Auditors - Frazier & Deeter, LLC C.P.A., Atlanta, Ga.
Transfer Agents - TSX Trust Company, Toronto, Ont.
FP500 Revenue Ranking - 795

Profile - (Ont. 2018) Acquires, owns, renovates and operates hotel properties in the United States, with a focus on select-service, limited-service and extended stay hotels.

At Mar 31, 2023, the trust's portfolio consisted of 10 properties, totaling 1,535 rooms, located across six major metropolitan statistical area markets in Oregon, Washington State, Texas, Florida, Tennessee and Utah in the select-service, limited-service and extended stay hospitality categories. Each property has a long-term franchise agreement with Hilton (Hilton Garden Inn, Double Tree, Homewood Suites and Hampton Inn & Suites), Hyatt, Marriott and InterContinental Hotels Group (Holiday Inn Express) brands. The trust's franchise agreements initially range from 10 to 20 years with various extension provisions. The expiry dates of the franchise agreements range from December 2029 to February 2042, subject to earlier extension.

Property Portfolio

Location	Hotels	Rooms
Oregon	1	101
Washington State	1	102
Texas	4	595
Florida	2	328
Tennessee	1	287
Utah	1	122
	10	1,535

The portfolio consists of DoubleTree (2), Homewood Suites (3), Hilton Gardens Inn, Holiday Inn Express, Marriott, Hyatt and Hampton Inn & Suites brands.

NexPoint Real Estate Advisors VI, L.P. is the trust's manager.

The company began the marketing process to sell the remaining two DoubleTree properties of Tigard and Olympia, as well as the Holiday Inn in Nashville. The company expected the transactions to close in the second and third quarters of 2023. The company targeted a sales price of US$125,000,000 for Holiday Inn property.

Recent Merger and Acquisition Activity

Status: pending **Announced:** Aug. 11, 2023
NexPoint Hospitality Trust agreed to sell Holiday Inn Express hotel property in Nashville, Tenn. to NF V Acquisitions, LLC, for US$120,000,000. The transaction is expected to close in the third quarter of 2023.

Status: pending **Revised:** Mar. 8, 2023
UPDATE: NexPoint signed a letter of intent to sell Tigard property for US$12,750,000, which is expected to close in the third quarter of 2023. Also expected the sale of Olympia property in the second or third quarter of 2023. PREVIOUS: NexPoint Hospitality Trust has awarded the purchase of all five properties in the DoubleTree Portfolio including Beaverton, Tigard, Vancouver, Bend and Olympia properties to four different third party buyers for undisclosed terms. The transaction is expected to close in the third quarter of 2022 or in October 2022 if extended. Aug. 19, 2022 - NexPoint decided to no longer sell Bend and Olympia hotel properties, and agreed to sell Beaverton, Tigard, Vancouver hotel properties for total consideration of US$43,600,000. Aug. 24, 2022 - NexPoint sold Vancouver property for US$14,500,000. Sep. 30, 2022 - NexPoint sold Beaverton property for US$14,500,000. Nov. 14, 2022 - NexPoint decided not to sell Olympia property. Dec. 12, 2022 - NexPoint sold Bend property for US$38,500,000. NexPoint also expected the sale of Tigard property before the end of 2023.

Trustees - James Dondero, chr. & CEO, Dallas, Tex.; Neil J. Labatte‡, Toronto, Ont.; M. Jerry Patava, Toronto, Ont.; Graham D. Senst, Toronto, Ont.

Oper. Subsid./Mgt. Co. Officers - Brian Mitts, CFO, treas. & corp. sec.; Matthew McGraner, chief invest. officer; Jesse Blair III, exec. v-p & head, lodging; Paul Richards, v-p, asset mgt.

‡ Lead trustee

Capital Stock

	Authorized (shs.)	Outstanding (shs.)[1]
Trust Unit	unlimited	29,352,055
Class B Unit	unlimited	205,597[2 3]

[1] At Mar. 31, 2023
[2] Classified as debt.
[3] Securities of NHT Operating Partnership, LLC

Trust Unit - The trust initially intends to make quarterly cash distributions, on an annual basis, representing 65% of estimated core funds from operations (Core FFO). One vote per trust unit.

Class B Unit - Issued by NHT Operating Partnership, LLC. Economic equivalent to trust units and redeemable for trust units on a 1-for-1 basis. Non-voting.

Major Shareholder - James Dondero held 73.96% interest at May 31, 2022.

Price Range - NHT.U/TSX-VEN

Year	Volume	High	Low	Close
2022	18,550	US$2.50	US$1.50	US$1.50
2021	107,050	US$4.00	US$1.00	US$2.10
2020	16,600	US$4.00	US$2.50	US$2.75
2019	73,750	US$5.25	US$4.00	US$4.00

Recent Close: US$0.50

Capital Stock Changes - There were no changes to capital stock during 2021 or 2022.

Wholly Owned Subsidiaries

NHT Intermediary, LLC, United States.
- 100% int. in **NHT Holdings, LLC**, United States.
  - 100% int. in **NHT Operating Partnership, LLC**, United States.
    - 100% int. in **NHT Bradenton, LLC**, Del.
    - 100% int. in **NHT DFW Portfolio, LLC**, United States.
    - 100% int. in **NHT Park City, LLC**, Del.
    - 100% int. in **NHT SP, LLC**, United States.
    - 100% int. in **NHT 2325 Stemmons, LLC**, United States.
    - 100% int. in **NREO NW Hospitality, LLC**, United States.
    - 100% int. in **NexPoint Multifamily Capital Trust, Inc.**, United States.

Note: The preceding list includes only the major related companies in which interests are held.

Financial Statistics

Periods ended:	12m Dec. 31/22[A]		12m Dec. 31/21[oA]
	US$000s	%Chg	US$000s
Operating revenue	**62,107**	**+72**	**36,040**
Cost of sales	18,354		12,733
Salaries & benefits	14,546		8,708
General & admin expense	15,450		10,449
Operating expense	**48,350**	**+52**	**31,890**
Operating income	**13,757**	**+231**	**4,150**
Deprec., depl. & amort.	14,605		10,652
Finance costs, gross	16,044		10,201
Write-downs/write-offs	829		38,162
Pre-tax income	**571**	**-98**	**24,513**
Income taxes	(1,414)		(800)
Net inc. bef. disc. opers	**1,985**	**-92**	**25,313**
Income from disc. opers	4,700		(1,042)
Net income	**6,685**	**-72**	**24,271**
Cash & equivalent	3,174		1,532
Accounts receivable	1,608		3,802
Current assets	28,605		14,962
Fixed assets, net	269,536		297,564
Right-of-use assets	3,240		2,129
Total assets	**308,205**	**-3**	**317,261**
Accts. pay. & accr. liabs	20,374		24,175
Current liabilities	40,091		129,659
Long-term debt, gross	195,967		238,548
Long-term debt, net	176,581		133,064
Long-term lease liabilities	1,063		1,224
Shareholders' equity	5,931		(754)
Cash from oper. activs	**23,387**	**+375**	**4,922**
Cash from fin. activs	(28,342)		4,304
Cash from invest. activs	6,597		(8,772)
Net cash position	**3,174**	**+107**	**1,532**
Capital expenditures	(3,451)		(5,436)
	US$		US$
Earns. per sh bef disc opers*	0.07		0.86
Earnings per share*	0.23		0.82
Cash flow per share*	0.78		0.17
	shs		shs
No. of shs. o/s*	29,901,742		29,901,742
Avg. no. of shs. o/s*	29,901,742		29,352,055
	%		%
Net profit margin	3.20		70.24
Return on equity	n.m.		n.m.
Return on assets	18.47		11.91
Foreign sales percent	100		100

* Trust Unit
[o] Restated
[A] Reported in accordance with IFRS

Latest Results

Periods ended:	3m Mar. 31/23[A]		3m Mar. 31/22[oA]
	US$000s	%Chg	US$000s
Operating revenue	19,582	+43	13,708
Net inc. bef. disc. opers	(3,756)	n.a.	830
Income from disc. opers	12		(484)
Net income	(3,744)	n.a.	346
	US$		US$
Earns. per sh. bef. disc. opers.*	(0.13)		0.03
Earnings per share*	(0.13)		0.01

* Trust Unit
[o] Restated
[A] Reported in accordance with IFRS

Historical Summary
(as originally stated)

Fiscal Year	Oper. Rev. US$000s	Net Inc. Bef. Disc. US$000s	EPS* US$
2022[A]	62,107	1,985	0.07
2021[A]	49,453	24,271	n.a.
2020[A]	31,991	(112,336)	n.a.
2019[A]	71,624	(7,289)	n.a.

* Trust Unit
[A] Reported in accordance with IFRS

N.45 Next Hydrogen Solutions Inc.

Symbol - NXH **Exchange** - TSX-VEN **CUSIP** - 65345D
Head Office - 6610 Edwards Blvd, Mississauga, ON, L5T 2V6
Telephone - (647) 578-6360
Website - nexthydrogen.com
Email - rafzaal@nexthydrogen.com
Investor Relations - Raveel Afzaal (647) 961-6620
Auditors - KPMG LLP C.A., Toronto, Ont.
Transfer Agents - TSX Trust Company, Toronto, Ont.
Employees - 43 at May 16, 2023

Profile - (B.C. 2014) Designs and manufactures electrolyzers that use water and electricity as inputs to generate clean hydrogen for use as an energy source.

The hydrogen generators' key component is a patented electrolyzer module, which is combined with various supporting and auxiliary components including power, controls, gas purification, closed loop cooling and water treatment. The system is automatically controlled and operates with minimal oversight. The system's resulting hydrogen is cleaned and sent to the user's production or hydrogen storage.

Product offerings consist of the NH-100, NH-300 (base model) and NH-500 hydrogen generation systems, with 0.6, 1.8 and 3 MW of power, respectively. The technology is being scaled up to deliver commercial solutions to decarbonize transportation and industrial sectors.

The company has a 27,000-sq.-ft. in-house assembly facility in Mississauga, Ont., which provides 40-MW capacity for product assembly, testing, product development and engineering.

Common reinstated on TSX-VEN, May 30, 2023.
Common suspended from TSX-VEN, May 9, 2023.

Predecessor Detail - Name changed from BioHEP Technologies Ltd., June 21, 2021, pursuant to the reverse takeover acquisition of Next Hydrogen Corporation.

Directors - Allan Mackenzie, chr., Alta.; Matthew Fairlie, exec. v-chr., Ont.; Raveel Afzaal, pres. & CEO, Ont.; Jens P. Clausen, Nev.; Anthony R. (Tony) Guglielmin, Vancouver, B.C.; Walter Q. Howard, Fairfield, Conn.; Susan Uthayakumar, West Palm Beach, Fla.

Other Exec. Officers - Jim Franchville, COO; Rohan Advani, CFO; Dr. Jim Hinatsu, chief product officer; Michael Stemp, chief tech. officer; James Davies, v-p, eng.; Shane Day, v-p, opers.

Capital Stock

	Authorized (shs.)	Outstanding (shs.)[1]
Common	unlimited	22,888,436

[1] At Aug. 14, 2023

Major Shareholder - Allan Mackenzie held 16.69% interest at Apr. 17, 2023.

Price Range - NXH/TSX-VEN

Year	Volume	High	Low	Close
2022	4,196,798	$3.44	$1.11	$1.20
2021	1,573,868	$10.25	$3.22	$3.39

Recent Close: $0.77

Capital Stock Changes - There were no changes to capital stock during 2022.

Wholly Owned Subsidiaries

Next Hydrogen Corporation, Mississauga, Ont.
Next Hydrogen USA, Inc.

Financial Statistics

Periods ended:	12m Dec. 31/22[A]		12m Dec. 31/21[□A1]
	$000s	%Chg	$000s
Operating revenue	**722**	**+306**	**178**
Cost of sales	644		82
Research & devel. expense	7,705		6,403
General & admin expense	6,174		6,139
Stock-based compensation	1,884		2,616
Operating expense	**16,407**	**+8**	**15,240**
Operating income	**(15,685)**	**n.a.**	**(15,062)**
Deprec., depl. & amort	708		279
Finance income	560		93
Finance costs, gross	248		359
Write-downs/write-offs	(790)		(5,911)
Pre-tax income	**(14,278)**	**n.a.**	**(26,613)**
Net income	**(14,278)**	**n.a.**	**(26,613)**
Cash & equivalent	22,085		39,197
Inventories	2,886		2,000
Accounts receivable	716		894
Current assets	26,084		43,437
Fixed assets, net	4,832		1,109
Right-of-use assets	1,706		1,903
Intangibles, net	941		1,139
Total assets	**33,728**	**-29**	**47,686**
Bank indebtedness	60		60
Accts. pay. & accr. liabs	1,094		2,321
Current liabilities	1,456		4,439
Long-term debt, gross	163		301
Long-term debt, net	86		164
Long-term lease liabilities	1,753		1,820
Shareholders' equity	23,906		36,188
Cash from oper. activs	**(12,636)**	**n.a.**	**(12,553)**
Cash from fin. activs	(440)		52,207
Cash from invest. activs	(4,036)		(1,548)
Net cash position	**22,085**	**-44**	**39,197**
Capital expenditures	(4,028)		(1,070)
	$		$
Earnings per share*	(0.62)		(1.36)
Cash flow per share*	(0.55)		(0.64)
	shs		shs
No. of shs. o/s*	22,888,436		22,888,436
Avg. no. of shs. o/s*	22,888,436		19,586,728
	%		%
Net profit margin	n.m.		n.m.
Return on equity	(46.28)		n.m.
Return on assets	(34.31)		(101.94)

* Common
□ Restated
[A] Reported in accordance with IFRS
[1] Results reflect the June 24, 2021, reverse takeover acquisition of Next Hydrogen Corporation.

Latest Results

Periods ended:	6m June 30/23[A]		6m June 30/22[A]
	$000s	%Chg	$000s
Operating revenue	90	+5	86
Net income	(6,335)	n.a.	(7,080)
	$		$
Earnings per share*	(0.28)		(0.31)

* Common
[A] Reported in accordance with IFRS

Historical Summary
(as originally stated)

Fiscal Year	Oper. Rev.	Net Inc. Bef. Disc.	EPS*
	$000s	$000s	$
2022[A]	722	(14,278)	(0.62)
2021[A]	178	(25,008)	(1.28)
2020[A1]	2	(6,851)	(0.77)
2019[A1]	58	(2,651)	(0.62)

* Common
[A] Reported in accordance with IFRS
[1] Results pertain to Next Hydrogen Corporation.

N.46 NexTech AR Solutions Corp.

Symbol - NTAR **Exchange** - NEO **CUSIP** - 65345C
Head Office - PO Box 64039 RPO Royal Bank Plaza, Toronto, ON, M5J 2T6 **Telephone** - (604) 788-5508 **Toll-free** - (866) 274-8493
Website - www.nextechar.com
Email - evan@nextechar.com
Investor Relations - Evan Gappelberg (866) 274-8493
Auditors - Davidson & Company LLP C.A., Vancouver, B.C.
Transfer Agents - Computershare Trust Company of Canada Inc., Vancouver, B.C.
Profile - (B.C. 2018) Develops and markets augmented reality (AR) platforms used in e-commerce, virtual events, higher education learning, corporate training, digital advertising and entertainment.

Products and services include ARitize 3D, a webAR solution for e-commerce and an end-to-end AR platform with content creation, hosting and viewing of AR/3D assets, which give users the ability to embed a 3D model in a product page on an e-commerce website. Available tools within the platform includes ARitize Swirl, a rotating 3D and AR banners on the header or page of an e-commerce website; ARitize Social Swirl, a social media AR filter designed to promote and visualize e-commerce products in an interactive and shareable way; ARitize Ads, an advertisement solution for captivating 3D ads that are interactive, engaging and memorable that can be run on social media and the service provides real-time ad analytics; ARitize CAD, which enables conversion of CAD files into 3D/AR models at scale; ARitize Decorator, which enables customers to virtually preview home furnishing and decor in a desired location, using a simple 2D photo of a room; ARitize Holograms, a human hologram creator mobile app; ARitize CPG (Consumer Packed Goods), an interactive consumer packaged goods AR hologram experience triggered by a visual anchor such as QR code placed on product packaging, in-store aisles or end-cap displays; and ARitize Labs, which allows users to design, build and publish a virtual learning lab, where students can interact and learn in 3D, mimicking a traditional lab environment. Also offers Nextech Event Solutions (formerly Map D), a self-serve visual events platform which allows organizers to create, host and manage live events for more than 100,000 attendees both online and in the company's branded native event application.

Affiliate **Arway Corporation** (48.82% owned) offers ARway.ai, a no-code spatial computing platform, with an augmented reality indoor wayfinding solution for large, multi-purpose venues activated with visual marker tracking.

Affiliate **Toggle3D.ai Inc.** (45.4% owned) offers Toggle3D, a web-based design studio which enables product designers, 3D artists, marketing professionals and e-commerce site owners to create, customize and publish high-quality 3D models and experiences.

In July 2023, the company announced its plan to change its name to **Nextech3D.ai, Inc.**

In June 2023, the company transferred the Toggle3D.ai CAD-3D design studio software-as-a-service (SaaS) platform to wholly owned **Toggle3D.ai Inc.** and spun out Toggle3D.ai Inc. to the company's shareholders. Toggle3D.ai Inc issued a total of 20,000,000 common shares, of which 13,000,000 were retained by the company, representing a 45.4% interest in Toggle3D.ai Inc.; 4,000,000 were distributed to the company's shareholders on a pro rata basis; and 3,000,000 were transferred by the company to certain service providers in consideration of past services and other indebtedness. Toggle3D.ai is an augmented reality (AR) enhanced standalone web application which enables product designers, 3D artists, marketing professionals and e-commerce site owners to create, customize and publish high-quality 3D models and experiences without any technical or 3D design knowledge required. The common shares of Toggle3D.ai Inc. commenced trading on the Canadian Securities Exchange on June 14, 2023.

In March 2023, the company sold its wholly owned **Infinite Pet, LLC**'s assets including infinitepetlife.com, an e-commerce platform that retails health supplements for pets, for US$150,000.

In December 2022, common shares were listed on OTCQX® Best Market under the symbol NEXCF.

The company incorporated wholly owned **Arway Corporation** on July 15, 2022, to facilitate the transfer of the company's ARway mobile application, an augmented reality spatial computing platform, and associated assets to Arway. The transfer was completed in October 2022 and the company spun out Arway, with the company receiving 15,999,900 Arway common shares and shareholders of the company receiving 4,000,000 common shares, which were distributed on a pro rata basis. Immediately following completion of the spin-out, the company transferred 3,000,000 of the Arway common shares to certain service providers; as a result, the company held 13,000,000 Arway common shares (inclusive of 100 shares previously held), representing a 48.82% interest. Arway's common shares commenced trading on the Canadian Securities Exchange effective Oct. 26, 2022.

In June 2022, the company's e-commerce operations that include vacuumcleanermarket.com, which retails residential vacuum cleaners and trulyfesupplements.com, which sells health supplements for humans, were wound down.

Recent Merger and Acquisition Activity

Status: terminated **Revised:** July 5, 2022
UPDATE: The transaction was terminated. PREVIOUS: PC 1 Corp. entered into a letter of intent for the Qualifying Transaction acquisition of the assets of NexTech AR Solutions Corp.'s U.K.-based wholly owned ARWAY Ltd. for issuance of 16,000,000 post-consolidated at a deemed price of 25¢ per share. ARWAY provides ARitize Maps, a smartphone application which allows users to spatially map their location and populate it with interactive 3D objects, navigations, wayfinding, audio and more.

Directors - Evan Gappelberg, founder, chr. & CEO, Fla.; Belinda Tyldesley, corp. sec., B.C.; Dr. David Cramb, Calgary, Alta.; Nidhi Kumra, Toronto, Ont.; Anthony Pizzonia, Toronto, Ont.

Other Exec. Officers - Reza Davariar, COO; Andrew Chan, CFO; Deta Constantine, chief HR officer; Dr. Nima Sarshar, chief tech. officer, visual computing & AI; Rob Christie, sr. v-p, product innovation; Max Hwang, sr. v-p, eng.; Feras Abutaha, v-p, opers.; Melea Guilbault, CEO, Nextech Event Solutions

Capital Stock

	Authorized (shs.)	Outstanding (shs.)[1]
Common	unlimited	109,874,662

[1] At May 18, 2023

Major Shareholder - Evan Gappelberg held 10% interest at Apr. 18, 2023.

Price Range - NTAR/NEO

Year	Volume	High	Low	Close
2022	30,175,950	$1.90	$0.31	$0.78
2021	20,243,938	$7.27	$1.20	$1.30
2020	84,682,097	$10.08	$0.78	$6.70
2019	22,296,153	$3.17	$0.47	$1.88
2018	4,873,662	$1.10	$0.24	$1.00

Recent Close: $0.33

Capital Stock Changes - In January 2023, public offering of 3,614,457 units (1 common share & 1 warrant) at 83¢ per unit was completed, with warrants exercisable at $1.03 per share for four years. In July 2023, private placement of 6,062,390 units (1 common share & 1 warrant) at 42¢ per unit was completed, with warrants exercisable at 52¢ per share for three years.

In January 2022, private placement of 8,130,082 units (1 common share & 1 warrant) at $1.23 per unit was completed. Also during 2022, common shares were issued as follows: 2,972,176 on exercise of warrants and 1,454,420 for services.

Wholly Owned Subsidiaries

AR Ecommerce, LLC, Del.
Arway Ltd., United Kingdom.
Jolokia Corporation, Santa Cruz, Calif.
NexTech AR Solutions USA LLC, Del.
1383947 B.C. Ltd., B.C.
1400330 B.C. Ltd., B.C.
Threedy.ai, Inc., Calif.

Investments

48.82% int. in **Arway Corporation**, Toronto, Ont. (see separate coverage)
45.4% int. in **Toggle3D.ai Inc.**, Toronto, Ont. (see separate coverage)

Financial Statistics

Periods ended:	12m Dec. 31/22[A]		12m Dec. 31/21[□A]
	$000s	%Chg	$000s
Operating revenue	**3,225**	**-52**	**6,690**
Cost of sales	63		nil
Salaries & benefits	11,618		17,883
Research & devel. expense	2,060		2,666
General & admin expense	10,135		10,996
Stock-based compensation	1,716		5,030
Operating expense	**25,592**	**-30**	**36,575**
Operating income	**(22,367)**	**n.a.**	**(29,885)**
Deprec., depl. & amort	2,855		2,210
Write-downs/write-offs	(3,178)		nil
Pre-tax income	**(26,674)**	**n.a.**	**(30,042)**
Income taxes	(637)		(177)
Net inc. bef. disc. opers	**(26,037)**	**n.a.**	**(29,864)**
Income from disc. opers	(1,341)		(2,788)
Net income	**(27,378)**	**n.a.**	**(32,652)**
Net inc. for equity hldrs	**(26,940)**	**n.a.**	**(32,652)**
Net inc. for non-cont. int	**(438)**	**n.a.**	**nil**
Cash & equivalent	3,777		7,237
Inventories	45		3,389
Accounts receivable	744		1,081
Current assets	5,968		12,843
Fixed assets, net	278		377
Right-of-use assets	830		1,079
Intangibles, net	10,060		15,210
Total assets	**17,136**	**-42**	**29,510**
Accts. pay. & accr. liabs	2,642		2,759
Current liabilities	3,394		3,658
Long-term debt, gross	nil		91
Long-term debt, net	nil		91
Long-term lease liabilities	583		787
Shareholders' equity	10,955		24,262
Non-controlling interest	2,174		nil
Cash from oper. activs	**(15,326)**	**n.a.**	**(24,666)**
Cash from fin. activs	12,622		18,894
Cash from invest. activs	(130)		2,568
Net cash position	**3,786**	**-48**	**7,237**
Capital expenditures	(102)		(179)
	$		$
Earns. per sh. bef disc opers*	(0.26)		(0.36)
Earnings per share*	(0.28)		(0.39)
Cash flow per share*	(0.15)		(0.29)
	shs		shs
No. of shs. o/s*	103,437,469		90,880,791
Avg. no. of shs. o/s*	100,201,691		83,888,487
	%		%
Net profit margin	(807.35)		(446.40)
Return on equity	(145.38)		(127.95)
Return on assets	(111.64)		(101.95)

* Common
□ Restated
[A] Reported in accordance with IFRS

Latest Results

Periods ended:	3m Mar. 31/23[A]		3m Mar. 31/22[□A]
	$000s	%Chg	$000s
Operating revenue	1,301	+155	510
Net inc. bef. disc. opers	(6,564)	n.a.	(6,861)
Income from disc. opers	nil		(589)
Net income	(6,564)	n.a.	(7,450)
Net inc. for equity hldrs	(5,864)	n.a.	(7,450)
Net inc. for non-cont. int	(699)		nil
	$		$
Earns. per sh. bef. disc. opers.*	(0.06)		(0.07)
Earnings per share*	(0.06)		(0.08)

* Common
[□] Restated
[A] Reported in accordance with IFRS

Historical Summary
(as originally stated)

Fiscal Year	Oper. Rev.	Net Inc. Bef. Disc.	EPS*
	$000s	$000s	$
2022[A]	3,225	(26,037)	(0.26)
2021[A]	25,935	(32,652)	(0.39)
2020[A]	17,686	(15,594)	(0.23)
2019[A1]	4,004	(5,297)	(0.10)
2019[A]	2,002	(4,668)	(0.11)

* Common
[A] Reported in accordance with IFRS
[1] 7 months ended Dec. 31, 2019.

N.47 NextGen Food Robotics Corp.

Symbol - NGRB **Exchange** - NEO **CUSIP** - 65344X
Head Office - 855 Terminal Ave, Vancouver, BC, V6A 2M9 **Telephone** - (236) 471-1357
Website - originalholycow.com
Email - privas@originalholycow.com
Investor Relations - Paul F. Rivas (236) 471-1357
Auditors - Crowe MacKay LLP C.A., Vancouver, B.C.
Transfer Agents - Odyssey Trust Company, Vancouver, B.C.
Employees - 2 at July 29, 2022
Profile - (B.C. 2016) Operates a commissary and ghost kitchen facility and provides co-packing and private label manufacturing services. Also produces and sells plant-based meat alternative products.

Operates a facility in Vancouver, B.C., which houses a commissary and ghost kitchen providing kitchen space for foodservice providers to prepare, cook, and store food and equipment in exchange for hourly or monthly rents; and as a site for providing co-packing and private label manufacturing services for foods, soups and sauces, including several packaging options such as glass bottles, stand-up pouches and small individual sachets.

Also manufactures products that are made of 50% plant-based and 50% conventional beef ingredients under the brand Holy Cow! which include 50/50 crumble, a ground beef alternative; 50/50 patties, a beef hamburger alternative; and 50/50 meatballs, a beef meatball alternative.

Predecessor Detail - Name changed from Holy Cow Foods Inc., Jan. 24, 2023.

Directors - Paul F. Rivas, pres., CEO & corp. sec., Vancouver, B.C.; Liam Breen, Vancouver, B.C.; Parimal Rana, Vancouver, B.C.; Connor Yuen, Vancouver, B.C.

Other Exec. Officers - Tas Mann, CFO

Capital Stock

	Authorized (shs.)	Outstanding (shs.)[1]
Common	unlimited	37,970,647

[1] At Dec. 15, 2022

Major Shareholder - Paul F. Rivas held 13.17% interest at June 30, 2022.

Price Range - NGRB/NEO

Year	Volume	High	Low	Close
2022	34,000	$0.79	$0.11	$0.15

Recent Close: $0.69

Capital Stock Changes - On Mar. 14, 2022, an initial public offering of 3,677,000 units (1 common share & ½ warrant) at 50¢ per unit was completed. Also in March 2022, 4,089,000 units (1 common share & 1 warrant) were issued without further consideration on exchange of special warrants sold in March 2021 at $0.10 each and 3,216,047 units (1 common share & 1 warrant) were issued without further consideration on exchange of special warrants sold in August 2021 at $0.85 each. Also during fiscal 2022, 30,500 common shares were issued on exercise of warrants.

Financial Statistics

Periods ended:	12m Apr. 30/22[A]		7m Apr. 30/21[A]
	$000s	%Chg	$000s
Salaries & benefits	174		5
General & admin expense	707		157
Stock-based compensation	nil		83
Other operating expense	50		nil
Operating expense	**757**	**n.a.**	**245**
Operating income	**(757)**	**n.a.**	**(245)**
Deprec., depl. & amort	163		nil
Finance income	7		1
Finance costs, gross	86		nil
Write-downs/write-offs	(189)		nil
Pre-tax income	**(1,361)**	**n.a.**	**(244)**
Net income	**(1,361)**	**n.a.**	**(244)**
Cash & equivalent	2,874		1,074
Inventories	nil		17
Accounts receivable	31		6
Current assets	3,142		1,100
Long-term investments	20		nil
Fixed assets, net	645		2
Right-of-use assets	947		nil
Total assets	**4,754**	**+331**	**1,102**
Accts. pay. & accr. liabs	198		40
Current liabilities	333		48
Long-term lease liabilities	722		nil
Shareholders' equity	3,698		1,054
Cash from oper. activs	**(1,196)**	**n.a.**	**(148)**
Cash from fin. activs	3,676		1,224
Cash from invest. activs	(681)		(2)
Net cash position	**2,874**	**+168**	**1,074**
Capital expenditures	(661)		(2)
	$		$
Earnings per share*	(0.05)		(0.01)
Cash flow per share*	(0.04)		(0.01)
	shs		shs
No. of shs. o/s*	37,968,147		26,955,600
Avg. no. of shs. o/s*	28,471,485		16,318,182
	%		%
Net profit margin	n.a.		...
Return on equity	(57.28)		...
Return on assets	(43.55)		...

* Common
[A] Reported in accordance with IFRS

Latest Results

Periods ended:	6m Oct. 31/22[A]		6m Oct. 31/21[A]
	$000s	%Chg	$000s
Operating revenue	44	n.a.	nil
Net income	(584)	n.a.	(523)
	$		$
Earnings per share*	(0.02)		(0.02)

* Common
[A] Reported in accordance with IFRS

N.48 Nextleaf Solutions Ltd.

Symbol - OILS **Exchange** - CSE **CUSIP** - 65347A
Head Office - 304-68 Water St, Vancouver, BC, V6B 1A4 **Telephone** - (604) 283-2301 **Fax** - (604) 357-1030
Website - www.nextleafsolutions.com
Email - paul@nextleafsolutions.com
Investor Relations - E. Paul Pedersen (604) 283-2301 ext. 205
Auditors - Davidson & Company LLP C.A., Vancouver, B.C.
Lawyers - Fasken Martineau DuMoulin LLP, Vancouver, B.C.; Beadle Raven LLP, Vancouver, B.C.
Transfer Agents - Odyssey Trust Company, Vancouver, B.C.
Profile - (B.C. 2016) Manufactures and distributes tetrahydrocannabinol and cannabidiol products using a proprietary technology for cannabinoid extraction, distillation and acetylation.

Has developed a proprietary technology for a closed-loop, industrial-scale process of producing purified cannabinoid distillate concentrate best suited for infusing premium value-added products. Distillate produced through the company's process is suitable for various formulations and cannabis products, such as vapes, beverages, edibles and topicals. The company commercializes its technology through licensing agreements with third parties; providing toll processing services to cannabis and hemp operators and supplying the produced cannabis oils to wholesale customers; and distribution of cannabis consumer products such as cannabinoid vapes, oils and softgels under the Glacial Gold™ and High Plains™ brand through retail and online channels.

Predecessor Detail - Name changed from Legion Metals Corp., Mar. 14, 2019, pursuant to reverse takeover acquisition of private Vancouver, B.C.-based Nextleaf Solutions Ltd. on a share-for-share basis.; basis 1 new for 3.5 old shs.

Directors - E. Paul Pedersen, pres. & CEO, Vancouver, B.C.; Kevin Keagan, CFO & corp. sec., Aurora, Ont.; Fred Bonner, Halifax, N.S.; Dr. Sherry Boodram, Toronto, Ont.

Other Exec. Officers - Ryan Ko, v-p, innov. & tech.

Capital Stock

	Authorized (shs.)	Outstanding (shs.)[1]
Common	unlimited	145,492,390

[1] At Jan. 30, 2023

Major Shareholder - Widely held at June 29, 2022.

Price Range - OILS/CSE

Year	Volume	High	Low	Close
2022	39,207,089	$0.21	$0.04	$0.05
2021	77,392,901	$0.42	$0.17	$0.18
2020	66,561,706	$0.45	$0.14	$0.18
2019	125,475,267	$0.83	$0.26	$0.40
2018	508,486	$0.74	$0.18	$0.60

Consolidation: 1-for-3.5 cons. in Mar. 2019
Recent Close: $0.05

Capital Stock Changes - In December 2021, public offering of 15,844,208 units (1 common share & ½ warrant) at 20¢ per unit was completed, including 2,376,631 common shares on exercise of over-allotment option. Also during fiscal 2022, common shares were issued as follows: 1,009,900 for services, 720,074 for debt settlement and 500,000 as finders' fee.

Wholly Owned Subsidiaries

Nextleaf Innovations Ltd., Vancouver, B.C.
Nextleaf Labs Ltd., B.C.

Financial Statistics

Periods ended:	12m Sept. 30/22[A]		12m Sept. 30/21[□A]
	$000s	%Chg	$000s
Operating revenue	**4,410**	**+31**	**3,379**
Cost of sales	3,659		3,387
Salaries & benefits	1,452		1,519
Research & devel. expense	11		38
General & admin expense	1,904		1,733
Stock-based compensation	7		430
Operating expense	**7,033**	**-1**	**7,107**
Operating income	**(2,623)**	**n.a.**	**(3,728)**
Deprec., depl. & amort	921		1,210
Finance costs, gross	476		381
Pre-tax income	**(3,487)**	**n.a.**	**(5,385)**
Net income	**(3,487)**	**n.a.**	**(5,385)**
Cash & equivalent	378		915
Inventories	1,538		1,824
Accounts receivable	839		1,060
Current assets	2,780		3,961
Fixed assets, net	3,900		4,693
Intangibles, net	324		481
Total assets	**7,152**	**-22**	**9,193**
Accts. pay. & accr. liabs	2,774		2,477
Current liabilities	3,819		5,407
Long-term debt, gross	1,044		2,892
Long-term debt, net	40		40
Long-term lease liabilities	278		319
Shareholders' equity	3,015		3,427
Cash from oper. activs	**(802)**	**n.a.**	**(2,870)**
Cash from fin. activs	373		2,819
Cash from invest. activs	(109)		(21)
Net cash position	**377**	**-59**	**915**
Capital expenditures	(109)		(66)
Capital disposals	nil		48
	$		$
Earnings per share*	(0.03)		(0.04)
Cash flow per share*	(0.01)		(0.02)
	shs		shs
No. of shs. o/s*	143,392,390		125,318,208
Avg. no. of shs. o/s*	138,365,006		122,921,939
	%		%
Net profit margin	(79.07)		(159.37)
Return on equity	(108.26)		(100.76)
Return on assets	(36.84)		(52.75)

* Common
[□] Restated
[A] Reported in accordance with IFRS

Historical Summary
(as originally stated)

Fiscal Year	Oper. Rev.	Net Inc. Bef. Disc.	EPS*
	$000s	$000s	$
2022[A]	4,410	(3,487)	(0.03)
2021[A]	3,379	(5,385)	(0.04)
2020[A]	691	(5,954)	(0.05)
2019[A1]	nil	(8,746)	(0.10)
2018[A2]	nil	(279)	(0.11)

* Common
[A] Reported in accordance with IFRS
[1] Results reflect the Mar. 14, 2019, reverse takeover acquisition of private Vancouver, B.C.-based Nextleaf Solutions Ltd.
[2] Results for fiscal 2018 and prior year pertain to Legion Metals Corp.
Note: Adjusted throughout for 1-for-3.5 cons. in Mar. 2019

N.49 NextPoint Financial Inc.

Symbol - NPF.U **Exchange** - TSX (S) **CUSIP** - 65345F
Head Office - 500 Grapevine Hwy, Suite 402, Hurst, TX, United States, 76054 **Telephone** - (914) 614-5626
Website - nextpointacquisition.com
Email - investorrelations@nxtpt.com
Investor Relations - Raymond Guba (914) 614-5626
Auditors - Deloitte LLP C.P.A., Richmond, Va.
Lawyers - Blake, Cassels & Graydon LLP, Toronto, Ont.
Transfer Agents - TSX Trust Company, Toronto, Ont.
Profile - (B.C. 2020) Provides financial services to consumers and small businesses.

Wholly owned **Liberty Tax** provides institutional tax preparation services in the U.S. and Canada. Liberty's core products include tax preparation for individuals and small businesses, and tax-related financial products such as prepaid debit cards and refund transfer products. Services are offered at 2,700 franchised and owned locations as well as through online solutions.

Wholly owned **LoanMe, Inc.** is a tech-enabled consumer and small business lender that has originated more than US$2 billion loans on behalf of more than 340,000 borrowers.

Common suspended from TSX, May 25, 2022.

Predecessor Detail - Name changed from NextPoint Acquisition Corp., July 2, 2021, pursuant to the Qualifying Acquisition of Liberty Tax and LoanMe, Inc.

Directors - Nik Ajagu, Calif.; Maryann Bruce, N.C.; William Minner, Pa.; Alicia Morga, Calif.; Logan Powell, R.I.; Dan Shribman, Conn.; Don Turkleson, Tex.

Other Exec. Officers - Scott Terrell, interim CEO & COO; Raymond (Randy) Guba, CFO; Ghazi Dakik, chief legal & compliance office; Juliet Diiorio, chief mktg. officer; Brooke Janousek, sr. v-p, brand mktg.; Kyle Sawai, sr. v-p, digital mktg.; Steve She, sr. v-p, analytics; Kevin Ortiz, v-p, corp. devel.; Jonathan Williams, pres., lending

Capital Stock

	Authorized (shs.)	Outstanding (shs.)[1]
Common	unlimited	20,565,849
Proportionate Vtg.	unlimited	168,550

[1] At Feb. 28, 2023

Common - One vote per share.

Proportionate Voting - Convertible, at the holder's option, into common shares on the basis of 100 common shares for 1 proportionate share. 100 votes per share.

Major Shareholder - Franchise Group, Inc. held 18.17% interest, Andrew (Andy) Neuberger held 11.78% interest and Omega Capital Partners, LP held 10.69% interest at Aug. 29, 2022.

Price Range - NPF.U/TSX (S)

Year	Volume	High	Low	Close
2022	366,370	US$5.67	US$1.79	US$3.00
2021	4,720,370	US$11.29	US$3.90	US$5.10
2020	2,557,786	US$10.00	US$9.50	US$9.99

Wholly Owned Subsidiaries

NPI Holdco LLC, Del.
- 100% int. in **Franchise Group Intermediate L1, LLC**, Del.
  - 100% int. in **Franchise Group Intermediate L2, LLC**, Del.
    - 100% int. in **JTH Tax LLC**, Del.
      - 100% int. in **Community Tax LLC**, Chicago, Ill.
      - 100% int. in **JTH Court Plaza, LLC**, Va.
      - 100% int. in **JTH Financial LLC**, Va.
        - 100% int. in **JTH Properties 1622, LLC**, Va.
      - 100% int. in **JTH Tax Office Properties LLC**, Va.
      - 100% int. in **LTS Properties LLC**, Va.
      - 100% int. in **LTS Software LLC**, Va.
      - 100% int. in **Liberty Credit Repair**, Va.
      - 100% int. in **Liberty Tax Holding Corporation**, Canada.
        - 40% int. in **Liberty Tax Service, Inc.**, Canada.
          - 18.3% int. in **Trilogy Software Inc.**, Calgary, Alta.
      - 60% int. in **Liberty Tax Service, Inc.**, Canada.
        - 18.3% int. in **Trilogy Software Inc.**, Calgary, Alta.
      - 100% int. in **360 Accounting Solutions, LLC**, Va.
      - 100% int. in **Wefile LLC**, Va.
    - 100% int. in **SiempreTax LLC**, Va.
- 100% int. in **NPLM Holdco LLC**, Del.
  - 100% int. in **LoanMe, LLC**, Del.
    - 100% int. in **InsightsLogic LLC**, Del.
    - 100% int. in **LM BP Holdings LLC**, Del.
      - 100% int. in **LM 2014 BP SPE LLC**, Del.
      - 100% int. in **LM 2014 BP II SPE LLC**, Del.
      - 100% int. in **LM 2015 BP SPE LLC**, Del.
    - 100% int. in **LM Retention Holdings LLC**, Del.
      - 27.65% int. in **LoanMe Trust Prime 2018-1**, Del.
      - 100% int. in **LoanMe Trust SBL 2019-1**, Del.
    - 100% int. in **LM 2014 BP III SPE LLC**, Del.
    - 100% int. in **LM 2014 HC SPE LLC**, Del.
    - 100% int. in **LM 2015 NLP SPE LLC**, Del.
    - 100% int. in **LM 2015 NLP II SPE LLC**, Del.
    - 100% int. in **LM 2015 PWB I LLC**, Del.
    - 100% int. in **LM 2016 NLP SPE LLC**, Del.
    - 100% int. in **LM 2017 NLP SPE LLC**, Del.
    - 100% int. in **LM 2020 CM I SPE LLC**, Del.
    - 100% int. in **LoanMe Funding, LLC**, Del.

N.50 Nexus Industrial REIT

Symbol - NXR.UN **Exchange** - TSX **CUSIP** - 65344U
Head Office - 211-1540 Cornwall Rd, Oakville, ON, L6J 7W5 **Telephone** - (416) 906-2379 **Fax** - (416) 863-2653
Website - www.nexusreit.com
Email - khanczyk@nexusreit.com
Investor Relations - Kelly C. Hanczyk (416) 906-2379
Auditors - PricewaterhouseCoopers LLP C.A., Toronto, Ont.
Lawyers - Blake, Cassels & Graydon LLP, Toronto, Ont.
Transfer Agents - TSX Trust Company, Toronto, Ont.
Managers - Edgefront Realty Advisors Limited Partnership, Toronto, Ont.
FP500 Revenue Ranking - 727
Employees - 19 at Dec. 31, 2022
Profile - (Ont. 2013) Owns and operates industrial, office and retail properties in western Canada, Ontario, Quebec, New Brunswick and Prince Edward Island, with a primary focus on industrial properties.

The trust's property portfolio consists of 82 industrial (including two properties held for development), 18 retail (includes 1 mixed-use property) and 13 office properties in western Canada, Ontario, Quebec and Atlantic Canada totaling 13,085,579 sq. ft., of which the trust's proportionate interest is 11,605,286 sq. ft.

Type	Sq. ft.
Industrial	10,187,717
Retail	2,117,784
Office	780,078
	13,085,579

Geographic composition at Mar. 31, 2023:

Location	Props.
Northwest Territories	1
British Columbia	5
Alberta	26
Saskatchewan	11
Quebec[1]	40
Ontario	25
New Brunswick	4
Manitoba	1
	113

[1] Includes 50% ownership interest in 25 properties.

In December 2022, the trust sold a retail property in Charlottetown, P.E.I., for $955,000.

In September 2022, the trust acquired a 34,800-sq.-ft. single-tenant industrial property in Cornwall, Ont., for $4,850,000.

In July 2022, the trust acquired a 80% interest in a property held for development in Hamilton, Ont., for $4,846,000.

Recent Merger and Acquisition Activity

Status: completed **Announced:** Apr. 26, 2023
Nexus Industrial REIT sold a retail property in Victoriaville, Que., for $40,300,000.

Status: completed **Announced:** Apr. 21, 2023
Nexus Industrial REIT acquired a 264,600-sq.-ft. industrial property in London, Ont., for $36,000,000.

Status: completed **Announced:** Mar. 7, 2023
Nexus Industrial REIT acquired a 532,000-sq.-ft. newly constructed distribution centre in Casselman, Ont., for $116,800,000.

Status: completed **Announced:** Nov. 1, 2022
Nexus Industrial REIT acquired three industrial properties in Windsor, Ont., and one industrial property in Tilbury, Ont., totalling 435,871 sq. ft. of gross leasable area, for $38,875,000.

Status: completed **Announced:** Oct. 4, 2022
Nexus Industrial REIT sold a retail property in Longueuil, Que., for $11,850,000.

Status: completed **Announced:** Sept. 8, 2022
Nexus Industrial REIT acquired a 74,681-sq.-ft. single-tenant industrial property in Baie-D'Urfe, Que., for $17,800,000.

Status: completed **Announced:** Aug. 3, 2022
Nexus Industrial REIT sold a retail property in Châteauguay, Que., for $8,300,000. The transaction was satisfied through assumption of mortgage financing and cash on hand.

Status: completed **Announced:** July 11, 2022
Nexus Industrial REIT acquired a 94,000-sq.-ft. single-tenant industrial property in St-Augustin-de-Desmaures, Que., for $18,875,000.

Status: completed **Announced:** June 22, 2022
Nexus Industrial REIT acquired a 80% interest in a a property held for development in Hamilton, Ont., for $17,760,000. The development is partially owned, and managed, by entities controlled by RFA Capital Partners Inc.(RFA), an entity related to a trustee of Nexus. Pursuant to the acquisition, the vendor provided financing in the amount of $15,360,000 repayable within 18 to 24 months.

Status: completed **Announced:** Mar. 1, 2022
Nexus Real Estate Investment Trust acquired three industrial properties totaling 340,320 sq. ft. in London, Ont., for $35,700,000, which partially satisfied through the issuance of 1,565,394 Class B LP units.

Status: completed **Announced:** Mar. 1, 2022
Nexus Real Estate Investment Trust acquired a 72,420-sq.-ft. industrial property in Edmonton, Alta., for $14,600,000.

Predecessor Detail - Name changed from Nexus Real Estate Investment Trust, Mar. 7, 2022.

Trustees - Ben Rodney, chr., Toronto, Ont.; Kelly C. Hanczyk, CEO, Oakville, Ont.; Floriana G. Cipollone, Mississauga, Ont.; Bradley (Brad) Cutsey, Mississauga, Ont.; Justine Delisle, Montréal, Qué.; Louie DiNunzio, Toronto, Ont.

Other Exec. Officers - Robert P. (Rob) Chiasson, CFO & corp. sec.

Capital Stock

	Authorized (shs.)	Outstanding (shs.)[1]
Trust Unit	unlimited	68,004,000
Special Voting Unit		19,862,000
Class B LP Unit		19,862,000[2]

[1] At May 12, 2023

[2] Securities of limited partnerships of REIT

Trust Unit - The trust will endeavour to make monthly cash distributions with a yield of 8% per annum. One vote per trust unit.

Special Voting Unit - Non-participating. Issued to holders of class B limited partnership units of limited partnerships of the trust. Each special voting unit entitles the holder to a number of votes at unitholder meetings equal to the number of trust units into which the class B limited partnership units are exchangeable.

Class B Limited Partnership Unit - Entitled to distributions equal to those provided to trust units or equivalent to 1.67 times of those to trust units. Directly exchangeable into trust units on a 1-for-1 basis at any time by holder. Puttable instruments classified as financial liabilities under IFRS.

Major Shareholder - 1803299 Ontario Inc. held 15.3% interest at Mar. 27, 2023.

Price Range - NXR.UN/TSX

Year	Volume	High	Low	Close
2022	35,285,001	$14.03	$8.15	$9.64
2021	24,024,582	$13.63	$7.50	$12.62
2020	8,038,461	$9.40	$4.36	$7.72
2019	10,409,069	$8.72	$7.08	$8.68
2018	4,105,653	$8.32	$7.24	$7.56

Consolidation: 1-for-4 cons. in Feb. 2021
Recent Close: $7.91

Capital Stock Changes - In December 2022, bought deal public offering of 8,225,000 trust units was completed at $10.30 per unit, including 925,000 trust units on exercise of over-allotment option. Also during 2022, trust units were issued as follows: 1,317,478 on exchange of a like number of class B limited partnership units, 277,649 under distribution reinvestment plan, 144,714 on exercise of options, 35,755 under restricted share unit plan and 19,419 under employee purchase plan.

Dividends

NXR.UN tr unit Ra $0.64 pa M est. Mar. 14, 2014**
Listed Feb 1/21.
1-for-4 cons eff. Feb. 1, 2021
** Reinvestment Option

Wholly Owned Subsidiaries

Edgefront Barrie GP Inc., Barrie, Ont.
- 0.01% int. in **Edgefront Barrie Limited Partnership**, Barrie, Ont.

Edgefront GP Inc., Ont.
- 0.01% int. in **Edgefront Limited Partnership**, Toronto, Ont.

Edgefront West GP Inc., Alta.
- 0.01% int. in **Edgefront West Limited Partnership**, Baden, Ont.
- 0.01% int. in **Edgefront West 2 L.P.**, Alta.

Nobel Real Estate Investment Trust, Montréal, Qué.
Nobel REIT GP Inc., Canada.
- 100% int. in **Nobel REIT Limited Partnership**, Montréal, Qué.
  - 100% int. in **Capital Nobel Inc.**, Montréal, Qué.
  - 100% int. in **Nexus Richmond GP Inc.**, Ont.
    - 100% int. in **Nexus Richmond LP**, Ont.
  - 50% int. in **9301-6897 Quebec Inc.**, Qué.
  - 100% int. in **RFA 844 Glancaster Road LP**, Ont.

1767366 Alberta Ltd.
1834585 Alberta Ltd., Alta.

Subsidiaries

99.99% int. in **Edgefront Barrie Limited Partnership**, Barrie, Ont.
99.99% int. in **Edgefront Limited Partnership**, Toronto, Ont.
- 100% int. in **Edgefront Realty Corp.**

99.99% int. in **Edgefront West Limited Partnership**, Baden, Ont.
99.99% int. in **Edgefront West 2 L.P.**, Alta.
99.99% int. in **RW Real Estate Holdings Limited Parnership**

Financial Statistics

Periods ended:	12m Dec. 31/22[A]		12m Dec. 31/21[A]
	$000s	%Chg	$000s
Total revenue	**137,121**	**+64**	**83,559**
Rental operating expense	41,313		27,607
General & admin. expense	6,517		4,855
Operating expense	**47,830**	**+47**	**32,462**
Operating income	**89,291**	**+75**	**51,097**
Investment income	1,797		917
Finance costs, net	42,171		24,161
Pre-tax income	**120,868**	**+29**	**93,539**
Net income	**120,868**	**+29**	**93,539**
Cash & equivalent	11,533		82,279
Accounts receivable	5,944		2,747
Current assets	107,681		97,516
Long-term investments	10,975		9,178
Income-producing props	1,822,639		1,545,866
Property interests, net	1,822,639		1,545,866
Right-of-use assets	993		1,086
Total assets	**1,967,501**	**+19**	**1,658,157**
Accts. pay. & accr. liabs	25,941		25,939
Current liabilities	132,878		87,220
Long-term debt, gross	1,012,423		924,026
Long-term debt, net	942,013		865,874
Long-term lease liabilities	10,495		3,597
Shareholders' equity	872,540		689,484
Cash from oper. activs	**41,530**	**+66**	**24,995**
Cash from fin. activs	203,451		512,545
Cash from invest. activs	(315,727)		(469,254)
Net cash position	**11,533**	**-86**	**82,279**
Capital expenditures	(11,213)		(5,373)
Increase in property	(312,233)		(477,176)
Decrease in property	7,719		13,295
	$		$
Earnings per share*	n.a.		n.a.
Cash flow per share*	0.62		0.44
Funds from opers. per sh.*	0.81		0.76
Adj. funds from opers. per sh.*	0.70		0.69
Cash divd. per share*	0.64		0.64
Total divd. per share*	**0.64**		**0.64**
	shs		shs
No. of shs. o/s*	67,322,644		57,302,629
	%		%
Net profit margin	88.15		111.94
Return on equity	15.48		18.91
Return on assets	6.67		7.90
No. of employees (FTEs)	19		15

* Trust Unit
[A] Reported in accordance with IFRS

Latest Results

Periods ended:	3m Mar. 31/23[A]		3m Mar. 31/22[A]
	$000s	%Chg	$000s
Total revenue	37,476	+18	31,699
Net income	3,717	-79	18,064
	$		$
Earnings per share*	n.a.		n.a.

[A] Reported in accordance with IFRS

Historical Summary
(as originally stated)

Fiscal Year	Total Rev. $000s	Net Inc. Bef. Disc. $000s	EPS* $
2022[A]	137,121	120,868	n.a.
2021[A]	83,559	93,539	n.a.
2020[A]	61,386	35,235	n.a.
2019[A]	60,010	42,388	n.a.
2018[A]	54,097	38,834	n.a.

* Trust Unit
[A] Reported in accordance with IFRS
Note: Adjusted throughout for 1-for-4 cons. in Feb. 2021

N.51 Nicholas Financial, Inc.

Symbol - NICK **Exchange** - NASDAQ **CUSIP** - 65373J
Head Office - 2454 McMullen Booth Rd, Bldg C, Suite 501-B, Clearwater, FL, United States, 33759 **Telephone** - (727) 726-0763 **Fax** - (727) 726-2140
Website - www.nicholasfinancial.com
Email - investorservices@nicfn.com
Investor Relations - Irina Nashtatik (727) 726-0763
Auditors - RSM US LLP C.P.A., Raleigh, N.C.
Lawyers - Hill Ward Henderson, Tampa, Fla.
Transfer Agents - Computershare Trust Company of Canada Inc., Vancouver, B.C.
Employees - 278 at Mar. 31, 2022
Profile - (B.C. 1986) Provides specialized consumer finance primarily in acquiring and servicing automobile finance instalment contracts for purchases of used and new automobiles and light trucks. Also offers direct consumer loans and sells consumer-finance related products.

Provides automobile financing through 47 branch offices in Alabama (2), Florida (11), Georgia (5), Idaho (1), Illinois (1), Indiana (2), Kentucky (3), Michigan (2), Missouri (2), Nevada (1), North Carolina (3), Ohio (6), Pennsylvania (1), South Carolina (3), Tennessee (1), Texas (1), Utah (1) and Wisconsin (1). Also operates non-branch expansion efforts in the Arizona, Kansas and Texas markets. At Mar. 31, 2022, the company held non-exclusive agreements with about 13,000 automobile dealers, of which 9,000 were active, to purchase instalment sales contracts. Active agreements are those purchased by the company within the last six months. At Mar. 31, 2022, average finance receivables, net of unearned interest, totaled US$178,686,000.

In addition, originates direct loans in Alabama, Florida, Georgia, Illionois, Indiana, Kansas, Kentucky, Michigan, Missouri, North Carolina, Ohio, Pennsylvania, South Carolina and Tennessee. These loans are originated directly with the consumer, typically range from US$500 to US$11,000, and are generally secured by a lien on an automobile, watercraft or other permissible tangible personal property.

In July 2022, the company announced the closure of 11 branches.

During fiscal 2022, the company opened a branch in Boise, Idaho, and Houston Tex.

Predecessor Detail - Name changed from Nicholas Data Services Ltd., Aug. 9, 1993.

Directors - Jeffrey C. Royal, chr., Omaha, Neb.; Mark Hutchins; Brendan Keating; Adam K. Peterson, Omaha, Neb.; Jeremy Q. Zhu, Los Angeles, Calif.

Other Exec. Officers - Michael (Mike) Rost, interim CEO; Irina Nashtatik, CFO

Capital Stock

	Authorized (shs.)	Outstanding (shs.)[1]
Preferred	5,000,000	nil
Common	50,000,000	12,600,000

[1] At July 26, 2022

Major Shareholder - Adam K. Peterson held 33.17% interest at July 29, 2022.

Price Range - NICK/NASDAQ

Year	Volume	High	Low	Close
2022	526,845	US$11.93	US$5.23	US$6.31
2021	663,354	US$12.48	US$8.17	US$11.79
2020	623,333	US$9.09	US$4.64	US$8.38
2019	542,755	US$11.28	US$8.07	US$8.24
2018	609,242	US$12.50	US$8.36	US$10.40

Capital Stock Changes - During fiscal 2022, common shares were issued as follows: 18,000 on grants of restricted share awards and 2,000 on exercise of options; 182,000 common shares were repurchased and held in treasury.

Wholly Owned Subsidiaries

Nicholas Data Services, Inc., Fla. Inactive.
- 100% int. in **Nicholas Financial, Inc.**, Fla.
  - 100% int. in **NF Funding I, LLC**, Fla.

Financial Statistics

Periods ended:	12m Mar. 31/22[A]		12m Mar. 31/21[oA]
	US$000s	%Chg	US$000s
Realized invest. gain (loss)	nil		1,809
Total revenue	**49,779**	**-11**	**56,020**
Salaries & benefits	20,050		19,083
General & admin. expense	13,951		12,517
Operating expense	**34,001**	**+8**	**31,600**
Operating income	**15,778**	**-35**	**24,420**
Deprec. & amort	401		244
Finance costs, gross	5,366		5,980
Pre-tax income	**4,046**	**-63**	**10,946**
Income taxes	1,048		2,595
Net income	**2,998**	**-64**	**8,351**
Cash & equivalent	4,775		22,022
Investments	168,600		170,318
Fixed assets, net	1,783		859
Right-of-use assets	4,277		3,392
Total assets	**183,570**	**-14**	**212,438**
Accts. pay. & accr. liabs	4,717		4,451
Debt	58,057		89,398
Lease liabilities	4,410		3,367
Shareholders' equity	116,386		115,222
Cash from oper. activs	**3,487**	**-76**	**14,403**
Cash from fin. activs	(35,551)		(36,191)
Cash from invest. activs	3,862		30,081
Net cash position	**4,775**	**-86**	**32,977**
Capital expenditures	(1,312)		(615)
Capital disposals	7		20
	US$		US$
Earnings per share*	0.39		1.09
Cash flow per share*	0.46		1.89
	shs		shs
No. of shs. o/s*	7,546,000		7,708,000
Avg. no. of shs. o/s*	7,572,000		7,626,000
	%		%
Net profit margin	6.02		14.91
Return on equity	2.59		7.50
Return on assets	3.52		5.72
No. of employees (FTEs)	278		261

* Common
[o] Restated
[A] Reported in accordance with U.S. GAAP

Latest Results

Periods ended:	3m June 30/22[A]		3m June 30/21[A]
	US$000s	%Chg	US$000s
Total revenue	11,277	-10	12,594
Net income	(1,777)	n.a.	1,729
	US$		US$
Earnings per share*	(0.24)		0.22

* Common
[A] Reported in accordance with U.S. GAAP

Historical Summary
(as originally stated)

Fiscal Year	Total Rev. US$000s	Net Inc. Bef. Disc. US$000s	EPS* US$
2022[A]	49,779	2,998	0.39
2021[A]	56,020	8,351	1.09
2020[A]	62,095	3,466	0.45
2019[A]	71,300	(3,648)	(0.46)
2018[A]	83,917	(1,098)	(0.14)

* Common
[A] Reported in accordance with U.S. GAAP

N.52 Nirvana Life Sciences Inc.

Symbol - NIRV **Exchange** - CSE **CUSIP** - 654652
Head Office - 2110-650 Georgia St W, Vancouver, BC, V6B 4N8 **Telephone** - (604) 401-8100
Website - nirvanalifescience.com
Email - ceoinfo@nirvanalifescience.com
Investor Relations - Bruce Clark (604) 401-8100
Auditors - Dale Matheson Carr-Hilton LaBonte LLP C.A., Vancouver, B.C.
Transfer Agents - Computershare Trust Company of Canada Inc., Vancouver, B.C.
Profile - (B.C. 2011) Develops novel therapeutic products derived from psychedelics for pain management as well as the treatment for ailments such as addiction, anxiety and depression.

Recent Merger and Acquisition Activity

Status: completed **Revised:** Mar. 17, 2022
UPDATE: The transaction was completed. Endocan changed its name to Nirvana Life Sciences Inc. and (old) Nirvana's name was changed to 1253766 B.C. Ltd. PREVIOUS: Endocan Solutions Inc. agreed to the reverse takeover acquisition of private Vancouver, B.C.-based Nirvana Life Sciences Inc., which develops novel therapeutic products derived from psychedelics for pain management as well as the treatment for

ailments such as addiction, anxiety and depression, on a share-for-share basis, which would result in the issuance of 39,827,095 common shares at a deemed price of 25¢ per share. Aug. 16, 2021 - Terms of the transaction were amended whereby Endocan would issue 39,455,095 common shares. Jan. 10, 2022 - Terms of the transaction were further amended whereby Endocan would issue 25,905,095 common shares.

Predecessor Detail - Name changed from Endocan Solutions Inc., Mar. 10, 2022, pursuant to the reverse takeover acquisition of (old) Nirvana Life Sciences Inc. (concurrently renamed 1253766 B.C. Ltd.).

Directors - Bruce Clark, pres. & CEO, Vancouver, B.C.; Annie Storey, CFO, Burnaby, B.C.; Sheldon Inwentash, Toronto, Ont.; Mark Marissen, Vancouver, B.C.

Other Exec. Officers - Michael McCune, COO; Dr. Sazzad Hossain, chief technical officer; Gordon J. (Gord) Fretwell, corp. sec.

Capital Stock

	Authorized (shs.)	Outstanding (shs.)[1]
Common	unlimited	34,033,010

[1] At Dec. 30, 2022

Major Shareholder - Dr. Sazzad Hossain held 11.81% interest at Mar. 17, 2022.

Price Range - NIRV/CSE

Year	Volume	High	Low	Close
2022	13,147,872	$0.95	$0.12	$0.15

Recent Close: $0.07

Capital Stock Changes - On Mar. 17, 2022, 25,905,095 common shares were issued pursuant to the reverse takeover acquisition of (old) Nirvana Life Sciences Inc. (concurrently renamed 1253766 B.C. Ltd.).

Wholly Owned Subsidiaries

1253766 B.C. Ltd., Vancouver, B.C.

Financial Statistics

Periods ended:	12m Apr. 30/22[A1]		10m Apr. 30/21[□A]
	$000s	%Chg	$000s
Research & devel. expense	321		328
General & admin expense	447		191
Operating expense	**768**	**n.a.**	**519**
Operating income	**(768)**	**n.a.**	**(519)**
Finance income	12		nil
Pre-tax income	**(5,657)**	**n.a.**	**(612)**
Net income	**(5,657)**	**n.a.**	**(612)**
Net inc. for equity hldrs	**(5,654)**	**n.a.**	**(612)**
Net inc. for non-cont. int	**(2)**	**n.a.**	**nil**
Cash & equivalent	36		625
Current assets	144		769
Fixed assets, net	343		434
Total assets	**487**	**-60**	**1,203**
Accts. pay. & accr. liabs	106		18
Current liabilities	648		18
Shareholders' equity	(162)		1,185
Cash from oper. activs	**(490)**	**n.a.**	**(544)**
Cash from fin. activs	2		1,727
Cash from invest. activs	(101)		(558)
Net cash position	**36**	**-94**	**625**
Capital expenditures	nil		(458)
	$		$
Earnings per share*	(0.16)		n.a.
Cash flow per share*	(0.01)		n.a.
	shs		shs
No. of shs. o/s*	33,020,139		n.a.
Avg. no. of shs. o/s*	36,520,229		n.a.
	%		%
Net profit margin	n.a.		...
Return on equity	n.m.		...
Return on assets	n.m.		...

* Common
□ Restated
[A] Reported in accordance with IFRS
[1] Results reflect the Mar. 17, 2022, reverse takeover acquisition of Nirvana Life Sciences Inc.

Latest Results

Periods ended:	6m Oct. 31/22[A]		6m Oct. 31/21[A]
	$000s	%Chg	$000s
Net income	(549)	n.a.	(369)
	$		$
Earnings per share*	(0.02)		n.a.

* Common
[A] Reported in accordance with IFRS

Historical Summary
(as originally stated)

Fiscal Year	Oper. Rev.	Net Inc. Bef. Disc.	EPS*
	$000s	$000s	$
2022[A]	nil	(5,657)	(0.16)
2021[A1]	nil	(254)	(0.05)
2020[A1]	nil	(314)	(0.07)
2019[A1]	nil	13	0.01

* Common
[A] Reported in accordance with IFRS
[1] Results pertain to Endocan Solutions Inc.

N.53 Noble Iron Inc.

Symbol - NIR.H **Exchange** - TSX-VEN **CUSIP** - 655056
Head Office - 330-7 871 Victoria St N, Kitchener, ON, N2B 3S4 **Telephone** - (519) 840-2123 **Toll-free** - (800) 361-1233 **Fax** - (519) 836-1738
Website - www.nobleiron.com
Email - mariam.chaudhry@nobleiron.com
Investor Relations - Mariam Chaudhry (866) 762-9475
Auditors - RSM Canada LLP C.A., Toronto, Ont.
Lawyers - Wildeboer Dellelce LLP, Toronto, Ont.
Transfer Agents - Computershare Trust Company of Canada Inc., Toronto, Ont.

Profile - (Ont. 2008; orig. B.C., 2000) Pursuing voluntary wind up.

On July 12, 2023, shareholders approved the voluntary liquidation and dissolution of the company. A return of capital distribution of 30¢ per share would be made on Aug. 8, 2023, to shareholders of record Aug. 1, 2023.

On Oct. 31, 2022, the company agreed to sell the preferred LP units it holds in **BP Tex Parent, LP**, back to **Banneker Partners LLC** via the sale to **Banneker Partners Fund II, L.P.**, an affiliate of **Banneker Partners LLC**, for Cdn$4,200,000 (US$3,257,797). BP Tex Parent is a private Delaware limited partnership formed by Banneker Partners to hold the Texada Software Canadian and Australia businesses acquired from the company in June 2022. The preferred LP units represent a 7.4% interest in BP Tex Parent. The company would used these proceeds and proceeds from sale of Texada Software to fund a return of capital totaling $27,267,479. Shareholders of record Dec. 19, 2022, would receive $1.00 per share return of capital distribution on Dec. 23, 2022.

In October 2022, a reduction in the stated capital of the company was proposed for the purpose of distributing to the shareholders certain of the proceeds of the sale of the Texada software business. The company initially plans to distribute about $1.00 per common share and plans to distribute additional capital to shareholders in 2023 of proceeds from sale of its investment in **BP Tex Parent, LP**.

Recent Merger and Acquisition Activity

Status: completed **Revised:** June 30, 2022
UPDATE: The transaction was completed. The sale represented all of Noble's operating activities. Concurrently, Noble completed its $4,200,000 investment in BP Tex Parent, LP, representing a 7.4% interest. PREVIOUS: Noble Iron Inc. agreed to sell wholly owned Systematic Computer Services Corporation, which operates Noble's Texada software business, to BP Tex Canada Amalco Corporation (BP Canada) for cash consideration of $36,200,000 and all of the assets of wholly owned Texada Software Pty Ltd. to BP Tex Australia Acquisition Corporation Pty Ltd. (BP Australia) for $1,000,000. BP Canada and BP Australia are indirectly wholly owned by private equity fund Banneker Partners. On closing, Noble Iron would use $4,200,000 of the purchase price acquire preferred LP units of BP Tex Parent, LP, a private Delaware limited partnership created by Banneker to hold all of the outstanding securities of BP Canada and BP Australia. Noble would hold preferred LP units representing 10% of the outstanding LP units. Nabil Kassam, who holds 10,237,903 Noble common shares (representing a 37.5% interest) and Zahra Kassam, who holds 3,653,840 Noble common shares (representing a 13.4% interest), have agreed to vote in favour of the transaction. Texada Software offers cloud or client-based software applications for equipment rental companies, equipment dealerships, construction companies, general contractors, and equipment operators, including mechanics, logistics managers and service technicians. On closing, the company plans to acquire or develop a new business that will meet Continued Listing Requirements of the TSX Venture Exchange.

Predecessor Detail - Name changed from Texada Software Inc., July 23, 2012; basis 1 new for 5 old shs.

Directors - Nabil Kassam, chr. & CEO, Calif.; Aly G. Mawji, Halifax, N.S.; Paul Strachman, N.Y.; Mary Van Santvoort, Ont.

Other Exec. Officers - Mariam Chaudhry, CFO

Capital Stock

	Authorized (shs.)	Outstanding (shs.)[1]
Preferred	100,000,000	nil
Common	unlimited	27,267,479

[1] At May 16, 2023

Major Shareholder - Nabil Kassam held 37.55% interest and Zahra Kassam held 13.4% interest at May 16, 2023.

Price Range - NIR.H/TSX-VEN

Year	Volume	High	Low	Close
2022	757,103	$1.23	$0.16	$0.20
2021	1,000,982	$1.05	$0.25	$0.71
2020	471,504	$0.35	$0.13	$0.30
2019	120,845	$0.32	$0.18	$0.18
2018	977,224	$0.40	$0.19	$0.33

Recent Close: $0.03

Wholly Owned Subsidiaries

Noble Equipment, Inc., United States.
Noble Iron (U.S.) Inc., United States.

Investments

7.4% int. in **BP Tex Parent, LP**, Del.

Financial Statistics

Periods ended:	12m Dec. 31/21[A]		12m Dec. 31/20[A]
	$000s	%Chg	$000s
Operating revenue	**6,740**	**+15**	**5,855**
Cost of sales	500		325
Research & devel. expense	1,781		1,327
General & admin expense	3,126		3,219
Other operating expense	1,024		852
Operating expense	**6,431**	**+8**	**5,939**
Operating income	**309**	**n.a.**	**(84)**
Deprec., depl. & amort	77		156
Finance costs, net	(7)		(138)
Pre-tax income	**269**	**n.a.**	**(102)**
Income taxes	1		1
Net income	**268**	**n.a.**	**(103)**
Cash & equivalent	5,497		5,471
Accounts receivable	654		552
Current assets	6,294		6,225
Fixed assets, net	18		57
Right-of-use assets	nil		57
Intangibles, net	14		35
Total assets	**6,325**	**-1**	**6,374**
Accts. pay. & accr. liabs	763		905
Current liabilities	960		1,167
Long-term debt, gross	230		246
Long-term debt, net	230		246
Long-term lease liabilities	nil		6
Shareholders' equity	5,136		4,955
Cash from oper. activs	**404**	**+28**	**315**
Cash from fin. activs	(60)		389
Cash from invest. activs	(9)		1
Net cash position	**5,498**	**0**	**5,471**
Capital expenditures	(11)		(6)
Capital disposals	nil		2
	$		$
Earnings per share*	0.01		(0.00)
Cash flow per share*	0.01		0.01
	shs		shs
No. of shs. o/s*	27,267,479		27,267,479
Avg. no. of shs. o/s*	27,267,479		27,267,479
	%		%
Net profit margin	3.98		(1.76)
Return on equity	5.31		(2.07)
Return on assets	4.22		(1.61)
Foreign sales percent	18		19

* Common
[A] Reported in accordance with IFRS

Latest Results

Periods ended:	6m June 30/22[A]		6m June 30/21[□A]
	$000s	%Chg	$000s
Net inc. bef. disc. opers	(1,780)	n.a.	(182)
Income from disc. opers	34,289		189
Net income	32,509	n.m.	8
	$		$
Earns. per sh. bef. disc. opers.*	(0.01)		nil
Earnings per share*	1.25		nil

* Common
□ Restated
[A] Reported in accordance with IFRS

Historical Summary
(as originally stated)

Fiscal Year	Oper. Rev.	Net Inc. Bef. Disc.	EPS*
	$000s	$000s	$
2021[A]	6,740	268	0.01
2020[A]	5,855	(103)	(0.00)
2019[A]	5,749	(3,760)	(0.14)
2018[A]	6,106	(3,099)	(0.11)
2017[A]	4,671	(2,618)	(0.10)

* Common
[A] Reported in accordance with IFRS

N.54 Norsemont Mining Inc.

Symbol - NOM **Exchange** - CSE **CUSIP** - 65652P
Head Office - 610-700 Pender St W, West Vancouver, BC, V6C 1G8 **Telephone** - (604) 669-9788 **Fax** - (604) 669-9768
Website - www.norsemont.com
Email - kulwant.sandher@gmail.com
Investor Relations - Kulwant Sandher (604) 669-9788
Auditors - Dale Matheson Carr-Hilton LaBonte LLP C.A., Vancouver, B.C.
Lawyers - Max Pinsky Personal Law Corporation, Vancouver, B.C.

Transfer Agents - Odyssey Trust Company, Vancouver, B.C.
Profile - (B.C. 2016; orig. Can., 2000) Holds formerly producing Choquelimpie gold-silver-copper project, 5,757 hectares, 185 km east of Arica, Chile.
Predecessor Detail - Name changed from Norsemont Capital Inc., Feb. 24, 2020.
Directors - Marc E. Levy, chr. & CEO, Vancouver, B.C.; Charles E. (Chuck) Ross†, Vancouver, B.C.; John M. Bean, West Vancouver, B.C.; Patrick J. Burns, Salta, Argentina; Arthur C. (Art) Freeze, Vancouver, B.C.; Allan Larmour, White Rock, B.C.; Nikolas Perrault, Lisbon, Portugal
Other Exec. Officers - Kulwant Sandher, CFO; John Currie, v-p, explor.
† Lead director

Capital Stock

	Authorized (shs.)	Outstanding (shs.)[1]
Common	unlimited	55,795,180

[1] At May 29, 2023

Major Shareholder - Widely held at July 25, 2022.

Price Range - NOM/CSE

Year	Volume	High	Low	Close
2022	10,649,170	$0.93	$0.30	$0.34
2021	24,735,601	$1.25	$0.45	$0.78
2020	26,412,489	$2.79	$0.25	$1.06
2019	758,299	$0.43	$0.25	$0.35
2018	298,608	$0.47	$0.32	$0.35

Recent Close: $0.18
Capital Stock Changes - During 2022, common shares were issued as follows: 850,000 by private placement, 349,250 under restricted share unit plan, 284,772 for debt settlement and 80,000 on exercise of warrants.

Wholly Owned Subsidiaries

Rosswoll Industries Inc., B.C.
Tavros Gold Corp., B.C.
- 100% int. in **Sociedad Contractual Minera Vilacollo**, Chile.

Financial Statistics

Periods ended:	12m Dec. 31/22[A]		12m Dec. 31/21[A]
	$000s	%Chg	$000s
Salaries & benefits	524		431
Exploration expense	2,734		6,216
General & admin expense	947		1,176
Stock-based compensation	1,022		1,617
Operating expense	**5,226**	**-45**	**9,440**
Operating income	**(5,226)**	**n.a.**	**(9,440)**
Deprec., depl. & amort.	37		26
Finance income	3		3
Finance costs, gross	134		8
Write-downs/write-offs	(32)		(38)
Pre-tax income	**(5,441)**	**n.a.**	**(9,464)**
Net income	**(5,441)**	**n.a.**	**(9,464)**
Cash & equivalent	25		2,602
Accounts receivable	10		16
Current assets	72		2,726
Fixed assets, net	51		88
Explor./devel. properties	27,477		27,477
Total assets	**27,629**	**-9**	**30,320**
Bank indebtedness	240		nil
Accts. pay. & accr. liabs.	2,004		1,425
Current liabilities	3,300		2,103
Long-term debt, gross	1,008		nil
Long-term lease liabilities	12		50
Shareholders' equity	24,317		28,167
Cash from oper. activs.	**(4,225)**	**n.a.**	**(6,556)**
Cash from fin. activs.	1,660		1,513
Net cash position	**25**	**-99**	**2,602**
	$		$
Earnings per share*	(0.10)		(0.18)
Cash flow per share*	(0.08)		(0.13)
	shs		shs
No. of shs. o/s*	55,548,055		53,984,033
Avg. no. of shs. o/s*	54,777,557		52,208,138
	%		%
Net profit margin	n.a.		n.a.
Return on equity	(20.73)		(30.16)
Return on assets	(18.32)		(28.79)

* Common
[A] Reported in accordance with IFRS

Historical Summary
(as originally stated)

Fiscal Year	Oper. Rev.	Net Inc. Bef. Disc.	EPS*
	$000s	$000s	$
2022[A]	nil	(5,441)	(0.10)
2021[A]	nil	(9,464)	(0.18)
2020[A]	nil	(5,563)	(0.17)
2019[A]	nil	(332)	(0.03)
2018[A]	nil	(251)	(0.02)

* Common
[A] Reported in accordance with IFRS

N.55 North American Construction Group Ltd.

Symbol - NOA **Exchange** - TSX **CUSIP** - 656811
Head Office - 27287 100 Ave, Acheson, AB, T7X 6H8 **Telephone** - (780) 960-7171 **Fax** - (780) 969-5599
Website - www.nacg.ca
Email - jveenstra@nacg.ca
Investor Relations - Jason W. Veenstra (780) 948-2009
Auditors - KPMG LLP C.A., Edmonton, Alta.
Lawyers - Fasken Martineau DuMoulin LLP, Toronto, Ont.; Bracewell LLP, Houston, Tex.
Transfer Agents - Computershare Trust Company of Canada Inc., Toronto, Ont.
FP500 Revenue Ranking - 385
Employees - 1,932 at Dec. 31, 2022
Profile - (Can. 2006 amalg.) Provides a wide range of mining and heavy construction services to customers in the resource development and industrial construction sectors within Canada, the U.S. and Australia.
The primary market is the Canadian oil sands region in Alberta, and principal oil sands customers include **Suncor Energy Inc., Fort Hills Energy LP, Syncrude Canada Ltd.** and **Imperial Oil Limited**. Services are typically provided pursuant to non-exclusive master service agreements or multiple use agreements with terms of three to five-year periods.
Provides surface mine services supporting the construction and operation, particularly in the oil sands, which include clearing; road construction; site preparation; underground utility installation; mine infrastructure construction such as tailings ponds, access roads, stabilized earth walls and earth dams; maintenance; upgrading; equipment and labour supply; overburden removal; material hauling; and land reclamation. In addition, provides mine management services for thermal coal mines in Wyoming and Texas. Wholly owned **DGI (Aust) Trading Pty Ltd.** sources and procures production-critical equipment components for customers in the mining and construction industry. Affiliate **Nuna Logistics Limited** provides construction, logistics, contract mining and support services to the resource industry in northern Canada.
At Dec. 31, 2022, the company operated 637 units of heavy equipment including mining trucks, dozers, excavators, loaders, graders, articulated trucks, shovels and packers, and a fleet of more than 850 ancillary vehicles including various service and maintenance vehicles. A major equipment maintenance facility is located in Acheson, Alta., and additional project management and equipment maintenance functions are carried out from regional facilities in Fort McMurray, Alta.
Subsequent to Dec. 31, 2022, affiliate **Dene North Site Services Partnership** (49% owned) was dissolved.

Recent Merger and Acquisition Activity

Status: completed **Announced:** Oct. 1, 2022
North American Construction Group Ltd. acquired private Fort McMurray, Alta.-based ML Northern Services Ltd., a heavy equipment company specializing in mobile fuel, lube and steaming services, for $15,000,000, which was funded through existing debt facilities.
Predecessor Detail - Name changed from North American Energy Partners Inc., Apr. 16, 2018.
Directors - Martin R. Ferron, chr., Houston, Tex.; Joseph C. (Joe) Lambert, pres. & CEO, Spruce Grove, Alta.; Bryan D. Pinney†, Calgary, Alta.; John J. Pollesel, Sudbury, Ont.; Maryse C. Saint-Laurent, Calgary, Alta.; Thomas P. (Tom) Stan, Calgary, Alta.; Kristina E. Williams, Edmonton, Alta.
Other Exec. Officers - Barry W. Palmer, COO; Jason W. Veenstra, exec. v-p & CFO; David G. Kallay, v-p, health, safety envir. & HR; Jordan A. Slator, v-p, gen. counsel & corp. sec.
† Lead director

Capital Stock

	Authorized (shs.)	Outstanding (shs.)[1]
Common	unlimited	26,414,780[2]
Non-vtg. Common	unlimited	nil

[1] At Feb. 10, 2023
[2] Excludes 1,412,502 shares held in trust.

Major Shareholder - Mawer Investment Management Limited held 14.7% interest at Mar. 15, 2023.

Price Range - NOA/TSX

Year	Volume	High	Low	Close
2022	17,176,445	$20.46	$12.65	$18.08
2021	21,275,869	$22.00	$11.48	$19.19
2020	33,905,968	$15.99	$5.81	$12.44
2019	18,536,291	$18.36	$11.77	$15.74
2018	13,039,628	$16.41	$5.11	$12.15

Recent Close: $33.23
Capital Stock Changes - During 2022, 2,195,646 common shares were repurchased under a Normal Course Issuer Bid.

Dividends

NOA com Ra $0.40 pa Q est. Apr. 6, 2023
Prev. Rate: $0.32 est. Oct. 7, 2022
Prev. Rate: $0.16 est. Oct. 4, 2019

Wholly Owned Subsidiaries

DGI (Aust) Trading Pty Ltd., N.S.W., Australia.
ML Northern Services Ltd., Fort McMurray, Alta.
NACG Acheson Ltd.
NACG Management Ltd., Alta.
NACG Properties Inc.
North American Engineering Inc., Alta.
North American Enterprises LP, Alta.
North American Fleet LP, Alta.
North American Maintenance Ltd., Alta.
North American Mining Inc.
North American Services Inc., Alta.
North American Site Development Ltd., Alta.

Investments

30% int. in **ASN Constructors, LLC**, Fargo, N.D.
50% int. in **BNA Remanufacturing Limited Partnership**
49% int. in **Mikisew North American Limited Partnership**
49% int. in **NAYL Realty Inc.**, Alta.
37.25% int. in **Nuna East Ltd.**
49% int. in **Nuna Logistics Limited**, B.C.
37.25% int. in **Nuna Pang Contracting Ltd.**
49% int. in **Nuna West Mining Ltd.**
15% int. in **Red River Valley Alliance LLC**, United States.

Financial Statistics

Periods ended:	12m Dec. 31/22[A]		12m Dec. 31/21[A]
	$000s	%Chg	$000s
Operating revenue	**769,539**	**+18**	**654,143**
Cost of sales	548,723		455,710
General & admin expense	29,855		35,374
Operating expense	**578,578**	**+18**	**491,084**
Operating income	**190,961**	**+17**	**163,059**
Deprec., depl. & amort.	119,268		108,016
Finance income	24		62
Finance costs, gross	24,567		19,094
Investment income	37,053		21,860
Pre-tax income	**84,445**	**+39**	**60,693**
Income taxes	17,073		9,285
Net income	**67,372**	**+31**	**51,408**
Cash & equivalent	69,144		16,601
Inventories	49,898		44,544
Accounts receivable	83,811		68,787
Current assets	230,359		147,179
Long-term investments	75,637		55,974
Fixed assets, net	645,810		640,950
Right-of-use assets	14,739		14,768
Intangibles, net	6,773		4,407
Total assets	**979,513**	**+13**	**869,278**
Accts. pay. & accr. liabs.	146,333		109,640
Current liabilities	192,303		161,034
Long-term debt, gross	420,541		380,448
Long-term debt, net	378,452		335,720
Long-term lease liabilities	12,376		11,461
Shareholders' equity	305,919		278,463
Cash from oper. activs.	**169,201**	**+2**	**165,180**
Cash from fin. activs.	(19,493)		(92,759)
Cash from invest. activs.	(97,469)		(99,269)
Net cash position	**69,144**	**+317**	**16,601**
Capital expenditures	(111,499)		(112,563)
Capital disposals	3,400		17,141
	$		$
Earnings per share*	2.46		1.81
Cash flow per share*	6.17		5.83
Cash divd. per share*	0.32		0.16
	shs		shs
No. of shs. o/s*	26,420,821		28,458,115
Avg. no. of shs. o/s*	27,406,140		28,325,489
	%		%
Net profit margin	8.75		7.86
Return on equity	23.06		19.51
Return on assets	9.41		8.13
No. of employees (FTEs)	1,932		2,042

* Common
[A] Reported in accordance with U.S. GAAP

Historical Summary
(as originally stated)

Fiscal Year	Oper. Rev.	Net Inc. Bef. Disc.	EPS*
	$000s	$000s	$
2022[A]	769,539	67,372	2.46
2021[A]	654,143	51,408	1.81
2020[A]	500,374	49,208	1.75
2019[A]	719,067	37,133	1.45
2018[A]	410,061	15,321	0.61

* Common
[A] Reported in accordance with U.S. GAAP

N.56 North American Financial 15 Split Corp.

Symbol - FFN **Exchange** - TSX **CUSIP** - 65685J
Head Office - c/o Quadravest Capital Management Inc., 2510-200 Front St W, PO Box 51, Toronto, ON, M5V 3K2 **Telephone** - (416) 304-4440 **Toll-free** - (877) 478-2372
Website - www.quadravest.com
Email - info@quadravest.com
Investor Relations - Shari Payne (877) 478-2372
Auditors - PricewaterhouseCoopers LLP C.A., Toronto, Ont.
Lawyers - Blake, Cassels & Graydon LLP, Toronto, Ont.
Transfer Agents - Computershare Trust Company of Canada Inc., Toronto, Ont.
Investment Managers - Quadravest Capital Management Inc., Toronto, Ont.
Managers - Quadravest Capital Management Inc., Toronto, Ont.

Profile - (Ont. 2004) Invests in a portfolio consisting primarily of common shares of 10 Canadian and five U.S. financial services companies.

The Canadian financial services companies consist of **Bank of Montreal**, **The Bank of Nova Scotia**, **Canadian Imperial Bank of Commerce**, **Royal Bank of Canada**, **The Toronto-Dominion Bank**, **National Bank of Canada**, **Manulife Financial Corporation**, **Sun Life Financial Inc.**, **Great-West Lifeco Inc.** and **CI Financial Corp.** The U.S. financial services companies consist of **Bank of America Corp.**, **Citigroup Inc.**, **Goldman Sachs Group Inc.**, **JPMorgan Chase & Co.** and **Wells Fargo & Co.** Shares held within the portfolio are expected to range between 4% and 8% in weight but may vary from time to time. The portfolio may hold up to 15% of its net asset value in equity securities of other issuers.

To supplement the dividends received on the investment portfolio and to reduce risk, the company may, from time to time, write covered call options in respect of all or part of the common shares in the portfolio.

The company will terminate on Dec. 1, 2024, or earlier at the discretion of the manager if the class A or preferred shares are delisted by the TSX or if the net asset value of the company declines to less than $5,000,000. At such time, all outstanding class A and preferred shares will be redeemed. The termination date may be extended beyond Dec. 1, 2024, for a further five years and thereafter for additional successive periods of five years as determined by the board of directors.

The investment manager receives a management fee at an annual rate equal to 0.65% of the net asset value of the company calculated and payable monthly in arrears. In addition, the manager receives an administration fee at an annual rate equal to 0.1% of the net asset value of the company calculated and payable monthly in arrears, as well as service fee payable to dealers on the class A shares at a rate of 0.5% per annum.

Top 10 holdings at Feb. 28, 2023 (as a percentage of net assets):

Holdings	Percentage
JPMorgan Chase & Co.	9.1%
Royal Bank of Canada	8.4%
Morgan Stanley	8.1%
Bank of America Corporation	7.9%
Goldman Sachs Group Inc	7.8%
Wells Fargo & Co.	7.6%
Citigroup Inc.	7.5%
The Toronto-Dominion Bank	5.5%
Sun Life Financial Inc.	5.0%
Manulife Financial Corporation	4.5%

Predecessor Detail - Name changed from Financial 15 Split Corp. II, Mar. 18, 2015.

Directors - S. Wayne Finch, chr., pres. & CEO, Caledon, Ont.; Laura L. Johnson, corp. sec., Oakville, Ont.; Peter F. Cruickshank, Oakville, Ont.; Michael W. Sharp, Toronto, Ont.; John D. Steep, Stratford, Ont.

Other Exec. Officers - Silvia Gomes, CFO

Capital Stock

	Authorized (shs.)	Outstanding (shs.)[1]
Preferred	unlimited	54,084,787[2]
Class B	1,000	1,000[2]
Class A	unlimited	55,220,987

[1] At May 15, 2023

[2] Classified as debt.

Preferred - Entitled to receive fixed cumulative preferential monthly dividends of $0.05625 per share (to yield 6.75% per annum on the original $10 issue price). Retractable at any time at a price per share equal to the lesser of: (i) $10; and (ii) 98% of the net asset value (NAV) per unit (one preferred share and one class A share) less the cost to the company of purchasing one class A share in the market for cancellation. Shareholders who concurrently retract one unit in October of each year are entitled to receive an amount equal to the NAV per unit less any expenses (to a maximum of 1% of the NAV per unit) related to liquidating the portfolio to pay such redemption. All outstanding preferred shares will be redeemed on Dec. 1, 2024, at $10 per share. Rank in priority to class A and class B shares with respect to the payment of dividends and the repayment of capital. Non-voting.

Class B - Not entitled to dividends. Retractable at $1.00 per share and are entitled to liquidation value of $1.00 per share. Rank subsequent to preferred shares and prior to class A shares with respect to the repayment of capital on the dissolution, liquidation or winding-up of the company. One vote per share.

Class A - The company will endeavour to pay monthly cash dividends targeted to be $0.11335 per share (to yield 8% per annum on the original $15 issue price). If, after such dividends are paid, any amounts remain available, a special dividend of such amount will be made to shareholders in November of each year. Retractable at any time at a price per share equal to 98% of the NAV per unit less the cost to the company of purchasing one preferred share in the market for cancellation. Shareholders who concurrently retract one unit in October of each year are entitled to receive an amount equal to the NAV per unit less any expenses (to a maximum of 1% of the NAV per unit) related to liquidating the portfolio to pay such redemption. All outstanding class A shares will be redeemed on Dec. 1, 2024, at $15 per share. Class A shareholders are also entitled to receive the balance, if any, of the value of the investment portfolio remaining after returning the original issue price to preferred and class A shareholders. Rank subordinate to preferred and class B shares with respect to payment of dividends and the repayment of capital. Non-voting.

Normal Course Issuer Bid - The company plans to make normal course purchases of up to 5,514,879 class A shares representing 10% of the public float. The bid commenced on May 29, 2023, and expires on May 28, 2024.

The company plans to make normal course purchases of up to 5,408,428 preferred shares representing 10% of the public float. The bid commenced on May 29, 2023, and expires on May 28, 2024.

Major Shareholder - Financial 15 Split Corp. II Holding Trust held 100% interest at Feb. 23, 2023.

Price Range - FFN/TSX

Year	Volume	High	Low	Close
2022	75,806,332	$7.97	$3.45	$4.22
2021	41,456,747	$7.71	$4.06	$7.44
2020	14,446,448	$7.80	$2.51	$4.10
2019	17,666,566	$8.59	$4.59	$6.99
2018	15,188,609	$10.38	$3.46	$5.00

Consolidation: 0.882239-for-1 cons. in Dec. 2019

Recent Close: $3.38

Capital Stock Changes - In January 2022, public offering of 5,364,000 preferred shares and 4,364,000 class A shares was completed at $10.05 and $7.75 per share, respectively. Also during fiscal 2022, 13,194,100 preferred shares and 14,724,300 class A shares were issued under an at-the-market equity program, and 1,987,276 preferred shares and 2,517,476 class A shares were retracted.

Dividends

FFN cl A N.V. omitted [1]

$0.11335	Mar. 10/23	$0.11335	Feb. 10/23
$0.11335	Dec. 9/22	$0.11335	May 10/22

Paid in 2023: $0.2267 2022: $0.6801 2021: $1.24685

FFN.PR.A pfd cum. ret. Ra $0.775 pa M

Prev. Rate: $0.675

[1] Monthly divd normally payable in Apr/23 has been omitted.

Financial Statistics

Periods ended:	12m Nov. 30/22[A]		12m Nov. 30/21[A]
	$000s	%Chg	$000s
Realized invest. gain (loss)	1,726		(948)
Unrealized invest. gain (loss)	(23,492)		82,995
Total revenue	**1,808**	**-98**	**93,144**
General & admin. expense	6,286		4,290
Other operating expense	2,805		1,546
Operating expense	**9,091**	**+56**	**5,836**
Operating income	**(7,283)**	**n.a.**	**87,308**
Finance costs, gross	38,725		20,586
Pre-tax income	**(46,009)**	**n.a.**	**66,722**
Net income	**(46,009)**	**n.a.**	**66,722**
Cash & equivalent	90,594		57,597
Accounts receivable	1,600		697
Investments	720,196		537,397
Total assets	**812,436**	**+36**	**595,691**
Accts. pay. & accr. liabs	602		730
Debt	522,813		357,105
Shareholders' equity	276,118		231,468
Cash from oper. activs	**(187,365)**	**n.a.**	**(241,639)**
Cash from fin. activs	220,451		276,140
Net cash position	**90,594**	**+57**	**57,597**
	$		$
Earnings per share*	(0.93)		2.59
Cash flow per share*	(3.79)		(9.39)
Net asset value per share*	5.28		6.48
Cash divd. per share*	0.68		1.25
	shs		shs
No. of shs. o/s*	52,281,187		35,710,363
Avg. no. of shs. o/s*	49,459,973		25,726,938
	%		%
Net profit margin	n.m.		71.63
Return on equity	(18.13)		45.03
Return on assets	(1.03)		21.08

* Class A

[A] Reported in accordance with IFRS

Note: Net income reflects increase/decrease in net assets from operations.

Historical Summary
(as originally stated)

Fiscal Year	Total Rev.	Net Inc. Bef. Disc.	EPS*
	$000s	$000s	$
2022[A]	1,808	(46,009)	(0.93)
2021[A]	93,144	66,722	2.59
2020[A]	(36,434)	(48,454)	(2.93)
2019[A]	41,214	27,170	1.64
2018[A]	(8,841)	(22,144)	(1.52)

* Class A

[A] Reported in accordance with IFRS

Note: Adjusted throughout for 0.882239-for-1 cons. in Dec. 2019

N.57 The North West Company Inc.*

Symbol - NWC **Exchange** - TSX **CUSIP** - 663278

Head Office - Gibraltar House, 77 Main St, Winnipeg, MB, R3C 2R1 **Telephone** - (204) 943-0881 **Toll-free** - (800) 563-0002 **Fax** - (204) 934-1317

Website - www.northwest.ca

Email - jking@northwest.ca

Investor Relations - John D. King (800) 782-0391

Auditors - PricewaterhouseCoopers LLP C.A., Winnipeg, Man.

Bankers - Bank of Montreal; The Toronto-Dominion Bank

Transfer Agents - TSX Trust Company, Montréal, Qué.

FP500 Revenue Ranking - 195

Employees - 7,311 at Jan. 31, 2023

Profile - (Can. 2011, amalg.) Retails food and general merchandise to rural communities and urban neighbourhoods in northern and western Canada, Alaska, the South Pacific and the Caribbean.

Canadian Operations - Operations consist of 119 Northern stores, five NorthMart stores, 28 Quickstop convenience stores, five Giant Tiger stores, two Valu Lots discount centres, one Motorsports store, one Solo Market store, one Inuulisautinut Niuvirvik concept store, and two stand-alone pharmacy and convenience stores. The communities served range in size from small remote settlements with populations of as few as 300 people to larger regional locations with populations of up to 8,000 people.

Northern and NorthMart stores feature a combination of perishable and non-perishable food and general merchandise, as well as services including fuel sales, post office, pharmacy, income tax preparation, proprietary credit programs and financial services such as cheque cashing, ATMs and prepaid card products. Quickstop convenience stores offer extended hours, ready-to-eat foods, fuel and related services. Giant Tiger stores are junior discount retail stores offering family fashion, household products and food. Other retail formats include Valu Lots, which are discount centres and direct-to-customer food distribution outlet; Motorsports, a dealership offering sales, service, parts and accessories for Ski-doo, Honda, Can-am and other brands; Solo Market, a full service grocery and pharmacy targeted to road accessible rural communities; and Inuulisautinut Niuvirvik, a wellness-focused concept store featuring grocery, booster juice, pharmacy and optical services.

In addition to its retail operations, the company operates: (i) Crescent Multi Foods, which is a full-line produce and fresh meat distributor serving the company's stores and third party grocery stores in Saskatchewan, Manitoba and northwestern Ontario; (ii) Amdocs, which provides isolated northern communities with physician services; (iii) North West Telepharmacy Solutions, which provides contract telepharmacist services to rural hospitals and health centres across Canada; (iv) **Transport Nanuk Inc.**, a 50%-owned shipping company servicing the eastern Arctic; and (v) **North Star Air Ltd.**, a Thunder Bay, Ont.-based airline, providing cargo and passenger services within northwestern Ontario, northern Manitoba and Nunavut through a fleet of 18 aircraft.

International Operations - Operations consist of 32 Alaska Commercial Company stores (AC), five Quickstop convenience stores, 11 Cost-U-Less stores, and nine Riteway Food Markets stores. AC stores are located in rural Alaska, serving communities with populations ranging from 375 to 9,000 people, and are operated on a similar format to the Canadian Northern and NorthMart stores. The AC operations also include Pacific Alaska Wholesale (formerly Frontier Expeditors and Span Alaska), which provide wholesale food and general merchandise to independent grocery stores, commercial accounts and individual households in rural Alaska. Cost-U-Less stores are operated as mid-sized warehouse style retail stores in the South Pacific and the Caribbean. Riteway Food Markets provide retailing and wholesale operations in the British Virgin Islands.

Distribution & Infrastructure - Canadian operations include both a wholly owned and third party distribution centre in Winnipeg, Man. The AC operations have distribution centres in Tacoma, Wash., and Anchorage, Alaska. The Cost-U-Less operation has a distribution centre in San Leandro, Calif., and uses other third party facilities in both Florida and California. The Riteway Food Market operations have a wholesale facility in Tortola, British Virgin Islands, and uses other third party facilities in Florida.

Stores are serviced by all available modes of transportation including sealift, long haul water transportation, barge, trucks including via winter roads, rail and air. The company's logistics network is supported by its interests in Transport Nanuk and North Star Air.

In April 2023, the company acquired Nickel City Motors, a full-service motorsports dealer in Thompson, Ma., and a store was acquired in Point Hope, Alaska.

In February 2023, a QuickStop convenience store was opened in Taloyoak, Nunavut and a store was acquired in Arviat, Nunavut offering motorsports, furniture, appliances and other general merchandise.

In February 2023, the company closed its Cost-U-Less store in Curacao.

During fiscal 2023, two Quickstop convenience stores and a Northern store were opened in Canada. In addition, two Alaska Commercial stores and a Quickstop convenience store were opened in Alaska.

In September 2022, the company acquired Owens Cash & Carry store in Little Grand Rapids, Man., for an undisclosed amount. The store is 2,770 sq. ft. with a convenience store-style offering of bread, milk, select groceries, chips and pop, limited general merchandise and fuel pumps.

Predecessor Detail - Succeeded North West Company Fund, Jan. 1, 2011, pursuant to plan of arrangement whereby The North West Company Inc. was formed to facilitate the conversion of the fund into a corporation and the fund was subsequently dissolved.

Directors - W. Brock Bulbuck, chr., Winnipeg, Man.; Daniel G. (Dan) McConnell, pres. & CEO, Winnipeg, Man.; Deepak Chopra, Toronto, Ont.; Frank J. Coleman, Corner Brook, N.L.; Stewart F. Glendinning, Ocean Ridge, Fla.; Rachel L. Huckle, Toronto, Ont.; Annalisa King, Vancouver, B.C.; Violet A. M. (Vi) Konkle, Ont.; Steven Kroft, Winnipeg, Man.; Jennefer Nepinak, Winnipeg, Man.; Victor Tootoo, Iqaluit, Nun.

Other Exec. Officers - Alison Coville, chief people officer; Vineet Gupta, CIO; John D. King, exec. v-p & CFO; Cole J. A. Akerstream, v-p, corp. devel.; Michael T. Beaulieu, v-p, Cdn. store opers.; David M. Chatyrbok, v-p, Cdn. procurement & mktg.; Leanne G. Flewitt, v-p, logistics, supply chain & distrib., Cdn. opers.; Matt D. Johnson, v-p, Cost-U-Less food procurement & mktg.; Laurie J. Kaminsky, v-p, NWC health products & srvcs.; Randy L. Roller, v-p & gen. mgr., facilities & store planning; Nicoals Sabogal, v-p, strategy, planning & analytics; Kevin T. Sie, v-p, fin.; Amanda E. Sutton, v-p, legal & corp. sec.; Jim R. Caldwell, pres., Cdn. retail; Kyle A. Hill, pres., Alaska Commercial Company; J. Kevin Proctor, pres., Cost-U-Less & Riteway; Frank W. Kelner, chr. & CEO, North Star Air Ltd.

Capital Stock

	Authorized (shs.)	Outstanding (shs.)[1]
Common Vtg. & Variable Vtg.	unlimited	47,827,659

[1] At Apr. 30, 2023

Variable Voting - Held by individuals who are not Canadians as defined in the Canada Transportation Act (CTA). Automatically convertible into common voting shares on a one-for-one basis if the shares become held by a qualified Canadian or foreign ownership restrictions in the CTA are repealed and not replaced with similar provisions. Convertible at option of holder if an offer is made for all or substantially all of the common voting shares. This conversion right is only exercisable for the purpose of depositing the resulting common voting shares in response to the offer. Entitled to one vote per share unless: (i) a single non-Canadian holder or non-Canadians authorized to provide an air service holds more than 25% of the total number of variable voting and common voting shares outstanding; or (ii) the total number of votes that would be cast by or on behalf of a single non-Canadian and non-Canadians authorized to provide an air service would exceed 49% of the total number votes that would be cast at any meeting. If either of the above noted thresholds would otherwise be surpassed at any time, the vote attached to each variable voting share will decrease proportionately automatically and without further act or formality such that: (i) the variable voting shares held by such single non-Canadian or non-Canadians authorized to provide an air service do not carry more than 25% of the total votes attached to all issued and outstanding variable voting and common voting shares; and (ii) the total number of votes cast by or on behalf of a single non-Canadian and non-Canadians authorized to provide an air service do not exceed 49% of the total number of votes cast.

Common Voting - Held by qualified Canadians under the CTA. Automatically convertible into variable voting shares on a one-for-one basis if the shares become held by a non-qualified Canadian unless the foreign ownership restrictions of the CTA are repealed and not replaced with similar restrictions. Convertible at option of holder if an offer is made for all or substantially all of the variable voting shares. This conversion right is only exercisable for the purpose of depositing the resulting variable voting shares in response to the offer. One vote per share.

Options - At Jan. 31, 2023, options were outstanding to purchase 1,684,739 common voting and variable voting shares at prices ranging from $23.80 to $35.83 per share with a weighted average remaining contractual life of up to 6.3 years.

Normal Course Issuer Bid - The company plans to make normal course purchases of up to 4,740,895 common voting and variable voting shares representing 10% of the public float. The bid commenced on Nov. 15, 2022, and expires on Nov. 14, 2023.

Major Shareholder - Widely held at Apr. 5, 2023.

Price Range - NWC/TSX

Year	Volume	High	Low	Close
2022	35,670,344	$40.08	$30.55	$35.57
2021	31,246,210	$38.20	$30.24	$34.24
2020	36,999,790	$36.92	$16.06	$32.44
2019	29,157,794	$33.16	$27.22	$27.33
2018	25,858,953	$32.07	$26.50	$31.42

Recent Close: $31.03

Capital Stock Changes - During fiscal 2023, 108,030 common voting and variable voting shares were issued under a share-based compensation plan and 236,075 common voting and variable voting shares were repurchased under a Normal Course Issuer Bid. In addition, 57,151 common voting and variable voting shares (net) were returned to trust for settlement of performance share units.

Dividends

NWC vtg & var vtg Ra $1.52 pa Q est. Oct. 14, 2022
Prev. Rate: $1.48 est. Oct. 15, 2021
Prev. Rate: $1.44 est. Oct. 15, 2020

Long-Term Debt - Outstanding at Jan. 31, 2023:

Revolv. loan facility due 2027[1]	$96,032,000
3.74% sr. notes due 2029	100,000,000
Sr. notes[2]	93,483,000
Note payable	535,000
	290,050,000
Less: Current portion	268,000
	289,782,000

[1] Borrowings drawn from $400,000,000 revolving loan facilities, bearing interest at bankers' acceptances rates plus stamping fees or the Canadian prime rate.

[2] Consist of US$35,000,000 bearing interest at 2.88% due June 2027 and US$35,000,000 bearing interest at 3.09% due June 2032.

Wholly Owned Subsidiaries

NWC GP Inc., Winnipeg, Man.
North West Company Holdings (BVI) Inc., British Virgin Islands.
- 77% int. in **Roadtown Wholesale Trading Ltd.**, British Virgin Islands.

North West Company Holdings Inc., Canada.
- 100% int. in **NWC (U.S.) Holdings Inc.**, Del.
  - 100% int. in **The North West Company (International) Inc.**, Del.
- 100% int. in **North Star Air Ltd.**, Thunder Bay, Ont.
- 50% int. in **Transport Nanuk Inc.**, Montréal, Qué.

The North West Company Limited Partnership, Winnipeg, Man.

Financial Statistics

Periods ended:	12m Jan. 31/23[A]		12m Jan. 31/22[A]
	$000s	%Chg	$000s
Operating revenue	**2,352,760**	**+5**	**2,248,796**
Cost of sales	1,604,845		1,511,045
General & admin expense	469,237		426,376
Operating expense	**2,074,082**	**+7**	**1,937,421**
Operating income	**278,678**	**-11**	**311,375**
Deprec., depl. & amort.	98,373		90,950
Finance income	1,016		1,101
Finance costs, gross	15,852		14,159
Pre-tax income	**165,469**	**-20**	**207,367**
Income taxes	39,633		49,916
Net income	**125,836**	**-20**	**157,451**
Net inc. for equity hldrs	**122,190**	**-21**	**154,802**
Net inc. for non-cont. int.	**3,646**	**+38**	**2,649**
Cash & equivalent	58,809		49,426
Inventories	293,835		247,988
Accounts receivable	113,798		99,241
Current assets	474,844		403,358
Long-term investments	16,220		14,456
Fixed assets, net	606,310		554,457
Right-of-use assets	102,632		100,844
Intangibles, net	81,125		82,596
Total assets	**1,336,890**	**+10**	**1,219,273**
Accts. pay. & accr. liabs	225,481		221,319
Current liabilities	248,606		294,490
Long-term debt, gross	290,050		235,640
Long-term debt, net	289,782		189,378
Long-term lease liabilities	93,833		96,015
Shareholders' equity	629,221		563,635
Non-controlling interest	18,679		16,569
Cash from oper. activs	**182,838**	**-18**	**224,135**
Cash from fin. activs	(68,298)		(170,196)
Cash from invest. activs	(106,802)		(75,861)
Net cash position	**58,809**	**+19**	**49,426**
Capital expenditures	(112,581)		(87,341)
Capital disposals	510		85
Unfunded pension liability	12,188		21,714
	$		$
Earnings per share*	2.55		3.21
Cash flow per share*	3.82		4.64
Cash divd. per share*	1.50		1.46
	shs		shs
No. of shs. o/s*	47,685,083		47,870,279
Avg. no. of shs. o/s*	47,865,000		48,268,000
	%		%
Net profit margin	5.35		7.00
Return on equity	20.49		29.35
Return on assets	10.79		13.96
Foreign sales percent	44		43
No. of employees (FTEs)	7,311		7,524

* Var. & com. vtg.
[A] Reported in accordance with IFRS

Latest Results

Periods ended:	3m Apr. 30/23[A]		3m Apr. 30/22[A]
	$000s	%Chg	$000s
Operating revenue	593,564	+8	552,016
Net income	22,197	-21	28,161
Net inc. for equity hldrs	20,894	-24	27,380
Net inc. for non-cont. int.	1,303		781
	$		$
Earnings per share*	0.44		0.57

* Var. & com. vtg.
[A] Reported in accordance with IFRS

Historical Summary
(as originally stated)

Fiscal Year	Oper. Rev.	Net Inc. Bef. Disc.	EPS*
	$000s	$000s	$
2023[A]	2,352,760	125,836	2.55
2022[A]	2,248,796	157,451	3.21
2021[A]	2,359,239	143,560	2.87
2020[A]	2,094,393	86,273	1.70
2019[A]	2,013,486	90,632	1.78

* Var. & com. vtg.
[A] Reported in accordance with IFRS

N.58 Northfield Capital Corporation

Symbol - NFD.A **Exchange** - TSX-VEN **CUSIP** - 66611D
Head Office - 301-141 Adelaide St W, Toronto, ON, M5H 3L5 **Telephone** - (416) 628-5901 **Fax** - (416) 628-5911
Website - www.northfieldcapital.com
Email - mike@northfieldcapital.com
Investor Relations - Michael G. Leskovec (647) 794-4360
Auditors - MNP LLP C.A., Toronto, Ont.
Lawyers - Cassels Brock & Blackwell LLP, Toronto, Ont.
Transfer Agents - TSX Trust Company, Toronto, Ont.

Profile - (Ont. 1981) Invests in public and private companies primarily in the mining, oil and gas, manufacturing and technology sectors. In addition, operates fly-in fishing camps in Ontario and provides chartered air, flight training and aircraft maintenance services; manufactures and sells wines; and has spirit distilling operations.

Investment portfolio at Mar. 31, 2023 (as a percentage of portfolio):

Investment type	Percentage
Equity - public	47%
Equity - private	47%
Cash & cash equivalents	6%

In addition, wholly owned **True North Airways Inc.** (formerly **Sudbury Aviation Limited**), **Omar Aviation Limited** and **369445 Ontario Limited** operates fly-in fishing camps in northern Ontario and provides chartered air, flight training and aircraft maintenance services; subsidiary **The Grange of Prince Edward Inc.** (56.7% owned) manufactures and sells wines through its vineyard and winery in Prince Edward cty., Ont.; and subsidiary **Distillery Network Inc.** (57.6% owned) has spirit distilling operations at Spirit of York distillery in Toronto, Ont.

In June 2023, name change to **Northfield & Company Inc.** and an up to 20-for-1 share split were proposed.

In April 2023, wholly owned **Spurce Goose Aviation Inc.** acquired a 2003 Israel aircraft industries gulfstream 100 for US$3,350,000.

Directors - Robert D. Cudney, founder, pres. & CEO, Toronto, Ont.; Maryke Ballard, Toronto, Ont.; The Hon. Ernie Eves, Caledon, Ont.; John D. McBride, Toronto, Ont.; Thomas J. (Tom) Pladsen, Toronto, Ont.; Morris J. Prychidny, Toronto, Ont.

Other Exec. Officers - Michael G. (Mike) Leskovec, CFO

Capital Stock

	Authorized (shs.)	Outstanding (shs.)[1]
Preference	200,000	nil
Class A Restricted Voting	unlimited	2,214,763
Class B Multiple Voting	unlimited	3,720

[1] At June 16, 2023

Class A Restricted Voting - One vote per share.

Class B Multiple Voting - Convertible into class A common shares on a 1-for-1 basis. 500 votes per share.

Normal Course Issuer Bid - The company plans to make normal course purchases of up to 110,738 class A restricted voting shares representing 5% of the total outstanding. The bid commenced on Jan. 23, 2023, and expires on Jan. 22, 2024.

Major Shareholder - Robert D. Cudney held 64.3% interest at June 16, 2023.

Price Range - NFD.A/TSX-VEN

Year	Volume	High	Low	Close
2022	7,000	$37.30	$31.00	$31.00
2021	24,680	$38.00	$32.00	$37.30
2020	60,680	$31.00	$26.00	$28.00
2019	112,390	$35.85	$27.00	$30.00
2018	71,336	$30.00	$24.00	$27.00

Recent Close: $35.00

Capital Stock Changes - During 2022, 6,900 class A restricted voting shares were repurchased under a Normal Course Issuer Bid.

Wholly Owned Subsidiaries

Spurce Goose Aviation Inc.
- 100% int. in **Omar Aviation Limited**
- 100% int. in **369445 Ontario Limited**
- 100% int. in **True North Airways Inc.**

2756189 Ontario Inc., Ont.

Subsidiaries

57.6% int. in **Distillery Network Inc.**
56.7% int. in **The Grange of Prince Edward Inc.**, Ont.
93% int. in **Northfield Aviation Group Inc.**

Note: The preceding list includes only the major related companies in which interests are held.

Financial Statistics

Periods ended:	12m Dec. 31/22[A]		12m Dec. 31/21[oA]
	$000s	%Chg	$000s
Realized invest. gain (loss)	2,191		3,949
Unrealized invest. gain (loss)	(10,809)		(5,668)
Total revenue	**(2,463)**	**n.a.**	**3,485**
Salaries & benefits	3,343		3,171
General & admin. expense	3,028		3,618
Operating expense	**6,786**	**0**	**6,789**
Operating income	**(9,249)**	**n.a.**	**(3,304)**
Deprec. & amort	2,038		1,670
Finance costs, gross	244		71
Write-downs/write-offs	nil		(820)
Pre-tax income	**(15,111)**	**n.a.**	**(8,214)**
Income taxes	131		(1,501)
Net income	**(15,242)**	**n.a.**	**(6,712)**
Net inc. for equity hldrs	**(14,023)**	**n.a.**	**(5,149)**
Net inc. for non-cont. int	**(1,218)**	**n.a.**	**(1,563)**
Cash & equivalent	6,270		612
Inventories	1,226		1,246
Accounts receivable	185		1,203
Investments	52,300		68,911
Fixed assets, net	18,238		19,268
Right-of-use assets	1,074		1,328
Total assets	**79,881**	**-14**	**92,793**
Accts. pay. & accr. liabs	1,740		2,230
Debt	5,870		2,701
Lease liabilities	1,245		1,468
Shareholders' equity	69,044		83,325
Non-controlling interest	1,680		2,899
Cash from oper. activs	**4,497**	**+78**	**2,527**
Cash from fin. activs	1,857		346
Cash from invest. activs	(696)		(4,407)
Net cash position	**6,270**	**+925**	**612**
Capital expenditures	(696)		(4,407)
	$		$
Earnings per share*	(6.32)		(2.31)
Cash flow per share*	2.03		1.13
	shs		shs
No. of shs. o/s*	2,218,483		2,225,383
Avg. no. of shs. o/s*	2,220,360		2,231,771
	%		%
Net profit margin	n.m.		(192.60)
Return on equity	(18.41)		(5.97)
Return on assets	(17.37)		(6.91)

* Class A & B
[o] Restated
[A] Reported in accordance with IFRS

Note: Operating revenue includes investment income and realized and unrealized gains (losses) on investments.

Latest Results

Periods ended:	3m Mar. 31/23[A]		3m Mar. 31/22[A]
	$000s	%Chg	$000s
Total revenue	4,178	n.a.	(2,793)
Net income	1,619	n.a.	(4,811)
Net inc. for equity hldrs	1,958	n.a.	(4,546)
Net inc. for non-cont. int	(339)		(266)
	$		$
Earnings per share*	0.88		(2.05)

* Class A & B
[A] Reported in accordance with IFRS

Historical Summary
(as originally stated)

Fiscal Year	Total Rev.	Net Inc. Bef. Disc.	EPS*
	$000s	$000s	$
2022[A]	(2,463)	(15,242)	(6.32)
2021[A]	3,485	(6,712)	(2.31)
2020[A]	15,317	(6,566)	(0.36)
2019[A]	8,953	6,355	2.71
2018[A]	(7,572)	(8,022)	(3.31)

* Class A & B
[A] Reported in accordance with IFRS

N.59 Northland Power Inc.*

Symbol - NPI **Exchange** - TSX **CUSIP** - 666511
Head Office - 1200-30 St. Clair Ave W, Toronto, ON, M4V 3A1
Telephone - (416) 962-6262 **Fax** - (416) 962-6266
Website - www.northlandpower.com
Email - investorrelations@northlandpower.com
Investor Relations - Adam Beaumont (647) 288-1929
Auditors - Ernst & Young LLP C.A., Toronto, Ont.
Bankers - Canadian Imperial Bank of Commerce, Toronto, Ont.
Lawyers - Borden Ladner Gervais LLP, Toronto, Ont.
Transfer Agents - Computershare Trust Company of Canada Inc., Toronto, Ont.
FP500 Revenue Ranking - 188
Employees - 1,339 at Dec. 31, 2022
Profile - (Ont. 2011, amalg.) Develops, constructs, owns and operates power generation facilities, including renewable and natural gas energy, in North America, Europe, Latin America and Asia. Also owns a regulated utility business in Colombia. At Mar. 31, 2023, operating facilities had generating capacity of 3,026 MW (2,616 MW net).

Wind Facilities

Owns and operates 2,021 MW (1,643 MW net) of wind generation. Offshore facilities consist of 60% interest in the 600-MW Gemini wind farm, 85 km off the coast of the Netherlands; and the 252-MW Deutsche Bucht and 85% interest in the 332-MW Nordsee One wind farms in the German North Sea. Onshore facilities consist of the 133-MW Jardin d'Eole wind farm near Matane, Que.; the 101-MW Mont Louis wind farm in the Gaspesie region of Quebec; 50% interest in the 60-MW McLean's Mountain wind farm in Manitoulin Island, Ont.; 50% interest in the 100-MW wind farm in Grand Bend, Ont.; and 14 wind farms, totaling 443 MW (435 MW net), in Spain.

Projects under construction or in various stages of development include three onshore wind projects in New York, consisting of the 108-MW Ball Hill, the 112-MW Bluestone; two offshore wind projects in Taiwan, consisting of 60% interest in the 1,044-MW Hai Long, which comprises the 300-MW Hai Long 2A, the 232-MW Hai Long 2B and the 512-MW Hai Long; 49% interest in the 1,200-MW Baltic Power offshore wind project in Poland; 50% interest in the 600-MW Chiba offshore wind project in Japan; 100% interest in up to 1,000-MW Dado Ocean, the 600-MW Bobae and the up to 1,800-MW Wando offshore wind projects in South Korea; 100% interest in the 2,340-MW Scotwind offshore wind project in Scotland; and the 400-MW Hecate offshore wind project in the Hecate Straight off the coast of British Columbia.

Solar Facilities

Owns and operates 262 MW (247 MW net) of solar facilities consisting of 13 individual 10-MW ground-mounted solar facilities, totaling 130 MW (115 MW net), in Ontario; 18 solar photovoltaic plants, totaling 66 MW, and a 50-MW concentrated solar facility in Spain; and the 16-MW Helios solar project in Colombia.

Projects under construction or development include the 1,400-MW Alberta Solar and 220-MW Jurassic solar projects in Alberta; the 130-MW La Lucha solar project in Durango, Mexico; and 50% interest in the 130-MW Suba solar projects in Colombia.

Battery Energy Storage Facility

Owns a majority interest in the 250-MW Oneida battery energy storage project, a mid- to late-development stage project in southern Ontario.

Efficient Natural Gas Facilities

Owns and operates 743 MW (726 MW net) of thermal generation facilities consisting of a 265-MW natural-gas fired cogeneration facility in Thorold, Ont.; an 86-MW natural-gas fired facility in Spy Hill, Sask.; a 260-MW natural-gas fired combined-cycle facility near North Battleford, Sask.; and 77% effective interest in a 102-MW natural-gas and biomass baseload power plant and a 30-MW natural gas peaking facility, both in Kirkland Lake, Ont.

Utility

Owns 99.4% interest in **Empresa de Energía de Boyacá S.A. E.S.P.** (EBSA), which holds the sole franchise rights for electricity distribution in the Boyacá region of Colombia and retails electricity for the regulated residential sector in the region.

In May 2023, the company agreed to sell a 24.5% interest in its Scotwind offshore wind project in Scotland to **Electricity Supply Board** (ESB) for an undisclosed amount.

In December 2022, the company agreed to develop a 250-MW late-stage, grid-connected battery energy storage project in southern Ontario, in partnership with **NRStor Inc.** and the **Six Nations of the Grand River Development Corporation**. The company would own a majority interest in the project and would take the lead role in the construction, financing and operations. The project was expected to commence commercial operations in 2025.

Periods ended:	12m Dec. 31/22	12m Dec. 31/21
Generating capacity, MW	2,616	2,817
Electric gen., GWh	10,139	8,879

Recent Merger and Acquisition Activity

Status: completed **Announced:** May 25, 2023
Northland Power Inc. sold its 49% ownership interest in the Nordsee offshore wind cluster portfolio (NSC) in Germany to its partner on the portfolio, RWE Offshore Wind GmbH (RWE), giving RWE 100% ownership of the projects, for a cash consideration of €35,000,000. NSC's total gross capacity consists of 1,560 MW of offshore wind projects including: Nordsee Two, Nordsee Three, Delta Nordsee and Godewind.

Status: pending **Announced:** Feb. 17, 2023
Northland Power Inc. agreed to sell the 100-MW Highbridge onshore wind project in New York for an undisclosed amount. The transaction was expected to close in the second half of 2023.

Status: completed **Announced:** Dec. 31, 2022
Northland Power Inc. acquired a solar and battery energy storage pipeline with more than 1.6 GW and 1.2 GWh, respectively, in Alberta for an undisclosed amount. The acquisition includes the 220-MW Jurassic solar project, a mid- to late-development stage project that was expected to commence commercial operations in 2025.

Status: pending **Announced:** Dec. 14, 2022
Northland Power Inc. agreed to sell 49% of its 60% interest in the 1,044-MW Hai Long offshore wind project in Taiwan to Gentari International Renewables Pte. Ltd. for equity consideration of Cdn$800,000,000. On closing, Genetari would hold a 29.4% indirect equity interest in the project. Final equity consideration remains subject to closing adjustments. The transaction was expected to close following the achievement of financial close of the project.

Status: completed **Announced:** Apr. 7, 2022
Northland Power Inc. sold its 120-MW Iroquois Falls and 110-MW Kingston natural-gas fired combined-cycle facilities in Ontario to Validus Power Corp. Terms were not disclosed.

Predecessor Detail - Succeeded Northland Power Income Fund, Jan. 1, 2011, pursuant to plan of arrangement whereby Northland Power Inc. was formed to facilitate the conversion of the fund into a corporation and the fund was subsequently dissolved.

Directors - John W. Brace, chr., Toronto, Ont.; Russell Goodman†, Mont-Tremblant, Qué.; Linda L. Bertoldi, Toronto, Ont.; Lisa J. Colnett, Toronto, Ont.; Kevin A. Glass, Toronto, Ont.; Keith Halbert, Toronto, Ont.; Helen M. Mallovy Hicks, Toronto, Ont.; Ian W. Pearce, Oakville, Ont.; Eckhardt Ruemmler, Neuss, Germany

Other Exec. Officers - Mike Crawley, pres. & CEO; Pauline Alimchandani, CFO; Wendy Franks, chief strategy officer & head, hydrogen bus. unit; Rachel Stephenson, chief people officer; Michelle Chislett, exec. v-p, onshore renewables; Yonni Fushman, exec. v-p, sustainability & chief legal officer; Calvin MacCormack, exec. v-p, thermal & utility; David Povall, exec. v-p, offshore wind

† Lead director

Capital Stock

	Authorized (shs.)	Outstanding (shs.)[1]
Preferred	unlimited	
Series 1	6,000,000	4,762,246
Series 2	6,000,000	1,237,754
Common	unlimited	252,210,890

[1] At May 9, 2023

Preferred - Issuable in series. Non-voting unless dividends are in arrears for at least two years.

Series 1 - Entitled to fixed cumulative preferential annual dividends of $0.8004 per share payable quarterly to Sept. 30, 2025, and thereafter at a rate reset every five years equal to the five-year Government of Canada bond yield plus 2.8%. Redeemable on Sept. 30, 2025, and on September 30 every five years thereafter at $25 per share plus declared and unpaid dividends. Convertible at the holder's option, on Sept. 30, 2025, and on September 30 every five years thereafter, into floating rate preferred series 2 shares on a share-for-share basis, subject to certain conditions.

Series 2 - Entitled to floating cumulative preferential annual dividends payable quarterly equal to the 90-day Canadian Treasury bill rate plus 2.8%. Redeemable on Sept. 30, 2025, and on September 30 every five years thereafter at $25 per share or at $25.50 per share on any other non-conversion date, plus declared and unpaid dividends on both cases. Convertible at the holder's option, on Sept. 30, 2025, and on September 30 every five years thereafter, into preferred series 1 shares on a share-for-share basis, subject to certain conditions.

Common - One vote per share.

Preferred Series 3 (old) - Were entitled to fixed cumulative preferential annual dividends of $1.27 per share payable quarterly to Dec. 31, 2022. Redeemed on Jan. 3, 2023, at $25 per share.

Major Shareholder - Widely held at Apr. 6, 2023.

Price Range - NPI/TSX

Year	Volume	High	Low	Close
2022	178,531,670	$47.13	$34.95	$37.13
2021	181,491,717	$51.45	$36.07	$37.95
2020	198,587,858	$47.62	$20.52	$45.67
2019	151,112,114	$28.13	$21.58	$27.20
2018	83,505,756	$25.33	$19.91	$21.70

Recent Close: $25.58

Capital Stock Changes - On Jan. 3, 2023, all 4,800,000 preferred series 3 shares were redeemed at $25 per share.

During 2022, common shares were issued as follows: 20,894,982 under an at-the-market program, 2,224,650 under the dividend reinvestment plan and 14,974 under the long-term incentive plan.

Dividends

NPI com Ra $1.20 pa M est. Jan. 15, 2018**
NPI.PR.A pfd ser 1 cum. red. exch. Adj. Ra $0.80 pa Q est. Dec. 31, 2020
NPI.PR.B pfd ser 2 cum. red. exch. Fltg. Ra pa Q

$0.4638	Sept. 29/23	$0.4587	June 30/23
$0.4272	Mar. 31/23	$0.3856	Dec. 30/22

Paid in 2023: $1.3497 2022: $1.0491 2021: $0.9084

pfd ser 3 cum. red. exch. Adj. Ra $1.27 pa Q est. Mar. 30, 2018[1]

[1] Redeemed Jan. 3, 2023 at $25 per sh. plus accr. divds. of $0.3175.
** Reinvestment Option

Long-Term Debt - Outstanding at Dec. 31, 2022:

Empresa de Energía de Boyacá:	
3.7% loans & borrowings due 2024	$518,847,000
New York wind:	
1.4% loans & borrowings due 2024	327,059,000
Nordsee One GmbH:	
2.3% loans & borrowings due 2026	535,382,000
Jardin LP:	
6% loans & borrowings due 2029	65,796,000
Kirkland Lake Power Corp.:	
4.2% loans & borrowings due 2030	45,955,000
Thorold CoGen LP:	
6.7% loans & borrowings due 2030	206,980,000
Buitengaats & ZeeEnergie (Gemini):	
3.5% loans & borrowings due 2031	1,919,470,000
Mont Louis LP:	
6.6% loan due 2031	58,482,000
Northland Deutsche Bucht GmbH:	
2.4% loans & borrowings due 2031	1,028,411,000
Solar facilities:	
Phase I - 4.4% loan due 2032	148,763,000
Phase II - 4.5% loans & borrow. due 2034	108,187,000
North Battleford LP:	
5% loans & borrowings due 2032	502,797,000
McLean's LP:	
6% loans & borrowings due 2034	100,143,000
Cochrane Solar:	
4.6% loans & borrowings due 2035	149,261,000
Grand Bend LP:	
4.2% loans & borrowings due 2035	281,136,000
Spy Hill LP:	
4.1% loan due 2036	119,584,000
Northland Power Spain Holdings, S.L.U.:	
2% loans & borrow. due to 2042	845,702,000
	6,961,955,000
Less: Current portion	784,114,000
	6,177,841,000

Principal payment requirements on subsidiary borrowings for the next five years were as follows:

2023	$805,268,000
2024-2025	2,179,040,000
2026-2027	1,473,817,000
Thereafter	2,823,094,000

Note - In March 2023, the maturity date of the Empresa de Energía de Boyacá (EBSA) term loan was extended from December 2024 to March 2026. In April 2023, the Thorold CoGen LP loan was restructured whereby the interest rate was decreased from 6.7% to 6.4%. In June 2023, private placement of $500,000,000 9.25% green subordinated notes, series 2023-A due June 30, 2083, was arranged.

Wholly Owned Subsidiaries

North Battleford Power Limited Partnership, Sask.
Northland Deutsche Bucht GmbH, Germany.
Thorold CoGen Limited Partnership, Thorold, Ont.

Subsidiaries

60% int. in **Buitengaats C.V.**, Netherlands.
99.4% int. in **Empresa de Energia de Boyaca S.A. E.S.P.**, Colombia.
60% int. in **Hai Long 3 Offshore Wind Power Co. Limited**, Republic of China.
60% int. in **Hai Long 2 Offshore Wind Power Co. Limited**, Republic of China.
85% int. in **Nordsee One GmbH**, Germany.
98.5% int. in **Northland Power Spain Holdings, S.L.U.**, Spain.
60% int. in **ZeeEnergie C.V.**, Netherlands.

Note: The preceding list includes only the major related companies in which interests are held.

Financial Statistics

Periods ended:	12m Dec. 31/22^A		12m Dec. 31/21^□A
	$000s	%Chg	$000s
Operating revenue	**2,448,815**	**+17**	**2,093,255**
Cost of sales	270,426		213,493
General & admin expense	162,180		145,343
Other operating expense	351,995		327,894
Operating expense	**784,601**	**+14**	**686,730**
Operating income	**1,664,214**	**+18**	**1,406,525**
Deprec., depl. & amort.	624,701		636,039
Finance income	24,792		18,451
Finance costs, gross	336,630		345,988
Write-downs/write-offs	nil		(29,981)
Pre-tax income	**1,260,119**	**+198**	**423,231**
Income taxes	304,662		153,352
Net income	**955,457**	**+254**	**269,879**
Net inc. for equity hldrs	**827,733**	**+337**	**189,559**
Net inc. for non-cont. int.	**127,724**	**+59**	**80,320**
Cash & equivalent	1,299,833		673,692
Inventories	43,783		35,945
Accounts receivable	397,771		383,308
Current assets	2,348,956		1,414,693
Long-term investments	441,565		138,726
Fixed assets, net	9,377,584		9,586,466
Intangibles, net	1,228,393		1,251,008
Total assets	**14,222,609**	**+10**	**12,871,816**
Accts. pay. & accr. liabs	835,993		461,172
Current liabilities	1,908,852		1,404,545
Long-term debt, gross	6,961,955		7,634,039
Long-term debt, net	6,177,841		6,956,661
Long-term lease liabilities	138,464		138,064
Preferred share equity	144,843		260,880
Shareholders' equity	4,391,182		2,756,879
Non-controlling interest	333,091		208,832
Cash from oper. activs	**1,832,983**	**+14**	**1,609,295**
Cash from fin. activs	(604,837)		(225,679)
Cash from invest. activs	(629,683)		(1,030,863)
Net cash position	**1,299,833**	**+93**	**673,692**
Capital expenditures	(452,576)		(469,793)
	$		$
Earnings per share*	3.46		0.82
Cash flow per share*	7.76		7.35
Cash divd. per share*	1.20		1.20
	shs		shs
No. of shs. o/s*	250,017,357		226,882,751
Avg. no. of shs. o/s*	236,156,878		218,861,235
	%		%
Net profit margin	39.02		12.89
Return on equity	24.22		9.38
Return on assets	8.94		4.04
Foreign sales percent	73		68
No. of employees (FTEs)	1,339		1,186

* Common
□ Restated
A Reported in accordance with IFRS

Latest Results

Periods ended:	3m Mar. 31/23^A		3m Mar. 31/22^A
	$000s	%Chg	$000s
Operating revenue	621,721	-11	695,054
Net income	107,137	-63	287,580
Net inc. for equity hldrs	69,894	-69	229,142
Net inc. for non-cont. int.	37,243		58,438
	$		$
Earnings per share*	0.27		0.99

* Common
A Reported in accordance with IFRS

Historical Summary
(as originally stated)

Fiscal Year	Oper. Rev.	Net Inc. Bef. Disc.	EPS*
	$000s	$000s	$
2022^A	2,448,815	955,457	3.46
2021^A	2,093,255	269,879	0.82
2020^A	2,060,627	485,057	1.76
2019^A	1,658,977	451,754	1.71
2018^A	1,555,587	405,508	1.50

* Common
A Reported in accordance with IFRS

N.60 Northstar Clean Technologies Inc.

Symbol - ROOF **Exchange** - TSX-VEN **CUSIP** - 66706T
Head Office - 7046 Brown St, Delta, BC, V4G 1G8 **Telephone** - (604) 569-2209
Website - www.northstarcleantech.com
Email - info@kincommunications.com
Investor Relations - Investor Relations (866) 684-6730
Auditors - MNP LLP C.A., Vancouver, B.C.
Transfer Agents - Computershare Trust Company of Canada Inc.

Profile - (B.C. 2017) Operates material recovery facilities that use a proprietary process for taking discarded asphalt shingles and extracting the liquid asphalt, aggregate sands and fibre for usage in new hot mix asphalt, construction products and other industrial applications.

Has a pilot facility in Delta, B.C., where asphalt shingle manufacturers, roofing companies, roofing contractors and waste haulers can dispose of single-use or defective asphalt shingle construction waste. The company's proprietary bitumen extraction and separation technology (BEST) uses a combination of reactions, which break the molecular bonds of the component parts and then separates the liquid asphalt, aggregate and fibre components. The liquid asphalt is stored in heated tanks for delivery to customers and the aggregate sands and fibre are stockpiled at the location and sold. The tipping fees charged to dispose of the shingles are offered at a meaningful discount to landfill tipping fees. These tipping fees are expected to supplement the company's income from the sale of finished product. The facility received its first truckload of landfill-bound asphalt shingles in November 2022.

In addition, the company plans to build and operate a 150- to 200-tonne-per-day asphalt shingle reprocessing scale facility in Calgary, Alta., as well as to explore opportunities to create an asphalt shingle reprocessing scale facility in Toronto, Ont.

The company has executed a definitive off-take agreement with **McAsphalt Industries Ltd.**, whereby the company has agreed to sell, and McAsphalt has agreed to purchase, 100% of the asphalt oil produced at the proposed Calgary, Alta., facility.

In October 2022, the company announced a partnership **Renewable U Energy Inc.** to fully fund its Phase 1 expansion program through financing of over $43,500,000, including the issuance of 4,875,000 common shares to Renewable U at $0.40 per share, secured three-year 6% convertible debentures, convertible after year two at $0.50 per share, debt of $36,000,000 for three facilities at $12,000,000 per facility, and the issuance of 4,500,000 warrants to acquire common shares of the company at $0.60 per share for a period of two years. The Phase 1 plan includes building three scale-up asphalt shingle reprocessing facilities in Calgary, the Greater Toronto Area and the Pacific Northwest region of the United States.

Predecessor Detail - Name changed from Northstar Venture Technologies Inc., Jan. 29, 2021.

Directors - James A. (Jim) Currie, exec. chr., Vancouver, B.C.; Aidan Mills, pres. & CEO, Calgary, Alta.; Gregg J. Sedun†, Vancouver, B.C.; Jeffrey D. (Jeff) Beyer, Mo.; James C. Borkowski, Vancouver, B.C.; Neil Currie, Vancouver, B.C.; Gordon Johnson, Delta, B.C.

Other Exec. Officers - Rosemary Pritchard, CFO; Kellie Johnston, chief sustainability officer & corp. counsel; Diana Mark, corp. sec.

† Lead director

Capital Stock

	Authorized (shs.)	Outstanding (shs.)[1]
Common	unlimited	126,196,270

[1] At June 28, 2023

Major Shareholder - Widely held at June 28, 2023.

Price Range - ROOF/TSX-VEN

Year	Volume	High	Low	Close
2022	35,449,943	$0.38	$0.11	$0.17
2021	47,157,206	$0.54	$0.25	$0.36

Recent Close: $0.15

Capital Stock Changes - In April 2023, private placement of 18,195,367 units (1 common share & 1 warrant) at 15¢ per unit was completed, with warrants exercisable at 20¢ per share for three years.

In August and October 2022, private placement of 1,875,000 common shares was completed at 40¢ per share.

Wholly Owned Subsidiaries

Empower Environmental Solutions Calgary Ltd., Alta.
Empower Environmental Solutions Ltd., Delta, B.C.
Empower Environmental Solutions Toronto West Ltd., Ont.
1284041 B.C. Ltd., B.C.

Financial Statistics

Periods ended:	12m Dec. 31/22[A]		12m Dec. 31/21[A]
	$000s	%Chg	$000s
Salaries & benefits	2,228		722
Research & devel. expense	1,576		633
General & admin expense	2,580		2,586
Stock-based compensation	657		2,357
Operating expense	**7,041**	**+12**	**6,298**
Operating income	**(7,041)**	**n.a.**	**(6,298)**
Deprec., depl. & amort.	1,076		462
Finance costs, gross	229		293
Pre-tax income	**(8,445)**	**n.a.**	**(7,208)**
Income taxes	(244)		nil
Net income	**(8,201)**	**n.a.**	**(7,208)**
Cash & equivalent	1,114		5,949
Current assets	1,486		6,786
Fixed assets, net	3,287		3,205
Right-of-use assets	1,341		1,800
Intangibles, net	26		nil
Total assets	**6,829**	**-45**	**12,375**
Accts. pay. & accr. liabs	1,238		760
Current liabilities	1,905		1,294
Long-term debt, gross	1,102		239
Long-term debt, net	975		149
Long-term lease liabilities	1,143		1,659
Shareholders' equity	2,785		9,273
Cash from oper. activs	**(5,687)**	**n.a.**	**(4,095)**
Cash from fin. activs	1,500		9,205
Cash from invest. activs	(648)		(1,140)
Net cash position	**1,114**	**-81**	**5,949**
Capital expenditures	(717)		(761)
Capital disposals	nil		24
	$		$
Earnings per share*	(0.08)		(0.08)
Cash flow per share*	(0.05)		(0.05)
	shs		shs
No. of shs. o/s*	108,000,903		106,125,903
Avg. no. of shs. o/s*	106,838,232		88,830,351
	%		%
Net profit margin	n.a.		n.a.
Return on equity	(136.03)		(123.96)
Return on assets	(83.09)		(80.24)

* Common
[A] Reported in accordance with IFRS

Latest Results

Periods ended:	3m Mar. 31/23[A]		3m Mar. 31/22[A]
	$000s	%Chg	$000s
Operating revenue	21	n.a.	nil
Net income	(1,689)	n.a.	(2,033)
	$		$
Earnings per share*	(0.02)		(0.02)

* Common
[A] Reported in accordance with IFRS

Historical Summary
(as originally stated)

Fiscal Year	Oper. Rev.	Net Inc. Bef. Disc.	EPS*
	$000s	$000s	$
2022[A]	nil	(8,201)	(0.08)
2021[A]	nil	(7,208)	(0.08)
2020[A]	nil	(6,597)	(0.16)
2019[A]	nil	(901)	(0.02)

* Common
[A] Reported in accordance with IFRS

N.61 NorthStar Gaming Holdings Inc.

Symbol - BET **Exchange** - TSX-VEN **CUSIP** - 66707K
Head Office - 200-220 King St W, Toronto, ON, M5H 1K4 **Telephone** - (647) 530-2387
Website - www.northstargaming.ca
Email - corey.goodman@northstargaming.ca
Investor Relations - Corey Goodman (647) 530-2387
Auditors - KPMG LLP C.A., Vaughan, Ont.
Transfer Agents - Odyssey Trust Company
Profile - (B.C. 2020) Owns and operates NorthStar Bets, an online casino and sportsbook gaming platform for Ontario residents.

Holds a licence from the Alcohol and Gaming Commission of Ontario (AGCO) to operate its online gaming site northstarbets.ca, which offers access to 37 monthly regulated sports betting markets, and more than 300 casino games, including slot games, blackjack, roulette, baccarat at a variety of stakes and live dealer games. Also offer its own mobile applications. iGaming Ontario, a subsidiary of the AGCO, deducts company 20% of gross gamming revenue to cover its tax burden as the legal operator of all gaming sites operating under an Ontario licence. At Mar. 3, 2023, the platform had a customer database of over 20,000 registered Ontario players and had more than 19,500 active users between May 9, 2022 (launch date) and Jan. 31, 2023.

In July 2022, option on Midway gold prospect in British Columbia was terminated and related costs written off.

Common listed on TSX-VEN, Mar. 8, 2023.

Common delisted from CSE, Mar. 2, 2023.

Recent Merger and Acquisition Activity

Status: completed **Revised:** Mar. 3, 2023

UPDATE: The transaction was completed. PREVIOUS: Baden Resources Inc. entered into a letter of intent for the reverse takeover acquisition of private NorthStar Gaming Inc, which owns and operates NorthStar Bets, a made-in-Ontario casino and sportsbook gaming platform. Baden would issue post-consolidated common shares on a to-be-determined basis. June 29, 2022 - A definitive agreement was entered into. The basis of consideration was one-for-one (following a 1-for-3.3333 share consolidation). A condition for completion of the transaction was NorthStar completing a private placement of up to 30,000,000 subscription receipts at 50¢ per receipt, each of which would be automatically exchanged without further consideration into 1 Baden post-consolidated common share. Oct. 5, 2022 - NorthStar had completed a private placement of a total of 10,150,000 subscription receipts.

Predecessor Detail - Name changed from Baden Resources Inc., Mar. 2, 2023, pursuant to the reverse takeover acquisition of NorthStar Gaming Inc.; basis 1 new for 3.33333 old shs.

Directors - Michael Moskowitz, CEO & chr., Ont.; Barry W. Shafran†, Toronto, Ont.; Vic Bertrand, Beaconsfield, Qué.; Brian Cooper, Ont.; Christopher D. (Chris) Hodgson, Markham, Ont.; Dean T. MacDonald, St. John's, N.L.; Chris McGinnis, United Kingdom; Sylvia Prentice, Ont.

Other Exec. Officers - Gil Steinfeld, COO; Jennifer Barber, CFO; Corey Goodman, exec. v-p, corp. devel., counsel & corp. sec.; Dante Anderson, v-p, mktg.; Chin Dhushenthen, v-p, fin. & compliance; Dean MacNeil, v-p, product & managed srvcs.; Maureen Rydzik, v-p, IT & vender rel.

† Lead director

Capital Stock

	Authorized (shs.)	Outstanding (shs.)[1]
Preferred	unlimited	78,000
Common	unlimited	156,569,109

[1] At Mar. 8, 2023

Preferred - A total of 66,300 shares are held by entities controlled by Jordan Bitove. Entitled to an annual non-cumulative dividend of 6% on the redemption value of $100 per share. Redeemable at the option of the company or holder. A total of 50,000 shares are convertible into common shares at $552.51 per share. Non-voting. Classified as a current liability.

Major Shareholder - Paul Rivett and Janis Wolfe held 23% interest, Jordan L. Bitove held 23% interest and Playtech plc held 15.65% interest at Mar. 8, 2023.

Price Range - BDN/CSE (D)

Year	Volume	High	Low	Close
2022	56,792	$0.77	$0.40	$0.67
2021	173,808	$0.67	$0.43	$0.50

Consolidation: 1-for-3.33333 cons. in Mar. 2023

Recent Close: $0.14

Capital Stock Changes - In March 2023, common shares were consolidated on a 1-for-3.3333 basis and 152,387,671 post-consolidated common shares were issued pursuant to the reverse takeover acquisition of NorthStar Gaming Inc., and 78,000 preferred shares were issued on conversion of a like number of NorthStar Gaming Inc. preferred shares.

In February 2022, private placement of 2,000,000 units (1 common share & 1 warrant) at 10¢ per unit was completed. Also during fiscal 2022, 2,100 common shares were issued on exercise of warrants.

Wholly Owned Subsidiaries

NorthStar Gaming Inc, Ont.
- 100% int. in **NorthStar Gaming (Ontario) Inc.**, Toronto, Ont.

Financial Statistics

Periods ended:	12m June 30/22[A1]		12m June 30/21[A]
	$000s	%Chg	$000s
General & admin expense	208		117
Stock-based compensation	nil		6
Operating expense	**208**	**+70**	**122**
Operating income	**(208)**	**n.a.**	**(122)**
Write-downs/write-offs	(203)		(67)
Pre-tax income	**(410)**	**n.a.**	**(188)**
Net income	**(410)**	**n.a.**	**(188)**
Cash & equivalent	294		403
Current assets	299		413
Explor./devel. properties	nil		70
Total assets	**299**	**-38**	**484**
Accts. pay. & accr. liabs	36		11
Current liabilities	36		11
Shareholders' equity	263		472
Cash from oper. activs	**(181)**	**n.a.**	**(128)**
Cash from fin. activs	(200)		343
Cash from invest. activs	(128)		(54)
Net cash position	**294**	**-27**	**403**
Capital expenditures	(133)		(49)
	$		$
Earnings per share*	(0.10)		(0.07)
Cash flow per share*	(0.05)		(0.04)
	shs		shs
No. of shs. o/s*	4,181,430		3,580,800
Avg. no. of shs. o/s*	3,788,469		3,390,033
	%		%
Net profit margin	n.a.		n.a.
Return on equity	(111.56)		(49.87)
Return on assets	(104.73)		(47.24)

* Common
[A] Reported in accordance with IFRS
[1] Results for the 12-month period ended June 30, 2022 and prior periods pertain to Baden Resources Inc.

Historical Summary
(as originally stated)

Fiscal Year	Oper. Rev.	Net Inc. Bef. Disc.	EPS*
	$000s	$000s	$
2022[A]	nil	(410)	(0.10)
2021[A]	nil	(188)	(0.07)
2020[A1]	nil	(54)	(0.07)

* Common
[A] Reported in accordance with IFRS
[1] 23 weeks ended June 30, 2020.

Note: Adjusted throughout for 1-for-3.333333 cons. in Mar. 2023

N.62 Northview Residential REIT

Symbol - NRR.UN **Exchange** - TSX **CUSIP** - 66719E
Head Office - 200-6131 6 St SE, Calgary, AB, T2H 1L9 **Telephone** - (403) 531-0720 **Fax** - (866) 939-2858
Website - www.rentnorthview.com
Email - swalker@nvreit.ca
Investor Relations - Sarah Walker (403) 531-0720
Auditors - KPMG LLP C.A., Calgary, Alta.
Bankers - Canadian Imperial Bank of Commerce
Lawyers - Blake, Cassels & Graydon LLP
Transfer Agents - TSX Trust Company, Toronto, Ont.
Managers - Starlight Investments CDN AM Group L.P.
Employees - 335 at Dec. 31, 2022
Profile - (Ont. 2020) Acquires, owns and operates income-producing multi-residential suites, commercial real estate and execusuites across Canada.

The multi-residential properties include apartments, townhomes and single-family rental suites.

The commercial properties consist of office, industrial and retail properties, including mixed-use buildings, located primarily in regions where the fund has residential operations. A majority of the properties are leased to federal and provincial government and high quality commercial tenants under long-term leases.

The executive suites offer apartment-style accommodation where the rental periods range from a few days to several months.

Geographic breakdown of property portfolio at Aug. 23, 2023:

Location	Residential Suites	Commercial (Sq. ft.)[1]
Northwest Territories	1,468[2]	529,998
Nunavut	1,218[3]	226,662
British Columbia	1,379	86,238
Alberta	4,479	56,307
Manitoba	845	100,963
Ontario	272	1,298
Nova Scotia	844	2,288
Saskatchewan	323	nil
Quebec	581	4,490
New Brunswick	1,338	17,680
Newfoundland & Labrador	1,875	225,449
	14,622	1,251,373

[1] Leasable commercial space.

[2] Includes 158 execusuites.
[3] Includes 42 execusuites.

Recent Merger and Acquisition Activity

Status: completed **Revised:** Aug. 21, 2023
UPDATE: The transaction was completed. PREVIOUS: Northview Fund agreed to acquire three portfolios of multi-family properties, consisting of 3,301 multi-family suites and 119,643 commercial sq. ft., for a total of $742,000,000 in exchange for Northview Fund units and redeemable units at an issue price of $15.06 per unit and assumption of existing debt. The acquisition would include 12 properties totaling 2,088 apartments and 7,148 sq. ft. of commercial space in Alberta, Ontario, Nova Scotia and Quebec, owned by Galaxy Value Add Fund LP; four properties totaling 368 housing units and 11,532 sq. ft. of commercial space in Brantford and Guelph, Ont., and Edmonton, Alta., owned by an affiliate of Starlight Investments; and five properties totaling 845 housing units and 100,963 sq. ft. of commercial space in Winnipeg, Man., from two global institutional investors. Upon completion, Northview Fund would internalize management and restructure as Northview Residential REIT, a TSX-listed, traditional open-ended, real estate investment trust, with all classes of trust units concurrently consolidated on a 1-for-1.75 basis. Northview Residential REIT would hold 14,622 residential suites and 1,251,373 commercial sq. ft. across nine provinces and two territories.

Predecessor Detail - Name changed from Northview Fund, Aug. 21, 2023, pursuant to the acquisition of three portfolios of multi-family properties and concurrent restructuring as an open-ended, real estate investment trust; basis 1 new for 1.75 old shs.

Trustees - Daniel Drimmer, chr., Toronto, Ont.; Todd R. Cook, CEO, Calgary, Alta.; Lawrence D. Wilder‡, Toronto, Ont.; Rob Kumer, Toronto, Ont.; Harry Rosenbaum, Toronto, Ont.; Kelly Smith, Toronto, Ont.

Oper. Subsid./Mgt. Co. Officers - Sarah Walker, CFO; Karl Bomhof, v-p, HR, legal & gen. counsel; Linay Freda, v-p, opers.
‡ Lead trustee

Capital Stock

	Authorized (shs.)	Outstanding (shs.)[1]
Class A Trust Unit	unlimited	6,261,556
Class C Trust Unit	unlimited	24,408,338
Class F Trust Unit	unlimited	3,774,887

[1] At June 30, 2023

Note: Number of post-restructuring/consolidation trust units have yet to be disclosed.

Class A Trust Unit - Includes a 3% selling concession. Convertible into class F trust units on a 1-for-1 basis, subject to continuing to satisfy the minimum listing requirements of the Toronto Stock Exchange. One vote per unit.

Class C Trust Unit - No agents' fee or other commissions are payable. Convertible into class A or class F trust units on a 1-for-1 basis. One vote per unit.

Class F Trust Unit - For fee-based accounts and do not include selling concession. Convertible into class A trust units on a 1-for-1 basis. One vote per unit.

Major Shareholder - Daniel Drimmer held 28.54% interest, KingSett Capital Inc. held 21.59% interest, AIMCo Realty Investors LP held 13.93% interest and TC Green Limited Partnership & Prairie MUR Limited Partnership together held 11.48% interest at Aug. 23, 2023.

Price Range - NRR.UN/TSX

Year	Volume	High	Low	Close
2022	896,672	$28.18	$15.72	$17.85
2021	1,195,890	$30.42	$23.28	$27.63
2020	513,857	$26.78	$20.56	$23.29

Consolidation: 1-for-1.75 cons. in Aug. 2023
Recent Close: $12.82

Capital Stock Changes - On Aug. 23, 2023, class A, C and F trust units were consolidated on a 1-for-1.75 basis.

During 2022, 544,000 class F trust units were issued on conversion of 529,000 class A trust units and 31,000 class C trust units.

Dividends

NRR.UN cl A tr unit Ra $1.093752 pa M est. Sept. 15, 2023
1-for-2 cons eff. Aug. 23, 2023
Prev. Rate: $0.62496 est. July 17, 2023
Prev. Rate: $1.25712 est. Dec. 15, 2020

Wholly Owned Subsidiaries

Northview Canadian HY Holdings GP Inc., Ont.
- 0.01% int. in **Northview Canadian HY Holdings L.P.**, Ont.
- 0.01% int. in **Northview Canadian HY Properties L.P.**, Ont.

Subsidiaries

99.99% int. in **Northview Canadian HY Holdings L.P.**, Ont.
- 100% int. in **Northview Canadian HY Properties GP Inc.**, Ont.
- 99.99% int. in **Northview Canadian HY Properties L.P.**, Ont.

Financial Statistics

Periods ended:	12m Dec. 31/22[A]		12m Dec. 31/21[A]
	$000s	%Chg	$000s
Total revenue	**198,210**	**+3**	**192,125**
Rental operating expense	70,974		64,637
Property taxes	14,728		14,819
Operating expense	**85,702**	**+8**	**79,456**
Operating income	**112,508**	**0**	**112,669**
Investment income	1,960		1,316
Deprec. & amort.	3,377		3,400
Non-operating overhead	13,514		13,529
Finance costs, net	48,839		34,641
Pre-tax income	**70,811**	**n.a.**	**(21,341)**
Net income	**70,811**	**n.a.**	**(21,341)**
Net inc. for equity hldrs	**70,431**	**n.a.**	**(21,364)**
Net inc. for non-cont. int	**380**	**n.m.**	**23**
Cash & equivalent	26,486		11,312
Accounts receivable	5,546		7,074
Current assets	44,742		27,725
Long-term investments	13,153		12,743
Fixed assets	32,043		35,000
Income-producing props	1,842,870		1,755,470
Properties for future devel	19,208		19,208
Property interests, net	1,894,121		1,809,678
Total assets	**1,954,529**	**+5**	**1,853,096**
Accts. pay. & accr. liabs	30,402		31,464
Current liabilities	826,064		787,507
Long-term debt, gross	1,354,333		1,322,519
Long-term debt, net	562,433		570,239
Shareholders' equity	564,869		494,438
Non-controlling interest	1,163		912
Cash from oper. activs	**41,030**	**-29**	**57,531**
Cash from fin. activs	(6,321)		(49,470)
Cash from invest. activs	(19,535)		(22,086)
Net cash position	**26,486**	**+134**	**11,312**
Capital expenditures	(408)		(239)
Capital disposals	560		67
Increase in property	20,737		(23,311)
	$		$
Earnings per share*	n.a.		n.a.
Cash flow per share*	2.08		2.92
Funds from opers. per sh.*	2.49		3.19
Adj. funds from opers. per sh.*	1.87		2.64
Cash divd. per share*	2.20		2.20
Total divd. per share*	**2.20**		**2.20**
	shs		shs
No. of shs. o/s*	19,697,714		19,706,857
	%		%
Net profit margin	35.73		(11.11)
Return on equity	13.30		(4.23)
Return on assets	3.72		(1.14)
No. of employees (FTEs)	335		344

* Cl.A, C & F Trust Un
[A] Reported in accordance with IFRS

Latest Results

Periods ended:	6m June 30/23[A]		6m June 30/22[A]
	$000s	%Chg	$000s
Total revenue	103,205	+6	97,538
Net income	(12,521)	n.a.	(7,024)
Net inc. for equity hldrs	(12,593)	n.a.	(7,118)
Net inc. for non-cont. int	72		94
	$		$
Earnings per share*	n.a.		n.a.

[A] Reported in accordance with IFRS

Historical Summary
(as originally stated)

Fiscal Year	Total Rev.	Net Inc. Bef. Disc.	EPS*
	$000s	$000s	$
2022[A]	198,210	70,811	n.a.
2021[A]	192,125	(21,341)	n.a.
2020[A1]	31,059	89,664	n.a.
2019[A2]	194,001	40,187	n.a.
2018[A]	189,151	90,799	n.a.

* Cl.A, C & F Trust Un
[A] Reported in accordance with IFRS
[1] 37 weeks ended Dec. 31, 2020.
[2] Results for 2019 and 2018 represent carve-out financial statements of initial property portfolio.
Note: Adjusted throughout for 1-for-1.75 cons. in Aug. 2023

N.63 NorthWest Healthcare Properties Real Estate Investment Trust

Symbol - NWH.UN **Exchange** - TSX **CUSIP** - 667495
Head Office - 1100-180 Dundas St W, Toronto, ON, M5G 1Z8
Telephone - (416) 366-2000 **Fax** - (416) 366-2433
Website - www.nwhreit.com
Email - mike.brady@nwhreit.com
Investor Relations - Michael Brady (416) 366-2000
Auditors - KPMG LLP C.A., Toronto, Ont.
Lawyers - Goodmans LLP, Toronto, Ont.
Transfer Agents - Computershare Trust Company of Canada Inc., Toronto, Ont.
FP500 Revenue Ranking - 486
Employees - 250 at Dec. 31, 2022

Profile - (Ont. 2010) Owns, develops and manages healthcare properties in the Americas, Europe and Asia-Pacific.

Property portfolio at Dec. 31, 2022:

Location	Props.	Sq. Ft.[1]
Canada	56	3,594,690
U.S.	26	1,237,103
Brazil	8	1,880,333
Germany	38	3,550,717
Netherlands	17	1,236,527
U.K.	14	666,393
Australia & New Zealand	74	6,469,820
	233	18,635,583

[1] Gross leasable area (GLA).

In Canada, the trust owned and managed 56 properties, consisting primarily of medical office buildings, located in Alberta (14), Manitoba (2), Ontario (23), Quebec (11), New Brunswick (2) and Nova Scotia (4), with GLA of 3,564,512 sq. ft. at Dec. 31, 2022. Tenants include regional health authorities, primary care networks, family health teams, medical and diagnostic imaging clinics, medical practitioners, pharmacies and laboratories, as well as institutional and non-healthcare tenants. Also has two redevelopment properties in Calgary, Alta., totaling 30,178 sq. ft. of GLA.

In the United States, the trust owned and managed 26 properties, consisting of seven hospitals, five micro-hospitals and 14 medical office buildings, in Illinois (5), Indiana, Texas (4), Florida (2), Arizona (9), California, Oklahoma, Colorado, Minnesota and Massachusetts, with GLA of 1,237,103 sq. ft. at Dec. 31, 2022.

In Brazil, the trust owned eight private hospitals in São Paulo (4), Brasilia (3) and Rio de Janeiro, with GLA of 1,880,333 sq. ft. at Dec. 31, 2022. Seven of the hospitals are operated by **Rede D'Or São Luiz S.A.**

In Germany, the trust owned and managed 38 medical office buildings and healthcare facilities, including 10 properties held through a joint venture, in Berlin (11), Königs Wusterhausen, Fulda (2), Ingolstadt, Hamburg (2), Leipzig (11), Bad Kissingen, Wilhelmshaven, Bad Wildungen, Lübeck, Schleswig-Holstein, Hauptstrasse 2, Bad Salzuflen, Bad Rothenfelde and Graal-Müritz (2), with GLA of 3,550,717 sq. ft. at Dec. 31, 2022.

In the Netherlands, the trust owned and managed 17 medical office buildings and healthcare facilities, including nine properties held through joint ventures, in Rotterdam (2), Hilversum (2), Eindhoven, Brunssum, Doetichem, Sliedrecht, Assen, Dordrecht (4), Amersfoort, s-Hertogenbosch, Arnhem and Utrecht, with GLA of 1,236,527 sq. ft. at Dec. 31, 2022.

In the United Kingdom, the trust owned 14 private hospitals in London (4), Lincoln, Lancaster, Huddersfield, Bury Saint Edmunds, Birmingham, Essex, Sheffield, Edinburgh, Woking and Cheshire, with GLA of 666,393 sq. ft. at Dec. 31, 2022.

In Australia and New Zealand, the trust owned and managed, including joint venture interests, a portfolio of 20 hospitals and healthcare facilities, four medical office buildings and two life sciences properties mainly in Sydney, Melbourne and Brisbane, Australia, totaling 3,157,920 sq. ft. of GLA at Dec. 31, 2022; and through affiliate **Vital Healthcare Property Trust**, owned a portfolio of 48 hospitals and healthcare facilities, medical office buildings and development sites in Australia and New Zealand, totaling 3,311,900 sq. ft. of GLA at Dec. 31, 2022.

In August 2022, the trust acquired 38,287-sq.-ft. Peninsula Private Hospital in Brisbane, Qld., for an undisclosed amount. Also during 2022, the trust acquired various development lands in Australia, New Zealand and Europe for $7,600,000.

Recent Merger and Acquisition Activity

Status: completed **Announced:** May 31, 2023
NorthWest Healthcare Properties Real Estate Investment Trust sold Bakersfield Hospital in California for $76,000,000.

Status: completed **Announced:** Sept. 30, 2022
NorthWest Healthcare Properties Real Estate Investment Trust sold Queenston Medical-Dental Centre, an 18,400-sq.-ft. medical office building in Hamilton, Ont., for $5,500,000.

Status: completed **Announced:** June 13, 2022
NorthWest Healthcare Properties Real Estate Investment Trust, through a 30%-owned joint venture, acquired a 43,090-sq.-ft. hospital in Utrecht, Netherlands, for $25,300,000.

Status: completed **Revised:** Apr. 14, 2022
UPDATE: The transaction was completed. PREVIOUS: NorthWest Healthcare Properties Real Estate Investment Trust entered into a binding agreement to acquire a U.S. portfolio of cure-focused healthcare assets for US$601,900,000 (Cdn$764,300,000). The portfolio is NorthWest's first U.S. acquisition. The portfolio is made up of 15 medical office buildings and 12 hospitals across 10 U.S. states totaling 1,200,000 sq. ft. The transaction was expected to close in the second quarter of 2022.

Status: completed **Announced:** Mar. 29, 2022
NorthWest Healthcare Properties Real Estate Investment Trust acquired a 59,151-sq.-ft. medical office building in Amersfoort, Netherlands, for $10,900,000.

Status: completed **Announced:** Mar. 1, 2022
NorthWest Healthcare Properties Real Estate Investment Trust, through a 30%-owned joint venture, acquired a 151,502-sq.-ft. children clinic

and a 252,952-sq.-ft. rehabilitation clinic in Graal-Müritz, Germany, for $18,400,000.

Trustees - Dale Klein, chr., Edmonton, Alta.; Robert Baron, Toronto, Ont.; Bernard W. Crotty, Toronto, Ont.; Laura King, London, Middx., United Kingdom; Dr. David Klein, Toronto, Ont.; Maureen O'Connell, N.Y.; Brian Petersen, Calgary, Alta.

Exec. Officers - Craig Mitchell, interim CEO; Michael (Mike) Brady, pres.; Gerson Amado, man. dir., Brazil; Dave Casimiro, man. dir., Canada; Shailen Chande, CFO; Peter Riggin, CAO; Jan Krizan, head, global funds; Sophie Morin, regl. gen. mgr., Que. & Atlantic; Terry Schmitt, regl. gen. mgr., western Canada

Capital Stock

	Authorized (shs.)	Outstanding (shs.)[1]
Trust Unit	unlimited	242,494,222[2]
Special Voting Unit	unlimited	1,710,000
Cl.B Exch. Unit	unlimited	1,710,000[3 4]

[1] At Apr. 17, 2023

[2] At May 31, 2023.

[3] Classified as debt.

[4] Securities of subsidiary NWI Healthcare Properties L.P.

Trust Unit - One vote per trust unit.

Special Voting Unit - Issued to holders of class B exchangeable units of subsidiary NWI Healthcare Properties L.P. Each special voting unit entitles the holder to a number of votes at unitholder meetings equal to the number of trust units into which the class B limited partnership units are exchangeable.

Class B Exchangeable Unit - Securities of subsidiary NWI Healthcare Properties L.P. Entitled to distributions equal to those provided to holders of trust units. Directly exchangeable into trust units on a 1-for-1 basis at any time by holder. Classified as a financial liability.

Normal Course Issuer Bid - The company plans to make normal course purchases of up to 22,224,257 trust units representing 10% of the public float. The bid commenced on June 12, 2023, and expires on June 11, 2024.

Major Shareholder - Widely held at Apr. 17, 2023.

Price Range - NWH.UN/TSX

Year	Volume	High	Low	Close
2022	140,927,994	$14.42	$9.30	$9.50
2021	124,885,740	$13.90	$12.32	$13.81
2020	125,108,510	$13.35	$6.27	$12.60
2019	95,253,667	$12.79	$9.35	$11.93
2018	44,631,874	$11.71	$9.27	$9.48

Recent Close: $6.84

Capital Stock Changes - In March 2022, bought deal public offering of 12,500,500 trust units was completed at $13.80 per unit, including 1,630,500 trust units on exercise of over-allotment option. In May 2022, private placement of 1,086,955 trust units was completed at $13.80 per unit. Also during 2022, trust units were issued as follows: 2,839,242 under distribution reinvestment plan and 93,757 under deferred unit plan.

Dividends

NWH.UN unit Ra $0.80004 pa M est. Aug. 15, 2023**[1]

[1] Distribution reinvestment plan implemented eff. Aug. 27/10.

** Reinvestment Option

Wholly Owned Subsidiaries

Fundo De Investimenttno Imobiliário NorthWest Investmentos Fund I Imobiliários Em Saúde, Brazil.
NHP Holdings Limited Partnership, Ont.
- 100% int. in **Healthcare Properties Limited Partnership**, Man.
  - 100% int. in **NorthWest Healthcare Properties Corporation**, Ont.

NWH Australia Asset Trust, Australia.
NWH Australia Hold Trust No. 3, Australia.
NWH Australia Hold Trust, Australia.
NWI Galaxy Investment Advisory S.a.r.l., Luxembourg.
NWI Galaxy JV Lux 2 S.a.r.l., Luxembourg.
NWI Gesundheitsimmobilien GmbH & Co KG, Germany.
NWI Gezondheid Vastgoed B.V., Netherlands.
NWI Healthcare Properties L.P., Ont.
- 100% int. in **NWI Healthcare Properties LLC**, Delaware, Ont.
- 100% int. in **NWI Management GmbH**, Germany.
- 100% int. in **NWI NZ Management Company**, New Zealand.
- 28.1% int. in **Vital Healthcare Property Trust**, Auckland, New Zealand.

NWI Jersey HC Ltd., Jersey.
NWI Jersey Ltd., United Kingdom.
NWI Luxembourg S.A.R.L., Luxembourg.
NWI Management UK Ltd., United Kingdom.
NWI UK REIT Ltd., United Kingdom.
NWI US Hospital REIT LLC, United States.
NWI US MOB REIT LLC, United States.
NWI US Management LLC, United States.
Northwest Healthcare Australia RE Ltd., Australia.
NorthWest Healthcare Properties Management Limited, New Zealand.
NorthWest Healthcare Properties Management Pty Ltd., Australia.
Northwest International II Investimentos Imobiliar S.A., Brazil.
Northwest International Investimentos Imobiliar S.A., Brazil.
NorthWest Investmentos Em Saúde Fund I Fundo de Investimento Multimercado, Brazil.

Investments

30% int. in **NWI Galaxy JV GmbH & Co. KG**, Netherlands.
30% int. in **NorthWest Australia HSO Trust**, Australia.
30% int. in **NorthWest Australia Hospital Investment Galaxy 2 Trust**, Australia.
30% int. in **NorthWest Australia Hospital Investment Trust**, Australia.
30% int. in **NorthWest Healthcare Properties Australia REIT**, Australia.

Financial Statistics

Periods ended:	12m Dec. 31/22[A]		12m Dec. 31/21[A]
	$000s	%Chg	$000s
Total revenue	**464,052**	**+16**	**401,508**
Rental operating expense	100,477		85,093
General & admin. expense	46,474		38,821
Other operating expense	3,430		9,441
Operating expense	**150,381**	**+13**	**133,355**
Operating income	**313,671**	**+17**	**268,153**
Investment income	20,604		107,483
Deprec. & amort.	1,396		1,382
Finance income	9,180		4,597
Finance costs, gross	157,755		121,333
Pre-tax income	**204,924**	**-72**	**736,068**
Income taxes	79,297		124,229
Net inc. bef. disc. opers	**125,627**	**-79**	**611,839**
Income from disc. opers	nil		51,346
Net income	**125,627**	**-81**	**663,185**
Net inc. for equity hldrs	**64,295**	**-85**	**434,879**
Net inc. for non-cont. int	**61,332**	**-73**	**228,306**
Cash & equivalent	87,987		62,700
Accounts receivable	17,381		51,137
Long-term investments	619,580		481,352
Fixed assets	4,701		2,536
Income-producing props	6,612,535		6,294,305
Property interests, net	6,617,236		6,296,841
Right-of-use assets	4,413		4,312
Intangibles, net	84,578		88,947
Total assets	**8,514,000**	**+21**	**7,064,401**
Accts. pay. & accr. liabs	133,308		89,963
Long-term debt, gross	3,697,376		2,967,785
Shareholders' equity	2,456,847		2,392,131
Non-controlling interest	1,285,128		1,131,443
Cash from oper. activs	**224,178**	**+79**	**124,967**
Cash from fin. activs	1,176,963		711,186
Cash from invest. activs	(1,356,719)		(914,834)
Net cash position	**87,987**	**+40**	**62,700**
Capital expenditures	(615)		(483)
Increase in property	(1,224,428)		(774,570)
Decrease in property	7,070		56,577
	$		$
Earnings per share*	n.a.		n.a.
Cash flow per share*	0.93		0.56
Funds from opers. per sh.*	0.71		0.86
Adj. funds from opers. per sh.*	0.73		0.87
Cash divd. per share*	0.80		0.80
Total divd. per share*	**0.80**		**0.80**
	shs		shs
No. of shs. o/s*	240,647,589		224,127,135
	%		%
Net profit margin	27.07		152.39
Return on equity	2.65		19.03
Return on assets	2.85		11.04
Foreign sales percent	n.a.		69
No. of employees (FTEs)	250		265

* Trust unit

[A] Reported in accordance with IFRS

Latest Results

Periods ended:	3m Mar. 31/23[A]		3m Mar. 31/22[oA]
	$000s	%Chg	$000s
Total revenue	146,049	+28	114,122
Net income	(89,155)	n.a.	123,335
Net inc. for equity hldrs	(97,486)	n.a.	88,254
Net inc. for non-cont. int	8,331		35,081
	$		$
Earnings per share*	n.a.		n.a.

[o] Restated

[A] Reported in accordance with IFRS

Historical Summary
(as originally stated)

Fiscal Year	Total Rev.	Net Inc. Bef. Disc.	EPS*
	$000s	$000s	$
2022[A]	464,052	125,627	n.a.
2021[A]	401,508	611,839	n.a.
2020[A]	385,484	381,414	n.a.
2019[A]	377,359	73,250	n.a.
2018[A]	356,148	128,740	n.a.

* Trust unit

[A] Reported in accordance with IFRS

N.64 Nova Cannabis Inc.

Symbol - NOVC **Exchange** - TSX **CUSIP** - 66980W
Head Office - 101-17220 Stony Plain Rd NW, Edmonton, AB, T5S 1K6 **Telephone** - (780) 497-3262 **Toll-free** - (855) 702-7400 **Fax** - (780) 702-1999
Website - novacannabis.ca
Email - investor@novacannabis.ca
Investor Relations - Marcie Kiziak (780) 497-3262
Auditors - PricewaterhouseCoopers LLP C.A., Edmonton, Alta.
Transfer Agents - Odyssey Trust Company, Calgary, Alta.
Employees - 679 at Dec. 31, 2022

Profile - (Alta. 2019; orig. B.C., 1987) Owns or operates cannabis retail stores in Alberta, Ontario and Saskatchewan primarily under the Value Buds banner.

At Aug. 9, 2023, the company had 92 cannabis retail locations in Alberta (61), Ontario (30) and Saskatchewan (1). Stores operate under the Value Buds and Firesale Cannabis banners in Alberta and Ontario, and under the Sweet Tree Cannabis Co. banner in Saskatchewan. **Spirit Leaf Ontario Inc.** owns the Ontario stores, and the company operates these stores and provides funding for capital investment and operations and is entitled to the economic upside of these stores, less a fee payable to Spirit Leaf.

On Apr. 6, 2023, the company announced the launch of a new retail pilot concept, Firesale Cannabis, which offers significant discounts on cannabis for value-conscious shoppers. The first Firesale location opened in Edmonton, Alta., on Apr. 18, 2023.

On Jan. 1, 2023, wholly owned **Alcanna Cannabis Stores Finance Ltd.**, **YSS Cannabis Corp.**, **2102012 Alberta Ltd.**, **Sweet Tree Modern Apothecary Ltd.**, **2472573 Alberta Inc.** and **YSS Cannabis SK Inc.** were amalgamated into the company.

Recent Merger and Acquisition Activity

Status: pending **Revised:** Aug. 24, 2023
UPDATE: Closing was extended to Sept. 30, 2023. PREVIOUS: SNDL Inc. announced a partnership with subsidiary Nova Cannabis Inc. which would include the sale of its existing 26 cannabis retail stores under the Spiritleaf and Superette banners in Ontario and Alberta to Nova. Nova would also have a right of first refusal on SNDL's Canadian cannabis retail pipeline. The existing management and administrative services agreement between SNDL's subsidiary, Alcanna Inc., and Nova would be amended and restated. For the first three years following this amendment and restatement, no fee shall be payable by Nova under the agreement. Following the three-year fee holiday, Nova would pay an annual fee of Cdn$2,000,000 thereafter. In addition, a total of 14,258,555 Nova common shares held by SNDL would be returned to Nova and cancelled. The cancelled shares are valued at Cdn$7,500,000. SNDL plans to reduce its equity ownership in Nova to below 20% through a capital distribution of Nova shares owned by SNDL to SNDL shareholders. As consideration, SNDL would receive the intellectual property rights to Nova's Value Buds banner of 88 stores and the licence to grant Nova to operate the Value Buds, Spiritleaf and Superette banners. In addition, Nova and SNDL would enter into a licence agreement pursuant to which Nova would utilize SNDL's brands' intellectual property and other intangible property in exchange for a licence fee at a rate of 5% to 15% of gross profits on each store commencing one year after the transaction. SNDL holds 63% interest in Nova. Closing was expected to occur in May 2023. Apr. 3, 2023 - The agreement was amended to increase the number of stores Nova would acquire to 31, including 12 in Alberta, 11 in Ontario, three in British Columbia, three in Saskatchewan and two in Manitoba; and decrease the number of Nova shares to be surrendered by SNDL for cancellation to 2,009,622 shares valued at Cdn$1,600,000. SNDL also agreed to increase the number of Nova shares to be distributed to its shareholders such that, upon completion of the transaction, SNDL would hold no more than 19.9% of the issued and outstanding Nova shares. May 5, 2023 - Nova shareholders approved the transaction, which was expected to close on or before June 30, 2023. June 30, 2023 - Closing was extended to July 25, 2023. July 25, 2023 - Closing was extended to Aug. 25, 2023.

Status: completed **Announced:** Mar. 31, 2022
Nova Cannabis Inc. sold its Ontario retail operations consisting of 21 cannabis stores (including already opened stores or planned to opened in the coming months) to Spirit Leaf Ontario Inc. for a purchase price of $11,000,000. Concurrently, Nova entered into a brand-licensing and services arrangement pursuant to which Spirit Leaf would continue to operate the Ontario retail stores under Nova's existing Value Buds banner and Nova would continue to provide the services of its management and retail operating personnel in compliance with applicable law. Nova was also granted a re-purchase option with regards to those same stores, exercisable once the regulatory prohibition is no longer an issue and ownership is permitted under applicable law. The sale of the stores was made to comply with the regulatory restrictions that prohibit Sundial Growers Inc, as a licensed producer of cannabis, from directly or indirectly owning or controlling more than a 25% interest in any licensed Ontario cannabis retailer. Sundial acquired 63% ownership in Nova through its acquisition of Alcanna Inc on Mar. 31, 2022.

Predecessor Detail - Name changed from YSS Corp., Mar. 22, 2021, following the acquisition of Alcanna Inc.'s wholly owned Alcanna Cannabis Stores GP Inc. and Alcanna Cannabis Stores Limited Partnership, resulting in the reverse takeover acquisition of YSS by Alcanna Inc.; basis 1 new for 18.353 old shs.

Directors - Zachary R. (Zach) George, chr., New Canaan, Conn.; Marcie Kiziak, pres. & CEO, Edmonton, Alta.; Anne Fitzgerald†, Toronto, Ont.; Jeffrey Dean, Ont.; Ron S. Hozjan, Calgary, Alta.; Shari Mogk-Edwards, Ont.; Christopher Pelyk, B.C.

Other Exec. Officers - Grant Sanderson, COO; Cameron R. (Cam) Sebastian, CFO & corp. sec.
† Lead director

Capital Stock

	Authorized (shs.)	Outstanding (shs.)[1]
Preferred	unlimited	nil
Common	unlimited	57,205,740

[1] At Aug. 9, 2023

Major Shareholder - SNDL Inc. held 63% interest at June 30, 2023.

Price Range - NOVC/TSX

Year	Volume	High	Low	Close
2022	8,750,516	$3.28	$0.34	$1.24
2021	13,900,952	$4.42	$1.93	$2.81
2020	1,943,861	$5.32	$1.01	$2.11
2019	3,841,452	$9.91	$2.66	$3.03
2018	1,367,168	$49.55	$3.30	$5.51

Consolidation: 1-for-18.353 cons. in Mar. 2021; 1-for-6 cons. in June 2019

Recent Close: $0.55

Capital Stock Changes - During 2022, common shares were issued as follows: 61,666 on vesting of restricted share units and 16,500 under an at-the-market offering.

Wholly Owned Subsidiaries

Nova Cannabis Stores GP Inc., Alta.
Nova Cannabis Stores Limited Partnership, Alta.

Note: The preceding list includes only the major related companies in which interests are held.

Financial Statistics

Periods ended:	12m Dec. 31/22[A]		12m Dec. 31/21[*A1]
	$000s	%Chg	$000s
Operating revenue	**226,420**	**+69**	**134,364**
Cost of sales	182,566		109,477
Salaries & benefits	21,505		15,526
General & admin expense	15,066		11,955
Stock-based compensation	871		1,043
Operating expense	**220,008**	**+59**	**138,001**
Operating income	**6,412**	**n.a.**	**(3,637)**
Deprec., depl. & amort.	10,948		10,227
Finance costs, gross	3,976		3,067
Write-downs/write-offs	(2,887)		(2,904)
Pre-tax income	**(11,205)**	**n.a.**	**(20,614)**
Net income	**(11,205)**	**n.a.**	**(20,614)**
Cash & equivalent	5,033		10,527
Inventories	11,668		8,733
Accounts receivable	1,323		1,159
Current assets	18,732		21,091
Fixed assets, net	30,356		30,172
Right-of-use assets	43,836		47,183
Intangibles, net	19,270		19,270
Total assets	**113,151**	**-5**	**118,696**
Bank indebtedness	8,676		nil
Accts. pay. & accr. liabs	6,095		7,876
Current liabilities	19,892		13,410
Long-term lease liabilities	45,443		46,520
Shareholders' equity	47,816		58,766
Cash from oper. activs	**(65)**	**n.a.**	**(9,978)**
Cash from fin. activs	2,979		31,442
Cash from invest. activs	(8,408)		(12,374)
Net cash position	**5,033**	**-52**	**10,527**
Capital expenditures	(8,408)		(11,695)
	$		$
Earnings per share*	(0.20)		(0.39)
Cash flow per share*	(0.00)		(0.19)
	shs		shs
No. of shs. o/s*	57,171,094		57,092,928
Avg. no. of shs. o/s*	57,132,383		52,348,154
	%		%
Net profit margin	(4.95)		(15.34)
Return on equity	(21.03)		n.m.
Return on assets	(6.24)		n.a.
No. of employees (FTEs)	679		548

* Common
[*] Restated
[A] Reported in accordance with IFRS
[1] Results reflect the Mar. 22, 2021, reverse takeover acquisition of Alcanna Inc.'s retail cannabis business.

Latest Results

Periods ended:	6m June 30/23[A]		6m June 30/22[A]
	$000s	%Chg	$000s
Operating revenue	124,205	+17	106,131
Net income	492	n.a.	(4,903)
	$		$
Earnings per share*	0.01		(0.09)

* Common
[A] Reported in accordance with IFRS

Historical Summary
(as originally stated)

Fiscal Year	Oper. Rev.	Net Inc. Bef. Disc.	EPS*
	$000s	$000s	$
2022[A]	226,420	(11,205)	(0.20)
2021[A]	134,364	(20,614)	(0.39)
2020[A1]	63,314	(2,073)	n.a.
2019[A2]	8,541	(2,702)	(0.42)
2018[A3]	nil	(16,086)	(5.13)

* Common
[A] Reported in accordance with IFRS
[1] Results pertain to Alcanna Cannabis Stores Limited Partnership (renamed Nova Cannabis Stores Limited Partnership).
[2] Results for 2019 and prior fiscal years pertain to YSS Corp.
[3] 11 months ended Dec. 31, 2018.

Note: Adjusted throughout for 1-for-18.353 cons. in Mar. 2021; 1-for-6 cons. in June 2019

N.65 Nova Leap Health Corp.

Symbol - NLH **Exchange** - TSX-VEN **CUSIP** - 66980G
Head Office - 3006-7071 Bayers Rd, Halifax, NS, B3L 2C2 **Telephone** - (902) 401-9480 **Fax** - (902) 446-2001
Website - www.novaleaphealth.com
Email - cdobbin@novaleaphealth.com
Investor Relations - Christopher Dobbin (902) 401-9480
Auditors - Grant Thornton LLP C.A., Halifax, N.S.
Transfer Agents - Computershare Trust Company of Canada Inc., Toronto, Ont.

Profile - (Can. 2015) Provides home care and home health care services in the United States and Canada.

Acquires, manages and builds home care services companies which provide services in private homes, assisted living communities, hospitals, nursing homes, hospices and rehabilitation centres. Services offered include dementia care, companionship, personal care, respite care, cooking and meal preparation, light housekeeping, activities of daily living, transportation services, medication reminders and medication administration by nursing staff. Operations are conducted in 11 U.S. states (Arkansas, Massachusetts, New Hampshire, Ohio, Oklahoma, Rhode Island, Vermont, South Carolina, Kentucky, Indiana and Texas) and Nova Scotia.

Directors - Dana M. Hatfield, chr., Halifax, N.S.; Christopher (Chris) Dobbin, pres. & CEO, Halifax, N.S.; Marie T. Mullally, Halifax, N.S.; R. Wayne Myles, N.B.; Michael A. (Mike) O'Keefe, Halifax, N.S.; Anne Whelan, St. John's, N.L.

Other Exec. Officers - Chris LeBlanc, CFO & corp. sec.

Capital Stock

	Authorized (shs.)	Outstanding (shs.)[1]
Common	unlimited	86,209,252

[1] At May 30, 2023

Major Shareholder - Wayne Fulcher held 19.92% interest at May 30, 2023.

Price Range - NLH/TSX-VEN

Year	Volume	High	Low	Close
2022	10,157,966	$0.70	$0.25	$0.25
2021	18,940,796	$0.99	$0.50	$0.61
2020	14,899,717	$0.78	$0.21	$0.75
2019	12,240,697	$0.45	$0.23	$0.43
2018	7,139,777	$0.45	$0.20	$0.32

Recent Close: $0.18

Capital Stock Changes - In September 2022, private placement of 6,814,445 common shares was completed at Cdn$0.35 per share. Also during 2022, 100,000 common shares were issued on exercise of options.

Financial Statistics

Periods ended:	12m Dec. 31/22[A]		12m Dec. 31/21[A]
	US$000s	%Chg	US$000s
Operating revenue	**28,205**	**+33**	**21,279**
Cost of sales	18,230		14,068
General & admin expense	9,317		7,207
Stock-based compensation	365		374
Operating expense	**27,912**	**+29**	**21,649**
Operating income	**293**	**n.a.**	**(370)**
Deprec., depl. & amort.	1,356		861
Finance costs, gross	271		401
Write-downs/write-offs	(514)		(606)
Pre-tax income	**(1,207)**	**n.a.**	**2,473**
Income taxes	(371)		713
Net income	**(836)**	**n.a.**	**1,761**
Cash & equivalent	1,273		1,733
Accounts receivable	1,753		2,171
Current assets	3,978		5,962
Fixed assets, net	1,494		1,294
Intangibles, net	17,131		18,785
Total assets	**23,949**	**-11**	**26,769**
Bank indebtedness	1,378		3,123
Accts. pay. & accr. liabs	1,242		1,309
Current liabilities	3,988		6,227
Long-term debt, gross	1,008		1,671
Long-term debt, net	118		896
Long-term lease liabilities	1,161		1,025
Shareholders' equity	18,682		18,480
Cash from oper. activs	**1,021**	**-53**	**2,180**
Cash from fin. activs	(1,414)		4,330
Cash from invest. activs	(56)		(7,402)
Net cash position	**1,273**	**-27**	**1,733**
	US$		US$
Earnings per share*	(0.01)		0.02
Cash flow per share*	0.01		0.03
	shs		shs
No. of shs. o/s*	86,209,252		79,294,807
Avg. no. of shs. o/s*	81,458,770		74,404,395
	%		%
Net profit margin	(2.96)		8.28
Return on equity	(4.50)		12.44
Return on assets	(2.56)		9.24
Foreign sales percent	86		81

* Common
[A] Reported in accordance with IFRS

Latest Results

Periods ended:	3m Mar. 31/23[A]		3m Mar. 31/22[A]
	US$000s	%Chg	US$000s
Operating revenue	6,396	-12	7,297
Net income	(297)	n.a.	(390)
	US$		US$
Earnings per share*	(0.00)		(0.00)

* Common
[A] Reported in accordance with IFRS

Historical Summary
(as originally stated)

Fiscal Year	Oper. Rev.	Net Inc. Bef. Disc.	EPS*
	US$000s	US$000s	US$
2022[A]	28,205	(836)	(0.01)
2021[A]	21,279	1,761	0.02
2020[A]	17,309	1,256	0.02
2019[A]	17,405	(1,056)	(0.02)
2018[A]	10,362	(961)	(0.02)

* Common
[A] Reported in accordance with IFRS

N.66 Nova Mentis Life Science Corp.

Symbol - NOVA **Exchange** - CSE **CUSIP** - 66980V
Head Office - 700-838 Hastings St W, Vancouver, BC, V6C 0A6 **Telephone** - (778) 819-0244 **Toll-free** - (833) 542-5323
Website - www.novamentis.ca
Email - will@novamentis.ca
Investor Relations - William Rascan (778) 819-0244
Auditors - Kreston GTA LLP C.A., Markham, Ont.
Lawyers - Tiffany & Company Law Corp., Vancouver, B.C.
Transfer Agents - Olympia Trust Company, Vancouver, B.C.

Profile - (B.C. 2004) Developing a portfolio of health and wellness businesses.

Wholly owned **Nova Mentis Biotech Corp.** researches and develops anti-inflammatory effects of psilocybin in underexplored metabolic indications such as obesity and diabetes.

Wholly owned **Pilz Bioscience Corp.** develops medicinal psychedelics for neuroinflammatory conditions.

During the first quarter of 2022, the company determined not to invest further in wholly owned **Signature Cannabis Retails Ltd.**

Predecessor Detail - Name changed from Liberty Leaf Holdings Ltd., June 26, 2020, pursuant to the acquisition of Nova Mentis Biotech Corp.; basis 1 new for 4 old shs.

Directors - Derek Ivany, exec. chr.; William (Will) Rascan, pres. & CEO, Vancouver, B.C.; Jacqueline McConnell, COO; Dr. Stephen Glazer, chief science officer

Other Exec. Officers - Rebecca Hudson, CFO; Kelly Pladson, corp. sec.

Capital Stock

	Authorized (shs.)	Outstanding (shs.)[1]
Common	unlimited	142,329,660

[1] At Nov. 10, 2022

Major Shareholder - Widely held at Nov. 10, 2022.

Price Range - NOVA/CSE

Year	Volume	High	Low	Close
2022	45,029,086	$0.12	$0.02	$0.10
2021	67,979,876	$0.31	$0.05	$0.06
2020	33,174,987	$0.44	$0.06	$0.22
2019	17,346,020	$0.94	$0.14	$0.20
2018	34,350,936	$4.00	$0.32	$0.36

Consolidation: 1-for-4 cons. in June 2020

Recent Close: $0.03

Capital Stock Changes - In March 2022, private placement of 29,670,000 units (1 common share & 1 warrant) at $0.05 per unit was completed, with warrants exercisable at $0.075 per share for 18 months.

Wholly Owned Subsidiaries

Nova Mentis Biotech Corp., Canada.

Pilz Bioscience Corp., Vancouver, B.C.

Financial Statistics

Periods ended:	12m Dec. 31/21[A]		12m Dec. 31/20[o][A]
	$000s	%Chg	$000s
Operating revenue	**nil**	**n.a.**	**11**
Cost of goods sold	nil		10
Research & devel. expense	860		48
General & admin expense	1,721		854
Stock-based compensation	348		894
Operating expense	**2,929**	**+62**	**1,806**
Operating income	**(2,929)**	**n.a.**	**(1,795)**
Deprec., depl. & amort.	5		7
Finance income	5		4
Write-downs/write-offs	nil		(5,667)
Pre-tax income	**(2,685)**	**n.a.**	**(25,233)**
Net income	**(2,685)**	**n.a.**	**(25,233)**
Cash & equivalent	219		2,141
Inventories	nil		5
Current assets	328		2,581
Long-term investments	nil		442
Fixed assets, net	18		23
Total assets	**881**	**-71**	**3,046**
Accts. pay. & accr. liabs	422		383
Current liabilities	422		383
Shareholders' equity	459		2,664
Cash from oper. activs	**(1,946)**	**n.a.**	**(857)**
Cash from invest. activs	30		2,905
Net cash position	**219**	**-90**	**2,135**
	$		$
Earnings per share*	(0.02)		(0.49)
Cash flow per share*	(0.02)		(0.02)
	shs		shs
No. of shs. o/s*	111,503,077		111,137,867
Avg. no. of shs. o/s*	111,104,785		51,153,928
	%		%
Net profit margin	n.a.		n.m.
Return on equity	(103.91)		(565.51)
Return on assets	(89.90)		(524.00)

* Common
[o] Restated
[A] Reported in accordance with IFRS

Latest Results

Periods ended:	9m Sept. 30/22[A]		9m Sept. 30/21[A]
	$000s	%Chg	$000s
Net income	(1,397)	n.a.	(2,441)
	$		$
Earnings per share*	(0.01)		(0.02)

* Common
[A] Reported in accordance with IFRS

Historical Summary
(as originally stated)

Fiscal Year	Oper. Rev.	Net Inc. Bef. Disc.	EPS*
	$000s	$000s	$
2021[A]	nil	(2,685)	(0.02)
2020[A]	11	(23,249)	(0.45)
2019[A]	7	(1,398)	(0.04)
2018[A]	nil	(3,573)	(0.12)
2017[A]	nil	(1,866)	(0.08)

* Common
[A] Reported in accordance with IFRS

Note: Adjusted throughout for 1-for-4 cons. in June 2020

N.67 Nova Net Lease REIT

Symbol - NNL.U **Exchange** - CSE **CUSIP** - 66981K

Head Office - North Tower, 1200-200 Bay St, Toronto, ON, M5J 2J2 **Telephone** - (416) 569-6487

Website - novanetleasereit.com

Email - sriffe@nnlreit.com

Investor Relations - Stacy Riffe (416) 569-6487

Auditors - MNP LLP C.A., Toronto, Ont.

Transfer Agents - Olympia Trust Company, Toronto, Ont.

Profile - (Ont. 2021) Acquires, owns and leases, on a triple-net basis, cannabis-related industrial and retail properties in the United States.

The trust is focused on specialized industrial and retail properties leased to experienced, state-licensed operators in the legal U.S. cannabis industry. Plans to acquire properties through sale-leaseback transactions and lease such properties on a triple-net lease basis for a targeted ten to 15 year term and strives to negotiate annual rental rate increases in the leases.

Target markets are Michigan, California, Nevada, New York, New Jersey, Arizona and Massachusetts and targeted diversification mix is 80% in cultivation/growth/processing and 20% retail/dispensary assets.

At January 2022, the trust owned a 70,000-sq.-ft. industrial cannabis facility in Kalamazoo, Mich., including 67,000 sq. ft. of cultivation space and a 3,000-sq.-ft. medical marijuana dispensary.

Trustees - Steve Dawson, chr., Ala.; Katie Barthmaier, v-chr., Brooklyn, N.Y.; Patrick (Pat) Burke, Toronto, Ont.; Edward Lowenthal, Saddle River, N.J.; Andrew L. Oppenheim, Calgary, Alta.; Andrew Shapack, Toronto, Ont.; T. Richard (Rick) Turner, West Vancouver, B.C.

Oper. Subsid./Mgt. Co. Officers - Tyson Macdonald, pres. & CEO; Potter Polk, exec. v-p & chief invest. officer; Stacy Riffe, exec. v-p & CFO

Capital Stock

	Authorized (shs.)	Outstanding (shs.)[1]
Trust Units	unlimited	6,815,493
Class B	unlimited	8,000,000[2]

[1] At Jan. 31, 2022
[2] Securities of wholly owned Nova Net Lease Operating, LLC

Trust Unit - The trust intends to pay initial monthly cash distributions of US$0.025 to US$0.03 per trust unit (to yield between 2% to 2.4% per annum). One voter per trust unit.

Class B Unit - Issued by wholly owned Nova Net Lease Operating, LLC. Economically equivalent to trust units. Entitled to receive distributions proportionately to the distributions made by the trust to the trust unitholders. Redeemable for cash or trust units on a 1-for-1 basis. Non-voting.

Major Shareholder - Widely held at Jan. 4, 2022.

Price Range - NNL.U/CSE

Year	Volume	High	Low	Close
2022	383,196	US$1.25	US$0.05	US$0.09

Recent Close: US$0.10

Capital Stock Changes - In January 2022, an initial public offering of 3,407,800 trust units was completed at US$1.25 per unit, including 240,322 trust units on exercise of over-allotment option.

Dividends

NNL.U unit Ra US$0.027 pa M est. Feb. 15, 2022
Listed Jan 4/22.
US$0.00225i......... Feb. 15/22
i Initial Payment

Wholly Owned Subsidiaries

Verdant Growth Properties Corp., United States.
- 100% int. in **Nova Net Lease Operating, LLC**, Denver, Colo.
  - 100% int. in **Nova Kalamazoo LLC**, Kalamazoo, Mich.

N.68 Nova Scotia Power Incorporated

CUSIP - 669816

Head Office - 600-1223 Lower Water St, PO Box 910, Halifax, NS, B3J 2W5 **Telephone** - (902) 428-6096 **Toll-free** - (800) 428-6230 **Fax** - (902) 428-6171

Website - www.nspower.ca

Email - brian.curry@nspower.ca

Investor Relations - Brian C. Curry (902) 428-6996

Auditors - Ernst & Young LLP C.A., Halifax, N.S.

Lawyers - Cox & Palmer LLP, Halifax, N.S.

Transfer Agents - Computershare Trust Company of Canada Inc.

FP500 Subsidiary Revenue Ranking - 48

Employees - 2,138 at Dec. 31, 2022

Profile - (N.S. 1984) Generates, transmits and distributes regulated electricity in Nova Scotia.

Provides the majority of electricity generation in Nova Scotia. Owns 2,420 MW generating capacity of which about 44% is coal-fired, 28% is oil and natural gas, 19% is hydro and wind, 7% is petroleum coke and 2% is biomass-fueled generation. Has contracts to purchase renewable energy from independent power producers (IPP) and community feed in tariff participants which owned 546 MW of wind, tidal, biogas and biomass fuelled generation capacity at Dec. 31, 2022. Also owns 5,000 km of transmission facilities and 28,000 km of distribution facilities. During 2022, generation and purchases totaled 11,134 GWh compared with 10,905 GWh during 2021.

In addition, wholly owned **NS Power Energy Marketing Incorporated** purchases and sells electricity and natural gas in the United States energy commodity market.

Periods ended:	12m Dec. 31/22	12m Dec. 31/21
Electric sales, GWh	10,456	10,196
Generating capacity, MW	2,966	2,966
Transmission lines, km	5,000	5,000
Distribution lines, km	28,000	28,000
Electric. customers	541,000	536,000

Predecessor Detail - Name changed from International Engineering Services Limited, Aug. 10, 1992.

Directors - Scott C. Balfour, chr., Halifax, N.S.; Peter Gregg, pres. & CEO, Halifax, N.S.; James D. (Jim) Eisenhauer†, Lunenburg, N.S.; J. Lee Bragg, Fall River, N.S.; Cassandra Dorrington, Halifax, N.S.; Sandra Greer, Halifax, N.S.; Raymond E. (Ray) Ivany, Wolfville, N.S.; Richard C. (Rick) Janega, Halifax, N.S.; Julia Rivard Dexter, Fall River, N.S.; J. Mark Rodger, Toronto, Ont.

Other Exec. Officers - David A. (Dave) Pickles, COO; Gregory W. (Greg) Blunden, CFO; R. Michael (Mike) Roberts, chief HR officer; Mark R. Sidebottom, chief clean energy officer; Judith F. Ferguson, exec. v-p, regulatory, legal & govt. rel.; Christopher H. C. Smith, exec. v-p, fin.; Tony Folkins, v-p, tech.; Rene Gallant, v-p, strategy & stakeholder engagement; Jamie MacDonald, v-p, power prod.; Lia MacDonald, v-p, cust. experience & innovation; Brian C. Curry, corp. sec.

† Lead director

Capital Stock

	Authorized (shs.)	Outstanding (shs.)[1]
First Preferred	unlimited	nil
Second Preferred	unlimited	nil
Common	unlimited	155,096,535

[1] At Mar. 27, 2023

Major Shareholder - Emera Incorporated held 100% interest at Mar. 27, 2023.

Capital Stock Changes - During 2022, 30,234 common shares were issued to parent Emera Incorporated for proceeds of $300,000.

Wholly Owned Subsidiaries

NS Power Energy Marketing Incorporated, N.S.

Financial Statistics

Periods ended:	12m Dec. 31/22[A]		12m Dec. 31/21[A]
	$000s	%Chg	$000s
Operating revenue	**1,675,000**	**+12**	**1,501,000**
Cost of sales	803,000		654,000
General & admin expense	377,000		329,000
Operating expense	**1,180,000**	**+20**	**983,000**
Operating income	**495,000**	**-4**	**518,000**
Deprec., depl. & amort.	259,000		246,000
Finance income	6,000		2,000
Finance costs, gross	142,000		134,000
Pre-tax income	**124,000**	**-18**	**152,000**
Income taxes	(7,000)		11,000
Net income	**131,000**	**-7**	**141,000**
Cash & equivalent	2,000		nil
Inventories	287,000		201,000
Accounts receivable	375,000		280,000
Current assets	870,000		651,000
Fixed assets, net	4,589,000		4,345,000
Total assets	**6,842,000**	**+12**	**6,087,000**
Bank indebtedness	nil		1,000
Accts. pay. & accr. liabs	342,000		245,000
Current liabilities	811,000		532,000
Long-term debt, gross	3,530,000		3,026,000
Long-term debt, net	3,530,000		3,026,000
Long-term lease liabilities	22,000		21,000
Shareholders' equity	1,492,000		1,488,000
Cash from oper. activs	**166,000**	**-55**	**369,000**
Cash from fin. activs	349,000		nil
Cash from invest. activs	(513,000)		(369,000)
Net cash position	**2,000**	**n.a.**	**nil**
Capital expenditures	(464,000)		(338,000)
Capital disposals	nil		1,000
Pension fund surplus	54,000		19,000
	$		$
Earnings per share*	n.a.		n.a.
Cash flow per share*	1.16		2.59
	shs		shs
No. of shs. o/s*	142,600,000		142,600,000
	%		%
Net profit margin	7.82		9.39
Return on equity	8.79		10.08
Return on assets	4.35		4.58
No. of employees (FTEs)	2,138		2,105

* Common
[A] Reported in accordance with U.S. GAAP

Historical Summary
(as originally stated)

Fiscal Year	Oper. Rev. $000s	Net Inc. Bef. Disc. $000s	EPS* $
2022[A]	1,675,000	131,000	n.a.
2021[A]	1,501,000	141,000	n.a.
2020[A]	1,494,000	125,000	n.a.
2019[A]	1,430,000	138,000	n.a.
2018[A]	1,440,000	131,000	n.a.

* Common
[A] Reported in accordance with U.S. GAAP

N.69 Novanta Inc.

Symbol - NOVT **Exchange** - NASDAQ **CUSIP** - 67000B
Head Office - 125 Middlesex Turnpike, Bedford, MA, United States, 01730 **Telephone** - (781) 266-5700 **Toll-free** - (800) 342-3757 **Fax** - (781) 266-5114
Website - www.novanta.com
Email - investorrelations@novanta.com
Investor Relations - Ray Nash (781) 266-5137
Auditors - PricewaterhouseCoopers LLP C.P.A., Boston, Mass.
Transfer Agents - Computershare Trust Company of Canada Inc., Toronto, Ont.
FP500 Revenue Ranking - 319
Employees - 3,000 at Dec. 31, 2022
Profile - (N.B. 1999; orig. Ont., 1970) Designs, manufactures and sells photonic, vision and precision motion technology components and subsystems to original equipment manufacturers (OEM) in the medical and advanced industrial markets.

Operations are organized into three segments: Photonics; Vision; and Precision Motion.

The **Photonics** segment designs, manufactures and markets photonics-based solutions, including laser scanning, laser beam delivery, CO_2 laser, solid state laser, ultrafast laser and optical light engine products, to customers worldwide. The segment serves highly demanding photonics-based applications for advanced industrial processes, metrology, medical and life science imaging, DNA sequencing, and medical laser procedures, particularly ophthalmology applications.

The **Vision** segment designs, manufactures and markets a range of medical grade technologies, including medical insufflators, pumps and related disposables; visualization solutions; wireless technologies, video recorders and video integration technologies for operating room integrations; optical data collection and machine vision technologies; radio frequency identification technologies; thermal chart recorders; and spectrometry technologies and embedded touch screen solutions, to customers worldwide.

The **Precision Motion** segment designs, manufactures and markets optical and inductive encoders, precision motors, servo drives and motion control solutions, integrated stepper motors, intelligent robotic end-of-arm technology solutions, air bearings and air bearing spindles to customers worldwide.

Production facilities are located in Marlborough, Conn.; Rocklin, Calif.; Bedford, Mass.; Apex, N.C.; Syracuse, N.Y.; Mukilteo, Wash.; Ludwigsstadt and Wackersdorf, Germany; Taunton and Manchester, U.K.; Prelouc, Czech Republic; and Suzhou, People's Republic of China.

Recent Merger and Acquisition Activity

Status: completed **Announced:** Aug. 11, 2022
Novanta Inc. acquired Czech Republic-based MPH Medical Devices s.r.o., which manufactures medical consumables with plastics specialization in making disposable tube-set-like products, for US$22,600,000.

Predecessor Detail - Name changed from GSI Group Inc., May 11, 2016.

Directors - Matthijs Glastra, chr. & CEO, Newton, Mass.; Lonny Carpenter†, Mich.; Barbara B. Hulit, Medina, Wash.; Maxine Mauricio, Greenwich, Conn.; Katherine A. Owen, Hingham, Mass.; Thomas N. Secor, New York, N.Y.; Dr. Darlene J. S. Solomon, Calif.; Frank A. Wilson, Wellesley, Mass.

Other Exec. Officers - Stephen W. Bershad, chr., emeritus; Robert J. Buckley, CFO; Brian Young, chief HR officer; Kitty Sahin, exec. v-p, strategy & bus. devel.; Peter L. Chang, v-p, chief acctg. officer & contr.; Michele D. Welsh, gen. counsel & corp. sec.; Heinrich Dreyer, pres., Minimally Invasive Surgery; Phil Martin, pres., Photonics; Leane Sinicki, pres., Precision Motion
† Lead director

Capital Stock

	Authorized (shs.)	Outstanding (shs.)[1]
Preferred	7,000,000	nil
Common	unlimited	35,800,445

[1] At Mar. 27, 2023

Major Shareholder - BlackRock, Inc. held 11.8% interest at Mar. 27, 2023.

Price Range - NOVT/NASDAQ

Year	Volume	High	Low	Close
2022	21,448,670	US$176.93	US$110.93	US$135.87
2021	11,612,173	US$184.44	US$116.84	US$176.33
2020	13,336,724	US$127.66	US$66.44	US$118.22
2019	13,355,385	US$96.26	US$60.20	US$88.44
2018	16,839,200	US$78.85	US$48.40	US$63.00

Capital Stock Changes - During 2022, 276,000 common shares were issued under a stock-based compensation plan, 84,000 common shares were repurchased and 82,000 common shares (net) were redeemed in settlement of vested stock award.

Wholly Owned Subsidiaries

ATI Automation Industrial S. de R.L. de C.V., Mexico.
ATI Industrial Automation Inc., Apex, N.C.
ATI Industrial Automation (Lang Fang) Co., Ltd., People's Republic of China.
ATI Industrial Mexico, LLC, N.C.
GSI Lumonics Asia Pacific Ltd., Hong Kong, Hong Kong, People's Republic of China.
Ingenia-CAT, S.L., Barcelona, Spain.
MGC Industrial, Inc., N.C.
Med X Change, Inc., Bradenton, Fla.
NDS Surgical Imaging, LLC, San Jose, Calif.
Novanta Ceská republika s.r.o., Czech Republic.
Novanta Corporation, Mich.
Novanta Distribution (USD) GmbH, Germany.
Novanta EMEA B.V., Netherlands.
Novanta Europe GmbH, Germany.
Novanta Holdings B.V., Netherlands.
Novanta Insurance Company, Ariz.
Novanta Italy S.r.l., Italy.
Novanta Japan Corporation, Japan.
Novanta Medical s.r.o., Czech Republic.
Novanta Medical Technologies Corp., Del.
Novanta Singapore Pte. Ltd., Singapore.
Novanta Technologies (Suzhou) Co., Ltd., People's Republic of China.
Novanta Technologies UK Limited, United Kingdom.
- 100% int. in **Laser Quantum GmbH**, Germany.
- 100% int. in **Laser Quantum Limited**, Stockport, Cheshire, United Kingdom.

Novanta UK Investments Holding Limited, United Kingdom.
World of Medicine Asia Ltd., Hong Kong, Hong Kong, People's Republic of China.
World of Medicine GmbH, Berlin, Germany.
World of Medicine USA, Inc., Fla.
Zettlex (UK) Limited, United Kingdom.

Financial Statistics

Periods ended:	12m Dec. 31/22[A]		12m Dec. 31/21[A]
	US$000s	%Chg	US$000s
Operating revenue	**860,903**	**+22**	**706,793**
Cost of sales	466,649		390,169
Research & devel. expense	83,356		70,228
General & admin expense	140,719		111,900
Stock-based compensation	23,108		25,606
Operating expense	**713,832**	**+19**	**597,903**
Operating income	**147,071**	**+35**	**108,890**
Deprec., depl. & amort.	39,608		29,865
Finance costs, net	15,616		7,387
Pre-tax income	**87,159**	**+55**	**56,172**
Income taxes	13,108		5,841
Net income	**74,051**	**+47**	**50,331**
Cash & equivalent	100,105		117,393
Inventories	167,997		125,657
Accounts receivable	137,697		115,617
Current assets	420,519		373,825
Fixed assets, net	103,186		87,439
Right-of-use assets	43,317		48,338
Intangibles, net	654,663		700,489
Total assets	**1,241,212**	**+1**	**1,227,883**
Accts. pay. & accr. liabs	75,225		68,514
Current liabilities	164,522		183,938
Long-term debt, gross	435,462		434,458
Long-term debt, net	430,662		429,361
Long-term lease liabilities	40,808		45,700
Shareholders' equity	577,586		521,291
Cash from oper. activs	**90,779**	**-4**	**94,625**
Cash from fin. activs	(60,154)		204,753
Cash from invest. activs	(42,541)		(306,704)
Net cash position	**100,105**	**-15**	**117,393**
Capital expenditures	(19,643)		(19,976)
Capital disposals	137		200
Pension fund surplus	2,012		2,789
	US$		US$
Earnings per share*	2.08		1.42
Cash flow per share*	2.55		2.67
	shs		shs
No. of shs. o/s*	35,711,000		35,601,000
Avg. no. of shs. o/s*	35,652,000		35,396,000
	%		%
Net profit margin	8.60		7.12
Return on equity	13.48		10.09
Return on assets	6.00		4.81
Foreign sales percent	100		100
No. of employees (FTEs)	3,000		2,700

* Common
[A] Reported in accordance with U.S. GAAP

Historical Summary
(as originally stated)

Fiscal Year	Oper. Rev. US$000s	Net Inc. Bef. Disc. US$000s	EPS* US$
2022[A]	860,903	74,051	2.08
2021[A]	706,793	50,331	1.42
2020[A]	590,623	44,521	1.27
2019[A]	626,099	40,773	1.16
2018[A]	614,337	51,095	1.46

* Common
[A] Reported in accordance with U.S. GAAP

N.70 Novra Technologies Inc.

Symbol - NVI **Exchange** - TSX-VEN **CUSIP** - 67010X
Head Office - 210-100 Innovation Dr, Winnipeg, MB, R3T 6G2 **Telephone** - (204) 989-4724 **Toll-free** - (888) 204-4630 **Fax** - (204) 989-4640
Website - www.novragroup.com
Email - harris@novra.com
Investor Relations - Harris Liontas (888) 204-4630
Auditors - Baker Tilly HMA LLP C.A., Winnipeg, Man.
Transfer Agents - Computershare Trust Company of Canada Inc., Vancouver, B.C.
Profile - (Can. 1997) Designs, manufactures and installs products and systems and provides support solutions for distribution of broadband multimedia content via satellite and hybrid networks.

Product lines consist of video distribution, which are products and systems for providing end-to-end solutions for traditional and non-traditional video networks; broadcast radio, which are end-to-end infrastructure solutions to small, medium and large broadcast radio networks; data distribution, which provides a broadband multimedia distribution technology for networks requiring fast, ultra reliable, secure delivery of data via satellite and via Internet or private IP network and offers additional advanced content distribution network (CDN) software solution; digital cinema, which consists of uplink equipment, content management and network management, and high-end appliances for cinemas as well as decoders for live events and alternative content in 2D and 3D; and satellite (DVB) and terrestrial (ATSC) broadband receivers, which provides a standalone communication getaways to local networks. Customer base consists of approximately 2,000 customers in more than 100 countries, including more than 200,000 installations since inception.

Predecessor Detail - Name changed from Century Gold Corp., July 6, 2001.

Directors - Peter J. Wintemute, chr., Winnipeg, Man.; Harris Liontas, pres. & CEO, Winnipeg, Man.; George (Brian) Eckhardt, acting CFO, Man.; Kelvin Maloney, Winnipeg, Man.

Other Exec. Officers - Patricia Gair, exec. v-p, bus. opers.; Diana Cantú, v-p, mktg. & sales

Capital Stock

	Authorized (shs.)	Outstanding (shs.)[1]
Class A Preferred	unlimited	nil
Class A Common	unlimited	33,420,293[2]

[1] At May 11, 2023
[2] Excludes 2,000,000 shares held by subsidiary Wegener Corporation.

Major Shareholder - Harris Liontas held 15.4% interest at May 11, 2023.

Price Range - NVI/TSX-VEN

Year	Volume	High	Low	Close
2022	2,271,757	$0.13	$0.06	$0.07
2021	15,936,978	$0.20	$0.06	$0.12
2020	3,324,273	$0.14	$0.05	$0.08
2019	4,600,121	$0.20	$0.08	$0.10
2018	8,899,945	$0.29	$0.12	$0.15

Recent Close: $0.07

Capital Stock Changes - There were no changes to capital stock during 2022.

Wholly Owned Subsidiaries

International Datacasting Corporation, Kanata, Ont.

Subsidiaries

51.6% int. in **Wegener Corporation**, Ga.

Financial Statistics

Periods ended:	12m Dec. 31/22[A]		12m Dec. 31/21[A]
	$000s	%Chg	$000s
Operating revenue	**7,603**	**+6**	**7,205**
Cost of sales	3,317		3,727
Research & devel. expense	1,363		1,342
General & admin expense	2,052		1,675
Operating expense	**6,732**	**0**	**6,744**
Operating income	**871**	**+89**	**461**
Deprec., depl. & amort.	1,290		1,132
Finance income	13		1,033
Finance costs, gross	166		177
Pre-tax income	**(474)**	**n.a.**	**180**
Net income	**(474)**	**n.a.**	**180**
Net inc. for equity hldrs	**(907)**	**n.a.**	**(119)**
Net inc. for non-cont. int	**433**	**+45**	**299**
Cash & equivalent	1,966		2,965
Inventories	2,031		1,677
Accounts receivable	698		1,124
Current assets	6,202		6,509
Fixed assets, net	22		29
Right-of-use assets	1,454		1,721
Intangibles, net	1,023		1,208
Total assets	**8,813**	**-7**	**9,467**
Accts. pay. & accr. liabs	1,711		1,558
Current liabilities	5,697		7,001
Long-term debt, gross	3,815		3,374
Long-term debt, net	3,598		2,490
Long-term lease liabilities	1,660		1,449
Shareholders' equity	(2,814)		(1,727)
Non-controlling interest	(27)		(460)
Cash from oper. activs	**1,337**	**+431**	**252**
Cash from fin. activs	(702)		(1,119)
Cash from invest. activs	(1,876)		nil
Net cash position	**1,966**	**-34**	**2,965**
	$		$
Earnings per share*	(0.03)		(0.00)
Cash flow per share*	0.04		0.01
	shs		shs
No. of shs. o/s*	33,420,293		33,420,293
Avg. no. of shs. o/s*	33,420,293		33,420,293
	%		%
Net profit margin	(6.23)		2.50
Return on equity	n.m.		n.m.
Return on assets	(3.37)		3.62
Foreign sales percent	94		94

* Common
[A] Reported in accordance with IFRS

Latest Results

Periods ended:	3m Mar. 31/23[A]		3m Mar. 31/22[A]
	$000s	%Chg	$000s
Operating revenue	1,087	+17	929
Net income	(324)	n.a.	(758)
Net inc. for equity hldrs	(333)	n.a.	(643)
Net inc. for non-cont. int	9		(115)
	$		$
Earnings per share*	(0.01)		(0.02)

* Common
[A] Reported in accordance with IFRS

Historical Summary
(as originally stated)

Fiscal Year	Oper. Rev.	Net Inc. Bef. Disc.	EPS*
	$000s	$000s	$
2022[A]	7,603	(474)	(0.03)
2021[A]	7,205	180	(0.00)
2020[A]	4,979	(2,426)	(0.05)
2019[A]	9,756	(1,702)	(0.05)
2018[A]	10,630	(553)	(0.02)

* Common
[A] Reported in accordance with IFRS

N.71 NowVertical Group Inc.

Symbol - NOW **Exchange** - TSX-VEN **CUSIP** - 67013H
Head Office - 545 King St W, Toronto, ON, M5V 1M1 **Telephone** - (647) 741-1996
Website - www.nowvertical.com
Email - alim.virani@nowvertical.com
Investor Relations - Alim Virani (647) 741-1996
Auditors - BDO Canada LLP C.A., Markham, Ont.
Transfer Agents - TSX Trust Company, Toronto, Ont.
Employees - 432 at Aug. 31, 2022
Profile - (Ont. 2018) Acquires and builds intelligence software and services companies.

The company's vertical intelligence software and services solutions address industry-specific needs in data transformation (including data fusion, mobilization and securitization), data visualization and analysis, and artificial intelligence and automation.

Proprietary software include NOW Fusion, NOW Privacy, NOW DataBench and NOW Affinio.

NOW Fusion, is a database fusion technology that brings together structured and unstructured data from both inside and outside an organization to drive enhanced business analysis; NOW Privacy, is a data discovery, management and workflow tool that accelerates data governance, data efficiency and data management to an entire organization's data set; NOW DataBench, is a data science platform that brings business intelligence tools into a single interface to empower more people in an organization to make informed decisions using their data; and NOW Affinio, is an audience intelligence platform that helps marketers create better campaigns by giving them deeper insight into their most valuable audiences.

Revenues are generated through sales of software licences and subscriptions, as well as charges for implementation services, maintenance and support, and analytics consulting services.

In January 2023, the company acquired London, U.K.-based **Acrotrend Solutions Limited** for US$4,100,000 cash and issuance of 750,000 class A subordinate voting shares plus an earn-out consideration based on certain EBITDA targets payable annually over three years. Acrotrend is a customer data and analytics consultancy with operations in the U.K. and India. Acrotrend has worked with global brands across multiple verticals including Reed Exhibitions, The Economist Group, The Walt Disney Company, Sky Group, Informa, Nuffield Health, GSK and Cancer Research UK.

Also in January 2023, the company acquired Milton Keynes, U.K.-based **Smartlytics Consultancy Limited** for US$1,000,000 cash, issuance of 600,000 class A subordinate voting shares plus an earn-out consideration based on certain EBITDA targets payable annually over three years. Smartlytics offers end-to-end data solutions and eliminates data silos, creating a single source of truth. Smartlytics has a cloud-native platform called Smartlytics Hub which allows self-serve development of enterprise data solutions. Smartlytics operates in the UK, Dubai and Cairo and has clients in the public and private sector.

On July 20, 2022, the company acquired Princeton, N.J.-based **Resonant Analytics LLC** for US$1,500,000 cash and issuance of 900,000 class A subordinate voting shares plus an earn-out consideration based on certain adjusted EBITDA targets payable annually over three years in cash and class A subordinate voting shares. Resonant is a guided solutions analytics firm providing customer relationship management program strategy, database marketing and business intelligence solutions to Fortune 500 companies.

In March 2022, the company acquired U.K.-based **Exonar Ltd.** for US$650,000 consisting of $150,000 cash and issuance of US$500,000 class A subordinate voting shares. Exonar offers software solutions that provide enterprise-scale, big data architecture and machine learning technology that handles diverse data sources and types to locate sensitive and vital information.

Recent Merger and Acquisition Activity

Status: completed **Revised:** Feb. 2, 2023
UPDATE: The transaction was completed. PREVIOUS: NowVertical Group Inc. agreed to acquire private Sao Paulo, Brazil-based Analytics 10 and Inteligencia de Negocios (collectively A10 Group) for US$5,500,000 consisting of US$4,950,000 cash and issuance of US$550,000 of class A subordinate voting shares. In addition, NowVertical would pay an earn-out consideration based on certain adjusted EBITDA targets payable over four years. A10 Group engages in business intelligence, visual analytics and data discovery projects across various sectors, helping businesses to arrive at intelligent, data-backed decisions.

Predecessor Detail - Name changed from Good2Go Corp., June 28, 2021, pursuant to the Qualifying Transaction reverse takeover acquisition of (old) NowVertical Group, Inc. and concurrent amalgamation of (old) NowVertical with wholly owned Good2Go (US) Corp.; basis 1 new for 4.5 old shs.

Directors - Elaine Kunda, chr., Toronto, Ont.; Sasha Grujicic, CEO; Andre Garber, exec. v-p, corp. devel. & legal affairs & corp. sec., Toronto, Ont.; John Adamovich, Ocean Ridge, Fla.; Darrell MacMullin, Toronto, Ont.; G. Scott Nirenberski, Toronto, Ont.

Other Exec. Officers - Alim Virani, CFO; Jennifer Carman, chief people officer; Cody Shankman, exec. v-p & chief mktg. officer

Capital Stock

	Authorized (shs.)	Outstanding (shs.)[1]
Cl.A Subordinate Vtg.	unlimited	53,694,817
Cl.B Proportionate Vtg.	unlimited	223,651

[1] At Mar. 7, 2023

Class A Subordinate Voting - Convertible, at the holder's option, into class B proportionate voting shares on the basis of 1 class B proportionate voting share for 100 class A subordinate voting shares. One vote per share.

Class B Proportionate Voting - Convertible, at the company's option, into class A subordinate voting shares on the basis of 100 class A subordinate voting shares for 1 class B proportionate voting share. 100 votes per share.

Major Shareholder - Daren Trousdell held 34.64% interest at June 3, 2022.

Price Range - NOW/TSX-VEN

Year	Volume	High	Low	Close
2022	18,422,369	$1.27	$0.39	$0.57
2021	11,725,049	$1.43	$0.77	$1.27
2019	6,222	$0.54	$0.45	$0.45
2018	30,600	$0.90	$0.50	$0.50

Consolidation: 1-for-4.5 cons. in July 2021
Recent Close: $0.26

Capital Stock Changes - On Feb. 28, 2023, bought deal offering of 9,631,500 units (1 common share & ½ warrant) at Cdn$0.52 per unit was completed, with warrants exercisable at Cdn$0.80 per share for three years.

Pursuant to the June 28, 2021, Qualifying Transaction reverse takeover acquisition of (old) NowVertical Group, Inc., common shares were consolidated on a 1-for-4.5 basis (effective on the TSX Venture Exchange on July 5, 2021) and were redesignated as class A subordinate voting shares, and a new class of class B proportionate voting shares was created. A total of 10,750,249 post-consolidated class A subordinate voting shares and 271,270 class B proportionate voting shares were issued for the NowVertical acquisition, and 1,778,000 post-consolidated class A subordinate voting shares were issued as finder's fee. In addition, 8,394,000 post-consolidated class A subordinate voting shares were issued without further consideration on exchange of subscription receipts sold previously by private placement at $1.00 each. In November 2021, bought deal offering of 10,894,756 units (1 post-consolidated class A subordinate voting share & ½ warrant) at Cdn$0.95 per unit was completed and 1,300,000 post-consolidated class A subordinate voting shares were issued pursuant to the acquisition of Affinio Inc. Also during 2022, post-consolidated class A subordinate voting shares were issued as follows: 2,370,400 on conversion of 23,704 class B proportionate voting shares, 555,556 pursuant to the acquisition of Integra Data and Analytic Solutions Corp. and 40,000 pursuant to the acquisition of substantially all of the assets of DocAuthority Ltd.

Wholly Owned Subsidiaries

Affinio Inc., Halifax, N.S.
- 100% int. in **Affinio Holdings Inc.**, Canada.

CoreBI S.A.S., Colombia.
NOW Guardian Inc., Del.
- 100% int. in **Allegient Defense Inc.**, Va.

NowVertical Canada, Inc., Canada.
- 10% int. in **CoreBI S.A.**, Argentina.

NowVertical Group, Inc., N.Y.
- 100% int. in **Integra Data and Analytic Solutions Corp.**, Alta.
- 100% int. in **Seafront Analytics, LLC**, Washington, D.C.
- 100% int. in **Signafire Technologies Inc.**, West Palm Beach, Fla.

NowVertical UK Ltd., United Kingdom.
- 100% int. in **Exonar Ltd.**, United Kingdom.

NowVertical US Holdings Inc., Del.
- 100% int. in **Resonant Analytics, LLC**, Del.

Robert Baratheon Ltd., Israel.

Subsidiaries

90% int. in **CoreBI S.A.**, Argentina.

Financial Statistics

Periods ended:	12m Dec. 31/21[A]
	US$000s
Operating revenue	**3,221**
Cost of sales	947
Salaries & benefits	3,649
Research & devel. expense	231
General & admin expense	2,462
Stock-based compensation	3,944
Operating expense	**11,233**
Operating income	**(8,012)**
Deprec., depl. & amort.	4
Finance costs, gross	348
Write-downs/write-offs	(570)
Pre-tax income	**(13,903)**
Income taxes	(43)
Net income	**(13,860)**
Cash & equivalent	9,103
Accounts receivable	518
Current assets	10,193
Fixed assets, net	16
Intangibles, net	10,872
Total assets	**21,081**
Accts. pay. & accr. liabs	2,749
Current liabilities	6,733
Long-term debt, gross	1,419
Long-term debt, net	654
Shareholders' equity	10,762
Cash from oper. activs	**(4,459)**
Cash from fin. activs	14,621
Cash from invest. activs	(2,390)
Net cash position	**9,103**
Capital expenditures	(3)
	US$
Earnings per share*	(0.35)
Cash flow per share*	(0.11)
	shs
No. of shs. o/s*	62,042,153
Avg. no. of shs. o/s*	40,139,296
	%
Net profit margin	(430.30)
Return on equity	n.m.
Return on assets	n.a.

* Cl.A Subord. Vtg.
[A] Reported in accordance with IFRS

Latest Results

Periods ended:	9m Sept. 30/22[A]		9m Sept. 30/21[A]
	US$000s	%Chg	US$000s
Operating revenue	18,617	+795	2,081
Net income	(5,991)	n.a.	(9,361)
	US$		US$
Earnings per share*	(0.10)		(0.19)

* Cl.A Subord. Vtg.
[A] Reported in accordance with IFRS
Note: Adjusted throughout for 1-for-4.5 cons. in July 2021

N.72 Nubeva Technologies Ltd.

Symbol - NBVA **Exchange** - TSX-VEN **CUSIP** - 67021Y
Head Office - 1080-789 Pender St W, Vancouver, BC, V6C 1H2 **Telephone** - (778) 895-0180
Website - www.nubeva.com
Email - srempel@nubeva.com
Investor Relations - Sheri Rempel (604) 428-7050
Auditors - Dale Matheson Carr-Hilton LaBonte LLP C.A., Vancouver, B.C.
Transfer Agents - Computershare Trust Company of Canada Inc., Vancouver, B.C.
Profile - (B.C. 2017) Provides cloud-based security solutions to enterprise customers in the U.S.

Develops and licenses software-based decryption solutions to businesses, governments and organizations. The solutions include Transport Layer Security (TLS) network decryption that broadens network traffic security and visibility for cybersecurity and application monitoring manufacturers; and Ransomware Reversal which decrypts files and data that are encrypted by ransomware attacks, without paying ransoms for faster and lower cost restoration of operations. Both solutions are powered by the company's proprietary and patented Session Key Intercept (SKI) technology that enables the discovery and copy of the keys used to encrypt network traffic or files at the moment of encryption.

TLS solutions include decryption for secure web gateways, secure access service edge, next-gen firewalls, intrusion prevention systems, network detection and response, intrusion detection system, application performance monitoring system, host-based network security, PCAP stores, sandbox and APT systems, network packet brokers and 5G monitoring.

Also offers Prisms, which are offered as a complementary utility to acquire the traffic for decryption when infrastructure taps, mirrors and packet brokering is not available or when it is cost prohibitive; and StratusEdge, a proprietary cloud-based security software platform. The company has an agreement with security systems reseller **Optiv IT LLC** to sell StratusEdge under the Optiv brand.

Predecessor Detail - Name changed from Sherpa Holdings Corp., Mar. 1, 2018, pursuant to Qualifying Transaction reverse takeover acquisition of Nubeva, Inc. and merger of Nubeva with wholly owned Sherpa USA Ltd.; basis 1 new for 5 old shs.

Directors - Greig Bannister, co-founder & chief technical officer, Sydney, N.S.W., Australia; Randy Chou, co-founder, pres. & CEO, San Jose, Calif.; David Warner, Palo Alto, Calif.; David Wu, Fremont, Calif.

Other Exec. Officers - Sheri Rempel, CFO & corp. sec.; Steve Perkins, chief mktg. officer

Capital Stock

	Authorized (shs.)	Outstanding (shs.)[1]
Restricted Vtg.	unlimited	14,770,967
Common	unlimited	53,349,487

[1] At Sept. 28, 2022

Restricted Voting - Convertible into common shares on a 1-for-1 basis, subject to conditions. One vote per share, except for the election or removal of the directors.

Common - One vote per share.

Major Shareholder - Randy Chou held 31.8% interest at Sept. 6, 2022.

Price Range - NBVA/TSX-VEN

Year	Volume	High	Low	Close
2022	17,109,998	$2.53	$0.60	$1.81
2021	43,365,656	$2.24	$0.37	$2.09
2020	25,794,019	$0.73	$0.03	$0.62
2019	11,695,468	$0.50	$0.04	$0.12
2018	22,452,705	$1.90	$0.27	$0.41

Recent Close: $0.99

Capital Stock Changes - During fiscal 2022, common shares were issued as follows: 3,363,572 by private placement, 2,575,953 on exercise of warrants, 1,091,557 on exercise of options and 102,443 for services.

Wholly Owned Subsidiaries

Nubeva, Inc., San Jose, Calif.
- 100% int. in **Nubeva Pty Ltd.**, Sydney, N.S.W., Australia.

Financial Statistics

Periods ended:	12m Apr. 30/22[A]		12m Apr. 30/21[A]
	US$000s	%Chg	US$000s
Operating revenue	**236**	**-88**	**1,965**
Research & devel. expense	1,205		1,160
General & admin expense	1,931		1,765
Stock-based compensation	419		327
Operating expense	**3,555**	**+9**	**3,252**
Operating income	**(3,319)**	**n.a.**	**(1,287)**
Finance income	2		3
Finance costs, gross	12		24
Write-downs/write-offs	(16)		nil
Pre-tax income	**(3,266)**	**n.a.**	**(762)**
Net income	**(3,266)**	**n.a.**	**(762)**
Cash & equivalent	3,992		2,280
Accounts receivable	140		335
Current assets	4,397		2,987
Fixed assets, net	4		nil
Total assets	**4,401**	**+47**	**2,987**
Accts. pay. & accr. liabs	183		199
Current liabilities	248		420
Long-term debt, gross	26		209
Long-term debt, net	25		26
Shareholders' equity	4,128		2,540
Cash from oper. activs	**(2,564)**	**n.a.**	**(1,568)**
Cash from fin. activs	4,274		1,931
Cash from invest. activs	(5)		nil
Net cash position	**3,992**	**+75**	**2,280**
Capital expenditures	(5)		nil
	US$		US$
Earnings per share*	(0.05)		(0.01)
Cash flow per share*	(0.04)		(0.03)
	shs		shs
No. of shs. o/s*	68,120,454		60,986,929
Avg. no. of shs. o/s*	64,071,847		56,845,264
	%		%
Net profit margin	n.m.		(38.78)
Return on equity	(97.96)		(39.23)
Return on assets	(88.09)		(28.00)

* Common
[A] Reported in accordance with IFRS

Latest Results

Periods ended:	3m July 31/22[A]		3m July 31/21[A]
	US$000s	%Chg	US$000s
Operating revenue	78	+144	32
Net income	(794)	n.a.	(852)
	US$		US$
Earnings per share*	(0.01)		(0.01)

* Common
[A] Reported in accordance with IFRS

Historical Summary
(as originally stated)

Fiscal Year	Oper. Rev. US$000s	Net Inc. Bef. Disc. US$000s	EPS* US$
2022[A]	236	(3,266)	(0.05)
2021[A]	1,965	(762)	(0.01)
2020[A]	158	(3,784)	(0.07)
2019[A]	846	(4,058)	(0.07)
2018[A1]	708	(4,929)	(0.10)

* Common
[A] Reported in accordance with IFRS
[1] Results prior to Feb. 28, 2018, pertain to and reflect the Qualifying Transaction reverse takeover acquisition of Nubeva, Inc.

N.73 NuGen Medical Devices Inc.

Symbol - NGMD **Exchange** - TSX-VEN **CUSIP** - 67054F
Head Office - 1400-18 King St E, Toronto, ON, M5C 1C4 **Toll-free** - (833) 285-2666
Website - www.nugenmd.com
Email - richard@nugenmd.com
Investor Relations - Richard Buzbuzian (833) 285-2666
Auditors - KPMG LLP C.A., Montréal, Qué.
Transfer Agents - Computershare Trust Company of Canada Inc., Vancouver, B.C.
Profile - (Ont. 2018) Researches, develops and commercializes needle-free injection devices and systems for the administration of subcutaneous medication.

Main product is InsuJet™, a self-administered needle-free injection system used by diabetics for insulin therapy and based on jet-stream administration of liquid drugs. The needle-free injection system is safe for use by both medical professionals and by patients in their homes, and could be safely used 5,000 times without the risk of needle-stick injury or cross-contamination. InsuJet™ is available for sale in 42 countries with active sales distribution agreements in 11 countries for diabetes treatment. Also offers PetJet™, which allow pet owners and veterinarians to safely and quickly inject various types of medication without the fear of hurting their pets with a traditional hypodermic needle.

In addition, the company is developing products using its novel needle-free delivery technology in fields including semaglutide, growth and fertility hormone, deoxyribonucleic acid (DNA) and conventional/paediatric vaccines; InsuJet™ V6, which is a re-design of V5 focusing on ergonomics and esthetics of the device; and InsuJet™ V8, which allows the injector to have a storage inside for a drug container that simplifies the drug aspiration step. Other potential applications for these devices are home healthcare markets, dental anaesthesia and cosmetic treatments.

In May 2023, the company announced plans to voluntary delist from the TSX Venture Exchange and to apply to list the company's common shares on one or more alternative stock exchanges in Canada or the United States.

Predecessor Detail - Name changed from BuzBuz Capital Corp., Oct. 15, 2021, pursuant to the Qualifying Transaction reverse takeover acquisition of Inolife R&D Inc. (renamed EPG Global Ltd.); basis 1 new for 2 old shs.

Directors - Anthony (Tony) Di Benedetto, exec. chr., Toronto, Ont.; Richard Buzbuzian, pres. & CEO, Toronto, Ont.; Karen Dunlap, interim chief cust. officer, La Quinta, Calif.; Philip Cortese, Qué.; Christopher O. (Chris) Irwin, Toronto, Ont.; John Leombruno, Mississauga, Ont.

Other Exec. Officers - Véronique Laberge, CFO & corp. sec.; Nicky Canton, exec. v-p & COO

Capital Stock

	Authorized (shs.)	Outstanding (shs.)[1]
Common	unlimited	171,285,682

[1] At May 30, 2023

Major Shareholder - Widely held at May 12, 2023.

Price Range - NGMD/TSX-VEN

Year	Volume	High	Low	Close
2022	10,222,266	$0.34	$0.04	$0.04
2021	10,466,986	$0.53	$0.25	$0.30
2020	96,500	$0.40	$0.06	$0.33
2019	112,600	$0.60	$0.30	$0.48

Consolidation: 1-for-2 cons. in Nov. 2021

Recent Close: $0.11

Capital Stock Changes - In February 2023, private placement of 50,000,000 units (1 common share & 1 warrant) at 5¢ per unit was completed, with warrants exercisable at 5¢ per share for two years. In April 2023, private placement of units 22,222,222 units (1 common share & 1 warrant) at 18¢ per unit was completed, with warrants exercisable at 24¢ per share for two years. In May 2023, a 1-for-30 share consolidation was proposed.

During 2022, common shares were issued as follows: 8,903,763 by private placement and 1,644,736 for debt settlement.

Wholly Owned Subsidiaries

European Pharma Group B.V., Netherlands.
- 100% int. in **European Pharma Group Hong Kong Ltd.**, Hong Kong, People's Republic of China.
- 100% int. in **European Pharma Group Shenzhen Ltd.**, Republic of China.

Financial Statistics

Periods ended:	12m Dec. 31/22[A]		12m Dec. 31/21[A1]
	$000s	%Chg	$000s
Operating revenue	**152**	**+10**	**138**
Cost of goods sold	53		45
Salaries & benefits	854		1,070
General & admin expense	2,955		2,879
Stock-based compensation	432		1,308
Operating expense	**4,294**	**-19**	**5,302**
Operating income	**(4,142)**	**n.a.**	**(5,164)**
Deprec., depl. & amort.	652		791
Finance costs, net	838		(568)
Pre-tax income	**(5,575)**	**n.a.**	**(7,104)**
Income taxes	3		3
Net income	**(5,578)**	**n.a.**	**(7,107)**
Cash & equivalent	131		1,750
Inventories	77		13
Accounts receivable	6		11
Current assets	567		2,146
Fixed assets, net	8		18
Right-of-use assets	155		nil
Intangibles, net	6,112		6,681
Total assets	**6,282**	**-6**	**6,699**
Accts. pay. & accr. liabs.	1,493		908
Current liabilities	1,730		1,233
Long-term debt, gross	7,246		5,608
Long-term debt, net	7,163		5,608
Shareholders' equity	(2,262)		1,658
Cash from oper. activs.	**(2,131)**	**n.a.**	**(4,095)**
Cash from fin. activs.	514		5,584
Cash from invest. activs.	(1)		2
Net cash position	**131**	**-93**	**1,750**
Capital expenditures	(1)		(4)
	$		$
Earnings per share*	(0.06)		(0.10)
Cash flow per share*	(0.02)		(0.06)
	shs		shs
No. of shs. o/s*	96,563,460		86,014,961
Avg. no. of shs. o/s*	90,102,067		68,674,502
	%		%
Net profit margin	n.m.		n.m.
Return on equity	n.m.		n.m.
Return on assets	(85.94)		(96.11)

* Common

[A] Reported in accordance with IFRS

[1] Results prior to Oct. 19, 2021, pertain to and reflect Qualifying Transaction reverse takeover acquisition of Inolife R&D Inc. (renamed as EPG Global Ltd.)

Latest Results

Periods ended:	3m Mar. 31/23[A]		3m Mar. 31/22[A]
	$000s	%Chg	$000s
Operating revenue	24	-65	68
Net income	(2,111)	n.a.	(1,493)
	$		$
Earnings per share*	(0.02)		(0.02)

* Common

[A] Reported in accordance with IFRS

Historical Summary
(as originally stated)

Fiscal Year	Oper. Rev.	Net Inc. Bef. Disc.	EPS*
	$000s	$000s	$
2022[A]	152	(5,578)	(0.06)
2021[A]	138	(7,107)	(0.10)
2020[A]	47	(3,478)	(0.04)
2019[A]	nil	(1,983)	(0.02)

* Common

[A] Reported in accordance with IFRS

Note: Adjusted throughout for 1-for-2 cons. in Nov. 2021

N.74 Numinus Wellness Inc.

Symbol - NUMI **Exchange** - TSX **CUSIP** - 67054W
Head Office - 801-33 Water St, Vancouver, BC, V6B 1R4 **Toll-free** - (833) 686-4687
Website - numinus.com
Email - jamie.kokoska@numinus.com
Investor Relations - Jamie Kokoska (833) 686-4687
Auditors - Davidson & Company LLP C.A., Vancouver, B.C.
Transfer Agents - Odyssey Trust Company, Vancouver, B.C.

Profile - (B.C. 1962) Develops proprietary, psychedelic-centred, therapeutic products and services through its own laboratory and research and development processes to be delivered through its network of clinics, digital solutions and partnerships.

The company's Numinus Bioscience business holds a controlled drugs and substances licence under Health Canada which allows the possession, production, assembly, sale, export and delivery for a wide variety of psychedelic compounds and natural source materials, including psilocybe mushroom fruiting bodies and extracts, psilocybin, psilocin, ketamine, LSD, DMT and mescaline. Services include standardized testing for control compounds; product development and formulation studies; psilocybe mushroom product development; spore bank; contract research laboratory; import, storage and distribution of controlled drugs and substances; provision of psilocybe mushroom fruiting bodies and extracts; and cannabis testing. Also provides contract research management services in the United States specializing in clinical trials and evidence-based research for psychedelic medicine in through two research clinics.

Also operates 12 wellness clinics in Vancouver, Toronto, Arizona (2), Montreal (3) and Utah (5). In addition, psychedelic studies are being conducted in four dedicated research clinics in Vancouver, Montreal and Salt Lake City (2). Services offered in the clinics include ketamine-assisted psychotherapy (KAP) for depression, neurological care and psychotherapy, and counselling by registered psychologists. The company develops KAP protocols for other clinical indications, psychedelic neurology programming and therapeutic protocols for other psychedelic substances.

Recent Merger and Acquisition Activity

Status: completed **Revised:** June 10, 2022
UPDATE: The transaction was completed. PREVIOUS: Numinus Wellness Inc. agreed to acquire Novamind Inc. on the basis of 0.84 Numinus common shares for each Novamind common share held for total consideration of $26,200,000. The offer values Novamind at $0.44 per share. The combined company would operate four clinical research sites and a bioanalytical laboratory and 13 wellness clinics in Canada and the United States. The transaction was expected to close in June 2022.

Predecessor Detail - Name changed from Rojo Resources Ltd., May 14, 2020, pursuant to reverse takeover acquisition of Salvation Botanicals Ltd.; basis 1 new for 2 old shs.

Directors - Payton Nyquvest, chr. & CEO, North Vancouver, B.C.; Michael Tan, pres. & COO, Nanaimo, B.C.; Edwin (Ed) Garner, Nanaimo, B.C.; Allen Morishita, North Vancouver, B.C.; Larry E. Timlick, West Vancouver, B.C.

Other Exec. Officers - Nikhil Handa, CFO; Dr. Reid Robison, chief clinical officer; Julie Saunders, chief mktg. officer; Dr. Paul Thielking, chief science officer; Paula Amy Hewitt, sr. v-p, gen. counsel & chief privacy officer; Jason Lapensee, sr. v-p, clinic opers.; Neil Barclay, v-p, product & protocol; Lea Bottoni, v-p, people & culture; Dr. Devon Christie, v-p, clinical & psychedelic srvcs.; Dr. Lindsay Farrell, v-p, indigenous initiatives & reconciliation; Dr. Joe Flanders, v-p, psychology; Danielle Hinan, v-p, mktg.; John Kaczmarowski, v-p, IT; Jamie L. Kokoska, v-p, IR & commun.; Dr. Evan C. Lewis, v-p, psychedelic neurology; Raseel Sehmi, v-p, bus. devel. & strategic partnerships; Pam Sethi, v-p, experience design & innovation; Sharan Sidhu, v-p, scientific research, innovation & laboratory opers.

Capital Stock

	Authorized (shs.)	Outstanding (shs.)[1]
Common	unlimited	264,546,188

[1] At Apr. 13, 2023

Major Shareholder - Widely held at Jan. 18, 2023.

Price Range - NUMI/TSX

Year	Volume	High	Low	Close
2022	91,108,131	$0.76	$0.17	$0.19
2021	277,032,711	$1.95	$0.48	$0.53
2020	292,079,823	$2.45	$0.19	$1.07
2019	294,766	$0.60	$0.20	$0.38

Consolidation: 1-for-2 cons. in May 2020
Recent Close: $0.19

Capital Stock Changes - In June 2022, 43,474,659 common shares were issued pursuant to the acquisition of Novamind Inc. Also during fiscal 2022, common shares were issued as follows: 4,352,160 on exercise of warrants, 2,000,000 as share-based compensation, 1,902,000 on exercise of options, 780,815 pursuant to the 2021 acquisition of Mindspace Services Inc. (formerly Mindspace Psychology Services Inc.), 444,444 for services and 206,228 pursuant to the acquisition of Neurology Centre of Toronto Inc.

Wholly Owned Subsidiaries

Mindspace Services Inc., Montréal, Qué. formerly Mindspace Psychology Services Inc.
Neurology Centre of Toronto Inc., Canada.
Novamind Inc., Toronto, Ont.
- 100% int. in **Novamind Ventures Inc.**, Toronto, Ont.
  - 100% int. in **Cedar Clinical Research, Inc.**, Utah
  - 100% int. in **Cedar Psychiatry, Inc.**, Utah
  - 100% int. in **Foundations for Change, Inc.**, Ariz.

Numinus Bioscience Inc., Nanaimo, B.C.
- 100% int. in **Numinus Health Corp.**, B.C.
- 100% int. in **Salvation Bioscience Inc.**, B.C.

1050086 B.C. Ltd., Canada.
1134337 B.C. Ltd., Canada.
1659070 Canada Inc., Canada. Inactive.

Financial Statistics

Periods ended:	12m Aug. 31/22[A]		12m Aug. 31/21[A]
	$000s	%Chg	$000s
Operating revenue	**6,494**	**+329**	**1,514**
Cost of sales	4,194		1,323
Research & devel. expense	1,885		1,401
General & admin expense	23,905		12,092
Stock-based compensation	3,455		1,822
Operating expense	**33,439**	**+101**	**16,638**
Operating income	**(26,945)**	**n.a.**	**(15,124)**
Deprec., depl. & amort.	1,506		717
Finance costs, gross	558		114
Write-downs/write-offs	(13,770)		(2,479)
Pre-tax income	**(44,916)**	**n.a.**	**(18,774)**
Income taxes	(34)		nil
Net income	**(44,882)**	**n.a.**	**(18,774)**
Cash & equivalent	33,044		59,293
Inventories	nil		3
Accounts receivable	1,602		516
Current assets	36,122		60,970
Fixed assets, net	11,385		3,150
Intangibles, net	2,515		nil
Total assets	**52,631**	**-18**	**64,144**
Accts. pay. & accr. liabs.	2,710		1,304
Current liabilities	4,583		1,913
Long-term debt, gross	277		nil
Long-term debt, net	213		nil
Long-term lease liabilities	6,195		1,201
Shareholders' equity	41,214		60,831
Cash from oper. activs.	**(26,230)**	**n.a.**	**(15,578)**
Cash from fin. activs.	7		73,983
Cash from invest. activs.	123		(739)
Net cash position	**33,044**	**-44**	**59,293**
Capital expenditures	(1,246)		(642)
Capital disposals	nil		299
	$		$
Earnings per share*	(0.21)		(0.11)
Cash flow per share*	(0.12)		(0.09)
	shs		shs
No. of shs. o/s*	256,237,380		203,077,074
Avg. no. of shs. o/s*	216,587,034		164,940,392
	%		%
Net profit margin	(691.13)		n.m.
Return on equity	(87.97)		n.m.
Return on assets	(75.91)		n.a.

* Common

[A] Reported in accordance with IFRS

Latest Results

Periods ended:	3m Nov. 30/22[A]		3m Nov. 30/21[A]
	$000s	%Chg	$000s
Operating revenue	5,668	+617	790
Net income	(6,297)	n.a.	(5,354)
	$		$
Earnings per share*	(0.02)		(0.03)

* Common

[A] Reported in accordance with IFRS

Historical Summary
(as originally stated)

Fiscal Year	Oper. Rev.	Net Inc. Bef. Disc.	EPS*
	$000s	$000s	$
2022[A]	6,494	(44,882)	(0.21)
2021[A]	1,514	(18,774)	(0.11)
2020[A1]	881	(9,601)	(0.15)
2019[A2]	nil	(174)	(0.06)
2018[A]	nil	(279)	(0.14)

* Common

[A] Reported in accordance with IFRS

[1] Results reflect the May 15, 2020, reverse takeover acquisition of Salvation Botanicals Ltd.

[2] Results for fiscal 2019 and prior fiscal periods pertain to Rojo Resources Ltd.

Note: Adjusted throughout for 1-for-2 cons. in May 2020

N.75 Nuran Wireless Inc.

Symbol - NUR **Exchange** - CSE **CUSIP** - 67059X
Head Office - 100-2150 rue Cyrille-Duquet, Québec, QC, G1N 2G3 **Telephone** - (418) 914-7484 **Toll-free** - (855) 914-7484 **Fax** - (418) 914-9477
Website - www.nuranwireless.com
Email - francis.letourneau@nuranwireless.com
Investor Relations - Francis Létourneau (418) 264-1337
Auditors - Jeremy Levi C.P.A., Westmount, Qué.
Transfer Agents - Capital Transfer Agency Inc., Toronto, Ont.

Profile - (B.C. 2014) Researches, develops, manufactures, markets and operates digital electronic circuits and wireless telecommunication products and services including radio access network (RAN), core network and backhaul products for the mobile telephony industry.

Supplies wireless infrastructure systems, which are mobile wireless infrastructure equipment (i.e. base station radios) that uses small cell solutions to deliver better coverage and have efficient power consumption at a lower installed cost for specific markets such as defence, utilities, industrial and machine-to-machine. Products are provided for indoor coverage, isolated rural communities, offshore platforms and ships.

Products are either sold to mobile network operators (MNOs), or marketed through a Network-as-a-Service (NaaS) model. Through the NaaS model, the company provides the network equipment, as well as finances, builds, operates and maintains the cellular sites for MNOs. The NaaS model allows MNOs to reach previously uneconomic markets and meet obligations to serve remote communities that are a requirement of their government licences without capital investment. At May 30, 2023, the company had 4,642 NaaS sites in the Republic of Cameroon, the Democratic Republic of the Congo, the Republic of Madagascar, the Republic of South Sudan, the Republic of Namibia, the Republic of the Sudan and the Republic of Côte d'Ivoire under contract with multiple telecommunication operators for a potential contract value of more than US$800,000,000.

In January 2023, the company entered into a 10-year Network-as-a-Service (NaaS) agreement with **Orange Madagascar S.A.** for the deployment of up to 500 rural networking telecommunication sites under the NaaS business model in the east coast of Madagascar. The telecommunication sites are expected to generate an annual gross revenue of more than US$90,000,000.

In October 2022, the company entered into a five-year agreement with **MTN Ivory Coast** for the deployment of up to 1,000 rural sites under the Network-as-a-Service (NaaS) model in Ivory Coast. The rural sites are expected to generate gross revenue of more than US$75,000,000.

On July 21, 2022, the company entered into a group framework agreement with **MTN Group** for up to 19,000 network sites in more than 15 countries in the Middle East and Africa. The company expects to have a significant amount of these sites be under contract.

Directors - Francis Létourneau, pres. & CEO, Québec, Qué.; James A. (Jim) Bailey, CFO, Newbury, Berks., United Kingdom; Kenneth (Ken) Campbell, Ottawa, Ont.; Vitor M. Fonseca, Toronto, Ont.; Hassan Kabbani, Beirut, Lebanon; Binyomin Posen, Toronto, Ont.; Brendan Purdy, Toronto, Ont.

Other Exec. Officers - Gaël Campan, COO; David Parsons, chief tech. officer; Denis Lambert, v-p, sales & bus. devel.

Capital Stock

	Authorized (shs.)	Outstanding (shs.)[1]
Common	unlimited	37,458,197

[1] At Mar. 31, 2023

Major Shareholder - Widely held at July 8, 2022.

Price Range - NUR/CSE

Year	Volume	High	Low	Close
2022	22,039,783	$1.64	$0.45	$0.53
2021	52,571,817	$3.50	$0.28	$1.41
2020	8,280,854	$1.50	$0.32	$0.38
2019	4,895,144	$3.25	$0.88	$1.25
2018	2,571,351	$5.88	$1.00	$1.38

Consolidation: 1-for-25 cons. in Oct. 2020

Recent Close: $0.25

Capital Stock Changes - During 2022, common shares were issued as follows: 1,500,000 on conversion of debentures, 905,000 on exercise of warrants and 182,840 as bonus shares.

Wholly Owned Subsidiaries

NuRAN Wireless (Africa) Holding, Mauritius.
NuRAN Wireless Cameroon Ltd., Cameroon.
Nuran Wireless DRC S.A.R.L.U., Democratic Republic of Congo.

Financial Statistics

Periods ended:	12m Dec. 31/22[A]		14m Dec. 31/21[A]
	$000s	%Chg	$000s
Operating revenue	**4,872**	**n.a.**	**2,138**
Cost of sales	2,710		1,647
Research & devel. expense	264		336
General & admin expense	8,661		7,149
Stock-based compensation	1,177		5,842
Operating expense	**12,812**	**n.a.**	**14,974**
Operating income	**(7,940)**	**n.a.**	**(12,836)**
Deprec., depl. & amort.	454		298
Finance costs, gross	1,036		499
Write-downs/write-offs	nil		(138)
Pre-tax income	**(9,892)**	**n.a.**	**(14,128)**
Income taxes	nil		(1,410)
Net income	**(9,892)**	**n.a.**	**(12,718)**
Cash & equivalent	183		731
Inventories	4,913		5,355
Accounts receivable	5,655		948
Current assets	11,323		8,229
Fixed assets, net	303		267
Right-of-use assets	562		676
Intangibles, net	6,549		5,864
Total assets	**18,738**	**+25**	**15,036**
Bank indebtedness	5,985		nil
Accts. pay. & accr. liabs	6,730		2,562
Current liabilities	14,145		4,430
Long-term lease liabilities	406		559
Shareholders' equity	4,187		10,047
Cash from oper. activs	**(6,799)**	**n.a.**	**(10,571)**
Cash from fin. activs	7,320		11,706
Cash from invest. activs	(1,069)		(469)
Net cash position	**183**	**-75**	**731**
Capital expenditures	(961)		(532)
Capital disposals	nil		64
	$		$
Earnings per share*	(0.30)		(0.58)
Cash flow per share*	(0.20)		(0.48)
	shs		shs
No. of shs. o/s*	35,008,197		32,420,357
Avg. no. of shs. o/s*	33,427,811		22,115,234
	%		%
Net profit margin	(203.04)		...
Return on equity	(138.99)		...
Return on assets	(52.44)		...
Foreign sales percent	99		75

* Common
[A] Reported in accordance with IFRS

Latest Results

Periods ended:	3m Mar. 31/23[A]		3m Mar. 31/22[A]
	$000s	%Chg	$000s
Operating revenue	672	-64	1,882
Net income	(3,366)	n.a.	(3,249)
	$		$
Earnings per share*	(0.09)		(0.10)

* Common
[A] Reported in accordance with IFRS

Historical Summary
(as originally stated)

Fiscal Year	Oper. Rev. $000s	Net Inc. Bef. Disc. $000s	EPS* $
2022[A]	4,872	(9,892)	(0.30)
2021[A1]	2,138	(12,718)	(0.58)
2020[A]	3,930	(1,894)	(0.27)
2019[A]	2,122	(3,549)	(0.50)
2018[A]	4,169	(3,497)	(0.75)

* Common
[A] Reported in accordance with IFRS
[1] 14 months ended Dec. 31, 2021.

Note: Adjusted throughout for 1-for-25 cons. in Oct. 2020

N.76 Nurcapital Corporation Ltd.

Symbol - NCL.H **Exchange** - TSX-VEN **CUSIP** - 67091V
Head Office - 801-1 Adelaide St E, Toronto, ON, M5C 2V9 **Telephone** - (416) 754-4135 **Fax** - (416) 869-0547
Email - info@nurcapital.ca
Investor Relations - John A. Ryan (416) 869-1234
Auditors - MNP LLP C.A., Toronto, Ont.
Lawyers - Garfinkle Biderman LLP, Toronto, Ont.
Transfer Agents - TSX Trust Company, Toronto, Ont.
Profile - (Ont. 2015) Capital Pool Company.

In May 2023, a proposed Qualifying Transaction business combination with **Caravel Resources Corp.** was terminated. Caravel held minor oil and gas interests in southern Alberta.

Common reinstated on TSX-VEN, Dec. 6, 2022.

Recent Merger and Acquisition Activity

Status: terminated **Revised:** July 13, 2022

UPDATE: The transaction was terminated. PREVIOUS: Nurcapital Corporation Ltd. entered into a letter of intent for the Qualifying Transaction reverse takeover acquisition of private Calgary, Alta.-based Green Sky Labs Inc. (GSL), which develops and commercializes disruptive technologies for the development of cannabinoid medicines, products and plant cultivation, on a share-for-share basis, which would result in the issuance of 100,460,538 Nurcapital post-consolidated common shares (following a 1-for-3.65 share consolidation). Upon completion, Nurcapital would change its name to Green Sky Labs Inc. Mar. 13, 2021 - The parties entered into a definitive agreement whereby GSL would amalgamate with a wholly owned subsidiary of Nurcapital. Oct. 27, 2021 - Closing of the transaction was extended to Jan. 31, 2022.

Directors - John A. Ryan, CEO, Puslinch, Ont.; Barry M. Polisuk, corp. sec., Vaughan, Ont.; Irshad Ali, Ont.; Nadeem Ansari, Scarborough, Ont.; Sharief Zaman, Mississauga, Ont.

Other Exec. Officers - Kyle Appleby, CFO

Capital Stock

	Authorized (shs.)	Outstanding (shs.)[1]
Common	unlimited	3,252,833

[1] At May 29, 2023

Major Shareholder - Widely held at Dec. 9, 2022.

Capital Stock Changes - During 2022, 33,333 common shares were issued by private placement.

N.77 NurExone Biologic Inc.

Symbol - NRX **Exchange** - TSX-VEN **CUSIP** - 67059R
Head Office - 9 Mezada St, BSR 3 Tower, 30 Floor, Bnei Brak, Israel, 5120109 **Overseas Tel** - 972-52-480-3034
Website - www.nurexone.com
Email - info@nurexone.com
Investor Relations - Eran Ovadya 972-52-480-3034
Auditors - BDO Ziv Haft C.P.A., Tel Aviv, Israel
Transfer Agents - Computershare Trust Company of Canada Inc., Toronto, Ont.
Profile - (Alta. 2011) Developing a biological extracellular vesicles-based technology drug platform to treat damage in the Central Nerve System (CNS).

Exosomes are natural membrane vesicles, secreted by various cells. Exosomes have different properties, such as cell-to-cell communication, they can migrate to damaged areas and they can be loaded with different molecules, such as proteins, lipids, and genetic materials. when intranasally administered, they can pass the blood-brain barrier and are better retained in injury sites than when delivered intravenously. Moreover, they can be loadable with an array of therapeutic cargos for specific diseases.

Potential uses of the company's technology is to treat spinal cord injury, traumatic brain injury and other brain and neurological indications. The company has been granted an exclusive worldwide licence to develop and commercialize the technology by the Technion - Israel Institute of Technology, Haifa and Tel Aviv University, both located in Israel. Also holds an exclusive global licence to an exosome manufacturing process developed at the Technion.

On May 31, 2022, the company completed the spin-out of wholly owned **1222150 B.C. Ltd.** (SpinCo) by way of a dividend-in-kind distribution of the shares of SpinCo held by the company pro rata to the company's shareholders. Each shareholder of record May 24, 2022, received one SpinCo common share for each common share the company held. The company transferred its Johan Beetz feldspar property in Quebec in April 2022 to SpinCo in exchange for 25,360,000 SpinCo common shares. SpinCo was acquired by the company in March 2022 for nominal consideration in order to facilitate the spin-out.

Recent Merger and Acquisition Activity

Status: completed **Revised:** June 15, 2022

UPDATE: The transaction was completed. PREVIOUS: EnerSpar Corp. entered into a definitive agreement for the reverse takeover acquisition of private Israel-based NurExone Biologic Ltd., a pharmaceutical company developing a treatment for the reversal or reduction in the harmful results of spinal cord injury. on the basis of 17 EnerSpar common shares for each Nurexone ordinary share held (following a 1-for-10 share consolidation). NurExone would complete a concurrent financing of convertible loans and equity for gross proceeds of $1,957,195 and the company plans to raise $4,000,000 via a private placement of subscription receipts. On closing, the company would change its name to NurExone Biologic Inc. and consolidate its common shares a 1-for-10 basis. As a condition of closing of the transaction, EnerSpar would complete the spin-out of wholly owned 1222150 B.C. Ltd., which would acquire EnerSpar's Johan Beetz feldspar property in Quebec.

Predecessor Detail - Name changed from EnerSpar Corp., June 15, 2022, following reverse takeover acquisition of private Israel-based NurExone Biologic Ltd.; basis 1 new for 10 old shs.

Directors - Yoram Drucker, chr. & v-p, strategic devel., Israel; Dr. Lior Shaltiel, CEO, Israel; Eyal Flom, legal counsel, Israel; Oded Orgil, Toronto, Ont.; James A. (Jay) Richardson, Toronto, Ont.; Dr. Gadi Riesenfeld

Other Exec. Officers - Eran Ovadya, CFO

Capital Stock

	Authorized (shs.)	Outstanding (shs.)[1]
Preferred	unlimited	nil
Common	unlimited	42,855,159

[1] At May 23, 2023

Major Shareholder - Widely held at June 22, 2022.

Price Range - NRX/TSX-VEN

Year	Volume	High	Low	Close
2022	598,903	$0.80	$0.35	$0.39
2019	67,444	$0.65	$0.50	$0.55
2018	2,943,351	$1.00	$0.30	$0.55

Consolidation: 1-for-10 cons. in June 2022

Recent Close: $0.22

Capital Stock Changes - In June 2022, common shares were consolidated on a 1-for-10 basis and 39,847,963 post-consolidated common shares were issued pursuant to the reverse takeover acquisition of NurExone Biologic Ltd.

Dividends

NRX com N.S.R.
Listed Jun 22/22.
1-for-10 cons eff. June 22, 2022
stk.[1]r.................... May 31/22
Paid in 2023: n.a. 2022: stk.r 2021: n.a.

[1] Stk. divd. of 1 1222150 BC Ltd com. sh. for ea. 1 sh. held.
r Return of Capital

Wholly Owned Subsidiaries

NurExone Biologic Ltd., Israel.

Financial Statistics

Periods ended:	12m Dec. 31/21[A1]		12m Dec. 31/20[A]
	$000s	%Chg	$000s
Exploration expense	2		nil
General & admin expense	163		82
Operating expense	**165**	**+101**	**82**
Operating income	**(165)**	**n.a.**	**(82)**
Pre-tax income	**(166)**	**n.a.**	**(28)**
Net income	**(166)**	**n.a.**	**(28)**
Cash & equivalent	1		9
Current assets	2,129		18
Total assets	**2,129**	**n.m.**	**18**
Accts. pay. & accr. liabs	143		93
Current liabilities	2,378		101
Shareholders' equity	(249)		(83)
Cash from oper. activs	**(96)**	**n.a.**	**(2)**
Cash from fin. activs	2,207		8
Cash from invest. activs	(2,119)		nil
Net cash position	**1**	**-89**	**9**
	$		$
Earnings per share*	(0.07)		(0.01)
Cash flow per share*	(0.04)		(0.00)
	shs		shs
No. of shs. o/s*	2,536,000		2,536,000
Avg. no. of shs. o/s*	2,536,000		2,536,000
	%		%
Net profit margin	n.a.		n.a.
Return on equity	n.m.		n.m.
Return on assets	(15.46)		(103.70)

* Common
[A] Reported in accordance with IFRS
[1] Results for 2021 and prior years pertain to EnerSpar Corp.

Historical Summary
(as originally stated)

Fiscal Year	Oper. Rev.	Net Inc. Bef. Disc.	EPS*
	$000s	$000s	$
2021[A]	nil	(166)	(0.07)
2020[A]	nil	(28)	(0.01)
2019[A]	nil	86	0.03
2018[A]	nil	136	0.06
2017[A]	nil	822	0.40

* Common
[A] Reported in accordance with IFRS
Note: Adjusted throughout for 1-for-10 cons. in June 2022

N.78 Nutrien Ltd.*

Symbol - NTR **Exchange** - TSX **CUSIP** - 67077M
Head Office - 1700-211 19 St E, Saskatoon, SK, S7K 5R6 **Telephone** - (306) 933-8500 **Toll-free** - (800) 667-0403 **Fax** - (306) 933-8877
Website - www.nutrien.com
Email - investors@nutrien.com
Investor Relations - Jeff Holzman (306) 933-8545
Auditors - KPMG LLP C.A., Calgary, Alta.
Transfer Agents - Computershare Trust Company of Canada Inc., Calgary, Alta.
FP500 Revenue Ranking - 12
Employees - 24,700 at Dec. 31, 2022

Profile - (Can. 2018; orig. Sask., 1953) Provides crop inputs and services to customers worldwide through an integrated retail network and production and processing facilities of potash, nitrogen and phosphate products.

Operates through four interrelated business segments: Nutrien Ag Solutions (Retail); Potash; Nitrogen; and Phosphate.

The **Nutrien Ag Solutions (Retail)** segment sells crop nutrients, crop protection products, seeds and merchandise, and provides services and solutions to farmers and retailers through more than 2,000 retail locations across the U.S., Canada, Australia and South America (Argentina, Brazil, Chile and Uruguay) under the Nutrien Ag Solutions© banner. Private label and proprietary product lines distributed include the Loveland Products® brand of crop protection products and nutritionals, and the Dyna-Gro®, Proven™ and Sementes Goiás seed brands. In addition, the retail segment offers merchandise including fencing, feed supplements, animal identification merchandise, animal health products and services, and storage and irrigation equipment. Services and other solutions provided include custom product application, soil and leaf testing, crop scouting and precision agriculture, digital tools, wool sales and marketing, livestock marketing and auction, water services, insurance, real estate agency services and financing solutions (through Nutrien Financial).

The **Potash** segment includes the conventional and solution mining and processing of potash, primarily used as fertilizer. Potash is produced in southern Saskatchewan from the Lanigan, Allan, Cory, Vanscoy, Rocanville and Patience Lake mines, with a combined annual nameplate capacity of 20,600,000 tonnes. The six mines cover 282,000 of the 383,000 total hectares leased from the Crown in Saskatchewan. Potash for sale outside Canada and the U.S. is sold exclusively to **Canpotex Limited** (50% owned).

The **Nitrogen** segment consists of the production of nitrogen agricultural fertilizer, industrial and feed products, including ammonia and upgraded ammonia products such as urea, ammonium nitrate, ammonium sulfate, nitric acid and nitrogen solutions, urea liquor and the controlled-release product Environmentally Smart Nitrogen®. Production facilities have a combined annual ammonia nameplate capacity of 7,100,000 tonnes and are located in Redwater, Carseland, Joffre and Fort Saskatchewan, Alta.; Augusta, Ga.; Geismar, La.; Lima, Ohio; Borger, Tex.; and Point Lisas, Trinidad. Upgrading facilities are located in Carseland, Granum and Standard, Alta.; Kennewick, Wash.; and New Madrid, Mo. The segment also includes 50% interest in **Profertil S.A.**, a nitrogen producer in Argentina.

The **Phosphate** segment includes the mining of phosphate ore and the manufacture of solid and liquid fertilizers, feed products and industrial products. Integrated mining and processing facilities are located in Aurora, N.C., which include a 5,400,000-tonne-per-year mine and plants capable of producing solid fertilizer monoammonium phosphate (MAP), liquid fertilizer, superphosphoric acid (SPA), purified acid, merchant-grade phosphoric acid (MGA), hydrofluosilicic acid (HFSA), defluorinated merchant-grade acid, low magnesium SPA (LOMAG) and anhydrous hydrogen fluoride; and White Springs, Fla., which include a 2,000,000-tonne-per-year mine and plants that produce SPA, MGA, LOMAG, HFSA, MAP and sulphur-enhanced MAP. Operations also include animal feed plants in Marseilles, Ill., Weeping Water, Neb., and Joplin, Mo.; and a phosphoric acid plant in Cincinnati, Ohio.

Production

Year ended Dec. 31	2022	2021
	tonnes	tonnes
Potash (finished product)	13,007,000	13,790,000
Nitrogen (total ammonia)	5,759,000	5,996,000
Phosphate (P_2O_5)	1,351,000	1,518,000

Sales

Year ended Dec. 31	2022	2021
Potash:		
Tonnes sold[1]	12,537,000	13,625,000
Price per tonne, US$	630	296
Nitrogen:		
Tonnes sold[1]	10,023,000	10,725,000
Price per tonne, US$	638	371
Phosphate:		
Tonnes sold[1]	2,378,000	2,619,000
Price per tonne, US$	872	622

[1] Manufactured products.

In May 2022, the company announced it was evaluating Geismar, La., as the site to build the world's largest clean ammonia production facility. A final investment decision was expected in the second half of 2023. If approved, construction of the US$2 billion facility would begin in 2024 with full production expected by 2027. The plant was expected to have an annual production capacity of 1,200,000 tonnes of clean ammonia and capture at least 90% of CO_2 emissions.

Recent Merger and Acquisition Activity

Status: completed **Revised:** Oct. 1, 2022
UPDATE: The transaction was completed for US$279,000,000. PREVIOUS: Nutrien Ltd. agreed to acquire Brazilian agriculture retailer Casa do Adubo S.A., which includes 39 retail locations, under the brand Casa do Adubo, and 10 distribution centres under the brand Agrodistribuidor Casal. Terms were not disclosed. The acquisition of Casa do Adubo was expected to result in additional run-rate sales of US$400,000,000, increasing total Nutrien Ag Solutions annual sales in Latin America to US$2.2 billion.

Predecessor Detail - Succeeded Potash Corporation of Saskatchewan Inc., Jan. 1, 2018, (new parent company) following merger with Agrium Corp. (2.23 Nutrien shs. for 1 Agrium sh.); basis 0.4 new for 1 old sh.

Directors - Russell K. (Russ) Girling, chr., Calgary, Alta.; Kenneth A. (Ken) Seitz, pres. & CEO, Saskatoon, Sask.; Christopher M. Burley, Calgary, Alta.; Maura J. Clark, New York, N.Y.; Michael J. Hennigan, West Chester, Pa.; Miranda C. Hubbs, Toronto, Ont.; Raj S. Kushwaha, Gig Harbor, Wash.; Alice D. Laberge, Vancouver, B.C.; Consuelo E. Madere, Destin, Fla.; Keith G. Martell, Sask.; Aaron W. Regent, Toronto, Ont.; Nelson L. C. Silva, Rio de Janeiro, Brazil

Other Exec. Officers - Noralee M. Bradley, exec. v-p, external affairs & chief sustainability & legal officer; Pedro Farah, exec. v-p & CFO; Andrew J. (Andy) Kelemen, exec. v-p & chief corp. devel. & strategy officer; Brent D. Poohkay, exec. v-p & chief tech. officer; Chris P. Reynolds, exec. v-p & pres., potash; Jeff M. Tarsi, exec. v-p & pres., global retail; Mark Thompson, exec. v-p & chief comml. officer; Candace J. Laing, sr. v-p & chief HR officer; Trevor Williams, interim pres., nitrogen & phosphate

Capital Stock

	Authorized (shs.)	Outstanding (shs.)[1]
Preferred	unlimited	nil
Common	unlimited	494,508,425

[1] At Aug. 1, 2023

Options - At Dec. 31, 2022, options were outstanding to purchase 3,885,478 common shares at exercise prices ranging from US$37.84 to US$109.45 per share with a weighted average remaining life of five years.

Normal Course Issuer Bid - The company plans to make normal course purchases of up to 24,962,194 common shares representing 5% of the total outstanding. The bid commenced on Mar. 1, 2023, and expires on Feb. 29, 2024.

Major Shareholder - Widely held at Mar. 20, 2023.

Price Range - NTR/TSX

Year	Volume	High	Low	Close
2022	411,499,724	$147.93	$85.28	$98.85
2021	312,310,595	$99.10	$61.61	$95.08
2020	413,325,907	$64.98	$34.80	$61.24
2019	310,057,444	$73.64	$60.52	$62.17
2018	283,220,814	$76.17	$55.27	$64.12

Recent Close: $82.91

Capital Stock Changes - During 2022, 3,066,148 common shares were issued on exercise of options and 53,312,559 common shares were repurchased under a Normal Course Issuer Bid.

Dividends

NTR com Ra US$2.12 pa Q est. Apr. 13, 2023**
Prev. Rate: US$1.92 est. Apr. 14, 2022
Prev. Rate: US$1.84 est. Apr. 15, 2021
Prev. Rate: US$1.80 est. Oct. 17, 2019
** Reinvestment Option

Long-Term Debt - Outstanding at Dec. 31, 2022:

Senior notes:	
1.9% due 2023	US$500,000,000
5.9% due 2024	500,000,000
3% due 2025	500,000,000
5.95% due 2025	500,000,000
4% due 2026	500,000,000
4.2% due 2029	750,000,000
2.95% due 2030	500,000,000
4.125% due 2035	450,000,000
7.125% due 2036	212,000,000
5.875% due 2036	500,000,000
5.625% due 2040	500,000,000
6.125% due 2041	401,000,000
4.9% due 2043	500,000,000
5.25% due 2045	489,000,000
5% due 2049	750,000,000
3.95% due 2050	500,000,000
7.8% debs. due 2027	120,000,000
Credit facilities	165,000,000
Other debt	7,000,000
Net unamort. fair value adjs	310,000,000
Less: Net unamort. debt costs	72,000,000
	8,582,000,000
Less: Current portion	542,000,000
	8,040,000,000

Note - In March 2023, offering of US$750,000,000 principal amount of 4.9% senior notes due Mar. 27, 2028, and US$750,000,000 principal amount of 5.8% senior notes due Mar. 27, 2053, was completed.

Wholly Owned Subsidiaries

Nutrien (Canada) Holdings ULC, B.C.
- 100% int. in **Agrium Canada Partnership**, Alta.
- 100% int. in **Agrium Potash Ltd.**, Calgary, Alta.
- 100% int. in **Cominco Fertilizer Partnership**, Tex.
- 100% int. in **Loveland Products, Inc.**, Frisco, Tex.
- 100% int. in **Nutrien Ag Solutions Argentina S.A.**, Buenos Aires, Argentina.
- 100% int. in **Nutrien Ag Solutions Limited**, W.A., Australia.
- 100% int. in **Nutrien US LLC**, Loveland, Colo.
  - 100% int. in **Nutrien Ag Solutions (Canada) Inc.**, Canada.
  - 100% int. in **Nutrien Ag Solutions, Inc.**, Greeley, Colo.
- 50% int. in **Profertil S.A.**, Buenos Aires, Argentina.

Potash Corporation of Saskatchewan Inc., Sask.
- 50% int. in **Canpotex Limited**, Saskatoon, Sask.
- 100% int. in **Nutrien Holding Company LLC**, Del.
- 100% int. in **PCS Nitrogen Fertilizer, L.P.**, Del.
- 100% int. in **PCS Nitrogen Ohio LP**, Del.
- 100% int. in **PCS Nitrogen Trinidad Limited**, Trinidad and Tobago.
- 100% int. in **PCS Phosphate Company, Inc.**, Del.
- 100% int. in **PCS Sales (USA) Inc.**, Del.
- 22% int. in **Sinofert Holdings Limited**, People's Republic of China.

Note: The preceding list includes only the major related companies in which interests are held.

Financial Statistics

Periods ended:	12m Dec. 31/22[A]	%Chg	12m Dec. 31/21[□A]
	US$000s	%Chg	US$000s
Operating revenue	**37,012,000**	**+38**	**26,861,000**
Cost of goods sold	20,416,000		16,267,000
General & admin expense	3,139,000		2,853,000
Stock-based compensation	63,000		198,000
Operating expense	**23,618,000**	**+22**	**19,318,000**
Operating income	**13,394,000**	**+78**	**7,543,000**
Deprec., depl. & amort.	2,012,000		1,951,000
Finance income	25,000		8,000
Finance costs, gross	588,000		621,000
Investment income	247,000		89,000
Write-downs/write-offs	768,000[1]		(59,000)
Pre-tax income	**10,246,000**	**+146**	**4,168,000**
Income taxes	2,559,000		989,000
Net income	**7,687,000**	**+142**	**3,179,000**
Net inc. for equity hldrs	**7,660,000**	**+143**	**3,153,000**
Net inc. for non-cont. int.	**27,000**	**+4**	**26,000**
Cash & equivalent	901,000		499,000
Inventories	7,632,000		6,328,000
Accounts receivable	6,050,000		5,143,000
Current assets	16,342,000		13,846,000
Long-term investments	843,000		703,000
Fixed assets, net	21,767,000		20,016,000
Intangibles, net	14,665,000		14,560,000
Total assets	**54,586,000**	**+9**	**49,954,000**
Bank indebtedness	2,142,000		1,560,000
Accts. pay. & accr. liabs	5,797,000		5,179,000
Current liabilities	14,280,000		12,443,000
Long-term debt, gross	8,582,000		8,066,000
Long-term debt, net	8,040,000		7,521,000
Long-term lease liabilities	899,000		934,000
Shareholders' equity	25,818,000		23,652,000
Non-controlling interest	45,000		47,000
Cash from oper. activs	**8,110,000**	**+109**	**3,886,000**
Cash from fin. activs	(4,731,000)		(3,003,000)
Cash from invest. activs	(2,901,000)		(1,807,000)
Net cash position	**901,000**	**+81**	**499,000**
Capital expenditures	(2,227,000)		(1,777,000)
Pension fund surplus	75,000		72,000
	US$		US$
Earnings per share*	14.22		5.53
Cash flow per share*	15.06		6.82
Cash divd. per share*	1.92		1.84
	shs		shs
No. of shs. o/s*	507,246,105		557,492,516
Avg. no. of shs. o/s*	538,475,000		569,664,000
	%		%
Net profit margin	20.77		11.84
Return on equity	30.97		13.70
Return on assets	15.55		7.52
Foreign sales percent	90		89
No. of employees (FTEs)	24,700		23,500

* Common
□ Restated
[A] Reported in accordance with IFRS
[1] Includes impairment reversals of US$450,000,000 and US$330,000,000 in phosphate operations at Aurora, N.C., and White Springs, Fla., respectively.

Latest Results

Periods ended:	6m June 30/23[A]	%Chg	6m June 30/22[A]
	US$000s	%Chg	US$000s
Operating revenue	17,310,000	-20	21,739,000
Net income	1,024,000	-79	4,986,000
Net inc. for equity hldrs	1,011,000	-80	4,971,000
Net inc. for non-cont. int.	13,000		15,000
	US$		US$
Earnings per share*	2.03		9.02

* Common
[A] Reported in accordance with IFRS

Historical Summary
(as originally stated)

Fiscal Year	Oper. Rev. US$000s	Net Inc. Bef. Disc. US$000s	EPS* US$
2022[A]	37,012,000	7,687,000	14.22
2021[A]	26,861,000	3,179,000	5.53
2020[A]	20,053,000	459,000	0.81
2019[A]	19,255,000	992,000	1.70
2018[A]	18,772,000	(31,000)	(0.05)

* Common
[A] Reported in accordance with IFRS

N.79 Nuvei Corporation*

Symbol - NVEI **Exchange** - TSX **CUSIP** - 67079A
Head Office - 900-1100 boul René-Lévesque O, Montréal, QC, H3B 4N4 **Telephone** - (514) 227-6890 **Toll-free** - (866) 687-3722
Website - nuvei.com
Email - lindsay.matthews@nuvei.com
Investor Relations - Lindsay Matthews (514) 313-1190
Auditors - PricewaterhouseCoopers LLP C.A., Montréal, Qué.
Transfer Agents - American Stock Transfer & Trust Company, LLC, New York, N.Y.; TSX Trust Company, Montréal, Qué.
FP500 Revenue Ranking - 325
Employees - 1,690 at Dec. 31, 2022
Profile - (Can. 2017) Provides payment technology solutions to merchants and partners worldwide.

The company's proprietary platform delivers a comprehensive suite of payment solutions designed to support the entire lifecycle of a transaction across mobile or in-app or third party platforms or software, online (via application programming interface or multi-feature cashier), unattended and in-store channels. The platform enables customers to accept payments worldwide regardless of their customers' location, device or preferred payment method. The platform is available in over 200 markets worldwide, with local acquiring in 47 markets, and supports more than 630 alternative payment methods (APMs), including cryptocurrencies, and nearly 150 currencies. Solutions provided include end-to-end processing, including multi-currency authorization, clearing and settlement; global gateway; turnkey payment solutions; smart routing technology; pay-in and payout support for cryptocurrencies; currency management solutions; risk and chargeback management and fraud prevention tools; banking as a service; end-to-end card issuing; transaction risk scoring to identify potentially fraudulent transactions; and artificial intelligence (AI)-based transaction guarantee solutions. Industries served include online retail, online marketplaces, digital goods and services, regulated online gaming, social gaming, financial services, government, utilities, healthcare, non-profit and travel.

In March 2023, the company acquired certain assets of a service provider for US$10,000 cash.

During 2022, the company obtained approvals to support the gaming industry in Kansas, Maryland and Washington. The company also received money transmitter licence in Puerto Rico.

Recent Merger and Acquisition Activity

Status: completed **Revised:** Feb. 22, 2023
UPDATE: The transaction was completed for US$1.4 billion. The cash consideration included the settlement by Nuvei of seller-related payments of US$51,900,000 paid by Paya immediately prior to closing. PREVIOUS: Nuvei Corporation agreed to acquire Paya Holdings Inc., a provider of integrated payment and commerce solutions in the United States, for US$9.75 per share for total consideration of US$1.3 billion. GTCR LLC, which holds 34% of the outstanding shares of Paya, has agreed to tender its shares to the offer. Following the successful completion of the tender offer, Nuvei would acquire all remaining shares not tendered in the tender offer through a second-step merger at the same price. The agreement includes a US$38,000,000 termination fee payable by Paya to Nuvei under specified circumstances, including acceptance of a superior proposal. The transaction was expected to close by the end of the first quarter of 2023.
Status: completed **Revised:** Apr. 7, 2022
UPDATE: The transaction was completed for US$39,751,000 cash. PREVIOUS: Nuvei Corporation received a put option exercise notice which obligates Nuvei to acquire the remaining 40% interest in subsidiary LoanPaymentPro, LLC, a payment acceptance platform provider based in Bloomingdale, Ill., that services the debt repayment industry.

Predecessor Detail - Name changed from Pivotal Development Corporation Inc., Nov. 27, 2018.

Directors - Philip Fayer, chr. & CEO, Hampstead, Qué.; Samir Zabaneh†, Toronto, Ont.; Timothy A. (Tim) Dent, Boston, Mass.; Maren (Hwei Chyun) Lau, São Paulo, Brazil; David Lewin, Saint-Jean-sur-Richelieu, Qué.; Daniela Mielke, Calif.; Pascal Tremblay, Candiac, Qué.

Other Exec. Officers - Yuval Ziv, pres.; David Schwartz, CFO; Max Attias, chief tech. officer; Vicky Bindra, chief product & opers. officer; Scott Calliham, chief strategy officer; Guillaume Conteville, chief mktg. officer; Neil Erlick, chief corp. devel. officer; Netanel Kabala, chief data & analytics officer, digital payments; Edi Kadashev, CIO, digital payments; Laura Miller, chief revenue officer & global head, eCommerce; Ofer Nissim, chief info. security officer, digital payments; Caitlin Shetter, chief people officer; Craig Ludwig, sr. v-p, products; Lindsay Matthews, gen. counsel & corp. sec.
† Lead director

Capital Stock

	Authorized (shs.)	Outstanding (shs.)[1]
Preferred	unlimited	nil
Multiple Vtg.	unlimited	76,064,619
Subordinate Vtg.	unlimited	62,997,248

[1] At Aug. 4, 2023

Preferred - Issuable in series.
Multiple Voting - Participate equally with subordinate voting shares. Convertible into subordinate voting shares on a 1-for-1 basis at the option of the holder and automatically under certain circumstances. Ten votes per share.
Subordinate Voting - One vote per share.
Options - At Dec. 31, 2022, options were outstanding to purchase 8,594,289 common shares at prices ranging from US$2.80 to US$127.33 per share with a weighted average remaining contractual term of 7.4 years.

Normal Course Issuer Bid - The company plans to make normal course purchases of up to 5,556,604 subordinate voting shares representing 10% of the public float. The bid commenced on Mar. 22, 2023, and expires on Mar. 21, 2024.
Major Shareholder - Novacap Investments Inc. held 37.12% interest, Philip Fayer held 33.84% interest and Caisse de dépôt et placement du Québec held 21.44% interest at Apr. 3, 2023.

Price Range - NVEI/TSX

Year	Volume	High	Low	Close
2022	88,968,348	$98.80	$32.20	$34.41
2021	85,002,520	$180.00	$54.47	$82.00
2020	9,185,476	$82.04	$42.00	$77.79

Recent Close: $22.17
Capital Stock Changes - During 2022, subordinate voting shares were issued as follows: 100,257 on exercise of options and 92,662 on vesting of restricted share units; 3,660,743 subordinate voting shares were repurchased under a Normal Course Issuer Bid.

Dividends

NVEI com S.V. Ra $0.40 pa Q est. Sept. 5, 2023
Long-Term Debt - At Dec. 31, 2022, outstanding long-term debt totaled US$510,754,000 (US$8,652,000 current) and consisted of US$498,199,000 in borrowings under term loan facilities due Sept. 28, 2025, bearing interest at the alternate base rate (ABR) plus 1.5% or the adjusted eurocurrency rate plus 2.5% for loans drawn in U.S. dollars and at the Canadian prime rate plus 1.5% or banker's acceptance rate plus 2.5% for loans drawn in Canadian dollars; and US$12,555,000 of lease liabilities.
Note - In February 2023, the company entered into an US$800,000,000 revolving credit facility due Sept. 28, 2025. The new credit facility bears interest at Term SOFR (including 0.1% credit spread adjustment) plus 3% or ABR plus 2% until the delivery of the company's financial statements for the quarter ending Sept. 30, 2023, and will bear interest at Term SOFR (including 0.1% credit spread adjustment) plus 2.5% to 3.25% or ABR plus 1.5% to 2.25% thereafter.

Wholly Owned Subsidiaries

Nuvei Technologies Corp., Montréal, Qué.
- 100% int. in **Nuvei Commerce, LLC**, United States.
- 100% int. in **Nuvei International Group Limited**, St. Peter Port, Guernsey.
  - 100% int. in **Nuvei Consulting Services (Israel) Ltd.**, Israel.
  - 100% int. in **Nuvei Limited**, Cyprus.
    - 100% int. in **Nuvei Technology & Services B.V.**, Netherlands.
      - 100% int. in **Nuvei Global Services B.V.**, Netherlands.
- 100% int. in **Nuvei Technologies Inc.**, United States.
  - 100% int. in **LoanPaymentPro, LLC**, Bloomingdale, Ill.
- 100% int. in **Nuvei US, LLC**, United States.
- 100% int. in **SimplexCC Ltd.**, Israel.

Paya Holdings Inc., Atlanta, Ga.
Note: The preceding list includes only the major related companies in which interests are held.

Financial Statistics

Periods ended:	12m Dec. 31/22[A]		12m Dec. 31/21[A]
	US$000s	%Chg	US$000s
Operating revenue	**843,323**	**+16**	**724,526**
Cost of goods sold	4,430		4,494
Cost of sales	166,995		143,261
Salaries & benefits	155,359		109,798
General & admin expense	195,012		177,497
Stock-based compensation	139,103		53,180
Operating expense	**660,899**	**+35**	**488,230**
Operating income	**182,424**	**-23**	**236,296**
Deprec., depl. & amort.	101,492		90,828
Finance income	13,694		2,859
Finance costs, gross	22,841		16,879
Pre-tax income	**87,537**	**-34**	**131,961**
Income taxes	25,582		24,916
Net income	**61,955**	**-42**	**107,045**
Net inc. for equity hldrs	**56,732**	**-45**	**102,293**
Net inc. for non-cont. int	**5,223**	**+10**	**4,752**
Cash & equivalent	751,686		748,576
Inventories	2,117		1,277
Accounts receivable	61,228		39,262
Current assets	1,655,871		1,526,632
Fixed assets, net	31,881		18,856
Intangibles, net	1,809,588		1,874,368
Total assets	**3,524,669**	**+2**	**3,455,470**
Accts. pay. & accr. liabs	125,533		101,848
Current liabilities	978,939		856,775
Long-term debt, gross	510,754		508,595
Long-term debt, net	502,102		501,246
Shareholders' equity	1,968,731		2,009,738
Non-controlling interest	10,759		12,102
Cash from oper. activs	**267,663**	**0**	**266,857**
Cash from fin. activs	(214,298)		706,075
Cash from invest. activs	(50,235)		(395,108)
Net cash position	**751,686**	**0**	**748,576**
Capital expenditures	(13,744)		(5,728)
	US$		US$
Earnings per share*	0.40		0.73
Cash flow per share*	1.89		1.91
	shs		shs
No. of shs. o/s*	139,526,227		142,994,051
Avg. no. of shs. o/s*	141,555,788		139,729,116
	%		%
Net profit margin	7.35		14.77
Return on equity	2.85		5.91
Return on assets	2.24		4.24
No. of employees (FTEs)	1,690		1,368

* M.V. & S.V.
[A] Reported in accordance with IFRS

Latest Results

Periods ended:	6m June 30/23[A]		6m June 30/22[A]
	US$000s	%Chg	US$000s
Operating revenue	563,524	+32	425,838
Net income	3,328	-92	39,597
Net inc. for equity hldrs	145	-100	36,982
Net inc. for non-cont. int	3,183		2,615
	US$		US$
Earnings per share*	0.00		0.26

* M.V. & S.V.
[A] Reported in accordance with IFRS

Historical Summary
(as originally stated)

Fiscal Year	Oper. Rev.	Net Inc. Bef. Disc.	EPS*
	US$000s	US$000s	US$
2022[A]	843,323	61,955	0.40
2021[A]	724,526	107,045	0.73
2020[A]	375,046	(103,670)	(1.08)
2019[A]	245,816	(69,465)	(0.41)
2018[A]	149,726	(30,962)	(0.18)

* M.V. & S.V.
[A] Reported in accordance with IFRS

O

O.1 ONEnergy Inc.

Symbol - OEG.H **Exchange** - TSX-VEN (S) **CUSIP** - 68268C
Head Office - PO Box 47584 RPO Don Mills, Toronto, ON, M3C 1S7 **Telephone** - (416) 444-4848 **Toll-free** - (855) 753-2525 **Fax** - (647) 253-2525
Website - www.onenergyinc.com
Email - rdeocampo@onenergyinc.com
Investor Relations - Ray de Ocampo (647) 253-2534
Auditors - BDO Canada LLP C.A., Markham, Ont.
Bankers - The Toronto-Dominion Bank, Toronto, Ont.
Lawyers - Fasken Martineau DuMoulin LLP, Toronto, Ont.
Transfer Agents - Computershare Trust Company of Canada Inc.
Profile - (Ont. 2015; orig. Can., 1999 amalg.) Seeking new business opportunities.

The company previously retailed natural gas and electricity to residential and commercial customers in Ontario and provided energy efficiency products and services in the U.S., until the divestiture of the business in 2019.

On May 30, 2023, the company filed a proposal under the Bankruptcy and Insolvency Act (Canada). **B Riley Farber Inc.** was appointed proposal trustee. The proposal would settle the company's unsecured liabilities in exchange for common share valued at no more the 100% of the company's current market capitalization.

Common suspended from TSX-VEN, June 5, 2023.

Predecessor Detail - Name changed from Look Communications Inc., July 12, 2013.

Directors - Stephen J. J. (Steve) Letwin, chr. & interim CEO, Calgary, Alta.; Dr. Ivan Bos, Grimsby, Ont.; Lawrence H. Silber, Ottawa, Ont.

Other Exec. Officers - Ray de Ocampo, CFO

Capital Stock

	Authorized (shs.)	Outstanding (shs.)[1]
Preference	unlimited	nil
Common	unlimited	23,975,000

[1] At June 30, 2022

Major Shareholder - Arthur Silber held 11.6% interest and Canyon Creek Management Inc. held 11.3% interest at June 25, 2021.

Price Range - OEG.H/TSX-VEN (S)

Year	Volume	High	Low	Close
2022	949,732	$0.24	$0.01	$0.09
2021	450,671	$0.12	$0.01	$0.10
2019	78,378	$0.08	$0.04	$0.06
2018	1,798,969	$0.36	$0.11	$0.20

Recent Close: $0.09

Wholly Owned Subsidiaries

10927040 Canada Inc., Canada.
ONEnergy USA Holdings Inc., United States.
Sunwave Gas & Power Inc., Toronto, Ont.
2594834 Ontario Inc., Ont.
0867893 B.C. Ltd., Vancouver, B.C. dbl PVL Projects

Financial Statistics

Periods ended:	12m Dec. 31/21[A]		12m Dec. 31/20[A]
	$000s	%Chg	$000s
Operating revenue	**nil**	**n.a.**	**1**
Cost of sales	nil		2
Salaries & benefits	374		298
General & admin expense	663		542
Operating expense	**1,037**	**+23**	**842**
Operating income	**(1,037)**	**n.a.**	**(841)**
Finance income	nil		3
Finance costs, gross	462		441
Pre-tax income	**(1,461)**	**n.a.**	**(1,224)**
Net income	**(1,461)**	**n.a.**	**(1,224)**
Cash & equivalent	33		114
Accounts receivable	6		7
Current assets	67		175
Total assets	**67**	**-62**	**175**
Bank indebtedness	6,237		5,274
Accts. pay. & accr. liabs	2,411		1,996
Current liabilities	8,856		7,507
Long-term debt, gross	47		43
Long-term debt, net	47		43
Shareholders' equity	(8,836)		(7,375)
Cash from oper. activs	**(582)**	**n.a.**	**(573)**
Cash from fin. activs	480		218
Cash from invest. activs	21		118
Net cash position	**33**	**-71**	**114**
	$		$
Earnings per share*	(0.06)		(0.05)
Cash flow per share*	(0.02)		(0.02)
	shs		shs
No. of shs. o/s*	23,975,000		23,975,000
Avg. no. of shs. o/s*	23,975,000		23,975,000
	%		%
Net profit margin	n.a.		n.m.
Return on equity	n.m.		n.m.
Return on assets	(825.62)		(217.50)

* Common
[A] Reported in accordance with IFRS

Latest Results

Periods ended:	6m June 30/22[A]		6m June 30/21[A]
	$000s	%Chg	$000s
Net income	458	n.a.	(683)
	$		$
Earnings per share*	0.02		(0.03)

* Common
[A] Reported in accordance with IFRS

Historical Summary
(as originally stated)

Fiscal Year	Oper. Rev. $000s	Net Inc. Bef. Disc. $000s	EPS* $
2021[A]	nil	(1,461)	(0.06)
2020[A]	1	(1,224)	(0.05)
2019[A]	74	(703)	(0.03)
2018[A]	195	(1,329)	(0.06)
2017[A]	2,004	(3,762)	(0.16)

* Common
[A] Reported in accordance with IFRS

O.2 OOOOO Entertainment Commerce Limited

Symbol - OOOO **Exchange** - TSX-VEN **CUSIP** - 670885
Head Office - c/o 1000-925 Georgia St W, Vancouver, BC, V6C 3L2 **Telephone** - (604) 692-3056 **Toll-free** - (855) 255-1785
Website - invest.ooooo.com
Email - sam@ooooo.com
Investor Relations - Samuel Jones (855) 255-1785
Auditors - MNP LLP C.A., Vancouver, B.C.
Transfer Agents - Odyssey Trust Company, Vancouver, B.C.
Profile - (B.C. 2012) Licenses a video marketplace software platform to commerce companies and retailers that can be delivered to end customers via a native app or through mobile web. Also operates Fanz.com, which offers live video commerce, non-fungible tokens (NFTs) and mobile gaming.

The platform enables retailers, brands and entrepreneurs to share product-based opinions to consumers through live, interactive, shoppable videos. The platform also offers gamification and social features which reward the community for helping to grow the user base, reducing the need for traditional ad networks. The company's video commerce technology is also available as a web-based commerce solution that allows partners to crowd source video content by approved creators and capture sales on their own commerce platform. The lighter, web-based software requires no technology build for clients and allows them to own customer information and the payment process.

Through subsidiary **Fanz Technologies Limited**, also offers football teams and athletes an interactive video commerce solution to sell memorabilia and merchandise to fans through shoppable videos at Fanz.com. The website also includes games, as well as allows athletes and teams to create and launch NFTs and smart contracts that can be sold on the website.

Predecessor Detail - Name changed from Evermount Ventures Inc., July 19, 2021, pursuant to the Qualifying Transaction reverse takeover acquisition of Video Commerce Group Ltd.; basis 1 new for 2 old shs.

Directors - Samuel (Sam) Jones, founder, chr. & CEO, Oxford, Oxon., United Kingdom; Denise Evans, Washington, D.C.; Phillip Lord; Eric Zhang, Shanghai, Shanghai, People's Republic of China

Other Exec. Officers - Xiao Qin (Mary) Ma, CFO

Capital Stock

	Authorized (shs.)	Outstanding (shs.)[1]
Preferred	unlimited	nil
Multiple Vtg.	unlimited	17,332,771
Subordinate Vtg.	unlimited	64,755,383

[1] At June 27, 2023

Multiple Voting - All held by Samuel Jones. Convertible into subordinate voting shares on a one-for-one basis and automatically under certain circumstances. Five votes per share.

Subordinate Voting - One vote per share.

Major Shareholder - Samuel (Sam) Jones held 58.49% interest at June 17, 2022.

Price Range - OOOO/TSX-VEN

Year	Volume	High	Low	Close
2022	6,047,877	$0.60	$0.03	$0.04
2021	8,916,707	$1.40	$0.40	$0.40
2020	107,500	$0.19	$0.07	$0.19
2019	500	$0.20	$0.20	$0.20
2018	1,000	$0.24	$0.23	$0.24

Consolidation: 1-for-2 cons. in July 2021
Recent Close: $0.02

Wholly Owned Subsidiaries

Video Commerce Group Ltd., Oxford, Oxon., United Kingdom.
- 100% int. in **OOOOO Ltd.**, United Kingdom.
- 100% int. in **Shanghai Oufon Network Technology Co., Ltd.**, People's Republic of China.

Subsidiaries

57.72% int. in **Fanz Technologies Limited**, United Kingdom.

Financial Statistics

Periods ended:	12m Oct. 31/21[A1]		32w Oct. 31/20[oA]
	$000s	%Chg	$000s
Operating revenue	**91**	**n.a.**	**nil**
Cost of sales	69		nil
Salaries & benefits	2,851		182
General & admin expense	5,874		716
Stock-based compensation	360		nil
Operating expense	**9,154**	**n.a.**	**897**
Operating income	**(9,063)**	**n.a.**	**(897)**
Finance costs, gross	18		nil
Pre-tax income	**(17,089)**	**n.a.**	**(898)**
Income taxes	4		2
Net income	**(17,093)**	**n.a.**	**(899)**
Cash & equivalent	7,396		140
Accounts receivable	246		92
Current assets	8,310		233
Fixed assets, net	37		8
Right-of-use assets	2,051		nil
Intangibles, net	706		1,258
Total assets	**11,529**	**+670**	**1,498**
Bank indebtedness	nil		225
Accts. pay. & accr. liabs	1,245		673
Current liabilities	1,385		1,200
Long-term debt, gross	nil		302
Long-term lease liabilities	1,922		nil
Shareholders' equity	8,222		296
Cash from oper. activs	**(8,968)**	**n.a.**	**(317)**
Cash from fin. activs	20,359		1,726
Cash from invest. activs	(3,992)		(1,266)
Net cash position	**7,396**	**n.m.**	**140**
Capital expenditures	(35)		(9)
	$		$
Earnings per share*	(0.76)		n.a.
Cash flow per share*	(0.40)		n.a.
	shs		shs
No. of shs. o/s*	78,760,981		n.a.
Avg. no. of shs. o/s*	22,503,137		n.a.
	%		%
Net profit margin	n.m.		...
Return on equity	(401.31)		...
Return on assets	(265.11)		...

* Common
[o] Restated
[A] Reported in accordance with IFRS
[1] Results reflect the July 19, 2021, reverse takeover acquisition of Video Commerce Group Ltd.

Latest Results

Periods ended:	9m July 31/22[A]		9m July 31/21[oA]
	$000s	%Chg	$000s
Operating revenue	358	n.m.	8
Net income	(11,557)	n.a.	(9,599)
Net inc. for equity hldrs	(10,714)	n.a.	(9,599)
Net inc. for non-cont. int	(843)		nil
	$		$
Earnings per share*	(0.15)		n.a.

* Common
[o] Restated
[A] Reported in accordance with IFRS
Note: Adjusted throughout for 1-for-2 cons. in July 2021

0.3 ORAGIN Foods Inc.

Symbol - OG.H **Exchange** - TSX-VEN (S) **CUSIP** - 684022
Head Office - 579 Kerr St, Oakville, ON, L6K 3E1 **Telephone** - (289) 644-5377
Website - oragin.webflow.io
Email - ir@oragin.com
Investor Relations - Bill Mitoulas (416) 479-9547
Auditors - Smythe LLP C.A., Vancouver, B.C.
Lawyers - ECS Law Professional Corporation, Toronto, Ont.
Transfer Agents - TSX Trust Company, Vancouver, B.C.
Profile - (B.C. 2011) Operates four grocery stores featuring natural and organic products in Toronto (2), Oakville and Thornhill, Ont., under the Organic Garage banner; and manufactures plant-based cheeses and plant-based cheese products.

Operations are segmented into two divisions: Retail and Consumer Packaged Goods (CPG).

Retail Division - Operates stores under Organic Garage banner featuring produce, dairy, bakery, bulk, grocery, meat, frozen foods, prepared foods, vitamins and supplements, and health and beauty departments. Products are also available online through Inabuggy platform, Cornershop app and Instacart platform.

CPG Division - Develops, acquires, grows and commercializes new and innovate food and beverage brands. Has one portfolio, its wholly owned **The Future of Cheese Inc.**, which develops, manufactures and markets plant-based cheeses and plant-based cheese products.

Common suspended from TSX-VEN, Nov. 25, 2022.

Predecessor Detail - Name changed from Organic Garage Ltd., Feb. 24, 2022.
Directors - Matt Lurie, chr., pres. & CEO, Toronto, Ont.

Capital Stock

	Authorized (shs.)	Outstanding (shs.)[1]
Common	unlimited	62,467,336

[1] At Sept. 28, 2022

Major Shareholder - Matt Lurie held 13.2% interest at June 10, 2022.

Price Range - OG.H/TSX-VEN (S)

Year	Volume	High	Low	Close
2022	18,374,918	$0.45	$0.03	$0.05
2021	69,790,229	$1.00	$0.28	$0.42
2020	28,258,725	$0.49	$0.05	$0.49
2019	11,054,703	$0.31	$0.06	$0.10
2018	28,186,892	$0.58	$0.19	$0.28

Recent Close: $0.05

Wholly Owned Subsidiaries

The Future of Cheese Inc., Toronto, Ont.
1047023 B.C. Ltd., B.C.
Organic Garage (Canada) Limited, Ont.
- 100% int. in **2347018 Ontario Inc.**, Ont.
- 100% int. in **2368123 Ontario Inc.**, Ont.
- 100% int. in **2412383 Ontario Inc.**, Ont.
- 100% int. in **2507158 Ontario Inc.**, Ont.
- 100% int. in **2557479 Ontario Inc.**, Ont.
- 100% int. in **2581751 Ontario Inc.**, Ont.

2664699 Ontario Ltd., Ont.

Financial Statistics

Periods ended:	12m Jan. 31/22[A]		12m Jan. 31/21[A]
	$000s	%Chg	$000s
Operating revenue	**25,712**	**-15**	**30,276**
Cost of sales	17,785		21,348
Salaries & benefits	2,910		3,317
General & admin expense	3,684		2,811
Stock-based compensation	1,091		8
Operating expense	**25,470**	**-7**	**27,485**
Operating income	**242**	**-91**	**2,791**
Deprec., depl. & amort	1,558		1,642
Finance income	4		3
Finance costs, gross	1,323		1,416
Pre-tax income	**(2,987)**	**n.a.**	**(263)**
Net income	**(2,987)**	**n.a.**	**(263)**
Cash & equivalent	2,200		1,629
Inventories	1,352		1,405
Accounts receivable	171		166
Current assets	4,061		3,221
Fixed assets, net	12,918		13,821
Intangibles, net	8,957		nil
Total assets	**26,232**	**+53**	**17,187**
Accts. pay. & accr. liabs	2,381		1,789
Current liabilities	5,835		2,260
Long-term debt, gross	2,920		2,820
Long-term debt, net	nil		2,820
Long-term lease liabilities	7,661		8,195
Shareholders' equity	12,736		3,912
Cash from oper. activs	**924**	**-24**	**1,212**
Cash from fin. activs	255		652
Cash from invest. activs	(608)		(430)
Net cash position	**2,200**	**+35**	**1,629**
Capital expenditures	(1,070)		(430)
Capital disposals	103		nil
	$		$
Earnings per share*	(0.05)		(0.01)
Cash flow per share*	0.02		0.03
	shs		shs
No. of shs. o/s*	61,216,722		44,007,982
Avg. no. of shs. o/s*	59,204,626		39,004,270
	%		%
Net profit margin	(11.62)		(0.87)
Return on equity	(35.88)		(7.78)
Return on assets	(7.66)		6.66

* Common
[A] Reported in accordance with IFRS

Latest Results

Periods ended:	6m July 31/22[A]		6m July 31/21[A]
	$000s	%Chg	$000s
Operating revenue	11,358	-18	13,823
Net income	(1,440)	n.a.	(1,260)
	$		$
Earnings per share*	(0.02)		(0.02)

* Common
[A] Reported in accordance with IFRS

Historical Summary
(as originally stated)

Fiscal Year	Oper. Rev.	Net Inc. Bef. Disc.	EPS*
	$000s	$000s	$
2022[A]	25,712	(2,987)	(0.05)
2021[A]	30,276	(263)	(0.01)
2020[A]	24,155	(5,084)	(0.14)
2019[A]	23,609	(2,018)	(0.06)
2018[A]	19,857	(1,251)	(0.04)

* Common
[A] Reported in accordance with IFRS

0.4 Ocean Shore Capital Corp.

Symbol - OCAP.P **Exchange** - TSX-VEN **CUSIP** - 67501T
Head Office - 250-750 Pender St W, Vancouver, BC, V6C 2T7 **Telephone** - (604) 685-7450
Email - ron@asi-accounting.com
Investor Relations - Ronald A. Schmitz (604) 685-7450
Auditors - Davidson & Company LLP C.A., Vancouver, B.C.
Transfer Agents - Odyssey Trust Company, Vancouver, B.C.
Profile - (B.C. 2020) Capital Pool Company.

On Mar. 10, 2023, the company entered into a letter of intent for the Qualifying Transaction reverse takeover acquisition of **Delicawash Care Corp.**, for issuance of up to 24,500,000 common shares and up to 3,362,000 warrants. Concurrently, the company would complete a private placement of common shares (or securities convertible into common shares) for minimum gross proceeds of $2,000,000 at a price of $0.12 per share. Delicawash Care has developed DelicaWash, a product that is an alternative to the mesh laundry bag for protecting delicate items in washing machines and driers.

Directors - Michael P. (Mike) Walsh, pres. & CEO, Vancouver, B.C.; Ronald A. (Ron) Schmitz, CFO & corp. sec., Vancouver, B.C.; Douglas F. (Doug) Besse, North Vancouver, B.C.; Geoff Reed, North Vancouver, B.C.

Capital Stock

	Authorized (shs.)	Outstanding (shs.)[1]
Common	unlimited	7,535,000

[1] At Oct. 26, 2022

Major Shareholder - Widely held at Oct. 17, 2022.

Price Range - OCAP.P/TSX-VEN

Year	Volume	High	Low	Close
2022	30,679	$0.32	$0.12	$0.30

Recent Close: $0.10

Capital Stock Changes - On Apr. 6, 2022, an initial public offering of 3,000,000 common shares was completed at 10¢ per share. Also during fiscal 2022, 2,335,000 common shares were issued by private placement.

0.5 Oceanic Wind Energy Inc.

Symbol - NKW.H **Exchange** - TSX-VEN **CUSIP** - 675252
Head Office - 1000-355 Burrard St, Vancouver, BC, V6C 2G8 **Telephone** - (604) 631-4483 **Fax** - (604) 685-4215
Website - www.oceanicwind.ca
Email - wlang@oceanicwind.ca
Investor Relations - Wilbur Lang (604) 631-4480
Auditors - Davidson & Company LLP C.A., Vancouver, B.C.
Lawyers - Borden Ladner Gervais LLP, Vancouver, B.C.
Transfer Agents - Computershare Trust Company of Canada Inc., Vancouver, B.C.
Profile - (B.C. 1957) Holds option to acquire up to 10% interest in **Northland Power Inc.**'s 400-MW NaiKun offshore wind farm, which is under development, located in the Hecate Strait off the northeastern coast of Haida Gwaii, B.C.
Predecessor Detail - Name changed from NaiKun Wind Energy Group Inc., May 28, 2020.
Directors - Philip G. Hughes, chr., Calgary, Alta.; Michael J. O'Connor, pres. & CEO, B.C.; Joseph S. (Joe) Houssian, B.C.; Peter Pastewka, Denver, Colo.; David L. (Dave) Rehn, Calgary, Alta.; Arthur H. Willms, Vancouver, B.C.
Other Exec. Officers - Wilbur Lang, v-p, fin., CFO & corp. sec.

Capital Stock

	Authorized (shs.)	Outstanding (shs.)[1]
First Preferred	20,000,000	nil
Common	unlimited	84,027,896

[1] At May 11, 2023

Major Shareholder - Joseph S. (Joe) Houssian held 20.1% interest at Feb. 21, 2023.

Price Range - NKW.H/TSX-VEN

Year	Volume	High	Low	Close
2022	4,034,584	$0.12	$0.03	$0.06
2021	7,742,124	$0.25	$0.09	$0.12
2020	9,708,451	$0.27	$0.03	$0.14
2019	11,500,004	$0.27	$0.04	$0.15
2018	3,695,222	$0.14	$0.07	$0.08

Recent Close: $0.05

Capital Stock Changes - In November 2022, private placement of 5,000,840 units (1 common share & 1 warrant) at 5¢ per unit was completed, with warrants exercisable at 7¢ per share for one year.

During fiscal 2022, 176,094 common shares were issued as share-based compensation.

Financial Statistics

Periods ended:	12m Sept. 30/22[A]		12m Sept. 30/21[A]
	$000s	%Chg	$000s
Salaries & benefits	148		150
General & admin expense	113		154
Stock-based compensation	171		197
Operating expense	**432**	**-14**	**501**
Operating income	**(432)**	**n.a.**	**(501)**
Finance costs, gross	nil		4
Pre-tax income	**(402)**	**n.a.**	**(295)**
Net income	**(402)**	**n.a.**	**(295)**
Cash & equivalent	50		238
Accounts receivable	1		1
Current assets	68		257
Total assets	**68**	**-75**	**273**
Accts. pay. & accr. liabs	75		61
Current liabilities	1,075		1,061
Long-term debt, gross	39		36
Long-term debt, net	39		36
Shareholders' equity	(1,068)		(848)
Cash from oper. activs	**(188)**	**n.a.**	**(134)**
Cash from fin. activs	nil		320
Net cash position	**50**	**-79**	**238**
	$		$
Earnings per share*	(0.01)		(0.00)
Cash flow per share*	(0.00)		(0.00)
	shs		shs
No. of shs. o/s*	79,027,056		78,850,962
Avg. no. of shs. o/s*	78,997,164		76,914,976
	%		%
Net profit margin	n.a.		n.a.
Return on equity	n.m.		n.m.
Return on assets	(235.78)		(157.72)

* Common
[A] Reported in accordance with IFRS

Latest Results

Periods ended:	6m Mar. 31/23[A]		6m Mar. 31/22[A]
	$000s	%Chg	$000s
Net income	(186)	n.a.	(201)
	$		$
Earnings per share*	(0.00)		(0.00)

* Common
[A] Reported in accordance with IFRS

Historical Summary
(as originally stated)

Fiscal Year	Oper. Rev.	Net Inc. Bef. Disc.	EPS*
	$000s	$000s	$
2022[A]	nil	(402)	(0.01)
2021[A]	nil	(295)	(0.00)
2020[A]	nil	(560)	(0.01)
2019[A]	nil	(1,255)	(0.02)
2018[A]	nil	(847)	(0.01)

* Common
[A] Reported in accordance with IFRS

0.6 Oceansix Future Paths Ltd.

Symbol - OSIX **Exchange** - TSX-VEN **CUSIP** - M7S19L
Head Office - Derech Menachem Begin 11, Ramat Gan, Israel, 5268104 **Overseas Tel** - 972-4-629-6250 **Overseas Fax** - 972-4-981-1019
Website - www.oceansix.com
Email - hello@oceansix.com
Investor Relations - Elad Hameiri 972-5-456-07935
Auditors - Kost Forer Gabbay & Kasierer C.A., Tel Aviv, Israel
Transfer Agents - TSX Trust Company, Toronto, Ont.
Profile - (Israel 2008) Manufactures and distributes recycled and non-recycled plastic industrial products in Europe.

Has developed a waste-to-product process for recycling post-consumed plastic bags and sheets into various plastic products including polyurethane sheets and geomembranes that are primarily utilized by the building and infrastructure industry. The sheets are used for underground water and gas sealing systems, surfaces and floor protection, and sub terrain barriers against roots.

Operates a thermoforming manufacturing site in Valencia, Spain, which transforms plastic boards and sheets into three dimensional plastic industrial products. Also operates a research and development centre in Valencia. The company ceased production of recycled plastic boards and sheets in Israel in November 2022 and was exploring options in Europe including an another production facility, utilizing subcontractors, making use of third party facilities and/or finding other suppliers for recycled plastic boards and sheet.

Wholly owned **Oceansix GmbH** is researching and developing technologically advanced plastic-based products mainly from post-consumed plastic waste. Oceansix plans to process these recycled plastics into products related to packaging, container shipping, agriculture, marine farming and energy storage.

In November 2022, the company ceased production and permanently closed its Israeli production site and transferred certain components of its Israeli production facility to Germany in January 2023. As a result, it suspended the manufacturing and sale of recycled boards and sheets.

On June 17, 2022, the company acquired Berlin, Germany-based **Oceansix GmbH** from **RAM.ON finance GmbH** for issuance of 20,295,037 ordinary shares at 0.01 Israeli New Shekel plus issuance of up to 148,166,312 ordinary shares upon achievement of certain milestones. Oceansix develops technologies and product solutions, and plans to process post-consumed recycled plastics into products related to packaging, container shipping, agriculture, marine farming and energy storage. RAM.ON is beneficially owned by Gat Ramon.

On June 13, 2022, the company acquired Valencia, Spain-based **Plasticos Flome S.L.** (Flome) for €1,632,000 cash and issuance of 1,514,973 ordinary shares valued at €180,000. Flome manufactures trays and packaging products using plastic sheets and boards as raw materials. Flome's products are used by the automotive, agriculture and beverage industries.

Predecessor Detail - Name changed from K.B. Recycling Industries Ltd., Mar. 29, 2023.
Directors - Gat Ramon, chr., Tel Aviv, Israel; Maximo Buch, Valencia, Spain; Arnon Eshed; Mordechai (Mota) Gorfung, Herzliya, Israel; Noah Hershcoviz, Tel Aviv, Israel; Yoav Horowitz, Israel; Leon Koffler, Israel; Renah A. Persofsky, Toronto, Ont.; Lenny Recanati, Tel Aviv, Israel
Other Exec. Officers - Elad Hameiri, CEO; Salvador Cabañas, CFO

Capital Stock

	Authorized (shs.)	Outstanding (shs.)[1]
Ordinary	500,000,000	153,693,074

[1] At June 9, 2023

Major Shareholder - RAM.ON GmbH held 20.52% interest, Lenny Recanati held 19.5% interest, Tedea Technological Development and Automation Ltd. held 19.44% interest and Clover Wolf held 13.12% interest at June 9, 2023.

Price Range - OSIX/TSX-VEN

Year	Volume	High	Low	Close
2022	16,095,069	$0.40	$0.07	$0.09
2021	35,369,940	$0.79	$0.32	$0.33

Recent Close: $0.06
Capital Stock Changes - On June 8, 2022, an increase of the authorized number of ordinary shares from 300,000,000 to 500,000,000 was approved. Also during 2022, 31,810,010 ordinary shares were issued for business acquisitions.

Wholly Owned Subsidiaries

Oceansix GmbH, Berlin, Germany.
Plasticos Flome S.L., Valencia, Spain.

Financial Statistics

Periods ended:	12m Dec. 31/22[A]		12m Dec. 31/21[oA]
	US$000s	%Chg	US$000s
Operating revenue	**685**	**n.a.**	**nil**
Cost of sales	359		nil
Salaries & benefits	540		168
Research & devel. expense	70		nil
General & admin expense	2,234		1,706
Operating expense	**3,203**	**+71**	**1,874**
Operating income	**(2,518)**	**n.a.**	**(1,874)**
Deprec., depl. & amort.	195		38
Finance income	2,188		nil
Finance costs, gross	129		1,793
Write-downs/write-offs	(512)		nil
Pre-tax income	**(771)**	**n.a.**	**(3,711)**
Income taxes	(296)		nil
Net inc. bef. disc. opers	**(475)**	**n.a.**	**(3,711)**
Income from disc. opers	(3,997)		(2,977)
Net income	**(4,472)**	**n.a.**	**(6,688)**
Cash & equivalent	488		5,909
Inventories	144		81
Accounts receivable	687		514
Current assets	1,754		6,819
Fixed assets, net	1,024		1,694
Right-of-use assets	900		1,001
Intangibles, net	4,325		nil
Total assets	**8,241**	**-14**	**9,599**
Bank indebtedness	177		nil
Accts. pay. & accr. liabs	641		406
Current liabilities	2,139		1,465
Long-term lease liabilities	802		1,023
Shareholders' equity	4,190		4,656
Cash from oper. activs	**(3,034)**	**n.a.**	**(4,159)**
Cash from fin. activs	(405)		8,299
Cash from invest. activs	(1,557)		(126)
Net cash position	**488**	**-92**	**5,909**
Capital expenditures	(44)		(122)
Capital disposals	nil		7
	US$		US$
Earns. per sh. bef disc opers*	(0.00)		(0.04)
Earnings per share*	(0.03)		(0.07)
Cash flow per share*	(0.02)		(0.04)
	shs		shs
No. of shs. o/s*	153,693,074		121,883,064
Avg. no. of shs. o/s*	139,068,000		102,360,000
	%		%
Net profit margin	(69.34)		n.a.
Return on equity	(10.74)		n.m.
Return on assets	(4.43)		(25.31)

* Ordinary
[o] Restated
[A] Reported in accordance with IFRS

Historical Summary
(as originally stated)

Fiscal Year	Oper. Rev.	Net Inc. Bef. Disc.	EPS*
	US$000s	US$000s	US$
2022[A]	685	(475)	(0.00)
2021[A]	1,158	(6,688)	(0.07)
2020[A]	955	(4,460)	(7.00)
2019[A]	1,510	(2,410)	(4.00)
2018[A]	1,578	(3,011)	(5.21)

* Ordinary
[A] Reported in accordance with IFRS

0.7 Oculus VisionTech Inc.

Symbol - OVT **Exchange** - TSX-VEN **CUSIP** - 67575Y
Head Office - 507-837 Hastings St W, Vancouver, BC, V6C 3N6 **Telephone** - (604) 685-1017 **Toll-free** - (800) 321-8564 **Fax** - (604) 685-5777
Website - www.ovtz.com
Email - ajd@ovtz.com
Investor Relations - Anton J. Drescher (604) 685-1017
Auditors - Davidson & Company LLP C.A., Vancouver, B.C.
Transfer Agents - Computershare Trust Company of Canada Inc., Calgary, Alta.
Profile - (Wyo. 1995; orig. Alta., 1986) Designs, develops and markets a suite of Software-as-a-Service cyber security, data privacy and data protection products for enterprise business customers.

The company's systems, services and delivery solutions include digital watermark solutions and video content production, content encoding, media asset management, media and application hosting, multi-mode content distribution, transaction data capture and reporting, e-commerce, specialized engineering services and Internet streaming hardware.

Products include: Cloud-DPS, which secures and protects digital documents (including text documents, photos, blueprints, etc.) from any modification, and/or attempted forgery by imperceptibly watermarking documents, using real-time image processing and watermarking algorithms, embedded into a secured/protected copy of a document; ForgetMeYes®, a data privacy tool which is a software-as-a-service platform that provides a single-source capability of continuous compliance by incorporating secure, automated policy-driven services guaranteeing sustained Right-to-be-Forgotten and Right-of-Erase compliance for subscribers; ComplyTrust®, a set of software tools specifically designed to address cloud-native data management and regulatory compliant data governance; ComplyScan®, which would address public cloud data governance compliance is under development.

Predecessor Detail - Name changed from USA Video Interactive Corp., Jan. 25, 2012; basis 1 new for 15 old shs.

Directors - Rowland Perkins, pres. & CEO, Alta.; Anton J. (Tony) Drescher, CFO & corp. sec., Vancouver, B.C.; Tom Perovic, chief tech. officer, Ont.; Fabrice Helliker, United Kingdom; Maurice Loverso, Qué.; Ron Wages, N.C.

Capital Stock

	Authorized (shs.)	Outstanding (shs.)[1]
Preferred	250,000,000	nil
Common	500,000,000	91,422,469

[1] At May 9, 2023

Major Shareholder - Anton J. (Tony) Drescher held 15.1% interest at Mar. 28, 2023.

Price Range - OVT/TSX-VEN

Year	Volume	High	Low	Close
2022	3,738,657	$1.35	$0.13	$0.15
2021	11,020,299	$2.08	$0.44	$1.23
2020	10,917,174	$0.70	$0.14	$0.54
2019	5,730,118	$0.17	$0.09	$0.17
2018	3,820,758	$0.15	$0.07	$0.12

Recent Close: $0.08

Capital Stock Changes - There were no changes to capital stock during 2022.

Wholly Owned Subsidiaries

ComplyTrust Inc., San Diego, Calif.

Financial Statistics

Periods ended:	12m Dec. 31/22[A]		12m Dec. 31/21[A]
	US$000s	%Chg	US$000s
Research & devel. expense	1,138		818
General & admin expense	399		431
Stock-based compensation	397		714
Other operating expense	135		24
Operating expense	**1,650**	**-17**	**1,987**
Operating income	**(1,650)**	**n.a.**	**(1,987)**
Finance income	5		nil
Pre-tax income	**(1,650)**	**n.a.**	**(1,987)**
Net income	**(1,650)**	**n.a.**	**(1,987)**
Cash & equivalent	688		2,208
Current assets	718		2,246
Total assets	**718**	**-68**	**2,246**
Accts. pay. & accr. liabs	302		123
Current liabilities	302		123
Shareholders' equity	415		2,124
Cash from oper. activs	**(1,484)**	**n.a.**	**(1,350)**
Cash from fin. activs	nil		3,062
Cash from invest. activs	5		nil
Net cash position	**688**	**-69**	**2,208**
	US$		US$
Earnings per share*	(0.02)		(0.02)
Cash flow per share*	(0.02)		(0.02)
	shs		shs
No. of shs. o/s*	91,422,569		91,422,569
Avg. no. of shs. o/s*	91,422,569		89,968,723
	%		%
Net profit margin	n.a.		n.a.
Return on equity	(129.97)		(162.07)
Return on assets	(111.34)		(144.93)

* Common

[A] Reported in accordance with U.S. GAAP

Latest Results

Periods ended:	3m Mar. 31/23[A]		3m Mar. 31/22[A]
	US$000s	%Chg	US$000s
Net income	(235)	n.a.	(581)
	US$		US$
Earnings per share*	(0.00)		(0.01)

* Common

[A] Reported in accordance with U.S. GAAP

Historical Summary
(as originally stated)

Fiscal Year	Oper. Rev.	Net Inc. Bef. Disc.	EPS*
	US$000s	US$000s	US$
2022[A]	nil	(1,650)	(0.02)
2021[A]	nil	(1,987)	(0.02)
2020[A]	nil	(2,772)	(0.04)
2019[A]	nil	(193)	(0.00)
2018[A]	nil	(183)	(0.00)

* Common

[A] Reported in accordance with U.S. GAAP

O.8 Ocumetics Technology Corp.

Symbol - OTC **Exchange** - TSX-VEN **CUSIP** - 67577H

Head Office - 1250-639 5 Ave SW, Calgary, AB, T2P 0M9 **Telephone** - (403) 650-7718

Website - ocumetics.com

Email - roger.jewett@gmail.com

Investor Relations - Roger M. Jewett (403) 650-7718

Auditors - MNP LLP C.A.

Bankers - Canadian Imperial Bank of Commerce

Lawyers - TingleMerrett LLP, Calgary, Alta.

Transfer Agents - Alliance Trust Company, Calgary, Alta.

Profile - (Alta. 2018) Develops and commercializes medical optics and refractive technologies.

Principal product under preclinical development is the Bionic Lens™, an expandable intraocular lensthat fits within the natural lens compartment of the eye to completely eliminate the need for corrective lenses.

On Aug. 17, 2022, common shares were listed on the Frankfurt Stock Exchange under the symbol 2QBO.

Predecessor Detail - Name changed from Quantum Blockchain Technologies Ltd., Aug. 27, 2021, pursuant to the Qualifying Transaction reverse takeover acquisition of (old) Ocumetics Technology Corp. and concurrent amalgamation of (old) Ocumetics with wholly owned 2321205 Alberta Ltd. (and continued as Ocumetics Technology Inc.).

Directors - Dr. Garth T. Webb, chr. & chief scientific officer, Alta.; Dean Burns, pres. & CEO; Roger M. Jewett, CFO, Calgary, Alta.; Sandi K. Gilbert, Calgary, Alta.; Dayton R. Marks, Ont.; Robert J. Quinn, Kingwood, Tex.

Other Exec. Officers - Dr. Doyle Stulting, CMO

Capital Stock

	Authorized (shs.)	Outstanding (shs.)[1]
Preferred	unlimited	nil
Common	unlimited	112,810,124

[1] At Mar. 31, 2023

Major Shareholder - Dr. Garth T. Webb held 39.72% interest at Apr. 25, 2022.

Price Range - OTC/TSX-VEN

Year	Volume	High	Low	Close
2022	6,947,240	$0.55	$0.24	$0.40
2021	3,083,158	$0.88	$0.34	$0.55
2020	172,200	$0.10	$0.02	$0.03
2019	346,250	$0.12	$0.05	$0.07
2018	493,500	$0.20	$0.08	$0.10

Recent Close: $0.33

Capital Stock Changes - In February 2023, private placement of 1,493,574 units (1 common share & ½ warrant) at 45¢ per unit was completed, with warrants exercisable at 90¢ per share for two years.

During 2022, common shares were issued as follows: 2.428.248 on exercise of warrants and 250,000 on exercise of options.

Wholly Owned Subsidiaries

Ocumetics Technology Inc., Langley, B.C.

Financial Statistics

Periods ended:	12m Dec. 31/22[A]		5m Dec. 31/21[oA]
	$000s	%Chg	$000s
Research & devel. expense	556		98
General & admin expense	1,036		514
Stock-based compensation	486		242
Operating expense	**2,078**	**n.a.**	**854**
Operating income	**(2,078)**	**n.a.**	**(854)**
Deprec., depl. & amort	102		40
Finance costs, gross	27		10
Pre-tax income	**(2,220)**	**n.a.**	**(1,475)**
Net income	**(2,220)**	**n.a.**	**(1,475)**
Cash & equivalent	602		1,843
Accounts receivable	41		52
Current assets	673		1,918
Intangibles, net	701		736
Total assets	**1,374**	**-48**	**2,654**
Accts. pay. & accr. liabs	167		184
Current liabilities	244		261
Shareholders' equity	837		2,127
Cash from oper. activs	**(1,619)**	**n.a.**	**(1,022)**
Cash from fin. activs	444		2,690
Cash from invest. activs	(67)		91
Net cash position	**602**	**-67**	**1,843**
	$		$
Earnings per share*	(0.02)		(0.01)
Cash flow per share*	(0.01)		(0.01)
	shs		shs
No. of shs. o/s*	111,191,550		108,513,302
Avg. no. of shs. o/s*	109,718,687		103,575,004
	%		%
Net profit margin	n.a.		...
Return on equity	(162.70)		...
Return on assets	(108.89)		...

* Common

[o] Restated

[A] Reported in accordance with IFRS

Latest Results

Periods ended:	3m Mar. 31/23[A]		3m Mar. 31/22[A]
	$000s	%Chg	$000s
Net income	(676)	n.a.	(518)
	$		$
Earnings per share*	(0.01)		(0.00)

* Common

[A] Reported in accordance with IFRS

Historical Summary
(as originally stated)

Fiscal Year	Oper. Rev.	Net Inc. Bef. Disc.	EPS*
	$000s	$000s	$
2022[A]	nil	(2,220)	(0.02)
2021[A1,2]	nil	(1,465)	(0.01)
2021[A]	nil	(598)	(0.03)
2020[A]	nil	(172)	(0.01)

* Common

[A] Reported in accordance with IFRS

[1] 5 months ended Dec. 31, 2021.

[2] Results prior to Aug. 27, 2021, pertain to and reflect the Qualifying Transaction reverse takeover of (old) Ocumetics Technology Corp.

O.9 Odd Burger Corporation

Symbol - ODD **Exchange** - TSX-VEN **CUSIP** - 67578E

Head Office - 505 Consortium Crt, London, ON, N6E 2S8 **Toll-free** - (800) 286-2145

Website - oddburger.com

Email - invest@oddburger.com

Investor Relations - James McInnes (800) 286-2145

Auditors - MNP LLP C.A., Toronto, Ont.

Transfer Agents - TSX Trust Company, Vancouver, B.C.

Profile - (B.C. 2015) Owns, operates and franchises vegan fast-food restaurants, as well as manufactures and distributes plant-based protein and dairy alternatives.

Operates six corporate-owned restaurants in Toronto, London, Windsor, Vaughan, Waterloo and Whitby, Ont., and has franchised restaurants in Hamilton and Tecumseh, Ont. Its locations have small store footprints optimized for delivery and takeout. Additional franchise locations have been announced for Oakville, Ottawa, Oshawa and Toronto Ont.; Edmonton, Alta.; Vancouver and Victoria, B.C.; and Regina, Sask.

In addition, operates a food production centre in London, Ont., which produces 8,000 lbs. of product per week under the brand Preposterous Foods including chickUn burgers, meatless wings, ground beef, gyro meat, breakfast sausages, dairy-free ranch dressing, honey mustard sauce, tzatziki sauce, eggless mayonnaise and dairy free-cheese sauce. The company estimates the facility could produce 40,000 lbs. of product per week once additional staff is added and equipment is upgraded.

In June 2023, the company signed an area representative agreement with B.C.-based **5th Group Holdings Ltd.** for the development of 20 restaurant locations in Washington, D.C., over an eight-year period.

In May 2023, the company signed a letter of intent with **14728696 Canada Inc.** (dba **Earthlings Canada Inc.**) to open 145 locations in India and five locations in Singapore over a 10-year period.

In December 2022, the company entered into a letter of intent with Switzerland-based **Angelpreneur AG** to develop 25 restaurant locations in Florida and 25 locations in Germany, Switzerland and Austria over an eight-year period.

In July 2022, the company acquired a 6-acre parcel of land in London, Ont., for an undisclosed amount. The land would initially house a 50,000-sq.-ft. food manufacturing facility that can be expanded to up to 150,000-sq.-ft. of building space, which would be used to produce plant-based proteins and dairy-free sauces and supply select products to external food service customers.

Recent Merger and Acquisition Activity

Status: terminated **Revised:** May 26, 2023

UPDATE: The transaction was terminated. PREVIOUS: Odd Burger Corporation signed a letter of intent to acquire Zoglo's Food Corp., which designs, develops, produces, distributes and sells plant-based appetizers, veggies and meat substitutes. Odd Burger would issue common shares whereby Zoglo's shareholders would hold 25% of the Odd Burger shares issued and outstanding upon completion of the transaction.

Predecessor Detail - Name changed from Globally Local Technologies Inc., July 5, 2021.

Directors - James McInnes, chr., pres. & CEO, London, Ont.; Vasiliki McInnes, COO, London, Ont.; Edward (Ted) Sehl, CFO, Guelph, Ont.; Francois Arbour, Montréal, Qué.; Utsang Desai, Saskatoon, Sask.; Michael Fricker, East York, Ont.; Marc Goodman

Other Exec. Officers - Avra Epstein, v-p, mktg.; Trevor P. Wong-Chor, corp. sec.

Capital Stock

	Authorized (shs.)	Outstanding (shs.)[1]
Preferred	unlimited	nil
Common	unlimited	91,419,417

[1] At Mar. 31, 2023

Major Shareholder - James McInnes held 26.16% interest, Vasiliki McInnes held 26.16% interest and BoxOne Ventures Inc. held 15.57% interest at Aug. 15, 2022.

Price Range - ODD/TSX-VEN

Year	Volume	High	Low	Close
2022	6,641,936	$0.80	$0.24	$0.29
2021	11,596,265	$1.78	$0.53	$0.75
2020	173,389	$0.24	$0.13	$0.14
2019	173,314	$0.33	$0.13	$0.13
2018	96,740	$0.50	$0.25	$0.33

Consolidation: 1-for-2.5 cons. in Apr. 2021
Recent Close: $0.22
Capital Stock Changes - In January and February 2023, private placement of 12,440,000 units (1 common share & 1 warrant) at 25¢ per unit was completed, with warrants exercisable at 40¢ per share for two years.
During fiscal 2022, 2,322,500 common shares were issued by private placement.

Wholly Owned Subsidiaries

Odd Burger Ltd., London, Ont. dba Globally Local.
- 100% int. in **Globally Local Real Estate Inc.**, Ont.
- 100% int. in **Odd Burger Franchise Inc.**, London, Ont.
- 100% int. in **Odd Burger Franchise (US) Inc.**, Del.
- 100% int. in **Odd Burger Restaurants Inc.**, London, Ont.
  - **Globally Local Real Estate (US) Inc.**, London, Ont.
  - 100% int. in **2794443 Ontario Inc.**, Ont.
  - 100% int. in **2794444 Ontario Inc.**, Ont.
  - 100% int. in **2794445 Ontario Inc.**, Ont.
  - 100% int. in **2794446 Ontario Inc.**, Ont.
  - 100% int. in **2794447 Ontario Inc.**, Ont.
  - 100% int. in **2835888 Ontario Inc.**, London, Ont.
  - 100% int. in **2835889 Ontario Inc.**, London, Ont.
  - 100% int. in **2835892 Ontario Inc.**, London, Ont.
  - 100% int. in **2835893 Ontario Inc.**, London, Ont.
  - 100% int. in **2835895 Ontario Inc.**, London, Ont.
- 100% int. in **Preposterous Foods Inc.**, London, Ont.

Financial Statistics

Periods ended:	12m Sept. 30/22[A]		12m Sept. 30/21[A1]
	$000s	%Chg	$000s
Operating revenue	**2,952**	**+153**	**1,169**
Cost of goods sold	1,134		1,007
Salaries & benefits	3,102		989
General & admin expense	2,146		4,368
Operating expense	**6,382**	**0**	**6,364**
Operating income	**(3,430)**	**n.a.**	**(5,195)**
Deprec., depl. & amort.	604		252
Finance costs, gross	239		100
Pre-tax income	**(4,286)**	**n.a.**	**(5,171)**
Net income	**(4,286)**	**n.a.**	**(5,171)**
Cash & equivalent	436		2,753
Inventories	229		139
Accounts receivable	156		474
Current assets	996		3,464
Fixed assets, net	2,711		2,303
Right-of-use assets	984		1,182
Total assets	**5,224**	**-26**	**7,026**
Accts. pay. & accr. liabs	1,506		1,585
Current liabilities	2,242		2,031
Long-term debt, gross	195		243
Long-term debt, net	143		137
Long-term lease liabilities	1,788		1,259
Shareholders' equity	1,051		3,599
Cash from oper. activs	**(2,522)**	**n.a.**	**(1,087)**
Cash from fin. activs	1,142		4,894
Cash from invest. activs	(937)		(1,507)
Net cash position	**436**	**-84**	**2,753**
Capital expenditures	(1,273)		(2,160)
Capital disposals	336		82
	$		$
Earnings per share*	(0.05)		(0.07)
Cash flow per share*	(0.03)		(0.02)
	shs		shs
No. of shs. o/s*	85,161,418		82,838,918
Avg. no. of shs. o/s*	83,516,206		70,892,356
	%		%
Net profit margin	(145.19)		(442.34)
Return on equity	(184.34)		n.m.
Return on assets	(66.07)		(123.96)

* Common
[A] Reported in accordance with IFRS
[1] Results prior to Apr. 13, 2021, pertain to and reflect the Qualifying Transaction reverse takeover acquisition of 2204901 Ontario Inc. (dba Globally Local).

Latest Results

Periods ended:	6m Mar. 31/23[A]		6m Mar. 31/22[A]
	$000s	%Chg	$000s
Operating revenue	1,531	+15	1,329
Net income	(2,231)	n.a.	(2,211)
	$		$
Earnings per share*	(0.03)		(0.03)

* Common
[A] Reported in accordance with IFRS

Historical Summary
(as originally stated)

Fiscal Year	Oper. Rev.	Net Inc. Bef. Disc.	EPS*
	$000s	$000s	$
2022[A]	2,952	(4,286)	(0.05)
2021[A]	1,169	(5,171)	(0.07)
2020[A]	1,069	(2,781)	(0.05)
2019[†A]	1,007	(597)	(0.01)

* Common
† Unaudited
[A] Reported in accordance with IFRS
Note: Adjusted throughout for 1-for-2.5 cons. in Apr. 2021

O.10 Odessa Capital Ltd.

Symbol - ALFA.P **Exchange** - TSX-VEN **CUSIP** - 675849
Head Office - 800-333 7 Ave SW, Calgary, AB, T2P 2Z1 **Telephone** - (514) 795-6955
Email - milass2610@gmail.com
Investor Relations - Michel Lassonde
Auditors - MNP LLP C.A., Calgary, Alta.
Transfer Agents - Computershare Trust Company of Canada Inc., Calgary, Alta.
Profile - (Alta. 2023) Capital Pool Company.
Common listed on TSX-VEN, Aug. 3, 2023.
Directors - Michel Lassonde, pres. & CEO, Saint-Bruno-de-Montarville, Qué.; Martin Grimard, CFO, treas. & corp. sec., Saint-Charles-sur-Richelieu, Qué.; Francois Beaudry, Qué.; Pierre Colas, Outremont, Qué.; Richard Morrison, Terrebonne, Qué.; Andre Verrier, Drummondville, Qué.

Capital Stock

	Authorized (shs.)	Outstanding (shs.)[1]
Common	unlimited	20,000,000

[1] At Aug. 3, 2023
Major Shareholder - Widely held at Aug. 3, 2023.
Recent Close: $0.15
Capital Stock Changes - On Aug. 3, 2023, an initial public offering of 15,000,000 common shares was completed at 10¢ per share.

O.11 Olive Resource Capital Inc.

Symbol - OC **Exchange** - TSX-VEN **CUSIP** - 680767
Head Office - 82 Richmond St E, Toronto, ON, M5C 1P1 **Telephone** - (416) 741-6284
Website - olive-resource.com
Email - derek@olive-resource.com
Investor Relations - Derek Macpherson (416) 294-6713
Auditors - McGovern Hurley LLP C.A., Toronto, Ont.
Bankers - National Bank of Canada, Montréal, Qué.
Transfer Agents - Computershare Trust Company of Canada Inc., Toronto, Ont.
Profile - (Can. 2008; orig. B.C., 1987) Invests in public and private junior resource companies.
Core publicly traded investments include **Nevada Zinc Corporation**, whose key project is Lone Mountain zinc property in Nevada; **Rockcliff Metals Corporation**, which holds mineral interests in the Snow Lake area of Manitoba; and **Minera Alamos Inc.**, which has mineral interests in Mexico including Santana and La Fortuna open-pit gold projects.
Other investments include **Capstone Mining Corp.**, **Copper Mountain Mining CP**, **Generic Gold Corp.**, **Petrowolf LLC**, **ThreeD Capital Corp.**, **X-Terra Resources Inc.**, **Guided Therapeutics, Inc.**, **Canadian Premium Sand Inc.**, **TAG Oil Ltd.**, **Gold79 Mines Ltd.**, **Radio Fuels Energy Corp.**, **Guided Therapeutics, Inc.**, **Stem Holdings, Inc.** and **Discover Wellness Solutions Inc.**
On July 29, 2022, the company acquired a portfolio of assets from **CannaIncome Fund Corporation** for issuance of 30,254,247 common shares at $0.0835 per share. The assets acquired are a combination of public equities, including common shares and warrants in **Guided Therapeutics, Inc.**, **Canadian Premium Sand Inc.**, **TAG Oil Ltd.**, **Gold79 Mines Ltd.** and **Radio Fuels Energy Corp.**; convertible debentures and debt instruments in **Guided Therapeutics, Inc.**, **Stem Holdings, Inc.** and **Discover Wellness Solutions Inc.**; and common shares and convertible debentures in a number of private companies. The assets have a deemed value of $2,525,259.
Predecessor Detail - Name changed from Norvista Capital Corporation, Dec. 30, 2021.
Directors - Derek Macpherson, exec. chr., Toronto, Ont.; Samuel (Sam) Pelaez, pres., CEO & chief invest. officer; Evelyn Foo, Toronto, Ont.; David A. Regan, Halifax, N.S.; Jeffrey Singer, Fla.
Other Exec. Officers - Paul J. Crath, man. dir. & corp. sec.; Carmelo (Carm) Marrelli, CFO

Capital Stock

	Authorized (shs.)	Outstanding (shs.)[1]
Common	unlimited	110,768,709

[1] At Dec. 14, 2022
Normal Course Issuer Bid - The company plans to make normal course purchases of up to 10,466,520 common shares representing 10% of the public float. The bid commenced on Dec. 16, 2022, and expires on Dec. 15, 2023.
Major Shareholder - Donald R. Sobey held 17.58% interest and Stanley W. L. (Stan) Spavold held 12.78% interest at June 3, 2020.

Price Range - OC/TSX-VEN

Year	Volume	High	Low	Close
2022	14,035,036	$0.10	$0.02	$0.04
2021	32,317,343	$0.23	$0.07	$0.08
2020	12,478,183	$0.19	$0.04	$0.16
2019	10,306,247	$0.13	$0.06	$0.07
2018	6,716,658	$0.15	$0.06	$0.06

Recent Close: $0.03
Capital Stock Changes - On July 29, 2022, 30,254,247 common shares were issued pursuant to the acquisition of a portfolio of assets.

Dividends

OC com N.S.R.
$0.03◆ Feb. 9/21
Paid in 2023: n.a. 2022: n.a. 2021: $0.03◆
◆ Special

Wholly Owned Subsidiaries

Norvista Capital General Partner Ltd., Ont.
Norvista Capital Management Corp., Ont.
Olive Resource Capital G.P. Ltd., Ont.

Investments

21.3% int. in **Rockcliff Metals Corporation**, Toronto, Ont. (see Survey of Mines)
Note: The preceding list includes only the major related companies in which interests are held.

Financial Statistics

Periods ended:	12m Dec. 31/21[A]		12m Dec. 31/20[A]
	$000s	%Chg	$000s
Realized invest. gain (loss)	964		3,155
Unrealized invest. gain (loss)	(1,322)		998
Total revenue	**(312)**	**n.a.**	**4,195**
Salaries & benefits	284		466
General & admin. expense	1,353		515
Stock-based compensation	157		59
Operating expense	**1,794**	**+72**	**1,040**
Operating income	**(2,106)**	**n.a.**	**3,155**
Deprec. & amort.	nil		66
Finance costs, gross	nil		8
Pre-tax income	**(2,101)**	**n.a.**	**3,079**
Income taxes	(293)		293
Net income	**(1,808)**	**n.a.**	**2,786**
Cash & equivalent	291		3,312
Accounts receivable	55		118
Long-term investments	8,490		9,104
Total assets	**8,953**	**-29**	**12,602**
Accts. pay. & accr. liabs	678		279
Current liabilities	678		572
Shareholders' equity	8,275		12,030
Cash from oper. activs	**(916)**	**n.a.**	**2,787**
Cash from fin. activs	(2,104)		(90)
Net cash position	**291**	**-91**	**3,312**
	$		$
Earnings per share*	(0.03)		0.04
Cash flow per share*	(0.01)		0.04
Extra divd. - cash*	0.03		...
	shs		shs
No. of shs. o/s*	70,140,501		70,140,501
Avg. no. of shs. o/s*	70,140,501		70,187,486
	%		%
Net profit margin	n.m.		66.41
Return on equity	(17.81)		26.26
Return on assets	(16.78)		25.43

* Common
[A] Reported in accordance with IFRS

Latest Results

Periods ended:	3m Mar. 31/22[A]		3m Mar. 31/21[A]
	$000s	%Chg	$000s
Total revenue	109	n.a.	(355)
Net income	(45)	n.a.	(487)
	$		$
Earnings per share*	(0.00)		(0.01)

* Common
[A] Reported in accordance with IFRS

Historical Summary
(as originally stated)

Fiscal Year	Total Rev.	Net Inc. Bef. Disc.	EPS*
	$000s	$000s	$
2021A	(312)	(1,808)	(0.03)
2020A	4,195	2,786	0.04
2019A	(5,065)	(5,518)	(0.08)
2018A	2,730	1,227	0.02
2017A	296	(562)	(0.01)

* Common
A Reported in accordance with IFRS

O.12 Olympia Financial Group Inc.

Symbol - OLY **Exchange** - TSX **CUSIP** - 681472
Head Office - 4000-520 3 Ave SW, Calgary, AB, T2P 0R3 **Telephone** - (403) 261-0900 **Toll-free** - (877) 565-0011 **Fax** - (403) 265-1455
Website - www.olympiafinancial.com
Email - urschelerj@olympiafinancial.com
Investor Relations - Jennifer Urscheler (877) 565-0011
Auditors - PricewaterhouseCoopers LLP C.A., Calgary, Alta.
Bankers - Canadian Imperial Bank of Commerce
Transfer Agents - Olympia Trust Company, Calgary, Alta.
Employees - 277 at Feb. 23, 2023
Profile - (Alta. 1994) Manages self-administered registered plans and tax-free savings accounts; provides currency exchange and payment services; offers self-insured private health services plans and other insurance products; provides information technology services to exempt market dealers, registrants and issuers; and provides transfer agency and corporate trust services to public and private companies.

The majority of business is conducted through wholly owned **Olympia Trust Company**, which is licensed to carry on trust business as a non-deposit taking trust company in all provinces of Canada except Ontario. Operations are conducted through five divisions:

The **Investment Account Services** (IAS) division - Olympia Trust acts as trustee for self-directed, non-registered and registered plan and tax-free savings account as permitted by the Income Tax Act (Canada). The division acts as trustee and administrator only and does not provide investment advice or recommendations to clients. Plans offered include individual and spousal Registered Retirement Savings Plans, individual and spousal Registered Retirement Income Funds, Registered Education Savings Plans, Tax-Free Savings Accounts, Locked-In Retirement Accounts, Life Income Funds, Prescribed Registered Retirement Income Fund, Locked-in Retirement Income Funds and non-registered investment accounts.

The **Currency and Global Payments** division - Olympia Trust offers foreign currency spot trades, forward contracts, and put and call options to corporations and private clients which have requirements for exchanging funds as part of their business operations.

The **Private Health Services Plan** (PHSP) division - Wholly owned **Olympia Benefits Inc.** markets, sells and administers PHSPs to business owners and self-employed individuals. Also sells out of province emergency medical coverage insurance, exceptional expense insurance and catastrophic drug insurance underwritten by third party insurance companies.

The **Exempt Edge** division - Olympia Benefits also develops, markets and licenses a suite of cloud-based software systems designed for participants in the Canadian private capital markets. Products include Dealer Edge for back office compliance and customer relationship management; Issuer Edge for ongoing administration requirements; and EdgeLink, which allows users to connect and transfer data.

The **Corporate and Shareholder Services** division - Olympia Trust provides transfer agent and registrar services to public and private companies across Canada, including administering dividend reinvestment plans, acting as depository and disbursing agent for corporate reorganizations, assisting with shareholders solicitations and scrutineering shareholder meetings.

Predecessor Detail - Name changed from Target Energy Inc., Jan. 24, 2002; basis 1 new for 250 old shs.

Directors - Richard (Rick) Skauge, chr., pres. & CEO, Calgary, Alta.; Craig K. Skauge, exec. v-p, Calgary, Alta.; Antony Balasubramanian, Calgary, Alta.; Gerard A. Janssen, Calgary, Alta.; Paul Kelly, Calgary, Alta.; Anthony (Tony) Lanzl, Calgary, Alta.; Brian R. Newman, Chestermere, Alta.

Other Exec. Officers - Jennifer Urscheler, CFO; Ryan McKenna, CIO; Jonathan Bahnuik, gen. counsel & corp. sec.; Kenneth (Ken) Fry, pres., Olympia Benefits

Capital Stock

	Authorized (shs.)	Outstanding (shs.)[1]
Preferred	unlimited	nil
Common	unlimited	2,406,336

[1] At May 11, 2023

Major Shareholder - Richard (Rick) Skauge held 29.54% interest at May 11, 2023.

Price Range - OLY/TSX

Year	Volume	High	Low	Close
2022	208,935	$70.25	$46.32	$69.01
2021	221,955	$54.75	$38.52	$46.53
2020	202,034	$55.06	$30.20	$39.75
2019	226,138	$56.00	$38.40	$51.27
2018	188,403	$51.41	$29.52	$38.46

Recent Close: $87.95

Capital Stock Changes - There were no changes to capital stock from 2020 to 2022, inclusive.

Dividends

OLY com Ra $5.40 pa M est. Mar. 31, 2023
Prev. Rate: $4.20 est. Dec. 30, 2022
Prev. Rate: $3.24 est. May 31, 2022
Prev. Rate: $2.76 est. Mar. 29, 2019

Wholly Owned Subsidiaries

Olympia Benefits Inc., Calgary, Alta.
Olympia Trust Company, Calgary, Alta.

Financial Statistics

Periods ended:	12m Dec. 31/22A		12m Dec. 31/21A
	$000s	%Chg	$000s
Operating revenue	**50,194**	**+21**	**41,383**
Cost of sales	3,925		4,131
Salaries & benefits	29,410		20,811
General & admin expense	16,913		11,897
Operating expense	**50,248**	**+36**	**36,839**
Operating income	**(54)**	**n.a.**	**4,544**
Deprec., depl. & amort.	2,552		2,207
Finance income	21,965		7,613
Write-downs/write-offs	(835)		(415)
Pre-tax income	**18,595**	**+119**	**8,503**
Income taxes	4,442		1,992
Net inc bef disc ops, eqhldrs	14,153		6,511
Net income	**14,153**	**+117**	**6,511**
Cash & equivalent	8,366		15,107
Inventories	nil		42
Accounts receivable	15,692		6,817
Current assets	28,513		24,786
Long-term investments	96		99
Fixed assets, net	529		454
Right-of-use assets	976		1,076
Intangibles, net	6,790		8,634
Total assets	**37,496**	**+3**	**36,557**
Bank indebtedness	4,953		12,382
Accts. pay. & accr. liabs.	1,433		780
Current liabilities	11,172		16,556
Long-term lease liabilities	1,001		1,227
Shareholders' equity	25,323		18,773
Cash from oper. activs.	**8,553**	**-28**	**11,877**
Cash from fin. activs.	(15,124)		13
Cash from invest. activs.	(170)		(7,179)
Net cash position	**8,366**	**-45**	**15,107**
Capital expenditures	(379)		(247)
Capital disposals	43		67
	$		$
Earnings per share*	5.88		2.71
Cash flow per share*	3.55		4.94
Cash divd. per share*	3.16		2.76
	shs		shs
No. of shs. o/s*	2,406,336		2,406,336
Avg. no. of shs. o/s*	2,406,336		2,406,336
	%		%
Net profit margin	28.20		15.73
Return on equity	64.19		34.56
Return on assets	38.22		19.37

* Common
A Reported in accordance with IFRS

Latest Results

Periods ended:	3m Mar. 31/23A		3m Mar. 31/22A
	$000s	%Chg	$000s
Operating revenue	11,840	-4	12,292
Net income	5,228	+129	2,280
	$		$
Earnings per share*	2.17		0.95

* Common
A Reported in accordance with IFRS

Historical Summary
(as originally stated)

Fiscal Year	Oper. Rev.	Net Inc. Bef. Disc.	EPS*
	$000s	$000s	$
2022A	50,194	14,153	5.88
2021A	41,383	6,511	2.71
2020A	36,364	7,866	3.32
2019A	35,580	9,326	3.92
2018A	38,597	9,902	4.14

* Common
A Reported in accordance with IFRS

O.13 Omni-Lite Industries Canada Inc.

Symbol - OML **Exchange** - TSX-VEN **CUSIP** - 681976
Head Office - 17210 Edwards Rd, Cerritos, CA, United States, 90703 **Telephone** - (562) 404-8510 **Toll-free** - (800) 577-6664 **Fax** - (562) 926-6913
Website - www.omni-lite.com
Email - d.robbins@omni-lite.com
Investor Relations - David Robbins (800) 577-6664
Auditors - MNP LLP C.A., Calgary, Alta.
Lawyers - Miles Davison LLP, Calgary, Alta.
Transfer Agents - Computershare Trust Company of Canada Inc., Calgary, Alta.
Profile - (Alta. 1997 amalg.) Designs, engineers, manufactures and markets forged precision components and fasteners, which are made from advanced alloys and composites and are processed through computer-controlled hot and cold forging techniques.

Products are used in manufacturing operations of a wide range of industries, including aerospace, defence, specialty automotive, and sports and recreational industries. Patented products are sold to a broad spectrum of Fortune 500 customers. Customers include **The Boeing Company**, **Airbus S.E.**, **Bombardier Inc.**, **Chrysler**, **Ford Motor Company**, **L3Harris Technologies**, **Lockheed Martin**, **Raytheon**, **Pratt and Whitney**, the U.S. military, **Nike, Inc.** and **Adidas AG**.

Head office, research and development, and production operations are located in Cerritos, Calif., and Brampton, Ont. In addition, the company has a facility in Nashua, N.H.

Predecessor Detail - Formed from Omni-Lite Industries Corp. in Alberta, Sept. 15, 1997, on amalgamation with Omni-Lite Industries Inc.; basis 1 new for 3 old shs.

Directors - David Robbins, CEO, Mass.; Roger Dent, Toronto, Ont.; Jan Holland, Ont.; Patrick Hutchins, Calif.; Charles (Chuck) Samkoff, New York, N.Y.

Other Exec. Officers - Vern Brown, pres.; Amy Vetrano-Palmer, CFO; Michael (Mike) Walker, v-p, R&D

Capital Stock

	Authorized (shs.)	Outstanding (shs.)[1]
Common	unlimited	15,412,564

[1] At Mar. 31, 2023

Major Shareholder - Widely held at Oct. 19, 2022.

Price Range - OML/TSX-VEN

Year	Volume	High	Low	Close
2022	1,223,091	$0.90	$0.46	$0.59
2021	3,563,141	$0.95	$0.70	$0.91
2020	1,840,286	$1.19	$0.65	$0.89
2019	1,402,860	$1.35	$0.81	$0.90
2018	1,709,247	$1.70	$0.85	$0.92

Recent Close: $0.51

Capital Stock Changes - In February 2022, private placement of 1,000,000 common shares was completed at Cdn$1.25 per share.

Wholly Owned Subsidiaries

Designed Precision Castings Inc., Brampton, Ont.
Marvel Acquisition Co. Ltd., Ont.
Monzite Corporation, Nashua, N.H.
- 100% int. in **Impellimax Inc.**, N.H.

Monzite Holding Co., Del.
Omni-Lite Industries California Inc., Calif.

Investments

19% int. in **California Nanotechnologies Corp.**, Cerritos, Calif. (see separate coverage)

Financial Statistics

Periods ended:	12m Dec. 31/22^A		12m Dec. 31/21^oA
	US$000s	%Chg	US$000s
Operating revenue	**11,137**	**+93**	**5,763**
Cost of goods sold	9,976		5,005
Research & devel. expense	145		224
General & admin expense	1,967		1,714
Stock-based compensation	102		122
Operating expense	**12,190**	**+73**	**7,065**
Operating income	**(1,053)**	**n.a.**	**(1,302)**
Deprec., depl. & amort.	1,260		853
Finance income	65		11
Finance costs, gross	577		119
Write-downs/write-offs	nil		7
Pre-tax income	**(2,537)**	**n.a.**	**(118)**
Income taxes	16		365
Net income	**(2,553)**	**n.a.**	**(483)**
Cash & equivalent	1,328		2,418
Inventories	3,422		4,011
Accounts receivable	2,268		2,352
Current assets	7,307		9,326
Long-term investments	488		426
Fixed assets, net	11,081		12,064
Intangibles, net	1,129		1,296
Total assets	**20,063**	**-13**	**23,159**
Accts. pay. & accr. liabs	1,329		1,890
Current liabilities	1,667		2,623
Long-term lease liabilities	5,919		6,298
Shareholders' equity	12,418		14,177
Cash from oper. activs	**(765)**	**n.a.**	**(827)**
Cash from fin. activs	(714)		5,325
Cash from invest. activs	521		(3,614)
Net cash position	**1,328**	**-45**	**2,418**
Capital expenditures	(465)		(330)
	US$		US$
Earnings per share*	(0.17)		(0.04)
Cash flow per share*	(0.05)		(0.07)
	shs		shs
No. of shs. o/s*	15,412,564		14,412,564
Avg. no. of shs. o/s*	15,412,564		11,435,072
	%		%
Net profit margin	(22.92)		(8.38)
Return on equity	(19.20)		(3.63)
Return on assets	(9.13)		0.02
Foreign sales percent	64		99

* Common
^o Restated
^A Reported in accordance with IFRS

Latest Results

Periods ended:	3m Mar. 31/23^A		3m Mar. 31/22^A
	US$000s	%Chg	US$000s
Operating revenue	2,730	+15	2,380
Net income	(136)	n.a.	(703)
	US$		US$
Earnings per share*	(0.01)		(0.05)

* Common
^A Reported in accordance with IFRS

Historical Summary
(as originally stated)

Fiscal Year	Oper. Rev.	Net Inc. Bef. Disc.	EPS*
	US$000s	US$000s	US$
2022^A	11,137	(2,553)	(0.17)
2021^A	5,763	(483)	(0.04)
2020^A	6,684	(618)	(0.05)
2019^A	9,318	(1,873)	(0.17)
2018^A	7,075	(4,524)	(0.43)

* Common
^A Reported in accordance with IFRS

O.14 Oncolytics Biotech Inc.*

Symbol - ONC **Exchange** - TSX **CUSIP** - 682310
Head Office - 804-322 11 Ave SW, Calgary, AB, T2R 0C5 **Telephone** - (403) 670-7377 **Fax** - (403) 283-0858
Website - www.oncolyticsbiotech.com
Email - jpatton@oncolytics.ca
Investor Relations - Jon Patton (858) 886-7813
Auditors - Ernst & Young LLP C.A., Calgary, Alta.
Lawyers - McCarthy Tétrault LLP, Calgary, Alta.
Transfer Agents - TSX Trust Company, Calgary, Alta.
Employees - 29 at Dec. 31, 2022
Profile - (Alta. 1998) Develops and discovers oncolytic viruses for the treatment of cancers that have not been successfully treated with conventional therapeutics.

Lead product candidate under Phase III clinical development is pelareorep, a first-in-class immuno-oncolytic virus developed from the reovirus and delivered though veins for the treatment of solid tumours and hematological malignancies. This virus has been demonstrated to replicate specifically in tumour cells bearing an activated RAS-pathway. RAS is a cellular protein that is a key relay in the transmission of growth signals from the outside of the cell to the cell's nucleus. In non-cancer cells, pelareorep enters the cells but is unable to replicate and the virus is actively cleared. In cancer cells, pelareorep selectively replicates in permissive cancer cells. Upon virus replication, cancer cells lyse/die releasing additional virus particles to infect nearby cancer cells. Pelareorep's anti-tumour activity is based on three modes of action consisting of selective viral replication in permissive cancer cells which leads to tumour cell lysis; activation of innate immunity in response to the infection, which results in a cascade of cytokines, causing natural killer (NK) cells to be activated and attack cancer cells; and a specific adaptive immune response targeted to tumour- and viral-associated antigens displayed by antigen-presenting cells, infected tumour cells and/or dendritic cells to T cells.

Has development programs for key immunotherapy combinations in which pelareorep has the potential to provoke a specific innate and adaptive immune responses when combined with checkpoint blockade therapy, chemotherapy and/or targeted therapies. Programs include pelareorep in combination with paclitaxel and avelumab (Bavencio®), a human anti-PD-L1 antibody, for breast cancer; F. Hoffmann-La Roche (Roche)'s anti-PD-L1 checkpoint inhibitor, atezolizumab (Tecentriq®), for treatment of breast and gastrointestinal cancer; retifanlimab, an anti-PD-1 checkpoint inhibitor, for triple-negative breast cancer; Merck's anti-PD1 checkpoint inhibitor pembrolizumab (Keytruda®) to treat pancreatic cancer; Bristol-Myers Squibb's anti-PD1 checkpoint inhibitor Opdivo® for multiple myoma; CAR T cells to improved persistence and efficacy; radiotherapy to increase the number of infiltrating anti-cancer CD8+ T cells and prolonged survival; and chemotherapeutic agent azacitidine for leukemia.

Has more than 243 issued patents throughout the world including 24 U.S. patents, 11 Canadian patents and issuances in other jurisdictions. Also has 16 patents pending in the U.S., Canada and other jurisdictions. The company's patent portfolio also includes methods for treating proliferative disorders using modified adenovirus, HSV, parapoxvirus and vaccinia virus. The company has contracted toll manufacturers for the production of pelareorep for human clinical trials.

Directors - Dr. Matthew C. (Matt) Coffey, co-founder, pres. & CEO, Calgary, Alta.; Wayne Pisano, chr., Pa.; Deborah M. Brown, Ont.; Angela Holtham, Mississauga, Ont.; James T. Parsons, Mississauga, Ont.; Jonathan Rigby, La.; Dr. Bernd R. Seizinger, N.J.

Other Exec. Officers - Kirk J. Look, CFO; Dr. Thomas C. Heineman, CMO; Allison Hagerman, v-p, product devel.; Andrew de Guttadauro, pres., Oncolytics Biotech (U.S.) Inc. & global head, bus. devel.

Capital Stock

	Authorized (shs.)	Outstanding (shs.)[1]
Common	unlimited	72,368,797

[1] At Aug. 8, 2023

Options - At Dec. 31, 2022, options were outstanding to purchase 5,963,185 common shares at a weighted average exercise price of $2.91 per share with a weighted average remaining contractual life of 2.548 years.

Major Shareholder - Widely held at Mar. 15, 2023.

Price Range - ONC/TSX

Year	Volume	High	Low	Close
2022	15,173,088	$3.10	$1.06	$2.22
2021	37,036,853	$6.06	$1.75	$1.75
2020	62,341,789	$6.26	$1.35	$3.02
2019	24,221,376	$7.84	$0.48	$6.15
2018	7,582,733	$10.65	$2.26	$2.51

Recent Close: $3.19

Capital Stock Changes - In August 2023, bought deal public offering of 6,667,000 units (1 common share & ½ warrant) at US$2.25 per unit was completed, with warrants exercisable at US$2.81 per share for five years. Net proceeds would be used to continue pelareorep clinical programs in metastatic breast cancer and pancreatic cancer and general corporate and working capital purposes.

During 2022, common shares were issued as follows: 6,235,232 pursuant to at-the-market sales agreement with Canaccord Genuity Inc., 40,560 as share-based payment and 8,333 on exercise of options.

Long-Term Debt - At Dec. 31, 2022, the company had no long-term debt.

Wholly Owned Subsidiaries

Oncolytics Biotech (Barbados) Inc., Barbados.
- 100% int. in **Oncolytics Biotech (U.S.) Inc.**, Del.

Financial Statistics

Periods ended:	12m Dec. 31/22^A		12m Dec. 31/21^oA
	$000s	%Chg	$000s
Salaries & benefits	8,853		7,187
Research & devel. expense	8,078		6,188
General & admin expense	7,223		8,582
Stock-based compensation	2,378		3,826
Operating expense	**26,532**	**+3**	**25,782**
Operating income	**(26,532)**	**n.a.**	**(25,782)**
Deprec., depl. & amort.	392		452
Finance income	608		190
Finance costs, gross	80		92
Pre-tax income	**(24,751)**	**n.a.**	**(26,255)**
Income taxes	84		49
Net income	**(24,835)**	**n.a.**	**(26,304)**
Cash & equivalent	32,138		41,262
Accounts receivable	521		866
Current assets	35,684		44,904
Fixed assets, net	356		392
Right-of-use assets	296		584
Total assets	**37,334**	**-19**	**45,880**
Accts. pay. & accr. liabs	3,650		1,988
Current liabilities	3,945		2,690
Long-term lease liabilities	157		361
Shareholders' equity	26,502		36,099
Cash from oper. activs	**(23,355)**	**n.a.**	**(22,433)**
Cash from fin. activs	12,205		33,015
Cash from invest. activs	(20,403)		(286)
Net cash position	**11,666**	**-72**	**41,262**
Capital expenditures	(55)		(286)
	$		$
Earnings per share*	(0.43)		(0.49)
Cash flow per share*	(0.40)		(0.42)
	shs		shs
No. of shs. o/s*	61,327,914		55,043,789
Avg. no. of shs. o/s*	58,029,745		53,513,225
	%		%
Net profit margin	n.a.		n.a.
Return on equity	(79.34)		(86.45)
Return on assets	(59.50)		(65.34)
No. of employees (FTEs)	29		26

* Common
^o Restated
^A Reported in accordance with IFRS

Latest Results

Periods ended:	3m Mar. 31/23^A		3m Mar. 31/22^A
	$000s	%Chg	$000s
Net income	(6,437)	n.a.	(6,779)
	$		$
Earnings per share*	(0.10)		(0.12)

* Common
^A Reported in accordance with IFRS

Historical Summary
(as originally stated)

Fiscal Year	Oper. Rev.	Net Inc. Bef. Disc.	EPS*
	$000s	$000s	$
2022^A	nil	(24,835)	(0.43)
2021^A	nil	(26,304)	(0.49)
2020^A	nil	(22,505)	(0.56)
2019^A	nil	(33,123)	(1.50)
2018^A	nil	(17,037)	(1.06)

* Common
^A Reported in accordance with IFRS

O.15 1933 Industries Inc.

Symbol - TGIF **Exchange** - CSE **CUSIP** - 65442F
Head Office - 300-1055 Hastings St W, Vancouver, BC, V6E 2E9 **Telephone** - (604) 674-4756
Website - www.1933industries.com
Email - alexia@1933industries.com
Investor Relations - Alexia Helgason (604) 728-4407 ext. 1
Auditors - MNP LLP C.A., Burlington, Ont.
Lawyers - Armstrong Simpson, Vancouver, B.C.
Transfer Agents - Odyssey Trust Company, Calgary, Alta.
Profile - (B.C. 2018; orig. Alta., 2008) Cultivates, produces, extracts, manufactures and distributes cannabis and cannabidiol (CBD) infused products in the United States.

Wholly owned **Infused Mfg. LLC** operates a 15,000-sq.-ft. facility in Las Vegas for development and manufacturing of hemp-based, cannabidiol (CBD) infused products, including topicals, lotions, creams, gummies, vapes, tinctures, elixirs, capsules, dabs, lip balms and pre and post workout recovery sports products, under the company's Canna Hemp™, Canna Hemp X™, Canna Hemp™ CGB and CBN Natural Line and Canna Hemp™ HEMP brands for sale in the U.S. through licensed dispensaries, other retail outlets and online.

Subsidiary **Alternative Medicine Association LLC** (AMA; 91% owned) operates a 67,750-sq.-ft. cultivation facility and a 10,000-sq.-ft. extraction and production facility in Las Vegas, Nev. AMA's wholesale cannabis products are sold under the AMA brand and Level X premium brand and include premium craft-style cannabis, infused pre-rolls, full spectrum oils, high quality distillates, proprietary blends of terpenes, vaporizer products and boutique concentrates such as shatter, crumble, batter, sugar wax, diamonds, and cured and live resins. Through licensing agreements, AMA also manufactures and sells third party brands including Cannabis, Bloom™, Gotti's Gold, Blonde™ and Viva La Buds. Products are sold to licensed dispensaries or retail stores in Nevada.

In September 2022, the company sold a vacant property in Las Vegas for USUS2,650,000.

Recent Merger and Acquisition Activity

Status: terminated **Revised:** May 11, 2022
UPDATE: The transaction was terminated. PREVIOUS: 1933 Industries Inc. entered into a letter of intent to acquire Los Angeles, Calif.-based Day One Beverages Inc., which manufactures cannabidiol (CBD)-infused sparkling water products, for issuance of 55,000,000 common shares.

Predecessor Detail - Name changed from Friday Night Inc., Sept. 26, 2018.

Directors - Paul Rosen, chr. & CEO, Toronto, Ont.; Brian Farrell, CFO, Edmonton, Alta.; Lisa Capparelli, New York, N.Y.; Curtis Floyd, Bakersfield, Calif.; D. Richard (Rick) Skeith, Calgary, Alta.

Other Exec. Officers - Ester Vigil, pres.; Caleb Zobrist, exec. v-p & gen. counsel, U.S.; Alexia Helgason, v-p, IR; Marion McGrath, corp. sec.

Capital Stock

	Authorized (shs.)	Outstanding (shs.)[1]
Preferred	unlimited	nil
Common	unlimited	461,233,870

[1] At June 29, 2023

Major Shareholder - Widely held at Mar. 24, 2023.

Price Range - TGIF/CSE

Year	Volume	High	Low	Close
2022	78,936,234	$0.06	$0.01	$0.02
2021	272,177,386	$0.17	$0.04	$0.04
2020	197,634,147	$0.23	$0.05	$0.07
2019	182,891,113	$0.62	$0.19	$0.21
2018	520,549,350	$1.29	$0.30	$0.34

Recent Close: $0.02

Capital Stock Changes - During fiscal 2022, 372,666 common shares were issued on conversion of debentures.

Wholly Owned Subsidiaries

FN Pharmaceuticals, United States.
- 100% int. in **AMA Production LLC**, United States.
- 91% int. in **Alternative Medicine Association LLC**, Las Vegas, Nev.

1080034 B.C. Ltd., Vancouver, B.C.
1933 Legacy Inc., United States.
1933 Management Services Inc., United States.
- 100% int. in **Infused Mfg. LLC**, Las Vegas, Nev.

Spire Secure Logistics Inc., Vancouver, B.C. Inactive

Financial Statistics

Periods ended:	12m July 31/22[A]		12m July 31/21[A]
	$000s	%Chg	$000s
Operating revenue	**12,538**	**+5**	**11,975**
Cost of sales	9,848		7,155
Salaries & benefits	866		1,497
General & admin expense	6,330		5,420
Stock-based compensation	12		1,025
Operating expense	**17,056**	**+13**	**15,097**
Operating income	**(4,518)**	**n.a.**	**(3,122)**
Deprec., depl. & amort.	500		498
Finance income	16		nil
Finance costs, gross	1,760		2,107
Write-downs/write-offs	(11,540)		(427)
Pre-tax income	**(17,517)**	**n.a.**	**(5,805)**
Income taxes	549		482
Net inc bef disc ops, eqhldrs	(17,807)		(6,470)
Net inc bef disc ops, NCI	(259)		183
Net income	**(18,066)**	**n.a.**	**(6,287)**
Net inc. for equity hldrs	**(17,807)**	**n.a.**	**(6,470)**
Net inc. for non-cont. int.	**(259)**	**n.a.**	**183**
Cash & equivalent	363		4,406
Inventories	5,861		4,200
Accounts receivable	1,343		934
Current assets	12,347		11,149
Fixed assets, net	12,171		18,678
Intangibles, net	4,492		15,527
Total assets	**29,010**	**-36**	**45,354**
Accts. pay. & accr. liabs	2,756		1,381
Current liabilities	8,671		2,710
Long-term debt, gross	4,574		4,235
Long-term debt, net	4,574		4,235
Long-term lease liabilities	12,816		13,177
Shareholders' equity	8,522		25,993
Non-controlling interest	(999)		(760)
Cash from oper. activs	**(5,085)**	**n.a.**	**(4,666)**
Cash from fin. activs	1,535		6,060
Cash from invest. activs	2		(456)
Net cash position	**363**	**-92**	**4,406**
Capital expenditures	(15)		(456)
	$		$
Earnings per share*	(0.04)		(0.02)
Cash flow per share*	(0.01)		(0.01)
	shs		shs
No. of shs. o/s*	450,699,319		450,326,653
Avg. no. of shs. o/s*	450,684,512		387,006,229
	%		%
Net profit margin	(144.09)		(52.50)
Return on equity	(103.18)		(27.92)
Return on assets	(43.71)		(8.71)
Foreign sales percent	100		100

* Common
[A] Reported in accordance with IFRS

Latest Results

Periods ended:	3m Oct. 31/22[A]		3m Oct. 31/21[A]
	$000s	%Chg	$000s
Operating revenue	5,636	+129	2,466
Net income	(1,167)	n.a.	(949)
Net inc. for equity hldrs	(1,064)	n.a.	(953)
Net inc. for non-cont. int.	(103)		4
	$		$
Earnings per share*	(0.00)		(0.00)

* Common
[A] Reported in accordance with IFRS

Historical Summary
(as originally stated)

Fiscal Year	Oper. Rev.	Net Inc. Bef. Disc.	EPS*
	$000s	$000s	$
2022[A]	12,538	(18,066)	(0.04)
2021[A]	11,975	(6,287)	(0.02)
2020[A]	11,963	(20,017)	(0.07)
2019[A]	18,060	(18,535)	(0.07)
2018[A]	12,650	(5,490)	(0.02)

* Common
[A] Reported in accordance with IFRS

0.16 1CM Inc.

Symbol - EPIC **Exchange** - CSE **CUSIP** - 68237A
Head Office - 802-625 Cochrane Dr, Markham, ON, L3R 9R9 **Telephone** - (416) 842-8408
Website - 1cminc.com
Email - tanvi@1cminc.com
Investor Relations - Tanvi Bhandari (416) 999-9599
Auditors - Clearhouse LLP C.A., Mississauga, Ont.
Transfer Agents - Computershare Trust Company of Canada Inc., Vancouver, B.C.

Profile - (Ont. 2011) Owns and operates retail cannabis stores in Canada and a cannabis technology provider.

The company operates 28 retail cannabis stores in British Columbia, Alberta, Saskatchewan, Ontario and New Brunswick under the brands T Cannabis and Cost Cannabis. Stores offer flower, pre-rolls, concentrates, edibles, beverages, vapes, topicals, seeds and accessories. Also has one Costcan Liquor store in Creighton, Sask.

Through wholly owned **One Cannabis Market Inc.** develops and provides technology products and services to the cannabis industry including: last mile delivery; in-house last mile delivery application optimizing fleet management; providing real-time order tracking; data analytics; and generally improving the customer delivery experience.

In June 2023, the company won the Saskatchewan Liquor and Gaming Authority auctions for six retail liquor store permits in Regina, Saskatoon, Watrous, Creighton, Assiniboia and Humboldt, Sask., for a combined purchase price of $4,555,600. The company plans to use these retail liquor permits to expand its retail operations in the province. Its first Costcan Liquor store in Creighton was opened in August 2023.

Also in June 2023, the company entered into an agreement with **Cannabis NB Ltd.**, a provincial Crown corporation responsible for cannabis in New Brunswick, to open two retail cannabis stores in Blackville and Bouctouche.

In April 2023, the company entered into a letter of intent to acquire **Nugget Data**, a data platform providing cannabis retailers and brands with real-time data analysis on pricing, distribution and inventory. Terms were not disclosed.

On Mar. 10, 2023, the company completed the sale of wholly owned **LCG Holdings Inc.**, which held its Colombian cannabis assets including property in Carmen de Viboral, for a purchase price of $1,050,000.

In December 2022, the company acquired **Fresh Cannabis Co. Inc.**, a retail cannabis store in Revelstoke, B.C., for $375,000 in cash, and **1267842 B.C. Ltd.** (operating as **Greenery Cannabis Boutique Ltd.**), a retail cannabis store in Salmon Arm, B.C., for $70,000.

In November 2022, the company completed the sale its 9.75-acre property and cannabis processing facility in Smith cty., Tenn., for total consideration of US$2,500,000.

In July 2022, the company acquired the remaining 35% interest in its Colombian operating subsidiary **LCG Holdings Inc.** for nominal consideration.

In June 2022, the company acquired **One Cannabis Market Inc.**, a technology platform for cannabis market that provides B2B and B2C solutions including last mile delivery, digital signage, big data analytics and wholesale clearing services, for issuance of 500,000 common shares.

Recent Merger and Acquisition Activity

Status: completed **Announced:** Aug. 31, 2022
1CM Inc. sold wholly owned Woodstock Biomed Inc. for total consideration of $5,000,000. Woodstock held a 30-acre property with a greenhouse production facility in Pelham, Ont. The property was leased to Medical Saints Ltd., a licensed producer of industrial hemp under Health Canada.

Status: completed **Revised:** Aug. 31, 2022
UPDATE: The transaction was completed. PREVIOUS: Leviathan Natural Products Inc. agreed to acquire private Tirthankar Ltd., which operates 10 retail cannabis stores in Ontario, with five more locations in development, for $1,800,000 cash and issuance of 15,750,000 common shares. The Tirthankar stores operate under its retail brands T CANNABIS and COST CANNABIS, offering a wide variety of cannabis brands and products including flower, pre-rolls, concentrates, edibles, beverages, vapes, topicals, seeds and accessories.

Predecessor Detail - Name changed from Leviathan Natural Products Inc., Sept. 6, 2022.

Directors - Tanvi Bhandari, CEO; Lucas Leone; Rupalee Mehta

Other Exec. Officers - Harshil Chovatiya, COO, CFO & corp. sec.; Luvlina Sanghera, chief mktg. officer & CEO, Jekyll & Hyde Brand Builders Inc.

Capital Stock

	Authorized (shs.)	Outstanding (shs.)[1]
Common	unlimited	114,403,602

[1] At May 1, 2023

Major Shareholder - Widely held at Aug. 2, 2022.

Price Range - EPIC/CSE

Year	Volume	High	Low	Close
2022	4,588,419	$1.65	$0.50	$1.64
2021	9,361,857	$0.77	$0.18	$0.58
2020	5,128,510	$0.35	$0.10	$0.25
2019	10,640,926	$0.70	$0.09	$0.22
2018	23,233,938	$2.32	$0.20	$0.40

Recent Close: $1.90

Capital Stock Changes - In November 2022, private placement of 4,000,000 common shares was completed at $1.45 per share. In June 2023, private placement of 3,333,333 common shares was arranged at $1.50 per share.

In March and April 2022, private placement of 8,333,333 common shares was completed at 60¢ per share. On Aug. 31, 2022, 15,750,000 common shares were issued pursuant to the acquisition of Tirthankar Ltd. Also during fiscal 2022, common shares were issued as follows: 751,666 on exercise of warrants, 500,000 on acquisition of One Cannabis Market Inc., 250,000 as retention bonus and 75,000 on exercise of options.

Wholly Owned Subsidiaries

Bathurst Resources Corp., Toronto, Ont. Inactive.
Cost Cannabis Inc. (BC), B.C.
- 100% int. in **Fresh Cannabis Co. Inc.**, Revelstoke, B.C.
- 100% int. in **1267842 B.C. Ltd.**, B.C.

Cost Cannabis Inc. (SK), Sask.
Jekyll & Hyde Brand Builders Inc., Toronto, Ont.
- 100% int. in **One Cannabis Market Inc.**, United States.

Tirthankar Limited, Canada.
- 100% int. in **T Cann Mgmt Corp.**, United States.
- 100% int. in **T Cannabis NW Inc.**, United States.

Financial Statistics

Periods ended:	12m Aug. 31/22[A]		12m Aug. 31/21[A]
	$000s	%Chg	$000s
Operating revenue	**842**	**+146**	**342**
Cost of sales	1,270		489
Salaries & benefits	810		1,162
General & admin expense	4,711		706
Stock-based compensation	1,312		2,084
Operating expense	**8,103**	**+82**	**4,441**
Operating income	**(7,261)**	**n.a.**	**(4,099)**
Deprec., depl. & amort.	583		665
Write-downs/write-offs	nil		(566)
Pre-tax income	**(4,995)**	**n.a.**	**(5,015)**
Net inc. bef. disc. opers	**(4,995)**	**n.a.**	**(5,015)**
Income from disc. opers	54		100
Net income	**(4,941)**	**n.a.**	**(4,915)**
Net inc. for equity hldrs	**(4,727)**	**n.a.**	**(4,558)**
Net inc. for non-cont. int.	**(214)**	**n.a.**	**(357)**
Cash & equivalent	2,237		162
Current assets	3,470		819
Long-term investments	25		4,450
Fixed assets, net	6,150		3,945
Intangibles, net	18,588		108
Total assets	**28,233**	**+203**	**9,322**
Accts. pay. & accr. liabs	666		908
Current liabilities	2,612		3,209
Long-term debt, gross	11,135		12,261
Long-term debt, net	9,440		10,567
Shareholders' equity	15,381		(3,852)
Non-controlling interest	nil		(602)
Cash from oper. activs	**(2,528)**	**n.a.**	**(1,995)**
Cash from fin. activs	2,851		2,304
Cash from invest. activs	1,751		(151)
Net cash position	**2,237**	**n.m.**	**162**
Capital expenditures	(218)		(13)
	$		$
Earnings per share*	(0.06)		(0.05)
Cash flow per share*	(0.03)		(0.02)
	shs		shs
No. of shs. o/s*	110,403,602		84,743,603
Avg. no. of shs. o/s*	89,041,180		84,763,603
	%		%
Net profit margin	(593.23)		n.m.
Return on equity	n.m.		n.m.
Return on assets	(26.60)		(52.22)

* Common
[A] Reported in accordance with IFRS

Latest Results

Periods ended:	6m Feb. 28/23[A]		6m Feb. 28/22[A]
	$000s	%Chg	$000s
Operating revenue	15,099	n.m.	381
Net income	(132)	n.a.	(2,194)
Net inc. for equity hldrs	(132)	n.a.	(2,057)
Net inc. for non-cont. int	nil		(136)
	$		$
Earnings per share*	(0.01)		(0.02)

* Common
[A] Reported in accordance with IFRS

Historical Summary
(as originally stated)

Fiscal Year	Oper. Rev.	Net Inc. Bef. Disc.	EPS*
	$000s	$000s	$
2022[A]	842	(4,995)	(0.06)
2021[A]	342	(5,015)	(0.05)
2020[A]	73	(3,029)	(0.03)
2019[A]	119	(28,562)	(0.34)
2018[A]	82	(6,378)	(0.13)

* Common
[A] Reported in accordance with IFRS

O.17 OneSoft Solutions Inc.

Symbol - OSS **Exchange** - TSX-VEN **CUSIP** - 68276J
Head Office - 4227-10230 Jasper Ave, Edmonton, AB, T5J 4P6 **Telephone** - (780) 248-5794 **Toll-free** - (800) 270-5024 **Fax** - (866) 315-7135
Website - www.onesoft.ca
Email - sean@sophiccapital.com
Investor Relations - Sean Peasgood (416) 565-2805
Auditors - Ernst & Young LLP C.A., Edmonton, Alta.
Bankers - ATB Financial, Edmonton, Alta.
Lawyers - Parlee McLaws LLP, Edmonton, Alta.
Transfer Agents - Computershare Trust Company of Canada Inc., Calgary, Alta.
Employees - 38 at Dec. 31, 2022

Profile - (Alta. 1996) Develops and markets cloud software-as-service (SaaS) solutions based on **Microsoft Corporation**'s Machine Learning, Data Science, Power Business Intelligence and Azure cloud technology platforms and services for the global oil and gas pipeline industry.

Wholly owned **OneBridge Solutions Inc.** markets Cognitive Integrity Management™ (CIM), a SaaS application that uses the Microsoft Azure cloud platform and services including machine learning, predictive analytics, business intelligence reporting and other data science components to assist pipeline companies to prevent pipeline failures. The CIM application also provides functionality to solve pipeline integrity management business problems regarding assessment planning, regulatory compliance, threat monitoring, business intelligence and pipeline excavation management module. In addition, OneBridge offers Integrity Management (IM) operations, which includes risk assessment that uses RIPL and RiskCAT softwares to identify sections of oil and gas pipeline systems that could impact high consequence areas (HCA).

The company's product is marketed to pipeline operators in North America and select international markets with primary focus on U.S. pipeline companies.

On June 30, 2022, indirect wholly owned **OneBridge Solutions Inc.** acquired the Integrity Management business unit from **MESA Products, Inc.** for US$375,000 cash and issuance of 1,828,125 common shares. The business includes intellectual property and assets associated with RIPL risk and high consequence area management software solutions.

Predecessor Detail - Name changed from Serenic Corporation, Aug. 1, 2014.

Directors - Douglas J. (Doug) Thomson, chr., Edmonton, Alta.; R. Dwayne Kushniruk, CEO, Edmonton, Alta.; Ronald W. Odynski, Edmonton, Alta.; Nizar J. Somji, Edmonton, Alta.; R. David Webster, Calgary, Alta.

Other Exec. Officers - Brandon Taylor, pres. & COO; Paul D. Johnston, CFO; David S. Tam, corp. sec.; Tim Edward, pres., OneBridge Canada

Capital Stock

	Authorized (shs.)	Outstanding (shs.)[1]
Preferred	unlimited	nil
Common	unlimited	121,033,314

[1] At Apr. 26, 2023

Major Shareholder - Widely held at Apr. 17, 2023.

Price Range - OSS/TSX-VEN

Year	Volume	High	Low	Close
2022	12,233,900	$0.55	$0.25	$0.40
2021	17,705,327	$0.87	$0.41	$0.51
2020	33,210,685	$0.72	$0.19	$0.58
2019	29,643,480	$1.03	$0.47	$0.62
2018	29,408,991	$0.63	$0.20	$0.47

Recent Close: $0.81

Capital Stock Changes - During 2022, common shares were issued as follows: 1,828,125 pursuant to the acquisition of the Integrity Management business unit and 374,667 on exercise of options.

Wholly Owned Subsidiaries

OneBridge Solutions Canada Inc., Alta.
OneBridge Solutions Inc., Del.

Financial Statistics

Periods ended:	12m Dec. 31/22[A]		12m Dec. 31/21[A]
	$000s	%Chg	$000s
Operating revenue	**6,889**	**+55**	**4,442**
Cost of sales	1,978		1,125
Salaries & benefits	5,398		4,550
Research & devel. expense	(391)		(289)
General & admin expense	2,054		1,531
Stock-based compensation	619		960
Operating expense	**9,658**	**+23**	**7,877**
Operating income	**(2,769)**	**n.a.**	**(3,435)**
Deprec., depl. & amort.	461		456
Finance income	67		24
Pre-tax income	**(2,972)**	**n.a.**	**(3,889)**
Net income	**(2,972)**	**n.a.**	**(3,889)**
Cash & equivalent	4,392		5,509
Accounts receivable	293		216
Current assets	4,821		5,875
Fixed assets, net	38		23
Intangibles, net	1,851		1,003
Total assets	**6,711**	**-3**	**6,901**
Accts. pay. & accr. liabs	1,098		838
Current liabilities	3,392		1,720
Shareholders' equity	3,086		4,879
Cash from oper. activs	**(902)**	**n.a.**	**(1,817)**
Cash from fin. activs	96		507
Cash from invest. activs	(386)		(436)
Net cash position	**4,392**	**-20**	**5,509**
Capital expenditures	(25)		(13)
	$		$
Earnings per share*	(0.02)		(0.03)
Cash flow per share*	(0.01)		(0.02)
	shs		shs
No. of shs. o/s*	120,666,939		118,464,147
Avg. no. of shs. o/s*	119,597,891		116,930,353
	%		%
Net profit margin	(43.14)		(87.55)
Return on equity	(74.63)		(64.42)
Return on assets	(43.67)		(50.68)
Foreign sales percent	96		97
No. of employees (FTEs)	38		31

* Common
[A] Reported in accordance with IFRS

Latest Results

Periods ended:	3m Mar. 31/23[A]		3m Mar. 31/22[A]
	$000s	%Chg	$000s
Operating revenue	2,200	+72	1,280
Net income	(652)	n.a.	(1,064)
	$		$
Earnings per share*	(0.01)		(0.01)

* Common
[A] Reported in accordance with IFRS

Historical Summary
(as originally stated)

Fiscal Year	Oper. Rev.	Net Inc. Bef. Disc.	EPS*
	$000s	$000s	$
2022[A]	6,889	(2,972)	(0.02)
2021[A]	4,442	(3,889)	(0.03)
2020[A]	4,056	(3,256)	(0.03)
2019[A]	2,712	(3,606)	(0.03)
2018[A1]	4,328	295	0.00

* Common
[A] Reported in accordance with IFRS
[1] 10 months ended Dec. 31, 2018.

O.18 Onex Corporation*

Symbol - ONEX **Exchange** - TSX **CUSIP** - 68272K
Head Office - TD Canada Trust Tower, Brookfield Place, 4900-161 Bay St, PO Box 700, Toronto, ON, M5J 2S1 **Telephone** - (416) 362-7711 **Fax** - (416) 362-5765
Website - www.onex.com
Email - adaly@onex.com
Investor Relations - Andrea E. Daly (416) 362-7711
Auditors - PricewaterhouseCoopers LLP C.A., Toronto, Ont.
Transfer Agents - TSX Trust Company, Toronto, Ont.
FP500 Revenue Ranking - 441
Employees - 597 at Dec. 31, 2022

Profile - (Ont. 1980) Acts as an investor and asset manager which invests capital on behalf of shareholders and clients around the world through its private equity and credit businesses.

Private Equity - Raises and invests capital, from third party investors or limited partners along with own investing capital, through Onex Partners and ONCAP funds. At Mar. 31, 2023, the company had US$24.6 billion of private equity assets under management (AUM), including US$10.3 billion of fee-generating AUM and US$5.9 billion from the company's own investing capital.

Through Onex Partners funds, makes control investments in middle to large-cap businesses organized or domiciled in the U.S., Canada and Europe that require at least US$125,000,000 of equity. Investments include **Advanced Integration Technology LP**, a provider of automation, factory integration and tooling dedicated to the global aerospace, defence and space launch industries; **WestJet Airlines Ltd.**, a provider of scheduled flights, vacation packages, charter and cargo services to more than 100 destinations across North America, Central America, the Caribbean and Europe; **WireCo WorldGroup**, a global manufacturer of mission-critical steel wire rope, synthetic rope, specialty wire and engineered products; **Parkdean Resorts UK Limited**, an owner and operator of caravan holiday parks in the U.K.; **BBAM Limited Partnership**, an aircraft manager and lessor; **Convex Group Limited**, a specialty insurer and reinsurer focused on complex risks; **Sedgwick Claims Management Services**, a provider of technology-enabled risk, benefits and integrated business solutions; **SCP Health**, a provider of emergency and hospital medicine physician practice management services in the U.S.; **ASM Global Parent, Inc.**, a provider of venue management and services; **Clarivate Plc**, an owner and operator of subscription-based businesses focused on scientific and academic research, patent analytics and regulatory standards, pharmaceutical and biotech intelligence, trademark protection and domain brand protection; **Emerald Holding, Inc.** (formerly **Emerald Expositions Events, Inc.**), an operator of business-to-business trade shows in the U.S.; **PowerSchool Group LLC**, a provider of K-12 software and cloud-based solutions; **Ryan, LLC**, a provider of global tax services and software; **Acacium Group Limited** (formerly **Independent Clinical Services Group Ltd.**), a specialized staffing, workforce management solutions, and health and social services business operating primarily in Europe and present across four continents globally; **Digital Insurance, LLC** (dba OneDigital), a provider of employee benefits insurance brokerage and retirement consulting services in the U.S.; **Imagine Learning LLC** (formerly **Weld North Education LLC**), a K-12 digital curriculum company in the U.S.; **Monroe Operations, LLC** (dba Newport Healthcare), an operator of healing centres in the U.S. offering residential, partial hospitalization and outpatient treatment programs for teens and young adults with primary mental health disorders; **Wealth Enhancement Group, LLC**, an independent wealth management firm offering comprehensive and customized financial planning and investment management services to clients across the U.S.; **Fidelity Engineering, LLC** (dba Fidelity Building Services Group), a provider of technical building solutions for the commercial and industrial facilities market in the U.S.; **Tes Global Limited**, a provider of recruitment services to the U.K. education sector as well as comprehensive software solutions for the global education sector; **Resource Environmental Solutions, LLC**, an ecological restoration firm providing public and private sector clients with solutions for environmental mitigation, stormwater, water quality, and climate and flooding resilience; and **Analytic Partners, Inc.**, a cloud-based, managed software and service platform specializing in marketing data analytics.

Through ONCAP funds, makes control investments in small and medium-sized businesses of less than US$250,000,000 of equity in businesses organized or domiciled in the U.S. and Canada. Investments include **AutoSavvy**, a used vehicle retailer specializing in branded title vehicles in the U.S.; **EnGlobe Corp.**, a provider of specialty environmental and engineering services to public and private sector clients in Canada, France and the U.K.; **Hopkins Manufacturing Corporation**, a designer, manufacturer and marketer of proprietary branded products for the automotive aftermarket; **Precision Concepts International, LLC**, a designer and manufacturer of specialty rigid packaging solutions as well as a custom injection molder of plastic components; **Komar Industries, Inc.**, a designer and manufacturer of industrial waste and recycling processing systems; **Precision Global**, a global manufacturer of pressurized dispensing solutions; **Venanpri Group**, a manufacturer of high-precision consumable wear components embedded into agricultural soil preparation implements as well as hand tools for the agriculture, construction and gardening end markets; **Walter Surface Technologies Inc.**, a provider of premium, consumable surface technology solutions for industrial users; **Chatters Canada**, a retailer of professional hair care products and a hair salon operator; **International Language Academy of Canada Inc.**, an English language school; **Mayzon Group Inc.**, a designer, manufacturer and marketer of bath accessories and home products sold to retailers in the U.S. and Canada; **PURE Canadian Gaming Corp.**, a casino operator; **Wyse Meter Solutions**, a provider of submetering and utility expense management solutions for the multi-residential, condominium and commercial markets in Canada; **Ontivity**, a Tier 1 provider of wireless infrastructure services to the telecommunication industry in the U.S.; **Merrithew International Inc.**, a developer, manufacturer and retailer of Pilates equipment, accessories, content and education worldwide; and **Ideal Dental Management Partners, LLC** (dba Image Specialty Partners), a provider of business and administrative services to independent specialty dental care practices on the West Coast.

The company also directly invests its capital outside of its private equity funds. Direct investments include interests in **Ryan Specialty Group Holdings, Inc.**, an international specialty insurance company with a wholesale brokerage firm and an underwriting management organization; and **Unanet, Inc.**, a provider of enterprise resource planning (ERP) and customer relationship management (CRM) solutions for government contractors and architecture, engineering and construction firms.

Credit - Through Onex Credit, raises and invests capital across private credit, liquid credit and public equity strategies. At Mar. 31, 2023, the company had US$26.6 billion of AUM, including US$24.3 billion of fee-generating AUM and US$742,000,000 from the company's own investing capital.

Also holds an investment in Flushing Town Center, a 3,000,000-sq.-ft. retail and residential development located on approximately 14 acres in Flushing, N.Y.

On May 25, 2023, the company completed a secondary offering of 8,200,000 class A common shares of **Ryan Specialty Group Holdings, Inc.**, for gross proceeds of US$355,000,000. The company continues to hold 4,100,000 class A common shares of Ryan.

In May 2023, shareholders approved a sunset clause whereby Gerald Schwartz would resign as chief executive officer of the company and all 100,000 multiple voting shares held by Mr. Schwartz would be redeemed at Cdn$1.00 per share on May 11, 2026, the third anniversary of his resignation. The multiple voting shares entitle him to 60% of aggregate votes attached to all shares of the company and to elect 60% of the board of directors.

On Mar. 24, 2023, the company announced an agreement to transfer its Gluskin Sheff private wealth management teams to **Royal Bank of Canada**'s Wealth Management division (RBC Wealth Management) and wind down its wealth management and wealth planning operations not transferred to RBC Wealth Management. All advisor team employees of Gluskin Sheff would be offered employment with RBC Wealth Management.

Recent Merger and Acquisition Activity

Status: completed **Revised:** Aug. 4, 2023
UPDATE:The offering was completed for net proceeds of US$133,000,000. On closing, Onex no longer held any shares in Celestica. PREVIOUS: Onex Corporation announced a secondary offering of 6,757,198 subordinate voting shares (SVS) of Celestica Inc., substantially all of which would be issued upon conversion of a corresponding number of Celestica's multiple voting shares into SVS.

Status: completed **Revised:** June 8, 2023
UPDATE: The transaction was completed. PREVIOUS: Onex Corporation announced a secondary offering of 12,000,000 subordinate voting shares (SVS) of Celestica Inc. at US$12.40 per share for gross proceeds of US$148,800,000. Of the SVS to be sold, 11,800,000 SVS would be issued upon conversion of a corresponding number of Celestica's multiple voting shares into SVS. Onex holds about 18,600,000 Celestica MVS, representing a 15% equity interest and an 82% voting interest. The offering was expected to close on June 8, 2023.

Status: completed **Announced:** Dec. 31, 2022
Onex Corporation invested US$99,000,000 in Virginia-based Unanet, Inc., a developer and marketer of project-based enterprise resource planning (ERP) and customer relationship management (CRM) solutions for government contractors, architecture, engineering, construction and professional services.

Status: completed **Announced:** Aug. 31, 2022
Onex Corporation, through affiliates Onex Partners IV LP and Onex Partners V LP, sold Netherlands-based Partou Holding B.V., a provider of childcare services in the Netherlands. Onex' share of the net proceeds was US$154,000,000, including carried interest of US$13,000,000 and net of management incentive programs. Onex held a 20% economic interest and 72% voting interest in Partou.

Status: completed **Revised:** Aug. 31, 2022
UPDATE: The transaction was completed. Onex' share of the sale proceeds was US$103,000,000. PREVIOUS: A private equity fund managed by Los Angeles, Calif.-based Ares Management Corporation agreed to acquire a significant minority interest in Ryan, LLC from Ryan's management team and Onex Corporation's affiliate, Onex Partners IV LP, which would retain a minority interest in Ryan. Dallas, Tex.-based Ryan provides global tax services and software. Terms were not disclosed.

Status: completed **Revised:** Aug. 31, 2022
UPDATE: The transaction was completed. Onex' share of the sale proceeds was US$36,000,000 and Onex' economic interest in AIT was reduced to 9%. PREVIOUS: Qatar Investment Authority (QIA), the sovereign wealth fund of the State of Qatar, through its affiliates, agreed to acquire a minority interest in Advanced Integration Technology LP (AIT) through a combination of primary capital and partial sales from AIT's two existing shareholders, AIT's founding management team and Onex Partners IV LP. Onex Corporation, through affiliate Onex Partners IV, owns a 13% economic interest in AIT. On closing, QIA, AIT's founding management team and Onex Partners IV would assume minority joint ownership of AIT. Terms were not disclosed. Plano, Tex.-based AIT provides automation, factory integration and tooling solutions for the global aerospace, defence and space launch vehicle industries, as well as new manufacturing solutions for commercial urban air mobility markets.

Status: completed **Announced:** July 5, 2022
Onex Corporation, through its middle-market private equity platform ONCAP, acquired a majority interest in West Sacramento, Calif.-based Ideal Dental Management Partners, LLC, a specialty dental service organization focused on providing business and administrative services to specialty dental service providers on the West Coast. Ideal Dental partners with and supports independent specialty dental care practices which provide orthodontic, pedodontics, oral surgery and other therapeutic services. Onex invested US$28,000,000 as part of ONCAP's investment.

Status: completed **Revised:** Apr. 30, 2022
UPDATE: The transaction was completed. Onex invested US$108,000,000 as part of Onex Partners V's investment. PREVIOUS: Onex Corporation, through affiliate Onex Partners V LP, agreed to invest in Miami, Fla.-based Analytic Partners, Inc., a consulting firm specializing in marketing data analytics. Analytic Partners utilizes a proprietary cloud-based software platform which delivers comprehensive end-to-end data integration, multi-dimensional modelling and insights. Terms were not disclosed.

Status: completed **Revised:** Mar. 31, 2022
UPDATE: The transaction was completed. Onex invested US$117,000,000 as part of Onex Partners V's investment. PREVIOUS: Onex Corporation, through affiliate Onex Partners V LP, agreed to invest in Bellaire, Tex.-based Resource Environmental Solutions, LLC (RES), an ecological restoration firm which designs, builds, maintains and sustains sites that preserve the environmental balance. RES serves public and private sector clients with solutions for environmental mitigation, stormwater, water quality, and climate and flooding resilience. Terms were not disclosed.

Directors - Gerald W. (Gerry) Schwartz, founder & chr., Toronto, Ont.; Ewout R. Heersink, v-chr., Oakville, Ont.; Robert M. (Bobby) Le Blanc, pres., CEO & head, Onex Partners LP, Newtown, Conn.; J. Robert S. Prichard†, Toronto, Ont.; Lisa Carnoy, New York, N.Y.; Mitchell (Mitch) Goldhar, Toronto, Ont.; The Hon. Sarabjit S. (Sabi) Marwah, Toronto, Ont.; John B. McCoy, Columbus, Ohio; Heather M. Reisman, Toronto, Ont.; Arni C. Thorsteinson, Winnipeg, Man.; Beth A. Wilkinson, Washington, D.C.

Other Exec. Officers - Anthony Munk, v-chr.; Christopher A. (Chris) Govan, sr. man. dir & CFO; Justin Ashley, man. dir., fin., wealth mgt.; Jamie Chamberland, man. dir., fin.; David W. Copeland, man. dir., fin.; Judy E. Cotte, man. dir. & head, ESG; Andrea E. Daly, man. dir., gen. counsel & corp. sec.; Yonah Feder, man. dir. & chief compliance officer; Terry Hickey, man. dir., tech., corp. srvcs. & innovation; Jill Homenuk, man. dir., shareholder rel. & commun.; Heather Hrousalas, man. dir., talent mgt.; John Mack, man. dir. & head, fund opers.; Derek Mackay, man. dir., fin.; David (Dave) Kelly, head, Gluskin Sheff + Associates Inc.; Robert Auld, v-p, tax.; Mahesh Bhaskara, v-p, invest. tech.; Joanne Coles, v-p, IT; Priya Gnanabhaskar, v-p, corp. tech.; Ivan Jovcevski, v-p, fin.; Ani Kirakosyan, v-p, fin.; Zev Korman, v-p, shareholder rel. & commun.; Janet Lumb, v-p, special projects; Marty Mailloux, v-p, fin.; Gord McCullough, v-p, talent mgt.; Matt Murphy, v-p, legal; Muhammad Niazi, v-p, fin.; Andrea Niles-Day, v-p, project mgt.; Kevin Northrup, v-p & head, data & analytics; Colin Sam, v-p & assoc. gen. counsel; Dan Shearholdt, v-p, fin.; Tim Traill, v-p & head, wealth tech.; Alan Tsang, v-p, internal audit; Sarah Veitch, v-p, fin.; James Willey, v-p, fin.

† Lead director

Capital Stock

	Authorized (shs.)	Outstanding (shs.)[1]
Senior Preferred	unlimited	nil
Junior Preferred	unlimited	nil
Multiple Voting	100,000	100,000
Subordinate Voting	unlimited	80,863,172

[1] At Apr. 30, 2023

Senior & Junior Preferred - Issuable in series.

Multiple Voting - Entitled, as a class, to 60% of aggregate votes attached to all shares of the company and to elect 60% of the board of directors. Should an event of change occur (such as Gerald W. Schwartz, chairman and chief executive officer, ceasing to hold, directly or indirectly, more than 5,000,000 subordinate voting shares), the multiple voting shares would be entitled to elect only 20% of the directors and cease to have any general voting rights, and the subordinate voting shares would then carry 100% of the general voting rights and be entitled to elect 80% of the directors. The multiple voting shares have no entitlement to a distribution on winding-up or dissolution other than the payment of their nominal paid-up value. Not entitled to receive dividends.

Subordinate Voting - Entitled, as a class, to 40% of aggregate votes attached to all shares of the company, to elect 40% of the board of directors and to appoint auditors. The subordinate voting shares are entitled, subject to the prior rights of other classes, to distributions of the residual assets on winding-up and to any declared but unpaid cash dividends. Entitled to receive cash dividends, dividends in kind and stock dividends as and when declared by the board of directors.

Options - At Dec. 31, 2022, options were outstanding to purchase 7,584,295 subordinate voting shares at prices ranging from Cdn$56.92 to Cdn$101.62 per share with a remaining contractual life of up to 6.5 years.

Normal Course Issuer Bid - The company plans to make normal course purchases of up to 6,644,936 subordinate voting shares representing 10% of the public float. The bid commenced on Apr. 18, 2023, and expires on Apr. 17, 2024.

Major Shareholder - Gerald W. (Gerry) Schwartz held 65% interest at Mar. 27, 2023.

Price Range - ONEX/TSX

Year	Volume	High	Low	Close
2022	38,947,889	$101.61	$61.33	$65.29
2021	33,052,886	$100.90	$67.57	$99.28
2020	62,221,966	$89.92	$37.00	$73.06
2019	37,031,577	$84.28	$72.17	$82.17
2018	34,753,591	$99.82	$71.28	$74.35

Recent Close: $81.80

Capital Stock Changes - During 2022, 42,473 subordinate voting shares were issued on exercise of options and 6,039,668 subordinate voting shares were repurchased under a Normal Course Issuer Bid.

Dividends

ONEX com S.V. Ra $0.40 pa Q est. July 31, 2019**
** Reinvestment Option

Long-Term Debt - At Dec. 31, 2022, the company had no debt.

Wholly Owned Subsidiaries

Gluskin Sheff + Associates Inc., Toronto, Ont.
Onex CLO Holdings LLC, United States.
Onex Credit Holdings LLC, United States.
Onex Private Equity Holdings LLC, United States.

Subsidiaries

88% int. in **Onex Real Estate Holdings Inc.** Holds 100% voting interest.

Investments

16% int. in **ASM Global Parent, Inc.**, Los Angeles, Calif. Holds 50% voting interest.
19% int. in **Acacium Group Limited**, London, Middx., United Kingdom. Holds 79% voting interest.
9% int. in **Advanced Integration Technology LP**, Plano, Tex. Holds 37% voting interest.
15% int. in **Analytic Partners, Inc.**, Miami, Fla. Holds 54% voting interest.
9% int. in **BBAM Limited Partnership**, United States.
Clarivate Plc, London, Middx., United Kingdom.
13% int. in **Convex Group Limited**, London, Middx., United Kingdom. Holds 96% voting interest.
12% int. in **Digital Insurance, LLC**, Atlanta, Ga. Holds 53% voting interest.
23% int. in **Emerald Holding, Inc.**, San Juan Capistrano, Calif. Holds 87% voting interest.
23% int. in **Fidelity Engineering, LLC**, Sparks, Md. Holds 82% voting interest.
10% int. in **Imagine Learning LLC**, Scottsdale, Ariz. Holds 40% voting interest.
25% int. in **Meridian Aviation Partners Limited**, Ireland. Holds 100% voting interest.
23% int. in **Monroe Operations, LLC**, Nashville, Tenn. Holds 92% voting interest.
47% int. in **ONCAP II L.P.**, Toronto, Ont. Holds 100% voting interest.
29% int. in **ONCAP III LP**, Toronto, Ont. Holds 100% voting interest.
39% int. in **ONCAP IV LP**, Toronto, Ont. Holds 100% voting interest.
22% int. in **Onex Partners III LP**, New York, N.Y.
22% int. in **Onex Partners IV LP**, New York, N.Y.
Onex Partners V LP, New York, N.Y.
27% int. in **Parkdean Resorts UK Limited**, Northumbs., United Kingdom. Holds 100% voting interest.
12% int. in **PowerSchool Group LLC**, Folsom, Calif. Holds 38% voting interest.
20% int. in **Resource Environmental Solutions, LLC**, Bellaire, Tex. Holds 76% voting interest.
10% int. in **Ryan, LLC**, Dallas, Tex.
Ryan Specialty Holdings, Inc., Chicago, Ill.
26% int. in **Tes Global Limited**, London, Middx., United Kingdom. Holds 95% voting interest.
Unanet, Inc., Va.
11% int. in **Wealth Enhancement Group, LLC**, Plymouth, Minn. Holds 37% voting interest.
20% int. in **WestJet Airlines Ltd.**, Calgary, Alta. Holds 76% voting interest.
21% int. in **WireCo WorldGroup Inc.**, Prairie Village, Kan. Holds 67% voting interest.

Note: The preceding list includes only the major related companies in which interests are held.

Financial Statistics

Periods ended:	12m Dec. 31/22^A		12m Dec. 31/21^A
	US$000s	%Chg	US$000s
Unrealized invest. gain (loss)	130,000		1,698,000
Total revenue	**442,000**	**-78**	**2,034,000**
Salaries & benefits	239,000		248,000
Stock-based compensation	(222,000)		205,000
Other operating expense	103,000		101,000
Operating expense	**120,000**	**-78**	**554,000**
Operating income	**322,000**	**-78**	**1,480,000**
Deprec. & amort.	66,000		59,000
Finance costs, gross	2,000		2,000
Pre-tax income	**234,000**	**-83**	**1,404,000**
Income taxes	(1,000)		(1,000)
Net inc bef disc ops, eqhldrs	235,000		1,405,000
Net income	**235,000**	**-83**	**1,405,000**
Cash & equivalent	111,000		547,000
Accounts receivable	544,000		369,000
Investments	10,927,000		11,284,000
Fixed assets, net	140,000		148,000
Intangibles, net	350,000		403,000
Total assets	**12,163,000**	**-6**	**12,887,000**
Accts. pay. & accr. liabs.	28,000		25,000
Lease liabilities	70,000		71,000
Shareholders' equity	8,250,000		8,374,000
Cash from oper. activs	**(384,000)**	**n.a.**	**361,000**
Cash from fin. activs	(282,000)		(465,000)
Cash from invest. activs	234,000		(55,000)
Net cash position	**111,000**	**-80**	**547,000**
Capital expenditures	(8,000)		nil
Capital disposals	4,000		nil
	US$		US$
Earnings per share*	2.77		15.79
Cash flow per share*	(4.52)		4.06
Cash divd. per share*	$0.40		$0.40
	shs		shs
No. of shs. o/s*	80,908,343		86,905,538
Avg. no. of shs. o/s*	85,000,000		89,000,000
	%		%
Net profit margin	53.17		69.08
Return on equity	2.83		17.99
Return on assets	1.89		11.37
Foreign sales percent	76		70
No. of employees (FTEs)	597		536

* Subord. vtg.
^A Reported in accordance with IFRS

Latest Results

Periods ended:	3m Mar. 31/23^A		3m Mar. 31/22^A
	US$000s	%Chg	US$000s
Total revenue	60,000	-62	158,000
Net income	(232,000)	n.a.	164,000
	US$		US$
Earnings per share*	(2.87)		1.90

* Subord. vtg.
^A Reported in accordance with IFRS

Historical Summary
(as originally stated)

Fiscal Year	Total Rev.	Net Inc. Bef. Disc.	EPS*
	US$000s	US$000s	US$
2022^A	442,000	235,000	2.77
2021^A	2,034,000	1,405,000	15.79
2020^A	1,141,000	730,000	7.64
2019^A	1,105,000	4,277,000	42.78
2018^A	24,323,000	(846,000)	(7.05)

* Subord. vtg.
^A Reported in accordance with IFRS

O.19 Ontario Power Generation Inc.

CUSIP - 68321Z
Head Office - 700 University Ave, Toronto, ON, M5G 1X6 **Telephone** - (416) 592-4008 **Toll-free** - (877) 592-4008 **Fax** - (416) 592-2178
Website - www.opg.com
Email - investor.relations@opg.com
Investor Relations - Investor Relations (877) 592-4008
Auditors - Ernst & Young LLP C.A., Toronto, Ont.
FP500 Revenue Ranking - 88
Employees - 9,565 at Dec. 31, 2022
Profile - (Ont. 1998) Generates and markets electricity to customers in the Ontario wholesale market and in the interconnected markets of Quebec, Manitoba and the northeastern and midwestern United States.

Operations are carried out through five segments:

The **Regulated - Nuclear Generation** business segment operates in Ontario, generating and selling electricity from the Darlington and Pickering nuclear generating stations, both owned and operated by the company. Also includes revenue under the terms of a long-term lease arrangement and related non-lease agreements with **Bruce Power Limited Partnership** related to the Bruce nuclear generating stations.

The **Regulated - Nuclear Sustainability Services** business segment consists of the management of used nuclear fuel and low and intermediate level waste (L&ILW), the decommissioning of the company's nuclear generating stations (including the stations leased to Bruce Power) and nuclear waste facilities, the management of the Nuclear Segregated Funds and related activities including the inspection and maintenance of the used nuclear fuel and L&ILW storage facilities.

The **Regulated - Hydroelectric Generation** business segment operates in Ontario, generating and selling electricity from most of the company's hydroelectric generating stations, and consists of 54 regulated hydroelectric generating stations located across a number of major river systems in the province.

The **Contracted Hydroelectric and Other Generation** business segment operates in Ontario and in the U.S., generating and selling electricity from the company's non-regulated generating stations. Primarily includes generating facilities that operate under energy supply agreements (ESAs) with the Independent Electricity System Operator (IESO) or other long-term contracts.

The **Atura Power** business segment operates in Ontario, generating and selling electricity from the company's four combined-cycle natural gas-fired generating stations, Napanee, Halton Hills, Portlands Energy Centre and Brighton Beach. All of the generating facilities operate under ESAs with the IESO or other long-term contracts.

At Mar. 31, 2023, the company owned and operated 75 generating stations in Ontario (66 hydroelectric, four combined-cycle natural gas-fired, two nuclear, two thermal and one solar). Through wholly owned U.S. subsidiaries, also wholly or jointly owned and operated 85 hydroelectric generating stations and held minority shareholdings in 14 hydroelectric and two solar facilities in the U.S. Also owns two nuclear generating stations which are leased on a long-term basis to Bruce Power. The company does not operate the Bruce nuclear generating stations and the minority-held facilities in the U.S.

In December 2022, the company announced plans to sell 22 hydroelectric generating stations with total capacity of approximately 47-MW, as well as two storage reservoirs in the U.S. The transaction was expected to close in the first half of 2023. Terms were not disclosed.

During 2022, the company completed the construction of two 115-MW generating units at its Sir Adam Beck I hydroelectric generating station which would replace its existing units. The budget for the projected was $128,000,000.

Periods ended:	12m Dec. 31/22	12m Dec. 31/21
Generating capacity, MW	18,225	18,958
Electric gen., GWh	78,500	77,600

Recent Merger and Acquisition Activity

Status: pending **Announced:** Feb. 13, 2023
Ontario Power Generation Inc. agreed to acquire the former General Motors (GM) of Canada head office building at 1908 Colonel Sam Drive in Oshawa, Ont., for an undisclosed amount. The building would serve as GM Canada's new corporate headquarters, with the 285,000-sq.-ft. office and amenity space to be retrofitted prior to occupancy in late 2024.

Status: completed **Announced:** Nov. 3, 2022
Ontario Power Generation Inc., through wholly owned OPG Eagle Creek Holdings LLC, acquired a 13.3-MW hydroelectric facility in Seattle, Wash. for an undisclosed amount. The facility is operated by Eagle Creek.

Status: completed **Announced:** Oct. 31, 2022
Ontario Power Generation Inc. sold its non-core premises at 800 Kipling Avenue in Etobicoke, Ont., to the City of Toronto and Kinectrics Inc. for $200,000,000. The Kipling site spanned 76 acres and included 750,000 sq. ft. of buildings, which housed offices, records storage and training spaces. The City of Toronto would utilize the southern parcel for the Toronto Transit Commission's (TTC's) future electric bus facility, and would also take ownership of lands to the north of Kinectrics' parcel for future City services. Kinectrics would continue to operate and grow its business at the site.

Status: terminated **Revised:** Mar. 31, 2022
UPDATE: The transaction was terminated following the Province of Ontario's decision to stop the sale, citing the municipality did not follow procedures through its newly proposed Centre of Realty Excellence (CORE) program. OPG was 100% owned by the Province of Ontario. UPDATE: The Municipality of Port Hope agreed to acquire 1,334 acres of land in the Wesleyville area of Port Hope, Ont., from Ontario Power Generation Inc. (OPG) for $18,600,000. The property included 700 acres of environmentally important land that could be available for parks, recreation, green space, and the protection of significant natural and cultural features, including heritage sites; 634 acres that could potentially be developed, with options including residential, commercial and employment lands; and 260 acres of developed industrial land in which OPG's original intent was to develop a power generating station, and which OPG would lease to the municipality and sub-lease to the current industrial tenants for the first seven years of the municipality's ownership. The property also included more than 18 acres located along 4 km of protected Lake Ontario shoreline, which represented 20% of the entire waterfront of Port Hope.

Directors - Wendy W. T. Kei, chr., Toronto, Ont.; Kenneth M. (Ken) Hartwick, pres. & CEO, Milton, Ont.; Maria Filippelli, Toronto, Ont.; John Herron, Punta Gorda, Fla.; Selma M. Lussenburg, Toronto, Ont.; Scott G. McDonald, Toronto, Ont.; Jill Pepall, Toronto, Ont.; Tracy Primeau, Kincardine, Ont.; E. James (Jim) Reinsch, Frederick, Md.; James (Joe) Sheppard, League City, Tex.; Dr. Anju Virmani, Toronto, Ont.

Other Exec. Officers - Nicolle Butcher, COO; Karen Fritz, chief supply officer; Steve Gregoris, chief nuclear officer; Mel Hogg, CAO; David Kaposi, chief invest. officer; Mike Martelli, chief project officer; Carlton D. Mathias, chief legal, ESG & governance officer; Christopher F. (Chris)

Ginther, exec. v-p, bus. strategy & comml. mgt.; Aida Cipolla, sr. v-p, fin. & CFO; Heather Ferguson, sr. v-p, bus. devel. & corp. affairs; Kim Lauritsen, sr. v-p, enterprise strategy & energy markets; Subo Sinnathamby, sr. v-p, nuclear refurbishment; Dr. Neal Simmons, pres. & CEO, Eagle Creek Renewable Energy, LLC

Capital Stock

	Authorized (shs.)	Outstanding (shs.)[1]
Common	unlimited	256,300,010
Class A Non-vtg.	unlimited	18,343,815

[1] At Mar. 31, 2023

Common - One vote per share.

Class A Non-Voting - Ranks equally with the common shares with respect to the right to receive dividends and upon any distribution of the assets of the company. Non-voting.

Major Shareholder - Province of Ontario held 100% interest at Dec. 31, 2022.

Capital Stock Changes - There were no changes to capital stock from 2019 to 2022, inclusive.

Wholly Owned Subsidiaries

Eagle Creek Renewable Energy, LLC, Morristown, N.J.

Subsidiaries

99.9% int. in **Brighton Beach Power L.P.**, Windsor, Ont.
50.2% int. in **Kennebec Water Power Company**, United States.
83% int. in **Little Falls Hydroelectric Associates, LP**, N.Y.
75% int. in **Lower Mattagami Limited Partnership**
80% int. in **Nanticoke Solar L.P.**, Ont.
67% int. in **PSS Generating Station LP**, Ont.

Investments

27.08% int. in **Benton Falls Associates**, United States.
11.25% int. in **Boltonville Hydro Associates**, United States.
24.19% int. in **Brassua TIC**, United States.
27.08% int. in **Briar Hydro Associates**, United States.
0.1% int. in **Brighton Beach Power Ltd.**, Windsor, Ont.
• 100% int. in **Brighton Beach Power L.P.**, Windsor, Ont.
26.94% int. in **Concord Hydro Associates**, United States.
26.8% int. in **Dodge Falls Associates, L.P.**, United States.
26.94% int. in **HCE-Dodge Falls, Inc.**, United States.
33% int. in **HMG, LLC**, United States.
26.8% int. in **Mesalonskee Stream Hydro, LLC**, United States.
27.08% int. in **New Hampshire Hydro Associates**, United States.
26.8% int. in **North Hartland, LLC**, United States.
50% int. in **Ontario Charging Network L.P.**, Ont.
0.05% int. in **Portlands Energy Centre Inc.**, Ont.
• 100% int. in **Portlands Energy Centre L.P.**, Ont.
49.95% int. in **Portlands Energy Centre L.P.**, Ont.
50% int. in **South Fork II Associates, LP**, United States.

Financial Statistics

Periods ended:	12m Dec. 31/22[A]		12m Dec. 31/21[A]
	$000s	%Chg	$000s
Operating revenue	**7,349,000**	**+7**	**6,877,000**
Other operating expense	4,083,000		3,811,000
Operating expense	**4,083,000**	**+7**	**3,811,000**
Operating income	**3,266,000**	**+7**	**3,066,000**
Deprec., depl. & amort.	1,124,000		1,132,000
Finance income	1,095,000		1,006,000
Finance costs, gross	240,000		272,000
Investment income	nil		1,000
Pre-tax income	**1,994,000**	**+26**	**1,583,000**
Income taxes	343,000		239,000
Net income	**1,651,000**	**+23**	**1,344,000**
Net inc. for equity hldrs.	**1,636,000**	**+23**	**1,325,000**
Net inc. for non-cont. int.	**15,000**	**-21**	**19,000**
Cash & equivalent	1,595,000		698,000
Inventories	358,000		350,000
Accounts receivable	484,000		558,000
Current assets	3,552,000		2,462,000
Long-term investments	2,070,600		19,849,000
Fixed assets, net	31,767,000		30,327,000
Intangibles, net	666,000		637,000
Total assets	**62,343,000**	**+2**	**61,153,000**
Bank indebtedness	65,000		182,000
Accts. pay. & accr. liabs.	1,772,000		1,441,000
Current liabilities	2,095,000		2,078,000
Long-term debt, gross	10,152,000		9,666,000
Long-term debt, net	10,109,000		9,487,000
Shareholders' equity	18,813,000		16,789,000
Non-controlling interest	176,000		178,000
Cash from oper. activs.	**2,997,000**	**+23**	**2,440,000**
Cash from fin. activs.	322,000		(546,000)
Cash from invest. activs.	(2,426,000)		(1,917,000)
Net cash position	**1,595,000**	**+129**	**698,000**
Capital disposals	162,000		nil
Unfunded pension liability	n.a.		2,459,000
Pension fund surplus	742,000		n.a.
	$		$
Earnings per share*	5.96		4.83
Cash flow per share*	10.91		8.88
	shs		shs
No. of shs. o/s*	274,643,825		274,643,825
Avg. no. of shs. o/s*	274,643,825		274,643,825
	%		%
Net profit margin	22.47		19.54
Return on equity	9.19		8.24
Return on assets	3.00		2.56
No. of employees (FTEs)	9,565		9,325

* Common
[A] Reported in accordance with U.S. GAAP

Latest Results

Periods ended:	3m Mar. 31/23[A]		3m Mar. 31/22[A]
	$000s	%Chg	$000s
Operating revenue	1,830,000	-7	1,958,000
Net income	433,000	-15	507,000
Net inc. for equity hldrs.	429,000	-15	503,000
Net inc. for non-cont. int.	4,000		4,000
	$		$
Earnings per share*	1.56		1.83

* Common
[A] Reported in accordance with U.S. GAAP

Historical Summary
(as originally stated)

Fiscal Year	Oper. Rev.	Net Inc. Bef. Disc.	EPS*
	$000s	$000s	$
2022[A]	7,349,000	1,651,000	5.96
2021[A]	6,877,000	1,344,000	4.83
2020[A]	7,240,000	1,376,000	4.96
2019[A]	6,022,000	1,143,000	4.10
2018[A]	5,537,000	1,213,000	4.37

* Common
[A] Reported in accordance with U.S. GAAP

0.20 Open Text Corporation*

Symbol - OTEX **Exchange** - TSX **CUSIP** - 683715
Head Office - 275 Frank Tompa Dr, Waterloo, ON, N2L 0A1 **Telephone** - (519) 888-7111 **Toll-free** - (800) 499-6544 **Fax** - (519) 888-0677
Website - www.opentext.com
Email - macedo@opentext.com
Investor Relations - Michael F. Acedo (905) 762-6001
Auditors - KPMG LLP C.A., Toronto, Ont.
Lawyers - Cleary Gottlieb Steen & Hamilton LLP, New York, N.Y.; Blake, Cassels & Graydon LLP, Toronto, Ont.
Transfer Agents - Computershare Trust Company of Canada Inc., Toronto, Ont.
FP500 Revenue Ranking - 131
Employees - 24,100 at June 30, 2023

Profile - (Can. 2005; orig. Ont., 1991) Designs, develops, markets, licenses and supports information management software products and services for businesses, governments and consumers worldwide.

Information management solutions manage the creation, capture, use, analysis and lifecycle of structured and unstructured data, and are deployed in private and public clouds, on-premise (off-cloud), in an application programming interface (API) cloud or in a hybrid and multi-cloud environment. Solutions are also available through professional and managed services in which the company provides full advisory, implementation, migration, operation and support services for clients. Portfolio of solutions are grouped into six business clouds: Content Cloud, Cybersecurity Cloud, Business Network Cloud, Information Technology (IT) Operations Management Cloud, Analytics and Artificial Intelligence (AI) Cloud, and Application Automation Cloud.

Content Cloud manages the lifecycle, distribution, use and analysis of information across the organization, from capture through archiving and disposition. Solutions include content collaboration, intelligent capture (capture of data from paper, electronic files and other sources and transforming it into digital content), records management, e-signatures and archiving. Solutions allow integration with other third party enterprise software systems and applications, and support a wide range of operating systems, databases, application servers and applications. Content Cloud also includes Experience Cloud, which offers customer experience solutions to deliver personalized content and engagements at every point of customer interaction. Experience Cloud solutions create, manage, track and optimize omnichannel customer interactions and include customer experience management, web content management, digital asset management, customer analytics, AI and insights, eDiscovery, digital fax, omnichannel communications, secure messaging, voice of customer, and customer journey, testing and segmentation.

Cybersecurity Cloud provides multiple layers of security solutions to protect, prevent, detect, respond and recover from threats across endpoints, network, applications, IT infrastructure and data. Products include Carbonite, Webroot, Zix and BrightCloud.

Business Network Cloud provides integration solutions for supply chain and global commerce operations that connect external business systems, including customers, suppliers, partners, third party data sources and devices, to internal business systems. Core product is Trading Grid, a unified integration platform which enables digital communication between trading partners, digitalization and automation of processes such as procure-to-pay and order-to-cash, integration with enterprise applications and real-time visibility of business processes and trading partner relationships.

IT Operations Management Cloud provides a holistic management of IT assets and applications across all types of infrastructure and environments. Solutions include IT service management for IT support and asset management, AI operations management including network operations management and connected data management and observability, server and network automation, and cloud management.

Analytics and AI Cloud enables organizations to process data of all types from anywhere and transform data into insights for predictive process automation and accelerated decision-making. Solutions feature capabilities such as data analytics, including text mining, natural language processing and machine learning, insights, unstructured data types and visualization which can be consumed as a full stack analytics engine or as API components embedded in other custom OEM solutions.

Application Automation Cloud helps customers streamline processes and adapt to complex requirements for improved customer and employee applications. Solutions include low-code development tools, drag-and-drop components and reusable building blocks for easy application building and deployment; performance testing, functional testing and lifecycle management of applications; and transitioning workloads from mainframes and older infrastructures to the cloud.

In addition to the six business clouds, offers **Developers Cloud**, a single source of API, cloud services and software development kits (SDKs) from the six business cloud offerings that help developers build, extend and customize information management applications. Services can be applied to expand the company's existing implementations or integrated into an organization's custom solutions.

During the third quarter of fiscal 2022, 81%-owned **EC1 Pte. Ltd.** was liquidated.

Recent Merger and Acquisition Activity

Status: completed **Revised:** Jan. 31, 2023

UPDATE: The transaction was completed for US$5.8 billion. PREVIOUS: Open Text Corporation agreed to acquire LSE-listed Micro Focus International plc for £5.32 per share in cash implying an enterprise value of US$6 billion on a fully diluted basis. Micro Focus is one of the world's largest enterprise software companies and serves thousands of organizations globally and had US$2.7 billion pro forma trailing twelve months revenue for the period ended Apr. 30, 2022. Open Text would fund the acquisition with US$4.6 billion in new debt, US$1.3 billion in cash and a US$600,000,000 draw on its existing revolving credit facility. The transaction was expected to close in the first quarter of calendar 2023.

Directors - P. Thomas (Tom) Jenkins, chr., George Town, Cayman Islands; Mark J. Barrenechea, v-chr., CEO & chief tech. officer, Calif.; Randy Fowlie, Waterloo, Ont.; Maj.-Gen. (ret.) David A. Fraser, Toronto, Ont.; Gail E. Hamilton, Tex.; Robert (Bob) Hau, Wis.; Ann M. Powell, Pa.; Stephen J. Sadler, Ont.; Michael Slaunwhite, Gloucester, Ont.; Katharine B. (Kate) Stevenson, Toronto, Ont.; Deborah L. (Debbie) Weinstein, Ottawa, Ont.

Other Exec. Officers - Michael F. Acedo, exec. v-p, chief legal officer & corp. sec.; Prentiss Donohue, exec. v-p, cybersecurity sales; Paul Duggan, exec. v-p & chief cust. officer; Simon (Ted) Harrison, exec. v-p, enterprise sales; Muhi S. Majzoub, exec. v-p & chief product officer;

James McGourlay, exec. v-p, intl. sales; Renee McKenzie, exec. v-p, IT & CIO; Sandy Ono, exec. v-p & chief mktg. officer; Douglas M. (Doug) Parker, exec. v-p, corp. devel.; Madhu Ranganathan, exec. v-p & CFO; Paul Rodgers, exec. v-p, sales opers.; Brian Sweeney, exec. v-p & chief HR officer; Cosmin Balota, sr. v-p & chief acctg. officer

Capital Stock

	Authorized (shs.)	Outstanding (shs.)[1]
First Preference	unlimited	nil
Common	unlimited	271,195,369

[1] At Aug. 3, 2023

Options - At June 30, 2023, options were outstanding to purchase 12,219,439 common shares at a weighted average exercise price of US$38.44 per share with a weighted average remaining contractual life of 4.68 years.

Major Shareholder - Widely held at Aug. 3, 2023.

Price Range - OTEX/TSX

Year	Volume	High	Low	Close
2022	164,879,742	$61.35	$34.72	$40.12
2021	123,509,571	$69.79	$54.67	$60.04
2020	172,314,137	$64.00	$42.30	$57.84
2019	140,021,709	$59.13	$42.38	$57.22
2018	141,885,028	$51.98	$41.34	$44.50

Recent Close: $53.13

Capital Stock Changes - During fiscal 2023, common shares were issued as follows: 1,134,697 under the employee share purchase plan and 245,235 on exercise of options; 170,045 (net) common shares held in treasury were re-issued.

During fiscal 2022, common shares were issued as follows: 949,645 on exercise of options and 841,798 under the employee share purchase plan; 3,809,559 common shares were repurchased under a Normal Course Issuer Bid and 2,138,756 (net) common shares were repurchased and returned to treasury.

Dividends

OTEX com Ra US$1.00 pa Q est. Sept. 22, 2023
Prev. Rate: US$0.97196 est. Dec. 22, 2022
Prev. Rate: US$0.8836 est. Sept. 24, 2021
Prev. Rate: US$0.8032 est. Dec. 22, 2020

Long-Term Debt - Outstanding at June 30, 2023:

Revolv. credit facility due 2024[1]	US$275,000,000
Term loan due 2025[2]	947,500,000
First lien term loan due 2030[3]	3,567,075,000
6.9% sr. notes due 2027	1,000,000,000
3.875% sr. notes due 2028	900,000,000
3.875% sr. notes due 2029	850,000,000
4.125% sr. notes due 2030	900,000,000
4.125% sr. notes due 2031	650,000,000
Less: Discount & issue costs	206,629,000
	8,882,946,000
Less: Current portion	320,850,000
	8,562,096,000

[1] Bears interest at a rate equal to term SOFR plus SOFR adjustment and margin ranging from 1.25% to 1.75%.

[2] Bears interest at a rate equal to term SOFR plus SOFR adjustment and margin of 1.75%.

[3] Bears interest at a rate equal to term SOFR plus SOFR adjustment and margin of 3.5%.

Note - In August 2023, the applicable margin on the term loan due 2030 was reduced by 0.75% and, as such, borrowings under the term loan bear interest at a rate equal to term SOFR plus SOFR adjustment and margin of 2.75%.

Wholly Owned Subsidiaries

Acquisition U.K. Limited, United Kingdom.
AppRiver, LLC, Fla.
Arm Research Labs, LLC, Fla.
Attachmate Corporation, Wash.
Borland Software Corporation, Scotts Valley, Calif.
CM2.COM, Inc., Wash.
Carbonite, Inc., Boston, Mass.
Chameleon Holdings Ltd., Israel.
CloudAlly Ltd., Israel.
Covisint Software Services (Shanghai) Co., Ltd., Shanghai, Shanghai, People's Republic of China.
EasyLink Services International Limited, United Kingdom.
8493642 Canada Inc., Canada.
Full 360, Inc., New York, N.Y.
GWAVA ULC, Canada.
GXS, Inc., Del.
GreenView Data, Inc., Mich.
ICCM Professional Services Ltd., United Kingdom.
Mailstore Software GmbH, Germany.
Micro Focus International Limited, Newbury, Berks., United Kingdom.
NetIQ Corporation, Houston, Tex.
Novell Holdings, Inc., Del.
Nstein Technologies Inc., Montréal, Qué.
Open Text AB, Sweden.
Open Text AG, Switzerland.
Open Text A/S, Denmark.
Open Text (Asia) Pte. Ltd., Singapore.
Open Text Canada Ltd., Canada.
Open Text Coöperatief U.A., Netherlands.
Open Text Corporation India Private Limited, India.
Open Text Document Technologies GmbH, Germany.
Open Text Holdings, Inc., Del.
Open Text (Hong Kong) Limited, Hong Kong, Hong Kong, People's Republic of China.
Open Text Inc., Del.
Open Text Ireland Limited, Ireland.
Open Text KK, Japan.
Open Text Korea Co., Ltd., South Korea.
Open Text New Zealand Limited, New Zealand.
Open Text Oy, Finland.
Open Text (Philippines), Inc., Makati City, Philippines.
Open Text Pty Limited, Australia.
Open Text Public Sector Solutions, Inc., Va.
Open Text S. de R.L. de C.V., Mexico.
Open Text SA ULC, N.S.
Open Text S.A.R.L., France.
Open Text Saudi Arabia LLC, Saudi Arabia.
Open Text Software Austria GmbH, Austria.
Open Text Software GmbH, Germany. Formerly Gauss Interprise AG
Open Text Software, S.L.U., Spain.
Open Text Software Technology (Malaysia) Sdn. Bhd., Malaysia.
Open Text Software Technology (Shanghai) Co., Ltd., People's Republic of China.
Open Text Sp.zo.o, Poland.
Open Text S.r.l., Italy.
Open Text s.r.o., Czech Republic.
Open Text Technologia Da Informação (Brasil) Ltda., Brazil.
Open Text Technologies India Private Limited, India.
Open Text UK Limited, United Kingdom.
Open Text ULC, N.S.
Open Text Unterstützungskasse e.V., Germany.
Open Text Venture Capital Investment Limited Partnership, Ont.
RecomMind GmbH, Germany.
Resonate KT Limited, United Kingdom.
Serena Software, Inc., Calif.
Sysgenics Limited, United Kingdom.
3304709 Nova Scotia Limited, N.S.
Total Defense, LLC, Del.
Vertica Systems, LLC, Burlington, Mass.
Vignette India Private Ltd., India.
Vignette Partnership, LP, Del.
Webroot Inc., Broomfield, Colo.
XMedius Solutions Inc., Montréal, Qué.
Zix Corporation, Dallas, Tex.

Subsidiaries

70% int. in **Open Text South Africa (Pty) Ltd.**, South Africa.

Note: The preceding list includes only the major related companies in which interests are held.

Financial Statistics

Periods ended:	12m June 30/23[A]		12m June 30/22[A]
	US$000s	%Chg	US$000s
Operating revenue	**4,484,980**	**+28**	**3,493,844**
Cost of sales	1,093,403		863,594
Research & devel. expense	680,587		440,448
General & admin expense	1,368,188		994,203
Operating expense	**3,142,178**	**+37**	**2,298,245**
Operating income	**1,342,802**	**+12**	**1,195,599**
Deprec., depl. & amort.	657,351		503,953
Finance income	53,486		4,637
Finance costs, gross	382,914		162,517
Investment income	(23,077)		58,702
Pre-tax income	**221,333**	**-57**	**516,011**
Income taxes	70,767		118,752
Net income	**150,566**	**-62**	**397,259**
Net inc. for equity hldrs	**150,379**	**-62**	**397,090**
Net inc. for non-cont. int.	**187**	**+11**	**169**
Cash & equivalent	1,231,625		1,693,741
Accounts receivable	682,517		426,652
Current assets	2,275,231		2,285,367
Long-term investments	187,832		173,205
Fixed assets, net	356,904		244,709
Right-of-use assets	285,723		198,132
Intangibles, net	12,743,482		6,319,861
Total assets	**17,089,200**	**+68**	**10,178,973**
Accts. pay. & accr. liabs	996,261		448,607
Current liabilities	3,219,614		1,468,258
Long-term debt, gross	8,882,946		4,219,567
Long-term debt, net	8,562,096		4,209,567
Long-term lease liabilities	271,579		198,695
Shareholders' equity	4,020,775		4,031,118
Non-controlling interest	1,329		1,142
Cash from oper. activs	**779,205**	**-21**	**981,810**
Cash from fin. activs	4,403,053		138,456
Cash from invest. activs	(5,651,420)		(970,959)
Net cash position	**1,233,952**	**-27**	**1,695,911**
Capital expenditures	(123,832)		(93,109)
Unfunded pension liability	130,816		63,480
	US$		US$
Earnings per share*	0.56		1.46
Cash flow per share*	2.88		3.62
Cash divd. per share*	0.97		0.88
	shs		shs
No. of shs. o/s*	267,366,196		265,816,219
Avg. no. of shs. o/s*	270,299,000		271,271,000
	%		%
Net profit margin	3.36		11.37
Return on equity	3.74		9.77
Return on assets	3.01		5.28
Foreign sales percent	96		95
No. of employees (FTEs)	24,100		14,800

* Common
[A] Reported in accordance with U.S. GAAP

Historical Summary
(as originally stated)

Fiscal Year	Oper. Rev. US$000s	Net Inc. Bef. Disc. US$000s	EPS* US$
2023[A]	4,484,980	150,566	0.56
2022[A]	3,493,844	397,259	1.46
2021[A]	3,386,115	310,864	1.14
2020[A]	3,109,736	234,368	0.86
2019[A]	2,868,755	285,637	1.06

* Common
[A] Reported in accordance with U.S. GAAP

0.21 Opensesame Acquisition Corp.

Symbol - OPEN.P **Exchange** - TSX-VEN **CUSIP** - 68372X
Head Office - 2500-700 Georgia St W, Vancouver, BC, V7Y 1B3 **Telephone** - (604) 671-0918
Email - scottkelly.ca@gmail.com
Investor Relations - Scott S. Kelly (604) 671-0918
Auditors - Davidson & Company LLP C.A., Vancouver, B.C.
Transfer Agents - Computershare Trust Company of Canada Inc., Vancouver, B.C.
Profile - (B.C. 2021) Capital Pool Company.
Directors - Scott S. Kelly, pres., CEO, CFO & corp. sec., North Vancouver, B.C.; Stephen P. (Steve) Kenwood, White Rock, B.C.

Capital Stock

	Authorized (shs.)	Outstanding (shs.)[1]
Common	unlimited	5,500,000

[1] At Apr. 12, 2023

Major Shareholder - Ronald K. (Ron) Husband held 12.73% interest, Scott S. Kelly held 12.73% interest and Stephen P. (Steve) Kenwood held 10.91% interest at July 27, 2022.

Price Range - OPEN.P/TSX-VEN

Year	Volume	High	Low	Close
2022	126,120	$0.30	$0.10	$0.11

Recent Close: $0.06

Capital Stock Changes - On July 27, 2022, an initial public offering of 3,000,000 common shares was completed at 10¢ per share.

O.22 Opsens Inc.

Symbol - OPS **Exchange** - TSX **CUSIP** - 683823
Head Office - 750 boul du Parc-Technologique, Québec, QC, G1P 4S3 **Telephone** - (418) 781-0333 **Fax** - (418) 781-0024
Website - www.opsens.com
Email - louis.laflamme@opsens.com
Investor Relations - Louis Laflamme (418) 781-0333
Auditors - Deloitte LLP C.A., Québec, Qué.
Lawyers - Stein Monast LLP, Québec, Qué.
Transfer Agents - TSX Trust Company, Toronto, Ont.
Employees - 294 at Aug. 31, 2022
Profile - (Que. 2006 amalg.) Develops and sells medical devices for diagnosis and management of coronary artery disease worldwide. Also designs, manufactures and installs fibre optic sensor systems for critical and demanding industrial applications.

Operations are organized into two segments: Medical and Industrial.

The **Medical** segment includes the measurement of Fractional Flow Reserve (FFR) and Diastolic Pressure Ratio (dPR); and the sensor-guided transcatheter aortic valve replacement (TAVR) solution. The FFR measurement is recognized as the standard in the diagnosis of the severity of coronary lesions, which leads to better outcomes for patients. Products include OptoWire, a modern pressure guidewire designed to assess stenoses in vessels such as coronary artery, powered by Fidela™, a patented second generation fiber optic sensor to measure physiologic indices including FFR and dPR; OptoMonitor, which can be connected directly to the cath lab hemodynamic system to display FFR directly on the cath lab monitor; Diastolic Pressure Ratio, a proprietary resting index which is designed to measure intracoronary pressure without the injection of stimulant drugs to diagnose coronary heart disease, which is available via the OptoMonitor and works in combination with the OptoWire; SavvyWire, a product that is developed specifically for TAVR and the first guidewire intended to both deliver a valvular prosthesis while allowing continuous hemodynamic pressure measurement during the procedure; and XTender, a new generation guiding catheter extension that offers support and access during complicated intervention. Also provides proprietary sensing technology in the form of customizable microscale fiber optic sensors for pressure and temperature, which can be used in a wide range of applications and are designed to be integrated seamlessly into medical devices and life science research environments.

The **Industrial** segment produces fibre optic sensors for the aeronautics, geotechnical, infrastructures, nuclear, mining and military markets. Products include temperature, pressure, strain and displacement sensors; extensometer; and signal conditioners and OEM boards.

Predecessor Detail - Formed from DCB Capital Inc. in Quebec, Oct. 3, 2006, following Qualifying Transaction reverse takeover acquisition of and amalgamation with Opsens inc.

Directors - Alan Milinazzo, exec. chr., Mass.; Louis Laflamme, pres. & CEO, Qué.; Gaétan Duplain, pres., Opsens Solutions Inc., Beauport, Qué.; Lori Chmura, Cumming, Ga.; Denis Harrington, Minneapolis, Minn.; Jean Lavigueur, Québec, Qué.; James P. (Pat) Mackin, Kennesaw, Ga.; Denis M. Sirois, Québec, Qué.

Other Exec. Officers - John Hannigan, CFO

Capital Stock

	Authorized (shs.)	Outstanding (shs.)[1]
Common	unlimited	115,029,233

[1] At Jan. 11, 2023

Major Shareholder - Widely held at Dec. 2, 2022.

Price Range - OPS/TSX

Year	Volume	High	Low	Close
2022	28,320,528	$3.22	$1.55	$1.88
2021	41,668,833	$3.74	$1.28	$3.10
2020	11,680,719	$1.40	$0.39	$1.33
2019	7,629,214	$1.05	$0.73	$0.89
2018	11,796,489	$1.35	$0.62	$0.80

Recent Close: $2.01

Capital Stock Changes - In December 2022, bought deal public offering of 6,052,632 common shares was completed at $1.90 per share, including 789,474 common shares on exercise of over-allotment option.

During fiscal 2022, 1,678,000 common shares were issued on exercise of options.

Wholly Owned Subsidiaries

OpSens B.V., Netherlands.
OpSens Medical Inc.
Opsens Solutions Inc., Edmonton, Alta.

Financial Statistics

Periods ended:	12m Aug. 31/22[A]		12m Aug. 31/21[A]
	$000s	%Chg	$000s
Operating revenue	**35,324**	**+2**	**34,464**
Cost of sales	17,523		15,783
Research & devel. expense	8,358		5,510
General & admin expense	18,580		12,348
Operating expense	**44,461**	**+32**	**33,641**
Operating income	**(9,137)**	**n.a.**	**822**
Deprec., depl. & amort.	1,818		1,774
Finance income	272		110
Finance costs, gross	583		1,027
Pre-tax income	**(11,335)**	**n.a.**	**(1,129)**
Income taxes	44		21
Net income	**(11,378)**	**n.a.**	**(1,150)**
Cash & equivalent	23,816		38,563
Inventories	6,672		6,115
Accounts receivable	5,855		4,135
Current assets	39,016		49,783
Fixed assets, net	2,683		2,732
Right-of-use assets	5,026		4,322
Intangibles, net	1,786		1,677
Total assets	**48,511**	**-17**	**58,512**
Accts. pay. & accr. liabs.	7,300		3,843
Current liabilities	8,601		7,395
Long-term debt, gross	1,110		7,397
Long-term debt, net	640		4,595
Long-term lease liabilities	5,012		4,193
Shareholders' equity	34,259		42,330
Cash from oper. activs.	**(8,781)**	**n.a.**	**2,839**
Cash from fin. activs.	(5,011)		25,875
Cash from invest. activs.	(973)		(937)
Net cash position	**23,816**	**-38**	**38,563**
Capital expenditures	(858)		(747)
	$		$
Earnings per share*	(0.11)		(0.01)
Cash flow per share*	(0.08)		0.03
	shs		shs
No. of shs. o/s*	108,835,039		107,157,039
Avg. no. of shs. o/s*	108,219,362		98,806,987
	%		%
Net profit margin	(32.21)		(3.34)
Return on equity	(29.71)		(3.99)
Return on assets	(20.17)		(0.23)
Foreign sales percent	90		91
No. of employees (FTEs)	294		163

* Common
[A] Reported in accordance with IFRS

Latest Results

Periods ended:	3m Nov. 30/22[A]		3m Nov. 30/21[A]
	$000s	%Chg	$000s
Operating revenue	10,193	+26	8,096
Net income	(3,638)	n.a.	(2,089)
	$		$
Earnings per share*	(0.03)		(0.02)

* Common
[A] Reported in accordance with IFRS

Historical Summary
(as originally stated)

Fiscal Year	Oper. Rev.	Net Inc. Bef. Disc.	EPS*
	$000s	$000s	$
2022[A]	35,324	(11,378)	(0.11)
2021[A]	34,464	(1,150)	(0.01)
2020[A]	29,453	(2,644)	(0.03)
2019[A]	32,752	(1,952)	(0.02)
2018[A]	24,070	(4,549)	(0.05)

* Common
[A] Reported in accordance with IFRS

O.23 Optima Medical Innovations Corp.

Symbol - OMIC **Exchange** - CSE (S) **CUSIP** - 68405M
Head Office - 209-5460 Yonge St, Toronto, ON, M2N 6K7 **Telephone** - (416) 250-1812 **Fax** - (416) 250-8245
Website - optimamed.ca
Email - info@optimamed.ca
Investor Relations - Ali Sakhavati (647) 607-9044
Auditors - Zeifmans LLP C.A., Toronto, Ont.
Transfer Agents - Computershare Trust Company of Canada Inc., Vancouver, B.C.
Profile - (B.C. 2007) Provides healthcare services specializing in multi-disciplinary pain management, and researches, develops, processes and distributes products and treatments for pain relief, as well as other cannabidiol (CBD) products.

Provides healthcare services through multidisciplinary specialty pain clinics under the Toronto Poly Clinic (TPC) brand with a focus on the treatment of chronic pain, including controlled applications of medical cannabis in North York and Thornhill, Ont. Through TPC, the company has developed and implemented medical cannabis education, research and best practice platform (MCERP) and medical cannabis opioid reduction program (MCORP).

Also researches and develops innovative CBD products for a broad range of symptoms and overall wellness. In addition, the company is involved in various high-profile research projects and collaborations associated with cannabis, ranging from cannabis beer to natural health products as well as collaborates with universities, clinical sites, and cannabis producers to develop and manufacture novel cannabinoid-based products.

Common suspended from CSE, May 9, 2022.

Predecessor Detail - Name changed from Tree of Knowledge International Corp., Nov. 18, 2021; basis 1 new for 5 old shs.

Directors - Ali Sakhavati, interim CEO & CFO; Dr. Kaivan Talachian, Toronto, Ont.

Other Exec. Officers - Jessie Lin, contr.

Capital Stock

	Authorized (shs.)	Outstanding (shs.)[1]
Common	unlimited	47,500,131

[1] At Aug. 23, 2023

Major Shareholder - Dr. Kevin Rod held 11.33% interest at Aug. 13, 2021.

Price Range - CTD.H/TSX-VEN (D)

Year	Volume	High	Low	Close
2022	1,275,450	$0.06	$0.03	$0.05
2021	14,809,336	$0.24	$0.05	$0.06
2020	10,830,131	$0.28	$0.05	$0.05
2019	20,318,336	$1.60	$0.13	$0.18
2018	1,111,200	$7.65	$0.88	$1.05

Consolidation: 1-for-5 cons. in Nov. 2021

Wholly Owned Subsidiaries

Toronto Poly Clinic Inc., Toronto, Ont.
Tree of Knowledge Canada Inc., Ont.

O.24 Optimi Health Corp.

Symbol - OPTI **Exchange** - CSE **CUSIP** - 68405H
Head Office - 330-1122 Mainland St, Vancouver, BC, V6B 5L1 **Telephone** - (778) 930-1321
Website - www.optimihealth.ca
Email - leah@optimihealth.ca
Investor Relations - Leah Hodges (604) 377-0403
Auditors - Smythe LLP C.A., Vancouver, B.C.
Lawyers - Miller Thomson LLP, Vancouver, B.C.
Transfer Agents - Endeavor Trust Corporation, Vancouver, B.C.
Profile - (B.C. 2020) Cultivates, extracts, processes and distributes psilocybin, psilocyn and other psychedelic substances as well as functional mushrooms for health and wellness markets.

Has two 10,000-sq.-ft. facilities in Princeton, B.C., which is licensed by Health Canada to produce and supply natural GMP-grade psilocybin, psilocin, 3,4-methylenedioxy-methamphetamine (MDMA) and other psychedelic substances as well as functional mushrooms. Functional mushroom products are sold through the company's e-commerce website platform as well as to other health food brands and to distributors under the optimi™ brand. Products include supplements, stress reliever and vitamins.

Also was granted a research exemption license for Phase IIa and IIb clinical trials investigating the treatment of mental illnes, addictions and other mental health conditions through psilocybin, psilocin, MDMA and other psychedelic substances.

Directors - John J. (JJ) Wilson, chr., Vancouver, B.C.; Bryan Safarik, COO, Vancouver, B.C.; Jacob Safarik, CFO, Vancouver, B.C.; Dane Stevens, chief mktg. officer, Vancouver, B.C.; Jonathan (Jon) Schintler, Vancouver, B.C.

Other Exec. Officers - William J. (Bill) Ciprick, CEO; Justin D. Kirkland, chief science officer; Leah Hodges, corp. sec.

Capital Stock

	Authorized (shs.)	Outstanding (shs.)[1]
Common	unlimited	86,774,316

[1] At Dec. 12, 2022

Major Shareholder - Widely held at Dec. 5, 2022.

Price Range - OPTI/CSE

Year	Volume	High	Low	Close
2022	18,771,091	$0.55	$0.20	$0.23
2021	49,041,708	$1.10	$0.43	$0.47

Recent Close: $0.20

Capital Stock Changes - In October 2022, private placement of 5,692,308 units (1 common share & ½ warrant) at $0.325 per unit was completed, with warrants exercisable at 50¢ per share for two years.

During fiscal 2022, common shares were issued as follows: 10,744,500 on exercise of warrants, 428,250 on vesting of restricted share rights and 50,000 as share-based compensation; 150,000 common shares were returned to treasury.

Wholly Owned Subsidiaries

Optimi Labs Inc., B.C.
Optimi Nutraceuticals Corp., B.C.

Financial Statistics

Periods ended:	12m Sept. 30/22[A]		12m Sept. 30/21[A]
	$000s	%Chg	$000s
Operating revenue	**81**	**n.a.**	**nil**
Cost of sales	27		nil
Salaries & benefits	1,371		284
Research & devel. expense	133		241
General & admin expense	4,641		4,222
Stock-based compensation	1,005		1,261
Operating expense	**6,172**	**+3**	**6,008**
Operating income	**(6,091)**	**n.a.**	**(6,008)**
Deprec., depl. & amort.	294		47
Finance income	67		55
Finance costs, gross	28		19
Pre-tax income	**(7,351)**	**n.a.**	**(6,020)**
Net income	**(7,351)**	**n.a.**	**(6,020)**
Cash & equivalent	1,889		12,433
Inventories	265		nil
Accounts receivable	99		188
Current assets	2,428		14,302
Fixed assets, net	12,247		8,671
Right-of-use assets	132		233
Total assets	**16,818**	**-28**	**23,463**
Accts. pay. & accr. liabs	640		2,145
Current liabilities	728		2,240
Long-term lease liabilities	69		155
Shareholders' equity	16,020		21,068
Cash from oper. activs	**(4,580)**	**n.a.**	**(6,023)**
Cash from fin. activs	1,187		19,178
Cash from invest. activs	(3,151)		(9,193)
Net cash position	**1,889**	**-78**	**8,433**
Capital expenditures	(7,151)		(4,936)
	$		$
Earnings per share*	(0.09)		(0.12)
Cash flow per share*	(0.06)		(0.12)
	shs		shs
No. of shs. o/s*	80,942,883		69,870,133
Avg. no. of shs. o/s*	77,939,707		51,922,761
	%		%
Net profit margin	n.m.		n.a.
Return on equity	(39.64)		(45.68)
Return on assets	(36.36)		(40.50)
No. of employees (FTEs)	n.a.		9

* Common
[A] Reported in accordance with IFRS

Historical Summary
(as originally stated)

Fiscal Year	Oper. Rev.	Net Inc. Bef. Disc.	EPS*
	$000s	$000s	$
2022[A]	81	(7,351)	(0.09)
2021[A]	nil	(6,020)	(0.12)
2020[A1,2]	nil	(169)	(0.01)

* Common
[A] Reported in accordance with IFRS
[1] 18 weeks ended Sept. 30, 2020.
[2] As shown in the prospectus dated Feb. 12, 2021.

0.25 Optimind Pharma Corp.

Symbol - OMND **Exchange** - CSE **CUSIP** - 68405U
Head Office - TD Centre, North Tower, 3000-77 King St W, PO Box 95, Toronto, ON, M5K 1G8 **Telephone** - (647) 891-9379
Website - optimindpharma.com
Email - mrakesh15@hotmail.com
Investor Relations - Rakesh Malhotra (647) 891-9379
Auditors - DNTW Toronto LLP C.A., Toronto, Ont.
Transfer Agents - Computershare Trust Company of Canada Inc., Calgary, Alta.
Profile - (Ont. 2022; orig. Alta., 2008) Operates the Redytogo Clinic in London, Ont., specializing in the prescription of medical cannabis and other alternative treatments for various medical ailments, as well as providing ketamine-assisted treatment for those suffering from post-traumatic stress disorder (PTSD), anxiety, depression, and other mental illnesses and disabilities.
In addition, affiliate **Manitari Pharma Corporation** (40% owned) has a collaborative license and R&D agreement with the Mohawk community in Quebec for the development of psilocybin products.

Recent Merger and Acquisition Activity

Status: completed **Revised:** July 28, 2022
UPDATE: The transaction was completed. The share consideration of 66,552,008 common shares were issued on a post-consolidated basis (following a 1-for-1.713084 consolidation). The post-consolidated common shares of Optimind Pharma Corp. commenced trading on the CSE effective Aug. 4, 2022. PREVIOUS: Loon Energy Corporation entered into a letter of intent for the reverse takeover acquisition of private Toronto, Ont.-based Optimind Pharma Inc., which operates a clinic for psychedelic-assisted psychotherapy for the treatment of depression, anxiety and post-traumatic stress disorder (PTSD). Nov. 30, 2021 - A definitive agreement was entered. The basis of consideration was one-for-one, which would result in the issuance of 66,552,008 Loon common shares. Upon completion, Optimind would amalgamate with Loon's wholly owned 1000033135 Ontario Inc., and Loon would change its name to Optimind Pharma Corp. Loon planned to voluntarily delist its common shares from the TSX Venture Exchange and seek a listing on the Canadian Securities Exchange (CSE). June 16, 2022 - Loon applied to list its common shares on the CSE. June 24, 2022 - Loon's common shares were delisted from the TSX Venture Exchange.
Predecessor Detail - Name changed from Loon Energy Corporation, July 27, 2022, pursuant to the reverse takeover acquisition of Optimind Pharma Inc. and concurrent amalgamation of (old) Optimind with wholly owned 1000033135 Ontario Inc.; basis 1 new for 1.71308 old shs.
Directors - Tomas (Tom) Sipos, pres. & CEO, Toronto, Ont.; Dr. Mike Hart, COO, London, Ont.; Tushar Arora, Toronto, Ont.; Marshall I. Morris, Toronto, Ont.
Other Exec. Officers - Rakesh Malhotra, CFO & corp. sec.

Capital Stock

	Authorized (shs.)	Outstanding (shs.)[1]
Preferred	unlimited	nil
Common	unlimited	75,201,991

[1] At Aug. 4, 2022
Major Shareholder - Widely held at Aug. 4, 2022.

Price Range - OMND/CSE

Year	Volume	High	Low	Close
2022	1,886,601	$0.20	$0.02	$0.03
2021	302,979	$0.43	$0.17	$0.21
2020	557,842	$0.72	$0.10	$0.24
2018	585,825	$1.03	$0.10	$0.27

Consolidation: 1-for-1.71308 cons. in July 2022; 1-for-4 cons. in Dec. 2020
Recent Close: $0.02
Capital Stock Changes - On July 28, 2022, common shares were consolidated on a 1-for-1.713084 basis (effective on the Canadian Securities Exchange on Aug. 4, 2022) and 66,552,008 post-consolidated common shares were issued pursuant to the reverse takeover acquisition of Optimind Pharma Inc.

Wholly Owned Subsidiaries

Optimind Pharma Inc., Toronto, Ont.
- 40% int. in **Manitari Pharma Corporation**, Canada.

Financial Statistics

Periods ended:	63w Feb. 28/22[A1]		12m Dec. 31/21[A2]
	$000s	%Chg	US$000s
Operating revenue	**125**	**nil**	
General & admin expense	593		63
Stock-based compensation	nil		66
Operating expense	**593**	**129**	
Operating income	**(469)**	**(129)**	
Deprec., depl. & amort.	36		nil
Finance costs, gross	21		9
Pre-tax income	**(527)**	**(137)**	
Income taxes	(179)		nil
Net income	**(347)**	**(137)**	
Cash & equivalent	1,352		1
Accounts receivable	2		nil
Current assets	1,861		17
Long-term investments	310		nil
Right-of-use assets	125		nil
Intangibles, net	1,521		nil
Total assets	**3,816**	**17**	
Bank indebtedness	nil		126
Accts. pay. & accr. liabs	132		23
Current liabilities	664		149
Long-term lease liabilities	109		nil
Shareholders' equity	3,040		(132)
Cash from oper. activs	**(292)**	**(65)**	
Cash from fin. activs	2,250		60
Cash from invest. activs	(100)		nil
Net cash position	**1,859**	**1**	
	$		US$
Earnings per share*	(0.02)		(0.02)
Cash flow per share*	(0.01)		(0.01)
	shs		shs
No. of shs. o/s*	n.a.		5,983,519
Avg. no. of shs. o/s*	43,591,749		5,983,519
	%		%
Net profit margin	...		n.a.
Return on equity	...		n.m.
Return on assets	...		(984.62)

* Common
[A] Reported in accordance with IFRS
[1] Results reflect the July 28, 2022, reverse takeover acquisition of Optimind Pharma Inc.
[2] Results for 2021 and prior years pertain to Loon Energy Corporation.

Latest Results

Periods ended:	3m Mar. 31/22[A]		3m Mar. 31/21[A]
	US$000s	%Chg	US$000s
Net income	(13)	n.a.	(54)
	US$		US$
Earnings per share*	(0.00)		(0.02)

* Common
[A] Reported in accordance with IFRS

Historical Summary
(as originally stated)

Fiscal Year	Oper. Rev.	Net Inc. Bef. Disc.	EPS*
	$000s	$000s	$
2022[A1]	125	(347)	(0.02)
	US$000s	US$000s	US$
2021[A]	nil	(137)	(0.02)
2020[A]	nil	98	0.03
2019[A]	nil	(19)	(0.01)
2018[A]	nil	(165)	(0.07)

* Common
[A] Reported in accordance with IFRS
[1] 63 weeks ended Feb. 28, 2022.
Note: Adjusted throughout for 1-for-1.713084 cons. in July 2022; 1-for-4 cons. in Dec. 2020

0.26 Optiva Inc.

Symbol - OPT **Exchange** - TSX **CUSIP** - 68403N
Head Office - East Tower, 302-2233 Argentia Rd, Mississauga, ON, L5N 2X7 **Telephone** - (905) 625-2622 **Fax** - (905) 625-2773
Website - www.optiva.com
Email - investors-relations@optiva.com
Investor Relations - Ali Mahdavi (905) 625-2622
Auditors - KPMG LLP C.A., Toronto, Ont.
Lawyers - Blake, Cassels & Graydon LLP, Toronto, Ont.
Transfer Agents - Computershare Trust Company of Canada Inc., Toronto, Ont.
FP500 Revenue Ranking - 798
Employees - 386 at Dec. 31, 2022
Profile - (Can. 2006) Provides cloud-native monetization and business support systems (BSS) products for private and public communications service providers (CSPs) worldwide.
The company's software products enable the CSP's to introduce new tariffs and marketing offerings, through its rating, charging and billing solutions, together with its complementing products such as payment solutions, policy control, wholesales billing, customer care and subscriber self-service applications. Customers served range from regional to multinational telecommunication operators and mobile virtual network operators (MVNOs) which require data monetization solutions for their service offerings, including premium messaging, mobile broadband, Voice over Internet Protocol (VoIP) and data-rich services such as video streaming. The company's offerings can be integrated into BSS or deployed as an end-to-end platform.
Software products and services include:
Optiva Charging Engine™ - A customizable, convergent, full cloud-enabled charging platform for the monetization of any transactions in real-time. This solution can be integrated into a customer's network and serve as a single platform for all service types, including 4G and 5G networks, Voice-over-LTE/Voice-over-New Radio, fixed line broadband, television, Machine-to-Machine, Internet of Things (IoT), cloud services and Over-the-Top offerings.
Optiva Policy Control - Provides a single solution which enables service providers to take control of network resource usage, assure the quality of experience for users, and offer personalized services and differentiated, service-specific charging.
Optiva Payment Solution - Provides different payment methods including voucher and voucher-less payment and top-up solutions.
Optiva BSS Platform™ - A fully managed, end-to-end, cloud-native charging and billing solution available on the private and public cloud. This platform offers unified rating and charging, billing, customer care and self-care, product catalog, payments and voucher management, collections and settlements, and dealer care.
Optiva Wholesale Billing™ - A cloud-based software solution which provides operators with comprehensive and cost-effective interconnect, wholesale, roaming, MVNO, franchise management, and content settlement software solution.
In May 2022, the company established a research and development centre in Osijek, Croatia to deliver innovation in the business support systems market.
Predecessor Detail - Name changed from Redknee Solutions Inc., Mar. 28, 2018; basis 1 new for 50 old shs.
Directors - Robert Stabile, chr. & interim CEO, Toronto, Ont.; Joseph L. (Lee) Matheson, v-chr., Toronto, Ont.; Patrick (Pat) DiPietro, Ottawa, Ont.; Anuroop S, Duggal, Toronto, Ont.; Matthew Kirk, Corte Madera, Calif.; John A. Meyer, Dallas, Tex.; Simon Parmar, Toronto, Ont.; Barry Symons, Toronto, Ont.; Birgit Troy, Port Moody, B.C.
Other Exec. Officers - Mary-Lynn Oke, CFO; Michele Campriani, chief revenue officer; Matthew Halligan, chief tech. officer; Craig Clapper, v-p, global managed srvcs. & support; Sönke Jens, v-p, srvcs.; Dinesh Sharma, v-p, fin.

Capital Stock

	Authorized (shs.)	Outstanding (shs.)[1]
Preferred	unlimited	nil
Series A		nil
Common	unlimited	6,177,581

[1] At May 10, 2023

Major Shareholder - EdgePoint Investment Group Inc. held 29.4% interest, Maple Rock Capital Partners Inc. held 21.2% interest and OceanLink Management Ltd. held 16.5% interest at May 20, 2022.

Price Range - OPT/TSX

Year	Volume	High	Low	Close
2022	225,065	$28.00	$17.00	$18.70
2021	1,231,458	$39.30	$19.00	$27.36
2020	395,034	$58.00	$17.50	$34.91
2019	568,102	$59.85	$37.83	$52.09
2018	630,728	$57.50	$42.50	$46.93

Recent Close: $6.00

Capital Stock Changes - There were no changes to capital stock during 2022.

Wholly Owned Subsidiaries

Optiva Canada Inc., Mississauga, Ont.
- 100% int. in **Optiva Malta Holdings Limited**, Malta.
  - 100% int. in **Optiva Software Limited**, Malta.
- 100% int. in **Optiva Solutions (UK) Limited**, United Kingdom.
  - 1% int. in **Optiva India Technologies Pvt. Ltd.**, India.
  - 1% int. in **PT Redknee Indonesia**, Indonesia.
  - 100% int. in **Redknee Global Operations Leadership Centre GmbH**, Germany.
  - 1% int. in **Redknee Maroc S.A.R.L.**, Morocco.
  - 100% int. in **Redknee Techcenter GmbH**, Germany.
- 99% int. in **PT Redknee Indonesia**, Indonesia.
- 100% int. in **Redknee (Australia) Pty Ltd.**, Australia.
  - 100% int. in **Argent Networks Pty Ltd.**, Australia.
- 100% int. in **Redknee (Germany) GmbH**, Munich, Germany.
  - 100% int. in **Redknee Germany OS GmbH**, Germany.
    - 99% int. in **Redknee India OS Private Ltd.**, India.
  - 1% int. in **Redknee India OS Private Ltd.**, India.
  - 1% int. in **Redknee OS Brasil Informatica Ltda.**, Brazil.
- 100% int. in **Redknee Holdings (Pty) Ltd.**, South Africa.
  - 80% int. in **Redknee South Africa Proprietary Limited**, South Africa.
    - 99% int. in **Redknee Mozambique Limitada**, Mozambique.
    - 99.99% int. in **Redknee Tanzania Limited**, Tanzania.
- 100% int. in **Redknee MEA SAL**, Lebanon.
- 99% int. in **Redknee Maroc S.A.R.L.**, Morocco.
- 1% int. in **Redknee Mozambique Limitada**, Mozambique.
- 99% int. in **Redknee OS Brasil Informatica Ltda.**, Brazil.
- 0.01% int. in **Redknee Tanzania Limited**, Tanzania.
- 100% int. in **Redknee (US) Limited**, Del.

Financial Statistics

Periods ended:	12m Dec. 31/22[A]		12m Dec. 31/21[A]
	US$000s	%Chg	US$000s
Operating revenue	**61,779**	**-5**	**65,236**
Cost of sales	5,455		5,606
Salaries & benefits	31,877		27,183
Research & devel. expense	3,653		2,930
General & admin expense	5,383		9,148
Stock-based compensation	1,947		3,790
Operating expense	**48,315**	**-1**	**48,657**
Operating income	**13,464**	**-19**	**16,579**
Deprec., depl. & amort.	1,956		1,621
Finance costs, net	7,510		(6,794)
Pre-tax income	**2,880**	**-87**	**22,019**
Income taxes	2,171		3,516
Net income	**709**	**-96**	**18,503**
Cash & equivalent	18,386		29,587
Accounts receivable	7,535		7,203
Current assets	50,110		53,228
Fixed assets, net	1,221		883
Intangibles, net	32,631		34,076
Total assets	**86,618**	**-7**	**92,660**
Accts. pay. & accr. liabs	14,771		14,989
Current liabilities	21,131		26,652
Long-term debt, gross	87,716		86,990
Long-term debt, net	87,716		86,990
Shareholders' equity	(26,080)		(35,064)
Cash from oper. activs	**(237)**	**n.a.**	**2,647**
Cash from fin. activs	(8,775)		10,891
Cash from invest. activs	(2,006)		(1,219)
Net cash position	**18,386**	**-38**	**29,587**
Unfunded pension liability	713		9,423
	US$		US$
Earnings per share*	0.11		3.12
Cash flow per share*	(0.04)		0.45
	shs		shs
No. of shs. o/s*	6,178,000		6,177,581
Avg. no. of shs. o/s*	6,178,000		5,927,744
	%		%
Net profit margin	1.15		28.36
Return on equity	n.m.		n.m.
Return on assets	0.79		21.76
No. of employees (FTEs)	386		374

* Common

[A] Reported in accordance with IFRS

Latest Results

Periods ended:	3m Mar. 31/23[A]		3m Mar. 31/22[A]
	US$000s	%Chg	US$000s
Operating revenue	12,651	-22	16,136
Net income	(2,776)	n.a.	1,837
	US$		US$
Earnings per share*	(0.45)		0.30

* Common

[A] Reported in accordance with IFRS

Historical Summary
(as originally stated)

Fiscal Year	Oper. Rev. US$000s	Net Inc. Bef. Disc. US$000s	EPS* US$
2022[A]	61,779	709	0.11
2021[A]	65,236	18,503	3.12
2020[A]	75,916	(41,520)	(7.81)
2019[A1]	120,883	(13,751)	(2.60)
2018[A]	121,627	(92,592)	(17.69)

* Common

[A] Reported in accordance with IFRS

[1] 15 months ended Dec. 31, 2019.

0.27 Ord Mountain Resources Corp.

Symbol - OMR.H **Exchange** - TSX-VEN **CUSIP** - 685743

Head Office - 758 Riverside Dr, Unit 46, Port Coquitlam, BC, V3B 7V8 **Telephone** - (604) 760-8755

Email - lmontaine@icloud.com

Investor Relations - Luke Montaine (604) 760-8755

Auditors - MNP LLP C.A., Vancouver, B.C.

Lawyers - Boughton Law Corporation, Vancouver, B.C.

Transfer Agents - Computershare Trust Company of Canada Inc., Vancouver, B.C.

Profile - (B.C. 2021; orig. B.C., 2009) Capital Pool Company.

Recent Merger and Acquisition Activity

Status: terminated **Revised:** Jan. 18, 2023

UPDATE: The transaction was terminated. PREVIOUS: Ord Mountain Resources Corp. entered into a letter of intent (LOI) for the Qualifying Transaction reverse takeover acquisition of British Columbia-based BluSky Aviation Group Inc., a special purpose acquisitions company, on a share-for-share basis, resulting in the issuance of 23,901,000 post-consolidated common shares (following a 1-for-2.5 share consolidation). BluSky focuses on the acquisition and restructuring of distressed or undervalued commercial aviation related assets and technologies in the Pacific Northwest, Western Canada and Alaska. Upon completion of the transaction, Ord would change its name to BluSky Management Group Inc. Sept. 16, 2021 - The LOI was revised and expanded to include the acquisition of both BluSky and Richmond, B.C.-based Cascadia Northern Air Inc. (CAS), the first acquisition target of BluSky and the parent of Cascadia Airways Inc. (dba Cascadia Air). Cascadia Air is a small commuter airline in British Columbia providing direct flights to and from Vancouver, the Tri-Cities, Vancouver Island and Okanagan Valley. Cascadia Air also provides private charter flights within the province. Holders of class A voting and class B non-voting common shares of BluSky and CAS would receive one Ord post-consolidated common share (following a 1-for-2 share consolidation). Ord would change its name to BluSky Group of Companies Inc. Dec. 7, 2021 - A formal binding amalgamation agreement was entered into.

Predecessor Detail - Name changed from Sino Environ-Energy Tech Corp., Feb. 15, 2012.

Directors - Luke Montaine, CEO & interim CFO, Vancouver, B.C.; Alexander (Alex) Klenman, Surrey, B.C.

Capital Stock

	Authorized (shs.)	Outstanding (shs.)[1]
Preferred	unlimited	nil
Common	unlimited	4,702,000

[1] At July 19, 2022

Major Shareholder - Widely held at July 6, 2020.

Price Range - OMR.H/TSX-VEN

Year	Volume	High	Low	Close
2020	169,000	$0.25	$0.06	$0.20
2019	83,000	$0.12	$0.08	$0.08

Recent Close: $0.06

Wholly Owned Subsidiaries

1080199 B.C. Ltd., B.C.

0.28 Organic Potash Corporation

Symbol - OPC **Exchange** - CSE **CUSIP** - 68619U

Head Office - 22-10 Wilkinson Rd, Brampton, ON, L6T 5B1 **Telephone** - (905) 452-8060 **Fax** - (905) 452-8135

Website - www.organicpotash.com

Email - heather.welner@organicpotash.com

Investor Relations - Heather Welner (905) 452-8060

Auditors - RSM Canada LLP C.A., Toronto, Ont.

Transfer Agents - Computershare Trust Company of Canada Inc., Toronto, Ont.

Profile - (Ont. 2011 amalg.) Owns a mini manufacturing plant in Tema, Ghana, which produced 99%+ pure potassium carbonate from cocoa husks using a patented production technology licensed from **GC Technology Limited**. Operations have been on hold since 2016 pending additional funding.

In November 2015, the company and **New Commodity Ventures** (NCV) entered into a joint venture agreement to incorporate a new company, with each of the company and NCV owning 50%. The new company would be granted an exclusive sublicence for the production and sale of potassium carbonate in the Ivory Coast. Pursuant to the agreement, the company would provide the licence, technology expertise, marketing and sales expertise, and such other support as may be appropriate with the design and implementation of a 25 tonne per day production facility and NCV would be responsible to raise all funds necessary for the start-up and continued operation of the joint venture, not to be less than US$2,000,000. As at September 30, 2022, the joint venture has not commenced operations.

Directors - Heather Welner, pres. & CEO, Caledon, Ont.; Augustus Tanoh, exec. v-p, Accra, Ghana; Dr. Jean-Marc Anga, Côte d'Ivoire; Dr. Graham Norval, Ont.; Wally Rudensky, Toronto, Ont.; Jayson Schwarz, Toronto, Ont.

Other Exec. Officers - Volodymyr (Vlad) Ivanov, CFO; Dr. Martin Woode, v-p, research

Capital Stock

	Authorized (shs.)	Outstanding (shs.)[1]
Common	unlimited	121,124,961

[1] At May 23, 2023

Major Shareholder - Widely held at May 23, 2023.

Price Range - OPC/CSE

Year	Volume	High	Low	Close
2022	21,526,573	$0.07	$0.01	$0.01
2021	17,684,163	$0.07	$0.01	$0.01
2020	6,528,300	$0.03	$0.01	$0.01
2019	3,611,342	$0.06	$0.01	$0.02
2018	3,923,634	$0.08	$0.02	$0.03

Recent Close: $0.01

Capital Stock Changes - There were no changes to capital stock during fiscal 2022.

Wholly Owned Subsidiaries

GC Purchasing Limited, Ghana.

Investments

45% int. in **GC Resources Limited**, Ghana.

Financial Statistics

Periods ended:	12m June 30/22^A		12m June 30/21^A
	$000s	%Chg	$000s
General & admin expense	64		77
Operating expense	**64**	**-17**	**77**
Operating income	**(64)**	**n.a.**	**(77)**
Finance costs, gross	13		13
Pre-tax income	**(50)**	**n.a.**	**(60)**
Net income	**(50)**	**n.a.**	**(60)**
Cash & equivalent	12		68
Current assets	13		69
Total assets	**13**	**-81**	**69**
Bank indebtedness	nil		14
Accts. pay. & accr. liabs	236		272
Current liabilities	366		416
Long-term debt, gross	130		130
Shareholders' equity	(788)		(733)
Cash from oper. activs	**(55)**	**n.a.**	**(80)**
Cash from fin. activs	nil		100
Net cash position	**12**	**-82**	**68**
	$		$
Earnings per share*	(0.00)		(0.00)
Cash flow per share*	(0.00)		(0.00)
	shs		shs
No. of shs. o/s*	117,674,961		117,674,961
Avg. no. of shs. o/s*	117,674,961		113,455,783
	%		%
Net profit margin	n.a.		n.a.
Return on equity	n.m.		n.m.
Return on assets	(90.24)		(78.99)

* Common
A Reported in accordance with IFRS

Latest Results

Periods ended:	3m Sept. 30/22^A		3m Sept. 30/21^A
	$000s	%Chg	$000s
Net income	(19)	n.a.	(18)
	$		$
Earnings per share*	(0.00)		(0.00)

* Common
A Reported in accordance with IFRS

Historical Summary
(as originally stated)

Fiscal Year	Oper. Rev. $000s	Net Inc. Bef. Disc. $000s	EPS* $
2022^A	nil	(50)	(0.00)
2021^A	nil	(60)	(0.00)
2020^A	nil	(97)	(0.00)
2019^A	nil	(26)	(0.00)
2018^A	nil	1,529	0.02

* Common
A Reported in accordance with IFRS

O.29 OrganiGram Holdings Inc.

Symbol - OGI **Exchange** - TSX **CUSIP** - 68620P
Head Office - 35 English Dr, Moncton, NB, E1E 3X3 **Telephone** - (506) 801-8986 **Toll-free** - (855) 961-9420 **Fax** - (855) 267-1386
Website - www.organigram.ca
Email - paolo.deluca@organigram.ca
Investor Relations - Paolo De Luca (855) 961-9420
Auditors - KPMG LLP C.A., Vaughan, Ont.
Lawyers - Goodmans LLP, Toronto, Ont.
Transfer Agents - VStock Transfer. LLC, Woodmere, N.Y.; TSX Trust Company, Vancouver, B.C.
FP500 Revenue Ranking - 710
Employees - 931 at Oct. 31, 2022
Profile - (Can. 2016; orig. B.C., 2010) Produces and sells medical and recreational cannabis and cannabis-derived products for the Canadian and international markets.

Produces and manufactures cannabis and cannabis-derived products from an indoor cultivation and production facility located on a 14-acre campus in Moncton, N.B., with more than 100 three-tiered cultivation rooms and annual production capacity of 85,000 kg of flower; a 51,000-sq.-ft. edibles manufacturing facility in Winnipeg, Man.; and a cultivation and derivatives processing facility in Lac-Supérieur, Que., with 6,800 sq. ft. of greenhouse cultivation area and capacity to produce 600 kg of flower and 1,000,000 units of hash annually. Expansion at the Lac-Supérieur facility is underway which would increase the cultivation area to 33,000 sq. ft. and annual capacity to 2,400 kg of flower and 2,000,000 units of hash.

Medical cannabis products are offered for sale to patients through a third-party online platform, as well as to wholesale customers. Recreational products are sold to approved retailers and wholesalers, and marketed under the brands Edison Cannabis Co., SHRED, Holy Mountain, Big Bag O' Buds, Monjour, Tremblant and Laurentian. Also exports medical cannabis to partners in Israel and Australia.

The company changed its fiscal year end to September 30 from August 31, effective Sept. 30, 2023.

In March 2023, the company announced an agreement with **Green Tank Technologies Corp.**, which designs, develops and manufactures vaporization technologies, to exclusively access Green Tank vape cartridge technology for use with cannabis, including the development of a custom all-in-one device proprietary to the company. The company also acquired preferred shares of Green Tank's parent company, **Weekend Holdings Corp.**, representing a 2.6% interest in Weekend, for US$4,000,000.

Predecessor Detail - Name changed from Inform Exploration Corp., Aug. 25, 2014, following reverse takeover acquisition of OrganiGram Inc.; basis 1 new for 0.883605 old shs.

Directors - Peter Amirault, chr., Mississauga, Ont.; Beena Goldenberg, CEO, Toronto, Ont.; Simon Ashton, Surrey, United Kingdom; Caroline Ferland; Dexter D. S. John, Whitby, Ont.; D. Geoffrey Machum, Halifax, N.S.; Ken Manget, Toronto, Ont.; Sherry Porter, Halifax, N.S.; Stephen A. (Steve) Smith, Toronto, Ont.; Marjorie A. (Marni) Wieshofer, Santa Monica, Calif.

Other Exec. Officers - Derrick W. West, CFO; Paolo De Luca, chief strategy officer; Timothy (Tim) Emberg, chief comml. officer; Helen Martin, chief legal officer & corp. sec.; Katrina McFadden, chief people officer; Geoff Riggs, CIO; Nathalie Batten, sr. v-p, opers.; Megan McCrae, sr. v-p, mktg. & commun.; Borna Zlamalik, sr. v-p, R&D & innovation; James Fletcher, pres., The Edibles and Infusions Corporation

Capital Stock

	Authorized (shs.)	Outstanding (shs.)[1]
Preferred	unlimited	nil
Common	unlimited	80,498,692

[1] At July 7, 2023

Major Shareholder - British American Tobacco plc held 19.43% interest at Jan. 16, 2023.

Price Range - OGI/TSX

Year	Volume	High	Low	Close
2022	46,263,280	$9.28	$3.84	$4.40
2021	166,991,936	$32.00	$6.80	$8.88
2020	84,096,152	$18.96	$5.40	$6.76
2019	83,766,992	$45.20	$10.56	$12.76
2018	83,586,768	$34.20	$13.04	$19.36

Consolidation: 1-for-4 cons. in July 2023
Recent Close: $1.88

Capital Stock Changes - On July 7, 2023, common shares were consolidated on a 1-for-4 basis.

On Dec. 21, 2021, 10,896,442 common shares were issued pursuant to the acquisition of Laurentian Organic Inc. Also during fiscal 2022, common shares were issued as follows: 2,659,716 by private placement, 1,039,192 as earn-out payment, 259,000 under restricted share unit plan, 100,799 on exercise of options and 74,331 under performance share unit plan.

Wholly Owned Subsidiaries

The Edibles and Infusions Corporation, Winnipeg, Man.
Laurentian Organic Inc., Mont-Tremblant, Qué.
10870277 Canada Inc., Canada.
- 25% int. in **alpha-cannabis Pharma GmbH**, Germany.
- 2.6% int. in **Weekend Holdings Corp.**, Toronto, Ont.

OrganiGram Inc., Moncton, N.B.

Financial Statistics

Periods ended:	12m Aug. 31/22^A		12m Aug. 31/21^{oA}
	$000s	%Chg	$000s
Operating revenue	**145,809**	**+84**	**79,163**
Cost of sales	94,632		79,000
Salaries & benefits	12,018		8,380
Research & devel. expense	5,962		3,645
General & admin expense	42,451		34,876
Stock-based compensation	4,745		3,215
Operating expense	**159,808**	**+24**	**129,116**
Operating income	**(13,999)**	**n.a.**	**(49,953)**
Deprec., depl. & amort.	24,907		31,033
Finance costs, gross	429		2,960
Investment income	123		(264)
Write-downs/write-offs	(4,495)		(16,079)
Pre-tax income	**(14,371)**	**n.a.**	**(130,704)**
Income taxes	(88)		nil
Net income	**(14,283)**	**n.a.**	**(130,704)**
Cash & equivalent	98,607		183,555
Inventories	50,314		36,696
Accounts receivable	46,372		21,035
Current assets	221,623		260,615
Long-term investments	6,288		5,028
Fixed assets, net	259,819		235,939
Intangibles, net	56,239		17,046
Total assets	**577,107**	**+4**	**554,017**
Accts. pay. & accr. liabs	40,864		18,952
Current liabilities	55,285		26,266
Long-term debt, gross	235		310
Long-term debt, net	155		230
Long-term lease liabilities	2,206		4,651
Shareholders' equity	508,058		479,805
Cash from oper. activs	**(36,211)**	**n.a.**	**(28,589)**
Cash from fin. activs	5,328		174,463
Cash from invest. activs	44,033		(115,109)
Net cash position	**68,515**	**+24**	**55,365**
Capital expenditures, net	(48,748)		(11,757)
	$		$
Earnings per share*	(0.18)		(2.04)
Cash flow per share*	(0.47)		(0.45)
	shs		shs
No. of shs. o/s*	78,453,876		74,696,506
Avg. no. of shs. o/s*	77,228,918		64,029,983
	%		%
Net profit margin	(9.80)		(165.11)
Return on equity	(2.89)		(33.54)
Return on assets	(2.45)		(25.83)
Foreign sales percent	10		nil
No. of employees (FTEs)	882		693

* Common
o Restated
A Reported in accordance with IFRS

Latest Results

Periods ended:	6m Feb. 28/23^A		6m Feb. 28/22^A
	$000s	%Chg	$000s
Operating revenue	82,814	+33	62,214
Net income	(2,159)	n.a.	(5,352)
	$		$
Earnings per share*	(0.03)		(0.07)

* Common
A Reported in accordance with IFRS

Historical Summary
(as originally stated)

Fiscal Year	Oper. Rev. $000s	Net Inc. Bef. Disc. $000s	EPS* $
2022^A	145,809	(14,283)	(0.18)
2021^A	79,163	(130,704)	(2.04)
2020^A	86,795	(136,157)	(3.16)
2019^A	80,413	(9,504)	(0.27)
2018^A	12,429	22,124	0.74

* Common
A Reported in accordance with IFRS
Note: Adjusted throughout for 1-for-4 cons. in July 2023

O.30 Organto Foods Inc.

Symbol - OGO **Exchange** - TSX-VEN **CUSIP** - 68621J
Head Office - 805-36 Toronto St, Toronto, ON, M5C 2C5 **Telephone** - (647) 629-0018 **Toll-free** - (888) 818-1364
Website - www.organto.com
Email - john.rathwell@organto.com
Investor Relations - John Rathwell (888) 818-1364
Auditors - Dale Matheson Carr-Hilton LaBonte LLP C.A., Vancouver, B.C.
Lawyers - McMillan LLP, Vancouver, B.C.
Transfer Agents - Computershare Trust Company of Canada Inc., Vancouver, B.C.

Employees - 40 at Dec. 31, 2022
Profile - (B.C. 2007) Sources, distributes and markets organic and value-added fruit and vegetable products for distribution primarily in Europe.

Operates an integrated asset light business model using third party sourcing and supply agreements with suppliers in various countries in Europe, North and South America and Africa.

Organic products include mangoes, avocados, bananas, herbs, green asparagus, ginger, apples, pears, limes, oranges, lemons, grapefruits, raspberries, blueberries, mushrooms, sweet potatoes, sugar snaps, snow peas and fine beans. Products are also offered under I AM Organic™ and =Awesome Fruits® brands which include fresh organic vegetables/fruit/herbs, fresh organic fruit (convenience/on-the-go), ready-to-cook/pre-cut fresh organic vegetable mixes and packaged fresh organic herbs.

In January 2023, the company acquired private Germany-based **NFG New Fruit Group GmbH** for €250,000 cash, issuance of 2,250,000 common shares and an earn-out of up to €650,000 based on pre-established growth targets over a three-year period. NFG supplies organic and non-genetically modified organism (GMO) banana, avocado and mango for customers in Germany, Italy, France and Denmark.

Predecessor Detail - Name changed from Columbus Exploration Corporation, Dec. 22, 2015.

Directors - Peter L. Gianulis, founder & exec. v-p, corp. devel., Key Biscayne, Fla.; Steven R. (Steve) Bromley, chr., pres. & co-CEO, Aurora, Ont.; Rients van der Wal, co-CEO & CEO, Organto Europe BV, Netherlands; Jeremy N. Kendall, Toronto, Ont.; Alejandro Maldonado, Mexico; Joseph (Joe) Riz, Toronto, Ont.; Gert Jan van Noortwijk, Netherlands; Joost Verrest, Netherlands

Other Exec. Officers - Bob Kouw, COO, global opers.; Ralf O. Langner, CFO & corp. sec.; John Rathwell, sr. v-p, IR & corp. devel.

Capital Stock

	Authorized (shs.)	Outstanding (shs.)[1]
Common	unlimited	285,483,826

[1] At May 30, 2023

Major Shareholder - Widely held at May 19, 2023.

Price Range - OGO/TSX-VEN

Year	Volume	High	Low	Close
2022	90,544,385	$0.24	$0.07	$0.14
2021	64,363,900	$0.58	$0.20	$0.24
2020	36,778,948	$0.32	$0.02	$0.31
2019	38,972,259	$0.10	$0.02	$0.06
2018	24,367,032	$0.17	$0.06	$0.08

Recent Close: $0.06

Capital Stock Changes - During 2022, common shares were issued as follows: 1,645,643 pursuant to the acquisition of Zimbabwe Marketing Services, 1,579,670 pursuant to the acquisition of Beeorganic B.V., 1,500,000 on exercise of options and 121,860 on exercise of warrants.

Wholly Owned Subsidiaries

Beeorganic B.V., Netherlands.
Fresh Organic Choice B.V., Netherlands.
I AM Organic B.V., Netherlands.
1067001 B.C. Ltd., B.C.
- 1% int. in **Organto Argentina S.A.**, Argentina.
- 1% int. in **Organto de Mexico, S.A.**, Mexico.
- 1% int. in **Organto Guatemala, S.A.**, Guatemala.

1184866 B.C. Ltd., Canada.
Organto Europe B.V., Netherlands.
Organto USA, Inc., United States.

Subsidiaries

99% int. in **Organto Argentina S.A.**, Argentina.
99% int. in **Organto de Mexico, S.A.**, Mexico.
99% int. in **Organto Guatemala, S.A.**, Guatemala.

Investments

Xebra Brands Ltd., Vancouver, B.C. (see separate coverage)

Financial Statistics

Periods ended:	12m Dec. 31/22[A]		12m Dec. 31/21[A]
	$000s	%Chg	$000s
Operating revenue	**22,124**	**+13**	**19,519**
Cost of sales	20,860		17,532
Salaries & benefits	3,413		2,426
General & admin expense	3,564		3,190
Stock-based compensation	917		1,321
Operating expense	**28,754**	**+18**	**24,469**
Operating income	**(6,630)**	**n.a.**	**(4,950)**
Deprec., depl. & amort.	119		48
Finance costs, net	1,594		1,544
Write-downs/write-offs	(1,470)		(4)
Pre-tax income	**(10,895)**	**n.a.**	**(6,341)**
Income taxes	(67)		nil
Net income	**(10,828)**	**n.a.**	**(6,341)**
Cash & equivalent	5,863		11,870
Inventories	235		316
Accounts receivable	2,290		3,162
Current assets	9,935		18,064
Long-term investments	nil		1,052
Intangibles, net	550		1,844
Total assets	**11,371**	**-46**	**20,960**
Accts. pay. & accr. liabs.	4,166		5,694
Current liabilities	7,068		8,381
Long-term debt, gross	8,981		5,755
Long-term debt, net	7,393		5,755
Shareholders' equity	(3,155)		6,692
Cash from oper. activs.	**(5,721)**	**n.a.**	**(5,916)**
Cash from fin. activs.	(312)		13,992
Cash from invest. activs.	(929)		(357)
Net cash position	**5,770**	**-51**	**11,870**
	$		$
Earnings per share*	(0.04)		(0.02)
Cash flow per share*	(0.02)		(0.02)
	shs		shs
No. of shs. o/s*	282,233,826		277,386,653
Avg. no. of shs. o/s*	281,589,127		257,097,090
	%		%
Net profit margin	(48.94)		(32.49)
Return on equity	n.m.		n.m.
Return on assets	(66.98)		(45.73)
Foreign sales percent	100		100
No. of employees (FTEs)	40		35

* Common
[A] Reported in accordance with IFRS

Latest Results

Periods ended:	3m Mar. 31/23[A]		3m Mar. 31/22[A]
	$000s	%Chg	$000s
Operating revenue	7,504	+7	7,000
Net income	(2,048)	n.a.	(2,329)
	$		$
Earnings per share*	(0.01)		(0.01)

* Common
[A] Reported in accordance with IFRS

Historical Summary
(as originally stated)

Fiscal Year	Oper. Rev.	Net Inc. Bef. Disc.	EPS*
	$000s	$000s	$
2022[A]	22,124	(10,828)	(0.04)
2021[A]	19,519	(6,341)	(0.02)
2020[A]	11,448	(7,055)	(0.04)
2019[A]	3,712	(2,547)	(0.02)
2018[A]	1,537	(5,502)	(0.04)

* Common
[A] Reported in accordance with IFRS

O.31 Origin Therapeutics Holdings Inc.

Symbol - ORIG **Exchange** - CSE **CUSIP** - 68622H
Head Office - 1570-505 Burrard St, Vancouver, BC, V7X 1M5
Telephone - (604) 416-4099
Website - originpsychedelics.com
Email - klee@k2capital.ca
Investor Relations - Kelvin Lee (604) 416-4099
Auditors - WDM Chartered Accountants C.A., Vancouver, B.C.
Transfer Agents - Olympia Trust Company, Vancouver, B.C.
Employees - 1 at May 11, 2022
Profile - (B.C. 2020) Invests in equity, debt or other securities of public and private companies in the psychedelics industry that research, design, develop, test, produce, distribute and sell psychedelics and services related thereto.

Recent Merger and Acquisition Activity

Status: pending **Revised:** Aug. 2, 2023
UPDATE: The companies entered into a definitive agreement and Safe Supply raised $2,386,000 via a private placement of 5,965,000 subscription receipts at $0.40 per receipt. PREVIOUS: Origin Therapeutics Holdings Inc. entered into a letter of intent for the reverse takeover acquisition of Safe Supply Streaming Co. Ltd., a streaming company in the legal narcotics sector. The transaction was anticipated to be completed by way of a three-cornered amalgamation of Safe Supply and a wholly owned subsidiary of Origin. A name change to Safe Supply Streaming Co. Ltd., and a 1-for-4 consolidation of common shares was expected to be completed by Origin. A financing of subscription receipts for proceeds of at least $3,000,000 and no greater than $4,000,000 was expected to be completed by Safe Supply.

Predecessor Detail - Name changed from 1278700 B.C. Ltd., Mar. 2, 2021.

Directors - Michael Galego, interim CEO, Toronto, Ont.; Brianna Davies, Toronto, Ont.; Jonathan Goldman

Other Exec. Officers - Kelvin Lee, CFO & corp. sec.

Capital Stock

	Authorized (shs.)	Outstanding (shs.)[1]
Common	unlimited	56,563,000

[1] At June 6, 2022

Major Shareholder - Widely held at June 6, 2022.

Price Range - ORIG/CSE

Year	Volume	High	Low	Close
2022	5,580,883	$0.16	$0.02	$0.02

Recent Close: $0.03

Financial Statistics

Periods ended:	42w Nov. 30/21[A1]
	$000s
General & admin expense	432
Stock-based compensation	755
Operating expense	**1,187**
Operating income	**(1,187)**
Finance costs, gross	1
Pre-tax income	**(846)**
Net income	**(846)**
Cash & equivalent	6,997
Current assets	7,059
Total assets	**7,059**
Accts. pay. & accr. liabs.	104
Current liabilities	180
Shareholders' equity	6,879
Cash from oper. activs.	**(312)**
Cash from fin. activs.	6,967
Cash from invest. activs.	(2,118)
Net cash position	**4,537**
	$
Earnings per share*	(0.04)
Cash flow per share*	(0.01)
	shs
No. of shs. o/s*	56,563,000
Avg. no. of shs. o/s*	23,323,122
	%

* Common
[A] Reported in accordance with IFRS
[1] As shown in the prospectus dated May 11, 2022.

O.32 Orion Nutraceuticals Inc.

Symbol - ORI **Exchange** - CSE **CUSIP** - 68629J
Head Office - 810-789 Pender St W, Vancouver, BC, V6C 1H2
Telephone - (604) 687-2038
Email - investors@orionnutra.ca
Investor Relations - Joel S. Dumaresq (604) 313-2768
Auditors - Dale Matheson Carr-Hilton LaBonte LLP C.A., Vancouver, B.C.
Transfer Agents - Computershare Trust Company of Canada Inc., Vancouver, B.C.
Profile - (B.C. 2017) Seeking new business opportunities.

Formerly held and invested in companies that produce medical cannabis and develop medical cannabis products.

Recent Merger and Acquisition Activity

Status: terminated **Revised:** Sept. 30, 2022
UPDATE: The letter of intent has expired. The transaction was terminated. PREVIOUS: Orion Nutraceuticals Inc. entered into a letter of intent for the reverse takeover acquisition of private 2740162 Ontario Inc. (dba August Therapeutics) for issuance of 60,000,000 common shares. August Therapeutics had a subscription earn-in agreement to earn common shares of InStatin, Inc., which was developing novel treatments that use inhaled statins for patients with chronic lung conditions such as asthma and chronic obstructive pulmonary disease. The letter of intent would expire on Dec. 31, 2021. Feb. 28, 2022 - The expiration of the letter of intent was extended to Apr. 30, 2022. May 31, 2022 - The expiration of the letter of intent was extended to Sept. 30, 2022.

Directors - Joel S. Dumaresq, CEO & CFO, Vancouver, B.C.; Amy Boudreau; Guy Bourgeois

Capital Stock

	Authorized (shs.)	Outstanding (shs.)[1]
Common	unlimited	29,307,965

[1] At Apr. 11, 2023

Major Shareholder - Widely held at Mar. 28, 2022.

Price Range - ORI/CSE

Year	Volume	High	Low	Close
2020............	1,110,343	$1.50	$0.14	$0.40
2019............	286,558	$11.25	$0.38	$1.00
2018............	23,063	$25.00	$6.38	$11.25

Consolidation: 1-for-25 cons. in May 2020

Capital Stock Changes - There were no changes to capital stock during fiscal 2022.

Subsidiaries

99% int. in **MedicOasis Inc.**, Dorval, Qué. Inactive.

Financial Statistics

Periods ended:	12m May 31/22^A		12m May 31/21^A
	$000s	%Chg	$000s
General & admin expense...............	278		542
Stock-based compensation............	4		10
Operating expense.......................	**282**	**-49**	**552**
Operating income.......................	**(282)**	**n.a.**	**(552)**
Write-downs/write-offs...................	(2,611)		nil
Pre-tax income............................	**(2,620)**	**n.a.**	**(883)**
Net income...................................	**(2,620)**	**n.a.**	**(883)**
Cash & equivalent..........................	9		280
Accounts receivable.......................	nil		100
Current assets...............................	9		2,429
Total assets...............................	**9**	**-100**	**2,429**
Bank indebtedness.........................	44		44
Accts. pay. & accr. liabs.................	602		405
Current liabilities...........................	646		449
Shareholders' equity......................	(635)		1,980
Non-controlling interest..................	(1)		(1)
Cash from oper. activs.................	**(83)**	**n.a.**	**(935)**
Cash from fin. activs.......................	nil		3,112
Cash from invest. activs..................	(188)		(2,398)
Net cash position.........................	**9**	**-97**	**280**
	$		$
Earnings per share*........................	(0.09)		(0.03)
Cash flow per share*......................	(0.00)		(0.04)
	shs		shs
No. of shs. o/s*..............................	29,307,965		29,307,965
Avg. no. of shs. o/s*........................	29,307,965		26,637,358
	%		%
Net profit margin............................	n.a.		n.a.
Return on equity.............................	n.m.		n.m.
Return on assets............................	(214.93)		(58.59)

* Common

^A Reported in accordance with IFRS

Latest Results

Periods ended:	6m Nov. 30/22^A		6m Nov. 30/21^A
	$000s	%Chg	$000s
Net income.....................................	68	-34	103
	$		$
Earnings per share*........................	0.00		0.00

* Common

^A Reported in accordance with IFRS

Historical Summary
(as originally stated)

Fiscal Year	Oper. Rev.	Net Inc. Bef. Disc.	EPS*
	$000s	$000s	$
2022^A....................	nil	(2,620)	(0.09)
2021^A....................	nil	(883)	(0.03)
2020^A....................	nil	(386)	(0.20)
2019^A....................	nil	(6,391)	(3.75)
2018^A1,2...............	nil	(206)	(0.50)

* Common

^A Reported in accordance with IFRS

[1] 29 weeks ended May 31, 2018.

[2] As shown in the prospecuts dated Sept. 27, 2018.

Note: Adjusted throughout for 1-for-25 cons. in May 2020

O.33 Osisko Green Acquisition Limited

Symbol - GOGR **Exchange** - TSX **CUSIP** - 68828K
Head Office - 1440-155 University Ave, Toronto, ON, M5H 3B7 **Telephone** - (416) 464-4067 **Fax** - (416) 363-7579
Website - www.osiskogreen.com
Email - adann@osiskogreen.com
Investor Relations - Alexander Dann (416) 464-4067
Auditors - PricewaterhouseCoopers LLP C.A., Montréal, Qué.
Lawyers - Bennett Jones LLP
Transfer Agents - TSX Trust Company, Toronto, Ont.

Profile - (B.C. 2021) A Special Purpose Acquisition Corporation formed for the purpose of effecting an acquisition of one or more businesses or assets by way of a merger, share exchange, asset acquisition, share purchase, reorganization or any other similar business combination involving the company.

The company has until Sept. 8, 2023 (as extended from the initial permitted timeline of 18 months from Sept. 8, 2021) to complete a Qualifying Acquisition or 36 months from Sept. 8, 2021, subject to approval of holders of class A restricted voting shares. The company plans to target businesses in the green energy commodities sector such as mining of battery minerals, refining and processing, technology and supply chains, with an aggregate enterprise value of between $500,000,000 and $1 billion. However, the company's search for a Qualifying Acquisition is not limited to a particular industry or geographic region.

In March 2023, the permitted timeline by which the company has to consummate a Qualifying Transaction was extended from Mar. 8, 2023, to Sept. 8, 2023.

Directors - Sean E. O. Roosen, chr. & CEO, Beaconsfield, Qué.; John F. Burzynski, Toronto, Ont.; Tara M. Christie, B.C.; Jason Ellefson, Ont.; Christina McCarthy, Toronto, Ont.; John W. Sabine, Toronto, Ont.; Robert P. Wares, Montréal, Qué.

Other Exec. Officers - Donald R. (Don) Njegovan, pres.; Alexander (Alex) Dann, CFO & corp. sec.

Capital Stock

	Authorized (shs.)	Outstanding (shs.)[1]
Cl.A Restricted Vtg.	unlimited	5,539,701
Class B	unlimited	6,454,250

[1] At May 12, 2023

Class A Restricted Voting - Automatically convertible into common shares upon closing of Qualifying Acquisition on a 1-for-1 basis. Not permitted to redeem more than 15% of class A restricted voting shares outstanding. Automatically redeemable if no Qualifying Acquisition is completed. One vote per share on all matters requiring shareholder approval including a proposed Qualifying Acquisition, but not on the election and/or removal of directors and/or auditors.

Class B - Non-redeemable. Automatically convertible into proportionate voting shares upon closing of Qualifying Acquisition on the basis of 1 proportionate voting share for 100 class B shares. One vote per share.

Common - Not issuable prior to closing of Qualifying Acquisition. Would be convertible, at the holder's option, into proportionate voting shares on the basis of 1 proportionate voting share for 100 common shares. One vote per share.

Proportionate Voting - Not issuable prior to closing of Qualifying Acquisition. Would be convertible, at the holder's option, into common shares on the basis of 100 common shares for 1 proportionate share. 100 votes per share.

Major Shareholder - Robert P. Wares held 13.9% interest at Mar. 29, 2023.

Price Range - GOGR/TSX

Year	Volume	High	Low	Close
2022............	1,704,730	$9.95	$9.50	$9.75
2021............	562,978	$9.78	$9.26	$9.61

Recent Close: $10.25

Capital Stock Changes - In March 2023, 20,277,299 class A restricted voting shares were redeemed.

There were no changes to capital stock during 2022.

O.34 Ostrom Climate Solutions Inc.

Symbol - COO **Exchange** - TSX-VEN **CUSIP** - 688604
Head Office - 300-948 Homer St, Vancouver, BC, V6B 2W7 **Telephone** - (604) 646-0400 **Fax** - (778) 945-0965
Website - ostromclimate.com
Email - david.rokoss@ostromclimate.com
Investor Relations - David M. Rokoss (604) 760-1997
Auditors - Davidson & Company LLP C.A., Vancouver, B.C.
Lawyers - Thomas, Rondeau LLP, Vancouver, B.C.
Transfer Agents - Computershare Trust Company of Canada Inc., Vancouver, B.C.

Profile - (B.C. 2005) Sources, finances, develops and commercializes sustainable commodities across the carbon and agro-forestry sectors, with primary focus on carbon; and provides advisory, technology and impact investment services to public and private organizations worldwide.

The company develops carbon offset projects, particularly involving forestry and agriculture land-use worldwide, including Canada, the U.S. and the Democratic Republic of the Congo. Revenue is generated through the development and sale of emissions reductions (carbon offsets) that are marketed to both voluntary (non-compliance) and regulated (compliance) buyers.

The company is headquartered in Vancouver, B.C.

Predecessor Detail - Name changed from NatureBank Asset Management Inc., Dec. 9, 2021.

Directors - Harry Assenmacher, chr., Bonn, Germany; Phil Cull, CEO, Vancouver, B.C.; Guy O'Loughnane, Vancouver, B.C.; Petrina Ooi; Eduard Weber-Bemnet, Frankfurt am Main, Germany; Alexander Zang, Frankfurt am Main, Germany

Other Exec. Officers - Paula Archilles, interim CFO

Capital Stock

	Authorized (shs.)	Outstanding (shs.)[1]
Common	unlimited	77,136,139

[1] At May 2, 2022

Major Shareholder - Forest Finance Service GmbH held 24.5% interest, WBZ GmbH held 18.7% interest, Ledcor Environmental Group held 14.8% interest and Guy O'Loughnane held 11.7% interest at Sept. 14, 2020.

Price Range - COO/TSX-VEN

Year	Volume	High	Low	Close
2022............	2,231,007	$0.13	$0.05	$0.06
2021............	15,972,428	$0.15	$0.06	$0.09
2020............	18,078,252	$0.28	$0.01	$0.06
2019............	1,696,464	$0.04	$0.02	$0.02
2018............	12,935,616	$0.06	$0.02	$0.02

Recent Close: $0.07

Wholly Owned Subsidiaries

Carbon Credit Corporation, Vancouver, B.C. Inactive.
ERA Ecosystem Restoration Associates Inc., North Vancouver, B.C.
ERA Ecosystem Services U.S. Inc., Nev. Inactive.
NatureBank Technology, Inc., B.C. Inactive.
Ostrom Climate Solutions (Canada) Inc., Vancouver, B.C.

Financial Statistics

Periods ended:	12m Dec. 31/21^A		12m Dec. 31/20^A
	$000s	%Chg	$000s
Operating revenue.......................	**3,619**	**+52**	**2,388**
Cost of goods sold..........................	2,262		857
Salaries & benefits.........................	1,217		878
General & admin expense...............	599		420
Stock-based compensation............	140		nil
Operating expense.......................	**4,218**	**+96**	**2,155**
Operating income.......................	**(599)**	**n.a.**	**233**
Deprec., depl. & amort....................	30		88
Finance costs, gross.......................	116		105
Pre-tax income............................	**(1,140)**	**n.a.**	**309**
Net income...................................	**(1,140)**	**n.a.**	**309**
Cash & equivalent..........................	1,787		817
Inventories......................................	155		677
Accounts receivable.......................	286		228
Current assets...............................	2,719		1,982
Fixed assets, net............................	28		20
Right-of-use assets........................	nil		19
Total assets...............................	**2,747**	**+36**	**2,021**
Accts. pay. & accr. liabs.................	1,399		664
Current liabilities...........................	3,916		2,287
Long-term debt, gross....................	961		933
Long-term debt, net........................	145		66
Equity portion of conv. debs............	97		74
Shareholders' equity......................	(1,506)		(529)
Cash from oper. activs.................	**1,023**	**n.m.**	**24**
Cash from fin. activs.......................	(33)		(40)
Cash from invest. activs..................	(20)		267
Net cash position.........................	**1,787**	**+119**	**817**
Capital expenditures.......................	(20)		(13)
	$		$
Earnings per share*........................	(0.02)		0.00
Cash flow per share*......................	0.02		0.00
	shs		shs
No. of shs. o/s*..............................	61,752,679		61,752,679
Avg. no. of shs. o/s*........................	61,752,679		61,752,679
	%		%
Net profit margin............................	(31.50)		12.94
Return on equity.............................	n.m.		n.m.
Return on assets............................	(42.95)		22.67
Foreign sales percent.....................	57		21

* Common

^A Reported in accordance with IFRS

Latest Results

Periods ended:	3m Mar. 31/22^A		3m Mar. 31/21^A
	$000s	%Chg	$000s
Operating revenue..........................	489	+4	471
Net income.....................................	(417)	n.a.	(329)
	$		$
Earnings per share*........................	(0.00)		(0.00)

* Common

^A Reported in accordance with IFRS

Historical Summary
(as originally stated)

Fiscal Year	Oper. Rev.	Net Inc. Bef. Disc.	EPS*
	$000s	$000s	$
2021^A....................	3,619	(1,140)	(0.02)
2020^A....................	2,388	309	0.01
2019^A....................	2,851	786	0.01
2018^A....................	3,041	381	0.01
2017^A....................	4,521	352	0.01

* Common

^A Reported in accordance with IFRS

O.35 Ovation Science Inc.

Symbol - OVAT **Exchange** - CSE **CUSIP** - 69016D
Head Office - 1140-625 Howe St, Vancouver, BC, V6C 2T6 **Telephone** - (604) 283-0903 **Fax** - (604) 685-9182
Website - www.ovationscience.com
Email - ir@ovationscience.com

Investor Relations - Logan B. Anderson (604) 283-0903
Auditors - Dale Matheson Carr-Hilton LaBonte LLP C.A., Vancouver, B.C.
Lawyers - Northwest Law Group, Vancouver, B.C.
Transfer Agents - National Securities Administrators Ltd., Vancouver, B.C.
Profile - (B.C. 2017) Holds the exclusive worldwide rights to manufacture, distribute, sell, market, sublicense and promote products formulated with Invisicare®, a patented drug delivery technology used in topical and transdermal skin products containing hemp seed oil, cannabinoids and cannabis products.

Develops formulas for skin product lines containing hemp seed oil and cannabis, and licenses rights to product formulations to manufacturers and/or marketers globally. Has developed topical and transdermal creams and lotions made with cannabidiol (CBD), tetrahydrocannabinol (THC) and combinations thereof plus hemp seed oil. All formulations are formulated with Invisicare® technology, which enhances drug delivery to the skin by delivering greater amounts and enhancing cannabinoid penetration to enter the blood stream as required. The company does not handle product formulas containing marijuana, and the production and testing of marijuana containing products is done at the licensed premises of its sublicensees or by third party analytical labs. The company formulates products and then licenses the formulations, following which the sublicensees manufacture the products and purchase their own ingredients, source their own marijuana and purchase the Invisicare® polymer from the company. The company's sole sublicence has been granted to **Lighthouse Strategies, LLC** to sell topical products containing THC and CBD exclusively in Nevada.

Also offers its own hemp-derived CBD anti-aging skin care line under the ARLO CBD Beauty brand; and a CBD health and wellness product line under the Invibe® MD brand. In addition, holds a licence from **Skinvisible Pharmaceuticals, Inc.** to manufacture and sell DermSafe® hand sanitizer, which uses chlorhexidine gluconate as ingredient that has a proven ability to kill bacteria and viruses.

Directors - Terry Howlett, pres. & CEO, Henderson, Nev.; Logan B. Anderson, CFO & corp. sec., North Vancouver, B.C.; Doreen McMorran, v-p, bus. devel. & COO, Henderson, Nev.; Joan Chyphya, Richmond Hill, Ont.; Ian Howard, North Vancouver, B.C.; David K. (Dave) Ryan, Langley, B.C.

Capital Stock

	Authorized (shs.)	Outstanding (shs.)[1]
Preferred	unlimited	nil
Common	unlimited	29,374,836

[1] At Sept. 19, 2022

Major Shareholder - Terry Howlett held 13% interest and Doreen McMorran held 13% interest at Sept. 19, 2022.

Price Range - OVAT/CSE

Year	Volume	High	Low	Close
2022	1,792,239	$0.08	$0.03	$0.03
2021	4,214,679	$0.38	$0.05	$0.06
2020	10,502,945	$0.65	$0.17	$0.36
2019	6,229,081	$0.65	$0.14	$0.20
2018	1,276,902	$0.54	$0.29	$0.30

Recent Close: $0.03

Wholly Owned Subsidiaries

Ovation Science USA Inc., Las Vegas, Nev.

Financial Statistics

Periods ended:	12m Dec. 31/21[A]		12m Dec. 31/20[A]
	$000s	%Chg	$000s
Operating revenue	**225**	**-70**	**750**
Cost of sales	37		202
General & admin expense	1,009		1,215
Stock-based compensation	nil		413
Operating expense	**1,046**	**-43**	**1,830**
Operating income	**(821)**	**n.a.**	**(1,080)**
Deprec., depl. & amort.	8		9
Finance income	5		14
Finance costs, gross	nil		16
Pre-tax income	**(2,402)**	**n.a.**	**(1,167)**
Net income	**(2,402)**	**n.a.**	**(1,167)**
Cash & equivalent	648		1,538
Inventories	4		886
Accounts receivable	94		50
Current assets	758		2,490
Fixed assets, net	12		20
Intangibles, net	nil		742
Total assets	**770**	**-76**	**3,252**
Accts. pay. & accr. liabs	64		143
Current liabilities	64		143
Shareholders' equity	706		3,108
Cash from oper. activs	**(886)**	**n.a.**	**(1,385)**
Cash from fin. activs	nil		2,050
Cash from invest. activs	1,158		(685)
Net cash position	**648**	**+70**	**381**
	$		$
Earnings per share*	(0.08)		(0.04)
Cash flow per share*	(0.03)		(0.05)
	shs		shs
No. of shs. o/s*	29,374,836		29,374,836
Avg. no. of shs. o/s*	29,374,836		26,667,047
	%		%
Net profit margin	n.m.		(155.60)
Return on equity	(125.96)		(50.89)
Return on assets	(119.44)		(45.21)

* Common
[A] Reported in accordance with IFRS

Latest Results

Periods ended:	6m June 30/22[A]		6m June 30/21[A]
	$000s	%Chg	$000s
Operating revenue	68	-55	150
Net income	(422)	n.a.	(366)
	$		$
Earnings per share*	(0.01)		(0.01)

* Common
[A] Reported in accordance with IFRS

Historical Summary
(as originally stated)

Fiscal Year	Oper. Rev.	Net Inc. Bef. Disc.	EPS*
	$000s	$000s	$
2021[A]	225	(2,402)	(0.08)
2020[A]	750	(1,167)	(0.04)
2019[A]	302	(836)	(0.05)
2018[A]	96	(508)	(0.03)
2017[A1,2]	13	(62)	(0.03)

* Common
[A] Reported in accordance with IFRS
[1] 24 weeks ended Dec. 31, 2017.
[2] As shown in the prospectus dated Oct. 26, 2018.

0.36 OverActive Media Corp.

Symbol - OAM **Exchange** - TSX-VEN **CUSIP** - 690161
Head Office - 41 Fraser Ave, Toronto, ON, M6K 1Y7 **Telephone** - (416) 993-6745
Website - overactivemedia.com
Email - rshah@oam.gg
Investor Relations - Rikesh Shah (647) 227-2636
Auditors - KPMG LLP C.A., Vaughan, Ont.
Transfer Agents - Olympia Trust Company, Calgary, Alta.
Profile - (B.C. 2018) Owns eSports teams based in Toronto, Ont.; Madrid, Spain; and Berlin, Germany.

Owns team franchises in: the Overwatch League, operating as the Toronto Defiant; the Call of Duty League, operating as the Toronto Ultra; the League of Legends European Championship, operating as the MAD Lions; and VALORANT Challengers League North America, operating as the MAD Lions.

Also operates both live and online events, operating as OAM Live. In addition, operates fan clubs and other fan-related activities that increase the reach of its brands.

The company is constructing a 7,000-seat entertainment facility in Toronto, Ont., which was expected to be completed in 2025. The facility is intended to be a venue for eSport, music and entertainment events, major city-wide conventions, corporate events, product launches and award shows. The facility would also be the home for Toronto Ultra and Toronto Defiant.

On Apr. 19, 2022, the company ceased operations of its Counter Strike: Global Offensive team, operating as the MAD Lions in Flashpoint, a franchised league operated by **B Site Inc.** The company held a minority interest in B Site Inc., the value of which was written down to nil during 2021.

Predecessor Detail - Name changed from Abigail Capital Corporation, July 9, 2021, pursuant to the Qualifying Transaction reverse takeover acquisition of (old) OverActive Media Corp. and concurrent amalgamation of (old) OverActive with wholly owned 13016838 Canada Inc. (and continued as OverActive Media Holdings Corp.).; basis 1 new for 9 old shs.

Directors - Sheldon M. Pollack, chr., Toronto, Ont.; Jamie Firsten, corp. sec., Toronto, Ont.; Christina Bianco, Stouffville, Ont.; Wende Cartwright, Ont.; Stewart Johnston, Ont.; Jeffrey Kimel, Toronto, Ont.; Michael Kimel, Toronto, Ont.

Other Exec. Officers - Adam E. Adamou, interim CEO; Rikesh Shah, CFO; Alyson Walker, chief comml. officer; Robert J. (Bob) Hunter, sr. v-p, venue devel.; Tyler Keenan, sr. v-p, partnerships & rev.; Matt McGlynn, v-p, mktg. & brand; Amy Williams, v-p, global partnerships

Capital Stock

	Authorized (shs.)	Outstanding (shs.)[1]
Common	unlimited	80,308,000

[1] At May 24, 2023

Major Shareholder - Westdale Construction Co. Limited held 16.5% interest at May 26, 2023.

Price Range - OAM/TSX-VEN

Year	Volume	High	Low	Close
2022	13,201,159	$1.40	$0.15	$0.28
2021	11,567,521	$2.70	$0.90	$1.44
2020	500	$1.80	$1.35	$1.80
2019	5,555	$1.80	$1.80	$1.80

Consolidation: 1-for-9 cons. in July 2021
Recent Close: $0.17

Capital Stock Changes - There were no changes to capital stock during 2022.

Wholly Owned Subsidiaries

OverActive Media Holdings Corp., Toronto, Ont.
- 100% int. in **Media XP Inc.**, Canada.
- 100% int. in **OAMLEC, S.L.U.**, Spain.
- 100% int. in **11335537 Canada Inc.**, Canada.
- 100% int. in **OverActive GP Inc.**, Ont.
  - 100% int. in **OverActive Limited Partnership**, Ont.
    - 100% int. in **Splyce, Inc.**, Rochester, N.Y.
      - 10% int. in **10859036 Canada Inc.**, Canada. dba Toronto Defiant.
    - 100% int. in **Splyce Ltd.**, Ireland.
- 100% int. in **OverActive Media Group Inc.**, Canada.
  - 90% int. in **10859036 Canada Inc.**, Canada. dba Toronto Defiant.
  - 100% int. in **11779079 Canada Limited**, Canada.
  - 100% int. in **OverActive Media Delaware LLC**, Del.

Financial Statistics

Periods ended:	12m Dec. 31/22[A]		12m Dec. 31/21[A1]
	$000s	%Chg	$000s
Operating revenue	**14,162**	**0**	**14,195**
Salaries & benefits	14,686		13,992
General & admin expense	5,841		4,646
Stock-based compensation	2,433		4,514
Other operating expense	4,881		3,562
Operating expense	**27,841**	**+4**	**26,714**
Operating income	**(13,679)**	**n.a.**	**(12,519)**
Deprec., depl. & amort.	2,320		1,971
Finance income	118		nil
Finance costs, gross	5,251		5,103
Write-downs/write-offs	(34,214)		nil
Pre-tax income	**(43,925)**	**n.a.**	**(20,610)**
Income taxes	(7,000)		(1,214)
Net income	**(36,925)**	**n.a.**	**(19,396)**
Cash & equivalent	13,557		29,577
Accounts receivable	6,589		4,906
Current assets	22,232		35,691
Fixed assets, net	2,531		2,698
Right-of-use assets	1,297		1,827
Intangibles, net	61,582		95,244
Total assets	**87,642**	**-35**	**135,460**
Bank indebtedness	63		63
Accts. pay. & accr. liabs	4,256		3,651
Current liabilities	8,678		15,903
Long-term debt, gross	391		536
Long-term debt, net	228		350
Long-term lease liabilities	349		955
Shareholders' equity	47,459		81,920
Cash from oper. activs	**(11,507)**	**n.a.**	**(10,772)**
Cash from fin. activs	(3,112)		35,690
Cash from invest. activs	(1,694)		(1,110)
Net cash position	**13,557**	**-54**	**29,577**
Capital expenditures	(857)		(2,011)
Capital disposals	505		442
	$		$
Earnings per share*	(0.46)		(0.28)
Cash flow per share*	(0.14)		(0.15)
	shs		shs
No. of shs. o/s*	80,308,000		80,308,000
Avg. no. of shs. o/s*	80,308,000		69,708,000
	%		%
Net profit margin	(260.73)		(136.64)
Return on equity	(57.08)		(27.09)
Return on assets	(29.14)		(11.64)
Foreign sales percent	37		38

* Common
[A] Reported in accordance with IFRS
[1] Results reflect the July 9, 2021, reverse takeover acquisition of (old) OverActive Media Corp.

Latest Results

Periods ended:	3m Mar. 31/23[A]		3m Mar. 31/22[A]
	$000s	%Chg	$000s
Operating revenue	1,617	-23	2,099
Net income	(5,739)	n.a.	(4,638)
	$		$
Earnings per share*	(0.07)		(0.06)

* Common
[A] Reported in accordance with IFRS

Historical Summary
(as originally stated)

Fiscal Year	Oper. Rev. $000s	Net Inc. Bef. Disc. $000s	EPS* $
2022[A]	14,162	(36,925)	(0.46)
2021[A]	14,195	(19,396)	(0.28)
2020[A1]	8,376	(6,261)	(0.12)
2019[A1]	2,228	(22,758)	(0.47)

* Common
[A] Reported in accordance with IFRS
[1] Results pertain to (old) OverActive Media Corp.
Note: Adjusted throughout for 1-for-9 cons. in July 2021

P

P.1 PC 1 Corp.

Symbol - PCAA.P **Exchange** - TSX-VEN **CUSIP** - 69323W
Head Office - 201-10 Wanless Ave, Toronto, ON, M4N 1V6 **Telephone** - (416) 481-2222
Email - aeisenberg@plazacapital.ca
Investor Relations - Aaron Eisenberg (416) 481-2222
Auditors - Clearhouse LLP C.A., Mississauga, Ont.
Lawyers - Garfinkle Biderman LLP, Toronto, Ont.
Transfer Agents - Capital Transfer Agency Inc., Toronto, Ont.
Profile - (Ont. 2021) Capital Pool Company.

Recent Merger and Acquisition Activity

Status: terminated **Revised:** July 5, 2022
UPDATE: The transaction was terminated. PREVIOUS: PC 1 Corp. entered into a letter of intent for the Qualifying Transaction acquisition of the assets of NexTech AR Solutions Corp.'s U.K.-based wholly owned ARWAY Ltd. for issuance of 16,000,000 post-consolidated at a deemed price of 25¢ per share. ARWAY provides ARitize Maps, a smartphone application which allows users to spatially map their location and populate it with interactive 3D objects, navigations, wayfinding, audio and more.

Status: terminated **Revised:** May 19, 2022
UPDATE: The transaction was terminated. PREVIOUS: PC 1 Corp. entered into a letter of intent for the Qualifying Transaction reverse takeover acquisition of private Cashtag Media Corp., which was developing an online media platform exclusively focused on investor communications, on the basis of 1.129090909 PC 1 common shares for each Cashtag share held, which would result in the issuance of 28,227,273 PC 1 common shares at a deemed price of $0.2125604 per share.

Directors - Aaron Eisenberg, CEO, CFO & corp. sec., Toronto, Ont.; Yaron Conforti, Toronto, Ont.; Jesse Kaplan, Toronto, Ont.; Yisroel (Sruli) Weinreb, Toronto, Ont.

Capital Stock

	Authorized (shs.)	Outstanding (shs.)[1]
Common	unlimited	10,350,000

[1] At June 22, 2023

Major Shareholder - Widely held at Dec. 2, 2021.

Price Range - PCAA.P/TSX-VEN

Year	Volume	High	Low	Close
2022	326,811	$0.12	$0.03	$0.04
2021	20,000	$0.11	$0.11	$0.11

Recent Close: $0.03

Capital Stock Changes - On Dec. 2, 2021, an initial public offering of 5,000,000 common shares was completed at 10¢ per share; 250,000 common shares were issued to brokers in connection with the offering.

P.2 PHX Energy Services Corp.*

Symbol - PHX **Exchange** - TSX **CUSIP** - 69338U
Head Office - 1600-215 9 Ave SW, Calgary, AB, T2P 1K3 **Telephone** - (403) 543-4466 **Toll-free** - (866) 607-4677 **Fax** - (403) 543-4485
Website - www.phxtech.com
Email - critchie@phxtech.com
Investor Relations - Cameron M. Ritchie (403) 543-4466
Auditors - KPMG LLP C.A., Calgary, Alta.
Bankers - HSBC Bank Canada, Calgary, Alta.
Lawyers - Burnet, Duckworth & Palmer LLP, Calgary, Alta.
Transfer Agents - Odyssey Trust Company, Calgary, Alta.
FP500 Revenue Ranking - 453
Employees - 843 at Dec. 31, 2022

Profile - (Alta. 2010) Provides horizontal and directional drilling services to oil and gas exploration and development companies in Canada, the United States, Albania and the Middle East regions; and develops and manufactures drilling technologies for internal operational use.

Operations are conducted in Canada through indirect wholly owned **Phoenix Technology Services L.P.**, with sales, research and development, service and operational centres in Calgary, Alta., and a service facility in Estevan, Sask.; and in the U.S. through indirect wholly owned **Phoenix Technology Services USA Inc.**, with sales and services facilities in Houston and Midland, Tex., Casper, Wyo., and Oklahoma City, Okla. The company also has sales offices and service facilities in Albania, and administrative offices in Nicosia, Cyprus, and Luxembourg City, Luxembourg. Also operates in the Middle East through an arrangement with **National Energy Services Reunited Corp.**

The company's licensed technology includes Velocity Real-Time System, which is equipped with unified telemetry which allows the system to send downhole data to the surface via electromagnetic telemetry (EM) and mud pulse telemetry; PowerDrive Orbit RSS, which is designed to drill directionally with continuous rotation from the surface, eliminating the need to pause the drill string rotation to steer the wellbore; Atlas High Performance Drilling Motor, which is designed to provide greater horsepower to the drilling operation, reliably perform under more aggressive drilling parameters, drill the multiple sections of a well continuously, and to extend downhole run life; At-Bit System, which is equipped with sensors to provide more accurate and precise downhole measurements; Echo System, which is an antenna that can detect Velocity's EM signal transmission from nearby active well and transmit the signal through the wireline to its surface receiver; E-360 EM MWD System, which transmits electric signals through geological formations to the surface rather than through the mud; P-360 EM MWD System, which is designed to withstand harsh environments and high drilling velocities and provides the ability to transmit data quickly via the drilling mud system; and 360RWD Resistivity While Drilling System, which provides real-time information about the resistive nature of the rock the customer is drilling through to ensure they drill in the most optimal location within the respective zone.

In June 2022, the company sold wholly owned **Phoenix TSR LLC**, representing the Russian division, to **WellTech Services Ltd.**, a company based in Russia which provides drilling services, for 240,000,000 Russian Ruble (Cdn$4,200,000).

Predecessor Detail - Succeeded Phoenix Technology Income Fund, Dec. 31, 2010, pursuant to plan of arrangement whereby PHX Energy Services Corp. was formed to facilitate the conversion of the fund into a corporation and the fund was subsequently dissolved.

Directors - John M. Hooks, chr. & CEO, Calgary, Alta.; Myron A. Tétreault†, Calgary, Alta.; Randolph M. (Randy) Charron, Calgary, Alta.; Karen David-Green, Tex.; Terry D. Freeman, Edmonton, Alta.; Lawrence M. (Larry) Hibbard, Houston, Tex.; Roger D. Thomas, Calgary, Alta.

Other Exec. Officers - Michael (Mike) Buker, pres.; Craig Brown, sr. v-p, eng. & tech.; Cameron M. Ritchie, sr. v-p, fin., CFO & corp. sec.; Jeffery Shafer, sr. v-p, sales & mktg.

† Lead director

Capital Stock

	Authorized (shs.)	Outstanding (shs.)[1]
Common	unlimited	51,068,936

[1] At May 9, 2023

Options - At Dec. 31, 2022, options were outstanding to purchase 1,133,334 common shares at a weighted average exercise price of $3.31 per share with a weighted average remaining contractual life of 2.69 years.

Normal Course Issuer Bid - The company plans to make normal course purchases of up to 3,552,810 common shares representing 10% of the public float. The bid commenced on Aug. 16, 2023, and expires on Aug. 15, 2024.

Major Shareholder - GMT Capital Corp. held 12.35% interest and John M. Hooks held 10.62% interest at Mar. 28, 2023.

Price Range - PHX/TSX

Year	Volume	High	Low	Close
2022	24,513,965	$8.93	$3.94	$7.77
2021	20,590,146	$5.70	$2.40	$4.46
2020	27,096,994	$2.88	$0.51	$2.53
2019	12,559,053	$3.50	$2.26	$2.83
2018	10,495,712	$3.31	$1.82	$2.36

Recent Close: $7.82

Capital Stock Changes - During 2022, 1,266,038 common shares were issued on exercise of options, 2,277,875 common shares were released from treasury pursuant to retention award plan and 626,400 common shares were returned to treasury.

Dividends

PHX com Ra $0.60 pa Q est. Jan. 16, 2023**[1]
Prev. Rate: $0.40 est. Oct. 17, 2022
Prev. Rate: $0.30 est. Apr. 18, 2022
Prev. Rate: $0.20 est. Jan. 17, 2022
[1] First divd. since last Jan/16
** Reinvestment Option

Long-Term Debt - At Dec. 31 2022, outstanding long-term debt totaled $22,731,389 (none current) and consisted of $731,389 of borrowings under an operating facility bearing interest at prime plus 0.5% and $22,000,000 of borrowings under a syndicated facility bearing interest at SOFR plus 1.5%, both due Dec. 12, 2025.

Wholly Owned Subsidiaries

Phoenix Technology Services Inc., Calgary, Alta.
- 100% int. in **Phoenix Technology Management Inc.**, Alta.
  - 1% int. in **Phoenix Technology Services L.P.**, Alta.
- 100% int. in **Phoenix Technology Services International Ltd.**, Cyprus.
- 99% int. in **Phoenix Technology Services L.P.**, Alta.
- 100% int. in **Phoenix Technology Services Luxembourg S.A.R.L.**, Luxembourg.
- 100% int. in **Phoenix Technology Services USA Inc.**, Del.
  - 100% int. in **Qualitas Oilfield Services Inc.**, Tex.

Investments

DEEP Earth Energy Production Corp., Sask.

Financial Statistics

Periods ended:	12m Dec. 31/22[A]		12m Dec. 31/21[◻A]
	$000s	%Chg	$000s
Operating revenue	**535,745**	**+58**	**339,946**
Research & devel. expense	3,723		2,774
General & admin expense	68,901		44,982
Other operating expense	390,753		241,440
Operating expense	**463,377**	**+60**	**289,196**
Operating income	**72,368**	**+43**	**50,750**
Deprec., depl. & amort.	35,354		29,197
Finance costs, gross	3,392		2,619
Write-downs/write-offs	13		281
Pre-tax income	**53,353**	**+99**	**26,876**
Income taxes	9,042		3,559
Net inc. bef. disc. opers	**44,311**	**+90**	**23,318**
Income from disc. opers	(14,558)		(593)
Net income	**29,753**	**+31**	**22,725**
Cash & equivalent	18,247		24,829
Inventories	63,119		36,691
Accounts receivable	125,836		76,478
Current assets	210,227		141,159
Long-term investments	3,001		3,001
Fixed assets, net	115,945		76,363
Right-of-use assets	29,336		25,708
Intangibles, net	15,668		16,137
Total assets	**375,224**	**+43**	**262,494**
Accts. pay. & accr. liabs	104,689		77,572
Current liabilities	115,888		83,286
Long-term debt, gross	22,731		nil
Long-term debt, net	22,731		nil
Long-term lease liabilities	36,768		32,639
Shareholders' equity	176,878		134,432
Cash from oper. activs	**37,082**	**-18**	**45,453**
Cash from fin. activs	2,706		(22,718)
Cash from invest. activs	(47,388)		(23,629)
Net cash position	**18,247**	**-27**	**24,829**
Capital expenditures	(73,525)		(35,281)
Capital disposals	27,459		12,340
	$		$
Earns. per sh. bef disc opers*	0.88		0.47
Earnings per share*	0.59		0.46
Cash flow per share*	0.74		0.92
Cash divd. per share*	0.40		0.15
	shs		shs
No. of shs. o/s*	50,896,175		47,978,662
Avg. no. of shs. o/s*	50,144,334		49,549,967
	%		%
Net profit margin	8.27		6.86
Return on equity	28.47		17.50
Return on assets	14.78		10.68
Foreign sales percent	80		81
No. of employees (FTEs)	843		707

* Common
◻ Restated
[A] Reported in accordance with IFRS

Latest Results

Periods ended:	3m Mar. 31/23[A]		3m Mar. 31/22[◻A]
	$000s	%Chg	$000s
Operating revenue	166,022	+52	109,304
Net inc. bef. disc. opers	22,417	n.a.	(2,315)
Income from disc. opers	nil		(1,908)
Net income	22,417	n.a.	(4,223)
	$		$
Earns. per sh. bef. disc. opers.*	0.44		(0.05)
Earnings per share*	0.44		(0.09)

* Common
◻ Restated
[A] Reported in accordance with IFRS

Historical Summary
(as originally stated)

Fiscal Year	Oper. Rev.	Net Inc. Bef. Disc.	EPS*
	$000s	$000s	$
2022[A]	535,745	44,311	0.88
2021[A]	349,920	22,725	0.46
2020[A]	233,734	(6,878)	(0.13)
2019[A]	362,057	(2,213)	(0.04)
2018[A]	317,135	(18,947)	(0.33)

* Common
[A] Reported in accordance with IFRS

P.3 PIMCO Global Income Opportunities Fund

Symbol - PGI.UN **Exchange** - TSX **CUSIP** - 72202T
Head Office - 2050-199 Bay St, Toronto, ON, M5L 1G2 **Telephone** - (416) 368-3217 **Toll-free** - (866) 341-3350 **Fax** - (416) 368-3576
Website - www.pimco.ca
Email - pimcocanadareporting@pimco.com
Investor Relations - Stuart Graham (416) 368-3217
Auditors - PricewaterhouseCoopers LLP C.A., Toronto, Ont.
Lawyers - Torys LLP, Toronto, Ont.
Transfer Agents - TSX Trust Company, Toronto, Ont.
Trustees - State Street Bank and Trust Company, Toronto, Ont.
Investment Advisors - Pacific Investment Management Company, LLC, Newport Beach, Calif.
Managers - PIMCO Canada Corp., Toronto, Ont.
Profile - (Ont. 2014) Invests in an actively managed portfolio consisting primarily of fixed income securities across multiple global fixed income sectors.

Investments will include mortgage-related securities, investment grade corporate securities, high yield securities, bank loans and emerging markets corporate securities. The fund, from time to time, may also invest in government securities and other fixed, variable and floating rate income-producing securities of global issuers.

Geographic distribution of investment portfolio at Mar. 31, 2023 (as a percentage of net asset value):

Country	Percentage
United States	90.3%
Luxembourg	10.2%
United Kingdom	4.9%
Spain	4.4%
Cayman Islands	3.8%
Netherlands	3.3%
Italy	3.2%
Other	16.6%
Total (long positions)	136.7%
Cash & cash equivalents	2.5%
Fin. deriv. (long positions)	(2.9%)
Fin. deriv. (short positions)	8.4%
Liabilities less other assets	(44.7%)
	100%

Oper. Subsid./Mgt. Co. Directors - Stuart Graham, pres., Toronto, Ont.; John Kirkowski, CFO, Calif.; David Flattum, Irvine, Calif.
Oper. Subsid./Mgt. Co. Officers - Mostafa Asadi, sr. v-p, counsel & head, legal & compliance

Capital Stock

	Authorized (shs.)	Outstanding (shs.)[1]
Class A Unit	unlimited	36,546,016

[1] At May 31, 2023

Class A Unit - Entitled to monthly cash distributions targeted to be $0.0963 per unit. Retractable in March of each year at a price equal to the net asset value (NAV) per unit, less any costs to fund the retraction. Retractable monthly at a price per unit equal to the lesser of: (i) 94% of the weighted average price per unit on TSX for the 10 trading days immediately preceding the retraction date; and (ii) the closing price per unit. One vote per unit.
Major Shareholder - Widely held at Feb. 28, 2022.

Price Range - PGI.UN/TSX

Year	Volume	High	Low	Close
2022	8,378,077	$9.80	$7.15	$7.42
2021	6,916,358	$10.34	$9.45	$9.80
2020	8,499,010	$11.41	$7.02	$9.74
2019	8,383,773	$11.08	$9.25	$10.93
2018	9,562,511	$10.73	$9.19	$9.29

Recent Close: $6.93
Capital Stock Changes - In March 2022, 3,176,392 class A units were retracted. Also during 2022, 107,000 class A units were issued under distribution reinvestment plan.

Dividends

PGI.UN cl A unit Var. Ra pa M**

$0.05688	Sept. 15/23	$0.05688	Aug. 15/23
$0.05688	July 14/23	$0.05688	June 14/23

Paid in 2023: $0.51192 2022: $0.68256 + $0.0957◆ 2021: $0.68256
** Reinvestment Option ◆ Special

Financial Statistics

Periods ended:	12m Dec. 31/22^A		12m Dec. 31/21^A
	$000s	%Chg	$000s
Realized invest. gain (loss)	(4,208)		18,641
Unrealized invest. gain (loss)	(72,437)		(18,903)
Total revenue	**(36,937)**	**n.a.**	**38,205**
General & admin. expense	6,944		8,792
Operating expense	**6,944**	**-21**	**8,792**
Operating income	**(43,881)**	**n.a.**	**29,413**
Finance costs, gross	4,384		2,084
Pre-tax income	**(48,265)**	**n.a.**	**27,329**
Net income	**(48,265)**	**n.a.**	**27,329**
Cash & equivalent	26		665
Accounts receivable	2,013		9,725
Investments	412,012		584,155
Total assets	**437,430**	**-28**	**609,617**
Accts. pay. & accr. liabs	4,012		25,768
Debt	151,336		196,656
Shareholders' equity	275,692		377,085
Cash from oper. activs	**112,264**	**+307**	**27,563**
Cash from fin. activs	(106,191)		(30,787)
Net cash position	**7,899**	**+324**	**1,863**
	$		$
Earnings per share*	(1.29)		0.69
Cash flow per share*	3.06		0.69
Net asset value per share*	7.50		9.47
Cash divd. per share*	0.68		0.68
Extra divd. - cash*	nil		0.10
Total divd. per share*	**0.68**		**0.78**
	shs		shs
No. of shs. o/s*	36,737,749		39,807,000
	%		%
Net profit margin	n.m.		71.53
Return on equity	(14.79)		7.22
Return on assets	(8.38)		4.79

* Cl.A Unit
^A Reported in accordance with IFRS

Historical Summary

(as originally stated)

Fiscal Year	Total Rev. $000s	Net Inc. Bef. Disc. $000s	EPS* $
2022^A	(36,937)	(48,265)	(1.29)
2021^A	38,205	27,329	0.69
2020^A	28,668	17,040	0.43
2019^A	57,058	42,009	1.05
2018^A	28,506	11,635	0.27

* Cl.A Unit
^A Reported in accordance with IFRS

P.4 PIMCO Multi-Sector Income Fund

Symbol - PIX.UN **Exchange** - TSX **CUSIP** - 72204T
Head Office - Commerce Court West, 2050-199 Bay St, Toronto, ON, M5L 1G2 **Telephone** - (416) 368-3350 **Fax** - (416) 368-3576
Website - www.pimco.ca
Email - agnes.crane@pimco.com
Investor Relations - Agnes Crane (347) 952-8954
Auditors - PricewaterhouseCoopers LLP C.A., Toronto, Ont.
Transfer Agents - TSX Trust Company, Toronto, Ont.
Managers - PIMCO Canada Corp., Toronto, Ont.
Portfolio Managers - PIMCO Canada Corp., Toronto, Ont.
Profile - (Ont. 2022) Invests in an actively managed portfolio consisting primarily of fixed income securities selected from multiple global fixed income sectors.

The fund manger uses a dynamic asset allocation strategy among multiple sectors in the global credit markets, including corporate debt, mortgage-related and other asset-backed securities, government and sovereign debt, taxable municipal bonds, other fixed-, variable- and floating-rate income-producing securities of U.S., and global issuers, including emerging market issuers, and real estate-related investments. The portfolio will include: (i) debt obligations and other income-producing securities and instruments of any type and credit quality with varying maturities and related derivatives, and (ii) real estate-related investments.

The fund is scheduled to terminate on or about Feb. 17, 2034.

Pacific Investment Management Company LLC is the subadvisor of the fund.

The manager is entitled to a management fee at an annual rate of 1.30% of net asset value, calculated daily and payable monthly in arrears.

Oper. Subsid./Mgt. Co. Directors - Stuart Graham, pres., Toronto, Ont.; John Kirkowski, CFO, Calif.; David Flattum, Irvine, Calif.
Oper. Subsid./Mgt. Co. Officers - Mostafa Asadi, sr. v-p & head, legal & compliance

Capital Stock

	Authorized (shs.)	Outstanding (shs.)[1]
Class A Unit	unlimited	25,613,000
Class P Unit	unlimited	nil

[1] At June 30, 2023

Class A Unit - Entitled to initial monthly cash distributions targeted to be $0.04583 to $0.05208 per unit (to yield 5.5% to 6.25% per annum on the initial issue price of $10). Retractable monthly at a price per unit equal to the lesser of: (i) 94% of the weighted average price per unit on TSX for the 10 trading days immediately preceding the retraction date; and (ii) the closing market price per unit. One vote per unit.

Price Range - PIX.UN/TSX

Year	Volume	High	Low	Close
2022	4,566,000	$9.98	$7.96	$8.41

Recent Close: $7.60
Capital Stock Changes - On Mar. 10, 2022, an initial public offering of 8,701,987 class A units at $10 per unit and 13,910,615 class F units at $9.83 per unit was completed, including 1,112,602 class A units on exercise of over-allotment option. Class F units were immediately reclassified as class A units. A concurrent private placement of 3,000,657 class P units was completed at $10 per unit. Class P units are reclassified as class A units on Sept. 12, 2022.

Dividends

PIX.UN cl A unit Ra $0.78456 pa M est. Sept. 15, 2022**
Listed Mar 10/22.
Prev. Rate: $0.62496 est. June 14, 2022
$0.05208**i** June 14/22
** Reinvestment Option **i** Initial Payment

Financial Statistics

Periods ended:	12m Dec. 31/22^A
	$000s
Realized invest. gain (loss)	(11,897)
Unrealized invest. gain (loss)	(15,536)
Total revenue	**(11,308)**
General & admin. expense	3,813
Operating expense	**3,813**
Operating income	**(15,121)**
Finance costs, gross	1,492
Pre-tax income	**(16,613)**
Net income	**(16,613)**
Accounts receivable	2,752
Investments	246,190
Total assets	**296,719**
Accts. pay. & accr. liabs	15,569
Debt	45,498
Shareholders' equity	227,137
Cash from oper. activs	**(264,891)**
Cash from fin. activs	25,461
Net cash position	**25,450**
	$
Earnings per share*	(0.68)
Earnings per share	(0.19)
Cash flow per share***	(10.34)
Net asset value per share*	8.87
Cash divd. per share*	0.48
	shs
No. of shs. o/s***	25,613,259
	%
Net profit margin	n.m.
Return on equity	n.m.
Return on assets	n.a.

* Cl.A Unit
^A Reported in accordance with IFRS

Latest Results

Periods ended:	6m June 30/23^A		6m June 30/22^A
	$000s	%Chg	$000s
Total revenue	10,653	n.a.	(13,225)
Net income	6,841	n.a.	(14,729)
	$		$
Earnings per share*	0.27		(0.58)
Earnings per share	n.a.		(0.57)

* Cl.A Unit
^A Reported in accordance with IFRS

P.5 PIMCO Tactical Income Fund

Symbol - PTI.UN **Exchange** - TSX **CUSIP** - 72202K
Head Office - Commerce Court West, 2050-199 Bay St, Toronto, ON, M5L 1G2 **Telephone** - (416) 368-3550 **Toll-free** - (866) 341-3350
Website - www.pimco.ca
Email - jkirkowski@pimco.com
Investor Relations - John Kirkowski (416) 368-3550
Auditors - PricewaterhouseCoopers LLP C.A., Toronto, Ont.
Transfer Agents - TSX Trust Company, Toronto, Ont.
Trustees - State Street Bank and Trust Company, Toronto, Ont.
Managers - PIMCO Canada Corp., Toronto, Ont.
Portfolio Managers - PIMCO Canada Corp., Toronto, Ont.
Profile - (Ont. 2020) Invests in an actively managed portfolio consisting primarily of fixed income securities selected from multiple global fixed income sectors.

The fund manager uses a dynamic asset allocation strategy among multiple sectors in the global credit markets, including corporate debt, mortgage-related and other asset-backed securities, government and sovereign debt, taxable municipal bonds, other fixed-, variable- and floating-rate income-producing securities of U.S., and global issuers, including emerging market issuers, and real estate-related investments.

The fund is scheduled to terminate the first business day after Sept. 25, 2032.

Pacific Investment Management Company LLC is the subadvisor of the fund.

Geographic distribution of investment portfolio at Mar. 31, 2023 (as a percentage of net asset value):

Country	Percentage
United States	71%
Luxembourg	12.8%
Cayman Islands	11.1%
Spain	8.5%
United Kingdom	5.0%
Italy	3.6%
France	3.1%
Other	12.5%
Total (long positions)	127.6%
Cash & cash equivalents	12.6%
Fin. deriv. (long positions)	(1.2%)
Fin. deriv. (short positions)	5.7%
Liabilities Less Other Assets	(44.7%)
	100%

Oper. Subsid./Mgt. Co. Directors - Stuart Graham, pres., Toronto, Ont.; John Kirkowski, CFO, Calif.; David Flattum, Irvine, Calif.

Oper. Subsid./Mgt. Co. Officers - Mostafa Asadi, sr. v-p, counsel & chief compliance officer

Capital Stock

	Authorized (shs.)	Outstanding (shs.)[1]
Class A Unit	unlimited	37,619,995

[1] At May 31, 2023

Class A Unit - Entitled to monthly cash distributions of $0.0558 per unit. Retractable monthly at a price per unit equal to the lesser of: (i) 94% of the weighted average price per unit on TSX for the 10 trading days immediately preceding the retraction date; and (ii) the closing market price per unit. One vote per unit.

Major Shareholder - RBC Dominion Securities Inc. and RBC Private Counsel (USA) Inc. held 13.8% interest at Feb. 28, 2022.

Price Range - PTI.UN/TSX

Year	Volume	High	Low	Close
2022	10,375,788	$10.59	$6.74	$7.00
2021	6,808,094	$11.64	$10.05	$10.05
2020	2,912,299	$10.81	$9.70	$10.50

Recent Close: $6.41

Capital Stock Changes - During 2022, 19,000 class A units were issued under distribution reinvestment plan.

Dividends

PTI.UN cl A unit Var. Ra pa M**

$0.0558	Sept. 15/23	$0.0558	Aug. 15/23
$0.0558	July 14/23	$0.0558	June 14/23

Paid in 2023: $0.5022 2022: $1.48887 2021: $0.62496**i** + $0.06669◆

** Reinvestment Option ◆ Special **i** Initial Payment

Financial Statistics

Periods ended:	12m Dec. 31/22[A]		12m Dec. 31/21[oA]
	$000s	%Chg	$000s
Realized invest. gain (loss)	(45,836)		27,707
Unrealized invest. gain (loss)	(39,103)		(29,211)
Total revenue	**(42,331)**	**n.a.**	**34,712**
General & admin. expense	7,058		9,051
Operating expense	**7,058**	**-22**	**9,051**
Operating income	**(49,389)**	**n.a.**	**25,661**
Finance costs, gross	3,717		1,939
Pre-tax income	**(53,106)**	**n.a.**	**23,722**
Net income	**(53,106)**	**n.a.**	**23,722**
Cash & equivalent	nil		1
Accounts receivable	57,235		28,380
Investments	355,324		558,398
Total assets	**480,430**	**-21**	**610,427**
Accts. pay. & accr. liabs	65,697		42,586
Debt	122,951		168,906
Shareholders' equity	279,916		357,167
Cash from oper. activs	**136,453**	**n.m.**	**5,182**
Cash from fin. activs	(103,565)		2,809
Net cash position	**43,017**	**+325**	**10,121**
	$		$
Earnings per share*	(1.42)		0.63
Cash flow per share*	3.63		0.14
Net asset value per share*	7.45		9.51
Cash divd. per share*	0.59		1.53
	shs		shs
No. of shs. o/s*	37,587,000		37,568,000
	%		%
Net profit margin	n.m.		68.34
Return on equity	(16.67)		n.m.
Return on assets	(9.06)		n.a.

* Cl.A Unit
[o] Restated
[A] Reported in accordance with IFRS

Note: Net income reflects increase/decrease in net assets from operations.

P.6 PIMCO Tactical Income Opportunities Fund

Symbol - PTO.UN **Exchange** - TSX **CUSIP** - 69356D

Head Office - c/o PIMCO Canada Corp., Commerce Court West, 2050-199 Bay St, PO Box 363 Stn Commerce Court, Toronto, ON, M5L 1G2 **Telephone** - (416) 368-3350 **Toll-free** - (866) 341-3350

Website - www.pimco.ca

Investor Relations - Mostafa Asadi (416) 368-3350

Auditors - PricewaterhouseCoopers LLP C.A., Toronto, Ont.

Lawyers - Blake, Cassels & Graydon LLP, Toronto, Ont.

Transfer Agents - TSX Trust Company, Toronto, Ont.

Trustees - State Street Bank and Trust Company, Toronto, Ont.

Investment Advisors - Pacific Investment Management Company, LLC, Newport Beach, Calif.

Managers - PIMCO Canada Corp., Toronto, Ont.

Portfolio Managers - PIMCO Canada Corp., Toronto, Ont.

Profile - (Ont. 2021) Invests in an actively managed portfolio consisting primarily of fixed income securities selected from multiple global fixed income sectors.

The fund manager uses a dynamic asset allocation strategy among multiple sectors in the global credit markets, including corporate debt, mortgage-related and other asset-backed securities, government and sovereign debt, taxable municipal bonds, other fixed-, variable- and floating-rate income-producing securities of U.S., and global issuers, including emerging market issuers, and real estate-related investments.

The fund will terminate on May 26, 2033, unless extended by the manager.

Geographic distribution of investment portfolio at Mar. 31, 2023 (as a percentage of net asset value):

Country	Percentage
United States	64.9%
Cayman Islands	9.8%
Luxembourg	8.3%
Spain	5.3%
United Kingdom	4.4%
France	3.0%
Other	15.9%
Total (long positions)	111.6%
Cash and Cash Equivalents	19.6%
Fin. deriv. (long positions)	0.7%
Fin. deriv. (short positions)	3.1%
Liabilities less other assets	(35.0%)
	100%

Oper. Subsid./Mgt. Co. Directors - Stuart Graham, pres., Toronto, Ont.; John Kirkowski, CFO, Calif.; David Flattum, Irvine, Calif.

Oper. Subsid./Mgt. Co. Officers - Mostafa Asadi, sr. v-p, counsel & chief compliance officer

Capital Stock

	Authorized (shs.)	Outstanding (shs.)[1]
Class A Unit	unlimited	34,476,468

[1] At May 31, 2023

Class A Unit - Entitled to monthly cash distributions of $0.05709 per unit. Retractable monthly at a price per unit equal to the lesser of: (i) 94% of the weighted average price per unit on TSX for the 10 trading days immediately preceding the retraction date; and (ii) the closing price per unit. One vote per unit.

Major Shareholder - Widely held at Mar. 23, 2022.

Price Range - PTO.UN/TSX

Year	Volume	High	Low	Close
2022	8,112,853	$10.15	$6.82	$7.15
2021	3,898,331	$10.92	$9.85	$10.15

Recent Close: $6.88

Capital Stock Changes - During 2022, 3,000 class A units were issued under distribution reinvestment plan.

Dividends

PTO.UN cl A unit Var. Ra pa M**
Listed Jun 17/21.

$0.05709	Sept. 15/23	$0.05709	Aug. 15/23
$0.05709	July 14/23	$0.05709	June 14/23

Paid in 2023: $0.51381 2022: $0.63545 + $0.16389◆ 2021: $0.20**i**

** Reinvestment Option ◆ Special **i** Initial Payment

Financial Statistics

Periods ended:	12m Dec. 31/22[A]		28w Dec. 31/21[oA]
	$000s	%Chg	$000s
Realized invest. gain (loss)	(33,372)		(3,511)
Unrealized invest. gain (loss)	(47,249)		(5,635)
Total revenue	**(41,914)**	**n.a.**	**10,558**
General & admin. expense	6,030		4,164
Operating expense	**6,030**	**n.a.**	**4,164**
Operating income	**(47,944)**	**n.a.**	**6,394**
Finance costs, gross	2,953		385
Pre-tax income	**(50,897)**	**n.a.**	**6,009**
Net income	**(50,897)**	**n.a.**	**6,009**
Accounts receivable	16,629		16,205
Investments	326,214		458,676
Total assets	**369,697**	**-27**	**506,516**
Accts. pay. & accr. liabs	5,255		33,876
Debt	83,851		123,874
Shareholders' equity	263,456		336,467
Cash from oper. activs	**53,133**	**n.a.**	**(448,609)**
Cash from fin. activs	(68,595)		460,795
Net cash position	**(3,276)**	**n.a.**	**12,142**
	$		$
Earnings per share*	(1.48)		0.17
Cash flow per share*	1.54		(13.01)
Net asset value per share*	7.64		9.76
Cash divd. per share*	0.64		0.25
Extra divd. - cash*	nil		0.16
Total divd. per share*	**0.64**		**0.41**
	shs		shs
No. of shs. o/s*	34,476,000		34,473,000
	%		%
Net profit margin	n.m.		...
Return on equity	(16.97)		...
Return on assets	(10.94)		...

* Cl.A Unit
[o] Restated
[A] Reported in accordance with IFRS

Note: Net income reflects increase/decrease in net assets from operations.

P.7 POCML 7 Inc.

Symbol - POC.P **Exchange** - TSX-VEN **CUSIP** - 69291G

Head Office - 2210-130 King St W, Toronto, ON, M5X 1E4 **Telephone** - (416) 643-3880

Email - ddonofrio@poweronecapital.com

Investor Relations - David M. D'Onofrio (416) 643-3880

Auditors - MNP LLP C.A., Toronto, Ont.

Lawyers - Irwin Lowy LLP, Toronto, Ont.

Transfer Agents - TSX Trust Company, Toronto, Ont.

Profile - (Ont. 2021) Capital Pool Company.

Common listed on TSX-VEN, Nov. 16, 2022.

Directors - Pasquale (Pat) DiCapo, founder, CEO, CFO & corp. sec., Toronto, Ont.; David M. D'Onofrio, Toronto, Ont.; Adam Parsons, Toronto, Ont.

Capital Stock

	Authorized (shs.)	Outstanding (shs.)[1]
Common	unlimited	11,000,000
Special	unlimited	nil

[1] At Nov. 16, 2022

Common - One vote per share.

Special - Issuable in series.

Major Shareholder - Pasquale (Pat) DiCapo held 63.64% interest at Nov. 16, 2022.

Price Range - POC.P/TSX-VEN

Year	Volume	High	Low	Close
2022	37,000	$0.30	$0.16	$0.30

Recent Close: $0.10

Capital Stock Changes - On Nov. 16, 2022, an initial public offering of 2,500,000 common shares was completed at 10¢ per share.

P.8 POET Technologies Inc.

Symbol - PTK **Exchange** - TSX-VEN **CUSIP** - 73044W
Head Office - 1107-120 Eglinton Ave E, Toronto, ON, M4P 1E2 **Telephone** - (416) 368-9411 **Fax** - (416) 322-5075
Website - www.poet-technologies.com
Email - tm@poet-technologies.com
Investor Relations - Thomas R. Mika (416) 368-9411
Auditors - Marcum LLP C.P.A., New Haven, Conn.
Lawyers - Bennett Jones LLP, Toronto, Ont.
Transfer Agents - TSX Trust Company, Toronto, Ont.
Employees - 53 at Dec. 31, 2022
Profile - (Ont. 2010; orig. B.C., 1972) Designs, develops, manufactures and sells integrated opto-electronic solutions for data communications, telecommunications and artificial intelligence markets.

Developed the proprietary POET Optical Interposer™ platform, a technology which allows the combination or integration of various electronic and photonic components into a single multi-chip module using advanced wafer-level semiconductor manufacturing techniques and packaging methods. The technology eliminates costly components and labour-intensive assembly, alignment, burn-in and testing methods employed in conventional photonics. Applications include wafer-scale photonic integration, data centre market, telecommunications, accelerators for artificial intelligence (AI), Internet of Things (IoT) and industrial sensing, automotive LIDAR and on-board optics. The company's focus is on the development of optical engines for transceivers used in data centres and AI. Transceivers are used to convert digital electronic signals into light signals and vice versa, and to transmit and receive those light signals via fibre optic cables within data centers and between data centers and metropolitan centers in a vast data and telecommunications network.

Products include POET Starlight™, a packaged light source solution for AI applications consisting of LightBar™ and LightBar-C™, which are multiplexed light source products operating in the O-band for data communications applications and the C-band for sensing and computing applications; POET Infinity™, a chiplet-based transmitter platform for 400G, 800G and 1.6T pluggable transceivers and co-packaged optics solutions; POET Legacy, consists of 100/200G CWDM4/FR4 product lines for data centre operations, including fully validated receive, transmit and integrated optical engines and 100G LR4 product line for high performance optical engines to meet the specifications for long-range (10 km) communications on the client side of long-haul networks with amonolithic 4-channel multiplexing and demultiplexing functionality built directly into the Optical Interposer waveguides; 400G DR4/FR4 product line integrated with a 400G silicon photonics-based high speed modulator and/or thin film lithium niobate-based modulator; and 800G 2xFR4, a 8-channel receiver optical engine.

Effective Mar. 14, 2022, the company's common shares commenced trading on the NASDAQ under the symbol POET.

Predecessor Detail - Name changed from OPEL Technologies Inc., July 23, 2013.

Directors - Dr. Suresh Venkatesan, exec. chr. & CEO, Los Gatos, Calif.; Peter D. Charbonneau†, Ottawa, Ont.; Theresa L. Ende, Los Gatos, Calif.; Michal Lipson, New York, N.Y.; Jean-Louis Malinge, Paris, France; Glen Riley, Ore.; Christopher (Chris) Tsiofas, Toronto, Ont.

Other Exec. Officers - Vivek Rajgarhia, pres. & gen. mgr.; Thomas R. Mika, exec. v-p & CFO; Dr. Jinyu Mo, sr. v-p, Asia; Richard Zoccolillo, sr. v-p, strategic mktg. & product mgt.; Kevin Barnes, v-p, fin. & admin., contr. & treas.; Dr. Robert Ditizio, v-p, intellectual prop.; Raju Kankipati, v-p, product line mgt.; Dan Meerovich, v-p, product eng.
† Lead director

Capital Stock

	Authorized (shs.)	Outstanding (shs.)[1]
Special Vtg.	1	nil
Common	unlimited	40,586,667

[1] At Aug. 11, 2023

Major Shareholder - Widely held at May 15, 2023.

Price Range - PTK/TSX-VEN

Year	Volume	High	Low	Close
2022	5,573,411	$13.65	$3.26	$4.09
2021	10,720,014	$15.80	$7.10	$9.00
2020	7,886,330	$8.70	$2.25	$8.10
2019	4,761,913	$4.65	$2.70	$3.75
2018	14,804,119	$7.90	$1.90	$2.70

Consolidation: 1-for-10 cons. in Feb. 2022
Recent Close: $4.90

Capital Stock Changes - On Feb. 28, 2022, common shares were consolidated on a 1-for-10 basis. In December 2022, private placement of 1,126,635 units (1 post-consolidated common share & ½ warrant) at Cdn$3.81 per unit was completed. Also during 2022, post-consolidated common shares were issued as follows: 143,437 on exercise of stock options, 72,500 on exercise of warrants and 5,422 for debt settlement; 252 post-consolidated common shares were cancelled.

Wholly Owned Subsidiaries

BB Photonics Inc., N.J.
Opel Solar Inc., Del.
- 100% int. in **ODIS Inc.**, Del.

POET Technologies Pte Ltd., Singapore.
- 100% int. in **POET Optoelectronics Shenzhen Co. Ltd.**, Shenzhen, Guangdong, People's Republic of China.
- 80.7% int. in **Super Photonics Xiamen Co., Ltd.**, People's Republic of China.

Financial Statistics

Periods ended:	12m Dec. 31/22[A]	%Chg	12m Dec. 31/21[◻A]
	US$000s	%Chg	US$000s
Operating revenue	**553**	**+165**	**209**
Research & devel. expense	10,747		8,165
General & admin expense	8,223		7,955
Operating expense	**18,970**	**+18**	**16,120**
Operating income	**(18,417)**	**n.a.**	**(15,911)**
Deprec., depl. & amort.	1,293		1,101
Finance costs, gross	50		365
Investment income	(3,212)		(1,142)
Pre-tax income	**(21,037)**	**n.a.**	**(15,669)**
Net income	**(21,037)**	**n.a.**	**(15,669)**
Cash & equivalent	9,230		21,309
Current assets	9,568		21,789
Long-term investments	nil		1,445
Fixed assets, net	5,071		3,064
Right-of-use assets	241		327
Intangibles, net	511		528
Total assets	**15,390**	**-43**	**27,154**
Accts. pay. & accr. liabs	3,362		1,791
Current liabilities	3,817		1,924
Long-term debt, gross	30		32
Long-term lease liabilities	128		258
Shareholders' equity	11,445		24,972
Cash from oper. activs	**(12,326)**	**n.a.**	**(11,233)**
Cash from fin. activs	3,435		26,554
Cash from invest. activs	(3,293)		(7,298)
Net cash position	**9,230**	**-38**	**14,942**
Capital expenditures	(3,012)		(772)
	US$		US$
Earnings per share*	(0.57)		(4.50)
Cash flow per share*	(0.34)		(3.25)
	shs		shs
No. of shs. o/s*	37,841,950		3,649,423
Avg. no. of shs. o/s*	36,739,857		3,454,575
	%		%
Net profit margin	n.m.		n.m.
Return on equity	(115.53)		(101.79)
Return on assets	(98.66)		(78.90)
No. of employees (FTEs)	53		46

* Common
◻ Restated
[A] Reported in accordance with IFRS

Latest Results

Periods ended:	6m June 30/23[A]	%Chg	6m June 30/22[A]
	US$000s	%Chg	US$000s
Operating revenue	358	+198	120
Net income	(9,660)	n.a.	(10,715)
	US$		US$
Earnings per share*	(0.25)		(0.29)

* Common
[A] Reported in accordance with IFRS

Historical Summary
(as originally stated)

Fiscal Year	Oper. Rev. US$000s	Net Inc. Bef. Disc. US$000s	EPS* US$
2022[A]	553	(21,037)	(0.57)
2021[A]	209	(15,669)	(0.45)
2020[A]	nil	(18,169)	(0.60)
2019[A]	nil	(11,435)	(0.40)
2018[A]	3,888	(16,323)	(0.60)

* Common
[A] Reported in accordance with IFRS
Note: Adjusted throughout for 1-for-10 cons. in Feb. 2022

P.9 POSaBIT Systems Corporation

Symbol - PBIT **Exchange** - CSE **CUSIP** - 737307
Head Office - 11915 124 Ave NE, Kirkland, WA, United States, 98034 **Telephone** - (855) 767-2248
Website - www.posabit.com
Email - investors@posabit.com
Investor Relations - Matthew A. Fowler (855) 767-2248
Auditors - Armanino LLP C.P.A., Bellevue, Wash.
Transfer Agents - Computershare Trust Company of Canada Inc., Vancouver, B.C.
Employees - 47 at Dec. 31, 2022
Profile - (B.C. 2017) Provides point of sale (POS) software-as-a-service (SaaS) and compliant cashless payment processors for the cannabis sector.

Offers the following services to retailers and dispensaries:

POSaBIT Point-of-Sale - A software-as-a-service product that allows merchants to offer integrated pin debit and ACH (Automated Clearing House) payment options. This solution is able to track all sales and integrate full customer history and preferences. Revenue generated from this solution consists of monthly or annual subscription fees per terminal or console; installation fees; hardware fees; license fees; and charges for stand and deliver support over the term of licensing agreement.

POSaBIT Payments Services - A solution allowing merchants to provide a compliant, normalized retail experience to their customers who wish to pay for products other than with cash. Revenue generated from this solution consists of non-cash adjustment fees; transaction fees; installation fees; and rental fees.

Recent Merger and Acquisition Activity

Status: terminated **Revised:** Apr. 5, 2023
UPDATE: The transaction was terminated. PREVIOUS: POSaBIT Systems Corporation agreed to acquire Denver, Colo.-based MJ Freeway, LLC and Toronto, Ont.-based Ample Organics Inc. from Akerna Corp. for US$4,000,000 cash. MJ Freeway develops a cloud-based seed-to-sale cannabis software platform, allowing entrepreneurs and multi-state operators to manage, scale and optimize more competitive operations. Ample Organics develops seed-to-sale software solutions that facilitate compliance with government regulations.

Status: completed **Announced:** Apr. 3, 2023
POSaBIT Systems Corporation acquired certain assets from Scottsdale, Ariz.-based Hypur Inc. for US$7,500,000 including issuance of 6,210,729 common shares and US$1,500,000 cash, as well as issuance of up to 1,242,146 common shares upon achievement of certain milestones. Hypur develops payment and bank compliance software solutions for high-risk industries including cannabis businesses. Solutions offered include redundant PIN debit payment processing; Hypur Pay, the leading cannabis ACH eCommerce and mobile payment solution; and Hypur Comply, compliance technology for financial institutions serving the cannabis industry. Assets acquired include Hypur Comply, Hypur Pay and Hypur's PIN debit merchant processing solution. POSaBIT now provides a one-stop shop for all payment and bank compliance needs for cannabis dispensaries, processors, cultivators, distributors and the financial institutions that serve them.

Predecessor Detail - Name changed from Foreshore Exploration Partners Corp., Mar. 28, 2019, pursuant to the Qualifying Transaction reverse takeover acquisition of POSaBIT, Inc. and concurrent amalgamation of (old) POSaBIT with wholly owned POSaBIT Merger Sub, Inc. with (old) POSaBIT renamed POSaBIT U.S., Inc.

Directors - Ryan Hamlin, pres. & CEO, Redmond, Wash.; Mike Apker, Incline Village, Nev.; Louis Camhi, Great Neck, N.Y.; Bruce Jaffe, New York, N.Y.; Donald J. (Don) Tringali, Phoenix, Ariz.

Other Exec. Officers - Matthew A. (Matt) Fowler, CFO & corp. sec.; Oscar Dahl, chief of staff; Sarah Mirsky-Terranova, chief compliance officer; Julie Solomon, chief revenue officer; Andrew Sweet, chief tech. officer; Christine Foster, v-p, product

Capital Stock

	Authorized (shs.)	Outstanding (shs.)[1]
Common	unlimited	149,783,724

[1] At May 31, 2023

Major Shareholder - Alex Sharp held 16.36% interest at May 31, 2023.

Price Range - PBIT/CSE

Year	Volume	High	Low	Close
2022	8,247,210	$1.85	$0.50	$1.01
2021	27,139,316	$2.40	$0.15	$1.68
2020	4,802,441	$0.21	$0.01	$0.15
2019	4,783,578	$1.18	$0.04	$0.06
2018	110,000	$0.20	$0.17	$0.20

Recent Close: $0.70

Capital Stock Changes - In January 2023, private placement of 4,533,333 units (1 common share & 0.95 warrant) at US$0.662 per unit was completed, with warrants exercisable at Cdn$1.25 per share for three years.

In June 2022, private placement of 5,861,941 units (1 common share & ¾ warrant) at Cdn$0.80 per unit was completed. Also during 2022, common shares were issued as follows: 1,216,427 on exercise of warrants and 834,375 on exercise of options.

Wholly Owned Subsidiaries

POSaBIT U.S., Inc., Wash.

Financial Statistics

Periods ended:	12m Dec. 31/22[A]		12m Dec. 31/21[ΩA]
	US$000s	%Chg	US$000s
Operating revenue	**49,772**	**+134**	**21,302**
Cost of sales	27,070		15,583
Salaries & benefits	7,542		3,916
General & admin expense	4,636		2,891
Stock-based compensation	2,229		764
Operating expense	**41,477**	**+79**	**23,153**
Operating income	**8,295**	**n.a.**	**(1,851)**
Deprec., depl. & amort.	213		250
Finance income	148		nil
Finance costs, gross	275		174
Write-downs/write-offs	(137)		(105)
Pre-tax income	**8,468**	**n.a.**	**(10,566)**
Income taxes	404		nil
Net income	**8,064**	**n.a.**	**(10,566)**
Cash & equivalent	3,076		4,419
Inventories	464		679
Accounts receivable	2,745		2,332
Current assets	7,590		7,565
Fixed assets, net	274		219
Total assets	**17,997**	**+128**	**7,904**
Accts. pay. & accr. liabs	2,460		5,874
Current liabilities	2,864		5,874
Long-term debt, gross	313		135
Long-term debt, net	313		135
Shareholders' equity	8,223		(8,707)
Cash from oper. activs	**(4,916)**	**n.a.**	**(2,190)**
Cash from fin. activs	3,904		5,903
Cash from invest. activs	(331)		(272)
Net cash position	**3,076**	**-30**	**4,419**
Capital expenditures	(331)		(246)
	US$		US$
Earnings per share*	0.06		(0.09)
Cash flow per share*	(0.04)		(0.02)
	shs		shs
No. of shs. o/s*	139,815,388		131,902,645
Avg. no. of shs. o/s*	135,434,137		116,346,410
	%		%
Net profit margin	16.20		(49.60)
Return on equity	n.m.		n.m.
Return on assets	64.29		(179.33)
Foreign sales percent	100		100
No. of employees (FTEs)	47		39

* Common
Ω Restated
A Reported in accordance with IFRS

Latest Results

Periods ended:	3m Mar. 31/23[A]		3m Mar. 31/22[ΩA]
	US$000s	%Chg	US$000s
Operating revenue	11,492	+82	6,319
Net income	(3,037)	n.a.	(470)
	US$		US$
Earnings per share*	(0.02)		(0.00)

* Common
Ω Restated
A Reported in accordance with IFRS

Historical Summary
(as originally stated)

Fiscal Year	Oper. Rev.	Net Inc. Bef. Disc.	EPS*
	US$000s	US$000s	US$
2022[A]	49,772	8,064	0.06
2021[A]	21,302	(10,566)	(0.09)
2020[A]	7,823	(1,148)	(0.01)
2019[A1]	4,175	(5,511)	(0.07)
2018[A2]	2,443	(3,895)	(0.10)

* Common
A Reported in accordance with IFRS
1 Results reflect the Apr. 3, 2019, Qualifying Transaction reverse takeover acquisition of POSaBIT, Inc.
2 Results pertain to POSaBIT, Inc.

P.10 PR Technology Inc.

Symbol - PRTI **Exchange** - CSE (S) **CUSIP** - 693692
Head Office - 1001-1166 Alberni St, Vancouver, BC, V6E 3Z3
Telephone - (778) 331-3813
Email - njryu74@prt-k.com
Investor Relations - Neon Jun Ryu (778) 331-3816
Auditors - Adam Sung Kim Ltd. C.A., Burnaby, B.C.
Transfer Agents - Endeavor Trust Corporation, Vancouver, B.C.
Profile - (B.C. 2019) Developing wireless power transmission (WPT) systems for factory automation and rail guided vehicles (RGVs) on the factory floor. Also offers wireless chargers for mobile devices and develops wireless charging products for home appliances, wireless charging stations for drones and wireless LED lights (Lightning Bug).

WPT refers to the transfer of energy from the transmitter device to the receiver device without the need of wire. Power transfer takes place across the air. WPT has a range of applications in consumer goods, automotive, healthcare, defence, industrial and other industries. The company has developed a wireless cell phone charger, based on magnetic resonance technology, which can charge a device from a distance of 3 cm regardless of any physical obstacles and can be installed in a table.

Also developing the following products:

WPT Systems for Factory Automation & RGVs - Primarily focused on developing WPT systems in the automobile industry for RGVs used on the factory floor in manufacturing faculties. Its RGV WPT technology is based on the magnetic resonance technology and includes transmitters and receivers. The receivers are installed on the RGVs and the transmitters are installed at certain locations along the rail lines. This removes the need for wired charging of the RGVs resulting in improved productivity and reduced wear and tear.

Wireless Charging for Home Appliances - Has developed a WPT system and wireless charger for home appliances including smart tables, electric toothbrushes, humidifiers, LED lights and Bluetooth speakers with a power range between 15 W and 200 W.

Wireless Drone Charging Systems - Its wireless charging station for drones enables drones to charge wirelessly by automatic sensor when they approach the station. Has a partnership with **LIG Nex1 Co., Ltd.**, a South Korean aerospace manufacturer and defence company, to jointly develop an aviation drone business. The company would be in charge of developing WPT systems for drones and unmanned aerial vehicles with LIG Nex1 in charge of overall development of the aviation drone field.

Wireless LED Lights - Has developed wireless LED lights for use in consumer products, mainly toys and fish tanks called the Lightning Bug.

Common suspended from CSE, May 9, 2023.

Directors - Neon Jun Ryu, COO, interim CEO, CFO & corp. sec.; Seok Min Kang; Seok Kyun Oh; Jong in Park, South Korea

Capital Stock

	Authorized (shs.)	Outstanding (shs.)[1]
Common	unlimited	11,256,000

1 At Nov. 1, 2022

Major Shareholder - PRH Co. Ltd. held 28.58% interest at Nov. 26, 2021.

Price Range - PRTI/CSE (S)

Year	Volume	High	Low	Close
2022	417,267	$3.60	$0.06	$0.06
2021	260,067	$6.75	$0.45	$3.60

Consolidation: 1-for-9 cons. in Aug. 2022
Recent Close: $0.10
Capital Stock Changes - On Aug. 10, 2022, common shares were consolidated on a 1-for-9 basis.

Wholly Owned Subsidiaries

PRT Korea Co., Ltd., South Korea.

Financial Statistics

Periods ended:	12m Dec. 31/21[A]
	$000s
Operating revenue	**5**
Cost of sales	5
Salaries & benefits	561
Research & devel. expense	597
General & admin expense	1,386
Stock-based compensation	220
Operating expense	**2,769**
Operating income	**(2,764)**
Deprec., depl. & amort.	630
Pre-tax income	**(3,397)**
Net income	**(3,397)**
Cash & equivalent	495
Inventories	23
Current assets	611
Fixed assets, net	269
Right-of-use assets	71
Intangibles, net	930
Total assets	**1,969**
Accts. pay. & accr. liabs	226
Current liabilities	280
Long-term lease liabilities	22
Shareholders' equity	1,613
Cash from oper. activs	**(2,338)**
Cash from fin. activs	(125)
Cash from invest. activs	65
Net cash position	**495**
Capital expenditures	(55)
	$
Earnings per share*	(0.54)
Cash flow per share*	(0.36)
	shs
No. of shs. o/s*	11,256,000
Avg. no. of shs. o/s*	6,482,165
	%
Net profit margin	n.m.
Return on equity	n.m.
Return on assets	n.a.

* Common
A Reported in accordance with IFRS

Latest Results

Periods ended:	9m Sept. 30/22[A]		9m Sept. 30/21[A]
	$000s	%Chg	$000s
Operating revenue	5	-38	8
Net income	(2,196)	n.a.	(2,226)
	$		$
Earnings per share*	(0.20)		(0.45)

* Common
A Reported in accordance with IFRS
Note: Adjusted throughout for 1-for-9 cons. in Aug. 2022

P.11 PRO Real Estate Investment Trust

Symbol - PRV.UN **Exchange** - TSX **CUSIP** - 742694
Head Office - 1000-2000 rue Mansfield, Montréal, QC, H3A 2Z7
Telephone - (514) 933-9552 **Fax** - (514) 933-9094
Website - www.proreit.com
Email - jbeckerleg@proreit.com
Investor Relations - James W. Beckerleg (514) 933-9552
Auditors - MNP LLP C.A., Montréal, Qué.
Lawyers - Osler, Hoskin & Harcourt LLP, Toronto, Ont.
Transfer Agents - TSX Trust Company, Toronto, Ont.
FP500 Revenue Ranking - 773
Employees - 80 at Dec. 31, 2022
Profile - (Ont. 2013) Holds a portfolio of diversified commercial real estate properties in Canada, with a focus on primary and secondary markets in Quebec, Atlantic Canada, Ontario and select markets in western Canada.

At Mar. 31, 2023, the trust owned 130 commercial properties in Atlantic Canada (76), Quebec (13), Ontario (15) and western Canada (26), totaling 6,531,305 sq. ft.

Property portfolio at Mar. 31, 2023:

Type	Props.	Area (sq. ft.)[1]
Industrial	86	5,216,121
Retail	35	885,775
Office	9	429,409
	130[2]	6,531,305

1 Gross leasable area.
2 88 are 100%-owned and 42 are 50%-owned.

In April 2023, the company sold 50,000-sq.ft. non-core office property for $2,100,000.

In December 2022, the trust sold a 3,500-sq.-ft. retail property in Quebec, for $1,625,000.

Recent Merger and Acquisition Activity

Status: completed **Announced:** Nov. 3, 2022

PRO Real Estate Investment Trust sold a retail property in Alberta, totaling 11,000 sq. ft. of gross leasable area, for $5,400,000.
Status: completed **Announced:** Sept. 27, 2022
PRO Real Estate Investment Trust sold nine non-core retail properties in western Canada, totaling 94,000 sq. ft. of gross leasable area, for $18,750,000.
Status: completed **Revised:** Aug. 5, 2022
UPDATE: The transaction was completed. PREVIOUS: PRO Real Estate Investment Trust and Crestpoint Real Estate Investments Ltd. agreed to each acquire a 50% interest in 21 industrial properties in Burnside Industrial Park, located in the Halifax Regional Municipality in Dartmouth, N.S., totaling 1,577,556 sq. ft. of gross leasable area, for a total purchase price of $228,000,000. PRO REIT would finance its $114,000,000 portion of the costs from proceeds of a 50% interest in $148,000,000 new fixed-rate mortgages and the balance of $40,000,000 would be satisfied with cash on hand, including cash from the proceeds of the proposed concurrent sale of a 50% interest in 21 existing industrial properties to Crestpoint.
Status: completed **Revised:** Aug. 5, 2022
UPDATE: The transaction was completed. The joint acquisition of the 21 industrial properties was also concurrently completed. PREVIOUS: PRO Real Estate Investment Trust agreed to sell a 50% interest in 21 existing industrial properties in Halifax (20), N.S., and Moncton (1), N.B., totaling 1,481,844 sq. ft. of gross leasable area (GLA), to Crestpoint Real Estate Investments Ltd. for $113,500,000 (representing a total value of $227,000,000 for the properties). The consideration would consist of $49,000,000 cash and Crestpoint assuming a 50% interest in $129,000,000 of fixed-rate mortgages held by PRO REIT. Upon completion of the transaction, along with the proposed concurrent joint acquisition of 21 industrial properties in Burnside Industrial Park, located in the Halifax Regional Municipality in Dartmouth, N.S., by PRO REIT and Crestpoint, each would hold a 50% in the 42 industrial properties, which totaled 3,059,400 sq. ft. of GLA.

Predecessor Detail - Succeeded Taggart Capital Corp., Mar. 11, 2013, pursuant to plan of arrangement whereby PRO Real Estate Investment Trust was formed to facilitate the conversion of the corporation into a trust.

Trustees - James W. Beckerleg, chr., Montréal, Qué.; Gordon G. Lawlor, pres. & CEO, Halifax, N.S.; Martin Coté‡, Montréal, Qué.; Vincent Chiara, Montréal, Qué.; Shenoor Jadavji, Vancouver, B.C.; Christine Pound, Halifax, N.S.; Deborah Shaffner, Wolfville, N.S.; Ronald E. (Ron) Smith, Yarmouth, N.S.

Other Exec. Officers - Alison Schafer, CFO & corp. sec.; Chris Andrea, pres., Compass Commercial Realty LP
‡ Lead trustee

Capital Stock

	Authorized (shs.)	Outstanding (shs.)[1]
Trust Unit	unlimited	59,047,809
Special Voting Unit	unlimited	1,399,421
Class B LP Unit	unlimited	1,399,421[2]

[1] At Apr. 17, 2023
[2] Classified as debt.

Trust Unit - The trust will endeavour to make monthly cash distributions. One vote per trust unit.

Special Voting Unit - Issued to holders of class B limited partnership units of subsidiary PRO REIT Limited Partnership. Each special voting unit entitles the holder to a number of votes at unitholder meetings equal to the number of trust units into which the class B limited partnership units are exchangeable.

Class B Limited Partnership Unit - Entitled to distributions equal to those provided to trust units. Directly exchangeable into trust units on a 1-for-1 basis at any time by holder. Classified as debt under IFRS.

Normal Course Issuer Bid - The company plans to make normal course purchases of up to 1,771,049 trust units representing 3% of the total outstanding. The bid commenced on Sept. 26, 2022, and expires on Sept. 25, 2023.

Major Shareholder - Collingwood Investments Incorporated held 19.11% interest at Apr. 17, 2023.

Price Range - PRV.UN/TSX

Year	Volume	High	Low	Close
2022	19,734,656	$7.64	$5.34	$5.96
2021	16,758,031	$7.25	$5.81	$6.79
2020	35,230,461	$7.85	$2.40	$6.06
2019	14,820,385	$7.50	$5.73	$7.38
2018	9,843,646	$7.35	$5.40	$5.73

Consolidation: 1-for-3 cons. in May 2019
Recent Close: $5.05

Capital Stock Changes - During 2022, 12,812 trust units were issued on exchange of a like number of class B limited partnership units of PRO REIT Limited Partnership.

Dividends

PRV.UN unit Ra $0.45 pa M est. May 15, 2020**
Prev. Rate: $0.21 est. Jan. 15, 2014
** Reinvestment Option

Wholly Owned Subsidiaries

PRO REIT GP Inc., Ont.

Subsidiaries

97.7% int. in **PRO REIT Limited Partnership**, Qué.
- 100% int. in **Compass Commercial Realty GP Inc.**, N.S.
  - 0.01% int. in **Compass Commercial Realty LP**, N.S.
- 37% int. in **Compass Commercial Realty LP**, N.S.
- 100% int. in **Compass Commercial Realty Trust**, N.S.
  - 63% int. in **Compass Commercial Realty LP**, N.S.
- 100% int. in **PRO REIT Management Inc.**, Ont.

Financial Statistics

Periods ended:	12m Dec. 31/22[A]		12m Dec. 31/21[A]
	$000s	%Chg	$000s
Total revenue	**97,210**	**+25**	**77,674**
Rental operating expense	39,473		31,392
General & admin. expense	5,160		4,347
Stock-based compensation	691		3,060
Operating expense	**45,324**	**+17**	**38,799**
Operating income	**51,886**	**+33**	**38,875**
Deprec. & amort.	789		729
Finance costs, gross	21,175		17,550
Pre-tax income	**84,494**	**+3**	**81,844**
Net income	**84,494**	**+3**	**81,844**
Cash & equivalent	7,531		5,944
Accounts receivable	2,733		2,133
Current assets	13,233		10,184
Fixed assets	1,116[1]		2,059
Income-producing props	1,017,965		974,700
Property interests, net	1,016,849		975,793
Intangibles, net	3,614		3,986
Total assets	**1,035,928**	**+5**	**989,963**
Bank indebtedness	36,818		14,738
Accts. pay. & accr. liabs	7,864		9,601
Long-term debt, gross	485,847		517,634
Long-term debt, net	420,986		496,285
Shareholders' equity	487,690		429,693
Cash from oper. activs	**28,235**	**-4**	**29,276**
Cash from fin. activs	(38,582)		252,015
Cash from invest. activs	11,934		(281,606)
Net cash position	**7,531**	**+27**	**5,944**
Capital expenditures	(440)		(273)
Increase in property	(123,745)		(296,899)
Decrease in property	138,008		18,339
	$		$
Earnings per share*	n.a.		n.a.
Cash flow per share*	0.48		0.50
Funds from opers. per sh.*	0.50		0.45
Adj. funds from opers. per sh.*	0.52		0.51
Cash divd. per share*	0.45		0.45
Total divd. per share*	**0.45**		**0.45**
	shs		shs
No. of shs. o/s*	59,047,809		59,034,997
	%		%
Net profit margin	86.92		105.37
Return on equity	18.42		24.33
Return on assets	10.43		12.24
No. of employees (FTEs)	80		70

* Trust unit
[A] Reported in accordance with IFRS
[1] Net of accumulated depreciation.

Latest Results

Periods ended:	3m Mar. 31/23[A]		3m Mar. 31/22[A]
	$000s	%Chg	$000s
Total revenue	25,278	+4	24,330
Net income	13,048	-72	46,522
	$		$
Earnings per share*	n.a.		n.a.

[A] Reported in accordance with IFRS

Historical Summary
(as originally stated)

Fiscal Year	Total Rev.	Net Inc. Bef. Disc.	EPS*
	$000s	$000s	$
2022[A]	97,210	84,494	n.a.
2021[A]	77,674	81,844	n.a.
2020[A]	69,810	21,072	n.a.
2019[A]	57,627	14,975	n.a.
2018[A]	40,889	18,770	n.a.

* Trust unit
[A] Reported in accordance with IFRS
Note: Adjusted throughout for 1-for-3 cons. in May 2019

P.12 PUDO Inc.

Symbol - PDO **Exchange** - CSE **CUSIP** - 386671
Head Office - 6600 Goreway Dr, Unit D, Mississauga, ON, L4V 1S6
Toll-free - (844) 300-8533 **Fax** - (905) 507-4177
Website - www.pudopoint.com
Email - elliott.etheredge@pudopoint.com
Investor Relations - Elliott K. Etheredge (844) 300-8533
Auditors - Clearhouse LLP C.A., Mississauga, Ont.
Lawyers - Warshaw Burstein, LLP, New York, N.Y.; WeirFoulds LLP, Toronto, Ont.
Transfer Agents - TSX Trust Company, Toronto, Ont.

Profile - (Ont. 1945) Provides a plug-and play, pay-as-you-go platform and a network of parcel pick-up and drop-off storefront counters known as PUDOpoint™ counters.

PUDOpoint™ provides consumers with carrier-neutral alternative convenient locations to pick-up and drop-off e-commerce parcels for parcel receipt certainty, early/late/weekend pick-up, return convenience and elimination of door-drop parcel theft through collaborations with online retailers, third party logistics (3PL) companies, software-as-a-service (SaaS) providers and courier companies. Existing businesses such as convenience stores and gas stations provide services as a PUDOpoint™ counter.

Predecessor Detail - Name changed from Grandview Gold Inc., July 13, 2015, following reverse takeover acquisition of My Courier Depot Inc.; basis 1 new for 20 old shs.

Directors - Richard H. Cooper, chr., Kleinburg, Ont.; Thomas F. (Tom) Bijou, Addison, Tex.; Tracy K. Bramlett, Dallas, Tex.; Murray Cook, Brampton, Ont.; Howard Westerman, Richardson, Tex.

Other Exec. Officers - Elliott K. Etheredge, CEO; Frank Coccia, pres. & COO; Douglas P. (Doug) Baker, CFO

Capital Stock

	Authorized (shs.)	Outstanding (shs.)[1]
Preference	unlimited	nil
Common	unlimited	27,271,007

[1] At July 28, 2023

Major Shareholder - Palm Holding Inc. held 27.87% interest at July 28, 2023.

Price Range - PDO/CSE

Year	Volume	High	Low	Close
2022	376,822	$1.35	$0.40	$0.77
2021	676,758	$1.80	$0.95	$0.95
2020	820,918	$2.99	$0.70	$1.60
2019	391,928	$1.80	$0.35	$1.55
2018	296,217	$2.99	$0.50	$0.70

Recent Close: $0.75

Capital Stock Changes - During fiscal 2023, common shares were issued as follows: 102,896 for debt settlement and 21,111 on exercise of options.

Wholly Owned Subsidiaries

Grandview Gold (USA) Inc.
PUDOpoint Inc.
Recuperacion Realzada, S.A.C.

Financial Statistics

Periods ended:	12m Feb. 28/23[A]		12m Feb. 28/22[A]
	$000s	%Chg	$000s
Operating revenue	**3,834**	**+77**	**2,162**
Cost of sales	2,356		1,465
Salaries & benefits	814		928
General & admin expense	627		690
Stock-based compensation	313		206
Operating expense	**4,110**	**+25**	**3,288**
Operating income	**(276)**	**n.a.**	**(1,126)**
Deprec., depl. & amort.	53		82
Pre-tax income	**(328)**	**n.a.**	**(1,211)**
Net income	**(328)**	**n.a.**	**(1,211)**
Cash & equivalent	178		135
Accounts receivable	277		325
Current assets	573		571
Fixed assets, net	4		23
Intangibles, net	35		67
Total assets	**612**	**-8**	**662**
Accts. pay. & accr. liabs	569		714
Current liabilities	569		714
Shareholders' equity	43		(52)
Cash from oper. activs	**52**	**n.a.**	**(589)**
Cash from fin. activs	nil		(13)
Cash from invest. activs	(2)		(7)
Net cash position	**178**	**+32**	**135**
Capital expenditures	(2)		(7)
	$		$
Earnings per share*	(0.01)		(0.04)
Cash flow per share*	0.00		(0.02)
	shs		shs
No. of shs. o/s*	27,271,007		27,147,000
Avg. no. of shs. o/s*	27,165,677		27,124,038
	%		%
Net profit margin	(8.56)		(56.01)
Return on equity	n.m.		n.m.
Return on assets	(51.49)		(117.86)
Foreign sales percent	3		3

* Common
[A] Reported in accordance with IFRS

Latest Results

Periods ended:	3m May 31/23[A]		3m May 31/22[A]
	$000s	%Chg	$000s
Operating revenue	783	-10	873
Net income	(209)	n.a.	(163)
	$		$
Earnings per share*	(0.01)		(0.01)

* Common
[A] Reported in accordance with IFRS

Historical Summary
(as originally stated)

Fiscal Year	Oper. Rev. $000s	Net Inc. Bef. Disc. $000s	EPS* $
2023[A]	3,834	(328)	(0.01)
2022[A]	2,162	(1,211)	(0.04)
2021[A]	1,671	(1,824)	(0.07)
2020[A]	1,121	(2,004)	(0.08)
2019[A]	833	(3,388)	(0.18)

* Common
[A] Reported in accordance with IFRS

P.13 P2Earn Inc.

Symbol - PXE **Exchange** - CSE **CUSIP** - 69379U
Head Office - 150-1090 Homer St, Vancouver, BC, V6B 2W9 **Telephone** - (604) 410-2277
Website - p2earn.io
Email - investors@p2earn.io
Investor Relations - Jesse Dylan (604) 265-7511
Auditors - GreenGrowth C.P.A., Los Angeles, Calif.
Transfer Agents - Computershare Trust Company of Canada Inc., Vancouver, B.C.
Profile - (B.C. 2018 amalg.) Provides podcasting platform for content creators, engages in carbon neutral cryptocurrency mining, building a blockchain gaming operation in the play-2-earn gaming space and develops blockchain technology that powers cryptocurrencies and finance related projects.

Podcast & Audio

Podkast.com provides an audio and video subscription-based platform that content creators use to secure their content behind a paywall and provide access to their fans. Revenue is generated by retaining 20% of the monthly subscription fee paid by the subscribers.

Bitcoin Mining

Has carbon neutral bitcoin mining operations using Bitmain Antminer S19 Pro 100 terahash per second mining rigs.

Blockchain

Developing AR Block application which accelerates the accounts receivable pay cycle for publishers through ensuring prompt payments to publishers without requiring third-party intermediaries such as factoring agents.

Jellyworks

Wholly owned **Jellyworks Inc.** operates a bitcoin mining operation and is building a revenue generating play-2-earn gaming guild, which is where players can earn digital tokens as a reward for playing a game of skill, for example, play-2-earn poker. These digital tokens can either be exchanged for fiat currency through certain exchanges or retained in digital format. Jellyworks operates by buying online gaming NFT's (non-fungible tokens) then delegating those NFT's to players around the world who play skill-based games and earn tokens. The tokens are then split 50/50 between the player and Jellyworks.

In August 2022, the company acquired the remaining 2% interest in **Podkast Entertainment Corp.** for issuance of 389,280 common shares at a deemed value of $42,820, increasing its interest to 100% from 98%.

Recent Merger and Acquisition Activity

Status: completed **Revised:** Nov. 1, 2022
UPDATE: The acquisition of 100% of Jellyworks was completed for issuance of 86,522,440 common shares. PREVIOUS: Aquarius AI Inc. agreed to acquire a minimum 70% interest in Jellyworks Inc. for issuance of 60,565,708 common shares. Jellyworks is a Web3 technology company that generates most of its revenues from bitcoin mining.

Predecessor Detail - Name changed from Aquarius AI Inc., Mar. 27, 2023; basis 1 new for 4 old shs.
Directors - Jesse Dylan, exec. chr., Whistler, B.C.; Alex Lineton, CEO, United Kingdom; Graham Martin, pres., London, Middx., United Kingdom; Eugene (Gene) Valaitis, Calif.
Other Exec. Officers - Leonard A. (Len) Schmidt, CFO

Capital Stock

	Authorized (shs.)	Outstanding (shs.)[1]
Preferred	unlimited	nil
Common	unlimited	69,540,908

[1] At May 30, 2023

Major Shareholder - Michael (Jesse Dylan) Woodman held 14.1% interest and Christopher Bradley held 11.89% interest at Apr. 28, 2023.

Price Range - PXE/CSE

Year	Volume	High	Low	Close
2022	8,926,131	$0.60	$0.04	$0.06
2021	27,990,392	$1.24	$0.24	$0.50
2020	2,479,541	$1.20	$0.20	$0.28
2019	2,059,378	$22.00	$0.40	$0.60
2018	1,748,210	$20.00	$4.00	$8.00

Consolidation: 1-for-4 cons. in Mar. 2023; 1-for-10 cons. in July 2020
Recent Close: $0.03
Capital Stock Changes - On Mar. 27, 2023, common shares were consolidated on a 1-for-4 basis. In April and May 2023, private placement of 12,566,663 post-consolidated common shares was completed at $0.075 per share.

In August 2022, 389,280 common shares were issued pursuant to the acquisition of the remaining 2% interest in Podkast Entertainment Corp. On Nov. 1, 2022, 86,522,440 common shares were issued pursuant to the acquisition of Jellyworks Inc. Also during 2022, 25,000 common shares were returned to treasury.

Wholly Owned Subsidiaries

Jellyworks Inc., Vancouver, B.C.
Lighthouse Digital Inc.
• 100% int. in **495 Communications, LLC**, New York, N.Y.
Podkast Entertainment Corp.

Financial Statistics

Periods ended:	12m Dec. 31/22[A]	%Chg	12m Dec. 31/21[A]
	$000s	%Chg	$000s
Operating revenue	**222**	**+41**	**157**
Cost of sales	145		180
General & admin expense	1,501		2,900
Operating expense	**1,646**	**-47**	**3,080**
Operating income	**(1,424)**	**n.a.**	**(2,922)**
Deprec., depl. & amort.	485		235
Finance costs, gross	14		11
Write-downs/write-offs	nil		(3,510)
Pre-tax income	**3,146**	**n.a.**	**(2,925)**
Net income	**3,146**	**n.a.**	**(2,925)**
Net inc. for equity hldrs	**3,149**	**n.a.**	**(2,923)**
Net inc. for non-cont. int.	**(3)**	**n.a.**	**(2)**
Cash & equivalent	62		668
Accounts receivable	47		335
Current assets	154		1,034
Intangibles, net	4,829		nil
Total assets	**6,404**	**+157**	**2,487**
Accts. pay. & accr. liabs	441		1,086
Current liabilities	1,128		2,026
Long-term lease liabilities	32		98
Shareholders' equity	4,807		(1,891)
Non-controlling interest	16		19
Cash from oper. activs	**1,129**	**n.a.**	**(4,775)**
Cash from fin. activs	71		6,702
Cash from invest. activs	(1,806)		(1,260)
Net cash position	**62**	**-91**	**668**
	$		$
Earnings per share*	0.08		(0.16)
Cash flow per share*	0.03		(0.29)
	shs		shs
No. of shs. o/s*	52,224,207		30,502,526
Avg. no. of shs. o/s*	37,701,857		16,347,909
	%		%
Net profit margin	n.m.		n.m.
Return on equity	n.m.		n.m.
Return on assets	71.08		(229.00)

* Common
[A] Reported in accordance with IFRS

Latest Results

Periods ended:	3m Mar. 31/23[A]	%Chg	3m Mar. 31/22[A]
	$000s	%Chg	$000s
Operating revenue	77	+8	71
Net income	(562)	n.a.	(733)
Net inc. for equity hldrs	(562)	n.a.	(731)
Net inc. for non-cont. int.	nil		(2)
	$		$
Earnings per share*	(0.01)		(0.04)

* Common
[A] Reported in accordance with IFRS

Historical Summary
(as originally stated)

Fiscal Year	Oper. Rev. $000s	Net Inc. Bef. Disc. $000s	EPS* $
2022[A]	222	3,146	0.08
2021[A]	157	(2,925)	(0.16)
2020[A]	nil	9,942	2.16
2019[A]	8,858	(24,894)	(11.86)
2018[A1]	20,077	(2,265)	(1.20)

* Common
[A] Reported in accordance with IFRS
[1] Results reflect the Jan. 26, 2018, Qualifying Transaction reverse takeover of (old) Good Life Networks Inc.

Note: Adjusted throughout for 1-for-4 cons. in Mar. 2023; 1-for-10 cons. in July 2020

P.14 Pacific GeoInfo Corp.

Symbol - PGO.H **Exchange** - TSX-VEN **CUSIP** - 69433R
Head Office - 600-777 Hornby St, Vancouver, BC, V6Z 1S4 **Telephone** - (604) 689-9113 **Fax** - (604) 689-9022
Email - info@pacificgeoinfo.com
Investor Relations - Luoxin Wang (604) 689-9113
Auditors - MNP LLP C.A., Vancouver, B.C.
Transfer Agents - Computershare Trust Company of Canada Inc., Vancouver, B.C.
Profile - (B.C. 2004; orig. Can., 1985) Seeking new business opportunities.

Previously provided airborne remote sensing and other geospatial services based in strategic locations throughout the People's Republic of China.
Predecessor Detail - Name changed from G.R. Pacific Resource Corp., Feb. 3, 2003.
Directors - Guo Qing (Paul) Liu, chr., Hong Kong, Hong Kong, People's Republic of China; Luoxin (Peter) Wang, pres. & CEO, New Westminster, B.C.; Zheng He, People's Republic of China; Dr. Lei Yin, People's Republic of China
Other Exec. Officers - Paul Stevenson, CFO; Bernard G. (Bernie) Poznanski, corp. sec.

Capital Stock

	Authorized (shs.)	Outstanding (shs.)[1]
Common	unlimited	37,234,777

[1] At Nov. 23, 2022

Major Shareholder - Guo Qing (Paul) Liu held 41.4% interest at Nov. 19, 2021.

Price Range - PGO.H/TSX-VEN

Year	Volume	High	Low	Close
2022	57,000	$0.02	$0.02	$0.02
2021	2,300	$0.02	$0.02	$0.02
2020	7,000	$0.01	$0.01	$0.01
2019	665,745	$0.03	$0.01	$0.01
2018	10,000	$0.01	$0.01	$0.01

Financial Statistics

Periods ended:	12m Dec. 31/21[A]	%Chg	12m Dec. 31/20[A]
	$000s	%Chg	$000s
Salaries & benefits	39		39
General & admin expense	88		79
Operating expense	**126**	**+7**	**118**
Operating income	**(126)**	**n.a.**	**(118)**
Pre-tax income	**(126)**	**n.a.**	**(118)**
Net income	**(126)**	**n.a.**	**(118)**
Cash & equivalent	117		103
Current assets	124		109
Total assets	**125**	**+15**	**109**
Accts. pay. & accr. liabs	8		16
Current liabilities	8		16
Shareholders' equity	117		93
Cash from oper. activs	**(136)**	**n.a.**	**(116)**
Cash from fin. activs	150		nil
Net cash position	**117**	**+14**	**103**
	$		$
Earnings per share*	(0.01)		(0.01)
Cash flow per share*	(0.01)		(0.01)
	shs		shs
No. of shs. o/s*	37,234,777		22,234,777
Avg. no. of shs. o/s*	23,275,873		22,234,777
	%		%
Net profit margin	n.a.		n.a.
Return on equity	(120.00)		(77.63)
Return on assets	(107.69)		(70.45)

* Common
[A] Reported in accordance with IFRS

Latest Results

Periods ended:	6m June 30/22[A]	%Chg	6m June 30/21[A]
	$000s	%Chg	$000s
Net income	(48)	n.a.	(52)
	$		$
Earnings per share*	(0.00)		(0.00)

* Common
[A] Reported in accordance with IFRS

Historical Summary
(as originally stated)

Fiscal Year	Oper. Rev. $000s	Net Inc. Bef. Disc. $000s	EPS* $
2021[A]	nil	(126)	(0.01)
2020[A]	nil	(118)	(0.01)
2019[A]	nil	(146)	(0.01)
2018[A]	nil	(191)	(0.01)
2017[A]	nil	(205)	(0.01)

* Common
[A] Reported in accordance with IFRS

P.15 Palisades Goldcorp Ltd.

Symbol - PALI **Exchange** - TSX-VEN **CUSIP** - 69639F
Head Office - 2500-700 Georgia St W, PO Box 10026 Pacific Centre South, Vancouver, BC, V7Y 1B3
Website - palisades.ca
Email - collin@palisades.ca
Investor Relations - Collin Kettell (301) 744-8774
Auditors - Deloitte LLP C.A., Vancouver, B.C.
Transfer Agents - Computershare Trust Company of Canada Inc.

Profile - (B.C. 2019) Operates as a resource investment company and merchant bank focused on junior companies in the resource and mining sector.

The company seeks to acquire equity participation in pre-initial public offering and early stage public resource companies with undeveloped or undervalued high quality projects. Focuses on companies that are in need of financial resources to realize their full potential, are undervalued in capital markets and/or operate in jurisdictions with low to moderate local political risk. At May 18, 2023, had a portfolio of equity investments, or securities convertible into equity investments, in more than 50 junior resource issuers.

At Mar. 31, 2023, the company held a 26.67% equity interest in **New Found Gold Corp.**, with a carrying value of $253,264,637, and an investment portfolio with a fair value of $15,176,688 compared with $18,049,860 at Dec. 31, 2022.

Investment	Fair Value
Equities	$6,699,339
Warrants	8,477,349
	15,176,688

Common listed on TSX-VEN, Feb. 6, 2023.

Predecessor Detail - Name changed from Palisades Acquisitions Corp., Apr. 14, 2020.

Directors - Collin Kettell, chr. & CEO, Puerto Rico; Gregor Gregersen, Singapore, Singapore; Elizabeth J. Harrison, Vancouver, B.C.; William B. Hayden, Sydney, N.S.W., Australia

Other Exec. Officers - Bassam Moubarak, CFO

Capital Stock

	Authorized (shs.)	Outstanding (shs.)[1]
Common	unlimited	49,345,977

[1] At May 18, 2023

Normal Course Issuer Bid - The company plans to make normal course purchases of up to 2,467,298 common shares representing 5% of the total outstanding. The bid commenced on Apr. 1, 2023, and expires on Mar. 31, 2024.

Major Shareholder - Collin Kettell held 27.44% interest at May 15, 2023.

Recent Close: $2.55

Capital Stock Changes - During 2022, 15,222,336 common shares were cancelled.

Investments

26.67% int. in **New Found Gold Corp.**, Vancouver, B.C. (see Survey of Mines)

Financial Statistics

Periods ended:	12m Dec. 31/22[A1]		12m Dec. 31/21[A]
	$000s	%Chg	$000s
Realized invest. gain (loss)	(8,472)		(9,593)
Unrealized invest. gain (loss)	(37,856)		17,174
Total revenue	**(46,146)**	**n.a.**	**7,850**
General & admin. expense	1,696		4,622
Stock-based compensation	nil		37,256
Other operating expense	1,297		55,338
Operating expense	**2,994**	**-97**	**97,230**
Operating income	**(49,140)**	**n.a.**	**(89,380)**
Deprec. & amort.	nil		237
Finance costs, gross	1		15
Write-downs/write-offs	(136,844)		(145,147)
Pre-tax income	**(206,958)**	**n.a.**	**361,398**
Income taxes	(58,797)		103,569
Net income	**(148,160)**	**n.a.**	**257,829**
Net inc. for equity hldrs	**(148,079)**	**n.a.**	**262,927**
Net inc. for non-cont. int	**(82)**	**n.a.**	**(5,097)**
Cash & equivalent	23,440		97,303
Current assets	25,480		116,387
Long-term investments	258,612		418,166
Total assets	**284,093**	**-47**	**534,604**
Accts. pay. & accr. liabs	178		15,270
Current liabilities	178		15,304
Shareholders' equity	217,379		393,979
Non-controlling interest	(2,586)		(13)
Cash from oper. activs	**(3,034)**	**n.a.**	**(42,700)**
Cash from fin. activs	nil		44,747
Cash from invest. activs	nil		(58,200)
Net cash position	**5,390**	**-36**	**8,424**
Capital expenditures	nil		(1,345)
	$		$
Earnings per share*	(3.00)		5.18
Cash flow per share*	(0.06)		(0.84)
	shs		shs
No. of shs. o/s*	49,345,977		64,568,368
Avg. no. of shs. o/s*	49,345,977		50,782,758
	%		%
Net profit margin	n.m.		n.m.
Return on equity	(48.44)		96.88
Return on assets	(36.19)		64.36

* Common

[A] Reported in accordance with IFRS

[1] All share and per share amounts adjusted to reflect a 1-for-2 share consolidation effective June 30, 2022.

Latest Results

Periods ended:	3m Mar. 31/23[A]		3m Mar. 31/22[A]
	$000s	%Chg	$000s
Total revenue	(2,978)	n.a.	(2,989)
Net income	(16,304)	n.a.	(2,684)
Net inc. for equity hldrs	(16,304)	n.a.	(2,602)
Net inc. for non-cont. int	nil		(82)
	$		$
Earnings per share*	(0.33)		(0.05)

* Common

[A] Reported in accordance with IFRS

Historical Summary

(as originally stated)

Fiscal Year	Total Rev.	Net Inc. Bef. Disc.	EPS*
	$000s	$000s	$
2022[A]	(46,146)	(148,160)	(3.00)
2021[A]	7,850	257,829	5.18
2020[A]	111,385	(2,517)	0.58

* Common

[A] Reported in accordance with IFRS

P.16 Pangea Natural Foods Inc.

Symbol - PNGA **Exchange** - CSE **CUSIP** - 69841D

Head Office - 8035 130 St, Surrey, BC, V3W 0H7 **Telephone** - (604) 765-8069

Website - www.pangeafood.com

Email - pratap@pangeafood.com

Investor Relations - Pratap Sandhu (604) 765-8069

Auditors - Baker Tilly WM LLP C.A., Vancouver, B.C.

Transfer Agents - Endeavor Trust Corporation, Vancouver, B.C.

Profile - (B.C. 2021) Produces and sells plant-based patties and nuggets, old fashioned ghee, mixed nuts, blueberry juice, nutritional drink mix, plant-based recovery drink and a vegan pre-work out supplement in Canada.

Products are manufactured at the company's facility in Surrey, B.C., and sold through multiple distribution channels including online sales platforms and retailers such as Loblaws, Save-on-Foods, Sobeys, IGA Marketplace, Fresh Street Market, Choices Markets, Whole Foods and on select Air Canada and WestJet flights.

In April 2023, the company agreed to acquire private Vancouver, B.C.-based **Glory Organic Juice Company Inc.** and **Glory Juice Co. Vancouver Ltd.** (collectively, Glory Juice) for issuance of 6,000,000 common shares. In addition, the company would cause Glory Juice to repay $1,800,000 outstanding loans to Glory Juice shareholders through issuance of promissory notes which would be payable in equal quarterly instalments over 56 months beginning on the closing date of the transaction. Glory Juice produces and sells cold-pressed juice, nut and seed mylks, ready-to-blend smoothies, wellness shots and more, and has retail locations in Vancouver. Glory Juice also offers franchising options, business-to-business partnerships with wholesale partners, co-branding and white-label capabilities.

Directors - Pratap Sandhu, CEO & corp. sec., B.C.; Mohammad S. (Mo) Fazil, Calgary, Alta.; Nahsir Virani, B.C.

Other Exec. Officers - Ruben Tse, CFO; Daryl Louie, chief mktg. officer

Capital Stock

	Authorized (shs.)	Outstanding (shs.)[1]
Common	unlimited	36,515,001

[1] At June 29, 2023

Major Shareholder - Pratap Sandhu held 36% interest at Mar. 28, 2023.

Price Range - PNGA/CSE

Year	Volume	High	Low	Close
2022	3,211,171	$0.45	$0.08	$0.13

Recent Close: $0.16

Capital Stock Changes - In February 2023, private placement of 7,650,000 units (1 common share & ½ warrant) at 10¢ per share was completed, with warrants exercisable at 20¢ per share for two years.

During fiscal 2022, common shares were issued as follows: 250,000 on exercise of warrants, 150,000 by private placement and 50,000 on exercise of options.

Financial Statistics

Periods ended:	12m Oct. 31/22[A]		29w Oct. 31/21[A]
	$000s	%Chg	$000s
Operating revenue	**698**	**n.a.**	**68**
Cost of sales	657		54
Salaries & benefits	161		81
General & admin expense	662		84
Stock-based compensation	76		nil
Operating expense	**1,556**	**n.a.**	**219**
Operating income	**(858)**	**n.a.**	**(151)**
Deprec., depl. & amort.	41		1
Write-downs/write-offs	nil		(22)
Pre-tax income	**(1,135)**	**n.a.**	**(173)**
Net income	**(1,135)**	**n.a.**	**(173)**
Cash & equivalent	76		808
Inventories	88		7
Accounts receivable	249		84
Fixed assets, net	23		23
Intangibles, net	8		37
Total assets	**620**	**-54**	**1,342**
Accts. pay. & accr. liabs	409		117
Current liabilities	409		117
Shareholders' equity	212		1,225
Cash from oper. activs	**(719)**	**n.a.**	**(530)**
Cash from fin. activs	(1)		1,398
Cash from invest. activs	(7)		(61)
Net cash position	**76**	**-91**	**808**
Capital expenditures	nil		(24)
	$		$
Earnings per share*	(0.04)		(0.04)
Cash flow per share*	(0.03)		(0.13)
	shs		shs
No. of shs. o/s*	27,635,001		27,185,001
Avg. no. of shs. o/s*	27,385,138		3,972,256
	%		%
Net profit margin	(162.61)		...
Return on equity	(157.97)		...
Return on assets	(115.70)		...

* Common

[A] Reported in accordance with IFRS

Latest Results

Periods ended:	6m Apr. 30/23[A]		6m Apr. 30/22[A]
	$000s	%Chg	$000s
Operating revenue	265	+27	209
Net income	(961)	n.a.	(366)
	$		$
Earnings per share*	(0.03)		(0.01)

* Common

[A] Reported in accordance with IFRS

P.17 PanGenomic Health Inc.

Symbol - NARA **Exchange** - CSE **CUSIP** - 69842E

Head Office - 102-3800 Westbrook Mall, Vancouver, BC, V6S 2L9 **Telephone** - (778) 743-4642

Website - www.pangenomic.com

Email - ir@pangenomic.com

Investor Relations - Tammy Gillis (778) 743-4642

Auditors - Saturna Group Chartered Accountants LLP C.A., Vancouver, B.C.

Transfer Agents - TSX Trust Company

Profile - (B.C. 2015) Has developed a self-care digital platform to deliver personalized, evidence-based information about natural treatments to support mental health.

The company's mobile app, Nara, provide consumers with a knowledge base tailored to an individual's unique user profile, leveraging input from mental health questionnaires, current drug treatment regimen, genomic sequence analysis, as well as their proteomics and microbiomic biomarker reports. Its digital therapeutics clinic platform, PlantGx, provides health practitioners with access to a consumer's Nara app data in order to assist them to optimize the identification of appropriate natural remedies and monitor a patient's prognosis during treatment.

Nara was expected to be launched in Canada and the United States in the third quarter of 2022 with a paid subscription version scheduled for release in the second quarter of 2023.

Initial revenue would be earned from monthly subscription fees and one-time fees paid by consumers for access to premium services on the Nara App. Revenue would also be earned from monthly subscription fees paid by health practitioners for access to an advanced knowledge base and treatment analytics, as well as fees earned for new patient and diagnostic test referrals.

Recent Merger and Acquisition Activity

Status: completed **Revised:** Dec. 12, 2022

UPDATE: The transaction was completed. PREVIOUS: PanGenomic Health Inc. agreed to acquire Mydecine Innovations Group, Inc.'s wholly owned Mindleap Health Inc., a telehealth platform for psychedelic integration available on the iOS and Android mobile stores, for $3,600,000 payable by the issuance of units (1 class common share & 1 warrant) at $0.20, with warrants exercisable at $0.30 per share for two years. Upon Closing, Mydecine was expected to hold 19.4% of the issued and outstanding common shares of PanGenomic.

Predecessor Detail - Name changed from Zetta Capital Corp., Dec. 6, 2021.

Directors - Robert (Rob) Nygren, exec. chr., Vancouver, B.C.; Maryam Marissen, pres. & CEO, Vancouver, B.C.; Peter Green, West Vancouver, B.C.; Vincent L. Lum, Vancouver, B.C.; Jonathan Lutz, B.C.

Other Exec. Officers - Tammy Gillis, CFO, treas. & corp. sec.; Kaidong Zhang, chief scientific officer

Capital Stock

	Authorized (shs.)	Outstanding (shs.)[1]
Preferred	unlimited	
Series 1 Preferred		nil
Common	unlimited	99,328,169

[1] At Mar. 10, 2023

Series 1 Preferred - Convertible into common shares on a 2.5-for-1 basis until July 28, 2022. Non-voting.

Common - One vote per share.

Major Shareholder - Widely held at Mar. 10, 2023.

Price Range - NARA/CSE

Year	Volume	High	Low	Close
2022	9,689,850	$0.30	$0.16	$0.27

Recent Close: $0.04

Capital Stock Changes - In July 2022, 7,365,999 units (1 common share & 1 warrant) were issued without further consideration on exchange of subscription receipts sold previously by private placement at 15¢ each.

Wholly Owned Subsidiaries

Mindleap Health Inc., Vancouver, B.C.
PanGenomic Technologies Corp., B.C.

Financial Statistics

Periods ended:	12m Dec. 31/21[A]		12m Dec. 31/20[A]
	$000s	%Chg	$000s
Salaries & benefits	35		nil
Research & devel. expense	130		nil
General & admin expense	330		137
Stock-based compensation	51		nil
Operating expense	**546**	**+299**	**137**
Operating income	**(546)**	**n.a.**	**(137)**
Deprec., depl. & amort.	2		nil
Finance income	16		nil
Finance costs, gross	2		3
Write-downs/write-offs	(1,794)		nil
Pre-tax income	**(2,649)**	**n.a.**	**(140)**
Net income	**(2,649)**	**n.a.**	**(140)**
Cash & equivalent	1,349		38
Accounts receivable	41		8
Current assets	1,670		147
Fixed assets, net	25		nil
Intangibles, net	850		nil
Total assets	**2,577**	**n.m.**	**147**
Bank indebtedness	nil		27
Accts. pay. & accr. liabs	171		52
Current liabilities	334		136
Shareholders' equity	2,242		11
Cash from oper. activs	**(1,059)**	**n.a.**	**(38)**
Cash from fin. activs	2,975		174
Cash from invest. activs	(605)		(100)
Net cash position	**1,349**	**n.m.**	**38**
Capital expenditures	(7)		nil
	$		$
Earnings per share*	(0.13)		(0.02)
Cash flow per share*	(0.05)		(0.01)
	shs		shs
No. of shs. o/s*	38,749,973		5,869,355
Avg. no. of shs. o/s*	19,779,471		5,869,355
	%		%
Net profit margin	n.a.		n.a.
Return on equity	(235.15)		n.m.
Return on assets	(194.35)		n.a.

* Common
[A] Reported in accordance with IFRS

P.18 Panorama Capital Corp.

Symbol - PANO.P **Exchange** - TSX-VEN **CUSIP** - 698613

Head Office - 301-1665 Ellis St, Kelowna, BC, V1Y 2B3 **Telephone** - (604) 312-4777

Email - csedun@annapurnaadvisors.com

Investor Relations - Carson Sedun (604) 655-0030

Auditors - MNP LLP C.A., Vancouver, B.C.

Transfer Agents - TSX Trust Company, Calgary, Alta.

Profile - (B.C. 2018) Capital Pool Company.

Directors - Carson Sedun, pres. & CEO, Vancouver, B.C.; Michael G. (Mick) Thomson, v-p, bus. devel. & corp. sec., Calgary, Alta.; Keith C. Inman, Kelowna, B.C.

Other Exec. Officers - Blaine Y. Bailey, CFO

Capital Stock

	Authorized (shs.)	Outstanding (shs.)[1]
Common	unlimited	11,227,685

[1] At May 27, 2022

Major Shareholder - Widely held at Mar. 31, 2021.

Price Range - PANO.P/TSX-VEN

Year	Volume	High	Low	Close
2022	597,800	$0.10	$0.03	$0.05
2021	693,100	$0.10	$0.05	$0.08
2020	328,000	$0.07	$0.04	$0.07
2019	252,440	$0.13	$0.06	$0.06

Recent Close: $0.04

Wholly Owned Subsidiaries

Panorama Capital USA Inc., United States.

P.19 ParcelPal Logistics Inc.

Symbol - PKG **Exchange** - CSE **CUSIP** - 69938P

Head Office - c/o Lions Corporate Secretarial, 620-1111 Melville St, Vancouver, BC, V6E 3V6 **Toll-free** - (866) 982-6348

Website - www.parcelpal.com

Email - rich@parcelpal.com

Investor Relations - Rich Wheeless (587) 883-9811

Auditors - BF Borgers CPA PC C.P.A., Lakewood, Colo.

Transfer Agents - Computershare Trust Company of Canada Inc., Vancouver, B.C.

Profile - (B.C. 2006; orig. Alta., 1997) Provides last-mile delivery service and logistics solutions for business-to-business (B2B), business-to-customer (B2C) and any other tailored creative solution partners may require with hubs to customers in the pharmacy and health, meal kit delivery, retail and grocery sectors in Canada and the western U.S.

Services include warehousing solutions, next and same-day delivery and e-commerce integration.

The company's ParcelPal On-Demand app allows customers to place orders from a list of retailers, restaurants, medical and recreational marijuana dispensaries, liquor stores and other available merchants, and pay online through ParcelPal's secure ordering platform. A courier is then requested for the pick-up and delivery of the order. The system also allows the use of phones' location as the drop off point. The company's e-commerce API for integration into online platforms include Magento and Shopify.

Some of the major partners include **Amazon.com Inc.**, **Bayshore Specialty Rx Ltd.** (subsidiary of **Bayshore HealthCare Ltd.**), **CareRx Corporation**, **Sysco Corporation**, **Oco Meals**, **Farmer's Meals**, **WeDoLaundry** and **FedEx**.

In June 2022, wholly owned **ParcelPal Logistics USA Inc.** acquired a customer contract between **Delta Express Delivery, Inc.** and **FedEx Ground Package System, Inc.** whereby ParcelPal would be an independent service provider for FedEx, for issuance of 13,473,358 common shares at a fair value of Cdn$269,467 (US$209,107) and US$336,834 cash. In addition, the company acquired a U.S. delivery service company for US$1,350,000, payable 50% in cash and 50% in common shares.

Common reinstated on CSE, May 18, 2023.

Common suspended from CSE, May 9, 2023.

Predecessor Detail - Name changed from ParcelPal Technology Inc., June 18, 2021.

Directors - Brian Storseth, acting chr., Alta.; Rich Wheeless, CEO & CFO, Ohio; Robert G. Faissal, Toronto, Ont.

Capital Stock

	Authorized (shs.)	Outstanding (shs.)[1]
Common	unlimited	196,374,591

[1] At Aug. 30, 2022

Major Shareholder - Widely held at Aug. 30, 2022.

Price Range - PKG/CSE

Year	Volume	High	Low	Close
2022	57,547,060	$0.07	$0.01	$0.01
2021	134,048,799	$0.30	$0.05	$0.06
2020	96,649,994	$0.20	$0.05	$0.16
2019	75,332,572	$0.38	$0.08	$0.11
2018	185,548,903	$0.59	$0.18	$0.24

Recent Close: $0.02

Wholly Owned Subsidiaries

ParcelPal Logistics USA, Inc., United States.

Subsidiaries

95% int. in **Web-to-door Trucking**, Nev.

Financial Statistics

Periods ended:	12m Dec. 31/21[A]		12m Dec. 31/20[A]
	$000s	%Chg	$000s
Operating revenue	**7,522**	**+19**	**6,317**
Cost of sales	5,907		5,559
Salaries & benefits	547		533
General & admin expense	3,585		2,913
Stock-based compensation	264		473
Operating expense	**10,302**	**+9**	**9,478**
Operating income	**(2,780)**	**n.a.**	**(3,161)**
Deprec., depl. & amort.	347		389
Finance costs, gross	755		324
Pre-tax income	**(4,103)**	**n.a.**	**(4,874)**
Net income	**(4,103)**	**n.a.**	**(4,874)**
Cash & equivalent	552		256
Accounts receivable	202		364
Current assets	904		656
Fixed assets, net	105		150
Right-of-use assets	547		194
Total assets	**5,489**	**+449**	**999**
Bank indebtedness	67		28
Accts. pay. & accr. liabs	833		1,053
Current liabilities	4,877		3,035
Long-term debt, gross	2,429		766
Long-term lease liabilities	405		120
Shareholders' equity	208		(2,156)
Cash from oper. activs	**(1,077)**	**n.a.**	**(927)**
Cash from fin. activs	2,908		999
Cash from invest. activs	(1,567)		(112)
Net cash position	**552**	**+116**	**256**
Capital expenditures	(62)		(112)
Capital disposals	43		nil
	$		$
Earnings per share*	(0.03)		(0.05)
Cash flow per share*	(0.01)		(0.01)
	shs		shs
No. of shs. o/s*	155,838,733		102,953,973
Avg. no. of shs. o/s*	152,119,211		91,147,886
	%		%
Net profit margin	(54.55)		(77.16)
Return on equity	n.m.		n.m.
Return on assets	(103.21)		(395.65)

* Common
[A] Reported in accordance with IFRS

Latest Results

Periods ended:	6m June 30/22[A]		6m June 30/21[A]
	$000s	%Chg	$000s
Operating revenue	5,179	+106	2,511
Net income	(1,798)	n.a.	(1,847)
	$		$
Earnings per share*	(0.01)		(0.02)

* Common
[A] Reported in accordance with IFRS

Historical Summary
(as originally stated)

Fiscal Year	Oper. Rev.	Net Inc. Bef. Disc.	EPS*
	$000s	$000s	$
2021[A]	7,522	(4,103)	(0.03)
2020[A]	6,317	(4,874)	(0.05)
2019[A]	4,783	(4,498)	(0.06)
2018[A]	3,370	(3,818)	(0.06)
2017[A]	374	(1,440)	(0.03)

* Common
[A] Reported in accordance with IFRS

P.20 Pardus Ventures Inc.

Symbol - PDVN.P **Exchange** - TSX-VEN **CUSIP** - 69945A

Head Office - 2250-1055 Hastings St W, Vancouver, BC, V6E 2E9 **Telephone** - (778) 331-2082

Email - herrick.lau@barongroupintl.com

Investor Relations - Herrick Lau (778) 331-2082

Auditors - MNP LLP C.A., Vancouver, B.C.

Transfer Agents - Computershare Trust Company of Canada Inc., Vancouver, B.C.

Profile - (B.C. 2022) Capital Pool Company.

Common listed on TSX-VEN, July 27, 2023.

Directors - Herrick Lau, CEO, CFO & corp. sec., Vancouver, B.C.; Jackie (Kai Yat) Lee, Hong Kong, Hong Kong, People's Republic of China; Kar Fai Leung, Hong Kong, Hong Kong, People's Republic of China

Capital Stock

	Authorized (shs.)	Outstanding (shs.)[1]
Common	unlimited	4,000,000

[1] At July 27, 2023

Major Shareholder - Jackie (Kai Yat) Lee held 23.75% interest and Kar Fai Leung held 23.75% interest at July 27, 2023.

Capital Stock Changes - On July 27, 2023, an initial public offering of 2,000,000 common shares was completed at 10¢ per share.

P.21 Park Lawn Corporation

Symbol - PLC **Exchange -** TSX **CUSIP -** 700563
Head Office - 705-2 St. Clair Ave E, Toronto, ON, M4T 2T5 **Telephone -** (416) 231-1462 **Toll-free -** (888) 636-6798 **Fax -** (416) 233-8155
Website - www.parklawncorp.com
Email - investors@parklawncorp.com
Investor Relations - Daniel Millett (416) 231-1462 ext. 221
Auditors - KPMG LLP C.A., Toronto, Ont.
Lawyers - Goodmans LLP, Toronto, Ont.
Transfer Agents - TSX Trust Company, Toronto, Ont.
FP500 Revenue Ranking - 503
Employees - 2,539 at Dec. 31, 2022
Profile - (Ont. 2010) Owns and operates cemeteries, crematoria and funeral homes across Canada and the U.S.

Operates 109 cemeteries, 140 funeral homes and 35 on-sites (where a funeral home is located at a cemetery) businesses in British Columbia, Ontario, Quebec and 19 U.S. states, and primarily generates revenue through cemetery property interment rights, merchandise and services, as well as funeral services and merchandise sales. The cemetery property interment rights offered includes developed lots, lawn crypts, mausoleum spaces, niches, and other cremation memorialization and interment options. Cemetery merchandise and services offered consist of memorials, markers and bases, outer burial containers, wreaths, flowers and floral placement, graveside services, merchandise installation, interments and other ancillary merchandise. Funeral services offered includes meeting with families, removing and preparing remains, embalming, arranging and directing funeral services, cremations and other ancillary funeral services. Merchandise sales offered for the funeral business consist primarily of the use of funeral home facilities for visitation, remembrance and transportation services, burial caskets, urns, outer burial containers, flowers, online and video tributes, memorialization products and other ancillary funeral and cremation merchandise.

On Apr. 10, 2023, the company acquired substantially all of the assets of Carson-Speaks Chapel, Speaks Buckner Chapel, Speaks Suburban Chapel, and Oak Ridge Memory Gardens (collectively Speaks) in Independence and Buckner, Mo., consisting of three stand-alone funeral homes and one stand-alone cemetery in Kansas City, Mo. Terms were not disclosed.

On Mar. 13, 2023, the company agreed to acquire substantially all of the assets of Meyer Brothers Funeral Homes (collectively Meyer), a business consisting of five stand-alone funeral homes located in Sioux City, Iowa, South Sioux City, Nebraska and Ponca, Neb. Terms were not disclosed.

On Dec. 12, 2022, the company acquired substantially all of the assets of Schrader, Aragon & Jacoby Funeral Home, Mountain View Memorial Park and Bustard & Jacoby Funerals, Cremation, Monuments and Receptions (collectively Jacoby), which consists of two-stand alone funeral homes and one stand-alone cemetery located in Cheyenne and Casper, Wyo. Terms were not disclosed.

On Nov. 28, 2022, the company acquired substantially all of the assets of Park Lawn Funeral Home and Memorial Park Cemetery & Green Lawn Cemetery, Park Lawn Northland Chapel and Glenridge Cemetery (collectively Park Lawn Missouri) in Kansas City and Liberty, Mo., which consists of one on-site, one stand alone funeral home and one stand-alone cemetery located in Kansas City, Mo. Terms were not disclosed.

On Nov. 15, 2022, the company acquired substantially all of the assets of Muehlebach Funeral Care, Skradski-Pierce Funeral Home and Assurance Cremation Society (collectively Muehleback), consisting of three stand-alone funeral homes located in Kansas City, Mo., and Kansas City, Kan. Terms were not disclosed.

On Nov. 9, 2022, the company acquired substantially all of the assets of Brown's Cremation & Funeral Service, a stand-alone funeral home located in Grand Junction, Colo.; and Taylor Funeral Home, consisting of three stand-alone funeral homes and one on-site funeral home and cemetery combination located in Delta, Cedaredge, Hotchkiss and Paonia, Colo. Terms were not disclosed.

In October 2022, the company acquired substantially all of the assets of Ertel Funeral Home & Crematory, a stand-alone funeral home located in Cortez, Colo. Terms were not disclosed.

On June 6, 2022, the company acquired substantially all of the assets of Hudson Funeral Home & Cremation Services (collectively Hudson), a business consisting of one stand-alone funeral home located in Durham, N.C. The purchase price was undisclosed and was funded by credit facility and available cash on hand.

On Apr. 18, 2022, the company acquired substantially all of the assets of Chancellor Funeral Home and Garden of Memories (collectively Chancellor), a business consisting of one stand-alone funeral home and one combination funeral home and cemetery property located in Byram and Florence, Miss., respectively. The purchase price was undisclosed and was funded by available cash on hand.

Recent Merger and Acquisition Activity

Status: completed **Announced:** Sept. 12, 2022
Park Lawn Corporation acquired substantially all of the assets of Shackelford Corporation, a group of businesses consisting of eight stand-alone funeral homes, two stand-alone cemeteries and one on-site funeral home and cemetery located in and around the Savannah, Tenn., for US$28,182,262.

Status: completed **Announced:** Aug. 8, 2022
Park Lawn Corporation acquired substantially all of the assets of Farris Funeral Service, Inc. and Affiliated Service Group, Inc. (collectively Farris), a group of businesses consisting of one stand-alone funeral home and one on-site funeral home and cemetery located in Abingdon, Va., for US$8,692,830.

Predecessor Detail - Succeeded Park Lawn Income Trust, Dec. 31, 2010, pursuant to plan of arrangement whereby Park Lawn Corporation was formed to facilitate the conversion of the fund into a corporation and the fund was subsequently dissolved.

Directors - Deborah Robinson, chr., Toronto, Ont.; J. Bradley (Brad) Green, CEO, Houston, Tex.; Jay D. Dodds, pres. & COO, Humble, Tex.; Marilyn Brophy, Toronto, Ont.; John A. Nies, Boston, Mass.; Steven R. Scott, Toronto, Ont.; Elijio V. Serrano, Houston, Tex.

Other Exec. Officers - Daniel Millett, CFO; Jennifer Hay, chief strategy officer & gen. counsel; Jeff Parker, chief tech. officer; Mathew Forastiere, sr. v-p, opers.; W. Clark Harlow, sr. v-p, operational fin. & acctg.; James D. (Jim) Price, sr. v-p, industry rel.; Linda Gilbert, v-p, corp. fin. & finl. reporting; Lorie Johnson, v-p, HR

Capital Stock

	Authorized (shs.)	Outstanding (shs.)[1]
Common	unlimited	34,272,395

[1] At Aug. 4, 2023

Normal Course Issuer Bid - The company plans to make normal course purchases of up to 3,391,575 common shares representing 10% of the public float. The bid commenced on Aug. 17, 2023, and expires on Aug. 16, 2024.

Major Shareholder - Widely held at Apr. 12, 2023.

Price Range - PLC/TSX

Year	Volume	High	Low	Close
2022	19,081,303	$42.13	$20.64	$25.85
2021	22,355,680	$42.04	$27.15	$41.50
2020	26,208,233	$31.77	$15.58	$27.94
2019	19,559,568	$30.62	$22.56	$29.29
2018	10,311,554	$27.95	$20.25	$23.06

Recent Close: $22.42

Capital Stock Changes - During 2022, common shares were issued as follows: 105,387 under dividend reinvestment plan and 104,542 under the equity incentive plan; 200,985 common shares were repurchased under a Normal Course Issuer Bid.

Dividends

PLC com Ra $0.456 pa Q est. Feb. 15, 2011**
PLC.U com Ra $1.368 pa M est. Apr. 15, 2022
Listed Feb 11/22.
$0.114**i**................ Apr. 15/22
** Reinvestment Option **i** Initial Payment

Wholly Owned Subsidiaries

Citadel Management LLC, Greenville, S.C.
Midwest Memorial Group, LLC, Beverly Hills, Mich.
PLC CMS Ltd., Del.
PLC Saber Ltd.
Park Lawn Limited Partnership, Toronto, Ont.
Signature Funeral and Cemetery Investments, LLC, Houston, Tex.
Note: The preceding list includes only the major related companies in which interests are held.

Financial Statistics

Periods ended:	12m Dec. 31/22[A]		12m Dec. 31/21[◻A]
	US$000s	%Chg	US$000s
Total revenue	**326,110**	**+11**	**294,772**
General & admin. expense	258,753		225,497
Stock-based compensation	4,642		3,809
Operating expense	**263,395**	**+15**	**229,306**
Operating income	**62,715**	**-4**	**65,466**
Deprec. & amort.	13,058		11,788
Finance costs, gross	8,330		7,643
Pre-tax income	**35,634**	**-9**	**38,955**
Income taxes	10,509		11,054
Net income	**25,125**	**-10**	**27,901**
Net inc. for equity hldrs	**25,125**	**-10**	**27,813**
Net inc. for non-cont. int	**nil**	**n.a.**	**88**
Cash & equivalent	30,278		20,786
Inventories	11,014		9,655
Accounts receivable	48,049		47,476
Current assets	92,995		82,372
Long-term investments	448,752		489,692
Fixed assets, net	260,564		271,454
Properties	32,943		40,151
Intangibles	461,705		408,009
Total assets	**1,479,007**	**+5**	**1,406,098**
Accts. pay. & accr. liabs	45,855		48,068
Current liabilities	65,369		43,613
Long-term debt, gross	236,852		162,943
Long-term debt, net	222,595		159,325
Long-term lease liabilities	4,262		3,870
Shareholders' equity	551,596		540,033
Cash from oper. activs	**68,890**	**+9**	**63,344**
Cash from fin. activs	48,578		70,078
Cash from invest. activs	(107,715)		(136,586)
Net cash position	**30,278**	**+46**	**20,786**
Capital expenditures	(20,052)		(18,677)
Capital disposals	2,943		1,736
	US$		US$
Earnings per share*	0.74		0.89
Cash flow per share*	2.02		2.04
Cash divd. per share*	$0.46		$0.46
	shs		shs
No. of shs. o/s*	33,939,153		33,930,209
Avg. no. of shs. o/s*	34,173,743		31,111,308
	%		%
Net profit margin	7.70		9.47
Return on equity	4.57		5.83
Return on assets	2.13		2.53
Foreign sales percent	90		89
No. of employees (FTEs)	2,539		2,340

* Common
◻ Restated
A Reported in accordance with IFRS

Latest Results

Periods ended:	3m Mar. 31/23[A]		3m Mar. 31/22[A]
	US$000s	%Chg	US$000s
Total revenue	86,736	+4	83,173
Net income	4,576	-47	8,702
	US$		US$
Earnings per share*	0.13		0.26

* Common
A Reported in accordance with IFRS

Historical Summary
(as originally stated)

Fiscal Year	Total Rev.	Net Inc. Bef. Disc.	EPS*
	US$000s	US$000s	US$
2022[A]	326,110	25,125	0.73
	$000s	$000s	$
2021[A]	369,540	34,976	1.12
2020[A]	334,153	19,338	0.64
2019[A]	244,259	7,286	0.25
2018[A]	161,421	7,120	0.33

* Common
A Reported in accordance with IFRS

P.22 Parkit Enterprise Inc.

Symbol - PKT **Exchange -** TSX-VEN **CUSIP -** 70137X
Head Office - 100 Canadian Rd, Toronto, ON, M1R 4Z5 **Toll-free -** (888) 627-9881 **Fax -** (647) 670-1223
Website - www.parkitenterprise.com
Email - joanne@parkitenterprise.com
Investor Relations - JoAnne Odette (888) 627-9881
Auditors - RSM Canada LLP C.A., Toronto, Ont.
Lawyers - Maitland & Company, Vancouver, B.C.
Transfer Agents - Computershare Trust Company of Canada Inc., Toronto, Ont.
Employees - 1 at Dec. 31, 2022

Profile - (Ont. 2021; orig. B.C., 2006) Owns, acquires and manages industrial properties across key urban markets in Canada, as well as parking facilities across the United States.

At Mar. 31, 2023, the company owned 23 industrial properties in the Greater Toronto Area and Ottawa, Ont., Montreal, Que., Winnipeg, Man., and Saskatchewan totaling 1,879,141 sq. ft. of gross leasable area with an additional 271,050 sq. ft. of planned future expansion. The industrial properties include warehouses, distribution facilities and light manufacturing facilities with a mix of single and multi-tenant properties.

Wholly owned **PAVe Nashville, LLC** holds Fly-Away Airport Parking, servicing Nashville International Airport in Tennessee. Affiliate **OP Holdings JV, LLC** holds a portfolio of parking facilities as follows: Canopy Airport Parking, servicing Denver International Airport in Colorado; Chapel Square in downtown New Haven, Conn.; and Z Airport Parking in East Granby, Conn., servicing Bradley International Airport.

The company's joint venture partners include **Parking Real Estate, LLC** and **Sculptor Capital Management**.

In May 2023, the company acquired the remaining 50% interest in Fly AwayAirport Parking in Nashville, Tenn., for US$3,550,000 cash. Fly Away Airport Parking is an off-airport parking lot with 1,204 parking spaces on an 8.5-acre land servicing the Nashville International Airport.

Recent Merger and Acquisition Activity

Status: completed **Revised:** Mar. 20, 2023

UPDATE: The transaction was completed. PREVIOUS: Parkit Enterprise Inc. agreed to acquire a portfolio of 10 industrial properties in Winnipeg, Man., and Saskatchewan, totaling 800,000 sq. ft., for a purchase price of $90,250,000, which would be funded with a mortgage and funds on hand. The portfolio includes six properties in Winnipeg, Manitoba, and 4 properties in Saskatchewan.

Status: completed **Revised:** May 25, 2022

UPDATE: The transaction was completed. Parkit acquired the 62,400-sq.-ft. industrial property on a 3-acre land at 1155 Lola St., Ottawa, Ont., for $17,600,000 payable through the assumption of $8,000,000 mortgage and the remaining through cash. PREVIOUS: Parkit Enterprise Inc. agreed to acquire three industrial properties, totaling 139,704-sq.-ft. on 13.8 acres of land in Ontario, for $40,280,000. May 12, 2022 - Parkit acquired the two industrial properties at 3455 Mainway Dr., and 5300 Harvester Rd. in Burlington, Ont., for $22,680,000 consisting of issuance of 5,885,238 common shares valued at $7,000,000, assumption of a $4,500,000 mortgage and $11,180,000 cash. The properties are 77,299 sq. ft. on a 10.8-acre land.

Predecessor Detail - Name changed from Greenscape Capital Group Inc., Sept. 11, 2013; basis 1 new for 10 old shs.

Directors - Steven R. Scott, chr., Toronto, Ont.; Iqbal Khan, CEO, Toronto, Ont.; David (Dave) Delaney, Toronto, Ont.; Bradley (Brad) Dunkley, Toronto, Ont.; Avrohom Y. (Avi) Geller, Spring Valley, N.Y.; R. Blair Tamblyn, Toronto, Ont.

Other Exec. Officers - Carey Chow, co-CFO; JoAnne Odette, co-CFO; Tamara Souglis, corp. sec.

Capital Stock

	Authorized (shs.)	Outstanding (shs.)[1]
Common	unlimited	233,845,162

[1] At May 11, 2023

Normal Course Issuer Bid - The company plans to make normal course purchases of up to 11,692,258 common shares representing 5% of the total outstanding. The bid commenced on Mar. 24, 2023, and expires on Mar. 23, 2024.

Major Shareholder - Steven R. Scott held 12.03% interest and NAWOC Holdings Limited held 10.92% interest at Apr. 14, 2023.

Price Range - PKT/TSX-VEN

Year	Volume	High	Low	Close
2022	27,775,479	$1.54	$0.87	$1.25
2021	49,137,329	$1.85	$0.59	$1.55
2020	10,946,824	$0.79	$0.07	$0.65
2019	3,120,651	$0.37	$0.16	$0.25
2018	6,277,617	$0.40	$0.25	$0.28

Recent Close: $0.68

Capital Stock Changes - During 2022, 7,885,982 common shares were issued on acquisition of industrial properties and 8,299,000 common shares were repurchased under a Normal Course Issuer Bid.

Wholly Owned Subsidiaries

Greenswitch Capital Ltd., B.C.
- 100% int. in **Greenswitch America Inc.**, Del.
  - 82.83% int. in **Parking Acquisition Ventures, LLC**, United States.
    - 29.45% int. in **OP Holdings JV, LLC**, United States.
  - 50% int. in **PAVe Admin, LLC**, United States.
  - 100% int. in **PAVe Nashville, LLC**, United States.

Financial Statistics

Periods ended:	12m Dec. 31/22[A]		12m Dec. 31/21[oA]
	$000s	%Chg	$000s
Total revenue	**11,069**	**+92**	**5,779**
Rental operating expense	5,186		2,456
Salaries & benefits	528		332
General & admin. expense	1,455		1,045
Stock-based compensation	1,196		3,175
Operating expense	**8,365**	**+19**	**7,008**
Operating income	**2,704**	**n.a.**	**(1,229)**
Investment income	199		(289)
Deprec. & amort.	4,588		1,967
Finance income	300		280
Finance costs, gross	2,175		770
Pre-tax income	**(3,560)**	**n.a.**	**(3,976)**
Income taxes	(80)		13
Net income	**(3,479)**	**n.a.**	**(3,988)**
Cash & equivalent	19,472		21,797
Accounts receivable	1,414		1,054
Long-term investments	11,780		13,218
Income-producing props	197,292		137,675
Properties under devel.	4,080		2,538
Property interests, net	201,372		140,214
Total assets	**239,634**	**+35**	**177,641**
Accts. pay. & accr. liabs	3,689		1,630
Long-term debt, gross	76,353		17,126
Long-term debt, net	76,353		17,126
Shareholders' equity	158,154		158,326
Cash from oper. activs	**1,566**	**-28**	**2,166**
Cash from fin. activs	35,780		110,178
Cash from invest. activs	(39,654)		(99,684)
Net cash position	**19,472**	**-11**	**21,797**
Increase in property	(41,291)		(99,512)
	$		$
Earnings per share*	(0.01)		(0.02)
Cash flow per share*	0.01		0.01
Funds from opers. per sh.*	0.01		0.01
	shs		shs
No. of shs. o/s*	234,050,662		234,463,680
Avg. no. of shs. o/s*	237,340,170		215,592,019
	%		%
Net profit margin	(31.43)		(69.01)
Return on equity	(2.20)		(4.59)
Return on assets	(0.65)		(3.33)
No. of employees (FTEs)	1		1

* Common
[o] Restated
[A] Reported in accordance with IFRS

Latest Results

Periods ended:	3m Mar. 31/23[A]		3m Mar. 31/22[A]
	$000s	%Chg	$000s
Total revenue	3,559	+69	2,110
Net income	(1,085)	n.a.	(493)
	$		$
Earnings per share*	(0.00)		(0.00)

* Common
[A] Reported in accordance with IFRS

Historical Summary
(as originally stated)

Fiscal Year	Total Rev.	Net Inc. Bef. Disc.	EPS*
	$000s	$000s	$
2022[A]	11,069	(3,479)	(0.01)
2021[A]	5,779	(3,988)	(0.02)
2020[A]	145	(5,328)	(0.15)
2019[A]	216	(879)	(0.03)
2018[A]	252	3,448	0.11

* Common
[A] Reported in accordance with IFRS

P.23 Parkland Corporation*

Symbol - PKI **Exchange** - TSX **CUSIP** - 70137W
Head Office - 1800-240 4 Ave SW, Calgary, AB, T2P 4H4 **Telephone** - (403) 567-2500 **Toll-free** - (877) 906-6644
Website - www.parkland.ca
Email - valerie.roberts@parkland.ca
Investor Relations - Valerie Roberts (403) 956-9282
Auditors - PricewaterhouseCoopers LLP C.A., Calgary, Alta.
Transfer Agents - Computershare Trust Company of Canada Inc., Calgary, Alta.
FP500 Revenue Ranking - 18
Employees - 6,284 at Dec. 31, 2022

Profile - (Alta. 2010) Supplies and markets fuel and petroleum products and operates convenience and food stores in Canada, the U.S., the Caribbean, and Central and South America.

Operations are grouped into four segments: Canada; International; USA; and Refining.

Canada - Owns, supplies and supports a coast-to-coast network of fuel and convenience stores, frozen food retail locations, cardlock sites, bulk fuel, propane, heating oil, lubricants and other related services to commercial, industrial and residential customers. The retail business operates and supplies a coast-to-coast network of 2,068 fuel and convenience stores, consisting of 863 company sites and 1,268 dealer sites. Retail fuel brands consist of Ultramar, Esso, Chevron, Pioneer, Fas Gas Plus, Husky and Crevier; and convenience store operations are conducted primarily under the On the Run/Marché Express brand. Retail operations also include a chain of specialty frozen foods stores under the M&M Food Market banner, with 313 franchise and company-owned stores and 2,903 third-party retailers who sell M&M Food Market products. The commercial business delivers bulk fuel, heating oil, lubricants and other related products and services to commercial, industrial and residential customers under the Ultramar, Bluewave Energy, Pipeline Commercial, Chevron, Columbia Fuels and Sparlings Propane brands. Commercial operations have a network of 170 cardlock sites which include commercial truck fuelling stations and marine fuel facilities. This segment is also responsible for managing fuel supply contracts, marketing fuel, transporting and distributing fuel through ships, rail and highway carriers, and storing fuel in owned and leased facilities. Also engages in low-carbon activities, such as emission credit and renewable fuel trading transactions and blending of biodiesel, ethanol and other fuels to produce renewable fuels resulting in emission credits.

International - Wholly owned **Sol Investments SEZC**, the largest independent fuel marketer in the Caribbean, operates across 23 countries and territories in the Caribbean and the northeast coast of South America through the following businesses: retail, which consists of 258 company-owned and operated and 232 dealer-owned and operated retail gas stations operating primarily under the Sol, Esso, Mobil, Shell and Texaco brands, and the operations of Sol Shop convenience stores; commercial and industrial, which delivers and supplies gasoline, diesel, fuel oil, propane and lubricants to customers in various sectors, including power, oil and gas, mining and hospitality; aviation, which operates at 16 airports, supplying aviation fuel and services to airlines; supply and distribution, which consists of a network of owned or leased infrastructure assets including import terminals, storage facilities, pipelines, marine berths and charter ships; and renewable energy, which provides commercial solar and other renewable energy solutions under the Sol Ecolution name. Sol Investments also owns a 29% interest in an 18,000-bbl-per-day refinery in Fort-De-France, Martinique; and 50% interest in **Isla Dominicana de Petroleo Corp.**, a joint venture consisting of 236 retail locations alongside an integrated commercial and aviation business in the Dominican Republic.

USA - Supplies and distributes refined petroleum products and other related products and services throughout Arizona, Colorado, Florida, Idaho, Minnesota, Montana, New Mexico, Nevada, North Dakota, Oregon, Utah and Wyoming. Operations are conducted through the following channels: retail; and commercial and wholesale. The retail business operates a network of 211 fuel and convenience stores under the On the Run, ARCO, Cenex, Chevron, Conoco, Exxon, Marathon, Mobil, Mr. Gas, Texaco, Phillips 66, Shell, U-Gas, 76, Superpumper, KJ's, Hart's, KB Express, Casey's Corner and U Shop brands. The commercial business delivers and supplies gasoline, diesel, marine fuel oil, propane, lubricants and ancillary products to customers in various sectors, as well as 429 independent dealer retail sites, which include multi-site dealer chains and branded and unbranded relationships, supported by a network of 48 cardlock sites. Commercial brands include Rhinehart Oil, Farstad Oil, Conrad & Bischoff, Tropic Oil and National Fuel Network (NFN). The wholesale business supplies gasoline, diesel and other fuels to wholesale customers and primarily operates under wholly owned **Parkland (U.S.) Supply Co.**

Refining - Owns and operates a refinery in Burnaby, B.C., which has a capacity of 55,000-bbl-per-day of light and medium crude oil with majority of production provided to the company's retail, commercial and wholesale networks. Refining is responsible for the refining of fuel products such as gasoline, diesel and jet fuel, and is also engaged in the renewable business activities, such as co-processing of bio-feedstocks (such as tallow, canola oil, tall oil and others).

On Mar. 1, 2023, wholly owned **Conrad & Bischoff, LLC** was amalgamated into wholly owned **Parkland USA Corporation**.

On July 1, 2022, subsidiary **Sol Investments SEZC** acquired **Gulfstream Petroleum, SRL** (GP) from **GB Group S.A.** for US$96,000,000. GP represented GB Group's retail, aviation, commercial, lubes and LPG businesses in Jamaica, including 65 retail sites and aviation fuelling at Montego Bay and Kingston airports.

On Apr. 1, 2022, wholly owned **Crevier Petroleum Inc.** was amalgamated into the company.

Recent Merger and Acquisition Activity

Status: completed **Revised:** Oct. 19, 2022

UPDATE: The transaction was completed. PREVIOUS: Parkland Corporation agreed to acquire the remaining 25% interest in Sol Investments SEZC from Simpson Oil Limited for issuance of 20,000,000 common shares. Sol operates in 23 countries and territories predominantly located in the Caribbean and the northern coast of South America, with over 600 retail services stations as well as commercial, industrial and aviation businesses. On closing, Simpson Oil would hold a 19.54% interest in Parkland.

Status: completed **Revised:** Sept. 13, 2022

UPDATE: The transaction was completed. PREVIOUS: Cenovus Energy Inc. agreed to sell 337 gas stations in its Husky retail fuels network to Parkland Corporation and Federated Co-operatives Limited (FCL) for $420,000,000, in which Parkland would pay $156,000,000 for 156 locations and FCL would pay $264,000,000 for 181 locations. Cenovus would retain its commercial fuels business, which included 170 cardlock, bulk plant and travel centre locations.

Status: completed **Revised:** June 1, 2022

UPDATE: The transaction was completed. PREVIOUS: Parkland Corporation agreed to acquire Vopak Terminals of Canada Inc. and Vopak Terminals of Eastern Canada Inc. from Royal Vopak N.V. for $168,000,000. The acquisition includes four product terminals in Montreal-Est, Montreal-Ouest and Quebec, Que., and Hamilton, Ont., with a total storage capacity of 780,000 cubic m.

Predecessor Detail - Name changed from Parkland Fuel Corporation, May 15, 2020.

Directors - Steven P. (Steve) Richardson, chr., Toronto, Ont.; Robert B. (Bob) Espey, pres. & CEO, Calgary, Alta.; Michael Christiansen, Cayman Islands; Lisa J. Colnett, Toronto, Ont.; Nora M. Duke, St. John's, N.L.; Mark Halley, Cayman Islands; Col. (honry.) Timothy W. (Tim) Hogarth, Burlington, Ont.; Richard Hookway, London, Middx., United Kingdom; Angela John, Houston, Tex.; Deborah S. (Debbie) Stein, Calgary, Alta.

Other Exec. Officers - James (Jim) Pantelidis, chr., emeritus; Marcel Teunissen, CFO; Ferio Pugliese, sr. v-p, people & culture; Darren Smart, sr. v-p, energy transition & corp. devel.; Pierre P. G. Magnan, pres., International; Donna Sanker, pres., USA; Ian White, pres., Parkland Canada

Capital Stock

	Authorized (shs.)	Outstanding (shs.)[1]
Preferred	unlimited	nil
Common	unlimited	175,518,000

[1] At Mar. 31, 2023

Options - At Dec. 31, 2022, options were outstanding to purchase 4,097,000 common shares at a weighted average exercise price of $32.56 per share with a weighted average remaining contractual life of four years.

Normal Course Issuer Bid - The company plans to make normal course purchases of up to 13,992,412 common shares representing 10% of the public float. The bid commenced on Dec. 1, 2022, and expires on Nov. 30, 2023.

Major Shareholder - Simpson Oil Limited held 20% interest at Mar. 27, 2023.

Price Range - PKI/TSX

Year	Volume	High	Low	Close
2022	127,847,993	$39.45	$24.25	$29.71
2021	100,853,599	$45.10	$32.78	$34.77
2020	120,141,354	$49.22	$17.57	$40.39
2019	105,250,954	$48.41	$34.03	$47.71
2018	101,387,614	$47.45	$26.70	$35.34

Recent Close: $36.35

Capital Stock Changes - In October 2022, 20,000,000 common shares were issued pursuant to the acquisition of the remaining 25% interest in Sol Investments SEZC. Also during 2022, common shares were issued as follows: 1,385,000 under the dividend reinvestment plan, 771,000 pursuant to business acquisitions, 421,000 on exercise of options and 128,000 on vesting of performance shares; 1,453,000 were repurchased under a Normal Course Issuer Bid.

Dividends

PKI com Ra $1.36 pa Q est. Apr. 14, 2023**[1]

Prev. Rate: $1.30 est. July 15, 2022

Prev. Rate: $1.2348 est. Apr. 15, 2021

Prev. Rate: $1.2144 est. Apr. 15, 2020

[1] Divds. paid monthly prior to July/22.

** Reinvestment Option

Long-Term Debt - Outstanding at Dec. 31, 2022:

Credit facility[1]	$1,702,000,000
3.875% sr. notes due 2026	600,000,000
5.875% sr. notes due 2027[2]	677,000,000
6% sr. notes due 2028	400,000,000
4.375% sr. notes due 2029	600,000,000
4.5% sr. notes due 2029[3]	1,083,000,000
4.625% sr. notes due 2030[3]	1,083,000,000
Lease obligs	828,000,000
Other notes	2,000,000
Redemption options	44,000,000
Less: Deferred fin. costs	47,000,000
	6,972,000,000
Less: Current portion	173,000,000
	6,799,000,000

[1] Consists of borrowings under a US$400,000,000 term loan due April 2024; and $1.594 billion Canadian syndicated revolving credit facility and a US$250,000,000 U.S. syndicated revolving credit facility, both due April 2027.

[2] US$500,000,000.

[3] US$800,000,000.

Wholly Owned Subsidiaries

Elbow River Marketing Ltd., Alta.

Estrella Holdings Limited, Cayman Islands.

- 100% int. in **Sol Investments SEZC**, Grand Cayman, Cayman Islands.
  - 100% int. in **Antilles Trading Company SEZC**, Cayman Islands.
  - 100% int. in **SOL Puerto Rico Limited**, United Kingdom.
  - 99.99% int. in **SOL St. Lucia Ltd.**, Saint Lucia.
  - 100% int. in **SOL Suriname N.V.**, Suriname.

M&M Meat Shops Ltd., Mississauga, Ont. dba M&MFood Market

Parkland Refining (B.C.) Ltd., B.C.

Parkland (U.S.) Supply Corporation, Del.

Parkland USA Corporation, N.D.

Rhinehart Oil Co., LLC, American Fork, Utah.

Superpumper Inc., N.D.

Tropic Oil Company, LLC, Miami, Fla.

Note: The preceding list includes only the major related companies in which interests are held.

Financial Statistics

Periods ended:	12m Dec. 31/22[A]		12m Dec. 31/21[A]
	$000s	%Chg	$000s
Operating revenue	**35,462,000**	**+65**	**21,468,000**
Cost of sales	31,441,000		18,512,000
Salaries & benefits	742,000		552,000
General & admin expense	225,000		160,000
Other operating expense	1,062,000		803,000
Operating expense	**33,470,000**	**+67**	**20,027,000**
Operating income	**1,992,000**	**+38**	**1,441,000**
Deprec., depl. & amort.	743,000		616,000
Finance costs, gross	331,000		323,000
Investment income	21,000		16,000
Pre-tax income	**416,000**	**+157**	**162,000**
Income taxes	70,000		36,000
Net income	**346,000**	**+175**	**126,000**
Net inc. for equity hldrs	**310,000**	**+220**	**97,000**
Net inc. for non-cont. int	**36,000**	**+24**	**29,000**
Cash & equivalent	716,000		284,000
Inventories	1,745,000		1,265,000
Accounts receivable	1,872,000		1,392,000
Current assets	4,574,000		3,127,000
Long-term investments	342,000		319,000
Fixed assets, net	5,141,000		4,429,000
Intangibles, net	3,839,000		3,274,000
Total assets	**14,288,000**	**+24**	**11,550,000**
Accts. pay. & accr. liabs	2,806,000		1,950,000
Current liabilities	3,286,000		2,253,000
Long-term debt, gross	6,972,000		5,556,000
Long-term debt, net	6,799,000		5,432,000
Shareholders' equity	3,037,000		1,970,000
Non-controlling interest	nil		362,000
Cash from oper. activs	**1,326,000**	**+47**	**904,000**
Cash from fin. activs	276,000		655,000
Cash from invest. activs	(1,227,000)		(1,513,000)
Net cash position	**716,000**	**+120**	**326,000**
Capital expenditures	(503,000)		(396,000)
Capital disposals	8,000		14,000
	$		$
Earnings per share*	1.94		0.64
Cash flow per share*	8.29		5.97
Cash divd. per share*	1.29		1.23
	shs		shs
No. of shs. o/s*	175,428,000		154,176,000
Avg. no. of shs. o/s*	159,867,000		151,451,000
	%		%
Net profit margin	0.98		0.59
Return on equity	12.38		4.99
Return on assets	4.81		3.65
Foreign sales percent	48		43
No. of employees (FTEs)	6,284		5,946

* Common

[A] Reported in accordance with IFRS

Latest Results

Periods ended:	3m Mar. 31/23[A]		3m Mar. 31/22[A]
	$000s	%Chg	$000s
Operating revenue	8,156,000	+7	7,606,000
Net income	77,000	+13	68,000
Net inc. for equity hldrs	77,000	+40	55,000
Net inc. for non-cont. int	nil		13,000
	$		$
Earnings per share*	0.44		0.36

* Common

[A] Reported in accordance with IFRS

Historical Summary
(as originally stated)

Fiscal Year	Oper. Rev.	Net Inc. Bef. Disc.	EPS*
	$000s	$000s	$
2022[A]	35,462,000	346,000	1.94
2021[A]	21,468,000	126,000	0.64
2020[A]	14,011,000	112,000	0.55
2019[A]	18,453,000	414,000	2.60
2018[A]	14,442,000	206,000	1.56

* Common

[A] Reported in accordance with IFRS

P.24 Partners Value Investments LP*

Symbol - PVF.UN **Exchange -** TSX-VEN **CUSIP -** 70214T

Head Office - Bay Wellington Tower, Brookfield Place, 300-181 Bay St, PO Box 762, Toronto, ON, M5J 2T3 **Telephone -** (416) 359-8620 **Fax -** (416) 365-9645

Website - www.pvii.ca

Email - jason.weckwerth@brookfield.com

Investor Relations - Jason Weckwerth (416) 956-5142

Auditors - Deloitte LLP C.A., Toronto, Ont.

Transfer Agents - TSX Trust Company, Montréal, Qué.

Profile - (Ont. 2016) An investment limited partnership whose principal investments are ownership interests in 134,000,000 class A limited voting shares of **Brookfield Corporation** (formerly **Brookfield Asset Management Inc.**) and 31,000,000 class A limited voting shares of **Brookfield Asset Management Ltd.** Also holds investments in other securities.

At Mar. 31, 2023, together with wholly owned **Partners Value Investments Inc.** and **Partners Value Split Corp.**, holds 133,722,910 class A limited voting shares of **Brookfield Corporation**, a global asset manager focused on renewable power and transition, infrastructure, private equity, real estate and credit; and 30,527,862 class A limited voting shares of **Brookfield Asset Management Ltd.**, an investment management firm focused on property development, renewable energy, infrastructure, insurance, and private equity. Also holds 2,875,370 limited partnership units of **Brookfield Business Partners L.P.**, which acquires, owns and operates the business services, infrastructure services and industrial sectors; and 915,000 Class A exchangeable limited voting shares of **Brookfield Reinsurance Ltd.**, which provides reinsurance and other capital-based services to the insurance industry.

Predecessor Detail - Succeeded Partners Value Investments Inc., June 30, 2016.

Trustees - Frank N. C. Lochan, chr., Oakville, Ont.; Brian D. Lawson, CEO, Toronto, Ont.; Danesh K. Varma, Kingston upon Thames, Surrey, United Kingdom; Ralph J. Zarboni, Toronto, Ont.

Oper. Subsid./Mgt. Co. Officers - Bahir Manios, pres.; Kathy Sarpash, man. dir., gen. counsel & corp. sec.; Jason Weckwerth, CFO; Kunal Dusad, sr. v-p

Capital Stock

	Authorized (shs.)	Outstanding (shs.)[1]	Par
Cl.A Preferred LP Unit	unlimited		
Series 1		16,035,461	US$25
General Partnership Unit	unlimited	1	
Equity Limited Partnership Unit	unlimited	66,097,961	

[1] At Mar. 31, 2023

Class A Preferred Limited Partnership Unit - Issuable in series. Non-voting. **Series 1 -** Entitled to fixed cumulative annual distributions of US$1.125 per unit payable quarterly less any amount required by law to be deducted and withheld. Redeemable by the limited partnership for US$25 per unit plus accrued and unpaid distributions. Exchangeable for equity limited partnership units in the event of any rights offering or a public offering of equity limited partnership units by the limited partnership. Can be used to satisfy the exercise price of warrants.

General Partnership Unit - Held by general partner PVI Management Trust, which is entitled to receive assets of the limited partnership upon dissolution.

Equity Limited Partnership Unit - Non-voting.

Normal Course Issuer Bid - The company plans to make normal course purchases of up to 3,369,353 equity limited partnership units representing 5% of the total outstanding. The bid commenced on Jan. 18, 2023, and expires on Jan. 17, 2024.

The company plans to make normal course purchases of up to 801,882 class A preferred LP units, series 1 representing 5% of the total outstanding. The bid commenced on Jan. 18, 2023, and expires on Jan. 17, 2024.

Price Range - PVF.UN/TSX-VEN

Year	Volume	High	Low	Close
2022	133,353	$80.00	$59.99	$65.00
2021	160,302	$81.00	$46.05	$81.00
2020	197,486	$69.79	$33.00	$50.05
2019	110,105	$55.10	$38.50	$52.00
2018	135,304	$43.00	$32.00	$38.50

Recent Close: $64.39

Capital Stock Changes - During 2022, 75,000 equity limited partnership units and 715 class A preferred limited partnership units, series 1 were repurchased under a Normal Course Issuer Bid.

Dividends

PVF.PR.U ser 1 pfd lp unit cum. Ra US$1.125 pa Q

Long-Term Debt - Outstanding at Dec. 31, 2022:

Corp. borrowings[1]	US$221,460,000
Partners Value Invests. LP cl.A:	
4% Ser.2 due 2026	50,797,000
4% Ser.3 due 2031	50,797,000
4% Ser.4 due 2036	50,812,000
Partners Value Split cl.AA:	
4.8% Ser.8 due 2024	110,717,000
4.75% Ser.11 due 2025	110,730,000
4.9% Ser.9 due 2026	110,671,000
4.7% Ser.10 due 2027	110,730,000
4.4% Ser.12 due 2028	127,340,000
4.45% Ser. 13 due 2029	110,730,000
PVI SIB LP cl.A:	
4% Ser.1 due 2026	28,125,000
4% Ser.2 due 2031	28,125,000
4% Ser.3 due 2036	28,125,000
Less: Deferred fin. costs	13,316,000
	1,125,843,000

[1] Consist of Cdn$150,000,000 of 4.375% senior notes due 2027 and Cdn$150,000,000 of 4% senior notes due 2028.

Wholly Owned Subsidiaries

Partners Value Investments Inc., Ont.
- 100% int. in **PVII Holdings I LP**, Ont.
- 100% int. in **PVII Subco Inc.**, Ont.
  - 100% int. in **PVI SIB LP**, Hamilton, Bermuda.
- 100% int. in **Partners Value Split Corp.**, Toronto, Ont. (see separate coverage)

Investments

Brookfield Asset Management Ltd., Toronto, Ont. (see separate coverage)
Brookfield Business Partners L.P., Hamilton, Bermuda. (see separate coverage)
Brookfield Corporation, Toronto, Ont. (see separate coverage)

Financial Statistics

Periods ended:	12m Dec. 31/22^A		12m Dec. 31/21^A
	US$000s	%Chg	US$000s
Total revenue	**1,137,988**	**+871**	**117,251**
Operating expense	**2,359**	**-27**	**3,249**
Operating income	**1,135,629**	**+896**	**114,002**
Finance costs, gross	52,905		46,594
Pre-tax income	**1,119,996**	**n.m.**	**38,702**
Income taxes	(1,449)		7,208
Net income	**1,121,445**	**n.m.**	**31,494**
Cash & equivalent	185,722		80,704
Accounts receivable	31,270		26,861
Investments	5,411,635		8,214,664
Total assets	**5,630,231**	**-33**	**8,360,786**
Accts. pay. & accr. liabs	7,354		7,693
Debt	1,125,843		1,071,532
Preferred share equity	153,049		153,054
Shareholders' equity	4,457,566		7,258,130
Non-controlling interest	9,962		nil
Cash from oper. activs	**53,110**	**n.a.**	**(5,410)**
Cash from fin. activs	115,469		(249,033)
Cash from invest. activs	(54,288)		16,372
Net cash position	**185,722**	**+130**	**80,704**
	US$		US$
Earnings per share*	16.84		0.34
Cash flow per share*	0.80		(0.07)
	shs		shs
No. of shs. o/s*	66,137,062		66,212,001
Avg. no. of shs. o/s*	66,169,783		72,953,504
	%		%
Net profit margin	98.55		26.86
Return on equity	19.54		0.43
Return on assets	16.79		0.96

* Eq. LP unit
^A Reported in accordance with IFRS

Note: Total revenue includes realized gains (losses) and unrealized gains (losses) on investments.

Latest Results

Periods ended:	3m Mar. 31/23^A		3m Mar. 31/22^A
	US$000s	%Chg	US$000s
Total revenue	25,065	-32	36,723
Net income	7,254	-27	9,979
	US$		US$
Earnings per share*	0.08		0.12

* Eq. LP unit
^A Reported in accordance with IFRS

Historical Summary
(as originally stated)

Fiscal Year	Total Rev.	Net Inc. Bef. Disc.	EPS*
	US$000s	US$000s	US$
2022^A	1,137,988	1,121,445	16.84
2021^A	117,251	31,494	0.34
2020^A	74,691	44,289	0.44
2019^A	72,289	(3,947)	(0.28)
2018^A	85,065	125,297	1.40

* Eq. LP unit
^A Reported in accordance with IFRS

P.25 Partners Value Split Corp.

CUSIP - 70214J
Head Office - Bay Wellington Tower, Brookfield Place, 300-181 Bay St, Box 762, Toronto, ON, M5J 2T3 **Telephone** - (647) 503-6516 **Fax** - (416) 365-9645
Website - www.partnersvaluesplit.com
Email - jason.weckwerth@brookfield.com
Investor Relations - Jason Weckwerth (416) 956-5142
Auditors - Deloitte LLP C.A., Toronto, Ont.
Lawyers - Torys LLP, Toronto, Ont.
Transfer Agents - TSX Trust Company, Toronto, Ont.
Investment Managers - Brookfield Public Securities Group LLC, New York, N.Y.
Managers - Brookfield Public Securities Group LLC, New York, N.Y.

Profile - (Ont. 2001) Holds a portfolio of class A limited voting shares of **Brookfield Corporation** (formerly **Brookfield Asset Management Inc.**), a global alternative asset manager; and **Brookfield Asset Management Ltd.**, an investment management firm, in order to generate a stable stream of dividend income for the holders of preferred shares and to enable the holders of capital shares to participate in any capital appreciation in the Brookfield shares.

At Dec. 31, 2022, the company held 119,611,449 class A limited voting shares of **Brookfield Corporation**; and 29,902,862 class A limited voting shares of **Brookfield Asset Management Ltd.**, with fair values totaling US$4.62 billion.

Predecessor Detail - Name changed from BAM Split Corp., Aug. 28, 2013.

Directors - Brian D. Lawson, chr. & CEO, Toronto, Ont.; Frank N. C. Lochan, Oakville, Ont.; Danesh K. Varma, Kingston upon Thames, Surrey, United Kingdom; Ralph J. Zarboni, Toronto, Ont.

Other Exec. Officers - Bahir Manios, pres.; Kathy Sarpash, man. dir., gen. counsel & corp. sec.; Jason Weckwerth, CFO; Kunal Dusad, sr. v-p

Capital Stock

	Authorized (shs.)	Outstanding (shs.)[1]
Class A Preferred	unlimited	nil
Class AA Preferred	unlimited	
Series 8		5,999,300[2]
Series 9		5,996,800[2]
Series 10		6,000,000[2]
Series 11		6,000,000[2]
Series 12		6,900,000[2]
Series 13		6,000,000[2]
Class AAA Preferred	unlimited	nil
Junior Preferred	unlimited	
Series 1		8,000,000[2]
Series 2		1,800,000[2]
Series 3		2,000,000[2]
Capital	unlimited	48,696,100
Class A Vtg.	unlimited	100

[1] At Dec. 31, 2022
[2] Classified as debt.

Class AA Preferred - Issuable in series. Rank prior to class AAA preferred, junior preferred and capital shares and on a pari passu basis with class A preferred shares with respect to dividends and return of capital in the event of the liquidation, dissolution or winding-up of the company. Non-voting. **Series 8** - Entitled to quarterly fixed cumulative preferential dividends of Cdn$0.30 per share to yield 4.8% per annum on the Cdn$25 issue price. Retractable at any time, at the lesser of: the NAV per unit and Cdn$25 plus accrued and unpaid dividends, for 4.9% series 6 debentures which mature on Sept. 30, 2024. Redeemable on or after Sept. 30, 2022, and prior to Sept. 30, 2024, at Cdn$25.50 per share plus accrued and unpaid dividends and which will decline by Cdn$0.50 on Sept. 30, 2023. All outstanding series 8 preferred shares will be redeemed on Sept. 30, 2024, at the lesser of: Cdn$25 plus accrued and unpaid dividends, and the NAV per unit. **Series 9** - Entitled to quarterly fixed cumulative preferential dividends of Cdn$0.3063 per share to yield 4.9% per annum on the Cdn$25 issue price. Retractable at any time, at the lesser of: the NAV per unit and Cdn$25 plus accrued and unpaid dividends, for 5% series 7 debentures which mature on Feb. 28, 2026. Redeemable on or after Feb. 28, 2024, and prior to Feb. 28, 2026, at Cdn$25.50 per share plus accrued and unpaid dividends and which will decline by Cdn$0.50 on Feb. 28, 2025. All outstanding series 9 preferred shares will be redeemed on Feb. 28, 2026, at the lesser of: Cdn$25 plus accrued and unpaid dividends, and the NAV per unit. **Series 10** - Entitled to quarterly fixed cumulative preferential dividends of Cdn$0.2938 per share to yield 4.7% per annum on the Cdn$25 issue price. Retractable at any time, at the lesser of: the NAV per unit and Cdn$25 plus accrued and unpaid dividends, for 4.8% series 8 debentures which mature on Feb. 28, 2027. Redeemable on or after Feb. 28, 2025, and prior to Feb. 28, 2027, at Cdn$25.50 per share plus accrued and unpaid dividends and which will decline by Cdn$0.50 on Feb. 28, 2026. All outstanding series 10 preferred shares will be redeemed on Feb. 28, 2027, at the lesser of: Cdn$25 plus accrued and unpaid dividends, and the NAV per unit. **Series 11** - Entitled to quarterly fixed cumulative preferential dividends of Cdn$0.2969 per share to yield 4.75% per annum on the Cdn$25 issue price. Retractable at any time, at the lesser of: the NAV per unit and Cdn$25 plus accrued and unpaid dividends, for 4.85% series 9 debentures which mature on Oct. 31, 2025. Redeemable on or after Oct. 31, 2023, and prior to Oct. 31, 2025, at Cdn$25.50 per share plus accrued and unpaid dividends and which will decline by Cdn$0.50 on Oct. 31, 2024. All outstanding series 11 preferred shares will be redeemed on Oct. 31, 2025, at the lesser of: Cdn$25 plus accrued and unpaid dividends, and the NAV per unit. **Series 12** - Entitled to quarterly fixed cumulative preferential dividends of Cdn$0.275 per share to yield 4.4% per annum on the Cdn$25 issue price. Retractable at any time, at the lesser of: the NAV per unit and Cdn$25 plus accrued and unpaid dividends, for 4.5% series 10 debentures which mature on Feb. 29, 2028. Redeemable on or after Feb. 28, 2026, and prior to Feb. 29, 2028, at Cdn$25.50 per share plus accrued and unpaid dividends and which will decline by Cdn$0.50 on Feb. 28, 2027. All outstanding series 12 preferred shares will be redeemed on Feb. 29, 2028, at the lesser of: Cdn$25 plus accrued and unpaid dividends, and the NAV per unit. **Series 13** - Entitled to quarterly fixed cumulative preferential dividends of Cdn$0.2781 per share to yield 4.45% per annum on the Cdn$25 issue price. Retractable at any time, at the lesser of: the NAV per unit and Cdn$25 plus accrued and unpaid dividends, for 4.55% series 11 debentures which mature on May 31, 2029. Redeemable on or after May 31, 2027, and prior to May 31, 2029, at Cdn$25.50 per share plus accrued and unpaid dividends and which will decline by Cdn$0.50 on May 31, 2028. All outstanding series 13 preferred shares will be redeemed on May 31, 2029, at the lesser of: Cdn$25 plus accrued and unpaid dividends, and the NAV per unit.

Junior Preferred - Issuable in series. Rank prior to capital shares and subsequent to class A preferred, class AA preferred, class AAA preferred and class A voting shares with respect to dividends and return of capital in the event of the liquidation, dissolution or winding-up of the company. Non-voting. **Series 1**, **Series 2** and **Series 3** - Entitled to non-cumulative quarterly dividend at an annual rate of 5% or Cdn$1.25 per share. Retractable at any time at the lesser of the NAV per unit and Cdn$25. Redeemable at any time at Cdn$25 per share plus accrued and unpaid dividends.

Capital - Rank subsequent to all preferred and class A voting shares with respect to dividends and return of capital in the event of the liquidation, dissolution or winding-up of the company. Entitled to dividends as and when declared by the board of directors of the company. Entitled to any appreciation in the market price of class A limited voting shares of Brookfield Asset Management Inc. upon redemption. Retractable at any time at a price per share equal to the amount by which 95% of the NAV exceeds the aggregate redemption price of all outstanding preferred shares divided by the number of capital shares then outstanding, less Cdn$1.00. Retractable with one preferred share as a unit (1 capital share and 1 preferred share) at a price per unit equal to the aggregate of: (i) the lesser of the redemption price for that class or series of preferred shares and 95% of the NAV per unit; and (ii) the amount by which 95% of the NAV per unit exceeds the redemption price for that class or series of preferred shares. Retractable with one preferred share as a unit under a special annual retraction on September 30 each year at a price per unit equal to the aggregate of: (i) the lesser of the redemption price for that class or series of preferred shares and the NAV per unit; and (ii) the amount by which the NAV per unit exceeds the redemption price for that class or series of preferred shares. Redeemable at any time at a price equal to the amount by which the NAV 20 days prior to the redemption date exceeds the aggregate redemption price of all outstanding preferred shares divided by the number of capital shares then outstanding. If any capital shares are tendered for retraction (other than a retraction where an equal number of preferred shares are also tendered), the company will redeem or purchase for cancellation in the open market preferred shares in order to ensure that the number of preferred shares outstanding does not exceed the number of capital shares outstanding. Non-voting.

Class A Voting - Not entitled to dividends while any preferred or capital shares are outstanding. Retractable and redeemable at any time at Cdn$1.00 per share. Rank prior to capital shares and all preferred shares with respect to return of capital in the event of the liquidation, dissolution or winding-up of the company. One vote per share.

Major Shareholder - Partners Value Investments LP held 100% interest at Mar. 30, 2023.

Capital Stock Changes - In March 2022, bought deal public offering of 6,000,000 class AA preferred series 13 shares was completed at Cdn$25 per share. The company's capital shares were subdivided to reflect this transaction.

Dividends

PVS.PR.F pfd AA ser 8 cum. red. ret. Ra $1.20 pa Q
PVS.PR.G pfd AA ser 9 cum. red. ret. Ra $1.225 pa Q
PVS.PR.H pfd AA ser 10 cum. red. ret. Ra $1.175 pa Q
PVS.PR.I pfd AA ser 11 cum. red. ret. Ra $1.1875 pa Q
$0.475**i**............... Mar. 5/21
PVS.PR.J pfd AA ser 12 cum. red. ret. Ra $1.10 pa Q
Listed Apr 12/21.
$0.1507**i**............... June 7/21
PVS.PR.K pfd AA ser 13 cum. red. ret. Ra $1.1125 pa Q
Listed Mar 25/22.
$0.2073**i**............... June 7/22
pfd AA ser 6 cum. red. ret. Ra $1.125 pa Q[1]
pfd AA ser 7 cum. red. ret. Ra $1.375 pa Q[2]
$0.3022**f**............... May 20/21

[1] Redeemed March 31, 2021 at $25.25 per sh. plus accr. divds. of $0.09272.
[2] Redeemed May 20, 2021 at $25 per sh. plus accr. divds. of $0.3022.
f Final Payment **i** Initial Payment

Financial Statistics

Periods ended:	12m Dec. 31/22[A]		12m Dec. 31/21[A]
	US$000s	%Chg	US$000s
Total revenue	**1,025,224**	**+872**	**105,479**
General & admin. expense	296		2,036
Operating expense	**296**	**-85**	**2,036**
Operating income	**1,024,928**	**+891**	**103,443**
Finance costs, gross	34,621		37,590
Pre-tax income	**(2,505,881)**	**n.a.**	**2,346,155**
Net income	**(2,505,881)**	**n.a.**	**2,346,155**
Cash & equivalent	35,527		248
Accounts receivable	16,746		15,550
Investments	4,620,291		7,222,139
Total assets	**4,672,564**	**-35**	**7,237,937**
Accts. pay. & accr. liabs	197		76
Debt	886,121		831,749
Shareholders' equity	3,786,246		6,406,112
Cash from oper. activs	**64,051**	**+6**	**60,296**
Cash from fin. activs	(28,772)		(198,248)
Net cash position	**35,527**	**n.m.**	**248**
	US$		US$
Earnings per share*	(52.94)		53.57
Cash flow per share*	1.35		1.38
Net asset value per share*	77.75		150.04
	shs		shs
No. of shs. o/s*	48,696,000		42,696,000
Avg. no. of shs. o/s*	47,300,000		43,800,000
	%		%
Net profit margin	(244.42)		n.m.
Return on equity	(49.17)		44.23
Return on assets	(41.50)		38.68

* Capital

[A] Reported in accordance with IFRS

Historical Summary
(as originally stated)

Fiscal Year	Total Rev.	Net Inc. Bef. Disc.	EPS*
	US$000s	US$000s	US$
2022[A]	1,025,224	(2,505,881)	(52.94)
2021[A]	105,479	2,346,155	53.57
2020[A]	57,663	337,133	8.39
2019[A]	51,461	1,546,718	45.63
2018[A]	48,393	(338,846)	(9.91)

* Capital

[A] Reported in accordance with IFRS

P.26 Parvis Invest Inc.

Symbol - PVIS **Exchange** - TSX-VEN **CUSIP** - 702168
Head Office - Five Bentall Centre, 1008-550 Burrard St, Vancouver, BC, V6C 2B5 **Telephone** - (604) 818-8131
Website - parvisinvest.com
Email - david@parvisinvest.com
Investor Relations - David Michaud (604) 818-8131
Auditors - MNP LLP C.A., Toronto, Ont.
Lawyers - DuMoulin Black LLP, Vancouver, B.C.
Transfer Agents - TSX Trust Company, Toronto, Ont.
Employees - 6 at Feb. 28, 2023
Profile - (B.C. 2021) Provides real estate investment opportunities through the Parvis platform.

The Parvis platform is a blockchain-backed digital platform that offers capital raising services for real estate developers and real estate investment opportunities for investors, as well as offers a secondary market that allows investors to resell their tokenized real estate assets at market value.

Revenue is generated by receiving a commission of between 3.5% to 5% of the amount raised for each project on the Parvis platform paid by the real estate partner and a performance fee of 2% of the total annual return to investors paid by the investors. In addition, a 1% commission is received on the sale of tokenized real estate assets on the Parvis secondary market.

Recent Merger and Acquisition Activity

Status: completed **Revised:** Mar. 3, 2023
UPDATE: The transaction was completed. Gravitas II issued 17,258,482 post-consolidated common shares at a deemed price of 50¢ per share. The (new) Parvis Invest common shares commenced trading on the TSX Venture Exchange effective Mar. 10, 2023. PREVIOUS: Gravitas II Capital Corp. entered into a letter of intent for the Qualifying Transaction reverse takeover acquisition of private Vancouver, B.C.-based Parvis Invest Inc., which provides real estate investment opportunities through the Parvis platform, on a share-for-share basis (following a 1-for-2.49 share consolidation). Upon completion, Parvis would amalgamate with Gravitas II's wholly owned 14492528 Canada Inc. to form Parvis Fintech Inc., and Gravitas II would change its name to Parvis Invest Inc. Nov. 1, 2022 - A definitive agreement was entered into.

Predecessor Detail - Name changed from Gravitas II Capital Corp., Mar. 3, 2023, pursuant to the Qualifying Transaction reverse takeover acquisition of (old) Parvis Invest Inc. and concurrent amalgamation of (old) Parvis with wholly owned 14492528 Canada Inc. (and continued as Parvis Fintech Inc.); basis 1 new for 2.49 old shs.

Directors - Drew Green, chr., Vancouver, B.C.; David Michaud, CEO, Qué.; Jas Bagry, CFO & corp. sec., B.C.; Kia Besharat, Nassau, Bahamas; Tirta Liu, B.C.; Jeff McCann; Blair McCreadie, Ont.

Capital Stock

	Authorized (shs.)	Outstanding (shs.)[1]
Common	unlimited	26,771,735

[1] At Mar. 10, 2023

Major Shareholder - Drew Green held 17.47% interest, David Michaud held 12.68% interest and Kia Besharat held 12.28% interest at Mar. 10, 2023.

Price Range - PVIS/TSX-VEN

Year	Volume	High	Low	Close
2022	595,276	$0.31	$0.20	$0.24
2021	526,104	$0.56	$0.30	$0.31

Consolidation: 1-for-2.49 cons. in Mar. 2023
Recent Close: $0.04
Capital Stock Changes - On Mar. 3, 2023, common shares were consolidated on a 1-for-2.49 basis (effective on the TSX Venture Exchange on Mar. 10, 2023) and 17,258,482 post-consolidated common shares were issued pursuant to the Qualifying Transaction reverse takeover acquisition of (old) Parvis Invest Inc.

On July 2, 2021, an initial public offering of 13,688,000 common shares was completed at 20¢ per share.

Wholly Owned Subsidiaries

Parvis Fintech Inc., Vancouver, B.C.
- 100% int. in **Parvis GP Inc.**, Ont.

Financial Statistics

Periods ended:	12m Oct. 31/22[A1]		12m Oct. 31/21[A1]
	$000s	%Chg	$000s
General & admin expense	1,386		65
Operating expense	**1,386**	**n.m.**	**65**
Operating income	**(1,386)**	**n.a.**	**(65)**
Finance income	17		1
Pre-tax income	**(1,392)**	**n.a.**	**(72)**
Net income	**(1,392)**	**n.a.**	**(72)**
Cash & equivalent	1,201		449
Current assets	1,206		474
Fixed assets, net	3		nil
Total assets	**1,209**	**+155**	**474**
Accts. pay. & accr. liabs	232		39
Current liabilities	232		252
Equity portion of conv. debs	nil		313
Shareholders' equity	977		222
Cash from oper. activs	**(1,156)**	**n.a.**	**(51)**
Cash from fin. activs	1,910		500
Cash from invest. activs	(3)		nil
Net cash position	**1,201**	**+167**	**449**
Capital expenditures	(3)		nil
	$		$
Earnings per share*	(0.17)		n.a.
Cash flow per share*	(0.14)		n.a.
	shs		shs
No. of shs. o/s	n.a.		n.a.
Avg. no. of shs. o/s*	7,974,882		n.a.
	%		%
Net profit margin	n.a.		n.a.
Return on equity	(232.19)		n.m.
Return on assets	(165.42)		n.a.

* Common

[A] Reported in accordance with IFRS

[1] Results pertain to (old) Parvis Invest Inc.

Note: Adjusted throughout for 1-for-2.49 cons. in Mar. 2023

P.27 Pason Systems Inc.*

Symbol - PSI **Exchange** - TSX **CUSIP** - 702925
Head Office - 6130 3 St SE, Calgary, AB, T2H 1K4 **Telephone** - (403) 301-3400 **Toll-free** - (877) 255-3158 **Fax** - (403) 301-3499
Website - www.pason.com
Email - celine.boston@pason.com
Investor Relations - Celine Boston (403) 301-3400
Auditors - Deloitte LLP C.A., Calgary, Alta.
Bankers - Royal Bank of Canada, Calgary, Alta.
Lawyers - Gowling WLG (Canada) LLP, Calgary, Alta.
Transfer Agents - Computershare Trust Company of Canada Inc., Calgary, Alta.
FP500 Revenue Ranking - 546
Employees - 674 at Dec. 31, 2022
Profile - (Alta. 1996 amalg.) Provides instrumentation systems for rent or sale to land-based and offshore drilling operations in the oil and gas industry, with products providing an integrated package of complex services including data acquisition, wellsite reporting, automation, remote communications, web-based information management and data analytics. Services are provided to oil and gas companies, drilling contractors and other service companies in Canada, the U.S., Argentina, Australia, Bolivia, Brazil, Colombia, Dubai, Ecuador, Mexico, Peru and Saudi Arabia. Also provides services to solar and energy storage developers.

Has three business units: North America (Canada and the U.S.) and International (Latin America, Mexico, Offshore, the Eastern Hemisphere and the Middle East) business units, both of which offer services to oil and gas industry, as well as solar and energy storage business unit. Products and services are organized into five product categories: Drilling Data; Mud Management and Safety; Communications; Drilling Intelligence; and Analytics and Other.

Drilling Data - Offers all products and services associated with the acquisition, display, storage and delivery of drilling data. Primary product is the Electronic Drilling Recorder (EDR), a complete system of drilling data acquisition, data networking, drilling management tools and reports that acts as a base with which all other wellsite instrumentation products are linked. The data collected is transmitted via LTE, high-speed wireless ground or broadband satellite to the company's DataHub, a data management system which collects, stores and displays drilling data, reports and real-time information.

Mud Management and Safety - Products include Pit Volume Totalizer (PVT), which monitor mud tank levels and mud flow rate out of the wellbore to detect and warn rig crews of impending kicks or lost circulation resulting from gas or fluids entering or escaping the wellbore while drilling; Gas Analyzer, which measures the hydrocarbon gases in the drilling fluid exiting the wellbore and then calculates the formation depth where the gases were produced; Hazardous Gas Alarm, which monitors lower explosive limit gases and displays the readings on the EDR; and Electronic Choke system, which regulates the rate at which excess gas pressure is bled out of manifold, as well as providing a means of remotely controlling the choke valve.

Communications - Offers a number of communication services including the provision of bandwidth through the company's automatically-aiming satellite system and terrestrial networks, which in turn provides high-speed Internet and wellsite communications for email and web-enabled tools.

Drilling Intelligence - Provides customers with drilling optimization and automation. Products include AutoDriller, which electronically controls the feed rate of the drill bit to various pre-set parameters such as weight on bit, differential pressure, torque and rate of penetration, providing greater precision, control and drilling speed; and Drilling Advisory System™, which uses a combination of patented algorithms that enable real-time decision-making to increase drilling speeds, save money on downhole equipment repairs, and produce a higher quality wellbore.

Analytics and Other - Includes the solar and energy storage business, which provides a suite of products primarily for solar and storage developers to model, control and measure economics and performance of solar energy and storage projects.

International operations include the offering of instrumentation systems for rent for both land and offshore applications in Australia and several Latin American countries, and in the Middle East through a joint venture in the Kingdom of Saudi Arabia and an office in Dubai.

Recent Merger and Acquisition Activity

Status: completed **Announced:** Dec. 15, 2022
Pason Systems Inc. invested an additional $7,900,000 in private Calgary, Alta.-based Intelligent Wellhead Systems Inc. (IWS) through the acquisition of common shares and agreed to invest up to $25,000,000 in IWS preferred shares. The preferred share investment consists of an initial subscription of $10,000,000, with up to a further $15,000,000 in future tranches of preferred shares subject to the continued growth and success of IWS. IWS develops and deploys wellsite control systems used in onshore and offshore critical well intervention operations.

Predecessor Detail - Formed from Mark 8 Ventures Inc. in Alberta, Nov. 1, 1996, on reverse takeover acquisition of Pason Systems Corp. and amalgamation with 698367 Alberta Ltd.

Directors - Marcel Kessler, chr., Victoria, B.C.; Jon Faber, pres. & CEO, Calgary, Alta.; Laura L. Schwinn†, Columbia, Md.; T. Jay Collins, Houston, Tex.; Judith M. (Judi) Hess, Vancouver, B.C.; Kenneth B. (Ken) Mullen, Calgary, Alta.

Other Exec. Officers - Celine Boston, CFO; Kevin Boston, v-p, comml.; Craig Bye, v-p, R&D - cloud platforms & applications; Natalie Fenez, v-p, legal & corp. sec.; Heather Hantos, v-p, HR; Bryce McLean, v-p, opers.; Lars Olesen, v-p, product & tech.; Russell Smith, v-p, intl.; Ryan Van Beurden, v-p, rigsite R&D

† Lead director

Capital Stock

	Authorized (shs.)	Outstanding (shs.)[1]
Preferred	unlimited	nil
Common	unlimited	80,069,168

[1] At Aug. 10, 2023

Options - At Dec. 31, 2022, options were outstanding to purchase 2,665,121 common shares at a weighted average exercise price of $14.31 per share with a weighted average remaining contractual life of 2.97 years.

Normal Course Issuer Bid - The company plans to make normal course purchases of up to 8,105,263 common shares representing 10% of the public float. The bid commenced on Dec. 20, 2022, and expires on Dec. 19, 2023.

Major Shareholder - Widely held at Mar. 15, 2023.

Price Range - PSI/TSX

Year	Volume	High	Low	Close
2022	51,769,837	$17.12	$10.98	$15.94
2021	44,960,924	$11.82	$7.50	$11.54
2020	76,902,371	$14.08	$4.74	$7.88
2019	40,952,630	$21.31	$12.45	$13.11
2018	31,597,740	$24.57	$16.05	$18.29

Recent Close: $13.83

Capital Stock Changes - During 2022, 303,553 common shares were issued on exercise of options and 970,650 common shares were repurchased under a Normal Course Issuer Bid.

Dividends

PSI com Ra $0.48 pa Q est. Dec. 30, 2022[1]
Prev. Rate: $0.20 est. Sept. 30, 2020
[1] Divds. paid semiannually prior to April/13.

Long-Term Debt - At Dec. 31, 2022, the company had no long-term debt.

Wholly Owned Subsidiaries

Pason Canada Holdings Corp., Alta.
- 100% int. in **Pason US Holdings Corp.**, Del.
  - 80% int. in **Energy Toolbase Software Inc.**, Del.
  - 100% int. in **Pason Systems USA Corp.**, Golden, Colo.
  - 100% int. in **Pason US Financial Corp.**, Del.
  - 100% int. in **Petron Industries Inc.**, Houston, Tex.

Pason Systems Corp., Alta.
- 100% int. in **Pason Australia Pty Limited**, Australia.
- 100% int. in **Pason Colombia S.A.S.**, Bogota, Colombia.
- 99% int. in **Pason DGS Ecuador S.A.**, Quito, Ecuador.
- 99% int. in **Pason DGS Peru S.A.C.**, Lima, Peru.
- 99% int. in **Pason DGS S.A.**, Argentina.
- 1% int. in **Pason de Mexico S.A. de C.V.**, Mexico.
- 92% int. in **Pason Sistemas de Perfuracao Ltda.**, Brazil.
- 50% int. in **Rawabi Pason Company Limited**, Saudi Arabia.

Verdazo Analytics Inc., Calgary, Alta.

Subsidiaries

99% int. in **Pason de Mexico S.A. de C.V.**, Mexico.

Investments

1% int. in **Pason DGS Ecuador S.A.**, Quito, Ecuador.
1% int. in **Pason DGS Peru S.A.C.**, Lima, Peru.
1% int. in **Pason DGS S.A.**, Argentina.
8% int. in **Pason Sistemas de Perfuracao Ltda.**, Brazil.

Note: The preceding list includes only the major related companies in which interests are held.

Financial Statistics

Periods ended:	12m Dec. 31/22^A		12m Dec. 31/21^A
	$000s	%Chg	$000s
Operating revenue	**334,998**	**+62**	**206,686**
Research & devel. expense	37,573		32,220
General & admin expense	27,746		24,181
Stock-based compensation	15,230		11,523
Other operating expense	109,879		76,662
Operating expense	**190,428**	**+32**	**144,586**
Operating income	**144,570**	**+133**	**62,100**
Deprec., depl. & amort.	20,842		25,689
Finance costs, net	(4,937)		1,526
Investment income	(290)		(1,103)
Pre-tax income	**139,131**	**+219**	**43,663**
Income taxes	33,405		11,738
Net income	**105,726**	**+231**	**31,925**
Net inc. for equity hldrs	**107,616**	**+218**	**33,845**
Net inc. for non-cont. int.	**(1,890)**	**n.a.**	**(1,920)**
Cash & equivalent	172,434		158,283
Inventories	15,641		nil
Accounts receivable	84,819		49,453
Current assets	284,776		226,565
Long-term investments	47,839		30,046
Fixed assets, net	97,695		82,265
Intangibles, net	39,618		41,065
Total assets	**469,928**	**+24**	**379,941**
Accts. pay. & accr. liabs	53,699		31,475
Current liabilities	70,877		42,482
Long-term lease liabilities	3,712		5,537
Shareholders' equity	386,481		311,475
Non-controlling interest	(5,519)		(3,694)
Cash from oper. activs	**104,414**	**+60**	**65,061**
Cash from fin. activs	(42,065)		(27,046)
Cash from invest. activs	(92,233)		(27,077)
Net cash position	**132,057**	**-17**	**158,283**
Capital expenditures	(34,010)		(10,237)
Capital disposals	874		1,132
	$		$
Earnings per share*	1.31		0.41
Cash flow per share*	1.27		0.79
Cash divd. per share*	0.36		0.20
	shs		shs
No. of shs. o/s*	81,526,954		82,194,051
Avg. no. of shs. o/s*	81,960,589		82,792,177
	%		%
Net profit margin	31.56		15.45
Return on equity	30.84		10.94
Return on assets	24.88		8.61
No. of employees (FTEs)	674		620

* Common
[A] Reported in accordance with IFRS

Latest Results

Periods ended:	6m June 30/23^A		6m June 30/22^A
	$000s	%Chg	$000s
Operating revenue	182,920	+24	148,076
Net income	60,416	+68	35,993
Net inc. for equity hldrs	61,312	+65	37,113
Net inc. for non-cont. int.	(896)		(1,120)
	$		$
Earnings per share*	0.76		0.45

* Common
[A] Reported in accordance with IFRS

Historical Summary
(as originally stated)

Fiscal Year	Oper. Rev.	Net Inc. Bef. Disc.	EPS*
	$000s	$000s	$
2022^A	334,998	105,726	1.31
2021^A	206,686	31,925	0.41
2020^A	156,636	5,134	0.08
2019^A	295,642	53,803	0.63
2018^A	306,393	62,944	0.74

* Common
[A] Reported in accordance with IFRS

P.28 Pathfinder Ventures Inc.

Symbol - RV **Exchange** - TSX-VEN **CUSIP** - 70323P
Head Office - 9451 Glover Rd, PO Box 610, Fort Langley, BC, V1M 2R9 **Telephone** - (604) 914-2575
Website - pathfinderventures.ca
Email - ir@pathfinderventures.ca
Investor Relations - Jennifer Lee (604) 914-2575
Auditors - Smythe LLP C.A.
Lawyers - Maxis Law Corporation, Vancouver, B.C.
Transfer Agents - Computershare Trust Company of Canada Inc., Vancouver, B.C.

Profile - (B.C. 2018) Owns, operates, acquires and develops recreational vehicle (RV) parks and campgrounds in British Columbia under the Pathfinder Camp Resorts name.

The company operates three RV parks and campgrounds in Agassiz-Harrison, Fort Langley and Parksville, B.C., which offer short and long-term accommodations year-round through camping and glamping in 327 sites and 10 mobile home lots. The company also plans to expand by providing RV and self-storage space solutions.

In May 2022, the company's letter of intent to acquire British Columbia-based **Black Sheep Income Corp.** was terminated. Black Sheep owns and operates two recreational vehicle (RV) and self-storage assets in Penticton and Nanaimo, B.C., and has contracts to purchase two existing RV resorts and campgrounds located along the Kootenay River in British Columbia and the North Saskatchewan River in Alberta.

In April 2022, the company acquired a 1.892-acre property, adjacent to its existing resort in Agassiz, B.C., for $750,000.

Predecessor Detail - Name changed from Discovery One Investment Corp., Oct. 20, 2021, pursuant the reverse takeover acquisition of Pacific Frontier Investments Inc. (PFI) and concurrent amalgamation of PFI and wholly owned 1231986 B.C. Ltd.; basis 1 new for 2.3 old shs.

Directors - Joseph (Joe) Bleackley, CEO & corp. sec., Chilliwack, B.C.; Dr. Leonard W. (Len) Brownlie, West Vancouver, B.C.; Catherine A. Butler, Alta.; Michael A. (Mike) Iverson, Langley, B.C.

Other Exec. Officers - Stan Duckworth, COO; Jennifer Lee, CFO

Capital Stock

	Authorized (shs.)	Outstanding (shs.)[1]
Preferred	unlimited	nil
Common	unlimited	55,926,803

[1] At Nov. 10, 2022

Major Shareholder - Canaccord Genuity Group Inc. held 27.07% interest and Haywood Securities Inc. held 12.77% interest at Nov. 19, 2021.

Price Range - RV/TSX-VEN

Year	Volume	High	Low	Close
2022	16,459,520	$0.23	$0.05	$0.05
2021	2,282,113	$0.35	$0.13	$0.16
2019	289,565	$0.37	$0.23	$0.25
2018	223,673	$0.46	$0.25	$0.43

Consolidation: 1-for-2.3 cons. in Oct. 2021
Recent Close: $0.04

Wholly Owned Subsidiaries

Pacific Frontier Investments Inc., Vancouver, B.C.
- 100% int. in **Duckworth Management Group Ltd.**, B.C.
- 100% int. in **Pathfinder Camp Resorts Inc.**, B.C.
- 100% int. in **Pathfinder Camp Resorts (Parksville) Inc.**, B.C.

Financial Statistics

Periods ended:	12m Dec. 31/21^A1		12m Dec. 31/20^A2
	$000s	%Chg	$000s
Operating revenue	**2,462**	**n.m.**	**109**
Cost of sales	165		1
Salaries & benefits	1,011		50
General & admin expense	1,861		608
Stock-based compensation	235		nil
Operating expense	**3,272**	**+397**	**659**
Operating income	**(810)**	**n.a.**	**(550)**
Deprec., depl. & amort.	497		12
Finance costs, gross	551		97
Write-downs/write-offs	nil		(2)
Pre-tax income	**(3,465)**	**n.a.**	**(667)**
Income taxes	(95)		1
Net income	**(3,370)**	**n.a.**	**(668)**
Cash & equivalent	2,093		1,111
Inventories	13		7
Accounts receivable	27		109
Current assets	2,279		1,563
Fixed assets, net	13,378		7,869
Total assets	**15,707**	**+67**	**9,432**
Bank indebtedness	278		300
Accts. pay. & accr. liabs	355		757
Current liabilities	2,779		5,661
Long-term debt, gross	9,041		4,189
Long-term debt, net	7,610		nil
Long-term lease liabilities	226		249
Shareholders' equity	5,091		3,522
Cash from oper. activs	**(768)**	**n.a.**	**(688)**
Cash from fin. activs	7,211		8,161
Cash from invest. activs	(5,461)		(6,364)
Net cash position	**2,093**	**+88**	**1,111**
Capital expenditures	(6,107)		(841)
Capital disposals	3		nil
	$		$
Earnings per share*	(0.07)		n.a.
Cash flow per share*	(0.02)		n.a.
	shs		shs
No. of shs. o/s*	55,926,803		n.a.
Avg. no. of shs. o/s*	47,097,393		n.a.
	%		%
Net profit margin	(136.88)		(612.84)
Return on equity	(78.25)		n.m.
Return on assets	(22.55)		n.a.

* Common
[A] Reported in accordance with IFRS
[1] Results reflect the Oct. 15, 2021, Qualifying Transaction reverse takeover acquisition of Pacific Frontier Investments Inc.
[2] Results pertain to Pacific Frontier Investments Inc.

Latest Results

Periods ended:	6m June 30/22^A		6m June 30/21^A
	$000s	%Chg	$000s
Operating revenue	1,376	+67	822
Net income	(1,150)	n.a.	(996)
	$		$
Earnings per share*	(0.02)		n.a.

* Common
[A] Reported in accordance with IFRS

Note: Adjusted throughout for 1-for-2.3 cons. in Oct. 2021

P.29 Pathway Health Corp.

Symbol - PHC **Exchange** - TSX-VEN (S) **CUSIP** - 70324L
Head Office - 203A-16 Four Seasons Pl, Etobicoke, ON, M9B 6E5 **Telephone** - (905) 505-0770 **Fax** - (866) 253-4111
Website - pathwayhealth.ca
Email - aura.balboa@pathwayhealth.ca
Investor Relations - Aura Balboa (647) 989-2872
Auditors - MNP LLP C.A., Mississauga, Ont.
Transfer Agents - TSX Trust Company, Calgary, Alta.

Profile - (Alta. 2014) Operates medical clinics in Canada that offer multi-disciplinary therapies to patients that suffer from chronic pain, including pharmaceutical and medical cannabis-related therapies. Also provides virtual care across Canada.

The company's clinical services are delivered in inter-disciplinary pain clinics and through virtual care by physicians and other health care providers, who are trained in managing chronic pain through assessment and multi-modality treatments including minimally-invasive approaches, intravenous therapies, allied health methods and the prescription of medical cannabis which is supplied to the patient directly by Health Canada-approved licensed producers.

The clinic network consisted of 11 clinics in Ontario, Manitoba (2), Alberta (3) and Quebec (5) operating under the trade names The Clinic Network, Slawner Ortho, Nature Medic and Silver Centre for Pain Care.

In October 2022, the company agreed to acquire the operating assets of **IRP Health Ltd.** from **Wellbeing Digital Sciences Inc.** for $107,000 cash.

Common suspended from TSX-VEN, Aug. 1, 2023.

Recent Merger and Acquisition Activity

Status: pending **Announced:** Dec. 22, 2022
Pathway Health Corp. entered into a letter of intent to acquire HEAL Global Holdings Corp. and The Newly Institute Inc., for issuance of 139,000,000 post-consolidated common shares (following a 1-for-5 share consolidation). HEAL Global provides personalized and curated healthcare. The Newly operates inter-disciplinary mental health clinics in Calgary, Fredericton and Edmonton.

Status: pending **Announced:** Mar. 4, 2022
Pathway Health Corp. entered into a letter of intent to acquire the operating assets of private Scarborough, Ont.-based National Cannabinoid Clinics Inc. (NCC), which would add 1,500 active patients to Pathway's existing base. Terms of the transaction were not disclosed.

Predecessor Detail - Name changed from Colson Capital Corp., May 31, 2021, pursuant to the Qualifying Transaction reverse takeover acquisition of (old) Pathway Health Corp. (renamed Pathway Health Services Corp.); basis 1 new for 2.941 old shs.

Capital Stock

	Authorized (shs.)	Outstanding (shs.)[1]
Preferred	unlimited	nil
Common	unlimited	93,722,085

[1] At May 30, 2023

Major Shareholder - The Clinic Network Canada, Inc. held 55.01% interest at June 10, 2022.

Price Range - PHC/TSX-VEN (S)

Year	Volume	High	Low	Close
2022	11,184,363	$0.20	$0.03	$0.05
2021	9,567,196	$0.55	$0.18	$0.18
2018	76,446	$0.59	$0.28	$0.28

Consolidation: 1-for-2.941 cons. in June 2021
Recent Close: $0.02

Wholly Owned Subsidiaries

Pathway Health Services Corp., Canada.
- 51% int. in **10030712 Manitobal Ltd.**, Man.
- 100% int. in **Slawner Ortho Ltée**, Qué.
- 100% int. in **2563367 Ontario Ltd.**, Ont.

Pathway Healthcare Technologies Corp., Canada.
- 100% int. in **1964433 Alberta Ltd.**, Alta.

Pathway Wellness Products Corp., Canada.

Financial Statistics

Periods ended:	12m Dec. 31/21[A1]
	$000s
Operating revenue	**10,895**
Cost of sales	5,013
Salaries & benefits	6,748
General & admin expense	3,842
Stock-based compensation	548
Operating expense	**16,151**
Operating income	**(5,256)**
Deprec., depl. & amort.	882
Finance costs, gross	601
Investment income	(138)
Write-downs/write-offs	(678)
Pre-tax income	**(8,892)**
Net income	**(8,892)**
Net inc. for equity hldrs	**(8,866)**
Net inc. for non-cont. int	**(26)**
Cash & equivalent	2,603
Inventories	340
Accounts receivable	812
Current assets	4,135
Long-term investments	476
Fixed assets, net	2,914
Intangibles, net	1,196
Total assets	**8,839**
Accts. pay. & accr. liabs	1,586
Current liabilities	2,152
Long-term debt, gross	68
Long-term debt, net	68
Long-term lease liabilities	2,293
Shareholders' equity	4,326
Cash from oper. activs	**(4,643)**
Cash from fin. activs	7,120
Cash from invest. activs	126
Net cash position	**2,603**
Capital expenditures	(100)
	$
Earnings per share*	(0.16)
Cash flow per share*	(0.08)
	shs
No. of shs. o/s*	93,647,085
Avg. no. of shs. o/s*	55,010,082
	%
Net profit margin	(81.62)
Return on equity	n.m.
Return on assets	n.a.
No. of employees (FTEs)	148

* Common
[A] Reported in accordance with IFRS
[1] Results reflect the May 31, 2021, Qualifying Transaction reverse takeover acquisition of Pathway Health Corp.

Latest Results

Periods ended:	9m Sept. 30/22[A]		9m Sept. 30/21[A]
	$000s	%Chg	$000s
Operating revenue	7,726	-6	8,226
Net income	(6,238)	n.a.	(5,728)
Net inc. for equity hldrs	(6,238)	n.a.	(5,702)
Net inc. for non-cont. int	nil		(26)
	$		$
Earnings per share*	(0.07)		(0.14)

* Common
[A] Reported in accordance with IFRS
Note: Adjusted throughout for 1-for-2.941 cons. in June 2021

P.30 Payfare Inc.

Symbol - PAY **Exchange** - TSX **CUSIP** - 70437C
Head Office - 551-40 University Ave, Toronto, ON, M5J 1T1
Telephone - (416) 985-6272
Website - corp.payfare.com
Email - investor@payfare.com
Investor Relations - Cihan Tuncay (888) 850-2713
Auditors - KPMG LLP C.A., Vaughan, Ont.
Lawyers - Gowling WLG (Canada) LLP
Transfer Agents - Odyssey Trust Company, Calgary, Alta.
Employees - 78 at Dec. 31, 2022

Profile - (B.C. 2021; orig. Ont., 2012) Provides digital banking and instant payout solutions, which include a payment card and loyalty-driven cashback rewards, through the Payfare platform to on-demand platforms including DoorDash, Uber and Lyft.

The Payfare platform is cloud-based and delivers near real-time transaction processing including ATM withdrawals, fund transfers, bill payments and savings wallet to gig workers and platforms. Services are enabled through partnerships with issuing banks, who are members of major payment networks including Visa® and Mastercard®, and other third parties in the value chain such as payment processors, ATM networks and card manufacturers. Operations are conducted in Canada, the U.S. and Mexico.

Directors - Marco Margiotta, co-founder, chr. & CEO, Ont.; Keith McKenzie, co-founder, Ont.; Paul Haber†, Toronto, Ont.; Hugo Chan, Shanghai, People's Republic of China; Kelly Graziadei, Tiburon, Calif.; Dmitry Shevelenko, San Francisco, Calif.; Matt Swann, Washington, D.C.

Other Exec. Officers - Ryan Deslippe, co-founder & chief revenue officer; Brian Miller, COO; Charles Park, CFO & corp. sec.; Su Chun, chief compliance officer; Kamran Haidari, chief tech. officer; Braulio Lam, chief product officer; Mark Lau, chief legal officer; Sonya Verheyden, v-p, mktg.
† Lead director

Capital Stock

	Authorized (shs.)	Outstanding (shs.)[1]
Class A Common	unlimited	47,683,354
Class B Common	unlimited	nil

[1] At May 11, 2023

Major Shareholder - Kingsferry Capital Management Group held 11.56% interest at May 11, 2023.

Price Range - PAY/TSX

Year	Volume	High	Low	Close
2022	21,840,121	$8.95	$3.77	$4.29
2021	26,782,806	$13.79	$4.51	$8.37

Recent Close: $6.66

Capital Stock Changes - During 2022, 1,010,819 class A common shares were issued on exercise of options, warrants and restricted share units, and 1,194,800 class A common shares were repurchased under a Normal Course Issuer Bid.

Wholly Owned Subsidiaries

Payfare International Inc., Del.
Payfare México Inc., S.A. de C.V., Mexico.

Financial Statistics

Periods ended:	12m Dec. 31/22[A]		12m Dec. 31/21[oA]
	$000s	%Chg	$000s
Operating revenue	**129,928**	**+210**	**41,967**
Cost of sales	104,051		36,319
Salaries & benefits	10,736		7,625
General & admin expense	10,129		9,902
Stock-based compensation	7,418		5,516
Operating expense	**132,334**	**+123**	**59,361**
Operating income	**(2,406)**	**n.a.**	**(17,394)**
Deprec., depl. & amort.	1,380		948
Finance income	852		249
Finance costs, gross	2		3,034
Write-downs/write-offs	(781)		(381)
Pre-tax income	**(2,874)**	**n.a.**	**(21,375)**
Income taxes	63		nil
Net income	**(2,936)**	**n.a.**	**(21,375)**
Cash & equivalent	42,586		40,930
Accounts receivable	3,631		2,505
Current assets	211,822		222,977
Fixed assets, net	161		218
Intangibles, net	3,325		1,098
Total assets	**217,073**	**-3**	**224,293**
Accts. pay. & accr. liabs	19,958		11,376
Current liabilities	167,448		176,386
Long-term lease liabilities	nil		35
Shareholders' equity	49,626		47,872
Cash from oper. activs	**7,870**	**n.a.**	**(14,721)**
Cash from fin. activs	(2,738)		55,099
Cash from invest. activs	(3,551)		(1,069)
Net cash position	**42,586**	**+4**	**40,930**
Capital expenditures	(86)		(152)
	$		$
Earnings per share*	(0.06)		(0.49)
Cash flow per share*	0.17		(0.34)
	shs		shs
No. of shs. o/s*	46,424,247		46,608,228
Avg. no. of shs. o/s*	46,053,238		43,297,932
	%		%
Net profit margin	(2.26)		(50.93)
Return on equity	(6.02)		n.m.
Return on assets	(1.33)		(14.33)
Foreign sales percent	99		97
No. of employees (FTEs)	78		70

* Cl.A Common
[o] Restated
[A] Reported in accordance with IFRS

Latest Results

Periods ended:	3m Mar. 31/23[A]		3m Mar. 31/22[□A]
	$000s	%Chg	$000s
Operating revenue	42,315	+76	24,029
Net income	1,289	n.a.	(2,705)
	$		$
Earnings per share*	0.03		(0.06)

* Cl.A Common
[□] Restated
[A] Reported in accordance with IFRS

Historical Summary
(as originally stated)

Fiscal Year	Oper. Rev. $000s	Net Inc. Bef. Disc. $000s	EPS* $
2022[A]	129,928	(2,936)	(0.06)
2021[A]	43,775	(21,375)	(0.49)
2020[A1]	13,450	(26,324)	(0.87)
2019[A1]	6,310	(23,903)	(1.03)
2018[A1]	3,588	(13,406)	(0.77)

* Cl.A Common
[A] Reported in accordance with IFRS
[1] Shares and per share figures adjusted to reflect 1-for-6.2771 share consolidation effective Mar. 9, 2021.

P.31 Peak Discovery Capital Ltd.

Symbol - HE.H **Exchange** - TSX-VEN **CUSIP** - 70470A
Head Office - 612-610 Granville St, Vancouver, BC, V6C 3T3 **Telephone** - (604) 685-2239 **Fax** - (604) 677-5579
Email - mma@hanweienergy.com
Investor Relations - Xiao Qin Ma (604) 685-2239
Auditors - Mao & Ying LLP C.A., Vancouver, B.C.
Transfer Agents - Computershare Trust Company of Canada Inc., Vancouver, B.C.
Profile - (B.C. 2005) Seeking new business opportunities.
Predecessor Detail - Name changed from Hanwei Energy Services Corp., Apr. 20, 2023.
Directors - Joanne F. Q. Yan, chr., Vancouver, B.C.; Xiao Qin (Mary) Ma, CEO, CFO & corp. sec., B.C.; S. Randall (Randy) Smallbone, Burlington, Ont.

Capital Stock

	Authorized (shs.)	Outstanding (shs.)[1]
Common	unlimited	19,420,123

[1] At Aug. 7, 2023

Major Shareholder - Fulai Lang held 17.89% interest at Mar. 23, 2023.

Price Range - HE.H/TSX-VEN

Year	Volume	High	Low	Close
2022	1,101,505	$0.30	$0.03	$0.07
2021	1,536,092	$0.35	$0.15	$0.15
2020	1,181,743	$0.25	$0.05	$0.20
2019	1,013,564	$0.30	$0.05	$0.10
2018	900,709	$0.55	$0.20	$0.20

Consolidation: 1-for-10 cons. in Oct. 2022
Recent Close: $0.07
Capital Stock Changes - On Oct. 21, 2022, common shares were consolidated on a 1-for-10 basis.
There were no changes to capital stock from fiscal 2016 to fiscal 2022, inclusive.

Financial Statistics

Periods ended:	12m Mar. 31/23[A]		12m Mar. 31/22[A]
	$000s	%Chg	$000s
Salaries & benefits	nil		180
General & admin expense	180		271
Stock-based compensation	29		68
Operating expense	**209**	**-60**	**519**
Operating income	**(209)**	**n.a.**	**(519)**
Finance costs, gross	1		128
Pre-tax income	**(109)**	**n.a.**	**(684)**
Net inc. bef. disc. opers	**(109)**	**n.a.**	**(684)**
Income from disc. opers	nil		13,906
Net income	**(109)**	**n.a.**	**13,222**
Cash & equivalent	1		88
Accounts receivable	6		17
Current assets	16		113
Total assets	**16**	**-86**	**113**
Bank indebtedness	30		nil
Accts. pay. & accr. liabs	62		110
Current liabilities	92		110
Long-term debt, gross	60		60
Long-term debt, net	60		60
Shareholders' equity	(137)		(57)
Cash from oper. activs	**(117)**	**n.a.**	**(2,364)**
Cash from fin. activs	30		(561)
Cash from invest. activs	nil		2,751
Net cash position	**1**	**-99**	**88**
	$		$
Earns. per sh. bef disc opers*	(0.01)		(0.04)
Earnings per share*	(0.01)		0.68
Cash flow per share*	(0.01)		(0.12)
	shs		shs
No. of shs. o/s*	19,420,123		19,420,123
Avg. no. of shs. o/s*	19,420,123		19,420,123
	%		%
Net profit margin	n.a.		n.a.
Return on equity	n.m.		n.m.
Return on assets	(167.44)		(5.63)

* Common
[A] Reported in accordance with IFRS

Historical Summary
(as originally stated)

Fiscal Year	Oper. Rev. $000s	Net Inc. Bef. Disc. $000s	EPS* $
2023[A]	nil	(109)	(0.01)
2022[A]	nil	(684)	(0.04)
2021[A]	9,370	(4,898)	(0.30)
2020[A]	10,029	(5,022)	(0.30)
2019[A]	10,402	(17,337)	(0.90)

* Common
[A] Reported in accordance with IFRS
Note: Adjusted throughout for 1-for-10 cons. in Oct. 2022

P.32 PeakBirch Commerce Inc.

Symbol - PKB **Exchange** - CSE (S) **CUSIP** - 70470T
Head Office - 400-837 Hastings St W, Vancouver, BC, V6C 3N6 **Telephone** - (604) 306-0068 **Fax** - (604) 687-3141
Email - investors@peakbirch.com
Investor Relations - Mohsen Rahimi (725) 218-3097
Auditors - Dale Matheson Carr-Hilton LaBonte LLP C.A., Vancouver, B.C.
Transfer Agents - Computershare Trust Company of Canada Inc.
Profile - (B.C. 2015) Sells and distributes vaporizers, cannabis-related accessories, ancillary and cannabidiol (CBD) products via e-commerce portals.

The company's e-commerce sites, which include Namastevaporizers.com, Everyonedoesit.com, LiftedCBD.com, Lifted.com, LeafScience.com, Greeny.com and Hotboxherb.com, offer a range of brand-name vaporizers, CBD products and are a source of both general and specific information, reviews and media regarding the industry and related products. In addition, through Hot Box Herb, the company distributes and sells its own organic branded CBD products, named New Era Wellness, consisting of a product line of topicals, edibles and flower. The company is also focusing on expanding into the non-psychoactive mushroom market via Shroommart.com.

Plans to commence the development of a non-fungible token (NFT) marketplace to allow digital content creators to buy, sell and trade NFTs are also underway.

In February 2023, the company agreed to acquire the assets used in connection the e-commerce herbal vaporizers and accessories retail business operated by **Kiaro Brands Inc.**, indirectly through **8651159 Canada Inc.** (formerly **Sculthorp SEO Inc.**) and Kiaro Australia Pty Ltd., for a purchase price of $250,000 in cash. The acquisition includes the domain names used in connection with the business under the brand names Vaped and Vaporizer Direct (being Vaped.com and Vaped.ca). The expected closing was June 30, 2023.

Common suspended from CSE, May 8, 2023.
Predecessor Detail - Name changed from Peakbirch Logic Inc., Feb. 23, 2022; basis 1 new for 3.3 old shs.
Directors - Mohsen Rahimi, interim CEO, B.C.; Usama (Sam) Chaudhry, CFO, Vancouver, B.C.; Ricardo De Barros, Montréal, Qué.; Kiranjit (Kiran) Sidhu, Wash.

Capital Stock

	Authorized (shs.)	Outstanding (shs.)[1]
Common	unlimited	8,331,416

[1] At Apr. 14, 2023

Major Shareholder - Widely held at Nov. 12, 2021.

Price Range - PKB/CSE (S)

Year	Volume	High	Low	Close
2022	1,371,137	$0.95	$0.05	$0.05
2021	1,214,366	$5.45	$0.50	$0.66
2020	60,574	$99.00	$3.96	$5.45
2019	2,579	$220.11	$37.95	$37.95
2018	14,698	$683.10	$34.16	$49.34

Consolidation: 1-for-10 cons. in Apr. 2023; 1-for-3.3 cons. in Feb. 2022; 1-for-23 cons. in Sept. 2020
Recent Close: $0.03
Capital Stock Changes - On Apr. 14, 2023, common shares were consolidated a 1-for-10 basis.
On Feb. 24, 2022, common shares were consolidated on a 1-for-3.3 basis and 27,272,727 post-consolidated common shares were issued pursuant to the acquisition of Greenlite Crowdfunding Corp.

Wholly Owned Subsidiaries

Canndora Delivery Ltd., Vancouver, B.C.
Greenlite Crowdfunding Corp., Canada.
Greeny Collaboration Group (Canada) Inc., Vancouver, B.C.
Greeny Collaboration Group Corp., New York, N.Y.
Lifted Innovations Inc., Vancouver, B.C.
- 100% int. in **Lifted Technology Inc.**, Del.

Stul Ltd., London, Middx., United Kingdom.

Financial Statistics

Periods ended:	12m Oct. 31/21[A]		12m Oct. 31/20[A1]
	US$000s	%Chg	US$000s
Operating revenue	**2,955**	**+97**	**1,499**
Cost of sales	2,214		1,225
Salaries & benefits	162		94
General & admin expense	1,617		3,882
Stock-based compensation	251		23,435
Operating expense	**4,244**	**-85**	**28,637**
Operating income	**(1,289)**	**n.a.**	**(27,138)**
Deprec., depl. & amort	313		106
Finance costs, gross	361		89
Write-downs/write-offs	(1,814)		(10)
Pre-tax income	**(3,790)**	**n.a.**	**(28,538)**
Net income	**(3,790)**	**n.a.**	**(28,538)**
Cash & equivalent	132		232
Inventories	59		7
Current assets	615		511
Fixed assets, net	5		3
Right-of-use assets	85		n.a.
Intangibles, net	145		2,124
Total assets	**850**	**-68**	**2,637**
Accts. pay. & accr. liabs	1,226		875
Current liabilities	2,016		1,287
Long-term debt, gross	881		1,033
Long-term debt, net	128		960
Long-term lease liabilities	49		n.a.
Shareholders' equity	(1,343)		391
Cash from oper. activs	**(885)**	**n.a.**	**(1,257)**
Cash from fin. activs	534		1,166
Cash from invest. activs	138		281
Net cash position	**132**	**-43**	**232**
	US$		US$
Earnings per share*	(0.99)		(14.19)
Cash flow per share*	(0.28)		(0.63)
	shs		shs
No. of shs. o/s*	3,837,319		2,845,522
Avg. no. of shs. o/s*	3,187,666		2,006,532
	%		%
Net profit margin	(128.26)		n.m.
Return on equity	n.m.		n.m.
Return on assets	(196.67)		n.m.

* Common
[A] Reported in accordance with IFRS
[1] Results reflect the Sept. 8, 2020, reverse takeover acquisition of 98.5% of Lifted Innovations Inc.

Latest Results

Periods ended:	9m July 31/22[A]		9m July 31/21[A]
	US$000s	%Chg	US$000s
Operating revenue	868	-70	2,846
Net income	(1,125)	n.a.	(1,066)
	US$		US$
Earnings per share*	(0.20)		(0.33)

* Common
[A] Reported in accordance with IFRS

Historical Summary
(as originally stated)

Fiscal Year	Oper. Rev.	Net Inc. Bef. Disc.	EPS*
	US$000s	US$000s	US$
2021[A]	2,955	(3,790)	(0.99)
2020[A]	1,499	(28,538)	(14.19)
	$000s	$000s	$
2020[A1]	nil	(417)	(30.36)
2019[A]	nil	(1,789)	(144.21)
2018[A]	nil	(2,642)	(440.22)

* Common
[A] Reported in accordance with IFRS
[1] Results for fiscal 2020 and prior periods pertain to Kootney Zinc Corp.
Note: Adjusted throughout for 1-for-10 cons. in Apr. 2023; 1-for-3.3 cons. in Feb. 2022; 1-for-23 cons. in Sept. 2020

P.33 Pearl River Holdings Limited

Symbol - PRH **Exchange** - TSX-VEN **CUSIP** - 704914
Head Office - 502-383 Richmond St, London, ON, N6A 3C4 **Telephone** - (519) 645-0267 **Fax** - (519) 679-1446
Email - george@lunick.ca
Investor Relations - George W. Lunick (519) 679-1200
Auditors - Crowe MacKay LLP C.A., Calgary, Alta.
Bankers - Bank of Montreal
Lawyers - DLA Piper (Canada) LLP, Calgary, Alta.
Transfer Agents - TSX Trust Company, Calgary, Alta.
Profile - (Can. 1997 amalg.) Operates a plastic products manufacturing and distribution enterprise in the People's Republic of China (PRC), Australia and the United States.
Manufactures proprietary plastic products for international niche markets including general household, bottles and containers, and PVC piping and fittings.
Predecessor Detail - Formed from Bayside Capital Corporation in Canada, June 18, 1997, following reverse takeover acquisition of and amalgamation with Pearl River Holdings Limited; basis 1 new for 2 old shs.
Directors - Jorge Enrique A. Ruix, chr., Mexico City, D.F., Mexico; George W. Lunick, pres. & CEO, London, Ont.; Dr. Imanol Belausteguigoitia, Mexico City, D.F., Mexico; Casandra N. Lunick, Toronto, Ont.
Other Exec. Officers - Anne Dang, CFO

Capital Stock

	Authorized (shs.)	Outstanding (shs.)[1]
First Preferred	unlimited	nil
Second Preferred	unlimited	nil
Common	unlimited	27,309,927

[1] At Mar. 31, 2022
Major Shareholder - Nacional de Aceros y Plasticos S.A. de C.V. held 21.8% interest at Feb. 28, 2022.

Price Range - PRH/TSX-VEN

Year	Volume	High	Low	Close
2022	768,252	$0.30	$0.17	$0.19
2021	750,307	$0.36	$0.18	$0.29
2020	944,473	$0.30	$0.10	$0.25
2019	146,102	$0.33	$0.15	$0.28
2018	620,391	$0.41	$0.10	$0.16

Recent Close: $0.16

Wholly Owned Subsidiaries
Pearl River Plastics Limited, British Virgin Islands.
- 100% int. in **Guangzhou Rodman Industrial Design Services Co. Ltd.**, People's Republic of China.
- 64% int. in **Guangzhou Rodman Plastics Company Limited**, People's Republic of China.
- 72.5% int. in **Red Door China Pty Limited**, Australia.
- 72.5% int. in **Red Door Enterprises Limited**, British Virgin Islands.
- 100% int. in **Rodman Enterprises Limited**, Hong Kong, People's Republic of China.
- 72.5% int. in **Rodman International Limited**, Hong Kong, People's Republic of China.
- 100% int. in **Rodman Plastics Company Limited**, Hong Kong, People's Republic of China.

Financial Statistics

Periods ended:	12m Dec. 31/21[A]		12m Dec. 31/20[A]
	Cn¥000s	%Chg	Cn¥000s
Operating revenue	**332,315**	**+3**	**321,303**
Cost of goods sold	250,197		226,424
General & admin expense	52,117		56,208
Operating expense	**302,314**	**+7**	**282,632**
Operating income	**30,001**	**-22**	**38,671**
Deprec., depl. & amort.	12,765		12,520
Finance income	332		365
Finance costs, gross	3,011		3,065
Pre-tax income	**8,849**	**-53**	**18,751**
Income taxes	208		2,306
Net income	**8,642**	**-47**	**16,446**
Net inc. for equity hldrs	**6,741**	**-40**	**11,284**
Net inc. for non-cont. int.	**1,900**	**-63**	**5,161**
Cash & equivalent	44,082		51,995
Inventories	47,335		33,358
Accounts receivable	58,194		64,986
Current assets	159,707		157,723
Fixed assets, net	26,944		25,475
Right-of-use assets	22,762		20,312
Total assets	**209,413**	**+3**	**203,510**
Bank indebtedness	9,250		7,000
Accts. pay. & accr. liabs	41,966		46,925
Current liabilities	57,614		58,345
Long-term lease liabilities	19,017		18,290
Shareholders' equity	87,153		82,572
Non-controlling interest	37,690		37,651
Cash from oper. activs	**9,423**	**-66**	**27,579**
Cash from fin. activs	(6,157)		(5,979)
Cash from invest. activs	(8,713)		(3,201)
Net cash position	**44,082**	**-15**	**51,995**
Capital expenditures	(8,896)		(3,395)
Capital disposals	183		194
	Cn¥		Cn¥
Earnings per share*	0.25		0.41
Cash flow per share*	0.35		1.01
	shs		shs
No. of shs. o/s*	27,309,927		27,309,927
Avg. no. of shs. o/s*	27,309,927		27,309,927
	%		%
Net profit margin	2.60		5.12
Return on equity	7.94		14.39
Return on assets	5.61		10.13
Foreign sales percent	100		100

* Common
[A] Reported in accordance with IFRS

Latest Results

Periods ended:	3m Mar. 31/22[A]		3m Mar. 31/21[A]
	Cn¥000s	%Chg	Cn¥000s
Operating revenue	84,316	+8	78,430
Net income	424	-87	3,254
Net inc. for equity hldrs	351	-85	2,326
Net inc. for non-cont. int	72		928
	Cn¥		Cn¥
Earnings per share*	0.01		0.09

* Common
[A] Reported in accordance with IFRS

Historical Summary
(as originally stated)

Fiscal Year	Oper. Rev.	Net Inc. Bef. Disc.	EPS*
	Cn¥000s	Cn¥000s	Cn¥
2021[A]	332,315	8,642	0.25
2020[A]	321,303	16,446	0.41
2019[A]	280,195	9,303	0.22
2018[A]	271,634	5,013	0.12
2017[A]	259,551	(2,012)	(0.11)

* Common
[A] Reported in accordance with IFRS

P.34 Peekaboo Beans Inc.

Symbol - BEAN **Exchange** - CSE (S) **CUSIP** - 70538A
Head Office - Unit 206, 5000 Canoe Pass Way, Tsawwassen, BC, V4M 0B3 **Telephone** - (604) 279-2326 **Toll-free** - (855) 692-3267
Website - www.pkbeans.com
Email - ir@peekaboobeans.com
Investor Relations - Traci Costa (604) 279-2326
Auditors - Dale Matheson Carr-Hilton LaBonte LLP C.A., Vancouver, B.C.
Transfer Agents - Computershare Trust Company of Canada Inc., Vancouver, B.C.
Profile - (B.C. 2005; orig. Alta., 1982) Designs and retails children's apparel in Canada and the U.S. retail stores, social platforms and online.
Products include children's apparel and non-medical masks designed to promote playful lifestyle which are being distributed through various channels such as e-commerce sites, social media and pop-up boutiques within large retailers.
In June 2022, the company would up its PK Beans apparel operations which sold second-hand clothing and repurposed items such as wall art, home decor, dog toys and scrunchies.
Common suspended from CSE, May 11, 2022.

Recent Merger and Acquisition Activity
Status: pending **Announced:** Mar. 21, 2022
Peekaboo Beans Inc. entered into a letter of intent for the reverse takeover acquisition of For Heroes Only (FHO), a transmedia production studio set on transforming the way kids engage with brands.
Predecessor Detail - Name changed from North Group Finance Limited, Sept. 23, 2016, following reverse takeover acquisition of (old) Peekaboo Beans Inc.; basis 1 new for 3 old shs.
Directors - Traci Costa, pres. & CEO, Surrey, B.C.; Darrell Kopke, West Vancouver, B.C.; Tamara Mimran, Ont.
Other Exec. Officers - David (Dave) Fong, CFO

Capital Stock

	Authorized (shs.)	Outstanding (shs.)[1]
Common	unlimited	80,607,771

[1] At Mar. 10, 2022
Major Shareholder - Widely held at Mar. 10, 2022.

Price Range - BEAN/TSX-VEN (D)

Year	Volume	High	Low	Close
2022	23,229,421	$0.06	$0.02	$0.02
2021	31,408,323	$0.14	$0.03	$0.04
2020	14,880,529	$0.06	$0.02	$0.04
2019	14,741,546	$0.29	$0.02	$0.05
2018	8,954,768	$0.99	$0.10	$0.13

Capital Stock Changes - In September and October 2021, private placement of 23,087,930 units (1 common share & 1 warrant) at 5¢ per unit was completed, with warrants exercisable at 10¢ per share for three years.

Wholly Owned Subsidiaries
Peekaboo Beans (Canada) Inc., Richmond, B.C.
Peekaboo Beans, Inc., Del.
Les Petits Terribles Inc., Qué.

P.35 Pembina Pipeline Corporation*

Symbol - PPL **Exchange** - TSX **CUSIP** - 706327
Head Office - 4000-585 8 Ave SW, Calgary, AB, T2P 1G1 **Telephone** - (403) 231-7500 **Toll-free** - (888) 428-3222 **Fax** - (403) 237-0254
Website - www.pembina.com
Email - investor-relations@pembina.com
Investor Relations - Investor Relations (855) 880-7404
Auditors - KPMG LLP C.A., Calgary, Alta.
Lawyers - Blake, Cassels & Graydon LLP, Calgary, Alta.
Transfer Agents - Computershare Trust Company of Canada Inc., Calgary, Alta.
FP500 Revenue Ranking - 52
Employees - 2,669 at Dec. 31, 2022
Profile - (Alta. 2007 amalg.) Owns and operates an integrated network of hydrocarbon liquids and natural gas pipelines, gas gathering and processing facilities, oil and NGL infrastructure and logistics business and export terminals in North America.
Operations are carried out through three divisions: Pipelines; Facilities; and Marketing & New Ventures.

Pipelines
This division provides pipeline transportation, terminalling, storage and rail services in Canada and the United States for crude oil, condensate, NGL and natural gas. Assets consist of conventional, oil sands and heavy oil, and transmission assets.
The conventional assets include pipelines and terminalling hubs which gather and transport crude oil, condensate and NGL in Alberta and British Columbia. Network consists of the 4,000-km Peace Pipeline system, which transports ethane mix, propane mix, crude oil and condensate from northwestern Alberta to Edmonton, Alta., and to Fort Saskatchewan, Alta.; the 700-km Northern Pipeline system, which transports NGL from Belloy to Fort Saskatchewan, Alta.; the 1,100-km Drayton Valley Pipeline system, which transports crude oil and condensate from the area southwest of Edmonton to Edmonton, Alta.; the 395-km NEBC Pipeline system, which transports NGL, crude oil and condensate from northeastern British Columbia to Taylor, B.C.; the 400-km Western Pipeline system, which transports crude oil from Taylor to Prince George, B.C.; the 400-km Liquids Gathering Pipeline system, which transports NGL from northeastern British Columbia to Gordondale, Alta.; the 500-km Brazeau NGL Pipeline system, which transports NGL from natural gas processing plants southwest of Edmonton to Fort Saskatchewan, Alta.; Canadian Diluent Hub (CDH), which includes 500,000 bbl of above ground storage; Edmonton North Terminal, which includes 900,000 bbl of above ground storage with access to crude oil and condensate supply transported on the company's operated pipelines and products from various third-party operated pipelines; and 13 truck terminals providing pipeline and market access for crude oil and condensate production that is not pipeline connected.
The oil sands and heavy oil assets transport heavy and synthetic crude oil within Alberta and offer associated storage, terminalling and rail services. Pipelines and terminals consist of the Syncrude Pipeline system, a 450-km, 389,000-bbl-per-day pipeline which transports synthetic crude oil for **Syncrude Canada Ltd.** to delivery points near Edmonton Alta.; the Horizon Pipeline system, a 525-km, 335,000-bbl-per-day pipeline which transports synthetic crude oil for **Canadian Natural Resources Limited**'s Horizon Oil Sands operation to delivery points near Edmonton Alta.; the Cheecham Lateral system,

a 50-km, 230,000-bbl-per-day pipeline which transports synthetic crude oil from the Syncrude and Horizon Pipelines to a terminalling facility near Cheecham, Alta.; the Nipisi Pipeline system, a 375-km, 100,000-bbl-per-day pipeline which was temporarily taken out of service in the fourth quarter of 2021, and expected to be reactivated in 2023 to transport crude oil from the Clearwater formation to Edmonton, Alta.; the Swan Hills Pipeline, a 425-km, 48,000-bbl-per-day pipeline which transports light sweet crude oil from the Swan Hills region of Alberta to delivery points near Edmonton, Alta.; the Edmonton South Terminal, which consists of 15 tanks leased from **Trans Mountain Corporation** totaling 5,100,000 bbl of storage capacity; the North 40 Terminal, which consists of nine tanks with a storage capacity of 2,150,000 bbl; 50% interest (**Keyera Corp.** 50%) in Base Line Terminal, which consists of 12 tanks with a storage capacity of 4,800,000 bbl; and 50% interest (**Imperial Oil Limited** 50%) in Edmonton South Rail Terminal, with a capacity of 210,000 bbl per day.

The transmission assets transport natural gas, ethane and condensate throughout Canada and the United States on pipelines linking various key market hubs. Pipelines include the Vantage Pipeline system, a 786-km, 69,000-bbl-per-day pipeline and laterals that link ethane supply from the North Dakota Bakken play to the petrochemical market in Alberta, originating from two gas plants in Tioga, N.D., extending northwest through Saskatchewan and terminating near Empress, Alta., where it is connected to the Alberta Ethane Gathering System (AEGS); the AEGS, a 1,336-km, 330,000-bbl-per-day pipeline which transports ethane within Alberta from extraction plants to petrochemical complexes located near Joffre and Fort Saskatchewan, Alta.; 50% interest (**Enbridge Inc.** 50%) in Alliance Pipeline system, a 3,849-km pipeline delivering 1.7-bcf-per-day of rich natural gas from the Western Canadian Sedimentary Basin and the Williston Basin in North Dakota to natural gas markets in Chicago, Ill., consisting of a 1,561-km mainline pipeline and 732 km of lateral pipelines for the Canadian portion and 1,556 km of infrastructure for the U.S. portion; the Cochin Pipeline system, a 2,452-km, 110,000-bbl-per-day pipeline extending from Kankakee cty., Ill., to Fort Saskatchewan, Alta., to transport light condensate;and the Jet Fuel Pipeline, a 40-km, 15,000-bbl-per-day pipeline which transports jet fuel from a refinery in Burnaby, B.C., and the Westridge Marine Terminal to the Vancouver International Airport. Operations also include 75% interest in Grand Valley wind farm in Ontario.

Facilities

This division includes natural gas processing and NGL fractionation facilities and related infrastructure, a liquefied propane export facility and a bulk marine terminal that provide natural gas, condensate and NGL services.

Gas services assets include the Younger NGL extraction facility, a 640-mmcf-per-day extraction and 10,000-net-bbl-per-day fractionation facility in British Columbia that supplies NGL products to local markets, as well as NGL mix supply transported on the company's pipeline systems to the Fort Saskatchewan, Alta., area for fractionation and sale, and condensate to the company's CDH; the Empress NGL extraction facility in Empress, Alta., which has 1.2 bcf per day of extraction capacity and 67,000 net bbl per day of ethane-plus fractionation; the 1,100,000-bbl Burstall ethane storage facility near Burstall, Sask.; and 60% interest (**KKR & Co. Inc.** 40%) in **Pembina Gas Infrastructure Inc.** (PGI), a gas processing entity in western Canada serving customers from central Alberta to northeastern British Columbia. PGI owns the Saturn, Sunrise and Tower sweet gas processing facilities near Dawson Creek, B.C., totaling 1.1 bcf per day of processing capacity, and including 800 km of gas gathering lines and three liquids hubs; the Cutbank Complex located near Grande Prairie, Alta., which has 805 mmcf per day of sweet gas processing capacity including 205 mmcf per day of sweet deep cut extraction capacity, and consists of four shallow cut sweet gas processing plants (Cutbank, 89% interest in Musreau I, Musreau II/III and 50% interest in Kakwa 1-35) and a deep cut sweet gas processing plant (Musreau Deep Cut), 450 km of gathering pipelines, nine field compression stations and centralized condensate stabilization; the Hythe and Steeprock sweet and sour gas processing facilities located northwest of Grande Prairie, Alta., with 641 mmcf per day of processing capacity and 480 km of associated gathering lines; the 435-mmcf-per-day Saturn Complex located near Hinton, Alta., which includes the Saturn I and Saturn II deep cut processing plants and 25 km of gathering pipelines; 98% interest in the 390-mmcf-per-day Patterson Creek sweet gas processing facility located southeast of Grande Prairie, Alta., with shallow cut NGL recovery and 482 km of gathering pipelines; 97% interest in the 375-mmcf-per-day Kaybob South 3 sour gas processing facility located south of Fox Creek, Alta., with shallow cut NGL recovery and 751 km of gathering pipelines; the Duvernay Complex located near Fox Creek, Alta., which includes three shallow cut sweet gas processing facilities (92% interest each in Duvernay I, Duvernay II and Duvernay III), the Duvernay sour gas treating facilities and Duvernay field hub, totaling 330 mmcf per day of shallow cut sweet gas processing capacity, 330 mmcf per day of inlet gas handling capability, 60,000 bbl per day of raw inlet condensate stabilization, 15,000 bbl per day of water handling, 150 mmcf per day of sour gas sweetening capacity, 300 mmcf per day of amine regeneration capability and up to 1 tonne of sulphur per day of acid incineration, as well as 12 km of sales gas pipeline and 35 km of gas gathering and fuel gas pipelines; 78% interest in the 300-mmcf-per-day Resthaven raw-to-deep cut sweet gas processing facility located near Grande Cache, Alta., including 30 km of gathering pipelines; the Kakwa River facility located near Grande Prairie, Alta., which has 200 mmcf per day of raw-to-deep cut sour gas processing capacity and 50 mmcf per day of shallow cut sweet gas capacity; 90% interest in the 220-mmcf-per-day Kaybob South Amalgamated sour gas processing facility located southwest of Fox Creek, Alta., with shallow cut NGL recovery and 239 km of gathering pipelines; the 200-mmcf-per-day Wapiti sour gas processing facility located southwest of Grande Prairie, Alta., with shallow cut NGL recovery and 420 km of gathering pipelines; the 60-mmcf-per-day Smoke Lake gas processing facility located near Fox Creek, Alta.; and the Saskatchewan Ethane Extraction Plant located near Viewfield, Sask., which has 54 mmcf per day of deep cut sweet gas processing capacity, up to 4,500 bbl per day of ethane, propane and butane fractionation capabilities and a 104-km ethane delivery pipeline.

NGL services assets include the Redwater Complex in Redwater, Alta., which includes two 73,000-bbl-per-day ethane-plus fractionation facilities, a 55,000-bbl-per-day propane-plus fractionator and 12,100,000 bbl of cavern storage as well as truck and rail terminals; the East NGL System, which includes 20,000 bbl per day of fractionation capacity and 1,200,000 bbl of cavern storage in Sarnia, Ont., storage and terminalling assets at Kerrobert, Sask., and Superior, Wisc., and 6,000,000 bbl of hydrocarbon storage, truck and rail loading facilities at Corunna, Ont.; the Prince Rupert Terminal, a propane export terminal located on Watson Island, B.C., with capacity of 20,000 bbl per day; the Vancouver Wharves, a 125-acre bulk marine import/export terminal in North Vancouver, B.C., with 1,000,000 tons of bulk storage capacity, 450,000 bbl of distillate storage capacity, four berths, facilities that can house up to 325 rail cars and connectivity to rail companies; and 50% interest in **Fort Corp.**, which has 27,500 tonnes of ethylene storage and 33,400 tonnes of ethane-plus NGL mix storage near Fort Saskatchewan, Alta.

Marketing & New Ventures

This division consists of marketing activities, including the operations of Aux Sable which consist of **Aux Sable Liquids Products Inc.**, **Aux Sable Liquid Products LP** and **Aux Sable Midstream LLC** (Aux Sable U.S.) and **Aux Sable Canada LP** and **Aux Sable Canada Ltd.** (Aux Sable Canada); and new ventures, which includes the development of new large-scale or value chain extending projects, including those that provide enhanced access to global markets and support a transition to a lower-carbon economy.

Marketing activities include buying and selling products (natural gas, ethane, propane, butane, condensate, crude oil and electricity), commodity arbitrage and optimizing storage opportunities. The marketing business enters into contracts for capacity on both the company's and third-party infrastructure, handles proprietary and customer volumes and aggregates production for onward sale.

Aux Sable U.S. (42.7% interest, Enbridge 42.7%, **The Williams Companies, Inc.** 14.6%) owns the 2.1-bcf-per-day Channahon facility in Channahon, Ill., which processes all the natural gas delivered via the Alliance Pipeline; the 80-mmcf-per-day Palermo conditioning plant in Palermo, N.D., which receives gas from gathering systems servicing nearby Bakken shale oil and gas production areas and removes the heavier hydrocarbon compounds while leaving majority of the NGL in the rich gas; and the 120-mmcf-per-day Prairie Rose Pipeline, which connects the Palermo conditioning plant to the Alliance Pipeline.

Aux Sable Canada (50% interest, Enbridge 50%) owns the 20-mmcf-per-day Heartland offgas extraction plant in Fort Saskatchewan, Alta., and the 350-mmcf-per-day Septimus Pipeline, which transports sweet, liquids rich gas from the Septimus and Wilder gas plants in northeastern British Columbia to the Alliance Pipeline for downstream processing at the Channahon facility.

New ventures projects consist of 49.9% interest (Haisla Nation 50.1%) in the Cedar liquefied natural gas (LNG) project, a proposed floating LNG facility with a liquefaction capacity of 3,000,000 tonnes of LNG per annum in Kitimat, B.C.; Alberta Carbon Grid, a carbon transportation and sequestration system with the capacity to transport and store more than 20,000,000 tonnes of CO_2 annually through several hubs across Alberta, to be jointly developed with **TC Energy Corporation**; and a partnership with various First Nations to pursue ownership of the Trans Mountain Pipeline.

Throughput

Year ended Dec. 31	2022	2021
Pipelines (BOE/d)		
Conventional	959,000	908,000
Oil Sands	976,000	1,036,000
Transmission	589,000	642,000
Facilities		
Gas Services (mcf/d)	3,918,000	4,014,000
NGL Services (BOE/d)	206,000	201,000
Mktg. & New Ventures		
(BOE/d)	190,000	190,000

On Mar. 31, 2022, **Ruby Pipeline, LLC**, a wholly owned subsidiary of **Ruby Pipeline Holding Company, LLC**, filed for bankruptcy protection as it lacked the sufficient liquidity to satisfy its obligations pertaining to US$475,000,000 principal amount of unsecured notes due Apr. 1, 2022. Through Ruby Pipeline, LLC and Ruby Pipeline Holding Company, LLC, the company and **Kinder Morgan Inc.** each held a 50% interest in the Ruby Pipeline system, a 1,094-km, 1.5-bcf-per-day natural gas transmission system delivering natural gas production from the Rockies Basin to western U.S. On Nov. 18, 2022, the company entered into a settlement agreement with Ruby Pipeline, LLC which released the company from any causes of action arising in connection with the bankruptcy in exchange for a US$102,000,000 payment by the company to Ruby Pipeline, LLC. On Jan. 13, 2023, pursuant to Ruby Pipeline, LLC's bankruptcy proceedings, the sale of Ruby Pipeline, LLC's reorganized equity was completed. As a result, the company ceased to have any ownership interest in the Ruby Pipeline system.

In October 2022, the company sold its minority interest in certain assets that were part of the Empress NGL extraction facility in Empress, Alta., including Empress I plant, Empress I plant expansion and Empress VI plant, to **Plains Midstream Canada ULC** in exchange for a processing agreement that provides the company the right to first priority for gas processing at all Plains-operated assets at Empress.

During the third quarter of 2022, the company and **Petrochemical Industries Company K.S.C.** of Kuwait, through their 50/50 joint venture entity **Canada Kuwait Petrochemical Corporation**, decided to cancel the proposed 550,000-tonne-per-annum integrated propane dehydrogenation plant and polypropylene upgrading facility that was to be located adjacent to the company's Redwater fractionation complex in Alberta. The project had been in a state of indefinite suspension since December 2020.

On Aug. 15, 2022, the company and private equity firm **KKR & Co. Inc.** completed a joint venture transaction to combine their respective western Canadian natural gas processing assets into a new joint venture entity, **Pembina Gas Infrastructure Inc.** (PGI), owned 60% by the company and 40% by KKR's global infrastructure funds. The transaction included the company's field-based natural gas processing assets (Cutbank, Saturn and Duvernay Complexes, Resthaven Facility and Saskatchewan Ethane Extraction Plant), the Veresen Midstream business (owned 55% by funds managed by KKR and 45% by the company), and the business carried on by **Energy Transfer Canada ULC** (ETC) (owned 49% by funds managed by KKR). PGI then acquired **Energy Transfer L.P.**'s remaining 51% interest in ETC. The total value of these transactions totaled $11.4 billion, excluding the value of assets under construction. The company's Empress, Younger and Burstall assets were excluded from the transaction.

Recent Merger and Acquisition Activity

Status: completed **Revised:** Apr. 26, 2023

UPDATE: The transaction was completed. PREVIOUS: Pembina Pipeline Corporation agreed to sell Pembina Gas Infrastructure Inc.'s 50% interest in the Key Access Pipeline System (KAPS) in Alberta to private equity firm Stonepeak Partners L.P. for $662,500,000. Pembina Gas Infrastructure was 60%-owned by Pembina, with the remaining 40% owned by KKR & Co. Inc. KAPS was under construction and would collect condensate and other petroleum liquids produced with natural gas in the Montney and Duvernay regions, and would bring it to the liquids processing and storage hub and Fort Saskatchewan. The pipeline would consist of 16-inch pipeline for condensate and a 12-inch pipeline for NGL mix. The transaction was expected to be completed in the first quarter of 2023, subject to approval by the Commissioner of Competition as well as other closing conditions.

Status: completed **Revised:** Aug. 15, 2022

UPDATE: The transaction was completed. The joint venture entity was named Pembina Gas Infrastructure Inc. PREVIOUS: Energy Transfer L.P. agreed to sell its 51% interest in Energy Transfer Canada ULC to a new joint venture entity that was to be owned 60% by Pembina Pipeline Corporation and 40% by global infrastructure funds managed by private equity firm KKR & Co. Inc. for gross proceeds of Cdn$340,000,000 (US$270,000,000). Energy Transfer Canada's assets included six natural gas processing plants that have a combined operating capacity of 1,290 mcf per day and a network of 848 miles of natural gas gathering and transportation infrastructure in the Western Canadian Sedimentary Basin. The transaction was expected to close by the third quarter of 2022.

Predecessor Detail - Succeeded Pembina Pipeline Income Fund, Oct. 1, 2010, pursuant to plan of arrangement whereby Pembina Pipeline Corporation was formed to facilitate the conversion of the fund into a corporation.

Directors - Henry W. Sykes, chr., Calgary, Alta.; J. Scott Burrows, pres. & CEO, Calgary, Alta.; Anne-Marie N. Ainsworth, Houston, Tex.; Cynthia B. Carroll, Naples, Fla.; Ana Dutra, Indian River Shores, Fla.; Robert G. (Bob) Gwin, Houston, Tex.; Dr. Maureen E. Howe, Vancouver, B.C.; Gordon J. Kerr, Calgary, Alta.; David M. B. LeGresley, Toronto, Ont.; Andy J. Mah, Calgary, Alta.; Leslie A. O'Donoghue, Calgary, Alta.; Bruce D. Rubin, Pa.

Other Exec. Officers - Eva M. Bishop, sr. v-p & corp. srvcs. officer; Cameron J. (Cam) Goldade, sr. v-p & CFO; Janet C. Loduca, sr. v-p, external affairs & chief legal & sustainability officer; Chris Scherman, sr. v-p & mktg. & strategy officer; Jaret A. Sprott, sr. v-p & COO; Stuart V. (Stu) Taylor, sr. v-p & corp. devel. officer

Capital Stock

	Authorized (shs.)	Outstanding (shs.)[1]
Class A Preferred	254,850,850	
Series 1		10,000,000
Series 3		6,000,000
Series 5		10,000,000
Series 7		10,000,000
Series 9		9,000,000
Series 15		8,000,000
Series 17		6,000,000
Series 19		8,000,000
Series 21		14,971,870
Series 22		1,028,130
Series 25		10,000,000
Series 2021-A		600,000
Class B Preferred	unlimited	nil
Common	unlimited	549,198,000

[1] At July 31, 2023

Class A Preferred Series 1 - Entitled to fixed cumulative annual dividends of $1.2265 per share payable quarterly to Dec. 1, 2023, and thereafter at a rate reset every five years equal to the five-year Government of Canada bond yield plus 2.47%. Redeemable on Dec. 1, 2023, and on December 1 every five years thereafter at $25 per share plus declared and unpaid dividends. Convertible at the holder's option, on Dec. 1, 2023, and on December 1 every five years thereafter, into cumulative redeemable floating rate class A preferred series 2 shares on a share-for-share basis, subject to certain conditions. The series 2 shares will pay a quarterly dividend equal to the 90-day Canadian Treasury bill rate plus 2.47%. Non-voting.

Class A Preferred Series 3 - Entitled to fixed cumulative annual dividends of $1.1195 per share payable quarterly to Mar. 1, 2024, and thereafter at a rate reset every five years equal to the five-year Government of Canada bond yield plus 2.6%. Redeemable on Mar. 1, 2024, and on March 1 every five years thereafter at $25 per share plus declared and unpaid dividends. Convertible at the holder's option, on Mar. 1, 2024, and on March 1 every five years thereafter, into cumulative redeemable floating rate class A preferred series 4 shares on a share-for-share basis, subject to certain conditions. The series 4 shares will pay a quarterly dividend equal to the 90-day Canadian Treasury bill rate plus 2.6%. Non-voting.

Class A Preferred Series 5 - Entitled to fixed cumulative annual dividends of $1.1433 per share payable quarterly to June 1, 2024, and thereafter at a rate reset every five years equal to the five-year Government of Canada bond yield plus 3%. Redeemable on June 1, 2024, and on June 1 every five years thereafter at $25 per share plus declared and unpaid dividends. Convertible at the holder's option, on June 1, 2024, and on June 1 every five years thereafter, into cumulative redeemable floating rate class A preferred series 6 shares on a share-for-share basis, subject to certain conditions. The series 6 shares will pay a quarterly dividend equal to the 90-day Canadian Treasury bill rate plus 3%. Non-voting.

Class A Preferred Series 7 - Entitled to fixed cumulative annual dividends of $1.095 per share payable quarterly to Dec. 1, 2024, and thereafter at a rate reset every five years equal to the five-year Government of Canada bond yield plus 2.94%. Redeemable on Dec. 1, 2024, and on December 1 every five years thereafter at $25 per share plus declared and unpaid dividends. Convertible at the holder's option, on Dec. 1, 2024, and on December 1 every five years thereafter, into cumulative redeemable floating rate class A preferred series 8 shares on a share-for-share basis, subject to certain conditions. The series 8 shares will pay a quarterly dividend equal to the 90-day Canadian Treasury bill rate plus 2.94%. Non-voting.

Class A Preferred Series 9 - Entitled to fixed cumulative annual dividends of $1.0755 per share payable quarterly to Dec. 1, 2025, and thereafter at a rate reset every five years equal to the five-year Government of Canada bond yield plus 3.91%. Redeemable on Dec. 1, 2025, and on December 1 every five years thereafter at $25 per share plus declared and unpaid dividends. Convertible at the holder's option, on Dec. 1, 2025, and on December 1 every five years thereafter, into cumulative redeemable floating rate class A preferred series 10 shares on a share-for-share basis, subject to certain conditions. The series 10 shares will pay a quarterly dividend equal to the 90-day Canadian Treasury bill rate plus 3.91%. Non-voting.

Class A Preferred Series 15 - Entitled to fixed cumulative annual dividends of $1.541 per share payable quarterly to Sept. 30, 2027, and thereafter at a rate reset every five years equal to the five-year Government of Canada bond yield plus 2.92%. Redeemable on Sept. 30, 2027, and on September 30 every five years thereafter at $25 per share plus declared and unpaid dividends. Convertible at the holder's option, on Sept. 30, 2027, and on September 30 every five years thereafter, into cumulative redeemable floating rate class A preferred series 16 shares on a share-for-share basis, subject to certain conditions. The series 16 shares will pay a quarterly dividend equal to the 90-day Canadian Treasury bill rate plus 2.92%. Non-voting.

Class A Preferred Series 17 - Entitled to fixed cumulative annual dividends of $1.2053 per share payable quarterly to Mar. 31, 2024, and thereafter at a rate reset every five years equal to the five-year Government of Canada bond yield plus 3.01%. Redeemable on Mar. 31, 2024, and on March 31 every five years thereafter at $25 per share plus declared and unpaid dividends. Convertible at the holder's option, on Mar. 31, 2024, and on March 31 every five years thereafter, into cumulative redeemable floating rate class A preferred series 18 shares on a share-for-share basis, subject to certain conditions. The series 18 shares will pay a quarterly dividend equal to the 90-day Canadian Treasury bill rate plus 3.01%. Non-voting.

Class A Preferred Series 19 - Entitled to fixed cumulative annual dividends of $1.171 per share payable quarterly to June 30, 2025, and thereafter at a rate reset every five years equal to the five-year Government of Canada bond yield plus 4.27%. Redeemable on June 30, 2025, and on June 30 every five years thereafter at $25 per share plus declared and unpaid dividends. Convertible at the holder's option, on June 30, 2025, and on June 30 every five years thereafter, into cumulative redeemable floating rate class A preferred series 20 shares on a share-for-share basis, subject to certain conditions. The series 20 shares will pay a quarterly dividend equal to the 90-day Canadian Treasury bill rate plus 4.27%. Non-voting.

Class A Preferred Series 21 - Entitled to fixed cumulative annual dividends of $1.5755 per share payable quarterly to Mar. 1, 2028, and thereafter at a rate reset every five years equal to the five-year Government of Canada bond yield plus 3.26% but not less than 4.9%. Redeemable on Mar. 1, 2028, and on March 1 every five years thereafter at $25 per share plus declared and unpaid dividends. Convertible at the holder's option, on Mar. 1, 2028, and on March 1 every five years thereafter, into cumulative redeemable floating rate class A preferred series 22 shares on a share-for-share basis, subject to certain conditions. Non-voting.

Class A Preferred Series 22 - Entitled to cumulative dividends payable quarterly equal to the 90-day Canadian Treasury bill rate plus 3.26%. Redeemable on Mar. 1, 2028, and on March 1 every five years thereafter at $25 per share plus declared and unpaid dividends or at $25.50 per share on any other non-conversion date. Convertible at the holder's option, on Mar. 1, 2028, and on March 1 every five years thereafter, into cumulative redeemable fixed rate class A preferred series 21 shares on a share-for-share basis, subject to certain conditions. Non-voting.

Class A Preferred Series 25 - Entitled to fixed cumulative annual dividends of $1.6203 per share payable quarterly to Feb. 15, 2028, and thereafter at a rate reset every five years equal to the five-year Government of Canada bond yield plus 3.51% but not less than 5.2%. Redeemable on Feb. 15, 2028, and on February 15 every five years thereafter at $25 per share plus declared and unpaid dividends. Convertible at the holder's option on Feb. 15, 2028, and on February 15 every five years thereafter, into cumulative redeemable floating rate class A preferred series 26 shares on a share-for-share basis, subject to certain conditions. The series 26 shares will pay a quarterly dividend equal to the 90-day Canadian Treasury bill rate plus 3.51%. Non-voting.

Class A Preferred Series 2021-A - Held in trust as treasury shares to satisfy the company's obligations under the indenture governing the subordinated hybrid notes, series 1. Not entitled to dividends prior to delivery to the holders of the hybrid notes following the occurrence of certain bankruptcy or insolvency events. Redeemable together with the redemption, cancellation or repayment of the hybrid notes.

Common - One vote per share.

Options - At Dec. 31, 2022, options were outstanding to purchase 12,085,000 common shares at prices ranging from $26.83 to $49.78 per share with a weighted average remaining life of up to five years.

Class A Preferred Series 23 (old) - Were entitled to fixed cumulative annual dividends of $1.3125 per share payable quarterly to Nov. 15, 2022. Redeemed on Nov. 15, 2022, at $25 per share.

Normal Course Issuer Bid - The company plans to make normal course purchases of up to 27,516,835 common shares representing 5% of the total outstanding. The bid commenced on Mar. 10, 2023, and expires on Mar. 9, 2024.

Major Shareholder - Widely held at Mar. 17, 2023.

Price Range - PPL/TSX

Year	Volume	High	Low	Close
2022	548,802,923	$53.58	$37.51	$45.96
2021	565,455,719	$43.00	$30.48	$38.37
2020	640,260,210	$53.79	$15.27	$30.10
2019	331,693,673	$50.65	$39.74	$48.13
2018	314,519,697	$47.84	$37.60	$40.51

Recent Close: $41.33

Capital Stock Changes - On Mar. 1, 2023, 1,028,130 class A preferred shares, series 22 were issued on conversion of a like number of class A preferred shares, series 21.

On Nov. 15, 2022, all 12,000,000 class A preferred shares, series 23 were redeemed at $25 per share. Also during 2022, 7,000,000 common shares were issued as share-based compensation and 7,154,000 common shares were repurchased under a Normal Course Issuer Bid.

Dividends

PPL com Ra $2.67 pa Q est. June 30, 2023[1]
Prev. Rate: $2.61 est. Oct. 14, 2022
Prev. Rate: $2.52 est. Feb. 14, 2020
PPL.PR.A pfd A ser 1 cum. red. exch. Adj. Ra $1.2265 pa Q est. Mar. 1, 2019
PPL.PR.C pfd A ser 3 cum. red. exch. Adj. Ra $1.1195 pa Q est. June 3, 2019
PPL.PR.E pfd A ser 5 cum. red. exch. Adj. Ra $1.14325 pa Q est. Sept. 3, 2019
PPL.PR.G pfd A ser 7 cum. red. exch. Adj. Ra $1.095 pa Q est. Mar. 2, 2020
PPL.PR.I pfd A ser 9 cum. red. exch. Adj. Ra $1.0755 pa Q est. Mar. 1, 2021
PPL.PR.O pfd A ser 15 cum. red. exch. Adj. Ra $1.541 pa Q est. Jan. 3, 2023
PPL.PR.Q pfd A ser 17 cum. red. exch. Adj. Ra $1.20525 pa Q est. July 2, 2019
PPL.PR.S pfd A ser 19 cum. red. exch. Adj. Ra $1.171 pa Q est. Sept. 30, 2020
PPL.PF.A pfd A ser 21 cum. red. exch. Adj. Ra $1.5755 pa Q est. June 1, 2023
PPL.PF.E pfd A ser 25 cum. red. exch. Adj. Ra $1.62025 pa Q est. May 15, 2023
PPL.PF.B pfd A ser 22 cum. red. exch. Fltg. Ra pa Q
Listed Mar 1/23.
$0.485836............ Sept. 1/23 $0.485584**i**....... June 1/23
Paid in 2023: $0.97142**i** 2022: n.a. 2021: n.a.

pfd A ser 11 cum. red. exch. Adj. Ra $1.4375 pa Q est. Mar. 1, 2016[2]
pfd A ser 13 cum. red. exch. Adj. Ra $1.4375 pa Q est. Sept. 1, 2016[3]
Delisted Jun 2/21.
$0.359375**f**........... June 1/21
pfd A ser 23 cum. red. exch. Adj. Ra $1.3125 pa Q est. Feb. 18, 2020[4]
$0.328125**f**........... Nov. 15/22

[1] Divds. paid monthly prior to Mar/23
[2] Redeemed March 1, 2021 at $25 per sh.
[3] Redeemed June 1, 2021 at $25 per sh.
[4] Redeemed Nov. 15, 2022 at $25 per sh.
f Final Payment **i** Initial Payment

Long-Term Debt - Outstanding at Dec. 31, 2022:

Credit facilities[1]	$768,000,000
Sr. medium-term notes:	
2.56% due 2023	600,000,000
2.99% due 2024	649,000,000
3.54% due 2025	449,000,000
3.71% due 2026	602,000,000
4.24% due 2027	499,000,000
4.02% due 2028	658,000,000
3.62% due 2029	653,000,000
3.31% due 2030	598,000,000
3.53% due 2031	497,000,000
4.75% due 2043	447,000,000
4.81% due 2044	597,000,000
4.74% due 2047	543,000,000
4.75% due 2048	839,000,000
4.54% due 2049	712,000,000
4.67% due 2050	397,000,000
4.49% due 2051	497,000,000
Subord. hybrid notes due 2081[2]	595,000,000
	10,600,000,000
Less: Current portion	600,000,000
	10,000,000,000

[1] Consist of borrowings under a $1.5 billion revolving credit facility due June 2027, a $1 billion sustainability linked revolving credit facility due June 2026, a US$250,000,000 non-revolving term loan due May 2025 and a $20,000,000 operating facility due May 2023. All bearing interest at prime, bankers' acceptance or LIBOR plus applicable margins.

[2] Bear fixed interest of 4.8% to Jan. 24, 2031, and thereafter at a rate reset every five years equal to the five-year Government of Canada yield plus: (i) 4.17% from, and including, Jan. 25, 2031, to, but excluding Jan. 25, 2051; and (ii) 4.92% from, and including, Jan. 25, 2051, to, but excluding Jan. 25, 2081.

Note - In June 2023, offering of $100,000,000 principal amount of 3.54% senior medium-term notes due February 2025, $300,000,000 principal amount of 5.72% senior medium-term notes due June 2026 and $100,000,000 principal amount of 4.24% senior medium-term notes due June 2027 was completed.

Wholly Owned Subsidiaries

Pembina Cochin LLC, Del.
Pembina Empress NGL Parnership, Alta.
Pembina Holding Canada L.P., Alta.
Pembina Infrastructure and Logistics LP, Alta.
Pembina Pipeline Partnership, Alta.
- 100% int. in **Pembina Midstream Limited Partnership**, Alta.
- 100% int. in **Pembina Oil Sands Pipeline L.P.**, Alta.

Subsidiaries

75% int. in **Grand Valley I Limited Partnership**, Canada.
60% int. in **Pembina Gas Infrastructure Inc.**, Calgary, Alta.
- 100% int. in **PGI Processing ULC**, Calgary, Alta.
- 100% int. in **Veresen Midstream Limited Partnership**, Canada.

Investments

50% int. in **Alliance Pipeline L.P.**, Del.
50% int. in **Alliance Pipeline Limited Partnership**, Calgary, Alta.
50% int. in **Aux Sable Canada Ltd.**, Canada.
50% int. in **Aux Sable Canada LP**, Alta.
42.7% int. in **Aux Sable Liquid Products L.P.**, Del.
42.7% int. in **Aux Sable Liquids Products Inc.**, United States.
42.7% int. in **Aux Sable Midstream LLC**, Del.

Note: The preceding list includes only the major related companies in which interests are held.

Financial Statistics

Periods ended:	12m Dec. 31/22[A]		12m Dec. 31/21[A]
	$000s	%Chg	$000s
Operating revenue	**11,611,000**	**+35**	**8,627,000**
General & admin expense	360,000		267,000
Other operating expense	8,233,000		5,450,000
Operating expense	**8,593,000**	**+50**	**5,717,000**
Operating income	**3,018,000**	**+4**	**2,910,000**
Deprec., depl. & amort.	683,000		723,000
Finance costs, gross	486,000		450,000
Investment income	361,000		281,000
Write-downs/write-offs	nil		(474,000)[1]
Pre-tax income	**3,219,000**	**+93**	**1,665,000**
Income taxes	248,000		423,000
Net income	**2,971,000**	**+139**	**1,242,000**
Cash & equivalent	94,000		43,000
Inventories	269,000		376,000
Accounts receivable	807,000		780,000
Current assets	1,362,000		1,245,000
Long-term investments	7,370,000		4,622,000
Fixed assets, net	15,518,000		18,193,000
Right-of-use assets	518,000		581,000
Intangibles, net	6,131,000		6,238,000
Total assets	**31,475,000**	**0**	**31,456,000**
Accts. pay. & accr. liabs	1,254,000		1,063,000
Current liabilities	2,046,000		2,390,000
Long-term debt, gross	10,600,000		11,239,000
Long-term debt, net	10,000,000		10,239,000
Long-term lease liabilities	596,000		635,000
Preferred share equity	2,208,000		2,517,000
Shareholders' equity	15,729,000		14,303,000
Non-controlling interest	60,000		60,000
Cash from oper. activs	**2,929,000**	**+11**	**2,650,000**
Cash from fin. activs	(2,720,000)		(1,665,000)
Cash from invest. activs	(154,000)		(1,039,000)
Net cash position	**94,000**	**+119**	**43,000**
Capital expenditures	(605,000)		(658,000)
Capital disposals	31,000		nil
Pension fund surplus	17,000		11,000
	$		$
Earnings per share*	5.14		2.00
Cash flow per share*	5.30		4.82
Cash divd. per share*	2.55		2.52
	shs		shs
No. of shs. o/s*	550,000,000		550,000,000
Avg. no. of shs. o/s*	553,000,000		550,000,000
	%		%
Net profit margin	25.59		14.40
Return on equity	22.46		9.23
Return on assets	10.87		5.02
No. of employees (FTEs)	2,669		2,349

* Common
[A] Reported in accordance with IFRS
[1] Consists of $424,000,000 related to the impairment of oil sands assets (Nipisi and Mitsue pipelines and the Edmonton South Rail Terminal) and $50,000,000 partial impairments of equity investments.

Latest Results

Periods ended:	6m June 30/23[A]		6m June 30/22[A]
	$000s	%Chg	$000s
Operating revenue	4,367,000	-29	6,133,000
Net income	732,000	-19	899,000
	$		$
Earnings per share*	1.21		1.51

* Common
[A] Reported in accordance with IFRS

Historical Summary
(as originally stated)

Fiscal Year	Oper. Rev.	Net Inc. Bef. Disc.	EPS*
	$000s	$000s	$
2022[A]	11,611,000	2,971,000	5.14
2021[A]	8,627,000	1,242,000	2.00
2020[A]	5,953,000	(316,000)	(0.86)
2019[A]	7,230,000	1,492,000	2.66
2018[A]	7,351,000	1,278,000	2.28

* Common
[A] Reported in accordance with IFRS

P.36 Penbar Capital Ltd.

Symbol - PEM.P **Exchange** - TSX-VEN **CUSIP** - 70662P
Head Office - 2250-1055 Hastings St W, Vancouver, BC, V6E 2E9 **Telephone** - (604) 688-9588
Email - queenie.kuang@barongroupintl.com
Investor Relations - Queenie Kuang (604) 688-9588
Auditors - Davidson & Company LLP C.A., Vancouver, B.C.
Lawyers - Capiche Legal LLP, Vancouver, B.C.
Transfer Agents - Olympia Trust Company, Vancouver, B.C.
Profile - (B.C. 2021) Capital Pool Company.
Directors - David A. Eaton, pres. & CEO, Vancouver, B.C.; Queenie Kuang, CFO & corp. sec., B.C.; Herrick Lau, Vancouver, B.C.; Denise Lok, Vancouver, B.C.; David Velisek, Vancouver, B.C.

Capital Stock

	Authorized (shs.)	Outstanding (shs.)[1]
Common	unlimited	4,000,000

[1] At Nov. 25, 2022

Major Shareholder - David A. Eaton held 10% interest, Queenie Kuang held 10% interest, Herrick Lau held 10% interest, Denise Lok held 10% interest and David Velisek held 10% interest at Nov. 8, 2022.

Price Range - PEM.P/TSX-VEN

Year	Volume	High	Low	Close
2022	724,500	$0.25	$0.08	$0.09

Recent Close: $0.06
Capital Stock Changes - On Jan. 27, 2022, an initial public offering of 2,000,000 common shares was completed at 10¢ per share.

P.37 Pender Growth Fund Inc.

Symbol - PTF **Exchange** - TSX-VEN **CUSIP** - 70671Q
Head Office - 1830-1066 Hastings St W, Vancouver, BC, V6E 3X2 **Telephone** - (604) 688-1511 **Toll-free** - (866) 377-4743 **Fax** - (604) 563-3199
Website - www.pendergrowthfund.com
Email - dbarr@penderfund.com
Investor Relations - David Barr (866) 377-4743
Auditors - KPMG LLP C.A., Vancouver, B.C.
Lawyers - Bennett Jones LLP, Vancouver, B.C.
Transfer Agents - TSX Trust Company, Vancouver, B.C.
Managers - PenderFund Capital Management Ltd.
Profile - (B.C. 1994) Invests in private and publicly traded companies in Canada and the U.S. primarily in the technology sector.
Top 10 holdings at Mar. 31, 2023 (as a percentage of net asset value):

Company	Percentage
Private unlisted companies	78.4%
Zillow Group, Inc.	2.7%
Peloton Interactive, Inc.	2.4%
ProntoForms Corporation	2.3%
Sangoma Technologies Corporation	2.2%
Copperleaf Technologies Inc.	1.9%
Quorum Information Technologies Inc.	1.6%
Tantalus Systems Holding Inc.	0.6%
GreenSpace Brands Inc.	0.5%
BuildDirect.com Technologies Inc.	0.1%

In August 2023, the fund acquired the remaining 2% interest in **Pender Private Investments Inc.** for $6.9418 cash per share. The total purchase price was $855,490.
Predecessor Detail - Name changed from Pender Growth Fund (VCC) Inc., Nov. 1, 2016.
Directors - J. Kelly Edmison, chr., Vancouver, B.C.; David Barr, pres. & CEO, North Vancouver, B.C.; Wendy Porter, West Vancouver, B.C.; Ian D. Power, Langley, B.C.
Oper. Subsid./Mgt. Co. Officers - Ginalee (Gina) Jones, CFO; Tony Rautava, corp. sec.

Capital Stock

	Authorized (shs.)	Outstanding (shs.)[1]
Preferred	unlimited	nil
Class C Common	unlimited	7,553,629

[1] At May 18, 2023

Normal Course Issuer Bid - The company plans to make normal course purchases of up to 663,045 class C common shares representing 10% of the public float. The bid commenced on Feb. 14, 2023, and expires on Feb. 13, 2024.
Major Shareholder - Widely held at May 18, 2023.

Price Range - PTF/TSX-VEN

Year	Volume	High	Low	Close
2022	544,922	$18.30	$5.65	$5.65
2021	798,273	$21.68	$4.00	$18.00
2020	1,211,191	$4.45	$2.50	$4.35
2019	792,955	$4.05	$2.91	$3.75
2018	348,675	$4.75	$3.01	$3.10

Recent Close: $6.50
Capital Stock Changes - During 2022, 46,600 class C common shares were repurchased under a Normal Course Issuer Bid.

Wholly Owned Subsidiaries

Pender Private Investments Inc., Vancouver, B.C.

Investments

25% int. in **Pender Technology Inflection Fund II Limited Partnership**, Canada.

Financial Statistics

Periods ended:	12m Dec. 31/22[A]		12m Dec. 31/21[A]
	$000s	%Chg	$000s
Realized invest. gain (loss)	13,557		52,500
Unrealized invest. gain (loss)	125,989		115,907
Total revenue	**(139,269)**	**n.a.**	**168,788**
General & admin. expense	(22,856)		38,968
Other operating expense	37		663
Operating expense	**(22,819)**	**n.a.**	**39,327**
Operating income	**(116,450)**	**n.a.**	**129,461**
Finance costs, gross	539		304
Pre-tax income	**(148,847)**	**n.a.**	**174,641**
Income taxes	(21,008)		22,545
Net income	**(127,839)**	**n.a.**	**152,097**
Cash & equivalent	1,553		10,009
Accounts receivable	163		198
Investments	66,300		208,351
Total assets	**76,464**	**-66**	**226,511**
Accts. pay. & accr. liabs	143		204
Shareholders' equity	70,239		198,644
Cash from oper. activs	**(7,402)**	**n.a.**	**3,881**
Cash from fin. activs	(1,052)		4,293
Net cash position	**1,553**	**-84**	**10,009**
	$		$
Earnings per share*	(16.85)		19.90
Cash flow per share*	(0.98)		0.51
Net asset value per share*	9.28		26.08
	shs		shs
No. of shs. o/s*	7,569,929		7,616,529
Avg. no. of shs. o/s*	7,588,183		7,642,298
	%		%
Net profit margin	n.m.		90.11
Return on equity	(95.09)		123.71
Return on assets	(84.08)		110.83

* Cl.C com.
[A] Reported in accordance with IFRS

Latest Results

Periods ended:	3m Mar. 31/23[A]		3m Mar. 31/22[A]
	$000s	%Chg	$000s
Total revenue	(3,646)	n.a.	(57,633)
Net income	(3,293)	n.a.	(51,822)
	$		$
Earnings per share*	(0.44)		(6.81)

* Cl.C com.
[A] Reported in accordance with IFRS

Historical Summary
(as originally stated)

Fiscal Year	Total Rev.	Net Inc. Bef. Disc.	EPS*
	$000s	$000s	$
2022[A]	(139,269)	(127,839)	(16.85)
2021[A]	168,788	152,097	19.90
2020[A]	16,795	14,475	1.84
2019[A]	3,142	2,063	0.31
2018[A]	(673)	(1,425)	(0.34)

* Cl.C com.
[A] Reported in accordance with IFRS

P.38 Pender Street Capital Corp.

Symbol - PCP.P **Exchange** - TSX-VEN **CUSIP** - 70672P
Head Office - 40440 Thunderbridge Ridge, Garibaldi Highlands, BC, V0N 1T0 **Telephone** - (778) 997-7573
Email - mark@vanrycap.com
Investor Relations - Mark Vanry (778) 997-7573
Auditors - D & H Group LLP C.A., Vancouver, B.C.
Transfer Agents - Odyssey Trust Company, Vancouver, B.C.
Profile - (B.C. 2021) Capital Pool Company.
Directors - Mark Vanry, CEO & CFO, Vancouver, B.C.; Cody Campbell, Smithers, B.C.; Steven E. (Steve) Vanry, Calgary, Alta.
Other Exec. Officers - Cory H. Kent, corp. sec.

Capital Stock

	Authorized (shs.)	Outstanding (shs.)[1]
Common	unlimited	6,000,001

[1] At May 30, 2023

Major Shareholder - Mark Vanry held 16.67% interest, Steven E. (Steve) Vanry held 15% interest, Craig Roberts held 11.67% interest and Ranjeet Sundher held 11.67% interest at Jan. 25, 2023.

Price Range - PCP.P/TSX-VEN

Year	Volume	High	Low	Close
2022	730,001	$0.19	$0.10	$0.11

Recent Close: $0.12
Capital Stock Changes - On Mar. 23, 2022, an initial public offering of 2,000,000 common shares was completed at 10¢ per share.

P.39 Pentagon I Capital Corp.

Symbol - PNTI.P **Exchange** - TSX-VEN **CUSIP** - 70962P
Head Office - 902-18 King St E, Toronto, ON, M5C 1C4 **Telephone** - (416) 962-3300
Email - am@spinnakercmi.com
Investor Relations - Ali Mahdavi (416) 962-3300
Auditors - McGovern Hurley LLP C.A., Toronto, Ont.
Transfer Agents - Marrelli Transfer Services Corp., Toronto, Ont.
Profile - (Ont. 2021) Capital Pool Company.
Directors - Ali Mahdavi, pres., CEO, CFO & corp. sec., Toronto, Ont.; Estanislao R. Auriemma, Buenos Aires, Argentina; Paul Fornazzari, Toronto, Ont.; James G. McVicar, Toronto, Ont.

Capital Stock

	Authorized (shs.)	Outstanding (shs.)[1]
Common	unlimited	5,800,000

[1] At June 29, 2023

Major Shareholder - Widely held at June 29, 2023.

Price Range - PNTI.P/TSX-VEN

Year	Volume	High	Low	Close
2022	75,000	$0.16	$0.10	$0.15

Recent Close: $0.11
Capital Stock Changes - On June 29, 2022, an initial public offering of 3,000,000 common shares was completed at 10¢ per share.

P.40 Perimeter Medical Imaging AI, Inc.

Symbol - PINK **Exchange** - TSX-VEN **CUSIP** - 71385D
Head Office - 511-555 Richmond St W, Toronto, ON, M5V 3B1 **Telephone** - (647) 360-0302 **Toll-free** - (877) 278-4614
Website - www.perimetermed.com
Email - investors@perimetermed.com
Investor Relations - Jodi Regts (888) 988-7465
Auditors - KPMG LLP C.A.
Transfer Agents - Computershare Trust Company of Canada Inc., Vancouver, B.C.
Profile - (B.C. 2020 amalg.) Commercializing Perimeter S-Series Optical Coherence Tomography (OCT) imaging system, an FDA-cleared point-of-care imaging system that allows surgeons, radiologists and pathologists to better assess microscopic tissue structures during a surgical procedure.

The Perimeter S-Series (OCT) imaging system provides cross-sectional images of tissues down to 2 mm depth, with 10-times higher image resolution than standard x-ray and ultrasound which gives physicians the ability to visualize microscopic tissue structures at the point-of-care which has the potential to result in better long-term outcomes for patients and lower costs to the healthcare system. The console of the OCT includes an intraoperative device for automated scanning of the specimen that provides a rapid subsurface map of up to a 10x10 cm surface area, a specimen-handling consumable designed to hold and maintain orientation of the specimen, and a proprietary imaging library and training set.

Also advancing the development of next-gen machine learning tools and artificial intelligence (AI) technology, called ImgAssist AI, through clinical development under its ATLAS AI project. ImgAssist AI has the potential to increase the efficiency of image review and be an additional tool when combined with Perimeter OCT to aid physicians with real-time margin visualization and assessment to improve surgical outcomes for patients and reduce the likelihood of needing additional surgeries. The company was granted by the U.S. Food and Drug Administration (FDA) an Investigational Device Exemption (IDE) in November 2021, enabling the ATLAS AI project to move into the next validation stage of clinical development by evaluating Perimeter B-Series OCT with ImgAssist AI within a pivotal study. A multi-center, randomized, two-arm clinical trial is underway to measure the effectiveness of the breakthrough-device-designated Perimeter B-Series OCT with ImgAssist AI in reducing the number of unaddressed positive margins in breast lumpectomy procedures when used in addition to standard intraoperative margin assessment. Completion of the study enrolment was expected by the end of 2023.

In October 2022, the company changed its reporting currency to U.S. dollars from Canadian dollars.

Predecessor Detail - Formed from New World Resource Corp. in British Columbia, June 29, 2020, on amalgamation with Perimeter Medical Imaging, Inc. (PMI), constituting a reverse takeover by PMI; basis 0.20833 new for 1 PMI sh. and 0.36499 new for 1 New World Resource sh.
Directors - Suzanne M. Foster, chr., N.H.; Hugh Cleland, Oakville, Ont.; Aaron Davidson, Huntsville, Ont.; Anantha Kancherla, Menlo Park, Calif.; Ian C. Mortimer, Burnaby, B.C.; Jeremy Sobotta, Dallas, Tex.; Josh Vose
Other Exec. Officers - Adrian Mendes, CEO; M. Thomas (Tom) Boon, COO; Russell Wagner, interim CFO; Steve Sapot, chief comml. officer; Andrew Berkeley, v-p, bus. devel.; Dr. Sarah Butler, v-p, clinical & medical affairs; Carl Gazdzinski, v-p, eng. & mfg.

Capital Stock

	Authorized (shs.)	Outstanding (shs.)[1]
Common	unlimited	64,467,700

[1] At May 25, 2023

Major Shareholder - Roadmap Capital, Inc. held 26.01% interest and SC Master Holdings, LLC held 22.54% interest at Sept. 20, 2022.

Price Range - PINK/TSX-VEN

Year	Volume	High	Low	Close
2022	11,146,559	$4.18	$1.10	$1.64
2021	24,106,943	$5.20	$2.00	$4.10
2020	8,087,834	$2.80	$1.46	$2.65
2019	355,402	$0.24	$0.17	$0.21
2018	3,176,358	$0.30	$0.13	$0.19

Recent Close: $1.48
Capital Stock Changes - In January 2022, private placement of 16,234,333 units (1 common share & 1 warrant) at $3.00 per unit was completed. Also during 2022, common shares were issued as follows: 1,546,989 on exercise of options, 960,716 on exercise of warrants and 434,000 as finder's fees.

Wholly Owned Subsidiaries

Perimeter Medical Imaging Corp., Del.

Financial Statistics

Periods ended:	12m Dec. 31/22[A]		12m Dec. 31/21[oA]
	US$000s	%Chg	US$000s
Operating revenue	**133**	**n.m.**	**9**
Cost of goods sold	32		5
Research & devel. expense	2,476		3,589
General & admin expense	10,282		9,206
Operating expense	**12,790**	**0**	**12,800**
Operating income	**(12,657)**	**n.a.**	**(12,791)**
Deprec., depl. & amort.	801		75
Finance income	2,353		8
Finance costs, net	178		538
Pre-tax income	**(9,906)**	**n.a.**	**(13,256)**
Net income	**(9,906)**	**n.a.**	**(13,256)**
Cash & equivalent	28,439		4,056
Inventories	43		5
Accounts receivable	72		nil
Current assets	31,495		6,101
Fixed assets, net	3,101		1,772
Intangibles, net	nil		1
Total assets	**34,596**	**+339**	**7,875**
Accts. pay. & accr. liabs.	1,753		1,462
Current liabilities	8,043		1,693
Long-term debt, gross	224		318
Long-term debt, net	10		128
Long-term lease liabilities	166		77
Shareholders' equity	26,106		5,855
Cash from oper. activs.	**(11,868)**	**n.a.**	**(10,924)**
Cash from fin. activs.	40,284		7,911
Cash from invest. activs.	(1,749)		(1,139)
Net cash position	**28,439**	**+664**	**3,723**
Capital expenditures	(1,991)		(1,671)
	US$		US$
Earnings per share*	(0.16)		(0.30)
Cash flow per share*	(0.20)		(0.25)
	shs		shs
No. of shs. o/s*	64,458,586		45,282,548
Avg. no. of shs. o/s*	60,615,594		44,109,772
	%		%
Net profit margin	n.m.		n.m.
Return on equity	(60.31)		(182.84)
Return on assets	(45.39)		(143.66)

* Common
[o] Restated
[A] Reported in accordance with IFRS

Latest Results

Periods ended:	3m Mar. 31/23[A]		3m Mar. 31/22[oA]
	US$000s	%Chg	US$000s
Operating revenue	110	n.a.	nil
Net income	(3,259)	n.a.	(5,087)
	US$		US$
Earnings per share*	(0.05)		(0.09)

* Common
[o] Restated
[A] Reported in accordance with IFRS

Historical Summary
(as originally stated)

Fiscal Year	Oper. Rev.	Net Inc. Bef. Disc.	EPS*
	US$000s	US$000s	US$
2022[A]	133	(9,906)	(0.16)
	$000s	$000s	$
2021[A]	11	(16,652)	(0.38)
2020[A1]	nil	(7,886)	(0.29)
2019[A2]	nil	(317)	(0.02)
2018[A]	nil	706	0.05

* Common
[A] Reported in accordance with IFRS
[1] Results reflect the June 29, 2020, reverse takeover of Perimeter Medical Imaging, Inc.
[2] Results for 2019 and prior periods pertain to New World Resource Corp.

P.41 Perk Labs Inc.

Symbol - PERK **Exchange** - CSE **CUSIP** - 71401N
Head Office - Two Bentall Centre, 1755-555 Burrard St, Box 240, Vancouver, BC, V7X 1M9 **Telephone** - (778) 819-1352 **Toll-free** - (855) 288-6044
Website - www.perklabs.io
Email - investors@perklabs.io
Investor Relations - Jonathan Hoyles (833) 338-0299
Auditors - Welch LLP C.A., Ottawa, Ont.
Transfer Agents - Computershare Trust Company of Canada Inc., Vancouver, B.C.
Profile - (B.C. 2014) Owns and operates the Getit and Perk Hero mobile applications which provide digital ordering, delivery and loyalty solutions.

The Getit application offers digital ordering via web and mobile for pickup, delivery, to-your-table, to-your-seat and events. Getit Local is a local marketplace for third-party sales and local delivery for small to medium-sized businesses. In addition, custom marketplace solutions are built for multi-vendor stadiums, venues, hotels and airports that digitalize their customer journey and ordering experience.

The Perk Hero application is a mobile and web-based ordering, payment and customer loyalty application that connects consumers with restaurants, specialty sellers and popular digital gift cards. The application has the ability to make quick secure payments from a mobile device, by QR Code or paying by photo, and includes features such as mobile pre-order, e-commerce dropshipping capabilities, gamified loyalty reward platform allowing users to earn virtual coins, Perk Points digital currency, Perks crypto rewards, merchant analytics, and dashboard and artificial intelligence powered receipt recognition. The all-in-one user and merchant app is integrated with Shopify, Apple Pay, Google Pay, BitPay and Alipay. The company generates revenue through commissions from merchants when users place an order or make a payment on the platform, franchising fees, and software-as-service licensing revenues.

In March 2023, the company acquired private Ottawa, Ont.-based **Getit Technologies Inc.** for issuance of 186,200,000 common shares at a deemed price of $0.025 per share. Getit owns and operates the Getit application which offers digital ordering via web and mobile for pickup, delivery, to-your-table, to-your-seat and events.

Predecessor Detail - Name changed from Glance Technologies Inc., Feb. 25, 2020.
Directors - Kirk Herrington, chr., West Vancouver, B.C.; Ryan Hardy, CEO, Ottawa, Ont.; Jonathan Hoyles, chief legal officer, Vancouver, B.C.; Benoit (Ben) Lacroix, Ottawa, Ont.; Larry E. Timlick, West Vancouver, B.C.
Other Exec. Officers - Andrew Bailes, interim CFO; Gary Zhang, chief tech. officer; Justin Strange, v-p, franchise sales & opers.

Capital Stock

	Authorized (shs.)	Outstanding (shs.)[1]
Common	unlimited	393,090,164

[1] At Mar. 2, 2023

Major Shareholder - Widely held at Feb. 28, 2022.

Price Range - PERK/CSE

Year	Volume	High	Low	Close
2022	30,082,265	$0.05	$0.01	$0.01
2021	96,332,104	$0.25	$0.05	$0.05
2020	71,416,988	$0.50	$0.04	$0.08
2019	36,303,982	$0.23	$0.03	$0.05
2018	174,289,866	$2.20	$0.11	$0.11

Recent Close: $0.01
Capital Stock Changes - In March 2023, 186,200,000 common shares were issued pursuant to the reverse takeover acquisition of Getit Technologies Inc.

In March and April 2022, private placement of 7,672,138 units (1 common share & 1 warrant) at $0.042 per unit was completed, with warrants exercisable at $0.05 per share for two years.

Wholly Owned Subsidiaries

Getit Technologies Inc., Ottawa, Ont.
Perk Hero Software Inc., Vancouver, B.C. formerly Glance Pay Inc.
- 100% int. in **Perk Hero USA, Inc.**, United States.

Perks Technologies Inc., Vancouver, B.C.

Investments

Better Plant Sciences Inc., Vancouver, B.C. (see separate coverage)
Hero Innovation Group Inc., Vancouver, B.C. (see separate coverage)

Financial Statistics

Periods ended:	12m Nov. 30/21[A]		12m Nov. 30/20[□A]
	$000s	%Chg	$000s
Operating revenue	**29**	**-55**	**64**
Cost of sales	27		68
Research & devel. expense	921		726
General & admin expense	1,726		1,846
Stock-based compensation	442		564
Operating expense	**3,117**	**-3**	**3,204**
Operating income	**(3,088)**	**n.a.**	**(3,140)**
Deprec., depl. & amort.	97		76
Finance income	5		9
Finance costs, gross	54		33
Pre-tax income	**(1,487)**	**n.a.**	**(4,491)**
Net income	**(1,487)**	**n.a.**	**(4,491)**
Cash & equivalent	2,275		1,071
Accounts receivable	30		57
Current assets	2,397		1,215
Long-term investments	652		192
Fixed assets, net	135		230
Total assets	**3,185**	**+95**	**1,637**
Accts. pay. & accr. liabs	302		347
Current liabilities	402		423
Long-term lease liabilities	57		157
Shareholders' equity	2,726		1,057
Cash from oper. activs	**(2,205)**	**n.a.**	**(2,224)**
Cash from fin. activs	2,442		460
Cash from invest. activs	267		630
Net cash position	**1,287**	**+64**	**784**
	$		$
Earnings per share*	(0.01)		(0.03)
Cash flow per share*	(0.01)		(0.02)
	shs		shs
No. of shs. o/s*	182,313,919		152,474,995
Avg. no. of shs. o/s*	173,653,486		141,770,052
	%		%
Net profit margin	n.m.		n.m.
Return on equity	(78.61)		(165.72)
Return on assets	(59.44)		(140.01)
No. of employees (FTEs)	17		16

* Common
[□] Restated
[A] Reported in accordance with IFRS

Latest Results

Periods ended:	3m Feb. 28/22[A]		3m Feb. 28/21[A]
	$000s	%Chg	$000s
Operating revenue	9	-40	15
Net income	(406)	n.a.	1,590
	$		$
Earnings per share*	(0.00)		0.01

* Common
[A] Reported in accordance with IFRS

Historical Summary
(as originally stated)

Fiscal Year	Oper. Rev.	Net Inc. Bef. Disc.	EPS*
	$000s	$000s	$
2021[A]	29	(1,487)	(0.01)
2020[A]	64	(4,491)	(0.03)
2019[A]	32	(8,079)	(0.06)
2018[A]	1,695	(13,030)	(0.10)
2017[A]	1,070	(9,756)	(0.12)

* Common
[A] Reported in accordance with IFRS

P.42 Personas Social Incorporated

Symbol - PRSN **Exchange** - TSX-VEN **CUSIP** - 71534M
Head Office - 302-155 University Ave, Toronto, ON, M5H 3B7 **Telephone** - (647) 988-7727
Website - www.personas.com
Email - mark@personas.com
Investor Relations - Mark Itwaru (647) 992-7727
Auditors - Zeifmans LLP C.A., Toronto, Ont.
Lawyers - TingleMerrett LLP, Calgary, Alta.
Transfer Agents - TSX Trust Company, Toronto, Ont.
Profile - (Alta. 2008; orig. B.C., 2004) Provides social media products and services for use by consumers and businesses, with a focus on mobile (iOS and Android) applications.

Primary product is the Peeks Social platform, a live streaming, mobile-enabled social commerce platform that provides broadcasters and content creators with a wide variety of proprietary content monetization services. The platform includes three main social media applications: Peeks Social, which allows users to view and interact with content or to livestream or broadcast themselves, send "likes", tip broadcasters, chat and interact with content providers in real-time; Personas, an enhanced ecommerce-enabled video conferencing app and web site (personas.com) which allows users to host video conferences and seminars, and to livestream them to social media sites; and WADSPro, an eGaming/eSports video streaming app.

Other services provided in the platform include Keek™, which offers users to share and connect content through both short-form and long-form videos; Get Popular, a self-promotion tool which allows broadcasters to purchase advertising units for themselves or for their content in the application's channels; OfferBox, a merchant tool which allows users to create live shopping channels; and AdShare Program, which allows content creators to select specific advertisements to promote based on their viewer demographics.

Services are monetized through the charging of platform fees on user transactions, which include tipping as well as paid broadcasting, where the broadcaster charges one-time or subscription fees for access to content. The company also derives revenue from payment processing which is earned as a percentage of fees charged by Personas conference hosts to attendees. During 2022, the average platform fee charged by the company on transactions in the Peeks Social service was approximately 31%.

Common reinstated on TSX-VEN, Feb. 14, 2023.

Predecessor Detail - Name changed from Peeks Social Ltd., July 15, 2020.

Directors - Mark Itwaru, chr., pres. & CEO, Toronto, Ont.; William (Bill) Lavin, CFO, Toronto, Ont.; Fareed M. Amin, Toronto, Ont.; W. James (Jim) Westlake, Toronto, Ont.

Capital Stock

	Authorized (shs.)	Outstanding (shs.)[1]
Preference	unlimited	nil
Common	unlimited	369,957,159

[1] At Mar. 31, 2023

Major Shareholder - Mark Itwaru held 54.5% interest at Sept. 28, 2022.

Price Range - PRSN/TSX-VEN

Year	Volume	High	Low	Close
2022	8,897,080	$0.06	$0.03	$0.03
2021	116,966,677	$0.26	$0.03	$0.04
2020	31,670,319	$0.15	$0.03	$0.03
2019	22,252,332	$0.12	$0.02	$0.02
2018	32,062,521	$0.46	$0.06	$0.10

Recent Close: $0.06

Capital Stock Changes - In June 2023, private placement of 19,166,666 units (1 common share & ½ warrant) at 6¢ per unit was completed, with warrants exercisable at 8¢ per share for two years.

In March 2022, private placement of 2,400,000 units (1 common share & ½ warrant) at 5¢ per unit was completed.

Wholly Owned Subsidiaries

Keek Inc., Ont.
Primary Petroleum Canada Corporation, Canada.
WASDPro Inc.

Financial Statistics

Periods ended:	12m Dec. 31/22[A]		12m Dec. 31/21[A]
	$000s	%Chg	$000s
Operating revenue	**4,459**	**+16**	**3,839**
Cost of sales	2,413		2,281
Salaries & benefits	310		724
General & admin expense	1,231		1,694
Operating expense	**3,954**	**-16**	**4,699**
Operating income	**505**	**n.a.**	**(860)**
Deprec., depl. & amort.	50		183
Finance income	nil		70
Finance costs, gross	53		266
Write-downs/write-offs	(277)		(3,036)
Pre-tax income	**103**	**n.a.**	**(3,897)**
Net income	**103**	**n.a.**	**(3,898)**
Cash & equivalent	32		100
Accounts receivable	123		294
Current assets	442		502
Fixed assets, net	174		62
Intangibles, net	2,522		2,799
Total assets	**3,137**	**-7**	**3,364**
Accts. pay. & accr. liabs	2,671		2,622
Current liabilities	5,770		6,315
Long-term lease liabilities	88		nil
Shareholders' equity	(4,046)		(4,269)
Cash from oper. activs	**(195)**	**n.a.**	**72**
Cash from fin. activs	127		(166)
Cash from invest. activs	nil		107
Net cash position	**32**	**-68**	**100**
Capital expenditures	nil		(76)
	$		$
Earnings per share*	0.00		(0.01)
Cash flow per share*	(0.00)		0.00
	shs		shs
No. of shs. o/s*	327,989,359		325,589,359
Avg. no. of shs. o/s*	326,728,687		325,087,989
	%		%
Net profit margin	2.31		(101.54)
Return on equity	n.m.		n.m.
Return on assets	4.80		(63.34)
Foreign sales percent	97		97

* Common
[A] Reported in accordance with IFRS

Latest Results

Periods ended:	3m Mar. 31/23[A]		3m Mar. 31/22[A]
	$000s	%Chg	$000s
Operating revenue	1,166	+14	1,020
Net income	108	n.m.	2
	$		$
Earnings per share*	0.00		0.00

* Common
[A] Reported in accordance with IFRS

Historical Summary
(as originally stated)

Fiscal Year	Oper. Rev.	Net Inc. Bef. Disc.	EPS*
	$000s	$000s	$
2022[A]	4,459	103	0.00
2021[A]	3,839	(3,898)	(0.01)
2020[A1]	3,200	(2,656)	(0.01)
2020[A]	2,880	(4,412)	(0.02)
2019[A2]	7,388	(24,294)	(0.11)

* Common
[A] Reported in accordance with IFRS
[1] 10 months ended Dec. 31, 2020.
[2] Results reflect the May 2, 2018, reverse takeover acquisition of Personas.com Corporation.

P.43 PesoRama Inc.

Symbol - PESO **Exchange** - TSX-VEN **CUSIP** - 715792
Head Office - TD North Tower, 700-77 King St W, Toronto, ON, M5K 1G8 **Telephone** - (416) 368-6200 **Fax** - (416) 368-0300
Website - pesorama.ca
Email - erica@joi.mx
Investor Relations - Erica Fattore (647) 471-6476
Auditors - MNP LLP C.A., Toronto, Ont.
Transfer Agents - TSX Trust Company, Toronto, Ont.
Profile - (Ont. 2018) Operates a chain of value retail stores in Mexico under the JOI Canadian Stores banner offering products at primarily a single price point.

All stores are corporate-owned and are located in high-traffic areas such as strip malls and shopping centres. Stores offer a broad range of consumer products and general merchandise such as household wares, kitchenware, home cleaning products, home décor products, seasonal products, stationary, toys and games, arts and crafts materials, electronics, souvenirs, novelties, jewelry, clothing, footwear, headwear, costumes, personal care products, health and beauty,cosmetics, food, beverages, snacks, confectionary, pet food and pet accessories, hardware, garden tools and other general merchandise. Products are sold in individual or multiple units at select fixed price points up to 50 pesos. At January 2023, owns and operates 21 stores in Mexico City and throughout Mexico State.

Predecessor Detail - Name changed from Skyscape Capital Inc., Feb. 7, 2022, pursuant to the Qualifying Transaction reverse takeover acquisition of (old) PesoRama Inc.

Directors - Rahim Bhaloo, exec. chr. & acting CFO, Mexico; Antonio Heredia, Mexico; Andrew Parks, Toronto, Ont.; Paul Pathak, Toronto, Ont.

Other Exec. Officers - Erica Fattore, pres. & CEO; Sebastian Avila, COO; Abdulmajeed Bawazeer, chief strategy officer

Capital Stock

	Authorized (shs.)	Outstanding (shs.)[1]
Common	unlimited	72,878,239

[1] At Dec. 22, 2022

Major Shareholder - Widely held at Feb. 24, 2022.

Price Range - PESO/TSX-VEN

Year	Volume	High	Low	Close
2022	8,375,886	$0.79	$0.09	$0.11
2019	16,000	$0.50	$0.50	$0.50
2018	31,000	$0.62	$0.50	$0.50

Recent Close: $0.28

Capital Stock Changes - In February 2022, 65,228,239 common shares were issued pursuant to the Qualifying Transaction reverse takeover acquisition of (old) PesoRama Inc., including 8,499,858 on conversion of (old) PesoRama debentures and 5,335,170 on exchange of (old) PesoRama subscription receipts issued previously at $1.00 per receipt. In addition, public offering of 4,700,000 units (1 common share & 1 warrant) at $1.00 per unit was completed, with warrants exercisable at $1.25 per share for two years. In January 2023, private placement of 5,939,333 units (1 common share & 1 warrant) at 15¢ per unit was completed, with warrants exercisable at 30¢ per share for three years.

Wholly Owned Subsidiaries

PesoRama Holdings Inc., Calgary, Alta.
- 100% int. in **Canmex Dollar Stores, S.A. de C.V.**, Mexico.
  - 100% int. in **Joi Canadian Stores, S.A. de C.V.**, Mexico.
    - 100% int. in **PesoRama Stores Services, S.A. de C.V.**, Mexico.
  - 100% int. in **PesoRama Consulting Services, S.A. de C.V.**, Mexico.

Financial Statistics

Periods ended:	12m Jan. 31/22[A1]		12m Jan. 31/21[rA]
	$000s	%Chg	$000s
Operating revenue	**9,350**	**+107**	**4,507**
Cost of sales	7,819		3,664
General & admin expense	6,185		5,583
Operating expense	**14,004**	**+51**	**9,247**
Operating income	**(4,654)**	**n.a.**	**(4,740)**
Deprec., depl. & amort.	2,619		1,468
Finance costs, net	2,023		724
Pre-tax income	**(11,073)**	**n.a.**	**(7,088)**
Net income	**(11,073)**	**n.a.**	**(7,088)**
Cash & equivalent	891		642
Inventories	2,528		4,294
Current assets	9,755		6,845
Fixed assets, net	3,972		2,937
Right-of-use assets	3,906		3,270
Intangibles, net	7		166
Total assets	**17,790**	**+33**	**13,370**
Accts. pay. & accr. liabs	5,137		3,334
Current liabilities	11,501		3,975
Long-term debt, gross	6,017		nil
Long-term debt, net	6,017		nil
Long-term lease liabilities	3,749		3,041
Shareholders' equity	(4,757)		6,355
Cash from oper. activs	**(2,236)**	**n.a.**	**(4,628)**
Cash from fin. activs	10,408		(521)
Cash from invest. activs	(2,389)		540
Net cash position	**6,226**	**+870**	**642**
Capital expenditures	(2,373)		(1,337)
	$		$
Earnings per share*	(0.23)		(0.15)
Cash flow per share*	(0.05)		(0.10)
	shs		shs
No. of shs. o/s*	49,643,211		47,139,610
Avg. no. of shs. o/s*	48,787,836		45,998,997
	%		%
Net profit margin	(118.43)		(157.27)
Return on equity	n.m.		(71.75)
Return on assets	(71.07)		(45.67)
Foreign sales percent	...		100

* Common
[r] Restated
[A] Reported in accordance with IFRS
[1] Results for fiscal 2022 and prior periods pertain to (old) PesoRama Inc.

Latest Results

Periods ended:	9m Oct. 31/22[A]		9m Oct. 31/21[A]
	$000s	%Chg	$000s
Operating revenue	9,376	+48	6,352
Net income	(12,700)	n.a.	(5,869)
	$		$
Earnings per share*	(0.18)		(0.12)

* Common
[A] Reported in accordance with IFRS

Historical Summary
(as originally stated)

Fiscal Year	Oper. Rev.	Net Inc. Bef. Disc.	EPS*
	$000s	$000s	$
2022[A]	9,350	(11,073)	(0.23)
2021[A]	4,507	(7,088)	(0.15)
2020[A]	1,701	(3,778)	(0.10)

* Common
[A] Reported in accordance with IFRS

P.44 Pet Valu Holdings Ltd.

Symbol - PET **Exchange** - TSX **CUSIP** - 71584R

Head Office - 130 Royal Crest Crt, Markham, ON, L3R 0A1 **Telephone** - (416) 319-9950

Website - investors.petvalu.com/overview/default.aspx

Email - investors@petvalu.com

Investor Relations - James Allison (289) 806-4559

Auditors - Ernst & Young LLP C.A., Toronto, Ont.

Transfer Agents - Computershare Trust Company of Canada Inc., Toronto, Ont.

FP500 Revenue Ranking - 353

Employees - 2,135 at Dec. 31, 2022

Profile - (B.C. 2016) Operates more than 740 pet stores across Canada primarily under the Pet Valu banner.

Specializes in the retail sale of pet food and pet-related supplies, as well as select services including full-service grooming salons and self-serve dog washes. Certain stores also sell live animals, including fish, birds, reptiles and other small animals, and facilitate the adoption of cats, dogs or other small animals on behalf of local animal welfare organizations. Product offering consists of more than 350 brands and more than 7,000 pet products specialized for dogs, cats, fish, birds, reptiles and small animals. Its own proprietary brand portfolio consists of more than 1,800 items available only at its stores and includes Performatrin Prime, Performatrin Ultra, Performatrin Ultra Limited, Performatrin Naturals, Lovibles, Barker's Complete, Fresh 4 Life, Bailey & Bella, Jump and Essentials Pet Expert Approved. Customers are offered with loyalty programs, Your Rewards/VIP Plus™ and Chico Privilege card, which consisted of 2,400,000 active members at Dec. 31, 2022.

At Dec. 31, 2022, the company had 744 system-wide stores across all 10 Canadian provinces, consisting of 225 corporate-owned stores and 519 franchised locations. Stores typically range in size from 2,000 to 6,000 sq. ft., and operate mainly under the Pet Valu banner. Other banners consist of Bosley's by Pet Valu, Tisol and Total Pet in British Columbia, the Paulmac's Pets banner in Ontario and the Chico banner in Quebec. The distribution centre network includes four warehouses in Delta, B.C., Calgary, Alta., Mississauga and Etobicoke, Ont., and Varennes, Que., and two forward deployment cross-dock centres in London and Ottawa, Ont.

On June 1, 2023, bought deal secondary offering of 4,690,000 common shares of the company by selling shareholders **PV Holdings S.A.R.L., Roark Capital Partners II AIV AG, L.P., RCPS Equity Cayman LP** and **Roark Capital Partners Parallel II AIV AG, L.P.** at $33.05 per share was completed. The company did not receive any proceeds from the offering. On closing, Roark's interest in the company was 47.5%.

During fiscal 2022, the company opened 45 net new stores compared with 28 new net stores during fiscal 2021. The company plans to open between 40 and 350 new locations during fiscal 2023.

In November 2022, bought deal secondary offering of 5,175,000 common shares of the company by selling shareholders **PV Holdings S.A.R.L., Roark Capital Partners II AIV AG, L.P., RCPS Equity Cayman LP** and **Roark Capital Partners Parallel II AIV AG, L.P.** at $37.40 per share was completed. The company did not receive any proceeds from the offering.

In September 2022, the company launched AutoShip, a subscription-based service which enables customers to automatically receive pet essentials on a recurring schedule.

Directors - Anthony Truesdale, chr., Ariz.; Richard Maltsbarger, pres. & CEO, N.C.; Danielle Barran, N.B.; Sarah R. Davis, Halton Hills, Ont.; Clayton Harmon, Ga.; Patrick Hillegass, Ga.; Kevin Hofmann, Ga.; Lawrence Molloy, Md.; Erin Young, Ont.

Other Exec. Officers - Linda Drysdale, CFO; Liliane Bedrossian, chief acctg. officer; Tanbir Grover, chief digital & mktg. officer; Catherine J. Johnston, chief legal officer, gen. counsel & corp. sec.; Kendalee MacKay, chief mdsg. officer; Christine A. Martin-Bevilacqua, CAO; Christine Schultz, CIO; Nico Weidel, chief supply chain officer; Gaylyn Craig, sr. v-p, corporate store operations; Adam Woodward, sr. v-p, franchise store operations

Capital Stock

	Authorized (shs.)	Outstanding (shs.)[1]
Preferred	unlimited	nil
Common	unlimited	71,029,578

[1] At May 8, 2023

Major Shareholder - Roark Capital Management, LLC held 47.5% interest at June 1, 2023.

Price Range - PET/TSX

Year	Volume	High	Low	Close
2022	16,973,349	$41.17	$27.41	$39.13
2021	8,544,616	$36.27	$24.00	$36.07

Recent Close: $25.56

Capital Stock Changes - During fiscal 2022, 892,482 common shares were issued on exercise of options.

Dividends

PET com Ra $0.40 pa Q est. Apr. 17, 2023
Listed Jun 24/21.
Prev. Rate: $0.24 est. Apr. 15, 2022
Prev. Rate: $0.04 est. Dec. 15, 2021
$0.01**i** Dec. 15/21
i Initial Payment

Wholly Owned Subsidiaries

Pet Valu Canada Holding Corporation, B.C.
- 100% int. in **Pet Holdings ULC**, B.C.
  - 100% int. in **Pet Valu Canada Inc.**, Markham, Ont.
    - 100% int. in **Pet Valu Canada Franchising Inc.**, Canada.
      - 100% int. in **Les Franchises Chico Inc.**, Qué.
        - 100% int. in **9353-0145 Quebec Inc.**, Qué.
      - 100% int. in **Pet Retail Brands North America Holdings ULC**, B.C.
        - 100% int. in **PV Management Services Inc.**, Ga.
          - 100% int. in **Pet Retail Brands US Holdings LLC**, Del.

Investments

19.9% int. in **HAFTAL LLC**, Del.

Financial Statistics

Periods ended:	52w Dec. 31/22[A]		52w Jan. 1/22[A]
	$000s	%Chg	$000s
Operating revenue	**951,697**	**+23**	**776,013**
Cost of sales	577,590		468,414
General & admin expense	175,394		144,462
Operating expense	**752,984**	**+23**	**612,876**
Operating income	**198,713**	**+22**	**163,137**
Deprec., depl. & amort.	38,073		33,714
Finance income	8,969		6,830
Finance costs, gross	29,447		53,703
Investment income	68		(8)
Write-downs/write-offs	(448)		(17)
Pre-tax income	**138,671**	**+11**	**125,085**
Income taxes	37,905		26,292
Net income	**100,766**	**+2**	**98,793**
Net inc. for equity hldrs	**100,766**	**+6**	**95,363**
Net inc. for non-cont. int	**nil**	**n.a.**	**3,430**
Cash & equivalent	63,034		50,068
Inventories	118,410		91,699
Accounts receivable	22,965		14,398
Current assets	256,498		193,218
Long-term investments	4,708		2,179
Fixed assets, net	91,774		62,067
Right-of-use assets	82,242		80,757
Intangibles, net	149,854		130,297
Total assets	**740,176**	**+24**	**599,173**
Accts. pay. & accr. liabs	103,782		86,977
Current liabilities	189,205		152,397
Long-term debt, gross	337,813		345,496
Long-term debt, net	320,063		336,621
Long-term lease liabilities	215,966		196,954
Shareholders' equity	376		(94,522)
Cash from oper. activs	**123,524**	**-11**	**138,159**
Cash from fin. activs	(92,804)		(163,342)
Cash from invest. activs	(17,325)		3,991
Net cash position	**63,034**	**+26**	**50,068**
Capital expenditures	(38,833)		(23,787)
Capital disposals	3,643		5,167
	$		$
Earnings per share*	1.43		1.36
Cash flow per share*	1.75		1.97
Cash divd. per share*	0.24		0.01
	shs		shs
No. of shs. o/s*	70,976,471		70,083,989
Avg. no. of shs. o/s*	70,450,000		69,987,000
	%		%
Net profit margin	10.59		12.73
Return on equity	n.m.		n.m.
Return on assets	18.24		24.32
No. of employees (FTEs)	2,135		1,815

* Common
[A] Reported in accordance with IFRS

Latest Results

Periods ended:	13w Apr. 1/23[A]		13w Apr. 2/22[A]
	$000s	%Chg	$000s
Operating revenue	250,292	+17	213,253
Net income	18,729	-17	22,621
	$		$
Earnings per share*	0.26		0.32

* Common
[A] Reported in accordance with IFRS

Historical Summary
(as originally stated)

Fiscal Year	Oper. Rev.	Net Inc. Bef. Disc.	EPS*
	$000s	$000s	$
2022[A]	951,697	100,766	1.43
2021[A]	776,013	98,793	1.36
2020[A1,2]	648,459	28,622	n.a.
2019[A2]	573,540	20,825	n.a.

* Common
[A] Reported in accordance with IFRS
[1] 53 weeks ended Jan. 2, 2021.
[2] Results represent carve-out financial statements as reported in prospectus date June 23, 2021.

P.45 PharmaCielo Ltd.

Symbol - PCLO **Exchange** - TSX-VEN **CUSIP** - 71716K
Head Office - 82 Richmond St E, Toronto, ON, M5C 1P1 **Telephone** - (647) 560-4640
Website - www.pharmacielo.com
Email - i.atacan@pharmacielo.com
Investor Relations - Ian D. Atacan (416) 562-3220
Auditors - BDO Canada LLP C.A., Vancouver, B.C.
Transfer Agents - Computershare Trust Company of Canada Inc., Vancouver, B.C.
Profile - (B.C. 2017) Cultivates, processes and distributes medicinal cannabis extracts and related products for the Colombian and international markets. Also offers a telemedicine platform in Colombia.

Wholly owned **PharmaCielo Colombia Holdings S.A.S.** owns and operates a cultivation and processing complex in Rionegro, Colombia, with 12 hectares of fully operational open-air greenhouses and a 3.6-hectare processing and extraction centre, which has a processing capacity of 360 tonnes per year of dried flowers. PharmaCielo Colombia's complex has licence from the Colombian Ministry of Health and Social Protection and the Colombian Ministry of Justice and Law to cultivate, produce, and distribute (domestically and internationally) both THC (tetrahydrocannabinol) and CBD (cannabidiol) medicinal cannabis flowers and extracts. Products produced are focused on oils, flowers, distillates and isolates which are distributed for the medical cannabis markets in Colombia and other international regions.

Wholly owned **Ubiquo Telemedicina S.A.S.** offers a telemedicine platform for Colombian medical practitioners and patients.

In May 2022, the company signed an investment agreement with **Soteria Holdings Limited**, whereby Soteria would apply for a number of licenses to import and wholesale the company's medical cannabis flower and extracts in the Polish market.

Predecessor Detail - Name changed from AAJ Capital 1 Corp., Jan. 15, 2019, pursuant to Qualifying Transaction reverse takeover acquisition of private Toronto, Ont.-based (old) PharmaCielo Ltd. on a share-for-share basis (post-consolidation); basis 1 new for 11.94 old shs.

Directors - Marc Lustig, chr. & CEO, Vancouver, B.C.; Ian D. Atacan, CFO, Toronto, Ont.; William B. (Bill) Petron†, Ariz.; Douglas H. (Doug) Bache, Burlington, Ont.

Other Exec. Officers - Andres F. Botero, COO
† Lead director

Capital Stock

	Authorized (shs.)	Outstanding (shs.)[1]
Preferred	unlimited	nil
Common	unlimited	156,078,139

[1] At May 29, 2023

Major Shareholder - Widely held at July 21, 2023.

Price Range - PCLO/TSX-VEN

Year	Volume	High	Low	Close
2022	20,212,018	$1.22	$0.15	$0.18
2021	49,410,404	$2.94	$0.81	$0.98
2020	61,054,174	$3.69	$0.41	$2.08
2019	49,135,195	$11.50	$2.51	$3.05
2018	15,178	$4.78	$2.39	$2.51

Consolidation: 1-for-11.94 cons. in Jan. 2019
Recent Close: $0.16
Capital Stock Changes - During 2022, common shares were issued as follows: 1,823,014 for debenture interest payment, 1,791,667 on vesting of restricted share units, 1,250,000 under deferred share unit plan, 701,943 for debt settlement and 128,000 on exercise of warrants.

Wholly Owned Subsidiaries

PharmaCielo Holdings Ltd., Toronto, Ont.
- 100% int. in **PharmaCielo Colombia Holdings S.A.S.**, Medellín, Colombia.
- 100% int. in **Ubiquo Telemedicina S.A.S.**, Medellín, Colombia.

Financial Statistics

Periods ended:	12m Dec. 31/22[A]		12m Dec. 31/21[A]
	$000s	%Chg	$000s
Operating revenue	**5,309**	**+173**	**1,945**
Cost of goods sold	4,481		4,373
Salaries & benefits	5,300		6,651
General & admin expense	4,153		5,679
Stock-based compensation	2,209		6,820
Other operating expense	146		220
Operating expense	**16,289**	**-31**	**23,743**
Operating income	**(10,980)**	**n.a.**	**(21,798)**
Deprec., depl. & amort.	453		1,319
Finance income	2		2
Finance costs, gross	1,595		561
Investment income	(841)		(472)
Write-downs/write-offs	(1,269)		(2,078)
Pre-tax income	**(14,516)**	**n.a.**	**(26,630)**
Net income	**(14,516)**	**n.a.**	**(26,630)**
Cash & equivalent	326		5,629
Inventories	2,132		2,281
Accounts receivable	671		565
Current assets	4,018		9,197
Long-term investments	473		640
Fixed assets, net	20,596		25,190
Right-of-use assets	29		930
Total assets	**25,116**	**-30**	**35,957**
Accts. pay. & accr. liabs.	6,111		7,733
Current liabilities	6,953		8,072
Long-term debt, gross	12,281		7,218
Long-term debt, net	11,729		7,138
Long-term lease liabilities	41		1,065
Shareholders' equity	6,392		19,326
Cash from oper. activs.	**9,708**	**n.a.**	**(20,073)**
Cash from fin. activs.	5,296		18,209
Cash from invest. activs.	725		(1,657)
Net cash position	**173**	**-97**	**5,338**
Capital expenditures	(522)		(1,138)
	$		$
Earnings per share*	(0.10)		(0.18)
Cash flow per share*	0.06		(0.14)
	shs		shs
No. of shs. o/s*	154,962,787		149,268,163
Avg. no. of shs. o/s*	150,977,119		145,638,254
	%		%
Net profit margin	(273.42)		n.m.
Return on equity	(112.89)		(116.87)
Return on assets	(42.31)		(65.19)
Foreign sales percent	100		100

* Common
[A] Reported in accordance with IFRS

Latest Results

Periods ended:	3m Mar. 31/23[A]		3m Mar. 31/22[A]
	$000s	%Chg	$000s
Operating revenue	786	-35	1,201
Net income	(3,559)	n.a.	(2,912)
	$		$
Earnings per share*	(0.02)		(0.02)

* Common
[A] Reported in accordance with IFRS

Historical Summary
(as originally stated)

Fiscal Year	Oper. Rev.	Net Inc. Bef. Disc.	EPS*
	$000s	$000s	$
2022[A]	5,309	(14,516)	(0.10)
2021[A]	1,945	(26,630)	(0.18)
2020[A]	2,654	(43,756)	(0.39)
2019[A]	787	(34,667)	(0.36)
	US$000s	US$000s	US$
2018[A1]	nil	(24,426)	(3.70)

* Common
[A] Reported in accordance with IFRS
[1] Results for 2018 and 2017 pertain to (old) PharmaCielo Ltd.
Note: Adjusted throughout for 1-for-11.94 cons. in Jan. 2019

P.46 Pharmadrug Inc.

Symbol - PHRX **Exchange** - CSE **CUSIP** - 71716W
Head Office - 2905-77 King St W, Toronto, ON, M5K 1H1 **Telephone** - (647) 202-1824
Website - www.pharmadrug.co
Email - dcohen@pharmadrug.co
Investor Relations - Daniel Cohen (647) 202-1824
Auditors - Clearhouse LLP C.A., Mississauga, Ont.
Transfer Agents - Capital Transfer Agency Inc., Toronto, Ont.
Profile - (Ont. 2018; orig. Can., 2011) Researches, develops and commercializes controlled-substances and naturally-derived approved drugs.

Wholly owned **Interrobang Ltd.** (dba Super Smart) operates slimwinkel.com, an e-commerce platform which sells functional mushrooms in the U.S. Also develops in-house premium blend of functional mushrooms under the WeRx brand sold through slimwinkel.com, a brick and mortar approach, and the Amazon store.

Wholly owned **Sairiyo Therapeutics Inc.** repurposes and develops improved formulations of naturally derived compounds for serious, rare and life-threatening diseases. Its lead drug candidate is Cepharanthine, a repurposed and reformulated naturally-derived compound for the potential treatment of cancer, neurological, inflammatory and infectious diseases.

In August 2022, the company sold wholly owned **Pharmadrug Production GmbH** to **Khiron Life Sciences Corp.** for issuance of 5,968,750 common shares at a deemed price of 16¢ per share and issuance of a $974,137 promissory note. Pharmadrug Production imports and distributes medical cannabis to pharmacies in Germany and the rest of the European Union, as markets become legalized.

During the second quarter of 2022, the company ceased all its European operations. As a result, the company no longer deals in any psilocybin products.

Common reinstated on CSE, May 17, 2023.
Common suspended from CSE, May 8, 2023.

Predecessor Detail - Name changed from Aura Health Inc., Oct. 22, 2019.

Directors - Daniel (Dan) Cohen, chr. & CEO, Toronto, Ont.; Michael Forbes, B.C.; Dr. David Kideckel, Ont.; Paul McClory, United Kingdom; Al Quong, Toronto, Ont.; Nikolai Vassev, Vancouver, B.C.

Other Exec. Officers - Keith Li, CFO; Harry Resin, pres., Super Smart

Capital Stock

	Authorized (shs.)	Outstanding (shs.)[1]
Common	unlimited	355,626,346

[1] At Aug. 26, 2022

Major Shareholder - Widely held at Feb. 8, 2021.

Price Range - PHRX/CSE

Year	Volume	High	Low	Close
2022	133,384,270	$0.07	$0.01	$0.02
2021	512,945,000	$0.21	$0.03	$0.04
2020	632,358,285	$0.15	$0.01	$0.08
2019	49,025,528	$0.32	$0.02	$0.03
2018	13,334,293	$0.65	$0.14	$0.25

Recent Close: $0.01
Capital Stock Changes - In May 2022, private placement of 7,000,000 units (1 common share & 1 warrant) at 4¢ per unit was completed, with warrants exercisable at 5¢ per share for two years.

Wholly Owned Subsidiaries

Aura Health Corp., Toronto, Ont.
- 100% int. in **Green Global Properties Inc.**, Del.

Interrobang Ltd., Ont.
Interrobang Online Ltd., Del.
Interrobang Tiel B.V., Netherlands.
Sairiyo Therapeutics Inc., Canada.

Investments

Khiron Life Sciences Corp., Vancouver, B.C. (see separate coverage)

Financial Statistics

Periods ended:	12m Dec. 31/21[A]		12m Dec. 31/20[A]
	$000s	%Chg	$000s
Operating revenue	**495**	**-28**	**684**
Cost of goods sold	394		502
Research & devel. expense	554		nil
General & admin expense	2,788		2,102
Stock-based compensation	600		775
Operating expense	**4,335**	**+28**	**3,379**
Operating income	**(3,840)**	**n.a.**	**(2,695)**
Deprec., depl. & amort.	1,283		1,297
Finance costs, gross	156		321
Pre-tax income	**(6,707)**	**n.a.**	**(5,903)**
Income taxes	(834)		(475)
Net income	**(5,874)**	**n.a.**	**(5,428)**
Net inc. for equity hldrs	**(5,626)**	**n.a.**	**(5,150)**
Net inc. for non-cont. int	**(247)**	**n.a.**	**(277)**
Cash & equivalent	958		2,135
Inventories	156		40
Accounts receivable	22		37
Current assets	1,594		4,686
Long-term investments	337		2,270
Fixed assets, net	100		122
Intangibles, net	17,827		8,881
Total assets	**19,520**	**+43**	**13,689**
Accts. pay. & accr. liabs	437		562
Current liabilities	480		619
Long-term debt, gross	786		1,033
Long-term debt, net	786		1,033
Long-term lease liabilities	37		36
Equity portion of conv. debs	249		249
Shareholders' equity	16,865		9,657
Non-controlling interest	nil		1,256
Cash from oper. activs	**(4,125)**	**n.a.**	**(1,803)**
Cash from fin. activs	777		132
Cash from invest. activs	1,481		3,781
Net cash position	**958**	**-55**	**2,135**
Capital expenditures	nil		(18)
	$		$
Earnings per share*	(0.02)		(0.04)
Cash flow per share*	(0.01)		(0.01)
	shs		shs
No. of shs. o/s*	340,816,383		241,632,183
Avg. no. of shs. o/s*	331,181,318		142,456,439
	%		%
Net profit margin	n.m.		(793.57)
Return on equity	(42.43)		(81.54)
Return on assets	(34.55)		(42.65)

* Common
[A] Reported in accordance with IFRS

Latest Results

Periods ended:	6m June 30/22[A]		6m June 30/21[oA]
	$000s	%Chg	$000s
Operating revenue	1	0	1
Net inc. bef. disc. opers	(2,485)	n.a.	(2,155)
Income from disc. opers	(4,956)		(912)
Net income	(7,441)	n.a.	(3,067)
Net inc. for equity hldrs	(7,441)	n.a.	(2,884)
Net inc. for non-cont. int	nil		(182)
	$		$
Earns. per sh. bef. disc. opers.*	(0.01)		(0.01)
Earnings per share*	(0.02)		(0.01)

* Common
[o] Restated
[A] Reported in accordance with IFRS

Historical Summary
(as originally stated)

Fiscal Year	Oper. Rev.	Net Inc. Bef. Disc.	EPS*
	$000s	$000s	$
2021[A]	495	(5,874)	(0.02)
2020[A]	684	(5,428)	(0.04)
2019[A]	611	(6,539)	(0.09)
2018[A1]	nil	(3,512)	(0.26)
2017[A2]	nil	(115)	(0.03)

* Common
[A] Reported in accordance with IFRS
[1] Results reflect the Aug. 9, 2018, reverse takeover acquisition of Aura Health Corp.
[2] Results for fiscal 2017 and prior years pertain to Lamêlée Iron Ore Ltd.

P.47 Pharmala Biotech Holdings Inc.

Symbol - MDMA **Exchange** - CSE **CUSIP** - 71719L
Head Office - 82 Richmond St E, Toronto, ON, M5C 1P1 **Toll-free** - (855) 444-6362
Website - pharmala.ca
Email - nick@pharmala.ca
Investor Relations - Nicholas Kadysh (855) 444-6362
Auditors - Clearhouse LLP C.A., Mississauga, Ont.
Transfer Agents - Marrelli Trust Company Limited, Vancouver, B.C.
Profile - (B.C. 2021) Manufactures the active pharmaceutical ingredients of psychedelic drug MDXX (substituted methylenedioxy-phenethylamines) class compounds including MDMA (ecstasy/molly, 3,4-Methylenedioxymethamphetamine).

Also plans to develop novel formulations of MDMA and the MDXX class of compounds as well as develop novel drug delivery pathways for these molecules.

Directors - Jodi L. H. Butts, chr., Ottawa, Ont.; Nicholas Kadysh, pres. & CEO, Toronto, Ont.; Dr. Harriet de Wit, Chicago, Ill.; Fraser Macdonald, Toronto, Ont.; Kevin Roy, Toronto, Ont.; Dr. Abdelmalik (Malik) Slassi, Mississauga, Ont.; Perry Tsergas, Ottawa, Ont.

Other Exec. Officers - Dr. Shane Morris, COO; Carmelo (Carm) Marrelli, CFO & corp. sec.; Harpreet Kaur, v-p, research

Capital Stock

	Authorized (shs.)	Outstanding (shs.)[1]
Common	unlimited	82,998,600

[1] At Jan. 24, 2023

Major Shareholder - Widely held at Jan. 24, 2023.

Price Range - MDMA/CSE

Year	Volume	High	Low	Close
2022	53,461,112	$0.44	$0.02	$0.03

Recent Close: $0.22

Capital Stock Changes - On Sept. 30, 2021, 40,689,600 common shares were issued without further consideration on exchange of special warrants sold previously by private placement at 75¢ each.

Wholly Owned Subsidiaries

Pharmala Biotech Inc., Vancouver, B.C.

Financial Statistics

Periods ended:	12m Aug. 31/22[A]		32w Aug. 31/21[A1]
	$000s	%Chg	$000s
Operating revenue	**78**	**n.a.**	**nil**
Cost of goods sold	2		nil
Salaries & benefits	104		13
General & admin expense	709		2,353
Stock-based compensation	237		143
Operating expense	**1,052**	**n.a.**	**2,509**
Operating income	**(974)**	**n.a.**	**(2,509)**
Deprec., depl. & amort.	12		nil
Pre-tax income	**(986)**	**n.a.**	**(2,509)**
Net income	**(986)**	**n.a.**	**(2,509)**
Cash & equivalent	852		2,472
Inventories	116		nil
Accounts receivable	23		nil
Current assets	1,085		2,532
Fixed assets, net	4		2
Intangibles, net	1,241		260
Total assets	**2,330**	**-17**	**2,794**
Accts. pay. & accr. liabs	372		138
Current liabilities	424		138
Shareholders' equity	1,906		2,655
Cash from oper. activs	**(625)**	**n.a.**	**(174)**
Cash from fin. activs	nil		2,017
Cash from invest. activs	(995)		629
Net cash position	**852**	**-66**	**2,472**
Capital expenditures	(3)		(3)
	$		$
Earnings per share*	(0.01)		(0.08)
Cash flow per share*	(0.01)		(0.01)
	shs		shs
No. of shs. o/s*	82,998,600		42,309,000
Avg. no. of shs. o/s*	79,756,846		30,231,272
	%		%
Net profit margin	n.m.		...
Return on equity	(43.24)		...
Return on assets	(38.49)		...

* Common
[A] Reported in accordance with IFRS
[1] Results reflect the Mar. 19, 2021, reverse takeover acquisition of Pharmala Biotech Inc.

Latest Results

Periods ended:	3m Nov. 30/22[A]		3m Nov. 30/21[A]
	$000s	%Chg	$000s
Net income	(289)	n.a.	(303)
	$		$
Earnings per share*	(0.00)		(0.00)

* Common
[A] Reported in accordance with IFRS

P.48 PharmaTher Holdings Ltd.

Symbol - PHRM **Exchange** - CSE **CUSIP** - 71716H
Head Office - 82 Richmond St E, Toronto, ON, M5C 1P1 **Toll-free** - (888) 846-3171 **Fax** - (416) 848-0790
Website - www.pharmather.com
Email - info@pharmather.com
Investor Relations - Fabio A. Chianelli (888) 846-3171
Auditors - Clearhouse LLP C.A., Mississauga, Ont.
Transfer Agents - Marrelli Transfer Services Corp., Toronto, Ont.
Profile - (B.C. 2019) Researches, develops and commercializes novel uses, formulations and delivery methods of psychedelics to treat mental illness, neurological and pain disorders.

Has an exclusive licence for an FDA-approved psychedelic drug, ketamine, as an individual or in combination with FDA-approved drugs to treat certain neuropsychiatric, neurological and neuromuscular diseases. Ketamine is a rapid-acting, nonbarbiturate general anesthetic approved by the Food and Drug Administration (FDA) in 1970 and is clinically used for analgesia, sedation, and anesthetic induction.

Products under development include KETAPATCH™, a ketamine microneedle patch for mental health and pain disorders; KETARX™ Pump, a ketamine hydrochloride injection U.S. patented (USP) product for anaesthesia, procedural sedation, pain and neurological disorders including Parkinson's and amyotrophic lateral sclerosis (ALS); and PHARAMAPATCH™, a novel microneedle patch technology solutions including hydrogel-forming microneedle and gelatin methacryloyl microneedle systems to deliver psychedelics (psilocybin, N,N-Dimethyltryptamine (DMT), 3,4-Methylenedioxy methamphetamine (MDMA) and lysergic acid diethylamide (LSD)) and potentially other drugs to treat infectious diseases.

Also holds licence for the development and commercialization of KETABET™, a combination drug of ketamine and betaine as treatment to mental health neurological and pain disorders, whereby betaine enhance the antidepressant effect while reducing the negative side effects of ketamine.

Predecessor Detail - Name changed from Newscope Capital Corporation, Apr. 7, 2021.

Directors - Fabio A. Chianelli, CEO, Toronto, Ont.; Dr. Beverly J. Inceldon, George Town, Cayman Islands; Carlo Sansalone, Vaughan, Ont.; Christian Scovenna, Etobicoke, Ont.

Other Exec. Officers - Carmelo (Carm) Marrelli, CFO; Andrew Todd, corp. sec.

Capital Stock

	Authorized (shs.)	Outstanding (shs.)[1]
Common	unlimited	88,169,065

[1] At Oct. 21, 2022

Major Shareholder - Fabio A. Chianelli held 17.45% interest at Oct. 21, 2022.

Price Range - PHRM/CSE

Year	Volume	High	Low	Close
2022	35,743,325	$0.41	$0.06	$0.07
2021	113,559,326	$1.24	$0.19	$0.34
2020	38,480,726	$0.55	$0.05	$0.32

Recent Close: $0.14

Capital Stock Changes - In September 2021, private placement of 15,625,000 units (1 common share & 1 warrant) at 64¢ per unit was completed. Also during fiscal 2022, common shares were issued as follows: 3,684,200 on exercise of warrants and 1,125,000 on exercise of options.

Wholly Owned Subsidiaries

PharmaTher Inc., Toronto, Ont.

Financial Statistics

Periods ended:	12m May 31/22[A]		12m May 31/21[A1]
	$000s	%Chg	$000s
Research & devel. expense	2,605		752
General & admin expense	1,124		1,988
Stock-based compensation	373		409
Operating expense	**4,102**	**+30**	**3,149**
Operating income	**(4,102)**	**n.a.**	**(3,149)**
Pre-tax income	**(4,236)**	**n.a.**	**2,889**
Income taxes	(225)		225
Net income	**(4,011)**	**n.a.**	**2,664**
Cash & equivalent	9,155		2,778
Accounts receivable	30		29
Current assets	12,162		5,940
Fixed assets, net	2		4
Total assets	**12,164**	**+105**	**5,944**
Accts. pay. & accr. liabs	328		134
Current liabilities	330		176
Shareholders' equity	11,834		5,583
Cash from oper. activs	**(3,511)**	**n.a.**	**922**
Cash from fin. activs	9,888		1,253
Cash from invest. activs	nil		215
Net cash position	**9,155**	**+230**	**2,778**
Capital expenditures	nil		(4)
	$		$
Earnings per share*	(0.05)		0.04
Cash flow per share*	(0.04)		0.01
	shs		shs
No. of shs. o/s*	88,169,065		67,734,865
Avg. no. of shs. o/s*	81,105,083		64,558,158
	%		%
Net profit margin	n.a.		n.a.
Return on equity	n.m.		92.07
Return on assets	n.a.		86.44

* Common
[A] Reported in accordance with IFRS
[1] Results reflect the June 10, 2020, reverse takeover acquisition of PharmaTher Inc.

Latest Results

Periods ended:	3m Aug. 31/22[A]		3m Aug. 31/21[A]
	$000s	%Chg	$000s
Net income	(1,788)	n.a.	(914)
	$		$
Earnings per share*	(0.02)		(0.01)

* Common
[A] Reported in accordance with IFRS

Historical Summary
(as originally stated)

Fiscal Year	Oper. Rev.	Net Inc. Bef. Disc.	EPS*
	$000s	$000s	$
2022[A]	nil	(4,011)	(0.05)
2021[A]	nil	2,664	0.04
2020[A]	nil	(283)	(0.06)

* Common
[A] Reported in accordance with IFRS

P.49 Picton Mahoney Tactical Income Fund

Symbol - PMB.UN **Exchange** - TSX **CUSIP** - 71989R
Head Office - 830-33 Yonge St, Toronto, ON, M5E 1G4 **Telephone** - (416) 955-4108 **Toll-free** - (866) 369-4108 **Fax** - (416) 955-4100
Website - www.pictonmahoney.com
Email - agalloway@pictonmahoney.com
Investor Relations - Arthur F. Galloway (416) 955-4108
Auditors - PricewaterhouseCoopers LLP C.A., Toronto, Ont.
Lawyers - McMillan LLP, Toronto, Ont.
Transfer Agents - TSX Trust Company, Toronto, Ont.
Trustees - TSX Trust Company, Toronto, Ont.
Investment Managers - Picton Mahoney Asset Management, Toronto, Ont.
Managers - Picton Mahoney Asset Management, Toronto, Ont.
Profile - (Ont. 2012) Invests in an actively-managed portfolio of high-yield and investment grade bonds and, to a more limited extent, government bonds, convertible bonds, preferred shares and dividend paying equities, with a focus on North American issuers.
The fund's top 10 long positions at Mar. 31, 2023 (as a percentage of net asset value):

Holding	Percentage
Cash	11.4%
Secure Energy SE 7.25%	3.1%
Freeport Minerals Corporation 7.125%	3.1%
Horizon Therapeutics USA 5.5%	2.7%
National Bank Of Canada 7.50%	2.5%
Parkland Corporation 3.875%	2.5%
Acadia Healthcare Company Inc. 5.50%	2.3%
Northriver Midstream Financials 5.625%	2.1%
American Airlines Inc. 11.75%	2.0%
IA Financial Corporation Inc. 6.61%	1.9%

Oper. Subsid./Mgt. Co. Officers - David K. Picton, pres. & CEO; Arthur F. Galloway, COO, CFO & corp. sec.; Catrina Duong, chief compliance officer

Capital Stock

	Authorized (shs.)	Outstanding (shs.)[1]
Class A Unit	unlimited	2,193,665
Class F Unit	unlimited	766,634

[1] At Dec. 31, 2022

Class A Unit - Entitled to a monthly cash distribution of $0.0300 per class A unit. Retractable in April of each year at a price equal to the net asset value (NAV) per class A unit less any costs associated with the retraction, including commissions. Retractable in any other month at a price equal to the lesser of: (i) 95% of the weighted average price of the class A units on the TSX during the 10 trading days preceding the retraction date; and (ii) the closing price per unit. Convertible into class F units at a ratio based on the NAV per class A unit divided by the NAV per class F unit. One vote per class A unit.
Class F Unit - Entitled to a monthly cash distribution of $0.0330 per class F unit. For fee-based accounts. Retractable in April of each year at a price equal to the NAV per class F unit less any costs associated with the retraction, including commissions. Retractable in any other month at a price equal to the product of: (i) the retraction amount per class A unit; and (ii) a fraction, the numerator of which is the most recently calculated NAV per class F unit and the denominator of which is the most recently calculated NAV per class A unit. Convertible into class A units on a weekly basis at a ratio based on the NAV per class F unit divided by the NAV per class A unit. One vote per class F unit.
Major Shareholder - Widely held at Mar. 1, 2023.

Price Range - PMB.UN/TSX

Year	Volume	High	Low	Close
2022	422,148	$7.89	$6.85	$6.87
2021	504,461	$8.19	$7.61	$7.75
2020	711,433	$7.96	$6.14	$7.85
2019	1,655,839	$8.06	$7.54	$7.70
2018	1,485,211	$8.97	$7.60	$7.61

Recent Close: $6.93
Capital Stock Changes - During 2022, 318 class A units were issued under distribution reinvestment plan, 63,746 class A units were exchanged for 57,900 class F units, and 240,468 class A units and 50,020 class F units were retracted.

Dividends

PMB.UN cl A Ra $0.36 pa M est. Feb. 22, 2023**
Prev. Rate: $0.3996 est. Feb. 22, 2022
Prev. Rate: $0.4068 est. Feb. 22, 2021
Prev. Rate: $0.4008 est. Feb. 22, 2019
** Reinvestment Option

Financial Statistics

Periods ended:	12m Dec. 31/22[A]		12m Dec. 31/21[oA]
	$000s	%Chg	$000s
Realized invest. gain (loss)	(1,933)		1,309
Unrealized invest. gain (loss)	(1,113)		(1,051)
Total revenue	**(583)**	**n.a.**	**1,785**
General & admin. expense	663		728
Operating expense	**663**	**-9**	**728**
Operating income	**(1,246)**	**n.a.**	**1,057**
Pre-tax income	**(1,247)**	**n.a.**	**1,057**
Income taxes	1		2
Net income	**(1,247)**	**n.a.**	**1,055**
Cash & equivalent	18,702		9,811
Accounts receivable	355		351
Investments	24,793		31,219
Total assets	**43,990**	**-2**	**44,978**
Accts. pay. & accr. liabs	183		210
Shareholders' equity	21,845		26,609
Cash from oper. activs	**4,000**	**+22**	**3,266**
Cash from fin. activs	(3,529)		(4,580)
Net cash position	**2,368**	**+30**	**1,824**
	$		$
Earnings per share*	(0.41)		0.30
Earnings per share**	(0.39)		0.33
Cash flow per share***	1.30		0.96
Net asset value per share*	7.19		7.99
Cash divd. per share*	0.40		0.41
	shs		shs
No. of shs. o/s***	2,960,299		3,256,315
Avg. no. of shs. o/s***	3,075,056		3,408,855
	%		%
Net profit margin	n.m.		59.10
Return on equity	(5.15)		3.72
Return on assets	(3.08)		2.41

* Class A unit
** Class F unit
*** Class A unit & Class F unit
[o] Restated
[A] Reported in accordance with IFRS
Note: Net income reflects increase/decrease in net assets from operations.

Historical Summary
(as originally stated)

Fiscal Year	Total Rev.	Net Inc. Bef. Disc.	EPS*
	$000s	$000s	$
2022[A]	(583)	(1,247)	(0.41)
2021[A]	1,785	1,055	0.30
2020[A]	2,730	1,703	0.39
2019[A]	3,215	2,243	0.39
2018[A]	(633)	(1,925)	(0.27)

* Class A unit
[A] Reported in accordance with IFRS

P.50 Pine Trail Real Estate Investment Trust

Symbol - PINE.UN **Exchange** - TSX-VEN **CUSIP** - 72288P
Head Office - 2700-161 Bay St, Toronto, ON, M5J 2S1 **Telephone** - (416) 583-5513
Website - www.pinereit.com
Investor Relations - Andrew Shapack (416) 532-2200
Auditors - McGovern Hurley LLP C.A., Toronto, Ont.
Lawyers - Dentons Canada LLP, Calgary, Alta.
Transfer Agents - TSX Trust Company, Calgary, Alta.
Profile - (Alta. 2017) Owns and acquires healthcare properties in Canada with a focus on medical office buildings and seniors housing.
The trust owns a 12,000-sq.-ft. medical office building in Picton, Ont., which is fully occupied by medical practitioners and a pharmacy and generates revenue of $20,000 per month.
Predecessor Detail - Name changed from Pine Trail Capital Trust, Nov. 27, 2018, pursuant to Qualifying Transaction acquisition of a medical office building in Picton, Ont.
Trustees - Andrew Shapack, CEO, Toronto, Ont.; Henry (Hank) Bulmash, Toronto, Ont.; Seldon (Jamie) James, Toronto, Ont.; Mohammed Atiq Nakrawala, Windsor, Ont.
Oper. Subsid./Mgt. Co. Officers - David Luu, CFO; Nicole Bacsalmasi, legal counsel & corp. sec.

Capital Stock

	Authorized (shs.)	Outstanding (shs.)[1]
Preferred Unit	unlimited	nil
Class A Trust Unit	unlimited	35,442,657

[1] At Mar. 31, 2023

Major Shareholder - Widely held at June 21, 2022.

Price Range - PINE.UN/TSX-VEN

Year	Volume	High	Low	Close
2022	3,378,840	$0.08	$0.05	$0.06
2021	2,781,512	$0.09	$0.06	$0.07
2020	2,367,466	$0.18	$0.02	$0.07
2019	676,534	$0.19	$0.11	$0.15
2018	305,000	$0.16	$0.11	$0.12

Recent Close: $0.07

Capital Stock Changes - There were no changes to capital stock during 2021 or 2022.

Dividends

PINE.UN tr unit Ra $0.0036 pa M est. Nov. 16, 2022**
Prev. Rate: $0.0072 est. Jan. 15, 2019
PINE.U US$ tr unit Ra $0.0036 pa M est. Mar. 15, 2023**
$0.0003**i**.............. Mar. 15/23
** Reinvestment Option **i** Initial Payment

Subsidiaries

99.9% int. in **Pine Trail Operating L.P.**, Alta.
• 100% int. in **Pine Trail Picton Inc.**, Ont.

Financial Statistics

Periods ended:	12m Dec. 31/22A		12m Dec. 31/21A
	$000s	%Chg	$000s
Total revenue	**399**	**-3**	**410**
Rental operating expense	95		91
General & admin. expense	88		136
Stock-based compensation	52		31
Property taxes	33		34
Operating expense	**304**	**+16**	**262**
Operating income	**95**	**-36**	**148**
Pre-tax income	**(136)**	**n.a.**	**768**
Net income	**(136)**	**n.a.**	**768**
Cash & equivalent	186		161
Income-producing props	3,400		3,650
Property interests, net	3,400		3,650
Total assets	**3,605**	**-6**	**3,822**
Accts. pay. & accr. liabs	197		205
Shareholders' equity	3,298		3,455
Cash from oper. activs	**78**	**-21**	**99**
Cash from invest. activs	(32)		nil
Net cash position	**186**	**+16**	**161**
Increase in property	32		nil
	$		$
Earnings per share*	n.a.		n.a.
Cash flow per share*	0.00		0.00
Cash divd. per share*	0.00		nil
	shs		shs
No. of shs. o/s*	35,442,657		35,442,657
	%		%
Net profit margin	(34.09)		187.32
Return on equity	(4.03)		25.01
Return on assets	(3.66)		22.27

* Cl.A Trust Unit
[A] Reported in accordance with IFRS

Latest Results

Periods ended:	3m Mar. 31/23A		3m Mar. 31/22A
	$000s	%Chg	$000s
Total revenue	107	+5	102
Net income	24	-38	39
	$		$
Earnings per share*	n.a.		n.a.

[A] Reported in accordance with IFRS

Historical Summary
(as originally stated)

Fiscal Year	Total Rev.	Net Inc. Bef. Disc.	EPS*
	$000s	$000s	$
2022A	399	(136)	n.a.
2021A	410	768	n.a.
2020A	408	148	n.a.
2019A	394	9	n.a.
2018A1	61	(187)	n.a.

* Cl.A Trust Unit
[A] Reported in accordance with IFRS
[1] Results reflect the Nov. 6, 2018, Qualifying Transaction acquisition of a medical office building in Picton, Ont.

P.51 Pinetree Capital Ltd.*

Symbol - PNP **Exchange** - TSX **CUSIP** - 723330
Head Office - 49 Leuty Ave, Toronto, ON, M4E 2R2 **Telephone** - (416) 941-9600 **Fax** - (416) 941-1090
Website - www.pinetreecapital.com
Email - jbouffard@pinetreecapital.com
Investor Relations - John Bouffard (416) 941-9600 ext. 200
Auditors - MNP LLP C.A., Toronto, Ont.
Lawyers - Cassels Brock & Blackwell LLP, Toronto, Ont.
Transfer Agents - TSX Trust Company, Toronto, Ont.
Employees - 3 at Dec. 31, 2022

Profile - (Ont. 1962) Owns and manages a portfolio of investments and provides merchant banking services focused on the technology sector.

Invests primarily in equity, as well as debt and convertible securities, held for both long-term capital appreciation and shorter-term gains. At June 30, 2023, the company's investment portfolio had a fair value of $42,412,000 compared with $39,950,000 at Dec. 31, 2022.

Predecessor Detail - Succeeded Genevest Inc., June 1, 2004, following reverse takeover acquisition of Genevest Inc. by Pinetree Capital Corp. and name change of Pinetree Capital Corp. to Pinetree Capital Ltd.; basis 1 new sh. for 1.75 old Pinetree shs. and 1 new sh. for 0.7955 Genevest shs.

Directors - Damien Leonard, chr. & pres., Ont.; Craig Miller†, Toronto, Ont.; Howard Riback, B.C.; Peter Tolnai, W.A., Australia

Other Exec. Officers - Shezad Okhai, chief invest. officer; John Bouffard, exec. v-p, CFO & corp. sec.

† Lead director

Capital Stock

	Authorized (shs.)	Outstanding (shs.)1
Common	unlimited	9,387,000

[1] At July 28, 2023

Major Shareholder - Damien Leonard and siblings held 35.4% interest at Apr. 10, 2023.

Price Range - PNP/TSX

Year	Volume	High	Low	Close
2022	430,404	$5.71	$2.51	$3.99
2021	1,089,623	$5.99	$3.32	$5.45
2020	791,659	$3.58	$1.70	$3.04
2019	292,836	$3.70	$2.40	$3.08
2018	463,954	$6.40	$2.42	$2.52

Consolidation: 1-for-2 cons. in July 2021

Recent Close: $4.11

Capital Stock Changes - There were no changes to capital stock during 2022.

Long-Term Debt - At Dec. 31, 2022, outstanding debt totaled $203,000 and consisted entirely of class C preferred shares issued by wholly owned Pinetree Capital Investment Corp. The class C preferred shares are redeemable and retractable at any time, and entitled to cumulative dividends at a rate of 8% per annum.

Wholly Owned Subsidiaries

Emerald Capital Corp., Alta.
Pinetree (Barbados) Inc., Barbados. Inactive.
Pinetree Capital Investment Corp., Ont.
Pinetree Income Partnership
Pinetree (Israel) Inc., Israel. Inactive.
Pinetree Resource Partnership Inactive.

Financial Statistics

Periods ended:	12m Dec. 31/22A		12m Dec. 31/21A
	$000s	%Chg	$000s
Realized invest. gain (loss)	2,224		(1,311)
Unrealized invest. gain (loss)	(340)		3,335
Total revenue	**2,289**	**-4**	**2,394**
General & admin. expense	891		755
Other operating expense	37		54
Operating expense	**928**	**+15**	**809**
Operating income	**1,361**	**-14**	**1,585**
Finance costs, gross	16		16
Pre-tax income	**1,154**	**-22**	**1,472**
Income taxes	(26)		13
Net income	**1,180**	**-19**	**1,459**
Cash & equivalent	6,045		9,939
Investments	33,905		28,858
Total assets	**40,062**	**+3**	**38,851**
Accts. pay. & accr. liabs	240		209
Debt	203		203
Shareholders' equity	39,619		38,439
Cash from oper. activs	**(3,894)**	**n.a.**	**(10,910)**
Cash from fin. activs	nil		17,879
Net cash position	**6,045**	**-39**	**9,939**
	$		$
Earnings per share*	0.13		0.19
Cash flow per share*	(0.41)		(1.43)
Net asset value per share*	4.22		4.09
	shs		shs
No. of shs. o/s*	9,387,000		9,387,000
Avg. no. of shs. o/s*	9,387,000		7,617,104
	%		%
Net profit margin	51.55		60.94
Return on equity	3.02		5.07
Return on assets	3.03		5.06
No. of employees (FTEs)	3		3

* Common
[A] Reported in accordance with IFRS

Latest Results

Periods ended:	6m June 30/23A		6m June 30/22A
	$000s	%Chg	$000s
Total revenue	3,047	n.a.	(228)
Net income	2,492	n.a.	(795)
	$		$
Earnings per share*	0.27		(0.08)

* Common
[A] Reported in accordance with IFRS

Historical Summary
(as originally stated)

Fiscal Year	Total Rev.	Net Inc. Bef. Disc.	EPS*
	$000s	$000s	$
2022A	2,289	1,180	0.13
2021A	2,394	1,459	0.19
2020A	1,678	1,203	0.26
2019A	2,489	1,918	0.42
2018A	(1,889)	(2,360)	(0.52)

* Common
[A] Reported in accordance with IFRS

Note: Adjusted throughout for 1-for-2 cons. in July 2021

P.52 Pioneer Media Holdings Inc.

Symbol - JPEG **Exchange** - NEO **CUSIP** - 723747
Head Office - Four Bentall Center, 3104-1055 Dunsmuir St, Vancouver, BC, V7X 1G4 **Telephone** - (604) 788-1348
Website - www.p1Oneer.com
Email - ir@p1Oneer.com
Investor Relations - Darcy Taylor (604) 373-5452
Auditors - De Visser Gray LLP C.A., Vancouver, B.C.
Transfer Agents - National Securities Administrators Ltd., Vancouver, B.C.

Profile - (B.C. 2017) Creates Web3 gaming ecosystem which includes content and game development; infrastructure and Web2 conversion; and distribution and global publishing using its proprietary MetaKit blockchain technology.

MetaKit is the company's core software technology and proprietary game infrastructure framework for developers that removes the friction of player onramps and increases each game's likelihood of success. The software includes Flex Connect, a single sign-on solution for blockchain games that allows users to play with NFTs across multiple wallets; Flex Marketplace, a platform which enables NFT rental with a plug-and-play rental marketplace and guild solution for blockchain games; Helix Pay, a Web3 payment solution that provides seamless in-game crypto payment processing and the real-time purchase of tokens; and Helix Subscriptions, a frictionless solution for subscriptions using a proprietary relay method that allows developers to implement reliable crypto subscriptions in just a few lines of code.

The company also operates wholly owned **Crowdform Ltd.**, a digital product and venture activation studio that creates innovative platforms, apps and websites for global brands and startups; **Kodoku Studios Limited**, which is developing The Pit, a platform for gamers to stake their NFTs which was launched in December 2021; **Roundhouse Media Pte. Ltd.**, which is developing Stonks: Tycoon, which would be a play-to-earn NFT game where users can potentially generate income through playing and may be rewarded with tokens or NFTs based on duration of play; **NGMI Labs Inc.**, which serves as an onramp into DAO and tokenized communities; and **Bark Ventures Ltd.**, which develops NFT play-to-earn games for niche communities.

In addition, holds certain investments in companies engaged in the gaming, eSports and Web3 sectors. At Nov. 30, 2022, the investment portfolio had a fair market value of $5,379,446.

In November 2021, the company sold its interest in U.K.-based **Blue Star Capital Plc**, which invests in new technologies, for $1,142,152. In addition, the company acquired CryptoPunk 8869, a non-fungible token, for US$438,041 which was subsequently sold in Apirl 2022 for US50,000.

In March 2022, the company acquired London, U.K.-based **Crowdform Ltd.** from Ewan Collinge and Léo Mercier for £601,994 (Cdn$987,968) cash paid on closing, with an additional £500,000 to be paid six months thereafter. In addition, Messrs. Collinge and Mercier would receive 4,460,303 common shares, which would be issued in four equal tranches every six months from closing. Crowdform creates innovative platforms, apps and websites for global brands and startups.

Predecessor Detail - Name changed from Haro Metals Corp., Oct. 25, 2019, pursuant to change of business from a mineral exploration company to an investment company with a focus on the gaming and eSport sector.

Directors - Darcy Taylor, CEO, West Vancouver, B.C.; Julia Becker, West Vancouver, B.C.; Olivia Edwards, B.C.; Mark Rutledge, Vancouver, B.C.

Other Exec. Officers - James M. (Jim) MacCallum, CFO

Capital Stock

	Authorized (shs.)	Outstanding (shs.)1
Common	unlimited	83,812,582

[1] At Jan. 9, 2023

Major Shareholder - Michael S. (Mike) Edwards held 16.9% interest at Dec. 12, 2022.

Price Range - JPEG/NEO

Year	Volume	High	Low	Close
2022	100,751	$1.90	$0.10	$0.10
2021	956,069	$2.03	$0.35	$1.80

Recent Close: $0.06

Capital Stock Changes - In November 2022, private placement of 5,800,000 units (1 common share & ½ warrant) at 10¢ per unit was completed, with warrants exercisable at 25¢ per share for two years.

During fiscal 2022, common shares were issued as follows: 8,000,000 pursuant to acquisition of Kodoku Studios Limited, 5,000,000 pursuant to acquisition of Roundhouse Media Pte. Ltd., 4,000,000 pursuant to acquisition of NGMI Labs Inc., 2,857,142 pursuant to acquisition of Bark Ventures Ltd. and 1,503,932 by private placement.

Wholly Owned Subsidiaries

Bark Ventures Ltd., Vancouver, B.C.

Crowdform Ltd., London, Middx., United Kingdom.
Kodoku Studios Limited, United Kingdom.
NGMI Labs Inc., B.C.
Roundhouse Media Pte. Ltd., Singapore.

Note: The preceding list includes only the major related companies in which interests are held.

Financial Statistics

Periods ended:	12m May 31/22[A]		12m May 31/21[rA]
	$000s	%Chg	$000s
Operating revenue	**482**	**n.a.**	**nil**
Cost of sales	101		nil
Research & devel. expense	370		nil
General & admin expense	1,546		336
Stock-based compensation	584		394
Operating expense	**2,601**	**+256**	**730**
Operating income	**(2,119)**	**n.a.**	**(730)**
Deprec., depl. & amort.	3,586		nil
Finance costs, net	71		(266)
Write-downs/write-offs	(15,588)		nil
Pre-tax income	**(28,629)**	**n.a.**	**5,379**
Income taxes	(1,141)		463
Net income	**(27,488)**	**n.a.**	**4,916**
Cash & equivalent	1,654		2,871
Accounts receivable	289		nil
Current assets	2,028		2,873
Long-term investments	8,930		17,590
Intangibles, net	4,605		nil
Total assets	**15,563**	**-24**	**20,463**
Accts. pay. & accr. liabs.	342		343
Current liabilities	1,823		575
Shareholders' equity	13,138		18,747
Cash from oper. activs.	**(2,143)**	**n.a.**	**1**
Cash from fin. activs.	1,438		7,083
Cash from invest. activs.	(511)		(4,309)
Net cash position	**1,654**	**-42**	**2,871**
	$		$
Earnings per share*	(0.42)		0.13
Cash flow per share*	(0.03)		nil
	shs		shs
No. of shs. o/s*	76,897,507		55,536,433
Avg. no. of shs. o/s*	64,977,683		36,468,080
	%		%
Net profit margin	n.m.		n.a.
Return on equity	(172.42)		38.79
Return on assets	(152.60)		35.28

* Common
[r] Restated
[A] Reported in accordance with IFRS

Latest Results

Periods ended:	6m Nov. 30/22[A]		6m Nov. 30/21[A]
	$000s	%Chg	$000s
Operating revenue	844	n.a.	nil
Net income	(6,765)	n.a.	(5,695)
	$		$
Earnings per share*	(0.09)		(0.10)

* Common
[A] Reported in accordance with IFRS

Historical Summary
(as originally stated)

Fiscal Year	Oper. Rev.	Net Inc. Bef. Disc.	EPS*
	$000s	$000s	$
2022[A]	482	(27,488)	(0.42)
2021[A]	nil	4,916	0.13
2020[A1]	nil	(748)	(0.10)
2019[A1]	nil	(52)	(0.22)

* Common
[A] Reported in accordance with IFRS
[1] As shown in the listing statement dated Apr. 6, 2021. Shares and per share figures adjusted to reflect 1-for-10 share consolidation effective Oct. 25, 2019, and 1-for-2 share consolidation effective May 28, 2020.

P.53 Pioneering Technology Corp.

Symbol - PTE **Exchange** - TSX-VEN **CUSIP** - 72403R
Head Office - Unit 7, 2400 Skymark Ave, Mississauga, ON, L4W 5K5 **Telephone** - (905) 712-2061 **Toll-free** - (800) 433-6026 **Fax** - (905) 712-3833
Website - www.pioneeringtech.com
Email - kcallahan@pioneeringtech.com
Investor Relations - Kevin R. Callahan (647) 945-7515
Auditors - KPMG LLP C.A., Hamilton, Ont.
Lawyers - Goodmans LLP, Toronto, Ont.
Transfer Agents - Computershare Trust Company of Canada Inc., Toronto, Ont.

Profile - (Ont. 2006 amalg.) Develops and engineers proprietary, energy-smart product innovations primarily focused on reducing and preventing cooking fire and false alarms.

Products include the Safe-T-element® (STE) cooking system, which is engineered to prevent stovetop cooking fires on electric coiled stoves before they start and reduce the amount of electricity required to cook; the SmartBurner™, an easy to install plug and play version of the STE that does not require a professional hardwired installation; the Safe-T-sensor™ (STS) or STS 2.0 (known as the Smart Micro™), which is designed to prevent microwave fires and false or nuisance alarms; the RangeMinder™, which is engineered to help prevent unattended cooking on both gas and electric rangetops; and the SmartRange™, which is engineered to help alert users to imminent danger via a low frequency alarm and would turn off the stove if not addressed.

The company licenses or sells its proprietary products and components to leading original equipment manufacturers (OEMs) in large mass market categories and through established distribution channels for the general public and B2B customers.

Predecessor Detail - Name changed from Pioneering Technology Inc., Sept. 18, 2008; basis 1 new for 10 old shs.

Directors - John Bergsma, chr., Waterdown, Ont.; Kevin R. Callahan, CEO, Toronto, Ont.; Meredith K. Appy, Portland, Ore.; Paul H. Harricks, Toronto, Ont.

Other Exec. Officers - Mark Weigel, CFO; Will Boake, exec. v-p, bus. devel.; Tim Mulroney, v-p, sales & mktg.

Capital Stock

	Authorized (shs.)	Outstanding (shs.)[1]
Series 1 Preferred	unlimited	20,533,133
Common	unlimited	56,041,746

[1] At Mar. 1, 2023

Series 1 Preferred - Not entitled to dividends. May be redeemed or purchased for cancellation at up to 6¢ per share. Non-voting.

Common - One vote per share.

Major Shareholder - David L. Dueck held 15.6% interest at Feb. 28, 2023.

Price Range - PTE/TSX-VEN

Year	Volume	High	Low	Close
2022	4,000,455	$0.05	$0.02	$0.02
2021	21,785,416	$0.14	$0.04	$0.05
2020	25,856,874	$0.15	$0.03	$0.08
2019	12,600,345	$0.13	$0.03	$0.04
2018	24,136,939	$0.85	$0.07	$0.08

Recent Close: $0.02

Capital Stock Changes - There were no changes to capital stock from fiscal 2019 to fiscal 2022, inclusive.

Financial Statistics

Periods ended:	12m Sept. 30/22[A]		12m Sept. 30/21[A]
	$000s	%Chg	$000s
Operating revenue	**2,438**	**-27**	**3,351**
Cost of goods sold	1,218		1,893
Research & devel. expense	94		92
General & admin expense	1,523		2,220
Other operating expense	97		72
Operating expense	**2,933**	**-31**	**4,276**
Operating income	**(495)**	**n.a.**	**(925)**
Deprec., depl. & amort.	201		219
Finance costs, gross	84		87
Pre-tax income	**(625)**	**n.a.**	**(1,316)**
Net income	**(625)**	**n.a.**	**(1,316)**
Cash & equivalent	890		1,495
Inventories	2,477		2,334
Accounts receivable	485		484
Current assets	3,941		4,596
Fixed assets, net	1,686		1,742
Intangibles, net	231		227
Total assets	**5,859**	**-11**	**6,565**
Accts. pay. & accr. liabs.	876		1,072
Current liabilities	968		1,156
Long-term lease liabilities	1,420		1,512
Shareholders' equity	3,472		3,898
Cash from oper. activs.	**(424)**	**n.a.**	**(365)**
Cash from fin. activs.	(164)		(160)
Cash from invest. activs.	(14)		(50)
Net cash position	**890**	**-40**	**1,495**
Capital expenditures	(14)		nil
	$		$
Earnings per share*	(0.01)		(0.02)
Cash flow per share*	(0.01)		(0.01)
	shs		shs
No. of shs. o/s*	56,041,746		56,041,746
Avg. no. of shs. o/s*	56,041,746		56,041,746
	%		%
Net profit margin	(25.64)		(39.27)
Return on equity	(16.96)		(28.26)
Return on assets	(8.71)		(15.98)
Foreign sales percent	88		84

* Common
[A] Reported in accordance with IFRS

Historical Summary
(as originally stated)

Fiscal Year	Oper. Rev.	Net Inc. Bef. Disc.	EPS*
	$000s	$000s	$
2022[A]	2,438	(625)	(0.01)
2021[A]	3,351	(1,316)	(0.02)
2020[A]	6,541	(883)	(0.02)
2019[A]	3,942	(3,856)	(0.07)
2018[A]	4,750	(3,305)	(0.06)

* Common
[A] Reported in accordance with IFRS

P.54 Pivotree Inc.

Symbol - PVT **Exchange** - TSX-VEN **CUSIP** - 72583B
Head Office - 6300 Northam Dr, Mississauga, ON, L4V 1H7 **Toll-free** - (877) 767-5577
Website - pivotree.com
Email - bill.dinardo@pivotree.com
Investor Relations - William Di Nardo (877) 767-5577
Auditors - BDO Canada LLP C.A., Markham, Ont.
Lawyers - Owens, Wright LLP, Toronto, Ont.
Transfer Agents - TSX Trust Company, Toronto, Ont.

Profile - (Ont. 2020; orig. Ont., 1998) Designs, integrates, deploys and manages digital platforms in commerce, data management and supply chain for major retail and branded manufacturers worldwide.

Operates through two segments: managed services and professional services.

Wholly owned **Thinkwrap Solutions Inc.** is a professional services provider that delivers strategy, design, software development and integration services to enterprise retailers, branded manufacturers, wholesalers and distributors, implementing, upgrading and enhancing their e-commerce platforms such as Oracle ATG, SAP Hybris and Shopify, or product information management (PIM) and master data management (MDM) solutions such as Stibo, EnterWorks, ContentServ, Riversand and Informatica.

Wholly owned **Pivotree USA Inc.** (formerly **Spark::red Inc.**) is a managed application service provider primarily focused on the Oracle Commerce platform, delivering high availability systems to large branded retailers and manufacturers. Services include infrastructure deployment and management, web and application hosting, 24/7 access to experts for system and application triage, application support, configuration management and security. The segment is primarily related to services provided by hosting/infrastructure providers such as AWS and Azure, and managed service/application providers.

In addition, wholly owned **Bridge Solutions Group Corp.** and **Codifyd Inc.** have been discontinued with all business being transacted under **Pivotree USA Inc.** Services include supply chain services including order management, warehouse management and application integration; and end-to-end digital services including Master Data Management (MDM) and Production Information Management (PIM) services, product content management and digital commerce solutions.

The company is headquartered in Toronto, Ont., with additional offices in Ottawa, Ont.; Redmond, Va.; Valencia, Spain; and Noida and Pune, India.

In January 2023, wholly owned **Bridge Solutions Group Corp.** and **Codifyd Inc.** were amalgamated into wholly owned **Pivotree USA Inc.**

Directors - Vernon Lobo, chr., Toronto, Ont.; William (Bill) Di Nardo, CEO, Toronto, Ont.; Ashlee Aldridge, Westerville, Ohio; Brian Beattie, Toronto, Ont.; Scott Bryan, Toronto, Ont.; William F. (Bill) Morris, Toronto, Ont.; Brian O'Neil, Toronto, Ont.

Other Exec. Officers - Todd Jurkuta, pres.; Ted Smith Jr., COO; Moataz (Mo) Ashoor, CFO, CAO & corp. sec.; Edgar Aranha, chief people & culture officer; Sarah Kirk-Douglas, v-p, mktg.

Capital Stock

	Authorized (shs.)	Outstanding (shs.)[1]
Common	unlimited	26,641,324

[1] At May 8, 2023

Normal Course Issuer Bid - The company plans to make normal course purchases of up to 1,924,014 common shares representing 10% of the public float. The bid commenced on Aug. 8, 2023, and expires on Aug. 7, 2024.

Major Shareholder - Widely held at May 8, 2023.

Price Range - PVT/TSX-VEN

Year	Volume	High	Low	Close
2022	2,584,598	$5.71	$3.03	$3.32
2021	5,756,280	$13.19	$3.15	$4.38
2020	3,986,745	$13.99	$9.00	$13.19

Recent Close: $2.18

Capital Stock Changes - During 2022, common shares were issued as follows: 811,018 on exercise of options, 572,466 were issued pursuant to the acquisition of Bridge Solutions Group Corp. and Codifyd Inc., and 20,279 on conversion of on vesting of restricted share units; 66,200 common shares were repurchased under a Normal Course Issuer Bid.

Wholly Owned Subsidiaries

Pivotree US Holdings Corp., Del.
- 100% int. in **Pivotree Solutions India Pvt. Ltd.**
- 100% int. in **Pivotree USA Inc.**, United States.

Thinkwrap Solutions Inc., Ottawa, Ont.

Financial Statistics

Periods ended:	12m Dec. 31/22^A		12m Dec. 31/21^A
	$000s	%Chg	$000s
Operating revenue	**101,693**	**+51**	**67,544**
Cost of sales	55,965		37,669
Research & devel. expense	4,203		1,919
General & admin expense	42,525		33,171
Stock-based compensation	926		1,118
Operating expense	**103,618**	**+40**	**73,876**
Operating income	**(1,924)**	**n.a.**	**(6,332)**
Deprec., depl. & amort.	8,621		5,494
Finance income	65		209
Finance costs, gross	349		422
Pre-tax income	**(10,299)**	**n.a.**	**(11,727)**
Income taxes	(1,212)		(134)
Net income	**(9,087)**	**n.a.**	**(11,593)**
Cash & equivalent	17,346		24,570
Accounts receivable	17,760		16,184
Current assets	37,800		43,340
Fixed assets, net	3,432		3,678
Right-of-use assets	1,252		1,392
Intangibles, net	41,163		45,769
Total assets	**83,753**	**-11**	**94,179**
Accts. pay. & accr. liabs.	11,489		9,064
Current liabilities	17,504		22,116
Long-term lease liabilities	775		887
Shareholders' equity	65,474		67,879
Cash from oper. activs	**(1,689)**	**n.a.**	**(8,165)**
Cash from fin. activs	(682)		(879)
Cash from invest. activs	(4,853)		(20,328)
Net cash position	**17,346**	**-29**	**24,570**
Capital expenditures	(706)		(571)
	$		$
Earnings per share*	(0.35)		(0.47)
Cash flow per share*	(0.06)		(0.33)
	shs		shs
No. of shs. o/s*	26,616,416		25,278,853
Avg. no. of shs. o/s*	26,180,606		24,900,192
	%		%
Net profit margin	(8.94)		(17.16)
Return on equity	(13.63)		(16.03)
Return on assets	(9.87)		(12.23)
Foreign sales percent	74		65

* Common
^A Reported in accordance with IFRS

Latest Results

Periods ended:	3m Mar. 31/23^A		3m Mar. 31/22^A
	$000s	%Chg	$000s
Operating revenue	25,046	+2	24,497
Net income	(1,418)	n.a.	(3,303)
	$		$
Earnings per share*	(0.05)		(0.13)

* Common
^A Reported in accordance with IFRS

Historical Summary
(as originally stated)

Fiscal Year	Oper. Rev.	Net Inc. Bef. Disc.	EPS*
	$000s	$000s	$
2022^A	101,693	(9,087)	(0.35)
2021^A	67,544	(11,593)	(0.47)
2020^A	63,596	(5,758)	(0.57)
2019^A1	59,686	(2,900)	n.a.
2018^A1	49,805	(2,076)	n.a.

* Common
^A Reported in accordance with IFRS
[1] As shown in the prospectus dated Oct. 23, 2020.

P.55 Pizza Pizza Royalty Corp.

Symbol - PZA **Exchange** - TSX **CUSIP** - 72585V
Head Office - 500 Kipling Ave, Toronto, ON, M8Z 5E5 **Telephone** - (416) 967-1010 **Fax** - (416) 967-9865
Website - www.pizzapizza.ca
Email - cdsylva@pizzapizza.ca
Investor Relations - Christine D'Sylva (416) 967-1010 ext. 393
Auditors - KPMG LLP C.A., Vaughan, Ont.
Lawyers - Torys LLP, Toronto, Ont.
Transfer Agents - TSX Trust Company, Toronto, Ont.
Profile - (Ont. 2012) Through subsidiary **Pizza Pizza Royalty Limited Partnership**, owns trademarks, trade names and other intellectual property and rights by **Pizza Pizza Limited** in its Pizza Pizza and Pizza 73 restaurants, and in its international franchising business.

Subsidiary **Pizza Pizza Royalty Limited Partnership** (PPRLP) has granted **Pizza Pizza Limited** (PPL) an exclusive 99-year licence to use the Pizza Pizza and Pizza 73 trademarks (granted in 2005 and 2007, respectively) in Canada for which PPL pays the PPRLP a royalty equal to 6% of the system sales of its Pizza Pizza restaurants in the royalty pool, and 9% of the system sales of its Pizza 73 restaurants in the royalty pool. In addition, PPL has a licence and royalty agreement with PPRLP for international franchising activities using the Pizza Pizza rights with an initial licence in Mexico, where PPL is required to pay PPRLP a fee calculated as 12.5% of the royalty received by PPL under its master franchise agreement. At Mar. 31, 2023, PPL indirectly held an effective 23.9% interest in the company through ownership of all class B and D units of the partnership.

At Mar. 31, 2023, royalties were payable to the company from 644 Pizza Pizza and 99 Pizza 73 restaurants.

Predecessor Detail - Succeeded Pizza Pizza Royalty Income Fund, Dec. 31, 2012, pursuant to plan of arrangement whereby Pizza Pizza Royalty Corp. was formed to facilitate the conversion of the fund into a corporation and the fund was dissolved.

Directors - Jay A. Swartz, chr., Toronto, Ont.; Neil Lester, Ont.; Edward P. H. (Ted) Nash, Ont.; Michelle R. Savoy, Toronto, Ont.; Kathryn A. (Kathy) Welsh, Stouffville, Ont.

Oper. Subsid./Mgt. Co. Officers - Paul Goddard, pres. & CEO; Philip Goudreau, COO; Christine D'Sylva, CFO

Capital Stock

	Authorized (shs.)	Outstanding (shs.)[1]
Preferred	5,500,000	nil
Common	unlimited	24,618,392
Class B Partnership Unit	unlimited	5,474,213
Class D Partnership Unit	unlimited	2,244,975

[1] At Mar. 31, 2023

Note: Partnership units of indirect subsidiary Pizza Pizza Royalty Limited Partnership are common equivalent securities.

Common - One vote per share.

Class B Partnership Unit - Entitled to vote and to receive monthly distributions based on the number of common shares for which class B units are exchangeable. Exchangeable into common shares on the basis of class B exchange multiplier applicable at the date of such exchange. The multiplier, adjusted on January 1 each year, is based on a defined calculation which is based in part on the franchise revenue from Pizza Pizza restaurants added to the royalty pool as well as the franchise revenue of Pizza Pizza restaurants in the royalty pool which are closed. At Jan. 1, 2023, the class B exchange multiplier was 2.118582. Pizza Pizza Limited holds all of the class B units.

Class D Partnership Unit - Entitled to vote and to receive monthly distributions based on the number of common shares for which class D units are exchangeable. Exchangeable into common shares on the basis of class D exchange multiplier applicable at the date of such exchange. The multiplier, adjusted on January 1 each year, is based on a defined calculation which is based in part on the franchise revenue from Pizza 73 restaurants added to the royalty pool as well as the franchise revenue of Pizza 73 restaurants in the royalty pool which are closed. At Jan. 1, 2023, the class D exchange multiplier was 22.44976. Pizza Pizza Limited holds all of the class D units.

Major Shareholder - Widely held at Apr. 11, 2023.

Price Range - PZA/TSX

Year	Volume	High	Low	Close
2022	11,769,950	$14.33	$11.05	$13.64
2021	13,279,323	$12.22	$9.05	$12.02
2020	19,014,383	$10.14	$5.26	$9.20
2019	14,708,931	$10.65	$8.82	$9.77
2018	13,968,896	$16.30	$8.30	$8.95

Recent Close: $14.73

Capital Stock Changes - There were no changes to capital stock during 2021 or 2022.

Dividends

PZA com Ra $0.90 pa M est. July 14, 2023
Prev. Rate: $0.87 est. Apr. 14, 2023
Prev. Rate: $0.84 est. Dec. 15, 2022
Prev. Rate: $0.81 est. Sept. 15, 2022
Prev. Rate: $0.78 est. Mar. 15, 2022
Prev. Rate: $0.72 est. Sept. 15, 2021
Prev. Rate: $0.66 est. Dec. 15, 2020

Subsidiaries

76.1% int. in **Pizza Pizza GP Inc.**, Toronto, Ont.
76.1% int. in **Pizza Pizza Royalty Limited Partnership**, Ont.

Financial Statistics

Periods ended:	12m Dec. 31/22^A		12m Dec. 31/21^A
	$000s	%Chg	$000s
Total revenue	**36,427**	**+14**	**31,919**
General & admin. expense	632		559
Operating expense	**632**	**+13**	**559**
Operating income	**35,795**	**+14**	**31,360**
Finance costs, gross	1,322		1,355
Pre-tax income	**34,555**	**+15**	**30,005**
Income taxes	7,005		6,082
Net income	**27,550**	**+15**	**23,923**
Cash & equivalent	7,936		6,157
Accounts receivable	3,646		3,184
Current assets	11,582		9,341
Long-term investments	353,716		353,716
Total assets	**367,831**	**+1**	**363,057**
Accts. pay. & accr. liabs.	1,246		1,213
Current liabilities	4,070		2,804
Long-term debt, gross	46,958		46,941
Long-term debt, net	46,958		46,941
Shareholders' equity	292,423		290,226
Cash from oper. activs	**28,989**	**+17**	**24,754**
Cash from fin. activs	(27,210)		(23,597)
Cash from invest. activs	(2,500)		(750)
Net cash position	**1,936**	**-27**	**2,657**
	$		$
Earnings per share*	0.86		0.74
Cash flow per share*	0.90		0.77
Cash divd. per share*	0.80		0.69
	shs		shs
No. of shs. o/s*	32,177,276		32,177,276
Avg. no. of shs. o/s*	32,177,276		32,177,276
	%		%
Net profit margin	75.63		74.95
Return on equity	9.46		8.27
Return on assets	7.83		6.90

* Common
^A Reported in accordance with IFRS

Latest Results

Periods ended:	3m Mar. 31/23^A		3m Mar. 31/22^A
	$000s	%Chg	$000s
Total revenue	9,135	+15	7,920
Net income	7,105	+19	5,964
	$		$
Earnings per share*	0.22		0.19

* Common
^A Reported in accordance with IFRS

Historical Summary
(as originally stated)

Fiscal Year	Total Rev.	Net Inc. Bef. Disc.	EPS*
	$000s	$000s	$
2022^A	36,427	27,550	0.86
2021^A	31,919	23,923	0.74
2020^A	31,789	24,474	0.76
2019^A	35,946	27,305	0.85
2018^A	35,408	26,886	0.85

* Common
^A Reported in accordance with IFRS

P.56 Plaintree Systems Inc.

Symbol - NPT **Exchange** - CSE **CUSIP** - 72663E
Head Office - 10 Didak Dr, Arnprior, ON, K7S 0C3 **Telephone** - (613) 623-3434 **Toll-free** - (800) 565-2743 **Fax** - (613) 623-9497
Website - www.plaintree.com
Email - lsaunders@plaintree.com
Investor Relations - Lynn E. Saunders (613) 623-3434 ext. 2223
Auditors - Welch LLP C.A., Ottawa, Ont.
Transfer Agents - Computershare Trust Company of Canada Inc.
Profile - (Can. 1991) Has proprietary technologies and manufacturing capabilities in structural design and aerospace, and manufactures vintage-inspired kitchen appliances.

Product lines are divided into two divisions: Specialty Structures and Electronics.

The **Specialty Structures** division consists of the Triodetic business, a design/build manufacturer of steel, aluminum and stainless steel specialty structures including commercial domes, free form structures, barrel vaults, space frames and industrial dome coverings; and wholly owned **Spotton Corporation**, which designs and manufactures custom hydraulic and pneumatic valves and cylinders for industrial, automation, and oil and gas markets.

The **Electronics** division consists of the Hypernetics business, which manufactures avionic components for various applications including aircraft antiskid braking, aircraft instrument indicators, solenoids and permanent magnet alternators; wholly owned **Summit Aerospace USA Inc.**, which provides machining of super-alloys for the aircraft and helicopter markets; and Elmira Stove Works business, which manufactures heritage and retro-styled kitchen appliances under the Northstar, Fireview and Heritage brands.

Operations are conducted from a 16,300-sq.-ft. facility in Pocono Summit, Pa.

In April 2022, wholly owned **Elmira Direct Limited** and **Hendrick Energy Systems Inc.** (collectively, Elmira Stove Works business) and **9366920 Canada Inc.** were amalgamated and continued under **Elmira Stove Works Inc.** In addition, operation of the Elmira Stove Works business was moved from Elmira, Ont., to the company's Arnprior, Ont., facilities.

On Mar. 30, 2022, the company acquired private Elmira, Ont.-based **Hendrick Energy Systems Inc.** and **Elmira Direct Limited** (collectively, Elmira Stove Works business) for $3,100,000 cash. Consideration consists of (i) three payments of $500,000 due on closing date, and six and 12 months thereafter; (ii) up to $500,000 of earnout payment based on Elmira Stove Works business' net sales; and (iii) the value of inventory on hand on closing date which is payable over 24 months following the closing and when the inventory is sold (estimated to be $1,100,000). The Elmira Stove Works business manufactures and sells direct to consumers and through dealers in Canada and the United States antique and retro-styled home kitchen appliances under the Northstar, Fireview and Antique brands.

Directors - Jerry S. Vickers, chr., Toronto, Ont.; W. David Watson II, pres. & CEO, Burritts Rapids, Ont.; Girvan L. Patterson, Ottawa, Ont.; Sean T. Watson, Pakenham, Ont.

Other Exec. Officers - Lynn E. Saunders, COO; Robert Turley, CFO; Gary Jessop, corp. sec.

Capital Stock

	Authorized (shs.)	Outstanding (shs.)[1]
Class A Preferred	unlimited	18,325
Common	unlimited	12,925,253

[1] At Feb. 20, 2023

Class A Preferred - Entitled to 8% cumulative dividends. Redeemable at the company's option at any time at $1,000 per share plus accrued dividends. Non-voting. At Mar. 31, 2022, accrued and unpaid dividends totaled $19,724,000.

Common - One vote per share.

Major Shareholder - Targa Group Inc. held 19.5% interest, W. David Watson II held 14.9% interest and Estate of Nora Watson held 12.2% interest at Aug. 15, 2022.

Price Range - NPT/CSE

Year	Volume	High	Low	Close
2022	376,471	$0.18	$0.08	$0.10
2021	546,988	$0.24	$0.10	$0.16
2020	382,409	$0.25	$0.06	$0.10
2019	645,911	$0.24	$0.07	$0.09
2018	1,479,563	$0.30	$0.12	$0.18

Recent Close: $0.08

Capital Stock Changes - There were no changes to capital stock from fiscal 2011 to fiscal 2022, inclusive.

Wholly Owned Subsidiaries

Elmira Stove Works Inc.
Spotton Corporation, Ont.
Summit Aerospace USA Inc., Pa.
Triodetic Inc., United States.
Triodetic Ltd.

Financial Statistics

Periods ended:	12m Mar. 31/22[A]		12m Mar. 31/21[A]
	$000s	%Chg	$000s
Operating revenue	**16,193**	**+28**	**12,660**
Cost of goods sold	11,249		8,146
Research & devel. expense	1,378		975
General & admin expense	2,034		1,413
Operating expense	**14,662**	**+39**	**10,534**
Operating income	**1,531**	**-28**	**2,126**
Deprec., depl. & amort.	1,439		1,002
Finance costs, gross	243		183
Write-downs/write-offs	(29)		nil
Pre-tax income	**(201)**	**n.a.**	**894**
Income taxes	1		50
Net income	**(202)**	**n.a.**	**844**
Cash & equivalent	1,911		2,067
Inventories	3,094		1,677
Accounts receivable	2,787		2,223
Current assets	10,143		8,016
Fixed assets, net	3,047		3,456
Right-of-use assets	2,429		nil
Intangibles, net	2,145		286
Total assets	**18,047**	**+50**	**12,048**
Bank indebtedness	50		50
Accts. pay. & accr. liabs	2,615		1,684
Current liabilities	8,101		3,202
Long-term debt, gross	3,183		1,407
Long-term debt, net	608		603
Long-term lease liabilities	1,891		538
Shareholders' equity	1,767		1,969
Cash from oper. activs	**1,289**	**-15**	**1,517**
Cash from fin. activs	(743)		(504)
Cash from invest. activs	(701)		(450)
Net cash position	**1,911**	**-8**	**2,067**
Capital expenditures	(453)		(428)
	$		$
Earnings per share*	(0.13)		(0.05)
Cash flow per share*	0.10		0.12
	shs		shs
No. of shs. o/s*	12,925,253		12,925,253
Avg. no. of shs. o/s*	12,925,253		12,925,253
	%		%
Net profit margin	(1.25)		6.67
Return on equity	(89.29)		n.m.
Return on assets	0.28		8.72
Foreign sales percent	48		55

* Common
[A] Reported in accordance with IFRS

Latest Results

Periods ended:	3m June 30/22[A]		3m June 30/21[A]
	$000s	%Chg	$000s
Operating revenue	5,447	+50	3,643
Net income	339	+29	262
	$		$
Earnings per share*	(0.00)		(0.01)

* Common
[A] Reported in accordance with IFRS

Historical Summary
(as originally stated)

Fiscal Year	Oper. Rev. $000s	Net Inc. Bef. Disc. $000s	EPS* $
2022[A]	16,193	(202)	(0.13)
2021[A]	12,660	844	(0.05)
2020[A]	17,356	(2,500)	(0.31)
2019[A]	17,003	(252)	(0.13)
2018[A]	19,006	2,005	0.04

* Common
[A] Reported in accordance with IFRS

P.57 Planet Based Foods Global Inc.

Symbol - PBF **Exchange** - CSE **CUSIP** - 72703G
Head Office - 2250-1055 Hastings St W, Vancouver, BC, V6E 2E9 **Telephone** - (805) 452-1359
Website - planetbasedfoods.com
Email - braelyn@planetbasedfoods.com
Investor Relations - Braelyn Davis (805) 452-1359
Auditors - MNP LLP C.A., Vancouver, B.C.
Transfer Agents - Computershare Trust Company of Canada Inc.
Profile - (B.C. 2017) Develops and produces plant-based meat substitutes including vegan burgers and sausage patties.

Products developed by the company include plant-based frozen burgers, breakfast sausages, burger crumbles and sausage crumbles. Online sales are expected to launch from the company's ecommerce site in February 2022. Future products are to include two new burgers, meatballs, empanadas and taquitos.

The company uses co-packers to manufacture and package its products for the wholesale market including sales to restaurants and to resellers of consumer packaged goods.

Predecessor Detail - Name changed from Digital Buyer Technologies Corp., Aug. 31, 2021, pursuant to reverse takeover acquisition of Planet Based Foods, Inc.

Directors - Braelyn Davis, pres. & CEO, Calif.; Theodore (Cash) Llewellyn, COO & interim CFO, Calif.; James Harris, v-p, bus. devel. & opers., Calif.; Scott Keeney, Los Angeles, Calif.

Other Exec. Officers - Robert Davis, chief innovation officer; Dave Wilbern, v-p, sales

Capital Stock

	Authorized (shs.)	Outstanding (shs.)[1]
Multiple Vtg.	unlimited	4,000,000
Subordinate Vtg.	unlimited	51,235,693

[1] At May 1, 2023

Multiple Voting - Convertible into subordinate voting shares on a 2-for-1 basis. Two votes per share.

Subordinate Voting - One voter per share.

Major Shareholder - Widely held at Jan. 11, 2022.

Price Range - PBF/CSE

Year	Volume	High	Low	Close
2022	12,327,433	$0.50	$0.09	$0.10

Recent Close: $0.04

Wholly Owned Subsidiaries

Planet Based Foods, Inc., San Diego, Calif.

P.58 Planet 13 Holdings Inc.

Symbol - PLTH **Exchange** - CSE **CUSIP** - 72706K
Head Office - 2548 West Desert Inn Rd, Las Vegas, NV, United States, 89109 **Telephone** - (702) 206-1313
Website - www.planet13holdings.com
Email - ir@planet13lasvegas.com
Investor Relations - Robert Groesbeck (702) 206-1313
Auditors - Davidson & Company LLP C.A., Vancouver, B.C.
Transfer Agents - Odyssey Trust Company, Vancouver, B.C.
FP500 Revenue Ranking - 728
Employees - 567 at Dec. 31, 2022
Profile - (B.C. 2019; orig. Can., 2002) Cultivates, produces, distributes and retails medical and recreational cannabis products in Nevada and California, and developing similar operations in Florida and Illinois.

Sells more than 123 different strains of cannabis (up to 35 of which are grown in-house), and owns and manufactures cannabis products under the brands HaHa (gummies and beverages), Dreamland (chocolates), TRENDI (flower, vapes and concentrates), Medizin (flower, vapes and concentrates) and Leaf & Vine (vapes).

In Nevada, operates a 16,100-sq.-ft. indoor cultivation and distribution facility in Las Vegas; a 45,000-sq.-ft. indoor cultivation and production facility in Las Vegas; a 500-sq.-ft. research and development, genetics testing and production facility in Beatty, located on 80 acres of land with potential for over 2,300,000 sq. ft. of greenhouse production; and a 2,300-sq.-ft. Medizin-branded dispensary in Las Vegas. Also operates the Planet 13 Las Vegas SuperStore, a cannabis production, retail and entertainment complex totaling 112,000 sq. ft. located adjacent to the Las Vegas strip, which includes an 18,500-sq.-ft. consumer-facing production facility, incorporating butane hash oil extraction, distillation equipment and microwave-assisted extraction equipment, a bottling and infused beverage line and an edibles line able to produce infused chocolates, infused gummies and other edible products; a 23,000-sq.-ft. dispensary; a restaurant with a liquor license; a non-cannabis retail store and event space, with plans to build out a cannabis consumption lounge; and the company's corporate office. Ten cannabis cultivation, production, distribution and dispensary licences are held in the state.

In California, operates a nursery, cultivation, processing, manufacturing and distribution campus in Coalinga, including a 35,875-sq.-ft. indoor cultivation facility and a 4,000-sq.-ft. production facility; and the Planet 13 OC SuperStore, totaling 33,000 sq. ft., in Santa Ana, including a 25,600-sq.-ft. dispensary and a 6,300-sq.-ft. distribution facility. Seven cannabis nursery, cultivation, processing, manufacturing, distribution and dispensary licences are held in the state.

In Florida, holds a Medical Marijuana Treatment Center licence; owns a 23-acre parcel of land and a 10,500-sq.-ft. building, near Ocala, intended for future cultivation operations; and has entered into leases for four proposed dispensary locations.

In Illinois, holds a conditional adultuse dispensary licence, and owns a proposed dispensary location in Waukegan, consisting of an 8,000-sq.-ft. building on 1.9 acres.

On Feb. 7, 2023, the company exercised an option to acquire the remaining 51% interest in **Planet 13 Illinois, LLC** for US$866,250 cash and issuance of 1,063,377 common shares valued at US$2,000,000. In July 2022, Planet 13 Illinois was awarded a conditional dispensary licence in the Chicago-Naperville-Elgin region.

On Feb. 3, 2023, the company completed the purchase of real property for a proposed dispensing location in Waukegan, Ill., for US$2,500,000.

In July 2022, the company acquired a 23-acre property, including a 10,500-sq.-ft. building, near Ocala, Fla., for US$3,300,000.

Recent Merger and Acquisition Activity

Status: completed **Revised:** Mar. 2, 2022
UPDATE: The transaction was completed and NGW amalgamated with Planet 13. PREVIOUS: Planet 13 Holdings Inc. agreed to acquire Next Green Wave Holdings Inc. (NGW) for 0.1081 Planet 13 common shares and Cdn$0.0001 cash for each NGW share held. The transaction was valued at Cdn$91,000,000, representing Cdn$0.465 per NGW share. NGW cultivates, processes and distributes cannabis products in

California. NGW's board of directors unanimously recommended that shareholders vote in favour of the transaction, which was expected to be completed in the first quarter of 2022. Feb. 25, 2022 - NGW's shareholders approved the transaction. The consideration was adjusted to 0.1145 Planet 13 common shares and Cdn$0.0001 cash for each NGW share held.

Predecessor Detail - Name changed from Carpincho Capital Corp., June 11, 2018, following reverse takeover acquisition of MM Development Company, Inc.

Directors - Robert Groesbeck, co-chr. & co-CEO, Henderson, Nev.; Larry Scheffler, co-chr. & co-CEO, Henderson, Nev.; Lee Fraser, Westlake Village, Calif.; Adrienne O'Neal, Las Vegas, Nev.

Other Exec. Officers - Dennis Logan, CFO; David Farris, v-p, sales & mktg.; Todd Hybels, v-p, Midwestern opers.; William (Bill) Vargas, v-p, fin.; Chris Wren, v-p, opers.; Leighton Koehler, gen. counsel & corp. sec.; Michael (Mike) Jennings, pres., East Coast opers.

Capital Stock

	Authorized (shs.)	Outstanding (shs.)[1]
Common	unlimited	222,247,854
Class A Restricted	unlimited	nil

[1] At June 30, 2023

Major Shareholder - Larry Scheffler held 17.96% interest and Robert Groesbeck held 17.66% interest at June 5, 2023.

Price Range - PLTH/CSE

Year	Volume	High	Low	Close
2022	30,613,223	$4.40	$0.83	$0.83
2021	63,768,491	$10.88	$3.70	$3.74
2020	94,447,663	$8.20	$0.99	$7.09
2019	72,932,882	$3.60	$1.44	$2.57
2018	48,697,282	$3.50	$0.66	$1.49

Recent Close: $0.69

Capital Stock Changes - On Feb. 7, 2023, 1,063,377 common shares were issued pursuant to the acquisition of the remaining 51% interest in Planet 13 Illinois, LLC.

In March 2022, 21,361,002 common shares were issued pursuant to the acquisition of Next Green Wave Holdings Inc. Also during 2022, common shares were issued as follows: 242,700 on exercise of warrants, 97,325 on exercise of options and 81,084 on vesting of restricted share units.

Wholly Owned Subsidiaries

BLC Management Company, LLC, Nev.
BLC NV Food, LLC, Nev.
- 100% int. in **By The Slice, LLC**, Nev. dba Trece Restaurant.

Club One Three, LLC, Nev. Inactive.
Crossgate Capital US Holdings Corp., Las Vegas, Nev.
- 100% int. in **Next Green Wave, LLC**, Visalia, Calif.

LBC CBD, LLC, Nev. dba Planet M.
MM Development Company, Inc., Las Vegas, Nev. dba Planet 13 and Medizin.
Newtonian Principles, Inc., Calif. dba Planet 13.
Planet 13 Chicago, LLC, Ill.
Planet 13 Florida, Inc., Fla.
Planet 13 Illinois, LLC, Ill.

Financial Statistics

Periods ended:	12m Dec. 31/22[A]		12m Dec. 31/21[A]
	US$000s	%Chg	US$000s
Operating revenue	**104,574**	**-12**	**119,493**
Cost of goods sold	53,306		51,607
Salaries & benefits	15,232		21,903
General & admin expense	30,208		28,419
Stock-based compensation	7,459		15,577
Other operating expense	2,745		2,608
Operating expense	**108,950**	**-9**	**120,114**
Operating income	**(4,376)**	**n.a.**	**(621)**
Deprec., depl. & amort.	11,631		7,213
Finance costs, net	(455)		17
Write-downs/write-offs	(32,750)		nil
Pre-tax income	**(40,228)**	**n.a.**	**(5,982)**
Income taxes	8,752		13,479
Net income	**(48,980)**	**n.a.**	**(19,461)**
Cash & equivalent	52,357		61,589
Inventories	13,005		14,225
Accounts receivable	1,327		1,216
Current assets	70,499		81,008
Fixed assets, net	71,466		50,778
Right-of-use assets	211,168		20,400
Intangibles, net	69,288		63,398
Total assets	**233,630**	**+8**	**216,809**
Accts. pay. & accr. liabs	11,185		10,299
Current liabilities	15,375		12,733
Long-term debt, gross	884		884
Long-term lease liabilities	25,833		23,134
Shareholders' equity	190,889		173,708
Cash from oper. activs	**3,802**	**n.a.**	**(380)**
Cash from fin. activs	1,142		64,538
Cash from invest. activs	(14,176)		(81,757)
Net cash position	**52,357**	**-15**	**61,589**
Capital expenditures	(16,675)		(25,910)
Capital disposals	1,050		nil
	US$		US$
Earnings per share*	(0.23)		(0.10)
Cash flow per share*	0.02		(0.00)
	shs		shs
No. of shs. o/s*	220,470,061		198,687,950
Avg. no. of shs. o/s*	216,586,621		195,126,972
	%		%
Net profit margin	(46.84)		(16.29)
Return on equity	(26.87)		(13.22)
Return on assets	(21.75)		(10.61)
Foreign sales percent	100		100
No. of employees (FTEs)	567		575

* Common
[A] Reported in accordance with U.S. GAAP

Note: Cost of Goods Sold is net of realized fair value amounts included in inventory sold and unrealized fair value gain on growth of biological assets.

Latest Results

Periods ended:	6m June 30/23[A]		6m June 30/22[A]
	US$000s	%Chg	US$000s
Operating revenue	50,748	-6	54,107
Net income	(10,654)	n.a.	(4,101)
	US$		US$
Earnings per share*	(0.05)		(0.02)

* Common
[A] Reported in accordance with U.S. GAAP

Historical Summary
(as originally stated)

Fiscal Year	Oper. Rev. US$000s	Net Inc. Bef. Disc. US$000s	EPS* US$
2022[A]	104,574	(48,980)	(0.23)
2021[A]	119,493	(19,461)	(0.10)
2020[B]	70,491	(7,942)	(0.05)
2019[B]	63,595	(6,658)	(0.05)
2018[B1]	21,167	(10,724)	(0.11)

* Common
[A] Reported in accordance with U.S. GAAP
[B] Reported in accordance with IFRS
[1] Results reflect the June 11, 2018, reverse takeover acquisition of MM Development Company, Inc.

P.59 Planet Ventures Inc.

Symbol - PXI **Exchange** - TSX-VEN **CUSIP** - 727053
Head Office - 303-750 Pender St W, Vancouver, BC, V6C 2T7
Telephone - (604) 681-0084 **Fax** - (604) 681-0094
Website - www.planetventuresinc.com
Email - info@planetventuresinc.com
Investor Relations - Christopher R. Cooper (604) 681-0084
Auditors - SHIM & Associates LLP C.A., Vancouver, B.C.
Lawyers - McMillan LLP, Vancouver, B.C.
Transfer Agents - Computershare Trust Company of Canada Inc., Vancouver, B.C.

Profile - (B.C. 2012; orig. Alta., 1996) Invests in disruptive industries primarily in eSports, eGaming and online sports betting. Also pursuing lithium interests in Quebec.

Portfolio includes **First Eleven Ltd.**, an eSports and sports media business with interests in an eSports gaming platform, talent management and an editorial platform; and **Cucu Sports Limited**, a mobile social media publishing platform featuring athletes and celebrities. Also owns Tier 1 betting licence, a U.K. gaming licence which allows live events, sports, pre-match betting, gaming software, pool betting and business-to-business (B2B) capabilities.

In August 2023, the company agreed to acquire Pow prospect, 413 claims, in Quebec for $125,000 cash and issuance of 1,000,000 common shares.

In June 2023, the company agreed to acquire Potier lithium prospect, 46,909 hecatres (consisting of separate properties known as Snap, Crackle and Pop), Leaf River South area, 200 km west-southwest of Kuujjuaq, Que., for $350,000 cash and issuance of 5,000,000 common shares.

Predecessor Detail - Name changed from Planet Mining Exploration Inc., June 28, 2017.

Directors - Desmond M. (Des) Balakrishnan, exec. dir., Vancouver, B.C.; Christopher R. (Chris) Cooper, CFO, Vancouver, B.C.; Craig Loverock, Toronto, Ont.

Other Exec. Officers - Alexander (Alex) Klenman, CEO; Cassandra Gee, corp. sec.

Capital Stock

	Authorized (shs.)	Outstanding (shs.)[1]
First Preferred	unlimited	nil
Second Preferred	unlimited	nil
Common	unlimited	110,625,674

[1] At July 29, 2023

Major Shareholder - Widely held at Nov. 10, 2022.

Price Range - PXI/TSX-VEN

Year	Volume	High	Low	Close
2022	6,858,052	$0.11	$0.03	$0.03
2021	16,370,003	$0.52	$0.09	$0.10
2020	11,228,912	$0.62	$0.10	$0.35
2019	6,995,265	$0.65	$0.23	$0.25
2018	7,554,799	$1.18	$0.28	$0.30

Consolidation: 1-for-5 cons. in Oct. 2020
Recent Close: $0.05

Capital Stock Changes - In March 2023, 55,312,836 common shares were issued at 2¢ per share pursuant to a rights offering.

In April 2021, private placement of 4,050,000 units (1 common share & 1 warrant) at $0.225 per unit was completed. Also during fiscal 2022, 75,000 common shares were issued on exercise of warrants and 70,000 common shares were repurchased under a Normal Course Issuer Bid.

Wholly Owned Subsidiaries

First Eleven Ltd., United Kingdom.
1261489 B.C. Ltd., B.C.
- 100% int. in **Cucu Sports Limited**, United Kingdom.

Planet Ventures Exploration Inc.

Financial Statistics

Periods ended:	12m Mar. 31/23^A		12m Mar. 31/22^A
	$000s	%Chg	$000s
Total revenue	**(1,679)**	**n.a.**	**(1,479)**
General & admin. expense	333		783
Stock-based compensation	nil		14
Operating expense	**333**	**-58**	**797**
Operating income	**(2,012)**	**n.a.**	**(2,276)**
Deprec. & amort.	75		74
Finance costs, gross	34		6
Pre-tax income	**(1,815)**	**n.a.**	**(1,797)**
Net income	**(1,815)**	**n.a.**	**(1,797)**
Cash & equivalent	3,717		3,848
Accounts receivable	50		56
Current assets	6,151		6,762
Long-term investments	nil		8
Right-of-use assets	295		370
Total assets	**6,475**	**-10**	**7,169**
Accts. pay. & accr. liabs	167		177
Current liabilities	408		311
Long-term lease liabilities	248		313
Shareholders' equity	5,820		6,544
Cash from oper. activs	**(1,131)**	**n.a.**	**6**
Cash from fin. activs	1,092		851
Cash from invest. activs	(92)		(88)
Net cash position	**3,717**	**-3**	**3,848**
	$		$
Earnings per share*	(0.03)		(0.03)
Cash flow per share*	(0.02)		0.00
	shs		shs
No. of shs. o/s*	110,625,674		55,312,838
Avg. no. of shs. o/s*	56,366,477		55,079,824
	%		%
Net profit margin	n.m.		n.m.
Return on equity	(29.36)		(25.64)
Return on assets	(26.11)		(23.57)

* Common
^A Reported in accordance with IFRS

Historical Summary
(as originally stated)

Fiscal Year	Total Rev.	Net Inc. Bef. Disc.	EPS*
	$000s	$000s	$
2023^A	(1,679)	(1,815)	(0.03)
2022^A	(1,479)	(1,797)	(0.03)
2021^A	(3,769)	(5,206)	(0.11)
2020^A	(1,553)	(1,946)	(0.10)
2019^A	(505)	(1,030)	(0.05)

* Common
^A Reported in accordance with IFRS
Note: Adjusted throughout for 1-for-5 cons. in Oct. 2020

P.60 Planet X Capital Corp.

Symbol - XOX.P **Exchange** - TSX-VEN **CUSIP** - 72706J
Head Office - HSBC Building, 2200-885 Georgia St W, Vancouver, BC, V6C 3E8 **Telephone** - (604) 618-4919
Email - bm@bmstrategiccapital.com
Investor Relations - Bassam Moubarak (604) 618-4919
Auditors - Crowe MacKay LLP C.A., Vancouver, B.C.
Lawyers - Cassels Brock & Blackwell LLP, Vancouver, B.C.
Transfer Agents - Odyssey Trust Company, Vancouver, B.C.
Profile - (B.C. 2021) Capital Pool Company.
Directors - Bassam Moubarak, pres., CEO, CFO & corp. sec., North Vancouver, B.C.; Paul F. Matysek, Vancouver, B.C.; Dino Minicucci, West Vancouver, B.C.

Capital Stock

	Authorized (shs.)	Outstanding (shs.)[1]
Common	unlimited	4,100,000

[1] At July 25, 2023

Major Shareholder - Paul F. Matysek held 17.07% interest, Dino Minicucci held 17.07% interest and Bassam Moubarak held 17.07% interest at June 2, 2022.

Price Range - XOX.P/TSX-VEN

Year	Volume	High	Low	Close
2022	237,000	$0.20	$0.13	$0.20

Recent Close: $0.14
Capital Stock Changes - There were no changes to capital stock during fiscal 2023.
On Feb. 10, 2022, an initial public offering of 2,000,000 common shares was completed at 10¢ per share.

P.61 Planet X II Capital Corp.

Symbol - PLXX.P **Exchange** - TSX-VEN **CUSIP** - 72706M
Head Office - HSBC Building, 2200-885 Georgia St W, Vancouver, BC, V6C 3E8 **Telephone** - (604) 618-4919
Email - bm@bmstrategiccapital.com
Investor Relations - Bassam Moubarak (604) 618-4919
Auditors - Crowe MacKay LLP C.A., Vancouver, B.C.
Lawyers - Cassels Brock & Blackwell LLP, Vancouver, B.C.
Transfer Agents - Odyssey Trust Company, Vancouver, B.C.
Profile - (B.C. 2021) Capital Pool Company.
Directors - Bassam Moubarak, pres., CEO, CFO & corp. sec., North Vancouver, B.C.; Paul F. Matysek, Vancouver, B.C.; Dino Minicucci, West Vancouver, B.C.

Capital Stock

	Authorized (shs.)	Outstanding (shs.)[1]
Common	unlimited	4,100,000

[1] At July 25, 2023

Major Shareholder - Paul F. Matysek held 17.07% interest, Dino Minicucci held 17.07% interest and Bassam Moubarak held 17.07% interest at June 2, 2022.

Price Range - PLXX.P/TSX-VEN

Year	Volume	High	Low	Close
2022	227,000	$0.20	$0.13	$0.15

Recent Close: $0.15
Capital Stock Changes - There were no changes to capital stock during fiscal 2023.
On Feb. 10, 2022, an initial public offering of 2,000,000 common shares was completed at 10¢ per share.

P.62 Plank Ventures Ltd.

Symbol - PLNK **Exchange** - CSE **CUSIP** - 72706P
Head Office - 401-750 Pender St W, Vancouver, BC, V6C 2T7 **Telephone** - (604) 428-7050 **Fax** - (604) 428-7052
Website - plank.ventures
Email - laurie@plank.ventures
Investor Relations - Laurie Baggio (604) 805-7498
Auditors - Dale Matheson Carr-Hilton LaBonte LLP C.A., Vancouver, B.C.
Transfer Agents - Odyssey Trust Company, Vancouver, B.C.
Profile - (B.C. 2013) Invests and acquires Internet software companies, with a focus on business-to-business software-as-a-service (SaaS) verticals.
At Oct. 31, 2022, the fair value of the investment portfolio totaled $3,616,531 which included investments in **Exahash Cryptomining Corp.**, **Votigo, Inc.**, **ThinkCX Technologies Inc.**, **SiteMax Systems Inc.**, **500 Startups Canada, L.P.**, **Sockeye Technologies Inc.**, **Shop and Shout Ltd.**, **CodeZero Technologies Inc.**, **East Side Games Group Inc.** and **Karve IT Ltd.**
In April 2022, affiliate **Votigo Inc.** acquired **Promotion Activators Management, LLC** which administers sweepstakes, games and contests, for US$1,650,000.
Predecessor Detail - Name changed from 0968998 B.C. Ltd., Oct. 26, 2018.
Directors - Laurie Baggio, pres. & CEO, Victoria, B.C.; Bradley Carlyle, North Vancouver, B.C.; Brian T. O'Neill, Port Coquitlam, B.C.
Other Exec. Officers - Carla Matheson, CFO & corp. sec.

Capital Stock

	Authorized (shs.)	Outstanding (shs.)[1]
Preferred	unlimited	nil
Common	unlimited	17,740,019

[1] At Dec. 29, 2022

Major Shareholder - Code Consulting Limited held 74.61% interest at Nov. 29, 2022.

Price Range - PLNK/CSE

Year	Volume	High	Low	Close
2022	105,428	$0.30	$0.09	$0.10
2021	276,809	$0.60	$0.15	$0.24

Recent Close: $0.03
Capital Stock Changes - There were no changes to capital stock during fiscal 2022.

Wholly Owned Subsidiaries

Exahash Cryptomining Corp., Vancouver, B.C.

Investments

34.44% int. in **Karve IT Ltd.**
40.62% int. in **Votigo, Inc.**, Boulder, Colo.
- 100% int. in **Laughton Marketing Communications, Inc.**, Rochester, N.Y. dba US Sweepstakes and Fulfillment Company.

Financial Statistics

Periods ended:	12m July 31/22^A		12m July 31/21^oA
	$000s	%Chg	$000s
Operating revenue	**4,197**	**+49**	**2,812**
Cost of sales	475		629
Salaries & benefits	2,357		1,982
General & admin expense	1,449		1,038
Stock-based compensation	51		11
Other operating expense	nil		1
Operating expense	**4,332**	**+18**	**3,661**
Operating income	**(135)**	**n.a.**	**(849)**
Deprec., depl. & amort.	291		236
Finance income	25		25
Finance costs, gross	639		487
Write-downs/write-offs	nil		(433)
Pre-tax income	**(1,764)**	**n.a.**	**(932)**
Income taxes	(298)		45
Net income	**(1,466)**	**n.a.**	**(977)**
Net inc. for equity hldrs	**(1,470)**	**n.a.**	**(831)**
Net inc. for non-cont. int	**4**	**n.a.**	**(146)**
Cash & equivalent	2,668		4,119
Accounts receivable	1,140		962
Current assets	4,002		5,297
Long-term investments	3,617		3,482
Fixed assets, net	2		2
Right-of-use assets	8		26
Intangibles, net	4,240		2,314
Total assets	**11,868**	**+7**	**11,121**
Accts. pay. & accr. liabs	3,039		1,862
Current liabilities	3,909		2,541
Long-term debt, gross	3,883		3,059
Long-term debt, net	3,874		3,047
Long-term lease liabilities	nil		7
Shareholders' equity	2,365		3,711
Non-controlling interest	1,321		1,348
Cash from oper. activs	**254**	**n.a.**	**(1,122)**
Cash from fin. activs	(335)		3,733
Cash from invest. activs	(2,038)		391
Net cash position	**1,495**	**-59**	**3,614**
	$		$
Earnings per share*	(0.08)		(0.12)
Cash flow per share*	0.01		(0.12)
	shs		shs
No. of shs. o/s*	17,740,019		17,740,019
Avg. no. of shs. o/s*	17,740,019		9,584,971
	%		%
Net profit margin	(34.93)		(34.74)
Return on equity	(48.39)		n.m.
Return on assets	(8.13)		(5.21)
Foreign sales percent	100		100

* Common
^o Restated
^A Reported in accordance with IFRS

Latest Results

Periods ended:	3m Oct. 31/22^A		3m Oct. 31/21^A
	$000s	%Chg	$000s
Operating revenue	1,476	+58	933
Net income	(87)	n.a.	(195)
Net inc. for equity hldrs	(309)	n.a.	(261)
Net inc. for non-cont. int	222		66
	$		$
Earnings per share*	(0.01)		(0.02)

* Common
^A Reported in accordance with IFRS

Historical Summary
(as originally stated)

Fiscal Year	Oper. Rev.	Net Inc. Bef. Disc.	EPS*
	$000s	$000s	$
2022^A	4,197	(1,466)	(0.08)
2021^A	2,812	(977)	(0.12)
2020^A1	1,140	51	0.03
2019^A1	6	(74)	(0.02)

* Common
^A Reported in accordance with IFRS
[1] Results adjusted to reflect 1-for-6 share consolidation effective Feb. 3, 2021.

P.63 Plant Veda Foods Ltd.

Symbol - MILK **Exchange** - CSE **CUSIP** - 727351
Head Office - Unit 313, 14640 64 Ave, Vancouver, BC, V3S 1X7 **Telephone** - (604) 200-3335
Website - www.plantveda.com
Email - sunny@plantveda.com
Investor Relations - Sunny Gurnani (604) 781-0385
Auditors - Dale Matheson Carr-Hilton LaBonte LLP C.A., Vancouver, B.C.

Transfer Agents - Endeavor Trust Corporation, Vancouver, B.C.
Profile - (B.C. 2019) Manufactures and produces plant-based dairy alternatives.

The company uses plant-based technology to create low processed, all natural, nutritional products and a blend of raw, heart-healthy cashews, fibre-rich gluten-free oats, and pea protein, cultured with billions of live probiotics good for the gut. Also offers maple sweetened and unsweetened options, along with antioxidant-rich blueberries and strawberries, and select healing and comforting herbs and spices from the traditional ayurvedic kitchen.

Products include coffee cream, probiotic lassi, cashew milk and yogurt. Products are sold in more than 100 premium retail grocery stores in British Columbia, online via its website and through a subscription service.

Products are manufactured from a 15,831-sq.-ft. warehouse and production facility, with 9,325 sq. ft. of office space.

In January 2023, the company acquired B.C.-based **Nora's Non-Dairy Ltd.**, a plant-based ice cream company, for issuance of 1,530,613 common shares at a deemed price of $0.196 per share.

Directors - Michael Yang, pres., Vancouver, B.C.; Geoffrey (Geoff) Balderson, CFO & corp. sec., Vancouver, B.C.; Mayur Sajnani, chief revenue officer, Surrey, B.C.; Claire Smith, Switzerland; Aaron Wong, Vancouver, B.C.

Other Exec. Officers - Sunny Gurnani, CEO; Greg Smith, v-p, global sales

Capital Stock

	Authorized (shs.)	Outstanding (shs.)[1]
Common	unlimited	33,286,427

[1] At May 30, 2023

Major Shareholder - Sunny Gurnani held 31.42% interest and Vanita Gurnani held 31.42% interest at Aug. 11, 2021.

Price Range - MILK/CSE

Year	Volume	High	Low	Close
2022	1,767,606	$1.43	$0.13	$0.16
2021	6,084,952	$1.88	$1.01	$1.14

Recent Close: $0.06

Capital Stock Changes - During 2022, common shares were issued as follows: 1,683,786 on exercise of warrants, 1,530,613 pursuant to the acquisition of Nora's Non-Dairy Ltd., 432,692 by private placement, 100,000 for financing fees and 20,000 on exercise of options.

Wholly Owned Subsidiaries

Nora's Non-Dairy Ltd., B.C.

Financial Statistics

Periods ended:	12m Dec. 31/22[A]		12m Dec. 31/21[A]
	$000s	%Chg	$000s
Operating revenue	**309**	**+36**	**227**
Cost of sales	337		211
Salaries & benefits	875		435
Research & devel. expense	57		nil
General & admin expense	1,396		3,599
Stock-based compensation	1,497		1,686
Operating expense	**4,162**	**-30**	**5,931**
Operating income	**(3,853)**	**n.a.**	**(5,705)**
Finance costs, gross	358		197
Write-downs/write-offs	(3)		nil
Pre-tax income	**(3,993)**	**n.a.**	**(6,000)**
Income taxes	(23)		nil
Net income	**(3,970)**	**n.a.**	**(6,000)**
Cash & equivalent	74		857
Inventories	111		62
Accounts receivable	136		109
Current assets	460		1,280
Fixed assets, net	1,181		1,166
Right-of-use assets	1,738		1,947
Total assets	**3,378**	**-23**	**4,392**
Accts. pay. & accr. liabs	677		446
Current liabilities	922		590
Long-term debt, gross	962		30
Long-term debt, net	892		30
Long-term lease liabilities	1,765		1,910
Shareholders' equity	(201)		1,861
Cash from oper. activs	**(1,723)**	**n.a.**	**(3,839)**
Cash from fin. activs	1,127		6,124
Cash from invest. activs	(187)		(1,473)
Net cash position	**74**	**-91**	**857**
Capital expenditures	(187)		(1,223)
	$		$
Earnings per share*	(0.13)		(0.31)
Cash flow per share*	(0.05)		(0.20)
	shs		shs
No. of shs. o/s*	33,286,427		29,519,336
Avg. no. of shs. o/s*	31,561,515		19,117,109
	%		%
Net profit margin	n.m.		n.m.
Return on equity	n.m.		(629.26)
Return on assets	(93.03)		(258.26)

* Common
[A] Reported in accordance with IFRS

Latest Results

Periods ended:	3m Mar. 31/23[A]		3m Mar. 31/22[A]
	$000s	%Chg	$000s
Operating revenue	215	+412	42
Net income	(409)	n.a.	(2,204)
	$		$
Earnings per share*	(0.01)		(0.07)

* Common
[A] Reported in accordance with IFRS

Historical Summary
(as originally stated)

Fiscal Year	Oper. Rev.	Net Inc. Bef. Disc.	EPS*
	$000s	$000s	$
2022[A]	309	(3,970)	(0.13)
2021[A]	227	(6,000)	(0.31)
2020[A]	118	(112)	(0.01)
2019[A1]	37	(93)	(0.01)

* Common
[A] Reported in accordance with IFRS
[1] 39 weeks ended Dec. 31, 2019.

P.64 PlantFuel Life Inc.

Symbol - FUEL **Exchange** - CSE **CUSIP** - 72748Q
Head Office - Unit 202, 2500 Meadowpine Blvd, Mississauga, ON, L5N 6C4 **Telephone** - (416) 669-9392 **Toll-free** - (877) 312-8900
Website - plantfuel.com
Email - ir@plantfuel.com
Investor Relations - Connor Yuen (888) 630-6938
Auditors - RSM Canada LLP C.A., Toronto, Ont.
Transfer Agents - Computershare Trust Company of Canada Inc., Toronto, Ont.
Profile - (B.C. 2014) Manufactures and distributes supplements, and nutritional and plant-based protein products. Also produces and sells branded bee pollen.

Products include All-in-One Nutrition, a 20 g plant-based protein on the go that has 29 fruits and vegetables, as well as Wellmune® beta-glucan targeted to improve immune system health; Performance Protein, a 20 g plant-based protein with added vegan-fermented Branched-Chain Amino Acids (BCAAs) as InstAminos® and Peak02® performance mushrooms; All-in-One Pre-Workout, which features patented 3D Pump Breakthrough™ with vegan-fermented citrulline, glycerol and Amla fruit extract designed to support exercise performance, recovery and nitric oxide, as well as 250 mg of Purcaf® Organic Caffeine and 85 mg of Dynamine® aimed to increase perceived energy and alertness; All-in-One Recovery, which provides vegan fermented BCAAs as InstAminos® with essential amino acids as vegan Amino9® plus vegan fermented Creatine and BetaPrime® to reduce soreness and recovery time and optimize muscle protein synthesis; and Daily Immunity + Hydration, which has ingredients aimed to strengthen the immune system and Aquamin™ calcified sea algae intended to provide superior hydration benefits; and Athlete's Superfood, which delivers the essential phytonutrient equivalents of three servings of fruits and vegetables, bioavailable magnesium, plus a revolutionary blend of probiotics and prebiotic fiber along with performance mushrooms and clinically proven, plant-based nutrients; Performance Pre-Workout, has ingredients clinically proven to increase energy and focus, reduce fatigue, lactic acid buildup, improve blood flow, nitric oxide, muscular endurance and ultimately to increase total training volume; and Clean Mass Gainer, a vegan mass gainer utilizing ingredients and macronutrients including low-glycemic carbohydrates formulated to support increased strength, size, recovery and athletic performance.

Products are marketed under the PlantFuel brand across North America, the United Kingdom, the Middle East and East Asia through various distributors and online channels.

Through wholly owned **BeeImmune Distribution Inc.**, produces and sells branded bee pollen.

On Apr. 11, 2023, the company acquired private British Columbia-based **1402105 B.C. Ltd.** (dba BeeImmune), which produces and sells branded bee pollen, on the basis of 1.045 common shares for each BeeImmune share held. Following completion, existing company shareholders and former BeeImmune shareholders held 55.2% and 44.8% of the common shares of the company, respectively. BeeImmune amalgamated with wholly owned **1406733 B.C. Ltd.** to form **BeeImmune Distribution Inc.**

Predecessor Detail - Name changed from Sire Bioscience Inc., Apr. 30, 2021.

Directors - Connor Yuen, CEO, Vancouver, B.C.; Andy Wu, CFO & corp. sec.; Cassidy McCord, Vancouver, B.C.; Alson Niu

Other Exec. Officers - Maria Dane, pres.; Dr. Anthony Galea, CMO; Derek West, v-p, sales

Capital Stock

	Authorized (shs.)	Outstanding (shs.)[1]
Preferred	unlimited	nil
Common	unlimited	9,629,910

[1] At June 7, 2023

Major Shareholder - Widely held at June 3, 2022.

Price Range - FUEL/CSE

Year	Volume	High	Low	Close
2022	1,677,899	$11.60	$0.70	$0.90
2021	1,991,848	$33.00	$3.30	$11.90
2020	117,749	$18.00	$3.00	$3.90
2019	75,781	$60.00	$12.00	$15.00
2018	61,271	$168.00	$15.00	$24.00

Consolidation: 1-for-10 cons. in June 2023; 1-for-6 cons. in Dec. 2021; 1-for-10 cons. in Oct. 2020

Recent Close: $0.07

Capital Stock Changes - From October to December 2022, private placement of 11,527,500 units (1 common share & ½ warrant) at 8¢ per unit was completed, with warrants exercisable at 20¢ per share for three years. On June 7, 2023, common shares were consolidated on a 1-for-6 basis.

In November 2021, private placement of 768,976 units (1 post-consolidated common share & ½ warrant) at $1.56 per unit was completed. On Dec. 23, 2021, common shares were consolidated on a 1-for-6 basis. In March 2022, private placement of 6,751,000 units (1 post-consolidated common share & ½ warrant) at 50¢ per unit was completed. Also during fiscal 2022, post-consolidated common shares were issued as follows: 500,000 for loan and 156,749 for services.

Wholly Owned Subsidiaries

BCP Holdings and Investments Inc.
BeeImmune Distribution Inc., B.C.
Best Cannabis Products Inc., Toronto, Ont.
Big Rock Technologies Inc., B.C.
Fusion Nutrition Incorporated, Guelph, Ont.
PlantFuel, Inc., Denver, Colo.

Financial Statistics

Periods ended:	12m Sept. 30/22[A]		12m Sept. 30/21[A]
	$000s	%Chg	$000s
Operating revenue	**907**	**-14**	**1,053**
Cost of goods sold	917		1,029
Salaries & benefits	1,465		815
Research & devel. expense	1,626		454
General & admin expense	6,421		3,314
Stock-based compensation	672		3,799
Operating expense	**11,102**	**+18**	**9,411**
Operating income	**(10,195)**	**n.a.**	**(8,358)**
Deprec., depl. & amort.	6,305		3,330
Finance income	nil		17
Finance costs, gross	217		314
Write-downs/write-offs	(21,187)[1]		(606)
Pre-tax income	**(37,935)**	**n.a.**	**(13,485)**
Income taxes	nil		(90)
Net income	**(37,935)**	**n.a.**	**(13,395)**
Cash & equivalent	5		297
Inventories	1,539		1,564
Accounts receivable	18		49
Current assets	2,199		3,935
Fixed assets, net	10		20
Right-of-use assets	1,938		31
Intangibles, net	nil		27,247
Total assets	**4,147**	**-87**	**31,233**
Accts. pay. & accr. liabs	2,773		1,288
Current liabilities	5,166		1,314
Long-term lease liabilities	1,972		3
Shareholders' equity	(2,991)		29,677
Cash from oper. activs	**(4,861)**	**n.a.**	**(7,212)**
Cash from fin. activs	4,570		7,431
Net cash position	**5**	**-98**	**297**
	$		$
Earnings per share*	(11.40)		(7.08)
Cash flow per share*	(1.46)		(3.82)
	shs		shs
No. of shs. o/s*	3,682,825		2,865,147
Avg. no. of shs. o/s*	3,339,913		1,890,975
	%		%
Net profit margin	n.m.		n.m.
Return on equity	n.m.		(88.09)
Return on assets	(213.22)		(68.11)
Foreign sales percent	100		4

* Common
[A] Reported in accordance with IFRS
[1] Represents impairment of intangible assets relating to wholly owned PlantFuel Inc.

Latest Results

Periods ended:	6m Mar. 31/23[A]		6m Mar. 31/22[A]
	$000s	%Chg	$000s
Operating revenue	47	-86	339
Net income	(1,091)	n.a.	(9,738)
	$		$
Earnings per share*	(0.20)		(3.20)

* Common
[A] Reported in accordance with IFRS

Historical Summary
(as originally stated)

Fiscal Year	Oper. Rev. $000s	Net Inc. Bef. Disc. $000s	EPS* $
2022[A]	907	(37,935)	(11.40)
2021[A]	1,053	(13,395)	(7.08)
2020[A]	492	(2,074)	(3.00)
2019[A1]	nil	(6,396)	(24.00)
2019[A2]	125	(1,884)	(12.00)

* Common
[A] Reported in accordance with IFRS
[1] Results reflect the Aug. 28, 2019, reverse takeover acquisition of Best Cannabis Products Inc.
[2] Results for fiscal 2019 and prior fiscal years pertain to Blox Labs Inc.
Note: Adjusted throughout for 1-for-10 cons. in June 2023; 1-for-6 cons. in Dec. 2021; 1-for-10 cons. in Oct. 2020

P.65 Plantify Foods, Inc.

Symbol - PTFY **Exchange** - TSX-VEN **CUSIP** - 72749H
Head Office - 2264 11 Ave E, Vancouver, BC, V5N 1Z6 **Telephone** - (604) 833-6820
Website - plantifyfoods.com
Email - gabi@plantifyfoods.com
Investor Relations - Gabriel Kabazo (604) 833-6820
Auditors - BDO Ziv Haft C.P.A., Tel Aviv, Israel
Lawyers - Stikeman Elliott LLP, Vancouver, B.C.
Transfer Agents - Computershare Trust Company of Canada Inc., Vancouver, B.C.
Profile - (B.C. 2018) Develops, produces and sells clean-label plant-based products including meat alternatives, dips and snacks.
Product line consists of plant-based burger patties and plant-based crispy veggie balls, with additional products being developed including alternative meat products with beef, chicken or fish textures, a clean-label cracker, and dips and spreads. Products are sold in Israel, Europe and the United States.
Has production facilities in Israel, which currently have a capacity of 176,000 kg per month. The company intends to build a North American production facility by 2024.

Recent Merger and Acquisition Activity

Status: completed **Revised:** July 29, 2022
UPDATE: The transaction was completed. Antalis issued a total of 132,065,783 common shares. PREVIOUS: Antalis Ventures Corp. entered into a letter of intent for the Qualifying Transaction reverse takeover acquisition of private Israel-based Peas of Bean Ltd. (POB), which develops and produces clean-label plant-based products including meat alternatives, dips and snacks, for issuance of 95,000,000 common shares. POB's products were sold in Israel and the U.S. Aug. 11, 2021 - A definitive agreement was entered into. Upon completion, POB would amalgamate with Antalis's wholly owned 1372632 B.C. Ltd., and Antalis would change its name to Plantify Foods, Inc.
Predecessor Detail - Name changed from Antalis Ventures Corp., July 28, 2022, pursuant to the Qualifying Transaction reverse takeover acquisition of private Israel-based Peas of Bean Ltd. (POB) and concurrent amalgamation of POB with wholly owned 1372632 B.C. Ltd.
Directors - Dr. Roy Borochov, pres. & CEO, Israel; Noam Ftecha, CEO, Peas of Bean Ltd., Israel; Israel Berenstein; Moshe Revach, Ramat Gan, Israel; L. Rowland Wallenius, White Rock, B.C.
Other Exec. Officers - Gabriel (Gabi) Kabazo, CFO & corp. sec.; Stanislav Levin, v-p, product devel.

Capital Stock

	Authorized (shs.)	Outstanding (shs.)[1]
Common	unlimited	183,560,000

[1] At June 1, 2023
Major Shareholder - Noam Ftecha held 15.37% interest, Yair Ginat held 15.37% interest, Stanislav Levin held 15.37% interest and Hama Fund, Limited Partnership held 11.62% interest at Aug. 4, 2022.

Price Range - PTFY/TSX-VEN

Year	Volume	High	Low	Close
2022	1,914,136	$0.18	$0.03	$0.04
2021	10,000	$0.10	$0.10	$0.10
2020	223,500	$0.14	$0.10	$0.10
2019	10,000	$0.11	$0.11	$0.11

Recent Close: $0.03
Capital Stock Changes - On July 29, 2022, 132,065,783 common shares were issued pursuant to the Qualifying Transaction reverse takeover acquisition of Peas of Bean Ltd. and 8,810,581 common shares were issued as finder's fee and corporate finance shares. Also during 2022, 1,341,280 common shares were issued for services.

Wholly Owned Subsidiaries

Peas of Bean Ltd., Israel.

Financial Statistics

Periods ended:	12m Dec. 31/22[A1]		12m Dec. 31/21[A]
	US$000s	%Chg	US$000s
Operating revenue	**374**	**-21**	**472**
Cost of sales	477		452
Salaries & benefits	654		477
Research & devel. expense	nil		13
General & admin expense	640		657
Operating expense	**1,771**	**+11**	**1,599**
Operating income	**(1,397)**	**n.a.**	**(1,127)**
Deprec., depl. & amort.	100		44
Finance income	nil		107
Finance costs, gross	543		30
Pre-tax income	**(4,670)**	**n.a.**	**(1,094)**
Net income	**(4,670)**	**n.a.**	**(1,094)**
Cash & equivalent	59		114
Inventories	88		48
Accounts receivable	176		277
Current assets	338		455
Fixed assets, net	1,523		312
Total assets	**1,893**	**+136**	**803**
Bank indebtedness	207		257
Accts. pay. & accr. liabs.	nil		511
Current liabilities	2,010		1,036
Long-term debt, gross	773		437
Long-term debt, net	178		287
Long-term lease liabilities	570		nil
Shareholders' equity	(865)		(520)
Cash from oper. activs.	**(2,227)**	**n.a.**	**(922)**
Cash from fin. activs.	2,942		1,076
Cash from invest. activs.	(844)		(172)
Net cash position	**59**	**-48**	**114**
Capital expenditures	(849)		(177)
Capital disposals	nil		5
	US$		US$
Earnings per share*	(0.04)		(0.16)
Cash flow per share*	(0.02)		(0.14)
	shs		shs
No. of shs. o/s*	147,317,644		n.a.
Avg. no. of shs. o/s*	120,557,361		6,691,712
	%		%
Net profit margin	n.m.		(231.78)
Return on equity	n.m.		n.m.
Return on assets	(306.16)		(163.32)
Foreign sales percent	100		100

* Common
[A] Reported in accordance with IFRS
[1] Results prior to July 29, 2022, pertain to and reflect the Qualifying Transaction reverse takeover acquisition of Peas of Bean Ltd.

Historical Summary
(as originally stated)

Fiscal Year	Oper. Rev. US$000s	Net Inc. Bef. Disc. US$000s	EPS* US$
2022[A]	374	(4,670)	(0.04)
2021[A]	472	(1,094)	(0.16)
2020[A]	356	(359)	(0.07)

* Common
[A] Reported in accordance with IFRS

P.66 The Planting Hope Company Inc.

Symbol - MYLK **Exchange** - TSX-VEN **CUSIP** - 72749F
Head Office - 4710 N. Sheridan Rd, Chicago, IL, United States, 60640 **Telephone** - (773) 492-2243
Website - plantinghopecompany.com
Email - julia@plantinghopecompany.com
Investor Relations - Julia Stamberger (773) 492-2243
Auditors - MNP LLP C.A., Calgary, Alta.
Lawyers - Miller Thomson LLP, Vancouver, B.C.
Transfer Agents - Endeavor Trust Corporation, Vancouver, B.C.
Profile - (B.C. 2020) Develops, produces, markets and distributes plant-based consumer packaged food and beverage products.
Product brands consist of: Hope & Sesame® (sesame-based plant milk); Veggicopia® (single serving dip cups and snack olives); Mozaics™ (real veggie chips); and RightRice® (rice and risotto made with vegetables).
Products are sold in retail supermarkets and natural foods stores in the U.S., Canada and globally; via e-commerce platforms including Amazon.com and Well.ca; and by foodservice operators and related distributor partners such as airlines and restaurant and coffee chains.
Directors - Julia Stamberger, chr. & CEO, Ill.; Saundra Linn†, Ind.; Shelley Diamond, N.Y.; Amanda Helming, Vt.; Kay Wong-Alafriz, B.C.
Other Exec. Officers - Susan Walters-Flood, COO; Kohmela Grier, CFO; Mara Ebert, chief sales officer; James Curley, exec. v-p, sales; Jeannie Andolena, sr. v-p, e-comm. & mktg.; Becky Harrison, v-p, food service; Kendra Low, corp. sec.
† Lead director

Capital Stock

	Authorized (shs.)	Outstanding (shs.)[1]
Subordinate Voting	unlimited	73,175,277
Multiple Voting	unlimited	406,428

[1] At May 23, 2023
Subordinate Voting - One vote per share.
Multiple Voting - Each convertible into 100 subordinate voting shares. 100 votes per share.
Major Shareholder - Widely held at May 23, 2023.

Price Range - MYLK/TSX-VEN

Year	Volume	High	Low	Close
2022	16,165,488	$1.23	$0.39	$0.50
2021	4,548,318	$1.15	$0.63	$1.06

Recent Close: $0.34
Capital Stock Changes - In March 2022, public offering of 10,062,500 subordinate voting shares was completed at Cdn$0.80 per share, including 1,312,500 shares on exercise of over-allotment option. In November 2022, 17,303,571 subordinate voting shares were issued on conversion of Cdn$4,825,000 of convertible notes. In December 2022, private placement of 2,000,272 units (1 common share & 1 warrant) at Cdn$0.50 per unit was completed. Also during 2022, 301,680 subordinate voting shares were issued on exercise of warrants.

Wholly Owned Subsidiaries

Planting Hope Brands, LLC, Chicago, Ill.

Financial Statistics

Periods ended:	12m Dec. 31/22[A]		12m Dec. 31/21[oA1]
	US$000s	%Chg	US$000s
Operating revenue	**8,981**	**+287**	**2,321**
Cost of goods sold	6,716		1,257
Salaries & benefits	3,401		1,775
General & admin expense	8,842		4,981
Stock-based compensation	730		2,611
Operating expense	**19,689**	**+85**	**10,624**
Operating income	**(10,708)**	**n.a.**	**(8,303)**
Deprec., depl. & amort.	684		32
Finance costs, gross	1,520		555
Pre-tax income	**(7,806)**	**n.a.**	**(17,600)**
Net income	**(7,806)**	**n.a.**	**(17,600)**
Cash & equivalent	237		5,811
Inventories	2,604		697
Accounts receivable	1,004		111
Current assets	4,074		6,970
Fixed assets, net	102		57
Right-of-use assets	448		565
Intangibles, net	5,217		nil
Total assets	**9,841**	**+30**	**7,592**
Bank indebtedness	2,900		nil
Accts. pay. & accr. liabs.	4,100		1,300
Current liabilities	7,257		11,382
Long-term debt, gross	718		2,864
Long-term debt, net	53		19
Long-term lease liabilities	372		478
Equity portion of conv. debs.	924		nil
Shareholders' equity	1,639		(4,287)
Cash from oper. activs.	**(8,511)**	**n.a.**	**(6,511)**
Cash from fin. activs.	(7,083)		11,151
Cash from invest. activs.	(4,076)		829
Net cash position	**237**	**-96**	**5,811**
Capital expenditures	(76)		(58)
	US$		US$
Earnings per share*	(0.08)		(0.89)
Cash flow per share*	(0.09)		(0.33)
	shs		shs
No. of shs. o/s*	111,968,971		82,300,948
Avg. no. of shs. o/s*	92,819,101		19,702,659
	%		%
Net profit margin	(86.92)		(758.29)
Return on equity	n.m.		n.m.
Return on assets	(72.12)		(416.04)
Foreign sales percent	98		99

* Subord. Vtg.
[o] Restated
[A] Reported in accordance with IFRS
[1] Results reflect the Aug. 25, 2021, reverse takeover acquisition of Planting Hope Brands, LLC.

Latest Results

Periods ended:	3m Mar. 31/23[A]		3m Mar. 31/22[A]
	US$000s	%Chg	US$000s
Operating revenue	3,237	+62	2,001
Net income	(2,457)	n.a.	(722)
	US$		US$
Earnings per share*	(0.02)		(0.01)

* Subord. Vtg.
[A] Reported in accordance with IFRS

Historical Summary
(as originally stated)

Fiscal Year	Oper. Rev.	Net Inc. Bef. Disc.	EPS*
	US$000s	US$000s	US$
2022[A]	8,981	(7,806)	(0.08)
2021[A]	2,321	(17,600)	(0.89)
2020[A1]	985	(2,530)	n.a.

* Subord. Vtg.
[A] Reported in accordance with IFRS
[1] Results pertain to Planting Hope Brands, LLC.

P.67 PlasCred Circular Innovations Inc.

Symbol - PLAS **Exchange** - CSE **CUSIP** - 727941
Head Office - 810-789 Pender St W, Vancouver, BC, V6C 1H2 **Telephone** - (604) 669-4771 **Fax** - (604) 669-4731
Website - plascred.com
Email - troy@plascred.com
Investor Relations - Troy Lupul (587) 430-3004
Auditors - Dale Matheson Carr-Hilton LaBonte LLP C.A., Vancouver, B.C.
Lawyers - Boughton Law Corporation, Vancouver, B.C.
Transfer Agents - Computershare Trust Company of Canada Inc., Vancouver, B.C.
Profile - (B.C. 2007) Has developed a patent-pending and proprietary upcycling process for transforming up to 80% of unsorted, unwashed waste plastic into condensate.

The company's Zero Sulphur Green Condensate™ can be mixed with heavy, sour crude oil to produce a marketable, lighter crude oil that can be easily shipped by pipeline to distant markets. Other potential commercial end products are carbon black and aromatics, which includes including hydrogen, propane and butane. Has a pilot facility in Calgary, Alta., for conducting beta testing of the process, which was brought online and commissioned in May 2023.

Has a partnership with **Canadian National Railway Company** for logistics and transportation of plastic waste to PlasCred upcycling plant locations and a partnership with **FibreCo Export Inc.** for investigating utilizing existing port location for importing plastic waste feedstock. The company aims to set up PlasCred plant sites in major cities including Sarnia, Ont., Houston, Tex., Chicago, Ill., Los Angeles, Calif., and Cushing, Okla.

Recent Merger and Acquisition Activity

Status: completed **Revised:** Aug. 3, 2023
UPDATE: The transaction was completed. PREVIOUS: Cover Technologies Inc. (COVE) entered into a letter of intent in which COVE would take assignment of an agreement between 1346487 B.C. Ltd. and PlasCred Inc., a private Alberta-based green technology company. COVE would issue 12,500,000 units (1 common share & 1 warrant) to 1346487 B.C. at 10¢ per share for the assignment, with warrants exercisable at 25¢ per share for two years. The assignment would allow COVE to acquire PlasCred, with consideration consisting of the issuance of 35,000,000 common shares at a deemed price of 10¢ per share. PlasCred has a patent-pending and proprietary process that enables true plastic waste removal to deliver a commercially viable plastic recycling process. The transaction would represent a fundamental change of business. Nov. 15, 2022 - COVE entered into a definitive agreement whereby it would issue 12,000,000 units to 1346487 for the assignment and 35,000,000 common shares at $0.10 per share to acquire PlasCred. Prior to closing, COVE would consolidate its common shares on a 1-for-2 basis. COVE would also complete a private placement for up to 13,333,333 post-consolidated common shares at a deemed price of $0.30 per share. Mar. 23, 2023 - COVE shareholders approved the transaction.
Predecessor Detail - Name changed from Cover Technologies Inc., Aug. 3, 2023, pursuant to reverse takeover acquisition of PlasCred Inc.; basis 1 new for 2 old shs.
Directors - Troy Lupul, pres. & CEO, Calgary, Alta.; James B. Cairns, Calgary, Alta.; Gerald N. (Gerry) Gilewicz, Calgary, Alta.
Other Exec. Officers - Brian Hearst, CFO & corp. sec.; Dr. Wayne Monnery, chief tech. officer

Capital Stock

	Authorized (shs.)	Outstanding (shs.)[1]
Class B Preferred	unlimited	nil
Common	unlimited	61,996,566

[1] At Aug. 8, 2023

Major Shareholder - Troy Lupul held 44.51% interest at Aug. 8, 2023.

Price Range - PLAS/CSE

Year	Volume	High	Low	Close
2022	1,800,497	$1.52	$0.03	$0.37
2021	2,755,784	$55.72	$1.10	$1.34
2020	180,429	$42.00	$4.20	$4.76
2019	32,375	$63.00	$5.60	$11.20
2018	17,537	$82.60	$12.60	$33.60

Consolidation: 1-for-2 cons. in Aug. 2023; 1-for-7 cons. in Dec. 2021; 1-for-20 cons. in Oct. 2020
Recent Close: $0.75
Capital Stock Changes - In May 2023, 12,000,000 post-consolidated common shares were issued to 1346487 B.C. Ltd. as consideration for assignment agreement. On Aug. 3, 2023, 35,000,000 post-consolidated common shares were issued on acquisition of PlasCred Inc., and private placement of 10,339,662 post-consolidated common shares at $0.30 per share. In addition,1,500,000 post-consolidated common shares were issued as finder's fee and 396,249 post-consolidated common shares were issued for debt settlement. On Aug. 8, 2023, common shares were consolidated on a 1-for-2 basis.

On Dec. 2, 2021, common shares were consolidated on a 1-for-7 basis. In February 2022, private placement of 1,453,431 post-consolidated common shares was completed at $0.255 per share.

Wholly Owned Subsidiaries

Mag One Operations Inc., Montréal, Qué.
- 100% int. in **North American Magnesium Products, LLC**, Oak Ridge, Tenn.

Mag One Operations Inc., United States.
PlasCred Inc., Calgary, Alta.

Financial Statistics

Periods ended:	12m Sept. 30/22[A1]		12m Sept. 30/21[A]
	$000s	%Chg	$000s
Research & devel. expense	50		6
General & admin expense	1,920		2,335
Stock-based compensation	159		1,677
Operating expense	**2,129**	**-47**	**4,018**
Operating income	**(2,129)**	**n.a.**	**(4,018)**
Finance costs, gross	31		33
Pre-tax income	**(2,360)**	**n.a.**	**(8,623)**
Net income	**(2,360)**	**n.a.**	**(8,623)**
Cash & equivalent	224		1,329
Current assets	314		2,122
Total assets	**314**	**-85**	**2,122**
Bank indebtedness	3		92
Accts. pay. & accr. liabs	515		354
Current liabilities	1,163		1,138
Long-term debt, gross	nil		58
Shareholders' equity	(849)		983
Cash from oper. activs	**(1,127)**	**n.a.**	**(3,134)**
Cash from fin. activs	224		4,475
Cash from invest. activs	(200)		(25)
Net cash position	**224**	**-83**	**1,329**
	$		$
Earnings per share*	(0.96)		(8.05)
Cash flow per share*	(0.45)		(2.92)
	shs		shs
No. of shs. o/s*	2,760,655		2,033,939
Avg. no. of shs. o/s*	2,483,906		1,071,462
	%		%
Net profit margin	n.a.		n.a.
Return on equity	n.m.		n.m.
Return on assets	(191.22)		(782.33)

* Common
[A] Reported in accordance with IFRS
[1] Results for fiscal 2022 and prior periods pertain to Cover Technologies Inc.

Latest Results

Periods ended:	6m Mar. 31/23[A]
	$000s
Net income	(150)
	$
Earnings per share*	(0.06)

* Common
[A] Reported in accordance with IFRS

Historical Summary
(as originally stated)

Fiscal Year	Oper. Rev.	Net Inc. Bef. Disc.	EPS*
	$000s	$000s	$
2022[A]	nil	(2,360)	(0.96)
2021[A]	nil	(8,623)	(8.05)
2020[A]	nil	(473)	(2.41)
2019[A]	nil	(1,278)	(8.40)
2018[A]	nil	(2,078)	(14.00)

* Common
[A] Reported in accordance with IFRS

Note: Adjusted throughout for 1-for-2 cons. in Aug. 2023; 1-for-7 cons. in Dec. 2021; 1-for-20 cons. in Oct. 2020

P.68 Platinex Inc.

Symbol - PTX **Exchange** - CSE **CUSIP** - 72765P
Head Office - 82 Richmond St E, Toronto, ON, M5C 1P1 **Telephone** - (905) 470-6400 **Fax** - (888) 470-6450
Website - www.platinex.com
Email - gferron@platinex.com
Investor Relations - Greg Ferron (416) 270-5042
Auditors - Baker Tilly WM LLP C.A., Vancouver, B.C.
Lawyers - Fogler, Rubinoff LLP, Toronto, Ont.
Transfer Agents - Computershare Trust Company of Canada Inc., Vancouver, B.C.
Profile - (Ont. 1998) Has mineral interests in Ontario.

Through 75%-owned **South Timmins Mining Mining Inc.**, holds Shining Tree gold property, 23,242 hectares, 120 km north of Sudbury, including formerly producing Ronda mine; Heenan gold prospect, 390 hectares, 120, km southwest of Timmins; nearby Mallard gold prospect, 5,104 hectares; and Dorothy gold prospect, 1,470 hectares.

Also holds W2 copper-nickel-PGE prospect, 22,094 hectares, 475 km northeast of Thunder Bay, including option to acquire 1,456-hectare claims; and option to acquire Muskrat Dam lithium project, 12,934 hectares, 600 km northwest of Thunder Bay.

On Mar. 15, 2023, the company completed a binding heads of agreement with **Fancamp Exploration Ltd.** to form a joint venture to advance gold mineral prospects in Ontario. Pursuant to the agreement, the company would transfer Shining Tree gold property in Ontario to **South Timmins Mining Inc.** (JVco) for 75% interest in JVco, and Fancamp would transfer Heenan, Mallard and Dorothy gold prospects for 25% interest in JVco. Fancamp would have an option to increase its ownership in JVco up to 50% interest, which may be exercised over a two-year period commencing on the date of approval of a Phase II Exploration Program by making staged cash payments to JVco totaling $1,500,000. Fancamp would also be granted 1% NSR royalty in Heenan, Mallard and Dorothy, subject to a decrease to 0.5% NSR royalty should Fancamp elect to exercise the option.
Directors - James R. (Jim) Trusler, chr., Newmarket, Ont.; Greg Ferron, pres. & CEO, Toronto, Ont.; Sam Kiri, Toronto, Ont.; Felix Lee, Toronto, Ont.; Christophe Vereecke, Paris, France
Other Exec. Officers - Graham C. Warren, CFO & corp. sec.; Lori Paradis, asst. sec.

Capital Stock

	Authorized (shs.)	Outstanding (shs.)[1]
Common	unlimited	272,563,062

[1] At May 30, 2023

Major Shareholder - Widely held at May 31, 2022.

Price Range - PTX/CSE

Year	Volume	High	Low	Close
2022	63,464,804	$0.06	$0.02	$0.04
2021	77,392,350	$0.09	$0.04	$0.04
2020	113,904,056	$0.13	$0.01	$0.08
2019	14,424,376	$0.07	$0.01	$0.01
2018	54,630,911	$0.30	$0.04	$0.05

Recent Close: $0.04
Capital Stock Changes - In April and May 2022, private placement of 16,021,667 flow-through units (1 common share & ½ warrant) at 6¢ per unit and 19,354,000 units (1 common share & ½ warrant) at 5¢ per unit was completed. Also during 2022, common shares were issued as follows: 4,875,000 on acquisition of mineral property and 2,330,000 for debt settlement.

Wholly Owned Subsidiaries

Cannabis Mall Inc. Inactive.
Endurance Elements Inc. Inactive.
PTX Nevada LLC, Nev. Inactive.
Platinex Investment Inc. Inactive.

Subsidiaries

75% int. in **South Timmins Mining Inc.**

Financial Statistics

Periods ended:	12m Dec. 31/22[A]		12m Dec. 31/21[A]
	$000s	%Chg	$000s
General & admin expense	1,289		790
Stock-based compensation	98		408
Operating expense	**1,387**	**+16**	**1,198**
Operating income	**(1,387)**	**n.a.**	**(1,198)**
Deprec., depl. & amort	nil		1
Finance costs, gross	36		9
Pre-tax income	**(1,423)**	**n.a.**	**(1,208)**
Net income	**(1,423)**	**n.a.**	**(1,208)**
Cash & equivalent	148		203
Accounts receivable	72		17
Current assets	484		245
Explor./devel. properties	3,002		2,147
Total assets	**3,487**	**+46**	**2,392**
Bank indebtedness	259		259
Accts. pay. & accr. liabs	479		246
Current liabilities	738		504
Long-term debt, gross	40		40
Long-term debt, net	40		40
Shareholders' equity	2,709		1,848
Cash from oper. activs	**(1,270)**	**n.a.**	**(719)**
Cash from fin. activs	1,833		302
Cash from invest. activs	(618)		(773)
Net cash position	**148**	**-27**	**203**
Capital expenditures	(618)		(773)
	$		$
Earnings per share*	(0.01)		(0.01)
Cash flow per share*	(0.01)		(0.00)
	shs		shs
No. of shs. o/s*	204,235,265		161,654,598
Avg. no. of shs. o/s*	192,696,444		158,308,358
	%		%
Net profit margin	n.a.		n.a.
Return on equity	(62.45)		(56.94)
Return on assets	(47.18)		(47.25)

* Common
[A] Reported in accordance with IFRS

Historical Summary
(as originally stated)

Fiscal Year	Oper. Rev. $000s	Net Inc. Bef. Disc. $000s	EPS* $
2022^A	nil	(1,423)	(0.01)
2021^A	nil	(1,208)	(0.01)
2020^A	nil	(772)	(0.01)
2019^A	nil	(457)	(0.00)
2018^A	nil	(3,393)	(0.03)

* Common
^A Reported in accordance with IFRS

P.69 Playgon Games Inc.

Symbol - DEAL **Exchange** - TSX-VEN **CUSIP** - 728123
Head Office - 1100-1199 Hastings St W, Vancouver, BC, V6E 3T5 **Telephone** - (604) 563-2640
Website - www.playgon.com
Email - mikem@playgon.com
Investor Relations - Michele N. Marrandino (604) 725-5225
Auditors - D & H Group LLP C.A., Vancouver, B.C.
Transfer Agents - Computershare Trust Company of Canada Inc., Vancouver, B.C.

Profile - (B.C. 2005; orig. B.C., 1985) Offers business-to-business (B2B) software-as-a-service (SaaS) products for online casinos, sportsbook operators, land-based operators, media groups and big database companies.

The Live Dealer Casino (LDC) software platform offers table and e-table games including Roulette, Odds UP Roulette™, Blackjack, Baccarat and Tiger Bonus Baccarat™ wherein a human dealer operates the game in real-time from a casino gaming table which can be seen via live streaming video link through the player's mobile or desktop device.

Daily Fantasy Sports (DFS) software and network offers a structured form of competition referred to as a contest where site end users pay an entry fee to participate and build a team of athletes in a certain sport while complying with different contest rules and win a share of a pre-determined prize pool.

Revenues are generated from licensing and use of the company's SaaS; and set-up fees for the integration, customization and branding of the customer site for the use of the company's products.

Predecessor Detail - Name changed from Global Daily Fantasy Sports Inc., July 31, 2020.

Directors - James R. Penturn, chr., London, Middx., United Kingdom; Darcy E. Krogh, CEO, Vancouver, B.C.; Guido Ganschow, pres., B.C.; Michele N. (Mike) Marrandino, Vancouver, B.C.; Robert J. (Bobby) Soper, Fort Lauderdale, Fla.

Other Exec. Officers - Steve Baker, COO; Harpreet (Harry) Nijjar, CFO

Capital Stock

	Authorized (shs.)	Outstanding (shs.)[1]
Common	unlimited	253,331,449

[1] At May 30, 2023

Major Shareholder - Kathleen Ann Crook held 12.37% interest and Guido Ganschow held 11.28% interest at Oct. 31, 2022.

Price Range - DEAL/TSX-VEN

Year	Volume	High	Low	Close
2022	40,701,414	$0.35	$0.04	$0.07
2021	48,469,385	$0.81	$0.25	$0.35
2020	49,064,539	$0.65	$0.16	$0.50
2019	13,391,606	$0.15	$0.06	$0.15
2018	33,583,879	$0.42	$0.07	$0.08

Recent Close: $0.06

Capital Stock Changes - There were no changes to capital stock during 2022.

Wholly Owned Subsidiaries

Playgon Distribution Limited, Cyprus.
Playgon Interactive Inc., Vancouver, B.C.
- 100% int. in **Bitrate Productions**, United States.
- 100% int. in **Cleebo Games Inc.**, Canada.

Playgon Malta Holding Limited, Malta.
- 100% int. in **Playgon Malta Limited**, Malta.

Financial Statistics

Periods ended:	12m Dec. 31/22^A		12m Dec. 31/21^{□A}
	$000s	%Chg	$000s
Operating revenue	**958**	**+499**	**160**
Salaries & benefits	8,274		6,164
General & admin expense	5,160		4,553
Stock-based compensation	614		1,219
Operating expense	**14,048**	**+18**	**11,936**
Operating income	**(13,090)**	**n.a.**	**(11,776)**
Deprec., depl. & amort.	3,340		3,117
Finance income	16		16
Finance costs, gross	255		163
Pre-tax income	**(16,823)**	**n.a.**	**(14,844)**
Net income	**(16,823)**	**n.a.**	**(14,844)**
Cash & equivalent	207		5,930
Accounts receivable	260		162
Current assets	882		6,948
Fixed assets, net	658		1,061
Right-of-use assets	191		574
Intangibles, net	6,042		8,498
Total assets	**8,213**	**-52**	**17,079**
Bank indebtedness	5,807		699
Accts. pay. & accr. liabs.	3,669		1,911
Current liabilities	9,715		3,043
Long-term debt, gross	920		60
Long-term debt, net	920		60
Long-term lease liabilities	nil		190
Shareholders' equity	(2,421)		13,787
Cash from oper. activs.	**(11,188)**	**n.a.**	**(11,212)**
Cash from fin. activs.	5,519		18,862
Cash from invest. activs.	(30)		(481)
Net cash position	**207**	**-97**	**5,930**
Capital expenditures	(30)		(481)
	$		$
Earnings per share*	(0.07)		(0.07)
Cash flow per share*	(0.04)		(0.05)
	shs		shs
No. of shs. o/s*	253,331,449		253,331,449
Avg. no. of shs. o/s*	253,331,449		213,391,696
	%		%
Net profit margin	n.m.		n.m.
Return on equity	n.m.		(129.94)
Return on assets	(131.01)		(95.45)

* Common
□ Restated
^A Reported in accordance with IFRS

Latest Results

Periods ended:	3m Mar. 31/23^A		3m Mar. 31/22^A
	$000s	%Chg	$000s
Operating revenue	288	+104	141
Net income	(3,994)	n.a.	(3,900)
	$		$
Earnings per share*	(0.02)		(0.02)

* Common
^A Reported in accordance with IFRS

Historical Summary
(as originally stated)

Fiscal Year	Oper. Rev. $000s	Net Inc. Bef. Disc. $000s	EPS* $
2022^A	958	(16,823)	(0.07)
2021^A	160	(14,844)	(0.07)
2020^A	nil	(6,391)	(0.05)
2019^A	51	(2,258)	(0.03)
2018^A	107	(7,917)	(0.15)

* Common
^A Reported in accordance with IFRS

P.70 Playground Ventures Inc.

Symbol - PLAY **Exchange** - CSE **CUSIP** - 72814U
Head Office - 1100-736 Granville St, Vancouver, BC, V6Z 1G3 **Toll-free** - (888) 449-4148
Website - playgroundventures.com
Email - investors@playgroundventures.com
Investor Relations - Jon D. Gill (416) 361-1913
Auditors - Jones & O'Connell LLP C.A., St. Catharines, Ont.
Lawyers - Irwin Lowy LLP, Toronto, Ont.
Transfer Agents - TSX Trust Company, Toronto, Ont.

Profile - (B.C. 2014) Develops platforms and publishes video games that are either developed internally or externally through engagement of video game developers.

The video games published by the company can be played by consumers on various platforms including personal computers (PC), mobile and console platforms, and the Internet. The video games are published through Steam® and gaming websites on PCs; Xbox Store and PlayStation Store on gaming consoles; and iOS App store, Google Play store and Amazon App stores on mobile.

Published video game is Skate Video Tycoon, a mobile game project licensed with the largest online skateboarding community. Video game projects in development include Heavy Gear Assault, a first person simulator where the player controls war machines called Gears via their in-game pilot characters; Sabotage, based on Matt Cook's best-selling novel of the same name; Modern Miner, based on mineral exploration; and The Campaign, where players follow stories as they manage and grow a political campaign.

On July 7, 2021, the company agreed to invest up to €1,000,000 in **GG Hub S.r.l.**, an Italian media gaming corporation, in exchange for up to 60% interest in GG Hub. As at June 30, 2022, the company had paid €500,000 for an ownership interest of 35%.

On May 27, 2022, wholly owned **Stompy Bot Productions Inc.** and **TokenPlay Inc.** were amalgamated into the company.

Common reinstated on CSE, Aug. 10, 2023.
Common suspended from CSE, May 8, 2023.

Predecessor Detail - Name changed from Blocplay Entertainment Inc., May 3, 2021.

Directors - Jon D. Gill, chr. & interim CFO, King City, Ont.; Christopher O. (Chris) Irwin, pres., CEO & corp. sec., Toronto, Ont.; Emma Fairhurst, B.C.; Harrison Reynolds, B.C.

Capital Stock

	Authorized (shs.)	Outstanding (shs.)[1]
Common	unlimited	80,237,785

[1] At Aug. 2, 2023

Major Shareholder - Emma Fairhurst held 45.96% interest at Mar. 10, 2022.

Price Range - PLAY/CSE

Year	Volume	High	Low	Close
2022	12,447,866	$0.15	$0.02	$0.03
2021	10,923,870	$0.63	$0.10	$0.14
2020	7,252,733	$0.30	$0.04	$0.16
2019	1,555,898	$0.20	$0.10	$0.10
2018	14,233,947	$5.20	$0.10	$0.20

Consolidation: 1-for-20 cons. in June 2020

Recent Close: $0.02

Capital Stock Changes - In February 2023, 17,477,199 common shares were issued at 5¢ per share for debt settlement.

On Jan. 27, 2022, 5,000,000 common shares were issued pursuant to the acquisition of 1281750 B.C. Ltd. Also during 2022, common shares were issued as follows: 1,308,349 for debt settlement and 550,000 on exercise of options.

Wholly Owned Subsidiaries

Countervail Games Ltd., B.C.
1279078 B.C. Ltd., B.C.
1281750 B.C. Ltd.
1296858 B.C. Ltd.
1296860 B.C. Ltd.

Investments

35% int. in **GG Hub S.r.l.**, Italy.
40% int. in **MotionPix Game Studio Inc.**, Vancouver, B.C.
40% int. in **WeatherGen Climate Partners Inc.**

Financial Statistics

Periods ended:	12m Dec. 31/22^A		12m Dec. 31/21^A
	$000s	%Chg	$000s
General & admin expense	835		1,220
Operating expense	**835**	**-32**	**1,220**
Operating income	**(835)**	**n.a.**	**(1,220)**
Finance income	nil		17
Finance costs, gross	247		665
Investment income	(1,032)		(41)
Write-downs/write-offs	(5,621)		nil
Pre-tax income	**(7,772)**	**n.a.**	**(1,913)**
Net income	**(7,772)**	**n.a.**	**(1,913)**
Cash & equivalent	3		55
Accounts receivable	30		61
Current assets	126		348
Long-term investments	nil		1,692
Intangibles, net	nil		4,577
Total assets	**126**	**-98**	**6,617**
Accts. pay. & accr. liabs.	646		593
Current liabilities	1,070		729
Shareholders' equity	(944)		5,888
Cash from oper. activs.	**(116)**	**n.a.**	**(881)**
Cash from fin. activs.	434		2,879
Cash from invest. activs.	(357)		(2,092)
Net cash position	**3**	**-95**	**55**
	$		$
Earnings per share*	(0.12)		(0.05)
Cash flow per share*	(0.00)		(0.02)
	shs		shs
No. of shs. o/s*	62,760,586		55,902,237
Avg. no. of shs. o/s*	62,255,630		40,529,482
	%		%
Net profit margin	n.a.		n.a.
Return on equity	n.m.		(52.96)
Return on assets	(223.19)		(30.58)

* Common
^A Reported in accordance with IFRS

Latest Results

Periods ended:	3m Mar. 31/23[A]		3m Mar. 31/22[A]
	$000s	%Chg	$000s
Net income	(10)	n.a.	(601)
	$		$
Earnings per share*	(0.00)		(0.01)

* Common
[A] Reported in accordance with IFRS

Historical Summary
(as originally stated)

Fiscal Year	Oper. Rev.	Net Inc. Bef. Disc.	EPS*
	$000s	$000s	$
2022[A]	nil	(7,772)	(0.12)
2021[A]	nil	(1,913)	(0.05)
2020[A]	nil	(149)	(0.01)
2019[A]	nil	(12)	(0.00)
2018[A]	nil	(3,119)	(0.34)

* Common
[A] Reported in accordance with IFRS
Note: Adjusted throughout for 1-for-20 cons. in June 2020

P.71 Playmaker Capital Inc.

Symbol - PMKR **Exchange** - TSX-VEN **CUSIP** - 72815P
Head Office - 601-2 St. Clair Ave W, Toronto, ON, M4V 1L5 **Telephone** - (416) 815-4993
Website - www.playmaker.fans
Email - jgnat@playmaker.fans
Investor Relations - Jordan Gnat (416) 815-4993
Auditors - MNP LLP C.A., Toronto, Ont.
Transfer Agents - Odyssey Trust Company, Toronto, Ont.
Profile - (Ont. 2018) Operates a diverse portfolio of digital sports media and technology brands, intended to deliver engaged audiences of sports fans to sports betting companies, leagues, teams and advertisers, with a focus on U.S., Latin American and Canadian markets.

The company plans to build a network of sports media brands with large and diverse fan bases, varieties of content, revenue and distribution channels, influencer networks and social channels, and the tools needed to attract and retain users. Its intended ecosystem consists of five principal customer categories and revenue streams: (i) sports betting and iGaming operators, (ii) traditional advertisers, (iii) content syndication, (iv) technical design and product development services, and (v) direct to consumer (e-commerce operations and streaming revenue sharing).

Principal subsidiaries include **Odenton Company S.A.** and **Futbol Sites LLC** (collectively Futbol Sites), a soccer-focused digital media group operating in the U.S., Argentina, Brazil, Colombia, Chile and Mexico under the brands BolaVip, Futbol Centro América and Redgol; **YB Media LLC** (dba Yardbarker), a California-based sports and entertainment media platform providing NFL, NBA, MLB, college sports and NHL content; and **Oilersnation.com Ltd.**, which operates The Nation Network, an Edmonton, Alta.-based digital media group focused on hockey content.

In April 2022, the company acquired the digital media assets of The Sports Drop, a U.S.-based sports media company that focuses on NFL, NBA and collegiate sports coverage. Terms were not disclosed.

Recent Merger and Acquisition Activity

Status: pending **Announced:** Oct. 17, 2022
Playmaker Capital Inc. acquired Glasgow, U.K.-based Wedge Traffic Limited, which has affiliate marketing relationships with 15 online sportsbooks and casinos, and is active in 16 states and in Ontario, for US$8,500,000 cash and issuance of 3,694,933 common shares at a deemed price of Cdn$0.75 per share (valued at US$2,000,000). In addition, contingent consideration of US$20,700,000 would be paid by Playmaker, in a combination of cash and common shares, in two separate earn-out payments upon Wedge achieving certain revenue and EBITDA thresholds during 2023 and 2024.

Status: completed **Announced:** Nov. 3, 2021
Playmaker Capital Inc. acquired Oilersnation.com Ltd. and its wholly owned DailyFaceoff.com Ltd. (collectively The Nation Network or TNN) for consideration of up to CAD$15,000,000. TNN operates a hockey-based digital network of fan community sites, podcasts and a hockey fantasy reference property. The price consisted of $6,000,000 cash and issuance of common shares valued at US$3,000,000, plus up to $3,000,000 in contingent consideration based on TNN's performance over the following 12 months.

Status: completed **Announced:** Aug. 31, 2021
Playmaker Capital Inc. acquired Two-Up Agency Ltd., which provides technical solutions to the online gaming industry, for consideration of up to US$5,750,000. The price consisted of US$750,000 cash and issuance of common shares valued at US$2,500,000, plus up to US$2,500,000 in contingent consideration based on Two-Up's performance over the following three years.

Predecessor Detail - Name changed from Apolo III Acquisition Corp., May 31, 2021, pursuant to the Qualifying Transaction reverse takeover acquisition of (old) Playmaker Capital Inc., with (old) Playmaker amalgamating with wholly owned 2830125 Ontario Inc. and then concurrently amalgamated into the company.; basis 1 new for 4.54 old shs.

Directors - Maryann Turcke, chr., Toronto, Ont.; Jordan Gnat, CEO, Toronto, Ont.; John L. Albright, Toronto, Ont.; Mark Harrison, Toronto, Ont.; Sebastian Siseles, Buenos Aires, Argentina; Sara Slane, Baltimore, Md.; Mark Trachuk, Toronto, Ont.

Other Exec. Officers - Jake Cassaday, COO; Michael (Mike) Cooke, CFO; Federico Grinberg, exec. v-p

Capital Stock

	Authorized (shs.)	Outstanding (shs.)[1]
Preferred	unlimited	nil
Common	unlimited	226,438,061

[1] At Dec. 31, 2022

Major Shareholder - Relay Ventures Fund III Capital Inc. held 15.5% interest and Jordan Gnat held 12.7% interest at Mar. 25, 2022.

Price Range - PMKR/TSX-VEN

Year	Volume	High	Low	Close
2022	21,261,589	$0.75	$0.30	$0.48
2021	32,077,721	$1.00	$0.36	$0.76
2020	37,444	$0.36	$0.14	$0.16
2019	50,110	$0.55	$0.23	$0.23
2018	115,473	$0.68	$0.45	$0.45

Consolidation: 1-for-4.54 cons. in June 2021
Recent Close: $0.45
Capital Stock Changes - On Oct. 17, 2022, 3,694,933 common shares were issued pursuant to the acquisition of Wedge Traffic Limited.

Wholly Owned Subsidiaries

Futbol Sites LLC, Hollywood, Fla.
- 1% int. in **Futbol Sites MX S.A. de C.V.**, Mexico.

Odenton Company S.A., Uruguay.
- 100% int. in **Aeris S.A.**, Uruguay.
- 100% int. in **Editora Flop Ltda.**, Brazil.
- 98.71% int. in **FSN S.R.L.**, Argentina.
- 100% int. in **Futbol Sites Colombia S.A.S.**, Colombia.
- 99% int. in **Futbol Sites MX S.A. de C.V.**, Mexico.
- 80% int. in **Sociedad Comercial Dale Ideas Limitada**, Chile.
- 99% int. in **Sociedad Comercial Futbol Sites Network Chile**, Chile.
  - 20% int. in **Sociedad Comercial Dale Ideas Limitada**, Chile.
- 100% int. in **Spkr Midias E Eventos Ltda.**, Brazil.

Oilersnation.com Ltd., Edmonton, Alta.
- 100% int. in **Dailyfaceoff.com Ltd.**, Canada.

12574837 Canada Inc., Canada.
PMKR US Inc., United States.
- 100% int. in **YB Media, LLC**, Burlingame, Calif.

Two-Up Agency Ltd., London, Middx., United Kingdom.
- 100% int. in **Two-Up Agency z.o.o**, Poland.

Note: The preceding list includes only the major related companies in which interests are held.

Financial Statistics

Periods ended:	12m Dec. 31/21[A]		12m Dec. 31/20[A]
	US$000s	%Chg	US$000s
Operating revenue	**14,820**	**n.a.**	**nil**
Cost of sales	1,190		nil
Salaries & benefits	5,798		93
General & admin expense	734		45
Stock-based compensation	577		30
Other operating expense	4,108		71
Operating expense	**12,407**	**n.m.**	**239**
Operating income	**2,413**	**n.a.**	**(239)**
Deprec., depl. & amort.	648		2
Finance costs, gross	130		nil
Pre-tax income	**(3,762)**	**n.a.**	**(266)**
Income taxes	(220)		nil
Net income	**(3,542)**	**n.a.**	**(266)**
Cash & equivalent	7,112		6,631
Inventories	19		nil
Accounts receivable	4,407		nil
Current assets	11,960		6,634
Fixed assets, net	301		1
Right-of-use assets	477		nil
Intangibles, net	45,808		nil
Total assets	**87,828**	**n.m.**	**6,635**
Accts. pay. & accr. liabs	568		nil
Current liabilities	16,385		88
Long-term debt, gross	61		nil
Long-term debt, net	47		nil
Long-term lease liabilities	415		nil
Shareholders' equity	56,058		6,547
Cash from oper. activs	**515**	**n.a.**	**(199)**
Cash from fin. activs	24,037		4,924
Cash from invest. activs	(23,726)		nil
Net cash position	**7,112**	**+7**	**6,631**
Capital expenditures	(246)		nil
	US$		US$
Earnings per share*	(0.03)		n.a.
Cash flow per share*	0.00		n.a.
	shs		shs
No. of shs. o/s*	212,061,061		n.a.
Avg. no. of shs. o/s*	128,850,587		n.a.
	%		%
Net profit margin	(23.90)		n.a.
Return on equity	(11.32)		n.m.
Return on assets	(7.24)		n.a.
Foreign sales percent	92		n.a.
No. of employees (FTEs)	312		n.a.

* Common
[A] Reported in accordance with IFRS

Latest Results

Periods ended:	3m Mar. 31/22[A]		3m Mar. 31/21[A]
	US$000s	%Chg	US$000s
Operating revenue	5,817	n.a.	nil
Net income	(3,399)	n.a.	(339)
	US$		US$
Earnings per share*	(0.02)		n.a.

* Common
[A] Reported in accordance with IFRS
Note: Adjusted throughout for 1-for-4.54 cons. in June 2021

P.72 Plaza Retail REIT

Symbol - PLZ.UN **Exchange** - TSX **CUSIP** - 72820F
Head Office - 98 Main St, Fredericton, NB, E3A 9N6 **Telephone** - (506) 451-1826 **Fax** - (506) 451-1802
Website - www.plaza.ca
Email - kim.strange@plaza.ca
Investor Relations - Kimberly A. Strange (506) 357-7901
Auditors - KPMG LLP C.A., Fredericton, N.B.
Lawyers - Goodmans LLP
Transfer Agents - TSX Trust Company, Calgary, Alta.
FP500 Revenue Ranking - 757
Employees - 88 at Dec. 31, 2022
Profile - (Ont. 2013) Acquires, develops and manages open-air centres and stand-alone retail real estate throughout Canada with a focus on Ontario, Quebec and Atlantic Canada.

At Dec. 31, 2022, the trust had interests in a portfolio of 251 properties, consisting of 117 open-air centres, three enclosed shopping centres and 131 single-use properties with quick service restaurants (59) or retail outlets (72).

Property portfolio at Dec. 31, 2022:

Location	Properties	Sq. ft.[1]
Quebec	83	2,344,231
Ontario	56	1,836,389
New Brunswick	53	1,928,719
Nova Scotia	33	1,249,948
Newfoundland & Labrador	12	829,274
Prince Edward Island	11	601,031
Alberta	2	34,238
Manitoba	1	17,018
	251	8,840,848

[1] Gross leasable area.

The trust had interests in projects under development or redevelopment totaling 1,283,025 sq. ft. at Dec. 31, 2022.

Top 10 tenants consist of Shoppers Drug Mart/Loblaw, Dollarama, KFC, TJX Group, Canadian Tire, Sobeys, Staples, Bulk Barn, Giant Tiger and RBI.

During 2022, the trust acquired two properties for development/redevelopment in Stewiacke, N.S., and Dieppe, N.B., for a total of $3,641,000.

In addition, the trust sold nine properties consisting of quick service restaurants and non-core assets in Digby, N.S., Hamilton, Ottawa,Wallaceburg, Ont., and Brossard, Lachute, Montreal, Pierrefonds and Victoriaville, Que., for a total of $8,355,000. Also, the trust sold its 50% interest in a non-core asset in Port Hope, Ont., for $3,993,000.

Recent Merger and Acquisition Activity

Status: completed **Announced:** July 28, 2022

Plaza Retail REIT acquired a 50% managing interest in Niagara Street Plaza, a 94,000-sq.-ft. open-air centre with future development potential in Welland, Ont., for $9,580,000.

Predecessor Detail - Succeeded Plazacorp Retail Properties Ltd., Jan. 1, 2014, pursuant to plan of arrangement whereby Plaza Retail REIT was formed to facilitate the conversion of the corporation into a trust.

Trustees - A. Douglas (Doug) McGregor, chr., Toronto, Ont.; Earl A. Brewer, v-chr., Fredericton, N.B.; Michael A. Zakuta, pres. & CEO, Montréal, Qué.; Stephen E. Johnson, Toronto, Ont.; S. Jane Marshall, Toronto, Ont.; Lynda M. Savoie, Fredericton, N.B.; Susan Taves, Waterloo, Ont.

Other Exec. Officers - Jim Drake, CFO; Mathieu Bordeleau, exec. v-p, Que./Ont.; Peter Mackenzie, exec. v-p & chief invest. officer; Stephen Penney, exec. v-p; Kimberly A. Strange, gen. counsel & corp. sec.

Capital Stock

	Authorized (shs.)	Outstanding (shs.)[1]
Preferred Unit	unlimited	nil
Trust Unit	unlimited	110,379,391
Special Voting Unit	unlimited	1,156,172
Class B LP Unit	n.a.	1,156,172[2]

[1] At Apr. 12, 2023

[2] Classified as debt.

Trust Unit - One vote per unit.

Special Voting Unit - Issued to holders of class B limited partnership units of a subsidiary of the trust. Each special voting unit entitles the holder to a number of votes at unitholder meetings equal to the number of trust units into which the class B limited partnership units are exchangeable.

Class B Limited Partnership Unit - Entitled to distributions equal to those provided to trust units. Exchangeable into trust units on a 1-for-1 basis. Classified as debt.

Normal Course Issuer Bid - The company plans to make normal course purchases of up to 6,478,960 trust units representing 10% of the public float. The bid commenced on Sept. 28, 2022, and expires on Sept. 27, 2023.

Major Shareholder - Morguard Corporation held 15.27% interest and Michael A. Zakuta held 12.29% interest at Apr. 12, 2023.

Price Range - PLZ.UN/TSX

Year	Volume	High	Low	Close
2022	12,438,748	$5.10	$3.88	$4.48
2021	18,016,978	$4.81	$3.54	$4.72
2020	32,585,307	$4.75	$2.65	$3.61
2019	18,373,764	$4.76	$3.86	$4.57
2018	19,656,941	$4.40	$3.68	$3.88

Recent Close: $3.98

Capital Stock Changes - In March 2023, bought deal public offering of 8,548,000 trust units was completed at $4.68 per unit. Underwriters were granted an over-allotment option to purchase up to an additional 1,282,200 trust units. Net proceeds would be used to fund the repayment of all of the trust's series E 5.10% convertible subordinated unsecured debentures.

During 2022, 15,000 trust units were issued under restricted unit plan and 19,000 trust units were repurchased under a Normal Course Issuer Bid.

Dividends

PLZ.UN unit Ra $0.28 pa M est. Apr. 16, 2018**[1]

[1] Plazacorp Retail Properties Ltd. com prior to Jan. 8, 2014. Distribution reinvestment plan suspended eff. Oct. 15, 2018.

** Reinvestment Option

Wholly Owned Subsidiaries

Bedford Commons 2 Property Holdings Inc.
LeMarchant Property Holdings Inc.
Northwest Plaza Commercial Trust
Plaza Group Management Limited
Plaza Master Limited Partnership, N.B.
Plaza Retail Limited Partnership #1
Plaza Tacoma Limited Partnership
Plazacorp - Shediac Limited Partnership
Scott's Acquisition Inc.
Scott's Real Estate Limited Partnership, Ont.
Spring Park Plaza Inc., P.E.I.

Subsidiaries

90% int. in **Exhibition Plaza Inc.**, Saint John, N.B.
90% int. in **Granville Street Properties Limited Partnership**, P.E.I.
80% int. in **Riverside Emerald (Timmins) Limited Partnership**, Timmins, Ont.
90% int. in **Stavanger Torbay Limited Partnership**
90% int. in **Wildan Properties Limited Partnership**, P.E.I.

Investments

50% int. in **CPRDL Limited Partnership**
10% int. in **Centennial Plaza Limited Partnership**
50% int. in **Fundy Retail Limited**
25% int. in **144 Denison East Limited Partnership**, Canada.
25% int. in **Plazacorp Ontario1 Limited Partnership**, Canada.
50% int. in **Plazacorp Ontario3 Limited Partnership**
50% int. in **Plazacorp Ontario4 Limited Partnership**
50% int. in **Plazacorp Ontario2 Limited Partnership**
50% int. in **RBEG Limited Partnership**
50% int. in **The Shoppes at Galway Limited Partnership**
25% int. in **Ste. Hyacinthe Limited Partnership**
15% int. in **Trois Rivieres Limited Partnership**
20% int. in **VGH Limited Partnership**

Financial Statistics

Periods ended:	12m Dec. 31/22[A]		12m Dec. 31/21[◻A]
	$000s	%Chg	$000s
Total revenue	**111,245**	**+1**	**110,632**
Rental operating expense	17,238		16,135
General & admin. expense	7,873		7,052
Property taxes	23,426		22,718
Operating expense	**48,537**	**+6**	**45,905**
Operating income	**62,708**	**-3**	**64,727**
Investment income	4,301		4,494
Finance costs, gross	23,150		28,836
Pre-tax income	**54,396**	**-46**	**101,259**
Income taxes	175		770
Net income	**54,221**	**-46**	**100,489**
Net inc. for equity hldrs	**53,891**	**-46**	**99,615**
Net inc. for non-cont. int	**330**	**-62**	**874**
Cash & equivalent	7,262		8,062
Accounts receivable	4,014		4,503
Current assets	45,112		24,239
Long-term investments	51,180		48,680
Income-producing props	1,025,249		1,017,733
Properties under devel	78,620		57,585
Property interests, net	1,169,075		1,141,304
Total assets	**1,269,011**	**+4**	**1,214,834**
Bank indebtedness	38,988		34,525
Accts. pay. & accr. liabs	18,510		16,636
Current liabilities	189,625		144,016
Long-term debt, gross	609,282		584,349
Long-term debt, net	484,921		498,934
Long-term lease liabilities	64,403		65,206
Shareholders' equity	518,900		493,521
Non-controlling interest	2,405		4,372
Cash from oper. activs	**38,469**	**-20**	**47,873**
Cash from fin. activs	1,147		(25,995)
Cash from invest. activs	(44,903)		(21,952)
Net cash position	**(30,538)**	**n.a.**	**(25,251)**
Increase in property	(50,260)		(32,967)
Decrease in property	8,579		13,102
	$		$
Earnings per share*	n.a.		n.a.
Cash flow per share*	0.38		0.47
Funds from opers. per sh.*	0.40		0.43
Adj. funds from opers. per sh.*	0.32		0.36
Cash divd. per share*	0.28		0.28
Total divd. per share*	**0.28**		**0.28**
	shs		shs
No. of shs. o/s*	101,800,000		101,804,000
	%		%
Net profit margin	48.74		90.83
Return on equity	10.65		21.75
Return on assets	6.22		10.97
No. of employees (FTEs)	88		84

* Trust Unit

◻ Restated

[A] Reported in accordance with IFRS

Historical Summary

(as originally stated)

Fiscal Year	Total Rev.	Net Inc. Bef. Disc.	EPS*
	$000s	$000s	$
2022[A]	111,245	54,221	n.a.
2021[A]	110,632	100,489	n.a.
2020[A]	106,898	(14,937)	n.a.
2019[A]	112,461	51,337	n.a.
2018[A]	104,017	12,212	n.a.

* Trust Unit

[A] Reported in accordance with IFRS

P.73 Pluribus Technologies Corp.

Symbol - PLRB **Exchange** - TSX-VEN **CUSIP** - 72942X

Head Office - 503-111 Peter St, Toronto, ON, M5V 2H1 **Toll-free** - (800) 851-9383

Website - www.pluribustechnologies.com

Email - investors@pluribustechnologies.com

Investor Relations - Richard D. Adair (800) 851-9383

Auditors - Ernst & Young LLP C.A., Toronto, Ont.

Transfer Agents - TSX Trust Company, Toronto, Ont.

Profile - (Ont. 2021) Acquires and grows small business-to-business (B2B) software companies from owners and investors that are seeking a succession plan.

Acquisitions are made in four different operating segments: eLearning, providing digital tools for companies and educators to create and deliver learning content and experiences online; Digital Enablement, enabling enterprises through digital business platforms to achieve efficient business processes; HealthTech, offering technology-enabled healthcare products and services; and eCommerce, providing tools to support small and medium-sized enterprises (SMEs) to optimize their websites and online stores to increase revenue.

The company is headquartered in Toronto, Ont., and has operating businesses in Alberta, North Carolina, California, Utah and the United Kingdom.

On May 16, 2022, the company acquired private Woburn, Mass.-based **Knowledge Strategies Inc.** (dba Tortal Training) for US$1,900,000, consisting of US$1,400,000 cash and issuance of 175,926 common shares. In addition, Tortal Training shareholders would be entitled to an earn-out consideration based on the achievement of future performance targets. Tortal Training provides learning management systems, employee training and eLearning program services to a broad customer base specializing in solutions for automotive (original equipment manufacturer, aftermarket and motorsport) and consumer products franchises, with a focus on organizations with distributed workforces.

Recent Merger and Acquisition Activity

Status: completed **Announced:** May 30, 2022

Pluribus Technologies Corp. acquired private Milton Keynes, U.K.-based Rowanwood Professional Service Limited for £3,600,000 (Cdn$5,800,000) cash plus an earn-out consideration based on the achievement of certain future performance targets. Rowanwood develops Apex Asset Management Solution, a housing asset management software designed to help organizations manage their property portfolio. Software features include cataloguing an inventory of assets and their condition, tracking investment planning and supplier allocation, and providing financial management and project audit, along with key performance indicator review.

Predecessor Detail - Name changed from Aumento Capital IX Corp., Jan. 13, 2022, pursuant to the Qualifying Transaction reverse takeover acquisition of Pluribus Technologies Inc. and concurrent amalgamation of Pluribus with wholly owned 13515630 Canada Inc. (and continued as Pluribus Technologies Holdings Inc.).; basis 1 new for 7.94118 old shs.

Directors - Elmer I. Kim, chr., Toronto, Ont.; Richard D. Adair, CEO, Toronto, Ont.; Alfred Apps, Toronto, Ont.; David Coombs, Kelowna, B.C.; Carolyn Currie, Mississauga, Ont.; James B. (Jim) Dunbar, Toronto, Ont.; Warner Sulz, Toronto, Ont.

Other Exec. Officers - Diane Pedreira, COO; Nancy Fahy, CFO; Jacqueline Yuen, sr. v-p, fin. & treas.

Capital Stock

	Authorized (shs.)	Outstanding (shs.)[1]
Common	unlimited	15,826,593

[1] At May 29, 2023

Major Shareholder - Widely held at May 24, 2023.

Price Range - PLRB/TSX-VEN

Year	Volume	High	Low	Close
2022	2,208,454	$6.69	$1.41	$1.56
2021	2,518	$4.37	$4.37	$4.37

Consolidation: 1-for-7.94118 cons. in Jan. 2022

Recent Close: $0.90

Capital Stock Changes - On Jan. 13, 2022, common shares were consolidated on a 1-for-7.94118 basis (effective on the TS Venture Exchange on Jan. 19, 2022), 15,065,998 post-consolidated common shares were issued pursuant to the Qualifying Transaction reverse takeover acquisition of Pluribus Technologies Inc. and 146,036 post-consolidated common shares were issued as finder's fee. On Jan. 28, 2022, 320,439 post-consolidated common shares were issued pursuant to the acquisition of Kesson Group Inc. On May 16, 2022, 175,926 post-consolidated common shares were issued pursuant to the acquisition of Knowledge Strategies Inc. (dba Tortal Training).

Wholly Owned Subsidiaries

Kesson Group Inc., Toronto, Ont.

Knowledge Strategies Inc., Woburn, Mass.
Pluribus Technologies Holdings Inc., Toronto, Ont.
- 100% int. in **Framework Technologies Inc.**
  - 100% int. in **TeleMED Diagnostic Management Inc.**, Toronto, Ont.
    - 100% int. in **TDM Telehealth Technology Inc.**
- 100% int. in **11273388 Canada Inc.**, Canada.
  - 100% int. in **Assured Software Limited**, Vancouver, B.C.
- 100% int. in **11273418 Canada Inc.**, Canada.
  - 100% int. in **Crescere Frameworks, LLC**, Irvine, Calif. The Learning Network.
    - 100% int. in **LogicBay Corporation**, Wilmington, N.C.
  - 100% int. in **ICOM Productions Inc.**, Calgary, Alta.
  - 100% int. in **Pathways Training & eLearning Inc.**, Toronto, Ont.
  - 100% int. in **SkilSure Inc.**, Canada.
    - 100% int. in **SkilSure Software Ltd.**, United Kingdom.
- 100% int. in **12742781 Canada Inc.**, Canada.
  - 100% int. in **POWR, Inc.**, San Francisco, Calif.
- 100% int. in **Pluribus Technologies Ltd.**, United Kingdom.
  - 100% int. in **Cranham Haig Limited**, Cheltenham, Gloucs., United Kingdom. dba CHL Software.

Rowanwood Professional Service Limited, Milton Keynes, Bucks., United Kingdom.
Veemo, Inc., Utah
- 100% int. in **Social5 Development Group, LLC**
- 100% int. in **Social5, LLC**

Financial Statistics

Periods ended:	12m Dec. 31/22[A1]		12m Dec. 31/21[□A]
	$000s	%Chg	$000s
Operating revenue	**38,120**	**+105**	**18,557**
Cost of sales	13,750		6,592
Research & devel. expense	6,899		2,804
General & admin expense	11,855		4,958
Stock-based compensation	2,004		34
Operating expense	**34,508**	**+275**	**9,196**
Operating income	**3,612**	**-61**	**9,361**
Deprec., depl. & amort.	5,153		2,295
Finance costs, net	2,379		914
Pre-tax income	**(10,498)**	**n.a.**	**(21,740)**
Income taxes	(1,691)		(748)
Net income	**(8,807)**	**n.a.**	**(20,992)**
Cash & equivalent	5,323		1,689
Accounts receivable	6,364		2,938
Current assets	13,222		29,832
Fixed assets, net	233		251
Right-of-use assets	236		434
Intangibles, net	82,146		55,825
Total assets	**95,837**	**+11**	**86,342**
Accts. pay. & accr. liabs	5,613		7,056
Current liabilities	18,395		43,246
Long-term debt, gross	26,227		19,515
Long-term debt, net	22,386		10,563
Long-term lease liabilities	73		212
Shareholders' equity	45,664		15,669
Cash from oper. activs	**(3,894)**	**n.a.**	**(329)**
Cash from fin. activs	27,900		31,959
Cash from invest. activs	(19,653)		(31,371)
Net cash position	**5,323**	**+215**	**1,689**
Capital expenditures	(82)		(57)
	$		$
Earnings per share*	(0.56)		(3.83)
Cash flow per share*	(0.25)		(0.06)
	shs		shs
No. of shs. o/s*	15,960,249		n.a.
Avg. no. of shs. o/s*	15,676,347		5,488,150
	%		%
Net profit margin	(23.10)		(113.12)
Return on equity	(28.72)		(238.11)
Return on assets	(9.67)		(41.80)
Foreign sales percent	62		55

* Common
□ Restated
A Reported in accordance with IFRS
1 Results reflect the Jan. 13, 2022, reverse takeover acquisition of Pluribus Technologies Inc.

Latest Results

Periods ended:	3m Mar. 31/23[A]		3m Mar. 31/22[□A]
	$000s	%Chg	$000s
Operating revenue	9,256	+13	8,158
Net income	(1,746)	n.a.	(4,620)
	$		$
Earnings per share*	(0.11)		(0.31)

* Common
□ Restated
A Reported in accordance with IFRS

Historical Summary
(as originally stated)

Fiscal Year	Oper. Rev. $000s	Net Inc. Bef. Disc. $000s	EPS* $
2022[A]	38,120	(8,807)	(0.56)
2021[A1]	18,557	(20,992)	(3.83)
2020[A]	5,429	(3,196)	(17.82)
2019[A]	2,092	(1,413)	(11.01)

* Common
A Reported in accordance with IFRS
1 Results pertain to Pluribus Technologies Inc.
Note: Adjusted throughout for 1-for-7.94118 cons. in Jan. 2022

P.74 Plurilock Security Inc.

Symbol - PLUR **Exchange** - TSX-VEN **CUSIP** - 72942L
Head Office - MNP Tower, 900-1021 Hastings St W, Vancouver, BC, V6E 0C3 **Telephone** - (604) 889-8476
Website - plurilock.com
Email - scott.meyers@plurilock.com
Investor Relations - Scott R. Meyers (604) 889-8476
Auditors - Mazars, LLP C.A., Montréal, Qué.
Transfer Agents - Computershare Trust Company of Canada Inc., Vancouver, B.C.
Profile - (B.C. 2018) Provides identity-centric cybersecurity solutions to businesses in Canada and the U.S.

Operations are organized into two divisions: Technology and Solutions.

Technology Division - Through wholly owned **Plurilock Security Solutions Inc.**, **Plurilock Security Corp.** and **Plurilock Security Private Limited**, provides core, multi-patent-protected technology that confirms user identity without password, numeric multi-factor authentication (MFA) codes, fingerprints and other common identity confirmation technologies. Products include Plurilock AI, a cybersecurity platform that implements advanced least privilege access management strategies which enables organizations to provide users the smallest possible amount of computing access needed to do their work. Plurilock AI has three configurations including Plurilock Cloud, an agentless solution that provides comprehensive suite of tools to enable cost-effective least privilege access management across enterprise's cloud universe, along with cloud-based data loss prevention (DLP) capabilities; Plurilock AI Cloud DLP, which pairs with Plurilock AI Cloud that enables end-point-based data loss prevention capability which ensures that least privilege strategies are maintained to protect sensitive data across employee workstations; and Plurilock AI Complete, provides real-time authentication and identifies confirmation as a signal to manage cloud and data access which is granted to the authorized user. Also offers Plurilock DEFEND, an enterprise continuous authentication platform that confirms user identity or alerts security teams to detect intrusions in real time, as regular work is carried out, without otherwise inconveniencing or interrupting users.

Solutions Division - Through wholly owned **Aurora Systems Consulting Inc.** and **Integra Networks Corporation**, resells cybersecurity industry products as well as provides enterprise service provision to manage these product deployments and their integration and operation.

In September 2022, wholly owned **Aurora Systems Consulting, Inc.** acquired U.S.-based **Atrion Communications, Inc.** for US$1,924,779 cash and issuance of 1,285,700 common shares at a deemed price of US$0.30 per share. Atrion provides consulting, cybersecurity and information technology solutions including procurement services, professional services and solutions integrations, managed services and cybersecurity consulting to customers in food service and facility management, pharmaceutical, hospitals and medical centers.

In August 2022, the company acquired India-based **CloudCodes Software Private Limited** for US$1,451,148 consisting of US$700,000 cash, issuance if US$300,000 promissory note maturing on Nov. 15, 2022 and issuance of 992,755 common shares at a deemed price of Cdn$0.59 per share. CloudCodes develops a Software-as-a-Service platform which protects email and group collaborations platforms like Microsoft 365 and Google Workspace while providing single-sign-on, multi-factor authentication and cloud data loss prevention functionality.

In March 2022, the company agreed to acquire ontario-based **Integra Networks Corporation** for $1,200,000 consisting of $600,000 cash, issuance of 476,190 common shares at a deemed price of 42¢ per share and issuance of $400,000 earn-out common shares. Integra provides cybersecurity, cloud computing, end-user computing and information technology infrastructure solutions for Canadian federal, provincial and local governments, as well as educational institutions, global healthcare organizations and world-class enterprise companies.

Predecessor Detail - Name changed from Libby K Industries Inc., Sept. 17, 2020, pursuant to the Qualifying Transaction reverse takeover acquisition of Plurilock Security Solutions Inc. and concurrent amalgamation of Plurilock with wholly owned 1243540 B.C. Ltd.; basis 1 new for 2 old shs.

Directors - Robert Kiesman, chr., Richmond, B.C.; Ian L. Paterson, CEO, Victoria, B.C.; Blake Corbet, B.C.; W. Edward (Ed) Hammersla III, Md.; V-Adm. (ret.) Mike McConnell, Middleburg, Va.; Jennifer Swindell, Idaho

Other Exec. Officers - Tucker Zengerle, COO; Scott R. Meyers, CFO & corp. sec.; Garr Stephenson Jr., chief revenue officer; Jord Tanner, chief tech. officer & CIO

Capital Stock

	Authorized (shs.)	Outstanding (shs.)[1]
Common	unlimited	87,328,732

1 At May 26, 2023

Major Shareholder - Widely held at May 16, 2023.

Price Range - PLUR/TSX-VEN

Year	Volume	High	Low	Close
2022	22,103,724	$0.47	$0.12	$0.13
2021	39,608,857	$0.85	$0.36	$0.50
2020	10,361,989	$0.45	$0.22	$0.40
2019	277,000	$0.40	$0.14	$0.16

Consolidation: 1-for-2 cons. in Sept. 2020
Recent Close: $0.13

Capital Stock Changes - In January 2023, private placement of 3,868,415 units (1 common share & 1 warrant) at 14¢ per unit was completed, with warrants exercisable at 25¢ per share for two years. In June 2023, private placement of 11,357,276 units (1 common share & 1 warrant) at $0.145 per unit was completed, with warrants exercisable at 20¢ per share for four years.

During 2022, common shares were issued as follows: 11,115,145 by private placement, 2,440,376 pursuant to the acquisition of Atrion Communications, Inc., 992,755 pursuant to the acquisition of CloudCodes Software Private Limited, 635,879 for services, 476,190 pursuant to the acquisition of Integra Networks Corporation and 12,808 on exercise of warrants.

Wholly Owned Subsidiaries

Atrion Communications, Inc., United States.
CloudCodes Software Private Limited, India.
Integra Networks Corporation, Canada.
Plurilock Security Solutions Inc., Victoria, B.C.
- 100% int. in **Plurilock Security Corp.**, United States.
  - 100% int. in **Aurora Systems Consulting, Inc.**, Calif.
- 0.01% int. in **Plurilock Security Private Limited**, India.

Subsidiaries

99.9% int. in **Plurilock Security Private Limited**, India.

Financial Statistics

Periods ended:	12m Dec. 31/22[A]		12m Dec. 31/21[A]
	$000s	%Chg	$000s
Operating revenue	**64,632**	**+76**	**36,625**
Cost of sales	59,650		34,142
Research & devel. expense	2,485		1,417
General & admin expense	2,924		5,515
Stock-based compensation	672		937
Operating expense	**65,731**	**+56**	**42,011**
Operating income	**(1,099)**	**n.a.**	**(5,386)**
Deprec., depl. & amort.	270		107
Finance costs, gross	599		348
Write-downs/write-offs	nil		(23)
Pre-tax income	**(8,451)**	**n.a.**	**(6,424)**
Income taxes	(5)		(146)
Net income	**(8,446)**	**n.a.**	**(6,277)**
Cash & equivalent	21,713		9,468
Inventories	316		734
Accounts receivable	12,020		6,096
Current assets	16,061		16,929
Fixed assets, net	139		65
Right-of-use assets	211		nil
Intangibles, net	7,076		1,475
Total assets	**23,608**	**+28**	**18,481**
Bank indebtedness	5,262		nil
Accts. pay. & accr. liabs	13,091		10,998
Current liabilities	19,182		11,326
Long-term debt, gross	1,191		202
Long-term debt, net	1,191		202
Long-term lease liabilities	137		nil
Shareholders' equity	2,801		6,930
Cash from oper. activs	**(9,837)**	**n.a.**	**(2,034)**
Cash from fin. activs	7,942		9,776
Cash from invest. activs	(4,670)		(5)
Net cash position	**2,853**	**-70**	**9,468**
Capital expenditures	(34)		(55)
	$		$
Earnings per share*	(0.12)		(0.10)
Cash flow per share*	(0.14)		(0.03)
	shs		shs
No. of shs. o/s*	85,360,725		69,687,572
Avg. no. of shs. o/s*	72,306,538		60,108,270
	%		%
Net profit margin	(13.07)		(17.14)
Return on equity	(173.59)		(145.86)
Return on assets	(37.29)		(57.33)

* Common
A Reported in accordance with IFRS

Latest Results

Periods ended:	3m Mar. 31/23[A]		3m Mar. 31/22[A]
	$000s	%Chg	$000s
Operating revenue	15,767	+127	6,953
Net income	(1,358)	n.a.	(2,379)
	$		$
Earnings per share*	(0.02)		(0.03)

* Common
A Reported in accordance with IFRS

Historical Summary
(as originally stated)

Fiscal Year	Oper. Rev.	Net Inc. Bef. Disc.	EPS*
	$000s	$000s	$
2022[A]	64,632	(8,446)	(0.12)
2021[A]	36,625	(6,277)	(0.10)
2020[A1]	479	(4,598)	(0.16)
2019[A]	647	(1,337)	n.a.
2018[A]	653	(1,432)	n.a.

* Common
[A] Reported in accordance with IFRS
[1] Results prior to Sept. 17, 2020, pertain to and reflect the Qualifying Transaction reverse takeover acquisition of Plurilock Security Solutions Inc.
Note: Adjusted throughout for 1-for-2 cons. in Sept. 2020

P.75 Poko Innovations Inc.

Symbol - POKO **Exchange** - CSE (S) **CUSIP** - 73087F
Head Office - 2700-1000 rue Sherbrooke O, Montréal, QC, H3A 3G4 **Telephone** - (514) 375-5172 **Toll-free** - (866) 228-1299 **Fax** - (514) 987-1213
Website - www.pokogroup.com
Email - ir@pokogroup.com
Investor Relations - David Hughes (866) 228-1299
Auditors - MNP LLP C.A., Ottawa, Ont.
Transfer Agents - Computershare Trust Company of Canada Inc., Calgary, Alta.
Profile - (Can. 2021; orig. Alta., 2006) Owns and operates a group of cannabidiol (CBD) and financial services focused businesses in the United Kingdom and Europe.
The company's business units are as follows:
LumiPay, a CBD-friendly and high-risk tolerant, payment processing service marketed to businesses with e-commerce needs; **The Extract**, a business-to-business (B2B) news and media website for the CBD and cannabis industry in the U,K., whose aim is to provide lead generation for the raw materials and marketplace sites; **Candid Magazine**, a business-to-consumer (B2C) lifestyle and culture magazine focused on the avid CBD and cannabis user whose purpose is to provide data intelligence on consumer behaviour and provide leads for the company's B2C focused brands Poko and Candid; **CBD Village**, an e-commerce site; **Social Channel Network**, consists of non-CBD focused pages; **Cannmed Products**, a wholesale premium white labelling and raw materials supplier in the U.K.; **Cannmed Marketplace**, a marketplace technology and licence which gives the company the technological capability of scaling to tens of thousands of suppliers and handling millions of orders; **Poko Skincare:** a B2C CBD-based skincare brand; and **Candid**, the company's second business-to-consumer CBD brand which offers a range of tinctures, gummies, softgels and hot beverages.
Common suspended from CSE, Nov. 7, 2022.
Predecessor Detail - Name changed from Brunswick Resources Inc., Aug. 10, 2021, pursuant to the reverse takeover acquisition of Poko Group Ltd.; basis 1 new for 5 old shs.
Directors - Michael Porter, chr., N.J.; Tim Henley, United Kingdom; Alex Leigh, Manchester, Lancs., United Kingdom; Simon Painter, N.S.
Other Exec. Officers - David Hughes, CEO; Justine O'Hanlon, COO; Senan Sexton, CFO

Capital Stock

	Authorized (shs.)	Outstanding (shs.)[1]
Preferred	unlimited	nil
Common	unlimited	80,201,562

[1] At Mar. 31, 2022
Major Shareholder - David Hughes held 54.71% interest at Aug. 19, 2021.

Price Range - BRU.H/TSX-VEN (D)

Year	Volume	High	Low	Close
2022	7,525,666	$0.11	$0.02	$0.03
2021	2,006,143	$0.36	$0.08	$0.11
2019	167,355	$0.15	$0.10	$0.13
2018	428,131	$0.23	$0.13	$0.18

Consolidation: 1-for-5 cons. in Aug. 2021
Recent Close: $0.03

Wholly Owned Subsidiaries
Poko Group Ltd., London, Middx., United Kingdom.

P.76 Polaris Northstar Capital Corp.

Symbol - POLE **Exchange** - CSE (S) **CUSIP** - 73108T
Head Office - 810-789 Pender St W, Vancouver, BC, V6C 1H2 **Telephone** - (604) 687-2038 **Fax** - (604) 536-2788
Email - info@globalcarecapital.com
Investor Relations - Charles Maddin (604) 687-2038
Auditors - Mao & Ying LLP C.A., Vancouver, B.C.
Bankers - Bank of Montreal
Lawyers - Stikeman Elliott LLP, Vancouver, B.C.
Transfer Agents - National Securities Administrators Ltd., Vancouver, B.C.
Profile - (B.C. 2004) Invests in early-stage private and public companies in the cryptocurrency, blockchain, healthcare and natural resource sectors.
At June 30, 2022, the investment portfolio consisted of three publicly traded investments and eight privately held investments with a total fair value of $3,264,046.
Primary investments include 100%-owned **1290369 B.C. Ltd.** (dba **CCM Technologies Inc.**), which provides infrastructure in digital asset technology; **ASIC Power Company**, which provides cryptocurrency mining market with expansion finance through royalty streaming contracts and access to application specific integrated circuit chips necessary for mining cryptocurrencies; **ViralClear Rapid Test Corp.**, which has developed a novel Coronavirus (COVID-19) Rapid IgM-IgG combined antibody test and launched its employee protection equipment (EPE) kit; **Healthview Technologies Inc.**, which provides an online solution and tool that employees and employment firms will be able to use to maintain wellness and provide support for staff; and 70%-owned **High Standard Health Care Ltd.**, which provides personal protective equipment globally to assist front line workers during the global pandemic.
Common suspended from CSE, May 9, 2023.
Predecessor Detail - Name changed from Global Care Capital Inc., Mar. 29, 2023; basis 1 new for 20 old shs.
Directors - Charles (Hugh) Maddin, interim CEO, West Vancouver, B.C.; Ho Hung (Ricky) Chung; Denis Hayes, Kelowna, B.C.; Maciej (Magic) Lis, Toronto, Ont.
Other Exec. Officers - Richard (Rick) Barnett, CFO; Bernice Wong, corp. sec.

Capital Stock

	Authorized (shs.)	Outstanding (shs.)[1]
Common	unlimited	64,687,309

[1] At Mar. 29, 2023
Major Shareholder - Widely held at Aug. 27, 2021.

Price Range - RIN/TSX (D)

Year	Volume	High	Low	Close
2022	13,686,887	$1.40	$0.06	$0.10
2021	30,498,618	$4.80	$0.80	$1.20
2020	15,906,755	$36.80	$0.30	$1.70
2019	200,717	$140.00	$2.50	$10.00
2018	26,785	$400.00	$40.00	$42.50

Consolidation: 1-for-20 cons. in Mar. 2023; 1-for-25 cons. in Mar. 2020
Recent Close: $0.04
Capital Stock Changes - On Mar. 29, 2023, common shares were consolidated on a 1-for-20 basis.

Wholly Owned Subsidiaries
ASIC Power Company, Toronto, Ont.
Health View Technologies Inc.
Metaverse Capital Corp., Vancouver, B.C.
1290369 B.C. Ltd., Canada. dba CCM Technologies Inc.
360 Life Sciences Corp.
Vancity Green List Inc., B.C.
ViralClear Rapid Test Corp., Vancouver, B.C.

Subsidiaries
70% int. in **High Standard Health Care Ltd.**, New York, N.Y.

Investments
Pembrook Copper Corp., Vancouver, B.C.

Financial Statistics

Periods ended:	12m Dec. 31/21[A]		12m Dec. 31/20[A]
	$000s	%Chg	$000s
Realized invest. gain (loss)	(209)		(5,238)
Unrealized invest. gain (loss)	(26,517)		(35,463)
Total revenue	**(26,727)**	**n.a.**	**(42,514)**
General & admin. expense	905		9,869
Stock-based compensation	479		1,754
Operating expense	**1,384**	**-88**	**11,623**
Operating income	**(28,111)**	**n.a.**	**(54,137)**
Pre-tax income	**(28,110)**	**n.a.**	**(53,380)**
Net income	**(28,110)**	**n.a.**	**(53,380)**
Cash & equivalent	618		322
Investments	2,343		390
Total assets	**2,961**	**+316**	**712**
Accts. pay. & accr. liabs	821		371
Shareholders' equity	2,139		(1,359)
Cash from oper. activs	**(344)**	**n.a.**	**(2,123)**
Cash from fin. activs	640		2,431
Net cash position	**618**	**+92**	**322**
	$		$
Earnings per share*	(2.00)		(16.80)
Cash flow per share*	(0.02)		(0.66)
	shs		shs
No. of shs. o/s*	17,032,878		5,277,162
Avg. no. of shs. o/s*	14,225,986		3,192,806
	%		%
Net profit margin	n.m.		n.m.
Return on equity	n.m.		n.m.
Return on assets	n.m.		n.m.

* Common
[A] Reported in accordance with IFRS

Latest Results

Periods ended:	6m June 30/22[A]		6m June 30/21[A]
	$000s	%Chg	$000s
Total revenue	921	+183	326
Net income	(520)	n.a.	(491)
	$		$
Earnings per share*	(0.03)		(0.04)

* Common
[A] Reported in accordance with IFRS

Historical Summary
(as originally stated)

Fiscal Year	Total Rev.	Net Inc. Bef. Disc.	EPS*
	$000s	$000s	$
2021[A]	(26,727)	(28,110)	(2.00)
2020[A]	(42,514)	(53,380)	(16.80)
2019[A]	82	(13,018)	(53.80)
2018[A]	(3,679)	(7,348)	(72.00)
2017[A]	230	(60)	(3.45)

* Common
[A] Reported in accordance with IFRS
Note: Adjusted throughout for 1-for-20 cons. in Mar. 2023; 1-for-25 cons. in Mar. 2020

P.77 Polaris Renewable Energy Inc.

Symbol - PIF **Exchange** - TSX **CUSIP** - 73108L
Head Office - 606-7 St. Thomas St, Toronto, ON, M5S 2B7 **Telephone** - (647) 245-7199
Website - polarisrei.com
Email - info@polarisrei.com
Investor Relations - Anthony Jelic (647) 245-7199
Auditors - PricewaterhouseCoopers LLP C.A., Toronto, Ont.
Lawyers - Stikeman Elliott LLP, Toronto, Ont.
Transfer Agents - TSX Trust Company, Toronto, Ont.
FP500 Revenue Ranking - 793
Employees - 208 at Feb. 23, 2023
Profile - (Ont. 2022; orig. B.C., 1984) Develops and operates geothermal, hydroelectric and solar energy projects in Latin America.
Owns and operates the 72-MW San Jacinto-Tizate geothermal project located 90 km northwest of Managua, Nicaragua, including the 10-MW organic rankine cycle (ORC) binary facility; three run-of-river hydroelectric projects in Peru, consisting of 5-MW Canchayllo facility in Canchayllo district, 8-MW El Carmen and 20-MW 8 de Agosto facilities in Monzón district; a 6-MW run-on-river hydroelectric facility in San Jose de Minas, Ecuador; and 25-MW defined conditions (MWdc) Canoa 1 photovoltaic solar plant in Barahona, Dominican Republic.
Other projects under various stages of construction and development include two solar plants totaling 10-MWdc located in the village of Vista Hermosa in Panama; 25-MWdc Canoa 2 photovoltaic solar plant in Barahona, Dominican Republic; 20-MW Karpa hydroelectric facility in Tantamayo district; and about 189 MW of other hydroelectric projects in pre-development stage, all in Peru.
During 2022, the 10-MW organic rankine cycle (ORC) geothermal binary facility in Nicaragua finished construction and achieved commercial operation on Dec. 31, 2022.
In March 2022, the company acquired two solar plants totaling 13.4 MW defined conditions (MWdc) located in the village of Vista Hermosa in Panama for US$600,000. The acquisition includes the licenses and permits required to complete the construction and to operate. The company would fund 100% of the costs to build two construction-ready solar plants, with a target commercial operation date of 9 to 10 months, for $10,000,000. In connection, the company would receive exclusive development rights for two additional solar development stage solar projects totaling 26 MWdc in Panama.

Periods ended:	12m Dec. 31/22	12m Dec. 31/21
Electric gen., GWh	650	644

Recent Merger and Acquisition Activity
Status: completed **Revised:** Sept. 7, 2022
UPDATE: The transaction was completed for US$16,300,000 cash and assumption of US$6,100,000 of debt. PREVIOUS: Polaris Renewable Energy Inc. agreed to acquire 83.16% interest in Hidroelectrica San Jose de Minas S.A. for US$20,400,000 and assumption of estimated debt of US$7,000,000. The transaction includes a 6-MW operational run-on-river hydroelectric facility, located along the Cubi River in San Jose de Minas, Ecuador and has been operating since June 2020. In addition, Polaris intends to acquire the remaining interest within one year and was working to formalize a development framework agreement with the vendor to jointly pursue further hydro projects in the Ecuadorian market. Hidroelectrica explores for and develops hydroelectric energy projects in Ecuador.
Status: completed **Revised:** June 28, 2022
UPDATE: The transaction was completed for US$20,300,000 cash and assumption of US$35,300,000 of debt. PREVIOUS: Polaris Infrastructure Inc. agreed to acquire Emerald Solar Energy S.R.L. for US$18,400,000 cash and assumption of project level debt of US$35,000,000. The transaction includes a 32-MW defined conditions (MWdc) operational photovoltaic solar plant (Canoa 1) and Canoa 2 expansion, located in Barahona, Dominican Republic. Emerald explores for and develops solar projects in the Dominican Republic.
Predecessor Detail - Name changed from Polaris Infrastructure Inc., July 5, 2022.

Directors - James Guillen, chr., London, Middx., United Kingdom; Marc Murnaghan, CEO, Ont.; Marcela Paredes de Vasquez, Panama City, Panama; James V. (Jim) Lawless, Auckland, New Zealand

Other Exec. Officers - Anthony (Anton) Jelic, CFO; Michael Kosianic, exec. v-p, project fin.; Alexis Osorno, sr. v-p, Latin America; Priscila Cortes, v-p, fin.; Guzman Fernandez, v-p, corp. devel.; Denise Parada, v-p, fin. transformation & governance; Alba Seisdedos, v-p, tax. & legal affairs

Capital Stock

	Authorized (shs.)	Outstanding (shs.)[1]
Common	unlimited	21,025,775

[1] At Aug. 2, 2023

Normal Course Issuer Bid - The company plans to make normal course purchases of up to 2,048,273 common shares representing 10% of the public float. The bid commenced on Aug. 23, 2023, and expires on Aug. 22, 2024.

Major Shareholder - Widely held at May 3, 2023.

Price Range - PIF/TSX

Year	Volume	High	Low	Close
2022	13,726,375	$23.05	$13.34	$14.07
2021	22,656,981	$24.41	$15.50	$16.86
2020	17,111,303	$19.88	$8.59	$17.71
2019	13,497,496	$15.83	$9.22	$12.25
2018	11,946,452	$20.75	$8.32	$10.30

Recent Close: $14.13

Capital Stock Changes - During 2022, common shares were issued as follows: 1,400,399 on conversion of debentures and 100,000 pursuant to the acquisition of Union Energy Group Corp.

Dividends

PIF com Ra US$0.60 pa Q est. Nov. 27, 2017

Wholly Owned Subsidiaries

Polaris Energy Peru Corp., Peru.
- 99.9% int. in **Andean Power Generation Ltd.**, British Virgin Islands.
  - 100% int. in **Andean Power Generation S.A.C.**, Peru.
    - 99.9% int. in **Generacion Andina S.A.C.**, Peru.
  - 100% int. in **Energias Renovables de los Andes S.A.C.**, Peru.
    - 99.9% int. in **Empresa de Generacion Electrica Canchayllo S.A.C.**, Peru.
- 99.9% int. in **Polaris Energy Services S.A.C.**, Peru.

Polaris International Holdings Inc., Canada.
- 100% int. in **Emerald Solar Energy S.R.L.**, Dominican Republic.

Polaris Renewable Energy Ecuador S.A.S., Ecuador.
- 83.16% int. in **Hidroelectrica San Jose de Minas S.A.**, Ecuador.

Polaris Renewable Energy S.A., Panama.
- 100% int. in **Panasolar Green Energy Corp.**, Panama.
- 100% int. in **Panasolar Green Power Corp.**, Panama.

Ram Power Inc., United States.

Sierra Power, Corp., Canada.

Subsidiaries

99.34% int. in **Polaris Energy Corp.**, Panama.
- 100% int. in **San Jacinto Power International Corporation**, Panama.
  - 99.99% int. in **Polaris Energy Nicaragua, S.A.**, Nicaragua.

Financial Statistics

Periods ended:	12m Dec. 31/22[A]		12m Dec. 31/21[A]
	US$000s	%Chg	US$000s
Operating revenue	**62,600**	**+5**	**59,517**
Cost of sales	11,658		10,699
General & admin expense	6,043		5,608
Stock-based compensation	383		875
Other operating expense	788		20
Operating expense	**18,872**	**+10**	**17,202**
Operating income	**43,728**	**+3**	**42,315**
Deprec., depl. & amort.	26,119		26,396
Finance income	677		374
Finance costs, gross	19,477		16,962
Pre-tax income	**969**	**-78**	**4,418**
Income taxes	(1,464)		3,876
Net income	**2,433**	**+349**	**542**
Net inc. for equity hldrs	**2,499**	**+399**	**501**
Net inc. for non-cont. int	**(66)**	**n.a.**	**41**
Cash & equivalent	35,325		97,930
Accounts receivable	11,239		9,324
Current assets	50,609		110,143
Fixed assets, net	389,138		348,657
Right-of-use assets	2,830		1,225
Intangibles, net	69,882		22,968
Explor./devel. properties	9,898		8,779
Total assets	**535,102**	**+6**	**502,700**
Accts. pay. & accr. liabs	14,931		10,743
Current liabilities	30,598		34,307
Long-term debt, gross	184,408		169,686
Long-term debt, net	169,466		146,571
Long-term lease liabilities	2,498		1,000
Shareholders' equity	269,677		262,759
Non-controlling interest	535		(1,935)
Cash from oper. activs	**33,506**	**-19**	**41,129**
Cash from fin. activs	(30,125)		6,891
Cash from invest. activs	(65,994)		(10,146)
Net cash position	**35,325**	**-64**	**97,930**
Capital expenditures	(32,482)		(8,413)
Capital disposals	nil		317
	US$		US$
Earnings per share*	0.12		0.03
Cash flow per share*	1.66		2.19
Cash divd. per share*	0.60		0.60
	shs		shs
No. of shs. o/s*	21,025,775		19,525,376
Avg. no. of shs. o/s*	20,127,720		18,805,465
	%		%
Net profit margin	3.89		0.91
Return on equity	0.94		0.20
Return on assets	9.89		0.53
Foreign sales percent	100		100

* Common

[A] Reported in accordance with IFRS

Historical Summary
(as originally stated)

Fiscal Year	Oper. Rev. US$000s	Net Inc. Bef. Disc. US$000s	EPS* US$
2022[A]	62,600	2,433	0.12
2021[A]	59,517	542	0.03
2020[A]	74,720	28,873	1.84
2019[A]	71,251	12,843	0.92
2018[A]	68,824	12,199	0.77

* Common

[A] Reported in accordance with IFRS

P.78 Pollard Banknote Limited

Symbol - PBL **Exchange** - TSX **CUSIP** - 73150R

Head Office - 140 Otter St, Winnipeg, MB, R3T 0M8 **Telephone** - (204) 474-2323 **Fax** - (204) 453-1375

Website - www.pollardbanknote.com

Email - rrose@pbl.ca

Investor Relations - Robert Rose (204) 474-2323 ext. 250

Auditors - KPMG LLP C.A., Winnipeg, Man.

Bankers - Canadian Western Bank, Edmonton, Alta.; Bank of Montreal, Calgary, Alta.; The Toronto-Dominion Bank, Winnipeg, Man.

Lawyers - Torys LLP, Toronto, Ont.

Transfer Agents - Computershare Trust Company of Canada Inc., Toronto, Ont.

FP500 Revenue Ranking - 477

Employees - 2,191 at Dec. 31, 2022

Profile - (Can. 2010) Provides products and services to lotteries and charitable organizations globally. Also designs, produces and services electronic games and devices to charitable and other gaming markets in North America.

The company serves more than 60 instant ticket lotteries including a number of the largest lotteries throughout the world. Manufacturing and warehousing facilities are located in Winnipeg, Man. (2); Barrhead, Alta.; Sault Ste. Marie and Stoney Creek, Ont.; Ypsilanti, Mich.; Council Bluffs and Adair, Iowa; Chatsworth, Calif; Jefferson City, Mo.; Omaha, Neb.; Mento, Ohio; London, Newcastle and Macclesfield, U.K.; Kópavogur, Iceland; Barcelona, Spain; and Belgrade, Serbia.

Operations are organized into two segments: Lotteries and Charitable Gaming; and eGaming Systems.

The **Lotteries and Charitable Gaming** segment manufactures and provides instant-win/scratch, pull-tab and draw tickets, Internet lottery services (iLottery), bingo paper, licensed games, lottery ticket dispensers and point-of-sale displays, lottery management services and information systems, interactive digital games and website development, pull-tab vending machines and ancillary products such as pull-tab counting machines. Charitable gaming products are principally sold in the U.S. under the American Games and International Gamco brands.

The **eGaming Systems** segment operates through wholly owned **Diamond Game Enterprises, Inc.**, which provides kiosk-based technologies NexPlay® and EZ Tab® that allow lotteries and charity gaming markets to expand their retailer base into less traditional establishments, such as bars, taverns, bingo halls and social clubs. The NexPlay® terminal provides self-service purchasing of instant and draw game tickets. In addition, Diamond Game's wholly owned **Compliant Gaming LLC** provides electronic pull-tab gaming systems and products to the charitable gaming market.

Product Sales

	2022	2021
Instant tickets[1]	15.1	15.1
Bingo cards[1]	2	1.9
Pull-tab tickets[1]	2.3	2.4
Vending machines	700	1,000
Charitable gaming machines[2]	3,100	3,800
Electronic pull-tab tablets[2]	3,100	2,000

[1] Billion.

[2] Leased.

Predecessor Detail - Succeeded Pollard Banknote Income Fund, May 14, 2010, following conversion of Pollard Banknote Income Fund into a corporation; basis 1 com. sh. for 1 fund unit and 1 com. sh. for 1 class B or class C limited partnership unit of Pollard Holdings Limited Partnership.

Directors - Gordon O. Pollard, exec. chr., Winnipeg, Man.; Douglas E. Pollard, co-CEO, Winnipeg, Man.; John S. Pollard, co-CEO, Winnipeg, Man.; David G. (Dave) Brown, Winnipeg, Man.; Lee Meagher, Winnipeg, Man.; Carmele N. Peter, Winnipeg, Man.

Other Exec. Officers - Steven Fingold, exec. v-p, charitable gaming; Paul Franzmann, exec. v-p, corp. devel.; Pedro Melo, exec. v-p, IT; Margaret Proven, exec. v-p, HR; Riva Richard, exec. v-p, legal affairs, gen. counsel & corp. sec.; Robert (Rob) Rose, exec. v-p, fin. & CFO; Jennifer Westbury, exec. v-p, sales & cust. devel.; Robert B. Young, exec. v-p, opers.

Capital Stock

	Authorized (shs.)	Outstanding (shs.)[1]
Preference	unlimited	nil
Common	unlimited	26,917,669

[1] At Apr. 6, 2023

Major Shareholder - The Pollard family held 64.3% interest at Apr. 6, 2023.

Price Range - PBL/TSX

Year	Volume	High	Low	Close
2022	5,644,229	$40.68	$15.77	$19.12
2021	8,181,158	$67.00	$32.08	$39.85
2020	2,446,514	$36.36	$12.06	$35.74
2019	1,317,836	$25.08	$19.06	$20.00
2018	2,784,815	$27.75	$16.91	$20.55

Recent Close: $26.48

Capital Stock Changes - There were no changes to capital stock during 2022.

Dividends

PBL com Ra $0.16 pa Q est. Oct. 15, 2021
Prev. Rate: $0.236 est. July 15, 2021
Prev. Rate: $0.16 est. Apr. 15, 2019

Wholly Owned Subsidiaries

Concuros y Promociones Pollard de Puerto Rico, Inc., Puerto Rico. Inactive.

mkodo Limited, London, Middx., United Kingdom.

Nacako Sdn. Bhd., Malaysia. Inactive.

Next Generation Lotteries AS, Oslo, Norway.
- 100% int. in **Pollard Digital Solutions GmbH**, Vienna, Austria.
  - 99.99% int. in **Next Generation Lotteries S.A.R.L.**, Tunis, Tunisia.
  - 100% int. in **Next Generation Lotteries S.L.**, Barcelona, Spain.
  - 100% int. in **Pollard Digital Solutions d.o.o. Beograd**, Belgrade, Serbia.
    - 0.01% int. in **Next Generation Lotteries S.A.R.L.**, Tunis, Tunisia.
  - 100% int. in **Pollard Digital Solutions ehf.**, Iceland.

PBL of Puerto Rico Inc., Puerto Rico. Inactive.

Pollard Holdings, Inc., Del.
- 100% int. in **Diamond Game Enterprises, Inc.**, Chatsworth, Calif.
  - 100% int. in **Compliant Gaming LLC**, Jamestown, R.I.
  - 100% int. in **Diamond Game Enterprises Canada ULC**, B.C.
- 50% int. in **NeoPollard Interactive LLC**, Del.
- 100% int. in **Pollard Games, Inc.**, Del.
  - 100% int. in **Intergity Bingo, LLC**, Ark.
- 100% int. in **Pollard iLottery Inc.**, Del.
- 100% int. in **Pollard (U.S.) Ltd.**, Del.
- 100% int. in **Schafer Systems (2018) Inc.**, Iowa

Schafer Systems (UK) Limited, United Kingdom.

Investments

50% int. in **2278943 Ontario Inc.**, Ont. Inactive.

Note: The preceding list includes only the major related companies in which interests are held.

Financial Statistics

Periods ended:	12m Dec. 31/22[A]		12m Dec. 31/21[A]
	$000s	%Chg	$000s
Operating revenue	**482,278**	**+5**	**459,014**
Cost of sales	400,455		367,912
General & admin expense	26,270		25,198
Operating expense	**426,725**	**+9**	**393,110**
Operating income	**55,553**	**-16**	**65,904**
Deprec., depl. & amort	40,982		39,554
Finance income	3,600		832
Finance costs, gross	15,579		7,234
Investment income	23,720		12,336
Pre-tax income	**22,215**	**-18**	**27,115**
Income taxes	2,938		7,414
Net income	**19,277**	**-2**	**19,701**
Cash & equivalent	1,479		3,517
Inventories	62,132		45,008
Accounts receivable	79,310		73,351
Current assets	184,933		153,166
Long-term investments	549		585
Fixed assets, net	100,620		104,590
Intangibles, net	210,618		202,480
Total assets	**499,266**	**+8**	**461,405**
Accts. pay. & accr. liabs	89,523		81,306
Current liabilities	105,029		90,970
Long-term debt, gross	121,655		115,130
Long-term debt, net	121,655		115,130
Long-term lease liabilities	7,539		10,419
Shareholders' equity	251,934		206,957
Cash from oper. activs	**56,537**	**0**	**56,537**
Cash from fin. activs	(7,728)		6,369
Cash from invest. activs	(24,572)		(60,589)
Net cash position	**1,479**	**-58**	**3,517**
Capital expenditures	(14,318)		(22,226)
Unfunded pension liability	n.a.		22,541
Pension fund surplus	988		n.a.
	$		$
Earnings per share*	0.72		0.73
Cash flow per share*	2.10		2.11
Cash divd. per share*	0.16		0.18
	shs		shs
No. of shs. o/s*	26,917,669		26,917,669
Avg. no. of shs. o/s*	26,917,669		26,743,919
	%		%
Net profit margin	4.00		4.29
Return on equity	8.40		11.28
Return on assets	6.83		5.76
Foreign sales percent	82		82
No. of employees (FTEs)	2,191		2,064

* Common

[A] Reported in accordance with IFRS

Latest Results

Periods ended:	3m Mar. 31/23[A]		3m Mar. 31/22[A]
	$000s	%Chg	$000s
Operating revenue	124,633	+9	113,872
Net income	4,826	-25	6,425
	$		$
Earnings per share*	0.18		0.24

* Common

[A] Reported in accordance with IFRS

Historical Summary
(as originally stated)

Fiscal Year	Oper. Rev. $000s	Net Inc. Bef. Disc. $000s	EPS* $
2022[A]	482,278	19,277	0.72
2021[A]	459,014	19,701	0.74
2020[A]	414,134	33,288	1.30
2019[A]	397,839	22,017	0.86
2018[A]	331,868	14,852	0.58

* Common

[A] Reported in accordance with IFRS

P.79 Pond Technologies Holdings Inc.

Symbol - POND **Exchange** - TSX-VEN **CUSIP** - 73238C
Head Office - Unit 8, 250 Shields Crt, Markham, ON, L3R 9W7 **Telephone** - (416) 287-3835 **Fax** - (416) 287-3808
Website - www.pondtech.com
Email - t.masney@pondtech.com
Investor Relations - Thomas Masney (416) 287-3835
Auditors - Baker Tilly WM LLP C.A., Vancouver, B.C.
Transfer Agents - Computershare Trust Company of Canada Inc., Calgary, Alta.

Profile - (Alta. 2002; orig. B.C., 1972) Develops and commercializes patented algae growing platform technology which converts carbon dioxide found in untreated stack gas of industrial emitters into algal-based commercial products including animal and human feeds, nutraceuticals and natural fertilizers.

Operates through two segments: Technology Services and Nutraceutical Products.

Technology Services - This segment includes the company's technology, which uses industrial emissions or clean carbon dioxide to grow algae for multiple applications including food, feed and nutraceutical ingredients as well as for reproductive medium for the expression of human anti-bodies and proteins. The company grows algae in large vessels (bioreactors), which are engineered to automatically regulate the inflow of carbon dioxide or nutrients while reducing the need for manual supervision. Raw stack gas emissions from heavy industrial emitters, such as cement, steel, oil, chemicals and power producers, are used to produce algae for bio-products including biofuels, bioplastics and fertilizers. Clean carbon dioxide sources are used in the production of algae superfoods such as astaxanthin, phycocyanin, chlorella and spirulina for the nutraceutical and food additive markets as well as algae that contains certain antigens related to SARs-COV-2 which can be used in rapid diagnostic tests. Also developing Algaerithm, which receives data from and controls the many sensors required to assist the achieving optimal real-time algae results and intended to be marketed as a licensed leased product.

Nutraceutical Products - This segment includes wholly owned **Pond Naturals Inc.** (dba Regenurex), which develops a line of products to help the body regenerate. It operates a 10,000-sq.-ft. production facility in Agassiz, B.C.; and sells microalgae, antioxidants, fermented ingredients, vegan proteins, natural energy, natural colours, fruits and vegetable powders and extracts, botanicals and teas, organic greens, and liquid extracts and concentrates.

Periods ended:	12m Dec. 31/21	12m Dec. 31/20
Avg. oil & NGL prod., bbl/d	n.a.	27
Avg. gas prod., mcf/d	n.a.	3
Avg. BOE prod., bbl/d	n.a.	31
Avg. oil & NGL price, $/bbl	n.a.	41.27
Avg. gas price, $/mcf	n.a.	2.17
Avg. BOE price, $/bbl	n.a.	38.05

Note: Remaining oil and gas assets sold in June 2021.

Predecessor Detail - Name changed from Ironhorse Oil & Gas Inc., Feb. 6, 2018, pursuant to reverse takeover acquisition of Pond Technologies Inc.; basis 1 new for 6.9 old shs.

Directors - Robert S. McLeese, chr., Toronto, Ont.; Grant Smith, CEO & pres., Pond Naturals Inc., Markham, Ont.; J. William Asselstine, Oakville, Ont.; Dr. John M. Farah Jr., Pa.

Other Exec. Officers - Dan O'Connor, COO; Thomas Masney, CFO; Peter Howard, v-p, project devel.; Emidio Di Pietro, gen. mgr., tech. div.

Capital Stock

	Authorized (shs.)	Outstanding (shs.)[1]
First Preferred	unlimited	nil
Common	unlimited	60,299,023

[1] At Aug. 2, 2022

Common - One vote per share.

Junior Preferred (old) - Were converted into common shares on a 0.2216-for-1 basis on Aug. 2, 2022.

Senior Preferred (old) - Were converted into common shares on a 0.625-for-1 basis on Aug. 2, 2022.

Major Shareholder - Robert S. McLeese held 11.65% interest at May 6, 2022.

Price Range - POND/TSX-VEN

Year	Volume	High	Low	Close
2022	16,736,496	$0.32	$0.08	$0.09
2021	15,955,814	$0.80	$0.25	$0.27
2020	4,524,660	$0.54	$0.16	$0.30
2019	2,643,618	$0.85	$0.43	$0.51
2018	4,037,739	$2.35	$0.56	$0.80

Recent Close: $0.04

Capital Stock Changes - In March 2022, private placement of 8,920,002 common shares was completed at 20¢ per share. On Aug. 2, 2022, all remaining 7,242,577 junior preferred shares and 3,219,198 senior preferred shares were converted into 3,617,167 common shares. In September and October 2022, private placement of 3,673,334 common shares was completed at 15¢ per share. In addition, private placement of up to 3,750,000 common shares at 12¢ per share was announced.

Wholly Owned Subsidiaries

PaiGE Growth Technologies Inc.
Pond Naturals Inc., B.C. dba Regenurex.
Pond Technologies Inc., Markham, Ont.

Financial Statistics

Periods ended:	12m Dec. 31/21[A]		12m Dec. 31/20[A]
	$000s	%Chg	$000s
Operating revenue	**5,133**	**+7**	**4,800**
Cost of sales	3,693		3,830
Salaries & benefits	1,186		1,119
General & admin expense	2,468		1,754
Stock-based compensation	744		381
Operating expense	**8,091**	**+14**	**7,084**
Operating income	**(2,958)**	**n.a.**	**(2,284)**
Deprec., depl. & amort	579		558
Finance income	1		1
Finance costs, gross	864		827
Write-downs/write-offs	(120)		(358)
Pre-tax income	**(4,520)**	**n.a.**	**(4,146)**
Income taxes	822		nil
Net inc. bef. disc. opers	**(5,342)**	**n.a.**	**(4,146)**
Income from disc. opers	268		(2,470)
Net income	**(5,074)**	**n.a.**	**(6,616)**
Cash & equivalent	1,067		156
Inventories	203		179
Accounts receivable	439		912
Current assets	2,240		1,380
Fixed assets, net	1,117		1,266
Right-of-use assets	230		237
Intangibles, net	1,673		1,942
Total assets	**5,260**	**-15**	**6,199**
Accts. pay. & accr. liabs	1,119		3,030
Current liabilities	2,378		6,474
Long-term debt, gross	4,018		4,805
Long-term debt, net	3,418		1,827
Long-term lease liabilities	176		174
Preferred share equity	2,170		2,821
Shareholders' equity	(712)		(2,380)
Cash from oper. activs	**(3,112)**	**n.a.**	**(1,432)**
Cash from fin. activs	4,373		663
Cash from invest. activs	(350)		(110)
Net cash position	**1,067**	**+584**	**156**
Capital expenditures	(77)		(29)
	$		$
Earns. per sh. bef disc opers*	(0.13)		(0.15)
Earnings per share*	(0.12)		(0.25)
Cash flow per share*	(0.07)		(0.06)
	shs		shs
No. of shs. o/s*	47,761,854		29,526,598
Avg. no. of shs. o/s*	42,460,798		25,954,540
	%		%
Net profit margin	(104.07)		(86.38)
Return on equity	n.m.		n.m.
Return on assets	(75.41)		(41.54)
Foreign sales percent	26		8
No. of employees (FTEs)	n.a.		20

* Common

[A] Reported in accordance with IFRS

Latest Results

Periods ended:	6m June 30/22[A]		6m June 30/21[A]
	$000s	%Chg	$000s
Operating revenue	2,048	-7	2,201
Net inc. bef. disc. opers	(2,506)	n.a.	(1,979)
Income from disc. opers	nil		239
Net income	(2,506)	n.a.	(1,740)
	$		$
Earnings per share*	(0.05)		(0.05)

* Common

[A] Reported in accordance with IFRS

Historical Summary
(as originally stated)

Fiscal Year	Oper. Rev. $000s	Net Inc. Bef. Disc. $000s	EPS* $
2021[A]	5,133	(5,342)	(0.13)
2020[A]	4,800	(4,146)	(0.15)
2019[A]	5,447	(9,092)	(0.42)
2018[A1]	2,704	(5,374)	(0.28)
2017[A2]	1,503	(6,120)	(1.52)

* Common

[A] Reported in accordance with IFRS

[1] Results reflect the Jan. 30, 2018, reverse takeover acquisition of Pond Technologies Inc.

[2] Results for 2017 and prior years pertain to Ironhorse Oil & Gas Inc.

Note: Adjusted throughout for 1-for-6.9 cons. in Feb. 2018

P.80 Pontus Protein Ltd.

Symbol - HULK **Exchange** - TSX-VEN (S) **CUSIP** - 732768
Head Office - 17686 66 A Ave, Surrey, BC, V3S 2A7 **Telephone** - (778) 999-3353
Website - pontuswaterlentils.com

Email - invest@pontuswaterlentils.com
Investor Relations - Avtar Dhaliwal (778) 214-6514
Auditors - MNP LLP C.A., Vancouver, B.C.
Transfer Agents - TSX Trust Company, Vancouver, B.C.
Profile - (B.C. 2018) Processes and manufactures plant-based protein powders. Also provides catering and product consultation services.

Focuses on delivering agricultural food from a closed and controlled environment using proprietary vertical farming and artificial intelligence (AI)-engineered robots. Principal product is Pontus Protein Powder™, an organic, 42.1% pure plant-based protein produced from water lentils which are manufactured at its 20,570-sq.-ft. manufacturing facility in Surrey, B.C.

Through wholly owned **Ephemere Catering & Consulting Inc.**, provides catering and product consultation services and operates private dining experiences.

In November 2022, the company agreed to sell all assets related to its aquaponic farming business to **CEVAS Technology Inc.** for $200,000 and up to $3,500,000 assumption in liabilities and obligations. The assets consist of closed-environment vertical aquaponics system (CEVAS) and all associated intellectual property; harvesting automated robotic vehicle (HARV) and all intellectual properties and patents associated with HARV; and all other formations and know-hows of the aquaponics business.

Common suspended from TSX-VEN, June 2, 2023.

Predecessor Detail - Name changed from AmWolf Capital Corp., Jan. 28, 2021, pursuant to the Qualifying Transaction reverse takeover acquisition of Pontus Water Lentils Ltd. and concurrent amalgamation of Pontus Water with wholly owned 1253044 B.C. Ltd. (and continued as 42 Protein Corp.).

Directors - Avtar Dhaliwal, interim CEO, B.C.; Steve McArthur, chief tech. officer, Victoria, B.C.; David Bentil; David M. (Dave) Jenkins, Langley, B.C.; Mohsen Rahimi, B.C.

Other Exec. Officers - Andy Wu, CFO; Alson Niu, exec. v-p

Capital Stock

	Authorized (shs.)	Outstanding (shs.)[1]
Common	unlimited	87,287,211

[1] At Aug. 31, 2022

Major Shareholder - Connor Yuen held 11.85% interest and Alson Niu held 11.23% interest at May 27, 2021.

Price Range - HULK/TSX-VEN (S)

Year	Volume	High	Low	Close
2022	16,000,954	$0.15	$0.01	$0.01
2021	53,114,773	$1.65	$0.12	$0.15
2019	3,101,909	$0.15	$0.08	$0.09

Recent Close: $0.01

Capital Stock Changes - In March 2022, private placement of 3,947,250 units (1 common share & 1 warrant) at 16¢ per unit was completed, with warrants exercisable at 30¢ per share for two years. In August 2022, private placement of 16,666,667 units (1 common share & 1 warrant) at 3¢ per unit was completed, with warrants exercisable at 5¢ per share for one year.

Wholly Owned Subsidiaries

Ephemere Catering & Consulting Inc., Vancouver, B.C.
42 Protein Corp., Victoria, B.C.

Financial Statistics

Periods ended:	12m Nov. 30/21[A1]		12m Nov. 30/20[□A]
	$000s	%Chg	$000s
Research & devel. expense	100		19
General & admin expense	1,608		705
Stock-based compensation	958		nil
Operating expense	**2,666**	**+268**	**724**
Operating income	**(2,666)**	**n.a.**	**(724)**
Deprec., depl. & amort.	217		17
Finance costs, gross	198		19
Write-downs/write-offs	(750)		nil
Pre-tax income	**(8,747)**	**n.a.**	**(693)**
Net income	**(8,747)**	**n.a.**	**(693)**
Cash & equivalent	12		10
Current assets	393		171
Fixed assets, net	5,331		2,111
Intangibles, net	nil		688
Total assets	**5,757**	**+92**	**2,997**
Accts. pay. & accr. liabs	1,535		375
Current liabilities	2,314		762
Long-term debt, gross	285		77
Long-term debt, net	27		25
Long-term lease liabilities	1,760		1,865
Shareholders' equity	1,657		346
Cash from oper. activs	**916**	**n.a.**	**(481)**
Cash from fin. activs	2,064		602
Cash from invest. activs	(3,281)		(111)
Net cash position	**12**	**+20**	**10**
Capital expenditures	(63)		nil
	$		$
Earnings per share*	(0.15)		(0.02)
Cash flow per share*	0.02		(0.02)
	shs		shs
No. of shs. o/s*	76,215,813		n.a.
Avg. no. of shs. o/s*	59,831,377		28,340,030
	%		%
Net profit margin	n.a.		n.a.
Return on equity	(873.39)		(176.56)
Return on assets	(195.32)		(36.58)

* Common
□ Restated
A Reported in accordance with IFRS
[1] Results prior to Jan. 26, 2021, pertain to and reflect the Qualifying Transaction reverse takeover acquisition of Pontus Water Lentils Ltd.

Latest Results

Periods ended:	9m Aug. 31/22[A]		9m Aug. 31/21[A]
	$000s	%Chg	$000s
Net income	(890)	n.a.	(3,303)
	$		$
Earnings per share*	(0.01)		(0.06)

* Common
A Reported in accordance with IFRS

Historical Summary
(as originally stated)

Fiscal Year	Oper. Rev.	Net Inc. Bef. Disc.	EPS*
	$000s	$000s	$
2021[A]	nil	(8,747)	(0.15)
2020[A]	nil	(693)	(0.02)
2019[A]	nil	(546)	(0.02)

* Common
A Reported in accordance with IFRS

P.81 Pool Safe Inc.

Symbol - POOL **Exchange** - TSX-VEN **CUSIP** - 73278C
Head Office - Unit 14, 401 Magnetic Dr, North York, ON, M3J 3H9
Telephone - (416) 630-2444
Website - www.poolsafeinc.com
Email - sglaser@poolsafeinc.com
Investor Relations - Steven Glaser (416) 630-2444
Auditors - Wasserman Ramsay C.A., Markham, Ont.
Lawyers - Garfinkle Biderman LLP, Toronto, Ont.
Transfer Agents - TSX Trust Company, Toronto, Ont.
Profile - (Can. 2009) Designs, manufactures and distributes Loungenie, a personal poolside safe for securing belongings for hotels, resorts, water parks and cruise ships.

Loungenie is placed next to pool lounge chairs and is a lockable storage space for guests to leave their belongings such as electronics. Each unit features a safe with a waterproof electronic key pad, a service call button that guests can use to bring a server to their location, a solar-powered charger for USB compatible devices and a storage compartment for food. The company also offers a touch screen application installed in a food and beverage area that alerts the staff when a guest has pressed the Loungenie call button. The Loungenie units can be customized to be wrapped in logos and imagery for branding purposes or for media advertising.

Has developed hardware and software technology that enables two-way communication between the Loungenie, its database gateway, and the cloud. This technology could collect usage information and deposit it into an archive in the cloud for later analysis and potential monetization. Also developing a tablet and an application that connects directly to the point of sale system of a resort and enables guests to place their own food and beverage orders, as well as gain access to other amenities offered at the resort or waterpark location.

Revenue is generated through direct sales as well as through a revenue-share partnership where there is no upfront capital cost to the company's customers.

At Mar. 31, 2023, the company had 771 Loungenie units in service.

Predecessor Detail - Name changed from Pounder Venture Capital Corp., Apr. 24, 2017, pursuant to Qualifying Transaction reverse takeover acquisition of (old) Pool Safe Inc.; basis 1 new for 4 old shs.

Directors - Nils A. Kravis, exec. chr., Ont.; David Berger, CEO, Toronto, Ont.; Steven Glaser, CFO, COO & corp. sec., Toronto, Ont.; Gillian F. J. Deacon, New York, N.Y.; Steven M. (Steve) Mintz, Toronto, Ont.; Robert Pratt, Vancouver, B.C.

Capital Stock

	Authorized (shs.)	Outstanding (shs.)[1]
Preferred	unlimited	nil
Common	unlimited	89,979,750

[1] At May 25, 2023

Major Shareholder - David Berger held 26.71% interest at Jan. 16, 2023.

Price Range - POOL/TSX-VEN

Year	Volume	High	Low	Close
2022	1,788,552	$0.04	$0.02	$0.03
2021	4,727,925	$0.07	$0.02	$0.04
2020	2,938,561	$0.07	$0.01	$0.02
2019	7,425,040	$0.14	$0.04	$0.05
2018	3,082,159	$0.14	$0.06	$0.12

Recent Close: $0.04

Capital Stock Changes - There were no changes to capital stock during 2022.

Wholly Owned Subsidiaries

1974134 Ontario Inc.

Financial Statistics

Periods ended:	12m Dec. 31/22[A]		12m Dec. 31/21[A]
	$000s	%Chg	$000s
Operating revenue	**707**	**+177**	**255**
Cost of sales	395		425
General & admin expense	757		343
Stock-based compensation	56		nil
Operating expense	**1,208**	**+57**	**768**
Operating income	**(501)**	**n.a.**	**(513)**
Deprec., depl. & amort.	20		38
Finance costs, gross	192		223
Pre-tax income	**(714)**	**n.a.**	**(619)**
Net income	**(714)**	**n.a.**	**(619)**
Cash & equivalent	221		29
Inventories	211		197
Accounts receivable	33		31
Current assets	465		257
Fixed assets, net	756		617
Total assets	**1,221**	**+40**	**874**
Accts. pay. & accr. liabs	258		202
Current liabilities	1,285		1,294
Long-term debt, gross	1,896		1,055
Long-term debt, net	903		nil
Long-term lease liabilities	45		78
Shareholders' equity	(1,012)		(498)
Cash from oper. activs	**(298)**	**n.a.**	**(326)**
Cash from fin. activs	910		623
Cash from invest. activs	(419)		(303)
Net cash position	**221**	**+662**	**29**
Capital expenditures	(419)		(303)
	$		$
Earnings per share*	(0.01)		(0.01)
Cash flow per share*	(0.00)		(0.00)
	shs		shs
No. of shs. o/s*	89,229,750		89,229,750
Avg. no. of shs. o/s*	89,229,750		81,461,153
	%		%
Net profit margin	(100.99)		(242.75)
Return on equity	n.m.		n.m.
Return on assets	(49.83)		(51.30)
Foreign sales percent	100		100

* Common
A Reported in accordance with IFRS

Latest Results

Periods ended:	3m Mar. 31/23[A]		3m Mar. 31/22[A]
	$000s	%Chg	$000s
Operating revenue	92	+31	70
Net income	(330)	n.a.	(157)
	$		$
Earnings per share*	(0.00)		(0.00)

* Common
[A] Reported in accordance with IFRS

Historical Summary
(as originally stated)

Fiscal Year	Oper. Rev.	Net Inc. Bef. Disc.	EPS*
	$000s	$000s	$
2022[A]	707	(714)	(0.01)
2021[A]	255	(619)	(0.01)
2020[A]	265	(632)	(0.01)
2019[A]	416	(715)	(0.01)
2018[A]	373	(997)	(0.02)

* Common
[A] Reported in accordance with IFRS

P.82 PopReach Corporation

Symbol - POPR **Exchange** - TSX-VEN **CUSIP** - 73319W
Head Office - 300-1 University Ave, Toronto, ON, M5J 2P1 **Telephone** - (416) 583-5918
Website - popreach.com
Email - jwalsh@popreach.com
Investor Relations - Jonathan Walsh (416) 583-5918
Auditors - MNP LLP C.A., Toronto, Ont.
Transfer Agents - TSX Trust Company, Toronto, Ont.
Employees - 153 at Dec. 31, 2022

Profile - (Ont. 2018) Acquires, integrates and manages a complementary portfolio of digital media businesses.

The company's digital media businesses include: **PopReach**, a free-to-play mobile game publisher with more than 25 games that are played by millions of users, and has a live operations studios in Vancouver, Bangalore, India and London, U.K.; **Notify AI**, is a provider of a push notification subscription and monetization platform for publishers, marketers and affiliates; **SCS**, a brand transformation service provider; **OpenMoves**, a performance and growth marketing platform which provides paid media (search and social), search engine optimization (SEO), email marketing services and creative services; **Q1Media**, an advertising and digital media service provider; **Contobox**, an e-commerce and creative advertising technology platform; and **Ubiquity**, an omnichannel marketing network and acquisition technology consortium.

Recent Merger and Acquisition Activity

Status: completed **Announced:** Apr. 26, 2023
PopReach Corporation acquired New York, N.Y.-based OpenMoves, LLC, which specializes in paid media (search and social), search engine optimization (SEO), email marketing services and creative services, for US$7,500,000, consisting of US$4,000,000 cash, issuance of 9,000,000 common shares valued at US$1,500,000 and issuance of a US$2,000,000 7% convertible debenture.

Status: completed **Announced:** Apr. 19, 2023
PopReach Corporation acquired Costa Mesa, Calif.-based Schiefer Chopshop, a brand transformation company, for US$14,900,000, consisting of US$2,000,000 cash, issuance of 4,400 class B non-voting shares of PopReach's wholly owned SCS Acquisition, Inc., issuance of a US$5,500,000 vendor take back note, issuance of a US$750,000 convertible debenture and inclusive of earn out payments of up to US$1,500,000 payable in each of the first two years following completion of the transaction based upon the achievement of certain financial performance objectives by Schiefer. Schiefer was a digital agency that brings media, creative and content together in a data-first offering that complements PopReach's services offerings delivered to brands and advertisers through Q1Media and Contobox.

Status: completed **Announced:** Sept. 9, 2022
PopReach Corporation acquired Boca Raton, Fla.-based Ubiquity Agency LLC, a user acquisition and marketing technology business, for US$44,300,000 consisting of US$18,700,000 in cash, issuance of 41,000,000 common shares at a deemed price of US$0.34 per share, issuance of a US$13,750,000 convertible debenture and the assumption of US$1,250,000 of existing liabilities. Ubiquity operates a digital agency and performance marketing network; a direct-to-consumer omnichannel marketing company; a full stack development and SaaS platform to support delivery, online engagement and analytics for SMS and email campaigns; and a data driven performance marketing company. For the 12 months ended June 30, 2022, Ubiquity generated revenue of US$51,280,000.

Status: completed **Revised:** Apr. 28, 2022
UPDATE: The transaction was completed. The net purchase price was Cdn$127,240,000, including the assumption of US$22,963,000 of Federated debt. Each Federated shareholder received 0.7541 PopReach common shares for each Federated share held, which resulted in the issuance of 159,053,948 PopReach common shares. PREVIOUS: PopReach Corporation entered into a letter of intent for the reverse takeover acquisition of private 2810735 Ontario Inc. (dba Federated Foundry), an acquirer and operator of digital technology companies, for issuance of 200,000,000 common shares at a deemed price of Cdn$0.80 per share. Federated's portfolio included two operating divisions: a push notification advertising platform operated by Denver, Colo.-based Notify AI, LLC; and Austin, Tex.-based Q1Media, LLC, an advertising and media service provider. Federated was also pursuing the acquisition of Toronto, Ont.-based Crucial Interactive Holdings Inc., which provides personalization, ecommerce and creative advertising technologies. Oct. 18, 2021 - A definitive agreement was entered into. Feb. 14, 2022 - The TSX Venture Exchange conditionally approved the transaction.

Predecessor Detail - Name changed from Mithrandir Capital Corp., July 8, 2020, pursuant to Qualifying Transaction reverse takeover acquisition of PopReach Incorporated; basis 1 new for 8 old shs.

Directors - Ted Hastings, exec. chr., Waterloo, Ont.; Jonathan (Jon) Walsh, CEO, Oakville, Ont.; Ben Colabrese, Oakville, Ont.; Natasha De Masi, Austin, Tex.; Iain Klugman, Kitchener, Ont.; Christopher Locke, Etobicoke, Ont.; Mike Vorhaus, Los Angeles, Calif.

Other Exec. Officers - Kevin Ferrell, pres.; Jeffrey D. (Jeff) Collins, COO & interim CFO; Amy Hastings, gen. counsel & corp. sec.

Capital Stock

	Authorized (shs.)	Outstanding (shs.)[1]
Common	unlimited	285,388,328

[1] At May 30, 2023

Major Shareholder - Michael Fitzgerald held 15.5% interest and James Mansfield held 15.49% interest at Mar. 6, 2023.

Price Range - POPR/TSX-VEN

Year	Volume	High	Low	Close
2022	8,902,953	$0.50	$0.22	$0.28
2021	9,672,412	$1.55	$0.56	$0.63
2020	19,639,969	$1.71	$0.74	$1.42
2019	114,875	$1.12	$0.72	$0.72

Consolidation: 1-for-8 cons. in July 2020
Recent Close: $0.21

Capital Stock Changes - On Apr. 26, 2023, 9,000,000 common shares were issued pursuant to the acquisition of OpenMoves, LLC.

On Apr. 28, 2022, 159,053,948 common shares were issued pursuant to the reverse takeover acquisition of 2810735 Ontario Inc. (dba Federated Foundry). In September 2022, 41,000,000 common shares were issued on acquisition of Ubiquity Agency LLC. Also during the 15-month period ended Dec. 31, 2022, 1,746,726 common shares were issued on exercise of options.

Wholly Owned Subsidiaries

OpenMoves, LLC, New York, N.Y.
PopReach Incorporated, Toronto, Ont.
- 100% int. in **PopReach Technologies Pvt. Ltd.**, India.
- 100% int. in **PopReach UK Limited**, United Kingdom.

SCS Acquisition, Inc.
- 100% int. in **Schiefer Chopshop**, Costa Mesa, Calif.

2810735 Ontario Inc., Ont. dba Federated Foundry.
- 100% int. in **Crucial Interactive Holdings Inc.**, Ont.
  - 100% int. in **Crucial Interactive Inc.**, Ont.
    - 100% int. in **Contobox U.S. Inc.**, Del.
  - 100% int. in **Media Xeo Inc.**, Qué.
    - 100% int. in **Okra Media Inc.**, Canada.
- 100% int. in **Notify AcquisitionCo Inc.**, Del.
  - 100% int. in **Notify AI, LLC**, Wyo.
- 100% int. in **Q1Media, Inc.**, Del.

Ubiquity Agency Acquisition, Inc., United States.
- 100% int. in **Ubiquity Agency LLC**, Boca Raton, Fla.
  - 100% int. in **BW Ventures LLC**, Del.
  - 100% int. in **Hippo Investments LLC**, Del.
  - 100% int. in **Jet Marketing Agency LLC**, Del.
  - 100% int. in **Mosten Media BV**, Netherlands.
  - 100% int. in **Sedulen LLC**, Fla.
  - 100% int. in **Verias LLC**, Del.

Financial Statistics

Periods ended:	15m Dec. 31/22[A1]		12m Dec. 31/21[A]
	US$000s	%Chg	US$000s
Operating revenue	**125,251**	**n.a.**	**17,074**
Cost of sales	71,968		6,245
Research & devel. expense	7,680		3,661
General & admin expense	35,642		6,185
Stock-based compensation	n.a.		200
Operating expense	**115,290**	**n.a.**	**16,292**
Operating income	**9,961**	**n.a.**	**782**
Deprec., depl. & amort.	12,505		1,907
Finance costs, gross	4,187		783
Write-downs/write-offs	(17,574)[2]		nil
Pre-tax income	**(23,804)**	**n.a.**	**1,685**
Income taxes	55		91
Net income	**(23,859)**	**n.a.**	**1,594**
Cash & equivalent	7,795		11,028
Accounts receivable	15,423		1,354
Current assets	24,310		13,183
Long-term investments	nil		43
Fixed assets, net	230		199
Right-of-use assets	472		545
Intangibles, net	96,830		12,020
Total assets	**124,491**	**+362**	**26,933**
Accts. pay. & accr. liabs	17,044		1,353
Current liabilities	29,110		6,738
Long-term debt, gross	47,411		4,905
Long-term debt, net	39,599		3,732
Long-term lease liabilities	148		156
Shareholders' equity	51,904		14,457
Cash from oper. activs	**8,360**	**n.a.**	**931**
Cash from fin. activs	4,506		(1,936)
Cash from invest. activs	(7,213)		(6,056)
Net cash position	**7,795**	**-29**	**11,028**
Capital expenditures	(93)		(107)
	US$		US$
Earnings per share*	(0.12)		0.02
Cash flow per share*	0.04		0.01
	shs		shs
No. of shs. o/s*	275,266,828		73,466,154
Avg. no. of shs. o/s*	205,446,007		73,134,374
	%		%
Net profit margin	...		9.34
Return on equity	...		7.42
Return on assets	...		5.03
No. of employees (FTEs)	153		248

* Common
[A] Reported in accordance with IFRS
[1] Results reflect the Apr. 28, 2022, reverse takeover acquisition of 2810735 Ontario Inc. (dba Federated Foundry).
[2] Includes goodwill impaiment of Notify totaling US$13,212,000.

Latest Results

Periods ended:	3m Mar. 31/23[A]		3m Mar. 31/22[oA]
	US$000s	%Chg	US$000s
Operating revenue	36,489	+152	14,480
Net income	(4,204)	n.a.	(820)
	US$		US$
Earnings per share*	(0.02)		(0.01)

* Common
[o] Restated
[A] Reported in accordance with IFRS

Historical Summary
(as originally stated)

Fiscal Year	Oper. Rev.	Net Inc. Bef. Disc.	EPS*
	US$000s	US$000s	US$
2022[A1]	125,251	(23,859)	(0.12)
2021[A]	17,074	1,594	0.02
2020[A2]	18,010	(6,301)	(0.13)
2019[A]	17,954	(4,436)	n.a.
2018[A]	1,447	(1,462)	n.a.

* Common
[A] Reported in accordance with IFRS
[1] 15 months ended Dec. 31, 2022.
[2] Results prior to June 30, 2020, pertain to and reflect the Qualifying Transaction reverse takeover acquisition of PopReach Incorporated.
Note: Adjusted throughout for 1-for-8 cons. in July 2020

P.83 Postmedia Network Canada Corp.

Symbol - PNC.A **Exchange** - TSX **CUSIP** - 73752W
Head Office - 1200-365 Bloor St E, Toronto, ON, M4W 3L4 **Telephone** - (416) 383-2300 **Fax** - (416) 442-2077
Website - www.postmedia.com
Email - mlavallee@postmedia.com
Investor Relations - Mary Anne Lavallee (416) 442-3448
Auditors - PricewaterhouseCoopers LLP C.A., Winnipeg, Man.

Lawyers - Paul, Weiss, Rifkind, Wharton & Garrison LLP; Goodmans LLP, Toronto, Ont.

Transfer Agents - Computershare Trust Company of Canada Inc., Toronto, Ont.

FP500 Revenue Ranking - 488

Employees - 2,098 at Aug. 31, 2022

Profile - (Can. 2010) Through wholly owned **Postmedia Network Inc.**, publishes Canadian daily national newspaper National Post, 15 Canadian daily metropolitan newspapers and several local community and specialty publications in Ontario, New Brunswick and western Canada, as well as operates digital media and online assets.

Publishing assets include National Post, a national daily newspaper in Canada; and 15 daily metropolitan newspapers including The Province (Vancouver), Edmonton Journal, Calgary Herald, Saskatoon StarPhoenix, Regina Leader-Post, Windsor Star, Ottawa Citizen, Montreal Gazette, The Vancouver Sun, London Free Press (London, Ont.) and Sun tabloid newspapers in Toronto, Ottawa, Winnipeg, Calgary and Edmonton. Other operations include 18 daily newspapers in smaller communities in Ontario (15) and New Brunswick (3); 80 non-daily community newspapers and shopping guides distributed in Ontario, Alberta, Manitoba, Saskatchewan and New Brunswick; various specialty publications and newspaper-related publications; Flyer Force, a distribution service for advertising flyers, which distributes insert packages to non-subscribers in Calgary and Edmonton, Alta., and Ottawa and London, Ont., providing extended market coverage for their associated Postmedia newspapers; and Postmedia Parcel Services, which offers trucking, sorting and distribution of small parcels by leveraging the corporation's national distribution network.

Digital media and online operations include the canada.com and canoe.com websites; each newspaper's online website; and various classified websites. In total, the company owns and operates over 130 destination websites. Also generates revenue through electronic licensing of content and subscriptions for corporate financial data through Financial Post and FPadvisor

Also provides sales representation services to third party owned publications and third party branded websites, digital marketing services such as website development, search engine optimization and search engine marketing, and programmatic digital advertising.

On July 10, 2023, the company confirmed that discussions with **Nordstar Capital LP** regarding a potential transaction have ceased. On June 27, 2023, the company announced it had entered into non-binding discussions with Nordstar Capital **LP**, owner of Metroland Media Group and the Toronto Star, to consider a combination of the company, together with the Metroland newspapers and certain operational assets of the Toronto Star, through a potential merger transaction. The merged entity would have been jointly owned and jointly controlled by Nordstar, which would have a 50% voting interest and 44% economic interest, and existing shareholders of the company, who would have a combined voting interest of 50% and a combined economic interest of 56%. The Toronto Star would maintain its editorial independence from the merged entity through the incorporation of a new company, **Toronto Star Inc.**, which would manage editorial operations of the Toronto Star. Nordstar would retain a 65% interest in Toronto Star Inc., and Jordan Bitove would remain publisher of the Toronto Star.

On Mar. 25, 2022, wholly owned **Brunswick News Inc.** was amalgamated into wholly owned **Postmedia Network Inc.**

Recent Merger and Acquisition Activity

Status: completed **Revised:** Mar. 25, 2022

UPDATE: The transaction was completed for issuance of 4,282,920 Postmedia variable voting shares valued at $7,602,000 and $7,500,000 in cash. PREVIOUS: Postmedia Network Canada Corp. agreed to acquire to acquire Brunswick News Inc. (BNI) from J. D. Irving, Limited (JDI) for $7,500,000 in cash and $8,600,000 in Postmedia variable voting shares at an implied price of $2.10 per variable voting share. The acquisition includes BNI's daily and weekly New Brunswick newspapers, digital properties and parcel delivery business. BNI daily and weekly newspapers include the Telegraph-Journal, Times Globe, Times & Transcript, The Daily Gleaner, Miramichi Leader, Woodstock Bugle-Observer, Bathurst Northern Light, Kings County Record, The Campbellton Tribune and The Victoria Star. Postmedia and JDI would enter into an agreement whereby JDI would be restricted from converting its Postmedia variable voting shares into voting shares, subject to certain exceptions.

Directors - L. Peter Sharpe†, interim chr., Toronto, Ont.; Andrew MacLeod, pres. & CEO, Kitchener, Ont.; John B. Bode, Naples, Fla.; Janet L. Ecker, Ajax, Ont.; Vincent Gasparro, Toronto, Ont.; Wendy Henkelman, Edmonton, Alta.; Mary E. Junck, Clayton, Mo.; Daniel Rotstein, Plantation, Fla.

Other Exec. Officers - Duncan Clark, chief content officer; Gillian Akai, exec. v-p, CAO, gen. counsel & corp. sec.; Mary Anne Lavallee, exec. v-p, CFO & chief transformation officer

† Lead director

Capital Stock

	Authorized (shs.)	Outstanding (shs.)[1]
Class C Voting	unlimited	67,167
Class NC Variable Voting	unlimited	98,750,682

[1] At July 11, 2023

Class C Voting - Rank equally with the class NC variable voting shares with respect to dividends and distribution of capital. Automatically convertible into class NC variable voting shares on a one-for-one basis if they become held by a non-Canadian. One vote per share.

Class NC Variable Voting - Rank equally with the class C voting shares with respect to dividends and distribution of capital. Automatically convertible into class C voting shares on a one-for-one basis if they become held by a Canadian. One vote per share unless (i) the number of outstanding class NC shares exceeds 49.9% of the total number of all shares outstanding or (ii) the total number of votes that may be cast by or on behalf of class NC shareholders present at any meeting of shareholders exceeds 49.9% of the total number of votes that may be cast at such meeting. In either case, the vote attached to each class NC share will decrease to equal the maximum permitted vote per share such that class NC shares as a class cannot carry more than 49.9% of the total votes.

Major Shareholder - Chatham Asset Management, LLC held 31.49% interest at Dec. 13, 2022.

Price Range - PNC.A/TSX

Year	Volume	High	Low	Close
2022	112,225	$2.81	$1.08	$1.36
2021	44,087	$2.55	$1.37	$1.61
2020	59,213	$3.61	$1.18	$1.50
2019	88,176	$4.50	$1.00	$1.52
2018	139,002	$2.05	$0.70	$1.30

Recent Close: $1.53

Capital Stock Changes - In March 2022, 4,282,920 class NC variable voting shares were issued pursuant to acquisition of Brunswick News Inc. Also during fiscal 2022, class C voting shares were issued as follows: 794,630 for financing fees and 500 (net) on conversion of a like number of class NC variable voting shares.

Wholly Owned Subsidiaries

Postmedia Network Inc., Toronto, Ont.

Financial Statistics

Periods ended:	12m Aug. 31/22[A]		12m Aug. 31/21[A]
	$000s	%Chg	$000s
Operating revenue	**458,224**	**+4**	**442,343**
Salaries & benefits	168,166		154,537
Stock-based compensation	1,403		645
Other operating expense	275,675		250,108
Operating expense	**445,244**	**+10**	**405,290**
Operating income	**12,980**	**-65**	**37,053**
Deprec., depl. & amort	20,340		20,953
Finance costs, gross	31,936		31,731
Write-downs/write-offs	(15,745)		(26,164)
Pre-tax income	**(74,712)**	**n.a.**	**33,726**
Net income	**(74,712)**	**n.a.**	**33,726**
Cash & equivalent	12,061		61,996
Inventories	4,950		3,348
Accounts receivable	49,118		41,255
Current assets	92,861		133,460
Fixed assets, net	66,747		76,390
Right-of-use assets	30,095		35,646
Intangibles, net	17,930		23,791
Total assets	**211,375**	**-23**	**276,201**
Accts. pay. & accr. liabs	39,440		49,599
Current liabilities	85,780		89,736
Long-term debt, gross	273,909		255,671
Long-term debt, net	260,909		248,262
Long-term lease liabilities	27,749		33,161
Shareholders' equity	(201,232)		(139,711)
Cash from oper. activs	**(21,464)**	**n.a.**	**39,021**
Cash from fin. activs	(21,618)		(38,764)
Cash from invest. activs	(6,853)		11,944
Net cash position	**12,061**	**-81**	**61,996**
Capital expenditures	(2,005)		(2,475)
Capital disposals	2,736		5,889
	$		$
Earnings per share*	(0.78)		0.36
Cash flow per share*	(0.22)		0.42
	shs		shs
No. of shs. o/s*	98,817,849		93,740,299
Avg. no. of shs. o/s*	95,869,801		93,740,299
	%		%
Net profit margin	(16.30)		7.62
Return on equity	n.m.		n.m.
Return on assets	(17.55)		21.35
No. of employees (FTEs)	2,098		2,006

* Cl.C & NC

[A] Reported in accordance with IFRS

Latest Results

Periods ended:	9m May 31/23[A]		9m May 31/22[A]
	$000s	%Chg	$000s
Operating revenue	347,209	+2	341,176
Net income	(61,524)	n.a.	(43,298)
	$		$
Earnings per share*	(0.62)		(0.46)

* Cl.C & NC

[A] Reported in accordance with IFRS

Historical Summary
(as originally stated)

Fiscal Year	Oper. Rev. $000s	Net Inc. Bef. Disc. $000s	EPS* $
2022[A]	458,224	(74,712)	(0.78)
2021[A]	442,343	33,726	0.36
2020[A]	508,406	(16,153)	(0.17)
2019[A]	619,638	(7,067)	(0.08)
2018[A]	676,293	(33,870)	(0.36)

* Cl.C & NC

[A] Reported in accordance with IFRS

P.84 Power Corporation of Canada*

Symbol - POW **Exchange** - TSX **CUSIP** - 739239

Head Office - 751 rue du Square-Victoria, Montréal, QC, H2Y 2J3

Telephone - (514) 286-7400 **Toll-free** - (800) 890-7440

Website - www.powercorporation.com

Email - guy@powercorporation.com

Investor Relations - Chantal Guy (514) 286-7400

Auditors - Deloitte LLP C.A., Montréal, Qué.

Lawyers - Blake, Cassels & Graydon LLP, Toronto, Ont.

Transfer Agents - Computershare Trust Company of Canada Inc., Montréal, Qué.

FP500 Revenue Ranking - 11

Employees - 37,300 at Dec. 31, 2022

Profile - (Can. 1925) International management and holding company focusing on the financial services sector, with primary holdings in insurance, retirement, wealth management and investment businesses, including alternative asset investment.

Publicly Traded Operating Companies

Holds controlling interests, through wholly owned **Power Financial Corporation**, in public companies as follows:

Great-West Lifeco Inc. (66.6% owned) - Owns **The Canada Life Assurance Company**, **Empower Annuity Insurance Company of America**, **Putnam Investments, LLC** and **Irish Life Group Limited**. The companies provide a wide range of life and health insurance, retirement and investment, asset management and reinsurance products and services in Canada, the U.S. and Europe.

IGM Financial Inc. (62.2% owned) - Provides wealth and asset management solutions in Canada, the U.S., Europe and Asia through **Investors Group Inc.**, **Mackenzie Financial Corporation** and **Investment Planning Counsel Inc.**

Groupe Bruxelles Lambert S.A. (GBL) - Wholly owned **Power Financial Europe S.A.** holds 50% interest in **Parjointco S.A.**, which in turn holds 29.8% equity interest (44% voting interest) in Belgian holding company, GBL. GBL has holdings in European-based global companies including 54.6% equity interest (68.1% voting interest) in **Imerys S.A.**, a French-based producer of mineral-based specialty solutions for industry; 2.1% interest in **Holcim Ltd.**, a Swiss-based global building materials company which offers cement, aggregates and concrete; 19.1% interest in **SGS S.A.**, a Swiss-based inspection, verification, testing and certification company; 7.6% interest in **adidas AG**, a German-based designer, developer, producer and distributor of sporting goods; 6.9% equity interest (11.5% voting interest) in **Pernod Ricard S.A.**, a French-based wines and spirits company; 15.9% interest in **Umicore N.V./S.A.**, a Belgian-based materials technology and precious metals recycling company; 20% interest in **Ontex Group N.V.**, a Belgian-based manufacturer of personal hygiene products; 6.3% interest in **GEA Group AG**, a German-based manufacturer of equipment for the processing industries primarily in the food and beverage sectors; 1.9% interest in **Mowi ASA**, a Norway-based producer of seafood, with focus on Atlantic salmon; 61.5% interest in **Webhelp SAS**, a French-based business process outsourcer, specializing in customer experience, sales and marketing and payment services; 23% interest in **Parques Reunidos Servicios Centrales, S.A.**, a leisure park operator based in Madrid, Spain; 48.2% interest in **Canyon Bicycles GmbH**, a German-based direct-to-consumer manufacturer of premium conventional and electric bicycles; 16.2% interest in **Voodoo SAS**, a French-based developer and publisher of mobiles games; 99.6% equity interest (100% voting interest) in **Affidea Group B.V.**, a Netherlands-based provider of advanced diagnostics and outpatient services; and 83.8% equity interest (63% voting interest) in **Sanoptis AG**, a Swiss-based owner and operator of ophthalmology clinics. GBL is also engaged in alternative asset management as well as provides third party asset management services.

Alternative Asset Investment Platforms & Other

Manages portfolios on behalf of the company and third party investors in several alternative asset classes primarily in North America, Europe and China.

Sagard Holdings Inc. (100% owned) - A multi-strategy alternative asset manager which invests in five assets classes (venture capital and growth, private equity, private credit, royalties and real estate) and also offers private wealth management services. In venture capital and growth, **Portag3 Ventures Limited Partnership**, **Portag3 Ventures II Limited Partnership**, **Portage Ventures III Limited Partnership**, **Portage Capital Solutions** and **Portage Fintech Acquisition Corporation** focus on financial technology (fintech) and financial services opportunities, including an investment in **Wealthsimple Financial Corp.**, which operates a digital investing platform. In private equity, manages investments under three strategies: Sagard Private Equity Canada, which invests in the Canadian middle market, with a focus on business and financial services as well as manufacturing; Sagard MidCap, which invests in the European middle-market business services, healthcare, food and consumer and industrial sectors; and Sagard NewGen, which invests in the European lower-middle-market primarily in technology and healthcare, with investment sizes between €10,000,000 and €50,000,000. In private credit, provides non-sponsored direct lending to public and private middle-market companies in Canada and the U.S. through Sagard Credit and Sagard Senior Lending. In royalties, Sagard Healthcare, a biopharmaceutical royalties investment strategy, invests in royalties and credit backed by approved and commercialized biopharmaceutical products, diagnostics and medical devices. In real estate, **EverWest Holdings Inc.** offers a full-service real estate investment platform operating in acquisitions, development, asset management and property management in specific sub-markets within the U.S. In private wealth management, **Grayhawk Wealth Holdings Inc.** offers investment solutions for Canadian families.

Power Sustainable Capital Inc. (100% owned) - A global multi-platform alternative asset manager investing in companies and projects that contribute to decarbonization, social progress and quality growth. Main platforms are **Power Sustainable Investment Management Inc.**, which invests in China's public equity markets; **Power Sustainable Energy Infrastructure**, which invests in the development, construction, financing and operation of renewable energy assets across North America; and **Power Sustainable Lios Inc.**, which invests in middle-market companies across the food value chain in North America that support the sustainability transformation occurring within the food system.

Standalone Businesses - Consist of interests in **Peak Achievement Athletics Inc.**, a designer and marketer of sports equipment and apparel for ice hockey and lacrosse; **LMPG Inc.**, a designer, developer and manufacturer of LED lighting solutions; and **The Lion Electric Company**, a designer and manufacturer of zero-emission vehicles sold throughout North America.

Recent Merger and Acquisition Activity

Status: completed **Revised:** Jan. 12, 2023

UPDATE: The transaction was completed. PREVIOUS: Power Corporation of Canada agreed to sell its 13.9% interest in China Asset Management Co., Ltd. (ChinaAMC) to Mackenzie Financial Corporation, owned by IGM Financial Inc., for $1.15 billion. As a result, IGM's indirect interest in ChinaAMC would increase to 27.8%. To partially fund the transaction, IGM would sell $575,000,000 of Great-West Lifeco Inc. common shares to Power Corporation, representing a 1.6% interest. The sale of the Great-West Lifeco shares was conditional on the purchase of the ChinaAMC shares. The transaction expected to be completed in the first half of 2022.

Status: completed **Revised:** June 28, 2022

UPDATE: The transaction was completed for US$20,300,000 cash and assumption of US$35,300,000 of debt. PREVIOUS: Polaris Infrastructure Inc. agreed to acquire Emerald Solar Energy S.R.L. for US$18,400,000 cash and assumption of project level debt of US$35,000,000. The transaction includes a 32-MW defined conditions (MWdc) operational photovoltaic solar plant (Canoa 1) and Canoa 2 expansion, located in Barahona, Dominican Republic. Emerald explores for and develops solar projects in the Dominican Republic.

Predecessor Detail - Name changed from Power Corporation of Canada, Limited, May 31, 1980.

Directors - Paul Desmarais Jr., chr., Westmount, Qué.; André Desmarais, deputy chr., Westmount, Qué.; R. Jeffrey Orr, pres. & CEO, Montréal, Qué.; Anthony R. Graham†, Toronto, Ont.; Pierre Beaudoin, Knowlton, Qué.; Marcel R. Coutu, Calgary, Alta.; The Hon. Gary A. Doer, Winnipeg, Man.; Sharon MacLeod, Georgetown, Ont.; Paula B. Madoff, New York, N.Y.; Isabelle Marcoux, Montréal, Qué.; Christian Noyer, Paris, France; T. Timothy Ryan Jr., Miami Beach, Fla.; Siim A. Vanaselja, Toronto, Ont.; Elizabeth D. (Beth) Wilson, Toronto, Ont.

Other Exec. Officers - Jocelyn Lefebvre, v-chr., Europe; Michel Plessis-Bélair, v-chr.; Claude Généreux, exec. v-p; Gregory D. Tretiak, exec. v-p & CFO; Olivier Desmarais, sr. v-p; Paul Desmarais III, sr. v-p; Dr. Paul C. Genest, sr. v-p; Charles Dumont, v-p, strategy; Stéphane Lemay, v-p, gen. counsel & sec.; Denis Le Vasseur, v-p & contr.; Yuhong (Henry) Liu, v-p; Patrick Mercier, v-p; Richard Pan, v-p & head, corp. fin.; Luc Reny, v-p, HR & admin.; Edouard Vo-Quang, asst. gen. counsel

† Lead director

Capital Stock

	Authorized (shs.)	Outstanding (shs.)[1]
First Preferred	unlimited	
Series A		6,000,000
Series B		8,000,000
Series C		6,000,000
Series D		10,000,000
Series G		8,000,000
Participating Preferred	unlimited	54,860,866
Subordinate Voting	unlimited	611,173,933

[1] At May 15, 2023

First Preferred Series A - Entitled to fixed non-cumulative preferential annual dividends of $1.40 per share payable quarterly. Redeemable at $25 per share. Non-voting.

First Preferred Series B - Entitled to fixed non-cumulative preferential annual dividends of $1.3375 per share payable quarterly. Redeemable at $25 per share. Non-voting.

First Preferred Series C - Entitled to fixed non-cumulative preferential annual dividends of $1.45 per share payable quarterly. Redeemable at $25 per share. Non-voting.

First Preferred Series D - Entitled to fixed non-cumulative preferential annual dividends of $1.25 per share payable quarterly. Redeemable at $25 per share. Non-voting.

First Preferred Series G - Entitled to fixed non-cumulative preferential annual dividends of $1.40 per share payable quarterly. Redeemable at $25 per share. Non-voting.

Participating Preferred - Entitled to non-cumulative preferential annual dividends of $0.009375 per share and to participate equally in any further dividends, in any year, after $0.009375 per share has been paid on the subordinate voting shares. Rank junior to the first preferred shares with respect to payment of dividends and distribution of assets. Holders of the participating preferred shares have the right, upon issuance by the company of additional subordinate voting shares in certain circumstances, to subscribe for an aggregate number of participating preferred shares that is equal to 12% of the number of subordinate voting proposed to be issued at the same price per share as that of the newly issued subordinate voting shares. Ten votes per share.

Subordinate Voting - Holders of the subordinate voting shares have the right, upon the issuance by the company of additional participating preferred shares in certain circumstances, to subscribe for an aggregate number of subordinate voting shares that is equal to 8.333 times the number of participating preferred shares proposed to be issued at the same price per share as the newly issued participating preferred shares. One vote per share.

Options - At Dec. 31, 2022, options were outstanding to purchase 25,567,243 subordinate voting shares at a weighted average exercise price of $31.86 per share with a weighted average remaining contractual life of 4.1 years.

First Preferred 1986 Series (old) - Were entitled to cumulative preferential annual dividends at a rate equal to 70% of the average of the prime rate of two major Canadian chartered banks payable quarterly. Redeemed at $50 per share on Jan. 15, 2022.

Normal Course Issuer Bid - The company plans to make normal course purchases of up to 30,000,000 subordinate voting shares representing 5.4% of the public float. The bid commenced on Mar. 1, 2023, and expires on Feb. 29, 2024.

Major Shareholder - Desmarais Family Residuary Trust held 51.34% interest at Mar. 17, 2023.

Price Range - POW/TSX

Year	Volume	High	Low	Close
2022	625,908,898	$43.45	$29.76	$31.85
2021	565,198,167	$44.53	$28.81	$41.80
2020	583,521,860	$35.13	$17.47	$29.23
2019	334,580,409	$35.15	$24.16	$33.45
2018	200,825,751	$32.66	$23.35	$24.53

Recent Close: $36.07

Capital Stock Changes - On Jan. 15, 2022, all 86,100 first preferred 1986 series shares were redeemed at $50 per share. Also during 2022, 1,683,043 subordinate voting shares were issued under the executive stock option plan and 11,219,400 subordinate voting shares were repurchased under a Normal Course Issuer Bid.

Dividends

POW com S.V. Ra $2.10 pa Q est. May 1, 2023
Prev. Rate: $1.98 est. Feb. 1, 2022
Prev. Rate: $1.79 est. May 1, 2020

POW.PR.E pfd part. M.V. Var. Ra pa Q

$0.525	Nov. 1/23	$0.525	Aug. 1/23
$0.525	May 1/23	$0.495	Feb. 1/23

Paid in 2023: $2.07 2022: $1.98 2021: $1.79

POW.PR.A pfd 1st ser A red. Ra $1.40 pa Q
POW.PR.B pfd 1st ser B red. Ra $1.3375 pa Q
POW.PR.C pfd 1st ser C red. Ra $1.45 pa Q
POW.PR.D pfd 1st ser D red. Ra $1.25 pa Q
POW.PR.G pfd 1st ser G red. Ra $1.40 pa Q
pfd 1st ser 1986 cum. red. Fltg. Ra pa Q[1]

$0.2144f	Jan. 15/22	$0.2144	Oct. 15/21
$0.2144	July 15/21	$0.2144	Apr. 15/21

Paid in 2023: n.a. 2022: $0.2144f 2021: $0.8576

[1] Redeemed Jan. 17, 2022 at $50 per sh.

f Final Payment

Long-Term Debt - Outstanding at Dec. 31, 2022:

Power Corp. debs.	$647,000,000
Power Financial debs.	250,000,000
Great-West Lifeco debs. & bonds	4,948,000,000
Great-West Lifeco other debt	5,561,000,000
IGM Financial debs.	2,100,000,000
Other subsidiaries debt	1,956,000,000
Less: Consolidation adj.	88,000,000
	15,374,000,000

Principal repayments of debentures and other debt in the next five years were reported as follows:

2023	$2,017,000,000
2024	100,000,000
2025	977,000,000
2026	823,000,000
2027	1,140,000,000
Thereafter	9,744,000,000

Wholly Owned Subsidiaries

Power Financial Corporation, Montréal, Qué. (see separate coverage)

Power Sustainable Capital Inc., Canada.

- 49.6% int. in **LMPG Inc.**, Longueuil, Qué.
- 35.4% int. in **The Lion Electric Company**, Saint-Jérôme, Qué. (see separate coverage)
- 100% int. in **Nautilus Solar Energy, LLC**, Summit, N.J.
- 100% int. in **Potentia Renewables Inc.**, Toronto, Ont.
- 39.4% int. in **Power Sustainable Energy Infrastructure Partnership**, Canada.
- 100% int. in **Power Sustainable Investment Management Inc.**, Montréal, Qué.

Sagard Holdings Inc., Canada.

- 42.6% int. in **Peak Achievement Athletics Inc.**, Canada. 50% voting interest.
- 4.7% int. in **Portag3 Ventures II Limited Partnership**, Toronto, Ont.
- 2.4% int. in **Portage Ventures III Limited Partnership**, Toronto, Ont.
- 80.9% int. in **Sagard Holdings Management Inc.**, Canada.

Note: The preceding list includes only the major related companies in which interests are held.

Financial Statistics

Periods ended:	12m Dec. 31/22[A]		12m Dec. 31/21[A]
	$000s	%Chg	$000s
Total revenue	**48,695,000**	**-30**	**69,561,000**
Salaries & benefits	5,605,000		5,680,000
General & admin. expense	3,211,000		3,118,000
Other operating expense	4,419,000		4,410,000
Operating expense	**42,899,000**	**-32**	**63,503,000**
Operating income	**5,796,000**	**-4**	**6,058,000**
Deprec. & amort.	877,000		778,000
Finance costs, gross	676,000		599,000
Pre-tax income	**4,024,000**	**-24**	**5,316,000**
Income taxes	481,000		643,000
Net income	**3,543,000**	**-24**	**4,673,000**
Net inc. for equity hldrs	**1,965,000**	**-34**	**2,969,000**
Net inc. for non-cont. int	**1,578,000**	**-7**	**1,704,000**
Cash & equivalent	9,848,000		9,509,000
Accounts receivable	7,528,000		6,845,000
Investments	243,676,000		214,077,000
Fixed assets, net	4,409,000		3,686,000
Intangibles, net	22,905,000		20,575,000
Total assets	**733,650,000**	**+11**	**661,633,000**
Bank indebtedness	274,000		407,000
Accts. pay. & accr. liabs	4,111,000		3,840,000
Debt	15,374,000		13,180,000
Lease liabilities	916,000		886,000
Preferred share equity	950,000		954,000
Shareholders' equity	24,021,000		24,339,000
Non-controlling interest	20,081,000		19,389,000
Cash from oper. activs	**7,502,000**	**-32**	**11,053,000**
Cash from fin. activs	(948,000)		(962,000)
Cash from invest. activs	(6,498,000)		(10,579,000)
Net cash position	**9,848,000**	**+4**	**9,509,000**
Unfunded pension liability	n.a.		700,000
Pension fund surplus	246,000		n.a.
	$		$
Earnings per share*	2.85		4.31
Cash flow per share*	11.19		16.33
Net asset value per share*	41.91		52.60
Cash divd. per share*	1.98		1.84
Cash divd. per share**	1.98		1.84
	shs		shs
No. of shs. o/s*	667,080,597		676,616,954
Avg. no. of shs. o/s*	670,600,000		676,800,000
	%		%
Net profit margin	7.28		6.72
Return on equity	8.24		13.07
Return on assets	0.59		0.81
Foreign sales percent	65		66
No. of employees (FTEs)	37,300		33,700

* Partic. pref. & S.V.
** Partic. pref.
[A] Reported in accordance with IFRS

Latest Results

Periods ended:	3m Mar. 31/23[A]		3m Mar. 31/22[oA]
	$000s	%Chg	$000s
Total revenue	13,472,000	n.a.	(2,607,000)
Net income	600,000	-57	1,411,000
Net inc. for equity hldrs	326,000	-63	875,000
Net inc. for non-cont. int	274,000		536,000
	$		$
Earnings per share*	0.47		1.28

* Partic. pref. & S.V.
[o] Restated
[A] Reported in accordance with IFRS

Historical Summary
(as originally stated)

Fiscal Year	Total Rev. $000s	Net Inc. Bef. Disc. $000s	EPS* $
2022[A]	48,695,000	3,543,000	2.85
2021[A]	69,561,000	4,673,000	4.31
2020[A]	64,616,000	3,534,000	3.08
2019[A]	48,841,000	3,043,000	2.53
2018[A]	48,098,000	3,467,000	2.77

* Partic. pref. & S.V.
[A] Reported in accordance with IFRS

P.85 Power Financial Corporation

CUSIP - 73927C
Head Office - 751 rue du Square-Victoria, Montréal, QC, H2Y 2J3 **Telephone** - (514) 286-7430 **Toll-free** - (800) 890-7440
Website - www.powerfinancial.com
Email - guy@powercorporation.com
Investor Relations - Chantal Guy (514) 286-7400
Auditors - Deloitte LLP C.A., Montréal, Qué.
Lawyers - Blake, Cassels & Graydon LLP, Montréal, Qué.
Transfer Agents - Computershare Trust Company of Canada Inc., Montréal, Qué.
Profile - (Can. 1986 amalg.) Holds interests in financial services and wealth and asset management businesses in Canada, the United States, Europe and Asia through controlling interests in **Great-West Lifeco Inc.** and **IGM Financial Inc.** Also has significant holdings in a portfolio of global companies based in Europe through an indirect investment in **Groupe Bruxelles Lambert S.A.**
Common delisted from TSX, Feb. 19, 2020.
Directors - Paul Desmarais Jr., chr., Westmount, Qué.; André Desmarais, deputy chr., Westmount, Qué.; R. Jeffrey Orr, pres. & CEO, Montréal, Qué.; The Hon. Gary A. Doer, Winnipeg, Man.; T. Timothy Ryan Jr., Miami Beach, Fla.; Siim A. Vanaselja, Toronto, Ont.
Other Exec. Officers - Gregory D. Tretiak, exec. v-p & CFO; Stéphane Lemay, v-p, gen. counsel & sec.; Denis Le Vasseur, v-p & contr.

Capital Stock

	Authorized (shs.)	Outstanding (shs.)[1]
First Preferred	unlimited	
Series A		4,000,000
Series D		6,000,000
Series E		8,000,000
Series F		6,000,000
Series H		6,000,000
Series K		10,000,000
Series L		8,000,000
Series O		6,000,000
Series P		9,657,516
Series Q		1,542,484
Series R		10,000,000
Series S		12,000,000
Series T		8,000,000
Series V		10,000,000
Series 23		8,000,000
Second Preferred	unlimited	nil
Third Preferred	unlimited	175,000,000
Common	unlimited	679,161,284
Class A Common	unlimited	nil

[1] At May 15, 2023

First Preferred - Issuable in series. Rank prior to second preferred, third preferred, common and class A common shares with respect to the payment of dividends and return of capital. Non-voting.
First Preferred Series A - Entitled to cumulative preferential annual dividends at a rate equal to 70% of the average of the prime rate of two major Canadian chartered banks payable quarterly. Redeemable at $25 per share.
First Preferred Series D - Entitled to non-cumulative preferential annual dividends of $1.375 per share payable quarterly. Redeemable at $25 per share.
First Preferred Series E - Entitled to non-cumulative preferential annual dividends of $1.3125 per share payable quarterly. Redeemable at $25 per share.
First Preferred Series F - Entitled to non-cumulative preferential annual dividends of $1.475 per share payable quarterly. Redeemable at $25 per share.
First Preferred Series H - Entitled to non-cumulative preferential annual dividends of $1.4375 per share payable quarterly. Redeemable at $25 per share.
First Preferred Series K - Entitled to non-cumulative preferential annual dividends of $1.2375 per share payable quarterly. Redeemable at $25 per share.
First Preferred Series L - Entitled to non-cumulative preferential annual dividends of $1.275 per share payable quarterly. Redeemable at $25 per share.
First Preferred Series O - Entitled to non-cumulative preferential annual dividends of $1.45 per share payable quarterly. Redeemable at $25 per share.
First Preferred Series P - Entitled to non-cumulative preferential annual dividends of $0.4995 per share payable quarterly to Jan. 31, 2026, and thereafter at a rate reset every five years equal to the five-year Government of Canada bond yield plus 1.6%. Redeemable on Jan. 31, 2026, and on January 31 every five years thereafter at $25 per share. Convertible at the holder's option on Jan. 31, 2026, and on January 31 every five years thereafter, into floating rate first preferred series Q shares on a share-for-share basis, subject to conditions.
First Preferred Series Q - Entitled to non-cumulative preferential annual dividends payable quarterly equal to the 90-day Canadian Treasury bill rate plus 1.6%. Redeemable on Jan. 31, 2026, and on January 31 every five years thereafter at $25 per share or at any other time at $25.50 per share. Convertible at the holder's option on Jan. 31, 2026, and on January 31 every five years thereafter, into floating rate first preferred series P shares on a share-for-share basis, subject to conditions.
First Preferred Series R - Entitled to non-cumulative preferential annual dividends of $1.375 per share payable quarterly. Redeemable at $25 per share.
First Preferred Series S - Entitled to non-cumulative preferential annual dividends of $1.20 per share payable quarterly. Redeemable at $25 per share.
First Preferred Series T - Entitled to non-cumulative preferential annual dividends of $1.0538 per share payable quarterly to Jan. 31, 2024, and thereafter at a rate reset every five years equal to the five-year Government of Canada bond yield plus 2.37%. Redeemable on Jan. 31, 2024, and on January 31 every five years thereafter at $25 per share. Convertible at the holder's option, on Jan. 31, 2024, and on January 31 every five years thereafter, into floating rate first preferred series U shares on a share-for-share basis, subject to conditions. The series U shares would pay a quarterly dividend equal to the 90-day Canadian Treasury bill rate plus 2.37%.
First Preferred Series V - Entitled to non-cumulative preferential annual dividends of $1.2875 per share payable quarterly. Redeemable at $26 per share and declining by 25¢ per share annually to July 31, 2026, and at $25 per share thereafter.
First Preferred Series 23 - Entitled to non-cumulative preferential annual dividends of $1.125 per share payable quarterly. Redeemable at $26 per share on or after Jan. 31, 2027, and declining by 25¢ per share annually to Jan. 31, 2031, and at $25 per share thereafter.
Second Preferred - Issuable in series. Rank subordinate to first preferred shares but prior to third preferred, common and class A common shares. Non-voting.
Third Preferred - Rank subordinate to first and second preferred shares but prior to common and class A common shares. Entitled to non-cumulative preferential annual dividends of 3¢ per share. Redeemable at $1.00 per share. Non-voting.
Common - One vote per share.
Class A Common - Rank equally with common shares. Convertible into common shares. One vote per share.
Major Shareholder - Power Corporation of Canada held 100% interest at Mar. 16, 2023.

Price Range - PWF/TSX (D)

Year	Volume	High	Low	Close
2020	34,062,650	$36.89	$33.93	$36.31
2019	187,910,803	$37.00	$25.38	$34.94
2018	132,422,891	$34.98	$25.05	$25.83

Capital Stock Changes - During 2022, 75,000,000 third preferred shares were redeemed at $1.00 per share and 15,064,778 common shares were issued to Power Corporation of Canada.

Dividends

PWF.PR.A pfd 1st ser A cum. red. Fltg. Ra pa Q
$0.29575............. Aug. 15/23 $0.290063........ May 15/23
$0.259875........... Feb. 15/23 $0.28125.......... Jan. 31/23
Paid in 2023: $1.126938 2022: $0.892507 2021: $0.428752

PWF.PR.E pfd 1st ser D red. Ra $1.375 pa Q
PWF.PR.F pfd 1st ser E red. Ra $1.3125 pa Q
PWF.PR.G pfd 1st ser F red. Ra $1.475 pa Q
PWF.PR.H pfd 1st ser H red. Ra $1.4375 pa Q
PWF.PR.K pfd 1st ser K red. Ra $1.2375 pa Q
PWF.PR.L pfd 1st ser L red. Ra $1.275 pa Q
PWF.PR.O pfd 1st ser O red. Ra $1.45 pa Q
PWF.PR.P pfd 1st ser P red. exch. Adj. Ra $0.4995 pa Q est. Apr. 30, 2021
PWF.PR.R pfd 1st ser R red. Adj. Ra $1.375 pa Q est. Apr. 30, 2012
PWF.PR.S pfd 1st ser S red. Ra $1.20 pa Q
PWF.PR.T pfd 1st ser T red. exch. Adj. Ra $1.05375 pa Q est. Apr. 30, 2019
PWF.PR.Q pfd 1st ser Q red. exch. Fltg. Ra pa Q
$0.411608........... Oct. 31/23 $0.378525........ July 31/23
$0.359843........... Apr. 30/23 $0.330952........ Jan. 31/23
Paid in 2023: $1.480928 2022: $0.601167 2021: $0.43058

PWF.PR.Z pfd 1st ser V red. Ra $1.2875 pa Q
PWF.PF.A pfd 1st ser 23 red. Ra $1.125 pa Q
Listed Oct 15/21.
$0.33288i............ Jan. 31/22
pfd 1st ser I red. Ra $1.50 pa Q[1]
$0.09041f............ Nov. 22/21
[1] Redeemed Nov. 22, 2021 at $25 per sh.
f Final Payment **i** Initial Payment

Wholly Owned Subsidiaries

Power Financial Europe S.A., Belgium.
- 50% int. in **Parjointco S.A.**, Belgium.
  - 29.8% int. in **Groupe Bruxelles Lambert S.A.**, Brussels, Belgium. 44% voting interest.
    - 7.6% int. in **adidas AG**, Germany.
    - 99.6% int. in **Affidea Group B.V.**, The Hague, Netherlands. 100% voting interest.
    - 48.2% int. in **Canyon Bicycles GmbH**, Germany.
    - 6.3% int. in **GEA Group AG**, Germany.
    - 2.1% int. in **Holcim Ltd.**, Zug, Switzerland.
    - 54.6% int. in **Imerys S.A.**, France. 68.1% voting interest.
    - 1.9% int. in **Mowi ASA**, Bergen, Norway.
    - 20% int. in **Ontex Group N.V.**, Belgium.
    - 23% int. in **Parques Reunidos Servicios Centrales, S.A.**, Madrid, Spain.
    - 6.9% int. in **Pernod Ricard S.A.**, Paris, France. 11.5% voting interest.
    - 19.1% int. in **SGS S.A.**, Geneva, Switzerland.
    - 83.8% int. in **Sanoptis AG**, Zug, Switzerland. 63% voting interest.
    - 15.9% int. in **Umicore N.V.**, Belgium.
    - 16.2% int. in **Voodoo SAS**, Paris, France.
    - 61.5% int. in **Webhelp SAS**, Paris, France.

Subsidiaries

66.6% int. in **Great-West Lifeco Inc.**, Winnipeg, Man. (see separate coverage)
62.2% int. in **IGM Financial Inc.**, Winnipeg, Man. (see separate coverage)
63% int. in **Portag3 Ventures Limited Partnership**, Toronto, Ont.

Investments

7.7% int. in **Portag3 Ventures II Limited Partnership**, Toronto, Ont.
13.5% int. in **Wealthsimple Financial Corp.**, Toronto, Ont.

P.86 PowerBand Solutions Inc.

Symbol - PBX **Exchange** - TSX-VEN **CUSIP** - 73934B
Head Office - 300-1100 Burloak Dr, Burlington, ON, L7L 6B2 **Toll-free** - (866) 768-7653
Website - www.powerbandsolutions.com
Email - darrin.swenson@powerbandsolutions.com
Investor Relations - Darrin Swenson (866) 768-7653
Auditors - MNP LLP C.A., Vancouver, B.C.
Transfer Agents - Computershare Investor Services Inc.
Profile - (B.C. 2009) Develops, markets and sells a suite of cloud-based finance portal and auction software tools to the automotive sector for buying, selling, leasing, trading, financing and auctioning vehicles from any location using smart phones or other online devices.
Primary product DrivrzFinancial, a new and used vehicle leasing portal, is offered through subsidiary **Drivrz Financial Holdings, LLC**, which streamlines leasing for consumers and dealers, as well as incorporates first-of-its-kind technology to navigate the underwriting, funding, and delivery process.
Also offers DrivrzXchange, an online auction platform in the U.S., through 50%-owned **D2D Auto Auctions LLC**, which features identity verification for all parties, payment handling and processing, transportation, inspection, financing as well as mechanical and detailing services. This segment was placed under maintenance on February 2023.
Effective Feb. 28, 2023, the company discontinued its operations of its wholly-owned **IntellaCar Solutions Inc, LLC** (dba DrivrzLane), a digital retailing solution that offers video and library of brochures of vehicles which enables customers to review vehicle details. In addition, DrivrzXchange, an inclusive multi-sided marketplace (web application) that allows buyers and sellers of all types to list and/or find vehicles, was placed on maintenance.
In December 2022, the company sold its 73.6% interest in **Motor One Canada Inc.** (formerly **DRIVRZ Financial Inc.**) to an arm's length third party for $633,150.
In December 2022, the company discontinued the operations of its subsidiary **2744915 Ontario Inc.**
In September 2022, the company entered into an agreement with John Canales and Bruce Polkes, former chairman and CEO, respectively, to transfer their 30% and 10% interest in **IntellaCar Solutions LLC**, to the company. The company now holds 100% interest in IntellaCar.
In April 2022, former president and CEO Kelly Jennings transferred all 44,188,828 common shares held of the company, representing a 21.97% interest, to an arm's length lender pursuant to a series of loan transactions with the lender. Kelly Jennings no longer held any common shares of the company. The loan agreements provide that the common shares be returned to Kelly Jennings upon loan repayment and assuming no uncured event of default.
Predecessor Detail - Name changed from Marquis Ventures Inc., Feb. 8, 2018, pursuant to Qualifying Transaction reverse takeover of PowerBand Global Dealer Services Inc.
Directors - Johnnie Bryan Hunt Jr., chr., Ark.; Joe Poulin, v-chr., Barbados; Darrin Swenson, interim pres. & interim CEO, Ark.; Geoffrey S. (Geoff) Belsher, Toronto, Ont.; Jerome Letter, N.Y.; Vassilis Stachtos, N.Y.
Other Exec. Officers - Shibu Abraham, CFO; Sean Severin, chief tech. officer; Sam Rizek, v-p, bus. devel.

Capital Stock

	Authorized (shs.)	Outstanding (shs.)[1]
Common	unlimited	299,282,129

[1] At May 30, 2023

Major Shareholder - Johnnie Bryan Hunt Jr. held 17.71% interest and Joe Poulin held 10.72% interest at Aug. 8, 2022.

Price Range - PBX/TSX-VEN

Year	Volume	High	Low	Close
2022	117,869,128	$0.92	$0.06	$0.07
2021	203,942,189	$1.49	$0.30	$0.91
2020	79,563,084	$0.32	$0.08	$0.29
2019	19,357,773	$0.22	$0.06	$0.10
2018	33,452,736	$0.40	$0.09	$0.13

Recent Close: $0.03
Capital Stock Changes - In June 2022, 15,113,640 common shares were issued for settlement of $4,534,092 of debt. In June and July 2022, private placement of 79,354,361 units (1 common share & 1 warrant) at 30¢ per unit was completed. Also during 2022, common

shares were issued as follows: 3,392,125 vesting of restricted share units, 2,100,000 on exercise of options and 578,276 on exercise of warrants.

Wholly Owned Subsidiaries

DRIVRZ Financial Inc., Ont.
IntellarCar Solutions LLC, United States.
PowerBand Global Dealer Services Inc., Burlington, Ont.

Subsidiaries

91% int. in **PBX Holdings LLC**, United States.
91% int. in **Powerband Solutions US Inc.**, United States.
- 65.52% int. in **DRIVRZ US, LLC**, United States.
- 94.6% int. in **Drivrz Financial Holdings, LLC**, Dallas, Tex.
  - 100% int. in **MUSA Auto Finance, LLC**, Dallas, Tex.

51% int. in **2744915 Ontario Inc.**, Canada.

Investments

7.5% int. in **CB Auto Group Inc.**, Atlanta, Ga.
50% int. in **D2D Auto Auction LLC**, Ark.

Financial Statistics

Periods ended:	12m Dec. 31/22[A]		12m Dec. 31/21[□A]
	$000s	%Chg	$000s
Operating revenue	**12,761**	**-47**	**23,937**
Cost of sales	6,118		12,297
Salaries & benefits	8,846		7,759
General & admin expense	8,446		9,869
Stock-based compensation	4,348		2,470
Operating expense	**28,158**	**-13**	**32,395**
Operating income	**(15,397)**	**n.a.**	**(8,458)**
Deprec., depl. & amort.	1,346		1,581
Finance costs, gross	1,131		1,058
Write-downs/write-offs	(13,518)[1]		nil
Pre-tax income	**(30,656)**	**n.a.**	**(15,973)**
Net inc. bef. disc. opers	**(30,656)**	**n.a.**	**(15,973)**
Income from disc. opers	117		(217)
Net income	**(30,539)**	**n.a.**	**(16,191)**
Net inc. for equity hldrs	**(27,305)**	**n.a.**	**(14,959)**
Net inc. for non-cont. int	**(3,234)**	**n.a.**	**(1,232)**
Cash & equivalent	10,299		6,368
Inventories	nil		7
Accounts receivable	891		1,547
Current assets	12,024		9,064
Long-term investments	443		195
Fixed assets, net	1,968		323
Right-of-use assets	2,727		3,320
Intangibles, net	nil		7,440
Total assets	**17,235**	**-16**	**20,411**
Accts. pay. & accr. liabs	4,905		5,105
Current liabilities	7,349		11,064
Long-term debt, gross	1,648		3,905
Long-term debt, net	nil		1,738
Long-term lease liabilities	2,516		3,075
Shareholders' equity	7,966		3,883
Non-controlling interest	(596)		652
Cash from oper. activs	**(10,740)**	**n.a.**	**(7,605)**
Cash from fin. activs	22,323		20,070
Cash from invest. activs	(8,562)		(7,407)
Net cash position	**10,299**	**+62**	**6,357**
Capital expenditures	(6,411)		(69)
	$		$
Earns. per sh. bef disc opers*	(0.11)		(0.09)
Earnings per share*	(0.11)		(0.08)
Cash flow per share*	(0.04)		(0.04)
	shs		shs
No. of shs. o/s*	298,765,462		...
Avg. no. of shs. o/s*	250,160,064		175,277,531
	%		%
Net profit margin	(240.23)		(66.73)
Return on equity	(462.86)		n.m.
Return on assets	(156.86)		(87.09)
Foreign sales percent	99		99

* Common
□ Restated
A Reported in accordance with IFRS
1 Includes $8,888,424 impairment of intangible assets and goodwill from discontinuing operations in DrivrzLane and product development costs for DrivrzFinancial and DrivrzXchange projects and $4,629,511 impairment of vehicle lease contracts that were repurchased.

Latest Results

Periods ended:	3m Mar. 31/23[A]		3m Mar. 31/22[□A]
	$000s	%Chg	$000s
Operating revenue	839	-86	5,962
Net inc. bef. disc. opers	(3,259)	n.a.	(5,592)
Income from disc. opers	13		(688)
Net income	(3,247)	n.a.	(6,280)
Net inc. for equity hldrs	(3,134)	n.a.	(5,939)
Net inc. for non-cont. int	(113)		(341)
	$		$
Earns. per sh. bef. disc. opers.*	(0.01)		(0.03)
Earnings per share*	(0.01)		(0.03)

* Common
□ Restated
A Reported in accordance with IFRS

Historical Summary
(as originally stated)

Fiscal Year	Oper. Rev.	Net Inc. Bef. Disc.	EPS*
	$000s	$000s	$
2022[A]	12,761	(30,656)	(0.11)
2021[A]	23,937	(16,191)	(0.09)
2020[A]	3,028	(12,843)	(0.11)
2019[A]	1,999	(8,050)	(0.11)
2018[A1]	282	(6,575)	(0.13)

* Common
A Reported in accordance with IFRS
1 Result prior to Feb. 8, 2018, pertain to and reflect the Qualifying Transaction reverse takeover acquisition of Powerband Global Dealer Services Inc.

P.87 PowerTap Hydrogen Capital Corp.

Symbol - MOVE **Exchange** - NEO **CUSIP** - 73939X
Head Office - 810-789 Pender St W, Vancouver, BC, V6C 1H2 **Telephone** - (604) 687-2038 **Toll-free** - (877) 360-0692
Website - powertapcapital.com
Email - raghu@hydrogenfueling.co
Investor Relations - Raghunath Kilambi (604) 687-2038
Auditors - SHIM & Associates LLP C.A., Vancouver, B.C.
Transfer Agents - National Securities Administrators Ltd., Vancouver, B.C.

Profile - (B.C. 2018; orig. B.C., 1980) Develops and installs hydrogen production and dispensing fueling infrastructure in the United States.

Wholly owned **PowerTap Hydrogen Fueling Corp.** has developed a patented, onsite hydrogen generating fuel station technology. Using renewable natural gas (biomethane or upgraded biogas) from landfills, animal manure, food scraps and wastewater sludge as feedstock, the onsite hydrogen production and dispensing unit uses steam methane reforming technology, coupled with an advanced CO_2 capture system, to produce blue hydrogen. The company is commercializing its blue hydrogen product, PowerTap 3.0, focusing on the refueling needs of the long-haul trucking market, and has a partnership with **Humboldt Petroleum, Inc.**, **Peninsula Petroleum, LLC** and **Colvin Oil I LLC** (collectively the Andretti Group) to install PowerTap modular hydrogenfueling stations initially in California.

Affiliate **Progressus Clean Technologies Inc.** (49% owned) owns exclusive rights and intellectual property pertaining to the Advanced Electrolyzer System (AES), a novel electrochemical technology that selectively recovers high purity hydrogen from dilute syngas streams.

In June 2023, the company entered into a letter of intent with **Cleantech Power Corp.** to pursue collaborative energy project development towards the adoption of low carbon intensity clean hydrogen and renewable energy solutions.

In September 2022, affiliate **Progressus Clean Technologies Inc.** terminated its June 23, 2022, letter of intent with **BioQuest Corp.** whereby BioQuest would acquire Progressus.

Predecessor Detail - Name changed from Clean Power Capital Corp., June 10, 2021.

Directors - Raghunath (Raghu) Kilambi, pres. & CEO, Calif.; Byron Berry, Ont.; John Martin, Geneva, Switzerland; John Zorbas, Athens, Greece

Other Exec. Officers - Margarito Rodriguez, CFO

Capital Stock

	Authorized (shs.)	Outstanding (shs.)[1]	Par
Common	unlimited	23,610,806	US$0.01

1 At June 15, 2023

Major Shareholder - Widely held at Apr. 18, 2023.

Price Range - MOVE/NEO

Year	Volume	High	Low	Close
2022	1,030,050	$10.00	$0.30	$0.50
2021	5,415,918	$69.40	$6.20	$6.20
2020	5,802,486	$39.40	$1.10	$36.40
2019	513,079	$85.40	$9.10	$9.80
2018	73,098	$113.40	$10.50	$33.60

Consolidation: 1-for-20 cons. in June 2023; 1-for-7 cons. in May 2020

Recent Close: $0.65

Capital Stock Changes - On June 15, 2023, common shares were consolidated on a 1-for-20 basis. Also in June 2023, private placement of up to 1,764,706 units (1 post-consolidated common share & ½ warrant) at 85¢ per unit was announced, with warrants exercisable at $1.15 per share for two years.

In July 2021 and January 2022, 40,000,000 common shares were issued pursuant to the acquisition of 49% interest in Progressus Clean Technologies Inc. Also during fiscal 2022, common shares were issued as follows: 35,900,000 on conversion of restricted stock units, 15,455,042 for sponsorship fees, 2,000,000 for finders fees, 1,653,327 for sales fees, 409,632 for consulting fees, 3,628,843 on exercise of warrants and 500,000 on exercise of options.

Wholly Owned Subsidiaries

Bendu Capital Limited, B.C.
Cubix Acquisitionco Inc., B.C. Inactive.
Pleasant Shores Ventures Ltd., British Virgin Islands. Inactive.
PowerTap Hydrogen Fueling Corp., Newport Beach, Calif.

Investments

C3 Center Holding Inc.
Cabral Gold Inc., Vancouver, B.C. (see Survey of Mines)
FusionOne Energy Corp.
49% int. in **Progressus Clean Technologies Inc.**, Canada.
2459160 Ontario Ltd., Ont. dba Toronto Wolfpack.
2591046 Ontario Corp., Toronto, Ont.

Financial Statistics

Periods ended:	12m June 30/22[A]		12m June 30/21[A]
	$000s	%Chg	$000s
Salaries & benefits	652		nil
General & admin expense	81,293		9,983
Stock-based compensation	66,914		6,607
Operating expense	**81,293**	**+390**	**16,590**
Operating income	**(81,293)**	**n.a.**	**(16,590)**
Investment income	(466)		nil
Write-downs/write-offs	(125,014)		(6)
Pre-tax income	**(219,495)**	**n.a.**	**(57,860)**
Net income	**(219,495)**	**n.a.**	**(57,860)**
Cash & equivalent	3,795		11,446
Current assets	6,189		14,780
Long-term investments	5,399		nil
Fixed assets, net	212		30
Intangibles, net	nil		108,571
Total assets	**12,814**	**-90**	**123,867**
Bank indebtedness	...		40
Accts. pay. & accr. liabs	656		1,123
Current liabilities	798		1,123
Shareholders' equity	11,976		122,704
Cash from oper. activs	**(8,173)**	**n.a.**	**(10,397)**
Cash from fin. activs	2,137		27,152
Cash from invest. activs	(619)		(9,431)
Net cash position	**1,083**	**-86**	**7,963**
Capital expenditures	(177)		(9)
	$		$
Earnings per share*	(11.80)		(5.60)
Cash flow per share*	(0.44)		(0.99)
	shs		shs
No. of shs. o/s*	20,567,732		15,590,390
Avg. no. of shs. o/s*	18,561,184		10,474,840
	%		%
Net profit margin	n.a.		n.a.
Return on equity	(325.95)		(90.46)
Return on assets	(321.18)		(89.42)

* Common
A Reported in accordance with IFRS

Latest Results

Periods ended:	9m Mar. 31/23[A]		9m Mar. 31/22[A]
	$000s	%Chg	$000s
Net income	(15,410)	n.a.	(69,612)
	$		$
Earnings per share*	(0.80)		(3.80)

* Common
A Reported in accordance with IFRS

Historical Summary
(as originally stated)

Fiscal Year	Oper. Rev.	Net Inc. Bef. Disc.	EPS*
	$000s	$000s	$
2022[A]	nil	(219,495)	(11.80)
2021[A]	nil	(57,860)	(5.60)
2020[A]	nil	(81,961)	(35.80)
2019[A]	nil	10,243	12.60
	US$000s	US$000s	US$
2018[A]	nil	(540)	(12.60)

* Common
A Reported in accordance with IFRS

Note: Adjusted throughout for 1-for-20 cons. in June 2023; 1-for-7 cons. in May 2020; 2-for-1 split in Oct. 2018

P.88 Precision Drilling Corporation*

Symbol - PD **Exchange** - TSX **CUSIP** - 74022D
Head Office - 800-525 8 Ave SW, Calgary, AB, T2P 1G1 **Telephone** - (403) 716-4500 **Fax** - (403) 264-0251
Website - www.precisiondrilling.com
Email - investorrelations@precisiondrilling.com
Investor Relations - Lavonne Zdunich (403) 716-4500
Auditors - KPMG LLP C.A., Calgary, Alta.
Bankers - Royal Bank of Canada, Calgary, Alta.
Lawyers - Osler, Hoskin & Harcourt LLP
Transfer Agents - Computershare Trust Company, N.A., Canton, Mass.; Computershare Trust Company of Canada Inc., Calgary, Alta.
FP500 Revenue Ranking - 253
Employees - 4,802 at Dec. 31, 2022
Profile - (Alta. 2010, amalg.) Provides onshore drilling, completion and production services to exploration and production companies in the oil and natural gas, and geothermal industries in Canada, the U.S. and the Middle East.

Operations are carried out through two segments: Contract Drilling Services; and Completion and Production Services.

In Canada, the Contract Drilling Services segment includes land drilling services, procurement and distribution of oilfield supplies, and manufacturing and refurbishment of drilling and service rig equipment. The Completion and Production Services segment includes service rigs for well completion and workover services, camp and catering services, rental of oilfield surface equipment and wellsite accommodations. At Dec. 31, 2022, segment equipment consisted of 111 land drilling rigs, 125 well completion and workover service rigs, 103 wellsite accommodation units, 782 drill camp beds, 654 base camp beds and three kitchen diners, and 1,900 oilfield rental items.

In the United States, the Contract Drilling Services segment includes land drilling services, turnkey drilling services, procurement and distribution of oilfield supplies, and manufacturing and refurbishment of drilling and service rig equipment. The Completion and Production Services segment includes service rigs for well completion and workover services. At Dec. 31, 2022, segment equipment consisted of 101 land drilling rigs and 10 well completion and workover service rigs

Internationally, the Contract Drilling Services segment consists of land drilling services. At Dec. 31, 2022, segment equipment consisted of four land drilling rigs in Saudi Arabia, six in Kuwait, two in Iraq and one in Georgia.

The company's drilling rig fleet is supported by its digitally enabled Alpha™ suite of technologies that includes AlphaAutomation™, AlphaApps™ and AlphaAnalytics™, which automate key processes of the drilling cycle and significantly improves the efficiency of the downhole function. The company also offers EverGreen™ suite of environmental solutions which is designed to reduce the environmental impact of oilfield operations. EverGreen™ solutions consists of EverGreen Monitoring™, an integrated power and emissions monitoring system that provides environmental insights as they occur, monitoring fuel consumption, power generation key performance indicators and real-time greenhouse gas emissions; EverGreenEnergy™, which provides clean, efficient and cost effective rig power sources; and EverGreen™ Fuel Cell converts blended green hydrogen into existing diesel or natural gas generators, which helps reduce greenhouse gas emissions. The company has tested, field hardened and implemented its battery energy storage system and fuel monitoring system which are both offered across North America.

Periods ended:	12m Dec. 31/22	12m Dec. 31/21
No. of drill rigs	225	227
Drill rig operating days	43,105	32,466
Drill rig rev. per oper. day $[1]	27,037	21,105
Drill rig rev. per oper. day US$[2]	27,309	21,213
Drill rig rev. per oper. day[3]	51,242	52,837
No. of service rigs	135	123
Service rig operating hrs	170,362	126,840
Service rig util. rate, %	42	28

[1] Canadian operations.
[2] U.S. operations.
[3] International operations (US$); primarily the Middle East.

Recent Merger and Acquisition Activity

Status: completed **Revised:** July 28, 2022
UPDATE: The transaction was completed. PREVIOUS: High Arctic Energy Services Inc. agreed to sell its Canadian well servicing business to Precision Drilling Corporation for a purchase price of $38,200,000 including $10,200,000 payable at closing with the balance payable in January 2023. High Arctic expects to retain around $3,000,000 in closing working capital. High Arctic plans to focus on its existing business in Papua New Guinea. High Arctic's Canadian well servicing fleet marketed under the Concord Well Servicing brand consists of 51 marketable rigs and 29 inactive and out of service rigs, as well as oilfield rental equipment associated with well servicing including 17 modern hydraulic catwalks. The sale of this business together with the sale of the Canadian snubbing business to Team Snubbing Services Inc., would result in the elimination of High Arctic's Production Services segment. Post-closing, High Arctic would retain in Canada its Ancillary Services segment consisting of the nitrogen pumping business and a smaller rentals business focused on pressure control under the HAES Rental Services branding.

Predecessor Detail - Succeeded Precision Drilling Trust, June 1, 2010, pursuant to plan of arrangement whereby Precision Drilling Corporation was formed to facilitate the conversion of the trust into a corporation and Precision Drilling Trust subsequently dissolved.

Directors - Steven W. Krablin, chr., Spring, Tex.; Kevin A. Neveu, pres. & CEO, Houston, Tex.; Michael R. Culbert, Calgary, Alta.; William T. Donovan, North Palm Beach, Fla.; Lori A. Lancaster, New York, N.Y.; Susan M. MacKenzie, Calgary, Alta.; Dr. Kevin O. Meyers, Anchorage, Alaska; David W. Williams, Houston, Tex.

Other Exec. Officers - Veronica H. Foley, chief legal & compliance office; Shuja U. Goraya, chief tech. officer; Darren J. Ruhr, CAO; Carey T. Ford, sr. v-p & CFO; Gene C. Stahl, pres., North American drilling

Capital Stock

	Authorized (shs.)	Outstanding (shs.)[1]
Preferred	unlimited	nil
Common	unlimited	13,607,739

[1] At June 30, 2023

Options - At Dec. 31, 2022, options were outstanding to purchase 23,055 common shares at a weighted average exercise price of Cdn$113.01 per share with a weighted average remaining contractual life of 1.7 years and 141,748 common shares at a weighted average exercise price of US$84.84 per share with a weighted average remaining contractual life of 1.64 years.

Major Shareholder - Fidelity Investments Inc. held 10.51% interest at Mar. 22, 2023.

Price Range - PD/TSX

Year	Volume	High	Low	Close
2022	27,273,231	$116.00	$46.60	$103.71
2021	30,149,480	$62.26	$20.72	$44.69
2020	19,640,071	$43.00	$7.70	$20.93
2019	17,549,918	$81.00	$26.40	$36.20
2018	25,746,618	$106.60	$45.00	$47.40

Consolidation: 1-for-20 cons. in Nov. 2020
Recent Close: $87.85
Capital Stock Changes - During 2022, common shares were issued as follows: 263,900 under performance share unit plan and 120,595 on exercise of options; 130,395 common shares were repurchased under a Normal Course Issuer Bid.

Long-Term Debt - Outstanding at Dec. 31, 2022:

Sr. sec. revolv. facility due June 2025[1]	$59,620,000
Real estate term facilities[2]	29,989,000
7.125% sr. notes due Jan. 2026[3]	471,225,000
6.875% sr. notes due Jan. 2029[4]	542,004,000
Less: Net unamort. debt issue costs	14,581,000
	1,088,257,000
Less: Current portion	2,287,000
	1,085,970,000

[1] Bears interest at either U.S. base rate, LIBOR, Canadian prime or CDOR plus a margin based on the company's consolidated total debt to EBITDA ratio.
[2] Consists of US$11,000,000 real estate term credit facility, bearing interest at LIBOR plus a margin and matures in November 2025, and Cdn$20,000,000 Canadian real estate term credit facility, bearing interest at CDOR rate plus margin and matures in March 2026.
[3] US$347,765,000.
[4] US$400,000,000.

Repayment requirements of long-term debt over the next five years were reported as follows:

2023	$2,287,000
2024	2,287,000
2025	71,367,000
2026	484,893,000
Thereafter	542,004,000

Wholly Owned Subsidiaries

Grey Wolf Drilling (Barbados) Ltd., Barbados.
Grey Wolf Drilling Limited, Barbados.
Precision Diversified Oilfield Services Corp., Alta.
Precision Drilling Canada Limited Partnership, Alta.
Precision Drilling (US) Corporation, Tex.
- 100% int. in **Precision Completion & Production Services Ltd.**, Del.
- 100% int. in **Precision Drilling Holdings Company**, Nev.
  - 100% int. in **Precision Drilling Company, LP**, Tex.

Precision Limited Partnership, Alta.

Investments

Cathedral Energy Services Ltd., Calgary, Alta. (see separate coverage)

Financial Statistics

Periods ended:	12m Dec. 31/22[A]		12m Dec. 31/21[A]
	$000s	%Chg	$000s
Operating revenue	**1,617,194**	**+64**	**986,847**
General & admin expense	180,988		95,931
Other operating expense	1,124,601		698,144
Operating expense	**1,305,589**	**+64**	**794,075**
Operating income	**311,605**	**+62**	**192,772**
Deprec., depl. & amort.	279,035		282,326
Finance income	323		210
Finance costs, gross	88,136		91,641
Investment income	12,452		(400)
Pre-tax income	**(14,143)**	**n.a.**	**(182,782)**
Income taxes	20,150		(5,396)
Net income	**(34,293)**	**n.a.**	**(177,386)**
Cash & equivalent	21,587		40,588
Inventories	35,158		23,429
Accounts receivable	413,925		255,740
Current assets	470,670		319,757
Long-term investments	20,451		7,382
Fixed assets, net	2,303,338		2,258,391
Right-of-use assets	60,032		51,440
Intangibles, net	19,575		23,915
Total assets	**2,876,123**	**+8**	**2,661,752**
Accts. pay. & accr. liabs	392,053		224,123
Current liabilities	410,029		238,120
Long-term debt, gross	1,088,257		1,109,017
Long-term debt, net	1,085,970		1,106,794
Long-term lease liabilities	52,978		45,823
Shareholders' equity	1,230,529		1,225,555
Cash from oper. activs	**237,104**	**+70**	**139,225**
Cash from fin. activs	(113,171)		(149,913)
Cash from invest. activs	(144,415)		(56,613)
Net cash position	**21,587**	**-47**	**40,588**
Capital expenditures	(184,250)		(75,941)
Capital disposals	37,198		13,086
	$		$
Earnings per share*	(2.53)		(13.32)
Cash flow per share*	17.50		10.46
	shs		shs
No. of shs. o/s*	13,558,525		13,304,425
Avg. no. of shs. o/s*	13,546,000		13,315,000
	%		%
Net profit margin	(2.12)		(17.98)
Return on equity	(2.79)		(13.48)
Return on assets	6.48		(3.18)
Foreign sales percent	54		55
No. of employees (FTEs)	4,802		3,350

* Common
[A] Reported in accordance with IFRS

Latest Results

Periods ended:	6m June 30/23[A]		6m June 30/22[A]
	$000s	%Chg	$000s
Operating revenue	984,229	+45	677,355
Net income	122,730	n.a.	(68,455)
	$		$
Earnings per share*	8.98		(5.06)

* Common
[A] Reported in accordance with IFRS

Historical Summary
(as originally stated)

Fiscal Year	Oper. Rev.	Net Inc. Bef. Disc.	EPS*
	$000s	$000s	$
2022[A]	1,617,194	(34,293)	(2.53)
2021[A]	986,847	(177,386)	(13.32)
2020[A]	935,753	(120,138)	(8.76)
2019[A]	1,541,320	6,618	0.46
2018[A]	1,541,189	(294,270)	(20.05)

* Common
[A] Reported in accordance with IFRS
Note: Adjusted throughout for 1-for-20 cons. in Nov. 2020

P.89 Predictiv AI Inc.

Symbol - PAI.H **Exchange** - TSX-VEN (S) **CUSIP** - 74036G
Head Office - 1100-20 Bay St, Toronto, ON, M5J 2N8 **Telephone** - (416) 792-9088
Website - www.predictiv.ai
Email - kqureshi@predictiv.ai
Investor Relations - Khurram R. Qureshi (647) 500-7371
Auditors - Olayinka Oyebola & Co. C.A., Lagos, Nigeria
Lawyers - Fogler, Rubinoff LLP, Toronto, Ont.
Transfer Agents - Computershare Trust Company of Canada Inc., Toronto, Ont.
Profile - (Ont. 2015; orig. Alta., 1994) Provides software solutions in the artificial intelligence (AI) and Internet of Things (IoT) markets using deep machine learning and data science techniques.

Operates through wholly owned **Weather Telematics Inc.**, which offers real-time advanced AI-based predictive road condition weather analytics for safer, connected and autonomous transportation including Alert Fleet sensor and software system, which provides fleet owners the tools they need to run significantly safer and more efficient fleets.

Also holds 51% interest in **New Hope IoT Intl. Inc.**, which is focused on converting big data through analytics by means of professional consultation and manufacturing process optimization to transform traditional manufacturing operations into advanced and smart industrial IoT enabled facilities. Its FreePoint's ShiftWorx platform measures real-time production flows and assesses inventory management in its facility in China.

Common suspended from TSX-VEN, June 7, 2022.

Predecessor Detail - Name changed from Internet of Things Inc., Sept. 1, 2020; basis 1 new for 5.5 old shs.

Directors - Jim Grimes, exec. chr., interim pres. & interim CEO, Toronto, Ont.; Millard Roth, Toronto, Ont.

Other Exec. Officers - Khurram R. Qureshi, CFO; Darryl Smith, chief tech. officer; Thomas (Tom) Park, v-p, govt. rel. & regulatory affairs; Rick Moscone, corp. sec.

Capital Stock

	Authorized (shs.)	Outstanding (shs.)[1]
First Preferred	unlimited	nil
Second Preferred	unlimited	nil
Common	unlimited	93,500,616

[1] At Dec. 24, 2021

Major Shareholder - Widely held at July 20, 2020.

Price Range - PAI.H/TSX-VEN (S)

Year	Volume	High	Low	Close
2022	11,371,600	$0.04	$0.02	$0.02
2021	76,532,143	$0.25	$0.03	$0.04
2020	107,855,605	$0.44	$0.03	$0.19
2019	7,869,923	$0.28	$0.03	$0.06
2018	10,898,981	$0.80	$0.11	$0.17

Consolidation: 1-for-5.5 cons. in Sept. 2020

Wholly Owned Subsidiaries

AI Labs Inc.

IoT Labs Inc.

Weather Telematics Inc., Ottawa, Ont.

Subsidiaries

51% int. in **New Hope IoT International Inc.**

Financial Statistics

Periods ended:	12m Jan. 31/21[A]		12m Jan. 31/20[A]
	$000s	%Chg	$000s
Operating revenue	**78**	**-76**	**330**
Cost of sales	131		111
Research & devel. expense	37		nil
General & admin expense	1,675		1,314
Stock-based compensation	1,214		78
Operating expense	**3,056**	**+103**	**1,503**
Operating income	**(2,978)**	**n.a.**	**(1,173)**
Deprec., depl. & amort.	127		124
Finance costs, net	58		52
Write-downs/write-offs	(296)		(662)
Pre-tax income	**(7,243)**	**n.a.**	**(2,052)**
Net income	**(7,243)**	**n.a.**	**(2,052)**
Cash & equivalent	173		43
Accounts receivable	10		75
Current assets	341		170
Fixed assets, net	117		6
Intangibles, net	nil		422
Total assets	**458**	**-23**	**598**
Bank indebtedness	nil		291
Accts. pay. & accr. liabs	200		864
Current liabilities	200		1,165
Long-term debt, gross	40		nil
Long-term debt, net	40		nil
Shareholders' equity	(2,050)		(583)
Cash from oper. activs	**(2,094)**	**n.a.**	**(677)**
Cash from fin. activs	2,834		465
Cash from invest. activs	(610)		(33)
Net cash position	**173**	**+302**	**43**
	$		$
Earnings per share*	(0.12)		(0.06)
Cash flow per share*	(0.03)		(0.02)
	shs		shs
No. of shs. o/s*	78,472,999		37,532,672
Avg. no. of shs. o/s*	61,764,836		37,219,010
	%		%
Net profit margin	n.m.		(621.82)
Return on equity	n.m.		n.m.
Return on assets	n.m.		(163.31)

* Common

[A] Reported in accordance with IFRS

Latest Results

Periods ended:	9m Oct. 31/21[A]		9m Oct. 31/20[A]
	$000s	%Chg	$000s
Operating revenue	17	-77	73
Net income	(679)	n.a.	(2,203)
	$		$
Earnings per share*	(0.01)		(0.03)

* Common

[A] Reported in accordance with IFRS

Historical Summary
(as originally stated)

Fiscal Year	Oper. Rev.	Net Inc. Bef. Disc.	EPS*
	$000s	$000s	$
2021[A]	78	(7,243)	(0.12)
2020[A]	330	(2,052)	(0.06)
2019[A]	222	(1,729)	(0.06)
2018[A]	nil	(1,294)	(0.06)
2017[A]	nil	(1,755)	(0.06)

* Common

[A] Reported in accordance with IFRS

Note: Adjusted throughout for 1-for-5.5 cons. in Sept. 2020

P.90 Predictmedix AI Inc.

Symbol - PMED **Exchange** - CSE **CUSIP** - 74040N

Head Office - 3000-77 King St W, Toronto, ON, M5K 1G8 **Telephone** - (647) 889-6916

Website - www.predictmedix.com

Email - rahul@predictmedix.com

Investor Relations - Dr. Rahul Kushwah (647) 889-6916

Auditors - Kreston GTA LLP C.A., Markham, Ont.

Transfer Agents - National Securities Administrators Ltd., Vancouver, B.C.

Profile - (B.C. 1987) Develops and markets artificial intelligence (AI)-based technologies for alcohol or cannabis impairment testing, mental illness screening, and remote patient monitoring and treatment plans.

The company's technologies use facial, thermal, video and audio recognition to determine when individuals are impaired, suffering from infectious disease or mental illness. Primary product being sold is Infectious Disease Symptom Screening Solutions, which focuses on mass screening for infectious diseases including influenza and COVID-19. Also offers MobileWellbeing™, a telemedicine AI-integrated remote patient monitoring platform which checks patient vitals through wearables and portable devices, provides options to clinicians, facilitates communications, and links up with clinician's patient management platform. Other products under development includes Mental Health Screening, which is capable of mass screening behavioural and physiological indicators of mental illness such as depression, dementia, autism and attention deficit hyperactivity disorder (ADHD); and Impairment Detection Screening, which is used for non-invasive and contactless screening of cannabis and alcohol impairment for use in workplace and law enforcement.

In February 2023, common shares were listed on the Frankfurt Stock Exchange under the symbol 3QP.

Predecessor Detail - Name changed from Predictmedix Inc., July 13, 2023.

Directors - Sheldon Kales, pres. & CEO, Toronto, Ont.; Dr. Rahul Kushwah, COO, Toronto, Ont.; Tomas (Tom) Sipos, Toronto, Ont.

Other Exec. Officers - Rakesh Malhotra, CFO & corp. sec.; Rajiv Muradia, v-p, tech.

Capital Stock

	Authorized (shs.)	Outstanding (shs.)[1]
Common	unlimited	145,646,292

[1] At July 17, 2023

Major Shareholder - Sheldon Kales held 26.6% interest at Apr. 2, 2022.

Price Range - PMED/CSE

Year	Volume	High	Low	Close
2022	13,560,822	$0.21	$0.03	$0.05
2021	40,227,131	$0.64	$0.14	$0.15
2020	96,185,202	$1.15	$0.06	$0.33
2019	3,595,690	$0.11	$0.04	$0.05

Recent Close: $0.13

Capital Stock Changes - In February 2023, private placement of 12,250,000 units (1 common share & 1 warrant) at 5¢ per unit was completed, with warrants exercisable at 10¢ per share for two years. In June 2023, private placement of 10,510,000 units (1 common share & 1 warrant) at 10¢ per unit was completed, with warrants exercisable at 15¢ per share for two years.

From August to November 2022, private placement of 9,900,000 units (1 common share & ½ warrant) at 5¢ per unit was completed. Also during fiscal 2023, 3,100,000 common shares were issued for services.

Wholly Owned Subsidiaries

Cultivar Holdings Ltd., Ont.

- 100% int. in **CannIP Holdings Inc.**, Ont.

Financial Statistics

Periods ended:	12m Jan. 31/23[A]		12m Jan. 31/22[A]
	$000s	%Chg	$000s
Operating revenue	**35**	**-74**	**135**
Cost of goods sold	8		50
Salaries & benefits	116		165
Research & devel. expense	83		73
General & admin expense	1,383		1,466
Stock-based compensation	351		183
Operating expense	**1,940**	**0**	**1,938**
Operating income	**(1,905)**	**n.a.**	**(1,803)**
Deprec., depl. & amort.	159		79
Pre-tax income	**(2,068)**	**n.a.**	**(1,882)**
Net income	**(2,068)**	**n.a.**	**(1,882)**
Cash & equivalent	79		211
Accounts receivable	38		381
Current assets	137		642
Fixed assets, net	135		76
Intangibles, net	446		519
Total assets	**718**	**-42**	**1,237**
Bank indebtedness	38		nil
Accts. pay. & accr. liabs	833		334
Current liabilities	871		350
Shareholders' equity	(153)		887
Cash from oper. activs	**(534)**	**n.a.**	**(1,532)**
Cash from fin. activs	547		1,682
Cash from invest. activs	(145)		(418)
Net cash position	**79**	**-63**	**211**
	$		$
Earnings per share*	(0.02)		(0.02)
Cash flow per share*	(0.00)		(0.01)
	shs		shs
No. of shs. o/s*	122,051,292		109,051,292
Avg. no. of shs. o/s*	114,168,278		107,925,066
	%		%
Net profit margin	n.m.		n.m.
Return on equity	n.m.		(214.47)
Return on assets	(211.56)		(167.96)

* Common

[A] Reported in accordance with IFRS

Latest Results

Periods ended:	3m Apr. 30/23[A]		3m Apr. 30/22[A]
	$000s	%Chg	$000s
Operating revenue	nil	n.a.	22
Net income	(478)	n.a.	(311)
	$		$
Earnings per share*	(0.00)		(0.00)

* Common

[A] Reported in accordance with IFRS

Historical Summary
(as originally stated)

Fiscal Year	Oper. Rev.	Net Inc. Bef. Disc.	EPS*
	$000s	$000s	$
2023[A]	35	(2,068)	(0.02)
2022[A]	135	(1,882)	(0.02)
2021[A]	nil	(1,931)	(0.02)
2020[A1]	nil	(2,311)	(0.02)
2019[A2]	nil	(42)	(0.01)

* Common

[A] Reported in accordance with IFRS

[1] Results reflect the Sept. 23, 2019, reverse takeover acquisition of Cultivar Holdings Ltd.

[2] Results for fiscal 2019 and prior fiscal years pertain to Admiral Bay Resources Inc.

P.91 Premier Diversified Holdings Inc.

Symbol - PDH **Exchange** - TSX-VEN **CUSIP** - 74051Q

Head Office - 680-1199 Pender St W, Vancouver, BC, V6E 2R1 **Telephone** - (604) 678-9115 **Fax** - (604) 678-9278

Website - www.pdh-inc.com

Email - sparsad@pdh-inc.com

Investor Relations - Sanjeev Parsad (604) 678-9115 ext. 205

Auditors - Davidson & Company LLP C.A., Vancouver, B.C.

Lawyers - Robertson Neil, LLP, Vancouver, B.C.

Transfer Agents - Computershare Trust Company of Canada Inc.

Profile - (B.C. 2010 amalg.) Operates as a holding company investing in private and publicly listed companies.

Holdings include **Purposely Platform Inc.** (47% owned), which develops an online social platform which can be used for volunteer management by organizations and to find relevant volunteer opportunities by individuals; and **MyCare MedTech Inc.** (42% owned), a telemedicine company which delivers virtual medical consultations with licensed health care providers for non-emergency conditions through its mobile app GOeVisit.

Investment portfolio at Mar. 31, 2023:

	Fair Value
Purposely Platform Inc.	$178,561
MyCare MedTech Inc.	973,151
	1,151,712

During fiscal 2021, the construction of **Arcola Developments Ltd.**'s residential housing complex project concluded, and a total distribution of $500,000 was distributed to the company in two equal instalments during fiscal 2022 and 2021. At Sept. 30, 2022, the company didn't hold any common shares of Arcola (Sept. 30, 2021 - 500,000 class B common shares, representing 4.6% interest)

In July 2022, the company was informed by the management of **ZED Therapeutics Inc.** that the management had decided to voluntarily dissolve ZED and its subsidiaries. At May 2022, the company held 42% interest in ZED. ZED's management advised that it does not expect to have any funds available for distribution to ZED shareholders once certain payments are made including closing costs and severance payments to employees. Zed Therapeutics Inc. engages in research and development of high-cannabidiol (CBD) USDA-compliant hemp genetics.

Predecessor Detail - Name changed from Premier Diagnostic Health Services Inc., Apr. 22, 2015.

Directors - Dr. Simon Sutcliffe, chr., Vancouver, B.C.; Sanjeev Parsad, pres. & CEO, Surrey, B.C.; Alnesh P. Mohan, CFO, Vancouver, B.C.; G. Andrew Cooke, Arlington, Va.; Pui Hong (Eric) Tsung, Vancouver, B.C.

Other Exec. Officers - Marta C. Davidson, corp. sec.; Daniel N. Waters, contr.

Capital Stock

	Authorized (shs.)	Outstanding (shs.)[1]
Common	unlimited	4,710,684

[1] At May 25, 2023

Major Shareholder - Corner Market Capital Corporation held 35.64% interest and Eric Ingman held 10.05% interest at Mar. 22, 2022.

Price Range - PDH/TSX-VEN

Year	Volume	High	Low	Close
2022	65,789	$0.35	$0.12	$0.12
2021	510,522	$3.25	$0.25	$0.25
2020	299,638	$2.00	$0.25	$0.75
2019	116,107	$2.25	$0.50	$0.75
2018	314,831	$3.75	$0.25	$0.75

Consolidation: 1-for-50 cons. in Sept. 2021

Recent Close: $0.06

Capital Stock Changes - There were no changes to capital stock during fiscal 2022.

Wholly Owned Subsidiaries

Premier Diagnostics (Hong Kong) Limited, Hong Kong, Hong Kong, People's Republic of China. Inactive.
- 100% int. in **Premier Diagnostic (China) Corporation**, Beijing, People's Republic of China. Inactive

Premier Investment (Hong Kong) Ltd., Hong Kong, People's Republic of China. Inactive.
- 100% int. in **Premier Investment Shanghai Ltd.**, People's Republic of China.

Investments

42% int. in **MyCare MedTech Inc.**, Calgary, Alta.
47% int. in **Purposely Platform Inc.**, B.C.

Financial Statistics

Periods ended:	12m Sept. 30/22[A]		12m Sept. 30/21[A]
	$000s	%Chg	$000s
Operating revenue	**nil**	**n.a.**	**2**
Salaries & benefits	174		309
General & admin expense	475		500
Stock-based compensation	21		68
Operating expense	**669**	**-24**	**877**
Operating income	**(669)**	**n.a.**	**(875)**
Deprec., depl. & amort	nil		1
Finance income	88		61
Finance costs, gross	335		265
Investment income	(416)		(273)
Pre-tax income	**(2,094)**	**n.a.**	**(458)**
Net income	**(2,094)**	**n.a.**	**(458)**
Net inc. for equity hldrs	**(2,094)**	**n.a.**	**(417)**
Net inc. for non-cont. int	**nil**	**n.a.**	**(41)**
Cash & equivalent	35		103
Accounts receivable	79		52
Current assets	2,263		1,661
Long-term investments	1,475		2,834
Total assets	**3,738**	**-17**	**4,495**
Bank indebtedness	3,474		2,228
Accts. pay. & accr. liabs	246		249
Current liabilities	3,720		2,476
Long-term debt, gross	34		34
Long-term debt, net	34		34
Shareholders' equity	(17)		1,984
Cash from oper. activs	**(686)**	**n.a.**	**(865)**
Cash from fin. activs	922		1,608
Cash from invest. activs	(305)		(695)
Net cash position	**35**	**-66**	**103**
	$		$
Earnings per share*	(0.44)		(0.11)
Cash flow per share*	(0.15)		(0.22)
	shs		shs
No. of shs. o/s*	4,710,684		4,710,684
Avg. no. of shs. o/s*	4,710,684		3,926,225
	%		%
Net profit margin	n.a.		n.m.
Return on equity	n.m.		(35.01)
Return on assets	(42.73)		(5.16)

* Common
[A] Reported in accordance with IFRS

Latest Results

Periods ended:	6m Mar. 31/23[A]		6m Mar. 31/22[A]
	$000s	%Chg	$000s
Net income	(469)	n.a.	(629)
	$		$
Earnings per share*	(0.10)		(0.13)

* Common
[A] Reported in accordance with IFRS

Historical Summary
(as originally stated)

Fiscal Year	Oper. Rev.	Net Inc. Bef. Disc.	EPS*
	$000s	$000s	$
2022[A]	nil	(2,094)	(0.44)
2021[A]	2	(458)	(0.11)
2020[A]	nil	(1,135)	(0.50)
2019[A]	977	(1,306)	(0.50)
2018[A]	1,567	(610)	(0.19)

* Common
[A] Reported in accordance with IFRS

Note: Adjusted throughout for 1-for-50 cons. in Sept. 2021

P.92 Premier Health of America Inc.

Symbol - PHA **Exchange** - TSX-VEN **CUSIP** - 74052G
Head Office - 1-1114 boul Curé-Labelle, Blainville, QC, J7C 2M9 **Toll-free** - (877) 822-9077
Website - www.premierhealthgroup.ca
Email - gdaoust@premierhealth.ca
Investor Relations - Guy D'Aoust (800) 231-9916
Auditors - Raymond Chabot Grant Thornton LLP C.A., Montréal, Qué.
Transfer Agents - TSX Trust Company, Montréal, Qué.
FP500 Revenue Ranking - 797

Profile - (Can. 2017) Provides healthcare staffing and outsourced solutions to governments, corporations and individuals in Canada.

Operations are conducted through the following business units:

Placement Premier Soin - Provides temporary or permanent resources, including registered nurses, registered practical nurses, registered therapists and personal support workers, to more than 480 public and private hospitals, medical clinics and retirement homes in Quebec.

Wholly owned **Premier Health Nordik Inc.** provides health consulting, nursing and healthcare services in remote communities in the northern regions of Canada through healthcare professionals. Services include community health programs, maternal and child monitoring, women's health, chronic disease monitoring, home care and medical evacuation.

Wholly owned **Solutions Nursing PHA Inc.** provides specially trained nursing staff to northern healthcare organizations and in remote areas of Quebec and Nunavut, including primary care assignments in isolated communities and in industrial settings such as mining or logging operations. The type of care covered includes community health programs, maternal and child monitoring, women's health, chronic disease monitoring, home care and medevac.

Code Bleu - Offers permanent and temporary placements to public and private clients in Quebec through 3,000 nurses, caregivers, dental staff and other health-related personnel.

Wholly owned **Canadian Health Care Agency Inc.** provides relief nursing services (registered nurses, advance practice primary care nurse practitioners and registered/licensed practical nurses) to remote and semi-remote communities in northern Ontario, northern Manitoba, Alberta and Yukon.

The company's services are provided through its proprietary LiPHe® platform, which enables centralized management of workforce recruitment and scheduling, customer requests and billing.

Recent Merger and Acquisition Activity

Status: pending **Announced:** July 4, 2023
Premier Health of America Inc. agreed to acquire private British Columbia-based Solutions Staffing Inc. (SSI), which provides specialized healthcare staffing services, for $21,000,000. Up to an additional $4,000,000 would be paid as a variable deferred cash consideration in the event SSI achieves 100% of its EBITDA objectives.

Status: completed **Revised:** Apr. 19, 2022
UPDATE: The transaction was completed. PREVIOUS: Premier Health of America Inc., through newly created wholly owned 13822214 Canada Inc., agreed to acquire private Umana Holdings Inc. for $10,500,000, with up to an additional $4,000,000 payable as deferred cash consideration upon the achievement of performance objectives. Umana, through Cambridge, Ont.-based wholly owned Canadian Health Care Agency Inc., provides relief nursing services (registered nurses, advance practice primary care nurse practitioners and registered/licensed practical nurses) to remote and isolated communities in northern Ontario, northern Manitoba, Alberta and Yukon.

Predecessor Detail - Name changed from Physinorth Acquisition Corporation Inc., Feb. 24, 2020, pursuant to reverse takeover acquisition of 6150977 Canada Inc. (dba Groupe Premier Soin).

Directors - Éric Chouinard, chr., Rosemère, Qué.; Martin Legault, CEO, Blainville, Qué.; Jean-Robert Pronovost, v-p, corp. devel., Mont-Tremblant, Qué.; Gilles Seguin, corp. sec., Montréal, Qué.; Anne Côté†, Montréal, Qué.; Joseph Cianci, Laval, Qué.; Marie-Andrée Lavoie, Montréal, Qué.; Hubert R. Marleau, Montréal, Qué.; Pierre-Luc Toupin, Montréal, Qué.

Other Exec. Officers - Guy D'Aoust, CFO; Eric Dupont, chief tech. officer

† Lead director

Capital Stock

	Authorized (shs.)	Outstanding (shs.)[1]
Common	unlimited	55,719,600

[1] At May 29, 2023

Normal Course Issuer Bid - The company plans to make normal course purchases of up to 1,428,571 common shares representing 7% of the total outstanding. The bid commenced on Nov. 18, 2022, and expires on Nov. 17, 2023.

Major Shareholder - Martin Legault held 38.68% interest at Feb. 16, 2023.

Price Range - PHA/TSX-VEN

Year	Volume	High	Low	Close
2022	9,614,228	$0.93	$0.31	$0.37
2021	17,126,087	$1.76	$0.70	$0.88
2020	2,253,795	$0.87	$0.25	$0.87
2019	21,970	$0.60	$0.20	$0.30

Recent Close: $0.40

Capital Stock Changes - During 2022, common shares were issued as follows: 1,875,052 on exercise of warrants and 412,622 on exercise of options.

Wholly Owned Subsidiaries

8961760 Canada Inc., Qué.
9104-8306 Québec Inc., Qué. dba Code Bleu Placement en Santé.
10544485 Canada Inc., Qué.
13822214 Canada Inc., Canada.
- 100% int. in **Umana Holdings Inc.**, Canada.
  - 100% int. in **Canada Health Care Agency Inc.**, Cambridge, Ont.

6150977 Canada Inc., Qué.
- 100% int. in **Premier Health Nordik Inc.**, Qué.

Solutions Nursing PHA Inc., Qué.

Financial Statistics

Periods ended:	12m Sept. 30/22[A]		12m Sept. 30/21[A]
	$000s	%Chg	$000s
Operating revenue	**80,507**	**+21**	**66,629**
Cost of sales	60,424		50,375
General & admin expense	14,658		10,533
Operating expense	**75,082**	**+23**	**60,907**
Operating income	**5,425**	**-5**	**5,722**
Deprec., depl. & amort.	3,089		2,282
Finance costs, gross	947		918
Pre-tax income	**1,241**	**-51**	**2,521**
Income taxes	1,352		1,025
Net income	**(112)**	**n.a.**	**1,497**
Cash & equivalent	5,125		2,683
Accounts receivable	19,334		10,763
Current assets	25,401		14,571
Fixed assets, net	3,290		3,640
Right-of-use assets	886		1,039
Intangibles, net	27,258		19,671
Total assets	**57,094**	**+46**	**39,128**
Bank indebtedness	60		nil
Accts. pay. & accr. liabs	8,620		4,920
Current liabilities	12,572		6,616
Long-term debt, gross	21,780		11,224
Long-term debt, net	21,264		10,895
Long-term lease liabilities	611		738
Shareholders' equity	18,469		17,317
Cash from oper. activs	**4,041**	**+105**	**1,975**
Cash from fin. activs	11,066		15,556
Cash from invest. activs	(12,666)		(16,081)
Net cash position	**5,125**	**+91**	**2,683**
Capital expenditures	(613)		(1,877)
Capital disposals	289		13
	$		$
Earnings per share*	(0.00)		0.03
Cash flow per share*	0.07		0.04
	shs		shs
No. of shs. o/s*	56,137,953		53,850,279
Avg. no. of shs. o/s*	55,220,139		49,652,559
	%		%
Net profit margin	(0.14)		2.25
Return on equity	(0.63)		14.13
Return on assets	(0.41)		8.53
No. of employees (FTEs)	n.a.		589

* Common
[A] Reported in accordance with IFRS

Latest Results

Periods ended:	6m Mar. 31/23[A]		6m Mar. 31/22[A]
	$000s	%Chg	$000s
Operating revenue	43,370	+20	36,000
Net income	(316)	n.a.	(459)
	$		$
Earnings per share*	(0.01)		(0.01)

* Common
[A] Reported in accordance with IFRS

Historical Summary
(as originally stated)

Fiscal Year	Oper. Rev.	Net Inc. Bef. Disc.	EPS*
	$000s	$000s	$
2022[A]	80,507	(112)	(0.00)
2021[A]	66,629	1,497	0.03
2020[A1]	20,740	28	0.00
2019[A]	11,618	424	n.a.

* Common
[A] Reported in accordance with IFRS
[1] Results reflect the Feb. 25, 2020, Qualifying Transaction reverse takeover acquisition of 6150977 Canada Inc. and its subsidiaries (dba Groupe Premier Soin).

P.93 Premium Brands Holdings Corporation*

Symbol - PBH **Exchange** - TSX **CUSIP** - 74061A
Head Office - 100-10991 Shellbridge Way, Richmond, BC, V6X 3C6 **Telephone** - (604) 656-3100 **Toll-free** - (855) 756-3100 **Fax** - (604) 656-3170
Website - www.premiumbrandsholdings.com
Email - investor@premiumbrandsgroup.com
Investor Relations - William D. Kalutycz (855) 756-3100
Auditors - PricewaterhouseCoopers LLP C.A., Vancouver, B.C.
Lawyers - Blake, Cassels & Graydon LLP; Ryan, Swanson & Cleveland, PLLC, Seattle, Wash.; Bryan & Company LLP, Edmonton, Alta.
Transfer Agents - TSX Trust Company, Toronto, Ont.
FP500 Revenue Ranking - 102
Employees - 12,593 at Dec. 31, 2022
Profile - (Can. 2007 amalg.) Owns specialty food manufacturing and food distribution and wholesale businesses with operations in British Columbia, Alberta, Saskatchewan, Manitoba, Ontario, Quebec, Nova Scotia, Arizona, Minnesota, Mississippi, Nevada, Ohio and Washington.

Operations are grouped into two segments: Specialty Foods and Premium Food Distribution.

The **Specialty Foods** segment consists of specialty manufacturing businesses including Harvest, Hempler's, Piller's, Grimm's, Freybe, Isernio's, Expresco, SJ Fine Foods, McSweeney's, Made-Rite Meat Products, Direct Plus, Oberto, Deli Chef, Belmont Meats, Conte Foods, SK Food Group, Oven Pride, Hygaard, Quality Fast Foods, HQ Fine Foods, Creekside, Stuyver's, Bread Garden Go, Audrey's Patisserie, Duso's, Gourmet Chef, Island City Baking, Skilcor Food Products, Leadbetter Foods, McLean Meats, Buddy's Kitchen, Raybern's, Partners Crackers, Shaw Bakers, Concord Meats, Country Prime Meats, Lou's Kitchen, Yorkshire Valley Frams, Maid-Rite and Golden Valley Farms. Specialty food products include processed meats, deli products, meat snacks, beef jerky, halal, sandwiches, pastries, gourmet, entrées, panini, wraps, subs, hamburgers, muffins, sushi, bread, pasta, salads, kettle and baking products. This segment has 59 facilities in Canada (39) and the U.S. (20), totaling 3,890,000 sq. ft.

The **Premium Food Distribution** segment consists of differentiated distribution and wholesale businesses including Centennial Foodservice, B&C Food Distributors, C&C Packing, Multi-National Foods, Westcadia, Maximum Seafood, Premier Foods, Harlan Fairbanks, Shahir, Eleven, Ocean Miracle, Hub City Fisheries, C2C Premium Seafood, Diana's Seafood, Interprovincial Meat Sales, Penguin Meat Supply, Frandon Seafood, Ready Seafood, Viandex, Allseas, Confederation Freezers Starboard, Mermax and Distribution Côte-Nord. The company distributes beef, pork, poultry, turkey, seafood and concession products. The company has exclusive use in certain defined geographical areas and market segments of several leading third party brands including: Sterling Silver, Primrose, Iron Chef America, 1855, Icee, Slush Puppie, Carpigiani, Cretors and Boyd's Coffee. This segment has 47 facilities in Canada (41) and the U.S. (6), totaling 2,090,000 sq. ft.

In addition, through 50%-owned **Clearwater Seafoods Incorporated**, sells seafood products that are harvested by its fleet of vessels, as well as those procured from other harvesters, manufacturers and/or distributors. Clearwater has processing facilities in Canada (6) and the U.K. (4).

Customers include large national and regional grocery chains, warehouse clubs, independent grocery and general stores, convenience stores, gas bars, ethnic food retailers, foodservice operators such as restaurants, bars, café's, concession operators, caterers, hotels, recreation facilities, schools and hospitals, foodservice distributors which purchases and delivers products to foodservice operators, and other food manufacturers and food brokers.

In October 2021, the company acquired the remaining 6% interest in **Interprovincial Meat Sales Limited**, a food distributor, for an undisclosed amount. As a result, the company now holds 100% interest in Interprovincial Meat.

In August 2022, the company acquired an additional 2.6% interest in **PB Bakery Group Inc.**, which produces and distributes baked goods, and Mediterranean and Italian foods, for an undisclosed amount. As a result, the company held 96.6% interest in PB Bakery.

Recent Merger and Acquisition Activity

Status: completed **Announced:** June 12, 2022
Premium Brands Holdings Corporation acquired private King's Command Foods LLC, which manufactures cooked meat products. Terms were not disclosed.

Status: completed **Announced:** May 10, 2022
Premium Brands Holdings Corporation acquired the remaining 50% interest in private Arthur, Ont.-based Golden Valley Farms Inc., which processes and manufactures deli meat sliced products. Terms were not disclosed.

Status: completed **Announced:** Mar. 4, 2022
Premium Brands Holdings Corporation acquired Toronto, Ont.-based Beechgrove Country Foods Inc., which produces a line of pizza toppings and other fully cooked meat ingredients for the pizza, frozen food and food service sectors, for an undisclosed amount. Beechgrove has a 50,000-sq.-ft. meat plant in Toronto.

Predecessor Detail - Name changed from Thallion Pharmaceuticals Inc., July 22, 2009, pursuant to plan of arrangement to convert Premium Brands Income Fund (PBIF) to a corp. resulting in PBIF and wholly owned Premium Brands Holdings Limited Partnership (PBHLP) becoming wholly owned subsids. of Premium Brands Holdings Corporation (PBHC). All assets and liabilities of Thallion Pharmaceuticals Inc. (old Thallion) were transferred to Thallion Pharmaceuticals Inc. (new Thallion) formed by way of amalgamation between 4504003 Canada Inc. and 4504011 Canada Inc. (both old Thallion subsids.).

Directors - Bruce Hodge, chr., West Vancouver, B.C.; George Paleologou, pres. & CEO, Surrey, B.C.; Sean Cheah, Toronto, Ont.; Johnny Ciampi, Vancouver, B.C.; Dr. Marie Y. Delorme, Calgary, Alta.; Kathleen L. Keller-Hobson, Niagara-on-the-Lake, Ont.; Hugh McKinnon, Surrey, B.C.; Dr. Mary K. Wagner, Mercer Island, Wash.

Other Exec. Officers - William D. (Will) Kalutycz, CFO; Douglas O. (Doug) Goss, gen. counsel & corp. sec.; Ronald Cons, CEO, C&C Packing Limited Partnership; Irving Teper, CEO, Concord Premium Meats Ltd.

Capital Stock

	Authorized (shs.)	Outstanding (shs.)[1]
Special Preferred	unlimited	nil
Redeemable Common	unlimited	nil
Common	unlimited	44,629,382

[1] At Aug. 11, 2023

Normal Course Issuer Bid - The company plans to make normal course purchases of up to 2,231,469 common shares representing 5% of the total outstanding. The bid commenced on July 31, 2023, and expires on July 30, 2024.

Major Shareholder - Mackenzie Financial Corporation held 14.81% interest at Mar. 15, 2023.

Price Range - PBH/TSX

Year	Volume	High	Low	Close
2022	18,605,883	$130.00	$77.36	$82.28
2021	12,850,545	$137.75	$99.77	$126.44
2020	24,621,796	$106.24	$62.79	$100.73
2019	26,773,753	$98.87	$69.01	$90.96
2018	28,611,603	$122.77	$66.99	$74.86

Recent Close: $103.68

Capital Stock Changes - During fiscal 2022, 167,086 common shares were repurchased under a Normal Course Issuer Bid.

Dividends

PBH com Ra $3.08 pa Q est. Apr. 14, 2023
Prev. Rate: $2.80 est. Apr. 19, 2022
Prev. Rate: $2.54 est. Apr. 15, 2021
Prev. Rate: $2.31 est. Apr. 15, 2020

Long-Term Debt - Outstanding at Dec. 31, 2022:

Unsec. revolv. term loan[1]	$1,414,400,000
Promissory notes[2]	9,100,000
IDR bond due 2036[3]	8,300,000
Conv. debs.[4]:	
4.65% due April 2025	172,000,000
4.2% due Sept. 2027	162,600,000
5.4% due Sept. 2029	144,000,000
Other term loans	600,000
Less: financing costs	4,500,000
	1,906,500,000
Less: Current portion	6,500,000
	1,900,000,000

[1] Bears interest at prime plus nil to 1.25% or banker's acceptance rate or SOFR plus 1% to 2.33%. Matures in November 2026.
[2] Bears interest between 1.5% and 6% and matures to December 2029.
[3] US$6,100,000. Industrial Development Revenue Bond. No principal payments until maturity. Bears interest at the weekly variable rate for such bonds, which averaged 1.04% for 2022.
[4] 4.65% debentures due 2025 are convertible into common shares at $182.51 per share; 4.2% debentures due 2027 are convertible into common shares at $142.40 per share; and 5.4% convertible debentures due 2029 are convertible into common shares at $160.25 per share.

Wholly Owned Subsidiaries

Allseas Fisheries Inc., Toronto, Ont.
Buddy's Kitchen Inc., Burnsville, Minn.
C&C Packing Limited Partnership, Ont.
Centennial General Partner Inc., Alta.
Concord Premium Meats Ltd., Ont.
Hempler Foods Group LLC, Wash.
King's Command Foods LLC, Del.
Maid-Rite Specialty Foods, LLC, Dunmore, Pa.
Maine Seafood Ventures, LLC, Me.
The Meat Factory Ltd., Ont.
Oberto Snacks Inc., Del.
Premium Brands Operating GP Inc., B.C.
- 100% int. in **Belmont Meats Products Limited**, Ont.
- 100% int. in **FG Deli Group Ltd.**, B.C.
- 100% int. in **Premium Brands Holdings Inc.**, Wash.

Premium Brands Operating Limited Partnership, Man.
- 70% int. in **Expresco Foods Inc.**, Montréal, Qué.

Premium Brands (USA) Holdings Corp., Del.
Ready Seafood Co., Portland, Me.
SK Food Group Inc., Seattle, Wash.
Viandex Inc., Québec, Qué.
Westmorland Fisheries Ltd., Cap-Pelé, N.B.

Subsidiaries

71.2% int. in **Medex Fish Importing & Exporting Co. Ltd.**, Toronto, Ont.

Investments

50% int. in **Clearwater Seafoods Incorporated**, Bedford, N.S.
Note: The preceding list includes only the major related companies in which interests are held.

Financial Statistics

Periods ended:	53w Dec. 31/22^A		52w Dec. 25/21^A
	$000s	%Chg	$000s
Operating revenue	**6,029,800**	**+22**	**4,931,700**
Cost of goods sold	4,926,100		4,029,800
General & admin expense	661,300		524,900
Operating expense	**5,587,400**	**+23**	**4,554,700**
Operating income	**442,400**	**+17**	**377,000**
Deprec., depl. & amort.	160,300		134,800
Finance costs, gross	105,900		60,500
Investment income	49,900		45,900
Pre-tax income	**201,500**	**+9**	**184,200**
Income taxes	41,400		51,500
Net income	**160,100**	**+21**	**132,700**
Cash & equivalent	11,400		16,500
Inventories	786,100		645,200
Accounts receivable	590,800		521,700
Current assets	1,426,300		1,212,000
Long-term investments	538,900		568,800
Fixed assets, net	862,200		617,300
Right-of-use assets	576,000		464,500
Intangibles, net	1,651,500		1,527,500
Total assets	**5,078,600**	**+15**	**4,408,900**
Bank indebtedness	37,300		35,000
Accts. pay. & accr. liabs	419,400		445,500
Current liabilities	564,800		581,200
Long-term debt, gross	1,906,500		1,409,600
Long-term debt, net	1,900,000		1,405,000
Long-term lease liabilities	589,300		477,400
Shareholders' equity	1,813,000		1,773,900
Cash from oper. activs	**96,500**	**+46**	**66,300**
Cash from fin. activs	242,000		396,100
Cash from invest. activs	(343,600)		(808,900)
Net cash position	**11,400**	**-31**	**16,500**
Capital expenditures	(228,400)		(143,200)
	$		$
Earnings per share*	3.59		3.05
Cash flow per share*	2.16		1.52
Cash divd. per share*	3.44		2.48
	shs		shs
No. of shs. o/s*	44,400,000		44,600,000
Avg. no. of shs. o/s*	44,600,000		43,500,000
	%		%
Net profit margin	2.66		2.69
Return on equity	8.93		7.87
Return on assets	5.15		4.43
Foreign sales percent	39		38
No. of employees (FTEs)	12,593		11,676

* Common
^A Reported in accordance with IFRS

Latest Results

Periods ended:	26w July 1/23^A		26w June 25/22^A
	$000s	%Chg	$000s
Operating revenue	3,061,400	+10	2,771,100
Net income	39,800	-54	85,700
	$		$
Earnings per share*	0.90		1.92

* Common
^A Reported in accordance with IFRS

Historical Summary
(as originally stated)

Fiscal Year	Oper. Rev.	Net Inc. Bef. Disc.	EPS*
	$000s	$000s	$
2022^A1	6,029,800	160,100	3.59
2021^A	4,931,700	132,700	3.05
2020^A	4,068,900	83,700	2.16
2019^A	3,649,400	84,200	2.35
2018^A	3,025,800	98,000	3.03

* Common
^A Reported in accordance with IFRS
[1] 53 weeks ended Dec. 31, 2022.

P.94 Premium Income Corporation

Symbol - PIC.A **Exchange** - TSX **CUSIP** - 740910
Head Office - c/o Mulvihill Capital Management Inc., Standard Life Centre, 2600-121 King St W, PO Box 113, Toronto, ON, M5H 3T9 **Telephone** - (416) 681-3966 **Toll-free** - (800) 725-7172 **Fax** - (416) 681-3901
Website - mulvihill.com
Email - jgermain@mulvihill.com
Investor Relations - John D. Germain (416) 681-3966
Auditors - Deloitte LLP C.A., Toronto, Ont.
Lawyers - Osler, Hoskin & Harcourt LLP, Toronto, Ont.
Transfer Agents - Computershare Trust Company of Canada Inc., Toronto, Ont.
Investment Managers - Mulvihill Capital Management Inc., Toronto, Ont.
Managers - Mulvihill Capital Management Inc., Toronto, Ont.
Profile - (Ont. 1996) Invests in a portfolio consisting primarily of common shares of **Bank of Montreal**, **The Bank of Nova Scotia**, **Canadian Imperial Bank of Commerce**, **National Bank of Canada**, **Royal Bank of Canada** and **The Toronto-Dominion Bank**.

At least 75% of the net asset value (NAV) is invested in common shares of **Bank of Montreal**, **The Bank of Nova Scotia**, **Canadian Imperial Bank of Commerce**, **Royal Bank of Canada** and **The Toronto-Dominion Bank** and up to 25% of the NAV in common shares of **National Bank of Canada**.

The company has a scheduled termination date of Nov. 1, 2024, which will be automatically extended for a further seven years and thereafter for additional successive periods of seven years. Upon termination, all outstanding preferred shares and class A shares will be redeemed.

The manager receives a management fee and an investment management fee at annual rates equal to 0.1% and 0.8%, respectively, of the net asset value of the company, calculated and payable monthly in arrears.

Portfolio holdings at Apr. 30, 2023 (as a percentage of net asset value):

Holdings	Percentage
Cash & short-term invests	21.5%
The Toronto-Dominion Bank	16.0%
Bank of Montreal	13.4%
Canadian Imperial Bank of Commerce	13.0%
Mulvihill Canadian Bank Enhanced Yield ETF	12.8%
National Bank of Canada	12.0%
The Bank of Nova Scotia	11.3%

Directors - John P. Mulvihill, chr., CEO & corp. sec., Toronto, Ont.; John D. Germain, sr. v-p & CFO, Toronto, Ont.; Dr. Robert (Bob) Bell, Toronto, Ont.; Robert G. (Bob) Bertram, Aurora, Ont.; R. Peter Gillin, Toronto, Ont.

Capital Stock

	Authorized (shs.)	Outstanding (shs.)[1]
Preferred	unlimited	13,872,791[2]
Class C Preferred	unlimited	nil
Class D Preferred	unlimited	nil
Class E Preferred	unlimited	nil
Class A	unlimited	13,872,791
Class B	1,000	1,000[2]
Class C	unlimited	nil
Class D	unlimited	nil
Class E	unlimited	nil

[1] At Apr. 30, 2023
[2] Classified as debt.

Preferred - Entitled to receive quarterly preferential cash dividends of $0.215625 per share, representing $0.8625 per annum to yield 5.75% on the original $15 subscription price. Retractable at any time at an amount equal to the lesser of: (A) the sum of (1) 96% of the lesser of (i) net asset value (NAV) per unit (one class A share and one preferred share) less the cost to the company of purchasing a class A share in the market and (ii) $15, and (2) any accrued and unpaid dividends thereon; and (B) the sum of (1) 96% of the lesser of (i) the unit market price less the cost to the company of purchasing a class A share in the market and (ii) $15, and (2) any accrued and unpaid dividends thereon. Retractable in October of each year, together with a class A share, at a price equal to the NAV per unit. Redeemable on Nov. 1, 2024, at the lesser of $15 or the NAV divided by the number of preferred shares then outstanding. Rank in priority to the class A and class B shares with respect to the payment of dividends and repayment of capital. Non-voting.

Class A - Entitled to receive quarterly cash dividends equal to the amount, if any, by which the net realized capital gains, dividends and option premiums (other than option premiums in respect of options outstanding at year end) earned on the portfolio in any year, net of expenses and loss carryforwards, exceed the amount of the dividends paid on the preferred shares. Once the NAV per unit exceeds $25, the class A share dividends will be based on 8% per annum of the NAV per class A share. Retractable at any time at an amount equal to the lesser of: (A) the sum of (1) 96% of the difference between (i) the NAV per unit and (ii) the cost to the company of purchasing a preferred share in the market, and (2) any accrued and unpaid dividends thereon; and (B) the sum of (1) 96% of the difference between (i) the unit market price and (ii) the cost to the company of purchasing a preferred share in the market, and (2) any accrued and unpaid dividends thereon. Redeemable on Nov. 1, 2024, at the greater of the NAV per unit minus $15, or nil. Rank in priority to the class B shares with respect to the payment of dividends and repayment of capital. Non-voting.

Class B - Not entitled to dividends. Retractable at $1.00 per share. One vote per share.

Normal Course Issuer Bid - The company plans to make normal course purchases of up to 1,350,429 class A shares representing 10% of the public float. The bid commenced on Feb. 1, 2023, and expires on Jan. 31, 2024.

The company plans to make normal course purchases of up to 1,350,999 preferred shares representing 10% of the public float. The bid commenced on Feb. 1, 2023, and expires on Jan. 31, 2024.

Major Shareholder - Mulvihill Capital Management Inc. held 100% interest at Jan. 13, 2023.

Price Range - PIC.A/TSX

Year	Volume	High	Low	Close
2022	4,909,365	$8.87	$6.08	$6.95
2021	5,017,238	$7.67	$4.69	$7.63
2020	5,535,459	$6.55	$3.04	$4.77
2019	5,791,548	$7.04	$5.82	$6.45
2018	4,271,365	$8.44	$5.75	$6.34

Recent Close: $4.19

Capital Stock Changes - During fiscal 2022, 137,100 preferred shares and 137,100 class A shares were issued for cash.

Dividends

PIC.A cl A red. N.V. Ra $0.81276 pa Q est. Apr. 30, 2021
Prev. Rate: $0.50 est. Jan. 29, 2021
Prev. Rate: $0.40 est. Apr. 30, 2020
PIC.PR.A pfd cum. red. ret. Ra $0.8625 pa Q

Financial Statistics

Periods ended:	12m Oct. 31/22^A		12m Oct. 31/21^A
	$000s	%Chg	$000s
Realized invest. gain (loss)	30,437		23,008
Unrealized invest. gain (loss)	(60,673)		79,476
Total revenue	**(17,627)**	**n.a.**	**113,466**
General & admin. expense	3,739		3,404
Operating expense	**3,739**	**+10**	**3,404**
Operating income	**(21,366)**	**n.a.**	**110,062**
Finance costs, gross	11,411		11,596
Pre-tax income	**(32,777)**	**n.a.**	**98,465**
Net income	**(32,777)**	**n.a.**	**98,465**
Cash & equivalent	2,561		3,398
Accounts receivable	1,365		1,164
Investments	249,830		298,555
Total assets	**256,843**	**-15**	**303,388**
Accts. pay. & accr. liabs	314		338
Debt	199,819		197,763
Shareholders' equity	56,708		99,423
Cash from oper. activs	**24,318**	**+6**	**23,010**
Cash from fin. activs	(25,155)		(21,438)
Net cash position	**2,561**	**-25**	**3,398**
	$		$
Earnings per share*	(2.48)		7.32
Cash flow per share*	1.84		1.71
Net asset value per share*	4.26		7.54
Cash divd. per share*	0.81		0.73
	shs		shs
No. of shs. o/s*	13,321,291		13,184,191
Avg. no. of shs. o/s*	13,227,443		13,443,578
	%		%
Net profit margin	n.m.		86.78
Return on equity	(41.99)		175.54
Return on assets	(7.63)		42.42

* Class A
^A Reported in accordance with IFRS

Latest Results

Periods ended:	6m Apr. 30/23^A		6m Apr. 30/22^oA
	$000s	%Chg	$000s
Total revenue	1,458	-31	2,124
Net income	(6,256)	n.a.	(5,517)
	$		$
Earnings per share*	(0.46)		(0.42)

* Class A
^o Restated
^A Reported in accordance with IFRS

Historical Summary
(as originally stated)

Fiscal Year	Total Rev.	Net Inc. Bef. Disc.	EPS*
	$000s	$000s	$
2022^A	(17,627)	(32,777)	(2.48)
2021^A	113,466	98,465	7.32
2020^A	(42,313)	(57,067)	(4.24)
2019^A	23,623	10,178	0.86
2018^A	(4,032)	(15,593)	(1.56)

* Class A
^A Reported in accordance with IFRS

P.95 Prestwick Capital Corporation Limited

Symbol - PWIK.P **Exchange** - TSX-VEN **CUSIP** - 741369
Head Office - 3000-421 7 Ave SW, Calgary, AB, T2P 4K9 **Telephone** - (403) 589-2468
Email - gordon@modernfinancelaw.com
Investor Relations - Gordon Chmilar (403) 589-2468
Auditors - Kenway Mack Slusarchuk Stewart LLP C.A., Calgary, Alta.
Transfer Agents - Alliance Trust Company, Calgary, Alta.
Profile - (Alta. 2021) Capital Pool Company.
Common listed on TSX-VEN, July 31, 2023.

Directors - Rufus Round, CEO, United Kingdom; Gordon Chmilar, CFO & corp. sec., Calgary, Alta.; Angus Campbell, United Kingdom; Rupert Williams, Godalming, Surrey, United Kingdom

Capital Stock

	Authorized (shs.)	Outstanding (shs.)[1]
Common	unlimited	11,050,100

[1] At July 31, 2023

Major Shareholder - Alan D. Brimacombe held 13.57% interest, Val Huxley held 13.57% interest, Robert W. Shewchuk held 13.57% interest and Rupert Williams held 13.57% interest at July 31, 2023.

Recent Close: $0.15

Capital Stock Changes - On July 31, 2023, an initial public offering of 2,000,000 common shares was completed at 10¢ per share.

P.96 PreveCeutical Medical Inc.

Symbol - PREV **Exchange** - CSE **CUSIP** - 74141E

Head Office - 2500-885 Cambie St, Vancouver, BC, V6B 0R6 **Telephone** - (604) 416-7777 **Toll-free** - (855) 416-7738 **Fax** - (778) 945-6290

Website - www.preveceutical.com

Email - ir@preveceutical.com

Investor Relations - Stephen Van Deventer (604) 306-9669

Auditors - Smythe LLP C.A., Vancouver, B.C.

Lawyers - Lotz & Company, Vancouver, B.C.

Transfer Agents - TSX Trust Company, Toronto, Ont.

Profile - (B.C. 2014) Researches and develops options for preventive and curative therapies utilizing organic and nature identical products.

Proprietary technologies under development include synthetic Nature Identical™ peptides from Caribbean Blue Scorpion venom to assist with cancer-targeted treatments, as well as to treat athletes who suffer from concussions (mild traumatic brain injury); sol-gel platform for nose-to-brain delivery of therapeutic compounds of medical cannabinoids for pain, inflammation, seizures and neurological disorders, as well as for treatment and/or prevention of COVID-19; disulfide linker technology in engineering non-addictive, analgesic peptides for moderate to severe pain and inflammatory conditions; and dual gene therapy technology for the treatment and prevention of diabetes and obesity.

Also holds licences to use, manufacture, distribute and sell three Health Canada-approved natural sleep aids consisting of Blissful Sleep, Blissful Sleep Ex and Skullcap Serenity.

In January 2023, the company entered into an agreement with **Sanity Group GmbH** pursuant to which Sanity would be granted an option to license the sol-gel technology for the delivery of cannabinoid products on an exclusive basis, for an initial payment of €1,000,000 and subsequent milestone payments.

Predecessor Detail - Name changed from Carrara Exploration Corp., July 14, 2017, following reverse takeover acquisition of (old) PreveCeutical Medical Inc. and subsequent amalgamation with wholly owned 1110607 B.C. Ltd.; basis 1 new for 3 old shs.

Directors - Stephen Van Deventer, chr., CEO & interim CFO, Vancouver, B.C.; Dr. Makarand (Mak) Jawadekar, pres. & chief science officer, Conn.; Evan Ballantyne; Dr. Linnéa Olofsson; Kathleen Rotika

Other Exec. Officers - Dr. Harendra (Harry) Parekh, chief research officer

Capital Stock

	Authorized (shs.)	Outstanding (shs.)[1]
Common	unlimited	535,303,359

[1] At May 30, 2023

Major Shareholder - Widely held at Mar. 21, 2022.

Price Range - PREV/CSE

Year	Volume	High	Low	Close
2022	49,389,501	$0.03	$0.02	$0.03
2021	104,780,038	$0.04	$0.02	$0.03
2020	269,803,482	$0.10	$0.01	$0.03
2019	186,599,247	$0.08	$0.01	$0.02
2018	566,973,038	$0.17	$0.03	$0.05

Recent Close: $0.03

Capital Stock Changes - During 2022, common shares were issued as follows: 22,000,000 on conversion of debt and 1,600,000 for debt settlement.

Wholly Owned Subsidiaries

PreveCeutical (Australia) Pty Ltd., Qld., Australia.

Financial Statistics

Periods ended:	12m Dec. 31/22[A]		12m Dec. 31/21[A]
	$000s	%Chg	$000s
Salaries & benefits	187		225
Research & devel. expense	78		62
General & admin expense	449		515
Stock-based compensation	334		90
Operating expense	**1,048**	**+17**	**892**
Operating income	**(1,048)**	**n.a.**	**(892)**
Deprec., depl. & amort.	10		5
Finance costs, gross	237		467
Write-downs/write-offs	(39)		nil
Pre-tax income	**(1,481)**	**n.a.**	**(1,747)**
Income taxes	nil		(20)
Net income	**(1,481)**	**n.a.**	**(1,727)**
Cash & equivalent	6		16
Accounts receivable	19		55
Current assets	63		83
Fixed assets, net	1		2
Intangibles, net	125		76
Total assets	**189**	**+17**	**161**
Bank indebtedness	361		398
Accts. pay. & accr. liabs	1,533		1,336
Current liabilities	4,824		2,589
Long-term debt, gross	2,930		2,531
Long-term debt, net	nil		1,676
Equity portion of conv. debs	nil		755
Shareholders' equity	(4,635)		(4,104)
Cash from oper. activs	**(223)**	**n.a.**	**(426)**
Cash from fin. activs	212		137
Cash from invest. activs	1		(53)
Net cash position	**7**	**-56**	**16**
Capital disposals	1		3
	$		$
Earnings per share*	(0.00)		(0.00)
Cash flow per share*	(0.00)		(0.00)
	shs		shs
No. of shs. o/s*	535,303,359		511,703,359
Avg. no. of shs. o/s*	521,789,934		507,953,238
	%		%
Net profit margin	n.a.		n.a.
Return on equity	n.m.		n.m.
Return on assets	(710.86)		(546.59)

* Common

[A] Reported in accordance with IFRS

Latest Results

Periods ended:	3m Mar. 31/23[A]		3m Mar. 31/22[A]
	$000s	%Chg	$000s
Net income	(381)	n.a.	(601)
	$		$
Earnings per share*	(0.00)		(0.00)

* Common

[A] Reported in accordance with IFRS

Historical Summary
(as originally stated)

Fiscal Year	Oper. Rev.	Net Inc. Bef. Disc.	EPS*
	$000s	$000s	$
2022[A]	nil	(1,481)	(0.00)
2021[A]	nil	(1,727)	(0.00)
2020[A]	nil	(3,801)	(0.01)
2019[A]	3	(3,579)	(0.01)
2018[A]	15	(11,884)	(0.04)

* Common

[A] Reported in accordance with IFRS

P.97 Primaris Real Estate Investment Trust

Symbol - PMZ.UN **Exchange** - TSX **CUSIP** - 74167K

Head Office - 400-26 Wellington St E, Toronto, ON, M5E 1S2 **Telephone** - (416) 642-7800 **Fax** - (416) 640-7698

Website - www.primarisreit.com

Email - rdavloor@primarisreit.com

Investor Relations - Raghunath Davloor (416) 645-3716

Auditors - KPMG LLP C.A., Toronto, Ont.

Lawyers - Blake, Cassels & Graydon LLP, Toronto, Ont.

Transfer Agents - TSX Trust Company, Toronto, Ont.

Employees - 400 at Feb. 28, 2023

Profile - (Ont. 2021) Owns, acquires and manages primarily regional enclosed shopping centres located in major urban markets and major secondary cities across Canada.

At Mar. 31, 2023, the trust owned 35 properties totaling 10,855,000 sq. ft. of gross leasable area in British Columbia, Alberta, Manitoba, Ontario, Quebec and New Brunswick. The portfolio includes 21 enclosed shopping centres and 14 unenclosed shopping centre and mixed-use properties.

Geographic diversification at Mar. 31, 2023:

Location	Area[1]
Ontario	4,405,000
Alberta	3,945,000
British Columbia	1,195,000
Manitoba	563,000
New Brunswick	442,000
Quebec	305,000
	10,855,000

[1] Gross leasable area (sq. ft.).

Trustees - Timothy (Tim) Pire, chr., Wis.; Patrick Sullivan, pres. & COO, Calgary, Alta.; Avtar T. Bains, Vancouver, B.C.; Anne Fitzgerald, Toronto, Ont.; Louis M. Forbes, Toronto, Ont.; Deborah Weinswig, N.Y.

Oper. Subsid./Mgt. Co. Officers - Alex Avery, CEO; Raghunath (Rags) Davloor, CFO; Mordecai Bobrowsky, sr. v-p, legal & corp. sec.; Leslie Buist, sr. v-p, fin.; Brenda Huggins, sr. v-p, HR; Graham Procter, sr. v-p, asset mgt.; Laurel Adamson, v-p, leasing western Canada; Joseph Martino, v-p, IT; Leigh Murray, v-p, leasing eastern Canada

Capital Stock

	Authorized (shs.)	Outstanding (shs.)[1]
REIT Units, Series A	unlimited	96,508,317
REIT Units, Series B	unlimited	n.a
Special Voting Unit	unlimited	nil
Class B Exch. LP Units	unlimited	nil

[1] At Mar. 31, 2023

REIT unit, Series A and B - Entitled initial monthly annual cash distributions of $0.0683 per unit. Redeemable at any time at a price equal to the lesser of: (i) 90% of the market price per unit during the 10-day trading period prior to the redemption date; (ii) and 100% of the market price on the redemption date. **Series A** - One vote per unit. **Series B** - Convertible at any time into REIT units, series A, on a one-for-one basis. Non-voting.

Class B Exchangeable LP Unit - Entitled to receive the economic equivalence of distributions on a per unit amount equal to a per unit amount provided to holders of REIT units. Convertible at any time into REIT units, series A, on a one-for-one basis. Classified as liabilities.

Special Voting Unit - Issued to holders of class B exchangeable units. Each special voting unit entitles the holder to a number of votes at unitholder meetings equal to the number of REIT units into which the exchangeable units are exchangeable.

Normal Course Issuer Bid - The company plans to make normal course purchases of up to 7,020,105 REIT units, series A representing 10% of the public float. The bid commenced on Mar. 9, 2023, and expires on Mar. 8, 2024.

Major Shareholder - Healthcare of Ontario Pension Plan held 26.97% interest at Feb. 28, 2023.

Price Range - PMZ.UN/TSX

Year	Volume	High	Low	Close
2022	88,108,308	$16.38	$11.93	$14.64

Recent Close: $13.15

Capital Stock Changes - In January 2022, all 3,336,016 class B limited partnership of a subsidiary held by H&R Real Estate Investment Trust were exchanged for a like number of REIT units, series A. Also during 2022, 10,511 REIT units, series A were issued under restricted trust unit plan and 3,885,700 REIT units, series A were repurchased under a Normal Course Issuer Bid.

Dividends

PMZ.UN ser A unit Ra $0.82 pa M est. Jan. 16, 2023
Listed Jan 5/22.
Prev. Rate: $0.80 est. Feb. 15, 2022
$0.0667**i** .... Feb. 15/22
i Initial Payment

Wholly Owned Subsidiaries

New Primaris Master GP Trust, Ont.
New Primaris Master LP, Ont.
- 100% int. in **Investor Retail GP Trust**, Ont.
- 100% int. in **Investor Retail LP**, Ont.
- 100% int. in **Primaris GP Trust**, Ont.
- 100% int. in **Primaris Limited Partnership**, Ont.

PRR Trust, Ont.
Primaris Management Inc., Ont.
Primaris Trustee Inc., Ont.

Financial Statistics

Periods ended:	12m Dec. 31/22[A]		12m Dec. 31/21[oA]
	$000s	%Chg	$000s
Total revenue	**380,064**	**+53**	**247,888**
Rental operating expense	168,277		106,294
General & admin. expense	27,826		13,272
Operating expense	**196,103**	**+64**	**119,566**
Operating income	**183,961**	**+43**	**128,322**
Deprec. & amort.	1,142		260
Finance income	3,657		2,510
Finance costs, gross	33,400		18,881
Pre-tax income	**(12,080)**	**n.a.**	**340,989**
Net income	**(12,080)**	**n.a.**	**340,989**
Cash & equivalent	10,954		5,636
Income-producing props	2,934,590		3,023,188
Properties under devel.	184,000		181,000
Property interests, net	3,118,590		3,204,188
Right-of-use assets	10,404		8,059
Total assets	**3,201,781**	**-1**	**3,247,842**
Accts. pay. & accr. liabs	49,553		56,883
Long-term debt, gross	1,007,515		834,622
Long-term lease liabilities	11,176		8,590
Shareholders' equity	2,087,629		2,191,326
Cash from oper. activs	**164,307**	**n.a.**	**(75,734)**
Cash from fin. activs	(46,381)		112,452
Cash from invest. activs	(112,608)		(46,090)
Net cash position	**10,954**	**+94**	**5,636**
Increase in property	(52,012)		(24,870)
Decrease in property	5,481		nil
	$		$
Earnings per share*	n.a.		n.a.
Cash flow per share*	1.64		(0.77)
Funds from opers. per sh.*	1.59		n.a.
Adj. funds from opers. per sh.*	1.23		n.a.
Cash divd. per share*	0.80		...
Total divd. per share*	**0.80**		**...**
	shs		shs
No. of shs. o/s*	97,712,717		98,251,890
Avg. no. of shs. o/s*	100,047,000		n.a.
	%		%
Net profit margin	(3.18)		137.56
Return on equity	(0.56)		21.36
Return on assets	0.66		13.37

* REIT Unit, Ser.A
[o] Restated
[A] Reported in accordance with IFRS

Latest Results

Periods ended:	3m Mar. 31/23[A]		3m Mar. 31/22[A]
	$000s	%Chg	$000s
Total revenue	96,369	+5	91,772
Net income	35,586	+18	30,031
	$		$
Earnings per share*	n.a.		n.a.

[A] Reported in accordance with IFRS

Historical Summary
(as originally stated)

Fiscal Year	Total Rev. $000s	Net Inc. Bef. Disc. $000s	EPS* $
2022[A]	380,064	(12,080)	n.a.
2021[A1]	253,979	340,989	n.a.
2020[A1]	270,230	(574,478)	n.a.

* REIT Unit, Ser.A
[A] Reported in accordance with IFRS
[1] Results were prepared on a carve-out basis reflecting the Primaris retail properties transferred from H&R Real Estate Investment Trust.

P.98 Prime Dividend Corp.

Symbol - PDV **Exchange** - TSX **CUSIP** - 74161F
Head Office - c/o Quadravest Capital Management Inc., 2510-200 Front St W, PO Box 51, Toronto, ON, M5V 3K2 **Telephone** - (416) 304-4440 **Toll-free** - (877) 478-2372
Website - www.quadravest.com
Email - info@quadravest.com
Investor Relations - Shari Payne (877) 478-2372
Auditors - PricewaterhouseCoopers LLP C.A., Toronto, Ont.
Lawyers - Blake, Cassels & Graydon LLP, Toronto, Ont.
Transfer Agents - Computershare Trust Company of Canada Inc., Toronto, Ont.
Investment Managers - Quadravest Capital Management Inc., Toronto, Ont.
Managers - Quadravest Capital Management Inc., Toronto, Ont.
Profile - (Ont. 2005) Invests in a diversified portfolio of equity securities of Canadian dividend-paying banks, life insurance, utilities and other, and investment management companies.

The investment portfolio includes the following companies: **Bank of Montreal**, **The Bank of Nova Scotia**, **Canadian Imperial Bank of Commerce**, **National Bank of Canada**, **Royal Bank of Canada**, **The Toronto-Dominion Bank**, **Great-West Lifeco Inc.**, **Manulife Financial Corporation**, **Sun Life Financial Inc.**, **AGF Management Ltd.**, **CI Financial Corp.**, **IGM Financial Inc.**, **BCE Inc.**, **TransAlta Corporation**, **TC Energy Corporation**, **Power Financial Corporation** and **TMX Group Limited**. Shares held within the portfolio are expected to range between 4% and 8% in weight but may vary from time to time. Up to 20% of the net asset value of the company may be invested in equity securities of issuers in the financial services or utilities sectors in Canada or the United States other than the core holdings.

To supplement the dividends received on the investment portfolio and to reduce risk, the company may, from time to time, write covered call options in respect of all or part of the common shares in the portfolio.

The company will terminate on Dec. 1, 2028, or earlier if the class A or preferred shares are delisted by the TSX or if the net asset value of the company declines to less than $5,000,000. At such time all outstanding class A and preferred shares will be redeemed. The termination date may be extended beyond Dec. 1, 2028, for a further five years and thereafter for additional successive periods of five years as determined by the board of directors.

The investment manager receives a management fee at an annual rate equal to 0.65% of the net asset value of the company calculated and payable monthly in arrears. In addition, the manager receives an administration fee at an annual rate equal to 0.2% of the net asset value of the company calculated and payable monthly in arrears, as well as service fee payable to dealers on the class A shares at a rate of 0.5% per annum.

Top 10 holdings at Feb. 28, 2023 (as a percentage of net assets):

Holdings	Percentage
National Bank of Canada	9.6%
TMX Group Limited	8.8%
The Toronto-Dominion Bank	7.9%
Manulife Financial Corporation	6.8%
TC Energy Corporation	6.2%
Royal Bank of Canada	6.1%
Canadian Imperial Bank of Commerce	6.0%
BCE Inc.	5.8%
Sun Life Financial Inc.	5.7%
Power Corporation of Canada	5.6%

In March 2023, the maturity date of the company's preferred shares and class A shares was extended a further five years, to Dec. 1, 2028.

Directors - S. Wayne Finch, chr., pres. & CEO, Caledon, Ont.; Laura L. Johnson, corp. sec., Oakville, Ont.; Peter F. Cruickshank, Oakville, Ont.; Michael W. Sharp, Toronto, Ont.; John D. Steep, Stratford, Ont.
Other Exec. Officers - Silvia Gomes, CFO

Capital Stock

	Authorized (shs.)	Outstanding (shs.)[1]
Preferred	unlimited	854,254[2]
Class B	1,000	1,000[2]
Class A	unlimited	854,254

[1] At Feb. 23, 2023
[2] Classified as debt.

Preferred - Entitled to receive floating rate cumulative monthly cash dividends equal to the prime rate plus 2.35%, with a minimum annual rate of 5% and a maximum annual rate of 8%. Retractable in any month at a price equal to the lesser of (i) $10; and (ii) 96% of the net asset value (NAV) per unit (one class A share and one preferred share) less the cost of the purchase of a class A share in the market for cancellation. Under a concurrent annual retraction in April of each year, a shareholder will receive, for each unit, an amount equal to the NAV per unit, less any costs (to a maximum of 1% of the NAV per unit) to fund the retraction. All outstanding preferred shares will be redeemed at $10 per share on Dec. 1, 2028. Rank in priority to class A and class B shares with respect to the payment of dividends and repayment of capital. Non-voting except in certain circumstances.

Class B - Not entitled to dividends. Retractable at $1.00 per share and have a liquidation entitlement of $1.00 per share. Rank subsequent to preferred shares and prior to class A shares with respect to repayment of capital. One vote per share.

Class A - Entitled to receive monthly non-cumulative distributions targeted to be 10% per annum of the volume-weighted average market price of the class A shares for the last five trading days of the preceding month. In addition, a special year-end dividend will be payable on the last day of November in each year if such funds are available. No regular monthly distributions will be paid if any dividends on the preferred shares are in arrears or if the NAV per unit is equal to or less than $15 and no special year-end dividends will be paid if after such payment the NAV per unit would be less than $25. Retractable in any month at a price equal 96% of the NAV per unit less the cost of the purchase of a preferred share in the market for cancellation. Under a special annual concurrent retraction in April of each year, shareholders will receive an amount equal to the NAV per unit, less any related commissions and expenses (to a maximum of 1% of the NAV per unit) to fund the retraction. The company will endeavour to redeem all outstanding class A shares at $15 per share on Dec. 1, 2028. Rank subsequent to preferred shares and class B shares with respect to the payment of dividends and repayment of capital. Non-voting except in certain circumstances.

Major Shareholder - Prime Dividend Corp. Holding Trust held 100% interest at Feb. 23, 2023.

Price Range - PDV/TSX

Year	Volume	High	Low	Close
2022	458,518	$9.48	$4.50	$7.00
2021	375,416	$9.24	$5.13	$8.50
2020	422,075	$7.65	$2.56	$5.70
2019	330,302	$7.69	$5.01	$6.98
2018	339,424	$11.11	$5.55	$5.85

Recent Close: $4.61

Capital Stock Changes - There were no changes to capital stock during fiscal 2022.

Dividends

PDV cl A N.V. omitted [1]

$0.04642	Aug. 10/23	$0.04533	July 10/23
$0.04992	June 9/23	$0.04883	May 10/23

Paid in 2023: $0.35158 2022: $0.78442 2021: $0.69093

PDV.PR.A pfd cum. ret. Fltg. Ra pa M

$0.06667	Sept. 8/23	$0.06667	Aug. 10/23
$0.06667	July 10/23	$0.06667	June 9/23

Paid in 2023: $0.60003 2022: $0.62418 2021: $0.50004

[1] Monthly divd normally payable in Nov/22 has been omitted.

Financial Statistics

Periods ended:	12m Nov. 30/22[A]		12m Nov. 30/21[A]
	$000s	%Chg	$000s
Realized invest. gain (loss)	240		372
Unrealized invest. gain (loss)	(1,220)		2,666
Total revenue	**(349)**	**n.a.**	**3,661**
General & admin. expense	279		299
Other operating expense	98		104
Operating expense	**377**	**-6**	**402**
Operating income	**(726)**	**n.a.**	**3,259**
Finance costs, gross	553		445
Pre-tax income	**(1,259)**	**n.a.**	**2,814**
Net income	**(1,259)**	**n.a.**	**2,814**
Cash & equivalent	751		300
Accounts receivable	23		32
Investments	12,836		15,161
Total assets	**13,610**	**-12**	**15,493**
Accts. pay. & accr. liabs	45		51
Debt	8,544		8,544
Shareholders' equity	4,866		6,795
Cash from oper. activs	**1,653**	**-13**	**1,892**
Cash from fin. activs	(1,202)		(2,538)
Net cash position	**751**	**+150**	**300**
	$		$
Earnings per share*	(1.47)		3.15
Cash flow per share*	1.94		2.12
Net asset value per share*	5.70		7.96
Cash divd. per share*	0.78		0.69
	shs		shs
No. of shs. o/s*	854,254		854,254
Avg. no. of shs. o/s*	854,254		893,167
	%		%
Net profit margin	n.m.		76.86
Return on equity	(21.59)		46.75
Return on assets	(4.85)		21.48

* Class A
[A] Reported in accordance with IFRS

Note: Net income reflects increase/decrease in net assets from operations.

Historical Summary
(as originally stated)

Fiscal Year	Total Rev. $000s	Net Inc. Bef. Disc. $000s	EPS* $
2022[A]	(349)	(1,259)	(1.47)
2021[A]	3,661	2,814	3.15
2020[A]	(535)	(1,425)	(1.51)
2019[A]	2,515	1,528	1.62
2018[A]	(1,064)	(2,113)	(2.19)

* Class A
[A] Reported in accordance with IFRS

Note: Adjusted throughout for 0.8083024-for-1 cons. in Dec. 2018

P.99 Prime Drink Group Corp.

Symbol - PRME **Exchange** - CSE **CUSIP** - 741957
Head Office - 609-1188 av Union, Montréal, QC, H3B 0E5 **Telephone** - (514) 394-7717
Website - www.prime-group.ca
Email - jean.gosselin@prime-group.ca
Investor Relations - Jean Gosselin (514) 707-0223
Auditors - MNP LLP C.A., Vancouver, B.C.
Transfer Agents - Computershare Trust Company of Canada Inc., Vancouver, B.C.
Profile - (Can. 2020 amalg.) Acquires and manages natural spring water sources in North America, with an initial focus on the development of water rights in Quebec.

The water rights consist of six primary water sources: Duhamel, Notre-Dame-du-Laus, St-Joseph de Coleraine, Sainte-Cécile-de-Witton,

Saint-Élie de-Caxton and Source St-Siméon, which represent access to more than 3.352 billion litres of spring water per year.

Predecessor Detail - Name changed from Dominion Water Reserves Corp., Nov. 23, 2022.

Directors - Raimondo Messina, chr., Laval, Qué.; Robert Dunn, v-chr., Montréal, Qué.; Alexandre Côté, pres. & CEO, Brossard, Qué.; Germain Turpin, pres., water div., Qué.; Michael Pesner, Montréal, Qué.; Dominique Primeau

Other Exec. Officers - Jean Gosselin, CFO; Alexandra Frank, v-p, mktg.

Capital Stock

	Authorized (shs.)	Outstanding (shs.)[1]
Common	unlimited	144,177,462

[1] At May 29, 2023

Major Shareholder - Olivier Primeau held 27.25% interest and Germain Turpin held 18.56% interest at Oct. 14, 2022.

Price Range - PRME/CSE

Year	Volume	High	Low	Close
2022	41,085,795	$0.22	$0.04	$0.15
2021	85,650,920	$0.23	$0.06	$0.06
2020	32,208,387	$0.50	$0.06	$0.08

Recent Close: $0.11

Capital Stock Changes - In July and September 2022, private placement of 41,687,500 units (1 common shares & $^{1}/_{10}$ warrant) at 8¢ per unit was completed. Also during 2022, 390,000 common shares were issued on exercise of warrants and 575,762 common shares were cancelled.

Wholly Owned Subsidiaries

Centre Piscicole Duhamel Inc., Qué.
11973002 Canada Inc., Canada.
6305768 Canada Inc., Canada.
Société Alto 2000 Inc., Qué.
Source Sainte-Cécile Inc., Qué.
3932095 Canada Inc., Qué.

Financial Statistics

Periods ended:	12m Dec. 31/22[A]		12m Dec. 31/21[A]
	$000s	%Chg	$000s
General & admin expense	778		843
Stock-based compensation	nil		692
Operating expense	**778**	**-49**	**1,535**
Operating income	**(778)**	**n.a.**	**(1,535)**
Deprec., depl. & amort.	26		21
Finance costs, gross	4		4
Pre-tax income	**(808)**	**n.a.**	**(1,559)**
Net income	**(808)**	**n.a.**	**(1,559)**
Cash & equivalent	2,421		197
Current assets	2,437		251
Fixed assets, net	529		382
Right-of-use assets	4		29
Intangibles, net	5,658		5,658
Total assets	**8,627**	**+37**	**6,320**
Accts. pay. & accr. liabs.	107		86
Current liabilities	110		113
Long-term lease liabilities	nil		3
Shareholders' equity	8,517		6,204
Cash from oper. activs	**(786)**	**n.a.**	**(848)**
Cash from fin. activs	3,157		1,175
Cash from invest. activs	(148)		(255)
Net cash position	**2,421**	**n.m.**	**197**
Capital expenditures	(148)		nil
	$		$
Earnings per share*	(0.01)		(0.02)
Cash flow per share*	(0.01)		(0.01)
	shs		shs
No. of shs. o/s*	137,657,396		96,155,658
Avg. no. of shs. o/s*	108,588,536		92,156,781
	%		%
Net profit margin	n.a.		n.a.
Return on equity	(10.98)		(27.68)
Return on assets	(10.76)		(26.62)

* Common
[A] Reported in accordance with IFRS

Latest Results

Periods ended:	3m Mar. 31/23[A]		3m Mar. 31/22[A]
	$000s	%Chg	$000s
Net income	(92)	n.a.	(162)
	$		$
Earnings per share*	(0.00)		(0.00)

* Common
[A] Reported in accordance with IFRS

Historical Summary
(as originally stated)

Fiscal Year	Oper. Rev.	Net Inc. Bef. Disc.	EPS*
	$000s	$000s	$
2022[A]	nil	(808)	(0.01)
2021[A]	nil	(1,559)	(0.02)
2020[A]	nil	(5,425)	(0.09)
2019[A1]	nil	(507)	(0.02)
2018[A1]	nil	(101)	(0.00)

* Common
[A] Reported in accordance with IFRS
[1] Results pertain to (old) Dominion Water Reserves Corp. (DWR). Shares outstanding and per share figures have been adjusted to reflect 1-for-3 share consolidation effected on Apr. 23, 2020, by (old) DWR.

P.100 Primo Water Corporation*

Symbol - PRMW **Exchange** - TSX **CUSIP** - 74167P
Head Office - 1200 Britannia Rd E, Mississauga, ON, L4W 4T5 **Telephone** - (905) 672-1900 **Toll-free** - (888) 260-3776 **Fax** - (905) 672-7504
Website - www.primowatercorp.com
Email - investorrelations@primowater.com
Investor Relations - Jon Kathol (813) 313-1732
Auditors - PricewaterhouseCoopers LLP C.P.A., Tampa, Fla.
Transfer Agents - Computershare Trust Company, N.A.; Computershare Trust Company of Canada Inc.
FP500 Revenue Ranking - 175
Employees - 9,240 at Dec. 31, 2022

Profile - (Ont. 2021; orig. Can., 1955) Provides water direct to consumers and water filtration services, as well as water dispensers, purified and spring bottled water, and self-service refill drinking water and office coffee services primarily in North America and Europe.

Offers a portfolio of water bottle brands such as Primo, Crystal Springs, Mountain Valley, Crystal Rock, Vermont Pure, Sparkletts, Hinckley Springs, Kentwood Springs, Canadian Springs, Labrador Source and Eden Springs, as well as Keurig®, Mars Alterra®, Starbucks® Coffee, Caribou Coffee®, Peet's Coffee & Tea®, Javarama® and Lavazza® for office coffee services.

Through its Water Direct business, the company offers a comprehensive selection of bottled water and beverage products delivered directly to homes or to commercial businesses. Through the company's Water Exchange business that is available in 17,500 locations, customers can return 3- and 5-gallon refillable/reusable Primo water bottles to the store and receive recycle tickets for discounts on next purchase of Primo water. Through its Water Refill business, customers refill empty bottles at 23,500 self-service refill drinking water machines. In addition, the company offers water filtration appliances that connect directly to existing water supply in homes or businesses to reduce potentially harmful impurities and other contaminants that may be found in tap water, as well as top-loading and bottom-loading water dispensers that are designed to dispense water from returnable 3- and 5-gallon bottles available in over 10,000 locations.

At Dec. 31, 2022, the company's business was supported by 63 manufacturing and production facilities across North America (43), Europe (16) and other locations (4) in the U.K. and Israel; and 318 branch distribution and warehouse facilities across North America (191), Europe (120) and other locations (7) in the U.K. and Israel.

In February 2023, the company acquired an additional spring water source adjacent to its current Mountain Valley spring in Garland cty, Ark., for an undisclosed amount.

In October 2022, the company, through wholly owned **Primo Water North America**, acquired substantially all the assets of Rhode Island-based **Crystal Spring Water Company**, which manufactures and distributes spring water to customers in Rhode Island and southeastern Massachusetts. Terms were not disclosed.

In September 2022, the company acquired France-based **Eureau Sources**, which packages spring water in 5-gallon returnable bottles for refrigerated water coolers; and **Defeaus S.A.R.L.**, which markets and distributes HERMES spring water to commercial and residential customers. Terms were not disclosed.

On July 19, 2022, the company exited its business in Russia.

In July 2022, the company, through wholly owned **Primo Water North America**, acquired Atlanta, Ga.-based **Highland Mountain Water**, which distributes the company's Mountain Valley® premium water. Terms were not disclosed.

During the second quarter of fiscal 2022, the company exited the North America single-use retail bottled water category consisting primarily of 1 gallon, 2.5 gallon and case-pack water. The exit did not affect the company's large format exchange, refill and dispenser business nor the company's Mountain Valley brand, which sells products primarily in glass bottles.

Recent Merger and Acquisition Activity

Status: completed **Announced:** Dec. 29, 2022
Primo Water Corporation sold and leased back two properties for US$50,100,000

Predecessor Detail - Name changed from Cott Corporation, Mar. 2, 2020, pursuant to acquisition of (old) Primo Water Corporation.

Directors - Jerry Fowden, chr., St. Petersburg, Fla.; Thomas J. Harrington, CEO, Tampa, Fla.; Britta Bomhard†, Princeton, N.J.; Susan E. Cates, Chapel Hill, N.C.; Eric J. Foss; Derek R. Lewis, Fla.; Lori T. Marcus, N.Y.; Billy D. Prim, Palm Beach Gardens, Fla.; Archana Singh, Wash.; Steven P. Stanbrook, Racine, Wis.

Other Exec. Officers - Cate Gutowski, COO; David W. Hass, CFO; Jason Ausher, chief acctg. officer; Shayron Barnes-Selby, chief diversity & inclusion officer; William (Jamie) Jamieson, CIO; Anne Melaragni, chief HR officer; Marni Morgan Poe, chief legal officer & corp. sec.; Mercedes Romero, chief procurement officer; Steven Kitching, exec. v-p, bus. devel., Europe; Jeff Johnson, sr. v-p, global operational excellence & srvc. optimization; Jon Kathol, v-p, IR
† Lead director

Capital Stock

	Authorized (shs.)	Outstanding (shs.)[1]
First Preferred	unlimited	nil
Series A		nil
Series B		nil
Second Preferred	unlimited	nil
Common	unlimited	159,134,534

[1] At Apr. 27, 2023

Options - At Dec. 31, 2022, options were outstanding to purchase 4,524,000 common shares at a weighted average exercise price of US$14.52 per share with a weighted average remaining contractual life of 5.2 years.

Major Shareholder - BlackRock, Inc. held 10.6% interest at Apr. 27, 2023.

Price Range - PRMW/TSX

Year	Volume	High	Low	Close
2022	22,311,924	$22.76	$15.66	$21.02
2021	29,412,846	$25.31	$17.94	$22.32
2020	44,680,663	$21.24	$9.23	$19.96
2019	39,940,121	$21.06	$15.62	$17.74
2018	41,848,275	$22.40	$17.81	$19.01

Recent Close: $20.46

Capital Stock Changes - During fiscal 2022, common shares were issued as follows: 906,000 under equity incentive plan, 126,000 under employee share purchase plan and 1,000 under dividend reinvestment plan; 1,753,479 common shares were repurchased under a Normal Course Issuer Bid and 259,521 common shares were cancelled.

Dividends

PRMW com Ra US$0.32 pa Q est. Mar. 27, 2023††
Prev. Rate: US$0.28 est. Mar. 28, 2022
Prev. Rate: US$0.24 est. June 18, 2014
†† Currency Option

Long-Term Debt - Outstanding at Dec. 31, 2022:

3.875% sr. notes due 2028	US$479,100,000
4.375% sr. notes due 2029	750,000,000
Other debt	2,400,000
Finance leases	84,000,000
Less: Unamort. issue costs	14,200,000
	1,301,300,000
Less: Current portion	17,500,000
	1,283,800,000

Repayment requirements of long-term debt over the next five years were reported as follows:

2023	US$229,800,000
2024	16,400,000
2025	16,300,000
2026	13,100,000
2027	7,000,000
Thereafter	1,245,200,000

Wholly Owned Subsidiaries

Aimia Foods Limited, United Kingdom.
AquaTerra Corporation, Mississauga, Ont.
Café Espresso Italia Ltd., Israel.
Carbon Luxembourg S.A.R.L., Luxembourg.
Chateau d'Eau S.A.S., France.
Chateaud'eau S.a.r.l., Luxembourg.
Clearwater Kereskedelmi és Szolgáltató Korlátolt Felelosségu Társaság, Hungary.
Cott (Barbados) IBC Ltd., Barbados.
Cott Beverages Luxembourg S.A.R.L., Luxembourg.
Cott Cayman, Cayman Islands.
Cott Retail Brands Limited, United Kingdom.
Cott Switzerland GmbH, Switzerland.
DS Services of America, Inc., Del.
Decantae Mineral Water Limited, United Kingdom.
Dispensing Coffee Club (IAI-2003) Ltd., Israel.
Distribution, Exploitation de Fontaine d'EAU de Source S.A.S., France.
Eden Springs i Porla Brunn A.B., Sweden.
Eden Springs (Denmark) A.S., Denmark.
Eden Springs (Deutschland) GmbH, Germany.
Eden Springs Espana S.A.U., Spain.
Eden Springs Estonia O.U., Estonia.
Eden Springs Latvia S.I.A., Latvia.
Eden Springs Nederlands B.V., Netherlands.
• 100% int. in **Sip-Well N.V.**, Belgium.
Eden Springs (Norway) A.S., Norway.
Eden Springs Oy, Finland.
Eden Springs Portugal S.A., Portugal.
Eden Springs Scandinavia A.B., Sweden.
Eden Springs Sp.zo.o, Poland.
Eden Springs (Sweden) A.B., Sweden.
Eden Springs (Switzerland) S.A., Switzerland.
Eden Springs UK Ltd., United Kingdom.
Eden Water and Coffee Deutschland GmbH, Germany.
Entrepure Industries LLC, Colo.
Eureau Sources Holding, France.
Eureau Sources, France.
Fairview HK Ltd., Hong Kong, Hong Kong, People's Republic of China.
Fonthill Waters Limited, United Kingdom.

GW Services, LLC, Calif.
Garraways Ltd., United Kingdom.
Hydropure Distribution Ltd., United Kingdom.
John Farrer & Company (Kendal) Limited, United Kingdom.
Kafevend Group Ltd., United Kingdom.
Kafevend Holdings Ltd., United Kingdom.
Mey Eden Ltd., Israel.
Nowa Woda Sp. Zo o., Poland.
OCS, SIA, Latvia.
Old WCS (Bottlers) Limited, United Kingdom.
Pauza Coffee Services Ltd., Israel.
Primo Customer Care, LLC, Del.
Primo European Central Services SL, Spain.
Primo Products, LLC, N.C.
Primo Refill, LLC, N.C.
Primo Water Europe S.L.U., Spain.
Primo Water Holdings Inc., Del.
Primo Water Holdings UK Limited, United Kingdom.
Pure Choice Watercoolers Ltd., United Kingdom.
SEMD, Société des eaux minérales de Dorénaz S.A., Switzerland.
The Shakespeare Coffee Company Ltd., United Kingdom.
TWS Bidco 1 Limited, United Kingdom.
Tea UK Limited, United Kingdom.
The Interesting Drinks Company Limited, United Kingdom.
UAB Eden Springs Lietuva, Lithuania.

Investments

10% int. in **Bibo Limited**, Oxon., United Kingdom.
34.5% int. in **Wax Water Limited**, London, Middx., United Kingdom.

Note: The preceding list includes only the major related companies in which interests are held.

Financial Statistics

Periods ended:	52w Dec. 31/22[A]		52w Jan. 1/22[A]
	US$000s	%Chg	US$000s
Operating revenue	**2,215,100**	**+7**	**2,073,300**
Cost of goods sold	675,600		693,400
General & admin expense	1,151,400		1,034,300
Operating expense	**1,827,000**	**+6**	**1,727,700**
Operating income	**388,100**	**+12**	**345,600**
Deprec., depl. & amort.	246,100		222,500
Finance costs, gross	69,800		68,800
Write-downs/write-offs	(29,100)		nil
Pre-tax income	**49,300**	**+683**	**6,300**
Income taxes	19,700		9,500
Net inc bef disc ops, eqhldrs	29,600		(3,200)
Net income	**29,600**	**n.a.**	**(3,200)**
Cash & equivalent	122,600		128,400
Inventories	112,100		94,600
Accounts receivable	258,600		261,600
Current assets	538,000		509,800
Fixed assets, net	714,400		718,100
Right-of-use assets	198,600		177,400
Intangibles, net	2,187,700		2,291,200
Total assets	**3,667,000**	**-2**	**3,723,400**
Bank indebtedness	212,300		222,100
Accts. pay. & accr. liabs	163,700		181,400
Current liabilities	690,600		709,800
Long-term debt, gross	1,301,300		1,338,800
Long-term debt, net	1,283,800		1,321,100
Long-term lease liabilities	174,500		148,700
Shareholders' equity	1,282,900		1,320,100
Cash from oper. activs	**281,600**	**+9**	**258,700**
Cash from fin. activs	(102,800)		(800)
Cash from invest. activs	(181,500)		(240,900)
Net cash position	**122,600**	**-5**	**128,400**
Capital expenditures	(207,700)		(152,000)
Capital disposals	54,200		1,900
Unfunded pension liability	4,300		7,900
	US$		US$
Earnings per share*	0.18		(0.02)
Cash flow per share*	1.75		1.61
Cash divd. per share*	0.28		0.24
	shs		shs
No. of shs. o/s*	159,752,299		160,732,552
Avg. no. of shs. o/s*	160,763,000		160,778,000
	%		%
Net profit margin	1.34		(0.15)
Return on equity	2.27		(0.24)
Return on assets	1.94		(1.04)
Foreign sales percent	97		97
No. of employees (FTEs)	9,240		9,230

* Common
[A] Reported in accordance with U.S. GAAP

Latest Results

Periods ended:	3m Apr. 1/23[A]		3m Apr. 2/22[A]
	US$000s	%Chg	US$000s
Operating revenue	546,500	+4	526,100
Net income	5,800	n.a.	(6,700)
	US$		US$
Earnings per share*	0.04		(0.04)

* Common
[A] Reported in accordance with U.S. GAAP

Historical Summary
(as originally stated)

Fiscal Year	Oper. Rev. US$000s	Net Inc. Bef. Disc. US$000s	EPS* US$
2022[A]	2,215,100	29,600	0.18
2021[A]	2,073,300	(3,200)	(0.02)
2020[A1]	1,953,500	(156,800)	(1.01)
2019[A]	2,394,500	(100)	(0.00)
2018[A]	2,372,900	28,900	0.21

* Common
[A] Reported in accordance with U.S. GAAP
[1] 53 weeks ended Jan. 2, 2021.

P.101 Principal Technologies Inc.

Symbol - PTEC **Exchange** - TSX-VEN **CUSIP** - 74260Q
Head Office - 2500-700 Georgia St W, Vancouver, BC, V7Y 1B3
Telephone - (604) 609-6112 **Fax** - (604) 609-6145
Website - www.principal-technologies.com
Email - office@principal-technologies.com
Investor Relations - Gerald Trent (604) 609-6112
Auditors - Dale Matheson Carr-Hilton LaBonte LLP C.A., Vancouver, B.C.
Transfer Agents - TSX Trust Company, Vancouver, B.C.
Profile - (B.C. 2018) Holds 80% interest in a global contract research organization based in Vienna, Austria.

E&E CRO Consulting GmbH specializes in tailored project management of international scale clinical studies primarily related to medical device technologies requiring regulatory approvals in various international jurisdictions including the European Union, the United States, Latin America and Oceania. E&E charges a fee for services and usually receives either monthly retainers or payments on monthly or quarterly basis. Services provided include concept development and project preparation; study submissions; on site implementation; final document archiving; and quality assurance and audting.

Common reinstated on TSX-VEN, Mar. 6, 2023.

Common suspended from TSX-VEN, Dec. 2, 2022.

Predecessor Detail - Name changed from Connaught Ventures Inc., Mar. 31, 2021.

Directors - Alfred von Liechtens, chr., Liechtenstein; Gerald Trent, pres. & CEO, Vienna, Austria; Dr. Leopold Specht, Vienna, Austria

Other Exec. Officers - Peter L. McKeown, CFO & corp. sec.

Capital Stock

	Authorized (shs.)	Outstanding (shs.)[1]
Common	unlimited	17,833,924

[1] At Dec. 20, 2021

Major Shareholder - Greenlslands Global Opportunities Fund held 68.09% interest at Aug. 6, 2021.

Price Range - PTEC/TSX-VEN

Year	Volume	High	Low	Close
2022	250,155	$0.25	$0.10	$0.11
2021	380,358	$0.17	$0.09	$0.12
2020	47,000	$0.18	$0.11	$0.16
2019	159,000	$0.16	$0.09	$0.10
2018	199,000	$0.21	$0.15	$0.15

Recent Close: $0.15

Capital Stock Changes - In March 2023, private placement of up to 7,000,000 units (1 common share & 1 warrant) at 10¢ per unit was arranged, with warrants exercisable at 12¢ per share for three years.

Wholly Owned Subsidiaries

Principal Technologies Capital Management GmbH, Austria.
- 80% int. in **E&E CRO Consulting GmbH**, Vienna, Austria.

Latest Results

Periods ended:	3m Oct. 31/21[A]		3m Oct. 30/20[A]
	$000s	%Chg	$000s
Operating revenue	110	n.a.	nil
Net income	(251)	n.a.	(38)
Net inc. for equity hldrs	(263)	n.a.	(38)
Net inc. for non-cont. int	12		nil
	$		$
Earnings per share*	(0.01)		(0.00)

* Common
[A] Reported in accordance with IFRS

P.102 Profound Medical Corp.

Symbol - PRN **Exchange** - TSX **CUSIP** - 74319B
Head Office - Unit 6, 2400 Skymark Ave, Mississauga, ON, L4W 5K5
Telephone - (647) 476-1350 **Fax** - (647) 847-3739
Website - www.profoundmedical.com
Email - skilmer@profoundmedical.com
Investor Relations - Stephen Kilmer (647) 872-4849 ext. 425
Auditors - PricewaterhouseCoopers LLP C.A., Oakville, Ont.
Lawyers - Torys LLP, Toronto, Ont.
Transfer Agents - TSX Trust Company, Toronto, Ont.
Employees - 131 at Mar. 7, 2023
Profile - (Ont. 2014) Develops and markets customizable, incision-free therapeutic systems for the image guided ablation of diseased tissue by combining real-time magnetic resonance imaging (MRI) with directional and focused ultrasound technology.

Technologies include TULSA-PRO®, which combines real-time MRI, robotically-driven transurethral sweeping-action thermal ultrasound with closed-loop temperature feedback control to ablate whole gland or physician defined region of malignant or benign prostate tissue, including prostate cancer and benign prostatic hyperplasia; and SONALLEVE®, a therapeutic platform that combines real-time MRI and thermometry with focused ultrasound delivered from the outside of the patient to enable precise and incision-free ablation of diseased tissue.

TULSA-PRO® has U.S. Food and Drug Administration (FDA) clearance as a class II device for thermal ablation of prescribed prostate tissue, using transurethral ultrasound ablation in the U.S., and CE marked in the European Union (EU) for ablation of targeted prostate tissue (benign or malignant). The TULSA-PRO system was approved by Health Canada in November 2019 as a class III device. In addition, SONAVELLE® is CE marked in the EU for the treatment of uterine fibroids and palliative pain relief associated with metastases in bone, has humanitarian device exemption from the U.S. FDA for treatment of osteoid osteoma, and has also been approved by the regulatory body in China for non-invasive treatment of uterine fibroids.

The company has operating facilities in Mississauga, Ont., and Vantaa, Finland. The company also generates revenue from the lease of medical devices, which requires certain consumables being sold also by the company.

Predecessor Detail - Name changed from Mira IV Acquisition Corp., June 3, 2015, pursuant to the Qualifying Transaction reverse takeover amalgamation of Profound Medical Inc. with wholly owned Mira IV Subco Inc.

Directors - Dr. Arun Menawat, chr. & CEO, Bonita Springs, Fla.; Brian Ellacott†, Sanibel, Fla.; Dr. Cynthia Lavoie, Gloucester, Ont.; Murielle Lortie, Pointe-Claire, Qué.; Arthur Rosenthal, Oro Valley, Ariz.; Krishan (Kris) Shah, Mississauga, Ont.

Other Exec. Officers - Rashed Dewan, CFO; Abbey Goodman, chief comml. officer, U.S.; Hartmut Warnken, chief comml. officer, OUS; Dr. Mathieu Burtnyk, sr. v-p, product leader, Tulsa-Pro; Jacques Cornet, sr. v-p, product leader, Sonalleve

† Lead director

Capital Stock

	Authorized (shs.)	Outstanding (shs.)[1]
Common	unlimited	21,115,632

[1] At May 10, 2023

Major Shareholder - Gagnon Securities LLC held 15% interest at Apr. 6, 2023.

Price Range - PRN/TSX

Year	Volume	High	Low	Close
2022	8,888,484	$15.74	$4.21	$14.48
2021	10,338,727	$36.73	$12.96	$14.26
2020	17,011,948	$29.58	$9.51	$26.19
2019	3,065,339	$15.90	$5.60	$14.75
2018	2,229,031	$12.50	$4.60	$5.50

Consolidation: 1-for-10 cons. in Oct. 2019

Recent Close: $10.76

Capital Stock Changes - During 2022, common shares were issued as follows; 62,738 on vesting of restricted share units and 40,542 on exercise of options

Wholly Owned Subsidiaries

Profound Medical Inc., Toronto, Ont.
- 100% int. in **Profound Medical GmbH**, Germany.
- 100% int. in **Profound Medical (U.S.) Inc.**, Del.
- 100% int. in **Profound Oy**, Finland.
- 100% int. in **2753079 Ontario Inc.**, Ont.
  - 100% int. in **Profound Medical Technology Services (Beijing) Co., Ltd.**, Beijing, People's Republic of China.

Financial Statistics

Periods ended:	12m Dec. 31/22^A		12m Dec. 31/21^oA
	US$000s	%Chg	US$000s
Operating revenue	**6,681**	**-3**	**6,873**
Cost of sales	2,397		2,738
Salaries & benefits	14,942		12,835
Research & devel. expense	2,839		3,358
General & admin expense	9,278		7,884
Stock-based compensation	4,238		7,205
Other operating expense	985		1,265
Operating expense	**34,679**	**-2**	**35,285**
Operating income	**(27,998)**	**n.a.**	**(28,412)**
Deprec., depl. & amort.	1,604		1,879
Finance income	n.a.		205
Finance costs, gross	n.a.		508
Finance costs, net	(3,744)		n.a.
Write-downs/write-offs	(2,524)		nil
Pre-tax income	**(28,382)**	**n.a.**	**(30,594)**
Income taxes	287		105
Net income	**(28,669)**	**n.a.**	**(30,699)**
Cash & equivalent	46,517		67,152
Inventories	7,941		7,413
Accounts receivable	6,344		1,412
Current assets	62,024		77,125
Fixed assets, net	899		788
Right-of-use assets	818		1,116
Intangibles, net	680		4,124
Total assets	**64,421**	**-26**	**86,775**
Accts. pay. & accr. liabs.	2,033		3,180
Current liabilities	4,185		4,155
Long-term debt, gross	7,174		nil
Long-term debt, net	6,651		nil
Long-term lease liabilities	817		1,127
Shareholders' equity	52,004		80,618
Cash from oper. activs	**(25,800)**	**n.a.**	**(22,360)**
Cash from fin. activs	7,031		5,948
Cash from invest. activs	nil		(593)
Net cash position	**46,517**	**-31**	**67,152**
Capital expenditures	nil		(32)
	US$		US$
Earnings per share*	(1.38)		(1.50)
Cash flow per share*	(1.24)		(1.09)
	shs		shs
No. of shs. o/s*	20,879,497		20,776,217
Avg. no. of shs. o/s*	20,829,861		20,464,168
	%		%
Net profit margin	(429.11)		(446.66)
Return on equity	(43.23)		(34.50)
Return on assets	(37.92)		(31.55)
Foreign sales percent	78		70

* Common
^o Restated
^A Reported in accordance with IFRS

Latest Results

Periods ended:	3m Mar. 31/23^A		3m Mar. 31/22^A
	US$000s	%Chg	US$000s
Operating revenue	1,860	+36	1,364
Net income	(6,741)	n.a.	(8,215)
	US$		US$
Earnings per share*	(0.32)		(0.40)

* Common
^A Reported in accordance with IFRS

Historical Summary
(as originally stated)

Fiscal Year	Oper. Rev.	Net Inc. Bef. Disc.	EPS*
	US$000s	US$000s	US$
2022^A	6,681	(28,669)	(1.38)
2021^A	6,873	(30,699)	(1.50)
2020^A	7,304	(21,622)	(1.25)
	$000s	$000s	$
2019^A	5,528	(20,192)	(1.82)
2018^A	2,602	(20,763)	(2.10)

* Common
^A Reported in accordance with IFRS
Note: Adjusted throughout for 1-for-10 cons. in Oct. 2019

P.103 Progressive Planet Solutions Inc.

Symbol - PLAN **Exchange** - TSX-VEN **CUSIP** - 74337Q
Head Office - 724 Sarcee St E, Kamloops, BC, V2H 1E7 **Telephone** - (604) 683-3995 **Toll-free** - (800) 910-3072 **Fax** - (604) 683-3988
Website - www.progressiveplanet.ca
Email - steve@harpurinc.com
Investor Relations - Stephen Harpur (800) 910-3072
Auditors - KPMG LLP C.A., Vancouver, B.C.
Lawyers - Richards Buell Sutton LLP, Vancouver, B.C.
Transfer Agents - Computershare Trust Company of Canada Inc., Toronto, Ont.
Profile - (B.C. 2006) Researches, designs, develops, manufactures and integrates advanced absorbent regenerative fertilizers, other farm products and eco-friendly cement products. Also has mineral interests in British Columbia.

Manufactures and supplies mineral-based products including regenerative fertilizer, which reduces the application of chemical fertilizer and pesticides, and creates supplementary materials with low-embodied carbon foot prints. Products are derived from diatomaceous earth, bentonite, leonardite and zeolite sourced from its Red Lake and Bud mining operations in Savona and Princeton, B.C., respectively.

Products include industrial absorbents, which are sold under the CanDry brand as well as under private label sold in more than 550 locations in Canada; cat litters, which are sold in western Canada under the WunderCat brand as well as under private label for most of the retailers in Canada; and animal husbandry, which are sold under many brands including the company's largest selling individual product marketed as Activated Barn Fresh, which neutralizes ammonia in chicken barns and enables the bird to breathe easier.

In addition, commercializes three supplementary cementitious materials (SCM) to replace up to 50% of Portland cement in concrete through an active development program focused on developing technologies to lower the carbon footprint of all the Portland cement powder. Products include PozGlass™ 100G, which is made from 100% post-consumer glass; PozDE™, which is made from waste fines from the company's Red Lake diatomaceous earth mine; and PozZeo, a finely ground powder derived from the coarse power which is a by-product of making two granular zeolite products.

Also holds Z1 zeolite property, 93 hectares, 3 km northeast of Cache Creek; option to acquire Heffley Creek nickel-chromium-natural pozzolan property, 69 claims; 23% interest [**International Zeolite Corp.** (IZ) 77%] in Bromley Creek zeolite prospect, 1,135 hectares, 9 km southwest of Princeton, with measured resources of 240,900 tonnes with average cation exchange capacity of 101.7 at August 2018; and 2.5% interest in (IZ 97.5%) in Sun Group zeolite prospect, 949 hectares, Similkameen mining district.

Has a research and manufacturing facilities in Kamloops, B.C. and Calgary, Alta.

In December 2022, the company entered into a joint development agreement with **Eco Health Industries Ltd.** and **High Brix Manufacturing Inc.** to develop three regenerative fertilizers that reduce the application of chemical nitrogen and other chemical fertilizers. Under the agreement, the company would own all the intellectual property rights.

In October 2021, option to acquire Z2 zeolite property in British Columbia was terminated and related costs written off.

In July 2022, the company dismantled its comminution plant in Spallumcheen, B.C., and all the industrial scale equipment from the plant was relocated to new fertilizer and cement production facilities in Kamloops, B.C. The comminution plant is being used to crush glass and blend it with Z1 natural pozzolan to supply test materials to various parties which are conducting testing on behalf of the company as it develops its first natural pozzolan product PozGlass™ SCM, a supplementary cementing material.

On May 2, 2022, wholly owned **Absorbent Products Ltd.**'s name was changed to **Progressive Planet Products Inc.**

Predecessor Detail - Name changed from Ashburton Ventures Inc., June 8, 2018.

Directors - Stephen Harpur, chr., pres. & CEO, Salmon Arm, B.C.; Edward (Ed) Beggs, B.C.; Suzanne Davis-Hall, Calgary, Alta.; Randy Gue

Other Exec. Officers - Ian Grant, COO; Chris Halsey-Brandt, CFO; Dr. Roger Mah, v-p, R&D

Capital Stock

	Authorized (shs.)	Outstanding (shs.)[1]
Common	unlimited	100,011,151

[1] At Nov. 22, 2022

Major Shareholder - George D. Richardson held 25.9% interest at Oct. 18, 2022.

Price Range - PLAN/TSX-VEN

Year	Volume	High	Low	Close
2022	14,951,002	$0.45	$0.22	$0.23
2021	23,199,525	$0.60	$0.08	$0.40
2020	10,752,444	$0.11	$0.02	$0.09
2019	9,698,360	$0.18	$0.05	$0.06
2018	18,016,332	$0.59	$0.11	$0.12

Consolidation: 1-for-3 cons. in Dec. 2019
Recent Close: $0.20

Capital Stock Changes - In February 2022, 3,428,570 common shares were issued pursuant to the acquisition of Progressive Planet Products Inc. (formerly Absorbent Products Ltd.) and private placement of 17,763,640 units (1 common share & 1 warrant) at 35¢ per unit was completed. Also during fiscal 2022, common shares were issued as follows; 6,764,564, on exercise of warrants, 713,333 on exercise of options and 6,667 on acquisition of mineral property.

Wholly Owned Subsidiaries

Progressive Planet Alberta Inc., Alta.
Progressive Planet Products Inc., Kamloops, B.C.
Progressive Planet US LLC, Ore.
0820443 B.C. Ltd., B.C.

Investments

Snow Lake Resources Ltd., Winnipeg, Man. (see Survey of Mines)
ZS2 Technologies Ltd.

Financial Statistics

Periods ended:	12m Apr. 30/22^A		12m Apr. 30/21^oA
	$000s	%Chg	$000s
Operating revenue	**3,833**	**n.a.**	**nil**
Cost of sales	3,242		nil
Salaries & benefits	793		276
Research & devel. expense	168		159
General & admin expense	2,210		629
Stock-based compensation	1,827		1,605
Operating expense	**8,240**	**+209**	**2,669**
Operating income	**(4,407)**	**n.a.**	**(2,669)**
Deprec., depl. & amort.	95		nil
Finance costs, gross	175		26
Pre-tax income	**(3,388)**	**n.a.**	**(2,392)**
Income taxes	(110)		nil
Net income	**(3,278)**	**n.a.**	**(2,392)**
Cash & equivalent	1,771		1,339
Inventories	3,380		nil
Accounts receivable	2,262		69
Current assets	8,012		1,441
Long-term investments	1,331		302
Fixed assets, net	14,987		969
Right-of-use assets	2,333		n.a.
Explor./devel. properties	1,632		1,545
Total assets	**28,295**	**+565**	**4,257**
Bank indebtedness	1,418		nil
Accts. pay. & accr. liabs.	1,732		237
Current liabilities	4,308		327
Long-term debt, gross	8,713		248
Long-term debt, net	8,066		219
Long-term lease liabilities	2,381		133
Shareholders' equity	11,262		3,578
Cash from oper. activs	**(3,354)**	**n.a.**	**(899)**
Cash from fin. activs	15,080		3,025
Cash from invest. activs	(11,294)		(894)
Net cash position	**1,771**	**+32**	**1,339**
Capital expenditures	(517)		(1,006)
	$		$
Earnings per share*	(0.05)		(0.06)
Cash flow per share*	(0.05)		(0.02)
	shs		shs
No. of shs. o/s*	59,774,377		59,774,377
Avg. no. of shs. o/s*	69,357,788		42,002,452
	%		%
Net profit margin	(85.52)		n.a.
Return on equity	(44.18)		(95.28)
Return on assets	(19.10)		(77.91)

* Common
^o Restated
^A Reported in accordance with IFRS

Latest Results

Periods ended:	6m Oct. 31/22^A		6m Oct. 31/21^A
	$000s	%Chg	$000s
Operating revenue	10,600	n.a.	nil
Net income	(396)	n.a.	(819)
	$		$
Earnings per share*	(0.00)		(0.01)

* Common
^A Reported in accordance with IFRS

Historical Summary
(as originally stated)

Fiscal Year	Oper. Rev.	Net Inc. Bef. Disc.	EPS*
	$000s	$000s	$
2022^A	3,833	(3,278)	(0.05)
2021^A	nil	(2,392)	(0.06)
2020^A	nil	(1,718)	(0.07)
2019^A	nil	(1,244)	(0.06)
2018^A	nil	(1,149)	(0.09)

* Common
^A Reported in accordance with IFRS
Note: Adjusted throughout for 1-for-3 cons. in Dec. 2019

P.104 ProMIS Neurosciences Inc.

Symbol - PMN **Exchange** - NASDAQ **CUSIP** - 74346M
Head Office - 200-1920 Yonge St, Toronto, ON, M4S 3E2 **Telephone** - (416) 847-6898 **Fax** - (416) 847-6899
Website - www.promisneurosciences.com
Email - gavin.malenfant@promisneurosciences.com
Investor Relations - Gavin T. Malenfant (617) 806-6597
Auditors - Baker Tilly US, LLP C.P.A.
Lawyers - McMillan LLP, Vancouver, B.C.
Transfer Agents - Computershare Trust Company of Canada Inc., Toronto, Ont.
Employees - 104 at Feb. 24, 2023
Profile - (Ont. 2023; orig. Can., 2005 amalg.) Developing antibody therapies, therapeutic vaccines, and diagnostics selectively targeting

toxic oligomers implicated in the development and progression of neurodegenerative diseases, in particular Alzheimer's disease (AD), amyotrophic lateral sclerosis (ALS) and multiple system atrophy (MSA).

The company's proprietary discovery platforms, ProMIS™ and Collective Coordinates, are used to predict novel disease specific epitopes (DSEs) on the molecular surface of abnormal, misfolded proteins, which are fundamental drivers of multiple neurodegenerative diseases.

Lead therapeutic program is PMN310, a monoclonal therapeutic antibody designed to treat AD by selectively targeting the toxic misfolded form of amyloid-beta. Other candidates are PMN442, an antibody targeting toxic misfolded alpha-synuclein (a-syn), a primary driver of MSA; and PMN267, an antibody targeting misfolded TAR-DNA binding protein 43 (TDP-43), a root cause of ALS.

The discovery platform is also being applied to other toxic proteins that drive neurodegenerative and other misfolded protein diseases including tau in AD, frontotemporal lobar degeneration, progressive supranuclear palsy, and corticobasal degeneration (CBD), Huntington's disease, disrupted in schizophrenia 1 (DISC1) in schizophrenia, and Receptor For Activated C Kinase 1 (RACK1) in ALS in order to potentially generate antibody therapies for these disorders.

Other development programs include a AD vaccine program capable of inducing an effective antibody response against toxic amyloid-beta oligomers.

On July 13, 2023, the company continued its jurisdiction from the Canada Business Corporations Act to Ontario.

Common delisted from TSX, July 24, 2023.

Predecessor Detail - Name changed from Amorfix Life Sciences Ltd., July 8, 2015.

Directors - Eugene Williams, chr., Mass.; Dr. Gail M. Farfel, CEO, San Francisco, Calif.; Dr. Neil Cashman, chief scientific officer, B.C.; Patrick D. Kirwin, Alta.; Joshua (Josh) Mandel-Brehm, Mass.; Dr. Maggie Shafmaster, Fla.; Neil K. Warma, Calif.; William Wyman, N.H.

Other Exec. Officers - Dr. Elliot Goldstein, pres.; Gavin T. Malenfant, COO; Daniel E. Geffken, CFO; Dr. Larry Altstiel, CMO; Dr. Johanne Kaplan, chief devel. officer; Dr. David Wishart, chief physics officer

Capital Stock

	Authorized (shs.)	Outstanding (shs.)[1]
Series 1 Preferred	unlimited	70,000,000
Common	unlimited	8,579,284

[1] At May 5, 2023

Series 1 Preferred - Convertible into common shares on a 1-for-1 basis. Automatically convert into common shares upon the closing of one or more sales of equity securities resulting in at least US$30,000,000 of gross proceeds to the company. Entitled to a liquidation preference in an amount per share equal to US$0.10. Non-voting.

Common - One vote per share.

Major Shareholder - Widely held at May 5, 2023.

Price Range - PMN/TSX (D)

Year	Volume	High	Low	Close
2022	819,177	$12.22	$5.70	$6.10
2021	1,421,567	$16.50	$4.80	$8.70
2020	1,374,838	$18.60	$4.80	$6.00
2019	1,041,704	$26.40	$9.90	$10.20
2018	2,055,398	$43.80	$11.40	$16.20

Consolidation: 1-for-60 cons. in June 2022

Capital Stock Changes - In June 2022, 70,000,000 series 1 preferred shares at US$0.10 per share to settle US$7,000,000 of debentures. On June 28, 2022, common shares were consolidated on a 1-for-60 basis. In October 2022, private placement of 1,383,755 units (1 post-consolidated common share & 1 warrant) at US$5.40 per unit was completed.

Wholly Owned Subsidiaries

ProMIS Neurosciences (US) Inc., Del.

Financial Statistics

Periods ended:	12m Dec. 31/22[A]		12m Dec. 31/21[□A]
	US$000s	%Chg	US$000s
Salaries & benefits	2,413		56
Research & devel. expense	14,473		4,482
General & admin expense	6,000		3,196
Stock-based compensation	488		516
Operating expense	**23,374**	**+204**	**7,679**
Operating income	**(23,374)**	**n.a.**	**(7,679)**
Deprec., depl. & amort.	6		41
Finance costs, gross	282		416
Pre-tax income	**(18,062)**	**n.a.**	**(9,790)**
Net income	**(18,062)**	**n.a.**	**(9,790)**
Cash & equivalent	5,907		16,977
Current assets	6,903		17,714
Fixed assets, net	nil		5
Intangibles, net	21		28
Total assets	**6,925**	**-61**	**17,747**
Accts. pay. & accr. liabs	6,413		929
Current liabilities	6,413		929
Long-term debt, gross	nil		3,906
Long-term debt, net	nil		3,906
Shareholders' equity	(1,348)		5,660
Cash from oper. activs	**(17,034)**	**n.a.**	**(9,305)**
Cash from fin. activs	6,495		25,523
Cash from invest. activs	(2)		95
Net cash position	**5,876**	**-65**	**16,944**
Capital expenditures	(2)		(6)
Capital disposals	nil		99
	US$		US$
Earnings per share*	(2.41)		(101.40)
Cash flow per share*	(2.27)		(96.50)
	shs		shs
No. of shs. o/s*	8,579,284		119,925
Avg. no. of shs. o/s*	7,502,609		96,427
	%		%
Net profit margin	n.a.		n.a.
Return on equity	n.m.		n.m.
Return on assets	(145.43)		(98.42)
No. of employees (FTEs)	6		n.a.

* Common
□ Restated
A Reported in accordance with IFRS

Latest Results

Periods ended:	3m Mar. 31/23[A]		3m Mar. 31/22[□A]
	US$000s	%Chg	US$000s
Net income	(4,959)	n.a.	(2,059)
	US$		US$
Earnings per share*	(0.58)		(17.40)

* Common
□ Restated
A Reported in accordance with IFRS

Historical Summary
(as originally stated)

Fiscal Year	Oper. Rev.	Net Inc. Bef. Disc.	EPS*
	US$000s	US$000s	US$
2022[A]	nil	(18,062)	(2.41)
	$000s	$000s	$
2021[A]	10	(11,784)	(1.80)
2020[A]	2	(5,662)	(1.20)
2019[A]	1	(7,396)	(1.80)
2018[A]	nil	(10,167)	(2.40)

* Common
A Reported in accordance with IFRS
Note: Adjusted throughout for 1-for-60 cons. in June 2022

P.105 ProntoForms Corporation

Symbol - PFM **Exchange -** TSX-VEN **CUSIP -** 74345T
Head Office - 250-2500 Solandt Rd, Ottawa, ON, K2K 3G5 **Telephone -** (613) 599-8288 **Toll-free -** (888) 282-4184
Website - www.prontoforms.com
Email - dcroucher@prontoforms.com
Investor Relations - David Croucher (613) 599-8288
Auditors - KPMG LLP C.A., Ottawa, Ont.
Transfer Agents - TSX Trust Company, Toronto, Ont.

Profile - (Ont. 2007) Researches, develops and markets mobile business software solutions to help automate field sales, field service and field data collection business processes.

The ProntoForms® platform is a no-code app development solutions which automates forms used by remote workers to collect data on mobile device, access company data in the field and automatically share results with the back-office systems, cloud services and people. ProntoForms® can be deployed using the do-it-yourself route or the 5-step onboarding methodology with the help or expertise of the company's professional service team. The company has a broad cross section of customers in diverse industries, with a prime focus in medical device manufacturing, heavy manufacturing, energy resources, construction and utilities.

The company sells directly to end-users and indirectly through resellers in North America, South America and Western Europe, as well as to certain system integrators, mobile device manufacturers and mobile operators.

In May 2023, name change to **TrueContext Corporation** was proposed.

Predecessor Detail - Name changed from TrueContext Mobile Solutions Corporation, June 19, 2013.

Directors - Dr. Terence H. (Terry) Matthews, chr., Ottawa, Ont.; Philip C. Deck, co-CEO, Toronto, Ont.; Alvaro Pombo, pres. & co-CEO, Ottawa, Ont.; D. Neil McDonnell, West Vancouver, B.C.; Catherine Sigmar, Ont.

Other Exec. Officers - David Croucher, CFO; Glenn Chenier, chief product officer; Michael W. Kramer, chief revenue officer; Mansell Nelson, sr. v-p, bus. devel.; Aly Mawani, v-p, client success & opers.; Lisa Scian, v-p, people & culture; Lise Snelgrove, v-p, mktg.; Cindy McGann, gen. counsel

Capital Stock

	Authorized (shs.)	Outstanding (shs.)[1]
Common	unlimited	132,799,621

[1] At May 9, 2023

Major Shareholder - PenderFund Capital Management Ltd. held 16.45% interest, Dr. Terence H. (Terry) Matthews held 15.66% interest and Topline Capital Management LLC held 12.7% interest at May 2, 2023.

Price Range - PFM/TSX-VEN

Year	Volume	High	Low	Close
2022	3,354,322	$0.96	$0.35	$0.47
2021	13,171,952	$1.65	$0.69	$0.86
2020	16,082,825	$1.00	$0.55	$0.99
2019	12,498,192	$0.65	$0.32	$0.55
2018	12,304,938	$0.40	$0.29	$0.33

Recent Close: $0.62

Capital Stock Changes - During 2022, 2,281,388 common shares were issued on exercise of options.

Wholly Owned Subsidiaries

ProntoForms Inc., Canada.
TrueContext Incorporated, United States.
TrueContext Limited, United Kingdom.

Financial Statistics

Periods ended:	12m Dec. 31/22[A]		12m Dec. 31/21[A]
	US$000s	%Chg	US$000s
Operating revenue	**21,327**	**+10**	**19,354**
Cost of sales	3,126		2,927
Research & devel. expense	6,617		6,882
General & admin expense	14,274		12,424
Stock-based compensation	1,234		866
Operating expense	**21,895**	**-5**	**22,952**
Operating income	**(568)**	**n.a.**	**(3,598)**
Deprec., depl. & amort.	401		416
Finance costs, gross	246		116
Write-downs/write-offs	(230)		(147)
Pre-tax income	**(4,449)**	**n.a.**	**(4,464)**
Net income	**(4,449)**	**n.a.**	**(4,464)**
Cash & equivalent	6,112		6,082
Accounts receivable	4,179		3,199
Current assets	12,045		10,701
Fixed assets, net	287		332
Right-of-use assets	149		403
Total assets	**12,671**	**+9**	**11,593**
Accts. pay. & accr. liabs	2,686		2,254
Current liabilities	9,368		8,249
Long-term debt, gross	6,008		3,262
Long-term debt, net	6,008		3,262
Long-term lease liabilities	nil		185
Shareholders' equity	(2,705)		(135)
Cash from oper. activs	**(3,152)**	**n.a.**	**(2,097)**
Cash from fin. activs	3,519		691
Cash from invest. activs	(101)		(86)
Net cash position	**6,112**	**0**	**6,082**
Capital expenditures	(101)		(86)
	US$		US$
Earnings per share*	(0.03)		(0.04)
Cash flow per share*	(0.02)		(0.02)
	shs		shs
No. of shs. o/s*	132,739,871		130,458,483
Avg. no. of shs. o/s*	128,289,657		125,869,247
	%		%
Net profit margin	(20.86)		(23.06)
Return on equity	n.m.		n.m.
Return on assets	(34.64)		(34.57)
Foreign sales percent	85		86

* Common
A Reported in accordance with IFRS

Latest Results

Periods ended:	3m Mar. 31/23[A]		3m Mar. 31/22[A]
	US$000s	%Chg	US$000s
Operating revenue	5,772	+15	5,041
Net income	(1,128)	n.a.	(1,544)
	US$		US$
Earnings per share*	(0.01)		(0.01)

* Common
[A] Reported in accordance with IFRS

Historical Summary
(as originally stated)

Fiscal Year	Oper. Rev. US$000s	Net Inc. Bef. Disc. US$000s	EPS* US$
2022[A]	21,327	(4,449)	(0.03)
2021[A]	19,354	(4,464)	(0.04)
2020[A]	17,666	(1,485)	(0.01)
2019[A]	15,104	(2,265)	(0.02)
2018[A]	12,133	(2,501)	(0.02)

* Common
[A] Reported in accordance with IFRS

P.106 Propel Holdings Inc.

Symbol - PRL **Exchange** - TSX **CUSIP** - 74349D
Head Office - 1500-69 Yonge St, Toronto, ON, M5E 1K3 **Telephone** - (647) 776-5479
Website - www.propelholdings.com
Email - jay.vaghela@propelholdings.com
Investor Relations - Jay Vaghela (647) 776-5479
Auditors - MNP LLP C.A., Toronto, Ont.
Transfer Agents - TSX Trust Company, Toronto, Ont.
FP500 Revenue Ranking - 569
Employees - 419 at Dec. 31, 2022
Profile - (Ont. 2011) Operates a proprietary online lending platform delivering instalment loans and lines of credit to underserved consumers in the United States under the MoneyKey™ and CreditFresh™ brands, and in Canada under the Fora Credit™ brand.

Operates as a direct lender and credit services organization or credit access business, and is also involved in multiple bank sponsorship programs where it provides certain services including marketing, technology, underwriting and loan servicing for bank originated loans facilitated through its mobile technology platform.

Primary focus are the millions of underserved U.S. and Canadian consumers who struggle to access credit from traditional credit providers, such as mainstream banks and credit unions, for a variety of reasons including low-to-moderate or volatile incomes and/or limited credit profiles. Earns interest revenue based on a stated annual percentage rate (APR) for closed-end instalment loans and a daily periodic rate of interest for open-ended lines of credit.

As at Mar. 31, 2023, the company has facilitated 998,600 personal, unsecured loans and lines of credit through its platform, with US$1.13 billion being advanced to customers. Operates in 27 U.S. states and three Canadian provinces.

Also has a partnership with for **Pathward, N.A.**, whereby Pathward would provide credit products in the U.S. through the company's Lending-as-a-Service (LaaS) platform. The company generates fee and service revenue for services provided to Pathward.

Directors - Michael L. Stein, chr., Toronto, Ont.; Clive Kinross, CEO, Ont.; Peter W. Anderson, Toronto, Ont.; Geoff Greenwade, Tex.; Karen L. Martin, Toronto, Ont.; Peter Monaco, Mass.; Prof. Poonam Puri, Toronto, Ont.

Other Exec. Officers - Gary Edelstein, pres.; Sarika Ahluwalia, sr. exec. v-p, corp. affairs & chief compliance officer; Noah Buchman, exec. v-p & pres., CreditFresh; Dr. Jonathan Goler, exec. v-p & chief risk officer; Sheldon Saidakovsky, exec. v-p & CFO; Jay Vaghela, sr. v-p, gen. counsel & corp. sec.; Robert Joe, v-p, fin.; Rachel Kaplan, v-p, product & analytics; Jonathan Krauklis, v-p, opers.; Bradley Sherk, v-p, opers. & shared srvcs.; Cindy Usprech, v-p, people & culture; Neal Weinstein, v-p, software devel.; Matthew Wiens, v-p, bank programs & legal affairs

Capital Stock

	Authorized (shs.)	Outstanding (shs.)[1]
Common	unlimited	34,325,320

[1] At June 30, 2023

Major Shareholder - Clive Kinross held 18.6% interest and Michael L. Stein held 18.6% interest at May 8, 2023.

Price Range - PRL/TSX

Year	Volume	High	Low	Close
2022	3,225,902	$13.43	$6.03	$7.45
2021	3,110,685	$14.79	$9.75	$13.63

Recent Close: $8.92

Capital Stock Changes - During 2022, 200 common shares were issued on exercise of options.

Dividends

PRL com Ra $0.40 pa Q est. June 7, 2023
Listed Oct 20/21.
Prev. Rate: $0.38 est. Dec. 8, 2021
$0.095**i** Dec. 8/21
i Initial Payment

Wholly Owned Subsidiaries

Credit Fresh Inc., Ont.
- 100% int. in **Credit Fresh DST I**, Del.

Fora Credit Inc., Ont.
MK Holdings Canada, Inc., Ont.
MoneyKey Inc., Ont.
- 100% int. in **MoneyKey - TX, Inc.**, Tex.

Financial Statistics

Periods ended:	12m Dec. 31/22[A]		12m Dec. 31/21[A]
	US$000s	%Chg	US$000s
Total revenue	**226,851**	**+75**	**129,649**
Salaries & benefits	26,710		21,377
General & admin. expense	8,845		4,649
Other operating expense	37,260		29,495
Operating expense	**72,814**	**+31**	**55,520**
Operating income	**154,037**	**+108**	**74,129**
Deprec. & amort.	3,377		2,913
Provision for loan losses	119,450		50,284
Finance costs, gross	10,164		5,758
Pre-tax income	**20,222**	**+151**	**8,064**
Income taxes	5,095		1,502
Net income	**15,127**	**+131**	**6,562**
Cash & equivalent	7,659		7,239
Accounts receivable	195,628		103,849
Fixed assets, net	525		500
Right-of-use assets	2,117		2,479
Intangibles, net	11,473		7,913
Total assets	**256,681**	**+72**	**149,499**
Accts. pay. & accr. liabs	18,458		19,697
Debt	148,900		46,870
Lease liabilities	2,672		3,184
Shareholders' equity	81,641		75,329
Cash from oper. activs	**(85,321)**	**n.a.**	**(51,833)**
Cash from fin. activs	91,014		56,590
Cash from invest. activs	(5,274)		(2,764)
Net cash position	**7,659**	**+6**	**7,239**
Capital expenditures	(183)		(104)
	US$		US$
Earnings per share*	0.44		0.24
Cash flow per share*	(2.49)		(1.89)
Cash divd. per share*	$0.38		$0.10
	shs		shs
No. of shs. o/s*	34,325,320		34,325,120
Avg. no. of shs. o/s*	34,325,137		27,459,552
	%		%
Net profit margin	6.67		5.06
Return on equity	19.27		15.67
Return on assets	11.19		9.84
No. of employees (FTEs)	419		415

* Common
[A] Reported in accordance with IFRS

Latest Results

Periods ended:	3m Mar. 31/23[A]		3m Mar. 31/22[A]
	US$000s	%Chg	US$000s
Total revenue	65,617	+30	50,517
Net income	7,415	+91	3,877
	US$		US$
Earnings per share*	0.22		0.11

* Common
[A] Reported in accordance with IFRS

Historical Summary
(as originally stated)

Fiscal Year	Total Rev. US$000s	Net Inc. Bef. Disc. US$000s	EPS* US$
2022[A]	226,851	15,127	0.44
2021[A]	129,649	6,562	0.24
2020[A]	73,462	7,333	0.62
2019[A]	67,970	1,995	0.17

* Common
[A] Reported in accordance with IFRS

P.107 Prophecy DeFi Inc.

Symbol - PDFI **Exchange** - CSE **CUSIP** - 74349R
Head Office - 100-87 Scollard St, Toronto, ON, M5R 1G4 **Telephone** - (416) 786-9031
Website - prophecydefi.com
Email - jmcmahon@prophecydefi.com
Investor Relations - John A. McMahon (416) 764-0314
Auditors - Kingston Ross Pasnak LLP C.A., Edmonton, Alta.
Transfer Agents - TSX Trust Company, Toronto, Ont.
Profile - (Ont. 1997) Invests funds in technology start-ups in the blockchain and decentralized finance (DeFi) sectors to fund innovation, elevate industry research and create new business opportunities in a coherent ecosystem.

Wholly owned **Layer2 Blockchain Inc.** manages capital, technology and infrastructure in the DeFi cryptocurrency sector focusing on scalable layer two DeFi protocols.

At Sept. 30, 2022, the company held $4,270,934 of digital currencies.

Predecessor Detail - Name changed from Bucephalus Capital Corp., June 23, 2021, pursuant to change in investment focus on Decentralized Finance.

Directors - John A. McMahon, chr. & CEO, Toronto, Ont.; Andy Dayes, Toronto, Ont.; Timothy (Tim) Diamond, Oakville, Ont.

Other Exec. Officers - Jon Cohen, CFO; Cameron Day, v-p

Capital Stock

	Authorized (shs.)	Outstanding (shs.)[1]
Common	unlimited	132,147,212

[1] At Sept. 30, 2022

Common - One vote per share.
Multiple Voting (old) - Were convertible into subordinate voting shares on a 1-for-1 basis at any time. Four votes per share.
Subordinate Voting (old) - Were convertible into multiple voting shares on a 1-for-1 basis in the event an offer is made to purchase multiple voting shares. One vote per share

Price Range - PDFI/CSE

Year	Volume	High	Low	Close
2022	32,670,883	$0.42	$0.02	$0.03
2021	70,400,431	$0.90	$0.04	$0.42
2020	596,534	$0.07	$0.02	$0.06
2019	915,938	$0.13	$0.03	$0.06
2018	832,360	$0.15	$0.07	$0.12

Recent Close: $0.02

Wholly Owned Subsidiaries

Layer2 Blockchain Inc., Canada.

Financial Statistics

Periods ended:	12m Dec. 31/21[A]		12m Dec. 31/20[A]
	$000s	%Chg	$000s
Total revenue	**1,341**	**n.a.**	**(53)**
Salaries & benefits	485		nil
General & admin. expense	4,414		322
Stock-based compensation	2,300		...
Operating expense	**7,199**	**n.m.**	**322**
Operating income	**(5,858)**	**n.a.**	**(375)**
Deprec. & amort.	75		nil
Finance costs, gross	29		nil
Pre-tax income	**(5,961)**	**n.a.**	**(375)**
Net income	**(5,961)**	**n.a.**	**(375)**
Cash & equivalent	12,841		18
Accounts receivable	nil		18
Investments	194		295
Fixed assets, net	998		nil
Intangibles, net	19,705		nil
Total assets	**33,817**	**n.m.**	**357**
Accts. pay. & accr. liabs	430		530
Debt	4,818		nil
Lease liabilities	617		nil
Shareholders' equity	27,953		(174)
Cash from oper. activs	**(3,221)**	**n.a.**	**(36)**
Cash from fin. activs	11,330		nil
Cash from invest. activs	(1,475)		nil
Net cash position	**6,653**	**n.m.**	**18**
Capital expenditures	(413)		nil
	$		$
Earnings per share*	(0.06)		(0.01)
Cash flow per share*	(0.04)		(0.00)
	shs		shs
No. of shs. o/s*	132,147,212		29,514,241
Avg. no. of shs. o/s*	84,289,264		29,514,241
	%		%
Net profit margin	(444.52)		n.m.
Return on equity	n.m.		n.m.
Return on assets	(34.72)		(92.71)

* M.V. & S.V.
[A] Reported in accordance with IFRS

Latest Results

Periods ended:	9m Sept. 30/22[A]		9m Sept. 30/21[oA]
	$000s	%Chg	$000s
Total revenue	(2,849)	n.a.	1,124
Net income	(5,252)	n.a.	(4,248)
	$		$
Earnings per share*	(0.06)		(0.04)

* M.V. & S.V.
[o] Restated
[A] Reported in accordance with IFRS

Historical Summary
(as originally stated)

Fiscal Year	Total Rev.	Net Inc. Bef. Disc.	EPS*
	$000s	$000s	$
2021A	1,341	(5,961)	(0.06)
2020A	(53)	(375)	(0.01)
2019A	(883)	(1,256)	(0.04)
2018A	(260)	(639)	(0.02)
2017A	76	(150)	(0.01)

* M.V. & S.V.
A Reported in accordance with IFRS

P.108 Prospect Park Capital Corp.

Symbol - PPK **Exchange** - CSE (S) **CUSIP** - 743523
Head Office - 1 First Canadian Place, 6000-100 King St W, Toronto, ON, M5X 1E2 **Telephone** - (416) 369-5265
Email - james_greig@hotmail.com
Investor Relations - James S. Greig (778) 788-2745
Auditors - DNTW Toronto LLP C.A., Toronto, Ont.
Lawyers - DLA Piper (Canada) LLP, Toronto, Ont.
Transfer Agents - Computershare Trust Company of Canada Inc., Toronto, Ont.
Profile - (Ont. 2012) Invests in technology companies with a focus on communications space in the areas of health and education.
Investment holdings consist of wholly owned **Diitalk Communications Inc.**, which operates a reward-based communication platform that features Voice over Internet Protocol (VoIP) calling, SMS messaging, analytics engine, mobile applications and advertisement engine; wholly owned **102130706 Saskatchewan Inc.** (dba Tutors on Demand), which operates a virtual marketplace through Tutors on Demand platform that enables connection of qualified tutors and student learners who are seeking additional educational support; and convertible debenture investment in **1289580 B.C. Ltd.** (dba GetTheSupport), which operates a communication platform for delivering mental help services.
Common suspended from CSE, Feb. 7, 2023.
Directors - James S. (Jim) Greig, CEO, Vancouver, B.C.; Toby R. Pierce, Vancouver, B.C.; Anthony Zelen, Coldstream, B.C.
Officers - Malcolm Davidson, CFO & corp. sec.

Capital Stock

	Authorized (shs.)	Outstanding (shs.)[1]
Common	unlimited	61,297,074

[1] At Aug. 29, 2022
Major Shareholder - James S. (Jim) Greig held 11.9% interest, Toby R. Pierce held 11.9% interest and Dr. Samuel Herschkowitz held 10.2% interest at Oct. 15, 2020.

Price Range - PPK/TSX-VEN (D)

Year	Volume	High	Low	Close
2022	7,895,325	$0.15	$0.01	$0.01
2021	4,619,976	$0.25	$0.07	$0.07
2020	6,781,989	$0.19	$0.04	$0.10
2019	512,160	$0.20	$0.04	$0.06
2018	1,633,960	$0.42	$0.04	$0.05

Split: 3-for-1 split in Feb. 2021; 1-for-5 cons. in Apr. 2020
Recent Close: $0.01
Capital Stock Changes - In February 2022, private placement of up to 10,000,000 common shares was announced at 10¢ per share.

Wholly Owned Subsidiaries
Diitalk Communications Inc., Vancouver, B.C.
102130706 Saskatchewan Inc., Sask. dba Tudors on Demand.

Financial Statistics

Periods ended:	12m Sept. 30/21A		12m Sept. 30/20A
	$000s	%Chg	$000s
Total revenue	**12**	**n.a.**	**nil**
General & admin. expense	287		83
Operating expense	**287**	**+246**	**83**
Operating income	**(275)**	**n.a.**	**(83)**
Finance costs, gross	2		9
Pre-tax income	**(277)**	**n.a.**	**54**
Net income	**(277)**	**n.a.**	**54**
Cash & equivalent	671		234
Total assets	**1,033**	**+341**	**234**
Bank indebtedness	nil		100
Accts. pay. & accr. liabs	31		49
Shareholders' equity	1,002		85
Cash from oper. activs	**(357)**	**n.a.**	**(146)**
Cash from fin. activs	1,094		372
Cash from invest. activs	(300)		nil
Net cash position	**671**	**+187**	**234**
	$		$
Earnings per share*	(0.01)		0.01
Cash flow per share*	(0.01)		(0.02)
	shs		shs
No. of shs. o/s*	32,347,074		14,222,472
Avg. no. of shs. o/s*	25,179,593		7,644,168
	%		%
Net profit margin	n.m.		n.a.
Return on equity	(50.97)		n.m.
Return on assets	(43.41)		52.28

* Common
A Reported in accordance with IFRS

Latest Results

Periods ended:	6m Mar. 31/22A		6m Mar. 31/21A
	$000s	%Chg	$000s
Total revenue	4	n.a.	nil
Net income	(418)	n.a.	(149)
	$		$
Earnings per share*	(0.01)		(0.01)

* Common
A Reported in accordance with IFRS

Historical Summary
(as originally stated)

Fiscal Year	Total Rev.	Net Inc. Bef. Disc.	EPS*
	$000s	$000s	$
2021A	12	(277)	(0.01)
2020A	nil	54	0.01
2019A	(115)	(157)	(0.03)
2018A	70	79	0.02
2017A	(12)	(125)	(0.02)

* Common
A Reported in accordance with IFRS
Note: Adjusted throughout for 3-for-1 split in Feb. 2021; 1-for-5 cons. in Apr. 2020

P.109 ProStar Holdings Inc.

Symbol - MAPS **Exchange** - TSX-VEN **CUSIP** - 74365J
Head Office - 760 Horizon Dr, Suite 200, Grand Junction, CO, United States, 81506 **Telephone** - (970) 242-4024
Website - www.prostarcorp.com
Email - investorrelations@prostarcorp.com
Investor Relations - Joel Sutherland (970) 822-4792
Auditors - Davidson & Company LLP C.A., Vancouver, B.C.
Lawyers - Armstrong Simpson, Vancouver, B.C.
Transfer Agents - Computershare Trust Company of Canada Inc., Vancouver, B.C.
Profile - (B.C. 2007) Develops precision mapping solutions and software designed to precisely capture, record and provide visualization of utility and pipelines that are placed below the Earth's surface.
The precision mapping solutions provide geospatial intelligence, location precision and transparency. The company's cloud and mobile solutions are Transparent Earth®, which is designed to improve the construction, maintenance and repair of underground infrastructure and to better protect the worker, the public and the environment; and the company's flagship product, PointMan®, is a patented cloud and mobile mapping software application that captures, records, and displays the location of buried utilities and pipelines with unprecedented precision, along with the associated metadata including the type, the depth and the depth of cover that works globally on Android and Apple iOS platforms. The conflated geospatial data view provides field workers with the information they need during construction and maintenance activities to avoid damage to assets, as well as personal injury and pollution. These solutions are used by various sectors including construction, municipalities and subsurface utility engineering.
Predecessor Detail - Name changed from Doxa Energy Ltd., Dec. 22, 2020, pursuant to reverse takeover acquisition of ProStar Geocorp Inc. and concurrent amalgamation of ProStar Geopcorp with wholly owned Doxa Merger Corp.; basis 1 new for 17 old shs.
Directors - Page Tucker, CEO, Grand Junction, Colo.; Vasanthan Dasan, COO, Boulder, Colo.; Pat Clawson, Naples, Fla.; Paul T. McKenzie, Vancouver, B.C.; Herb McKim, N.C.; Wayne L. Moore, United States
Other Exec. Officers - Jonathan R. Richards, CFO; Matthew Breman, sr. v-p, mktg.; Joel Sutherland, v-p, corp. devel. & IR

Capital Stock

	Authorized (shs.)	Outstanding (shs.)[1]
Common	unlimited	116,861,084

[1] At May 12, 2023
Major Shareholder - Widely held at Sept. 8, 2022.

Price Range - MAPS/TSX-VEN

Year	Volume	High	Low	Close
2022	13,095,006	$0.49	$0.12	$0.23
2021	14,880,847	$1.00	$0.36	$0.47
2018	126,541	$0.43	$0.17	$0.26

Consolidation: 1-for-17 cons. in Jan. 2021
Recent Close: $0.31
Capital Stock Changes - During 2022, 16,000 common shares were issued on exercise of warrants.

Wholly Owned Subsidiaries
ProStar Geocorp Inc., Del.

Financial Statistics

Periods ended:	12m Dec. 31/22A		12m Dec. 31/21A
	US$000s	%Chg	US$000s
Operating revenue	**757**	**+1**	**750**
Cost of sales	187		145
Salaries & benefits	261		216
General & admin expense	4,536		4,712
Stock-based compensation	711		1,277
Operating expense	**5,695**	**-10**	**6,349**
Operating income	**(4,938)**	**n.a.**	**(5,599)**
Deprec., depl. & amort	149		140
Finance income	49		4
Finance costs, gross	10		18
Pre-tax income	**(5,044)**	**n.a.**	**(5,706)**
Net income	**(5,044)**	**n.a.**	**(5,706)**
Cash & equivalent	2,205		7,025
Accounts receivable	225		99
Current assets	2,430		7,125
Fixed assets, net	35		204
Intangibles, net	8		9
Total assets	**2,474**	**-66**	**7,337**
Accts. pay. & accr. liabs	230		294
Current liabilities	470		715
Long-term lease liabilities	nil		36
Shareholders' equity	2,003		6,587
Cash from oper. activs	**(4,422)**	**n.a.**	**(4,600)**
Cash from fin. activs	(135)		8,217
Cash from invest. activs	(6)		(19)
Net cash position	**2,205**	**-69**	**7,025**
Capital expenditures	(6)		(19)
Capital disposals	1		nil
	US$		US$
Earnings per share*	(0.05)		(0.06)
Cash flow per share*	(0.04)		(0.05)
	shs		shs
No. of shs. o/s*	116,861,084		116,845,084
Avg. no. of shs. o/s*	116,860,909		93,512,577
	%		%
Net profit margin	(666.31)		(760.80)
Return on equity	(117.44)		n.m.
Return on assets	(102.62)		n.a.

* Common
A Reported in accordance with IFRS

Latest Results

Periods ended:	3m Mar. 31/23A		3m Mar. 31/22A
	US$000s	%Chg	US$000s
Operating revenue	231	+22	189
Net income	(1,112)	n.a.	(1,227)
	US$		US$
Earnings per share*	(0.01)		(0.01)

* Common
A Reported in accordance with IFRS

Historical Summary
(as originally stated)

Fiscal Year	Oper. Rev.	Net Inc. Bef. Disc.	EPS*
	US$000s	US$000s	US$
2022[A]	757	(5,044)	(0.05)
2021[A]	750	(5,706)	(0.06)
2020[A1]	1,123	(6,728)	(0.95)
2019[A2]	nil	(122)	(0.06)
2018[A]	nil	(307)	(0.15)

* Common
[A] Reported in accordance with IFRS
[1] Results reflect the Dec. 29, 2020, reverse takeover acquisition of ProStar Geocorp Inc.
[2] Results for 2019 and prior periods pertain to Doxa Energy Ltd.
Note: Adjusted throughout for 1-for-17 cons. in Jan. 2021

P.110 Proton Capital Corp.

Symbol - PTN.P **Exchange** - TSX-VEN **CUSIP** - 74373X
Head Office - 3603 Selinger Cres, Regina, SK, S4V 2H7 **Telephone** - (306) 536-3771
Email - simpsonvideo@sasktel.net
Investor Relations - Alan A. Simpson (306) 536-3771
Auditors - MNP LLP C.A., Calgary, Alta.
Transfer Agents - TSX Trust Company, Calgary, Alta.
Profile - (Alta. 2021) Capital Pool Company.
In April 2023, the company entered into a letter of intent with **PharmaChoice Canada Inc.** whereby it would acquire and operate a PharmaChoice-branded pharmacy or pharmacies, with such acquisition constituting its Qualifying Transaction. Terms were not disclosed.
Directors - Alan A. Simpson, pres., CEO, CFO & corp. sec., Regina, Sask.; Kimberly Carroll, Regina, Sask.; Glenn E. Fradette, Regina, Sask.

Capital Stock

	Authorized (shs.)	Outstanding (shs.)[1]
Preferred	unlimited	nil
Common	unlimited	40,200,000

[1] At Mar. 31, 2023
Major Shareholder - Alan A. Simpson held 12.19% interest and Dwayne A. Anderson held 11.19% interest at Feb. 21, 2023.

Price Range - PTN.P/TSX-VEN

Year	Volume	High	Low	Close
2022	147,000	$0.60	$0.12	$0.60

Recent Close: $0.21
Capital Stock Changes - On May 16, 2022, an initial public offering of 20,000,000 common shares was completed at 10¢ per share.

P.111 PsyBio Therapeutics Corp.

Symbol - PSYB **Exchange** - TSX-VEN **CUSIP** - 693697
Head Office - 1624 Washington St, Denver, CO, United States, 80203 **Telephone** - (513) 449-9585
Website - www.psybiolife.com
Email - noah@psybiolife.com
Investor Relations - Noah Davis (513) 449-9585
Auditors - MNP LLP C.A., Toronto, Ont.
Transfer Agents - Odyssey Trust Company
Employees - 4 at Mar. 2, 2022
Profile - (B.C. 2021; orig. Ont., 2009) Researches, develops and commercializes novel psychedelic-inspired regulated therapeutics for the treatment of mental illness and neurological disorders.
Has developed a proprietary technology platform that enables the rapid generation of its formulation for its lead compound psilocybin, biosynthetic psilocybin, and other targeted tryptamines through a biosynthetic process using genetically modified bacteria. Laboratory research is conducted at Miami University in Oxford, Ohio, on more than 20 psychedelically inspired compounds from different fungi and plants with unique psychoactive properties. Its initial focus is on the treatment of cancer patients with depression.
Predecessor Detail - Name changed from Leo Acquisitions Corp., Feb. 25, 2021, pursuant to the Qualifying Transaction reverse takeover acquisition of PsyBio Therapeutics, Inc., and concurrent amalgamation of (old) PsyBio Therapeutics with wholly owned ELUSS, Inc.; basis 1 new for 1.6667 old shs.
Directors - Evan M. Levine, CEO, Calif.; Noah Davis, CFO & corp. sec., Tex.; Ross Carmel, chief legal officer, N.J.; Nitin Kaushal, Richmond Hill, Ont.; Bob Oliver, Pa.
Other Exec. Officers - Dr. Michael Spigarelli, CMO & chief scientific officer

Capital Stock

	Authorized (shs.)	Outstanding (shs.)[1]
Subordinate Vtg.	unlimited	61,960,306
Multiple Vtg.	unlimited	49,378

[1] At Aug. 29, 2022
Subordinate Voting - One vote per share.
Multiple Voting - Convertible into subordinate voting shares on a 1,000-for-1 basis, subject to restrictions. 1,000 votes per share.
Major Shareholder - Evan M. Levine held 14% interest and Rob Nathan held 12% interest at June 17, 2022.

Price Range - PSYB/TSX-VEN

Year	Volume	High	Low	Close
2022	19,458,025	$0.26	$0.02	$0.04
2021	21,703,257	$0.90	$0.20	$0.20

Consolidation: 1-for-1.6667 cons. in Feb. 2021
Recent Close: $0.02

Wholly Owned Subsidiaries
PsyBio Therapeutics, Inc., United States.

Financial Statistics

Periods ended:	12m Dec. 31/21[A1]		49w Dec. 31/20[A2]
	US$000s	%Chg	US$000s
Research & devel. expense	623		50
General & admin expense	8,089		2,275
Stock-based compensation	2,130		3,530
Other operating expense	65		44
Operating expense	**10,905**	**+85**	**5,900**
Operating income	**(10,905)**	**n.a.**	**(5,900)**
Pre-tax income	**(11,019)**	**n.a.**	**(5,899)**
Net income	**(11,019)**	**n.a.**	**(5,899)**
Cash & equivalent	3,805		270
Current assets	3,995		286
Total assets	**4,008**	**n.m.**	**286**
Accts. pay. & accr. liabs.	441		523
Current liabilities	1,041		1,023
Shareholders' equity	2,718		(737)
Cash from oper. activs.	**(6,950)**	**n.a.**	**(792)**
Cash from fin. activs.	10,368		1,061
Cash from invest. activs.	(3,564)		nil
Net cash position	**124**	**-54**	**270**
	US$		US$
Earnings per share*	(0.10)		n.a.
Cash flow per share*	(0.07)		n.a.
	shs		shs
No. of shs. o/s*	112,960,796		n.a.
Avg. no. of shs. o/s*	106,935,260		n.a.
	%		%
Net profit margin	n.a.		n.a.
Return on equity	n.m.		n.m.
Return on assets	(513.23)		n.a.

* Subord. Vtg.
[A] Reported in accordance with IFRS
[1] Results reflect the Feb. 19, 2022, Qualifying Transaction reverse takeover acquisition of PsyBio Therapeutics Inc.
[2] Results pertain to PsyBio Therapeutics Inc.

Latest Results

Periods ended:	6m June 30/22[A]		6m June 30/21[A]
	US$000s	%Chg	US$000s
Net income	(3,022)	n.a.	(6,407)
	US$		US$
Earnings per share*	(0.03)		(0.06)

* Subord. Vtg.
[A] Reported in accordance with IFRS
Note: Adjusted throughout for 1-for-1.6667 cons. in Feb. 2021

P.112 Psyched Wellness Ltd.

Symbol - PSYC **Exchange** - CSE **CUSIP** - 74447P
Head Office - 2905-77 King St W, Toronto, ON, M5K 1A2 **Telephone** - (647) 400-8494 **Fax** - (416) 941-8852
Website - www.psyched-wellness.com
Email - jstevens@psyched-wellness.com
Investor Relations - Jeffrey J. Stevens (647) 400-8494
Auditors - Clearhouse LLP C.A., Mississauga, Ont.
Transfer Agents - TSX Trust Company, Toronto, Ont.
Profile - (Ont. 1981) Researches, develops and produces products made from the medicinal properties of the Amanita muscaria mushroom.
Amanita muscaria is not classified as a scheduled drug in North America and is considered a food. The company's flagship product, Calm, is an Amanita muscaria-derived extract in liquid supplement which aids stress relief and relaxation. Calm is approved for sale in the U.S., as food supplement. Also developing other formulations such as teas, gummies and capsules to assist with sleeping and to support mood. Products are distributed in the U.S., through brick-and-mortar retail stores and online via e-commerce marketplaces and the company's website, shop.psyched-wellness.com.
In May 2022, the company sold two non-core legacy properties located in the Red Lake District, Ont. for gross proceeds of $226,500.
Predecessor Detail - Name changed from Duncan Park Holdings Corporation, July 13, 2020.
Directors - Michael Nederhoff, chr., Saskatoon, Sask.; Jeffrey J. (Jeff) Stevens, CEO, Scarborough, Ont.; Harrison Aaron, Calif.; Terrence (Terry) Booth, Edmonton, Alta.; Nicholas Kadysh, Toronto, Ont.; Prof. David J. Nutt, London, Middx., United Kingdom; Janeen Stodulski, Ont.
Other Exec. Officers - David Shisel, COO; Keith Li, CFO & corp. sec.; Matthew Singh, chief comml. officer

Capital Stock

	Authorized (shs.)	Outstanding (shs.)[1]
Common	unlimited	145,374,695

[1] At July 31, 2023
Major Shareholder - Widely held at June 6, 2023.

Price Range - PSYC/CSE

Year	Volume	High	Low	Close
2022	25,446,950	$0.18	$0.03	$0.06
2021	107,837,065	$0.75	$0.10	$0.12
2020	57,566,209	$0.44	$0.10	$0.27
2019	350,027	$0.50	$0.07	$0.10
2018	471,258	$0.80	$0.20	$0.20

Consolidation: 1-for-40 cons. in Feb. 2019
Recent Close: $0.07
Capital Stock Changes - During fiscal 2022, 5,200,000 common shares were issued on vesting of restricted share units.

Wholly Owned Subsidiaries
AME Wellness Inc., Del.
Psyched Wellness Corp., Toronto, Ont.

Financial Statistics

Periods ended:	12m Nov. 30/22[A]		12m Nov. 30/21[A]
	$000s	%Chg	$000s
Operating revenue	**14**	**n.a.**	**nil**
Cost of goods sold	7		nil
Research & devel. expense	952		539
General & admin expense	1,924		2,950
Stock-based compensation	1,204		957
Operating expense	**4,087**	**-8**	**4,446**
Operating income	**(4,073)**	**n.a.**	**(4,446)**
Deprec., depl. & amort.	1		nil
Write-downs/write-offs	(449)		nil
Pre-tax income	**(4,296)**	**n.a.**	**(4,498)**
Net income	**(4,296)**	**n.a.**	**(4,498)**
Cash & equivalent	2,568		5,530
Inventories	267		nil
Accounts receivable	64		56
Current assets	3,191		5,905
Fixed assets, net	24		nil
Intangibles, net	95		477
Total assets	**3,311**	**-48**	**6,383**
Accts. pay. & accr. liabs.	175		178
Current liabilities	198		178
Shareholders' equity	3,113		6,204
Cash from oper. activs.	**(3,090)**	**n.a.**	**(3,007)**
Cash from fin. activs.	nil		6,506
Cash from invest. activs.	127		(29)
Net cash position	**2,568**	**-54**	**5,530**
	$		$
Earnings per share*	(0.03)		(0.04)
Cash flow per share*	(0.02)		(0.02)
	shs		shs
No. of shs. o/s*	135,789,695		130,589,695
Avg. no. of shs. o/s*	134,631,133		124,642,240
	%		%
Net profit margin	n.m.		n.a.
Return on equity	(92.22)		(95.91)
Return on assets	(88.63)		(93.77)
Foreign sales percent	100		n.a.

* Common
[A] Reported in accordance with IFRS

Latest Results

Periods ended:	6m May 31/23[A]		6m May 31/22[A]
	$000s	%Chg	$000s
Operating revenue	164	n.a.	nil
Net income	(1,803)	n.a.	(2,520)
	$		$
Earnings per share*	(0.01)		(0.02)

* Common
[A] Reported in accordance with IFRS

Historical Summary
(as originally stated)

Fiscal Year	Oper. Rev.	Net Inc. Bef. Disc.	EPS*
	$000s	$000s	$
2022[A]	14	(4,296)	(0.03)
2021[A]	nil	(4,498)	(0.04)
2020[A]	nil	(2,073)	(0.03)
2019[A]	nil	(350)	(0.09)
2018[A]	nil	(248)	(0.08)

* Common
[A] Reported in accordance with IFRS
Note: Adjusted throughout for 1-for-40 cons. in Feb. 2019

P.113 Psyence Group Inc.

Symbol - PSYG **Exchange** - CSE **CUSIP** - 74449Q
Head Office - 1300-121 Richmond St W, Toronto, ON, M5H 2K1 **Telephone** - (416) 854-0456
Website - www.psyence.com
Email - ir@psyence.com
Investor Relations - Warwick Corden-Lloyd (416) 477-1708
Auditors - MNP LLP C.A., Mississauga, Ont.
Transfer Agents - Odyssey Trust Company, Toronto, Ont.

Profile - (Ont. 1994 amalg.) Produces and supplies medicinal-grade psilocybin mushroom products to the global legal psychedelic research, medical and nutraceutical industries.

Operations are segmented into three divisions: Psyence Therapeutics; Psyence Function; and Psyence Production.

Psyence Therapeutics - Provides standardized natural psilocybin products to clinicians, research centres, and universities undertaking research and clinical trials in the use of natural psilocybin for the treatment of a range of mental health disorders and other medical conditions. Develops therapeutic dosages to help heal psychological trauma and the diagnosable disorders that can result, including anxiety, depression, PTSD, grief and bereavement, especially in the context of palliative care. Clinical trial includes the use of **Filament Health Corp.**'s botanical drug candidate PEX010, containing 25 mg of psilocybin per oral capsule, to treat anxiety and depression in the U.K.

Psyence Function - Developing over-the-counter non-psilocybin containing functional mushroom nutraceutical products. Builds category-disruptive brands and establishes a vibrant and vital channel mix for global wellness products including GOODMIND, a functional mushroom product that does not contain psilocybin. GOODMIND™ functional mushroom sachets, which blend with coffee and other beverages, are available for sale through 300 stores of Vide e Caffè retail chains in Africa. GOODMIND™ franchise is a nutraceutical mental wellness collection that supports improved focus, calm, and sleep.

Psyence Production - Builds and operates one of the first federally licensed commercial psilocybin cultivation and production facilities in the world, located in Lesotho, southern Africa. Focuses on the production of certified, pharmaceutical-quality psilocybin/psilocin- yielding mushrooms. The company's production facility is licensed to import, cultivate, produce, market and export psilocybin and psilocybin mushroom products.

In April 2022, the company entered into an exclusive licensing agreement with **Filament Health Corp.**, whereby Filament would license its proprietary botanical drug candidate PEX010, containing 25 mg of psilocybin per oral capsule, and the associated intellectual property to the company for use in the company's upcoming clinical trials to treat anxiety and depression, which would be conducted in the U.K.

Recent Merger and Acquisition Activity

Status: pending **Announced:** Jan. 9, 2023

Psyence Biomed Corp., a wholly owned subsidiary of Psyence Group Inc., agreed to the reverse takeover acquisition of Oakland, Calif.-based Newcourt Acquisition Corp, a Special Purpose Acquisition Corporation. Terms of the transaction would be subsequently disclosed. Upon completion, and assuming redemptions of shares by its public shareholders, Psyence Biomed would expect to receive a minimum of US$20,000,000 of cash held in trust. The transaction reflected a pre-money equity value of US$50,000,000 for Psyence Biomed. Upon completion, Psyence Biomed would seek to list as a public company in the U.S., with Psyence Group retaining a significant ownership stake.

Predecessor Detail - Name changed from Cardinal Capital Partners Inc., Jan. 19, 2021, pursuant to the reverse takeover acquisition of Mindhealth Biomed Corp. and concurrent amalgamation of Mindhealth with wholly owned 1264216 B.C. Ltd. (and continued as Psyence Biomed Corp.).; basis 1 new for 19.24 old shs.

Directors - Jody Aufrichtig, co-founder & exec. chr., Cape Town, South Africa; Dr. Neil Maresky, CEO, Ont.; Christopher Bull; Alan Friedman, Toronto, Ont.; Marvin J. Singer, Toronto, Ont.

Other Exec. Officers - Warwick Corden-Lloyd, CFO; Tony Budden, chief strategy officer; Dr. Justin Grant, chief scientific officer; Mary-Elizabeth Gifford, exec. v-p, public affairs & corp. social responsibility; Taryn Vos, gen. counsel

Capital Stock

	Authorized (shs.)	Outstanding (shs.)[1]
Preferred	unlimited	nil
Common	unlimited	95,295,299

[1] At Mar. 1, 2023

Major Shareholder - Widely held at Nov. 9, 2021.

Price Range - PSYG/CSE

Year	Volume	High	Low	Close
2022	4,578,867	$0.19	$0.01	$0.11
2021	13,253,564	$0.62	$0.10	$0.18

Consolidation: 1-for-19.24 cons. in Jan. 2021

Recent Close: $0.08

Capital Stock Changes - In November and December 2022, private placement of 17,918,214 common shares was completed at 12¢ per share.

There were no changes to capital stock during fiscal 2022.

Wholly Owned Subsidiaries

Psyence Biomed Corp., Toronto, Ont.
- 50% int. in **Good Psyence (Pty) Ltd.**, South Africa.
- 100% int. in **Mind Health (Pty) Ltd.**, Lesotho.
- 100% int. in **Psyence Jamaica Limited**, Jamaica.
- 100% int. in **Psyence South Africa (Pty) Ltd.**, South Africa.
- 100% int. in **Psyence Therapeutics Corp.**, Ont.
- 100% int. in **Psyence UK Group Ltd.**, United Kingdom.
- 50% int. in **Pure Psyence Corp.**, Vancouver, B.C.

Financial Statistics

Periods ended:	12m Mar. 31/22[A]		10m Mar. 31/21[A1]
	$000s	%Chg	$000s
Research & devel. expense	116		22
General & admin expense	4,340		3,141
Operating expense	**4,456**	**n.a.**	**3,163**
Operating income	**(4,456)**	**n.a.**	**(3,163)**
Deprec., depl. & amort.	53		24
Finance costs, gross	1		1
Investment income	(85)		nil
Pre-tax income	**(4,601)**	**n.a.**	**(11,284)**
Net income	**(4,601)**	**n.a.**	**(11,284)**
Cash & equivalent	3,495		6,096
Accounts receivable	142		182
Current assets	3,799		6,321
Fixed assets, net	511		392
Intangibles, net	22		18
Total assets	**4,355**	**-35**	**6,731**
Accts. pay. & accr. liabs	315		228
Current liabilities	1,591		237
Long-term debt, gross	1,273		nil
Long-term lease liabilities	53		55
Shareholders' equity	2,711		6,439
Cash from oper. activs	**(3,560)**	**n.a.**	**(2,203)**
Cash from fin. activs	1,270		8,672
Cash from invest. activs	(311)		(373)
Net cash position	**3,495**	**-43**	**6,096**
Capital expenditures	(164)		(358)
	$		$
Earnings per share*	(0.05)		(0.22)
Cash flow per share*	(0.04)		(0.04)
	shs		shs
No. of shs. o/s*	85,528,931		85,528,931
Avg. no. of shs. o/s*	85,528,931		51,205,555
	%		%
Net profit margin	n.a.		...
Return on equity	(100.57)		...
Return on assets	(82.99)		...

* Common

[A] Reported in accordance with IFRS

[1] Results reflect the Jan. 19, 2021, reverse takeover acquisition of MindHealth Biomed Corp.

Latest Results

Periods ended:	3m June 30/22[A]		3m June 30/21[A]
	$000s	%Chg	$000s
Net income	(1,180)	n.a.	(1,207)
	$		$
Earnings per share*	(0.01)		(0.01)

* Common

[A] Reported in accordance with IFRS

Historical Summary
(as originally stated)

Fiscal Year	Oper. Rev. $000s	Net Inc. Bef. Disc. $000s	EPS* $
2022[A]	nil	(4,601)	(0.05)
2021[A1]	nil	(11,284)	(0.22)
2020[A2]	nil	(93)	(1.15)
2019[A3]	nil	(19)	(0.01)
2018[A]	nil	(13)	(0.02)

* Common

[A] Reported in accordance with IFRS

[1] 10 months ended Mar. 31, 2021.

[2] Results pertain to Cardinal Capital Partners Inc.

[3] Results for 2019 and prior years pertain to Cardinal Capital Partners Inc.

Note: Adjusted throughout for 1-for-19.24 cons. in Jan. 2021

P.114 Pulse Seismic Inc.*

Symbol - PSD **Exchange** - TSX **CUSIP** - 74586Q

Head Office - 2700-421 7 Ave SW, Calgary, AB, T2P 4K9 **Telephone** - (403) 237-5559 **Toll-free** - (877) 460-5559

Website - www.pulseseismic.com

Email - pamela.wicks@pulseseismic.com

Investor Relations - Pamela Wicks (877) 460-5559

Auditors - MNP LLP C.A., Calgary, Alta.

Bankers - The Toronto-Dominion Bank, Calgary, Alta.

Lawyers - McCarthy Tétrault LLP, Calgary, Alta.

Transfer Agents - Computershare Trust Company of Canada Inc., Calgary, Alta.

Employees - 16 at Dec. 31, 2022

Profile - (Can. 1985) Acquires, markets and licenses two-dimensional (2D) and three-dimensional (3D) seismic data for the energy sector in western Canada.

Owns and controls the largest licensable seismic data library in the Western Canadian Sedimentary Basin (WCSB), consisting of 829,207 net km of 2D seismic data and 65,310 net km^2 of 3D seismic data spanning Alberta, northeastern British Columbia, Saskatchewan, Manitoba, Montana and portions of the Northwest Territories and Yukon. The library extensively covers the WCSB where most of Canada's oil and natural gas exploration and development occur. Seismic data is used by oil and natural gas and development companies to identify portions of geological formations that have the potential to hold hydrocarbons.

The company acquires seismic data to grow its data library through two main methods: purchasing proprietary rights to complementary 2D and 3D seismic data sets; and conducting 3D participation surveys in areas complementary to its current data library. Customers include Canadian oil and gas exploration and development companies; and companies exploring for non-traditional forms of energy and related resources such as lithium, geothermal, carbon and helium.

In January 2023, the company licensed $4,000,000 of 3D seismic data located in a fairway in west-central Alberta.

Predecessor Detail - Name changed from Pulse Data Inc., May 28, 2009.

Directors - Robert E. Robotti, chr., New York, N.Y.; Neal Coleman, pres. & CEO, Calgary, Alta.; Paul A. Crilly, Calgary, Alta.; Dallas L. Droppo, Carefree, Ariz.; Patrick R. (Pat) Ward, Calgary, Alta.; Melanie Westergaard, Golden, Colo.

Other Exec. Officers - Trevor Meier, v-p, sales & mktg.; Pamela Wicks, v-p, fin. & CFO; Catherine M. Samuel, corp. sec.

Capital Stock

	Authorized (shs.)	Outstanding (shs.)[1]
Preferred	unlimited	nil
Common	unlimited	53,280,621

[1] At July 25, 2023

Normal Course Issuer Bid - The company plans to make normal course purchases of up to 3,070,659 common shares representing 10% of the public float. The bid commenced on Nov. 16, 2022, and expires on Nov. 15, 2023.

Major Shareholder - EdgePoint Investment Group Inc. held 27.7% interest and Ravenswood Management Company, LLC held 16.3% interest at Mar. 20, 2023.

Price Range - PSD/TSX

Year	Volume	High	Low	Close
2022	6,736,635	$2.91	$1.61	$1.82
2021	8,355,593	$2.60	$0.94	$2.19
2020	7,700,433	$2.17	$0.61	$0.96
2019	4,079,530	$2.92	$1.36	$1.94
2018	4,671,900	$3.21	$1.29	$1.49

Recent Close: $1.97

Capital Stock Changes - During 2022, 157,848 common shares were repurchased under a Normal Course Issuer Bid.

Dividends

PSD com N.S.R.

$0.15◆	Aug. 22/23	$0.01375	Aug. 22/23
$0.01375	May 24/23	$0.0125	Mar. 20/23
$0.0125	Nov. 22/22		

Paid in 2023: $0.04 + $0.15◆ 2022: $0.05 2021: $0.0125 + $0.04◆

◆ Special

Long-Term Debt - At Dec. 31, 2022, the company had no long-term debt.

Wholly Owned Subsidiaries

1334130 Alberta Ltd., Calgary, Alta.

777747 Alberta Ltd., Alta.
- 0.01% int. in **Pulse Seismic GP**, Alta.

Subsidiaries

99.99% int. in **Pulse Seismic GP**, Alta.

95% int. in **ReQuest Seismic Surveys LP**, Alta.

Financial Statistics

Periods ended:	12m Dec. 31/22A		12m Dec. 31/21A
	$000s	%Chg	$000s
Operating revenue	**9,570**	**-81**	**49,150**
Salaries & benefits	3,898		4,302
General & admin expense	2,770		1,905
Stock-based compensation	572		311
Operating expense	**7,240**	**+11**	**6,518**
Operating income	**2,330**	**-95**	**42,632**
Deprec., depl. & amort.	10,075		10,624
Finance income	103		62
Finance costs, gross	198		1,889
Write-downs/write-offs	(295)		nil
Pre-tax income	**(8,135)**	**n.a.**	**30,181**
Income taxes	(228)		8,667
Net income	**(7,907)**	**n.a.**	**21,514**
Cash & equivalent	5,822		nil
Accounts receivable	1,088		15,030
Current assets	7,738		15,393
Fixed assets, net	14		50
Right-of-use assets	18		228
Intangibles, net	27,410		37,228
Total assets	**35,222**	**-33**	**52,899**
Accts. pay. & accr. liabs	1,077		2,593
Current liabilities	1,145		5,644
Long-term debt, gross	nil		2,265
Long-term debt, net	nil		2,265
Long-term lease liabilities	nil		21
Shareholders' equity	33,496		44,141
Cash from oper. activs	**11,992**	**-60**	**29,799**
Cash from fin. activs	(6,158)		(29,441)
Cash from invest. activs	(12)		(358)
Net cash position	**5,822**	**n.a.**	**nil**
Capital expenditures	(12)		(358)
	$		$
Earnings per share*	(0.15)		0.40
Cash flow per share*	0.22		0.55
Cash divd. per share*	0.05		0.01
Extra divd. - cash*	nil		0.04
Total divd. per share*	**0.05**		**0.05**
	shs		shs
No. of shs. o/s*	53,626,869		53,784,717
Avg. no. of shs. o/s*	53,703,039		53,792,984
	%		%
Net profit margin	(82.62)		43.77
Return on equity	(20.37)		61.99
Return on assets	(17.51)		41.70
No. of employees (FTEs)	16		16

* Common
[A] Reported in accordance with IFRS

Latest Results

Periods ended:	6m June 30/23A		6m June 30/22A
	$000s	%Chg	$000s
Operating revenue	17,163	+247	4,953
Net income	6,307	n.a.	(4,284)
	$		$
Earnings per share*	0.12		(0.08)

* Common
[A] Reported in accordance with IFRS

Historical Summary
(as originally stated)

Fiscal Year	Oper. Rev.	Net Inc. Bef. Disc.	EPS*
	$000s	$000s	$
2022A	9,570	(7,907)	(0.15)
2021A	49,150	21,514	0.40
2020A	11,349	(6,786)	(0.13)
2019A	24,155	(3,411)	(0.06)
2018A	10,188	(1,730)	(0.03)

* Common
[A] Reported in accordance with IFRS

P.115 Pure Extracts Technologies Corp.

Symbol - PULL **Exchange** - CSE **CUSIP** - 74624U
Head Office - Unit 6, 7341 Industrial Way, Pemberton, BC, V0N 2K0 **Telephone** - (604) 345-2724
Website - pureextractscorp.com
Email - yana@pureextractscorp.com
Investor Relations - Yana Popova (604) 328-5598
Auditors - Davidson & Company LLP C.A., Vancouver, B.C.
Profile - (B.C. 2009; orig. Can., 2006) Extracts and processes cannabis, hemp, and functional mushrooms as a third-party service to licensed producers for toll processing or white label processing and for its own private label of products containing THC (tetrahydrocannabinol) and CBD (cannabidiol)-based extracted oils.

Holds a standard processing licence from Health Canada and has a fully-built carbon dioxide extraction facility in Pemberton, B.C., built to European Union Good Manufacturing Practices (EU-GMP) standards, which will allow it, subject to obtaining the necessary permits, to export its products to international markets where cannabis is legal for recreational use.

Wholly owned **Pure Mushrooms Corp.**, once granted licence by Health Canada, would be permitted to cultivate and/or purchase psychedelic mushrooms, and extract and sell compounds such as psilocybin.

Predecessor Detail - Name changed from Big Sky Petroleum Corporation, Oct. 28, 2020, pursuant to the reverse takeover acquisition of Pure Extracts Technologies Inc. and concurrent amalgamation of Pure Extracts with wholly owned 1270233 B.C. Ltd. (and continued as Pure Extracts Manufacturing Corp.).; basis 1 new for 6 old shs.

Directors - Ben Nikolaevsky, CEO, Toronto, Ont.; Doug Benville, COO, Whistler, B.C.; Yana Popova, CFO & corp. sec., Vancouver, B.C.; Sean Bromley, Vancouver, B.C.; Dwight Duncan, Windsor, Ont.

Other Exec. Officers - Andy Gauvin, dir., sales; Alexander Logie, dir., bus. devel.

Capital Stock

	Authorized (shs.)	Outstanding (shs.)[1]
Common	unlimited	116,766,811

[1] At May 30, 2023

Major Shareholder - Widely held at Sept. 27, 2021.

Price Range - PULL/CSE

Year	Volume	High	Low	Close
2022	36,843,407	$0.13	$0.01	$0.01
2021	83,268,349	$0.83	$0.10	$0.11
2020	17,146,250	$0.89	$0.30	$0.64
2019	49,266	$0.90	$0.33	$0.39
2018	12,706	$0.90	$0.30	$0.48

Consolidation: 1-for-6 cons. in Oct. 2020
Recent Close: $0.01

Capital Stock Changes - In July 2022, 5,937,001 units (1 common share & ½ warrant) were issued without further consideration on exchange of special warrants sold previously by private placement at $0.075 each, with warrants exercisable at 15¢ per share for two years.

During fiscal 2022, common shares were issued as follows: 3,400,000 on exercise of warrants, 2,752,448 for debt settlement, 2,576,167 on exercise of options and 2,281,500 on exercise of performance securities.

Wholly Owned Subsidiaries

Pure Extracts Manufacturing Corp., Pemberton, B.C.
Pure Extracts USA Inc., Mich.
Pure Mushrooms Corp., B.C.

Financial Statistics

Periods ended:	12m June 30/22A		12m June 30/21A1
	$000s	%Chg	$000s
Operating revenue	**1,229**	**n.m.**	**102**
Cost of goods sold	1,100		160
Salaries & benefits	1,601		1,625
Research & devel. expense	nil		35
General & admin expense	2,214		6,251
Stock-based compensation	426		8,200
Operating expense	**5,341**	**-67**	**16,271**
Operating income	**(4,112)**	**n.a.**	**(16,169)**
Deprec., depl. & amort.	751		686
Finance income	3		1
Finance costs, gross	149		205
Write-downs/write-offs	(149)		(664)
Pre-tax income	**(5,240)**	**n.a.**	**(20,693)**
Net income	**(5,240)**	**n.a.**	**(20,693)**
Cash & equivalent	111		1,629
Inventories	1,443		720
Accounts receivable	187		219
Current assets	2,197		3,286
Fixed assets, net	3,078		2,773
Right-of-use assets	884		2,274
Total assets	**6,322**	**-26**	**8,498**
Accts. pay. & accr. liabs	1,770		590
Current liabilities	3,156		1,017
Long-term debt, gross	965		nil
Long-term lease liabilities	682		1,313
Shareholders' equity	2,484		6,168
Cash from oper. activs	**(2,796)**	**n.a.**	**(9,445)**
Cash from fin. activs	1,312		11,731
Cash from invest. activs	(35)		(791)
Net cash position	**111**	**-93**	**1,629**
Capital expenditures	(35)		nil
	$		$
Earnings per share*	(0.05)		(0.32)
Cash flow per share*	(0.03)		(0.15)
	shs		shs
No. of shs. o/s*	108,849,810		97,839,695
Avg. no. of shs. o/s*	102,794,753		64,107,846
	%		%
Net profit margin	(426.36)		n.m.
Return on equity	n.m.		n.m.
Return on assets	n.a.		(316.98)

* Common
[A] Reported in accordance with IFRS
[1] Results reflect the Oct. 28, 2020, reverse takeover acquisition of Pure Extracts Technologies Inc.

Historical Summary
(as originally stated)

Fiscal Year	Oper. Rev.	Net Inc. Bef. Disc.	EPS*
	$000s	$000s	$
2022A	1,229	(5,240)	(0.05)
2021A	102	(20,693)	(0.32)
	US$000s	US$000s	US$
2019A1	nil	(59)	(0.06)
2018A	nil	(88)	(0.12)

* Common
[A] Reported in accordance with IFRS
[1] Results for 2019 and prior years pertain to Big Sky Petroleum Corp.
Note: Adjusted throughout for 1-for-6 cons. in Oct. 2020

P.116 Pure to Pure Beauty Inc.

Symbol - PPB **Exchange** - CSE **CUSIP** - 74622P
Head Office - 650-1231 Pacific Blvd, Vancouver, BC, V6Z 0E2 **Telephone** - (604) 339-0339
Website - www.p2pbeauty.com
Email - simonchengnow@gmail.com
Investor Relations - Yee Sing Cheng (604) 339-0339
Auditors - SHIM & Associates LLP C.A., Vancouver, B.C.
Transfer Agents - Computershare Trust Company of Canada Inc., Vancouver, B.C.
Profile - (B.C. 2014) Develops and sells consumer product goods, including health and wellness products, under its Pure to Pure brand.

Products are manufactured by **Deserving Health International Corp.** (DHI) in Richmond, B.C., and a German production company. DHI produces the Pure to Pure shampoo and foaming hand wash while the German supplier produces the company's face serum with aloe vera and jojoba oil. The company is also seeking to acquire the right or intellectual property for dietary supplements, as well as actively sourcing additional contract manufacturers for additional products.

Products are sold on the company's website, as well as third party websites. Principal markets are Canada, the U.S. and Germany.

On May 3, 2023, common shares were listed on the Frankfurt Stock Exchange under the stock symbol 3QG0.

In March 2023, the company entered into a letter of intent to acquire a 51% interest in the SunSeal™ brand of products from **Corium Health Limited**, a developer of skin care brands specifically in the sun care market, for issuance of 5,000,000 common shares.

Common listed on CSE, Sept. 1, 2022.

Predecessor Detail - Name changed from P2P Info Inc., May 10, 2021.

Directors - Yee Sing (Simon) Cheng, CEO, Calgary, Alta.; Steven Pearce, Singapore, Singapore

Other Exec. Officers - Tak Tsan (Simon) Tso, CFO

Capital Stock

	Authorized (shs.)	Outstanding (shs.)[1]
Common	unlimited	53,076,882

[1] At May 11, 2023

Major Shareholder - Widely held at Sept. 1, 2022.

Price Range - PPB/CSE

Year	Volume	High	Low	Close
2022	314,402	$0.46	$0.02	$0.06

Recent Close: $0.04

Capital Stock Changes - There were no changes to capital stock during fiscal 2022.

Financial Statistics

Periods ended:	12m Sept. 30/22^A		12m Sept. 30/21^A
	$000s	%Chg	$000s
Operating revenue	**27**	**n.a.**	**nil**
Cost of sales	12		nil
Salaries & benefits	nil		1
Research & devel. expense	1		...
General & admin expense	220		61
Operating expense	**233**	**+282**	**61**
Operating income	**(206)**	**n.a.**	**(61)**
Deprec., depl. & amort.	5		1
Finance costs, gross	1		nil
Pre-tax income	**(212)**	**n.a.**	**(61)**
Net income	**(212)**	**n.a.**	**(61)**
Cash & equivalent	316		521
Accounts receivable	11		9
Current assets	327		530
Intangibles, net	44		49
Total assets	**370**	**-36**	**578**
Accts. pay. & accr. liabs.	34		26
Current liabilities	34		30
Long-term debt, gross	75		75
Long-term debt, net	75		75
Shareholders' equity	262		474
Cash from oper. activs.	**(205)**	**n.a.**	**(40)**
Cash from fin. activs.	nil		560
Net cash position	**316**	**-39**	**521**
	$		$
Earnings per share*	(0.00)		(0.00)
Cash flow per share*	(0.00)		(0.00)
	shs		shs
No. of shs. o/s*	53,076,882		53,076,882
Avg. no. of shs. o/s*	53,076,882		35,792,171
	%		%
Net profit margin	(785.19)		n.a.
Return on equity	(57.61)		n.m.
Return on assets	(44.51)		(21.07)

* Common
^A Reported in accordance with IFRS

Latest Results

Periods ended:	6m Mar. 31/23^A		6m Mar. 31/22^A
	$000s	%Chg	$000s
Net income	(82)	n.a.	(116)
	$		$
Earnings per share*	(0.00)		(0.00)

* Common
^A Reported in accordance with IFRS

Historical Summary
(as originally stated)

Fiscal Year	Oper. Rev.	Net Inc. Bef. Disc.	EPS*
	$000s	$000s	$
2022^A	27	(212)	(0.00)
2021^A	nil	(61)	(0.00)
2020^A	nil	(18)	(0.00)

* Common
^A Reported in accordance with IFRS

P.117 Pushfor Tech Inc.

Symbol - PUSH **Exchange** - CSE **CUSIP** - 74643G
Head Office - 210-9648 128 St, Surrey, BC, V3T 2K9 **Telephone** - (604) 357-4730 **Fax** - (604) 592-6882
Website - pushfortech.com
Email - lucky@jandagroup.ca
Investor Relations - Lakhwindar Janda (604) 357-4730
Auditors - Mao & Ying LLP C.A., Vancouver, B.C.
Bankers - Bank of Montreal, Vancouver, B.C.
Transfer Agents - Odyssey Trust Company, Vancouver, B.C.
Profile - (B.C. 2007) Wholly owned **AFX Networks Inc.** provides an integrated cloud platform ecosystem which eliminates data redundancy, allows immediate payment settlements, provides end-to-end supply chain visibility and mitigates fraud for the third party logistics and freight broker industry.
Investment **Education Revolution LLC** (15% owned) provides the Socrates learning system, a multi-stage and multi-language educational technology learning platform.
Predecessor Detail - Name changed from Pushfor Investments Inc., June 9, 2022; basis 1 new for 10 old shs.
Directors - Lakhwindar (Lucky) Janda, pres., CEO & interim CFO, Richmond, B.C.; Parmjeet (Parm) Johal, Surrey, B.C.; Harpreet (Harp) Sangha
Other Exec. Officers - Kyle Lucas, v-p & chief tech. officer

Capital Stock

	Authorized (shs.)	Outstanding (shs.)[1]
Preferred	unlimited	nil
Common	unlimited	9,261,002

[1] At Jan. 11, 2022

Major Shareholder - Widely held at Apr. 7, 2022.

Price Range - PUSH/CSE

Year	Volume	High	Low	Close
2022	1,508,809	$1.60	$0.04	$0.10
2021	1,301,477	$10.20	$0.80	$1.20
2020	132,094	$7.00	$0.50	$0.70
2019	318,848	$50.80	$4.80	$5.80
2018	366,244	$37.00	$8.00	$36.80

Consolidation: 1-for-2 cons. in Jan. 2023; 1-for-10 cons. in June 2022
Recent Close: $0.05
Capital Stock Changes - On Jan. 12, 2023, common shares were consolidated on a 1-for-2 basis.
In January 2022, 1,500,000 post-consolidated common shares were issued pursuant to the acquisition of AFX Networks Inc. and 700,000 post-consolidated common shares were issued pursuant to the acquisition of a 15% interest in Education Revolution LLC. On June 9, 2022, common shares were consolidated on a 1-for-10 basis.

Wholly Owned Subsidiaries

AFX Networks Inc.
114611 B.C. Ltd., Canada. Inactive.

Investments

15% int. in **Education Revolution LLC**, United States.

Financial Statistics

Periods ended:	12m Sept. 30/21^A		12m Sept. 30/20^A
	$000s	%Chg	$000s
General & admin. expense	496		727
Stock-based compensation	2,128		700
Operating expense	**2,624**	**+84**	**1,427**
Operating income	**(2,624)**	**n.a.**	**(1,427)**
Finance costs, gross	11		1
Pre-tax income	**(2,620)**	**n.a.**	**(2,815)**
Net inc. bef. disc. opers.	**(2,620)**	**n.a.**	**(2,815)**
Income from disc. opers.	nil		(1,942)
Net income	**(2,620)**	**n.a.**	**(4,758)**
Cash & equivalent	1,242		4
Accounts receivable	91		nil
Current assets	1,369		4
Total assets	**1,369**	**n.m.**	**4**
Accts. pay. & accr. liabs.	209		148
Current liabilities	209		148
Shareholders' equity	1,160		(144)
Cash from oper. activs.	**(450)**	**n.a.**	**(284)**
Cash from fin. activs.	1,768		187
Cash from invest. activs.	(84)		85
Net cash position	**1,240**	**n.m.**	**1**
	$		$
Earns. per sh. bef disc opers*	(0.40)		(0.40)
Earnings per share*	(0.40)		(0.80)
Cash flow per share*	(0.07)		(0.05)
	shs		shs
No. of shs. o/s*	7,826,022		6,034,022
Avg. no. of shs. o/s*	6,868,419		6,032,509
	%		%
Net profit margin	n.a.		n.a.
Return on equity	n.m.		n.m.
Return on assets	(380.04)		(98.12)

* Common
^A Reported in accordance with IFRS

Latest Results

Periods ended:	9m June 30/22^A		9m June 30/21^A
	$000s	%Chg	$000s
Net income	(1,366)	n.a.	(213)
	$		$
Earnings per share*	(0.16)		(0.03)

* Common
^A Reported in accordance with IFRS

Historical Summary
(as originally stated)

Fiscal Year	Total Rev.	Net Inc. Bef. Disc.	EPS*
	$000s	$000s	$
2021^A	nil	(2,620)	(0.40)
2020^A	nil	(2,815)	(0.40)
2019^A	35	(3,177)	(0.40)
2018^A	nil	(2,491)	(0.40)
2017^A	nil	227	0.07

* Common
^A Reported in accordance with IFRS

Note: Adjusted throughout for 1-for-2 cons. in Jan. 2023; 1-for-10 cons. in June 2022; 2-for-1 split in Dec. 2017

P.118 PyroGenesis Canada Inc.

Symbol - PYR **Exchange** - TSX **CUSIP** - 74734T
Head Office - 200-1744 rue William, Montréal, QC, H3J 1R4 **Telephone** - (514) 937-0002 **Fax** - (514) 937-5757
Website - www.pyrogenesis.com
Email - ir@pyrogenesis.com
Investor Relations - Rodayna Kafal (514) 937-0002
Auditors - Raymond Chabot Grant Thornton LLP C.A., Montréal, Qué.
Transfer Agents - American Stock Transfer & Trust Company, LLC, New York, N.Y.; TSX Trust Company, Montréal, Qué.
Employees - 116 at Dec. 31, 2022
Profile - (Can. 2011 amalg.) Designs, develops, manufactures and commercializes advanced plasma processes and products to reduce greenhouse gases.
Offers plasma systems and processes, and technology development services to the defence, metallurgical, mining, environmental, oil and gas industries, as well as plasma atomized powders for the additive manufacturing (AM) industry, specifically 3D printing.
Products and services are as follows:
Plasma torch systems used for replacing fossil fuel burners in industrial iron ore induration (pelletization) process in mining and metallurgy sectors.
Waste destruction and waste-to-energy systems including Plasma Arc Waste Destruction System (PAWDS), for waste destruction onboard ships; Steam Plasma Arc Refrigerant Cracking (SPARC), for the destruction of refrigerants such as chlorofluorocarbons (CFCs), hydrofluorocarbons (HFCs) and hydrochlorofluorocarbons (HCFCs); Plasma Arc Chemical Warfare Agent Destruction System (PACWADS), a mobile system for the onsite destruction of chemical warfare agents; Plasma Resource Recovery System (PRRS), for land-based waste destruction and waste-to-energy applications; and Plasma Arc Gasification and Vitrification (PAGV), which converts incinerator ash and other hazardous inorganic material to an inert slag.
Systems for the recovery of aluminum and other metal from dross (a residue generated by primary and secondary metal producers, as well as metal parts casters) through its DROSRITE™ process, which systems are predominantly offered to customers in the metallurgical industry. DROSRITE™ is a salt-free, sustainable process for maximizing metal recovery from dross without any hazardous by-products.
Production of high purity spherical metal powders, including titanium alloy powders, through its plasma atomization process known as NEXGEN®, which are predominantly offered to customers in the AM industry. NEXGEN® provides an improved yield in the finer size cuts, along with a higher production rate.
In partnership with **HPQ Silicon Inc.**, the company is developing PUREVAP™ Quartz Reduction Reactor (QRR), which uses a plasma arc within a vacuum furnace to produce high purity metallurgical grade silicon and solar grade silicon from quartz; PUREVAP™ Nano Silicon Reactor (NSiR), which transforms silicon of different purities into spherical silicon nanopowders and nanowires for use in lithium-ion batteries. In addition, the company is developing processes to produce high purity silicon metals through its PUREVAP™ process, and nano powders and nanowires through its PUREVAP™ NSiR process.
Through wholly owned **Pyro Green-Gas Inc.** offers equipment which combines different technologies for the removal of contaminants from biogas and landfill gas, such as hydrogen sulfide, oxygen nitrogen, volatile organic compounds (VOCs) and moisture. Pryo Green also offer individual equipment and fully integrated turnkey systems for gas purification and air emission controls.
In partnership with HPQ, the company is developing a fumed silica reactor, a plasma-based process which allows a direct quartz to fumed silica transformation, removing the usage of hazardous chemical in the making of fumed silica and eliminating the hydrogen chloride gas associated with its manufacturing.
The company also offers installation, commissioning and start-up services typically quoted as an option in equipment sales contracts, as well as after sales services such as sale of spare parts, consumable parts and onsite or remote service on installed systems; and research and development services (internal and external funded projects by customers).
In September 2022, the company sold to **HPQ Silicon Inc.** an intellectual property relating exclusively for carbon emission reduction in the production of silicon for $3,600,000.
In June 2022, a name change to **PyroGenesis Inc.** was approved.
Predecessor Detail - Formed from Industrial Growth Income Corporation in Canada, July 11, 2011, pursuant to Qualifying Transaction amalgamation with (old) PyroGenesis Canada Inc.; basis 1 new sh. for 1 old PyroGenesis sh. and 0.32298 new shs. for 1 Industrial Growth sh.
Directors - Alan R. Curleigh, chr., Pointe-Claire, Qué.; P. Peter Pascali Jr., pres. & CEO, Montréal, Qué.; Maj.-Gen. (ret.) Robert M. Radin†, S.C.; Andrew Abdalla, Qué.; Dr. Virendra Jha, Qué.; Ben Naccarato, Ga.; Nannette Ramsey, Fla.
Other Exec. Officers - Andre Mainella, CFO; Pierre Carabin, chief tech. officer & chief strategist; Massimo Dattilo, v-p, sales; Rodayna Kafal, v-p, IR & strategic bus. devel.; Steve McCormick, v-p, corp. affairs; Mark Paterson, gen. counsel
† Lead director

Capital Stock

	Authorized (shs.)	Outstanding (shs.)[1]
Class A Common	unlimited	178,580,395

[1] At May 15, 2023

Major Shareholder - P. Peter Pascali Jr. held 45.14% interest at May 5, 2023.

Price Range - PYR/TSX

Year	Volume	High	Low	Close
2022	66,634,216	$3.90	$0.84	$1.03
2021	107,991,737	$12.14	$2.91	$3.33
2020	84,705,257	$6.43	$0.19	$3.61
2019	19,781,085	$0.77	$0.40	$0.46
2018	22,355,573	$0.84	$0.38	$0.52

Recent Close: $0.91

Capital Stock Changes - In March 2023, private placement of 5,000,000 units (1 class A common share & ½ warrant) at $1.00 per unit was completed, with warrants exercisable at $1.25 per share for two years.

During 2022, class A common shares were issued as follows: 2,440,000 on exercise of options and 1,014,600 by private placement.

Wholly Owned Subsidiaries

Pyro Green-Gas Inc., Montréal, Qué.
- 90% int. in **Air Science Italia S.r.l.**, Italy.
- 100% int. in **Air Science Technologies Pvt. Ltd.**, India.
- 100% int. in **Alga-Labs Inc.**, Canada.

Investments

Beauce Gold Fields Inc., Montréal, Qué. (see Survey of Mines)
HPQ Silicon Inc., Montréal, Qué. (see separate coverage)

Financial Statistics

Periods ended:	12m Dec. 31/22[A]		12m Dec. 31/21[A]
	$000s	%Chg	$000s
Operating revenue	**19,014**	**-39**	**31,068**
Cost of sales	9,992		18,171
Research & devel. expense	2,318		2,536
General & admin expense	23,306		26,311
Operating expense	**35,616**	**-24**	**47,017**
Operating income	**(16,602)**	**n.a.**	**(15,949)**
Deprec., depl. & amort.	2,118		1,392
Finance income	118		133
Finance costs, gross	669		537
Write-downs/write-offs	(4,480)		nil
Pre-tax income	**(32,091)**	**n.a.**	**(39,172)**
Income taxes	76		(740)
Net income	**(32,167)**	**n.a.**	**(38,432)**
Cash & equivalent	3,446		12,203
Inventories	1,876		888
Accounts receivable	18,625		17,640
Current assets	27,448		38,759
Long-term investments	6,243		14,902
Fixed assets, net	3,393		3,713
Right-of-use assets	4,819		5,766
Intangibles, net	4,765		5,435
Total assets	**47,667**	**-32**	**69,771**
Bank indebtedness	992		nil
Accts. pay. & accr. liabs	10,116		10,069
Current liabilities	25,797		24,752
Long-term debt, gross	390		191
Long-term debt, net	320		108
Long-term lease liabilities	2,861		2,390
Shareholders' equity	16,869		40,769
Cash from oper. activs	**(11,129)**	**n.a.**	**(18,113)**
Cash from fin. activs	2,641		9,474
Cash from invest. activs	(368)		2,723
Net cash position	**3,446**	**-72**	**12,203**
Capital expenditures	(396)		(1,502)
	$		$
Earnings per share*	(0.19)		(0.23)
Cash flow per share*	(0.07)		(0.11)
	shs		shs
No. of shs. o/s*	173,580,395		170,125,796
Avg. no. of shs. o/s*	170,953,374		166,645,546
	%		%
Net profit margin	(169.18)		(123.70)
Return on equity	(111.62)		(76.72)
Return on assets	(53.64)		(52.54)
Foreign sales percent	37		76
No. of employees (FTEs)	116		87

* Cl.A Common
[A] Reported in accordance with IFRS

Latest Results

Periods ended:	3m Mar. 31/23[A]		3m Mar. 31/22[oA]
	$000s	%Chg	$000s
Operating revenue	2,592	-38	4,207
Net income	(6,139)	n.a.	(4,107)
	$		$
Earnings per share*	(0.03)		(0.02)

* Cl.A Common
[o] Restated
[A] Reported in accordance with IFRS

Historical Summary
(as originally stated)

Fiscal Year	Oper. Rev.	Net Inc. Bef. Disc.	EPS*
	$000s	$000s	$
2022[A]	19,014	(32,167)	(0.19)
2021[A]	31,068	(38,432)	(0.23)
2020[A]	17,775	41,768	0.28
2019[A]	4,814	(9,171)	(0.07)
2018[A]	5,030	(7,846)	(0.06)

* Cl.A Common
[A] Reported in accordance with IFRS

Q

Q.1 Q4 Inc.

Symbol - QFOR **Exchange** - TSX **CUSIP** - 74738R
Head Office - 469A King St W, Toronto, ON, M5V 1K4 **Telephone** - (647) 278-7959 **Toll-free** - (877) 545-1241
Website - www.q4inc.com
Email - ir@q4inc.com
Investor Relations - Edward Miller (877) 545-1241
Auditors - PricewaterhouseCoopers LLP C.A., Toronto, Ont.
Transfer Agents - Computershare Shareholder Services, Inc.
Employees - 555 at Apr. 24, 2023
Profile - (Ont. 2016 amalg.) Provides Q4 Capital Connect™, a capital markets communication cloud-based software platform that connects publicly listed companies, investment banks and investment managers along a variety of workflows including investor relations, corporate access, deal management and research.

Q4 Capital Connect™ provides corporate customers with critical technology infrastructure and data that may be used to support their investor relations teams through its website, virtual events, analytics and customer relationship management (CRM) products. Provides sell-side (investment banks) customers with a platform solution that enables corporate access teams to build and manage complex virtual and hybrid investor events, as well as the technology infrastructure, data and analytics to enable their customers' corporate access teams to build and manage complex investor conference schedules, and manage hundreds of concurrent meetings between public companies and investors. Provides buy-side (investment managers) customers with access to corporate information, corporate events and direct communication with issuers.

Customers have the option to purchase products on a per product basis or in tiered subscription bundles. Generates revenue from the sale of products in its platform through an annual subscription fee that is typically prepaid on an annual or quarterly basis with the majority of contracts being one to three years in length. Major channel partners of the company include S&P Global Market Intelligence, a division of **S&P Global Inc.**, New York Stock Exchange (NYSE), Level Access/eSSENTIAL Accessibility and BusinessWire, all of whom recommend the company's products to their customers.

Headquarters are in Toronto, Ont., with offices in New York, N.Y., London, U.K., and Copenhagen, Denmark.

Predecessor Detail - Name changed from Q4 Web Systems Inc., Mar. 2, 2016, following amalgamation with 1955312 Ontario Inc.

Directors - Colleen M. Johnston, chr., Toronto, Ont.; Darrell F. Heaps, pres. & CEO, Ont.; Daniel Kittredge, Conn.; Ned May, Conn.; W. Neil Murdoch, Oakville, Ont.; Julie E. Silcock, Tex.

Other Exec. Officers - Keith Reed, COO; Donna de Winter, CFO; Dorothy Arturi, chief people officer; Warren Faleiro, chief tech. officer; Lorie Coulombe, sr. v-p, mktg. & commun.; Kenneth Szeto, gen. counsel & corp. sec.

Capital Stock

	Authorized (shs.)	Outstanding (shs.)[1]
Preferred	unlimited	nil
Common	unlimited	39,960,119

[1] At Apr. 3, 2023

Normal Course Issuer Bid - The company plans to make normal course purchases of up to 2,134,343 common shares representing 10% of the public float. The bid commenced on Mar. 31, 2023, and expires on Mar. 30, 2024.

Major Shareholder - Ten Coves Capital, LP held 25.7% interest at Apr. 3, 2023.

Price Range - QFOR/TSX

Year	Volume	High	Low	Close
2022	5,027,504	$8.82	$1.88	$3.21
2021	2,755,542	$12.05	$7.90	$8.50

Recent Close: $4.02

Capital Stock Changes - During 2022, common shares were issued as follows: 273,127 on exercise of options, 225,081 on exercise of warrants, 34,344 under deferred share unit plan and 3,569 under restricted share unit plan; 378,600 common shares were repurchased under a Normal Course Issuer Bid.

Wholly Owned Subsidiaries

Kiufor Mexico, Mexico.
Q4 Denmark, ApS, Denmark.
Q4 London Limited, United Kingdom.
Q4 Software Holdings ULC, Alta.
Q4 US, LLC, Del.

Financial Statistics

Periods ended:	12m Dec. 31/22[A]		12m Dec. 31/21[A]
	US$000s	%Chg	US$000s
Operating revenue	**56,075**	**+1**	**55,388**
Cost of sales	22,889		23,800
Research & devel. expense	18,208		11,084
General & admin expense	44,938		36,154
Other operating expense	2,709		440
Operating expense	**88,744**	**+24**	**71,478**
Operating income	**(32,669)**	**n.a.**	**(16,090)**
Deprec., depl. & amort.	3,702		3,969
Finance income	72		23
Finance costs, gross	72		1,246
Pre-tax income	**(36,080)**	**n.a.**	**(26,833)**
Income taxes	289		48
Net income	**(36,369)**	**n.a.**	**(26,881)**
Cash & equivalent	29,143		63,283
Accounts receivable	9,824		9,328
Current assets	46,497		78,471
Fixed assets, net	1,209		914
Right-of-use assets	1,040		1,676
Intangibles, net	24,549		27,087
Total assets	**73,832**	**-32**	**109,117**
Accts. pay. & accr. liabs	4,354		5,457
Current liabilities	21,248		22,349
Long-term lease liabilities	513		1,273
Shareholders' equity	44,374		78,703
Cash from oper. activs	**(32,200)**	**n.a.**	**(12,360)**
Cash from fin. activs	(277)		73,620
Cash from invest. activs	(8,099)		(671)
Net cash position	**21,536**	**-66**	**63,283**
Capital expenditures	(820)		(460)
	US$		US$
Earnings per share*	(0.91)		(1.71)
Cash flow per share*	(0.81)		(0.78)
	shs		shs
No. of shs. o/s*	39,780,108		39,622,587
Avg. no. of shs. o/s*	39,752,981		15,749,813
	%		%
Net profit margin	(64.86)		(48.53)
Return on equity	(59.10)		(194.52)
Return on assets	(39.68)		(31.45)
No. of employees (FTEs)	567		528

* Common
[A] Reported in accordance with IFRS

Historical Summary
(as originally stated)

Fiscal Year	Oper. Rev. US$000s	Net Inc. Bef. Disc. US$000s	EPS* US$
2022[A]	56,075	(36,369)	(0.91)
2021[A]	55,388	(26,881)	(1.71)
2020[A]	40,381	(13,119)	(0.32)
2019[A]	22,400	(11,053)	(0.28)

* Common
[A] Reported in accordance with IFRS

Q.2 QYOU Media Inc.

Symbol - QYOU **Exchange** - TSX-VEN **CUSIP** - 77584B
Head Office - 601-154 University Ave, Toronto, ON, M5H 3Y9 **Telephone** - (416) 204-9788 **Fax** - (888) 809-0059
Website - www.qyoumedia.com
Email - curt@qyoutv.com
Investor Relations - Curt Marvis (647) 559-2700
Auditors - MNP LLP C.A., Burlington, Ont.
Lawyers - Wildeboer Dellelce LLP, Toronto, Ont.
Transfer Agents - Computershare Trust Company of Canada Inc., Toronto, Ont.
Profile - (Alta. 1993) Curates, produces and distributes content created by social media stars and digital content creators, and primarily operates in India and the U.S. Also a casual mobile games application.

Operations are organized into two segments: QYOU India and QYOU USA.

QYOU India - The company curates, produces and distributes premium content including television networks and video on demand (VOD) for cable and satellite television, over-the-top (OTT) and mobile platforms. The company has Indian channels consisting of The Q (mass entertainment in Hindi language), Q Marathi (regional content in Marathi language), Q Kahaniyan (animated content), Q Comedistaan (comedy content), Sadhguru TV and Q-GameX (live gaming). All channels are advertiser-supported and deliver digital programming from social media stars and digital video creators targeting young Indian audiences. The channels have a growing library of more than 1,300 programs and reaches more than 800,000,000 audiences via 125,000,000 television homes with partners including DD Free Dish, TATA Sky, DISH TV, SitiNetworks, Den Networks, Hathaway, and d2h and GTPL; as well as 675,000,000 OTT, mobile, app based and smart TV users via platforms including MX Player, JioTV, Snap, Chingari, Samsung TV Plus, Xiaomi MiTV and Amazon FireStick TV. The company also has an influencer marketing division in India, operating through subsidiary **Chatterbox Technologies Pvt Ltd.** (dba Chtrbox). Chtrbox enables brands to discover and collaborate with content creators, social media influencers, bloggers and passionate fans of their brand. Chtrbox also provides brands with services including micro-videos and personlized brand storytelling that would empower brands to become digital creators themselves. Also offers Q GAMESMELA, a casual mobile games application and that could be downloaded from the Google Play store for Android phone users.

QYOU USA - The company's U.S.-based influencer marketing business manages campaigns for major film studios, game publishers and other consumer brands. These contents are distributed on various large scale social platforms including TikTok, YouTube, Instagram, Snapchat and Twitter. Services offered include creative strategy, influencer deals, in-house production, media amplification and channel management.

In January 2023, the company acquired 51% interest in **Maxamtech Digital Ventures Private Limited** for an undisclosed amount. Maxamtech operates through its proprietary platform, Gaming 360, which hosts a variety of mobile gaming destinations for companies including Vodafone, Disney India, Sony, Viacom 18, Zee5, Ooredoo, Glance and SpiceJet.

Predecessor Detail - Name changed from Galleria Opportunities Ltd., Mar. 13, 2017, pursuant to reverse takeover acquisition of (old) QYOU Media Inc. and amalgamation of wholly owned 2561287 Ontario Ltd. with (old) QYOU Media (deemed acquiror); basis 1 new for 2 old shs.

Directors - Curt Marvis, co-founder & CEO, Los Angeles, Calif.; G. Scott Paterson, chr., Toronto, Ont.; Steven (Steve) Beeks, Calif.; Damian Lee, Toronto, Ont.; Raj Mishra, India; Catherine Warren, Vancouver, B.C.

Other Exec. Officers - Krishna Menon, COO; Kevin Williams, interim CFO; Jace Sparks, chief product officer; Robert N. Spiegel, corp. sec.; Glenn Ginsburg, pres., QYOU USA Inc.

Capital Stock

	Authorized (shs.)	Outstanding (shs.)[1]
Common	unlimited	456,424,962

[1] At June 5, 2023

Major Shareholder - Widely held at June 5, 2023.

Price Range - QYOU/TSX-VEN

Year	Volume	High	Low	Close
2022	64,940,181	$0.26	$0.09	$0.09
2021	396,148,823	$0.52	$0.10	$0.23
2020	154,067,761	$0.14	$0.03	$0.11
2019	46,925,668	$0.11	$0.05	$0.06
2018	45,967,339	$0.43	$0.07	$0.09

Recent Close: $0.11

Capital Stock Changes - In November 2022, public offering of 25,600,000 units (1 common share & ½ warrant) at $0.125 per unit and private placement of 1,840,000 common shares at $0.125 per share was completed. Also during 2022, common shares were issued as follows: 16,428,163 on exercise of warrants, 6,783,335 on vesting of restricted share units and 41,660 on exercise of options.

Wholly Owned Subsidiaries

QYOU Limited, Dublin, Ireland.
- 100% int. in **QYOU USA Inc.**, Del.
- 100% int. in **QYOUTV International Limited**, Ireland.

QYOU Productions Inc., Canada.

Subsidiaries

98% int. in **Chatterbox Technologies Pvt Ltd.**, Mumbai, India.
51% int. in **Maxamtech Digital Ventures Private Limited**, Pune, India.
88% int. in **QYOU Media India Pvt. Ltd.**, India.

Financial Statistics

Periods ended:	12m Dec. 31/22^A		6m Dec. 31/21^A
	$000s	%Chg	$000s
Operating revenue	**27,170**	**n.a.**	**10,311**
Salaries & benefits	5,649		2,008
General & admin expense	26,660		10,379
Stock-based compensation	3,286		2,284
Operating expense	**35,595**	**n.a.**	**14,671**
Operating income	**(8,425)**	**n.a.**	**(4,360)**
Deprec., depl. & amort.	659		132
Finance costs, gross	85		48
Write-downs/write-offs	(3,270)[1]		nil
Pre-tax income	**(11,254)**	**n.a.**	**(4,734)**
Income taxes	97		46
Net income	**(11,351)**	**n.a.**	**(4,780)**
Net inc. for equity hldrs	**(11,349)**	**n.a.**	**(4,888)**
Net inc. for non-cont. int	**(2)**	**n.a.**	**108**
Cash & equivalent	3,511		6,549
Accounts receivable	6,904		4,131
Current assets	13,529		15,027
Fixed assets, net	145		105
Right-of-use assets	361		753
Intangibles, net	916		4,398
Total assets	**16,070**	**-22**	**20,612**
Accts. pay. & accr. liabs	6,962		4,700
Current liabilities	7,697		6,070
Long-term debt, gross	65		61
Long-term debt, net	57		53
Long-term lease liabilities	164		558
Shareholders' equity	(7,848)		12,369
Non-controlling interest	(445)		(443)
Cash from oper. activs	**(4,846)**	**n.a.**	**(5,462)**
Cash from fin. activs	3,483		3,193
Cash from invest. activs	(1,768)		(381)
Net cash position	**3,511**	**-46**	**6,549**
Capital expenditures	(111)		(62)
	$		$
Earnings per share*	(0.03)		(0.01)
Cash flow per share*	(0.01)		(0.01)
	shs		shs
No. of shs. o/s*	452,087,472		401,394,314
Avg. no. of shs. o/s*	418,462,283		394,204,814
	%		%
Net profit margin	(41.78)		...
Return on equity	n.m.		...
Return on assets	(61.42)		...
Foreign sales percent	99		98

* Common
^A Reported in accordance with IFRS
[1] Pertains to goodwill impairment.

Latest Results

Periods ended:	3m Mar. 31/23^A		3m Mar. 31/22^A
	$000s	%Chg	$000s
Operating revenue	7,046	+35	5,235
Net income	(1,503)	n.a.	(2,308)
Net inc. for equity hldrs	(1,422)	n.a.	(2,225)
Net inc. for non-cont. int	(81)		(83)
	$		$
Earnings per share*	(0.00)		(0.01)

* Common
^A Reported in accordance with IFRS

Historical Summary
(as originally stated)

Fiscal Year	Oper. Rev.	Net Inc. Bef. Disc.	EPS*
	$000s	$000s	$
2022^A	27,170	(11,351)	(0.03)
2021^A1	10,311	(4,780)	(0.01)
2021^A	4,183	(7,307)	(0.02)
2020^A	2,802	(6,548)	(0.04)
2019^A	4,718	(6,123)	(0.06)

* Common
^A Reported in accordance with IFRS
[1] 6 months ended Dec. 31, 2021.

Q.3 Quantum eMotion Corp.

Symbol - QNC **Exchange** - TSX-VEN **CUSIP** - 74767K
Head Office - 209-2300 boul Alfred Nobel, Montréal, QC, H4S 2A4 **Telephone** - (514) 894-4324
Website - www.quantumemotion.com
Email - mrousseau@lvrcapital.ca
Investor Relations - Marc Rousseau (514) 886-0045
Auditors - KPMG LLP C.A., Montréal, Qué.
Lawyers - McMillan LLP, Montréal, Qué.
Transfer Agents - Computershare Trust Company of Canada Inc., Montréal, Qué.

Profile - (Ont. 2007) Developing quantum random number generator technologies, and related products including a quantum-safe messenger platform and quantum-operating blockchain wallet.

The company's quantum random number generator technological project (international patent application number PCT/CA2015/050408) provides a simple, low-cost, compact and adaptable quantum random number generator (QRNG) that exploits the built-in unpredictability of quantum mechanics to produce random numbers. The technology makes use of random signals that can be obtained from a random tunnelling of charges from one conductor to another conductor across a quantum tunnelling barrier. The random signal can be amplified and associated to a random number and association can be performed repetitively to generate a sequence of random numbers. The QRNG2 is the first commercial version of its quantum number generator capable of delivering entropy at 1.5 gigabits per second and has multiple commercial applications including mobile and Internet transactions, Internet of Things (IoT) communications, machine-to-machine connections, networking equipment, cloud-based applications and blockchain technologies.

Has been granted patents in the U.S., Russia, Europe, the People's Republic of China (PRC), Australia, Canada, Brazil and South Korea, and has patent pending applications in Thailand and India, for the use of quantum tunnelling to produce random numbers. Has also been granted patents in Europe, the U.S., Indonesia and Russia, and has patent pending applications in Australia, Brazil, India, Japan, Canada, PRC, Thailand and South Korea, for a technology developed to ensure that the random numbers are purely random and entirely based on quantum processes.

TransferTech Sherbrooke, a partnership that manages the intellectual property arising from research at the Université de Sherbrooke, holds a royalty of 5% of all future sales of commercial applications incorporating the technology. The company has an option to buy back the royalty in the future at terms and conditions to be agreed upon by both parties.

In addition, has developed Sentry-Q, a quantum-safe messenger platform designed for the secure communication of large and complex messages, including entire database structures. Sentry-Q has the potential to perform as a cloud-based solution or as a physical hardware device. Also has a patent application for a new method to operate a blockchain wallet that benefits from the protection provided by QRNG2.

Predecessor Detail - Name changed from Quantum Numbers Corp., June 14, 2021.

Directors - Dr. Edward L. (Larry) Moore, chr. & chief tech. officer, Hudson, Qué.; Dr. Francis Bellido, pres. & CEO, Qué.; Tullio Panarello, Qué.; Scott Rickards, Portsmouth, N.H.; Wayne Teeple, Ont.

Other Exec. Officers - Marc Rousseau, CFO & corp. sec.; Abder Benrabah, v-p, quality & compliance; Pierre Cardinal, v-p, devel. & commercialization

Capital Stock

	Authorized (shs.)	Outstanding (shs.)[1]
Class A Preference	unlimited	nil
Class B Preference	unlimited	nil
Class C Preference	unlimited	nil
Class D Preference	unlimited	nil
Special Non-voting	unlimited	nil
Common	unlimited	135,502,838

[1] At May 30, 2023

Major Shareholder - Widely held at May 11, 2023.

Price Range - QNC/TSX-VEN

Year	Volume	High	Low	Close
2022	183,417,117	$0.49	$0.07	$0.09
2021	189,386,762	$0.48	$0.10	$0.16
2020	47,701,237	$0.30	$0.03	$0.10
2019	21,956,408	$0.20	$0.08	$0.19
2018	56,435,427	$0.24	$0.06	$0.11

Recent Close: $0.07

Capital Stock Changes - During 2022, common shares were issued as follows: 21,240,000 on exercise of warrants and 250,000 on exercise of options.

Financial Statistics

Periods ended:	12m Dec. 31/22^A		12m Dec. 31/21^A
	$000s	%Chg	$000s
Salaries & benefits	96		28
Research & devel. expense	272		118
General & admin expense	1,260		1,141
Stock-based compensation	542		264
Operating expense	**2,170**	**+40**	**1,551**
Operating income	**(2,170)**	**n.a.**	**(1,551)**
Deprec., depl. & amort.	22		22
Finance income	77		1
Finance costs, gross	25		9
Pre-tax income	**(2,805)**	**n.a.**	**(1,563)**
Net income	**(2,805)**	**n.a.**	**(1,563)**
Cash & equivalent	2,594		2,036
Current assets	3,664		2,144
Intangibles, net	374		957
Total assets	**4,038**	**+30**	**3,101**
Accts. pay. & accr. liabs	338		334
Current liabilities	378		334
Long-term debt, gross	40		54
Long-term debt, net	nil		54
Shareholders' equity	3,660		2,711
Cash from oper. activs	**(1,618)**	**n.a.**	**(1,467)**
Cash from fin. activs	3,211		3,809
Cash from invest. activs	(21)		(1,340)
Net cash position	**2,594**	**+154**	**1,022**
	$		$
Earnings per share*	(0.02)		(0.02)
Cash flow per share*	(0.01)		(0.01)
	shs		shs
No. of shs. o/s*	135,502,838		114,012,838
Avg. no. of shs. o/s*	134,474,811		103,961,043
	%		%
Net profit margin	n.a.		n.a.
Return on equity	(88.06)		(106.58)
Return on assets	(77.88)		(82.35)

* Common
^A Reported in accordance with IFRS

Latest Results

Periods ended:	3m Mar. 31/23^A		3m Mar. 31/22^A
	$000s	%Chg	$000s
Net income	(504)	n.a.	(692)
	$		$
Earnings per share*	(0.00)		(0.00)

* Common
^A Reported in accordance with IFRS

Historical Summary
(as originally stated)

Fiscal Year	Oper. Rev.	Net Inc. Bef. Disc.	EPS*
	$000s	$000s	$
2022^A	nil	(2,805)	(0.02)
2021^A	nil	(1,563)	(0.02)
2020^A	nil	(799)	(0.01)
2019^A	nil	(663)	(0.01)
2018^A	nil	(916)	(0.02)

* Common
^A Reported in accordance with IFRS

Q.4 Quarterhill Inc.*

Symbol - QTRH **Exchange** - TSX **CUSIP** - 747713
Head Office - 1101-25 King St W, Toronto, ON, M5L 2A1 **Telephone** - (416) 247-9652
Website - www.quarterhill.com
Email - ir@quarterhill.com
Investor Relations - Dave Mason (416) 247-9652
Auditors - Ernst & Young LLP C.A., Toronto, Ont.
Bankers - Canadian Imperial Bank of Commerce, Ottawa, Ont.; Royal Bank of Canada, Ottawa, Ont.
Lawyers - Norton Rose Fulbright Canada LLP, Ottawa, Ont.
Transfer Agents - Computershare Trust Company of Canada Inc., Toronto, Ont.
FP500 Revenue Ranking - 561
Employees - 604 at Dec. 31, 2022

Profile - (Can. 2007; orig. Alta., 1992) Provides tolling and enforcement systems and services in the intelligent transportation systems (ITS) industry.

Through wholly owned **Electronic Transaction Consultants, LLC** (ETC), **International Road Dynamics Inc.** (IRD) and IRD's subsidiaries provides systems, products, solutions and services to the ITS industry. ETC provides smart mobility solutions, including intelligent transportation systems, electronic tolling and congestion management (back-office solutions, and roadside solutions) and related operations and maintenance services to governmental toll authorities and contractors in the U.S. ETC offers customers mobility solutions through its riteSuite™ software platform, which include all-electronic tolling, dynamic pricing, agency interoperability, hosted mobility solutions and machine learning. IRD's portfolio of integrated hardware and software solutions, which are centered on detection, measurement and analysis of transportation metrics such as weigh-in-motion and vehicle measurement technologies that detect, classify and weigh vehicles at highway speeds are offered to government transportation agencies, traffic engineering consultants and operators, city and municipal agencies, concessionaires and industrial, mining and transportation service companies worldwide. IRD's automated systems are used for commercial vehicle operations at truck weigh stations, border crossings, highway traffic data collection, smart cities and highway toll collection systems.

Holds 10% interest in **Wi-LAN Inc.**, which develops, acquires and commercializes patented technologies, with patents licensed to more than 350 companies.

Recent Merger and Acquisition Activity

Status: completed **Announced:** June 15, 2023
Quarterhill Inc. sold its intellectual property licensing business, Wi-LAN Inc., for gross proceeds of up to $71,400,000. On closing, Wi-LAN would be owned 10% by Quarterhill and Owlpoint IP Opportunities JVF LP, a joint venture between Arena Investors, LP and Owlpoint Capital Management, LLC, would hold 90%. Consideration consists of $48,000,00 in cash, $8,000,000 as an earnout and $15,400,000 pursuant to an unsecured promissory note, which earn out and note are payable on Wi-LAN achieving certain revenue milestones. Quarterhill's 10% ownership interest can be repurchased by Wi-LAN for between $13,000,000 and $16,000,000 subject to Wi-LAN meeting certain revenue milestones. Wi-LAN owns, directly or indirectly, more than 3,374 patents and patent applications in many different countries, for many of which it has granted licences to more than 350 companies in many technology markets around the world.

Predecessor Detail - Name changed from Wi-LAN Inc., June 1, 2017.

Directors - Rusty Lewis, chr., Pa.; Roxanne Anderson, Ottawa, Ont.; William F. (Bill) Morris, Toronto, Ont.; Chuck Myers, Calif.; Pamela Steer, Toronto, Ont.; Anna M. Tosto, Ottawa, Ont.

Other Exec. Officers - John K. Gillberry, interim pres. & interim CEO; James M. Childress, chief tech. officer; Prashant Watchmaker, sr. v-p, gen. counsel & corp. sec.; Kyle Chriest, v-p, corp. fin. & interim CFO; Kevin Holbert, pres. & CEO, Electronic Transaction Consultants, LLC; Rish Malhotra, pres. & CEO, International Road Dynamics Inc.; Andrew Parolin, pres. & CEO, Wi-LAN Inc.

Capital Stock

	Authorized (shs.)	Outstanding (shs.)[1]
Special Preferred	6,351	nil
Preferred	unlimited	nil
Common	unlimited	114,705,169

[1] At June 30, 2023

Options - At Dec. 31, 2022, options were outstanding to purchase 8,669,951 common shares at prices ranging from $1.33 to $2.99 per share (weighted average exercise price of $2.15 per share) with a weighted average remaining term of 4.07 years.

Major Shareholder - Widely held at Mar. 21, 2023.

Price Range - QTRH/TSX

Year	Volume	High	Low	Close
2022	33,860,764	$2.72	$1.45	$1.58
2021	47,317,680	$3.11	$2.17	$2.70
2020	73,099,465	$2.87	$1.30	$2.56
2019	32,500,634	$1.92	$1.17	$1.67
2018	74,572,129	$2.44	$1.16	$1.33

Recent Close: $1.47

Capital Stock Changes - During 2022, common shares were issued as follows: 608,335 on exercise of options, 131,316 under restricted share unit plan and 19,196 under performance share unit plan.

Dividends

QTRH com omitted [1]

$0.0125	Apr. 11/23	$0.0125	Jan. 9/23
$0.0125	Oct. 7/22	$0.0125	July 8/22

Paid in 2023: $0.025 2022: $0.05 2021: $0.05

[1] Quarterly divd normally payable in July/23 has been omitted.

Long-Term Debt - At Dec. 31, 2022, outstanding long-term debt totaled $77,671,000 ($29,292,000 current and net of $2,013,000 debt issuance costs) and consisted of borrowings under a $50,000,000 revolving term credit facility, bearing interest at 6.91%; and $48,379,000 6% subordinated convertible debentures due Oct. 30, 2026, convertible into common shares at $3.80 per share.

Wholly Owned Subsidiaries

Quarterhill ITS Inc., Canada.

- 100% int. in **International Road Dynamics Inc.**, Saskatoon, Sask.
  - 100% int. in **Icoms Detections S.A.**, Belgium.
  - 100% int. in **International Road Dynamics Europe GmbH**, Germany.
  - 100% int. in **PAT Traffic Ltda.**, Santiago, Chile.
  - 100% int. in **Sensor Line GmbH**, Germany.
  - 100% int. in **VDS Verkehrstechnik GmbH**, Löbau, Germany.
  - 50% int. in **Xuzhou-PAT Control Technologies Limited**, Xuzhou, Jiangsu, People's Republic of China.
- 100% int. in **Quarterhill USA, Inc.**, Del.
  - 100% int. in **Electronic Transaction Consultants, LLC**, Richardson, Tex.

Investments

10% int. in **Wi-LAN Inc.**, Ottawa, Ont.

Note: The preceding list includes only the major related companies in which interests are held.

Financial Statistics

Periods ended:	12m Dec. 31/22[A]		12m Dec. 31/21[A]
	$000s	%Chg	$000s
Operating revenue	**305,690**	**+143**	**125,695**
Cost of sales	188,154		88,260
Research & devel. expense	2,539		2,372
General & admin expense	51,640		31,384
Stock-based compensation	1,875		1,955
Operating expense	**244,208**	**+97**	**123,971**
Operating income	**61,482**	**n.m.**	**1,724**
Deprec., depl. & amort.	29,612		23,379
Finance income	1,083		164
Finance costs, gross	10,024		2,328
Pre-tax income	**13,819**	**n.a.**	**(26,729)**
Income taxes	11,053		(4,546)
Net income	**2,766**	**n.a.**	**(22,183)**
Cash & equivalent	67,907		72,597
Inventories	13,671		13,731
Accounts receivable	23,277		30,176
Current assets	159,999		161,102
Long-term investments	7,751		7,458
Fixed assets, net	6,926		5,694
Right-of-use assets	10,312		7,761
Intangibles, net	197,720		204,420
Total assets	**411,944**	**-4**	**427,195**
Accts. pay. & accr. liabs.	45,630		40,584
Current liabilities	88,490		56,044
Long-term debt, gross	77,671		108,108
Long-term debt, net	48,379		104,927
Long-term lease liabilities	9,655		5,626
Shareholders' equity	257,660		241,116
Cash from oper. activs.	**39,613**	**n.a.**	**(13,340)**
Cash from fin. activs.	(42,888)		108,263
Cash from invest. activs.	(10,298)		(158,091)
Net cash position	**66,357**	**-6**	**70,746**
Capital expenditures	(2,943)		(1,149)
Capital disposals	234		117
	$		$
Earnings per share*	0.02		(0.19)
Cash flow per share*	0.35		(0.12)
Cash divd. per share*	0.05		0.05
	shs		shs
No. of shs. o/s*	114,639,700		113,880,853
Avg. no. of shs. o/s*	114,389,608		114,013,610
	%		%
Net profit margin	0.90		(17.65)
Return on equity	1.11		(8.65)
Return on assets	1.14		(5.54)
Foreign sales percent	99		98
No. of employees (FTEs)	604		562

* Common
[A] Reported in accordance with IFRS

Latest Results

Periods ended:	6m June 30/23[A]		6m June 30/22[oA]
	$000s	%Chg	$000s
Operating revenue	90,180	+17	77,007
Net inc. bef. disc. opers.	(25,960)	n.a.	(30,221)
Income from disc. opers.	(22,174)		62,790
Net income	(48,134)	n.a.	32,569
	$		$
Earns. per sh. bef. disc. opers.*	(0.23)		(0.26)
Earnings per share*	(0.42)		0.29

* Common
[o] Restated
[A] Reported in accordance with IFRS

Historical Summary
(as originally stated)

Fiscal Year	Oper. Rev.	Net Inc. Bef. Disc.	EPS*
	$000s	$000s	$
2022[A]	305,690	2,766	0.02
2021[A]	125,695	(22,183)	(0.19)
2020[A]	144,526	4,428	0.04
	US$000s	US$000s	US$
2019[B]	146,720	10,528	0.09
2018[B]	77,401	(49,120)	(0.41)

* Common
[A] Reported in accordance with IFRS
[B] Reported in accordance with U.S. GAAP

Q.5 Quebecor Inc.*

Symbol - QBR.B **Exchange -** TSX **CUSIP -** 748193
Head Office - 612 rue Saint-Jacques, Montréal, QC, H3C 4M8 **Telephone -** (514) 380-1999 **Toll-free -** (866) 380-1999 **Fax -** (514) 954-0052
Website - www.quebecor.com
Email - hugues.simard@quebecor.com
Investor Relations - Hugues Simard (866) 380-1999
Auditors - Ernst & Young LLP C.A., Montréal, Qué.
Transfer Agents - TSX Trust Company
FP500 Revenue Ranking - 125
Employees - 8,832 at Dec. 31, 2022

Profile - (Que. 1965, via letters patent) Operates telecommunication and media businesses primarily through wholly owned **Quebecor Media Inc.** with activities in mobile and wireline telecommunications; Internet access; television; over-the-top (OTT) video; business telecommunications solutions; broadcasting; soundstage and equipment rental; audiovisual content production and distribution; newspaper publishing and distribution; digital news and entertainment platforms; book and magazine publishing and distribution; music production and distribution; out-of-home advertising; operation and management of a world-class arena and entertainment venues; ownership and management of hockey teams; and production, management and promotion of concerts and sporting and cultural events.

Telecommunications

Wholly owned **Vidéotron Ltée** offers wireline (cable), mobile telephony, over-the-top (OTT) video and business telecommunications services. Vidéotron's wireline network covers about 83% of Quebec's 4,100,000 residential premises and serves 2,600,000 customers. Wireline services include Internet access; digital multiplatform television, including video-on-demand, pay-per-view and pay television; wireline telephony; and Helix, a platform which offers Internet, Internet Protocol television (IPTV) and home automation services. Mobile services are offered to more than 3,500,000 customers across Quebec and in Ottawa, Ont., under the Vidéotron and Fizz brands, and in Ontario, Alberta and British Columbia under the Freedom Mobile brand, and include mobile Internet access, wireless voice and enhanced voice features, text and email, global voice and data roaming, and advanced wireless solutions for businesses. OTT video services, marketed under the Club illico and Vrai names, are subscription-based platforms which offer a varied selection of unlimited, on-demand French language content. Business telecommunications solutions include mobile telephony, Internet access, telephony and television solutions, as well as fibre connectivity, private network connectivity, Wi-Fi, managed services and security solutions which are provided to small, medium and large-size businesses as well as telecommunications carriers.

Media

Subsidiary **TVA Group Inc.** owns and operates six of the 10 television stations that make up the Réseau TVA (TVA Network) in Quebec, consisting of CFTM-TV (Montreal), CFCM-TV (Quebec City), CHLT-TV (Sherbrooke), CHEM-TV (Trois-Rivieres), CFER-TV (Rimouski-Matane-Sept-Iles) and CJPM-TV (Saguenay/Lac St-Jean), and a portfolio of specialty channels. TVA holds interests in the other four stations in the TVA Network through affiliates. In addition to linear television, TVA Network and the specialty channels broadcast on-demand and stream content over multiplatform and mobile applications. TVA also provides commercial production and custom publishing services. TVA owns MELS, a provider of soundstage, mobile and equipment rental, post-production, visual effects, virtual production, dubbing, subtitling and described video services to the film and television industries. TVA also produces and distributes television programs, movies and television series for the world market. TVA also publishes French- and English-language magazines, available in print and digitally, which cover various categories, including show business, television, fashion and beauty, food, travel and lifestyle.

Wholly owned **MediaQMI Inc.** publishes two paid daily newspapers, Le Journal de Montréal and Le Journal de Québec. Newspaper content are available through traditional print format and related websites.

Wholly owned **NumériQ Inc.** creates digital platforms and content for the company as wells as for external clients. NumériQ also operates a number of other digital brands, including Le Guide de l'auto, Le sac de chips, Pèse sur Start, Silo 57 and 24heures.ca. In addition, owns QUB radio, an online and mobile audio platform with a live radio stream and a library of podcasts; and QUB, an online and mobile platform which consolidates all the company's live and on-demand news and entertainment content in a customizable feed based on user interest.

This segment is also engaged in commercial printing of newspapers from a facility in Mirabel, Que., serving the company and third parties; distribution of newspapers and magazines to dealers and households; and out-of-home advertising through installation, maintenance and management of out-of-home advertisement, including on transit and bus shelters. In addition, this segment includes QMI Agency, a news agency that provides content to all Quebecor Media properties; Quebecor Media Expertise, which offers integrated, diversified and complete advertising services; Quebecor Content, which contributes to the creation, development, acquisition and distribution of television content and formats; and Elmire, a digital marketing agency.

Sports and Entertainment

This segment includes the management and operation of the Videotron Centre under an agreement between Quebecor Media and Quebec City for usage and naming rights to the arena through 2040. In addition, owns Théâtre Capitole, a performance venue in Quebec City. Also operates Gestev, which produces, promotes and manages live shows and various sporting, cultural and corporate events. Gestev also manages Baie de Beauport, a beach in Quebec City; Cabaret du Casino de Montréal, a multipurpose hall; and Théâtre du Casino Lac-Leamy in Gatineau. This segment also owns and manages two Quebec Major Junior Hockey League (QMJHL) teams: Armada de Blainville-Boisbriand (73.3%) and Remparts de Québec (100%). Book distribution and publishing are conducted through wholly owned **CEC Publishing Inc.**, which publishes academic books; wholly owned **Sogides Group Inc.**, which publishes general literature through its 18 publishing houses; and wholly owned **Messageries A.D.P. Inc.**, which distributes physical and digital books. This segment also creates and produces music recordings, videos, live performances, shows and concerts through the Disques Musicor, MP3 Disques, Audiogram and Musicor Spectacles divisions.

In February 2023, the company announced the discontinuation of its music streaming platform, QUB musique, which was launched in May 2020 as a Quebec alternative to Spotify and Apple Music. QUB musique would cease its activities to merge with the French online music platform, Qobuz.

On Feb. 16, 2023, the company announced the elimination of 240 positions at **TVA Group Inc.**, **NumériQ Inc.**, Quebecor Media Expertise and Quebecor Content, including 140 positions at TVA Group. The positions represented 10% of the combined workforce of the four entities.

In January 2023, the company acquired spectrum licences in the 600 MHz band in Manitoba and in the 3500 MHz band in Quebec for $10,000,000. The acquisition was made in the auction of residual spectrum licences that concluded on Jan. 25, 2023.

Periods ended:	12m Dec. 31/22	12m Dec. 31/21
Wireless subscribers	1,710,400	1,601,900
Digital cable subscribers	1,396,100	1,418,600
Internet subscribers	1,904,200	1,840,800
Cable telephony lines	751,200	824,900

Recent Merger and Acquisition Activity

Status: completed **Revised:** Apr. 3, 2023
UPDATE: The transaction was completed. PREVIOUS: Rogers Communications Inc. and Shaw Communications Inc. announced an agreement to sell Shaw's Freedom Mobile Inc. to Quebecor Inc. for an enterprise value of $2.85 billion. The agreement provides for the sale of all of Freedom branded wireless and Internet customers as well as all of Freedom's infrastructure, spectrum and retail locations. It also includes a long-term undertaking by Shaw and Rogers to provide Quebecor transport services (including backhaul and backbone) and roaming services. The transaction requires approvals under the Competition Act and the approval of the Minister of Innovation, Science and Industry (ISED) and would close substantially concurrent with closing of Rogers acquisition of Shaw. Aug. 12, 2022 - The companies entered into definitive agreement for the sale of Freedom Mobile to Quebecor subsidiary Videotron Ltd. Oct. 27, 2022 - A settlement was not reached with the Commissioner of Competition to eliminate concerns on the proposed merger of Rogers and Shaw, including the sale of Freedom Mobile to Videotron. As a result, the proposed transactions would enter a hearing before the Competition Tribunal. Dec. 31, 2022 - The Competition Tribunal dismissed the Commissioner of Competition's application to block Rogers' proposed acquisition of Shaw and the divestiture of Freedom Mobile to Videotron. The only required regulatory approval remaining is the approval from the Minister of Innovation, Science and Industry for the transfer of Freedom Mobile's wireless spectrum licences to Videotron. Jan. 24, 2023 - The Federal Court of Appeal dismissed the Commissioner of Competition's appeal of the Competition Tribunal decision's on Dec. 31, 2022, which rejected the Commissioner's challenge of the proposed acquisition of Freedom Mobile and subsequent acquisition of Shaw by Rogers. Jan. 30, 2023 - The outside date to close the transaction was extended to Feb. 17, 2023. Feb. 17, 2023 - The outside date to close the transaction was further extended to Mar. 31, 2023. Mar. 31, 2023 - Minister of Innovation, Science and Industry provided final approval to transfer Shaw's spectrum licences to Videotron.

Status: completed **Announced:** July 28, 2022
Quebecor Inc. acquired VMedia Inc., a provider of VoIP telephone, Internet, IPTV and home security services in Canada. Terms were not disclosed.

Directors - The Rt. Hon. Brian Mulroney, chr., Montréal, Qué.; Sylvie Lalande†, v-chr., Lachute, Qué.; Chantal Bélanger, Blainville, Qué.; André P. Brosseau, Montréal, Qué.; Michèle Colpron, Saint-Lambert, Qué.; Lise Croteau, Mont-Tremblant, Qué.; Érik Péladeau, Sainte-Adèle, Qué.; Jean B. Péladeau, Montréal, Qué.

Other Exec. Officers - Pierre Karl Péladeau, pres. & CEO; Hugues Simard, CFO; Jonathan Lee Hickey, sr. v-p, legal affairs & corp. secretariat; Véronique Mercier, v-p, commun.; Jean-François Parent, v-p & treas.; Denis Sabourin, v-p & contr.; Sophie Riendeau, dir., legal affairs & corp. sec.

† Lead director

Capital Stock

	Authorized (shs.)	Outstanding (shs.)[1]
Class A	unlimited	76,970,888
Class B	unlimited	153,965,202

[1] At Aug. 1, 2023

Class A - Entitled to 10 votes per share and to elect 75% of the directors, unless the number of class A shares outstanding is less than 12.5% of the total number of class A shares and class B shares outstanding. In that event, the holders of class A shares will vote together with the holders of the class B shares to elect 75% of the directors, with the holders of class A shares entitled to 10 votes per share and the holders of class B shares entitled to one vote per share.

If the Péladeau Group or an acceptable successor does not own a number of class A shares equal to at least 40% of all class A shares then outstanding, or does not own at least 32,000,000 class A shares, then the class A shares shall carry one vote per share and all members of the board of directors shall be elected by the holders of the class A shares and class B shares voting together as a single class.

The company defined an "acceptable successor" as any person or persons who acquired class A shares from the Péladeau Group or from another acceptable successor (i) at a price not exceeding the then average market price of the class A shares or the class B shares (whichever is lower), plus the margin of variation determined in accordance with the provisions of the Securities Act (Quebec) governing takeover bids at the time of acquisition (presently 15%); or (ii) in a transaction which includes the making of a takeover bid for class B shares, at a price equal to that paid for the class A shares, on a share for share basis, and for all class B shares or that number of class B voting shares equal to the number of class A shares acquired in such transactions or series of transactions multiplied by 10.

Each class A share may, at any time, at the holder's option, be converted into one class B share.

Class B - Entitled to one vote per share and to elect 25% of the directors. Class B shareholders are also entitled to participate, in certain circumstances (as outlined above), in a takeover bid for the class A shares, on the same conditions as the holders of the class A shares.

Options - At Dec. 31, 2022, options were outstanding to purchase 3,693,733 class B shares at a weighted average exercise price of $29.54 per share with a weighted average remaining contractual life of 7.9 years.

Normal Course Issuer Bid - The company plans to make normal course purchases of up to 1,000,000 class A shares representing 1.3% of the total outstanding. The bid commenced on Aug. 15, 2023, and expires on Aug. 14, 2024.

The company plans to make normal course purchases of up to 2,000,000 class B shares representing 1.3% of the total outstanding. The bid commenced on Aug. 15, 2023, and expires on Aug. 14, 2024.

Major Shareholder - Pierre Karl Péladeau held 75.74% interest at Mar. 7, 2023.

Price Range - QBR.B/TSX

Year	Volume	High	Low	Close
2022	164,920,504	$32.72	$23.85	$30.20
2021	154,003,987	$36.26	$27.33	$28.55
2020	124,756,216	$34.55	$25.00	$32.76
2019	130,759,132	$33.99	$28.51	$33.14
2018	121,487,839	$29.89	$22.88	$28.74

Recent Close: $31.01

Capital Stock Changes - During 2022, 8,321,451 class B shares were repurchased under a Normal Course Issuer Bid.

Dividends

QBR.A cl A M.V. Ra $1.20 pa Q est. Apr. 5, 2022
Prev. Rate: $1.10 est. Apr. 6, 2021
Prev. Rate: $0.80 est. Apr. 21, 2020
QBR.B cl B S.V. Ra $1.20 pa Q est. Apr. 5, 2022
Prev. Rate: $1.10 est. Apr. 6, 2021
Prev. Rate: $0.80 est. Apr. 21, 2020

Long-Term Debt - Outstanding at Dec. 31, 2022:

4% conv. debs. due 2024[1]	$150,000,000
Quebecor Media Inc.	
5.75% sr. notes due 2023	1,152,100,000
TVA Group Inc.	
Revolv. credit facility due 2023[2]	9,000,000
Vidéotron Ltée	
Revolv. credit facility due 2026[3]	77,500,000
Sr. notes due to 2031[4]	5,279,100,000
Less: Fair value hedge	5,600,000
Less: Fin. fees, net of amort.	33,300,000
	6,628,800,000
Less: Current portion	1,161,100,000
	5,467,700,000

[1] Convertible into class B shares at a floor price of $24.62 per share and a ceiling price of $30.77 per share. The cap and floor conversion price features are presented as embedded derivatives in other liabilities.

[2] Bears interest at banker's acceptance rate, Canadian or U.S. prime plus a variable spread.

[3] Bears interest at banker's acceptance rate, SOFR, Canadian or U.S. prime plus a variable spread.

[4] Bear interest at rates ranging from 3.125% to 5.75%.

Principal payments on long-term debt, excluding convertible debentures, were reported as follows:

2023	$1,161,100,000
2024	813,200,000
2025	400,000,000
2026	452,200,000
2027	813,200,000
Thereafter	2,877,700,000

Note - In February 2023, maturity of TVA's revolving credit facility was extended to February 2024.

Wholly Owned Subsidiaries

Quebecor Media Inc., Montréal, Qué.
- 100% int. in **CEC Publishing Inc.**, Qué.
- 100% int. in **Event Management Gestev Inc.**, Beaupré, Qué.
- 100% int. in **MediaQMI Inc.**, Canada.
- 100% int. in **NumériQ Inc.**, Canada.
- 100% int. in **QMI Spectacles Inc.**, Qué.
- 100% int. in **Quebecor Media Network Inc.**, Canada.
- 100% int. in **Quebecor Media Printing (2015) Inc.**, Canada.
- 100% int. in **Québecor Sports et Divertissements Inc.**, Canada.
- 100% int. in **Select Music Inc.**, Canada.
- 100% int. in **Sogides Group Inc.**, Canada.
- 68.37% int. in **TVA Group Inc.**, Montréal, Qué. Holds 99.97% voting interest. (see separate coverage)
- 100% int. in **Vidéotron Ltée**, Montréal, Qué.
  - 100% int. in **Fizz Mobile & Internet Inc.**, Qué.
  - 100% int. in **Freedom Mobile Inc.**, Toronto, Ont.
  - 100% int. in **VMedia Inc.**, Toronto, Ont.

Note: The preceding list includes only the major related companies in which interests are held.

Financial Statistics

Periods ended:	12m Dec. 31/22[A]		12m Dec. 31/21[oA]
	$000s	%Chg	$000s
Operating revenue	**4,531,900**	**0**	**4,554,400**
Salaries & benefits	696,900		685,000
Other operating expense	1,900,500		1,896,200
Operating expense	**2,597,400**	**+1**	**2,581,200**
Operating income	**1,934,500**	**-2**	**1,973,200**
Deprec., depl. & amort.	767,700		783,800
Finance costs, gross	323,000		333,400
Write-downs/write-offs	(3,700)		(1,500)
Pre-tax income	**810,100**	**+3**	**785,400**
Income taxes	213,400		197,000
Net inc bef disc ops, eqhldrs	599,700		578,400
Net inc bef disc ops, NCI	(3,000)		10,000
Net income	**596,700**	**+1**	**588,400**
Net inc. for equity hldrs	**599,700**	**+4**	**578,400**
Net inc. for non-cont. int	**(3,000)**	**n.a.**	**10,000**
Cash & equivalent	45,900		227,100
Inventories	406,200		282,600
Accounts receivable	840,700		745,100
Current assets	1,810,100		1,523,500
Long-term investments	151,000		159,300
Fixed assets, net	2,897,600		3,058,700
Right-of-use assets	155,400		152,300
Intangibles, net	5,001,000		5,062,600
Total assets	**10,625,300**	**-1**	**10,763,000**
Bank indebtedness	10,100		nil
Accts. pay. & accr. liabs	932,800		846,100
Current liabilities	2,534,800		1,473,100
Long-term debt, gross	6,628,800		6,674,400
Long-term debt, net	5,467,700		6,617,900
Long-term lease liabilities	149,200		147,100
Shareholders' equity	1,357,300		1,255,600
Non-controlling interest	126,200		123,200
Cash from oper. activs	**1,262,700**	**+7**	**1,182,600**
Cash from fin. activs	(812,600)		281,900
Cash from invest. activs	(631,300)		(1,374,100)
Net cash position	**45,900**	**-80**	**227,100**
Capital expenditures	(395,100)		(429,300)
Capital disposals	7,000		7,700
Unfunded pension liability	n.a.		59,300
Pension fund surplus	119,300		n.a.
	$		$
Earnings per share*	2.55		2.38
Cash flow per share*	5.37		4.86
Cash divd. per share*	1.20		1.10
	shs		shs
No. of shs. o/s*	230,936,090		239,257,541
Avg. no. of shs. o/s*	235,200,000		243,500,000
	%		%
Net profit margin	13.17		12.92
Return on equity	45.90		48.85
Return on assets	7.80		8.13
No. of employees (FTEs)	8,832		9,172

* Class A & B
[o] Restated
[A] Reported in accordance with IFRS

Latest Results

Periods ended:	3m Mar. 31/23[A]		3m Mar. 31/22[A]
	$000s	%Chg	$000s
Operating revenue	1,115,600	+3	1,088,000
Net income	113,500	-3	117,100
Net inc. for equity hldrs	120,900	0	121,400
Net inc. for non-cont. int	(7,400)		(4,300)
	$		$
Earnings per share*	0.52		0.51

* Class A & B
[A] Reported in accordance with IFRS

Historical Summary
(as originally stated)

Fiscal Year	Oper. Rev.	Net Inc. Bef. Disc.	EPS*
	$000s	$000s	$
2022[A]	4,531,900	596,700	2.55
2021[A]	4,554,400	588,400	2.38
2020[A]	4,317,800	584,200	2.28
2019[A]	4,293,800	560,800	2.17
2018[A]	4,181,000	435,400	1.66

* Class A & B
[A] Reported in accordance with IFRS

Q.6 Queen's Road Capital Investment Ltd.

Symbol - QRC **Exchange** - TSX **CUSIP** - G7315B
Head Office - Cheung Kong Centre, 2 Queen's Road Central, Suite 2006, Hong Kong, People's Republic of China **Overseas Tel** - 852-2759-2022
Website - www.queensrdcapital.com
Email - info@queensrdcapital.com
Investor Relations - Alex Granger 852-2759-2022
Auditors - KPMG LLP C.A., Vancouver, B.C.
Lawyers - Fang & Associates, Vancouver, B.C.
Transfer Agents - Computershare Trust Company of Canada Inc., Vancouver, B.C.
Profile - (Cayman Islands 2020; orig. B.C., 2011) Invests in equity and debt of privately held and publicly traded resource companies.
Investments include **NexGen Energy Ltd.**, which holds uranium interests in Saskatchewan and Nunavut; **IsoEnergy Ltd.**, which holds uranium prospects in Saskatchewan and Nunavut; **Adriatic Metals plc**, which holds Vares silver project in Bosnia and Herzegovina; **Los Andes Copper Ltd.**, which holds the Vizcachitas copper-molybdenum project in Putaendo, Chile; **Contango ORE, Inc.**, which holds an interest in Peak Gold project in Alaska; **Challenger Exploration Ltd.**, holds Hualilan gold project in Argentina and El Guayabo gold-copper project in Ecuador; and **Osisko Green Acquisition Ltd.**, a Special Purpose Acquisition Corporation.
At Nov. 30, 2022, the fair value of investment portfolio totaled $216,112,823 compared with $196,751,187 at Aug. 31, 2022.
Predecessor Detail - Name changed from Lithion Energy Corp., Feb. 5, 2020, pursuant to change of business from a resource company to an investment company.
Directors - Warren P. Gilman, chr. & CEO, Hong Kong, Hong Kong, People's Republic of China; Alex Granger, pres., Hong Kong, Hong Kong, People's Republic of China; Peter Chau, Hong Kong, Hong Kong, People's Republic of China; Michael (Mike) Cowin, B.C.; Donald J. (Don) Roberts, Hong Kong, Hong Kong, People's Republic of China
Other Exec. Officers - Vicki Cook, CFO; Monita Farris, corp. sec.

Capital Stock

	Authorized (shs.)	Outstanding (shs.)[1]	Par
Common	5,000,000,000	452,266,991	$0.001

[1] At Jan. 13, 2023

Normal Course Issuer Bid - The company plans to make normal course purchases of up to 22,126,121 common shares representing 5% of the total outstanding. The bid commenced on Nov. 22, 2022, and expires on Nov. 21, 2023.
Major Shareholder - Wyloo Metals Pty Ltd. held 25.3% interest, Corom Pty Ltd. held 15.8% interest and BBRC International Pte Ltd. held 13.5% interest at Nov. 25, 2022.

Price Range - QRC/TSX

Year	Volume	High	Low	Close
2022	10,222,186	$0.90	$0.60	$0.68
2021	11,261,875	$0.94	$0.60	$0.78
2020	15,590,208	$0.79	$0.30	$0.77
2019	7,046,523	$0.47	$0.05	$0.47
2018	2,959,973	$0.14	$0.05	$0.06

Recent Close: $0.62
Capital Stock Changes - In February 2022, private placement of 156,250,000 common shares was completed at Cdn$0.64 per share. Also during fiscal 2022, common shares were issued as follows: 8,000,000 on exercise of options and 4,393,303 under dividend reinvestment plan; 2,339,578 common shares were returned to treasury.

Dividends

QRC com N.S.R. **
Listed Jul 6/22.
$0.017................. Nov. 17/22 $0.015**i**............ Nov. 19/21
Paid in 2023: n.a. 2022: $0.017 2021: $0.015**i**

com special N.S.R. **
Delisted Jul 6/22.
$0.015**i**................ Nov. 19/21
** Reinvestment Option **i** Initial Payment

Wholly Owned Subsidiaries

QRC Nexgen Investment Ltd., Cayman Islands.
Note: The preceding list includes only the major related companies in which interests are held.

Financial Statistics

Periods ended:	12m Aug. 31/22[A]		12m Aug. 31/21[A]
	US$000s	%Chg	US$000s
Total revenue	**8,498**	**-88**	**71,392**
General & admin. expense	3,322		1,963
Stock-based compensation	7,532		2,449
Operating expense	**10,854**	**+146**	**4,412**
Operating income	**(2,356)**	**n.a.**	**66,980**
Deprec. & amort.	78		nil
Finance costs, gross	683		nil
Write-downs/write-offs	nil		19
Pre-tax income	**(3,482)**	**n.a.**	**67,025**
Net income	**(3,482)**	**n.a.**	**67,025**
Cash & equivalent	34,509		2,158
Accounts receivable	721		621
Current assets	35,341		2,829
Long-term investments	196,751		146,396
Right-of-use assets	482		n.a.
Total assets	**232,574**	**+56**	**149,225**
Accts. pay. & accr. liabs	1,000		173
Current liabilities	1,181		173
Long-term lease liabilities	316		n.a.
Shareholders' equity	231,077		149,052
Cash from oper. activs	**638**	**+2**	**628**
Cash from fin. activs	77,676		nil
Cash from invest. activs	(45,614)		(23,565)
Net cash position	**34,509**	**n.m.**	**2,158**
	US$		US$
Earnings per share*	(0.01)		0.24
Cash flow per share*	0.00		0.00
Cash divd. per share*	$0.02		$nil
	shs		shs
No. of shs. o/s*	443,556,376		277,252,651
Avg. no. of shs. o/s*	366,017,026		277,252,651
	%		%
Net profit margin	(40.97)		93.88
Return on equity	(1.83)		58.28
Return on assets	(1.47)		58.11

* Common
[A] Reported in accordance with IFRS

Latest Results

Periods ended:	3m Nov. 30/22[A]		3m Nov. 30/21[A]
	US$000s	%Chg	US$000s
Total revenue	2,589	-82	14,551
Net income	459	-97	13,887
	US$		US$
Earnings per share*	0.00		0.05

* Common
[A] Reported in accordance with IFRS

Historical Summary
(as originally stated)

Fiscal Year	Total Rev.	Net Inc. Bef. Disc.	EPS*
	US$000s	US$000s	US$
2022[A]	8,498	(3,482)	(0.01)
2021[A]	71,392	67,025	0.24
	$000s	$000s	$
2020[A]	22,357	6,667	0.04
2019[A]	nil	(1,252)	(0.04)
2018[A]	nil	(247)	(0.01)

* Common
[A] Reported in accordance with IFRS

Q.7 Quest PharmaTech Inc.

Symbol - QPT **Exchange** - TSX-VEN **CUSIP** - 74836M
Head Office - 8123 Roper Rd NW, Edmonton, AB, T6E 6S4 **Telephone** - (780) 448-1400 **Fax** - (780) 416-0324
Website - www.questpharmatech.com
Email - madi@questpharmatech.com
Investor Relations - Dr. Ragupathy Madiyalakan (780) 448-1400 ext. 204
Auditors - Kingston Ross Pasnak LLP C.A., Edmonton, Alta.
Bankers - The Toronto-Dominion Bank
Lawyers - Miller Thomson LLP, Edmonton, Alta.
Transfer Agents - Computershare Trust Company of Canada Inc., Toronto, Ont.
Profile - (Alta. 1996) Developing antibody MAb AR9.6 for targeted cancer therapy applications and holds investments in pharmaceutical companies.
MAb AR9.6 is an antibody licensed from the University of Nebraska that is used against truncated O-glycans on MUC16 for targeted cancer therapy applications. The potential cancer targets include pancreatic, colon, leukemia, ovarian and breast cancer. Also developing SonoLight, a photodynamic therapy technology for oncology and dermatology applications.
Investments include 42.52% interest in **OncoQuest Inc.**, which develops combinatorial immunotherapy products for the treatment of cancer; and 10.67% interest in **OncoVent Co., Ltd.**, which manufactures and commercializes cancer immunotherapy products within the People's Republic of China with pancreatic cancer as its first target as well as holds the licence for OncoQuest's immunotherapy portfolio for the greater China market.
In September 2022, the company sold its 20% interest in **BioCeltran Co., Ltd.**, which develops skin penetrating active molecules using Protein Transduction Domain (PTD) drug delivery technology for cosmetic and pharmaceutical use, for $300,000. As a result, BioCeltran also returned its licence to the company's photodynamic therapy technology, SonoLight, for oncology and dermatology applications.
Predecessor Detail - Name changed from Altachem Pharma Ltd., Oct. 5, 2005.
Directors - Dr. Ragupathy (Madi) Madiyalakan, CEO, Edmonton, Alta.; J. Mark Lievonen, Stouffville, Ont.; Jeffrey Shon, Edmonton, Alta.
Other Exec. Officers - Pierre Vermette, CFO; Thomas Woo, v-p, product devel.

Capital Stock

	Authorized (shs.)	Outstanding (shs.)[1]
First Preferred	unlimited	nil
Second Preferred	unlimited	nil
Common	unlimited	168,929,247

[1] At Sept. 26, 2022

Major Shareholder - Hepalink USA Inc. held 14.8% interest at June 13, 2022.

Price Range - QPT/TSX-VEN

Year	Volume	High	Low	Close
2022	4,197,218	$0.17	$0.05	$0.07
2021	10,327,186	$0.24	$0.06	$0.10
2020	5,274,249	$0.32	$0.06	$0.23
2019	5,495,579	$0.20	$0.08	$0.13
2018	14,418,590	$0.19	$0.10	$0.10

Recent Close: $0.07

Wholly Owned Subsidiaries

Madenco BioSciences Inc., Edmonton, Alta.
SonoLight Pharmaceuticals Corp., Edmonton, Alta.

Investments

42.52% int. in **OncoQuest, Inc.**, Edmonton, Alta.
• 23% int. in **OncoVent Co., Ltd.**, People's Republic of China.
10.67% int. in **OncoVent Co., Ltd.**, People's Republic of China.

Financial Statistics

Periods ended:	12m Jan. 31/22[A]		12m Jan. 31/21[oA]
	$000s	%Chg	$000s
Salaries & benefits	205		171
Research & devel. expense	157		201
General & admin expense	390		659
Operating expense	**752**	**-27**	**1,031**
Operating income	**(752)**	**n.a.**	**(1,031)**
Deprec., depl. & amort.	39		39
Finance income	nil		2
Finance costs, gross	13		8
Investment income	(84,503)		62,605
Pre-tax income	**(85,039)**	**n.a.**	**190,064**
Net income	**(85,039)**	**n.a.**	**190,064**
Cash & equivalent	264		199
Accounts receivable	nil		33
Current assets	288		281
Long-term investments	90,714		175,267
Fixed assets, net	16		55
Total assets	**91,029**	**-48**	**175,614**
Bank indebtedness	500		250
Accts. pay. & accr. liabs	109		85
Current liabilities	623		375
Long-term lease liabilities	nil		14
Shareholders' equity	90,406		175,224
Cash from oper. activs	**(171)**	**n.a.**	**(2,515)**
Cash from fin. activs	250		299
Cash from invest. activs	(14)		262
Net cash position	**264**	**+33**	**199**
	$		$
Earnings per share*	(0.51)		1.11
Cash flow per share*	(0.00)		(0.02)
	shs		shs
No. of shs. o/s*	168,239,247		168,239,247
Avg. no. of shs. o/s*	168,239,247		167,789,576
	%		%
Net profit margin	n.a.		n.a.
Return on equity	(64.03)		n.m.
Return on assets	(63.78)		211.11

* Common
[o] Restated
[A] Reported in accordance with IFRS

Latest Results

Periods ended:	6m July 31/22[A]		6m July 31/21[A]
	$000s	%Chg	$000s
Net income	(1,662)	n.a.	(137)
	$		$
Earnings per share*	(0.01)		(0.00)

* Common
[A] Reported in accordance with IFRS

Historical Summary
(as originally stated)

Fiscal Year	Oper. Rev. $000s	Net Inc. Bef. Disc. $000s	EPS* $
2022[A]	nil	(85,039)	(0.51)
2021[A1]	nil	190,064	1.13
2020[A]	nil	(13,254)	(0.04)
2019[A]	nil	(8,641)	(0.03)
2018[A]	38	(9,112)	(0.03)

* Common
[A] Reported in accordance with IFRS
[1] Results include $128,321,402 gain on deconsolidation of ownership of OncoQuest, Inc.

Q.8 Questor Technology Inc.

Symbol - QST **Exchange** - TSX-VEN **CUSIP** - 747946
Head Office - 2240-140 4 Ave SW, Calgary, AB, T2P 3N3 **Telephone** - (403) 571-1530 **Toll-free** - (844) 478-3786 **Fax** - (403) 571-1539
Website - www.questortech.com
Email - aosinski@questortech.com
Investor Relations - Ann-Marie Osinski (403) 539-4371
Auditors - PricewaterhouseCoopers LLP C.A., Calgary, Alta.
Bankers - HSBC Bank Canada, Calgary, Alta.
Lawyers - Field LLP, Calgary, Alta.
Transfer Agents - Computershare Trust Company of Canada Inc., Calgary, Alta.
Profile - (Alta. 1994) Designs, manufactures and services high efficiency waste gas combustion systems. Also provides power generation solutions utilizing waste heat.

The company's combustion technology destroys harmful pollutants, including methane, hydrogen sulfide gas, volatile organic hydrocarbons, hazardous air pollutants and benzene, toluene, ethylbenzene and xylene (BTEX) gases. This enables its clients to meet emission regulations, reduce greenhouse gas emissions, address community concerns and improve safety at industrial sites. The company has three product lines: Q-Series, Q-Power and Q-Insights.

Q-Series consists of incineration optimized based upon waste gas composition and flow rate to achieve a combustion efficiency of greater than 99.99%. It collects waste gas through its patented natural flow design which has no fans, blowers, or moving parts and is capable of accepting multiple gas streams to ensure lower maintenance and higher efficiency. The incinerators vary in size, ranging from 20 mcf per day to 5,000 mcf per day to accommodate small to large amounts of gas handling. The incinerators also vary in automation and instrumentation depending on the client's requirements.

Q-Power is a power generation solution designed to efficiently transform otherwise wasted high and low temperature heat into valuable electricity power. Q-Power is based on Organic Rankine Cycle (ORC) technology utilizing an axial turbine expander coupled to a synchronous generator via a gearbox and have an evaporator, condenser, economizer-heat exchanger, centrifugal refrigerant pump, and Programmable Logic Controller (PLC). Q-Power products are installed at petroleum and manufacturing client sites, and can be used in many other industries to process all types of waste gas including agriculture, rail car loading, mining, water treatment, landfill biogas, syngas, waste engine exhaust, geothermal and solar, and cement plant waste heat.

Q-Insights is a cloud-based product to provide continuous and real-time emissions data monitoring and analysis. Q-Insights, via the Gas Emissions Methane Monitoring and Analysis (GEMMA) product, provides monitoring and emissions tracking continuously and in real-time for distributed waste gas systems of various types. This helps small and mid-sized waste gas producers more effectively monetize pollution reduction activities through carbon offsets and trading, as well as reducing equipment issues and maintenance costs.

In addition, wholly owned **ClearPower Systems, Inc.** developed heat to power generation technology and offers solutions for landfill biogas, syngas, waste engine exhaust, geothermal and solar, cement plant waste heat, and oil and gas projects internationally.

Also, the company researches and develops data solutions to deliver an integrated system that amalgamates all of the emission detection data available and demonstrates how the company's clean combustion and power generation technologies can be used to help clients achieve zero emission targets.

Directors - A. Stewart (Stew) Hanlon, chr., Calgary, Alta.; Derek O'Malley-Keyes, interim pres. & interim CEO, Colo.; James Inkster, Dawson Creek, B.C.; Glenn Leroux, Calgary, Alta.
Other Exec. Officers - Ann-Marie Osinski, CFO & corp. sec.; Ryan Pilsner, v-p, global opers. & cust. experience

Capital Stock

	Authorized (shs.)	Outstanding (shs.)[1]
Common	unlimited	27,933,299

[1] At May 23, 2023

Major Shareholder - Audrey Mascarenhas held 17.19% interest and Claret Asset Management Corporation held 17.07% interest at Apr. 28, 2023.

Price Range - QST/TSX-VEN

Year	Volume	High	Low	Close
2022	5,186,975	$1.89	$0.77	$1.03
2021	13,992,543	$3.64	$1.16	$1.60
2020	27,193,027	$5.68	$1.18	$2.44
2019	12,093,330	$5.36	$3.21	$4.96
2018	14,972,698	$4.55	$2.05	$3.34

Recent Close: $0.83

Capital Stock Changes - During 2022, common shares were issued as follows: 103,623 under restricted share unit plan and 57,818 under performance share unit plan.

Wholly Owned Subsidiaries

ClearPower Systems, Inc., United States.
Questor Solutions & Technology Inc., United States.

Financial Statistics

Periods ended:	12m Dec. 31/22[A]		12m Dec. 31/21[oA]
	$000s	%Chg	$000s
Operating revenue	**8,381**	**+52**	**5,504**
Cost of sales	3,837		3,727
Salaries & benefits	2,175		2,380
Research & devel. expense	470		316
General & admin expense	1,267		1,151
Stock-based compensation	385		341
Operating expense	**8,134**	**+3**	**7,915**
Operating income	**247**	**n.a.**	**(2,411)**
Deprec., depl. & amort.	2,423		2,382
Finance costs, net	(195)		(68)
Write-downs/write-offs	(839)		(230)
Pre-tax income	**(2,487)**	**n.a.**	**(5,236)**
Income taxes	(761)		(1,248)
Net income	**(1,726)**	**n.a.**	**(3,988)**
Cash & equivalent	15,198		14,660
Inventories	1,623		1,184
Accounts receivable	1,556		3,068
Current assets	18,866		19,565
Fixed assets, net	11,841		13,790
Right-of-use assets	499		588
Intangibles, net	2,374		958
Total assets	**33,873**	**-3**	**35,048**
Accts. pay. & accr. liabs	971		894
Current liabilities	3,860		3,290
Long-term lease liabilities	257		401
Shareholders' equity	29,195		30,482
Cash from oper. activs	**1,522**	**n.a.**	**(1,130)**
Cash from fin. activs	638		88
Cash from invest. activs	(7,900)		(602)
Net cash position	**8,944**	**-39**	**14,660**
Capital expenditures	(111)		(45)
Capital disposals	21		26
	$		$
Earnings per share*	(0.06)		(0.15)
Cash flow per share*	0.05		(0.04)
	shs		shs
No. of shs. o/s*	27,923,299		27,761,858
Avg. no. of shs. o/s*	27,792,459		27,470,254
	%		%
Net profit margin	(20.59)		(72.46)
Return on equity	(5.78)		(12.37)
Return on assets	(5.01)		(10.92)
Foreign sales percent	40		58

* Common
[o] Restated
[A] Reported in accordance with IFRS

Latest Results

Periods ended:	3m Mar. 31/23[A]		3m Mar. 31/22[A]
	$000s	%Chg	$000s
Operating revenue	1,839	-29	2,588
Net income	(175)	n.a.	(366)
	$		$
Earnings per share*	(0.01)		(0.01)

* Common
[A] Reported in accordance with IFRS

Historical Summary
(as originally stated)

Fiscal Year	Oper. Rev. $000s	Net Inc. Bef. Disc. $000s	EPS* $
2022[A]	8,381	(1,726)	(0.06)
2021[A]	5,504	(3,988)	(0.15)
2020[A]	9,211	(1,830)	(0.07)
2019[A]	30,194	7,429	0.28
2018[A]	23,473	7,138	0.27

* Common
[A] Reported in accordance with IFRS

Q.9 Quinsam Capital Corporation

Symbol - QCA **Exchange** - CSE **CUSIP** - 748747
Head Office - Toronto Dominion Centre, 2905-77 King St W, PO Box 121, Toronto, ON, M5K 1H1 **Telephone** - (647) 993-5475
Website - www.quinsamcapital.com
Email - roger@quinsamcapital.com
Investor Relations - Roger Dent (647) 993-5475
Auditors - MNP LLP C.A., Toronto, Ont.
Lawyers - Fogler, Rubinoff LLP, Toronto, Ont.
Transfer Agents - Computershare Trust Company of Canada Inc., Vancouver, B.C.
Profile - (Can. 2004) Operates as a merchant bank focused on the small-cap market with early-stage investments in the technology, healthcare, mining and exploration, e-sports, and cannabis markets. Activities include acquisitions, advisory services, lending activities and portfolio investments.

Investments consist of equity, warrants, debt and convertible securities. Also holds non-cannabis related investments in its portfolio.

At Mar. 31, 2022, the company held cannabis investments with a fair value of $17,135,896 and non-cannabis investments with a fair value of $10,311,942.

Directors - Eric E. V. Szustak, chr. & corp. sec., Oakville, Ont.; Roger Dent, CEO, Toronto, Ont.; Ross Geddes, Oakville, Ont.; Susan Lambie, Ont.; Anthony R. (Tony) Roodenburg, Toronto, Ont.
Other Exec. Officers - Keith Li, CFO

Capital Stock

	Authorized (shs.)	Outstanding (shs.)[1]
Preferred	unlimited	nil
Common	unlimited	100,307,230

[1] At May 25, 2022

Major Shareholder - Roger Dent held 12.93% interest at Oct. 19, 2021.

Price Range - QCA/CSE

Year	Volume	High	Low	Close
2022	10,624,974	$0.15	$0.07	$0.08
2021	34,425,309	$0.21	$0.14	$0.15
2020	36,871,724	$0.18	$0.05	$0.17
2019	46,042,736	$0.31	$0.09	$0.11
2018	116,343,008	$1.19	$0.19	$0.25

Recent Close: $0.05

Dividends

QCA com Ra $0.005 pa Q est. Nov. 25, 2016

Investments

17% int. in **Budd Hutt Inc.**, Ont.
10.9% int. in **City View Green Holdings Inc.**, Toronto, Ont. (see separate coverage)
11.09% int. in **Nevada Organic Phosphate Inc.**, West Vancouver, B.C. (see Survey of Mines)

Financial Statistics

Periods ended:	12m Dec. 31/21[A]		12m Dec. 31/20[A]
	$000s	%Chg	$000s
Realized invest. gain (loss)	1,874		(2,934)
Unrealized invest. gain (loss)	(4,206)		3,317
Total revenue	**(303)**	**n.a.**	**3,096**
Salaries & benefits	214		370
General & admin. expense	378		367
Stock-based compensation	312		347
Operating expense	**905**	**-17**	**1,084**
Operating income	**(1,208)**	**n.a.**	**2,012**
Pre-tax income	**(2,016)**	**n.a.**	**2,240**
Income taxes	467		(200)
Net income	**(2,484)**	**n.a.**	**2,440**
Cash & equivalent	58		1,116
Accounts receivable	1,822		1,961
Investments	30,050		31,757
Total assets	**31,930**	**-8**	**34,834**
Accts. pay. & accr. liabs	109		236
Shareholders' equity	30,753		34,174
Cash from oper. activs	**348**	**-81**	**1,813**
Cash from fin. activs	(1,405)		(1,371)
Net cash position	**58**	**-95**	**1,116**
	$		$
Earnings per share*	(0.02)		0.02
Cash flow per share*	0.00		0.02
Cash divd. per share*	0.00		0.00
	shs		shs
No. of shs. o/s*	100,043,106		104,992,106
Avg. no. of shs. o/s*	103,494,480		109,376,974
	%		%
Net profit margin	n.m.		78.81
Return on equity	(7.65)		7.29
Return on assets	(7.44)		7.04

* Common
[A] Reported in accordance with IFRS

Latest Results

Periods ended:	3m Mar. 31/22^A		3m Mar. 31/21^A
	$000s	%Chg	$000s
Total revenue	(1,537)	n.a.	4,577
Net income	(1,651)	n.a.	3,581
	$		$
Earnings per share*	(0.02)		0.03

* Common
A Reported in accordance with IFRS

Historical Summary
(as originally stated)

Fiscal Year	Total Rev. $000s	Net Inc. Bef. Disc. $000s	EPS* $
2021^A	(303)	(2,484)	(0.02)
2020^A	3,096	2,440	0.02
2019^A	(10,038)	(10,078)	(0.09)
2018^A	17,633	10,591	0.09
2017^A	3,954	1,688	0.05

* Common
A Reported in accordance with IFRS

Q.10 Quinto Resources Inc.

Symbol - QIT.H **Exchange** - TSX-VEN (S) **CUSIP** - 74877T
Head Office - 4000-1 Place Ville Marie, Montréal, QC, H3B 4M4 **Telephone** - (514) 232-3344
Email - marcel.bergeron1@videotron.ca
Investor Relations - Marcel Bergeron (514) 232-3344
Auditors - Petrie Raymond LLP C.A., Montréal, Qué.
Lawyers - Séguin Racine Attorneys Ltd., Laval, Qué.
Transfer Agents - Computershare Trust Company of Canada Inc., Toronto, Ont.
Profile - (Can. 2010) Seeking new business opportunities.
Class A suspended from TSX-VEN, June 11, 2021.
Predecessor Detail - Name changed from Quinto Real Capital Corporation, Aug. 18, 2017.
Directors - Philippe Frère, chr., acting pres. & acting CEO, Saint-Lambert, Qué.; Marcel Bergeron, CFO, Montréal, Qué.; The Hon. Christian Paradis, Qué.

Capital Stock

	Authorized (shs.)	Outstanding (shs.)[1]
Class A Common	unlimited	41,779,998

[1] At May 31, 2022

Price Range - QIT.H/TSX-VEN (S)

Year	Volume	High	Low	Close
2020	10,971,803	$0.08	$0.02	$0.08
2019	12,395,513	$0.09	$0.04	$0.05
2018	20,989,451	$0.14	$0.02	$0.07

Financial Statistics

Periods ended:	12m Jan. 31/22^A		12m Jan. 31/21^A
	$000s	%Chg	$000s
General & admin expense	71		444
Operating expense	**71**	**-84**	**444**
Operating income	**(71)**	**n.a.**	**(444)**
Pre-tax income	**(71)**	**n.a.**	**(140)**
Net income	**(71)**	**n.a.**	**(140)**
Cash & equivalent	25		71
Current assets	74		136
Total assets	**74**	**-46**	**136**
Accts. pay. & accr. liabs	635		625
Current liabilities	635		627
Shareholders' equity	(561)		(490)
Cash from oper. activs	**(45)**	**n.a.**	**(181)**
Cash from invest. activs	nil		230
Net cash position	**25**	**-65**	**71**
	$		$
Earnings per share*	(0.00)		(0.00)
Cash flow per share*	(0.00)		(0.00)
	shs		shs
No. of shs. o/s*	41,779,998		41,779,998
Avg. no. of shs. o/s*	41,779,998		41,779,998
	%		%
Net profit margin	n.a.		n.a.
Return on equity	n.m.		n.m.
Return on assets	(67.62)		(166.67)

* Cl.A Common
A Reported in accordance with IFRS

Historical Summary
(as originally stated)

Fiscal Year	Oper. Rev. $000s	Net Inc. Bef. Disc. $000s	EPS* $
2022^A	nil	(71)	(0.00)
2021^A	nil	(140)	(0.00)
2020^A	nil	(410)	(0.01)
2019^A	nil	(450)	(0.01)
2018^A	nil	(652)	(0.02)

* Cl.A Common
A Reported in accordance with IFRS

Q.11 Quipt Home Medical Corp.*

Symbol - QIPT **Exchange** - TSX **CUSIP** - 74880P
Head Office - 1019 Town Dr, Wilder, KY, United States, 41076 **Telephone** - (859) 878-2220 **Toll-free** - (877) 811-9690 **Fax** - (859) 441-1107
Website - quipthomemedical.com
Email - cole.stevens@myquipt.com
Investor Relations - Cole Stevens (859) 300-6455
Auditors - BDO USA LLP C.P.A., Cincinnati, Ohio
Lawyers - DLA Piper (Canada) LLP
Transfer Agents - Computershare Trust Company of Canada Inc., Toronto, Ont.
FP500 Revenue Ranking - 681
Employees - 800 at Sept. 30, 2022
Profile - (B.C. 2013; orig. Alta., 1997) Delivers and services home-based medical equipment including oxygen therapy, sleep apnoea treatment and mobility equipment, as well as medical supplies to patients in the United States.
Provides in-home medical equipment and supplies, and disease management services focusing on patients with heart or pulmonary disease, sleep disorders, reduced mobility and other chronic health conditions. The company has more than 270,000 active patients across 115 locations in the U.S., including Missouri, Arkansas, California, Mississippi, Maine, New Hampshire, Virginia, South Carolina, Georgia, Florida, Tennessee, Kentucky, Illinois, Indiana and Ohio with 32,500 referring physicians. Product line consists of daily and ambulatory aides, power mobility, respiratory equipment rental, oxygen therapy, sleep apnoea and positive airway pressure treatment, home ventilation and equipment solutions. Products are offered under various brands including Quipt, West Home Healthcare, Riverside Medical, Resource Medical Group, Patient Aids, Legacy Oxygen, Cooley Medical, Coastal Med Tech, Care Medical, Black Bear Medical, Acadia Medical Supply, Halsom Home Care, Health Technology Resources, Mayhugh's Medical, Sleepwell, Care Plus, Med Supply Plus, Heckman Healthcare, Medical West Healthcare Center, Access Respiratory Homecare Sleep & Wellness Center, Thrift Home Care, At Home Health Equipment, GoodNight Medical, NorCal Respiratory and Hometown Medical.
In June 2022, the company acquired **NorCal Respiratory, Inc.**, which has three locations in northern California, for US$3,100,000.
Common delisted from TSX-VEN, June 21, 2023.
Common listed on TSX, June 21, 2023.

Recent Merger and Acquisition Activity

Status: completed **Announced:** Dec. 31, 2022
Quipt Home Medical Corp. acquired Great Elm Healthcare, LLC, a division of Great Elm Group, Inc., for a purchase price of US$80,000,000 consisting of US$73,000,000 in cash, US$5,000,000 in assumed debt and 431,966 Quipt common shares at a deemed price of US$4.63 per share. Great Elm Healthcare operates a complete line of respiratory related durable medical equipment service locations across eight states in the Midwest, Southwest and Pacific Northwest.
Status: completed **Announced:** July 11, 2022
Quipt Home Medical Corp. acquired Hometown Medical, LLC, a respiratory product business with operations in Mississippi with unaudited trailing 12-month annual revenues of US$7,000,000. The acquisition consists of two locations in Mississippi with over 1,000 referring physicians bringing Quipt's referring network base to over 21,600, and increases Quipt's active patient count by over 11,000, bringing Quipt's total to over 200,000 active patients.
Status: completed **Announced:** June 21, 2022
Quipt Home Medical Corp. acquired Access Respiratory Homecare, LLC, which offers respiratory services and equipment in two locations in Louisiana. Terms were not disclosed.
Status: completed **Announced:** Apr. 17, 2022
Quipt Home Medical Corp. acquired Ohio-based Good Night Medical, LLC, which provides sleep medicine and home ventilation for sleep apnoea patients, for US$6,105,000. The acquisition added 10,000 active patients, and encompassed locations across seven U.S. states including Arkansas, Georgia, Massachusetts, North Carolina, Ohio, Texas and California.
Predecessor Detail - Name changed from Protech Home Medical Corp., May 13, 2021; basis 1 new for 4 old shs.
Directors - Gregory (Greg) Crawford, chr., pres. & CEO, Fort Thomas, Ky.; Dr. Kevin A. Carter, Bellbrook, Ohio; Mark Greenberg, Cincinnati, Ohio; Brian J. Wessel, San Antonio, Tex.
Other Exec. Officers - Hardik Mehta, CFO; David Bachelder, exec. v-p, opers.; Thomas Roehrig, exec. v-p, fin.; Will Childers, v-p, bus. devel.; Jerry Kim, v-p, opers.; Mark Miles, v-p, IT; Cole Stevens, v-p, corp. devel.; Robbie Grossman, corp. sec.

Capital Stock

	Authorized (shs.)	Outstanding (shs.)[1]
Preferred	unlimited	nil
Common	unlimited	42,072,469

[1] At June 21, 2023

Options - At Sept. 30, 2022, options were outstanding to purchase 3,751,000 common shares at a weighted average exercise price of Cdn$4.24 per share for employee, director and consultant options.
Major Shareholder - Widely held at Feb. 1, 2023.

Price Range - QIPT/TSX-VEN (D)

Year	Volume	High	Low	Close
2022	10,674,798	$7.63	$5.14	$6.32
2021	19,178,151	$10.16	$6.08	$7.08
2020	23,625,304	$7.16	$1.88	$6.44
2019	13,367,886	$4.76	$2.20	$3.88
2018	14,840,586	$4.10	$1.50	$2.40

Consolidation: 1-for-4 cons. in May 2021; 1-for-5 cons. in Dec. 2018
Recent Close: $7.46
Capital Stock Changes - In April 2023, bought deal public offering of 5,129,000 common shares at $7.85 per share, including 669,000 shares on exercise of over-allotment option, and private placement of 280,000 common shares at $7.85 per share were completed. Net proceeds would be used for repayment of debt, potential future acquisitions, working capital and general corporate purposes.
In September 2022, 1,879,038 common shares were issued on conversion of $9,771,000 of debentures. Also during fiscal 2022, common shares were issued as follows: 227,962 on conversion of debentures and 148,000 on exercise of options.
Long-Term Debt - Outstanding at Sept. 30, 2022:

Senior credit facility[1]	US$10,235,000
SBA loan[2]	120,000
Equipment loans	5,707,000
	16,062,000
Less: Current portion	12,330,000
	3,732,000

[1] Consists of US$5,000,000 term loan bearing interest at 5.7% as at Sept. 30, 2022, and US$7,000,000 revolving credit facility bearing interest at 7% as at Sept. 30, 2022, all due in 2027.
[2] Bears interest at stated interest rate plus 3.75%.

Wholly Owned Subsidiaries

Quipt Home Medical Inc., Del.
- 100% int. in **Great Elm Healthcare, LLC**, Mesa, Ariz.
- 100% int. in **Patient Home Monitoring, Inc.**, Wash.
- 100% int. in **QHM Holdings Inc.**, Del. formerly Healthcare Logistics Corporation.
  - 100% int. in **Acadia Medical Supply, Inc.**, Me.
  - 100% int. in **Access Respiratory Homecare, LLC**, La.
  - 100% int. in **At Home Health Equipment, Inc.**, Ind.
  - 100% int. in **Black Bear Medical Group, Inc.**, Me.
    - 100% int. in **Black Bear Medical, Inc.**, Me.
    - 100% int. in **Black Bear Medical NH, Inc.**, N.H.
    - 100% int. in **Coastal Med-Tech Corp.**, Me.
  - 100% int. in **Care Medical Partners, LLC**, Ga.
    - 100% int. in **Care Medical Atlanta, LLC**, Ga.
    - 100% int. in **Care Medical of Athens, Inc.**, Ga.
    - 100% int. in **Care Medical of Augusta, LLC**, Ga.
    - 100% int. in **Care Medical of Gainesville, LLC**, Ga.
    - 100% int. in **Care Medical Savannah, LLC**, Ga.
  - 100% int. in **Central Oxygen, Inc.**, Ind.
  - 100% int. in **Cooley Medical, Inc.**, Ky.
  - 100% int. in **Good Night Medical, LLC**, Ohio
  - 100% int. in **Health Technology Resources, LLC**, Ill.
  - 100% int. in **Heckman Healthcare Service & Supplies Inc.**, Ill.
  - 100% int. in **Hometown Medical, LLC**, Miss.
  - 100% int. in **Legacy Oxygen & Home Care Equipment, LLC**, Ky.
  - 100% int. in **Mayhugh's Drugs Inc.**, Fla.
  - 100% int. in **Med Supply Center, Inc.**, Miss.
  - 100% int. in **Medical West Healthcare Center, LLC**, Mo.
  - 100% int. in **NorCal Respiratory, Inc.**, Calif.
  - 100% int. in **Oxygen Plus Inc.**, Calif.
  - 100% int. in **Patient-Aids Inc.**, Ky.
  - 100% int. in **Resource Medical, Inc.**, S.C.
    - 100% int. in **Resource Medical Group, LLC**, North Charleston, S.C.
    - 100% int. in **Resource Medical Group of Charleston, LLC**, S.C.
  - 100% int. in **Riverside Medical, Inc.**, Tenn.
  - 100% int. in **Semo Drugs - Care Plus of MO, Inc.**, Mo.
    - 100% int. in **100 W. Commercial Street, LLC**, Mo.
  - 100% int. in **Sleepwell, LLC**, Ga.
    - 100% int. in **Tuscan, Inc.**, Ohio
  - 100% int. in **Thrift Home Care, Inc.**, Miss.
  - 100% int. in **West Home Healthcare, Inc.**, Richmond, Va.

Financial Statistics

Periods ended:	12m Sept. 30/22[A]		12m Sept. 30/21[DA]
	US$000s	%Chg	US$000s
Operating revenue	**139,862**	**+37**	**102,351**
Cost of sales	33,213		28,172
Salaries & benefits	41,456		29,549
General & admin expense	22,286		14,251
Stock-based compensation	5,493		4,952
Other operating expense	1,461		1,005
Operating expense	**103,909**	**+33**	**77,929**
Operating income	**35,953**	**+47**	**24,422**
Deprec., depl. & amort.	23,040		17,786
Finance costs, net	1,796		7,869
Write-downs/write-offs	(12,225)		(7,957)
Pre-tax income	**2,935**	**n.a.**	**(9,329)**
Income taxes	(1,904)		(3,155)
Net income	**4,839**	**n.a.**	**(6,174)**
Cash & equivalent	8,516		34,612
Inventories	15,585		9,253
Accounts receivable	16,383		11,938
Current assets	41,536		57,233
Fixed assets, net	33,497		23,506
Intangibles, net	57,095		27,330
Total assets	**132,214**	**+22**	**108,573**
Accts. pay. & accr. liabs	17,292		13,044
Current liabilities	41,740		32,737
Long-term debt, gross	16,062		19,289
Long-term debt, net	3,732		12,297
Long-term lease liabilities	7,195		4,784
Shareholders' equity	79,547		58,622
Cash from oper. activs	**26,344**	**+48**	**17,761**
Cash from fin. activs	(9,851)		4,840
Cash from invest. activs	(42,493)		(17,838)
Net cash position	**8,516**	**-75**	**34,612**
Capital expenditures	(9,161)		(5,046)
Capital disposals	193		98
	US$		US$
Earnings per share*	0.14		(0.20)
Cash flow per share*	0.78		0.58
	shs		shs
No. of shs. o/s*	35,605,000		33,350,000
Avg. no. of shs. o/s*	33,647,000		30,438,000
	%		%
Net profit margin	3.46		(6.03)
Return on equity	7.00		(13.90)
Return on assets	4.02		(6.66)
Foreign sales percent	100		100
No. of employees (FTEs)	800		623

* Common
[D] Restated
[A] Reported in accordance with IFRS

Latest Results

Periods ended:	6m Mar. 31/23[A]		6m Mar. 31/22[A]
	US$000s	%Chg	US$000s
Operating revenue	98,935	+57	63,077
Net income	(425)	n.a.	2,905
	US$		US$
Earnings per share*	(0.01)		0.09

* Common
[A] Reported in accordance with IFRS

Historical Summary
(as originally stated)

Fiscal Year	Oper. Rev.	Net Inc. Bef. Disc.	EPS*
	US$000s	US$000s	US$
2022[A]	139,862	4,839	0.14
2021[A]	102,351	(6,174)	(0.20)
	$000s	$000s	$
2020[A]	97,755	(5,597)	(0.25)
2019[A]	80,967	(9,141)	(0.44)
2018[A]	76,863	(6,967)	(0.37)

* Common
[A] Reported in accordance with IFRS

Note: Adjusted throughout for 1-for-4 cons. in May 2021; 1-for-5 cons. in Dec. 2018

Q.12 Quisitive Technology Solutions, Inc.

Symbol - QUIS **Exchange** - TSX-VEN **CUSIP** - 74881G
Head Office - TD Canada Trust Tower, 2325-161 Bay St, Toronto, ON, M5J 2S1 **Telephone** - (647) 317-5337
Website - www.quisitive.com
Email - tami.anders@quisitive.com
Investor Relations - Tami Anders (972) 573-0995
Auditors - KPMG LLP C.A., Vaughan, Ont.
Transfer Agents - Computershare Trust Company of Canada Inc., Vancouver, B.C.
FP500 Revenue Ranking - 615

Profile - (B.C. 2017; orig. Alta., 2011) Provides Microsoft solutions that help enterprises move, operate and innovate in the three Microsoft clouds, including Microsoft Azure, Microsoft Dynamics business applications and Microsoft Office 365. Also provides software-as-a-service (SaaS) solutions and products that complement the Microsoft platform.

Operations are organized into two segments: Cloud Solutions and Payment Solutions.

Cloud Solutions - Products and services are organized into three approaches: cloud services, which include infrastructure, digital workplace, data and analytics, security, application development, managed and licensing services; IP solutions, which include MazikCare, a set of healthcare-ready business solutions, PowerGov, a community development application for state and local government, emPerform™, an employee performance management solution for human resource and talent management, Spyglass, a security solution which provides advanced threat detection and automated response capabilities, allowing organizations to quickly respond to security incidents, ShopFloor, a management solution that gives access to dashboards to track project and process flows and MazikThings, a manufacturing solution that helps teams simplify supply chain, workforce, operations and facilities on one integrated platform built on Microsoft Dynamics; and business applications, which include budgeting and financial planning, enterprise resource planning, human resource and talent management, and sales and customer relationship management.

Cloud Solutions segment earns revenue from professional services, recurring managed services and recurring SaaS licensing fees.

Payment Solutions - Products and services include PayiQ, a cloud-based payment processing and payments intelligence platform that processes non-cash payments from retail merchants which features full credit and debit processing directly connected to Visa, Mastercard, AMEX, Discover and key debit networks, gift card activation and management, stored value card management, loyalty program management, card issuance push-to-card, rules engine to trigger targeted promotions and react to potential fraud; and merchant services which offers credit card processing products and services that has the ability to accept payments online through a payment gateway, in store with a credit card terminal, over the phone via virtual terminal or on the go using a mobile credit card processing application.

Payment Solutions segment earns revenue from transaction-based fees, data fees and residual payment processing on all the transactions in its merchant portfolio.

Predecessor Detail - Name changed from Nebo Capital Corp., Aug. 8, 2018, following Qualifying Transaction reverse takeover acquisition of Fusion Agiletech Partners Inc.

Directors - Michael (Mike) Reinhart, founder, chr. & CEO, Southlake, Tex.; Amy Brandt, Southlake, Tex.; Laurie M. Goldberg, Winnipeg, Man.; David D. (Dave) Guebert, Calgary, Alta.; Philip Sorgen, Bellevue, Wash.

Other Exec. Officers - Scott Meriwether, CFO & corp. sec.; Tami Anders, chief of staff; Steven Balusek, sr. v-p, global IT & innovation; Terri Burmeister, pres., global cloud srvcs. & applications; Jana Schmidt, pres., global payments solutions

Capital Stock

	Authorized (shs.)	Outstanding (shs.)[1]
Preferred	unlimited	nil
Common	unlimited	399,240,941

[1] At July 7, 2023

Major Shareholder - Widely held at May 23, 2023.

Price Range - QUIS/TSX-VEN

Year	Volume	High	Low	Close
2022	36,190,670	$1.19	$0.48	$0.77
2021	91,695,644	$1.97	$0.86	$1.17
2020	43,994,967	$1.26	$0.24	$1.09
2019	19,057,018	$0.27	$0.07	$0.25
2018	7,782,281	$0.35	$0.09	$0.20

Recent Close: $0.35

Capital Stock Changes - In June 2023, bought deal offering of 19,780,000 common shares was completed at $0.35 per share.

During 2022, common shares were issued as follows: 11,554,968 as contingent consideration, 1,179,460 under restricted share unit plan and 15,000 on exercise of options; 310,558 common shares were settled for tax liabilities on restricted share units.

Wholly Owned Subsidiaries

Corporate Renaissance Group Inc., Canada.
Menlo Technologies Acquisition Inc., Del.
- 100% int. in **Menlo Technologies, Inc.**, Menlo Park, Calif.
  - 100% int. in **Menlo Software India Private Limited**, India.
  - 100% int. in **MidTech Software Solutions, Inc.**, United States.
  - 100% int. in **Support Solutions, Inc.**, United States.

Quisitive Ltd., Del.
- 100% int. in **Catapult Systems, LLC**, Austin, Tex.
- 100% int. in **Mazik Global Inc.**, Chicago, Ill.
- 100% int. in **Quisitive, LLC**, Irving, Tex.
- 100% int. in **Quisitive Payment Solutions, Inc**, Del.
  - 100% int. in **BankCard USA Merchant Services, Inc.**, Westlake Village, Calif.
  - 80% int. in **LedgerPay, Inc.**, Del.

Financial Statistics

Periods ended:	12m Dec. 31/22[A]		12m Dec. 31/21[A]
	US$000s	%Chg	US$000s
Operating revenue	**187,262**	**+94**	**96,678**
Cost of sales	110,706		60,161
General & admin expense	49,952		22,659
Stock-based compensation	3,325		1,247
Operating expense	**163,983**	**+95**	**84,067**
Operating income	**23,279**	**+85**	**12,611**
Deprec., depl. & amort.	19,241		12,444
Finance costs, gross	4,709		4,806
Pre-tax income	**(9,146)**	**n.a.**	**(19,011)**
Income taxes	132		(2,208)
Net income	**(9,278)**	**n.a.**	**(16,803)**
Net inc. for equity hldrs	**(8,372)**	**n.a.**	**(16,315)**
Net inc. for non-cont. int	**(906)**	**n.a.**	**(488)**
Cash & equivalent	9,408		13,516
Inventories	1,745		1,783
Accounts receivable	28,039		23,631
Current assets	41,727		41,599
Fixed assets, net	4,768		6,793
Intangibles, net	281,090		293,125
Total assets	**327,935**	**-4**	**341,867**
Accts. pay. & accr. liabs	16,598		16,789
Current liabilities	46,936		46,302
Long-term debt, gross	76,936		78,555
Long-term debt, net	67,508		70,427
Long-term lease liabilities	2,593		3,806
Shareholders' equity	201,532		200,918
Non-controlling interest	(1,122)		(216)
Cash from oper. activs	**18,272**	**+190**	**6,297**
Cash from fin. activs	(17,002)		159,215
Cash from invest. activs	(5,378)		(162,979)
Net cash position	**(9,408)**	**n.a.**	**13,516**
Capital expenditures	(323)		(607)
	US$		US$
Earnings per share*	(0.02)		(0.06)
Cash flow per share*	0.05		0.02
	shs		shs
No. of shs. o/s*	368,753,749		356,314,879
Avg. no. of shs. o/s*	361,002,113		283,293,387
	%		%
Net profit margin	(4.95)		(17.38)
Return on equity	(4.16)		(14.34)
Return on assets	(1.34)		(6.19)
Foreign sales percent	n.a.		91

* Common
[A] Reported in accordance with IFRS

Historical Summary
(as originally stated)

Fiscal Year	Oper. Rev.	Net Inc. Bef. Disc.	EPS*
	US$000s	US$000s	US$
2022[A]	187,262	(9,278)	(0.02)
2021[A]	96,678	(16,803)	(0.06)
2020[A]	49,764	(9,908)	(0.07)
2019[A]	18,525	(7,377)	(0.08)
2018[A]	12,607	(6,610)	(0.09)

* Common
[A] Reported in accordance with IFRS

Q.13 Quizam Media Corporation

Symbol - QQ **Exchange** - CSE **CUSIP** - 749057
Head Office - 650-609 Granville St, PO Box 10381, Vancouver, BC, V7Y 1G6 **Telephone** - (604) 683-0020 **Toll-free** - (800) 425-3276 **Fax** - (604) 683-0045
Website - www.quizammedia.com
Email - russ123@quizam.com
Investor Relations - Russell L. Rossi (800) 425-3276
Auditors - Manning Elliott LLP C.A., Vancouver, B.C.
Transfer Agents - Computershare Trust Company of Canada Inc., Vancouver, B.C.

Profile - (B.C. 2000) Operates four retail cannabis dispensaries in British Columbia, and produces, aggregates and markets media for corporate online learning and entertainment in Canada and the U.K.

Wholly owned **Quantum 1 Cannabis Corp.** holds provincial cannabis dispensary licence for British Columbia, and operates four retail stores in Keremeos, Vernon, Vancouver and North Vancouver.

Wholly owned **On-Track Computer Training Ltd.** provides corporate learning through ontracktv.com and ontrackTV.co.uk in Canada and the U.K., respectively. Within On-Track there are 3 divisions: On-Track Corporate Training (face to face consulting), On-Track Online Live (face to face but online) and OntrackTV (a large library of short vignettes). Online training courses include information technology computer training, soft skill training for corporations (including customer service, conflict resolution, project management and workplace assertiveness) and courses on cannabis and trades.

Predecessor Detail - Name changed from Torq Media Corporation, May 18, 2005; basis 1 new for 4 old shs.

Directors - Russell L. (Russ) Rossi, pres. & CEO, Vancouver, B.C.; James (Jim) Rosevear, CFO & corp. sec., Burnaby, B.C.; Stephen Alexander, London, Middx., United Kingdom; Michael Skellern, B.C.

Capital Stock

	Authorized (shs.)	Outstanding (shs.)[1]
Common	unlimited	33,777,678

[1] At Oct. 28, 2022

Major Shareholder - Widely held at Dec. 18, 2018.

Price Range - QQ/CSE

Year	Volume	High	Low	Close
2022	2,232,697	$0.21	$0.03	$0.05
2021	2,818,206	$0.90	$0.18	$0.20
2020	1,765,456	$0.96	$0.21	$0.38
2019	557,117	$1.80	$0.72	$0.72
2018	1,269,165	$2.82	$0.48	$1.56

Consolidation: 1-for-12 cons. in May 2020

Recent Close: $0.03

Capital Stock Changes - In June 2022, private placement of 4,000,000 units (1 common share & ½ warrant) at 6¢ per unit was completed, with warrants exercisable at 20¢ per share for two years. In August 2022, private placement of 4,000,000 units (1 common share & ½ warrant) at 5¢ per unit was completed, with warrants exercisable at 10¢ per share for two years.

During fiscal 2022, common shares were issued as follows: 6,000,000 by private placement, 434,783 for pre-operating costs, 337,500 on exercise of warrants, 285,424 for services and 6,000 on exercise of options.

Wholly Owned Subsidiaries

On-Track Computer Training Ltd.

Quantum 1 Cannabis Corp., B.C.

Quizam Entertainment LLC, United States. Inactive.

Financial Statistics

Periods ended:	12m May 31/22[A]		12m May 31/21[A]
	$000s	%Chg	$000s
Operating revenue	**6,878**	**+69**	**4,064**
Salaries & benefits	886		569
Research & devel. expense	473		382
General & admin expense	7,136		4,065
Stock-based compensation	106		275
Operating expense	**8,601**	**+63**	**5,291**
Operating income	**(1,723)**	**n.a.**	**(1,227)**
Deprec., depl. & amort.	512		230
Finance costs, gross	132		59
Pre-tax income	**(2,470)**	**n.a.**	**(1,935)**
Net income	**(2,470)**	**n.a.**	**(1,935)**
Cash & equivalent	279		922
Inventories	270		121
Accounts receivable	48		68
Current assets	685		1,200
Fixed assets, net	2,137		868
Total assets	**2,822**	**+36**	**2,068**
Accts. pay. & accr. liabs	786		383
Current liabilities	1,487		735
Long-term debt, gross	60		60
Long-term debt, net	40		60
Long-term lease liabilities	1,624		455
Shareholders' equity	(329)		817
Cash from oper. activs	**(1,105)**	**n.a.**	**(1,613)**
Cash from fin. activs	555		2,610
Cash from invest. activs	(92)		(82)
Net cash position	**279**	**-70**	**922**
Capital expenditures	(92)		(82)
	$		$
Earnings per share*	(0.12)		(0.14)
Cash flow per share*	(0.05)		(0.11)
	shs		shs
No. of shs. o/s*	25,277,679		18,213,971
Avg. no. of shs. o/s*	21,221,000		14,170,000
	%		%
Net profit margin	(35.91)		(47.61)
Return on equity	n.m.		n.m.
Return on assets	(95.62)		(122.29)

* Common

[A] Reported in accordance with IFRS

Latest Results

Periods ended:	3m Aug. 31/22[A]		3m Aug. 31/21[A]
	$000s	%Chg	$000s
Operating revenue	1,906	+19	1,605
Net income	(83)	n.a.	(448)
	$		$
Earnings per share*	(0.00)		(0.02)

* Common

[A] Reported in accordance with IFRS

Historical Summary
(as originally stated)

Fiscal Year	Oper. Rev.	Net Inc. Bef. Disc.	EPS*
	$000s	$000s	$
2022[A]	6,878	(2,470)	(0.12)
2021[A]	4,064	(1,935)	(0.14)
2020[A]	819	(1,678)	(0.32)
2019[A]	890	(2,390)	(0.60)
2018[A]	631	(1,128)	(0.84)

* Common

[A] Reported in accordance with IFRS

Note: Adjusted throughout for 1-for-12 cons. in May 2020

Q.14 Quorum Information Technologies Inc.

Symbol - QIS **Exchange** - TSX-VEN **CUSIP** - 749093

Head Office - B28-6020 2 St SE, Calgary, AB, T2H 2L8 **Telephone** - (403) 777-0036 **Toll-free** - (877) 770-0036 **Fax** - (403) 777-0039

Website - quoruminformationsystems.com

Email - maury.marks@quoruminfotech.com

Investor Relations - Maury Marks (877) 770-0036

Auditors - Deloitte LLP C.A., Calgary, Alta.

Bankers - HSBC Bank Canada, Calgary, Alta.

Lawyers - McLeod Law LLP, Calgary, Alta.

Transfer Agents - Olympia Trust Company, Calgary, Alta.

Profile - (Alta. 2000) Provides software products and services to automotive dealerships and original equipment manufacturers in Canada and the U.S.

Key products and services include: Quorum DMS, a fully integrated digital service and modernized sales solution to streamlines key processes across all departments, to improve revenue generation and customer satisfaction; DealerMine CRM, a single platform to analyze data, discover opportunities and manage customer communications: Autovance, a desking and digital retailing tool; MyDeal, a digital retailing system which allows dealers and customers to interact online for vehicle sales; Accessible Accessories, a digital retailing platform which allows franchised dealerships to sell accessories; PowerLane, a mobile service lane inspection tool that provides touchless, transparent media capture capabilities allowing customers to review a video of any necessary repairs; and QAnalytics, a reporting tool which provides dealership-critical metrics and provides the ROI calculations for individual products and the full suite. At Mar. 31, 2023, the company had a customer base of 1,433 dealerships (roofstops) at an average SaaS revenue per month of $1,634 per rooftop.

In September 2022, the company entered into a definitive agreement to sell the Advantage Complete Dealership Management System (DMS) software to **Vitali Auto Group** for a nominal amount.

In April 2022, the company acquired private Medicine Hat, Alta.-based **Accessible Accessories Ltd.**, which develops, implements and supports a web-based platform that allows franchised dealerships to sell accessories, for $4,500,000. Accessible had more than 680 automotive franchised dealership customers across Canada.

Predecessor Detail - Name changed from QIS Ventures Inc., Oct. 23, 2001.

Directors - D. Neil McDonnell, chr., West Vancouver, B.C.; Maury Marks, pres. & CEO, Calgary, Alta.; Joseph L. (Joe) Campbell, Fla.; Scot Eisenfelder, Parkland, Fla.; Jon Hook, Ore.; Damien Leonard, Ont.; William Nurthen, Wis.; Gregory I. (Greg) Pollard, Alta.

Other Exec. Officers - Marilyn Bown, CFO; Bruce Atkinson, v-p, opers.; Rick Johnston, v-p, product; Yossi Ronnen, v-p, software devel.; Jane Webb, v-p, sales & mktg.

Capital Stock

	Authorized (shs.)	Outstanding (shs.)[1]
Preferred	unlimited	nil
Common	unlimited	73,237,048

[1] At Mar. 31, 2023

Major Shareholder - Voss Capital LLC held 19.94% interest and Burgundy Asset Management Ltd. held 13.88% interest at June 23, 2022.

Price Range - QIS/TSX-VEN

Year	Volume	High	Low	Close
2022	5,505,021	$1.19	$0.60	$0.79
2021	4,304,427	$1.50	$0.93	$1.13
2020	7,672,710	$1.65	$0.65	$1.05
2019	6,524,211	$1.29	$0.62	$1.29
2018	9,317,144	$0.70	$0.48	$0.69

Recent Close: $0.63

Capital Stock Changes - During 2022, 108,328 common shares were issued as stock-based compensation.

Wholly Owned Subsidiaries

Accessible Accessories Ltd., Alta.

Autovance Technologies Inc., Lethbridge, Alta.

DealerMine Inc., Saint John, N.B.

- 100% int. in **DealerMine USA Holdings Inc.**
- 100% int. in **DealerMine USA Inc.**

Quorum Advantage Limited, London, Ont.

Quorum Information Systems Inc.

Quorum Information Technologies (US) Inc.

Financial Statistics

Periods ended:	12m Dec. 31/22[A]		12m Dec. 31/21[A]
	$000s	%Chg	$000s
Operating revenue	**38,804**	**+8**	**36,051**
Cost of sales	20,141		19,642
Research & devel. expense	2,625		1,413
General & admin expense	11,316		10,527
Stock-based compensation	180		388
Operating expense	**34,262**	**+7**	**31,970**
Operating income	**4,542**	**+11**	**4,081**
Deprec., depl. & amort.	4,110		4,091
Finance income	30		12
Finance costs, gross	1,569		1,544
Write-downs/write-offs	nil		(1,668)
Pre-tax income	**(1,107)**	**n.a.**	**(3,210)**
Income taxes	306		(498)
Net income	**(1,413)**	**n.a.**	**(2,711)**
Cash & equivalent	4,870		6,478
Inventories	13		14
Accounts receivable	3,383		3,576
Current assets	9,559		11,011
Fixed assets, net	696		1,015
Right-of-use assets	2,138		2,672
Intangibles, net	28,682		23,676
Total assets	**47,128**	**+4**	**45,173**
Accts. pay. & accr. liabs	2,454		2,682
Current liabilities	3,339		3,397
Long-term debt, gross	12,268		8,936
Long-term debt, net	11,804		8,632
Long-term lease liabilities	2,440		2,892
Shareholders' equity	26,577		27,767
Cash from oper. activs	**3,507**	**+114**	**1,640**
Cash from fin. activs	(1,440)		(1,161)
Cash from invest. activs	(3,698)		(3,254)
Net cash position	**4,870**	**-25**	**6,478**
Capital expenditures	(213)		(511)
	$		$
Earnings per share*	(0.02)		(0.04)
Cash flow per share*	0.05		0.02
	shs		shs
No. of shs. o/s*	73,237,048		73,128,720
Avg. no. of shs. o/s*	73,140,364		72,840,494
	%		%
Net profit margin	(3.64)		(7.52)
Return on equity	(5.20)		(9.38)
Return on assets	1.28		(2.97)
Foreign sales percent	11		12

* Common

[A] Reported in accordance with IFRS

Latest Results

Periods ended:	3m Mar. 31/23[A]		3m Mar. 31/22[A]
	$000s	%Chg	$000s
Operating revenue	9,906	+7	9,286
Net income	(560)	n.a.	(598)
	$		$
Earnings per share*	(0.01)		(0.01)

* Common

[A] Reported in accordance with IFRS

Historical Summary
(as originally stated)

Fiscal Year	Oper. Rev.	Net Inc. Bef. Disc.	EPS*
	$000s	$000s	$
2022[A]	38,804	(1,413)	(0.02)
2021[A]	36,051	(2,711)	(0.04)
2020[A]	30,856	(1,859)	(0.03)
2019[A]	32,841	(1,106)	(0.02)
2018[A]	16,441	(711)	(0.01)

* Common

[A] Reported in accordance with IFRS

R

R.1 R&R Real Estate Investment Trust

Symbol - RRR.UN **Exchange** - TSX-VEN **CUSIP** - 74979N
Head Office - 500-5090 Explorer Dr, Mississauga, ON, L4W 4T9 **Telephone** - (905) 206-7100 **Fax** - (905) 206-7114
Email - bob.choo@whg.com
Investor Relations - Bob Choo (905) 206-7102
Auditors - MNP LLP C.A., Toronto, Ont.
Lawyers - Blake, Cassels & Graydon LLP, Toronto, Ont.
Transfer Agents - TSX Trust Company, Toronto, Ont.
Profile - (Ont. 2014) Owns and acquires hotel properties in the U.S.
Owns 17 hotels (at Sept. 30, 2022), totaling 2,093 rooms, which operate primarily under the Red Roof Inn brand.
Predecessor Detail - Succeeded WestCap Investments Corp., Aug. 25, 2014, pursuant to Qualifying Transaction plan of arrangement acquisition of a hotel property in Maryland.
Trustees - Majid Mangalji, exec. chr., Wimbledon, Surrey, United Kingdom; Graham Blyth‡, Toronto, Ont.; Louise Dermott, Toronto, Ont.; Irfan Lakha, Toronto, Ont.; L. Geoffrey (Geoff) Morphy, Toronto, Ont.
Other Exec. Officers - Michael Klingher, pres. & CEO; Bob Choo, CFO & corp. sec.
‡ Lead trustee

Capital Stock

	Authorized (shs.)	Outstanding (shs.)[1]
Trust Unit	unlimited	37,324,318
Special Voting Unit	unlimited	245,070,857
Class B LP Unit	unlimited	58,035,650[2,3]
Class B LP Unit	unlimited	72,031,112[2,4]
Class B LP Unit	unlimited	63,595,200[2,5]
US Class B LP Unit	unlimited	51,408,895[2,6]

[1] At Sept. 30, 2022
[2] Classified as debt.
[3] Securities of R&R Ironhound Limited Partnership and R&R Unencumbered LP
[4] Securities of R&R 3650 Limited Partnership
[5] Securities of a newly formed limited partnership.
[6] Securities of R&R (US) Limited Partnership

Trust Unit - Redeemable at a price per unit equal to the lesser of (i) 90% of the weighted average price per unit during the 20-trading day period immediately following the date on which the units were surrendered for redemption and (ii) an amount equal to (a) the closing price of the units on the redemption date; (b) the average of the highest and lowest prices of the units on the redemption date; or (c) the average of the last bid and ask prices if there was no trading on the redemption date. One vote per trust unit.
Special Voting Unit - Issued to holders of class B limited partnership units of subsidiaries R&R 3650 Limited Partnership, R&R Ironhound Limited Partnership and R&R Unencumbered Limited Partnership (Class B LP units) and class B limited partnership units of indirect subsidiary R&R (US) Limited Partnership (US Class B LP units). Non-participating and have no economic entitlement in the trust. Each special voting unit entitles the holder to a vote at meetings of the trust equal to the number of trust units into which the Class B LP units and US Class B LP units are exchangeable. Upon the exchange or surrender of a Class B LP Unit or a US Class B LP Unit for a trust unit, the special voting unit attached to such Class B LP Unit or US Class B LP Unit will automatically be redeemed and cancelled for no consideration.
Class B LP Unit & US Class B LP Unit - Economic equivalent of trust units, entitled to distributions equivalent to those paid to trust units and exchangeable for trust units on a 1-for-1 basis. Not transferable other than in connection with an exercise of exchange rights.
Major Shareholder - Majid Mangalji held 79.97% interest and Michael Klingher held 10.56% interest at Sept. 30, 2022.

Price Range - RRR.UN/TSX-VEN

Year	Volume	High	Low	Close
2022	5,269,604	$0.12	$0.04	$0.10
2021	3,194,970	$0.10	$0.04	$0.05
2020	1,601,919	$0.10	$0.01	$0.04
2019	1,688,045	$0.15	$0.06	$0.10
2018	1,670,805	$0.11	$0.07	$0.08

Recent Close: $0.16

Wholly Owned Subsidiaries

R&R Ironhound Limited Partnership, Del.
R&R Limited Partnership, Ont.
- 100% int. in **R&R (US) Limited Partnership**, Del.
  - 99.5% int. in **R&R (BWI) LP**, Del.
  - 99.5% int. in **R&R (US) BWI LP**, Del.
    - 0.5% int. in **R&R (BWI) LP**, Del.

R&R Nat LP, Del.
R&R 3650 Limited Partnership
R&R Unencumbered Limited Partnership, Del.

Financial Statistics

Periods ended:	12m Dec. 31/21[A]		12m Dec. 31/20[A]
	US$000s	%Chg	US$000s
Total revenue	**34,180**	**+12**	**30,647**
Rental operating expense	20,657		19,854
General & admin. expense	585		591
Property taxes	1,850		1,947
Operating expense	**23,092**	**+3**	**22,393**
Operating income	**11,088**	**+34**	**8,254**
Deprec. & amort.	4,444		4,706
Finance income	2		4
Finance costs, gross	4,147		4,757
Pre-tax income	**2,661**	**n.m.**	**227**
Income taxes	49		(130)
Net income	**2,612**	**+632**	**357**
Cash & equivalent	9,252		9,454
Accounts receivable	435		511
Current assets	10,781		14,521
Fixed assets	107,426		107,488
Property interests, net	91,627		95,830
Total assets	**107,557**	**-7**	**115,502**
Accts. pay. & accr. liabs	3,360		4,415
Current liabilities	8,051		20,387
Long-term debt, gross	79,205		86,076
Long-term debt, net	74,782		74,129
Long-term lease liabilities	2,893		1,854
Shareholders' equity	21,831		19,132
Cash from oper. activs	**4,909**	**+5**	**4,679**
Cash from fin. activs	(10,893)		(1,774)
Cash from invest. activs	5,782		(3,110)
Net cash position	**9,252**	**-2**	**9,454**
Capital expenditures	(2,528)		(3,274)
Capital disposals	8,308		nil
	US$		US$
Earnings per share*	0.07		0.01
Cash flow per share*	0.14		0.14
Funds from opers. per sh.*	$0.20		$0.11
Adj. funds from opers. per sh.*	$0.17		$0.08
	shs		shs
No. of shs. o/s*	37,324,318		35,351,428
Avg. no. of shs. o/s*	35,448,721		34,182,925
	%		%
Net profit margin	7.64		1.16
Return on equity	12.75		1.89
Return on assets	5.99		6.45
Foreign sales percent	100		100

* Trust Unit
[A] Reported in accordance with IFRS

Latest Results

Periods ended:	9m Sept. 30/22[A]		9m Sept. 30/21[A]
	US$000s	%Chg	US$000s
Total revenue	27,095	+4	25,937
Net income	(12)	n.a.	941
	US$		US$
Earnings per share*	(0.00)		0.03

* Trust Unit
[A] Reported in accordance with IFRS

Historical Summary
(as originally stated)

Fiscal Year	Total Rev. US$000s	Net Inc. Bef. Disc. US$000s	EPS* US$
2021[A]	34,180	2,612	0.07
2020[A]	30,647	357	0.01
2019[A]	23,039	(3,961)	(0.12)
2018[A]	15,518	5,199	0.16
2017[A]	4,671	(1,513)	(0.05)

* Trust Unit
[A] Reported in accordance with IFRS

R.2 RB Global, Inc.*

Symbol - RBA **Exchange** - TSX **CUSIP** - 74935Q
Head Office - 9500 Glenlyon Pky, Burnaby, BC, V5J 0C6 **Telephone** - (778) 331-5500 **Toll-free** - (800) 663-1739 **Fax** - (778) 331-5501
Website - investor.rbglobal.com
Email - srathod@rbglobal.com
Investor Relations - Sameer Rathod (510) 381-7584
Auditors - Ernst & Young LLP C.A., Vancouver, B.C.
Lawyers - McCarthy Tétrault LLP, Vancouver, B.C.
Transfer Agents - Computershare Trust Company, N.A., New York, N.Y.; Computershare Trust Company of Canada Inc., Vancouver, B.C.
FP500 Revenue Ranking - 200
Employees - 7,600 at May 9, 2023
Profile - (Can. 1997) Sells a broad range of primarily used commercial and industrial assets through unreserved on site auctions, online marketplaces, listings and private brokerage services. Additional services include equipment financing, assets appraisals and inspection, online equipment listing, logistical services and equipment refurbishment. Through IAA, operates an omnichannel digital marketplace connecting vehicle buyers and sellers.
Has operations in 13 countries including the United States, Canada, Australia, the United Arab Emirates and the Netherlands, and maintains presence in 42 countries where customers are able to sell from their own yards. The company's auction site network consists of 41 main auction sites and 22 local satellite yards, as well as 28 yards serving the U.S. military. IAA's network includes over 210 yards globally with a significant presence in the U.S., Canada and Europe.
The company's brands offering auctions, marketplace and brokerage services consist of Ritchie Bros. Auctioneers, which offers live unreserved on site auctions with live online simulcast where the company has care, custody and control of consignors' assets; IronPlanet, an online marketplace with featured weekly auctions and provides exclusive IronClad Assurance® equipment condition certification; Marketplace-E, an online marketplace offering multiple price and timing options; GovPlanet, an online marketplace for the sale of government and military assets; and Ritchie Bros. Private Treaty, which offers confidential, negotiated sale of large equipment. Other services include equipment financing and leasing; appraisal services; inspection services; online listing services; repair, paint and other make-ready services; logistical services, which provides end-to-end transportation and customs clearance solution for sellers and buyers with shipping needs; data services, which provides construction equipment market intelligence; software services, which provides cloud-based platform to manage end-to-end disposition; and a digital marketplace connecting equipment owners with parts manufacturers.
IAA's global digital marketplace facilitates the marketing and sale of total-loss, damage and low-value vehicles for a full spectrum of sellers including insurance carriers, dealerships, fleet lease and rental car companies and charitable organizations. Offers sellers a comprehensive suite of services including commerce, logistics and vehicle-processing and provides buyers with multiple bidding and buying digital channels, innovative vehicle merchandising and efficient evaluation service.

Total Auction Metrics

	2022	2021
Total lots sold[1]	520,959	493,371
Bids per lot sold[2]	28	28

[1] Lot is a single asset to be sold or a group of assets bundled for sale as one unit.
[2] Total number of bids received for a lot divided by the total number of lots sold.

Note - GovPlanet business metrics are excluded.
During 2022, the company discontinued the Kruse Energy brand, which previously offered event-based sales of used energy equipment.

Recent Merger and Acquisition Activity

Status: completed **Revised:** Mar. 20, 2023
UPDATE: The transaction was completed. PREVIOUS: Ritchie Bros. Auctioneers Incorporated agreed to acquire NYSE-listed IAA, Inc. for US$7.3 billion, including assumption of US$ 1 billion of net debt. IAA shareholders would receive US$10 in cash and 0.5804 Ritchie Bros. common shares for each IAA common share held, for a purchase price of US$46.88. IAA is a global digital marketplace connecting vehicle buyers and sellers with more than 210 facilities across the United States, Canada and Europe. Its platform facilitates the marketing and sale of total-loss, damaged and low-value vehicles. Ritchie Bros. would continue to be legally incorporated in Canada and retain its offices and employee base in Burnaby, B.C., and IAA's Chicago, Illinois offices would serve as the official headquarters of the combined company. The transaction was expected to close in the first half of 2023. Dec. 20, 2022 - All regulatory clearances have been received. Jan. 23, 2023 - Terms were amended pursuant to which IAA shareholders would now receive US$12.80 per share in cash and 0.5252 Ritchie Bros. common shares for each IAA share held. Ritchie also plans to pay a one-time special dividend to its shareholders of US$1.08 per share prior to closing. Ancora Alternatives, IAA's top shareholder, has now agreed to support the transaction. Mar. 6, 2023 - Independent proxy voting advisory firms Institutional Shareholder Services Inc. and Glass, Lewis & Co. each recommended that Ritchie Bros. shareholders vote against the proposed acquisition of IAA. Independent proxy advisory firm Egan-Jones Proxy Services recommended that Ritchie Bros. shareholders vote for the transaction. Mar. 14, 2023 - Ritchie Bros. shareholders approved the transaction.

Status: completed **Revised:** Mar. 17, 2023
UPDATE: The transaction was completed for Cdn$23,100,000. PREVIOUS: Ritchie Bros. Auctioneers Incorporated agreed to acquire a property in Amaranth, Ont., for US$22,000,000. Ritchie Bros. plans to relocate its auction operations from its recently acquired property in

Bolton, Ont., to the Amaranth property once the acquisition and development of Amaranth is completed.

Status: completed **Announced:** Jan. 3, 2023

Ritchie Bros. Auctioneers Incorporated acquired 8,889,766 units of Tampa, Fla.-based VeriTread, LLC from VeriTread unitholders for US$25,000,000 and 1,056,338 units through an investment of US$3,000,000 cash. VeriTread develops an online marketplace for open deck transportation where shippers can list their freight while transportation providers submit competing bids for the shipment. As a result, Ritchie Bros increased its holdings in VeriTread from 11% to 75% interest. Concurrently, Ritchie Bros entered into a put/call agreement with one of the minority unitholders of VeriTread for their remaining units.

Status: terminated **Revised:** June 28, 2022

UPDATE: The transaction was terminated. PREVIOUS: Ritchie Bros. Auctioneers Incorporated agreed to acquire Euro Auctions group which consists of Northern Ireland-based companies including Euro Auctions Limited, William Keys & Sons Holdings Limited, Equipment & Plant Services Ltd. and Equipment Sales Ltd. for an enterprise value of £775,000,000 cash. Euro Auctions conducts unreserved heavy equipment auctions with onsite and online bidding under the brands Euro Auctions and Yoder & Frey. During 2020, Euro Auctions conducted 60 auctions, selling close to 90,000 items for over £484,000,000 across nine locations in the U.K., Northern Ireland, Germany, Spain, the United Arab Emirates, Australia and the U.S. Euro Auctions also sells items through a timed auction format and a daily marketplace with buy now and make offer options. Mar. 4, 2022 - The United Kingdom Competition and Markets Authority (CMA) notified Ritchie Bros. that it intends to refer the proposed transaction to a phase 2 review process. Apr. 29, 2022 - Ritchie Bros. decided to discontinue the phase 2 review by the CMA. As a result, the transaction would automatically terminate on June 28, 2022.

Status: completed **Announced:** Mar. 17, 2022

Ritchie Bros. Auctioneers Incorporated completed a sale-leaseback transaction for a property in Bolton, Ont., consisting of a parcel of land with buildings for $208,195,000. Ritchie Bros. continued to use the property for auction operations under the operating leaseback agreement until the completion of the acquisition and development of a replacement property and auction site in Amaranth, Ont.

Predecessor Detail - Name changed from Ritchie Bros. Auctioneers Incorporated, May 23, 2023.

Directors - Erik Olsson, chr., Scottsdale, Ariz.; James (Jim) Kessler, CEO, Pa.; Brian Bales, Scottsdale, Ariz.; William (Bill) Breslin, San Antonio, Tex.; Adam DeWitt, Chicago, Ill.; Robert G. (Bob) Elton, Vancouver, B.C.; Timothy J. (Tim) O'Day, Chicago, Ill.; Sarah E. Raiss, Calgary, Alta.; Michael Sieger, Miami, Fla.; Jeffrey C. Smith, Boca Raton, Fla.; Carol M. Stephenson, London, Ont.

Other Exec. Officers - Matt Ackley, chief digital officer; Baron Concors, chief product & tech. officer; Kevin Geisner, chief strategy officer; James J. (Jeff) Jeter, chief revenue officer; Carmen Thiede, chief transformation & people officer; Karl W. Werner, chief bus. devel. officer; Darren J. Watt, sr. v-p, gen. counsel & corp. sec.; Megan Cash, principal fin. & acctg. officer

Capital Stock

	Authorized (shs.)	Outstanding (shs.)[1]	Par
Ser.A Sr. Preferred	unlimited	485,000,000	US$1.00
Junior Preferred	unlimited	nil	
Common	unlimited	182,140,903	

[1] At Aug. 2, 2023

Senior Preferred - Issuable in series.

Series A - Entitled to receive dividends at the rate of 5.5% per annum and entitled to participate on an as-converted basis in common share dividends, subject to a US$0.27 per share per quarter floor. Convertible into a number of common shares equal to the face amount of such preferred shares multiplied by the then-applicable conversion rate. On Feb. 1, 2027, preferred holders will have the right to increase the preferential dividend rate to 7.5%, and on Feb. 1, 2032, preferred holders will have the right to increase the preferential dividend rate to a fixed percentage equal to the greater of (x) 600 basis points over the daily simple SOFR as then in effect and (y) 10.50%, subject, in each case, to the company's right to redeem the preferred shares for which a dividend rate increase has been demanded. Entitled to number of votes equal to the number of common shares into which senior preferred series A shares would be convertible.

Junior Preferred - Issuable in series. Non-voting.

Common - One vote per share.

Options - At Dec. 31, 2022, options were outstanding to purchase 2,730,295 common shares at a weighted average exercise price of US$46.88 per share with a weighted average remaining contractual term of 7.3 years.

Major Shareholder - Widely held at Apr. 5, 2023.

Price Range - RBA/TSX

Year	Volume	High	Low	Close
2022	50,614,709	$94.18	$62.02	$78.21
2021	38,150,709	$94.96	$64.17	$77.41
2020	65,559,506	$101.93	$37.76	$88.48
2019	31,230,404	$58.51	$42.64	$55.72
2018	39,180,130	$50.66	$37.08	$44.66

Recent Close: $80.68

Capital Stock Changes - On Feb. 1, 2023, private placement of 485,000,000 senior preferred series A shares at US$1.00 per share and 251,163 common shares at US$59.722 per share was completed with Starboard Value LP. On Mar. 20, 2023, 71,100,000 common shares were issued pursuant to acquisition of IAA, Inc.

During 2022, common shares were issued as follows: 159,920 on exercise of options and 103,394 on vesting of share units.

Dividends

RBA com Ra US$1.08 pa Q est. Sept. 14, 2022
Prev. Rate: US$1.00 est. Sept. 15, 2021
Prev. Rate: US$0.88 est. Sept. 16, 2020
US$1.08◆............ Mar. 28/23
Paid in 2023: US$0.81 + US$1.08◆ 2022: US$1.04 2021: US$0.94
◆ Special

Long-Term Debt - Outstanding at Dec. 31, 2022:

Term loan[1]	US$85,523,000
5.375% sr. unsec. notes due 2025	500,000,000
Less: Unamort. debt issue costs	4,026,000
	581,497,000
Less: Current portion	4,386,000
	577,111,000

[1] Bearing interest at a weighted average rate of 5.86% and due on September 2026.

Principal repayments of long-term debt were reported as follows:

2023	US$4,386,000
2024	4,386,000
2025	504,386,000
2026	72,365,000

Note - In February 2023, $550,000,000 principal amount of 6.750% senior secured notes due Mar. 15, 2028, and $800,000,000 principal amount of 7.750% senior notes due Mar. 15, 2031, were issued.

Wholly Owned Subsidiaries

IAA, Inc., Westchester, Ill.
IronPlanet Canada Ltd., Canada.
IronPlanet, Inc., Del.
IronPlanet Limited, Ireland.
IronPlanet Mexico, S. de R.L. de C.V., Mexico.
IronPlanet Motors, LLC, Del.
IronPlanet UK Limited, United Kingdom.
Kruse Energy & Equipment Auctioneers, LLC, Tex.
Leake Auction Company, Tulsa, Okla.
Mascus A/S, Netherlands.
Mascus International B.V., Netherlands.
Mascus International Holding B.V., Amsterdam, Netherlands.
Mascus IP B.V., Netherlands.
R.B. Holdings S.A.R.L., France.
R.B. Properties EURL, France.
R.B. Services S.A.R.L., France.
RBA Holdings Inc., Del.
• 100% int. in **AssetNation, Inc.**, Del.
Ritchie Auction (Beijing) Co. Ltd., People's Republic of China.
Ritchie Bros. Asset Solutions Inc., Fla.
Ritchie Bros. Auctioneers (Beijing) Co. Ltd., People's Republic of China.
Ritchie Bros. Auctioneers Comercial de Equipamentos Industriais Ltda, Brazil.
Ritchie Bros. Auctioneers de Mexico, S. de R.L. de C.V., Mexico.
Ritchie Bros. Auctioneers France S.A.S., France.
Ritchie Bros. Auctioneers India Private Limited, India.
Ritchie Bros. Auctioneers (Japan) K.K., Japan.
Ritchie Bros. Auctioneers (ME) Limited, Cyprus.
Ritchie Bros. Auctioneers Mexico Services, S. de R.L. de C.V., Mexico.
Ritchie Bros. Auctioneers (Panama) S.A., Panama.
Ritchie Bros. Auctioneers Pte. Ltd., Singapore.
Ritchie Bros. Auctioneers Pty Ltd., Australia.
Ritchie Bros. Auctioneers (Spain) S.L.U., Spain.
Ritchie Bros. B.V., Netherlands.
Ritchie Bros. Deutschland GmbH, Germany.
Ritchie Bros. Finance Ltd., Canada.
Ritchie Bros. Financial Services (America) Inc., Nev.
Ritchie Bros. Financial Services Ltd., Canada.
Ritchie Bros. Finland Oy, Finland.
Ritchie Bros. Holdings B.V., Netherlands.
Ritchie Bros. Holdings Inc., Wash.
• 100% int. in **Ritchie Bros. Auctioneers (America) Inc.**, Wash.
• 100% int. in **Ritchie Bros. Properties Inc.**, Wash.
Ritchie Bros. Holdings Ltd., Canada.
• 100% int. in **Ritchie Bros. Auctioneers (Canada) Ltd.**, Canada.
• 100% int. in **Ritchie Bros. Properties Ltd.**, Canada.
Ritchie Bros. Holdings Pty Ltd., Australia.
Ritchie Bros. Investment Holdings (Luxembourg) S.A.R.L., Cyprus.
Ritchie Bros. Italia S.r.l., Italy.
Ritchie Bros. (NZ) Limited, New Zealand.
Ritchie Bros. Polska Sp.zo.o, Poland.
Ritchie Bros. Properties B.V., Netherlands.
Ritchie Bros. Properties Japan KK, Japan.
Ritchie Bros. Properties Pty Ltd., Australia.
Ritchie Bros. Properties, S. de R.L. de C.V., Mexico.
Ritchie Bros. Properties S.r.l., Italy.
Ritchie Bros. Properties (Spain) S.L.U., Spain.
Ritchie Bros. Real Estate Service Ltd., Canada.
Ritchie Bros. Shared Services B.V., Netherlands.
Ritchie Bros. Sweden AB, Sweden.
Ritchie Bros. UK Holdings Limited, Milton Keynes, Bucks., United Kingdom.
Ritchie Bros. UK Limited, United Kingdom.
Rouse Analytics LLC, Calif.
Rouse Appraisals LLC, Calif.
Rouse Sales LLC, Calif.
Rouse Services Canada Ltd., Canada.
Rouse Services LLC, Beverly Hills, Calif.
SalvageSale De Mexico S. de R.L. de C.V., Mexico.
SalvageSale Servicios, S. de R.L. de C.V., Mexico.
SmartEquip, Inc., Del.
Xcira LLC, Del.

Subsidiaries

75.2% int. in **VeriTread, LLC**, Tampa, Fla.

Note: The preceding list includes only the major related companies in which interests are held.

Financial Statistics

Periods ended:	12m Dec. 31/22[A]		12m Dec. 31/21[A]
	US$000s	%Chg	US$000s
Operating revenue	**1,733,808**	**+22**	**1,416,971**
Cost of goods sold	710,620		544,371
Salaries & benefits	426,728		367,449
General & admin expense	179,286		147,562
Operating expense	**1,316,634**	**+24**	**1,059,382**
Operating income	**417,174**	**+17**	**357,589**
Deprec., depl. & amort.	97,155		87,889
Finance income	6,971		1,402
Finance costs, gross	57,880		36,993
Pre-tax income	**405,988**	**+98**	**205,232**
Income taxes	86,230		53,378
Net income	**319,758**	**+111**	**151,854**
Net inc. for equity hldrs	**319,657**	**+110**	**151,868**
Net inc. for non-cont. int	**101**	**n.a.**	**(14)**
Cash & equivalent	494,324		326,113
Inventories	103,050		102,494
Accounts receivable	183,180		146,499
Current assets	963,117		762,222
Fixed assets, net	459,137		449,087
Right-of-use assets	122,934		114,414
Intangibles, net	1,271,468		1,298,231
Total assets	**2,863,727**	**-20**	**3,592,914**
Bank indebtedness	29,118		6,147
Accts. pay. & accr. liabs	698,431		552,021
Current liabilities	795,290		588,419
Long-term debt, gross	581,497		1,737,438
Long-term debt, net	577,111		1,733,940
Long-term lease liabilities	127,220		123,865
Shareholders' equity	1,289,609		1,070,675
Non-controlling interest	466		388
Cash from oper. activs	**463,055**	**+46**	**317,586**
Cash from fin. activs	(1,258,122)		960,908
Cash from invest. activs	77,332		(214,066)
Net cash position	**625,946**	**-54**	**1,362,452**
Capital expenditures	(31,972)		(9,816)
Capital disposals	165,542		1,911
	US$		US$
Earnings per share*	2.89		1.38
Cash flow per share*	4.18		2.88
Cash divd. per share*	1.04		0.94
	shs		shs
No. of shs. o/s*	110,881,363		110,618,049
Avg. no. of shs. o/s*	110,781,282		110,315,782
	%		%
Net profit margin	18.44		10.72
Return on equity	27.09		14.62
Return on assets	11.32		6.03
Foreign sales percent	78		80
No. of employees (FTEs)	2,800		2,700

* Common
[A] Reported in accordance with U.S. GAAP

Latest Results

Periods ended:	6m June 30/23[A]		6m June 30/22[A]
	US$000s	%Chg	US$000s
Operating revenue	1,618,900	+84	878,467
Net income	58,600	-75	231,512
Net inc. for equity hldrs	58,800	-75	231,459
Net inc. for non-cont. int	(200)		53
	US$		US$
Earnings per share*	0.29		2.09

* Common
[A] Reported in accordance with U.S. GAAP

Historical Summary
(as originally stated)

Fiscal Year	Oper. Rev. US$000s	Net Inc. Bef. Disc. US$000s	EPS* US$
2022[A]	1,733,808	319,758	2.89
2021[A]	1,416,971	151,854	1.38
2020[A]	1,377,260	170,358	1.56
2019[A]	1,318,641	149,140	1.37
2018[A]	1,170,026	121,506	1.12

* Common
[A] Reported in accordance with U.S. GAAP

R.3 RDARS Inc.

Symbol - RDRS **Exchange** - CSE **CUSIP** - 75526A
Head Office - 507-2 Covington Rd, North York, ON, M6A 3E2 **Telephone** - (786) 564-5602
Website - www.rdars.com
Email - charles.zwebner@rdars.com
Investor Relations - Charles Zwebner (786) 564-5602
Auditors - Zeifmans LLP C.A., North York, Ont.
Transfer Agents - Endeavor Trust Corporation, Vancouver, B.C.
Profile - (Ont. 2019) Developing various autonomous technologies including a drone which augments security systems for residential, commercial and industrial applications.

Flagship product is the Eagle Watch platform, which consists of Eagle Eye, a drone; Eagle Nest, a drone station; Eagle Rover, an indoor robotic system; and Eagle Watch Command & Control Software, a suite of software applications which maintain, control and secure the communications and data received from these autonomous systems. When an alarm is triggered, the indoor Eagle Rover or outdoor Eagle Eye drone will autonomously travel and/or fly to the zone where the alarm was triggered and provide real time visual and audio to the company's trained response personnel at the Command and Control Center in Miami, Fla. Live video and audio are captured, recorded and streamed to allow personnel to assess the situation, allowing such personnel to dispatch appropriate emergency first responders including police, fire and ambulance, as necessary.

Production level designs for the products are in the final stages of development. First production run of Eagle Eye and Eagle Nest was completed in October 2022. Development of Eagle Rover has been deferred to the third quarter of fiscal 2023.

In October 2022, the company opened a UAS (Unmanned Aerial System) Command and Control Center in Miami, Fla., to allow drone operators using the company's Eagle Watch platform to manage its global fleet of autonomous systems. Eagle Watch platform consists of a drone, a drone station and indoor robotic system and a software application that acts as a command-and-control environment to manage, maintain and control all remote systems.

In September 2022, the company opened a manufacturing facility in Pickering, Ont., for the production of Eagle Eye and Eagle Nest products. These products are part of the company's Eagle Watch platform, which consists of a drone, a drone station and indoor robotic system and a software application that acts as a command-and-control environment to manage, maintain and control all remote systems.

Common listed on CSE, Sept. 7, 2022.

Directors - Charles Zwebner, founder, CEO & corp. sec., Toronto, Ont.; Anthony Heller, Toronto, Ont.; Binyomin Posen, Toronto, Ont.
Other Exec. Officers - Bennett Kurtz, CFO; Jason Braverman, chief tech. officer

Capital Stock

	Authorized (shs.)	Outstanding (shs.)[1]
Common	unlimited	17,721,287

[1] At June 6, 2023

Major Shareholder - Widely held at Apr. 25, 2023.

Price Range - RDRS/CSE

Year	Volume	High	Low	Close
2022	1,074,558	$1.20	$0.30	$0.40

Consolidation: 1-for-20 cons. in June 2023
Recent Close: $0.12
Capital Stock Changes - On June 6, 2023, common shares were consolidated on a 1-for-20 basis.

In July 2022, 53,650,000 units (1 common share & 1 warrant) were issued without further consideration on exchange of subscription receipts sold previously by private placement at 5¢ each. In August 2022, 34,380,817 common shares were issued on conversion of debentures. Also during fiscal 2022, common shares were issued as follows: 17,740,000 on exercise of warrants, 1,510,000 as finders' fees and 919,328 on conversion of debentures.

Financial Statistics

Periods ended:	12m Nov. 30/22[A]		12m Nov. 30/21[A1]
	$000s	%Chg	$000s
General & admin expense	2,242		1,313
Stock-based compensation	1,020		...
Operating expense	**3,263**	**+149**	**1,313**
Operating income	**(3,263)**	**n.a.**	**(1,313)**
Deprec., depl. & amort.	1		nil
Finance income	4		nil
Finance costs, gross	395		224
Pre-tax income	**(3,025)**	**n.a.**	**(1,984)**
Net income	**(3,025)**	**n.a.**	**(1,984)**
Cash & equivalent	575		91
Current assets	927		294
Fixed assets, net	8		nil
Intangibles, net	1,253		793
Total assets	**2,187**	**+101**	**1,087**
Bank indebtedness	nil		279
Accts. pay. & accr. liabs	830		1,069
Current liabilities	1,440		1,728
Long-term debt, gross	1,206		2,180
Long-term debt, net	596		1,800
Equity portion of conv. debs	166		14
Shareholders' equity	151		(2,441)
Cash from oper. activs	**(2,617)**	**n.a.**	**(1,330)**
Cash from fin. activs	3,570		1,496
Cash from invest. activs	(468)		(76)
Net cash position	**575**	**+532**	**91**
Capital expenditures	(9)		nil
	$		$
Earnings per share*	(0.20)		(0.16)
Cash flow per share*	(0.19)		(0.11)
	shs		shs
No. of shs. o/s*	17,721,287		12,311,280
Avg. no. of shs. o/s*	13,752,606		12,311,280
	%		%
Net profit margin	n.a.		n.a.
Return on equity	n.m.		n.m.
Return on assets	(160.66)		(184.29)

* Common
[A] Reported in accordance with IFRS
[1] As shown in the prospectus dated Aug. 26, 2022. Shares and per share figures adjusted to reflect 60-for-1 split effective Dec. 30, 2021.

Latest Results

Periods ended:	3m Feb. 28/23[A]		3m Feb. 28/22[A]
	$000s	%Chg	$000s
Net income	(619)	n.a.	(384)
	$		$
Earnings per share*	(0.03)		(0.03)

* Common
[A] Reported in accordance with IFRS

Historical Summary
(as originally stated)

Fiscal Year	Oper. Rev.	Net Inc. Bef. Disc.	EPS*
	$000s	$000s	$
2022[A]	nil	(3,025)	(0.20)
2021[A1]	nil	(1,984)	(0.16)
2020[A1]	nil	(1,199)	(0.10)

* Common
[A] Reported in accordance with IFRS
[1] As shown in the prospectus dated Aug. 26, 2022. Shares and per share figures adjusted to reflect 60-for-1 split effective Dec. 30, 2021.
Note: Adjusted throughout for 1-for-20 cons. in June 2023

R.4 RE Royalties Ltd.

Symbol - RE **Exchange** - TSX-VEN **CUSIP** - 75527Q
Head Office - 1400-1040 Georgia St W, Vancouver, BC, V6E 4H1 **Telephone** - (778) 374-2000 **Toll-free** - (800) 667-2114 **Fax** - (604) 684-8092
Website - www.reroyalties.com
Email - taliabeckett@reroyalties.com
Investor Relations - Talia Beckett (778) 374-2000
Auditors - Deloitte LLP C.A., Vancouver, B.C.
Transfer Agents - Computershare Trust Company of Canada Inc., Vancouver, B.C.
Employees - 8 at Dec. 31, 2022
Profile - (B.C. 2016) Holds royalty interests in renewable energy generation facilities and projects, and other clean energy technologies in North America and Europe.

Acquires royalties from renewable power generation facility and other clean energy technology owners, operators and developers by providing non-dilutive financing. The royalties represent an ongoing economic interest in the production or future production of electricity from a project.

Has a portfolio of 110 royalties on solar (70), battery storage (23), wind (14), energy efficiency (2) and renewable natural gas (1) projects in Canada, the United States, Mexico and Romania with a total generating capacity of 376 MW.

In May 2023, the company acquired a royalty on a 100-MW wind project in Alberta from a major independent power producer with a power purchase agreement with a large corporate off taker for $940,000. The company would receive an average annual royalty payments of approximately $132,000 per year payable monthly for 12 years.

In February 2023, the company acquired a gross revenue royalty on the 27-MWdc (20-MWac) Jackson Center solar project phase 2 in Mercer cty., Penn., from **Teichos Energy LLC** in exchange for a US$1,800,000 secured term loan. The company would receive a 1% gross revenue royalty on the project for a period of 15 years once it reaches commercial operation, and could increase to an up to 2% gross royalty if loan term is extended.

In May 2022, the company acquired a 1% and 5% gross revenue royalty on six operational solar projects in Mexico from **ReVolve Renewable Power Corp.** in exchange for a $1,600,000 secured 24-month 10% loan. Subsequently in September 2022, the company agreed to finance Revolve Renewable's purchase of three battery storage development projects in Mexico with a $1,860,000 secured two-year 12% loan in exchange for a 5% gross revenue royalty on the projects.

In August 2022, the company financed **Switch Power Ontario Battery Operations Corp.**'s acquisition of a 0.38-MW operational rooftop solar generation project in Vaughan, Ont., with $1,300,000 six-month 10% loan in exchange for a 1% gross revenue royalty on the project.

In April 2022, the company acquired a 3.5% gross revenue royalty on six development battery storage projects in Vermont from **Nomad Transportable Power Systems Inc.** in exchange for a US$5,600,000 five-year 12% secured working capital loan.

Predecessor Detail - Name changed from Baetis Ventures Ltd., Nov. 6, 2018, pursuant to Qualifying Transaction reverse takeover acquisition of (old) RE Royalties Ltd.; basis 1 new for 3 old shs.
Directors - Marchand Snyman, co-founder & chr., West Vancouver, B.C.; Bernard Tan, founder & CEO, Richmond, B.C.; René G. Carrier, West Vancouver, B.C.; Stephen Cheeseman, North Vancouver, B.C.; Gordon J. (Gord) Fretwell, Vancouver, B.C.; Paul A. Larkin, Vancouver, B.C.; Jill D. Leversage, Vancouver, B.C.
Other Exec. Officers - Peter Leighton, COO; Luqman Khan, CFO; Bryce Anderson, v-p, invests.; Talia Beckett, v-p, commun. & sustainability; Shane Grovue, v-p, growth & impact/ESG; Alistair Howard, v-p, corp. devel.

Capital Stock

	Authorized (shs.)	Outstanding (shs.)[1]
Preferred	unlimited	nil
Common	unlimited	43,127,607

[1] At May 26, 2023

Major Shareholder - CTR Holdings Ltd. held 12.51% interest at Aug. 25, 2022.

Price Range - RE/TSX-VEN

Year	Volume	High	Low	Close
2022	2,456,714	$1.05	$0.65	$0.75
2021	1,817,352	$1.63	$0.94	$1.02
2020	1,114,327	$1.80	$0.85	$1.53
2019	1,114,534	$1.01	$0.70	$0.97
2018	312,995	$1.10	$0.51	$0.99

Recent Close: $0.56
Capital Stock Changes - In June 2022, public offering of 9,837,680 units (1 common share & 1 warrant) at 82¢ per unit was completed.

Dividends

RE com Ra $0.04 pa Q est. Aug. 23, 2023

Wholly Owned Subsidiaries

RE Royalties (Canada) Ltd.
RE Royalties USA Inc., Del.
- 96.68% int. in **FP OCEP Invest LLC**, Del.
- 98% int. in **FP Puerto Rico Invest, LLC**, Del.

Investments

23.3% int. in **RER US 1 LLC**, Del.

Financial Statistics

Periods ended:	12m Dec. 31/22[A]		12m Dec. 31/21[A]
	$000s	%Chg	$000s
Operating revenue	**4,237**	**+150**	**1,696**
Salaries & benefits	758		625
General & admin expense	1,603		1,198
Stock-based compensation	89		853
Other operating expense	50		51
Operating expense	**2,500**	**-8**	**2,727**
Operating income	**1,737**	**n.a.**	**(1,031)**
Deprec., depl. & amort.	364		304
Finance costs, gross	1,868		1,026
Investment income	508		nil
Write-downs/write-offs	(473)		nil
Pre-tax income	**(223)**	**n.a.**	**(2,130)**
Income taxes	211		nil
Net income	**(434)**	**n.a.**	**(2,130)**
Net inc. for equity hldrs	**(726)**	**n.a.**	**(2,130)**
Net inc. for non-cont. int.	**292**	**n.a.**	**nil**
Cash & equivalent	4,598		10,472
Accounts receivable	750		711
Current assets	18,667		21,129
Long-term investments	23,688		13,889
Right-of-use assets	65		84
Total assets	**42,610**	**+21**	**35,195**
Accts. pay. & accr. liabs	402		186
Current liabilities	2,597		201
Long-term debt, gross	19,443		20,516
Long-term debt, net	21,488		20,516
Long-term lease liabilities	53		72
Shareholders' equity	20,388		14,406
Cash from oper. activs	**142**	**-1**	**143**
Cash from fin. activs	4,363		7,643
Cash from invest. activs	(17,397)		616
Net cash position	**7,580**	**-62**	**20,102**
	$		$
Earnings per share*	(0.02)		(0.06)
Cash flow per share*	0.00		0.00
Cash divd. per share*	0.04		0.04
	shs		shs
No. of shs. o/s*	43,127,607		33,289,927
Avg. no. of shs. o/s*	38,653,484		33,289,927
	%		%
Net profit margin	(10.24)		(125.59)
Return on equity	(4.17)		(13.56)
Return on assets	8.23		(3.52)
No. of employees (FTEs)	8		4

* Common
[A] Reported in accordance with IFRS

Latest Results

Periods ended:	3m Mar. 31/23[A]		3m Mar. 31/22[A]
	$000s	%Chg	$000s
Operating revenue	1,824	+229	554
Net income	558	n.a.	(550)
Net inc. for equity hldrs	166	n.a.	(550)
Net inc. for non-cont. int.	392		...
	$		$
Earnings per share*	0.00		(0.02)

* Common
[A] Reported in accordance with IFRS

Historical Summary
(as originally stated)

Fiscal Year	Oper. Rev.	Net Inc. Bef. Disc.	EPS*
	$000s	$000s	$
2022[A]	4,237	(434)	(0.02)
2021[A]	1,696	(2,130)	(0.06)
2020[A]	2,371	(447)	(0.01)
2019[A]	1,380	(412)	(0.01)
2018[A1]	1,019	(3,199)	(0.17)

* Common
[A] Reported in accordance with IFRS
[1] Results reflect the Nov. 6, 2018, Qualifying Transaction reverse takeover acquisition of (old) RE Royalties Ltd.

R.5 RESAAS Services Inc.

Symbol - RSS **Exchange** - TSX-VEN **CUSIP** - 76083V
Head Office - 2600-595 Burrard St, Vancouver, BC, V7X 1L3 **Telephone** - (604) 558-2929 **Toll-free** - (888) 929-7227
Website - www.resaas.com
Email - don.mosher@resaas.com
Investor Relations - Donald A. Mosher (604) 617-5448
Auditors - Smythe LLP C.A.
Lawyers - TroyGould PC, Los Angeles, Calif.; Blake, Cassels & Graydon LLP, Vancouver, B.C.
Transfer Agents - Computershare Investor Services Inc.

Profile - (B.C. 2009) Provides a cloud-based technology platform for the real estate industry.

Developed a platform that is integrated with a suite of tools including a global referral network, lead generation engine, listing management, client engagement modules, customer relationship management tools, analytics, file sharing, an advertising engine and payment system. The platform services real estate brokerage, multiple listing services (MLS), franchises and real estate agents on a business to business basis, and allow them to communicate with other agents globally, find leads, send and receive referrals, create pre-market property listings before it is made available to the MLS, create off-market property listings for a closed group and create on-market property listings.

Directors - Pierre Chadi, chr., Montréal, Qué.; Thomas (Tom) Rossiter, pres. & CEO, B.C.; Adrian Barrett, B.C.; Randall Miles, N.Y.

Other Exec. Officers - Sascha Williams, COO; Donald A. (Don) Mosher, v-p, capital markets

Capital Stock

	Authorized (shs.)	Outstanding (shs.)[1]	Par
Class A Preferred	unlimited	nil	$0.01
Class B Preferred	unlimited	nil	
Common	unlimited	75,347,002	

[1] At May 1, 2023

Major Shareholder - Craig Barton held 11.62% interest at Mar. 23, 2023.

Price Range - RSS/TSX-VEN

Year	Volume	High	Low	Close
2022	4,877,541	$1.10	$0.10	$0.19
2021	9,901,381	$1.88	$0.60	$0.84
2020	8,836,900	$0.65	$0.16	$0.64
2019	7,741,882	$0.50	$0.15	$0.23
2018	6,185,035	$0.90	$0.18	$0.32

Recent Close: $0.16

Capital Stock Changes - During 2022, common shares were issued as follows: 2,000,000 by private placement and 249,000 on exercise of options.

Wholly Owned Subsidiaries

RESAAS USA Inc., Calif.
Real Block Inc., Ont.

Financial Statistics

Periods ended:	12m Dec. 31/22[A]		12m Dec. 31/21[A]
	$000s	%Chg	$000s
Operating revenue	**374**	**-33**	**560**
General & admin expense	1,353		1,730
Stock-based compensation	(26)[1]		1,459
Operating expense	**1,327**	**-58**	**3,190**
Operating income	**(953)**	**n.a.**	**(2,630)**
Deprec., depl. & amort.	183		178
Finance income	2		nil
Finance costs, gross	2		nil
Write-downs/write-offs	(35)		(38)
Pre-tax income	**(1,189)**	**n.a.**	**(2,834)**
Net income	**(1,189)**	**n.a.**	**(2,834)**
Cash & equivalent	241		152
Accounts receivable	59		19
Current assets	304		230
Fixed assets, net	3		4
Right-of-use assets	56		7
Intangibles, net	12		206
Total assets	**400**	**-10**	**446**
Accts. pay. & accr. liabs	434		518
Current liabilities	791		701
Preferred share equity	42		nil
Shareholders' equity	(433)		(255)
Cash from oper. activs	**(1,118)**	**n.a.**	**(1,176)**
Cash from fin. activs	1,209		1,201
Cash from invest. activs	(4)		(3)
Net cash position	**240**	**+58**	**152**
Capital expenditures	(4)		(3)
	$		$
Earnings per share*	(0.02)		(0.04)
Cash flow per share*	(0.02)		(0.02)
	shs		shs
No. of shs. o/s*	75,147,002		72,898,002
Avg. no. of shs. o/s*	74,515,386		71,670,249
	%		%
Net profit margin	(317.91)		(506.07)
Return on equity	n.m.		n.m.
Return on assets	(280.61)		(508.34)

* Common
[A] Reported in accordance with IFRS
[1] Includes stock-based compensation recovery of $77,560 from revaluation of options.

Latest Results

Periods ended:	3m Mar. 31/23[A]		3m Mar. 31/22[A]
	$000s	%Chg	$000s
Operating revenue	81	-10	90
Net income	(1,277)	n.a.	(304)
	$		$
Earnings per share*	(0.02)		(0.00)

* Common
[A] Reported in accordance with IFRS

Historical Summary
(as originally stated)

Fiscal Year	Oper. Rev.	Net Inc. Bef. Disc.	EPS*
	$000s	$000s	$
2022[A]	374	(1,189)	(0.02)
2021[A]	560	(2,834)	(0.04)
2020[A]	657	(2,780)	(0.04)
2019[A]	802	(3,126)	(0.06)
2018[A]	618	(5,845)	(0.13)

* Common
[A] Reported in accordance with IFRS

R.6 RF Capital Group Inc.*

Symbol - RCG **Exchange** - TSX **CUSIP** - 74971G
Head Office - 2500-100 Queens Quay E, Toronto, ON, M5E 1Y3 **Telephone** - (416) 943-6696 **Toll-free** - (866) 263-0818 **Fax** - (416) 943-6691
Website - richardsonwealth.com
Email - twilson@rfcapgroup.com
Investor Relations - Timothy Wilson (416) 943-6169
Auditors - KPMG LLP C.A., Toronto, Ont.
Lawyers - Goodmans LLP
Transfer Agents - TSX Trust Company, Toronto, Ont.
FP500 Revenue Ranking - 533
Employees - 890 at Dec. 31, 2022

Profile - (Ont. 2009) Operates wealth management business focused on providing wealth advice and investment solutions for high net worth private clients in Canada.

Wholly owned **Richardson Wealth Limited** is the company's full-service investment brokerage, operating as Richardson Wealth and in the francophone market as Patrimoine Richardson, which focuses on guiding high net worth private investors across Canada in wealth preservation, income and growth strategies. Richardson Wealth provides wealth planning and investment products, including externally and internally managed account programs and discretionary investment management.

The company had $35.8 billion in client assets at June 30, 2023, administered by 158 investment advisory teams through 21 offices across Canada. Operations also include wholly owned **RF Securities Clearing LP**, which provides clearing services to Richardson Wealth and **Stifel Nicolaus Canada Inc.**'s Canadian capital markets operations. These services include trade execution, clearing and settlement of securities, custodial services, record keeping, trade confirmations and tax slips. The company also operates a securities borrowing and lending business.

Predecessor Detail - Name changed from GMP Capital Inc., Nov. 20, 2020.

Directors - Donald A. (Don) Wright, chr., Toronto, Ont.; Kishore (Kish) Kapoor, pres. & CEO, Toronto, Ont.; Nathalie Bernier, Montréal, Qué.; David G. (Dave) Brown, Winnipeg, Man.; Vincent Duhamel, Westmount, Qué.; David C. Ferguson, Ajax, Ont.; David G. Leith, Toronto, Ont.; Jane Mowat, Toronto, Ont.; David J. Porter, Edmonton, Alta.; H. Sanford (Sandy) Riley, Winnipeg, Man.

Oper. Subsid./Mgt. Co. Officers - Krista Coburn, sr. v-p, gen. counsel & corp. sec.; Timothy (Tim) Wilson, sr. v-p & CFO; Julie Burnham, v-p, strategic commun.

Capital Stock

	Authorized (shs.)	Outstanding (shs.)[1]
Preferred	unlimited	
Series B	4,600,000	4,600,000
Series C	4,600,000	nil
Common	unlimited	15,800,000

[1] At Aug. 2, 2023

Preferred Series B - Entitled to cumulative preferential annual dividends of $0.9325 per share payable quarterly to Mar. 31, 2026, and thereafter at a rate reset every five years equal to the five-year Government of Canada bond yield plus 2.89%. Redeemable on Mar. 31, 2026, and on March 31 every five years thereafter at $25 per share plus declared and unpaid dividends. Convertible at the holder's option on Mar. 31, 2026, and on March 31 every five years thereafter, into floating rate preferred series C shares on a share-for-share basis, subject to certain conditions. Non-voting.

Common - One vote per share.

Options - At Dec. 31, 2022, options were outstanding to purchase 50,000 common shares at prices ranging from $18 to $20.5 per share with a weighted average remaining contractual life of up to 0.61 year.

Preferred Series C (old) - Were entitled to cumulative preferential annual dividends payable quarterly equal to the 90-day Government of Canada bond yield plus 2.89%. Converted into preferred series B shares on a share-for-share basis on Mar. 31, 2021.

Major Shareholder - Richardson Financial Group Limited held 44.18% interest at Mar. 20, 2023.

Price Range - RCG/TSX

Year	Volume	High	Low	Close
2022	1,139,311	$19.50	$10.24	$11.50
2021	1,178,999	$25.20	$16.20	$19.00
2020	2,170,615	$21.30	$10.70	$17.40
2019	2,103,478	$28.40	$17.30	$19.30
2018	2,868,558	$46.40	$17.60	$18.80

Consolidation: 1-for-10 cons. in Mar. 2022

Recent Close: $6.70

Capital Stock Changes - On Mar. 30, 2022, common shares were consolidated on a 1-for-10 basis. During 2022, 9,717 post-consolidated common shares were cancelled and 61,102 post-consolidated common shares were repurchased under a Normal Course Issuer Bid.

Dividends

RCG com N.S.R. [1]

1-for-10 cons eff. Mar. 30, 2022

$0.23313............. Jan. 3/23

Paid in 2023: $0.23313 2022: n.a. 2021: n.a.

RCG.PR.B pfd ser B cum. red. exch. Adj. Ra $0.925 pa Q est. June 30, 2021

pfd ser C cum. red. exch. Fltg. Ra pa Q

Delisted Apr 1/21.

$0.181788............ Mar. 31/21

Paid in 2023: n.a. 2022: n.a. 2021: $0.181788

[1] Quarterly divd normally payable in June/20 has been omitted.

Long-Term Debt - At Dec. 31, 2022, outstanding debt totaled $110,922,000 and consisted of $80,500,000 drawn under a revolving credit facility due September 2023 and $30,422,000 liability in connection with preferred share ownership in wholly owned Richardson Wealth Limited.

Note - In May 2023, maturity of the revolving credit facility was extended from September 2023 to May 2025.

Wholly Owned Subsidiaries

RF Securities Clearing LP, Toronto, Ont.

Richardson Wealth Limited, Toronto, Ont.

Financial Statistics

Periods ended:	12m Dec. 31/22^A		12m Dec. 31/21^A
	$000s	%Chg	$000s
Total revenue	**353,972**	**+8**	**328,519**
Salaries & benefits	78,538		77,134
General & admin. expense	64,035		58,019
Other operating expense	158,382		164,001
Operating expense	**300,955**	**+1**	**299,154**
Operating income	**53,017**	**+81**	**29,365**
Deprec. & amort.	45,331		42,539
Finance costs, gross	10,797		6,631
Pre-tax income	**(3,111)**	**n.a.**	**(19,805)**
Income taxes	1,692		347
Net income	**(4,803)**	**n.a.**	**(20,152)**
Cash & equivalent	367,848		518,099
Accounts receivable	464,770		707,531
Investments	673		62,355
Fixed assets, net	37,452		15,541
Right-of-use assets	52,809		19,547
Intangibles, net	337,581		348,152
Total assets	**1,699,654**	**-23**	**2,216,015**
Bank indebtedness	nil		13,625
Accts. pay. & accr. liabs.	1,110,424		1,638,336
Debt	110,922		110,922
Lease liabilities	62,448		23,256
Preferred share equity	112,263		112,263
Shareholders' equity	346,921		354,890
Cash from oper. activs.	**(107,402)**	**n.a.**	**(14,207)**
Cash from fin. activs.	(13,802)		(14,637)
Cash from invest. activs.	(29,043)		(9,335)
Net cash position	**367,848**	**-29**	**518,099**
Capital expenditures	(26,387)		(5,979)
	$		$
Earnings per share*	(0.95)		(3.30)
Cash flow per share*	(11.19)		(1.94)
Cash divd. per share*	0.23		nil
	shs		shs
No. of shs. o/s*	15,570,000		15,640,000
Avg. no. of shs. o/s*	9,601,000		7,320,200
	%		%
Net profit margin	(1.36)		(6.13)
Return on equity	(3.81)		(9.55)
Return on assets	0.61		(0.62)
No. of employees (FTEs)	890		890

* Common

^A Reported in accordance with IFRS

Latest Results

Periods ended:	6m June 30/23^A		6m June 30/22^A
	$000s	%Chg	$000s
Total revenue	176,532	-2	179,513
Net inc. bef. disc. opers.	(6,756)	n.a.	(3,089)
Income from disc. opers.	(2,064)		nil
Net income	(8,820)	n.a.	(3,089)
	$		$
Earns. per sh. bef. disc. opers.*	(0.71)		(0.55)
Earnings per share*	(0.88)		(0.55)

* Common

^A Reported in accordance with IFRS

Historical Summary
(as originally stated)

Fiscal Year	Total Rev.	Net Inc. Bef. Disc.	EPS*
	$000s	$000s	$
2022^A	353,972	(4,803)	(0.95)
2021^A	328,519	(20,152)	(3.30)
2020^A	84,119	29,408	3.50
2019^A	36,840	(13,710)	(2.60)
2018^A	177,804	15,173	1.60

* Common

^A Reported in accordance with IFRS

Note: Adjusted throughout for 1-for-10 cons. in Mar. 2022

R.7 RIV Capital Inc.

Symbol - RIV **Exchange** - CSE **CUSIP** - 768014

Head Office - 2504-40 King St W, Toronto, ON, M5H 3Y2 **Telephone** - (647) 475-0437 **Toll-free** - (855) 227-8639

Website - www.rivcapital.com

Email - matt@rivcapital.com

Investor Relations - Matthew Mundy (416) 583-5945

Auditors - MNP LLP C.A., Mississauga, Ont.

Transfer Agents - Odyssey Trust Company, Toronto, Ont.

Employees - 12 at June 10, 2022

Profile - (Ont. 2017) Acquires, invests in and develops cannabis operators and brands across the U.S.

Operations are organized into two segments:

U.S. Cannabis Platform - Focused on the cultivation, manufacturing, distribution and sale of cannabis products in the U.S. Through wholly owned **Etain IP LLC** and control of **Etain, LLC**, operates a 12,000-sq.-ft. indoor cultivation and processing facility in Chestertown and four medical cannabis dispensaries under the Etain banner in Manhattan, Kingston, Syracuse and Yonkers, all in New York. Etain manufactures a portfolio of medical cannabis products, including dried flower, vaporizers, capsules, tinctures, powders, lozenges, lotions and oral sprays, which are offered under the Balance, Dolce, Forte and Mezzo brands. Etain also plans to develop a 75,000-sq.-ft. indoor cultivation and manufacturing facility in Buffalo, N.Y.

Minority Portfolio - Holds a legacy portfolio of venture capital investments which include **Agripharm Corp.** (royalty), which cultivates, processes and sells cannabis and cannabis edibles, extracts and topicals in Canada; **BioLumic Ltd.** (preferred shares), a New Zealand-based developer of a UV light crop yield enhancement technology; **Dynaleo Inc.** (common shares and warrants), a manufacturer and distributor of edible cannabis gummies for the Canadian market; **Headset, Inc.** (preferred shares), which develops and markets business intelligence and analytics software platform for the cannabis industry in the U.S. and Canada; **High Beauty, Inc.** (preferred shares and warrants), a manufacturer and distributor of cannabis-based beauty products; **LeafLink Services International ULC** (common shares), which operates a business-to-business e-commerce and supply chain platform for cannabis markets outside the U.S.; **NOYA Holdings Inc.** and **NOYA Cannabis Inc.** (common shares, royalty, convertible debenture and warrants), which cultivate, process and sell cannabis and cannabis oils in Canada; and **ZeaKal, Inc.** (preferred shares) a California-based developer of a plant genetics technology that increases photosynthesis, improves plant yield and enhances nutritional profiles.

On June 20, 2022, the company sold all its interest in **10831425 Canada Ltd.** (dba Greenhouse Juice Company), which manufactures and distributes plant-based beverages in Canada, for US$4,260,000. The company held 3,830,412 preferred shares of Greenhouse Juice, representing a 16% equity interest on a non-diluted basis, Cdn$6,000,000 of convertible debentures and a control warrant.

The company changed its reporting currency to U.S. dollars from Canadian dollars, effective Apr. 1, 2022.

During fiscal 2022, agreement to sell the company's royalty investment in **Agripharm Corp.** to **TREC Brands Inc.** was terminated.

Recent Merger and Acquisition Activity

Status: pending **Revised:** Apr. 22, 2022

UPDATE: The initial closing was completed. RIV acquired the non-regulated portion of the Etain companies (Etain IP LLC) for US$169,775,000 cash and issuance of 21,092,335 class A common shares. PREVIOUS: RIV Capital Inc. agreed to acquire ownership and control of Etain, LLC and Etain IP LLC, owners and operators of licensed cannabis cultivation and retail dispensaries in New York, for US$247,006,000, consisting of US$212,219,000 cash and issuance of 26,365,419 class A common shares valued at US$34,787,000. Etain has a cultivation and processing facility in Chestertown and four retail dispensaries in Manhattan, Kingston, Syracuse and Westchester. The acquisition would serve as the first step in the execution of RIV's strategy, shifting from an investor in the cannabis value chain to a full-fledged operator of licensed cultivation and dispensary facilities in the U.S. The acquisition would close in two stages, with the initial closing expected in the second quarter of 2022 and the final closing in the second half of 2022. On closing, former owners of Etain were expected to hold 16% interest in RIV. The cash portion of the consideration would be financed in part by RIV through issuance of US$25,000,000 convertible note to The Hawthorne Collective, Inc.

Predecessor Detail - Name changed from Canopy Rivers Inc., Feb. 23, 2021.

Directors - Joseph (Joe) Mimran, chr., Toronto, Ont.; Laura Curran, N.Y.; Christopher (Chris) Hagedorn, Vt.; Richard P. (Rick) Mavrinac, Toronto, Ont.; Amy Peckham, N.Y.; Dawn Sweeney, Fla.

Other Exec. Officers - Mike Totzke, COO & interim CEO; Edward Lucarelli, CFO; Matthew Mundy, chief strategy officer, gen. counsel & corp. sec.

Capital Stock

	Authorized (shs.)	Outstanding (shs.)[1]
Class A Common	unlimited	163,844,998

[1] At Aug. 29, 2022

Major Shareholder - JW Asset Management, LLC and certain funds its manages held 20.4% interest and BrandCo HoldCo, LLC held 12.87% interest at Aug. 22, 2022.

Price Range - RIV/CSE

Year	Volume	High	Low	Close
2022	15,075,462	$1.87	$0.19	$0.21
2021	77,023,160	$3.60	$1.20	$1.45
2020	49,948,466	$1.68	$0.54	$1.17
2019	107,818,563	$6.14	$1.02	$1.14
2018	69,195,019	$11.82	$2.40	$3.07

Recent Close: $0.11

Capital Stock Changes - In April 2022, 21,092,335 class A common shares were issued pursuant to the acquisition of Etain IP LLC.

During fiscal 2022, class A common shares were issued as follows: 253,342 on vesting of performance share units, 157,266 on vesting of restricted share units and 97,272 on exercise of options.

Wholly Owned Subsidiaries

Etain IP LLC, Calif.

RIV Capital Corporation, Ont.

- 100% int. in **2683922 Ontario Inc.**, Ont.

RIV Capital US Corporation, United States.

- 100% int. in **RIV Capital US Holdings LLC**, United States.
- 100% int. in **RIV Capital US Real Estate LLC**, United States.
- 100% int. in **RIV Capital US Services LLC**, United States.

Note: The preceding list includes only the major related companies in which interests are held.

Financial Statistics

Periods ended:	12m Mar. 31/22^A		12m Mar. 31/21^A
	$000s	%Chg	$000s
Total revenue	**(46,089)**	**n.a.**	**(134,937)**
General & admin. expense	8,242		7,435
Stock-based compensation	1,452		934
Other operating expense	4,961		nil
Operating expense	**14,655**	**+75**	**8,369**
Operating income	**(60,744)**	**n.a.**	**(143,306)**
Deprec. & amort.	221		183
Finance costs, gross	7,217		28
Pre-tax income	**(65,204)**	**n.a.**	**(152,354)**
Income taxes	(12,473)		(18,474)
Net income	**(52,731)**	**n.a.**	**(133,880)**
Cash & equivalent	398,255		127,882
Accounts receivable	1,043		3,068
Current assets	412,606		131,731
Long-term investments	43,029		194,614
Right-of-use assets	251		402
Total assets	**457,615**	**+36**	**335,362**
Accts. pay. & accr. liabs.	4,767		2,944
Current liabilities	4,932		23,638
Long-term debt, gross	100,453		nil
Long-term debt, net	100,453		nil
Long-term lease liabilities	99		264
Equity portion of conv. debs.	68,803		nil
Shareholders' equity	330,784		311,460
Cash from oper. activs.	**(28,394)**	**n.a.**	**(8,093)**
Cash from fin. activs.	187,162		1,019
Cash from invest. activs.	110,318		88,232
Net cash position	**398,255**	**+211**	**127,882**
	$		$
Earnings per share*	(0.37)		(0.72)
Cash flow per share*	(0.20)		(0.04)
	shs		shs
No. of shs. o/s*	142,592,403		142,084,523
Avg. no. of shs. o/s*	142,420,017		186,028,610
	%		%
Net profit margin	n.m.		n.m.
Return on equity	(16.42)		(43.91)
Return on assets	(11.83)		(42.11)
No. of employees (FTEs)	12		12

* Cl.A. Common

^A Reported in accordance with IFRS

Latest Results

Periods ended:	3m June 30/22^A		3m June 30/21^□A
	US$000s	%Chg	US$000s
Total revenue	1,341	n.a.	nil
Net income	(3,474)	n.a.	(24,510)
	US$		US$
Earnings per share*	(0.02)		(0.17)

* Cl.A. Common
□ Restated
A Reported in accordance with IFRS

Historical Summary
(as originally stated)

Fiscal Year	Total Rev. $000s	Net Inc. Bef. Disc. $000s	EPS* $
2022^A	(46,089)	(52,731)	(0.37)
2021^A	(134,937)	(133,880)	(0.72)
2020^A	(22,654)	(40,566)	(0.22)
2019^A	38,477	3,918	0.03
2018^A1	50,211	36,361	9.83

* Cl.A. Common
A Reported in accordance with IFRS
1 48 weeks ended Mar. 31, 2018.
Note: Adjusted throughout for 1-for-26.565 cons. in Sept. 2018

R.8 RIWI Corp.

Symbol - RIWI **Exchange** - TSX-VEN **CUSIP** - 749601
Head Office - 500-33 Bloor St E, Toronto, ON, M4W 3H1 **Telephone** - (416) 205-9984 **Toll-free** - (888) 505-7494
Website - www.riwi.com
Email - investors@riwi.com
Investor Relations - Greg Wong (888) 505-7494
Auditors - KPMG LLP C.A., Toronto, Ont.
Lawyers - Stikeman Elliott LLP
Transfer Agents - Computershare Trust Company of Canada Inc.
Profile - (Can. 2009) Provides global trend-tracking and prediction technology featuring tracking surveys, continuous risk monitoring, predictive analytics and advertising effectiveness tests globally without collecting any personally identifiable data.

The company's cloud-based software solutions provide a global digital intelligence platform to clients seeking real-time consumer and citizen sentiment data to improve business performance, evaluate program effectiveness, enhance customer engagement, and to monitor and reduce emerging threats and violent conflict. Clients include the United States Department of State, G7 agencies, the United Nations World Food Programme, Harvard University, the United States Agency for International Aid and Development, one Central Bank, and Global Health Crisis Coordination Center. Data marketplace partners include Battlefin, Bloomberg, Datarade, data.world, Inc., Esri, Eagle Alpha, Freedom House, Knoema and ThinkData Works.

On July 1, 2022, the company acquired Paris, France-based **Research on Mobile S.A.S.U.** (ROM) for US$525,000 plus potential earn-out consideration. ROM has developed proprietary survey software that profiles respondents and dynamically matches them to research marketplaces from which commercial customers buy data.

Common reinstated on TSX-VEN, May 18, 2023.
Common suspended from TSX-VEN, May 8, 2023.

Directors - Neil L. Seeman, founder, Toronto, Ont.; Annette Cusworth, chr., Burnaby, B.C.; Greg Wong, pres. & CEO, Toronto, Ont.; David Kincaid, Ont.; Leonard (Lenny) Murphy, Ky.
Other Exec. Officers - Travis Campbell, CFO; Alton Ing, chief tech. officer; Danielle Goldfarb, v-p & gen. mgr., global affairs, economics & public policy; Natasha Hsi, v-p & gen. mgr., intl. devel.; Amber Schaefer, corp. sec.

Capital Stock

	Authorized (shs.)	Outstanding (shs.)[1]
Common	unlimited	18,004,428

1 At May 24, 2023

Major Shareholder - RIWI Hold Inc. held 34.8% interest at May 23, 2023.

Price Range - RIWI/TSX-VEN

Year	Volume	High	Low	Close
2022	1,972,098	$1.69	$0.50	$0.73
2021	3,601,005	$3.00	$1.05	$1.15
2020	2,506,986	$5.00	$1.50	$2.74
2019	1,603,720	$3.50	$1.35	$2.35
2018	546,449	$2.25	$1.00	$1.35

Recent Close: $0.45
Capital Stock Changes - There were no changes to capital stock during 2021 or 2022.

Wholly Owned Subsidiaries
Research on Mobile S.A.S.U., Paris, France.

Financial Statistics

Periods ended:	12m Dec. 31/22^A		12m Dec. 31/21^□A
	US$000s	%Chg	US$000s
Operating revenue	**2,787**	**-33**	**4,136**
Salaries & benefits	1,266		1,868
General & admin expense	2,852		2,620
Stock-based compensation	259		210
Operating expense	**4,377**	**-7**	**4,698**
Operating income	**(1,590)**	**n.a.**	**(562)**
Deprec., depl. & amort.	80		65
Finance costs, net	(38)		5
Pre-tax income	**(1,692)**	**n.a.**	**(627)**
Income taxes	(1)		(87)
Net income	**(1,691)**	**n.a.**	**(541)**
Cash & equivalent	2,351		4,254
Accounts receivable	836		265
Current assets	3,342		4,906
Fixed assets, net	5		10
Right-of-use assets	18		61
Intangibles, net	483		67
Total assets	**3,847**	**-24**	**5,044**
Accts. pay. & accr. liabs	341		360
Current liabilities	662		442
Long-term lease liabilities	nil		22
Shareholders' equity	3,148		4,580
Cash from oper. activs	**(1,475)**	**n.a.**	**260**
Cash from fin. activs	(50)		(53)
Cash from invest. activs	(381)		(13)
Net cash position	**2,351**	**-45**	**4,254**
	US$		US$
Earnings per share*	(0.09)		(0.03)
Cash flow per share*	(0.08)		0.01
	shs		shs
No. of shs. o/s*	18,004,428		18,004,428
Avg. no. of shs. o/s*	18,004,428		18,004,428
	%		%
Net profit margin	(60.67)		(13.08)
Return on equity	(43.76)		(11.40)
Return on assets	(38.04)		(10.29)
Foreign sales percent	82		73

* Common
□ Restated
A Reported in accordance with IFRS

Latest Results

Periods ended:	3m Mar. 31/23^A		3m Mar. 31/22^A
	US$000s	%Chg	US$000s
Operating revenue	1,201	+34	897
Net income	(128)	n.a.	(175)
	US$		US$
Earnings per share*	(0.01)		(0.01)

* Common
A Reported in accordance with IFRS

Historical Summary
(as originally stated)

Fiscal Year	Oper. Rev. US$000s	Net Inc. Bef. Disc. US$000s	EPS* US$
2022^A	2,787	(1,691)	(0.09)
2021^A	4,136	(541)	(0.03)
2020^A	4,581	657	0.04
2019^A	3,111	910	0.05
2018^A	2,668	417	0.02

* Common
A Reported in accordance with IFRS

R.9 RYAH Group, Inc.

Symbol - RYAH **Exchange** - CSE (S) **CUSIP** - 78349C
Head Office - 11654 Plaza America Dr, Suite 776, Reston, VA, United States, 20190 **Telephone** - (917) 210-0543
Website - ryahgroup.com
Email - fdesrosiers@ryah.com
Investor Relations - François C. Desrosiers (438) 874-0558
Auditors - Dale Matheson Carr-Hilton LaBonte LLP C.A., Vancouver, B.C.
Transfer Agents - Computershare Trust Company of Canada Inc.
Employees - 6 at June 15, 2023
Profile - (Can. 2004) Offers a suite of Internet of Things (IoT) dose measuring devices combined with an artificial intelligence-powered analytics platform that predicts the efficacy of plant-based medicines, including cannabis, and other substances in order to control dosing regimens and capture vital data.

Dose measuring devices include the RYAH Smart Patch and Inhaler, each of which have their own mobile app. The RYAH MD platform enables doctors to remotely monitor and control their patients' dosing regimen with use the devices. The target market for the company's technology is researchers, clinical trials, growers, dispensaries and patients.

Sub vtg suspended from CSE, July 6, 2022.
Predecessor Detail - Name changed from Prime Blockchain Inc., Oct. 28, 2020, pursuant to pending reverse takeover acquisition of Potbotics Inc.
Directors - Dr. David R. (Dave) Richards, CEO, Va.; François C. Desrosiers, CFO & corp. sec., Qué.; Tanvir M. Mukhtar; Binyomin Posen, Toronto, Ont.
Other Exec. Officers - C. Jordan Medley, v-p, global product

Capital Stock

	Authorized (shs.)	Outstanding (shs.)[1]
Cl.A Subord. Vtg.	unlimited	448,131,390
Cl.B Super Vtg.	unlimited	717,486

1 At Sept. 30, 2022

Class A Subordinate Voting - Convertible into super voting shares on a 1-for-100 basis. One vote per share.
Class B Super Voting - Convertible into subordinate voting shares on a 100-for-1 basis. 100 votes per share.
Major Shareholder - Dr. Boris Goldstein held 13.19% interest at May 7, 2021.

Price Range - RYAH/CSE (S)

Year	Volume	High	Low	Close
2022	24,885,535	$0.05	$0.02	$0.03
2021	108,247,406	$0.20	$0.03	$0.05

Capital Stock Changes - In early 2022, 760,859 class B super voting shares were converted into 76,085,900 class A subordinate voting shares.

Wholly Owned Subsidiaries
PotBotics Inc., New York, N.Y. Inactive.
RYAH MedTech, Inc., Fla.

Financial Statistics

Periods ended:	12m Dec. 31/21^A1		12m Dec. 31/20^□A2
	$000s	%Chg	$000s
Operating revenue	**168**	**+300**	**42**
Cost of sales	44		29
Salaries & benefits	313		232
Research & devel. expense	392		132
General & admin expense	2,859		823
Stock-based compensation	958		455
Operating expense	**4,566**	**+173**	**1,671**
Operating income	**(4,398)**	**n.a.**	**(1,629)**
Deprec., depl. & amort.	6		30
Finance costs, gross	78		828
Pre-tax income	**(16,218)**	**n.a.**	**(2,490)**
Net income	**(16,218)**	**n.a.**	**(2,490)**
Cash & equivalent	489		153
Inventories	116		145
Accounts receivable	69		nil
Current assets	490		305
Fixed assets, net	1		8
Total assets	**491**	**+57**	**313**
Accts. pay. & accr. liabs	776		837
Current liabilities	940		1,306
Long-term debt, gross	20		784
Long-term debt, net	nil		727
Shareholders' equity	(449)		(1,721)
Cash from oper. activs	**(3,165)**	**n.a.**	**(487)**
Cash from fin. activs	3,185		605
Net cash position	**227**	**+48**	**153**
	$		$
Earnings per share*	(0.03)		n.a.
Cash flow per share*	(0.01)		n.a.
	shs		shs
No. of shs. o/s*	501,228,650		n.a.
Avg. no. of shs. o/s*	528,766,589		n.a.
	%		%
Net profit margin	n.m.		n.m.
Return on equity	n.m.		n.m.
Return on assets	n.m.		(612.15)

* S.V.
□ Restated
A Reported in accordance with IFRS
1 Results reflect the Apr. 19, 2021, reverse takeover acqusition of Potbotics Inc.
2 Results pertain to Potbotics Inc.

Latest Results

Periods ended:	9m Sept. 30/22		9m Sept. 30/21
	$000s	%Chg	$000s
Operating revenue	56	-44	100
Net income	(1,532)	n.a.	(20,176)
	$		$
Earnings per share*	(0.00)		(0.05)

* S.V.

Historical Summary
(as originally stated)

Fiscal Year	Oper. Rev.	Net Inc. Bef. Disc.	EPS*
	$000s	$000s	$
2021[A]	168	(16,218)	(0.03)
2020[A1]	42	(2,490)	n.a.
2019[A1]	6	(2,290)	n.a.
2019[A2]	nil	(503)	(0.03)
2018[A]	nil	(701)	(0.07)

* S.V.
[A] Reported in accordance with IFRS
[1] Results pertain to Potbotics Inc.
[2] Results for Aug. 31, 2019, and prior periods pertain to Prime Blockchain Inc.

R.10 RYU Apparel Inc.

Symbol - RYU **Exchange** - TSX-VEN (S) **CUSIP** - 74979J
Head Office - 55 Town Centre Crt, Scarborough, ON, M1P 4X4 **Telephone** - (647) 451-6459 **Toll-free** - (844) 535-2880
Email - investors@ryu.com
Investor Relations - Cesare Fazari (844) 535-2880
Auditors - Smythe LLP C.A.
Lawyers - Clark Wilson LLP, Vancouver, B.C.
Transfer Agents - Computershare Trust Company of Canada Inc., Vancouver, B.C.
Profile - (B.C. 2014) Designs, markets and distributes performance and lifestyle athletic apparel, bags and accessories in Canada, Europe, the U.K. and the U.S., under the RYU brand.

Products include tops, bottoms, outerwear, sports bras, backpacks, duffle bags and other athletic accessories. Products are produced through third party manufacturers in North America and Asia; and are sold through the company's flagship retail store (at Mar. 31, 2022) in British Columbia, wholesale channels, and online via ecommerce sites, ryu.com and ryu.ca, which are also accessible in Europe and the U.K.

The company is currently in a strategic move to rebuild into omni-channel business, rebrand and focus on ecommerce, craft world-class products and generate demand for those products.

During the first quarter of 2022, the company closed its retail stores at Williamsburg in Brooklyn, N.Y. and Queen Street West in Toronto, Ont., in relation to its continued shifts in digital preferences. With the closure of these two stores, the company intends to concentrate on co-located shop-in-shops and store partnerships, predominantly in the U.S.

Common suspended from TSX-VEN, Dec. 6, 2022.

Predecessor Detail - Succeeded Respect Your Universe, Inc., Feb. 20, 2015, pursuant to a plan of arrangement with Respect Your Universe continuing as a wholly owned subsid. of RYU Apparel.

Directors - Cesare Fazari, chr., CEO & interim CFO, Toronto, Ont.; Bill Marcus, Glencoe, Ill.

Other Exec. Officers - Ryan Lindholm, sr. v-p, mktg. & innovation; Alex Briglio, v-p, sales & mktg.

Capital Stock

	Authorized (shs.)	Outstanding (shs.)[1]
Common	unlimited	210,336,766

[1] At May 30, 2022

Major Shareholder - Cesare Fazari held 12.87% interest at May 2, 2022.

Price Range - RYU/TSX-VEN (S)

Year	Volume	High	Low	Close
2022	37,079,692	$0.09	$0.02	$0.02
2021	42,957,320	$0.26	$0.05	$0.06
2020	21,136,675	$0.40	$0.05	$0.15
2019	13,291,224	$1.20	$0.20	$0.30
2018	29,832,864	$3.25	$1.00	$1.15

Consolidation: 1-for-10 cons. in July 2020
Recent Close: $0.02

Wholly Owned Subsidiaries

Respect Your Universe, Inc., Nev.

Financial Statistics

Periods ended:	12m Dec. 31/21[A]	%Chg	12m Dec. 31/20[A]
	$000s	%Chg	$000s
Operating revenue	**1,273**	**-19**	**1,567**
Cost of sales	1,277		905
Salaries & benefits	1,543		1,973
General & admin expense	4,506		2,997
Stock-based compensation	2,838		1,262
Operating expense	**10,164**	**+42**	**7,136**
Operating income	**(8,891)**	**n.a.**	**(5,569)**
Deprec., depl. & amort.	192		149
Finance costs, gross	838		796
Write-downs/write-offs	(1,313)		nil
Pre-tax income	**(10,040)**	**n.a.**	**(1,858)**
Net income	**(10,040)**	**n.a.**	**(1,858)**
Cash & equivalent	681		771
Inventories	1,812		1,842
Accounts receivable	72		147
Current assets	2,917		4,260
Long-term investments	nil		1,313
Fixed assets, net	9		59
Total assets	**3,010**	**-48**	**5,783**
Bank indebtedness	1,007		11
Accts. pay. & accr. liabs	4,668		5,708
Current liabilities	6,420		6,767
Long-term debt, gross	2,846		nil
Long-term debt, net	2,846		nil
Long-term lease liabilities	3,272		3,385
Shareholders' equity	(9,528)		(4,369)
Cash from oper. activs	**(4,607)**	**n.a.**	**(3,340)**
Cash from fin. activs	4,521		5,342
Cash from invest. activs	(3)		(1,313)
Net cash position	**681**	**-12**	**771**
Capital expenditures	(3)		nil
	$		$
Earnings per share*	(0.05)		(0.02)
Cash flow per share*	(0.02)		(0.04)
	shs		shs
No. of shs. o/s*	205,270,100		179,193,537
Avg. no. of shs. o/s*	196,053,373		85,159,923
	%		%
Net profit margin	(788.69)		(118.57)
Return on equity	n.m.		n.m.
Return on assets	(209.30)		(24.65)
Foreign sales percent	38		27

* Common
[A] Reported in accordance with IFRS

Latest Results

Periods ended:	3m Mar. 31/22[A]	%Chg	3m Mar. 31/21[A]
	$000s	%Chg	$000s
Operating revenue	348	+75	199
Net income	2,604	n.a.	(3,935)
	$		$
Earnings per share*	0.01		(0.03)

* Common
[A] Reported in accordance with IFRS

Historical Summary
(as originally stated)

Fiscal Year	Oper. Rev.	Net Inc. Bef. Disc.	EPS*
	$000s	$000s	$
2021[A]	1,273	(10,040)	(0.05)
2020[A]	1,567	(1,858)	(0.02)
2019[A]	5,618	(28,894)	(0.52)
2018[A]	5,048	(19,327)	(0.40)
2017[A]	3,020	(9,201)	(0.40)

* Common
[A] Reported in accordance with IFRS
Note: Adjusted throughout for 1-for-10 cons. in July 2020

R.11 Radial Research Corp.

Symbol - RAD **Exchange** - CSE **CUSIP** - 750232
Head Office - 600-890 Pender St W, Vancouver, BC, V6C 1J9 **Telephone** - (604) 332-3707 **Fax** - (604) 332-3709
Website - radial-research.com
Email - chris.haill@radial-research.com
Investor Relations - Chris Haill (778) 999-7030
Auditors - Smythe LLP C.A., Vancouver, B.C.
Lawyers - Beadle Raven LLP, Vancouver, B.C.
Transfer Agents - TSX Trust Company, Vancouver, B.C.
Profile - (B.C. 2017) Develops online and download technologies and services, including software, websites and smartphone applications.

Developing and exploring business opportunities related to its Zoompages, an e-commerce sales funnel content management system; and Chatvertizer, a complementary software platform that allows consumer brands to interact with their customers and boost sales capability using an automated platform. Also seeking other opportunities in e-commerce, Internet and smartphone-based technologies.

Also has launched Zoom NFT (non-fungible token) software, a fully customizable influencer pages, allowing influencers and celebrities to interact with their fans and followers, before, during and after NFT auctions.

Directors - Chris Haill, CEO, London, Middx., United Kingdom; Jason Argall, Panama City, Panama; Andrew King, Vancouver, B.C.

Other Exec. Officers - Daniel Hejcman, CFO & corp. sec.

Capital Stock

	Authorized (shs.)	Outstanding (shs.)[1]
Common	unlimited	27,838,189

[1] At Sept. 15, 2022

Major Shareholder - Widely held at Aug. 4, 2021.

Price Range - RAD/CSE

Year	Volume	High	Low	Close
2022	1,894,844	$0.04	$0.02	$0.02
2021	678,764	$0.15	$0.04	$0.04
2020	386,922	$0.20	$0.05	$0.07
2019	513,925	$0.35	$0.05	$0.05
2018	1,060,000	$0.16	$0.12	$0.15

Recent Close: $0.01

Capital Stock Changes - There were no changes to capital stock during fiscal 2022.

Financial Statistics

Periods ended:	12m May 31/22[A]	%Chg	12m May 31/21[A]
	$000s	%Chg	$000s
General & admin expense	144		150
Stock-based compensation	nil		20
Operating expense	**144**	**-15**	**170**
Operating income	**(144)**	**n.a.**	**(170)**
Deprec., depl. & amort.	123		45
Finance income	nil		9
Finance costs, gross	67		66
Write-downs/write-offs	(447)		nil
Pre-tax income	**(780)**	**n.a.**	**(653)**
Net income	**(780)**	**n.a.**	**(653)**
Cash & equivalent	524		681
Accounts receivable	11		11
Current assets	542		699
Intangibles, net	nil		569
Total assets	**542**	**-57**	**1,268**
Accts. pay. & accr. liabs	91		79
Current liabilities	581		79
Long-term debt, gross	490		448
Long-term debt, net	nil		448
Equity portion of conv. debs	478		478
Shareholders' equity	(39)		742
Cash from oper. activs	**(157)**	**n.a.**	**(142)**
Net cash position	**524**	**-23**	**681**
	$		$
Earnings per share*	(0.03)		(0.03)
Cash flow per share*	(0.01)		(0.01)
	shs		shs
No. of shs. o/s*	27,838,189		27,838,189
Avg. no. of shs. o/s*	27,838,189		23,535,723
	%		%
Net profit margin	n.a.		n.a.
Return on equity	n.m.		(93.02)
Return on assets	(78.78)		(48.59)

* Common
[A] Reported in accordance with IFRS

Historical Summary
(as originally stated)

Fiscal Year	Oper. Rev.	Net Inc. Bef. Disc.	EPS*
	$000s	$000s	$
2022[A]	nil	(780)	(0.03)
2021[A]	nil	(653)	(0.03)
2020[A]	nil	(215)	(0.01)
2019[A]	nil	(173)	(0.01)
2018[A1,2]	nil	(134)	(0.02)

* Common
[A] Reported in accordance with IFRS
[1] 49 weeks ended May 31, 2018.
[2] As shown in the prospectus dated Aug. 31, 2018.

R.12 Radient Technologies Inc.

Symbol - RTI **Exchange** - TSX-VEN (S) **CUSIP** - 75034P
Head Office - 4035 101 St NW, Edmonton, AB, T6E 0A4 **Telephone** - (780) 465-1318 **Fax** - (780) 465-1381
Website - www.radientinc.com
Email - phariharan@radientinc.com
Investor Relations - Prakash Hariharan (780) 465-1318
Auditors - McGovern Hurley LLP C.A., Toronto, Ont.
Lawyers - Fasken Martineau DuMoulin LLP, Vancouver, B.C.
Transfer Agents - Odyssey Trust Company, Calgary, Alta.
Profile - (Can. 2014 amalg.) Formulates and manufactures value-added cannabis extracts, derivatives and packaged products.

Products include high-purity cannabinoid extracts that contain a greater concentration of active compounds and retain nearly full cannabinoid and terpene profiles which are extracted using the company's MAP™ technology, an extraction platform that extracts cannabinoids from cannabis and hemp biomass at industrial scale volumes, achieving up to 99% recovery of active compounds; cannabis formulations for cannabis derivative products such as standardized oils, solid powders stable water soluble and water dispersible powders, tinctures, topicals and sub-lingual sprays; cannabinoid-based ingredients which improves the taste and shelf life of cannabis-infused beverages as well as reproducibly ensure exact strength and potency for use in natural food and beverage products, personal care, and nutraceutical and pharmaceutical products; and cannabis infused products.

The company's 23,000-sq.-ft. Edmonton I manufacturing facility in Edmonton, Alta., is currently operating at an annual capacity of 56,000 kg of cannabis biomass. In addition, licensed space at the company's Edmonton II facility is currently being utilized for manufacturing and packaging activities. Construction of the 100,000-sq.-ft. Edmonton III facility which would have annual capacity of 280,000 kg of cannabis biomass and 2,800,000 kg of hemp biomass, as well as Edmonton II retrofit have been deferred as of Oct. 5, 2021.

In August 2022, the company terminated the proposed acquisition of **PBR Laboratories Inc.**, which provides analytical and contract research services to public and private sector clients in the cannabis, pharmaceutical, biotechnology, food, natural health product and agriculture industries.

Common suspended from TSX-VEN, Mar. 8, 2023.

Predecessor Detail - Formed from Madison Capital Corporation in Canada, May 22, 2014, on Qualifying Transaction amalgamation with (old) Radient Technologies Inc. (deemed acquiror); basis 1 new for 10 old shs.

Directors - Jocelyne F. Lafrenière, interim chr., Qué.; Dr. Steven Splinter, interim CEO & corp. sec., Vancouver, B.C.; Dimitris Tzanis, Zurich, Switzerland; Danesh K. Varma, Kingston upon Thames, Surrey, United Kingdom

Other Exec. Officers - Prakash Hariharan, CFO; Zachary Riauka, sr. v-p, opers.

Capital Stock

	Authorized (shs.)	Outstanding (shs.)[1]
Common	unlimited	539,868,021

[1] At Nov. 29, 2022

Major Shareholder - Widely held at Nov. 15, 2021.

Price Range - RTI/TSX-VEN (S)

Year	Volume	High	Low	Close
2022	68,247,743	$0.08	$0.01	$0.01
2021	73,243,545	$0.18	$0.04	$0.04
2020	106,541,229	$0.45	$0.07	$0.09
2019	100,364,344	$1.20	$0.35	$0.43
2018	256,707,757	$2.28	$0.60	$0.74

Recent Close: $0.01

Capital Stock Changes - In December 2021, private placement of 20,880,714 units (1 common share & 1 warrant) at 6¢ per unit was completed. On Jan. 28, 2022, 70,000,000 common shares were issued pursuant to the acquisition of Tunaaaa Room Xtracts Inc. Also during fiscal 2022, common shares were issued as follows: 7,179,974 for debt settlement and 261,133 for services.

Wholly Owned Subsidiaries

1631807 Alberta Ltd., Alta.
Radient Technologies (Cannabis) Inc.
Radient Technologies Innovations Inc.
Tunaaaa Room Xtracts Inc., Alta.

Financial Statistics

Periods ended:	12m Mar. 31/22[A]		12m Mar. 31/21[A]
	$000s	%Chg	$000s
Operating revenue	**3,622**	**+46**	**2,489**
Cost of sales	3,433		2,985
Research & devel. expense	61		390
General & admin expense	4,986		9,253
Stock-based compensation	37		1,571
Operating expense	**8,517**	**-40**	**14,199**
Operating income	**(4,895)**	**n.a.**	**(11,710)**
Deprec., depl. & amort.	1,714		2,156
Finance income	(68)		162
Finance costs, gross	2,290		2,945
Write-downs/write-offs	(2,498)		(24,601)
Pre-tax income	**(12,930)**	**n.a.**	**(42,266)**
Net income	**(12,930)**	**n.a.**	**(42,266)**
Cash & equivalent	32		486
Inventories	2,122		1,394
Accounts receivable	117		446
Current assets	2,599		3,021
Fixed assets, net	22,252		24,845
Right-of-use assets	380		644
Intangibles, net	2,356		604
Total assets	**27,735**	**-5**	**29,295**
Bank indebtedness	1,245		1,000
Accts. pay. & accr. liabs.	18,192		15,358
Current liabilities	37,700		31,455
Long-term debt, gross	10,810		9,583
Long-term lease liabilities	161		369
Shareholders' equity	(10,126)		(2,530)
Cash from oper. activs.	**(177)**	**n.a.**	**(6,968)**
Cash from fin. activs.	1,302		7,323
Cash from invest. activs.	(1,578)		(14)
Net cash position	**32**	**-93**	**486**
Capital expenditures	(1,578)		(120)
Capital disposals	nil		16
	$		$
Earnings per share*	(0.03)		(0.13)
Cash flow per share*	(0.00)		(0.02)
	shs		shs
No. of shs. o/s*	530,868,021		432,546,200
Avg. no. of shs. o/s*	452,591,046		325,351,377
	%		%
Net profit margin	(356.99)		n.m.
Return on equity	n.m.		n.m.
Return on assets	(37.31)		(90.16)

* Common
[A] Reported in accordance with IFRS

Latest Results

Periods ended:	6m Sept. 30/22[A]		6m Sept. 30/21[A]
	$000s	%Chg	$000s
Operating revenue	1,920	+4	1,846
Net income	(3,847)	n.a.	(3,632)
	$		$
Earnings per share*	(0.01)		(0.01)

* Common
[A] Reported in accordance with IFRS

Historical Summary
(as originally stated)

Fiscal Year	Oper. Rev. $000s	Net Inc. Bef. Disc. $000s	EPS* $
2022[A]	3,622	(12,930)	(0.03)
2021[A]	2,489	(42,266)	(0.13)
2020[A]	18,405	(37,418)	(0.14)
2019[A]	214	(27,856)	(0.11)
2018[A]	451	(14,048)	(0.07)

* Common
[A] Reported in accordance with IFRS

R.13 Radius Gold Inc.

Symbol - RDU **Exchange** - TSX-VEN **CUSIP** - 750468
Head Office - 650-200 Burrard St, Vancouver, BC, V6C 3L6 **Telephone** - (604) 801-5432 **Toll-free** - (888) 627-9378 **Fax** - (604) 662-8829
Website - radiusgold.com
Email - sallyw@goldgroup.com
Investor Relations - Sally Whittall (888) 627-9378
Auditors - Smythe LLP C.A., Vancouver, B.C.
Lawyers - Blake, Cassels & Graydon LLP, Vancouver, B.C.
Transfer Agents - Computershare Trust Company of Canada Inc., Toronto, Ont.

Profile - (B.C. 2004 amalg.) Has mineral interests in Mexico and Guatemala, and invests in companies which hold mineral property interests.

In Mexico, holds 35% (**Pan American Silver Corp.** 65%) interest in Amalia gold-silver project, 10,250 hectares, 25 km southwest of Guadalupe y Calvo mining district in Chihuahua state, including Palmillas prospect; Rambler gold-silver prospect, 10,379 hectares, Sierra Madre Mountains; option to acquire Maricela gold-silver prospect, 155 hectares, Sonora state, requiring payment of US$1,250,000 over three years to March 2024; Plata Verde silver prospect, 800 hectares, Chihuahua state, consisting of option to acquire Don Benja concession, requiring payment of US$1,201,000 over four years to 2024, and option to acquire Don Jose concession; and option to acquire Tropico silver-gold prospect, 200 hectares, 30 km northwest of Fresnillo city, requiring payment of US$5,400,0000 over four years to March 2027.

In southeastern Guatemala, holds silver-gold properties, 15 km south of Chiquimula, including Holly and Banderas prospects, and Montagua Norte prospect, 240,000 hectares. **Volcanic Gold Mines Inc.** holds option to earn 60% interest in Holly and Banderas prospects, requiring exploration expenditures of US$7,000,000 over four years to March 2025.

The company's investments include **Medgold Resources Corp.**, **Rackla Metals Inc.**, and **Volcanic Gold Mines Inc.**

Predecessor Detail - Formed from Radius Explorations Ltd. in British Columbia, July 1, 2004, on amalgamation with Pilagold Inc. with Radius the deemed acquiror; basis 1 new for 2.25 Pilagold shs.

Directors - Simon T. Ridgway, founder & exec. chr., Vancouver, B.C.; Bruce Smith, pres. & CEO, Cooks Beach, New Zealand; William Katzin, West Vancouver, B.C.; Mario D. Szotlender, Caracas, Venezuela

Other Exec. Officers - Kevin Bales, CFO; Javier Castaneda, chief geologist; Adam Buchanan, v-p, corp. devel.; Sally Whittall, corp. sec.

Capital Stock

	Authorized (shs.)	Outstanding (shs.)[1]
Common	unlimited	98,418,533

[1] At June 30, 2023

Major Shareholder - Sprott entities and their fully managed accounts held 11.51% interest at June 30, 2023.

Price Range - RDU/TSX-VEN

Year	Volume	High	Low	Close
2022	9,693,378	$0.40	$0.16	$0.19
2021	15,820,314	$0.38	$0.20	$0.36
2020	22,925,936	$0.38	$0.11	$0.32
2019	55,021,954	$0.47	$0.09	$0.25
2018	25,321,267	$0.19	$0.09	$0.12

Recent Close: $0.17

Capital Stock Changes - In May 2023, private placement of 11,149,983 units (1 common share & 1 warrant) at $0.175 per unit was completed, with warrants exercisable at $0.35 per share for two years.

During 2022, 25,000 common shares were issued on exercise of options.

Wholly Owned Subsidiaries

Radius (Cayman) Inc., Cayman Islands.
- 100% int. in **Geometales del Norte-Geonorte, S.A. de C.V.**, Mexico.

Radius Gold (U.S.) Inc., Nev.
- 100% int. in **Minerales Sierra Pacifico S.A.**, Guatemala.

Investments

Medgold Resources Corp., Vancouver, B.C. (see Survey of Mines)
Rackla Metals Inc., Vancouver, B.C. (see Survey of Mines)
Volcanic Gold Mines Inc., Vancouver, B.C. (see Survey of Mines)

Financial Statistics

Periods ended:	12m Dec. 31/22^A		12m Dec. 31/21^A
	$000s	%Chg	$000s
Salaries & benefits	149		103
Exploration expense	732		690
General & admin expense	246		249
Stock-based compensation	47		175
Operating expense	**1,174**	**-4**	**1,217**
Operating income	**(1,174)**	**n.a.**	**(1,217)**
Deprec., depl. & amort.	63		78
Finance costs, gross	18		24
Investment income	10		3
Write-downs/write-offs	nil		(118)
Pre-tax income	**1,076**	**n.a.**	**(892)**
Net income	**1,076**	**n.a.**	**(892)**
Cash & equivalent	3,289		2,272
Accounts receivable	80		32
Current assets	3,423		2,364
Fixed assets, net	7		9
Right-of-use assets	121		182
Explor./devel. properties	38		127
Total assets	**3,711**	**+32**	**2,804**
Accts. pay. & accr. liabs	100		84
Current liabilities	173		149
Long-term lease liabilities	82		155
Shareholders' equity	3,457		2,500
Cash from oper. activs	**(1,098)**	**n.a.**	**(1,086)**
Cash from fin. activs	(61)		(38)
Cash from invest. activs	1,046		433
Net cash position	**1,420**	**-7**	**1,533**
Capital expenditures	(941)		(254)
Capital disposals	12		63
	$		$
Earnings per share*	0.01		(0.01)
Cash flow per share*	(0.01)		(0.01)
	shs		shs
No. of shs. o/s*	87,268,550		87,243,550
Avg. no. of shs. o/s*	87,252,523		87,227,112
	%		%
Net profit margin	n.a.		n.a.
Return on equity	36.13		(30.34)
Return on assets	33.58		(26.48)

* Common
[A] Reported in accordance with IFRS

Latest Results

Periods ended:	3m Mar. 31/23^A		3m Mar. 31/22^A
	$000s	%Chg	$000s
Net income	(373)	n.a.	(288)
	$		$
Earnings per share*	(0.00)		(0.00)

* Common
[A] Reported in accordance with IFRS

Historical Summary
(as originally stated)

Fiscal Year	Oper. Rev.	Net Inc. Bef. Disc.	EPS*
	$000s	$000s	$
2022[A]	nil	1,076	0.01
2021[A]	nil	(892)	(0.01)
2020[A]	nil	(893)	(0.01)
2019[A]	nil	(2,563)	(0.03)
2018[A]	nil	(1,566)	(0.02)

* Common
[A] Reported in accordance with IFRS

R.14 Raffles Financial Group Limited

Symbol - RICH **Exchange** - CSE (S) **CUSIP** - G7353K
Head Office - #11-01H, 3 Shenton Way, Singapore, Singapore, 068805
Overseas Tel - 65-6909-8765
Website - www.rafflesfinancial.co
Email - monica@rafflesfinancial.co
Investor Relations - Monica Kwok 65-6909-8765
Auditors -
Transfer Agents - TSX Trust Company
Profile - (Cayman Islands 2020; orig. B.C., 2011) Provides corporate finance advisory and related services for family trusts, family offices and investment funds to companies in the People's Republic of China (PRC), Singapore, Canada, Switzerland and other countries in and throughout Asia.

Through wholly owned **Raffles Financial Pte. Ltd.**, provides advice on a full range of transactions, including mergers, sales, acquisitions, leveraged buyouts, joint ventures, raid defences, spin-offs, divestitures and other restructurings. Its head office is in downtown business district of Singapore as well as smaller regional offices in Sydney, Beijing and Hong Kong. Also, Raffles Financial is represented in Australia, Canada, the PRC, Europe, Hong Kong and Singapore, and has the resources to serve the aims of the Japanese firms seeking funding and resources through their public listings outside Japan.

Through wholly owned **Raffles Financial AG**, provides advisory and brokerage services for cash listings, corporate financing and restructuring and fund investment advice in Switzerland.

In November 2022, the company agreed to acquire Singapore-based **Financial Technology (Asia) Pte. Ltd.** and Hong Kong-based **Raffles Financial Technology (China) Ltd.**

In October 2022, the company proposed a reorganization whereby it would incorporate a company in Wyoming (USCo) which would setup a Singapore-based wholly owned subsidiary (SGCo) that would carry on the company's financial licensing-as-a-service business. The company would receive 50,150,000 common shares of USCo, representing the same amount of the total issued shares of the company, and which would be distributed to shareholders of the company on a one-for-one basis. USCO plans to apply for a U.S. listing.

In March 2022, the company and **The Joseph Sassoon Group** agreed to form joint venture company **Sassoon Raffles Financial** to serve clients in the Americas and Europe with corporate finance advisory and public listing services.

Common suspended from CSE, Jan. 6, 2022.

Predecessor Detail - Name changed from Explorex Resources Inc., Apr. 28, 2020, pursuant to reverse takeover acquisition of Raffles Financial Pte. Ltd.; basis 1 new for 25.9466 old shs.

Directors - Li Ying (Abigail) Zhang, chief invest. officer, Singapore, Singapore; David Anthony Bruzzisi, Vancouver, B.C.; Dr. Chang Sheng (Victor) Liu, Singapore, Singapore; Haopu (Lily) Ren, Vancouver, B.C.; David Wong

Other Exec. Officers - Chuan Huang, CEO; Dong H. (Don) Shim, CFO; Monita Faris, corp. sec.

Capital Stock

	Authorized (shs.)	Outstanding (shs.)[1]
Common	unlimited	50,105,000

[1] At Aug. 24, 2023

Major Shareholder - Nany Sing (Charlie) In held 32.3% interest, Dr. Chang Sheng (Victor) Liu held 32.3% interest and Li Ying (Abigail) Zhang held 16.2% interest at Dec. 3, 2020.

Price Range - EX/TSX-VEN (D)

Year	Volume	High	Low	Close
2022	5,202	$3.00	$2.85	$2.85
2021	193,331	$10.50	$3.50	$4.05
2020	353,778	$10.09	$3.49	$10.07
2019	242,468	$10.38	$3.89	$4.67
2018	304,141	$11.68	$5.97	$8.69

Consolidation: 1-for-25.9466 cons. in May 2020

Dividends

com N.S.R.
$0.090809◆......... June 23/21
Paid in 2023: n.a. 2022: n.a. 2021: $0.090809◆
◆ Special

Wholly Owned Subsidiaries

Changsheng Investment Development Limited, Hong Kong, People's Republic of China.
Marvel Earn Limited, Hong Kong, People's Republic of China.
Raffles Financial AG, Switzerland.
Raffles Financial Pte. Ltd., Singapore, Singapore.

R.15 Raging Rhino Capital Corp.

Symbol - RRCC.P **Exchange** - TSX-VEN **CUSIP** - 750648
Head Office - 480-1500 Georgia St W, Vancouver, BC, V6G 2Z5
Telephone - (604) 684-4535
Email - eric.tsung@quantumllp.com
Investor Relations - Pui Hong Tsung (604) 684-4535
Auditors - Davidson & Company LLP C.A., Vancouver, B.C.
Lawyers - David Smalley Law Corporation, Vancouver, B.C.
Transfer Agents - Odyssey Trust Company, Vancouver, B.C.
Profile - (B.C. 2021) Capital Pool Company.
Common listed on TSX-VEN, May 24, 2023.

Directors - Michael B. Harrison, CEO, Indonesia; Vladimiro G. Cernetig, Vancouver, B.C.; Edward T. L. Cheung, Hong Kong, People's Republic of China; John P. Conlon, Toronto, Ont.; Gary V. O'Connor, Georgetown, Ont.

Other Exec. Officers - Pui Hong (Eric) Tsung, CFO & corp. sec.

Capital Stock

	Authorized (shs.)	Outstanding (shs.)[1]
Common	unlimited	6,790,200

[1] At May 24, 2023

Major Shareholder - Widely held at May 24, 2023.

Capital Stock Changes - On May 24, 2023, an initial public offering of 2,500,000 common shares was completed at 10¢ per share.

R.16 Railtown AI Technologies Inc.

Symbol - RAIL **Exchange** - CSE **CUSIP** - 750763
Head Office - 104-8337 Eastlake Dr, Burnaby, BC, V5A 4W2
Telephone - (604) 690-3797
Website - www.railtown.ai
Email - rebecca@railtown.ai
Investor Relations - Rebecca Kerswell (604) 690-3797
Auditors - Crowe MacKay LLP C.A., Vancouver, B.C.
Transfer Agents - National Securities Administrators Ltd., Vancouver, B.C.
Profile - (B.C. 2011) Developing software-as-a-service (SaaS) artificial intelligence (AI) solutions that help software development teams detect, analyze and fix errors quickly in their development projects.

The Railtown AI platform is built specifically to discover, track, monitor and notify software developers about critical bugs and errors in their software development projects. The platform allows for real-time exception monitoring and alerting which permits developers, team managers and executives to quickly locate, understand and correct errors in their software development projects and their root causes, thereby preventing system and application downtimes. The platform tracks efficiency gains across entire development teams as well as the status and health of applications. It can also track team efficiency and performance over time, and visualize areas of application, team and process improvement.

Has three versions of the Railtown AI platform including the Start-up Edition, which is a limited version that is free to use and is meant to be used by students, teachers and solo developers but with fewer features and functions; a full-featured Teams Edition; and the Enterprise Edition, which is a customized version of the Teams Edition designed to be used by large organizations.

The company has developed AI co-pilot solutions such as Root Cause Analysis, which connects to ticketing systems, build servers and logging services and matches tickets to builds in each environment pointing directly to any code change that it recognizes as the root cause of any issue, error, bug or exception; Release Notes, which generates release notes from developer tickets; and Scrum Master Chat, which provides developers with accurate and reason-based answers to any questions about the application and the team working on it.

Predecessor Detail - Name changed from Railtown Capital Corp., Aug. 15, 2019.

Directors - Cory Brandolini, pres. & CEO, B.C.; Paul Woodward, CFO, B.C.; Marwan Haddad, chief tech. officer, B.C.; Robert (Rob) Goehring, Coquitlam, B.C.; Anna-Marie Parente, B.C.

Capital Stock

	Authorized (shs.)	Outstanding (shs.)[1]
Common	unlimited	76,607,999

[1] At May 29, 2023

Major Shareholder - Marwan Haddad held 26.19% interest, Cory Brandolini held 22.59% interest and Dr. Elliot Holtham held 10.12% interest at May 18, 2023.

Price Range - RAIL/CSE

Year	Volume	High	Low	Close
2022	3,283,822	$0.33	$0.09	$0.12
2021	1,068,625	$0.55	$0.26	$0.33

Recent Close: $0.18

Capital Stock Changes - On Nov. 30, 2021, public offering of 5,568,700 common shares was completed at 40¢ per share. Also during fiscal 2022, 625,000 common shares were issued as finder's fee.

Financial Statistics

Periods ended:	12m Sept. 30/22^A		12m Sept. 30/21^oA
	$000s	%Chg	$000s
Salaries & benefits	842		782
General & admin expense	878		465
Stock-based compensation	142		586
Operating expense	**1,862**	**+2**	**1,833**
Operating income	**(1,862)**	**n.a.**	**(1,833)**
Deprec., depl. & amort.	20		9
Finance income	nil		1
Finance costs, gross	7		nil
Pre-tax income	**(1,391)**	**n.a.**	**(1,743)**
Net income	**(1,391)**	**n.a.**	**(1,743)**
Cash & equivalent	678		275
Accounts receivable	45		13
Current assets	750		317
Fixed assets, net	12		14
Right-of-use assets	162		nil
Total assets	**924**	**+179**	**331**
Accts. pay. & accr. liabs	116		175
Current liabilities	142		175
Long-term lease liabilities	140		nil
Shareholders' equity	643		155
Cash from oper. activs	**(1,523)**	**n.a.**	**(1,034)**
Cash from fin. activs	1,932		1,067
Cash from invest. activs	(6)		(10)
Net cash position	**678**	**+147**	**275**
Capital expenditures	(6)		(10)
	$		$
Earnings per share*	(0.02)		(0.03)
Cash flow per share*	(0.02)		(0.01)
	shs		shs
No. of shs. o/s*	76,507,999		70,314,299
Avg. no. of shs. o/s*	75,472,887		69,372,682
	%		%
Net profit margin	n.a.		n.a.
Return on equity	(348.62)		(871.50)
Return on assets	(220.56)		(578.11)

* Common
[o] Restated
[A] Reported in accordance with IFRS

Latest Results

Periods ended:	6m Mar. 31/23[A]		6m Mar. 31/22[A]
	$000s	%Chg	$000s
Net income	(995)	n.a.	(1,027)
	$		$
Earnings per share*	(0.01)		(0.01)

* Common
[A] Reported in accordance with IFRS

Historical Summary
(as originally stated)

Fiscal Year	Oper. Rev. $000s	Net Inc. Bef. Disc. $000s	EPS* $
2022[A]	nil	(1,391)	(0.02)
2021[A]	nil	(1,743)	(0.03)
2020[A]	nil	(1,434)	(0.02)
2019[A]	nil	nil	nil

* Common
[A] Reported in accordance with IFRS

R.17 Railtown Capital Corp.

Symbol - RLT.P **Exchange** - TSX-VEN **CUSIP** - 75076L
Head Office - 2200-885 Georgia St W, Vancouver, BC, V6C 3E8 **Telephone** - (604) 765-2601
Email - cam@caliber.vc
Investor Relations - W. D. Cameron White (604) 765-2601
Auditors - MNP LLP C.A., Vancouver, B.C.
Lawyers - Cassels Brock & Blackwell LLP, Vancouver, B.C.
Transfer Agents - Odyssey Trust Company, Vancouver, B.C.
Profile - (Can. 2020) Capital Pool Company.

Recent Merger and Acquisition Activity

Status: terminated **Revised:** Apr. 25, 2022
UPDATE: The transaction was terminated. PREVIOUS: Railtown Capital Corp. entered into a letter of intent for the Qualifying Transaction reverse takeover acquisition of Selten Metal Corp., which holds option from NexOptic Technology Corp. to acquire THOR Heavy & Light rare earth element project in Nevada. Under the agreement, Selten common shares would be exchanged by Railtown common shares on a share-for-share basis at a deemed price of 20¢ per share. Selten would complete a private placement of 15,000,0000 common shares at 15¢ per share. Upon completion, Railtown would change its name to Selten Metal Corp.

Directors - W. D. Cameron (Cam) White, pres., CEO & corp. sec., Surrey, B.C.; Claudia Tornquist, CFO, Vancouver, B.C.; Graeme Barker, B.C.; Timothy (Tim) Gamble, Vancouver, B.C.

Capital Stock

	Authorized (shs.)	Outstanding (shs.)[1]
Common	unlimited	13,000,000

[1] At July 13, 2023

Major Shareholder - Widely held at Apr. 14, 2022.

Price Range - RLT.P/TSX-VEN

Year	Volume	High	Low	Close
2022	55,000	$0.28	$0.18	$0.28
2021	458,515	$0.25	$0.17	$0.20

Recent Close: $0.13

R.18 Rakovina Therapeutics Inc.

Symbol - RKV **Exchange** - TSX-VEN **CUSIP** - 75103L
Head Office - 105-1008 Beach Ave, Vancouver, BC, V6E 1T7 **Fax** - (604) 631-3309
Website - www.rakovinatherapeutics.com
Email - ir@rakovinatherapeutics.com
Investor Relations - David Hyman (403) 613-1453
Auditors - Davidson & Company LLP C.A., Vancouver, B.C.
Lawyers - Blake, Cassels & Graydon LLP
Transfer Agents - Computershare Trust Company of Canada Inc., Vancouver, B.C.; Odyssey Trust Company, Vancouver, B.C.
Profile - (B.C. 2019) Researches and develops new cancer treatments based on novel DNA-damage response technologies.

Holds worldwide rights, excluding the People's Republic of China, Hong Kong and Taiwan, to develop and commercialize the kt-2000 series of PARP inhibitors, as well as the exclusive option to evaluate the potential commercial value of the kt-3000 and kt-4000 series drug candidates prior to negotiating terms of an exclusive worldwide license to the technology. kt-2000 series drug candidates are being optimized around potential differentiating factors and competitive advantages, including PARP-1 selectivity and the ability to cross the blood brain barrier. kt-3000 series are bi-functional small-molecule drug candidates designed to potently inhibit PARP and histone deacetylase (HDAC) and have the potential to overcome acquired treatment resistance to FDA-approved PARP inhibitors. kt-4000 series are small-molecule drug candidates that have been engineered to cause targeted DNA-damage to a tumor cell's DNA while simultaneously inhibiting the tumor's DNA damage response.

Predecessor Detail - Name changed from Vincero Capital Corp., Mar. 25, 2021, pursuant to the Qualifying Transaction reverse takeover acquisition of (old) Rakovina Therapeutics Inc. and concurrent amalgamation of (old) Rakovina with wholly owned 1260541 B.C. Ltd. (and continued as Rakovina Research Ltd.).

Directors - Jeffrey A. Bacha, exec. chr., Vancouver, B.C.; Alfredo De Lucrezia, v-chr., North Vancouver, B.C.; Dr. Dennis Brown, Menlo Park, Calif.; Michael Liggett, Vancouver, B.C.

Other Exec. Officers - Dr. Mads Daugaard, pres. & chief scientific officer; John Langlands, COO; David Hyman, CFO & corp. sec.

Capital Stock

	Authorized (shs.)	Outstanding (shs.)[1]
Common	unlimited	69,829,500

[1] At May 30, 2023

Major Shareholder - Edison Oncology Holding Corp. held 34.7% interest at May 24, 2023.

Price Range - RKV/TSX-VEN

Year	Volume	High	Low	Close
2022	5,247,721	$0.25	$0.12	$0.18
2021	7,511,876	$0.40	$0.16	$0.22
2020	185,000	$0.20	$0.10	$0.20

Recent Close: $0.11

Capital Stock Changes - During 2022, 21,500 common shares were issued on exercise of options.

Wholly Owned Subsidiaries

Rakovina Research Ltd., Vancouver, B.C.

Financial Statistics

Periods ended:	12m Dec. 31/22[A]		12m Dec. 31/21[A1]
	$000s	%Chg	$000s
Research & devel. expense	1,238		853
General & admin expense	785		3,891
Stock-based compensation	259		370
Operating expense	**2,281**	**-55**	**5,113**
Operating income	**(2,281)**	**n.a.**	**(5,113)**
Deprec., depl. & amort.	536		413
Finance income	28		9
Pre-tax income	**(2,791)**	**n.a.**	**(5,521)**
Net income	**(2,791)**	**n.a.**	**(5,521)**
Cash & equivalent	897		2,812
Accounts receivable	15		74
Current assets	1,070		3,071
Intangibles, net	5,051		5,587
Total assets	**6,121**	**-29**	**8,658**
Accts. pay. & accr. liabs	28		40
Current liabilities	107		114
Shareholders' equity	6,014		8,544
Cash from oper. activs	**(1,917)**	**n.a.**	**(2,308)**
Cash from fin. activs	2		4,320
Cash from invest. activs	nil		800
Net cash position	**897**	**-68**	**2,812**
	$		$
Earnings per share*	(0.04)		(0.10)
Cash flow per share*	(0.03)		(0.04)
	shs		shs
No. of shs. o/s*	69,829,500		69,808,000
Avg. no. of shs. o/s*	69,828,794		53,622,734
	%		%
Net profit margin	n.a.		n.a.
Return on equity	(38.34)		n.m.
Return on assets	(37.77)		n.a.

* Common
[A] Reported in accordance with IFRS
[1] Results reflect the Mar. 25, 2021, Qualifying Transaction reverse takeover acquisition of (old) Rakovina Therapeutics Inc. (renamed Rakovina Research Ltd.).

Latest Results

Periods ended:	3m Mar. 31/23[A]		3m Mar. 31/22[A]
	$000s	%Chg	$000s
Net income	(642)	n.a.	(712)
	$		$
Earnings per share*	(0.01)		(0.01)

* Common
[A] Reported in accordance with IFRS

R.19 Ramm Pharma Corp.

Symbol - RAMM **Exchange** - CSE **CUSIP** - 75150G
Head Office - World Trade Center, Montevideo Torre 2 #2306, Cr. Luis E. Lecueder 3536, Montevideo, Uruguay, 11300 **Overseas Tel** - 598-25-139-958
Website - www.rammpharma.com
Email - investors@rammpharma.com
Investor Relations - José Roldan 598-92-223-131
Auditors - Zeifmans LLP C.A., Toronto, Ont.
Transfer Agents - Odyssey Trust Company, Toronto, Ont.
Profile - (Can. 1987) Develops and commercializes pharmaceutical, cosmetic and nutraceutical products in Uruguay, Peru, Brazil, Italy and Poland, as well as provides medical services in Uruguay and Italy.

Sells medical devices and consumables, pharmaceutical products and cosmetics, as well as offers medical devices sterilization services. Products include Xalex™ 10 oral solution, a prescription pharmaceutical formulation of highly purified, plant-derived cannabidiol (CDB) free of tetrahydrocannabinol (THC), for the treatment of refractory epilepsy, chronic pain, multiple sclerosis and other medical conditions; Epifractán CBD extract, an approved treatment for children and teens for seizures caused by refractory epilepsy; CannabiPiel™ cream with 1% CBD, an over-the-counter treatment for joint pain and inflammation and a variety of skin disorders; Ultrapiel™ cream with vitamin A, urea and allantoin, and free of parabens; Psoricur™, a soothing and conditioning cream for the skin, without corticosteroids and free of parabens; NettaPet™, a brand of cannabis-based products focused on nutrition for pets and animals including dog foods specially formulated for various stages of a dog's life; and NettaVet™, a line of specialized CBD veterinary and medicinal products for animals.

Also sells a line of personal care products including, liquid soap, sanitizer, ethyl alcohols, cosmetics and disposable medical products in Uruguay under Bioset brand; as well as wellness and cosmetic products in Italy under Marishanti brand. In addition, manufactures and markets premium hemp-derived CBD products, including oils, capsules, skincare and supplements, in Poland, and plans on developing CBD-infused cosmetics, skincare and beauty products for the Italian cosmetics market.

Operations include 35,000 sq. ft. of production and storage facilities in Montevideo, Uruguay; 734,000 sq. ft. of agricultural land with 145,000 sq. ft. of operating greenhouses in Salto, Uruguay; and 1,000 hectares of extraction plant in Italy for manufacturing and processing of CBD oil, distillates and isolates to be used in pharmaceutical, wellness and cosmetic products.

In September 2022, the company acquired Poland-based **HemPoland Sp.zo.o**, a manufacturer and marketer of premium hemp-derived cannabidiol (CBD) products in Europe, from **BZAM Ltd.** (formerly **The Green Organic Dutchman Holdings Ltd.**) for $1,350,000.

Predecessor Detail - Name changed from MTC Growth Fund-I Inc., Oct. 28, 2019, pursuant to reverse takeover acquisition of Medic Plast S.A., and Yurelan S.A.

Directors - Jackie P. (Jack) Burnett, chr. & CEO, Montevideo, Uruguay; Daniel Augereau, Paris, France; Eric R. Klein, Toronto, Ont.

Other Exec. Officers - José Roldan, interim CFO & corp. sec.; Dr. Leticia Cuñetti, CMO; Edelma Ros, chief technical officer

Capital Stock

	Authorized (shs.)	Outstanding (shs.)[1]
Common	unlimited	121,802,317

[1] At May 8, 2023

Major Shareholder - Jackie P. (Jack) Burnett held 16.15% interest at May 8, 2023.

Price Range - RAMM/CSE

Year	Volume	High	Low	Close
2022	28,747,266	$0.40	$0.01	$0.14
2021	30,801,095	$1.19	$0.21	$0.38
2020	14,300,413	$0.94	$0.33	$0.65
2019	7,601,927	$0.94	$0.45	$0.93

Recent Close: $0.05

Capital Stock Changes - During fiscal 2022, 1,048,500 common shares were repurchased under a Normal Course Issuer Bid.

Wholly Owned Subsidiaries

Canapar Corp., Toronto, Ont.
- 100% int. in **Canapar S.r.l.**, Italy.
  - 100% int. in **Canapar Farming Societa' Agricola S.r.l.**, Italy.
  - 100% int. in **Canapar Iberica Sl.**, Italy.
  - 100% int. in **Canapar Marishanti S.r.l.**, Italy.

Glediser S.A., Uruguay.
HemPoland Sp.zo.o, Poland.
- 100% int. in **Green Absolutes sp.z.o.o**, Poland.
- 100% int. in **PHK sp.z.o.o**, Poland.

Medic Plast S.A., Uruguay.
Ramm Pharma Holdings Corp., Toronto, Ont.
Yurelan S.A., Uruguay.

Financial Statistics

Periods ended:	12m Oct. 31/22[A]		12m Oct. 31/21[oA]
	$000s	%Chg	$000s
Operating revenue	**3,897**	**-5**	**4,116**
Cost of sales	2,666		3,301
Salaries & benefits	2,981		2,665
General & admin expense	4,773		3,361
Stock-based compensation	384		699
Operating expense	**10,804**	**+8**	**10,026**
Operating income	**(6,907)**	**n.a.**	**(5,910)**
Deprec., depl. & amort.	1,020		733
Finance income	163		374
Finance costs, gross	14		13
Pre-tax income	**(20,952)**	**n.a.**	**(7,101)**
Income taxes	8		6
Net income	**(20,960)**	**n.a.**	**(7,107)**
Cash & equivalent	9,773		17,155
Inventories	4,019		3,049
Accounts receivable	2,915		4,072
Current assets	16,713		24,281
Fixed assets, net	18,983		19,306
Right-of-use assets	727		30
Intangibles, net	803		14,317
Total assets	**39,306**	**-34**	**59,798**
Accts. pay. & accr. liabs.	3,031		3,281
Current liabilities	3,267		3,315
Long-term lease liabilities	454		2
Shareholders' equity	35,585		56,390
Cash from oper. activs	**(5,913)**	**n.a.**	**(3,831)**
Cash from fin. activs	(354)		(178)
Cash from invest. activs	(1,152)		(6,833)
Net cash position	**9,773**	**-43**	**17,155**
Capital expenditures	(168)		(430)
Capital disposals	38		27
	$		$
Earnings per share*	(0.17)		(0.07)
Cash flow per share*	(0.05)		(0.04)
	shs		shs
No. of shs. o/s*	122,400,317		123,448,817
Avg. no. of shs. o/s*	122,773,204		108,460,225
	%		%
Net profit margin	(537.85)		(172.67)
Return on equity	(45.58)		(15.41)
Return on assets	(42.31)		(14.63)
Foreign sales percent	100		100

* Common
[o] Restated
[A] Reported in accordance with IFRS

Latest Results

Periods ended:	3m Jan. 31/23[A]		3m Jan. 31/22[A]
	$000s	%Chg	$000s
Operating revenue	1,327	+41	943
Net income	(1,661)	n.a.	(1,923)
	$		$
Earnings per share*	(0.01)		(0.02)

* Common
[A] Reported in accordance with IFRS

Historical Summary
(as originally stated)

Fiscal Year	Oper. Rev.	Net Inc. Bef. Disc.	EPS*
	$000s	$000s	$
2022[A]	3,897	(20,960)	(0.17)
2021[A]	4,116	(7,107)	(0.07)
2020[A]	5,445	(7,431)	(0.07)
2019[A1]	5,611	(6,820)	(0.14)
	US$000s	US$000s	US$
2018[A2]	6,485	(532)	n.a.

* Common
[A] Reported in accordance with IFRS
[1] Results reflect the Oct. 28, 2019, reverse takeover acquisition of Medic Plast S.A., Yurelan S.A. and Ramm Pharma Holdings Corp.
[2] Results for fiscal 2018 and 2017 pertain to Medic Plast S.A.

R.20 Rapid Dose Therapeutics Corp.

Symbol - DOSE **Exchange** - CSE **CUSIP** - 75339A
Head Office - Unit 3A, 1121 Walkers Line, Burlington, ON, L7N 2G4 **Telephone** - (416) 477-1052
Website - www.rapid-dose.com
Email - mupsdell@rapid-dose.com
Investor Relations - Mark Upsdell (416) 477-1020
Auditors - SRCO Professional Corporation C.A., Richmond Hill, Ont.
Transfer Agents - Capital Transfer Agency Inc., Toronto, Ont.
Profile - (Ont. 2009) Owns a proprietary, oral fast-dissolving drug delivery system, named QuickStrip™, capable of rapidly releasing active ingredients into the blood stream of pharmaceuticals, emulsified oils and over-the-counter medicines. Also provides packaged goods for cannabis edibles and cannabis infused health and wellness products as well as product innovation, production and consultation to the nutraceutical, cannabis healthcare and pharmaceutical manufacturing industries.

QuickStrip™ is based on an inert fabrication of a film-forming polymer and is designed to provide a stable base for an active ingredient that may be a pharmaceutical product, a nutraceutical product, a cannabinoid product, or any product that would provide enhanced bioavailability in the human body by means of oral dissolution to achieve direct and effective delivery of the active ingredient into the bloodstream, and without the necessity of breakdown through digestive processes. Also holds cannabidiol (CBD) to tetrahydrocannabinol (THC) conversion technology.

Products include QuickStrip™ Energy, which delivers energizing caffeine to keep you alert and focused; QuickStrip™ B12, which delivers vitamin B12 to your system, assisting with metabolism and physical energy; QuickStrip™ Sleep, which delivers melatonin to your system, inducing natural and healthy sleep - refreshing body and mind; and QuickSips™, a biodegradable infused straws with active ingredient on the inside that dissolves quickly and is taken up in just a few sips of liquid. Also offers dental products including Xylitol, which addresses dry mouth; and Lidocaine, an alternative pain therapy which manages pain during dental procedures. In addition, products that are in the process of launching include Tadalafil and Sildenafil, which are erectile dysfunction molecules that would be available to doctors, pharmacists and hospitals.

Also has pending licence application under the Cannabis Act and a fully approved research and development cannabis licence. Research and development includes QuickStrip™ for administering vaccines orally as a convenient and safe alternative to injection with needles; and a new nicotine product.

In addition, has distribution and sale agreements with **ANCAR Canada Limited**, **Oakland Health**, and **Cannmart Inc.** for the sale of the company's nutraceutical products in Canada, the U.K. and the European Union; Managed Strip Services Agreement with **Skycare Compounding Labs**, for the production of oral thin strips of approved pharmaceuticals for the medical and dental industry; and manufacturing agreements with **THRIVE Cannabis Inc.**, **Aphria Inc.**, **Phoena Holdings**, and **Rose Life**, whereby the company produce private label QuickStrip™ products for the Canadian market at its facilities located in Burlington, Ont. Also manufactures and sells vape line of products under agreement with **OG Laboratories LLC.**

Also provides packaged goods for cannabis edibles and cannabis infused health and wellness products, as well as product innovation, production and consultation to the nutraceutical, cannabis healthcare and pharmaceutical manufacturing industries.

In April 2023, the company agreed to terminate its distribution agreement with **MapleX Naturals Inc.**, whereby MapleX would assist in the production, purchase and sales process for the company's MapleX branded castile soap body wash product line.

Common reinstated on CSE, May 4, 2023.
Common suspended from CSE, Aug. 29, 2022.

Predecessor Detail - Name changed from ACME Resources Corp., Dec. 10, 2018, following reverse takeover acquisition of Rapid Dose Therapeutics Inc.

Directors - Mark Upsdell, pres. & CEO, Burlington, Ont.; Marisa Cornacchia, Ont.; Andrew Duckman, Ont.; Peter T. Hasler, Munich, Germany; Christine J. Hrudka, Saskatoon, Sask.; John M. McKimm, Toronto, Ont.

Other Exec. Officers - Douglas (Doug) Hyland, interim CFO; Jason Lewis, sr. v-p, bus. devel.

Capital Stock

	Authorized (shs.)	Outstanding (shs.)[1]
Common	unlimited	103,574,267

[1] At July 27, 2023

Major Shareholder - Mark Upsdell held 11.5% interest at June 27, 2023.

Price Range - DOSE/CSE

Year	Volume	High	Low	Close
2022	4,553,761	$0.51	$0.07	$0.09
2021	22,859,558	$0.70	$0.17	$0.52
2020	4,614,012	$0.55	$0.18	$0.32
2019	7,524,784	$1.33	$0.29	$0.38
2018	766,318	$1.23	$0.60	$0.92

Recent Close: $0.11

Capital Stock Changes - In April 2022, private placement of 506,157 units (1 common share & 1 warrant) at 30¢ per unit was completed.

Wholly Owned Subsidiaries

Consolidated Consumer Brands Inc., Ont.
Rapid Dose Therapeutics Inc., Burlington, Ont.
• 100% int. in **RDT Therapeutics Inc.**, Del.
Rapid Dose Therapeutics (UK) Limited, United Kingdom.

Financial Statistics

Periods ended:	12m Feb. 28/23[A]		12m Feb. 28/22[A]
	$000s	%Chg	$000s
Operating revenue	**718**	**-59**	**1,752**
Cost of sales	346		407
Salaries & benefits	1,391		1,590
Research & devel. expense	93		359
General & admin expense	1,083		1,239
Stock-based compensation	707		1,533
Operating expense	**3,620**	**-29**	**5,128**
Operating income	**(2,902)**	**n.a.**	**(3,376)**
Deprec., depl. & amort.	627		766
Finance costs, gross	264		133
Write-downs/write-offs	nil		(4,085)[1]
Pre-tax income	**(3,810)**	**n.a.**	**(8,487)**
Net income	**(3,810)**	**n.a.**	**(8,487)**
Cash & equivalent	28		34
Inventories	145		237
Accounts receivable	146		183
Current assets	420		614
Fixed assets, net	1,514		1,853
Right-of-use assets	312		601
Total assets	**2,247**	**-27**	**3,068**
Bank indebtedness	1,060		500
Accts. pay. & accr. liabs.	2,780		1,361
Current liabilities	4,701		2,452
Long-term debt, gross	187		nil
Long-term debt, net	187		nil
Long-term lease liabilities	29		364
Shareholders' equity	(2,670)		252
Cash from oper. activs	**(864)**	**n.a.**	**(3,000)**
Cash from fin. activs	857		1,127
Cash from invest. activs	nil		1,855
Net cash position	**28**	**-18**	**34**
Capital expenditures	nil		(40)
Capital disposals	nil		1
	$		$
Earnings per share*	(0.04)		(0.08)
Cash flow per share*	(0.01)		(0.03)
	shs		shs
No. of shs. o/s*	103,574,267		103,068,110
Avg. no. of shs. o/s*	103,416,180		100,216,232
	%		%
Net profit margin	(530.64)		(484.42)
Return on equity	n.m.		n.m.
Return on assets	(133.43)		(242.14)

* Common
[A] Reported in accordance with IFRS
[1] Pertains to impairment of goodwill acquisition of 2544737 Ontario Limited

Latest Results

Periods ended:	3m May 31/23[A]		3m May 31/22[A]
	$000s	%Chg	$000s
Operating revenue	241	+289	62
Net income	(567)	n.a.	(1,008)
	$		$
Earnings per share*	(0.01)		(0.01)

* Common
[A] Reported in accordance with IFRS

Historical Summary
(as originally stated)

Fiscal Year	Oper. Rev.	Net Inc. Bef. Disc.	EPS*
	$000s	$000s	$
2023[A]	718	(3,810)	(0.04)
2022[A]	1,752	(8,487)	(0.08)
2021[A]	263	(2,298)	(0.03)
2020[A1]	101	(7,965)	(0.10)
2019[A]	nil	(11,398)	(0.18)

* Common
[A] Reported in accordance with IFRS
[1] Results reflect the Dec. 7, 2018, reverse takeover acquisition of Rapid Dose Therapeutics Inc.

R.21 Ravensource Fund

Symbol - RAV.UN **Exchange** - TSX **CUSIP** - 754402
Head Office - c/o Stornoway Portfolio Management Inc., 901-30 St. Clair Ave W, Toronto, ON, M4V 3A1 **Telephone** - (416) 250-2845 **Fax** - (416) 250-6330
Website - www.ravensource.ca
Email - sreid@stornowayportfolio.com
Investor Relations - Scott R. Reid (416) 250-2845
Auditors - KPMG LLP C.A., Toronto, Ont.
Transfer Agents - Computershare Trust Company of Canada Inc., Toronto, Ont.
Trustees - Computershare Trust Company of Canada Inc., Toronto, Ont.

Investment Managers - Stornoway Portfolio Management Inc., Toronto, Ont.

Managers - Stornoway Portfolio Management Inc., Toronto, Ont.

Profile - (Ont. 1997) Invests in North American alternative credit and distressed debt securities, and in special situation equity securities.

Sector allocation at Dec. 31, 2022 (as a percentage of net assets):

Sector	Percentage
Litigation Finance	27.2%
Financial	17%
Oil & Gas	16.5%
Steel	14.2%
Media & Publishing	9.2%
Real Estate	8.2%
Technology	5.1%
Industrial	2.5%

Predecessor Detail - Name changed from The First Asia Income Fund, Oct. 8, 2003.

Oper. Subsid./Mgt. Co. Directors - Scott R. Reid, pres., Toronto, Ont.

Oper. Subsid./Mgt. Co. Officers - Daniel T. Metrikin, exec. v-p, invests.

Capital Stock

	Authorized (shs.)	Outstanding (shs.)[1]	Par
Trust Unit	unlimited	1,050,695	$10

[1] At Dec. 31, 2022

Trust Unit - Entitled to semiannual distributions which, on an annual basis, will be at least equal to the net capital gains plus the net income of the fund for that year. Redeemable on annual redemption date being the valuation date following August 31 in any year. One vote per trust unit.

Major Shareholder - Widely held at Mar. 29, 2023.

Price Range - RAV.UN/TSX

Year	Volume	High	Low	Close
2022	111,346	$16.50	$13.25	$14.62
2021	44,005	$17.35	$15.01	$16.02
2020	45,518	$18.00	$13.65	$15.00
2019	51,540	$20.00	$15.32	$17.85
2018	31,829	$16.75	$14.01	$16.75

Recent Close: $16.01

Capital Stock Changes - During 2022, 146,639 trust units were redeemed.

Dividends

RAV.UN tr unit omitted pa S[1]

[1] Semiannual divd normally payable in June/23 has been omitted.

Financial Statistics

Periods ended:	12m Dec. 31/22[A]		12m Dec. 31/21[A]
	$000s	%Chg	$000s
Realized invest. gain (loss)	(827)		546
Unrealized invest. gain (loss)	(1,627)		2,508
Total revenue	**(1,972)**	**n.a.**	**3,179**
General & admin. expense	448		561
Operating expense	**448**	**-20**	**561**
Operating income	**(2,420)**	**n.a.**	**2,618**
Finance costs, gross	178		nil
Pre-tax income	**(2,598)**	**n.a.**	**2,618**
Net income	**(2,598)**	**n.a.**	**2,618**
Cash & equivalent	1,808		387
Accounts receivable	85		22
Investments	20,193		25,813
Total assets	**22,207**	**-16**	**26,300**
Accts. pay. & accr. liabs	140		112
Debt	6,347		5,305
Shareholders' equity	15,690		20,864
Cash from oper. activs	**3,015**	**n.a.**	**(3,930)**
Cash from fin. activs	(1,533)		983
Net cash position	**1,808**	**+367**	**387**
	$		$
Earnings per share*	(2.27)		1.94
Cash flow per share*	2.63		(2.91)
Net asset value per share*	14.93		17.43
Cash divd. per share*	0.30		0.30
	shs		shs
No. of shs. o/s*	1,050,695		1,197,334
Avg. no. of shs. o/s*	1,144,606		1,348,861
	%		%
Net profit margin	n.m.		82.35
Return on equity	(14.21)		12.06
Return on assets	(9.98)		10.69

* Trust unit

[A] Reported in accordance with IFRS

Note: Net income reflects increase/decrease in net assets from operations.

Historical Summary
(as originally stated)

Fiscal Year	Total Rev. $000s	Net Inc. Bef. Disc. $000s	EPS* $
2022[A]	(1,972)	(2,598)	(2.27)
2021[A]	3,179	2,618	1.94
2020[A]	(2,194)	(2,776)	(1.74)
2019[A]	2,056	1,406	0.84
2018[A]	5,721	4,262	2.55

* Trust unit

[A] Reported in accordance with IFRS

R.22 Razor Energy Corp.

Symbol - RZE **Exchange** - TSX-VEN **CUSIP** - 75525M

Head Office - 800-500 5 Ave SW, Calgary, AB, T2P 3L5 **Telephone** - (403) 262-0242

Website - www.razor-energy.com

Email - dbailey@razor-energy.com

Investor Relations - Douglas Bailey (403) 262-0242

Auditors - KPMG LLP C.A., Calgary, Alta.

Bankers - National Bank of Canada, Calgary, Alta.

Lawyers - McCarthy Tétrault LLP, Calgary, Alta.

Transfer Agents - Alliance Trust Company, Calgary, Alta.

FP500 Revenue Ranking - 750

Employees - 87 at Dec. 31, 2022

Profile - (Alta. 2017; orig. Ont., 2010) Explores for, develops and produces oil and gas in Alberta, with a focus on light oil; operates and develops renewable power generation projects; and provides oilfield services in west-central Alberta.

Principal areas of interest are Swan Hills, Kaybob and District South in Alberta.

At Dec. 31, 2022, the company had 281 gross (160 net) producing oil wells, 114 gross (87 net) producing gas wells, 984 gross (728 net) non-producing oil wells, 217 gross (134 net) non-producing gas wells and 516 gross (342 net) other non-producing wells. Undeveloped land holdings totaled 51,400 gross (33,031 net) acres and developed land holdings totaled 275,293 gross (199,124 net) acres at Dec. 31, 2022.

In addition, wholly owned **FutEra Power Corp.** operates a 21-MW co-produced geothermal and natural gas hybrid energy project in Swan Hills, Alta.; and wholly owned **Blade Energy Services Corp.** provides oilfield services, including crude oil hauling, road maintenance, earthworks and well site reclamation.

On May 1, 2023, the company announced a recapitalization plan which included the settlement of Cdn$63,200,000 of debt owed by the company to **Alberta Investment Management Corporation** (AIMCo) in exchange for the transfer of 70% and 100% of the common and preferred shares, respectively, of wholly owned **FutEra Power Corp.** to AIMCo. In addition, the company announced an up to Cdn$10,000,000 rights offering to fund certain production enhancement activities and general working capital purposes. On closing, FutEra would assume the US$7,900,000 senior secured debt owed by the company to **Arena Investors, LP** and create a new class of convertible voting preferred shares. The transaction was expected to be completed in June 2023.

Periods ended:	12m Dec. 31/22	12m Dec. 31/21
Avg. oil prod., bbl/d	2,673	2,250
Avg. NGL prod., bbl/d	898	572
Avg. gas prod., mcf/d	4,324	4,209
Avg. BOE prod., bbl/d	4,291	3,524
Avg. light oil price, $/bbl	117.5	80.7
Avg. heavy oil price, $/bbl	92.34	68.45
Avg. NGL price, $/bbl	49.47	31.18
Avg. gas price, $/mcf	5.93	3.43
Avg. BOE price, $/bbl	88.65	60.26
Oil reserves, net, mbbl	9,923	13,199
NGL reserves, net, mbbl	3,649	3,185
Gas reserves, net, mmcf	10,460	8,428
BOE reserves, net, mbbl	15,315	17,789

Predecessor Detail - Name changed from Vector Resources Inc., Jan. 31, 2017, following Qualifying Transaction reverse takeover acquisition of (old) Razor Energy Corp.; basis 1 new for 20 old shs.

Directors - Douglas (Doug) Bailey, pres. & CEO, Calgary, Alta.; Shahin (Sonny) Mottahed, Calgary, Alta.; Frank P. Muller, Calgary, Alta.; Sean Phelan, Calgary, Alta.

Other Exec. Officers - Michael Blair, COO; Kevin Braun, CFO; Lisa Mueller, v-p, new ventures & pres. & CEO, FutEra Power Corp.; Devin K. Sundstrom, v-p, prod.; Stephen Sych, v-p, opers.

Capital Stock

	Authorized (shs.)	Outstanding (shs.)[1]
Preferred	unlimited	nil
Common	unlimited	25,275,250

[1] At May 8, 2023

Major Shareholder - Alberta Investment Management Corporation held 18.25% interest at May 8, 2023.

Price Range - RZE/TSX-VEN

Year	Volume	High	Low	Close
2022	27,319,043	$4.14	$0.73	$1.33
2021	12,072,429	$1.06	$0.20	$0.70
2020	7,950,711	$1.00	$0.09	$0.27
2019	2,519,747	$2.85	$0.80	$0.99
2018	3,810,947	$3.30	$1.38	$2.25

Recent Close: $0.63

Capital Stock Changes - In May 2022, 1,960,784 flow-through common shares were issued at $2.55 per share pursuant to a rights offering.

Wholly Owned Subsidiaries

Blade Energy Services Corp., Alta.

FutEra Power Corp., Alta.

- 100% int. in **Swan Hills Geothermal Power Corp.**, Alta.

Razor Holdings GP Corp.

Razor Resources Corp., Alta.

Razor Royalties Limited Partnership

Financial Statistics

Periods ended:	12m Dec. 31/22[A]		12m Dec. 31/21[A]
	$000s	%Chg	$000s
Operating revenue	**114,485**	**+72**	**66,581**
Cost of sales	86,333		60,256
General & admin expense	6,239		4,656
Stock-based compensation	456		283
Operating expense	**93,028**	**+43**	**65,195**
Operating income	**21,457**	**n.m.**	**1,386**
Deprec., depl. & amort.	22,014		14,678
Finance income	295		645
Finance costs, gross	20,375		11,212
Write-downs/write-offs	706		24,125
Pre-tax income	**(22,310)**	**n.a.**	**14,115**
Income taxes	310		(3,623)
Net income	**(22,620)**	**n.a.**	**17,738**
Cash & equivalent	2,424		2,841
Inventories	660		747
Accounts receivable	13,545		16,367
Current assets	21,291		22,108
Fixed assets, net	179,074		217,058
Total assets	**200,761**	**-16**	**239,166**
Accts. pay. & accr. liabs	50,518		43,798
Current liabilities	146,577		57,219
Long-term debt, gross	89,309		73,192
Long-term debt, net	632		64,047
Long-term lease liabilities	2,015		435
Shareholders' equity	(52,597)		(34,771)
Cash from oper. activs	**26,997**	**+235**	**8,060**
Cash from fin. activs	(716)		13,343
Cash from invest. activs	(26,529)		(19,623)
Net cash position	**2,424**	**-15**	**2,841**
Capital expenditures	(28,774)		(21,626)
Capital disposals	nil		530
	$		$
Earnings per share*	(0.92)		0.83
Cash flow per share*	1.10		0.38
	shs		shs
No. of shs. o/s*	25,275,250		23,314,466
Avg. no. of shs. o/s*	24,571,517		21,491,178
	%		%
Net profit margin	(19.76)		26.64
Return on equity	n.m.		n.m.
Return on assets	(0.89)		15.80
No. of employees (FTEs)	87		62

* Common

[A] Reported in accordance with IFRS

Historical Summary
(as originally stated)

Fiscal Year	Oper. Rev. $000s	Net Inc. Bef. Disc. $000s	EPS* $
2022[A]	114,485	(22,620)	(0.92)
2021[A]	66,581	17,738	0.83
2020[A]	47,091	(46,197)	(2.19)
2019[A]	73,131	(29,573)	(1.75)
2018[A]	107,193	4,239	0.27

* Common

[A] Reported in accordance with IFRS

R.23 React Gaming Group Inc.

Symbol - RGG **Exchange** - TSX-VEN (S) **CUSIP** - 75526E

Head Office - 107-2020 rte Transcanadienne, Dorval, QC, H9P 2N4 **Telephone** - (514) 861-1881 **Toll-free** - (866) 632-7217

Website - www.reactgaming.ca

Email - info@reactgaming.ca

Investor Relations - Leigh Hughes (866) 632-7217

Auditors -

Lawyers - BCF LLP, Montréal, Qué.

Transfer Agents - TSX Trust Company, Montréal, Qué.

Profile - (Can. 2003; orig. Alta., 2001) Offers fully licensed, safe and secure online platforms in the eSports and iGaming industry.

Portfolio includes LOOT.BET, an online gaming and live eSports betting platform with more than 500,000 registered users; Compete.gg (formerly HypeX.gg), a social gaming platform specializing in eSports tournaments and wagering; Team BH, a top-tier Canadian Fortnite team; Generationz Gaming Entertainment, which offers partners the opportunity to build their own online/mobile iGaming and eSports business with the company's completely customizable betting platform; and Parabelleum ESports, a Toronto, Ont.-based professional eSports organization that competes in titles such as Rainbow 6, Rocket League, Super Smash

Bros Ultimate, CSGO and iRacing, and operates Northern Shield Academy, which gives amateur players coaching, mentorships and paths to move their eSports career forward.

In April 2022, the company discontinued its eFlyermaker business.

Common suspended from TSX-VEN, June 2, 2023.

Predecessor Detail - Name changed from Intema Solutions Inc., Apr. 12, 2022.

Directors - Normand Bellemare; Michael (Mike) Curtis, Deux-Montagnes, Qué.; Jessica N. Di Rito, Toronto, Ont.; Arthur (Art) Manteris, Boulder City, Nev.; Philip Nolan, Outremont, Qué.

Other Exec. Officers - Leigh Hughes, interim pres. & CEO; Claude Théoret, COO; Scott R. Meyers, CFO; Laura Klauber, exec. v-p, opers.; Sébastien Plourde, exec. v-p & chief tech. officer; Daniel Drouet, v-p, products

Capital Stock

	Authorized (shs.)	Outstanding (shs.)[1]
Common	unlimited	167,439,734

[1] At Nov. 28, 2022

Major Shareholder - Widely held at Oct. 18, 2022.

Price Range - RGG/TSX-VEN (S)

Year	Volume	High	Low	Close
2022	26,256,077	$0.36	$0.07	$0.08
2021	51,777,075	$0.80	$0.21	$0.31
2020	48,331,568	$0.37	$0.02	$0.35
2019	12,759,636	$0.21	$0.02	$0.13
2018	29,367,652	$0.22	$0.02	$0.02

Consolidation: 1-for-2 cons. in Sept. 2019

Recent Close: $0.04

Capital Stock Changes - In February 2022, 20,014,000 common shares were issued without further consideration on exchange of subscription receipts sold previously by private placement at 50¢ each. In November 2022, a 1-for-4 share consolidation was approved.

Wholly Owned Subsidiaries

Champion Esports Inc., Canada.
GGWP, Belarus.
Generationz Gaming Entertainment Inc., Chicago, Ill.
HypeX.gg Plateforme de Jeux Sociaux Inc.
Intema Solutions Inc., Canada.
Livestream eSports Limited, Isle of Man.
Livestream Gaming Ltd., Belize City, Belize.
Livestream Ltd., Cyprus.
Livestream Services Limited, Isle of Man.
Parabellum Media Inc., Ont.
Team BloodHounds Inc., Ont.
Zubrsoft LLC, Belarus.

Financial Statistics

Periods ended:	12m Dec. 31/21[A]		12m Dec. 31/20[□A]
	$000s	%Chg	$000s
Operating revenue	**127**	**-12**	**144**
Cost of sales	nil		48
General & admin expense	4,738		1,134
Stock-based compensation	260		nil
Operating expense	**4,998**	**+323**	**1,182**
Operating income	**(4,871)**	**n.a.**	**(1,038)**
Deprec., depl. & amort.	200		100
Finance costs, gross	17		17
Write-downs/write-offs	94		nil
Pre-tax income	**(5,183)**	**n.a.**	**(1,106)**
Net income	**(5,183)**	**n.a.**	**(1,106)**
Cash & equivalent	2,950		301
Accounts receivable	164		120
Current assets	13,241		898
Fixed assets, net	44		32
Right-of-use assets	161		85
Intangibles, net	826		75
Total assets	**14,287**	**n.m.**	**1,100**
Bank indebtedness	nil		125
Accts. pay. & accr. liabs	603		193
Current liabilities	10,942		825
Long-term debt, gross	362		283
Long-term debt, net	140		86
Shareholders' equity	3,205		189
Cash from oper. activs	**(4,531)**	**n.a.**	**(641)**
Cash from fin. activs	7,374		422
Cash from invest. activs	(194)		19
Net cash position	**2,950**	**+880**	**301**
Capital expenditures	(46)		nil
	$		$
Earnings per share*	(0.04)		(0.02)
Cash flow per share*	(0.04)		(0.01)
	shs		shs
No. of shs. o/s*	135,823,174		91,753,790
Avg. no. of shs. o/s*	115,485,297		70,938,178
	%		%
Net profit margin	n.m.		(768.06)
Return on equity	(305.42)		(336.68)
Return on assets	(67.15)		(104.66)

* Common
[□] Restated
[A] Reported in accordance with IFRS

Latest Results

Periods ended:	9m Sept. 30/22[A]		9m Sept. 30/21[□A]
	$000s	%Chg	$000s
Operating revenue	1,972	n.m.	96
Net income	(7,004)	n.a.	(2,885)
	$		$
Earnings per share*	(0.04)		(0.03)

* Common
[□] Restated
[A] Reported in accordance with IFRS

Historical Summary
(as originally stated)

Fiscal Year	Oper. Rev.	Net Inc. Bef. Disc.	EPS*
	$000s	$000s	$
2021[A]	127	(5,183)	(0.04)
2020[A]	144	(1,106)	(0.02)
2019[A]	509	(585)	(0.01)
2018[A]	604	(1,006)	(0.02)
2017[A]	817	(974)	(0.02)

* Common
[A] Reported in accordance with IFRS

Note: Adjusted throughout for 1-for-2 cons. in Sept. 2019

R.24 The Real Brokerage Inc.

Symbol - REAX **Exchange** - NASDAQ **CUSIP** - 75585H

Head Office - 302-133 Richmond St W, Toronto, ON, M5H 2L3 **Telephone** - (647) 920-6383

Website - joinreal.com

Email - investors@therealbrokerage.com

Investor Relations - Jason Lee (908) 280-2515

Auditors - Brightman Almagor Zohar & Co. C.P.A., Tel Aviv, Israel

Transfer Agents - Computershare Trust Company of Canada Inc., Toronto, Ont.

FP500 Revenue Ranking - 468

Employees - 118 at Dec. 31, 2022

Profile - (B.C. 2018) Offers a digital real estate brokerage platform for agents across the United States and Canada.

The cloud-based platform is used improve efficiencies and empower real estate agents to provide a seamless end-to-end experience for home buyers and sellers. Features of the platform include customer relationship management, broker support, technical support, interactive training, education, transaction management, transaction support, documents library, contract templates, paperless file sharing, virtual signature tools, business dashboard and weekly educational webinars and conference calls. To aid agents in marketing, each agent joining the platform receives a personal branded mobile app, personal branded website, access to a print portal to enable ordering of business cards, yard signs, marketing materials, designer assistance, access to marketing webinars, as well as agents buyer and seller leads. Agents are also offered access to the company's app and desktop-based community where they can socialize, celebrate success, ask questions, cooperate, market properties, exchange leads, transact business with colleagues, share information and view company announcements.

The company does not maintain physical locations (unless required by local laws) and uses proprietary mobile applications, as well as other technology platforms to distribute its services. Revenue consists primarily of commissions from the processing of real estate transactions. A portion of commissions received are paid to the agents and brokers.

At Mar. 16, 2023, the company operated in 45 U.S. states, the District of Columbia, and in Alberta, British Columbia and Ontario with more than 9,300 real estate professionals, who are independent contractors.

In December 2022, the company acquired **LemonBrew Lending Corp.** from **LemonBrew Technologies Corp.** for US$1,250,000 consisting of US$800,000 cash and issuance of 351,837 common shares at US$1.279 per share. LemonBrew Lending is licensed to provide a full suite of mortgage services across 20 states in the U.S. including Texas, California and Florida.

In November 2022, the company acquired private B.C.-based **Redline Real Estate Group (BC) Inc.** for Cdn$1.00 cash. Redline is a real estate company with 90 agents serving clients throughout the provinces of Alberta, Ontario and British Columbia.

Common delisted from TSX, Aug. 14, 2023.

Predecessor Detail - Name changed from ADL Ventures Inc., June 12, 2020, pursuant to Qualifying Transaction reverse takeover acquisition of Real Technology Broker Ltd.

Directors - Tamir Poleg, chr. & CEO, Tel Aviv, Israel; Vikki Bartholomae, Winter Garden, Fla.; Guy Gamzu, Tel Aviv, Israel; Larry Klane, Westport, Conn.; Atul Malhotra Jr., West Hollywood, Calif.; Laurence Rose, Toronto, Ont.; Susanne Greenfield Sandler

Other Exec. Officers - Sharran Srivatsaa, pres.; Michelle Ressler, CFO & corp. sec.; Pritesh Damani, chief tech. officer; Dre Madden, chief mktg. officer; Sheila Dunagan, exec. v-p, brokerage opers.; Alexandra Lumpkin, gen. counsel

Capital Stock

	Authorized (shs.)	Outstanding (shs.)[1]
Common	unlimited	180,130,539

[1] At May 18, 2023

Normal Course Issuer Bid - The company plans to make normal course purchases of up to 9,006,526 common shares representing 5% of the total outstanding. The bid commenced on May 29, 2023, and expires on May 28, 2024.

Major Shareholder - Insight Holdings Group, LLC held 19.2% interest and Magma Venture Capital funds held 13.61% interest at Apr. 24, 2023.

Price Range - REAX/TSX (D)

Year	Volume	High	Low	Close
2022	4,831,129	$4.70	$1.28	$1.44
2021	15,764,757	$5.20	$0.90	$4.61
2020	10,668,505	$2.64	$0.16	$1.18
2019	108,500	$0.10	$0.08	$0.08
2018	153,000	$0.18	$0.10	$0.18

Split: 4-for-1 split in July 2021; 1-for-4 cons. in June 2021

Capital Stock Changes - During fiscal 2022, common shares were issued as follows: 2,504,000 on vesting of restricted share units, 1,389,000 on exercise of options and 351,837 on acquisition of LemonBrew Lending Corp.; and 3,800,000 common shares were repurchased under a Normal Course Issuer Bid.

Wholly Owned Subsidiaries

Real Broker BC Ltd., B.C.
- 100% int. in **Real Broker AB Ltd.**, Alta.
- 100% int. in **Real Broker ON Ltd.**, Ont.
  - 100% int. in **Real Broker Ontario Ltd.**, Ont.

Real PIPE, LLC, Del.
Real Technology Broker Ltd., Israel.
- 100% int. in **Real Broker LLC**, Tex.
  - 100% int. in **LemonBrew Lending Corp.**, N.J.
  - 100% int. in **Real Broker CT, LLC**, Conn.
  - 100% int. in **Real Broker Commercial LLC**, Tex.
  - 100% int. in **Real Broker MA, LLC**, Mass.
  - 100% int. in **Real Broker NY, LLC**, Del.
  - 100% int. in **Real Brokerage Technologies Inc.**, Calif.
  - 100% int. in **The Real Title Inc.**, Miami, Fla. formerly Expetitle, Inc.
    - 51% int. in **Beycome Title, LLC**, Fla.
    - 100% int. in **Real Escrow of California, Inc.**, Fla.
    - 100% int. in **Real Title Abstract Group, LLC**, Fla.
    - 88% int. in **Real Title Agency, LLC**, Fla.
    - 100% int. in **Real Title Closing Services, LLC**, Fla.
    - 100% int. in **Real Title Great Lakes, LLC**, Fla.
    - 100% int. in **Real Title Mountain West, LLC**, Fla.
    - 100% int. in **Real Title Open Agency, LLC**, Fla.
    - 99% int. in **Real Title Open Group, LLC**, Fla.
    - 51% int. in **Real Title Quality Closing, LLC**, Fla.

Financial Statistics

Periods ended:	12m Dec. 31/22[A]		12m Dec. 31/21[□A]
	US$000s	%Chg	US$000s
Operating revenue	**381,756**	**+214**	**121,681**
Cost of sales	349,806		110,587
Salaries & benefits	14,223		4,915
Research & devel. expense	2,643		1,594
General & admin expense	25,987		10,431
Stock-based compensation	8,510		5,207
Operating expense	**401,169**	**+202**	**132,734**
Operating income	**(19,413)**	**n.a.**	**(11,053)**
Deprec., depl. & amort.	333		213
Finance costs, net	1,167		662
Pre-tax income	**(20,335)**	**n.a.**	**(11,679)**
Net income	**(20,335)**	**n.a.**	**(11,679)**
Net inc. for equity hldrs	**(20,577)**	**n.a.**	**(11,679)**
Net inc. for non-cont. int	**242**	**n.a.**	**nil**
Cash & equivalent	18,738		37,893
Accounts receivable	1,621		277
Current assets	28,369		38,665
Fixed assets, net	1,350		170
Right-of-use assets	73		109
Intangibles, net	13,970		1,053
Total assets	**43,762**	**+9**	**39,997**
Accts. pay. & accr. liabs	12,340		8,872
Current liabilities	21,105		12,314
Long-term lease liabilities	nil		40
Shareholders' equity	22,152		27,004
Non-controlling interest	263		nil
Cash from oper. activs	**5,995**	**+256**	**1,684**
Cash from fin. activs	(7,849)		7,267
Cash from invest. activs	(9,048)		(1,271)
Net cash position	**18,327**	**-37**	**29,129**
Capital expenditures	(1,408)		(172)
	US$		US$
Earnings per share*	(0.12)		(0.07)
Cash flow per share*	0.03		0.01
	shs		shs
No. of shs. o/s	n.a.		n.a.
Avg. no. of shs. o/s*	178,201,000		170,483,000
	%		%
Net profit margin	(5.33)		(9.60)
Return on equity	(83.72)		(70.82)
Return on assets	(48.56)		(37.73)
No. of employees (FTEs)	118		n.a.

* Common
[□] Restated
[A] Reported in accordance with IFRS

Latest Results

Periods ended:	3m Mar. 31/23[A]		3m Mar. 31/22[A]
	US$000s	%Chg	US$000s
Operating revenue	107,845	+75	61,649
Net income	(7,315)	n.a.	(4,252)
Net inc. for equity hldrs	(7,395)	n.a.	(4,313)
Net inc. for non-cont. int	80		61
	US$		US$
Earnings per share*	(0.04)		(0.03)

* Common
[A] Reported in accordance with IFRS

Historical Summary
(as originally stated)

Fiscal Year	Oper. Rev.	Net Inc. Bef. Disc.	EPS*
	US$000s	US$000s	US$
2022[A]	381,756	(20,335)	(0.12)
2021[A]	121,681	(11,679)	(0.07)
2020[A1]	16,559	(3,621)	(0.04)
2019[A2]	15,751	(2,251)	n.a.
2018[A]	8,444	(2,524)	n.a.

* Common
[A] Reported in accordance with IFRS
[1] Results reflect the June 5, 2020, Qualifying Transaction reverse takeover acquisition of Real Technology Broker Ltd.
[2] Results for 2019 and 2018 pertain to Real Technology Broker Ltd.
Note: Adjusted throughout for 4-for-1 split in July 2021; 1-for-4 cons. in June 2021

R.25 Real Estate Split Corp.

Symbol - RS **Exchange** - TSX **CUSIP** - 75602C
Head Office - c/o Middlefield Limited, 1 First Canadian Place, 5800-100 King St W, PO Box 192, Toronto, ON, M5X 1A6 **Telephone** - (416) 362-0714 **Toll-free** - (888) 890-1868 **Fax** - (416) 362-7925
Website - www.middlefield.com
Email - sroberts@middlefield.com
Investor Relations - Sarah Roberts (416) 847-5355
Auditors - Deloitte LLP C.A., Toronto, Ont.
Transfer Agents - TSX Trust Company
Investment Advisors - Middlefield Capital Corporation, Toronto, Ont.
Managers - Middlefield Limited, Calgary, Alta.
Profile - (Ont. 2020) Invests in a diversified, actively managed portfolio of dividend paying securities of issuers operating in the real estate or related sectors, including real estate investment trusts, that the advisor believes are well-positioned to benefit from low interest rates, the rapid adoption of e-commerce, the growth of data infrastructure as well as attractive valuations in various areas of the real estate sector.

The company has a scheduled termination date of Dec. 31, 2025, subject to extension for successive terms of up to five years.

Top 10 holdings at Mar. 31, 2023 (as a percentage of net asset value):

Holding	Percentage
Dream Industrial REIT	9.8%
Granite REIT	9.1%
H&R REIT	6.8%
First Capital REIT	6.6%
Canadian Apartment Properties REIT	6.3%
Choice Properties REIT	6.1%
Boardwalk REIT	6.0%
RioCan REIT	5.9%
SmartCentres REIT	5.8%
Killam Apartment REIT	5.7%

Predecessor Detail - Name changed from Real Estate & E-Commerce Split Corp., Jan. 1, 2022.
Oper. Subsid./Mgt. Co. Directors - Dean Orrico, pres. & CEO, Vaughan, Ont.; Craig Rogers, CFO & corp. sec., Toronto, Ont.; Jeremy T. Brasseur, Toronto, Ont.; Wendy Teo, Toronto, Ont.

Capital Stock

	Authorized (shs.)	Outstanding (shs.)[1]
Preferred	unlimited	5,652,912
Class A	unlimited	5,744,812
Class M	unlimited	100

[1] At June 28, 2023

Preferred - Entitled to fixed cumulative preferential quarterly cash distributions of $0.13125 per share to yield 5.25% per annum on the original $10 issue price. Retractable monthly for a price per share equal to 96% of the lesser of: (i) the net asset value (NAV) per unit (1 class A share and 1 preferred share) less the cost to the company for purchasing a class A share in the market for cancellation; and (ii) $10. Retractable in November of each year together with a class A share for a price equal to the NAV per unit less any retraction costs, including commissions. All outstanding preferred shares will be redeemed on Dec. 31, 2025, at a price per share equal to the lesser of: (i) the NAV per share; and (ii) $10 plus accrued and unpaid dividends. Rank in priority to the class A and class M shares with respect to the payment of distributions and the repayment of capital on the dissolution, liquidation or winding-up of the company. Non-voting.

Class A - Entitled to non-cumulative monthly cash distributions of $0.10 per share to yield 8% per annum on the original $15 issue price. No distributions will be paid if the distributions payable on the preferred shares are in arrears or in respect of a cash distribution, after payment of the distribution, the NAV per unit would be less than $15. Retractable monthly for a price per share equal to 96% of the difference between: (i) the NAV per unit; and (ii) the cost to the company of purchasing a preferred share in the market for cancellation. If the NAV per unit is less than $10, plus accrued and unpaid dividends on a preferred share, the class A retraction price will be nil. Retractable in November of each year together with a preferred share for a price equal to the NAV per unit less any retraction costs, including commissions. All outstanding class A shares will be redeemed on Dec. 31, 2025, at a price per share equal to the greater of: (i) the NAV per unit minus the sum of $10 plus accrued dividends and unpaid dividends per preferred share; and (ii) nil. Rank subsequent to the preferred shares but in priority to the class M shares with respect to the payment of distributions and the repayment of capital on the dissolution, liquidation or winding-up of the company. Non-voting.

Class M - Not entitled to receive distributions. Retractable and redeemable at any time at $1.00 per share. Rank subsequent to both preferred and class A shares with respect to distributions on the dissolution, liquidation or winding-up of the company. One vote per share.

Major Shareholder - Real Estate & E-Commerce Split Corp. Holding Trust held 100% interest at Mar. 31, 2023.

Price Range - RS/TSX

Year	Volume	High	Low	Close
2022	3,815,445	$19.69	$13.65	$14.00
2021	2,183,146	$22.78	$12.45	$19.00
2020	71,307	$14.95	$13.86	$14.50

Recent Close: $13.99

Capital Stock Changes - In March 2023, public offering of 383,500 preferred shares and 340,500 class A shares was completed at $9.65 and $14.60 per share, respectively. In June 2023, public offering of 500,500 preferred shares and 393,700 class A shares was completed at $9.35 and $14.25 per share, respectively.

In February 2022, public offering of 550,425 preferred shares and 550,425 class A shares was completed at $10.55 and $19.10 per share, respectively. In May 2022, public offering of 539,600 preferred shares and 539,600 class A shares was completed at $10.10 and $18 per share, respectively. In June 2022, public offering of 397,800 preferred shares and 397,800 class A shares was completed at $10.12 and $15.30 per share, respectively. In October 2022, public offering of 489,950 preferred shares and 489,950 class A shares was completed at $9.80 and $14.40 per share, respectively. In November 2022, public offering of 644,400 preferred shares and 644,400 class A shares was completed at $9.45 and $13.90 per share, respectively. Also during 2022, 850 preferred shares and 850 class A shares were retracted.

Dividends

RS cl A Ra $1.56 pa M est. Sept. 15, 2021**
Prev. Rate: $1.20 est. Jan. 15, 2021
$0.10**i** .... Jan. 15/21
RS.PR.A pfd Ra $0.525 pa Q
Prev. Rate: $0.2454
$0.06135**i** .... Jan. 15/21
** Reinvestment Option **i** Initial Payment

Financial Statistics

Periods ended:	12m Dec. 31/22[A]		12m Dec. 31/21[A]
	$000s	%Chg	$000s
Realized invest. gain (loss)	(789)		2,146
Unrealized invest. gain (loss)	(16,119)		10,971
Total revenue	**(13,783)**	**n.a.**	**14,393**
General & admin. expense	1,319		904
Operating expense	**1,319**	**+46**	**904**
Operating income	**(15,102)**	**n.a.**	**13,489**
Finance costs, gross	2,209		1,120
Pre-tax income	**(17,312)**	**n.a.**	**12,368**
Income taxes	26		67
Net income	**(17,338)**	**n.a.**	**12,302**
Cash & equivalent	5,363		3,710
Accounts receivable	482		299
Investments	115,247		74,549
Total assets	**121,094**	**+54**	**78,558**
Accts. pay. & accr. liabs	142		93
Debt	52,622		26,909
Shareholders' equity	66,455		50,866
Cash from oper. activs	**(57,825)**	**n.a.**	**(26,412)**
Cash from fin. activs	59,473		27,750
Net cash position	**5,363**	**+45**	**3,710**
	$		$
Earnings per share*	(4.48)		6.27
Cash flow per share*	(14.95)		(13.46)
Net asset value per share*	12.63		19.26
Cash divd. per share*	1.56		1.35
	shs		shs
No. of shs. o/s*	5,262,212		2,640,887
Avg. no. of shs. o/s*	3,868,980		1,962,786
	%		%
Net profit margin	n.m.		85.47
Return on equity	(29.56)		n.m.
Return on assets	(15.15)		n.a.

* Class A
[A] Reported in accordance with IFRS

R.26 Real Luck Group Ltd.

Symbol - LUCK **Exchange** - TSX-VEN **CUSIP** - 75602A
Head Office - 3400-350 7 Ave SW, Calgary, AB, T2P 3N9 **Telephone** - (403) 613-7310
Website - www.realluckgroup.com
Email - nik@sophiccapital.com
Investor Relations - Nikhil Thadani (647) 670-2882
Auditors - Baker Tilly WM LLP C.A., Toronto, Ont.
Transfer Agents - TSX Trust Company, Calgary, Alta.
Employees - 33 at Apr. 27, 2023
Profile - (Alta. 2018) Provides a fully licensed eSports and traditional sports, and online casino wagering platform under the Luckbox brand which enable users to bet, watch and chat in a safe environment on desktop and mobile devices.

Has developed a technology platform offering an online, general betting book with fixed odds to bet on professional competitive video game events and matches across 14 game titles, 10 traditional sports, and casino games.Wholly owned **Real Time Games Holdings Limited** has an Isle of Man (IOM) gaming licence which enables it to operate an online casino and other casino games, as well as the online general betting book using the domain name www.luckbox.com. An IOM licence permits licence holders to accept players who are residents of a wide range of countries and does not restrict Luckbox from any specific market. Customers from certain countries such as the United Kingdom and the United States are not accepted but the company plans to enter multiple additional licensed jurisdictions.

Predecessor Detail - Name changed from Elephant Hill Capital Inc., Dec. 7, 2020, pursuant to Qualifying Transaction reverse takeover acquisition of Esports Limited (dba Luckbox); basis 1 new for 4.2 old shs.
Directors - Drew Green, chr., Vancouver, B.C.; Thomas Rosander, CEO, Malta; Lloyd Melnick, Douglas, Isle of Man; Maruf Raza, Toronto, Ont.; Bo Wänghammar, Malta
Other Exec. Officers - Benn Timbury, COO; William Moore, CFO; Jo-Anne Archibald, corp. sec.

Capital Stock

	Authorized (shs.)	Outstanding (shs.)[1]
Preferred	unlimited	nil
Common	unlimited	68,900,548

[1] At Aug. 14, 2023

Major Shareholder - Widely held at June 22, 2022.

Price Range - LUCK/TSX-VEN

Year	Volume	High	Low	Close
2022	19,247,969	$0.25	$0.08	$0.11
2021	57,859,577	$1.80	$0.18	$0.23
2020	5,565,434	$1.04	$0.36	$0.88
2019	154,190	$0.42	$0.21	$0.42
2018	49,523	$0.63	$0.38	$0.42

Consolidation: 1-for-4.2 cons. in Dec. 2020
Recent Close: $0.03
Capital Stock Changes - During 2022, 119,048 common shares were issued for services.

Wholly Owned Subsidiaries

Esports Limited, Isle of Man.
- 100% int. in **Esports Tech Limited**, Isle of Man.
- 100% int. in **Real Time Games Holdings Limited**, Isle of Man.
  - 100% int. in **Real Time Games Services Ltd.**, Isle of Man.
    - 100% int. in **Real Time Games Development Limited**, Bulgaria.

Real Luck Group Holdings Limited, Canada.

Financial Statistics

Periods ended:	12m Dec. 31/22[A]		12m Dec. 31/21[oA]
	$000s	%Chg	$000s
Operating revenue	**160**	**+540**	**25**
Cost of sales	672		290
Salaries & benefits	2,037		1,736
General & admin expense	5,511		4,724
Stock-based compensation	916		1,890
Operating expense	**9,136**	**+6**	**8,640**
Operating income	**(8,976)**	**n.a.**	**(8,615)**
Deprec., depl. & amort.	81		79
Finance income	31		41
Finance costs, gross	64		70
Write-downs/write-offs	(27)		nil
Pre-tax income	**(9,110)**	**n.a.**	**(8,625)**
Income taxes	7		6
Net income	**(9,117)**	**n.a.**	**(8,631)**
Cash & equivalent	6,070		14,398
Accounts receivable	152		137
Current assets	6,805		14,953
Fixed assets, net	50		87
Right-of-use assets	22		61
Intangibles, net	26		13
Total assets	**6,912**	**-54**	**15,124**
Accts. pay. & accr. liabs	1,069		1,000
Current liabilities	1,085		1,040
Long-term lease liabilities	11		24
Shareholders' equity	5,816		14,060
Cash from oper. activs	**(8,222)**	**n.a.**	**(6,934)**
Cash from fin. activs	(39)		17,566
Cash from invest. activs	(24)		(51)
Net cash position	**6,070**	**-58**	**14,398**
Capital expenditures	(14)		(21)
Capital disposals	2		nil
	$		$
Earnings per share*	(0.13)		(0.14)
Cash flow per share*	(0.12)		(0.11)
	shs		shs
No. of shs. o/s*	68,900,548		68,781,500
Avg. no. of shs. o/s*	68,825,531		61,457,032
	%		%
Net profit margin	n.m.		n.m.
Return on equity	(91.74)		(99.88)
Return on assets	(82.17)		(88.13)
Foreign sales percent	100		100

* Common
[o] Restated
[A] Reported in accordance with IFRS

Latest Results

Periods ended:	3m Mar. 31/23[A]		3m Mar. 31/22[A]
	$000s	%Chg	$000s
Operating revenue	625	n.m.	19
Net income	(4,165)	n.a.	(2,070)
	$		$
Earnings per share*	(0.06)		(0.03)

* Common
[A] Reported in accordance with IFRS

Historical Summary
(as originally stated)

Fiscal Year	Oper. Rev.	Net Inc. Bef. Disc.	EPS*
	$000s	$000s	$
2022[A]	160	(9,117)	(0.13)
2021[A]	25	(8,631)	(0.14)
2020[A1]	75	(5,496)	(0.18)
	€000s	€000s	€
2019[A]	2	(2,971)	n.a.
2018[A]	nil	(3,684)	n.a.

* Common
[A] Reported in accordance with IFRS
[1] Results prior to Dec. 14, 2020, pertain to and reflect the Qualifying Transaction reverse takeover acquisition of Esports Limited (dba Luckbox).
Note: Adjusted throughout for 1-for-4.2 cons. in Dec. 2020

R.27 Real Matters Inc.*

Symbol - REAL **Exchange** - TSX **CUSIP** - 75601Y
Head Office - 401-50 Minthorn Blvd, Markham, ON, L3T 7X8 **Toll-free** - (877) 739-2212 **Fax** - (905) 739-1222
Website - www.realmatters.com
Email - lbeauregard@realmatters.com
Investor Relations - Lyne Beauregard (416) 994-5930
Auditors - Deloitte LLP C.A., Toronto, Ont.
Lawyers - Osler, Hoskin & Harcourt LLP, Toronto, Ont.
Transfer Agents - TSX Trust Company, Toronto, Ont.
FP500 Revenue Ranking - 498
Employees - 424 at Sept. 30, 2022

Profile - (Can. 2004) Provides appraisal services to the mortgage lending industry in the U.S. and Canada and title services to the mortgage lending industry in the U.S., all through its Solidifi brand. Also provides insurance inspection services to property and casualty insurers in Canada through its iv3 brand.

Operations are organized into three segments: U.S. Appraisal; U.S. Title; and Canada.

The **U.S. Appraisal** segment provides residential real estate appraisal services to the largest mortgage lenders in the U.S., including all Tier 1 mortgage lenders, for purchase origination, refinance origination, home equity, default and real estate owned (REO) transactions. Clients primarily order residential appraisals for mortgage loan assessment purposes and for compliance with government sponsored entities (GSE) requirements. Residential appraisal products include complete home appraisals by a duly accredited professional real estate appraiser indicating their opinion on the value of a specific property, including interior and/or exterior inspections; desktop appraisals from a qualified appraiser which does not include any inspection of the property; quantitative appraisal reports based on observations of the interior and/or exterior conditions of a property from a site visit by the appraiser or third-party inspector as well as from public record or local market data; broker price opinions; interior and exterior property condition reports; property evaluation report; automated valuation model (AVM) reports, which are computer-generated reports that use mathematical modeling combined with databases of existing properties and transactions to estimate the value of a specific property; enhanced AVM reports, which are completed by a qualified appraiser based on the output of an AVM; and flood determination reports.

The **U.S. Title** segment offers and/or coordinates various title services for refinance, purchase, short sale and REO transactions to financial institutions across the U.S., with a focus on Tier 1, 2 and 3 mortgage lenders. Services include handling of all title curative, settlement, closing coordination and escrow functions on behalf of lender clients for origination (refinance or purchase) and REO, resulting in a title insurance policy; title search and examination, curative, escrow services and accounting for a refinance, purchase or REO transaction on behalf of a client; second-position lender searches, taxes and reporting relating to legal vesting and encumbrances as part of clients' home equity lending to consumers; searching and reporting on the status of the land records, which could be sold to clients or bundled into another product, such as foreclosure reports; and title insurance quotes as well as recording and transfer tax fees to clients.

The **Canada** segment provides residential mortgage appraisal services to the majority of the big five Canadian banks for purchase, refinance and home equity transactions. In addition, provides residential and commercial property insurance inspection services to some of North America's largest insurance companies. Insurance inspections include residential property inspection services, which includes evaluation reports based on room-by-room inspections of entire dwellings, premium plan reports for high value homes, exterior-only hazards identification inspections and supplementary reports covering wood stoves, out-structures, water damage prevention, fuel storage tanks, home-based business and rental units, and on-site recommendations; commercial property and liability surveys and risk inspection services for commercial properties; and FarmSafe inspection services, which provides customized reports that help clients accurately underwrite farms, including site plans, building measurements and sketches, property valuations, residential farm home inspections and large working farms, to confirm that the condition and use of the property is accurately reflected.

The company is headquartered in Markham, Ont., and has principal offices in Buffalo, N.Y., and Middletown, R.I.

Directors - Jason Smith, founder & exec. chr., Ont.; Brian Lang, CEO, Ont.; Garry M. Foster†, Ont.; Karen L. Martin, Toronto, Ont.; Frank V. McMahon, Calif.; Lisa Melchior, Toronto, Ont.; Peter M. Vukanovich, Oakville, Ont.

Other Exec. Officers - Colleen McCafferty, chief compliance officer; Loren Cooke, exec. v-p & pres., Solidifi U.S. Inc.; Kim Montgomery, exec. v-p & pres., Solidifi Title & Closing, LLC; Rodrigo Pinto, exec. v-p & CFO; Ryan Smith, exec. v-p & chief tech. officer; Lisa Allen, v-p, risk & internal controls; Lyne Beauregard, v-p, IR & corp. commun.; Jay Greenspoon, gen. counsel & corp. sec.
† Lead director

Capital Stock

	Authorized (shs.)	Outstanding (shs.)[1]
Preferred	unlimited	nil
Common	unlimited	72,801,000

[1] At July 27, 2023

Options - At Sept. 30, 2022, options were outstanding to purchase 4,426,000 common shares at a weighted average exercise price of Cdn$8.47 per share with a weighted average remaining contractual life of 3.75 years.

Major Shareholder - Burgundy Asset Management Ltd. held 11.9% interest at Dec. 13, 2022.

Price Range - REAL/TSX

Year	Volume	High	Low	Close
2022	61,049,163	$8.29	$3.80	$4.18
2021	117,232,399	$20.58	$7.17	$8.30
2020	146,465,078	$33.01	$7.74	$19.21
2019	63,458,710	$13.85	$3.32	$12.32
2018	46,589,521	$10.32	$2.95	$3.30

Recent Close: $6.71

Capital Stock Changes - During fiscal 2022, common shares were issued as follows: 97,000 on exercise of options and 77,000 on exercise of warrants; 6,526,000 common shares were repurchased under a Normal Course Issuer Bid.

Long-Term Debt - At Sept. 30, 2022, the company had no long-term debt.

Wholly Owned Subsidiaries

Redihive Inc., Markham, Ont.
Solidifi Corp., Markham, Ont.
- 100% int. in **Solidifi U.S. Inc.**, United States.
  - 100% int. in **RM Ventures LLC**, United States.
    - 100% int. in **RM Title LLC**, United States.
      - 100% int. in **Solidifi Title & Closing, LLC**, R.I.

Note: The preceding list includes only the major related companies in which interests are held.

Financial Statistics

Periods ended:	12m Sept. 30/22[A]		12m Sept. 30/21[A]
	US$000s	%Chg	US$000s
Operating revenue	**339,642**	**-33**	**504,107**
Salaries & benefits	61,244		83,385
General & admin expense	14,423		18,013
Stock-based compensation	1,535		2,408
Other operating expense	256,596		343,508
Operating expense	**333,798**	**-25**	**447,314**
Operating income	**5,844**	**-90**	**56,793**
Deprec., depl. & amort.	4,530		5,045
Finance income	134		151
Finance costs, gross	264		430
Write-downs/write-offs	(17,296)[1]		nil
Pre-tax income	**(12,349)**	**n.a.**	**46,118**
Income taxes	(3,084)		13,038
Net income	**(9,265)**	**n.a.**	**33,080**
Net inc. for equity hldrs	**(9,272)**	**n.a.**	**32,992**
Net inc. for non-cont. int	**7**	**-92**	**88**
Cash & equivalent	46,142		60,213
Accounts receivable	19,831		46,021
Current assets	69,733		109,090
Fixed assets, net	6,964		11,087
Intangibles, net	48,173		66,705
Total assets	**137,004**	**-30**	**194,340**
Accts. pay. & accr. liabs	16,138		26,095
Current liabilities	17,686		27,810
Long-term lease liabilities	4,312		6,328
Shareholders' equity	114,891		159,443
Non-controlling interest	115		108
Cash from oper. activs	**17,567**	**-30**	**25,021**
Cash from fin. activs	(30,424)		(94,050)
Cash from invest. activs	(1,080)		(2,878)
Net cash position	**46,142**	**-23**	**60,213**
Capital expenditures	(1,015)		(3,025)
	US$		US$
Earnings per share*	(0.12)		0.40
Cash flow per share*	0.23		0.30
	shs		shs
No. of shs. o/s*	72,696,000		79,048,000
Avg. no. of shs. o/s*	76,514,000		82,772,000
	%		%
Net profit margin	(2.73)		6.56
Return on equity	(6.76)		17.91
Return on assets	(5.47)		15.04
Foreign sales percent	85		90
No. of employees (FTEs)	424		809

* Common
[A] Reported in accordance with IFRS
[1] Pertains to goodwill impairment of the U.S. Title segment.

Latest Results

Periods ended:	9m June 30/23[A]		9m June 30/22[A]
	US$000s	%Chg	US$000s
Operating revenue	121,725	-57	281,442
Net income	(7,818)	n.a.	703
Net inc. for equity hldrs	(7,795)	n.a.	688
Net inc. for non-cont. int	(23)		15
	US$		US$
Earnings per share*	(0.11)		0.01

* Common
[A] Reported in accordance with IFRS

Historical Summary
(as originally stated)

Fiscal Year	Oper. Rev.	Net Inc. Bef. Disc.	EPS*
	US$000s	US$000s	US$
2022[A]	339,642	(9,265)	(0.12)
2021[A]	504,107	33,080	0.40
2020[A]	455,945	42,798	0.50
2019[A]	322,537	10,094	0.10
2018[A]	281,451	(4,015)	(0.05)

* Common
[A] Reported in accordance with IFRS

R.28 Realia Properties Inc.

Symbol - RLP **Exchange** - TSX-VEN (S) **CUSIP** - 75605D
Head Office - 1100-151 Yonge St, Toronto, ON, M5C 2W7 **Telephone** - (647) 775-8337 **Fax** - (647) 775-8301
Website - www.realiaproperties.com
Email - eric.fazilleau@inovalis.com
Investor Relations - Eric Fazilleau (647) 775-8337
Auditors - Smythe LLP C.A.
Lawyers - Richards Buell Sutton LLP, Vancouver, B.C.
Transfer Agents - TSX Trust Company, Vancouver, B.C.
Profile - (Can. 2008) Acquires retail shopping centres primarily in southwestern U.S.

Holds Martin Downs Town Center, a 36,252-sq.-ft. (gross leasable area, GLA) retail shopping centre in Palm City, Fla.; 116th Street Centre, a 44,839-sq.-ft. (GLA) retail shopping centre in Carmel, Ind.; and Metro Gateway Shopping Center, a 73,146-sq.-ft. (GLA) retail shopping centre in Phoenix, Ariz.

Common suspended from TSX-VEN, May 9, 2023.
Predecessor Detail - Name changed from TitanStar Properties Inc., Oct. 22, 2019.
Directors - Jean-Daniel Cohen, chr., Luxembourg; Lawrence A. (Larry) Goldberg, corp. sec., Toronto, Ont.; Stéphane J. Amine, Paris, France
Other Exec. Officers - Eric Fazilleau, CEO; Krya Dorn, CFO

Capital Stock

	Authorized (shs.)	Outstanding (shs.)[1]
Preferred	unlimited	nil
Common	unlimited	255,221,137

[1] At May 27, 2022

Major Shareholder - Hoche Partners Private Equity Investors S.A.R.L. held 65.15% interest and Inovalis S.A. held 21.91% interest at May 25, 2022.

Price Range - RLP/TSX-VEN (S)

Year	Volume	High	Low	Close
2022	7,187,076	$0.02	$0.01	$0.01
2021	9,646,853	$0.03	$0.01	$0.02
2020	8,097,499	$0.03	$0.01	$0.01
2019	2,334,541	$0.02	$0.01	$0.01
2018	2,384,619	$0.04	$0.01	$0.01

Recent Close: $0.02

Wholly Owned Subsidiaries

Realia Hospitality Inc., Canada.
Realia Properties U.S., Inc.
- 100% int. in **Martin Downs NSC LLC**, Fla.
- 100% int. in **TSP Metro Gateway LLC**, Nev.
- 100% int. in **TSP 116th Street, LLC**, Carmel, Ind.

TSP GP Holdings Inc., B.C.
TSP LP Holdings Inc., B.C.
TitanStar DSC Holdings Inc., Canada.
Note: The preceding list includes only the major related companies in which interests are held.

Financial Statistics

Periods ended:	12m Dec. 31/21[A]		12m Dec. 31/20[A]
	$000s	%Chg	$000s
Total revenue	**5,179**	**+14**	**4,555**
Rental operating expense	1,582		1,460
General & admin. expense	325		543
Operating expense	**1,906**	**-5**	**2,003**
Operating income	**3,273**	**+28**	**2,552**
Deprec. & amort.	1,287		1,546
Finance costs, gross	1,954		2,558
Pre-tax income	**2,077**	**n.a.**	**(1,236)**
Net income	**2,077**	**n.a.**	**(1,236)**
Net inc. for equity hldrs	**2,077**	**n.a.**	**(1,235)**
Net inc. for non-cont. int	**nil**	**n.a.**	**(1)**
Cash & equivalent	1,154		2,137
Accounts receivable	351		816
Current assets	1,569		3,059
Income-producing props	36,399		37,861
Property interests, net	35,112		36,314
Total assets	**37,855**	**-6**	**40,471**
Bank indebtedness	nil		1,273
Accts. pay. & accr. liabs	568		729
Current liabilities	3,522		28,127
Long-term debt, gross	27,567		31,663
Long-term debt, net	27,190		8,223
Equity portion of conv. debs	149		269
Shareholders' equity	5,634		3,856
Non-controlling interest	nil		69
Cash from oper. activs	**3,738**	**+82**	**2,056**
Cash from fin. activs	(4,126)		(121)
Cash from invest. activs	(223)		(563)
Net cash position	**1,154**	**-46**	**2,137**
Capital expenditures	(183)		(542)
	$		$
Earnings per share*	0.01		(0.00)
Cash flow per share*	0.01		0.01
	shs		shs
No. of shs. o/s*	255,221,137		255,221,137
Avg. no. of shs. o/s*	255,221,137		255,221,137
	%		%
Net profit margin	40.10		(27.14)
Return on equity	43.77		(27.78)
Return on assets	10.29		3.27

* Common
[A] Reported in accordance with IFRS

Latest Results

Periods ended:	3m Mar. 31/22[A]		3m Mar. 31/21[A]
	$000s	%Chg	$000s
Total revenue	1,121	-45	2,056
Net income	(237)	n.a.	1,141
	$		$
Earnings per share*	(0.00)		0.00

* Common
[A] Reported in accordance with IFRS

Historical Summary
(as originally stated)

Fiscal Year	Total Rev. $000s	Net Inc. Bef. Disc. $000s	EPS* $
2021[A]	5,179	2,077	0.01
2020[A]	4,555	(1,236)	(0.00)
2019[A]	4,691	(2,326)	(0.01)
2018[A]	2,941	1,743	0.01
2017[A]	2,524	(6,239)	(0.03)

* Common
[A] Reported in accordance with IFRS

R.29 Reco International Group Inc.

Symbol - RGI **Exchange** - TSX-VEN **CUSIP** - 756224
Head Office - 100-2051 Viceroy Pl, Richmond, BC, V6V 1Y9 **Telephone** - (604) 273-2932 **Fax** - (604) 270-2923
Email - hugh@recodeco.com
Investor Relations - Yu Guang Zhen (604) 273-2932
Auditors - RSM Alberta LLP C.A., Edmonton, Alta.
Transfer Agents - Computershare Trust Company of Canada Inc., Vancouver, B.C.
Profile - (Alta. 1999) Provides commercial and residential construction and millwork services in British Columbia.

Services provided include interior design, millwork, construction of upholstered furniture, general and custom renovation, custom-built furniture, as well as other related construction services for specific requirements.
Predecessor Detail - Name changed from Cosmo Capital Corp., Dec. 17, 2004.
Directors - Yu Guang (Hugh) Zhen, chr., pres. & CEO, Burnaby, B.C.; Lyn T. Jones, Delta, B.C.; Hubert Lau, Edmonton, Alta.; David A. Malicki, Vancouver, B.C.; James M. Smith, Longwood, Fla.
Other Exec. Officers - William Harper, interim CFO

Capital Stock

	Authorized (shs.)	Outstanding (shs.)[1]
Preferred	unlimited	nil
Common	unlimited	49,635,635

[1] At Feb. 27, 2023

Major Shareholder - Yu Guang (Hugh) Zhen held 24.13% interest and Quin Quang Sie held 11.71% interest at Jan. 27, 2023.

Price Range - RGI/TSX-VEN

Year	Volume	High	Low	Close
2022	3,371,753	$0.07	$0.01	$0.02
2021	722,726	$0.08	$0.03	$0.04
2020	629,500	$0.05	$0.02	$0.03
2019	591,966	$0.06	$0.03	$0.05
2018	2,054,839	$0.14	$0.04	$0.05

Recent Close: $0.02

Capital Stock Changes - In June 2022, private placement of 24,000,000 common shares was completed at 5¢ per share.

Wholly Owned Subsidiaries

Reco Decoration Group Inc., Richmond, B.C.
Z & Z Holdings Ltd., B.C.

Financial Statistics

Periods ended:	12m Sept. 30/22[A]		12m Sept. 30/21[oA]
	$000s	%Chg	$000s
Operating revenue	**2,603**	**+70**	**1,531**
Salaries & benefits	733		861
General & admin expense	2,241		1,029
Stock-based compensation	110		nil
Operating expense	**3,084**	**+63**	**1,890**
Operating income	**(481)**	**n.a.**	**(359)**
Deprec., depl. & amort.	169		129
Finance costs, gross	35		15
Pre-tax income	**(805)**	**n.a.**	**(492)**
Net income	**(805)**	**n.a.**	**(492)**
Accounts receivable	894		432
Current assets	1,686		461
Fixed assets, net	79		100
Right-of-use assets	640		68
Total assets	**2,425**	**+278**	**641**
Bank indebtedness	73		73
Accts. pay. & accr. liabs	75		452
Current liabilities	2,163		1,295
Long-term debt, gross	70		70
Long-term debt, net	70		70
Shareholders' equity	(252)		(724)
Cash from oper. activs	**(65)**	**n.a.**	**(43)**
Cash from fin. activs	855		(106)
Cash from invest. activs	(42)		(57)
Net cash position	**676**	**n.a.**	**(73)**
Capital expenditures	nil		(1)
	$		$
Earnings per share*	(0.02)		(0.02)
Cash flow per share*	(0.00)		(0.00)
	shs		shs
No. of shs. o/s*	49,635,635		25,635,635
Avg. no. of shs. o/s*	34,376,731		25,635,635
	%		%
Net profit margin	(30.93)		(32.14)
Return on equity	n.m.		n.m.
Return on assets	(50.23)		(50.08)

* Common
[o] Restated
[A] Reported in accordance with IFRS

Latest Results

Periods ended:	3m Dec. 31/22[A]		3m Dec. 31/21[A]
	$000s	%Chg	$000s
Operating revenue	248	-68	784
Net income	(349)	n.a.	276
	$		$
Earnings per share*	(0.01)		0.01

* Common
[A] Reported in accordance with IFRS

Historical Summary
(as originally stated)

Fiscal Year	Oper. Rev. $000s	Net Inc. Bef. Disc. $000s	EPS* $
2022[A]	2,603	(805)	(0.02)
2021[A]	1,531	(492)	(0.02)
2020[A]	3,630	(444)	(0.02)
2019[A]	2,495	(223)	(0.01)
2018[A]	3,685	290	0.01

* Common
[A] Reported in accordance with IFRS

R.30 RecycLiCo Battery Materials Inc.

Symbol - AMY **Exchange** - TSX-VEN **CUSIP** - 75629Y
Head Office - Unit 2, 17942 55 Ave, Surrey, BC, V3S 6C8 **Telephone** - (778) 574-4444
Website - recyclico.com
Email - zmeseldzija@amymn.com
Investor Relations - Zarko Meseldzija (778) 574-4444
Auditors - De Visser Gray LLP C.A., Vancouver, B.C.
Transfer Agents - Endeavor Trust Corporation, Vancouver, B.C.
Profile - (B.C. 1987) Owns the patented RecycLiCo™ process for recycling cathode material in spent lithium-ion batteries, and holds mineral interests in British Columbia and Arizona.

Focused on commercializing its flagship RecycLiCo™ process, a closed-loop hydrometallurgical process which involves the recovery of cathode metals, such as lithium, cobalt, nickel, manganese and aluminum, from spent lithium-ion batteries while converting these materials back to fresh cathode materials suitable for manufacturing new lithium-ion batteries.

Owns a 6,700-sq.-ft. demonstration plant facility in Vancouver, B.C., with a 500-kg-per-day demonstration recycling plant and a 5-tonne-per-day commercial recycling plant using the RecycLiCo™ process.

Also holds mineral interests consisting of Rocher Deboule polymetallic property, 1,016 hectares, 8 km south of New Hazelton, B.C.; Lonnie-Virgil niobium-lanthanum prospect, 674 hectares, 6 km northeast of Manson Creek, B.C., carried at nominal value; and Artillery Peak manganese property, 600 acres, Mohave cty., Ariz., with indicated resource of 65,700,000 tonnes grading 2.2% manganese at September 2012, carried at nominal value.

In January 2023, the company signed a memorandum of understanding with **Sonid Inc.** to develop a lithium-ion battery recycling facility in South Korea. Sonid manufactures and distributes electronic products such as optical clear resins (OCRs), resins, silver pastes, etchant, near field communication (NFC) antennas and radio frequency identification (RFID) tags.

During fiscal 2022, Lonnie-Virgil niobium-lanthanum prospect in British Columbia was written down by $116,452 to nominal value.

Predecessor Detail - Name changed from American Manganese Inc., Oct. 3, 2022.

Directors - Dr. Paul Hildebrand, interim chr., Vancouver, B.C.; Zarko Meseldzija, interim CEO & chief technical officer, B.C.; Shaheem Ali, CFO; Andris Kikauka, Vancouver, B.C.; Edward F. (Ed) Skoda, Guadalajara, Jal., Mexico

Capital Stock

	Authorized (shs.)	Outstanding (shs.)[1]
Common	unlimited	252,212,827

[1] At Oct. 31, 2022

Major Shareholder - Widely held at June 1, 2022.

Price Range - AMY/TSX-VEN

Year	Volume	High	Low	Close
2022............	33,375,583	$0.94	$0.26	$0.28
2021............	154,290,511	$2.86	$0.46	$0.52
2020............	54,865,500	$0.72	$0.10	$0.49
2019............	35,504,051	$0.31	$0.13	$0.19
2018............	41,889,478	$0.30	$0.13	$0.15

Recent Close: $0.43

Capital Stock Changes - In October 2021, private placement of 20,000,000 units (1 common share & 1 warrant) at $1.00 per unit was completed. Also during fiscal 2022, common shares were issued as follows: 6,982,604 on exercise of warrants and 3,345,300 on exercise of options.

Wholly Owned Subsidiaries

Rocher Manganese Inc., Nev.

Financial Statistics

Periods ended:	12m July 31/22[A]		12m July 31/21[A]
	$000s	%Chg	$000s
Salaries & benefits........................	572		355
Research & devel. expense.............	4,091		939
General & admin expense...............	721		702
Stock-based compensation............	6,191		11,383
Operating expense.......................	**11,575**	**-13**	**13,379**
Operating income........................	**(11,575)**	**n.a.**	**(13,379)**
Finance income..............................	102		nil
Finance costs, gross.......................	2		4
Write-downs/write-offs....................	(116)		nil
Pre-tax income...........................	**(11,313)**	**n.a.**	**(13,064)**
Net income..................................	**(11,313)**	**n.a.**	**(13,064)**
Cash & equivalent..........................	21,295		5,906
Accounts receivable.......................	205		119
Current assets...............................	21,621		6,840
Explor./devel. properties.................	647		562
Total assets.................................	**...**	**n.a.**	**7,444**
Accts. pay. & accr. liabs..................	198		545
Current liabilities...........................	198		545
Shareholders' equity.......................	22,088		6,898
Cash from oper. activs..................	**(4,706)**	**n.a.**	**(2,155)**
Cash from fin. activs.......................	20,311		7,862
Cash from invest. activs..................	(216)		(58)
Net cash position.........................	**21,318**	**+260**	**5,929**
Capital expenditures.......................	(239)		(58)
	$		$
Earnings per share*........................	(0.05)		(0.07)
Cash flow per share*.......................	(0.02)		(0.01)
	shs		shs
No. of shs. o/s*...............................	248,246,347		217,918,443
Avg. no. of shs. o/s*.......................	240,395,056		200,009,020
	%		%
Net profit margin............................	n.a.		n.a.
Return on equity.............................	(78.06)		(343.11)
Return on assets.............................	n.m.		(314.51)

* Common
[A] Reported in accordance with IFRS

Historical Summary
(as originally stated)

Fiscal Year	Oper. Rev.	Net Inc. Bef. Disc.	EPS*
	$000s	$000s	$
2022[A]...................	nil	(11,313)	(0.05)
2021[A]...................	nil	(13,064)	(0.07)
2020[A]...................	nil	375	0.00
2019[A]...................	nil	(8,055)	(0.05)
2018[A]...................	nil	(2,426)	(0.02)

* Common
[A] Reported in accordance with IFRS

R.31 Red Light Holland Corp.

Symbol - TRIP **Exchange** - CSE **CUSIP** - 75671E
Head Office - 801-1 Adelaide St E, Toronto, ON, M5C 2V9 **Telephone** - (647) 204-7129 **Fax** - (416) 869-0547
Website - www.redlight.co
Email - todd@redlight.co
Investor Relations - Todd Shapiro (647) 643-8747
Auditors - Clearhouse LLP C.A., Mississauga, Ont.
Lawyers - Garfinkle Biderman LLP, Toronto, Ont.
Transfer Agents - Odyssey Trust Company
Profile - (Ont. 1988; orig. B.C., 1982) Cultivates, produces, distributes and sells psilocybin (magic) truffles for recreational use in the Netherlands and functional mushrooms and mushroom home grow kits in North America and Europe. Also developing psychedelic operations in St. Vincent and the Grenadines and develops and offers psychedelic technologies.

In Europe, the company produces psychedelic truffle microdosing kits as well as mushroom fruiting extracts, capsules and tinctures under the iMicrodose brand, and magic truffles under the Maka brand. These products are sold only within the Netherlands via wholesale channels through wholly owned **SR Wholesale B.V.**, e-commerce platforms and retail stores/smart shops, including two stores owned by the company which are located in Utrecht and Oss. Production of truffle products are conducted at the company's 3,000-sq.-ft. indoor growing, production and distribution facility in Horst, Netherlands. In addition, the company operates a separate home grow mushroom farm in Horst, which specializes in the sale of grow-at-home mushroom kits across Europe. Wholly owned SR Wholesale distributes the company's products as well as third party products, including psychedelics and cannabis related products, in legal jurisdictions within Europe.

In Canada, operations include 80% interest in **316747 Nova Scotia Limited** (dba Happy Caps), a gourmet mushroom farm in Halifax, N.S., selling grow-at-home mushroom kits, mushroom plug spawn and wholesale fresh mushrooms in Canada and the U.S.; 51% interest in **Acadian Exotic Mushrooms Ltd.**, a 22,000-sq.-ft. gourmet mushroom production facility in Eel River Crossing, N.B.; and 100 acres of farmland near Peterborough, Ont., where the company intends to build two mushroom production facilities totaling 65,000 sq. ft.

Also holds wholly owned **Scarlette Lillie Science and Innovation Inc.**, which holds a licence in St. Vincent and the Grenadines allowing for psychedelic product research and development, opening of treatment clinics, cultivation, extraction and processing, importation and exportation of psychedelic compounds, such as psilocybin, ayahuasca, MDMA, DMT, peyote and ketamine, and many other natural based plants; and wholly owned **Radix Motion Inc.**, which develops embodied technology based on neuroscience, including augmented reality (AR), virtual reality (VR) and interactive holograms. Radix Motion has developed Meu, an AR/VR interactive hologram messenger; Wisdom, a VR application explaining the effects of psychedelics on the brain; the iMicro web application and digital care platform, which allows users to journal their microdosing session, take physiological measurements of their body to assess their energy level and includes telecounseling with a therapist, group messaging and event notifications; and Wisdom Truffle, a companion figurine to be produced in three different models with different sizes and capabilities as smart home devices and meditation and mindfulness technology.

In October 2022, the company acquired **MiniChamp B.V.**, a mushroom farm in Horst, Netherlands, selling mushroom grow home kits with distribution channels across the European Union, for €550,000 cash and issuance of 981,466 common shares.

On Aug. 1, 2022, the company acquired two smart shops in Utrecht and Oss, Netherlands. Total consideration was €300,000, consisting of €210,000 cash and issuance of 1,423,963 common shares.

On June 29, 2022, the company entered into an intellectual property licensing agreement with **Mistercap, LLC** whereby Mistercap granted the company an exclusive licence to develop, cultivate, process, package, distribute and sell mushroom and/or truffle-related products under the wellness brand Mistercap in exchange for $250,000 cash and issuance of $1,000,000 of common shares.

In June 2022, the company and **Halo Collective Inc.** dissolved their 50/50 joint venture, **Red Light Oregon, Inc.**, which was formed in April 2021 to develop a commercialization strategy for psilocybin services in Oregon.

On June 20, 2022, the company acquired 100 acres of farmland near Peterborough, Ont., for $1,850,000 which would be developed into 65,000 sq. ft. of two mushroom production facilities.

Predecessor Detail - Name changed from Added Capital Inc., Apr. 24, 2020, pursuant to reverse takeover acquisition of Red Light Holland Financing Inc. and Red Light Holland Debt Inc.

Directors - Brad J. Lamb, chr., Toronto, Ont.; Todd Shapiro, CEO, Toronto, Ont.; Ann C. Barnes, Toronto, Ont.; Binyomin Posen, Toronto, Ont.

Other Exec. Officers - David J. Ascott, CFO; Ridley Doolittle, chief mktg. officer; Sarit (Sarah) Hashkes, chief tech. innovation officer; Russell Peters, chief creative officer; Shai Ramsahai, v-p; Hans Derix, pres., RLH Netherlands B.V.

Capital Stock

	Authorized (shs.)	Outstanding (shs.)[1]
Preference	2,000,000	nil
Common	unlimited	386,941,930

[1] At Feb. 6, 2023

Normal Course Issuer Bid - The company plans to make normal course purchases of up to 19,762,354 common shares representing 5% of the total outstanding. The bid commenced on July 4, 2023, and expires on July 4, 2024.

Major Shareholder - Widely held at Feb. 6, 2023.

Price Range - TRIP/CSE

Year	Volume	High	Low	Close
2022............	96,209,094	$0.17	$0.07	$0.09
2021............	548,861,080	$0.70	$0.12	$0.14
2020............	558,520,083	$0.55	$0.07	$0.31
2019............	5,132	$0.80	$0.40	$0.50
2018............	12,865	$4.00	$0.40	$0.40

Consolidation: 1-for-20 cons. in Feb. 2020

Recent Close: $0.07

Capital Stock Changes - In June 2021, 12,701,742 and 1,290,323 common shares were issued pursuant to the acquisitions of Radix Motion Inc. and 80% interest in 4316747 Nova Scotia Limited, respectively. In August 2021, 700,000 common shares were issued pursuant to the acquisition of Mera Life Sciences LLC (renamed Scarlette Lillie Science and Innovation Inc.). In September 2021, 3,065,135 common shares were issued pursuant to the acquisition of 51% interest in Acadian Exotic Mushrooms Ltd. Also during fiscal 2022, common shares were issued as follows: 4,222,000 on vesting of restricted share units, 2,166,667 on exercise of options, 933,333 on exercise of warrants and 197,318 for services.

Wholly Owned Subsidiaries

RLH Netherlands B.V., Netherlands.
- 100% int. in **MiniChamp B.V.**, Netherlands.
- 100% int. in **SR Wholesale B.V.**, Netherlands.

Red Light Acquisition Inc., United States.
- 100% int. in **Radix Motion Inc.**, San Francisco, Calif.

Red Light Holland (Subco 1) Inc., Canada.
Red Light Holland (Subco 2) Inc., Canada.
Scarlette Lillie Science and Innovation Inc., Saint Vincent and the Grenadines.
Wellness World Oss B.V., Netherlands.
Wellness World Utrecht B.V., Netherlands.

Subsidiaries

51% int. in **Acadian Exotic Mushrooms Ltd.**, N.B.
80% int. in **4316747 Nova Scotia Limited**, N.S.

Financial Statistics

Periods ended:	12m Mar. 31/22[A]		12m Mar. 31/21[ºA1]
	$000s	%Chg	$000s
Operating revenue	**2,326**	**n.m.**	**111**
Cost of sales	1,708		92
Research & devel. expense	753		15
General & admin expense	5,218		3,032
Stock-based compensation	3,199		1,583
Operating expense	**10,877**	**+130**	**4,721**
Operating income	**(8,551)**	**n.a.**	**(4,610)**
Deprec., depl. & amort.	524		36
Finance income	64		17
Finance costs, gross	50		11
Write-downs/write-offs	(5,937)		nil
Pre-tax income	**(14,942)**	**n.a.**	**(1,645)**
Income taxes	(246)		nil
Net income	**(14,695)**	**n.a.**	**(1,645)**
Net inc. for equity hldrs	**(14,367)**	**n.a.**	**(1,645)**
Net inc. for non-cont. int.	**(328)**	**n.a.**	**nil**
Cash & equivalent	26,622		32,681
Inventories	382		438
Accounts receivable	381		186
Current assets	27,749		33,775
Long-term investments	682		100
Fixed assets, net	2,877		122
Right-of-use assets	202		150
Intangibles, net	1,318		2,148
Total assets	**32,939**	**-9**	**36,295**
Bank indebtedness	905		nil
Accts. pay. & accr. liabs	1,383		1,072
Current liabilities	2,732		1,125
Long-term debt, gross	385		714
Long-term debt, net	nil		714
Long-term lease liabilities	150		100
Shareholders' equity	28,477		34,055
Non-controlling interest	681		nil
Cash from oper. activs	**(4,876)**	**n.a.**	**(3,360)**
Cash from fin. activs	452		32,783
Cash from invest. activs	(583)		(202)
Net cash position	**26,094**	**-16**	**31,185**
Capital expenditures	(407)		(87)
	$		$
Earnings per share*	(0.04)		(0.01)
Cash flow per share*	(0.01)		(0.02)
	shs		shs
No. of shs. o/s*	358,165,282		332,888,764
Avg. no. of shs. o/s*	351,398,544		210,836,814
	%		%
Net profit margin	(631.77)		n.m.
Return on equity	(45.95)		n.m.
Return on assets	(42.31)		(8.12)
Foreign sales percent	87		100

* Common
º Restated
[A] Reported in accordance with IFRS
[1] Results reflect the May 22, 2020, reverse takeover acquisition of Red Light Holland Financing Inc. and Red Light Holland Debt Inc.

Latest Results

Periods ended:	6m Sept. 30/22[A]		6m Sept. 30/21[A]
	$000s	%Chg	$000s
Operating revenue	1,522	+41	1,081
Net income	(2,840)	n.a.	(5,298)
Net inc. for equity hldrs	(2,767)	n.a.	(5,298)
Net inc. for non-cont. int.	(73)		nil
	$		$
Earnings per share*	(0.01)		(0.02)

* Common
[A] Reported in accordance with IFRS

Historical Summary
(as originally stated)

Fiscal Year	Oper. Rev.	Net Inc. Bef. Disc.	EPS*
	$000s	$000s	$
2022[A]	2,326	(14,695)	(0.04)
2021[A]	111	(1,645)	(0.01)
2020[A1]	nil	(325)	(0.38)
2019[A]	11	(180)	(0.20)
2018[A]	41	(309)	(0.40)

* Common
[A] Reported in accordance with IFRS
[1] Results for fiscal 2020 and prior fiscal periods pertain to Added Capital Inc.
Note: Adjusted throughout for 1-for-20 cons. in Feb. 2020

R.32 Red Rock Capital Corp.

Symbol - RCC.H **Exchange** - TSX-VEN **CUSIP** - 75700U
Head Office - 2200-885 Georgia St W, Vancouver, BC, V6C 3E8 **Telephone** - (604) 990-1012
Email - rchisholm@emprisecapital.com
Investor Relations - Robert Chisholm (778) 331-8505
Auditors - Manning Elliott LLP C.A., Vancouver, B.C.
Lawyers - McMillan LLP, Vancouver, B.C.
Transfer Agents - Computershare Trust Company of Canada Inc., Vancouver, B.C.
Profile - (B.C. 2012) Capital Pool Company.
In March 2022, the company entered into a letter of intent with **Bay Capital Markets Inc.** whereby the company would be granted an option to acquire Gosselin and Normetal South prospects in Quebec. Terms were not disclosed. The transaction would constitute the company's Qualifying Transaction.
Directors - Aleem Nathwani, CEO, Vancouver, B.C.; Robert (Rob) Chisholm, CFO & corp. sec., Vancouver, B.C.; Morgan Tincher, Vancouver, B.C.

Capital Stock

	Authorized (shs.)	Outstanding (shs.)[1]
Preferred	unlimited	nil
Common	unlimited	22,520,366

[1] At Mar. 31, 2022
Major Shareholder - Widely held at Feb. 22, 2019.

Price Range - RCC.H/TSX-VEN

Year	Volume	High	Low	Close
2022	225,163	$0.27	$0.13	$0.16
2021	907,269	$0.29	$0.14	$0.23
2020	1,411,423	$0.43	$0.08	$0.21
2019	100,850	$0.78	$0.04	$0.08

Consolidation: 1-for-2.75 cons. in Jan. 2022
Capital Stock Changes - On Jan. 20, 2022, common shares were consolidated on a 1-for-2.75 basis.

R.33 Red White & Bloom Brands Inc.

Symbol - RWB **Exchange** - CSE **CUSIP** - 75704R
Head Office - 810-789 Pender St W, Vancouver, BC, V6C 1H2 **Telephone** - (604) 687-2038 **Fax** - (604) 687-3141
Website - www.redwhitebloom.com
Email - ir@redwhitebloom.com
Investor Relations - Edoardo Mattei (604) 687-2038
Auditors - Macias Gini & O'Connell LLP C.P.A., Los Angeles, Calif.
Lawyers - Gowling WLG (Canada) LLP, Toronto, Ont.
Transfer Agents - National Securities Administrators Ltd., Vancouver, B.C.
Profile - (B.C. 1980) Has cannabis and hemp cultivation, processing and dispensary operations in the United States.
Owns and operates a 113,550-sq.-ft. cannabis cultivation and processing facility in Sanderson, Fla.; and a 45,000-sq.-ft. cannabis greenhouse facility in Apopka, Fla. Also operates a dispensary in Spring Hill, Fla.
In addition, the company holds three cannabis licences, two of which are for cultivation and one is for processing, and 2.8 acres of development land in Massachusetts; and investments in **PharmaCo, Inc.**, which has three indoor cultivation facilities totaling 110,000 sq. ft., 10 acres of outdoor cultivation, two processing locations and eight provisioning centres (dispensaries), all in Michigan.
Brands include the proprietary Platinum Vape/PV and Mid-American brands and the licensed High Times brand.
Common reinstated on CSE, May 18, 2023.
Common suspended from CSE, May 9, 2023.

Recent Merger and Acquisition Activity

Status: terminated **Revised:** July 14, 2023
UPDATE: The transaction was terminated. PREVIOUS: Red White & Bloom Brands Inc. (RWB) agreed to acquire Aleafia Health Inc. on the basis of 0.35 RWB common share for each Aleafia common share held. As part of the agreement, the loan agreement between Aleafia and NE SPC II LP was assigned by NE SPC II LP to RWB.
Status: completed **Announced:** Apr. 14, 2022
Red White & Bloom Brands Inc. sold its 3,613,000-sq.-ft. greenhouse facility in Granville, Ill., associated real estate and certain greenhouse equipment to New Branches LLC of California for a purchase price of $56,100,000.
Predecessor Detail - Name changed from Tidal Royalty Corp., Apr. 24, 2020, pursuant to reverse takeover acquisition of MichiCann Medical Inc. (dba Red White & Bloom); basis 1 new for 16 old shs.
Directors - Brad Rogers, chr. & CEO, Pickering, Ont.; William (Bill) Dawson, Ont.; Michael Marchese, Ont.; Brendan Purdy, Toronto, Ont.; Johannes P. M. (Theo) van der Linde, North Vancouver, B.C.
Other Exec. Officers - Edoardo (Eddie) Mattei, CFO & corp. sec.

Capital Stock

	Authorized (shs.)	Outstanding (shs.)[1]
Preferred	unlimited	
Series 1	unlimited	3,181,250
Series 2	unlimited	nil
Common	unlimited	443,900,084

[1] At Nov. 29, 2022
Series 1 Preferred - Convertible into common shares on a 1-for-1 basis. Non-voting.
Common - One vote per share.
Series 2 Preferred (old) - Were entitled to a fixed dividend equal to 5% per annum, calculated monthly and payable in series 2 preferred shares. Automatically converted into common shares on two-year anniversary of issuance (Apr. 24, 2022).
Major Shareholder - Widely held at Dec. 20, 2021.

Price Range - RWB/CSE

Year	Volume	High	Low	Close
2022	80,455,134	$0.68	$0.06	$0.10
2021	112,463,763	$2.00	$0.38	$0.42
2020	81,607,263	$1.35	$0.49	$0.76

EGC/TSX (D)

Year	Volume	High	Low	Close
2019	3,743,101	US$4.88	US$1.52	US$4.16
2018	9,113,691	US$13.28	US$1.44	US$1.84

Consolidation: 1-for-16 cons. in Apr. 2020
Recent Close: $0.05
Capital Stock Changes - In April 24, 2022, all 93,139,265 outstanding series 2 preferred shares were automatically converted into common shares on a 1-for-1 basis.

Wholly Owned Subsidiaries

GC Ventures 2, LLC, Mich.
MichiCann Medical Inc., Vaughan, Ont.
- 100% int. in **Mid-American Growers, Inc.**, United States.
  - 100% int. in **Mid-American Cultivation LLC**, United States.

1251881 B.C. Ltd., B.C.
PV CBD LLC, Calif.
RWB Freedom Flower, LLC, Ill.
RWB Illinois Inc., Ill.
RWB Licensing Inc., B.C.
RWB Michigan LLC, Mich.
RWB Platinum Vape Inc., Calif.
Royalty USA Corp., Del.
- 100% int. in **RLTY Beverage 1 LLC**, Del.
- 100% int. in **RLTY Development MA 1 LLC**, Del.
  - 100% int. in **RLTY Development Orange LLC**, Mass.
  - 100% int. in **RLTY Development Springfield LLC**, Mass.

Vista Prime Management, LLC, Calif.
Vista Prime 3, Inc., Calif.
Vista Prime 2, Inc., Calif.

Subsidiaries

77% int. in **RWB Florida LLC**, Fla.
- 100% int. in **Red White & Bloom Florida, Inc.**, Fla.

R.34 RediShred Capital Corp.

Symbol - KUT **Exchange** - TSX-VEN **CUSIP** - 757489
Head Office - 202-2233 Argentia Rd, Mississauga, ON, L5N 2X7 **Telephone** - (416) 490-8600 **Toll-free** - (866) 379-5028 **Fax** - (905) 812-9448
Website - www.proshred.com
Email - harjit.brar@proshred.com
Investor Relations - Harjit Brar (416) 986-7028
Auditors - KPMG LLP C.A., Vaughan, Ont.
Transfer Agents - Computershare Trust Company of Canada Inc., Montréal, Qué.
Employees - 296 at Dec. 31, 2022
Profile - (Can. 2006) Operates and franchises the right in the U.S. and internationally to sell on-site services for the destruction, disposal and recycling of documents and other confidential materials under the trademark PROSHRED®.
At Dec. 31, 2022, there were 30 PROSHRED® locations in the U.S., consisting of 15 corporate and 15 franchised locations. The company has one international master licence to operate in the Middle East and North Africa.
In August 2022, the company acquired the assets a of **Tech Shredders LLC**, electronic waste recycling and hard drive shredding business in Roseland, N.J., for an undisclosed amount.
In June 2022, the company acquired the assets and clients of **SafeGuard Document Destruction**, a shredding company in New Jersey and Fort Lauderdale, Fla., for an undisclosed amount.
In March 2022, the company acquired the assets of **Mobile Document Destruction**, a shredding company in Illinois, for $500,000.

Recent Merger and Acquisition Activity

Status: completed **Announced:** Nov. 1, 2022
RediShred Capital Corp. acquired the Proshred Philadelphia business from its franchisee for US$7,100,000. Proshred Philadelphia offers paper and hard drive shredding, product destruction and paper recycling services. The acquisition included on-site paper and hard drive shredding trucks, box trucks, containers, client relationships, paper baling equipment and other assets used in the shredding and paper recycling business. Proshred Philadelphia earned US$2,800,000 in revenue during fiscal 2021.
Directors - Robert M. Crozier, chr., Dartmouth, N.S.; Jeffrey I. Hasham, CEO, Mississauga, Ont.; Brad E. Foster, Pickering, Ont.; Phillip H. (Phil) Gaunce, Halifax, N.S.; Robert G. Kay, Moncton, N.B.; James C. Lawley, Halifax, N.S.; Mark J. MacMillan, Halifax, N.S.; Robert G. Richardson, Halifax, N.S.
Other Exec. Officers - Harjit Brar, sr. v-p, CFO & corp. sec.; Katherina (Kasia) Pawluk, sr. v-p, fin. & acqs.

Capital Stock

	Authorized (shs.)	Outstanding (shs.)[1]
Preferred	unlimited	nil
Common	unlimited	18,304,372

[1] At May 4, 2023
Normal Course Issuer Bid - The company plans to make normal course purchases of up to 987,800 common shares representing 10%

of the public float. The bid commenced on May 8, 2023, and expires on May 7, 2024.

Major Shareholder - Moray Tawse held 13.8% interest and Donville Kent Asset Management Inc. held 13.5% interest at Apr. 20, 2023.

Price Range - KUT/TSX-VEN

Year	Volume	High	Low	Close
2022	1,814,810	$4.95	$3.15	$3.70
2021	3,550,685	$5.00	$2.60	$4.40
2020	4,446,802	$4.50	$1.83	$2.70
2019	1,917,614	$5.70	$3.00	$4.50
2018	890,706	$3.75	$2.50	$3.30

Consolidation: 1-for-5 cons. in Aug. 2022

Recent Close: $3.55

Capital Stock Changes - On Aug. 23, 2022, common shares were consolidated on a 1-for-5 basis. During 2022, 127,515 post-consolidated common shares were issued on exercise of options.

Wholly Owned Subsidiaries

American Security Shredding Corp., New York, N.Y.

Redishred Holdings US Inc., Del.
- 100% int. in **Proshred Franchising Corp.**, Del.
- 100% int. in **Redishred Acquisition Inc.**, Del.
  - 100% int. in **Proshred Charlotte Inc.**, Del.
- 100% int. in **Redishred Chicago Inc.**, Del.
- 100% int. in **Redishred Holdings US Inc.**, Del.
- 100% int. in **Redishred Kansas Inc.**, Del.
- 100% int. in **Redishred New England Inc.**, Mass.
  - 100% int. in **Pleasant Point Partners Corp.**, Conn.

Financial Statistics

Periods ended:	12m Dec. 31/22^A		12m Dec. 31/21^oA
	$000s	%Chg	$000s
Operating revenue	**57,226**	**+58**	**36,199**
Salaries & benefits	22,730		15,688
General & admin expense	15,503		8,495
Stock-based compensation	302		117
Operating expense	**38,535**	**+59**	**24,300**
Operating income	**18,691**	**+57**	**11,899**
Deprec., depl. & amort.	9,592		7,212
Finance income	47		13
Finance costs, gross	1,904		1,236
Pre-tax income	**7,626**	**+259**	**2,127**
Income taxes	1,752		769
Net income	**5,874**	**+333**	**1,358**
Cash & equivalent	6,919		9,848
Accounts receivable	8,778		4,894
Current assets	16,702		15,301
Fixed assets, net	24,746		18,271
Intangibles, net	55,288		44,808
Total assets	**97,811**	**+23**	**79,334**
Accts. pay. & accr. liabs	4,452		3,147
Current liabilities	16,694		11,324
Long-term debt, gross	31,812		36,557
Long-term debt, net	24,973		21,867
Long-term lease liabilities	4,760		2,301
Shareholders' equity	47,281		40,360
Cash from oper. activs	**11,587**	**+38**	**8,403**
Cash from fin. activs	2,140		13,334
Cash from invest. activs	(16,861)		(15,014)
Net cash position	**6,696**	**-31**	**9,660**
	$		$
Earnings per share*	0.32		0.09
Cash flow per share*	0.64		0.53
	shs		shs
No. of shs. o/s*	18,243,872		17,999,371
Avg. no. of shs. o/s*	18,200,572		15,850,676
	%		%
Net profit margin	10.26		3.75
Return on equity	13.40		3.84
Return on assets	8.29		3.11
Foreign sales percent	100		100
No. of employees (FTEs)	296		215

* Common
o Restated
A Reported in accordance with IFRS

Latest Results

Periods ended:	3m Mar. 31/23^A		3m Mar. 31/22^oA
	$000s	%Chg	$000s
Operating revenue	16,996	+36	12,517
Net income	735	+169	273
	$		$
Earnings per share*	0.04		0.10

* Common
o Restated
A Reported in accordance with IFRS

Historical Summary
(as originally stated)

Fiscal Year	Oper. Rev. $000s	Net Inc. Bef. Disc. $000s	EPS* $
2022^A	57,226	5,874	0.32
2021^A	36,199	1,358	0.09
2020^A	25,437	276	0.02
2019^A	22,407	(779)	(0.05)
2018^A	14,660	2,712	0.25

* Common
A Reported in accordance with IFRS

Note: Adjusted throughout for 1-for-5 cons. in Aug. 2022

R.35 Reem Capital Corp.

Symbol - REEM.P **Exchange** - TSX-VEN **CUSIP** - 75846C
Head Office - Roslyn Building, 300-400 5 Ave SW, Calgary, AB, T2P 0L6 **Telephone** - (403) 999-7808
Email - arthur_h_kwan@hotmail.com
Investor Relations - Arthur H. Kwan (403) 999-7808
Auditors - SRCO Professional Corporation C.A., Richmond Hill, Ont.
Lawyers - Borden Ladner Gervais LLP, Calgary, Alta.
Transfer Agents - Endeavor Trust Corporation, Vancouver, B.C.
Profile - (B.C. 2021) Capital Pool Company.

Recent Merger and Acquisition Activity

Status: pending **Revised:** Dec. 29, 2022
UPDATE: Completion of the transaction was extended to Mar. 15, 2023. PREVIOUS: Reem Capital Corp. entered into a letter of intent for the Qualifying Transaction reverse takeover acquisition of private Ramat Gan, Israel-based Kalron Holdings Ltd. on a share-for-share basis, following a share consolidation on such basis as is necessary to result in the deemed value of the Reem common shares being equal to $2,000,000. Kalron, through wholly owned Seegnal eHealth Ltd., provides patient-tailored Software-as-a-Service (SaaS)-based platform for one-glance managing and mitigating drug related problems while providing decision support to healthcare professionals at the point of care. Kalron would complete a concurrent $3,000,000 private placement of subscription receipts as part of the transaction. Upon completion of the transaction, Reem would change its name to Seegnal eHealth Ltd.

Directors - Arthur H. Kwan, CEO, Calgary, Alta.; Jonathan Held, CFO, Toronto, Ont.; Michael J. Saliken, corp. sec., Calgary, Alta.; Jonathan Holmes, Windsor, Ont.; Ronnie (Ronen) Jaegermann, Tel Aviv, Israel

Capital Stock

	Authorized (shs.)	Outstanding (shs.)[1]
Preferred	unlimited	nil
Common	unlimited	7,900,000

[1] At Jan. 27, 2023

Major Shareholder - Jonathan Held held 12.66% interest, Arthur H. Kwan held 12.66% interest, Ronnie (Ronen) Jaegermann held 11.39% interest and Jonathan Holmes held 10.13% interest at Feb. 11, 2022.

Price Range - REEM.P/TSX-VEN

Year	Volume	High	Low	Close
2022	75,000	$0.11	$0.08	$0.08

Capital Stock Changes - On Feb. 11, 2022, an initial public offering of 3,500,000 common shares was completed at 10¢ per share.

R.36 ReGen III Corp.

Symbol - GIII **Exchange** - TSX-VEN **CUSIP** - 75888V
Head Office - 1750-400 Burrard St, Vancouver, BC, V6C 3A6 **Telephone** - (604) 806-5275 **Fax** - (604) 806-4875
Website - www.regeniii.com
Email - lvanhatten@regeniii.com
Investor Relations - Larry Van Hatten (604) 806-5275
Auditors - Ernst & Young LLP C.A., Vancouver, B.C.
Lawyers - DLA Piper (Canada) LLP, Vancouver, B.C.
Transfer Agents - Computershare Trust Company of Canada Inc., Toronto, Ont.

Profile - (Alta. 2017; orig. B.C., 1984) Developed a patented technology process for re-refining used motor oil (UMO) into base lubricating oils.

The proprietary ReGen™ technology is capable of recycling UMOs to produce base oils such as Group II and II+, and Group III synthetic grade base lubricating oil, light oil, as well as vacuum tower asphalt extender used in the roofing and road asphalt industries. The company intends to use the technology to produce Group III base lubricating oils, which sells for 65% more than Group II base lubricating oils. Base lubricating oils are the main component in lubricants for motor vehicles and a wide range of other applications. These base oils are defined by their quality and fall into three categories: Group I (lowest quality), Group II (mid-range) or Group III (highest quality) that can be produced from minerals. The company holds 14 ReGen™ patents and 18 ReGen™ patent applications pending worldwide.

The company proposed the development and construction of a UMO re-refinery facility (USGC facility) that uses the ReGen™ technology in the U.S. Golf Coast in Texas, Tex. The USGC facility has a design capacity of 5,600-bbl-per-day UMO and an estimated output design capacity of 4,200 to 4,400 bbl per day of base oil production, which would result in an annual 81,000,000 gallons of used lubricating oils being processed. The company intends to use the site provided by **Advario North America, LLC** (formerly **Oiltanking North America, LLC**) at Advario Galveston County Terminal in Texas, Tex., for the USGC facility.

Also exploring opportunities to develop ReGen™ re-refinery facilities at other locations in Canada, the United States, Mexico, South America, Europe, Australia and other markets, as well as investigating opportunities to license the ReGen™ technology in order to access non-core markets and to accelerate the market penetration of the technology.

In April 2023, the company announced the termination of multi-year offtake agreement with **BP Products North America Inc.**, a North American subsidiary of **BP plc.**, whereby BP would have acquired all of the company's future production of base oils from a proposed 5,600-bbl-per-day re-refining terminal facility in or near Houston, Tex.

In July 2022, the company entered into an amended equity agreement with a private equity firm (PE firm) for the development, construction, financing and ownership of the company's used motor oil (UMO) re-refinery facility in Texas as well as a partnership framework for future financing projects. Under the transaction, the PE firm's designated affiliate would commit up to US$150,000,000 to the company's recycling project and would receive 14.4% preferred return on funds invested plus 50% interest in the project.

Predecessor Detail - Name changed from GEN III Oil Corporation, May 17, 2021.

Directors - Gregory M. (Greg) Clarkes, chr. & CEO, Vancouver, B.C.; Larry Van Hatten†, West Vancouver, B.C.; Catherine Banat, N.Y.; Bob Rennie, B.C.; Jose Luis Salinas, Panama; Brad White, Toronto, Ont.

Other Exec. Officers - Mark Redcliffe, pres.; Thomas Lawlor, COO; Rick Low, CFO; Grant Brown, exec. v-p; Christine O'Grady, exec. v-p, supply, origination & bus. devel.; Kimberly Hedlin, v-p, corp. fin.

† Lead director

Capital Stock

	Authorized (shs.)	Outstanding (shs.)[1]
Preferred	unlimited	nil
Common	unlimited	118,355,547

[1] At May 26, 2023

Major Shareholder - Widely held at June 21, 2022.

Price Range - GIII/TSX-VEN

Year	Volume	High	Low	Close
2022	15,670,542	$2.07	$0.68	$0.77
2021	51,199,184	$1.97	$0.47	$1.68
2020	31,118,670	$0.47	$0.13	$0.47
2019	20,431,839	$0.40	$0.12	$0.19
2018	16,423,587	$0.82	$0.24	$0.30

Recent Close: $0.33

Capital Stock Changes - In March 2023, private placement of 3,692,502 units (1 common share & ½ warrant) at 75¢ per unit was completed, with warrants exercisable at $1.25 per share for two years.

In April 2022, private placement of 1,435,480 common shares was completed at $1.70 per share. Also during 2022, 1,620,000 common shares were issued on exercise of options.

Wholly Owned Subsidiaries

ReGen III (USGC) Corporation, Del.
- 100% int. in **RG3 Texas Holdings LLC**, Del.
  - 100% int. in **RG3 Texas LLC**, Del.

ReGen IIII (Alberta) Inc., Alta.

Financial Statistics

Periods ended:	12m Dec. 31/22[A]		12m Dec. 31/21[A]
	$000s	%Chg	$000s
Salaries & benefits	1,983		1,572
General & admin expense	8,982		5,458
Stock-based compensation	1,472		2,520
Operating expense	**12,437**	**+30**	**9,550**
Operating income	**(12,437)**	**n.a.**	**(9,550)**
Deprec., depl. & amort.	136		382
Finance income	53		42
Finance costs, gross	48		896
Pre-tax income	**(12,468)**	**n.a.**	**(4,728)**
Net income	**(12,468)**	**n.a.**	**(4,728)**
Cash & equivalent	718		7,735
Accounts receivable	27		32
Current assets	890		8,025
Long-term investments	38		42
Fixed assets, net	8		8
Right-of-use assets	295		432
Total assets	**1,232**	**-86**	**8,507**
Accts. pay. & accr. liabs	1,595		474
Current liabilities	1,991		800
Long-term debt, gross	40		38
Long-term debt, net	nil		38
Long-term lease liabilities	212		369
Shareholders' equity	(971)		7,300
Cash from oper. activs	**(9,576)**	**n.a.**	**(6,800)**
Cash from fin. activs	2,560		13,179
Net cash position	**718**	**-91**	**7,735**
	$		$
Earnings per share*	(0.11)		(0.04)
Cash flow per share*	(0.08)		(0.06)
	shs		shs
No. of shs. o/s*	114,463,045		111,407,565
Avg. no. of shs. o/s*	113,769,987		105,597,787
	%		%
Net profit margin	n.a.		n.a.
Return on equity	n.m.		n.m.
Return on assets	(255.06)		(38.70)

* Common
[A] Reported in accordance with IFRS

Latest Results

Periods ended:	3m Mar. 31/23[A]		3m Mar. 31/22[A]
	$000s	%Chg	$000s
Net income	(1,439)	n.a.	(6,927)
	$		$
Earnings per share*	(0.01)		(0.06)

* Common
[A] Reported in accordance with IFRS

Historical Summary
(as originally stated)

Fiscal Year	Oper. Rev.	Net Inc. Bef. Disc.	EPS*
	$000s	$000s	$
2022[A]	nil	(12,468)	(0.11)
2021[A]	nil	(4,728)	(0.04)
2020[A]	nil	(4,742)	(0.06)
2019[A]	nil	(5,965)	(0.08)
2018[A]	nil	(7,708)	(0.12)

* Common
[A] Reported in accordance with IFRS

R.37 Regent Pacific Properties Inc.

Symbol - RPP **Exchange** - TSX-VEN **CUSIP** - 75900R
Head Office - 2607 Ellwood Dr SW, Edmonton, AB, T6X 0P7 **Telephone** - (780) 424-9898 **Fax** - (780) 437-9899
Email - eyu@cassel.ca
Investor Relations - David S. Tam (780) 423-8662
Auditors - Kenway Mack Slusarchuk Stewart LLP C.A., Calgary, Alta.
Lawyers - Parlee McLaws LLP, Edmonton, Alta.
Transfer Agents - Computershare Trust Company of Canada Inc., Calgary, Alta.
Profile - (Alta. 2007) Owns and acquires income-producing commercial and residential properties in Alberta.

Portfolio consists of a 72,675-sq.-ft. three-story commercial office tower and attached single-story bays with underground parking facility in Edmonton.

Directors - Eddie W. W. Yu, chr., pres. & CEO, Edmonton, Alta.; David S. Tam, corp. sec., Edmonton, Alta.; Edward K. (Ted) Power, Edmonton, Alta.

Other Exec. Officers - William Harper, interim CFO

Capital Stock

	Authorized (shs.)	Outstanding (shs.)[1]
Preferred	unlimited	nil
Common	unlimited	40,039,000

[1] At Nov. 30, 2022

Major Shareholder - Eddie W. W. Yu held 75.82% interest at Nov. 30, 2022.

Price Range - RPP/TSX-VEN

Year	Volume	High	Low	Close
2022	127,248	$0.04	$0.02	$0.02
2021	529,219	$0.06	$0.02	$0.04
2020	177,550	$0.07	$0.05	$0.06
2019	206,057	$0.09	$0.07	$0.07
2018	1,275,300	$0.14	$0.05	$0.11

Recent Close: $0.02

Wholly Owned Subsidiaries

Cassel Centre Ltd., Edmonton, Alta.
1572587 Alberta Ltd.

Financial Statistics

Periods ended:	12m Dec. 31/21[A]		12m Dec. 31/20[A]
	$000s	%Chg	$000s
Total revenue	**1,557**	**-10**	**1,725**
Rental operating expense	1,000		1,003
General & admin. expense	194		210
Other operating expense	(898)		(836)
Operating expense	**295**	**-22**	**376**
Operating income	**1,262**	**-6**	**1,349**
Deprec. & amort.	4		5
Finance income	61		17
Finance costs, gross	621		736
Pre-tax income	**(476)**	**n.a.**	**(2,171)**
Income taxes	60		(136)
Net income	**(536)**	**n.a.**	**(2,035)**
Accounts receivable	85		19
Current assets	85		19
Fixed assets	82		82
Income-producing props	22,250		23,500
Property interests, net	22,267		23,521
Total assets	**23,656**	**-5**	**24,783**
Bank indebtedness	815		829
Accts. pay. & accr. liabs	225		255
Current liabilities	18,029		18,715
Long-term debt, gross	16,979		17,585
Shareholders' equity	3,839		4,375
Cash from oper. activs	**1,237**	**-17**	**1,487**
Cash from fin. activs	(1,274)		(1,922)
Cash from invest. activs	(1)		nil
Net cash position	**(287)**	**n.a.**	**(249)**
Increase in property	(1)		nil
	$		$
Earnings per share*	(0.01)		(0.05)
Cash flow per share*	0.03		0.04
	shs		shs
No. of shs. o/s*	40,039,000		40,039,000
Avg. no. of shs. o/s*	40,039,000		40,039,000
	%		%
Net profit margin	(34.43)		(117.97)
Return on equity	(13.05)		(37.73)
Return on assets	0.67		(4.91)

* Common
[A] Reported in accordance with IFRS

Latest Results

Periods ended:	6m June 30/22[A]		6m June 30/21[A]
	$000s	%Chg	$000s
Total revenue	780	+5	745
Net income	366	+14	322
	$		$
Earnings per share*	0.01		0.01

* Common
[A] Reported in accordance with IFRS

Historical Summary
(as originally stated)

Fiscal Year	Total Rev.	Net Inc. Bef. Disc.	EPS*
	$000s	$000s	$
2021[A]	1,557	(536)	(0.01)
2020[A]	1,725	(2,035)	(0.05)
2019[A]	1,982	(489)	(0.01)
2018[A]	2,129	990	0.02
2017[A]	1,945	1,843	0.05

* Common
[A] Reported in accordance with IFRS

R.38 Reitmans (Canada) Limited*

Symbol - RET.A **Exchange** - TSX-VEN **CUSIP** - 759404
Head Office - 250 rue Sauvé O, Montréal, QC, H3L 1Z2 **Telephone** - (514) 384-1140 **Toll-free** - (877) 385-2666 **Fax** - (514) 385-2669
Website - www.reitmanscanadalimited.com
Email - riwait@reitmans.com
Investor Relations - Richard Wait (514) 384-1140 ext. 23050
Auditors - KPMG LLP C.A., Montréal, Qué.
Transfer Agents - Computershare Trust Company of Canada Inc., Montréal, Qué.
FP500 Revenue Ranking - 378
Profile - (Can. 1947) Operates a retail chain of women's wear stores and e-commerce sites in Canada under the banners Reitmans, Penningtons (PENN.) and RW&CO.

At Apr. 29, 2023, the company operated 406 stores consisting of 235 Reitmans, 91 Penningtons and 80 RW&CO.

Reitmans stores, averaging 4,700 sq. ft., offer a targeted assortment of current fashions designed to appeal to budget-conscious and fashion-conscious women. Penningtons stores, averaging 5,800 sq. ft., offer a wide selection of affordable plus-size women's apparel, such as dresses, shirts, capri, shorts, underwear, footwear, bags and accessories. RW&CO. stores, averaging 4,500 sq. ft., cater to men and women with an urban mindset, featuring fashion that blends the latest trends with style, quality and attention to detail. Products are also available online at reitmans.com, penningtons.com and rw-co.com.

Merchandise sold by the company is produced by manufacturers primarily in Asia. While some branded merchandise is sold by the company, most of the merchandise consist of items produced for the company's private labels. Distribution is conducted through a 566,000-sq.-ft. distribution centre in Montreal, Que., where all merchandise is received and processed for distribution to all banner stores throughout Canada, primarily by common carrier.

During the first quarter of fiscal 2023, the company opened two new stores and closed two stores.

During fiscal 2023, the company opened eight new stores and closed six stores.

Directors - Daniel Rabinowicz, chr., Saint-Lambert, Qué.; Stephen F. Reitman, pres. & CEO, Montréal, Qué.; Bruce J. Guerriero, Montréal, Qué.; David J. Kassie, Toronto, Ont.; Samuel Minzberg, Montréal, Qué.; Gillian Reitman, N.Y.; Anita Sehgal, Tex.; Theresa (Terry) Yanofsky, Westmount, Qué.

Other Exec. Officers - Gale Blank, CIO; Richard Wait, exec. v-p & CFO; Diane Archibald, v-p, store planning, design & facilities mgt.; Aldo Battista, v-p, fin.; Domenic Carbone, v-p, distrib. & logistics; Caroline Goulian, v-p, finl. performance & analysis; Randi Haimovitz, v-p, HR; Harpreet Heer, v-p, global sourcing; Marc Laurent-Atthalin, v-p, data & digital media; Katia Lombardi, v-p, real estate; Alain Murad, v-p, legal & corp. sec.; Lisa Reitman, v-p, cust. experience; Michael Strachan, pres., Penningtons & RW&CO.; Jacqueline (Jackie) Tardif, pres., Reitmans

Capital Stock

	Authorized (shs.)	Outstanding (shs.)[1]
Class A Non-vtg.	unlimited	35,427,322
Common	unlimited	13,440,000

[1] At June 14, 2023

Class A Non-Voting - Ranks equally and pari passu with the common shares with respect to the right to receive dividends and upon any distribution of the assets of the company. However, in the case of stock dividends, the class A non-voting shareholders shall have the right to receive class A non-voting shares. Non-voting.

Common - One vote per share.

Options - At Jan. 28, 2023, options were outstanding to purchase 1,635,000 class A non-voting shares at prices ranging from $1.50 to $6.75 per share with a weighted average remaining contractual life of 2.08 years.

Major Shareholder - Stephen F. Reitman, heirs of the late Jeremy H. Reitman and certain associates held 49.85% interest at May 11, 2023.

Price Range - RET.A/TSX-VEN

Year	Volume	High	Low	Close
2022	11,741,463	$2.38	$0.75	$2.21
2021	24,628,009	$2.38	$0.16	$2.09
2020	28,181,131	$1.32	$0.06	$0.24
2019	9,790,023	$4.14	$0.91	$1.16
2018	6,936,794	$4.53	$3.40	$3.93

Recent Close: $3.00

Capital Stock Changes - There were no changes to capital stock from fiscal 2021 to fiscal 2023, inclusive.

Long-Term Debt - At Jan. 28, 2023, the company had no long-term debt.

Financial Statistics

Periods ended:	52w Jan. 28/23[A]		52w Jan. 29/22[A]
	$000s	%Chg	$000s
Operating revenue	**800,627**	**+21**	**661,952**
Cost of goods sold	351,979		308,787
General & admin expense	47,991		32,885
Other operating expense	309,313		228,800
Operating expense	**709,283**	**+24**	**570,472**
Operating income	**91,344**	**0**	**91,480**
Deprec., depl. & amort.	43,745		47,585
Finance income	2,713		3,725
Finance costs, gross	5,384		4,067
Write-downs/write-offs	(739)		(1,611)
Pre-tax income	**45,569**	**-68**	**142,804**
Income taxes	(32,098)		(420)
Net inc. bef. disc. opers	**77,667**	**-46**	**143,224**
Income from disc. opers	nil		15,032
Net income	**77,667**	**-51**	**158,256**
Cash & equivalent	103,004		25,502
Inventories	142,302		118,972
Accounts receivable	3,241		7,606
Current assets	265,857		194,670
Fixed assets, net	63,833		65,970
Right-of-use assets	79,894		44,978
Intangibles, net	2,638		5,613
Total assets	**444,530**	**+41**	**314,274**
Bank indebtedness	nil		29,634
Accts. pay. & accr. liabs	81,087		34,478
Current liabilities	122,946		99,027
Long-term lease liabilities	60,758		31,419
Shareholders' equity	260,826		183,828
Cash from oper. activs	**149,967**	**n.a.**	**(24,729)**
Cash from fin. activs	(63,359)		(9,192)
Cash from invest. activs	(10,651)		(15,222)
Net cash position	**103,004**	**+304**	**25,502**
Capital expenditures, net	(10,651)		(15,222)
Pension fund surplus	1,099		100
	$		$
Earns. per sh. bef disc opers*	1.59		2.93
Earnings per share*	1.59		3.24
Cash flow per share*	3.07		(0.51)
	shs		shs
No. of shs. o/s*	48,867,000		48,867,000
Avg. no. of shs. o/s*	48,867,000		48,867,000
	%		%
Net profit margin	9.70		21.64
Return on equity	34.93		139.38
Return on assets	22.89		41.41

* Cl.A & com.
[A] Reported in accordance with IFRS

Latest Results

Periods ended:	13w Apr. 29/23[A]		13w Apr. 30/22[A]
	$000s	%Chg	$000s
Operating revenue	165,018	+7	153,859
Net income	(3,840)	n.a.	(1,717)
	$		$
Earnings per share*	(0.08)		(0.04)

* Cl.A & com.
[A] Reported in accordance with IFRS

Historical Summary
(as originally stated)

Fiscal Year	Oper. Rev.	Net Inc. Bef. Disc.	EPS*
	$000s	$000s	$
2023[A]	800,627	77,667	1.59
2022[A]	661,952	143,224	2.93
2021[A]	533,362	(100,036)	(2.05)
2020[A]	869,497	(87,426)	(1.56)
2019[A]	923,018	6,765	0.11

* Cl.A & com.
[A] Reported in accordance with IFRS

R.39 Reklaim Ltd.

Symbol - MYID **Exchange** - TSX-VEN **CUSIP** - 759402
Head Office - 2200-145 King St W, Toronto, ON, M5H 4G2 **Telephone** - (647) 360-3691 **Toll-free** - (855) 908-3282
Website - investors.reklaimyours.com
Email - investorrelations@reklaimyours.com
Investor Relations - Sean Peasgood (855) 908-3282
Auditors - MNP LLP C.A., Ottawa, Ont.
Lawyers - Minden Gross LLP, Toronto, Ont.
Transfer Agents - Computershare Trust Company of Canada Inc., Vancouver, B.C.
Profile - (Ont. 2019; orig. Alta., 2004 amalg.) Offers Reklaim (formerly Killi™) mobile application which allows users to opt in to sell their personal data to brands, agencies, platforms and data companies in exchange for monetary compensation.

The Reklaim app is available for Android and iPhone users in Canada, the U.S., Australia, Singapore and New Zealand. Users of Reklaim can choose to share their data such as profile attributes including gender, zip code, interests, household information, device, browsing and purchases; data about the user's device including device model, operating system, mobile service provider, IP address and installed apps; browsing history; purchases on credit or debit cards; and survey polls which users can answer. Users of Reklaim are compensated with cash or cryptocurrency for the use of their data.

The company also acquires consented data through partnerships with publishers and data companies. After integrating data from its partners, the company attempts to contact each account to notify them of how they can access their data while allowing them to take advantage of the income opportunities offered in the company's ecosystem. Through the company's My Footprint, which was introduced in 2021, users can see what data companies are purchasing and for how much. The company offers consumers access to the data that has historically been collected and sold without their participation. Upon joining the Reklaim platform, the company recognizes such an account as active and is integrated into the company's ecosystem. If the account opts out, the account is removed from the company's platform.

Has over 320,000,000 accounts on its platform through strategic partnerships with data companies, security firms and publishers.

Predecessor Detail - Name changed from Killi Ltd., Nov. 4, 2021.

Directors - Neil Sweeney, chr. & CEO, Toronto, Ont.; Andrew L. Elinesky, Toronto, Ont.; Robert Ferincola, Mississauga, Ont.; Jason R. B. Maguire, Toronto, Ont.; Brad Marks, Toronto, Ont.; Kevin Shea, Brighton, Ont.

Other Exec. Officers - Ira Levy, CFO; Alan Chapell, chief privacy officer; Jake Phillips, chief tech. officer; Marla Baum, head, people; Laura Jordan, v-p, fin.

Capital Stock

	Authorized (shs.)	Outstanding (shs.)[1]
Preferred	unlimited	nil
Class A Common	unlimited	88,669,466

[1] At July 5, 2022

Major Shareholder - Neil Sweeney held 33% interest at July 5, 2022.

Price Range - MYID/TSX-VEN

Year	Volume	High	Low	Close
2022	9,061,045	$0.30	$0.02	$0.03
2021	14,891,951	$1.05	$0.21	$0.27
2020	14,823,074	$1.55	$0.05	$0.60
2019	4,060,317	$1.18	$0.20	$0.28
2018	1,346,906	$1.06	$0.61	$0.67

Consolidation: 1-for-5 cons. in Apr. 2021; 1-for-2.22786 cons. in June 2019

Recent Close: $0.11

Capital Stock Changes - In June and July 2022, private placement of 23,185,146 units (1 class A common share & 1 warrant) at $0.0675 per unit was completed, with warrants exercisable at 10¢ per share for three years.

Wholly Owned Subsidiaries

Reklaim Inc., Toronto, Ont.
- 100% int. in **Reklaim Holdings Ltd.**, Ont.
- 100% int. in **Reklaim USA Inc.**, Del.

Financial Statistics

Periods ended:	12m Dec. 31/21[A]		12m Dec. 31/20[A]
	$000s	%Chg	$000s
Operating revenue	**1,000**	**+462**	**178**
Cost of sales	1,440		392
Research & devel. expense	1,033		1,676
General & admin expense	4,994		2,650
Operating expense	**7,468**	**+58**	**4,718**
Operating income	**(6,467)**	**n.a.**	**(4,540)**
Deprec., depl. & amort.	24		26
Finance income	11		8
Pre-tax income	**(6,323)**	**n.a.**	**(4,328)**
Net inc. bef. disc. opers	**(6,323)**	**n.a.**	**(4,328)**
Income from disc. opers	nil		(327)
Net income	**(6,323)**	**n.a.**	**(4,655)**
Cash & equivalent	464		1,520
Accounts receivable	352		382
Current assets	1,027		2,095
Fixed assets, net	53		51
Total assets	**1,080**	**-50**	**2,146**
Accts. pay. & accr. liabs	1,458		849
Current liabilities	1,477		875
Long-term debt, gross	42		57
Long-term debt, net	23		31
Shareholders' equity	(420)		1,240
Cash from oper. activs	**(5,727)**	**n.a.**	**(4,324)**
Cash from fin. activs	4,526		3,153
Cash from invest. activs	131		234
Net cash position	**464**	**-69**	**1,520**
Capital expenditures	(26)		(7)
	$		$
Earns. per sh. bef disc opers*	(0.10)		(0.09)
Earnings per share*	(0.10)		(0.09)
Cash flow per share*	(0.09)		(0.09)
	shs		shs
No. of shs. o/s*	67,377,894		60,204,382
Avg. no. of shs. o/s*	66,039,645		50,084,557
	%		%
Net profit margin	(632.30)		n.m.
Return on equity	n.m.		n.m.
Return on assets	(392.00)		n.a.
Foreign sales percent	100		100

* Cl.A Common
[A] Reported in accordance with IFRS

Latest Results

Periods ended:	3m Mar. 31/22[A]		3m Mar. 31/21[A]
	$000s	%Chg	$000s
Operating revenue	391	+218	123
Net income	(2,064)	n.a.	(1,242)
	$		$
Earnings per share*	(0.03)		(0.02)

* Cl.A Common
[A] Reported in accordance with IFRS

Historical Summary
(as originally stated)

Fiscal Year	Oper. Rev.	Net Inc. Bef. Disc.	EPS*
	$000s	$000s	$
2021[A]	1,000	(6,323)	(0.10)
2020[A]	178	(4,328)	(0.09)
2019[A1]	3,456	(9,055)	(0.25)
2018[A2]	nil	(235)	(0.05)
2017[A]	nil	(436)	(0.11)

* Cl.A Common
[A] Reported in accordance with IFRS
[1] Results reflect the June 14, 2019, reverse takeover acquisition of Freckle I.O.T. Ltd.
[2] Results prior to June 14, 2019, pertain to Knol Resources Corp.
Note: Adjusted throughout for 1-for-5 cons. in Apr. 2021; 1-for-2.2278588 cons. in June 2019

R.40 Reko International Group Inc.*

Symbol - REKO **Exchange** - TSX-VEN **CUSIP** - 75941H
Head Office - 469 Silver Creek Industrial Dr, Lakeshore, ON, N8N 4W2 **Telephone** - (519) 727-3287 **Fax** - (519) 727-6681
Website - www.rekointl.com
Email - dreko@rekointl.com
Investor Relations - Diane M. Reko (866) 492-9983
Auditors - PricewaterhouseCoopers LLP C.A., Waterloo, Ont.
Bankers - Bank of Montreal, Windsor, Ont.; Comerica Bank, N.A., Detroit, Mich.; The Toronto-Dominion Bank
Lawyers - Bartlet & Richardes LLP, Windsor, Ont.
Transfer Agents - TSX Trust Company, Montréal, Qué.
Profile - (Ont. 1976) Designs and manufactures a variety of engineered products and services including factory automation and precision machining solutions.

Products include specialty machines and lean cell factory automation solutions and robotics integration; and high precision, custom machining of very large critical components and assemblies. For the automotive industry, the company conceptualizes, designs and builds specialty machines for plastic punch and weld applications, for gas tank assembly lines, material handling applications and varied work cell solutions. For the transportation, capital equipment and oil and gas industries, the company machines customer supplied metal castings and fabrications to customer indicated specifications.

Operations are carried out at three manufacturing plants in Lakeshore, Ont., a suburb of Windsor.

Directors - Diane M. Reko, chr., CEO & sec.-treas., Lakeshore, Ont.; Dr. Andrew J. Szonyi†, Toronto, Ont.; John Sartz, Ajax, Ont.; Maria A. Thompson, Mich.; Roy Verstraete, Ont.

Other Exec. Officers - Gregory (Greg) Yzerman, COO; Kim Marks, CFO; Christine Ferrari, contr.

† Lead director

Capital Stock

	Authorized (shs.)	Outstanding (shs.)[1]
Class A Preference	unlimited	nil
Class B Preference	unlimited	nil
Common	unlimited	5,699,313

[1] At Apr. 30, 2023

Options - At July 31, 2022, options were outstanding to purchase 230,800 common shares at a weighted average exercise price of $3.12 per share expiring on various dates to 2027.

Normal Course Issuer Bid - The company plans to make normal course purchases of up to 286,420 common shares representing 5% of the total outstanding. The bid commenced on Jan. 9, 2023, and expires on Jan. 8, 2024.

Major Shareholder - The Reko family held 67.62% interest at Oct. 31, 2022.

Price Range - REKO/TSX-VEN

Year	Volume	High	Low	Close
2022............	220,776	$5.38	$4.14	$4.95
2021............	211,374	$5.14	$3.02	$5.12
2020............	265,224	$3.52	$2.00	$3.02
2019............	200,988	$4.00	$2.83	$3.40
2018............	335,692	$4.10	$2.53	$2.75

Recent Close: $5.37

Capital Stock Changes - During fiscal 2022, 67,800 common shares were issued on exercise of options and 291,300 common shares were repurchased under a Normal Course Issuer Bid.

Dividends

REKO com N.S.R.

$0.25◆................ Jan. 13/23 $0.25◆............ Dec. 2/21

Paid in 2023: $0.25◆ 2022: n.a. 2021: $0.25◆

◆ Special

Long-Term Debt - Outstanding at July 31, 2022:

2.04% mtge. due 2023............................	$3,252,000
4.31% mtge. due 2023............................	2,372,000
Fltg. rate mtge. due 2025[1]........................	3,097,000
2.78% equip. lease due 2027..................	1,488,000
3.99% equip. lease due 2027..................	1,292,000
5.23% equip. lease due 2029..................	1,484,000
Less: Unamort. finance fees......................	17,000
	12,968,000
Less: Current portion..............................	9,489,000
	3,479,000

[1] Bears interest at 3.06% plus a credit spread of up to 2.75%. At July 31, 2022, effective all-in rate was 5%.

Wholly Owned Subsidiaries

Concorde Precision Machining Inc., Ont.
Concorde USA, LLC, Mich.
Reko International Holdings Inc., Mich.
Reko International Services, Inc., Mich.
Reko Manufacturing Group Inc., Lakeshore, Ont.

Financial Statistics

Periods ended:	12m July 31/22[A]		12m July 31/21[A]
	$000s	%Chg	$000s
Operating revenue........................	**53,884**	**+37**	**39,196**
Cost of sales..................................	41,788		31,251
General & admin expense...............	6,399		5,405
Operating expense........................	**48,187**	**+31**	**36,656**
Operating income.........................	**5,697**	**+124**	**2,540**
Deprec., depl. & amort....................	3,370		3,120
Finance costs, gross.......................	354		339
Pre-tax income.............................	**2,609**	**+255**	**735**
Income taxes..................................	488		(129)
Net income....................................	**2,121**	**+145**	**864**
Cash & equivalent...........................	14,023		10,709
Inventories......................................	9,222		10,846
Accounts receivable........................	11,629		9,617
Current assets.................................	35,757		32,327
Fixed assets, net.............................	29,024		27,141
Total assets...................................	**66,891**	**+7**	**62,361**
Accts. pay. & accr. liabs..................	6,818		4,750
Current liabilities............................	17,000		12,053
Long-term debt, gross.....................	12,968		9,080
Long-term debt, net.........................	3,479		3,252
Shareholders' equity........................	46,412		47,056
Cash from oper. activs..................	**7,805**	**+35**	**5,782**
Cash from fin. activs........................	797		(1,252)
Cash from invest. activs..................	(788)		(2,762)
Net cash position..........................	**14,023**	**+126**	**6,209**
Capital expenditures........................	(5,364)		(3,093)
Capital disposals.............................	76		17
	$		$
Earnings per share*.........................	0.36		0.14
Cash flow per share*.......................	1.31		0.94
Extra divd. - cash*...........................	0.25		nil
	shs		shs
No. of shs. o/s*...............................	5,780,350		6,003,850
Avg. no. of shs. o/s*........................	5,949,875		6,121,025
	%		%
Net profit margin.............................	3.94		2.20
Return on equity..............................	4.54		1.84
Return on assets.............................	3.73		2.04

* Common
[A] Reported in accordance with IFRS

Latest Results

Periods ended:	9m Apr. 30/23[A]		9m Apr. 30/22[A]
	$000s	%Chg	$000s
Operating revenue..........................	35,768	-8	38,882
Net income......................................	1,242	-15	1,458
	$		$
Earnings per share*.........................	0.22		0.25

* Common
[A] Reported in accordance with IFRS

Historical Summary
(as originally stated)

Fiscal Year	Oper. Rev.	Net Inc. Bef. Disc.	EPS*
	$000s	$000s	$
2022[A]...................	53,884	2,121	0.36
2021[A]...................	39,196	864	0.14
2020[A]...................	40,226	763	0.12
2019[A]...................	47,989	1,577	0.25
2018[A]...................	42,272	2,035	0.32

* Common
[A] Reported in accordance with IFRS

R.41 Relevium Technologies Inc.

Symbol - RLV **Exchange** - TSX-VEN (S) **CUSIP** - 75942W
Head Office - 2700-1000 rue Sherbrooke O, Montréal, QC, H3A 3G4 **Telephone** - (514) 562-1374 **Toll-free** - (888) 528-8687 **Fax** - (514) 987-1213
Website - www.releviumtechnologies.com
Email - auseche@releviumcorp.com
Investor Relations - Aurelio Useche (514) 824-8559
Auditors - Richter LLP C.A.
Transfer Agents - Computershare Trust Company of Canada Inc., Montréal, Qué.

Profile - (Can. 2012) Markets dietary supplements, nutraceuticals, sports nutrition and nutri-cosmeceuticals in the U.S., Latin America and Europe; and has a pending application under Health Canada's Cannabis Act for the cultivation, processing, extraction, formulation, research and development, and encapsulation of medical cannabis products.

Through wholly owned **BGX E-Health LLC**, markets dietary supplements, nutraceuticals, sports nutrition and cosmeceuticals under the Bioganix®, Bioganix® Clean Care™ and Push & Pull System® brands in the U.S. and Europe. Bioganix® products are sold through the BioGanix e-commerce site (www.bioganix.com) and other third party e-commerce sites, such as Walmart.com and Amazon.com. BGX also offers a line of organic health and wellness products formulated with hemp extracts marketed under the LeefLyfe® brand in the U.S., Latin America and Europe. Products include weight-loss, anti-inflammatory, heart, vision, beauty and fitness supplements including alcohol and hand sanitizers.

In addition, BGX, through a partnership with **H-Source Holdings Ltd.**, an online secure and trusted personal protective equipment (PPE) platform, develops, sources and supplies global PPE requirements due to COVID-19; and holds a license for patented science based nutraceutical formulation that addresses major points of viral invasion, replication and toxicities to be sold under the Bioganix® brand.

Through wholly owned **Biocannabix Health Corporation**, has a pending application under Health Canada's Cannabis Act for its 93,000-sq.-ft. cultivation and processing facility in Montreal, Que.; and is developing a line of pediatric endo-medicinal nutraceuticals to be sold under the Cannakids brand exclusive in Canada. Also developing geriatric products targeting inflammatory conditions including joints, heart and brain to be sold under Relevium Senior® brand and pediatric products of nutraceuticals and oral nutritional supplements under the Relevium Kids® brand.

Common suspended from TSX-VEN, Feb. 9, 2022.

Predecessor Detail - Name changed from BIOflex Technologies Inc., Dec. 18, 2015.

Directors - André Godin, chr., Laval, Qué.; Aurelio Useche, pres. & CEO, Verdun, Qué.; Michel Timperio, Saint-Charles-sur-Richelieu, Qué.

Other Exec. Officers - Mark A. Billings, CFO; Dr. Wolfgang Renz, chief scientific officer; Kosta Kostic, corp. sec.

Capital Stock

	Authorized (shs.)	Outstanding (shs.)[1]
Preferred	unlimited	
Series A		nil
Series B		nil
Common	unlimited	329,492,346

[1] At Aug. 30, 2022

Major Shareholder - Widely held at Aug. 30, 2022.

Price Range - RLV/TSX-VEN (S)

Year	Volume	High	Low	Close
2022............	563,444	$0.02	$0.02	$0.02
2021............	148,928,505	$0.05	$0.01	$0.02
2020............	290,061,025	$0.09	$0.01	$0.04
2019............	90,288,455	$0.13	$0.03	$0.04
2018............	177,805,761	$0.32	$0.05	$0.11

Capital Stock Changes - In August 2022, an up to 1-for-25 share consolidation was proposed.

In September 2021, 121,721,958 common shares were issued at 2¢ per share for debt settlement.

Wholly Owned Subsidiaries

BGX E-Health LLC, United States.
Biocannabix Health Corporation, Canada.
Ovid Acquisition Corp., Canada.
Relevium E-Health Inc., Canada.

R.42 Reliq Health Technologies Inc.

Symbol - RHT **Exchange** - TSX-VEN **CUSIP** - 75955T
Head Office - 406A-175 Longwood Rd S, Hamilton, ON, L8P 0A1 **Toll-free** - (888) 701-6390 **Fax** - (647) 317-1929
Website - www.reliqhealth.com
Email - ir@reliqhealth.com
Investor Relations - Dr. Lisa Crossley (888) 869-1362
Auditors - KPMG LLP C.A., Hamilton, Ont.
Transfer Agents - Endeavor Trust Corporation, Vancouver, B.C.

Profile - (B.C. 2005) Develops and markets a software platform for remote patient monitoring, chronic care management, principal care management, behavioral health management, telemedicine, transitional care management, remote therapeutic monitoring and wound care solutions for care coordination and community-based healthcare.

Products include iUGO Care platform, an integrated wearables, sensors, voice technology, and intuitive mobile apps and desktop user interface for patients, clinicians and healthcare administrators to provide real-time access to remote patient monitoring data and allow timely interventions by the care team to prevent costly hospital readmissions and ER visits which features a secure messaging, telehealth, medication management, family sharing, notifications, tailored education and health trends; iUGO Home solution, which uses a wearable personal emergency response system device in watch or pendant form to connect patients to their care team using a two-way communication, sensors and automated alerts; and iUGO Voice, a multilingual interactive voice recognition product.

Predecessor Detail - Name changed from Moseda Technologies, Inc., May 10, 2016.

Directors - Brian Storseth, chr., Alta.; Dr. Lisa Crossley, CEO, Ont.; Eugene Beukman, North Vancouver, B.C.

Other Exec. Officers - Michael Frankel, CFO; Dr. Joyce Johnson, CMO; Dave McKay, chief tech. & innovation officer; Chris Ryan, chief strategy officer; Lucas Smithen, chief product officer; Ron Manno, v-p, tech.; Leanne Ratzlaff, corp. sec.

Capital Stock

	Authorized (shs.)	Outstanding (shs.)[1]
Preferred	unlimited	nil
Common	unlimited	196,760,195

[1] At Nov. 29, 2022

Major Shareholder - Widely held at Nov. 16, 2022.

Price Range - RHT/TSX-VEN

Year	Volume	High	Low	Close
2022	80,575,771	$1.24	$0.36	$0.49
2021	204,153,803	$1.33	$0.38	$1.05
2020	103,327,126	$0.63	$0.20	$0.50
2019	159,916,956	$0.72	$0.17	$0.45
2018	270,244,388	$2.62	$0.22	$0.36

Recent Close: $0.47

Capital Stock Changes - During fiscal 2022, common shares were issued as follows: 14,571,500 on exercise of options and 757,119 on exercise of warrants.

Wholly Owned Subsidiaries

iUGOHealth Inc., Canada. formerly CareKit Health Corporation.
MobSafety, Inc., Vancouver, B.C.

Financial Statistics

Periods ended:	12m June 30/22[A]		12m June 30/21[A]
	$000s	%Chg	$000s
Operating revenue	**8,773**	**+445**	**1,611**
Cost of sales	3,251		604
Salaries & benefits	1,691		2,168
Research & devel. expense	2,222		1,732
General & admin expense	3,323		4,097
Stock-based compensation	5,507		4,362
Operating expense	**15,994**	**+23**	**12,964**
Operating income	**(7,221)**	**n.a.**	**(11,353)**
Deprec., depl. & amort.	115		126
Finance income	77		nil
Finance costs, gross	35		47
Write-downs/write-offs	(738)		(6)
Pre-tax income	**(8,171)**	**n.a.**	**(11,781)**
Net income	**(8,171)**	**n.a.**	**(11,781)**
Cash & equivalent	233		326
Inventories	272		546
Accounts receivable	2,266		2,161
Current assets	6,969		3,178
Right-of-use assets	176		284
Total assets	**10,267**	**+197**	**3,462**
Accts. pay. & accr. liabs	3,591		2,057
Current liabilities	3,712		2,238
Long-term debt, gross	40		40
Long-term debt, net	40		40
Long-term lease liabilities	144		181
Shareholders' equity	6,371		1,002
Cash from oper. activs	**(8,028)**	**n.a.**	**(7,106)**
Cash from fin. activs	7,934		7,297
Cash from invest. activs	nil		23
Net cash position	**133**	**-41**	**226**
	$		$
Earnings per share*	(0.04)		(0.07)
Cash flow per share*	(0.04)		(0.05)
	shs		shs
No. of shs. o/s*	188,580,796		173,252,177
Avg. no. of shs. o/s*	183,085,929		157,891,120
	%		%
Net profit margin	(93.14)		(731.28)
Return on equity	(221.65)		(1,174.58)
Return on assets	(118.52)		(380.67)
Foreign sales percent	100		100

* Common
[A] Reported in accordance with IFRS

Latest Results

Periods ended:	3m Sept. 30/22[A]		3m Sept. 30/21[A]
	$000s	%Chg	$000s
Operating revenue	3,472	+116	1,608
Net income	(122)	n.a.	(4,210)
	$		$
Earnings per share*	(0.00)		(0.02)

* Common
[A] Reported in accordance with IFRS

Historical Summary
(as originally stated)

Fiscal Year	Oper. Rev.	Net Inc. Bef. Disc.	EPS*
	$000s	$000s	$
2022[A]	8,773	(8,171)	(0.04)
2021[A]	1,611	(11,781)	(0.07)
2020[A]	1,143	(11,122)	(0.08)
2019[A]	182	(13,004)	(0.11)
2018[A]	2,269	(13,797)	(0.14)

* Common
[A] Reported in accordance with IFRS

R.43 RenoWorks Software Inc.

Symbol - RW **Exchange** - TSX-VEN **CUSIP** - 759887
Head Office - 2721 Hopewell Pl NE, Calgary, AB, T1Y 7J7 **Telephone** - (403) 296-3880 **Toll-free** - (877) 980-3880 **Fax** - (403) 296-3886
Website - www.renoworks.com
Email - doug.vickerson@renoworks.com
Investor Relations - Doug Vickerson (877) 980-3880
Auditors - RSM Alberta LLP C.A., Calgary, Alta.
Lawyers - Lindsey MacCarthy LLP, Calgary, Alta.
Transfer Agents - Computershare Trust Company of Canada Inc., Toronto, Ont.

Profile - (Alta. 2002 amalg.) Develops and distributes digital visualization software for the remodelling and new home construction industries focusing in the U.S. and Canada.

Provides custom developed applications or desktop software solutions to manufacturers, contractors, builders and retailers. Products include RenoWorks Pro, a photo rendering software and sales tool that enables dealers/contractors to input digital images of a customer's home and apply exterior and interior building and remodelling products and supply a photo-quality printout of what the customer's home will look like after the remodelling projects are complete; RenoWorks Design Services, which allows clients to design their home projects without learning any software; RenoWorks FastTrack, a design and measurement software for building product manufacturers that automatically generates accurate measurement reports for their contractors and lets clients design their home; and RenoWorks API (application programming interface), an open visualization platform that allow agencies and development teams access its API to build unique homeowner experiences that blend seamlessly with their brand.

Predecessor Detail - Formed from SNC Equity Inc. in Alberta, Aug. 31, 2002, on Qualifying Transaction amalgamation with RenoWorks Software Inc. which constituted a reverse takeover by RenoWorks; basis 0.35 new for 1 old sh.

Directors - Greg Martineau, founder & chr., Calgary, Alta.; Doug Vickerson, CEO, Calgary, Alta.; Nairn Nerland, Okotoks, Alta.; Dr. Robert (Bob) Schultz, Calgary, Alta.

Other Exec. Officers - Debbie (Deb) Carter-Ross, CFO; Brad Finck, sr. v-p, bus. devel.

Capital Stock

	Authorized (shs.)	Outstanding (shs.)[1]
Preferred	unlimited	nil
Common	unlimited	40,662,635

[1] At May 30, 2022

Major Shareholder - Dr. Robert (Bob) Schultz held 13.56% interest and Nairn Nerland held 13.55% interest at May 13, 2022.

Price Range - RW/TSX-VEN

Year	Volume	High	Low	Close
2022	4,126,125	$0.52	$0.18	$0.19
2021	8,235,591	$0.60	$0.37	$0.46
2020	6,052,986	$0.60	$0.20	$0.60
2019	3,461,609	$0.45	$0.21	$0.30
2018	3,780,665	$0.50	$0.15	$0.42

Recent Close: $0.15

Financial Statistics

Periods ended:	12m Dec. 31/21[A]		12m Dec. 31/20[A]
	$000s	%Chg	$000s
Operating revenue	**5,553**	**+8**	**5,132**
Cost of sales	796		696
Salaries & benefits	3,383		3,001
Research & devel. expense	936		811
General & admin expense	744		175
Stock-based compensation	114		91
Operating expense	**5,972**	**+25**	**4,774**
Operating income	**(419)**	**n.a.**	**359**
Deprec., depl. & amort.	97		94
Finance income	2		3
Finance costs, gross	32		51
Write-downs/write-offs	22		23
Pre-tax income	**(609)**	**n.a.**	**124**
Net income	**(609)**	**n.a.**	**124**
Cash & equivalent	1,189		524
Accounts receivable	596		617
Current assets	1,901		1,262
Fixed assets, net	77		51
Right-of-use assets	64		141
Total assets	**2,214**	**+44**	**1,534**
Accts. pay. & accr. liabs	167		152
Current liabilities	1,430		986
Long-term debt, gross	nil		37
Long-term lease liabilities	nil		85
Shareholders' equity	572		204
Cash from oper. activs	**94**	**-48**	**182**
Cash from fin. activs	712		(147)
Cash from invest. activs	(140)		(12)
Net cash position	**1,189**	**+127**	**524**
Capital expenditures	(45)		(12)
	$		$
Earnings per share*	(0.02)		0.00
Cash flow per share*	0.00		0.00
	shs		shs
No. of shs. o/s*	38,985,968		36,610,507
Avg. no. of shs. o/s*	37,829,136		36,610,507
	%		%
Net profit margin	(10.97)		2.42
Return on equity	(156.96)		n.m.
Return on assets	(30.79)		11.98
Foreign sales percent	96		96

* Common
[A] Reported in accordance with IFRS

Latest Results

Periods ended:	3m Mar. 31/22[A]		3m Mar. 31/21[A]
	$000s	%Chg	$000s
Operating revenue	1,316	-7	1,421
Net income	10	-77	43
	$		$
Earnings per share*	0.00		0.00

* Common
[A] Reported in accordance with IFRS

Historical Summary
(as originally stated)

Fiscal Year	Oper. Rev.	Net Inc. Bef. Disc.	EPS*
	$000s	$000s	$
2021[A]	5,553	(609)	(0.02)
2020[A]	5,132	124	0.00
2019[A]	4,264	(686)	(0.02)
2018[A]	3,843	(475)	(0.01)
2017[A]	3,074	(837)	(0.03)

* Common
[A] Reported in accordance with IFRS

R.44 Repare Therapeutics Inc.

Symbol - RPTX **Exchange** - NASDAQ **CUSIP** - 760273
Head Office - 100-7210 rue Frederick-Banting, Saint-Laurent, QC, H4S 2A1 **Telephone** - (514) 803-0544
Website - www.reparerx.com
Email - investor@reparerx.com
Investor Relations - Steve Forte (514) 286-4777
Auditors - Ernst & Young LLP C.A., Montréal, Qué.
Lawyers - Stikeman Elliott LLP, Montréal, Qué.
Transfer Agents - Computershare Trust Company of Canada Inc., Montréal, Qué.
Employees - 180 at Feb. 24, 2023

Profile - (Can. 2016) Discovers and develops highly targeted cancer therapies focused on genomic instability, including DNA damage repair, using its proprietary genome-wide, CRISPR-enabled SNIPRx platform to identify novel synthetic lethal (SL) gene pairs.

Lead SL product candidate is camonsertib (RP-3500 or RG6526), a potent and selective oral small molecule inhibitor of Ataxia-Telangiectasia and Rad3-related protein kinase (ATR) for the treatment of solid tumours with specific DNA damage repair-related genomic alterations, including those in the Ataxia-Telangiectasia mutated kinase gene, which is under Phase Ib/II clinical trial. Also developing a portfolio of SL product candidates to treat cancers with a high unmet medical need. Other products include RP-6306, a first-in-class, oral protein kinase membrane-associated tyrosine- and theonine- specific cdc-2 inhibitory kinase (PKMYT1) inhibitor as a monotheraphy and in combinations in multiple early clinical studies to treat tumours with genetic alterations characterized by amplification of CCNE1 and tumours with heterogeneity of copy number in ovarian, uterine and breast cancers; and polymerase theta (RP-2119), an SL target associated with BRCA mutations as well as other genomic alterations.

Has a collaboration and license agreement with New York, N.Y.-based **Bristol-Myers Squibb Company** to research and develop potential new product candidates for the treatment of cancer; and Japan-based **Ono Pharmaceutical Company Ltd.** to research and develop potential new product candidates targeting polymerase theta.

In June 2022, the company entered into a collaboration and license agreement with **Hoffman-La Roche Inc.** and **F. Hoffman-La Roche Ltd.** regarding the development and commercialization of the company's product candidate camonsertib (RP-3500) and specified other Ataxia-Telangiectasia and Rad3-related protein kinase inhibitors products. Under the agreement, the company would retain an option to enter into a U.S. co-development and profit share arrangement with Roche exercisable prior to the commencement of the first pivotal clinical trial of camonsertib. The company also received an upfront payment of US$125,000,000.

Directors - Thomas Civik, chr., N.Y.; Lloyd M. Segal, pres. & CEO, Montréal, Qué.; Dr. David P. Bonita, N.Y.; Todd Foley, Wyo.; Dr. Samantha Kulkarni, Mass.; Susan Molineaux, Calif.; Dr. Briggs W. Morrison, Pa.; Ann D. Rhoads, Mont.; Carol A. Schafer, Fla.

Other Exec. Officers - Dr. Daniel Durocher, co-founder; Dr. Agnel Sfeir, co-founder; Dr. Frank Sicheri, co-founder; Dr. Laurence F. Akiyoshi, exec. v-p, org. & leadership devel.; Daniel Bélanger, exec. v-p, HR; Dr. Cameron Black, exec. v-p, discovery; Steve Forte, exec. v-p & CFO; Philip (Phil) Herman, exec. v-p, comml. & new product devel.; Dr. Maria Koehler, exec. v-p & CMO; Dr. Kim Seth, exec. v-p & head, bus. & corp. devel.; Dr. Michael Zinda, exec. v-p & chief scientific officer

Capital Stock

	Authorized (shs.)	Outstanding (shs.)[1]
Preferred	unlimited	nil
Common	unlimited	42,088,446

[1] At May 1, 2023

Major Shareholder - the Biotechnology Value funds held 19.7% interest at Apr. 15, 2023.

Price Range - RPTX/NASDAQ

Year	Volume	High	Low	Close
2022	19,370,297	US$22.06	US$8.13	US$14.71
2021	11,372,073	US$46.44	US$18.38	US$21.09
2020	5,724,663	US$39.69	US$21.46	US$34.30

Capital Stock Changes - During 2022, common shares were issued as follows: 148,116 on exercise of options and 37,915 under employee share purchased plan

Wholly Owned Subsidiaries

Repare Therapeutics USA Inc., Del.

Financial Statistics

Periods ended:	12m Dec. 31/22[A]		12m Dec. 31/21[A]
	US$000s	%Chg	US$000s
Operating revenue	**131,830**	**n.m.**	**7,600**
Research & devel. expense	119,066		90,047
General & admin expense	10,891		11,913
Stock-based compensation	19,691		12,829
Operating expense	**149,648**	**+30**	**114,789**
Operating income	**(17,818)**	**n.a.**	**(107,189)**
Deprec., depl. & amort	1,978		1,471
Finance income	5,631		259
Pre-tax income	**(13,900)**	**n.a.**	**(108,586)**
Income taxes	15,147		(1,678)
Net income	**(29,047)**	**n.a.**	**(106,908)**
Cash & equivalent	343,941		341,866
Accounts receivable	1,518		654
Current assets	353,979		351,414
Fixed assets, net	4,228		5,604
Right-of-use assets	5,371		7,491
Total assets	**364,075**	**-1**	**368,715**
Accts. pay. & accr. liabs	22,106		20,924
Current liabilities	78,619		35,089
Long-term lease liabilities	3,257		5,592
Shareholders' equity	279,517		288,421
Cash from oper. activs	**322**	**n.a.**	**(85,796)**
Cash from fin. activs	880		95,557
Cash from invest. activs	(175,778)		(1,676)
Net cash position	**159,521**	**-52**	**334,427**
Capital expenditures	(602)		(1,690)
Capital disposals	nil		40
	US$		US$
Earnings per share*	(0.69)		(2.83)
Cash flow per share*	0.01		(2.27)
	shs		shs
No. of shs. o/s*	42,036,193		41,850,162
Avg. no. of shs. o/s*	41,922,042		37,818,115
	%		%
Net profit margin	(22.03)		n.m.
Return on equity	(10.23)		(37.17)
Return on assets	(7.93)		(29.46)

* Common

[A] Reported in accordance with U.S. GAAP

Latest Results

Periods ended:	3m Mar. 31/23[A]		3m Mar. 31/22[A]
	US$000s	%Chg	US$000s
Operating revenue	5,678	n.m.	408
Net income	(34,941)	n.a.	(34,757)
	US$		US$
Earnings per share*	(0.83)		(0.83)

* Common

[A] Reported in accordance with U.S. GAAP

Historical Summary
(as originally stated)

Fiscal Year	Oper. Rev.	Net Inc. Bef. Disc.	EPS*
	US$000s	US$000s	US$
2022[A]	131,830	(29,047)	(0.69)
2021[A]	7,600	(106,908)	(2.83)
2020[A]	135	(53,417)	(2.66)
2019[A1]	nil	(27,216)	(17.81)
2018[A1]	nil	(14,283)	(9.35)

* Common

[A] Reported in accordance with U.S. GAAP

[1] As shown in the prospectus dated June 17, 2020.

R.45 RepliCel Life Sciences Inc.

Symbol - RP **Exchange** - TSX-VEN **CUSIP** - 76027P

Head Office - 900-570 Granville St, Vancouver, BC, V6C 3P1 **Telephone** - (604) 248-8730 **Toll-free** - (800) 248-5255 **Fax** - (604) 248-8690

Website - www.replicel.com

Email - lee@replicel.com

Investor Relations - Robert L. Buckler (604) 248-8693

Auditors - Mao & Ying LLP C.A., Vancouver, B.C.

Lawyers - Clark Wilson LLP, Vancouver, B.C.

Transfer Agents - Computershare Trust Company of Canada Inc., Vancouver, B.C.

Profile - (B.C. 2011; orig. Ont., 1967) Researches and develops injection technologies and autologous cell therapies that treat functional cellular deficits for aesthetic and orthopaedic conditions, including chronic tendinosis, skin aging and androgenetic alopecia.

Has developed DermaPrecise™, a dermal electronic injection device which delivers programmable volumes of injectable substances into the skin and subcutaneous tissue allowing for consistency and control over depth, dose and the pressure involved in delivery. Compatible substances include dermal fillers, toxins, enzymes, drugs and biologics. The device is in the prototype and testing stage.

Additional products under development include: RCT-01 (tendon repair), a treatment for chronic tendinosis made from a procedure using collagen-producing fibroblasts isolated from non-bulbar dermal sheath (NBDS) cells within the hair follicle that are replicated in culture; RCS-01 (skin rejuvenation), which provides a platform that treats intrinsically and extrinsically aged/damaged skin by providing UV-naïve collagen-producing fibroblast cells directly to the affected area; and RCH-01 (hair restoration), a minimally invasive cell therapy using dermal sheath cup (DSC) cells isolated from the hair follicle for the treatment of androgenetic alopecia.

Predecessor Detail - Name changed from Newcastle Resources Ltd., June 22, 2011, following reverse takeover acquisition of TrichoScience Innovations Inc.

Directors - David M. Hall, chr., Vancouver, B.C.; Andrew Schutte, pres. & CEO, Ariz.; Gary Boddington, West Vancouver, B.C.; Robert L. (Lee) Buckler, B.C.; Peter W. Lewis, Vancouver, B.C.; Peter Lowry, Auckland, New Zealand; Jamie MacKay, Wyo.

Other Exec. Officers - Ben Austring, COO & corp. sec.; David Kwok, CFO; Dr. Rolf Hoffmann, CMO; Dr. Kevin McElwee, chief scientific officer

Capital Stock

	Authorized (shs.)	Outstanding (shs.)[1]
Cl.A Preference	unlimited	1,089,125
Common	unlimited	65,001,560

[1] At May 30, 2023

Class A Preference - Entitled to a fixed dividend rate which shall accrue on a daily basis at a rate of 7% per annum. Convertible into common shares at any time prior to Sept. 12, 2024, at a conversion price of 33¢ per share. Redeemable at (i) $0.468 per share through the first anniversary; (ii) $0.536 per share after the first anniversary through the second anniversary; (iii) $0.604 per share after the second anniversary through the third anniversary; (iv) $0.672 per share after the third anniversary through the fourth anniversary; and (v) 74¢ per share after the fourth anniversary through the fifth anniversary. Priority over all or other class of shares of the company as to dividends and upon liquidation. Non voting.

Common - One vote per share.

Major Shareholder - Andrew Schutte held 26.77% interest and Jamie MacKay held 15.44% interest at Apr. 25, 2023.

Price Range - RP/TSX-VEN

Year	Volume	High	Low	Close
2022	1,640,858	$0.29	$0.07	$0.09
2021	4,527,281	$0.58	$0.20	$0.23
2020	4,461,429	$0.39	$0.10	$0.23
2019	3,268,695	$0.42	$0.16	$0.26
2018	10,553,292	$0.68	$0.30	$0.37

Recent Close: $0.13

Capital Stock Changes - In January 2023, private placement of 8,419,650 units (1 common share & ½ warrant) at 10¢ per unit was completed, with warrants exercisable at 20¢ per share for three years. In March 2023, private placement of 10,131,000 units (1 common share & ½ warrant) at 10¢ per unit was completed, with warrants exercisable at 20¢ per share for four years.

In May 2022, private placement of 4,218,470 units (1 common share & ½ warrant) at 18¢ per unit was completed. In December 2022, private placement of 8,419,650 units (1 common share & ½ warrant) at 10¢ per unit was completed.

Wholly Owned Subsidiaries

TrichoScience Innovations Inc., Vancouver, B.C.

Financial Statistics

Periods ended:	12m Dec. 31/22[A]		12m Dec. 31/21[A]
	$000s	%Chg	$000s
Operating revenue	**354**	**0**	**354**
Research & devel. expense	624		1,149
General & admin expense	1,090		1,469
Stock-based compensation	69		472
Operating expense	**1,783**	**-42**	**3,090**
Operating income	**(1,429)**	**n.a.**	**(2,736)**
Deprec., depl. & amort.	36		37
Finance costs, gross	85		147
Pre-tax income	**(743)**	**n.a.**	**(4,073)**
Net income	**(743)**	**n.a.**	**(4,073)**
Cash & equivalent	413		221
Accounts receivable	47		26
Current assets	636		393
Fixed assets, net	2		3
Total assets	**798**	**+35**	**592**
Accts. pay. & accr. liabs	1,030		709
Current liabilities	2,073		1,674
Long-term debt, gross	730		646
Long-term debt, net	41		34
Shareholders' equity	(5,915)		(6,842)
Cash from oper. activs	**(1,409)**	**n.a.**	**(2,514)**
Cash from fin. activs	1,601		2,701
Net cash position	**413**	**+87**	**221**
	$		$
Earnings per share*	(0.02)		(0.13)
Cash flow per share*	(0.04)		(0.08)
	shs		shs
No. of shs. o/s*	47,597,327		34,959,207
Avg. no. of shs. o/s*	37,767,620		32,486,770
	%		%
Net profit margin	(209.89)		n.m.
Return on equity	n.m.		n.m.
Return on assets	(94.68)		(775.12)
No. of employees (FTEs)	nil		1

* Common
[A] Reported in accordance with IFRS

Latest Results

Periods ended:	3m Mar. 31/23[A]		3m Mar. 31/22[A]
	$000s	%Chg	$000s
Operating revenue	88	0	88
Net income	(963)	n.a.	(787)
	$		$
Earnings per share*	(0.01)		(0.02)

* Common
[A] Reported in accordance with IFRS

Historical Summary
(as originally stated)

Fiscal Year	Oper. Rev.	Net Inc. Bef. Disc.	EPS*
	$000s	$000s	$
2022[A]	354	(743)	(0.02)
2021[A]	354	(4,073)	(0.13)
2020[A]	354	(1,580)	(0.06)
2019[A]	253	(2,954)	(0.11)
2018[A]	121	(2,769)	(0.12)

* Common
[A] Reported in accordance with IFRS

R.46 Reservoir Capital Corp.

Symbol - REO **Exchange** - CSE (S) **CUSIP** - 761125
Head Office - 1000-595 Howe St, Vancouver, BC, V6C 2T5 **Telephone** - (604) 662-8448 **Fax** - (604) 688-1157
Website - www.reservoircapitalcorp.com
Email - mhutchins@dsacorp.ca
Investor Relations - Monique Hutchins (416) 848-4501
Auditors - PKF Antares Professional Corporation C.A., Calgary, Alta.
Transfer Agents - Computershare Trust Company of Canada Inc., Vancouver, B.C.
Profile - (B.C. 2007; orig. Alta., 2006) Invests in clean power companies and clean power assets primarily in Africa and Latin America.
Investments include **Mainstream Energy Solutions Limited** (4% interest), a Nigerian power company which owns and operates two hydroelectric power generation plants on the Niger River in Nigeria with aggregate operating capacity of 922 MW; and **North South Power Company Ltd.**, a Nigerian power generation company with 630 MW operating hydro capacity which includes the 600 MW Shiroro hydropower plant and the 30 MW Gurara hydro power plant, both located on the Kaduna River in Nigeria.
Common suspended from CSE, May 10, 2022.
Directors - Mohammad S. (Mo) Fazil, Calgary, Alta.; Eric Olo, Lagos, Nigeria; Scott M. Reeves, Calgary, Alta.
Other Exec. Officers - André Ayotte Jr., interim CFO; Monique Hutchins, corp. sec.

Capital Stock

	Authorized (shs.)	Outstanding (shs.)[1]
Preferred	unlimited	nil
Common	unlimited	5,753,474

[1] At Aug. 24, 2023

Major Shareholder - Tunde Joseph Afolabi held 38.23% interest and Vincent Gueneau held 23.6% interest at May 3, 2022.

Price Range - REO/TSX-VEN (D)

Year	Volume	High	Low	Close
2022	4,786	$1.80	$1.01	$1.65
2021	14,365	$2.98	$1.76	$1.76
2020	25,870	$5.00	$2.00	$2.25
2019	75,668	$7.50	$2.00	$5.00
2018	39,159	$7.00	$1.00	$3.00

Consolidation: 1-for-100 cons. in Aug. 2020

Wholly Owned Subsidiaries

Kainji Power Holding Limited, Port Louis, Mauritius.
- 4% int. in **Mainstream Energy Solutions Limited**, Abuja, Nigeria.
- 100% int. in **OLOCORP Nigeria Ltd**, Nigeria.
  - **North South Power Company Ltd**, Abuja, Nigeria.

Reservoir Capital (BVI) Corp., British Virgin Islands.

R.47 Restaurant Brands International Inc.*

Symbol - QSR **Exchange** - TSX **CUSIP** - 76131D
Head Office - 300-130 King St W, PO Box 339, Toronto, ON, M5X 1E1
Telephone - (905) 845-6511 **Fax** - (905) 845-0265
Website - www.rbi.com
Email - mkeusch@rbi.com
Investor Relations - Michele Keusch (905) 339-6011
Auditors - KPMG LLP C.P.A., Miami, Fla.
Lawyers - Torys LLP, Toronto, Ont.
Transfer Agents - Computershare Trust Company, N.A., Denver, Colo.; Computershare Trust Company of Canada Inc., Toronto, Ont.
FP500 Revenue Ranking - 77
Employees - 6,400 at Dec. 31, 2022
Profile - (Can. 2014; orig. B.C., 2014) The company is the sole general partner of **Restaurant Brands International Limited Partnership**, the indirect parent of **Burger King Worldwide, Inc.**, which franchises and operates fast food hamburger restaurants under the Burger King® brand; **The TDL Group Corp.** (operating as Tim Hortons), which franchises and operates quick service restaurants serving premium coffee and other beverage and food products under the Tim Hortons® brand; **Popeyes Louisiana Kitchen, Inc.**, which franchises and operates chicken quick service restaurants under the Popeyes® brand; and **FRG, LLC**, which franchises and operates quick service restaurants serving hot gourmet submarine sandwiches under the Firehouse Subs® brand.
At Dec. 31, 2022, the company franchised or owned 30,722 restaurants, consisting of 19,789 Burger King® restaurants, 5,600 Tim Hortons® restaurants, 4,091 Popeyes® restaurants and 1,242 Firehouse Subs® restaurants, in more than 100 countries and U.S. territories.
Restaurant footprint at Dec. 31, 2022:

	Franchised	Company
Burger King®	19,739	50
Tim Hortons®	5,593	7
Popeyes®	4,050	41
Firehouse Subs®	1,203	39

Burger King® restaurants feature flame-grilled hamburgers such as the flagship Whopper® sandwich, chicken and other specialty sandwiches, french fries, soft drinks and other affordably-priced food items. Tim Hortons® offers premium blend coffee, tea, espresso-based hot and cold specialty drinks, fresh baked goods, including donuts, Timbits®, bagels, muffins, cookies and pastries, grilled paninis, classic sandwiches, wraps, soups and other food products. Popeyes® offers Louisiana style menu which includes fried chicken, chicken tenders, fried shrimp and other seafood, red beans and rice, and other regional items. Firehouse Subs® offers hot and hearty subs piled high with quality meats and cheeses, as well as chopped salads, chili and soups, signature and other sides, soft drinks and local specialties.
Revenues consist of supply chain sales, which represent sales of products, supplies and restaurant equipment to franchisees; sales to retailers and sales at company owned restaurants; franchise revenues, which is primarily from royalties based on a percentage of sales reported by franchise restaurants and franchise fees paid by franchisees; property revenues from leased and subleased properties to franchisees; and advertising revenues and other services, which is primarily from advertising fund contributions based on a percentage of sales reported by franchise restaurants.
During 2022, the company entered into master franchise agreements in Indonesia, New Zealand, Poland, the Czech Republic and Taiwan for the Popeyes® brand; in Poland, the Czech Republic and Romania for the Burger King® brand; and in Pakistan for the Tim Hortons® brand. In addition, development agreements were entered in Singapore, Dominican Republic, Puerto Rico, Kazakhstan and Honduras for the Popeyes® brand.
Directors - J. Patrick Doyle, exec. chr., United States; Paul J. Fribourg†, N.Y.; Alexandre Behring, Rio de Janeiro, Brazil; Maximilien de Limburg Stirum, Brussels, Belgium; Cristina Farjallat; Ali G. Hedayat, Toronto, Ont.; Marc Lemann, São Paulo, Brazil; Jason Melbourne, Toronto, Ont.; Daniel S. Schwartz, Fla.; Thecla Sweeney, Ont.
Other Exec. Officers - Joshua (Josh) Kobza, CEO; Matthew (Matt) Dunnigan, CFO; Jacqueline Friesner, chief acctg. officer & contr.; Duncan S. A. Fulton, chief corp. officer; Jill Granat, gen. counsel & corp. sec.; Tom Curtis IV, pres., Burger King, U.S. & Canada; Mike Hancock, pres., Firehouse Subs; Axel Schwan, pres., Tim Hortons, Americas; David Shear, pres., intl.; Sami Siddiqui, pres., Popeyes, Americas; Jeff Housman, chief people & srvcs. officer
† Lead director

Capital Stock

	Authorized (shs.)	Outstanding (shs.)[1]
Class A Preferred	68,530,939	nil
Common	unlimited	312,283,429
Special Vtg.	1	1
Cl.B Exch. LP Unit	unlimited	140,758,781[2]

[1] At Aug. 1, 2023
[2] Securities of Restaurant Brands International LP. Classified as non-controlling interest.

Common - One vote per share.
Special Voting - Held by a trustee. Entitles the trustee to a number of votes equal to the number of outstanding class B exchangeable limited partnership units of Restaurant Brands International Limited Partnership. Exchangeable unitholders have the right to direct the trustee to vote on their behalf in all voting matters presented to the company's common shareholders.
Class B Exchangeable Limited Partnership Unit - Entitled to distributions in an amount equal to any dividends or distributions declared and payable on common shares of the company. Have the benefit of a voting trust agreement pursuant to which a trustee holds a special voting share of the company that entitles the trustee to a number of votes equal to the number of outstanding class B exchangeable limited partnership units on all matters submitted to a vote of the common shareholders. Exchangeable into common shares on a 1-for-1 basis, subject to the company's right to determine to settle any such exchange for a cash payment in lieu of common shares.
Options - At Dec. 31, 2022, options were outstanding to purchase 7,494,000 common shares at a weighted average exercise price of US$58 with a weighted average remaining contractual term of 6.1 years.
Major Shareholder - 3G Capital Partners Ltd. held 28.9% interest at Apr. 10, 2023.

Price Range - QSR/TSX

Year	Volume	High	Low	Close
2022	190,653,329	$92.65	$60.37	$87.57
2021	177,103,792	$87.32	$69.42	$76.70
2020	254,826,944	$89.32	$36.48	$77.83
2019	145,252,224	$105.93	$69.00	$82.78
2018	131,018,784	$85.71	$67.55	$71.32

Recent Close: $92.36
Capital Stock Changes - During 2022, Restaurant Brands International Limited Partnership exchanged 1,996,818 class B exchangeable limited partnership units for a like number of common shares of the company. In addition, common shares were issued as follows: 1,737,934 for cash and 483,980 on exercise of options; 6,101,364 common shares were cancelled.

Dividends

QSR com Ra US$2.20 pa Q est. Apr. 5, 2023
Prev. Rate: US$2.16 est. Jan. 4, 2023

Long-Term Debt - Outstanding at Dec. 31, 2022:

Term loan facility due 2026[1]	US$1,250,000,000
Term loan facility due 2026[2]	5,190,000,000
5.75% sr. notes due 2025	500,000,000
3.875% sr. notes due 2028	1,550,000,000
4.375% sr. notes due 2028	750,000,000
3.5% sr. notes due 2029	750,000,000
4% sr. notes due 2030	2,900,000,000
Other	155,000,000
Finance leases	343,000,000
Less: Def. fin. costs & debt disc.	111,000,000
	13,277,000,000
Less: Current portion	127,000,000
	13,150,000,000

[1] Bears interest, at the company's option, at either a base rate, subject to a floor of 1%, plus 0% to 0.5% or adjusted term SOFR, subject to a floor of 0%, plus 0.75% to 1.5%. At Dec. 31, 2022, interest rate was 5.44%.
[2] Bears interest, at the company's option, at either a base rate, subject to a floor of 1%, plus 0.75% or a Eurocurrency rate, subject to a floor of 0%, plus 1.75%. At Dec. 31, 2022, interest rate was 6.13%.

Aggregate maturities of long-term debt for the next five years, excluding finance leases:

2023	US$97,000,000
2024	107,000,000
2025	741,000,000
2026	6,148,000,000
2027	nil
Thereafter	5,952,000,000

Future minimum finance lease commitments are as follows:

2023	US$49,000,000
2024	48,000,000
2025	44,000,000
2026	41,000,000
2027	38,000,000
Thereafter	244,000,000

Wholly Owned Subsidiaries

Restaurant Brands International Limited Partnership, Toronto, Ont.
Represents sole general partnership interest. (see separate coverage)

Note: The preceding list includes only the major related companies in which interests are held.

Financial Statistics

Periods ended:	12m Dec. 31/22[A]		12m Dec. 31/21[A]
	US$000s	%Chg	US$000s
Operating revenue	**6,505,000**	**+13**	**5,739,000**
Cost of sales	2,122,000		1,689,000
General & admin expense	1,708,000		1,470,000
Other operating expense	518,000		489,000
Operating expense	**4,348,000**	**+19**	**3,648,000**
Operating income	**2,157,000**	**+3**	**2,091,000**
Deprec., depl. & amort.	190,000		201,000
Finance income	7,000		3,000
Finance costs, gross	540,000		519,000
Investment income	(44,000)		(4,000)
Pre-tax income	**1,365,000**	**0**	**1,363,000**
Income taxes	(117,000)		110,000
Net income	**1,482,000**	**+18**	**1,253,000**
Net inc. for equity hldrs	**1,008,000**	**+20**	**838,000**
Net inc. for non-cont. int.	**474,000**	**+14**	**415,000**
Cash & equivalent	1,178,000		1,087,000
Inventories	133,000		96,000
Accounts receivable	614,000		547,000
Current assets	2,048,000		1,816,000
Long-term investments	249,000		274,000
Fixed assets, net	1,950,000		2,035,000
Right-of-use assets	1,082,000		1,130,000
Intangibles, net	16,679,000		17,423,000
Total assets	**22,746,000**	**-2**	**23,246,000**
Accts. pay. & accr. liabs.	758,000		614,000
Current liabilities	2,116,000		1,878,000
Long-term debt, gross	13,277,000		13,345,000
Long-term debt, net	13,150,000		13,249,000
Long-term lease liabilities	1,027,000		1,070,000
Shareholders' equity	2,499,000		2,237,000
Non-controlling interest	1,769,000		1,616,000
Cash from oper. activs.	**1,490,000**	**-14**	**1,726,000**
Cash from fin. activs.	(1,307,000)		(1,093,000)
Cash from invest. activs.	(64,000)		(1,103,000)
Net cash position	**1,178,000**	**+8**	**1,087,000**
Capital expenditures	(100,000)		(106,000)
	US$		US$
Earnings per share*	3.28		2.71
Cash flow per share*	4.85		5.57
Cash divd. per share*	2.16		2.12
	shs		shs
No. of shs. o/s*	307,142,436		309,025,068
Avg. no. of shs. o/s*	307,000,000		310,000,000
	%		%
Net profit margin	22.78		21.83
Return on equity	42.57		38.06
Return on assets	8.99		7.52
Foreign sales percent	47		47
No. of employees (FTEs)	6,400		5,700

* Common

[A] Reported in accordance with U.S. GAAP

Latest Results

Periods ended:	6m June 30/23[A]		6m June 30/22[A]
	US$000s	%Chg	US$000s
Operating revenue	3,365,000	+9	3,090,000
Net income	628,000	+2	616,000
Net inc. for equity hldrs	430,000	+3	419,000
Net inc. for non-cont. int.	198,000		197,000
	US$		US$
Earnings per share*	1.39		1.36

* Common

[A] Reported in accordance with U.S. GAAP

Historical Summary
(as originally stated)

Fiscal Year	Oper. Rev. US$000s	Net Inc. Bef. Disc. US$000s	EPS* US$
2022[A]	6,505,000	1,482,000	3.28
2021[A]	5,739,000	1,253,000	2.71
2020[A]	4,968,000	750,000	1.61
2019[A]	5,603,000	1,111,000	2.40
2018[A]	5,357,000	1,144,000	2.46

* Common

[A] Reported in accordance with U.S. GAAP

R.48 Restaurant Brands International Limited Partnership

Symbol - QSP.UN **Exchange** - TSX **CUSIP** - 76090H
Head Office - 300-130 King St W, PO Box 339, Toronto, ON, M5X 1E1 **Telephone** - (905) 339-5724 **Fax** - (905) 845-2931
Website - www.rbi.com
Email - mkeusch@rbi.com
Investor Relations - Michele Keusch (905) 339-6011
Auditors - KPMG LLP C.P.A.
Transfer Agents - Computershare Trust Company of Canada Inc.

Profile - (Can. 2014) Indirect parent of **Burger King Worldwide, Inc.**, which franchises and operates fast food hamburger restaurants under the Burger King® brand; **The TDL Group Corp.** (operating as Tim Hortons), which franchises and operates quick service restaurants serving premium coffee and other beverage and food products under the Tim Hortons® brand; **Popeyes Louisiana Kitchen, Inc.**, which franchises and operates chicken quick service restaurants under the Popeyes® brand; and **FRG, LLC**, which franchises and operates quick service restaurants serving hot gourmet submarine sandwiches under the Firehouse Subs® brand.

The limited partnership does not prepare separate financial statements due to an exemption from the continuous disclosure requirements under the Securities Act. One of the conditions of the exemption is that the company is required to file with the Canadian securities commissions all documents filed by parent company **Restaurant Brands International Inc.** (RBI; see separate coverage) with the U.S. Securities Exchange Commission.

RBI is the sole general partner of the limited partnership.

Capital Stock

	Authorized (shs.)	Outstanding (shs.)[1]
Preferred Partnership Unit	unlimited	nil
Cl.A Common Unit	unlimited	202,006,067[2]
Cl.B Exchangeable LP Unit	unlimited	140,758,781

[1] At Aug. 1, 2023

[2] Held by Restaurant Brands International Inc.

Class A Common Unit - Represents the interest of the general partner, Restaurant Brands International Inc. (RBI), in the limited partnership. Entitled to distributions in an amount equal to those declared and payable on RBI common shares.

Class B Exchangeable Limited Partnership Unit - Represents the interests of the limited partners in the limited partnership. Entitled to distributions in an amount equal to any dividends or distributions declared and payable on RBI common shares. Have the benefit of a voting trust agreement pursuant to which a trustee holds a special voting share of RBI that entitles the trustee to a number of votes equal to the number of outstanding class B exchangeable limited partnership units on all matters submitted to a vote of RBI common shareholders. Exchangeable into RBI common shares on a 1-for-1 basis, subject to RBI's right to determine to settle any such exchange for a cash payment in lieu of common shares.

Major Shareholder - Restaurant Brands International Inc. held 100% interest at Feb. 14, 2023.

Price Range - QSP.UN/TSX

Year	Volume	High	Low	Close
2022	116,250	$91.48	$59.47	$87.07
2021	160,804	$85.88	$69.70	$77.34
2020	762,915	$89.17	$37.79	$77.87
2019	192,712	$104.20	$69.24	$84.20
2018	47,663	$86.01	$68.98	$71.64

Recent Close: $94.00

Capital Stock Changes - During 2022, 1,996,818 class B exchangeable limited partnership units were exchanged for a like number of Restaurant Brands International Inc. common shares.

Dividends

QSP.UN exch unit Var. Ra pa Q
US$0.55............... Oct. 4/23 US$0.55........... July 6/23
US$0.55............... Apr. 5/23 US$0.54........... Jan. 4/23
Paid in 2023: US$2.19 2022: US$2.15 2021: US$2.11

Wholly Owned Subsidiaries

1011778 B.C. Unlimited Liability Company, B.C.
- 100% int. in **Burger King Worldwide, Inc.**, Miami, Fla.
- 100% int. in **FRG, LLC**, Jacksonville, Fla.
- 100% int. in **Popeyes Louisiana Kitchen, Inc.**, Atlanta, Ga.
- 100% int. in **The TDL Group Corp.**, Toronto, Ont.

Note: The preceding list includes only the major related companies in which interests are held.

R.49 Resverlogix Corp.

Symbol - RVX **Exchange** - TSX **CUSIP** - 76128M
Head Office - 300-4820 Richard Rd SW, Calgary, AB, T3E 6L1 **Telephone** - (403) 254-9252 **Fax** - (403) 256-8495
Website - www.resverlogix.com
Email - don@resverlogix.com
Investor Relations - Donald J. McCaffrey (403) 254-9252 ext. 234
Auditors - RSM Canada LLP C.A., Toronto, Ont.
Bankers - Bank of Montreal, Calgary, Alta.
Lawyers - Borden Ladner Gervais LLP, Calgary, Alta.
Transfer Agents - Computershare Trust Company of Canada Inc., Toronto, Ont.
Employees - 19 at Dec. 31, 2022

Profile - (Alta. 2000) Researches and develops technology focusing on epigenetic candidate apabetalone (RVX-208) which can regulate disease-causing genes for patients with chronic disease.

Lead drug candidate is apabetalone/RVX-208, which targets Bromodomain (BD2) and Extra Terminal domain (BET) proteins to impact biological processes that drive high risk chronic vascular diseases such as cardiovascular diseases (CVD), diabetes mellitus (DM) and chronic kidney disease (CKD) namely vascular inflammation, acute phase response, vascular calcification, complement and coagulation and reverse cholesterol transport. Apabetalone also limits the ability of severe acute respiratory syndrome coronavirus 2 (SARS-CoV-2) to infect human cells and reduces hyperinflammatory responses to the virus. RVX-208 is under Phase III clinical trial development for the secondary prevention of major adverse cardiovascular events in high-risk CVD patients with a DM co-morbidity, and under Phase II/III clinical trial for post COVID-19 conditions. In addition, the company is exploring the potential of apabetalone to modulate disease-related pathology in other indications including end-stage renal disease, vascular cognitive impairment and orphan diseases such as pulmonary arterial hypertension. Apabetalone has been granted Breakthrough Therapy Designation by U.S. FDA, in combination with top standard of care, including high-intensity statins, for the secondary prevention of major adverse cardiovascular events in patients with Type 2 diabetes mellitus and recent acute coronary syndrome.

In May 2022, the company has been granted by the U.S. FDA a Type C meeting in early August 2022 to review the clinical trial protocol for its Phase 3 study of apabetalone in high risk COVID-19 outpatients.

Predecessor Detail - Name changed from Apsley Management Group Inc., Apr. 25, 2003, following Qualifying Transaction acquisition of Resverlogix Inc.

Directors - Donald J. McCaffrey, chr., pres., CEO & corp. sec., Calgary, Alta.; Shawn Lu, Toronto, Ont.; Kelly B. McNeill, Winnipeg, Man.; Siu Lun (Dicky) To, Hong Kong, People's Republic of China; Kenneth J. Zuerblis, Sarasota, Fla.

Other Exec. Officers - A. Brad Cann, CFO; Dr. Ewelina Kulikowski, chief scientific officer; Dr. Jan O. Johansson, sr. v-p, medical affairs; Dr. Michael T. Sweeney, sr. v-p, clinical devel.; Dr. Henrik C. Hansen, v-p, intellectual prop.; Dr. Ravi Jahagirdar, v-p, pharmacology, toxicology & safety

Capital Stock

	Authorized (shs.)	Outstanding (shs.)[1]
Series A Preferred	unlimited	nil
Royalty Preferred	75,202,620	75,202,620[2 3]
Common	unlimited	268,521,296

[1] At May 11, 2023

[2] Classified as debt.

[3] All held by Zenith Epigenetics Corp.

Royalty Preferred - Issuable in series. Entitled to dividends in the amount of 6 to 12% of net Apo revenue. Non-participating, non-voting and not entitled to any claim on the company's residual net assets. All held by Zenith Epigenetics Corp. Classified as a liability.

Common - One vote per share.

Major Shareholder - Shenzhen Hepalink Pharmaceutical Co., Ltd. held 31.8% interest and Eastern Capital Limited held 10.3% interest at May 10, 2023.

Price Range - RVX/TSX

Year	Volume	High	Low	Close
2022	14,405,567	$0.82	$0.12	$0.14
2021	12,933,783	$1.12	$0.41	$0.51
2020	16,723,416	$1.53	$0.56	$0.94
2019	32,582,986	$4.94	$0.35	$1.23
2018	21,634,957	$4.31	$1.11	$3.29

Recent Close: $0.09

Capital Stock Changes - During 2022, common shares were issued as follows: 18,711,902 by private placement, 3,315,597 under long term incentive plan, 334,730 under deferred share unit plan and 101,356 on exercise of warrant.

Wholly Owned Subsidiaries

Resverlogix Inc., Del.

Financial Statistics

Periods ended:	12m Dec. 31/22[A]		12m Dec. 31/21[A]
	US$000s	%Chg	US$000s
Salaries & benefits	2,799		3,373
Research & devel. expense	2,787		1,367
General & admin expense	3,836		7,453
Stock-based compensation	2,392		2,622
Operating expense	**11,814**	**-20**	**14,815**
Operating income	**(11,814)**	**n.a.**	**(14,815)**
Deprec., depl. & amort.	1,007		1,106
Finance costs, gross	1,669		853
Pre-tax income	**(3,592)**	**n.a.**	**(24,759)**
Income taxes	18		12
Net income	**(3,610)**	**n.a.**	**(24,771)**
Cash & equivalent	40		6
Inventories	2,371		2,453
Current assets	2,888		2,953
Fixed assets, net	66		141
Right-of-use assets	360		898
Intangibles, net	2,205		3,428
Total assets	**8,115**	**-19**	**9,982**
Bank indebtedness	5,858		5,839
Accts. pay. & accr. liabs	14,095		8,703
Current liabilities	22,734		17,420
Long-term debt, gross	43,700		50,700
Long-term debt, net	43,700		50,700
Long-term lease liabilities	nil		442
Shareholders' equity	(59,281)		(59,870)
Cash from oper. activs	**(3,541)**	**n.a.**	**(8,024)**
Cash from fin. activs	4,063		8,807
Cash from invest. activs	(473)		(833)
Net cash position	**40**	**+567**	**6**
	US$		US$
Earnings per share*	(0.01)		(0.10)
Cash flow per share*	(0.01)		(0.03)
	shs		shs
No. of shs. o/s*	265,673,607		243,210,022
Avg. no. of shs. o/s*	254,422,707		239,867,716
	%		%
Net profit margin	n.a.		n.a.
Return on equity	n.m.		n.m.
Return on assets	(21.36)		(231.22)
No. of employees (FTEs)	19		22

* Common
[A] Reported in accordance with IFRS

Latest Results

Periods ended:	3m Mar. 31/23[A]		3m Mar. 31/22[A]
	US$000s	%Chg	US$000s
Net income	(5,155)	n.a.	2,332
	US$		US$
Earnings per share*	(0.02)		0.01

* Common
[A] Reported in accordance with IFRS

Historical Summary
(as originally stated)

Fiscal Year	Oper. Rev.	Net Inc. Bef. Disc.	EPS*
	US$000s	US$000s	US$
2022[A]	nil	(3,610)	(0.01)
2021[A]	nil	(24,771)	(0.10)
2020[A1]	nil	1,643	0.01
2020[A]	nil	118,025	0.57
2019[A]	nil	(162,798)	(0.87)

* Common
[A] Reported in accordance with IFRS
[1] 8 months ended Dec. 31, 2020.

R.50 Revitalist Lifestyle and Wellness Ltd.

Symbol - CALM **Exchange** - CSE (S) **CUSIP** - 76151T
Head Office - 10608 Flickenger Lane, Knoxville, TN, United States, 37922 **Toll-free** - (865) 585-8414
Website - revitalist.com
Email - kathryn.walker@revitalistclinic.com
Investor Relations - Kathryn Walker (865) 585-8414
Auditors - Davidson & Company LLP C.A., Vancouver, B.C.
Transfer Agents - Endeavor Trust Corporation, Vancouver, B.C.
Employees - 90 at May 25, 2022
Profile - (B.C. 2018) Operates medical clinics offering ketamine-enhanced psychotherapy for the treatment of chronic mood and pain disorders.

Ketamine is presently the only legal psychedelic medicine generally available to be prescribed by healthcare practitioners in Canada and the United States. At Sept. 30, 2022, the company had nine clinics in Knoxville (2), Johnson City and Chattanooga, Tenn.; Louisville, Ky.; Raleigh, N.C.; Detroit, Mich.; Washington, D.C.; and Jacksonville, Fla. Services offered include intravenous ketamine infusions; ketamine-assisted psychotherapy; Transcranial Magnetic Stimulation (TMS) for depression and obsessive-compulsive disorders (OCD); administration of Spravato, an FDA-approved ketamine-based nasal spray; medication infusions; vitamin infusions; and acupuncture.

During the third quarter of 2022, the company put the development of virtual clinics in the Metaverse on hold.

In May 2022, the company opened two ketamine-enhanced psychotherapy clinics in Johnson City and Chattanooga, Tenn.

In March 2022, the company agreed to acquire **Alchemy Wellness**, a ketamine-enhanced psychotherapy clinic in Richmond, Va., for US$800,000, consisting of US$40,000 cash, assumption of US$190,000 debt and US$570,000 in common shares.

Common suspended from CSE, May 9, 2023.

Predecessor Detail - Name changed from Deadpool Capital Corp., Jan. 19, 2021.

Directors - Kathryn Walker, co-founder & CEO, Knoxville, Tenn.; Kevin Murray, interim CFO; Corby Marshall, Savannah, Ga.

Other Exec. Officers - Dr. William Walker, co-founder & CMO; Paul Auchterlonie, COO; Dr. Robert Long, v-p, neuroscience research

Capital Stock

	Authorized (shs.)	Outstanding (shs.)[1]
Common	unlimited	80,470,631

[1] At Feb. 2, 2023

Major Shareholder - Widely held at May 16, 2022.

Price Range - CALM/CSE (S)

Year	Volume	High	Low	Close
2022	26,404,480	$0.29	$0.03	$0.03
2021	14,676,729	$0.88	$0.16	$0.19

Recent Close: $0.02

Capital Stock Changes - In February 2023, private placement of 11,900,000 units (1 common share & 1 warrant) at 5¢ per unit was completed, with warrants exercisable at 5¢ per share for five years.

Wholly Owned Subsidiaries

Ketamine Holdings Ltd., B.C.
- 100% int. in **Ketamine Holdings (USA) Ltd.**, Del.
  - 100% int. in **Revitalist, LLC**, Nashville, Tenn.

Subsidiaries

60% int. in **Revitaland Meta Tech Inc.**, B.C.

Financial Statistics

Periods ended:	12m Dec. 31/21[A1]		12m Dec. 31/20[¤A]
	$000s	%Chg	$000s
Operating revenue	**2,067**	**n.a.**	**nil**
Salaries & benefits	4,581		nil
Research & devel. expense	418		nil
General & admin expense	3,058		2
Stock-based compensation	5,490		nil
Operating expense	**13,547**	**n.m.**	**2**
Operating income	**(11,480)**	**n.a.**	**(2)**
Deprec., depl. & amort.	662		nil
Finance costs, gross	453		nil
Pre-tax income	**(12,777)**	**n.a.**	**(2)**
Net income	**(12,777)**	**n.a.**	**(2)**
Net inc. for equity hldrs	**(12,609)**	**n.a.**	**(2)**
Net inc. for non-cont. int.	**(167)**	**n.a.**	**nil**
Cash & equivalent	3,887		nil
Accounts receivable	153		nil
Current assets	4,166		nil
Fixed assets, net	407		nil
Right-of-use assets	5,221		nil
Intangibles, net	1,789		nil
Total assets	**11,745**	**n.a.**	**nil**
Accts. pay. & accr. liabs	687		5
Current liabilities	3,283		5
Long-term lease liabilities	4,806		nil
Shareholders' equity	3,824		(5)
Non-controlling interest	(168)		nil
Cash from oper. activs	**(3,525)**	**n.a.**	**nil**
Cash from fin. activs	8,467		nil
Cash from invest. activs	(1,055)		nil
Net cash position	**3,887**	**n.a.**	**nil**
	$		$
Earnings per share*	(0.24)		(0.03)
Cash flow per share*	(0.07)		nil
	shs		shs
No. of shs. o/s*	67,712,580		n.a.
Avg. no. of shs. o/s*	53,136,496		70,356
	%		%
Net profit margin	(618.14)		n.a.
Return on equity	(644.50)		n.m.
Return on assets	(207.90)		n.m.
Foreign sales percent	100		nil

* Common
[¤] Restated
[A] Reported in accordance with IFRS
[1] Results reflect the Feb. 19, 2021, reverse takeover acquisition of Ketamine Holdings Ltd.

Latest Results

Periods ended:	9m Sept. 30/22[A]		9m Sept. 30/21[A]
	$000s	%Chg	$000s
Operating revenue	3,723	+234	1,116
Net income	(8,279)	n.a.	(8,821)
Net inc. for equity hldrs	(8,219)	n.a.	(8,821)
Net inc. for non-cont. int.	(60)		nil
	$		$
Earnings per share*	(0.12)		(0.18)

* Common
[A] Reported in accordance with IFRS

Historical Summary
(as originally stated)

Fiscal Year	Oper. Rev.	Net Inc. Bef. Disc.	EPS*
	$000s	$000s	$
2021[A]	2,067	(12,777)	(0.24)
	US$000s	US$000s	US$
2020[A1]	815	75	n.a.
2019[A]	686	18	n.a.

* Common
[A] Reported in accordance with IFRS
[1] Results for 2020 and 2019 pertain to Revitalist, LLC.

R.51 Revive Therapeutics Ltd.

Symbol - RVV **Exchange** - CSE **CUSIP** - 761516
Head Office - 82 Richmond St E, Toronto, ON, M5C 1P1 **Toll-free** - (888) 901-0036
Website - www.revivethera.com
Email - mfrank@revivethera.com
Investor Relations - Michael Frank (888) 901-0036
Auditors - Clearhouse LLP C.A., Mississauga, Ont.
Lawyers - Peterson & Company LLP, Toronto, Ont.
Transfer Agents - Computershare Trust Company of Canada Inc., Toronto, Ont.
Profile - (Ont. 2012) Researches and develops therapeutics for infectious diseases and rare disorders.

Product pipeline includes Bucillamine, an anti-rheumatic drug used in Japan and South Korea, which is being repurposed for the treatment of infectious diseases primarily mild to moderate COVID-19, which is under Phase III clinical trial; psychedelic therapeutics focused on the use of psilocybin, a psychedelic prodrug compound produced by various mushroom species, to treat methamphetamine use disorder (under Phase I/II clinical study), traumatic brain injury and stroke (under clinical study), mental illness, substance abuse and neurological disorders, as an individual or in combination with FDA-approved drugs; and cannabinoid pharmaceuticals focused on the use of cannabidiol (CBD) for the treatment of autoimmune hepatitis (AIH), a rare liver disease, and ischemia and reperfusion injury (IRI) resulting from solid organ transplantation, such as liver, kidney, heart and lung. The U.S. FDA has granted the company orphan drug designations for CBD to treat AIH and IRI.

Also developing simple and efficient method for rapidly producing natural products, such as psilocybin, using an engineered enzymatic pathway in E. coli; psychedelic-assisted therapies including its tannin-chitosan delivery system to pioneer the clinical research and development of psychedelics in Antigua and Barbuda; proprietary psilocybin oral thin film strip in collaboration with **LTS Lohmann Therapie-Systeme AG**; and medicinal mushroom Ganoderma Lucidum to treat cancer under license agreement with **Puerto Rico Science Technology and Research Trust**.

The company's psilocybin and cannabinoid-based products would be formulated and delivered utilizing the company's novel delivery technology that allows natural and synthetic psychedelics and cannabinoids to be delivered in various ways including topical gels, creams or ointments, oral or transdermal patches, oral dosages and foams.

Predecessor Detail - Name changed from Mercury Capital II Limited, Dec. 30, 2013, pursuant to Qualifying Transaction reverse takeover acquisition of Revive Therapeutics Inc.

Directors - Michael Frank, chr. & CEO, Toronto, Ont.; Joshua Herman, Toronto, Ont.; William J. (Bill) Jackson, Hamilton, Ont.; Andrew Lindzon, Toronto, Ont.; Christian Scovenna, Etobicoke, Ont.

Other Exec. Officers - Carmelo (Carm) Marrelli, CFO

Capital Stock

	Authorized (shs.)	Outstanding (shs.)[1]
Common	unlimited	357,646,841

[1] At Mar. 31, 2023

Major Shareholder - Widely held at Mar. 31, 2023.

Price Range - RVV/CSE

Year	Volume	High	Low	Close
2022	84,349,605	$0.49	$0.10	$0.12
2021	220,907,947	$0.76	$0.32	$0.34
2020	600,610,496	$0.92	$0.04	$0.62
2019	25,645,957	$0.18	$0.03	$0.06
2018	58,837,220	$0.51	$0.09	$0.09

Recent Close: $0.05

Wholly Owned Subsidiaries

Psilocin Pharma Corp., Ont.
Revive Therapeutics Inc., Vaughan, Ont.

Investments

Herman Holdings Limited, Canada.
Red Light Holland Corp., Toronto, Ont. (see separate coverage)

Financial Statistics

Periods ended:	12m June 30/21[A]		12m June 30/20[A]
	$000s	%Chg	$000s
Salaries & benefits	n.a.		158
Research & devel. expense	6,705		455
General & admin expense	3,319		1,851
Stock-based compensation	8,568		1,191
Operating expense	**18,592**	**+409**	**3,655**
Operating income	**(18,592)**	**n.a.**	**(3,655)**
Deprec., depl. & amort.	1		28
Finance income	103		49
Finance costs, gross	85		91
Pre-tax income	**(20,119)**	**n.a.**	**(5,382)**
Net income	**(20,119)**	**n.a.**	**(5,382)**
Cash & equivalent	16,600		1,481
Current assets	16,795		2,158
Long-term investments	250		250
Fixed assets, net	2		3
Intangibles, net	12,500		5,500
Total assets	**29,806**	**+261**	**8,261**
Accts. pay. & accr. liabs	509		302
Current liabilities	598		372
Long-term debt, gross	60		40
Long-term debt, net	60		40
Long-term lease liabilities	268		356
Shareholders' equity	28,807		7,429
Cash from oper. activs	**(8,307)**	**n.a.**	**(2,516)**
Cash from fin. activs	26,244		3,280
Cash from invest. activs	(2,719)		142
Net cash position	**16,600**	**n.m.**	**1,381**
	$		$
Earnings per share*	(0.08)		(0.05)
Cash flow per share*	(0.03)		(0.02)
	shs		shs
No. of shs. o/s*	317,958,751		199,889,511
Avg. no. of shs. o/s*	267,491,089		106,877,828
	%		%
Net profit margin	n.a.		n.a.
Return on equity	(111.04)		(128.30)
Return on assets	(105.26)		(110.88)

* Common
[A] Reported in accordance with IFRS

Latest Results

Periods ended:	3m Sept. 30/21[A]		3m Sept. 30/20[A]
	$000s	%Chg	$000s
Net income	(4,870)	n.a.	(4,523)
	$		$
Earnings per share*	(0.02)		(0.02)

* Common
[A] Reported in accordance with IFRS

Historical Summary
(as originally stated)

Fiscal Year	Oper. Rev. $000s	Net Inc. Bef. Disc. $000s	EPS* $
2021[A]	nil	(20,119)	(0.08)
2020[A]	nil	(5,382)	(0.05)
2019[A]	nil	(1,344)	(0.02)
2018[A]	nil	(1,791)	(0.03)
2017[A]	nil	(1,616)	(0.03)

* Common
[A] Reported in accordance with IFRS

R.52 RevoluGROUP Canada Inc.

Symbol - REVO **Exchange** - TSX-VEN **CUSIP** - 76156R
Head Office - 211-4388 Still Creek Dr, Burnaby, BC, V5C 6C6 **Telephone** - (604) 687-3376 **Toll-free** - (800) 567-8181 **Fax** - (604) 687-3119
Website - www.revolugroup.com
Email - info@revolugroup.com
Investor Relations - Jason Tong (800) 567-8181
Auditors - SHIM & Associates LLP C.A., Vancouver, B.C.
Lawyers - McMillan LLP
Transfer Agents - Computershare Trust Company of Canada Inc., Toronto, Ont.
Profile - (B.C. 1980) Offers remittance and payment systems worldwide, travel marketing, electronic reservations, exclusive travel membership sales, online booking solutions, an invoice factoring platform and a sports betting platform.

Operations are segmented into two divisions: FinTec and Travel.

The **FinTech** division operates RevoluPAY®, which offers a banking licensed proprietary remittance and payment app, and an app-linked Visa® card, powered by blockchain protocols; RevoluCHARGE, a proprietary worldwide phone top-up service which allows anyone to send pay-as-you-go minute, SMS and data credits from 283 operators in 163 countries, to family and friends utilizing RevoluPAY® for payments; RevoluREALTY, a real estate payment platform which would assist property buyers worldwide with instant online payments via RevoluPAY®; RevoluEGAME, which provides worldwide selection and payment of entire mobile/console-based games and in-game play credits exclusively through RevoluPAY®; RevolUTILITY, an online payment service that is used to buy credits, software, E-game credits and gifts cards, and pay utility bills from businesses around the world; RevoluSEND, which provides instant worldwide remittances; RevoluTRANSFER, an online money transfer service that allows customers to send money abroad at low foreign exchange rates in up to 50 different currencies; RevoluEX, a digital currency exchange which allows RevoluPAY® users to convert more than 100 major cryptocurrencies into fiat money for instant deposit into their RevoluPAY® e-wallet; RevoluPOS, a point-of-sale platform linked to RevoluPAY® that would allow anyone to accept digital payments worldwide; RevoluFIN, a web-based factoring platform which enables third party financiers to directly finance outstanding secured receivables while obtaining above market interest returns; RevoluESPORTS, which offers eSports event ticket purchase and event organizer integrated stadium payment systems; RevoluMED, which leverages the RevoluPAY® payment application for healthcare appointment scheduling and insurance and pharmacy payments; and RevoluBet, a legal sports betting platform, which would act as a principal financial conduit through its varied financial licenses.

The **Travel** division operates through wholly owned **Travelucion S.L.** (dba RevoluVIP), which owns a portfolio of Caribbean-focused web assets with 432 websites in up to six languages collectively generating over 30,000,000 page views per year, and manages 182 worldwide travel websites known as the VIP collection, all directing traffic to the main travel booking and e-commerce sites. The VIP collection forms part of wholly owned **RevoluVIP International Inc.**, a members-only travel club that provides discounts to its three levels of membership. The websites cover all facets of over 130 countries including tourist destination visitor tips, cruises, hotels and resorts, golf, spas, restaurants, car rentals, culture, health, commerce and dining. Its online booking system determines the lowest price and best travel options from various travel suppliers which includes bookings for hotels, bed and breakfasts (B&B), car rentals, tours and a variety of other types of bookings.

In January 2023, the company signed a memorandum of understanding for a share equity acquisition by a European financially regulated entity allied to a U.A.E.-based financial consultancy firm.

In July 2022, the company acquired 182 travel websites (VIP collection) from Stephen Marshall for issuance of 2,638,184 common shares valued at $0.195 per share. The company's The RevoluVIP Travel Club operates the VIP collection, which is a group of worldwide domain name properties, most online for over 20 years, featuring 106 countries, 27 specific high-traffic tourist destinations and seven generic websites.

Predecessor Detail - Name changed from CUV Ventures Corp., Nov. 11, 2019.

Directors - Gavin M. McMillan, interim CEO, B.C.; Daniel (Danny) Hernandez Rodriguez, Spain; Bernard Lonis, Spain; Alfredo Manresa Ruiz, Barcelona, Spain

Other Exec. Officers - Jason Tong, CFO; Derek Sobel, corp. sec. & contr.

Capital Stock

	Authorized (shs.)	Outstanding (shs.)[1]
Common	unlimited	193,585,376

[1] At Apr. 28, 2023

Major Shareholder - Stephen (Steve) Marshall held 12.07% interest at Nov. 10, 2022.

Price Range - REVO/TSX-VEN

Year	Volume	High	Low	Close
2022	41,102,043	$0.43	$0.18	$0.27
2021	80,329,056	$0.44	$0.19	$0.25
2020	170,917,867	$0.66	$0.10	$0.37
2019	237,605,777	$0.75	$0.12	$0.15
2018	163,981,677	$0.42	$0.06	$0.27

Recent Close: $0.04

Capital Stock Changes - In February 2022, private placement of 10,939,100 units (1 common share & 1 warrant) at 20¢ per unit was completed. Also during fiscal 2022, 1,050,000 common shares were issued on exercise of options.

Wholly Owned Subsidiaries

RP Payment Services S.L., Barcelona, Spain.
RevoluFIN Inc., Panama.
RevoluGroup USA Inc., Miami, Fla.
RevoluPAY S.L., Barcelona, Spain.
RevoluVIP International Inc., Vancouver, B.C.
Travelucion S.L., Spain.

Financial Statistics

Periods ended:	12m May 31/22[A]		12m May 31/21[A]
	$000s	%Chg	$000s
Operating revenue	**206**	**+48**	**139**
Cost of sales	55		74
General & admin expense	2,063		1,991
Stock-based compensation	388		400
Operating expense	**2,506**	**+2**	**2,465**
Operating income	**(2,300)**	**n.a.**	**(2,326)**
Deprec., depl. & amort.	166		193
Finance costs, gross	92		41
Pre-tax income	**(2,557)**	**n.a.**	**(2,460)**
Net income	**(2,557)**	**n.a.**	**(2,460)**
Cash & equivalent	1,307		1,290
Current assets	2,140		1,864
Fixed assets, net	272		431
Total assets	**2,412**	**+5**	**2,295**
Accts. pay. & accr. liabs	575		418
Current liabilities	681		488
Long-term lease liabilities	53		168
Shareholders' equity	1,678		1,639
Cash from oper. activs	**(2,058)**	**n.a.**	**(1,934)**
Cash from fin. activs	2,194		1,722
Cash from invest. activs	(20)		45
Net cash position	**1,307**	**+1**	**1,290**
Capital expenditures	(20)		(55)
	$		$
Earnings per share*	(0.02)		(0.02)
Cash flow per share*	(0.01)		(0.01)
	shs		shs
No. of shs. o/s*	186,969,692		174,980,592
Avg. no. of shs. o/s*	178,503,025		169,473,304
	%		%
Net profit margin	n.m.		n.m.
Return on equity	(154.18)		(140.61)
Return on assets	(104.74)		(109.01)

* Common
[A] Reported in accordance with IFRS

Latest Results

Periods ended:	3m Aug. 31/22[A]		3m Aug. 31/21[A]
	$000s	%Chg	$000s
Operating revenue	91	+406	18
Net income	(440)	n.a.	(516)
	$		$
Earnings per share*	(0.00)		(0.00)

* Common
[A] Reported in accordance with IFRS

Historical Summary
(as originally stated)

Fiscal Year	Oper. Rev. $000s	Net Inc. Bef. Disc. $000s	EPS* $
2022[A]	206	(2,557)	(0.02)
2021[A]	139	(2,460)	(0.02)
2020[A]	1,181	(2,826)	(0.02)
2019[A]	725	(4,222)	(0.03)
2018[A]	1,618	(3,104)	(0.03)

* Common
[A] Reported in accordance with IFRS

R.53 ReVolve Renewable Power Corp.

Symbol - REVV **Exchange** - TSX-VEN **CUSIP** - 76157B
Head Office - Bushfield House 57, Bushfield Sq, Philipsburgh Ave, Dublin, Ireland
Website - revolve-renewablepower.com
Email - steve@revolve-renewablepower.com
Investor Relations - Stephen Dalton (778) 885-5550
Auditors - Davidson & Company LLP C.A., Vancouver, B.C.
Lawyers - DLA Piper (Canada) LLP, Vancouver, B.C.
Transfer Agents - Computershare Trust Company, Inc.
Employees - 10 at Mar. 14, 2022
Profile - (B.C. 2018; orig. Alta., 1989) Develops renewable electricity generation projects in North America.

Operations are organized into two segments: Utility Scale and Distributed Generation assets.

The **Utility Scale** assets consist of active project development portfolio consisting of twelve individual projects, totaling 3.6 GW, across both Mexico and that U.S. as at Nov. 10, 2022. Its four material projects are the 103.4-MW El 24 wind project in Tamaulipas, Mexico; the 400-MW Presa Nueva wind project in Nuevo Leon, Mexico; the 1,000-MW Bouse solar and storage project in La Paz cty., Ariz.; and the 225-MW Lordsburg solar and storage project in Hidalgo cty., N.M. Also has a pipeline of greenfield project development opportunities totaling 1.1 GW of potential new project capacity across wind, solar and battery storage.

The **Distributed Generation** assets consist of the distributed generation market and sub 20 MW renewable energy projects. This segment targets both "behind the meter" and grid-connected wind, rooftop solar, ground-mounted solar, battery storage and related energy efficiency projects both in the U.S. and Mexico. As at Nov. 10, 2022, the segment has an operating portfolio of 2.85 MW with an additional 6.2 MW under construction phase.

In May 2022, the company entered into an agreement with **RE Royalties Ltd.** for a $1,600,000 24-month 10% secured loan in exchange for a 1% and 5% gross revenue royalty on six operational solar projects of the company in Mexico. Subsequently in September 2022, RE Royalties agreed to finance the purchase of three battery storage development projects in Mexico with a $1,860,000 two-year 12% secured loan in exchange for a 5% gross revenue royalty on the projects.

In August 2022, the company acquired **Centrica Business Solutions Mexico S.A. de C.V.** (CBS Mexico) for US$1,424,428. CBS Mexico owns and operates six distributed generation projects, totaling 2.85 MW, with a seventh project under development, in Mexico.

During fiscal 2022, the company sold wholly owned **Pacific Metals Canada Philippines Inc.**, which held its Malitao and Dilong copper-gold prospects in the Philippines, to Peter Draper for nominal consideration of $1.00. In addition, wholly owned **Philippine Metals (Guernsey) Ltd.** and **Volcano Metals (Guernsey) Ltd.** were released to Peter Draper, who acquired Pacific Metals. Also during fiscal 2022, wholly owned **Philippine Metals Corp.** was dissolved.

Recent Merger and Acquisition Activity

Status: completed **Revised:** Mar. 7, 2022

UPDATE: The transaction was completed. Shares of the resulting issuer commenced trading on TSX Venture Exchange on Mar. 17, 2022. PREVIOUS: Philippine Metals Inc. (PMI) entered into a letter of intent for the reverse takeover acquisition of private Dublin, Ireland-based ReVolve Renewable Power Limited for issuance of 35,100,000 post-consolidated common shares of PMI (following a 1-for-4 shares consolidation). ReVolve has a portfolio of renewable energy generation projects in North America with a focus on solar, wind and battery storage technologies. The portfolio consists of 2.23 GW of projects under development and 1.16 GW of greenfield opportunities. In addition, ReVolve would complete a private placement of up to 6,134,969 units (1 common share & 1 warrant) at €0.815 per unit, each of which would be exchanged into 2.5 post-consolidated shares of PMI. PMI would also complete a separate financing of Cdn$1,500,000 of subscription receipts. PMI plans to dispose of its mineral interests in the Philippines. Sept. 7, 2021 - ReVolve has completed private placement of 3,837,219 units (1 common share & 1 warrant) at €0.815 per unit, which would be exchanged into further 9,593,048 post-consolidated units of PMI (1 common share & 1 warrant). Feb. 17, 2022 - Conditional TSX Venture Exchange approval was received.

Predecessor Detail - Name changed from Philippine Metals Inc., Mar. 7, 2022, pursuant to the reverse takeover acquisition of ReVolve Renewable Power Limited.; basis 1 new for 4 old shs.

Directors - Stephen (Steve) Dalton, co-founder & CEO, Dublin, Ireland; Dr. Roger Norwich, chr., United Kingdom; Omar Bojorquez, pres., Gto., Mexico; Jonathan Clare, Surrey, United Kingdom; Craig T. Lindsay, Vancouver, B.C.; Finn Lyden, Dublin, Ireland; JP Maguire, Dublin, Ireland; Joseph O'Farrell, Dublin, Ireland

Other Exec. Officers - Nicholas (Nick) Furber, CFO; Sunita Prasad, v-p, corp. devel. & IR; Janet Bates, corp. sec.

Capital Stock

	Authorized (shs.)	Outstanding (shs.)[1]
Preferred	unlimited	nil
Common	unlimited	54,905,565

[1] At Nov. 29, 2022

Major Shareholder - Joseph O'Farrell held 14.75% interest and Dr. Roger Norwich held 13.95% interest at Mar. 8, 2022.

Price Range - REVV/TSX-VEN

Year	Volume	High	Low	Close
2022............	2,228,263	$0.60	$0.20	$0.52
2021............	677,541	$0.40	$0.20	$0.40
2020............	345,304	$0.46	$0.08	$0.22
2019............	396,408	$0.54	$0.14	$0.32
2018............	565,407	$0.60	$0.16	$0.16

Consolidation: 1-for-4 cons. in Mar. 2022

Recent Close: $0.32

Capital Stock Changes - On Mar. 7, 2022, common shares were consolidated on a 1-for-4 basis (effective on the TSX Venture Exchange on Mar. 17, 2022) and 49,873,816 post-consolidated common shares were issued pursuant to the reverse takeover acquisition of ReVolve Renewable Power Limited.

Wholly Owned Subsidiaries

ReVolve Renewable Power Limited, Dublin, Ireland.
- 10% int. in **EPM Eólica 24 S.A. de C.V.**, Mexico.
- 10% int. in **EPM Solar, S.A. de C.V.**, Mexico. Inactive.
- 98% int. in **Emerald Power Mexico S.A. de C.V.**, Mexico.
- 10% int. in **Eólica El Mentillo S.A. de C.V.**, Mexico.
- 10% int. in **Eólica La Florida S.A. de C.V.**, Mexico.
- 10% int. in **Eólicse, S.A.P.I. de C.V.**, Mexico. Inactive.
- 100% int. in **MRE Mamulique Solar Limited**, Ireland. Inactive.
  - 90% int. in **EPM Solar, S.A. de C.V.**, Mexico. Inactive.
- 90% int. in **MRE US Wind & Solar Inc.**, Wyo.
  - 100% int. in **ReVolve Afton Solar LLC**, N.M.
  - 100% int. in **ReVolve Lordsburg Solar LLC**, N.M.
  - 100% int. in **ReVolve Parker Solar AZ LLC**, Ariz.
  - 100% int. in **ReVolve Renewable Power AZ LLC**, Ariz.
  - 100% int. in **ReVolve Vernal BESS LLC**, Utah
- 100% int. in **MSE Eólicse Wind Limited**, Ireland. Inactive.
  - 2% int. in **Emerald Power Mexico S.A. de C.V.**, Mexico.
  - 90% int. in **Eólicse, S.A.P.I. de C.V.**, Mexico.
- 10% int. in **Presa Nueva Eólica S.A. de C.V.**, Mexico.
- 100% int. in **ReVolve El Mentillo Wind DAC**, Ireland.
  - 90% int. in **Eólica El Mentillo S.A. de C.V.**, Mexico.
- 100% int. in **ReVolve El 24 Wind DAC**, Ireland.
  - 90% int. in **EPM Eólica 24 S.A. de C.V.**, Mexico.
- 100% int. in **ReVolve Florida Wind DAC**, Ireland.
  - 90% int. in **Eólica La Florida S.A. de C.V.**, Mexico.
- 100% int. in **ReVolve Presa Nueva Wind DAC**, Ireland.
  - 90% int. in **Presa Nueva Eólica S.A. de C.V.**, Mexico.

ReVolve Renewable Power Canada Inc., Canada.
- 99.99% int. in **Centrica Business Solutions Mexico, S.A. de C.V.**, Mexico.

Investments

0.01% int. in **Centrica Business Solutions Mexico, S.A. de C.V.**, Mexico.

Financial Statistics

Periods ended:	12m June 30/22[A1]		12m June 30/21[¤A]
	US$000s	%Chg	US$000s
Research & devel. expense.............	1,224		439
General & admin expense................	1,553		710
Stock-based compensation............	699		nil
Operating expense.......................	**3,476**	**+203**	**1,149**
Operating income........................	**(3,476)**	**n.a.**	**(1,149)**
Write-downs/write-offs...................	nil		(6)
Pre-tax income.............................	**(6,456)**	**n.a.**	**308**
Net income.....................................	**(6,456)**	**n.a.**	**308**
Net inc. for equity hldrs................	**(6,340)**	**n.a.**	**335**
Net inc. for non-cont. int..............	**(116)**	**n.a.**	**(26)**
Cash & equivalent...........................	2,567		127
Accounts receivable.......................	nil		9
Current assets................................	4,167		388
Fixed assets, net.............................	100		6
Total assets...................................	**4,565**	**+588**	**664**
Bank indebtedness.........................	1,242		nil
Accts. pay. & accr. liabs.................	398		103
Current liabilities............................	1,640		103
Shareholders' equity.......................	3,082		587
Cash from oper. activs..................	**(2,929)**	**n.a.**	**(58)**
Cash from fin. activs.......................	4,922		nil
Cash from invest. activs..................	669		(250)
Net cash position..........................	**2,547**	**n.m.**	**127**
Capital expenditures.......................	(100)		nil
	US$		US$
Earnings per share*........................	(0.21)		n.a.
Cash flow per share*......................	(0.10)		n.a.
	shs		shs
No. of shs. o/s*...............................	54,905,565		n.a.
Avg. no. of shs. o/s*........................	28,981,477		n.a.
	%		%
Net profit margin.............................	n.a.		n.a.
Return on equity.............................	(345.60)		n.m.
Return on assets.............................	(246.93)		77.51

* Common
¤ Restated
[A] Reported in accordance with IFRS
[1] Results reflect the Mar. 7, 2022, reverse takeover acquisition of ReVolve Renewable Power Limited.

Latest Results

Periods ended:	3m Sept. 30/22[A]		3m Sept. 30/21[¤A]
	US$000s	%Chg	US$000s
Operating revenue...........................	25	n.a.	nil
Net income.....................................	(573)	n.a.	(620)
Net inc. for equity hldrs..................	(558)	n.a.	(582)
Net inc. for non-cont. int.................	(15)		(38)
	US$		US$
Earnings per share*........................	(0.01)		(0.04)

* Common
¤ Restated
[A] Reported in accordance with IFRS

Historical Summary
(as originally stated)

Fiscal Year	Oper. Rev.	Net Inc. Bef. Disc.	EPS*
	US$000s	US$000s	US$
2022[A1].................	nil	(6,456)	(0.21)
	$000s	$000s	$
2021[A2].................	nil	(18)	(0.00)
2020[A]...................	nil	(144)	(0.04)
2019[A]...................	nil	(209)	(0.08)
2018[A]...................	nil	(79)	(0.04)

* Common
[A] Reported in accordance with IFRS
[1] Results reflect the Mar. 7, 2022, reverse takeover acquisition of ReVolve Renewable Power Limited.
[2] Results for fiscal 2021 and prior fiscal years pertain to Philippine Metals Inc.
Note: Adjusted throughout for 1-for-4 cons. in Mar. 2022

R.54 Richards Packaging Income Fund

Symbol - RPI.UN **Exchange** - TSX **CUSIP** - 763102
Head Office - 6095 Ordan Dr, Mississauga, ON, L5T 2M7 **Telephone** - (905) 670-7760 **Toll-free** - (800) 361-6453 **Fax** - (905) 670-1960
Website - www.richardspackaging.com
Email - edigennaro@richardspackaging.com
Investor Relations - Enzio Di Gennaro (905) 670-7760 ext. 10388
Auditors - PricewaterhouseCoopers LLP C.A., Toronto, Ont.
Lawyers - McMillan LLP, Toronto, Ont.
Transfer Agents - TSX Trust Company, Toronto, Ont.
FP500 Revenue Ranking - 492
Employees - 652 at Dec. 31, 2022

Profile - (Ont. 2004) Designs, manufactures and distributes packaging solutions in glass and plastic containers and closures to small and medium-sized North American businesses.

Provides more than 8,000 types of packaging containers and related components sourced from more than 900 suppliers and its own in-house plastics manufacturing facilities. Products are sold to more than 17,000 small and medium-sized retailers and manufacturers of food and beverage, cosmetics, specialty chemical, pharmaceutical, healthcare and other products. Complementary services include comprehensive packaging design and development services, sourcing capabilities and logistics management.

Operations are carried out through 20 facilities (1,063,600-sq.-ft. at Dec. 31, 2022) throughout North America, all of which are leased. The locations in Langley, B.C., Cambridge, Ont., and Tacoma, Wash., are manufacturing facilities, with 39 blow moulding machines which produce plastic containers using polyvinyl chloride (PVC), high-density polyethylene (HDPE) and polyethylene terephthalate (PET). During 2022, 6% of sales were supplied by the manufacturing facilities.

Products are marketed under the Dispill™ trademark in Canada and McKernan™ trademark in the U.S. In addition, the fund holds the patent for the Dispill™ pill dispensing products.

Trustees - Donald A. (Don) Wright, chr., Toronto, Ont.; Susan Allen, Mississauga, Ont.; Darlene Dasent, Ajax, Ont.; Gerry Glynn, Grand Cayman, Cayman Islands; Rami E. Younes, Toronto, Ont.

Oper. Subsid./Mgt. Co. Officers - David L. Prupas, pres. & COO; Enzio Di Gennaro, CFO

Capital Stock

	Authorized (shs.)	Outstanding (shs.)[1]
Fund Unit	unlimited	10,955,007
Special Voting Unit	n.a.	463,006[2]
Exchangeable	n.a.	463,006[2 3]

[1] At Mar. 23, 2023
[2] Classified as debt.
[3] Shares of wholly owned Richards Packaging Holdings Inc. or Richards Packaging Holdings (US) Inc.

Fund Unit - Each unit represents an equal undivided beneficial interest in any distributions of the fund and in the net assets of the fund. Transferable and not subject to future calls or assessments. One vote per fund unit.

Special Voting Unit - Issued to holders of wholly owned Richards Packaging Holdings Inc. and Richards Packaging Holdings (US) Inc.'s exchangeable shares. Each special voting unit entitles the holder to a number of votes at unitholder meetings equal to the number of fund units into which the exchangeable shares are exchangeable. The exchangeable shares are exchangeable into fund units on a 1-for-1 basis and are entitled to receive distributions equal to those provided to fund units. The exchangeable shares have been classified as minority interest. The number of special voting units outstanding will be equal to the number of exchangeable shares outstanding.

Exchangeable - Shares of wholly owned Richards Packaging Holdings Inc. or Richards Packaging Holdings (US) Inc. Exchangeable at the holder's option at any time into fund units on a 1-for-1 basis. Redeemable on the fifth anniversary of their issue date, or prior to that date in limited circumstances. The exchangeable shares issued as consideration for the McKernan acquisition are retractable on a limited basis by the holder in increments of up to US$2,000,000 at the end of each issue anniversary, however the fund has the option to settle the redemption in cash. Redeemable by the company on the fifth anniversary of their issue date, or earlier under certain circumstances. One vote per exchangeable share.

Major Shareholder - Gerry Glynn held 19.8% interest and Mawer Investment Management Limited held 11.8% interest at Mar. 23, 2023.

Price Range - RPI.UN/TSX

Year	Volume	High	Low	Close
2022	1,880,646	$61.80	$41.46	$43.40
2021	1,616,788	$79.00	$53.01	$61.76
2020	2,450,656	$86.28	$27.51	$76.85
2019	983,275	$47.68	$33.50	$45.59
2018	1,484,879	$40.88	$30.00	$35.00

Recent Close: $30.85

Capital Stock Changes - There were no changes to capital stock during 2022.

Dividends

RPI.UN unit Ra $1.32 pa M est. Apr. 14, 2017
$0.38† Mar. 24/23 $0.69◆ Mar. 18/22
Paid in 2023: $0.99 + $0.38† 2022: $1.32 + $0.69◆ 2021: $1.32

† Extra ◆ Special

Wholly Owned Subsidiaries

Richards Packaging Holdings Inc., Mississauga, Ont.
- 100% int. in **Richards Packaging Holdings 3 Inc.**, Ont.
- 100% int. in **Richards Packaging Inc.**, Mississauga, Ont.
  - 100% int. in **Clarion Medical Technologies Inc.**, Cambridge, Ont.
    - 100% int. in **Accutech Medical Technologies Inc.**, Ont.
    - 100% int. in **Luvo Medical Technologies Inc.**, Ont.
  - 100% int. in **Healthmark Services Ltd.**, Saint-Laurent, Qué.
  - 50% int. in **Vision Plastics Inc.**, Langley, B.C.

Richards Packaging Holdings 2 Inc., Ont.
- 100% int. in **Richards Packaging Holdings (US) Inc.**, Del.
  - 100% int. in **Richards Packaging, Inc.**, Wash.
    - 100% int. in **The E.J. McKernan Company**, Ill.
      - 90% int. in **McKernan Packaging - Richards de Mexico, S.A. de C.V.**, Mexico.
    - 10% int. in **McKernan Packaging - Richards de Mexico, S.A. de C.V.**, Mexico.

Financial Statistics

Periods ended:	12m Dec. 31/22[A]		12m Dec. 31/21[A]
	$000s	%Chg	$000s
Operating revenue	**446,896**	**-1**	**451,438**
Cost of sales	351,306		350,087
General & admin expense	21,737		21,471
Operating expense	**373,043**	**0**	**371,558**
Operating income	**73,853**	**-8**	**79,880**
Deprec., depl. & amort.	12,387		12,420
Finance costs, gross	7,068		5,603
Investment income	126		112
Pre-tax income	**59,355**	**+195**	**20,104**
Income taxes	14,183		18,036
Net income	**45,172**	**n.m.**	**2,068**
Cash & equivalent	5,445		8,420
Inventories	97,770		100,724
Accounts receivable	57,334		50,259
Current assets	170,526		172,187
Long-term investments	725		688
Fixed assets, net	4,970		5,993
Right-of-use assets	32,733		38,056
Intangibles, net	140,937		139,974
Total assets	**349,891**	**-2**	**356,898**
Accts. pay. & accr. liabs	56,615		75,480
Current liabilities	87,847		161,821
Long-term debt, gross	84,738		51,110
Long-term debt, net	64,817		22,688
Long-term lease liabilities	29,564		34,505
Shareholders' equity	161,500		130,833
Cash from oper. activs	**43,152**	**-24**	**56,870**
Cash from fin. activs	4,754		(44,947)
Cash from invest. activs	(51,051)		(11,489)
Net cash position	**5,445**	**-35**	**8,420**
Capital expenditures	(856)		(1,807)
	$		$
Earnings per share*	4.12		0.19
Cash flow per share*	3.94		5.09
Cash divd. per share*	1.32		1.32
Extra divd. - cash*	0.69		...
Total divd. per share*	**2.01**		**1.32**
	shs		shs
No. of shs. o/s*	10,995,007		10,955,007
Avg. no. of shs. o/s*	10,955,007		11,165,774
	%		%
Net profit margin	10.11		0.46
Return on equity	30.90		1.42
Return on assets	14.30		0.75
Foreign sales percent	38		44
No. of employees (FTEs)	652		695

* Fund unit
[A] Reported in accordance with IFRS

Historical Summary
(as originally stated)

Fiscal Year	Oper. Rev.	Net Inc. Bef. Disc.	EPS*
	$000s	$000s	$
2022[A]	446,896	45,172	4.12
2021[A]	451,438	2,068	0.19
2020[A]	489,235	50,143	4.47
2019[A]	334,148	21,734	1.97
2018[A]	318,058	24,120	2.21

* Fund unit
[A] Reported in accordance with IFRS

R.55 Richco Investors Inc.

Symbol - RII.H **Exchange** - TSX-VEN **CUSIP** - 76329P
Head Office - 3882 Lawrence Pl, North Vancouver, BC, V7K 2X2 **Telephone** - (604) 389-5861 **Fax** - (604) 408-8515
Email - robertgsmiley@hotmail.com
Investor Relations - Robert G. Smiley (604) 689-4407
Auditors - Crowe MacKay LLP C.A., Vancouver, B.C.
Transfer Agents - Computershare Trust Company of Canada Inc., Vancouver, B.C.

Profile - (Ont. 1994; orig. B.C., 1980) Provides financial, management and other administrative services to early development stage businesses.

Creates or helps businesses fulfill their potential through strategic planning, capital infusion and corporate restructuring. May also invest extensively in emerging growth companies which are in the development stage or in companies investing in such.

Predecessor Detail - Name changed from Consolidated Hale Resources Ltd., Jan. 21, 1994.

Directors - Christopher (Chris) Tsakok, pres., CEO & CFO, Vancouver, B.C.; Robert G. Smiley, West Vancouver, B.C.; Sandra Tsakok, Vancouver, B.C.

Capital Stock

	Authorized (shs.)	Outstanding (shs.)[1]
Preference	unlimited	nil
Multiple Voting	unlimited	5,310,191
Subordinate Voting	unlimited	23,863,463

[1] At May 27, 2022

Multiple Voting - Convertible at any time into subordinate voting shares on a share-for-share basis. 100 votes per share.

Subordinate Voting - One vote per share.

Major Shareholder - Raoul N. Tsakok held 74.67% interest at Mar. 8, 2022.

Price Range - RII.H/TSX-VEN

Year	Volume	High	Low	Close
2020	316,505	$0.02	$0.01	$0.02
2018	14,000	$0.04	$0.02	$0.04

Investments

Drucker, Inc.
IQ Webquest Inc.
UNIREX Corporation, Huntsville, Ala.

Financial Statistics

Periods ended:	12m Dec. 31/21[A]		12m Dec. 31/20[A]
	$000s	%Chg	$000s
Total revenue	**13**	**0**	**13**
General & admin. expense	29		33
Operating expense	**29**	**-12**	**33**
Operating income	**(16)**	**n.a.**	**(20)**
Finance costs, gross	3		11
Pre-tax income	**(353)**	**n.a.**	**(31)**
Net income	**(353)**	**n.a.**	**(31)**
Cash & equivalent	68		97
Accounts receivable	nil		323
Current assets	70		424
Total assets	**70**	**-83**	**424**
Accts. pay. & accr. liabs	44		45
Current liabilities	44		45
Shareholders' equity	(213)		140
Cash from oper. activs	**(29)**	**n.a.**	**(74)**
Cash from fin. activs	nil		89
Net cash position	**68**	**-30**	**97**
	$		$
Earnings per share*	(0.01)		(0.00)
Cash flow per share*	(0.00)		(0.00)
	shs		shs
No. of shs. o/s*	23,863,463		23,863,463
Avg. no. of shs. o/s*	23,863,463		21,878,444
	%		%
Net profit margin	n.m.		(238.46)
Return on equity	n.m.		n.m.
Return on assets	(141.70)		(5.59)

* M.V. & S.V.
[A] Reported in accordance with IFRS

Latest Results

Periods ended:	3m Mar. 31/22[A]		3m Mar. 31/21[A]
	$000s	%Chg	$000s
Total revenue	nil	n.a.	3
Net income	(9)	n.a.	(9)
	$		$
Earnings per share*	(0.00)		(0.00)

* M.V. & S.V.
[A] Reported in accordance with IFRS

Historical Summary
(as originally stated)

Fiscal Year	Total Rev.	Net Inc. Bef. Disc.	EPS*
	$000s	$000s	$
2021[A]	13	(353)	(0.01)
2020[A]	13	(31)	(0.00)
2019[A]	2	(28)	(0.00)
2018[A]	1	(26)	(0.00)
2017[A]	1	(26)	(0.00)

* M.V. & S.V.
[A] Reported in accordance with IFRS

R.56 Richelieu Hardware Ltd.*

Symbol - RCH **Exchange** - TSX **CUSIP** - 76329W
Head Office - 200-7900 boul Henri-Bourassa O, Saint-Laurent, QC, H4S 1V4 **Telephone** - (514) 336-4144 **Toll-free** - (800) 361-6000 **Fax** - (514) 336-4002
Website - www.richelieu.com
Email - aauclair@richelieu.com
Investor Relations - Antoine Auclair (514) 336-4144
Auditors - Ernst & Young LLP C.A., Montréal, Qué.
Lawyers - Osler, Hoskin & Harcourt LLP
Transfer Agents - Computershare Trust Company of Canada Inc., Montréal, Qué.
FP500 Revenue Ranking - 235
Employees - 2,800 at Nov. 30, 2022

Profile - (Que. 1968) Distributes, imports and manufactures specialty hardware and related products for kitchen and bathroom cabinet, storage and closet, home furnishing and office furniture, door and window manufacturers, residential and commercial woodworking industry, and hardware retailers including improvement superstores.

Product selection consists of more than 130,000 items. Main product categories include furniture, glass and building decorative and functional hardware, lighting systems, finishing and decorative products, ergonomic workstation components, kitchen and closet storage solutions, sliding door systems, decorative and functional panels, high-pressure laminates, railing and baluster, and floor protection products as well as accessories for power tools.

Manufacturing operations are carried out through wholly owned **Les Industries Cedan Inc.** in Longueuil, Que., and subsidiary **Menuiserie des Pins Ltée** in Notre-Dame-des-Pins, Que., which manufacture a variety of veneer sheets and edge banding products and a selection of decorative mouldings and components for the window and door industry; and wholly owned **Unigrav Inc.** and **Usimm Inc.** in Drummondville and Montreal Que., respectively, which offers digitization services including computer numerical control (CNC) cutting, 3D scanning and printing for the architectural and industrial markets. Products are manufactured according to specifications and those of its customers.

The company serves more than 110,000 customers from 112 distribution centres in Canada (50) and the U.S. (62), the company's website and the three manufacturing plants in Quebec.

In April 2023, the company acquired the principal net assets of specialized hardware distributors **Maverick Hardware Inc.**, which operates a distribution centre in Eugene, Ore., and **Westlund Distributing Inc.**, which operates a distribution centre in Monticello, Minn.

On Sept. 2, 2022, the company acquired **Quincaillerie Deno**, a distributor of specialized hardware products operating a distribution centre in Anjou, Que.

Recent Merger and Acquisition Activity

Status: completed **Announced:** Jan. 19, 2023
Richelieu Hardware Ltd. acquired four companies including Quincaillerie Rabel Inc., which distributes specialty hardware products and operates a distribution centre in Terrebonne, Que.; Trans-World Distributing Ltd., which distributes industrial fasteners and operates a distribution centre in Dartmouth, N.S.; Unigrav Inc. and Usimm Inc., which supplies custom products, including digitization services such as computer numerical control (CNC) cutting, 3D scanning and printing, in Drummondville and Montreal, Que., respectively. Total consideration was $19,500,000.

Directors - Sylvie Vachon, chr., Longueuil, Qué.; Richard Lord, pres. & CEO, Saint-Laurent, Qué.; Lucie Chabot, Montréal, Qué.; Robert Courteau, Montréal, Qué.; Marie Lemay, Qué.; Luc Martin, Laval, Qué.; Pierre Pomerleau, Montréal, Qué.; Marc Poulin, Outremont, Qué.

Other Exec. Officers - Antoine Auclair, v-p & CFO; Alain Charron, v-p, supply chain & logistics; Jeff Crews, v-p, bus. devel., retailers market, Canada; Denis Gagnon, v-p, IT; Guy Grenier, v-p, sales & mktg., ind.; Larry Lucyshyn, v-p, sales, U.S. retailers; Marjolaine Plante, v-p, HR; Craig Ratchford, v-p & gen. mgr., U.S.; Eric Daignault, gen. mgr., div.; Marion Kloibhofer, gen. mgr., central Canada div.; John G. Statton, gen. mgr., western Canada & western U.S.; Yannick Godeau, mgr., legal affairs & corp. sec.

Capital Stock

	Authorized (shs.)	Outstanding (shs.)[1]
Preferred	unlimited	nil
Common	unlimited	55,879,385

[1] At May 31, 2023

Options - At Nov. 30, 2022, options were outstanding to purchase 1,680,000 common shares at exercise prices ranging from $12.71 to $43.57 per share with a weighted average remaining life of 6.16 years.

Normal Course Issuer Bid - The company plans to make normal course purchases of up to 1,500,000 common shares representing 2.7% of the total outstanding. The bid commenced on Dec. 30, 2022, and expires on Dec. 29, 2023.

Major Shareholder - Widely held at Jan. 19, 2023.

Price Range - RCH/TSX

Year	Volume	High	Low	Close
2022	29,546,018	$51.52	$32.35	$36.21
2021	21,979,519	$46.55	$32.60	$43.63
2020	28,478,733	$41.25	$20.51	$33.04
2019	22,458,464	$28.25	$20.03	$27.13
2018	24,253,134	$34.65	$20.98	$22.69

Recent Close: $41.96

Capital Stock Changes - During fiscal 2022, 271,000 common shares were issued on exercise of options and 327,329 common shares were repurchased and cancelled under a Normal Course Issuer Bid.

Dividends

RCH com Ra $0.60 pa Q est. Feb. 16, 2023[1]
Prev. Rate: $0.52 est. Feb. 17, 2022
Prev. Rate: $0.28 est. Aug. 5, 2021
$0.0667◆ Feb. 18/21
Paid in 2023: $0.45 2022: $0.52 2021: $0.28 + $0.0667◆

[1] Quarterly divd normally payable in May/20 has been omitted.
◆ Special

Long-Term Debt - At Nov. 30, 2022, outstanding long-term debt totaled $6,067,000 ($5,208,000 current) and consisted entirely of a non-interest bearing business acquisition considerations payable.

Wholly Owned Subsidiaries

Distributions 20-20 Inc., Québec, Qué.
Les Industries Cedan Inc., Longueuil, Qué.
Quincaillerie Rabel Inc., Terrebonne, Qué.
Richelieu America Ltd., Del.
Richelieu Finances Ltd., Montréal, Qué.
- 100% int. in **Richelieu Hardware Canada Ltd.**, Mississauga, Ont.
  - 100% int. in **Euro Ornamental Forgings Inc.**, Ont.
  - 75% int. in **Inter-Co Division 10 Inc.**, Canada.

Trans-World Distributing Ltd., Dartmouth, N.S.
Unigrav Inc., Drummondville, Qué.
Usimm Inc., Montréal, Qué.

Subsidiaries

85% int. in **Menuiserie des Pins Ltée**, Qué.
85% int. in **Provincial Woodproducts Inc.**, N.S.

Financial Statistics

Periods ended:	12m Nov. 30/22[A]		12m Nov. 30/21[A]
	$000s	%Chg	$000s
Operating revenue	**1,802,787**	**+25**	**1,440,416**
Operating expense	**1,515,345**	**+26**	**1,206,018**
Operating income	**287,442**	**+23**	**234,398**
Deprec., depl. & amort.	48,646		36,957
Finance costs, net	7,144		2,700
Pre-tax income	**231,652**	**+19**	**194,741**
Income taxes	61,703		52,410
Net income	**169,949**	**+19**	**142,331**
Net inc. for equity hldrs	**168,390**	**+19**	**141,764**
Net inc. for non-cont. int	**1,559**	**+175**	**567**
Cash & equivalent	21,220		58,707
Inventories	660,242		395,464
Accounts receivable	222,238		199,585
Current assets	910,771		659,179
Fixed assets, net	54,832		46,239
Right-of-use assets	116,204		87,013
Intangibles, net	194,060		164,686
Total assets	**1,283,865**	**+33**	**964,180**
Bank indebtedness	133,208		nil
Accts. pay. & accr. liabs	169,913		155,009
Current liabilities	348,223		202,803
Long-term debt, gross	6,067		6,439
Long-term debt, net	859		1,100
Long-term lease liabilities	95,705		71,880
Shareholders' equity	817,157		666,442
Non-controlling interest	2,665		2,495
Cash from oper. activs	**(36,169)**	**n.a.**	**104,406**
Cash from fin. activs	(66,641)		(53,691)
Cash from invest. activs	(66,833)		(66,490)
Net cash position	**(111,988)**	**n.a.**	**58,707**
Capital expenditures	(22,578)		(17,054)
	$		$
Earnings per share*	3.01		2.54
Cash flow per share*	(0.65)		1.87
Cash divd. per share*	0.52		0.28
Extra divd. - cash*	nil		0.07
Total divd. per share*	**0.52**		**0.35**
	shs		shs
No. of shs. o/s*	55,784,790		55,841,119
Avg. no. of shs. o/s*	55,925,000		55,896,000
	%		%
Net profit margin	9.43		9.88
Return on equity	22.70		23.29
Return on assets	15.12		16.40
Foreign sales percent	40		34
No. of employees (FTEs)	2,800		2,500

* Common
[A] Reported in accordance with IFRS

Latest Results

Periods ended:	6m May 31/23[A]		6m May 31/22[A]
	$000s	%Chg	$000s
Operating revenue	875,112	0	872,401
Net income	53,776	-31	77,510
Net inc. for equity hldrs	53,104	-31	77,082
Net inc. for non-cont. int	672		428
	$		$
Earnings per share*	0.95		1.38

* Common
[A] Reported in accordance with IFRS

Historical Summary
(as originally stated)

Fiscal Year	Oper. Rev.	Net Inc. Bef. Disc.	EPS*
	$000s	$000s	$
2022[A]	1,802,787	169,949	3.01
2021[A]	1,440,416	142,331	2.54
2020[A]	1,127,840	85,611	1.51
2019[A]	1,041,647	67,733	1.19
2018[A]	1,004,400	67,964	1.18

* Common
[A] Reported in accordance with IFRS

R.57 Ridgewood Canadian Investment Grade Bond Fund

Symbol - RIB.UN **Exchange** - TSX **CUSIP** - 76622W
Head Office - 1020-55 University Ave, Toronto, ON, M5J 2H7
Telephone - (416) 842-0227 **Toll-free** - (888) 789-8957 **Fax** - (416) 479-2750
Website - www.ridgewoodcapital.ca
Email - jsimpson@ridgewoodcapital.ca
Investor Relations - John H. Simpson (888) 789-8957
Auditors - Deloitte LLP C.A., Toronto, Ont.
Lawyers - Fasken Martineau DuMoulin LLP, Toronto, Ont.
Transfer Agents - TSX Trust Company, Toronto, Ont.
Trustees - Ridgewood Capital Asset Management Inc., Toronto, Ont.
Managers - Ridgewood Capital Asset Management Inc., Toronto, Ont.
Portfolio Advisors - Ridgewood Capital Asset Management Inc., Toronto, Ont.

Profile - (Ont. 2009) Invests primarily in Canadian investment grade bonds.

The investment portfolio consists primarily of debt securities and term loans that are generally rated at or above BBB- from Standard & Poor's, or Baa3 or higher from **Moody's Investor Services Inc.**, or a similar rating from different qualified rating agencies. The fund may also invest up to 35% of the portfolio in non-Canadian investment grade bonds.

Top 10 holdings at Mar. 31, 2023 (as a percentage of net asset value):

Issuer, coupon rate, maturity	Percentage
Bank of Canada, 1.75%, 2053	11.9%
Bell Canada, 5.15%, 2053	6.0%
REALT 2019-HBC, 4.352%, 2024	5.9%
Manulife Financial Corp., 7.117%, 2027	5.4%
Pembina Pipeline Corp, 4.80%, 2030	4.9%
Cameco Corp., 5.09%, 2042	4.7%
Transalta Corp., 7.30%, 2029	4.5%
Transalta Corp., 6.90%, 2030	4.0%
Great-West Lifeco Inc., 3.60%, 2026	4.0%
Manulife Financial Corp., 4.10%, 2027	4.0%

Oper. Subsid./Mgt. Co. Directors - John H. Simpson, chr., man. dir., CEO, chief compliance officer & corp. sec., Creemore, Ont.; Paul W. Meyer, pres., man. dir., chief invest. officer & CFO, Oakville, Ont.; Mark J. Carpani, sr. v-p, Oakville, Ont.

Capital Stock

	Authorized (shs.)	Outstanding (shs.)[1]
Trust Unit	unlimited	18,575,820

[1] At Feb. 28, 2023

Trust Unit - Entitled to a monthly cash distribution of $0.053 per unit (5.3% per annum based on an issue price of $12 per unit). Retractable in December of each year at a price equal to the net asset value (NAV) per unit, less any costs associated with the retraction. Retractable in any other month at a price equal to the least of: (i) 96% of the weighted average price per unit on TSX during the 10 trading days prior to the monthly retraction date; (ii) the closing price per unit, being either (a) the closing price on TSX if there was a trade on the monthly retraction date, (b) the average of the highest and lowest prices on TSX on the monthly retraction date if there was trading and only the highest and lowest prices are provided or (c) the average of the last bid and the last asking prices on TSX if there was no trading on the monthly retraction date; and (iii) the NAV per unit at the monthly retraction date, less any costs associated with the retraction. One vote per trust unit.

Major Shareholder - Ridgewood Capital Asset Management Inc. held 75.7% interest at Feb. 28, 2023.

Price Range - RIB.UN/TSX

Year	Volume	High	Low	Close
2022	761,533	$17.43	$14.49	$14.90
2021	505,181	$17.60	$16.70	$17.19
2020	630,331	$17.93	$14.26	$17.00
2019	721,455	$17.20	$14.47	$16.84
2018	833,406	$15.11	$14.80	$14.88

Recent Close: $14.20

Capital Stock Changes - There were no changes to capital stock during 2022.

Dividends

RIB.UN unit Ra $0.636 pa M est. Feb. 15, 2013
$0.086818◆ Jan. 13/23 stk.[1]◆g Jan. 14/22
$0.190566◆ Jan. 14/22
Paid in 2023: $0.477 + $0.086818◆ 2022: $0.636 + $0.190566◆ + stk.◆g 2021: $0.636

[1] Distribution will be automatically reinvested and the units will be consolidated immediately after distribution. Equiv to $0.103884.
◆ Special **g** Capital Gain

Financial Statistics

Periods ended:	12m Dec. 31/22^A		12m Dec. 31/21^A
	$000s	%Chg	$000s
Realized invest. gain (loss)	(20,632)		3,036
Unrealized invest. gain (loss)	(40,397)		(7,515)
Total revenue	**(43,240)**	**n.a.**	**13,857**
General & admin. expense	1,825		2,074
Operating expense	**1,825**	**-12**	**2,074**
Operating income	**(45,065)**	**n.a.**	**11,783**
Finance costs, gross	2,275		1,230
Pre-tax income	**(47,340)**	**n.a.**	**10,553**
Net income	**(47,340)**	**n.a.**	**10,553**
Cash & equivalent	15		202
Accounts receivable	2,306		3,281
Investments	250,510		452,614
Total assets	**252,832**	**-45**	**456,097**
Accts. pay. & accr. liabs	202		370
Debt	14,715		155,118
Shareholders' equity	235,317		296,084
Cash from oper. activs	**155,570**	**n.a.**	**(71,033)**
Cash from fin. activs	(155,757)		71,229
Net cash position	**15**	**-93**	**202**
	$		$
Earnings per share*	(2.55)		0.60
Cash flow per share*	8.37		(4.04)
Net asset value per share*	12.67		15.94
Cash divd. per share*	0.64		0.64
Extra divd. - cash*	0.09		0.19
Extra stk. divd. - cash equiv.*	nil		0.10
Total divd. per share*	**0.72**		**0.93**
	shs		shs
No. of shs. o/s*	18,575,820		18,575,820
Avg. no. of shs. o/s*	18,575,820		17,561,730
	%		%
Net profit margin	n.m.		76.16
Return on equity	(17.82)		3.76
Return on assets	(12.71)		2.84

* Trust unit
^A Reported in accordance with IFRS

Historical Summary
(as originally stated)

Fiscal Year	Total Rev. $000s	Net Inc. Bef. Disc. $000s	EPS* $
2022^A	(43,240)	(47,340)	(2.55)
2021^A	13,857	10,553	0.60
2020^A	29,987	26,889	1.77
2019^A	30,883	26,937	1.92
2018^A	7,097	3,839	0.31

* Trust unit
^A Reported in accordance with IFRS

R.58 Rift Valley Resources Corp.

Symbol - RVR **Exchange** - CSE (S) **CUSIP** - 766544
Head Office - 400-1681 Chestnut St, Vancouver, BC, V6J 4M6 **Telephone** - (604) 682-7339
Website - www.riftvalleyresources.ca
Email - vernporter21@gmail.com
Investor Relations - Thomas J. Kennedy (604) 682-2928
Auditors - Davidson & Company LLP C.A., Vancouver, B.C.
Lawyers - DLA Piper (Canada) LLP, Vancouver, B.C.
Transfer Agents - National Securities Administrators Ltd., Vancouver, B.C.
Profile - (B.C. 2009) Constructing a wireless broadband network in Crockett, Tex., and Bend Ore., to provide Internet access to rural areas. Also pursuing acquisition of a development stage rural wireless broadband service company.

The company, through a collaboration agreement with **ARK Multicasting, Inc.**, a low power TV broadcaster with licences in the U.S., provides for the companies to collaborate with technical and market trials for a wireless broadband Internet Service Provider using a combination of radio frequencies including TV White Space (TVWS) technology in the 500 MHz bands, 3.5 GHz Citizens Broadband Radio Service spectrum and 5.7 GHz Unlicensed National Information Infrastructure band spectrum. The company began the construction of a wireless broadband network in Crockett, Tex., in December 2019, the first of a proposed 130 regional rural networks throughout the U.S. The company also has initiated construction of a second wireless broadband network in Bend, Ore.

In September 2022, the company entered into a letter of intent to acquire private **Ruralink Broadband Inc.**, a Washington-based development stage rural wireless broadband service provider for issuance of 46,659,205 post-consolidated common shares (following a 1-for-2 share consolidation). The company holds certain convertible notes and debentures of Ruralink that if converted would result in the company owning 43% interest in Ruralink. The transaction would be structured to acquire the remaining interest following conversion of the notes and debentures. As part of the transaction, Ruralink would complete a private placement of a minimum of $1,500,000.

Common suspended from CSE, May 9, 2023.

Directors - Thomas J. (Tom) Kennedy, CEO, Vancouver, B.C.; Donald A. (Don) Gordon, CFO & corp. sec., North Vancouver, B.C.; Nadwynn Sing, Vancouver, B.C.
Other Exec. Officers - Warren D. Robb, v-p, explor.; Thomas Robertson, v-p

Capital Stock

	Authorized (shs.)	Outstanding (shs.)[1]
Common	unlimited	104,348,807

[1] At Aug. 29, 2022

Major Shareholder - Stephen Edward Martin held 20.52% interest at Oct. 19, 2021.

Price Range - RVR/CSE (S)

Year	Volume	High	Low	Close
2022	7,106,513	$0.08	$0.04	$0.05
2021	23,618,631	$0.13	$0.05	$0.08
2020	29,212,282	$0.13	$0.03	$0.07
2019	22,164,160	$0.10	$0.03	$0.06
2018	6,967,521	$0.14	$0.05	$0.08

Recent Close: $0.05

Wholly Owned Subsidiaries

Rural Wireless Inc., B.C.

Investments

Ruralink Broadband, Inc.

Financial Statistics

Periods ended:	12m Dec. 31/21^A		12m Dec. 31/20^oA
	$000s	%Chg	$000s
General & admin expense	847		904
Stock-based compensation	35		383
Operating expense	**882**	**-31**	**1,287**
Operating income	**(882)**	**n.a.**	**(1,287)**
Finance income	121		17
Pre-tax income	**(826)**	**n.a.**	**(1,345)**
Net income	**(826)**	**n.a.**	**(1,345)**
Cash & equivalent	3		134
Current assets	35		153
Long-term investments	237		237
Total assets	**1,942**	**+107**	**937**
Accts. pay. & accr. liabs	150		100
Current liabilities	150		100
Shareholders' equity	1,771		816
Cash from oper. activs	**(811)**	**n.a.**	**(1,022)**
Cash from fin. activs	1,745		1,791
Cash from invest. activs	(1,066)		(634)
Net cash position	**3**	**-98**	**134**
	$		$
Earnings per share*	(0.01)		(0.03)
Cash flow per share*	(0.01)		(0.02)
	shs		shs
No. of shs. o/s*	104,348,807		75,898,698
Avg. no. of shs. o/s*	92,172,220		48,006,769
	%		%
Net profit margin	n.a.		n.a.
Return on equity	(63.86)		n.m.
Return on assets	(57.38)		(230.51)

* Common
^o Restated
^A Reported in accordance with IFRS

Latest Results

Periods ended:	6m June 30/22^A		6m June 30/21^A
	$000s	%Chg	$000s
Net income	(23)	n.a.	(572)
	$		$
Earnings per share*	(0.00)		(0.01)

* Common
^A Reported in accordance with IFRS

Historical Summary
(as originally stated)

Fiscal Year	Oper. Rev. $000s	Net Inc. Bef. Disc. $000s	EPS* $
2021^A	nil	(826)	(0.01)
2020^A	nil	(1,345)	(0.03)
2019^A	nil	(754)	(0.03)
2018^A	nil	(1,471)	(0.07)
2017^A	nil	(321)	(0.03)

* Common
^A Reported in accordance with IFRS

R.59 Right Season Investments Corp.

Symbol - LITT **Exchange** - TSX-VEN **CUSIP** - 76658Q
Head Office - 800-1199 Hastings St W, Vancouver, BC, V6E 3T5 **Telephone** - (604) 687-2038 **Toll-free** - (800) 406-6185
Website - rightseasoninvestmentcorp.com
Email - luke@rightseasoninvestmentcorp.com
Investor Relations - Luke Montaine (604) 687-2038
Auditors - GreenGrowth C.P.A., Los Angeles, Calif.
Transfer Agents - Computershare Trust Company of Canada Inc., Vancouver, B.C.
Profile - (B.C. 2007) Invests in private and public companies in a broad range of sectors including financial technology, education, natural resources, healthcare, and consumer retail services.

Investment portfolio includes wholly owned **Hard Rock Lithium Corp.**, which holds the Ingraham Trail lithium prospect, 132 hectares, 40 km east of Yellowknife, N.W.T.; wholly owned **CLOV Biopharma Corp.**, which conducts research and development of cedar leaf oil vapour for the purposes of preventing the spread of Coronavirus and other respiratory viruses such as influenza; 50.5%-owned **Bellini Fine Art Inc.**, which exhibits, markets, purchases and sells graphic art of cultural merit; **bettermoo(d) Food Corporation**, a beverage company which distributes products through online and in-store retail platforms; **Grounded People Apparel Inc.**, which designs, develops and produces unisex canvas sneakers made from sustainable, ethically sourced and produced materials, and manufactured by fair trade workers.; **1254571 BC Ltd.**, which holds licences to conduct research and development, as well as, formulate, produce and export psychedelic compounds; **Cicino Corporation**, an operator of a luxury brand concept boutique in Vancouver, B.C.; **Deserving Health International Corp.**, which develops proprietary formulations and innovative natural skin care and personal care products; **Yaletown Energy Capital Corp.**, which rehabilitates suspended oil wells in the Canadian Western Sedimentary Basin using innovative analytical and recovery technologies; **BoardSuite Corp.**, operator of BoardSuite online board portal which organizes and manages information and tasks; **Lions Bay Holdings Inc.**, which owns two hop farms in British Columbia; and **Desource Mining Corp.**

Also holds a Future Token Equity agreement with **Pinmo Creative Technology Ltd.** whereby the company has the right to acquire Pinmo Creative Token cryptographic tokens.

In January 2023, the company acquired 4,464,286 units of **Grounded People Apparel Inc.** (1 Grounded People common share & 1 warrant) at 56¢ per unit via private placement. As a result, the company's interest in Grounded People increased to 20.73% from 1.86%. Grounded People is a sustainable fashion company which produces handmade clothing using recycled materials in its vegan factory in Brazil.

In December 2022, the company acquired 16,186 common shares of **1254571 BC Ltd.** for $200,000 via private placement. 1254571 BC Ltd. holds licences to conduct research and development, as well as, formulate, produce and export psychedelic compounds.

In August 2022, the company acquired 271,739 common shares of **bettermoo(d) Food Corporation** for 9,000,000 common shares at a deemed price of $0.05 per share. bettermoo(d) is a beverage company which distributes products through online and in-store retail platforms.

Predecessor Detail - Name changed from Roadman Investments Corp., Jan. 3, 2023.
Directors - Tyler Lewis, CEO, B.C.; Luke Montaine, interim CFO, Vancouver, B.C.; Constantine Carmichel; Sam Shahrokhi
Other Exec. Officers - Larry Yen, corp. sec.

Capital Stock

	Authorized (shs.)	Outstanding (shs.)[1]
Preferred	unlimited	nil
Common	unlimited	131,541,265

[1] At Jan. 3, 2023

Major Shareholder - Widely held at Oct. 3, 2022.

Price Range - LITT/TSX-VEN

Year	Volume	High	Low	Close
2022	10,762,829	$0.20	$0.03	$0.05
2021	56,034,920	$2.30	$0.15	$0.20
2020	22,640,712	$0.80	$0.15	$0.25
2019	13,573,640	$2.20	$0.15	$0.20
2018	517,145	$3.50	$0.20	$0.60

Consolidation: 1-for-10 cons. in Jan. 2022
Recent Close: $0.04
Capital Stock Changes - In November 2022, private placement of 50,300,000 units (1 common share & ½ warrant) at 5¢ per unit and 30,103,000 units (1 common share & ½ warrant) at $0.035 per unit was completed, with warrants exercisable at $0.075 per share for two year sand 5¢ per share for three years, respectively.

On Jan. 24, 2022, common shares were consolidated on a 1-for-10 basis. Also during fiscal 2022, post-consolidated common shares were issued as follows: 1,145,384 for debt settlement and 151,200 for services.

Wholly Owned Subsidiaries

CLOV Biopharma Corp.
Genesis Fintech Inc., B.C. Inactive.
Hard Rock Lithium Corp., Canada.
1137182 B.C. Ltd., B.C.

Subsidiaries

50.5% int. in **Bellini Fine Art Inc.**
- 50% int. in **Art Flow Through Limited Partnership**

Financial Statistics

Periods ended:	12m June 30/22[A]		12m June 30/21[A]
	$000s	%Chg	$000s
Realized invest. gain (loss)	155		43
Unrealized invest. gain (loss)	(1,266)		644
Total revenue	**(1,111)**	**n.a.**	**686**
General & admin. expense	1,568		1,902
Stock-based compensation	nil		1,261
Operating expense	**1,568**	**-50**	**3,163**
Operating income	**(2,679)**	**n.a.**	**(2,477)**
Deprec. & amort.	nil		1
Finance costs, gross	1		18
Pre-tax income	**(2,662)**	**n.a.**	**(2,592)**
Net income	**(2,662)**	**n.a.**	**(2,592)**
Cash & equivalent	486		2,351
Accounts receivable	2		2
Current assets	509		2,756
Long-term investments	310		168
Total assets	**819**	**-72**	**2,924**
Bank indebtedness	184		14
Accts. pay. & accr. liabs	634		398
Current liabilities	829		423
Shareholders' equity	16		2,527
Non-controlling interest	(26)		(26)
Cash from oper. activs	**(755)**	**n.a.**	**(1,989)**
Cash from fin. activs	194		3,541
Cash from invest. activs	(339)		(622)
Net cash position	**112**	**-89**	**1,011**
	$		$
Earnings per share*	(0.13)		(0.20)
Cash flow per share*	(0.04)		(0.13)
	shs		shs
No. of shs. o/s*	21,224,148		19,927,564
Avg. no. of shs. o/s*	20,047,406		14,989,117
	%		%
Net profit margin	n.m.		(377.84)
Return on equity	(209.36)		n.m.
Return on assets	(142.19)		(157.62)

* Common
[A] Reported in accordance with IFRS

Latest Results

Periods ended:	3m Sept. 30/22[A]		3m Sept. 30/21[A]
	$000s	%Chg	$000s
Total revenue	(235)	n.a.	(321)
Net income	(472)	n.a.	(720)
	$		$
Earnings per share*	(0.02)		(0.04)

* Common
[A] Reported in accordance with IFRS

Historical Summary
(as originally stated)

Fiscal Year	Total Rev.	Net Inc. Bef. Disc.	EPS*
	$000s	$000s	$
2022[A]	(1,111)	(2,662)	(0.13)
2021[A]	686	(2,592)	(0.20)
2020[A]	(783)	(2,692)	(0.20)
2019[A]	(2,047)	(4,162)	(0.70)
2018[A]	90	(203)	(0.05)

* Common
[A] Reported in accordance with IFRS
Note: Adjusted throughout for 1-for-10 cons. in Jan. 2022

R.60 RioCan Real Estate Investment Trust*

Symbol - REI.UN **Exchange** - TSX **CUSIP** - 766910
Head Office - RioCan Yonge Eglinton Centre, 500-2300 Yonge St, PO Box 2386, Toronto, ON, M4P 1E4 **Telephone** - (416) 866-3033 **Toll-free** - (800) 465-2733 **Fax** - (416) 866-3020
Website - www.riocan.com
Email - klee@riocan.com
Investor Relations - Kim Lee (800) 465-2733
Auditors - Ernst & Young LLP C.A., Toronto, Ont.
Lawyers - Goodmans LLP, Toronto, Ont.
Transfer Agents - TSX Trust Company, Toronto, Ont.
FP500 Revenue Ranking - 345
Employees - 563 at Dec. 31, 2022
Profile - (Ont. 1981) Owns, manages and develops retail and mixed-use properties in Canada.

At June 30, 2023, the trust's portfolio consisted of 193 retail and mixed-use properties, including office, residential rental and 11 development properties, totaling 33,545,000 sq. ft. of net leasable area. The properties are concentrated in Greater Toronto Area and Ottawa, Ont.; Calgary and Edmonton, Alta.; Montreal, Que.; and Vancouver, B.C. Properties are also located in secondary markets across Canada. Of these properties, 45 properties, including seven under development, are held through co-ownership arrangements.

Income producing properties are classified into grocery anchored centres, mixed-use/urban and open air centres. Grocery anchored centres are properties with a grocery anchor tenant or shadow grocery anchors. Mixed-use/urban consists of assets with more than one type of use, such as retail, office and residential, located in major markets, and non mixed-use assets that are located in high-density urban areas. The trust's residential portfolio, under the RioCan Living brand, includes purpose-built residential rental buildings, townhouses and condominiums. Open air centres are community shopping centres with little or no enclosed component that often include high-quality anchor tenants such as pharmacies, liquor stores, home improvement stores and banks.

Property portfolio at June 30, 2023:

	Retail[1]	Office[1]	Residential Rental[1]
Income producing props.[2]	29,074,000	2,545,000	1,050,000
Props. under devel.[2]	502,000	81,000	293,000
	29,576,000	2,626,000	1,343,000

[1] Net leasable area (sq. ft.).
[2] Consisted of 182 income producing properties and 11 development properties, totaling 32,669,000 and 876,000 sq. ft. of net leasable area, respectively.

	% Area[1]
Grocery anchored centre	65.8%
Mixed-use/urban	19.3%
Open air centre	14.9%
	100%

[1] Net leasable area (sq. ft.).

In addition, the trust had partial interests in 15 properties held through joint ventures.

During the second quarter of 2023, the trust's ownership interest in its joint venture with **Hudson's Bay Company** increased to 22% from 20.2%.

In March and April 2023, the trust acquired 508 Lansdowne Avenue for $2,209,000 and 1303 Bloor Street West for $3,675,000. Both properties formed part of the trust's Bloor Street West and Lansdowne Avenue land assembly under development in Toronto, Ont.

In February 2023, the trust sold 5,000-sq.-ft. Hamilton Highbury Plaza in London, Ont., for $115,000.

In August 2022, the trust acquired 4980 Boulevard des Sources, a 3,000-sq.-ft. property in Pierrefonds, Que., for $1,072,000.

In July 2022, the trust sold 107th Avenue Northwest, a 12,000-sq.-ft. property in Edmonton, Alta., for $3,400,000.

In March 2022, the trust sold a 50% interest in 100,000-sq.-ft. Timiskaming Square in New Liskeard, Ont., for $1,650,000; and 97th Street Northwest, a 12,000-sq.-ft. property in Edmonton, Alta., for $2,000,000.

Recent Merger and Acquisition Activity

Status: completed **Announced:** June 29, 2023
RioCan Real Estate Investment Trust acquired 18154-18162 Yonge Street, a 16,000-sq.-ft. property in Toronto, Ont., for $8,214,000.

Status: completed **Announced:** June 26, 2023
RioCan Real Estate Investment Trust acquired a 50% interest in King & Sherbourne portfolio in Toronto, Ont., totaling 16,000 sq. ft., for $10,613,000, including assumption of mortgage payable and vendor-take-back mortgage payable of $2,799,000.

Status: completed **Revised:** May 29, 2023
UPDATE: RioCan acquired Bellevue phases one, two and four. PREVIOUS: RioCan Real Estate Investment Trust agreed to acquire three phases (phases one, two and four) of Bellevue, a four phase new build residential rental complex in Montreal, Que., for $55,300,000. Phases one and two consist of 124 units and phase four consists of a vacant lot zoned for residential. Closing of the transaction was expected by the end of May 2023. RioCan also agreed to acquire phase three, consisting of 60 units, with closing expected no later than March 2026.

Status: completed **Announced:** May 1, 2023
RioCan Real Estate Investment Trust sold 164,000-sq.-ft. RioCan West Ridge in Orillia, Ont., for $25,041,000.

Status: completed **Announced:** May 1, 2023
RioCan Real Estate Investment Trust sold a property in Orillia, Ont., for $23,500,000.

Status: completed **Announced:** Jan. 16, 2023
RioCan Real Estate Investment Trust sold 132,000-sq.-ft. Southland Crossing Shopping Centre in Calgary, Alta., for $42,000,000.

Status: completed **Announced:** Jan. 13, 2023
RioCan Real Estate Investment Trust acquired the parking lease at RioCan Hall in Toronto, Ont., for $26,638,000.

Status: completed **Announced:** Dec. 19, 2022
RioCan Real Estate Investment Trust sold 220,000-sq.-ft. Abbotsford Power Centre in Abbotsford, B.C., for $53,000,000.

Status: completed **Announced:** Dec. 15, 2022
RioCan Real Estate Investment Trust sold 455,000-sq.-ft. Mill Woods Town Centre in Edmonton, Alta., for $68,739,000.

Status: completed **Announced:** Dec. 6, 2022
RioCan Real Estate Investment Trust sold 97,000-sq.-ft. Fallingbrook Shopping Centre in Ottawa, Ont., for $38,856,000, including a vendor take-back mortgage of $22,300,000.

Status: completed **Announced:** Dec. 1, 2022
RioCan Real Estate Investment Trust sold 89,000-sq.-ft. Shoppes on Queen West in Toronto, Ont., for $51,218,000.

Status: completed **Announced:** Nov. 28, 2022
RioCan Real Estate Investment Trust sold 173,000-sq.-ft. Chahko Mika Mall in Nelson, B.C., for $28,312,000.

Status: completed **Announced:** Nov. 22, 2022
RioCan Real Estate Investment Trust acquired a commercial building at South Cambridge Shopping Centre in Cambridge, Ont., for $5,011,000.

Status: completed **Announced:** Sept. 13, 2022
RioCan Real Estate Investment Trust sold 370,000-sq.-ft. Parkwood Place in Prince George, B.C., for $30,500,000.

Status: completed **Announced:** Sept. 8, 2022
RioCan Real Estate Investment Trust sold RioCan Greenfield, a 341,000-sq.-ft. strip mall in Greenfield Park, Que., for $47,838,000.

Status: completed **Announced:** Aug. 29, 2022
RioCan Real Estate Investment Trust sold 182,000-sq.-ft. Trinity Conception Square in Carbonear, Nfld., for $14,900,000.

Status: completed **Announced:** June 6, 2022
RioCan Real Estate Investment Trust sold 285,000-sq.-ft. Lethbridge Walmart Centre in Lethbridge, Alta., for $27,625,000.

Status: completed **Announced:** May 3, 2022
RioCan Real Estate Investment Trust sold a parcel of land in Vaughan, Ont., for $9,300,000.

Status: completed **Revised:** Mar. 30, 2022
UPDATE: The transaction was completed. PREVIOUS: RioCan Real Estate Investment Trust agreed to sell a 50% interest in Mega Centre Notre-Dame, a 500,000-sq.-ft. outdoor commercial centre in Laval, Que., to Harden Group for $34,500,000.

Status: completed **Announced:** Mar. 29, 2022
RioCan Real Estate Investment Trust sold 71,000-sq.-ft. Highbury Shopping Plaza in London, Ont., for $10,750,000.

Status: completed **Announced:** Mar. 14, 2022
RioCan Real Estate Investment Trust sold a 50% interest in 180,000-sq.-ft. Eastcourt Mall in Cornwall, Ont., for $6,945,000.

Status: completed **Announced:** Mar. 14, 2022
RioCan Real Estate Investment Trust sold 85 Bloor Street West, a 13,800-sq.-ft. retail property in Toronto, Ont., to a newly formed 50/50 joint venture (JV) with Parallax Development Corporation for $35,000,000. The property would be used as part of the JV's planned mixed-use residential project.

Status: completed **Announced:** Mar. 14, 2022
RioCan Real Estate Investment Trust and Parallax Development Corporation, through their 50/50 joint venture, acquired four adjacent properties (83, 89-91, 95 and 95 A Bloor Street) for $105,000,000. The JV plans to develop a mixed-use residential project situated on the properties.

Predecessor Detail - Name changed from Counsel Real Estate Investment Trust, July 21, 1995.

Trustees - Edward Sonshine, founder & chr., Toronto, Ont.; Jonathan Gitlin, pres. & CEO, Toronto, Ont.; Siim A. Vanaselja‡, Toronto, Ont.; Bonnie R. Brooks, Keswick, Ont.; Richard Dansereau, Toronto, Ont.; Janice R. Fukakusa, Toronto, Ont.; Marie-Josée Lamothe, Montréal, Qué.; Dale H. Lastman, Toronto, Ont.; S. Jane Marshall, Toronto, Ont.; Charles M. (Chuck) Winograd, Toronto, Ont.

Oper. Subsid./Mgt. Co. Officers - John Ballantyne, COO; Dennis Blasutti, CFO; Andrew Duncan, chief invest. officer; Terri Andrianopoulos, sr. v-p, people & brand; Oliver Harrison, sr. v-p, leasing & tenant experience; Franca X. Smith, sr. v-p, fin.; Jennifer Suess, sr. v-p, gen. counsel, ESG & corp. sec.; Moshe Batalion, v-p, natl. leasing; Stuart Craig, v-p, devel.; Roberto DeBarros, v-p, const.; George Ho, v-p, IT; Xi Huang, v-p, invests.; Kalliopi Karkas, v-p, RioCan Living; Anton Katipunan, v-p, devel.; Rocky Kim, v-p, finl. planning & analysis & treasury; Kim Lee, v-p, IR; John McKinnon, v-p, asset mgt.; Pradeepa Nadarajah, v-p, prop. acctg.; Thayaparan (Paran) Namasivayam, v-p, recovery acctg.; Stephen (Steve) Roberts, v-p, analytics; Renee Simms, v-p, insce.; Jonathan Sonshine, v-p, tenant experience; Jeffrey Stephenson, v-p, natl. prop. mgt.; Naftali Sturm, v-p, real estate fin.; Kimberly Valliere, v-p, devel. const.; Jason Wong, v-p, corp. tax
‡ Lead trustee

Capital Stock

	Authorized (shs.)	Outstanding (shs.)[1]
Preferred Unit	50,000,000	
Series A	5,000,000	nil
Series B	5,000,000	nil
Series C	5,980,000	nil
Series D	5,980,000	nil
Trust Unit	unlimited	300,400,000
Exch. LP Unit	n.a.	499,754[2]

[1] At Aug. 1, 2023
[2] Issued by subsidiary limited partnerships.

Preferred Unit - Issuable in series. Fully and unconditionally guaranteed by the trust. Non-voting.

Trust Unit - One vote per trust unit.

Exchangeable Limited Partnership Unit - Issued by subsidiary limited partnerships to vendors as partial consideration in connection with property acquisitions. Entitled to distributions equivalent to the distributions paid on the trust units into which they may be exchanged. Exchangeable into trust units on a 1-for-1 basis. Non-voting.

Options - At Dec. 31, 2022, options were outstanding to purchase 5,691,000 trust units at a weighted average exercise price of $25.03 per unit with a weighted average remaining contractual life of three years.

Normal Course Issuer Bid - The company plans to make normal course purchases of up to 30,247,803 trust units representing 10% of the public float. The bid commenced on Nov. 7, 2022, and expires on Nov. 6, 2023.

Major Shareholder - Widely held at Apr. 28, 2023.

Price Range - REI.UN/TSX

Year	Volume	High	Low	Close
2022	225,926,160	$26.11	$17.85	$21.13
2021	268,894,096	$23.22	$16.30	$22.94
2020	470,212,290	$27.82	$12.41	$16.75
2019	159,624,666	$27.92	$23.51	$26.76
2018	200,131,092	$25.82	$22.97	$23.80

Recent Close: $19.32

Capital Stock Changes - During 2022, trust units were issued as follows: 88,000 under the unit-based compensation plan and 14,000 under the direct purchase plan; 9,540,000 trust units were repurchased under a Normal Course Issuer Bid.

Dividends

REI.UN tr unit Ra $1.08 pa M est. Mar. 7, 2023[1]
Prev. Rate: $1.02 est. Mar. 7, 2022
Prev. Rate: $0.96 est. Feb. 5, 2021
Prev. Rate: $1.44 est. Feb. 7, 2018
[1] Distribution reinvestment plan suspended eff. Nov. 1/17.

Long-Term Debt - Outstanding at Dec. 31, 2022:

Mtges. payable[1]	$2,659,180,000
Operating line of credit[2]	131,601,000
Credit facilities[3]	699,823,000
Const. lines & other loans[4]	309,688,000
Debs.:	
3.73% Ser.T due 2023	200,000,000
3.21% Ser.AA due 2023	300,000,000
3.29% Ser.W due 2024	300,000,000
2.58% Ser.AB due 2025	500,000,000
5.95% Ser.I due 2026	100,000,000
1.97% Ser.AD due 2026	500,000,000
2.36% Ser.AC due 2027	350,000,000
2.83% Ser.AE due 2028	450,000,000
4.63% Ser.AF due 2029	250,000,000
Less: Fin. costs, net	7,949,000
	6,742,343,000

[1] Bear interest at a weighted average effective rate of 3.29% inclusive of bond forward hedges (weighted average contractual rate of 3.39%). Due between 2023 and 2034.
[2] Bears a weighted average contractual interest rate of 6.34%. Due May 31, 2027.
[3] Bear all-in fixed interest rates between 3.53% and 3.68% through interest rate swaps. Due between 2023 and 2024.
[4] Bear a weighted average contractual interest rate of 5.89%. Due between 2023 and 2026.

Minimum mortgage repayments were reported as follows:

2023	$320,177,000
2024	238,713,000
2025	527,991,000
2026	138,440,000
2027	197,623,000
Thereafter	1,241,696,000

Minimum debentures repayments were reported as follows:

2023	$500,000,000
2024	300,000,000
2025	500,000,000
2026	600,000,000
2027	350,000,000
Thereafter	700,000,000

Note - In March 2023, offering of $200,000,000 principal amount of 5.611% series AG senior unsecured debentures due Oct. 6, 2027, was completed. In June 2023, offering of $300,000,000 principal amount of 5.962% series AH senior unsecured debentures due Oct. 1, 2029, was completed.

Wholly Owned Subsidiaries

RC Bloor-Lansdowne LP, Canada.
RC Clarkson LP, Canada.
RC Condo Development Trust, Canada.
RC Condo Management Trust, Canada.
RC Coxwell LP, Ont.
RC Dufferin LP, Toronto, Ont.
RC Durham Centre LP, Canada.
RC Eglinton Avenue LP, Canada.
RC Elmvale Acres LP, Toronto, Ont.
RC Grand Park LP, Canada.
RC Holding I LP, Canada.
RC Holding II LP, Canada.
RC Kirkland Trust, Canada.
RC Lachine Trust, Canada.
RC Lender LP, Ont.
RC Lincoln Fields LP, Canada.
RC Mill Woods LP, Toronto, Ont.
RC NA Property 5 LP, Toronto, Ont.
RC Pierrefonds Trust, Canada.
RC Rental IPP LP, Canada.
RC Sandalwood LP, Canada.
RC Scarborough Centre LP, Canada.
RC Sheppard Centre LP, Canada.
RC Strawberry Hills LP, Toronto, Ont.
RC 3180 Dufferin LP, Canada.
RC 2290 Lawrence (White Shield) LP, Canada.
RC Well Commercial LP, Canada.
RC Westgate LP, Toronto, Ont.
RC Windfield Farms LP, Canada.
RC Yonge Roehampton LP, Toronto, Ont.
RC Yorkville LP, Canada.
RioCan (Bloor/St. Thomas) LP, Canada.
RioCan (Festival Hall) Trust, Canada.
RioCan (GH) Limited Partnership, Toronto, Ont.
RioCan (KS) Management LP, Canada.
RioCan Living LP, Canada.
RioCan Management (BC) Inc., Vancouver, B.C.
RioCan Management Inc., Toronto, Ont.
RioCan Property Services Trust, Ont.
RioCan Realty Investments Partnership Eleven LP, Toronto, Ont.
RioCan Realty Investments Partnership Fifteen LP, Toronto, Ont.
RioCan Realty Investments Partnership Four LP, Canada.
RioCan Realty Investments Partnership Seven LP, Canada.
RioCan Realty Investments Partnership Twelve LP, Toronto, Ont.
RioCan Realty Investments Partnership Twenty-Eight LP, Toronto, Ont.
RioCan Realty Investments Partnership Twenty-Five LP, Toronto, Ont.
RioCan Realty Investments Partnership Twenty-Four LP, Toronto, Ont.
RioCan Realty Investments Partnership Twenty LP, Ont.
RioCan Realty Investments Partnership Twenty-Six LP, Canada.
RioCan Realty Investments Partnership Twenty-Three LP, Toronto, Ont.
RioCan Realty Investments Partnership Twenty-Two LP, Toronto, Ont.
RioCan White Shield Limited Partnership, Canada.
Shoppers World Brampton Investment Trust, Canada.
Timmins Square Limited Partnership, Canada.

Note: The preceding list includes only the major related companies in which interests are held.

Financial Statistics

Periods ended:	12m Dec. 31/22[A]		12m Dec. 31/21[A]
	$000s	%Chg	$000s
Total revenue	**991,779**	**-25**	**1,315,522**
Rental operating expense	404,869		408,050
Cost of real estate sales	96,286		65,346
Salaries & benefits	26,228		23,823
General & admin. expense	16,437		12,975
Stock-based compensation	6,998		10,580
Operating expense	**550,818**	**+6**	**520,774**
Operating income	**440,961**	**-45**	**794,748**
Investment income	2,349		19,189
Deprec. & amort.	4,774		4,022
Finance costs, gross	180,365		171,521
Pre-tax income	**237,693**	**-60**	**598,330**
Income taxes	921		(59)
Net income	**236,772**	**-60**	**598,389**
Cash & equivalent	86,229		77,758
Accounts receivable	60,629		71,052
Long-term investments	634,231		565,125
Income-producing props.	12,635,332		12,573,286
Properties under devel.	1,172,408		1,448,052
Residential inventory	272,005		217,043
Property interests, net	14,079,745		14,238,381
Total assets	**15,101,859**	**0**	**15,177,463**
Accts. pay. & accr. liabs	393,684		345,847
Long-term debt, gross	6,742,343		6,610,618
Long-term lease liabilities	36,572		37,975
Shareholders' equity	7,728,892		7,911,344
Cash from oper. activs	**506,124**	**+3**	**490,397**
Cash from fin. activs	(417,968)		(745,487)
Cash from invest. activs	(79,685)		94,392
Net cash position	**86,229**	**+11**	**77,758**
Capital expenditures	(392,973)		(463,879)
Increase in property	(90,026)		(17,177)
Decrease in property	420,970		659,979
Unfunded pension liability	10,100		13,600
	$		$
Earnings per share*	0.77		1.89
Cash flow per share*	1.65		1.55
Funds from opers. per sh.*	1.71		1.60
Adj. funds from opers. per sh.*	1.51		1.40
Cash divd. per share*	1.02		0.96
Total divd. per share*	**1.02**		**0.96**
	shs		shs
No. of shs. o/s*	300,359,000		309,797,000
Avg. no. of shs. o/s*	306,069,000		317,201,000
	%		%
Net profit margin	23.87		45.49
Return on equity	3.03		7.65
Return on assets	2.75		5.06
No. of employees (FTEs)	563		600

* Trust unit
[A] Reported in accordance with IFRS

Latest Results

Periods ended:	6m June 30/23[A]		6m June 30/22[A]
	$000s	%Chg	$000s
Total revenue	544,879	-10	602,945
Net income	229,971	-4	238,518
	$		$
Earnings per share*	0.77		0.77

* Trust unit
[A] Reported in accordance with IFRS

Historical Summary
(as originally stated)

Fiscal Year	Total Rev.	Net Inc. Bef. Disc.	EPS*
	$000s	$000s	$
2022[A]	991,779	236,772	0.77
2021[A]	1,315,522	598,389	1.89
2020[A]	639,706	(64,780)	(0.20)
2019[A]	1,598,597	775,834	2.52
2018[A]	1,197,914	527,362	1.68

* Trust unit
[A] Reported in accordance with IFRS

R.61 Rivalry Corp.

Symbol - RVLY **Exchange** - TSX-VEN **CUSIP** - 76803P
Head Office - 701-116 Spadina Ave, Toronto, ON, M5V 2K6 **Telephone** - (416) 565-4713
Website - rivalrycorp.com
Email - ss@rivalry.com
Investor Relations - Steven Salz (416) 565-4713
Auditors - Macias Gini & O'Connell LLP C.P.A., Los Angeles, Calif.
Transfer Agents - Odyssey Trust Company, Calgary, Alta.
Employees - 53 at May 1, 2023

Profile - (Ont. 2016) Offers fully regulated online wagering on eSports, traditional sports and casino games globally in jurisdictions where permitted.

Has developed an in-house technology platform offering fixed odds sports betting on both eSports and traditional sports, in addition to an originally developed casino game called Rushlane, and casino platform called Casino.exe. It holds an Isle of Man (IOM) licence, which allows it to offer multiple forms of wagering, and operates in a number of jurisdictions under the IOM licence, which allows licensed operators to accept bets from global markets where it is legal to do so. The company was granted a sports bookmaker licence in the Northern Territories, Australia in February 2022 and is a fully registered operator of Internet gaming and sports betting in Ontario, where legalized online gaming launched on Apr. 4, 2022.

The company does not plan to operate in countries where it is illegal to take bets or where a local licence is required, such as the United Kingdom and the United States, or countries with current United Nations sanctions. It plans to accept cryptocurrencies such as bitcoin and ethereum as a payment for certain products or services on its platform.

Predecessor Detail - Name changed from PMML Corp., Sept. 21, 2021.

Directors - Steven Salz, co-founder & CEO, Ont.; Ryan White, co-founder & chief tech. officer, Ont.; Kevin Wimer, co-founder & COO, Ohio; Steven G. Isenberg, Toronto, Ont.; Stephen Rigby, Toronto, Ont.; Kristine Stewart, Calif.

Other Exec. Officers - Kejda Qorri, CFO

Capital Stock

	Authorized (shs.)	Outstanding (shs.)[1]
Subordinate Voting	unlimited	64,489,741
Multiple Voting	unlimited	2,222,220

[1] At May 23, 2023

Subordinate Voting - One vote per share.

Multiple Voting - Convertible into subordinate voting shares on a 1-for-1 basis at any time at the option of the holder and automatically in certain other circumstances. 100 votes per share.

Major Shareholder - Ryan White & Kevin Wimer, together, held 39.52% interest, Steven G. Isenberg held 21.53% interest and Steven Salz held 18.51% interest at May 23, 2023.

Price Range - RVLY/TSX-VEN

Year	Volume	High	Low	Close
2022	10,444,440	$2.44	$0.65	$0.90
2021	6,313,840	$3.80	$1.50	$1.61

Recent Close: $1.65

Capital Stock Changes - In May 2023, private placement of 4,866,012 subordinate voting shares was completed at $1.50 per share.

During 2022, 1,343,702 subordinate voting shares were issued on vesting of restricted share units.

Wholly Owned Subsidiaries

PMML Advisors Corp., Ont.
PMML Dev Corp., Ont.
PMML IP Corp., Ont.
Pick Winn Earn Corp., Ont.
Rivalry Australia Pty Ltd., Australia.
Rivalry Limited, Isle of Man.
Rivalry Ontario Corp., Ont.
Rivalry Service Limited, Isle of Man.

Financial Statistics

Periods ended:	12m Dec. 31/22[A]		12m Dec. 31/21[□A]
	$000s	%Chg	$000s
Operating revenue	**26,634**	**+140**	**11,079**
Cost of sales	16,827		8,893
General & admin expense	31,565		14,738
Stock-based compensation	8,163		10,512
Operating expense	**56,556**	**+66**	**34,142**
Operating income	**(29,921)**	**n.a.**	**(23,063)**
Deprec., depl. & amort.	221		213
Finance costs, net	3		7
Write-downs/write-offs	nil		(1,542)
Pre-tax income	**(31,124)**	**n.a.**	**(24,305)**
Net income	**(31,124)**	**n.a.**	**(24,305)**
Cash & equivalent	112,192		35,451
Accounts receivable	12		1,930
Current assets	16,596		39,986
Fixed assets, net	207		122
Right-of-use assets	622		213
Intangibles, net	135		135
Total assets	**18,056**	**-55**	**40,455**
Accts. pay. & accr. liabs	2,870		1,333
Current liabilities	3,029		1,454
Long-term lease liabilities	326		18
Shareholders' equity	14,701		38,983
Cash from oper. activs	**(21,276)**	**n.a.**	**(10,381)**
Cash from fin. activs	(124)		45,296
Cash from invest. activs	(606)		(59)
Net cash position	**12,192**	**-66**	**35,451**
Capital expenditures	(110)		(59)
	$		$
Earnings per share*	(0.53)		(0.57)
	shs		shs
No. of shs. o/s*	59,878,728		58,535,026
Avg. no. of shs. o/s*	58,799,439		42,776,715
	%		%
Net profit margin	(116.86)		(219.38)
Return on equity	(115.95)		(106.15)
Return on assets	(106.39)		(101.11)
No. of employees (FTEs)	51		n.a.

* Subord. Vtg.
[□] Restated
[A] Reported in accordance with IFRS

Latest Results

Periods ended:	3m Mar. 31/23[A]		3m Mar. 31/22[A]
	$000s	%Chg	$000s
Operating revenue	11,968	+151	4,766
Net income	(3,259)	n.a.	(6,555)
	$		$
Earnings per share*	(0.05)		(0.11)

* Subord. Vtg.
[A] Reported in accordance with IFRS

Historical Summary
(as originally stated)

Fiscal Year	Oper. Rev.	Net Inc. Bef. Disc.	EPS*
	$000s	$000s	$
2022[A]	26,634	(31,124)	(0.53)
2021[A]	11,079	(24,721)	(0.57)
2020[A1]	1,545	(6,900)	(0.11)
2019[A]	518	(3,786)	n.a.

* Subord. Vtg.
[A] Reported in accordance with IFRS
[1] Adjusted for 1-for-4.5 share consolidation on Sept. 21, 2021

R.62 Riverwalk Acquisition Corp.

Symbol - RAC.P **Exchange** - TSX-VEN **CUSIP** - 76952A
Head Office - 478-6647 Fraser St, Vancouver, BC, V5X 0K3 **Telephone** - (604) 998-1395
Email - riverwalk-ir@outlook.com
Investor Relations - Vincent Wong (604) 998-1395
Auditors - Baker Tilly HMA LLP C.A., Winnipeg, Man.
Transfer Agents - Endeavor Trust Corporation, Vancouver, B.C.
Profile - (B.C. 2021) Capital Pool Company.
Directors - Vincent Wong, chr., CEO & corp. sec., Vancouver, B.C.; Robert (Rob) Goehring, Coquitlam, B.C.; Warren Jung, Vancouver, B.C.; Ryan Maarschalk, Kelowna, B.C.; Dr. Jeffrey R. (Jeff) Wilson, Vancouver, B.C.
Other Exec. Officers - Charles E. (Chuck) Jenkins, CFO

Capital Stock

	Authorized (shs.)	Outstanding (shs.)[1]
Common	unlimited	6,800,001

[1] At June 26, 2023

Major Shareholder - Warren Jung held 17.6% interest and Vincent Wong held 12.1% interest at Mar. 27, 2023.

Price Range - RAC.P/TSX-VEN

Year	Volume	High	Low	Close
2022	26,000	$0.18	$0.10	$0.10

Recent Close: $0.09
Capital Stock Changes - On June 16, 2022, an initial public offering of 3,000,000 common shares was completed at 10¢ per share.

R.63 Rockport Capital Corp.

Symbol - R.P **Exchange** - TSX-VEN **CUSIP** - 77382L
Head Office - 59 Burtch's Lane, Rockport, ON, K0E 1V0
Email - hbarr@newagemetals.com
Investor Relations - Harry G. Barr (604) 685-1870
Auditors - SHIM & Associates LLP C.A., Vancouver, B.C.
Lawyers - Borden Ladner Gervais LLP, Calgary, Alta.
Transfer Agents - Computershare Trust Company of Canada Inc., Vancouver, B.C.
Profile - (B.C. 2021) Capital Pool Company.

Recent Merger and Acquisition Activity

Status: pending **Revised:** Jan. 11, 2023
UPDATE: GME completed a $865,000 private placement. PREVIOUS: Rockport Capital Corp. entered into a letter of intent for the Qualifying Transaction reverse takeover acquisition of GME Metals Limited, a private British Columbia mineral exploration company, for issuance of 80,000,000 common shares. GME Metals holds rights and licenses to develop the Arran Carbonatite property, 140 km northwest of Johannesburg, South Africa, prospective for magnetite, phosphate rock and rare earth oxides.
Directors - Harry G. Barr, chr., CEO & corp. sec., Vancouver, B.C.; Gordon Chunnett, pres., Cape Town, South Africa; John W. Londry, Stittsville, Ont.
Other Exec. Officers - Robert Guanzon, CFO

Capital Stock

	Authorized (shs.)	Outstanding (shs.)[1]
Preferred	unlimited	nil
Common	unlimited	8,300,000

[1] At Feb. 21, 2023

Major Shareholder - Harry G. Barr held 24.1% interest and Gordon Chunnett held 24.1% interest at Aug. 10, 2021.

Price Range - R.P/TSX-VEN

Year	Volume	High	Low	Close
2022	40,000	$0.11	$0.05	$0.06
2021	62,000	$0.14	$0.11	$0.11

Capital Stock Changes - On Aug. 10, 2021, an initial public offering of 4,000,000 common shares was completed at 10¢ per share.

R.64 Rocky Mountain Liquor Inc.

Symbol - RUM **Exchange** - TSX-VEN **CUSIP** - 77472P
Head Office - 11478 149 St, Edmonton, AB, T5M 1W7 **Telephone** - (780) 863-2326 **Fax** - (780) 483-6525
Website - www.ruminvestor.com
Email - allisonr@rockymountainliquor.ca
Investor Relations - Allison Radford (780) 483-8183
Auditors - Grant Thornton LLP C.A., Edmonton, Alta.
Lawyers - McInnes Cooper
Transfer Agents - Computershare Trust Company of Canada Inc., Calgary, Alta.
Profile - (Can. 2007) Owns and operates 25 retail liquor stores in Alberta under various banners including Great Canadian Liquor.
Products include beer, spirits, wine and ready-to-drink liquor products, as well as ancillary items such as juice, ice, mix and giftware. Stores are located in Athabasca (2), Beaumont (2), Cochrane, Devon (2), Edmonton, Fairview, Fort Macleod, Fort McMurray, Gibbons, Grand Prairie, Lac La Biche, Lethbridge (2), Morinville (2), Rocky Mountain House, Slave Lake, St. Paul (2), Sylvan Lake (2) and Wetaskiwin.
During 2022, the company sold one liquor store.
Predecessor Detail - Name changed from Humber Capital Corporation, Sept. 21, 2009.
Directors - Peter J. Byrne, exec. chr., Edmonton, Alta.; Allison Radford, acting CEO, Edmonton, Alta.; Frank J. Coleman†, Corner Brook, N.L.; Courtney Burton, Calgary, Alta.; Robert A. (Rob) Normandeau, Bedford, N.S.
Other Exec. Officers - Sarah T. Stelmack, CFO
† Lead director

Capital Stock

	Authorized (shs.)	Outstanding (shs.)[1]
Common	unlimited	47,827,775

[1] At Aug. 16, 2023

Major Shareholder - Peter J. Byrne held 22.24% interest, Camac Partners, LLC & Camac Fund, LP held 17.67% interest and Jonathan Armoyan held 10.13% interest at May 8, 2023.

Price Range - RUM/TSX-VEN

Year	Volume	High	Low	Close
2022	8,027,538	$0.22	$0.11	$0.14
2021	25,926,567	$0.23	$0.12	$0.20
2020	24,035,502	$0.16	$0.03	$0.14
2019	13,523,347	$0.33	$0.04	$0.04
2018	2,147,333	$0.73	$0.18	$0.20

Consolidation: 1-for-5 cons. in Sept. 2019
Recent Close: $0.12
Capital Stock Changes - During 2022, 337,838 common shares were issued on exercise of options.

Wholly Owned Subsidiaries

Andersons Liquor Inc., Edmonton, Alta.

Financial Statistics

Periods ended:	12m Dec. 31/22[A]		12m Dec. 31/21[A]
	$000s	%Chg	$000s
Operating revenue	**41,981**	**-6**	**44,789**
Cost of sales	32,505		34,740
General & admin expense	6,795		6,778
Stock-based compensation	59		nil
Operating expense	**39,359**	**-5**	**41,518**
Operating income	**2,622**	**-20**	**3,271**
Deprec., depl. & amort.	1,396		1,352
Finance costs, gross	893		962
Pre-tax income	**330**	**-65**	**946**
Income taxes	52		(196)
Net income	**278**	**-76**	**1,143**
Cash & equivalent	147		118
Inventories	4,652		4,951
Accounts receivable	444		433
Current assets	5,488		5,671
Fixed assets, net	1,229		1,424
Right-of-use assets	10,728		12,449
Intangibles, net	6,188		6,215
Total assets	**23,778**	**-8**	**25,956**
Accts. pay. & accr. liabs	471		596
Current liabilities	4,130		4,812
Long-term debt, gross	1,471		2,203
Long-term debt, net	952		1,388
Long-term lease liabilities	10,209		11,607
Shareholders' equity	8,486		8,150
Cash from oper. activs	**2,517**	**-11**	**2,832**
Cash from fin. activs	(2,452)		(2,713)
Cash from invest. activs	(38)		(148)
Net cash position	**147**	**+25**	**118**
Capital expenditures	(88)		(148)
Capital disposals	51		nil
	$		$
Earnings per share*	0.01		0.02
Cash flow per share*	0.05		0.06
	shs		shs
No. of shs. o/s*	47,827,775		47,489,937
Avg. no. of shs. o/s*	47,706,524		47,489,937
	%		%
Net profit margin	0.66		2.55
Return on equity	3.34		15.08
Return on assets	4.14		8.74

* Common
[A] Reported in accordance with IFRS

Latest Results

Periods ended:	3m Mar. 31/23[A]		3m Mar. 31/22[A]
	$000s	%Chg	$000s
Operating revenue	8,382	-3	8,643
Net income	(290)	n.a.	(212)
	$		$
Earnings per share*	(0.01)		(0.00)

* Common
[A] Reported in accordance with IFRS

Historical Summary
(as originally stated)

Fiscal Year	Oper. Rev.	Net Inc. Bef. Disc.	EPS*
	$000s	$000s	$
2022[A]	41,981	278	0.01
2021[A]	44,789	1,143	0.02
2020[A]	48,428	1,521	0.03
2019[A]	43,971	2,838	0.10
2018[A]	44,068	(1,217)	(0.10)

* Common
[A] Reported in accordance with IFRS
Note: Adjusted throughout for 1-for-5 cons. in Sept. 2019

R.65 Rogers Communications Inc.*

Symbol - RCI.B **Exchange** - TSX **CUSIP** - 775109
Head Office - 1000-333 Bloor St E, Toronto, ON, M4W 1G9 **Telephone** - (416) 935-2303 **Fax** - (416) 935-3548
Website - www.rogers.com
Email - glenn.brandt@rci.rogers.com
Investor Relations - Glenn A. Brandt (844) 801-4792
Auditors - KPMG LLP C.A., Toronto, Ont.
Transfer Agents - American Stock Transfer & Trust Company, LLC, New York, N.Y.; TSX Trust Company, Toronto, Ont.
FP500 Revenue Ranking - 38
Employees - 22,000 at Dec. 31, 2022
Profile - (B.C. 1987; orig. Can., 1920) Provides wireless voice and data communications, high-speed Internet access, cable and satellite television and other video services, telephony and information technology services to Canadian consumers and businesses. Also

operates sports, television and radio broadcasting, televised and online shopping, and digital media businesses in Canada.

Wireless

Provides wireless voice and data communication products and services to about 10,600,000 individual consumers and businesses across Canada over its Fifth Generation/Long-Term Evolution/High Speed Packet Access/Global System for Mobile Communications (5G/LTE/HSPA/GSM) wireless networks. The company's 5G and LTE networks cover 82% and 96% of the population, respectively. The company's network is supported by roaming agreements with domestic and international carriers in more than 200 destinations, as well as through network sharing agreements with wireless operators in urban and rural Canada.

Wireless solutions include mobile Internet access, device financing, device protection, global voice and data roaming, wireless home phone, advanced business wireless solutions, and machine-to-machine and Internet of Things (IoT) solutions. Products and services are marketed under the Rogers, Fido and chatr brands and are distributed through a nationwide network of company-owned stores, third party dealer and retail locations, including outlets of 50%-owned mobile phone retailer **GLENTEL Inc.** (50% **BCE Inc.**), contact centres, outbound telemarketing and online and self-serve channels.

Cable

Provides Internet, television and other video, satellite, telephony and smart home monitoring services to consumers and businesses, and network connectivity solutions for the business, public sector and carrier wholesale markets in Canada.

Residential customers in Ontario, New Brunswick, Nova Scotia and Newfoundland are offered with high-speed broadband and fixed wireless Internet access through the Rogers Ignite and Fido Internet brands; Rogers Smart Home Monitoring, a real-time home monitoring, automation and security service; television solutions including local and network TV through traditional digital or the Internet Protocol (IP)-based Ignite TV, on-demand television, cloud-based digital video recorders (DVRs), personal video recorders (PVRs), the Ignite Streaming service, linear and time-shifted programming, digital specialty channels, 4K television programming, and the Ignite TV app, which delivers content on smartphones, tablets, laptops and computers; and local and long-distance telephone services.

Enterprise network and communication services are offered across Canada to business customers, including government and other telecommunications service providers. Solutions include voice; data networking; IP; Ethernet; optical wave; Internet; multi-protocol label switching services; information technology (IT) and network technology solutions such as collocation, cloud and managed services; cable access network services for primary, bridging and back-up connectivity; and telecommunications technical consulting for Internet service providers (ISPs). Operations include a transcontinental network of 85,000 km of fibre optic infrastructure with key connections to the U.S., and nine data centres across Canada.

Residential products and services are distributed through company-owned stores, online and self-serve channels, contact centres, outbound telemarketing, door-to-door agents and major retail chains. Business and wholesale customers are served through the company's sales team and third party channel distributors.

Media

Operations include sports media and entertainment, television and radio broadcasting, and digital media.

The sports media and entertainment group owns the Toronto Blue Jays Major League Baseball Club as well as Rogers Centre event venue in Toronto, Ont.; and 37.5% interest (BCE Inc. 37.5%, **Kilmer Van Nostrand Co. Limited** 25%) in **Maple Leaf Sports & Entertainment Ltd.**, owner of Scotiabank Arena in Toronto, the NHL's Toronto Maple Leafs, the NBA's Toronto Raptors, the MLS' Toronto FC, the CFL's Toronto Argonauts, the AHL's Toronto Marlies and associated real estate holdings. Also has a 12-year exclusive licensing agreement to broadcast National Hockey League games within Canada in multiple languages on all platforms until the end of the 2025-2026 season.

The broadcasting group consists of 23 television stations and specialty channels including Sportsnet, Citytv, OMNI, FX Canada, FXX Canada, OLN (formerly Outdoor Life Network) and nationally televised shopping channel TSC (Today's Shopping Choice); and 54 AM and FM radio stations across Canada.

Digital assets include sportsnet.ca, SN NOW, Citytv NOW, TSC online retail platform, and a range of other websites, apps, podcasts and digital products associated with the company's various brands and businesses.

In March 2022, the company acquired **Cross Country T.V. Limited**, a small regional provider of Internet, television and home phone services in Nova Scotia. Terms were not disclosed.

Periods ended:	12m Dec. 31/22	12m Dec. 31/21
Wireless subscribers[1]	10,647,000	10,013,000
Digital cable subscribers	1,525,000[2]	1,491,000[2]
Internet subscribers	2,284,000	2,229,000
Cable telephony lines	836,000	911,000

[1] Includes postpaid and prepaid.
[2] Includes IPTV and other video subscribers.

Recent Merger and Acquisition Activity

Status: completed **Revised:** Apr. 24, 2023
UPDATE:The transaction was completed. PREVIOUS: Rogers Communications Inc. agreed to acquire the Canadian operations of Sydney, Australia-based BAI Communications for an undisclosed amount. BAI held the exclusive rights to build the Toronto Transit Commission's (TTC) wireless network. The acquisition would allow Rogers to build out a 5G network throughout the entire TTC subway system, including access to 911 for all riders.

Status: completed **Revised:** Apr. 3, 2023
UPDATE: The transaction was completed. PREVIOUS: Rogers Communications Inc. and Shaw Communications Inc. announced an agreement to sell Shaw's Freedom Mobile Inc. to Quebecor Inc. for an enterprise value of $2.85 billion. The agreement provides for the sale of all of Freedom branded wireless and Internet customers as well as all of Freedom's infrastructure, spectrum and retail locations. It also includes a long-term undertaking by Shaw and Rogers to provide Quebecor transport services (including backhaul and backbone) and roaming services. The transaction requires approvals under the Competition Act and the approval of the Minister of Innovation, Science and Industry (ISED) and would close substantially concurrent with closing of Rogers acquisition of Shaw. Aug. 12, 2022 - The companies entered into definitive agreement for the sale of Freedom Mobile to Quebecor subsidiary Videotron Ltd. Oct. 27, 2022 - A settlement was not reached with the Commissioner of Competition to eliminate concerns on the proposed merger of Rogers and Shaw, including the sale of Freedom Mobile to Videotron. As a result, the proposed transactions would enter a hearing before the Competition Tribunal. Dec. 31, 2022 - The Competition Tribunal dismissed the Commissioner of Competition's application to block Rogers' proposed acquisition of Shaw and the divestiture of Freedom Mobile to Videotron. The only required regulatory approval remaining is the approval from the Minister of Innovation, Science and Industry for the transfer of Freedom Mobile's wireless spectrum licences to Videotron. Jan. 24, 2023 - The Federal Court of Appeal dismissed the Commissioner of Competition's appeal of the Competition Tribunal decision's on Dec. 31, 2022, which rejected the Commissioner's challenge of the proposed acquisition of Freedom Mobile and subsequent acquisition of Shaw by Rogers. Jan. 30, 2023 - The outside date to close the transaction was extended to Feb. 17, 2023. Feb. 17, 2023 - The outside date to close the transaction was further extended to Mar. 31, 2023. Mar. 31, 2023 - Minister of Innovation, Science and Industry provided final approval to transfer Shaw's spectrum licences to Videotron.

Status: completed **Revised:** Apr. 3, 2023
UPDATE: The transaction was completed. Shaw amalgamated with Rogers. PREVIOUS: Rogers Communications Inc. agreed to acquire Shaw Communications Inc. for $40.50 cash per share. The transaction was valued at $26 billion, including $6 billion of Shaw debt. The Shaw Family Living Trust, Shaw's controlling shareholder, and certain members of the Shaw family, would receive $16.20 cash and 0.417206775 of Rogers class B shares for each of their shares. The transaction requires approval of two thirds of the votes cast by the holders of Shaw's class A shares and class B shares at a special shareholders meeting to be held in May 2021, voting separately as a class, as well as majority of the minority approval. The Shaw Family Living Trust has agreed to vote all of its class A shares and class B shares in favour of the transaction. The transaction was subject to other customary closing conditions including court and stock exchange approval, as well as approvals from Canadian regulators. Subject to receipt of all required approvals, the transaction was expected to occur in the first half of 2022. Under the agreement, Rogers has the right to cause Shaw to redeem its outstanding preferred shares on June 30, 2021, in accordance with their terms by providing written notice to Shaw. Rogers' board of directors unanimously approved the transaction. A special committee of independent directors of Shaw unanimously recommended the transaction, and Shaw's board of directors unanimously approved the transaction and unanimously recommended that Shaw shareholders (other than the Shaw Family Living Trust) approve it. Shaw's directors and management agreed to vote of all of their shares in favour of the transaction. May 20, 2021 - Shaw shareholders voted in favour of the transaction. May 25, 2021 - Alberta Court approval was received for the transaction. Mar. 24, 2022 - CRTC approved the transfer of Shaw's licensed broadcasting undertakings to Rogers. May 6, 2022 - The Commissioner of Competition Bureau announced it plans to oppose the transaction. Rogers and Shaw plans to oppose the application to prevent the transaction to be made by the Commissioner of Competition. The companies have offered to address concerns regarding the possible impact of the transaction on Canada's competitive wireless market by proposing the full sale of Shaw's wireless business, Freedom Mobile. The companies have agreed to extend the outside date of the transaction to July 31, 2022. May 30, 2022 - The companies have agreed to not proceed with closing their proposed transaction until either a negotiated settlement is agreed with the Commissioner of Competition or the Competition Tribunal has ruled on the matter. June 17, 2022 - Rogers and Shaw agreed to sell Shaw's Freedom Mobile business to Videotron Ltd. July 6, 2022 - The companies announced that early mediation with the Commissioner of Competition on July 4 and July 5, 2022, did not result in a resolution of the Commissioner's objections to the proposed transaction. July 27, 2022 - The outside date to complete the transaction was extended to Dec. 31, 2022, which may be further extended to Jan. 31, 2023, at the option of Rogers or Shaw. Oct. 27, 2022 - The mediation with the Commissioner of Competition did not yield a negotiated settlement to eliminate concerns on the proposed merger, including the sale of Freedom Mobile to Quebecor. As a result, the proposed transactions would enter a hearing before the Competition Tribunal. Dec. 31, 2022 - The Competition Tribunal dismissed the Commissioner of Competition's application to block Rogers' proposed acquisition of Shaw and the divestiture of Freedom Mobile to Videotron. The only required regulatory approval remaining is the approval from the Minister of Innovation, Science and Industry for the transfer of Freedom Mobile's wireless spectrum licences to Videotron. The outside date to close the transaction was extended to Jan. 31, 2023. Jan. 24, 2023 - The Federal Court of Appeal dismissed the Commissioner of Competition's appeal of the Competition Tribunal decision's on Dec. 31, 2022 which rejected the Commissioner's challenge of the proposed divestiture of Freedom Mobile and subsequent acquisition of Shaw by Rogers. Jan. 30, 2023 - The outside date to complete the transaction was extended to Feb. 17, 2023. Feb. 17, 2023 - The outside date to close the transaction was further extended to Mar. 31, 2023

Predecessor Detail - Name changed from Rogers Cablesystems Inc., Apr. 2, 1986.

Directors - Edward S. Rogers, chr., Toronto, Ont.; Melinda M. Rogers-Hixon, deputy chr., Toronto, Ont.; Anthony (Tony) Staffieri, pres. & CEO, Toronto, Ont.; Robert J. Gemmell†, Oakville, Ont.; Jack L. Cockwell, Toronto, Ont.; Michael J. Cooper, Toronto, Ont.; Trevor English, Calgary, Alta.; Ivan Fecan, Vancouver, B.C.; Jan L. Innes, Toronto, Ont.; John C. (Jake) Kerr, Vancouver, B.C.; Dr. Mohamed Lachemi, Mississauga, Ont.; David A. Robinson, Toronto, Ont.; Lisa Rogers, B.C.; Martha L. Rogers, Toronto, Ont.; Bradley S. (Brad) Shaw, Calgary, Alta.

Other Exec. Officers - Glenn A. Brandt, CFO; The Hon. Navdeep Bains, chief corp. affairs officer; Bret D. Leech, chief HR officer; Ron McKenzie, chief tech. & info. officer; Zoran Stakic, chief transformation officer; Terrie L. Tweddle, chief brand & commun. officer; Mahes S. Wickramasinghe, chief comml. officer; Marisa L. Wyse, chief legal & regulatory officer & corp. sec.; Lisa L. Durocher, exec. v-p, finl. & emerging srvcs.; Robert Dépatie, pres. & COO, residential & bus.; Philip J. (Phil) Hartling, pres., wireless; Colette S. Watson, pres., Rogers sports & media

† Lead director

Capital Stock

	Authorized (shs.)	Outstanding (shs.)[1]
Preferred	400,000,000	nil
Class A Vtg.	112,474,388	111,152,011
Class B Non-vtg.	1,400,000,000	417,414,747

[1] At June 30, 2023

Preferred - Issuable in series and non-voting.

Class A Voting - Convertible into class B non-voting shares on a one-for-one basis. Fifty votes per share.

Class B Non-voting - Non-voting.

Options - At Dec. 31, 2022, options were outstanding to purchase 9,860,208 class B non-voting shares at prices ranging from $42.85 to $73 per share with a weighted average remaining contractual life of 6.95 years.

Major Shareholder - Rogers Control Trust held 97.53% interest at Feb. 24, 2023.

Price Range - RCI.B/TSX

Year	Volume	High	Low	Close
2022	395,205,198	$80.85	$50.53	$63.37
2021	369,575,175	$67.59	$54.69	$60.23
2020	292,400,891	$67.34	$46.81	$59.26
2019	267,359,373	$73.82	$60.06	$64.48
2018	229,761,937	$72.45	$55.63	$69.96

Recent Close: $53.41

Capital Stock Changes - On Apr. 3, 2023, 23,641,441 class B non-voting shares were issued pursuant to the acquisition of Shaw Communications Inc.

During 2022, 1,400 class B non-voting shares were issued on conversion of a like number of class A voting shares.

Dividends

RCI.B cl B N.V. Ra $2.00 pa Q est. Apr. 1, 2019**
RCI.A cl A M.V. Ra $2.00 pa Q est. Apr. 1, 2019**
** Reinvestment Option

Long-Term Debt - Outstanding at Dec. 31, 2022:

3% sr. notes due 2023[1]	$677,000,000
4.1% sr. notes due 2023[2]	1,151,000,000
4% sr. notes due 2024	600,000,000
2.95% sr. notes due 2025[3]	1,354,000,000
3.1% sr. notes due 2025	1,250,000,000
3.625% sr. notes due 2025[4]	948,000,000
2.9% sr. notes due 2026[1]	677,000,000
3.65% sr. notes due 2027	1,500,000,000
3.2% sr. notes due 2027[5]	1,761,000,000
3.75% sr. notes due 2029	1,000,000,000
3.25% sr. notes due 2029	1,000,000,000
3.8% sr. notes due 2032[6]	2,709,000,000
4.25% sr. notes due 2032	1,000,000,000
8.75% sr. debs. due 2032[7]	271,000,000
7.5% sr. notes due 2038[8]	474,000,000
6.68% sr. notes due 2039	500,000,000
6.11% sr. notes due 2040	800,000,000
6.56% sr. notes due 2041	400,000,000
4.5% sr. notes due 2042[9]	1,016,000,000
4.5% sr. notes due 2043[1]	677,000,000
5.45% sr. notes due 2043[10]	880,000,000
5% sr. notes due 2044[11]	1,422,000,000
4.3% sr. notes due 2048[9]	1,016,000,000
4.35% sr. notes due 2049[12]	1,693,000,000
3.7% sr. notes due 2049[3]	1,354,000,000
4.55% sr. notes due 2052[6]	2,709,000,000
5.25% sr. notes due 2052	1,000,000,000
5% subord. notes due 2081	2,000,000,000
5.25% subord. notes due 2082[9]	1,016,000,000
Less: Def. trans. costs & discounts	1,122,000,000
	31,733,000,000
Less: Current portion	1,828,000,000
	29,905,000,000

[1] US$500,000,000.
[2] US$850,000,000.
[3] US$1 billion.

[4] US$700,000,000.
[5] US$1.3 billion.
[6] US$2 billion.
[7] US$200,000,000.
[8] US$350,000,000.
[9] US$750,000,000.
[10] US$650,000,000.
[11] US$1.05 billion.
[12] US$1.25 billion.

Principal repayments for the next five years were reported as follows:

2023	$1,828,000,000
2024	600,000,000
2025	3,552,000,000
2026	3,693,000,000
2027	3,261,000,000
Thereafter	19,921,000,000

Note - In July 2023, an exchange offer was completed whereby $996,349,000 principal amount of 2.95% senior notes due 2025, $1.289 billion principal amount of 3.2% senior notes due 2027, $1.949 billion principal amount of 3.8% senior notes due 2032, $749,970,000 principal amount of 4.5% senior notes due 2042 and $1.997 billion principal amount of 4.55% senior notes due 2052 were exchanged for new notes that are substantially identical to the terms of the old notes.

Wholly Owned Subsidiaries

Fido Solutions Inc., B.C.
Rogers Communications Canada Inc., Toronto, Ont.
Rogers Media Inc., Toronto, Ont.
- 100% int. in **Blue Jays Holdco Inc.**, Ont.

Shaw Cablesystems Limited, Calgary, Alta.
- 100% int. in **Shaw Cablesystems G.P.**, Alta.

Shaw Envision Inc., Calgary, Alta.
Shaw Satellite Services Inc., Mississauga, Ont.
- 100% int. in **Shaw Satellite G.P.**, Alta.
- 100% int. in **Star Choice Television Nework Incorporated**, Fredericton, N.B.

Shaw Telecom Inc., Calgary, Alta.
- 100% int. in **Shaw Telecom G.P.**, Alta.

Investments

COGECO Inc., Montréal, Qué. (see separate coverage)
Cogeco Communications Inc., Montréal, Qué. (see separate coverage)
50% int. in **GLENTEL Inc.**, Burnaby, B.C.
37.5% int. in **Maple Leaf Sports & Entertainment Ltd.**, Toronto, Ont.

Note: The preceding list includes only the major related companies in which interests are held.

Financial Statistics

Periods ended:	12m Dec. 31/22^A		12m Dec. 31/21^A
	$000s	%Chg	$000s
Operating revenue	**15,396,000**	**+5**	**14,655,000**
Cost of goods sold	235,000		271,000
Cost of sales	2,141,000		2,161,000
Salaries & benefits	2,159,000		2,121,000
Stock-based compensation	67,000		60,000
Other operating expense	4,401,000		4,155,000
Operating expense	**9,003,000**	**+3**	**8,768,000**
Operating income	**6,393,000**	**+9**	**5,887,000**
Deprec., depl. & amort.	2,576,000		2,585,000
Finance income	281,000		42,000
Finance costs, gross	1,468,000		849,000
Investment income	(31,000)		(44,000)
Pre-tax income	**2,289,000**	**+8**	**2,127,000**
Income taxes	609,000		569,000
Net income	**1,680,000**	**+8**	**1,558,000**
Cash & equivalent	13,300,000		715,000
Inventories	438,000		535,000
Accounts receivable	4,184,000		3,847,000
Current assets	19,283,000		5,829,000
Long-term investments	2,088,000		2,493,000
Fixed assets, net	15,574,000		14,666,000
Intangibles, net	16,282,000		16,305,000
Total assets	**55,655,000**	**+33**	**41,963,000**
Bank indebtedness	2,985,000		2,200,000
Accts. pay. & accr. liabs	3,722,000		3,416,000
Current liabilities	9,549,000		8,619,000
Long-term debt, gross	31,733,000		18,688,000
Long-term debt, net	29,905,000		17,137,000
Long-term lease liabilities	1,666,000		1,621,000
Shareholders' equity	10,092,000		10,532,000
Cash from oper. activs	**4,493,000**	**+8**	**4,161,000**
Cash from fin. activs	11,355,000		203,000
Cash from invest. activs	(3,263,000)		(6,133,000)
Net cash position	**13,300,000**	**n.m.**	**715,000**
Capital expenditures	(3,075,000)		(2,788,000)
Pension fund surplus	340,000		27,000
	$		$
Earnings per share*	3.33		3.09
Cash flow per share*	8.90		8.24
Cash divd. per share*	2.00		2.00
	shs		shs
No. of shs. o/s*	504,925,317		504,925,318
Avg. no. of shs. o/s*	504,925,317		504,925,318
	%		%
Net profit margin	10.91		10.63
Return on equity	16.29		15.50
Return on assets	5.65		5.39
No. of employees (FTEs)	22,000		23,000

* Class A & B
^A Reported in accordance with IFRS

Latest Results

Periods ended:	6m June 30/23^A		6m June 30/22^A
	$000s	%Chg	$000s
Operating revenue	8,881,000	+19	7,487,000
Net income	620,000	-23	801,000
	$		$
Earnings per share*	1.20		1.59

* Class A & B
^A Reported in accordance with IFRS

Historical Summary
(as originally stated)

Fiscal Year	Oper. Rev.	Net Inc. Bef. Disc.	EPS*
	$000s	$000s	$
2022^A	15,396,000	1,680,000	3.33
2021^A	14,655,000	1,558,000	3.09
2020^A	13,916,000	1,592,000	3.15
2019^A	15,073,000	2,043,000	3.99
2018^A	15,096,000	2,059,000	4.00

* Class A & B
^A Reported in accordance with IFRS

R.66 Rogers Sugar Inc.*

Symbol - RSI **Exchange** - TSX **CUSIP** - 77519R
Head Office - 123 Rogers St, Vancouver, BC, V6B 3V2 **Telephone** - (604) 253-1131 **Toll-free** - (800) 661-5350 **Fax** - (604) 253-2517
Website - www.lanticrogers.com
Email - jscouillard@lantic.ca
Investor Relations - Jean-Sébastien Couillard (514) 940-4350
Auditors - KPMG LLP C.A., Montréal, Qué.
Lawyers - Davies Ward Phillips & Vineberg LLP, Montréal, Qué.
Transfer Agents - Computershare Trust Company of Canada Inc., Toronto, Ont.
Administrators - Lantic Inc., Montréal, Qué.
FP500 Revenue Ranking - 340

Employees - 869 at Oct. 1, 2022
Profile - (Can. 2010) Refines, produces and markets sugar products and bottles and distributes maple syrup and related maple products primarily in Canada.

Operations are organized into two product segments: Sugar and Maple.

Sugar

Wholly owned **Lantic Inc.** operates cane sugar refineries in Montreal, Que., and Vancouver, B.C., as well as a beet sugar processing facility in Taber, Alta., with a combined annual nominal production capacity of 1,000,000 tonnes. Operations also include a distribution centre and blending and packaging facility in Toronto, Ont. Products are marketed under the Lantic trademark in eastern Canada and the Rogers trademark in western Canada. Products include granulated, icing, cube, yellow and brown sugars, liquid sugars and specialty syrups.

Maple

Wholly owned **The Maple Treat Corporation** (TMTC) operates maple syrup bottling plants in Granby, Dégelis and St-Honoré-de-Shenley, Que., and Websterville, Vt., and has partnerships with more than 1,400 maple syrup producers primarily in Quebec and Vermont. Products include bottled maple syrup, bulk maple syrup, maple sugar and flakes, and ancillary or derived maple products sold under the TMTC, Highland Sugarworks, Uncle Luke's, Decacer and Great Northern brands.

Sales Volume

	Fiscal 2022	Fiscal 2021
Sugar (tonnes)	794,600	779,505
Maple syrup (lbs.)	47,063,000	52,255,000

In August 2023, the company's board of directors approved the expansion of the production and logistic capacity of its eastern sugar refining operations in Montreal, Que., and Toronto, Ont. The expansion, which would cost $200,000,000, is expected to provide 100,000 tonnes of incremental refined sugar capacity. The company expects the incremental production and logistic capacity to be in service in two years.

Predecessor Detail - Succeeded Rogers Sugar Income Fund, Jan. 1, 2011, pursuant to plan of arrangement whereby Rogers Suger Inc. was formed to facilitate the conversion of the fund into a corporation and the fund was subsequently dissolved.

Directors - M. Dallas H. Ross, chr., Vancouver, B.C.; Dean J. Bergmame, Montréal, Qué.; Gary M. Collins, Vancouver, B.C.; Daniel L. Lafrance, Kirkland, Qué.; Shelley Potts, Oro-Medonte, Ont.; Stephanie Wilkes, Ont.

Other Exec. Officers - Michael M. (Mike) Walton, pres. & CEO; Jean-Sébastien Couillard, v-p, fin., CFO & corp. sec.

Capital Stock

	Authorized (shs.)	Outstanding (shs.)[1]
Preferred	unlimited	nil
Common	unlimited	105,096,120

[1] At Aug. 11, 2023

Major Shareholder - Belkorp Industries Inc. held 10.9% interest at Dec. 21, 2022.

Price Range - RSI/TSX

Year	Volume	High	Low	Close
2022	39,117,709	$6.59	$5.65	$5.69
2021	47,603,108	$6.12	$5.15	$5.95
2020	54,694,640	$5.83	$3.85	$5.61
2019	34,634,049	$6.17	$4.54	$4.92
2018	38,786,737	$6.49	$5.18	$5.44

Recent Close: $5.71

Capital Stock Changes - During fiscal 2022, 685,122 common shares were issued on exercise of options.

Dividends

RSI com Ra $0.36 pa Q est. July 20, 2012

Long-Term Debt - Outstanding at Oct. 1, 2022:

Revolv. credit facility due 2026[1]	$126,000,000
5% conv. debs. due 2024[2]	57,425,000
4.75% conv. debs. due 2025[3]	97,575,000
3.49% sr. notes due 2031	98,901,000
Accretion exp. equity component	4,164,000
Less: Def. fin. fees	2,535,000
Less: Pre-tax equity component	6,930,000
	374,600,000
Less: Current portion	26,000,000
	348,600,000

[1] Bears interest at prime rate, LIBOR or bankers' acceptance plus 0.2% to 2.5%.
[2] Convertible into common shares at $8.26 per share. Equity component totaling $1,953,000 was classified as part of shareholders' equity.
[3] Convertible into common shares at $8.85 per share. Equity component totaling $3,132,000 was classified as part of shareholders' equity.

Note - In January 2023, principal amount of the revolving credit facility increased from $200,000,000 to $265,000,000.

Wholly Owned Subsidiaries

Lantic Inc., Montréal, Qué.
- 100% int. in **The Maple Treat Corporation**, Granby, Qué. Formerly L.B. Maple Treat Corporation.
  - 100% int. in **Highland Sugarworks Inc.**, Canada.

Financial Statistics

Periods ended:	12m Oct. 1/22^A		12m Oct. 2/21^A
	$000s	%Chg	$000s
Operating revenue	**1,006,134**	**+13**	**893,931**
Cost of sales	855,217		735,194
General & admin expense	39,747		30,737
Other operating expense	21,709		18,292
Operating expense	**916,673**	**+17**	**784,223**
Operating income	**89,461**	**-18**	**109,708**
Deprec., depl. & amort.	26,148		25,211
Finance costs, net	17,567		19,439
Write-downs/write-offs	(50,000)		nil
Pre-tax income	**(4,254)**	**n.a.**	**65,058**
Income taxes	12,314		17,531
Net income	**(16,568)**	**n.a.**	**47,527**
Cash & equivalent	151		15,643
Inventories	246,706		180,291
Accounts receivable	120,207		95,546
Current assets	390,610		302,232
Fixed assets, net	247,969		241,713
Right-of-use assets	22,932		18,526
Intangibles, net	257,271		311,041
Total assets	**937,956**	**+7**	**879,930**
Accts. pay. & accr. liabs	168,042		110,608
Current liabilities	216,572		129,926
Long-term debt, gross	374,600		346,527
Long-term debt, net	348,600		346,527
Long-term lease liabilities	19,198		15,443
Equity portion of conv. debs	5,085		5,085
Shareholders' equity	291,419		318,958
Cash from oper. activs	**21,552**	**-73**	**78,577**
Cash from fin. activs	(13,554)		(40,158)
Cash from invest. activs	(23,730)		(24,678)
Net cash position	**151**	**-99**	**15,643**
Capital expenditures, net	(23,635)		(24,320)
Unfunded pension liability	6,682		14,294
	$		$
Earnings per share*	(0.16)		0.46
Cash flow per share*	0.21		0.76
Cash divd. per share*	0.36		0.36
	shs		shs
No. of shs. o/s*	104,372,045		103,686,923
Avg. no. of shs. o/s*	103,904,615		103,581,358
	%		%
Net profit margin	(1.65)		5.32
Return on equity	(5.43)		16.13
Return on assets	(1.82)		5.38
Foreign sales percent	22		25
No. of employees (FTEs)	869		884

* Common
^A Reported in accordance with IFRS

Latest Results

Periods ended:	9m July 1/23^A		9m July 2/22^A
	$000s	%Chg	$000s
Operating revenue	796,677	+8	738,728
Net income	39,913	+38	28,934
	$		$
Earnings per share*	0.38		0.28

* Common
^A Reported in accordance with IFRS

Historical Summary
(as originally stated)

Fiscal Year	Oper. Rev.	Net Inc. Bef. Disc.	EPS*
	$000s	$000s	$
2022^A	1,006,134	(16,568)	(0.16)
2021^A	893,931	47,527	0.46
2020^A	860,801	35,419	0.34
2019^A	794,292	(8,167)	(0.08)
2018^A	805,201	48,729	0.46

* Common
^A Reported in accordance with IFRS

R.67 Ronin Ventures Corp.

Symbol - RVC.P **Exchange** - TSX-VEN **CUSIP** - 776331
Head Office - 228-1122 Mainland St, Vancouver, BC, V6B 5L1 **Telephone** - (778) 388-5258
Email - anthonyzelen88@gmail.com
Investor Relations - Anthony Zelen (778) 388-5258
Auditors - Crowe MacKay LLP C.A., Vancouver, B.C.
Transfer Agents - Computershare Trust Company of Canada Inc., Vancouver, B.C.
Profile - (B.C. 2022) Capital Pool Company.
In February 2023, the company's proposed Qualifying Transaction reverse takeover acquisition of **HerdWhistle Technologies Inc.** was terminated. HerdWhistle provide electronic livestock identification and traceability products to facilitate livestock animal monitoring and create livestock animal health data analytics.
Directors - Anthony Zelen, CEO, CFO & corp. sec., Coldstream, B.C.; Robert L. (Rob) Birmingham, North Vancouver, B.C.; Lance Morginn, Vancouver, B.C.

Capital Stock

	Authorized (shs.)	Outstanding (shs.)[1]
Common	unlimited	4,500,000

[1] At Aug. 11, 2022

Major Shareholder - Lance Morginn held 20% interest, Anthony Zelen held 20% interest and Kristina Loganchuk held 11.1% interest at Aug. 11, 2022.

Price Range - RVC.P/TSX-VEN

Year	Volume	High	Low	Close
2022	7,000	$0.11	$0.11	$0.11

Recent Close: $0.07
Capital Stock Changes - On Aug. 11, 2022, an initial public offering of 2,000,000 common shares was completed at 10¢ per share.

R.68 Roots Corporation*

Symbol - ROOT **Exchange** - TSX **CUSIP** - 776652
Head Office - 1400 Castlefield Ave, Toronto, ON, M6B 4C4 **Telephone** - (416) 781-3574 **Toll-free** - (800) 208-0521
Website - www.roots.com
Email - khonsberger@roots.com
Investor Relations - Kaleb Honsberger (416) 781-3574
Auditors - KPMG LLP C.A., Toronto, Ont.
Transfer Agents - Computershare Trust Company of Canada Inc., Toronto, Ont.
FP500 Revenue Ranking - 590
Employees - 2,033 at Jan. 28, 2023
Profile - (Can. 2015) Designs, markets and sells men's, women's, children and gender-free apparel, leather goods, footwear and accessories under the Roots brand through corporate retail stores, an e-commerce website and international operating partners.
At Jan. 28, 2023, the company's retail network consisted of 107 corporate stores in Canada, two corporate stores in the U.S., 12 temporary pop-up locations in Canada, more than 100 partner-operated stores in Asia, an e-commerce platform, www.roots.com and a Roots-branded storefront on business-to-consumer marketplace website in the People's Republic of China.
The company's international operating partner in Taiwan and the PRC is Branded Lifestyle (BLS), an affiliate of **Fung Retailing Limited**.
The company has a 68,364-sq.-ft. head office, a 45,436-sq.-ft. leather factory and 209,948-sq.-ft. distribution facility, all in Toronto, Ont. Most of the company's apparel products are manufactured outside of North America and majority of leather products are made at the Toronto facility.
During the fiscal year ended Jan. 28, 2023, the company opened one store and closed one store.
Directors - Erol Uzumeri, chr., Ont.; Meghan Roach, pres. & CEO, Ont.; Dale H. Lastman†, Toronto, Ont.; Phil Bacal, Ont.; Mary Ann Curran, Ont.; Gregory David, Toronto, Ont.; Richard P. (Rick) Mavrinac, Toronto, Ont.; Dexter Peart, Qué.; Joel Teitelbaum, Qué.
Other Exec. Officers - Leon Wu, CFO; Karuna Scheinfeld, chief product officer; Kaleb Honsberger, sr. v-p, gen. counsel & corp. sec.; Michelle Lettner, sr. v-p, HR; Ron Ijack, v-p, info. strategy & sys.; Karl Kowalewski, v-p, leather factory; Joseph Mangattoor, v-p, opers.; Melinda McDonald, v-p, wholesale & bus. devel.; Sonya Thomas, v-p, e-commerce & cust. experience
† Lead director

Capital Stock

	Authorized (shs.)	Outstanding (shs.)[1]
Preferred	unlimited	nil
Common	unlimited	40,907,413

[1] At June 7, 2023

Options - At Jan. 28, 2023, options were outstanding to purchase 2,295,073 common shares at a weighted average exercise price of $3.09 per share.
Major Shareholder - Searchlight Capital Partners, L.P. held 50.16% interest and Kernwood Limited held 12.34% interest at June 7, 2023.

Price Range - ROOT/TSX

Year	Volume	High	Low	Close
2022	6,688,901	$3.95	$2.33	$2.75
2021	11,823,445	$4.39	$2.04	$3.19
2020	13,382,687	$2.63	$0.62	$2.43
2019	26,036,408	$4.77	$1.85	$2.06
2018	30,508,375	$13.55	$2.91	$3.15

Recent Close: $2.90
Capital Stock Changes - During fiscal 2023, common shares were issued as follows: 21,337 under restricted share unit plan and 18,334 on exercise of options; 631,869 common shares were repurchased under a Normal Course Issuer Bid.
Long-Term Debt - At Jan. 28, 2023, outstanding long-term debt totaled $56,726,000 ($4,613,000 current) and consisted entirely of amounts drawn on credit facilities bearing interest (according to the type of borrowing advanced) at the U.S. base rate or Canadian prime plus 1.75% to 3%, or LIBOR or bankers' acceptances rate plus 2.75% to 4%, and due Sept. 6, 2024.
Note - In April 2023, the company extended its $60,000,000 facility agreement from Sept. 6, 2024, to Sept. 6, 2026. Also, the terms of the agreement would transition from LIBOR to SOFR.

Wholly Owned Subsidiaries

Roots International ULC, B.C.
Roots Leasing Corporation, Toronto, Ont. Inactive.

Financial Statistics

Periods ended:	52w Jan. 28/23^A		52w Jan. 29/22^oA
	$000s	%Chg	$000s
Operating revenue	**272,116**	**-1**	**273,834**
Cost of goods sold	115,140		110,977
General & admin expense	108,486		91,552
Stock-based compensation	380		655
Operating expense	**224,006**	**+10**	**203,184**
Operating income	**48,110**	**-32**	**70,650**
Deprec., depl. & amort.	29,324		29,994
Finance income	263		53
Finance costs, gross	9,019		8,861
Write-downs/write-offs	(435)		(649)
Pre-tax income	**9,595**	**-69**	**31,199**
Income taxes	2,902		8,436
Net income	**6,693**	**-71**	**22,763**
Cash & equivalent	31,921		34,161
Inventories	54,990		41,256
Accounts receivable	5,684		5,984
Current assets	96,155		86,473
Fixed assets, net	39,170		42,847
Right-of-use assets	62,484		68,000
Intangibles, net	194,083		196,385
Total assets	**391,892**	**0**	**393,705**
Accts. pay. & accr. liabs	38,414		28,307
Current liabilities	75,032		68,152
Long-term debt, gross	56,726		60,779
Long-term debt, net	52,113		56,166
Long-term lease liabilities	57,575		65,947
Shareholders' equity	188,042		186,057
Cash from oper. activs	**29,298**	**-48**	**56,467**
Cash from fin. activs	(25,190)		(27,064)
Cash from invest. activs	(6,348)		(4,408)
Net cash position	**31,921**	**-7**	**34,161**
Capital expenditures	(6,348)		(4,408)
	$		$
Earnings per share*	0.16		0.54
Cash flow per share*	0.70		1.34
	shs		shs
No. of shs. o/s*	41,461,863		42,054,061
Avg. no. of shs. o/s*	41,739,504		42,221,249
	%		%
Net profit margin	2.46		8.31
Return on equity	3.58		13.00
Return on assets	3.31		7.46
No. of employees (FTEs)	2,033		2,044

* Common
^o Restated
^A Reported in accordance with IFRS

Latest Results

Periods ended:	13w Apr. 29/23^A		13w Apr. 30/22^A
	$000s	%Chg	$000s
Operating revenue	41,496	-4	43,072
Net income	(7,966)	n.a.	(5,261)
	$		$
Earnings per share*	(0.19)		(0.13)

* Common
^A Reported in accordance with IFRS

Historical Summary
(as originally stated)

Fiscal Year	Oper. Rev.	Net Inc. Bef. Disc.	EPS*
	$000s	$000s	$
2023^A	272,116	6,693	0.16
2022^A	273,834	22,763	0.54
2021^A	240,506	13,080	0.31
2020^A	329,865	(62,029)	(1.47)
2019^A	329,028	11,400	0.27

* Common
^A Reported in accordance with IFRS

R.69 Roshni Capital Inc.

Symbol - ROSH.P **Exchange** - TSX-VEN **CUSIP** - 77815W
Head Office - 2185 Rosemount Cres, Oakville, ON, L6M 3P4 **Telephone** - (905) 510-7636
Email - psingh@thesiscapital.ca
Investor Relations - Pritpal Singh (905) 510-7636
Auditors - MNP LLP C.A., Toronto, Ont.
Transfer Agents - Odyssey Trust Company, Toronto, Ont.
Profile - (Ont. 2021) Capital Pool Company.
Directors - Pritpal Singh, CEO, Oakville, Ont.; Eyal Ofir, CFO & corp. sec., Toronto, Ont.; Michael Rennie, Toronto, Ont.; Pardeep S. Sangha, Vancouver, B.C.

Capital Stock

	Authorized (shs.)	Outstanding (shs.)[1]
Common	unlimited	8,000,000

[1] At Apr. 24, 2023

Major Shareholder - Pardeep S. Sangha held 12.5% interest and Pritpal Singh held 12.5% interest at Dec. 8, 2021.

Price Range - ROSH.P/TSX-VEN

Year	Volume	High	Low	Close
2022	100,000	$0.10	$0.04	$0.04
2021	45,000	$0.10	$0.10	$0.10

Recent Close: $0.10

Capital Stock Changes - There were no changes to capital stock during 2022.

R.70 Route1 Inc.

Symbol - ROI **Exchange** - TSX-VEN **CUSIP** - 77929Q
Head Office - 1801-8 King St E, Toronto, ON, M5C 1B5 **Telephone** - (416) 848-8391 **Toll-free** - (866) 286-7330 **Fax** - (416) 848-8394
Website - www.route1.com
Email - tony.busseri@route1.com
Investor Relations - Tony P. Busseri (416) 509-1496
Auditors - MNP LLP C.A., Mississauga, Ont.
Transfer Agents - Computershare Trust Company of Canada Inc., Toronto, Ont.

Profile - (Ont. 2004; orig. Alta., 1994) Provides security and identity management solutions to private and public sector clients worldwide enabling access to digital resources and sensitive data at anytime from anywhere. Also supplies rugged mobile devices to automotive manufacturers and suppliers, other manufacturing and distribution companies, and local and state government in the southeastern and southwestern U.S.

Products offered are organized into three groups: Automatic License Plate Recognition; Surveillance and Video Intelligence; and Data Security and User Authentications.

Automatic License Plate Recognition - Includes Genetec Security Center AutoVu, a camera device used to capture and identifies incensed plates and vehicle-based evidence in all weather conditions; and MobiLPR which extends AutoVu camera on a mobile device.

Surveillance and Video Intelligence - Includes Omnicast, a unified platform which can view all monitored areas and data analytics which uses video analytics and advanced perimeter protection capabilities to locate threats and notify relevant personnel as well as store video evidence which can be accessed by authorized personnel; Stratocast, which provides real-time video intelligence monitored from one unified platform which utilizes cloud-based management system for the storage of the data; Body-worn Cameras, which are used for evidence without context or data which allows for a better understanding of events that officers are confronted with daily; in-car video, a rear and front-facing dash cams; and Synergis Access Control, an IP access control which connects to a large selection of third-party access control devices and unifies video and other security systems to deliver operational and security insights.

Data Security and User Authentications - Includes MobiKEY, a remote access technology device which uses smartcard and Public Key Infrastructure (PKI)-based multifactor authentication to securely connect the organization's assets with authorized employees and contractors and provide access to data anytime and anywhere and on any device; DerivID, which validates the identity of mobile user without the need of external card reader; MobiNET, a universal identity management and service delivery platform which identifies and authenticates users within all levels of classified and unclassified networks; DEFIMNET™, a military version of MobiNET®, resides in all levels of classified and unclassified networks and interacts with other defence network systems; PocketVault P-3X, an encrypted solid-state disk (SSD) drive which includes embedded PKI smartcard for multi-factor authentication that protects data which can be used anywhere like USB drive; and NcryptNshare, which creates a personal secure vault on each user's personal computer that cannot be accessed or viewed without the user's PocketVault P-3X generated token that protects the encryption and authentication/signature keys in wholly owned **Spyrus Solutions, Inc.**,'s Rosetta, a FIPS 140-2 Level 3 validated controller chip embedded in all PocketVault.

Also provides technology and application engineering services including advisory and analysis, design and engineering, hardware and software procurement, project management, installation and configuration, operations optimization, technology life-cycle maintenance and support, and admin user and admin training.

Through its Group Mobile division, offers end-to-end mobile technology solutions to guide mobile projects through their entire lifecycle. Solutions offered are rugged mobile hardware, in-vehicle system integration, project service support, pre-deployment and post-deployment services, asset management and customer support helpdesk for use in a wide range of applications in the utilities, telecommunications, field services, insurance, healthcare, Fire/EMT, police and public safety sectors, as well as state and local government.

Through wholly owned subsidiary **Portable Computer Systems, Inc.**, resells computer with expertise in mobile data applications which include wireless products for in-vehicle use. Solutions offered are rugged devices and applications which include Panasonic Toughbook mobile computers, Xplore and Getac rugged tablets, Genetec license plate recognition solutions, and accessories from Gamber-Johnson and Havis for use in a wide range of applications for various industries.

Through wholly owned **DataSource Mobility, LLC**, resells ruggedized tablets and laptops along with associated accessories as well as offers guidance and mobile devices for a wide range of sectors including public safety, utilities, field services, logistics, healthcare, and state and local governments.

Through wholly owned **Spyrus Solutions**, develops and manufactures cryptographic products including encryption, authentication and digital content security products to U.S. defence and civilian agencies, international government, financial and healthcare enterprises. Spyrus's products include the SPYCOS smart card operating system, which enables strong protection for data-in-motion, data-at-rest and data-in-process.

Predecessor Detail - Name changed from The Prospectus Group Inc., Oct. 21, 2004, following reverse takeover acquisition of IP Co. Limited.

Directors - Michael D. Harris, chr., East York, Ont.; Tony P. Busseri, CEO & CFO, Oakville, Ont.; Peter F. Chodos, exec. v-p, corp. devel., Toronto, Ont.; Michael F. Doolan, Mississauga, Ont.; John Marino, Leesburg, Va.

Other Exec. Officers - Jerry S. Iwanski, exec. v-p & COO; Alex Shpurov, sr. v-p & chief tech. officer; Elton Crawford, v-p, opers.

Capital Stock

	Authorized (shs.)	Outstanding (shs.)[1]
Preferred	unlimited	nil
Common	unlimited	39,709,463

[1] At Sept. 30, 2022

Major Shareholder - Widely held at Oct. 17, 2022.

Price Range - ROI/TSX-VEN

Year	Volume	High	Low	Close
2022	8,615,833	$0.32	$0.02	$0.06
2021	16,534,026	$1.14	$0.25	$0.30
2020	13,936,210	$1.09	$0.32	$0.90
2019	4,350,561	$0.80	$0.25	$0.39
2018	7,931,941	$0.65	$0.15	$0.55

Consolidation: 1-for-10 cons. in Aug. 2019
Recent Close: $0.05

Wholly Owned Subsidiaries

DataSource Mobility, LLC, Tenn.
• 100% int. in **VetSource Mobility, LLC**, Tenn.
Group Mobile Int'l LLC, Chandler, Ariz.
Portable Computer Systems, Inc., Denver, Colo.
Route1 Security Corporation
Spyrus Solutions, Inc., San Jose, Calif.

Financial Statistics

Periods ended:	12m Dec. 31/21[A]		12m Dec. 31/20[A]
	$000s	%Chg	$000s
Operating revenue	**27,271**	**-8**	**29,707**
Cost of goods sold	16,446		18,635
Research & devel. expense	906		763
General & admin expense	8,906		7,849
Stock-based compensation	568		497
Operating expense	**26,826**	**-3**	**27,744**
Operating income	**445**	**-77**	**1,963**
Deprec., depl. & amort.	1,316		1,323
Finance costs, gross	277		163
Pre-tax income	**210**	**n.a.**	**(1,711)**
Income taxes	(12)		(3)
Net income	**222**	**n.a.**	**(1,707)**
Cash & equivalent	63		1,137
Inventories	682		679
Accounts receivable	4,397		3,311
Current assets	5,726		6,408
Fixed assets, net	908		893
Right-of-use assets	1,635		2,152
Intangibles, net	5,344		3,238
Total assets	**15,097**	**+6**	**14,176**
Bank indebtedness	1,827		777
Accts. pay. & accr. liabs	4,564		4,063
Current liabilities	10,563		9,779
Long-term debt, gross	1,162		1,015
Long-term debt, net	nil		257
Long-term lease liabilities	1,352		1,740
Shareholders' equity	2,728		2,141
Cash from oper. activs	**1,047**	**+309**	**256**
Cash from fin. activs	6		1,315
Cash from invest. activs	(2,202)		(458)
Net cash position	**63**	**-94**	**1,137**
Capital expenditures	(553)		(373)
Capital disposals	77		3
	$		$
Earnings per share*	0.01		(0.05)
Cash flow per share*	0.03		0.01
	shs		shs
No. of shs. o/s*	39,709,463		38,694,020
Avg. no. of shs. o/s*	39,553,980		35,499,546
	%		%
Net profit margin	0.81		(5.75)
Return on equity	9.12		(109.39)
Return on assets	3.52		(11.52)
Foreign sales percent	99		99

* Common
[A] Reported in accordance with IFRS

Latest Results

Periods ended:	9m Sept. 30/22[A]		9m Sept. 30/21[A]
	$000s	%Chg	$000s
Operating revenue	18,657	-8	20,237
Net income	9	-98	537
	$		$
Earnings per share*	0.00		0.01

* Common
[A] Reported in accordance with IFRS

Historical Summary
(as originally stated)

Fiscal Year	Oper. Rev.	Net Inc. Bef. Disc.	EPS*
	$000s	$000s	$
2021[A]	27,271	222	0.01
2020[A]	29,707	(1,707)	(0.05)
2019[A]	24,010	(554)	(0.02)
2018[A]	26,231	(434)	(0.01)
2017[A]	6,070	(610)	(0.02)

* Common
[A] Reported in accordance with IFRS
Note: Adjusted throughout for 1-for-10 cons. in Aug. 2019

R.71 Royal Bank of Canada*

Symbol - RY **Exchange** - TSX **CUSIP** - 780087
Head Office - 1 Place Ville Marie, Montréal, QC, H3B 3A9 **Telephone** - (514) 874-2110 **Toll-free** - (888) 212-5533 **Fax** - (514) 874-6582
Website - www.rbc.com
Email - nadine.ahn@rbc.com
Investor Relations - Nadine Ahn (416) 955-7804
Auditors - PricewaterhouseCoopers LLP C.A., Toronto, Ont.
Transfer Agents - Computershare Investor Services plc, Bristol, Gloucs. United Kingdom; Computershare Trust Company, N.A., Canton, Mass.; Computershare Trust Company of Canada Inc., Montréal, Qué.
FP500 Revenue Ranking - 3
Employees - 91,427 at Oct. 31, 2022

Profile - (Can. 1871, via Bank Act; orig. N.S., 1869) A Schedule I Canadian chartered bank providing personal and commercial banking, wealth management, insurance, investor and treasury services and capital markets products and services to 17,000,000 clients through offices in Canada, the U.S. and 27 other countries.

Personal & Commercial Banking

Provides banking, investing and financing products and services to personal and business customers in Canada, the Caribbean and the U.S.

Canadian Banking offers personal and business banking to over 14,000,000 clients through a network of 1,162 branches, 4,028 automated teller machines (ATMs) and mobile sales channels. Personal banking provides financing and investment products and services, including home equity financing, personal lending, chequing and savings accounts, private banking, indirect lending (including automobile financing), mutual funds and self-directed brokerage accounts, guaranteed investment certificates (GICs), credit cards, and payment products and solutions to individual clients. Business banking provides lending, leasing, deposit, investment, foreign exchange, cash management, automobile dealer financing, trade products and services to small and medium-sized commercial businesses.

Caribbean and U.S. Banking offers banking products and services, international financing and trade promotion services in nine countries and territories in the Caribbean, and serves the needs of the bank's Canadian retail and small business clients in all 50 U.S. states. The bank operates a network of 38 branches and 269 ATMs.

Wealth Management

Provides investment, estate and trust, banking, credit and other wealth management and asset management products and services to affluent, high net worth and ultra high net worth individual and institutional clients in Canada, the U.S., the U.K., Europe and Asia.

Canadian Wealth Management offers full-service wealth advisory through over 1,950 investment advisors, and provides discretionary investment management and estate and trust services through over 100 investment counsellors and over 100 trust professionals.

U.S. Wealth Management consists of the private client group business, which offers full-service wealth advisory through over 2,100 financial advisors; and the clearing and custody business, which provides clearing and execution services for small to medium-sized independent broker-dealers and registered investment advisor firms. Operations also include wholly owned **City National Bank**, a private and commercial bank which provides lending, deposit, cash management, equipment financing, wealth management and other products and services to affluent individuals, entrepreneurs, professionals, their businesses and their families.

Global Asset Management provides investment management services and solutions through mutual, pooled and private funds, fee-based accounts and separately managed portfolios to individual and institutional investors in Canada, the U.K., the U.S., Europe and Asia. Products and services are distributed to clients directly and through the bank's branches, self-directed and full-service wealth advisory businesses, independent third party advisors and private banks.

International Wealth Management provides customized and integrated wealth management solutions to individual and corporate clients in key financial centres in the U.K., Ireland, the Channel Islands and Asia.

Insurance

Provides insurance and reinsurance solutions in Canada and internationally. Canadian Insurance serves individual and business clients with life, health, travel, wealth accumulation solutions and annuities, as well as home and automobile insurance through a distribution agreement with Aviva Canada. Products and services are offered through advice centres, the bank's insurance stores, mobile advisors, digital platforms, independent brokers and partners. International Insurance operates in reinsurance and retrocession markets globally offering life, disability and longevity reinsurance products.

Investor & Treasury Services

Provides asset, payment and treasury services to financial institutions and asset owners worldwide. Products and services offered include custody, fund administration, shareholder services, private capital services, middle office, transaction banking (including trade finance, insourced solutions and services to broker dealers) and treasury and market services (including cash and liquidity management, foreign exchange and securities finance).

Capital Markets

Provides advisory and origination, sales and trading, and lending and financing to corporations, institutional clients, asset managers, private equity firms and governments through 63 offices in 18 countries across North America, the U.K. and Europe, Australia, Asia and other regions. Operations consist of Corporate and Investment Banking, which includes corporate lending, municipal finance, loan syndication, debt and equity origination, and mergers and acquisitions advisory services; and Global Markets, which includes the sales and trading businesses covering fixed income, foreign exchange, commodities and equities, as well as the repurchase agreements and secured financing products. Operations also include a legacy portfolio, which consists of the bank's U.S. commercial mortgage-backed securities (MBS), bank-owned life insurance (BOLI) derivative contracts and structured rates in Asia.

Recent Merger and Acquisition Activity

Status: pending **Announced:** Nov. 29, 2022

Royal Bank of Canada (RBC) agreed to acquire HSBC Holdings plc's Canadian banking business, HSBC Bank Canada, for $13.5 billion in cash. HSBC Bank Canada is a Canadian personal and commercial bank focused on globally connected clients. At Sept. 30, 2022, HSBC Bank Canada had $134 billion in assets, more than 130 branches, over 780,000 retail and commercial customers and 4,200 full-time equivalent employees. RBC would also acquire all of existing preferred shares and subordinated debt of HSBC Bank Canada held by HSBC Holdings plc at par value. The transaction was expected to close in late 2023.

Status: pending **Announced:** Oct. 17, 2022

Royal Bank of Canada and CACEIS, the asset servicing banking group of Crédit Agricole S.A. and Banco Santander, S.A., signed a Memorandum of Understanding with a view for CACEIS to acquire the European asset servicing activities of RBC Investor Services and its associated Malaysian centre of excellence. Terms were not disclosed. The transaction would include custody, global custody foreign exchange, fund administration, transfer agency, middle office and securities lending. RBC Investor Services is a provider of asset services and holds assets under administration (AUA) in Europe of €1.2 trillion and assets under custody in Europe of €0.5 trillion. The completion of the contemplated transaction was expected to take place by the end of the third quarter of the 2023 calendar year.

Status: completed **Announced:** Oct. 4, 2022

Royal Bank of Canada acquired MDBilling.ca, a cloud-based platform that automates medical billing for physicians in Ontario and British Columbia. Terms of the transaction were not disclosed.

Status: completed **Revised:** Sept. 27, 2022

UPDATE: The transaction was completed. PREVIOUS: Royal Bank of Canada agreed to acquire London, U.K.-based Brewin Dolphin Holdings plc for £5.15 cash per share, in a transaction valued at £1.6 billion (Cdn$2.6 billion). Brewin was a London Stock Exchange-listed company that provides wealth and investment management services in the U.K., the Channel Islands and Ireland, with more than 30 offices and £59 billion in assets under management (AUM). Brewin's board of directors planned to recommend the transaction to shareholders, which was expected to be completed by the end of the third quarter of 2022. The transaction was subject to customary closing conditions, including regulatory approvals and Brewin shareholder approval. The acquisition would create a wealth manager with £64 billion of AUM and, based on 2021 earnings, combined annual revenue of £545,000,000.

Predecessor Detail - Name changed from The Royal Bank of Canada, Nov. 1, 1990.

Directors - Jacynthe Côté, chr., Candiac, Qué.; David I. McKay, pres. & CEO, Toronto, Ont.; Mirko Bibic, Toronto, Ont.; Andrew A. Chisholm, Toronto, Ont.; Toos N. Daruvala, New York, N.Y.; Cynthia J. Devine, Toronto, Ont.; Roberta L. Jamieson, Ohsweken, Ont.; Maryann Turcke, Toronto, Ont.; Thierry Vandal, Mamaroneck, N.Y.; Bridget A. van Kralingen, Point Pleasant Beach, N.J.; Frank M. Vettese, Toronto, Ont.; Jeffery W. Yabuki, Incline Village, Nev.

Other Exec. Officers - Nadine Ahn, CFO; Maria Douvas, chief legal officer; Graeme Hepworth, chief risk officer; Christoph Knoess, chief administrative & strategy officer; Kelly Pereira, chief HR officer; Douglas A. (Doug) Guzman, grp. head, wealth mgt., insce. & investor & treasury srvcs.; Neil McLaughlin, grp. head, personal & comml. banking; Derek Neldner, grp. head, capital markets & CEO, RBC Capital Markets; Bruce B. Ross, grp. head, tech. & opers.; Janet Boyle, sr. v-p, unsecured & indirect lending & specialized segments; Karen E. McCarthy, sr. v-p, assoc. gen. counsel & corp. sec.; Kathleen Novak, sr. mtge. specialist

Capital Stock

	Authorized (shs.)	Outstanding (shs.)[1]
First Preferred	unlimited	
Series AZ		20,000,000
Series BB		20,000,000
Series BD		24,000,000
Series BF		12,000,000
Series BH		6,000,000
Series BI		6,000,000
Series BO		14,000,000
Series BT		750,000
Series C-2		15,000
Second Preferred	unlimited	nil
Limited Recourse Capital Notes	n.a.	[2]
Series 1		1,750,000
Series 2		1,250,000
Series 3		1,000,000
Common	unlimited	1,395,266,075[3]

[1] At Aug. 18, 2023

[2] Number of shares represent the number of notes issued.

[3] Net of treasury shares held of 969,114.

First Preferred - Total authorized amount is an unlimited number of shares without nominal or par value; the aggregate consideration for which all first preferred shares may be issued shall not exceed $20 billion. Non-voting. Issuable in series. Each series of first preferred shares shall rank on a parity with every other series of first preferred shares and in priority to the second preferred and common shares with respect to the payment of dividends and the distribution of capital in the event of liquidation, dissolution or winding-up of the bank.

Series AZ - Entitled to non-cumulative annual dividends of $0.925 payable quarterly to May 24, 2024, and thereafter at a rate reset every five years equal to the five-year Government of Canada bond yield plus 2.21%. Redeemable on May 24, 2024, and on May 24 every five years thereafter at $25 per share. Convertible at the holder's option, on May 24, 2024, and on May 24 every five years thereafter, into floating rate first preferred series BA shares on a share-for-share basis, subject to certain conditions. The series BA shares would pay a quarterly dividend equal to the 90-day Canadian Treasury bill rate plus 2.21%. Convertible into common shares upon occurrence of certain trigger events related to financial viability. The contingent conversion formula is 1.0 multiplied by $25 plus declared and unpaid dividends divided by the greater of (i) a floor price of $5.00; and (ii) current market price of the common shares.

Series BB - Entitled to non-cumulative annual dividends of $0.9125 payable quarterly to Aug. 24, 2024, and thereafter at a rate reset every five years equal to the five-year Government of Canada bond yield plus 2.26%. Redeemable on Aug. 24, 2024, and on August 24 every five years thereafter at $25 per share. Convertible at the holder's option, on Aug. 24, 2024, and on August 24 every five years thereafter, into floating rate first preferred series BC shares on a share-for-share basis, subject to certain conditions. The series BC shares would pay a quarterly dividend equal to the 90-day Canadian Treasury bill rate plus 2.26%. Convertible into common shares upon occurrence of certain trigger events related to financial viability. The contingent conversion formula is 1.0 multiplied by $25 plus declared and unpaid dividends divided by the greater of (i) a floor price of $5.00; and (ii) current market price of the common shares.

Series BD - Entitled to non-cumulative annual dividends of 80¢ payable quarterly to May 24, 2025, and thereafter at a rate reset every five years equal to the five-year Government of Canada bond yield plus 2.74%. Redeemable on May 24, 2025, and on May 24 every five years thereafter at $25 per share. Convertible at the holder's option, on May 24, 2025, and on May 24 every five years thereafter, into floating rate first preferred series BE shares on a share-for-share basis, subject to certain conditions. The series BE shares would pay a quarterly dividend equal to the 90-day Canadian Treasury bill rate plus 2.74%. Convertible into common shares upon occurrence of certain trigger events related to financial viability. The contingent conversion formula is 1.0 multiplied by $25 plus declared and unpaid dividends divided by the greater of (i) a floor price of $5.00; and (ii) current market price of the common shares.

Series BF - Entitled to non-cumulative annual dividends of 75¢ payable quarterly to Nov. 24, 2025, and thereafter at a rate reset every five years equal to the five-year Government of Canada bond yield plus 2.62%. Redeemable on Nov. 24, 2025, and on November 24 every five years thereafter at $25 per share. Convertible at the holder's option, on Nov. 24, 2025, and on November 24 every five years thereafter, into floating rate first preferred series BG shares on a share-for-share basis, subject to certain conditions. The series BG shares would pay a quarterly dividend equal to the 90-day Canadian Treasury bill rate plus 2.62%. Convertible into common shares upon occurrence of certain trigger events related to financial viability. The contingent conversion formula is 1.0 multiplied by $25 plus declared and unpaid dividends divided by the greater of (i) a floor price of $5.00; and (ii) current market price of the common shares.

Series BH - Entitled to non-cumulative annual dividends of $1.225 payable quarterly. Redeemable at $25.50 per share, and declining by 25¢ per share annually (on Nov. 24) to Nov. 24, 2024, and at $25 per share thereafter. Convertible into common shares upon occurrence of certain trigger events related to financial viability. The contingent conversion formula is 1.0 multiplied by $25 plus declared and unpaid dividends divided by the greater of (i) a floor price of $5.00; and (ii) current market price of the common shares.

Series BI - Entitled to non-cumulative annual dividends of $1.225 payable quarterly. Redeemable at $25.50 per share, and declining by 25¢ per share annually (on Nov. 24) to Nov. 24, 2024, and at $25 per share thereafter. Convertible into common shares upon occurrence of certain trigger events related to financial viability. The contingent conversion formula is 1.0 multiplied by $25 plus declared and unpaid dividends divided by the greater of (i) a floor price of $5.00; and (ii) current market price of the common shares.

Series BO - Entitled to non-cumulative annual dividends of $1.20 payable quarterly to Feb. 24, 2024, and thereafter at a rate reset every five years equal to the five-year Government of Canada bond yield plus 2.38%. Redeemable on Feb. 24, 2024, and on February 24 every five years thereafter at $25 per share. Convertible at the holder's option, on Feb. 24, 2024, and on February 24 every five years thereafter, into floating rate first preferred series BP shares on a share-for-share basis, subject to certain conditions. The series BP shares would pay a quarterly dividend equal to the 90-day Canadian Treasury bill rate plus 2.38%. Convertible into common shares upon occurrence of certain trigger events related to financial viability. The contingent conversion formula is 1.0 multiplied by $25 plus declared and unpaid dividends divided by the greater of (i) a floor price of $5.00; and (ii) current market price of the common shares.

Series BT - Entitled to non-cumulative annual dividends of $42 payable semi-annually to Feb. 24, 2027, and thereafter at a rate reset every five years equal to the five-year Government of Canada bond yield plus 2.71%. Redeemable during the period from January 24 to and including February 24, commencing Jan. 24, 2027, and every five years thereafter at $1,000 per share. Convertible into common shares upon occurrence of certain trigger events related to financial viability. The contingent conversion formula is 1.0 multiplied by $1,000 plus declared and unpaid dividends divided by the greater of (i) a floor price of $5.00; and (ii) current market price of the common shares.

Series C-2 - Entitled to non-cumulative annual dividends of US$67.50 payable quarterly to Nov. 7, 2023, and thereafter at a rate equal to the three-month LIBOR plus 4.052%. Redeemable at US$1,000 per share on or after Nov. 7, 2023.

Second Preferred - Total authorized amount is an unlimited number of shares without nominal or par value; the aggregate consideration for which all second preferred shares may be issued shall not exceed $5 billion. Non-voting. Issuable in series. Each series of second preferred shares shall rank junior to the first preferred shares, on a parity with every other series of second preferred shares and in priority to the common shares with respect to the payment of dividends and the distribution of capital in the event of liquidation, dissolution or winding-up of the bank.

Limited Recourse Capital Notes (LRCNs) - Notes with recourse limited to assets held by a third party trustee in a consolidated trust. **LRCN Series 1** - Bear interest at 4.5% per annum until Nov. 24, 2025, and thereafter at an annual rate reset every five years equal to the five-year Government of Canada bond yield plus 4.137% until maturity on Nov. 24, 2080. Trust assets consist of non-cumulative five-year reset first preferred series BQ shares. **LRCN Series 2** - Bear interest at 4% per annum until Feb. 24, 2026, and thereafter at an annual rate reset every five years equal to the five-year Government of Canada bond yield plus 3.617% until maturity on Feb. 24, 2081. Trust assets consist of non-cumulative five-year reset first preferred series BR shares. **LRCN Series 3** - Bear interest at 3.65% per annum until Nov. 24, 2026, and thereafter at an annual rate reset every five years equal to the five-year Government of Canada bond yield plus 2.665% until maturity on Nov. 24, 2081. Trust assets consist of non-cumulative five-year reset first preferred series BS shares.

Common - An unlimited number of shares without nominal or par value may be issued. One vote per share.

Options - At Oct. 31, 2022, options were outstanding to purchase an aggregate of 7,509,000 common shares at prices ranging from $48.22 to $129.99 per share with a weighted average remaining contractual life of 5.91 years.

First Preferred Series BK (old) - Were entitled to non-cumulative annual dividends of $1.375 payable quarterly. Redeemed on May 24, 2021, at $25 per share.

First Preferred Series BM (old) - Were entitled to non-cumulative annual dividends of $1.375 payable quarterly. Redeemed on Aug. 24, 2021, at $25 per share.

First Preferred Series BJ (old) - Were entitled to non-cumulative annual dividends of $1.3125 payable quarterly. Redeemed on Feb. 24, 2022, at $25.75 per share.

Major Shareholder - Widely held at Mar. 13, 2023.

Price Range - RY/TSX

Year	Volume	High	Low	Close
2022	952,225,395	$149.60	$116.75	$127.30
2021	967,010,721	$135.34	$103.22	$134.25
2020	1,070,131,994	$109.42	$72.00	$104.59
2019	670,106,352	$109.68	$92.26	$102.75
2018	583,491,641	$108.52	$90.10	$93.44

Recent Close: $121.02

Capital Stock Changes - In November 2021, public offering of 750,000 first preferred series BT shares was completed at $1,000 per share. On Feb. 24, 2022, all 6,000,000 first preferred series BJ shares were redeemed at $25.75 per share. Also during fiscal 2022, 1,270,000 common shares were issued on exercise of options and 40,866,000 common shares were repurchased under a Normal Course Issuer Bid. In addition, 2,018,000 (net) common shares were returned to treasury and 152,000 (net) preferred shares were released from treasury.

Dividends

RY com Ra $5.40 pa Q est. Aug. 24, 2023**
Prev. Rate: $5.28 est. Feb. 24, 2023
Prev. Rate: $5.12 est. Aug. 24, 2022
Prev. Rate: $4.80 est. Feb. 24, 2022
Prev. Rate: $4.32 est. May 22, 2020
RY.PR.Z pfd 1st ser AZ red. exch. Adj. Ra $0.925 pa Q est. Aug. 23, 2019**
RY.PR.H pfd 1st ser BB red. exch. Adj. Ra $0.9125 pa Q est. Nov. 22, 2019**
RY.PR.J pfd 1st ser BD red. exch. Adj. Ra $0.80 pa Q est. Aug. 24, 2020**
RY.PR.M pfd 1st ser BF red. exch. Adj. Ra $0.75 pa Q est. Feb. 24, 2021**
RY.PR.N pfd 1st ser BH red. exch. Ra $1.225 pa Q**
RY.PR.O pfd 1st ser BI red. exch. Ra $1.225 pa Q**
RY.PR.S pfd 1st ser BO red. exch. Adj. Ra $1.20 pa Q est. Feb. 22, 2019
pfd 1st ser BJ red. exch. Ra $1.3125 pa Q**[1]
$0.328125f.......... Feb. 24/22
pfd 1st ser BK red. exch. Adj. Ra $1.375 pa Q est. May 24, 2016**[2]
$0.34375f............ May 21/21
pfd 1st ser BM red. exch. Adj. Ra $1.375 pa Q est. Aug. 24, 2016**[3]
$0.34375f............ Aug. 24/21

[1] Redeemed Feb. 23, 2022 at $25.75 per sh.
[2] Redeemed May. 24, 2021 at $25 per sh.
[3] Redeemed Aug. 24, 2021 at $25 per sh.
** Reinvestment Option **f** Final Payment

Long-Term Debt - All bank debentures are direct unsecured and subordinated to deposits and other liabilities.

Outstanding at Oct. 31, 2022:

Subord. debs.	
Fixed rate:	
9.3% due 2023	$110,000,000
4.65% due 2026[1]	1,884,000,000
4.75% due 2027[2]	60,000,000
Floating rate:	
2.74% due 2029[3]	1,415,000,000
2.88% due 2029[4]	1,412,000,000
2.09% due 2030[5]	1,250,000,000
2.14% due 2031[6]	1,637,000,000
2.94% due 2032[7]	932,000,000
1.67% due 2033[8]	875,000,000
Due 2083[9]	224,000,000
Due 2085[10]	237,000,000
Less: Def. fin. costs	11,000,000
	10,025,000,000

[1] US$1.5 billion.
[2] TT$300,000,000.
[3] Bears interest at 2.74% to July 25, 2024; thereafter, at the three-month CDOR plus 0.98%.
[4] Bears interest at 2.88% to Dec. 23, 2024; thereafter, at the three-month CDOR plus 0.89%.
[5] Bears interest at 2.09% to June 30, 2025; thereafter, at the three-month CDOR plus 1.31%.
[6] Bears interest at 2.14% to Nov. 3, 2026; thereafter, at the three-month CDOR plus 0.61%.
[7] Bears interest at 2.94% to May 3, 2027; thereafter, at the three-month CDOR plus 0.76%.
[8] Bears interest at 1.67% to Jan. 28, 2028; thereafter, at the three-month CDOR plus 0.55%.
[9] Bears interest at the 30-day bankers' acceptance rate plus 0.4%.
[10] US$174,000,000. Bears interest at the US$ three-month LIMEAN plus 0.25%.

The aggregate maturities of the debentures, based on the maturity dates under the terms of issue, were as follows:

Within one year	$110,000,000
One to five years	1,884,000,000
Five to 10 years	6,706,000,000
Thereafter	1,336,000,000

Note - In November 2022, all TT$300,000,000 of 4.75% subordinated debentures due 2027 were redeemed. In January 2023, offering of $1.5 billion of 5.01% subordinated debentures due 2033 was completed, bearing interest at 5.01% until Feb. 1, 2028, and thereafter at the Daily Compounded Canadian Overnight Repo Rate Average (CORRA) plus 2.12%.

Wholly Owned Subsidiaries

RBC Dominion Securities Limited, Toronto, Ont. Carrying value of voting shares owned by the bank at Oct. 31, 2022, totaled $13,535,000,000.
- 100% int. in **RBC Dominion Securities Inc.**, Toronto, Ont.

RBC Europe Limited, London, Middx., United Kingdom. Carrying value of voting shares owned by the bank at Oct. 31, 2022, totaled $2,669,000,000.

RBC U.S. Group Holdings LLC, Toronto, Ont. Carrying value of voting shares owned by the bank at Oct. 31, 2022, totaled $27,655,000,000.
- 100% int. in **RBC USA Holdco Corporation**, New York, N.Y.
  - 100% int. in **City National Bank**, Los Angeles, Calif.
  - 100% int. in **RBC Capital Markets, LLC**, New York, N.Y.

Royal Bank Holding Inc., Toronto, Ont. Carrying value of voting shares owned by the bank at Oct. 31, 2022, totaled $77,914,000,000.
- 100% int. in **Capital Funding Alberta Limited**, Calgary, Alta.
  - 100% int. in **RBC Global Asset Management Inc.**, Toronto, Ont.
- 100% int. in **Investment Holdings (Cayman) Limited**, George Town, Cayman Islands.
  - 100% int. in **RBC (Barbados) Funding Ltd.**, St. Michael, Barbados.
- 100% int. in **RBC (Barbados) Trading Bank Corporation**, St. James, Barbados.
- 100% int. in **RBC Direct Investing Inc.**, Toronto, Ont.
- 100% int. in **R.B.C. Holdings (Bahamas) Limited**, Nassau, Bahamas.
  - 100% int. in **RBC Caribbean Investments Limited**, George Town, Cayman Islands.
    - 100% int. in **Royal Bank of Canada Insurance Company Ltd.**, Grand Cayman, Cayman Islands.
- 100% int. in **RBC Insurance Holdings Inc.**, Mississauga, Ont.
  - 100% int. in **RBC Life Insurance Company**, Mississauga, Ont.
- 100% int. in **RBC Investor Services Bank S.A.**, Esch-sur-Alzette, Luxembourg.
- 100% int. in **RBC Investor Services Trust**, Toronto, Ont.

Royal Bank Mortgage Corporation, Toronto, Ont. Carrying value of voting shares owned by the bank at Oct. 31, 2022, totaled $5,604,000,000.

The Royal Trust Company, Montréal, Qué. Carrying value of voting shares owned by the bank at Oct. 31, 2022, totaled $1,215,000,000.

Royal Trust Corporation of Canada, Toronto, Ont. Carrying value of voting shares owned by the bank at Oct. 31, 2022, totaled $486,000,000.

Note: The preceding list includes only the major related companies in which interests are held.

Financial Statistics

Periods ended:	12m Oct. 31/22[A]		12m Oct. 31/21[A]
	$000s	%Chg	$000s
Interest income	**40,771,000**	**+45**	**28,145,000**
Interest expense	18,054,000		8,143,000
Net interest income	**22,717,000**	**+14**	**20,002,000**
Provision for loan losses	484,000		(753,000)
Other income	26,268,000		29,691,000
Salaries & pension benefits	16,528,000		16,539,000
Non-interest expense	28,392,000		29,815,000
Pre-tax income	**20,109,000**	**-3**	**20,631,000**
Income taxes	4,302,000		4,581,000
Net income	**15,807,000**	**-2**	**16,050,000**
Net inc. for equity hldrs	**15,794,000**	**-2**	**16,038,000**
Net inc. for non-cont. int.	**13,000**	**+8**	**12,000**
Cash & equivalent	180,408,000		193,484,000
Securities	318,223,000		284,724,000
Net non-performing loans	1,530,000		1,611,000
Total loans	1,137,810,000		1,025,478,000
Fixed assets, net	7,214,000		7,424,000
Total assets	**1,917,219,000**	**+12**	**1,706,323,000**
Deposits	1,208,814,000		1,100,831,000
Other liabilities	590,205,000		497,137,000
Subordinated debt	10,025,000		9,593,000
Preferred share equity	7,318,000		6,684,000
Shareholders' equity	108,064,000		98,667,000
Non-controlling interest	111,000		95,000
Cash from oper. activs	**21,942,000**	**-64**	**61,044,000**
Cash from fin. activs	(2,185,000)		(5,928,000)
Cash from invest. activs	(57,054,000)		(57,348,000)
Pension fund surplus	3,125,000		2,382,000
	$		$
Earnings per share*	11.08		11.08
Cash flow per share*	15.63		42.86
Cash divd. per share*	4.96		4.32
	shs		shs
No. of shs. o/s*	1,382,911,000		1,424,525,000
Avg. no. of shs. o/s*	1,403,654,000		1,424,343,000
	%		%
Basel III Common Equity Tier 1	12.60		13.70
Basel III Tier 1	13.80		14.90
Basel III Total	15.40		16.70
Net profit margin	32.27		32.30
Return on equity	16.13		18.28
Return on assets	0.87		0.96
Foreign sales percent	40		41
No. of employees (FTEs)	91,427		85,301

* Common
[A] Reported in accordance with IFRS

Latest Results

Periods ended:	9m July 31/23[A]		9m July 31/22[A]
	$000s	%Chg	$000s
Net interest income	18,587,000	+13	16,435,000
Net income	10,735,000	-10	11,925,000
Net inc. for equity hldrs	10,730,000	-10	11,918,000
Net inc. for non-cont. int.	5,000		7,000
	$		$
Earnings per share*	7.61		8.33

* Common
[A] Reported in accordance with IFRS

Historical Summary
(as originally stated)

Fiscal Year	Int. Inc. $000s	Net Inc. Bef. Disc. $000s	EPS* $
2022[A]	40,771,000	15,807,000	11.08
2021[A]	28,145,000	16,050,000	11.08
2020[A]	34,883,000	11,437,000	7.84
2019[A]	41,333,000	12,871,000	8.78
2018[A]	33,021,000	12,431,000	8.39

* Common
[A] Reported in accordance with IFRS

R.72 Royal Wins Corporation

Symbol - SKLL **Exchange** - CSE (S) **CUSIP** - 78075B
Head Office - 2704-401 Bay St, Box 4, Toronto, ON, M5H 2Y4 **Telephone** - (416) 642-1807
Website - royalwins.com
Email - catherine@grovecorp.ca
Investor Relations - Catherine Beckett (416) 642-1807
Auditors - Clearhouse LLP C.A., Mississauga, Ont.
Transfer Agents - Capital Transfer Agency Inc., Toronto, Ont.

Profile - (Can. 2017) Designs, develops and operates wagering and betting real money pure skill games for online and mobile wagering markets.

The company's lead game is Kash Karnival, the world's first pure skill gaming app that allows players to bet and win in casual mobile games of skill rather than chance or odds-based casino games. Operates on both the Android and iOS mobile platforms. In addition, plans to launch Kash Royale (tournaments which will include player-vs-player and multi-player games). Holds a licence from the Kahnawake Gaming Commission located in the Mohawk Territory of Kahnawake in Quebec, to operate pure skill games online for real money.

Future plans include expansion into eSports tournament wagering and development of a framework and platform for a centralized app store for real money pure skill games, subject to ensuring full regulatory compliance.

Common suspended from CSE, June 6, 2022.

Predecessor Detail - Name changed from 10557510 Canada Corp., Mar. 25, 2021.

Directors - Robert Fong, co-founder & COO, N.S.W., Australia; Charles Vycichl, chr., Geneva, Switzerland; Peter Gan, pres. & CEO, Sydney, N.S.W., Australia; Stephen Coates, Toronto, Ont.; Daniel (Dan) Fuoco, Vaughan, Ont.

Other Exec. Officers - Lukie Ali, co-founder & chief tech. officer; Geoff Kritzinger, CFO; Catherine Beckett, corp. sec.

Capital Stock

	Authorized (shs.)	Outstanding (shs.)[1]
Common	unlimited	123,962,143

[1] At Feb. 28, 2022

Major Shareholder - Robert Fong held 20.92% interest and Lukie Ali held 10.81% interest at Nov. 2, 2021.

Price Range - SKLL/CSE (S)

Year	Volume	High	Low	Close
2022	11,688,875	$0.31	$0.05	$0.09
2021	13,740,869	$0.40	$0.14	$0.25

Capital Stock Changes - In July 2021, 11,223,331 common shares were issued without further consideration on exchange of subscription receipts sold previously by private placement at 30¢ each.

Wholly Owned Subsidiaries

Antics Gaming LLC, Las Vegas, Nev.
Royal Wins Pty Ltd., Sydney, N.S.W., Australia.

Financial Statistics

Periods ended:	12m June 30/21[A]		12m June 30/20[°A]
	$000s	%Chg	$000s
Operating revenue	**413**	**+88**	**220**
Salaries & benefits	472		256
General & admin expense	1,400		943
Stock-based compensation	694		71
Operating expense	**2,566**	**+102**	**1,270**
Operating income	**(2,153)**	**n.a.**	**(1,050)**
Deprec., depl. & amort.	27		1
Pre-tax income	**(11,340)**	**n.a.**	**(1,063)**
Net income	**(11,340)**	**n.a.**	**(1,063)**
Cash & equivalent	495		336
Accounts receivable	nil		8
Current assets	4,425		344
Fixed assets, net	5		6
Intangibles, net	24		50
Total assets	**4,454**	**n.m.**	**400**
Bank indebtedness	30		nil
Accts. pay. & accr. liabs	416		229
Current liabilities	4,338		229
Shareholders' equity	116		171
Cash from oper. activs	**(1,359)**	**n.a.**	**(987)**
Cash from fin. activs	1,517		1,236
Net cash position	**495**	**+47**	**336**
	$		$
Earnings per share*	(0.14)		n.a.
	shs		shs
No. of shs. o/s*	104,147,045		n.a.
Avg. no. of shs. o/s*	78,845,312		n.a.
	%		%
Net profit margin	n.m.		(483.18)
Return on equity	(7,910.27)		n.m.
Return on assets	(467.28)		(392.71)

* Common
° Restated
[A] Reported in accordance with IFRS

Latest Results

Periods ended:	3m Sept. 30/21[A]		3m Sept. 30/20[A]
	$000s	%Chg	$000s
Operating revenue	2	-99	147
Net income	(902)	n.a.	(115)
	$		$
Earnings per share*	(0.01)		n.a.

* Common
[A] Reported in accordance with IFRS

Historical Summary
(as originally stated)

Fiscal Year	Oper. Rev.	Net Inc. Bef. Disc.	EPS*
	$000s	$000s	$
2021[A]	413	(11,340)	(0.14)
	A$000s	A$000s	A$
2020[A1]	244	(1,181)	n.a.
2019[A]	283	(2,558)	n.a.

* Common
[A] Reported in accordance with IFRS
[1] Results for fiscal 2020 and prior periods pertain to Royal Wins Pty Ltd.

R.73 Royalties Inc.

Symbol - RI **Exchange** - CSE **CUSIP** - 780764
Head Office - 1805-55 University Ave, Toronto, ON, M5J 2H7 **Telephone** - (416) 925-0090
Website - www.royaltiesinc.com
Email - neil@steenberglaw.ca
Investor Relations - Neil J. F. Steenberg (416) 362-8243
Auditors - McGovern Hurley LLP C.A., Toronto, Ont.
Lawyers - Neil J.F. Steenberg, Toronto, Ont.
Transfer Agents - TSX Trust Company, Toronto, Ont.
Profile - (Ont. 2009; orig. B.C., 2007) Holds gold, silver and copper royalties and invests in royalties in various industries including media and entertainment. Also has mineral interests in north-central Mexico.

Holds mineral royalty interests including a 1.5% NSR royalty on four mining concessions consisting the bulk of the Bilbao polymetallic property; and various legal or royalty interests in certain mineral properties in Mexico, including the Bilbao polymetallic property and an asserted claim to a 2% NSR royalty on six mining concessions located adjacent to the Cozamin mine in Zacatecas operated by **Capstone Mining Corp.** held through subsidiary **Minera Portree de Zacatecas, S.A. de C.V.**

In addition, holds interest in **Music Royalties Inc.**, which acquires passive music royalties from rights holders (including but not limited to artists, producers and songwriters) and holds a portfolio of 25 cash-flowing music royalties.

Holds Bilbao polymetallic property, 1,407 hectares, 500 km northwest of Mexico City. A preliminary economic assessment released in April 2014 contemplated average annual production of 720,000 tonnes over an 8-year mine life. Initial capital costs were estimated at US$91,170,948. Indicated resource was 6,125,227 tonnes grading 2.31% zinc, 1.81% lead, 0.19% copper, and 65 g/t silver.

Also holds La Laguna Pedernalillo silver-gold-mercury tailings project, 5 km east of Zacatecas, with proven and probable reserves of 6,799,000 tonnes grading 57.92 g/t silver, 0.31 g/t gold and 328.92 g/t mercury at February 2008.

In April 2023, change of business from a mineral resource exploration company to a diversified royalties company was completed.

In December 2022, the company acquired 2,000,000 common shares of **Music Royalties Inc.** (MRI), a Canadian-based private company that acquires passive music royalties from rights holders and holds a portfolio of 25 cash-flowing music royalties, for issuance of 20,000,000 common shares at a price of $0.05 per share. The MRI shares had a value of $1,000,000 and are expected to yield $5,000 of dividends per month.

Common delisted from TSX-VEN, Apr. 12, 2023.
Common listed on CSE, Apr. 12, 2023.

Predecessor Detail - Name changed from Xtierra Inc., Feb. 27, 2023, pursuant to change of business from a mineral resource exploration company to a diversified royalties company.

Directors - Timothy D. (Tim) Gallagher, chr., pres. & CEO, Toronto, Ont.; Gerald J. Gauthier, Ont.; Paul O'Brien, Toronto, Ont.; Andrew Robertson, Toronto, Ont.

Other Exec. Officers - Jacqueline Logan, CFO; Neil J. F. Steenberg, corp. sec.

Capital Stock

	Authorized (shs.)	Outstanding (shs.)[1]
Common	unlimited	201,293,057

[1] At Apr. 12, 2023

Major Shareholder - Buchans Resources Limited held 21.36% interest and Timothy D. (Tim) Gallagher held 17.08% interest at Apr. 12, 2023.

Price Range - XAG/TSX-VEN (D)

Year	Volume	High	Low	Close
2022	2,996,100	$0.05	$0.02	$0.03
2021	13,272,439	$0.21	$0.03	$0.04
2020	10,510,375	$0.23	$0.03	$0.10
2019	9,435,802	$0.08	$0.03	$0.05
2018	37,831,240	$0.08	$0.02	$0.06

Recent Close: $0.05

Wholly Owned Subsidiaries

Orca Minerals Limited, Ont.
- 100% int. in **Orca Gold International Limited**, Bahamas.
  - 100% int. in **Bilbao Mining S.A. de C.V.**, Mexico.
  - 100% int. in **Bilbao Resources S.A. de C.V.**, Mexico.
  - 100% int. in **Minera Orca S.A. de C.V.**, Mexico.
  - 100% int. in **Orca Mining Exploration S.A. de C.V.**, Mexico.

Subsidiaries

88% int. in **Minera Portree de Zacatecas, S.A. de C.V.**, Mexico.

Investments

Music Royalties Inc., Canada.

Financial Statistics

Periods ended:	12m Dec. 31/21[A]		12m Dec. 31/20[A]
	US$000s	%Chg	US$000s
Exploration expense	254		148
General & admin expense	144		123
Stock-based compensation	30		128
Operating expense	**428**	**+8**	**398**
Operating income	**(428)**	**n.a.**	**(398)**
Finance costs, gross	6		nil
Pre-tax income	**(661)**	**n.a.**	**(563)**
Net income	**(661)**	**n.a.**	**(563)**
Cash & equivalent	39		524
Accounts receivable	1		15
Current assets	40		578
Total assets	**227**	**-70**	**765**
Bank indebtedness	198		796
Accts. pay. & accr. liabs	91		143
Current liabilities	2,289		2,940
Shareholders' equity	(2,082)		(2,195)
Non-controlling interest	21		21
Cash from oper. activs	**(404)**	**n.a.**	**(225)**
Cash from fin. activs	nil		758
Cash from invest. activs	(81)		(47)
Net cash position	**39**	**-93**	**524**
	US$		US$
Earnings per share*	(0.00)		(0.00)
Cash flow per share*	(0.00)		(0.00)
	shs		shs
No. of shs. o/s*	175,693,057		162,693,057
Avg. no. of shs. o/s*	171,525,934		151,140,180
	%		%
Net profit margin	n.a.		n.a.
Return on equity	n.m.		n.m.
Return on assets	(132.06)		(136.32)

* Common
[A] Reported in accordance with IFRS

Historical Summary
(as originally stated)

Fiscal Year	Oper. Rev.	Net Inc. Bef. Disc.	EPS*
	US$000s	US$000s	US$
2021[A]	nil	(661)	(0.00)
2020[A]	nil	(563)	(0.00)
2019[A]	nil	(168)	(0.00)
2018[A]	nil	(882)	(0.01)
2017[A]	nil	(461)	(0.00)

* Common
[A] Reported in accordance with IFRS

R.74 Rubicon Organics Inc.

Symbol - ROMJ **Exchange** - TSX-VEN **CUSIP** - 78112W
Head Office - 505-744 Hastings St W, Vancouver, BC, V6C 1A5 **Telephone** - (604) 331-1296
Website - www.rubiconorganics.com
Email - ir@rubiconorganics.com
Investor Relations - Margaret Brodie (604) 687-5744
Auditors - PricewaterhouseCoopers LLP C.A., Vancouver, B.C.
Lawyers - Borden Ladner Gervais LLP, Vancouver, B.C.
Transfer Agents - Odyssey Trust Company, Vancouver, B.C.
Profile - (B.C. 2015) Cultivates, processes and sells cannabis products for the recreational and medical-use markets in Canada.

Owns and operates a 125,000-sq.-ft. hybrid greenhouse facility, with annual production capacity of 11,000 kg of organic certified cannabis, and 11-acre outdoor grow site in Delta, B.C. Products are marketed across Canada under the proprietary brands Simply Bare™ Organic, Lab Theory™, 1964 Supply Co.™ and Homestead Cannabis Supply™. Also holds license to produce and sell cannabidiol (CBD) relief sticks and cool sticks in Canada under the Wildflower™ brand. In the international market, the company has a supply agreement for the distribution of its products to the German medical cannabis market with commercial exports to commence upon completion of EU-GMP certification.

In October 2022, the company acquired the Wildflower™ brand and related trademarks for the sale of cannabis-infused wellness products in Canada for $500,000.

Directors - Margaret Brodie, interim CEO & CFO, Vancouver, B.C.; Melanie Ramsey, chief comml. officer, Vancouver, B.C.; David Donnan†, Ill.; Michael E. Detlefsen, Toronto, Ont.; John Pigott, Ont.

Other Exec. Officers - Peter Dierx, v-p, opers.; Monika Mascitti, v-p, people; Benoit Pinsonneault, v-p, sales; Janis Risbin, v-p, fin.

† Lead director

Capital Stock

	Authorized (shs.)	Outstanding (shs.)[1]
Common	unlimited	56,124,994

[1] At May 19, 2023

Major Shareholder - Jesse McConnell held 21.09% interest, Eric Savics held 17.48% interest and Pierre Lassonde held 10.19% interest at Nov. 1, 2022.

Price Range - ROMJ/TSX-VEN

Year	Volume	High	Low	Close
2022	3,595,562	$1.95	$0.55	$0.77
2021	9,980,629	$4.30	$1.65	$1.85
2020	7,062,047	$4.40	$1.50	$3.62
2019	7,188,083	$3.47	$1.28	$1.84
2018	3,068,059	$5.25	$1.60	$1.89

Recent Close: $0.47

Capital Stock Changes - During 2022, common shares were issued as follows: 75,000 on exercise of deferred share units and 66,667 on vesting of restricted share units.

Wholly Owned Subsidiaries

Rubicon Holdings Corp., B.C.
West Coast Marketing Corporation, B.C.

Financial Statistics

Periods ended:	12m Dec. 31/22^A		12m Dec. 31/21^A
	$000s	%Chg	$000s
Operating revenue	**35,518**	**+57**	**22,612**
Cost of sales	18,124		17,322
Salaries & benefits	8,362		7,420
General & admin expense	4,663		5,023
Stock-based compensation	3,042		2,140
Operating expense	**34,191**	**+7**	**31,905**
Operating income	**1,327**	**n.a.**	**(9,293)**
Deprec., depl. & amort.	3,050		2,396
Finance costs, gross	1,023		1,255
Write-downs/write-offs	(866)		(1,651)
Pre-tax income	**(3,856)**	**n.a.**	**(14,521)**
Net income	**(3,856)**	**n.a.**	**(14,521)**
Cash & equivalent	8,294		11,583
Inventories	10,509		8,441
Accounts receivable	4,781		4,156
Current assets	27,695		27,174
Fixed assets, net	25,956		25,094
Right-of-use assets	75		208
Intangibles, net	2,382		1,882
Total assets	**56,107**	**+2**	**54,841**
Accts. pay. & accr. liabs.	7,202		5,794
Current liabilities	8,373		6,938
Long-term debt, gross	10,160		9,605
Long-term debt, net	9,401		8,945
Long-term lease liabilities	nil		59
Shareholders' equity	38,333		38,899
Cash from oper. activs	**1,952**	**n.a.**	**(10,442)**
Cash from fin. activs	(839)		(15,305)
Cash from invest. activs	(4,451)		(5,497)
Net cash position	**8,294**	**-28**	**11,583**
Capital expenditures	(4,101)		(5,497)
	$		$
Earnings per share*	(0.07)		(0.26)
Cash flow per share*	0.03		(0.19)
	shs		shs
No. of shs. o/s*	56,124,994		55,983,327
Avg. no. of shs. o/s*	56,239,058		54,917,756
	%		%
Net profit margin	(10.86)		(64.22)
Return on equity	(9.99)		(42.87)
Return on assets	(5.11)		(25.05)

* Common

^A Reported in accordance with IFRS

Latest Results

Periods ended:	3m Mar. 31/23^A		3m Mar. 31/22^A
	$000s	%Chg	$000s
Operating revenue	8,800	+71	5,148
Net income	(575)	n.a.	(1,492)
	$		$
Earnings per share*	(0.01)		(0.03)

* Common

^A Reported in accordance with IFRS

Historical Summary
(as originally stated)

Fiscal Year	Oper. Rev.	Net Inc. Bef. Disc.	EPS*
	$000s	$000s	$
2022^A	35,518	(3,856)	(0.07)
2021^A	22,612	(14,521)	(0.26)
2020^A	9,387	(14,350)	(0.33)
2019^A	nil	(11,105)	(0.29)
2018^A	2,029	(29,875)	(0.89)

* Common

^A Reported in accordance with IFRS

R.75 Rumbu Holdings Ltd.

Symbol - RMB.P **Exchange** - TSX-VEN **CUSIP** - 781391
Head Office - 1605-400 Eau Claire Ave SW, Calgary, AB, T2P 4X2 **Telephone** - (403) 585-3737
Email - ross@drysdalelaw.com
Investor Relations - Ross O. Drysdale (403) 585-3737
Auditors - Kenway Mack Slusarchuk Stewart LLP C.A., Calgary, Alta.
Transfer Agents - TSX Trust Company, Toronto, Ont.
Profile - (Alta. 2021) Capital Pool Company.
Directors - Ross O. Drysdale, pres., CEO & corp. sec., Calgary, Alta.; Shelina Hirji, CFO, Vancouver, B.C.; Daryl Lockyer, Lethbridge, Alta.; J. Michael Sullivan, Calgary, Alta.; Shane A. Wylie, Calgary, Alta.

Capital Stock

	Authorized (shs.)	Outstanding (shs.)[1]
Common	unlimited	6,500,000

[1] At Dec. 10, 2021

Major Shareholder - Widely held at Dec. 10, 2021.

Price Range - RMB.P/TSX-VEN

Year	Volume	High	Low	Close
2022	193,500	$0.16	$0.02	$0.08

Recent Close: $0.08
Capital Stock Changes - On Dec. 10, 2021, an initial public offering of 4,000,000 common shares was completed at 10¢ per share.

R.76 Rupert's Crossing Capital Inc.

Symbol - RUCC.P **Exchange** - TSX-VEN **CUSIP** - 78165Y
Head Office - 1250-639 5 Ave SW, Calgary, AB, T2P 0M9 **Telephone** - (403) 777-1188
Email - jdsilva@ruperts.ca
Investor Relations - Jason D'Silva (403) 777-1188
Auditors - Kenway Mack Slusarchuk Stewart LLP C.A., Calgary, Alta.
Lawyers - TingleMerrett LLP, Calgary, Alta.
Transfer Agents - Odyssey Trust Company, Calgary, Alta.
Profile - (Alta. 2021) Capital Pool Company.
Directors - Jason D'Silva, pres., CEO, CFO & sec.-treas., Calgary, Alta.; Maria Binnion, Calgary, Alta.; Michael R. Binnion, Calgary, Alta.

Capital Stock

	Authorized (shs.)	Outstanding (shs.)[1]
Common	unlimited	5,000,000

[1] At Aug. 30, 2022

Major Shareholder - Maria Binnion held 20% interest, Michael R. Binnion held 20% interest and Jason D'Silva held 20% interest at Dec. 23, 2021.

Price Range - RUCC.P/TSX-VEN

Year	Volume	High	Low	Close
2022	45,000	$0.20	$0.12	$0.12
2021	75,000	$0.15	$0.13	$0.15

Recent Close: $0.11
Capital Stock Changes - On Dec. 23, 2021, an initial public offering of 2,000,000 common shares was completed at 10¢ per share.

R.77 Russel Metals Inc.*

Symbol - RUS **Exchange** - TSX **CUSIP** - 781903
Head Office - 6600 Financial Dr, Mississauga, ON, L5N 7J6 **Telephone** - (905) 819-7777 **Toll-free** - (800) 268-0750 **Fax** - (905) 819-7409
Website - www.russelmetals.com
Email - info@russelmetals.com
Investor Relations - Martin L. Juravsky (905) 819-7361
Auditors - Deloitte LLP C.A., Toronto, Ont.
Lawyers - Davies Ward Phillips & Vineberg LLP, Toronto, Ont.
Transfer Agents - TSX Trust Company, Toronto, Ont.
FP500 Revenue Ranking - 112
Employees - 3,350 at Dec. 31, 2022
Profile - (Can. 2002 amalg.) Distributes metals across North America with a focus on value-added processing, operating in three segments: metals service centers, energy field stores and steel distributors.

Metals Service Centres

Has 45 metals service centres in Canada and 23 in the U.S. which sell plate, flat rolled carbon and other general line carbon steel products, as well as stainless steel, aluminum and other non-ferrous specialty metal products in a wide range of sizes, shapes and specifications. General line steel products, consisting of plate, structural shapes, bars, sheet, pipe, tubing and hollow structural steel tubing, are utilized by end users in a wide variety of industries. These centres also provide customized value-added processing services to satisfy specifications established by end users. Products and services are provided to end users in machinery and equipment manufacturing, construction, shipbuilding and natural resources, such as mining and petroleum.

Energy Field Stores

This segment distributes flanges, valves, fittings and tubular goods primarily to the energy industry in western Canada and the U.S., through its Field stores consisting of 44 facilities in Canada and 14 in the U.S.

Steel Distributors

Operations are conducted through wholly owned **Wirth Steel** in Canada and wholly owned **Sunbelt Group L.P.** in the U.S. which sell steel in large volumes to other steel service centres and large equipment manufacturers mainly on an "as is" basis and offer cut-to-length applications through **Arrow Steel**, a division of Sunbelt Group. The company's steel distributors source their steel domestically and offshore. The company sources carbon steel plate, beams, channel, flat rolled products, rail and pipe products. Sales commitments for a portion of these products are obtained prior to their purchase or while the product is in production and transit. Products for which sales commitments have not been obtained are held in public warehouses for resale to North American service centres and other customers.

Recent Merger and Acquisition Activity

Status: completed **Announced:** Mar. 31, 2022
Russel Metals Inc. sold wholly owned Apex Western Fiberglass Inc., which supplies and installs firbreglass pipe and tubing products, for $10,000,000 cash. Apex Western Fibreglass was part of Russel Metals' Energy segment.

Predecessor Detail - Name changed from Federal Industries Ltd., June 1, 1995.
Directors - James F. (Jim) Dinning, chr., Calgary, Alta.; John G. Reid, pres. & CEO, Tenn.; Linh J. Austin, Chattanooga, Tenn.; John M. Clark, Etobicoke, Ont.; Brian R. Hedges, Toronto, Ont.; Cynthia Johnston, Victoria, B.C.; Alice D. Laberge, Vancouver, B.C.; William M. (Bill) O'Reilly, Toronto, Ont.; Roger D. Paiva, Bowmanville, Ont.; Annie Thabet, Ile-des-Soeurs, Qué.
Other Exec. Officers - Martin L. Juravsky, exec. v-p, CFO & corp. sec.; Lesley M. S. Coleman, v-p, contr. & asst. sec.; Ryan W. MacDermid, v-p, risk mgt. & legal; John F. Maclean, v-p, srvc. centre opers.; Catherine Milne, v-p, HR; Dan Schmelzer, v-p, IT; Sherri McKelvey, asst. sec.

Capital Stock

	Authorized (shs.)	Outstanding (shs.)[1]
Class I Preferred	unlimited	nil
Class II Preferred	unlimited	nil
Common	unlimited	61,307,326

[1] At Aug. 11, 2023

Options - At Dec. 31, 2022, options were outstanding to purchase 575,785 common shares at prices ranging from $14.61 to $31.46 per share with a weighted average remaining contractual life of 2.9 years.
Normal Course Issuer Bid - The company plans to make normal course purchases of up to 6,076,625 common shares representing 10% of the public float. The bid commenced on Aug. 16, 2023, and expires on Aug. 15, 2024.
Major Shareholder - Widely held at Mar. 2, 2023.

Price Range - RUS/TSX

Year	Volume	High	Low	Close
2022	60,266,493	$36.15	$23.80	$28.78
2021	65,050,994	$37.57	$22.33	$33.63
2020	69,596,744	$23.09	$10.97	$22.73
2019	51,865,579	$25.22	$18.47	$22.17
2018	49,516,725	$32.65	$19.72	$21.33

Recent Close: $39.72
Capital Stock Changes - During 2022, 12,000 common shares were issued on exercise of options and 1,000,000 common shares were repurchased under a Normal Course Issuer Bid.

Dividends

RUS com Ra $1.60 pa Q est. June 15, 2023
Prev. Rate: $1.52 est. Sept. 15, 2014

Long-Term Debt - At Dec. 31, 2022, outstanding long-term debt totaled $296,000,000 (none current) and consisted of $147,800,000 5.75% senior unsecured notes due Oct. 27, 2025, and $148,200,000 6% senior unsecured notes due Mar. 16, 2026.

Wholly Owned Subsidiaries

Apex Distribution Inc., Calgary, Alta.
Boyd Metals Inc., Alta.
Elite Supply Partners Inc., Tex.
FIL (US) Inc., Alaska
Fedmet Enterprises Corporation, Del.
JMS Russel Metals Corp., Del.
Pioneer Steel & Tube Corp., Del.
Russel Metals Williams Bahcall Inc., Del.
Sunbelt Group L.P., Del.
Wirth Steel, a general partnership, Qué.

Investments

50% int. in **TriMark Tubulars Ltd.**, Canada.
Note: The preceding list includes only the major related companies in which interests are held.

Financial Statistics

Periods ended:	12m Dec. 31/22[A]		12m Dec. 31/21[◻A]
	$000s	%Chg	$000s
Operating revenue	**5,070,600**	**+20**	**4,208,500**
Cost of goods sold	3,937,400		2,988,900
Salaries & benefits	402,500		397,400
General & admin expense	183,700		162,000
Operating expense	**4,523,600**	**+27**	**3,548,300**
Operating income	**547,000**	**-17**	**660,200**
Deprec., depl. & amort.	66,100		57,900
Finance costs, gross	25,300		26,000
Investment income	31,000		6,100
Write-downs/write-offs	nil		(2,600)
Pre-tax income	**487,500**	**-16**	**580,100**
Income taxes	115,600		147,900
Net income	**371,900**	**-14**	**432,200**
Cash & equivalent	363,000		133,100
Inventories	956,500		986,000
Accounts receivable	497,900		554,100
Current assets	1,869,500		1,719,600
Long-term investments	46,600		37,600
Fixed assets, net	313,800		302,400
Right-of-use assets	102,700		86,700
Intangibles, net	126,500		132,200
Total assets	**2,506,900**	**+8**	**2,314,500**
Accts. pay. & accr. liabs.	482,000		557,700
Current liabilities	501,500		640,200
Long-term debt, gross	296,000		294,800
Long-term debt, net	296,000		294,800
Long-term lease liabilities	112,200		93,700
Shareholders' equity	1,559,300		1,248,300
Cash from oper. activs.	**359,900**	**+18**	**304,500**
Cash from fin. activs.	(139,100)		(93,500)
Cash from invest. activs.	(6,500)		(107,200)
Net cash position	**363,000**	**+173**	**133,100**
Capital expenditures	(41,500)		(28,800)
Capital disposals	3,200		1,100
Pension fund surplus	42,000		27,900
	$		$
Earnings per share*	5.91		6.90
Cash flow per share*	5.72		4.86
Cash divd. per share*	1.52		1.52
	shs		shs
No. of shs. o/s*	62,112,220		63,100,220
Avg. no. of shs. o/s*	62,891,611		62,667,618
	%		%
Net profit margin	7.33		10.27
Return on equity	26.49		40.91
Return on assets	16.23		23.09
Foreign sales percent	39		36
No. of employees (FTEs)	3,350		3,300

* Common
[◻] Restated
[A] Reported in accordance with IFRS

Latest Results

Periods ended:	3m Mar. 31/23[A]		3m Mar. 31/22[A]
	$000s	%Chg	$000s
Operating revenue	1,186,700	-11	1,338,600
Net income	73,900	-25	98,700
	$		$
Earnings per share*	1.19		1.56

* Common
[A] Reported in accordance with IFRS

Historical Summary
(as originally stated)

Fiscal Year	Oper. Rev.	Net Inc. Bef. Disc.	EPS*
	$000s	$000s	$
2022[A]	5,070,600	371,900	5.91
2021[A]	4,208,500	432,200	6.90
2020[A]	2,688,300	24,500	0.39
2019[A]	3,675,900	76,600	1.23
2018[A]	4,165,000	219,000	3.53

* Common
[A] Reported in accordance with IFRS

S

S.1 S Split Corp.

Symbol - SBN **Exchange** - TSX **CUSIP** - 784732
Head Office - c/o Mulvihill Capital Management Inc., Standard Life Centre, 2600-121 King St W, PO Box 113, Toronto, ON, M5H 3T9 **Telephone** - (416) 681-3966 **Toll-free** - (800) 725-7172 **Fax** - (416) 681-3901
Website - www.mulvihill.com
Email - jgermain@mulvihill.com
Investor Relations - John D. Germain (416) 681-3966
Auditors - Deloitte LLP C.A., Toronto, Ont.
Lawyers - Osler, Hoskin & Harcourt LLP, Toronto, Ont.
Transfer Agents - Computershare Trust Company of Canada Inc., Toronto, Ont.
Trustees - RBC Investor Services Trust, Toronto, Ont.
Investment Managers - Mulvihill Capital Management Inc., Toronto, Ont.
Managers - Mulvihill Capital Management Inc., Toronto, Ont.
Profile - (Ont. 2007) Holds common shares of **The Bank of Nova Scotia** in order to provide preferred shareholders with monthly distributions on a fixed, cumulative and preferential basis and class A shareholders with leveraged exposure to the performance of the bank's common shares including increases or decreases in value and dividends paid.

At Dec. 31, 2022, the company held 870,800 common shares of the **The Bank of Nova Scotia** with a fair value of $5,824,652.

The company has a scheduled termination date of Nov. 30, 2028, which will be automatically extended for a further seven years and thereafter for additional successive periods of seven years. Upon termination, all outstanding preferred shares and class A shares will be redeemed.

The manager receives a management fee and an investment management fee at annual rates equal to 0.1% and 1.55%, respectively, of the net asset value of the company, calculated and payable monthly in arrears.

Directors - John P. Mulvihill, chr., CEO & corp. sec., Toronto, Ont.; John D. Germain, sr. v-p & CFO, Toronto, Ont.; Dr. Robert (Bob) Bell, Toronto, Ont.; Robert G. (Bob) Bertram, Aurora, Ont.; R. Peter Gillin, Toronto, Ont.

Capital Stock

	Authorized (shs.)	Outstanding (shs.)[1]
Preferred	unlimited	450,029[2]
Class A	unlimited	450,029
Class J	unlimited	100[2]

[1] At Dec. 31, 2022
[2] Classified as debt.

Preferred - Entitled to fixed cumulative preferential monthly cash distributions of $0.04375 per share to yield 5.25% per annum on the original $10 issue price. Retractable in November of each year, together with a class A share, at a price equal to the net asset value (NAV) per unit (1 class A share and 1 preferred share). Retractable in any other month, without a class A share, at a price equal to 95% of the lesser of: (i) the NAV per unit less the cost to purchase a class A share in the market for cancellation; (ii) the sum of the weighted average price per class A share and the weighted average price per preferred share on TSX for the 10 trading days prior the retraction date less the cost to purchase a class A share in the market for cancellation; and (iii) $10. All outstanding preferred shares will be redeemed on Nov. 30, 2028, at a price per share equal to the lesser of: (i) the NAV per share; and (ii) $10 plus any accrued and unpaid dividends. Rank in priority to the class A and class J shares with respect to the payment of distributions and the repayment of capital on the dissolution, liquidation or winding-up of the company. Non-voting.

Class A - Entitled to non-cumulative monthly cash distributions targeted to be 6% per annum of the NAV per share. No distributions will be paid if the distributions payable on the preferred shares are in arrears or, after payment of the distribution, the NAV per unit would be less than $16.50. In addition, no special distributions will be paid if, after payment of the distribution, the NAV per unit would be less than $25 unless the company has to make such distributions to fully recover refundable taxes. Retractable in November of each year, together with a preferred share, at a price equal to the NAV per unit. Retractable in any other month, without a preferred share, at a price equal to 95% of the lesser of: (i) the difference between (a) the NAV per unit and (b) the cost to purchase a preferred share in the market for cancellation; and (ii) the difference between (a) the sum of the weighted average price per class A share and the weighted average price per preferred share on TSX for the 10 trading days prior the retraction date and (b) the cost to purchase a preferred share in the market for cancellation. If the NAV per unit is less than $10, the class A retraction price will be nil. All outstanding class A shares will be redeemed on Nov. 30, 2028, at a price per share equal to the greater of: (i) the NAV per unit minus the sum of $10 plus accrued and unpaid dividends per preferred share; and (ii) nil. Rank subordinate to the preferred shares but in priority to the class J shares with respect to the payment of distributions and the repayment of capital on the dissolution, liquidation or winding-up of the company. Non-voting.

Class J - Not entitled to receive distributions. Retractable and redeemable at any time at $1.00 per share. Rank subordinate to both preferred and class A shares with respect to distributions on the dissolution, liquidation or winding-up of the company. One vote per share.

Major Shareholder - S Split Trust held 100% interest at Mar. 27, 2023.

Price Range - SBN/TSX

Year	Volume	High	Low	Close
2022	170,529	$7.70	$2.54	$3.33
2021	310,939	$6.98	$3.51	$6.98
2020	199,953	$6.08	$0.70	$3.67
2019	105,501	$6.61	$4.70	$5.31
2018	188,529	$8.38	$4.81	$5.00

Recent Close: $2.66
Capital Stock Changes - During 2022, 58,509 preferred shares and 58,509 class A shares were retracted.

Dividends

SBN cl A N.V. omitted [1]

$0.03605	June 30/22	$0.0402	Apr. 29/22
$0.04355	Mar. 31/22	$0.04385	Feb. 28/22

Paid in 2023: n.a. 2022: $0.2051 2021: $0.2055

SBN.PR.A pfd cum. red. ret. Ra $0.525 pa M
[1] No set frequency divd normally payable in Aug/23 has been omitted.

Financial Statistics

Periods ended:	12m Dec. 31/22[A]		12m Dec. 31/21[A]
	$000s	%Chg	$000s
Realized invest. gain (loss)	421		1,285
Unrealized invest. gain (loss)	(2,722)		1,566
Total revenue	**(1,991)**	**n.a.**	**3,573**
General & admin. expense	387		499
Operating expense	**387**	**-22**	**499**
Operating income	**(2,378)**	**n.a.**	**3,074**
Finance costs, gross	264		418
Pre-tax income	**(2,643)**	**n.a.**	**2,656**
Net income	**(2,643)**	**n.a.**	**2,656**
Cash & equivalent	118		323
Accounts receivable	nil		101
Investments	5,825		9,080
Total assets	**5,943**	**-37**	**9,505**
Accts. pay. & accr. liabs	79		82
Debt	4,500		5,085
Shareholders' equity	1,363		4,337
Cash from oper. activs	**3,354**	**+244**	**975**
Cash from fin. activs	(1,181)		(5,749)
Net cash position	**118**	**-63**	**323**
	$		$
Earnings per share*	(5.22)		3.30
Cash flow per share*	6.58		1.21
Net asset value per share*	3.03		8.53
Cash divd. per share*	0.21		0.21
	shs		shs
No. of shs. o/s*	450,029		508,538
Avg. no. of shs. o/s*	509,966		805,878
	%		%
Net profit margin	n.m.		74.34
Return on equity	(92.74)		64.61
Return on assets	(30.80)		28.38

* Class A
[A] Reported in accordance with IFRS

Note: Net income reflects increase/decrease in net assets from operations.

Historical Summary
(as originally stated)

Fiscal Year	Total Rev. $000s	Net Inc. Bef. Disc. $000s	EPS* $
2022[A]	(1,991)	(2,643)	(5.22)
2021[A]	3,573	2,656	3.30
2020[A]	(544)	(1,423)	(1.60)
2019[A]	1,724	691	0.72
2018[A]	(1,981)	(3,062)	(3.13)

* Class A
[A] Reported in accordance with IFRS

S.2 SATO Technologies Corp.

Symbol - SATO **Exchange** - TSX-VEN **CUSIP** - 78435J
Head Office - 289 Dugas St, Joliette, QC, J6E 4H1 **Telephone** - (450) 756-3636
Website - bysato.com
Email - rnouzareth@bysato.com
Investor Relations - Romain Nouzareth (450) 756-3636
Auditors - Raymond Chabot Grant Thornton LLP C.A., Montréal, Qué.
Transfer Agents - Computershare Trust Company of Canada Inc., Calgary, Alta.
Employees - 14 at Dec. 31, 2022
Profile - (Ont. 2008) Engages in Bitcoin mining.

Has a 20-MW Bitcoin mining centre with a hash rate of 0.6 exahashes per second (EH/s), and a 0.5-MW Bitcoin mining centre, which are both located in Joliette, Que., and powered by hydroelectricity. It is designed to support blockchain infrastructure cryptocurrency mining, artificial intelligence deployments and other computationally-intensive processes.

Predecessor Detail - Name changed from Canada Computational Unlimited Corp., June 16, 2022.
Directors - Romain Nouzareth, chr. & CEO, N.Y.; Frank Di Tomaso, Montréal, Qué.; Mathieu Nouzareth, Calif.; Dominique Payette, Montréal, Qué.; Frederick T. (Fred) Pye, Pointe-Claire, Qué.
Other Exec. Officers - Fanny Philip, COO; Kyle Appleby, CFO; Damian Di Zeo, v-p, tech.; Cedric Gaden, v-p, infrastructure & project; Alasdair Federico, gen. counsel & corp. sec.

Capital Stock

	Authorized (shs.)	Outstanding (shs.)[1]
Common	unlimited	72,585,465

[1] At May 26, 2023

Major Shareholder - Romain Nouzareth held 15.26% interest, True Global Ventures 4 Plus Fund Pte Ltd. held 12.75% interest and Mathieu Nouzareth held 11.47% interest at May 26, 2023.

Price Range - SATO/TSX-VEN

Year	Volume	High	Low	Close
2022	3,209,644	$1.14	$0.11	$0.12
2021	4,001,930	$2.20	$0.15	$0.93
2020	81,898	$0.22	$0.03	$0.15
2019	106,845	$0.49	$0.10	$0.10
2018	63,208	$0.43	$0.19	$0.22

Consolidation: 1-for-2.7 cons. in Sept. 2021
Recent Close: $0.45
Capital Stock Changes - In January 2022, private placement of 3,912,481 common shares was completed at 84¢ per share. Also during 2022, 1,803,236 common shares were issued on exercise of warrants.

Wholly Owned Subsidiaries

Canada Computational Unlimited Inc., Joliette, Qué.
SATO Corp., Del.

Financial Statistics

Periods ended:	12m Dec. 31/22[A]		12m Dec. 31/21[◻A]
	$000s	%Chg	$000s
Operating revenue	**10,621**	**+74**	**6,118**
Salaries & benefits	208		233
General & admin expense	4,494		2,245
Stock-based compensation	1,822		250
Other operating expense	6,196		2,247
Operating expense	**12,720**	**+156**	**4,975**
Operating income	**(2,099)**	**n.a.**	**1,143**
Deprec., depl. & amort.	1,886		820
Finance costs, gross	394		514
Write-downs/write-offs	(769)		nil
Pre-tax income	**(7,948)**	**n.a.**	**(1,726)**
Income taxes	53		4
Net income	**(8,001)**	**n.a.**	**(1,730)**
Cash & equivalent	1,350		4,048
Accounts receivable	1,704		500
Current assets	3,237		5,096
Fixed assets, net	9,120		5,869
Right-of-use assets	2,461		1,248
Intangibles, net	264		66
Total assets	**15,514**	**+24**	**12,503**
Accts. pay. & accr. liabs.	1,892		2,968
Current liabilities	6,101		3,527
Long-term debt, gross	3,778		88
Long-term debt, net	2,382		47
Long-term lease liabilities	2,258		1,097
Shareholders' equity	4,774		7,822
Cash from oper. activs.	**649**	**n.a.**	**(2,729)**
Cash from fin. activs.	6,300		6,758
Cash from invest. activs.	(3,501)		(3,501)
Net cash position	**360**	**-55**	**794**
Capital expenditures	(6,998)		(3,423)
	$		$
Earnings per share*	(0.11)		(0.03)
Cash flow per share*	0.01		(0.04)
	shs		shs
No. of shs. o/s*	72,585,465		66,869,748
Avg. no. of shs. o/s*	70,606,459		66,869,748
	%		%
Net profit margin	(75.33)		(28.28)
Return on equity	(127.04)		(40.45)
Return on assets	(54.28)		(15.65)
No. of employees (FTEs)	14		10

* Common
◻ Restated
[A] Reported in accordance with IFRS

Latest Results

Periods ended:	3m Mar. 31/23[A]		3m Mar. 31/22[A]
	$000s	%Chg	$000s
Operating revenue	3,909	+129	1,709
Net income	511	n.a.	(2,107)
	$		$
Earnings per share*	0.01		(0.03)

* Common
[A] Reported in accordance with IFRS

Historical Summary
(as originally stated)

Fiscal Year	Oper. Rev.	Net Inc. Bef. Disc.	EPS*
	$000s	$000s	$
2022[A]	10,621	(8,001)	(0.11)
2021[A1]	6,118	(1,730)	(0.03)
2020[A]	1,860	(959)	(0.54)
2019[A]	2,309	(1,006)	(0.57)
2018[A]	633	(671)	(0.54)

* Common
[A] Reported in accordance with IFRS
[1] Results prior to Sept. 7, 2021, pertain to and reflect the Qualifying Transaction reverse takeover acquisition of Canada Computational Unlimited Corp. (dba CCU.ai).
Note: Adjusted throughout for 1-for-2.7 cons. in Sept. 2021

S.3 SBD Capital Corp.

Symbol - SBD **Exchange** - CSE **CUSIP** - 78412Y
Head Office - 401-217 Queen St W, Toronto, ON, M5V 0R2 **Telephone** - (416) 361-2515
Email - cburk@irwinlowy.com
Investor Relations - Carly Burk (416) 361-2515
Auditors - Jones & O'Connell LLP C.A., St. Catharines, Ont.
Transfer Agents - TSX Trust Company, Toronto, Ont.
Profile - (Ont. 1979) Produces, manufactures and distributes rum in Canada and the United States.

Wholly owned **Secret Barrel Distillery Corporation** produces, markets and distributes craft rum in Alberta, Saskatchewan, Manitoba and the United States under the Secret Barrel Rum brand. The company imports from Guyana, Jamaica, and Trinidad and Tobago to High River, Alta., for blending and bottling. Products include White rum, 7 and 10 year-aged Demerara, Spiced rum, Cinnamon rum and cocktails.

Also holds rights to distribute rum products from Guyana under the XM Rum brand. Products include XM 5, 10, 12 and 15 year-aged rums.

Common reinstated on CSE, Oct. 14, 2022.

Predecessor Detail - Name changed from White Pine Resources Inc., Sept. 26, 2017.

Directors - Christopher O. (Chris) Irwin, CEO, Toronto, Ont.; Trumbull G. Fisher, Oakville, Ont.; Richard Paolone Jr., Toronto, Ont.

Other Exec. Officers - Arvin Ramos, CFO; Carly Burk, corp. sec.

Capital Stock

	Authorized (shs.)	Outstanding (shs.)[1]
Special	unlimited	nil
Preference	500,000	nil
Common	unlimited	4,724,341

[1] At Dec. 23, 2022

Price Range - SBD/CSE

Year	Volume	High	Low	Close
2022	1,687,007	$0.48	$0.12	$0.12
2021	3,244,552	$1.08	$0.24	$0.36
2020	1,251,153	$1.44	$0.24	$0.24
2019	1,294,410	$4.68	$0.60	$1.38
2018	420,771	$6.60	$0.60	$2.52

Consolidation: 1-for-12 cons. in Dec. 2022
Recent Close: $0.08

Capital Stock Changes - On Dec. 23, 2022, common shares were consolidated on a 1-for-12 basis.

In April 2021, private placement of 30,000,000 units (1 common share & 1 warrant) at $0.025 per unit was completed. In December 2021, private placement of 1,800,000 units (1 common share & 1 warrant) at $0.025 per unit was completed.

Wholly Owned Subsidiaries

Secret Barrel Distillery Corporation, Calgary, Alta.

Financial Statistics

Periods ended:	12m Mar. 31/22[A]		12m Mar. 31/21[◻A]
	$000s	%Chg	$000s
Operating revenue	**15**	**-38**	**24**
Cost of goods sold	16		18
General & admin expense	164		201
Operating expense	**180**	**-18**	**219**
Operating income	**(165)**	**n.a.**	**(195)**
Finance costs, gross	1		2
Pre-tax income	**(886)**	**n.a.**	**(185)**
Net income	**(886)**	**n.a.**	**(185)**
Cash & equivalent	14		29
Inventories	nil		11
Accounts receivable	54		51
Current assets	68		90
Total assets	**68**	**-24**	**90**
Accts. pay. & accr. liabs.	242		466
Current liabilities	286		905
Shareholders' equity	(218)		(815)
Cash from oper. activs.	**(79)**	**n.a.**	**(42)**
Cash from fin. activs.	64		52
Net cash position	**14**	**-52**	**29**
	$		$
Earnings per share*	(0.24)		(0.12)
Cash flow per share*	(0.02)		(0.02)
	shs		shs
No. of shs. o/s*	4,724,341		2,074,341
Avg. no. of shs. o/s*	4,516,670		2,074,341
	%		%
Net profit margin	n.m.		(770.83)
Return on equity	n.m.		n.m.
Return on assets	n.m.		(140.23)

* Common
◻ Restated
[A] Reported in accordance with IFRS

Historical Summary
(as originally stated)

Fiscal Year	Oper. Rev.	Net Inc. Bef. Disc.	EPS*
	$000s	$000s	$
2022[A]	15	(886)	(0.24)
2021[A]	24	(200)	(0.12)
2020[A]	35	(621)	(0.36)
2019[A]	131	(1,319)	(0.60)
2018[A]	16	(232)	(0.24)

* Common
[A] Reported in accordance with IFRS
Note: Adjusted throughout for 1-for-12 cons. in Dec. 2022

S.4 SIQ Mountain Industries Inc.

Symbol - SIQ.H **Exchange** - TSX-VEN **CUSIP** - 82964L
Head Office - 13966 18B Ave, South Surrey, BC, V4A 8J1 **Telephone** - (604) 802-7372 **Toll-free** - (877) 464-8592
Website - www.siqmountain.com
Email - bond@siqmountain.com
Investor Relations - James R. Bond
Auditors - De Visser Gray LLP C.A., Vancouver, B.C.
Lawyers - Clark Wilson LLP, Vancouver, B.C.
Transfer Agents - Computershare Trust Company of Canada Inc., Vancouver, B.C.
Profile - (B.C. 2016) Seeking new business opportunities.

Predecessor Detail - Name changed from Snobro Enterprises Inc., Oct. 3, 2017, following Qualifying Transaction acquisition of snow-bike technology.

Directors - James R. (Rik) Bond†, pres. & CEO, Kelowna, B.C.; Richard (Rick) Lee, CFO & corp. sec., Surrey, B.C.; Kathy Love, Burnaby, B.C.
† Lead director

Capital Stock

	Authorized (shs.)	Outstanding (shs.)[1]
Preferred	unlimited	nil
Common	unlimited	25,133,433

[1] At Feb. 2, 2023

Major Shareholder - Widely held at Feb. 2, 2023.

Price Range - SIQ.H/TSX-VEN

Year	Volume	High	Low	Close
2022	1,499,300	$0.06	$0.03	$0.06
2021	2,445,415	$0.07	$0.03	$0.06
2020	1,201,980	$0.11	$0.06	$0.07
2019	627,200	$0.17	$0.04	$0.10
2018	1,481,190	$0.28	$0.12	$0.14

Recent Close: $0.05

Capital Stock Changes - There were no changes to capital stock during fiscal 2022.

Wholly Owned Subsidiaries

SiQ Mountain Studios Inc., B.C. Formerly SiQ Ride Rentals Inc.

Financial Statistics

Periods ended:	12m Aug. 31/22[A]		12m Aug. 31/21[A]
	$000s	%Chg	$000s
General & admin expense	28		52
Stock-based compensation	nil		1
Operating expense	**28**	**-47**	**53**
Operating income	**(28)**	**n.a.**	**(53)**
Finance income	nil		3
Finance costs, gross	1		2
Pre-tax income	**(30)**	**n.a.**	**(52)**
Net income	**(30)**	**n.a.**	**(52)**
Cash & equivalent	2		21
Accounts receivable	2		1
Current assets	5		24
Total assets	**8**	**-67**	**24**
Accts. pay. & accr. liabs.	87		77
Current liabilities	87		77
Shareholders' equity	(82)		(52)
Cash from oper. activs.	**(18)**	**n.a.**	**(50)**
Cash from fin. activs.	nil		50
Net cash position	**2**	**-90**	**21**
	$		$
Earnings per share*	(0.00)		(0.00)
Cash flow per share*	(0.00)		(0.00)
	shs		shs
No. of shs. o/s*	25,133,433		25,133,433
Avg. no. of shs. o/s*	25,133,433		25,106,036
	%		%
Net profit margin	n.a.		n.a.
Return on equity	n.m.		n.m.
Return on assets	(181.25)		(185.19)

* Common
[A] Reported in accordance with IFRS

Latest Results

Periods ended:	3m Nov. 30/22[A]		3m Nov. 30/21[A]
	$000s	%Chg	$000s
Net income	(5)	n.a.	(7)
	$		$
Earnings per share*	(0.00)		(0.00)

* Common
[A] Reported in accordance with IFRS

Historical Summary
(as originally stated)

Fiscal Year	Oper. Rev.	Net Inc. Bef. Disc.	EPS*
	$000s	$000s	$
2022[A]	nil	(30)	(0.00)
2021[A]	nil	(52)	(0.00)
2020[A]	nil	(433)	(0.02)
2019[A]	nil	(1,051)	(0.05)
2018[A]	nil	(855)	(0.04)

* Common
[A] Reported in accordance with IFRS

S.5 SIR Royalty Income Fund

Symbol - SRV.UN **Exchange** - TSX **CUSIP** - 829636
Head Office - 200-5360 South Service Rd, Burlington, ON, L7L 5L1
Telephone - (905) 681-2997 **Fax** - (905) 681-0394
Website - www.sircorp.com
Email - jgood@sircorp.com
Investor Relations - Jeffrey Good (905) 681-2997
Auditors - PricewaterhouseCoopers LLP C.A., Toronto, Ont.
Lawyers - Stikeman Elliott LLP, Toronto, Ont.
Transfer Agents - Computershare Trust Company of Canada Inc., Toronto, Ont.
Administrators - SIR Royalty Limited Partnership
Profile - (Ont. 2004) Owns directly certain debt and indirectly, through **SIR Royalty Limited Partnership**, the Canadian trademarks of **SIR Corp.**, which creates, owns and operates full service restaurants in Canada under the banners Jack Astor's Bar and Grill®, Scaddabush Italian Kitchen & Bar®, REDS® Wine Tavern, Reds® Kitchen + Wine Bar Fallsview REDS® Square One, The Loose Moose Tap & Grill®, Abbey's Bakehouse® and Duke's Refresher® & Bar.

SIR Royalty Limited Partnership has granted **SIR Corp.** a 99-year licence, commencing Oct. 12, 2004, to use the trademarks related to the SIR Corp. restaurants in Canada in consideration for a royalty payment equal to 6% of the revenue of the restaurants included in the royalty pool. At Mar. 31, 2023, the fund holds an investment in SIR Royalty Limited Partnership through indirect ownership of all its class A and ordinary limited partnership units valued at $50,984,321; and a $40,000,000 principal amount of loan, bearing interest at 7.5% per annum, owed by SIR Corp.

At Mar. 31, 2023, 51 restaurants were included in the royalty pool.

During 2022, the company permanently closed and converted its remaining Canyon Creek® restaurants in Niagara Falls and Etobicoke, Ont., into new Reds Kitchen + Wine Bar Fallsview and Scaddabush Italian Kitchen & Bar, respectively. Subsequently, the two new restaurants were added to the Royalty Pooled restaurants effective Jan. 1, 2023.

Trustees - Norman (Norm) Mayr, chr., Port Moody, B.C.; Stephen Dewis, London, Ont.; Michael Fisher, North York, Ont.; Lembit Janes, Toronto, Ont.; Sandra Levy, Toronto, Ont.

Oper. Subsid./Mgt. Co. Officers - Peter Fowler, CEO; Paul J. Bognar, pres. & COO; Jeffrey (Jeff) Good, CFO & corp. sec.

Capital Stock

	Authorized (shs.)	Outstanding (shs.)[1]
Fund Unit	unlimited	8,375,567[2]
Class A LP Unit	unlimited	3,018,900
Ordinary LP Unit	unlimited	5,356,667
Ordinary GP Unit	unlimited	100
Class A GP Unit	unlimited	1,291,618[3]
Class B GP Unit	unlimited	96,284,667
Class C GP Unit	unlimited	4,000,000

[1] At Mar. 22, 2022
[2] At Apr. 25, 2022.
[3] At Apr. 25, 2022.

Note: Class A LP units, ordinary LP units, ordinary GP units, class A GP units, class B GP units and class C GP units are securities of SIR Royalty Limited Partnership.

Fund Unit - The fund will endeavour to make monthly cash distributions equal to a pro rata share of interest and (if applicable) principal repayments on the SIR Loan and the trust notes and distributions on or in respect of the trust units of SIR Holdings Trust owned by the fund, less amounts which are paid, payable, incurred or provided for in such period in connection with: (i) administrative expenses and other obligations of the fund; (ii) amounts which may be paid by the fund in connection with any cash redemptions of fund units; (iii) any interest expense incurred by the fund; and (iv) such reasonable reserves as may be established by the trustees in their sole discretion, which are expected to be nominal. Redeemable on demand by holders at the lesser of: (i) 90% of the average market price of the fund units during the 10 trading days preceding the redemption date; and (ii) 100% of the closing market price of the fund units on the redemption date. One vote per fund unit.

Class A and Ordinary LP Unit - All indirectly owned by the fund through SIR Holdings Trust.

Ordinary GP Unit - Held by SIR GP Inc. and SIR Corp.

Class A, B and C GP Unit - All held by SIR Corp. Class A general partner units are exchangeable for fund units on a 1-for-1 basis, and are entitled to vote together with fund units as to the number of fund units they would receive if exchanged. Class B general partner units are exchangeable, on a 1-for-1 basis, for class A general partner units in an amount to be determined on January 1 of each year based on a formula related to the number of new restaurants added to the SIR royalty pool and revenue generated by such restaurants. Class A general partner units may be reconverted to class B general partner units, on a 1-for-1 basis, based on a formula for the closure of restaurants in the SIR royalty pool. Class C general partner units are entitled to receive a cumulative preferential monthly cash distribution equal to $0.063 per unit, payable on the dates that distributions are paid on fund units.

Major Shareholder - Lembit Janes held 17.36% interest and Mary Irvine held 11.61% interest at Apr. 14, 2023.

Price Range - SRV.UN/TSX

Year	Volume	High	Low	Close
2022	2,432,190	$17.84	$10.50	$17.84
2021	5,652,235	$13.88	$3.12	$11.58
2020	8,165,654	$8.63	$1.31	$3.05
2019	4,665,045	$16.92	$7.76	$8.15
2018	2,034,369	$16.18	$13.15	$14.69

Recent Close: $16.00

Capital Stock Changes - There were no changes to capital stock from 2017 to 2022, inclusive.

Dividends

SRV.UN unit Ra $1.14 pa M est. Mar. 31, 2023
$0.05◆ .... Dec. 30/22 $0.135◆ .... July 29/22
$0.10◆ .... Dec. 31/21
Paid in 2023: $0.76 2022: $1.095 + $0.185◆ 2021: $0.50 + $0.10◆
◆ Special

Wholly Owned Subsidiaries

SIR Holdings Trust, Burlington, Ont.
• 87.5% int. in **SIR Royalty Limited Partnership**, Ont.

Subsidiaries

80% int. in **SIR GP Inc.**, Burlington, Ont.

Financial Statistics

Periods ended:	12m Dec. 31/22[A]		12m Dec. 31/21[A]
	$000s	%Chg	$000s
Total revenue	**18,885**	**+167**	**7,064**
General & admin. expense	625		569
Operating expense	**625**	**+10**	**569**
Operating income	**18,260**	**+181**	**6,495**
Write-downs/write-offs	30,066		60
Pre-tax income	**48,326**	**+637**	**6,555**
Income taxes	3,917		1,645
Net income	**44,409**	**+804**	**4,910**
Cash & equivalent	2,275		1,413
Current assets	5,487		5,872
Long-term investments	77,734		43,608
Total assets	**83,221**	**+68**	**49,481**
Accts. pay. & accr. liabs.	190		131
Current liabilities	4,888		4,877
Shareholders' equity	76,274		42,586
Cash from oper. activs.	**11,583**	**+84**	**6,300**
Cash from fin. activs.	(10,721)		(5,025)
Net cash position	**2,275**	**+61**	**1,413**
	$		$
Earnings per share*	5.30		0.59
Cash flow per share*	1.38		0.63
Cash divd. per share*	1.10		0.50
Extra divd. - cash*	0.19		0.10
Total divd. per share*	**1.28**		**0.60**
	shs		shs
No. of shs. o/s*	8,375,567		8,375,567
Avg. no. of shs. o/s*	8,375,567		8,375,567
	%		%
Net profit margin	235.15		69.51
Return on equity	74.72		11.51
Return on assets	66.93		10.02

* Fund unit
[A] Reported in accordance with IFRS

Latest Results

Periods ended:	3m Mar. 31/23[A]		3m Mar. 31/22[A]
	$000s	%Chg	$000s
Total revenue	1,291	-13	1,479
Net income	300	-72	1,055
	$		$
Earnings per share*	0.04		0.13

* Fund unit
[A] Reported in accordance with IFRS

Historical Summary
(as originally stated)

Fiscal Year	Total Rev.	Net Inc. Bef. Disc.	EPS*
	$000s	$000s	$
2022[A]	18,885	44,409	5.30
2021[A]	7,064	4,910	0.59
2020[A]	(12,604)	(44,002)	(5.25)
2019[A]	16,781	12,644	1.51
2018[A]	7,990	5,115	0.61

* Fund unit
[A] Reported in accordance with IFRS

S.6 SLANG Worldwide Inc.

Symbol - SLNG **Exchange** - CSE **CUSIP** - 831006
Head Office - 50 Carroll St, Toronto, ON, M4M 3G3 **Toll-free** - (833) 752-6499
Website - www.slangww.com
Email - investors@slangww.com
Investor Relations - Mikel Rutherford (833) 752-6499
Auditors - MNP LLP C.A.
Lawyers - Dentons Canada LLP
Transfer Agents - Odyssey Trust Company, Toronto, Ont.
Employees - 122 at Apr. 27, 2022
Profile - (Can. 2017) Acquires, develops and creates cannabis consumer brands.

Owns, licenses and markets brands, including O.pen, Alchemy Naturals, CeresMED, Firefly and District Edibles, for various product categories consisting of flower, inhalable concentrates, and ingestibles. The company cultivates, brands, manufactures and distributes medical and recreational cannabis products to wholesale and retail customers in Colorado and Vermont. Operations include a 28,000-sq.-ft. cultivation, processing and distribution facility, three medical dispensaries and a recreational cannabis store, all in Vermont. Products are also licensed to cannabis cultivators, manufacturers, distributors, retailers and e-commerce distribution platforms in Florida, Maine, New Mexico, Massachusetts, Michigan, Ohio, Pennsylvania, Washington, West Virginia, Maryland and Puerto Rico.

Revenues are generated primarily through sales of finished products and certain product components and ingredients, such as flavouring concentrates/bases, packaging and hardware; and licensing and consulting fees from partners and licensees.

Recent Merger and Acquisition Activity

Status: completed **Revised:** Apr. 12, 2022
UPDATE: The transaction was completed for issuance of 708,326 post-consolidated common shares and 1,062,490 post-consolidated restricted voting shares of SLANG. PREVIOUS: SLANG Worldwide Inc. agreed to acquire NS Holdings Inc., the parent company of GNT Oregon, LLC, which produces O.pen, Bakked and District Edibles branded cannabis products and operates a carbon dioxide extraction and manufacturing facility in Portland, Ore. Consideration would consist of issuance of 358,667 post-consolidated common shares and 531,250 post-consolidated restricted voting shares (following a 1-for-6 share consolidation) of SLANG within the next 10 days as deposit and issuance of 354,167 post-consolidated common shares and 438,282 post-consolidated restricted voting shares of SLANG upon closing. SLANG may issue additional shares to the NS Holdings vendors upon achievement of certain performance milestones. Closing of the transaction was expected to occur in the third quarter of 2021. June 2021 - SLANG issued 354,166 post-consolidated common shares and 531,249 post-consolidated restricted voting shares as a deposit on signing of the agreement.

Predecessor Detail - Name changed from Fire Cannabis Inc., Nov. 26, 2018.

Directors - Ruth Chun, chr., Campbellville, Ont.; Kevin K. Albert, N.Y.; Todd Boudreau, Mass.; Adam Crocker, Calif.; Sandra Levy, Toronto, Ont.; Felicia Snyder, Ont.

Other Exec. Officers - Johnathan (John) Moynan, CEO, gen. counsel & corp. sec.; Mikel Rutherford, CFO; Brittany Hallett, v-p, mktg.; Matt Melnick, v-p, opers.

Capital Stock

	Authorized (shs.)	Outstanding (shs.)[1]
Preferred	unlimited	nil
Common	unlimited	88,894,073
Restricted Vtg.	unlimited	32,245,170

[1] At Nov. 28, 2022

Preferred - Redeemable by the company at any time on payment of a redemption price per share, plus all declared and unpaid non-cumulative cash dividends. One vote per share at meetings of the shareholders, except a meeting of holders of a particular class of shares other than the preferred shares who are entitled to vote separately as a class at such meeting.

Common - One vote per share.

Restricted Voting - Convertible into common shares, at the holder's option, on a one-for-one basis as follows: at any time that is not a restricted period, which means any time at which the board of directors reasonably believes that the company is a domestic issuer under applicable U.S. securities laws; following the date that is the three-year anniversary of the date of issuance; with consent of the board; or if there is an offer to purchase the common shares. Entitled to one vote per share provided that holders will not be entitled to vote for the election or removal of the directors of the company.

Major Shareholder - Widely held at May 12, 2022.

Price Range - SLNG/CSE

Year	Volume	High	Low	Close
2022	10,741,421	$0.51	$0.03	$0.04
2021	13,912,070	$4.50	$0.39	$0.42
2020	25,879,038	$2.70	$0.66	$1.92
2019	27,445,396	$17.40	$1.98	$2.85

Consolidation: 1-for-6 cons. in Mar. 2022
Recent Close: $0.05
Capital Stock Changes - On Mar. 3, 2022, common shares and restricted voting shares were consolidated on a 1-for-6 basis.

Wholly Owned Subsidiaries

Allied Concessions Group, Inc., Denver, Colo.
Pleasant Valley Ranch, LLC, Carbondale, Colo.
SLANG Investments, Inc., B.C.
SLANG NonPT Holdco, Inc., Del.
• 100% int. in **National Concessions Group, Inc.**, Colo.

- 100% int. in **SLANG Colorado RE1, LLC**, Colo.
- 100% int. in **Slang Colorado RE, Inc.**, Del.

SLANG Oregon Holdings Inc., Colo.

- 100% int. in **Oregon OV, LLC**, Ore.
  - 100% int. in **GNT Oregon, LLC**, Ore.

SLANG PT Holdco, Inc., Del.

- 100% int. in **SLANG Colorado, Inc.**, Colo.
  - 100% int. in **SLANG Colorado Cultivation, Inc.**, Colo.
  - 100% int. in **SLANG Colorado Distribution, Inc.**, Denver, Colo.
  - 100% int. in **SLANG Colorado Manufacturing, Inc.**, Colo.
- 100% int. in **SLANG Oregon, Inc.**, Ore.
  - 100% int. in **CHC Laboratories, Inc.**, Ore.
  - 100% int. in **Hydra Oregon, LLC**, Ore.
  - 100% int. in **LBA CBD, LLC**, Ore.
- 100% int. in **SLANG Vermont, Inc.**, Vt.
  - 100% int. in **Ceres LLC**, Vt.
  - 100% int. in **Champlain Valley Dispensary, Inc.**, Vt.

Investments

20% int. in **Agripharm Corp.**, Creemore, Ont.

Financial Statistics

Periods ended:	12m Dec. 31/21[A]		12m Dec. 31/20[oA]
	$000s	%Chg	$000s
Operating revenue	**37,273**	**+57**	**23,741**
Cost of goods sold	22,049		12,647
Research & devel. expense	90		108
General & admin expense	22,053		19,701
Stock-based compensation	8,849		9,415
Operating expense	**53,040**	**+27**	**41,871**
Operating income	**(15,767)**	**n.a.**	**(18,130)**
Deprec., depl. & amort.	7,849		6,453
Finance costs, net	(10,921)		(14,044)
Write-downs/write-offs	(53,260)[1]		(4,122)
Pre-tax income	**(51,864)**	**n.a.**	**(16,420)**
Income taxes	(535)		(2,285)
Net inc. bef. disc. opers	**(51,329)**	**n.a.**	**(14,135)**
Income from disc. opers	(4,756)		74
Net income	**(56,086)**	**n.a.**	**(14,061)**
Cash & equivalent	17,028		6,477
Inventories	8,730		4,583
Accounts receivable	2,510		2,594
Current assets	40,953		18,581
Long-term investments	nil		33
Fixed assets, net	1,670		7,528
Right-of-use assets	4,487		3,489
Intangibles, net	28,377		71,716
Total assets	**79,290**	**-26**	**107,611**
Accts. pay. & accr. liabs	6,766		11,115
Current liabilities	16,047		17,843
Long-term debt, gross	9,240		2,271
Long-term debt, net	8,553		826
Long-term lease liabilities	4,515		3,466
Shareholders' equity	38,168		66,750
Cash from oper. activs	**(11,977)**	**n.a.**	**(15,417)**
Cash from fin. activs	29,245		(17,668)
Cash from invest. activs	(3,256)		13,165
Net cash position	**20,831**	**+215**	**6,609**
Capital expenditures	(749)		(54)
Capital disposals	27		64
	$		$
Earns. per sh. bef disc opers*	(0.60)		(0.24)
Earnings per share*	(0.66)		(0.24)
Cash flow per share*	(0.14)		(0.29)
	shs		shs
No. of shs. o/s*	92,881,690		63,874,495
Avg. no. of shs. o/s*	84,943,902		53,608,343
	%		%
Net profit margin	(137.71)		(59.54)
Return on equity	(97.85)		(26.32)
Return on assets	(54.93)		(13.56)
Foreign sales percent	99		95
No. of employees (FTEs)	152		99

* Common
[o] Restated
[A] Reported in accordance with IFRS
[1] Includes impairment of $35,873,320 of goodwill, $11,228,125 of various intangible assets, $4,836,876 of property, plant and equipment, and $1,321,522 of equipment deposit.

Latest Results

Periods ended:	9m Sept. 30/22[A]		9m Sept. 30/21[oA]
	$000s	%Chg	$000s
Operating revenue	26,248	-8	28,637
Net inc. bef. disc. opers	(13,920)	n.a.	(18,149)
Income from disc. opers	(740)		(1,501)
Net income	(14,661)	n.a.	(19,650)
	$		$
Earns. per sh. bef. disc. opers.*	(0.14)		(0.22)
Earnings per share*	(0.15)		(0.24)

* Common
[o] Restated
[A] Reported in accordance with IFRS

Historical Summary
(as originally stated)

Fiscal Year	Oper. Rev.	Net Inc. Bef. Disc.	EPS*
	$000s	$000s	$
2021[A]	37,273	(51,329)	(0.60)
2020[A]	25,106	(14,061)	(0.24)
2019[A]	28,178	(200,336)	(5.22)
2018[A]	4,774	(28,279)	(2.22)
2018[A1,2]	1,999	(23,298)	(2.04)

* Common
[A] Reported in accordance with IFRS
[1] 8 months ended Aug. 31, 2018.
[2] As shown in the listing statement dated Jan. 17, 2019.
Note: Adjusted throughout for 1-for-6 cons. in Mar. 2022

S.7 SNC-Lavalin Group Inc.*

Symbol - SNC **Exchange** - TSX **CUSIP** - 78460T
Head Office - 455 boul René-Lévesque O, Montréal, QC, H2Z 1Z3
Telephone - (514) 393-1000 **Fax** - (514) 866-0795
Website - www.snclavalin.com
Email - denis.jasmin@snclavalin.com
Investor Relations - Denis Jasmin (514) 393-8000 ext. 57553
Auditors - Deloitte LLP C.A., Montréal, Qué.
Transfer Agents - Computershare Trust Company of Canada Inc., Montréal, Qué.
FP500 Revenue Ranking - 86
Employees - 33,876 at Dec. 31, 2022
Profile - (Can. 1967) Provides consulting, advisory and environmental services, intelligent networks and cybersecurity, design and engineering, procurement, project and construction management, operations and maintenance, decommissioning and capital services.

Operations are organized into six reportable segments: Engineering Services, Nuclear, Operations & Maintenance (O&M) and Linxon (SNCL Services line of business); LSTK Projects; and Capital.

SNCL Services

Engineering Services includes all consultancy, engineering, design and project management services around the world. Projects are mainly in transportation (including rail, mass transit, roads and airports), building and places, defence, water, industrial and mining and power and renewables markets. A significant portion of Engineering services revenues are derived from the public sector, including national, provincial, state and local, and municipal authorities.

Nuclear supports clients across the entire nuclear life cycle with the full spectrum of services including consultancy, engineering, procurement and construction management (EPCM) services, field services, technology services, spare parts, reactor support and decommissioning, and waste management. Also provides new-build and full refurbishment services of CANDU (Canada Deuterium Uranium) reactors.

O&M provides operations, maintenance and asset management solutions for bridges, transit systems, highways, buildings and industrial plants including power plants, water supply and treatment systems and desalination plants, as well as postal services and ships.

Linxon offers engineering, procurement, management and construction services for execution of large, complex alternative current power substations including expansions and electrification, primarily through repetitive engineering, procurement and construction offerings in the utilities, renewable, conventional generation, transportation and data center markets.

LSTK Projects

The segment includes the remaining lump-sum turnkey (LSTK) construction contracts of the company, particularly mass transit projects in Canada and one mining and metallurgy project in the Middle East. Also includes the financial results of legacy warranty costs and claims from completed LSTK projects.

Capital

The company's investment, financing and asset management arm responsible for developing projects, arranging financing, investing equity, undertaking complex financial modeling and managing its infrastructure investments for optimal returns. Activities are primarily concentrated in infrastructure for public services such as bridges, highways, mass transit systems, power facilities, energy infrastructure, water treatment plants and social infrastructure. Also includes 20% interest in **SNC-Lavalin Infrastructure Partners LP**, which holds investments in infrastructure assets in Canada.

In January 2023, wholly owned **SNC-Lavalin GEM Quebec Inc.** was amalgamated into wholly owned **SNC-Lavalin Inc.**

In December 2022, the company sold its 4.5% interest in **Carlyle Global Infrastructure Opportunity Fund L.P.**, which holds investments in infrastructure projects related to energy, power and other natural resources, for US$52,100,000.

Recent Merger and Acquisition Activity

Status: pending **Announced:** July 7, 2023
SNC-Lavalin Group Inc. agreed to sell its Scandinavian engineering business to Paris, France-based SYSTRA Group for £80,000,000 (Cdn$136,000,000). The Scandinavian segment generated Cdn$95,000,000 in revenue annually, representing less than 2% of SNC's annual total. The division employed 750 workers in Denmark, Sweden and Norway. The transaction was expected to close in late 2023, subject to regulatory approvals and customary closing conditions.

Predecessor Detail - Name changed from The SNC Group Inc., June 7, 1993.

Directors - William L. (Bill) Young, chr., Lexington, Mass.; Ian L. Edwards, pres. & CEO, Montréal, Qué.; Gary C. Baughman, Charlotte, N.C.; Mary-Ann Bell, Montréal, Qué.; Christie J. B. (Chris) Clark, Toronto, Ont.; Ruby McGregor-Smith, Ascot, Berks., United Kingdom; Steven L. Newman, Holladay, Utah; Robert Paré, Westmount, Qué.; Michael B. (Mike) Pedersen, Toronto, Ont.; Benita M. Warmbold, Toronto, Ont.

Other Exec. Officers - Jeffrey A. (Jeff) Bell, exec. v-p & CFO; Andrée-Claude Bérubé, exec. v-p & gen. counsel; James Cullens, exec. v-p, HR; Erik J. Ryan, exec. v-p, strategy, mktg. & external rel.; Nigel W. M. White, exec. v-p, project oversight; Denis Jasmin, v-p, IR; Robert E. (Bob) Alger, pres., major projects; Philip Hoare, pres., eng. srvcs., U.K., Europe, Middle East, India & Canada; Stephen (Steve) Morriss, pres., eng. srvcs., U.S., Asia Pacific & mining & metallurgy; Joseph (Joe) St. Julian, pres., nuclear; Stéphanie Vaillancourt, pres., capital & opers. & maint.

Capital Stock

	Authorized (shs.)	Outstanding (shs.)[1]
First Preferred	unlimited	nil
Second Preferred	unlimited	nil
Common	unlimited	175,554,252

[1] At July 25, 2023

First Preferred - Issuable in series and non-voting.
Second Preferred - Issuable in series and non-voting.
Common - One vote per share.

Normal Course Issuer Bid - The company plans to make normal course purchases of up to 1,500,000 common shares representing 0.9% of the total outstanding. The bid commenced on Mar. 8, 2023, and expires on Mar. 7, 2024.

Major Shareholder - Caisse de dépôt et placement du Québec held 19.9% interest and Jarislowsky, Fraser Limited held 11.6% interest at Mar. 20, 2023.

Price Range - SNC/TSX

Year	Volume	High	Low	Close
2022	99,812,878	$33.11	$21.27	$23.86
2021	115,210,955	$38.25	$21.11	$30.91
2020	170,759,074	$34.36	$17.50	$21.73
2019	264,201,222	$48.88	$15.47	$29.95
2018	101,783,146	$61.54	$43.73	$45.92

Recent Close: $42.92

Capital Stock Changes - There were no changes to capital stock from 2019 to 2022, inclusive.

Dividends

SNC com Ra $0.08 pa Q est. Aug. 29, 2019

Long-Term Debt - Outstanding at Dec. 31, 2022:

Revolving facility	$176,339,000
Term loan[1]	499,156,000
Debs.:	
3.235% ser.4 due Mar. 2023	199,963,000
3.8% ser.6 due Aug. 2024	298,649,000
7% ser.7 due June 2026	296,453,000
CDPQ loan due 2024	400,000,000
Subsidiary sr. notes due 2026	22,157,000
Unsec. loan of Linxon[3]	11,769,000
TransitNEXT credit facility[4]	143,738,000
Other	8,173,000
	2,056,397,000
Less: Current portion	547,286,000
	1,509,111,000

[1] Bears interest at prime rate loan or acceptances, due May 2025.
[2] Bears interest at a base rate, which is the greater of the CDOR rate and 0.9% plus an applicable margin.
[3] Non-recourse share of debt of Linxon Pvt Ltd. consisting of principal amount of US$9,300,000 interest-free loan due 2023.
[4] Non-recourse share of debt of TransitNEXT General Partnership consisting of principal amount of $149,000,000 credit facility, bearing interest at CDOR rate plus an applicable margin, due 2024.

Minimum repayments of recourse, limited recourse and non-recourse long-term debt were reported as follows:

2023	$552,675,000
2024	707,620,000
2025	507,620,000
2026	300,272,000

Note - During the second quarter of 2023, the maturity of its term loan was extended from May 2025 to May 2026. In July 2023, the maturity of its CDPQ loan was extended from July 2024 to July 2026.

Wholly Owned Subsidiaries

Atkins China Limited, Hong Kong, People's Republic of China.
Atkins Denmark A/S, Denmark.
Atkins International Holdings Limited, United Kingdom.

Atkins Limited, United Kingdom.
The Atkins North America Holdings Corporation, Fla.
Atkins North America, Inc., Fla.
Atkins Nuclear Secured Holdings Corporation
Atkins US Holdings Inc., Del.
Candu Energy Inc., Canada.
Faithful + Gould Limited, United Kingdom.
Isotek Systems, LLC, United States.
Kentz Canada Holdings Limited, Canada.
Linxon Saudi Arabia Co. Ltd., Saudi Arabia.
Linxon Sweden AB, Sweden.
Linxon Switzerland Ltd., Switzerland.
Linxon UK Ltd., United Kingdom.
Linxon U.S. LLC, United States.
Protrans B.C. Operations Ltd., B.C.
SNC-Lavalin ATP Inc., Montréal, Qué.
SNC-Lavalin Algérie EURL, Algeria.
SNC-Lavalin Arabia LLC, Saudi Arabia.
SNC-Lavalin Capital Inc., Canada.
SNC-Lavalin Construction Inc., Canada.
SNC-Lavalin Construction (Ontario) Inc., Canada.
SNC-Lavalin Constructors Inc., Del.
SNC-Lavalin Constructors International Inc., Canada.
SNC-Lavalin Constructors (Pacific) Inc., Canada.
The SNC-Lavalin Corporation, Del.
SNC-Lavalin Europe B.V., Netherlands.
SNC-Lavalin (GB) Holdings Limited, United Kingdom.
SNC-Lavalin (GB) Limited, United Kingdom.
SNC-Lavalin (Guernsey) Holdings Ltd., Guernsey.
SNC-Lavalin Highway Holdings Inc., Canada.
SNC-Lavalin Inc., Montréal, Qué.
SNC-Lavalin International Inc., Canada.
SNC-Lavalin International S.A.S., France.
SNC-Lavalin Investments Inc., Canada.
SNC-Lavalin Major Projects Inc., Canada.
SNC-Lavalin Nuclear Inc., Canada.
SNC-Lavalin Operations & Maintenance Inc., Canada.
SNC-Lavalin Peru S.A., Peru.
SNC-Lavalin Projetos Industriais Ltda., Brazil.
SNC-Lavalin Rail & Transit Limited, United Kingdom.
SNC Lavalin Romania S.A., Romania.
SNC-Lavalin Stavibel Inc., Canada.
TransitNEXT General Partnership, Ont.
WS Atkins International Limited, Australia.
WS Atkins Limited, London, Middx., United Kingdom.

Subsidiaries

51% int. in **Faithful + Gould Saudi Arabia Limited**, Saudi Arabia.
99% int. in **Linxon India Private Limited**, India.
51% int. in **Linxon Pvt Ltd.**, United Kingdom.
51% int. in **TC Dôme S.A.S.**, France.

Investments

50% int. in **Canadian National Energy Alliance Ltd.**, Canada.
22% int. in **Central Plateau Cleanup Company LLC**, Del.
25% int. in **Crosslinx Transit Solutions Constructors G.P.**, Alta.
25% int. in **Crosslinx Transit Solutions General Partnership**, Toronto, Ont.
50% int. in **407 East Construction General Partnership**, Canada.
50% int. in **407 East Development Group Partnership**, Ont.
6.76% int. in **407 International Inc.**, Woodbridge, Ont.
49% int. in **Linxon Gulf LLC**, United Arab Emirates.
42% int. in **Mid-America Conversion Services, LLC**, United States.
25.5% int. in **Myah Tipaza S.p.A.**, Algeria.
24% int. in **NouvLR General Partnership**, Canada.
40% int. in **Rideau Transit Group Partnership**, Canada.
40% int. in **SLN-Aecon JV**, Canada.
40% int. in **SNC-Dragados-Pennecon G.P.**, Canada.
26% int. in **Shariket Kahraba Hadjret en Nouss S.p.A.**, Algeria.
50% int. in **Signature on the Saint-Laurent Group G.P.**, Qué.
45% int. in **Signature on the Saint Lawrence Construction G.P.**, Qué.
40% int. in **Washington River Protection Solutions LLC**, United States.

Financial Statistics

Periods ended:	12m Dec. 31/22[A]		12m Dec. 31/21[A]
	$000s	%Chg	$000s
Operating revenue	**7,549,031**	**+2**	**7,371,252**
General & admin expense	123,970		145,073
Other operating expense	6,968,727		6,700,110
Operating expense	**7,092,697**	**+4**	**6,845,183**
Operating income	**456,334**	**-13**	**526,069**
Deprec., depl. & amort.	251,459		271,314
Finance income	12,648		3,406
Finance costs, gross	128,397		113,856
Write-downs/write-offs	nil		1,348
Pre-tax income	**(20,738)**	**n.a.**	**83,648**
Income taxes	(27,757)		(22,031)
Net inc bef disc ops, eqhldrs	16,640		100,186
Net inc bef disc ops, NCI	(9,621)		5,493
Net inc. bef. disc. opers	**7,019**	**-93**	**105,679**
Disc. opers., equity hldrs	(6,890)		566,377
Income from disc. opers	(6,890)		566,377
Net income	**129**	**-100**	**672,056**
Net inc. for equity hldrs	**9,750**	**-99**	**666,563**
Net inc. for non-cont. int	**(9,621)**	**n.a.**	**5,493**
Cash & equivalent	570,279		608,446
Inventories	17,411		17,037
Accounts receivable	1,177,388		1,145,932
Current assets	3,361,556		3,632,300
Long-term investments	477,809		493,640
Fixed assets, net	334,554		333,493
Right-of-use assets	287,795		355,637
Intangibles, net	3,716,251		3,828,659
Total assets	**9,459,986**	**-4**	**9,875,964**
Accts. pay. & accr. liabs	1,704,352		1,652,514
Current liabilities	3,934,676		3,951,304
Long-term debt, gross	2,056,397		1,664,171
Long-term debt, net	1,509,111		1,553,297
Long-term lease liabilities	348,660		405,741
Shareholders' equity	2,869,514		2,973,367
Non-controlling interest	9,571		20,092
Cash from oper. activs	**(245,360)**	**n.a.**	**134,198**
Cash from fin. activs	283,118		(192,535)
Cash from invest. activs	(82,470)		(263,707)
Net cash position	**570,279**	**-7**	**610,610**
Capital expenditures	(109,827)		(106,291)
Unfunded pension liability	4,113		n.a.
Pension fund surplus	n.a.		29,415
	$		$
Earns. per sh. bef disc opers*	0.09		0.57
Earnings per share*	0.06		3.80
Cash flow per share*	(1.40)		0.76
Cash divd. per share*	0.08		0.08
	shs		shs
No. of shs. o/s*	175,554,000		175,554,000
Avg. no. of shs. o/s*	175,554,000		175,554,000
	%		%
Net profit margin	0.09		1.43
Return on equity	0.57		3.62
Return on assets	(0.38)		2.47
Foreign sales percent	69		68
No. of employees (FTEs)	33,876		30,989

* Common
[A] Reported in accordance with IFRS

Latest Results

Periods ended:	6m June 30/23[A]		6m June 30/22[A]
	$000s	%Chg	$000s
Operating revenue	4,154,601	+11	3,759,553
Net income	92,130	+263	25,365
Net inc. for equity hldrs	92,243	+250	26,329
Net inc. for non-cont. int	(113)		(964)
	$		$
Earnings per share*	0.53		0.15

* Common
[A] Reported in accordance with IFRS

Historical Summary
(as originally stated)

Fiscal Year	Oper. Rev.	Net Inc. Bef. Disc.	EPS*
	$000s	$000s	$
2022[A]	7,549,031	7,019	0.09
2021[A]	7,371,252	105,679	0.57
2020[A]	7,007,501	(346,929)	(2.03)
2019[A]	9,515,610	330,587	1.87
2018[A]	10,084,006	(1,316,295)	(7.50)

* Common
[A] Reported in accordance with IFRS

S.8 SNDL Inc.

Symbol - SNDL **Exchange** - NASDAQ **CUSIP** - 83307B
Head Office - 300-919 11 Ave SW, Calgary, AB, T2R 1P3 **Telephone** - (403) 948-5227 **Toll-free** - (844) 249-6746
Website - sndl.com
Email - spilon@sundialgrowers.com
Investor Relations - Sophie Pilon (587) 327-2017
Auditors - Marcum LLP C.P.A., New York, N.Y.
Transfer Agents - Odyssey Trust Company, Toronto, Ont.
FP500 Revenue Ranking - 395
Employees - 1,346 at Dec. 31, 2022
Profile - (Alta. 2006) Operates a network of corporate-owned retail liquor stores under the Wine and Beyond, Liquor Depot and Ace Liquor banners, and corporate-owned and franchised retail cannabis stores primarily under the Spiritleaf and Value Buds banner in Canada. Also produces, distributes and sells cannabis products in Canada, and invests in the global cannabis sector.

Liquor Retail

Owns and operates 170 retail liquor stores (at May 12, 2023) in Alberta (169) and Kelowna, B.C., under the Ace Liquor (138), Liquor Depot (20) and Wine and Beyond (12) banners.

Cannabis Retail

The company franchises, owns and operates (at May 12, 2023) 104 locations in Alberta, British Columbia, Manitoba and Ontario under the retail banners Spiritleaf (99) and Superette (5) and subsidiary **Nova Cannabis Inc.** owns or operates 91 Value Bud and two Firesale Cannabis stores Alberta, Ontario and Saskatchewan.

Cannabis Operations

Cultivation and processing activities are conducted from a 448,000-sq.-ft. facility in Olds, Alta., including 428,000 sq. ft. of indoor cultivation and a 20,000-sq.-ft. processing facility; a 380,000-sq.-ft. indoor cultivation facility in Atholville, N.B.; a 25,000-sq.-ft. extraction, post-processing and analytical testing facility, a 42,000-sq.-ft. white label, extraction and manufacturing facility and a 10,500-sq.-ft. manufacturing facility, all in Kelowna, B.C.; and a 30,000-sq.-ft. beverage facility in the Bolton, Ont. Products include dried flower, pre-rolls, vapes, concentrates and edibles which are marketed under the Top Leaf, Citizen Stash, Contraband, Sundial, Palmetto, Bon Jak, Spiritleaf Selects, Versus, Value Buds, Vacay and Grasslands brands primarily for the recreational market. Is the preferred business-to-business partner to 21 licensed cannabis producers in Canada.

Distributes cannabis-derived medical products in Australia through distribution relationships and third-party manufacturing with local partners through wholly owned **Valens Australia Pty Ltd.**

Green Roads, Inc., acquired in the acquisition of Valens, manufactured, distributed and sold CBD products in the United States. Green Roads filed for bankruptcy on Mar. 6, 2023, a successful bid of USD$3,100,000 was accepted and the sale was approved at a court hearing on May 10, 2023.

Investments

Through **SunStream Bancorp Inc.**, a 50/50 joint venture with **SAF Group**, invests in the Canadian and international cannabis industry, including debt, equity and hybrid investments. Investment portfolio consists of six credit investments.

In March 2023, the company obtained two liquor retail licences in Regina and Saskatoon, Sask., through the Saskatchewan Liquor and Gaming Authority auction. The company plans to expand its Wine and Beyond banner into the province.

On Feb. 7, 2023, the company completed the acquisition of all of the business and assets of Superette Inc. through proceedings under the Companies' Creditors Arrangement Act (Canada). Consideration was the extinguishment of a promissory note. The assets included five cannabis stores in Ontario under the Suprette banner.

During the second quarter of 2022, the company sold its property in Merritt, B.C., for $3,500,000. The company was previously developing a 35,000-sq.-ft. indoor cultivation and extraction facility on the property, but suspended the construction during 2020.

In March 2021, the company and **SAF Opportunities LP**, a member of the Canadian alternative investment management firm **SAF Group**, formed **SunStream Bancorp Inc.**, a 50/50 joint venture focused on cannabis opportunities and investments in Canada and internationally. In July 2021, the company increased its commitment to SunStream to $538,000,000 from the previously announced commitment of $188,000,000. At June 30, 2022, the company had contributed $497,800,000 to SunStream.

Recent Merger and Acquisition Activity

Status: pending **Revised:** Aug. 24, 2023
UPDATE: Closing was extended to Sept. 30, 2023. PREVIOUS: SNDL Inc. announced a partnership with subsidiary Nova Cannabis Inc. which would include the sale of its existing 26 cannabis retail stores under the Spiritleaf and Superette banners in Ontario and Alberta to Nova. Nova would also have a right of first refusal on SNDL's Canadian cannabis retail pipeline. The existing management and administrative services agreement between SNDL's subsidiary, Alcanna Inc., and Nova would be amended and restated. For the first three years following this amendment and restatement, no fee shall be payable by Nova under the agreement. Following the three-year fee holiday, Nova would pay an annual fee of Cdn$2,000,000 thereafter. In addition, a total of 14,258,555 Nova common shares held by SNDL would be returned to Nova and cancelled. The cancelled shares are valued at Cdn$7,500,000. SNDL plans to reduce its equity ownership in Nova to below 20% through a capital distribution of Nova shares owned by SNDL to SNDL shareholders. As consideration, SNDL would receive the intellectual property rights to Nova's Value Buds banner of 88 stores and the licence to grant Nova to operate the Value Buds, Spiritleaf and Superette

banners. In addition, Nova and SNDL would enter into a licence agreement pursuant to which Nova would utilize SNDL's brands' intellectual property and other intangible property in exchange for a licence fee at a rate of 5% to 15% of gross profits on each store commencing one year after the transaction. SNDL holds 63% interest in Nova. Closing was expected to occur in May 2023. Apr. 3, 2023 - The agreement was amended to increase the number of stores Nova would acquire to 31, including 12 in Alberta, 11 in Ontario, three in British Columbia, three in Saskatchewan and two in Manitoba; and decrease the number of Nova shares to be surrendered by SNDL for cancellation to 2,009,622 shares valued at Cdn$1,600,000. SNDL also agreed to increase the number of Nova shares to be distributed to its shareholders such that, upon completion of the transaction, SNDL would hold no more than 19.9% of the issued and outstanding Nova shares. May 5, 2023 - Nova shareholders approved the transaction, which was expected to close on or before June 30, 2023. June 30, 2023 - Closing was extended to July 25, 2023. July 25, 2023 - Closing was extended to Aug. 25, 2023.

Status: pending **Announced:** Mar. 28, 2023
SNDL Inc. agreed to acquire four cannabis retail stores operating under the Dutch Love Cannabis banner in British Columbia (3) and Ontario (1) from Lightbox Enterprises Ltd. for $7,800,000. The combined assets generated annual revenue of $11,500,000 in 2022.

Status: completed **Revised:** Jan. 17, 2023
UPDATE: The transaction was completed. PREVIOUS: SNDL Inc. agreed to acquire The Valens Company Inc. on the basis of 0.3334 SNDL common shares for each Valens share held, representing an implied value of $1.26 per Valens share, for total consideration of $138,000,000. Valens manufactures and sells cannabis products in Canada and cannabidiol (CBD) products in the U.S., and distributes medical cannabis in Australia. Valens' board of directors unanimously approved the transaction, which was expected to be completed in January 2023. Nov. 29, 2022 - Valens' shareholders voted in favour of the transaction.

Status: completed **Revised:** Nov. 1, 2022
UPDATE: The transaction was completed. The Stellarton facility would be sold. PREVIOUS: Sundial Growers Inc. entered into a purchase agreement, in the form of a stalking horse bid, to acquire Zenabis Global Inc. and the business and assets of Zenabis' wholly owned subsidiaries. Zenabis has filed a petition for protection under the Companies' Creditors Arrangement Act (CCAA) and Ernst & Young Inc. has been appointed as the Monitor to oversee the CCAA proceedings. The assets covered by the agreement include a 380,000-sq.-ft. indoor cultivation facility in Atholville, N.B., and a non-operational 255,000-sq.-ft. indoor facility in Stellarton, N.S., which was used for processing, manufacturing and packaging. The agreement is subject to the approval by the Québec Superior Court supervising the CCAA proceedings, and to potential alternative bids pursuant to bidding procedures that would follow. Zenabis is wholly owned by HEXO Corp., and the CCAA petition is limited to Zenabis and neither HEXO nor any of its subsidiaries, other than the members of the Zenabis, are petitioners or parties to the CCAA proceedings. Sundial, through a special purpose vehicle, holds $51,900,000 principal amount of senior secured debt of Zenabis.

Status: completed **Revised:** July 6, 2022
UPDATE: The transaction was completed. REVIOUS: Sundial Growers Inc. agreed to sell its 33,000-sq.-ft. fully licensed cultivation and processing facility in Rocky View County, Alta., to Simply Solventless Concentrates Ltd. (SSC) for $1,500,000 cash and a $3,500,000 mortgage in favour of Sundial. The transaction was expected to be completed in the first quarter of 2022 upon receipt of SSC's Health Canada licences. SSC was pursuing a going-public transaction via a Qualifying Transaction reverse takeover acquisition of SSC by Dash Capital Corp.

Status: completed **Revised:** Mar. 31, 2022
UPDATE: The transaction was completed for total consideration of $320,000,000. Shares of Alcanna were delisted from TSX on Apr. 1, 2022. PREVIOUS: Sundial Growers Inc. agreed to acquire Alcanna Inc. on the basis of 10.69 Sundial common shares for each Alcanna common share held, representing a deemed value of Cdn$9.12 per Alcanna share for a fully diluted consideration of Cdn$346,000,000. Alcanna operates liquor stores in Alberta and British Columbia and owns a 63% interest in Canadian cannabis retailer, Nova Cannabis Inc. The agreement includes a Cdn$10,000,000 termination fee payable to Sundial from Alcanna in the event the transaction is terminated in certain specified circumstances. The closing of the transaction was expected to be in December 2021 or in the first quarter of 2022. Dec. 13, 2021 - The date of Alcanna special shareholders meeting to vote on proposal was postponed to Jan. 7, 2022, due to current voting results showing lack of sufficient support to reach the necessary 66% threshold of votes cast. Jan. 6, 2022 - Sundial has amended the consideration to 8.85 Sundial common shares and $1.50 in cash for each Alcanna common share held. The revised offer values Alcanna at $8.43 per share. Jan. 7, 2022 - Alcanna shareholders approved the proposed transaction. Jan. 19, 2022 - A final court order was obtained approving the transaction. Feb. 25, 2022 - The outside date for closing the transaction was extended to Mar. 30, 2022.

Predecessor Detail - Name changed from Sundial Growers Inc., July 26, 2022; basis 1 new for 10 old shs.

Directors - Greg Mills, chr., Toronto, Ont.; Zachary R. (Zach) George, CEO, New Canaan, Conn.; Lori S. Ell, Calgary, Alta.; Frank Krasovec, Austin, Tex.; Bryan D. Pinney, Calgary, Alta.; Gregory G. (Greg) Turnbull, Calgary, Alta.

Other Exec. Officers - Alberto Paredero-Quiros, CFO; Ryan Hellard, chief strategy officer; Robbie Madan, chief info. & digital officer; Deanna Garand, v-p, HR; Matthew Husson, gen. counsel & corp. sec.; Marcie Kiziak, pres., cannabis retail; A. Tyler Robson, pres., cannabis; Taranvir (Tank) Vander, pres., liquor retail

Capital Stock

	Authorized (shs.)	Outstanding (shs.)[1]
Preferred	unlimited	nil
Common	unlimited	260,495,996

[1] At Mar. 1, 2023

Normal Course Issuer Bid - The company plans to make normal course purchases of up to 11,800,000 common shares representing 5% of the total outstanding. The bid commenced on Nov. 21, 2022, and expires on Nov. 20, 2023.

Major Shareholder - Widely held at Mar. 1, 2023.

Price Range - SNDL/NASDAQ

Year	Volume	High	Low	Close
2022	200,774,726	US$8.68	US$1.96	US$2.09
2021	634,016,960	US$39.50	US$4.70	US$5.78
2020	223,654,784	US$38.75	US$1.38	US$4.74
2019	2,926,020	US$132.20	US$18.85	US$30.10

Consolidation: 1-for-10 cons. in July 2022

Capital Stock Changes - In January 2023, 26,918,563 common shares were issued pursuant to acquisition of The Valens Company Inc.

In March 2022, 32,060,135 post-consolidated common shares were issued pursuant to acquisition of Alcanna Inc. On July 26, 2022, common shares were consolidated on a 1-for-10 basis.

Wholly Owned Subsidiaries

Alcanna Inc., Edmonton, Alta.
- 100% int. in **Canadian Liquor Retailers Alliance GP Inc.**
- 100% int. in **Liquor Depot Acquisitions Inc.**, Alta.
- 100% int. in **Liquor Stores GP Inc.**, Canada.
- 100% int. in **Liquor Stores Limited Partnership**, Alta.
- 63% int. in **Nova Cannabis Inc.**, Edmonton, Alta. (see separate coverage)

Inner Spirit Holdings Ltd., Calgary, Alta.
- 100% int. in **Spirit Leaf Corporate Inc.**, Canada.
- 100% int. in **Spirit Leaf Inc.**, Calgary, Alta.

KamCan Products Inc., Alta.
NGBA-BC Holdings Ltd., B.C.
Sundial Deutschland GmbH, Germany.
Sundial Insurance (Bermuda) Ltd., Bermuda.
2657408 Ontario Inc., Ont.
The Valens Company Inc., Kelowna, B.C.
Zenabis Global Inc., Vancouver, B.C.

Investments

15.5% int. in **Indiva Limited**, Ottawa, Ont. (see separate coverage)
25% int. in **Pathway Rx Inc.**, Alta.
50% int. in **SunStream Bancorp Inc.**, Canada.
50% int. in **Vines of Riverbend GP Inc.**, Alta.
50% int. in **Vines of Riverbend Limited Partnership**, Alta.

Financial Statistics

Periods ended:	12m Dec. 31/22[A]		12m Dec. 31/21[oA]
	$000s	%Chg	$000s
Operating revenue	**712,197**	**n.m.**	**56,128**
Cost of sales	557,807		44,476
Salaries & benefits	80,134		18,675
Research & devel. expense	2,448		2,446
General & admin expense	68,451		24,411
Stock-based compensation	9,671		12,307
Operating expense	**718,511**	**+602**	**102,315**
Operating income	**(6,314)**	**n.a.**	**(46,187)**
Deprec., depl. & amort.	47,948		8,962
Finance income	884		573
Finance costs, gross	42,198		4,329
Investment income	(91,427)		1,561
Write-downs/write-offs	(203,045)[1]		(76,978)[2]
Pre-tax income	**(379,770)**	**n.a.**	**(234,698)**
Income taxes	(7,342)		(7,914)
Net inc bef disc ops, eqhldrs	(335,114)		(226,984)
Net inc bef disc ops, NCI	(37,314)		200
Net income	**(372,428)**	**n.a.**	**(226,784)**
Net inc. for equity hldrs	**(335,114)**	**n.a.**	**(226,984)**
Net inc. for non-cont. int.	**(37,314)**	**n.a.**	**200**
Cash & equivalent	301,512		641,975
Inventories	127,782		29,503
Accounts receivable	22,636		10,865
Current assets	501,483		728,175
Long-term investments	609,957		483,356
Fixed assets, net	143,409		56,472
Right-of-use assets	134,154		6,717
Intangibles, net	142,145		122,644
Total assets	**1,559,350**	**+9**	**1,427,660**
Accts. pay. & accr. liabs	48,153		38,452
Current liabilities	89,361		65,853
Long-term lease liabilities	139,625		27,769
Shareholders' equity	1,306,499		1,329,304
Non-controlling interest	21,156		229
Cash from oper. activs	**(6,711)**	**n.a.**	**(155,752)**
Cash from fin. activs	(41,790)		1,149,916
Cash from invest. activs	(230,164)		(496,280)
Net cash position	**279,586**	**-50**	**558,251**
Capital expenditures	(10,666)		(3,793)
Capital disposals	4,000		194
	$		$
Earnings per share*	(1.46)		(1.22)
Cash flow per share*	(0.03)		(0.84)
	shs		shs
No. of shs. o/s*	235,194,236		206,040,836
Avg. no. of shs. o/s*	229,871,000		186,038,000
	%		%
Net profit margin	(52.29)		(404.05)
Return on equity	(25.46)		(28.47)
Return on assets	(22.19)		(25.85)
No. of employees (FTEs)	1,346		184

* Common
[o] Restated
[A] Reported in accordance with IFRS
[1] Includes $172,300,000 of impairment on goodwill and intangible assets of the cannabis retail segment, $15,209,000 of impairment on property, plant and equipment and $7,012,000 of inventory obsolescence.
[2] Includes $16,978,000 of inventory obsolescence and $60,000,000 impairment of cultivation and processing facility in Olds, Alta.

Latest Results

Periods ended:	3m Mar. 31/23[A]		3m Mar. 31/22[A]
	$000s	%Chg	$000s
Operating revenue	202,452	n.m.	17,597
Net inc. bef. disc. opers	(34,778)	n.a.	(38,040)
Income from disc. opers	(1,365)		nil
Net income	(36,143)	n.a.	(38,040)
Net inc. for equity hldrs	(35,568)	n.a.	(37,904)
Net inc. for non-cont. int	(575)		(136)
	$		$
Earnings per share*	(0.14)		(0.18)

* Common
[A] Reported in accordance with IFRS

Historical Summary
(as originally stated)

Fiscal Year	Oper. Rev.	Net Inc. Bef. Disc.	EPS*
	$000s	$000s	$
2022[A]	712,197	(372,428)	(1.46)
2021[A]	56,128	(230,182)	(1.20)
2020[A]	60,918	(206,317)	(9.50)
2019[A]	75,860	(271,629)	(31.70)
2018[A1,2]	nil	(56,526)	(8.20)

* Common
[A] Reported in accordance with IFRS
[1] 10 months ended Dec. 31, 2018.
[2] Per share and share amounts adjusted to reflect 1.6-for-1 share split on July 22, 2019.
Note: Adjusted throughout for 1-for-10 cons. in July 2022

S.9 SOL Global Investments Corp.

Symbol - SOL **Exchange** - CSE **CUSIP** - 78471G
Head Office - 5600-100 King St W, Toronto, ON, M5X 1C9 **Telephone** - (416) 366-9192 **Fax** - (647) 556-2110
Website - www.solglobal.com
Email - info@solglobal.com
Investor Relations - Paul L. Kania (212) 729-9208
Auditors - Kreston GTA LLP C.A., Markham, Ont.
Transfer Agents - Odyssey Trust Company, Toronto, Ont.
Profile - (Ont. 2005) Invests in small and mid-capitalization public and private companies in the retail, agriculture, quick service restaurant (QSR) and hospitality, media technology and gaming, and new age wellness industries.

At May 31, 2022, the fair value of the investment portfolio totaled $214,681,968 and included common shares, commercial assets (real estate), warrants, promissory notes and convertible debentures of public and private companies. Equity and commercial asset investments in cannabis and cannabis-related businesses in the U.S. totaled $36,939,017, and non-U.S. cannabis, cannabis-related and non-cannabis businesses totaled $163,686,430.

Type	Fair Value
Common shares	$167,337,855
Commercial assets	31,677,318
Warrants	1,610,274
Promissory notes	9,150,239
Convertible debentures	4,906,282
	214,681,968

Portfolio of investments include interests in **House of Lithium Ltd.**, which holds a portfolio of electric vehicle, green technology and clean technology investments; **Casters Holdings Inc.**, which develops and markets a suite of compliance cloud software and services built to overcome the complexities of highly regulated industries; **Captor Capital Corp.**, which distributes and retails recreational and medical cannabis products in the U.S.; **Simply Better Brands Corp.**, an omni-channel platform with diversified assets in the plant-based and holistic wellness consumer product categories, including CBD, plant-based food and beverage, pet care and skin care; **Common C Holdings LP**, which cultivates, processes, retails and distributes cannabis products in Michigan and across the U.S.; **KWESST Micro Systems Inc.**, which develops and markets intelligent tactical systems and proprietary technology for applications in the military and homeland security market; **Jones Soda Co.**, which develops, produces, markets and distributes beverages across North America and internationally; **Livwrk SOL Wynwood LLC**, which develops and operates commercial properties in Miami, Fla.; **Marsico AXS CS LLC**, which holds an investment in **Core Scientific, Inc.**, a large-scale net carbon-neutral blockchain infrastructure provider and miner of digital assets in North America; **Kings Entertainment Group Inc.**, an international online service provider of lottery, casino and sportsbook gambling; **Andretti Acquisition Corp.**, a special purpose acquisition company (SPAC) formed for the purpose of effecting a business combination with one or more businesses or entities, with a focus on the automotive industry; and **Build A Rocket Boy Ltd.**, a video game developer.

Predecessor Detail - Name changed from Scythian Biosciences Corp., Oct. 25, 2018.
Directors - Deena Siblock, v-p, Toronto, Ont.; Mehdi Azodi, Toronto, Ont.; Jason Batista
Other Exec. Officers - Paul L. Kania, interim CEO & CFO

Capital Stock

	Authorized (shs.)	Outstanding (shs.)[1]
Common	unlimited	54,411,981

[1] At May 1, 2023

Major Shareholder - Andrew (Andy) DeFrancesco held 19.99% interest at Oct. 19, 2022.

Price Range - SOL/CSE

Year	Volume	High	Low	Close
2022	14,065,921	$3.01	$0.14	$0.16
2021	67,745,529	$7.00	$2.60	$3.00
2020	76,536,232	$3.11	$0.14	$2.62
2019	56,048,361	$4.13	$0.38	$0.60
2018	67,682,206	$8.61	$1.02	$2.25

Recent Close: $0.18
Capital Stock Changes - In December 2021, 7,407,404 common shares were repurchased under a Substantial Issuer Bid.

Subsidiaries
58.6% int. in **House of Lithium Ltd.**, Canada.

Financial Statistics

Periods ended:	12m Nov. 30/22[‡A]		12m Nov. 30/21[A]
	$000s	%Chg	$000s
Total revenue	**(234,934)**	**n.a.**	**306,991**
Salaries & benefits	...		48,306
General & admin. expense	...		11,242
Stock-based compensation	...		7,886
Operating expense	**...**	**n.a.**	**67,434**
Operating income	**...**	**n.a.**	**239,557**
Deprec. & amort.	...		1,123
Finance costs, gross	7,096		9,464
Pre-tax income	**...**	**n.a.**	**160,470**
Income taxes	...		1,250
Net income	**(297,020)**	**n.a.**	**159,220**
Cash & equivalent	...		15,431
Investments	...		433,621
Fixed assets, net	...		3,157
Right-of-use assets	...		3,686
Total assets	**153,125**	**-69**	**489,158**
Accts. pay. & accr. liabs	...		21,848
Debt	22,220		48,708
Lease liabilities	...		3,802
Shareholders' equity	41,831		366,994
Cash from oper. activs	**42,835**	**+4**	**41,306**
Cash from fin. activs	...		(23,186)
Cash from invest. activs	...		(2,805)
Net cash position	**...**	**n.a.**	**15,431**
Capital expenditures	...		(2,805)
	$		$
Earnings per share*	(5.46)		3.06
Cash flow per share*	0.79		0.79
Net asset value per share*	...		6.29
	shs		shs
No. of shs. o/s*	54,441,981		52,018,533
Avg. no. of shs. o/s*	54,441,981		52,018,533
	%		%
Net profit margin	n.m.		51.86
Return on equity	(145.30)		55.07
Return on assets	n.m.		42.83

* Common
‡ Preliminary
[A] Reported in accordance with IFRS

Note: Total revenue includes gains (losses) on investments, realized/unrealized gains (losses) on investments and interest and other income.

Historical Summary
(as originally stated)

Fiscal Year	Total Rev.	Net Inc. Bef. Disc.	EPS*
	$000s	$000s	$
2022[‡A]	(234,934)	(297,020)	(5.46)
2021[A]	306,991	159,220	3.06
2020[A]	139,004	98,014	1.79
2019[A1]	(113,220)	(103,728)	(1.91)
2019[A]	152,415	94,986	2.38

* Common
‡ Preliminary
[A] Reported in accordance with IFRS
[1] 8 months ended Nov. 30, 2019.

S.10 SPARQ Systems Inc.

Symbol - SPRQ **Exchange** - TSX-VEN **CUSIP** - 84657W
Head Office - Innovation Park, 945 Princess St, Box 212, Kingston, ON, K7L 0E9 **Toll-free** - (855) 947-7277
Website - www.sparqsys.com
Email - pjain@sparqsys.com
Investor Relations - Dr. Praveen K. Jain (343) 477-1158
Auditors - MNP LLP C.A., Calgary, Alta.
Lawyers - Aird & Berlis LLP, Toronto, Ont.
Transfer Agents - TSX Trust Company, Toronto, Ont.
Profile - (Ont. 2018) Designs, develops and manufactures single-phase microinverters for residential and commercial solar electric applications.

Has developed the Quad, a proprietary photovoltaic (PV) solution which optimizes four solar panels with a single microinverter compared with traditional microinverters that have one PV module. The Quad microinverters are compact units installed on PV racks, and utilize proprietary and patented technology to convert direct current (DC) electricity to alternating current (AC) electricity to supply energy to the electrical grid.

Product portfolio includes Q1200 Grid-Tied microinverter, which connects four PV panels, up to 400W, to the AC power grid; Q1200 Dual Mode microinverter, which operates both in grid-tied and off-grid modes, with and without batteries, and connects four PV panels, up to 400W, to the AC power grid; Q2000 microinverter, a high powered version which connects four PV panels, up to 550W, to the AC power grid and operates in grid-tied, standalone or dual-mode PV applications; and a multi-purpose microinverter for solar water pump applications in farms, capable of working on-grid and off-grid.

Solutions are sold primarily through distributors, as well as through direct sales to solar equipment installers and developers of third-party solar finance offerings. Research, planning and development is conducted in-house in Kingston, Ont., and products are produced by third party manufacturers in Ottawa, Ont., and Guangdong province, People's Republic of China.

Predecessor Detail - Name changed from SPARQ Corp., Jan. 1, 2023.
Directors - Ravi Sood, chr., Toronto, Ont.; Dr. Praveen K. Jain, CEO, Kingston, Ont.; Dr. Nishith Goel, Ottawa, Ont.; BaoJun (Robbie) Luo, Shenzhen, Guangdong, People's Republic of China; Dr. Arul Shanmugasundaram, India
Other Exec. Officers - Kyle Appleby, CFO; Muhammad Ikram, v-p, fin.; Pankaj Jain, v-p, opers.; Dr. Hassan Kojori, v-p, program mgt.; Majid Pahlevaninezhad, v-p, tech.; Dr. Shangzhi Pan, v-p, eng.; Haibo Zhang, v-p, mfg.; Richard M. Kimel, corp. sec.

Capital Stock

	Authorized (shs.)	Outstanding (shs.)[1]
Common	unlimited	82,444,752

[1] At Jan. 3, 2023

Major Shareholder - Dr. Praveen K. Jain held 19.53% interest, Highchart Investments Limited held 17.11% interest and Greg Steers held 12.15% interest at Apr. 29, 2022.

Price Range - SPRQ/TSX-VEN

Year	Volume	High	Low	Close
2022	1,758,754	$0.51	$0.25	$0.31
2021	37,200	$0.23	$0.14	$0.23
2020	124,560	$0.22	$0.08	$0.16

Consolidation: 1-for-1.25 cons. in Jan. 2022
Recent Close: $0.13

Wholly Owned Subsidiaries
SPARQ Systems Inc., Ont.
- 100% int. in **Sparq Systems (USA), Inc.**, United States.

Financial Statistics

Periods ended:	12m Dec. 31/21[A1]		12m Dec. 31/20[A]
	$000s	%Chg	$000s
Operating revenue	**nil**	**n.a.**	**1**
Cost of sales	45		98
Research & devel. expense	972		887
General & admin expense	7,020		289
Stock-based compensation	403		434
Operating expense	**8,440**	**+394**	**1,707**
Operating income	**(8,440)**	**n.a.**	**(1,706)**
Deprec., depl. & amort.	18		22
Finance income	2		1
Pre-tax income	**(7,806)**	**n.a.**	**(1,092)**
Net income	**(7,806)**	**n.a.**	**(1,092)**
Cash & equivalent	9,298		1,347
Inventories	529		178
Accounts receivable	83		18
Current assets	10,247		1,924
Fixed assets, net	40		22
Total assets	**10,287**	**+429**	**1,946**
Accts. pay. & accr. liabs	607		76
Current liabilities	607		76
Long-term debt, gross	38		30
Long-term debt, net	38		30
Shareholders' equity	9,641		1,840
Cash from oper. activs	**(906)**	**n.a.**	**(332)**
Cash from fin. activs	8,728		1,624
Cash from invest. activs	130		(2)
Net cash position	**9,298**	**+590**	**1,347**
Capital expenditures	(36)		(2)
	$		$
Earnings per share*	(0.19)		(0.01)
Cash flow per share*	(0.02)		n.a.
	shs		shs
No. of shs. o/s*	82,444,752		n.a.
Avg. no. of shs. o/s*	42,110,808		n.a.
	%		%
Net profit margin	n.a.		n.m.
Return on equity	(135.98)		n.m.
Return on assets	(127.62)		(72.92)

* Common
[A] Reported in accordance with IFRS
[1] Results reflect the Dec. 31, 2021, Qualifying Transaction reverse takeover acquisition of SPARQ Systems Inc.

Latest Results

Periods ended:	6m June 30/22[A]		6m June 30/21[A]
	$000s	%Chg	$000s
Net income	(1,725)	n.a.	(559)
	$		$
Earnings per share*	(0.02)		(0.00)

* Common
[A] Reported in accordance with IFRS

Historical Summary
(as originally stated)

Fiscal Year	Oper. Rev.	Net Inc. Bef. Disc.	EPS*
	$000s	$000s	$
2021^A	nil	(7,806)	(0.19)
2020^A	1	(1,092)	(0.01)
2019^A	591	(1,010)	(0.01)

* Common
^A Reported in accordance with IFRS
Note: Adjusted throughout for 1-for-1.25 cons. in Jan. 2022

S.11 SPoT Coffee (Canada) Ltd.

Symbol - SPP **Exchange** - TSX-VEN **CUSIP** - 84921K
Head Office - 1007-141 Adelaide St W, Toronto, ON, M5H 3L5 **Telephone** - (416) 368-2220 **Fax** - (416) 368-4469
Website - www.spotcoffee.com
Email - rkoroll@spotcoffee.com
Investor Relations - Randy Koroll (416) 662-9455
Auditors - DNTW Toronto LLP C.A., Toronto, Ont.
Bankers - The Bank of Nova Scotia
Lawyers - TingleMerrett LLP, Calgary, Alta.
Transfer Agents - Computershare Trust Company of Canada Inc.
Profile - (Ont. 2007) Designs, builds, operates and franchises community-oriented cafés and express cafés in the U.S. under the SPoT Coffee brand; and distributes and retails roasted coffee beans.

The company has cafes that are operating and in development in New York and Connecticut, including six corporate-owned cafes in Buffalo, Rochester, Saratoga Springs, Elmwood, Glens Falls and Orchard Park; 11 operating franchise cafes in Kenmore, Hertel, West Hartford, Hamburg, Roswell Park, Clarence, Williamsville, Waterfront Village, Amherst, West Seneca and Niagara Falls; five SPoT Tops cafe locations; and two Express cafes operating under licence to Chartwells at the Buffalo State College.

Full-scale locations are at least 2,500 sq. ft. in size while the SPoT Express cafe locations are less than 1,500 sq. ft. in size and offer a quick service alternative to a full scale cafe franchise.

The cafes offer beverages including brewed coffee, iced coffee, teas, hot chocolate, smoothie and shake, as well as muffins, bagels, sandwiches, wraps, pizzas, soups and salads. Roasted coffee beans are also sold to food service and grocery chains, business offices and resellers such as universities and hospitals.

Predecessor Detail - Name changed from Award Capital Corp., July 23, 2009, following amalgamation of a wholly owned subsid. with SPoT Coffee (Canada) Inc., constituting a Qualifying Transaction reverse takeover acquisition of SPoT Coffee (Canada) Inc.

Directors - John Lorenzo, exec. chr., Toronto, Ont.; Anton Ayoub, pres. & CEO, Toronto, Ont.; Glenn Abadir, San Diego, Calif.; Mario Giorgio, Toronto, Ont.; Raymond J. Stapell, Buffalo, N.Y.

Other Exec. Officers - Daniel M. (Dan) Hensley, COO; Randy Koroll, CFO; Tamara T. Ballanti, v-p, HR; Richard Gress, v-p, global opers. & CEO, U.S. opers.; Paul A. Bolger, corp. sec.; Robert Burchett, contr.

Capital Stock

	Authorized (shs.)	Outstanding (shs.)[1]
Common	unlimited	161,226,670

[1] At May 30, 2023

Major Shareholder - Glenn Abadir held 15.67% interest at May 23, 2023.

Price Range - SPP/TSX-VEN

Year	Volume	High	Low	Close
2022	8,319,920	$0.08	$0.03	$0.08
2021	14,062,782	$0.06	$0.03	$0.04
2020	12,414,014	$0.09	$0.02	$0.04
2019	9,856,599	$0.17	$0.06	$0.08
2018	13,596,884	$0.18	$0.06	$0.06

Recent Close: $0.05

Capital Stock Changes - There were no changes to capital stock during 2022.

Wholly Owned Subsidiaries

SPoT Orchard Park, LLC, Orchard Park, N.Y.
SPoT Tonawanda, LLC, Buffalo, N.Y.
SPoT Coffee Buffalo Inc., Buffalo, N.Y.
SPoT Coffee International Inc., Buffalo, N.Y.
Spot Coffee Transit Inc., New York, N.Y.
Valshire SPoT Inc., Rochester, N.Y.

Subsidiaries

51% int. in **SPoT Coffee Elmwood Inc.**, Buffalo, N.Y.
74% int. in **SPoT Coffee Glen, LLC**, Glens Falls, N.Y.
60% int. in **SPoT Coffee Saratoga LLC**, Saratoga Springs, N.Y.

Financial Statistics

Periods ended:	12m Dec. 31/22^A		12m Dec. 31/21^{oA}
	$000s	%Chg	$000s
Operating revenue	**8,022**	**+29**	**6,223**
Cost of sales	2,555		1,755
Salaries & benefits	3,973		2,477
General & admin expense	1,956		1,502
Operating expense	**8,484**	**+48**	**5,735**
Operating income	**(462)**	**n.a.**	**488**
Deprec., depl. & amort	712		715
Finance costs, gross	769		407
Write-downs/write-offs	nil		(1,002)
Pre-tax income	**(784)**	**n.a.**	**1,058**
Net income	**(784)**	**n.a.**	**1,058**
Net inc. for equity hldrs	**(809)**	**n.a.**	**492**
Net inc. for non-cont. int	**25**	**-96**	**566**
Cash & equivalent	nil		38
Inventories	184		171
Accounts receivable	1,803		623
Current assets	2,560		1,287
Fixed assets, net	278		310
Right-of-use assets	2,311		1,528
Total assets	**6,086**	**+43**	**4,247**
Bank indebtedness	1,496		1,400
Accts. pay. & accr. liabs	2,942		1,456
Current liabilities	4,684		4,684
Long-term debt, gross	1,442		1,182
Long-term debt, net	255		302
Long-term lease liabilities	3,459		2,845
Shareholders' equity	(4,736)		(3,988)
Non-controlling interest	414		404
Cash from oper. activs	**764**	**+458**	**137**
Cash from fin. activs	(786)		347
Cash from invest. activs	(138)		(167)
Net cash position	**(76)**	**n.a.**	**38**
Capital expenditures	(39)		(47)
	$		$
Earnings per share*	(0.00)		0.01
Cash flow per share*	0.00		0.00
	shs		shs
No. of shs. o/s*	159,576,670		159,576,670
Avg. no. of shs. o/s*	159,567,670		146,864,146
	%		%
Net profit margin	(9.77)		17.00
Return on equity	n.m.		n.m.
Return on assets	(0.29)		37.23
Foreign sales percent	100		100

* Common
^o Restated
^A Reported in accordance with IFRS

Latest Results

Periods ended:	3m Mar. 31/23^A		3m Mar. 31/22^A
	$000s	%Chg	$000s
Operating revenue	2,064	+30	1,587
Net income	(530)	n.a.	(584)
Net inc. for equity hldrs	(554)	n.a.	(580)
Net inc. for non-cont. int	24		(4)
	$		$
Earnings per share*	(0.00)		(0.00)

* Common
^A Reported in accordance with IFRS

Historical Summary
(as originally stated)

Fiscal Year	Oper. Rev.	Net Inc. Bef. Disc.	EPS*
	$000s	$000s	$
2022^A	8,022	(784)	(0.01)
2021^A	6,223	1,058	0.01
2020^A	4,098	(2,718)	(0.02)
2019^A	8,465	(2,534)	(0.02)
2018^A	8,368	(273)	(0.00)

* Common
^A Reported in accordance with IFRS

S.12 SQI Diagnostics Inc.

Symbol - SQD **Exchange** - TSX-VEN **CUSIP** - 78466B
Head Office - 36 Meteor Dr, Toronto, ON, M9W 1A4 **Telephone** - (416) 674-9500 **Toll-free** - (888) 829-0849 **Fax** - (416) 674-9300
Website - www.sqidiagnostics.com
Email - mreddock@sqidiagnostics.com
Investor Relations - Morlan Reddock (416) 674-9500 ext. 277
Auditors - RSM Canada LLP C.A., Toronto, Ont.
Lawyers - Gowling WLG (Canada) LLP, Toronto, Ont.; McCarthy Tétrault LLP, Toronto, Ont.
Transfer Agents - Computershare Trust Company of Canada Inc., Toronto, Ont.

Profile - (Can. 2003) Discovers, develops, manufactures and commercializes innovative rapid diagnostic testing for healthcare providers, patients and consumers worldwide.

The company's advanced diagnostic targets COVID-19 testing, organ transplant and autoimmune disease.

The **COVID-19 Testing** includes Biomeme SARS-CoV-2 test, a Health Canada-approved mobile COVID-19 testing solution that provides rapid results in one hour using real-time PCR technology; Sofia® SARS Antigen Fluorescent Immunoassay, which provides automated and objective results in 15 minutes, allowing for testing of patients suspected of COVID-19 in near-patient testing environments; TripleLock™ Test Strips, a rapid, point-of-need diagnostic RT-PCR test able to provide accurate results for 9 samples in just 60 minutes; EXACT COVID-19 HOME antibody test, which identifies the presence of IgM, IgA and IgG antibodies of SARS-CoV-2 in individuals suspected to have been infected with COVID-19 through simple finger-prick blood sample collection which mailed to the testing laboratory; RALI-dx™ COVID-19 severity triage test, which measures critical biomarkers including IL-6 in approximately 50 minutes to assist in identifying severe inflammatory response in patients with suspected SARS-CoV-2 (or influenza) viral infection and to help clinicians determine whether patients require hospital admission or not; and the COVID-19 RALI-fast™ severity triage point-of-care (POC) test, which measures the key critical biomarker IL-6 in 15 minutes.

The **Organ Transplant** diagnostics include the development of an advanced diagnostic test that increases the chance of successful lung transplant by assessing the health of the donor organ prior to transplant surgery. Product includes TORdx™ Lung Test, which can detect inflammation at the molecular level enabling surgeons to make a decision on initiating transplantation. The company also plans to develop Liver and Kidney transplant Dx, which are markers and matrix similar to TORdx™ Lung Test, for liver and kidney transplant as well as a lung oncology biopsy screen (POC).

The **Autoimmune Disease** testing include the company's direct-to-consumer celiac disease and a rheumatoid arthritis (RA) test, which helps to identify and confirm RA symptoms for early care. The celiac test is the only test that confirms the disease and also validate the effectiveness of dietary and lifestyle changes to confirm the autoimmune response is improving. The company offers three different platforms to run and analyze microarray plates including sqidworks™ diagnostic platform, a high-throughput, fully automated microarray processing and analytical instrument ideal for high-volume labs; sqidlite™ diagnostic system, a fully automated, bench-top microarray processing and analytical system capable of processing over 1,000 results per hour; and sqid-X™ system, a semi-automated, bench-top platform that incorporates all of the company's technology with the exception of automated fluidics handling. Also developed QuantiSpot™ (marketed as IgX PLEX Rheumatoid Arthritis Assay (Quantitative) in Europe) test kit for detecting the four predominant biomarkers for rheumatoid arthritis; the Ig_plex™ CHEX technology which provides multiple in-microarray checks to ensure that the test has been completed without system, control, calibration or microarray-relates errors; and the Ig_plex™ Celiac DGP panel, a tool which provides clinicians with a fast method to measure the levels of multiple key biomarkers associated with celiac disease. Other autoimmune assays in the Ig_plex™ product pipeline include panels for the diagnosis of lupus, vasculitis and Crohn's disease.

Predecessor Detail - Name changed from Emblem Capital Inc., Apr. 26, 2007, followed by Qualifying Transaction amalgamation of wholly owned 6701914 Canada Inc. with umedik, Inc.; basis 1 new for 6 old shs.

Directors - Gerald R. (Gerry) Connor, Toronto, Ont.; Wilmot L. Matthews, Toronto, Ont.; Claude Ricks, Barrie, Ont.

Other Exec. Officers - Morlan Reddock, CFO; Russell (Russ) Peloquin, v-p, global comml. opers.

Capital Stock

	Authorized (shs.)	Outstanding (shs.)[1]
Common	unlimited	407,170,550

[1] At May 30, 2023

Major Shareholder - Wilmot L. Matthews held 25.74% interest, Cumberland Private Wealth Management Inc. held 25.26% interest and Clive J. Beddoe held 24.06% interest at May 30, 2023.

Price Range - SQD/TSX-VEN

Year	Volume	High	Low	Close
2022	10,067,336	$0.22	$0.07	$0.12
2021	24,397,445	$0.55	$0.14	$0.16
2020	50,819,658	$0.29	$0.06	$0.24
2019	13,286,002	$0.18	$0.05	$0.08
2018	13,190,921	$0.30	$0.05	$0.07

Recent Close: $0.02

Capital Stock Changes - In November 2021, private placement of 26,932,895 units (1 common share & 1 warrant) at 19¢ per unit was completed, with warrants exercisable at 25¢ per share for five years. In February 2022, 4,171,779 common shares were issued pursuant to the acquisition of substantially all of the assets underlying Precision Biomonitoring Inc.'s human diagnostic COVID-19 PCR testing business and its TripleLock™ molecular diagnostic testing technology.

Wholly Owned Subsidiaries

SQI Diagnostics Systems Inc.
SQI US, Inc., United States.

Financial Statistics

Periods ended:	12m Sept. 30/21[A]		12m Sept. 30/20[A]
	$000s	%Chg	$000s
Operating revenue	**917**	**-10**	**1,023**
Cost of goods sold	150		232
Salaries & benefits	4,476		3,131
Research & devel. expense	3,516		967
General & admin expense	1,881		2,929
Stock-based compensation	180		856
Operating expense	**10,203**	**+26**	**8,115**
Operating income	**(9,286)**	**n.a.**	**(7,092)**
Deprec., depl. & amort.	753		800
Finance costs, gross	518		679
Pre-tax income	**(10,557)**	**n.a.**	**(8,571)**
Net income	**(10,557)**	**n.a.**	**(8,571)**
Cash & equivalent	2,295		2,596
Inventories	898		364
Accounts receivable	204		477
Current assets	3,638		3,668
Fixed assets, net	2,658		1,180
Right-of-use assets	2,377		2,838
Intangibles, net	391		384
Total assets	**9,064**	**+12**	**8,070**
Accts. pay. & accr. liabs	2,474		1,041
Current liabilities	2,952		1,465
Long-term debt, gross	2,204		2,148
Long-term lease liabilities	2,382		2,731
Shareholders' equity	1,526		1,726
Cash from oper. activs	**(8,645)**	**n.a.**	**(6,961)**
Cash from fin. activs	9,953		6,295
Cash from invest. activs	(1,609)		(182)
Net cash position	**2,295**	**-12**	**2,596**
Capital expenditures	(1,504)		(152)
Capital disposals	26		nil
	$		$
Earnings per share*	(0.03)		(0.03)
Cash flow per share*	(0.03)		(0.03)
	shs		shs
No. of shs. o/s*	362,530,000		308,095,000
Avg. no. of shs. o/s*	338,454,000		266,943,000
	%		%
Net profit margin	n.m.		(837.83)
Return on equity	(649.26)		(526.64)
Return on assets	(117.18)		(110.05)
Foreign sales percent	84		60

* Common
[A] Reported in accordance with IFRS

Latest Results

Periods ended:	3m Dec. 31/21[A]		3m Dec. 31/20[A]
	$000s	%Chg	$000s
Operating revenue	59	-63	161
Net income	(3,433)	n.a.	(3,718)
	$		$
Earnings per share*	(0.01)		(0.01)

* Common
[A] Reported in accordance with IFRS

Historical Summary
(as originally stated)

Fiscal Year	Oper. Rev.	Net Inc. Bef. Disc.	EPS*
	$000s	$000s	$
2021[A]	917	(10,557)	(0.03)
2020[A]	1,023	(8,571)	(0.03)
2019[A]	1,891	(8,021)	(0.04)
2018[A]	1,335	(7,437)	(0.06)
2017[A]	968	(5,929)	(0.06)

* Common
[A] Reported in accordance with IFRS

S.13 SQID Technologies Limited

Symbol - SQID **Exchange** - CSE **CUSIP** - Q8700M
Head Office - 440 Collins St, Level 14, Melbourne, VIC, Australia, 3000 **Overseas Tel** - 61-7-3393-9187
Website - https://sqidtechnologies.com/
Email - athan@sqidpayments.com.au
Investor Relations - Athan Lekkas 61-3-8620-6400
Auditors - Pitcher Partners BA&A Pty Ltd. C.A., Brisbane, Qld. Australia
Transfer Agents - Computershare Trust Company of Canada Inc., Vancouver, B.C.
Profile - (Australia 2006) Provides merchant services and transaction processing to business merchants and e-commerce customers across both business-to-business (B2B) and business-to-consumer (B2C) segments in Australia. Also invests in eSports gaming.

Operates a payment processing software platform that facilitates the communication of transaction information for online debit or credit card purchases. The platform has the ability to offer ApplePay, GooglePay, BPAY, electronic fund transfer, multi-currency processing and instant funds to its customers.

Wholly owned **ICON Esports Pty Ltd.** runs the Chiefs Esports platform, a premier electronic sports club in Australia, and markets Icon branded nutritional supplements and apparel.

Directors - Athan Lekkas, chr. & CEO, Adelaide, S.A., Australia; Michael R. Clarke, Adelaide, S.A., Australia; Andrew S. Sterling, Qld., Australia
Other Exec. Officers - Mark Pryn, CFO & corp. sec.

Capital Stock

	Authorized (shs.)	Outstanding (shs.)[1]
Ordinary	unlimited	14,416,827

[1] At Mar. 31, 2023

Major Shareholder - First Growth Funds Limited held 14.2% interest at Sept. 30, 2022.

Price Range - SQID/CSE

Year	Volume	High	Low	Close
2022	29,000	$0.25	$0.05	$0.05
2021	133,287	$1.25	$0.26	$0.50
2020	43,515	$2.00	$0.20	$0.51

Recent Close: $0.01

Wholly Owned Subsidiaries

ICON Esports Pty Ltd., Australia.
- 100% int. in **The Chiefs Esports Pty Ltd.**, Australia.
- 100% int. in **Tainted Minds E-Sports Pty Ltd.**, Australia.
- 100% int. in **Team Icon Pty Ltd.**, Australia.

SQID Payments Pty Ltd., Australia.

Investments

MSM Corporation International Limited, Australia.
Vello Technologies Pty Ltd., Australia.
- 100% int. in **Vello Technologies Inc.**, Melbourne, Vic., Australia.

Financial Statistics

Periods ended:	12m Dec. 31/21[A]		12m Dec. 31/20[ΩA]
	A$000s	%Chg	A$000s
Operating revenue	**1,015**	**-86**	**7,199**
Cost of goods sold	842		4,319
Salaries & benefits	481		537
General & admin expense	1,533		1,985
Operating expense	**2,856**	**-58**	**6,841**
Operating income	**(1,841)**	**n.a.**	**358**
Deprec., depl. & amort.	502		58
Finance income	nil		22
Write-downs/write-offs	(797)		(124)
Pre-tax income	**(3,300)**	**n.a.**	**535**
Income taxes	121		462
Net income	**(3,421)**	**n.a.**	**72**
Net inc. for equity hldrs	**(3,122)**	**n.a.**	**72**
Net inc. for non-cont. int	**(299)**	**n.a.**	**nil**
Cash & equivalent	1,806		3,352
Inventories	68		nil
Accounts receivable	150		285
Current assets	2,089		3,877
Intangibles, net	60		nil
Total assets	**2,149**	**-53**	**4,602**
Accts. pay. & accr. liabs	400		214
Current liabilities	605		1,376
Shareholders' equity	1,526		3,210
Cash from oper. activs	**(2,583)**	**n.a.**	**44**
Cash from fin. activs	659		nil
Cash from invest. activs	732		1,276
Net cash position	**1,806**	**-40**	**2,998**
Capital expenditures	nil		(6)
	A$		A$
Earnings per share*	(0.35)		0.01
Cash flow per share*	(0.29)		0.01
	shs		shs
No. of shs. o/s*	14,416,827		7,973,456
Avg. no. of shs. o/s*	8,960,849		7,920,355
	%		%
Net profit margin	(337.04)		1.00
Return on equity	(131.84)		2.30
Return on assets	(101.35)		1.53
Foreign sales percent	100		100

* Ordinary
[Ω] Restated
[A] Reported in accordance with IFRS

Latest Results

Periods ended:	9m Sept. 30/22[A]		9m Sept. 30/21[A]
	A$000s	%Chg	A$000s
Operating revenue	766	+5	729
Net income	(925)	n.a.	(2,160)
Net inc. for equity hldrs	(925)	n.a.	(1,872)
Net inc. for non-cont. int	nil		(288)
	A$		A$
Earnings per share*	(0.06)		(0.23)

* Ordinary
[A] Reported in accordance with IFRS

Historical Summary
(as originally stated)

Fiscal Year	Oper. Rev.	Net Inc. Bef. Disc.	EPS*
	A$000s	A$000s	A$
2021[A]	1,015	(3,421)	(0.35)
2020[A]	7,199	72	0.01
2019[A1]	3,457	196	0.02
2019[A2]	5,355	807	0.10
2018[A2]	3,120	449	0.07

* Ordinary
[A] Reported in accordance with IFRS
[1] 6 months ended Dec. 31, 2019.
[2] Share and per share figures adjusted to reflect 1-for-2 share consolidation effected Sept. 5, 2019. As shown in the prospectus dated Dec. 18, 2019.

S.14 SSC Security Services Corp.

Symbol - SECU **Exchange** - TSX-VEN **CUSIP** - 85236T
Head Office - 300-1914 Hamilton St, Regina, SK, S4P 3N6 **Telephone** - (306) 347-3006 **Fax** - (306) 352-4110
Website - securityservicescorp.ca
Email - brad@securityservicescorp.ca
Investor Relations - Bradley D. Farquhar (306) 347-7202
Auditors - MNP LLP C.A., Regina, Sask.
Bankers - Canadian Imperial Bank of Commerce, Regina, Sask.
Lawyers - McKercher LLP, Regina, Sask.
Transfer Agents - TSX Trust Company, Calgary, Alta.
Employees - 2,750 at Sept. 30, 2022
Profile - (Sask. 2013; orig. Ont., 2012) Provides physical, cyber and electronic security services to corporate and public sector clients across Canada.

Physical security services include on-site security guards, remote continuous video monitoring, mobile patrol and investigative services. Cyber security services include Managed Security Services (MSS), vulnerability and risk analysis, cyber security consulting services, CISO consulting and cyber security staff augmentation services. Electronic security services include security risk assessments and analysis, electronic security system design and installation services, and ongoing remote monitoring of camera and other Internet of Things (IoT) sensors and systems. Clients include federal and provincial governments, Crown corporations, and many high profile corporate and public sector clients such as hospitals, airports, utility companies and police forces.

Recent Merger and Acquisition Activity

Status: completed **Revised:** June 1, 2022
UPDATE: The transaction was completed. PREVIOUS: SSC Security Services Corp. agreed to acquire Toronto, Ont.-based Logixx Security Inc., a provider of security protection (including security guards and patrols) for enterprise and commercial clients across Canada, from Avante Logixx Inc. for $23,950,000. The transaction was entered into as an alternative to SSC's proposed acquisition of Avante, which was concurrently terminated.

Status: terminated **Revised:** Mar. 30, 2022
UPDATE: The transaction was terminated. PREVIOUS: SSC Security Services Corp. agreed to acquire Avante Logixx Inc. for 52¢ cash and 0.4155 SSC common shares for each Avante share held, which implied a total consideration of $1.75 per Avante share. The transaction was valued at $46,500,000, including the assumption of $9,400,000 of Avante debt. Avante provides and develops technology-enabled security systems and services for residential and commercial clients. Avante's operating subsidiaries are Avante Security Inc., and Logixx Security Inc.

Predecessor Detail - Name changed from Input Capital Corp., Oct. 1, 2021, pursuant to change of business to security services provider; basis 1 new for 3 old shs.

Directors - Douglas A. (Doug) Emsley, chr., pres. & CEO, Regina, Sask.; Bradley D. (Brad) Farquhar, exec. v-p & CFO, Regina, Sask.; David A. Brown†, Gilford, Ont.; Dr. Lorne H. Hepworth, London, Ont.; David H. Laidley, Montréal, Qué.; Laurie Powers, Kelowna, B.C.

Other Exec. Officers - Blair W. Ross, COO & pres. & COO, SRG Security Resource Group Inc.; Patricia J. F. Warsaba, corp. sec.; Brett Leonard, dir., fin. & admin.

† Lead director

Capital Stock

	Authorized (shs.)	Outstanding (shs.)[1]
Common	unlimited	19,453,721

[1] At Mar. 31, 2023

Normal Course Issuer Bid - The company plans to make normal course purchases of up to 1,200,000 common shares representing 10% of the public float. The bid commenced on Jan. 4, 2023, and expires on Jan. 3, 2024.

Major Shareholder - Douglas A. (Doug) Emsley held 23.5% interest at Dec. 28, 2022.

Price Range - SECU/TSX-VEN

Year	Volume	High	Low	Close
2022	3,543,817	$3.20	$2.25	$2.75
2021	2,599,613	$3.40	$2.34	$2.87
2020	5,315,311	$5.22	$1.25	$2.58
2019	4,175,912	$3.60	$1.71	$2.13
2018	5,390,705	$4.89	$2.19	$2.55

Consolidation: 1-for-3 cons. in Oct. 2021
Recent Close: $2.58

Capital Stock Changes - On Oct. 1, 2021, common shares were consolidated on a 1-for-3 basis. During fiscal 2022, 79,766 post-consolidated common shares were issued on exercise of options and 749,700 post-consolidated common shares were repurchased under a Normal Course Issuer Bid.

Dividends

SECU com Ra $0.12 pa Q est. Jan. 16, 2017
1-for-3 cons eff. Oct. 1, 2021

Wholly Owned Subsidiaries

Logixx Security Inc., Toronto, Ont.
SRG Security Resource Group Inc., Canada.

Financial Statistics

Periods ended:	12m Sept. 30/22[A]		12m Sept. 30/21[oA]
	$000s	%Chg	$000s
Operating revenue	**49,697**	**+171**	**18,308**
Cost of sales	41,227		15,268
Salaries & benefits	4,144		1,759
General & admin expense	5,607		2,218
Stock-based compensation	114		92
Operating expense	**51,092**	**+164**	**19,336**
Operating income	**(1,395)**	**n.a.**	**(1,028)**
Deprec., depl. & amort.	1,765		665
Finance income	605		1,968
Finance costs, gross	51		242
Write-downs/write-offs	(820)		7
Pre-tax income	**(1,314)**	**n.a.**	**2,590**
Income taxes	(333)		701
Net income	**(981)**	**n.a.**	**1,889**
Cash & equivalent	11,195		28,796
Inventories	349		nil
Accounts receivable	20,889		4,773
Current assets	37,657		40,039
Fixed assets, net	3,157		865
Intangibles, net	34,524		19,674
Total assets	**87,669**	**+3**	**84,888**
Accts. pay. & accr. liabs.	11,766		4,518
Current liabilities	13,198		6,883
Long-term debt, gross	nil		2,540
Long-term debt, net	nil		277
Long-term lease liabilities	769		295
Shareholders' equity	70,645		75,867
Cash from oper. activs.	**(4,202)**	**n.a.**	**1,118**
Cash from fin. activs.	(7,126)		(9,033)
Cash from invest. activs.	(6,273)		9,476
Net cash position	**11,195**	**-61**	**28,796**
Capital expenditures	(985)		(100)
	$		$
Earnings per share*	(0.05)		0.10
Cash flow per share*	(0.21)		0.06
Cash divd. per share*	0.12		0.15
	shs		shs
No. of shs. o/s*	19,618,338		20,288,285
Avg. no. of shs. o/s*	19,864,604		19,184,584
	%		%
Net profit margin	(1.97)		10.32
Return on equity	(1.34)		2.57
Return on assets	(1.09)		2.48
No. of employees (FTEs)	2,750		625

* Common
[o] Restated
[A] Reported in accordance with IFRS

Latest Results

Periods ended:	6m Mar. 31/23[A]		6m Mar. 31/22[A]
	$000s	%Chg	$000s
Operating revenue	53,237	+368	11,384
Net income	245	n.a.	(762)
	$		$
Earnings per share*	0.01		(0.04)

* Common
[A] Reported in accordance with IFRS

Historical Summary
(as originally stated)

Fiscal Year	Oper. Rev.	Net Inc. Bef. Disc.	EPS*
	$000s	$000s	$
2022[A]	49,697	(981)	(0.05)
2021[A]	18,308	1,889	0.09
2020[A]	22,084	(731)	(0.03)
2019[A]	39,446	(2,235)	(0.09)
2018[A]	37,056	(1,383)	(0.06)

* Common
[A] Reported in accordance with IFRS
Note: Adjusted throughout for 1-for-3 cons. in Oct. 2021

S.15 STEP Energy Services Ltd.

Symbol - STEP **Exchange** - TSX **CUSIP** - 85859H
Head Office - Bow Valley Square 2, 1200-205 5 Ave SW, Calgary, AB, T2P 2V7 **Telephone** - (403) 457-1772 **Fax** - (403) 457-2747
Website - www.stepenergyservices.com
Email - klaas.deemter@step-es.com
Investor Relations - Klaas Deemter (587) 390-0761
Auditors - KPMG LLP C.A., Calgary, Alta.
Bankers - ATB Financial, Calgary, Alta.
Lawyers - Stikeman Elliott LLP, Calgary, Alta.
Transfer Agents - TSX Trust Company, Calgary, Alta.
FP500 Revenue Ranking - 346
Employees - 1,439 at Dec. 31, 2022

Profile - (Alta. 2011) Provides coiled tubing, fluid and nitrogen pumping, and hydraulic fracturing services to oil and gas operators in Canada and the U.S.

In Alberta and northeastern British Columbia, provides coiled tubing designed to service deepest wells in the region and offers fracturing services predominantly in the deeper, more technically challenging plays, with a focus primarily on the Montney, Duvernay, Viking and Deep Basin.

In the U.S., provides coiled tubing and fracturing services in the Permian Basin and Eagle Ford Shale Play in Texas along with coiled tubing services in the Bakken Shale Play in North Dakota and the Uinta-Piceance and Niobrara-DJ Basin in Utah and Colorado, respectively.

At Dec. 31, 2022, Canadian operations consisted of 282,500 horsepower (HP), of which 132,000 HP has dual-fuel capability, and 16 purposed-built coiled tubing spreads; and U.S. operations consisted of 207,500 HP, of which 80,000 HP is Tier 4 diesel and 50,250 HP has direct-injected dual-fuel, and 19 coiling tubing spreads.

The company is headquartered in Calgary, Alta., with the Canadian operations conducted out of Red Deer, Blackfalds, Grande Prairie and Medicine Hat, Alta.; and Fort St. John, B.C. The U.S. operations are based out of San Antonio, Tex., and conducted out of Houston, Floresville and Midland, Tex.; Windsor, Colo.; and Williston, N.D.

Operating Statistics

Year ended Dec. 31	2022	2021
Coiled Tubing		
Operating days[1]	1,964	1,569
Revenue per operating day[1]	$58,160	$51,278
Operating days[2]	2,374	1,738
Revenue per operating day[2]	$52,421	$39,726
Fracturing		
Operating days[1]	1,194	977
Revenue per operating day[1]	$379,909	$283,599
Operating days[2]	848	704
Revenue per operating day[2]	$349,920	$155,874

[1] Reflects Canadian operations.
[2] Reflects U.S. operations.

Recent Merger and Acquisition Activity

Status: completed **Announced:** Sept. 1, 2022
STEP Energy Services Ltd. acquired four high-spec, ultra-deep capacity coiled tubing units and ancillary equipment from ProPetro Holding Corp., a Permian Basin energy services company, for $17,200,000. The units were capable of handling 30,000 ft. of 2-3/8" and 2-5/8" strings of coiled tubing.

Directors - Stephen (Steve) Glanville, co-founder, pres. & CEO, Calgary, Alta.; Douglas C. Freel, chr., Calgary, Alta.; Donna Garbutt†, Calgary, Alta.; Evelyn M. Angelle, Houston, Tex.; Jeremy Gackle, Calgary, Alta.; D. James Harbilas, Cochrane, Alta.; Jason E. Skehar, Chestermere, Alta.

Other Exec. Officers - Rory Thompson, COO; Klaas Deemter, CFO; Tara Boucher, v-p, HR; Michael (Mike) Burvill, v-p, bus. devel. & innovation; Joshua Kane, v-p, legal & gen. counsel; Bradley McFarlane, v-p, fin.

† Lead director

Capital Stock

	Authorized (shs.)	Outstanding (shs.)[1]
Preferred	unlimited	nil
Common	unlimited	71,617,464

[1] At May 10, 2023

Major Shareholder - ARC Energy Fund 8 held 37.23% interest and ARC Energy Fund 6 held 18.98% interest at Mar. 1, 2023.

Price Range - STEP/TSX

Year	Volume	High	Low	Close
2022	60,625,548	$6.85	$1.60	$5.33
2021	16,156,309	$2.23	$0.76	$1.61
2020	18,637,330	$1.70	$0.28	$0.74
2019	42,420,906	$2.96	$0.86	$1.57
2018	47,656,566	$12.99	$1.65	$1.94

Recent Close: $3.66

Capital Stock Changes - In September 2022, 2,616,460 common shares were issued pursuant to the acquisition of coiled tubing units and ancillary equipment from ProPetro Holding Corp. Also during 2022, 816,185 common shares were issued on exercise of restricted share units and performance share units.

Wholly Owned Subsidiaries

STEP Finance Ltd., Alta.
- 100% int. in **STEP Energy Services LLC**, Del.
- 100% int. in **STEP Energy Services (USA) Ltd.**, Del.
  - 100% int. in **STEP Energy Services (Leasing) LLC**, Del.
  - 100% int. in **STEP Two Energy Services Ltd.**, Del.
    - 100% int. in **STEP Energy Services Holdings Ltd.**, Kan.
    - 100% int. in **STEP Technologies (U.S.A.) Ltd.**, Tex.

Financial Statistics

Periods ended:	12m Dec. 31/22[A]		12m Dec. 31/21[A]
	$000s	%Chg	$000s
Operating revenue	**989,018**	**+84**	**536,309**
Cost of goods sold	305,300		164,533
Cost of sales	234,446		142,220
Salaries & benefits	240,752		158,275
General & admin expense	9,238		8,868
Stock-based compensation	20,824		6,717
Operating expense	**810,560**	**+69**	**480,613**
Operating income	**178,458**	**+220**	**55,696**
Deprec., depl. & amort.	87,969		73,381
Finance income	12		nil
Finance costs, gross	10,589		14,624
Write-downs/write-offs	38,388		550
Pre-tax income	**120,642**	**n.a.**	**(30,625)**
Income taxes	25,861		(2,498)
Net income	**94,781**	**n.a.**	**(28,127)**
Cash & equivalent	2,785		3,698
Inventories	46,410		32,732
Accounts receivable	199,004		86,644
Current assets	256,361		133,255
Fixed assets, net	402,482		335,499
Right-of-use assets	23,528		14,788
Intangibles, net	161		306
Total assets	**682,532**	**+41**	**483,848**
Accts. pay. & accr. liabs.	165,869		95,183
Current liabilities	189,781		129,343
Long-term debt, gross	140,794		189,857
Long-term debt, net	140,794		162,007
Long-term lease liabilities	13,860		9,163
Shareholders' equity	306,033		177,442
Cash from oper. activs.	**122,601**	**+108**	**58,846**
Cash from fin. activs.	(57,775)		(25,671)
Cash from invest. activs.	(66,438)		(30,708)
Net cash position	**2,785**	**-25**	**3,698**
Capital expenditures	(82,984)		(37,242)
Capital disposals	6,393		1,104
	$		$
Earnings per share*	1.37		(0.41)
Cash flow per share*	1.77		0.87
	shs		shs
No. of shs. o/s*	71,589,626		68,156,981
Avg. no. of shs. o/s*	69,412,087		68,007,878
	%		%
Net profit margin	9.58		(5.24)
Return on equity	39.21		(14.73)
Return on assets	17.68		(3.05)
Foreign sales percent	43		33
No. of employees (FTEs)	1,439		1,175

* Common
[A] Reported in accordance with IFRS

Historical Summary
(as originally stated)

Fiscal Year	Oper. Rev.	Net Inc. Bef. Disc.	EPS*
	$000s	$000s	$
2022[A]	989,018	94,781	1.37
2021[A]	536,309	(28,127)	(0.41)
2020[A]	368,945	(119,358)	(1.77)
2019[A]	668,297	(143,883)	(2.16)
2018[A]	781,763	(39,304)	(0.60)

* Common
[A] Reported in accordance with IFRS

S.16 SWMBRD Sports Inc.

Symbol - SWIM **Exchange** - CSE **CUSIP** - 78502J
Head Office - 1450-789 Pender St W, Vancouver, BC, V6C 1H2 **Telephone** - (778) 870-1497
Website - swmbrd.com
Email - matthew.schroenn@swmbrd.com
Investor Relations - Matthew Schroenn (604) 375-4664
Auditors - De Visser Gray LLP C.A., Vancouver, B.C.
Transfer Agents - Odyssey Trust Company

Profile - (B.C. 2015) Developing the SWMBRD aquatic sports board.

SWMBRD (the swimboard) is a human-powered aquatic sports board that can closely approximate the action of swimming, combined with the range-of-operation and security of a stand-up paddle board (SUP) or kayak. The swimboard will be less than four feet in length and 10 lbs. in weight. Prototypes were expected to be produced by March 2022 and production of the first 500 swimboards was expected by December 2022. Principal methods by which products will be sold and distributed: resorts and commercial sales; resort retail outlets; and online sales through its own e-commerce store. The company does not plan to retail its products through traditional brick-and-mortar retailers.

Predecessor Detail - Name changed from Zambezi Sports Inc., July 9, 2021.

Directors - Justin Schroenn, pres. & CEO, B.C.; Gareth Schroenn, v-p & treas., B.C.; Matthew (Matt) Schroenn, v-p & corp. sec., B.C.; J. Christopher (Chris) Grove, North Vancouver, B.C.; Michael (Mike) Hodge, B.C.

Other Exec. Officers - Dong H. (Don) Shim, CFO

Capital Stock

	Authorized (shs.)	Outstanding (shs.)[1]
Common	unlimited	82,457,000

[1] At Jan. 26, 2023

Major Shareholder - Zimtu Capital Corp. held 18.15% interest at Feb. 16, 2022.

Price Range - SWIM/CSE

Year	Volume	High	Low	Close
2022	6,319,871	$0.50	$0.03	$0.06

Recent Close: $0.03

Financial Statistics

Periods ended:	12m Feb. 28/21[A]		12m Feb. 29/20[A]
	$000s	%Chg	$000s
General & admin expense	120		20
Other operating expense	24		nil
Operating expense	**144**	**+620**	**20**
Operating income	**(144)**	**n.a.**	**(20)**
Deprec., depl. & amort.	25		25
Write-downs/write-offs	(6)		nil
Pre-tax income	**(176)**	**n.a.**	**(45)**
Net income	**(176)**	**n.a.**	**(45)**
Cash & equivalent	920		nil
Current assets	1,239		2
Fixed assets, net	1		1
Intangibles, net	70		98
Total assets	**1,310**	**n.m.**	**101**
Accts. pay. & accr. liabs	34		9
Current liabilities	44		19
Shareholders' equity	1,266		83
Cash from oper. activs	**(121)**	**n.a.**	**8**
Cash from fin. activs	1,044		nil
Cash from invest. activs	(3)		(8)
Net cash position	**920**	**n.a.**	**nil**
	$		$
Earnings per share*	(0.01)		(0.00)
	shs		shs
No. of shs. o/s*	61,170,220		14,320,083
Avg. no. of shs. o/s*	20,652,417		14,320,083
	%		%
Net profit margin	n.a.		n.a.
Return on equity	(26.09)		n.m.
Return on assets	(24.95)		n.a.

* Common
[A] Reported in accordance with IFRS

Latest Results

Periods ended:	6m Aug. 31/21[A]		6m Aug. 31/20[A]
	$000s	%Chg	$000s
Net income	(548)	n.a.	(13)
	$		$
Earnings per share*	(0.01)		(0.00)

* Common
[A] Reported in accordance with IFRS

S.17 Sabio Holdings Inc.

Symbol - SBIO **Exchange** - TSX-VEN **CUSIP** - 78570Q
Head Office - Brookfield Place, 4400-181 Bay St, Toronto, ON, M5J 2T3 **Toll-free** - (844) 974-2662
Website - www.sabio.inc
Email - aideen@sabioholding.com
Investor Relations - Aideen McDermott (844) 974-2662
Auditors - MNP LLP C.A., Toronto, Ont.
Transfer Agents - TSX Trust Company, Toronto, Ont.
Profile - (Ont. 2017) Offers a suite of advertising and analytics technology and services to brands and advertisement agencies, including ad delivery and analytics insights (App Science®).

Has two primary business lines: digital ad media delivery, and digital media analytics (App Science analytics). The media delivery business focuses on working with brands and agencies to run their advertising campaigns targeting audiences on both mobile and Connected TV (CTV) devices. Add delivery is provided in two ways: Managed Service, and Programmatic. The company charges customers for these campaigns and purchases media inventory from publishers to execute these campaigns. Over 90% of the company's revenue in 2020 was from its mobile advertising business. Its App Science analytics business consists of wholly owned **AppScience, Inc.**, which offers App Science®, a proprietary machine learning platform that pairs observations of consumer behaviour with corresponding data to inform marketing decisions. App Science is intended to operate via a Software-as-a-Service (SaaS) business model.

Revenue is generated from managed service, programmatic sales, connectedTV, and App Science® insights. The company sells digital advertising directly to marketers or through advertising agencies. Revenue from advertising is mostly generated through video and display advertising delivered through advertising impressions.

On Apr. 4, 2022, the company acquired substantially all of the assets of **Vidillion Inc.**, a U.S.-based streaming TV supply side platform, for US$3,000,000, consisting of US$1,250,000 cash and issuance of 1,685,079 common shares at a deemed price of Cdn$1.30 per share (valued at US$1,750,000).

Predecessor Detail - Name changed from Spirit Banner II Capital Corp., pursuant to the Qualifying Transaction reverse takeover acquisition of Sabio Mobile, Inc.; basis 1 new for 15.9091 old shs.

Directors - Aziz Rahimtoola, CEO, Los Angeles, Calif.; Jennifer Cabalquinto; Carl Farrell, Toronto, Ont.; Muizz Kheraj, Los Angeles, Calif.; Paula Madison, Los Angeles, Calif.

Other Exec. Officers - Sajid Premji, CFO; Joe Camacho, chief mktg. officer; Humera Kassem, chief people officer; Tim Russell, chief revenue officer; Jon Stimmel, chief growth officer; Simon Wong, exec. v-p; Jessica Ackerman, sr. v-p, sales; Joao Machado, sr. v-p, mktg.; Jason Tong, sr. v-p, eng.; Jessica Gailys, v-p, product mktg.; Meghna Kothari, v-p, culture & commun.; Sudha Reddy, v-p, product innovation & gen. mgr., India; Kendra Low, corp. sec.

Capital Stock

	Authorized (shs.)	Outstanding (shs.)[1]
Common	unlimited	15,091,425
Restricted Vtg.	unlimited	31,755,764

[1] At Feb. 15, 2023

Common - One vote per share.

Restricted Voting - Held by residents of the United States. Convertible into common shares by the holder under certain circumstances and by the company at any time and from time-to-time. One vote per share, excluding for the election of the board of directors.

Normal Course Issuer Bid - The company plans to make normal course purchases of up to 754,571 common shares representing 5% of the total outstanding. The bid commenced on Mar. 22, 2023, and expires on Mar. 21, 2024.

Major Shareholder - Aziz Rahimtoola held 54.45% interest at Nov. 26, 2021.

Price Range - SBIO/TSX-VEN

Year	Volume	High	Low	Close
2022	3,243,006	$1.58	$0.65	$0.80
2021	338,425	$1.85	$1.35	$1.55
2020	18,857	$1.59	$0.64	$1.19
2019	11,440	$2.39	$0.88	$1.43
2018	9,805	$3.18	$1.59	$1.91

Consolidation: 1-for-15.9091 cons. in Nov. 2021
Recent Close: $0.55

Capital Stock Changes - On Apr. 4, 2022, 1,685,079 common shares were issued pursuant to the acquisition of substantially all of the assets of Vidillion Inc. In December 2022, 5,646,807 common shares were exchanged for a like number of restricted voting shares.

Wholly Owned Subsidiaries

Sabio Mobile, Inc., Los Angeles, Calif.
- 100% int. in **AppScience, Inc.**, N.Y.
- 100% int. in **Sabio, Inc.**, United States.
- 99.99% int. in **Sabio Mobile India Pvt. Ltd.**, India.

S.18 Sagen MI Canada Inc.

CUSIP - 786688
Head Office - 300-2060 Winston Park Dr, Oakville, ON, L6H 5R7 **Telephone** - (905) 287-5300 **Toll-free** - (800) 511-8888 **Fax** - (905) 287-5472
Website - www.sagen.ca
Email - philip.mayers@sagen.ca
Investor Relations - Philip Mayers (905) 287-5393
Auditors - Ernst & Young LLP C.A., Toronto, Ont.
Lawyers - Blake, Cassels & Graydon LLP, Toronto, Ont.
Transfer Agents - TSX Trust Company, Toronto, Ont.
FP500 Subsidiary Revenue Ranking - 66
Employees - 250 at Dec. 31, 2022
Profile - (Can. 2009) Provides private residential mortgage insurance in Canada through wholly owned **Sagen Mortgage Insurance Company Canada** (operating as Sagen™).

All federally regulated financial institutions in Canada must purchase mortgage insurance on residential mortgages whenever the loan-to-value ratio exceeds 80% at time of origination. The company's major competitors are **Canada Mortgage and Housing Corporation** (CMHC), a Crown corporation, and **Canada Guaranty Mortgage Insurance Company**, the company's only private sector mortgage insurance competitor.

Mortgages originated with a ratio of greater than 80% are known as high loan-to-value mortgages and those with loan-to-value ratios of below 80% are known as low loan-to-value mortgages. The company offers high loan-to-value mortgage insurance and low loan-to-value insurance.

At Dec. 31, 2022, the company's mortgage insurer capital adequacy test ratio was 178% and loss ratio was 3%.

The company actively manages an investment portfolio which consists primarily of fixed income securities, including federal and provincial government bonds, collateralized loan obligations, corporate bonds and Canadian preferred shares. At Dec. 31, 2022, the fair value of the portfolio, including cash and cash equivalents, was $6.1 billion.

Common delisted from TSX, Apr. 6, 2021.

Recent Merger and Acquisition Activity

Status: completed **Announced:** Oct. 19, 2022
Sagen MI Canada Inc. acquired an additional 8.81% interest in private India Mortgage Guarantee Corporation Pvt. Ltd. (IMGC) for $9,036,000. IMGC offers mortgage guarantees against borrower defaults on housing loans from mortgage lenders in India.

Status: completed **Announced:** June 8, 2022
Sagen MI Canada Inc. acquired a 31.39% interest in private India Mortgage Guarantee Corporation Pvt. Ltd. (IMGC) for $31,632,000. IMGC offers mortgage guarantees against borrower defaults on housing loans from mortgage lenders in India.

Predecessor Detail - Name changed from Genworth MI Canada Inc., Feb. 5, 2021.

Directors - Erson Olivan, chr., Ont.; Stuart Levings, pres. & CEO, Ont.; Fredric J. (Fred) Tomczyk†, Ont.; Dana Ades-Landy, Montréal, Qué.; Sophia Chen, Ont.; Sharon T. Giffen, B.C.; Lyndsay Hatlelid, Toronto, Ont.; David Latour, Qué.; Neil Parkinson, Cambridge, Ont.; David Planques, Toronto, Ont.; Rajinder (Raj) Singh, N.C.

Other Exec. Officers - Mary-Jo Hewat, sr. v-p, HR & facilities; Winsor Macdonell, sr. v-p, gen. counsel & corp. sec.; Philip Mayers, sr. v-p & CFO; Ed Orlik, sr. v-p & CIO; Jim Spitali, sr. v-p, sales & mktg.; Craig Sweeney, sr. v-p & chief risk officer

† Lead director

Capital Stock

	Authorized (shs.)	Outstanding (shs.)[1]
Class A Preferred	unlimited	
Series 1		4,000,000
Class A Common	unlimited	1,009,590

[1] At June 30, 2023

Class A Preferred, Series 1 - Entitled to fixed non-cumulative annual dividends of $1.35 per share payable quarterly. Redeemable at $26 per share on or after Mar. 31, 2026, and declining by 25¢ per share annually to Mar. 31, 2030, and at $25 per share thereafter. 0.1431 vote per share.

Common - One vote per share.

Major Shareholder - Brookfield Business Partners L.P. held 65% interest at Apr. 21, 2023.

Price Range - MIC/TSX (D)

Year	Volume	High	Low	Close
2021	14,116,170	$44.00	$43.17	$43.48
2020	62,505,320	$61.39	$24.02	$43.41
2019	43,575,836	$58.81	$39.44	$56.82
2018	47,868,355	$46.75	$38.00	$40.20

Capital Stock Changes - During 2022, 6,087 class A common shares were issued as part of reorganization undertaken for tax purposes.

Dividends

MIC.PR.A pfd A ser 1 red. Ra $1.35 pa Q
Listed Feb 18/21.
$0.48822**i**............ June 30/21
com Ra $2.16 pa Q est. Nov. 27, 2019
Delisted Apr 6/21.
i Initial Payment

Wholly Owned Subsidiaries

MIC Holdings K Company, Ont.
Sagen Holdings I Company, N.S.
- 93% int. in **Sagen Mortgage Insurance Company Canada**, Oakville, Ont.
  - 100% int. in **MIC Insurance Company Canada**, Canada.

Sagen Holdings II Company, N.S.
- 7% int. in **Sagen Mortgage Insurance Company Canada**, Oakville, Ont.

Sagen International Holdings Inc., Ont.

Investments

40.2% int. in **India Mortgage Guarantee Corporation Pvt. Ltd.**, India.

Financial Statistics

Periods ended:	12m Dec. 31/22^A		12m Dec. 31/21^A
	$000s	%Chg	$000s
Net premiums earned	866,066		800,393
Net investment income	208,051		181,854
Total revenue	**1,074,117**	**+9**	**982,247**
Salaries & benefits	53,747		51,572
General & admin. expense	28,113		28,066
Premium taxes	59,518		87,431
Other operating expense	27,107		(66,341)
Operating expense	**168,485**	**+67**	**100,728**
Operating income	**905,632**	**+3**	**881,519**
Deprec. & amort.	5,971		6,049
Finance costs, gross	38,588		38,552
Pre-tax income	**854,165**	**+3**	**828,475**
Income taxes	217,208		208,536
Net income	**636,957**	**+3**	**619,939**
Cash & equivalent	362,919		387,157
Securities investments	5,899,195		6,591,261
Total investments	5,899,195		6,591,261
Total assets	**6,867,519**	**-7**	**7,373,176**
Accts. pay. & accr. liabs	166,814		105,819
Claims provisions	72,231		89,499
Debt	891,637		1,102,013
Long-term lease liabilities	7,734		7,630
Preferred share equity	97,907		97,907
Shareholders' equity	2,647,950		3,092,181
Cash from oper. activs	**611,299**	**-33**	**914,750**
Cash from fin. activs	(890,804)		(911,226)
Cash from invest. activs	179,291		(184,022)
Net cash position	**256,595**	**-28**	**356,809**
Capital expenditures	(6,145)		(6,451)
Unfunded pension liability	18,424		25,491
	$		$
Earnings per share*	n.a.		n.a.
Cash flow per share*	605.49		911.56
Cash divd. per share*	nil		205.54
Extra divd. - cash*	nil		518.19
Total divd. per share*	**nil**		**723.73**
	shs		shs
No. of shs. o/s*	1,009,590		1,003,503
	%		%
Net profit margin	59.30		63.11
Return on equity	22.78		17.92
Return on assets	9.35		8.74
No. of employees (FTEs)	250		260

* Common
^A Reported in accordance with IFRS

Latest Results

Periods ended:	6m June 30/23^A		6m June 30/22^{oA}
	$000s	%Chg	$000s
Total revenue	421,518	+2	412,987
Net income	213,086	-11	238,956
	$		$
Earnings per share*	n.a.		n.a.

^o Restated
^A Reported in accordance with IFRS

Historical Summary
(as originally stated)

Fiscal Year	Total Rev.	Net Inc. Bef. Disc.	EPS*
	$000s	$000s	$
2022^A	1,074,117	636,957	n.a.
2021^A	982,247	619,939	n.a.
2020^A	874,146	440,976	5.11
2019^A	857,818	426,262	4.92
2018^A	869,724	451,551	5.04

* Common
^A Reported in accordance with IFRS

S.19 Sagicor Financial Company Ltd.

Symbol - SFC **Exchange** - TSX **CUSIP** - 78669Q
Head Office - Cecil F De Caires Building, Wildey, St. Michael, Barbados, 15096 **Telephone** - (246) 467-7500 **Fax** - (246) 436-8829
Website - www.sagicor.com
Email - george_sipsis@sagicor.com
Investor Relations - George Sipsis (800) 342-0719
Auditors - PricewaterhouseCoopers SRL, St. Michael, Barbados
Transfer Agents - TSX Trust Company, Toronto, Ont.
Employees - 4,775 at Dec. 31, 2022
Profile - (Bermuda 2019; orig. Ont., 2017) Provides insurance and other financial services, including asset management and banking, in the Caribbean primarily in Jamaica, Barbados and Trinidad and Tobago, and the United States.

The company has operations in 20 countries offering a wide range of products and services including life and health insurance, annuities, pension investment and administration, property and casualty insurance, asset management, and commercial and investment banking. The company operates through three main business segments: Sagicor Jamaica, Sagicor Life, and Sagicor USA.

Sagicor Jamaica

The company operates in Jamaica through its controlled subsidiary **Sagicor Group Jamaica Ltd.** (Sagicor Jamaica), a full service financial institution offering insurance and non-insurance solutions. Primary insurance products are individual life insurance and employee benefits, which consists of both group health and group pension. Non-insurance solutions include commercial banking operations conducted through 15 bank branches, and investment banking focused on securities trading, asset management, stock brokerage, corporate finance, advisory services, underwriting, cash management and custody services. Sagicor Jamaica also includes operations in the Cayman Islands and Costa Rica, and hospitality and real estate interests in select regions.

Sagicor Life

Wholly owned **Sagicor Life Inc.** provides life and health insurance, property and casualty insurance, pensions, annuities and asset management products and services in Barbados, Trinidad and Tobago, Eastern Caribbean, Dutch Caribbean, Bahamas, Belize and Panama. Sagicor Life's operations in the Eastern Caribbean are conducted in six territories (Antigua, the Commonwealth of Dominica, St. Lucia, Grenada, St. Kitts and Nevis, and St. Vincent) through three branches (Antigua, Grenada, and St. Lucia) and three agencies (Dominica, St.Kitts and Nevis, and St. Vincent). Sagicor Life offers its solutions to individual and group customers through its network of advisors and brokers.

Sagicor USA

Wholly owned **Sagicor USA, Inc.** and **Sagicor Life Insurance Company** offer life insurance and annuities in 45 U.S. states and the District of Columbia through third party marketing firms, financial institutions, independent agents, managing general agents and individual distributors as well as direct-to-consumer platforms. Products are primarily offered to individuals and small businesses in the middle market segment.

On Oct. 5, 2022, the company agreed to sell its insurance operations in Curacao and St. Maarten, subject to receipt of regulatory approval. Terms were not disclosed.

In March and September 2022, subsidiary **Sagicor Group Jamaica Ltd.** sold its entire holdings in **Sagicor Real Estate X-Fund Limited**, which had interests in hospitality and real estate activities in the Caribbean and the U.S., for total proceeds of US$35,300,000.

On Sept. 20, 2022, wholly owned **Sage Distribution, LLC** and **Sage Partners, LLC** were dissolved.

In August 2022, subsidiary **Sagicor Group Jamaica Ltd.** acquired the securities dealer book of business of **Alliance Investment Management Limited**, a Kingston, Jamaica-based licensed securities dealer offering asset management, securities trading and financial advisory services, for US$100,000.

On Apr. 1, 2022, subsidiary **Sagicor Group Jamaica Ltd.** acquired Kingston, Jamaica-based **Alliance Financial Services Limited**, a provider of cambio and remittance services in Jamaica, for US$16,800,000 plus contingent consideration of up to US$22,600,000 based on specified performance criteria.

Recent Merger and Acquisition Activity

Status: pending **Announced:** Aug. 24, 2022
Sagicor Financial Company Ltd. agreed to acquire Toronto, Ont.-based ivari Holdings ULC from Wilton Re Ltd. for Cdn$325,000,000, expected to be financed with new debt and cash on hand. ivari provides insurance and investment products and services to middle-market customers in Canada, with a focus on individual universal and term life insurance. ivari had 700,000 policyholders and Cdn$13.9 billion in total assets at Dec. 31, 2021. The transaction was expected to close within six to 12 months.

Predecessor Detail - Name changed from Alignvest Acquisition II Corporation, Dec. 9, 2019, pursuant to the Qualifying Acquisition of Sagicor Financial Corporation Limited.

Directors - Mahmood Khimji, chr., Irving, Tex.; Andre Mousseau, pres. & CEO, Toronto, Ont.; Sir Hilary Beckles, St. Thomas, Barbados; Dr. Archibald Campbell, Kingston, Jamaica; Peter E. Clarke, Maraval, Trinidad and Tobago; Keith Duncan, Kingston, Jamaica; Monish K. Dutt, Washington, D.C.; Stephen Facey, Kingston, Jamaica; Dennis L. Harris, Kingston, Jamaica; Dr. Dodridge D. Miller, Fla.; Gilbert S. (Gil) Palter, Toronto, Ont.; Alan Ryder, Ont.; Reza Satchu, Toronto, Ont.; Aviva Shneider, N.Y.

Other Exec. Officers - Kathryn (Kathy) Jenkins, CFO; Anthony Chandler, chief finl. contr.; Lynda Gauthier, chief risk officer & chief sustainability officer; Nari T. Persad, chief actuary; Ronald Blitstein, exec. v-p & CIO; Althea Hazzard, exec. v-p, gen. counsel & corp. sec.; George Sipsis, exec. v-p, corp. devel. & capital markets; Keston D. Howell, pres. & CEO, Sagicor General Insurance Inc.; Robert Trestrail, pres. & CEO, Sagicor Life Inc.; Christopher (Chris) Zacca, pres. & CEO, Sagicor Group Jamaica Ltd.; Donald S. Austin, CEO, Sagicor Life (Eastern Caribbean) Inc.; J. Andrew (Andy) Gallagher, CEO, Sagicor Reinsurance Bermuda Ltd.

Capital Stock

	Authorized (shs.)	Outstanding (shs.)[1]	Par
Preference	10,000,000,000	nil	US$0.01
Common	10,000,000,000	142,564,230	US$0.01

[1] At June 14, 2023

Normal Course Issuer Bid - The company plans to make normal course purchases of up to 8,840,727 common shares representing 10% of the public float. The bid commenced on June 24, 2023, and expires on June 23, 2024.

Major Shareholder - JMMB Group Limited held 23.33% interest at Apr. 19, 2023.

Price Range - SFC/TSX

Year	Volume	High	Low	Close
2022	2,506,341	$6.75	$5.47	$5.48
2021	6,055,564	$7.00	$5.25	$6.25
2020	5,584,427	$9.75	$4.88	$6.40
2019	11,247,311	$10.96	$7.89	$9.75
2018	6,597,676	$10.01	$9.62	$10.00

Recent Close: $4.32

Capital Stock Changes - During 2022, 768,000 common shares were issued for cash and 1,184,000 common shares were repurchased under a Normal Course Issuer Bid.

Dividends

SFC com Ra US$0.225 pa Q est. May 29, 2020
Prev. Rate: US$0.226 est. Feb. 28, 2020

Wholly Owned Subsidiaries

Sagicor Bank (Barbados) Limited, Barbados.
Sagicor Financial Corporation Limited, St. Michael, Barbados.

- 100% int. in **Sagicor Life Inc.**, Barbados.
  - 100% int. in **LOJ Holdings Ltd.**, Jamaica.
    - 32.45% int. in **Sagicor Group Jamaica Ltd.**, Jamaica.
  - 16.66% int. in **Sagicor Group Jamaica Ltd.**, Jamaica.
- 100% int. in **Sagicor Reinsurance Bermuda Ltd.**, Bermuda.
- 100% int. in **Sagicor USA, Inc.**, Del.
  - 100% int. in **Sagicor Life Insurance Company**, Tex.

Note: The preceding list includes only the major related companies in which interests are held.

Financial Statistics

Periods ended:	12m Dec. 31/22^A		12m Dec. 31/21^A
	US$000s	%Chg	US$000s
Net premiums earned	2,048,076		1,713,150
Net investment income	317,994		429,797
Total revenue	**2,540,252**	**+8**	**2,359,094**
Policy benefits & claims	1,666,521		1,531,407
Commissions	137,471		135,998
General & admin. expense	392,912		349,787
Premium taxes	17,659		17,524
Operating expense	**548,042**	**+9**	**503,309**
Operating income	**325,689**	**0**	**324,378**
Deprec. & amort.	30,950		32,701
Finance costs, gross	39,626		45,054
Pre-tax income	**262,904**	**-1**	**264,733**
Income taxes	93,302		68,257
Net income	**169,602**	**-14**	**196,476**
Net inc. for equity hldrs	**115,565**	**-13**	**133,179**
Net inc. for non-cont. int	**53,871**	**-16**	**63,919**
Net inc. for partic policyhldrs	**166**	**n.a.**	**(622)**
Cash & equivalent	368,137		359,975
Accounts receivable	60,809		59,168
Securities investments	7,412,281		7,122,702
Mortgages	617,044		449,923
Real estate	77,359		75,954
Total investments	9,108,852		8,629,310
Total assets	**10,765,871**	**+4**	**10,377,932**
Bank indebtedness	1,737		761
Accts. pay. & accr. liabs	248,393		253,521
Claims provisions	362,912		341,441
Debt	632,535		683,388
Long-term lease liabilities	33,294		32,836
Policy liabilities & claims	5,182,739		4,792,627
Partic. policyhldrs.' equity	181		581
Shareholders' equity	1,084,244		1,133,970
Non-controlling interest	418,427		531,662
Cash from oper. activs	**(154,503)**	**n.a.**	**124,882**
Cash from fin. activs	(65,266)		140,473
Cash from invest. activs	(26,620)		36,155
Net cash position	**592,737**	**-29**	**836,791**
Capital expenditures	(17,634)		(10,919)
Capital disposals	188		281
Unfunded pension liability	12,019		25,945
	US$		US$
Earnings per share*	0.81		0.92
Cash flow per share*	(1.08)		0.86
Cash divd. per share*	$0.23		$0.23
	shs		shs
No. of shs. o/s*	142,768,612		143,184,643
Avg. no. of shs. o/s*	142,905,000		144,892,000
	%		%
Net profit margin	6.68		8.33
Return on equity	10.42		11.87
Return on assets	1.85		2.34
Foreign sales percent	100		100
No. of employees (FTEs)	4,775		4,669

* Common
^A Reported in accordance with IFRS

Latest Results

Periods ended:	3m Mar. 31/23[A]		3m Mar. 31/22[□A]
	US$000s	%Chg	US$000s
Total revenue	418,311	+555	63,867
Net income	9,184	n.a.	(82,298)
Net inc. for equity hldrs	1,409	n.a.	(81,024)
Net inc. for non-cont. int	7,775		(1,274)
	US$		US$
Earnings per share*	0.01		(0.57)

* Common
□ Restated
[A] Reported in accordance with IFRS

Historical Summary
(as originally stated)

Fiscal Year	Total Rev.	Net Inc. Bef. Disc.	EPS*
	US$000s	US$000s	US$
2022[A]	2,540,252	169,602	0.81
2021[A]	2,359,094	196,476	0.92
2020[A]	1,878,367	(15,130)	(0.02)
2019[A1]	1,867,326	103,574	0.57
2018[A2]	1,484,261	95,821	n.a.

* Common
[A] Reported in accordance with IFRS
[1] Results reflect the Dec. 5, 2019, reverse takeover acquisition of Sagicor Financial Corporation Limited.
[2] Results for fiscal 2018 and 2017 pertain to Sagicor Financial Corporation Limited.

S.20 St. Davids Capital Inc.

Symbol - SDCI.P **Exchange** - TSX-VEN **CUSIP** - 78927W
Head Office - TD Centre, North Tower, 3000-77 King St W, PO Box 95, Toronto, ON, M5K 1G8 **Telephone** - (416) 953-7012
Email - rocrac80@gmail.com
Investor Relations - Rocco Racioppo (416) 953-7012
Auditors - Jones & O'Connell LLP C.A., St. Catharines, Ont.
Transfer Agents - TSX Trust Company, Toronto, Ont.
Profile - (Ont. 2021) Capital Pool Company.
Common listed on TSX-VEN, Oct. 14, 2022.
Directors - Rocco Racioppo, pres., CEO & corp. sec., Toronto, Ont.; Philip M. Hampson, CFO, Toronto, Ont.; Douglas (Doug) Harris, Aurora, Ont.; William C. Kennedy, Toronto, Ont.

Capital Stock

	Authorized (shs.)	Outstanding (shs.)[1]
Common	unlimited	5,078,500

[1] At July 4, 2023
Major Shareholder - Rocco Racioppo held 39.38% interest at Feb. 17, 2023.

Price Range - SDCI.P/TSX-VEN

Year	Volume	High	Low	Close
2022	1,400	$0.10	$0.10	$0.10

Recent Close: $0.07
Capital Stock Changes - On Oct. 14, 2022, an initial public offering of 2,178,500 common shares was completed at 10¢ per share.

S.21 Salona Global Medical Device Corporation

Symbol - SGMD **Exchange** - TSX-VEN **CUSIP** - 79549X
Head Office - 6160 Innovation Way, Carlsbad, CA, United States, 92009 **Toll-free** - (800) 760-6826
Website - www.salonaglobal.com
Email - info@salonaglobal.com
Investor Relations - Michael Seckler (800) 760-6826
Auditors - SRCO Professional Corporation C.A., Richmond Hill, Ont.
Transfer Agents - Computershare Trust Company of Canada Inc., Toronto, Ont.
Employees - 144 at Dec. 31, 2022
Profile - (B.C. 2010; orig. Can., 2013) Develops, manufactures and sells proprietary and white label medical devices for pain management and physical therapy treatments as well as wearable technology and other products used for prevention, treatment, and rehabilitation of the human body.

The company acquires smaller U.S.-based private medical device companies with a focus on the business of recovery science technologies that help individuals recover from surgery and prevent disease.

Wholly owned **South Dakota Partners, Inc.** (SDP) develops and manufactures white label medical devices for an array of global businesses from a facility in Clear Lake, S.D.

Wholly owned **Simbex, LLC** operates as a product design and development firm for primarily U.S. medical device and consumer health companies with product ranging from wearable technology to products for physical stability.

Wholly owned **ALG Health PLus, LLC** sells medical devices and supplies to small, independent hospitals and group purchasing organizations that offer devices and supplies to small medical offices and clinics.

Wholly owned **Mio-Guard, LLC** distributes sports medicine products and equipment focused on preventative care and rehabilitation to the athletic training, physical therapy and orthopedic markets across the United States.

Wholly owned **DaMar Plastics Manufacturing Inc.** designs, produces and sells specialty plastics to the medical and consumer industries.

Wholly owned **Biodex Medical Systems Inc.** sells orthopedic and sports medicine devices and technology.

Wholly owned **Arrowhead Medical, LLC** sells and distributes recovery science medical devices.

In May 2023, the company acquired **Arrowhead Medical, LLC**, which sells and distributes recovery science medical devices, for issuance of $1,000,000 class A non-voting shares, assumption of $250,000 bank debt and an up to $2,000,000 contingent earnout for two years.

In December 2022, the company changed its fiscal year end to December 31 from February 28.

In March 2022, the company acquired Michigan-based **Mio-Guard, LLC**, which sells and markets medical devices in the United States, for 1,300,000 class B units on closing and 125,000 class B units per quarter for eight consecutive quarters immediately following closing. Additionally the company would issue up to 4,000,000 class B units upon achieving certain milestones. Class B units are exchangeable into class A non-voting common shares on a 1-for-1 basis.

Recent Merger and Acquisition Activity

Status: completed **Revised:** Apr. 3, 2023
UPDATE: The transaction was completed for total consideration of $8,000,000, consisting of $1,000,000 cash and three installment payments totaling $7,000,000 payable on July 1, 2023 ($2,000,000), on Oct. 1, 2023 ($3,000,000) and on Jan. 1, 2024 ($3,000,000). PREVIOUS: Salona Global Medical Device Corporation entered into a letter of intent to acquire certain rehabilitation and sports medicine device assets from Biodex Medical Systems Inc., which sells orthopedic and sports medicine devices and technology, for US$8,000,000, consisting of US$6,000,000 upon closing and US$2,000,000 on the one-year anniversary of closing. Nov. 29, 2022 - Salona Global Medical Device has executed a definitive asset purchase agreement to acquire the physical medicine assets of Biodex. Mar. 15, 2023 - Salona Global Medical Device entered into a stock purchase agreement to acquire all of outstanding shares of Biodex Medical Systems for total consideration of $8,000,000, which replaces the previously disclosed asset purchase agreement covering the same business that was first announced on November 29, 2022. The transaction is expected to close on Apr. 3, 2023.

Status: completed **Revised:** Sept. 26, 2022
UPDATE: The transaction was completed for US$3,200,000 and issuance of 1,576,609 common shares. PREVIOUS: Salona Global Medical Device Corporation agreed to acquire El Cajon, Calif.-based DaMar Plastics Manufacturing Inc., which provides precision plastics molding technology to the medical and consumer industries, for US$3,000,000 and issuance of 1,600,000 common shares and up to US$5,500,000 or issuance of up to 5,000,000 common shares pursuant to an earn-out provision based on performance of DaMar Plastics during the 12-month period ending Feb. 28, 2024.

Status: pending **Announced:** June 9, 2022
Salona Global Medical Device Corporation agreed to acquire a U.S.-based medical device business, which provides medical devices and equipment for physical therapy clinics, for US$14,000,000, consisting of US$9,000,000 cash, issuance of 3,300,000 common shares and a US$3,000,000 subordinated note.

Predecessor Detail - Name changed from Brattle Street Investment Corp., Dec. 15, 2020; basis 1 new for 1.35685 old shs.
Directors - Leslie H. (Les) Cross, exec. chr., Del Mar, Calif.; Lana Newishy, v-chr., Miami, Fla.; Michael (Mike) Seckler, CEO, Warren, N.J.; Dr. Kenneth B. (Ken) Kashkin, Sparta, N.J.; Kyle Wilks, Huntington Beach, Calif.
Other Exec. Officers - Dennis Nelson, CFO

Capital Stock

	Authorized (shs.)	Outstanding (shs.)[1]
Common	unlimited	56,423,091[2]
Class A	unlimited	15,717,656

[1] At May 9, 2023
[2] At July 7, 2023.
Common - One vote per share.
Class A - Convertible into common shares on a one-for-one basis, subject to certain terms and conditions. Non-voting.
Major Shareholder - MMCAP International Inc. held 10.8% interest at July 7, 2023.

Price Range - SGMD/TSX-VEN

Year	Volume	High	Low	Close
2022	13,397,742	$0.95	$0.44	$0.45
2021	20,445,284	$1.49	$0.42	$0.64
2020	6,894,281	$0.19	$0.11	$0.16
2019	11,312,980	$0.20	$0.14	$0.16
2018	12,151,527	$0.35	$0.14	$0.16

Consolidation: 1-for-1.35685 cons. in Dec. 2020
Recent Close: $0.22
Capital Stock Changes - In September 2022, 1,576,609 common shares were issued pursuant to the acquisition of DaMar Plastics Inc. Also during the 10-month period ended Dec. 31, 2022, common shares were issued as follows: 454,817 on exercise of warrants, 281,726 for financing fees, 260,921 for debt settlement and 28,154 on exercise of options. In addition, 143,000 class A non-voting shares were issued on conversion of a like number of common shares.

Wholly Owned Subsidiaries

ALG Health Plus, LLC, United States.
Arrowhead Medical, LLC
Biodex Medical Systems Inc., N.Y.
Brattle Acquisition I Corp.
DaMar Plastics Manufacturing Inc., El Cajon, Calif.
Inspira Financial Company, Wash.
- 100% int. in **DaMar Acquisition Corporation**
- 100% int. in **Mio-Guard, LLC**, United States.

Inspira SAAS Billing Inc., United States.
Mio-Tech Parent LLC
1077863 B.C. Ltd., B.C.
Pan Novus Hospital Sales Group, LLC
Simbex Acquisition Parent I Corporation
Simbex Acquisition Parent Corporation
Simbex, LLC, N.H.
South Dakota Partners, Inc., S.D.

Financial Statistics

Periods ended:	10m Dec. 31/22[A]		12m Feb. 28/22[A]
	$000s	%Chg	$000s
Operating revenue	**33,595**	**n.a.**	**18,312**
Cost of sales	23,034		12,350
General & admin expense	10,124		4,532
Stock-based compensation	1,279		1,196
Operating expense	**34,438**	**n.a.**	**18,078**
Operating income	**(843)**	**n.a.**	**234**
Deprec., depl. & amort.	1,808		842
Finance costs, gross	590		388
Write-downs/write-offs	nil		(5,521)
Pre-tax income	**(19,031)**	**n.a.**	**(4,474)**
Income taxes	(3,134)		(102)
Net income	**(15,896)**	**n.a.**	**(4,372)**
Cash & equivalent	1,928		8,057
Inventories	8,103		4,969
Accounts receivable	6,353		6,596
Current assets	16,601		20,035
Fixed assets, net	3,400		1,460
Right-of-use assets	7,782		3,942
Intangibles, net	23,071		16,760
Total assets	**52,050**	**n.a.**	**42,682**
Accts. pay. & accr. liabs	6,641		3,679
Current liabilities	30,161		23,156
Long-term debt, gross	5,933		6,353
Long-term debt, net	575		682
Long-term lease liabilities	5,983		3,934
Shareholders' equity	15,332		13,153
Cash from oper. activs	**(219)**	**n.a.**	**(3,704)**
Cash from fin. activs	(220)		3,935
Cash from invest. activs	(5,597)		(4,618)
Net cash position	**1,928**	**n.a.**	**8,057**
Capital expenditures	(639)		(55)
	$		$
Earnings per share*	(0.29)		(0.10)
Cash flow per share*	(0.00)		(0.08)
	shs		shs
No. of shs. o/s*	53,707,780		52,539,162
Avg. no. of shs. o/s*	54,841,014		43,627,051
	%		%
Net profit margin	...		(23.88)
Return on equity	...		(39.90)
Return on assets	...		(9.26)
Foreign sales percent	100		100
No. of employees (FTEs)	144		99

* Common
[A] Reported in accordance with U.S. GAAP

Latest Results

Periods ended:	3m Mar. 31/23[A]		3m Mar. 31/22[A]
	$000s	%Chg	$000s
Operating revenue	10,683	+23	8,668
Net income	(1,663)	n.a.	(594)
	$		$
Earnings per share*	(0.03)		(0.01)

* Common
[A] Reported in accordance with U.S. GAAP

Historical Summary
(as originally stated)

Fiscal Year	Oper. Rev.	Net Inc. Bef. Disc.	EPS*
	$000s	$000s	$
2022[A1]	33,595	(15,896)	(0.29)
2022[A]	18,312	(4,372)	(0.10)
2021[A2]	12,603	(4,161)	(0.10)
2021[A]	(34)	(2,667)	(0.08)
2020[B]	352	(1,768)	(0.05)

* Common
[A] Reported in accordance with U.S. GAAP
[B] Reported in accordance with IFRS
[1] 10 months ended Dec. 31, 2022.
[2] 10 months ended Dec. 31, 2021.
Note: Adjusted throughout for 1-for-1.3568521 cons. in Dec. 2020

S.22 Samurai Capital Corp.

Symbol - SSS.P **Exchange** - TSX-VEN **CUSIP** - 79607E
Head Office - 228-1122 Mainland St, Vancouver, BC, V6B 5L1 **Telephone** - (604) 808-2865 **Fax** - (604) 608-5442
Email - rcheung@mcpa.ca
Investor Relations - Ryan E. Cheung (604) 808-2865
Auditors - Crowe MacKay LLP C.A., Vancouver, B.C.
Lawyers - AFG Law LLP, Vancouver, B.C.
Transfer Agents - TSX Trust Company, Vancouver, B.C.
Profile - (B.C. 2020) Capital Pool Company.

Recent Merger and Acquisition Activity

Status: terminated **Revised:** Apr. 23, 2023
UPDATE: The transaction was terminated. PREVIOUS:Samurai Capital Corp. entered into a letter of intent for the Qualifying Transaction reverse takeover acquisition of Home Run Oil & Gas Inc., which holds oil and gas interests in the Ante Creek North area of west-central Alberta. Terms were not disclosed.

Directors - Anthony Zelen, CEO, Coldstream, B.C.; Craig Taylor, Vancouver, B.C.; David Weinkauf, Calgary, Alta.
Other Exec. Officers - Ryan E. Cheung, CFO & corp. sec.

Capital Stock

	Authorized (shs.)	Outstanding (shs.)[1]
Common	unlimited	4,400,000

[1] At June 27, 2023

Major Shareholder - Craig Taylor held 18.18% interest and Anthony Zelen held 18.18% interest at July 14, 2022.

Price Range - SSS.P/TSX-VEN

Year	Volume	High	Low	Close
2022	286,539	$0.13	$0.05	$0.06
2021	766,430	$0.30	$0.10	$0.14

Recent Close: $0.10
Capital Stock Changes - There were no changes to capital stock during fiscal 2023.

S.23 Sangoma Technologies Corporation*

Symbol - STC **Exchange** - TSX **CUSIP** - 80100R
Head Office - 100-100 Renfrew Dr, Markham, ON, L3R 9R6 **Telephone** - (905) 474-1990 **Toll-free** - (800) 388-2475 **Fax** - (905) 474-9223
Website - www.sangoma.com
Email - lstock@sangoma.com
Investor Relations - Larry Stock (800) 388-2475
Auditors - KPMG LLP C.A., Vaughan, Ont.
Lawyers - Caravel Law Professional Corporation, Toronto, Ont.
Transfer Agents - Computershare Trust Company of Canada Inc., Toronto, Ont.
FP500 Revenue Ranking - 574
Employees - 726 at June 30, 2022
Profile - (Ont. 2000; orig. Alta., 1995) Provides Communications-as-a-Service (CaaS) solutions and cloud-based Managed Service Provider (MSP) for small to medium-sized businesses (SMBs), enterprises, original equipment manufacturers (OEMs), carriers and service providers worldwide.

Primary solutions, which are typically offered with monthly, yearly or multi-year contracts, include UCaaS, Session Initiation Protocol (SIP) Trunking-as-a-Service (TaaS), Contact Center-as-a-Service (CCaaS), Communications Platform-as-a-Service (CPaaS), Video Meetings-as-a-Service (MaaS), Collaboration-as-a-Service (Collab aaS), Desktop-as-a-Service (DaaS) and Access-Control-as-a-Service (ACaaS).

UCaaS are business communication systems that can be deployed on-premise or hosted in the cloud. These include cloud-based and on-premise business phone solutions. Cloud-based solutions provide businesses with contact centre, mobility, softphone, call control and productivity features. On-premise business phone solutions include IP deskphones which work with the company's cloud and on-premise system and has a high-definition voice and plug-and-play deployment feature; headsets which work in conjunction with the desktop phones or to the company's desktop soft client; and UC clients and softphones which are available as an application on smartphones or computer and enables employees to work remotely by enabling phone calls to customers and other employees as if they were in a physical office.

SIP TaaS includes retail SIP trunking service offered through SIPStation which provides predictable monthly expenses with pricing based per trunk; and Wholesale SIP trunking primarily offered to large businesses or service provides who resell SIP trunks.

CCaaS is a cloud-based contact center, or customer experience, offering which provides robust contact center capabilities running in various ways: either standalone, in conjunction with other cloud services (such as UCaaS), or integrated inside UCaaS product in a simplified version.

CPaaS includes APIdaze platform which enables the company, its integrator/developer partners, and advanced customers to build new communications services based on voice, rest Application Program Interface (APIs), WebRTC and SMS.

MaaS includes Sangoma Meet, a video conferencing and collaboration service accessible from any device which enables file sharing on screen as well as integrates seamlessly with the user's calendar and enables Public Switched Telephone Network (PSTN) phone calls.

Collab aaS includes Team Hub, which allows users to interact using any of various forms of communications, including chatting, calling, and video.

DaaS provides companies with a secure method for staff to access their tools and applications from any location to do their work. It also delivers simplified IT administration and cuts down on the capital expenditures of deploying PCs.

ACaaS includes SmartOffice Access, a cloud-based wireless solution which allows employees to control door access completely from a smartphone app.

Also offers cloud-based Managed Service Provider (MSP) that includes Managed Security, which is called Unified Threat Management, whereby the customers network, including voice and data traffic, are secured by intrusion prevention and detection capabilities; Managed SD-WAN, which enables network redundancy through the ability to manage multiple Internet connections from multiple providers, which is seen as one seamless connection for the customer; and Managed Access, which provides a robust broadband connectivity solution, including network monitoring, analytic backup and a fully PCI-compliant offering for payment card and credit card transactions.

Has network interconnection products including Session Border Controllers (SBCs) which addresses issues of provider-to-provider connections, provider-to-enterprise connection, and enterprise-to-enterprise connections; VoIP gateways which are used by businesses to connect their traditional phone systems to a VoIP provider; and PSTN interface and media processing boards which are primarily used by communications solution developers in PC/server based telecommunications systems that connect to the PSTN that perform a very similar task to VoIP gateways, but are installed inside the server rather than being stand-alone devices. In addition, offers open source software products including Asterisk® and FreePBX®.

Recent Merger and Acquisition Activity

Status: completed **Announced:** Mar. 29, 2022
Sangoma Technologies Corporation acquired Delaware-based NetFortis Corporation, which provides Unified Communications and Unified-Communications-as-a-Service (UCaaS) and cloud-based, fully managed service provider (MSP) solutions for businesses of all sizes across all industries in North America, for US$48,800,000 cash, issuance of US$19,200,000 common shares, and up to US$12,000,000 milestone payment.

Predecessor Detail - Name changed from Sangoma.com Inc., Oct. 18, 2001.
Directors - Norman A. Worthington III, chr., Fla.; Allan J. Brett†, Kleinburg, Ont.; Al Guarino, Etobicoke, Ont.; Marc Lederman, Pa.; Joanne Moretti, Tex.
Other Exec. Officers - Larry Stock, CFO; Nenad Corbic, chief tech. officer; James (Jim) Machi, chief product & mktg. officer; Jamie Minner, chief revenue officer; Samantha Reburn, gen. counsel & corp. sec.
† Lead director

Capital Stock

	Authorized (shs.)	Outstanding (shs.)[1]
Common	unlimited	33,038,367

[1] At May 11, 2023

Options - At June 30, 2022, options were outstanding to purchase 261,252 common shares at prices ranging from US$3.01 to US$27 per share with a weighted average remaining contractual life of 2.71 years.
Major Shareholder - Widely held at Nov. 8, 2022.

Price Range - STC/TSX

Year	Volume	High	Low	Close
2022	5,895,830	$21.99	$4.70	$6.35
2021	9,461,402	$38.50	$18.55	$21.82
2020	7,452,951	$26.32	$7.56	$24.85
2019	4,661,440	$18.69	$7.70	$17.43
2018	3,218,521	$10.08	$4.90	$8.19

Consolidation: 1-for-7 cons. in Nov. 2021
Recent Close: $5.23
Capital Stock Changes - On Nov. 8, 2021, common shares were consolidated on a 1-for-7 basis. During fiscal 2022, post-consolidated common shares were issued as follows: 1,494,536 pursuant to the acquisition of NetFortis Corporation, 857,142 pursuant to the acquisition of StarBlue Inc. and 66,340 on exercise of options; 28 post-consolidated common shares were cancelled.
Long-Term Debt - At June 30, 2022, outstanding long-term debt totaled US$104,625,000 (US$17,700,000 current) and consisted of amounts of drawn on credit facilities.

Wholly Owned Subsidiaries

Sangoma Technologies Inc., Markham, Ont.
- 100% int. in **Sangoma U.S. Inc.**, Del.
  - 100% int. in **Sangoma Technologies U.S. Inc.**, Del.
    - 100% int. in **Digium, Inc.**, Huntsville, Ala.
    - 100% int. in **NetFortis Corporation**, Dallas, Tex.
      - 100% int. in **Fonality Inc.**, Del.
      - 100% int. in **NetFortis Acquisition Co., Inc.**, Del.
      - 100% int. in **NetFortis Operation Co., Inc.**, Del.
    - 100% int. in **StarBlue Inc.**, Sarasota, Fla.
      - 100% int. in **Star2Star Communications, LLC**, Del.
    - 100% int. in **VoIP Innovations, LLC**, Pittsburgh, Pa.
- 100% int. in **VoIP Supply, LLC**, Buffalo, N.Y.

Financial Statistics

Periods ended:	12m June 30/22[A]		12m June 30/21[□A]
	US$000s	%Chg	US$000s
Operating revenue	**224,352**	**+71**	**131,383**
Cost of sales	65,600		41,741
Research & devel. expense	34,158		21,438
General & admin expense	80,840		41,946
Stock-based compensation	9,929		3,758
Operating expense	**190,527**	**+75**	**108,883**
Operating income	**33,825**	**+50**	**22,500**
Deprec., depl. & amort.	39,351		16,830
Finance income	12		38
Finance costs, gross	3,875		1,946
Write-downs/write-offs	(91,685)		nil
Pre-tax income	**(104,390)**	**n.a.**	**4,384**
Income taxes	6,390		4,102
Net income	**(110,780)**	**n.a.**	**282**
Cash & equivalent	12,702		22,096
Inventories	17,426		11,820
Accounts receivable	23,943		14,734
Current assets	61,008		53,349
Fixed assets, net	10,274		7,653
Right-of-use assets	16,974		13,530
Intangibles, net	401,378		461,367
Total assets	**498,533**	**-8**	**540,347**
Accts. pay. & accr. liabs.	28,568		22,360
Current liabilities	78,406		55,173
Long-term debt, gross	104,625		74,963
Long-term debt, net	86,925		60,413
Long-term lease liabilities	14,397		11,821
Shareholders' equity	293,808		376,154
Cash from oper. activs.	**21,057**	**+14**	**18,517**
Cash from fin. activs.	25,366		91,830
Cash from invest. activs.	(55,817)		(108,246)
Net cash position	**12,702**	**-43**	**22,096**
Capital expenditures	(1,868)		(1,133)
	US$		US$
Earnings per share*	(3.52)		0.01
Cash flow per share*	0.67		0.64
	shs		shs
No. of shs. o/s*	21,439,632		19,021,644
Avg. no. of shs. o/s*	31,475,255		28,944,216[1]
	%		%
Net profit margin	(49.38)		0.21
Return on equity	(33.20)		0.13
Return on assets	(20.58)		0.12
Foreign sales percent	98		97
No. of employees (FTEs)	726		570

* Common
□ Restated
[A] Reported in accordance with IFRS
[1] Includes shares to be issued.

Latest Results

Periods ended:	9m Mar. 31/23[A]		9m Mar. 31/22[□A]
	US$000s	%Chg	US$000s
Operating revenue	188,850	+19	158,051
Net income	(5,396)	n.a.	(11,533)
	US$		US$
Earnings per share*	(0.17)		(0.36)

* Common
□ Restated
[A] Reported in accordance with IFRS

Historical Summary
(as originally stated)

Fiscal Year	Oper. Rev.	Net Inc. Bef. Disc.	EPS*
	US$000s	US$000s	US$
2022[A]	224,352	(110,780)	(3.52)
	$000s	$000s	$
2021[A]	167,345	767	0.03
2020[A]	131,418	3,905	0.39
2019[A]	109,648	1,538	0.21
2018[A]	57,362	2,453	0.46

* Common
[A] Reported in accordance with IFRS
Note: Adjusted throughout for 1-for-7 cons. in Nov. 2021

S.24 Sanibel Ventures Corp.

Symbol - SBEL.P **Exchange** - TSX-VEN (S) **CUSIP** - 80101U
Head Office - 67 5 Ave E, Vancouver, BC, V5T 1G7 **Telephone** - (778) 588-7139
Email - richard@barksdalecapital.com
Investor Relations - Richard S. Silas (778) 588-7139
Auditors - De Visser Gray LLP C.A., Vancouver, B.C.
Transfer Agents - Computershare Trust Company of Canada Inc., Vancouver, B.C.
Profile - (B.C. 2017) Capital Pool Company.

On Mar. 13, 2023, the company entered into a letter of intent for the Qualifying Transaction reverse takeover acquisition of **JM Resources Corp.**, which has mineral interests in Utah. Terms are to be entered into by the companies.

Common suspended from TSX-VEN, July 30, 2020.

Directors - Richard S. Silas, CEO, CFO & corp. sec., Vancouver, B.C.; Jeffrey M. (Jeff) O'Neill, Vancouver, B.C.; Rose Zanic, Vancouver, B.C.

Capital Stock

	Authorized (shs.)	Outstanding (shs.)[1]
Common	unlimited	4,040,000

[1] At Aug. 19, 2022

Major Shareholder - Jeffrey M. (Jeff) O'Neill held 23.51% interest and Richard S. Silas held 23.51% interest at May 21, 2021.

Price Range - SBEL.P/TSX-VEN (S)

Year	Volume	High	Low	Close
2020............	160,000	$0.22	$0.11	$0.19
2019............	190,500	$0.32	$0.12	$0.12
2018............	228,500	$0.43	$0.16	$0.19

Capital Stock Changes - There were no changes to capital stock during fiscal 2022.

S.25 Saputo Inc.*

Symbol - SAP **Exchange** - TSX **CUSIP** - 802912
Head Office - 6869 boul Métropolitain E, Montréal, QC, H1P 1X8 **Telephone** - (514) 328-6662 **Fax** - (514) 328-3364
Website - www.saputo.com
Email - investors@saputo.com
Investor Relations - Nicholas Estrela (866) 648-5902
Auditors - KPMG LLP C.A., Montréal, Qué.
Lawyers - Stikeman Elliott LLP, Montréal, Qué.
Transfer Agents - Computershare Trust Company of Canada Inc., Montréal, Qué.
FP500 Revenue Ranking - 39
Employees - 19,200 at Mar. 31, 2023

Profile - (Can. 1992 amalg.) Produces, markets and distributes a wide variety of dairy products, including cheeses, fluid milk, extended shelf-life milk and cream products, cultured products and dairy ingredients, as well as dairy alternative cheeses and beverages to the retail, foodservice and industrial markets. Products are sold in more than 60 countries under various brand names.

Operations are organized into four geographic sectors: Canada, consisting of the Dairy Division (Canada); USA, consisting of the Dairy Division (USA); International, consisting of the Dairy Division (Australia) and Dairy Division (Argentina); and Europe, consisting of the Dairy Division (U.K.).

Canada

The company produces, markets and distributes in Canada a variety of cheeses including everyday cheeses such as mozzarella and cheddar; specialty cheeses such as ricotta, provolone, parmesan, goat cheese, feta, havarti and soft cheeses; and processed cheeses. Cheese products are sold under brand names such as Saputo, Armstrong, Alexis de Portneuf, Bari, Cogruet, DuVillage 1860, Kingsey, Shepherd Gourmet Dairy, Stella and Woolwich Goat Dairy, as well as under customer brand names. In addition, the company distributes fine imported cheeses to specialty stores as well as various dairy and non-dairy products manufactured by third parties that are complementary to the products manufactured by the company.

The company also produces, markets and distributes fluid milk, cream, yogurt, sour cream, cottage cheese and ice cream mixes. Fluid milk is sold under the brands Dairyland in western Canada, Neilson in Ontario, Nutrilait in Quebec and Baxter and Scotsburn in Atlantic Canada. Value-added milk is marketed under the brands Trutaste, Milk2Go/Lait's Go and Joyya.

Other dairy and non-dairy products include butter under the Dairyland, Neilson, Saputo, Baxter and Scotsburn brands, flavoured cream under the Baileys brand, and dips under the Heluva Good brand. In addition, numerous dairy ingredients including milk powder, whey powder, lactose and whey protein concentrates are produced and marketed for the Canadian and international markets.

The company operates 18 manufacturing facilities in Canada, all of which are owned by the company except one.

USA

The company produces, markets and distributes in the U.S. a wide array of products including cheese, extended shelf-life and aseptic dairy and non-dairy fluid products, cultured products and dairy ingredients.

Cheese portfolio includes various everyday and specialty cheeses such as mozzarella, string cheese, blue cheese, goat cheese, provolone, snacking, ricotta, parmesan, feta, cheddar and romano, as well as dairy alternative cheeses. Cheeses are sold under various brand names including Black Creek, Frigo, Frigo Cheese Heads, Great Midwest, Montchevre, Organic Creamery, Salemville, Saputo, Saputo Gold, Stella, Treasure Cave and Vitalite, as well as under customer brand names. The company also holds import licences for the sale and distribution of a broad range of specialty cheeses manufactured abroad.

Extended shelf-life and cultured dairy products portfolio includes ice cream mixes, half and half, whipping cream, value-added beverages, dairy and non-dairy creamers, coffee beverages, aerosol whipped toppings, almond milk, oat milk, aseptic food products and beverages, sour cream and cottage cheese. These products are sold under customer brand names, as well as under the company's own brands such as DairyStar and Friendship Dairies.

Dairy ingredient products include whey powder, whey protein concentrates, lactose, goat whey and dairy ingredient blends which are produced and marketed for the U.S. and international markets.

The company operates 29 manufacturing facilities in the U.S., all of which are owned by the company except two, as well as a commercial culinary innovation facility.

International

In Australia, the company produces, markets and distributes for the Australian and international markets a full range of dairy products, including cheeses, butter and butter blends, milk, cream and dairy beverages. Products are sold under brand names such as CHEER, Cracker Barrel, Devondale, Fred Walker, Great Ocean Road, King Island Dairy, Liddells, Mersey Valley, Mil Lel, Murray Goulburn Ingredients, Warrnambool, South Cape, Sungold and Tasmanian Heritage. The company also offers dairy ingredients and nutritional products, including milk powder, whey protein concentrates, lactoferrin and infant formula.

In Argentina, the company produces, markets and distributes for the Argentinean and international markets a variety of cheeses, butter and cream under various brands such as La Paulina, Molfino, Saputo, Stella and Ricrem. In addition, the company produces dairy ingredients, including milk powder, casein and whey protein.

The company operates 12 manufacturing facilities in Australia (10) and Argentina (2), all of which are owned by the company except two.

Europe

The company produces, markets and distributes in the U.K. a variety of cheeses, butter, spreads and oils under brands names such as Cathedral City, Clover, Country Life, Davidstow, Frylight and Wensleydale Creamery; non-dairy spreads under the Vitalite brand; dairy alternative cheeses under the Cathedral City, Sheese and Vitalite brands; and dairy ingredients such as demineralized whey powder and galacto-oligosaccharide (GOS).

The company operates seven manufacturing facilities in the U.K., all of which are owned by the company except two.

During fiscal 2023, the company announced capital investments and consolidation initiatives to streamline and enhance its manufacturing operations. These included: closure of the cheese packing facility in Frome, U.K., to consolidate all cheese packing into the facility in Nuneaton, U.K.; conversion of the mozzarella cheese manufacturing facility in Reedsburg, Wisc., to a goat cheese manufacturing plant, and closure of the goat cheese manufacturing facility in Belmont, Wisc.; closure of a facility in Maffra, Vic., and streamlining activities at facilities in Leongatha, Vic., and Mil-Lel, S.A.; construction of a new cut-and-wrap facility in Franklin, Wisc., to consolidate packaging operations from other manufacturing sites in the U.S. Midwest, leading to the closure of facilities in Big Stone, S.D., and Green Bay, Wisc.; and conversion of a former cut-and-wrap facility in Tulare, Calif., into a string cheese packaging facility, resulting in the closure of the South Gate, Calif., facility.

Recent Merger and Acquisition Activity

Status: pending **Announced:** Apr. 1, 2023
Saputo Inc. agreed to sell two fresh milk processing facilities in Australia to Coles Group Limited, an Australian-based supermarket, retail and consumer services chain, for A$105,000,000 (Cdn$95,000,000). The facilities were located in Laverton North, Vic., and Erskine Park, N.S.W. The transaction was subject to customary conditions, including the clearance from the Australian Competition and Consumer Commission, and was expected to be completed in the second half of 2023.

Predecessor Detail - Name changed from Saputo Group Inc., Oct. 19, 2000.

Directors - Emmanuele A. (Lino) Saputo Jr., chr., pres. & CEO, Montréal, Qué.; Anthony M. (Tony) Fata†, Montréal, Qué.; Henry E. Demone, Lunenburg, N.S.; Olu Fajemirokun-Beck, N.J.; Annalisa King, Vancouver, B.C.; Karen A. Kinsley, Ottawa, Ont.; Diane Nyisztor, Saint-Lambert, Qué.; Franziska Ruf, Qué.; Annette M. Verschuren, Toronto, Ont.

Other Exec. Officers - Maxime Therrien, CFO & corp. sec.; Martin Gagnon, chief acq. & strategic devel. officer; Gaétane Wagner, chief HR officer; Tom Atherton, pres. & COO, dairy div., U.K.; Marcelo Cohen, pres. & COO, dairy div., Argentina; Carl Colizza, pres. & COO, North America; Leanne Cutts, pres. & COO, intl. & Europe; Frank Guido, pres. & COO, dairy div., U.S.A.; Haig Poutchigian, pres. & COO, dairy div., Canada; Richard Wallace, pres. & COO, dairy div., Australia

† Lead director

Capital Stock

	Authorized (shs.)	Outstanding (shs.)[1]
Common	unlimited	422,646,292

[1] At July 31, 2023

Options - At Mar. 31, 2023, options were outstanding to purchase 19,988,303 common shares at a weighted average exercise price of $38.02 per share expiring up to 2033.

Major Shareholder - Emanuele (Lino) Saputo held 32.2% interest and Francesco Saputo held 10.1% interest at May 31, 2023.

Price Range - SAP/TSX

Year	Volume	High	Low	Close
2022............	131,397,624	$36.05	$24.61	$33.52
2021............	123,470,765	$42.42	$27.54	$28.50
2020............	123,671,373	$41.95	$29.31	$35.63
2019............	116,826,716	$46.41	$37.38	$40.20
2018............	104,867,819	$45.76	$35.56	$39.19

Recent Close: $28.86

Capital Stock Changes - During fiscal 2023, common shares were issued as follows: 3,182,091 under dividend reinvestment plan and 1,684,724 on exercise of options.

During fiscal 2022, common shares were issued as follows: 2,783,718 under dividend reinvestment plan and 1,620,752 on exercise of options.

Dividends

SAP com Ra $0.74 pa Q est. Sept. 15, 2023**[1]
Prev. Rate: $0.72 est. Sept. 17, 2021
Prev. Rate: $0.70 est. Oct. 2, 2020

[1] Dividend reinvestment plan implemented eff. May 28, 2020.
** Reinvestment Option

Long-Term Debt - Outstanding at Mar. 31, 2023:

Term loans[1]...	$497,000,000
2.83% sr. notes due Nov. 2023................	300,000,000
2.88% sr. notes due Nov. 2024................	400,000,000
3.6% sr. notes due Aug. 2025..................	350,000,000
1.42% sr. notes due June 2026................	350,000,000
2.24% sr. notes due June 2027................	700,000,000
2.3% sr. notes due June 2028..................	300,000,000
5.25% sr. notes due Nov. 2029................	300,000,000
Other debt..	54,000,000
	3,251,000,000
Less: Current portion................................	307,000,000
	2,944,000,000

[1] Bear interest at prime rates plus up to 1%, or bankers' acceptance rates, Australian bank bill rate or SOFR plus 0.8% to 2%, depending on the company's credit ratings. Due June 2025.

Principal repayments are due as follows:

Fiscal 2024...	$307,000,000
Fiscal 2025...	413,000,000
Fiscal 2026...	847,000,000
Fiscal 2027...	350,000,000
Fiscal 2028...	734,000,000
Thereafter..	600,000,000

Wholly Owned Subsidiaries

Dairy Crest Limited, Esher, Surrey, United Kingdom.
Molfino Hermanos S.A., Argentina.
Saputo Cheese USA, Inc., Del.
Saputo Dairy Australia Pty Ltd., Australia.
- 100% int. in **Warrnambool Cheese and Butter Factory Company Holdings Limited**, Vic., Australia.

Saputo Dairy Products Canada G.P., Qué.

Note: The preceding list includes only the major related companies in which interests are held.

Financial Statistics

Periods ended:	12m Mar. 31/23^A		12m Mar. 31/22^A
	$000s	%Chg	$000s
Operating revenue	**17,843,000**	**+19**	**15,035,000**
Cost of goods sold	12,433,000		10,365,000
Salaries & benefits	2,108,000		1,877,000
General & admin expense	1,749,000		1,638,000
Operating expense	**16,290,000**	**+17**	**13,880,000**
Operating income	**1,553,000**	**+34**	**1,155,000**
Deprec., depl. & amort.	582,000		560,000
Finance costs, gross	101,000		70,000
Write-downs/write-offs	(65,000)		(118,000)
Pre-tax income	**775,000**	**+91**	**405,000**
Income taxes	153,000		131,000
Net income	**622,000**	**+127**	**274,000**
Cash & equivalent	263,000		165,000
Inventories	2,872,000		2,503,000
Accounts receivable	1,621,000		1,500,000
Current assets	4,851,000		4,295,000
Long-term investments	36,000		35,000
Fixed assets, net	4,286,000		3,962,000
Right-of-use assets	446,000		475,000
Intangibles, net	4,621,000		4,559,000
Total assets	**14,425,000**	**+5**	**13,683,000**
Bank indebtedness	356,000		419,000
Accts. pay. & accr. liabs.	2,149,000		1,952,000
Current liabilities	3,002,000		2,780,000
Long-term debt, gross	3,251,000		3,375,000
Long-term debt, net	2,944,000		3,075,000
Long-term lease liabilities	342,000		386,000
Shareholders' equity	7,140,000		6,505,000
Cash from oper. activs.	**1,025,000**	**+48**	**693,000**
Cash from fin. activs.	(369,000)		(72,000)
Cash from invest. activs.	(632,000)		(799,000)
Net cash position	**263,000**	**+59**	**165,000**
Capital expenditures	(617,000)		(453,000)
Capital disposals	9,000		70,000
Pension fund surplus	75,000		235,000
	$		$
Earnings per share*	1.49		0.66
Cash flow per share*	2.45		1.67
Cash divd. per share*	0.72		0.72
	shs		shs
No. of shs. o/s*	421,604,856		416,738,041
Avg. no. of shs. o/s*	418,620,009		414,137,462
	%		%
Net profit margin	3.49		1.82
Return on equity	9.12		4.23
Return on assets	5.00		2.40
Foreign sales percent	74		72
No. of employees (FTEs)	19,200		18,600

* Common
^A Reported in accordance with IFRS

Latest Results

Periods ended:	3m June 30/23^A		3m June 30/22^A
	$000s	%Chg	$000s
Operating revenue	4,207,000	-3	4,327,000
Net income	141,000	+1	139,000
	$		$
Earnings per share*	0.33		0.33

* Common
^A Reported in accordance with IFRS

Historical Summary
(as originally stated)

Fiscal Year	Oper. Rev.	Net Inc. Bef. Disc.	EPS*
	$000s	$000s	$
2023^A	17,843,000	622,000	1.49
2022^A	15,035,000	274,000	0.66
2021^A	14,293,900	625,600	1.53
2020^A	14,943,500	582,800	1.46
2019^A	13,501,900	755,300	1.94

* Common
^A Reported in accordance with IFRS

S.26 Saskatchewan Power Corporation

CUSIP - 417990
Head Office - 2025 Victoria Ave, Regina, SK, S4P 0S1 **Telephone** - (306) 566-2121 **Toll-free** - (888) 757-6937 **Fax** - (306) 566-2548
Website - www.saskpower.com
Email - tking@saskpower.com
Investor Relations - Troy King (306) 566-2872
Auditors - Deloitte LLP C.A., Regina, Sask.
FP500 Subsidiary Revenue Ranking - 35
Employees - 3,057 at Mar. 31, 2022
Profile - (Sask. 1950) Provincial Crown corporation that generates, purchases, transmits, distributes and sells electricity and related products and services in the Province of Saskatchewan.

Operates seven natural gas stations, three coal-fired power stations, five hydroelectric stations and two wind generation facilities with an aggregate generating capacity of 3,968 MW. Also buys power from various independent power producers, with an aggregate generating capacity of 1,081 MW, including the gas-fired North Battleford generating station, the gas-fired Meridian cogeneration station at Lloydminister, the gas-fired Spy Hill generating station near Esterhazy, the Riverhurst wind energy project southwest of Riverhurst, the Red Lily wind energy project near Moosomin, the SunBridge wind power project near Swift Current, the Western Lily wind energy project near Grenfell, the Morse wind energy project, the SunBridge wind power project, the Golden South wind energy project south of Assiniboia and the Highfield solar energy project east of Swift Current. In addition, has customer-generated solar capacity of 44 MW, two import power purchase agreements with Manitoba Hydro for a total of 125 MW, and total capacity of 28 MW from small independent power producers (includes flare gas, waste heat recovery, landfill gas and wind), bringing its total available generating capacity to 5,246 MW (at Mar. 31, 2022).

Periods ended:	12m Mar. 31/22	12m Mar. 31/21
Electric sales, GWh	23,995	22,903
Generating capacity, MW	5,246	4,987
Avg. electric price, $/MWh	110	111
Transmission lines, km	14,673	14,600
Distribution lines, km	142,713	142,972
Electric. customers	549,940	545,179

Directors - Chief Darcy Bear, chr., Saskatoon, Sask.; Bryan Leverick, v-chr., Saskatoon, Sask.; Don Atchison, Saskatoon, Sask.; A. Terence (Terry) Bergan, Saskatoon, Sask.; Amber Biemans, Humboldt, Sask.; Bevra Fee, Sask.; Shawn Grice, Regina, Sask.; Jim Hopson, Regina, Sask.; Cherilyn Jolly-Nagel, Mossbank, Sask.; Fred Matheson, Prince Albert, Sask.; Robert (Rob) Nicolay, Estevan, Sask.; Jeff Richards, Weyburn, Sask.; The Hon. Vaughn Solomon Schofield, Sask.; Tammy Van Lambalgen, Saskatoon, Sask.; Stephanie Yong, Saskatoon, Sask.
Other Exec. Officers - Rupen Pandya, pres. & CEO; Kory Hayko, exec. v-p, COO & pres. & CEO, NorthPoint Energy Solutions Inc.; Troy King, exec. v-p & chief strategy, tech. & finl. officer; Kathryn Pollack, exec. v-p, people, safety & indigenous & corp. rel.; Rachelle Verret Morphy, exec. v-p, legal & corp. srvcs. & gen. counsel; Tim Eckel, v-p, energy transition & asset mgt.; Howard Matthews, v-p, generation; Shawn Schmidt, v-p, trans. & distrib.; Neil Henneberg, corp. sec.
Major Shareholder - Crown Investments Corporation of Saskatchewan held 100% interest at Mar. 31, 2022.

Wholly Owned Subsidiaries
NorthPoint Energy Solutions Inc., Sask.

Financial Statistics

Periods ended:	12m Mar. 31/22^A		12m Mar. 31/21^A
	$000s	%Chg	$000s
Operating revenue	**2,885,000**	**+4**	**2,771,000**
Salaries & benefits	346,000		346,000
Operating expense	**1,744,000**	**+16**	**1,507,000**
Operating income	**1,141,000**	**-10**	**1,264,000**
Deprec., depl. & amort.	612,000		595,000
Finance income	15,000		25,000
Finance costs, gross	416,000		451,000
Pre-tax income	**11,000**	**-93**	**160,000**
Net income	**11,000**	**-93**	**160,000**
Cash & equivalent	32,000		98,000
Inventories	293,000		251,000
Accounts receivable	362,000		433,000
Current assets	754,000		811,000
Fixed assets, net	10,133,000		9,816,000
Right-of-use assets	516,000		565,000
Intangibles, net	77,000		68,000
Total assets	**12,229,000**	**+1**	**12,133,000**
Accts. pay. & accr. liabs.	692,000		567,000
Current liabilities	1,690,000		1,301,000
Long-term debt, gross	6,495,000		6,741,000
Long-term debt, net	6,239,000		6,501,000
Long-term lease liabilities	904,000		946,000
Shareholders' equity	2,960,000		2,853,000
Cash from oper. activs.	**738,000**	**-9**	**814,000**
Cash from fin. activs.	108,000		(294,000)
Cash from invest. activs.	(912,000)		(658,000)
Net cash position	**32,000**	**-67**	**98,000**
Capital expenditures	(876,000)		(660,000)
Capital disposals	8,000		2,000
Unfunded pension liability	86,000		162,000
	$		$
Earnings per share*	n.a.		n.a.
	shs		shs
No. of shs. o/s	n.a.		n.a.
	%		%
Net profit margin	0.38		5.77
Return on equity	0.38		5.71
Return on assets	3.51		5.02
No. of employees (FTEs)	3,057		3,036

^A Reported in accordance with IFRS

Historical Summary
(as originally stated)

Fiscal Year	Oper. Rev.	Net Inc. Bef. Disc.	EPS*
	$000s	$000s	$
2022^A	2,885,000	11,000	n.a.
2021^A	2,771,000	160,000	n.a.
2020^A	2,772,000	205,000	n.a.
2019^A	2,722,000	197,000	n.a.
2018^A	2,586,000	146,000	n.a.

* Common
^A Reported in accordance with IFRS

S.27 Satellos Bioscience Inc.

Symbol - MSCL **Exchange** - TSX-VEN **CUSIP** - 80401L
Head Office - Royal Bank Plaza, South Tower, 2800-200 Bay St, Toronto, ON, M5J 2J1 **Telephone** - (647) 660-1780
Website - satellos.com
Email - fgleeson@satellos.com
Investor Relations - Frank Gleeson (905) 336-6128
Auditors - MNP LLP C.A., Toronto, Ont.
Transfer Agents - Computershare Trust Company of Canada Inc., Vancouver, B.C.
Employees - 3 at Dec. 31, 2022
Profile - (Can. 2021) Develops novel therapeutics that stimulate or restore muscle regeneration in severe disorders, with a lead program focused on an oral therapeutic drug for Duchenne muscular dystrophy, a fatal genetic disorder diagnosed in childhood.

The company applies its proprietary MyoReGenX™ discovery platform to identify regulatory pathways and drug candidates to treat muscle disorders where stem cell polarity is dysregulated.

Lead product candidates include SAT-3153, a small molecule designed to inhibit a particular kinase protein which controls Notch polarity within muscle stem cells to treat Duchenne muscular dystrophy; and Project Gamma, which has a potential to be modulated by small molecule drugs to affect symmetric muscle stem cell divisions to enhance regeneration.

Also owns legacy assets including the Oral AmpB Delivery System (OralTrans™) (Phase I), which treats systemic fungal infections in immune-compromised patients (in HIV/AIDS, cancer, transplant recipients, diabetes) and certain parasitical infections in the developing world such as visceral leishmaniasis; and iCo-008 (Bertilimumab), a human monoclonal antibody which treats bullous pemphigoid and may have utility in atopic dermatitis, gastrointestinal conditions including inflammatory bowel disease/ulcerative colitis, vernal keratoconjunctivitis, asthma and age-related macular degeneration.

NW Micelle Therapeutics Inc. (15% owned) is developing an oral formulation of cannabidiol (CBD) using OralTrans™ technology for the treatment of insomnia.

In October 2022, wholly owned **Amphotericin B Technologies, Inc.** and **NW PharmaTech Limited** established **NW Micelle Therapeutics Inc.**, to develop an oral formulation of cannabidiol (CBD) using the company's OralTrans™ technology for the treatment of insomnia. Amphotericin B and NW PharmaTech holds 15% and 85% interest in NW Micelle, respectively.

Predecessor Detail - Succeeded iCo Therapeutics Inc., Aug. 13, 2021, pursuant to the reverse takeover acquisition of (old) Satellos Bioscience Inc.; basis 1 new for 20 old shs.
Directors - Geoff MacKay, chr., Me.; Frank Gleeson, pres. & CEO, Markham, Ont.; William Jarosz, exec. dir., Mont.; Dr. Rima Al-awar, Ont.; Franklin M. Berger, New York, N.Y.; Brian M. Bloom, Toronto, Ont.; Dr. William (Bill) McVicar, Mass.; Adam Mostafa, Mass.
Other Exec. Officers - Warren Whitehead, CFO; Dr. Alan K. Jacobs, CMO; Philip Lambert, chief tech. officer; Dr. Michael Rudnicki, chief scientific officer; J. Robert (Rob) Hall, v-p, fin. & admin.; Dr. Sridhar Narayan, v-p, drug discovery & program leadership

Capital Stock

	Authorized (shs.)	Outstanding (shs.)[1]
Common	unlimited	112,791,658

[1] At May 30, 2023

Major Shareholder - Widely held at May 29, 2023.

Price Range - MSCL/TSX-VEN

Year	Volume	High	Low	Close
2022	10,351,421	$1.20	$0.22	$0.22
2021	13,396,547	$3.20	$1.00	$1.00
2020	6,111,036	$1.70	$0.40	$1.20
2019	4,924,897	$2.90	$0.90	$1.60
2018	14,369,714	$5.50	$0.60	$1.00

Consolidation: 1-for-20 cons. in Aug. 2021
Recent Close: $0.41
Capital Stock Changes - In May 2023, public offering of 70,297,200 common shares was completed at 50¢ per share.

In September 2022, public offering of 8,750,000 units (1 common share & ½ warrant) at 40¢ per unit was completed. Also during 2022, 50,000 on acquisition of intellectual property.

Wholly Owned Subsidiaries
Amphotericin B Technologies, Inc.
- 15% int. in **NW Micelle Therapeutics Inc.**

iCo Therapeutics Australia Pty Ltd., Australia.

Financial Statistics

Periods ended:	12m Dec. 31/22[A]		12m Dec. 31/21[◻A]
	$000s	%Chg	$000s
Research & devel. expense	2,587		2,004
General & admin expense	3,999		1,669
Stock-based compensation	1,440		972
Operating expense	**8,026**	**+73**	**4,645**
Operating income	**(8,026)**	**n.a.**	**(4,645)**
Deprec., depl. & amort.	337		166
Finance income	21		8
Finance costs, gross	nil		985
Investment income	42		nil
Pre-tax income	**(11,317)**	**n.a.**	**(15,506)**
Income taxes	5		nil
Net income	**(11,322)**	**n.a.**	**(15,506)**
Cash & equivalent	1,924		4,871
Accounts receivable	nil		2
Current assets	2,233		5,443
Long-term investments	42		nil
Fixed assets, net	8		8
Intangibles, net	3,916		7,135
Total assets	**6,199**	**-51**	**12,586**
Accts. pay. & accr. liabs	2,830		2,104
Current liabilities	2,830		2,104
Shareholders' equity	3,369		10,482
Cash from oper. activs	**(5,713)**	**n.a.**	**(5,034)**
Cash from fin. activs	2,775		7,451
Cash from invest. activs	(3)		1,738
Net cash position	**1,924**	**-61**	**4,871**
Capital expenditures	(3)		(7)
	$		$
Earnings per share*	(0.32)		(0.64)
Cash flow per share*	(0.16)		(0.21)
	shs		shs
No. of shs. o/s*	41,797,613		32,997,613
Avg. no. of shs. o/s*	35,680,113		24,076,457
	%		%
Net profit margin	n.a.		n.a.
Return on equity	(163.48)		n.m.
Return on assets	(120.54)		(221.15)
No. of employees (FTEs)	3		3

* Common
◻ Restated
[A] Reported in accordance with IFRS

Latest Results

Periods ended:	3m Mar. 31/23[A]		3m Mar. 31/22[A]
	$000s	%Chg	$000s
Net income	(1,666)	n.a.	(2,116)
	$		$
Earnings per share*	(0.04)		(0.06)

* Common
[A] Reported in accordance with IFRS

Historical Summary
(as originally stated)

Fiscal Year	Oper. Rev.	Net Inc. Bef. Disc.	EPS*
	$000s	$000s	$
2022[A]	nil	(11,322)	(0.32)
2021[A1]	nil	(15,506)	(0.64)
2020[A]	nil	(1,488)	(0.20)
2019[A]	nil	(1,938)	(0.40)
2018[A]	nil	(1,703)	(0.40)

* Common
[A] Reported in accordance with IFRS
[1] Results reflect the Aug. 13, 2021, reverse takeover acquisition of Satellos Bioscience Inc. (old)

Note: Adjusted throughout for 1-for-20 cons. in Aug. 2021

S.28 Savanna Capital Corp.

Symbol - SAC.P **Exchange** - TSX-VEN **CUSIP** - 804675
Head Office - 198 Davenport Rd, Toronto, ON, M5R 1J2 **Telephone** - (416) 861-2267
Email - kenny.choi@fmresources.ca
Investor Relations - Kenny Choi (416) 861-2262
Auditors - McGovern Hurley LLP C.A., Toronto, Ont.
Lawyers - Double Diamond Law Corporation, Whistler, B.C.
Transfer Agents - Computershare Trust Company of Canada Inc., Vancouver, B.C.
Profile - (B.C. 2017) Capital Pool Company.
On Mar. 1, 2022, the company agreed to the Qualifying Transaction reverse takeover acquisition of private Ontario-based **1000090242 Ontario Inc.** (San Luis ON), which holds the 1,217-hectare formerly producing San Luis silver-copper-zinc property in Mexico, on a share-for-share basis, which would result in the issuance of 40,000,000 common shares, inclusive of a private placement San Luis ON plans to complete of 10,000,000 units (1 common share & 1 warrant) at 15¢ per unit prior to closing of the transaction. Upon completion, San Luis ON would amalgamate with a wholly owned subsidiary of the company, and the company would change its name to **Plata Corp.**
Directors - Alexandros (Alexander) Tzilios, pres., CEO & corp. sec., North Vancouver, B.C.; Deborah (Deb) Battiston, Fort Erie, Ont.; Frederic W. R. (Fred) Leigh, Toronto, Ont.; Brent Lokash, Vancouver, B.C.
Other Exec. Officers - Ryan Ptolemy, CFO

Capital Stock

	Authorized (shs.)	Outstanding (shs.)[1]
Preferred	unlimited	nil
Common	unlimited	4,615,000

[1] At July 17, 2023

Major Shareholder - Frederic W. R. (Fred) Leigh held 21.67% interest and Alexandros (Alexander) Tzilios held 17.33% interest at Feb. 25, 2022.

Price Range - SAC.P/TSX-VEN

Year	Volume	High	Low	Close
2022	2,500	$0.05	$0.05	$0.05
2019	712,000	$0.12	$0.10	$0.11
2018	997,250	$0.24	$0.07	$0.10

Capital Stock Changes - There were no changes to capital stock during 2021 or 2022.

S.29 Savaria Corporation

Symbol - SIS **Exchange** - TSX **CUSIP** - 805112
Head Office - 4350 aut 13, Laval, QC, H7R 6E9 **Telephone** - (450) 681-5655 **Toll-free** - (800) 931-5655 **Fax** - (450) 628-4500
Website - www.savaria.com
Email - nrimbert@savaria.com
Investor Relations - Nicolas Rimbert (800) 931-5655
Auditors - KPMG LLP C.A., Montréal, Qué.
Bankers - National Bank of Canada, Montréal, Qué.
Lawyers - Blake, Cassels & Graydon LLP, Montréal, Qué.; McLeod Law LLP, Calgary, Alta.
Transfer Agents - Computershare Trust Company of Canada Inc., Montréal, Qué.
FP500 Revenue Ranking - 380
Employees - 2,300 at Mar. 15, 2023
Profile - (Alta. 1999) Provides accessibility solutions for the elderly and physically challenged individuals in Canada, the United States and internationally.
Operations are carried out through three segments: Accessibility; Patient Care (formerly Patient Handling); and Adapted Vehicles.
The **Accessibility** segment designs, manufactures, distributes and installs accessibility products for individuals with mobility impairments, such as stairlifts for both straight and curved stairs, vertical and inclined wheelchair lifts, and elevators for home and commercial use. Products are distributed worldwide through a network of more than 1,500 dealers as well as 30 direct sales offices.
The **Patient Care** segment, carried out through wholly owned **Span-America Medical Systems, Inc.**, designs and manufactures medical beds, therapeutic support surfaces and pressure management products used in healthcare facilities such as long-term care and nursing homes; and through wholly owned **Silvalea Ltd.**, manufactures patient transfer slings and accessories.Products include patient positioners, mattress overlays, wheelchair cushions and other foam products.
The **Adapted Vehicles** segment, carried out through wholly owned **Van-Action (2005) Inc.** and **Freedom Motors Inc.**, designs and manufactures lowered-floor wheelchair accessible conversions for selected brands of minivans. Wholly owned **Silver Cross Automotive Inc.** distributes converted vehicles in the Ontario, Alberta and British Columbia retail markets.
Operates a global manufacturing network with 16 plants in Canada (6), the U.S. (2), Mexico (1), Europe (5) and the People's Republic of China (2).
In November 2022, the company agreed to sell wholly owned **Handicare AS** to **Drive AS**, a subsidiary of an automotive company **Cognia AS**, for terms not yet disclosed. The transaction is expected to closed in late March or early April 2023. Handicare has service depots across Norway and focuses on commercial adaptations including emergency-use police, fire and rescue, and paramedic vehicles.
Predecessor Detail - Name changed from Jessian Capital Corp., Mar. 1, 2002, following Qualifying Transaction acquisition of Services Industriels Savaria Inc.
Directors - Marcel Bourassa, founder, chr., pres. & CEO, Georgetown, Ont.; Sebastien Bourassa, COO, Burlington, Ont.; Peter Drutz†, Richmond Hill, Ont.; Caroline Bérubé, Singapore, Singapore; Jean-Marie Bourassa, Montréal, Qué.; Jean-Louis Chapdelaine, Pointe-Claire, Qué.; Sylvain Dumoulin, L'Ile-Bizard, Qué.; Anne Le Breton, Qué.; Alain Tremblay, Terrebonne, Qué.
Other Exec. Officers - Stephen Reitknecht, CFO; Sylvain Aubry, chief legal officer & corp. sec.; Les Teague, grp. pres., patient care; Clare Brophy, exec. v-p, comml. Europe; Alexandre Bourassa, v-p, sales; Laureen Cushing, v-p, HR; Vince Sciamanna, pres., Garaventa Canada Ltd.
† Lead director

Capital Stock

	Authorized (shs.)	Outstanding (shs.)[1]
First Preferred	unlimited	
Series A	7,000,000	nil
Second Preferred	unlimited	nil
Common	unlimited	64,513,987

[1] At Mar. 28, 2023

Major Shareholder - Marcel Bourassa held 20.5% interest at Mar. 28, 2023.

Price Range - SIS/TSX

Year	Volume	High	Low	Close
2022	21,091,780	$19.26	$12.02	$13.99
2021	32,380,709	$22.63	$14.29	$19.16
2020	34,114,913	$16.42	$7.31	$14.46
2019	36,583,290	$15.45	$10.55	$13.95
2018	32,543,740	$20.95	$11.41	$13.06

Recent Close: $15.88
Capital Stock Changes - During 2022, 221,832 common shares were issued on exercise of options.

Dividends

SIS com Ra $0.5196 pa M est. July 7, 2023[1]
Prev. Rate: $0.52 est. Oct. 7, 2022
Prev. Rate: $0.50 est. Oct. 8, 2021
Prev. Rate: $0.48 est. Oct. 8, 2020
[1] Divds. paid quarterly prior to Oct. 2017.

Wholly Owned Subsidiaries

Companion Stairlifts Limited, United Kingdom.
Florida Lifts LLC, Boynton Beach, Fla.
Freedom Motors Inc., Ont.
Garaventa Accessibility AG, Switzerland.
Garaventa (Canada) Ltd., Canada.
Garaventa Lift S.r.l., Italy.
Garaventa USA Inc., Ill.
Savaria Concord Lifts Inc., Brampton, Ont.
Savaria (Huizhou) Mechanical Equipment Manufacturing Co., People's Republic of China.
Savaria Sales Installation and Services Inc., London, Ont.
Savaria USA Inc, Vt.
Silvalea Ltd., Devon, United Kingdom.
Silver Cross Automotive Inc.
Silver Cross Franchising Inc., Brampton, Ont.
Span-America Medical Systems, Inc., Greenville, S.C.
• 100% int. in **Span Medical Products Canada ULC**, B.C.
Ultron Technologies Ltd., United Kingdom.
Van-Action (2005) Inc., Saint-Laurent, Qué.

Subsidiaries

95.2% int. in **Handicare Group AB**, Kista, Sweden.
• 100% int. in **Handicare Accessibility Limited**, United Kingdom.
• 100% int. in **Handicare Accessibility LLC**, Del.
• 100% int. in **Handicare AS**, Norway.
• 100% int. in **Handicare Canada Ltd.**, Ont.
• 100% int. in **Handicare Stairlifts B.V.**, Netherlands.
• 100% int. in **Handicare USA LLC**, Del.

Financial Statistics

Periods ended:	12m Dec. 31/22[A]		12m Dec. 31/21[A]
	$000s	%Chg	$000s
Operating revenue	**789,091**	**+19**	**660,983**
Cost of sales	534,722		445,447
General & admin expense	134,144		115,286
Stock-based compensation	1,862		1,747
Operating expense	**670,728**	**+19**	**562,480**
Operating income	**118,363**	**+20**	**98,503**
Deprec., depl. & amort.	49,102		49,323
Finance income	426		105
Finance costs, gross	16,895		15,861
Pre-tax income	**47,472**	**+136**	**20,128**
Income taxes	12,161		8,593
Net income	**35,311**	**+206**	**11,535**
Cash & equivalent	44,725		63,494
Inventories	144,261		128,496
Accounts receivable	99,450		102,497
Current assets	327,314		320,726
Fixed assets, net	59,168		54,831
Right-of-use assets	41,796		51,248
Intangibles, net	649,177		659,072
Total assets	**1,109,963**	**0**	**1,106,920**
Accts. pay. & accr. liabs.	99,171		107,251
Current liabilities	182,439		166,411
Long-term debt, gross	366,882		379,991
Long-term debt, net	365,717		378,933
Long-term lease liabilities	35,031		42,430
Shareholders' equity	452,969		434,600
Cash from oper. activs.	**90,742**	**+58**	**57,277**
Cash from fin. activs.	(83,253)		351,796
Cash from invest. activs.	(21,583)		(396,439)
Net cash position	**44,725**	**-30**	**63,494**
Capital expenditures	(11,509)		(6,565)
Capital disposals	322		230
Unfunded pension liability	639		6,556
	$		$
Earnings per share*	0.55		0.19
Cash flow per share*	1.41		0.93
Cash divd. per share*	0.51		0.49
	shs		shs
No. of shs. o/s*	64,433,986		64,212,154
Avg. no. of shs. o/s*	64,337,514		61,832,773
	%		%
Net profit margin	4.47		1.75
Return on equity	7.96		3.23
Return on assets	4.32		2.64
Foreign sales percent	83		82
No. of employees (FTEs)	2,300		2,250

* Common

[A] Reported in accordance with IFRS

Historical Summary
(as originally stated)

Fiscal Year	Oper. Rev. $000s	Net Inc. Bef. Disc. $000s	EPS* $
2022[A]	789,091	35,311	0.55
2021[A]	660,983	11,535	0.19
2020[A]	354,496	26,463	0.52
2019[A]	374,340	25,747	0.53
2018[A]	286,034	17,658	0.40

* Common

[A] Reported in accordance with IFRS

S.30 Sayward Capital Corp.

Symbol - SAWC.P **Exchange** - TSX-VEN **CUSIP** - 805841
Head Office - 1900-520 3 Ave SW, Calgary, AB, T2P 0Z3 **Telephone** - (403) 510-2423
Email - manhas.rick@gmail.com
Investor Relations - Rick Manhas (403) 510-2423
Auditors - MNP LLP C.A., Calgary, Alta.
Transfer Agents - Odyssey Trust Company, Calgary, Alta.
Profile - (Alta. 2020) Capital Pool Company.

Recent Merger and Acquisition Activity

Status: pending **Revised:** June 13, 2023
UPDATE: The parties entered into a definitive agreement. Upon completion, Midex would amalgamate with 2372845 Alberta Ltd., a wholly owned subsidiary of Sayward, and Sayward would consolidate its shares on a 1-for-2 basis and change its name to Midex Resources Inc. PREVIOUS: Sayward Capital Corp. entered into a letter of intent for the Qualifying Transaction reverse takeover acquisition of private Toronto, Ont.-based Midex Resources Ltd., which holds five lithium properties in northwestern Ontario including the Berens North and Crescent Lake projects.

Status: terminated **Revised:** Mar. 24, 2022
UPDATE: The transaction was terminated. PREVIOUS: Sayward Capital Corp. entered into a letter of intent for the Qualifying Transaction reverse takeover acquisition of Field Safe Solutions Inc., a private Alberta company that provides a worker safety app which connects workers, improves safety, optimizes operations and lowers costs. Sept. 21, 2021 - The companies entered into a definitive agreement whereby Field Safe would amalgamate with a wholly owned subsidiary of Sayward. A consolidation of Sayward common shares would be carried out such that each Sayward share would be exchanged for such number of pre-consolidated share equal to the product of 6.4138 and the purchase price per Field Safe subscription receipt. The private placement of Field Safe subscription receipts is intended to be completed prior to the completion of the transaction. Sayward also plans to change its name to Field Safe Solutions Ltd. Nov. 2, 2021 - Sayward's shareholders approved the transaction. Nov. 8, 2021 - A conditional acceptance for the transaction was received from the TSX Venture Exchange. Dec. 7, 2021 - Field Safe's shareholders approved the transaction.

Directors - Rick Manhas, pres., CEO, CFO & corp. sec., Calgary, Alta.; Luke Caplette, Calgary, Alta.; Jason Joseph, B.C.

Capital Stock

	Authorized (shs.)	Outstanding (shs.)[1]
Preferred	unlimited	nil
Common	unlimited	8,000,000

[1] At June 19, 2023

Major Shareholder - Luke Caplette held 12.5% interest and Rick Manhas held 12.5% interest at June 19, 2023.

Price Range - SAWC.P/TSX-VEN

Year	Volume	High	Low	Close
2022	259,111	$0.11	$0.03	$0.09
2021	27,500	$0.20	$0.15	$0.15

Recent Close: $0.13

Capital Stock Changes - There were no changes to capital stock during 2022.

Wholly Owned Subsidiaries

2372845 Alberta Ltd., Alta.

S.31 Scaling Capital 1 Corp.

Symbol - SKAL.P **Exchange** - TSX-VEN **CUSIP** - 80589D
Head Office - 800-333 7 Ave SW, Calgary, AB, T2P 1Z1
Email - vkeelmann@ninepoint.com
Investor Relations - Vello Keelmann (416) 922-2822
Auditors - Crowe MacKay LLP C.A., Calgary, Alta.
Lawyers - DS Lawyers Canada LLP, Calgary, Alta.
Transfer Agents - Odyssey Trust Company, Calgary, Alta.
Profile - (Alta. 2021) Capital Pool Company.
Common listed on TSX-VEN, Feb. 10, 2023.
Directors - Kirstin H. McTaggart, corp. sec., Mississauga, Ont.; James R. Fox, Toronto, Ont.; John Wilson, Toronto, Ont.
Other Exec. Officers - Alex Tapscott, pres. & CEO; Shirin Kabani, CFO

Capital Stock

	Authorized (shs.)	Outstanding (shs.)[1]
Preferred	unlimited	nil
Common	unlimited	17,000,000

[1] At Feb. 10, 2023

Major Shareholder - James R. Fox held 29.41% interest and John Wilson held 11.76% interest at Feb. 10, 2023.

Recent Close: $0.08

Capital Stock Changes - On Feb. 10, 2023, an initial public offering of 4,500,000 common shares was completed at 10¢ per share.

S.32 Sceptre Ventures Inc.

Symbol - SVP.H **Exchange** - TSX-VEN **CUSIP** - 806215
Head Office - 1450-789 Pender St W, Vancouver, BC, V6C 1H2
Telephone - (604) 688-4219 **Fax** - (604) 688-4215
Website - sceptreventures.com
Email - mhodge@savilleres.com
Investor Relations - Michael Hodge (604) 688-4219
Auditors - De Visser Gray LLP C.A., Vancouver, B.C.
Transfer Agents - Computershare Trust Company of Canada Inc., Vancouver, B.C.
Profile - (B.C. 2008) Capital Pool Company.
Directors - Michael (Mike) Hodge, pres. & CEO, B.C.; Jody Bellefleur, CFO & corp. sec., Surrey, B.C.; Sean Charland, Whistler, B.C.; Alicia Milne, Burnaby, B.C.; Frances Petryshen, Vancouver, B.C.
Other Exec. Officers - Graham Abbott, v-p, bus. devel.; Jaime Stallwood, v-p, bus. devel.

Capital Stock

	Authorized (shs.)	Outstanding (shs.)[1]
Common	unlimited	12,008,277

[1] At May 10, 2023

Major Shareholder - Zimtu Capital Corp. held 35.83% interest at July 27, 2022.

Price Range - SVP.H/TSX-VEN

Year	Volume	High	Low	Close
2022	325,251	$0.09	$0.04	$0.04
2021	9,268	$0.32	$0.06	$0.06

Consolidation: 1-for-4 cons. in Jan. 2022

Recent Close: $0.03

Capital Stock Changes - In July 2022, 6,806,192 common shares were issued at a deemed price of 6¢ per share for debt settlement.

On Jan. 24, 2022, common shares were consolidated on a 1-for-4 basis.

S.33 Schwabo Capital Corporation

Symbol - SBO.H **Exchange** - TSX-VEN **CUSIP** - 808526
Head Office - c/o Harmony Corporate Services Ltd., 1000-409 Granville St, Vancouver, BC, V6C 1T2 **Telephone** - (604) 602-0001 **Fax** - (604) 608-5448
Email - gb@harmonycs.ca
Investor Relations - Geoffrey Balderson (604) 602-0001
Auditors - Dale Matheson Carr-Hilton LaBonte LLP C.A., Vancouver, B.C.
Transfer Agents - Computershare Trust Company of Canada Inc., Toronto, Ont.
Profile - (Alta. 2007) Capital Pool Company.
Directors - Charles E. (Chuck) Ross, pres. & CEO, Vancouver, B.C.; Vitaly Melnikov, Vancouver, B.C.
Other Exec. Officers - Geoffrey (Geoff) Balderson, CFO

Capital Stock

	Authorized (shs.)	Outstanding (shs.)[1]
Preferred	unlimited	nil
Common	unlimited	8,153,751

[1] At June 26, 2023

Price Range - SBO.H/TSX-VEN

Year	Volume	High	Low	Close
2022	224,758	$0.26	$0.15	$0.15
2021	256,600	$0.38	$0.16	$0.35
2020	342,500	$0.34	$0.10	$0.18
2019	155,000	$0.23	$0.08	$0.08
2018	166,500	$0.22	$0.09	$0.10

Recent Close: $0.15

Capital Stock Changes - There were no changes to capital stock during fiscal 2022.

S.34 Scope Carbon Corp.

Symbol - SCPE **Exchange** - CSE **CUSIP** - 80914P
Head Office - 200-550 Denman St, Vancouver, BC, V6G 3H1 **Telephone** - (604) 683-0911 **Fax** - (604) 684-0642
Website - scopecarboncorp.com
Email - darienlattanzi@outlook.com
Investor Relations - Darien Lattanzi (604) 683-0911
Auditors - Mao & Ying LLP C.A., Vancouver, B.C.
Lawyers - Norton Rose Fulbright Canada LLP, Vancouver, B.C.
Transfer Agents - Endeavor Trust Corporation, Vancouver, B.C.
Profile - (B.C. 2018) Developing the Scope Analysis software, an Artificial Intelligence (AI)-driven image recognition technology used for the identification and estimation of carbon-based lifeforms and carbon emissions, both key components in the identification of carbon credits.

The company is focused on the commercial development of the software through its research and development program to expand the software's capabilities and to provide a one-tool solution in carbon mapping.

Common listed on CSE, Sept. 6, 2022.

Recent Merger and Acquisition Activity

Status: pending **Announced:** Apr. 27, 2023
Scope Carbon Corp. entered into a letter of intent to acquire Tempe, Ariz.-based Farm Flight, Inc., which provides an image-based crop intelligence platform that combines data collection services, unmanned aircraft systems (UAS) technology and various machine learning products into a single solution for customers throughout the supply chain, for issuance of 12,351,662 common shares valued at US$14,500,000.

Directors - Sean Prescott, chr., Schwyz, Switzerland; James Y. Liang, CEO, Vancouver, B.C.; Michael Zenko, COO, Surrey, B.C.; Alan Tam, CFO, Vancouver, B.C.; Darien Lattanzi, Vancouver, B.C.

Capital Stock

	Authorized (shs.)	Outstanding (shs.)[1]
Preferred	unlimited	nil
Common	unlimited	37,000,001

[1] At May 23, 2023

Major Shareholder - Widely held at Sept. 6, 2022.

Price Range - SCPE/CSE

Year	Volume	High	Low	Close
2022	2,874,167	$1.85	$0.16	$1.55

Recent Close: $2.02

Capital Stock Changes - On Sept. 6, 2022, an initial public offering of 10,500,000 common shares was completed at 10¢ per share.

Financial Statistics

Periods ended:	12m Sept. 30/22[A]		12m Sept. 30/21[A]
	$000s	%Chg	$000s
Research & devel. expense	9		nil
General & admin expense	363		3
Operating expense	**372**	**n.m.**	**3**
Operating income	**(372)**	**n.a.**	**(3)**
Finance income	2		nil
Finance costs, gross	nil		2
Pre-tax income	**(369)**	**n.a.**	**(5)**
Income taxes	nil		(1)
Net income	**(369)**	**n.a.**	**(4)**
Cash & equivalent	194		nil
Current assets	nil		10
Long-term investments	1,002		nil
Total assets	**1,216**	**n.m.**	**10**
Bank indebtedness	nil		10
Accts. pay. & accr. liabs	130		nil
Current liabilities	130		10
Shareholders' equity	1,087		nil
Cash from oper. activs	**(254)**	**n.a.**	**(38)**
Cash from fin. activs	1,448		10
Cash from invest. activs	(1,000)		28
Net cash position	**194**	**n.a.**	**nil**
	$		$
Earnings per share*	(0.02)		n.a.
Cash flow per share*	(0.01)		n.a.
	shs		shs
No. of shs. o/s*	37,000,001		n.a.
Avg. no. of shs. o/s*	17,529,590		n.a.
	%		%
Net profit margin	n.a.		n.a.
Return on equity	n.m.		n.m.
Return on assets	(60.20)		(12.63)

* Common
[A] Reported in accordance with IFRS

Latest Results

Periods ended:	3m Dec. 31/22[A]		3m Dec. 31/21[A]
	$000s	%Chg	$000s
Net income	(369)	n.a.	(4)
	$		$
Earnings per share*	(0.02)		n.a.

* Common
[A] Reported in accordance with IFRS

Historical Summary
(as originally stated)

Fiscal Year	Oper. Rev.	Net Inc. Bef. Disc.	EPS*
	$000s	$000s	$
2022[A]	nil	(369)	(0.02)
2021[A]	nil	(4)	n.a.
2020[A]	nil	(75)	n.a.

* Common
[A] Reported in accordance with IFRS

S.35 Scryb Inc.

Symbol - SCYB **Exchange** - CSE **CUSIP** - 81111V
Head Office - 202-65 International Blvd, Etobicoke, ON, M9W 6L9 **Telephone** - (647) 872-9982 **Toll-free** - (844) 247-6633 **Fax** - (647) 438-6246
Website - www.scryb.ai
Email - info@scryb.ai
Investor Relations - W. Clark Kent (844) 247-6633
Auditors - Jackson & Co., LLP C.A., Toronto, Ont.
Transfer Agents - TSX Trust Company, Toronto, Ont.
Profile - (Ont. 2014; orig. B.C., 1987) Develops and commercializes a suite of products in the digital health, diagnostics and manufacturing sectors.

Primay products include Fionet platform, an end-to-end, rapid testing and tracking solution operated by 33%-owned **Fionet Rapid Response Group** which handles scheduling and registration via phone app at home, on-site check-in, rapid, on-the-spot antigen testing, data integration with other testing devices, result notification, public health notification as appropriate, and anonymized data and stats for dashboards for authorized stakeholders; Pharmatrac technology, a UX-centric (User Experience) system which predicts medication behaviour, and delivers actionable recommendations for the care team, to improve medication adherence of patients; HemoPalm™ system which consists of a disposable cartridge and a handheld blood analyzer that measures co-oximetry, blood gases and electrolytes in a patient's blood to assess acid-base and oxygenation status at the point of care; and Cybeats, an integrated security platform designed to secure and protect high-valued connected devices.

Recent Merger and Acquisition Activity

Status: completed **Revised:** Nov. 11, 2022
UPDATE: The transaction was completed. PREVIOUS: Scryb Inc. entered into a letter of intent to sell wholly owned Cybeats Technologies Inc., which provides a cybersecurity platform designed to secure and protect high-valued connected devices, to private Toronto, Ont.-based Pima Zinc Corp. Terms of the transaction were to be subsequently disclosed. Aug. 11, 2022 - A definitive agreement was entered into. Pima would issue 60,000,000 common shares at a deemed price of 50¢ per share. Upon completion, Cybeats would amalgamate with Pima's wholly owned 2635212 Ontario Inc., and Pima would change its name to Cybeats Technologies Corp.

Predecessor Detail - Name changed from Relay Medical Corp., Dec. 8, 2021.

Directors - W. Clark Kent, pres., Ont.; Michael Minder, Bermuda; Medhanie Tekeste, Ont.; Sudhir (Sid) Thomas, Ont.; Gregory J. (Greg) Van Staveren, Etobicoke, Ont.

Other Exec. Officers - Yoav Raiter, CEO; Christopher J. (Chris) Hopkins, CFO; Dr. Tom Glawdel, chief scientific officer; Bob Lyle, chief revenue officer; iGAL Roytblat, chief tech. officer; John Solonika, sr. v-p, acqs. & exits; Chris Blask, v-p, strategy; Paul Glavina, v-p, in vitro diagnostics; Vadim Kositsky, v-p, artificial intelligence & data science

Capital Stock

	Authorized (shs.)	Outstanding (shs.)[1]
Common	unlimited	257,012,672

[1] At May 30, 2023

Major Shareholder - Widely held at Jan. 18, 2023.

Price Range - SCYB/CSE

Year	Volume	High	Low	Close
2022	31,327,582	$0.21	$0.09	$0.14
2021	201,809,213	$0.93	$0.17	$0.19
2020	65,968,727	$0.35	$0.14	$0.35
2019	15,464,872	$0.26	$0.18	$0.18
2018	21,093,197	$0.75	$0.19	$0.23

Recent Close: $0.07

Capital Stock Changes - In March and April 2023, private placement of 17,320,000 units (1 common share & 1 warrant) at $0.125 per unit was completed, with warrants exercisable at 15¢ per share for 18 months.

During fiscal 2022, 1,586,001 common shares were repurchased under a Normal Course Issuer Bid

Wholly Owned Subsidiaries

HemoPalm Corp., Canada.
Osprey Device Networks Corp., Canada.
UX Data Sciences Corp., Ottawa, Ont.

Investments

33% int. in **Fionet Rapid Response Group**, Ont.

Financial Statistics

Periods ended:	12m Sept. 30/22[A]		12m Sept. 30/21[oA]
	$000s	%Chg	$000s
Operating revenue	**145**	**+15**	**126**
Salaries & benefits	5,191		1,942
Research & devel. expense	724		526
General & admin expense	3,848		7,224
Stock-based compensation	213		7,943
Operating expense	**9,976**	**-43**	**17,635**
Operating income	**(9,830)**	**n.a.**	**(17,509)**
Deprec., depl. & amort	950		840
Finance costs, net	82		125
Investment income	(792)		203
Pre-tax income	**(11,144)**	**n.a.**	**(17,253)**
Net income	**(11,144)**	**n.a.**	**(17,253)**
Cash & equivalent	368		5,687
Accounts receivable	3,204		2,908
Current assets	3,831		9,082
Long-term investments	1,368		2,363
Fixed assets, net	36		51
Right-of-use assets	411		300
Intangibles, net	5,497		6,197
Total assets	**11,220**	**-38**	**18,066**
Accts. pay. & accr. liabs	1,326		644
Current liabilities	1,544		851
Long-term debt, gross	173		183
Long-term debt, net	113		123
Long-term lease liabilities	105		235
Shareholders' equity	5,741		16,857
Cash from oper. activs	**(4,832)**	**n.a.**	**(10,705)**
Cash from fin. activs	(460)		16,645
Cash from invest. activs	(26)		(1,149)
Net cash position	**368**	**-94**	**5,687**
Capital expenditures	(348)		(49)
	$		$
Earnings per share*	(0.05)		(0.08)
Cash flow per share*	(0.02)		(0.05)
	shs		shs
No. of shs. o/s*	239,692,672		241,278,673
Avg. no. of shs. o/s*	240,051,037		210,112,140
	%		%
Net profit margin	n.m.		n.m.
Return on equity	(98.63)		(194.64)
Return on assets	(76.10)		(164.97)

* Common
[o] Restated
[A] Reported in accordance with IFRS

Latest Results

Periods ended:	6m Mar. 31/23[A]		6m Mar. 31/22[A]
	$000s	%Chg	$000s
Operating revenue	525	+720	64
Net income	(11,087)	n.a.	(5,407)
Net inc. for equity hldrs	(7,212)	n.a.	(5,407)
Net inc. for non-cont. int	(3,876)		nil
	$		$
Earnings per share*	(0.03)		(0.02)

* Common
[A] Reported in accordance with IFRS

Historical Summary
(as originally stated)

Fiscal Year	Oper. Rev.	Net Inc. Bef. Disc.	EPS*
	$000s	$000s	$
2022[A]	145	(11,144)	(0.05)
2021[A]	126	(17,253)	(0.08)
2020[A]	nil	(7,119)	(0.05)
2019[A]	nil	(8,091)	(0.07)
2018[A]	nil	(8,104)	(0.09)

* Common
[A] Reported in accordance with IFRS

S.36 Searchlight Innovations Inc.

Symbol - SLX.P **Exchange** - TSX-VEN **CUSIP** - 81223J
Head Office - Bentall 5, 2300-550 Burrard St, Vancouver, BC, V6C 2B5 **Telephone** - (604) 999-4456
Email - fayyaz@zabinacapital.com
Investor Relations - Fayyaz Alimohamed (604) 999-4456
Auditors - Davidson & Company LLP C.A., Vancouver, B.C.
Lawyers - Gowling WLG (Canada) LLP, Vancouver, B.C.
Transfer Agents - Odyssey Trust Company, Vancouver, B.C.
Profile - (B.C. 2021) Capital Pool Company.
Directors - Fayyaz Alimohamed, CEO, CFO & corp. sec., North Vancouver, B.C.; Bradley (Brad) Humphrey, Toronto, Ont.; Frederic W. R. (Fred) Leigh, Toronto, Ont.

Capital Stock

	Authorized (shs.)	Outstanding (shs.)[1]
Common	unlimited	5,100,000

[1] At May 24, 2023

Major Shareholder - Fayyaz Alimohamed held 19.6% interest and Frederic W. R. (Fred) Leigh held 19.6% interest at Feb. 14, 2023.

Price Range - SLX.P/TSX-VEN

Year	Volume	High	Low	Close
2022	64,500	$0.21	$0.15	$0.21

Recent Close: $0.21

Capital Stock Changes - On Aug. 8, 2022, an initial public offering of 3,000,000 common shares was completed at 10¢ per share.

S.37 Secure Energy Services Inc.*

Symbol - SES **Exchange** - TSX **CUSIP** - 81373C
Head Office - Brookfield Place, 2300-225 6 Ave SW, Calgary, AB, T2P 1N2 **Telephone** - (403) 984-6100 **Fax** - (403) 984-6101
Website - www.secure-energy.com
Email - cmagus@secure-energy.com
Investor Relations - Chad Magus (403) 984-6100
Auditors - KPMG LLP C.A., Calgary, Alta.
Bankers - The Toronto-Dominion Bank; Bank of Montreal; Canadian Imperial Bank of Commerce; National Bank of Canada; ATB Financial, Calgary, Alta.
Lawyers - Bennett Jones LLP, Calgary, Alta.
Transfer Agents - Odyssey Trust Company, Calgary, Alta.
FP500 Revenue Ranking - 79
Employees - 2,124 at Dec. 31, 2022
Profile - (Alta. 2007 amalg.) Provides midstream infrastructure as well as environmental and fluid management services, primarily to oil and gas companies in western Canada and North Dakota.

Operations are organized into two operating segments: Midstream Infrastructure; and Environmental and Fluid Management.

The **Midstream Infrastructure** segment includes a network of processing, waste treatment, disposal and storage facilities, and crude oil and water pipelines throughout western Canada and North Dakota. Services include clean oil terminalling and storage, custom treating of crude oil, crude oil marketing, produced and waste water disposal, oilfield waste processing, and oil purchase and resale services. Midstream infrastructure solutions are provided at 65 locations in Alberta (41), Saskatchewan (11), British Columbia (8), North Dakota (4) and Oklahoma.

The **Environmental and Fluid Management** segment includes a network of industrial landfills, hazardous and non hazardous waste management and disposal; onsite abandonment; environmental solutions for site remediation and reclamation; bio-remediation and technologies; water treatment and recycling; emergency response; rail services; metal recycling services; a suite of comprehensive environmental management solutions provided by the company to a diversified customer base; and drilling, completion and production fluid operations management for oil and gas producers in western Canada. Services offered include secure disposal of oilfield and industrial solid wastes into the company's owned or managed landfill network located in western Canada and North Dakota; pipeline integrity projects (inspection, excavation, repair, replacement and rehabilitation), demolition and decommissioning; remediation and reclamation; environmental construction projects (landfills, containment ponds and subsurface containment walls); naturally occurring radioactive material (NORM) management; waste container services; and emergency response services. The company's fluid operations management includes drilling services, production services and onsite integrated fluid solutions (water management, recycling, pumping and storage).

In March 2023, the company announced that the Competition Tribunal issued its decision in connection with the company's July 2021 acquisition of **Tervita Corporation**. The tribunal issued an order requiring the company to divest of 17 treatment, recovery and disposal facilities, six landfills, four water disposal wells and two disposal caverns all formerly owned by Tervita. This represented 29 of the 103 facilities acquired in the acquisition of Tervita. The company filed a notice of appeal and received a partial stay of the Tribunal's order.

Recent Merger and Acquisition Activity

Status: completed **Announced:** May 16, 2022

Secure Energy Services Inc. acquired Brooks Industrial Metals Ltd.'s metals recycling business, which sells and offers metals recycling services to over 100 clients through a scrap recycling yard in Brooks, Alta., for $6,000,000. Brooks Industrial sells and fabricates steel for welding, mechanic and repair, agriculture, machine shops, oilfield construction and custom projects.

Directors - Michael H. (Mick) Dilger, chr., Calgary, Alta.; Rene Amirault, CEO, Calgary, Alta.; Mark R. Bly, Incline Village, Nev.; Wendy L. Hanrahan, Calgary, Alta.; Joseph Lenz, New York, N.Y.; Bradley R. (Brad) Munro, Saskatoon, Sask.; Susan L. (Sue) Riddell Rose, Calgary, Alta.; Deanna L. Zumwalt, Calgary, Alta.

Other Exec. Officers - Allen Gransch, pres.; Corey Higham, COO; Chad Magus, CFO; James Anderson, sr. v-p, fluids mgt.; David (Dave) Engel, sr. v-p, landfill solutions; Michael Parnetta, v-p, people & cultue; Rhonda Rudnitski, v-p, envir., social & governance; Michael Callihoo, gen. counsel & corp. sec.

Capital Stock

	Authorized (shs.)	Outstanding (shs.)[1]
Preferred	unlimited	nil
Common	unlimited	293,629,841

[1] At July 26, 2023

Normal Course Issuer Bid - The company plans to make normal course purchases of up to 22,055,749 common shares representing 10% of the public float. The bid commenced on Dec. 14, 2022, and expires on Dec. 13, 2023.

Major Shareholder - Angelo, Gordon & Co., LP held 16.9% interest at Mar. 15, 2023.

Price Range - SES/TSX

Year	Volume	High	Low	Close
2022	178,249,468	$7.85	$5.02	$7.03
2021	226,115,996	$6.58	$2.40	$5.26
2020	235,469,003	$5.20	$0.64	$2.46
2019	98,019,668	$9.44	$4.02	$5.06
2018	88,737,191	$9.82	$6.25	$7.01

Recent Close: $7.29

Capital Stock Changes - During 2022, common shares were issued as follows: 976,997 under performance unit plan and 863,464 under restricted share unit plan; 617,700 common shares were repurchased under a Normal Course Issuer Bid.

Dividends

SES com Ra $0.40 pa Q est. Jan. 16, 2023[1]

Prev. Rate: $0.03 est. May 15, 2020

[1] Divds. paid monthly prior to Oct/20.

Long-Term Debt - Outstanding at Dec. 31, 2022:

Revolv. credit facility[1]	$352,000,000
11% sr. sec. notes due 2025	219,000,000
7.25% sr. unsec. notes due 2026	340,000,000
Premium on issuance of notes	19,000,000
Less: Unamort. fin. cost	11,000,000
	919,000,000
Less: Current portion	nil
	919,000,000

[1] Bears interest at either Canadian prime, U.S. base rate plus 0.625% to 2.5%, bankers' acceptance rate or SOFR plus 1.625% to 3.5%.

Wholly Owned Subsidiaries

Secure Energy (Drilling Services) Inc., Calgary, Alta.
- 100% int. in **SES USA Holdings Inc.**, Del.
  - 100% int. in **Secure Energy Services USA LLC**, Colo.
    - 27% int. in **Barcas Pipeline Ventures LLC**, Okla.

Secure Energy Inc., Alta.
- 0.01% int. in **Secure Energy**, Canada.

Subsidiaries

99.99% int. in **Secure Energy**, Canada.

Financial Statistics

Periods ended:	12m Dec. 31/22[A]		12m Dec. 31/21[A]
	$000s	%Chg	$000s
Operating revenue	**8,002,000**	**+112**	**3,766,000**
Cost of sales	7,167,000		3,282,000
Salaries & benefits	249,000		159,000
General & admin expense	28,000		41,000
Stock-based compensation	19,000		13,000
Operating expense	**7,463,000**	**+114**	**3,495,000**
Operating income	**539,000**	**+99**	**271,000**
Deprec., depl. & amort.	178,000		173,000
Finance costs, gross	97,000		60,000
Write-downs/write-offs	nil		(269,000)[1]
Pre-tax income	**252,000**	**n.a.**	**(273,000)**
Income taxes	68,000		(69,000)
Net income	**184,000**	**n.a.**	**(204,000)**
Net inc. for equity hldrs	**184,000**	**n.a.**	**(203,000)**
Net inc. for non-cont. int	**nil**	**n.a.**	**(1,000)**
Cash & equivalent	12,000		10,000
Inventories	100,000		100,000
Accounts receivable	449,000		345,000
Current assets	576,000		466,000
Fixed assets, net	1,513,000		1,646,000
Right-of-use assets	71,000		71,000
Intangibles, net	514,000		529,000
Total assets	**2,840,000**	**-3**	**2,937,000**
Accts. pay. & accr. liabs	404,000		279,000
Current liabilities	459,000		333,000
Long-term debt, gross	919,000		1,207,000
Long-term debt, net	919,000		1,207,000
Long-term lease liabilities	84,000		82,000
Shareholders' equity	1,266,000		1,106,000
Cash from oper. activs	**411,000**	**+455**	**74,000**
Cash from fin. activs	(346,000)		(26,000)
Cash from invest. activs	(58,000)		(43,000)
Net cash position	**12,000**	**+20**	**10,000**
Capital expenditures	(96,000)		(43,000)
Capital disposals	56,000		8,000
	$		$
Earnings per share*	0.59		(0.87)
Cash flow per share*	1.33		0.32
Cash divd. per share*	0.12		0.02
	shs		shs
No. of shs. o/s*	309,381,452		308,158,691
Avg. no. of shs. o/s*	309,637,322		234,226,176
	%		%
Net profit margin	2.30		(5.42)
Return on equity	15.51		(22.69)
Return on assets	8.82		(7.30)
Foreign sales percent	1		4
No. of employees (FTEs)	2,124		2,050

* Common

[A] Reported in accordance with IFRS

[1] Includes $144,000,000 impairment on sites in the midstream processing facilities and landfills cash generating units that were either suspended or closed or planned to be suspended or closed in 2021 and 2022.

Latest Results

Periods ended:	6m June 30/23[A]		6m June 30/22[A]
	$000s	%Chg	$000s
Operating revenue	3,689,000	-4	3,828,000
Net income	89,000	-3	92,000
	$		$
Earnings per share*	0.30		0.30

* Common

[A] Reported in accordance with IFRS

Historical Summary
(as originally stated)

Fiscal Year	Oper. Rev.	Net Inc. Bef. Disc.	EPS*
	$000s	$000s	$
2022[A]	8,002,000	184,000	0.59
2021[A]	3,766,000	(204,000)	(0.87)
2020[A]	1,823,656	(87,187)	(0.55)
2019[A]	3,072,480	191	0.01
2018[A]	2,937,453	19,929	0.12

* Common

[A] Reported in accordance with IFRS

S.38 Sekur Private Data Ltd.

Symbol - SKUR **Exchange** - CSE **CUSIP** - 81607F

Head Office - First Canadian Place, 5600-100 King St W, Toronto, ON, M5X 1C9 **Telephone** - (416) 644-8690

Website - www.sekurprivatedata.com

Email - corporate@sekurprivatedata.com

Investor Relations - Alain M. Ghiai-Chamlou (416) 644-8690

Auditors - De Visser Gray LLP C.A., Vancouver, B.C.

Transfer Agents - National Securities Administrators Ltd., Vancouver, B.C.

Profile - (B.C. 2017) Designs, develops and distributes secure cloud-based storage, disaster recovery, document management, encrypted e-mails and secure communication tools which are hosted in Switzerland.

Offers Sekur®, an encrypted email, messaging and file transfer solution bundle with features including SekurSend®, which allows users to send an email to any other recipient in full privacy and security; SekurReply®, which allow users to reply in same manner as to SekurSend®; SekurVPN®, secures Internet Protocol (IP) address from hackers and keeps users' information private without sharing their data with third party service providers; and SekurMail®, which provides full control of email delivery, automatic data export for large enterprises and an automatic data loss prevention technology with real time continuous archiving. Also offers SekurSafe®, a cloud-based product suite which allow users to securely manage and create encrypted passwords, store and share notes and documents of all types, with the protection of Swiss privacy laws using military grade encryption; SekurPro®, which provides voice and video conferencing encryption, over the web; SekurMessenger® for encrypted messaging, voice recording transfer and file share only; SekurEmail® which is the secure email without messaging; PrivaTalk, a secure communications application offering secure and private audio/video calling, chat, self deleting chat, file transfer and email via any mobile device, tablet or desktop; PrivaTalk Messenger, which includes encrypted messaging with self-destruct timer; and Custodia, a secure email platform for enterprises.

Products are sold worldwide through the company's online store (via websites sekur.com and sekursuite.com), direct sales force, approved wholesalers, distributors and telecommunications companies.

The products were developed by **GlobeX Data S.A.**, a private Swiss-based cyber security and secure communications company, and licensed to the company.

Predecessor Detail - Name changed from GlobeX Data Ltd., Apr. 14, 2022.

Directors - Alain M. Ghiai-Chamlou, pres., CEO & corp. sec., Geneva, Switzerland; Claudio Alberti, Geneva, Switzerland; Amir Assar, B.C.; Henry Sjoman, Monaco

Other Exec. Officers - Scott C. Davis, CFO

Capital Stock

	Authorized (shs.)	Outstanding (shs.)[1]
Common	unlimited	117,025,441

[1] At May 25, 2023

Major Shareholder - Alain M. Ghiai-Chamlou held 26.63% interest at Sept. 28, 2022.

Price Range - SKUR/CSE

Year	Volume	High	Low	Close
2022	24,618,145	$0.51	$0.04	$0.06
2021	60,857,715	$0.60	$0.15	$0.47
2020	16,195,005	$0.19	$0.09	$0.16
2019	348,744	$0.30	$0.01	$0.15

Recent Close: $0.13

Capital Stock Changes - In April 2022, private placement of 2,321,585 units (1 common share & 1 warrant) at 35¢ per unit was completed. Also during 2022, common shares were issued as follows: 852,668 on exercise of warrants and 150,000 for services.

Wholly Owned Subsidiaries

GlobeX Data Inc., Del.

Financial Statistics

Periods ended:	12m Dec. 31/22^A		12m Dec. 31/21^A
	$000s	%Chg	$000s
Operating revenue	**464**	**+220**	**145**
General & admin expense	6,740		4,963
Stock-based compensation	nil		4,556
Operating expense	**6,740**	**-29**	**9,518**
Operating income	**(6,276)**	**n.a.**	**(9,373)**
Deprec., depl. & amort.	137		6
Finance income	66		7
Pre-tax income	**(6,390)**	**n.a.**	**(9,412)**
Net income	**(6,390)**	**n.a.**	**(9,412)**
Cash & equivalent	4,039		8,812
Accounts receivable	34		49
Current assets	4,253		9,636
Fixed assets, net	752		667
Intangibles, net	2,553		2,553
Total assets	**7,558**	**-41**	**12,856**
Accts. pay. & accr. liabs	171		78
Current liabilities	210		130
Shareholders' equity	7,348		12,725
Cash from oper. activs	**(5,508)**	**n.a.**	**(4,906)**
Cash from fin. activs	956		13,884
Cash from invest. activs	(223)		(673)
Net cash position	**4,039**	**-54**	**8,812**
Capital expenditures	(223)		(673)
	$		$
Earnings per share*	(0.06)		(0.11)
Cash flow per share*	(0.05)		(0.06)
	shs		shs
No. of shs. o/s*	117,025,441		113,701,188
Avg. no. of shs. o/s*	116,003,853		87,769,397
	%		%
Net profit margin	n.m.		n.m.
Return on equity	(63.67)		(118.90)
Return on assets	(62.60)		(117.28)
Foreign sales percent	100		100

* Common
^A Reported in accordance with IFRS

Latest Results

Periods ended:	3m Mar. 31/23^A		3m Mar. 31/22^A
	$000s	%Chg	$000s
Operating revenue	132	+50	88
Net income	(1,237)	n.a.	(1,708)
	$		$
Earnings per share*	(0.01)		(0.01)

* Common
^A Reported in accordance with IFRS

Historical Summary
(as originally stated)

Fiscal Year	Oper. Rev.	Net Inc. Bef. Disc.	EPS*
	$000s	$000s	$
2022^A	464	(6,390)	(0.06)
2021^A	145	(9,412)	(0.11)
2020^A	27	(1,319)	(0.02)
2019^A	32	(1,124)	(0.02)
2018^A1	25	(1,286)	(0.03)

* Common
^A Reported in accordance with IFRS
[1] As shown in the prospectus dated May 8, 2019.

S.39 Sensible Meats Inc.

Symbol - HOTD **Exchange** - NEO **CUSIP** - 81742R
Head Office - 300-4723 1 St SW, Calgary, AB, T2G 4Y8 **Toll-free** - (825) 800-0115
Website - sensiblehotdogs.com
Email - hello@sensiblehotdogs.com
Investor Relations - Shawn Balaghi (825) 800-0115
Auditors - Dale Matheson Carr-Hilton LaBonte LLP C.A., Vancouver, B.C.
Transfer Agents - Endeavor Trust Corporation, Vancouver, B.C.
Profile - (B.C. 2020) Develops plant-based meat food alternatives, with a planned initial product line of plant-based hot dogs.
The company (dba Sensible Hot Dogs) plans to distribute and sell its products through two main sales channels: Food service, and Retail. At July 2023, the company was reviewing its options for co-manufacturing its products.
Common listed on NEO, Dec. 22, 2022.
Directors - Shawn Balaghi, CEO, Coquitlam, B.C.; Christopher P. (Chris) Cherry, CFO, Vancouver, B.C.; Chris Jackson, West Vancouver, B.C.; Zahara (Zara) Kanji, Vancouver, B.C.; Scott M. Reeves, Calgary, Alta.
Other Exec. Officers - Lindsay Hamelin-Vendel, corp. sec.

Capital Stock

	Authorized (shs.)	Outstanding (shs.)[1]
Cl.A Vtg. Common	unlimited	52,300,000

[1] At May 31, 2023
Major Shareholder - Widely held at Dec. 22, 2022.

Price Range - HOTD/NEO

Year	Volume	High	Low	Close
2022	34,000	$0.15	$0.12	$0.14

Recent Close: $0.14
Capital Stock Changes - During fiscal 2022, one class A voting common share was repurchased.

Financial Statistics

Periods ended:	12m Nov. 30/22^A		11m Nov. 30/21^A
	$000s	%Chg	$000s
Salaries & benefits	181		31
General & admin expense	671		396
Stock-based compensation	290		53
Operating expense	**1,141**	**+138**	**480**
Operating income	**(1,141)**	**n.a.**	**(480)**
Deprec., depl. & amort.	40		10
Finance income	97		nil
Finance costs, gross	18		5
Pre-tax income	**(1,077)**	**n.a.**	**(489)**
Net income	**(1,077)**	**n.a.**	**(489)**
Cash & equivalent	7,128		8,155
Accounts receivable	174		129
Current assets	8,590		9,338
Fixed assets, net	90		119
Total assets	**10,685**	**-7**	**11,501**
Accts. pay. & accr. liabs	93		55
Current liabilities	172		122
Long-term lease liabilities	66		145
Shareholders' equity	10,447		11,235
Cash from oper. activs	**(932)**	**n.a.**	**(3,507)**
Cash from fin. activs	(85)		11,353
Cash from invest. activs	(11)		(26)
Net cash position	**7,128**	**-13**	**8,155**
Capital expenditures	(11)		(26)
	$		$
Earnings per share*	(0.02)		(0.01)
Cash flow per share*	(0.02)		(0.11)
	shs		shs
No. of shs. o/s*	52,300,000		52,300,001
Avg. no. of shs. o/s*	52,300,000		32,953,257
	%		%
Net profit margin	n.a.		n.a.
Return on equity	(9.93)		n.m.
Return on assets	(9.55)		n.a.

* Cl.A Vtg. Com.
^A Reported in accordance with IFRS

Latest Results

Periods ended:	6m May 31/23^A		6m May 31/22^A
	$000s	%Chg	$000s
Net income	(331)	n.a.	(389)
	$		$
Earnings per share*	(0.01)		(0.01)

* Cl.A Vtg. Com.
^A Reported in accordance with IFRS

S.40 Senvest Capital Inc.*

Symbol - SEC **Exchange** - TSX **CUSIP** - 81731L
Head Office - 2400-1000 rue Sherbrooke O, Montréal, QC, H3A 3G4 **Telephone** - (514) 281-8082 **Fax** - (514) 281-0166
Website - www.senvest.com
Email - gmalikotsis@senvest.com
Investor Relations - George Malikotsis (514) 281-8082
Auditors - PricewaterhouseCoopers LLP C.A., Montréal, Qué.
Lawyers - Blake, Cassels & Graydon LLP, Montréal, Qué.
Transfer Agents - Computershare Trust Company of Canada Inc., Montréal, Qué.
Employees - 32 at Dec. 31, 2022
Profile - (Can. 1968) Operates as a holding company with interests in merchant banking, asset management, real estate investments and electronic security.
Equity Investments - Invests in both publicly traded and private companies. Holdings are principally in small- and mid-capitalization companies located primarily in the U.S. and are at varying levels of participation. Prior to making any investment, the company conducts extensive industry- and company-specific research, including an in-depth analysis of the senior management and its long-term strategy. The company's strategy is to focus on long-term growth as opposed to quarterly results. Also provides services to funds which are targeted toward institutions and high net worth individuals.
Real Estate Holdings - Holds a portfolio of U.S. real estate investments consisting primarily of office, research and development, and telecommunications properties. Has also invested in real estate properties in Argentina and self-storage properties in Spain.
Predecessor Detail - Name changed from Sensormatic Canada Limited, May 21, 1991.
Directors - Victor Mashaal, chr., pres. & CEO, Montréal, Qué.; Richard R. Mashaal, v-p, Montréal, Qué.; Frank Daniel, sec.-treas., Montréal, Qué.; David E. Basner, New York, N.Y.; Eileen Bermingham, New York, N.Y.; Jeffrey L. Jonas, Boston, Mass.
Other Exec. Officers - George Malikotsis, v-p, fin. & CFO

Capital Stock

	Authorized (shs.)	Outstanding (shs.)[1]
Common	unlimited	2,474,724

[1] At Aug. 4, 2023
Normal Course Issuer Bid - The company plans to make normal course purchases of up to 100,000 common shares representing 4% of the total outstanding. The bid commenced on Aug. 16, 2023, and expires on Aug. 15, 2024.
Major Shareholder - Victor Mashaal held 48.08% interest at Apr. 30, 2023.

Price Range - SEC/TSX

Year	Volume	High	Low	Close
2022	47,931	$420.00	$279.00	$324.00
2021	259,605	$415.00	$175.65	$410.00
2020	82,560	$183.00	$100.00	$174.00
2019	105,002	$201.87	$156.01	$172.25
2018	104,413	$250.05	$159.99	$161.01

Recent Close: $325.00
Capital Stock Changes - During 2022, 24,400 common shares were repurchased under a Normal Course Issuer Bid.
Long-Term Debt - At Dec. 31, 2022, the company had no debt.

Wholly Owned Subsidiaries

Argentina Capital Inc., Canada.
Coldstream S.L., Spain.
Pennsylvania Properties Inc., United States.
Senvest Global (KY) L.P., Cayman Islands.
Senvest Global L.P., United States.

Subsidiaries

75% int. in **Senvest Cyprus Recovery Investment Fund, L.P.**, Cayman Islands.

Investments

39% int. in **Senvest Master Fund, L.P.**, Cayman Islands.
49% int. in **Senvest Technology Partners Master Fund, L.P.**, Cayman Islands.

Financial Statistics

Periods ended:	12m Dec. 31/22^A		12m Dec. 31/21^A
	$000s	%Chg	$000s
Unrealized invest. gain (loss)	(810,022)		2,423,815
Total revenue	**(730,345)**	**n.a.**	**2,482,176**
Salaries & benefits	40,953		156,403
Other operating expense	47,182		42,382
Operating expense	**88,135**	**-56**	**198,785**
Operating income	**(818,480)**	**n.a.**	**2,283,391**
Finance costs, gross	51,780		15,552
Pre-tax income	**(367,832)**	**n.a.**	**836,822**
Income taxes	(40,507)		100,950
Net income	**(327,325)**	**n.a.**	**735,872**
Net inc. for equity hldrs	**(326,083)**	**n.a.**	**732,988**
Net inc. for non-cont. int	**(1,242)**	**n.a.**	**2,884**
Cash & equivalent	42,531		52,189
Investments	5,415,036		6,403,786
Total assets	**5,653,153**	**-14**	**6,563,902**
Bank indebtedness	532		253
Accts. pay. & accr. liabs	26,926		93,140
Lease liabilities	2,768		3,707
Shareholders' equity	1,576,258		1,804,644
Non-controlling interest	17,513		11,009
Cash from oper. activs	**257,308**	**-56**	**590,301**
Cash from fin. activs	(250,380)		(398,217)
Cash from invest. activs	(19,184)		(151,261)
Net cash position	**42,531**	**-19**	**52,189**
	$		$
Earnings per share*	(130.98)		289.32
Cash flow per share*	103.35		233.00
	shs		shs
No. of shs. o/s*	2,478,624		2,503,024
Avg. no. of shs. o/s*	2,489,652		2,533,466
	%		%
Net profit margin	n.m.		29.65
Return on equity	(19.29)		50.50
Return on assets	(4.60)		14.10
No. of employees (FTEs)	32		27

* Common
^A Reported in accordance with IFRS

Latest Results

Periods ended:	6m June 30/23[A]		6m June 30/22[A]
	$000s	%Chg	$000s
Total revenue	298,833	n.a.	(932,661)
Net income	67,262	n.a.	(362,182)
Net inc. for equity hldrs	64,972	n.a.	(361,401)
Net inc. for non-cont. int	2,290		(781)
	$		$
Earnings per share*	26.24		(144.84)

* Common
[A] Reported in accordance with IFRS

Historical Summary
(as originally stated)

Fiscal Year	Total Rev.	Net Inc. Bef. Disc.	EPS*
	$000s	$000s	$
2022[A]	(730,345)	(327,325)	(130.98)
2021[A]	2,482,176	735,872	289.32
2020[A]	739,405	238,319	80.66
2019[A]	426,150	116,664	39.16
2018[A]	(316,619)	(164,397)	(51.72)

* Common
[A] Reported in accordance with IFRS

S.41 Sernova Corp.

Symbol - SVA **Exchange** - TSX **CUSIP** - 81732W
Head Office - 114-700 Collip Cir, London, ON, N6G 4X8 **Telephone** - (519) 858-5177 **Toll-free** - (877) 299-4603 **Fax** - (519) 858-5099
Website - www.sernova.com
Email - christopher.barnes@sernova.com
Investor Relations - Christopher Barnes (519) 902-7923
Auditors - KPMG LLP C.A., Vancouver, B.C.
Bankers - Bank of Montreal
Lawyers - McMillan LLP, Vancouver, B.C.
Transfer Agents - TSX Trust Company, Vancouver, B.C.
Profile - (Can. 2001; orig. B.C., 1998) Researches and develops novel technologies to treat chronic diseases using therapeutic cells transplanted into an implanted medical device, the Cell Pouch™.

Lead product, the Cell Pouch™, is a scalable, implantable medical device for the transplantation and engraftment of therapeutic cells (human donor, xenogeneic or stem cell-derived cells) which then release proteins and/or hormones for the long-term treatment of a number of serious, chronic, debilitating diseases such as insulin-dependent diabetes, hemophilia A and hypothyroid disease. Local immune protection technologies such as microencapsulation protect the therapeutic cells within the Cell Pouch™ from immune system attack reducing or eliminating the need for antirejection drugs. The Cell Pouch™ System, including the Cell Pouch™, which is a novel, proprietary, scalable, implantable macro-encapsulation device solution designed for the long-term survival and function of therapeutic cells, is ongoing Phase I/II clinical trial for type 1 diabetes (T1D). Also has ongoing pre-clinical trials of the Cell Pouch™ System for the treatment of hemophilia A and hypothyroid disease.

Has exclusive worldwide license with the University of Miami for the commercial rights to novel conformal coating immune protection technologies.

Predecessor Detail - Name changed from Pheromone Sciences Corp., Sept. 20, 2006.

Directors - Brett A. Whalen, chr., Markham, Ont.; Dr. Philip M. Toleikis, pres., CEO & chief tech. officer, Ont.; Dr. Daniel Mahony, Cambs., United Kingdom; James T. Parsons, Mississauga, Ont.; Dr. Steven Sangha, Richmond, B.C.; Bertram T. von Plettenberg

Other Exec. Officers - David Swetlow, CFO; Christopher Barnes, v-p, IR; Frank Shannon, v-p, clinical devel. & regulatory affairs

Capital Stock

	Authorized (shs.)	Outstanding (shs.)[1]
Common	unlimited	303,332,686

[1] At Mar. 8, 2023

Major Shareholder - Widely held at Mar. 8, 2023.

Price Range - SVA/TSX

Year	Volume	High	Low	Close
2022	48,968,030	$2.22	$0.69	$0.79
2021	157,557,826	$2.87	$0.54	$1.82
2020	87,111,937	$0.74	$0.10	$0.67
2019	95,203,016	$0.29	$0.15	$0.17
2018	44,276,352	$0.51	$0.17	$0.20

Recent Close: $0.75

Capital Stock Changes - During fiscal 2022, common shares were issued as follows: 28,817,024 on exercise of warrants, 12,944,904 by private placement and 437,500 on exercise of options.

Financial Statistics

Periods ended:	12m Oct. 31/22[A]		12m Oct. 31/21[A]
	$000s	%Chg	$000s
Salaries & benefits	2,986		2,000
Research & devel. expense	10,948		3,010
General & admin expense	2,929		1,440
Stock-based compensation	7,451		218
Operating expense	**24,314**	**+265**	**6,669**
Operating income	**(24,314)**	**n.a.**	**(6,669)**
Deprec., depl. & amort	440		267
Finance income	577		71
Finance costs, gross	118		58
Pre-tax income	**(24,421)**	**n.a.**	**(6,966)**
Net income	**(24,421)**	**n.a.**	**(6,966)**
Cash & equivalent	49,776		27,874
Accounts receivable	1,147		449
Current assets	51,091		28,327
Fixed assets, net	402		176
Right-of-use assets	251		388
Intangibles, net	517		717
Total assets	**52,485**	**+76**	**29,820**
Accts. pay. & accr. liabs	4,600		1,358
Current liabilities	4,740		1,476
Long-term lease liabilities	136		276
Shareholders' equity	47,609		28,068
Cash from oper. activs	**(14,421)**	**n.a.**	**(6,844)**
Cash from fin. activs	36,665		30,997
Cash from invest. activs	(46,341)		(229)
Net cash position	**3,776**	**-86**	**27,874**
Capital expenditures	(329)		(17)
	$		$
Earnings per share*	(0.09)		(0.03)
Cash flow per share*	(0.05)		(0.03)
	shs		shs
No. of shs. o/s*	303,332,686		261,133,258
Avg. no. of shs. o/s*	273,593,143		245,522,770
	%		%
Net profit margin	n.a.		n.a.
Return on equity	(64.54)		(43.25)
Return on assets	(59.06)		(38.87)

* Common
[A] Reported in accordance with IFRS

Latest Results

Periods ended:	3m Jan. 31/23[A]		3m Jan. 31/22[A]
	$000s	%Chg	$000s
Net income	(8,015)	n.a.	(5,459)
	$		$
Earnings per share*	(0.03)		(0.02)

* Common
[A] Reported in accordance with IFRS

Historical Summary
(as originally stated)

Fiscal Year	Oper. Rev.	Net Inc. Bef. Disc.	EPS*
	$000s	$000s	$
2022[A]	nil	(24,421)	(0.09)
2021[A]	nil	(6,966)	(0.03)
2020[A]	nil	(5,321)	(0.04)
2019[A]	nil	(3,971)	(0.02)
2018[A]	nil	(3,699)	(0.02)

* Common
[A] Reported in accordance with IFRS

S.42 Seven Oaks Capital Corp.

Symbol - SEVN.P **Exchange** - TSX-VEN **CUSIP** - 81788J
Head Office - 1712-8 King St E, Toronto, ON, M5C 1B5 **Telephone** - (416) 910-3401
Website - seven-oaks.ca
Email - gmcleod@seven-oaks.ca
Investor Relations - Grant McLeod (416) 910-3401
Auditors - Segal GCSE LLP C.A., Toronto, Ont.
Transfer Agents - TSX Trust Company, Toronto, Ont.
Profile - (Ont. 2021) Capital Pool Company.

Recent Merger and Acquisition Activity

Status: terminated **Revised:** June 5, 2023
UPDATE: The transaction was terminated. PREVIOUS: Seven Oaks Capital Corp. agreed to acquire to the Qualifying Transaction reverse takeover acquisition of Israel-based Rimon Hedge Funds Ltd., which primarily trades in contracts for difference with underlying assets typically forex pairs, select commodities and indices tied to the real economy through its two hedge funds, Hetmed Hedge Fund Limited Partnership and Mango Hedge Fund Limited Partnership. On closing, Seven Oaks plans to change its name to Rimon Funds Ltd. Rimon plains to raise minimum proceeds of US$5,000,000 via a private placement of subscription receipts convertible into common shares of resulting issuer and up to an additional US$15,000,000, but no less than US$2,500,000 convertible into preferred shares of the resulting issuer.

Directors - Grant McLeod, CEO, Toronto, Ont.; Monique Hutchins, Toronto, Ont.; Dexter D. S. John, Whitby, Ont.

Other Exec. Officers - Myles Fontaine, pres., COO & corp. sec.; David (Dave) Redekop, CFO

Capital Stock

	Authorized (shs.)	Outstanding (shs.)[1]
Common	unlimited	11,600,000

[1] At May 22, 2023

Major Shareholder - Integrity Enterprises Inc. held 46.6% interest, Grant McLeod & Myles Fontaine held 34% interest and Canaccord Genuity Corp. held 17.2% interest at July 12, 2022.

Price Range - SEVN.P/TSX-VEN

Year	Volume	High	Low	Close
2022	219,300	$0.12	$0.10	$0.11

Recent Close: $0.08

Capital Stock Changes - On Apr 5, 2022, an initial public offering of 3,500,000 common shares was completed at 10¢ per share.

S.43 Sharc International Systems Inc.

Symbol - SHRC **Exchange** - CSE **CUSIP** - 81948A
Head Office - 1443 Spitfire Pl, Port Coquitlam, BC, V3C 6L4 **Telephone** - (604) 475-7710 **Fax** - (778) 262-0120
Website - www.sharcenergy.com
Email - hanspaul.pannu@sharcenergy.com
Investor Relations - Hanspaul Pannu (604) 475-7710 ext. 4
Auditors - Davidson & Company LLP C.A., Vancouver, B.C.
Lawyers - McMillan LLP
Transfer Agents - Computershare Trust Company of Canada Inc., Toronto, Ont.
Profile - (B.C. 2011) Provides wastewater energy transfer (WET) products and services.

Products include SHARC™ WET system, an industrial-sized wastewater heat recovery and filtration system that filters high volumes of wastewater flow for the purposes of extracting or rejecting thermal energy from or into wastewater for WET district energy, micro-grids, large commercial and mixed-use building developments, and industrial applications; and PIRANHA™ WET system, a self-contained heat pump that can offset electric or natural gas boilers used in hot water production up to 100% while providing some air conditioning as a by-product of hot water production.

In April 2023, the company entered into a five-year partnership with **Subterra Capital Partners Inc.** whereby the company and Subterra would co-develop up to $200,000,000 of qualified projects that consist of either the acquisition of existing systems active in the field or the development of systems requiring capital to design, build, own, operate and maintain. Upon completion of the deployment of $200,000,000 or expiration of the term, Subterra would receive a first right of refusal on any similar relationship for one year. The company would not maintain an ownership interest in the projects but would receive fees on qualified projects that range from 2.5% to 5% of the total acquisition or installed cost of the systems based on certain milestones. In addition, the company would receive 35% of any net cash flows from Subterra on a development project for a period of five years from beginning of commercial operation of the systems.

During 2022, wholly owned **2336882 Ontario Inc.** was dissolved.

Predecessor Detail - Name changed from International Wastewater Systems Inc., Sept. 11, 2017; basis 1 new for 3.5 old shs.

Directors - Lynn Mueller, chr. & CEO, Richmond, B.C.; Daryle Anderson, B.C.; Eleanor Chiu, Alta.; Sasko Despotovski, Oslo, Norway; The Hon. Michael F. (Mike) Harcourt, Vancouver, B.C.; Allen G. (Al) Saurette, Alta.

Other Exec. Officers - Hanspaul Pannu, CFO, COO & corp. sec.; Michael Albertson, pres., SHARC Energy (US) Systems Inc.

Capital Stock

	Authorized (shs.)	Outstanding (shs.)[1]
Preferred	unlimited	nil
Common	unlimited	146,705,563

[1] At May 26, 2023

Major Shareholder - Widely held at May 25, 2022.

Price Range - SHRC/CSE

Year	Volume	High	Low	Close
2022	17,951,451	$0.38	$0.28	$0.29
2021	32,064,163	$0.69	$0.28	$0.33
2020	28,726,610	$0.40	$0.07	$0.33
2019	17,482,571	$0.34	$0.03	$0.07
2018	11,649,713	$0.59	$0.25	$0.30

Recent Close: $0.24

Capital Stock Changes - During the first half of 2023, 27,538,333 common shares were issued on conversion of $3,395,500 of debt.

During 2022, common shares were issued as follows: 3,787,292 on conversion of debt, 1,940,714 on exercise of warrants, 716,667 on exercise of options and 349,701 under restricted share unit plan.

Wholly Owned Subsidiaries

SHARC Energy (US) Systems Inc., Del. Inactive.
Sharc Energy Systems Inc., Canada.

Financial Statistics

Periods ended:	12m Dec. 31/22^A		12m Dec. 31/21^A
	$000s	%Chg	$000s
Operating revenue	**1,941**	**-28**	**2,697**
Cost of sales	1,381		1,706
Salaries & benefits	1,709		1,072
Research & devel. expense	136		72
General & admin expense	1,517		1,307
Stock-based compensation	897		374
Operating expense	**5,640**	**+25**	**4,530**
Operating income	**(3,699)**	**n.a.**	**(1,833)**
Deprec., depl. & amort.	162		157
Finance income	16		5
Finance costs, gross	860		1,096
Pre-tax income	**(4,819)**	**n.a.**	**(3,064)**
Income taxes	(1)		(19)
Net income	**(4,818)**	**n.a.**	**(3,045)**
Cash & equivalent	1,070		3,151
Inventories	971		962
Accounts receivable	522		1,355
Current assets	2,644		5,530
Fixed assets, net	409		390
Total assets	**3,154**	**-47**	**5,970**
Accts. pay. & accr. liabs	1,003		461
Current liabilities	4,873		2,184
Long-term debt, gross	3,734		4,687
Long-term debt, net	nil		3,066
Long-term lease liabilities	141		202
Equity portion of conv. debs	684		757
Shareholders' equity	(1,946)		457
Cash from oper. activs	**(1,559)**	**n.a.**	**(2,594)**
Cash from fin. activs	(401)		2,777
Cash from invest. activs	(121)		(134)
Net cash position	**1,070**	**-66**	**3,151**
Capital expenditures	(121)		(109)
	$		$
Earnings per share*	(0.05)		(0.03)
Cash flow per share*	(0.01)		(0.03)
	shs		shs
No. of shs. o/s*	107,499,566		100,705,192
Avg. no. of shs. o/s*	104,622,238		91,564,625
	%		%
Net profit margin	(248.22)		(112.90)
Return on equity	n.m.		n.m.
Return on assets	(86.76)		(37.83)

* Common
^A Reported in accordance with IFRS

Latest Results

Periods ended:	3m Mar. 31/23^A		3m Mar. 31/22^A
	$000s	%Chg	$000s
Operating revenue	734	-17	884
Net income	(755)	n.a.	(837)
	$		$
Earnings per share*	(0.01)		(0.01)

* Common
^A Reported in accordance with IFRS

Historical Summary
(as originally stated)

Fiscal Year	Oper. Rev.	Net Inc. Bef. Disc.	EPS*
	$000s	$000s	$
2022^A	1,941	(4,818)	(0.05)
2021^A	2,697	(3,045)	(0.03)
2020^A	631	(2,894)	(0.05)
2019^A	144	(3,295)	(0.08)
2018^A	2,136	(5,896)	(0.17)

* Common
^A Reported in accordance with IFRS

S.44 Shawcor Ltd.*

Symbol - MATR **Exchange** - TSX **CUSIP** - 820439
Head Office - 25 Bethridge Rd, Toronto, ON, M9W 1M7 **Telephone** - (416) 743-7111 **Fax** - (416) 743-7199
Website - www.shawcor.com
Email - meghan.maceachern@shawcor.com
Investor Relations - Meghan MacEachern (437) 341-1848
Auditors - KPMG LLP C.A., Toronto, Ont.
Bankers - The Toronto-Dominion Bank, Toronto, Ont.
Lawyers - McMillan LLP, Toronto, Ont.; Stikeman Elliott LLP, Toronto, Ont.
Transfer Agents - TSX Trust Company, Toronto, Ont.
FP500 Revenue Ranking - 297
Employees - 3,937 at Dec. 31, 2022
Profile - (Can. 2013 amalg.) Manufactures, builds and supplies composite pipes and underground storage tanks, heat shrink products and devices, engineered wires and cables, and offshore pipe coatings, as well as provides pipeline girth weld inspection services for oil and gas, water and wastewater, fuel, transportation and industrial applications.

Operations are carried out through three business segments: Composite Technologies, which consists of Composite Production Systems division; Connection Technologies, which consists of Connection Systems division; and Pipeline and Pipe Services, which consists of Pipeline Performance Group and Shaw Pipeline Services divisions.

Composite Technologies

The **Composite Production Systems** division manufactures and installs composite linepipes for oil and gas gathering, enhanced oil recovery, CO_2 injection or water transportation application; composite tanks made of premium resin and glass that are used for fuel, water, and oil and gas storage; and a combined line of corrosion-resistant fibreglass tanks with treatment, filtration, storage and infiltration options for stormwater management systems. Operations include a manufacturing and distribution centre in Calgary, Alta., tank manufacturing facilities across North America and a 3D glass fabric weaving manufacturing facility in the Netherlands, as well as sales offices and service depots in Alberta, Saskatchewan, Texas, Colorado, Utah, California and North Dakota. The products are sold internationally through direct sales and a global network of agents and distributors.

Connection Technologies

The **Connection Systems** division includes DSG Canusa, a global manufacturer of heat-shrinkable products including tubing, sleeves and moulded products, as well as heat-shrink accessories and equipment; Shawflex, a manufacturer of highly engineered, low-voltage wire, cable, connector and harness solutions for control, instrumentation, thermocouple, power, and industrial applications; and Kanata Electronics, a manufacturer and supplier of specialty cable assemblies and wire harnesses for the nuclear and aerospace industries. DSG-Canusa products are manufactured and distributed through facilities located in Canada, the United States, Germany and The People's Republic of China, and are sold directly to end-users or through distributors and agents throughout North America, Europe and Asia. Shawflex products are manufactured in Toronto, Ont., and are sold direct to end-users or through distributors and agents throughout North America. Kanata Electronics products are also manufactured in Toronto, and are sold directly to end-users or through distributors and agents throughout North America, South America, Europe and Asia.

Pipeline and Pipe Services

The **Pipeline Performance Group** division offers specialized internal anti-corrosion and flow efficiency pipe coating systems, insulation coating systems, weight coating systems and custom coating and field joint application services for onshore and offshore pipeline. The division has 12 plants operating in most major energy producing markets, and the capability to install temporary project-specific plants anywhere, with customers consisting of major private and government-owned oil and gas producers, pipe mills, pipeline owners and pipeline construction contractors. In addition, the division has logistics capabilities that assist customers in reducing freight costs by allowing them to efficiently source and move pipes around the world.

During the second quarter of 2023, the company agreed to sell an idle facility in Pozzallo, Italy. The transaction was expected to close in the third quarter of 2023.

In June 2023, the company announced plans for two new operating facilities which, in combination, would replace its existing Greater Toronto Area (GTA) manufacturing site that was sold and leased-back in June of 2022. Its Shawflex business (custom wire and cable products) would be relocating to a larger facility in Vaughan, Ont., which would also house **Kanata Electronic Services Ltd.** Its DSG-Canusa business (heat and cold shrink tubing) would be relocating from the GTA to Fairfield, Ohio. The Fairfield site would also house the business' North American distribution hub, which would relocate from Loveland, Ohio.

In June 2023, the company was rebranded as Mattr Infratech reflecting the change from an energy services company into a materials technology company. Previously, the company commenced a review of strategic alternatives for its Pipeline Performance Group, Shaw Pipeline Services and Oilfield Asset Management operating units. A range of options are under consideration, including the potential sale of all three operating units. A name change to **Mattr Corp.** was also approved in May 2023.

In May 2023, the company sold the specialty pipe coating business and related assets in Ellon, Scotland, which is under the Pipeline and Pipe Services segment, for $500,000.

In April 2023, the company announced plans to spend $60,000,000 to add two new composite systems operating facilities. An additional production facility at its Flexpipe® business in Texas and an additional production facility for its Xerxes® business in South Carolina would be added.

On May 19, 2022, the company announced today that it had secured an early exit from its leased facility, which formerly housed the FlexFlow operations, in Calgary's Oxford Airport Business Park. This exit would be completed during the third quarter of 2022 and would result in net savings of $15,000,000 over the course of the next seven years. The company would incur one-time restructuring costs of $2,000,000 to execute this transaction, which would be reflected in the second quarter of 2022 financial results.

Recent Merger and Acquisition Activity

Status: completed **Announced:** June 1, 2023
Shawcor Ltd. sold its Shaw Pipeline Services (SPS) operating unit to a U.S.-based investor group which includes Achieve Capital LLC and members of current SPS management. Terms were not disclosed. SPS provides ultrasonic and radiographic pipeline girth weld inspection services to pipeline operators and construction contractors worldwide for both onshore and offshore pipeline applications.

Status: completed **Announced:** Mar. 1, 2023
Shawcor Ltd. acquired the assets of private Brighton, Mich.-based Triton Stormwater Solutions, a fabricator of highly engineered, lightweight, composite materials-based underground infiltration chamber products, used primarily within stormwater management solutions, for $14,600,000. The product line would be consolidated into the water management arm of Shawcor's Composite Systems segment.

Status: completed **Announced:** Dec. 20, 2022
Shawcor Ltd. sold subsidiary Socotherm Americas S.A. for Cdn$6,600,000 net of working capital adjustments. Socotherm Americas provides external and internal anti-corrosion coating and thermal insulation coating to the Argentine and regional pipeline, and oilfield tubular markets from its base in Escobar.

Status: completed **Announced:** Dec. 6, 2022
Shawcor Ltd. acquired private Etobicoke, Ont.-based Kanata Electronic Services Limited, which designs, manufactures and supplies specialty cable assemblies and wire harnesses for the aerospace, nuclear, military, medical and commercial industries. Terms of the transaction were not disclosed.

Status: completed **Announced:** Nov. 18, 2022
Shawcor Ltd. sold its Oilfield Asset Management (OAM) business to Force Inspection Services Inc. for $15,000,000. OAM offers oilfield tubular management services which include in-plant and mobile inspection, repair, machining, manufacturing, recertification, pressure testing and inventory management to the oil and gas industry in western Canada. OAM had six locations in Nisku, Grande Prairie, Lloydminster and Brooks, Alta.; Fort St. John, B.C.; and Estevan, Sask. Shawcor retained the OAM real estate and leased the properties to Force.

Status: completed **Announced:** Sept. 1, 2022
Shawcor Ltd. sold wholly owned Lake Superior Consulting, LLC to a private investment group, including members of Lake Superior management, for $5,900,000. Lake Superior offers engineering, consulting and field inspection services to the U.S. onshore pipeline and energy infrastructure markets, with facilities in Minnesota, Texas, Nebraska, Tennessee and Pennsylvania.

Status: completed **Revised:** June 28, 2022
UPDATE: The transaction was completed for net proceeds of $49,000,000. PREVIOUS: Shawcor Ltd. entered into a letter of intent to sell and leaseback its Rexdale property in Toronto, Ont., to a third party. The sale would generate net proceeds in excess of $45,000,000. The transaction was expected to be completed in the first half of 2022.

Status: completed **Announced:** May 31, 2022
Shawcor Ltd. sold its Global Poly business, which manufactures and offers a wide variety of high density polyethylene pressure pipe and HDPE liners, for $5,800,000.

Predecessor Detail - Name changed from ShawCor Ltd., Feb. 1, 2016.

Directors - Derek S. Blackwood, chr., Houston, Tex.; Michael E. Reeves, pres. & CEO, Houston, Tex.; Laura A. Cillis, Nelson, B.C.; Kathleen J. Hall, Pa.; Alan R. Hibben, Yorks., United Kingdom; Kevin L. Nugent, Calgary, Alta.; Dr. Ramesh Ramachandran, Princeton, N.J.; Katherine A. Rethy, Huntsville, Ont.

Other Exec. Officers - Frank Cistrone, grp. pres., automotive & ind.; Chris V. Havern, grp. pres., integrity mgt.; Martin N. Perez, grp. pres., composite sys.; Kevin D. Reizer, grp. pres., pipeline performance grp.; Thomas R. (Tom) Holloway, sr. v-p, fin. & CFO; Timothy J. (Tim) Hutzul, sr. v-p, gen. counsel & corp. sec.; Geoff W. Smith, sr. v-p & chief people & HSE officer; Shannon Glover, v-p, legal & asst. corp. sec.

Capital Stock

	Authorized (shs.)	Outstanding (shs.)[1]
Common	unlimited	69,409,720

[1] At Aug. 11, 2023

Options - At Dec. 31, 2022, options were outstanding to purchase 1,486,551 common shares at a weighted average exercise price of $18.41 per share with a remaining contractual life of 5.94 years.

Normal Course Issuer Bid - The company plans to make normal course purchases of up to 3,442,233 common shares representing 10% of the public float. The bid commenced on June 28, 2023, and expires on June 27, 2024.

Major Shareholder - The Turtle Creek Group held 19.17% interest at Mar. 31, 2023.

Price Range - MATR/TSX

Year	Volume	High	Low	Close
2022	69,522,465	$14.42	$4.44	$13.74
2021	117,639,454	$7.73	$3.51	$4.91
2020	243,612,485	$13.23	$0.64	$3.52
2019	29,191,890	$22.46	$11.60	$12.53
2018	25,047,209	$29.50	$15.11	$16.58

Recent Close: $19.63

Capital Stock Changes - During 2022, common shares were issued as follows: 174,009 on exercise of restricted share units and 116,740 on exercise of stock options; 514,300 common shares were repurchased under a Normal Course Issuer Bid.

Long-Term Debt - At Dec. 31, 2022, outstanding long-term debt totaled $210,832,000 (none current and net of $8,168,000 of deferred transaction costs) and consisted of a $69,000,000 unsecured committed bank credit facility due 2026 and $150,000,000 9% senior unsecured notes due 2026.

Wholly Owned Subsidiaries

DSG-Canusa GmbH, Germany.

J.M. Sales Associates, Inc., Brighton, Mich.
Shawcor Canada Holdings Ltd., Calgary, Alta.
- 100% int. in **Shawcor International Cooperatie U.A. Netherlands**, Netherlands.
  - 100% int. in **Bredero Shaw International B.V.**, Netherlands.
    - 95% int. in **PT Bredero Shaw Indonesia**, Indonesia.
    - 100% int. in **Shawcor Norway AS**, Norway.
  - 100% int. in **Bredero Shaw Mexico S.A. de C.V.**, Mexico.
  - 100% int. in **Fineglade Unlimited Company**, Ireland.
  - 5% int. in **PT Bredero Shaw Indonesia**, Indonesia.
  - 100% int. in **Shawcor Inc.**, Nev.
    - 100% int. in **Flexpipe Systems (US) LLC**, Del.
    - 100% int. in **Shawcor Pipe Protection LLC**, Del.
    - 100% int. in **ZCL Acquisition Corp.**, Minneapolis, Minn.
      - 100% int. in **Xerxes Corporation**, United States.

Note: The preceding list includes only the major related companies in which interests are held.

Financial Statistics

Periods ended:	12m Dec. 31/22[A]		12m Dec. 31/21[A]
	$000s	%Chg	$000s
Operating revenue	**1,255,289**	**+10**	**1,143,000**
Cost of goods sold	890,584		824,877
Research & devel. expense	8,782		8,104
General & admin expense	234,653		202,378
Operating expense	**1,134,019**	**+10**	**1,035,359**
Operating income	**121,270**	**+13**	**107,641**
Deprec., depl. & amort.	71,416		77,767
Finance income	893		208
Finance costs, gross	22,608		22,421
Investment income	nil		1,770
Write-downs/write-offs	(22,433)		(57,328)
Pre-tax income	**(50,254)**	**n.a.**	**(68,560)**
Income taxes	(19,278)		12,060
Net income	**(30,976)**	**n.a.**	**(80,620)**
Net inc. for equity hldrs	**(29,989)**	**n.a.**	**(79,111)**
Net inc. for non-cont. int	**(987)**	**n.a.**	**(1,509)**
Cash & equivalent	263,990		124,449
Inventories	181,964		122,740
Accounts receivable	223,779		184,041
Current assets	740,349		492,254
Fixed assets, net	297,101		311,354
Right-of-use assets	50,286		50,222
Intangibles, net	387,856		387,968
Total assets	**1,549,090**	**+22**	**1,267,752**
Accts. pay. & accr. liabs	237,397		184,664
Current liabilities	506,125		260,069
Long-term debt, gross	210,832		292,140
Long-term debt, net	210,832		292,140
Long-term lease liabilities	33,635		41,048
Shareholders' equity	699,378		639,275
Non-controlling interest	275		2,798
Cash from oper. activs	**211,103**	**+226**	**64,684**
Cash from fin. activs	(111,647)		(163,532)
Cash from invest. activs	19,502		3,832
Net cash position	**263,990**	**+112**	**124,449**
Capital expenditures	(50,083)		(25,072)
Capital disposals	58,179		8,726
Pension fund surplus	n.a.		3,468
	$		$
Earnings per share*	(0.43)		(1.12)
Cash flow per share*	3.00		0.92
	shs		shs
No. of shs. o/s*	70,258,163		70,481,714
Avg. no. of shs. o/s*	70,460,000		70,467,000
	%		%
Net profit margin	(2.47)		(7.05)
Return on equity	(4.48)		(11.70)
Return on assets	(1.21)		(3.88)
Foreign sales percent	67		71
No. of employees (FTEs)	3,937		4,273

* Common
[A] Reported in accordance with IFRS

Latest Results

Periods ended:	6m June 30/23[A]		6m June 30/22[A]
	$000s	%Chg	$000s
Operating revenue	765,037	+33	574,812
Net income	38,251	+198	12,831
Net inc. for equity hldrs	38,292	+186	13,410
Net inc. for non-cont. int	(41)		(579)
	$		$
Earnings per share*	0.55		0.19

* Common
[A] Reported in accordance with IFRS

Historical Summary
(as originally stated)

Fiscal Year	Oper. Rev.	Net Inc. Bef. Disc.	EPS*
	$000s	$000s	$
2022[A]	1,255,289	(30,976)	(0.43)
2021[A]	1,143,000	(80,620)	(1.12)
2020[A]	1,178,482	(234,555)	(3.33)
2019[A]	1,489,489	(33,295)	(0.47)
2018[A]	1,408,872	26,179	0.37

* Common
[A] Reported in accordance with IFRS

S.45 Shellron Capital Ltd.

Symbol - SHLL.P **Exchange** - TSX-VEN **CUSIP** - 82281V
Head Office - 1090 Hamilton St, Vancouver, BC, V6B 2R9 **Telephone** - (604) 634-0970
Email - daniela@columbusgroup.com
Investor Relations - Daniela V. Freitas (604) 634-0970
Auditors - Saturna Group Chartered Accountants LLP C.A., Vancouver, B.C.
Lawyers - S. Paul Simpson Law Corporation, Vancouver, B.C.
Transfer Agents - Computershare Trust Company of Canada Inc., Vancouver, B.C.
Profile - (B.C. 2021) Capital Pool Company.

In August 2022, the company entered into a letter of intent for the Qualifying Transaction reverse takeover acquisition of private Vancouver, B.C.-based **Launchtrip Technologies Corp.** on a share-for-share basis. Launchtrip offers a travel booking app which focuses on group trips to destinations and events around the world and includes a full split payment feature. The transaction would be completed by way of a three-cornered amalgamation between a wholly owned subsidiary of the company and Launchtrip. As part of the transaction, Launchtrip would complete a debenture offering of $500,000 and a concurrent financing to be determined. Closing of the transaction was expected to close no later than Jan. 31, 2023.

Recent Merger and Acquisition Activity

Status: terminated **Revised:** Mar. 24, 2023
UPDATE: The transaction was terminated. PREVIOUS: Shellron Capital Ltd. entered into a letter of intent for the Qualifying Transaction reverse takeover acquisition of private Vancouver, B.C.-based Launchtrip Technologies Corp., which provides a travel booking application that focuses on group trips to destinations and events worldwide, on a share-for-share basis. Upon completion, Launchtrip would amalgamate with a wholly owned subsidiary of Shellron.

Directors - Andrew Yau, CEO & CFO, Vancouver, B.C.; Robin Beynon, B.C.; Robert F. Giustra, West Vancouver, B.C.; Julian Ing, B.C.; Jorge Martínez, Vancouver, B.C.
Other Exec. Officers - Daniela V. Freitas, corp. sec.

Capital Stock

	Authorized (shs.)	Outstanding (shs.)[1]
Common	unlimited	8,539,000

[1] At Mar. 8, 2023

Major Shareholder - Robert F. Giustra held 11.13% interest at Aug. 3, 2022.

Price Range - SHLL.P/TSX-VEN

Year	Volume	High	Low	Close
2022	402,985	$0.22	$0.08	$0.14
2021	87,100	$0.20	$0.15	$0.16

Recent Close: $0.04
Capital Stock Changes - On Nov. 22, 2021, an initial public offering of 4,289,000 common shares was completed at 10¢ per share.

S.46 Sherritt International Corporation*

Symbol - S **Exchange** - TSX **CUSIP** - 823901
Head Office - East Tower, Bay Adelaide Centre, 4220-22 Adelaide St W, Toronto, ON, M5H 4E3 **Telephone** - (416) 924-4551 **Toll-free** - (800) 704-6698 **Fax** - (416) 924-5015
Website - www.sherritt.com
Email - lucy.chitilian@sherritt.com
Investor Relations - Lucy Chitilian (800) 704-6698
Auditors - Deloitte LLP C.A., Toronto, Ont.
Lawyers - Torys LLP, Toronto, Ont.
Transfer Agents - TSX Trust Company, Toronto, Ont.
FP500 Revenue Ranking - 680
Employees - 3,310 at Dec. 31, 2022
Profile - (Can. 2016; orig. N.B., 1995) Mines and refines nickel and cobalt from lateritic ores with projects and operations in Canada and Cuba. The company is the largest independent energy producer in Cuba, with extensive oil and power operations across the island. Also licenses proprietary technologies and provides metallurgical services to mining and refining operations worldwide.

Metals operations are conducted through a 50% interest (**General Nickel Company S.A.** 50%) in the Moa joint venture (nickel and cobalt mining, processing, refining and marketing), with operations carried on through three companies: **Moa Nickel S.A.**, which holds Moa nickel-cobalt project, 12,100 hectares, as well as mining and processing facilities in Moa, Cuba; **The Cobalt Refinery Company Inc.**, which operates refineries at Fort Saskatchewan, Alta., with a combined annual capacity of 38,200 tonnes of nickel and cobalt; and **International Cobalt Company Inc.**, which acquires nickel and cobalt feed materials for refining from Moa Nickel and third parties as well as markets and sells commodity nickel and cobalt. At Dec. 31, 2022, proven and probable reserves were 116,000,000 tonnes grading 1.01% nickel and 0.12% cobalt.

Also owns and operates fertilizer, utilities and storage facilities (Fort Site) in Fort Saskatchewan, Alta., which produces ammonia, sulphuric acid and utilities for use in the hydrometallurgical process as well as crystalline ammonium sulphate, a fertilizer produced as a by-product of nickel and cobalt refining which is sold primarily in western Canada.

Oil and gas operations include interests in two production sharing contracts covering areas in the north coast of Cuba, all of which are in the exploration phase. Also holds working interest in several oil fields and related production platform including 14.5% working interest in Casablanca, 15.6% working interest in Rodaballo, 29% working interest in Boquerón and 18.4% working interest in Barracuda oil fields, all in the Gulf of Valencia, offshore Spain. These fields ceased production on June 15, 2021, and are in the abandonment and reclamation phase.

Power operations include one-third interest in **Energas S.A.**, a joint venture that generates electricity for sale to the national grid system in Cuba, and operates integrated gas treatment/power generating facilities near the Varadero, Boca de Jaruco and Puerto Escondido oil fields with a total capacity of 506 MW.

Technologies division develops industry solutions that can be commercialized externally to improve operational performance and product quality, reduce carbon emissions and improve profitability, or applied internally to support growth initiatives including de-bottlenecking production, evaluating expansion opportunities and increasing mineral reserves. The technologies division provides technical support, process optimization and technology development services to the Moa joint venture and Fort Site operations, as well as provides a comprehensive suite of services for the mining industry including process development; metallurgical testing and analytical services; and engineering design and technical support from a project's inception to commercialization.

The company's share of sales volumes were reported as follows:

Year ended Dec. 31	2022	2021
Nickel (tonnes)	15,879	15,603
Cobalt (tonnes)	1,379	1,775
Fertilizers (tonnes)	170,427	168,782
Power (MWh)	568,000	450,000

Average realized prices were reported as follows:

Year ended Dec. 31	2022	2021
Moa JV		
Nickel, $/lb	14.93	10.30
Cobalt, $/lb	34.26	25.88
Fertilizers, $/tonne	759.91	438.75
Cuba, $/bbl	n.a.	42.24
Electricity, $/MWh	56.47	54.05

Directors - Sir Richard Lapthorne, chr., Bucks., United Kingdom; Maryse Bélanger, deputy chr., Vancouver, B.C.; Leon Binedell, pres. & CEO, Ont.; Dr. Peter Hancock, Halifax, N.S.; Anna M. Ladd-Kruger, B.C.; Chih-Ting Lo, Vancouver, B.C.; John M. Warwick, Toronto, Ont.
Other Exec. Officers - Yasmin Gabriel, CFO; Gregory (Greg) Honig, chief comml. officer; Chad Ross, chief HR officer; Daniel (Dan) Rusnell, sr. v-p, metals; Elvin Saruk, sr. v-p, oil & gas & power & head, growth projects; Edward A. (Ward) Sellers, sr. v-p, gen. counsel & corp. sec.

Capital Stock

	Authorized (shs.)	Outstanding (shs.)[1]
Common	unlimited	397,288,680

[1] At July 26, 2023

Options - At Dec. 31, 2022, options were outstanding to purchase 2,701,741 common shares at prices ranging from $0.68 to $5.14 per share with a weighted average remaining contractual life of 3.2 years.
Major Shareholder - Clearwater Capital Management Inc. held 10.5% interest at Mar. 17, 2023.

Price Range - S/TSX

Year	Volume	High	Low	Close
2022	208,158,308	$0.85	$0.31	$0.52
2021	137,337,837	$0.70	$0.36	$0.41
2020	166,557,444	$0.44	$0.07	$0.41
2019	282,077,753	$0.53	$0.17	$0.19
2018	345,201,315	$1.87	$0.37	$0.45

Recent Close: $0.46
Capital Stock Changes - There were no changes to capital stock during 2022.
Long-Term Debt - Outstanding at Dec. 31, 2022:

Syndicated revolv. credit facility[1]	$46,500,000
8.5% notes due 2026	233,600,000
10.75% notes due 2029	70,800,000
	350,900,000
Less: Current portion	46,500,000
	304,400,000

[1] Bears interest at bankers' acceptance plus 4%. Due Apr. 30, 2024.

Wholly Owned Subsidiaries

SICOG Oil and Gas Limited, Barbados.
Sherritt International Oil and Gas Limited, Alta.

Investments

50% int. in **The Cobalt Refinery Company Inc.**, Fort Saskatchewan, Alta.
33.33% int. in **Energas S.A.**, Cuba.
50% int. in **International Cobalt Company Inc.**, Bahamas.
50% int. in **Moa Nickel S.A.**, Cuba.

Financial Statistics

Periods ended:	12m Dec. 31/22^A		12m Dec. 31/21^ΩA
	$000s	%Chg	$000s
Operating revenue	**178,800**	**+62**	**110,200**
Cost of sales	66,100		46,900
Salaries & benefits	87,000		86,400
General & admin expense	2,300		4,900
Stock-based compensation	17,500		13,900
Operating expense	**172,900**	**+14**	**152,100**
Operating income	**5,900**	**n.a.**	**(41,900)**
Deprec., depl. & amort.	26,000		35,000
Finance costs, net	55,400		20,800
Investment income	140,800		86,500
Write-downs/write-offs	(2,000)		(1,100)
Pre-tax income	**63,300**	**n.a.**	**(12,300)**
Income taxes	(400)		1,100
Net inc. bef. disc. opers	**63,700**	**n.a.**	**(13,400)**
Income from disc. opers	(200)		(5,000)
Net income	**63,500**	**n.a.**	**(18,400)**
Cash & equivalent	123,900		145,600
Inventories	37,700		30,300
Accounts receivable	186,400		190,700
Current assets	429,300		390,000
Long-term investments	756,000		642,400
Fixed assets, net	148,600		150,900
Intangibles, net	6,500		17,400
Explor./devel. properties	7,300		6,900
Total assets	**1,555,600**	**+11**	**1,398,000**
Accts. pay. & accr. liabs	209,700		196,000
Current liabilities	367,600		221,900
Long-term debt, gross	350,900		444,500
Long-term debt, net	304,400		444,500
Long-term lease liabilities	12,600		14,200
Shareholders' equity	694,900		585,000
Cash from oper. activs	**88,700**	**n.a.**	**(4,400)**
Cash from fin. activs	(93,300)		(6,900)
Cash from invest. activs	(23,400)		(9,900)
Net cash position	**123,900**	**-15**	**145,600**
Capital expenditures	(28,500)		(10,700)
Capital disposals	1,300		nil
	$		$
Earns. per sh. bef disc opers*	0.16		(0.03)
Earnings per share*	0.16		(0.05)
Cash flow per share*	0.22		(0.01)
	shs		shs
No. of shs. o/s*	397,288,680		397,288,680
Avg. no. of shs. o/s*	397,300,000		397,300,000
	%		%
Net profit margin	35.63		(12.16)
Return on equity	9.95		(2.25)
Return on assets	4.31		(0.97)
No. of employees (FTEs)	3,310		3,311

* Common
Ω Restated
A Reported in accordance with IFRS

Latest Results

Periods ended:	6m June 30/23^A		6m June 30/22^A
	$000s	%Chg	$000s
Operating revenue	152,100	+52	100,000
Net inc. bef. disc. opers	13,900	-86	97,900
Income from disc. opers	(300)		(1,100)
Net income	13,600	-86	96,800
	$		$
Earns. per sh. bef. disc. opers.*	0.03		0.25
Earnings per share*	0.03		0.24

* Common
A Reported in accordance with IFRS

Historical Summary
(as originally stated)

Fiscal Year	Oper. Rev. $000s	Net Inc. Bef. Disc. $000s	EPS* $
2022^A	178,800	63,700	0.16
2021^A	110,200	(13,400)	(0.03)
2020^A	119,800	(85,700)	(0.22)
2019^A	137,600	(364,700)	(0.92)
2018^A	152,900	(80,200)	(0.21)

* Common
A Reported in accordance with IFRS

S.47 ShiftCarbon Inc.

Symbol - SHFT **Exchange** - CSE (S) **CUSIP** - G8126P
Head Office - Craigmuir Chambers, PO Box 71, Road Town, Tortola, British Virgin Islands, VG 1110 **Telephone** - (284) 494-3399 **Fax** - (284) 494-3041
Website - www.shiftcarbon.io
Email - mark@shiftcarbon.io
Investor Relations - Mark Leung (778) 655-4242
Auditors - Dale Matheson Carr-Hilton LaBonte LLP C.A., Vancouver, B.C.
Lawyers - Buttonwood Law Corporation, Vancouver, B.C.
Transfer Agents - Computershare Trust Company of Canada Inc., Vancouver, B.C.

Profile - (British Virgin Islands 2013; orig. B.C., 2011 amalg.) Provides a full suite of carbon management platform for carbon accounting, offsetting and measurement, reporting and verification (MRV) automation of carbon offsets. Also develops Internet of Things (IoT)-enabled technology devices for large-scale industrial and enterprise operations and holds investments in 5G-focused wireless technology.

ShiftCarbon is a carbon management platform which operates three verticals including ShiftCarbon Measure, which features carbon accounting, benchmarking, integration and goal tracking; ShiftCarbon Offset, which allows businesses to purchase carbon offsets certified through third party audits; and MRV automation of carbon offsets, which integrates with the company's IoT sensor technology and modular software to create and measure carbon credits at scale.

Also operates TRACEsafe, which develops IoT enabled technology solutions that transforms large-scale industrial and enterprise operations with wearables, industrial-grade sensors and analytics platform as well as offers gateways to connect theses wearables together including WiFi Gateway and LTE-M Gateway.

On Oct. 18, 2022, the company changed its business focus to managed decarbonization and in accordance began operating under the name **ShiftCarbon**.

In July 2022, the company acquired Offsety, a carbon offset marketplace for individuals to reduce their carbon footprint by investing in offset credits, for issuance of 2,000,000 common shares at a fair value of Cdn$270,000.

Common suspended from CSE, May 8, 2023.

Predecessor Detail - Name changed from TraceSafe Inc., Dec. 20, 2022.

Directors - James C. Passin, chr., Ill.; Wayne Lloyd, pres. & CEO, Vancouver, B.C.; Jeremy L. Gardner, Fla.; Gregory Kallinikos, Singapore; Murray Tevlin, B.C.

Other Exec. Officers - Mark Leung, CFO; Suresh Singamsetty, chief tech. officer; Gordon (Gord) Zeilstra, chief revenue officer; Chris Leung, v-p, global opers. & cust. success; Susanne MacKillop, v-p, sales; Marcin Samiec, v-p, tech. & chief privacy officer; Betty Anne Loy, corp. sec.; Dr. Dennis Kwan, CEO, Tracesafe Technologies Inc.

Capital Stock

	Authorized (shs.)	Outstanding (shs.)[1]
Preferred	unlimited	nil
Common	unlimited	56,364,647

[1] At Dec. 20, 2022

Major Shareholder - James C. Passin held 16.36% interest at July 13, 2021.

Price Range - SHFT/CSE (S)

Year	Volume	High	Low	Close
2022	15,269,625	$0.64	$0.06	$0.07
2021	38,689,228	$1.90	$0.38	$0.50
2020	19,834,403	$1.70	$0.17	$0.63
2019	2,307,967	$0.91	$0.11	$0.20
2018	115,651	$2.40	$0.12	$0.45

Recent Close: $0.04

Capital Stock Changes - In November 2022, private placement of 6,560,000 units (1 common share & 1 warrant) at US$0.10 per unit was completed, with warrants exercisable at US$0.25 per share for two years.

Wholly Owned Subsidiaries

TraceSafe Canada Inc., B.C.
TraceSafe Technologies Inc., Nev.
Wishland Properties Limited, British Virgin Islands.
- **Airbeam Wireless Technologies Inc.**
  - **Airbeam 60 GHz Holdings Ltd.**, B.C.

Subsidiaries

70% int. in **TraceSafe Asia Pacific Pte Ltd.**, Singapore.

Financial Statistics

Periods ended:	12m Dec. 31/21^A		12m Dec. 31/20^A
	US$000s	%Chg	US$000s
Operating revenue	**12,953**	**+264**	**3,560**
Cost of goods sold	7,447		2,021
Salaries & benefits	n.a.		1,027
Research & devel. expense	1,852		1,166
General & admin expense	7,018		2,269
Stock-based compensation	328		1,634
Operating expense	**16,645**	**+105**	**8,117**
Operating income	**(3,692)**	**n.a.**	**(4,557)**
Deprec., depl. & amort.	250		149
Finance costs, gross	687		223
Write-downs/write-offs	(4,485)		(20)
Pre-tax income	**(8,990)**	**n.a.**	**(7,739)**
Net income	**(8,990)**	**n.a.**	**(7,739)**
Net inc. for equity hldrs	**(1,108)**	**n.a.**	**(3,840)**
Net inc. for non-cont. int	**(7,882)**	**n.a.**	**(3,900)**
Cash & equivalent	357		557
Accounts receivable	510		2,018
Current assets	2,028		3,446
Long-term investments	2,202		3,103
Fixed assets, net	64		nil
Intangibles, net	nil		4,617
Total assets	**4,295**	**-62**	**11,166**
Bank indebtedness	756		1,468
Accts. pay. & accr. liabs	2,388		1,329
Current liabilities	4,299		2,852
Shareholders' equity	6,212		4,799
Non-controlling interest	(6,216)		3,514
Cash from oper. activs	**561**	**n.a.**	**(4,569)**
Cash from fin. activs	(710)		5,422
Cash from invest. activs	(46)		(301)
Net cash position	**357**	**-36**	**557**
Capital expenditures	(46)		nil
	US$		US$
Earnings per share*	(0.26)		(0.13)
Cash flow per share*	0.01		(0.15)
	shs		shs
No. of shs. o/s*	45,711,255		35,765,784
Avg. no. of shs. o/s*	42,896,772		30,074,853
	%		%
Net profit margin	(69.40)		(217.39)
Return on equity	(20.13)		(143.35)
Return on assets	(107.41)		(124.51)

* Common
A Reported in accordance with IFRS

Latest Results

Periods ended:	6m June 30/22^A		6m June 30/21^A
	US$000s	%Chg	US$000s
Operating revenue	2,074	-56	4,686
Net income	(2,994)	n.a.	(5,825)
Net inc. for equity hldrs	(2,581)	n.a.	(3,278)
Net inc. for non-cont. int	(413)		(2,547)
	US$		US$
Earnings per share*	(0.06)		(0.08)

* Common
A Reported in accordance with IFRS

Historical Summary
(as originally stated)

Fiscal Year	Oper. Rev. US$000s	Net Inc. Bef. Disc. US$000s	EPS* US$
2021^A	12,953	(8,990)	(0.26)
2020^A	3,560	(7,739)	(0.13)
2019^A	nil	(660)	(0.03)
2018^A	nil	(1,432)	(0.16)
2017^A	nil	(346)	(0.05)

* Common
A Reported in accordance with IFRS
Note: Adjusted throughout for 1-for-10 cons. in May 2018

S.48 Shine Box Capital Corp.

Symbol - RENT.P **Exchange** - TSX-VEN **CUSIP** - 824561
Head Office - East Tower, Centennial Place, 1900-520 3 Ave SW, Calgary, AB, T2P 0R3 **Telephone** - (416) 628-8589
Email - ndobrijevic@realcannareit.com
Investor Relations - Nebojsa Dobrijevic (416) 628-8589
Auditors - MNP LLP C.A., Calgary, Alta.
Transfer Agents - TSX Trust Company, Calgary, Alta.
Profile - (Can. 2018) Capital Pool Company.

Recent Merger and Acquisition Activity

Status: pending **Announced:** Feb. 16, 2023
Shine Box Capital Corp. entered into a letter of intent for the Qualifying Transaction reverse takeover acquisition of private Toronto, Ont.-based Electro Metals and Mining Inc., which has mineral interests in Quebec, on a share-for-share basis (following a 1-for-1.5 share consolidation).

Shine Box would issue 33,146,560 common shares at a deemed value of 30¢ per share. Electro proposed to complete a private placement of $3,500,000 to $5,500,000 in conjunction with the transaction. Upon completion, Shine Box would change its name to Electro Metals and Mining Inc.

Directors - Daniele Forigo, CEO, Calgary, Alta.; Nebojsa Dobrijevic, CFO & corp. sec., Toronto, Ont.; Gopikannan (Gopi) Pillai, Oakville, Ont.

Capital Stock

	Authorized (shs.)	Outstanding (shs.)[1]
Common	unlimited	6,000,000

[1] At Feb. 24, 2023

Major Shareholder - Noel C. O'Brien held 16.67% interest at Jan. 10, 2022.

Price Range - RENT.P/TSX-VEN

Year	Volume	High	Low	Close
2021	184,400	$0.10	$0.05	$0.09
2020	181,422	$0.14	$0.01	$0.14
2019	8,000	$0.15	$0.15	$0.15

Capital Stock Changes - There were no changes to capital stock during fiscal 2021 or fiscal 2022.

S.49 Shiny Health & Wellness Corp.

Symbol - SNYB **Exchange** - TSX-VEN **CUSIP** - 82464L
Head Office - 1008-150 York St, Toronto, ON, M5H 3S5 **Telephone** - (416) 583-2501 **Toll-free** - (888) 833-1260
Website - www.shinyhealthandwellness.com
Email - mike@snybcorp.com
Investor Relations - Michael Nadeau (437) 222-7047
Auditors - BDO Canada LLP C.A., Toronto, Ont.
Lawyers - Bennett Jones LLP
Transfer Agents - Computershare Trust Company of Canada Inc., Vancouver, B.C.
Employees - 173 at Oct. 31, 2022
Profile - (Can. 2022; orig. B.C., 2021) Owns and operates licensed recreational cannabis retail stores in Ontario and pursing acquisition of community pharmacies in Ontario.

Wholly owned **Shiny Bud Inc.** owns 28 stores operating under the ShinyBud, BudgetBud and Mihi banners; an additional 13 cannabis retail stores are owned and operated by third parties under the ShinyBud brand pursuant to trademark licence agreements. Cannabis products are purchased directly or indirectly from licensed producers in Canada. The stores range in size from 400 to 4,500 sq. ft.

Through wholly owned **mihi Health & Wellness Inc.**, the company plans to build a network of community pharmacies across Ontario. At October 2022, mihi owned an independent pharmacy in Cornwall, Ont.

In October 2022, the company acquired Cotton Mill Pharmacy, an independent no-banner pharmacy in Cornwall, Ont., for $900,000.

Common reinstated on TSX-VEN, July 5, 2023.
Common suspended from TSX-VEN, June 7, 2023.

Predecessor Detail - Name changed from ShinyBud Corp., Aug. 15, 2022.

Directors - Micah (Mike) Dass, exec. v-chr., Qué.; Michael (Mike) Nadeau, CEO, Ont.; Lyn Christensen, Calif.; Richard Espinos, Vaughan, Ont.; Bradley R. (Brad) Kipp, Mississauga, Ont.; Meris Kott, Fla.; Donald B. (Don) Schroeder, Burlington, Ont.; Roland M. Walton, Oakville, Ont.

Other Exec. Officers - Dominic Lavallée, interim CFO

Capital Stock

	Authorized (shs.)	Outstanding (shs.)[1]
Common	unlimited	10,657,799

[1] At June 28, 2023

Major Shareholder - Micah (Mike) Dass held 65.47% interest at June 28, 2023.

Price Range - SNYB/TSX-VEN

Year	Volume	High	Low	Close
2022	402,466	$6.25	$1.10	$1.70

Recent Close: $0.25

Wholly Owned Subsidiaries

mihi Health & Wellness Inc., Ont.
- 49% int. in **1000209217 Ontario Ltd.**, Ont.

Shiny Bud Inc., Toronto, Ont.
- 75.1% int. in **Mihi Express Inc.**, Ont.
- 100% int. in **SNYB Franchising Inc.**, Canada.
- 100% int. in **ShinyBud AdFund Corp.**, Canada.

Financial Statistics

Periods ended:	12m Jan. 31/22[A1]		12m Jan. 31/21[A2]
	$000s	%Chg	$000s
Operating revenue	**20,647**	**+95**	**10,582**
Cost of sales	12,999		6,581
Salaries & benefits	5,576		895
General & admin expense	2,146		902
Operating expense	**20,721**	**+147**	**8,378**
Operating income	**(74)**	**n.a.**	**2,204**
Deprec., depl. & amort.	1,273		363
Finance costs, gross	1,229		383
Write-downs/write-offs	(136)		nil
Pre-tax income	**(5,765)**	**n.a.**	**1,465**
Income taxes	26		414
Net income	**(5,791)**	**n.a.**	**1,051**
Cash & equivalent	4,527		151
Inventories	1,547		754
Accounts receivable	199		nil
Current assets	7,115		980
Fixed assets, net	6,692		2,065
Right-of-use assets	8,201		2,251
Intangibles, net	13,089		nil
Total assets	**35,578**	**+538**	**5,574**
Accts. pay. & accr. liabs	3,219		725
Current liabilities	8,255		2,285
Long-term debt, gross	2,070		nil
Long-term debt, net	2,070		nil
Long-term lease liabilities	7,685		2,181
Shareholders' equity	15,527		967
Cash from oper. activs	**(1,329)**	**n.a.**	**1,450**
Cash from fin. activs	8,352		509
Cash from invest. activs	(2,646)		(1,848)
Net cash position	**4,527**	**n.m.**	**151**
Capital expenditures	(2,309)		(1,676)
	$		$
Earnings per share*	(0.79)		n.a.
Cash flow per share*	(0.18)		n.a.
	shs		shs
No. of shs. o/s*	10,657,808		n.a.
Avg. no. of shs. o/s*	7,343,485		n.a.
	%		%
Net profit margin	(28.05)		9.93
Return on equity	(70.22)		n.m.
Return on assets	(22.14)		n.a.
No. of employees (FTEs)	144		n.a.

* Common
[A] Reported in accordance with IFRS
[1] Results reflect the Jan. 20, 2022, Qualifying Transaction reverse takeover acquisition of Shiny Bud Inc. and Mihi Inc.
[2] Results pertain to Shiny Bud Inc.

Latest Results

Periods ended:	3m Apr. 30/22[A]		3m Apr. 30/21[A]
	$000s	%Chg	$000s
Operating revenue	7,575	+74	4,342
Net income	(1,758)	n.a.	364
	$		$
Earnings per share*	(0.16)		n.a.

* Common
[A] Reported in accordance with IFRS

Note: Adjusted throughout for 1-for-42.748 cons. in Feb. 2022

S.50 Shooting Star Acquisition Corp.

Symbol - SSSS.P **Exchange** - TSX-VEN **CUSIP** - 82505P
Head Office - 1000-409 Granville St, Vancouver, BC, V6C 1T2 **Telephone** - (604) 602-0001
Email - gb@harmonycs.ca
Investor Relations - Geoffrey Balderson (604) 602-0001
Auditors - Crowe MacKay LLP C.A., Vancouver, B.C.
Transfer Agents - Odyssey Trust Company, Vancouver, B.C.
Profile - (B.C. 2018) Capital Pool Company.

In November 2022, proposed acquisition of option from **Eagle Plains Resources Ltd.** to earn 60% interest in the Eldridge gold prospect in Saskatchewan was terminated. The acquisition would have constituted the company's Qualifying Transaction.

Recent Merger and Acquisition Activity

Status: terminated **Revised:** Dec. 29, 2022
UPDATE: The transaction was terminated. PREVIOUS: Shooting Star Acquisition Corp. entered into a letter of intent for the Qualifying Transaction reverse takeover acquisition of private Golden Mountain Technologies Inc., which holds an option to acquire the 3,100-hectare Cabot copper prospect in the northwest corner of the Baie Verte Peninsula, N.L., on a share-for-share basis, which would result in the issuance of 28,708,454 Shooting Star post-consolidated common shares at a deemed price of 20¢ per share (following a 1-for-4 share consolidation).

Directors - Geoffrey (Geoff) Balderson, pres., CEO, CFO & corp. sec., Vancouver, B.C.; Stephen R. Gatensbury, Vancouver, B.C.; Gregory F. (Greg) Smith, North Vancouver, B.C.

Capital Stock

	Authorized (shs.)	Outstanding (shs.)[1]
Common	unlimited	4,540,000

[1] At May 26, 2023

Major Shareholder - Geoffrey (Geoff) Balderson held 20.7% interest at Mar. 20, 2023.

Price Range - SSSS.P/TSX-VEN

Year	Volume	High	Low	Close
2022	112,530	$0.12	$0.06	$0.06
2021	90,900	$0.14	$0.09	$0.09
2019	49,000	$0.15	$0.05	$0.06

Capital Stock Changes - There were no changes to capital stock during fiscal 2021 or fiscal 2022.

S.51 Shopify Inc.*

Symbol - SHOP **Exchange** - TSX **CUSIP** - 82509L
Head Office - Ground Flr, 151 O'Connor St, Ottawa, ON, K2P 2L8 **Telephone** - (613) 241-2828
Website - www.shopify.com
Email - ir@shopify.com
Investor Relations - Carrie Gillard (613) 241-2828
Auditors - PricewaterhouseCoopers LLP C.A., Ottawa, Ont.
Lawyers - Skadden, Arps, Slate, Meagher & Flom LLP, New York, N.Y.; Stikeman Elliott LLP, Toronto, Ont.
Transfer Agents - Computershare Trust Company, N.A., Canton, Mass.; Computershare Trust Company of Canada Inc., Toronto, Ont.
FP500 Revenue Ranking - 90
Employees - 11,600 at Dec. 31, 2022
Profile - (Can. 2004) Designs, develops and provides a cloud-based commerce platform for merchants of all sizes to start, grow, market and manage their retail operations across multiple sales channels.

The company's commerce platform provides merchants with a single view of their business and customers across all of their sales channels, including web and mobile storefronts, physical retail locations, pop-up shops, business-to-business (B2B), social media storefronts, native mobile applications, buy buttons, and marketplaces such as Amazon and eBay. The platform enables merchants to manage products and inventory, process orders and payments, fulfill and ship orders, discover new buyers and build customer relationships, source products, leverage analytics and reporting, manage cash, payments and transactions, and access financing. Merchants from more than 175 countries use the company's platform.

Year ended Dec. 31	2022	2021
	US$000s	US$000s
Monthly recurring revenue	109,510	102,022
Gross mdse. volume	197,166,882	175,361,814

In May 2023, the company announced it will reduce its head count by 20%, representing approximately 1,800 employees. This resulted in US$148,000,000 of severance related costs in the second quarter of 2023.

On July 26, 2022, the company announced staff reductions, representing 10% of its workforce.

On June 9, 2022, a plan of arrangement was completed whereby the company issued a founder share to co-founder and major shareholder Tobias Lütke that has a variable number of votes that, when combined with his other holdings, represents 40% of the total voting power attached to all of the company's outstanding voting shares. The founder share would not be transferable and would sunset if Lütke no longer serves the company in certain capacities (as an executive officer, board member or consultant whose primary engagement is with the company) or Lütke, his immediately family and his affiliates no longer hold a number of class A and class B shares equal to at least 30% of the class B shares held as of Apr. 11, 2022. In the event of a sunset of the founder share, Lütke would also convert his remaining class B shares into class A shares.

Recent Merger and Acquisition Activity

Status: completed **Revised:** June 6, 2023
UPDATE: The transaction was completed. Equity representing a 13% interest in Flexport was received, increasing Shopify's interest to 17% at closing. PREVIOUS: Shopify Inc. agreed to sell its logistics business unit, including last-mile delivery startup Deliverr, to San Francisco, Calif.-based Flexport Inc. Shopify would receive common shares that represented a 13% equity interest in Flexport. Upon completion, Flexport would become Shopify's official logistics provider, while Shopify would retain its Shopify Fulfillment Network application where merchants manage their logistics process.

Status: completed **Announced:** Aug. 19, 2022
Shopify Inc. acquired San Francisco, Calif.-based Remix Software Inc., a developer of a full-stack web framework for building websites and applications, for an undisclosed amount which included the issuance of 251,972 class A subordinate voting shares.

Status: completed **Revised:** July 8, 2022
UPDATE: The transaction was completed. PREVIOUS: Shopify Inc. agreed to acquire San Francisco, Calif.-based Deliverr, Inc., an e-commerce fulfillment company providing an end-to-end software and logistics platform that was integrated with e-commerce marketplaces including Amazon, eBay, Etsy and Walmart, for US$2.1 billion, consisting of US$1.7 billion cash and US$400,000,000 of Shopify class A subordinate voting shares. Deliverr's technology offers scalable logistics infrastructure for end-to-end inventory orchestration to millions of merchants, allowing them to offer and achieve fast (two-day) delivery promises across multiple channels including online stores, search and

social channels, and the e-commerce marketplaces, as well as removes the complexity of fragmented supply chain management.

Directors - Tobias (Tobi) Lütke, co-founder, chr. & CEO, Ont.; Robert G. (Rob) Ashe†, Ottawa, Ont.; Gail Goodman, Mass.; Colleen M. Johnston, Toronto, Ont.; Jeremy Levine, N.Y.; Tobyn Shannan, Perth, Ont.; Fidji Simo, Calif.; Bret Taylor, Calif.

Other Exec. Officers - Harley Finkelstein, pres.; Jeff Hoffmeister, CFO; John Asante, chief info. security officer; Allan Leinwand, chief tech. officer; Luc Levesque, chief growth officer; Bobby Morrison, chief revenue officer; Tia Silas, chief HR officer; Kasra (Kaz) Nejatian, v-p, product & COO; Jessica Hertz, gen. counsel & corp. sec.

† Lead director

Capital Stock

	Authorized (shs.)	Outstanding (shs.)[1]
Preferred	unlimited	nil
Cl.A Subord. Vtg.	unlimited	1,203,499,789
Cl.B Restricted Vtg.	unlimited	79,272,851
Founder	1	1

[1] At July 28, 2023

Class A Subordinate Voting - One vote per share.

Class B Restricted Voting - Convertible into class A subordinate voting shares on a one-for-one basis at any time at the option of the holder and automatically in certain other circumstances. Ten votes per share.

Founder - Held by Tobias Lütke. When combined with the class B restricted voting shares and class A subordinate voting shares held by Lütke, his immediately family and his affiliates, represents 40% of the total voting power attached to all of the company's outstanding voting shares, provided that the voting power of Lütke, his immediately family and his affiliates does not exceed 49.9% of the total voting power attached to all of the company's outstanding voting shares. Sunsets if Lütke no longer serves the company in certain capacities or Lütke, his immediate family and his affiliates no longer hold a number of class A subordinate voting shares and class B restricted voting shares equal to at least 2,367,556, representing 30% of the class B restricted voting shares held by Lütke, his immediate family and his affiliates as of Apr. 11, 2022.

Options - At Dec. 31, 2022, options were outstanding to purchase 1,038,218 class B restricted voting shares and 12,970,543 class A subordinate voting shares at a weighted average exercise price of US$36.55 per share with a remaining contractual life of 6.71 years.

Major Shareholder - Tobias (Tobi) Lütke held 40.03% interest at Apr. 28, 2023.

Price Range - SHOP/TSX

Year	Volume	High	Low	Close
2022	919,517,836	$174.24	$33.00	$47.01
2021	417,832,800	$222.87	$124.86	$174.17
2020	704,242,240	$165.88	$43.50	$143.73
2019	750,870,464	$54.40	$17.46	$51.63
2018	826,331,136	$23.27	$12.67	$18.88

Split: 10-for-1 split in June 2022

Recent Close: $75.57

Capital Stock Changes - Effective June 9, 2022, a plan of arrangement was completed whereby the authorized capital was amended to include one founder share, which was issued to Tobias Lütke for cash consideration of Cdn$10, all 3,750,000 pre-split class B multiple voting shares held by Klister Credit Corp. were converted into a like number of class A subordinate voting shares, and class B multiple voting shares were renamed as class B restricted voting shares. On June 29, 2022, class A subordinate voting shares and class B restricted voting shares were split on a 10-for-1 basis. In July 2022, 5,397,628 post-split class A subordinate voting shares were issued pursuant to the acquisition of Deliverr, Inc. Also during 2022, 7,380,507 post-split class A subordinate voting shares were issued on vesting of restricted share units, 3,126,869 post-split class A subordinate voting shares and class B restricted voting shares were issued on exercise of options and 251,972 post-split class A subordinate voting shares were issued pursuant to the acquisition of Remix Software Inc.

Long-Term Debt - At Dec. 31, 2022, outstanding long-term debt totaled US$913,312,000 (nil current and net of US$6,688,000 unamortized offering costs) and consisted entirely of 0.125% convertible senior notes due Nov. 1, 2025, convertible into class A subordinate voting shares at US$144.01 per share, subject to certain adjustments and circumstances.

Wholly Owned Subsidiaries

Shopify Commerce Singapore Pte. Ltd., Singapore.

Shopify Holdings (USA) Inc., Del.

- 100% int. in **Shopify (USA) Inc.**, Del.

Shopify International Limited, Ireland.

Shopify LLC, Del.

Investments

17% int. in **Flexport Inc.**, San Francisco, Calif.

Note: The preceding list includes only the major related companies in which interests are held.

Financial Statistics

Periods ended:	12m Dec. 31/22[A]		12m Dec. 31/21[◻A]
	US$000s	%Chg	US$000s
Operating revenue	**5,599,864**	**+21**	**4,611,856**
Cost of sales	2,784,752		2,099,869
Research & devel. expense	1,098,858		618,822
General & admin expense	1,679,648		1,115,589
Stock-based compensation	549,142		330,763
Operating expense	**6,112,400**	**+47**	**4,165,043**
Operating income	**(512,536)**	**n.a.**	**446,813**
Deprec., depl. & amort.	90,520		66,308
Finance income	79,141		15,356
Finance costs, gross	3,499		3,493
Write-downs/write-offs	(84,314)		(30,145)
Pre-tax income	**(3,622,848)**	**n.a.**	**3,140,592**
Income taxes	(162,430)		225,933
Net income	**(3,460,418)**	**n.a.**	**2,914,659**
Cash & equivalent	5,052,950		7,768,093
Accounts receivable	273,055		192,209
Current assets	6,050,473		8,539,320
Long-term investments	1,953,460		3,955,545
Fixed assets, net	130,821		105,526
Right-of-use assets	355,145		196,388
Intangibles, net	2,226,430		495,024
Total assets	**10,757,151**	**-19**	**13,340,172**
Accts. pay. & accr. liabs.	517,021		450,762
Current liabilities	856,008		702,733
Long-term debt, gross	913,312		910,963
Long-term debt, net	913,312		910,963
Long-term lease liabilities	465,135		246,776
Shareholders' equity	8,238,889		11,133,341
Cash from oper. activs.	**(136,448)**	**n.a.**	**535,711**
Cash from fin. activs.	17,549		1,649,762
Cash from invest. activs.	(718,567)		(2,379,073)
Net cash position	**1,649,328**	**-34**	**2,502,992**
Capital expenditures	(50,018)		(50,788)
	US$		US$
Earnings per share*	(2.73)		2.34
Cash flow per share*	(0.11)		0.43
	shs		shs
No. of shs. o/s*	1,275,128,567		1,258,971,590
Avg. no. of shs. o/s*	1,266,268,155		1,246,588,910
	%		%
Net profit margin	(61.79)		63.20
Return on equity	(35.73)		33.25
Return on assets	(28.69)		27.65
Foreign sales percent	94		93
No. of employees (FTEs)	11,600		10,000

* Cl.A & B Vtg.

◻ Restated

[A] Reported in accordance with U.S. GAAP

Latest Results

Periods ended:	6m June 30/23[A]		6m June 30/22[A]
	US$000s	%Chg	US$000s
Operating revenue	3,202,000	+28	2,498,686
Net income	(1,243,000)	n.a.	(2,678,315)
	US$		US$
Earnings per share*	(0.97)		(2.12)

* Cl.A & B Vtg.

[A] Reported in accordance with U.S. GAAP

Historical Summary
(as originally stated)

Fiscal Year	Oper. Rev. US$000s	Net Inc. Bef. Disc. US$000s	EPS* US$
2022[A]	5,599,864	(3,460,418)	(2.73)
2021[A]	4,611,856	2,914,659	2.34
2020[A]	2,929,491	319,509	0.27
2019[A]	1,578,173	(124,842)	(0.11)
2018[A]	1,073,229	(64,553)	(0.06)

* Cl.A & B Vtg.

[A] Reported in accordance with U.S. GAAP

Note: Adjusted throughout for 10-for-1 split in June 2022

S.52 Sienna Senior Living Inc.

Symbol - SIA **Exchange** - TSX **CUSIP** - 82621K

Head Office - 300-302 Town Centre Blvd, Markham, ON, L3R 0E8

Telephone - (905) 477-4006 **Fax** - (905) 415-7623

Website - www.siennaliving.ca

Email - nancy.webb@siennaliving.ca

Investor Relations - Nancy Webb (905) 489-0254

Auditors - Deloitte LLP C.A., Toronto, Ont.

Lawyers - Goodmans LLP, Toronto, Ont.

Transfer Agents - Computershare Trust Company of Canada Inc., Toronto, Ont.

FP500 Revenue Ranking - 398

Employees - 12,000 at Dec. 31, 2022

Profile - (Ont. 2010) Owns and operates 93 seniors' living residences in Ontario, British Columbia and Saskatchewan offering a full range of seniors' living options, including independent and assisted living, long-term and residential care, and specialized programs and services. Also provides related management services.

The long-term care (LTC) homes provide essential health services in the form of 24-hour registered nursing support, assistance with activities of daily living and mobility, to individuals with complex physical and medical care needs who may otherwise require hospital care. These residences also provide specialized services such as dementia care, continence management, skin and wound care, palliation and end of life care.

Retirement residences focus on independent living, independent supportive living, assisted living (AL), and in some cases, memory care, and generally provide studio, one-bedroom or two-bedroom accommodation suites and amenity space. Suites are rented to residents on a monthly basis, and provide for meals, snacks, leisure activities, transportation and AL services.

At Dec. 31 2022, the company's portfolio consisted of 93 facilities, of which 80 were either wholly or partially owned and 13 were managed on behalf of third parties.

The company's portfolio of owned communities consisted of:

	Residences	Suites/Beds
LTC	46	7,281[1, 2]
Retirement[3]	47	5,202
	93	12,483

[1] 180 of the long-term care beds are privately funded.

[2] Includes 256 beds which are 40%-owned and 118 beds which are 77%-owned.

[3] Includes 12 residences which are 50%-owned.

In December 2022, the company announced the closure of one of its long-term care residences in Ontario, incurring restructuring costs of $6,600,000.

Recent Merger and Acquisition Activity

Status: completed **Revised:** Jan. 3, 2023

UPDATE: The transaction was completed for a purchase price of $26,300,000. Sienna Senior Living Inc. agreed to acquire Woods Park Care Centre in Barrie, Ont., which offers a continuum of care, for $26,000,000. Woods Park consists of 55 private-pay independent living retirement suites and 123 government-funded class A long-term care beds. The transaction was expected to be completed in the second half of 2022.

Status: completed **Revised:** June 1, 2022

Sienna Senior Living Inc. agreed to acquire a 50% interest in The Village at Stonebridge in Saskatoon, Sask., a retirement residence consisting of 159 independent living suites and 27 assisted living suites, for $35,800,000. Sabra Health Care REIT, Inc., based in Irvine, Calif., would acquire the remaining 50% interest, with Sienna acting as the manager of the property.

Status: completed **Revised:** May 16, 2022

UPDATE: The transaction was completed. PREVIOUS: Extendicare Inc. agreed to sell its Espirt retirement living operations consisting of 1,050 retirement living suites across 11 retirement communities in Ontario (7) and Saskatchewan (4), to Sienna-Sabra LP, a 50/50 partnership formed between Sienna Senior Living Inc. and Irvine, Calif.-based Sabra Health Care REIT, Inc., for a purchase price of $307,500,000, subject to customary closing adjustments. Sienna would partially fund its portion of the acquisition price with proceeds from a proposed bought deal public offering. The portfolio consisted of 840 independent living suites, 51 assisted living suites and 157 memory care suites. Extendicare plans to focus on its long-term care and home health care segments.

Status: completed **Revised:** Mar. 31, 2022

UPDATE: The transaction was completed. PREVIOUS: Sienna Senior Living Inc. agreed to sell Camilla Care Community in Mississauga, Ont., a long-term care facility consisting of 236 beds, for $19,875,000.

Predecessor Detail - Name changed from Leisureworld Senior Care Corporation, May 1, 2015.

Directors - Shelly L. Jamieson, chr., Norwood, Ont.; Nitin Jain, pres. & CEO, Toronto, Ont.; Paul A. Boniferro, Toronto, Ont.; Dr. Gina P. Cody, Toronto, Ont.; Brian K. Johnston, Toronto, Ont.; Paula Jourdain Coleman, Oakville, Ont.; Stephen L. Sender, Thornhill, Ont.

Other Exec. Officers - Jennifer Anderson, exec. v-p, long-term care opers.; Teresa Fritsch, exec. v-p & chief corp. officer; Olga Giovanniello, exec. v-p & chief HR officer; David Hung, exec. v-p & CFO; Mark A. Lugowski, exec. v-p, retirement opers.; Adam Walsh, sr. v-p, gen. counsel & corp. sec.; Nancy Webb, sr. v-p, public affairs & mktg.

Capital Stock

	Authorized (shs.)	Outstanding (shs.)[1]
Preferred	unlimited	nil
Common	unlimited	72,967,166

[1] At June 12, 2023

Normal Course Issuer Bid - The company plans to make normal course purchases of up to 3,648,358 common shares representing 5% of the total outstanding. The bid commenced on June 20, 2023, and expires on June 19, 2024.

Major Shareholder - Widely held at Mar. 13, 2023.

Price Range - SIA/TSX

Year	Volume	High	Low	Close
2022	68,098,618	$15.78	$10.61	$10.90
2021	65,860,675	$16.85	$12.72	$15.03
2020	96,224,279	$19.72	$8.85	$14.14
2019	40,396,136	$20.35	$15.65	$18.26
2018	47,174,932	$18.49	$15.44	$15.74

Recent Close: $11.76

Capital Stock Changes - In March 2022, bought deal public offering of 5,750,000 common shares was completed at $15 per share, including 750,000 common shares on exercise of over-allotment option. Also during 2022, 150,818 common shares were issued under a stock-based compensation plan.

Dividends

SIA com Ra $0.936 pa M est. Oct. 15, 2019**
** Reinvestment Option

Wholly Owned Subsidiaries

Leisureworld Senior Care LP, Ont.
- 100% int. in **2063412 Investment LP**, Ont.
- 100% int. in **2063414 Investment LP**, Ont.
- 100% int. in **2063415 Investment LP**, Ont.
- 100% int. in **2067475 Investment LP**, Ont.
- 100% int. in **Vigour Limited Partnership**, Ont.

The Royale Development LP, Ont.
The Royale LP, Ont.
The Royale West Coast LP, Ont.
SSLI1 Development LP, Ont.
Sienna Baltic Development LP, Ont.
Sienna Baltic LP, Ont.
Sienna Management LP, Ont.
Sienna Ontario RH 2017 LP, Ont.
2371281 Investment LP, Ont.

Investments

50% int. in **Sienna-Sabra LP**, Ont.

Financial Statistics

Periods ended:	12m Dec. 31/22[A]		12m Dec. 31/21[oA]
	$000s	%Chg	$000s
Operating revenue	**718,590**	**+7**	**668,494**
Cost of sales	588,481		526,353
General & admin expense	37,419		29,830
Stock-based compensation	1,951		1,440
Operating expense	**627,851**	**+13**	**557,623**
Operating income	**90,739**	**-18**	**110,871**
Deprec., depl. & amort.	47,337		53,069
Finance income	1,838		1,725
Finance costs, gross	27,527		29,105
Investment income	(11,275)		(30)
Write-downs/write-offs	(12,788)		nil
Pre-tax income	**11,181**	**-60**	**28,033**
Income taxes	513		7,385
Net income	**10,668**	**-48**	**20,648**
Cash & equivalent	38,050		29,053
Accounts receivable	17,498		21,469
Current assets	83,755		114,741
Long-term investments	159,073		6,297
Fixed assets, net	1,064,880		1,102,791
Intangibles, net	357,188		363,581
Total assets	**1,680,428**	**+4**	**1,609,189**
Accts. pay. & accr. liabs	125,622		126,789
Current liabilities	336,706		237,989
Long-term debt, gross	977,964		950,284
Long-term debt, net	851,865		899,134
Shareholders' equity	434,692		405,853
Cash from oper. activs	**106,077**	**+8**	**98,516**
Cash from fin. activs	37,646		(147,094)
Cash from invest. activs	(134,726)		(18,046)
Net cash position	**38,050**	**+31**	**29,053**
Capital expenditures	(55,642)		(40,296)
Capital disposals	49,789		nil
	$		$
Earnings per share*	0.15		0.31
Cash flow per share*	1.48		1.47
Cash divd. per share*	0.94		0.94
	shs		shs
No. of shs. o/s*	72,939,941		67,039,123
Avg. no. of shs. o/s*	71,589,104		67,039,123
	%		%
Net profit margin	1.48		3.09
Return on equity	2.54		4.84
Return on assets	2.25		2.56
No. of employees (FTEs)	12,000		12,000

* Common
[o] Restated
[A] Reported in accordance with IFRS

Latest Results

Periods ended:	3m Mar. 31/23[A]		3m Mar. 31/22[A]
	$000s	%Chg	$000s
Operating revenue	192,054	+10	174,282
Net income	(340)	n.a.	26,020
	$		$
Earnings per share*	(0.00)		0.39

* Common
[A] Reported in accordance with IFRS

Historical Summary
(as originally stated)

Fiscal Year	Oper. Rev.	Net Inc. Bef. Disc.	EPS*
	$000s	$000s	$
2022[A]	718,590	10,668	0.15
2021[A]	668,494	20,648	0.31
2020[A]	664,233	(24,487)	(0.37)
2019[A]	669,733	7,547	0.11
2018[A]	641,984	9,883	0.15

* Common
[A] Reported in accordance with IFRS

S.53 Silo Wellness Inc.

Symbol - SILO **Exchange** - CSE **CUSIP** - 827124
Head Office - 702-200 Consumers Rd, Toronto, ON, M2J 4R4 **Telephone** - (416) 861-5882 **Toll-free** - (855) 937-4561 **Fax** - (416) 861-8165
Website - www.silowellness.com
Email - mike@silowellness.com
Investor Relations - C. Michael Arnold (541) 797-0110
Auditors - Zeifmans LLP C.A., Toronto, Ont.
Lawyers - CP LLP, Toronto, Ont.
Transfer Agents - TSX Trust Company, Toronto, Ont.
Profile - (Ont. 2017) Operates as psychedelics company focused on the development and online sale of functional mushroom tinctures (including under the Marley One™ brand), development of a psilocybin nasal spray, and offering of psilocybin and ketamine-assisted wellness retreats in Jamaica and Oregon, respectively. Also has psychedelic mushroom cultivation operations in Jamaica.

In October 2022, the company acquired **Dyscovry Science Ltd.**, a private Toronto, Ont.-based biotechnology company focused on biosynthetic manufacturing of psilocybin and its derivatives to treat irritable bowel syndrome, for issuance of 12,762,325 common shares, which represented a 49% interest in the company.

Common reinstated on CSE, Apr. 11, 2023.

Common suspended from CSE, Mar. 7, 2023.

Predecessor Detail - Name changed from Yukoterre Resources Inc., Feb. 26, 2021, pursuant to reverse takeover acquisition of FlyOverture Equity Inc., and concurrent amalgamation of FlyOverture with wholly owned 1261466 B.C. Inc.

Directors - C. Michael (Mike) Arnold, chr., pres. & interim CEO, Springfield, Ore.; Michael Hartman, COO, Millbrae, Calif.; Dr. Simon R. Bababeygy, Los Angeles, Calif.; Gregory Biniowsky, Vancouver, B.C.

Other Exec. Officers - Yongbiao (Winfield) Ding, CFO

Capital Stock

	Authorized (shs.)	Outstanding (shs.)[1]
Common	unlimited	129,926,994

[1] At Mar. 2, 2023

Major Shareholder - Widely held at May 12, 2022.

Price Range - SILO/CSE

Year	Volume	High	Low	Close
2022	41,559,748	$2.00	$0.01	$0.02
2021	1,021,059	$7.60	$0.70	$0.90
2020	6,312	$4.00	$3.20	$4.00
2019	20,725	$6.40	$3.60	$3.60

Consolidation: 1-for-20 cons. in June 2022; 0.5-for-1 cons. in Feb. 2021

Recent Close: $0.01

Capital Stock Changes - On June 17, 2022, common shares were consolidated on a 1-for-20 basis. In October 2022, 12,762,325 post-consolidated common shares were issued pursuant to the acquisition of Dyscovry Science Ltd.

Wholly Owned Subsidiaries

Dyscovry Science Ltd., Toronto, Ont.
SW Holdings, Inc., Ore.
Silo Psychedelics Inc., B.C.

Financial Statistics

Periods ended:	12m Oct. 31/21[A1]		12m Oct. 31/20[oA]
	US$000s	%Chg	US$000s
Operating revenue	**120**	**n.m.**	**6**
Cost of sales	389		49
General & admin expense	4,045		1,020
Stock-based compensation	621		nil
Operating expense	**5,055**	**+373**	**1,069**
Operating income	**(4,935)**	**n.a.**	**(1,063)**
Deprec., depl. & amort.	55		327
Finance costs, gross	69		2
Pre-tax income	**(6,209)**	**n.a.**	**(1,386)**
Net income	**(6,209)**	**n.a.**	**(1,386)**
Cash & equivalent	98		118
Inventories	90		7
Current assets	613		260
Intangibles, net	nil		55
Total assets	**613**	**+19**	**515**
Bank indebtedness	58		101
Accts. pay. & accr. liabs	687		118
Current liabilities	972		350
Shareholders' equity	(359)		(36)
Cash from oper. activs	**(3,798)**	**n.a.**	**(615)**
Cash from fin. activs	(3,781)		731
Net cash position	**98**	**-17**	**118**
	US$		US$
Earnings per share*	(2.00)		(2.40)
Cash flow per share*	(1.23)		(1.10)
	shs		shs
No. of shs. o/s*	3,570,125		n.a.
Avg. no. of shs. o/s*	3,096,855		558,718
	%		%
Net profit margin	n.m.		n.m.
Return on equity	n.m.		n.m.
Return on assets	n.m.		(305.14)

* Common
[o] Restated
[A] Reported in accordance with IFRS
[1] Results reflect the Mar. 1, 2021, reverse takeover acquisition of FlyOverture Equity Inc.

Latest Results

Periods ended:	6m Apr. 30/22[A]		6m Apr. 30/21[A]
	US$000s	%Chg	US$000s
Operating revenue	175	+257	49
Net income	(1,987)	n.a.	(3,714)
	US$		US$
Earnings per share*	(0.60)		(1.60)

* Common
[A] Reported in accordance with IFRS

Historical Summary
(as originally stated)

Fiscal Year	Oper. Rev.	Net Inc. Bef. Disc.	EPS*
	US$000s	US$000s	US$
2021[A]	120	(6,209)	(2.00)
	$000s	$000s	$
2020[A1]	nil	(664)	(2.40)
2019[A]	nil	(215)	(1.20)
2018[A2]	nil	(61)	(0.40)
2017[A2,3]	nil	(41)	(0.80)

* Common
[A] Reported in accordance with IFRS
[1] Results for fiscal 2020 and prior fiscal years pertain to Yukoterre Resources Inc.
[2] As shown in the prospectus dated June 26, 2019.
[3] 38 weeks ended Oct. 31, 2017.

Note: Adjusted throughout for 1-for-20 cons. in June 2022; 0.5-for-1 cons. in Feb. 2021

S.54 Silver Bullet Mines Corp.

Symbol - SBMI **Exchange** - TSX-VEN **CUSIP** - 827459
Head Office - 200-3310 South Service Rd, Burlington, ON, L7N 3J3 **Telephone** - (905) 302-3843
Website - www.silverbulletmines.com
Email - johncarter@silverbulletmines.com
Investor Relations - A. John Carter (905) 302-3843
Auditors - Grant Thornton LLP C.A., Toronto, Ont.
Transfer Agents - Capital Transfer Agency Inc., Toronto, Ont.
Profile - (Ont. 2018) Has mineral interests in Arizona, Idaho and Nevada.

In Arizona, holds Black Diamond prospect, 4,793 acres, 10 miles north of Globe, which includes formerly producing McMorris, McClellan, Silver Seven and La Plata silver mines, and lease on formerly producing Buckeye silver mine; and a 125-tonne-per-day silver pilot plant near Globe that was commissioned in July 2022.

In Idaho, holds Washington Mines gold prospect, 119 acres, 48 hectares, Boise cty.

In Nevada, holds Siolfor gold prospect, 200 acres, 15 miles west of Tonopah; and Ophir Canyon gold prospect, 150 acres, 15 miles north of Round Mountain.

On June 21, 2022, amalgamation of wholly owned **Silver Bullet Mining Inc.** with the company and name change to **Silver Bullet Mines Inc.** were approved.

Common reinstated on TSX-VEN, Nov. 15, 2022.

Common suspended from TSX-VEN, Nov. 9, 2022.

Predecessor Detail - Name changed from Pinehurst Capital I Inc., Dec. 6, 2021, pursuant to the Qualifying Transaction reverse takeover acquisition of Silver Bullet Mines Inc.; basis 1 new for 2.14286 old shs.

Directors - A. John Carter, CEO, Oakville, Ont.; Ron Wortel, pres., King City, Ont.; Peter M. Clausi, v-p, capital markets, St. Catharines, Ont.; Ron Murphy, v-p, min., Ariz.; Eric Balog, Toronto, Ont.; J. Birks Bovaird, Toronto, Ont.; Jonathan (Jon) Wiesblatt, Thornhill, Ont.

Other Exec. Officers - Brian L. Crawford, CFO & corp. sec.

Capital Stock

	Authorized (shs.)	Outstanding (shs.)[1]
Common	unlimited	64,892,962

[1] At Nov. 9, 2022

Major Shareholder - A. John Carter held 24.04% interest at Apr. 28, 2022.

Price Range - SBMI/TSX-VEN

Year	Volume	High	Low	Close
2022	18,776,090	$0.59	$0.14	$0.21
2021	2,331,801	$0.45	$0.25	$0.32
2020	103,133	$0.13	$0.04	$0.11
2019	18,858	$0.26	$0.26	$0.26

Consolidation: 1-for-2.14286 cons. in Dec. 2021

Recent Close: $0.14

Capital Stock Changes - In December 2021, common shares were consolidated on a 1-for-2.142857 basis and 51,484,705 post-consolidated common shares were issued pursuant to the Qualifying Transaction reverse takeover acquisition of Silver Bullet Mines Inc. In February and March 2022, private placement of 6,797,258 units (1 post-consolidated common share & 1 warrants) at 40¢ per unit was completed. Also during fiscal 2022, post-consolidated common shares were issued as follows: 1,500,000 as finder's fees, 140,000 on exercise of warrants and 166,666 on exercise of options.

Wholly Owned Subsidiaries

Silver Bullet Mining Inc., Ariz.
- 100% int. in **Black Diamond Exploration Inc.**
- 100% int. in **Silver Bullet Arizona Inc.**, United States.
  - 100% int. in **Silver Bullet Arizona LLC**, United States.
- 100% int. in **Silver Bullet Holdings Inc.**, United States.
- 100% int. in **Silver Bullet Idaho Inc.**, United States.
  - 100% int. in **Silver Bullet Mines LLC**, United States.

Financial Statistics

Periods ended:	12m June 30/22[A1]		12m June 30/21[A]
	$000s	%Chg	$000s
Exploration expense	2,972		586
General & admin expense	2,442		628
Stock-based compensation	591		337
Operating expense	**6,004**	**+287**	**1,551**
Operating income	**(6,004)**	**n.a.**	**(1,551)**
Finance costs, gross	21		340
Pre-tax income	**(6,072)**	**n.a.**	**(1,890)**
Net income	**(6,072)**	**n.a.**	**(1,890)**
Cash & equivalent	285		3,505
Current assets	530		3,984
Fixed assets, net	3,090		1,141
Total assets	**3,620**	**-29**	**5,125**
Accts. pay. & accr. liabs	264		357
Current liabilities	264		369
Long-term debt, gross	274		230
Long-term debt, net	274		230
Shareholders' equity	3,082		4,526
Cash from oper. activs	**(4,107)**	**n.a.**	**(1,267)**
Cash from fin. activs	2,802		5,871
Cash from invest. activs	(1,874)		(1,099)
Net cash position	**285**	**-92**	**3,505**
Capital expenditures	(1,955)		(1,029)
	$		$
Earnings per share*	(0.11)		(0.05)
Cash flow per share*	(0.07)		(0.04)
	shs		shs
No. of shs. o/s*	62,421,962		n.a.
Avg. no. of shs. o/s*	56,162,000		34,602,000
	%		%
Net profit margin	n.a.		n.a.
Return on equity	(159.62)		n.m.
Return on assets	(138.39)		(58.27)

* Common

[A] Reported in accordance with IFRS

[1] Results prior to Dec. 2, 2021, pertain to and reflect the reverse takeover acquisition of Silver Bullet Mines Inc.

Historical Summary
(as originally stated)

Fiscal Year	Oper. Rev. $000s	Net Inc. Bef. Disc. $000s	EPS* $
2022[A]	nil	(6,072)	(0.11)
2021[A]	nil	(1,890)	(0.05)
2020[A1]	nil	(4,145)	n.a.

* Common

[A] Reported in accordance with IFRS

[1] 7 months ended Nov. 30, 2020.

Note: Adjusted throughout for 1-for-2.142857 cons. in Dec. 2021

S.55 Simply Better Brands Corp.

Symbol - SBBC **Exchange** - TSX-VEN **CUSIP** - 82888R

Head Office - 206-595 Howe St, Vancouver, BC, V6C 2T5 **Toll-free** - (855) 883-7441

Website - www.simplybetterbrands.com

Email - ir@simplybetterbrands.com

Investor Relations - Brian Meadows (855) 553-7441

Auditors - Marcum LLP C.P.A., New York, N.Y.

Transfer Agents - Odyssey Trust Company

Profile - (B.C. 2018) Produces and sells consumer health and wellness products primarily in the U.S., including cannabidiol (CBD) tinctures, capsules, gummies, macarons, candies, sprays, vape pens, pet treats, pet wellness products, bath bombs, skincare products, petcare products and nutritious snack bars. Also offers brand management services.

Through 50.1%-owned **PureKana, LLC**, sells hemp-based CBD products in the U.S. including tinctures, capsules, topicals, patches and gummies for humans and dogs. PureKana's primary source of revenue is from its PureKana.com e-commerce website; however, it has been expanding its sales to select retail stores.

Through 82.54%-owned **No B.S. Life, LLC** produces skin care products made with plant-based and scientifically proven ingredients, and no synthetic fragrances and harmful chemicals like parabens, sulfates or phthalates. Product line includes caffeine eye cream and retinol night cream, charcoal peel-off masks, moisturizers, serums, toner, cleanser and acne patches.

Through wholly owned **TRU Brands Inc.** of Colorado, produces dessert-inspired protein bars made with plant-based ingredients.

Through wholly owned **Nirvana Group, LLC** of Florida, offers a portfolio of global brands that offer sustainable health and wellness products including BudaPets, which offers all-natural pet wellness products; CBD 4 YOU, an online CBD marketplace; and Dr. Soul, which offers a line of CBD products that combines herbal medicine with potent effects of hemp oil.

Through 60% interest in **Crisp Management Group Inc.**, sells and distributes CBD and hemp products through an e-commerce platform, and also holds the exclusive rights to market CBD and hemp products at Breakaway Music Festivals throughout North America.

Through wholly owned **Hervé Edibles Limited**, develops, produces and sells a variety of cannabis-infused sweets including hard candies, gummies, macarons and other desserts.

Through wholly owned **The BRN Group Inc.**, provides total brand management services including strategic brand planning, digital presence mapping, and online and offline distribution. Brands under BRN include Seventh Sense, a topical CBD brand, and Vibez Wellness, a brand of Keto products which was launched by the company in the U.S. in exchange of an earn-out consideration.

Recent Merger and Acquisition Activity

Status: terminated **Revised:** June 7, 2022

UPDATE: The transaction was terminated. PREVIOUS: Simply Better Brands Corp. (SBBC) agreed to acquire Jones Soda Co. for US$0.75 per share payable in SBBC common shares. In addition, SBBC would assume all outstanding debt of Jones and exchange any dilutive securities of Jones for materially similar securities of SBBC based on an implied ratio of 0.20548 SBBC common shares for each Jones share held, with the aggregate value being of the transaction being approximately US$98,902,257. Upon completion, SBBC planned to change its name to Jones Soda or something similar.

Status: pending **Announced:** Apr. 25, 2022

Simply Better Brands Corp. entered into a letter of intent to acquire private Longmont, Colo.-based CFH Limited for issuance of US$14,320,000 of common shares. CFH researches, develops, extracts, manufactures and distributes cannabis products including hemp flower oil extracts, hemp flower oil soft gels, edibles and topicals for its own brands and its white label operation.

Status: completed **Revised:** Apr. 1, 2022

UPDATE: The transaction was completed for issuance of 2,729,763 common shares valued at US$10,000,000. PREVIOUS: Simply Better Brands Corp. entered into a letter of intent to acquire private Toronto, Ont.-based The BRN Group Inc., which provides total brand management services including strategic brand planning, digital presence mapping, and online and offline distribution, for issuance of US$10,000,000 of common shares.

Status: completed **Announced:** Mar. 18, 2022

Simply Better Brands Corp. acquired private Toronto, Ont.-based Hervé Edibles Limited for issuance of 1,705,755 common shares valued at Cdn$8,000,000. Hervé develops, produces and sells a variety of cannabis-infused sweets including hard candies, gummies, macarons and other desserts.

Predecessor Detail - Name changed from PureK Holdings Corp., May 3, 2021.

Directors - Paul Norman, chr., Miami, Fla.; Kathy Casey, CEO, Mich.; Michael B. Galloro, Toronto, Ont.; Richard C. Kellam, Toronto, Ont.; J. R. Kingsley Ward, Toronto, Ont.

Other Exec. Officers - Brian Meadows, CFO & corp. sec.; Joe Wichser, v-p, sales

Capital Stock

	Authorized (shs.)	Outstanding (shs.)[1]
Series 1 Preferred	unlimited	nil[2]
Common	unlimited	71,724,489

[1] At May 30, 2023

[2] Classified as debt.

Common - One vote per share.

Series 1 Preferred (old) - Converted into common shares during 2021.

Major Shareholder - Widely held at Mar. 29, 2023.

Price Range - SBBC/TSX-VEN

Year	Volume	High	Low	Close
2022	48,546,472	$5.06	$0.18	$0.24
2021	4,924,127	$7.15	$3.27	$5.00
2020	103,512	$4.50	$0.80	$3.50
2019	12,315	$3.20	$1.47	$1.47

Split: 3-for-1 split in Mar. 2021; 1-for-40 cons. in Dec. 2020

Recent Close: $0.30

Capital Stock Changes - In February 2023, private placement of 28,000,000 units (1 common share & ½ warrant) at 25¢ per unit was completed, with warrants exercisable at 45¢ per share for two years.

In March 2022, 1,705,755 common shares were issued pursuant to the acquisition of Hervé Edibles Limited. In April 2022, 2,701,669 common shares were issued pursuant to the acquisition of The BRN Group Inc. In July and August 2022, private placement of 10,646,928 common shares was completed at Cdn$0.295 per share. Also during 2022, common shares were issued as follows: 329,443 for services, 309,000 on vesting of restricted share units, 283,527 on conversion of notes, 213,219 pursuant to the acquisition of Hervé Edibles Limited and 140,351 for debt settlement.

Wholly Owned Subsidiaries

BRN Brands Redemption Group LLC, United States.
The BRN Group Inc., Toronto, Ont.
Delysees Luxury Desserts, United States.
The French Dessert Company, United States.
Hervé Edibles Limited, Toronto, Ont.
Nirvana Group LLC, Fla.
Tru Brands Snack Company, Canada.
Tru Brands US Corp., United States.

Subsidiaries

60% int. in **Crisp Management Group Inc.**, United States.
65% int. in **No B.S. Life, LLC**, Del.
50.1% int. in **PureKana, LLC**, Paradise Valley, Ariz.
- 35% int. in **No B.S. Life, LLC**, Del.

Financial Statistics

Periods ended:	12m Dec. 31/22[A]	%Chg	12m Dec. 31/21[A]
	US$000s	%Chg	US$000s
Operating revenue	**65,414**	**+319**	**15,626**
Cost of sales	20,853		5,917
Salaries & benefits	4,366		3,194
General & admin expense	40,767		9,982
Stock-based compensation	4,302		5,615
Operating expense	**70,288**	**+184**	**24,708**
Operating income	**(4,874)**	**n.a.**	**(9,082)**
Deprec., depl. & amort	4,735		655
Finance income	nil		20
Finance costs, gross	1,398		2,341
Write-downs/write-offs	(2,649)		(2,604)
Pre-tax income	**(13,381)**	**n.a.**	**(12,869)**
Income taxes	(1,032)		(44)
Net income	**(12,349)**	**n.a.**	**(12,825)**
Cash & equivalent	2,343		2,235
Inventories	3,555		1,981
Accounts receivable	4,616		400
Current assets	15,137		6,668
Fixed assets, net	12		1
Right-of-use assets	nil		29
Intangibles, net	21,152		14,770
Total assets	**36,630**	**+68**	**21,805**
Accts. pay. & accr. liabs	6,122		2,083
Current liabilities	24,473		18,511
Long-term debt, gross	19,155		20,628
Long-term debt, net	1,016		4,318
Shareholders' equity	12,594		(650)
Non-controlling interest	(1,453)		(1,404)
Cash from oper. activs	**(4,764)**	**n.a.**	**(4,980)**
Cash from fin. activs	1,488		(380)
Cash from invest. activs	3,346		(713)
Net cash position	**2,343**	**+5**	**2,235**
Capital expenditures	(6)		nil
	US$		US$
Earnings per share*	(0.36)		(0.57)
Cash flow per share*	(0.14)		(0.22)
	shs		shs
No. of shs. o/s*	42,488,379		26,066,432
Avg. no. of shs. o/s*	34,504,543		22,626,969
	%		%
Net profit margin	(18.88)		(82.07)
Return on equity	n.m.		n.m.
Return on assets	(37.85)		(61.91)

* Common
[A] Reported in accordance with IFRS

Latest Results

Periods ended:	3m Mar. 31/23[A]	%Chg	3m Mar. 31/22[oA]
	US$000s	%Chg	US$000s
Operating revenue	24,626	+104	12,080
Net income	(2,684)	n.a.	(3,167)
	US$		US$
Earnings per share*	(0.05)		(0.12)

* Common
[o] Restated
[A] Reported in accordance with IFRS

Historical Summary
(as originally stated)

Fiscal Year	Oper. Rev.	Net Inc. Bef. Disc.	EPS*
	US$000s	US$000s	US$
2022[A]	65,414	(12,349)	(0.36)
2021[A]	15,626	(12,825)	(0.57)
2020[A1]	13,768	(1,982)	(0.10)
2019[A2]	25,308	5,774	n.a.

* Common
[A] Reported in accordance with IFRS
[1] Results reflect the Dec. 8, 2020, reverse takeover acquisition of 50.1% interest in PureKana, LLC.
[2] Results pertain to PureKana, LLC.
Note: Adjusted throughout for 3-for-1 split in Mar. 2021; 1-for-40 cons. in Dec. 2020

S.56 Sirona Biochem Corp.

Symbol - SBM **Exchange** - TSX-VEN **CUSIP** - 82967M
Head Office - c/o WeWork, 595 Burrard St, Vancouver, BC, V7X 1L4 **Telephone** - (604) 641-4466 **Toll-free** - (888) 747-6621 **Fax** - (604) 608-5471
Website - www.sironabiochem.com
Email - chopton@sironabiochem.com
Investor Relations - Christopher D. Hopton (888) 747-6621
Auditors - De Visser Gray LLP C.A., Vancouver, B.C.
Lawyers - McMillan LLP, Vancouver, B.C.
Transfer Agents - Computershare Trust Company of Canada Inc., Vancouver, B.C.

Profile - (B.C. 2006) Develops cosmetic and pharmaceutical active ingredients which are licensed to third parties.

Owns a proprietary technology to develop and identify carbohydrate-based compounds by stabilizing carbohydrate molecules through fluorination. Carbohydrate-based compounds are used for development of active ingredients in cosmetic and pharmaceutical applications. The company's lead compounds are TFC-1067, a skin lightening compound that is a safer and superior alternative to other skin lightening agents such as hydroquinone, and developed for treatment of dyschromia; and TFC-039, a sodium-glucose cotransporter-2 (SGLT) inhibitor for the treatment human and animal diabetes. Other projects include the development of anti-aging/anti-wrinkle compounds, including TFC-1326; keloid and scar therapies; antiviral compounds; and cellulite treatment.

The compounds are licensed to third parties in return for upfront licensing fees, milestone fees and ongoing royalty payments.

In January 2023, the company terminated its five-year agreement with San Francisco, Calif.-based skincare company **Rodan & Fields, LLC** (R&F) for the non-exclusive use of the company's skin lightening compound TFC-1067 in R&F's products in the U.S., Canada, Australia and Japan.

In June 2022, the company entered into a global licensing agreement with **Abbvie Inc.** for the development and commercialization of topical skin care treatments based on active ingredients derived from the company's patents for TFC-1067 and related family compounds. The company would receive upfront and milestone payments as well as royalties on product sales.

Predecessor Detail - Name changed from High Rider Capital Inc., May 4, 2009, following Qualifying Transaction license agreement with TFChem S.A.R.L.

Directors - Dr. Howard J. Verrico, chr., CEO & corp. sec., Maple Ridge, B.C.; Christopher D. (Chris) Hopton, CFO, Vancouver, B.C.; Dr. Géraldine Deliencourt-Godefroy, chief scientific officer, France; Dr. Alex Marazzi, Abbotsford, B.C.; Jason Tian, Shanghai, Shanghai, People's Republic of China

Other Exec. Officers - Michelle Seltenrich, v-p, opers.

Capital Stock

	Authorized (shs.)	Outstanding (shs.)[1]
Common	unlimited	252,223,526

[1] At June 29, 2023

Major Shareholder - Widely held at Nov. 25, 2022.

Price Range - SBM/TSX-VEN

Year	Volume	High	Low	Close
2022	18,088,752	$0.35	$0.11	$0.12
2021	22,588,512	$0.56	$0.14	$0.18
2020	26,551,259	$0.51	$0.18	$0.33
2019	102,802,716	$0.69	$0.07	$0.44
2018	24,018,755	$0.19	$0.07	$0.09

Recent Close: $0.11

Capital Stock Changes - During fiscal 2022, common shares were issued as follows: 14,008,960 on exercise of warrants and 1,655,000 on exercise of options.

Wholly Owned Subsidiaries

TFChem S.A.R.L., Rouen, France.

Financial Statistics

Periods ended:	12m Oct. 31/22[A]	%Chg	12m Oct. 31/21[A]
	$000s	%Chg	$000s
Operating revenue	**672**	**+151**	**268**
Salaries & benefits	146		142
Research & devel. expense	1,080		1,154
General & admin expense	1,510		928
Stock-based compensation	1,465		331
Operating expense	**4,201**	**+64**	**2,555**
Operating income	**(3,529)**	**n.a.**	**(2,287)**
Deprec., depl. & amort	9		9
Finance income	6		8
Finance costs, gross	27		3
Pre-tax income	**(3,552)**	**n.a.**	**(2,312)**
Income taxes	6		(6)
Net income	**(3,558)**	**n.a.**	**(2,306)**
Cash & equivalent	422		778
Accounts receivable	54		86
Current assets	1,272		1,260
Fixed assets, net	19		28
Total assets	**1,291**	**0**	**1,287**
Accts. pay. & accr. liabs	491		403
Current liabilities	865		741
Long-term debt, gross	429		769
Long-term debt, net	91		469
Long-term lease liabilities	5		44
Shareholders' equity	215		(97)
Cash from oper. activs	**(2,178)**	**n.a.**	**(2,158)**
Cash from fin. activs	2,037		1,450
Net cash position	**422**	**-46**	**778**
	$		$
Earnings per share*	(0.01)		(0.01)
Cash flow per share*	(0.01)		(0.01)
	shs		shs
No. of shs. o/s*	251,731,526		236,067,566
Avg. no. of shs. o/s*	241,039,380		229,216,426
	%		%
Net profit margin	(529.46)		(860.45)
Return on equity	n.m.		n.m.
Return on assets	(273.93)		(134.52)

* Common
[A] Reported in accordance with IFRS

Latest Results

Periods ended:	6m Apr. 30/23[A]	%Chg	6m Apr. 30/22[A]
	$000s	%Chg	$000s
Operating revenue	60	n.a.	nil
Net income	(1,386)	n.a.	(2,813)
	$		$
Earnings per share*	(0.01)		(0.01)

* Common
[A] Reported in accordance with IFRS

Historical Summary
(as originally stated)

Fiscal Year	Oper. Rev.	Net Inc. Bef. Disc.	EPS*
	$000s	$000s	$
2022[A]	672	(3,558)	(0.01)
2021[A]	268	(2,306)	(0.01)
2020[A]	106	(4,134)	(0.02)
2019[A]	136	(4,550)	(0.02)
2018[A]	1,279	(1,273)	(0.01)

* Common
[A] Reported in accordance with IFRS

S.57 Sixth Wave Innovations Inc.

Symbol - SIXW **Exchange** - CSE **CUSIP** - 83011Y
Head Office - 110-210 Waterfront Dr, Bedford, NS, B4A 0H3 **Telephone** - (902) 835-0403 **Toll-free** - (866) 869-8072 **Fax** - (888) 691-0529
Website - sixthwave.com
Email - investors@sixthwave.com
Investor Relations - Dr. Jonathan Gluckman (866) 869-8072
Auditors - Davidson & Company LLP C.A., Vancouver, B.C.
Transfer Agents - Computershare Trust Company of Canada Inc., Vancouver, B.C.

Profile - (B.C. 2007) Developing nanotechnologies focused on extraction and detection of target substances at the molecular level.

The company uses its patented molecularly imprinted polymers (MIPs) technology which consist of durable polymer beads imprinted with adsorption micropores which match the molecular geometry of organic materials such as cannabinoids, pathogens and inorganic materials such as metals. The company's products are in various stages of development and includes:

IXOS® Gold Extraction - a line of extraction polymers used for the extraction of gold. IXOS® nanotech beads have completed extensive testing in laboratory and field trials with one of the world's largest gold mining companies, with confirmatory testing completed by independent mine sites, independent laboratories, and two major chemical corporations. Subsidiary **Geolithic Corp.** holds a licence to use the company's proprietary nanotechnology to extract lithium and other value elements from geothermal brines in the Salton Sea in California.

Affinity™ Cannabinoid Purification System - designed to separate and purify cannabinoids from crude cannabis extracts. The Affinity™ unit houses the Affinity™ beads and a flow control system that controls the delivery of diluted distillate oil to the beads. The baseline system is capable to process approximately 14 kg of high purity distillate every 10 hours of operation, or in excess of 30 kg per day.

Accelerated Molecularly Imprinted Polymer System (AMIPs™) - a rapid virus test for the selective identification of viruses such as COVID-19, other viruses and bacterial pathogens that can give results within minutes. AMIP is designed to identify the virus directly using physical characteristics such as molecular size, shape and surface structures. The company intends to incorporate the AMIPs technology into several rapid-detection products including rapid virus test kits, air and water monitoring systems and Pathogenic Amines Detection System (PADS™) is a sensing technology for detection of biomarkers associated with food spoilage.

The company is in the process of a commercial rollout of Affinity™ and IXOS® while the AMIPs is in the development stages.

Predecessor Detail - Name changed from Atom Energy Inc., Aug. 26, 2019.

Directors - Dr. Jonathan (Jon) Gluckman, pres., CEO & acting CFO, N.S.; Sherman McGill, exec. v-p & chief devel. officer, Tenn.; Dr. David Fransen, Ont.; Sokhie S. Puar, Vancouver, B.C.; Patricia Steadman, B.C.

Other Exec. Officers - John Cowan, COO; Dr. Aristotle Kalivretenos, chief science officer; Dr. Garrett Kraft, v-p, innovations

Capital Stock

	Authorized (shs.)	Outstanding (shs.)[1]
Preferred	unlimited	nil
Common	unlimited	136,693,529

[1] At Apr. 28, 2023

Major Shareholder - Widely held at Feb. 7, 2023.

Price Range - SIXW/CSE

Year	Volume	High	Low	Close
2022	27,314,860	$0.24	$0.03	$0.03
2021	37,472,367	$0.53	$0.20	$0.20
2020	48,536,527	$1.20	$0.23	$0.30
2018	173,941	$0.40	$0.25	$0.25

Recent Close: $0.01

Capital Stock Changes - In December 2021, private placement of 5,160,000 units (1 common share & 1 warrant) at 20¢ per unit was completed. In March 2022, private placement of 12,200,000 units (1 common share & 1 warrant) at 12¢ per unit was completed. Also during fiscal 2022, 761,598 common shares were issued for debt settlement.

Wholly Owned Subsidiaries

6th Wave Innovations Corp., Salt Lake City, Utah.
- 100% int. in **Geolithic Corp.**, Salt Lake City, Utah.

Financial Statistics

Periods ended:	12m Aug. 31/22[A]		12m Aug. 31/21[A]
	$000s	%Chg	$000s
Research & devel. expense	1,113		1,309
General & admin expense	3,751		4,808
Stock-based compensation	480		1,101
Operating expense	**5,344**	**-26**	**7,218**
Operating income	**(5,344)**	**n.a.**	**(7,218)**
Deprec., depl. & amort.	608		630
Finance income	100		112
Finance costs, gross	536		584
Write-downs/write-offs	(1,050)		(7,709)
Pre-tax income	**(8,831)**	**n.a.**	**(16,236)**
Net income	**(8,831)**	**n.a.**	**(16,236)**
Cash & equivalent	13		1,068
Current assets	406		1,737
Fixed assets, net	253		557
Right-of-use assets	39		158
Intangibles, net	1,178		2,648
Total assets	**2,048**	**-60**	**5,100**
Bank indebtedness	333		nil
Accts. pay. & accr. liabs	2,082		448
Current liabilities	3,689		618
Long-term debt, gross	1,997		1,612
Long-term debt, net	914		1,612
Long-term lease liabilities	nil		47
Equity portion of conv. debs	417		417
Shareholders' equity	(2,718)		2,556
Cash from oper. activs	**(2,781)**	**n.a.**	**(7,087)**
Cash from fin. activs	1,451		7,487
Cash from invest. activs	274		(52)
Net cash position	**13**	**-99**	**1,068**
Capital expenditures	nil		(35)
Capital disposals	274		nil
	$		$
Earnings per share*	(0.07)		(0.16)
Cash flow per share*	(0.02)		(0.07)
	shs		shs
No. of shs. o/s*	135,429,586		117,307,988
Avg. no. of shs. o/s*	126,356,954		98,934,346
	%		%
Net profit margin	n.a.		n.a.
Return on equity	n.m.		(359.56)
Return on assets	(232.09)		(176.04)

* Common
[A] Reported in accordance with IFRS

Latest Results

Periods ended:	6m Feb. 28/23[A]		6m Feb. 28/22[A]
	$000s	%Chg	$000s
Net income	(2,732)	n.a.	(3,709)
	$		$
Earnings per share*	(0.02)		(0.03)

* Common
[A] Reported in accordance with IFRS

Historical Summary
(as originally stated)

Fiscal Year	Oper. Rev. $000s	Net Inc. Bef. Disc. $000s	EPS* $
2022[A]	nil	(8,831)	(0.07)
2021[A]	nil	(16,236)	(0.16)
2020[A]	nil	(20,973)	(0.34)
2019[A]	nil	(7,172)	(0.22)
2018[A]	nil	(821)	(0.05)

* Common
[A] Reported in accordance with IFRS

S.58 Sixty Six Capital Inc.

Symbol - SIX **Exchange** - CSE **CUSIP** - 83013J
Head Office - 15 Percy St, London, MDX, United Kingdom, W1T 1DS
Website - sixtysixcapital.com
Email - ndemare@chasemgt.com
Investor Relations - Nick DeMare (604) 685-9316
Auditors - Davidson & Company LLP C.A., Vancouver, B.C.
Transfer Agents - Capital Transfer Agency Inc., Toronto, Ont.

Profile - (B.C. 2007) Invests in cryptocurrency mining companies.

Owns 338,273 shares of **Northern Data AG**, a Germany-based high performance computing (HPC) operator with facilities in Canada, the U.S., Norway and Sweden.

Also reviewing additional green energy investment and business opportunities within the financial technology (FinTech) space.

Predecessor Detail - Name changed from Hydro66 Holdings Corp., Apr. 13, 2021.

Directors - David Rowe, founder, chr. & CEO, London, Middx., United Kingdom; Alex Johnstone, CFO, London, Middx., United Kingdom; Richard Croft, chief legal officer, London, Middx., United Kingdom; Michael R. Hudson, Vic., Australia; Richard J. Patricio, Toronto, Ont.

Other Exec. Officers - Christaan Keet, chief technical officer; Paul Morrison, chief comml. officer; Nick DeMare, corp. sec.

Capital Stock

	Authorized (shs.)	Outstanding (shs.)[1]
Common	unlimited	130,649,950

[1] At Aug. 26, 2022

Major Shareholder - David Rowe held 39.21% interest and Robert Keith held 28.72% interest at Jan. 15, 2021.

Price Range - SIX/CSE

Year	Volume	High	Low	Close
2022	6,659,672	$0.15	$0.01	$0.02
2021	14,042,573	$0.33	$0.09	$0.11
2020	12,969,871	$0.50	$0.07	$0.23
2019	10,125,399	$0.70	$0.15	$0.18
2018	1,351,170	$0.95	$0.25	$0.38

Recent Close: $0.03

Wholly Owned Subsidiaries

Megamining Limited, United Kingdom.

Investments

Northern Data AG, Frankfurt am Main, Germany.

Financial Statistics

Periods ended:	12m Dec. 31/21[A]		12m Dec. 31/20[A]
	$000s	%Chg	$000s
Operating revenue	**1,778**	**-51**	**3,619**
Cost of sales	652		1,766
Salaries & benefits	256		1,338
General & admin expense	980		2,027
Stock-based compensation	885		242
Other operating expense	81		270
Operating expense	**2,855**	**-49**	**5,643**
Operating income	**(1,077)**	**n.a.**	**(2,025)**
Deprec., depl. & amort.	488		2,197
Finance costs, net	502		564
Write-downs/write-offs	114		27
Pre-tax income	**24,414**	**n.a.**	**(6,896)**
Net income	**24,414**	**n.a.**	**(6,896)**
Cash & equivalent	105		199
Accounts receivable	nil		152
Current assets	123		1,407
Long-term investments	37,036		nil
Fixed assets, net	nil		15,758
Right-of-use assets	nil		2,120
Intangibles, net	nil		19
Total assets	**39,114**	**+103**	**19,304**
Bank indebtedness	58		1,087
Accts. pay. & accr. liabs	89		2,164
Current liabilities	146		3,734
Long-term debt, gross	5,913		5,436
Long-term debt, net	5,913		5,436
Long-term lease liabilities	nil		1,687
Shareholders' equity	30,893		5,627
Cash from oper. activs	**(785)**	**n.a.**	**(4,207)**
Cash from fin. activs	8		1,977
Cash from invest. activs	1,085		1,591
Net cash position	**105**	**-47**	**199**
Capital expenditures	(545)		(1,573)
	$		$
Earnings per share*	0.19		(0.04)
Cash flow per share*	(0.01)		(0.03)
	shs		shs
No. of shs. o/s*	130,649,950		130,649,950
Avg. no. of shs. o/s*	130,649,950		130,649,950
	%		%
Net profit margin	n.m.		(190.55)
Return on equity	133.70		(83.10)
Return on assets	83.58		(36.61)

* Common
[A] Reported in accordance with IFRS

Note: Share and per share information not adjusted for 1-for-76.3945 share consolidation in June 2018.

Latest Results

Periods ended:	6m June 30/22[A]		6m June 30/21[¤A]
	$000s	%Chg	$000s
Operating revenue	nil	n.a.	1,778
Net income	(27,298)	n.a.	27,142
	$		$
Earnings per share*	(0.21)		0.35

* Common
[¤] Restated
[A] Reported in accordance with IFRS

Historical Summary
(as originally stated)

Fiscal Year	Oper. Rev.	Net Inc. Bef. Disc.	EPS*
	$000s	$000s	$
2021[A]	1,778	24,414	0.19
2020[A]	3,619	(6,896)	(0.04)
2019[A]	4,273	(5,273)	(0.04)
2018[A1]	7,644	(6,336)	(0.06)
2017[A2]	nil	784	0.01

* Common
[A] Reported in accordance with IFRS
[1] Results reflect the June 8, 2018, reverse takeover acquisition of Arctic Blockchain Ltd.
[2] Results for 2017 and prior years pertain to Caza Gold Corp.

S.59 Siyata Mobile Inc.

Symbol - SYTA **Exchange** - NASDAQ **CUSIP** - 83013Q
Head Office - A414-1001 rue Lenoir, Montréal, QC, H4C 2Z6 **Telephone** - (514) 500-1181 **Toll-free** - (888) 316-3747
Website - www.siyatamobile.com
Email - gerry@siyatamobile.com
Investor Relations - Gerald Bernstein (514) 824-7357
Auditors - Barzily & Co. C.P.A.
Transfer Agents - Computershare Trust Company of Canada Inc., Vancouver, B.C.
Employees - 27 at Mar. 31, 2022
Profile - (B.C. 1986) Develops, manufactures, markets and sells cellular-based communications solutions over advanced 4G/LTE mobile networks under the Uniden® Cellular and Siyata brands.

Products are grouped into rugged handheld mobile devices, in-vehicle communications solutions and cellular amplifiers.

Rugged handheld mobile devices are 4G/LTE connected Push-to-Talk (PTT) over Cellular (PoC) smartphone devices for industrial users, including enterprise customers, first responders, construction workers, security guards, government agencies, utilities, transportation and waste management, amusement parks and mobile workers. Products include Siyata SD7, a mission critical PTT handset suited for use in harsh environments; Uniden® UR5, a rugged, all-in-one smartphone in a convenient compact form factor; and Uniden® UR7, a rugged smart phone in a clamshell form factor.

In-Vehicle communications solutions consist of connected-vehicle devices and accessories specifically designed for enterprise customers and professional vehicles such as trucks, vans, buses, emergency service vehicles and government cars. Products include Uniden® UV350, a 4G/LTE all-in-one vehicle communication device that incorporates cellular voice calls, PoC, data, fleet management and other Android-based professional applications; Uniden® CP250, a 4G/LTE all-in-one tablet style fleet communications device designed to be installed on the dash or mounted on a windshield, with cellular voice calls, PoC, navigation, data applications, built in camera and DVR; and Siyata VK7, a car kit with an integrated speaker designed for use with the company's SD7 device.

Cellular amplifiers consist of a portfolio of cellular signal boosters and accessories designed for homes, buildings and vehicles.

The company's customer base includes cellular network operators and their dealers, as well as commercial vehicle technology distributors for fleets of all sizes in the U.S., Canada, Europe, Australia, the Middle East and other international markets.

Predecessor Detail - Name changed from Teslin River Resources Corp., July 24, 2015, following reverse takeover acquisition of (old) Siyata Mobile Inc.; basis 1 new for 2.2 old shs.

Directors - Peter Goldstein, chr., B.C.; Marc Seelenfreund, CEO, Ra'anana, Israel; Lourdes Felix, Calif.; Michael J. Kron, Montréal, Qué.; Stephen Ospalak, Toronto, Ont.

Other Exec. Officers - Gerald Bernstein, CFO; Gidi Bracha, v-p, tech.; Glenn Kennedy, v-p, intl. sales & mktg.; Daniel Kim, v-p, corp. devel.

Capital Stock

	Authorized (shs.)	Outstanding (shs.)[1]
Preferred	unlimited	nil
Common	unlimited	45,601,649

[1] At Oct. 27, 2022

Major Shareholder - Widely held at Mar. 31, 2022.

Price Range - SYTA/NASDAQ

Year	Volume	High	Low	Close
2022	619,425	US$428.00	US$10.50	US$15.30
2021	530,047	US$1,565.00	US$250.00	US$370.00
2020	15,272	US$1,190.00	US$390.00	US$1,077.00

SIM/TSX-VEN (D)

Year	Volume	High	Low	Close
2020	7,956	$5,075.00	$525.00	$650.00
2019	4,869	$8,700.00	$3,770.00	$4,785.00
2018	3,108	$8,990.00	$4,785.00	$6,235.00

Consolidation: 1-for-100 cons. in Aug. 2023

Capital Stock Changes - In January 2022, public offering of 7,215,652 units (1 common share & 1 warrant) at US$2.30 per unit was completed, with warrants exercisable at US$2.30 per share for five years. In October 2022, public offering of 15,810,000 units (1 common share & 1 warrant) at US$0.23 per unit was completed, with warrants exercisable at US$0.23 per share for five years.

Wholly Owned Subsidiaries

Queensgate Resources Corporation, B.C.
- 100% int. in **Queensgate Resources US Corp.**, Nev.

Signifi Mobile Inc., Montréal, Qué.
- 100% int. in **ClearRF Nevada Inc.**, Nev.
  - 100% int. in **ClearRF, LLC**, Spokane, Wash.

Siyata Mobile (Canada) Inc., B.C.
- 100% int. in **Siyata Mobile Israel Ltd.**, Israel.

Financial Statistics

Periods ended:	12m Dec. 31/21[A]		12m Dec. 31/20[A]
	US$000s	%Chg	US$000s
Operating revenue	**7,545**	**+26**	**5,990**
Cost of sales	5,677		4,410
Salaries & benefits	3,363		2,395
Research & devel. expense	846		560
General & admin expense	6,074		4,154
Stock-based compensation	1,339		518
Operating expense	**17,299**	**+44**	**12,037**
Operating income	**(9,754)**	**n.a.**	**(6,047)**
Deprec., depl. & amort.	1,008		1,280
Finance income	6		23
Finance costs, gross	1,990		1,768
Write-downs/write-offs	(9,610)		(3,395)
Pre-tax income	**(23,626)**	**n.a.**	**(13,591)**
Net income	**(23,626)**	**n.a.**	**(13,591)**
Cash & equivalent	1,620		5,469
Inventories	2,397		2,410
Accounts receivable	1,544		2,737
Current assets	6,186		23,095
Fixed assets, net	268		55
Right-of-use assets	1,078		377
Intangibles, net	4,351		7,351
Total assets	**12,051**	**-61**	**31,092**
Bank indebtedness	27		438
Accts. pay. & accr. liabs	2,646		2,622
Current liabilities	6,855		9,405
Long-term debt, gross	3,343		6,269
Long-term debt, net	1,921		52
Long-term lease liabilities	788		214
Shareholders' equity	2,487		21,279
Cash from oper. activs	**(12,569)**	**n.a.**	**(9,990)**
Cash from fin. activs	1,006		25,349
Cash from invest. activs	(3,116)		(1,535)
Net cash position	**1,620**	**-90**	**16,465**
Capital expenditures	(225)		(21)
	US$		US$
Earnings per share*	(487.00)		(915.00)
Cash flow per share*	(259.19)		(672.77)
	shs		shs
No. of shs. o/s*	52,767		46,633
Avg. no. of shs. o/s*	48,493		14,849
	%		%
Net profit margin	(313.13)		(226.89)
Return on equity	(198.82)		(95.59)
Return on assets	(100.30)		(52.33)
Foreign sales percent	78		72
No. of employees (FTEs)	27		25

* Common
[A] Reported in accordance with IFRS

Latest Results

Periods ended:	9m Sept. 30/22[A]		9m Sept. 30/21[A]
	US$000s	%Chg	US$000s
Operating revenue	4,370	-22	5,608
Net income	(8,711)	n.a.	(18,646)
	US$		US$
Earnings per share*	(59.00)		(389.00)

* Common
[A] Reported in accordance with IFRS

Historical Summary
(as originally stated)

Fiscal Year	Oper. Rev.	Net Inc. Bef. Disc.	EPS*
	US$000s	US$000s	US$
2021[A]	7,545	(23,626)	(487.00)
2020[A]	5,990	(13,591)	(915.00)
	$000s	$000s	$
2019[A]	13,020	(10,160)	(1,305.00)
2018[A]	14,221	(11,528)	(1,740.00)
2017[A]	17,753	(5,058)	(870.00)

* Common
[A] Reported in accordance with IFRS
Note: Adjusted throughout for 1-for-100 cons. in Aug. 2023; 1-for-145 cons. in Sept. 2020

S.60 Skychain Technologies Inc.

Symbol - SCT **Exchange** - TSX-VEN (S) **CUSIP** - 83084Q
Head Office - 500-1112 Pender St W, Vancouver, BC, V6E 2S1 **Telephone** - (604) 456-0608
Website - www.skychaintechnologiesinc.com
Email - info@skychaintechnologiesinc.com
Investor Relations - Dr. Weichong Du (604) 688-5464
Auditors - Bassi & Karimjee LLP C.A., Brampton, Ont.
Lawyers - Steve Veitch Law Corporation, Vancouver, B.C.
Transfer Agents - Endeavor Trust Corporation, Vancouver, B.C.
Profile - (B.C. 1977) Offers blockchain infrastructure solutions including provision of warehouse space, low-cost electricity, and maintenance and hosting services to cryptominers in Canada.

Wholly owned **MiningSky Technology Ltd.**, **MiningSky Technologies (Manitoba) Inc.** and **10117749 Manitoba Ltd.** provide Bitcoin mining energy and rapid deployment solutions for miners and mining farms, as well as miner hosting and colocation services. MiningSky transforms shipping containers into turn-key crypto-mining systems that can be quickly delivered to the power supply site/hosting location where it is essentially plugged in. Each container is modified with rack/shelving, wiring and heat mitigation technology and fitted with customer supplied mining machines. In addition, markets and sells MiningSky 8-GPU, a proprietary GPU-based cryptocurrency mining rig designed to mine Ethereum and other cryptocurrencies.

MiningSky owns a four-acre property in Melita, Man., which would be used to construct and operate a cryptocurrenct mining hosting facility.

Affiliate **MiningSky Container Ltd.** manufactures and markets containers for use in cryptocurrency mining.

In September 2022, the company sold its 25% interest in **Miningsky Container Ltd.** to the 70% equity holder of MiningSky Container for $1.00.

In March 2022, lease agreement with **2558239 Ontario Ltd**. on the Birtle, Man., property was terminated and construction on the cryptomining facility was ceased. The agreement included an option to purchase the 1.6-acre parcel of leased land.

Common suspended from TSX-VEN, Aug. 8, 2022.

Predecessor Detail - Name changed from Green Valley Mine Incorporated, Sept. 21, 2018.

Directors - William Ying, chr., B.C.; Dr. Weichong (Richard) Du, pres.; Wing Mou (Bernard) Fung; Xi (Walson) Wang, Los Angeles, Calif.

Other Exec. Officers - Donald A. (Don) Gordon, CEO; West Ma, COO; Lindley Huang, CFO; John Yang, chief strategy officer

Capital Stock

	Authorized (shs.)	Outstanding (shs.)[1]
Common	unlimited	26,835,601

[1] At Dec. 31, 2022

Major Shareholder - 1151152 B.C. Ltd. held 16.34% interest and The9 Limited held 13.75% interest at Nov. 5, 2021.

Price Range - SCT/TSX-VEN (S)

Year	Volume	High	Low	Close
2022	444,365	$0.40	$0.04	$0.04
2021	2,725,183	$1.81	$0.28	$0.35
2020	1,251,269	$0.63	$0.06	$0.63
2019	291,590	$0.98	$0.05	$0.05
2018	286,400	$2.50	$0.28	$0.28

Consolidation: 1-for-5 cons. in Feb. 2019

Capital Stock Changes - In June 2021, private placement of 2,631,579 units (1 common share & 1 warrant) at 76¢ per unit was completed. In December 2021 and January 2022, private placement of 7,519,380 common shares was completed at 42¢ per share. Also during fiscal 2022, common shares were issued as follows: 1,455,901 by private placement, 420,734 for debt settlement and 25,000 on exercise of warrants.

Wholly Owned Subsidiaries

MiningSky Technologies (Manitoba) Inc., Man.
Miningsky Technology Ltd., Vancouver, B.C.
- 100% int. in **MiningSky USA, Inc.**, Wash. Inactive.

10117749 Manitoba Ltd., Man.
RBN Digitech Labs Inc., B.C.
- 33.33% int. in **Peterific Studios, Inc.**, B.C.

Financial Statistics

Periods ended:	12m Mar. 31/22^A		12m Mar. 31/21^A
	$000s	%Chg	$000s
Operating revenue	**nil**	**n.a.**	**2,565**
Cost of goods sold	nil		49
Salaries & benefits	1,539		682
General & admin expense	1,813		495
Stock-based compensation	814		nil
Other operating expense	nil		2,720
Operating expense	**4,166**	**+6**	**3,946**
Operating income	**(4,166)**	**n.a.**	**(1,381)**
Deprec., depl. & amort.	237		304
Finance income	nil		2
Finance costs, gross	220		54
Write-downs/write-offs	2,237[1]		nil
Pre-tax income	**(6,635)**	**n.a.**	**(1,241)**
Net income	**(6,635)**	**n.a.**	**(1,241)**
Cash & equivalent	3,162		3
Accounts receivable	310		58
Current assets	3,563		113
Fixed assets, net	2,998		890
Right-of-use assets	17		45
Total assets	**7,261**	**+378**	**1,518**
Bank indebtedness	nil		594
Accts. pay. & accr. liabs	5,395		1,274
Current liabilities	6,749		2,659
Long-term debt, gross	1,136		31
Long-term debt, net	nil		31
Equity portion of conv. debs	999		nil
Shareholders' equity	511		(1,172)
Cash from oper. activs	**(476)**	**n.a.**	**(869)**
Cash from fin. activs	7,258		461
Cash from invest. activs	(3,623)		288
Net cash position	**3,162**	**n.m.**	**3**
Capital expenditures	(2,354)		(74)
Capital disposals	nil		347
	$		$
Earnings per share*	(0.33)		(0.09)
Cash flow per share*	(0.02)		(0.06)
	shs		shs
No. of shs. o/s*	26,835,601		14,783,007
Avg. no. of shs. o/s*	19,957,156		14,090,048
	%		%
Net profit margin	n.a.		(48.38)
Return on equity	n.m.		n.m.
Return on assets	(146.14)		(72.84)

* Common
^A Reported in accordance with IFRS
[1] Includes bad debt and impairment of assets, infrastructure and investment.

Historical Summary
(as originally stated)

Fiscal Year	Oper. Rev.	Net Inc. Bef. Disc.	EPS*
	$000s	$000s	$
2022^A	nil	(6,635)	(0.33)
2021^A	2,565	(1,241)	(0.09)
2020^A	2,747	(1,342)	(0.17)
2019^A	977	(3,401)	(0.65)
2018^A	nil	(15)	(0.00)

* Common
^A Reported in accordance with IFRS
Note: Adjusted throughout for 1-for-5 cons. in Feb. 2019

S.61 Skylight Health Group Inc.

Symbol - SLHG **Exchange** - TSX-VEN (S) **CUSIP** - 83086L
Head Office - 402-5520 Explorer Dr, Mississauga, ON, L4W 5L1
Telephone - (416) 642-1807 **Toll-free** - (855) 874-4999
Website - www.skylighthealthgroup.com
Email - investors@skylighthealthgroup.com
Investor Relations - Jackie Kelly (416) 301-2949
Auditors -
Transfer Agents - Capital Transfer Agency Inc., Toronto, Ont.
Profile - (Can. 2017) Offers medical services and contact research and development, and technology and data analytics solutions.

Operations are organized into two segments: Medical Services and Software.

Medical Services - Provides medical services under the Skylight Health Group name through a virtual telemedicine platform and 32 medical clinics located across U.S. states. Services provided include a broad range of integrated health services, such as primary and urgent medical care, consultative specialist care, alternative health, wellness and multi-disciplinary services. Also offers turnkey contract research organization (CRO) services to support all phases of drug development of third parties including pharmaceutical companies, academia and research organizations. Services include feasibility studies, clinical trial designs, regulatory and drug applications, protocol development and ethics/institutional review board (IRB) approval, patient clinical site recruitment, site monitoring and adverse events reporting, medical writing and publication submission.

Software - Utilizes cloud infrastructure to combine data from hundreds of data sources to provide a framework to improve patient care. Also includes the company's primary proprietary platform Sail, an electronic database management and patient record platform which allows practitioners and other clinical staff to schedule appointments, manage patient files, evaluate patients for integrative therapies and where necessary, create the required documents to submit to regulatory bodies on behalf of patients.

Common suspended from TSX-VEN, May 8, 2023.

Recent Merger and Acquisition Activity

Status: completed **Revised:** May 6, 2022
UPDATE: The transaction was completed. PREVIOUS: Skylight Health Group Inc. agreed to acquire NeighborMD, Inc., which owns and operates nine clinics offering primary care services to more than 5,000 people in Florida, for US$8,000,000.

Predecessor Detail - Name changed from CB2 Insights Inc., Nov. 23, 2020.

Directors - Pradyum (Prad) Sekar, CEO, Oakville, Ont.; Kashaf Qureshi, pres., Milton, Ont.; Tom Brogan, Ottawa, Ont.; Peter Cummins, Guelph, Ont.; Norton Singhavon, Kelowna, B.C.

Other Exec. Officers - Farooq Akhter, interim CFO; Dr. Kit Brekhus, CMO; Dan Thompson, chief commun. officer; Stephanie Gluhacki, sr. v-p, compliance; Greg Sieman, sr. v-p, mktg. & commun.; Catherine Beckett, corp. sec.

Capital Stock

	Authorized (shs.)	Outstanding (shs.)[1]
Preferred	unlimited	
Series A		275,000
Common	unlimited	39,822,269

[1] At Nov. 15, 2022

Series A Preferred - Entitled to cumulative dividends of 9.25% payable monthly. Redeemable, at the company's option, at US$25 per share at any time on or after three years from closing. Non-voting.
Common - One vote per share.
Major Shareholder - Merida Capital Partners II LP, Merida Capital Partners III LP & Merida Capital Partners III QP LP held 12.87% interest at May 13, 2022.

Price Range - SLHG/TSX-VEN (S)

Year	Volume	High	Low	Close
2022	10,999,184	$1.74	$0.30	$0.33
2021	34,372,627	$9.50	$1.58	$1.65
2020	17,593,678	$6.75	$0.28	$5.85
2019	11,524,695	$2.50	$0.28	$0.50

Consolidation: 1-for-5 cons. in May 2021
Recent Close: $0.02

Wholly Owned Subsidiaries

MVC Technologies Inc., Ont.
- 100% int. in **MVC Technologies USA Inc.**, United States.
  - 100% int. in **Quantum Fuel Systems, LLC**
- 100% int. in **Skylight Health Group, Inc.**, Del.
  - 100% int. in **Skylight Health Group CO, LLC**, Colo.
    - 100% int. in **Infinite Care LLC**
  - 100% int. in **Skylight Health Group Management of Florida, LLC**, Fla.
  - 100% int. in **Skylight Health Group Management of Massachusetts, LLC**, Mass.
  - 100% int. in **Skylight Health Group Management of New Jersey, LLC**, N.J.
  - 100% int. in **Skylight Health Group Management of Pennsylvania, LLC**, Pa.

NeighborMD, Inc., Fla.

Financial Statistics

Periods ended:	12m Dec. 31/21^A		12m Dec. 31/20^◊A
	$000s	%Chg	$000s
Operating revenue	**27,157**	**n.m.**	**689**
Cost of sales	12,071		419
Salaries & benefits	15,376		2,633
General & admin expense	13,499		2,059
Stock-based compensation	2,051		4,313
Operating expense	**42,997**	**+356**	**9,424**
Operating income	**(15,840)**	**n.a.**	**(8,735)**
Deprec., depl. & amort.	4,618		1,094
Finance costs, net	285		2,324
Write-downs/write-offs	(1,408)		nil
Pre-tax income	**(22,151)**	**n.a.**	**(12,153)**
Net inc bef disc ops, eqhldrs	(22,310)		(12,153)
Net inc bef disc ops, NCI	159		nil
Net inc. bef. disc. opers	**(22,151)**	**n.a.**	**(12,153)**
Disc. opers., equity hldrs	8,563		2,672
Income from disc. opers	8,563		2,672
Net income	**(13,588)**	**n.a.**	**(9,481)**
Net inc. for equity hldrs	**(13,747)**	**n.a.**	**(9,481)**
Net inc. for non-cont. int	**159**	**n.a.**	**nil**
Cash & equivalent	11,653		20,052
Inventories	nil		31
Accounts receivable	5,858		529
Current assets	21,081		21,361
Fixed assets, net	766		88
Right-of-use assets	15,695		1,325
Intangibles, net	23,612		8,698
Total assets	**65,447**	**+108**	**31,472**
Accts. pay. & accr. liabs	6,687		1,123
Current liabilities	11,302		2,715
Long-term debt, gross	317		762
Long-term debt, net	nil		316
Long-term lease liabilities	14,528		804
Preferred share equity	6,237		nil
Shareholders' equity	37,895		27,637
Non-controlling interest	712		nil
Cash from oper. activs	**(11,309)**	**n.a.**	**(1,887)**
Cash from fin. activs	18,971		23,995
Cash from invest. activs	(15,777)		(2,392)
Net cash position	**11,653**	**-42**	**20,052**
Capital expenditures	(134)		(11)
Capital disposals	4		nil
	$		$
Earns. per sh. bef disc opers*	(0.59)		(0.56)
Earnings per share*	(0.36)		(0.43)
Cash flow per share*	(0.30)		(0.09)
	shs		shs
No. of shs. o/s*	39,133,000		35,069,989
Avg. no. of shs. o/s*	37,449,000		21,884,219
	%		%
Net profit margin	(81.57)		n.m.
Return on equity	(75.25)		(83.74)
Return on assets	(45.71)		(59.35)
Foreign sales percent	99		65
No. of employees (FTEs)	259		n.a.

* Common
◊ Restated
^A Reported in accordance with IFRS

Latest Results

Periods ended:	9m Sept. 30/22^A		9m Sept. 30/21^◊A
	$000s	%Chg	$000s
Operating revenue	44,638	+152	17,748
Net inc. bef. disc. opers	(17,799)	n.a.	(13,964)
Income from disc. opers	nil		2,633
Net income	(17,799)	n.a.	(11,331)
Net inc. for equity hldrs	(18,022)	n.a.	(11,338)
Net inc. for non-cont. int	223		7
	$		$
Earns. per sh. bef. disc. opers.*	(0.45)		(0.38)
Earnings per share*	(0.45)		(0.31)

* Common
◊ Restated
^A Reported in accordance with IFRS

Historical Summary
(as originally stated)

Fiscal Year	Oper. Rev. $000s	Net Inc. Bef. Disc. $000s	EPS* $
2021[A]	27,157	(22,151)	(0.59)
2020[A]	13,141	(9,481)	(0.43)
2019[A1]	13,424	(10,974)	(0.71)
2018[A2]	10,768	(3,657)	n.a.
2017[A]	280	(1,257)	n.a.

* Common
[A] Reported in accordance with IFRS
[1] Results reflect the Feb. 27, 2019, reverse takeover acqusition of MVC Technologies Inc.
[2] Results for 2018 and prior years pertain to MVC Technologies Inc.
Note: Adjusted throughout for 1-for-5 cons. in May 2021

S.62 Slate Grocery REIT

Symbol - SGR.UN **Exchange** - TSX **CUSIP** - 831062
Head Office - 200-121 King St W, Toronto, ON, M5H 3T9 **Telephone** - (416) 644-4264 **Fax** - (416) 947-9366
Website - www.slategroceryreit.com
Email - ir@slateam.com
Investor Relations - Andrew Agatep (416) 583-1782
Auditors - Deloitte LLP C.A., Toronto, Ont.
Lawyers - McCarthy Tétrault LLP, Toronto, Ont.
Transfer Agents - TSX Trust Company, Toronto, Ont.
Managers - Slate Asset Management LP, Toronto, Ont.
FP500 Revenue Ranking - 628
Profile - (Ont. 2012) Acquires, owns and leases grocery-anchored retail properties in major metropolitan statistical areas in the United States.

At Mar. 31, 2023, the trust owned a portfolio of 117 grocery-anchored retail properties, totaling 15,284,170 sq. ft. of gross leasable area, in 24 U.S. states. The properties are anchored by large, established retailers including Kroger, Walmart, Ahold Delhaize, Albertsons and Tops Markets.

In August 2022, the company sold East Little Creek, a 68,770-sq.-ft. Kroger-anchored shopping centre located at 230 East Little Creek Road in Norfolk, Va., for US$2,000,000.

In June 2022, the trust entered into a joint venture agreement with **Slate North American Essential Real Estate Income Fund L.P.** (NA Essential Fund), whereby NA Essential Fund would invest US$180,000,000 in exchange for a 9.2% interest in the trust's wholly owned **Slate Grocery One L.P.** and **Slate Grocery Investments U.S. L.P.** Upon closing of the agreement, NA Essential Fund would own 18.4% interest in the trust's total retail assets.

Recent Merger and Acquisition Activity

Status: completed **Announced:** Nov. 21, 2022
Slate Grocery REIT sold Hilliard Rome Commons, a 106,571-sq.-ft. Burlington-anchored retail centre located in Columbus, Ohio, for US$15,600,000.

Status: completed **Announced:** Nov. 10, 2022
Slate Grocery REIT sold Westminster Plaza, a 98,975-sq.-ft. VASA Fitness-anchored shopping centre located in Westminster, Md., for US$20,000,000.

Status: completed **Announced:** Oct. 27, 2022
Slate Grocery REIT sold Bloomingdale Plaza, a 83,237-sq.-ft. grocery-anchored retail centre in Brandon, Fla., for US$13,200,000.

Status: completed **Announced:** Oct. 24, 2022
Slate Grocery REIT sold Stadium Center, a 92,538-sq.-ft. Kroger-anchored retail centre in Port Huron, Mich., for US$5,800,000.

Status: completed **Revised:** July 15, 2022
UPDATE: The transaction was completed. PREVIOUS: Slate Grocery REIT agreed to acquire a grocery-anchored portfolio consisting of 14 properties totaling 2,449,010 sq. ft. across seven U.S. states for US$425,000,000. The consideration would be funded through a US$275,000,000 term loan and US$180,000,000 investment from Slate North American Real Estate Income Fund L.P. June 30, 2022 - Acquisition of 151,548 sq. ft. property in Greeley, Colo., was completed for US$37,550,000.

Predecessor Detail - Name changed from Slate Retail REIT, Aug. 21, 2020.

Trustees - Andrea M. Stephen, chr., Toronto, Ont.; Blair Welch, interim CEO, Chicago, Ill.; Colum P. Bastable, Toronto, Ont.; Christopher Chee, Los Angeles, Calif.; Patrick Flatley, Etobicoke, Ont.; Marc Rouleau, Saint-Lambert, Qué.; Mary D. Vitug, Toronto, Ont.; Brady Welch, London, Middx., United Kingdom

Other Exec. Officers - Andrew Agatep, CFO; Ramsey Ali, gen. counsel & corp. sec.

Capital Stock

	Authorized (shs.)	Outstanding (shs.)[1]
Class A Unit	unlimited	146,214
Class I Unit	unlimited	18,369
Class U Unit	unlimited	59,962,000
Special Voting Unit	unlimited	132,561
Exch. LP Unit	unlimited	132,561[2 3]
Cl.B LP1 Unit	unlimited	28,158[2 4]
Cl.B LP2 Unit	unlimited	823,785[2 5]

[1] At Mar. 31, 2023
[2] Classified as debt.
[3] U.S. Grocery-Anchored Retail (1B) limited partnership units. Classified as non-controlling interest
[4] Slate Grocery One limited partnership units.
[5] Slate Grocery Two limited partnership units.

Class U Unit - Entitled to monthly cash distributions of US$0.072 per unit. One vote per unit.

Class A Unit - Entitled to monthly cash distributions in an amount equal to Canadian dollar equivalent of class U distribution multiplied by 1.0078. Convertible at anytime into class U units on 1-for-1 basis. One vote per unit.

Class I Unit - Entitled to monthly cash distributions in an amount equal to class U distribution multiplied by 1.0554. Convertible at anytime into class U units on 1-for-1 basis. One vote per unit.

Class B Limited Partnership 1 Unit - Issued by Slate Grocery One L.P. Entitled to distributions equal to those provided to class U trust units. Directly exchangeable into class U trust units on a 1-for-1 basis at any time by holder. Classified as financial liabilities under IFRS

Class B Limited Partnership 2 Unit - Issued by Slate Grocery Two L.P. Entitled to distributions equal to those provided to class U trust units. Directly exchangeable into class U trust units on a 1-for-1 basis at any time by holder. Classified as financial liabilities under IFRS.

Exchangeable Limited Partnership Unit - Issued by U.S. Grocery-Anchored Retail (1B) Limited Partnership. Entitled to distributions equal to those provided to class U trust units. Directly exchangeable into class U trust units on a 1-for-1 basis at any time by holder. Classified as financial liabilities under IFRS.

Special Voting Unit - Issued to holders of exchangeable limited partnership units of U.S. Grocery-Anchored Retail (1B) Limited Partnership. Each special voting unit entitles the holder to a number of votes at unitholder meetings equal to the number of trust units into which the limited partnership units are exchangeable.

Normal Course Issuer Bid - The company plans to make normal course purchases of up to 5,655,086 class U units representing 10% of the public float. The bid commenced on Feb. 1, 2023, and expires on Jan. 31, 2024.

Major Shareholder - Widely held at Mar. 15, 2023.

Price Range - SGR.UN/TSX

Year	Volume	High	Low	Close
2022	35,918,092	$17.51	$12.74	$15.11
2021	33,333,385	$14.49	$11.15	$14.43
2020	20,140,294	$13.60	$4.95	$11.27
2019	10,234,862	$13.30	$11.51	$13.13
2018	10,297,421	$13.20	$11.20	$11.75

Recent Close: $12.95

Capital Stock Changes - During 2022, class U trust units were issued as follows: 1,425,000 for cash and 438,000 on exchange of a like number of class A, class I and limited partnership units.

Dividends

SGR.UN cl U unit Ra US$0.864 pa M est. Jan. 15, 2020**
SGR.U cl U unit Ra US$0.864 pa M est. Jan. 15, 2020**
** Reinvestment Option

Wholly Owned Subsidiaries

Slate Grocery Investment L.P., Ont.
- 100% int. in **Slate Grocery One L.P.**, Del.
  - 100% int. in **Slate Grocery Two L.P.**, Del.

Slate Grocery Investments Inc.
- 100% int. in **Slate Grocery Investments US L.P.**

U.S. Grocery Anchored Retail (1B) Limited Partnership, Ont.

Financial Statistics

Periods ended:	12m Dec. 31/22[A]		12m Dec. 31/21[A]
	US$000s	%Chg	US$000s
Total revenue	**177,485**	**+28**	**138,275**
Rental operating expense	50,071		37,417
General & admin. expense	14,067		9,730
Operating expense	**64,138**	**+36**	**47,147**
Operating income	**113,347**	**+24**	**91,128**
Investment income	29,270		20,489
Finance costs, net	47,005		41,591
Write-downs/write-offs	(884)		(691)
Pre-tax income	**173,713**	**+37**	**127,210**
Income taxes	34,038		35,818
After-tax income (expense)	(802)		(3,964)
Net income	**138,873**	**+59**	**87,428**
Net inc. for equity hldrs	**128,002**	**+47**	**86,905**
Net inc. for non-cont. int	**10,871**	**n.m.**	**523**
Cash & equivalent	20,392		14,038
Accounts receivable	23,649		17,573
Current assets	55,907		39,757
Long-term investments	109,456		87,304
Income-producing props	2,087,432		1,608,655
Property interests, net	2,087,432		1,608,655
Total assets	**2,270,400**	**+31**	**1,737,162**
Accts. pay. & accr. liabs	38,373		30,039
Current liabilities	134,651		52,441
Long-term debt, gross	1,142		950,046
Long-term debt, net	1,050		941,520
Shareholders' equity	740,510		619,020
Non-controlling interest	190,592		4,901
Cash from oper. activs	**58,986**	**+16**	**50,804**
Cash from fin. activs	329,111		151,725
Cash from invest. activs	(381,743)		(190,853)
Net cash position	**20,392**	**+45**	**14,038**
Increase in property	(443,014)		(151,253)
Decrease in property	54,277		4,059
	US$		US$
Earnings per share*	n.a.		n.a.
Cash flow per share*	0.98		0.87
Funds from opers. per sh.*	1.09		1.03
Adj. funds from opers. per sh.*	0.90		0.86
Cash divd. per share*	0.86		0.86
Total divd. per share*	**0.86**		**0.86**
	shs		shs
No. of shs. o/s*	60,205,000		58,342,000
	%		%
Net profit margin	78.24		63.23
Return on equity	18.83		16.22
Return on assets	6.93		5.71
Foreign sales percent	100		100

* Cl.U Unit
[A] Reported in accordance with IFRS

Latest Results

Periods ended:	3m Mar. 31/23[A]		3m Mar. 31/22[A]
	US$000s	%Chg	US$000s
Total revenue	50,789	+30	38,966
Net income	(14,831)	n.a.	27,425
Net inc. for equity hldrs	(12,100)	n.a.	27,109
Net inc. for non-cont. int	(2,731)		316
	US$		US$
Earnings per share*	n.a.		n.a.

[A] Reported in accordance with IFRS

Historical Summary
(as originally stated)

Fiscal Year	Total Rev. US$000s	Net Inc. Bef. Disc. US$000s	EPS* US$
2022[A]	177,485	138,873	n.a.
2021[A]	138,275	87,428	n.a.
2020[A]	126,130	41,605	n.a.
2019[A]	141,315	26,323	n.a.
2018[A]	144,213	2,461	n.a.

* Cl.U Unit
[A] Reported in accordance with IFRS

S.63 Slate Office Real Estate Investment Trust

Symbol - SOT.UN **Exchange** - TSX **CUSIP** - 831021
Head Office - 200-121 King St W, Toronto, ON, M5H 3T9 **Telephone** - (416) 644-4264 **Fax** - (416) 947-9366
Website - www.slateofficereit.com
Email - brady@slateam.com
Investor Relations - Brady Welch (416) 644-4264
Auditors - KPMG LLP C.A., Toronto, Ont.
Lawyers - McCarthy Tétrault LLP, Toronto, Ont.
Transfer Agents - TSX Trust Company, Toronto, Ont.
Managers - Slate Asset Management LP, Toronto, Ont.
FP500 Revenue Ranking - 659

Profile - (Ont. 2012) Owns and operates office properties in Canada, the U.S. and Ireland.

At Dec. 31, 2022, the trust owned or had interests in 54 properties, consisting of 44 office, seven industrial, two retail and one data centre, totaling 7,520,247 sq. ft. of gross leaseable area.

Property portfolio at Dec. 31, 2022:

Location	Props.	Sq. ft.[1]
Ontario	9[2]	2,265,877
Manitoba	5[3]	377,963
Saskatchewan	1	84,862
New Brunswick	7	1,392,137
Nfld. & Labrador	4	603,866
Nova Scotia	2	606,817
Illinois	3	1,226,681
Ireland	12	437,301
	54	7,520,247

[1] Gross leaseable area.

[2] Includes a 250-room Delta Brunswick Hotel in St. John, N.B.

[3] Includes a seven-storey office building, a three-storey multi-family residential building, two parking lots and a 63,439-sq.-ft. retail property.

Recent Merger and Acquisition Activity

Status: completed **Revised:** Nov. 1, 2022

UPDATE: The transaction was completed. PREVIOUS: Slate Office Real Estate Investment Trust agreed to acquire a class A office property in Chicago, Ill., for US$19,800,000, which would be funded with proceeds from a bought deal public offering of convertible debentures. The property consisted of 197,527 rentable sq. ft.

Status: completed **Announced:** Oct. 4, 2022

Slate Office Real Estate Investment Trust sold the property at 95-105 Moatfield Drive in Toronto, Ont., for $97,000,000.

Predecessor Detail - Name changed from FAM Real Estate Investment Trust, Mar. 16, 2015.

Trustees - Monty Baker, interim chr., Burlington, Ont.; Brady Welch, interim CEO, London, Middx., United Kingdom; Jean-Charles Angers, Westmount, Qué.; George S. Armoyan, Halifax, N.S.; Lori-Ann Beausoleil, Toronto, Ont.; Michael Fitzgerald, Edmonton, Alta.; Meredith Michetti, Toronto, Ont.; Blair Welch, Chicago, Ill.

Other Exec. Officers - Bozena Jankowska, man. dir. & global head, ESG; Robert Armstrong, CFO; Ramsey Ali, gen. counsel & corp. sec.

Capital Stock

	Authorized (shs.)	Outstanding (shs.)[1]
Preferred Unit	unlimited	nil
Trust Unit	unlimited	80,023,409
Special Voting Unit	unlimited	5,285,160
Slate Office I Class B LP Unit	unlimited	2,977,132[2]
Slate Office II Class B LP Unit	unlimited	2,308,028[2]

[1] At Mar. 20, 2023

[2] Classified as debt.

Trust Unit - The trust intends to make monthly cash distributions equal to approximately 95% of the trust's adjusted funds from operations. One vote per trust unit.

Special Voting Unit - Issued to holders of class B limited partnership units of subsidiaries Slate Office I L.P. and Slate Office II L.P. Each special voting unit entitles the holder to a number of votes at unitholder meetings equal to the number of trust units into which the class B limited partnership units are exchangeable.

Class B Limited Partnership Unit - Entitled to distributions equal to those provided to trust units. Directly exchangeable into trust units on a 1-for-1 basis at any time by holder. All held by Slate Asset Management LP. Classified as long-term debt under IFRS.

Major Shareholder - G2S2 Capital Inc. held 16.62% interest at Mar. 20, 2023.

Price Range - SOT.UN/TSX

Year	Volume	High	Low	Close
2022	47,082,948	$5.30	$4.21	$4.32
2021	45,475,809	$5.48	$4.03	$5.00
2020	48,948,508	$5.94	$2.50	$4.14
2019	48,425,349	$6.91	$5.71	$5.85
2018	46,226,717	$8.38	$5.65	$5.97

Recent Close: $1.61

Capital Stock Changes - In February 2022, 11,225,000 trust units were issued without further consideration on exchange of subscription receipts sold previously by bought deal public offering at $4.90 each and private placement of 1,183,800 trust units was completed at $4.90 per unit. Also during 2022, 150,800 trust units were repurchased under a Normal Course Issuer Bid.

Dividends

SOT.UN tr unit Ra $0.12 pa M est. May 15, 2023**

Prev. Rate: $0.40 est. Apr. 15, 2019

** Reinvestment Option

Wholly Owned Subsidiaries

Slate Office GP Inc., Ont.
- 100% int. in **Slate Office I L.P.**, Ont. Class A limited partnership units.
- 100% int. in **Slate Office II L.P.**, Ont. Class A limited partnership units.

Slate Office Investment Holdings Inc., Canada.
- 100% int. in **Slate Office Ireland Investment Ltd.**, Ireland.
  - 100% int. in **Slate Office Ireland YG Limited**, Ireland.

Slate Office U.S. Inc., Del.

Note: The preceding list includes only the major related companies in which interests are held.

Financial Statistics

Periods ended:	12m Dec. 31/22[A]		12m Dec. 31/21[A]
	$000s	%Chg	$000s
Total revenue	**196,515**	**+14**	**172,650**
Rental operating expense	104,117		94,106
General & admin. expense	9,867		7,714
Operating expense	**113,984**	**+12**	**101,820**
Operating income	**82,531**	**+17**	**70,830**
Deprec. & amort.	966		1,022
Finance income	3,542		3,751
Finance costs, gross	55,056		46,201
Write-downs/write-offs	(1,324)		(319)
Pre-tax income	**(17,440)**	**n.a.**	**49,368**
Income taxes	(821)		2,728
Net income	**(16,619)**	**n.a.**	**46,640**
Cash & equivalent	19,905		9,909
Accounts receivable	10,344		9,808
Current assets	39,497		165,785
Income-producing props.	1,754,338		1,591,958
Property interests, net	1,754,338		1,591,958
Total assets	**1,869,362**	**+3**	**1,808,907**
Accts. pay. & accr. liabs.	36,871		34,248
Current liabilities	416,566		256,467
Long-term debt, gross	1,176,085		1,071,968
Long-term debt, net	802,058		909,759
Shareholders' equity	644,366		621,967
Cash from oper. activs.	**49,563**	**+30**	**38,232**
Cash from fin. activs.	49,753		97,441
Cash from invest. activs.	(88,368)		(134,268)
Net cash position	**19,905**	**+101**	**9,909**
Capital expenditures	(22,924)		(24,698)
Increase in property	(223,308)		nil
Decrease in property	85,493		35,089
	$		$
Earnings per share*	n.a.		n.a.
Cash flow per share*	0.62		0.56
Funds from opers. per sh.*	0.48		0.54
Adj. funds from opers. per sh.*	0.47		0.52
Cash divd. per share*	0.40		0.40
Total divd. per share*	**0.40**		**0.40**
	shs		shs
No. of shs. o/s*	80,023,409		67,765,409
	%		%
Net profit margin	(8.46)		27.01
Return on equity	(2.62)		7.60
Return on assets	1.95		5.18
Foreign sales percent	32		25

* Trust Unit

[A] Reported in accordance with IFRS

Historical Summary
(as originally stated)

Fiscal Year	Total Rev. $000s	Net Inc. Bef. Disc. $000s	EPS* $
2022[A]	196,515	(16,619)	n.a.
2021[A]	172,650	46,640	n.a.
2020[A]	183,586	13,648	n.a.
2019[A]	215,520	62,441	n.a.
2018[A]	209,899	77,137	n.a.

* Trust Unit

[A] Reported in accordance with IFRS

S.64 Sleep Country Canada Holdings Inc.*

Symbol - ZZZ **Exchange** - TSX **CUSIP** - 83125J

Head Office - 7920 Airport Rd, Brampton, ON, L6T 4N8 **Telephone** - (289) 748-0206 **Fax** - (905) 790-9379

Website - www.sleepcountry.ca

Email - craig.depratto@sleepcountry.ca

Investor Relations - Craig De Pratto (289) 748-0206

Auditors - PricewaterhouseCoopers LLP C.A., Toronto, Ont.

Bankers - The Toronto-Dominion Bank, Toronto, Ont.

Lawyers - Davies Ward Phillips & Vineberg LLP, Toronto, Ont.

Transfer Agents - Computershare Trust Company of Canada Inc., Toronto, Ont.

FP500 Revenue Ranking - 358

Employees - 1,600 at Dec. 31, 2022

Profile - (Can. 2015) Retails mattresses and complementary sleep related products across Canada through retail stores and e-commerce platforms.

Offers a large selection of mattresses and a wide assortment of sleep related products and accessories including bed frames, bases, boxsprings, pillows, pillowcases, sheets, blankets, throws, quilts, duvets, duvet covers, mattress toppers, mattress protectors, pet beds, cushions, weighted blankets, headboards, footboards, storage benches and platforms through retail stores and websites under the banners Dormez-vous™ in Quebec, Casper™, Sleep Country™, Endy™, Silk & Snow™ and Hush™ for the rest of Canada.

At June 30, 2023, the company's retail network consisted of 295 mattress stores, which average 5,000 sq. ft., and 19 warehouses across Canada. E-commerce platforms include sleepcountry.ca, dormezvous.com, endy.com, hush.ca, hushblankets.com, silkandsnow.com and casper.ca. Additionally, partnerships have been established by the company to offer mattresses and sleep accessories at **Walmart Canada** superstores, as well as on **Walmart Canada**'s, **Best Buy Canada**'s, and **Loblaw Companies Ltd.**'s online marketplaces.

Subsidiary **Hush Blankets Inc.** (52% owned) retails sleep products online, including weighted blankets, pillows, sheets and mattresses.

Wholly owned **Silk & Snow Inc.** operates www.silkandsnow.com, which offers high-quality sleep and lifestyle products including bed sheets, mattresses, bed frames, weighted blankets and other home essentials, as well as bath products such as towels and robes.

Recent Merger and Acquisition Activity

Status: completed **Revised:** Apr. 14, 2023

UPDATE: The transaction was completed. PREVIOUS: Sleep Country Canada Holdings Inc. agreed to acquire the Canadian operations of Casper Sleep Inc., an online retailer of sleep products including mattresses, pillows, bedding and furniture, for US$20,600,000. Sleep Country would also receive a cumulative US$4,500,000 marketing transition fee from Casper over the next four years and receive three-year warrants which would convert into a 1% interest in Casper upon exercise. In addition, Sleep Country invested US$20,000,000 in five-year convertible notes which would have the option of converting into 5% of Casper's shares.

Status: completed **Revised:** Jan. 4, 2023

UPDATE: The transaction was completed. PREVIOUS: Sleep Country Canada Holdings Inc. agreed to acquire private Toronto, Ont.-based Silk & Snow Inc. for $24,000,000, which would be financed with cash on hand and a revolving credit facility. Sleep Country agreed to pay up to an additional $19,450,000 in early 2026 based on Silk & Snow achieving certain grown and profitability targets in aggregate for fiscal years 2023, 2024 and 2025. Silk & Snow operates www.silkandsnow.com, which offers high-quality sleep and lifestyle products including bed sheets, mattresses, bed frames, weighted blankets and other home essentials, as well as bath products such as towels and robes. Silk & Snow would operate as an independent entity within Sleep Country.

Directors - Christine A. Magee†, chr., Toronto, Ont.; Stewart Schaefer, pres. & CEO, Ont.; John M. Cassaday, Toronto, Ont.; Mandeep Chawla, Ont.; Zabeen Hirji, Ont.; Andrew R. G. Moor, Toronto, Ont.; Stacey Mowbray, Ont.; David R. Shaw, Ont.

Other Exec. Officers - Craig De Pratto, CFO & corp. sec.; Lynne Feldman, chief people officer; Alexandra Voyevodina-Wang, pres. & gen. mgr., Endy Canada Inc.

† Lead director

Capital Stock

	Authorized (shs.)	Outstanding (shs.)[1]
Common	unlimited	34,789,130
Class A Common	unlimited	nil

[1] At Aug. 10, 2023

Options - At Dec. 31, 2022, options were outstanding to purchase 1,038,790 common shares at a weighted average exercise price of $25.46 per share with a weighted average remaining life of six years.

Normal Course Issuer Bid - The company plans to make normal course purchases of up to 2,675,550 common shares representing 10% of the public float. The bid commenced on Mar. 9, 2023, and expires on Mar. 8, 2024.

Major Shareholder - Mawer Investment Management Limited held 10.44% interest and Mackenzie Financial Corporation held 10.19% interest at Mar. 30, 2023.

Price Range - ZZZ/TSX

Year	Volume	High	Low	Close
2022	24,988,324	$39.82	$19.66	$22.98
2021	24,650,164	$41.97	$25.15	$37.53
2020	37,795,118	$27.63	$7.75	$26.47
2019	26,897,708	$22.70	$16.01	$20.21
2018	33,371,018	$37.24	$18.79	$19.97

Recent Close: $23.53

Capital Stock Changes - During 2022, common shares were issued as follows: 156,675 on exercise of options and 106,690 under performance share unit plan; 2,339,409 common shares were repurchased under a Normal Course Issuer Bid.

Dividends

ZZZ com Ra $0.948 pa Q est. May 31, 2023[1]

Prev. Rate: $0.86 est. May 30, 2022

[1] Quarterly divd. normally payable in May/2020 has been omitted.

Long-Term Debt - At Dec. 31, 2022, outstanding long-term debt totaled $99,082,000 (none current) and consisted entirely of borrowings under a senior secured credit facility due October 2026.

Wholly Owned Subsidiaries

14577973 Canada Inc., Brampton, Ont. dba Silk & Snow
- 100% int. in **Silk & Snow Inc.**, Toronto, Ont.

SCC USA Inc., United States.

Sleep Country Canada Inc., Toronto, Ont.
- 100% int. in **Endy Canada Inc.**, Toronto, Ont.

Subsidiaries

52% int. in **Hush Blankets Inc.**, North York, Ont.
- 100% int. in **Hush USA Inc.**, United States.

Investments

25% int. in **Sleepout Inc.**, Toronto, Ont.

Note: The preceding list includes only the major related companies in which interests are held.

Financial Statistics

Periods ended:	12m Dec. 31/22[A]		12m Dec. 31/21[A]
	$000s	%Chg	$000s
Operating revenue	**928,657**	**+1**	**920,194**
Cost of sales	417,590		433,769
Salaries & benefits	164,989		158,503
General & admin expense	133,166		124,006
Operating expense	**715,745**	**0**	**716,278**
Operating income	**212,912**	**+4**	**203,916**
Deprec., depl. & amort.	65,634		60,726
Finance costs, gross	n.a.		16,837
Finance costs, net	(889)		n.a.
Write-downs/write-offs	(2,417)		(4,367)
Pre-tax income	**146,042**	**+20**	**121,844**
Income taxes	35,346		32,862
Net inc bef disc ops, eqhldrs	110,471		88,603
Net inc bef disc ops, NCI	225		379
Net income	**110,696**	**+24**	**88,982**
Net inc. for equity hldrs	**110,471**	**+25**	**88,603**
Net inc. for non-cont. int.	**225**	**-41**	**379**
Cash & equivalent	78,318		36,546
Inventories	98,691		91,539
Accounts receivable	14,303		16,678
Current assets	201,633		154,592
Fixed assets, net	63,676		71,674
Right-of-use assets	263,149		273,097
Intangibles, net	488,152		484,231
Total assets	**1,021,719**	**+3**	**988,035**
Accts. pay. & accr. liabs	95,251		106,494
Current liabilities	192,782		179,231
Long-term debt, gross	99,082		61,895
Long-term debt, net	99,082		61,895
Long-term lease liabilities	275,170		284,338
Shareholders' equity	412,794		404,186
Non-controlling interest	7,284		5,778
Cash from oper. activs	**163,060**	**+4**	**156,143**
Cash from fin. activs	(103,044)		(94,808)
Cash from invest. activs	(18,224)		(63,106)
Net cash position	**78,318**	**+114**	**36,546**
Capital expenditures	(7,557)		(19,317)
	$		$
Earnings per share*	3.04		2.41
Cash flow per share*	4.49		4.24
Cash divd. per share*	0.84		0.78
	shs		shs
No. of shs. o/s*	34,837,943		36,913,987
Avg. no. of shs. o/s*	36,316,000		36,810,000
	%		%
Net profit margin	11.92		9.67
Return on equity	27.04		23.23
Return on assets	11.02		10.72
No. of employees (FTEs)	1,600		1,577

* Common
[A] Reported in accordance with IFRS

Latest Results

Periods ended:	6m June 30/23[A]		6m June 30/22[A]
	$000s	%Chg	$000s
Operating revenue	423,694	-3	434,603
Net income	24,060	-41	40,935
Net inc. for equity hldrs	24,015	-42	41,078
Net inc. for non-cont. int.	45		(143)
	$		$
Earnings per share*	0.69		1.11

* Common
[A] Reported in accordance with IFRS

Historical Summary
(as originally stated)

Fiscal Year	Oper. Rev.	Net Inc. Bef. Disc.	EPS*
	$000s	$000s	$
2022[A]	928,657	110,696	3.04
2021[A]	920,194	88,982	2.41
2020[A]	757,699	63,307	1.73
2019[A]	712,372	55,460	1.50
2018[A]	622,977	59,641	1.61

* Common
[A] Reported in accordance with IFRS

S.65 Sleeping Giant Capital Corp.

Symbol - SSX.P **Exchange** - TSX-VEN **CUSIP** - 83126J
Head Office - 4000-421 7 Ave SW, Calgary, AB, T2P 4K9 **Telephone** - (403) 875-8167
Investor Relations - Jonah D. Nguyen (403) 875-8167
Auditors - RSM Alberta LLP C.A., Calgary, Alta.
Lawyers - McCarthy Tétrault LLP, Calgary, Alta.
Transfer Agents - Odyssey Trust Company, Calgary, Alta.
Profile - (Alta. 2021) Capital Pool Company.
Directors - Terence S. (Terry) Meek, CEO, Calgary, Alta.; Jonah D. Nguyen, CFO; John F. (Jack) Elliott, Calgary, Alta.; Gregory G. (Greg) Turnbull, Calgary, Alta.
Other Exec. Officers - Gordon Cameron, corp. sec.

Capital Stock

	Authorized (shs.)	Outstanding (shs.)[1]
Common	unlimited	7,800,000

[1] At May 30, 2023

Major Shareholder - Widely held at Sept. 30, 2022.

Price Range - SSX.P/TSX-VEN

Year	Volume	High	Low	Close
2022	297,000	$0.11	$0.06	$0.09
2021	348,000	$0.14	$0.10	$0.10

Recent Close: $0.06
Capital Stock Changes - There were no changes to capital stock during 2022.

S.66 Small Pharma Inc.

Symbol - DMT **Exchange** - TSX-VEN **CUSIP** - 831664
Head Office - 6-8 Bonhill St, 3rd Flr, London, MDX, United Kingdom, EC2A 4BX **Overseas Tel** - 44-77-9237-6485
Website - smallpharma.co.uk
Email - david.steel@smallpharma.co.uk
Investor Relations - David Steel 44-77-9237-6485
Auditors - MNP LLP C.A., Toronto, Ont.
Transfer Agents - Odyssey Trust Company, Vancouver, B.C.
Employees - 19 at Aug. 9, 2022
Profile - (B.C. 2018) Developing new generation of treatments for mental health conditions, in particular depression, through the development of psychedelic and non-psychedelic medicines.

Psychedelic-based development programs include SPL026, which is the evaluation of N,N-dimethyltryptamine (DMT) with talk therapy for the treatment of depression under Phase 1/IIa clinical trial, and was granted a fast-track innovation passport designation from the U.K. Medicines and Healthcare products Regulatory Agency; SPL028, an injectable formulation of deuterated DMT designed to deliver a more prolonged psychedelic experience; and SPL029, an oral formulation of tryptamine to offer an alternative way to deliver the treatment to patients in clinic. The company has 10 patents granted and 71 patent applications pending and is actively pursuing to expand its portfolio.

The non-psychedelic based program includes SPL801B, an oral formulation of 6-hydroxynorketamine, a ketamine metabolite, which had shown in early pre-clinical studies to have signs of rapid antidepressant effects with an improved side effect profile to ketamine.

Predecessor Detail - Name changed from Unilock Capital Corp., Apr. 28, 2021, pursuant to the Qualifying Transaction reverse takeover acquisition of Small Pharma Ltd.; basis 1 new for 4.6 old shs.
Directors - Lyne Fortin, chr., Val-David, Qué.; George Tziras, CEO, London, Middx., United Kingdom; Marie Layzell, chief mfg. & devel. officer & head, CMC, Surrey, United Kingdom; Paul Maier, Williamsburg, Va.; Michael A. Wolfe, Toronto, Ont.
Other Exec. Officers - Dr. Alastair Riddell, COO; David Steel, CFO; Dr. Carol Routledge, chief medical & scientific officer; Richard M. Kimel, corp. sec.

Capital Stock

	Authorized (shs.)	Outstanding (shs.)[1]
Common	unlimited	321,562,487

[1] At June 28, 2023

Major Shareholder - Peter Rands held 27.7% interest at June 13, 2022.

Price Range - DMT/TSX-VEN

Year	Volume	High	Low	Close
2022	31,509,779	$0.40	$0.08	$0.09
2021	16,186,853	$1.10	$0.25	$0.32
2020	9,130	$0.74	$0.64	$0.69
2019	8,369	$0.92	$0.55	$0.64
2018	6,521	$0.92	$0.55	$0.64

Consolidation: 1-for-4.6 cons. in May 2021
Recent Close: $0.09

Wholly Owned Subsidiaries

Small Pharma Ltd., London, Middx., United Kingdom.
- 100% int. in **Small Pharma (US) Inc.**, Del.

Financial Statistics

Periods ended:	12m Feb. 28/22[A1]		12m Feb. 28/21[oA]
	$000s	%Chg	$000s
Operating revenue	**nil**	**n.a.**	**78**
Salaries & benefits	6,807		1,432
Research & devel. expense	4,828		1,920
General & admin expense	5,593		1,731
Stock-based compensation	704		610
Operating expense	**17,932**	**+215**	**5,693**
Operating income	**(17,932)**	**n.a.**	**(5,615)**
Finance costs, net	434		485
Pre-tax income	**(22,921)**	**n.a.**	**(7,029)**
Income taxes	(655)		7
Net income	**(22,266)**	**n.a.**	**(7,035)**
Cash & equivalent	40,656		5,778
Accounts receivable	1,214		476
Current assets	43,012		6,515
Fixed assets, net	62		72
Total assets	**45,574**	**+592**	**6,587**
Accts. pay. & accr. liabs	4,497		1,572
Current liabilities	4,497		12,357
Long-term debt, gross	nil		8,827
Shareholders' equity	41,077		(5,770)
Cash from oper. activs	**(16,235)**	**n.a.**	**(4,249)**
Cash from fin. activs	53,891		9,408
Cash from invest. activs	(2,404)		(71)
Net cash position	**40,656**	**+604**	**5,778**
Capital expenditures	(13)		(71)
	$		$
Earnings per share*	(0.07)		n.a.
Cash flow per share*	(0.05)		n.a.
	shs		shs
No. of shs. o/s*	319,625,487		n.a.
Avg. no. of shs. o/s*	311,599,658		n.a.
	%		%
Net profit margin	n.a.		n.m.
Return on equity	n.m.		n.m.
Return on assets	(85.40)		(190.75)

* Common
[o] Restated
[A] Reported in accordance with IFRS
[1] Results prior to Apr. 29, 2021, pertain to and reflect the Qualifying Transaction reverse takeover acquisition of Small Pharma Ltd.

Latest Results

Periods ended:	3m May 31/22[A]		3m May 31/21[oA]
	$000s	%Chg	$000s
Net income	(5,782)	n.a.	(8,312)
	$		$
Earnings per share*	(0.02)		(0.03)

* Common
[o] Restated
[A] Reported in accordance with IFRS

Historical Summary
(as originally stated)

Fiscal Year	Oper. Rev.	Net Inc. Bef. Disc.	EPS*
	$000s	$000s	$
2022[A]	nil	(22,266)	(0.07)
	£000s	£000s	£
2021[A]	45	(4,077)	n.a.
2020[A]	94	(327)	n.a.

* Common
[A] Reported in accordance with IFRS
Note: Adjusted throughout for 1-for-4.6 cons. in May 2021

S.67 SmartCentres Real Estate Investment Trust*

Symbol - SRU.UN **Exchange** - TSX **CUSIP** - 83179X
Head Office - 3200 Hwy 7, Vaughan, ON, L4K 5Z5 **Telephone** - (905) 326-6400 **Fax** - (905) 326-0783
Website - www.smartcentres.com
Email - pslan@smartcentres.com
Investor Relations - Peter Slan (905) 326-6400 ext. 7571
Auditors - PricewaterhouseCoopers LLP C.A., Toronto, Ont.
Bankers - The Bank of Nova Scotia; Canadian Imperial Bank of Commerce; Royal Bank of Canada; Bank of Montreal; The Toronto-Dominion Bank
Lawyers - Osler, Hoskin & Harcourt LLP, Toronto, Ont.
Transfer Agents - Computershare Trust Company of Canada Inc., Toronto, Ont.
FP500 Revenue Ranking - 377
Employees - 417 at Dec. 31, 2022
Profile - (Alta. 2001) Develops, leases, constructs, owns and operates income-producing retail properties across Canada, targeting major urban centres and shopping centres that are dominant in their trade area. **Walmart Canada Corp.** leases 40.8% of the gross leasable area of the trust's properties.

At Dec. 31, 2022, the property portfolio consisted of 155 retail properties, four offices, six self-storage properties, one residential property and 19 development properties totaling 34,750,379 sq. ft. of net rentable area, excluding undeveloped lands.

Geographic mix of portfolio at Dec. 31, 2022:

Location	Props.
British Columbia	15
Alberta	7
Saskatchewan	5
Manitoba	3
Ontario	116
Quebec	28
New Brunswick	2
Nova Scotia	2
Prince Edward Island	1
Newfoundland and Labrador	6
	185

In addition, the trust operates a property development and leasing management business of primarily open format retail centres across Canada. Services are provided to the Penguin group of companies and other parties.

In February 2023, the trust sold a 2.64-acre parcel of land in Chilliwack, B.C., for $4,800,000 cash.

In January 2023, the trust contributed its interest in a 1.41-acre parcel of land in Whitby, Ont., to **Whitby Self Storage LP**, with the intention to develop and operate a self-storage facility.

In December 2022, the trust contributed its interest in a 2.31-acre parcel of land in Vaughan, Ont., with a value of $25,000,000 to **Vaughan NW RR PropCo LP**, a 50/50 joint venture with **Revera Inc.**, for the development of a retirement residence.

In May 2022, the trust and **SmartStop Asset Management, LLC** formed a 50/50 joint venture, **Regent Self Storage Limited Partnership**, with each party contributing $3,490,000 into the joint venture to fund the acquisition of a 0.89-acre parcel of land in Burnaby, B.C., with the intention to develop and operate a self-storage facility.

Recent Merger and Acquisition Activity

Status: completed **Announced:** Feb. 8, 2023
SmartCentres Real Estate Investment Trust sold its interests in a 6.4-acre parcel of land in Vaughan, Ont., for $58,371,000 consisting of $42,321,000 relating to SmartCentres' 66.67% interest in the 4.3-acre western part of the land and $16,050,000 relating to SmartCentres' 50% interest in the 2.1-acre eastern part of the land.

Status: completed **Announced:** Sept. 30, 2022
SmartCentres Real Estate Investment Trust sold a 6.86-acre parcel of land in London, Ont., for $15,180,000.

Status: completed **Announced:** June 30, 2022
SmartCentres Real Estate Investment Trust acquired 38 acres of industrial lands in Pickering, Ont., for $16,635,000. The property has received approval for the construction of 241,000 sq. ft. of industrial space for the 16-acre phase 1 development.

Status: completed **Announced:** Apr. 30, 2022
SmartCentres Real Estate Investment Trust sold a 6.48-acre parcel of land in Stouffville, Ont., for $18,365,000.

Status: completed **Announced:** Mar. 31, 2022
SmartCentres Real Estate Investment Trust sold a 4.62-acre parcel of land in Laval East, Que., for $5,600,000.

Predecessor Detail - Name changed from Smart Real Estate Investment Trust, Oct. 20, 2017.

Trustees - Mitchell (Mitch) Goldhar, exec. chr. & CEO, Toronto, Ont.; Michael D. Young‡, Dallas, Tex.; Janet Bannister, Ont.; Garry M. Foster, Ont.; Gregory J. Howard, Ont.; Sylvie Lachance, Ont.; Jamie M. McVicar, Canmore, Alta.; Sharm Powell, Ont.

Other Exec. Officers - Peter Slan, CFO; Paula Bustard, exec. v-p, devel.; Rudy Gobin, exec. v-p, portfolio mgt. & invests.; Allan Scully, exec. v-p, devel.; Fernando Vescio, sr. v-p, HR & corp. srvcs.

‡ Lead trustee

Capital Stock

	Authorized (shs.)	Outstanding (shs.)[1]
Variable Voting Unit	unlimited	144,625,322[2]
Special Voting Unit	unlimited	33,542,795[3]
Class B LP Unit	unlimited	
Series 1		14,746,176
Series 2		957,822
Series 3		720,432
Class D LP Unit	unlimited	
Series 1		311,022[4]
Series 2		nil
Class F LP Unit	unlimited	
Series 3		8,708[4]
Class B LP II Unit	unlimited	756,525
Class B LP III Unit	unlimited	
Series 4		706,591
Series 5		583,535
Series 6		640,059
Series 7		434,598
Series 8		1,698,018
Class B LP IV Unit	unlimited	
Series 1		3,112,565
Class B Oshawa South LP Unit	unlimited	
Series 1		710,416
Class D Oshawa South LP Unit	unlimited	
Series 1		260,417[4]
Class B Oshawa Taunton LP Unit	unlimited	
Series 1		374,223
Class D Oshawa Taunton LP Unit	unlimited	
Series 1		nil[4]
Class B Boxgrove LP Unit	unlimited	nil
Series 1		170,000
Class B ONR LP Unit	unlimited	1,248,140[4]
Class B ONR LP I Unit	unlimited	
Series 1		132,881[4]
Series 2		139,302[4]
Class D SmartVMC West LP Unit	unlimited	5,797,101[4]

[1] At Dec. 31, 2022
[2] At Mar. 31, 2023.
[3] At Mar. 31, 2023.
[4] Classified as debt.

Note: Class B, D and F limited partnership units are securities of Smart Limited Partnership, class B limited partnership II units are securities of Smart Limited Partnership II, class B limited partnership III units are securities of Smart Limited Partnership III, class B limited partnership IV units are securities of Smart Limited Partnership IV, class B and D Oshawa South limited partnership units are securities of Smart Oshawa South Limited Partnership, class B and D Oshawa Taunton limited partnership units are securities of Smart Oshawa Taunton Limited Partnership, class B Boxgrove limited partnership units are securities of Smart Boxgrove Limited Partnership, class B ONR limited partnership units are securities of ONR Limited Partnership, class B ONR limited partnership I units are securities of ONR Limited Partnership I and class D SmartVMC West limited partnership units are securities of SmartVMC West Limited Partnership. All limited partnership units are classified as non-controlling interest under equity, except class D series 1 limited partnership units, class F series 3 limited partnership units, class D series 1 Oshawa South limited partnership units, class D series 1 Oshawa Taunton limited partnership units, class B ONR limited partnership units, class B series 1 and series 2 ONR limited partnership I units and class D SmartVMC West limited partnership units which are classified as debt.

Variable Voting Unit - One vote per unit.

Special Voting Unit - Entitled to provide voting rights to holders of class B, D and F limited partnership units of Smart Limited Partnership, holders of class B limited partnership II units of Smart Limited Partnership II, holders of class B limited partnership III units of Smart Limited Partnership III, holders of class B limited partnership IV units of Smart Limited Partnership IV, holders of class B and D limited partnership units of Smart Oshawa South Limited Partnership, holders of class B and D limited partnership units of Smart Oshawa Taunton Limited Partnership, holders of class B limited partnership units of Smart Boxgrove Limited Partnership, holders of class B limited partnership units of ONR Limited Partnership, holders of class B limited partnership I units of ONR Limited Partnership I and holders of class D limited partnership units of SmartVMC West Limited Partnership. Not entitled to any interest or share in the distributions or net assets of the trust. Each special voting unit entitles the holder to the number of votes at any meeting of unitholders of the trust, which is equal to the number of variable voting units into which the exchangeable security is exchangeable or convertible. Units are cancelled on the issuance of variable voting units on exercise, conversion or cancellation of the corresponding exchangeable securities. One vote per special voting unit.

Class B Limited Partnership Unit - Issued by Smart Limited Partnership. Issuable in series. Non-transferable, except under limited certain circumstances. Exchangeable into an equal number of variable voting units at the holder's option. Entitled to receive distributions equivalent to the distributions on variable voting units. Non-voting.

Class D Limited Partnership Unit - Issued by Smart Limited Partnership. Issuable in series. Non-transferable, except under limited certain circumstances. Exchangeable into an equal number of variable voting units at the holder's option. Entitled to receive distributions equivalent to the distributions on variable voting units. Non-voting.

Class F Limited Partnership Unit - Issued by Smart Limited Partnership. Issuable in series. Non-transferable, except under limited certain circumstances. Exchangeable into an equal number of variable voting units at the holder's option. Entitled to receive distributions equivalent to the 65.5% of the distributions on variable voting units. Non-voting.

Class B Limited Partnership II Unit - Issued by Smart Limited Partnership II. Non-transferable, except under limited certain circumstances. Exchangeable into an equal number of variable voting units at the holder's option. Entitled to receive distributions equivalent to the distributions on variable voting units. Non-voting.

Class B Limited Partnership III Unit - Issued by Smart Limited Partnership III. Issuable in series. Non-transferable, except under limited certain circumstances. Exchangeable into an equal number of variable voting units at the holder's option. Entitled to receive distributions equivalent to the distributions on variable voting units. Non-voting.

Class B Limited Partnership IV Unit - Issued by Smart Limited Partnership IV. Non-transferable, except under limited certain circumstances. Exchangeable into an equal number of variable voting units at the holder's option. Entitled to receive distributions equivalent to the distributions on variable voting units. Non-voting.

Class B Oshawa South Limited Partnership Unit - Issued by Smart Oshawa South Limited Partnership. Non-transferable, except under limited certain circumstances. Exchangeable into an equal number of variable voting units at the holder's option. Entitled to receive distributions equivalent to the distributions on variable voting units. Non-voting.

Class D Oshawa South Limited Partnership Unit - Issued by Smart Oshawa South Limited Partnership. Non-transferable, except under limited certain circumstances. Exchangeable into an equal number of variable voting units at the holder's option. Entitled to receive distributions equivalent to the distributions on variable voting units. Non-voting.

Class B Oshawa Taunton Limited Partnership Unit - Issued by Smart Oshawa Taunton Limited Partnership. Non-transferable, except under limited certain circumstances. Exchangeable into an equal number of variable voting units at the holder's option. Entitled to receive distributions equivalent to the distributions on variable voting units. Non-voting.

Class D Oshawa Taunton Limited Partnership Unit - Issued by Smart Oshawa Taunton Limited Partnership. Non-transferable, except under limited certain circumstances. Exchangeable into an equal number of variable voting units at the holder's option. Entitled to receive distributions equivalent to the distributions on variable voting units. Non-voting.

Class B Boxgrove Limited Partnership Unit - Issued by Smart Boxgrove Limited Partnership. Non-transferable, except under limited certain circumstances. Exchangeable into an equal number of variable voting units at the holder's option. Entitled to receive distributions equivalent to the distributions on variable voting units. Non-voting.

Class B ONR Limited Partnership Unit - Issued by ONR Limited Partnership. Issuable in series. Non-transferable, except under limited certain circumstances. Exchangeable into an equal number of variable voting units at the holder's option. Entitled to receive distributions equivalent to the distributions on variable voting units. Non-voting.

Class B ONR Limited Partnership I Unit - Issued by ONR Limited Partnership I. Issuable in series. Non-transferable, except under limited certain circumstances. Exchangeable into an equal number of variable voting units at the holder's option. Entitled to receive distributions equivalent to the distributions on variable voting units. Non-voting.

Class D SmartVMC West Limited Partnership Unit - Issued by SmartVMC West Limited Partnership. Issuable in series. Non-transferable, except under limited certain circumstances. Exchangeable into an equal number of variable voting units at the holder's option. Entitled to receive distributions equivalent to the distributions on variable voting units. Non-voting.

Major Shareholder - Mitchell (Mitch) Goldhar held 25% interest at Mar. 31, 2023.

Price Range - SRU.UN/TSX

Year	Volume	High	Low	Close
2022	77,493,593	$33.48	$24.94	$26.78
2021	102,531,869	$32.50	$22.76	$32.19
2020	163,311,969	$32.49	$14.58	$23.08
2019	73,532,814	$35.23	$30.38	$31.21
2018	58,517,626	$32.42	$28.14	$30.83

Recent Close: $24.34

Capital Stock Changes - During 2022, 18,655 class B series 1 limited partnership IV units, 12,419 class B series 6 limited partnership III units and 11,198 class B series 5 limited partnership III units were issued on exercise of earn-out options.

Dividends

SRU.UN var vtg unit Ra $1.85 pa M est. Nov. 15, 2019**
** Reinvestment Option

Long-Term Debt - Outstanding at Dec. 31, 2022:

Secured debt[1]	$969,054,000
Credit facility[2]	996,238,000
Operating facility[3]	81,283,000
3.985% ser.I debs. due May 2023	200,000,000
2.987% ser.O debs. due Aug. 2024	100,000,000
3.556% ser.N debs. due Feb. 2025	160,000,000
1.74% ser.X debs. due Dec. 2025	350,000,000
3.444% ser.P debs. due Aug. 2026	250,000,000
3.192% ser.V debs. due June 2027	300,000,000
3.834% ser.S debs. due Dec. 2027	250,000,000
2.307% ser.Y debs. due Dec. 2028	300,000,000
3.526% ser.U debs. due Dec. 2029	450,000,000
3.648% ser.W debs. due Dec. 2030	300,000,000
Class B, D & F LP units[4]	211,497,000
TRS debt[5]	143,232,000
Other	141,131,000
Less: Unamort. fin. costs	7,673,000
	5,194,762,000
Less: Current portion	459,278,000
	4,735,484,000

[1] Bears interest at a weighted average interest rate of 3.91% at Dec. 31, 2022, and due between 2023 and 2031.

[2] Consists of $170,000,000 non-revolving facility bearing interest at 3.146% and due June 2024; $80,000,000 non-revolving facility bearing interest at 2.98% and due January 2025; $150,000,0000 non-revolving facility bearing interest at 3.52% and due July 2026; $100,000,000 non-revolving facility bearing interest at 4.37% and due December 2025; $100,000,000 non-revolving facility bearing interest at banker's acceptance rate plus 1.2% and due December 2025; $100,000,000 non-revolving facility bearing interest at banker's acceptance rate plus 1.2% or Canadian prime rate and due December 2025; and $300,000,000 non-revolving facility bearing interest at banker's acceptance rate plus 1.2% and due January 2027.

[3] Consists of $500,000,000 revolving facility bearing interest at banker's acceptance rate plus 1.2% and due August 2026; and $150,000,000 bearing interest at US$ LIBOR rate plus 1.2% and due February 2024.

[4] Consists of class D LP unit, series 1; class F LP unit, series 3; class D Oshawa South LP unit, series 1; class B ONR LP unit; class B ONR LP 1 unit, series 1; class B ONR LP 1 unit, series 2; class D SmartVMCWest LP unit, series 1; and class D SmartVMCWest LP units, series 2.

[5] Bearing interest at CDOR plus 1.06%.

Minimum term mortgage repayments were reported as follows:

2023	$239,894,000
2024	151,032,000
2025	411,341,000
2026	98,121,000
2027	5,473,000
Thereafter	64,376,000

Note - In May 2023, offering of $300,000,000 principal amount of 5.354% series Z senior unsecured debentures due May 29, 2028, was completed.

Wholly Owned Subsidiaries

ONR Limited Partnership I, Ont.
ONR Limited Partnership, Ont.
Smart Boxgrove Limited Partnership
Smart Limited Partnership II, Alta.
Smart Limited Partnership III, Alta.
Smart Limited Partnership IV
Smart Limited Partnership, Alta.
Smart Oshawa South Limited Partnership
Smart Oshawa Taunton Limited Partnership
SmartVMC West Limited Partnership

Note: The preceding list includes only the major related companies in which interests are held.

Financial Statistics

Periods ended:	12m Dec. 31/22[A]		12m Dec. 31/21[oA]
	$000s	%Chg	$000s
Total revenue	**804,598**	**+3**	**780,796**
Rental operating expense	290,350		276,422
General & admin. expense	23,829		22,548
Other operating expense	15,092		14,882
Operating expense	**329,271**	**+5**	**313,852**
Operating income	**475,327**	**+2**	**466,944**
Investment income	4,199		211,420
Deprec. & amort.	9,440		9,374
Finance income	18,036		12,341
Finance costs, gross	148,702		144,540
Write-downs/write-offs	3,448		(3,652)
Pre-tax income	**635,965**	**-36**	**987,676**
Net income	**635,965**	**-36**	**987,676**
Net inc. for equity hldrs	**516,049**	**-38**	**827,976**
Net inc. for non-cont. int.	**119,916**	**-25**	**159,700**
Cash & equivalent	35,255		62,235
Accounts receivable	57,124		49,542
Current assets	276,140		223,412
Long-term investments	919,098		999,531
Fixed assets	2,874		1,622
Income-producing props.	8,496,893		8,395,077
Properties under devel.	1,711,178		1,452,001
Property interests, net	10,212,481		9,851,976
Intangibles, net	43,807		45,139
Total assets	**11,702,153**	**+4**	**11,293,248**
Accts. pay. & accr. liabs	86,592		78,518
Current liabilities	720,400		931,484
Long-term debt, gross	5,194,762		5,108,750
Long-term debt, net	4,735,484		4,430,344
Long-term lease liabilities	10,486		11,837
Shareholders' equity	5,126,197		4,877,961
Non-controlling interest	1,036,904		963,354
Cash from oper. activs	**370,762**	**0**	**371,624**
Cash from fin. activs	(276,349)		(690,809)
Cash from invest. activs	(121,393)		(413,174)
Net cash position	**35,255**	**-43**	**62,235**
Capital expenditures	(1,589)		(349)
Increase in property	(259,446)		(407,392)
Decrease in property	41,822		81,403
	$		$
Earnings per share*	n.a.		n.a.
Cash flow per share*	2.08		2.16
Funds from opers. per sh.*	2.09		2.20
Cash divd. per share*	1.85		1.85
Total divd. per share*	**1.85**		**1.85**
	shs		shs
No. of shs. o/s*	170,236,282		170,194,010
Avg. no. of shs. o/s*	178,121,149		172,447,334
	%		%
Net profit margin	79.04		126.50
Return on equity	10.32		18.01
Return on assets	6.82		10.28
No. of employees (FTEs)	417		378

* Var. Vtg. Unit
[o] Restated
[A] Reported in accordance with IFRS

Note: Variable voting units outstanding include LP, LP II and LP III units converted into variable voting units based on the conversion ratio.

Latest Results

Periods ended:	3m Mar. 31/23[A]		3m Mar. 31/22[oA]
	$000s	%Chg	$000s
Total revenue	210,594	+4	202,828
Net income	112,861	-70	370,110
Net inc. for equity hldrs	91,530	-70	300,452
Net inc. for non-cont. int.	21,331		69,658
	$		$
Earnings per share*	n.a.		n.a.

[o] Restated
[A] Reported in accordance with IFRS

Historical Summary
(as originally stated)

Fiscal Year	Total Rev.	Net Inc. Bef. Disc.	EPS*
	$000s	$000s	$
2022[A]	804,598	635,965	n.a.
2021[A]	780,758	987,676	n.a.
2020[A]	781,253	89,940	n.a.
2019[A]	806,412	374,203	n.a.
2018[A]	790,178	402,947	n.a.

* Var. Vtg. Unit
[A] Reported in accordance with IFRS

S.68 Smartcool Systems Inc.

Symbol - SSC.H **Exchange** - TSX-VEN (S) **CUSIP** - 83171N
Head Office - 7155 Kingsway, PO Box 54523, Highgate PO, Burnaby, BC, V5E 4J6 **Telephone** - (604) 669-1388 **Toll-free** - (888) 669-1388 **Fax** - (604) 602-0674
Website - www.smartcool.net
Email - ted.konyi@smartcool.net
Investor Relations - Theodore H. Konyi (888) 669-1388
Auditors - MNP LLP C.A., Vancouver, B.C.
Lawyers - Richards Buell Sutton LLP, Vancouver, B.C.
Transfer Agents - Computershare Trust Company of Canada Inc., Vancouver, B.C.

Profile - (Can. 2000) Develops and distributes energy saving technologies for air conditioning, refrigeration and heat pump systems.

Principal revenue streams include the sale and installation of the Energy Savings Modules (ESM™) and ECO3™.

The ESM™ is manufactured by a third party in Australia and is designed to reduce the electricity consumption and demand of refrigeration and air conditioning compressors by improving their performance and maintaining temperature control. The ESM™ uses microprocessor technology and software algorithms.

The ECO3™ is manufactured in the People's Republic of China and is a retrofit product that can be installed on any air conditioning, heat pump or refrigeration unit with one or two compressors, which achieves the same energy efficiency gains as the ESM™ for smaller systems.

Also manufactures and sells proprietary Power Factor Correction (PFC) products through wholly owned **Total Energy Concepts Inc.** directly to commercial customers and resellers. The two principal products have been engineered to provide PFC for grid connected and locally generated power.

The company distributes directly to clients in the food retail, telecommunications, commercial real estate and hospitality industries, and through a network of distributors with businesses in Australia, India, the U.A.E., Saudi Arabia, eastern Europe, Germany, France, South Africa and the U.S.

Common suspended from TSX-VEN, July 18, 2019.

Predecessor Detail - Name changed from Citotech Systems Inc., July 20, 2004; basis 1 new for 3 old shs.

Directors - Theodore H. (Ted) Konyi, founder, chr., pres. & CEO, Vancouver, B.C.; Haiwen (Helen) Qian, exec. v-p, bus. devel., B.C.; Dalton L. Larson, Surrey, B.C.; Malcolm Leggett, B.C.

Other Exec. Officers - Kulwant Sandher, CFO; Steven Martin, exec. v-p; Frank Lawrence, sr. v-p, cold chain; Don Iannucci, v-p, bus. devel., residential; Allan Thompson, corp. sec.

Capital Stock

	Authorized (shs.)	Outstanding (shs.)[1]
Preferred	unlimited	nil
Series A		300,000
Common	unlimited	252,473,165

[1] At Aug. 24, 2023

Series A Preferred - Entitled to cumulative dividends at a rate of 8% per annum. Upon liquidation, winding-up or dissolution, entitled to a liquidation preference of US$1.00 per share. Convertible at holder's option into common shares and automatically in May 2021. Non-voting.

Common - One vote per share.

Major Shareholder - Widely held at Nov. 9, 2018.

Price Range - SSC.H/TSX-VEN (S)

Year	Volume	High	Low	Close
2019	13,288,867	$0.07	$0.04	$0.05
2018	55,346,058	$0.09	$0.04	$0.05

Wholly Owned Subsidiaries

Lenten Street Ltd., United Kingdom.
Smartcool International Inc., St. Michael, Barbados.
Smartcool Systems GmbH, Germany.
Smartcool Systems (USA) Inc., Nev.
Total Energy Concepts Inc., Minn.

S.69 Smartset Services Inc.

Symbol - SMAR.P **Exchange** - TSX-VEN **CUSIP** - 83191T
Head Office - 2500-700 Georgia St W, Vancouver, BC, V7Y 1B3
Email - drcliff@telusplanet.net
Investor Relations - J. Randolph Clifford (778) 362-3037
Auditors - Saturna Group Chartered Accountants LLP C.A., Vancouver, B.C.
Lawyers - Farris LLP, Vancouver, B.C.
Transfer Agents - Computershare Trust Company of Canada Inc., Vancouver, B.C.

Profile - (B.C. 2018; orig. Alta., 2013) Capital Pool Company.

Recent Merger and Acquisition Activity

Status: terminated **Revised:** Feb. 6, 2023
UPDATE: The transaction was terminated. PREVIOUS: Smartset Services Inc. entered into a letter of intent (LOI) for the Qualifying Transaction acquisition of a portfolio of five gold and copper exploration-stage properties in eastern Australia for issuance of 30,647,727 post-consolidated common shares (following a 0.75-for-1 share consolidation). Under the terms of the transaction, Smartset would acquire Mount Morgan claims in Queensland from GBM Resources Ltd. for issuance of 20,079,545 post-consolidated common shares; and all issued shares of Vancouver, B.C.-based Great Southern Gold Corp. (GSG), which owns Bingara, Nundle, Bonalbo and Klondyke projects in New South Wales, for issuance of 10,568,182 post-consolidated common shares. July 13, 2021 - The parties amended the terms of the LOI to add EPM 17850, a 4,091-hectare exploration claim that is contiguous to GBM's Mount Morgan claims, in the portfolio. Smartset

would acquire EPM 17850 from GBM for issuance of 380,000 post consolidated common shares, Cdn$32,500 for the option payment and other transaction related expenses (up to Cdn$10,000) incurred by GBM to acquire EPM 17850. Aug. 29, 2022 -The parties entered into a definitive agreement whereby Smartset would acquire Mount Morgan claims from GBM for issuance of 20,459,545 post-consolidated common shares; and all issued shares of GSG for issuance of 11,625,000 post-consolidated common shares.

Directors - J. Randolph (Randy) Clifford, CEO, CFO & corp. sec., Kamloops, B.C.; Leonidas (Leo) Karabelas, Toronto, Ont.; Tyson King, Vancouver, B.C.

Capital Stock

	Authorized (shs.)	Outstanding (shs.)[1]
Preferred	unlimited	nil
Common	unlimited	15,500,000

[1] At Jan. 12, 2023

Major Shareholder - Widely held at Apr. 19, 2022.

Price Range - SMAR.P/TSX-VEN

Year	Volume	High	Low	Close
2021	185,500	$0.35	$0.11	$0.26
2020	188,000	$0.10	$0.02	$0.10
2019	21,500	$0.40	$0.05	$0.06
2018	2,000	$0.40	$0.40	$0.40

Recent Close: $0.03

Capital Stock Changes - In May 2021, private placement of 3,500,000 common shares was completed at 10¢ per share.

Wholly Owned Subsidiaries

Australis Metals Pty Ltd.

S.70 Smithe Resources Corp.

Symbol - SMTH.P **Exchange** - TSX-VEN **CUSIP** - 83222R

Head Office - 1201-1166 Alberni St, Vancouver, BC, V6E 3Z3 **Telephone** - (604) 722-9633

Email - andrewlau@evariscapital.com

Investor Relations - Andrew Lau (604) 722-9633

Auditors - Crowe MacKay LLP C.A., Vancouver, B.C.

Lawyers - Woods & Company, West Vancouver, B.C.

Transfer Agents - National Securities Administrators Ltd., Vancouver, B.C.

Profile - (B.C. 2021) Capital Pool Company.

Recent Merger and Acquisition Activity

Status: pending **Announced:** Aug. 4, 2022

Smithe Resources Corp. entered into a letter of intent for the Qualifying Transaction reverse takeover acquisition of private Texas-based Indie Power Storage Corp. (IPS BC) and its wholly owned Nevada-based subsidiary, IPS Systems Inc. (IPS NV), by way of a three-cornered amalgamation of IPS BC, IPS NV and newly created wholly owned British Columbia and Nevada subsidiaries of Smithe. As consideration, each of IPS BC and IPS NV would receive Smithe common shares, resulting in the issuance of 63,053,924 post-consolidated Smithe common shares (following a 1-for-2 share consolidation). Upon closing, Smithe would continue under a name to be determined by the companies.

Directors - Anthony Balic, Burnaby, B.C.; Matthew (Matt) Roma, North Vancouver, B.C.; Sam K. Wong, Burnaby, B.C.

Other Exec. Officers - Andrew Lau, CEO, CFO & corp. sec.

Capital Stock

	Authorized (shs.)	Outstanding (shs.)[1]
Common	unlimited	7,400,000

[1] At Sept. 2, 2022

Major Shareholder - Widely held at June 21, 2022.

Price Range - SMTH.P/TSX-VEN

Year	Volume	High	Low	Close
2022	235,500	$0.17	$0.05	$0.13
2021	22,538	$0.20	$0.08	$0.11

Capital Stock Changes - On Oct. 21, 2021, an initial public offering of 5,000,000 common shares was completed at 10¢ per share.

S.71 Snipp Interactive Inc.

Symbol - SPN **Exchange** - TSX-VEN (S) **CUSIP** - 83306Y

Head Office - 1700-666 Burrard St, Vancouver, BC, V6C 2X8 **Toll-free** - (888) 997-6477 **Fax** - (866) 545-6785

Website - www.snipp.com

Email - investors@snipp.com

Investor Relations - Jaisun Garcha (888) 997-6477

Auditors - RSM Canada LLP C.A., Calgary, Alta.

Transfer Agents - Computershare Trust Company of Canada Inc., Toronto, Ont.

Profile - (B.C. 2010) Develops and provides marketing technology solutions including shopper marketing promotions, loyalty, rewards, rebates and receipt processing primarily to advertising agencies, brands and related marketing and promotion agencies.

The company's marketing technology platform analyzes and processes user data according to the client's desired sales and marketing tactics and provides two-way communication and delivery of content such as video, text, voice and web links to users via mobile phones, email or Internet.

Solutions include SnippCheck, a mobile receipt processing solution for customized purchase-based promotions and loyalty programs; SnippRewards, a rewards and incentive platform offering a wide variety of digital, data and physical rewards; SnippLoyalty, a scalable and customizable loyalty engine which allows clients to reward consumers for purchase and non-purchase transactions; SnippRebates, a platform enabling clients to create and manage their own rebate programs as well as providing consumers a digitized rebates experience; SnippWin, a promotions and sweepstakes platform which provides a full range of promotions from contests and simple sweepstakes to instant win programs and tiered, multi-level games; SnippResearch, a research platform that collects and analyzes valuable data from multiple industries at various points along the entire path to purchase; SnippInsights, a data analytics program which gathers data from marketing programs and enables clients to better understand their customers and optimize their promotional programs; SnippRx, which allows medical practitioners to distribute incentives like coupons and pay-no-more cards direct to patients rapidly and economically via text or email; Snipp Mobile Influencer Platform, which enables you to track rep activity and incentive code usage as well as measure the ROI on your influencer investment; and Snipp Solutions for Alcohol Industry, which provides compliant promotions and loyalty programs for the beer, wine and spirits industry.

Also provides services to design, execute and promote client marketing programs.

As at Mar. 31, 2022, the company's bookings backlog was US$10,800,000. Operations are located in the U.S., Canada, Ireland, Switzerland and India.

Common suspended from TSX-VEN, July 18, 2023.

Predecessor Detail - Name changed from Alya Ventures Ltd., Mar. 6, 2012, pursuant to Qualifying Transaction acquisition of Consumer Impulse, Inc.

Directors - Sarfarz Haji, chr., Ont.; Atul Sabharwal, CEO, Bethesda, Md.; Sina Miri; Brian Tunick

Other Exec. Officers - Dr. Niamh O'Riordan, COO; Jaisun Garcha, CFO & corp. sec.; Christopher Cubba, chief revenue officer; Tom Treanor, chief mktg. officer; Wayne Wang, chief tech. officer; Christian Hausammann, exec. v-p, loyalty & man. dir., Germany, Switzerland & Austria; Rahoul Roy, exec. v-p, corp. devel. & chief legal officer; Anthony Aguiar, v-p, sales & bus. devel.; Mario Invernizzi, v-p, sales, EMEA; Mark Ross, v-p, sales; Thomas J. (Tom) Burgess, pres., SnippMEDIA

Capital Stock

	Authorized (shs.)	Outstanding (shs.)[1]
Preferred	unlimited	
Series 1 Vtg.	unlimited	nil
Common	unlimited	282,337,829

[1] At Nov. 29, 2022

Major Shareholder - Lark Investments Inc. held 22.6% interest at Nov. 12, 2021.

Price Range - SPN/TSX-VEN (S)

Year	Volume	High	Low	Close
2022	20,018,154	$0.31	$0.12	$0.13
2021	58,929,051	$0.31	$0.06	$0.29
2020	42,416,792	$0.08	$0.01	$0.06
2019	28,326,537	$0.08	$0.02	$0.02
2018	113,268,921	$0.19	$0.05	$0.05

Recent Close: $0.13

Capital Stock Changes - In February 2022, 20,524,925 common shares were issued pursuant to the acquisition of Gambit Digital Promotions Inc. In April 2022, private placement of 25,000,000 common shares was completed at US$0.20 per share.

Wholly Owned Subsidiaries

Gambit Digital Promotions Inc., United States.
- 100% int. in **Gambit Rewards Inc.**, Del.

SNIPP Interactive Inc., Del.
Snipp Interactive AG, Switzerland.
Snipp Interactive (India) Private Limited, India.
Snipp Interactive Limited, Ireland.

Financial Statistics

Periods ended:	12m Dec. 31/21[A]		12m Dec. 31/20[A]
	US$000s	%Chg	US$000s
Operating revenue	**15,276**	**+76**	**8,692**
Salaries & benefits	5,897		5,091
General & admin expense	7,567		3,255
Stock-based compensation	104		115
Operating expense	**13,568**	**+60**	**8,461**
Operating income	**1,708**	**+639**	**231**
Deprec., depl. & amort.	1,167		1,602
Finance costs, gross	7		19
Pre-tax income	**2,152**	**n.a.**	**(1,293)**
Income taxes	19		30
Net income	**2,133**	**n.a.**	**(1,323)**
Cash & equivalent	1,745		1,916
Accounts receivable	2,237		1,244
Current assets	4,890		3,581
Fixed assets, net	19		18
Intangibles, net	2,244		2,675
Total assets	**7,453**	**+19**	**6,273**
Bank indebtedness	nil		295
Accts. pay. & accr. liabs	1,954		2,740
Current liabilities	3,890		4,794
Shareholders' equity	3,563		1,479
Cash from oper. activs	**1,020**	**-31**	**1,473**
Cash from fin. activs	220		294
Cash from invest. activs	(1,095)		(778)
Net cash position	**1,745**	**-9**	**1,916**
Capital expenditures	(9)		(19)
	US$		US$
Earnings per share*	0.01		(0.01)
Cash flow per share*	0.00		0.01
	shs		shs
No. of shs. o/s*	235,218,238		234,830,571
Avg. no. of shs. o/s*	234,923,840		229,313,267
	%		%
Net profit margin	13.96		(15.22)
Return on equity	84.61		(67.97)
Return on assets	31.18		(19.97)
Foreign sales percent	81		95

* Common
[A] Reported in accordance with IFRS

Latest Results

Periods ended:	3m Mar. 31/22[A]		3m Mar. 31/21[A]
	US$000s	%Chg	US$000s
Operating revenue	4,205	+64	2,570
Net income	25	n.a.	(182)
	US$		US$
Earnings per share*	0.00		(0.00)

* Common
[A] Reported in accordance with IFRS

Historical Summary
(as originally stated)

Fiscal Year	Oper. Rev.	Net Inc. Bef. Disc.	EPS*
	US$000s	US$000s	US$
2021[A]	15,276	2,133	0.01
2020[A]	8,692	(1,323)	(0.01)
2019[A]	8,644	(7,022)	(0.03)
2018[A]	12,151	(3,096)	(0.01)
2017[A]	12,879	(4,444)	(0.03)

* Common
[A] Reported in accordance with IFRS

S.72 Softchoice Corporation*

Symbol - SFTC **Exchange** - TSX **CUSIP** - 83405M

Head Office - 200-173 Dufferin St, Toronto, ON, M6K 3H7 **Telephone** - (416) 588-9000 **Toll-free** - (800) 268-7638 **Fax** - (416) 588-9001

Website - www.softchoice.com

Email - habeeb.syed@softchoice.com

Investor Relations - Habeeb Syed (416) 583-7489

Auditors - KPMG LLP C.A., Vaughan, Ont.

Bankers - Bank of Montreal

Lawyers - Stikeman Elliott LLP

Transfer Agents - TSX Trust Company, Toronto, Ont.

FP500 Revenue Ranking - 307

Employees - 2,000 at Mar. 29, 2023

Profile - (Can. 2019; orig. Can., 2002 amalg.) Provides IT solutions including designing, procuring, implementing and managing complex multi-vendor IT environments to private and public sector customers in North America.

The company focuses on three sub-sectors: hybrid multi-cloud solutions; collaboration and digital workplaces; and software asset management. Hybrid multi-cloud solutions leverage on-premise hardware, private cloud and/or public cloud, depending on each customer's specific workload requirements, including cloud security and governance, mass migrations, application modernization and performance monitoring, streamlining software operations and data estate management and modernization, with more than 600 public and 600 private cloud certifications. Collaboration and digital workplaces involves designing, deploying and managing IT solutions that allow the company's customers employees to work more effectively together, including secure collaboration, virtual desktops, training and adoption. Software asset management involves providing IT solutions to track and manage complex software assets.

At Mar. 29, 2023, the company had more than 2,000 team members with a physical presence across multiple markets in the U.S. and Canada, including sales professionals and technical experts.

Predecessor Detail - Formed from Ukraine Enterprise Corporation in Canada, May 15, 2002, pursuant to amalgamation with Softchoice Corporation (deemed acquiror); basis 1 new for 10 old shs.

Directors - Vincent R. (Vince) De Palma, exec. chr., Toronto, Ont.; Andrew Caprara, pres. & CEO, Toronto, Ont.; Félix-Etienne Lebel†, Ont.; Amy Cappellanti-Wof, Calif.; Anthony (Tony) Gibbons, Ont.; Lawrence A. Pentland, Toronto, Ont.; Sylvie Marie Claire Veilleux, S.D.; Christopher Voorpostel, Ont.

Other Exec. Officers - Jonathan Roiter, CFO; Sean Denomey, sr. v-p, srvcs. & cust. srvcs.; Jeff Knowlton, sr. v-p, sales; Maria Odoardi, sr. v-p, org. effectiveness & chief of staff; Jeff Reis, sr. v-p, IT & workplace; Karen Scott, sr. v-p, people & culture; Habeeb Syed, sr. v-p, legal, gen. counsel & corp. sec.; Deepa (Dipali) Chander, v-p, fin. opers.; Yota Skederidis, v-p, finl. reporting & tax

† Lead director

Capital Stock

	Authorized (shs.)	Outstanding (shs.)[1]
Preferred	unlimited	nil
Common	unlimited	57,856,131

[1] At Aug. 10, 2023

Options - At Dec. 31, 2022, options were outstanding to purchase 3,441,784 common shares at a weighted average exercise price of Cdn$3.06 per share.

Normal Course Issuer Bid - The company plans to make normal course purchases of up to 2,901,668 common shares representing 5% of the total outstanding. The bid commenced on Mar. 13, 2023, and expires on Mar. 12, 2024.

Major Shareholder - Birch Hill Equity Partners Management Inc. held 46.9% interest and Mawer Investment Management Limited held 13.9% interest at Apr. 11, 2023.

Price Range - SFTC/TSX

Year	Volume	High	Low	Close
2022	12,547,569	$28.66	$13.57	$18.26
2021	16,498,957	$45.74	$19.71	$21.35

Recent Close: $16.58

Capital Stock Changes - During 2022, 894,170 common shares were issued on exercise of options and 2,378,783 common shares were repurchased under a Normal Course Issuer Bid.

Dividends

SFTC com Ra $0.44 pa Q est. Apr. 14, 2023
Listed May 27/21.
Prev. Rate: $0.36 est. Apr. 14, 2022
Prev. Rate: $0.28 est. Jan. 14, 2022
Prev. Rate: $0.372 est. Oct. 15, 2021
$0.093**i** Oct. 15/21
i Initial Payment

Long-Term Debt - At Dec. 31, 2022, outstanding long-term debt totaled US$89,742,000 (none current and net of US$1,141,000 deferred financing costs) and consisted entirely of a credit facility bearing interest at LIBOR plus 2% interest, due June 2026.

Wholly Owned Subsidiaries

Softchoice L.P., Canada.
- 100% int. in **Softchoice Canada Inc.**, Toronto, Ont.
- 100% int. in **Softchoice EmployeeCo Inc.**, Ont.
- 100% int. in **Softchoice US Holdings ULC**
  - 100% int. in **Softchoice Corporation**, Chicago, Ill.

Financial Statistics

Periods ended:	12m Dec. 31/22[A]		12m Dec. 31/21[A1]
	US$000s	%Chg	US$000s
Operating revenue	**928,214**	**+3**	**903,066**
Cost of sales	615,883		616,084
Salaries & benefits	203,193		197,650
General & admin expense	33,935		38,562
Stock-based compensation	1,971		26,355
Operating expense	**854,982**	**-3**	**878,651**
Operating income	**73,232**	**+200**	**24,415**
Deprec., depl. & amort.	19,391		21,167
Finance income	169		1,941
Finance costs, gross	21,535		11,876
Pre-tax income	**32,331**	**n.a.**	**(9,360)**
Income taxes	10,561		605
Net income	**21,770**	**n.a.**	**(9,965)**
Net inc. for equity hldrs	**21,770**	**n.a.**	**(11,506)**
Net inc. for non-cont. int.	**nil**	**n.a.**	**1,541**
Cash & equivalent	1,735		2,748
Inventories	465		425
Accounts receivable	357,684		377,541
Current assets	412,859		421,624
Fixed assets, net	6,042		5,004
Right-of-use assets	12,973		15,899
Intangibles, net	178,098		193,192
Total assets	**615,328**	**-4**	**641,287**
Accts. pay. & accr. liabs	393,710		410,324
Current liabilities	456,182		484,658
Long-term debt, gross	89,742		66,832
Long-term debt, net	89,742		66,832
Long-term lease liabilities	13,048		16,944
Shareholders' equity	40,108		58,230
Cash from oper. activs	**40,049**	**-25**	**53,730**
Cash from fin. activs	(35,804)		(49,774)
Cash from invest. activs	(4,149)		(1,911)
Net cash position	**1,735**	**-37**	**2,748**
Capital expenditures	(3,393)		(1,826)
	US$		US$
Earnings per share*	0.37		(0.22)
Cash flow per share*	0.68		1.00
Cash divd. per share*	$0.36		$0.16
	shs		shs
No. of shs. o/s*	58,037,889		59,522,502
Avg. no. of shs. o/s*	58,961,733		53,406,543
	%		%
Net profit margin	2.35		(1.10)
Return on equity	44.28		n.m.
Return on assets	5.77		0.43
Foreign sales percent	46		47

* Common
[A] Reported in accordance with IFRS
[1] Private company from June 2013 to June 2021.

Latest Results

Periods ended:	6m June 30/23[A]		6m June 30/22[A]
	US$000s	%Chg	US$000s
Operating revenue	416,371	-13	477,232
Net income	18,647	+62	11,517
	US$		US$
Earnings per share*	0.32		0.19

* Common
[A] Reported in accordance with IFRS

Historical Summary
(as originally stated)

Fiscal Year	Oper. Rev.	Net Inc. Bef. Disc.	EPS*
	US$000s	US$000s	US$
2022[A]	928,214	21,770	0.37
2021[A]	903,066	(9,965)	(0.22)
2020[A]	836,751	2,094	(0.01)
2019[A]	953,822	1,803	(0.07)
	$000s	$000s	$
2018[A]	950,240	(10,646)	(0.27)

* Common
[A] Reported in accordance with IFRS

S.73 Solar Alliance Energy Inc.

Symbol - SOLR **Exchange -** TSX-VEN **CUSIP -** 83418C
Head Office - 620-1111 Melville St, Vancouver, BC, V6E 4L4
Telephone - (604) 288-9051 **Fax -** (604) 684-2722
Website - www.solaralliance.com
Email - mclark@solaralliance.com
Investor Relations - Michael Clark (416) 848-7744
Auditors - KPMG LLP C.A., Toronto, Ont.
Transfer Agents - Computershare Trust Company of Canada Inc., Vancouver, B.C.

Profile - (B.C. 2017) Provides energy solutions focused on residential, commercial and industrial solar installations.

Develops, markets and installs residential, commercial and industrial rooftop solar systems primarily in California, Tennessee, Illinois, North and South Carolina, New York and Kentucky.

Operates on three business units: Large scale commercial, which involves construction of large solar commercial projects; Mid-sized commercial, which involves construction and installation of commercial solar project ranging from 30 kW to 150 kW projects; and SunBox, which offers standardized solar systems primarily for residential customers and consist of panels, optimizers, inverter, battery storage, racking and an optional generator.

Large scale commercial projects include a 56-MW solar project for data centre in Illinois for **Green Data Center Real Estate Inc.**; a 519-kW combined rooftop and carport solar project in Manhattan Beach, Calif., whereby the rooftop portion was completed in March 2020 for **Onni Contracting Ltd.**; a 4.57-MW ground and roof mount solar project in Murphysboro, Ill., for Green Data Center; a 3.84-MW ground and roof mount solar project in Murphysboro, Ill., including an electric vehicle charging hub for **NuYen Blockchain Inc.**; 350-kW and 389-kW solar projects, both in New York, for **Abundant Solar Power Inc.**; a 115-kW solar project in Kentucky for **Todd County Pallet, LLC**; and up to 14 solar projects in the U.K. with a total capacity of 2.8 MW for **Empire Cinemas Ltd.**

Also offers Powershed, a patent pending solar powered charging station for robotic lawn mowers that simplifies and improves the operation and use of robotic lawn mowers; Electric Vehicle Charger Installation, which offers electric vehicle charger installation for Tesla, GM, Jaguar, BMW and Land Rover as an option on the company's SunBox residential solar system and also install standalone charging systems; and generators.

In June 2021, the company completed the construction of a 1-MW commercial solar project in Kentucky for **PPL Corporation**. Terms were not disclosed. Subsequently in July 2022, the company completed the construction of a 500-kW commercial solar project also in Kentucky.

Predecessor Detail - Name changed from Finavera Solar Energy Inc., Jan. 29, 2016.

Directors - Brian Timmons, chr., London, Middx., United Kingdom; Michael (Myke) Clark, pres. & CEO, Toronto, Ont.; Robert J. (Bob) Miller, Nev.; Anton Shihoff, Dublin, Ireland; Ken Stadlin, Md.

Other Exec. Officers - Christina Wu, CFO; Harvey Abouelata, v-p, comml. solar; Monique Hutchins, corp. sec.

Capital Stock

	Authorized (shs.)	Outstanding (shs.)[1]
Common	unlimited	274,984,848

[1] At Aug. 25, 2022

Major Shareholder - Thomas (Tom) Anderson held 35.61% interest at Dec. 31, 2021.

Price Range - SOLR/TSX-VEN

Year	Volume	High	Low	Close
2022	47,965,972	$0.20	$0.05	$0.07
2021	410,923,522	$0.81	$0.12	$0.13
2020	123,630,056	$0.11	$0.02	$0.10
2019	102,602,393	$0.14	$0.03	$0.04
2018	47,216,458	$0.13	$0.03	$0.03

Recent Close: $0.06

Wholly Owned Subsidiaries

Abundant Solar Power (VC1) LLC, N.Y.
Finavera Solar Holdings, Inc., British Virgin Islands.
Solar Alliance Energy DevCo LLC, Del.
Solar Alliance of America, Inc., San Diego, Calif.
Solar Alliance Services, Inc., Del.
Solar Alliance Southeast, LLC, Tenn.
Wildmare Wind Energy Corp., B.C. Inactive.

Subsidiaries

85% int. in **Wildmare Wind Energy Limited Partnership** Inactive.

Financial Statistics

Periods ended:	12m Dec. 31/21[A]		12m Dec. 31/20[A]
	$000s	%Chg	$000s
Operating revenue	**3,666**	**+5**	**3,501**
Cost of goods sold	3,003		2,587
Salaries & benefits	1,812		1,064
General & admin expense	1,183		814
Stock-based compensation	105		158
Operating expense	**6,104**	**+32**	**4,622**
Operating income	**(2,438)**	**n.a.**	**(1,121)**
Deprec., depl. & amort.	28		53
Finance income	82		27
Finance costs, gross	48		154
Write-downs/write-offs	(69)		nil
Pre-tax income	**(449)**	**n.a.**	**(1,370)**
Net income	**(449)**	**n.a.**	**(1,370)**
Cash & equivalent	2,169		2
Inventories	58		152
Accounts receivable	596		74
Current assets	2,833		542
Fixed assets, net	90		5
Right-of-use assets	nil		9
Total assets	**3,056**	**+426**	**581**
Accts. pay. & accr. liabs	1,914		4,855
Current liabilities	1,990		5,999
Long-term debt, gross	60		402
Long-term debt, net	60		230
Shareholders' equity	904		(5,750)
Cash from oper. activs	**(3,635)**	**n.a.**	**(380)**
Cash from fin. activs	5,981		336
Cash from invest. activs	(178)		nil
Net cash position	**2,169**	**n.m.**	**2**
Capital expenditures	(104)		nil
	$		$
Earnings per share*	(0.00)		(0.01)
Cash flow per share*	(0.01)		(0.00)
	shs		shs
No. of shs. o/s*	274,984,848		233,114,037
Avg. no. of shs. o/s*	269,819,601		223,774,169
	%		%
Net profit margin	(12.25)		(39.13)
Return on equity	n.m.		n.m.
Return on assets	(22.05)		(126.01)
No. of employees (FTEs)	24		24

* Common
[A] Reported in accordance with IFRS

Latest Results

Periods ended:	6m June 30/22[A]		6m June 30/21[A]
	$000s	%Chg	$000s
Operating revenue	1,628	-19	2,003
Net income	(1,178)	n.a.	(921)
	$		$
Earnings per share*	(0.00)		(0.00)

* Common
[A] Reported in accordance with IFRS

Historical Summary
(as originally stated)

Fiscal Year	Oper. Rev.	Net Inc. Bef. Disc.	EPS*
	$000s	$000s	$
2021[A]	3,666	(449)	(0.00)
2020[A]	3,501	(1,370)	(0.01)
2019[A]	2,204	(2,764)	(0.01)
2018[A]	1,983	(2,336)	(0.02)
2017[A]	4,603	(7,477)	(0.09)

* Common
[A] Reported in accordance with IFRS

S.74 SolarBank Corporation

Symbol - SUNN **Exchange** - CSE **CUSIP** - 83417Y
Head Office - 803-505 Consumers Rd, Toronto, ON, M2J 4Z2 **Telephone** - (416) 494-9559
Website - solarbankcorp.com
Email - tracy.zheng@solarbankcorp.com
Investor Relations - Xiaohong Zheng (416) 494-9559
Auditors - MSLL CPA LLP C.P.A., Vancouver, B.C.
Lawyers - DLA Piper (Canada) LLP
Transfer Agents - Endeavor Trust Corporation, Vancouver, B.C.
Employees - 8 at June 30, 2022

Profile - (Ont. 2013) Develops and operates solar photovoltaic (PV) power generation projects in Canada and the United States, with a focus on New York, Maryland and Ontario.

The company originates, develops, engineers, procures and constructs, and operates solar assets that sell electricity to utilities, commercial, industrial, municipal and residential off-takers. Specializes in behind-the-meter (BTM) solar plants, grid-connected community solar gardens and utility-scale solar farms. Manages more than 100 solar plants with a capacity of more than 60 MW.

The company plans to shift its model from that of a developer to ownership of solar projects as an Independent Power Producer (IPP)

At Sept. 30, 2022, the company had six solar projects, totaling 12 MW, in New York and nine projects under development in New York totaling 42 MW and one 4.5-MW solar project under development in Alberta.

Common listed on CSE, Mar. 2, 2023.

Predecessor Detail - Name changed from Abundant Solar Energy Inc., Oct. 7, 2022.

Directors - Dr. Richard Lu, pres. & CEO, Toronto, Ont.; Olen Aasen, Vancouver, B.C.; Paul Pasalic, London, Middx., United Kingdom; C. Paul Sparkes, Toronto, Ont.

Other Exec. Officers - Andrew van Doorn, COO; Sam Sun, CFO; Xiaohong (Tracey) Zheng, CAO

Capital Stock

	Authorized (shs.)	Outstanding (shs.)[1]
Common	unlimited	26,550,000

[1] At Mar. 2, 2023

Major Shareholder - Widely held at Mar. 2, 2023.

Recent Close: $7.20

Capital Stock Changes - On Mar. 2, 2023, an initial public offering of 8,050,000 common shares was completed at $0.75 per share, including 1,050,000 common shares on exercise of over-allotment option. Concurrently, 2,500,000 common shares were issued on conversion of a $1,250,000 convertible bridge loan.

Wholly Owned Subsidiaries

Abundant Construction Inc., Ont.
Abundant Solar Power Inc., Rochester, N.Y.

Investments

49% int. in **2467264 Ontario Inc.**, Ont.

Note: The preceding list includes only the major related companies in which interests are held.

Financial Statistics

Periods ended:	12m June 30/22[A]		12m June 30/21[A]
	$000s	%Chg	$000s
Operating revenue	**10,198**	**+39**	**7,347**
Cost of goods sold	8,231		4,814
Salaries & benefits	1,175		1,937
General & admin expense	565		440
Operating expense	**9,971**	**+39**	**7,191**
Operating income	**227**	**+46**	**156**
Deprec., depl. & amort.	8		3
Finance costs, gross	159		335
Pre-tax income	**(307)**	**n.a.**	**(108)**
Income taxes	(118)		49
Net income	**(188)**	**n.a.**	**(157)**
Cash & equivalent	932		1,400
Inventories	196		594
Accounts receivable	1,857		5,633
Current assets	8,983		10,255
Fixed assets, net	25		29
Right-of-use assets	186		nil
Total assets	**9,195**	**-11**	**10,283**
Bank indebtedness	568		1,513
Accts. pay. & accr. liabs	1,951		2,806
Current liabilities	3,366		4,731
Long-term debt, gross	1,342		1,058
Long-term debt, net	1,231		1,021
Long-term lease liabilities	154		nil
Shareholders' equity	4,485		4,454
Non-controlling interest	(45)		(45)
Cash from oper. activs	**172**	**n.a.**	**(2,685)**
Cash from fin. activs	(679)		2,324
Cash from invest. activs	(11)		(3)
Net cash position	**932**	**-33**	**1,400**
Capital expenditures	(11)		(3)
	$		$
Earnings per share*	(0.01)		(0.01)
Cash flow per share*	0.01		(0.17)
	shs		shs
No. of shs. o/s*	16,000,000		16,000,000
Avg. no. of shs. o/s*	16,000,000		16,000,000
	%		%
Net profit margin	(1.84)		(2.14)
Return on equity	(4.21)		n.m.
Return on assets	(0.93)		n.a.

* Common
[A] Reported in accordance with IFRS

Latest Results

Periods ended:	3m Sept. 30/22[A]		3m Sept. 30/21[A]
	$000s	%Chg	$000s
Operating revenue	5,480	+111	2,602
Net income	226	n.a.	(88)
	$		$
Earnings per share*	0.01		(0.01)

* Common
[A] Reported in accordance with IFRS

S.75 Solarvest BioEnergy Inc.

Symbol - SVS **Exchange** - TSX-VEN **CUSIP** - 83416D
Head Office - 301-1228 Hamilton St, Vancouver, BC, V6B 6L2 **Telephone** - (604) 684-3323 **Fax** - (604) 684-3350
Website - www.solarvest.ca
Email - claes.ellegaard@solarvest.ca
Investor Relations - Claes Ellegaard
Auditors - Arsenault Best Cameron Ellis C.A., Charlottetown, P.E.I.
Lawyers - Cawkell Brodie Glaister LLP, Vancouver, B.C.
Transfer Agents - Computershare Trust Company of Canada Inc., Vancouver, B.C.

Profile - (B.C. 2005) Develops algal-based production system to produce nutritional nutraceutical products, oils and biologic active ingredients and therapies.

Through wholly owned **Eversea Inc.**, has developed a proprietary process for the production of organic Omega-3 fatty acids to human therapeutic proteins which is used by food enhancement and nutraceutical markets as well as an algae strain that can produce Bone Morphogenetic Protein (BMP), which is applied during orthopaedic surgery for bone repair. Also developing a genetically modified algae strain that can be used to produce hydrogen, through its patent-pending biological splitting of water into hydrogen and oxygen by microalgae; and algae strains that can produce other therapeutic protein targets including cannabinoids, recombinant viral antigens/immune stimulating proteins, antimicrobial peptide/protein and enzymes.

Research and development is carried out from a 5,000-sq.-ft. laboratory facility in Summerville, P.E.I.

The company's United States Department of Agriculture (USDA) and European Union (EU)-certified products include Organic Omega-3, the only vegan and organic Omega-3 nutraceutical on the market, which is being used to create cream, powder and organic gummy fruit; Nanuq™ Omega-3 powdered supplement, which has been approved as new dietary ingredient; and Eversea™ gummy products. Products are sold through the company's own and third party online platforms.

Predecessor Detail - Name changed from GCH Capital Partners Inc., Sept. 19, 2008, following Qualifying Transaction acquistion of Phycobiologics (Europe) Limited.

Directors - Dr. William M. (Bill) Cheliak, chr., Pembroke, Ont.; Donal V. Carroll, Etobicoke, Ont.; Gregory Drohan, Etobicoke, Ont.; Gerri J. Greenham, Stouffville, Ont.

Other Exec. Officers - Claes Ellegaard, CEO; Garth Greenham, COO; Leslie Auld, CFO; Dr. Raymond Surzycki, chief scientific officer

Capital Stock

	Authorized (shs.)	Outstanding (shs.)[1]
Common	unlimited	55,336,372

[1] At Oct. 31, 2022

Major Shareholder - Gerri J. Greenham held 17.1% interest at Sept. 16, 2022.

Price Range - SVS/TSX-VEN

Year	Volume	High	Low	Close
2022	8,199,488	$0.21	$0.04	$0.10
2021	27,253,837	$0.55	$0.11	$0.16
2020	3,814,974	$0.22	$0.02	$0.19
2019	2,576,149	$0.35	$0.12	$0.15
2018	1,410,600	$0.26	$0.15	$0.20

Recent Close: $0.03

Capital Stock Changes - There were no changes to capital stock during fiscal 2022.

Wholly Owned Subsidiaries

Eversea America Inc., P.E.I.
Eversea America, Inc.
Eversea Inc., P.E.I.
Phycobiologics (Europe) Limited, United Kingdom.

Investments

FSD Pharma Inc., Toronto, Ont. (see separate coverage)

Financial Statistics

Periods ended:	12m July 31/22[A]		12m July 31/21[oA]
	$000s	%Chg	$000s
Operating revenue	**1**	**-50**	**2**
Research & devel. expense	993		1,022
General & admin expense	461		838
Stock-based compensation	nil		435
Operating expense	**1,454**	**-37**	**2,295**
Operating income	**(1,453)**	**n.a.**	**(2,293)**
Deprec., depl. & amort.	87		94
Finance costs, gross	92		109
Pre-tax income	**(1,628)**	**n.a.**	**(3,460)**
Net income	**(1,628)**	**n.a.**	**(3,460)**
Cash & equivalent	16		1,388
Inventories	410		103
Accounts receivable	13		20
Current assets	471		1,529
Fixed assets, net	537		565
Intangibles, net	181		205
Total assets	**1,189**	**-48**	**2,299**
Accts. pay. & accr. liabs	701		542
Current liabilities	1,248		941
Long-term debt, gross	2,755		2,699
Long-term debt, net	2,694		2,681
Long-term lease liabilities	245		288
Shareholders' equity	(4,031)		(2,403)
Cash from oper. activs	**(1,522)**	**n.a.**	**(2,461)**
Cash from fin. activs	184		2,659
Cash from invest. activs	(34)		643
Net cash position	**16**	**-99**	**1,388**
Capital expenditures	(34)		(23)
	$		$
Earnings per share*	(0.03)		(0.07)
Cash flow per share*	(0.03)		(0.05)
	shs		shs
No. of shs. o/s*	55,336,372		55,336,372
Avg. no. of shs. o/s*	55,336,372		48,253,221
	%		%
Net profit margin	n.m.		n.m.
Return on equity	n.m.		n.m.
Return on assets	(88.07)		(124.90)

* Common
[o] Restated
[A] Reported in accordance with IFRS

Latest Results

Periods ended:	3m Oct. 31/22[A]		3m Oct. 31/21[A]
	$000s	%Chg	$000s
Net income	(378)	n.a.	(384)
	$		$
Earnings per share*	(0.01)		(0.01)

* Common
[A] Reported in accordance with IFRS

Historical Summary
(as originally stated)

Fiscal Year	Oper. Rev.	Net Inc. Bef. Disc.	EPS*
	$000s	$000s	$
2022[A]	1	(1,628)	(0.03)
2021[A]	2	(3,460)	(0.07)
2020[A]	nil	(1,541)	(0.04)
2019[A]	nil	(1,393)	(0.05)
2018[A]	nil	(1,273)	(0.05)

* Common
[A] Reported in accordance with IFRS

S.76 Solid Impact Investments Corp.

Symbol - SOLI.P **Exchange** - TSX-VEN **CUSIP** - 83422P
Head Office - 501-3292 Production Way, Burnaby, BC, V5A 4R4 **Telephone** - (604) 833-6820
Email - gkabazo@gmail.com
Investor Relations - Gabriel Kabazo (604) 833-6820
Auditors - Dale Matheson Carr-Hilton LaBonte LLP C.A., Vancouver, B.C.
Lawyers - MacDonald Tuskey Corporate & Securities Lawyers, North Vancouver, B.C.
Transfer Agents - Odyssey Trust Company, Vancouver, B.C.
Profile - (B.C. 2021) Capital Pool Company.

Recent Merger and Acquisition Activity

Status: pending **Announced:** July 18, 2023
Solid Impact Investments Corp. entered into a letter of intent for the Qualifying Transaction reverse takeover acquisition of Allied Critical Metals Corp. (ACM), which has an agreement to acquire Tungsten projects in Portugal. ACM has agreed to acquire Pan Metals Unipessola Ltda., which holds 90% interest in Borralha and Vila Verde tungsten projects, from Pan Iberia Limited. Consideration includes US$4,500,000 consisting of cash, promissory note, convertible debenture and ACM shares. ACM also plans to complete a financing of units to raise between $3,000,000 and $5,000,000. Following the closing of the acquisition and financing, Solid would acquire ACM by way of a three-cornered amalgamation between a wholly owned subsidiary of Solid and ACM to continue as ACM Holdings Ltd. Solid would change its name to Allied Critical Metals Corp.

Directors - Itamar David, pres. & CEO, Vancouver, B.C.; Gilad Bebzuck, Burnaby, B.C.; Meghan Brown, Vancouver, B.C.; Andrew M. Gertler, Westmount, Qué.
Other Exec. Officers - Gabriel (Gabi) Kabazo, CFO

Capital Stock

	Authorized (shs.)	Outstanding (shs.)[1]
Common	unlimited	5,600,000

[1] At Oct. 3, 2022

Major Shareholder - Itamar David held 28.57% interest at Oct. 3, 2022.

Price Range - SOLI.P/TSX-VEN

Year	Volume	High	Low	Close
2022	112,001	$0.40	$0.11	$0.14

Recent Close: $0.10
Capital Stock Changes - On Apr. 12, 2022, an initial public offering of 3,000,000 common shares was completed at 10¢ per share. Also during fiscal 2022, 2,600,000 common shares were issued to officers and directors and 1 common share was cancelled.

S.77 Solution Financial Inc.

Symbol - SFI **Exchange** - TSX **CUSIP** - 83439G
Head Office - Unit 137, 8680 Cambie Rd, Richmond, BC, V6X 4K1 **Telephone** - (604) 233-1937 **Fax** - (604) 233-1939
Website - www.solution.financial
Email - sean.hodgins@solution.financial
Investor Relations - Sean P. Hodgins (778) 318-1514
Auditors - Davidson & Company LLP C.A., Vancouver, B.C.
Transfer Agents - Computershare Trust Company of Canada Inc., Vancouver, B.C.
Employees - 15 at Jan. 27, 2023
Profile - (B.C. 2007) Provides lease financing for luxury and exotic vehicles, yachts and other high value assets throughout Canada to clients who prefer more flexible leasing options than those traditionally offered by banks and other lease providers.

Specializes in leasing both new and used luxury and exotic automobiles. Also a registered auto dealer which sells vehicles in the wholesale market when leasing opportunities are not available. Also leases yachts and other business assets. The company works with high-end auto dealers in Canada. Also provides unique leasing experience whereby it partners with its clients to help source limited edition and difficult to acquire vehicles as well as providing white glove services to clients for insuring, maintaining, upgrading, and reselling their vehicles. Customers are typically affluent new immigrants and/or international students with limited or no credit history in Canada, or business owners. Average lease term is 18 months with many customers electing to upgrade their vehicles prior to expiry of leases. The company's revenue consists of brokerage commissions for sales facilitated through partner dealers, in-house or finance lease vehicle sales, and interest and fee income from direct leases and loans. Has license to operate in Ontario from Ontario's Vehicle Sales Regulator.

At Oct. 31, 2022, the company's operating lease portfolio had a book value of $12,028,119.

Predecessor Detail - Name changed from Shelby Ventures Inc., June 22, 2018, pursuant to Qualifying Transaction reverse takeover acquisition of (old) Solution Financial Inc.; basis 1 new for 2.451 old shs.

Directors - Randy Smyth, chr., B.C.; Bryan Pang, pres. & CEO, Richmond, B.C.; Sean P. Hodgins, CFO & corp. sec., Richmond, B.C.; Vincent Lau, v-p, opers., B.C.; Desmond M. (Des) Balakrishnan, Vancouver, B.C.; John Gowans, B.C.; Kerry Meier, North Vancouver, B.C.
Other Exec. Officers - Jhonny Lau, contr.

Capital Stock

	Authorized (shs.)	Outstanding (shs.)[1]
Preferred	unlimited	nil
Common	unlimited	87,290,273

[1] At Feb. 17, 2023

Normal Course Issuer Bid - The company plans to make normal course purchases of up to 4,364,513 common shares representing 5% of the total outstanding. The bid commenced on Feb. 27, 2023, and expires on Feb. 26, 2024.
Major Shareholder - Bryan Pang held 59.64% interest at Jan. 27, 2023.

Price Range - SFI/TSX

Year	Volume	High	Low	Close
2022	4,254,680	$0.45	$0.27	$0.34
2021	2,128,046	$0.60	$0.32	$0.43
2020	2,281,772	$0.60	$0.29	$0.48
2019	2,473,461	$0.49	$0.25	$0.35
2018	4,442,491	$0.50	$0.17	$0.41

Recent Close: $0.29
Capital Stock Changes - During fiscal 2022, 1,814,000 common shares were repurchased under a Normal Course Issuer Bid.

Dividends

SFI com Ra $0.004 pa Q est. Sept. 16, 2019
Listed Sep 8/21.

Wholly Owned Subsidiaries

Solution Financial (Canada) Inc., B.C.

Financial Statistics

Periods ended:	12m Oct. 31/22[A]		12m Oct. 31/21[A]
	$000s	%Chg	$000s
Operating revenue	**20,348**	**-1**	**20,452**
Cost of sales	11,358		10,799
Salaries & benefits	532		421
General & admin expense	2,394		2,418
Stock-based compensation	nil		74
Operating expense	**14,284**	**+4**	**13,712**
Operating income	**6,064**	**-10**	**6,741**
Deprec., depl. & amort.	4,079		5,124
Finance costs, gross	626		436
Pre-tax income	**1,106**	**-4**	**1,151**
Income taxes	268		244
Net income	**838**	**-8**	**907**
Cash & equivalent	1,805		3,380
Inventories	473		426
Accounts receivable	234		505
Current assets	7,211		5,469
Long-term investments	22,247		27,465
Fixed assets, net	266		276
Right-of-use assets	68		43
Intangibles, net	45		39
Total assets	**29,836**	**-10**	**33,293**
Bank indebtedness	8,417		9,970
Accts. pay. & accr. liabs	436		221
Current liabilities	9,675		10,901
Long-term debt, gross	2,997		3,161
Long-term debt, net	2,997		3,161
Long-term lease liabilities	17		47
Equity portion of conv. debs	191		67
Shareholders' equity	13,493		13,434
Cash from oper. activs	**(9,308)**	**n.a.**	**6,249**
Cash from fin. activs	(2,640)		2,305
Cash from invest. activs	10,374		(7,701)
Net cash position	**1,805**	**-47**	**3,380**
Capital expenditures	(49)		(53)
	$		$
Earnings per share*	0.01		0.01
Cash flow per share*	(0.10)		0.07
Cash divd. per share*	0.00		0.00
	shs		shs
No. of shs. o/s*	87,630,273		89,444,273
Avg. no. of shs. o/s*	88,796,706		83,932,125
	%		%
Net profit margin	4.12		4.43
Return on equity	6.22		7.60
Return on assets	4.16		4.01

* Common
[A] Reported in accordance with IFRS

Historical Summary
(as originally stated)

Fiscal Year	Oper. Rev.	Net Inc. Bef. Disc.	EPS*
	$000s	$000s	$
2022[A]	20,348	838	0.01
2021[A]	20,452	907	0.01
2020[A]	14,299	400	0.01
2019[A]	9,640	182	0.00
2018[A1]	4,811	(1,918)	(0.03)

* Common
[A] Reported in accordance with IFRS
[1] Results reflect the June 22, 2018, Qualifying Transaction reverse takeover acquisition of (old) Solution Financial Inc.

S.78 Solvbl Solutions Inc.

Symbol - SOLV **Exchange** - CSE **CUSIP** - 834442
Head Office - First Canadian Place, 5700-100 King St W, Toronto, ON, M5X 1C7 **Toll-free** - (833) 722-7668 **Fax** - (416) 946-1007
Website - solvbl.com
Email - investors@solvbl.com
Investor Relations - Paul Carroll (416) 450-5995
Auditors - MNP LLP C.A., Burlington, Ont.
Transfer Agents - TSX Trust Company, Toronto, Ont.
Profile - (B.C. 2017) Develops and deploys cybersecurity and data authentication technology utilizing a proprietary blockchain solution. Also operates a content production and consumer marketplace business for the film and digital entertainment industries.

The company's flagship product is Q by SoLVBL™, a patented cryptographic cybersecurity product that allows users to authenticate their data in real-time and ensures that the data has not been subject to unauthorized modifications. Outside users can also perform the same checks and receive the same assurances in real-time. The company is targeting four verticals for Q by SoLVBL™ including financial institutions, the healthcare sector, critical Internet of Things (IoT) infrastructure and digital content production and distribution in the film and TV industry.

Wholly owned **Darkhorse Films Limited** operates a blockchain-powered movie digital content studio and an e-commerce business that runs in the decentralized Web3 and Film3 digital environment. The film content is financed and produced exclusively and non-exclusively for Darkhorse Films' and its partners' sales platforms and digital marketplaces. Revenue is generated from movie content distribution as well as traditional and digital e-commerce. Darkhorse specializes in the deployment of digital assets to the movie and television industries and digital asset enthusiasts, and its e-commerce operations include a digital content sales platform and digital marketplace.

Common reinstated on CSE, June 30, 2023.

Common suspended from CSE, May 8, 2023.

Recent Merger and Acquisition Activity

Status: completed **Revised:** Oct. 26, 2022

UPDATE: The transaction was completed. PREVIOUS: Solvbl Solutions Inc. entered into a letter of intent to acquire U.K.-based Darkhorse Films Limited, which operates a blockchain-powered movie digital content studio and e-commerce business, for Cdn$10,150,000, consisting of Cdn$2,537,500 cash and issuance of Cdn$7,612,500 of Solvbl restricted shares. Darkhorse generated revenue from movie content distribution, specializing in the deployment of digital assets to the movie and television industries. Darkhorse's e-commerce operations included a digital content sales platform and digital marketplace. Oct. 4, 2022 - A definitive agreement was entered into whereby the consideration of Cdn$10,150,000 would be paid through issuance of 115,384,615 Solvbl restricted shares at a deemed price of Cdn$0.065 per share, representing 43% interest in Solvbl, and Cdn$2,650,000 cash, payable in tranches and upon achievement of certain operational and financing milestones.

Predecessor Detail - Name changed from Stowe One Investments Corp., Feb. 11, 2021.

Directors - Vikas Gupta, chr., Oakville, Ont.; Khurram R. Qureshi, CFO, Toronto, Ont.; Brenda M. Brown, Toronto, Ont.; Alan Rootenberg, Toronto, Ont.; David Van Herwaarde

Other Exec. Officers - Paul Carroll, pres. & interim CEO; Terry Stone, sr. v-p, film prod.

Capital Stock

	Authorized (shs.)	Outstanding (shs.)[1]
Common	unlimited	267,917,678

[1] At Jan. 1, 2023

Major Shareholder - Widely held at Apr. 29, 2022.

Price Range - SOLV/CSE

Year	Volume	High	Low	Close
2022	35,257,463	$0.07	$0.02	$0.03
2021	31,833,602	$0.80	$0.04	$0.07

Recent Close: $0.01

Capital Stock Changes - In October 2022, 115,384,615 common shares were issued pursuant to the acquisition of Darkhorse Films Limited.

Wholly Owned Subsidiaries

Darkhorse Films Limited, London, Middx., United Kingdom.

1191212 BC Ltd., B.C.

Financial Statistics

Periods ended:	12m Dec. 31/21[A1]		12m Dec. 31/20[□A]
	$000s	%Chg	$000s
Operating revenue	**nil**	**n.a.**	**10**
Salaries & benefits	469		430
General & admin expense	1,941		535
Stock-based compensation	130		108
Operating expense	**2,543**	**+139**	**1,063**
Operating income	**(2,543)**	**n.a.**	**(1,053)**
Deprec., depl. & amort.	14		32
Finance costs, net	154		(51)
Pre-tax income	**(2,396)**	**n.a.**	**(613)**
Net income	**(2,396)**	**n.a.**	**(613)**
Cash & equivalent	1,278		225
Current assets	2,252		634
Fixed assets, net	6		8
Right-of-use assets	nil		12
Total assets	**2,257**	**+245**	**654**
Accts. pay. & accr. liabs	116		501
Current liabilities	318		540
Long-term debt, gross	58		305
Long-term debt, net	nil		305
Shareholders' equity	1,939		(191)
Cash from oper. activs	**(1,787)**	**n.a.**	**(728)**
Cash from fin. activs	3,490		938
Cash from invest. activs	(650)		nil
Net cash position	**1,279**	**+402**	**255**
	$		$
Earnings per share*	(0.02)		(0.01)
Cash flow per share*	(0.02)		(0.01)
	shs		shs
No. of shs. o/s*	152,533,063		n.a.
Avg. no. of shs. o/s*	112,019,504		76,024,191
	%		%
Net profit margin	n.a.		n.m.
Return on equity	n.m.		n.m.
Return on assets	(164.62)		(146.48)

* Common

□ Restated

[A] Reported in accordance with IFRS

[1] Results reflect the Feb. 10, 2021, reverse takeover acquisition of Agile Blockchain Corp.

Latest Results

Periods ended:	9m Sept. 30/22[A]		9m Sept. 30/21[A]
	$000s	%Chg	$000s
Net income	(1,417)	n.a.	(1,844)
	$		$
Earnings per share*	(0.01)		(0.02)

* Common

[A] Reported in accordance with IFRS

Historical Summary

(as originally stated)

Fiscal Year	Oper. Rev.	Net Inc. Bef. Disc.	EPS*
	$000s	$000s	$
2021[A]	nil	(2,396)	(0.02)
2020[A1]	10	(613)	(0.01)
2019[A]	nil	(1,277)	(0.02)
2018[A]	nil	(1,312)	(0.02)

* Common

[A] Reported in accordance with IFRS

[1] Results for 2020 and prior periods pertain to Agile Blockchain Corp.

S.79 Sona Nanotech Inc.

Symbol - SONA **Exchange** - CSE **CUSIP** - 83541C

Head Office - Purdy's Tower II, 2001-1969 Upper Water St, Halifax, NS, B3J 3R7 **Telephone** - (902) 482-1240 **Fax** - (902) 491-4281

Website - www.sonanano.com

Email - david@sonanano.com

Investor Relations - David A. Regan (902) 536-1932

Auditors - Manning Elliott LLP C.A., Vancouver, B.C.

Lawyers - Cox & Palmer LLP, Halifax, N.S.

Transfer Agents - Computershare Trust Company of Canada Inc., Montréal, Qué.

Profile - (Can. 2018 amalg.) Develops and commercializes gold nanoparticles (nanorods) and photothermal devices for diagnostic testing and medical treatment applications.

The company's rod-shaped gold nanorods (GNRs) are developed without the use of CTAB (cetyltrimethylammonium bromide) for use as reagents in both in-vitro and in-vivo applications such as lateral flow diagnostics and cell imaging, respectively. Its gold nanorod products are Gemini™ for diagnostic testing devices, primarily lateral flow assays; and Omni™ for medical applications such as drug delivery, photothermal therapy and cell imaging for detection and treatment of diseases.

The company is focused on the development of rapid diagnostic tests and biologic reagents and the advancement of its GNR intellectual property towards important medical in vivo applications. Products under development include bovine tuberculosis (bTB) rapid test, a rapid, lateral flow assay to identify the presence of bTB bacteria and to differentiate whether the bacteria is present due to ongoing infection or as a result of vaccination; and concussion test, which detects the presence of Glial fibrillary acidic protein (GFAP), a biological marker associated with concussions, typically released into the blood stream within minutes of an impact to the head.

Also through wholly owned **Siva Therapeutics, Inc.**, develops proprietary Targeted Hyperthermia Therapy™ (THT), a photothermal device that uses GNRs for cancer therapy, resulting in a less destructive treatment.

In March 2023, the company acquired U.S.-based **Siva Therapeutics, Inc.** for issuance of 15,107,457 common shares at a deemed value of $0.1824 per share plus a contingent consideration of $6,650,000 of common shares upon Siva's future achievement milestones. Siva develops proprietary Targeted Hyperthermia Therapy™ (THT), a photothermal device used for cancer treatment.

In November 2022, the company entered into a memorandum of understanding with U.K.-based **Biotangents Limited**, to commercialize its bovine tuberculosis (bTB) rapid test. Under the agreement, Biotangents would provide the company with consultation and execution of appropriate clinical evaluation studies to determine the performance of test prototype. In addition, Biotangents would be granted first right of refusal to license the company's bTB upon commercialization.

Predecessor Detail - Formed from Stockport Exploration Inc. in Canada, Aug. 8, 2018, pursuant to the reverse takeover acquisition of and amalgamation with Sona Nanotech Ltd. (deemed acquiror); basis 1 new Sona sh. for 4 Stockport shs. and 1 new Sona sh. for 1.5802 old Sona shs.

Directors - J. Mark Lievonen, chr., Stouffville, Ont.; Dr. Leonard Pagliaro, chief strategy officer; Neil Fraser, B.C.; Dr. Michael (Mike) Gross, Halifax, N.S.; James (Jim) Megann, Fall River, N.S.; Dr. Walter Strapps, Mass.

Other Exec. Officers - David A. Regan, CEO; Robert (Rob) Randall, CFO & corp. sec.; Darren Rowles, head, diagnostics

Capital Stock

	Authorized (shs.)	Outstanding (shs.)[1]
Common	unlimited	95,095,361

[1] At June 28, 2023

Major Shareholder - Widely held at Mar. 14, 2023.

Price Range - SONA/CSE

Year	Volume	High	Low	Close
2022	17,156,953	$0.55	$0.02	$0.08
2021	96,262,034	$4.44	$0.23	$0.44
2020	170,309,804	$16.05	$0.10	$3.68
2019	4,293,189	$0.34	$0.01	$0.13
2018	1,276,563	$0.30	$0.17	$0.25

Recent Close: $0.21

Capital Stock Changes - In February 2023, private placement of 11,000,000 common shares was completed at 10¢ per share. In March 2023, 15,107,457 common shares were issued pursuant to the acquisition of Siva Therapeutics, Inc.

In January 2022, 2,556,276 common shares were issued for settlement of $1,452,724 of debt. Also during fiscal 2022, common shares were issued as follows: 1,147,000 under an at-the-market offering and 100,000 on exercise of options.

Wholly Owned Subsidiaries

Siva Therapeutics, Inc., United States.

Financial Statistics

Periods ended:	12m Oct. 31/22[A]		12m Oct. 31/21[□A]
	$000s	%Chg	$000s
Salaries & benefits	1,007		1,341
Research & devel. expense	71		154
General & admin expense	735		1,067
Stock-based compensation	1,469		8,241
Operating expense	**3,282**	**-70**	**10,803**
Operating income	**(3,282)**	**n.a.**	**(10,803)**
Deprec., depl. & amort.	60		66
Finance costs, gross	4		21
Pre-tax income	**(2,361)**	**n.a.**	**(10,367)**
Net income	**(2,361)**	**n.a.**	**(10,367)**
Cash & equivalent	164		1,196
Current assets	470		1,412
Fixed assets, net	51		111
Total assets	**521**	**-66**	**1,523**
Accts. pay. & accr. liabs.	332		576
Current liabilities	420		2,046
Long-term debt, gross	608		1,336
Long-term debt, net	608		701
Shareholders' equity	(508)		(1,223)
Cash from oper. activs	**(1,805)**	**n.a.**	**(3,813)**
Cash from fin. activs	778		4,894
Net cash position	**155**	**-87**	**1,183**
	$		$
Earnings per share*	(0.03)		(0.16)
Cash flow per share*	(0.03)		(0.06)
	shs		shs
No. of shs. o/s*	68,987,904		65,184,628
Avg. no. of shs. o/s*	68,408,299		64,052,177
	%		%
Net profit margin	n.a.		n.a.
Return on equity	n.m.		n.m.
Return on assets	(230.63)		(920.46)

* Common
□ Restated
[A] Reported in accordance with IFRS

Latest Results

Periods ended:	6m Apr. 30/23[A]		6m Apr. 30/22[A]
	$000s	%Chg	$000s
Net income	(925)	n.a.	(2,490)
	$		$
Earnings per share*	(0.01)		(0.04)

* Common
[A] Reported in accordance with IFRS

Historical Summary
(as originally stated)

Fiscal Year	Oper. Rev.	Net Inc. Bef. Disc.	EPS*
	$000s	$000s	$
2022[A]	nil	(2,361)	(0.03)
2021[A]	nil	(10,367)	(0.16)
2020[A]	nil	(6,272)	(0.10)
2019[A]	nil	(2,521)	(0.05)
2018[A1]	nil	(5,196)	(0.19)

* Common
[A] Reported in accordance with IFRS
[1] Results reflect the Aug. 8, 2018, reverse takeover acquisition of and amalgamation with Sona Nanotech Ltd.

S.80 Sonor Investments Limited

CUSIP - 835640
Head Office - 2120-130 Adelaide St W, Toronto, ON, M5H 3P5 **Telephone** - (416) 369-1499 **Fax** - (416) 369-0280
Email - kmurray@fairwater.ca
Investor Relations - Kelly Murray (416) 369-1499
Auditors - Deloitte LLP C.A., Toronto, Ont.
Transfer Agents - TSX Trust Company, Toronto, Ont.
Profile - (Ont. 1960) Invests in public and private equity and fixed income securities with the objective of preserving its capital and growing it over a long term.

Holds all 35,596 outstanding first preference shares of **Fairwater Capital Corporation**, a private investment holding company which has the same directors as the company. The shares have a fair value of $35,596,000.

The articles of the company provide that, so long as any of the company's 195,600 first preference shares are outstanding, the company must meet two tests with respect to the value of assets and qualified investments. The aggregate value of the net assets of the company must not, at any time, be less than eight times the number of outstanding first preference shares times $5.00. In addition, the aggregate market value of qualified investments of the company and Fairwater must not, at any time, be less than two times the number of outstanding first preference shares times $5.00. The company has continuously met the obligations of these tests since December 1982 when these tests were established.

In addition, the company has investments in **Bank of Montreal**, **Intact Financial Corp.**, **Toronto Dominion Bank**, **Royal Bank of Canada**, **Canadian Imperial Bank of Commerce**, **Enbridge Inc.**, **Telus Corporation**, **Power Corp. of Canada**, **Emera Inc.** and **TC Energy Corporation**. Also holds investments in 10 other public and private companies.

Directors - Michael R. Gardiner, chr. & CEO, Toronto, Ont.; Glen G. MacArthur, Toronto, Ont.; Thomas C. MacMillan, Toronto, Ont.; David N. Middleton, Toronto, Ont.
Other Exec. Officers - Rosabell Chung Hun, CFO & treas.; Kelly Murray, corp. sec.

Capital Stock

	Authorized (shs.)	Outstanding (shs.)[1]
First Preference	195,600	195,600[2]
Second Preference	unlimited	nil
Class A Common	unlimited	nil
Class B Common	unlimited	nil
Common	unlimited	1,861,730

[1] At Apr. 25, 2023
[2] Classified as debt.

9% First Preference - Cumulative. Retractable at $5.00 per share. 15 votes per share.
9% Second Preference - Non-cumulative. Redeemable at $100 per share. Non-voting.
Class A Common - Convertible at any time into class B common shares on a share-for-share basis. Non-voting.
Class B Common - Redeemable at a price determined by the board of directors. Non-voting.
Common - Convertible at any time on a share-for-share basis into either class A common shares or class B common shares. One vote per share.
Major Shareholder - Michael R. Gardiner held 38.9% interest at Apr. 25, 2023.
Capital Stock Changes - There were no changes to capital stock from 2005 to 2022, inclusive.

Dividends

SNI.PR.A pfd 9% cum. red. M.V. Ra $0.45 pa S

Financial Statistics

Periods ended:	12m Dec. 31/22[A]		12m Dec. 31/21[A]
	$000s	%Chg	$000s
Realized invest. gain (loss)	1,076		372
Unrealized invest. gain (loss)	(1,838)		2,393
Total revenue	**3,504**	**-47**	**6,665**
General & admin. expense	489		333
Operating expense	**489**	**+47**	**333**
Operating income	**3,015**	**-52**	**6,332**
Finance costs, gross	88		88
Pre-tax income	**2,927**	**-53**	**6,244**
Income taxes	(96)		306
Net income	**3,023**	**-49**	**5,938**
Cash & equivalent	1,801		13,911
Accounts receivable	373		178
Current assets	2,174		17,471
Long-term investments	66,781		55,402
Total assets	**68,955**	**-5**	**72,873**
Accts. pay. & accr. liabs.	75		143
Current liabilities	253		3,787
Long-term debt, gross	978		978
Long-term debt, net	978		978
Shareholders' equity	67,724		68,108
Cash from oper. activs	**3,426**	**+2**	**3,348**
Cash from fin. activs	(3,395)		(3,382)
Cash from invest. activs	(12,141)		(6,375)
Net cash position	**1,801**	**-87**	**13,911**
	$		$
Earnings per share*	1.62		3.19
Cash flow per share*	1.84		1.80
	shs		shs
No. of shs. o/s*	1,861,730		1,861,730
Avg. no. of shs. o/s*	1,861,730		1,861,730
	%		%
Net profit margin	86.27		89.09
Return on equity	4.45		8.89
Return on assets	4.39		8.63

* Common
[A] Reported in accordance with IFRS

Latest Results

Periods ended:	3m Mar. 31/23[A]		3m Mar. 31/22[A]
	$000s	%Chg	$000s
Total revenue	582	-20	726
Net income	419	-25	562
	$		$
Earnings per share*	0.23		0.30

* Common
[A] Reported in accordance with IFRS

Historical Summary
(as originally stated)

Fiscal Year	Total Rev.	Net Inc. Bef. Disc.	EPS*
	$000s	$000s	$
2022[A]	3,504	3,023	1.62
2021[A]	6,665	5,938	3.19
2020[A]	3,571	3,087	1.66
2019[A]	5,059	4,425	2.38
2018[A]	3,106	2,674	1.44

* Common
[A] Reported in accordance with IFRS

S.81 Source Energy Services Ltd.

Symbol - SHLE **Exchange** - TSX **CUSIP** - 83615X
Head Office - 500-1060 7 St SW, Calgary, AB, T2R 0C4 **Telephone** - (403) 262-1312 **Fax** - (403) 800-9101
Website - www.sourceenergyservices.com
Email - dnewell@sourceenergyservices.com
Investor Relations - Derren Newell (403) 262-1312
Auditors - Ernst & Young LLP C.A., Calgary, Alta.
Transfer Agents - Odyssey Trust Company, Calgary, Alta.
FP500 Revenue Ranking - 508
Employees - 409 at Dec. 31, 2022
Profile - (Alta. 2017) Produces and distributes frac sand primarily to oil and gas operators in the Western Canadian Sedimentary Basin (WCSB).

Owns and operates a Northern White frac sand mine and related closed-loop wet processing plant near Sumner, Wisc.; a Northern White frac sand mine and related closed-loop wet processing plant, dry processing plant, storage and rail load out facility in Blair, Wisc.; adjacent Preston, a Northern White frac sand mine and related closed-loop wet processing plant, dry processing plant and rail load out facility; and a dry processing plant, storage and rail load out facility in Weyerhaeuser, Wisc. Also operates frac sand mine and wet and dry processing facilities in Peace River, Alta. These facilities have direct access to **Canadian National Railway Company**'s rail lines, which are used to transport the product to the company's transload terminals in the WCSB. The company's rail fleet includes approximately 3,400 two-pocket covered hopper cars to deliver its product.

The company's terminal network consists of nine in-basin terminals in Alberta and British Columbia to serve the Montney, Duvernay and Deep Basin regions. The terminals have a total storage capacity of over 170,000 tonnes, on-track storage of more than 60,000 tonnes and throughput capacity of over 5,000,000 tonnes per year. Select terminals also provide storage and logistics services for other bulk oil and gas well completion materials. Also offers Sahara, a proprietary mobile wellsite sand storage and handling system with a storage capacity of 1,800 tonnes.

Operating Data

At Dec. 31	2022	2021
Sales volumes (tonnes)	2,845,600	2,483,362
Sand revenue per tonne	$120.07	$104.11
Gross margin per tonne	$20.43	$15.84
Adj. gross margin per tonne	$27.75	$24.33

Directors - Christopher A. (Chris) Johnson, chr., Toronto, Ont.; Scott Melbourn, pres. & CEO, Calgary, Alta.; Jeff Belford, Calgary, Alta.; Carrie Lonardelli, Calgary, Alta.; Steven Sharpe, Toronto, Ont.
Other Exec. Officers - Derren Newell, exec. v-p & CFO; Kurtis Kisio, v-p, sales & mktg.; Jarett Finney, pres., distrib.; Shawn Furlong, pres., prod.

Capital Stock

	Authorized (shs.)	Outstanding (shs.)[1]
Common	unlimited	13,545,055
Class B	unlimited	nil

[1] At May 4, 2023

Major Shareholder - Mackenzie Investments Corporation held 15.22% interest and TriWest IV Canada Fund LP, TriWest IV US Fund LP, SES Canada LP, SES Canada 2 LP and SES Canada 3 LP held 10.26% interest at Mar. 23, 2023.

Price Range - SHLE/TSX

Year	Volume	High	Low	Close
2022	3,683,484	$3.00	$1.09	$1.89
2021	6,003,617	$3.80	$1.10	$1.60
2020	6,010,293	$4.80	$0.60	$1.56
2019	1,245,759	$21.12	$1.62	$2.88
2018	1,903,722	$115.80	$12.48	$15.48

Consolidation: 1-for-12 cons. in Jan. 2021
Recent Close: $4.08
Capital Stock Changes - There were no changes to capital stock during 2022.

Wholly Owned Subsidiaries

Source Energy Services Canada L.P., Calgary, Alta.
- 100% int. in **Source Energy Services Canada Holdings Ltd.**, Alta.
- 100% int. in **Source Energy Services Canadian Chemical LP**, Alta.
- 100% int. in **Source Energy Services Canadian Logistics LP**, Alta.

Source Energy Services U.S. L.P., Alta.
- 100% int. in **CSP Property Holdings LLC**, Wis.
- 100% int. in **Sand Products Wisconsin, LLC**, Mich.
  - 100% int. in **Sand Products Rail LLC**, Mich.
  - 100% int. in **Spartan Sand LLC**, Mich.
- 100% int. in **Source Energy Services Logistic U.S. LP**, Del.
- 100% int. in **Source Energy Services Proppants LP**, Del.

Financial Statistics

Periods ended:	12m Dec. 31/22^A		12m Dec. 31/21^A
	$000s	%Chg	$000s
Operating revenue	**415,912**	**+30**	**319,861**
Cost of sales	322,902		248,802
Salaries & benefits	30,000		25,580
General & admin expense	14,147		10,844
Stock-based compensation	947		643
Operating expense	**367,996**	**+29**	**285,869**
Operating income	**47,916**	**+41**	**33,992**
Deprec., depl. & amort.	31,382		30,975
Finance costs, gross	33,147		30,320
Pre-tax income	**(8,770)**	**n.a.**	**(24,403)**
Net income	**(8,770)**	**n.a.**	**(24,403)**
Inventories	72,533		56,337
Accounts receivable	42,304		43,499
Current assets	122,545		106,745
Fixed assets, net	135,159		131,935
Right-of-use assets	58,300		26,814
Total assets	**326,897**	**+23**	**266,031**
Accts. pay. & accr. liabs	68,425		29,336
Current liabilities	87,453		50,308
Long-term debt, gross	176,518		183,031
Long-term debt, net	176,518		175,531
Long-term lease liabilities	50,722		26,078
Shareholders' equity	5,657		6,526
Cash from oper. activs	**80,173**	**+472**	**14,011**
Cash from fin. activs	(66,275)		(8,011)
Cash from invest. activs	(13,898)		(6,000)
Capital expenditures	(14,799)		(6,517)
Capital disposals	1,511		75
	$		$
Earnings per share*	(0.65)		(1.80)
Cash flow per share*	5.92		1.03
	shs		shs
No. of shs. o/s*	13,545,055		13,545,055
Avg. no. of shs. o/s*	13,545,055		13,545,055
	%		%
Net profit margin	(2.11)		(7.63)
Return on equity	(143.97)		(124.46)
Return on assets	8.22		2.22
Foreign sales percent	3		nil
No. of employees (FTEs)	409		351

* Common
^A Reported in accordance with IFRS

Latest Results

Periods ended:	3m Mar. 31/23^A		3m Mar. 31/22^A
	$000s	%Chg	$000s
Operating revenue	163,724	+69	96,969
Net income	7,879	n.a.	(6,640)
	$		$
Earnings per share*	0.58		(0.49)

* Common
^A Reported in accordance with IFRS

Historical Summary
(as originally stated)

Fiscal Year	Oper. Rev.	Net Inc. Bef. Disc.	EPS*
	$000s	$000s	$
2022^A	415,912	(8,770)	(0.65)
2021^A	319,861	(24,403)	(1.80)
2020^A	249,878	(185,466)	(36.84)
2019^A	332,956	(89,955)	(17.64)
2018^A	415,027	(2,865)	(0.48)

* Common
^A Reported in accordance with IFRS
Note: Adjusted throughout for 1-for-12 cons. in Jan. 2021

S.82 Southern Arc Minerals Inc.

Symbol - SA.H **Exchange** - TSX-VEN **CUSIP** - 842200
Head Office - 650-669 Howe St, Vancouver, BC, V6C 0B4 **Telephone** - (778) 725-1490 **Fax** - (604) 428-1124
Website - www.southernarcminerals.com
Email - eau@sarcmin.com
Investor Relations - John G. Proust (778) 725-1482
Auditors - KPMG LLP C.A., Vancouver, B.C.
Lawyers - Morton Law, LLP, Vancouver, B.C.
Transfer Agents - Computershare Trust Company of Canada Inc., Vancouver, B.C.
Profile - (B.C. 2004) Holds investments in resource companies with a focus on gold and copper-gold.
Investments consist of **Japan Gold Corp.**, **Rise Gold Corp.** and **Adriatic Metals Plc.**
Directors - John G. Proust, exec. chr. & CEO, Vancouver, B.C.; Dr. Michael J. (Mike) Andrews, St. Ouen, Jersey; John Carlile, St. Brélade, Jersey; Robert J. (Bob) Gallagher, Deerfield Beach, Fla.; Morris Klid, Oakville, Ont.
Other Exec. Officers - Vincent (Vince) Boon, CFO & contr.; Eileen Au, corp. sec.

Capital Stock

	Authorized (shs.)	Outstanding (shs.)[1]
Class A	unlimited	22,898,283

[1] At Nov. 17, 2022

Major Shareholder - John G. Proust held 25.03% interest, Neil S. Subin held 15.3% interest and Dr. Michael J. (Mike) Andrews held 14.3% interest at Nov. 4, 2022.

Price Range - SA.H/TSX-VEN

Year	Volume	High	Low	Close
2022	556,140	$0.18	$0.06	$0.06
2021	1,833,516	$0.27	$0.13	$0.14
2020	2,182,475	$0.93	$0.11	$0.19
2019	830,843	$0.62	$0.30	$0.36
2018	900,663	$0.64	$0.27	$0.45

Recent Close: $0.05
Capital Stock Changes - There were no changes to capital stock during fiscal 2022.

Investments

Adriatic Metals plc, Cheltenham, Gloucs., United Kingdom.
Japan Gold Corp., Vancouver, B.C. (see Survey of Mines)
Rise Gold Corp., Vancouver, B.C. (see Survey of Mines)

Financial Statistics

Periods ended:	12m June 30/22^A		12m June 30/21^A
	$000s	%Chg	$000s
General & admin expense	428		764
Operating expense	**428**	**-44**	**764**
Operating income	**(428)**	**n.a.**	**(764)**
Deprec., depl. & amort.	1		26
Finance income	1		29
Investment income	nil		(152)
Pre-tax income	**(1,399)**	**n.a.**	**5,093**
Income taxes	nil		(177)
Net income	**(1,399)**	**n.a.**	**5,270**
Cash & equivalent	1,122		1,482
Accounts receivable	10		12
Current assets	1,150		1,514
Long-term investments	nil		1,046
Fixed assets, net	3		4
Total assets	**1,153**	**-55**	**2,564**
Accts. pay. & accr. liabs	50		61
Current liabilities	50		61
Shareholders' equity	1,104		2,503
Cash from oper. activs	**(452)**	**n.a.**	**(774)**
Cash from fin. activs	nil		1,137
Cash from invest. activs	867		(83)
Net cash position	**1,045**	**+66**	**630**
Capital expenditures	nil		(5)
	$		$
Earnings per share*	(0.06)		0.24
Cash flow per share*	(0.02)		(0.04)
	shs		shs
No. of shs. o/s*	22,768,283		22,768,283
Avg. no. of shs. o/s*	22,768,283		21,797,371
	%		%
Net profit margin	n.a.		n.a.
Return on equity	(77.57)		59.68
Return on assets	(75.28)		58.91

* Class A
^A Reported in accordance with IFRS

Historical Summary
(as originally stated)

Fiscal Year	Oper. Rev.	Net Inc. Bef. Disc.	EPS*
	$000s	$000s	$
2022^A	nil	(1,399)	(0.06)
2021^A	nil	5,270	0.24
2020^A	nil	53	0.00
2019^A	nil	4,622	0.38
2018^A	nil	(3,985)	(0.14)

* Class A
^A Reported in accordance with IFRS

S.83 Space Kingdom Digital Capital Corp.

Symbol - YSK.P **Exchange** - TSX-VEN **CUSIP** - 84616A
Head Office - Royal Centre, 1500-1055 Georgia St W, PO Box 11117, Vancouver, BC, V6E 4N7 **Telephone** - (604) 250-1060
Email - chris@taipanconsulting.co.uk
Investor Relations - Christopher Farnworth (604) 250-1060
Auditors - MNP LLP C.A., Toronto, Ont.
Transfer Agents - Odyssey Trust Company, Calgary, Alta.
Profile - (B.C. 2022) Capital Pool Company.
Common listed on TSX-VEN, July 27, 2023.
Directors - Xingtao Zhou, chr., Guangzhou, Guangdong, People's Republic of China; Christopher (Chris) Farnworth, CEO, CFO & corp. sec., London, Middx., United Kingdom; Harold C. Davidson, Surrey, B.C.; Stephen R. Gatensbury, Vancouver, B.C.; John Wallace, Philadelphia, Pa.

Capital Stock

	Authorized (shs.)	Outstanding (shs.)[1]
Common	unlimited	4,300,000

[1] At Aug. 18, 2023

Major Shareholder - Xingtao Zhou held 37.2% interest at July 27, 2023.
Capital Stock Changes - On July 27, 2023, an initial public offering of 2,000,000 common shares was completed at 10¢ per share.

S.84 Spacefy Inc.

Symbol - SPFY **Exchange** - CSE **CUSIP** - 84624Q
Head Office - 300-1 University Ave, Toronto, ON, M5J 2P1 **Toll-free** - (844) 277-2233
Website - www.spacefy.com
Email - michael@spacefy.com
Investor Relations - Michael J. Bradley (844) 277-2233
Auditors - MNP LLP C.A., Mississauga, Ont.
Lawyers - Stikeman Keeley Spiegel LLP, Toronto, Ont.
Transfer Agents - Computershare Trust Company of Canada Inc., Toronto, Ont.
Profile - (Ont. 2014) Operates Spacefy, an online marketplace for listing and booking residential, commercial or non-traditional space or locations for rent to people in the creative industries in certain urban centres in North America.
The company has two market segments: space owners, which are property owners and managers of venues, including houses and condos, restaurants and bars, professional photography and music studios, vacant retail shops, event venues and farms; and creatives, which are individuals and businesses in the creative industries such as photographers, filmmakers, advertising agencies and their agents, event planners, musicians and other members of the arts community that are interested in renting any of the spaces for their projects, productions and events. The company derives revenues from commissions (from space owners) and processing fees (from creatives) charged on the total amount of a successful booking, typically earning a 15% premium from each transaction.
Directors - Judeh Siwady, co-founder, Toronto, Ont.; Michael J. Bradley, chr., interim pres., interim CEO & treas., Toronto, Ont.; John R. Anderson, Toronto, Ont.; Peter C. McRae, Toronto, Ont.; Kelly Payne, Ont.
Other Exec. Officers - Alyas A. Ali, co-founder, v-p, growth & corp. sec.; Kyle Appleby, CFO; Moya Semaan, v-p

Capital Stock

	Authorized (shs.)	Outstanding (shs.)[1]
Preferred	unlimited	nil
Common	unlimited	45,458,608

[1] At May 30, 2023

Price Range - SPFY/CSE

Year	Volume	High	Low	Close
2022	2,874,342	$0.05	$0.01	$0.01
2021	14,293,034	$0.13	$0.02	$0.04
2020	8,145,666	$0.09	$0.01	$0.03
2019	30,630,838	$0.37	$0.04	$0.07
2018	2,490,950	$0.18	$0.14	$0.17

Recent Close: $0.01
Capital Stock Changes - There were no changes to capital stock from 2020 to 2022, inclusive.

Financial Statistics

Periods ended:	12m Dec. 31/22[A]		12m Dec. 31/21[A]
	$000s	%Chg	$000s
Operating revenue	**1**	**-50**	**2**
Salaries & benefits	36		36
General & admin expense	95		72
Operating expense	**131**	**+21**	**108**
Operating income	**(130)**	**n.a.**	**(106)**
Pre-tax income	**(129)**	**n.a.**	**(106)**
Net income	**(129)**	**n.a.**	**(106)**
Cash & equivalent	8		35
Accounts receivable	10		13
Current assets	29		53
Total assets	**29**	**-45**	**53**
Bank indebtedness	60		60
Accts. pay. & accr. liabs	298		271
Current liabilities	565		466
Shareholders' equity	(542)		(413)
Cash from oper. activs	**(99)**	**n.a.**	**(59)**
Cash from fin. activs	72		80
Net cash position	**8**	**-77**	**35**
	$		$
Earnings per share*	(0.00)		(0.00)
Cash flow per share*	(0.00)		(0.00)
	shs		shs
No. of shs. o/s*	45,458,608		45,458,608
Avg. no. of shs. o/s*	45,458,608		45,458,608
	%		%
Net profit margin	n.m.		n.m.
Return on equity	n.m.		n.m.
Return on assets	(314.63)		(238.20)

* Common
[A] Reported in accordance with IFRS

Latest Results

Periods ended:	3m Mar. 31/23[A]		3m Mar. 31/22[A]
	$000s	%Chg	$000s
Operating revenue	nil	n.a.	1
Net income	(26)	n.a.	(21)
	$		$
Earnings per share*	(0.00)		(0.00)

* Common
[A] Reported in accordance with IFRS

Historical Summary
(as originally stated)

Fiscal Year	Oper. Rev.	Net Inc. Bef. Disc.	EPS*
	$000s	$000s	$
2022[A]	1	(129)	(0.00)
2021[A]	2	(106)	(0.00)
2020[A]	4	(666)	(0.01)
2019[A]	5	(2,154)	(0.05)
2018[A]	4	(876)	(0.05)

* Common
[A] Reported in accordance with IFRS

S.85 Spackman Equities Group Inc.

Symbol - SQG **Exchange** - TSX-VEN **CUSIP** - 846311
Head Office - Scotia Plaza, 2502-40 King St W, Toronto, ON, M5H 3Y2 **Telephone** - (416) 304-1233 **Fax** - (416) 216-3960
Website - www.spackmanequities.com
Email - info@spackmanequities.com
Investor Relations - Alexander Falconer (416) 587-6227
Auditors - HDCPA Professional Corporation C.A., Mississauga, Ont.
Lawyers - Norton Rose Fulbright Canada LLP, Toronto, Ont.
Transfer Agents - Computershare Trust Company of Canada Inc., Toronto, Ont.
Profile - (Can. 2006) Invests in and develops small/medium-sized growth companies that possess industry-specific know-how or proprietary technologies, primarily in Asia.

Holdings include 7.55% interest in Singapore-based **Spackman Entertainment Group Limited**, an entertainment production company engaged in the independent development, production, presentation and financing of theatrical motion pictures in South Korea and production of Korean television dramas; 0.41% interest in Hong Kong-based **Spackman Media Group Limited**, an entertainment talent agency in Korea; and wholly owned **SEGI Investments Limited**, an investment company that invests in non-public equities.

Predecessor Detail - Name changed from Centiva Capital Inc., Sept. 30, 2011.
Directors - Richard Lee, chr., interim CEO & head of bus. devel., Spackman Entertainment Group Limited, Singapore; Douglas Babcook, Nanoose Bay, B.C.; William Hale, Saskatoon, Sask.; Kyoungwon Na, Singapore
Other Exec. Officers - Alexander (Alex) Falconer, CFO

Capital Stock

	Authorized (shs.)	Outstanding (shs.)[1]
Common	unlimited	14,899,972

[1] At Mar. 31, 2022

Major Shareholder - Widely held at June 1, 2021.

Price Range - SQG/TSX-VEN

Year	Volume	High	Low	Close
2022	555,656	$0.08	$0.01	$0.03
2021	4,031,758	$0.30	$0.05	$0.07
2020	2,286,799	$0.25	$0.05	$0.10
2019	1,030,344	$0.35	$0.10	$0.15
2018	2,928,627	$0.65	$0.20	$0.30

Consolidation: 1-for-10 cons. in Aug. 2021
Recent Close: $0.04

Wholly Owned Subsidiaries

SEGI Investments Limited, British Virgin Islands.

Investments

7.55% int. in **Spackman Entertainment Group Limited**, Hong Kong, People's Republic of China.
- 100% int. in **Constellation Agency Pte. Ltd.**, Singapore.
  - 100% int. in **The P Factory Co. Ltd.**, South Korea.
  - 100% int. in **Platform Media Group Co., Ltd.**, South Korea.
- 100% int. in **Greenlight Content Limited**, Cayman Islands.
  - 100% int. in **Greenlight Content Co. Ltd.**, South Korea.
- 60.2% int. in **noon pictures Co., Ltd.**, South Korea.
- 51% int. in **Novus Mediacorp Co., Ltd.**, South Korea.
- 100% int. in **Simplex Films Limited**, Hong Kong, Hong Kong, People's Republic of China.
  - 100% int. in **Simplex Films Co., Ltd.**, South Korea.
- 43.88% int. in **Spackman Media Group Limited**, Hong Kong, People's Republic of China.
- 100% int. in **Take Pictures Pte. Ltd.**, Singapore.
  - 100% int. in **Studio Take Co., Ltd.**, South Korea.
- 100% int. in **Zip Cinema (HK) Limited**, Hong Kong, People's Republic of China.
  - 100% int. in **Spackman Entertainment Korea Inc.**, South Korea.
    - 94.38% int. in **Upper West Inc.**, South Korea.
  - 100% int. in **Spackman Equities Limited**, Hong Kong, People's Republic of China.

Financial Statistics

Periods ended:	12m Dec. 31/21[A]		12m Dec. 31/20[A]
	$000s	%Chg	$000s
Unrealized invest. gain (loss)	(307)		(1,624)
Total revenue	**(307)**	**n.a.**	**(1,624)**
General & admin. expense	191		202
Operating expense	**191**	**-5**	**202**
Operating income	**(498)**	**n.a.**	**(1,826)**
Finance costs, gross	48		30
Pre-tax income	**(559)**	**n.a.**	**(1,844)**
Net income	**(559)**	**n.a.**	**(1,844)**
Cash & equivalent	73		83
Investments	691		1,037
Total assets	**764**	**-32**	**1,120**
Accts. pay. & accr. liabs	235		138
Debt	848		741
Shareholders' equity	(319)		240
Cash from oper. activs	**(143)**	**n.a.**	**(201)**
Cash from fin. activs	133		189
Net cash position	**73**	**-12**	**83**
	$		$
Earnings per share*	(0.04)		(0.10)
Cash flow per share*	(0.01)		(0.01)
	shs		shs
No. of shs. o/s*	14,889,972		14,890,018
Avg. no. of shs. o/s*	14,889,972		14,890,018
	%		%
Net profit margin	n.m.		n.m.
Return on equity	n.m.		(158.69)
Return on assets	(54.25)		(93.89)

* Common
[A] Reported in accordance with IFRS

Latest Results

Periods ended:	3m Mar. 31/22[A]		3m Mar. 31/21[A]
	$000s	%Chg	$000s
Net income	(65)	n.a.	(58)
	$		$
Earnings per share*	(0.00)		(0.00)

* Common
[A] Reported in accordance with IFRS

Historical Summary
(as originally stated)

Fiscal Year	Total Rev.	Net Inc. Bef. Disc.	EPS*
	$000s	$000s	$
2021[A]	(307)	(559)	(0.04)
2020[A]	(1,624)	(1,844)	(0.10)
2019[A]	(1,210)	(1,480)	(0.10)
2018[A]	(9,992)	(10,878)	(0.70)
2017[A]	(13,354)	(11,928)	(0.80)

* Common
[A] Reported in accordance with IFRS
Note: Adjusted throughout for 1-for-10 cons. in Aug. 2021

S.86 Sparc AI Inc.

Symbol - SPAI **Exchange** - CSE **CUSIP** - 846501
Head Office - Level 8, 90 Collins St, Melbourne, VIC, Australia, 30000 **Overseas Tel** - 61-3-966-6338
Website - www.sparcai.co
Email - anoosh@shape.capital
Investor Relations - Anoosh Manzoori 61-3-966-6338
Auditors - Smythe LLP C.A., Vancouver, B.C.
Lawyers - Joanne S. McClusky, Vancouver, B.C.
Transfer Agents - Computershare Trust Company of Canada Inc., Toronto, Ont.
Profile - (B.C. 2018) Developed Spatial Predictive Approximation and Radial Convolution (SPARC), an artificial intelligence (AI) technology that can determine the location of any distant object without the use of the Internet, GPS or satellite.

The company is working to embed SPARC AI algorithms modules into a microchip, which can be installed in drones and unmanned aerial vehicles (UAVs), fixed camera devices, motor vehicles, sensors and wearables. SPARC AI is 100% covert and can be used for a variety of commercial applications ideal for military, surveillance, target acquisition, asset protection and situational awareness.

Holds seven global patents registered in the U.S., Canada, Japan, South Korea, the People's Republic of China, Australia and New Zealand. The patents include a set of proprietary algorithms that calculates a camera xyz coordinates combined with the Earth's terrain model to predict the location of distant objects that may be hundreds of metres away.

Revenue is earned through a one-time chip fee and a recurring annual fee for updates, advanced features, integration to third-party data and systems.

Recent Merger and Acquisition Activity

Status: completed **Revised:** Aug. 4, 2023
EYEFI Group Technologies Inc. (EGTI) completed a restructuring which included EGTI's assets, consisting of the Sparc Algorithms and Sparc Patents (IP) being assigned from wholly owned EYEFI Pty Ltd. (EYEFI Australia) to EGTI. Thereafter, EGTI sold its shares of EYEFI Australia to a group of six shareholders led by the former CEO and director, Simon Langdon, for a purchase price of $5,042,659 including the transfer of 18,951,061 EYEFI Group common shares held by Langdon to EGTI plus a deferred consideration of $2,200,000. These shares will be returned to EGTI's treasury and then cancelled. EYEFI Australia was granted a licence of the SPARC IP. In the event EYEFI Australia needs to use the SPARC technology in the future for any new customer, it must pay 10% of the licence fee to EGTI on commercial terms. SPARC is a predicative set of algorithms allowing one to determine the location of any object without the need for satellite, GPS or Internet connection.

Predecessor Detail - Name changed from EYEFI Group Technologies Inc., Aug. 9, 2023.
Directors - Justin A. Hanka, chr., Vic., Australia; Anoosh Manzoori, CEO, Melbourne, Vic., Australia; Anthony Haberfield
Other Exec. Officers - Ben Dunne, COO; John Dinan, CFO

Capital Stock

	Authorized (shs.)	Outstanding (shs.)[1]
Common	unlimited	9,090,536

[1] At Aug. 10, 2023

Major Shareholder - Simon M. Langdon held 53.68% interest at Aug. 9, 2022.

Price Range - SPAI/CSE

Year	Volume	High	Low	Close
2022	852,499	$0.59	$0.20	$0.33
2021	2,825,768	$1.50	$0.41	$0.50
2020	136,173	$0.60	$0.08	$0.45

Recent Close: $0.15
Capital Stock Changes - In August 2023, 18,951,061 common shares were cancelled.

Wholly Owned Subsidiaries

Conxsme Pty Ltd., Melbourne, Vic., Australia.

Financial Statistics

Periods ended:	12m Dec. 31/21[A]		12m Dec. 31/20[A1]
	$000s	%Chg	$000s
Operating revenue	**501**	**+112**	**236**
Cost of sales	523		189
Salaries & benefits	696		367
Research & devel. expense	(377)[2]		(220)
General & admin expense	760		832
Stock-based compensation	75		22
Operating expense	**1,677**	**+41**	**1,190**
Operating income	**(1,176)**	**n.a.**	**(954)**
Deprec., depl. & amort	99		58
Finance costs, gross	104		46
Pre-tax income	**(1,373)**	**n.a.**	**(884)**
Net income	**(1,373)**	**n.a.**	**(884)**
Cash & equivalent	355		655
Accounts receivable	49		85
Current assets	825		997
Fixed assets, net	34		36
Right-of-use assets	231		13
Intangibles, net	41		51
Total assets	**336**	**+104**	**165**
Accts. pay. & accr. liabs	178		177
Current liabilities	645		651
Long-term debt, gross	nil		854
Long-term debt, net	nil		854
Long-term lease liabilities	172		nil
Shareholders' equity	340		(342)
Cash from oper. activs	**(1,297)**	**n.a.**	**(718)**
Cash from fin. activs	1,108		1,287
Cash from invest. activs	(10)		(9)
Net cash position	**355**	**-46**	**655**
Capital expenditures	(10)		(3)
	$		$
Earnings per share*	(0.05)		(0.04)
Cash flow per share*	(0.05)		(0.04)
	shs		shs
No. of shs. o/s*	27,555,600		23,005,600
Avg. no. of shs. o/s*	26,444,093		19,731,612
	%		%
Net profit margin	(274.05)		(374.58)
Return on equity	n.m.		n.m.
Return on assets	(506.59)		(439.90)

* Common

[A] Reported in accordance with IFRS

[1] Results reflect the May 27, 2020, reverse takeover acquisition of EYEFI Pty Ltd.

[2] Contains research and development tax credits.

Latest Results

Periods ended:	6m June 30/22[A]		6m June 30/21[A]
	$000s	%Chg	$000s
Operating revenue	245	-18	297
Net income	(497)	n.a.	(620)
	$		$
Earnings per share*	(0.00)		(0.03)

* Common

[A] Reported in accordance with IFRS

Historical Summary
(as originally stated)

Fiscal Year	Oper. Rev.	Net Inc. Bef. Disc.	EPS*
	$000s	$000s	$
2021[A]	501	(1,373)	(0.05)
2020[A]	236	(884)	(0.04)
2019[A]	260	(361)	(0.02)

* Common

[A] Reported in accordance with IFRS

S.87 Spark Power Group Inc.

Symbol - SPG **Exchange** - TSX **CUSIP** - 84651C
Head Office - 200-1337 North Service Rd E, Oakville, ON, L6H 1A7 **Telephone** - (905) 829-3336
Website - www.sparkpowercorp.com
Email - rperry@sparkpowercorp.com
Investor Relations - Richard Perri (905) 829-3336 ext. 127
Auditors - BDO Canada LLP C.A., Toronto, Ont.
Transfer Agents - TSX Trust Company, Toronto, Ont.
FP500 Revenue Ranking - 589
Employees - 1,212 at Dec. 31, 2022

Profile - (Ont. 2017) Provides end-to-end electrical contracting, operations and maintenance services and solutions to the commercial, industrial, utility and renewable asset markets in Canada and the U.S.

Operations are organized into two segments: Technical Services and Renewables.

The **Technical Services** segment focuses on pole-to-product electrical services and solutions including low, medium and high voltage services, engineering and new and used equipment sales and service in western and eastern Canada, as well as in the U.S. Low voltage services include electric contracting services, industrial automation, systems integration, custom control panel design and assembly, electronic repair and 24/7 emergency services. Medium and high voltage services include power on services, sub-station construction and maintenance, power line construction and maintenance, equipment installation, commissioning, thermography services and transformer maintenance. Engineering services include power systems engineering, protection and control engineering, sub-station engineering, supervisory control and data acquisition (SCADA) engineering and arc flash studies. Power equipment services include buying, refurbishing and reselling used electrical equipment; selling and renting power transformers; selling medium voltage electrical switchgear; and operating a full capability fabrication shop.

The **Renewables** segment includes 24/7 monitoring and analytics from central operating centre, and fence to fence, onsite operations and maintenance to wide range of solar sites for solar assets; in-construction services, asset monitoring, operations and maintenance, and commissioning for wind assets; engineering, procurement and construction, operations and maintenance, and commissioning for battery energy storage systems; and construction, operations and maintenance for electric vehicles.

As at Mar. 28, 2023, the company has 16 registered trademarks and 13 pending trademark applications in Canada and the U.S. Brands include Spark Power, Power, Pole to Product, Rondar, Pelikan, Tiltran, Taltrees, Orbis, Lizco, New Electric, 3-Phase Electric and One Wind.

In January 2023, wholly owned **Northwind Solutions Group Inc.**, **One Wind Services Inc.** and **Spark Power Solutions Ltd.** were amalgamated and continued as **Spark Power Renewables Canada Inc.** In addition, wholly owned **Northwind Solutions Group (USA), Inc.** and **One Wind Services (US), Inc.** amalgamated and continued as **Spark Power Renewables (USA) Inc.**

Recent Merger and Acquisition Activity

Status: completed **Announced:** Dec. 1, 2022
Spark Power Group Inc. sold indirect wholly owned Bullfrog Power Inc., a green energy retailer that offers its customers power from renewable energy sources such as wind, solar, low-impact hydro and green natural gas, to Envest Corp. for an undisclosed amount. The transaction included Bullfrog's U.S. business, which was carried on through Bullfrog Solutions USA Inc.

Predecessor Detail - Name changed from Canaccord Genuity Acquisition Corp., Aug. 31, 2018, following Qualifying Transaction reverse takeover acquisition of Spark Power Corp.

Directors - Andrew Clark, Toronto, Ont.; Daniel Péloquin, Chambly, Qué.; Joseph D. (Joe) Quarin, Toronto, Ont.; Jason Sparaga, Burlington, Ont.; Eric Waxman, Dundas, Ont.

Other Exec. Officers - Richard Jackson, pres. & CEO; Richard Perri, exec. v-p & CFO; April Currey, v-p, sales & mktg.; Michael Mah, v-p, IT; Najlaa Rauf, v-p, people & culture; Helen Yuan, v-p, fin.; Cody Zaitsoff, v-p & gen. mgr., U.S.; Philip R. (Phil) Lefko, chief legal counsel

Capital Stock

	Authorized (shs.)	Outstanding (shs.)[1]
Common	unlimited	91,036,613

[1] At Apr. 14, 2023

Major Shareholder - Jason Sparaga, Erix Waxman and Andrew Clark held 41.24% interest at Apr. 14, 2023.

Price Range - SPG/TSX

Year	Volume	High	Low	Close
2022	8,939,867	$1.51	$0.40	$0.48
2021	17,014,495	$2.89	$1.20	$1.25
2020	6,650,938	$2.25	$1.00	$1.45
2019	3,595,606	$2.60	$0.90	$1.20
2018	1,489,016	$3.40	$2.40	$2.50

Recent Close: $0.50

Capital Stock Changes - In January 2022, 24,674,133 common shares were issued at $1.20 per share pursuant to a rights offering and private placement of 8,333,333 common share was completed at $1.20 per share. Also during 2022, 551,434 common shares were issued under restricted share unit plan.

Wholly Owned Subsidiaries

Spark Power Corp., Oakville, Ont.
- 100% int. in **Spark Power Services Corp.**, Ont.
  - 100% int. in **Lizco Sales & Rental Group Inc.**, Ont.
  - 100% int. in **Orbis Engineering Field Services Ltd.**, Edmonton, Alta.
  - 100% int. in **Spark Power High Voltage Services Inc.**, Ont.
  - 100% int. in **Spark Power Low Voltage Services Inc.**, Ont.
  - 100% int. in **Spark Power Renewables Canada Inc.**, Ont.
  - 100% int. in **3-Phase Electrical Ltd.**, Winnipeg, Man.
  - 100% int. in **2552095 Ontario Inc.**, Ont.
- 100% int. in **Spark Power Solutions Inc.**, Ont.
  - 100% int. in **Canadian REC Wholesale Inc.**, Ont.
  - 100% int. in **New Electric Holdings Inc.**, Ont.
  - 100% int. in **Spark Solar Management Inc.**, Ont.
  - 100% int. in **Spark Solar Services Corp.**, Ont.
- 100% int. in **Spark Power (USA) Corp.**, United States.
  - 100% int. in **Spark Power, LLC**, Calif.
  - 100% int. in **Spark Power (Midwest USA) Corp.**, United States.
  - 100% int. in **Spark Power (Northeast USA) Corp.**, United States.
  - 100% int. in **Spark Power (Southeast USA) Corp.**, Del.
  - 100% int. in **Spark Power (Southwest USA) Corp.**, United States.
    - 100% int. in **Spark Power Renewables (USA) Inc.**, Del.

Note: The preceding list includes only the major related companies in which interests are held.

Financial Statistics

Periods ended:	12m Dec. 31/22[A]		12m Dec. 31/21[oA]
	$000s	%Chg	$000s
Operating revenue	**272,277**	**+11**	**244,624**
Cost of sales	204,602		187,811
General & admin expense	48,171		47,991
Operating expense	**177,256**	**-25**	**235,802**
Operating income	**95,021**	**+977**	**8,822**
Deprec., depl. & amort	20,641		19,443
Finance costs, gross	8,423		7,126
Write-downs/write-offs	(1,500)		(4,000)
Pre-tax income	**(15,639)**	**n.a.**	**(28,703)**
Income taxes	(4,640)		(2,180)
Net inc. bef. disc. opers	**(10,999)**	**n.a.**	**(26,523)**
Income from disc. opers	18,804		5,230
Net income	**7,805**	**n.a.**	**(21,293)**
Inventories	8,365		8,167
Accounts receivable	67,995		63,510
Current assets	114,273		103,384
Fixed assets, net	48,424		33,272
Intangibles, net	49,794		67,079
Total assets	**218,776**	**+4**	**210,885**
Bank indebtedness	24,921		28,142
Accts. pay. & accr. liabs	44,174		54,730
Current liabilities	92,281		172,256
Long-term debt, gross	35,602		72,700
Long-term debt, net	28,602		nil
Long-term lease liabilities	27,475		13,984
Shareholders' equity	70,418		23,549
Cash from oper. activs	**(12,006)**	**n.a.**	**9,074**
Cash from fin. activs	(9,383)		(3,475)
Cash from invest. activs	21,389		(5,599)
Capital expenditures	(4,548)		(5,599)
	$		$
Earns. per sh. bef disc opers*	(0.12)		(0.47)
Earnings per share*	0.09		(0.38)
Cash flow per share*	(0.13)		0.16
	shs		shs
No. of shs. o/s*	90,493,135		56,934,235
Avg. no. of shs. o/s*	89,560,957		56,564,958
	%		%
Net profit margin	(4.04)		(10.84)
Return on equity	(23.41)		(87.10)
Return on assets	(2.36)		(9.65)
No. of employees (FTEs)	1,212		1,377

* Common

[o] Restated

[A] Reported in accordance with IFRS

Latest Results

Periods ended:	3m Mar. 31/23[A]		3m Mar. 31/22[oA]
	$000s	%Chg	$000s
Operating revenue	65,809	-1	66,225
Net income	(2,344)	n.a.	(5,070)
	$		$
Earnings per share*	(0.03)		(0.05)

* Common

[o] Restated

[A] Reported in accordance with IFRS

Historical Summary
(as originally stated)

Fiscal Year	Oper. Rev.	Net Inc. Bef. Disc.	EPS*
	$000s	$000s	$
2022[A]	272,277	(10,999)	(0.12)
2021[A]	255,815	(20,818)	(0.37)
2020[A]	228,153	(1,679)	(0.03)
2019[A]	188,591	1,176	0.03
2018[A1]	119,759	(64,635)	(1.44)

* Common

[A] Reported in accordance with IFRS

[1] Results reflect the Aug. 31, 2018, Qualifying Acquisition of Spark Power Corp.

S.88 Sparta Capital Ltd.

Symbol - SAY **Exchange** - TSX-VEN **CUSIP** - 846905
Head Office - Dome Tower, 1600-333 7 Ave SW, Calgary, AB, T2P 2Z1 **Telephone** - (587) 400-2730 **Toll-free** - (855) 539-9146
Website - www.spartagroup.ca
Email - jobireck@spartacapital.com
Investor Relations - John O'Bireck (905) 751-8004
Auditors - Zeifmans LLP C.A., Toronto, Ont.
Transfer Agents - TSX Trust Company, Toronto, Ont.

Profile - (Alta. 1988) Holds investments in companies focusing on capturing lost waste energy, converting existing waste for other uses and into new consumable forms, and optimizing energy efficiencies.

Has three divisions under the Sparta Group™ brand: Sparta Energy; Sparta Environmental; and Sparta Innovation.

The **Sparta Energy** division focuses on upcycling lost or wasted energy and includes peak power mitigation systems through energy storage technology which eliminates black-out and brown-out conditions while significantly reducing global adjustment charges; power-factor and harmonic mitigation that brings plant voltages and currents back in sync while cleaning the electronic power systems; LED lighting retrofits which cuts consumption by 60% to 80%; photoluminescent safety products that provide required safety lighting systems with zero energy costs; and Internet of Things monitoring systems that can measure, monitor and optimize various energy systems in commercial and manufacturing facilities.

The **Sparta Environmental** division includes investments in **Re-ECO Tech Conversion Technologies Ltd.**, which focuses on sequestering carbon dioxide emissions through waste diversion and converting biomass waste into consumables; **Re-ECO Tech Electronic Conversions Ltd.**, which focuses on upcycling end-of-life electronic components resulting from increasing rate of change in electronic technology; and **Picton Heights Ltd.**, which utilizes earnings and implements the technologies from other business units into environmentally responsible community developments.

The **Sparta Innovation** division focuses on developing green initiatives related to transportation sector and storage technology. The segment includes TruckSuite Canada™, which offers fleet owners or operators comprehensive maintenance including roadside emergency assistance, emergency repair, complete warranty coverage and TreeFrog Transportation Optimization System™, an integrated vehicle health and safety management system that presents vital information in an easy-to-understand format saving both time and money; and Sparta Health Group, which provides a more streamlined process for accessing personal protective equipment and has expanded to help bring solutions developed within the TruckSuite Canada™ division to additional market verticals. Also includes minority investment in **SBL Testing Technologies™ (USA) Inc.**, a provider of on-site rapid testing technologies and support tools that help employers manage risk and maintain worker safety.

Predecessor Detail - Name changed from Mac-Mel Financial Corporation Inc., June 6, 1996.

Directors - Peter Quattrociocchi, chr. & CEO, Beaumaris, Ont.; John O'Bireck, pres. & chief tech. officer, Aurora, Ont.; Shawn Leon, Toronto, Ont.; Martin Marshall, Toronto, Ont.

Other Exec. Officers - Alyn D. Patterson, CFO; Revett Eldred, v-p, mktg. & bus. devel.

Capital Stock

	Authorized (shs.)	Outstanding (shs.)[1]
Preferred	50,000,000	nil
Common	unlimited	234,153,923
Special non-voting	unlimited	nil

[1] At Mar. 31, 2023

Major Shareholder - Widely held at Nov. 23, 2020.

Price Range - SAY/TSX-VEN

Year	Volume	High	Low	Close
2022	36,526,392	$0.06	$0.02	$0.03
2021	307,414,151	$0.31	$0.04	$0.05
2020	61,941,636	$0.13	$0.01	$0.04
2019	14,816,477	$0.06	$0.02	$0.04
2018	10,075,731	$0.18	$0.04	$0.06

Recent Close: $0.03

Capital Stock Changes - During fiscal 2022, common shares were issued as follows: 1,100,000 on exercise of options and 1,000,000 on exercise of warrants.

Wholly Owned Subsidiaries

Newport Environmental Technologies Ltd., Wyo. Inactive.
Sparta Technologies 4 Mining Ltd., Canada.
SuperNova Performance Technologies Ltd., Ont.

Subsidiaries

51% int. in **Illumineris Inc.**

Investments

10% int. in **Illumineris Power Systems Ltd.**
9% int. in **Picton Heights Ltd.**, Toronto, Ont.
20% int. in **Re-ECO Tech Electronic Conversions Ltd.**, Toronto, Ont.
10% int. in **Sparta Health Group Ltd.**

Financial Statistics

Periods ended:	12m Sept. 30/22[A]		12m Sept. 30/21[A]
	$000s	%Chg	$000s
Operating revenue	**5,975**	**+15**	**5,190**
Salaries & benefits	1,809		1,477
General & admin expense	4,482		3,099
Stock-based compensation	22		315
Operating expense	**6,312**	**+29**	**4,891**
Operating income	**(337)**	**n.a.**	**299**
Deprec., depl. & amort.	435		417
Finance costs, gross	194		191
Write-downs/write-offs	(522)		(195)
Pre-tax income	**(1,548)**	**n.a.**	**(629)**
Income taxes	(27)		27
Net income	**(1,521)**	**n.a.**	**(657)**
Net inc. for equity hldrs	**(970)**	**n.a.**	**(609)**
Net inc. for non-cont. int.	**(551)**	**n.a.**	**(47)**
Cash & equivalent	541		845
Inventories	8		35
Accounts receivable	511		880
Current assets	1,176		1,799
Fixed assets, net	136		201
Right-of-use assets	619		869
Total assets	**2,026**	**-34**	**3,064**
Bank indebtedness	2,197		1,788
Accts. pay. & accr. liabs	694		627
Current liabilities	3,313		2,820
Long-term debt, gross	245		125
Long-term debt, net	245		125
Long-term lease liabilities	221		531
Shareholders' equity	(973)		(182)
Non-controlling interest	(780)		(229)
Cash from oper. activs	**(515)**	**n.a.**	**210**
Cash from fin. activs	201		37
Cash from invest. activs	11		(15)
Net cash position	**541**	**-36**	**845**
Capital expenditures	nil		(15)
Capital disposals	11		nil
	$		$
Earnings per share*	(0.00)		(0.00)
Cash flow per share*	(0.00)		0.00
	shs		shs
No. of shs. o/s*	213,720,590		211,620,590
Avg. no. of shs. o/s*	213,266,744		206,964,289
	%		%
Net profit margin	(25.46)		(12.66)
Return on equity	n.m.		n.m.
Return on assets	(52.27)		(15.03)

* Common
[A] Reported in accordance with IFRS

Latest Results

Periods ended:	6m Mar. 31/23[A]		6m Mar. 31/22[A]
	$000s	%Chg	$000s
Operating revenue	4,853	+64	2,953
Net income	213	n.a.	(368)
Net inc. for equity hldrs	(163)	n.a.	(240)
Net inc. for non-cont. int.	376		(127)
	$		$
Earnings per share*	0.00		(0.00)

* Common
[A] Reported in accordance with IFRS

Historical Summary
(as originally stated)

Fiscal Year	Oper. Rev.	Net Inc. Bef. Disc.	EPS*
	$000s	$000s	$
2022[A]	5,975	(1,521)	(0.01)
2021[A]	5,190	(657)	(0.00)
2020[A]	5,277	(836)	(0.01)
2019[A]	11,011	(846)	(0.01)
2018[A]	11,331	(2,181)	(0.01)

* Common
[A] Reported in accordance with IFRS

S.89 Sparton Resources Inc.

Symbol - SRI **Exchange** - TSX-VEN **CUSIP** - 847243
Head Office - Unit 216, 81A Front St E, Toronto, ON, M5E 1Z7 **Telephone** - (647) 344-7734
Website - www.spartonres.ca
Email - info@spartonres.ca
Investor Relations - A. Lee Barker (647) 344-7734
Auditors - NVS Chartered Accountants Professional Corporation C.A., Markham, Ont.
Lawyers - Beach, Hepburn LLP, Toronto, Ont.
Transfer Agents - TSX Trust Company, Toronto, Ont.

Profile - (Ont. 1982) Has mineral interests in Quebec and Ontario, a gas interest in Nova Scotia, a contract drilling business in Canada, and an interest in a vanadium flow battery manufacturer.

In Quebec, holds Bruell gold prospect, 51 claims, Vauquelin twp., 75% optioned to **Eldorado Gold Corporation**.

In Ontario, holds Sir Harry Oakes gold prospect, 736 hectares, Matachewan area; and option to acquire Pense polymetallic prospect, 865 hectares, 25 km east of Englehart.

In Nova Scotia, holds 6.5% working interest in Chebucto gas field, 40 km southeast of Sable Island, carried at nominal value.

In addition, wholly owned **EDCOR Drilling Services Inc.** provides contract drilling services; and subsidiary **VanSpar Mining Inc.** (87.46% owned) holds 9.8% interest in **VRB Energy Inc.**, a manufacturer of vanadium redox battery (VRB) systems with a factory in Tongzhou (Beijing), PRC. VRB systems are used for energy storage related to clean renewable electricity generation.

Directors - A. Lee Barker, pres. & CEO, Whitby, Ont.; Denise Cummings-Luckie; G. Wesley (Wes) Roberts, Toronto, Ont.; Richard D. (Rick) Williams, Uxbridge, Ont.

Other Exec. Officers - Yongbiao (Winfield) Ding, CFO

Capital Stock

	Authorized (shs.)	Outstanding (shs.)[1]
Common	unlimited	148,341,537

[1] At May 29, 2023

Major Shareholder - Widely held at May 15, 2023.

Price Range - SRI/TSX-VEN

Year	Volume	High	Low	Close
2022	28,942,413	$0.12	$0.05	$0.06
2021	237,275,692	$0.21	$0.04	$0.07
2020	29,510,219	$0.08	$0.02	$0.05
2019	17,832,062	$0.08	$0.02	$0.03
2018	45,956,250	$0.12	$0.04	$0.05

Recent Close: $0.03

Capital Stock Changes - In December 2022, private placement of 1,100,000 flow-through units (1 common share & ½ warrant) at 8¢ per unit was completed. Also during 2022, 300,000 common shares were issued on acquisition of mineral property.

Wholly Owned Subsidiaries

EDCOR Drilling Services Inc., Canada.
Sparton International Holdings Inc., British Virgin Islands.
- 90% int. in **VanSpar Mining Inc.**, British Virgin Islands.
  - 9.8% int. in **VRB Energy Inc.**, Vancouver, B.C.

Financial Statistics

Periods ended:	12m Dec. 31/22[A]		12m Dec. 31/21[A]
	$000s	%Chg	$000s
Operating revenue	**1,142**	**+142**	**471**
Cost of sales	809		415
Exploration expense	350		122
General & admin expense	195		171
Stock-based compensation	112		87
Operating expense	**1,466**	**+85**	**794**
Operating income	**(324)**	**n.a.**	**(323)**
Deprec., depl. & amort.	22		9
Finance costs, gross	5		11
Investment income	(5)		7
Pre-tax income	**(356)**	**n.a.**	**(360)**
Income taxes	(2)		nil
Net income	**(353)**	**n.a.**	**(360)**
Cash & equivalent	85		246
Accounts receivable	162		123
Current assets	259		379
Long-term investments	1,587		1,494
Fixed assets, net	97		51
Total assets	**1,943**	**+1**	**1,923**
Accts. pay. & accr. liabs	149		91
Current liabilities	615		553
Long-term debt, gross	224		241
Shareholders' equity	978		1,025
Non-controlling interest	351		345
Cash from oper. activs	**(155)**	**n.a.**	**(296)**
Cash from fin. activs	68		479
Cash from invest. activs	(69)		(49)
Net cash position	**81**	**-66**	**236**
Capital expenditures	(68)		(49)
	$		$
Earnings per share*	(0.00)		(0.00)
Cash flow per share*	(0.00)		(0.00)
	shs		shs
No. of shs. o/s*	148,341,537		146,941,537
Avg. no. of shs. o/s*	147,039,071		142,965,924
	%		%
Net profit margin	(30.91)		(76.43)
Return on equity	(35.25)		(43.24)
Return on assets	(18.00)		(19.74)

* Common
[A] Reported in accordance with IFRS

Latest Results

Periods ended:	3m Mar. 31/23[A]		3m Mar. 31/22[A]
	$000s	%Chg	$000s
Operating revenue	nil	n.a.	267
Net income	(98)	n.a.	(83)
	$		$
Earnings per share*	(0.00)		(0.00)

* Common
[A] Reported in accordance with IFRS

Historical Summary
(as originally stated)

Fiscal Year	Oper. Rev.	Net Inc. Bef. Disc.	EPS*
	$000s	$000s	$
2022[A]	1,142	(353)	(0.00)
2021[A]	471	(360)	(0.00)
2020[A]	nil	(653)	(0.00)
2019[A]	47	(216)	(0.00)
2018[A]	75	(612)	(0.00)

* Common
[A] Reported in accordance with IFRS

S.90 Sparx Technology Inc.

Symbol - SPRX **Exchange** - TSX-VEN **CUSIP** - 84724T
Head Office - 1300-1500 Georgia St W, Vancouver, BC, V6G 2Z6
Website - www.sparxtechnology.com
Email - al@sparxtechnology.com
Investor Relations - Alan Thorgeirson (403) 471-3503
Auditors - MNP LLP C.A., Vancouver, B.C.
Lawyers - Cassels Brock & Blackwell LLP, Vancouver, B.C.
Transfer Agents - Endeavor Trust Corporation, Vancouver, B.C.

Profile - (B.C. 2021) Licenses its patented platform to media and entertainment companies and sports teams to engage audiences via smart phones, tablets or computers anywhere in the world, in real time.

Has designed and developed multiple interactive TV and video experiences including: live predictive gaming for sports, mobile trivia, virtual events, and Video on Demand (VoD) gamification. All are designed to engage viewers longer, drive ratings and generate new revenue streams. Has two product offerings: Sparx Studio and Predictive gaming. Sparx Studio is an all-in-one platform that allows customers to access all features including watch parties, gamification, trivia, contesting, and more. This product can be used for charity events, meetings, annual general meetings (AGMs) and conferences. Predictive gaming, its gaming platform, can be fully integrated into any media platform be it live or pre-recorded. This white label platform has been used by NBA, NHL and NFL teams and was used for the Academy Awards.

Recent Merger and Acquisition Activity

Status: completed **Revised:** Mar. 23, 2022
UPDATE: The transaction was completed. PREVIOUS: ECC Ventures 3 Corp. entered into a letter of intent for the Qualifying Transaction reverse takeover acquisition of Los Angeles, Calif.-based Sparx Technology Inc., which offers the patented Sparx platform that enables broadcasters, streamers and video producers to connect directly with consumers through sponsorship integration on both the main broadcast and second screen, for issuance of 52,800,000 post-split common shares at a deemed price of 25¢ per share (following a 1.2-for-1 share split), including the settlement of $200,000 of Sparx liabilities on the same terms. Upon completion, (old) Sparx Technology Inc. would amalgamate with ECC's wholly owned 13255841 Canada Ltd. to continue as Sparx Technology Corp., and ECC would change its name to Sparx Technology Inc. Dec. 2, 2021 - A definitive agreement was entered into.

Predecessor Detail - Name changed from ECC Ventures 3 Corp., Mar. 23, 2022, pursuant to the Qualifying Transaction reverse takeover acquisition of (old) Sparx Technology Inc. and concurrent amalgamation of (old) Sparx with wholly owned 13255841 Canada Ltd. (and continued as Sparx Technology Corp.); basis 1.2 new for 1 old sh.

Directors - Andy Batkin, exec. chr.; Brian Brady, Mich.; Drew Craig, North Vancouver, B.C.

Other Exec. Officers - Alan (Al) Thorgeirson, pres. & CEO; Spencer Trentini, CFO & corp. sec.; Alexandra Breukels, contr.

Capital Stock

	Authorized (shs.)	Outstanding (shs.)[1]
Common	unlimited	73,102,329

[1] At Oct. 28, 2022

Major Shareholder - Drew Craig held 24.02% interest, Brian Brady held 19.61% interest and Richard Hubbard held 19.61% interest at Mar. 23, 2022.

Price Range - SPRX/TSX-VEN

Year	Volume	High	Low	Close
2022	7,415,618	$0.40	$0.02	$0.02
2021	192,000	$0.11	$0.11	$0.11

Split: 1.2-for-1 split in Mar. 2022
Recent Close: $0.02

Capital Stock Changes - In March 2022, common shares were split on a 1.2-for-1 basis and 52,000,000 post-split common shares were issued pursuant to the Qualifying Transaction reverse takeover acquisition of (old) Sparx Technology Inc. In addition, 10,616,000 post-split common shares were issued without further consideration on exchange of subscription receipts sold previously by private placement at 25¢ each, 2,148,329 post-split common shares were issued on conversion of debentures shareholder loans and 1,558,000 post-split common shares were issued as finder's fee.

Wholly Owned Subsidiaries

Sparx Technology Corp., Los Angeles, Calif.
- 100% int. in **iPowow USA Inc.**, United States.

Financial Statistics

Periods ended:	12m June 30/22[A1]		12m June 30/21[oA]
	$000s	%Chg	$000s
Operating revenue	**931**	**+33**	**698**
Salaries & benefits	782		776
General & admin expense	3,740		1,075
Stock-based compensation	823		nil
Operating expense	**5,346**	**+188**	**1,859**
Operating income	**(4,415)**	**n.a.**	**(1,161)**
Deprec., depl. & amort.	1		2
Finance costs, gross	110		2,609
Pre-tax income	**(4,464)**	**n.a.**	**(3,638)**
Net income	**(4,464)**	**n.a.**	**(3,638)**
Cash & equivalent	936		101
Accounts receivable	105		46
Current assets	1,250		197
Fixed assets, net	3		2
Total assets	**1,253**	**+530**	**199**
Bank indebtedness	nil		211
Accts. pay. & accr. liabs	419		648
Current liabilities	519		1,500
Long-term debt, gross	110		463
Long-term debt, net	110		nil
Shareholders' equity	624		(1,337)
Cash from oper. activs	**(1,842)**	**n.a.**	**(1,111)**
Cash from fin. activs	2,672		1,046
Cash from invest. activs	19		(2)
Net cash position	**936**	**+827**	**101**
Capital expenditures	(3)		(2)
	$		$
Earnings per share*	(0.08)		(0.07)
Cash flow per share*	(0.03)		(0.02)
	shs		shs
No. of shs. o/s*	73,102,329		n.a.
Avg. no. of shs. o/s*	57,329,371		50,158,474
	%		%
Net profit margin	(479.48)		(521.20)
Return on equity	n.m.		n.m.
Return on assets	(599.72)		(568.51)

* Common
[o] Restated
[A] Reported in accordance with IFRS
[1] Results prior to Mar. 23, 2022, pertain to and reflect the Qualifying Transaction reverse takeover acquisition of (old) Sparx Technology Inc.

Historical Summary
(as originally stated)

Fiscal Year	Oper. Rev.	Net Inc. Bef. Disc.	EPS*
	$000s	$000s	$
2022[A]	931	(4,464)	(0.08)
2021[A]	698	(3,638)	(0.07)
2020[A]	679	(2,229)	(0.03)

* Common
[A] Reported in accordance with IFRS
Note: Adjusted throughout for 1.2-for-1 split in Mar. 2022

S.91 Spearmint Resources Inc.

Symbol - SPMT **Exchange** - CSE **CUSIP** - 847381
Head Office - 2905-700 Georgia St W, Vancouver, BC, V7Y 1K8
Telephone - (604) 646-6903 **Fax** - (604) 689-1733
Website - www.spearmintresources.ca
Email - info@spearmintresources.ca
Investor Relations - James Nelson (604) 646-6903
Auditors - Davidson & Company LLP C.A., Vancouver, B.C.
Lawyers - Clark Wilson LLP, Vancouver, B.C.
Transfer Agents - Computershare Trust Company of Canada Inc., Vancouver, B.C.

Profile - (B.C. 2009) Has mineral interests in Nevada and Quebec.

In Nevada, holds McGee lithium clay prospect, 880 acres; Elon lithium brine prospect, 280 acres; and Green Clay lithium prospect, 2,004 acres, all in Clayton Valley. At June 2022, indicated resource at McGee totaled 320,000,000 tonnes grading 803 ppm lithium.

In Quebec, holds Perron-East gold prospect, 11,608 acres, southeast of Val-Paradis; and Chibougamau vanadium prospect, 6,990 acres, Lac Chibougamau area.

During fiscal 2023, Gold Goose gold prospect in Newfoundland and Escape Lake North PGM prospect in Ontario were abandoned and related costs written off.

Predecessor Detail - Name changed from Indefinitely Capital Corp., Feb. 7, 2012, pursuant to Qualifying Transaction acquisition of Otter precious metals prospect.

Directors - James (Jim) Nelson, pres., CEO & corp. sec., Coquitlam, B.C.; Dennis Aalderink, B.C.; Negar Adam, Vancouver, B.C.; G. Franklin (Frank) Bain, Ariz.

Other Exec. Officers - Seth Kay, COO; Yangping (Cindy) Cai, CFO

Capital Stock

	Authorized (shs.)	Outstanding (shs.)[1]
Common	unlimited	261,043,583

[1] At Apr. 30, 2023

Major Shareholder - Widely held at Oct. 25, 2022.

Price Range - SPMT/CSE

Year	Volume	High	Low	Close
2022	88,313,184	$0.18	$0.04	$0.05
2021	367,463,426	$0.27	$0.05	$0.15
2020	294,304,865	$0.10	$0.01	$0.06
2019	53,178,536	$0.04	$0.01	$0.02
2018	347,539,916	$0.14	$0.02	$0.03

Recent Close: $0.05

Capital Stock Changes - During fiscal 2023, common shares were issued as follows: 2,640,000 on vesting of restricted share units, 2,000,000 on acquisition of mineral property, 1,200,000 on exercise of warrants and 250,000 on exercise of options.

Wholly Owned Subsidiaries

Mathers Lithium Corp., United States.
1177905 B.C. Ltd., Canada.

Financial Statistics

Periods ended:	12m Jan. 31/23[A]		12m Jan. 31/22[A]
	$000s	%Chg	$000s
General & admin expense	417		892
Stock-based compensation	648		867
Operating expense	**1,065**	**-39**	**1,758**
Operating income	**(1,065)**	**n.a.**	**(1,758)**
Finance income	19		8
Write-downs/write-offs	(429)		(361)
Pre-tax income	**(1,412)**	**n.a.**	**(1,914)**
Net income	**(1,412)**	**n.a.**	**(1,914)**
Cash & equivalent	933		2,330
Accounts receivable	5		34
Current assets	938		2,374
Explor./devel. properties	3,361		3,154
Total assets	**4,316**	**-22**	**5,544**
Accts. pay. & accr. liabs	62		721
Current liabilities	66		782
Shareholders' equity	4,250		4,761
Cash from oper. activs	**(482)**	**n.a.**	**(971)**
Cash from fin. activs	73		2,126
Cash from invest. activs	(988)		(787)
Net cash position	**933**	**-60**	**2,330**
Capital expenditures	(988)		(784)
	$		$
Earnings per share*	(0.01)		(0.01)
Cash flow per share*	(0.00)		(0.00)
	shs		shs
No. of shs. o/s*	261,043,583		254,953,583
Avg. no. of shs. o/s*	257,473,720		248,426,714
	%		%
Net profit margin	n.a.		n.a.
Return on equity	(31.34)		(45.23)
Return on assets	(28.64)		(40.18)

* Common
[A] Reported in accordance with IFRS

Historical Summary
(as originally stated)

Fiscal Year	Oper. Rev.	Net Inc. Bef. Disc.	EPS*
	$000s	$000s	$
2023[A]	nil	(1,412)	(0.01)
2022[A]	nil	(1,914)	(0.01)
2021[A]	nil	(779)	(0.00)
2020[A]	nil	(579)	(0.00)
2019[A]	nil	(769)	(0.01)

* Common
[A] Reported in accordance with IFRS

S.92 Spectra Products Inc.

Symbol - SSA **Exchange** - TSX-VEN **CUSIP** - 84757D
Head Office - Unit 2, 41 Horner Ave, Etobicoke, ON, M8Z 4X4
Telephone - (416) 252-2355 **Toll-free** - (888) 381-2355 **Fax** - (416) 252-2410
Website - www.spectraproducts.ca
Email - andy@spectraproducts.ca
Investor Relations - Andrew J. Malion (888) 381-2355
Auditors - AGT Partners LLP C.A., Woodbridge, Ont.
Lawyers - Miller Thomson LLP, Toronto, Ont.; Burnet, Duckworth & Palmer LLP, Calgary, Alta.
Transfer Agents - Computershare Trust Company of Canada Inc., Toronto, Ont.

Profile - (Alta. 1994) Manufactures and distributes safety and productivity products to the commercial transportation industry.

Oroduct line includes a visual brake stroke indicator called Brake Safe®, that permits vehicle drivers and maintenance personnel to visually determine the brake adjustment condition of a truck, trailer or bus equipped with an air activated brake system. an air activated brake system. The electronic version of Brake Safe® is an air brake diagnostic system called Brake Inspector®, which provides an in-cab display of air brake status and permits diagnosis of various existing and potential brake problems with the foundation brakes of trucks, trailers and buses. Additional products include Termin-8r®, an extreme pressure lubricant and penetrant use for protecting electrical vehicle charging ports and charging stations which are prone to corrosion; Zafety Lug Lock®, a device that prevents wheel-end lug nuts from loosening to avoid wheel damage or wheel loss; and Hub Alert®, a heat sensitive label which provides an early warning of critical temperature threshold levels. Also holds licensing rights to manufacture and sell the Anti-Seize Cotter Pin™, a product that keeps clevis pins from seizing in slack adjusters. A seized clevis pin can cause brake binding and loss of brake force.

Products are sold to the transportation industry through distributors, dealers and directly to fleets.

Also has a reseller agreement with Optimum Fleet Health, which offers predictive and prescriptive maintenance solution, using artificial intelligence to reduce or eliminate unplanned repairs and downtime in the transportation industry. The solution is presented to the company's existing fleet customers and dealers in North America.

Predecessor Detail - Name changed from Spectra Inc., Jan. 1, 2020, following vertical amalgamation of wholly owned Spectra Products Inc. into the company.

Directors - Andrew J. (Andy) Malion, chr., pres. & CEO, Toronto, Ont.; Aidan Bolger, Oakville, Ont.; Robert Moran

Other Exec. Officers - Ankit Bhandari, CFO

Capital Stock

	Authorized (shs.)	Outstanding (shs.)[1]
First Preferred	unlimited	nil
Second Preferred	unlimited	
Series 1	540,000	nil
Third Preferred	unlimited	nil
Fourth Preferred	unlimited	nil
Common	unlimited	14,650,895

[1] At Mar. 23, 2023

Normal Course Issuer Bid - The company plans to make normal course purchases of up to 732,545 common shares representing 5% of the total outstanding. The bid commenced on Mar. 27, 2023, and expires on Mar. 26, 2024.

Major Shareholder - B.E.S.T. Venture Opportunities Fund Inc. held 23.52% interest at Nov. 15, 2021.

Price Range - SSA/TSX-VEN

Year	Volume	High	Low	Close
2022	3,018,118	$0.25	$0.13	$0.18
2021	4,271,620	$0.43	$0.18	$0.20
2020	2,334,114	$0.35	$0.13	$0.25
2019	2,482,027	$0.40	$0.15	$0.25
2018	3,567,968	$0.28	$0.13	$0.15

Consolidation: 1-for-5 cons. in Oct. 2022

Recent Close: $0.25

Capital Stock Changes - On Oct. 31, 2022, common shares were consolidated on a 1-for-5 basis.

Investments

AgeX Therapeutics, Inc., United States.
Foremost Lithium Resource & Technology Ltd., Vancouver, B.C. (see Survey of Mines)
ImmunoPrecise Antibodies Ltd., Victoria, B.C. (see separate coverage)
Lineage Cell Therapeutics, Inc., Calif.
The Miso Brothers, Inc., United States.
SuperBuzz Inc., Toronto, Ont. (see separate coverage)
Unity Biotechnology, Inc.

Financial Statistics

Periods ended:	12m Dec. 31/21[A]		12m Dec. 31/20[A]
	$000s	%Chg	$000s
Operating revenue	**1,693**	**+6**	**1,594**
Cost of sales	738		675
General & admin expense	522		399
Operating expense	**1,261**	**+17**	**1,074**
Operating income	**432**	**-17**	**520**
Deprec., depl. & amort.	39		27
Finance costs, gross	6		7
Pre-tax income	**388**	**-20**	**487**
Income taxes	125		131
Net income	**262**	**-26**	**355**
Cash & equivalent	1,208		1,083
Inventories	177		156
Accounts receivable	247		170
Current assets	1,655		1,413
Fixed assets, net	nil		13
Right-of-use assets	156		183
Total assets	**2,064**	**+6**	**1,948**
Accts. pay. & accr. liabs	124		83
Current liabilities	149		107
Long-term lease liabilities	151		176
Shareholders' equity	1,763		1,665
Cash from oper. activs	**435**	**-17**	**521**
Cash from fin. activs	(24)		(29)
Cash from invest. activs	(103)		(53)
Net cash position	**878**	**+54**	**570**
	$		$
Earnings per share*	0.02		0.05
Cash flow per share*	0.03		0.03
	shs		shs
No. of shs. o/s*	15,421,994		15,421,994
Avg. no. of shs. o/s*	15,421,994		15,421,994
	%		%
Net profit margin	15.48		22.27
Return on equity	15.29		26.04
Return on assets	13.26		21.31
Foreign sales percent	53		48

* Common
[A] Reported in accordance with IFRS

Latest Results

Periods ended:	3m Mar. 31/22[A]		3m Mar. 31/21[A]
	$000s	%Chg	$000s
Operating revenue	357	-27	490
Net income	32	-45	58
	$		$
Earnings per share*	0.00		0.00

* Common
[A] Reported in accordance with IFRS

Historical Summary
(as originally stated)

Fiscal Year	Oper. Rev. $000s	Net Inc. Bef. Disc. $000s	EPS* $
2021[A]	1,693	262	0.02
2020[A]	1,594	355	0.05
2019[A]	2,036	873	0.05
2018[A]	2,046	495	0.05
2017[A]	1,781	223	0.01

* Common
[A] Reported in accordance with IFRS
Note: Adjusted throughout for 1-for-5 cons. in Oct. 2022

S.93 Spectral Medical Inc.

Symbol - EDT **Exchange -** TSX **CUSIP -** 847577
Head Office - 2-135 The West Mall, Toronto, ON, M9C 1C2 **Telephone** - (416) 626-3233 **Toll-free -** (888) 426-4264 **Fax -** (416) 626-7383
Website - www.spectraldx.com
Email - bmcinnis@spectraldx.com
Investor Relations - Blair McInnis (416) 626-3233
Auditors - PricewaterhouseCoopers LLP C.A., Oakville, Ont.
Lawyers - Stikeman Elliott LLP, Toronto, Ont.
Transfer Agents - Computershare Trust Company of Canada Inc., Toronto, Ont.
Employees - 32 at Dec. 31, 2022

Profile - (Ont. 1991) Developing Toraymyxin™, a therapeutic device for the treatment of septic shock, utilizing EAA™, the company's FDA approved rapid diagnostic test for the early identification of sepsis. Also manufactures and sells certain proprietary reagents.

Has developed Endotoxin Activity Assay (EAA™), a rapid in-vitro diagnostic test that measures endotoxin activity in a whole blood sample for sepsis, allowing hospital laboratories to respond quickly to the needs of intensive care units and other critical care settings. EAA™ is cleared for sale in the U.S., Canada and Europe.

Also seeking U.S. FDA approval for the treatment of patients with septic shock using Toraymyxin™ (Polymyxin B-Hemoperfusion, PMX), a therapeutic hemoperfusion device that removes endotoxin, a main trigger of sepsis, from the bloodstream. PMX is marketed worldwide including Japan, Europe and Canada, and is undergoing a Phase III clinical study in the U.S. A Breakthrough Device Designation was granted for the company's PMX device by U.S. FDA, which provide patients and health care providers with timely access to PMX by speeding up the development, assessment and review, while preserving the statutory standards for premarket approval, 510(k) clearance and De Novo marketing authorization.

Also maintains its legacy business of manufacturing and selling recombinant cardiac proteins, antibodies and calibrators sold for use in research and development as well as in products manufactured by other diagnostic companies

The EAA™ product is manufactured at the company's leased 10,500-sq.-ft. facility in Toronto, Ont.; and the PMX device is manufactured by **Toray Industries, Inc.**

In addition, holds 30% interest in **i-Dialco Inc.**, which develops and commercializes the Spectral Apheresis Machine (SAMI),a stand-alone pump for use in continuous renal replacement therapy (CRRT), therapeutic plasma exchange (TPE) as well as for hemoperfusion (HP), a modality specifically designed to facilitate patient treatment with the PMX cartridge; and an easy-to-use home hemodialysis and RRT machine, DIMI, built on the same platform as SAMI. SAMI and DIMI are approved for sale in the U.S, Canada and Europe.

In December 2022, the company entered into a joint venture agreement with **Informed S.A.**, which develops and manufactures blood purification devices, to create **i-Dialco Inc.**, a company which would focused on advancing the commercialization of Spectral Apheresis Machine (SAMI) and easy-to-use home hemodialysis and RRT machine, DIMI. Under the agreement, the company would contribute SAMI and DIMI regulatory approvals, as well as transfer its Medical Device Single Audit Program certification to i-Dialco, while Informed would contribute all hardware, software, and certain other intellectual property to further develop the SAMI and DIMI platforms. The company and Informed would own 30% and 70% interest, respectively, in i-Dialco.

Predecessor Detail - Name changed from Spectral Diagnostics Inc., Dec. 31, 2014.

Directors - Anthony P. Bihl III, chr., Ridgefield, Conn.; Chrisopher (Chris) Seto, CEO, Toronto, Ont.; Janelle (Jan) D'Alvise, Calif.; Dr. David W. Feigal Jr.; Jun Hayakawa, Tokyo, Japan; John E. Nosenzo, N.J.; William C. Stevens, Toronto, Ont.; Dr. Paul M. Walker, Toronto, Ont.

Other Exec. Officers - Blair McInnis, CFO; John Kellum, CMO; Debra (M.) Foster, v-p, clinical devel.; Samuel Amory, pres., Dialco Medical Inc.

Capital Stock

	Authorized (shs.)	Outstanding (shs.)[1]
Common	unlimited	278,547,804

[1] At May 5, 2023

Major Shareholder - Toray Industries, Inc. held 16.4% interest and Birch Hill Equity Partners Management Inc. held 13% interest at May 5, 2023.

Price Range - EDT/TSX

Year	Volume	High	Low	Close
2022	16,244,283	$0.62	$0.23	$0.37
2021	29,657,054	$0.76	$0.15	$0.22
2020	21,531,418	$0.85	$0.35	$0.41
2019	15,402,200	$0.80	$0.26	$0.72
2018	14,286,409	$0.44	$0.20	$0.29

Recent Close: $0.41

Capital Stock Changes - In November 2022, public offering of 10,061,250 units (1 common share & ½ warrant) at 40¢ per unit was completed. Also during 2022, common shares were issued as follows: 331,349 on vesting of restricted share units and 268,797 on exercise of options.

Wholly Owned Subsidiaries

Dialco Medical Inc., Ont.
- 100% int. in **Dialco Medical (US) Inc.**, Del.
  - 30% int. in **i-Dialco Inc.**, Ont.

Spectral Diagnostics (U.S.) Inc., Del. Formerly CarePoint Cardiac Corp.
Spectral Medical (US) Inc., Del.

Financial Statistics

Periods ended:	12m Dec. 31/22[A]		12m Dec. 31/21[□A]
	$000s	%Chg	$000s
Operating revenue	**1,667**	**-16**	**1,996**
Cost of goods sold	684		789
Salaries & benefits	3,767		3,009
General & admin expense	4,241		3,350
Stock-based compensation	1,197		1,259
Operating expense	**9,889**	**+18**	**8,407**
Operating income	**(8,222)**	**n.a.**	**(6,411)**
Deprec., depl. & amort.	225		246
Finance costs, gross	104		28
Write-downs/write-offs	nil		(162)
Pre-tax income	**(7,597)**	**n.a.**	**(6,959)**
Net inc. bef. disc. opers	**(7,597)**	**n.a.**	**(6,959)**
Income from disc. opers	(3,653)		(1,826)
Net income	**(11,250)**	**n.a.**	**(8,785)**
Cash & equivalent	8,414		8,890
Inventories	340		293
Accounts receivable	1,056		205
Current assets	10,086		10,263
Long-term investments	998		nil
Fixed assets, net	237		532
Right-of-use assets	464		532
Intangibles, net	211		228
Total assets	**11,996**	**+4**	**11,555**
Accts. pay. & accr. liabs	3,167		1,522
Current liabilities	3,959		2,303
Long-term debt, gross	6,129		nil
Long-term debt, net	6,129		nil
Long-term lease liabilities	420		490
Shareholders' equity	(2,523)		4,083
Cash from oper. activs	**(9,928)**	**n.a.**	**(8,701)**
Cash from fin. activs	9,485		12,165
Cash from invest. activs	(33)		(325)
Net cash position	**8,414**	**-5**	**8,890**
Capital expenditures	(33)		(483)
Capital disposals	nil		158
	$		$
Earns. per sh. bef disc opers*	(0.03)		(0.03)
Earnings per share*	(0.04)		(0.03)
Cash flow per share*	(0.04)		(0.03)
	shs		shs
No. of shs. o/s*	278,547,804		267,886,408
Avg. no. of shs. o/s*	269,843,447		252,464,462
	%		%
Net profit margin	(455.73)		(348.65)
Return on equity	n.m.		n.m.
Return on assets	(63.63)		(70.30)
Foreign sales percent	100		100
No. of employees (FTEs)	32		31

* Common
□ Restated
A Reported in accordance with IFRS

Latest Results

Periods ended:	3m Mar. 31/23[A]		3m Mar. 31/22[□A]
	$000s	%Chg	$000s
Operating revenue	530	+10	484
Net inc. bef. disc. opers	(1,734)	n.a.	(2,036)
Income from disc. opers	(43)		(649)
Net income	(1,777)	n.a.	(2,685)
	$		$
Earnings per share*	(0.01)		(0.01)

* Common
□ Restated
A Reported in accordance with IFRS

Historical Summary
(as originally stated)

Fiscal Year	Oper. Rev.	Net Inc. Bef. Disc.	EPS*
	$000s	$000s	$
2022[A]	1,667	(7,597)	(0.03)
2021[A]	2,052	(8,785)	(0.03)
2020[A]	2,101	(9,098)	(0.04)
2019[A]	2,868	(4,860)	(0.02)
2018[A]	3,840	(2,489)	(0.01)

* Common
A Reported in accordance with IFRS

S.94 Spectra7 Microsystems Inc.

Symbol - SEV **Exchange** - TSX-VEN **CUSIP** - 84761T
Head Office - 202-110 Cochrane Dr, Markham, ON, L3R 9S1
Telephone - (905) 480-9109 **Fax** - (905) 480-9484
Website - www.spectra7.com
Email - ir@spectra7.com
Investor Relations - Bonnie Tomei (669) 212-1089
Auditors - MNP LLP C.A., Toronto, Ont.
Lawyers - Aird & Berlis LLP, Toronto, Ont.
Transfer Agents - Computershare Trust Company of Canada Inc., Toronto, Ont.
Employees - 30 at May 2, 2022

Profile - (Can. 2010) Develops high performance analog semiconductors that delivers consumer connectivity at ultra-high bandwidth, speed and resolution to enable disruptive industrial design for leading electronics manufacturers in data centres, virtual reality (VR), augmented reality (AR) and other connectivity markets.

Products feature a patented signal processing technology used in the design of active cables and specialty interconnects which enable longer, thinner and lighter interconnects. The company serves data center operators and original equipment manufacturers (OEMs), both directly and through distributors, which applies the technology into data centre cables, VR, AR and consumer cables (HDMI, USB, DisplayPort). Products include VR7050, VR7100, AR-Connect™, DreamWeVR™ product line including VR8181, VR8050, VR8200 and VR8300, GaugeChanger™ product line, and USB 3.2 consumer interconnects. As at March 31, 2023, the company holds 55 patents relating to its products.

Trademarks include Spectra7, JTX, DisplayDirect, SpectraTune, Crystal Clear, Picture Perfect, Redmere, GaugeChanger, GaugeChanger Plus, DreamWeVR and HomeTheater.

The company is headquartered in San Jose, Calif., with design centre in Cork, Ireland, and a sales office in Dongguan, People's Republic of China.

Predecessor Detail - Name changed from Chrysalis Capital VIII Corporation, Feb. 5, 2013, pursuant to Qualifying Transaction reverse takeover acquisitions of Fresco Microchip Inc. (deemed acquiror) and RedMere Technology Limited; basis 1 new for 3.86364 old shs.

Directors - Ronald J. (Ron) Pasek, chr., Calif.; Raouf Halim, pres. & CEO, Calif.; Roger Maggs, Tetbury, Gloucs., United Kingdom; Christopher (Chris) Morgan, Ont.

Other Exec. Officers - Bonnie Tomei, CFO; John Mitchell, chief mktg. officer; Dr. Andrew Kim, v-p, eng. & chief technical officer; Richard M. Kimel, corp. sec.

Capital Stock

	Authorized (shs.)	Outstanding (shs.)[1]
Common	unlimited	39,827,304

[1] At May 1, 2023

Major Shareholder - Pathfinder Asset Management Limitied held 11.18% interest at May 1, 2023.

Price Range - SEV/TSX-VEN

Year	Volume	High	Low	Close
2022	4,763,551	$2.64	$0.33	$0.42
2021	11,473,961	$3.03	$1.00	$2.38
2020	4,376,773	$3.75	$0.50	$1.75
2019	1,627,704	$6.50	$0.25	$1.00
2018	1,492,152	$22.25	$3.50	$4.00

Consolidation: 1-for-50 cons. in Aug. 2021
Recent Close: $0.65

Capital Stock Changes - In March 2023, private placement of 5,990,000 units (1 common share & 1 warrant) at Cdn$1.00 per unit was completed, with warrants exercisable at Cdn$1.18 per share for five years.

During 2022, common shares were issued as follows: 607,904 under restricted share unit plan, 4,592 for debt settlement and 2,500 on exercise of options.

Wholly Owned Subsidiaries

Spectra7 Microsystems Corp., Markham, Ont.
- 100% int. in **Si Bai Ke Te (Dongguan) Electronics Trading Co. Ltd.**, Republic of China.
- 100% int. in **Spectra7 Microsystems Ltd.**, Del.

Spectra7 Microsystems (Ireland) Limited, Ireland.

Financial Statistics

Periods ended:	12m Dec. 31/22[A]		12m Dec. 31/21[A]
	US$000s	%Chg	US$000s
Operating revenue	**11,294**	**+107**	**5,461**
Cost of sales	5,544		2,256
Research & devel. expense	3,686		3,262
General & admin expense	4,245		2,746
Stock-based compensation	2,535		1,865
Operating expense	**16,010**	**+58**	**10,130**
Operating income	**(4,716)**	**n.a.**	**(4,669)**
Deprec., depl. & amort.	931		761
Finance costs, gross	1,495		1,555
Pre-tax income	**(7,257)**	**n.a.**	**(5,785)**
Income taxes	(216)		nil
Net income	**(7,041)**	**n.a.**	**(5,785)**
Cash & equivalent	772		5,944
Inventories	3,524		885
Accounts receivable	2,527		2,673
Current assets	7,748		10,957
Fixed assets, net	401		344
Right-of-use assets	80		320
Intangibles, net	70		597
Total assets	**8,307**	**-32**	**12,221**
Accts. pay. & accr. liabs	1,932		2,387
Current liabilities	2,088		8,579
Long-term debt, gross	5,640		5,947
Long-term debt, net	5,640		nil
Long-term lease liabilities	nil		87
Equity portion of conv. debs	1,514		911
Shareholders' equity	579		3,555
Cash from oper. activs	**(4,947)**	**n.a.**	**(10,330)**
Cash from fin. activs	(246)		17,341
Cash from invest. activs	(167)		(718)
Net cash position	**772**	**-87**	**5,944**
Capital expenditures	(196)		(272)
Capital disposals	nil		7
	US$		US$
Earnings per share*	(0.21)		(0.29)
Cash flow per share*	(0.15)		(0.49)
	shs		shs
No. of shs. o/s*	33,689,934		33,074,937
Avg. no. of shs. o/s*	33,463,639		21,248,369
	%		%
Net profit margin	(62.34)		(105.93)
Return on equity	(340.64)		n.m.
Return on assets	(54.47)		(64.24)
No. of employees (FTEs)	n.a.		25

* Common
A Reported in accordance with IFRS

Latest Results

Periods ended:	3m Mar. 31/23[A]		3m Mar. 31/22[A]
	US$000s	%Chg	US$000s
Operating revenue	3,134	+50	2,084
Net income	(1,090)	n.a.	(2,762)
	US$		US$
Earnings per share*	(0.03)		(0.08)

* Common
A Reported in accordance with IFRS

Historical Summary
(as originally stated)

Fiscal Year	Oper. Rev.	Net Inc. Bef. Disc.	EPS*
	US$000s	US$000s	US$
2022[A]	11,294	(7,041)	(0.21)
2021[A]	5,461	(5,785)	(0.29)
2020[A]	1,031	(6,158)	(0.50)
2019[A]	4,645	(11,042)	(2.00)
2018[A]	4,221	(15,189)	(4.00)

* Common
A Reported in accordance with IFRS
Note: Adjusted throughout for 1-for-50 cons. in Aug. 2021

S.95 Spectre Capital Corp.

Symbol - SOO.P **Exchange** - TSX-VEN **CUSIP** - 84763J
Head Office - 1000-409 Granville St, Vancouver, BC, V6C 1T2
Telephone - (604) 602-0001
Email - gb@harmonycs.ca
Investor Relations - Geoffrey Balderson (604) 602-0001
Auditors - Crowe MacKay LLP C.A., Vancouver, B.C.
Transfer Agents - Odyssey Trust Company, Vancouver, B.C.
Profile - (B.C. 2018) Capital Pool Company.

Recent Merger and Acquisition Activity

Status: terminated **Revised:** Mar. 25, 2022
UPDATE: The transaction was terminated. PREVIOUS: Spectre Capital Corp. entered into a letter of intent for the Qualifying Transaction reverse takeover acquisition of private Vancouver, B.C.-based Hemptown Organics Corp., which manufactures cannabinoid-based products from

a cultivation facility in Oregon, on a share-for-share basis (following a 1-for-2.5 share consolidation). In addition, Spectre would create a new class of class A shares that would be exchanged for Hemptown's class A shares. May 27, 2021 - Hemptown announced a private placement of up to 8,823,530 subscription receipts at 85¢ per receipt; each subscription receipt would automatically convert into 1 Spectre post-consolidation common share upon completion of the transaction. Jan. 25, 2022 - Terms of a definitive agreement continued to be negotiated.

Directors - Geoffrey (Geoff) Balderson, pres., CEO, CFO & corp. sec., Vancouver, B.C.; Stephen R. Gatensbury, Vancouver, B.C.; Robert W. Shewchuk, Calgary, Alta.

Capital Stock

	Authorized (shs.)	Outstanding (shs.)[1]
Common	unlimited	7,160,001

[1] At Jan. 25, 2022

Major Shareholder - Geoffrey (Geoff) Balderson held 17.88% interest and Robert W. Shewchuk held 13.97% interest at Feb. 21, 2020.

Price Range - SOO.P/TSX-VEN

Year	Volume	High	Low	Close
2022	763,750	$0.21	$0.05	$0.21
2020	615,500	$0.40	$0.09	$0.40

Recent Close: $0.13

S.96 Spetz Inc.

Symbol - SPTZ **Exchange** - CSE **CUSIP** - 848403
Head Office - Unit 1A, 200 Cochrane Dr, Markham, ON, L3R 8E7
Telephone - (416) 312-9698
Website - www.spetz.app
Email - ofir@spetz.app
Investor Relations - Ofir Friedman
Auditors - Clearhouse LLP C.A., Mississauga, Ont.
Transfer Agents - Marrelli Trust Company Limited

Profile - (Ont. 1998) Operates Spetz, a mobile application marketplace platform that connects consumers to nearby rated service providers in around 30 seconds.

Spetz marketplace platform has more than 400 job categories to choose from. Users can be connected with a specialist in their area immediately or at any scheduled time. The app is available in the United States, United Kingdom, Australia and Israel.

Also has legacy cryptocurrency-related operations. Through wholly owned **DataNavee Corporation** (DNV) provides "predictive analytics as a service" solutions to companies in variety of industries including retail, healthcare and financial services and through wholly owned **DigiMax Capital Corp.** offers clients with experienced international consultants who can help companies change or improve their business plan, and to seek new business partnerships that can enhance the value of their businesses prior to raising capital. As a registered broker dealer in Ontario (referred to an Exempt market Dealer), assists companies in attracting accredited investors in Ontario, and through its global network of other registered broker dealers, from around the world.

AI-based products include Projected Personality Interpreter, a platform which assesses personality traits of existing and potential employees and CryptoHawk.Ai, a subscription-based information tool that determines when price trend changes are likely to occur for Bitcoin and Ethereum.

Recent Merger and Acquisition Activity

Status: completed **Revised:** Aug. 17, 2022
UPDATE: The transaction was completed. DigiMax plan to shift in focus to Spetz app from cryptocurrency-related activities. PREVIOUS: DigiMax Global Inc. agreed to acquire Israel-based Spetz Tech Ltd., which has developed an artificial intelligence (AI) software to operate a mobile application that connects members of the public to available, top-rated trades people, service providers and professionals in their area immediately or at any scheduled time, for issuance of 250,000,000 common shares. The mobile application has been operational in Israel for four years, the U.K. for two years and Australia for one year, and has generated more than 400,000 service calls, and has connected members of the public to almost 10,000 service providers worldwide.

Predecessor Detail - Name changed from DigiMax Global Inc., Dec. 9, 2022, following to acquisition of Spetz Tech Ltd.

Directors - Yossi Nevo, chr. & CEO, Tel Aviv, Israel; Ofir Friedman, chief mktg. officer, Rehovot, Israel; On Freund; Bhavuk Kaul; Michael J. Kron, Montréal, Qué.

Other Exec. Officers - David Bhumgara, CFO; Yoav Sivan, chief tech. officer

Capital Stock

	Authorized (shs.)	Outstanding (shs.)[1]
Common	unlimited	505,211,520

[1] At Dec. 9, 2022

Major Shareholder - Yossi Nevo held 27.88% interest at Oct. 11, 2022.

Price Range - SPTZ/CSE

Year	Volume	High	Low	Close
2022	70,562,303	$0.09	$0.02	$0.03
2021	606,970,739	$0.66	$0.07	$0.09
2020	191,903,115	$0.24	$0.01	$0.18
2019	12,596,484	$0.10	$0.02	$0.02

Recent Close: $0.01

Capital Stock Changes - In August 2022, 230,146,518 common shares were issued pursuant to the acquisition of Spetz Tech Ltd.

Wholly Owned Subsidiaries

Darwin Ecosystem LLC, Tex.
DataNavee Corporation, Markham, Ont.
DigiMax Capital Corp., Ont.
Spetz Tech Ltd., Israel.
2618249 Ontario Corp., Ont. dba DigiCrypts.

Financial Statistics

Periods ended:	12m Jan. 31/22[A]		12m Jan. 31/21[oA]
	$000s	%Chg	$000s
Operating revenue	**92**	**-67**	**279**
Research & devel. expense	321		128
General & admin expense	5,325		1,192
Stock-based compensation	4,259		621
Operating expense	**9,905**	**+410**	**1,941**
Operating income	**(9,813)**	**n.a.**	**(1,662)**
Deprec., depl. & amort.	2,293		246
Finance income	39		nil
Finance costs, gross	18		326
Write-downs/write-offs	(2,021)		nil
Pre-tax income	**(15,222)**	**n.a.**	**(2,415)**
Net inc. bef. disc. opers	**(15,222)**	**n.a.**	**(2,415)**
Income from disc. opers	(229)		239
Net income	**(15,452)**	**n.a.**	**(2,176)**
Cash & equivalent	5,342		1,242
Current assets	14,591		2,000
Right-of-use assets	96		nil
Intangibles, net	nil		3,787
Total assets	**14,687**	**+154**	**5,787**
Accts. pay. & accr. liabs	531		188
Current liabilities	681		377
Long-term debt, gross	96		nil
Long-term lease liabilities	51		nil
Shareholders' equity	13,955		5,410
Cash from oper. activs	**(4,072)**	**n.a.**	**(1,207)**
Cash from fin. activs	18,271		2,154
Cash from invest. activs	(10,100)		nil
Net cash position	**5,342**	**+330**	**1,242**
	$		$
Earnings per share*	(0.06)		(0.02)
Cash flow per share*	(0.02)		(0.01)
	shs		shs
No. of shs. o/s*	271,065,013		188,791,365
Avg. no. of shs. o/s*	262,011,013		97,096,430
	%		%
Net profit margin	n.m.		(865.59)
Return on equity	(157.21)		n.m.
Return on assets	(148.52)		(68.51)

* Common
[o] Restated
[A] Reported in accordance with IFRS

Latest Results

Periods ended:	6m July 31/22[A]		6m July 30/21[A]
	$000s	%Chg	$000s
Operating revenue	72	+50	48
Net inc. bef. disc. opers	(2,450)	n.a.	(5,001)
Income from disc. opers	nil		(50)
Net income	(2,450)	n.a.	(5,051)
	$		$
Earnings per share*	(0.01)		(0.02)

* Common
[A] Reported in accordance with IFRS

Historical Summary
(as originally stated)

Fiscal Year	Oper. Rev.	Net Inc. Bef. Disc.	EPS*
	$000s	$000s	$
2022[A]	92	(15,222)	(0.06)
2021[A]	551	(2,176)	(0.02)
2020[A]	167	(828)	(0.02)
2019[A1]	nil	(1,706)	(0.03)

* Common
[A] Reported in accordance with IFRS
[1] Results reflect the Mar. 29, 2018, reverse takeover acquisition of 2618249 Ontario Corp. (dba DigiCrypts). Figures adjusted to reflect 1-for-4 share consolidation on Dec. 27, 2018.

S.97 Sphere 3D Corporation

Symbol - ANY **Exchange** - NASDAQ **CUSIP** - 84841L
Head Office - Bldg 2, 900-895 Don Mills Rd, Toronto, ON, M3C 1W3
Telephone - (416) 749-5999 **Fax** - (905) 282-9966
Website - www.sphere3d.com
Email - kurt.kalfleisch@sphere3d.com
Investor Relations - Kurt L. Kalbfleisch (858) 495-4211
Auditors - MaloneBailey, LLP C.P.A., Houston, Tex.
Lawyers - Meretsky Law Firm, Toronto, Ont.
Transfer Agents - Continental Stock Transfer & Trust Company, New York, N.Y.; TSX Trust Company, Toronto, Ont.

Profile - (Ont. 2007) Owns and operates carbon-neutral cryptocurrency miners; and provides data management, and desktop and application virtualization solutions via hybrid cloud, cloud and on-premises implementations through its own global reseller network and professional services organization. Also provides water production and purification solutions in three island communities in Turks and Caicos.

The company commenced mining Bitcoin in January 2022. As of Sept. 30, 2022, the company operates 1,000 S19j Pros miners with a production capacity of 100 petahashes per second (PH/s).

Primary products include HVE-STACK high density server, which provides the computer and storage appliance for the data centre ideally for high performance computing, cloud computing and virtual desktop infrastructure (VDI); HVE-VELOCITY High Availability Dual Enclosure storage area network, which provides data reliability and integrity for optimal data storage, protection and recovery; HVE 3DGFX, a VDI solution which offers hardware and software technologies to provide an appliance that can handle from eight up to 128 high demand users in a single 2U appliance; HVE STAGE Server Virtaluzation platform, a purpose-built server that has been optimized for server virtualization; and HVE Vault backup and compute appliance, which is designed to handle requirements for backup and replication storage.

In addition, offers on-site service and installation, round-the-clock phone access to solutions experts, and proof of concept and architectural design services. Also through wholly owned **101250 Investments Ltd.**, holds an exclusive rights to deliver the **Rainmaker Worldwide Inc.**'s Water-as-a-Service production and purification solution to three island communities in Turks and Caicos.

In September 2021, the company entered into an agreement with **FuFu Technology Limited** (BitFuFu) whereby the company committed to purchase 60,000 Bitcoin Antminer S19j Pros for an aggregate value of US$305,700,000 through December 2022. As of June 30, 2022, the company had paid US$107,000,00 to BitFuFu. The agreement was restructured subsequently in October 2022 whereby the US$107,000,000 paid by the company would be applied to the delivery by BitFuFu of 1.7 EEH/s of S19j Pros to the company. The miners are expected to be delivered at the end of November 2022.

In June 2022, the company terminated its agreement with **NuMiner Global, Inc.** whereby the company would purchase 60,000 units of NW440 machines for the purpose of digital asset mining for a total purchase price of up US$1.7 billion, subject to certain conditions.

In April 2022, the company entered into an agreement with **Bluesphere Ventures Inc.** for the right to acquire up to 1,040,000 carbon credits over 14 months. As part of the agreement, the company issued 1,350,000 common shares.

Recent Merger and Acquisition Activity

Status: terminated **Revised:** Apr. 4, 2022
UPDATE: The transaction was terminated. PREVIOUS: Sphere 3D Corporation agreed to the reverse takeover acquisition of Las Vegas, Nev.-based Gryphon Digital Mining, Inc., which mines bitcoin using renewable energy, for issuance of 111,000,000 common shares. Upon completion, Sphere 3D would change its name to Gryphon Digital Mining, Inc. The boards of directors of both companies approved the transaction, which was expected to be completed in the third quarter of 2021.

Predecessor Detail - Name changed from T.B. Mining Ventures Inc., Dec. 21, 2012, following Qualifying Transaction amalgamation of Sphere 3D Inc. with wholly owned 8283729 Canada Inc., constituting a reverse takeover by Sphere 3D; basis 1 new for 4 old shs.

Directors - Duncan J. McEwan, chr., Ont.; Patricia Trompeter, CEO, Conn.; Vivekanand (Vic) Mahadevan†, San Diego, Calif.; David C. Danziger, Toronto, Ont.; Timothy P. (Tim) Hanley, Fla.; Susan S. Harnett, Colo.

Other Exec. Officers - Joseph L. O'Daniel, pres.; Kurt L. Kalbfleisch, sr. v-p, interim CFO & corp. sec.; Jenny C. Yeh, sr. v-p & gen. counsel
† Lead director

Capital Stock

	Authorized (shs.)	Outstanding (shs.)[1]
Preferred		
Series B	unlimited	nil
Series C	unlimited	nil
Series D	unlimited	nil
Series E	unlimited	nil
Series G	unlimited	nil
Series H	unlimited	96,000
Common	unlimited	11,038,085

[1] At June 29, 2023

Preferred - Issuable in series. Non-voting.

series H - Convertible, at the holder's option, into common shares on a 1,000-for-1 basis provided that after such conversion, together with all the common shares held by the shareholder in the aggregate would not exceed 9.99% of the company's common shares outstanding.

Common - One vote per share.

series B (old) - Were entitled to cumulative cash dividends at a rate of 8% if the company receives any cash dividends on its equity investment in **Silicon Valley Technology Partners, Inc.**, and after Nov. 13, 2020, entitled to fixed, preferential cumulative cash dividends at a rate of 8%. All held by **FBC Holdings SARL**. Redeemed on Aug. 9, 2021.

series C (old) - Were convertible into common shares at a conversion rate in effect on the date of conversion, provided that after such conversion. All held by **Overland Storage, Inc.** Redeemed on Mar. 3, 2021.

Series D (old) - Convertible into common shares at US$0.65 per share provided that after such conversion, the common shares issuable, together with all the common shares held by the shareholder in the aggregate would not exceed 9.9% of the company's common shares outstanding.

Series E (old) - Entitled to dividends at a rate of 8% per annum, payable quarterly. Convertible into common shares at a conversion price equal to the lower of 70% of the average of the three lowest weighted average price of common share during 10 trading days but not including the conversion date; and US$2; however, in no event shall the conversion price be lower than US$1 per share. Non-voting.

Series G (old) - Entitled to dividends at a rate of 8% per annum, payable quarterly. Convertible into common shares at a conversion price equal to the lower of 80% of the average of the three lowest weighted average price of common share during 10 trading days but not including the conversion date; and US$2.75; however, in no event shall the conversion price be lower than US$1 per share. Non-voting.

Major Shareholder - Widely held at Nov. 19, 2021.

Price Range - ANY/NASDAQ

Year	Volume	High	Low	Close
2022	10,184,400	US$26.67	US$1.67	US$1.96
2021	49,081,052	US$83.79	US$9.00	US$21.84
2020	1,742,605	US$38.64	US$2.31	US$10.01
2019	994,524	US$27.93	US$4.67	US$5.39
2018	4,358,075	US$169.68	US$7.39	US$21.35

Consolidation: 1-for-7 cons. in June 2023

Capital Stock Changes - On June 29, 2023, common shares were consolidated on a 1-for-7 basis.

Wholly Owned Subsidiaries

HVE Inc., Del.
Minority Equality Opportunities Acquisition, LLC, Del.
101250 Investments Ltd., Turks and Caicos Islands.
S3D Nevada Inc., Nev.
Sphere GDM Corp., Del.
Sphere 3D Inc., Mississauga, Ont.
Sphere 3D Mining Corp., Del.
Sustainable Earth Acquisition Opportunities Sponsor, LLC, Del.
V3 Systems Holdings, Inc., Del.

Financial Statistics

Periods ended:	12m Dec. 31/21[A]		12m Dec. 31/20[A]
	US$000s	%Chg	US$000s
Operating revenue	**3,720**	**-23**	**4,848**
Cost of sales	2,022		2,599
Research & devel. expense	971		1,199
General & admin expense	13,574		5,753
Stock-based compensation	366		5
Operating expense	**16,933**	**+77**	**9,556**
Operating income	**(13,213)**	**n.a.**	**(4,708)**
Deprec., depl. & amort.	5,685		971
Finance income	2,930		n.a.
Finance costs, gross	516		728
Write-downs/write-offs	(820)		(286)
Pre-tax income	**(17,304)**	**n.a.**	**(5,775)**
Income taxes	(15)		4
Net income	**(17,289)**	**n.a.**	**(5,779)**
Cash & equivalent	54,355		461
Inventories	nil		558
Accounts receivable	181		264
Current assets	78,422		2,090
Long-term investments	19,949		2,100
Intangibles, net	63,017		3,993
Total assets	**275,924**	**n.m.**	**11,833**
Bank indebtedness	nil		406
Accts. pay. & accr. liabs	4,701		3,227
Current liabilities	5,208		5,805
Long-term debt, gross	nil		2,097
Long-term debt, net	nil		672
Preferred share equity	42,350		11,769
Shareholders' equity	269,626		5,009
Cash from oper. activs	**(28,518)**	**n.a.**	**(2,582)**
Cash from fin. activs	205,105		4,896
Cash from invest. activs	(122,693)		(2,000)
Net cash position	**54,355**	**n.m.**	**461**
Capital expenditures	(102,238)		nil
	US$		US$
Earnings per share*	(4.06)		(6.86)
Cash flow per share*	(6.47)		(3.07)
	shs		shs
No. of shs. o/s*	9,080,915		1,123,884
Avg. no. of shs. o/s*	4,408,930		840,651
	%		%
Net profit margin	(464.76)		(119.20)
Return on equity	(16.16)		n.m.
Return on assets	(11.66)		(49.91)
No. of employees (FTEs)	25		32

* Common
[A] Reported in accordance with U.S. GAAP

Latest Results

Periods ended:	6m June 30/22[A]		6m June 30/21[A]
	US$000s	%Chg	US$000s
Operating revenue	3,293	+80	1,834
Net income	(55,334)	n.a.	(5,253)
	US$		US$
Earnings per share*	(5.95)		(3.08)

* Common
[A] Reported in accordance with U.S. GAAP

Historical Summary
(as originally stated)

Fiscal Year	Oper. Rev.	Net Inc. Bef. Disc.	EPS*
	US$000s	US$000s	US$
2021[A]	3,720	(17,289)	(4.06)
2020[A]	4,848	(5,779)	(6.86)
2019[A]	5,579	(4,281)	(11.13)
2018[A]	9,030	(12,686)	(53.55)
2017[A]	81,523	(26,184)	(294.56)

* Common
[A] Reported in accordance with U.S. GAAP

Note: Adjusted throughout for 1-for-7 cons. in June 2023; 1-for-8 cons. in Nov. 2018

S.98 Spin Master Corp.*

Symbol - TOY **Exchange** - TSX **CUSIP** - 848510
Head Office - 200-225 King St W, Toronto, ON, M5V 3M2 **Telephone** - (416) 364-6002 **Toll-free** - (800) 622-8339 **Fax** - (416) 364-5097
Website - www.spinmaster.com
Email - sophiab@spinmaster.com
Investor Relations - Sophia Bisoukis (416) 364-6002
Auditors - Deloitte LLP C.A., Toronto, Ont.
Lawyers - Torkin Manes LLP, Toronto, Ont.
Transfer Agents - Computershare Trust Company of Canada Inc., Toronto, Ont.
FP500 Revenue Ranking - 182
Employees - 2,400 at Dec. 31, 2022

Profile - (Ont. 2015 amalg.) Creates, designs, manufactures, licenses and markets toys, entertainment properties and digital games.

Toys - Creates, designs, manufactures, licenses, markets and sells a diversified portfolio of toys, games and products based on owned intellectual property (IP) as well as brands licensed from third parties, majority of which are entertainment companies. Product portfolio is organized into four categories: wheels and action; preschool, and dolls and interactive; activities, games and puzzles, and plush; and outdoor. Primary brands include PAW Patrol, Rubik's, Bakugan, Tech Deck, Air Hogs, Hatchimals, Kinetic Sand, Etch A Sketch, Cool Maker, Meccano, Orbeez, GUND, SwimWays, Aerobie, Coop and Kelsyus as well as licensed brands including Disney, DC, Wizarding World, Monster Jam, Supercross, League of Legends, Gabby's Dollhouse and PlayStation.

Entertainment - Creates and produces multi-platform entertainment content, stories and characters through its in-house studio in Toronto, Ont., and partnerships with outside creators. This segment has created and produced original shows, short-form series and feature films for a variety of distribution channels, including television, streaming and digital platforms, and large-screen formats. Properties include PAW Patrol, Bakugan, Sago Mini Friends, Mighty Express and Abby Hatcher.

Digital Games - Develops and markets digital games and applications for children. Studios include Sago Mini in Toronto, Ont., Toca Boca, Noid and Nordlight in Stockholm, Sweden, and Originator in San Francisco, Calif., which offer open-ended and creative games and educational play.

Products are manufactured at an owned facility in Calais, France, and at third party manufacturers in the People's Republic of China as well as in Vietnam, India and Mexico. Products are distributed in more than 100 countries, supported by sales and marketing offices located in Toronto, Ont.; Los Angeles and San Francisco, Calif.; New York, N.Y.; Bentonville, Ark.; London, U.K.; Paris, France; Amsterdam, Netherlands; Munich, Germany; Milan, Italy; Mexico City, Mexico; Warsaw, Poland; Sydney, Australia; and Hong Kong.

In April 2023, the company acquired certain intellectual property of Hungary-based games and puzzles company **Mondrian Blocks** for US$3,000,000.

During the first quarter of 2023, the company announced a planned reduction to its global workforce as well as the intention to close its manufacturing facility in Calais, France.

In November 2022, bought deal secondary offering of 1,900,000 subordinate voting shares of the company by selling shareholder Anton Rabie, a co-founder and member of the company's board of directors, was completed at Cdn$32.10 per share. The offered shares were converted from multiple voting shares on a one-for-one basis. The shares represent 6.1% of Mr. Rabie's total fully diluted share ownership in the company. Upon closing, Mr. Rabie held 28,506,873 multiple voting shares and 281,249 subordinate voting shares, representing a 39.6% voting interest. The company did not receive any proceeds from the offering.

In July 2022, the company entered into a global licensing agreement with **Sony Interactive Entertainment Inc.** (SIE) which granted the company global master toy and collectible merchandising rights to SIE's PlayStation brand and game titles, including but not limited to God of War, Horizon Zero Dawn, The Last of Us and UNCHARTED.

Recent Merger and Acquisition Activity

Status: completed **Revised:** Feb. 1, 2023
UPDATE: The transaction was completed for US$16,000,000. PREVIOUS: Spin Master Corp. agreed to acquire the HEXBUG brand, a line of creatures and playsets featuring robotic technology, from Innovation First International, Inc., for an undisclosed amount.

Status: completed **Revised:** Jan. 17, 2023
UPDATE: Spin Master acquired the intellectual property of 4D Brands for US$20,200,000. PREVIOUS: Spin Master Corp. agreed to acquire private Toronto, Ont.-based 4D Brands International Inc., which manufactures three-dimensional (3D) model construction kits, for an undisclosed amount. 4D's kits included cityscapes, well-known landmarks as well as collectibles from franchises including Star Wars, Disney, Harry Potter, Marvel Universe and DC Comics. The transaction was expected to be completed in January 2023.

Status: completed **Announced:** Aug. 8, 2022
Spin Master Corp. acquired the remaining 81.47% interest in Nordlight Games AB, a digital game studio based in Stockholm, Sweden, for US$2,500,000. Spin Master acquired 18.53% of the shares of Nordlight in August 2021.

Status: completed **Announced:** Aug. 2, 2022
Spin Master Corp. acquired intellectual property from Tulsa, Okla.-based SolidRoots, LLC, a creator of family tabletop games such as Mind the Gap and Game of Phones, for US$8,600,000 plus contingent consideration of US$2,200,000 for future royalties payable upon the achievement of key performance indicators over a five-year period.

Directors - Ronnen Harary, co-founder & chr., Toronto, Ont.; Anton Rabie, co-founder, Ont.; Ben Varadi, co-founder, exec. v-p & chief creative officer, Ont.; Dr. W. Edmund (Ed) Clark, deputy chr., Toronto, Ont.; Max Rangel, pres. & CEO, Ont.; Charles M. (Chuck) Winograd†, Toronto, Ont.; Michael Blank, Calif.; Jeffrey I. Cohen, Ont.; Reginald (Reggie) Fils-Aimé, Wash.; Kevin A. Glass, Toronto, Ont.; Dina R. Howell, Fla.; Christina Miller, N.Y.; Christi L. Strauss, Minneapolis, Minn.

Other Exec. Officers - Paul Blom, exec. v-p, global opers. & supply chain; Tara Deakin, exec. v-p & chief people officer; Christopher Harris, exec. v-p, gen. counsel & corp. sec.; Mark L. Segal, exec. v-p & CFO; Jeremy Tucker, exec. v-p & chief mktg. officer; Jason Wilson, exec. v-p & CIO; Christopher (Chris) Beardall, pres., Spin Master toys; Jennifer Dodge, pres., entertainment; Fredrik Loving, pres., digital games
† Lead director

Capital Stock

	Authorized (shs.)	Outstanding (shs.)[1]
Preferred	unlimited	nil
Multiple Vtg.	unlimited	68,700,000
Subord. Vtg.	unlimited	34,900,000

[1] At Aug. 2, 2023

Multiple Voting - Participate equally with subordinate voting shares. Convertible into subordinate voting shares on a 1-for-1 basis at the option of the holder and automatically under certain circumstances. Ten votes per share.

Subordinate Voting - One vote per share.

Options - At Dec. 31, 2022, options were outstanding to purchase 483,426 subordinate voting shares at a weighted average exercise price of Cdn$34.97 per share with a weighted average remaining life of 4.3 years.

Normal Course Issuer Bid - The company plans to make normal course purchases of up to 2,845,904 subordinate voting shares representing 10% of the public float. The bid commenced on Jan. 9, 2023, and expires on Jan. 8, 2024.

Major Shareholder - Ronnen Harary held 42.02% interest, Anton Rabie held 39.57% interest and Ben Varadi held 13.73% interest at Mar. 13, 2023.

Price Range - TOY/TSX

Year	Volume	High	Low	Close
2022	19,105,280	$51.41	$30.63	$33.32
2021	22,163,347	$54.18	$25.54	$47.94
2020	44,768,534	$40.28	$9.73	$29.01
2019	26,459,567	$46.61	$34.82	$39.54
2018	24,918,251	$61.76	$34.93	$38.39

Recent Close: $35.44

Capital Stock Changes - During 2022, 1,900,000 multiple voting shares were converted into a like number of subordinate voting shares in conjunction with a bought deal secondary offering and 500,000 subordinate voting shares were issued under long-term incentive plan.

Dividends

TOY sub vtg S.V. Ra $0.24 pa Q est. Oct. 14, 2022
$0.06**i** Oct. 14/22
i Initial Payment

Long-Term Debt - At Dec. 31, 2022, the company had no long-term debt.

Wholly Owned Subsidiaries

Spin Master Ltd., Toronto, Ont.
- 100% int. in **Spin Master Europe Holdings B.V.**, Netherlands.
  - 100% int. in **Spin Master Far East Services Limited**, Hong Kong, People's Republic of China.
  - 100% int. in **Spin Master International B.V.**, Netherlands.
  - 100% int. in **Spin Master Toys Far East Limited**, Hong Kong, People's Republic of China.
  - 100% int. in **Spin Master Toys UK Limited**, United Kingdom.
  - 100% int. in **Toca Boca AB**, Sweden.
- 100% int. in **Spin Master US Holdings, Inc.**, Del.
  - 100% int. in **Spin Master, Inc.**, Del.

Note: The preceding list includes only the major related companies in which interests are held.

Financial Statistics

Periods ended:	12m Dec. 31/22[A]		12m Dec. 31/21[◻A]
	US$000s	%Chg	US$000s
Operating revenue	**2,020,300**	**-1**	**2,042,400**
Cost of sales	873,300		900,800
Salaries & benefits	236,900		230,300
Research & devel. expense	31,100		27,400
General & admin expense	500,400		476,100
Stock-based compensation	17,600		15,300
Operating expense	**1,659,300**	**+1**	**1,649,900**
Operating income	**361,000**	**-8**	**392,500**
Deprec., depl. & amort.	68,200		111,900
Finance costs, net	2,900		10,200
Investment income	100		600
Write-downs/write-offs	(3,000)		(4,500)
Pre-tax income	**340,400**	**+30**	**262,000**
Income taxes	79,100		63,400
Net income	**261,300**	**+32**	**198,600**
Cash & equivalent	644,300		562,700
Inventories	105,100		137,400
Accounts receivable	360,500		391,200
Current assets	1,132,200		1,119,700
Long-term investments	12,700		6,300
Fixed assets, net	36,000		39,800
Right-of-use assets	62,900		65,200
Intangibles, net	446,200		400,300
Total assets	**1,792,500**	**+3**	**1,736,700**
Accts. pay. & accr. liabs	334,800		476,400
Current liabilities	424,300		561,900
Long-term lease liabilities	54,900		59,700
Shareholders' equity	1,242,500		1,052,400
Cash from oper. activs	**249,300**	**-41**	**419,100**
Cash from fin. activs	(20,300)		(18,300)
Cash from invest. activs	(109,200)		(153,200)
Net cash position	**644,300**	**+15**	**562,700**
Capital expenditures	(30,400)		(26,400)
Capital disposals	9,200		nil
	US$		US$
Earnings per share*	2.54		1.94
Cash flow per share*	2.42		4.10
Cash divd. per share*	0.12		nil
	shs		shs
No. of shs. o/s*	102,900,000		102,400,000
Avg. no. of shs. o/s*	102,900,000		102,300,000
	%		%
Net profit margin	12.93		9.72
Return on equity	22.77		20.96
Return on assets	14.81		12.90
Foreign sales percent	95		96
No. of employees (FTEs)	2,400		2,300

* M.V. & S.V.

[◻] Restated

[A] Reported in accordance with IFRS

Latest Results

Periods ended:	6m June 30/23[A]		6m June 30/22[A]
	US$000s	%Chg	US$000s
Operating revenue	692,100	-26	930,500
Net income	26,100	-80	133,700
	US$		US$
Earnings per share*	0.25		1.30

* M.V. & S.V.

[A] Reported in accordance with IFRS

Historical Summary
(as originally stated)

Fiscal Year	Oper. Rev.	Net Inc. Bef. Disc.	EPS*
	US$000s	US$000s	US$
2022[A]	2,020,300	261,300	2.54
2021[A]	2,042,400	198,600	1.94
2020[A]	1,570,600	45,500	0.45
2019[A]	1,581,600	64,300	0.63
2018[A]	1,631,537	154,904	1.52

* M.V. & S.V.

[A] Reported in accordance with IFRS

S.99 Spirit Blockchain Capital Inc.

Symbol - SPIR **Exchange** - CSE **CUSIP** - 84859H
Head Office - One Bentall Centre, 1570-505 Burrard St, Vancouver, BC, V7X 1M5 **Telephone** - (604) 757-0331
Website - spiritblockchain.com
Email - info@spiritblockchain.com
Investor Relations - Raymond O'Neill (604) 757-0331
Auditors - MNP LLP C.A., Vancouver, B.C.
Transfer Agents - Olympia Trust Company, Vancouver, B.C.
Profile - (B.C. 2021) Holds a portfolio of cryptocurrencies, primarily Bitcoin and Ethereum, and invests in other blockchain companies.

Primary business activities are: royalties and streams by lending capital to blockchain companies, with repayment of the notional and interest paid in the form of cryptocurrency assets; advisory and research services; treasury management through investment in major cryptocurrency assets with cold storage in Switzerland; and providing IT solutions to the blockchain sector in the areas of compliance, anti-money laundering, forensics and risk reporting.

Common listed on CSE, Sept. 14, 2022.

Predecessor Detail - Name changed from 1284696 B.C. Ltd., July 29, 2021, pursuant to the reverse takeover acquisition of (old) Spirit Blockchain Capital Inc. and concurrent amalgamation of (old) Spirit with wholly owned 1302186 B.C. Ltd. (and continued as Spirit Blockchain Holdings Inc.).

Directors - Erich Perroulaz, chr., pres. & interim CFO, Switzerland; Lewis Bateman, CEO, Toronto, Ont.; Raymond O'Neill, Ireland; Denis G. Silva, Burnaby, B.C.

Other Exec. Officers - Antony John Turner, COO

Capital Stock

	Authorized (shs.)	Outstanding (shs.)[1]
Common	unlimited	85,817,000

[1] At Nov. 28, 2022

Major Shareholder - Erich Perroulaz held 21.25% interest and Gabriela S. Kühne-Hunkeler held 19.81% interest at Sept. 14, 2022.

Price Range - SPIR/CSE

Year	Volume	High	Low	Close
2022	2,958,412	$0.12	$0.03	$0.03

Recent Close: $0.04

Wholly Owned Subsidiaries

Spirit Blockchain Holdings Inc., Vancouver, B.C.
- 100% int. in **Spirit Blockchain AG**, Switzerland.

Financial Statistics

Periods ended:	12m Dec. 31/21[A1]		12m Dec. 31/20[A]
	$000s	%Chg	$000s
General & admin expense	930		99
Stock-based compensation	507		nil
Operating expense	**1,438**	**n.m.**	**99**
Operating income	**(1,438)**	**n.a.**	**(99)**
Finance costs, gross	1		1
Pre-tax income	**(10,187)**	**n.a.**	**(68)**
Income taxes	1		1
Net income	**(10,188)**	**n.a.**	**(69)**
Cash & equivalent	1,324		89
Accounts receivable	9		5
Current assets	4,043		396
Total assets	**4,043**	**+921**	**396**
Accts. pay. & accr. liabs	279		33
Current liabilities	279		33
Shareholders' equity	3,765		363
Cash from oper. activs	**(668)**	**n.a.**	**(43)**
Cash from fin. activs	3,404		250
Cash from invest. activs	(2,127)		(131)
Net cash position	**685**	**+670**	**89**
	$		$
Earnings per share*	(0.18)		(0.00)
Cash flow per share*	(0.01)		(0.00)
	shs		shs
No. of shs. o/s*	85,817,000		n.a.
Avg. no. of shs. o/s*	57,384,233		36,477,350
	%		%
Net profit margin	n.a.		n.a.
Return on equity	(493.60)		n.m.
Return on assets	(458.98)		n.a.

* Common

[A] Reported in accordance with IFRS

[1] Results reflect the July 29, 2021, reverse takeover acquisition of (old) Spirit Blockchain Capital Inc.

Latest Results

Periods ended:	6m June 30/22[A]
	$000s
Net income	(2,173)
	$
Earnings per share*	(0.03)

* Common

[A] Reported in accordance with IFRS

S.100 Spitfyre Capital Inc.

Symbol - FYRE.P **Exchange** - TSX-VEN **CUSIP** - 84862K
Head Office - 1 First Canadian Place, 1600-100 King St W, Toronto, ON, M5X 1G5 **Telephone** - (905) 484-7698
Website - spitfyrecapital.com
Email - matthew@spitfyrecapital.com
Investor Relations - Matthew McMillan (905) 484-7698
Auditors - MNP LLP C.A., Toronto, Ont.
Lawyers - Gowling WLG (Canada) LLP, Toronto, Ont.
Transfer Agents - Odyssey Trust Company, Toronto, Ont.
Profile - (Ont. 2021) Capital Pool Company.

Recent Merger and Acquisition Activity

Status: pending **Announced:** June 28, 2023
Spitfyre Capital Inc. entered into a letter of intent for the Qualifying Transaction reverse takeover acquisition of private NeoTerrex Corporation for issuance of 59,744,000 common shares of Spitfyre. NeoTerrex holds rare earths and lithium prospects in Quebec, including the Mount Discovery property. Upon completion, Spitfyre would change its name to NeoTerrex Corporation.

Directors - Matthew McMillan, CEO & corp. sec., Oakville, Ont.; Simon Sokol, CFO, Toronto, Ont.; Ralph Garcea, Caledon, Ont.; Gordon A. McMillan, Oakville, Ont.; Ben Sokol, Toronto, Ont.

Capital Stock

	Authorized (shs.)	Outstanding (shs.)[1]
Common	unlimited	5,750,000

[1] At May 26, 2023

Major Shareholder - Matthew McMillan held 15.65% interest, Pasquale (Pat) DiCapo held 13.91% interest, Ralph Garcea held 13.91% interest, Bülent Z. Pakdil held 13.91% interest, Ben Sokol held 13.91% interest and Gordon A. McMillan held 13.51% interest at Nov. 11, 2022.

Price Range - FYRE.P/TSX-VEN

Year	Volume	High	Low	Close
2022	359,500	$0.27	$0.22	$0.27

Recent Close: $0.27

Capital Stock Changes - On June 22, 2022, an initial public offering of 1,250,000 common shares was completed at 20¢ per share.

S.101 SponsorsOne Inc.

Symbol - SPO **Exchange** - CSE (S) **CUSIP** - 849113
Head Office - 820-2 Campbell Dr, Uxbridge, ON, L9P 1H6 **Telephone** - (647) 400-6927
Website - www.sponsorsone.com
Email - gbartholomew@sponsorsone.com
Investor Relations - Gary Bartholomew (647) 400-6927
Auditors - Clearhouse LLP C.A., Mississauga, Ont.
Lawyers - Gardiner Roberts LLP, Toronto, Ont.
Transfer Agents - TSX Trust Company, Toronto, Ont.
Profile - (Ont. 1965) Operates a proprietary digital marketing platform and a digital currency to offer incentives and compensation to the users of social networks for engaging with and promoting brands within their social networks. Also offers a line of premium and ready to drink spirits, and builds wholesale and retail distribution channels for brands focused on craft alcohol, functional beverage and hemp sectors.

Wholly owned **MXM Nation Inc.** has developed SponsorCoin™, an e-commerce platform which integrates with social networks and enables the delivery of social media marketing campaigns. It is designed to support the exchange of goods and services between brand owners and influencers using the company's SponsorCoins digital currency. The SponsorCoins digital currency is used to compensate the influencers for interacting, engaging and creating social media content around a brand's campaign. Influencers could also earn cash commission for influencing sales through authentic content creation and engagement which is tracked through the SponsorCoin network.

Wholly owned **S1 Brands Inc.** builds wholesale and retail distribution channels for brands acting as a master distributor. S1 Brands provides sales and marketing on behalf of the brand to its network of national wholesalers and retailers, and also provides purchase order financing to assist the brand in fulfilling every order.

Wholly owned **Premiere Beverage Consortium LLC**, which focuses on the spirits market, has a line of premium and ready to drink spirits consisting of Doc Wylder's line of infused lemonades, which includes lemonade infused with vodka, lemonade infused with tequila, lemonade and berry infused with vodka and a lemonade infused with bourbon; Smithville line of premium whiskey, which includes six-year bourbon, four-year bourbon, rye whiskey and a four grain whiskey; Four Corners Vodka, which is a premium vodka made from a proprietary four-grain blend; and Riverview Gin, which is branded as a Texas gin made from a compilation of proprietary local and statewide botanicals.

Wholly owned **HS Brands Inc.** develops products for the hemp smokes marketplace focusing on launching pre-rolled smokable hemp within the U.S. and internationally. HS Brands' product line up of hemp smokes include Primero, Suede and Reign brands.

In March 2023, name change to **SponsorsOne Brands Inc.** and 1-for-30 share consolidation were proposed.

Common suspended from CSE, May 8, 2023.

Predecessor Detail - Name changed from New International Infopet Systems Ltd., Jan. 8, 2014, following the Dec. 19, 2013, reverse takeover acquisition of MXM Nation Inc.

Directors - Gary Bartholomew, exec. chr., Waterloo, Ont.; Myles Bartholomew, pres. & CEO, Waterloo, Ont.; Douglas (Doug) Beynon, Waterloo, Ont.; Witold Ostrenko, Ont.

Other Exec. Officers - Ricardo Camargo, chief brand officer; Dr. Jaidip Chatterjee, chief patent officer; Brett Johnson, chief mktg. officer; Kevin Swadish, chief revenue officer; Guy Zajonc, pres., SponsorsOne Media Inc.

Capital Stock

	Authorized (shs.)	Outstanding (shs.)[1]
Preferred	unlimited	nil
Common	unlimited	1,993,742,722

[1] At Mar. 15, 2023

Major Shareholder - Widely held at Feb. 26, 2021.

Price Range - SPO/CSE (S)

Year	Volume	High	Low	Close
2022	206,291,686	$0.01	$0.01	$0.01
2021	1,693,688,775	$0.14	$0.01	$0.01
2020	261,945,149	$0.10	$0.01	$0.01
2019	8,190,483	$0.13	$0.03	$0.07
2018	13,227,113	$0.35	$0.08	$0.09

Recent Close: $0.01

Capital Stock Changes - In February 2022, private placement of 305,202,187 common shares was completed at $0.01 per share.

Wholly Owned Subsidiaries

MXM Nation Inc., Waterloo, Ont.
S1 Brands, Inc., Del.
- 100% int. in **HS Brands Inc.**, Del.
- 100% int. in **Premier Beverage Consortium LLC**, Redondo Beach, Calif.

Verve Beverage Company

Financial Statistics

Periods ended:	12m Dec. 31/21^A		12m Dec. 31/20^A
	$000s	%Chg	$000s
Operating revenue	**256**	**n.a.**	**nil**
Cost of goods sold	273		nil
Research & devel. expense	43		4
General & admin expense	23,581		7,523
Stock-based compensation	716		1,276
Operating expense	**24,614**	**+180**	**8,803**
Operating income	**(24,358)**	**n.a.**	**(8,803)**
Deprec., depl. & amort.	47		23
Finance costs, gross	25		24
Write-downs/write-offs	(2,404)		nil
Pre-tax income	**(26,834)**	**n.a.**	**(8,638)**
Net income	**(26,834)**	**n.a.**	**(8,638)**
Cash & equivalent	4		63
Inventories	349		nil
Accounts receivable	29		nil
Current assets	498		210
Fixed assets, net	67		115
Total assets	**565**	**+74**	**324**
Bank indebtedness	740		90
Accts. pay. & accr. liabs	1,535		1,488
Current liabilities	2,326		1,679
Long-term debt, gross	50		50
Shareholders' equity	(1,761)		(1,354)
Cash from oper. activs	**(5,955)**	**n.a.**	**(368)**
Cash from fin. activs	5,896		430
Net cash position	**4**	**-94**	**63**
	$		$
Earnings per share*	(0.02)		(0.05)
Cash flow per share*	(0.00)		(0.00)
	shs		shs
No. of shs. o/s*	1,688,540,535		419,504,269
Avg. no. of shs. o/s*	1,202,089,549		169,417,260
	%		%
Net profit margin	n.m.		n.a.
Return on equity	n.m.		n.m.
Return on assets	n.m.		n.m.

* Common
^A Reported in accordance with IFRS

Latest Results

Periods ended:	3m Mar. 31/22^A		3m Mar. 31/21^A
	$000s	%Chg	$000s
Operating revenue	26	n.a.	nil
Net income	(732)	n.a.	(8,506)
	$		$
Earnings per share*	(0.00)		(0.01)

* Common
^A Reported in accordance with IFRS

Historical Summary
(as originally stated)

Fiscal Year	Oper. Rev.	Net Inc. Bef. Disc.	EPS*
	$000s	$000s	$
2021^A	256	(26,834)	(0.02)
2020^A	nil	(8,638)	(0.05)
2019^A	29	(4,124)	(0.08)
2018^A	nil	(1,198)	(0.03)
2017^A	nil	(602)	(0.02)

* Common
^A Reported in accordance with IFRS

S.102 SpotLite360 IOT Solutions, Inc.

Symbol - LITE **Exchange** - CSE **CUSIP** - 84921X
Head Office - 810-789 Pender St W, Vancouver, BC, V6C 1H2 **Telephone** - (604) 687-2038 **Fax** - (604) 687-3141
Website - www.spotlite360.com
Email - ir@spotlite360.com
Investor Relations - Tim Harvie (720) 830-6120
Auditors - Reliant CPA PC C.P.A., Newport Beach, Calif.
Transfer Agents - Endeavor Trust Corporation, Vancouver, B.C.

Profile - (B.C. 2014) Offers Spotlite360, a Software-as-a-Service (SaaS)-based asset management and supply chain execution platform for enterprise clients in the pharmaceutical, healthcare and agriculture industries, as well as provides engineering services for the agricultural/cannabis environmental space. Also provides digital marketing services for brands and businesses.

The Spotlite360 platform leverages blockchain and a broad array of Internet of Things (IoT) technologies to seamlessly track the movement of a product. The platform integrates with systems of all major stakeholders in a supply chain from stakeholders engaged in raw material production to end consumers. This enables clients to realize improved visibility, a reduction in loss and theft, increased supply chain velocity, labour efficiency, improved asset utilization and support of their global sustainability initiatives.

Through subsidiary **E3 Service Group, LLC** (51% owned), develops, designs and builds cannabis cultivation facilities, with a primary focus on optimally configuring heating, ventilation and air conditioning (HVAC) equipment to create an ideal environment for growing cannabis plants. E3 has more than 300 engineering projects in 13 states.

Through wholly owned **Back to the Digital, Inc.**, provides digital marketing services for brands and businesses including concept creation, script development, filming in-studio or on-location, and posting on social media network accounts. Services offered deliver a complete production process that creates unique and original digital content that entertains, engages and interacts with audience.

In August 2022, the company acquired private United States-based **Reti Capital Corp.** for issuance of 13,250,000 common shares at Cdn$0.08 per share. Reti has an exclusive global licence with **Encapsa Technology Ventures, Inc.** to leverage Encapsa's patented data storage technology that brings together all forms of structured and unstructured data, and makes that data searchable and available to all members of an enterprise. Upon the acquisition of Reti, the company acquired private Denver, Colo.-based **Back to the Digital, Inc.** (BTTD) for issuance of 1,000,000 common shares at Cdn$0.08 per share and US$50,000 cash, and assumed the letter of intent between Reti and BTTD. BTTD offers digital marketing services for brands and businesses including concept creation, script development, filming in-studio or on-location, and posting on social media network accounts.

Recent Merger and Acquisition Activity

Status: pending **Announced:** Dec. 7, 2022
SpotLite360 IOT Solutions, Inc. entered into a letter of intent to acquire TrackX Holdings Inc. Terms of a definitive agreement were to be finalized. SpotLite360 already holds a software licence to TrackX's supply chain technology platform for use within the healthcare, pharmaceutical and agriculture industries.

Status: completed **Revised:** Mar. 10, 2022
UPDATE: The transaction was completed. SpotLite360 acquired a 51% interest in E3. PREVIOUS: SpotLite360 IOT Solutions, Inc. entered into a letter of intent to acquire a majority interest in Thornton, Colo.-based E3 Service Group, LLC, which develops, designs and builds cannabis cultivation facilities, with a primary focus on engineering heating, ventilation and air conditioning (HVAC) equipment to optimize equipments in which cannabis plants are grown. Terms of the transaction were not disclosed. Mar. 2, 2022 - A definitive agreement was entered into. Consideration would be US$1,000,000 cash and issuance of 20,000,000 SpotLite360 common shares at a deemed price of Cdn$0.20 per share.

Predecessor Detail - Name changed from Spotlite360 Technologies, Inc., Aug. 20, 2021.

Directors - Gene E. McConnell, CFO & corp. sec., Denver, Colo.; Dr. Billy Joe Page, Castle Rock, Colo.; Dr. Eddie Shek, Sherman Oaks, Calif.

Other Exec. Officers - Tim Harvie, interim pres. & interim CEO

Capital Stock

	Authorized (shs.)	Outstanding (shs.)[1]
Preferred	unlimited	nil
Common	unlimited	115,424,850

[1] At Nov. 28, 2022

Major Shareholder - Widely held at Aug. 19, 2022.

Price Range - LITE/CSE

Year	Volume	High	Low	Close
2022	45,596,059	$0.29	$0.07	$0.10
2021	137,311,489	$1.60	$0.09	$0.09

Recent Close: $0.03

Capital Stock Changes - In February 2022, private placement of 17,640,725 units (1 common share & ½ warrant) at 10¢ per unit was completed, with warrants exercisable at 15¢ per share for three years. On Mar. 10, 2022, 20,000,000 common shares were issued pursuant to the acquisition of a 51% interest in E3 Service Group, LLC. On Aug. 25, 2022, 13,250,000 common shares were issued pursuant to the acquisition of Reti Capital Corp.

Wholly Owned Subsidiaries

Back to the Digital, Inc., Denver, Colo.
Captios, LLC, Denver, Colo.
- 100% int. in **Spotlite360, Inc.**, Del.

Reti Capital Corp., United States. Inactive.

Subsidiaries

51% int. in **E3 Service Group, LLC**, Thornton, Colo.

Financial Statistics

Periods ended:	12m Dec. 31/21^A		12m Dec. 31/20^A
	$000s	%Chg	$000s
Operating revenue	**205**	**n.a.**	**nil**
Cost of sales	149		nil
Salaries & benefits	217		nil
General & admin expense	1,912		138
Stock-based compensation	1,445		516
Operating expense	**3,723**	**+469**	**654**
Operating income	**(3,518)**	**n.a.**	**(654)**
Finance costs, gross	2		1
Pre-tax income	**(4,117)**	**n.a.**	**(670)**
Income taxes	(107)		nil
Net income	**(4,010)**	**n.a.**	**(670)**
Cash & equivalent	268		352
Accounts receivable	144		nil
Current assets	704		608
Fixed assets, net	14		nil
Intangibles, net	1,454		nil
Total assets	**7,751**	**n.m.**	**608**
Bank indebtedness	17		16
Accts. pay. & accr. liabs	762		106
Current liabilities	1,030		122
Shareholders' equity	5,830		485
Cash from oper. activs	**(2,443)**	**n.a.**	**(98)**
Cash from fin. activs	2,727		450
Cash from invest. activs	(363)		nil
Net cash position	**268**	**-24**	**352**
Capital expenditures	(16)		nil
	$		$
Earnings per share*	(0.10)		(0.04)
Cash flow per share*	(0.06)		(0.01)
	shs		shs
No. of shs. o/s*	54,813,601		20,362,864
Avg. no. of shs. o/s*	42,001,204		16,690,078
	%		%
Net profit margin	n.m.		n.a.
Return on equity	(127.00)		n.m.
Return on assets	(95.90)		n.m.

* Common
^A Reported in accordance with IFRS

Latest Results

Periods ended:	9m Sept. 30/22^A		9m Sept. 30/21^A
	$000s	%Chg	$000s
Operating revenue	13,899	n.m.	6
Net income	(2,357)	n.a.	(2,924)
	$		$
Earnings per share*	(0.01)		(0.08)

* Common
^A Reported in accordance with IFRS

Historical Summary
(as originally stated)

Fiscal Year	Oper. Rev.	Net Inc. Bef. Disc.	EPS*
	$000s	$000s	$
2021^A	205	(4,010)	(0.10)
2020^A	nil	(670)	(0.04)
2019^A	nil	(92)	(0.05)

* Common
^A Reported in accordance with IFRS

S.103 Sprott Inc.*

Symbol - SII **Exchange** - TSX **CUSIP** - 852066
Head Office - South Tower, Royal Bank Plaza, 2600-200 Bay St, PO Box 27, Toronto, ON, M5J 2J1 **Telephone** - (416) 943-8099 **Toll-free** - (855) 943-8099 **Fax** - (416) 943-6497
Website - www.sprott.com
Email - gwilliams@sprott.com
Investor Relations - Glen Williams (416) 943-4394
Auditors - KPMG LLP C.A., Toronto, Ont.
Lawyers - Stikeman Elliott LLP, Toronto, Ont.
Transfer Agents - Continental Stock Transfer & Trust Company, New York, N.Y.; TSX Trust Company, Toronto, Ont.
FP500 Revenue Ranking - 669
Employees - 173 at Dec. 31, 2022

Profile - (Ont. 2008) Provides asset management, resource financing and wealth management services in Canada and the U.S. At Dec. 31, 2022, assets under management totaled US$23.4 billion.

The company has five operating segments: Exchange-listed Products; Managed Equities; Private Strategies; Brokerage; and Corporate.

The **Exchange-listed Products** segment consists of the company's closed-ended physical trusts and exchange-traded funds (ETFs), which are both actively traded on public securities exchanges. Wholly owned **Sprott Asset Management L.P.** (SAM) manages the segment, which offers physical bullion and commodity trusts, mining ETFs, gold bullion ETFs and managed equity strategies as well as managed funds. SAM earns revenue in the form of management fees and performance fees earned through the management of the funds and managed accounts.

The **Managed Equities** segment includes alternative investment strategies, and in-house and sub-advised products of SAM; wholly owned **Resource Capital Investments Corp.** (RCIC), which manages assets for closed-ended pooled investment vehicles with remaining durations between one to two years, and open-ended limited partnerships that invest in natural resource companies; and wholly owned **Sprott Asset Management U.S.A. Inc.** (SAM U.S.A.), which provides segregated managed accounts for institutional and high-net worth clients. RCIC earns revenue in the form of management fees and carried interests and performance fees through the management of the limited partnerships; and SAM U.S.A. earns in the form of management fees and performance fees from the management of managed accounts.

The **Private Strategies** (formerly **Lending**) segment consists of wholly owned **Sprott Resource Lending Corp.** (SRLC), which provides loan facilities to, and invests in, debt instruments of companies in the natural resource sector through its lending funds; and wholly owned **Sprott Resource Streaming and Royalty Corp.** (SRSR), which provides specialized forms of capital to the natural resource sector through its streaming fund. SRLC and SRSR earn revenue in the form of management fees and finance income.

The **Brokerage** segment, through wholly owned **Sprott Capital Partners LP** (SCP), provides focused advice and capital raising services to corporate clients; and investment management and administrative services to high net worth individuals and institutions. SCP revenue streams include commissions earned on capital raising services; fees earned on advisory deals; structured fees from structured flow-through transactions; commissions from trading, private placements and underwriting; and finance income from retail accounts. This segment also includes wholly owned **Sprott Global Resource Investments Ltd.** (SGRIL), a full service U.S. brokerage firm providing personalized brokerage services to investors in the natural resource sector. SGRIL had 3,048 client accounts at Dec. 31, 2022. SGRIL earns commissions and other fees from the sale and purchase of stocks by its clients, from new and follow-on offerings of limited partnerships managed by RCIC and from the sale of private placements to its clients.

The **Corporate** includes capital, balance sheet management and shared services provided to the company's subsidiaries.

Assets under management (AUM) at Dec. 31, 2022:

Product	$AUM[1]	Percentage
Exchange-listed products:		
Physical Trusts	16,849	72%
ETFs	1,206	5%
Managed equities	2,753	12%
Private strategies	1,880	8%
Non-core AUM[2]	745	3%
	23,433	100%

[1] US$ millions.

[2] This AUM is related to wholly owned **Sprott Korea Corporation** which co-manages a 10-year private equity fund for South Korea's National Pension Service.

Subsequent to 2022, the company announced its plan to sell its Canadian broker-dealer operations to the current management team as the company continues to focus on its core asset management businesses. The company would migrate its charity flow-through operations into its managed equities segment. The transaction was expected to close by June 2023.

Recent Merger and Acquisition Activity

Status: completed **Revised:** June 29, 2023

UPDATE: The transaction was completed and restructured as a sale to Sprott of a US$150,000,000 secured note. The note, bearing interest at 6.5% prior to maturity, would be repaid at maturity by a 1% NSR on all metals produced at KSM. The note matures on the earlier of: commercial production being achieved at KSM; and either Mar. 24, 2032, or, if the environmental assessment certificate (EAC) expires and Sprott does not exercise its right to put the note to the company, Mar. 24, 2035. PREVIOUS: Seabridge Gold Inc. agreed to sell a 1.2% NSR royalty on all metals produced at its KSM gold-copper-silver-molybdenum project in British Columbia, subject to certain adjustments, to Sprott Resource Streaming and Royalty Corp., a wholly owned subsidiary of Sprott Inc., for US$150,000,000.

Status: pending **Announced:** June 12, 2023

Sprott Resource Streaming and Royalty Corp. agreed to acquire 3% NSR royalty on Talisker Resources Ltd.'s 100%-owned Bralorne gold project in British Columbia for US$18,750,000 in two payments, to fund drilling, engineering, mobilization and site infrastructure. Talisker would have option to increase the NSR royalty by a further 2% to 5% for an additional US$12,500,000, available as needed for site infrastructure, mine start-up capital and working capital. The agreement includes a 50% buy-back provision.

Status: completed **Revised:** Dec. 19, 2022

UPDATE: The transaction was completed: PREVIOUS: First Mining Gold Corp. agreed to sell its 1.5% NSR royalty on Treasury Metals Inc.'s Goldlund gold project in northwestern Ontario to Sprott Resource Streaming and Royalty Corp. for $9,500,000.

Status: completed **Revised:** Apr. 25, 2022

UPDATE: The transaction was completed for US$10,500,000 cash and issuance of 72,464 common shares valued at US$4,000,000. PREVIOUS: Sprott Inc. agreed to acquire certain assets relating to managing the North Shore Global Uranium Mining ETF (URNM) from Exchange Traded Concepts, LLC. (ETC). Terms were not disclosed. Wholly owned Sprott Asset Management LP would license from North Shore Indices, Inc. the North Shore Global Uranium Mining Index, which is tacked by URNM and URNM would be reorganized into a newly created series of the Sprott Funds Trust, the Sprott Uranium Miners ETF. The reorganization was expected to close in the first half of 2022. Nov. 22, 2021 - The board of trustees of ETC approved the transaction.

Status: completed **Revised:** Apr. 11, 2022

UPDATE: The transaction was completed. PREVIOUS: Treasury Metals Inc. agreed to sell a 2.2% NSR royalty on the Goliath Gold Complex in northwestern Ontario to Sprott Inc. for US$20,000,000. Treasury Metals has an option to buy back 50% interest based on a buy-down schedule. Upon the achievement of 1,500,000 oz. of gold production, the royalty would be reduced by 50% for no additional consideration by Treasury Metals. In addition, Treasury Metals has a one-time option to reduce the applicable NSR percentage by 50% and 50% of any remaining minimum payments. Sprott would also have a right to participate up to 40% or US$40,000,000 potential metals streaming or royalty contract entered by Treasury Metals as part of a larger project financing for the Goliath Gold Complex.

Directors - Ronald (Ron) Dewhurst, chr., Vic., Australia; Whitney George, pres. & CEO, Darien, Conn.; Dr. Graham Birch, Dorset, United Kingdom; Barbara Connolly Keady, Conn.; Judith W. O'Connell, Mass.; Catherine P. Raw, Hereford., United Kingdom

Other Exec. Officers - Eric S. Sprott, founder & chr., emeritus; Greg Caione, sr. man. partner & man. partner, private strategies; John Ciampaglia, sr. man. partner; Edward C. Coyne, sr. man. partner & head, global sales; Arthur Einav, sr. man. partner, co-head, enterprise shared srvcs. grp., gen. counsel & corp. sec.; Peter F. Grosskopf, sr. man. partner; Kevin Hibbert, sr. man. partner, CFO & co-head, enterprise shared srvcs. grp.

Capital Stock

	Authorized (shs.)	Outstanding (shs.)[1]
Common	unlimited	25,225,210

[1] At Mar. 31, 2023

Options - At Dec. 31, 2022, options were outstanding to purchase 12,500 common shares at a weighted average exercise price of Cdn$27.30 per share with a weighted average remaining contractual life of 3.4 years.

Normal Course Issuer Bid - The company plans to make normal course purchases of up to 648,908 common shares representing 2.5% of the total outstanding. The bid commenced on Mar. 3, 2023, and expires on Mar. 2, 2024.

Major Shareholder - Arthur R. (Rick) Rule IV held 10.33% interest at Feb. 23, 2023.

Price Range - SII/TSX

Year	Volume	High	Low	Close
2022	13,973,614	$71.70	$41.60	$45.04
2021	12,780,496	$59.64	$35.86	$57.08
2020	18,619,947	$57.53	$19.00	$36.96
2019	6,970,856	$39.90	$23.60	$29.80
2018	7,839,301	$36.20	$24.20	$25.70

Consolidation: 1-for-10 cons. in May 2020

Recent Close: $43.71

Capital Stock Changes - During 2022, common shares were issued as follows: 324,568 on vesting of equity incentive plan, 115,102 on exercise of options, 80,345 on vesting of restricted share units, 72,464 pursuant to acquisition of North Shore Global Uranium Mining ETF and 3,927 under dividend reinvestment program; 180,594 common shares were purchased for equity incentive plan and 81,538 common shares were repurchased under a Normal Course Issuer Bid.

Dividends

SII com Ra US$1.00 pa Q est. Dec. 8, 2020[1]

Prev. Rate: US$0.92 est. Sept. 1, 2020

[1] Divds. paid in Cdn$ prior to Sept. 2020.

Long-Term Debt - At Dec. 31, 2022, outstanding long-term debt totaled US$54,437,000 (none current) and consisted entirely of amounts drawn on credit facility due December 2025, bearing interest at prime rate or banker's acceptance rate plus 1.7% for amounts drawn in Canadian dollars and base rate for amounts drawn in U.S. dollars.

Wholly Owned Subsidiaries

Sprott Asset Management L.P., Toronto, Ont.

Sprott Canada Holdings Inc., Ont.
- 100% int. in **Sprott Capital Partners LP**, Toronto, Ont. Formerly Sprott Private Wealth LP.

Sprott Inc. 2011 Employee Profit Sharing Plan Trust

Sprott Korea Corporation, South Korea.

Sprott Private Resource Streaming and Royalty (Management) Corp.

Sprott Resource Lending Corp., Toronto, Ont. Formerly Quest Capital Corporation.

Sprott Resource Streaming and Royalty Corp., Toronto, Ont.

Sprott U.S. Holdings Inc.
- 100% int. in **Resource Capital Investments Corp.**, Carlsbad, Calif.
- 100% int. in **SGRIL Holdings Inc.**, Calif.
  - 100% int. in **Sprott Global Resource Investments Ltd.**, Carlsbad, Calif. Formerly Global Resource Investments Ltd.
- 100% int. in **Sprott Asset Management USA Inc.**, Carlsbad, Calif. Formerly Terra Resource Investment Management Inc.

Note: The preceding list includes only the major related companies in which interests are held.

Financial Statistics

Periods ended:	12m Dec. 31/22[A]	%Chg	12m Dec. 31/21[A]
	US$000s	%Chg	US$000s
Total revenue	**145,182**	**-12**	**164,645**
Salaries & benefits	60,076		73,071
General & admin. expense	15,978		14,697
Stock-based compensation	17,041		3,650
Other operating expense	10,539		9,745
Operating expense	**103,634**	**+2**	**101,163**
Operating income	**41,548**	**-35**	**63,482**
Deprec. & amort.	3,355		4,552
Finance costs, gross	2,923		1,161
Pre-tax income	**25,079**	**-45**	**45,190**
Income taxes	7,447		12,005
Net income	**17,632**	**-47**	**33,185**
Cash & equivalent	55,026		55,938
Accounts receivable	10,967		13,183
Current assets	76,963		77,527
Long-term investments	73,573		68,765
Fixed assets, net	12,496		16,479
Intangibles	197,762		189,210
Total assets	**383,748**	**+5**	**365,873**
Accts. pay. & accr. liabs	10,703		9,362
Current liabilities	25,752		28,118
Long-term debt, gross	54,437		29,769
Long-term debt, net	54,437		29,769
Shareholders' equity	277,271		291,219
Cash from oper. activs	**32,496**	**-37**	**51,246**
Cash from fin. activs	(3,897)		(24,188)
Cash from invest. activs	(23,492)		(20,634)
Net cash position	**51,678**	**+4**	**49,805**
Capital expenditures	(128)		(693)
	US$		US$
Earnings per share*	0.70		1.33
Cash flow per share*	1.30		2.06
Cash divd. per share*	1.00		1.00
	shs		shs
No. of shs. o/s*	25,325,894		24,991,620
Avg. no. of shs. o/s*	25,066,000		24,878,000
	%		%
Net profit margin	12.14		20.16
Return on equity	6.20		11.40
Return on assets	5.25		9.16
Foreign sales percent	10		11
No. of employees (FTEs)	173		173

* Common

[A] Reported in accordance with IFRS

Latest Results

Periods ended:	3m Mar. 31/23[A]	%Chg	3m Mar. 31/22[A]
	US$000s	%Chg	US$000s
Total revenue	40,606	-4	42,463
Net income	7,638	+18	6,473
	US$		US$
Earnings per share*	0.30		0.26

* Common

[A] Reported in accordance with IFRS

Historical Summary
(as originally stated)

Fiscal Year	Total Rev.	Net Inc. Bef. Disc.	EPS*
	US$000s	US$000s	US$
2022[A]	145,182	17,632	0.70
2021[A]	164,645	33,185	1.33
2020[A]	121,776	26,978	1.10
	$000s	$000s	$
2019[A]	96,201	13,532	0.60
2018[A]	109,269	31,379	1.30

* Common

[A] Reported in accordance with IFRS

Note: Adjusted throughout for 1-for-10 cons. in May 2020

S.104 Sprott Physical Gold and Silver Trust*

Symbol - CEF **Exchange** - TSX **CUSIP** - 85208R

Head Office - South Tower, Royal Bank Plaza, 2600-200 Bay St, Toronto, ON, M5J 2J1 **Telephone** - (416) 943-8099 **Toll-free** - (855) 943-8099 **Fax** - (416) 943-6497

Website - www.sprott.com

Email - gwilliams@sprott.com

Investor Relations - Glen Williams (416) 943-4394

Auditors - KPMG LLP C.A., Toronto, Ont.

Lawyers - Skadden, Arps, Slate, Meagher & Flom LLP, Toronto, Ont.; Stikeman Elliott LLP, Toronto, Ont.

Transfer Agents - TSX Trust Company, Toronto, Ont.

Trustees - RBC Investor Services Trust, Toronto, Ont.

Managers - Sprott Asset Management L.P., Toronto, Ont.

Profile - (Ont. 2017) Invests in and holds physical gold and silver bullion.

The trust will invest and hold a minimum of 90% of its net assets in physical gold and silver bullion. Gold and silver bullion will be fully allocated and stored at the **Royal Canadian Mint**. Unitholders hold option to retract trust units on a monthly basis for physical gold and silver bullion at a price equal to the net asset value per unit, less any retraction and delivery expenses.

At Apr. 28, 2023, the trust's holdings totaled 1,422,859 oz. of physical gold bullion with a market value of US$2.83 billion and 58,229,276 oz. of physical silver bullion with a market value of US$1.46 billion.

Predecessor Detail - Succeeded Central Fund of Canada Limited, Jan. 16, 2018, pursuant to plan of arrangement whereby Sprott Physical Gold and Silver Trust was formed to facilitate Sprott Inc.'s acquisition of common shares of Central Fund of Canada Limited (CFCL) and exchange of CFCL class A shares for trust units.

Oper. Subsid./Mgt. Co. Directors - John Ciampaglia, CEO, Caledon, Ont.; Whitney George, Darien, Conn.; Kevin Hibbert, Toronto, Ont.

Oper. Subsid./Mgt. Co. Officers - Varinder (Vinny) Bhathal, CFO; Lara Misner, chief compliance officer; Maria Smirnova, chief invest. officer

Capital Stock

	Authorized (shs.)	Outstanding (shs.)[1]
Trust Unit	unlimited	214,947,991

[1] At Apr. 3, 2023

Trust Unit - The trust does not intend to make regular cash distributions. Retractable monthly for cash at a price equal to 95% of the lesser of: (i) the volume-weighted average price per unit on the NYSE Arca or, if trading has been suspended, the trading price on the TSX for the last five days on which the respective exchange was open for trading for the month in which the retraction request is processed; and (ii) the net asset value (NAV) per unit on the last trading day of the month on the NYSE Arca for the month in which the retraction request is processed. Retractable monthly for physical gold and silver bullion for a price equal to 100% of the NAV per unit on the last trading day of the month on the NYSE Arca, less any retraction and delivery expenses. Retraction requests for gold and silver must be for a minimum of 100,000 trust units, provided that if 100,000 trust units is not at least equivalent to the aggregate value of (i) one London Good Delivery bar of gold, which weighs between 350 and 430 troy ounces of gold, (ii) such number of London Good Delivery bars of silver, which weighs between 750 and 1,000 troy ounces of silver, with an aggregate value that is proportionate to the aggregate value of one London Good Delivery bar of gold based on the proportionate value of physical gold bullion and silver bullion held by the trust and (iii) applicable expenses, the minimum retraction amount shall be such number of trust units as are at least equivalent to the aggregate value (i) one London Good Delivery bar of gold, (ii) such number of London Good Delivery bars of silver with an aggregate value that is proportionate to the aggregate value of one London Good Delivery bar of gold based on the proportionate value of physical gold bullion and silver bullion held by the trust, and (iii) applicable expenses. The amount of physical gold and silver bullion a unitholder is entitled to receive would be determined by the manager, who would allocate the retraction amount to physical gold and silver bullion in direct proportion to the value of physical gold and silver bullion held by the trust at the time of retraction. One vote per unit.

Major Shareholder - Widely held at Mar. 17, 2023.

Price Range - CEF/TSX

Year	Volume	High	Low	Close
2022	6,438,289	$26.32	$20.27	$24.23
2021	7,041,671	$25.75	$21.40	$22.46
2020	13,781,507	$28.60	$16.20	$24.61
2019	5,506,092	$20.60	$16.18	$19.03
2018	3,468,590	$17.52	$14.84	$17.11

CEF.A/TSX (D)

Year	Volume	High	Low	Close
2018	252,915	$17.11	$16.64	$16.90

Recent Close: $24.94

Capital Stock Changes - During 2022, 796,849 trust units were issued under an at-the-market offering program and 6,584,884 trust units were retracted.

Long-Term Debt - At Dec. 31, 2022, the trust had no long-term debt.

Financial Statistics

Periods ended:	12m Dec. 31/22^A		12m Dec. 31/21^A
	US$000s	%Chg	US$000s
Realized invest. gain (loss)	24,121		10,784
Unrealized invest. gain (loss)	(448)		(300,318)
Total revenue	**23,724**	**n.a.**	**(289,534)**
General & admin. expense	17,944		19,696
Other operating expense	1,047		1,471
Operating expense	**18,991**	**-10**	**21,167**
Operating income	**4,733**	**n.a.**	**(310,701)**
Pre-tax income	**4,727**	**n.a.**	**(310,700)**
Net income	**4,727**	**n.a.**	**(310,700)**
Cash & equivalent	3,999,515		4,094,436
Total assets	**3,999,515**	**-2**	**4,094,436**
Accts. pay. & accr. liabs	783		62
Shareholders' equity	3,998,326		4,094,374
Cash from oper. activs	**(17,819)**	**n.a.**	**(21,229)**
Cash from fin. activs	9,784		15,352
Cash from invest. activs	10,760		5,156
Net cash position	**3,404**	**+401**	**679**
	US$		US$
Earnings per share*	0.02		(1.41)
Cash flow per share*	(0.08)		(0.10)
Net asset value per share*	18.60		18.55
	shs		shs
No. of shs. o/s*	214,949,762		220,737,797
Avg. no. of shs. o/s*	217,714,815		220,847,830
	%		%
Net profit margin	19.92		n.m.
Return on equity	0.12		(7.30)
Return on assets	0.12		(7.30)

* Trust Unit

^A Reported in accordance with IFRS

Latest Results

Periods ended:	3m Mar. 31/23^A		3m Mar. 31/22^A
	US$000s	%Chg	US$000s
Total revenue	215,419	-13	246,918
Net income	210,450	-13	241,889
	US$		US$
Earnings per share*	0.98		1.10

* Trust Unit

^A Reported in accordance with IFRS

Historical Summary
(as originally stated)

Fiscal Year	Total Rev. US$000s	Net Inc. Bef. Disc. US$000s	EPS* US$
2022^A	23,724	4,727	0.02
2021^A	(289,534)	(310,700)	(1.41)
2020^A	1,026,915	1,008,043	4.81
2019^A	439,138	419,468	2.13
2018^A	(235,345)	(257,000)	(1.11)

* Trust Unit

^A Reported in accordance with IFRS

S.105 Sprott Physical Gold Trust

Symbol - PHYS **Exchange** - TSX **CUSIP** - 85207H

Head Office - c/o Sprott Asset Management Inc., South Tower, Royal Bank Plaza, 2600-200 Bay St, PO Box 27, Toronto, ON, M5J 2J1 **Telephone** - (416) 362-7172 **Toll-free** - (888) 362-7172 **Fax** - (416) 943-6497

Website - www.sprott.com

Email - gwilliams@sprott.com

Investor Relations - Glen Willams (416) 943-4394

Auditors - KPMG LLP C.A., Toronto, Ont.

Lawyers - Stikeman Elliott LLP, Toronto, Ont.; Seward & Kissel LLP, Washington, D.C.

Transfer Agents - TSX Trust Company, Toronto, Ont.

Trustees - RBC Investor Services Trust, Toronto, Ont.

Managers - Sprott Asset Management L.P., Toronto, Ont.

Profile - (Ont. 2009) Invests in and holds physical gold bullion.

The trust will invest and hold a minimum of 90% of its net assets in physical gold bullion. Gold bullion will be fully allocated and stored at the **Royal Canadian Mint**. Unitholders hold option to retract trust units on a monthly basis for physical gold bullion at a price equal to the net asset value per unit, less any retraction and delivery expenses.

At Feb. 28, 2023, the trust held a total of 3,133,593 oz. of physical gold bullion with a market value of US$5.72 billion.

Oper. Subsid./Mgt. Co. Directors - John Ciampaglia, CEO, Caledon, Ont.; Whitney George, Darien, Conn.; Kevin Hibbert, Toronto, Ont.

Oper. Subsid./Mgt. Co. Officers - Varinder (Vinny) Bhathal, CFO; Lara Misner, chief compliance officer; Maria Smirnova, chief invest. officer

Capital Stock

	Authorized (shs.)	Outstanding (shs.)[1]
Trust Unit	unlimited	397,033,885

[1] At Apr. 3, 2023

Trust Unit - The trust does not intend to make regular cash distributions. Retractable monthly for cash at a price equal to 95% of the lesser of: (i) the volume-weighted average price per unit on the NYSE Arca or, if trading has been suspended, the trading price on the TSX for the last five days on which the respective exchange was open for trading for the month in which the retraction request is processed; and (ii) the net asset value (NAV) per unit on the last trading day of the month on the NYSE Arca for the month in which the retraction request is processed. Retractable monthly for physical gold bullion for a price equal to 100% of the NAV per unit on the last trading day of the month on the NYSE Arca, less any retraction and delivery expenses. Retraction requests for gold must be for amounts that are at least equivalent in value to one London Good Delivery bar, which weighs between 350 and 430 troy ounces of gold, or an integral multiple thereof plus applicable expenses. Any fractional amount of retraction proceeds in excess of a London Good Delivery bar or an integral multiple thereof would be paid in cash at a rate equal to 100% of the NAV per unit of such excess amount. One vote per unit.

Major Shareholder - Widely held at Mar. 17, 2023.

Price Range - PHYS/TSX

Year	Volume	High	Low	Close
2022	18,323,668	$20.86	$17.01	$19.06
2021	13,866,931	$19.58	$16.71	$18.16
2020	19,712,289	$22.13	$15.65	$19.19
2019	2,905,055	$16.57	$13.55	$15.81
2018	1,088,010	$14.69	$12.19	$14.10

Recent Close: $20.31

Capital Stock Changes - During 2022, 54,043,669 trust units were issued under an at-the-market offering program and 13,719 trust units were retracted.

Financial Statistics

Periods ended:	12m Dec. 31/22^A		12m Dec. 31/21^A
	US$000s	%Chg	US$000s
Realized invest. gain (loss)	324		6,945
Unrealized invest. gain (loss)	(60,006)		(184,975)
Total revenue	**(59,645)**	**n.a.**	**(178,030)**
General & admin. expense	21,621		18,868
Other operating expense	1,193		1,096
Operating expense	**22,814**	**+14**	**19,964**
Operating income	**(82,459)**	**n.a.**	**(197,994)**
Pre-tax income	**(82,470)**	**n.a.**	**(197,994)**
Net income	**(82,470)**	**n.a.**	**(197,994)**
Cash & equivalent	294		6,982
Investments	5,745,945		5,001,081
Total assets	**5,746,239**	**+15**	**5,008,063**
Accts. pay. & accr. liabs	144		40
Shareholders' equity	5,746,095		5,008,023
Cash from oper. activs	**(22,684)**	**n.a.**	**(20,110)**
Cash from fin. activs	820,542		346,877
Cash from invest. activs	(804,546)		(324,190)
Net cash position	**294**	**-96**	**6,982**
	US$		US$
Earnings per share*	(0.21)		(0.59)
Cash flow per share*	(0.06)		(0.06)
Net asset value per share*	14.46		14.59
	shs		shs
No. of shs. o/s*	397,346,037		343,316,087
Avg. no. of shs. o/s*	385,920,497		333,582,565
	%		%
Net profit margin	n.m.		n.m.
Return on equity	(1.53)		(4.00)
Return on assets	(1.53)		(4.00)

* Trust Unit

^A Reported in accordance with IFRS

Historical Summary
(as originally stated)

Fiscal Year	Total Rev. US$000s	Net Inc. Bef. Disc. US$000s	EPS* US$
2022^A	(59,645)	(82,470)	(0.21)
2021^A	(178,030)	(197,994)	(0.59)
2020^A	763,870	747,127	2.72
2019^A	371,265	360,214	1.83
2018^A	(46,297)	(56,173)	(0.27)

* Trust Unit

^A Reported in accordance with IFRS

S.106 Sprott Physical Platinum and Palladium Trust

Symbol - SPPP **Exchange** - TSX **CUSIP** - 85207Q

Head Office - c/o Sprott Asset Management Inc., South Tower, Royal Bank Plaza, 2600-200 Bay St, PO Box 27, Toronto, ON, M5J 2J1 **Telephone** - (406) 203-2310 **Toll-free** - (877) 403-2310 **Fax** - (416) 943-6497

Website - www.sprottphysicalsilvertrust.com

Email - gwilliams@sprott.com

Investor Relations - Glen Williams (416) 943-4394

Auditors - KPMG LLP C.A., Toronto, Ont.

Lawyers - Stikeman Elliott LLP, Toronto, Ont.; Seward & Kissel LLP, Washington, D.C.

Transfer Agents - TSX Trust Company, Toronto, Ont.
Trustees - RBC Investor Services Trust, Toronto, Ont.
Managers - Sprott Asset Management L.P., Toronto, Ont.
Profile - (Ont. 2011) Invests in and holds physical platinum and palladium bullion.

The trust will invest and hold a minimum of 90% of its net assets in physical platinum and palladium bullion. Platinum and palladium bullion will be fully allocated and stored at the **Royal Canadian Mint**. Unitholders hold option to retract trust units on a monthly basis for physical platinum and palladium bullion at a price equal to the net asset value per unit, less any retraction and delivery expenses.

At Feb. 28, 2023, the trust held a total of 60,102 oz. of physical platinum bullion with a market value of US$57,460,000 and 42,800 oz. of physical palladium bullion with a market value of US$60,710,000.

Oper. Subsid./Mgt. Co. Directors - John Ciampaglia, CEO, Caledon, Ont.; Whitney George, Darien, Conn.; Kevin Hibbert, Toronto, Ont.
Oper. Subsid./Mgt. Co. Officers - Varinder (Vinny) Bhathal, CFO; Lara Misner, chief compliance officer; Maria Smirnova, chief invest. officer

Capital Stock

	Authorized (shs.)	Outstanding (shs.)[1]
Trust Unit	unlimited	9,885,942

[1] At Apr. 3, 2023

Trust Unit - The trust does not intend to make regular cash distributions. Retractable monthly for cash at a price equal to 95% of the lesser of: (i) the volume-weighted average price per unit on the NYSE Arca or, if trading has been suspended, the trading price on the TSX for the last five days on which the respective exchange was open for trading for the month in which the retraction request is processed; and (ii) the net asset value (NAV) per unit on the last trading day of the month on the NYSE Arca for the month in which the retraction request is processed. Retractable monthly for physical platinum and palladium bullion for a price equal to 100% of the NAV per unit on last trading day of the month on the NYSE Arca, less any retraction and delivery expenses. Retraction requests for platinum and palladium must be for a minimum of 25,000 trust units. The amount of physical platinum and palladium bullion a unitholder is entitled to receive would be determined by the manager, who would allocate the retraction amount to physical platinum and palladium bullion in direct proportion to the value of physical platinum and palladium bullion held by the trust at the time of retraction. One vote per unit.

Major Shareholder - Widely held at Mar. 17, 2023.

Price Range - SPPP/TSX

Year	Volume	High	Low	Close
2022	859,375	$27.33	$16.41	$18.45
2021	899,141	$26.50	$15.75	$17.62
2020	253,216	$25.36	$13.82	$22.72
2019	70,045	$19.40	$12.90	$18.67
2018	14,105	$13.50	$10.16	$13.50

Recent Close: $15.08

Capital Stock Changes - During 2022, 1,403,774 trust units were issued under an at-the-market offering program and 901,220 trust units were retracted.

Financial Statistics

Periods ended:	12m Dec. 31/22[A]		12m Dec. 31/21[A]
	US$000s	%Chg	US$000s
Realized invest. gain (loss)	2,280		nil
Unrealized invest. gain (loss)	(6,293)		(30,125)
Total revenue	**(4,008)**	**n.a.**	**(30,125)**
General & admin. expense	1,299		1,431
Other operating expense	45		86
Operating expense	**1,344**	**-11**	**1,517**
Operating income	**(5,352)**	**n.a.**	**(31,642)**
Pre-tax income	**(5,354)**	**n.a.**	**(31,642)**
Net income	**(5,354)**	**n.a.**	**(31,642)**
Cash & equivalent	375		892
Investments	137,972		131,525
Total assets	**138,347**	**+4**	**132,483**
Accts. pay. & accr. liabs	59		267
Shareholders' equity	138,288		131,845
Cash from oper. activs	**(1,854)**	**n.a.**	**(1,119)**
Cash from fin. activs	24,371		36,673
Cash from invest. activs	(23,034)		(35,823)
Net cash position	**375**	**-58**	**892**
	US$		US$
Earnings per share*	(0.54)		(3.81)
Cash flow per share*	(0.19)		(0.13)
Net asset value per share*	14.37		14.46
	shs		shs
No. of shs. o/s*	9,622,518		9,119,964
Avg. no. of shs. o/s*	9,901,240		8,299,012
	%		%
Net profit margin	n.m.		n.m.
Return on equity	(3.96)		(24.47)
Return on assets	(3.95)		(24.38)

* Trust Unit
[A] Reported in accordance with IFRS

Historical Summary
(as originally stated)

Fiscal Year	Total Rev.	Net Inc. Bef. Disc.	EPS*
	US$000s	US$000s	US$
2022[A]	(4,008)	(5,354)	(0.54)
2021[A]	(30,125)	(31,642)	(3.81)
2020[A]	24,847	23,404	3.35
2019[A]	39,350	37,770	4.39
2018[A]	7,567	6,524	0.58

* Trust Unit
[A] Reported in accordance with IFRS

S.107 Sprott Physical Silver Trust

Symbol - PSLV **Exchange** - TSX **CUSIP** - 85207K
Head Office - c/o Sprott Asset Management Inc., South Tower, Royal Bank Plaza, 2600-200 Bay St, PO Box 27, Toronto, ON, M5J 2J1 **Telephone** - (416) 943-6707 **Toll-free** - (855) 943-8099 **Fax** - (416) 943-6497
Website - www.sprott.com
Email - gwilliams@sprott.com
Investor Relations - Glen Williams (855) 943-8099
Auditors - KPMG LLP C.A., Toronto, Ont.
Lawyers - Stikeman Elliott LLP, Toronto, Ont.; Seward & Kissel LLP, Washington, D.C.
Transfer Agents - TSX Trust Company, Toronto, Ont.
Trustees - RBC Investor Services Trust, Toronto, Ont.
Managers - Sprott Asset Management L.P., Toronto, Ont.
Profile - (Ont. 2010) Invests in and holds physical silver bullion.

The trust will invest and hold a minimum of 90% of its net assets in physical silver bullion. Silver bullion will be fully allocated and stored at the **Royal Canadian Mint**. Unitholders hold option to retract trust units on a monthly basis for physical silver bullion at a price equal to the net asset value per unit, less any retraction and delivery expenses.

At Feb. 28, 2023, the trust held a total of 170,530,589 oz. of physical silver bullion with a fair value of US$3.57 billion.

Oper. Subsid./Mgt. Co. Directors - John Ciampaglia, CEO, Caledon, Ont.; Whitney George, Darien, Conn.; Kevin Hibbert, Toronto, Ont.
Oper. Subsid./Mgt. Co. Officers - Varinder (Vinny) Bhathal, CFO; Lara Misner, chief compliance officer; Maria Smirnova, chief invest. officer

Capital Stock

	Authorized (shs.)	Outstanding (shs.)[1]
Trust Unit	unlimited	491,967,048

[1] At Apr. 3, 2023

Trust Unit - The trust does not intend to make regular cash distributions. Retractable monthly for cash at a price equal to 95% of the lesser of: (i) the volume-weighted average price per unit on the NYSE Arca or, if trading has been suspended, the trading price on the TSX for the last five days on which the respective exchange was open for trading for the month in which the retraction request is processed; and (ii) the net asset value (NAV) per unit on the last trading day of the month on the NYSE Arca for the month in which the retraction request is processed. Retractable monthly for physical silver bullion for a price equal to 100% of the NAV per unit on the last trading day of the month on the NYSE Arca, less any retraction and delivery expenses. Retraction requests for silver must be for amounts that are at least equivalent in value to 10 London Good Delivery bars, which each weighs between 750 and 1,100 troy ounces of silver, or an integral multiple of one bar in excess thereof plus applicable expenses. Any fractional amount of retraction proceeds in excess of 10 London Good Delivery bars or an integral multiple of one bar in excess thereof would be paid in cash at a rate equal to 100% of the NAV per unit of such excess amount. One vote per unit.

Major Shareholder - Widely held at Mar. 17, 2023.

Price Range - PSLV/TSX

Year	Volume	High	Low	Close
2022	22,172,359	$12.00	$8.10	$11.15
2021	44,241,932	$14.10	$9.51	$10.15
2020	17,291,256	$13.94	$6.26	$11.85
2019	2,335,436	$9.52	$6.92	$8.51
2018	1,308,717	$8.66	$6.57	$7.63

Recent Close: $11.28

Capital Stock Changes - During 2022, 50,578,176 trust units were issued under an at-the-market offering program and 60,447 trust units were retracted.

Financial Statistics

Periods ended:	12m Dec. 31/22[A]		12m Dec. 31/21[A]
	US$000s	%Chg	US$000s
Unrealized invest. gain (loss)	123,466		(527,962)
Total revenue	**123,634**	**n.a.**	**(527,962)**
General & admin. expense	19,406		20,297
Other operating expense	997		1,261
Operating expense	**20,403**	**-5**	**21,558**
Operating income	**103,231**	**n.a.**	**(549,520)**
Pre-tax income	**103,219**	**n.a.**	**(549,515)**
Net income	**103,219**	**n.a.**	**(549,515)**
Cash & equivalent	15,992		3,191
Investments	4,084,962		3,597,211
Total assets	**4,100,987**	**+14**	**3,600,588**
Accts. pay. & accr. liabs	140		477
Shareholders' equity	4,091,249		3,600,111
Cash from oper. activs	**(10,833)**	**n.a.**	**(21,547)**
Cash from fin. activs	387,919		1,741,811
Cash from invest. activs	(364,285)		(1,719,695)
Net cash position	**15,992**	**+401**	**3,191**
	US$		US$
Earnings per share*	0.23		(1.41)
Cash flow per share*	(0.02)		(0.06)
Net asset value per share*	8.47		8.32
	shs		shs
No. of shs. o/s*	483,129,478		432,611,749
Avg. no. of shs. o/s*	455,153,130		389,573,558
	%		%
Net profit margin	83.49		n.m.
Return on equity	2.68		(18.29)
Return on assets	2.68		(18.29)

* Trust Unit
[A] Reported in accordance with IFRS

Historical Summary
(as originally stated)

Fiscal Year	Total Rev.	Net Inc. Bef. Disc.	EPS*
	US$000s	US$000s	US$
2022[A]	123,634	103,219	0.23
2021[A]	(527,962)	(549,515)	(1.41)
2020[A]	733,141	722,828	3.39
2019[A]	132,401	126,098	0.82
2018[A]	(81,561)	(87,657)	(0.58)

* Trust Unit
[A] Reported in accordance with IFRS

S.108 Sprout AI Inc.

Symbol - BYFM **Exchange** - CSE **CUSIP** - 85209X
Head Office - International Business Park, Unit 5B, Bldg. 3860, Panama Pacifico, Panama **Overseas Tel** - 507-6384-8734
Website - sproutai.solutions
Email - cbolton@theracann.solutions
Investor Relations - Christopher Bolton 507-6384-8734
Auditors - Segal GCSE LLP C.A., Toronto, Ont.
Transfer Agents - Endeavor Trust Corporation, Vancouver, B.C.
Profile - (B.C. 2020) Plans, designs, manufactures and/or assembles vertical urban and controlled environment agriculture and farming cultivation equipment.

The company's business model is to plan, design, implement, and support vertical automated fogponic grow habitats designed to operate within high-density urban settings with access to limited power and water. Manufacturing facilities are located in Panama.

The equipment provided consists of multi-level rolling racks that have self-contained and environment-controlled habitats using proprietary systems and technologies. Each habitat is equipped to manage air temperature, humidity, water temperature, nutrient level, light duration and CO_2 duration, which are remotely controlled via a web-based software interface module. The habitats are designed to manage multiple crops including leafy green, micro-green, berries and other fruits The number of plants cultivated within each habitat depends primarily on the size of the plant grow; on average, a minimum of 32 plants can be grown per habitat.

Common reinstated on CSE, Dec. 28, 2022.

Recent Merger and Acquisition Activity

Status: pending **Announced:** June 2, 2023
Sprout AI Inc. agreed to the reverse takeover acquisition of Theracann International Benchmark Corporation, a Panama-based provider of turnkey cultivation and technology solutions offering a suite of products and services that support agricultural companies. Under the agreement, Sprout AI would consolidate its shares on a 1-for-3.333 basis and issue about 63,680,000 post-consolidated shares to TheraCann shareholders. Upon completion, TheraCann would amalgamate with Sprout AI S.A., a wholly owned Panamanian subsidiary of Sprout AI and Sprout AI would change its name to TheraCann Beyond Farming Inc. As TheraCann currently owns 53% interest in Sprout AI, the transaction requires the approval of Sprout AI's minority shareholders.

Predecessor Detail - Name changed from 1262803 B.C. Ltd., May 31, 2021, pursuant to the reverse takeover acquisition of Sprout AI, S.A.

Directors - Christopher (Chris) Bolton, chr., CEO & corp. sec., Panama Pacifico, Panama; Tom Andrews, Alta.; Dr. Toni Rinow, Laval, Qué.

Other Exec. Officers - Carlos Zapata, COO; Dean Callaway, interim CFO; Kathia Jimenez, contr.

Capital Stock

	Authorized (shs.)	Outstanding (shs.)[1]
Common	unlimited	90,264,806

[1] At June 2, 2023

Major Shareholder - Theracann International Benchmark Corporation held 53% interest at June 2, 2023.

Price Range - BYFM/CSE

Year	Volume	High	Low	Close
2022	12,737,751	$0.16	$0.04	$0.05
2021	114,528,212	$1.05	$0.12	$0.13

Recent Close: $0.05

Capital Stock Changes - There were no changes to capital stock during fiscal 2023.

Wholly Owned Subsidiaries

Sprout AI Australia Pty Ltd., Australia.
Sprout AI, S.A., Panama Pacifico, Panama.

Financial Statistics

Periods ended:	12m Jan. 31/23[A]		15m Jan. 31/22[oA1]
	US$000s	%Chg	US$000s
Operating revenue	**884**	**n.a.**	**113**
Cost of sales	303		nil
Salaries & benefits	734		345
General & admin expense	733		1,202
Operating expense	**1,770**	**n.a.**	**1,547**
Operating income	**(886)**	**n.a.**	**(1,434)**
Deprec., depl. & amort.	335		401
Finance costs, gross	190		241
Pre-tax income	**(1,329)**	**n.a.**	**(6,462)**
Net income	**(1,329)**	**n.a.**	**(6,462)**
Cash & equivalent	28		342
Inventories	31		167
Accounts receivable	1		43
Current assets	375		885
Fixed assets, net	211		368
Right-of-use assets	741		928
Intangibles, net	743		476
Total assets	**2,110**	**-21**	**2,657**
Accts. pay. & accr. liabs	852		329
Current liabilities	3,770		3,250
Long-term debt, gross	502		nil
Long-term debt, net	452		nil
Long-term lease liabilities	753		943
Shareholders' equity	(2,865)		(1,536)
Cash from oper. activs	**(28)**	**n.a.**	**(777)**
Cash from fin. activs	(35)		218
Cash from invest. activs	(251)		901
Net cash position	**28**	**-92**	**342**
Capital expenditures	(5)		(205)
Capital disposals	61		nil
	US$		US$
Earnings per share*	(0.01)		(0.09)
Cash flow per share*	(0.00)		(0.01)
	shs		shs
No. of shs. o/s*	90,964,806		90,964,806
Avg. no. of shs. o/s*	90,964,806		71,661,230
	%		%
Net profit margin	(150.34)		...
Return on equity	n.m.		...
Return on assets	(47.79)		...

* Common
[o] Restated
[A] Reported in accordance with IFRS
[1] Results reflect the May 31, 2021, reverse takeover acquisition of Sprout AI, S.A.

Historical Summary
(as originally stated)

Fiscal Year	Oper. Rev.	Net Inc. Bef. Disc.	EPS*
	US$000s	US$000s	US$
2023[A]	884	(1,329)	(0.01)
2022[A1]	113	(6,462)	(0.09)
2020[A2]	nil	(769)	n.a.
2019[A2,3]	nil	(1,067)	n.a.

* Common
[A] Reported in accordance with IFRS
[1] 15 months ended Jan. 31, 2022.
[2] Results pertain to Sprout AI, S.A.
[3] 50 weeks ended Oct. 31, 2019.

S.109 Sprouty Canada, Inc.

Symbol - SPR **Exchange** - CSE (S) **CUSIP** - 85209J
Head Office - 112-1020 Mainland St, Vancouver, BC, V6B 2T5
Telephone - (778) 945-6868
Website - www.sproutly.ca
Email - craig.loverock@sproutly.ca
Investor Relations - Craig Loverock (778) 945-6868
Auditors - Crowe MacKay LLP C.A., Vancouver, B.C.
Lawyers - DuMoulin Black LLP, Vancouver, B.C.
Transfer Agents - TSX Trust Company

Profile - (B.C. 2012) Holds licence from Health Canada to produce, manufacture, process and sell cannabis and related products. Also commercializing a patent-pending technology to produce ready-to-consume ingredients for the cannabis beverage and edibles market.

Wholly owned **Toronto Herbal Remedies Inc.** (THR) holds a licence to produce and sell medical marijuana and cannabis oil and related products under the provisions of the Cannabis Act from a 16,600-sq.-ft. facility in Toronto, Ont. THR also holds licence to manufacture and sell cannabis 2.0 products directly to provincial distributors and other authorized Canadian retail supply channels; and licence to sell dried cannabis flower products under the CALIBER brand in Alberta, New Brunswick, Manitoba, Saskatchewan, British Columbia and Ontario.

Wholly owned **Infusion Biosciences Canada Inc.** holds exclusive rights for Aqueous Phytorecovery Process (APP) technology in Canada, Europe, Australia, Jamaica and Israel. The technology uses proprietary reagents to produce ready-to-consume ingredients including Infuz$_2$O, a naturally water-soluble cannabis solution which fully dissolves in water and Bio Natural Oil, which are natural oils from cannabis plants infused into natural carrier oils for edible products. The company intends to commercialize the APP technology via the production, formulation, and sale of specialized ingredients made using Infuz$_2$O and Bio Natural Oils. The company has completed the formulation of its initial cannabis-infused edible gummy and beverage products utilizing cannabis extracts produced by the APP technology, and has filed with Health Canada its Notice of New Cannabis Product (NNCP) notification to sell these products.

Common suspended from CSE, Sept. 7, 2022.

Predecessor Detail - Name changed from Stone Ridge Exploration Corp., July 6, 2018, following reverse takeover acquisition of Sproutly Inc. by way of an amalgamation with a wholly owned subsidiary; basis 1 new for 2 old shs.

Directors - Dr. Arup Sen, chr. & CEO, Fla.; Craig Loverock, CFO & corp. sec., Toronto, Ont.; Con Constandis, Ont.; Paul Marcellino, Okla.

Other Exec. Officers - Melise Panetta, chief comml. officer; Alan Brosseau, exec. v-p

Capital Stock

	Authorized (shs.)	Outstanding (shs.)[1]
Common	unlimited	371,843,081

[1] At June 2, 2023

Major Shareholder - Infusion Biosciences Inc. held 14.32% interest at Oct. 4, 2021.

Price Range - SPR/CSE (S)

Year	Volume	High	Low	Close
2022	43,818,760	$0.05	$0.01	$0.02
2021	126,178,325	$0.11	$0.03	$0.04
2020	111,888,540	$0.23	$0.04	$0.05
2019	164,898,392	$1.08	$0.19	$0.21
2018	46,052,103	$1.20	$0.25	$0.41

Recent Close: $0.02

Capital Stock Changes - In March and April 2021, private placement of 26,966,037 units (1 common share & 1 warrant) at 5¢ per unit was completed, with warrants exercisable at 7¢ per share for two years.

Wholly Owned Subsidiaries

Infusion Biosciences Canada Inc., Ont.
SSM Partners Inc., Barbados.
Sproutly Inc., Vancouver, B.C.
- 100% int. in **Toronto Herbal Remedies Inc.**, Toronto, Ont.

Financial Statistics

Periods ended:	12m Feb. 28/21[A]		12m Feb. 29/20[A]
	$000s	%Chg	$000s
Operating revenue	**316**	**-66**	**927**
Cost of sales	376		(815)
Salaries & benefits	662		2,215
General & admin expense	1,058		4,319
Stock-based compensation	220		1,507
Operating expense	**2,315**	**-68**	**7,226**
Operating income	**(1,999)**	**n.a.**	**(6,299)**
Deprec., depl. & amort.	117		564
Finance costs, gross	2,958		3,350
Write-downs/write-offs	(12,000)		(52,438)
Pre-tax income	**(16,829)**	**n.a.**	**(62,748)**
Income taxes	(417)		(1,137)
Net income	**(16,412)**	**n.a.**	**(61,611)**
Cash & equivalent	172		32
Inventories	468		476
Accounts receivable	95		258
Current assets	918		1,422
Fixed assets, net	3,226		3,455
Right-of-use assets	nil		87
Intangibles, net	nil		11,628
Total assets	**4,198**	**-75**	**16,593**
Accts. pay. & accr. liabs	2,650		1,679
Current liabilities	9,702		9,745
Long-term debt, gross	7,029		10,536
Long-term debt, net	48		2,496
Long-term lease liabilities	61		73
Shareholders' equity	(5,614)		3,863
Cash from oper. activs	**(1,137)**	**n.a.**	**(6,532)**
Cash from fin. activs	1,220		2,483
Cash from invest. activs	19		(5,563)
Net cash position	**172**	**+438**	**32**
Capital expenditures	(7)		(588)
Capital disposals	26		nil
	$		$
Earnings per share*	(0.06)		(0.30)
Cash flow per share*	(0.00)		(0.03)
	shs		shs
No. of shs. o/s*	326,910,820		227,951,248
Avg. no. of shs. o/s*	270,522,467		205,112,854
	%		%
Net profit margin	n.m.		n.m.
Return on equity	n.m.		n.m.
Return on assets	(130.13)		n.a.

* Common
[A] Reported in accordance with IFRS

Latest Results

Periods ended:	6m Aug. 31/21[A]		6m Aug. 31/20[oA]
	$000s	%Chg	$000s
Operating revenue	343	+85	185
Net income	(796)	n.a.	(3,770)
	$		$
Earnings per share*	(0.00)		(0.02)

* Common
[o] Restated
[A] Reported in accordance with IFRS

Historical Summary
(as originally stated)

Fiscal Year	Oper. Rev.	Net Inc. Bef. Disc.	EPS*
	$000s	$000s	$
2021[A]	316	(16,412)	(0.06)
2020[A]	927	(61,611)	(0.30)
2019[A1]	nil	(12,628)	(0.10)
2018[A2]	nil	(356)	(0.04)
2017[A]	nil	(187)	(0.02)

* Common
[A] Reported in accordance with IFRS
[1] Results reflect the July 6, 2018, reverse takeover acquisition of Sproutly Inc.
[2] Results for fiscal 2018 and prior periods pertain to Stone Ridge Exploration Corp.
Note: Adjusted throughout for 1-for-2 cons. in July 2018

S.110 St-Georges Eco-Mining Corp.

Symbol - SX **Exchange** - CSE **CUSIP** - 85235Q
Head Office - 2700-1000 rue Sherbrooke O, Montréal, QC, H3A 3G4
Telephone - (514) 933-1503 **Fax** - (514) 933-9871
Website - www.st-georgescorp.com
Email - neha_tally@dumasbancorp.com
Investor Relations - Neha Tally (514) 996-6342
Auditors - Kingston Ross Pasnak LLP C.A., Edmonton, Alta.
Bankers - The Bank of Nova Scotia
Lawyers - McMillan LLP, Montréal, Qué.

Transfer Agents - Computershare Trust Company of Canada Inc., Montréal, Qué.

Profile - (Can. 2002) Has mineral interests in Quebec and Iceland and is pursuing the development of lithium processing and battery recycling technologies.

In Quebec, holds Manicouagan nickel-copper-PGE prospect, 13,611 hectares, 350 km northwest of Baie-Comeau; Julie nickel prospect, 16,227 hectares, Baie-Comeau city; 90% interest (**Lepidco Ltd.** 10%) in Le Royal lithium prospect, 286 hectares, 30 km of Val-d'Or; Villebon prospect, 84 claims; and Notre Dome prospect, 35 claims, near Notre-Dame de Lorette.

In Iceland, holds Thormodsdalur gold prospect, 20 km east Reykjavik; Vopnafjorour gold prospect, 59,850 hectares; and Trollaskagi gold prospect, 101,800 hectares.

Also developing a lithium processing technology for lithium-in-clay mineral deposits and an electric vehicle battery recycling technology. The company also plans to construct a battery recycling plant in Baie-Comeau, Que., to produce nickel ingots and recycle batteries. Also holds rights to access **Wintech Energy Corp.**'s green hydrogen technology to create value-added products for the company using clean hydrogen production.

Also holds 15% interest in **Íslenk Vatnsorka ehf.**, which is developing the 10 to 20-MW Hagavatnsvirkjun hydroelectric dam project in Iceland.

Wholly owned **Borealis Commodities Exchange ehf.** has developed a blockchain-based derivative marketplace platform. Government licenses to operate the exchange are required to move forward.

Effective Mar. 31, 2022, the company changed its fiscal year end from December 31 to March 31.

Predecessor Detail - Name changed from St-Georges Platinum and Base Metals Inc., Dec. 22, 2017.

Directors - Mark A. Billings, chr., Montréal, Qué.; Herb Duerr, pres. & CEO, Reno, Nev.; Enrico Di Cesare, v-p, R&D, Pierrefonds, Qué.; Keturah M. Nathe, Pitt Meadows, B.C.; Kristin Olafsdóttir; James C. Passin, Ill.

Other Exec. Officers - Richard (Rick) Barnett, CFO; Dr. Sabin Boily, v-p, intellectual property strategy; François (Frank) Dumas, v-p, bus. devel.; Neha Tally, corp. sec.

Capital Stock

	Authorized (shs.)	Outstanding (shs.)[1]
Preferred	unlimited	nil
Common	unlimited	244,820,928

[1] At Mar. 1, 2023

Major Shareholder - Widely held at Aug. 3, 2021.

Price Range - SX/CSE

Year	Volume	High	Low	Close
2022	70,307,989	$0.52	$0.15	$0.19
2021	291,285,143	$1.19	$0.09	$0.45
2020	67,537,218	$0.16	$0.03	$0.10
2019	80,837,151	$0.25	$0.06	$0.10
2018	472,084,618	$2.90	$0.04	$0.13

Recent Close: $0.10

Capital Stock Changes - In September 2022, private placement of up to $4,500,000 flow-through units (1 common share & 1 warrant) at $0.325 per unit was announced, with warrants exercisable at 36¢ per share for three years.

Wholly Owned Subsidiaries

Borealis Commodities Exchange ehf., Iceland.
EVSX Corp.
H2SX Corp., Canada.
Melmi ehf., Iceland.
St-Georges Metallurgy Corp.

Investments

BWA Group Plc, United Kingdom.
Iconic Minerals Ltd., Vancouver, B.C. (see Survey of Mines)
ThreeD Capital Inc., Toronto, Ont. (see separate coverage)
27.3% int. in **ZeU Gaming Inc.**, Canada.
27.3% int. in **ZeU Technologies, Inc.**, Montréal, Qué. (see separate coverage)
27.3% int. in **ZeUPay AS**, Norway.
27.3% int. in **ZeUPay Inc.**, Canada.

Financial Statistics

Periods ended:	15m Mar. 31/22[A]		12m Dec. 31/20[A]
	$000s	%Chg	$000s
Salaries & benefits	198		nil
Research & devel. expense	1,657		588
General & admin expense	4,770		2,072
Stock-based compensation	3,755		1,187
Operating expense	**10,380**	**n.a.**	**3,847**
Operating income	**(10,380)**	**n.a.**	**(3,847)**
Finance costs, gross	2,371		431
Write-downs/write-offs	(13,756)[1]		(2,661)
Pre-tax income	**(23,278)**	**n.a.**	**(14,096)**
Net income	**(23,278)**	**n.a.**	**(14,096)**
Cash & equivalent	4,265		539
Accounts receivable	906		59
Current assets	5,672		1,126
Long-term investments	nil		35
Fixed assets, net	8		11
Right-of-use assets	83		149
Explor./devel. properties	15,656		3,301
Total assets	**21,418**	**n.a.**	**4,622**
Bank indebtedness	4,382		3,520
Accts. pay. & accr. liabs	2,656		2,251
Current liabilities	7,155		6,143
Long-term debt, gross	5,629		4,715
Long-term debt, net	5,620		4,418
Shareholders' equity	21,768		20
Non-controlling interest	(13,181)		(6,190)
Cash from oper. activs	**(6,693)**	**n.a.**	**(2,170)**
Cash from fin. activs	22,155		1,996
Cash from invest. activs	(11,851)		121
Net cash position	**3,937**	**n.a.**	**326**
Capital expenditures	(11,828)		(312)
	$		$
Earnings per share*	(0.11)		(0.10)
Cash flow per share*	(0.03)		(0.01)
	shs		shs
No. of shs. o/s*	225,520,928		166,188,936
Avg. no. of shs. o/s*	206,590,087		147,044,881
	%		%
Net profit margin	...		n.a.
Return on equity	...		(277.23)
Return on assets	...		(83.23)

* Common
[A] Reported in accordance with IFRS
[1] Includes $13,320,813 impairment of goodwill and $435,000 allowance for doubtful account.

Historical Summary
(as originally stated)

Fiscal Year	Oper. Rev.	Net Inc. Bef. Disc.	EPS*
	$000s	$000s	$
2022[A1]	nil	(23,278)	(0.11)
2020[A]	nil	(14,096)	(0.10)
2019[A]	nil	(4,815)	(0.04)
2018[A]	nil	(7,884)	(0.08)

* Common
[A] Reported in accordance with IFRS
[1] 15 months ended Mar. 31, 2022.

S.111 Stack Capital Group Inc.

Symbol - STCK **Exchange** - TSX **CUSIP** - 85236X
Head Office - 3140-155 Wellington St W, Toronto, ON, M5V 3H1
Telephone - (647) 280-3307
Website - www.stackcapitalgroup.com
Email - brian@stackcapitalgroup.com
Investor Relations - Brian Viveiros (647) 280-3307
Auditors - PricewaterhouseCoopers LLP C.A., Toronto, Ont.
Lawyers - Fogler, Rubinoff LLP, Toronto, Ont.
Transfer Agents - Computershare Trust Company of Canada Inc., Toronto, Ont.
Managers - SC Partners Ltd., Toronto, Ont.

Profile - (Can. 2021) Invests in equity, debt and/or other securities of innovative and disruptive growth to late stage private operating businesses.

Will not invest in private operating businesses smaller than $100,000,000 in enterprise value, as well as will not invest in land, cryptocurrencies, metals or similar natured assets or businesses who earn a majority of their revenue from such assets.

Investment portfolio includes **Varo Money, Inc.** (common shares), a San Francisco, Calif.-based all-digital bank in the U.S.; **FNEX Ventures, LLC - Series 103** (limited partnership units), a special purpose vehicle primarily invested in preferred shares of Hawthorne, Calif.-based **Space Exploration Technologies Corp.** (SpaceX), a designer and manufacturer of rockets and spacecraft providing space transportation and tourism services, as well as a provider of satellite communications under the Starlink brand; **Bolt Financial, Inc.** (preferred shares), a San Francisco, Calif.-based software developer of the one-click checkout process and fraud protection for online retailers; **Prove Identity, Inc.** (preferred and common shares), a New York, N.Y.-based software developer of identity verification and authentication solutions; **Hopper, Inc.** (preferred shares), a Montreal, Que.-based developer of travel technology platforms, including mobile application for flights, hotels, car rental and home rental, financial technology (fintech) offerings and business-to-business cloud solutions; **Newfront Insurance Holdings, Inc.** (preferred shares), a San Francisco, Calif.-based provider of insurance, retirement solutions and employee benefits thought its software-driven platform; **GoEuro Corp.** (preferred shares), a Berlin, Germany-based operator of a multi-modal travel booking platform, Omio, which allows travellers in Europe, the U.S. and Canada to compare, plan and book trains, buses, ferries and flights; and **Locus Robotics Corp.** (preferred shares), a Wilmington, Mass.-based developer and manufacturer of autonomous mobile robots for warehouse fulfillment and distribution facilities of third party logistics, retail, e-commerce, healthcare and industrial clients.

Directors - John K. Bell, chr., Cambridge, Ont.; Jeffrey Parks, CEO, Ont.; Laurie M. Goldberg, Winnipeg, Man.; Dr. Geraldine B. (Gerri) Sinclair, Vancouver, B.C.

Other Exec. Officers - Demetrios (Jimmy) Vaiopoulos, CFO; Jason Meiers, chief invest. officer; Brian Viveiros, v-p, corp. devel. & IR & corp. sec.

Capital Stock

	Authorized (shs.)	Outstanding (shs.)[1]
Common	unlimited	9,047,574

[1] At May 10, 2023

Normal Course Issuer Bid - The company plans to make normal course purchases of up to 461,500 common shares representing 5% of the total outstanding. The bid commenced on Nov. 17, 2022, and expires on Nov. 16, 2023.

Major Shareholder - TD Waterhouse Canada Inc. held 15.3% interest at May 5, 2023.

Price Range - STCK/TSX

Year	Volume	High	Low	Close
2022	2,783,600	$10.07	$5.15	$5.85
2021	3,054,725	$11.20	$8.71	$9.09

Recent Close: $6.75

Capital Stock Changes - During 2022, 139,440 common shares were issued for additional investment in Prove Identity, Inc. and 81,800 common shares were repurchased under a Normal Course Issuer Bid.

Financial Statistics

Periods ended:	12m Dec. 31/22[A]		9m Dec. 31/21[A]
	$000s	%Chg	$000s
Unrealized invest. gain (loss)	1,579		928
Total revenue	**2,406**	**n.a.**	**1,150**
General & admin. expense	3,297		1,769
Stock-based compensation	2		nil
Operating expense	**3,299**	**n.a.**	**1,769**
Operating income	**(893)**	**n.a.**	**(619)**
Pre-tax income	**(849)**	**n.a.**	**(577)**
Net income	**(849)**	**n.a.**	**(577)**
Cash & equivalent	31,393		76,338
Investments	70,688		26,443
Total assets	**102,429**	**-1**	**102,985**
Accts. pay. & accr. liabs	215		478
Shareholders' equity	102,058		102,363
Cash from oper. activs	**(44,513)**	**n.a.**	**(26,643)**
Cash from fin. activs	(478)		102,940
Net cash position	**31,393**	**-59**	**76,338**
	$		$
Earnings per share*	(0.09)		(0.09)
Cash flow per share*	(4.87)		(4.06)
	shs		shs
No. of shs. o/s*	9,150,974		9,093,334
Avg. no. of shs. o/s*	9,133,646		6,557,683
	%		%
Net profit margin	(35.29)		...
Return on equity	(0.83)		...
Return on assets	(0.83)		...

* Common
[A] Reported in accordance with IFRS

Latest Results

Periods ended:	3m Mar. 31/23[A]		3m Mar. 31/22[A]
	$000s	%Chg	$000s
Total revenue	(207)	n.a.	7,176
Net income	(971)	n.a.	6,283
	$		$
Earnings per share*	(0.11)		0.69

* Common
[A] Reported in accordance with IFRS

S.112 StageZero Life Sciences Ltd.

Symbol - SZLS **Exchange** - TSX **CUSIP** - 852540
Head Office - 30-70 East Beaver Creek Rd, Markham, ON, L4B 3B2
Telephone - (905) 209-2030 **Toll-free** - (866) 375-0442
Website - www.stagezerolifesciences.com
Email - jht@stagezerols.com
Investor Relations - James R. Howard-Tripp (855) 240-7140 ext. 1

Auditors - SRCO Professional Corporation C.A., Richmond Hill, Ont.
Lawyers - Fasken Martineau DuMoulin LLP, Toronto, Ont.
Transfer Agents - TSX Trust Company, Toronto, Ont.
Profile - (Ont. 1997) Develops and commercializes blood-based molecular diagnostic tests for early disease detection and personalized health management, with a primary focus on cancer-related indications. Also offers multiple types of COVID-19 tests.

The company's core technology, Sentinel Principle®, allows for the detection, diagnosis and staging of a variety of diseases from a simple blood sample. Tests are being developed for cancer, arthritis, cardiovascular disease and neurological disorders. Products include Aristotle®, which has the ability to detect multiple cancers from a single sample of blood and is accessed through AVRT™, a physician-driven telehealth program for the early detection of cancer and other chronic illnesses; and ColonSentry®, is a blood-based molecular test to measure gene expression in white blood cells for assessing an individual's current risk of having colorectal cancer.

Wholly owned **Care Oncology, Inc.** operates on a global telehealth platform and provides clinical consultations, interventions and monitoring services for patients diagnosed with cancer through TREAT program which provides adjuvant therapeutic solutions. Telemedicine-based clinical services are offered through Care Oncology business units in the United Kingdom and the United States.

Also has partnered with its current and new service providers to offer COVID-19 testing solutions, a polymerase chain reaction (PCR) and antigen test which identifies an active infection through saliva and nasopharygeal specimens, and an antibody test which identifies antibodies in the blood that are indicative of a past infection.

Predecessor Detail - Name changed from GeneNews Limited, June 26, 2019.

Directors - James R. Howard-Tripp, exec. chr. & CEO, Burlington, Ont.; Harry Glorikian, Arlington, Mass.; Garth A. C. MacRae, Toronto, Ont.; Rory Riggs, New York, N.Y.

Other Exec. Officers - Carl Solomon, interim CFO & corp. sec.

Capital Stock

	Authorized (shs.)	Outstanding (shs.)[1]
Preference	unlimited	nil
Special	unlimited	nil
Common	unlimited	106,391,882

[1] At Apr. 18, 2023

Major Shareholder - Widely held at Apr. 28, 2023.

Price Range - SZLS/TSX

Year	Volume	High	Low	Close
2022	32,295,804	$0.32	$0.06	$0.06
2021	103,203,220	$1.65	$0.25	$0.30
2020	89,406,075	$1.40	$0.20	$0.75
2019	31,995,238	$1.64	$0.28	$0.36
2018	8,489,080	$1.88	$0.20	$0.36

Consolidation: 1-for-8 cons. in Sept. 2020
Recent Close: $0.07

Capital Stock Changes - In March 2022, private placement of 10,000,000 units (1 common share & 1 warrant) at Cdn$0.187 per unit was completed, with warrants exercisable at US$0.2206 per share for four years.

Wholly Owned Subsidiaries

Clinics Operations Limited, United Kingdom.
StageZero Holdings, Inc., Del.
- 100% int. in **Care Oncology, Inc.**, United States.
- 100% int. in **SZ Physicians Holdings, Inc.**, United States.
- 100% int. in **StageZero Life Sciences Inc.**, Del.
  - 49% int. in **COC Physicians, PC**, United States.

Investments

10% int. in **GeneNews Diagnostics Sdn. Bhd.**, Malaysia. Inactive.
49% int. in **GeneNews Technologies Inc.**, People's Republic of China. Inactive.

Financial Statistics

Periods ended:	12m Dec. 31/21[A]		12m Dec. 31/20[oA]
	US$000s	%Chg	US$000s
Operating revenue	**5,068**	**+22**	**4,152**
Cost of goods sold	2,004		2,569
Salaries & benefits	4,463		2,273
Research & devel. expense	775		219
General & admin expense	5,256		1,554
Stock-based compensation	391		637
Operating expense	**12,889**	**+78**	**7,252**
Operating income	**(7,821)**	**n.a.**	**(3,100)**
Deprec., depl. & amort.	566		255
Finance costs, gross	1,436		664
Pre-tax income	**(7,484)**	**n.a.**	**(6,864)**
Net income	**(7,484)**	**n.a.**	**(6,864)**
Cash & equivalent	1,725		6,597
Inventories	409		355
Accounts receivable	127		74
Current assets	2,385		7,222
Fixed assets, net	526		716
Right-of-use assets	346		544
Intangibles, net	7,364		nil
Total assets	**10,646**	**+25**	**8,508**
Accts. pay. & accr. liabs.	2,073		2,522
Current liabilities	4,745		5,556
Long-term debt, gross	941		928
Long-term debt, net	582		580
Long-term lease liabilities	194		415
Shareholders' equity	2,762		(1,233)
Cash from oper. activs	**(8,955)**	**n.a.**	**(3,064)**
Cash from fin. activs	4,103		9,663
Cash from invest. activs	(21)		(72)
Net cash position	**1,725**	**-74**	**6,597**
Capital expenditures	(148)		(72)
Capital disposals	46		nil
	US$		US$
Earnings per share*	(0.11)		(0.15)
Cash flow per share*	(0.13)		(0.07)
	shs		shs
No. of shs. o/s*	90,733,283		60,716,595
Avg. no. of shs. o/s*	70,715,834		44,820,966
	%		%
Net profit margin	(147.67)		(165.32)
Return on equity	n.m.		n.m.
Return on assets	(63.15)		(118.40)
Foreign sales percent	95		89
No. of employees (FTEs)	80		51

* Common
[o] Restated
[A] Reported in accordance with IFRS

Latest Results

Periods ended:	9m Sept. 30/22[A]		9m Sept. 30/21[A]
	US$000s	%Chg	US$000s
Operating revenue	3,119	-13	3,566
Net income	(1,917)	n.a.	(5,189)
	US$		US$
Earnings per share*	(0.02)		(0.06)

* Common
[A] Reported in accordance with IFRS

Historical Summary
(as originally stated)

Fiscal Year	Oper. Rev.	Net Inc. Bef. Disc.	EPS*
	US$000s	US$000s	US$
2021[A]	5,068	(7,484)	(0.11)
2020[A]	4,152	(6,864)	(0.15)
2019[A]	139	(3,482)	(0.16)
2018[A]	186	(3,944)	(0.24)
2017[A]	412	(2,947)	(0.24)

* Common
[A] Reported in accordance with IFRS
Note: Adjusted throughout for 1-for-8 cons. in Sept. 2020

S.113 Stampede Drilling Inc.

Symbol - SDI **Exchange** - TSX-VEN **CUSIP** - 852813
Head Office - South Tower, 2600-700 9 Ave SW, Calgary, AB, T2P 3V7 **Telephone** - (403) 984-5042 **Fax** - (403) 984-5097
Website - www.stampededrilling.com
Email - lylewhitmarsh@stampededrilling.com
Investor Relations - Lyle C. Whitmarsh (403) 984-5062
Auditors - PricewaterhouseCoopers LLP C.A., Calgary, Alta.
Bankers - ATB Financial, Calgary, Alta.
Lawyers - Burnet, Duckworth & Palmer LLP, Calgary, Alta.
Transfer Agents - Computershare Trust Company of Canada Inc., Calgary, Alta.
Employees - 23 at Dec. 31, 2022

Profile - (Alta. 2011 amalg.) Provides land based contract drilling rig services for the oil and gas industry in the Western Canadian Sedimentary Basin.

Drilling rig services are performed using drilling rigs and auxiliary equipment pursuant to contracts with exploration and production companies.

At May 11, 2023, the company had 18 telescopic double drilling rigs and one high spec triple drilling rig.

In addition, the company holds 50% interest in **2391764 Alberta Ltd.** (UBC Drillco), which specializes in engineering, manufacturing and supply of fully integrated under balanced coil drilling rigs (UBC drilling rigs) and corresponding support equipment for the oil and gas industry.

Periods ended:	12m Dec. 31/22	12m Dec. 31/21
Drill rig operating days	2,674	1,620
Drill rig rev. per oper. day $	25,011	19,854
Drill rig util. rate, %	60	44

Recent Merger and Acquisition Activity

Status: completed **Revised:** Aug. 23, 2022
UPDATE: The transaction was completed. PREVIOUVS: Stampede Drilling Inc. agreed to acquire six drilling rigs and related assets for $21,500,000, which would be funded with proceeds from a bought deal public offering that would be completed concurrent with the completion of the transaction. The drilling rigs consisted of two doubles, three heavy doubles and one super spec triple, which were suited to work in several of the most active oil and gas plays in western Canada.
Status: completed **Announced:** Apr. 21, 2022
Stampede Drilling Inc. acquired three telescopic double drilling rigs, two top drives and ancillary equipment from a third party for $5,000,000 cash.

Predecessor Detail - Name changed from MATRRIX Energy Technologies Inc., June 5, 2019.

Directors - Lyle C. Whitmarsh, chr., pres. & CEO, Cochrane, Alta.; Thane Russell†, Calgary, Alta.; Tim A. Beatty, Alta.; Kerri Beuk, Alta.; Diane Brickner, Edmonton, Alta.; Murray R. Hinz, Calgary, Alta.; Terrance J. (Terry) Owen, Calgary, Alta.; Drew Ross, Alta.

Other Exec. Officers - Terry Kuiper, COO, Canada; Jeff Schab, CFO & corp. sec.

† Lead director

Capital Stock

	Authorized (shs.)	Outstanding (shs.)[1]
Preferred	unlimited	nil
Common	unlimited	228,589,000

[1] At May 11, 2023

Normal Course Issuer Bid - The company plans to make normal course purchases of up to 21,872,232 common shares representing 10% of the public float. The bid commenced on June 1, 2023, and expires on May 31, 2024.

Major Shareholder - Widely held at Apr. 14, 2023.

Price Range - SDI/TSX-VEN

Year	Volume	High	Low	Close
2022	28,684,210	$0.50	$0.17	$0.32
2021	7,141,711	$0.29	$0.11	$0.17
2020	4,397,825	$0.21	$0.06	$0.13
2019	10,389,137	$0.45	$0.14	$0.20
2018	12,228,009	$0.50	$0.15	$0.20

Recent Close: $0.25

Capital Stock Changes - In August 2022, bought deal public offering of 83,202,000 common shares was completed at 32¢ per share, including 5,077,000 common shares on exercise of over-allotment option. Also during 2022, common shares were issued as follows: 952,000 on conversion of debentures and 608,000 on exercise of options.

Wholly Owned Subsidiaries

Stampede Drilling (U.S.) Inc., Del.

Investments

50% int. in **2391764 Alberta Ltd.**, Alta. 66.7% voting rights.

Financial Statistics

Periods ended:	12m Dec. 31/22^A		12m Dec. 31/21^{□A}
	$000s	%Chg	$000s
Operating revenue	**66,879**	**+108**	**32,163**
Cost of sales	44,564		20,135
Salaries & benefits	4,129		2,175
General & admin expense	2,881		1,492
Stock-based compensation	1,029		515
Operating expense	**52,603**	**+116**	**24,317**
Operating income	**14,276**	**+82**	**7,846**
Deprec., depl. & amort.	4,747		4,486
Finance costs, gross	1,246		670
Pre-tax income	**8,210**	**+188**	**2,852**
Net income	**8,210**	**+188**	**2,852**
Cash & equivalent	703		665
Accounts receivable	13,908		6,773
Current assets	14,926		7,651
Fixed assets, net	87,047		42,289
Right-of-use assets	1,846		354
Intangibles, net	461		461
Total assets	**108,280**	**+113**	**50,755**
Bank indebtedness	6,794		6,998
Accts. pay. & accr. liabs	7,652		2,574
Current liabilities	19,753		10,176
Long-term debt, gross	13,386		4,432
Long-term debt, net	8,575		4,032
Long-term lease liabilities	1,403		234
Equity portion of conv. debs	43		46
Shareholders' equity	72,831		36,179
Non-controlling interest	5,646		nil
Cash from oper. activs	**10,155**	**+67**	**6,093**
Cash from fin. activs	32,077		(2,276)
Cash from invest. activs	(42,181)		(3,832)
Net cash position	**703**	**+6**	**665**
Capital expenditures	(41,122)		(4,086)
Capital disposals	596		381
	$		$
Earnings per share*	0.05		0.02
Cash flow per share*	0.06		0.05
	shs		shs
No. of shs. o/s*	216,933,000		132,171,000
Avg. no. of shs. o/s*	162,505,000		132,171,000
	%		%
Net profit margin	12.28		8.87
Return on equity	15.06		8.27
Return on assets	11.89		7.15
No. of employees (FTEs)	23		13

* Common
□ Restated
A Reported in accordance with IFRS

Latest Results

Periods ended:	3m Mar. 31/23^A		3m Mar. 31/22^A
	$000s	%Chg	$000s
Operating revenue	25,697	+76	14,568
Net income	3,765	+62	2,322
	$		$
Earnings per share*	0.02		0.02

* Common
A Reported in accordance with IFRS

Historical Summary
(as originally stated)

Fiscal Year	Oper. Rev.	Net Inc. Bef. Disc.	EPS*
	$000s	$000s	$
2022^A	66,879	8,210	0.05
2021^A	32,163	2,852	0.02
2020^A	14,394	(4,042)	(0.03)
2019^A	23,697	(1,247)	(0.01)
2018^A	20,873	(4,124)	(0.03)

* Common
A Reported in accordance with IFRS

S.114 Standard Mercantile Acquisition Corp.

Symbol - SMA **Exchange** - TSX **CUSIP** - 85361A
Head Office - 1800-181 Bay St, Toronto, ON, M5J 2T9 **Telephone** - (416) 972-1741
Website - www.standardmercantileacquisition.com
Email - jordan.kupinsky@windsorgp.com
Investor Relations - Jordan M. Kupinsky (416) 972-1741
Auditors - Davidson & Company LLP C.A., Vancouver, B.C.
Lawyers - Fasken Martineau DuMoulin LLP, Vancouver, B.C.
Transfer Agents - Computershare Trust Company of Canada Inc., Toronto, Ont.
Profile - (Can. 2012) Undergoing an orderly wind-up.

The company's mortgage portfolio was invested in first ranking mortgages. The company continues to maintain mortgage investments but has ceased originating new loans and all mortgage renewal activity, subject to contractual rights. At Mar. 31, 2023, the company's mortgage portfolio consisted of two mortgages totaling an aggregate principal amount of $7,918,662, with a weighted average interest rate of 8.67% and a weighted average loan-to-value of 86.22%.

Predecessor Detail - Name changed from Trez Capital Senior Mortgage Investment Corporation, June 10, 2021.

Directors - Jonathon Cowan, chr., Vancouver, B.C.; Jordan M. Kupinsky, CEO, Toronto, Ont.; Kenneth R. (Ken) Wiener, Toronto, Ont.

Other Exec. Officers - Jack Z. Tasse, CFO

Capital Stock

	Authorized (shs.)	Outstanding (shs.)[1]
Class A Common	unlimited	7,298,567
Class B Common	unlimited	nil

[1] At May 2, 2023

Normal Course Issuer Bid - The company plans to make normal course purchases of up to 451,933 class A common shares representing 10% of the public float. The bid commenced on Dec. 20, 2022, and expires on Dec. 19, 2023.

Major Shareholder - Jordan M. Kupinsky held 20% interest and Neil Stratton held 17.73% interest at May 5, 2023.

Price Range - SMA/TSX

Year	Volume	High	Low	Close
2022	731,333	$1.60	$0.89	$0.89
2021	1,987,563	$2.44	$1.22	$1.28
2020	1,676,703	$2.85	$1.69	$2.07
2019	1,321,701	$2.63	$2.12	$2.41
2018	2,239,604	$2.88	$2.16	$2.24

Recent Close: $0.20

Capital Stock Changes - There were no changes to capital stock from 2018 to 2022, inclusive.

Dividends

SMA cl A N.S.R.

$0.40◆r	Aug. 17/23	$0.397◆	June 28/23
$0.45◆r	Dec. 29/22	$0.66◆r	Dec. 29/21

Paid in 2023: $0.397◆ + $0.40◆r 2022: $0.45◆r 2021: $0.478◆ + $0.66◆r

◆ Special **r** Return of Capital

Financial Statistics

Periods ended:	12m Dec. 31/22^A		12m Dec. 31/21^A
	$000s	%Chg	$000s
Total revenue	**776**	**-19**	**959**
General & admin. expense	463		444
Stock-based compensation	67		236
Operating expense	**530**	**-22**	**680**
Operating income	**246**	**-12**	**279**
Pre-tax income	**475**	**-21**	**605**
Net income	**475**	**-21**	**605**
Cash & equivalent	354		946
Investments	7,887		9,958
Total assets	**8,226**	**-25**	**10,920**
Accts. pay. & accr. liabs	96		86
Shareholders' equity	8,084		10,834
Cash from oper. activs	**(282)**	**n.a.**	**(310)**
Cash from fin. activs	3,293		(8,328)
Cash from invest. activs	2,984		3,977
Net cash position	**354**	**-63**	**946**
	$		$
Earnings per share*	0.06		0.08
Cash flow per share*	(0.04)		(0.04)
Cash divd. per share*	0.45		0.66
Extra divd. - cash*	0.45		1.14
Total divd. per share*	**0.90**		**1.80**
	shs		shs
No. of shs. o/s*	7,318,067		7,318,067
Avg. no. of shs. o/s*	7,318,067		7,318,067
	%		%
Net profit margin	61.21		63.09
Return on equity	5.02		4.15
Return on assets	4.96		4.13

* Cl.A Common
A Reported in accordance with IFRS

Latest Results

Periods ended:	3m Mar. 31/23^A		3m Mar. 31/22^A
	$000s	%Chg	$000s
Total revenue	201	+10	183
Net income	82	+46	56
	$		$
Earnings per share*	0.01		0.01

* Cl.A Common
A Reported in accordance with IFRS

Historical Summary
(as originally stated)

Fiscal Year	Total Rev.	Net Inc. Bef. Disc.	EPS*
	$000s	$000s	$
2022^A	776	475	0.06
2021^A	959	605	0.08
2020^A	1,242	4,046	0.55
2019^A	1,379	(486)	(0.07)
2018^A	1,228	604	0.08

* Cl.A Common
A Reported in accordance with IFRS

S.115 Stantec Inc.*

Symbol - STN **Exchange** - TSX **CUSIP** - 85472N
Head Office - 400-10220 103 Ave NW, Edmonton, AB, T5J 0K4 **Telephone** - (780) 917-7000 **Toll-free** - (866) 782-6832 **Fax** - (780) 917-7330
Website - www.stantec.com
Email - jess.nieukerk@stantec.com
Investor Relations - Jess Nieukerk (403) 569-5389
Auditors - PricewaterhouseCoopers LLP C.A.
Bankers - Canadian Imperial Bank of Commerce, Edmonton, Alta.
Lawyers - Norton Rose Fulbright LLP; Paul, Weiss, Rifkind, Wharton & Garrison LLP
Transfer Agents - Computershare Trust Company of Canada Inc., Calgary, Alta.
FP500 Revenue Ranking - 105
Employees - 26,000 at Dec. 31, 2022
Profile - (Can. 1984) Provides consulting services in engineering, architecture, interior design, landscape architecture, surveying, environmental sciences, project management and project economics for infrastructure and facilities projects. Services are provided in Canada, the U.S., the Caribbean, the U.K., Australia, New Zealand, South and Central America, Europe and Asia.

Operations are carried out through five business units: Infrastructure; Environmental Services; Water; Buildings; and Energy and Resources.

The **Infrastructure** business unit consists of evaluation, planning and designing infrastructure services for transportation, community development and urban spaces that are resilient and community friendly.

The **Environmental Services** business unit consists of provision of permitting, conservation, ecosystem restoration, health sciences and environmental, social and governance (ESG) strategy services to preserve and minimize impacts to environmental, cultural and social resources.

The **Water** business unit consists of designing solutions to provide resilience and improve health and quality of life through clean, safe water. This business unit supports the needs of communities and industry throughout the water lifecycle with tailored solutions for sustainable water resources, planning, management and infrastructure.

The **Buildings** business unit consists of integrated architecture, engineering, interior design and planning solutions to create lower-carbon innovations.

The **Energy and Resources** business consists of provision of safe and sustainable solutions for energy and resource needs globally and supports the energy transition with a focus on renewable sources.

In February 2023, the company was selected as the prime consultant for **Higland Fairview**'s US$25 billion World Logistics Center project in Moreno Valley, Calif. The company would provide civil engineering, industrial buildings architecture, geomatics, water and wastewater design, landscape architecture, urban planning, smart mobility and AV consulting, funding consulting, as well as energy and innovation design. Project design is underway, with construction slated to start in 2023.

In October 2022, the company acquired **L2, Inc.** and **Partridge Architects, Inc.** (collectively L2P), a 40-person Philadelphia-based architecture, interior design and planning firm, for an undisclosed amount. L2P provides services to the science and technology, commercial workplace, higher education, residential and hospitality markets.

In July 2022, the company has been selected as the program management consultant (PMC) for the Iona Island wastewater treatment plant (IIWWTP) projects in Vancouver, B.C. The $9.9 billion multi-year program includes construction of a new tertiary treatment facility and a range of ecological restoration and off-site works projects that will improve the connection between infrastructure, the community, and the environment. Completion of the IIWWTP projects is currently scheduled for 2038 with tertiary treatment commissioning in 2035.

Recent Merger and Acquisition Activity

Status: completed **Revised:** June 30, 2023
UPDATE: The transaction was completed. PREVIOUS: Stantec Inc. agreed to acquire private Chicago, Ill.-based Environmental Systems Design, Inc. (ESD) for $137,200,000 consisting of $86,700,000 cash and $50,500,000 in notes payable. ESD provides building engineering consulting services, specializing in mission critical and data centre services.

Status: completed **Announced:** Apr. 1, 2022
Stantec Inc. acquired Barton Willmore Holdings Limited and the assets of Barton Willmore LLP (collectively Barton Willmore) in the United Kingdom for an undisclosed amount. Barton Willmore provides planning and design services across all development sectors, with expertise in the residential space. Barton Willmore strengthens Stantec's infrastructure operations.

Predecessor Detail - Name changed from Stanley Technology Group Inc., Nov. 3, 1998.

Directors - Douglas K. Ammerman, chr., Laguna Beach, Calif.; Gordon A. (Gord) Johnston, pres. & CEO, Edmonton, Alta.; Martin A. à Porta,

Zug, Switzerland; Shelley A. M. Brown, Saskatoon, Sask.; Angeline G. Chen, Bethesda, Md.; Dr. Patricia D. Galloway, Cle Elum, Wash.; Robert J. (Bob) Gomes, Edmonton, Alta.; Donald J. (Don) Lowry, Edmonton, Alta.; Marie-Lucie Morin, Ottawa, Ont.; Celina J. Wang Doka, Newport Beach, Calif.

Other Exec. Officers - Steve M. Fleck, exec. v-p & chief practice & project officer; Theresa B. Y. Jang, exec. v-p & CFO; Stuart E. (Stu) Lerner, exec. v-p & COO, North America; Asifa Samji, exec. v-p & chief people & inclusion officer; Catherine M. (Cath) Schefer, exec. v-p & COO, global; John D. Take, exec. v-p & chief growth & innovation officer; Paul J. D. Alpern, sr. v-p, gen. counsel & corp. sec.

Capital Stock

	Authorized (shs.)	Outstanding (shs.)[1]
Preferred	unlimited	nil
Common	unlimited	110,958,545

[1] At Aug. 9, 2023

Options - At Dec. 31, 2022, options were outstanding to purchase 281,061 common shares at a weighted average exercise price of $32.98 per share which would expire on May 15, 2023.

Normal Course Issuer Bid - The company plans to make normal course purchases of up to 5,538,309 common shares representing 5% of the total outstanding. The bid commenced on Nov. 16, 2022, and expires on Nov. 15, 2023.

Major Shareholder - Mackenzie Financial Corporation held 12.17% interest at Mar. 20, 2023.

Price Range - STN/TSX

Year	Volume	High	Low	Close
2022	59,881,900	$71.31	$53.12	$64.88
2021	61,891,627	$73.10	$40.75	$71.07
2020	74,054,955	$44.85	$31.00	$41.28
2019	55,712,705	$37.26	$26.67	$36.70
2018	57,580,673	$36.83	$29.03	$29.91

Recent Close: $90.22

Capital Stock Changes - During 2022, 561,217 common shares were issued on exercise of options and 1,085,676 common shares were repurchased under a Normal Course Issuer Bid.

Dividends

STN com Ra $0.78 pa Q est. Apr. 17, 2023
Prev. Rate: $0.72 est. Apr. 18, 2022
Prev. Rate: $0.66 est. Apr. 15, 2021
Prev. Rate: $0.62 est. Apr. 15, 2020

Long-Term Debt - Outstanding at Dec. 31, 2022:

Notes payable due to 2025[1]	$62,400,000
Rev. credit facility due 2027[2 3]	533,000,000
Term loan due to 2027[3]	307,200,000
2.048% sr. unsecured notes due 2027	298,600,000
Software fin. obligs. due to 2027[4]	34,600,000
	1,235,800,000
Less: Current portion	52,200,000
	1,183,600,000

[1] Bears interest at a weighted average rate of 1.6%. Aggregate maturity value of notes is $62,800,000, with $22,800,000 (A$24,700,000) of the notes carrying value payable in Australian dollars, $28,600,000 (£17,500,000) in British pounds, and $11,400,000 in other foreign currencies.

[2] At Dec. 31, 2022, $376,000,000 was payable in Canadian funds and $157,000,000 (US$116,000,000) was payable in U.S. funds.

[3] Bears interest at an average rate of 6.09% at Dec. 31, 2022.

[4] Bears interest at rates of up to 5.94%.

Note - In June 2023, private offering of $250,000,000 principal amount of 5.393% senior unsecured notes due June 27, 2030, was completed.

Wholly Owned Subsidiaries

Cardno Consulting, LLC, Del.
International Insurance Group Inc., Barbados.
Mustang Acquisition Holdings Inc., Del.
Stantec Australia Holdings No. 1 Pty Ltd., Australia.
Stantec Australia Pty Limited, Australia.
Stantec Consulting Caribbean Ltd., Barbados.
Stantec Consulting International Ltd., Canada.
Stantec Consulting International LLC, Ariz.
Stantec Consulting Ltd., Canada.
Stantec Consulting Michigan Inc., Mich.
Stantec Consulting Services Inc., N.Y.
Stantec Delaware V LLC, Del.
Stantec Global Capital Limited, United Kingdom.
Stantec Holding (2017) Limited, United Kingdom.
Stantec Holdings LP, Alta.
Stantec Holdings ULC, Alta.
Stantec International Consulting, Inc., Del.
Stantec International Inc., Pa.
Stantec New Zealand, New Zealand.
Stantec Technology International Inc., Del.
Stantec UK Limited, United Kingdom.

Investments

Stantec Architecture Inc., N.C.
Stantec Architecture Ltd., Canada.
50% int. in **Stantec Geomatics Ltd.**, Alta.

Note: The preceding list includes only the major related companies in which interests are held.

Financial Statistics

Periods ended:	12m Dec. 31/22[A]		12m Dec. 31/21[A]
	$000s	%Chg	$000s
Operating revenue	**5,677,200**	**+24**	**4,576,800**
Cost of sales	1,220,000		940,700
Salaries & benefits	3,243,200		2,644,600
Stock-based compensation	26,000		46,700
Other operating expense	419,700		327,800
Operating expense	**5,002,400**	**+24**	**4,037,100**
Operating income	**674,800**	**+25**	**539,700**
Deprec., depl. & amort.	283,500		221,800
Finance income	5,600		4,800
Finance costs, gross	78,800		48,100
Investment income	n.a.		1,800
Write-downs/write-offs	5,500		(24,800)
Pre-tax income	**325,100**	**+24**	**263,000**
Income taxes	78,100		62,300
Net income	**247,000**	**+23**	**200,700**
Cash & equivalent	148,300		193,900
Accounts receivable	1,028,000		823,700
Current assets	1,937,800		1,664,400
Long-term investments	7,800		7,400
Fixed assets, net	250,700		233,700
Right-of-use assets	470,400		476,500
Intangibles, net	2,666,800		2,557,600
Total assets	**5,652,900**	**+8**	**5,226,400**
Bank indebtedness	65,400		7,200
Accts. pay. & accr. liabs.	755,700		634,700
Current liabilities	1,410,000		1,179,400
Long-term debt, gross	1,235,800		1,245,100
Long-term debt, net	1,183,600		1,194,100
Long-term lease liabilities	522,400		545,000
Shareholders' equity	2,286,000		2,001,700
Non-controlling interest	400		500
Cash from oper. activs.	**304,300**	**-23**	**397,000**
Cash from fin. activs.	(296,700)		276,500
Cash from invest. activs.	(73,800)		(764,800)
Net cash position	**148,300**	**-21**	**186,700**
Capital expenditures	(68,500)		(45,800)
Unfunded pension liability	n.a.		25,800
Pension fund surplus	40,400		n.a.
	$		$
Earnings per share*	2.23		1.80
Cash flow per share*	2.74		3.57
Cash divd. per share*	0.72		0.66
	shs		shs
No. of shs. o/s*	110,809,020		111,333,479
Avg. no. of shs. o/s*	110,936,481		111,242,658
	%		%
Net profit margin	4.35		4.39
Return on equity	11.52		10.21
Return on assets	5.64		4.94
Foreign sales percent	76		73
No. of employees (FTEs)	26,000		25,000

* Common
[A] Reported in accordance with IFRS

Latest Results

Periods ended:	6m June 30/23[A]		6m June 30/22[A]
	$000s	%Chg	$000s
Operating revenue	3,177,400	+18	2,690,500
Net income	152,900	+45	105,500
	$		$
Earnings per share*	1.38		0.95

* Common
[A] Reported in accordance with IFRS

Historical Summary
(as originally stated)

Fiscal Year	Oper. Rev. $000s	Net Inc. Bef. Disc. $000s	EPS* $
2022[A]	5,677,200	247,000	2.23
2021[A]	4,576,800	200,700	1.80
2020[A]	4,730,100	159,100	1.43
2019[A]	4,827,300	194,400	1.74
2018[A]	4,283,800	171,300	1.51

* Common
[A] Reported in accordance with IFRS

S.116 Star Navigation Systems Group Ltd.

Symbol - SNA **Exchange** - CSE **CUSIP** - 855157
Head Office - 11 Kenview Blvd, Brampton, ON, L6T 5G5 **Telephone** - (416) 252-2889 **Fax** - (416) 252-3963
Website - www.star-navigation.com
Email - randy.koroll@star-navigation.com
Investor Relations - Randy Koroll (416) 662-9455
Auditors - Richter LLP C.A., Toronto, Ont.
Bankers - The Toronto-Dominion Bank, Toronto, Ont.
Lawyers - Fogler, Rubinoff LLP, Toronto, Ont.
Transfer Agents - Capital Transfer Agency Inc., Toronto, Ont.

Profile - (Ont. 1993) Provides hardware and software platforms to assist aviation and other transport related operators worldwide.

Has developed Star-ISMS®, an on-board flight safety monitoring system which provides real-time monitoring and analysis of aircraft from a secure ground location. Star-A.D.S.® is an end-to-end solution which allows automated capture and delivery of the results of real-time, in-flight analysis of an agreed set of parameters. Other products include Star-T.T.T.™, an in-flight tracking and communication system incorporating two-way voice and data; Star V-trk™, a small-scale tracking and monitoring system that can be installed on smaller vehicles such as boats, marine, trains and trucks; Star-ISAMM™, an in-flight transmission system which transmits medical data concerning an on-board emergency patient to a hospital; and Star-LSAMM™, a variant of Star-ISAMM™, which transmits medical data from devices aboard air or land ambulances to a decision-making hub such as a hospital or dispatch center. Markets include commercial aviation, medical evacuation, search and rescue operations, military and shipping.

The Star-M.M.I.™ division designs, manufactures, repairs and sells on-board LCD flat screen displays for the defence and commercial aviation industries.

Subsidiary **Star-Isoneo Inc.**, a specialized software firm, develops complex solutions in engineering, simulation and development for Canadian customers.

Predecessor Detail - Name changed from Aztech New Media Corp., Aug. 23, 2002, pursuant to reverse takeover acquisition of Star Navigation Systems Inc. and amalgamation of Star with a wholly owned subsidiary; basis 1 new for 13.7907 old shs.

Directors - Gurdip (Gary) Panaich, chr., Ont.; Anoop Brar, interim CEO & COO, B.C.; Pawandeep Athwal, Ont.; Dr. Darren T. Milne, Ont.; Karl Reichert, Ont.

Other Exec. Officers - Randy Koroll, CFO & corp. sec.; Kevin Dhugga, v-p, mktg. & sales; Jean-Louis Larmor, v-p, corp. devel. & pres., Star-Isoneo Inc.; Barney Lassche, v-p, HR; Aman Siddiqui, v-p, eng.; Roger S. Peacock, gen. counsel

Capital Stock

	Authorized (shs.)	Outstanding (shs.)[1]
First Preferred	unlimited	
Series I	615,000	615,000
Series II	350,000	nil
Second Preferred	unlimited	nil
Common	unlimited	829,366,222

[1] At June 30, 2022

First Preferred - Redeemable at $1.00 per share. Non-voting. **Series I** - Entitled to non-cumulative dividends at 7% per annum. **Series II** - Entitled to cumulative dividends at 9% per annum and exchangeable for common shares at the rates of five common shares, 3.33 common shares and 2.5 common shares for each series II preferred share in each of the first, second and third years after issue, respectively.

Common - One vote per share.

Major Shareholder - Widely held at May 21, 2021.

Price Range - SNA/CSE

Year	Volume	High	Low	Close
2022	85,831,887	$0.05	$0.02	$0.04
2021	16,120,157	$0.07	$0.03	$0.04
2019	52,680,879	$0.09	$0.03	$0.03
2018	125,146,552	$0.14	$0.04	$0.07

Recent Close: $0.02

Capital Stock Changes - In October 2022, private placement of 101,328,571 units (1 common share & 1 warrant) at $0.021 per unit was completed, with warrants exercisable at 5¢ per share for one year.

In January 2022, private placement of 68,166,667 units (1 common share & 1 warrant) at 3¢ per unit was completed. Also during fiscal 2022, common shares were issued as follows: 130,043,723 for debt settlement and 8,180,000 as finders' fees.

Wholly Owned Subsidiaries

Star Navigation Systems Inc.
Star Navigation Systems (Quebec) Inc., Qué. Inactive.
Star Navigation Systems (U.K.) Ltd., United Kingdom. Inactive.

Subsidiaries

80% int. in **Star-Isoneo Inc.**, Montréal, Qué.

Financial Statistics

Periods ended:	12m June 30/22[A]	%Chg	12m June 30/21[oA]
	$000s	%Chg	$000s
Operating revenue	**25**	**-77**	**109**
Cost of goods sold	6		53
Salaries & benefits	1,701		901
Research & devel. expense	51		45
General & admin expense	2,022		1,103
Stock-based compensation	343		nil
Operating expense	**4,123**	**+96**	**2,102**
Operating income	**(4,098)**	**n.a.**	**(1,993)**
Deprec., depl. & amort.	129		97
Finance costs, gross	210		427
Pre-tax income	**(4,440)**	**n.a.**	**(446)**
Net income	**(4,440)**	**n.a.**	**(446)**
Cash & equivalent	nil		277
Inventories	38		nil
Accounts receivable	27		nil
Current assets	386		652
Fixed assets, net	56		63
Right-of-use assets	689		795
Intangibles, net	55		nil
Total assets	**1,187**	**-21**	**1,511**
Bank indebtedness	38		nil
Accts. pay. & accr. liabs	1,316		972
Current liabilities	2,879		3,852
Long-term debt, gross	427		1,548
Long-term debt, net	120		120
Long-term lease liabilities	864		967
Preferred share equity	615		615
Shareholders' equity	(2,677)		(3,428)
Cash from oper. activs	**(2,468)**	**n.a.**	**(2,080)**
Cash from fin. activs	2,185		2,343
Cash from invest. activs	(71)		(16)
Net cash position	**nil**	**n.a.**	**277**
Capital expenditures	(16)		(16)
	$		$
Earnings per share*	(0.01)		(0.00)
Cash flow per share*	(0.00)		(0.00)
	shs		shs
No. of shs. o/s*	829,366,222		622,975,832
Avg. no. of shs. o/s*	714,378,374		605,088,078
	%		%
Net profit margin	n.m.		(409.17)
Return on equity	n.m.		n.m.
Return on assets	(313.57)		(1.28)

* Common
[o] Restated
[A] Reported in accordance with IFRS

Historical Summary
(as originally stated)

Fiscal Year	Oper. Rev.	Net Inc. Bef. Disc.	EPS*
	$000s	$000s	$
2022[A]	25	(4,440)	(0.01)
2021[A]	109	(446)	(0.00)
2020[A]	110	(2,598)	(0.01)
2019[A]	463	(3,204)	(0.01)
2018[A]	175	(2,506)	(0.01)

* Common
[A] Reported in accordance with IFRS

S.117 Starlight U.S. Multi-Family (No. 2) Core Plus Fund

Symbol - SCPT.A **Exchange** - TSX-VEN **CUSIP** - 85554C
Head Office - Centre Tower, 1400-3280 Bloor St W, Toronto, ON, M8X 2X3 **Telephone** - (416) 234-8444 **Toll-free** - (866) 782-7536 **Fax** - (416) 234-8445
Website - www.starlightinvest.com
Email - mliddell@starlightinvest.com
Investor Relations - Martin Liddell (647) 729-2588
Auditors - BDO Canada LLP C.A., Toronto, Ont.
Transfer Agents - TSX Trust Company, Toronto, Ont.
Managers - Starlight Group Property Holdings Inc., Toronto, Ont.
Profile - (Ont. 2021) Acquires, owns and operates multi-family residential properties in the U.S.

The fund's primary markets consist of Arizona, California, Colorado, Florida, Georgia, Idaho, Nevada, North Carolina, Oregon, South Carolina, Tennessee, Texas, Utah and Washington.

The fund's portfolio consists of Montane, 23 garden-style buildings totaling 400 units in a suburb of Denver, Colo.; Hudson East, eight garden-style three-storey buildings and 10 garden-style two-storey buildings totaling 275 units near Orlando, Fla.; and Summermill, 10 garden-style buildings totaling 320 units in Raleigh, N.C.

The term of the fund is three years, with two one-year extensions at the option of the manager **Starlight Group Property Holdings Inc.**

Recent Merger and Acquisition Activity

Status: completed **Revised:** Apr. 27, 2022
UPDATE: The transaction was completed. PREVIOUS: Starlight U.S. Multi-Family (No. 2) Core Plus Fund acquired Summermill, a 320-suite class A multi-family property in Raleigh, N.C., for US$106,000,000, which would be financed with cash on hand and a new first mortgage on the property.

Directors - Daniel Drimmer, CEO, Toronto, Ont.; Harry Rosenbaum†, Toronto, Ont.; Kelly Smith, Toronto, Ont.
Other Exec. Officers - Evan Kirsh, pres.; Martin Liddell, CFO; David Hanick, corp. sec.
† Lead director

Capital Stock

	Authorized (shs.)	Outstanding (shs.)[1]
Class A LP Unit	unlimited	2,941,000
Class C LP Unit	unlimited	2,436,000
Class D LP Unit	unlimited	2,668,000
Class E LP Unit	unlimited	188,000
Class F LP Unit	unlimited	1,765,000
Class G LP Unit	unlimited	549,000
Class U LP Unit	unlimited	335,000

[1] At Mar. 31, 2023

Class A Limited Partnership Unit - For investors who want to make their investments and receive distributions in Canadian dollars. Includes a 3% selling concession. Convertible into class D limited partnership units at a fixed exchange rate. One vote per unit.

Class C Limited Partnership Unit - For senior management of the parent of the manager. Convertible into class A limited partnership units at a fixed exchange rate. One vote per unit.

Class D Limited Partnership Unit - For fee-based accounts. For investors who want to make their investments and receive distributions in U.S. dollars. Convertible into class U limited partnership units at a fixed exchange rate. One vote per unit.

Class E Limited Partnership Unit - For fee-based accounts. For investors who want to make their investments and receive distributions in U.S. dollars. Convertible into class U limited partnership units at a fixed exchange rate. One vote per unit.

Class F Limited Partnership Unit - For fee-based accounts. Convertible into class A limited partnership units at a fixed exchange rate. One vote per unit.

Class G Limited Partnership Unit - For institutional investors. Includes a 3% selling concession. Convertible into class A limited partnership units at a fixed exchange rate. One vote per unit.

Class U Limited Partnership Unit - For investors who want to make their investments and receive distributions in U.S. dollars. Includes a 3% selling concession. Convertible into class G limited partnership units. One vote per unit.

Major Shareholder - Daniel Drimmer held 27.8% interest at Mar. 31, 2021.

Price Range - SCPT.A/TSX-VEN

Year	Volume	High	Low	Close
2022	304,548	$11.01	$7.00	$8.00
2021	470,051	$11.50	$9.36	$10.50

Recent Close: $3.75

Capital Stock Changes - During 2022, 535,000 (net) class D limited partnership units and 5,000 (net) class G limited partnership units were issued due to conversions; and 497,000 (net) class A limited partnership units, 1,000 (net) class E limited partnership units, 38,000 (net) class F limited partnership units and 4,000 (net) class U limited partnership units were converted.

Dividends

SCPT.A cl A ltd ptnrshp unit Ra $0.40 pa M est. May 17, 2021
Listed Mar 31/21.
$0.03333i............ May 17/21
SCPT.U cl U ltd ptnrshp unit Ra US$0.40 pa M est. May 17, 2021
Listed Mar 31/21.
US$0.03333i......... May 17/21
i Initial Payment

Wholly Owned Subsidiaries

Starlight U.S. Multi-Family (No. 2) Core Plus REIT Inc.
Starlight U.S. Multi-Family (No. 2) Core Plus Holding LP
Starlight U.S. Multi-Family (No. 2) Core Plus Investment LP

Financial Statistics

Periods ended:	12m Dec. 31/22[A]	%Chg	12m Dec. 31/21[A]
	US$000s	%Chg	US$000s
Total revenue	**18,238**	**+81**	**10,104**
Rental operating expense	4,428		2,464
Other operating expense	1,351		859
Operating expense	**5,779**	**+74**	**3,323**
Operating income	**12,459**	**+84**	**6,781**
Finance costs, gross	7,266		6,111
Pre-tax income	**(5,201)**	**n.a.**	**37,816**
Income taxes	1,013		14,046
Net income	**(6,214)**	**n.a.**	**23,770**
Cash & equivalent	4,229		6,445
Current assets	6,693		7,610
Income-producing props	355,500		255,200
Total assets	**368,927**	**+40**	**263,166**
Accts. pay. & accr. liabs	2,004		1,541
Current liabilities	10,675		41,304
Long-term debt, gross	241,252		130,419
Long-term debt, net	234,333		91,411
Shareholders' equity	98,855		105,069
Cash from oper. activs	**10,129**	**+61**	**6,276**
Cash from fin. activs	98,300		205,596
Cash from invest. activs	(110,650)		(205,439)
Net cash position	**4,229**	**-34**	**6,445**
Increase in property	(110,650)		(205,439)
	US$		US$
Earnings per share*	n.a.		n.a.
Cash flow per share*	0.97		0.58
Funds from opers. per sh.*	$0.05		$0.21
Adj. funds from opers. per sh.*	$0.09		$0.28
Cash divd. per share*	$0.33		$0.30
Total divd. per share*	**$0.33**		**$0.30**
	shs		shs
No. of shs. o/s*	10,432,000		10,432,000
	%		%
Net profit margin	(34.07)		235.25
Return on equity	(6.09)		n.m.
Return on assets	0.78		n.a.

* Cl.A LP Unit
[A] Reported in accordance with IFRS

Latest Results

Periods ended:	3m Mar. 31/23[A]	%Chg	3m Mar. 31/22[A]
	US$000s	%Chg	US$000s
Total revenue	5,279	+53	3,453
Net income	(1,872)	n.a.	8,820
	US$		US$
Earnings per share*	n.a.		n.a.

[A] Reported in accordance with IFRS

S.118 Starlight U.S. Residential Fund

Symbol - SURF.A **Exchange** - TSX-VEN **CUSIP** - 85555B
Head Office - c/o Starlight Group Property Holdings Inc., Centre Tower, 1400-3280 Bloor St W, Toronto, ON, M8X 2X3 **Telephone** - (416) 234-8444 **Fax** - (416) 234-8445
Website - www.starlightinvest.com
Email - ekirsh@starlightus.com
Investor Relations - Evan Kirsh (647) 725-0417
Auditors - BDO Canada LLP C.A., Toronto, Ont.
Transfer Agents - TSX Trust Company, Toronto, Ont.
Managers - Starlight Group Property Holdings Inc., Toronto, Ont.
Profile - (Ont. 2021) Acquires, owns and operates income-producing residential properties located primarily in Arizona, California, Colorado, Florida, Georgia, Idaho, Nevada, North Carolina, Oregon, South Carolina, Tennessee, Texas, Utah and Washington.

The term of the fund is three years, with two one-year extensions at the option of the manager **Starlight Group Property Holdings Inc.**

The fund's portfolio consists of Bainbridge Sunlake in Tampa, Fla., consisting of 268 multi-family residential suites in 11 three-storey buildings and a central clubhouse; Eight at East in Orlando, Fla., consisting of 264 multi-family residential suites in 20 garden-style two and three storey buildings; Indigo Apartments located 25 km northwest of downtown Raleigh, N.C., consisting of 489 multi-family residential suites in 52 two and three-storey buildings and a central clubhouse; Lyric Apartments in Las Vegas, Nev., consisting of 376 multi-residential suites in 31 two-storey buildings and a central clubhouse; Emerson at Buda in Austin, Tex., consisting of 304 multi-family residential suites in 22 garden-style two-storey buildings; 90% interest in The Ventura in Phoenix, Ariz., consisting of 272 multi-family suites in 37 two storey buildings; and 42 single-family residential properties in Atlanta, Ga.

During the nine-month ended Sept. 30, 2022, the fund acquired 49 single-family rental homes in Atlanta, Ga., for total consideration of US$11,042,000.

Recent Merger and Acquisition Activity

Status: completed **Revised:** June 2, 2023
UPDATE: The transaction was completed. PREVIOUS: Starlight U.S. Residential Fund agreed to sell 56 out of its 98 single-family homes in

the suburban area of Atlanta, Ga., to an institutional investor for US$13,770,000. The transaction is scheduled to close on or about June 1, 2023.

Status: completed **Revised:** May 25, 2022

UPDATE: The transaction was completed. PREVIOUS: Starlight U.S. Residential Fund agreed to acquire a 90% interest in The Ventura, a 272-suite class A institutional multi-family property in Phoenix, Ariz., for US$117,500,000. The remaining 10% would be acquired by Daniel Drimmer.

Status: completed **Revised:** Apr. 27, 2022

UPDATE: The transaction was completed. PREVIOUS: Starlight U.S. Residential Fund agreed to acquire Eight at East, a 264-suite class A institutional multi-family property in Orlando, Fla., for US$91,750,000.

Trustees - Harry Rosenbaum, chr., Toronto, Ont.; Daniel Drimmer, CEO, Toronto, Ont.; Kelly Smith, Toronto, Ont.

Oper. Subsid./Mgt. Co. Officers - Evan Kirsh, pres.; Martin Liddell, CFO; David Hanick, corp. sec.

Capital Stock

	Authorized (shs.)	Outstanding (shs.)[1]
Class A Unit	unlimited	2,675,000
Class B LP Unit	unlimited	750,000[2]
Class C Unit	unlimited	2,680,000
Class D Unit	unlimited	11,848,000
Class E Unit	unlimited	694,000
Class F Unit	unlimited	6,386,000
Class G Unit	unlimited	918,000
Class I Unit	unlimited	3,500,000
Class U Unit	unlimited	1,077,000
Special Vtg. Unit	unlimited	750,000
U.S. REIT series A		250[3 4]

[1] At Mar. 31, 2023

[2] Units of certain subsidiary limited partnerships of the fund.

[3] Classified as debt.

[4] Shares of wholly owned U.S. MF REIT and U.S. SF REIT.

Class A Unit - Convertible into class D units. One vote per unit.

Class B Limited Partnership Unit - Convertible into class C units. One vote per unit. All owned by Daniel Drimmer.

Class C Unit - For senior management of the manager. Convertible into class A units. One vote per unit.

Class D Unit - Convertible into class A units. One vote per unit.

Class E Unit - For fee-based accounts. For investors who want to make their investments and receive distributions in U.S. dollars. Convertible into class U units. One vote per unit.

Class F Unit - For fee-based accounts. Convertible into class A units. One vote per unit.

Class G Unit - For investors who want to make their investments and receive distributions in U.S. dollars. Convertible into class U units. One vote per unit.

Class I Unit - For institutional investors. Convertible into class A units. One vote per unit.

Class U Unit - For investors who want to make their investments and receive distributions in U.S. dollars. Convertible into class G units. One vote per unit.

Special Voting Unit - Only issued in connection with the issuance of class B limited partnership units. Non-transferable. Will automatically be redeemed and cancelled upon the exchange or surrender of a class B limited partnership unit. One voter per unit. All owned by Daniel Drimmer.

U.S. REIT series A preferred - Issued by wholly owned **Starlight U.S. Residential (Multi-Family) REIT Inc.** (U.S. MF REIT) and **Starlight U.S. Residential (Single-Family) REIT Inc.** (U.S. SF REIT). Entitled to 12% cumulative dividends payable semi-annually. Redeemable at $1.00 per share. Non-voting.

Major Shareholder - Widely held at Nov. 15, 2021.

Price Range - SURF.A/TSX-VEN

Year	Volume	High	Low	Close
2022	703,368	$10.78	$6.02	$7.00
2021	89,891	$10.88	$9.58	$9.71

Recent Close: $4.20

Capital Stock Changes - During 2022, 884,000 (net) class D units and 116,000 (net) class G units were issued; and 795,000 (net) class A units, 6,000 (net) class E units, 88,000 (net) class F units and 111,000 (net) class U units were cancelled due to conversions. In addition, 250 U.S. REIT series A preferred shares were issued.

Dividends

SURF.A cl A unit Ra $0.39216 pa M est. Feb. 15, 2022
Listed Nov 15/21.
Prev. Rate: $0.39221 est. Jan. 17, 2022
$0.04943**i**............ Jan. 17/22
SURF.U cl U unit Ra US$0.39216 pa M est. Feb. 15, 2022
Listed Nov 15/21.
Prev. Rate: US$0.39221 est. Jan. 17, 2022
US$0.04943**i**......... Jan. 17/22
i Initial Payment

Wholly Owned Subsidiaries

Starlight U.S. Residential (Multi-Family) Holding L.P., United States.
Starlight U.S. Residential (Multi-Family) Investment L.P., United States.
Starlight U.S. Residential (Multi-Family) REIT Inc., United States.
Starlight U.S. Residential (Single-Family) Holding L.P., United States.
Starlight U.S. Residential (Single-Family) Investment L.P., United States.
Starlight U.S. Residential (Single-Family) REIT Inc., United States.

Financial Statistics

Periods ended:	12m Dec. 31/22[A]
	US$000s
Total revenue	**34,876**
Rental operating expense	8,470
Property taxes	3,034
Other operating expense	2,683
Operating expense	**14,187**
Operating income	**20,689**
Finance costs, gross	15,148
Pre-tax income	**(22,693)**
Income taxes	925
Net income	**(23,618)**
Net inc. for equity hldrs	**(21,709)**
Net inc. for non-cont. int	**(1,909)**
Cash & equivalent	7,628
Accounts receivable	578
Current assets	12,170
Income-producing props	672,026
Property interests, net	672,026
Total assets	**691,638**
Accts. pay. & accr. liabs	3,561
Current liabilities	25,825
Long-term debt, gross	464,944
Long-term debt, net	445,387
Shareholders' equity	216,685
Non-controlling interest	2,175
Cash from oper. activs	**18,303**
Cash from fin. activs	217,230
Cash from invest. activs	(238,312)
Net cash position	**7,628**
Capital expenditures	(5,859)
Increase in property	(236,537)
	US$
Earnings per share*	n.a.
Cash flow per share*	0.58
Funds from opers. per sh.*	$ (0.04)
Adj. funds from opers. per sh.*	$ (0.02)
Cash divd. per share*	$0.33
Total divd. per share*	**$0.33**
	shs
No. of shs. o/s	n.a.
Avg. no. of shs. o/s*	31,819,924
	%
Net profit margin	(67.72)
Return on equity	n.m.
Return on assets	n.a.
Foreign sales percent	100

* Cl.A Unit

[A] Reported in accordance with IFRS

Latest Results

Periods ended:	3m Mar. 31/23[A]		3m Mar. 31/22[A]
	US$000s	%Chg	US$000s
Total revenue	10,063	+53	6,577
Net income	(4,563)	n.a.	10,299
Net inc. for equity hldrs	(4,462)	n.a.	10,299
Net inc. for non-cont. int	(101)		nil
	US$		US$
Earnings per share*	n.a.		n.a.

[A] Reported in accordance with IFRS

S.119 Starrex International Ltd.

Symbol - STX **Exchange** - CSE **CUSIP** - 855679

Head Office - 1250-639 5 Ave SW, Calgary, AB, T2P 0M9 **Telephone** - (281) 406-8337

Website - www.starrexintl.com

Email - dmerritt@starrexintl.com

Investor Relations - Dr. Deborah Merritt (281) 406-8621

Auditors - McGovern Hurley LLP C.A., Toronto, Ont.

Bankers - Bank of Montreal

Lawyers - Dickinson Wright LLP, Toronto, Ont.

Transfer Agents - Reliable Stock Transfer Inc., Toronto, Ont.

Profile - (Can. 1982) Provides real estate services in the U.S., including consumer credit reporting and title services.

Through wholly owned **MFI Credit Solutions, LLC**, provides consumer credit reports to mortgage lenders, mortgage brokers and credit unions for home buyers considering the purchase or refinance of a home. Also provides risk mitigation, flood and verification services.

Through wholly owned **All American Title Co., Inc.**, provides services required to transfer title to property in real estate transactions in Minnesota and Wisconsin. Such services include as searching, abstracting, examining, closing and insuring the condition of the title to the property.

Recent Merger and Acquisition Activity

Status: pending **Announced:** May 1, 2023

Starrex International, Ltd. entered into a letter of intent to acquire four U.S. entities (Magnolia Title Arkansas, LLC, Magnolia Title Florida, LLC, Coast to Coast Title, LLC and Sol City Title, LLC) (collectively Magnolia Title) for US$18,600,000 plus potential performance-based consideration. A shareholder of Starrex holds about 24% interest in Magnolia Title and Starrex has advanced about US$3,000,000 to Magnolia Title. Magnolia Title provides title and escrow services from 21 offices in Texas, Florida and Arkansas.

Status: completed **Announced:** Mar. 17, 2023

Starrex International Ltd. acquired All American Title Co., Inc., AmeriFirst Title, LLC, AAT Holdings, LLC, Ameripine, LLC and Amcap Title, LLC for US$10,359,160 consisting of US$1,800,000 cash, a US$4,500,000 secured promissory note due 12 months after closing, US$2,700,000 in 6% secured convertible notes due 36 months after closing, 250,000 common shares of Starrex at US$1.20 per share, and 200,000 options to purchase common shares of Starrex. The acquired companies provided real estate title services in Minnesota and Wisconsin. The businesses and net assets of the acquired companies were concurrently consolidated within All American Title Co., Inc.

Status: completed **Revised:** Nov. 8, 2022

UPDATE: The transaction was completed. The final purchase price was US$9,847,000 after adjustments. PREVIOUS: Starrex International Ltd. agreed to sell the net assets and businesses of wholly owned Property Interlink, LLC and Reliable Valuation Service, LLC to Chicago, Ill.-based StoicLane Inc. for US$9,800,000. Property Interlink conducted Starrex's real estate appraisal management business and Reliable Valuation conducted Starrex's residential appraisal business. Starrex's board of directors unanimously approved the transaction.

Predecessor Detail - Name changed from Starrex Mining Corporation Ltd., May 1, 2014.

Directors - Matthew D. Hill, chr., pres. & CEO, Tomball, Tex.; Charles M. Burns, Maple, Ont.; P. Garrett Clayton, Houston, Tex.; Scott M. Reeves, Calgary, Alta.

Other Exec. Officers - Dr. Deborah (Debbie) Merritt, CFO

Capital Stock

	Authorized (shs.)	Outstanding (shs.)[1]
Common	unlimited	16,546,113

[1] At Mar. 31, 2023

Major Shareholder - The Clayton Legacy Foundation held 19.86% interest and Tyrrell L. Garth held 19.77% interest at Oct. 4, 2022.

Price Range - STX/CSE

Year	Volume	High	Low	Close
2022	272,811	$2.26	$0.65	$2.20
2021	352,018	$1.65	$0.60	$1.65
2020	652,357	$0.84	$0.36	$0.84
2019	226,942	$1.45	$0.65	$0.70
2018	103,874	$2.00	$0.51	$1.49

Recent Close: $0.75

Capital Stock Changes - During 2022, 543,588 common shares were issued for services.

Wholly Owned Subsidiaries

All American Title Co., Inc., Blaine, Minn.
MFI Credit Solutions, LLC, Wyo.
Property Interlink, LLC, Colo. Inactive.
Reliable Valuation Service, LLC, Wyo. Inactive.
Starrex Holdings, Inc.
Starrex Insurance Holdings, Inc.
Starrex Technical Services, LLC

Financial Statistics

Periods ended:	12m Dec. 31/22[A]		12m Dec. 31/21[□A]
	US$000s	%Chg	US$000s
Total revenue	**3,809**	**-29**	**5,374**
Salaries & benefits	807		607
General & admin. expense	1,184		1,115
Other operating expense	2,339		3,540
Operating expense	**4,330**	**-18**	**5,262**
Operating income	**(521)**	**n.a.**	**112**
Deprec. & amort.	291		171
Finance costs, gross	15		nil
Write-downs/write-offs	(377)		nil
Pre-tax income	**(1,221)**	**n.a.**	**(66)**
Income taxes	nil		49
Net inc. bef. disc. opers	**(1,221)**	**n.a.**	**(114)**
Income from disc. opers	5,377		649
Net income	**4,156**	**+677**	**535**
Cash & equivalent	7,857		2,172
Accounts receivable	479		992
Current assets	10,446		3,278
Fixed assets, net	264		318
Right-of-use assets	170		290
Intangibles	576		1,813
Total assets	**11,455**	**+101**	**5,699**
Bank indebtedness	850		nil
Accts. pay. & accr. liabs	773		1,635
Current liabilities	3,175		2,022
Long-term lease liabilities	86		207
Shareholders' equity	8,195		3,470
Cash from oper. activs	**(1,243)**	**n.a.**	**1,047**
Cash from fin. activs	733		(65)
Cash from invest. activs	6,195		(303)
Net cash position	**7,857**	**+262**	**2,172**
Capital expenditures	(53)		(268)
	US$		US$
Earns. per sh. bef disc opers*	(0.08)		(0.01)
Earnings per share*	0.26		0.03
Cash flow per share*	(0.08)		0.07
	shs		shs
No. of shs. o/s*	16,296,113		15,752,525
Avg. no. of shs. o/s*	15,832,968		15,741,840
	%		%
Net profit margin	(32.06)		(2.12)
Return on equity	n.m.		n.m.
Return on assets	n.a.		n.a.

* Common
[□] Restated
[A] Reported in accordance with IFRS

Latest Results

Periods ended:	3m Mar. 31/23[A]		3m Mar. 31/22[□A]
	US$000s	%Chg	US$000s
Total revenue	1,276	0	1,278
Net inc. bef. disc. opers	(441)	n.a.	(90)
Income from disc. opers	nil		96
Net income	(441)	n.a.	6
	US$		US$
Earns. per sh. bef. disc. opers.*	(0.03)		(0.01)
Earnings per share*	(0.03)		0.00

* Common
[□] Restated
[A] Reported in accordance with IFRS

Historical Summary
(as originally stated)

Fiscal Year	Total Rev.	Net Inc. Bef. Disc.	EPS*
	US$000s	US$000s	US$
2022[A]	3,809	(1,221)	(0.08)
2021[A]	20,716	535	0.03
2020[A]	17,051	1,689	0.11
2019[A]	12,076	(1,040)	(0.07)
2018[A]	9,655	(812)	(0.06)

* Common
[A] Reported in accordance with IFRS

S.120 StateHouse Holdings Inc

Symbol - STHZ **Exchange** - CSE **CUSIP** - 85754G
Head Office - 1295 West Morena Blvd, San Diego, CA, United States, 92110 **Toll-free** - (800) 892-4209
Website - statehouseholdings.com
Email - ir@statehouseholdings.com
Investor Relations - John H. Nichols (800) 892-4209
Auditors - Armanino LLP C.P.A., San Ramon, Calif.
Transfer Agents - Odyssey Trust Company, Toronto, Ont.
Profile - (Ont. 2011; orig. Alta., 2001) Cultivates, manufactures, distributes and sells wholesale and retail medicinal and/or recreational cannabis and cannabis products in California and Oregon.

Operations include 13 dispensaries in northern and southern California and one in Oregon, distribution facilities in San Jose and Los Angeles, Calif., and integrated cultivation/production facilities in Salinas and Greenfield, Calif. Product brands include Fuzzies, Sublime, KEY Harborside Farms, Kingpen, Urban Leaf, Loudpack, Dimebag and Smokiez. Retail brands are Urban Leaf, Harborside and Terpene Station.

In April 2022, the company acquired **LPF JV Corporation** (dba Loudpack), a manufacturer, cultivator and distributor of cannabis brands in California, for issuance of 90,752,139 subordinate voting shares, 2,000,000 warrants, the restructuring and assumption of US$50,000,000 of debt and US$5,000,000 in cash.

On Mar. 1, 2022, the company acquired **UL Holdings Inc.** (dba Urban Leaf), a California cannabis retailer, for issuance of 60,000,000 subordinate voting shares and the restructuring and assumption of UL debt.

Predecessor Detail - Name changed from Harborside Inc., July 25, 2022.

Directors - Matthew K. (Matt) Hawkins, chr., Dallas, Tex.; Edward M. (Ed) Schmults, CEO, R.I.; Marc Ravner, pres., integration, N.Y.; J. Roy Pottle, Fla.; James E. (Jim) Scott, Colo.; Felicia Snyder, Ont.

Other Exec. Officers - Kavi Bhai, CFO; Robert Bacchi, chief tech. officer; Will Senn, chief corp. devel. officer; Travis Higginbotham Jr., v-p, prod.; Keith Li, v-p, fin.; Angela Pih, v-p, mktg.; Marian Robinson, v-p, HR; John H. (Jack) Nichols, gen. counsel & corp. sec.

Capital Stock

	Authorized (shs.)	Outstanding (shs.)[1]
Common	unlimited	252,589,611

[1] At Nov. 22, 2022

Common (formerly **Subordinate Voting**) - One vote per share.
Multiple Voting (old) - Were each convertible into 100 subordinate voting shares. 100 votes per share. Mandatory conversion into common shares on a 100-for-1 basis on Mar. 31, 2022.
Major Shareholder - Andrew Sturner held 11.06% interest and Matthew K. (Matt) Hawkins held 11% interest at Apr. 25, 2022.

Price Range - STHZ/CSE

Year	Volume	High	Low	Close
2022	9,542,651	$0.81	$0.08	$0.10
2021	23,862,067	$3.19	$0.42	$0.46
2020	10,217,650	$2.22	$0.29	$1.96
2019	8,916,361	$6.28	$0.50	$0.67
2018	1,463,018	$20.28	$6.48	$6.90

Consolidation: 1-for-41.8182 cons. in June 2019
Recent Close: $0.05
Capital Stock Changes - On Mar. 1, 2022, 60,000,000 subordinate voting shares were issued pursuant to the acquisition of UL Holdings Inc. On Mar. 31, 2022, all 425,791 multiple voting shares were converted into subordinate voting shares on a 100-for-1 basis. Effective July 25, 2022, subordinate voting shares were reclassified as common shares.

Wholly Owned Subsidiaries

Accucanna LLC, Desert Hot Springs, Calif.
Encinal Productions RE, LLC, Calif.
FLRish, Inc., Calif.
- 100% int. in **FLRish Farms Management & Security Services, LLC**, Calif.
- 100% int. in **FLRish Flagship Enterprises, Inc.**, Calif.
- 100% int. in **FLRish IP, LLC**, Calif.
- 100% int. in **FLRish Retail Affiliates, LLC**, Calif.
- 100% int. in **FLRish Retail, LLC**, Calif.
  - 100% int. in **FLRish Retail JV, LLC**, Calif.
  - 100% int. in **FLRish Retail Management & Security Services, LLC**, Calif.
    - 100% int. in **FLRish Farms Cultivation 7, LLC**, Calif.
    - 100% int. in **FLRish Farms Cultivation 2, LLC**, Calif.
- 100% int. in **Savature, Inc.**, Calif.
  - 100% int. in **SaVaca, LLC**, Calif.
    - 100% int. in **FFC1, LLC**, Calif.

Haight Acquisition Corporation, Del.
- 21% int. in **FGW Haight, Inc.**, Calif.

LPF JV Corporation, Los Angeles, Calif.
Patients Mutual Assistance Collective Corporation, Calif.
- 100% int. in **San Jose Wellness Solutions Corp.**, Calif.
  - 100% int. in **San Leandro Wellness Solutions Corp.**, Calif.

Sublimation Inc., Oakland, Calif.
UL Holdings Inc., Calif.
Unite Capital Corp., Toronto, Ont.
- 100% int. in **LGC Holdings USA Inc.**, Nev.
  - 100% int. in **LGC Operations LLC**, Nev.
    - 100% int. in **Lineage GCL California LLC**, Calif.
    - 100% int. in **Lineage GCL Oregon Corp.**, Ore.
      - 100% int. in **LGCLORDIS1 LLC**, Ore.
        - 100% int. in **LGCLORDIS2 LLC**, Ore.

Note: The preceding list includes only the major related companies in which interests are held.

Financial Statistics

Periods ended:	12m Dec. 31/21[A]		12m Dec. 31/20[A]
	US$000s	%Chg	US$000s
Operating revenue	**60,301**	**+1**	**59,954**
Cost of goods sold	37,959[1]		30,360
Salaries & benefits	11,320		11,219
General & admin expense	19,080		15,881
Stock-based compensation	788		1,059
Operating expense	**69,147**	**+18**	**58,518**
Operating income	**(8,846)**	**n.a.**	**1,436**
Deprec., depl. & amort.	2,164		997
Finance costs, net	3,225		4,708
Write-downs/write-offs	(25,117)		(3,908)
Pre-tax income	**(28,146)**	**n.a.**	**(5,832)**
Income taxes	(1,778)		6,115
Net income	**(26,368)**	**n.a.**	**(11,947)**
Net inc. for equity hldrs	**(26,158)**	**n.a.**	**(11,947)**
Net inc. for non-cont. int	**(209)**	**n.a.**	**nil**
Cash & equivalent	8,775		10,459
Inventories	6,414		3,786
Accounts receivable	4,546		1,932
Current assets	27,124		19,808
Long-term investments	2,458		250
Fixed assets, net	23,516		17,910
Right-of-use assets	4,433		4,708
Intangibles, net	95,899		72,274
Total assets	**153,821**	**+34**	**114,969**
Accts. pay. & accr. liabs	23,693		17,199
Current liabilities	70,615		63,466
Long-term debt, gross	11,846		11,200
Long-term debt, net	11,846		10,726
Long-term lease liabilities	5,615		5,959
Shareholders' equity	44,756		15,565
Non-controlling interest	2,857		3,067
Cash from oper. activs	**(15,284)**	**n.a.**	**(1,746)**
Cash from fin. activs	27,707		(108)
Cash from invest. activs	(13,917)		(855)
Net cash position	**9,091**	**-13**	**10,459**
Capital expenditures	(3,309)		(755)
	US$		US$
Earnings per share*	(0.38)		(0.28)
Cash flow per share*	(0.22)		(0.04)
	shs		shs
No. of shs. o/s*	82,122,480		44,445,250
Avg. no. of shs. o/s*	68,158,181		42,505,013
	%		%
Net profit margin	(43.73)		(19.93)
Return on equity	(86.73)		n.m.
Return on assets	(19.62)		n.a.
No. of employees (FTEs)	230		200

* Subord. Vtg.
[A] Reported in accordance with IFRS
[1] Net of biological asset adjustments.

Latest Results

Periods ended:	9m Sept. 30/22[A]		9m Sept. 30/21[A]
	US$000s	%Chg	US$000s
Operating revenue	82,712	+83	45,241
Net income	(44,523)	n.a.	1,436
Net inc. for equity hldrs	(43,967)	n.a.	1,581
Net inc. for non-cont. int	(556)		(145)
	US$		US$
Earnings per share*	(0.22)		0.03

* Subord. Vtg.
[A] Reported in accordance with IFRS

Historical Summary
(as originally stated)

Fiscal Year	Oper. Rev.	Net Inc. Bef. Disc.	EPS*
	US$000s	US$000s	US$
2021[A]	60,301	(26,368)	(0.38)
2020[A]	59,954	(11,947)	(0.28)
2019[A1]	47,341	(49,458)	(1.49)
	$000s	$000s	$
2019[A2]	679	(6,328)	(4.47)
2018[A]	nil	(2,592)	(3.30)

* Subord. Vtg.
[A] Reported in accordance with IFRS
[1] Results reflect the May 30, 2019, reverse takeover acquisition of FLRish Inc. (dba Harborside).
[2] Results for fiscal 2019 and prior fiscal years pertain to Lineage Grow Company Ltd.
Note: Adjusted throughout for 1-for-41.818182 cons. in June 2019

S.121 Steep Hill Inc.

Symbol - STPH **Exchange** - CSE **CUSIP** - 85832P
Head Office - 30 Commercial Rd, Toronto, ON, M4G 1Z4 **Telephone** - (647) 501-1688
Website - www.steephill.com
Email - sameet.kanade@steephill.com
Investor Relations - Sameet Kanade (416) 847-7312
Auditors - MNP LLP C.A., Burlington, Ont.
Transfer Agents - Capital Transfer Agency Inc., Toronto, Ont.
Profile - (Can. 2018) Seeking new business opportunities.

Prior to April 2023, the company provided analytical testing services for the hemp and cannabis sectors in the U.S. from a laboratory in Berkeley, Calif. Services included testing for pesticides, mycotoxins, heavy metals, residual solvents, microbial, water activity, vitamin E Acetate and hemp analysis, as well as homogeneity testing, foreign matter inspection, terpenes and cannabinoids (potency) analysis.

In June 2023, sale of substantially all remaining assets of the company, consisting of a licensed mark in the U.S., to **Overlook Partners, LLC** was proposed.

In April 2023, wholly owned **Steep Hill Inc.** terminated its remaining license agreements in the U.S., negotiated settlement and release agreements thereby ending its contractual obligations with such licensees, and laid off the remainder of its U.S.-based employees and consultants. As a result, the company had no operations in the U.S.

On Feb. 28 2023, wholly owned subsidiary **Steep Hill Inc.** (Steep Hill US) terminated its license agreements with **Green Analytics MD, LLC, Green Analytics Massachusetts LLC, Green Analytics East LLC, Green Analytics North LLC, Green Analytics Virginia, LLC, Green Analytics West Virginia, LLC** and **Green Analytics New York, LLC.** In consideration and in settlement of all royalty and other amounts owing, the Green Analytics companies agreed to pay US$2,000,000 to Steep Hill US.

On Dec. 1, 2022, subsidiary **Canbud D2385NR Inc.** was dissolved.

On Oct. 21, 2022, wholly owned **MSC Corp.** and its wholly owned **Steep Hill Canada Inc.** filed for bankruptcy proceedings in Canada and these subsidiaries were deconsolidated from the company's accounts.

In September 2022, the company closed its analytical testing facility in Scarborough, Ont.

On July 31, 2022, the company terminated its lease on 55 acres of farm land in Lakefield, Ont., where it held a hemp licence for the growing and harvesting of hemp CBD flowers for processing into CBD and other cannabinoids extracts.

On July 19, 2022, subsidiaries **Canbud D580H124 Inc., Canbud D1726KC Inc., Canbud DEPL Corp.** and **Empathy Plant Co.** were dissolved.

Predecessor Detail - Name changed from Canbud Distribution Corporation, Feb. 28, 2022.

Directors - Sameet Kanade, CEO, Ont.; Ian Morton, Ont.; Anthony Viele, Woodbridge, Ont.; Dr. Jane Wright-Mitchell, Ont.

Other Exec. Officers - Patricia Militello, interim CFO

Capital Stock

	Authorized (shs.)	Outstanding (shs.)[1]
Common	unlimited	242,844,610

[1] At June 13, 2023

Major Shareholder - Widely held at June 13, 2023.

Price Range - STPH/CSE

Year	Volume	High	Low	Close
2022	53,152,601	$0.05	$0.01	$0.01
2021	44,180,225	$0.28	$0.04	$0.04
2020	15,229,884	$0.24	$0.04	$0.16

Recent Close: $0.01

Capital Stock Changes - In June 2023, a share consolidation of up to 1-for-15 was proposed.

On Jan. 31, 2022, 82,000,000 common shares were issued pursuant to the acquisition of (old) Steep Hill Inc. Also during 2022, 2,870,000 common shares were issued for services and 1,126,883 common shares were cancelled and returned to treasury.

Wholly Owned Subsidiaries

MSC Corp., Toronto, Ont.
• 100% int. in **Steep Hill Canada Inc.**
Steep Hill Inc., United States.

Financial Statistics

Periods ended:	12m Dec. 31/22[A]		12m Dec. 31/21[◻A]
	$000s	%Chg	$000s
Operating revenue	**3,073**	**+227**	**939**
Salaries & benefits	2,505		583
General & admin expense	2,518		2,560
Stock-based compensation	127		749
Operating expense	**2,077**	**-47**	**3,892**
Operating income	**996**	**n.a.**	**(2,953)**
Deprec., depl. & amort	826		522
Finance costs, gross	45		53
Write-downs/write-offs	(4,737)		(371)
Pre-tax income	**(7,249)**	**n.a.**	**(4,544)**
Income taxes	(135)		nil
Net income	**(7,114)**	**n.a.**	**(4,544)**
Net inc. for equity hldrs	**(7,122)**	**n.a.**	**(4,531)**
Net inc. for non-cont. int	**7**	**n.a.**	**(14)**
Cash & equivalent	1,913		2,584
Accounts receivable	649		276
Current assets	2,474		2,911
Fixed assets, net	34		2,726
Intangibles, net	408		1,164
Total assets	**3,016**	**-59**	**7,434**
Bank indebtedness	nil		146
Accts. pay. & accr. liabs	1,790		1,007
Current liabilities	2,151		1,279
Long-term debt, gross	40		37
Long-term lease liabilities	23		446
Shareholders' equity	842		5,770
Non-controlling interest	nil		(61)
Cash from oper. activs	**(1,817)**	**n.a.**	**(1,570)**
Cash from fin. activs	(254)		4,045
Cash from invest. activs	1,475		(337)
Net cash position	**1,913**	**-26**	**2,576**
Capital expenditures	nil		(1)
Capital disposals	750		nil
	$		$
Earnings per share*	(0.03)		(0.05)
Cash flow per share*	(0.01)		(0.01)
	shs		shs
No. of shs. o/s*	242,844,610		159,101,493
Avg. no. of shs. o/s*	236,763,356		90,799,699
	%		%
Net profit margin	(231.50)		(483.92)
Return on equity	(215.40)		(130.02)
Return on assets	(135.31)		(98.30)
No. of employees (FTEs)	...		14

* Common
◻ Restated
[A] Reported in accordance with IFRS

Latest Results

Periods ended:	3m Mar. 31/23[A]		3m Mar. 31/22[◻A]
	$000s	%Chg	$000s
Operating revenue	nil	n.a.	417
Net inc. bef. disc. opers	(143)	n.a.	(665)
Income from disc. opers	2,156		(222)
Net income	2,012	n.a.	(888)
	$		$
Earns. per sh. bef. disc. opers.*	(0.00)		(0.00)
Earnings per share*	0.01		(0.01)

* Common
◻ Restated
[A] Reported in accordance with IFRS

Historical Summary
(as originally stated)

Fiscal Year	Oper. Rev.	Net Inc. Bef. Disc.	EPS*
	$000s	$000s	$
2022[A]	3,073	(7,114)	(0.03)
2021[A]	939	(4,544)	(0.04)
2020[A]	nil	(2,120)	(0.05)
2019[A1]	nil	(471)	(0.02)

* Common
[A] Reported in accordance with IFRS
[1] 15 months ended Dec. 31, 2019.

S.122 Steer Technologies Inc.

Symbol - STER **Exchange** - TSX-VEN **CUSIP** - 858335
Head Office - Unit 16, 44 East Beaver Creek Rd, Richmond Hill, ON, L4B 1G8 **Telephone** - (905) 944-6536 **Toll-free** - (888) 300-2228 **Fax** - (905) 944-6520
Website - www.steeresg.com
Email - suman@steeresg.com
Investor Relations - Suman Pushparajah (905) 944-6536
Auditors - SRCO Professional Corporation C.A., Richmond Hill, Ont.
Transfer Agents - Odyssey Trust Company, Toronto, Ont.

Profile - (Ont. 2019; orig. Alta., 2018) Offers environmental, socially-conscious and governance-oriented (ESG) technology platform offering on-demand and subscription-based mobility and delivery services.

The company's offerings fall into two categories: Subscription-based offerings led by its flagship electric vehicle subscription business, STEER EV, providing car subscription services in Toronto, Ont., Vancouver, B.C., Washington, D.C., Austin, Tex, and Tampa, Fla.; and On-demand offerings incorporating delivery, business-to-business (B2B) marketplace (STEER Business), Delivery-as-a-Service (DaaS), health technology and rideshare services.

The company's platform is powered by EcoCRED, its big data, analytics and machine learning engine which seeks to capture, analyze, parse and report on key data points in ways that measure the company's impact on carbon reductions and offsets.

Recent Merger and Acquisition Activity

Status: completed **Revised:** Mar. 30, 2023
UPDATE: The transaction was completed. As a result, a group of investors held 37.5% interest in B2B marketplace for a post-money valuation of approximately $47,140,000. Steer received proceeds of $6,000,000 from the spin-off and retains a 62.5% interest in FoodsUp Inc. PREVIOUS: Steer Technologies Inc. agreed to sell a 37.5% interest in STEER Business, a Toronto, Ont.-based restaurant supplies wholesaler, which is currently indirectly held through wholly owned Food Hwy Canada Inc., to a group of investors for $18,000,000 in cash. The business would be transferred to a newly formed company FoodsUp Inc., of which proceeds of $12,000,000 would be injected directly into Newco. The business involves the sale and delivery of just-in-time supplies to restaurants on a business-to-business basis.

Predecessor Detail - Name changed from Facedrive Inc., Oct. 4, 2022.

Directors - Junaid Razvi, chr. & corp. sec., Toronto, Ont.; Suman Pushparajah, CEO, Toronto, Ont.; Mujir A. Muneeruddin, exec. v-p, M&A & strategy & chief legal officer, Oakville, Ont.; Dr. Hamilton Jeyaraj, Toronto, Ont.; Susan Uthayakumar, West Palm Beach, Fla.

Other Exec. Officers - Weiming (Jason) Xie, CFO

Capital Stock

	Authorized (shs.)	Outstanding (shs.)[1]
Preferred	unlimited	nil
Common	unlimited	132,944,615

[1] At May 30, 2023

Major Shareholder - Sayan Navaratnam held 24.3% interest at June 12, 2022.

Price Range - STER/TSX-VEN

Year	Volume	High	Low	Close
2022	25,415,602	$1.27	$0.29	$0.36
2021	116,163,427	$60.00	$0.87	$0.91
2020	28,883,712	$28.00	$1.96	$16.25
2019	682,624	$2.38	$0.55	$2.30
2018	93,640	$0.98	$0.58	$0.85

Split: 10-for-1 split in Oct. 2019; 1-for-50 cons. in Sept. 2019
Recent Close: $0.15

Capital Stock Changes - In March 2022, private placement of 7,343,750 units (1 common share & 1 warrant) at 64¢ per unit was completed. In April 2022, private placement of 29,661,016 units (1 common share & 1 warrant) at 59¢ per unit was completed. Also during 2022, common shares were issued as follows: 167,441 on vesting of restricted share units and 89,025 as share-based compensation; 38,116 were clawed back as a result of post-closing adjustment for the acquisition of Food Hwy Canada Inc.

Wholly Owned Subsidiaries

EcoCRED, LLC, United States.
Facedrive Food Inc., Richmond Hill, Ont.
Facedrive Health Inc., Ont.
Facedrive USA LLC, United States.
Food Hwy Canada Inc., Markham, Ont.
• 62.5% int. in **FoodsUp Inc.**, Canada.
HiRide Share Ltd.
Steer EV Canada Inc., Canada.
Steer Holdings LLC, United States.

Financial Statistics

Periods ended:	12m Dec. 31/22[A]	%Chg	12m Dec. 31/21[A]
	$000s	%Chg	$000s
Operating revenue	**54,921**	**+116**	**25,416**
Cost of sales	55,969		25,471
Salaries & benefits	15,137		11,859
Research & devel. expense	712		955
General & admin expense	3,037		5,979
Stock-based compensation	1,828		2,671
Operating expense	**76,684**	**+63**	**46,935**
Operating income	**(21,763)**	**n.a.**	**(21,518)**
Deprec., depl. & amort.	6,144		5,093
Finance income	3		38
Finance costs, gross	1,381		811
Write-downs/write-offs	(2,055)		(68)
Pre-tax income	**(33,380)**	**n.a.**	**(29,520)**
Income taxes	60		(209)
Net income	**(33,440)**	**n.a.**	**(29,311)**
Cash & equivalent	2,064		2,229
Inventories	2,932		5,433
Accounts receivable	667		1,915
Current assets	6,013		9,942
Fixed assets, net	760		399
Right-of-use assets	19,148		9,877
Intangibles, net	3,146		6,460
Total assets	**32,033**	**+8**	**29,533**
Accts. pay. & accr. liabs.	9,715		7,037
Current liabilities	14,562		10,602
Long-term debt, gross	110		99
Long-term debt, net	nil		99
Long-term lease liabilities	17,011		8,718
Shareholders' equity	460		10,114
Cash from oper. activs.	**(17,412)**	**n.a.**	**(19,887)**
Cash from fin. activs.	18,042		18,858
Cash from invest. activs.	(738)		(447)
Net cash position	**2,229**	**-40**	**3,711**
Capital expenditures	(4,481)		(1,314)
Capital disposals	3,835		883
	$		$
Earnings per share*	(0.27)		(0.31)
Cash flow per share*	(0.14)		(0.21)
	shs		shs
No. of shs. o/s*	132,944,615		95,721,499
Avg. no. of shs. o/s*	123,902,409		95,251,514
	%		%
Net profit margin	(60.89)		(115.32)
Return on equity	(632.49)		(230.70)
Return on assets	(104.14)		(99.26)

* Common
[A] Reported in accordance with IFRS

Latest Results

Periods ended:	3m Mar. 31/23[A]	%Chg	3m Mar. 31/22[A]
	$000s	%Chg	$000s
Operating revenue	15,229	+42	10,735
Net income	30,300	n.a.	(8,182)
	$		$
Earnings per share*	0.24		(0.08)

* Common
[A] Reported in accordance with IFRS

Historical Summary
(as originally stated)

Fiscal Year	Oper. Rev.	Net Inc. Bef. Disc.	EPS*
	$000s	$000s	$
2022[A]	54,921	(33,440)	(0.27)
2021[A]	25,416	(29,311)	(0.31)
2020[A]	3,934	(17,756)	(0.19)
2019[A]	599	(6,942)	(0.08)
2018[A1]	14	(1,934)	n.a.

* Common
[A] Reported in accordance with IFRS
[1] Results pertain to (old) Facedrive Inc.

Note: Adjusted throughout for 10-for-1 split in Oct. 2019; 1-for-50 cons. in Sept. 2019

S.123 Stelco Holdings Inc.*

Symbol - STLC **Exchange** - TSX **CUSIP** - 858522
Head Office - 386 Wilcox St, Hamilton, ON, L8L 8K5 **Telephone** - (905) 528-2511
Website - www.stelco.com
Email - paul.scherzer@stelco.com
Investor Relations - Paul D. Scherzer (905) 577-4432
Auditors - KPMG LLP C.A., Hamilton, Ont.
Transfer Agents - Computershare Trust Company of Canada Inc., Toronto, Ont.
FP500 Revenue Ranking - 157
Employees - 2,313 at Dec. 31, 2022

Profile - (Can. 2017) Produces steel products, such as hot-rolled, cold-rolled and coated sheet steel, as well as pig iron and metallurgical coke used primarily in the construction, automotive, energy, appliance, and pipe and tube industries across in Canada and the United States.

Operations consist of two facilities in Ontario: Lake Erie Works (LEW), on the shores of Lake Erie, near Nanticoke; and Hamilton Works (HW) in Hamilton. The LEW facility consists of a coke battery, a blast furnace, a pig iron caster, two steelmaking vessels, a steel ladle treatment system, an RHOB (Rheinstahl Heraus Oxygen Blowing) vacuum steel degassing facility, a twin-strand slab caster, a hot strip mill and three pickling lines. LEW produces hot-rolled coil and hot-rolled pickled steel that are either sold to third-parties or sent on to HW for further processing. HW consists of a coke battery, a cold-rolling mill, a continuous galvanizing line, a galvanizing and galvannealing Z-Line, batch annealing furnaces and a temper mill. HW is supplied with hot-rolled pickled steel from LEW and produces high quality cold-rolled and coated steel products as well as coke that is supplied to LEW to fuel its blast furnace and could be sold to third-parties.

Also owns 50% interest in **Baycoat Limited Partnership**, a provider of metal coating services in Hamilton; 50% interest in **D.C. Chrome Limited**, a provider of chrome plating services in Stoney Creek, Ont.; and 40% interest in **Hamilton Sports Group**, the owner of the Hamilton Tiger-Cats of the Canadian Football League and Hamilton's Forge FC of the Canadian Premier League, as well as the master lease of Tim Hortons Field stadium in Hamilton, Ont.

Shipping Volumes

Year ended Dec. 31	2022	2021
	net tons	net tons
Hot Rolled Sheet	1,881,000	1,973,000
Coated Sheet	455,000	498,000
Cold Rolled Sheet	82,000	63,000
Other[1]	209,000	156,000

[1] Includes other steel products: pig iron, slabs and non-prime steel sales.

Recent Merger and Acquisition Activity

Status: completed **Announced:** June 1, 2022
Stelco Holdings Inc. sold its interest in the 800-acre parcel of land it occupies on the shores of Hamilton Harbour in Hamilton, Ont., to Slate Asset Management for gross consideration of $518,000,000. In conjunction with the sale, Stelco entered into a long-term lease arrangement for certain portions of the lands to continue its cokemaking and value-added steel finishing operations at its Hamilton Works site in Hamilton, Ont.

Status: completed **Announced:** June 1, 2022
Slate Asset Management LP acquired an 800-acre industrial land and buildings in Hamilton, Ont. from Stelco Inc. for an undisclosed amount.

Status: completed **Revised:** Mar. 25, 2022
UPDATE: The transaction was completed. PREVIOUS: Stelco Holdings Inc. agreed to acquire a 40% interest in Hamilton Sports Group (HSG), which owns the Hamilton Tiger-Cats of the Canadian Football League and Hamilton's Forge FC of the Canadian Premier League, as well as the master lease of Tim Hortons Field stadium in Hamilton, Ont. Consideration was estimated to be $20,000,000. The transaction was subject to certain conditions and was expected to close in the first quarter of 2022.

Directors - Alan Kestenbaum, exec. chr. & CEO, Fla.; Heather D. Ross†, Toronto, Ont.; Monty Baker, Burlington, Ont.; Michael W. Dees, N.Y.; Michael J. Mueller, Windsor, Ont.; Dr. Indira V. Samarasekera, Vancouver, B.C.; Daryl C. F. Wilson, Burlington, Ont.

Other Exec. Officers - Sujit Sanyal, COO; Paul D. Scherzer, CFO; Paul Simon, gen. counsel & corp. sec.

† Lead director

Capital Stock

	Authorized (shs.)	Outstanding (shs.)[1]
Preferred	unlimited	nil
Common	unlimited	55,128,694

[1] At Aug. 9, 2023

Normal Course Issuer Bid - The company plans to make normal course purchases of up to 3,344,284 common shares representing 10% of the public float. The bid commenced on Feb. 28, 2023, and expires on Feb. 27, 2024.

Major Shareholder - Fairfax Financial Holdings Limited held 23.57% interest and Alan Kestenbaum held 15.73% interest at May 10, 2023.

Price Range - STLC/TSX

Year	Volume	High	Low	Close
2022	103,546,826	$56.99	$30.20	$44.29
2021	102,787,950	$51.09	$19.67	$41.22
2020	35,544,918	$23.55	$3.24	$22.73
2019	42,531,138	$20.01	$8.60	$10.91
2018	27,160,733	$28.00	$13.93	$15.06

Recent Close: $38.38

Capital Stock Changes - In January 2022, 4,441,023 common shares were repurchased under a Substantial Issuer Bid. In September 2022, 5,165,133 common shares were repurchased under a Substantial Issuer Bid. In October 2022, 8,226,997 common shares were repurchased under a Substantial Issuer Bid. Also during 2022, 4,353,418 common shares were repurchased under a Normal Course Issuer Bid.

Dividends

STLC com Ra $1.68 pa Q est. May 23, 2023[1]
$3.00◆ Dec. 1/22
Paid in 2023: $1.26 2022: $1.32 + $3.00◆ 2021: $0.62

[1] Quarterly divd normally payable in May/20 has been omitted.
◆ Special

Long-Term Debt - At Dec. 31, 2022, outstanding long-term debt totaled $69,000,000 ($15,000,000 current) and consisted entirely of non-revolving term loan under an asset-based lending (ABL) facility maturing on June 18, 2026. The weighted average finance rate for amounts drawn under the facility for the year ended Dec. 31, 2022, was 5.18% (Dec. 31, 2021 - 3.75%).

Wholly Owned Subsidiaries

Stelco Inc., Hamilton, Ont.
- 50% int. in **Baycoat Limited Partnership**, Hamilton, Ont.
- 50% int. in **D.C. Chrome Limited**, Ont.

Investments

40% int. in **Hamilton Sports Group**, Hamilton, Ont.

Financial Statistics

Periods ended:	12m Dec. 31/22[A]	%Chg	12m Dec. 31/21[A]
	$000s	%Chg	$000s
Operating revenue	**3,463,000**	**-16**	**4,123,000**
Cost of goods sold	2,213,000		2,013,000
General & admin expense	75,000		58,000
Operating expense	**2,288,000**	**+10**	**2,071,000**
Operating income	**1,175,000**	**-43**	**2,052,000**
Deprec., depl. & amort.	90,000		69,000
Finance income	8,000		(33,000)
Finance costs, gross	78,000		162,000
Investment income	1,000		nil
Write-downs/write-offs	(5,000)		(1,000)
Pre-tax income	**1,260,000**	**-29**	**1,782,000**
Income taxes	263,000		173,000
Net income	**997,000**	**-38**	**1,609,000**
Cash & equivalent	809,000		955,000
Inventories	789,000		617,000
Accounts receivable	147,000		412,000
Current assets	1,796,000		2,015,000
Long-term investments	18,000		2,000
Fixed assets, net	1,199,000		1,008,000
Intangibles, net	8,000		8,000
Total assets	**3,131,000**	**-3**	**3,237,000**
Accts. pay. & accr. liabs.	663,000		717,000
Current liabilities	906,000		1,258,000
Long-term debt, gross	69,000		84,000
Long-term debt, net	54,000		69,000
Long-term lease liabilities	369,000		44,000
Shareholders' equity	1,405,000		1,438,000
Cash from oper. activs.	**587,000**	**-63**	**1,607,000**
Cash from fin. activs.	(925,000)		(466,000)
Cash from invest. activs.	154,000		(248,000)
Net cash position	**809,000**	**-15**	**955,000**
Capital expenditures	(195,000)		(236,000)
Capital disposals	353,000		nil
Unfunded pension liability	11,000		11,000
	$		$
Earnings per share*	14.64		19.08
Cash flow per share*	8.62		19.05
Cash divd. per share*	1.32		0.62
Extra divd. - cash*	3.00		nil
Total divd. per share*	**4.32**		**0.62**
	shs		shs
No. of shs. o/s*	55,128,000		77,315,000
Avg. no. of shs. o/s*	68,118,000		84,341,000
	%		%
Net profit margin	28.79		39.02
Return on equity	70.14		187.20
Return on assets	33.25		69.99
Foreign sales percent	41		35
No. of employees (FTEs)	2,313		2,285

* Common
[A] Reported in accordance with IFRS

Latest Results

Periods ended:	6m June 30/23[A]	%Chg	6m June 30/22[A]
	$000s	%Chg	$000s
Operating revenue	1,528,000	-21	1,943,000
Net income	106,000	-87	816,000
	$		$
Earnings per share*	1.92		11.14

* Common
[A] Reported in accordance with IFRS

Historical Summary
(as originally stated)

Fiscal Year	Oper. Rev.	Net Inc. Bef. Disc.	EPS*
	$000s	$000s	$
2022[A]	3,463,000	997,000	14.64
2021[A]	4,123,000	1,609,000	19.08
2020[A]	1,517,000	(159,000)	(1.79)
2019[A]	1,841,000	20,000	0.23
2018[A]	2,460,000	253,000	2.85

* Common
[A] Reported in accordance with IFRS

S.124 Stella-Jones Inc.*

Symbol - SJ **Exchange** - TSX **CUSIP** - 85853F
Head Office - 300-3100 boul de la Côte-Vertu, Saint-Laurent, QC, H4R 2J8 **Telephone** - (514) 934-8666 **Fax** - (514) 934-5327
Website - www.stella-jones.com
Email - stravaglini@stella-jones.com
Investor Relations - Silvana Travaglini (514) 934-8660
Auditors - PricewaterhouseCoopers LLP C.A., Montréal, Qué.
Lawyers - Dentons Cohen & Grigsby P.C., Pittsburgh, Pa.; Foley & Lardner LLP, Chicago, Ill.; Fasken Martineau DuMoulin LLP, Montréal, Qué.
Transfer Agents - Computershare Trust Company of Canada Inc., Montréal, Qué.
FP500 Revenue Ranking - 166
Employees - 2,615 at Dec. 31, 2022
Profile - (Can. 1992) Manufactures pressure-treated wood products, specializing in the production of utility poles for electrical utilities and telecommunications companies, and railway ties and timbers for railroad operators. Also manufactures and distributes residential lumber and accessories to Canadian and U.S. retailers for outdoor applications, as well as industrial products including wood for railway bridges and crossings, marine and foundation pilings, construction timbers and coal tar-based products.

Operations are located in Canada and the United States.

Specializes in five major product categories: utility poles for utility and telecommunication companies; railway ties for rail transportation companies; pressure treated residential lumber products; industrial products for construction and marine applications; and logs and lumber.

Utility poles are used by regional telecommunication and electrical utility companies to support transmission and distribution lines . Poles are typically sold through multi-year contracts and in response to public tenders issued by customers, primarily regional electrical and telecommunication companies.

Railway ties and timbers are sold to North American class 1 railroad operators as well as to short-line railroads, commercial railroad operators and contractors that install and repair rail lines.

Residential lumber consists primarily of pressure treated lumber products to retailers for use in patios, decks, fences and other outdoor applications. Also distributes residential lumber accessories.

Industrial products include railway bridge and crossing timbers, foundation and marine pilings, construction timbers, crane mats, fence posts and highway guardrail posts. Creosote, a wood preservative, is also manufactured for use in wood treating activities, as well as other coal tar-based products such as roof pitch and road tar which are sold to third party customers.

Logs and lumber include harvested logs which are determined to be unsuitable for use as utility poles. The company also resells excess lumber to local home building markets.

The manufacturing process involves at least two stages: drying which is accomplished by air-seasoning, kiln drying or a conditioning process; and impregnation with preservatives through hydraulic pressure. The company operates 16 wood treating plants in Canada, located in Alberta, British Columbia (3), Manitoba, Nova Scotia, Ontario (6) and Quebec (4); and 27 wood treating plants in the U.S., located in Alabama (3), Arizona, Arkansas (2), Georgia, Indiana, Kentucky, Louisiana (3), Mississippi, Nevada, Oregon (2), Pennsylvania (2), South Carolina, Texas (2), Virginia (2), Washington (2) and Wisconsin (2). Creosote is produced at a coal tar distillery in Tennessee. The company operates 13 pole peeling facilities in Canada and the U.S., and is also serviced by numerous pole peeling sites operated by third parties in both Canada and the U.S.

The company holds forest licences in British Columbia that provide for an allowable annual cut of 138,913 m^3 for 15 years; in Manitoba that provide for an allowable annual cut of 15,567 m^3 for up to five years; and in Quebec that provide an allowable cut of 3,600 m^3 for five years. The remainder of the company's raw material requirements are met through supply agreements with major licensees and private woodland owners in British Columbia, Ontario and Quebec; purchasing timber sales in Washington, Wisconsin, Oregon, Idaho and British Columbia; and open market purchases in Canada and the U.S. In order to have access to as many areas of timber land as possible, the company enters in trade agreements with a number of sawmilling and forest products companies in British Columbia, Ontario and Quebec.

In December 2022, wholly owned **Cahaba Pressure Treated Forest Products, Inc.** and **Cahaba Timber, Inc.** merged with and into wholly owned **Stella-Jones Corporation**.

Recent Merger and Acquisition Activity

Status: completed **Announced:** July 14, 2023
Stella-Jones Inc. acquired substantially all of the assets of the wood utility pole manufacturing business of Baldwin Pole and Piling Company, Inc., Baldwin Pole Mississippi, LLC and Baldwin Pole & Piling, Iowa Coraporation (collectively, Baldwin) for US$48,000,000. Baldwin had manufacturing facilities in Bay Minette, Ala., and Wiggins, Miss.

Status: completed **Announced:** June 16, 2023
Stella-Jones Inc. acquired substantially all of the operating assets of Balfour Pole Co., LLC, which specialized in pole peeling and drying southern yellow pine poles in Bacnton, Ga., for US$15,000,000.

Status: completed **Announced:** Feb. 14, 2023
Stella-Jones Inc. acquired substantially all of the operating assets of IndusTREE Pole & Piling, LLC for US$13,000,000. IndusTREE specialized in procuring, peeling and drying southern yellow pine poles at its facility in Goodwater, Ala.

Status: completed **Revised:** Nov. 1, 2022
UPDATE: The transaction was completed. PREVIOUS: Stella-Jones Inc. agreed to acquire all wood utility pole manufacturing assets of Texas Electric Cooperatives, Inc., which produces southern yellow pine utility poles using creosote and CCA preservatives at its wood treating facility in Jasper, Tex., for US$31,000,000.

Status: completed **Announced:** July 22, 2022
Stella-Jones Inc. acquired substantially all of the operating assets of the Dinsmore Trucking group, a specialty poles and logs carrier and transportation business, for $9,000,000. Dinsmore provides services across Canada and parts of the U.S., with operations principally located in Ontario and Alberta.

Directors - Katherine A. (Kate) Lehman, chr., New York, N.Y.; Éric Vachon, pres. & CEO, Pointe-Claire, Qué.; Robert Coallier, Montréal, Qué.; Anne E. Giardini, Rome, Italy; Rhodri J. Harries, Westmount, Qué.; Karen A. Laflamme, Boucherville, Qué.; James A. Manzi Jr., Tampa, Fla.; Dr. Douglas W. (Doug) Muzyka, Philadelphia, Pa.; Sara O'Brien, Westmount, Qué.; Simon Pelletier, Atlanta, Ga.

Other Exec. Officers - Richard Cuddihy, sr. v-p & chief people officer; Ian Jones, sr. v-p, utility poles & U.S. residential lumber; Patrick Kirkham, sr. v-p, railway ties; Silvana Travaglini, sr. v-p & CFO; Sylvain Couture, v-p, utility pole & residential lumber opers., eastern Canada; Marla Eichenbaum, v-p, gen. counsel & corp. sec.; Brian Grant, v-p, Canada residential lumber sales & procurement; Steve Larocque, v-p, IT; Gordon Murray, v-p, R&D

Capital Stock

	Authorized (shs.)	Outstanding (shs.)[1]
Preferred	unlimited	nil
Common	unlimited	57,784,177

[1] At Aug. 8, 2023

Options - At Dec. 31, 2022, options were outstanding to purchase 30,000 common shares at a weighted average exercise price of $49.01 per share expiring on various dates to 2025.

Normal Course Issuer Bid - The company plans to make normal course purchases of up to 5,000,000 common shares representing 9.6% of the public float. The bid commenced on Nov. 14, 2022, and expires on Nov. 13, 2023.

Major Shareholder - Caisse de dépôt et placement du Québec held 12.9% interest at Mar. 14, 2023.

Price Range - SJ/TSX

Year	Volume	High	Low	Close
2022	41,246,308	$50.90	$30.54	$48.52
2021	43,453,116	$54.09	$38.58	$40.01
2020	47,590,783	$47.37	$23.34	$46.28
2019	41,236,251	$48.28	$36.00	$37.52
2018	32,767,967	$52.22	$37.40	$39.61

Recent Close: $64.69

Capital Stock Changes - During 2022, 39,019 common shares were issued under the employee share purchase plan and 4,696,312 common shares were repurchased under a Normal Course Issuer Bid.

Dividends

SJ com Ra $0.92 pa Q est. Apr. 21, 2023
Prev. Rate: $0.80 est. Apr. 22, 2022
Prev. Rate: $0.72 est. Apr. 24, 2021
Prev. Rate: $0.60 est. Apr. 24, 2020

Long-Term Debt - Outstanding at Dec. 31, 2022:

Revolv. credit facility[1]	$394,000,000
Sr. notes[2]	204,000,000
Term loan facility[3]	338,000,000
Promissory notes due to 2028	5,000,000
	941,000,000
Less: Current portion	1,000,000
	940,000,000

[1] Consists of borrowings under a US$400,000,000 revolving facility due Feb. 27, 2026, and under a US$100,000,000 revolving facility due Apr. 29, 2026.

[2] Consist of a US$75,000,000 3.54% series A senior note due Jan. 17, 2024, and a US$75,000,000 3.81% series B senior note due Jan. 17, 2027.

[3] Consist of US$125,000,000 (variable rate equal to LIBOR plus 1.725%) due in June 2028, US$100,000,000 fixed rates ranging from 3.27% to 4.47%, with quarterly amortization payments starting in 2026, due in November 2029 and March 2030 and a US$25,000,000 fixed rate of 4.52% due in March 2029.

Repayment requirements on long-term debt over the next five years were as follows:

2023	$1,000,000
2024	103,000,000
2025	1,000,000
2026	426,000,000
2027	136,000,000
Thereafter	274,000,000

Note - In March 2023, the company's US$350,000,000 credit facilities under the U.S. Farm Credit agreement was increased to US$550,000,000 and its term extended from Apr. 29, 2026, to Mar. 3, 2028.

Wholly Owned Subsidiaries

Stella-Jones U.S. Holding Corporation, Del.
- 100% int. in **Stella-Jones Corporation**, Pittsburgh, Pa.

Note: The preceding list includes only the major related companies in which interests are held.

Financial Statistics

Periods ended:	12m Dec. 31/22[A]		12m Dec. 31/21[A]
	$000s	%Chg	$000s
Operating revenue	**3,065,000**	**+11**	**2,750,000**
Cost of sales	2,467,000		2,231,000
General & admin expense	142,000		116,000
Operating expense	**2,609,000**	**+11**	**2,347,000**
Operating income	**456,000**	**+13**	**403,000**
Deprec., depl. & amort.	89,000		74,000
Finance costs, gross	33,000		23,000
Pre-tax income	**326,000**	**+8**	**303,000**
Income taxes	85,000		76,000
Net income	**241,000**	**+6**	**227,000**
Inventories	1,238,000		1,106,000
Accounts receivable	287,000		230,000
Current assets	1,583,000		1,388,000
Fixed assets, net	755,000		629,000
Right-of-use assets	160,000		138,000
Intangibles, net	540,000		499,000
Total assets	**3,073,000**	**+15**	**2,665,000**
Accts. pay. & accr. liabs	201,000		162,000
Current liabilities	259,000		242,000
Long-term debt, gross	941,000		734,000
Long-term debt, net	940,000		701,000
Long-term lease liabilities	126,000		109,000
Shareholders' equity	1,557,000		1,448,000
Cash from oper. activs	**255,000**	**+2**	**251,000**
Cash from fin. activs	(101,000)		(58,000)
Cash from invest. activs	(154,000)		(193,000)
Capital expenditures	(97,000)		(48,000)
Unfunded pension liability	(5,000)		(10,000)
	$		$
Earnings per share*	3.93		3.49
Cash flow per share*	4.15		3.86
Cash divd. per share*	0.80		0.72
	shs		shs
No. of shs. o/s*	59,115,959		63,773,252
Avg. no. of shs. o/s*	61,400,000		65,000,000
	%		%
Net profit margin	7.86		8.25
Return on equity	16.04		16.09
Return on assets	9.25		9.59
Foreign sales percent	69		64
No. of employees (FTEs)	2,615		2,402

* Common
[A] Reported in accordance with IFRS

Latest Results

Periods ended:	6m June 30/23[A]		6m June 30/22[A]
	$000s	%Chg	$000s
Operating revenue	1,682,000	+8	1,558,000
Net income	160,000	+14	140,000
	$		$
Earnings per share*	2.73		2.23

* Common
[A] Reported in accordance with IFRS

Historical Summary
(as originally stated)

Fiscal Year	Oper. Rev.	Net Inc. Bef. Disc.	EPS*
	$000s	$000s	$
2022[A]	3,065,000	241,000	3.93
2021[A]	2,750,000	227,000	3.49
2020[A]	2,551,000	210,000	3.12
2019[A]	2,169,023	163,078	2.37
2018[A]	2,123,893	137,597	1.98

* Common
[A] Reported in accordance with IFRS

S.125 Stem Holdings, Inc.

Symbol - STEM **Exchange** - CSE **CUSIP** - 85858U
Head Office - 2201 Corporate Blvd NW, Suite 205, Boca Raton, FL, United States, 33431 **Telephone** - (561) 237-2931 **Fax** - (561) 482-9405
Website - www.stemholdings.com
Email - mauria@stemholdings.com
Investor Relations - Mauria Betts (971) 266-1908
Auditors - L J Soldinger Associates, LLC
Transfer Agents - Odyssey Trust Company, Vancouver, B.C.
Profile - (Nev. 2016) Has cannabis cultivation, processing, extraction, retail and distribution operations in the United States.

Cultivation and processing facilities include a 28,000-sq.-ft. indoor cultivation facility in Springfield, Ore.; greenhouse cultivation site on a 14-acre lot in Mulino, Ore.; 40-acre outdoor cultivation site in Jacksonville, Ore.; 30,000-sq.-ft. extraction, edibles, processing and distribution facilities in Eugene, Ore.; a 10,000-sq.-ft. indoor cultivation facility in Hillsboro, Ore.; and a 5,450-sq.-ft. cultivation, extraction, edibles, processing and distribution facility in North Las Vegas, Nev. Also has hemp cultivation and research and development operations in New York; and a 12,000-sq.-ft. and a 28,000-sq.-ft. cultivation and processing facilities under development in San Diego, Calif., and Northampton, Mass., respectively.

Dispensaries are located in Eugene (three locations under the TJ's on Willamette, TJ's Provisions and TJ's on 7th banners), Portland (TJ's on Powell banner) and Salem (TJ's on Broadway banner), Ore.; Great Barrington, Mass. (Rebelle banner); and Sacramento, Calif. (Foothills Health & Wellness banner).

Brands include TJ's Gardens, TravisxJames and Yerba Buena (flower and extracts), Cannavore (edibles) and Doseology (CBD).

Directors - Matthew J. Cohen, co-founder, CEO & CFO; Brian Hayek, chief compliance officer; Garrett M. Bender, Fla.; Robert L. B. Diener; Rajiv (Roger) Rai, Toronto, Ont.; Daryl Simon; Lindy Snider, Pa.; Salvador Villanueva III

Capital Stock

	Authorized (shs.)	Outstanding (shs.)[1]	Par
Series A Preferred	50,000,000	nil	US$0.001
Series B Preferred	50,000,000	nil	US$0.001
Common	750,000,000	221,762,330	US$0.001

[1] At Aug. 16, 2021

Major Shareholder - Widely held at Dec. 31, 2020.

Price Range - STEM/CSE

Year	Volume	High	Low	Close
2022	16,496,125	$0.18	$0.02	$0.03
2021	52,316,894	$1.75	$0.11	$0.13
2020	5,980,898	$1.30	$0.26	$0.55
2019	2,807,715	$3.58	$1.02	$1.10
2018	148,665	$4.48	$2.20	$2.80

Recent Close: $0.01

Wholly Owned Subsidiaries

Consolidated Ventures of Oregon, Inc., Ore.
Driven Deliveries, Inc., Calif.
- 100% int. in **Budee, Inc.**, Calif.
- 100% int. in **Ganjarunner, Inc.**, Calif.

Opco Holdings, Inc., Ore.
Opco, LLC, United States.
Stem Group Oklahoma, Inc., Okla.
Stem Holdings Agri, Inc., Fla.
Stem Holdings IP, Inc., United States.
Stem Holdings Oregon, Inc., Ore.
2236034 Alberta Ltd., Alta.
- 100% int. in **Seven Leaf Ventures Corp.**, Calgary, Alta.
  - 100% int. in **7LV USA Corporation**, Calif.

Subsidiaries

63.75% int. in **NVD RE Corp.**, Nev.

Investments

50% int. in **YMY Ventures, LLC**, Nev.

Note: The preceding list includes only the major related companies in which interests are held.

S.126 Stingray Group Inc.

Symbol - RAY.A **Exchange** - TSX **CUSIP** - 86084H
Head Office - 800-730 rue Wellington, Montréal, QC, H3C 1T4 **Telephone** - (514) 664-1244 **Fax** - (514) 664-1143
Website - www.stingray.com
Email - mpeloquin@stingray.com
Investor Relations - Mathieu Péloquin (514) 664-1244 ext. 2362
Auditors - KPMG LLP C.A., Montréal, Qué.
Lawyers - Davies Ward Phillips & Vineberg LLP, Montréal, Qué.
Transfer Agents - TSX Trust Company, Montréal, Qué.
FP500 Revenue Ranking - 575
Employees - 975 at Apr. 30, 2023

Profile - (Can. 2006) Provides direct-to-consumer and business-to-business multi-platform music products and services, including audio television channels, radio stations, subscription video-on-demand (SVOD) content, 4K UHD television channels, free ad-supported streaming television (FAST) channels, karaoke products, digital signage, in-store music and music applications, to entertainment content providers and commercial clients worldwide.

Has two operating segments: Broadcasting and Commercial Music; and Radio.

The **Broadcasting and Commercial Music** segment specializes in the broadcast of music and videos on multiple platforms and digital signage experiences, and generates revenues from subscriptions or contracts. Music broadcasting services include television music broadcasting, satellite and streaming. The television music broadcasting alternative provides listeners with easy access to a number of high-quality curated music channels, offering music, music videos and concerts, which are included within the listener's TV subscription and distributed by pay television providers. In addition, offers commercial music as an in-store media solution, which is implemented across diversified industries including retail, restaurants, hotels and airports.

The **Radio** segment operates more than 100 traditional radio (AM/FM bands) stations across Canada in a variety of music formats including country, Top 40, rock, news/talk and classic hits. Radio broadcasting operations are conducted in Newfoundland and Labrador, New Brunswick, Nova Scotia, Prince Edward Island, Ontario, Alberta and British Columbia.

The company is headquartered in Montreal, Que., with additional leased facilities across the world, including in the U.S., the U.K., the Netherlands, Israel, Mexico and Australia.

In March 2023, the company acquired the assets and business of Montreal, Que.-based **Ultimate Trivia Network** for an undisclosed amount. Ultimate Trivia Network would initially launch as an ad-supported linear channel dedicated to trivia, providing an endless stream of questions across a wide range of categories and themes including geography, history, sports, arts and entertainment, sciences and nature, Hollywood, trending topics and technology.

Predecessor Detail - Name changed from Stingray Digital Group Inc., Dec. 1, 2018.

Directors - Eric Boyko, co-founder, pres. & CEO, Montréal, Qué.; François-Charles Sirois, co-founder, Montréal, Qué.; Mark L. Pathy, chr., Montréal, Qué.; Claudine Blondin, Westmount, Qué.; Karinne Bouchard, Montréal, Qué.; Mélanie Dunn, Montréal, Qué.; Frédéric Lavoie, Santa Monica, Calif.; Gary S. Rich, South Salem, N.Y.; Robert G. Steele, Bedford, N.S.; Pascal Tremblay, Candiac, Qué.

Other Exec. Officers - Jean-Pierre Trahan, CFO; David Purdy, chief revenue officer; Mario Dubois, sr. v-p & chief tech. officer; Lloyd P. Feldman, sr. v-p, gen. counsel & corp. sec.; Mathieu Péloquin, sr. v-p, mktg. & commun.; Valérie Héroux, v-p, content acq. & programming; Ian S. Lurie, pres., Stingray Radio Inc.

Capital Stock

	Authorized (shs.)	Outstanding (shs.)[1]
Multiple Vtg.	unlimited	17,941,498
Subord. Vtg.	unlimited	50,981,050[2]
Variable Subord. Vtg.	unlimited	388,852

[1] At Aug. 4, 2023

[2] Includes 19,569 shares held in trust through employee share purchase plan

Multiple Voting - Convertible, at the holder's option, into subordinate voting shares on a one-for-one basis. Ten votes per share.

Subordinate Voting - Entitled to quarterly dividends of $0.075 per share. Convertible automatically into variable subordinate voting shares on a one-for-one basis if such subordinate voting share is or becomes owned or controlled by a non-Canadian. One vote per share.

Variable Subordinate Voting - Entitled to quarterly dividends of $0.075 per share. Convertible automatically into subordinate voting shares on a one-for-one basis if such variable subordinate voting share is or becomes owned or controlled by a Canadian. One vote per share.

Normal Course Issuer Bid - The company plans to make normal course purchases of up to 2,868,124 subord. vtg. shares & variable subord. vtg. shares representing 10% of the public float. The bid commenced on Sept. 27, 2022, and expires on Sept. 26, 2023.

Major Shareholder - Eric Boyko held 58.2% interest and Telesystem Ltd. held 21.9% interest at June 12, 2023.

Price Range - RAY.A/TSX

Year	Volume	High	Low	Close
2022	9,909,798	$7.77	$4.10	$4.87
2021	14,981,129	$8.30	$6.50	$6.98
2020	26,732,469	$7.16	$3.18	$6.59
2019	18,517,934	$7.94	$5.51	$7.14
2018	12,581,635	$11.05	$5.92	$6.75

Recent Close: $5.13

Capital Stock Changes - During fiscal 2023, 786,100 subordinate voting shares and variable subordinate voting shares were repurchased under a Normal Course Issuer Bid. In addition, the total unvested subordinate voting shares held in trust for stock-based compensation plan was decreased by 9,974 subordinate voting shares.

During fiscal 2022, 95,000 subordinate voting shares and variable subordinate voting shares were issued on exercise of options and 2,106,000 subordinate voting shares and variable subordinate voting shares were repurchased under a Normal Course Issuer Bid. In addition, the total unvested subordinate voting shares held in trust for stock-based compensation plan was increased by 4,664 subordinate voting shares.

Dividends

RAY.A sub vtg S.V. Ra $0.30 pa Q est. Mar. 16, 2020
Prev. Rate: $0.28 est. Sept. 13, 2019
RAY.B var sub vtg S.V. Ra $0.30 pa Q est. Mar. 16, 2020
Prev. Rate: $0.28 est. Sept. 13, 2019

Wholly Owned Subsidiaries

Calm Radio Corp., Toronto, Ont.
DJ-Matic N.V., Belgium.
4445694 Canada Inc., Canada.
Music Choice Europe Limited
Pop Radio LLC, Princeton, N.J.
SBA Music Pty Ltd., Australia.
Stingray Digital International Ltd., United Kingdom.
Stingray Europe B.V., United Kingdom.
Stingray Music, S.A. de C.V.
Stingray Music USA Inc., Del.
Stingray Radio Inc., Dartmouth, N.S.
Transmedia Communications S.A.
- 100% int. in **Classica GmBH**
  - 100% int. in **Classica Asia GmBH**
  - 100% int. in **Think inside the box LLC**
- 100% int. in **Digital Music Distribution Pty Ltd.**, Australia.
- 100% int. in **9076-3392 Québec Inc.**

2144286 Ontario Inc., Ont.
- 0.01% int. in **Pay Audio Services Limited Partnership**, Ont.

Subsidiaries

99.99% int. in **Pay Audio Services Limited Partnership**, Ont.

Financial Statistics

Periods ended:	12m Mar. 31/23[A]		12m Mar. 31/22[oA]
	$000s	%Chg	$000s
Operating revenue	**323,944**	**+15**	**282,626**
Cost of sales	212,272		189,954
Operating expense	**212,272**	**+12**	**189,954**
Operating income	**111,672**	**+21**	**92,672**
Deprec., depl. & amort.	32,980		35,544
Finance costs, net	26,835		6,119
Pre-tax income	**39,659**	**-6**	**42,300**
Income taxes	9,540		9,013
Net income	**30,119**	**-10**	**33,287**
Cash & equivalent	15,453		14,563
Inventories	5,704		5,200
Accounts receivable	71,251		66,666
Current assets	115,983		99,913
Long-term investments	8,295		6,431
Fixed assets, net	38,792		39,931
Right-of-use assets	23,271		25,944
Intangibles, net	702,710		703,905
Total assets	**895,202**	**+1**	**884,076**
Accts. pay. & accr. liabs	74,826		67,391
Current liabilities	135,179		115,332
Long-term debt, gross	386,443		383,645
Long-term debt, net	378,943		376,145
Long-term lease liabilities	21,533		24,147
Shareholders' equity	286,269		273,529
Cash from oper. activs	**86,949**	**+4**	**83,663**
Cash from fin. activs	(65,454)		(59,510)
Cash from invest. activs	(20,605)		(18,630)
Net cash position	**15,453**	**+6**	**14,563**
Capital expenditures	(8,234)		(9,061)
	$		$
Earnings per share*	0.43		0.47
Cash flow per share*	1.25		1.18
Cash divd. per share*	0.30		0.30
	shs		shs
No. of shs. o/s*	69,319,798		70,095,924
Avg. no. of shs. o/s*	69,640,151		70,968,954
	%		%
Net profit margin	9.30		11.78
Return on equity	10.76		12.14
Return on assets	3.39		3.90
Foreign sales percent	42		37

* S.V., V.S.V. & M.V.
[o] Restated
[A] Reported in accordance with IFRS

Latest Results

Periods ended:	3m June 30/23[A]		3m June 30/22[A]
	$000s	%Chg	$000s
Operating revenue	78,992	+1	78,136
Net income	14,118	+50	9,397
	$		$
Earnings per share*	0.20		0.13

* S.V., V.S.V. & M.V.
[A] Reported in accordance with IFRS

Historical Summary
(as originally stated)

Fiscal Year	Oper. Rev.	Net Inc. Bef. Disc.	EPS*
	$000s	$000s	$
2023[A]	323,944	30,119	0.43
2022[A]	282,626	33,287	0.47
2021[A]	249,468	45,104	0.62
2020[A]	306,721	13,970	0.18
2019[A]	212,650	(11,988)	(0.19)

* S.V., V.S.V. & M.V.
[A] Reported in accordance with IFRS

S.127 Stock Trend Capital Inc.

Symbol - PUMP **Exchange** - CSE **CUSIP** - 86102Q
Head Office - 810-750 Pender St W, Vancouver, BC, V6C 2T7 **Telephone** - (604) 473-9569 **Toll-free** - (855) 207-4491
Email - anthony@firstrepubliccapital.com
Investor Relations - Anthony J. Durkacz (416) 720-4360
Auditors - Dale Matheson Carr-Hilton LaBonte LLP C.A., Vancouver, B.C.
Transfer Agents - Endeavor Trust Corporation, Vancouver, B.C.

Profile - (B.C. 2004; orig. B.C., 1965) Invests in private and public companies in the Canadian cannabis industry.

Effective Feb. 27, 2023, the company completed a change of business from a cannabis company to an investment company.

In February 2023, the company invested $750,000 in **The Hash Corporation** by way of a 5% secured convertible debenture which matures on May 31, 2023, and convertible at the company's option into common shares at $0.05 per share.

On Apr. 29, 2022, the company sold wholly owned **Soma Labs Scientific Inc.** to **CannaWorld Ventures Inc.** for issuance of 15,000,000 common shares. Soma designed, manufactured and supplied extraction and processing equipment and technology to produce cannabis and hemp oils, concentrates and derivative products. Previously, wholly owned **1323194 B.C. Ltd.** was amalgamated into Soma Labs.

Predecessor Detail - Name changed from World Class Extractions Inc., Feb. 27, 2023, pursuant to change of business to an investment company.

Directors - Anthony J. Durkacz, chr. & CEO, Toronto, Ont.; Navchand (Chand) Jagpal, CFO, Surrey, B.C.; Richard Buzbuzian, Toronto, Ont.; Michael B. Galloro, Toronto, Ont.

Other Exec. Officers - Shimmy Posen, corp. sec.

Capital Stock

	Authorized (shs.)	Outstanding (shs.)[1]
Common	unlimited	625,196,572

[1] At Feb. 27, 2023

Major Shareholder - Widely held at Mar. 21, 2022.

Price Range - PUMP/CSE

Year	Volume	High	Low	Close
2022	122,426,717	$0.02	$0.01	$0.01
2021	287,346,309	$0.06	$0.01	$0.02
2020	288,206,215	$0.06	$0.01	$0.02
2019	652,761,032	$0.23	$0.05	$0.06
2018	1,733,982	$0.25	$0.05	$0.05

Split: 3-for-1 split in Mar. 2019

Recent Close: $0.01

Capital Stock Changes - There were no changes to capital stock during fiscal 2021 or fiscal 2022.

Wholly Owned Subsidiaries

1230167 B.C. Ltd., B.C. Inactive.

Investments

CannaWorld Ventures Inc.

Financial Statistics

Periods ended:	12m Apr. 30/22[A]		12m Apr. 30/21[◻A]
	$000s	%Chg	$000s
General & admin expense	1,059		2,234
Stock-based compensation	nil		438
Operating expense	**1,059**	**-91**	**12,128**
Operating income	**(1,059)**	**n.a.**	**(12,128)**
Deprec., depl. & amort.	19		51
Finance income	9		n.a.
Finance costs, gross	5		n.a.
Finance costs, net	n.a.		202
Write-downs/write-offs	(232)		(508)
Pre-tax income	**(6,604)**	**n.a.**	**(2,394)**
Net inc. bef. disc. opers	**(6,604)**	**n.a.**	**(2,394)**
Income from disc. opers	(1,616)		(2,092)
Net income	**(8,220)**	**n.a.**	**(4,486)**
Net inc. for equity hldrs	**(6,856)**	**n.a.**	**(4,241)**
Net inc. for non-cont. int	**(1,363)**	**n.a.**	**(245)**
Cash & equivalent	2,534		2,378
Inventories	nil		100
Accounts receivable	61		1,776
Current assets	2,696		4,615
Fixed assets, net	nil		972
Right-of-use assets	nil		613
Intangibles, net	nil		9,445
Total assets	**3,744**	**-76**	**15,646**
Accts. pay. & accr. liabs	214		1,015
Current liabilities	216		5,028
Long-term debt, gross	nil		2,495
Long-term debt, net	37		96
Long-term lease liabilities	nil		782
Shareholders' equity	3,491		4,556
Non-controlling interest	nil		5,184
Cash from oper. activs	**(1,076)**	**n.a.**	**(2,419)**
Cash from fin. activs	(155)		(288)
Cash from invest. activs	1,387		(548)
Net cash position	**2,534**	**+7**	**2,378**
Capital expenditures	nil		(448)
Capital disposals	nil		1
	$		$
Earnings per share*	(0.01)		(0.01)
Cash flow per share*	(0.00)		(0.00)
	shs		shs
No. of shs. o/s*	625,196,572		625,196,572
Avg. no. of shs. o/s*	625,196,572		625,196,572
	%		%
Net profit margin	n.a.		n.a.
Return on equity	(130.26)		(33.28)
Return on assets	(68.07)		(13.35)

* Common
◻ Restated
[A] Reported in accordance with IFRS

Latest Results

Periods ended:	6m Oct. 31/22[A]		6m Oct. 31/21[◻A]
	$000s	%Chg	$000s
Net inc. bef. disc. opers	(621)	n.a.	(641)
Income from disc. opers	nil		(733)
Net income	(621)	n.a.	(1,374)
	$		$
Earns. per sh. bef. disc. opers.*	(0.00)		(0.00)
Earnings per share*	(0.00)		(0.00)

* Common
◻ Restated
[A] Reported in accordance with IFRS

Historical Summary
(as originally stated)

Fiscal Year	Oper. Rev.	Net Inc. Bef. Disc.	EPS*
	$000s	$000s	$
2022[A]	nil	(6,604)	(0.01)
2021[A]	9,643	(4,486)	(0.01)
2020[A]	1,108	(48,359)	(0.08)
2019[A1,2]	nil	(8,236)	(0.02)
2018[A2,3]	nil	(4,139)	(0.18)

* Common
[A] Reported in accordance with IFRS
[1] 4 months ended Apr. 30, 2019.
[2] Reflects the Mar. 11, 2019, three-cornered amalgamation between CBD MED Research Corp. and private World Class Extractions Inc.
[3] 48 weeks ended Dec. 31, 2018.

Note: Adjusted throughout for 3-for-1 split in Mar. 2019

S.128 StorageVault Canada Inc.

Symbol - SVI **Exchange** - TSX **CUSIP** - 86212H

Head Office - 100 Canadian Rd, Toronto, ON, M1R 4Z5 **Toll-free** - (877) 622-0205 **Fax** - (416) 352-1744

Website - www.storagevaultcanada.com

Email - ir@storagevaultcanada.com

Investor Relations - Iqbal Khan (877) 622-0205

Auditors - MNP LLP C.A., Calgary, Alta.

Bankers - Bank of Montreal

Lawyers - DLA Piper (Canada) LLP, Calgary, Alta.

Transfer Agents - TSX Trust Company, Calgary, Alta.

FP500 Revenue Ranking - 595

Employees - 800 at Feb. 23, 2023

Profile - (Alta. 2007) Owns, operates and rents self-storage and portable storage space to individual and commercial customers, with locations in British Columbia, Alberta, Saskatchewan, Manitoba, Ontario, Quebec and Nova Scotia.

Self-storage involves the customer renting space at the company's property, typically on a weekly or monthly basis. Units are used by individuals for furniture, household appliances, personal belongings, motor vehicles, boats, campers, motorcycles and other household goods storage. Commercial customers use the space for storage of excess inventory, business records, seasonal goods, equipment and fixtures. Portable storage involves delivering portable storage units to customers, with options to keep the unit at their location or have it moved to another location. Also offers FlexSpace Logistics, a last mile end to end technology platform that offers storage space, logistics and inventory management solutions to businesses across Canada.

At Dec. 31, 2022, operations consisted of 206 self-storage stores and 4,527 portable storage units, covering 11,422,068 sq. ft. and totaling 101,303 rental units across Canada operating under the Access Storage, Depotium Mini-Entrepots and Sentinel Storage brands for self-storage stores, and Cubeit and PUPS brands for portable storage. Also operates and manages 32 stores that are owned by third parties; and has an information and record management business operating under the RecordXpress brand which stores, shreds and manages documents and records for customers.

In September 2022, the company acquired a storage store in Alberta for $4,100,000.

Recent Merger and Acquisition Activity

Status: completed **Announced:** June 2, 2023
Automotive Properties Real Estate Investment Trust (50%) and StorageVault Canada Inc. (50%) jointly acquired a 50,415-sq.-ft. automotive dealership property located at 9425 Taschereau Boulevard in Brossard, Que., for $16,100,000 (each having funded 50% of the acquisition price). StorageVault owned a self-storage property adjacent to the dealership.

Status: pending **Announced:** Mar. 29, 2023
Storage Vault Canada Inc. agreed to acquire three storage locations located in Nova Scotia (2) and Alberta (1) for a total of $21,825,000, including the issuance of up to $4,500,000 of StorageVault common shares. The cash consideration would be financed with cash on hand, promissory notes or consisting debt of one of the stores being acquired. The acquisition was being completed with three vendor groups, of which one was with Access Self Storage Inc. The acquisitions were expected to close during the first and second quarters of 2023.

Status: completed **Announced:** Dec. 16, 2022
StorageVault Canada Inc. acquired two complementary shredding businesses to its records and information business, RecordXpress Inc., for $8,750,000.

Status: completed **Revised:** Dec. 16, 2022
UPDATE: The transaction was completed. PREVIOUS: StorageVault Canada Inc. agreed to acquire two storage locations in Edmonton, Alta., purchase price of $14,160,000. The consideration would be financed with cash on hand and first mortgages.

Status: completed **Revised:** June 30, 2022
UPDATE: The transaction was completed. As part of the consideration, StorageVault issued 814,686 common shares valued at $5,000,000. PREVIOUS: Storage Vault Canada Inc. agreed to acquire six storage stores located in Ontario for a total of $167,500,000, including the issuance of up to $5,000,000 of StorageVault common shares. The cash consideration would be financed with cash on hand, first mortgages and mortgage assumptions. The acquisition was being completed with five vendor groups, of which one was with Access Self Storage Inc.

Directors - Alan A. Simpson, co-founder, Regina, Sask.; Steven R. Scott, chr. & CEO, Toronto, Ont.; Iqbal Khan, CFO, Toronto, Ont.; Jay Lynne Fleming, Vancouver, B.C.; Benjamin Harris, N.Y.; Mary D. Vitug, Toronto, Ont.

Other Exec. Officers - Tamara Souglis, corp. sec.; Andrew Brown, pres., RecordXpress Inc.

Capital Stock

	Authorized (shs.)	Outstanding (shs.)[1]
Preferred	unlimited	nil
Series 1 Preferred	unlimited	nil
Common	unlimited	377,914,292

[1] At Apr. 5, 2023

Normal Course Issuer Bid - The company plans to make normal course purchases of up to 18,905,000 common shares representing 5% of the total outstanding. The bid commenced on Mar. 18, 2023, and expires on Mar. 17, 2024.

Major Shareholder - Access Self Storage Inc. held 36.17% interest at Apr. 4, 2023.

Price Range - SVI/TSX

Year	Volume	High	Low	Close
2022	107,491,273	$7.39	$5.28	$6.02
2021	33,323,881	$7.22	$3.68	$7.21
2020	38,456,184	$4.29	$1.90	$4.04
2019	58,022,860	$3.87	$2.26	$3.71
2018	46,590,783	$2.89	$2.26	$2.37

Recent Close: $4.52

Capital Stock Changes - During 2022, common shares were issued as follows: 4,171,246 on acquisition of various storage assets, 661,151 on exercise of options, 306,499 under dividend reinvestment plan and 94,421 under restricted and deferred share unit plan; 1,852,400 common shares were repurchased under a Normal Course Issuer Bid.

Dividends

SVI com Ra $0.01138 pa Q est. July 17, 2023**
Listed Jan 26/22.
Prev. Rate: $0.011324 est. Apr. 17, 2023
Prev. Rate: $0.011268 est. Jan. 16, 2023
Prev. Rate: $0.011212 est. Oct. 17, 2022
Prev. Rate: $0.011156 est. July 15, 2022
Prev. Rate: $0.011044 est. Jan. 17, 2022
Prev. Rate: $0.010992 est. Oct. 15, 2021
Prev. Rate: $0.010936 est. July 15, 2021
Prev. Rate: $0.01088 est. Apr. 15, 2021
Prev. Rate: $0.010828 est. Jan. 15, 2021
** Reinvestment Option

Wholly Owned Subsidiaries

Spyhill Ltd., Toronto, Ont.

Note: The preceding list includes only the major related companies in which interests are held.

Financial Statistics

Periods ended:	12m Dec. 31/22[A]		12m Dec. 31/21[A]
	$000s	%Chg	$000s
Operating revenue	**261,828**	**+25**	**208,661**
General & admin expense	106,843		87,478
Stock-based compensation	13,631		11,288
Operating expense	**120,474**	**+22**	**98,766**
Operating income	**141,354**	**+29**	**109,894**
Deprec., depl. & amort.	104,127		93,189
Finance costs, gross	78,466		52,366
Pre-tax income	**(50,827)**	**n.a.**	**(43,688)**
Income taxes	(9,585)		(7,823)
Net income	**(41,242)**	**n.a.**	**(35,865)**
Cash & equivalent	22,535		25,144
Accounts receivable	6,640		4,101
Fixed assets, net	1,803,531		1,625,647
Intangibles, net	173,399		168,764
Total assets	**2,020,752**	**+10**	**1,836,156**
Accts. pay. & accr. liabs.	20,860		18,508
Long-term debt, gross	1,655,403		1,460,027
Long-term lease liabilities	80,519		77,095
Shareholders' equity	207,155		222,207
Cash from oper. activs.	**67,310**	**+18**	**57,024**
Cash from fin. activs.	179,581		198,250
Cash from invest. activs.	(249,500)		(255,659)
Net cash position	**22,535**	**-10**	**25,144**
Capital expenditures	(35,600)		(29,012)
Capital disposals	185		20
	$		$
Earnings per share*	(0.11)		(0.10)
Cash flow per share*	0.18		0.15
Cash divd. per share*	0.01		0.01
	shs		shs
No. of shs. o/s*	378,017,360		374,636,443
Avg. no. of shs. o/s*	378,051,496		370,267,629
	%		%
Net profit margin	(15.75)		(17.19)
Return on equity	(19.21)		(16.59)
Return on assets	1.16		0.42
No. of employees (FTEs)	800		n.a.

* Common
[A] Reported in accordance with IFRS

Historical Summary
(as originally stated)

Fiscal Year	Oper. Rev. $000s	Net Inc. Bef. Disc. $000s	EPS* $
2022[A]	261,828	(41,242)	(0.11)
2021[A]	208,661	(35,865)	(0.10)
2020[A]	155,464	(33,282)	(0.09)
2019[A]	134,963	(46,118)	(0.13)
2018[A]	96,384	(24,151)	(0.07)

* Common
[A] Reported in accordance with IFRS

S.129 Strategem Capital Corporation

Symbol - SGE **Exchange** - TSX-VEN **CUSIP** - 86269P
Head Office - 210-240 11 Ave SW, Calgary, AB, T2R 0C3 **Toll-free** - (833) 743-4743
Website - www.strategemcapital.com
Email - info@strategemcapital.com
Investor Relations - Jo-Anne O'Connor (416) 567-7573
Auditors - De Visser Gray LLP C.A., Vancouver, B.C.
Lawyers - McMillan LLP
Transfer Agents - Computershare Trust Company of Canada Inc., Vancouver, B.C.
Profile - (B.C. 1994) Invests in public and private resource exploration and development, mining, energy production and agricultural companies.

Holds certain money market funds and public company securities with a fair value totaling $10,867,000 at Mar. 31, 2023.

Predecessor Detail - Name changed from Dexton Technologies Corporation, Nov. 19, 2001.

Directors - The Hon. Stockwell B. Day, chr., Vancouver, B.C.; Desmond M. (Des) Balakrishnan, Vancouver, B.C.; Matthew Cicci, B.C.; J. Gordon Flatt, Hamilton, Bermuda; Dickson Gould, Man.

Other Exec. Officers - Jo-Anne O'Connor, pres. & CEO; Carol Fozo, CFO & corp. sec.

Capital Stock

	Authorized (shs.)	Outstanding (shs.)[1]
Class A Preference	unlimited	nil
Class A Common	unlimited	9,226,728
Class B Common	unlimited	220

[1] At May 16, 2023

Class A Common - One vote per share.

Class B Common - Exchangeable for class A common shares on a share-for-share basis plus a cash payment of $1.75 per share. One vote per share.

Normal Course Issuer Bid - The company plans to make normal course purchases of up to 467,576 class A common shares representing 5% of the total outstanding. The bid commenced on Sept. 23, 2022, and expires on Sept. 22, 2023.

Major Shareholder - J. Gordon Flatt held 34.43% interest and 2023378 Ontario Inc. held 34.19% interest at May 9, 2023.

Price Range - SGE/TSX-VEN

Year	Volume	High	Low	Close
2022	270,624	$3.25	$1.00	$1.00
2021	174,192	$2.80	$2.10	$2.75
2020	798,392	$2.45	$1.50	$2.30
2019	144,480	$1.77	$1.60	$1.60
2018	124,280	$2.40	$1.76	$1.76

Recent Close: $0.78

Capital Stock Changes - During 2022, 127,400 common shares were repurchased under a Normal Course Issuer Bid.

Financial Statistics

Periods ended:	12m Dec. 31/22[A]		12m Dec. 31/21[A]
	$000s	%Chg	$000s
Realized invest. gain (loss)	108		521
Unrealized invest. gain (loss)	(20,154)		11,118
Total revenue	**(19,575)**	**n.a.**	**11,986**
Salaries & benefits	305		129
General & admin. expense	430		1,328
Operating expense	**735**	**-50**	**1,457**
Operating income	**(20,310)**	**n.a.**	**10,529**
Pre-tax income	**(20,352)**	**n.a.**	**10,537**
Income taxes	(2,725)		2,254
Net income	**(17,627)**	**n.a.**	**8,283**
Cash & equivalent	11,649		33,080
Accounts receivable	nil		38
Current assets	11,649		33,118
Total assets	**11,649**	**-65**	**33,118**
Accts. pay. & accr. liabs.	42		36
Current liabilities	47		936
Shareholders' equity	11,602		29,457
Cash from oper. activs.	**(114)**	**n.a.**	**(14,476)**
Cash from fin. activs.	(228)		11,825
Net cash position	**1,780**	**-16**	**2,122**
	$		$
Earnings per share*	(1.88)		1.10
Cash flow per share*	(0.01)		(1.93)
	shs		shs
No. of shs. o/s*	9,309,528		9,437,148
Avg. no. of shs. o/s*	9,376,493		7,503,000
	%		%
Net profit margin	n.m.		69.11
Return on equity	(85.86)		42.69
Return on assets	(78.75)		38.93

* Cl.A & B com.
[A] Reported in accordance with IFRS

Latest Results

Periods ended:	3m Mar. 31/23[A]		3m Mar. 31/22[A]
	$000s	%Chg	$000s
Total revenue	1,365	n.a.	(5,394)
Net income	1,141	n.a.	(4,112)
	$		$
Earnings per share*	0.12		(0.44)

* Cl.A & B com.
[A] Reported in accordance with IFRS

Historical Summary
(as originally stated)

Fiscal Year	Total Rev. $000s	Net Inc. Bef. Disc. $000s	EPS* $
2022[A]	(19,575)	(17,627)	(1.88)
2021[A]	11,986	8,283	1.10
2020[A]	113	(1,700)	(0.39)
2019[A]	696	252	0.06
2018[A]	(896)	(784)	(0.18)

* Cl.A & B com.
[A] Reported in accordance with IFRS

S.130 Stria Lithium Inc.

Symbol - SRA **Exchange** - TSX-VEN **CUSIP** - 86330Y
Head Office - 945 Princess St, Kingston, ON, K7L 0E9 **Telephone** - (613) 241-4040 **Fax** - (613) 241-8632
Website - www.strialithium.com
Email - dhanisch@strialithium.com
Investor Relations - Dean Hanisch (613) 612-6060
Auditors - MNP LLP C.A., Ottawa, Ont.
Transfer Agents - Computershare Trust Company of Canada Inc., Montréal, Qué.
Profile - (Can. 2011) Has mineral interests in Quebec and developing a lithium extraction technology.

Holds Pontax lithium prospect, 3,613 hectares, 350 km north of Matagami, up to 70% optioned to **Cygnus Gold Limited**, requiring exploration expenditures of $4,000,000 by January 2024 to earn an initial 51% interest; option to acquire nearby Pontax 2 lithium prospect, 5,535 hectares; and Romer polymetallic prospect, 2,592 hectares, Labrador Trough.

In addition, the company, together with **Grafoid Inc.**, is developing an alternative to conventional methods of recovering lithium from salt with higher yields of commercial lithium and potential fresh water supply. This technology is a graphene based filtration membrane used in the desalination process to efficiently separate lithium from salt. Lithium extracted would be used as ready supply for battery production.

On Aug. 11, 2022, the company acquired the 2,592-hectare Romer polymetallic prospect in Quebec from **Braille Energy Systems Inc.** for $125,000 cash and issuance of 7,500,000 common shares at a deemed price of 5¢ per share.

Predecessor Detail - Name changed from Stria Capital Inc., May 9, 2014.

Directors - Jeffrey (Jeff) York, chr., Ottawa, Ont.; Dean Hanisch, pres. & CEO, Ottawa, Ont.; Robin B. Dow, West Vancouver, B.C.; Harry Martyniuk, Ont.

Other Exec. Officers - Judith T. Mazvihwa-MacLean, CFO & corp. sec.

Capital Stock

	Authorized (shs.)	Outstanding (shs.)[1]
Common	unlimited	25,821,036

[1] At May 25, 2023

Major Shareholder - Jeffrey (Jeff) York held 18.6% interest at Feb. 14, 2023.

Price Range - SRA/TSX-VEN

Year	Volume	High	Low	Close
2022	6,871,353	$0.45	$0.12	$0.22
2021	4,130,065	$0.90	$0.20	$0.40
2020	977,641	$0.25	$0.05	$0.20
2019	1,030,418	$0.40	$0.05	$0.05
2018	1,867,197	$0.80	$0.20	$0.25

Consolidation: 1-for-10 cons. in May 2022

Recent Close: $0.21

Capital Stock Changes - On May 16, 2022, common shares were consolidated on a 1-for-10 basis. In August 2022, 4,274,999 units (1 post-consolidated common share & ½ warrant) at 15¢ per unit was completed. Also during fiscal 2022, post-consolidated common shares were issued as follows: 1,453,000 for debt settlement, 750,000 on acquisition of mineral properties and 200,000 on exercise of warrants.

Wholly Owned Subsidiaries

Pueblo Lithium LLC, United States. Inactive.

Financial Statistics

Periods ended:	12m Sept. 30/22[A]		12m Sept. 30/21[oA]
	$000s	%Chg	$000s
General & admin expense	359		375
Stock-based compensation	916		nil
Operating expense	**1,275**	**+240**	**375**
Operating income	**(1,275)**	**n.a.**	**(375)**
Finance costs, gross	61		64
Pre-tax income	**(1,333)**	**n.a.**	**(439)**
Net income	**(1,333)**	**n.a.**	**(439)**
Cash & equivalent	2,735		1,106
Current assets	2,979		1,734
Explor./devel. properties	2,241		1,926
Total assets	**5,220**	**+43**	**3,660**
Accts. pay. & accr. liabs.	147		344
Current liabilities	1,539		1,109
Long-term debt, gross	nil		10
Long-term debt, net	nil		10
Shareholders' equity	3,681		2,541
Cash from oper. activs.	**(546)**	**n.a.**	**(454)**
Cash from fin. activs.	961		2,021
Cash from invest. activs.	1,213		(655)
Net cash position	**2,735**	**+147**	**1,106**
Capital expenditures	(376)		(655)
	$		$
Earnings per share*	(0.08)		(0.47)
Cash flow per share*	(0.03)		(0.49)
	shs		shs
No. of shs. o/s*	21,236,036		1,455,804
Avg. no. of shs. o/s*	16,334,519		930,868
	%		%
Net profit margin	n.a.		n.a.
Return on equity	(42.85)		(23.72)
Return on assets	(28.65)		(11.65)

* Common
[o] Restated
[A] Reported in accordance with IFRS

Historical Summary
(as originally stated)

Fiscal Year	Oper. Rev.	Net Inc. Bef. Disc.	EPS*
	$000s	$000s	$
2022[A]	nil	(1,333)	(0.08)
2021[A]	nil	(439)	(0.05)
2020[A]	nil	19	0.00
2019[A]	nil	(214)	(0.03)
2018[A]	nil	(358)	(0.06)

* Common
[A] Reported in accordance with IFRS
Note: Adjusted throughout for 1-for-10 cons. in May 2022

S.131 Strong Global Entertainment, Inc.

Symbol - SGE **Exchange** - NYSE MKT **CUSIP** - 86335G
Head Office - 5960 Fairview Rd, Suite 275, Charlotte, NC, United States, 28210 **Telephone** - (704) 471-6784
Website - strong-entertainment.com
Email - ir@fg.group
Investor Relations - Mark D. Roberson (709) 944-8279
Auditors - Haskell & White LLP C.P.A., Irvine, Calif.
Transfer Agents - Broadridge Corporate Issuer Solutions, Inc., New York, N.Y.
Profile - (B.C. 2021) Manufactures and distributes large format projection screens, as well as provides managed services, technical support, and related products and services primarily to cinema exhibitors, theme parks, educational institutions and similar venues worldwide.
Operates through three businesses:
Wholly owned **Strong/MDI Screen Systems, Inc.** supplies screen and projection coatings worldwide, including the Eclipse curvilinear screens which are specifically designed for theme parks, immersive exhibitions, as well as simulation applications. Manufacturing operations of screen systems are conducted at an 80,000-sq.-ft. facility in Joliette, Que.
Wholly owned **Strong Technical Services, Inc.** offers a suite of cinema-focused services, including maintenance, repair, installation, network support services and other services to exhibitors throughout the U.S., as well as distributes cinema equipment.
Wholly owned **Strong Studios, Inc.** develops and produces original feature films and television series, and also acquires third-party rights to distribute content globally.
Class A listed on NYSE MKT, May 16, 2023.
Directors - D. Kyle Cerminara, chr., N.C.; Mark D. Roberson, CEO; Dr. Richard E. Govignon Jr., N.J.; Dr. Marsha G. King; John W. Struble, N.C.
Other Exec. Officers - Ray F. Boegner, pres.; Todd R. Major, CFO, corp. sec. & treas.

Capital Stock

	Authorized (shs.)	Outstanding (shs.)[1]
Preferred	150,000,000	nil
Cl.A Common Vtg.	150,000,000	7,000,000
Cl.B Common Vtg.	100	100[2]

[1] At May 18, 2023
[2] All held by FG Group Holdings Inc.

Preferred - Issuable in series.
Class A Common Voting - One vote per share.
Class B Common Voting - Not entitled to dividends. Redeemable and retractable at US$1.00 per share upon certain conditions being met. Holders are entitled to: elect or appoint at least 50% of the total number of the company's directors; remove any class B director; and elect or appoint a director to fill any vacancy left by a class B director. Holders are not entitled to vote on any other matter.
Major Shareholder - FG Group Holdings Inc. held 79% interest at May 18, 2023.
Capital Stock Changes - On May 18 2023, an initial public offering of 1,000,000 class A common voting shares was completed at US$4.00 per share.

Wholly Owned Subsidiaries
Strong/MDI Screen Systems, Inc., B.C.
Strong Technical Services, Inc., Neb.
- 100% int. in **Strong Studios, Inc.**, Del.

Financial Statistics

Periods ended:	12m Dec. 31/22[A]		12m Dec. 31/21[A]
	US$000s	%Chg	US$000s
Operating revenue	**39,867**	**+53**	**25,972**
Cost of goods sold	22,729		14,078
Cost of sales	7,592		4,526
General & admin expense	7,727		6,168
Operating expense	**38,048**	**+54**	**24,772**
Operating income	**1,819**	**+52**	**1,200**
Finance costs, net	134		107
Pre-tax income	**2,235**	**+89**	**1,181**
Income taxes	535		360
Net income	**1,700**	**+107**	**821**
Cash & equivalent	3,615		4,494
Inventories	3,389		3,272
Accounts receivable	6,148		4,631
Current assets	17,699		15,663
Fixed assets, net	4,607		5,207
Right-of-use assets	843		299
Intangibles, net	2,389		1,011
Total assets	**25,538**	**+15**	**22,199**
Accts. pay. & accr. liabs	8,592		6,679
Current liabilities	14,937		12,320
Long-term debt, gross	2,636		3,103
Long-term debt, net	126		105
Long-term lease liabilities	736		298
Shareholders' equity	9,204		8,810
Cash from oper. activs	**157**	**-97**	**4,831**
Cash from fin. activs	(69)		(3,334)
Cash from invest. activs	(712)		(394)
Net cash position	**3,615**	**-20**	**4,494**
Capital expenditures	(253)		(394)
	US$		US$
Earnings per share*	n.a.		n.a.
	shs		shs
No. of shs. o/s	n.a.		n.a.
	%		%
Net profit margin	4.26		3.16
Return on equity	18.87		n.m.
Return on assets	7.12		n.a.

[A] Reported in accordance with U.S. GAAP

S.132 Sun Life Financial Inc.*

Symbol - SLF **Exchange** - TSX **CUSIP** - 866796
Head Office - 1 York St, Toronto, ON, M5J 0B6 **Telephone** - (416) 979-9966 **Toll-free** - (877) 786-5433
Website - www.sunlife.com
Email - david.garg@sunlife.com
Investor Relations - David Garg (416) 408-8649
Auditors - Deloitte LLP C.A., Toronto, Ont.
Transfer Agents - American Stock Transfer & Trust Company, LLC, New York, N.Y.; Computershare Hong Kong Investor Services Limited, Hong Kong, Hong Kong People's Republic of China; Rizal Commercial Banking Corporation, Makati City, Philippines; Link Asset Services, Beckenham, Kent United Kingdom; TSX Trust Company, Toronto, Ont.
FP500 Revenue Ranking - 23
Employees - 29,162 at Dec. 31, 2022
Profile - (Can. 1999) Offers insurance, health, wealth and asset management products and services to individual and institutional customers primarily in Canada, the U.S. and Asia.
Has global operations through direct and indirect subsidiaries in Canada, the U.S., the U.K., Ireland, Hong Kong, the Philippines, Japan, Indonesia, India, the People's Republic of China (PRC), Australia, Singapore, Vietnam, Malaysia and Bermuda. Operations are organized into five business segments: Canada, United States, Asset Management, Asia and Corporate.
Canada - Provides protection, health, asset management and wealth products and services to 6,300,000 individual and group clients. This segment is divided into three business units: individual insurance and wealth, Sun Life Health and group retirement services. The individual insurance and wealth unit offers a broad range of life and health insurance and investment products to individual clients through a multi-channel distribution network, including the company's proprietary advisory network, third-party channels such as independent brokers and broker-dealers, and direct to consumers. The Sun Life Health unit provides group benefits including group insurance products to employers, such as life, dental, extended health care, disability and critical illness, and voluntary benefits solutions to individual plan members, including post-employment life and health plans, as well as personalized and on-demand digital health solutions. Sun Life Health products and services are distributed by sales representatives, independent advisors, benefits consultants and the company's proprietary advisory network. The group retirement services unit provides defined contribution pension plans and defined benefit solutions to employers, as well as voluntary savings plans, including post-employment plans, to members exiting their employer-sponsored plans, with products and services distributed by sales representatives, pension consultants and advisors.
U.S. - Consists of three business units: group benefits, dental and in-force management. The group benefits unit includes employee benefits, which provides group insurance products and services, including life, long-term and short-term disability, absence management, and voluntary and supplemental health insurance such as hospital indemnity, accident and critical illness, as well as turnkey risk management solutions for insurers and health plans; and health and risk solutions, which include medical stop-loss insurance and health care navigation services. Group benefits serves nearly 60,000 small, medium and large-sized employers and 17,000,000 members with products and services distributed through more than 32,000 independent brokers and benefits consultants, supported by about 175 employed sales representatives. The dental unit serves 37,000,000 members through Medicaid and Medicare Advantage dental benefits and commercial group dental and vision solutions for employers, and has a network of more than 70 oral health practices, which are located in underserved communities to help increase access to dental care to deliver direct patient care in rural and underserved communities. The in-force management unit is a run-off block with no new sales, managing 85,000 individual life insurance policies, primarily universal life and participating whole life insurance.
Asset Management - Consists of the MFS Investment Management and SLC Management businesses, providing asset management products and services to clients worldwide. MFS offers a comprehensive selection of financial products and services to retail and institutional investors, including pension plans, sovereign wealth funds, monetary authorities, endowments and foundations. SLC Management offers fixed income and alternative investment solutions, including public and private fixed income, real estate, debt and infrastructure, to institutional investors through indirect subsidiaries, including **Sun Life Capital Management (U.S.) LLC**, **Sun Life Capital Management (Canada) Inc.**, **BentallGreenOak**, **InfraRed Capital Partners Limited** and **Crescent Capital Group LP**, and to high-net-worth retail investors through subsidiary **Advisors Asset Management, Inc.** Retail products are distributed through financial advisors, brokerages and other professionals, and institutional products are distributed by an internal sales force supported by a network of independent consultants.
Asia - Consists of five business units: ASEAN, Hong Kong, Joint Ventures, High-Net-Worth and Regional Office. The local markets unit provides asset management, wealth, protection and health solutions to individual, business and institutional clients in the Philippines, Indonesia, Vietnam, Malaysia, India and the PRC through a multi-channel distribution network. Products and services include individual and group life and health insurance, savings, pension and retirement, individual and institutional asset management, passive third-party asset management and debt financing. The international hubs unit consists of operations in Hong Kong, which offer individual and group life and health insurance, mandatory provident funds (the government-legislated pension system) and pension administration to individuals and businesses; international operations, which provide individual life insurance solutions for high-net-worth clients in markets outside the U.S. and Canada, and manages a block of international wealth investment products closed to new sales; and Singapore operations, which provide individual life insurance solutions for high-net-worth clients in Asia.
Corporate - Includes the company's run-off reinsurance business, which has medical, guaranteed minimum income and death benefit coverage as well as group long-term disability and personal accident policies.

Assets Under Management

At Dec. 31	2022	2021
	$millions	$millions
General funds	205,614	205,374
Segregated funds	125,292	139,996
Retail, institutional & managed funds	994,953	1,099,358
	1,325,859	1,444,728

On Jan. 20, 2023, the company entered into a 15-year exclusive bancassurance partnership in Hong Kong with **Dah Sing Bank, Limited** effective July 1, 2023. The company would pay an initial HK$1.5 billion for the exclusive arrangement, with ongoing variable payments based on the success of the partnership.

Recent Merger and Acquisition Activity

Status: pending **Announced:** July 26, 2023
Sun Life Financial Inc. agreed to acquire all issued common shares of Dialogue Health Technologies Inc., other than certain common shares currently owned by Sun Life's affiliates and members of Dialogue executive management, for $5.15 per share in cash for a total equity value of $365,000,000. Dialogue's executive management would maintain a minority interest in Dialogue following closing. Dialogue would operate as a standalone entity of Sun Life Canada. The directors and certain members of Dialogue executive management, owning 8.7% of the common shares, and Portag3 Ventures LP, Portag3 Ventures II Investments LP and WSC IV LP, collectively holding 21%, have entered into customary support and voting agreements to vote in favour of the transaction. Certain members of Dialogue executive management have also agreed to roll a portion of their equity in Dialogue and would remain as Dialogue shareholders, owning a 3% interest with Sun Life owning the remaining 97%. The transaction was expected to close in the fourth quarter of 2023.

Status: completed **Revised:** Apr. 3, 2023
UPDATE: The transaction was completed. PREVIOUS: Sun Life Financial Inc. agreed to sell its wholly owned closed book business in the U.K., SLF of Canada UK Limited (Sun Life UK), to Phoenix Group Holdings plc for £248,000,000, funded from Phoenix's existing cash resources. Sun Life UK has been closed to new business since December 2010 and has been operating as a run-off business managing life and pension policies and annuity blocks for clients in the U.K. At Dec. 31, 2021, Sun Life UK had 480,000 in-force policies and £10 billion of assets under administration. Sun Life would retain its economic interest in Sun Life

UK's payout annuities business and would continue to manage through its asset management businesses, MFS Investment Management and SLC Management, Cdn$9 billion of Sun Life UK's general account upon the close of the sale. The transaction was expected to close during the first half of 2023, subject to receipt of regulatory approvals and satisfaction of customary closing conditions.

Status: completed **Revised:** Feb. 1, 2023
UPDATE: The transaction was completed. PREVIOUS: Sun Life Financial Inc. agreed to acquire a 51% interest in Monument, Colo.-based Advisors Asset Management, Inc. (AAM), which provides products and solutions to financial advisors at wirehouses, registered investment advisors and independent broker-dealers, including unit investment trusts, mutual funds and managed accounts, for US$214,000,000. Sun Life has a put/call option to acquire the remaining 49% interest in AAM starting in 2028. AAM oversaw US$41.4 billion in assets as of July 31, 2022. The transaction was expected to be completed in the first half of 2023, subject to receipt of regulatory approvals and satisfaction of customary closing conditions.

Status: completed **Revised:** Feb. 1, 2023
UPDATE: The transaction was completed. PREVIOUS: Sun Life Financial Inc. agreed to sell its sponsored markets business to Canadian Premier Life Insurance Company for an undisclosed amount. Upon completion, Sun Life expected to generate a one-time after-tax gain of $65,000,000. The business included a variety of association and affinity, and group creditor clients. The transaction would result in more than 100 sponsors and 1,500,000 insured clients and plan members/customers move from Sun Life to Canadian Premier. The transaction was expected to be completed in early 2023, subject to satisfaction of customary closing conditions, including receipt of regulatory approvals.

Status: completed **Revised:** June 1, 2022
UPDATE: The transaction was completed. PREVIOUS: Sun Life Financial Inc. agreed to acquire Boston, Mass.-based DentaQuest Group, Inc., which provides Medicaid dental benefits in the U.S., for US$2.475 billion (Cdn$3.1 billion), which would be financed using a combination of cash and debt. DentaQuest had more than 33,000,000 members in 36 states. Upon completion, DentaQuest would become a part of Sun Life's U.S. business. The transaction was expected to be completed in the first half of 2022, subject to receipt of regulatory approvals and satisfaction of customary closing conditions.

Predecessor Detail - Name changed from Sun Life Financial Services of Canada Inc., July 4, 2003.

Directors - Scott F. Powers, chr., Boston, Mass.; Kevin D. Strain, pres. & CEO, Mississauga, Ont.; Deepak Chopra, Toronto, Ont.; Stephanie L. Coyles, Toronto, Ont.; Ashok K. Gupta, London, Middx., United Kingdom; M. Marianne Harris, Toronto, Ont.; David H. Y. Ho, Shenzhen, Guangdong, People's Republic of China; Laurie G. Hylton, Newburyport, Mass.; Helen M. Mallovy Hicks, Toronto, Ont.; Marie-Lucie Morin, Ottawa, Ont.; Joseph M. (Joe) Natale, Toronto, Ont.; Barbara G. Stymiest, Toronto, Ont.

Other Exec. Officers - Linda M. Dougherty, exec. v-p & chief strategy & enablement officer; Melissa J. Kennedy, exec. v-p & chief legal & public policy officer; Laura A. Money, exec. v-p & chief info. & tech. innovation officer; Thomas P. (Tom) Murphy, exec. v-p & chief risk officer; Helena J. Pagano, exec. v-p & chief people & culture officer; Manjit Singh, exec. v-p & CFO; Christopher B. (Chris) Wei, exec. v-p & chief client & innovation officer; Remi Benoit, sr. v-p, tax; Alanna Boyd, sr. v-p & chief sustainability officer; Natalie Brady, sr. v-p, strategic fin. initiatives; Patricia Callon, sr. v-p & gen. counsel, corp.; Leigh Chalmers, sr. v-p & head, corp. fin. & capital mgt.; David Garg, sr. v-p, corp. devel. & IR; Brennan Kennedy, sr. v-p, global asset liability mgt.; Larry R. Madge, sr. v-p, finl. & insce. risk mgt.; Kevin Morrissey, sr. v-p & chief actuary; Julie O'Neill, sr. v-p, enterprise & operational risk mgt.; Shelley Peterson, sr. v-p, total rewards; Patrick R. Romain, sr. v-p & chief credit risk officer; Samiha Sachedina, sr. v-p & chief auditor; Kent Savage, sr. v-p & chief compliance officer; Emily Schur, sr. v-p, global talent; Aishling Cullen, v-p, corp. commun.; Troy Krushel, v-p, assoc. gen. counsel & corp. sec.; Daniel R. (Dan) Fishbein, pres., Sun Life U.S.; Jacques Goulet, pres., Sun Life Canada; Ingrid G. Johnson, pres., Sun Life Asia; Stephen C. (Steve) Peacher, pres., SLC Management

Capital Stock

	Authorized (shs.)	Outstanding (shs.)[1]
Class A Preferred	unlimited	
Series 3		10,000,000
Series 4		12,000,000
Series 5		10,000,000
Series 8R		6,217,331
Series 9QR		4,982,669
Series 10R		6,838,672
Series 11QR		1,161,328
Class B Preferred	unlimited	nil
Limited Recouse Capital Notes	n.a.	
Series 2021-1		1,000,000
Common	unlimited	586,937,220

[1] At July 28, 2023

Class A Preferred - Issuable in series. Non-voting.

Series 3 - Entitled to fixed non-cumulative preferential annual dividends of $1.1125 per share payable quarterly. Redeemable at $25 per share.

Series 4 - Entitled to fixed non-cumulative preferential annual dividends of $1.1125 per share payable quarterly. Redeemable at $25 per share.

Series 5 - Entitled to fixed non-cumulative preferential annual dividends of $1.125 per share payable quarterly. Redeemable at $25 per share.

Series 8R - Entitled to fixed non-cumulative preferential annual dividends of $0.45625 per share payable quarterly to June 30, 2025, and thereafter at a rate reset every five years equal to the five-year Government of Canada yield plus 1.41%. Redeemable on June 30, 2025, and on June 30 every five years thereafter at $25 per share plus accrued dividends. Convertible at the holder's option, on June 30, 2025, and on June 30 every five years thereafter, into non-cumulative floating rate class A preferred series 9QR shares on a share-for-share basis, subject to certain conditions.

Series 9QR - Entitled to non-cumulative preferential dividends payable quarterly equal to the 90-day Canadian Treasury bill rate plus 1.41%. Redeemable on June 30, 2025, and on June 30 every five years thereafter at $25 per share plus accrued dividends, or at $25.50 per share plus accrued dividends on any other date. Convertible at the holder's option, on June 30, 2025, and on June 30 every five years thereafter, into class A preferred series 8R shares on a share-for-share basis, subject to certain conditions.

Series 10R - Entitled to fixed non-cumulative preferential annual dividends of $0.74175 per share payable quarterly to Sept. 29, 2026, and thereafter at a rate reset every five years equal to the five-year Government of Canada yield plus 2.17%. Redeemable on Sept. 30, 2026, and on September 30 every five years thereafter at $25 per share plus accrued dividends. Convertible at the holder's option, on Sept. 30, 2026, and on September 30 every five years thereafter, into non-cumulative floating rate class A preferred series 11QR shares on a share-for-share basis, subject to certain conditions.

Series 11QR - Entitled to non-cumulative preferential dividends payable quarterly equal to the 90-day Canadian Treasury bill rate plus 2.17%. Redeemable on Sept. 30, 2026, and on September 30 every five years thereafter at $25 per share plus accrued dividends, or at $25.50 per share plus accrued dividends on any other date. Convertible at the holder's option, on Sept. 30, 2026, and on September 30 every five years thereafter, into class A preferred series 10R shares on a share-for-share basis, subject to certain conditions.

Class B Preferred - Entitled to preference over the common shares and any other shares ranking junior to the class B preferred shares, but are subordinate to the class A preferred shares and any other shares ranking senior to the class B preferred shares, all with respect to the payment of dividends and return of capital. Issuable in series. Non-voting.

Limited Recourse Capital Notes Series 2021-1 Subordinated Debentures (Series 2021-1 Notes) - Notes with recourse limited to assets held by a third party trustee in a consolidated trust. Bear interest at 3.6% per annum until June 30, 2026, and thereafter at an annual rate reset every five years equal to the five-year Government of Canada yield plus 2.604% until maturity on June 30, 2081. Trust assets consist of non-cumulative five-year reset class A preferred series 14 shares.

Common - One vote per share.

Options - At Dec. 31, 2022, options were outstanding to purchase 3,589,000 common shares at prices ranging from $36.98 to $68.12 per share with a weighted average contractual remaining life of 6.18 years.

Normal Course Issuer Bid - The company plans to make normal course purchases of up to 17,000,000 common shares representing 2.9% of the total outstanding. The bid commenced on Aug. 29, 2023, and expires on Aug. 28, 2024.

Major Shareholder - Widely held at Mar. 17, 2023.

Price Range - SLF/TSX

Year	Volume	High	Low	Close
2022	555,183,562	$74.22	$52.97	$62.85
2021	513,402,107	$71.73	$55.92	$70.41
2020	528,294,132	$66.44	$35.43	$56.60
2019	358,523,488	$61.91	$44.43	$59.21
2018	289,075,666	$56.09	$43.13	$45.29

Recent Close: $64.59

Capital Stock Changes - During 2022, 400,000 common shares were issued on exercise of options.

Dividends

SLF com Ra $3.00 pa Q est. June 30, 2023**
Prev. Rate: $2.88 est. Dec. 30, 2022
Prev. Rate: $2.76 est. June 30, 2022
Prev. Rate: $2.64 est. Dec. 31, 2021
Prev. Rate: $2.20 est. Dec. 31, 2019
SLF.PR.C pfd A ser 3 red. exch. Ra $1.1125 pa Q**
SLF.PR.D pfd A ser 4 red. exch. Ra $1.1125 pa Q**
SLF.PR.E pfd A ser 5 red. exch. Ra $1.125 pa Q**
SLF.PR.G pfd A ser 8R red. exch. Adj. Ra $0.45625 pa Q est. Sept. 30, 2020**
SLF.PR.H pfd A ser 10R red. exch. Adj. Ra $0.74175 pa Q est. Dec. 31, 2021**
SLF.PR.J pfd A ser 9QR red. exch. Fltg. Ra pa Q**

$0.376381	Sept. 29/23	$0.372352	June 30/23
$0.341692	Mar. 31/23	$0.297929	Dec. 30/22

Paid in 2023: $1.090425 2022: $0.701123 2021: $0.382422

SLF.PR.K pfd A ser 11QR red. exch. Fltg. Ra pa Q**

$0.424271	Sept. 29/23	$0.419722	June 30/23
$0.388541	Mar. 31/23	$0.345819	Dec. 30/22

Paid in 2023: $1.232534 2022: $0.891122 2021: $0.57242

pfd A ser 1 red. exch. Ra $1.1875 pa Q**[1]
$0.296875f Sept. 29/21
pfd A ser 2 red. exch. Ra $1.20 pa Q**[1]
$0.30f Sept. 29/21
pfd A ser 12R red. exch. Adj. Ra $0.9515 pa Q est. Mar. 31, 2017**[2]
$0.237875f Dec. 31/21

[1] Redeemed Sept. 29, 2021 at $25 per sh.
[2] Redeemed Dec. 31, 2021 at $25 per sh.
** Reinvestment Option **f** Final Payment

Long-Term Debt - Outstanding at Dec. 31, 2022:

Subordinated debt:	
6.3% due 2028	$150,000,000
3.05% due 2028[1]	999,000,000
2.38% due 2029[2]	749,000,000
2.46% due 2031[3]	498,000,000
2.58% due 2032[4]	996,000,000
2.8% due 2033[5]	996,000,000
4.78% due 2034[6]	646,000,000
2.06% due 2035[7]	746,000,000
3.15% due 2036[8]	498,000,000
5.4% due 2042[9]	398,000,000
Senior debentures:	
7.09% due 2052	200,000,000
	6,876,000,000

[1] From Sept. 19, 2023, interest is payable at CDOR plus 1.85%.
[2] From Aug. 13, 2024, interest is payable at CDOR plus 0.85%.
[3] From Nov. 18, 2026, interest is payable at CDOR plus 0.44%.
[4] From May 10, 2027, interest is payable at CDOR plus 1.66%.
[5] From Nov. 21, 2028, interest is payable at CDOR plus 0.69%.
[6] From Aug. 10, 2029, interest is payable at Canadian Overnight Repo Rate Average (CORRA) plus 1.96%.
[7] From Oct. 1, 2030, interest is payable at CDOR plus 1.03%.
[8] From Nov. 18, 2031, interest is payable at CDOR plus 0.91%.
[9] From May 29, 2037, interest is payable at CDOR plus 1%.

Note - In July 2023, offering of $500,000,000 principal amount of series 2023-1 subordinated unsecured 5.5% fixed/floating debentures due 2035 was completed and all $1 billion principal amount of series 2016-2 subordinated unsecured 3.05% fixed/floating debentures due 2028 were called for redemption on Sept. 19, 2023.

Wholly Owned Subsidiaries

SLGI Asset Management Inc., Toronto, Ont. Book value of voting shares owned by the company at Dec. 31, 2022, totaled $78,000,000.

Sun Life Assurance Company of Canada, Toronto, Ont. Book value of voting shares owned by the company at Dec. 31, 2022, totaled $25.775 billion.

- 100% int. in **BestServe Financial Limited**, Hong Kong, Hong Kong, People's Republic of China. Book value of voting shares owned by the company at Dec. 31, 2022, totaled $120,000,000.
- 100% int. in **PT Sun Life Financial Indonesia**, Jakarta, Indonesia. Book value of voting shares owned by the company at Dec. 31, 2022, totaled $705,000,000.
- 100% int. in **Sun Life and Health Insurance Company (U.S.)**, Mich. Book value of voting shares owned by the company at Dec. 31, 2022, totaled $535,000,000.
- 100% int. in **Sun Life Assurance Company of Canada (U.K.) Limited**, Basingstoke, Hants., United Kingdom. Book value of voting shares owned by the company at Dec. 31, 2022, totaled $369,000,000.
- 24.99% int. in **Sun Life Everbright Life Insurance Company Limited**, Tianjin, Tianjin, People's Republic of China.
- 100% int. in **Sun Life Financial Distributors (Canada) Inc.**, Waterloo, Ont. Book value of voting shares owned by the company at Dec. 31, 2022, totaled $8,000,000.
- 100% int. in **Sun Life Financial (India) Insurance Investments Inc.**, Toronto, Ont.
  - 49% int. in **Aditya Birla Sun Life Insurance Company Limited**, Mumbai, India.
- 100% int. in **Sun Life Financial Investment Services (Canada) Inc.**, Waterloo, Ont. Book value of voting shares owned by the company at Dec. 31, 2022, totaled $70,000,000.
- 100% int. in **Sun Life Financial of Canada (U.K.) Overseas Investments Limited**, Basingstoke, Hants., United Kingdom.
  - 100% int. in **Sun Life of Canada (Netherlands) B.V.**, Rotterdam, Netherlands.
    - 100% int. in **Sun Life Financial Philippine Holding Company, Inc.**, Manila, Philippines.
      - 49% int. in **Sun Life Grepa Financial, Inc.**, Philippines.
  - 100% int. in **Sun Life of Canada (Philippines), Inc.**, Manila, Philippines. Book value of voting shares owned by the company at Dec. 31, 2022, totaled $1.478 billion.
- 100% int. in **Sun Life Financial Trust Inc.**, Waterloo, Ont. Book value of voting shares owned by the company at Dec. 31, 2022, totaled $99,000,000.
- 100% int. in **Sun Life Hong Kong Limited**, Hong Kong, People's Republic of China. Book value of voting shares owned by the company at Dec. 31, 2022, totaled $2.449 billion.
- 100% int. in **Sun Life (India) AMC Investments Inc.**, Toronto, Ont.
  - 36.49% int. in **Aditya Birla Sun Life AMC Limited**, Mumbai, India.
- 100% int. in **Sun Life Insurance (Canada) Limited**, Toronto, Ont. Book value of voting shares owned by the company at Dec. 31, 2022, totaled $2.291 billion.
- 49% int. in **Sun Life Malaysia Assurance Bhd.**, Kuala Lumpur, Malaysia.

- 49% int. in **Sun Life Malaysia Takaful Bhd.**, Kuala Lumpur, Malaysia.
- 100% int. in **Sun Life Vietnam Insurance Company Limited**, Ho Chi Minh City, Vietnam. Book value of voting shares owned by the company at Dec. 31, 2022, totaled $895,000,000.

Sun Life Capital Management (Canada) Inc., Canada. Book value of voting shares owned by the company at Dec. 31, 2022, totaled $29,000,000.

Sun Life Global Investments Inc., Canada.

- 100% int. in **BK Canada Holdings Inc.**, Canada.
  - 51% int. in **BentallGreenOak (Canada) Limited Partnership**, Toronto, Ont. Book value of voting shares owned by the company at Dec. 31, 2022, totaled $358,000,000.
    - 71% int. in **BGO Holdings (Cayman), LP**, Grand Cayman, Cayman Islands. Book value of voting shares owned by the company at Dec. 31, 2022, totaled $73,000,000.

Sun Life 2007-1 Financing Corp., Toronto, Ont.

- 100% int. in **Sun Life Assurance Company of Canada - U.S. Operations Holdings, Inc.**, Del.
  - 100% int. in **DentaQuest Group, Inc.**, Boston, Mass.
    - 100% int. in **DentaQuest, LLC**, Boston, Mass. Book value of voting shares owned by the company at Dec. 31, 2022, totaled $3.706 billion.
  - 100% int. in **Sun Life Financial (U.S.) Holdings, Inc.**, Del.
    - 100% int. in **Sun Life Financial (U.S.) Investments LLC**, Del.
      - 100% int. in **Sun Life Institutional Distributors (U.S.) LLC**, Del. Book value of voting shares owned by the company at Dec. 31, 2022, totaled $1,000,000.
      - 100% int. in **Sun Life Investment Management U.S., Inc.**, Del.
        - 100% int. in **SL Investment US-RE Holdings 2009-1, Inc.**, Del.
          - 51% int. in **BentallGreenOak (U.S.) Limited Partnership**, New York, N.Y. Book value of voting shares owned by the company at Dec. 31, 2022, totaled $478,000,000.
        - 100% int. in **Sun Life Capital Management (U.S.) LLC**, Del. Book value of voting shares owned by the company at Dec. 31, 2022, totaled $122,000,000.
      - 99.93% int. in **Sun Life of Canada (U.S.) Financial Services Holdings, Inc.**, Del.
        - 95.14% int. in **Massachusetts Financial Services Company**, Boston, Mass. Book value of voting shares owned by the company at Dec. 31, 2022, totaled $978,000,000.
      - 100% int. in **Sun Life of Canada (U.S.) Holdings, Inc.**, Del.
        - 100% int. in **Independence Life and Annuity Company**, Del. Book value of voting shares owned by the company at Dec. 31, 2022, totaled $432,000,000.
        - 100% int. in **Professional Insurance Company**, Tex. Book value of voting shares owned by the company at Dec. 31, 2022, totaled $55,000,000.
        - 100% int. in **Sun Life Financial (U.S.) Services Company, Inc.**, Wilmington, Del. Book value of voting shares owned by the company at Dec. 31, 2022, totaled $102,000,000.
- 100% int. in **Sun Life (U.S.) HoldCo 2020, Inc.**, Del.
  - 51% int. in **Crescent Capital Group LP**, Los Angeles, Calif. Book value of voting shares owned by the company at Dec. 31, 2022, totaled $59,000,000.
  - 100% int. in **InfraRed (UK) Holdco 2020 Ltd.**, United Kingdom.
    - 80% int. in **InfraRed Partners LLP**, United Kingdom. Book value of voting shares owned by the company at Dec. 31, 2022, totaled $81,000,000.

Note: The preceding list includes only the major related companies in which interests are held.

Financial Statistics

Periods ended:	12m Dec. 31/22[A]		12m Dec. 31/21[A]
	$000s	%Chg	$000s
Net premiums earned	26,863,000		23,053,000
Net investment income	(11,587,000)		4,633,000
Total revenue	**23,322,000**	**-35**	**35,688,000**
Policy benefits & claims	9,879,000		21,223,000
Commissions	2,836,000		2,809,000
Salaries & benefits	4,846,000		4,320,000
Stock-based compensation	227,000		757,000
Premium taxes	487,000		429,000
Other operating expense	(37,000)		279,000
Operating expense	**8,359,000**	**-3**	**8,594,000**
Operating income	**5,084,000**	**-13**	**5,871,000**
Deprec. & amort.	528,000		438,000
Finance costs, gross	445,000		327,000
Write-downs/write-offs	(188,000)		(9,000)
Pre-tax income	**3,923,000**	**-23**	**5,097,000**
Income taxes	621,000		727,000
Net income	**3,302,000**	**-24**	**4,370,000**
Net inc. for equity hldrs	**3,130,000**	**-22**	**4,035,000**
Net inc. for non-cont. int.	**56,000**	**n.a.**	**nil**
Net inc. for partic policyhldrs	**116,000**	**-65**	**335,000**
Cash & equivalent	11,219,000		12,278,000
Accounts receivable	3,675,000		2,269,000
Securities investments	83,050,000		97,840,000
Mortgages	56,261,000		51,692,000
Real estate	10,102,000		9,109,000
Total investments	166,073,000		172,244,000
Segregated fund assets	125,292,000		139,996,000
Total assets	**330,906,000**	**-4**	**345,370,000**
Bank indebtedness	2,345,000		574,000
Accts. pay. & accr. liabs	2,639,000		1,866,000
Debt	6,876,000		6,625,000
Long-term lease liabilities	952,000		850,000
Policy liabilities & claims	143,732,000		151,179,000
Segregated fund liabilities	125,292,000		139,996,000
Partic. policyhldrs.' equity	1,837,000		1,700,000
Preferred share equity	2,239,000		2,239,000
Shareholders' equity	27,450,000		26,314,000
Non-controlling interest	90,000		59,000
Cash from oper. activs	**4,311,000**	**n.a.**	**(1,857,000)**
Cash from fin. activs	(71,000)		(260,000)
Cash from invest. activs	(2,863,000)		(803,000)
Net cash position	**9,372,000**	**+22**	**7,693,000**
Capital expenditures, net	71,000		(81,000)
Unfunded pension liability	n.a.		193,000
Pension fund surplus	36,000		n.a.
	$		$
Earnings per share*	5.22		6.72
Cash flow per share*	7.36		(3.17)
Cash divd. per share*	2.76		2.31
	shs		shs
No. of shs. o/s*	586,400,000		586,000,000
Avg. no. of shs. o/s*	586,000,000		586,000,000
	%		%
Net profit margin	14.16		12.25
Return on equity	12.42		17.00
Return on assets	1.09		1.39
Foreign sales percent	48		46
No. of employees (FTEs)	29,162		24,589

* Common
[A] Reported in accordance with IFRS

Latest Results

Periods ended:	6m June 30/23[A]		6m June 30/22[o][A]
	$000s	%Chg	$000s
Total revenue	19,651,000	n.a.	(7,626,000)
Net income	1,658,000	-4	1,729,000
Net inc. for equity hldrs	1,506,000	-7	1,627,000
Net inc. for non-cont. int.	68,000		18,000
Net inc. for partic policyhldrs	84,000		84,000
	$		$
Earnings per share*	2.50		2.72

* Common
[o] Restated
[A] Reported in accordance with IFRS

Historical Summary
(as originally stated)

Fiscal Year	Total Rev.	Net Inc. Bef. Disc.	EPS*
	$000s	$000s	$
2022[A]	23,322,000	3,302,000	5.22
2021[A]	35,688,000	4,370,000	6.72
2020[A]	43,337,000	2,792,000	4.11
2019[A]	39,679,000	2,947,000	4.42
2018[A]	26,997,000	2,914,000	4.16

* Common
[A] Reported in accordance with IFRS

S.133 Sun Residential Real Estate Investment Trust

Symbol - SRES **Exchange** - TSX-VEN **CUSIP** - 86687A
Head Office - Exchange Tower, 2300-130 King St W, Toronto, ON, M5X 1C8 **Telephone** - (416) 729-7592
Website - sunresreit.com
Email - jsherman@sunresreit.com
Investor Relations - Jeffrey D. Sherman (416) 214-2228
Auditors - PricewaterhouseCoopers LLP C.A., Toronto, Ont.
Bankers - Royal Bank of Canada, Toronto, Ont.
Lawyers - Stikeman Elliott LLP
Transfer Agents - Computershare Trust Company of Canada Inc., Toronto, Ont.

Profile - (Ont. 2019) Acquires, owns and operates multi-family residential properties primarily in the sunbelt region of the United States.

Holds a 51% interest in Evergreen at Southwood, a garden-style multi-family residential apartment community consisting of 12 buildings, totaling 288 rental units, with 276,664 sq. ft. of net rentable area, in Tallahassee, Fla. The average apartment is 968 sq. ft., and the average rent per unit is US$1,209 per month.

Trustees - Daniel N. Argiros, interim chr., Toronto, Ont.; Robert C. Wetenhall Jr., CEO, Newport Beach, Calif.; Robert G. (Rob) Goodall, Toronto, Ont.; Gordon Vollmer, Ajax, Ont.; Gordon M. (Gord) Wiebe, Winnipeg, Man.

Other Exec. Officers - Jeffrey D. Sherman, CFO & corp. sec.; Faruq Rashid, contr.

Capital Stock

	Authorized (shs.)	Outstanding (shs.)[1]
Trust Unit	unlimited	203,338,999

[1] At Aug. 1, 2023

Major Shareholder - Dynamic Income Opportunities Fund, Dynamic Alternative Yield Fund and Dynamic Global Real Estate Fund held 19.9% interest at Mar. 17, 2023.

Price Range - SRES/TSX-VEN

Year	Volume	High	Low	Close
2022	5,980,636	$0.11	$0.06	$0.07
2021	24,857,022	$0.10	$0.06	$0.06
2020	4,272,811	$0.32	$0.08	$0.09
2019	497,100	$0.20	$0.11	$0.14

Recent Close: $0.06

Capital Stock Changes - There were no changes to capital stock during 2021 or 2022.

Dividends

SRES tr unit Ra $0.0038 pa Q est. Mar. 31, 2023
$0.00095**i**............ Mar. 31/23
i Initial Payment

Wholly Owned Subsidiaries

SunResREIT US Inc., Del.

Subsidiaries

51% int. in **Westdale Evergreen Southwood, LLC**, Del.

Financial Statistics

Periods ended:	12m Dec. 31/22[A]		12m Dec. 31/21[A]
	US$000s	%Chg	US$000s
Total revenue	**5,460**	**+10**	**4,946**
Rental operating expense	1,667		1,340
General & admin. expense	394		399
Property taxes	792		738
Operating expense	**2,854**	**+15**	**2,477**
Operating income	**2,606**	**+6**	**2,469**
Finance costs, gross	1,122		1,122
Pre-tax income	**6,688**	**-51**	**13,769**
Income taxes	752		1,648
Net income	**5,936**	**-51**	**12,121**
Net inc. for equity hldrs	**2,482**	**-52**	**5,174**
Net inc. for non-cont. int	**3,454**	**-50**	**6,948**
Cash & equivalent	4,684		4,473
Current assets	4,951		4,740
Income-producing props	70,600		64,950
Property interests, net	70,600		64,950
Total assets	**75,551**	**+8**	**69,690**
Accts. pay. & accr. liabs	371		212
Current liabilities	371		212
Long-term debt, gross	31,440		31,440
Long-term debt, net	31,440		31,440
Shareholders' equity	21,802		19,462
Non-controlling interest	19,539		16,928
Cash from oper. activs	**1,536**	**+25**	**1,229**
Cash from fin. activs	(843)		(647)
Cash from invest. activs	(480)		(17)
Net cash position	**4,684**	**+5**	**4,473**
Capital expenditures	(480)		(17)
	US$		US$
Earnings per share*	n.a.		n.a.
Cash flow per share*	0.01		0.01
Funds from opers. per sh.*	$0.00		$0.00
Adj. funds from opers. per sh.*	$0.00		$0.00
	shs		shs
No. of shs. o/s*	203,338,999		203,338,999
Avg. no. of shs. o/s*	203,338,999		203,338,999
	%		%
Net profit margin	108.72		245.07
Return on equity	12.03		30.65
Return on assets	9.55		20.76
Foreign sales percent	100		100

* Trust Unit

[A] Reported in accordance with IFRS

Historical Summary
(as originally stated)

Fiscal Year	Total Rev.	Net Inc. Bef. Disc.	EPS*
	US$000s	US$000s	US$
2022[A]	5,460	5,936	n.a.
2021[A]	4,946	12,121	n.a.
2020[A]	4,357	235	n.a.
	$000s	$000s	$
2019[A1]	nil	(901)	(0.05)

* Trust Unit

[A] Reported in accordance with IFRS

[1] 49 weeks ended Dec. 31, 2019.

S.134 Suncor Energy Inc.*

Symbol - SU **Exchange** - TSX **CUSIP** - 867224
Head Office - 150 6 Ave SW, PO Box 2844, Calgary, AB, T2P 3E3 **Telephone** - (403) 296-8000 **Toll-free** - (866) 786-2671 **Fax** - (403) 296-3030
Website - www.suncor.com
Email - invest@suncor.com
Investor Relations - Arlene Strom (403) 296-6636
Auditors - KPMG LLP C.A., Calgary, Alta.
Lawyers - Paul, Weiss, Rifkind, Wharton & Garrison LLP, New York, N.Y.; Blake, Cassels & Graydon LLP, Calgary, Alta.
Transfer Agents - Computershare Trust Company, N.A.; Computershare Trust Company of Canada Inc.
FP500 Revenue Ranking - 7
Employees - 16,558 at Dec. 31, 2022

Profile - (Can. 2009 amalg.) Produces bitumen recovered from the Athabasca oil sands in Alberta through mining and in situ technology which is upgraded into synthetic crude oil and other products. Explores for, develops, produces and markets crude oil and natural gas in Canada and internationally. Transports and refines crude oil and markets petroleum and petrochemical products in Canada and the U.S. Conducts energy trading activities focused principally on marketing, supply and trading of crude oil, natural gas, byproducts, refined products and power. Participates in low-emission business opportunities through development and operation of renewable energy facilities and investments in clean energy.

Operations are carried out through three business segments: Oil Sands; Exploration and Production, including East Coast Canada and International; and Refining and Marketing. Operations not attributable directly to an operating business are reported under Corporate and Eliminations.

Oil Sands operations based near Fort McMurray, Alta., recover bitumen through oil sands mining and in situ technology, which is then upgraded into synthetic crude oil (SCO), diesel fuel and other byproducts or blended with diluent for refinery feedstock or direct sale to market. Mining operations consist of the Millennium and North Steepbank sites which include two integrated upgrading facilities with a combined capacity of 350,000 bbl per day of SCO; and the Base Mine Extension and Audet development sites. Additional mining operations include 68.76% interest (**TotalEnergies EP Canada Ltd.** 31.23%) in and operatorship of the Fort Hills mining project; and 58.74% interest (**Imperial Oil Limited** 25%, **Sinopec Oil Sands Partnership** 9.03%, **CNOOC Oil Sands Canada** 7.23%) in and operatorship of the Syncrude mining and upgrading joint venture, with operations at Mildred Lake and Aurora North. In situ operations consist of Firebag and MacKay River projects which use steam-assisted gravity drainage (SAGD) to separate bitumen from oil sands deposits that are too deep to be mined economically. Firebag complex consists of central processing facilities with total bitumen processing capacity of 215,000 bbl per day. Central processing facilities at MacKay River have a nameplate capacity of 38,000 bbl of bitumen per day. Other in situ holdings include Lewis, Meadow Creek (75% interest), Gregoire, OSLO (77.78% interest), Chard (25% to 50% interests) and Kirby (10% interest). In addition, owns and operates East Tank Farm (51% interest), a bitumen and diluent storage, blending and cooling facility located north of Fort McMurray.

Exploration and Production (E&P) operations in the east coast area of Canada are based in St. John's, Nfld., and focus primarily on offshore production and development in Terra Nova (48% interest; offline since late 2019), Hibernia (20% interest), Hibernia southern extension unit (19.485% interest), White Rose (40% interest), White Rose extensions (38.6% interest) and Hebron (21.034% interest). International operations include 29.89% interest in producing Buzzard field and 40% interest in Rosebank development project, both in the U.K. portion of the North Sea; working interests in onshore oilfields in the Sirte Basin in Libya (intermittent production since 2013); and an interest in Ebla onshore gas development in the Ash Shaer and Cherrife areas in Syria (under force majeure and indefinite suspension since early 2011).

Refining and Marketing consists of two primary operations: refining and supply; and marketing. Crude oil from the company's oil sands operations and third party producers is refined into a range of petroleum and petrochemical products at facilities in eastern and western North America. Eastern North America includes refineries in Montreal, Que., and Sarnia, Ont., with combined capacity of 222,000 bbl per day. Western North America includes refineries in Edmonton, Alta., and Commerce City, Colo., with combined capacity of 244,000 bbl per day. Other assets include a petrochemical plant (through 51% interest in **ParaChem Chemicals L.P.**) and a sulphur recovery facility, both in Montreal; the St. Clair ethanol plant in Ontario; and pipelines and product terminals in Canada and the U.S. Marketing operations sell refined petroleum products to retail, commercial and industrial customers through a combination of company-owned retail sites and branded dealers in Canada, Colorado and Wyoming, a nationwide commercial road transportation network in Canada and wholesale channels in Canada and the U.S. At Dec. 31, 2022, the company had 1,589 retail service stations under the Petro-Canada™ brand and one under the Sunoco™ brand across Canada, including a coast-to-coast network of electric vehicle charging stations (Electric Highway™); 44 owned or leased retail service stations in Colorado under the Shell™, Exxon™ and Mobil™ brands; and 323 Petro-Canada™ wholesale cardlock sites (PETRO-PASS™) in Canada. The company also supplies wholesale fuel to 174 Shell™, Exxon™ and Mobil™ branded sites in Colorado and Wyoming. Other wholesale customers include farm, home heating, paving, industrial and commercial markets and independent marketers.

The company's other businesses include energy trading activities, which provide crude oil, natural gas, transportation fuels, specialty products and feedstock, and electricity supply, transportation, storage and pricing solutions for mid- to large-sized commercial and industrial consumers, utility companies and energy producers, as well as to the company's own operations. Also has investments in **Enerkem Inc.** (waste-to-biofuels and renewable chemicals), **LanzaJet, Inc.** (sustainable aviation fuel and renewable diesel), **Svante Inc.** (carbon capture) and the Varennes Carbon Recycling facility in Quebec; participation in the Pathways Alliance, a consortium of Canada's six largest oil sands producers pursuing technologies and projects together with federal and provincial governments to address climate change; and partnership with **Canadian Utilities Limited** to build a proposed hydrogen facility in Alberta.

Oil Sands

Year ended Dec. 31	2022	2021
Production		
Upgraded (SCO & diesel), bbl/d		
Oil Sands[1]	303,100	301,600
Syncrude	176,900	167,000
	480,000	468,600
Non-upgraded bitumen, bbl/d		
Oil Sands[1]	100,400	124,900
Fort Hills	84,800	50,700
	185,200	175,600
Sales		
Upgraded (SCO & diesel), bbl/d	482,600	465,700
Non-upgraded bitumen, bbl/d	180,700	183,800
	663,300	649,500
Average Realized Price		
Upgraded (SCO & diesel), $/bbl	118.88	77.73
Non-upgraded bitumen, $/bbl	84.63	53.80
All products, $/bbl	109.57	70.96

[1] Excluding Fort Hills and Syncrude.

Exploration and Production

Year ended Dec. 31	2022	2021
East Coast Canada		
Production, bbl/d	50,200	54,400
Sales, bbl/d	51,400	53,100
Avg. price, $/bbl	128.07	84.70
International		
Production, BOE/d[1]	27,800	33,100
Sales, BOE/d	29,200	29,700
Avg. price, $/BOE[1]	126.61	82.16

[1] Excluding Libya.

At Dec. 31, 2022, the company had 573 gross (497.4 net) producing oil wells, 473 gross (243.4 net) non-producing oil wells and 6 non-producing gas wells. During 2022, the company drilled 41 gross (22 net) exploratory wells and 759 gross (513.1 net) development wells, consisting of 793 gross (533.6 net) in the oil sands segment, 3 gross (0.6 net) in East Coast Canada and 4 gross (0.9 net) in the U.K. North Sea. Undeveloped land holdings totaled 5,535,785 gross (2,556,073 net) hectares at Dec. 31, 2022.

Refinery Operations

Year ended Dec. 31	2022	2021
Eastern North America		
Refined prod. sales, bbl/d	259,300	256,200
Processed, bbl/d	206,200	202,800
Avg. utilization rate (%)	93	91
Western North America		
Refined prod. sales, bbl/d	294,300	272,200
Processed, bbl/d	227,000	212,700
Avg. utilization rate (%)	93	87

On May 3, 2023, the company announced a new partnership between its Petro-Canada business and **Canadian Tire Corporation, Limited** (CTC). The partnership includes a partnership between CTC's Triangle Rewards loyalty program, with more than 11,000,000 active members, and the company's Petro-Points loyalty program, with more than 3,000,000 active members; the rebranding of more than 200 Canadian Tire Gas+ retail fuel sites to Petro-Canada sites; and the company becoming the primary fuel provider to CTC's retail fuel network over time, eventually supplying more than 1 billion litres of fuel to the Canadian Tire retail fuel station network annually. Each company would retain full ownership and control of its respective loyalty program.

On Nov. 29, 2022, the company announced that following a comprehensive review it has decided to retain and continue to optimize the Petro-Canada retail business. This would include continued optimization of the Petro-Canada retail sites across the network as well as continued expansion of strategic partnerships in non-fuel related businesses such as quick service restaurants, convenience stores, loyalty partnerships and energy transition offerings.

During the third quarter of 2022, the 11-MW SunBridge wind farm in Saskatchewan was decommissioned following the end of the power purchase agreement with **Saskatchewan Power Corporation**. The facility began operations in February 2002 and was 50/50 owned by the company and **Enbridge Inc.**

Periods ended:	12m Dec. 31/22	12m Dec. 31/21
Oil reserves, gross, mbbl	6,565,000	6,838,000
Oil reserves, net, mbbl	5,482,000	5,780,000
Gas reserves, gross, mmcf	3,000	19,000
Gas reserves, net, mmcf	3,000	19,000
BOE reserves, gross, mbbl	6,565,000	6,841,000
BOE reserves, net, mbbl	5,483,000	5,783,000

Recent Merger and Acquisition Activity

Status: pending **Revised:** May 26, 2023
UPDATE: ConocoPhillips Canada exercised its right of first refusal with respect to TotalEnergies' 50% working interest in the Surmont project. Suncor's acquisition of TotalEnergies' Canadian operations was conditional upon ConocoPhillips waiving its right of first refusal in respect of the Surmont working interest. As a result, each of the parties have the right to terminate the transaction. PREVIOUS: Suncor Energy Inc. agreed to acquire the Canadian operations of Paris, France-based TotalEnergies SE, through the acquisition of TotalEnergies' wholly owned TotalEnergies EP Canada Ltd., for $5.5 billion, with additional payments of up to an aggregate maximum of $600,000,000, conditional upon Western Canadian Select benchmark and certain production targets. The transaction would include the acquisition of the remaining 31.23% interest in the Fort Hills oil sands mining project and a 50% interest in the Surmont in situ oil sand project, both in northeastern Alberta; the other 50% interest in the Surmont project was held by Houston, Tex.-based ConocoPhillips. The acquisition would add 135,000 bbl per day of net bitumen production capacity and 2.1 billion bbl of proved and probable reserves to Suncor's oil sands portfolio.

Status: pending **Announced:** Mar. 2, 2023
Suncor Energy Inc. agreed to sell wholly owned Suncor Energy UK Limited, which holds Suncor's non-operated offshore interests in the U.K. portion of the North Sea, to Equinor UK Limited for Cdn$1.2 billion, excluding working capital adjustments and including contingent consideration of Cdn$338,000,000 that is conditional upon the submission of the Rosebank development application to the regulator. The transaction includes Suncor's non-operated stakes in the producing Buzzard field (29.89%) and the Rosebank development project (40%). Equinor UK Limited is owned by Equinor ASA. The transaction was expected to close mid-2023.

Status: completed **Revised:** Feb. 2, 2023
UPDATE: The acquisition by Suncor of Teck's remaining 14.65% working interest was completed. PREVIOUS: Suncor Energy Inc. agreed to acquire Teck Resources Limited's 21.3% working interest in the Fort Hills oil sands project in Alberta and associated sales and logistics agreements

for $1 billion. Upon completion, Suncor's interest in the project would increase to 75.42%, with TotalEnergies EP Canada Ltd. continuing to hold the remaining 24.58% interest. The transaction was expected close in the first quarter of 2023. TotalEnergies EP Canada was wholly owned by Paris, France-based TotalEnergies SE, which announced in September 2022 its plan to exit the Canadian oil sands by spinning off TotalEnergies EP Canada in 2023. Jan. 27, 2023 - TotalEnergies EP Canada exercised its pre-emption right to acquire an additional 6.65% interest in the Fort Hills project for $312,000,000, thereby increasing its interest to 31.23%. As a result, Suncor would acquire Teck's remaining 14.65% working interest in the project for $688,000,000, which would increase its interest in the project to 68.76%.

Status: completed **Revised:** Jan. 3, 2023

UPDATE: The transaction was completed. Canadian Utilities acquired Adelaide and Forty Mile wind farms as well as the 1,500-MW development pipeline for $713,000,000. Existing partners of Suncor on the Chin Chute and Magrath wind farms opted to acquire the additional interest in these facilities. Suncor received total proceeds of $730,000,000 for its entire wind and solar assets. PREVIOUS: Suncor Energy Inc. agreed to sell its wind and solar energy assets, consisting of 252 MW of operational wind facilities and more than 1,500 MW of wind and solar projects at various stages of development located in Alberta and Ontario, to Canadian Utilities Limited, a subsidiary of ATCO Ltd., for $730,000,000. The sale includes interest in the 30-MW Magrath (33.3%), 30-MW Chin Chute (33.3%) and 40-MW Adelaide (75%) wind farms, as well as the 202-MW Forty Mile wind farm which was expected to be operating by the end of 2022, and development stage renewable power assets. Suncor plans to focus on areas of energy expansion, hydrogen and renewable fuels.

Status: completed **Revised:** Sept. 30, 2022

UPDATE: The transaction was completed for $430,000,000. PREVIOUS: Suncor Energy Inc. agreed to sell its exploration and production (E&P) assets in Norway for $410,000,000. The assets include 30% interest in producing Oda (formerly Butch) field in the Norwegian sector of the North Sea and 17.5% interest in Fenja development project in the Norwegian Sea. The transaction had an effective date of Mar. 1, 2022.

Status: completed **Announced:** May 31, 2022

Suncor Energy Inc. and its joint venture partners have agreed to restart work on the West White Rose project, located offshore Newfoundland and Labrador. As a result, Suncor increased its ownership in the White Rose project to 40% from 27.5% and in the West White Rose project (White Rose extensions) to 38.6% from 26.1% in exchange for a $50,000,000 cash payment by Cenovus Energy Inc. to Suncor. Cenovus' working interest in the original field decreased to 60% from 72.5% and the satellite extension to 56.375% from 68.875%. The White Rose asset joint venture owners are Cenovus (operator) and Suncor. The West White Rose project joint venture owners are Cenovus (operator), Suncor and Nalcor Energy.

Predecessor Detail - Name changed from Suncor Inc., Apr. 18, 1997.

Directors - Michael M. (Mike) Wilson, chr., Bragg Creek, Alta.; Richard M. (Rich) Kruger, pres. & CEO, Calgary, Alta.; Ian R. Ashby, San Jose, Calif.; Patricia M. Bedient, Sammamish, Wash.; Russell K. (Russ) Girling, Calgary, Alta.; Jean Paul (JP) Gladu, Greenstone, Ont.; Dennis M. Houston, Spring, Tex.; Brian P. MacDonald, Naples, Fla.; Lorraine Mitchelmore, Calgary, Alta.; Daniel (Dan) Romasko, Blanco, Tex.; Christopher (Chris) Seasons, Calgary, Alta.; M. Jacqueline (Jackie) Sheppard, Calgary, Alta.; Eira M. Thomas, West Vancouver, B.C.

Other Exec. Officers - Paul Gardner, chief people officer; Karen Keegans, chief HR officer; Jacqueline S. (Jacquie) Moore, chief legal officer, gen. counsel & corp. sec.; Arlene Strom, chief sustainability officer; Bruno Y. Francoeur, exec. v-p, bus. & opers. srvcs.; Dave Oldreive, exec. v-p, downstream; Kristopher P. (Kris) Smith, exec. v-p, corp. devel. & CFO; Peter D. Zebedee, exec. v-p, oil sands; Shelley Powell, sr. v-p, operational improvement & support srvcs.

Capital Stock

	Authorized (shs.)	Outstanding (shs.)[1]
Senior Preferred	unlimited	nil
Junior Preferred	unlimited	nil
Common	unlimited	1,300,418,024

[1] At Aug. 11, 2023

Options - At Dec. 31, 2022, options were outstanding to purchase 21,068,000 common shares at a weighted average exercise price of $38.55 per share with a weighted average remaining contractual life of three years.

Normal Course Issuer Bid - The company plans to make normal course purchases of up to 132,900,000 common shares representing 10% of the public float. The bid commenced on Feb. 17, 2023, and expires on Feb. 16, 2024.

Major Shareholder - Widely held at Feb. 27, 2023.

Price Range - SU/TSX

Year	Volume	High	Low	Close
2022	2,769,944,511	$53.62	$32.08	$42.95
2021	2,399,669,521	$34.35	$21.07	$31.65
2020	2,322,943,845	$45.12	$14.02	$21.35
2019	914,021,819	$46.50	$36.32	$42.56
2018	841,176,821	$55.47	$35.53	$38.13

Recent Close: $44.77

Capital Stock Changes - During 2022, 13,158,000 common shares were issued on exercise of options, 116,908,000 common shares were repurchased under a Normal Course Issuer Bid and 30,000 common shares were cancelled.

Dividends

SU com Ra $2.08 pa Q est. Dec. 23, 2022
Prev. Rate: $1.88 est. June 24, 2022
Prev. Rate: $1.68 est. Dec. 24, 2021
Prev. Rate: $0.84 est. June 25, 2020

Long-Term Debt - Outstanding at Dec. 31, 2022:

Medium-term notes:	
3% ser.5 due 2026	$115,000,000
3.1% ser.6 due 2029	79,000,000
5% ser.7 due 2030	154,000,000
5.39% ser.4 due 2037	279,000,000
4.34% ser.5 due 2046	300,000,000
3.95% ser.8 due 2051	493,000,000
Notes:	
8.2% due 2027	61,000,000
7.15% due 2032	676,000,000
5.35% due 2033	161,000,000
5.95% due 2034	675,000,000
5.95% due 2035	268,000,000
6.5% due 2038	1,553,000,000
6.8% due 2038	1,235,000,000
6.85% due 2039	1,013,000,000
6% due 2042	35,000,000
4% due 2047	1,011,000,000
3.75% due 2051	1,009,000,000
Debentures:	
7.875% due 2026	381,000,000
7% due 2028	342,000,000
Less: Deferred fin. costs	40,000,000
	9,800,000,000
Less: Current portion	nil
	9,800,000,000

Credit Facilities - At Dec. 31, 2022, the company had available $7.227 billion in credit facilities, of which $3.272 billion was unutilized.

Wholly Owned Subsidiaries

Suncor Energy Marketing Inc., Alta.
Suncor Energy Oil Sands Limited Partnership, Alta.
Suncor Energy Products Partnership, Alta.
Suncor Energy UK Limited, United Kingdom.
Suncor Energy (U.S.A.) Inc., Denver, Colo.
Suncor Energy (U.S.A.) Marketing Inc., Del.
Suncor Energy Ventures Corporation, Alta.
- 99.99% int. in **Canadian Oil Sands Partnership #1**
  - 36.74% int. in **Syncrude Canada Ltd.**, Fort McMurray, Alta.
- 100% int. in **1506627 Alberta Ltd.**, Alta.
  - 0.01% int. in **Canadian Oil Sands Partnership #1**

Suncor Energy Ventures Partnership, Alta.
- 22% int. in **Syncrude Canada Ltd.**, Fort McMurray, Alta.

Subsidiaries

68.76% int. in **Fort Hills Energy Limited Partnership**, Canada.

Investments

Enerkem Inc., Montréal, Qué.
LanzaJet, Inc., Deerfield, Ill.
Svante Inc., Burnaby, B.C.

Note: The preceding list includes only the major related companies in which interests are held.

Financial Statistics

Periods ended:	12m Dec. 31/22[A]		12m Dec. 31/21[A]
	$000s	%Chg	$000s
Operating revenue	**58,336,000**	**+49**	**39,165,000**
Cost of sales	12,306,000		7,482,000
Salaries & benefits	n.a.		3,562,000
Exploration expense	56,000		47,000
Stock-based compensation	501,000		322,000
Other operating expense	22,446,000		15,270,000
Operating expense	**35,309,000**	**+32**	**26,683,000**
Operating income	**23,027,000**	**+84**	**12,482,000**
Deprec., depl. & amort.	6,034,000		6,071,000
Finance income	100,000		64,000
Finance costs, gross	2,011,000		1,255,000
Write-downs/write-offs	(2,752,000)[1]		221,000[2]
Pre-tax income	**12,316,000**	**+121**	**5,570,000**
Income taxes	3,239,000		1,451,000
Net income	**9,077,000**	**+120**	**4,119,000**
Cash & equivalent	1,980,000		2,205,000
Inventories	5,058,000		4,110,000
Accounts receivable	6,068,000		4,534,000
Current assets	14,536,000		10,977,000
Long-term investments	758,000		391,000
Fixed assets, net	62,654,000		65,546,000
Intangibles, net	3,586,000		3,523,000
Explor./devel. properties	1,995,000		2,226,000
Total assets	**84,618,000**	**+1**	**83,739,000**
Bank indebtedness	2,807,000		1,284,000
Accts. pay. & accr. liabs	8,167,000		6,503,000
Current liabilities	12,869,000		10,399,000
Long-term debt, gross	9,800,000		14,220,000
Long-term debt, net	9,800,000		13,989,000
Long-term lease liabilities	2,695,000		2,540,000
Shareholders' equity	39,367,000		36,614,000
Cash from oper. activs	**15,680,000**	**+33**	**11,764,000**
Cash from fin. activs	(11,228,000)		(7,464,000)
Cash from invest. activs	(4,789,000)		(3,977,000)
Net cash position	**1,980,000**	**-10**	**2,205,000**
Capital expenditures	(4,987,000)		(4,555,000)
Capital disposals	315,000		335,000
Unfunded pension liability	n.a.		602,000
Pension fund surplus	129,000		n.a.
	$		$
Earnings per share*	6.54		2.77
Cash flow per share*	11.31		7.91
Cash divd. per share*	1.88		1.05
	shs		shs
No. of shs. o/s*	1,337,471,000		1,441,251,000
Avg. no. of shs. o/s*	1,387,000,000		1,488,000,000
	%		%
Net profit margin	15.56		10.52
Return on equity	23.89		11.38
Return on assets	12.54		6.00
Foreign sales percent	16		17
No. of employees (FTEs)	16,558		16,922

* Common
[A] Reported in accordance with IFRS
[1] Includes $3.397 billion impairment on share of the Fort Hills oil sands assets, $715,000,000 impairment reversal on share of the West White Rose project and $70,000,000 impairment on exploration and production assets in Norway.
[2] Represents impairment reversal on share of Terra Nova project as a result of the Asset Life Extension Project moving forward and the benefit of royalty and financial support from the Government of Newfoundland and Labrador.

Latest Results

Periods ended:	6m June 30/23[A]		6m June 30/22[A]
	$000s	%Chg	$000s
Operating revenue	23,633,000	-20	29,472,000
Net income	3,931,000	-43	6,945,000
	$		$
Earnings per share*	2.98		4.89

* Common
[A] Reported in accordance with IFRS

Historical Summary
(as originally stated)

Fiscal Year	Oper. Rev. $000s	Net Inc. Bef. Disc. $000s	EPS* $
2022[A]	58,336,000	9,077,000	6.54
2021[A]	39,165,000	4,119,000	2.77
2020[A]	24,763,000	(4,319,000)	(2.83)
2019[A]	38,344,000	2,899,000	1.86
2018[A]	38,684,000	3,293,000	2.03

* Common
[A] Reported in accordance with IFRS

S.135 Sunniva Inc.

Symbol - SNN **Exchange** - CSE (S) **CUSIP** - 86745H
Head Office - Waterfront Centre, 1200-200 Burrard St, PO Box 48600, Vancouver, BC, V7X 1T2 **Telephone** - (587) 430-0680
Website - www.sunniva.com
Email - ir@sunniva.com
Investor Relations - Dr. Anthony F. Holler (587) 430-0680
Auditors - GreenGrowth C.P.A., Los Angeles, Calif.
Transfer Agents - Odyssey Trust Company, Calgary, Alta.
Profile - (Can. 2014) Ceased operations.

On Sept. 22, 2022, the company and its subsidiaries ceased operations as a result of losing an arbitration against **Bobs LLC** regarding the company's rights to and leasehold interests in the cannabis extraction facility in Cathedral City, Calif. As settlement, the company transferred a cannabis licence to Bobs in lieu of the US$8,600,000 monetary damages awarded to Bobs.

Common suspended from CSE, June 23, 2020.

Directors - Dr. Anthony F. (Tony) Holler, chr. & CEO, Penticton, B.C.; Norman (Norm) Mayr, Port Moody, B.C.; Ian A. Webb, Vancouver, B.C.
Other Exec. Officers - Duncan Gordon, COO

Capital Stock

	Authorized (shs.)	Outstanding (shs.)[1]
Common	unlimited	795,750,102

[1] At June 18, 2021

Major Shareholder - Widely held at July 10, 2019.

Price Range - SNN/CSE (S)

Year	Volume	High	Low	Close
2020	10,094,859	$0.32	$0.10	$0.16
2019	37,130,590	$5.66	$0.19	$0.28
2018	40,291,735	$17.93	$2.83	$3.30

Wholly Owned Subsidiaries

11111035 Canada Inc., Vancouver, B.C.
Sun CA Holdings, Inc., Calif.
- 100% int. in **A1 Perez, LLC**, Del.
- 100% int. in **CP Logistics, LLC**, N.C.
  - 100% int. in **LTYR Logistics, LLC**, San Diego, Calif.
  - 100% int. in **Sun Ramon, LLC**, Cathedral City, Calif.
- 100% int. in **Sunny People, LLC**, Calif.

Sun Holdings Management, LLC, Del.
- 100% int. in **Sunniva Full Scale Distributors Corporation**, Calif.
  - 100% int. in **Full Scale Distributors, LLC**, Fla.

Sunniva Medical Inc., Vancouver, B.C.
- 100% int. in **1167025 B.C. Ltd.**, Vancouver, B.C.

S.136 SunOpta Inc.

Symbol - SOY **Exchange** - TSX **CUSIP** - 8676EP
Head Office - West Tower, 401-2233 Argentia Rd, Mississauga, ON, L5N 2X7 **Telephone** - (905) 821-8669
Website - www.sunopta.com
Email - scott.huckins@sunopta.com
Investor Relations - Scott E. Huckins (952) 838-3248
Auditors - Ernst & Young LLP C.P.A.
Lawyers - Stoel Rives LLP, Minneapolis, Minn.; Wildeboer Dellelce LLP, Toronto, Ont.
Transfer Agents - American Stock Transfer & Trust Company, LLC, New York, N.Y.; TSX Trust Company, Toronto, Ont.
FP500 Revenue Ranking - 303
Employees - 1,453 at Dec. 31, 2022
Profile - (Can. 1973) Processes and packages plant-based and fruit-based foods and beverages for retailers, foodservice operators, branded food companies and food manufacturers.

Operates its business in two reportable segments: Plant-Based Foods and Beverages; and Fruit-Based Foods and Beverages.

The **Plant-Based Foods and Beverages** segment offers plant-based beverages and liquid and powder ingredients using almond, soy, coconut, rice, oat, hemp and other bases, as well as broths, teas and nutritional beverages.

The **Fruit-Based Foods and Beverages** segment offers individually quick frozen (IQF) fruits for retail including strawberries, blueberries, mango, pineapple, and other berries and blends; and IQF and bulk frozen fruits for foodservice including toppings, purées, and smoothies. Also sells fruit snacks including bars, twists, ropes and bite-sized varieties, as well as fruit smoothie bowls.

The company operates 10 processing facilities in six U.S. states, Mexico and Canada, as well as owns innovation centre and pilot plant in Eden Prairie, Minn.

Recent Merger and Acquisition Activity

Status: completed **Announced:** Oct. 11, 2022
SunOpta Inc. sold it sunflower and roasted snacks business to Pacific Avenue Capital Partners LLC for US$16,000,000. The business formed part of SunOpta's Plant-Based Foods and Beverages segment and included three facilities in Crookston and Breckenridge, Minn., and Grace City, N.D., which processed sunflowers for inshell, kernel, bird food, and roasted products such as sunflower and chickpeas.

Status: completed **Announced:** Aug. 26, 2022
SunOpta Inc. sold its frozen fruit processing facility in Oxnard, Calif., for net cash proceeds of US$16,100,000.

Predecessor Detail - Name changed from Stake Technology Ltd., Oct. 31, 2003.

Directors - R. Dean Hollis, chr., Neb.; Joseph D. Ennen, CEO, Minn.; Dr. Albert D. (Al) Bolles, Mich.; Rebecca Fisher, Tex.; Katrina L. (Kathy) Houde, Toronto, Ont.; Leslie S. Keating, Tex.; Diego Reynoso, Ill.; Mahes S. Wickramasinghe, Toronto, Ont.

Other Exec. Officers - Scott E. Huckins, CFO; Jill Barnett, CAO, gen. counsel & corp. sec.; Rob Duchscher, CIO; Michael Buick, sr. v-p & gen. mgr., plant-based food & beverage; Bryan Clark, sr. v-p, R&D & food safety & quality; Chad Hagen, sr. v-p, sales; Barend Reijn, sr. v-p, global sourcing; Chris Whitehair, sr. v-p, supply chain

Capital Stock

	Authorized (shs.)	Outstanding (shs.)[1]
Series B-1 Preferred	n.a.	15,000[2]
Common	unlimited	115,607,935

[1] At Aug. 4, 2023
[2] Issued by wholly owned SunOpta Foods Inc.

Series B-1 Preferred - All held by Oaktree Capital Management, L.P., via funds it manages. Pay a cumulative dividend of 8% of the liquidation preference per year prior to Sept. 30, 2029, that may be paid-in-kind or cash, and 10% thereafter; any dividends not paid in cash after Sept. 30, 2029, will be an event of non-compliance. Exchangeable into common shares of the company at US$2.50 per share. Redeemable by the company on or after Apr. 24, 2025, at the amount equal to the liquidation preference plus accrued and unpaid dividends. Entitled to vote on an as-exchanged basis, subject to a permanent 19.99% voting cap.

Common - One vote per share.

Series 2 Special (old) - One vote per share. Non-transferable. Attached to 15,000 series B-1 preferred shares held by Engaged Capital, LLC to allow Engaged to vote together with common shares on shareholder meetings. Redeemed on Mar. 3, 2023.

Major Shareholder - Oaktree Capital Management, L.P. held 18.1% interest at Mar. 24, 2023.

Price Range - SOY/TSX

Year	Volume	High	Low	Close
2022	27,770,841	$15.90	$5.44	$11.38
2021	43,568,905	$21.63	$7.48	$8.77
2020	20,223,600	$14.96	$1.82	$14.87
2019	18,230,083	$6.33	$1.70	$3.23
2018	9,147,869	$11.97	$4.94	$5.28

Recent Close: $5.70

Capital Stock Changes - In March 2023, all 15,000 series B-1 preferred shares held by Engaged Capital, LLC were converted into 6,089,331 common shares.

During fiscal 2022, common shares were issued as follows: 462,000 on exercise of options and 88,000 under the employee share purchase plan.

Wholly Owned Subsidiaries

Citrusource, LLC, United States.
Cooperatie SunOpta U.A., Netherlands.
Farm Capital Incorporated, Del.
Pacific Ridge Farms, LLC, Ind.
SunOpta Companies Inc., Minn.
SunOpta Financing Canada ULC, Alta.
SunOpta Financing 2017 LLC, Del.
SunOpta Foods Inc., Del.
- 100% int. in **Servicios SunOpta, S. de R.L. de C.V.**, Mexico.
- 100% int. in **SunOpta Africa (Proprietary) Limited**, South Africa.
- 100% int. in **SunOpta de Mexico, S. de R.L. de C.V.**, Mexico.
- 100% int. in **SunOpta Global Organic Ingredients, Inc.**, Calif.
- 100% int. in **SunOpta Grains and Foods Inc.**, Minneapolis, Minn.

SunOpta Holdings LLC, Del.
SunOpta Investments Ltd., Canada.
SunOpta Mx, S.A. de C.V., Mexico.
Sunrise Growers, Inc., Del.
Sunrise Growers Mexico, S.R.L. de C.V., Mexico.
Sunrise Holdings (Delaware), Inc., Calif.

Investments

18.7% int. in **Enchi Corporation**, Del.

Financial Statistics

Periods ended:	52w Dec. 31/22[A]		52w Jan. 1/22[¤A]
	US$000s	%Chg	US$000s
Operating revenue	**934,662**	**+15**	**812,624**
Cost of goods sold	784,417		690,213
General & admin expense	89,312		76,599
Operating expense	**873,729**	**+14**	**766,812**
Operating income	**60,933**	**+33**	**45,812**
Deprec., depl. & amort.	37,673		34,641
Finance income	347		269
Finance costs, gross	15,441		9,038
Write-downs/write-offs	(1,812)		(3,206)
Pre-tax income	**(11,858)**	**n.a.**	**(7,600)**
Income taxes	(2,340)		(6,428)
Net inc. bef. disc. opers	**(9,518)**	**n.a.**	**(1,172)**
Income from disc. opers	4,677		nil
Net income	**(4,841)**	**n.a.**	**(1,172)**
Cash & equivalent	679		227
Inventories	207,047		219,778
Accounts receivable	74,903		84,702
Current assets	302,357		329,604
Fixed assets, net	322,391		219,537
Right-of-use assets	82,564		47,245
Intangibles, net	139,644		152,438
Total assets	**855,852**	**+13**	**754,754**
Accts. pay. & accr. liabs	108,511		121,155
Current liabilities	161,033		143,118
Long-term debt, gross	308,484		224,603
Long-term debt, net	269,993		214,843
Long-term lease liabilities	77,557		39,028
Shareholders' equity	319,207		313,328
Cash from oper. activs	**60,575**	**n.a.**	**(21,432)**
Cash from fin. activs	46,701		115,858
Cash from invest. activs	(106,824)		(94,450)
Net cash position	**679**	**+199**	**227**
Capital expenditures	(128,626)		(58,297)
Capital disposals	20,293		2,300
	US$		US$
Earns. per sh. bef disc opers*	(0.12)		(0.05)
Earnings per share*	(0.07)		(0.05)
Cash flow per share*	0.56		(0.21)
	shs		shs
No. of shs. o/s*	107,909,792		107,359,826
Avg. no. of shs. o/s*	107,659,000		104,098,000
	%		%
Net profit margin	(1.02)		(0.14)
Return on equity	(4.05)		(2.02)
Return on assets	0.36		0.03
Foreign sales percent	99		98
No. of employees (FTEs)	1,453		1,380

* Common
¤ Restated
[A] Reported in accordance with U.S. GAAP

Latest Results

Periods ended:	26w July 1/23[A]		26w July 2/22[¤A]
	US$000s	%Chg	US$000s
Operating revenue	431,689	-11	483,704
Net inc. bef. disc. opers	(17,461)	n.a.	3,287
Income from disc. opers	nil		2,752
Net income	(17,461)	n.a.	6,039
	US$		US$
Earns. per sh. bef. disc. opers.*	(0.16)		0.02
Earnings per share*	(0.16)		0.04

* Common
¤ Restated
[A] Reported in accordance with U.S. GAAP

Historical Summary
(as originally stated)

Fiscal Year	Oper. Rev. US$000s	Net Inc. Bef. Disc. US$000s	EPS* US$
2022[A]	934,662	(9,518)	(0.12)
2021[A]	812,624	(4,144)	(0.08)
2020[A1]	789,213	(47,302)	(0.65)
2019[A]	1,190,022	(604)	(0.10)
2018[A]	1,260,852	(109,143)	(1.34)

* Common
[A] Reported in accordance with U.S. GAAP
[1] 53 weeks ended Jan. 2, 2021.

S.137 Sunshine Agri-Tech Inc.

Symbol - SAI.H **Exchange** - TSX-VEN **CUSIP** - 867777
Head Office - c/o Fasken Martineau DuMoulin LLP, 2900-550 Burrard St, Vancouver, BC, V6C 0A3 **Telephone** - (604) 631-3131
Email - xpang@ls-qyyl.com
Investor Relations - Xiaozhu Pang (778) 865-2296
Auditors - MNP LLP C.A., Vancouver, B.C.

Lawyers - Clark Wilson LLP, Vancouver, B.C.

Transfer Agents - Computershare Trust Company of Canada Inc., Vancouver, B.C.

Profile - (B.C. 2009) Seeking new business opportunities.

Predecessor Detail - Name changed from Osia Ventures Ltd., July 27, 2010, pursuant to Qualifying Transaction reverse takeover acquisition of Sunscape (Hong Kong) Limited.

Directors - Dr. Baojun Zhang, pres. & CEO, Dalian, Liaoning, People's Republic of China; Xiang (George) Gao, Toronto, Ont.; Shun Yui (Raymond) Lu, B.C.; Xuexian Wang, Dalian, Liaoning, People's Republic of China; Hengwei Zhang, Beijing, People's Republic of China

Other Exec. Officers - Xiaozhu Pang, CFO; Jingchun Cui, chief tech. officer

Capital Stock

	Authorized (shs.)	Outstanding (shs.)[1]
Preferred	unlimited	nil
Common	unlimited	72,006,250

[1] At Aug. 30, 2022

Major Shareholder - Dr. Baojun Zhang held 51.83% interest at Nov. 9, 2020.

Price Range - SAI.H/TSX-VEN

Year	Volume	High	Low	Close
2022	1,254,997	$0.02	$0.01	$0.01
2021	4,173,814	$0.05	$0.01	$0.02
2020	2,359,183	$0.02	$0.01	$0.02
2019	1,399,199	$0.03	$0.01	$0.01
2018	9,166,566	$0.25	$0.02	$0.04

Recent Close: $0.02

Financial Statistics

Periods ended:	12m Dec. 31/21^A		12m Dec. 31/20^A
	$000s	%Chg	$000s
General & admin expense	83		119
Operating expense	**83**	**-30**	**119**
Operating income	**(83)**	**n.a.**	**(119)**
Deprec., depl. & amort.	nil		29
Finance costs, gross	nil		1
Pre-tax income	**(83)**	**n.a.**	**(148)**
Net inc. bef. disc. opers	**(83)**	**n.a.**	**(148)**
Income from disc. opers	nil		109
Net income	**(83)**	**n.a.**	**(39)**
Cash & equivalent	11		49
Accounts receivable	11		1,107
Current assets	27		1,165
Total assets	**27**	**-98**	**1,165**
Accts. pay. & accr. liabs	53		1,077
Current liabilities	116		1,171
Shareholders' equity	(89)		(5)
Cash from oper. activs	**(7)**	**n.a.**	**472**
Cash from fin. activs	(31)		(149)
Cash from invest. activs	nil		(280)
Net cash position	**11**	**-78**	**49**
Capital expenditures	nil		(27)
	$		$
Earns. per sh. bef disc opers*	(0.00)		(0.00)
Earnings per share*	(0.00)		(0.00)
Cash flow per share*	(0.00)		0.01
	shs		shs
No. of shs. o/s*	72,006,250		72,006,250
Avg. no. of shs. o/s*	72,006,250		72,006,250
	%		%
Net profit margin	n.a.		n.a.
Return on equity	n.m.		n.m.
Return on assets	(13.93)		(15.70)

* Common

^A Reported in accordance with IFRS

Latest Results

Periods ended:	6m June 30/22^A		6m June 30/21^A
	$000s	%Chg	$000s
Net income	(18)	n.a.	(67)
	$		$
Earnings per share*	(0.00)		(0.00)

* Common

^A Reported in accordance with IFRS

Historical Summary
(as originally stated)

Fiscal Year	Oper. Rev.	Net Inc. Bef. Disc.	EPS*
	$000s	$000s	$
2021^A	nil	(83)	(0.00)
2020^A	nil	(148)	(0.00)
2019^A	500	(540)	(0.01)
2018^A	641	(159)	(0.00)
2017^A	15,970	(666)	(0.01)

* Common

^A Reported in accordance with IFRS

S.138 SuperBuzz Inc.

Symbol - SPZ **Exchange** - TSX-VEN **CUSIP** - 868041

Head Office - c/o Garfinkle Biderman LLP, 801-1 Adelaide St E, Toronto, ON, M5C 2V9 **Telephone** - (416) 869-1234

Website - www.superbuzz.io

Email - liran@superbuzz.io

Investor Relations - Liran Brenner

Auditors - Bassi & Karimjee LLP C.A., Brampton, Ont.

Transfer Agents - TSX Trust Company, Toronto, Ont.

Profile - (Ont. 2020) Provides a real-time marketing automation platform that increases customer engagement through dynamic push notification campaigns that deliver relevant, personalized messages in micro-moments across mobile and desktop platforms.

Recent Merger and Acquisition Activity

Status: completed **Revised:** July 7, 2022

UPDATE: The transaction was completed. Cross Border issued a total of 29,641,860 common shares at a deemed price of Cdn$0.40 per share. PREVIOUS: Cross Border Capital I Inc. entered into a letter of intent for the Qualifying Transaction reverse takeover acquisition of Israel-based Message Notify Ltd. (dba SuperBuzz) on a share-for-share basis. SuperBuzz provides a real-time marketing automation platform that increases customer engagement through dynamic push notification campaigns that deliver relevant, personalized messages in micro-moments across mobile and desktop platforms. Jan. 6, 2022 - A definitive agreement was entered into. Upon completion, Cross Border would change its name to SuperBuzz Inc.

Predecessor Detail - Name changed from Cross Border Capital I Inc., July 7, 2022, pursuant to the Qualifying Transaction reverse takeover acquisition of Israel-based Message Notify Ltd. (dba SuperBuzz).

Directors - Liran Brenner, CEO, Tel Aviv, Israel; Sophie Galper-Komet, Toronto, Ont.; Tzafrir Peles, Tel Aviv, Israel; Nahum Segal, Tel Aviv, Israel

Other Exec. Officers - Igor Kostioutchenko, CFO; Ohad Avraham Alon, chief tech. officer; Netta L. Sadeh, chief revenue officer; Ahmed Kawasmi, v-p, R&D; Grant Duthie, corp. sec.

Capital Stock

	Authorized (shs.)	Outstanding (shs.)[1]
Common	unlimited	35,922,454

[1] At Dec. 31, 2022

Major Shareholder - Dror Erez held 23.11% interest at July 14, 2022.

Price Range - SPZ/TSX-VEN

Year	Volume	High	Low	Close
2022	1,093,008	$0.30	$0.03	$0.17
2021	153,449	$0.29	$0.15	$0.15
2020	23,328	$0.22	$0.18	$0.20

Recent Close: $0.03

Capital Stock Changes - On July 7, 2022, 29,641,860 common shares were issued pursuant to the Qualifying Transaction reverse takeover acquisition of Message Notify Ltd. (dba SuperBuzz).

Wholly Owned Subsidiaries

Message Notify Ltd., Israel. dba SuperBuzz.

Financial Statistics

Periods ended:	12m Dec. 31/21^A1		12m Dec. 31/20^A
	US$000s	%Chg	US$000s
Operating revenue	**594**	**+114**	**278**
Cost of sales	425		266
Salaries & benefits	167		198
Research & devel. expense	64		63
General & admin expense	225		113
Stock-based compensation	389		8
Operating expense	**1,270**	**+96**	**648**
Operating income	**(676)**	**n.a.**	**(370)**
Deprec., depl. & amort.	2		nil
Finance costs, gross	2,720		423
Pre-tax income	**(3,381)**	**n.a.**	**(812)**
Net income	**(3,381)**	**n.a.**	**(812)**
Cash & equivalent	11		29
Accounts receivable	184		40
Current assets	200		70
Fixed assets, net	nil		2
Total assets	**200**	**+178**	**72**
Bank indebtedness	402		1,031
Accts. pay. & accr. liabs	291		475
Current liabilities	693		1,506
Shareholders' equity	(493)		(1,434)
Cash from oper. activs	**(964)**	**n.a.**	**(231)**
Cash from fin. activs	950		199
Cash from invest. activs	(4)		4
Net cash position	**11**	**-62**	**29**
	US$		US$
Earnings per share*	(0.22)		(0.10)
Cash flow per share*	(0.06)		(0.03)
	shs		shs
No. of shs. o/s	n.a.		n.a.
Avg. no. of shs. o/s*	15,258,069		8,156,714
	%		%
Net profit margin	(569.19)		(292.09)
Return on equity	n.m.		n.m.
Return on assets	(486.03)		n.a.

* Common

^A Reported in accordance with IFRS

[1] Results prior to July 7, 2022, pertain to and reflect the Qualifying Transaction reverse takeover acquisition of Message Notify Ltd. (dba SuperBuzz).

S.139 Superior Plus Corp.*

Symbol - SPB **Exchange** - TSX **CUSIP** - 86828P

Head Office - 401-200 Wellington St W, Toronto, ON, M5V 3C7 **Telephone** - (416) 345-8050 **Toll-free** - (866) 490-7587 **Fax** - (416) 340-6030

Website - www.superiorplus.com

Email - rdorran@superiorplus.com

Investor Relations - Rob Dorran (866) 490-7587

Auditors - Ernst & Young LLP C.A., Toronto, Ont.

Lawyers - Torys LLP, Calgary, Alta.

Transfer Agents - Computershare Trust Company of Canada Inc., Calgary, Alta.

FP500 Revenue Ranking - 160

Employees - 4,620 at Dec. 31, 2022

Profile - (Can. 2008) Distributes and markets propane, compressed natural gas, renewable energy and related products and services, serving the retail and wholesale markets in the U.S. and Canada.

The company has four operating segments: U.S. Retail Propane Distribution, Canadian Retail Propane Distribution, North American Wholesale Propane Distribution and Certarus Ltd.

U.S. Retail Propane Distribution - Distributes and sells propane gas and liquid fuels; and installs, maintains and repairs propane and heating oil equipment in more than 24 states across the U.S. East Coast, Midwest region and California. Products and services are offered to 740,000 retail and commercial propane and heating oil/distillate customers, including residential, agricultural and construction companies, municipalities and schools. Primary trade names include Superior Plus Propane, Downeast Energy, Eastern Propane, Rymes Propane and Oil, Kamps Propane, Griffith Energy, Quarles, Earhart Propane, Virginia Propane, Champagne's Energy, Freeman Gas and Electric, Co., Osterman Propane, Atlantic Propane, Western Propane and Williams Energy Group. Operations include 212 service centres, 315 terminals, bulk plants and secondary offices, and 2,826 vehicles.

Canadian Retail Propane Distribution - Distributes and sells propane, lubricants and propane-consuming equipment; rents tanks, cylinders and other equipment; supplies, installs and repairs equipment; and offers equipment warranties and maintenance programs across Canada. Products and services are provided in 196,000 customer locations, including residential, commercial, agricultural, industrial and automotive customers, under the trade names Caledon Propane, Canwest Propane, Highlands Propane, Miller Propane, Pomerleau Gaz, Propane Stittco Energy, McRobert Propane and Superior Propane. Operations include 37 offices, 186 satellite locations and storage yards, and 1,050 vehicles.

North American Wholesale Propane Distribution - Operating under the Superior Gas Liquids (SGL) division, distributes, markets and supplies propane gas and other natural gas liquids to wholesale customers across Canada and the U.S.; and supplies propane gas for the company's Canadian and U.S. retail businesses. SGL manages the supply, transportation, storage and risk management requirements of third party customers and the company's retail operations. During 2022, the Canadian and U.S. retail propane distribution businesses represented 46% and 5%, respectively, of SGL's total sales. Trade names include Superior Gas Liquids, Superior Gas Liquids USA, United Pacific Energy and Kiva Energy. Operations include two offices, 14 satellite locations and storage yards, and 110 vehicles.

Certarus Ltd. (acquired in May 2023) - Transports and supplies compressed natural gas (CNG), renewable natural gas (RNG) and hydrogen to industrial and commercial customers in regional energy markets across North America through a network of CNG compression stations and a fleet of carbon fibre delivery trailers.

Operating Statistics

Year ended Dec. 31	2022	2021
Sales Volumes:		
U.S. retail propane[1]	1,533	1,327
Canadian retail propane[1]	1,219	1,168
Wholesale propane[1]	1,320	936
Sales Margin:		
U.S. retail propane, ¢/litre	46.8	40.7
Canadian retail propane, ¢/litre	29.4	28.8

[1] Millions of litres.

On Feb. 1, 2023, the company acquired **ACME Propane, Inc.**, a residential and commercial retail propane distributor in Lincoln, Calif., for US$3,300,000.

In January 2023, the company sold the $125,000,000 6% unsecured promissory note due October 2026 received as part of the purchase price from the sale of the Specialty Chemicals business in 2021 to **ERCO Worldwide LP**, an affiliate of **Birch Hill Equity Partners Management Inc.**, the acquiror of the Specialty Chemicals business, for $128,000,000.

On Sept. 9, 2022, the company acquired the propane distribution assets of **Reed Oil Company**, a retail propane supplier and distributor in North Carolina, for US$3,500,000.

On May 19, 2022, the company acquired the retail propane distribution assets of **DT Denton Gas Co. Inc.**, a retail propane distributor in South Carolina, for US$1,800,000.

In May 2022, the company signed a definitive agreement with **Charbone Corporation**, wholly owned by **Charbone Hydrogen Corporation**, to provide green hydrogen to commercial and industrial customers initially in Quebec. Charbone would provide the company with green hydrogen from its facility in Sorel-Tracy, Que., with initial deliveries expected in the third quarter of 2022. The company would deliver hydrogen directly from Charbone's facility to its customers.

In March 2022, the company acquired the retail propane distribution assets of Rock Hill, S.C.-based **Reid Gas, Inc.** for US$1,300,000.

Recent Merger and Acquisition Activity

Status: pending **Announced:** May 31, 2023
Superior Plus Corp. agreed to sell eight propane distribution hubs in northern Ontario, including customer contracts and associated operating assets at each location, to address the concerns of the Competition Bureau about Superior's acquisition of Certarus Ltd. Terms of the transaction were not disclosed. The sale would be made to an independent purchaser to be approved by the commissioner of competition. The federal competition regulator concluded that Superior's acquisition of Certarus would result in a substantial lessening of competition for the retail supply of portable heating fuels (propane and natural gas) for industrial customers in northern Ontario.

Status: completed **Revised:** May 31, 2023
UPDATE: The transaction was completed. Consideration consisted of 48,600,000 common shares valued at $498,000,000 and $353,000,000 in cash. In order to receive consent from the Canadian Competition Bureau, Superior agreed to divest eight retail propane distribution locations and related assets in northern Ontario. PREVIOUS: Superior Plus Corp. agreed to acquire private Calgary, Alta.-based Certarus Ltd., which distributes compressed natural gas, renewable natural gas and hydrogen, for $1.05 billion, consisting of $353,000,000 cash, issuance of 48,780,487 common shares at a deemed price of $10.25 per share (representing a value of $500,000,000) and assumption of $196,000,000 of debt. Superior would finance a portion of the purchase price with incremental drawings from its expanded senior credit facilities. Certarus had 18 hubs throughout Canada and the U.S. The transaction was expected to be completed in the first quarter of 2023.

Status: completed **Announced:** Nov. 9, 2022
Superior Plus Corp. acquired the assets of McRobert Fuels, a Strathroy, Ont.-based retail propane and distillates distributor, for $16,000,000.

Status: completed **Announced:** Oct. 3, 2022
Superior Plus Corp. acquired the propane distribution assets of Mountain Flame Propane, Inc., a residential, commercial and retail propane supplier and distributor in California, for US$7,400,000.

Status: completed **Revised:** June 1, 2022
UPDATE: The transaction was completed. The final purchase price was US$144,000,000, which was paid with funds drawn from Superior's existing credit facility. PREVIOUS: Superior Plus Corp. agreed to acquire the retail propane distribution and refined fuels assets of Fredericksburg, Va.-based Quarles Petroleum, Inc. (dba Quarles Delivered Fuels) for US$145,000,000. Quarles services 55,000 residential and commercial customers primarily in Virginia. Quarles had 29 propane bulk plants, one rail terminal, 3,000,000 gallons of storage capacity and a fleet of 197 vehicles. The transaction, which was subject to customary regulatory and commercial closing conditions, was anticipated to be completed in the second quarter of 2022.

Status: completed **Announced:** Apr. 1, 2022
Superior Plus Corp. acquired the assets of Heartland Industries, LLC, a retail propane distributor in Ohio, for US$7,100,000.

Status: completed **Revised:** Mar. 23, 2022
UPDATE: The transaction was completed. PREVIOUS: Superior Plus Corp. agreed to acquire equity interests in Kamps Propane, Inc., High Country Propane, Inc., Pick Up Propane, Inc., Kiva Energy, Inc., Competitive Capital, Inc. and Propane Construction and Meter Services (collectively, Kamps) for US$240,000,000. Kamps is a retail and wholesale propane distributor based in California servicing 45,000 residential, commercial and wholesale customers. Kamps has 14 retail branch offices, five company-operated rail terminals, over 375 vehicles and 280 employees. The transaction is expected to close during the third quarter of 2021. Sept. 23, 2021 - Superior and Kamps received a request for additional information from the United States Federal Trade Commission in connection with the pending acquisition.

Predecessor Detail - Succeeded Ballard Power Systems Inc., Dec. 31, 2008, pursuant to plan of arrangement to convert Superior Plus Income Fund (SPIF) to a corp. resulting in SPIF's wholly owned subsids. Superior Plus Limited Partnership and Superior Plus General Partner Inc. becoming wholly owned subsids. of Superior Plus Corp., with trust units of SPIF exchanged for common shares of Superior Plus Corp. on a 1-for-1 basis. All assets and liabilities of (old) Ballard Power Systems Inc. were transferred to (new) Ballard Power Systems Inc. which was spun out as a new public entity on a sh.-for-sh. basis.

Directors - David P. Smith, chr., Parry Sound, Ont.; Allan A. MacDonald, pres. & CEO, Toronto, Ont.; Catherine M. (Kay) Best, Calgary, Alta.; Eugene V. N. Bissell, Wayne, Pa.; Patrick E. Gottschalk, Scottsdale, Ariz.; Douglas J. (Doug) Harrison, Burlington, Ont.; Calvin B. (Cal) Jacober, Calgary, Alta.; Mary B. Jordan, Vancouver, B.C.; Angelo R. Rufino, New York, N.Y.

Other Exec. Officers - Andrew (Andy) Peyton, COO, North American propane distrib.; Elizabeth A. (Beth) Summers, exec. v-p & CFO; Jason Fortin, sr. v-p, bus. transformation; Darren Hribar, sr. v-p & chief legal officer; Inder Minhas, sr. v-p, M&A; Shawn B. Vammen, sr. v-p, Superior Gas Liquids; Brian DeMille, v-p, fin.; Rob Dorran, v-p, capital markets; Graham F. Fisher, v-p, HR; Harry Kanwar, v-p, risk & compliance; Ash Rajendra, v-p & CIO; Erin Seaman, v-p, tax; Rick Carron, pres., Superior Propane

Capital Stock

	Authorized (shs.)	Outstanding (shs.)[1]
Preferred	unlimited	
Series 1	260,000	260,000
Series 1 Special Vtg.	unlimited	30,002,837
Series 2	260,000	nil
Common	unlimited	249,300,000

[1] At June 30, 2023

Series 1 Preferred - Issued by wholly owned Superior Plus U.S. Holdings Inc. to Brookfield Corporation. Entitled to a cash dividend of 7.25% per annum payable monthly until June 30, 2027, and thereafter increasing by 0.75% per annum until June 30, 2031, to a maximum dividend of 10.25% per annum. Entitled to an equivalent amount for any dividends paid on common shares in excess of Cdn$0.06 per month. Redeemable at the company's option after June 13, 2027, at US$1,000 per share plus accrued and unpaid dividends. Exchangeable at Brookfield's option into common shares at US$8.67 per share at a ratio equal to US$1,000 per share plus accrued and unpaid dividends divided by US$8.67 per share, subject to adjustments. In the event of a liquidation, winding-up or dissolution of the company, entitled to receive an amount equal to the greater of (i) US$1,400 per share plus accrued and unpaid dividends or (ii) the amount receivable had the series 1 preferred shares been exchanged for common shares immediately prior to the liquidation event. Classified as non-controlling interest.

Series 1 Special Voting Preferred - Issued together with series 1 preferred shares of wholly owned Superior Plus U.S. to allow holders to vote, through a trustee, at shareholder meetings. Not entitled to dividends. Redeemable at Cdn$0.00001 per share. One vote per share.

Common - One vote per share.

Normal Course Issuer Bid - The company plans to make normal course purchases of up to 10,085,599 common shares representing 5% of the total outstanding. The bid commenced on Oct. 13, 2022, and expires on Oct. 12, 2023.

Major Shareholder - Marquard & Bahls AG held 18.3% interest and Brookfield Corporation held 15.9% interest at Apr. 17, 2023.

Price Range - SPB/TSX

Year	Volume	High	Low	Close
2022	136,508,965	$13.47	$9.44	$11.23
2021	127,665,522	$16.24	$11.97	$13.00
2020	165,920,461	$12.91	$5.97	$12.18
2019	135,285,041	$13.70	$9.58	$12.56
2018	103,721,931	$13.56	$9.17	$9.68

Recent Close: $10.25

Capital Stock Changes - In May 2023, 48,600,000 common shares were issued pursuant to the acquisition of Certarus Ltd.

In April 2022, bought deal public offering of 25,670,300 common shares was completed at $11.20 per share, including 3,348,300 common shares on exercise of over-allotment option. Also during 2022, 994,542 common shares were repurchased under a Normal Course Issuer Bid.

Dividends

SPB com Ra $0.72 pa Q est. Dec. 15, 2014**
** Reinvestment Option

Long-Term Debt - Outstanding at Dec. 31, 2022:

Bankers' acceptances due June 2027[1]	$93,000,000
SOFR loans due June 2027[1]	494,700,000
4.25% sr. notes due May 2028	500,000,000
4.5% sr. notes due Mar. 2029[2]	813,200,000
Other debt	45,100,000
Less: Def. fin. fees & discounts	19,900,000
	1,926,100,000
Less: Current portion	14,800,000
	1,911,300,000

[1] Bear interest at bankers' acceptance/SOFR plus 1.7%.
[2] US$600,000,000.

Minimum long-term debt repayments were reported as follows:

2023	$14,800,000
2024	11,200,000
2025	8,900,000
2026	6,200,000
2027	589,400,000
Thereafter	1,315,500,000

Wholly Owned Subsidiaries

Certarus Ltd., Calgary, Alta.
SP Reinsurance Company Limited, Bermuda.
Superior General Partner Inc., Toronto, Ont.
- 100% int. in **Cal-Gas Inc.**, Calgary, Alta.
- 100% int. in **Stittco Utilities Man Ltd.**, Man.
- 100% int. in **Stittco Utilities NWT Ltd.**, N.W.T.
- 1% int. in **Superior Gas Liquids Partnership**, Alta.
- 0.1% int. in **Superior Plus LP**, Toronto, Ont.

Superior Plus Canada Financing Inc., Toronto, Ont.

Subsidiaries

99.9% int. in **Superior Plus LP**, Toronto, Ont.
- 99% int. in **Superior Gas Liquids Partnership**, Alta.
- 100% int. in **Superior International Inc.**, Calgary, Alta.
  - 100% int. in **Superior Hungary Kft.**, Hungary.
  - 100% int. in **Superior Luxembourg S.A.R.L.**, Luxembourg.
  - 100% int. in **Superior Plus U.S. Holdings Inc.**, Del.
    - 100% int. in **Superior Plus Energy Services Inc.**, N.Y.
      - 100% int. in **Kamps Propane, Inc.**, Calif.
      - 100% int. in **Kiva Energy, Inc.**, Carson City, Nev.
      - 100% int. in **NGL Propane, LLC**, United States.
        - 100% int. in **Osterman Propane, LLC**, United States.
      - 100% int. in **Sheldon Gas Company**, Suisun City, Calif.
        - 100% int. in **Sheldon Oil Company**, Calif.
        - 51% int. in **Sheldon United Terminals, LLC**, United States.
      - 100% int. in **United Liquid Gas Company, Inc.**, Reno, Nev.
        - 49% int. in **Sheldon United Terminals, LLC**, United States.
    - 100% int. in **Superior Plus U.S. Capital Corp.**, Del.
    - 100% int. in **Superior Plus U.S. Financing Inc.**, Del.

Note: The preceding list includes only the major related companies in which interests are held.

Financial Statistics

Periods ended:	12m Dec. 31/22[A]		12m Dec. 31/21[◻A]
	$000s	%Chg	$000s
Operating revenue	**3,379,800**	**+41**	**2,392,600**
Cost of sales	2,190,000		1,479,900
Salaries & benefits	444,900		357,900
General & admin expense	321,000		217,300
Operating expense	**2,955,900**	**+44**	**2,055,100**
Operating income	**423,900**	**+26**	**337,500**
Deprec., depl. & amort.	238,900		201,100
Finance income	7,500		5,300
Finance costs, gross	89,300		160,300
Write-downs/write-offs	(9,800)		nil
Pre-tax income	**(124,900)**	**n.a.**	**22,900**
Income taxes	(37,000)		5,700
Net inc bef disc ops, eqhldrs	(112,500)		(6,600)
Net inc bef disc ops, NCI	24,600		23,800
Net inc. bef. disc. opers	**(87,900)**	**n.a.**	**17,200**
Disc. opers., equity hldrs	nil		189,500
Income from disc. opers	nil		189,500
Net income	**(87,900)**	**n.a.**	**206,700**
Net inc. for equity hldrs	**(112,500)**	**n.a.**	**182,900**
Net inc. for non-cont. int	**24,600**	**+3**	**23,800**
Cash & equivalent	58,400		28,400
Inventories	153,000		111,500
Accounts receivable	405,700		319,400
Current assets	855,300		555,700
Fixed assets, net	1,365,000		1,078,100
Intangibles, net	2,217,200		1,762,200
Total assets	**4,476,900**	**+26**	**3,553,100**
Accts. pay. & accr. liabs	547,300		425,100
Current liabilities	736,800		528,000
Long-term debt, gross	1,926,100		1,456,300
Long-term debt, net	1,911,300		1,444,900
Long-term lease liabilities	175,700		129,600
Shareholders' equity	1,108,100		983,600
Non-controlling interest	352,400		328,600
Cash from oper. activs	**248,700**	**+7**	**232,000**
Cash from fin. activs	410,900		(399,600)
Cash from invest. activs	(632,100)		172,000
Net cash position	**58,400**	**+106**	**28,400**
Capital expenditures	(117,300)		(105,100)
Capital disposals	7,900		6,800
Pension fund surplus	6,700		7,000
	$		$
Earns. per sh. bef disc opers*	(0.58)		(0.04)
Earnings per share*	(0.58)		0.99
Cash flow per share*	1.28		1.32
Cash divd. per share*	0.72		0.72
	shs		shs
No. of shs. o/s*	200,700,000		176,000,000
Avg. no. of shs. o/s*	194,900,000		176,000,000
	%		%
Net profit margin	(2.60)		0.72
Return on equity	(10.76)		(0.68)
Return on assets	(0.62)		3.73
Foreign sales percent	64		63
No. of employees (FTEs)	4,620		4,125

* Common
◻ Restated
A Reported in accordance with IFRS

Latest Results

Periods ended:	6m June 30/23[A]		6m June 30/22[A]
	$000s	%Chg	$000s
Operating revenue	1,836,900	+2	1,799,000
Net income	107,300	+92	56,000
Net inc. for equity hldrs	94,600	+115	43,900
Net inc. for non-cont. int	12,700		12,100
	$		$
Earnings per share*	0.45		0.23

* Common
A Reported in accordance with IFRS

Historical Summary
(as originally stated)

Fiscal Year	Oper. Rev.	Net Inc. Bef. Disc.	EPS*
	$000s	$000s	$
2022[A]	3,379,800	(87,900)	(0.58)
2021[A]	2,392,600	17,200	(0.04)
2020[A]	2,394,300	86,800	0.43
2019[A]	2,852,900	142,600	0.82
2018[A]	2,726,700	(34,000)	(0.22)

* Common
A Reported in accordance with IFRS

S.140 Supremex Inc.

Symbol - SXP **Exchange** - TSX **CUSIP** - 86863R
Head Office - 7213 rue Cordner, LaSalle, QC, H8N 2J7 **Telephone** - (514) 595-0555 **Toll-free** - (800) 361-6659 **Fax** - (514) 595-1112
Website - www.supremex.com
Email - vente@supremex.com
Investor Relations - Stewart Emerson (514) 595-0555 ext. 2316
Auditors - Ernst & Young LLP C.A., Montréal, Qué.
Lawyers - Stikeman Elliott LLP, Montréal, Qué.
Transfer Agents - Computershare Trust Company of Canada Inc.
FP500 Revenue Ranking - 588
Employees - 1,050 at Dec. 31, 2022
Profile - (Can. 2006) Manufactures and distributes stock and custom envelopes as well as paper-based packaging solutions and specialty products, including folding carton packaging, e-commerce fulfillment packaging solutions and labels, in Canada and the U.S.

Other packaging and specialty products include Conformer Products®, pressure sensitive labels, polyethylene bags for courier applications, bubble mailers and Enviro-logiX®.

Manufacturing facilities are located in Richmond, B.C.; Winnipeg, Man.; LaSalle, Lachine, Laval (2), Saint-Laurent and Saint-Hyacinthe, Que.; Etobicoke, Mississauga and Concord, Ont.; Niagara Falls, N.Y.; Douglas, Mass.; Indianapolis (2), Ind.; and Chicago and Naperville, Ill. Distribution facilities are located in Moncton, N.B. and Buffalo, N.Y. Customers include large corporations, direct mailers, nationwide resellers, government bodies, paper merchants, and solution and process providers.

In August 2022, the company announced a plan to move its folding carton plant in Mount Royal, Que., to the Durabox corrugated packaging facility in Lachine, Que. The Durabox operations would be wound down.

Recent Merger and Acquisition Activity

Status: completed **Announced:** Jan. 16, 2023
Supremex Inc. acquired Impression Paragraph Inc., an integrated provider of paper-based packaging, print and point of sale products for a broad range of commercial markets, for $26,600,000 cash. Paragraph operates two facilities located in Ville-Saint-Laurent and Saint-Hyacinthe, Qué., and generated sales of $38,600,000 for the 12-month period ended Oct. 31, 2022.

Status: completed **Announced:** Nov. 1, 2022
Supremex Inc. acquired substantially all of the assets of Chicago, Ill.-based Royal Envelope Corporation, an envelope manufacturer and lithography company, for US$18,700,000 cash plus US$2,000,000 for manufacturing equipment that was recently commissioned. Royal Envelope operated two facilities in Chicago, focusing primarily on higher-end, specialized, highly decorated envelopes in special format, coloured envelopes for direct mail applications. During the 12-month period ended June 30, 2022, Royal Envelope generated sales of US$38,800,000.

Predecessor Detail - Succeeded Supremex Income Fund, Jan. 1, 2011, pursuant to plan of arrangement whereby the fund was converted into a corporation and subsequently dissolved.

Directors - Robert B. Johnston, chr., Isle of Palms, S.C.; Stewart Emerson, pres. & CEO, Pickering, Ont.; Nicole L. Boivin, Brantford, Ont.; Georges Kobrynsky, Montréal, Qué.; Dany Paradis, Montréal, Qué.; Steven P. (Steve) Richardson, Toronto, Ont.; Warren J. White, Dollard-des-Ormeaux, Qué.

Other Exec. Officers - François Bolduc, CFO & corp. sec.; Murray Rundle, v-p, mktg. & innovation; Steven Perreault, contr.; Joe Baglione, pres., envelope; Simon Provencher, pres., packaging

Capital Stock

	Authorized (shs.)	Outstanding (shs.)[1]
Common	unlimited	25,977,069

[1] At May 9, 2023

Normal Course Issuer Bid - The company plans to make normal course purchases of up to 1,301,713 common shares representing 5% of the total outstanding. The bid commenced on Aug. 31, 2022, and expires on Aug. 30, 2023.

Major Shareholder - Article 6 Marital Trust created under the First Amended and Restated Jerry Zucker Revocable Trust held 23.7% interest and George Christopoulos held 10.4% interest at Mar. 31, 2023.

Price Range - SXP/TSX

Year	Volume	High	Low	Close
2022	12,342,474	$6.23	$2.75	$5.80
2021	12,268,803	$2.84	$1.81	$2.75
2020	13,424,379	$2.51	$1.10	$2.04
2019	9,720,497	$3.59	$2.24	$2.42
2018	9,284,303	$4.83	$2.14	$2.45

Recent Close: $4.25

Capital Stock Changes - During 2022, 438,400 common shares were repurchased under a Normal Course Issuer Bid.

Dividends

SXP com N.S.R. [1]

$0.035	Sept. 22/23	$0.035	June 23/23
$0.035	Apr. 7/23	$0.03	Dec. 23/22

Paid in 2023: $0.105 2022: $0.135 2021: n.a.

[1] First divd. since Apr/20.

Wholly Owned Subsidiaries

Impression Paragraph Inc., Qué.
Supremex USA Inc., United States.
- 100% int. in **Buffalo Envelope LLC**, Del.
- 100% int. in **Classic Envelope LLC**, Douglas, Mass.
- 100% int. in **Supremex Midwest LLC**, Del.

Vista Graphic Communications, LLC, Indianapolis, Ind.

Financial Statistics

Periods ended:	12m Dec. 31/22[A]		12m Dec. 31/21[A]
	$000s	%Chg	$000s
Operating revenue	**272,467**	**+20**	**226,430**
Cost of sales	109,105		92,914
Salaries & benefits	74,451		66,334
Other operating expense	33,156		28,305
Operating expense	**216,712**	**+16**	**187,553**
Operating income	**55,755**	**+43**	**38,877**
Deprec., depl. & amort.	14,090		13,524
Finance income	408		nil
Finance costs, net	2,572		2,226
Write-downs/write-offs	(1,410)		(2,074)
Pre-tax income	**38,093**	**+81**	**21,053**
Income taxes	9,657		5,301
Net income	**28,436**	**+81**	**15,752**
Cash & equivalent	1,929		6,365
Inventories	44,872		24,924
Accounts receivable	39,334		32,983
Current assets	88,702		65,640
Fixed assets, net	42,185		34,141
Right-of-use assets	32,028		21,796
Intangibles, net	31,699		22,889
Total assets	**260,556**	**+26**	**206,371**
Accts. pay. & accr. liabs	34,838		27,449
Current liabilities	42,669		40,389
Long-term debt, gross	54,996		44,351
Long-term debt, net	54,731		40,851
Long-term lease liabilities	29,569		18,995
Shareholders' equity	124,318		97,405
Cash from oper. activs	**26,914**	**-10**	**29,996**
Cash from fin. activs	(49)		(20,022)
Cash from invest. activs	(31,723)		(6,611)
Net cash position	**1,929**	**-70**	**6,365**
Capital expenditures	(2,723)		(3,356)
Capital disposals	543		53
Pension fund surplus	14,678		12,441
	$		$
Earnings per share*	1.09		0.58
Cash flow per share*	1.03		1.10
Cash divd. per share*	0.14		nil
	shs		shs
No. of shs. o/s*	25,977,069		26,415,469
Avg. no. of shs. o/s*	26,152,557		27,194,848
	%		%
Net profit margin	10.44		6.96
Return on equity	25.65		17.86
Return on assets	12.18		8.02
Foreign sales percent	43		39
No. of employees (FTEs)	1,050		825

* Common
A Reported in accordance with IFRS

Latest Results

Periods ended:	3m Mar. 31/23[A]		3m Mar. 31/22[A]
	$000s	%Chg	$000s
Operating revenue	88,422	+40	63,269
Net income	9,496	+51	6,302
	$		$
Earnings per share*	0.37		0.24

* Common
A Reported in accordance with IFRS

Historical Summary
(as originally stated)

Fiscal Year	Oper. Rev.	Net Inc. Bef. Disc.	EPS*
	$000s	$000s	$
2022[A]	272,467	28,436	1.09
2021[A]	226,430	15,752	0.58
2020[A]	204,604	7,495	0.27
2019[A]	191,669	7,088	0.25
2018[A]	195,087	(4,793)	(0.17)

* Common
A Reported in accordance with IFRS

S.141 SureNano Science Ltd.

Symbol - SURE **Exchange** - CSE **CUSIP** - 86867L
Head Office - 350-1650 2 Ave W, Vancouver, BC, V6J 1H4 **Telephone** - (604) 428-5171
Website - surenano.com
Email - info@surenano.com
Investor Relations - Charles MaLette (604) 428-5171
Auditors - Buckley Dodds C.P.A., Vancouver, B.C.
Transfer Agents - Endeavor Trust Corporation, Vancouver, B.C.
Profile - (B.C. 2021) Sells and distributes the SureNano™ surfactant under an exclusive licence in Canada, Oklahoma and Colorado.

SureNano™ is a ready-to-mix food grade compound that provides the base for high performance nano-emulsions to create homogeneous and stable products while maximizing bioavailability, clarity and taste, and can be used in other applications requiring the mixing of oil and water including pet food, fertilizers, cosmetics and skin care. SureNano™ is manufactured and supplied by private Mississauga, Ont.-based **Caldic Canada Inc.**

Also holds an exclusive licence to distribute a new powder nano-emulsion product which is being developed by **1150641 B.C. Ltd.**

In September 2022, the company entered into a joint venture for the purpose of developing and marketing a new powder nano-emulsion. In addition, the company's current licences for Canada and Colorado were expanded to include the new powder nano-emulsion product which is being developed by **1150641 B.C. Ltd.** The company and 1150641 agreed to make contributions to a common fund for the purpose of developing and marketing worldwide the new powder nano-emulsion product and sharing equally in the profits thereof.

In June 2022, the company signed a licensing agreement with **1150641 B.C. Ltd.** for the exclusive rights to sell and distribute all current and future products developed by 1150641 in the state of Oklahoma. Under the agreement, the company would pay $10,000 and would also pay quarterly a 20% royalty on all net sales for an initial term of 10 years.

Directors - Charles (Bud) MaLette, pres., CEO & corp. sec., B.C.; James Bordian, CFO, B.C.; Douglas C. (Doug) Bachman, St. Albert, Alta.; Peter Chapman, B.C.

Other Exec. Officers - George Brooks, v-p, sales

Capital Stock

	Authorized (shs.)	Outstanding (shs.)[1]
Common	unlimited	21,457,800

[1] At Nov. 23, 2022

Major Shareholder - Charles (Bud) MaLette held 31.05% interest at Oct. 7, 2022.

Price Range - SURE/CSE

Year	Volume	High	Low	Close
2022	597,745	$0.30	$0.09	$0.12
2021	4,000	$0.30	$0.30	$0.30

Recent Close: $0.08

Capital Stock Changes - In December 2021, 1,757,700 common shares were issued without further consideration on exchange of special warrants sold previously by private placement at 25¢ each.

Financial Statistics

Periods ended:	12m Mar. 31/22[A]
	$000s
Operating revenue	**14**
Cost of goods sold	1
Research & devel. expense	102
General & admin expense	616
Stock-based compensation	411
Operating expense	**1,131**
Operating income	**(1,117)**
Pre-tax income	**(1,118)**
Income taxes	1
Net income	**(1,119)**
Cash & equivalent	667
Accounts receivable	17
Current assets	686
Total assets	**686**
Accts. pay. & accr. liabs	21
Current liabilities	36
Shareholders' equity	650
Cash from oper. activs	**(670)**
Cash from fin. activs	408
Net cash position	**667**
	$
Earnings per share*	(0.06)
Cash flow per share*	(0.03)
	shs
No. of shs. o/s*	21,457,800
Avg. no. of shs. o/s*	20,239,449
	%
Net profit margin	n.m.
Return on equity	n.m.
Return on assets	n.a.

* Common

[A] Reported in accordance with IFRS

Latest Results

Periods ended:	6m Sept. 30/22[A]		6m Sept. 30/21[A]
	$000s	%Chg	$000s
Operating revenue	nil	n.a.	14
Net income	(247)	n.a.	(748)
	$		$
Earnings per share*	(0.01)		(0.04)

* Common

[A] Reported in accordance with IFRS

S.142 Sustainable Innovation & Health Dividend Fund

Symbol - SIH.UN **Exchange** - TSX **CUSIP** - 86934T

Head Office - c/o Middlefield Limited, 1 First Canadian Place, 5800-100 King St W, PO Box 192, Toronto, ON, M5X 1A6 **Telephone** - (416) 362-0714 **Toll-free** - (888) 890-1868 **Fax** - (416) 362-7925

Website - www.middlefield.com

Email - sroberts@middlefield.com

Investor Relations - Sarah Roberts (416) 847-5355

Auditors - Deloitte LLP C.A., Toronto, Ont.

Lawyers - Fasken Martineau DuMoulin LLP

Transfer Agents - TSX Trust Company

Trustees - Middlefield Limited, Calgary, Alta.

Investment Advisors - Middlefield Capital Corporation, Toronto, Ont.

Managers - Middlefield Limited, Calgary, Alta.

Profile - (Alta. 2020) Invests primarily in dividend paying securities of global technology and healthcare companies, including initially those which the fund's advisor believes are positioned to benefit long-term from the trends and changing consumer behaviours resulting from the COVID-19 global pandemic.

The fund's portfolio may initially include securities of issuers whose operations may be related to e-commerce, work from home, digital health and life sciences, as well as those whose operations may fall within traditional technology and healthcare subsectors. Up to 20% of the portfolio will be invested in securities of private issuers.

The manager is entitled to a management fee at an annual rate of 1.25% of net asset value, calculated and payable monthly.

The fund may borrow against the assets to a maximum of 25% of total assets for various purposes, including acquiring additional securities for the portfolio.

Top 10 holdings at Mar.31, 2023 (as a percentage of net asset value):

Holdings	Percentage
Sagard Healthcare Royalty Partners	8.5%
AbbVie Inc.	5.2%
Alphabet Inc.	4.9%
Astrazeneca plc	4.7%
UnitedHealth Group Inc.	4.3%
Apple Inc.	3.9%
Thermo Fisher Scientific Inc.	3.9%
El Lilly and Company	3.9%
Merk & Co.	3.9%
Pfizer Inc.	3.7%

Oper. Subsid./Mgt. Co. Directors - Jeremy T. Brasseur, exec. chr., Toronto, Ont.; Dean Orrico, pres. & CEO, Vaughan, Ont.; Craig Rogers, COO & chief compliance officer, Toronto, Ont.

Capital Stock

	Authorized (shs.)	Outstanding (shs.)[1]
Fund Unit	unlimited	6,060,822

[1] At Dec. 31, 2022

Fund Unit - Entitled to initial monthly cash distributions targeted to be $0.03333 per unit (to yield 4% per annum based on an issue price of $10 per unit). Retractable in August of each year for an amount equal to the net asset value per unit, less any costs to fund the retraction. Retractable in any other month at a price per unit equal to the lesser of: (i) 94% of the weighted average trading price on TSX during the 15 trading days immediately preceding the monthly retraction date; and (ii) the closing market price, less retraction costs. One vote per unit.

Normal Course Issuer Bid - The company plans to make normal course purchases of up to 788,740 fund units representing 10% of the public float. The bid commenced on Sept. 1, 2022, and expires on Aug. 31, 2023.

Major Shareholder - Widely held at Mar. 10, 2023.

Price Range - SIH.UN/TSX

Year	Volume	High	Low	Close
2022	2,441,245	$11.91	$8.03	$9.45
2021	4,445,650	$11.98	$8.65	$11.65
2020	1,594,701	$10.60	$8.88	$9.93

Recent Close: $9.51

Capital Stock Changes - During 2022, fund units were issued as follows: 14,800 for cash and 401 were released from treasury; 1,622,879 fund units were retracted, 404,900 fund units were repurchased under a Normal Course Issuer Bid and 78,100 fund units were repurchased in the market in accordance with the declaration of trust.

Dividends

SIH.UN unit Ra $0.39996 pa M est. Nov. 13, 2020**[1]

[1] Dividend reinvestment plan implemented eff. August 14, 2020.

** Reinvestment Option

Financial Statistics

Periods ended:	12m Dec. 31/22[A]		12m Dec. 31/21[A]
	$000s	%Chg	$000s
Realized invest. gain (loss)	(981)		2,764
Unrealized invest. gain (loss)	(13,366)		18,340
Total revenue	**(13,153)**	**n.a.**	**21,918**
General & admin. expense	1,280		1,744
Other operating expense	65		51
Operating expense	**1,345**	**-25**	**1,795**
Operating income	**(14,498)**	**n.a.**	**20,123**
Finance costs, gross	186		161
Pre-tax income	**(14,683)**	**n.a.**	**19,961**
Income taxes	103		137
Net income	**(14,786)**	**n.a.**	**19,825**
Cash & equivalent	6,079		9,582
Accounts receivable	62		71
Investments	58,280		103,368
Total assets	**64,424**	**-43**	**113,043**
Accts. pay. & accr. liabs	140		388
Debt	4,000		15,000
Shareholders' equity	60,082		97,383
Cash from oper. activs	**30,141**	**n.a.**	**(2,418)**
Cash from fin. activs	(33,753)		4,406
Net cash position	**6,079**	**-37**	**9,582**
	$		$
Earnings per share*	(1.98)		2.33
Cash flow per share*	4.04		(0.28)
Net asset value per share*	9.91		11.95
Cash divd. per share*	0.40		0.40
	shs		shs
No. of shs. o/s*	6,060,822		8,151,500
Avg. no. of shs. o/s*	7,467,049		8,498,882
	%		%
Net profit margin	n.m.		90.45
Return on equity	(18.78)		21.39
Return on assets	(16.45)		19.82

* Fund Unit

[A] Reported in accordance with IFRS

Note: Net income reflects increase/decrease in net assets from operations.

Historical Summary
(as originally stated)

Fiscal Year	Total Rev.	Net Inc. Bef. Disc.	EPS*
	$000s	$000s	$
2022[A]	(13,153)	(14,786)	(1.98)
2021[A]	21,918	19,825	2.33
2020[A1]	5,996	5,095	0.57

* Fund Unit

[A] Reported in accordance with IFRS

[1] 4 months ended Dec. 31, 2020.

S.143 Sustainable Power & Infrastructure Split Corp.

Symbol - PWI **Exchange** - TSX **CUSIP** - 86934R

Head Office - c/o Brompton Group Limited, Bay Wellington Tower, Brookfield Place, 2930-181 Bay St, PO Box 793, Toronto, ON, M5J 2T3 **Telephone** - (416) 642-9061 **Toll-free** - (866) 642-6001 **Fax** - (416) 642-6001

Website - www.bromptongroup.com/product/sustainable-power-infrastructure-split-corp

Email - wong@bromptongroup.com

Investor Relations - Ann P. Wong (416) 642-9061

Auditors - PricewaterhouseCoopers LLP C.A., Toronto, Ont.

Lawyers - Osler, Hoskin & Harcourt LLP, Toronto, Ont.

Transfer Agents - TSX Trust Company, Toronto, Ont.

Managers - Brompton Funds Limited, Toronto, Ont.

Portfolio Managers - Brompton Funds Limited, Toronto, Ont.

Profile - (Ont. 2021) Invests in a globally diversified and actively managed portfolio consisting primarily of dividend-paying securities of power and infrastructure companies, whose assets, products and services the manager believes are facilitating the multi-decade transition toward decarbonization and environmental sustainability.

The portfolio may include investments in companies operating in the areas of renewable power, green transportation, energy efficiency and communications with a market capitalization of at least $2 billion. In addition, up to 25% of the portfolio may be invested indirectly through exchange-traded funds, including funds managed by the manager.

The company has a scheduled termination date of May 29, 2026, subject to extension for successive terms of up to five years.

The manager receives a management fee at an annual rate equal to 0.75% of the net asset value calculated and payable monthly in arrears.

Top 10 holdings at Mar. 31, 2023 (as a percentage of net asset value):

Holdings	Percentage
Brompton Sustain. Real Assets Divid. ETF	4.6%
ONEOK, Inc.	4.4%
Schneider Electric SE	3.9%
Nextera Energy, Inc.	3.9%
Hitachi Ltd.	3.8%
Roper Technologies Inc.	3.6%
T-Mobile US Inc.	3.6%
Exelon Corporation	3.4%
Canadian Pacific Railway Ltd.	3.4%
Waste Management Inc.	3.4%

Oper. Subsid./Mgt. Co. Directors - Mark A. Caranci, pres. & CEO, Toronto, Ont.; Ann P. Wong, CFO & chief compliance officer, Toronto, Ont.; Christopher S. L. Hoffmann, Toronto, Ont.; Raymond R. Pether, Toronto, Ont.

Oper. Subsid./Mgt. Co. Officers - Laura Lau, chief invest. officer; Kathryn A. H. Banner, sr. v-p & corp. sec.; Michael D. Clare, sr. v-p & sr. portfolio mgr.; Christopher Cullen, sr. v-p; Manith (Manny) Phanvongsa, sr. v-p; Michelle L. Tiraborelli, sr. v-p

Capital Stock

	Authorized (shs.)	Outstanding (shs.)[1]
Preferred	unlimited	3,732,166[2]
Class A	unlimited	3,732,166
Class B	unlimited	nil
Class C	unlimited	nil
Class J	unlimited	100[2]

[1] At June 21, 2023

[2] Classified as debt.

Preferred - Entitled to fixed cumulative preferential quarterly distributions of $0.125 per share (representing 5% per annum). Retractable in May of each year at a price per unit equal to the net asset value (NAV) per unit (one class A share and one preferred share), less any costs associated with the retraction. Retractable in any other month at a price per share equal to 96% of the lesser of: (i) the NAV per unit less the cost to the company to purchase a class A share for cancellation; and (ii) $10. All outstanding preferred shares will be redeemed on May 29, 2026, at a price per share equal to the lesser of: (i) $10 plus any accrued and unpaid distributions; and (ii) the NAV per preferred share. Rank in priority to class A shares and class J shares with respect to payment of distributions and repayment of capital on the dissolution, liquidation or winding up of the company. Non-voting.

Class A - Entitled to monthly non-cumulative cash distributions targeted to be $0.06667 per share (representing 8% per annum). No distributions will be paid if the distributions payable on the preferred shares are in arrears, or, in respect of a cash distribution, after payment of the distribution, the NAV per unit would be less than $15. Retractable in May of each year along with an equal number of preferred shares at a price per share equal to the NAV per unit, less any costs associated with the retraction, including commissions. Retractable in any other month at a price per share equal to 96% of the difference between: (i) the NAV per unit on the retraction date; and (ii) the cost to the company to purchase a preferred share for cancellation. All outstanding class A shares will be redeemed on May 29, 2026, at a price per share equal to the greater of: (i) the NAV per unit minus $10 and any accrued and unpaid distributions on a preferred share; and (ii) nil. Rank subsequent to preferred shares but in priority to class J shares with respect to payment of distributions and repayment of capital on the dissolution, liquidation or winding up of the company. Non-voting.

Class J - Not entitled to dividends. Redeemable and retractable at $1.00 per share. Rank subsequent to both the preferred and class A shares with respect to the payment of dividends and the repayment of capital on the dissolution, liquidation or winding up of the company. One vote per share.

Class B & C - Issuable in series. Rank subsequent to preferred shares.

Major Shareholder - Brompton Funds Limited held 100% interest at Mar. 23, 2023.

Price Range - PWI/TSX

Year	Volume	High	Low	Close
2022	2,555,641	$9.95	$5.89	$7.55
2021	1,756,125	$10.41	$9.02	$9.87

Recent Close: $6.05

Capital Stock Changes - On Aug. 17, 2022, public offering of 510,500 preferred shares and 510,500 class A shares was completed at $10.50 and $8.95 per share, respectively.

Dividends

PWI cl A Ra $0.80004 pa M est. July 15, 2021
Listed May 21/21.
$0.06667**i**............ July 15/21
PWI.PR.A pfd Ra $0.50 pa Q
Listed May 21/21.
$0.05632**i**............ July 15/21
i Initial Payment

Financial Statistics

Periods ended:	12m Dec. 31/22[A]		32w Dec. 31/21[A]
	$000s	%Chg	$000s
Realized invest. gain (loss)	(5,742)		(2,701)
Unrealized invest. gain (loss)	(3,936)		6,960
Total revenue	**(7,940)**	**n.a.**	**5,713**
General & admin. expense	739		558
Operating expense	**739**	**n.a.**	**558**
Operating income	**(8,679)**	**n.a.**	**5,155**
Finance costs, gross	1,864		1,896
Pre-tax income	**(10,699)**	**n.a.**	**3,183**
Net income	**(10,699)**	**n.a.**	**3,183**
Cash & equivalent	243		370
Accounts receivable	174		127
Investments	61,015		65,188
Total assets	**61,735**	**-6**	**65,711**
Accts. pay. & accr. liabs	84		56
Debt	37,322		32,217
Shareholders' equity	23,449		32,504
Cash from oper. activs	**(6,881)**	**n.a.**	**(61,381)**
Cash from fin. activs	6,750		61,752
Net cash position	**243**	**-34**	**370**
	$		$
Earnings per share*	(3.13)		0.99
Cash flow per share*	(2.02)		(19.05)
Net asset value per share*	6.28		10.09
Cash divd. per share*	0.80		0.47
	shs		shs
No. of shs. o/s*	3,732,166		3,221,666
Avg. no. of shs. o/s*	3,413,278		3,221,666
	%		%
Net profit margin	n.m.		...
Return on equity	(38.24)		...
Return on assets	(13.86)		...

* Class A

[A] Reported in accordance with IFRS

S.144 Sustainable Real Estate Dividend Fund

Symbol - MSRE.UN **Exchange** - TSX **CUSIP** - 86934J

Head Office - c/o Middlefield Capital Corporation, 3100-8 Spadina Ave, Toronto, ON, M5V 0S8 **Telephone** - (416) 362-0714 **Toll-free** - (888) 890-1868 **Fax** - (416) 362-7925

Website - www.middlefield.com

Email - sroberts@middlefield.com

Investor Relations - Sarah Roberts (416) 362-0714

Auditors - Deloitte LLP C.A., Toronto, Ont.

Transfer Agents - TSX Trust Company

Investment Advisors - Middlefield Capital Corporation, Toronto, Ont.

Managers - Middlefield Limited, Calgary, Alta.

Profile - (Ont. 2022) Invests in a diversified, actively managed portfolio consisting primarily of dividend paying securities of international issuers focused on, involved in, or that derive a significant portion of their revenue from business models that are creating and transforming the green property and related sectors by employing or developing sustainable property management practices or materials

The fund's investment advisor will integrate Environmental, Social & Governance (ESG) considerations to complement fundamental analysis in selecting investments believed to have sustainable competitive advantages.

The manager is entitled to a management fee at an annual rate of 1.25% of net asset value, calculated and payable monthly.

The fund may borrow against the assets to a maximum of 25% of total assets for various purposes, including acquiring additional securities for the portfolio.

Oper. Subsid./Mgt. Co. Directors - Jeremy T. Brasseur, exec. chr., Toronto, Ont.; Dean Orrico, pres. & CEO, Vaughan, Ont.

Oper. Subsid./Mgt. Co. Officers - Craig Rogers, COO & chief compliance officer

Capital Stock

	Authorized (shs.)	Outstanding (shs.)[1]
Fund Unit	unlimited	2,301,647

[1] At Apr. 3, 2022

Fund Unit - Entitled to initial monthly cash distributions targeted to be $0.04167 per unit (to yield 5% per annum based on an issue price of $10 per unit). Retractable in March of each year, commencing in 2024, for an amount equal to the net asset value per unit, less any costs to fund the retraction. Retractable in any other month at a price per unit equal to the lesser of: (i) 94% of the weighted average trading price on TSX during the 15 trading days immediately preceding the monthly retraction date; and (ii) the closing market price, less retraction costs. One vote per unit.

Normal Course Issuer Bid - The company plans to make normal course purchases of up to 226,704 fund units representing 10% of the public float. The bid commenced on Apr. 13, 2023, and expires on Apr. 12, 2024.

Price Range - MSRE.UN/TSX

Year	Volume	High	Low	Close
2022	1,302,996	$9.98	$6.14	$7.39

Recent Close: $7.10

Capital Stock Changes - On Mar. 30, 2022, an initial public offering of 2,500,000 fund units was completed at $10 per unit.

Dividends

MSRE.UN unit Ra $0.50004 pa M est. June 15, 2022
Listed Mar 30/22.
$0.04167**i**............ June 15/22
i Initial Payment

S.145 Swarmio Media Holdings Inc.

Symbol - SWRM **Exchange** - CSE (S) **CUSIP** - 87000A

Head Office - 1430-800 Pender St W, Vancouver, BC, V6C 2V6 **Telephone** - (604) 638-8063

Website - swarmio.media/investors

Email - investors@swarmio.media

Investor Relations - Sean Peasgood (437) 253-9222

Auditors - Clearhouse LLP C.A., Mississauga, Ont.

Lawyers - LaBarge Weinstein LLP, Ottawa, Ont.

Transfer Agents - Odyssey Trust Company, Vancouver, B.C.

Employees - 60 at Nov. 1, 2022

Profile - (B.C. 2021) Provides a proprietary turnkey gaming and eSports platform, Ember, which enables telecommunications operators to engage and monetize gamers. Focus is on Asia, Middle East and North Africa (MENA) and Latin America markets.

Ember is a plug-and-play platform that can be integrated with major telecommunications operations, allowing telecommunications operators (telecos) to engage and monetize gaming subscribers who don't have access to credit cards. Ember provides a proprietary digital hub for gaming communities, allowing gamers to access an ultra-low-latency playing experience, competitive challenges and tournaments, exclusive gaming content, managed communities, gamification and points system, online store (Swarmio Store), gamer e-wallet (Swarmio Pay), and customized digital content.

The company shares 20% to 50% of the revenue from the game publishers with the telecos. Revenue streams include recurring revenues from gaming and eSports subscriptions, on-demand revenues from the sale of in-game tokens, contents and skins, and revenues from payment gateway services for game publishers and developers.

On June 22, 2023, the company filed for protection under the Companies' Creditor Arrangement Act (CCAA) and **Grant Thornton Limited** was appointed monitor.

Common suspended from CSE, Aug. 15, 2023.

Predecessor Detail - Name changed from 1283332 B.C. Ltd., Apr. 16, 2021.

Directors - Vijai Karthigesu, chr., pres. & CEO, Ajax, Ont.; Sorin Stoian, chief tech. officer, Ajax, Ont.; Andrew Ray, Halifax, N.S.

Other Exec. Officers - Jonathan Visva, CFO; Tesh Kapadia, exec. v-p, global sales; John Smith, exec. v-p, srvc. delivery; Vinicius Esteves, sr. v-p, fintech; Aseef Khan, v-p, gaming & esports

Capital Stock

	Authorized (shs.)	Outstanding (shs.)[1]
Common	unlimited	110,453,430

[1] At Nov. 4, 2022

Major Shareholder - Widely held at Aug. 15, 2022.

Price Range - SWRM/CSE (S)

Year	Volume	High	Low	Close
2022	23,863,765	$0.41	$0.04	$0.05
2021	1,395,322	$0.90	$0.31	$0.36

Recent Close: $0.01

Capital Stock Changes - In May 2022, private placement of 11,661,407 common shares was completed at 10¢ per share.

In November 2021, 59,218,800 common shares were issued pursuant to the reverse takeover acquisition of Swarmio Inc. and 17,904,284 common shares were issued without further consideration on exchange of subscription receipts sold previously by private placement at 35¢ each. Also during fiscal 2022, common shares were issued as follows: 4,083,794 as finders' fees, 2,000,000 for services and 945,145 on exercise of warrants.

Wholly Owned Subsidiaries

Swarmio IO Media ME Computer Systems, United Arab Emirates.
Swarmio Inc., Whitby, Ont.
- 100% int. in **Battlehive Inc.**, Ont.
- 100% int. in **Battlehive USA Inc.**, Del.
- 100% int. in **Swarmio Media Inc.**, Ont.
  - 100% int. in **Swarmio Media of Bahrain W.L.L.**, Bahrain.

Swarmio Media Singapore Pte. Ltd., Singapore.
Swarmio Tunisia, Tunisia.

Financial Statistics

Periods ended:	12m Mar. 31/22[A1]		12m Mar. 31/21[A2]
	$000s	%Chg	$000s
Operating revenue	**596**	**n.m.**	**4**
Salaries & benefits	1,720		477
General & admin expense	3,990		1,229
Stock-based compensation	2,152		420
Other operating expense	30		4
Operating expense	**7,892**	**+271**	**2,130**
Operating income	**(7,296)**	**n.a.**	**(2,126)**
Deprec., depl. & amort.	(17)		(47)
Finance costs, gross	1,219		1,203
Write-downs/write-offs	(269)		(69)
Pre-tax income	**(6,583)**	**n.a.**	**(4,684)**
Net income	**(6,583)**	**n.a.**	**(4,684)**
Cash & equivalent	1,628		2,434
Accounts receivable	7		25
Current assets	2,830		3,147
Fixed assets, net	17		17
Right-of-use assets	13		28
Intangibles, net	208		nil
Total assets	**3,068**	**-4**	**3,193**
Accts. pay. & accr. liabs.	1,098		1,339
Current liabilities	1,794		15,404
Long-term debt, gross	1,962		14,472
Long-term debt, net	1,284		977
Long-term lease liabilities	nil		17
Equity portion of conv. debs.	nil		516
Shareholders' equity	(9)		(13,205)
Cash from oper. activs.	**(6,766)**	**n.a.**	**(1,501)**
Cash from fin. activs.	6,170		3,860
Cash from invest. activs.	(210)		(9)
Net cash position	**1,628**	**-33**	**2,434**
Capital expenditures	(2)		(9)
	$		$
Earnings per share*	(0.14)		(0.34)
Cash flow per share*	(0.14)		(0.11)
	shs		shs
No. of shs. o/s*	98,792,023		n.a.
Avg. no. of shs. o/s*	48,414,113		13,732,404
	%		%
Net profit margin	n.m.		n.m.
Return on equity	n.m.		n.m.
Return on assets	(171.35)		(141.53)

* Common
[A] Reported in accordance with IFRS
[1] Results reflect the Nov. 5, 2021, reverse takeover acquisition of Swarmio Inc.
[2] Results for fiscal 2021 and prior period pertain to Swarmio Inc.

Latest Results

Periods ended:	6m Sept. 30/22[A]		6m Sept. 30/21[A]
	$000s	%Chg	$000s
Operating revenue	449	n.m.	1
Net income	(4,759)	n.a.	2,876
	$		$
Earnings per share*	(0.04)		0.19

* Common
[A] Reported in accordance with IFRS

Historical Summary
(as originally stated)

Fiscal Year	Oper. Rev.	Net Inc. Bef. Disc.	EPS*
	$000s	$000s	$
2022[A]	596	(6,583)	(0.14)
2021[A]	4	(4,684)	(0.34)
2020[A]	85	(3,885)	(0.39)

* Common
[A] Reported in accordance with IFRS

S.146 Sweet Earth Holdings Corporation

Symbol - SE **Exchange** - CSE **CUSIP** - 87039X
Head Office - 903-700 Pender St W, Vancouver, BC, V6C 1G8
Telephone - (604) 423-4499 **Fax** - (604) 909-2679
Website - sweetearthcbdcorp.com
Email - contact@sweetearthcbd.com
Investor Relations - Christopher R. Cooper (604) 307-8290
Auditors - SHIM & Associates LLP C.A., Vancouver, B.C.
Lawyers - McMillan LLP
Transfer Agents - Odyssey Trust Company

Profile - (B.C. 2014; orig. Alta., 2005) Cultivates organic hemp in Oregon and produces hemp and cannabidiol (CBD)-based products for the U.S. and global market.

Operations include about 100 acres of leased outdoor cultivation agricultural land in Applegate, Ore., with access to indoor greenhouses, totaling 35,000 sq. ft., where the company's own proprietary hemp strain is grown. The company also maintains 22 acres of leased irrigable land in Los Barrios, Spain.

Hemp and CBD products consist of skin and body care products, that include facial, men's, spa, hemp and muscle products, and pet treats sold under the Sweet Earth brand and CBD cigarettes/pre-rolls marketed under the Sweet Earth Smooth brand. Products are sold online, with skin and body care products also available through high-end retailers, such as supermarkets, spas, clinics and boutiques. The company also produces its products as a wholesaler and white label provider.

In May 2022, the company entered into a letter of intent with **ST Group of Companies** to explore the amalgamation of various assets and businesses of ST Group into the company. ST Group is an incubator company engaged in the pharmaceutical therapeutics, cannabidiol, cosmetics and lifestyle industries. The transaction was expected to provide the company an access to 1,000 dispensaries in the European Union and North America.

Predecessor Detail - Name changed from Seaway Energy Services Inc., May 19, 2020, pursuant to reverse takeover acquisition of (old) Sweet Earth Holdings Corporation; basis 1 new for 2.5 old shs.

Directors - Robert Dubeau, pres. & CEO, B.C.; Christopher R. (Chris) Cooper, CFO & corp. sec., Vancouver, B.C.; Sergio Guzman, Panama; Amiel (Ami) Seaton, B.C.

Capital Stock

	Authorized (shs.)	Outstanding (shs.)[1]
Preferred	unlimited	nil
Common	unlimited	2,802,956

[1] At Apr. 24, 2023

Major Shareholder - Widely held at Mar. 1, 2023.

Price Range - SE/CSE

Year	Volume	High	Low	Close
2022	440,967	$2.00	$0.08	$0.24
2021	1,514,977	$18.60	$1.60	$1.60
2020	848,633	$12.00	$5.20	$7.60
2019	441	$20.00	$16.00	$16.00
2018	57,988	$110.00	$14.50	$16.00

Consolidation: 1-for-8 cons. in Apr. 2023; 1-for-5 cons. in June 2022; 1-for-2.5 cons. in May 2020
Recent Close: $0.25

Capital Stock Changes - On Apr. 24, 2023, common shares were consolidated on a 1-for-8 basis.

In October 2021, private placement of 2,424,000 units (1 post-consolidated common share & 1 warrant) at 50¢ per unit was completed. On June 20, 2022, common shares were consolidated on a 1-for-5 basis.

Wholly Owned Subsidiaries

Sweet Earth Colombia S.A.S., Colombia.
Sweet Earth Holdings Corp. S.L., Spain.
TSN Agricorp Ltd., Ore.
- 100% int. in **Sweet Earth, LLC**, Ore.

Financial Statistics

Periods ended:	12m June 30/22[A]		12m June 30/21[A]
	$000s	%Chg	$000s
Operating revenue	**88**	**-56**	**201**
Cost of sales	50		93
Salaries & benefits	3		10
General & admin expense	802		3,440
Stock-based compensation	264		393
Other operating expense	24		94
Operating expense	**1,143**	**-72**	**4,031**
Operating income	**(1,055)**	**n.a.**	**(3,830)**
Deprec., depl. & amort.	233		248
Finance costs, gross	67		88
Write-downs/write-offs	(1,821)		(752)
Pre-tax income	**(3,147)**	**n.a.**	**(4,918)**
Net income	**(3,147)**	**n.a.**	**(4,918)**
Cash & equivalent	135		85
Inventories	40		54
Current assets	245		201
Fixed assets, net	1,039		2,798
Intangibles, net	nil		185
Total assets	**1,283**	**-60**	**3,184**
Bank indebtedness	nil		28
Accts. pay. & accr. liabs.	918		967
Current liabilities	1,131		1,239
Long-term lease liabilities	992		1,065
Shareholders' equity	(840)		881
Cash from oper. activs.	**(864)**	**n.a.**	**(3,570)**
Cash from fin. activs.	1,031		3,645
Cash from invest. activs.	(19)		nil
Net cash position	**135**	**+59**	**85**
Capital expenditures	(19)		nil
	$		$
Earnings per share*	(1.12)		(2.40)
Cash flow per share*	(0.32)		(1.82)
	shs		shs
No. of shs. o/s*	2,802,956		2,499,957
Avg. no. of shs. o/s*	2,714,132		1,962,494
	%		%
Net profit margin	n.m.		n.m.
Return on equity	n.m.		n.m.
Return on assets	(137.90)		n.a.

* Common
[A] Reported in accordance with IFRS

Latest Results

Periods ended:	3m Sept. 30/22[A]		3m Sept. 30/21[A]
	$000s	%Chg	$000s
Operating revenue	10	-55	22
Net income	(128)	n.a.	(225)
	$		$
Earnings per share*	(0.05)		(0.09)

* Common
[A] Reported in accordance with IFRS

Historical Summary
(as originally stated)

Fiscal Year	Oper. Rev.	Net Inc. Bef. Disc.	EPS*
	$000s	$000s	$
2022[A]	88	(3,147)	(1.12)
2021[A]	201	(4,918)	(2.40)
2020[A1]	nil	(3,340)	(2.00)
2019[A2]	nil	(616)	(2.00)
2018[A]	nil	(1,374)	(6.00)

* Common
[A] Reported in accordance with IFRS
[1] Results reflect the May 19, 2020, reverse takeover acquisition of (old) Sweet Earth Holdings Corporation.
[2] Results for fiscal 2019 and prior fiscal periods pertain to Seaway Energy Services Inc.
Note: Adjusted throughout for 1-for-8 cons. in Apr. 2023; 1-for-5 cons. in June 2022; 1-for-2.5 cons. in May 2020

S.147 Sweet Poison Spirits Inc.

Symbol - SPS **Exchange** - CSE **CUSIP** - 87043J
Head Office - 750-580 Hornby St, Box 113, Vancouver, BC, V6C 3B6
Telephone - (604) 602-4935 **Fax** - (604) 602-4936
Website - www.ystem.ca
Email - rob.e@ystem.ca
Investor Relations - Robert Eadie (604) 618-3400
Auditors - Kingston Ross Pasnak LLP C.A., Edmonton, Alta.
Transfer Agents - TSX Trust Company, Vancouver, B.C.

Profile - (B.C. 2018) Holds worldwide distribution rights to **Sweet Poison Spirits S. de R.L. de C.V.**'s and **Sweet Poison Spirits LLC**'s premium tequila and mescal products under the Sweet Poison brand names for an initial 10-year period.

On Nov. 3, 2022, the company was granted the worldwide distribution rights to the Sweet Poison brand of tequila and mescal products for an initial 10-year period. The company would issue a total of 5,000,000 common shares at a deemed price of US$0.20 per share over a two-year period.

In September 2022, the company ceased its cryptocurrency mining operations. The company continued to own the mining rigs.

In June 2022, a change of business from growing and processing hemp into CBD products to cryptocurrency miming received final Canadian Securities Exchange approval. The company has arranged to acquire 150 Siacoin mining rigs for US$525,000 from **Enigma Data Technologies LLC** and engaged Enigma to set-up, host and operate the 150 rigs and oversee the cryptocurrency mining activities, in exchange for issuance of 2,668,000 common shares of the company at a deemed value of $0.25 per share. The company would be responsible for ongoing operating costs, to be at an all-in cost of US$0.055 per KWh per mining rig.

In March 2022, the company sold wholly owned subsidiary **Hemp for Health H4H S.R.L.** and all Italian hemp operations for a nominal value.

Predecessor Detail - Name changed from Yellow Stem Tech Inc., June 1, 2023, following the grant of the worldwide distribution rights to the Sweet Poison brand of tequila and mescal products.

Directors - Robert Eadie, pres. & CEO, Mexico City, D.F., Mexico; Gary Arca, CFO & corp. sec., Delta, B.C.; Tanya Lutzke, Surrey, B.C.; Gina Pala, Victoria, B.C.

Capital Stock

	Authorized (shs.)	Outstanding (shs.)[1]
Common	unlimited	30,623,451

[1] At May 1, 2023

Major Shareholder - Robert Eadie held 24.94% interest at May 1, 2023.

Price Range - SPS/CSE

Year	Volume	High	Low	Close
2022	1,699,229	$0.36	$0.02	$0.03
2021	926,798	$0.40	$0.10	$0.15
2020	2,870,535	$1.10	$0.18	$0.22
2019	93,625	$1.20	$0.60	$0.68

Consolidation: 1-for-2 cons. in May 2023; 1-for-2 cons. in Dec. 2021

Recent Close: $0.03

Capital Stock Changes - On May 1, 2023, common shares were consolidated on a 1-for-2 basis and 4,155,200 post-consolidated common shares were issued for debt settlement. Also in May 2023, private placement of up to 10,000,000 units (1 post-consolidated common share & ½ warrant) at 10¢ per unit was arranged, with warrants exercisable at 25¢ per share for two years.

In December 2021 8,002,500 post-consolidated common shares were issue to settle $400,125 of debt. On Dec. 2, 2021, common shares were consolidated on a 1-for-2 basis. In December and February 2022, private placement of 23,950,000 units (1 post-consolidated common share & ½ warrant) at 5¢ per unit was completed.

Financial Statistics

Periods ended:	12m Apr. 30/22[A]		12m Apr. 30/21[A]
	$000s	%Chg	$000s
Research & devel. expense	420		662
General & admin expense	255		435
Operating expense	**675**	**-38**	**1,097**
Operating income	**(675)**	**n.a.**	**(1,097)**
Deprec., depl. & amort.	2		2
Pre-tax income	**(589)**	**n.a.**	**(1,508)**
Net income	**(589)**	**n.a.**	**(1,508)**
Cash & equivalent	270		12
Accounts receivable	2		1
Current assets	276		25
Fixed assets, net	5		6
Total assets	**954**	**n.m.**	**31**
Bank indebtedness	374		283
Accts. pay. & accr. liabs	96		212
Current liabilities	470		494
Shareholders' equity	484		(463)
Cash from oper. activs	**(636)**	**n.a.**	**(985)**
Cash from fin. activs	1,567		283
Cash from invest. activs	(673)		nil
Net cash position	**270**	**n.m.**	**12**
	$		$
Earnings per share*	(0.06)		(0.24)
Cash flow per share*	(0.06)		(0.16)
	shs		shs
No. of shs. o/s*	22,016,751		6,040,500
Avg. no. of shs. o/s*	11,574,367		6,040,500
	%		%
Net profit margin	n.a.		n.a.
Return on equity	n.m.		n.m.
Return on assets	(119.59)		(256.90)

* Common
[A] Reported in accordance with IFRS

Latest Results

Periods ended:	3m July 31/22[A]		3m July 31/21[A]
	$000s	%Chg	$000s
Net income	(92)	n.a.	(42)
	$		$
Earnings per share*	(0.00)		(0.01)

* Common
[A] Reported in accordance with IFRS

Historical Summary
(as originally stated)

Fiscal Year	Oper. Rev. $000s	Net Inc. Bef. Disc. $000s	EPS* $
2022[A]	nil	(589)	(0.06)
2021[A]	nil	(1,508)	(0.24)
2020[A]	nil	(2,126)	(0.40)
2019[A1]	nil	(237)	(0.16)

* Common
[A] Reported in accordance with IFRS
[1] 30 weeks ended Apr. 30, 2019.

Note: Adjusted throughout for 1-for-2 cons. in May 2023; 1-for-2 cons. in Dec. 2021

S.148 Swiss Water Decaffeinated Coffee Inc.

Symbol - SWP **Exchange** - TSX **CUSIP** - 871003
Head Office - 7750 Beedie Way, Delta, BC, V4G 0A5 **Telephone** - (604) 420-4050 **Toll-free** - (800) 667-6181 **Fax** - (604) 420-8711
Website - www.swisswater.com
Email - icarswell@swisswater.com
Investor Relations - Iain Carswell (800) 667-6181
Auditors - MNP LLP C.A., Vancouver, B.C.
Lawyers - Cassels Brock & Blackwell LLP
Transfer Agents - Computershare Trust Company of Canada Inc.
FP500 Revenue Ranking - 683
Employees - 90 at Dec. 31, 2022

Profile - (Can. 2010) Manufactures, using the Swiss Water® process, chemical-free decaffeinated green coffee in British Columbia, and markets the coffee and offers a complete range of coffee handling and storage services across North America and Europe.

The Swiss Water® process is a chemical-free green coffee decaffeinator. The company decaffeinates coffee owned by customers under toll arrangements and also buys its own premium quality Arabica coffee, which it decaffeinates and sells to the specialty coffee trade. The decaffeinated green coffee is sold to various specialty roaster retailers, specialty coffee importers and commercial coffee roasters in North America. The coffee is also marketed in other international markets through regional distributors. Operations are conducted from a 38,000-sq.-ft. leased facility in Burnaby, B.C., and a 96,000-sq.-ft. leased facility in Delta B.C. A second production line at its Delta location is under construction which is expected to be completed and fully commissioned in late 2023.

Wholly owned **Seaforth Supply Chain Solutions Inc.** provides green coffee logistics services, including devanning coffee received from origin; inspecting, weighing and sampling coffees; and storing, handling and preparing green coffee for outbound shipments. Also handles and stores coffees for several other coffee importers and brokers in Metro Vancouver. Seaforth operates out of one leased warehouse in Delta.

Predecessor Detail - Name changed from Ten Peaks Coffee Company Inc., Sept. 28, 2018, upon the concurrent amalgamation of wholly owned Swiss Water Decaffeinated Coffee Company Inc. into the company.

Directors - Alan C. Wallace, chr., B.C.; Frank A. Dennis, pres. & CEO, Vancouver, B.C.; Justin Jacobs, Fla.; Robert B. Johnston, Isle of Palms, S.C.; Nancy L. McKenzie, Lions Bay, B.C.; Donald J. (Don) Tringali, Phoenix, Ariz.; Roland W. Veit, Fla.

Other Exec. Officers - Marisol Pinzon, man. dir., trading & devel.; Iain Carswell, CFO; Barry Close, v-p, opers.; Emmanuel Dias, v-p, Europe; Dylan Easterbrook, contr.

Capital Stock

	Authorized (shs.)	Outstanding (shs.)[1]
Preferred	unlimited	
Class A		nil
Class B		nil
Common	unlimited	9,212,955

[1] At Mar. 29, 2023

Major Shareholder - Widely held at Mar. 29, 2023.

Price Range - SWP/TSX

Year	Volume	High	Low	Close
2022	1,232,772	$3.40	$2.27	$2.31
2021	2,464,747	$3.87	$2.83	$3.11
2020	4,756,614	$7.00	$2.30	$3.06
2019	3,364,811	$7.33	$4.85	$6.92
2018	3,299,245	$7.24	$4.51	$4.97

Recent Close: $2.70

Capital Stock Changes - In May 2022, new classes of an unlimited number of class A and class B preferred shares were created. Also during 2022, 36,142 common shares were issued under restricted share unit plan.

Wholly Owned Subsidiaries

Seaforth Supply Chain Solutions Inc., Coquitlam, B.C.
Swiss Water Decaffeinated Coffee Co. USA, Inc., Wash.
Swiss Water Decaffeinated Coffee Europe S.A.R.L., France.

Financial Statistics

Periods ended:	12m Dec. 31/22[A]		12m Dec. 31/21[A]
	$000s	%Chg	$000s
Operating revenue	**176,935**	**+41**	**125,076**
Cost of sales	144,347		101,865
General & admin expense	12,189		10,317
Operating expense	**156,536**	**+40**	**112,182**
Operating income	**20,399**	**+58**	**12,894**
Deprec., depl. & amort.	7,018		6,208
Finance income	509		442
Finance costs, gross	5,567		4,364
Pre-tax income	**3,206**	**+219**	**1,005**
Income taxes	819		509
Net income	**2,387**	**+381**	**496**
Cash & equivalent	3,761		4,250
Inventories	60,248		35,308
Accounts receivable	20,732		14,075
Current assets	90,412		60,168
Fixed assets, net	128,123		106,654
Intangibles, net	110		375
Total assets	**219,039**	**+30**	**168,245**
Accts. pay. & accr. liabs	35,229		15,260
Current liabilities	40,728		41,867
Long-term debt, gross	95,754		66,852
Long-term debt, net	95,563		43,436
Long-term lease liabilities	18,256		19,926
Shareholders' equity	54,906		55,595
Cash from oper. activs	**(1,042)**	**n.a.**	**(6,377)**
Cash from fin. activs	25,158		21,594
Cash from invest. activs	(24,605)		(13,716)
Net cash position	**3,761**	**-12**	**4,250**
Capital expenditures	(25,966)		(13,716)
	$		$
Earnings per share*	0.26		0.05
Cash flow per share*	(0.11)		(0.70)
	shs		shs
No. of shs. o/s*	9,165,815		9,129,673
Avg. no. of shs. o/s*	9,158,161		9,122,283
	%		%
Net profit margin	1.35		0.40
Return on equity	4.32		0.91
Return on assets	3.37		1.72
Foreign sales percent	74		69
No. of employees (FTEs)	90		90

* Common
[A] Reported in accordance with IFRS

Historical Summary
(as originally stated)

Fiscal Year	Oper. Rev. $000s	Net Inc. Bef. Disc. $000s	EPS* $
2022[A]	176,935	2,387	0.26
2021[A]	125,076	496	0.05
2020[A]	97,571	2,949	0.32
2019[A]	97,230	2,944	0.32
2018[A]	89,939	4,531	0.50

* Common
[A] Reported in accordance with IFRS

S.149 Sylogist Ltd.

Symbol - SYZ **Exchange** - TSX **CUSIP** - 87132P
Head Office - 102-5 Richard Way SW, Calgary, AB, T3E 7M8 **Telephone** - (403) 266-4808 **Toll-free** - (888) 330-3875 **Fax** - (403) 233-0845
Website - www.sylogist.com
Email - rudy.shirra@sylogist.com
Investor Relations - Rudy Shirra (888) 266-4808
Auditors - KPMG LLP C.A., Calgary, Alta.
Bankers - The Toronto-Dominion Bank, Edmonton, Alta.
Lawyers - Borden Ladner Gervais LLP, Calgary, Alta.
Transfer Agents - Computershare Trust Company of Canada Inc., Calgary, Alta.
Employees - 200 at Dec. 31, 2022

Profile - (Alta. 1993) Provides Software-as-a-Service (SaaS) solutions across government, nonprofit and education sectors worldwide.

Core platforms include: SylogistMission, a dollar raised to dollar delivered modular suite that includes enterprise resource planning (ERP), donor and volunteer engagement, fundraising, grants management, outcomes measurement, analytics and online giving for non-profit and non-governmental organizations; SylogistEd, an ERP, student information, scheduling and grading, lunchroom, fees and payments platform for the education market; and SylogistGov, a SaaS municipal government and citizen engagement platform which includes a fully integrated ERP, taxation, utility billing, asset management, budgeting, citizen engagement, permits and licensing, analytics and online payment solution for local governments, as well as criminal justice case management.

Also offers Portal Connector, a modern low/no code solution enabling clients to build and integrate customer-facing web applications with

Microsoft Dynamics; SylogistPay, which provides payment card industry and Europay, MasterCard, and Visa and PCI-compliant payment processing services, including card-not-present transactions, ACH and EMV payments; NaviPayroll, a fully-integrated, add-in payroll and human resources software solution for use with the SylogistMission ERP platform and Microsoft Dynamics 365 Business Central; SAVIN 360, a victim notification solution for state-level criminal justice agencies; Grants Manager Plus, which simplifies the grants process from initial solicitation through review, scoring, award, payment processing and post award reporting; GovCon, which uses Dynamic 365 to automate business processes, capture market intelligence & administer proposal management; Bellamy platform, an ERP and payroll solution for municipalities, school districts, and rural electrification associations in western Canada; SunPac platform, an ERP and payroll solution for local education agencies in North Carolina; NaviTrak, a materials synchronization solution for manufacturing operations that provides work order status by tracking the availability and movement of materials assigned to production work orders; NaviNet, a data collection service that captures data from a wide variety of shop floor systems and data collection devices, thereafter distributing processed data to a multitude of systems, including ERP and enterprise systems; NaviBridge, a suite of robust integration and administration tools to setup, integrate, monitor and manage data transfers between ERP (SAP, Oracle, and others) and legacy systems, distributed mobile systems and web-based applications; NaviView Terminal, an industrial-strength touch-screen terminal that securely runs any application, including NaviTrak manufacturing or warehousing solutions, or an ERP, CRM, supply chain management or warehouse management system; and professional services, which offers configuring solutions, integrating customers with other systems, and training customers in their use.

The company is headquartered in Calgary, Alta., with additional offices in Barrie, Ont.; Littleton, Colo.; Shawnee, Okla.; Washington, D.C.; and Oxford, U.K.

In January 2023, wholly owned **FPA Group Inc.** and **The Pavlik Group Inc.** were amalgamated into the company.

In November 2022, the company changed its year end to December 31 from September 30.

In October 2022, wholly owned **Mission CRM Ltd.** was amalgamated into the company.

Predecessor Detail - Name changed from Sylogist Inc., Dec. 4, 2002; basis 1 new for 7 old shs.

Directors - Barry D. A. Foster, chr., Ont.; William C. (Bill) Wood, pres. & CEO, Mass.; Taylor Gray, Alta.; Ian M. McKinnon, Toronto, Ont.; Errol Olsen, B.C.; Craig O'Neill, Ont.

Other Exec. Officers - Sujeet Kini, CFO & corp. sec.; Theresa (Terry) LoPresti, chief tech. & innovation officer; Grant McLarnon, chief revenue officer; Donna Smiley, chief cust. officer; Tracey Harder, v-p, talent & engagement; Xavier Shorter, v-p, fin. & opers.

Capital Stock

	Authorized (shs.)	Outstanding (shs.)[1]
Common	unlimited	23,634,877

[1] At May 19, 2023

Normal Course Issuer Bid - The company plans to make normal course purchases of up to 2,281,177 common shares representing 10% of the public float. The bid commenced on Nov. 17, 2022, and expires on Nov. 16, 2023.

Major Shareholder - PenderFund Capital Management Ltd. held 14.03% interest and Seymour Investment Management Ltd. held 10.06% interest at May 19, 2023.

Price Range - SYZ/TSX

Year	Volume	High	Low	Close
2022	12,838,401	$12.95	$4.08	$6.16
2021	17,587,211	$18.18	$9.80	$12.89
2020	8,265,052	$12.30	$6.16	$11.80
2019	3,142,596	$14.15	$9.21	$9.85
2018	4,021,793	$14.76	$8.75	$12.51

Recent Close: $7.82

Capital Stock Changes - During 2022, 15,000 common shares were issued on exercise of options and 86,100 common shares were repurchased under a Normal Course Issuer Bid.

Dividends

SYZ com Ra $0.04 pa Q est. Dec. 14, 2022
Listed Mar 31/21.
Prev. Rate: $0.50 est. Sept. 10, 2020

Wholly Owned Subsidiaries

Serenic Software (UK) Limited, United Kingdom.
Sylogist U.S.A. Inc.
- 100% int. in **Information Strategies, Inc.**, Washington, D.C.
- 100% int. in **Municipal Accounting Systems, Inc.**, Okla.
- 100% int. in **Serenic Software, Inc.**, Lakewood, Colo.
- 100% int. in **Serenic Software (US) Corporation**, Wash.

Financial Statistics

Periods ended:	15m Dec. 31/22[A]		12m Sept. 30/21[A]
	$000s	%Chg	$000s
Operating revenue	**69,000**	**n.a.**	**38,675**
Cost of sales	25,446		10,710
Research & devel. expense	5,363		1,881
General & admin expense	17,297		8,931
Stock-based compensation	1,081		2,778
Operating expense	**49,187**	**n.a.**	**24,300**
Operating income	**19,813**	**n.a.**	**14,375**
Deprec., depl. & amort.	12,929		6,669
Finance income	50		15
Finance costs, gross	1,428		247
Pre-tax income	**2,948**	**n.a.**	**6,276**
Income taxes	407		1,903
Net income	**2,541**	**n.a.**	**4,373**
Cash & equivalent	14,544		29,588
Inventories	211		218
Accounts receivable	6,394		1,985
Current assets	24,456		33,567
Fixed assets, net	985		817
Right-of-use assets	691		796
Intangibles, net	73,912		62,853
Total assets	**100,044**	**n.a.**	**98,033**
Bank indebtedness	21,210		18,210
Accts. pay. & accr. liabs	4,640		3,491
Current liabilities	47,893		39,774
Long-term lease liabilities	491		570
Shareholders' equity	39,905		46,694
Cash from oper. activs	**13,967**	**n.a.**	**18,822**
Cash from fin. activs	(11,319)		7,774
Cash from invest. activs	(17,685)		(38,398)
Net cash position	**14,544**	**n.a.**	**29,588**
Capital expenditures	(242)		(88)
	$		$
Earnings per share*	0.11		0.18
Cash flow per share*	0.58		0.79
Cash divd. per share*	0.51		0.50
	shs		shs
No. of shs. o/s*	23,829,777		23,900,877
Avg. no. of shs. o/s*	23,908,268		23,849,461
	%		%
Net profit margin	...		11.31
Return on equity	...		8.87
Return on assets	...		5.38
Foreign sales percent	63		56
No. of employees (FTEs)	200		100

* Common
[A] Reported in accordance with IFRS

Latest Results

Periods ended:	3m Mar. 31/23[A]
	$000s
Operating revenue	15,925
Net income	103
	$
Earnings per share*	0.00

* Common
[A] Reported in accordance with IFRS

Historical Summary
(as originally stated)

Fiscal Year	Oper. Rev.	Net Inc. Bef. Disc.	EPS*
	$000s	$000s	$
2022[A1]	69,000	2,541	0.11
2021[A]	38,675	4,373	0.18
2020[A]	38,079	1,924	0.08
2019[A]	37,612	10,009	0.44
2018[A]	38,192	13,172	0.59

* Common
[A] Reported in accordance with IFRS
[1] 15 months ended Dec. 31, 2022.

S.150 Symphony Floating Rate Senior Loan Fund

Symbol - SSF.UN **Exchange** - TSX **CUSIP** - 87158A
Head Office - c/o Brompton Group Limited, Bay Wellington Tower, Brookfield Place, 2930-181 Bay St, PO Box 793, Toronto, ON, M5J 2T3 **Telephone** - (416) 642-9061 **Toll-free** - (866) 642-6001 **Fax** - (416) 642-6001
Website - www.bromptongroup.com
Email - wong@bromptongroup.com
Investor Relations - Ann P. Wong (866) 642-6001
Auditors - PricewaterhouseCoopers LLP C.A., Toronto, Ont.
Transfer Agents - TSX Trust Company, Toronto, Ont.
Trustees - TSX Trust Company, Toronto, Ont.
Investment Managers - Symphony Asset Management LLC, San Francisco, Calif.
Managers - Brompton Funds Limited, Toronto, Ont.
Portfolio Managers - Brompton Funds Limited, Toronto, Ont.

Profile - (Ont. 2011) Invests in an actively managed portfolio of short-duration floating rate senior secured loans and other senior debt obligations of North American non-investment grade corporate borrowers.

Senior loans have a first-priority secured claim on repayment ahead of other debt and equity, are secured by the borrower's assets, and offer a high level of income and low interest rate risk compared to traditional fixed income asset classes. These loans are typically used to finance mergers and acquisitions, leverage buyouts, recapitalizations, refinancings, capital expenditure and for other general corporate purposes. Senior loans are usually originated by a bank or other financial institution and syndicated to a pool of lenders that collaborate to provide financing for the borrower. Once the loan is issued, lenders have the option to hold their portion for the life of the loan or to sell it to other investors in the secondary market.

Up to 20% of the portfolio may be invested in other non-investment grade corporate debt instruments including second lien loans, high yield bonds and other investments. The fund does not have a fixed termination date but may be terminated upon the approval of the unitholders.

Portfolio allocation at Mar. 31, 2023 (as a percentage of net asset value):

Sector	Percentage
Senior loans	139.4%
Fixed income investments	4.7%
Equities	13.7%
Cash & short-term investments	3.3%
Currency forward contracts	(0.2%)
Other net liabilities	(60.9%)

Oper. Subsid./Mgt. Co. Directors - Mark A. Caranci, pres. & CEO, Toronto, Ont.; Ann P. Wong, CFO, Toronto, Ont.; Christopher S. L. Hoffmann, Toronto, Ont.; Raymond R. Pether, Toronto, Ont.

Oper. Subsid./Mgt. Co. Officers - Laura Lau, chief invest. officer; Kathryn A. H. Banner, sr. v-p & corp. sec.; Michael D. Clare, sr. v-p & sr. portfolio mgr.; Christopher Cullen, sr. v-p; Manith (Manny) Phanvongsa, sr. v-p; Michelle L. Tiraborelli, sr. v-p

Capital Stock

	Authorized (shs.)	Outstanding (shs.)[1]
Class A Unit	unlimited	7,447,776
Class U Unit	unlimited	251,996
Class B Unit	unlimited	nil
Class C Unit	unlimited	nil
Class F Unit	unlimited	nil

[1] At Dec. 31, 2022

Class A and U Unit - Entitled to monthly cash distributions of Cdn$0.04 per class A unit and US$0.04 per class U unit, respectively (representing a yield of 4.8% per annum on the original issue price). Retractable in March of each year at a price equal to the net asset value (NAV) per unit less any costs associated with the retraction. Class A units are retractable in any other month at a price equal to the lesser of: (i) 94% of the weighted average price per unit on the TSX for the 10 trading days immediately preceding the retraction date; and (ii) the closing price per unit. Class U units are retractable in any other month for an amount equal to the U.S. dollar equivalent of the product of: (i) the class A monthly retraction amount; and (ii) a fraction, the numerator of which is the most recently calculated NAV per class U unit and the denominator of which is the most recently calculated NAV per class A unit. Class U units are convertible into class A units on a weekly basis at a ratio based on the NAV per class U unit divided by the NAV per class A unit. Class A units are for investors wishing to make their investment in Canadian dollars and class U units are for investors wishing to make their investment in U.S. dollars. One vote per unit.

Class B, C and F Unit - Entitled to monthly distributions of Cdn$0.045 per unit. Retractable in March of each year at a price equal to the NAV per unit less any costs associated with the retraction. Retractable in any other month at a price equal to the lesser of: (i) 94% of the weighted average price per class A unit on the TSX for the 10 trading days immediately preceding the retraction date; and (ii) the closing price per class A unit. Convertible into class A units on the first and 10th business day of each month at a ratio based on the NAV per class B, class C or class F unit divided by the NAV per class A unit. One vote per unit.

Normal Course Issuer Bid - The company plans to make normal course purchases of up to 741,000 class A units representing 10% of the public float. The bid commenced on Nov. 21, 2022, and expires on Nov. 20, 2023.

Major Shareholder - Richardson Wealth Limited held 10.5% interest at Mar. 1, 2023.

Price Range - SSF.UN/TSX

Year	Volume	High	Low	Close
2022	1,335,443	$8.98	$6.19	$6.56
2021	1,444,842	$8.39	$7.11	$7.85
2020	2,336,108	$8.36	$3.10	$7.12
2019	2,313,015	$8.62	$7.80	$8.11
2018	2,562,412	$9.08	$7.85	$7.92

Recent Close: $6.56

Capital Stock Changes - In June 2022, public offering of 526,535 class A units and 195,590 class F units was completed at $7.65 and $7.5259 per unit, respectively; the class F units were immediately converted into class A units on a 1-for-1 basis. Also during 2022, 6,372 class A units were issued under dividend reinvestment plan and 71,728 class A units were issued on conversion of 5,937 class U and 33,500 class C units and 26,500 class F units. In addition, 209,541 class A and 5,000 class F units were retracted and 127,300 class A units were repurchased under Normal Course Issuer Bid.

Dividends

SSF.UN cl A unit Ra $0.60 pa M est. Aug. 15, 2022**
Prev. Rate: $0.51 est. May 13, 2022
Prev. Rate: $0.48 est. Aug. 17, 2020
** Reinvestment Option

Financial Statistics

Periods ended:	12m Dec. 31/22[A]		12m Dec. 31/21[A]
	$000s	%Chg	$000s
Realized invest. gain (loss)	(2,393)		(805)
Unrealized invest. gain (loss)	(2,554)		6,414
Total revenue	**(1,865)**	**n.a.**	**9,747**
General & admin. expense	1,048		1,127
Operating expense	**1,048**	**-7**	**1,127**
Operating income	**(2,913)**	**n.a.**	**8,620**
Finance costs, gross	983		536
Pre-tax income	**(3,921)**	**n.a.**	**8,084**
Net income	**(3,921)**	**n.a.**	**8,084**
Cash & equivalent	476		nil
Accounts receivable	8,401		6,638
Investments	87,950		89,800
Total assets	**96,962**	**-1**	**98,358**
Bank indebtedness	nil		1,400
Accts. pay. & accr. liabs	8,769		8,496
Debt	33,173		29,347
Shareholders' equity	52,605		57,877
Cash from oper. activs	**1,465**	**-88**	**12,672**
Cash from fin. activs	346		(18,770)
Net cash position	**476**	**n.a.**	**(1,400)**
	$		$
Earnings per share*	(0.54)		1.02
Earnings per share**	(0.38)		1.00
Cash flow per share***	0.19		1.64
Net asset value per share*	6.76		7.85
Cash divd. per share*	0.55		0.48
	shs		shs
No. of shs. o/s***	7,699,772		7,242,315
Avg. no. of shs. o/s***	7,582,804		7,726,691
	%		%
Net profit margin	n.m.		82.94
Return on equity	(7.10)		12.80
Return on assets	(3.01)		8.43

* Cl.A Unit
** Cl.U Unit
*** Cl.A Unit & Cl.U Unit
[A] Reported in accordance with IFRS

Historical Summary
(as originally stated)

Fiscal Year	Total Rev.	Net Inc. Bef. Disc.	EPS*
	$000s	$000s	$
2022[A]	(1,865)	(3,921)	(0.54)
2021[A]	9,747	8,084	1.02
2020[A]	(5,128)	(7,158)	(0.72)
2019[A]	11,515	7,825	0.70
2018[A]	3,873	(18)	(0.05)

* Cl.A Unit
[A] Reported in accordance with IFRS

S.151 Synex Renewable Energy Corporation*

Symbol - SXI **Exchange** - TSX **CUSIP** - 87168M
Head Office - 4248 Broughton Ave, Niagara Falls, ON, L2E 0A4
Telephone - (604) 688-8271 **Fax** - (604) 688-1286
Website - www.synex.com
Email - daniel.russell@synex.com
Investor Relations - Daniel J. Russell (905) 329-5000
Auditors - Dale Matheson Carr-Hilton LaBonte LLP C.A., Vancouver, B.C.
Bankers - Bank of Montreal, Toronto, Ont.
Lawyers - Dentons Canada LLP, Vancouver, B.C.
Transfer Agents - Computershare Trust Company of Canada Inc., Vancouver, B.C.
Employees - 5 at Sept. 28, 2022

Profile - (B.C. 1982) Owns and operates three hydroelectric facilities totaling 11 MW and a regulated electrical distribution utility; holds a minority interest in a 6.5-MW hydroelectric plant; and owns 17 investigative wind licences, all in British Columbia. Also provides consulting engineering services in water resources and hydropower development.

Operations are carried out through four wholly owned subsidiaries: **Synex Energy Resources Ltd.** and **Kyuquot Power Ltd.**, which represent the Power Division; **Sea Breeze Power Corp.**, which represents the Wind Division; and **Sigma Engineering Ltd.**, which represents the Engineering Division.

The **Power Division** consists of the 3.8-MW Mears Creek and the 2.8-MW Cypress Creek hydroelectric plants near Gold River; the 4.4-MW Barr Creek hydroelectric plant (80% owned) near Zeballos; 12.5% interest in **Upnit Power Limited Partnership**, which owns and operates the 6.5-MW China Creek hydroelectric plant near Port Alberni on Vancouver Island; and the distribution and sale of electricity near Kyuquot on Vancouver Island. The remaining 20% interest in Barr Creek is held by Ehattesaht First Nation.

Projects under development include the 5.2-MW McKelvie Creek hydroelectric project near Tahsis; the 4.4-MW Newcastle Creek hydroelectric project near Sayward; and the 9.9-MW Victoria Lake hydroelectric project near Port Alice, all on Vancouver Island.

The **Wind Division** consists of 17 investigative licences suitable for wind, solar and storage sites located in four regions of British Columbia: Northern Vancouver Island, Central coast, Okanagan and East Kootenay. The licences have a potential power of up to 4,850 MW.

The **Engineering Division** focuses on the management and development of the company's power assets and development sites.

Periods ended:	12m June 30/22	12m June 30/21
Electric sales, GWh	35	39

Predecessor Detail - Name changed from Synex International Inc., Jan. 31, 2022; basis 1 new for 10 old shs.

Directors - Tanya L. DeAngelis, chr. & corp. sec., Ont.; Daniel J. Russell, pres. & CEO, Burlington, Ont.; Richard McGivern, Alta.; Adarsh Mehta, Ont.; Paul J. O'Sullivan, Gabriola, B.C.; Danny Sgro, Ont.

Other Exec. Officers - Hari Rupawala, CFO

Capital Stock

	Authorized (shs.)	Outstanding (shs.)[1]
Common	100,000,000	4,175,189

[1] At May 15, 2023

Options - At June 30, 2022, 55,000 options were outstanding to purchase common shares at a weighted average price of $3.64 per share with a weighted average remaining life of 19 months.

Major Shareholder - Daniel J. Russell held 56.96% interest at Oct. 20, 2022.

Price Range - SXI/TSX

Year	Volume	High	Low	Close
2022	439,076	$3.28	$2.40	$2.70
2021	613,188	$4.60	$2.25	$2.90
2020	56,815	$2.90	$1.40	$2.20
2019	133,800	$4.10	$1.35	$2.20
2018	579,258	$5.10	$3.00	$3.55

Consolidation: 1-for-10 cons. in Feb. 2022
Recent Close: $1.83

Capital Stock Changes - In June 2023, private placement of 167,597 common shares was completed at $1.79 per share.

On Feb. 3, 2022, common shares were consolidated on a 1-for-10 basis. During fiscal 2022, 59,000 post-consolidated common shares were issued on exercise of options.

Long-Term Debt - At June 30, 2022, outstanding long-term debt totaled $14,612,407 ($878,505 current) and consisted of various loans bearing interest at rates ranging from 4.26% to 4.767% due to June 2045.

Minimum long-term debt repayments were reported as follows:

2023	$878,505
2024	635,192
2025	487,905
2026	517,994
Thereafter	12,092,811

Wholly Owned Subsidiaries

Sigma Engineering Ltd., St. John's, N.L.
Synex Energy Resources Ltd., B.C.
- 80% int. in **Barr Creek Hydro Ltd.**, Canada.
- 80% int. in **Barr Creek Limited Partnership**
- 100% int. in **Kyuquot Power Ltd.**, B.C.
- 100% int. in **Sea Breeze Power Corp.**, Vancouver, B.C.
- 12.5% int. in **Upnit Power Limited Partnership**
- 50% int. in **Victoria Lake Hyrdo Ltd. Partnership**, Canada.

Note: The preceding list includes only the major related companies in which interests are held.

Financial Statistics

Periods ended:	12m June 30/22[A]		12m June 30/21[A]
	$000s	%Chg	$000s
Operating revenue	**3,346**	**-5**	**3,532**
Salaries & benefits	727		999
General & admin expense	1,492		968
Stock-based compensation	nil		58
Other operating expense	159		260
Operating expense	**2,378**	**+4**	**2,285**
Operating income	**968**	**-22**	**1,247**
Deprec., depl. & amort	940		896
Finance income	nil		5
Finance costs, gross	738		1,386
Pre-tax income	**(673)**	**n.a.**	**(874)**
Net income	**(673)**	**n.a.**	**(874)**
Net inc. for equity hldrs	**(664)**	**n.a.**	**(849)**
Net inc. for non-cont. int	**(9)**	**n.a.**	**(25)**
Cash & equivalent	626		1,074
Accounts receivable	539		829
Current assets	1,249		1,965
Long-term investments	172		134
Fixed assets, net	18,548		19,224
Total assets	**21,727**	**-6**	**23,132**
Accts. pay. & accr. liabs	703		572
Current liabilities	1,684		1,504
Long-term debt, gross	14,612		15,442
Long-term debt, net	13,734		14,612
Shareholders' equity	4,546		5,076
Non-controlling interest	483		597
Cash from oper. activs	**568**	**n.a.**	**(364)**
Cash from fin. activs	(802)		2,101
Cash from invest. activs	(272)		73
Net cash position	**2,165**	**-19**	**2,670**
Capital expenditures	(271)		(198)
	$		$
Earnings per share*	(0.17)		(0.22)
Cash flow per share*	0.14		(0.09)
	shs		shs
No. of shs. o/s*	4,011,511		3,952,514
Avg. no. of shs. o/s*	3,992,859		3,947,807
	%		%
Net profit margin	(20.11)		(24.75)
Return on equity	(13.80)		(15.54)
Return on assets	0.29		2.28

* Common
[A] Reported in accordance with IFRS

Latest Results

Periods ended:	9m Mar. 31/23[A]		9m Mar. 31/22[A]
	$000s	%Chg	$000s
Operating revenue	1,489	-37	2,353
Net income	(1,613)	n.a.	(435)
Net inc. for equity hldrs	(1,544)	n.a.	(458)
Net inc. for non-cont. int	(69)		23
	$		$
Earnings per share*	(0.38)		(0.11)

* Common
[A] Reported in accordance with IFRS

Historical Summary
(as originally stated)

Fiscal Year	Oper. Rev.	Net Inc. Bef. Disc.	EPS*
	$000s	$000s	$
2022[A]	3,346	(673)	(0.17)
2021[A]	3,532	(874)	(0.22)
2020[A]	3,326	(157)	(0.05)
2019[A]	2,879	(8,255)	(2.10)
2018[A]	3,315	(1,145)	(0.30)

* Common
[A] Reported in accordance with IFRS
Note: Adjusted throughout for 1-for-10 cons. in Feb. 2022

T

T.1 TC Energy Corporation*

Symbol - TRP **Exchange** - TSX **CUSIP** - 87807B
Head Office - TC Energy Tower, 450 1 St SW, Calgary, AB, T2P 5H1
Telephone - (403) 920-2000 **Toll-free** - (800) 661-3805
Website - www.tcenergy.com
Email - investor_relations@tcenergy.com
Investor Relations - Gavin Wylie (800) 361-6522
Auditors - KPMG LLP C.A., Calgary, Alta.
Lawyers - Mayer Brown LLP, Chicago, Ill.; Blake, Cassels & Graydon LLP, Calgary, Alta.
Transfer Agents - Computershare Trust Company, Inc., Golden, Colo.; Computershare Trust Company of Canada Inc., Calgary, Alta.
FP500 Revenue Ranking - 41
Employees - 7,477 at Dec. 31, 2022
Profile - (Can. 2003) Holds all outstanding common shares of **TransCanada PipeLines Limited**, a company engaged in natural gas and liquids transmission, electric power generation and storage facilities in Canada, the United States and Mexico.

Operations are carried out through five business segments: Canadian Natural Gas Pipelines; U.S. Natural Gas Pipelines; Mexico Natural Gas Pipelines; Liquids Pipelines; and Power and Energy Solutions.

Canadian Natural Gas Pipelines

Pipelines include the following: (i) the 24,631-km NGTL system which receives, transports and delivers natural gas within Alberta and British Columbia and connects with the Canadian Mainline and Foothills pipelines and with third party pipelines; (ii) the 14,082-km Canadian Mainline system which transports natural gas from the Alberta/Saskatchewan border and the Ontario/U.S. border, serving eastern Canada and interconnects to the U.S.; (iii) the 1,237-km Foothills system which carries natural gas for export from central Alberta to the U.S. border, serving markets in the U.S. Midwest, Pacific Northwest, California and Nevada; (iv) 50% interest in **Trans Québec & Maritimes Pipeline Inc.** (TQM), a 649-km pipeline system which connects with the Canadian Mainline pipeline near the Ontario/Quebec border to transport natural gas to the Montreal to Quebec City corridor, and interconnects with the Portland pipeline system; (v) **Ventures LP**, a 133-km pipeline which transports natural gas to the oil sands region near Fort McMurray, Alta.; and (vi) the 60-km Great Lakes Canada pipeline which transports natural gas from the Great Lakes pipeline system in the U.S. to a point near Dawn, Ont.

Projects under various stages of development include 35% interest in the 670-km Coastal GasLink pipeline which would transport natural gas from the Montney gas-producing region near Dawson Creek, B.C., to **LNG Canada Development Inc.**'s liquefied natural gas processing and export facility under construction in Kitimat, B.C.; and expansion programs on the NGTL and Foothills systems.

U.S. Natural Gas Pipelines

Pipelines include the following: (i) the 18,768-km Columbia Gas system which transports natural gas supply primarily from the Appalachian Basin to markets and pipeline interconnects throughout the U.S. Northeast, Midwest and Atlantic regions, and includes underground natural gas storage facilities with a capacity of 285 bcf; (ii) the 15,075-km ANR system which transports natural gas from various supply basins to markets throughout the U.S. Midwest and Gulf Coast, and includes underground natural gas storage facilities with a capacity of 247 bcf; (iii) the 5,419-km Columbia Gulf system which transports natural gas to various markets and pipeline interconnects in the southern U.S. and Gulf Coast; (iv) the 3,404-km Great Lakes system which connects with the Canadian Mainline pipeline near Emerson, Man., and to the Great Lakes Canada pipeline near St. Clair, Ont., and interconnects with the ANR pipeline at Crystal Falls and Farwell, Mich., serving markets in eastern Canada and the U.S. Midwest; (v) 50% interest in the 2,272-km Northern Border system which connects with the Foothills and Bison pipelines to transport natural gas from Western Canada, Bakken and U.S. Rocky Mountains regions to the U.S. Midwest; (vi) the 2,216-km Gas Transmission Northwest (GTN) system which transports natural gas from Western Canada and the U.S. Rocky Mountains region to Washington, Oregon and California, and connects with the Foothills and Tuscarora pipelines; (vii) 50% interest in the 669-km Iroquois system which connects with the Canadian Mainline pipeline and delivers natural gas to customers in New York; (viii) the 491-km Tuscarora pipeline which transports natural gas from the GTN system at Malin, Ore., to northeastern California and northwestern Nevada; (ix) the 488-km Bison pipeline which transports natural gas from the Powder River Basin in Wyoming to the Northern Border pipeline in North Dakota; (x) 61.7% interest in the 475-km Portland system which connects with the TQM pipeline near East Hereford, Que., to deliver natural gas to customers in the northeastern U.S. and Canadian Maritimes; (xi) 47.5% interest in the 424-km Millennium pipeline which delivers natural gas primarily from the Marcellus play to markets across southern New York and the lower Hudson Valley, as well as to New York City through pipeline interconnections; (xii) the 325-km Crossroads pipeline which operates in Indiana and Ohio with multiple interconnects to other pipelines; and (xiii) the 138-km North Baja system which extends from Ehrenberg, Ariz., to a point near Ogilby, Calif., and connects with a third party pipeline system on the California/Mexico border.

Projects under various stages of development include the 68-km Gillis Access pipeline which would connect supplies from the Haynesville Basin at Gillis, La., to markets elsewhere in Louisiana; expansion of the North Baja, GTN and Columbia Gulf systems through compressor station modifications and additions (North Baja XPress, GTN XPress and East Lateral XPress projects); and replacement and upgrading of certain facilities along the ANR and Columbia Gas systems.

Mexico Natural Gas Pipelines

Holds (i) 60% interest in the 770-km Sur de Texas pipeline which runs offshore in the Gulf of Mexico at the border point near Brownsville, Tex., and ends in Tuxpan, Veracruz state, connecting with the Tamazunchale and Tula pipelines and other third party facilities; (ii) the 572-km Topolobampo pipeline which transports natural gas to El Oro and Topolobampo, Sinaloa state, from interconnects with third party pipelines in El Oro, Sinaloa state, and El Encino, Chihuahua state; (iii) the 430-km Mazatlán pipeline which delivers natural gas from El Oro to Mazatlán, Sinaloa state, and connects to the Topolobampo pipeline at El Oro; (iv) the 370-km Tamazunchale pipeline which extends from Naranjos, Veracruz state, to Tamazunchale, San Luis Potosí state, and on to El Sauz, Querétaro state; (v) the 313-km Guadalajara pipeline which transports natural gas bidirectionally between Manzanillo, Colima state, and Guadalajara, Jalisco state; (vi) the 114-km east section of the 314-km Tula pipeline which receives natural gas from the Sur de Texas pipeline for transport to power plants in Tuxpan; and (vii) the 206-km north section of the 436-km bidirectional Villa de Reyes pipeline which interconnects with the Tamazunchale pipeline and third party systems, supporting natural gas deliveries to a power plant in Villa de Reyes, San Luis Potosí state.

Projects under construction include the 230-km lateral and south sections of the Villa de Reyes pipeline which would connect to the operational north section of the pipeline and the Tula pipeline; the 200-km central and west sections of the Tula pipeline which would interconnect the completed east segment with the Villa de Reyes pipeline at Tula, Hidalgo state, to supply natural gas to combined-cycle power generating facilities in central Mexico; and the 715-km offshore Southeast Gateway pipeline which would connect to the Tula pipeline and transport natural gas to delivery points in Coatzacoalcos, Veracruz state, and Paraíso, Tabasco state.

Liquids Pipelines

Holds the 4,324-km Keystone pipeline which transports crude oil from Hardisty, Alta., to U.S. markets at Wood River and Patoka, Ill., Cushing, Okla., and the U.S. Gulf Coast; the Marketlink pipeline along the Keystone pipeline which transports crude oil from the market hub at Cushing to the U.S. Gulf Coast refining markets; 50% interest in the 460-km Grand Rapids pipeline which connects producing areas northwest of Fort McMurray, Alta., to the Edmonton/Heartland market region of Alberta; and the 72-km White Spruce pipeline which transports crude oil from **Canadian Natural Resources Limited**'s Horizon facility in northeastern Alberta to the Grand Rapids pipeline.

Power and Energy Solutions

This segment includes electrical power generation plants and non-regulated natural gas storage facilities in Canada, as well as interests in new energy solutions, such as hydrogen, pumped storage, carbon capture utilization and storage (CCUS) and renewable natural gas (RNG) projects.

Electrical power generation plants in aggregate represent 4,339 MW of net power generation capacity. Operating facilities include natural gas-fired cogeneration plants at Bear Creek (100 MW), Carseland (95 MW), MacKay River (207 MW) and Redwater (46 MW), all in Alberta; the 550-MW Bécancour natural gas-fired cogeneration plant near Trois-Rivières, Que.; the 90-MW Grandview natural gas-fired cogeneration plant in Saint John, N.B.; and the 6,550-MW Bruce Power (48.3% partnership interest) nuclear power generation facility in Tiverton, Ont., which has eight operating reactors. The Saddlebrook solar and storage project is under construction in Aldersyde, Alta., consisting of an 81-MW solar-generating facility that would operate in conjunction with a 7-MW/40-MWh battery energy storage system.

Unregulated natural gas storage holdings include the 68-bcf Crossfield facility in Crossfield, Alta., and the 50-bcf Edson facility near Edson, Alta., both underground facilities connected to the NGTL system.

New energy projects include 30% interest in an RNG production facility under construction in Lynchburg, Tenn.; the 1,000-MW Ontario pumped storage project, an energy storage facility near Meaford, Ont.; the 75-MW Canyon Creek pumped storage project near Hinton, Alta.; Alberta Carbon Grid, a carbon transportation and sequestration system; and hydrogen production hubs in the U.S. and Canada.

On July 27, 2023, the company announced plans to spin-off its liquids pipelines business into a separate publicly traded company. The company plans that the initial combined dividends of the two companies will be equivalent to its annual dividend immediately prior to the completion of the transaction. Shareholders of the company would retain their current ownership in the company's common shares and receive a pro rata allocation of common shares in the new liquids pipelines company, Closing of the transaction was expected in the second half of 2024.

On Feb. 1, 2023, the company announced updated cost estimates for its 35%-owned 670-km Coastal GasLink pipeline. The estimated costs to complete the project increased to $14.5 billion, excluding potential cost recoveries and includes contingencies for certain factors outside of the company's control. As a result, a pre-tax impairment charge of $3.048 billion ($2.643 billion after-tax) was recognized by the company in the fourth quarter of 2022. The project was targeted to achieve mechanical completion by the end of 2023, with commissioning and clean-up work continuing into 2024 and 2025.

On Aug. 4, 2022, the company and Comisión Federal de Electricidad (CFE), Mexico's state-owned electric utility, announced a strategic partnership to develop natural gas infrastructure in Mexico. The alliance consolidates the existing Transportadora de Gas Natural de la Huasteca (TGNH) assets, including the Tamazunchale, Tula-Villa de Reyes (TVDR) and Tuxpan-Tula (TXTL) pipelines, under a single, U.S. dollar-denominated, take-or-pay Transportation Service Agreement (TSA) that extends through 2055. The parties agreed to mutually terminate presently suspended international arbitrations related to TXTL and TVDR, and subject to final investment decision (FID), complete the TXTL pipeline. The company and the CFE have undertaken an FID to jointly develop and construct the TGNH Southeast Gateway Pipeline, a 1.3-bcf-per-day, 715-km offshore natural gas pipeline, to serve southeast Mexico at a cost of US$4.5 billion. The project was anticipated to be in-service by mid-2025.

On Apr. 25, 2022, the company and **GreenGasUSA**, a portfolio of companies which develop, own and operate renewable natural gas (RNG) assets, announced a strategic collaboration to explore development of a network of natural gas transportation hubs, including RNG. These hubs would provide centralized access to existing energy transportation infrastructure for RNG sources, such as farms, wastewater treatment facilities and landfills. GreenGasUSA would originate RNG and transport it to the RNG hub, while the company would build, own and operate the RNG transportation hubs. The hubs were targeted to be under development in several U.S. states along the company's natural gas pipeline system within the next four years.

Recent Merger and Acquisition Activity

Status: pending **Announced:** July 24, 2023
TC Energy Corporation agreed to sell a 40% interest in Columbia Gas Transmission, LLC and Columbia Gulf Transmission, LLC to Global Infrastructure Partners (GIP) for $5.2 billion. The Columbia Gas and Columbia Gulf pipelines span more than 15,000 miles across North America. Wholly owned Columbia Pipeline Group, Inc. would contribute all of its equity interests in Columbia Gas and Columbia Gulf to newly formed Columbia Pipelines Operating Company, LLC (CPOC), which would be held by newly formed Columbia Pipelines Holding Company, LLC (CPHC), CPHC represents the entity through which TC Energy and GIP would each hold their equity interest. The transaction was expected to close in the fourth quarter of 2023.

Status: completed **Revised:** Feb. 1, 2023
UPDATE: The transaction was completed. PREVIOUS: TC Energy Corporation agreed to acquire the assets of KO Transmission Company for US$80,000,000. The assets consist of an interstate natural gas pipeline system, totaling 89 miles, originating in Means, Ky., and extending to Hamilton, Ohio, and Campbell, Ky. TC Energy would integrate the assets into its Columbia Gas pipeline system.

Status: completed **Announced:** Oct. 17, 2022
TC Energy Corporation acquired a 30% interest in the Lynchburg renewable fuels project, a renewable natural gas (RNG) production facility near the Jack Daniel Distillery in Lynchburg, Tenn., for US$29,300,000. The project was being developed by 3 Rivers Energy Partners, LLC, also an owner of the project, and would produce RNG from a byproduct of the Jack Daniel's distilling process. Completion of the project was expected in 2024.

Status: pending **Announced:** Mar. 9, 2022
TC Energy Corporation signed option agreements to sell a 10% equity interest in Coastal GasLink Pipeline Limited Partnership, which was constructing the $6.6 billion Coastal GasLink Pipeline Project in British Columbia, to Indigenous communities across the project corridor. Terms of the transaction were not disclosed. The Coastal GasLink project consists of the construction of 670 km of pipeline and associated facilities that would have an initial capacity of 2.1 bcf per day and connect Western Canadian Sedimentary Basin natural gas supply from the Dawson Creek, B.C., area to LNG Canada Development Inc.'s liquefaction and export facility being constructed in Kitimat, B.C. The project was 63% complete. The option was exercisable after commercial in-service of the pipeline, subject to regulatory approvals and consents, including the consent of LNG Canada. Upon completion, TC Energy would retain a 25% interest in Coastal GasLink.

Predecessor Detail - Name changed from TransCanada Corporation, May 9, 2019.

Directors - Siim A. Vanaselja, chr., Toronto, Ont.; François L. Poirier, pres. & CEO, Calgary, Alta.; Cheryl F. Campbell, Monument, Colo.; Michael R. Culbert, Calgary, Alta.; William D. (Bill) Johnson, Knoxville, Tenn.; Susan C. Jones, Calgary, Alta.; John E. Lowe, Houston, Tex.; David MacNaughton, Toronto, Ont.; Una M. Power, Vancouver, B.C.; Mary Pat Salomone, Naples, Fla.; Dr. Indira V. Samarasekera, Vancouver, B.C.; Thierry Vandal, Mamaroneck, N.Y.; Dheeraj (D) Verma, Houston, Tex.

Other Exec. Officers - Stanley G. (Stan) Chapman III, exec. v-p & COO, natural gas pipelines; Dawn E. de Lima, exec. v-p, corp. srvcs. & chief inclusion & diversity officer; Corey N. Hessen, exec. v-p & pres., power & energy solutions; Joel E. Hunter, exec. v-p & CFO; Patrick M. Keys, exec. v-p & gen. counsel; Annesley Wallace, exec. v-p, strategy, corp. devel. & energy transition planning; Bevin M. Wirzba, exec. v-p, strategy & corp. devel. & grp. exec., Cdn. natural gas & liquids pipelines; Jawad A. Masud, sr. v-p, technical centre; Patrick C. Muttart, sr. v-p, external rel.; Gloria L. Hartl, v-p, risk mgt.; Dennis P. Hebert, v-p, tax.; Nancy A.

Johnson, v-p & treas.; Christine R. Johnston, v-p, law & corp. sec.; G. Glenn Menuz, v-p & contr.; Jonathan E. (Jon) Wrathall, v-p, fin. & eval.; Gavin Wylie, v-p, IR

Capital Stock

	Authorized (shs.)	Outstanding (shs.)[1]
First Preferred	unlimited	
Series 1		14,577,184
Series 2		7,422,816
Series 3		9,997,177
Series 4		4,002,823
Series 5		12,070,593
Series 6		1,929,407
Series 7		24,000,000
Series 9		18,000,000
Series 11		10,000,000
Second Preferred	unlimited	nil
Common	unlimited	1,029,000,000

[1] At June 30, 2023

First Preferred - Issuable in series and non-voting.

Series 1 - Entitled to cumulative preferential annual dividends of $0.8698 per share payable quarterly to Dec. 31, 2024, and thereafter at a rate reset every five years equal to the five-year Government of Canada bond yield plus 1.92%. Redeemable on Dec. 31, 2024, and on December 31 every five years thereafter at $25 per share plus declared and unpaid dividends. Convertible at the holder's option on Dec. 31, 2024, and on December 31 every five years thereafter, into floating rate first preferred series 2 shares on a share-for-share basis, subject to certain conditions.

Series 2 - Entitled to cumulative preferential dividends payable quarterly equal to the 90-day Canadian Treasury bill rate plus 1.92%. Redeemable on Dec. 31, 2024, and on December 31 every five years thereafter at $25 per share, or at $25.50 per share in the case of redemptions on any other date, plus declared and unpaid dividends. Convertible at the holder's option on Dec. 31, 2024, and on December 31 every five years thereafter, into first preferred series 1 shares on a share-for-share basis, subject to certain conditions.

Series 3 - Entitled to cumulative preferential annual dividends of $0.4235 per share payable quarterly to June 30, 2025, and thereafter at a rate reset every five years equal to the five-year Government of Canada bond yield plus 1.28%. Redeemable on June 30, 2025, and on June 30 every five years thereafter at $25 per share plus declared and unpaid dividends. Convertible at the holder's option on June 30, 2025, and on June 30 every five years thereafter, into floating rate first preferred series 4 shares on a share-for-share basis, subject to certain conditions.

Series 4 - Entitled to cumulative preferential dividends payable quarterly equal to the 90-day Canadian Treasury bill rate plus 1.28%. Redeemable on June 30, 2025, and on June 30 every five years thereafter at $25 per share, or at $25.50 per share in the case of redemptions on any other date, plus declared and unpaid dividends. Convertible at the holder's option on June 30, 2025, and on June 30 every five years thereafter, into first preferred series 3 shares on a share-for-share basis, subject to certain conditions.

Series 5 - Entitled to cumulative preferential annual dividends of $0.4873 per share payable quarterly to Jan. 30, 2026, and thereafter at a rate reset every five years equal to the five-year Government of Canada bond yield plus 1.54%. Redeemable on Jan. 30, 2026, and on January 30 every five years thereafter at $25 per share plus declared and unpaid dividends. Convertible at the holder's option on Jan. 30, 2026, and on January 30 every five years thereafter, into floating rate first preferred series 6 shares on a share-for-share basis, subject to certain conditions.

Series 6 - Entitled to cumulative preferential dividends payable quarterly equal to the 90-day Canadian Treasury bill rate plus 1.54%. Redeemable on Jan. 30, 2026, and on January 30 every five years thereafter at $25 per share, or at $25.50 per share in the case of redemptions on any other date, plus declared and unpaid dividends. Convertible at the holder's option on Jan. 30, 2026, and on January 30 every five years thereafter, into first preferred series 5 shares on a share-for-share basis, subject to certain conditions.

Series 7 - Entitled to cumulative preferential annual dividends of $0.9758 per share payable quarterly to Apr. 30, 2024, and thereafter at a rate reset every five years equal to the five-year Government of Canada bond yield plus 2.38%. Redeemable on Apr. 30, 2024, and on April 30 every five years thereafter at $25 per share plus declared and unpaid dividends. Convertible at the holder's option on Apr. 30, 2024, and on April 30 every five years thereafter, into floating rate first preferred series 8 shares on a share-for-share basis, subject to certain conditions. The series 8 shares would pay a quarterly dividend equal to the 90-day Canadian Treasury bill rate plus 2.38%.

Series 9 - Entitled to cumulative preferential annual dividends of $0.9405 per share payable quarterly to Oct. 30, 2024, and thereafter at a rate reset every five years equal to the five-year Government of Canada bond yield plus 2.35%. Redeemable on Oct. 30, 2024, and on October 30 every five years thereafter at $25 per share plus declared and unpaid dividends. Convertible at the holder's option on Oct. 30, 2024, and on October 30 every five years thereafter, into floating rate first preferred series 10 shares on a share-for-share basis, subject to certain conditions. The series 10 shares would pay a quarterly dividend equal to the 90-day Canadian Treasury bill rate plus 2.35%.

Series 11 - Entitled to cumulative preferential annual dividends of $0.8378 per share payable quarterly to Nov. 28, 2025, and thereafter at a rate reset every five years equal to the five-year Government of Canada bond yield plus 2.96%. Redeemable on Nov. 28, 2025, and on November 28 every five years thereafter at $25 per share plus declared and unpaid dividends. Convertible at the holder's option on Nov. 28, 2025, and on November 28 every five years thereafter, into floating rate first preferred series 12 shares on a share-for-share basis, subject to certain conditions. The series 12 shares would pay a quarterly dividend equal to the 90-day Canadian Treasury bill rate plus 2.96%.

Second Preferred - Issuable in series and non-voting.

Common - One vote per share.

Options - At Dec. 31, 2022, options were outstanding to purchase 6,109,000 common shares at a weighted average exercise price of $63.86 per share with a weighted average remaining contractual life of 4.4 years.

Reserved - At Dec. 31, 2022, an additional 3,656,518 common shares were reserved for future issuance under the option plan.

First Preferred Series 15 (old) - Were entitled to cumulative preferential annual dividends of $1.225 per share payable quarterly to May 31, 2022. Redeemed on May 31, 2022, at $25 per share.

Major Shareholder - Widely held at Mar. 17, 2023.

Price Range - TRP/TSX

Year	Volume	High	Low	Close
2022	1,308,815,602	$74.44	$53.36	$53.98
2021	1,107,302,863	$68.20	$51.26	$58.83
2020	840,240,885	$76.58	$47.05	$51.75
2019	592,328,383	$70.64	$47.98	$69.16
2018	522,198,975	$62.24	$47.90	$48.75

Recent Close: $48.07

Capital Stock Changes - On May 31, 2022, all 40,000,000 first preferred series 15 shares were redeemed at $25 per share. In August 2022, bought deal public offering of 28,400,000 common shares was completed at $63.50 per share. Also during 2022, common shares were issued as follows: 5,916,000 under the dividend reinvestment and share purchase plan and 2,830,000 on exercise of options.

Dividends

TRP com Ra $3.72 pa Q est. Apr. 28, 2023††**
Prev. Rate: $3.60 est. Apr. 29, 2022
Prev. Rate: $3.48 est. Apr. 30, 2021
Prev. Rate: $3.24 est. Apr. 30, 2020

TRP.PR.A pfd 1st ser 1 cum. red. exch. Adj. Ra $0.86975 pa Q est. Mar. 31, 2020**

TRP.PR.B pfd 1st ser 3 cum. red. exch. Adj. Ra $0.4235 pa Q est. Sept. 30, 2020**

TRP.PR.C pfd 1st ser 5 cum. red. exch. Adj. Ra $0.48725 pa Q est. Apr. 30, 2021**

TRP.PR.D pfd 1st ser 7 cum. red. exch. Adj. Ra $0.97575 pa Q est. July 30, 2019**

TRP.PR.E pfd 1st ser 9 cum. red. exch. Adj. Ra $0.9405 pa Q est. Jan. 30, 2020**

TRP.PR.F pfd 1st ser 2 cum. red. exch. Fltg. Ra pa Q**

$0.404077	Sept. 29/23	$0.40414	June 30/23
$0.377276	Mar. 31/23	$0.330066	Dec. 30/22

Paid in 2023: $1.185493 2022: $0.826108 2021: $0.509971

TRP.PR.G pfd 1st ser 11 cum. red. exch. Adj. Ra $0.83775 pa Q est. Feb. 26, 2021**

TRP.PR.H pfd 1st ser 4 cum. red. exch. Fltg. Ra pa Q**

$0.364187	Sept. 29/23	$0.364249	June 30/23
$0.337386	Mar. 31/23	$0.289737	Dec. 30/22

Paid in 2023: $1.065822 2022: $0.666546 2021: $0.349973

TRP.PR.I pfd 1st ser 6 cum. red. exch. Fltg. Ra pa Q**

$0.407825	Oct. 30/23	$0.370669	July 31/23
$0.360185	May 1/23	$0.327167	Jan. 30/23

Paid in 2023: $1.465846 2022: $0.58575 2021: $0.415393

pfd 1st ser 13 cum. red. exch. Adj. Ra $1.375 pa Q est. May 31, 2016**[1]
$0.34375f .... May 31/21

pfd 1st ser 15 cum. red. exch. Adj. Ra $1.225 pa Q est. Feb. 28, 2017**[2]
$0.30625f .... May 31/22

[1] Redeemed May 31, 2021 at $25 per sh.

[2] Redeemed May 31, 2022 at $25 per sh.

†† Currency Option ** Reinvestment Option f Final Payment

Long-Term Debt - Outstanding at Dec. 31, 2022:

TransCanada PipeLines Limited:	
4.9% US$ sr. notes due to 2049	$21,032,000,000
4.5% Cdn$ med.-term notes due to 2052	13,966,000,000
US$ jr. subord. notes due 2067[1]	1,353,000,000
US$ jr. subord. notes due 2075[2]	1,015,000,000
US$ jr. subord. notes due 2076[3]	1,624,000,000
US$ jr. subord. notes due 2077[4]	2,030,000,000
Cdn$ jr. subord. notes due 2077[5]	1,500,000,000
US$ jr. subord. notes due 2079[6]	1,488,000,000
Cdn$ jr. subord. notes due 2081[7]	500,000,000
US$ jr. subord. notes due 2082[8]	1,083,000,000
NOVA Gas Transmission Ltd.:	
7.9% US$ debs. & notes due 2023	271,000,000
9.9% Cdn$ debs. & notes due 2024	100,000,000
7.5% US$ med.-term notes due 2026	44,000,000
7.4% Cdn$ med.-term notes due to 2030	504,000,000
Columbia Pipeline Group, Inc.:	
4.9% US$ sr. notes due to 2045	2,030,000,000
TC PipeLines, LP:	
4.2% US$ sr. notes due to 2027	1,150,000,000
ANR Pipeline Company:	
4.1% US$ sr. notes due to 2037	1,587,000,000
Gas Transmission Northwest LLC:	
4.3% US$ sr. notes due to 2035	440,000,000
Great Lakes Gas Trans. LP:	
7.6% US$ sr. notes due to 2030	198,000,000
Portland Natural Gas Trans. System:	
2.8% US$ sr. notes due to 2031	338,000,000
Tuscarora Gas Trans. Company:	
6.5% US$ term loan due 2024	46,000,000
Fair value adjustments	76,000,000
Less: Unamort. debt disc. & issue costs	337,000,000
	52,038,000,000
Less: Current portion	1,898,000,000
	50,140,000,000

[1] US$1 billion. Bear interest at a floating rate, reset quarterly to three-month LIBOR plus 2.21%.

[2] US$750,000,000. Bear a fixed interest rate of 5.875% until May 20, 2025, converting to a floating rate thereafter.

[3] US$1.2 billion. Bear a fixed interest rate of 6.125% until Aug. 15, 2026, converting to a floating rate thereafter.

[4] US$1.5 billion. Bear a fixed interest rate of 5.55% until Mar. 15, 2027, converting to a floating rate thereafter.

[5] Cdn$1.5 billion. Bear a fixed interest rate of 4.9% until May 18, 2027, converting to a floating rate thereafter.

[6] US$1.1 billion. Bear a fixed interest rate of 5.75% until Sept. 15, 2029, converting to a floating rate thereafter.

[7] Cdn$500,000,000. Bear a fixed interest rate of 4.45% until Mar. 4, 2031, resetting every five years thereafter.

[8] US$800,000,000. Bear a fixed interest rate of 5.85% until Mar. 7, 2032, resetting every five years thereafter.

Principal repayments for the next five years were reported as follows (excluding junior subordinated notes of TransCanada PipeLines Limited):

2023	$1,898,000,000
2024	2,782,000,000
2025	2,827,000,000
2026	2,278,000,000
2027	3,113,000,000

Wholly Owned Subsidiaries

TransCanada PipeLines Limited, Calgary, Alta.

- 35% int. in **Coastal GasLink Pipeline Limited Partnership**, B.C.
- 100% int. in **NOVA Gas Transmission Ltd.**, Calgary, Alta.
- 100% int. in **701671 Alberta Ltd.**, Alta.
  - 100% int. in **TransCanada Energy Ltd.**, Canada.
    - 100% int. in **TransCanada Energy Investment Ltd.**
      - 48.3% int. in **Bruce Power Limited Partnership**, Tiverton, Ont.
- 50% int. in **Trans Québec & Maritimes Pipeline Inc.**, Montréal, Qué.
- 100% int. in **TransCanada Mexican Investments Ltd.**, Alta.
- 100% int. in **TransCanada PipeLine USA Ltd.**, Nev.
  - 100% int. in **Columbia Pipeline Group, Inc.**, Houston, Tex.
    - 100% int. in **Columbia Energy Group**, Wilmington, Del.
      - 84.3% int. in **CPG OpCo LP**
        - 100% int. in **Columbia Energy Ventures, LLC**
        - 100% int. in **Columbia Gas Transmission, LLC**
        - 100% int. in **Columbia Gulf Transmission, LLC**
      - 100% int. in **CPP GP LLC**
    - 100% int. in **Columbia Pipeline Group Services Company**
      - 100% int. in **CPG OpCo GP LLC**
      - 15.7% int. in **CPG OpCo LP**
    - 100% int. in **Crossroads Pipeline Company**
  - 100% int. in **TransCanada American Investments Ltd.**, Del.
    - 50% int. in **Grand Rapids Pipeline Limited Partnership**, Calgary, Alta.
    - 61.7% int. in **Portland Natural Gas Transmission System Partnership**, United States.
    - 100% int. in **TC PipeLines, LP**, Mass.
  - 100% int. in **TransCanada Oil Pipelines Inc.**, Del.
    - 100% int. in **TransCanada Keystone Pipeline, LLC**, Del.
- 100% int. in **TransCanada PipeLines Services Ltd.**, Alta.

Financial Statistics

Periods ended:	12m Dec. 31/22[A]		12m Dec. 31/21[A]
	$000s	%Chg	$000s
Operating revenue	**14,977,000**	**+12**	**13,387,000**
Other operating expense	6,314,000		4,959,000
Operating expense	**6,314,000**	**+27**	**4,959,000**
Operating income	**8,663,000**	**+3**	**8,428,000**
Deprec., depl. & amort.	2,584,000		2,522,000
Finance costs, net	2,258,000		1,893,000
Investment income	1,054,000		898,000
Write-downs/write-offs	(3,619,000)		(3,126,000)
Pre-tax income	**1,374,000**	**-37**	**2,166,000**
Income taxes	589,000		120,000
Net income	**785,000**	**-62**	**2,046,000**
Net inc. for equity hldrs	**748,000**	**-62**	**1,955,000**
Net inc. for non-cont. int	**37,000**	**-59**	**91,000**
Cash & equivalent	620,000		673,000
Inventories	936,000		724,000
Accounts receivable	3,624,000		3,092,000
Current assets	7,332,000		7,423,000
Long-term investments	11,643,000		10,623,000
Fixed assets, net	75,940,000		70,182,000
Intangibles, net	12,843,000		12,582,000
Total assets	**114,348,000**	**+10**	**104,218,000**
Bank indebtedness	6,262,000		5,166,000
Accts. pay. & accr. liabs	4,665,000		4,464,000
Current liabilities	16,907,000		13,041,000
Long-term debt, gross	52,038,000		47,600,000
Long-term debt, net	50,140,000		46,280,000
Long-term lease liabilities	379,000		380,000
Preferred share equity	2,499,000		3,487,000
Shareholders' equity	33,990,000		33,271,000
Non-controlling interest	126,000		125,000
Cash from oper. activs	**6,375,000**	**-7**	**6,890,000**
Cash from fin. activs	487,000		(88,000)
Cash from invest. activs	(7,009,000)		(7,712,000)
Net cash position	**620,000**	**-8**	**673,000**
Capital expenditures	(6,727,000)		(5,924,000)
Capital disposals	nil		35,000
Pension fund surplus	400,000		118,000
	$		$
Earnings per share*	0.64		1.87
Cash flow per share*	6.41		7.08
Cash divd. per share*	3.60		3.48
	shs		shs
No. of shs. o/s*	1,017,962,000		980,816,000
Avg. no. of shs. o/s*	995,000,000		973,000,000
	%		%
Net profit margin	5.24		15.28
Return on equity	2.09		6.35
Return on assets	0.72		2.00
Foreign sales percent	67		66
No. of employees (FTEs)	7,477		7,017

* Common

[A] Reported in accordance with U.S. GAAP

Latest Results

Periods ended:	6m June 30/23[A]		6m June 30/22[A]
	$000s	%Chg	$000s
Operating revenue	7,758,000	+9	7,137,000
Net income	1,626,000	+22	1,331,000
Net inc. for equity hldrs	1,609,000	+23	1,311,000
Net inc. for non-cont. int	17,000		20,000
	$		$
Earnings per share*	1.53		1.27

* Common

[A] Reported in accordance with U.S. GAAP

Historical Summary
(as originally stated)

Fiscal Year	Oper. Rev.	Net Inc. Bef. Disc.	EPS*
	$000s	$000s	$
2022[A]	14,977,000	785,000	0.64
2021[A]	13,387,000	2,046,000	1.87
2020[A]	12,999,000	4,913,000	4.74
2019[A]	13,255,000	4,433,000	4.28
2018[A]	13,679,000	3,517,000	3.92

* Common

[A] Reported in accordance with U.S. GAAP

T.2 TDb Split Corp.

Symbol - XTD **Exchange** - TSX **CUSIP** - 87234Y

Head Office - c/o Quadravest Capital Management Inc., 2510-200 Front St W, PO Box 51, Toronto, ON, M5V 3K2 **Telephone** - (416) 304-4440 **Toll-free** - (877) 478-2372

Website - www.tdbsplit.com

Email - info@quadravest.com

Investor Relations - Shari Payne (877) 478-2372

Auditors - PricewaterhouseCoopers LLP C.A., Toronto, Ont.

Lawyers - Blake, Cassels & Graydon LLP, Toronto, Ont.

Transfer Agents - Computershare Trust Company of Canada Inc., Toronto, Ont.

Investment Managers - Quadravest Capital Management Inc., Toronto, Ont.

Managers - Quadravest Capital Management Inc., Toronto, Ont.

Profile - (Ont. 2007) Holds common shares of **The Toronto-Dominion Bank** (TD Bank) in order to provide a stable yield and downside protection for priority equity shareholders and to enable class A shareholders to participate in any capital appreciation of TD Bank's common shares and to benefit from any increases in the dividends paid by TD Bank on its common shares.

At Nov. 30, 2022, the company held 903,310 common shares of **The Toronto-Dominion Bank** (TD Bank) with a fair value of $80,873,344. To supplement the dividends earned on the investment portfolio and to reduce risk, the company may, from time to time, write covered call options in respect of all or a part of the common shares of TD Bank it holds.

The company has adopted a priority equity protection plan intended to repay the original issue price in full to priority equity shareholders on Dec. 1, 2024. Under the plan, if the net asset value of the company falls below a specified level, the investment manager would sell some of its TD Bank common shares and use the proceeds to acquire (i) qualifying debt securities; or (ii) certain securities and enter into a forward agreement in order to repay priority equity holders the original issue price in the event of further declines in the net asset value of the company.

The company terminates on Dec. 1, 2024, or earlier at the discretion of the manager if the priority equity shares or class A shares are delisted by the TSX or if the net asset value of the company declines to less than $5,000,000. At such time all outstanding priority equity shares and class A shares will be redeemed. The termination date may be extended beyond Dec. 1, 2024, for a further five years and thereafter for additional successive periods of five years as determined by the board of directors.

The investment manager receives a management fee at an annual rate equal to 0.55% of the net asset value of the company calculated and payable monthly in arrears. In addition, the manager receives an administration fee at an annual rate equal to 0.1% of the net asset value of the company calculated and payable monthly in arrears, as well as service fee payable to dealers on the class A shares at a rate of 0.5% per annum.

Directors - S. Wayne Finch, chr., pres. & CEO, Caledon, Ont.; Laura L. Johnson, corp. sec., Oakville, Ont.; Peter F. Cruickshank, Oakville, Ont.; Michael W. Sharp, Toronto, Ont.; John D. Steep, Stratford, Ont.

Other Exec. Officers - Silvia Gomes, CFO

Capital Stock

	Authorized (shs.)	Outstanding (shs.)[1]
Priority Equity	unlimited	6,545,660[2]
Class B	1,000	1,000[2]
Class A	unlimited	6,739,060

[1] At Feb. 23, 2023

[2] Classified as debt.

Priority Equity - Entitled to receive monthly fixed cumulative preferential cash dividends of $0.04375 per share (to yield 5.25% per annum on the original $10 issue price). Retractable at any time for an amount per share equal to the lesser of: (i) $10; and (ii) 98% of the net asset value (NAV) per unit (1 priority equity share and 1 class A share), less the cost to the company of purchasing a class A share in the market for cancellation. Shareholders who concurrently retract a priority equity share and a class A share in December of each year will receive an amount equal to the NAV per unit. All outstanding priority equity shares will be redeemed on Dec. 1, 2024, for an amount equal to the lesser of: (i) $10; and (ii) the NAV per priority share. Rank in priority to class A shares with respect to payment of dividends and in priority to class A and class B shares with respect to repayment of capital on the dissolution, liquidation or winding-up of the company. Non-voting.

Class B - Not entitled to receive dividends. Retractable at $1.00 per share and have a liquidation entitlement of $1.00 per share. Rank subsequent to priority equity and prior to class A shares with respect to repayment of capital on the dissolution, liquidation or winding-up of the company. One vote per share.

Class A - The company will endeavour to pay monthly dividends targeted to be 5¢ per share (to yield 6% per annum on the original $10 issue price). No monthly dividends will be paid as long as any dividends on the priority equity share are in arrears or the NAV per unit is less than or equal to $12.50. Retractable at any time for an amount per share equal to 98% of the NAV per unit less the cost to the company of purchasing a priority equity share in the market for cancellation. Shareholders who concurrently retract a priority equity share and a class A share in December of each year will receive an amount equal to the NAV per unit. All outstanding class A shares will be redeemed on or about Dec. 1, 2024, for an amount equal to the greater of: (i) the difference between the NAV per unit and $10; and (ii) nil. Rank subordinate to priority equity shares with respect to payment of dividends and subordinate to priority equity and class B shares with respect to the repayment of capital on the dissolution, liquidation or winding-up of the company. Non-voting.

Major Shareholder - TDb Split Corp. Holding Trust held 100% interest at Feb. 23, 2023.

Price Range - XTD/TSX

Year	Volume	High	Low	Close
2022	3,931,045	$5.87	$4.35	$4.60
2021	4,601,686	$5.59	$3.06	$5.19
2020	3,803,805	$6.14	$0.99	$3.07
2019	1,492,184	$6.65	$5.66	$5.98
2018	1,595,755	$7.09	$5.10	$5.70

Recent Close: $3.93

Capital Stock Changes - During fiscal 2022, 534,000 priority equity shares and 592,600 class A shares were issued under an at-the-market equity program.

Dividends

XTD cl A N.V. N.S.R. [1]

$0.05	Sept. 8/23	$0.05	Aug. 10/23
$0.05	June 9/23	$0.05	May 10/23

Paid in 2023: $0.35 2022: $0.60 2021: $0.55

XTD.PR.A priority equity sh cum. ret. Ra $0.525 pa M

[1] Monthly divd normally payable in Apr/23 has been omitted.

Financial Statistics

Periods ended:	12m Nov. 30/22[A]		12m Nov. 30/21[A]
	$000s	%Chg	$000s
Realized invest. gain (loss)	1,429		(685)
Unrealized invest. gain (loss)	(2,195)		17,002
Total revenue	**2,500**	**-87**	**19,001**
General & admin. expense	756		730
Other operating expense	193		177
Operating expense	**949**	**+5**	**907**
Operating income	**1,551**	**-91**	**18,094**
Finance costs, gross	3,407		3,303
Pre-tax income	**(1,857)**	**n.a.**	**14,791**
Net income	**(1,857)**	**n.a.**	**14,791**
Cash & equivalent	8,871		1,978
Accounts receivable	1		1
Investments	80,873		85,084
Total assets	**89,745**	**+3**	**87,063**
Accts. pay. & accr. liabs	86		118
Debt	64,758		59,419
Shareholders' equity	24,112		26,906
Cash from oper. activs	**5,845**	**n.a.**	**(19,995)**
Cash from fin. activs	1,048		8,603
Net cash position	**8,871**	**+348**	**1,978**
	$		$
Earnings per share*	(0.30)		2.64
Cash flow per share*	0.95		(3.56)
Net asset value per share*	3.69		4.53
Cash divd. per share*	0.60		0.55
	shs		shs
No. of shs. o/s*	6,534,360		5,941,760
Avg. no. of shs. o/s*	6,144,748		5,612,760
	%		%
Net profit margin	(74.28)		77.84
Return on equity	(7.28)		79.25
Return on assets	1.75		24.52

* Class A

[A] Reported in accordance with IFRS

Note: Net income reflects increase/decrease in net assets from operations.

Historical Summary
(as originally stated)

Fiscal Year	Total Rev.	Net Inc. Bef. Disc.	EPS*
	$000s	$000s	$
2022[A]	2,500	(1,857)	(0.30)
2021[A]	19,001	14,791	2.64
2020[A]	(13,529)	(17,736)	(3.63)
2019[A]	4,169	1,714	0.51
2018[A]	2,441	(56)	(0.02)

* Class A

[A] Reported in accordance with IFRS

T.3 TECSYS Inc.*

Symbol - TCS **Exchange** - TSX **CUSIP** - 878950

Head Office - 800-1 Place Alexis Nihon, Montréal, QC, H3Z 3B8 **Telephone** - (514) 866-0001 **Toll-free** - (800) 922-8649 **Fax** - (514) 866-1805

Website - www.tecsys.com

Email - investor@tecsys.com

Investor Relations - Mark J. Bentler (514) 866-0001

Auditors - KPMG LLP C.A., Montréal, Qué.

Bankers - National Bank of Canada, Montréal, Qué.

Lawyers - McCarthy Tétrault LLP, Montréal, Qué.

Transfer Agents - Computershare Trust Company of Canada Inc., Toronto, Ont.

FP500 Revenue Ranking - 726

Employees - 745 at Apr. 30, 2023

Profile - (Can. 1983) Develops, markets and sells enterprise-wide supply chain management software for distribution, warehousing, transportation logistics, point-of-use and order management to customers in the healthcare, services parts, third-party logistics, retail and general wholesale high volume distribution industries. Also provides related consulting, education and support services.

Vertical markets targeted by the company are healthcare industry, which includes hospitals and hospital supply networks or health systems, healthcare products distributors and healthcare third-party logistics providers; high-volume third-party logistics and complex distribution industry, which includes warehouse-centric distribution operations, omnichannel distributors, giftware and import-to-retail distributors, industrial manufacturers and distributors, general high-volume distributors and third-party logistics providers; and retail industry, which includes omnichannel and multi-channel retailers, and brand owners with direct-to-consumer operations. Software products offer following functionalities: distribution enterprise resource planning, warehouse management, demand planning, order management, procurement, financial management, requisition management, supply management, transportation management, mobile delivery management, radio frequency identification, electronic commerce, business intelligence and value-added services. The company's products run on an open systems platform and therefore support complementary software modules from third parties.

The company also offers related services including implementation, support, advisory and system enhancement, as well as third-party and proprietary hardware products, and complementary third-party software modules.

Revenues generated include Software-as-a-Service subscription fees, which represent the right to access the software platforms in a hosted and managed environment for a period of time; maintenance and support service fees, which are sold with perpetual licences and hardware maintenance services; professional service fees, which includes implementation consulting and training services to clients; licence fees; and hardware sales.

In May 2022, wholly owned **OrderDynamics Corporation** was amalgamated into the company.

Directors - David (Dave) Brereton, exec. chr., Sainte-Anne-de-Bellevue, Qué.; Peter Brereton, pres. & CEO, Pointe-Claire, Qué.; Vernon Lobo†, Toronto, Ont.; David Booth, Va.; Rani Hublou, Los Gatos, Calif.; Kathleen Miller, Fla.; Steve Sasser, Dallas, Tex.

Other Exec. Officers - Mark J. Bentler, CFO & corp. sec.; Vito Calabretta, chief cust. officer; Nancy Cloutier, chief HR officer; Shannon Karl, chief mktg. officer; Bill King, chief revenue officer; Greg MacNeill, sr. v-p, worldwide sales; Martin Schryburt, sr. v-p, product & tech.; Charles Kierpiec, v-p & gen. counsel

† Lead director

Capital Stock

	Authorized (shs.)	Outstanding (shs.)[1]
Class A Preferred	unlimited	nil
Common	unlimited	14,694,143

[1] At July 21, 2023

Major Shareholder - David Brereton & Kathryn Ensign-Brereton collectively held 14.34% interest and Fiera Capital Corporation held 11.9% interest at June 29, 2023.

Price Range - TCS/TSX

Year	Volume	High	Low	Close
2022	4,819,626	$53.72	$24.27	$26.53
2021	5,826,164	$66.58	$39.18	$52.61
2020	4,853,867	$51.00	$13.23	$49.82
2019	1,586,344	$22.58	$10.30	$21.37
2018	1,244,969	$18.48	$11.50	$12.36

Recent Close: $25.86

Capital Stock Changes - During fiscal 2023, 19,942 common shares were issued on exercise of options.

During fiscal 2022, 57,800 common shares were issued on exercise of options.

Dividends

TCS com Ra $0.30 pa Q est. Jan. 6, 2023
Prev. Rate: $0.28 est. Jan. 7, 2022
Prev. Rate: $0.26 est. Jan. 8, 2021

Long-Term Debt - At Apr. 30, 2023, the company had no long-term debt.

Wholly Owned Subsidiaries

Logi-D Holding Inc., Laval, Qué.
- 100% int. in **Logi D Corp.**, Del.
- 100% int. in **Logi D Inc.**, Canada.

TECSYS Europe Limited, London, Middx., United Kingdom.
TECSYS U.S. Inc., Ohio
Tecsys Denmark Holdings ApS, Denmark.
- 100% int. in **Tecsys A/S**, Denmark. Formerly PCSYS A/S.

Financial Statistics

Periods ended:	12m Apr. 30/23[A]		12m Apr. 30/22[A]
	$000s	%Chg	$000s
Operating revenue	**152,424**	**+11**	**137,200**
Cost of sales	82,951		73,895
Research & devel. expense	23,400		19,458
General & admin expense	38,631		34,407
Operating expense	**144,982**	**+13**	**127,760**
Operating income	**7,442**	**-21**	**9,440**
Deprec., depl. & amort.	3,874		4,064
Finance income	686		474
Finance costs, gross	541		999
Pre-tax income	**3,713**	**-32**	**5,424**
Income taxes	1,624		946
Net income	**2,089**	**-53**	**4,478**
Cash & equivalent	37,070		43,243
Inventories	2,768		2,385
Accounts receivable	23,423		17,196
Current assets	76,792		74,440
Fixed assets, net	1,802		2,064
Right-of-use assets	1,708		4,547
Intangibles, net	26,754		27,164
Total assets	**126,916**	**+1**	**125,844**
Accts. pay. & accr. liabs	21,669		16,971
Current liabilities	52,850		43,522
Long-term debt, gross	nil		8,400
Long-term debt, net	nil		7,200
Long-term lease liabilities	2,120		5,181
Shareholders' equity	70,438		68,683
Cash from oper. activs	**7,760**	**+57**	**4,944**
Cash from fin. activs	(8,423)		(5,307)
Cash from invest. activs	(1,106)		(2,385)
Net cash position	**21,235**	**-8**	**23,004**
Capital expenditures	(850)		(733)
	$		$
Earnings per share*	0.14		0.31
Cash flow per share*	0.53		0.34
Cash divd. per share*	0.29		0.27
	shs		shs
No. of shs. o/s*	14,582,837		14,562,895
Avg. no. of shs. o/s*	14,567,839		14,541,263
	%		%
Net profit margin	1.37		3.26
Return on equity	3.00		6.60
Return on assets	1.89		4.16
Foreign sales percent	82		79
No. of employees (FTEs)	745		719

* Common
[A] Reported in accordance with IFRS

Historical Summary
(as originally stated)

Fiscal Year	Oper. Rev.	Net Inc. Bef. Disc.	EPS*
	$000s	$000s	$
2023[A]	152,424	2,089	0.14
2022[A]	137,200	4,478	0.31
2021[A]	122,946	7,188	0.50
2020[A]	102,943	2,346	0.18
2019[A]	74,390	(741)	(0.06)

* Common
[A] Reported in accordance with IFRS

T.4 TELUS Corporation*

Symbol - T **Exchange** - TSX **CUSIP** - 87971M
Head Office - 2300-510 Georgia St W, Vancouver, BC, V6B 0M3
Telephone - (604) 695-6420 **Fax** - (604) 899-9228
Website - www.telus.com
Email - ir@telus.com
Investor Relations - Robert Mitchell (800) 667-4871
Auditors - Deloitte LLP C.A., Vancouver, B.C.
Lawyers - Paul, Weiss, Rifkind, Wharton & Garrison LLP, New York, N.Y.; Norton Rose Fulbright Canada LLP, Toronto, Ont.
Transfer Agents - Computershare Trust Company of Canada Inc., Calgary, Alta.
FP500 Revenue Ranking - 30
Employees - 108,500 at Dec. 31, 2022

Profile - (B.C. 1998) Provides telecommunications technology solutions including mobile and fixed voice and data telecommunications services and products, healthcare software and technology solutions, data management and data analytics-driven smart-food chain and consumer goods services, digitally led customer experiences and related equipment, and customer care and business services. Data services include Internet Protocol (IP), television, hosting, managed information technology and cloud-based services, and home and business security.

Mobile products and services are provided for consumers and businesses across Canada, including data and voice, devices and Internet of Things (IoT). Data and voice services are provided via the company's 4G and 5G network available to over 99% and 83% of Canadians, respectively, at Dec. 31, 2022, for video, social networking, messaging and mobile applications under the TELUS, Koodo Mobile and Public Mobile brands. Devices offered include smartphones, tablets, mobile Internet keys, mobile Wi-Fi devices, machine-to-machine (M2M) modems, digital life devices and wearable technology, such as smart watches and LivingWell Companion®. IoT solutions include M2M connectivity to support Canadian businesses locally and internationally, including asset tracking, fleet management, device estate management, connected worker, remote monitoring, digital signage, premises security, smart hospital solutions, intelligent traffic solutions and data analytics.

Fixed products and services including residential services provided in British Columbia, Alberta and eastern Quebec; business services, automation and security solutions provided across Canada; and healthcare, agriculture and consumer solutions provided globally. Residential services include Internet, offering secure TELUS PureFibre high-speed access with a comprehensive suite of security solutions; Television, offering HD entertainment service with personal video recorder (PVR), video-on-demand and pay-per-view services through Optik TV™ and Pik TV™; and Voice, offering fixed phone service with long distance and advanced calling features, and voice over IP (VoIP). Home and business security and automation services offer 24/7 real-time central monitoring station, guard response service, wireless and hard-wired security accessibility that is integrated with smart devices. IP connectivity for businesses include converged voice, video, data and Internet services on a high performing network; cloud and managed IT services, which offers a suite of hybrid IT solutions providing traditional and cloud technologies, network connectivity, security, managed IT and cloud advisory services; security consulting and managed services, offering cloud and on-premise solutions to secure data, email, websites, networks and applications; unified communications conferencing and collaboration, offering a range of equipment and application solutions to support meetings and webcasts using phone, video and the Internet. Healthcare services, provided through TELUS Health, include virtual care, virtual pharmacy, electronic medical records (EMR), pharmacy management systems, claims management solutions, personal health records, remote patient monitoring, personal emergency response services, mental health support, comprehensive primary care and employee wellness, and curation of health content. Agriculture and Consumer Goods, which include record-keeping and recommendations, rebate management services, supplier management, animal health solutions, food traceability and quality assurance, cold chain tracking, data management and software solutions for trade and promotion, optimization and analytics, retail execution, supply chain solutions and analytics capabilities.

Subsidiary **TELUS International (Cda) Inc.** provides customer care and business services in over 50 languages from 69 delivery locations across 30 countries in North America, Central America, Europe and Asia. Solutions offered include digital experience (DX), customer experience, AI data solutions, and content moderation, serving clients across multiple industry verticals including tech and games, communications and media, ecommerce and fintech, healthcare and travel and hospitality.

In June 2023, the company announced a partnership with Australian electric vehicle (EV) charging company, **Jolt Energy Limited** (JOLT), to install up to 5,000 public DC fast chargers across Canada, running on the company's network. Across the JOLT EV charging network, all electric vehicle drivers would be able to use their JOLT app to access 7 kWh of free charging per day, which equates to 40 to 50 km of range and 15 to 20 minutes of charge time, depending on the vehicle.

In May 2023, the company acquired an additional 2,500,000 multiple voting shares of **TELUS International (Cda) Inc.** held by **Baring Private Equity Asia Pvt. Ltd.** for a purchase price of US$16.90 per share for total consideration of US$42,250,000. The shares represented 1.3% of the outstanding multiple voting shares of TELUS International and 0.9% of all outstanding shares. After giving effect to the purchase, the company held 152,004,019 multiple voting shares and 1,438,013 subordinate voting shares of TELUS International, representing 56.1% of the outstanding shares, 76% of the outstanding multiple voting shares and 73.4% of the outstanding voting rights.

In June 2022, the company acquired an additional 3,000,000 multiple voting shares of **TELUS International (Cda) Inc.** held by **Baring Private Equity Asia Pvt. Ltd.** for a purchase price of US$22 per share for total consideration of US$66,000,000. The shares represent 1.5% of the outstanding multiple voting shares of TELUS International and 1.1% of all outstanding shares. After giving effect to the purchase, the company held 149,504,019 multiple voting shares and no subordinate voting shares of TELUS International, representing 56.17% of the outstanding shares, 74.78% of the outstanding multiple voting shares and 72.38% of the outstanding voting rights.

Periods ended:	12m Dec. 31/22	12m Dec. 31/21
Network access services[1]	1,096,000	1,123,000
Wireless subscribers	12,159,000	11,424,000
Internet subscribers	2,413,000	2,271,000
IPTV subscribers	1,325,000	1,265,000

[1] Excludes business network access services.

Recent Merger and Acquisition Activity

Status: completed **Revised:** Sept. 1, 2022

UPDATE: The transaction was completed. The aggregate consideration payable was paid $1.033 billion in cash and through the issuance of 34,000,000 TELUS common shares. LifeWorks' common shares were delisted from the TSX effective at the close of Sept. 2, 2022. PREVIOUS: TELUS Corporation, through its TELUS Health division, agreed to acquire LifeWorks Inc. for $33 per common share in cash or 1.0642 TELUS common share for each LifeWorks common share held, representing total offer consideration of $2.3 billion, and the assumption of net debt of $600,000,000. Elections to receive the cash or share consideration would be subject to pro-ration to ensure aggregate cash and share consideration each represent 50% of the total transaction consideration.

The agreement provides for a termination fee of $94,000,000, payable by LifeWorks under specified circumstances, as well as a reverse termination fee of $140,000,000, payable by TELUS under other specified circumstances. LifeWorks is a provider of employee and family assistance programs and benefits administration services. The transaction was expected to close in the fourth quarter of 2022. Aug. 4, 2022 - LifeWorks shareholders approved the transaction.

Status: completed **Announced:** June 8, 2022
TELUS Corporation acquired the Canadian customers, assets and operations of Utah-based Vivint Smart Home, Inc., which offers a range of products and services, including home security systems, home automation devices, and energy management systems in the United States and Canada, for $104,000,000.

Status: completed **Announced:** Mar. 29, 2022
TELUS Corporation acquired private Toronto, Ont.-based Sprout Wellness Solutions Inc., which offers a software platform providing health and wellbeing solutions, for an undisclosed amount. The platform, which was incorporated into and available as part of the TELUS Health suite of services, inspires employees to get fit and empowers employers across various industries and countries to manage and quantify their corporate wellness.

Predecessor Detail - Name changed from BCT.TELUS Communications Inc., May 8, 2000.

Directors - The Hon. John P. Manley, chr., Ottawa, Ont.; Darren Entwistle, pres. & CEO, Vancouver, B.C.; Raymond T. (Ray) Chan, Vancouver, B.C.; Hazel Claxton, Toronto, Ont.; Lisa de Wilde, Toronto, Ont.; Victor G. Dodig, Toronto, Ont.; Thomas E. Flynn, Toronto, Ont.; Dr. Mary Jo Haddad, Niagara-on-the-Lake, Ont.; Kathy Kinloch, Vancouver, B.C.; Christine A. Magee, Toronto, Ont.; David L. (Dave) Mowat, Vancouver, B.C.; Marc Parent, Montréal, Qué.; Denise M. Pickett, Toronto, Ont.; W. Sean Willy, Saskatoon, Sask.

Other Exec. Officers - Jill Schnarr, chief commun. & brand officer; Andrea Wood, chief legal & governance officer; Navin Arora, exec. v-p & pres., TELUS bus. solutions; Doug French, exec. v-p & CFO; Tony Geheran, exec. v-p & COO; Zainul Mawji, exec. v-p & pres., consumer solutions; Sandy McIntosh, exec. v-p, people & culture & chief HR officer; Jim Senko, exec. v-p; Gopi Chande, sr. v-p & treas.; Sudhakar (Sid) Kosaraju, pres., TELUS Health; John M. Raines, pres., TELUS Agriculture & consumer goods

Capital Stock

	Authorized (shs.)	Outstanding (shs.)[1]
First Preferred	1,000,000,000	nil
Second Preferred	1,000,000,000	nil
Common	4,000,000,000	1,454,000,000

[1] At July 31, 2023

Major Shareholder - Widely held at Mar. 6, 2023.

Price Range - T/TSX

Year	Volume	High	Low	Close
2022	687,588,996	$34.65	$25.94	$26.13
2021	658,252,067	$30.04	$24.93	$29.79
2020	667,136,443	$27.74	$18.55	$25.21
2019	540,038,144	$25.72	$22.26	$25.14
2018	499,601,920	$24.58	$21.94	$22.63

Split: 2-for-1 split in Mar. 2020

Recent Close: $23.35

Capital Stock Changes - On Sept. 1, 2022, 34,000,000 common shares were issued pursuant to the acquisition of LifeWorks Inc. Also during 2022, common shares were issued as follows: 23,000,000 under dividend reinvestment plan and 4,000,000 as share-based compensation.

Dividends

T com Ra $1.4544 pa Q est. July 4, 2023**
Prev. Rate: $1.4044 est. Jan. 3, 2023
Prev. Rate: $1.3544 est. July 4, 2022
Prev. Rate: $1.3096 est. Jan. 4, 2022
Prev. Rate: $1.2648 est. July 2, 2021
Prev. Rate: $1.2448 est. Jan. 4, 2021
** Reinvestment Option

Long-Term Debt - Outstanding at Dec. 31, 2022:

Comml. paper due 2023	$1,458,000,000
8.8% ser. B debs. due 2025	199,000,000
Credit facilities due to 2028[1]	2,059,000,000
Notes due to 2051[2]	18,660,000,000
Other	321,000,000
Lease liabs.	2,340,000,000
	25,037,000,000
Less: Current portion	2,541,000,000
	22,496,000,000

[1] Consists of US$800,000,000 revolving loans and US$1.2 billion term loans, bearing interest at prime, US$ base rate, banker's acceptance rate or SOFR, plus applicable margins; and $2.75 billion bank credit facility bearing interest at prime, US$ base rate, banker's acceptance rate or LIBOR, plus applicable margins.

[2] Consists of $500,000,000 3.35% series CJ notes due March 2023; $1.1 billion 3.35% series CK notes due April 2024; $800,000,000 3.75% series CQ notes due January 2025; $600,000,000 3.75% series CV notes due March 2026; $800,000,000 2.75% series CZ notes due July 2026; US$600,000,000 2.8% notes due February 2027; US$500,000,000 3.7% notes due September 2027; $600,000,000 2.35% series CAC notes due January 2028; $600,000,000 3.625% series CX notes due March 2028; $1 billion 3.3% series CY notes due May 2029; $350,000,000 5% series CAI notes due September 2029; $600,000,000 3.15% series CAA notes due February 2030; $500,000,000 2.05% series CAD notes due October 2030; $750,000,000 2.85% sustainability-linked series CAF notes due November 2031; US$900,000,000 3.4% sustainability-linked notes due May 2032; $1.1 billion 5.25% sustainability-linked series CAG notes due November 2032; $600,000,000 4.4% series CL notes due April 2043; $400,000,000 5.15% series CN notes due November 2043; $900,000,000 4.85% series CP notes due April 2044; $400,000,000 4.75% series CR notes due January 2045; $500,000,000 4.4% series CU notes due January 2046; $475,000,000 4.7% series CW notes March 2048; US$750,000,000 4.6% notes due November 2048; US$500,000,000 4.3% notes due June 2049; $800,000,000 3.95% series CAB notes due February 2050; $500,000,000 4.1% series CAE notes due April 2051; and $550,000,000 5.65% series CAH notes due September 2052. All values represent the principal amount of the respective note.

Minimum long-term debt repayments, including lease obligations, were reported as follows:

2023	$2,523,000,000
2024	2,762,000,000
2025	1,368,000,000
2026	1,688,000,000
2027	1,707,000,000
2028-2032	7,877,000,000
Thereafter	7,126,000,000

Note - In March 2023, offering of $500,000,000 4.95% sustainability-linked series CAJ notes due March 2033 was completed.

Wholly Owned Subsidiaries

TELUS Communications Inc., Vancouver, B.C.

- 56.1% int. in **TELUS International (Cda) Inc.**, Vancouver, B.C. 73.4% voting interest. (see separate coverage)

Note: The preceding list includes only the major related companies in which interests are held.

Financial Statistics

Periods ended:	12m Dec. 31/22[A]		12m Dec. 31/21[¤A]
	$000s	%Chg	$000s
Operating revenue	**18,292,000**	**+9**	**16,838,000**
Cost of sales	7,107,000		6,699,000
Salaries & benefits	4,484,000		3,814,000
Stock-based compensation	194,000		236,000
Operating expense	**12,006,000**	**+9**	**10,968,000**
Operating income	**6,286,000**	**+7**	**5,870,000**
Deprec., depl. & amort.	3,452,000		3,216,000
Finance income	17,000		16,000
Finance costs, gross	649,000		812,000
Investment income	4,000		4,000
Pre-tax income	**2,322,000**	**+2**	**2,278,000**
Income taxes	604,000		580,000
Net income	**1,718,000**	**+1**	**1,698,000**
Net inc. for equity hldrs	**1,615,000**	**-2**	**1,655,000**
Net inc. for non-cont. int	**103,000**	**+140**	**43,000**
Cash & equivalent	974,000		723,000
Inventories	537,000		448,000
Accounts receivable	3,297,000		2,671,000
Current assets	6,092,000		5,032,000
Long-term investments	608,000		496,000
Fixed assets, net	17,084,000		15,926,000
Intangibles, net	28,347,000		24,755,000
Total assets	**54,046,000**	**+13**	**47,983,000**
Bank indebtedness	104,000		114,000
Accts. pay. & accr. liabs	3,947,000		3,705,000
Current liabilities	8,281,000		8,273,000
Long-term debt, gross	25,037,000		20,852,000
Long-term debt, net	22,496,000		17,925,000
Shareholders' equity	16,569,000		15,116,000
Non-controlling interest	1,089,000		943,000
Cash from oper. activs	**4,811,000**	**+10**	**4,388,000**
Cash from fin. activs	848,000		953,000
Cash from invest. activs	(5,408,000)		(5,466,000)
Net cash position	**974,000**	**+35**	**723,000**
Capital expenditures	(3,647,000)		(3,097,000)
Capital disposals	16,000		508,000
Unfunded pension liability	392,000		643,000
Pension fund surplus	307,000		453,000
	$		$
Earnings per share*	1.16		1.23
Cash flow per share*	3.45		3.26
Cash divd. per share*	1.36		1.27
	shs		shs
No. of shs. o/s*	1,431,000,000		1,370,000,000
Avg. no. of shs. o/s*	1,396,000,000		1,346,000,000
	%		%
Net profit margin	9.39		10.08
Return on equity	10.19		12.17
Return on assets	4.31		5.04
No. of employees (FTEs)	108,500		90,800

* Common
¤ Restated
[A] Reported in accordance with IFRS

Latest Results

Periods ended:	6m June 30/23[A]		6m June 30/22[A]
	$000s	%Chg	$000s
Operating revenue	9,859,000	+14	8,629,000
Net income	420,000	-53	902,000
Net inc. for equity hldrs	417,000	-51	853,000
Net inc. for non-cont. int	3,000		49,000
	$		$
Earnings per share*	0.29		0.62

* Common
[A] Reported in accordance with IFRS

Historical Summary
(as originally stated)

Fiscal Year	Oper. Rev.	Net Inc. Bef. Disc.	EPS*
	$000s	$000s	$
2022[A]	18,292,000	1,718,000	1.16
2021[A]	16,838,000	1,698,000	1.23
2020[A]	15,341,000	1,260,000	0.95
2019[A]	14,589,000	1,776,000	1.45
2018[A]	14,095,000	1,624,000	1.34

* Common
[A] Reported in accordance with IFRS

Note: Adjusted throughout for 2-for-1 split in Mar. 2020

T.5 TELUS International (Cda) Inc.

Symbol - TIXT **Exchange** - TSX **CUSIP** - 87975H

Head Office - 700-510 Georgia St W, Vancouver, BC, V6B 0M3 **Telephone** - (604) 695-3455

Website - www.telusinternational.com

Email - ir@telusinternational.com

Investor Relations - Jason Mayr (604) 695-3455

Auditors - Deloitte LLP C.A., Vancouver, B.C.

Lawyers - Osler, Hoskin & Harcourt LLP

Transfer Agents - Computershare Trust Company of Canada Inc., Vancouver, B.C.; Computershare Trust Company, N.A., Canton, Ohio

FP500 Subsidiary Revenue Ranking - 27

Employees - 73,142 at Dec. 31, 2022

Profile - (B.C. 2016) Provides customer care and business services, as well as strategy and innovation, IT services and digital customer experience (CX) process and delivery solutions, to companies globally across many industry verticals.

Designs, builds and delivers next-generation digital solutions for global and disruptive brands. Operates from 69 delivery locations in 30 countries in North America, Central America, Europe and Asia, and has more than 74,000 team members serving clients across multiple industry verticals including tech and games, communications and media, e-commerce and fintech, healthcare, and travel and hospitality. Services are provided over multiple time zones and in more than 50 languages. Solutions offered include digital experience (DX), customer experience, artificial intelligence (AI) data solutions and content moderation.

In May 2023, **TELUS Corporation** acquired an additional 2,50,000 multiple voting shares of the company held by **Baring Private Equity Asia Pvt. Ltd.** for a purchase price of US$16.90 per share for total consideration of US$42,250,000. The shares represented 1.3% of the outstanding multiple voting shares and 0.9% of all outstanding shares. After giving effect to the purchase, TELUS Corporation held 152,004,019 multiple voting shares and 1,438,013 subordinate voting shares, representing 56.1% of the outstanding shares, 76% of the outstanding multiple voting shares and 73.4% of the outstanding voting rights.

In June 2022, **TELUS Corporation** acquired 3,000,000 multiple voting shares of the company held by **Baring Private Equity Asia Pvt. Ltd.** for a purchase price of US$22 per share for total consideration of US$66,000,000. The shares represent 1.5% of the outstanding multiple voting shares of the company and 1.1% of all outstanding shares. After giving effect to the purchase, TELUS Corporation held 149,504,019 multiple voting shares and no subordinate voting shares of the company, representing 56.17% of the outstanding shares, 74.78% of the outstanding multiple voting shares and 72.38% of the outstanding voting rights.

Recent Merger and Acquisition Activity

Status: completed **Revised:** Jan. 3, 2023
UPDATE: The transaction was completed. WillowTree would operate as WillowTree, a TELUS International Company. PREVIOUS: TELUS International (Cda) Inc. agreed to acquire Charlottesville, Va.-based WillowTree, LLC, a full-service digital product provider focused on end user experiences, such as native mobile applications and unified web interfaces, for US$1.225 billion, including the assumption of US$210,000,000 of debt, of which US$125,000,000 would be settled in TELUS International subordinate voting shares, US$160,000,000 would be reinvested by certain eligible management team members and settled subject to certain performance-based criteria, and the remainder paid in cash. The cash consideration would be financed, in part, from borrowings under TELUS International's non-recourse credit facilities. WillowTree operates 13 global studios across the U.S., Canada, Brazil, Portugal, Spain, Poland and Romania, and works with clients including FOX, CBC, PepsiCo, Anheuser-Busch InBev, Synchrony, Manulife and Marriott. Insignia Capital Group, L.P. is a majority shareholder in WillowTree. The transaction was expected to be completed in January 2023, subject to customary closing condition and regulatory approvals.

Directors - Darren Entwistle, chr., Vancouver, B.C.; Josh Blair, v-chr., Vancouver, B.C.; Jeffrey Puritt, pres. & CEO, Las Vegas, Nev.; Madhuri Andrews, Tex.; Olin Anton, B.C.; Navin Arora, Calgary, Alta.; Doug French, Whitby, Ont.; Tony Geheran, Vancouver, B.C.; Susan I. (Sue) Paish, Vancouver, B.C.; Carolyn Slaski, Fla.; Sandra J. Stuart, Vancouver, B.C.

Other Exec. Officers - Vanessa Kanu, CFO; Michel E. Belec, chief legal officer & corp. sec.; Beth Howen, chief transformation officer; Maria Pardee, chief comml. officer; Michael Ringman, CIO; Marilyn Tyfting, sr. v-p & chief corp. officer; Tobias Dengel, pres., WillowTree

Capital Stock

	Authorized (shs.)	Outstanding (shs.)[1]
Preferred	unlimited	nil
Multiple Vtg.	unlimited	199,931,876
Subordinate Vtg.	unlimited	73,202,309

[1] At Mar. 31, 2023

Multiple Voting - All held by TELUS Corporation and funds managed by Baring Private Equity Asia Pvt. Ltd. Convertible into subordinate voting shares on a one-for-one basis at the option of holder and automatically upon occurrence of certain events. Ten votes per share.

Subordinate Voting - Non-convertible. One vote per share.

Major Shareholder - TELUS Corporation held 72.2% interest and Baring Private Equity Asia Pvt. Ltd. held 24.3% interest at Mar. 13, 2023.

Price Range - TIXT/TSX

Year	Volume	High	Low	Close
2022	35,632,728	$43.78	$24.11	$26.73
2021	25,545,097	$49.43	$34.00	$41.80

Recent Close: $12.08

Capital Stock Changes - On Jan. 3, 2023, 6,500,000 subordinate voting shares were issued pursuant to the acquisition of WillowTree, LLC.

During 2022, 1,000,000 subordinate voting shares were issued as share-based compensation.

Wholly Owned Subsidiaries

CallPoint New Europe EAD, Sofia, Bulgaria.
TELUS International AI Inc., Las Vegas, Nev.
TELUS International Germany GmbH, Berlin, Germany.
TELUS International Philippines, Inc., Philippines.
TELUS International Services Limited, Dublin, Ireland.
TELUS International (U.S.) Corp., Las Vegas, Nev.
Voxpro Limited, Cork, Ireland.
WillowTree, LLC, Charlottesville, Va.
Xavient Digital LLC, Simi Valley, Calif.

Financial Statistics

Periods ended:	12m Dec. 31/22[A]		12m Dec. 31/21[oA]
	US$000s	%Chg	US$000s
Operating revenue	**2,468,000**	**+12**	**2,194,000**
Cost of sales	468,000		432,000
Salaries & benefits	1,393,000		1,222,000
Stock-based compensation	25,000		75,000
Other operating expense	40,000		23,000
Operating expense	**1,926,000**	**+10**	**1,752,000**
Operating income	**542,000**	**+23**	**442,000**
Deprec., depl. & amort.	258,000		257,000
Finance costs, gross	41,000		44,000
Pre-tax income	**250,000**	**+76**	**142,000**
Income taxes	67,000		64,000
Net income	**183,000**	**+135**	**78,000**
Cash & equivalent	125,000		115,000
Accounts receivable	428,000		414,000
Current assets	695,000		627,000
Fixed assets, net	449,000		405,000
Intangibles, net	2,358,000		2,538,000
Total assets	**3,556,000**	**-2**	**3,626,000**
Accts. pay. & accr. liabs	290,000		336,000
Current liabilities	552,000		807,000
Long-term debt, gross	964,000		1,148,000
Long-term debt, net	881,000		820,000
Shareholders' equity	1,838,000		1,655,000
Cash from oper. activs	**437,000**	**+41**	**311,000**
Cash from fin. activs	(300,000)		(235,000)
Cash from invest. activs	(119,000)		(110,000)
Net cash position	**125,000**	**+9**	**115,000**
Capital expenditures	(105,000)		(99,000)
	US$		US$
Earnings per share*	0.69		0.30
Cash flow per share*	1.64		1.18
	shs		shs
No. of shs. o/s*	267,000,000		266,000,000
Avg. no. of shs. o/s*	266,000,000		264,000,000
	%		%
Net profit margin	7.41		3.56
Return on equity	10.48		5.64
Return on assets	5.93		2.77
No. of employees (FTEs)	73,142		62,141

* M.V. & S.V.
[o] Restated
[A] Reported in accordance with IFRS

Latest Results

Periods ended:	3m Mar. 31/23[A]		3m Mar. 31/22[A]
	US$000s	%Chg	US$000s
Operating revenue	686,000	+15	599,000
Net income	14,000	-59	34,000
	US$		US$
Earnings per share*	0.05		0.13

* M.V. & S.V.
[A] Reported in accordance with IFRS

Historical Summary
(as originally stated)

Fiscal Year	Oper. Rev.	Net Inc. Bef. Disc.	EPS*
	US$000s	US$000s	US$
2022[A]	2,468,000	183,000	0.69
2021[A]	2,194,000	78,000	0.30
2020[A1]	1,581,600	102,900	0.46
2019[A1]	1,019,600	69,000	0.36
2018[A1]	834,600	47,100	0.25

* M.V. & S.V.
[A] Reported in accordance with IFRS
[1] Shares and per share figures adjusted to reflect 4.5-for-1 share split effective Feb. 5, 2021 (concurrent with the company's initial public offering).

T.6 TFI International Inc.*

Symbol - TFII **Exchange** - TSX **CUSIP** - 87241L
Head Office - 500-8801 aut Transcanadienne, Saint-Laurent, QC, H4S 1Z6 **Telephone** - (514) 331-4000 **Fax** - (514) 337-4200
Website - www.tfiintl.com
Email - abedard@tfiintl.com
Investor Relations - Alain Bédard (647) 729-4079
Auditors - KPMG LLP C.A., Montréal, Qué.
Bankers - U.S. Bank National Association; PNC Bank Canada Branch; J.P. Morgan Chase Bank (Canada); Bank of America Canada; Caisse centrale Desjardins; Bank of Montreal; Royal Bank of Canada; National Bank of Canada
Transfer Agents - Computershare Trust Company, N.A., Canton, Mass.; Computershare Trust Company of Canada Inc., Montréal, Qué.
FP500 Revenue Ranking - 53
Employees - 25,836 at Dec. 31, 2022
Profile - (Can. 2008) Provides transportation and logistics services through a trucking network across Canada and the United States.

Operations are carried out through four segments:

Package & Courier - Offers pickup, transport and delivery of items across North America.

Less-Than-Truckload - Offers pickup, consolidation, transport and delivery of smaller loads across North America.

Truckload - Provides full loads carried directly from the customer to the destination using a closed van or specialized equipment to meet customers' specific needs including expedited transportation, flatbed, tank container, dedicated services and truckload brokerage.

Logistics - Provides a wide range of asset-light logistics services including brokerage, freight forwarding and transportation management, as well as small parcel delivery.

At June 30, 2023, the company owned or leased 11,754 trucks and 34,018 trailers and had 7,298 independent contractors, with 247 terminals in eastern Canada (164) and western Canada (83), and 301 terminals in the U.S.

In October 2022, the company acquired Quebec-based **Quévrac Ltée**, which provides dry bulk transportation, principally cement, in Quebec and Ontario. Terms were not disclosed.

Recent Merger and Acquisition Activity

Status: completed **Revised:** Aug. 16, 2023
UPDATE: The transaction was completed. PREVIOUS: TFI International Inc. agreed to acquire Wisconsin-based JHT Holdings, Inc., which provides transportation services related to the delivery of large commercial trucks in North America, and also provides third-party logistics trust transport, car haul and other specialized services. Terms of the transaction were not disclosed. JHT generated annual revenues of more than US$500,000,000, and operated a terminal network consisting of 25 facilities, of which eight were owned, throughout the U.S. and Canada.

Status: completed **Revised:** July 13, 2023
UPDATE: The transaction was completed for US$79,600,000. PREVIOUS: TFI International Inc. agreed to acquire private Saskatoon, Sask.-based Siemens Transportation Group Inc., a less-than-truckload business that has 11 terminals in Canada and four in the U.S. Terms of the transaction were not disclosed.

Status: completed **Announced:** May 21, 2023
TFI International Inc. acquired Montreal, Que.-based Les Placements Jonadagi Inc., a provider of truckload services to eastern Canada, for an undisclosed amount.

Status: completed **Announced:** Apr. 30, 2023
TFI International Inc. acquired Minnesota-based Launch Logistix Inc., an independent agent of TForce Worldwide, a division of TFI, providing logistics services in the Greater Minneapolis and Saint Paul area. Terms were not disclosed.

Status: completed **Announced:** Apr. 2, 2023
TFI International Inc. acquired Blenheim, Ont.-based SM Freight Inc., which provides refrigerated and temperature-controlled less-than-truckload and truckload services throughout North America, as well as freight management and warehousing services. Terms were not disclosed.

Status: completed **Announced:** Mar. 20, 2023
UPDATE: The transaction was completed. PREVIOUS: TFI International Inc. agreed to acquire Wisconsin-based Hot-Line Freights Systems, Inc. and Hot-Line Logistics, LLC for an undisclosed amount. Hot-Line Freights Systems provides less-than-truckload freight services across the midwestern U.S., and Hot-Line Logistics provides logistics and freight management services in the U.S.

Status: completed **Announced:** Feb. 21, 2023
TFI International Inc. acquired Saint-Hubert, Que.-based Axsun Inc. (dba Axsun Group) for an undisclosed amount. Axsun provides an integrated mix of intermodal services and freight brokerage services including over-the-road highway, drayage, logistics and warehousing across Canada, the U.S. and Mexico. Axsun operates a fleet of 20 tractors and 300 trailers, generating annualized revenues of Cdn$90,000,000.

Status: completed **Announced:** Feb. 5, 2023
TFI International Inc. acquired Saint-Honoré-de-Shenley, Que.-based D.M. Breton Inc., which transports freight, lumber and paper products between Canada and the U.S. Terms were not disclosed.

Status: completed **Announced:** Jan. 9, 2023
TFI International Inc. acquired certain assets of Brooklyn, N.Y.-based Stallion Express, LLC, a provider of courier services to long-term care pharmacies in the eastern United States. Terms were not disclosed.

Status: completed **Announced:** Nov. 20, 2022
TFI International Inc. acquired 0806434 B.C. Ltd, OTM Express Trucking & Logistics 2013 Ltd., 2234360 Alberta Ltd. and 557317 B.C. Ltd. (collectively T-Lane) for an undisclosed amount. T-Lane provides specialized truckload services across Canada and the U.S.

Status: completed **Announced:** Sept. 30, 2022
TFI International Inc. acquired Mission, Kan.-based LLL Transport Inc. (dba Girton LLL Transport), which transports bulk liquid commodities across the U.S. Terms were not disclosed.

Status: completed **Announced:** Sept. 13, 2022
TFI International Inc. acquired certain assets of Groupe Boutin Inc., V. Boutin Express Inc., Frontenac Express Inc., Transport Jean Beaudry Inc. and Transnat Express Inc. (collectively Boutin), which specializes in truckload and dedicated truckload transportation, for an undisclosed amount. The transaction includes a fleet of 70 tractors, 394 trailers and the trucking facilities in Plessisville and Boucherville, Que.

Status: completed **Revised:** Aug. 31, 2022
UPDATE: The transaction was completed. PREVIOUS: TFI International Inc. agreed to sell its Contract Freighters, Inc. (CFI) non-dedicated U.S. dry van and temperature control truckload business and CFI Logistica operations in Mexico (CFI TL, TC & MX business) to Heartland Express, Inc. for US$525,000,000, subject to certain agreed upon adjustments. The CFI TL, TC & MX business operates primarily in the U.S.-based conventional TL operating segment of TFI's Truckload segment and provides truckload service offerings, including time definite dry-van truckload, long-haul and short-haul freight transportation, reefer transportation and Mexico-based non-asset logistics services. The CFI TL, TC & MX business has 2,000 tractors, 7,800 trailers and 2,800 employees. CFI's Mexican logistics business has a network of nearly 200 C-TPAT certified Mexico carrier partners. TFI would retain its CFI Dedicated and CFI U.S. Logistics businesses.

Status: completed **Announced:** Aug. 28, 2022
TFI International Inc. acquired Saint-Michel, Que.-based Transport St-Michel Inc. and related companies, which provides a full range of transportation services in Canada and the U.S., including general and specialized transport, storage and warehousing services. Terms were not disclosed.

Status: completed **Announced:** July 10, 2022
TFI International Inc. acquired Port Reading, N.J.-based HO-RO Trucking Company, Inc., a provider of flatbed trucking services primarily focusing on delivery of building materials in the northeastern U.S. Terms were not disclosed.

Status: completed **Announced:** July 3, 2022
TFI International Inc. acquired certain assets of L'Ange-Gardien, Que.-based Transport St-Amour, a provider of food grade tank services. Terms were not disclosed.

Status: completed **Announced:** June 17, 2022
TFI International Inc. acquired certain assets of Cedar Creek Express, LLC and DDW Transportation, LLC (collectively Cedar Creek), which provides food grade tank services in the U.S. Midwest. Terms were not disclosed.

Status: completed **Announced:** June 10, 2022
TFI International Inc. acquired certain assets of Premium Ventures Inc., a specialized carrier of oversized and overweight freight in Orangeville, Ont. Terms were not disclosed.

Status: completed **Announced:** May 27, 2022
TFI International Inc. acquired Sandusky, Ohio-based South Shore Transportation Company, Inc., a provider of flatbed truckload services primarily to building material retailers and wholesalers in the U.S. Midwest. South Shore has terminals in Ohio, Pennsylvania and Michigan. Terms were not disclosed.

Status: completed **Announced:** May 16, 2022
TFI International Inc. sold an underutilized terminal in southern California for US$83,000,000.

Status: completed **Announced:** Mar. 19, 2022
TFI International Inc. acquired California-based Unity Courier Services, Inc., a provider of regularly scheduled same-day service and short-term delivery solutions for the U.S. west coast, for US$22,200,000.

Predecessor Detail - Name changed from TransForce Inc., Dec. 23, 2016.

Directors - Alain Bédard, chr., pres. & CEO, Lac-Brome, Qué.; André Bérard†, Montréal, Qué.; Leslie Abi-Karam, Palm Beach Gardens, Fla.; William T. England, Burr Ridge, Ill.; Diane Giard, Shefford, Qué.; Debra

Kelly-Ennis, Palm Beach Gardens, Fla.; Neil D. Manning, Edmonton, Alta.; Sébastien Martel, Qué.; John Pratt, Kenilworth, Ill.; Joey Saputo, Montréal, Qué.; Rosemary Turner, Las Vegas, Nev.

Other Exec. Officers - David Saperstein, CFO; Daniel Auger, CIO; Steven A. (Steve) Brookshaw, sr. exec. v-p; Kal Atwal, exec. v-p; Kristen Fess, exec. v-p; Rick Hashie, exec. v-p; Robert McGonigal, exec. v-p; Junior Roy, exec. v-p; Christopher Traikos, exec. v-p; Ping Yan, sr. v-p, opers.; Norman Brazeau, v-p, real estate; Daniel Chevalier, v-p, fin., operational reporting; Patrick Croteau, v-p, fin. & control; Johanne Dean, v-p, mktg. & commun.; Sylvain Desaulniers, v-p, HR; Paul Freund, v-p, IT, security; David Gatti, v-p, bus. devel.; Josiane-Mélanie Langlois, v-p, legal affairs & corp. sec.; Sylvain Lemay, v-p, IT; Chantal Martel, v-p, insce. & compliance; Suri Musiri, v-p, internal audit; Bill Preece, v-p, envir.; Martin Quesnel, v-p, fin.; Ken Tourangeau, v-p, tax; Eric Anson, pres., TA dedicated; Larry Fuaco, pres., TForce Integrated Solutions, TForce Logistics Canada & AC Logistics Canada; Thomas Griffin, pres., TForce Worldwide; Wayne Gruszka, pres., TST-CF Express & TST Expedited; Paul Hoelting, pres., TForce Freight; Dan Leslie, pres., TForce Logistics U.S.; James (Jim) McKay, pres., Loomis Express & Canpar Express; Justin Paul, pres., TF Energy Solutions; Laurie Stoneburgh, pres., ICS Courier; Sean Watson, pres., Vitran Express

† Lead director

Capital Stock

	Authorized (shs.)	Outstanding (shs.)[1]
Preferred	unlimited	nil
Common	unlimited	85,801,479

[1] At July 31, 2023

Options - At Dec. 31, 2022, options were outstanding to purchase 1,302,000 common shares at a weighted average exercise price of US$27.89 per share with a weighted average remaining contractual life of 2.5 years.

Normal Course Issuer Bid - The company plans to make normal course purchases of up to 6,370,199 common shares representing 10% of the public float. The bid commenced on Nov. 2, 2022, and expires on Nov. 1, 2023.

Major Shareholder - Capital Research Global Investors held 10.7% interest and Capital International Investors held 10.5% interest at Mar. 15, 2023.

Price Range - TFII/TSX

Year	Volume	High	Low	Close
2022	66,122,342	$148.94	$93.63	$135.61
2021	89,700,218	$148.63	$64.74	$141.87
2020	87,937,095	$68.88	$23.21	$65.53
2019	61,033,502	$46.34	$33.36	$43.77
2018	77,260,191	$49.00	$29.09	$35.30

Recent Close: $173.30

Capital Stock Changes - During 2022, 754,988 common shares were issued on exercise of options and 6,368,322 common shares were repurchased under a Normal Course Issuer Bid.

Dividends

TFII com Ra US$1.40 pa Q est. Jan. 16, 2023[1]

Prev. Rate: US$1.08 est. Jan. 17, 2022

Prev. Rate: US$0.92 est. Apr. 15, 2021

Prev. Rate: $1.16 est. Jan. 15, 2021

[1] Divds. paid in Cdn$ prior to April 2021.

Long-Term Debt - Outstanding at Dec. 31, 2022:

Debs. due 2024[1]	US$147,233,000
Sales contracts due to 2024[2]	92,822,000
Sr. notes due to 2037[3]	1,075,702,000
	1,315,757,000
Less: Current portion	37,087,000
	1,278,670,000

[1] Bear interest at rates varying from 3.32% to 4.22%.

[2] Bear interest at rates varying from 1.45% to 5.28%.

[3] Bear interest at rates varying from 2.87% to 3.85%.

Wholly Owned Subsidiaries

TForce Holdings Inc.

- 100% int. in **AC Logistics Canada Inc.**, Ont.
- 100% int. in **CK Logistics GP Inc.**, Canada.
  - 49% int. in **CK Logistics HP L.P.**
- 100% int. in **Canpar Express Inc.**, Canada.
- 100% int. in **Cavalier Transportation Services Inc.**, Bolton, Ont.
- 100% int. in **Clarke Transport Inc.**, Montréal, Qué.
- 100% int. in **Contrans Corp.**, Woodstock, Ont.
  - 100% int. in **Contrans Flatbed Group GP Inc.**, Ont.
  - 100% int. in **Contrans Realty Holdings Inc.**
  - 100% int. in **Contrans Tank Group GP Inc.**, Ont.
  - 100% int. in **Cornerstone Logistics GP Inc.**, Ont.
  - 100% int. in **Cornerstone Logistics USA GP Inc.**, Del.
  - 100% int. in **Laidlaw Carriers Bulk GP Inc.**, Ont.
  - 100% int. in **Laidlaw Carriers Van GP Inc.**, Ont.
  - 100% int. in **Tri-Line Carriers GP Inc.**, Ont.
  - 100% int. in **Tripar Transportation GP Inc.**, Ont.
  - 100% int. in **Tripar Transportation USA GP Inc.**, Del.
- 100% int. in **Contrans Vrac Inc.**, Qué.
- 100% int. in **Craler Inc.**, Qué.
- 100% int. in **La Crete Transport 79 Ltd.**, Edmonton, Alta.
- 100% int. in **Direct Service Network Ltd.**, Mississauga, Ont.
- 100% int. in **Driving Force Decks Int'l Ltd.**, Abbotsford, B.C.
- 100% int. in **F.K.D. Contracting (Alta) Ltd.**, Hythe, Alta.
- 100% int. in **Fleetway Transport Inc.**, Ont.
- 100% int. in **4186397 Canada Inc.**, Canada.
  - 100% int. in **2231599 Alberta Ltd.**, Alta.
- 100% int. in **Freightline Carrier Systems Inc.**, Ont.
- 100% int. in **G.H.L. Inc.**, Anjou, Qué.
- 100% int. in **Gorski Bulk Transport**, Ont.
- 100% int. in **Gunter Transportation Ltd.**, Woodstock, Ont.
- 100% int. in **Gusgo Transport GP Inc.**, Ont.
- 100% int. in **Information Communication Services (ICS) Inc.**, Canada.
- 100% int. in **Laser Transport Inc.**, Windsor, Ont.
- 100% int. in **Logikit Inc.**, Qué.
- 100% int. in **McMurray Serv-U Expediting Ltd.**, Fort McMurray, Alta.
- 100% int. in **Normandin Transit Inc.**, Qué.
- 100% int. in **1040135 Ontario Inc.**, Ont. Dba TTL.
- 100% int. in **11009915 Canada Inc.**, Canada.
- 100% int. in **11447556 Canada Inc.**, Canada.
- 100% int. in **12068338 Canada Inc**, Canada.
  - 100% int. in **Clarke North America Inc.**
- 100% int. in **13454983 Canada Inc.**, Etobicoke, Ont.
- 100% int. in **175638 Canada Inc.**, Saint-Laurent, Qué.
- 100% int. in **Patriot Freight Services Inc.**, Montréal, Qué.
- 100% int. in **S.G.T. 2000 Inc.**, Saint-Germain-de-Grantham, Qué.
- 100% int. in **Les Services JAG Inc.**, Qué.
  - 100% int. in **Gestion G. Girard Inc.**, Qué.
- 100% int. in **613734 Saskatchewan Ltd.**, Sask. Dba Timeline Logistic International.
- 100% int. in **6422217 Canada Inc.**, Canada.
- 100% int. in **6586856 Canada Inc.**, Canada.
- 100% int. in **South Shore Transportation Company, Inc.**, Sandusky, Ohio.
- 100% int. in **TF TLH Canada GP Inc.**, Canada.
- 100% int. in **TF TLH Canada Inc.**, Canada.
- 100% int. in **TFH Canada G.P. Inc.**, Canada.
- 100% int. in **TFI Transport 4 Inc.**, Canada. Dba Kingsway Vrac.
- 100% int. in **TFI Transport 1 Inc.**, Canada.
- 100% int. in **TFI Transport 11 Inc.**, Canada.
- 100% int. in **TForce US Holdco, Inc.**, Del.
  - 100% int. in **TForce Holdings USA, Inc.**, Del.
    - 100% int. in **Quik X Transportation (US) Inc.**, Ill.
    - 100% int. in **TFH USA GP, LLC**, United States.
    - 100% int. in **TFH USA 1, LLC**, United States.
    - 100% int. in **TForce Properties, Inc.**, Del.
    - 100% int. in **TForce Direct, Inc.**, Del.
    - 100% int. in **TForce Freight, Inc.**, Va.
    - 100% int. in **TForce Logistics, Inc.**, Del.
      - 100% int. in **TF Dedicated, LLC**, Del.
      - 100% int. in **TForce Logistics West, LLC**, Del.
        - 100% int. in **Drive Force West, LLC**, Del.
      - 100% int. in **TForce Logistics Canada Inc.**, N.S.
      - 100% int. in **TForce Logistics East, LLC**, Del.
        - 100% int. in **Drive Force East, LLC**, Del.
    - 100% int. in **TForce Premier Distribution, Inc.**, Calif.
    - 100% int. in **TForce Worldwide, Inc.**, United States.
    - 100% int. in **Westfreight Holdings (U.S.A.) Inc.**, Nev.
  - 100% int. in **TForce TL Holdings USA, Inc.**, Del.
    - 100% int. in **Bulk Transport Company East, Inc.**, Mo.
      - 100% int. in **BTC Dedicated, Inc.**, Mo.
      - 100% int. in **BTC Solutions, Inc.**, Mo.
      - 100% int. in **CBTC Transport, LLC**, Mo.
      - 100% int. in **Coastal Transport Authority, LLC**, Missouri City, Tex.
      - 100% int. in **HO-RO Trucking Company, Inc.**, Woodbridge, N.J.
    - 100% int. in **Bulk Transport Company West, Inc.**, Neb.
    - 100% int. in **Cavalier Transportation Services Corp.**, N.Y.
    - 100% int. in **Coderre Investment USA, L.L.C.**, Houston, Tex.
    - 100% int. in **Freightline Carrier Systems USA, Inc.**, Tenn.
    - 100% int. in **Gorski Bulk Transport USA, Inc.**, Mich.
    - 100% int. in **Piston Tank Corporation**, Fenton, Mo.
    - 100% int. in **SGT 2000 Motor Freight, Inc.**, Houston, Tex.
    - 100% int. in **TF TLH USA GP, LLC**, United States.
    - 100% int. in **TF TLH USA 1, LLC**, United States.
    - 100% int. in **TF TLH USA 3, LLC**, United States.
      - 100% int. in **CFI Dedicated, Inc.**, Eagan, Minn.
    - 100% int. in **Transportation Resources, Inc.**, Mo.
      - 100% int. in **Contract Freighters, Inc.**, Mo.
        - 100% int. in **CFI Logistics, LLC**, Jefferson City, Mo.
        - 100% int. in **D&D Sexton, Inc.**, Carthage, Mo.
- 100% int. in **TST Expedited Services Inc.**, Del.
- 100% int. in **TForce Freight Canada Inc.**, Mississauga, Ont.
- 100% int. in **Tombro Trucking Limited**, Milton, Ont.
- 100% int. in **Trans2D Logistics Inc.**
- 100% int. in **TransForce Administration Inc.**, Canada.
- 100% int. in **TransForce Capital Insurance Company Limited**, Barbados.
- 100% int. in **Transport SAF Inc.**, Canada.
- 100% int. in **2801124 Canada Inc.**, Canada.
- 100% int. in **Unity Courier Services, Inc.**, Calif.
- 100% int. in **Vitran Express Canada Inc.**, Ont.
  - 100% int. in **Southern Express Lines of Ontario Limited**, Canada.
- 100% int. in **Westfreight Systems Inc.**, Calgary, Alta.

Note: The preceding list includes only the major related companies in which interests are held.

Financial Statistics

Periods ended:	12m Dec. 31/22[A]		12m Dec. 31/21[¤A]
	US$000s	%Chg	US$000s
Operating revenue	**8,812,491**	**+22**	**7,220,429**
Cost of sales	4,592,191		3,815,453
Salaries & benefits	2,362,856		1,974,081
Other operating expense	492,291		380,342
Operating expense	**7,447,338**	**+21**	**6,169,876**
Operating income	**1,365,153**	**+30**	**1,050,553**
Deprec., depl. & amort.	430,593		393,032
Finance income	1,750		5,127
Finance costs, gross	82,147		78,145
Pre-tax income	**1,065,641**	**+18**	**906,211**
Income taxes	242,409		151,806
Net income	**823,232**	**+9**	**754,405**
Cash & equivalent	147,117		19,292
Inventories	24,181		24,402
Accounts receivable	1,030,726		1,056,023
Current assets	1,263,563		1,162,258
Long-term investments	85,964		31,391
Fixed assets, net	2,131,955		2,455,141
Right-of-use assets	381,640		398,533
Intangibles, net	1,592,110		1,792,921
Total assets	**5,505,830**	**-6**	**5,883,663**
Accts. pay. & accr. liabs	678,479		837,027
Current liabilities	966,681		1,406,120
Long-term debt, gross	1,315,757		1,608,094
Long-term debt, net	1,278,670		1,244,508
Long-term lease liabilities	297,105		313,862
Shareholders' equity	2,463,070		2,310,355
Cash from oper. activs	**971,645**	**+14**	**855,351**
Cash from fin. activs	(1,067,242)		322,301
Cash from invest. activs	223,422		(1,162,657)
Net cash position	**147,117**	**+663**	**19,292**
Capital expenditures	(350,824)		(268,656)
Capital disposals	128,821		92,842
Unfunded pension liability	n.a.		66,877
Pension fund surplus	4,359		n.a.
	US$		US$
Earnings per share*	9.21		8.11
Cash flow per share*	10.87		9.19
Cash divd. per share*	1.51		0.96
	shs		shs
No. of shs. o/s*	86,539,559		92,152,893
Avg. no. of shs. o/s*	89,359,582		93,054,245
	%		%
Net profit margin	9.34		10.45
Return on equity	35.16		36.80
Return on assets	15.75		16.84
Foreign sales percent	69		67
No. of employees (FTEs)	25,836		29,539

* Common

¤ Restated

[A] Reported in accordance with IFRS

Latest Results

Periods ended:	6m June 30/23[A]		6m June 30/22[A]
	US$000s	%Chg	US$000s
Operating revenue	3,641,443	-21	4,613,836
Net income	240,152	-43	424,548
	US$		US$
Earnings per share*	2.78		4.65

* Common

[A] Reported in accordance with IFRS

Historical Summary

(as originally stated)

Fiscal Year	Oper. Rev.	Net Inc. Bef. Disc.	EPS*
	US$000s	US$000s	US$
2022[A]	8,812,491	823,232	9.21
2021[A]	7,220,429	664,361	7.14
2020[A]	3,781,134	275,675	3.09
	$000s	$000s	$
2019[A]	5,178,864	324,476	3.89
2018[A]	5,123,208	291,994	3.32

* Common

[A] Reported in accordance with IFRS

T.7 TGS Esports Inc.

Symbol - TGS **Exchange** - TSX-VEN (S) **CUSIP** - 87250P

Head Office - 4211 No. 3 Rd, Richmond, BC, V6X 2C3 **Telephone** - (604) 551-7831 **Fax** - (604) 676-2767

Website - www.thegamingstadium.com

Email - skhouri@thegamingstadium.com

Investor Relations - Spiro Khouri (604) 562-0606

Auditors - Dale Matheson Carr-Hilton LaBonte LLP C.A., Vancouver, B.C.

Transfer Agents - Odyssey Trust Company, Vancouver, B.C.

Profile - (B.C. 2018) Offers an eSports platform, which includes online and in-person tournaments and events, broadcast production, tournament software and scholastic eSports programs.

Owns and operates Pepper, an online eSports platform to host and facilitate events and tournaments; and The Gaming Stadium, a 7,000-sq.-ft. leased eSports arena in Richmond, B.C., which provides and hosts online and in-person eSports events, tournaments and leagues as well as provides broadcast production for any event.

In addition, wholly owned **Volcanic Media Inc.**, the company's scholastic division, provides eSports events, leagues, scholarship programs and educational curriculums for high schools and post-secondary institutions; and wholly owned **Even Matchup Gaming Inc.** organizes and broadcasts eSports events, including its owned Get On My Level (GOML) tournament in Canada and Let's Make Moves event in New York.

In November 2022, the company acquired the assets of **Lazarus Esports Inc.**, which is a professional eSports organization that competes in a variety of areas, from **Tiidal Gaming Group Corp.**

Common suspended from TSX-VEN, Nov. 4, 2022.

Recent Merger and Acquisition Activity

Status: pending **Announced:** Jan. 31, 2023

Midnight Gaming Corporation agreed to acquire TGS Esports Inc. for $0.135 cash per share, representing total consideration of $18,824,969. Midnight was a Shaumburg, Ill.-based company that owns and operates Gaming Television, a global eSports and gaming entertainment network.

Predecessor Detail - Name changed from Brockton Ventures Inc., July 30, 2020, pursuant to the Qualifying Transaction reverse takeover of Myesports Ventures Ltd. and concurrent amalgamation of Myesports with wholly owned 1231527 B.C. Ltd.

Directors - Spiro Khouri, CEO & interim CFO, Surrey, B.C.; Chi Yan (Carolina) Li, Richmond, B.C.; Spencer Smyl, Vancouver, B.C.

Other Exec. Officers - Dallas B. (Ben) Hoffman, chief tech. officer; Jackson Warren, chief product officer; Matthew (Matt) Low, v-p, opers.

Capital Stock

	Authorized (shs.)	Outstanding (shs.)[1]
Common	unlimited	139,444,213

[1] At Aug. 24, 2023

Major Shareholder - Lipont International Development Ltd. held 13.89% interest at Oct. 27, 2021.

Price Range - TGS/TSX-VEN (S)

Year	Volume	High	Low	Close
2022	3,246,721	$0.09	$0.05	$0.06
2021	33,024,454	$0.32	$0.06	$0.08
2020	19,604,014	$0.45	$0.10	$0.21
2019	184,000	$0.09	$0.07	$0.07
2018	71,250	$0.20	$0.11	$0.11

Capital Stock Changes - In October 2022, private placement of 1,000,000 common shares was completed at 20¢ per share.

Wholly Owned Subsidiaries

Even Matchup Gaming Inc., Toronto, Ont.
Myesports Ventures Ltd., Vancouver, B.C.
Pepper Esports Inc., Burnaby, B.C.
Volcanic Media Inc., B.C.

Investments

25% int. in **Mountainside Games Ltd.**, B.C.
Unlearning Network Inc., Vancouver, B.C.
Vancouver Street Battle Enterprises Ltd., Vancouver, B.C.

Financial Statistics

Periods ended:	12m June 30/21[A1]		12m June 30/20[oA2]
	$000s	%Chg	$000s
Operating revenue	**283**	**+53**	**185**
Cost of sales	113		324
Salaries & benefits	1,366		521
General & admin expense	1,665		1,090
Stock-based compensation	1,198		nil
Operating expense	**4,342**	**+124**	**1,936**
Operating income	**(4,059)**	**n.a.**	**(1,751)**
Deprec., depl. & amort.	166		316
Finance income	2		nil
Finance costs, gross	195		349
Write-downs/write-offs	(9,536)[3]		(2,208)
Pre-tax income	**(14,398)**	**n.a.**	**(4,599)**
Net income	**(14,398)**	**n.a.**	**(4,599)**
Cash & equivalent	851		54
Inventories	13		13
Accounts receivable	199		181
Current assets	1,124		285
Long-term investments	68		20
Fixed assets, net	302		394
Intangibles, net	778		nil
Total assets	**2,272**	**+225**	**699**
Bank indebtedness	15		77
Accts. pay. & accr. liabs	788		1,799
Current liabilities	1,610		1,990
Long-term debt, gross	536		495
Long-term debt, net	57		495
Long-term lease liabilities	878		1,009
Shareholders' equity	(272)		(2,795)
Cash from oper. activs	**(3,368)**	**n.a.**	**(143)**
Cash from fin. activs	3,976		407
Cash from invest. activs	190		(453)
Net cash position	**851**	**n.m.**	**54**
Capital expenditures	(13)		(648)
	$		$
Earnings per share*	(0.17)		(0.12)
Cash flow per share*	(0.04)		(0.00)
	shs		shs
No. of shs. o/s*	136,475,402		n.a.
Avg. no. of shs. o/s*	84,435,315		37,381,700
	%		%
Net profit margin	n.m.		n.m.
Return on equity	n.m.		n.m.
Return on assets	(956.11)		(318.59)

* Common
o Restated
[A] Reported in accordance with IFRS
[1] Results reflect the July 30, 2020, Qualifying Transaction reverse takeover acquisition of Myesports Ventures Ltd.
[2] Results pertain to Myesports Ventures Ltd.
[3] Includes goodwill impairment for wholly owned Pepper Esports Inc. and Volcanic Media Inc. totaling $9,540,749.

Latest Results

Periods ended:	3m Sept. 30/21[A]		3m Sept. 30/20[A]
	$000s	%Chg	$000s
Operating revenue	299	n.m.	9
Net income	(775)	n.a.	(1,990)
	$		$
Earnings per share*	(0.01)		(0.03)

* Common
[A] Reported in accordance with IFRS

Historical Summary
(as originally stated)

Fiscal Year	Oper. Rev.	Net Inc. Bef. Disc.	EPS*
	$000s	$000s	$
2021[A]	283	(14,398)	(0.17)
2020[A1]	185	(4,599)	(0.12)
2019[A1,2]	38	(1,247)	(0.06)

* Common
[A] Reported in accordance with IFRS
[1] Results pertain to Myesports Ventures Ltd.
[2] 49 weeks ended June 30, 2019.

T.8 THC BioMed Intl Ltd.

Symbol - THC **Exchange** - CSE **CUSIP** - 87243W
Head Office - 1-2550 Acland Rd, Kelowna, BC, V1X 7L4 **Telephone** - (250) 870-2512 **Toll-free** - (844) 842-6337 **Fax** - (888) 422-4718
Website - www.thcbiomed.com
Email - jm@thcmeds.ca
Investor Relations - John Miller (250) 870-2512
Auditors - Baker Tilly WM LLP C.A., Vancouver, B.C.
Lawyers - Owen Bird Law Corporation, Vancouver, B.C.
Transfer Agents - Computershare Trust Company of Canada Inc., Vancouver, B.C.
Employees - 35 at Nov. 24, 2022

Profile - (B.C. 1982) Cultivates, processes and sells medical and recreational marijuana in Canada.

Wholly owned **THC BioMed Ltd.** holds a licence from Health Canada to produce and sell medical and recreational marijuana from its facilities in Kelowna, B.C. Products include dried and live plant of genetic strains of medical marijuana, cannabis extracts, edibles, beverages, pre-rolls, topicals and cannabis oil products. Primary products are sold under the brands Pure Cannabis Sticks, THC Kiss Beverage Shot, THC Kiss Gummies, THC Kiss Biscuits, THC Sativa Landrace, THC Indica Landrace, THC Hybrid Landrace, CDB Indica Landrace, CDB Sativa Landrace and Smoke That Thunders. THC BioMed was also granted a licence to grow, produce and sell cannabis products on a large scale under the Cannabis Act.

Wholly owned **Clone Shipper Ltd.** manufactures Clone Shipper™ container, a packaging product used for the transportation of live plants which support the health of clones or young live plants and hold them securely for transport purposes.

Wholly owned **THC BioMed Victoria Falls Ltd.** holds a license for production of cannabis for medicinal and scientific use in Zimbabwe.

In November 2022, the company acquired a 40% share in an Asian company that is licensed to grow and sell medical cannabis in that country. The company would bring its intellectual property and fund the construction of the grow facility as well as being the financer for running the business.

In April 2022, the company sold its head office location on St. Paul Street, Kelowna, B.C. for a total of $2,715,000.

Predecessor Detail - Name changed from Thelon Capital Ltd., Mar. 23, 2015.

Directors - John Miller, pres. & CEO, Kelowna, B.C.; Hee Jung Chun, CFO, Kelowna, B.C.; Dr. Ashish Dave, Kelowna, B.C.; Penelope Laine, Whistler, B.C.

Capital Stock

	Authorized (shs.)	Outstanding (shs.)[1]
Common	unlimited	163,938,556

[1] At Nov. 24, 2022

Major Shareholder - John Miller held 19.21% interest at Nov. 24, 2022.

Price Range - THC/CSE

Year	Volume	High	Low	Close
2022	13,168,630	$0.10	$0.02	$0.03
2021	42,492,367	$0.34	$0.07	$0.08
2020	43,425,176	$0.25	$0.08	$0.10
2019	82,975,705	$0.75	$0.12	$0.16
2018	188,284,843	$3.36	$0.25	$0.32

Recent Close: $0.03

Capital Stock Changes - During fiscal 2022, 100,000 common shares were issued on exercise of options.

Wholly Owned Subsidiaries

Clone Shipper Ltd., Ariz.
THC Biomed Lesotho Ltd., Lesotho. Inactive
THC BioMed Ltd., B.C.
THC BioMed Victoria Falls Ltd., Canada.
THC2GO Dispensaries Ltd. Inactive

Financial Statistics

Periods ended:	12m July 31/22[A]		12m July 31/21[A]
	$000s	%Chg	$000s
Operating revenue	**3,340**	**-11**	**3,774**
Cost of sales	4,370		6,949
General & admin expense	1,107		1,110
Stock-based compensation	137		671
Operating expense	**5,614**	**-36**	**8,730**
Operating income	**(2,274)**	**n.a.**	**(4,955)**
Deprec., depl. & amort.	929		980
Finance costs, gross	501		422
Pre-tax income	**(3,066)**	**n.a.**	**(6,359)**
Net income	**(3,066)**	**n.a.**	**(6,359)**
Cash & equivalent	484		111
Inventories	1,719		1,961
Accounts receivable	447		553
Current assets	4,292		4,271
Fixed assets, net	10,405		13,125
Total assets	**14,746**	**-15**	**17,396**
Accts. pay. & accr. liabs	3,250		3,041
Current liabilities	6,845		5,968
Long-term debt, gross	4,277		3,880
Long-term debt, net	858		1,606
Long-term lease liabilities	110		39
Shareholders' equity	6,933		9,783
Cash from oper. activs	**(1,857)**	**n.a.**	**(1,010)**
Cash from fin. activs	(250)		767
Cash from invest. activs	2,480		(397)
Net cash position	**484**	**+336**	**111**
Capital expenditures	(160)		(369)
	$		$
Earnings per share*	(0.02)		(0.04)
Cash flow per share*	(0.01)		(0.01)
	shs		shs
No. of shs. o/s*	163,938,556		163,838,556
Avg. no. of shs. o/s*	163,902,392		163,565,571
	%		%
Net profit margin	(91.80)		(168.49)
Return on equity	(36.68)		(51.58)
Return on assets	(15.96)		(30.31)

* Common
[A] Reported in accordance with IFRS

Latest Results

Periods ended:	3m Oct. 31/22[A]		3m Oct. 31/21[A]
	$000s	%Chg	$000s
Operating revenue	668	-41	1,137
Net income	(331)	n.a.	25
	$		$
Earnings per share*	(0.00)		0.00

* Common
[A] Reported in accordance with IFRS

Historical Summary
(as originally stated)

Fiscal Year	Oper. Rev.	Net Inc. Bef. Disc.	EPS*
	$000s	$000s	$
2022[A]	3,340	(3,066)	(0.02)
2021[A]	3,774	(6,359)	(0.04)
2020[A]	4,178	(162)	(0.00)
2019[A]	1,490	(12,699)	(0.10)
2018[A]	925	(12,459)	(0.11)

* Common
[A] Reported in accordance with IFRS

T.9 TILT Holdings Inc.

Symbol - TILT **Exchange** - NEO **CUSIP** - 88688R
Head Office - 2801 E Camelback Rd, Suite 180, Phoenix, AZ, United States, 85016 **Telephone** - (623) 887-4990
Website - www.tiltholdings.com
Email - lricci@tiltholdings.com
Investor Relations - Lynn Ricci
Auditors - Macias Gini & O'Connell LLP C.P.A., San Francisco, Calif.
Transfer Agents - Odyssey Trust Company, Calgary, Alta.
FP500 Revenue Ranking - 631
Employees - 434 at Dec. 31, 2022
Profile - (B.C. 2018; orig. Nev., 2018) Operates in the cannabis industry with businesses engaged in inhalation technology, hardware, cultivation, manufacturing, processing, brand development and retail.
Operations are organized into two business segments: Inhalation Technology; and Cannabis.
Inhalation Technology - This segment develops, manufactures and distributes electronic vaping devices and systems for cannabis clients and brands across 37 U.S. states, as well as Canada, Israel, South America and the European Union.
Cannabis - This segment includes the production, cultivation, extraction and sale of cannabis products, including flower, vape cartridges, concentrates, capsules, oil syringes, tinctures, edibles and topicals, to wholesale and retail customers. Operations include a 100,000-sq.-ft. cultivation and processing facility and co-located dispensary in Taunton and two dispensaries in Brockton and Cambridge, all Massachusetts; a 33,500-sq.-ft. greenhouse cultivation and production facility in White Haven, Pa.; and a 21,000-sq.-ft. processing and extraction facility outside of Cleveland, Ohio. Also owns a 75% interest in a joint venture with the Shinnecock Indian Nation of Long Island, N.Y., which provides management services for the planning, construction and management of Shinnecock Nation's vertical cannabis operations, including a 60,000-sq.-ft. cultivation, processing, extraction and packaging facility, a dispensary and wellness lounge.
In May 2022, the company acquired its leased facility in Taunton, Mass., consisting of a 100,000-sq.-ft. building for cultivation, processing and manufacturing and a 3,000-sq.-ft. dispensary, for US$13,000,000. Concurrently, the company completed a sale and leaseback transaction for the facility with **Innovative Industrial Properties Inc.** for US$40,000,000.
In April 2022, the company entered into a sale and leaseback transaction with **Innovative Industrial Properties Inc.** for its 33,500-sq.-ft. cultivation and production facility in White Haven, Pa., for US$15,000,000.
Directors - John Barravecchia, chr., Ariz.; Tim Conder, interim CEO, Nev.; Adam R. Draizin; George Odden; Arthur (Art) Smuck
Other Exec. Officers - Brad Hoch, interim CFO & chief acctg. officer; Chris Kelly, chief revenue officer; Darryl K. Henderson, sr. v-p, HR; Lynn Ricci, v-p, IR & corp. commun.; Roseann Valencia-Fernandez, v-p, mktg.; Mark Higgins, deputy gen. counsel

Capital Stock

	Authorized (shs.)	Outstanding (shs.)[1]
Common	unlimited	334,064,756
Compressed	unlimited	nil
LP Unit	n.a.	43,821,379[2]

[1] At Apr. 11, 2023
[2] Securities of Jimmy Jang, L.P.

Common - One vote per share.
Compressed - Convertible, at the holder's option, into common shares on a 100-for-1 basis. Not convertible into common shares if the aggregate number of compressed shares and common shares held of record, directly or indirectly, by residents of the U.S., would exceed 40% of the aggregate number of compressed shares and common shares issued and outstanding after giving effect to such conversions. 100 votes per share.
Limited Partnership Unit - Securities of subsidiary Jimmy Jang, L.P. Convertible into common shares on a one-for-one basis.
Major Shareholder - Widely held at Apr. 11, 2023.

Price Range - TILT/NEO

Year	Volume	High	Low	Close
2022	4,315,500	$0.42	$0.04	$0.06
2021	41,919,500	$0.94	$0.25	$0.28
2020	86,329,467	$0.82	$0.16	$0.37
2019	163,721,146	$3.95	$0.23	$0.36
2018	7,877,981	$4.00	$1.51	$3.71

Recent Close: $0.03

Wholly Owned Subsidiaries

Jimmy Jang Holdings Inc., B.C.
Jimmy Jang, L.P., Del.
- 100% int. in **Baker Technologies, Inc.**, Denver, Colo.
  - 100% int. in **Standard Farms, LLC**, Pa.
  - 100% int. in **Standard Farms Ohio, LLC**, Ohio
- 100% int. in **Jupiter Research, LLC**, Phoenix, Ariz.
- 100% int. in **SFNY Holdings, Inc.**, Del.
  - 75% int. in **CGSF Group, LLC**, Del.
- 100% int. in **Santé Veritas Holdings Inc.**, Toronto, Ont.
- 100% int. in **Sea Hunter Therapeutics, LLC**, Boston, Mass.
  - 100% int. in **Commonwealth Alternative Care, Inc.**, Mass.

Financial Statistics

Periods ended:	12m Dec. 31/22[A]		12m Dec. 31/21[oA]
	US$000s	%Chg	US$000s
Operating revenue	**174,188**	**-14**	**202,705**
Cost of goods sold	130,441		147,921
Salaries & benefits	22,045		17,407
General & admin expense	23,163		20,530
Stock-based compensation	3,327		3,804
Operating expense	**178,976**	**-6**	**189,662**
Operating income	**(4,788)**	**n.a.**	**13,043**
Deprec., depl. & amort.	23,931		22,438
Finance income	215		593
Finance costs, gross	14,241		10,367
Write-downs/write-offs	(61,446)[1]		(30,398)
Pre-tax income	**(104,458)**	**n.a.**	**(49,029)**
Income taxes	3,006		(13,903)
Net income	**(107,464)**	**n.a.**	**(35,126)**
Net inc. for equity hldrs	**(107,455)**	**n.a.**	**(35,126)**
Net inc. for non-cont. int.	**(9)**	**n.a.**	**nil**
Cash & equivalent	2,202		4,221
Inventories	52,909		55,583
Accounts receivable	26,698		32,393
Current assets	85,927		100,613
Long-term investments	6,402		6,698
Fixed assets, net	67,937		62,360
Right-of-use assets	5,091		10,417
Intangibles, net	123,465		199,315
Total assets	**293,978**	**-23**	**381,348**
Accts. pay. & accr. liabs	58,170		49,482
Current liabilities	130,238		99,497
Long-term debt, gross	99,750		86,613
Long-term debt, net	35,631		45,855
Long-term lease liabilities	4,946		10,246
Shareholders' equity	121,351		225,490
Non-controlling interest	166		175
Cash from oper. activs	**8,612**	**n.a.**	**(8,599)**
Cash from fin. activs	4,783		6,514
Cash from invest. activs	(16,837)		186
Net cash position	**3,500**	**-50**	**6,952**
Capital expenditures	(15,142)		(3,064)
Capital disposals	9		1,233
	US$		US$
Earnings per share*	(0.29)		(0.09)
Cash flow per share*	0.02		(0.02)
	shs		shs
No. of shs. o/s*	333,694,012		330,261,380
Avg. no. of shs. o/s*	375,502,610		370,002,378
	%		%
Net profit margin	(61.69)		(17.33)
Return on equity	(60.50)		(13.81)
Return on assets	(26.18)		(6.83)
Foreign sales percent	93		93
No. of employees (FTEs)	434		361

* Common
[o] Restated
[A] Reported in accordance with U.S. GAAP
[1] Includes impairment of US$49,794,000 on goodwill and US$11,351,000 on intangible assets.

Historical Summary
(as originally stated)

Fiscal Year	Oper. Rev.	Net Inc. Bef. Disc.	EPS*
	US$000s	US$000s	US$
2022[A]	174,188	(107,464)	(0.29)
2021[B]	202,705	(45,121)	(0.12)
2020[B]	158,409	(52,107)	(0.14)
2019[B]	152,938	(133,374)	(0.37)
2018[B]	3,502	(550,119)	(18.14)

* Common
[A] Reported in accordance with U.S. GAAP
[B] Reported in accordance with IFRS

T.10 TMX Group Limited*

Symbol - X **Exchange** - TSX **CUSIP** - 87262K
Head Office - 300-100 Adelaide St W, Toronto, ON, M5H 1S3 **Toll-free** - (888) 873-8392 **Fax** - (416) 947-4727
Website - www.tmx.com
Email - amin.mousavian@tmx.com
Investor Relations - Amin Mousavian (888) 873-8392
Auditors - KPMG LLP C.A., Toronto, Ont.
Transfer Agents - TSX Trust Company, Toronto, Ont.
FP500 Revenue Ranking - 320
Employees - 1,693 at Dec. 31, 2022
Profile - (Ont. 2011) Owns and operates the Toronto Stock Exchange (TSX), serving the Canadian senior equity market; the TSX Venture Exchange (TSXV), serving the Canadian public venture equity market; the TSX Alpha Exchange, an alternative trading system for TSX and TSXV listed securities; the Canadian Depository for Securities (CDS), an automated facility for the clearing and settlement of equities and fixed income transactions and custody of securities; the Montreal

Exchange (MX), a financial derivatives exchange; the Canadian Derivatives Clearing Corporation, a clearinghouse for options and futures contracts and certain financial instruments; and Trayport, a connectivity network and data and analytics platform for the wholesale energy markets, to provide listing markets, trading markets, clearing facilities, depository services, technology solutions, data products and other services to the global financial community.

Capital Formation - Owns and operates Toronto Stock Exchange (TSX), the senior equities market in Canada, and TSX Venture Exchange (TSXV), the venture equities market in Canada. TSXV also has a board for issuers that have fallen below its ongoing listing standards, referred to as NEX. In general, established issuers initially list on TSX in connection with their initial public offerings (IPOs), by graduating from TSXV, or by seeking a secondary listing in addition to their existing listing venue. Venture stage companies generally list on TSXV in connection with an IPO or through alternative methods, such as TSXV's Capital Pool Company program or a reverse takeover. Issuers pay initial listing fees, annual sustaining listing fees, and additional listing fees for subsequent capital market transactions, such as private placements and public offerings. Wholly owned **TSX Trust Company** provides corporate trust, transfer agency, registrar and other services for equity and debt issuers and private companies.

Equities and Fixed Income Trading & Clearing - Facilitates fully electronic trading of securities on its equities markets, TSX, TSXV and TSX Alpha Exchange. Fixed income trading is conducted through wholly owned **Shorcan Brokers Limited**, an interdealer broker specializing in Canadian fixed income products, including bonds, repurchase agreements and swaps. Wholly owned **The Canadian Depository for Securities Limited** (CDS) is Canada's national securities depository, clearing and settlement hub for domestic and cross-border depository-eligible securities. CDS's clearing and settlement services support Canada's equity, fixed income and money markets as well as derivative transactions in depository-eligible securities, and offer related services such as buy-ins, risk controls and reporting and facilitating trades of eligible securities before they are publicly distributed through CDSX, the multilateral clearing and settlement system of CDS. CDS's depository services include the safe custody and movement of depository-eligible domestic and international securities, recordkeeping, processing post-trade transactions, and collecting and distributing entitlements related to securities deposited by participants. CDS also offers other services such as the issuance of International Security Identification Numbers (ISINs), depository eligibility, securities registration, and entitlement and corporate action event management.

Derivatives Trading & Clearing - Through wholly owned **Montréal Exchange Inc.** (MX), operates Canada's standardized financial derivatives exchange, which offers trading in interest rate, index, equity and currency derivatives to Canadian and international market participants. **Canadian Derivatives Clearing Corporation** (CDCC), wholly owned by MX, acts as the central clearing counterparty for exchange-traded derivative products in Canada and for a range of customized financial instruments. CDCC provides clearing and settlement services for MX transactions and certain over-the-counter derivatives, including fixed income repurchase and reverse repurchase agreement transactions. CDCC is also the issuer of options traded on MX markets. MX subsidiary **BOX Options Market LLC** operates an equity options exchange in the U.S.

Global Solutions, Insights & Analytics - Through its information services division, TMX Datalinx, provides a broad range of real-time, historical and other data products and services to customers worldwide. Real-time and historical data products include market information derived from TSX, TSXV, TSX Alpha Exchange and MX and are delivered to end users directly or via Canadian and global redistributors that sell data feeds and desktop market data. TMX Datalinx also offers a comprehensive suite of S&P/TSX Index products as well as market insights and analytics through an integrated set of financial content, tools and applications. This segment also provides co-location services, which allow clients to locate their trading and data applications in the company's data centres and obtain low-latency access to the company's trading engines and data feeds as well as to other capital market clients, financial content providers and technology providers. Through wholly owned **Trayport Holdings Limited**, offers technology solutions focused on the European and global wholesale energy markets for price discovery, trade execution, post-trade transparency and post-trade straight through processing. Trayport customers include energy traders, brokers and exchanges.

In June 2022, the company acquired a minority interest in London, U.K.-based **Ventriks Ltd.**, which offers a platform for data acquisition, integration and business intelligence. Terms were not disclosed.

Recent Merger and Acquisition Activity

Status: completed **Announced:** Apr. 21, 2023
TMX Group Limited sold wholly owned SigmaLogic, Inc. to affiliate VettaFi Holdings LLC in exchange for additional common shares of VettaFi. As a result, TMX increased its interest in VettaFi to 22.3% from 21.3%. SigmaLogic, a U.S.-based fintech firm, owns the LOGICLY platform which offers analytics and portfolio tools to the wealth management industry and investment fund manufacturers.

Status: completed **Announced:** Feb. 16, 2023
TMX Group Limited acquired the remaining interest in New York, N.Y.-based SigmaLogic, Inc. (dba LOGICLY; formerly ETFLogic), a provider of a comprehensive web-based investment research, analytics and portfolio management platform for wealth advisors, for US$4,500,000.

Status: completed **Announced:** Jan. 9, 2023
TMX Group Limited acquired a 21.3% interest in New York, N.Y.-based VettaFi Holdings LLC for US$175,000,000. Vettafi provides exchange-traded fund (ETF) services including data, analytics, indexing and digital distribution to financial advisors, asset managers and institutional investors.

Status: completed **Revised:** Nov. 9, 2022
UPDATE: The transaction was completed. PREVIOUS: TMX Group Limited agreed to acquire Woburn, Mass.-based Wall Street Horizon, Inc. (WSH) for US$14,400,000 plus a contingent consideration of up to US$10,000,000 based on the achievement of certain revenue targets in 2023 and 2024. WSH provides corporate event information, including earnings dates, dividend dates, options expiration dates, splits, spinoffs and a variety of investor-related conferences, to traders, portfolio managers, academics and others. WSH covered 9,000 publicly traded companies worldwide.

Predecessor Detail - Succeeded TMX Group Inc., Sept. 14, 2012, pursuant to plan of arrangement resulting in acquisition of the remaining 20% interest in TMX Group Inc. by TMX Group Limited (formerly Maple Group Acquisition Corporation) on a sh.-for-sh. basis. Maple Group acquired an initial 80% interest in TMX Group Inc. on Aug. 10, 2012, for $50 per share.

Directors - Luc Bertrand, chr., Montréal, Qué.; John McKenzie, CEO, Burlington, Ont.; Nicolas Darveau-Garneau, Los Gatos, Calif.; Martine M. Irman, Toronto, Ont.; Moe Kermani, Vancouver, B.C.; William (Bill) Linton, Toronto, Ont.; Audrey Mascarenhas, Calgary, Alta.; Monique Mercier, Montréal, Qué.; Kevin M. Sullivan, Toronto, Ont.; Claude Tessier, Laval, Qué.; Eric M. Wetlaufer, Newton, Mass.; Ava G. Yaskiel, Toronto, Ont.

Other Exec. Officers - Jayakumar (Jay) Rajarathinam, COO; David Arnold, CFO; Cindy Bush, chief HR officer; Cheryl Graden, chief legal & enterprise corp. affairs officer & corp. sec.; Luc Fortin, pres. & CEO, Montreal Exchange Inc. & global head, trading; Loui Anastasopoulos, CEO, Toronto Stock Exchange & global head, capital formation; Peter Conroy, CEO, Trayport Limited

Capital Stock

	Authorized (shs.)	Outstanding (shs.)[1]
Preference	unlimited	nil
Common	unlimited	278,664,835

[1] At July 24, 2023

Common - The company's articles of incorporation provide for restrictions on voting share ownership. Ownership of a person or company (or combination of persons or companies acting jointly or in concert) is restricted to a maximum of 10% of the voting shares of the company. The Ontario Securities Commission and Autorité des marchés financiers have the power to change the share ownership restrictions threshold in the future. One vote per share.

Options - At Dec. 31, 2022, options were outstanding to purchase 925,964 common shares at prices ranging from $40 to $132.10 per share with a weighted average remaining contractual life of 4.8 years.

Normal Course Issuer Bid - The company plans to make normal course purchases of up to 2,800,000 post-split common shares representing 1% of the total outstanding. The bid commenced on Mar. 3, 2023, and expires on Mar. 2, 2024.

Major Shareholder - Widely held at Mar. 13, 2023.

Price Range - X/TSX

Year	Volume	High	Low	Close
2022	153,343,632	$28.58	$24.28	$27.10
2021	140,410,416	$29.14	$24.03	$25.65
2020	228,754,208	$28.99	$16.90	$25.43
2019	199,736,560	$24.10	$14.01	$22.49
2018	122,619,872	$18.07	$13.77	$14.15

Split: 5-for-1 split in June 2023
Recent Close: $29.51

Capital Stock Changes - On June 14, 2023, common shares were split on a 5-for-1 basis.

During 2022, 358,238 common shares were issued on exercise of options and 560,000 common shares were repurchased under a Normal Course Issuer Bid.

Dividends

X com Ra $0.72 pa Q est. Aug. 25, 2023
5-for-1 split eff. June 14, 2023
Prev. Rate: $3.48 est. Mar. 10, 2023
Prev. Rate: $3.32 est. Mar. 11, 2022
Prev. Rate: $3.08 est. June 11, 2021
Prev. Rate: $2.80 est. Sept. 4, 2020

Long-Term Debt - Outstanding at Dec. 31, 2022:

4.461% ser.B debs. due Oct. 2023	$249,900,000
2.997% ser.D debs. due Dec. 2024	299,500,000
3.779% ser.E debs. due June 2028	199,400,000
2.016% ser.F debs. due Feb. 2031	248,900,000
	997,700,000
Less: Current portion	249,900,000
	747,800,000

Wholly Owned Subsidiaries

Alpha Exchange Inc., Canada.
The Canadian Depository for Securities Limited, Toronto, Ont.
- 100% int. in **CDS Clearing and Depository Services Inc.**, Canada.
- 100% int. in **CDS Innovations Inc.**, Canada.

Montréal Exchange Inc., Montréal, Qué.
- 100% int. in **Canadian Derivatives Clearing Corporation**, Toronto, Ont.
- 100% int. in **MX US 1 Inc.**, Del.
  - 100% int. in **MX US 2 Inc.**, Del.
    - 20% int. in **BOX Exchange LLC**, Del.
    - 47.89% int. in **BOX Holdings Group LLC**, Del. Voting interest of 51.43%
      - 100% int. in **Box Options Market LLC**, Del.

Shorcan Brokers Limited, Toronto, Ont.
TMX Investor Solutions Inc., Toronto, Ont.
TSX Inc., Toronto, Ont.
- 100% int. in **TSX Venture Exchange Inc.**, Calgary, Alta.

TSX Trust Company, Toronto, Ont.
Trayport Holdings Limited, United Kingdom.
- 100% int. in **Trayport Limited**, London, Middx., United Kingdom.
  - 100% int. in **Trayport Austria GmbH**, Vienna, Austria.
  - 100% int. in **Trayport Germany GmbH**, Bremen, Germany.
  - 100% int. in **Trayport Pte. Ltd.**, Singapore.

Financial Statistics

Periods ended:	12m Dec. 31/22[A]		12m Dec. 31/21[A]
	$000s	%Chg	$000s
Operating revenue	**1,116,600**	**+14**	**980,700**
Cost of sales	90,900		64,600
Salaries & benefits	274,700		253,500
General & admin expense	112,700		84,300
Operating expense	**478,300**	**+19**	**402,400**
Operating income	**638,300**	**+10**	**578,300**
Deprec., depl. & amort.	113,800		87,100
Finance income	7,100		1,600
Finance costs, gross	37,900		37,700
Investment income	(1,300)		24,200
Pre-tax income	**670,300**	**+40**	**479,300**
Income taxes	88,500		140,800
Net income	**581,800**	**+72**	**338,500**
Net inc. for equity hldrs	**542,700**	**+60**	**338,500**
Net inc. for non-cont. int	**39,100**	**n.a.**	**nil**
Cash & equivalent	493,100		341,600
Accounts receivable	156,500		132,600
Current assets	50,262,500		57,800,300
Long-term investments	15,500		45,800
Fixed assets, net	60,700		64,300
Right-of-use assets	79,700		84,300
Intangibles, net	5,517,600		5,156,900
Total assets	**55,983,100**	**-11**	**63,199,400**
Bank indebtedness	14,100		2,000
Accts. pay. & accr. liabs	365,500		332,800
Current liabilities	50,012,400		57,519,000
Long-term debt, gross	997,700		997,100
Long-term debt, net	747,800		997,100
Long-term lease liabilities	87,600		88,300
Shareholders' equity	3,987,200		3,706,100
Non-controlling interest	220,200		nil
Cash from oper. activs	**444,100**	**+1**	**441,400**
Cash from fin. activs	(292,900)		(194,800)
Cash from invest. activs	(41,400)		(203,900)
Net cash position	**375,700**	**+42**	**264,300**
Capital expenditures	(51,900)		(51,200)
Pension fund surplus	22,100		21,300
	$		$
Earnings per share*	1.95		1.21
Cash flow per share*	1.59		1.57
Cash divd. per share*	0.66		0.60
	shs		shs
No. of shs. o/s*	278,401,860		279,410,670
Avg. no. of shs. o/s*	278,729,125		280,492,300
	%		%
Net profit margin	52.10		34.52
Return on equity	14.11		9.25
Return on assets	1.03		0.74
Foreign sales percent	40		31
No. of employees (FTEs)	1,693		1,576

* Common
[A] Reported in accordance with IFRS

Latest Results

Periods ended:	6m June 30/23[A]		6m June 30/22[□A]
	$000s	%Chg	$000s
Operating revenue	605,300	+6	572,400
Net income	202,400	-47	379,700
Net inc. for equity hldrs	186,300	-48	359,500
Net inc. for non-cont. int	16,100		20,200
	$		$
Earnings per share*	0.67		1.29

* Common
[□] Restated
[A] Reported in accordance with IFRS

Historical Summary
(as originally stated)

Fiscal Year	Oper. Rev. $000s	Net Inc. Bef. Disc. $000s	EPS* $
2022[A]	1,116,600	581,800	1.95
2021[A]	980,700	338,500	1.21
2020[A]	865,100	279,700	0.99
2019[A]	806,900	247,600	0.88
2018[A]	817,100	286,000	1.03

* Common
[A] Reported in accordance with IFRS
Note: Adjusted throughout for 5-for-1 split in June 2023

T.11 TRYP Therapeutics Inc.

Symbol - TRYP **Exchange** - CSE **CUSIP** - 89854F
Head Office - 301-1665 Ellis St, Kelowna, BC, V1Y 2B3 **Telephone** - (250) 717-1840 **Toll-free** - (833) 811-8797
Website - trypttherapeutics.com
Email - pmolloy@tryptherapeutics.com
Investor Relations - Peter Molloy (833) 811-8797
Auditors - Smythe LLP C.A., Vancouver, B.C.
Lawyers - Pushor Mitchell LLP, Kelowna, B.C.
Transfer Agents - Computershare Trust Company of Canada Inc., Vancouver, B.C.
Profile - (B.C. 2019) Developing psilocybin and psilocin-based drug products for the treatment of diseases with unmet medical needs such as chronic pain and eating disorders.

The company's Psilocybin-For-Neuropsychiatric disorders (PFN™) program is designed to treat neuropsychiatric disorders using the oral administration of synthetic psilocybin, TRP-8802, which is in the Phase 2a clinical trial with the University of Florida to evaluate for binge eating disorder and Phase 2a clinical trial to evaluate for fibromyalgia with the University of Michigan would commence in early 2023. The other primary indications are in the areas of chronic pain including phantom limb pain and complex regional pain syndrome; and eating disorders including hypothalamic obesity.

Also developing its proprietary psilocybin-based product, TRP-8803, which would be administered through intravenous infusion and is designed to enhance the positive effects of psilocybin and psilocybin-related compounds whereby reducing the limitations of psilocybin dosed through other routes of administration, including oral, nasal and sublingual.

Directors - P. Gage Jull, chr., Ont.; Peter Molloy, chief bus. officer, New York, N.Y.; Dr. James Kuo, La Jolla, Calif.; Chris Ntoumenopoulos, Australia; David L. Tousley, Wake Forest, N.C.
Other Exec. Officers - Dr. James (Jim) Gilligan, pres., interim CEO & chief science officer; Sidney Taubenfeld, COO; James (Jim) O'Neill, CFO; Dr. Peter Guzzo, v-p, drug devel.

Capital Stock

	Authorized (shs.)	Outstanding (shs.)[1]
Preferred	unlimited	nil
Common	unlimited	96,419,347

[1] At Jan. 25, 2023

Major Shareholder - Dr. William J. (Bill) Garner held 40.26% interest at May 17, 2022.

Price Range - TRYP/CSE

Year	Volume	High	Low	Close
2022	15,040,910	$0.28	$0.06	$0.10
2021	49,603,065	$1.20	$0.21	$0.27
2020	12,152,015	$0.90	$0.65	$0.75

Recent Close: $0.08

Capital Stock Changes - In February 2022, private placement of 5,000,000 common shares was completed at 20¢ per share. In April 2022, private placement of 20,000,000 units (1 common share & ½ warrant) at 15¢ per unit was completed. Also during fiscal 2022, common shares were issued as follows: 3,570,588 for services, 1,000,000 by private placement and 180,000 on exercise of options.

Wholly Owned Subsidiaries
Tryp Therapeutics (USA) Inc., Del.

Financial Statistics

Periods ended:	12m Aug. 31/22[A]		12m Aug. 31/21[oA]
	$000s	%Chg	$000s
Research & devel. expense	2,964		1,281
General & admin expense	4,125		3,546
Stock-based compensation	275		2,462
Operating expense	**7,364**	**+1**	**7,288**
Operating income	**(7,364)**	**n.a.**	**(7,288)**
Finance income	3		11
Write-downs/write-offs	nil		(961)
Pre-tax income	**(7,495)**	**n.a.**	**(8,255)**
Net income	**(7,495)**	**n.a.**	**(8,255)**
Cash & equivalent	1,882		3,692
Current assets	2,175		4,083
Intangibles, net	163		25
Total assets	**2,339**	**-43**	**4,108**
Accts. pay. & accr. liabs	1,195		185
Current liabilities	1,195		185
Shareholders' equity	1,143		3,923
Cash from oper. activs	**(5,809)**	**n.a.**	**(5,063)**
Cash from fin. activs	4,137		4,137
Cash from invest. activs	(138)		(25)
Net cash position	**1,882**	**-49**	**3,692**
	$		$
Earnings per share*	(0.10)		(0.14)
Cash flow per share*	(0.07)		(0.09)
	shs		shs
No. of shs. o/s*	96,419,347		96,419,347
Avg. no. of shs. o/s*	78,064,602		57,512,239
	%		%
Net profit margin	n.a.		n.a.
Return on equity	(295.89)		(286.38)
Return on assets	(232.51)		(268.76)

* Common
[o] Restated
[A] Reported in accordance with IFRS

Latest Results

Periods ended:	3m Nov. 30/22[A]		3m Nov. 30/21[A]
	$000s	%Chg	$000s
Net income	(1,634)	n.a.	(3,001)
	$		$
Earnings per share*	(0.02)		(0.05)

* Common
[A] Reported in accordance with IFRS

Historical Summary
(as originally stated)

Fiscal Year	Oper. Rev. $000s	Net Inc. Bef. Disc. $000s	EPS* $
2022[A]	nil	(7,495)	(0.10)
2021[A]	nil	(8,255)	(0.14)
2020[A1,2]	nil	(423)	(0.02)

* Common
[A] Reported in accordance with IFRS
[1] 49 weeks ended Aug. 31, 2020.
[2] As shown in the prospectus dated Dec. 8, 2020.

T.12 TUGA Innovations, Inc.

Symbol - TUGA **Exchange** - CSE **CUSIP** - 89904W
Head Office - 1000-409 Granville St, Vancouver, BC, V6C 1T2 **Telephone** - (604) 602-0001
Website - tugainnovations.com
Email - faizaanlalani17@gmail.com
Investor Relations - Faizaan Lalani (604) 602-0001
Auditors - Crowe MacKay LLP C.A., Vancouver, B.C.
Transfer Agents - Odyssey Trust Company
Profile - (B.C. 2021) Developing an electric three-wheeled vehicle under the TUGA brand.

The TUGA is an urban commuter vehicle built on a flexible, modular platform that can be configured for the leisure, commuter, delivery, taxi, rental and ride share market. The vehicle has two seats and is no wider than a motorcycle and designed to deliver an estimated 160 km range, have an estimated top speed of 140 km per hour. TUGA model line up includes TUGA Thunder and TUGA Falcon, which are the limited-edition and high-performance model options; TUGA Commuter and TUGA Deliver, which are the introductory models that include swappable body parts, additional safety components and a Mobility-as-a-Service (MaaS) package; and TUGA Cargo and TUGA Pickup, which offers full-time fully extended chassis with 600 litres of cargo space in a vehicle only 88 cm wide, combined with an expanded rear wheelbase of 128cm.

In November 2022, the company entered into a letter of intent to form a manufacturing consortium to produce the initial TUGA commercial prototypes, limited series product line and for the continued advancements towards future production vehicles. The consortium consists of the company, **VANGEST Group** and **Optimal Structural Solutions**. Pursuant to the letter of intent, the consortium would engage in engineering design, dynamic and structural simulations, body moulding, interior design and fabrication, EU regulatory homologation, and integration of subsystems and components of the vehicles. The consortium would also model, design, and implement standards of quality for planned future production and assembly of TUGA models at anticipated regional production units within specified sales territories across the globe.

Directors - John Hagie, chr. & CEO, Portugal; Faizaan Lalani, CFO & corp. sec., Vancouver, B.C.; César Barbosa, v-p, Portugal; António Câmara, Portugal; Lucas Leonardi, France

Capital Stock

	Authorized (shs.)	Outstanding (shs.)[1]
Common	unlimited	44,495,021

[1] At Dec. 22, 2022

Major Shareholder - César Barbosa held 12.84% interest and Kraig Schultz held 12.84% interest at Oct. 26, 2022.

Price Range - TUGA/CSE

Year	Volume	High	Low	Close
2022	4,745,366	$1.12	$0.05	$0.10
2021	719,244	$0.85	$0.56	$0.72

Recent Close: $0.04

Capital Stock Changes - In December 2021, 11,118,750 units (1 common share & ½ warrant) were issued without further consideration on exchange of subscription receipts sold previously by private placement at 40¢ each. Also during fiscal 2022, common shares were issued as follows: 2,080,000 on vesting of restricted share units, 99,939 on exercise of warrants and 20,000 on exercise of options.

Wholly Owned Subsidiaries
TUGA-Global Inc., Grand Haven, Mich.

Financial Statistics

Periods ended:	12m July 31/22[A]		11m July 31/21[A]
	$000s	%Chg	$000s
Research & devel. expense	1,045		172
General & admin expense	2,568		346
Stock-based compensation	2,195		nil
Other operating expense	nil		40
Operating expense	**5,808**	**+941**	**558**
Operating income	**(5,808)**	**n.a.**	**(558)**
Deprec., depl. & amort.	3		nil
Pre-tax income	**(5,810)**	**n.a.**	**(558)**
Net income	**(5,810)**	**n.a.**	**(558)**
Cash & equivalent	855		472
Accounts receivable	77		7
Current assets	948		479
Fixed assets, net	45		nil
Intangibles, net	12		11
Total assets	**1,005**	**+105**	**490**
Accts. pay. & accr. liabs	142		114
Current liabilities	142		114
Shareholders' equity	863		376
Cash from oper. activs	**(3,671)**	**n.a.**	**(484)**
Cash from fin. activs	4,116		672
Cash from invest. activs	(48)		293
Net cash position	**855**	**+81**	**472**
Capital expenditures	(48)		nil
	$		$
Earnings per share*	(0.15)		(0.05)
Cash flow per share*	(0.09)		(0.04)
	shs		shs
No. of shs. o/s*	44,495,021		31,176,332
Avg. no. of shs. o/s*	39,486,159		10,796,491
	%		%
Net profit margin	n.a.		n.a.
Return on equity	(937.85)		n.m.
Return on assets	(777.26)		n.a.

* Common
[A] Reported in accordance with IFRS

Latest Results

Periods ended:	3m Oct. 31/22[A]		3m Oct. 31/21[A]
	$000s	%Chg	$000s
Net income	(623)	n.a.	(481)
	$		$
Earnings per share*	(0.01)		(0.02)

* Common
[A] Reported in accordance with IFRS

T.13 TUP Capital Inc.

Symbol - TUP.P **Exchange** - TSX-VEN **CUSIP** - 89979H
Head Office - 1 First Canadian Place, 3400-100 King St W, Toronto, ON, M5X 1A4 **Telephone** - (613) 232-1567
Email - paul@hypernet.ca
Investor Relations - Paul Barbeau (613) 218-5319
Auditors - MNP LLP C.A., Toronto, Ont.
Transfer Agents - TSX Trust Company, Toronto, Ont.
Profile - (B.C. 2020) Capital Pool Company.
Common reinstated on TSX-VEN, Sept. 20, 2022.

Recent Merger and Acquisition Activity

Status: pending **Announced:** June 16, 2023

TUP Capital Inc. entered into a letter of intent (LOI) for the Qualifying Transaction reverse takeover acquisition of Delaware-based Orthoforge, Inc., which has developed a wearable sensor patch that utilizes acoustics to quantify the stage of bone fracture and soft tissue injuries, for issuance of common shares at a deemed price of 20¢ per share. The transaction was valued at $10,750,000. Upon completion, TUP Capital would change its name to Orthoforge Inc.

Status: terminated **Revised:** May 2, 2022

UPDATE: The LOI expired and was not extended. PREVIOUS: TUP Capital Inc. entered into a letter of intent (LOI) for the Qualifying Transaction reverse takeover acquisition of Michigan-based BeyondChipz LLC, which develops, markets and sells tortilla chips and related products that are made with plant-based pea protein food ingredients, for issuance of post-consolidated common shares at a deemed price of 35¢ per share (following a 1-for-2.3 share consolidation). The transaction was valued at $14,000,000.

Directors - Paul Barbeau, chr., CEO & corp. sec., Ottawa, Ont.; Michael L. Labiak, La Salle, Ont.; Kirby McBride, Mass.; Sarton Molnar-Fenton, Mass.; William H. (Bill) Pound, Ont.

Other Exec. Officers - David R. Chow, CFO

Capital Stock

	Authorized (shs.)	Outstanding (shs.)[1]
Common	unlimited	11,900,000

[1] At May 31, 2023

Major Shareholder - Widely held at May 31, 2021.

Price Range - TUP.P/TSX-VEN

Year	Volume	High	Low	Close
2022............	186,000	$0.06	$0.03	$0.03
2021............	160,000	$0.10	$0.07	$0.08

Recent Close: $0.04

Capital Stock Changes - There were no changes to capital stock during fiscal 2023.

T.14 TUT Fitness Group Inc.

Symbol - GYM **Exchange** - TSX-VEN **CUSIP** - 90109P

Head Office - 2050-1055 Georgia St W, Vancouver, BC, V6E 3P3 **Toll-free** - (800) 674-5641

Website - tutfitnessgroup.com

Email - robs@tutfitnessgroup.com

Investor Relations - Robert Smith (800) 674-5641

Auditors - Dale Matheson Carr-Hilton LaBonte LLP C.A., Vancouver, B.C.

Transfer Agents - Computershare Trust Company of Canada Inc., Vancouver, B.C.

Profile - (B.C. 2019) Produces and sells portable home gym equipment and offers paid-subscription training mobile application.

Flagship products are TUT Trainer™, a wall-attachable gym equipment; and TUT Rower™, a portable rowing machine that can be used in combination with the TUT Trainer™. Both products utilize stackable resistance bands called TUT Plates™ that enable users to load incremental resistance, offering a total of more than 300 exercises that don't put excessive strain on joints and tendons. Equipment are manufactured by a contract manufacturer in China, shipped to warehouses in Van Nuys, Calif., and Vancouver, B.C., and sold in the United States and Canada.

Also offers subscriptions to its TUT training app which is powered by software developer, Trainerize. The app includes on-demand training content and live connectivity.

Predecessor Detail - Name changed from AAJ Capital 2 Corp., Sept. 29, 2021, pursuant to the Qualifying Transaction reverse takeover acquisition of TUT Fitness Group Limited; basis 1 new for 2 old shs.

Directors - Robert Smith, CEO, Vancouver, B.C.; Praveen K. Varshney, CFO & corp. sec., Vancouver, B.C.; Satnam Brar, Surrey, B.C.; Capt. Mervyn J. Pinto, Surrey, B.C.

Other Exec. Officers - Tima Fader, COO; Costa Dedegikas, chief mktg. officer; Mitchell Malandrino, v-p, corp. devel.; Stefan Sillner, v-p, intl. sales & distribution

Capital Stock

	Authorized (shs.)	Outstanding (shs.)[1]
Common	unlimited	30,716,461

[1] At July 10, 2023

Major Shareholder - Aaron Fader held 13.92% interest, Varshney Capital Corp. held 11.8% interest and Ever & Ever Investments And Development Limited held 10.26% interest at July 10, 2023.

Price Range - GYM/TSX-VEN

Year	Volume	High	Low	Close
2022............	3,426,569	$0.24	$0.03	$0.05
2021............	1,458,535	$0.50	$0.20	$0.22
2020............	267,750	$0.42	$0.24	$0.32
2019............	16,000	$0.36	$0.23	$0.23

Consolidation: 1-for-2 cons. in Sept. 2021

Recent Close: $0.04

Capital Stock Changes - During fiscal 2022, 1,000 common shares were issued on exercise of options.

Wholly Owned Subsidiaries

1195143 B.C. Ltd., B.C.

TUT Fitness Group Limited, Surrey, B.C.

Financial Statistics

Periods ended:	12m Sept. 30/22[A]		12m Sept. 30/21[A1]
	US$000s	%Chg	US$000s
Operating revenue........................	**108**	**+200**	**36**
Cost of goods sold..........................	112		28
Salaries & benefits..........................	45		34
Research & devel. expense..............	37		28
General & admin expense...............	1,059		809
Stock-based compensation.............	27		222
Operating expense........................	**1,280**	**+14**	**1,121**
Operating income.........................	**(1,172)**	**n.a.**	**(1,085)**
Deprec., depl. & amort.....................	116		9
Finance income..............................	nil		4
Finance costs, gross........................	15		10
Write-downs/write-offs.....................	(435)		6
Pre-tax income.............................	**(1,665)**	**n.a.**	**(2,146)**
Net income...................................	**(1,665)**	**n.a.**	**(2,146)**
Cash & equivalent...........................	392		2,434
Inventories.....................................	566		113
Accounts receivable........................	35		24
Current assets................................	1,059		2,764
Fixed assets, net.............................	181		8
Intangibles, net...............................	638		1,199
Total assets..................................	**1,879**	**-53**	**3,971**
Accts. pay. & accr. liabs..................	70		448
Current liabilities............................	104		461
Long-term lease liabilities...............	107		nil
Shareholders' equity........................	1,668		3,511
Cash from oper. activs..................	**(1,751)**	**n.a.**	**(986)**
Cash from fin. activs........................	(155)		3,429
Cash from invest. activs..................	(94)		(20)
Net cash position..........................	**392**	**-84**	**2,434**
Capital expenditures........................	(48)		(10)
	US$		US$
Earnings per share*.........................	(0.05)		(0.12)
Cash flow per share*.......................	(0.06)		(0.06)
	shs		shs
No. of shs. o/s*................................	30,716,461		30,715,461
Avg. no. of shs. o/s*........................	30,716,099		17,452,176
	%		%
Net profit margin.............................	n.m.		n.m.
Return on equity..............................	(64.30)		n.m.
Return on assets.............................	(56.41)		(104.96)

* Common

[A] Reported in accordance with IFRS

[1] Results prior to Sept. 29, 2021, pertain to and reflect the Qualifying Transaction reverse takeover of TUT Fitness Group Limited.

Latest Results

Periods ended:	6m Mar. 31/23[A]		6m Mar. 31/22[A]
	US$000s	%Chg	US$000s
Operating revenue..........................	134	+97	68
Net income.....................................	(500)	n.a.	(895)
	US$		US$
Earnings per share*.........................	(0.02)		(0.03)

* Common

[A] Reported in accordance with IFRS

Historical Summary
(as originally stated)

Fiscal Year	Oper. Rev.	Net Inc. Bef. Disc.	EPS*
	US$000s	US$000s	US$
2022[A]...................	108	(1,665)	(0.05)
2021[A]...................	36	(2,146)	(0.12)
2020[A]...................	29	(78)	n.a.
2019[A]...................	30	(153)	n.a.

* Common

[A] Reported in accordance with IFRS

Note: Adjusted throughout for 1-for-2 cons. in Sept. 2021

T.15 TVA Group Inc.*

Symbol - TVA.B **Exchange** - TSX **CUSIP** - 872948

Head Office - 1600 boul de Maisonneuve E, Montréal, QC, H2L 4P2 **Telephone** - (514) 526-9251 **Fax** - (514) 598-6085

Website - www.groupetva.ca

Email - marjorie.daoust@tva.ca

Investor Relations - Marjorie Daoust (514) 526-9251

Auditors - Ernst & Young LLP C.A., Montréal, Qué.

Lawyers - Norton Rose Fulbright Canada LLP

Transfer Agents - TSX Trust Company, Toronto, Ont.

FP500 Subsidiary Revenue Ranking - 84

Employees - 1,327 at Dec. 31, 2022

Profile - (Que. 1960) Operates broadcast television stations, provides film production and audiovisual services to the film and television industries, publishes magazines primarily for the French-language market in Canada, and produces and distributes television programs and movies for the world market.

Broadcasting - Creates, broadcasts and produces entertainment, sports, news and public affairs television programs for the French-language market in Canada. Owns and operates six of the 10 television stations that make up the TVA Network, including CFTM-TV (Montreal), CFCM-TV (Quebec City), CHLT-TV (Sherbrooke), CHEM-TV (Trois-Rivières), CFER-TV (Rimouski-Matane-Sept-Iles) and CJPM-TV (Saguenay/Lac St-Jean). An additional four stations in the TVA Network are owned through affiliates **RNC Media Inc.**, owner of CHOT-TV (Gatineau) and CFEM-TV (Rouyn); and **Télé Inter-Rives Ltée** (45% owned), owner of CIMT-TV (Rivière-du-Loup) and CHAU-TV (Carleton). The company also owns nine specialty channels Le Canal Nouvelles (LCN), ADDIK, Prise 2, CASA, YOOPA, TVA Sports, MOI ET CIE, Évasion and Zeste. The TVA Network and specialty channels have associated digital applications, including video-on-demand, online and mobile platforms, that allow access to programs and content on demand. Operations also include commercial production and custom publishing services.

Film Production & Audiovisual Services - Through wholly owned **Mels Studios and Postproduction G.P.** and **Mels Dubbing Inc.**, provides services for the film and television industries including complete soundstage, mobile and equipment leasing services, post-production services, visual effects, virtual production, and media accessibility services such as dubbing, subtitling and described video. Also offers asset management for distribution and broadcast via film, television, Internet and mobile telephony networks. Facilities include 212,000 sq. ft. of 18 rental purpose built stages in Montreal and St-Hubert, Que., used for both local and foreign film and television productions, including American blockbusters.

Magazines - Publishes French-language magazines primarily in Quebec as well as English-language titles in Canada focusing on the arts, entertainment, television, fashion and decorating through wholly owned **TVA Publications Inc.** Numerous magazines, including regular, special, thematic and seasonal issues, are published with a focus on two market niches: entertainment, which consists of 7 Jours, La Semaine, Échos Vedettes, Star Système, DH, Cool! and TV Hebdo; and monthly, which consists of Canadian Living, Coup de pouce, Clin d'oeil, Style at Home, Les idées de ma maison and Espaces. In addition to print publications, contents are also accessible on different digital platforms, including websites and mobile applications. Content is either produced internally by the company's employees or freelancers, or purchased on the market.

Production & Distribution - Produces and distributes television shows, movies and television series for the Canadian and international markets through wholly owned **Incendo Media Inc.** and the TVA Films division. Films, audiovisual productions and television broadcast formats are distributed on different platforms, including movie theatres, video-on-demand, DVD and digital and television.

In February 2023, the company announced the elimination of 140 positions as a result of reductions in operating expenses in all of the company's segments.

Predecessor Detail - Name changed from Télé-Métropole Inc., Feb. 17, 1998.

Directors - Sylvie Lalande, chr., Lachute, Qué.; A. Michel Lavigne, v-chr., Laval, Qué.; Jacques Dorion, Saint-Laurent, Qué.; Nathalie Elgrably-Levy, Côte Saint-Luc, Qué.; Régine Laurent, Montréal, Qué.; Jean-Marc Léger, Repentigny, Qué.; Annick Mongeau, Montréal, Qué.; Daniel Paillé, Montréal, Qué.

Exec. Officers - Pierre Karl Péladeau, interim pres. & interim CEO; Jonathan Lee Hickey, sr. v-p, legal affairs & corp. secretariat; Patrick Jutras, sr. v-p & chief advtg. officer; Marjorie Daoust, v-p, fin.; Denis Dubois, v-p, original content, Quebecor Content; Claude Foisy, v-p, mktg.; Martin Picard, v-p & COO, content; Lyne Robitaille, v-p, TVA publications; Sophie Riendeau, corp. sec.; Vanessa Romano, asst. sec.

Capital Stock

	Authorized (shs.)	Outstanding (shs.)[1]	Par
Preferred	unlimited	nil	$10
Class A Common	unlimited	4,320,000	n.p.v.
Class B	unlimited	38,885,535	n.p.v.

[1] At July 14, 2023

Preferred - Issuable in series, non-participating and non-voting.

Class A Common - Subject to prior rights of the preferred shareholders, class A and B shares participate share-for-share in any distribution of dividends and in all distributions of the assets of the company. One vote per share.

Class B - Ranks equally with class A shares. Non-voting.

Options - At Dec. 31, 2022, options were outstanding to purchase 519,503 class B shares at a weighted average exercise price of $2.29 per share with a weighted average remaining contractual life of 7.41 years.

Major Shareholder - Quebecor Inc. held 99.97% interest at Mar. 7, 2023.

Price Range - TVA.B/TSX

Year	Volume	High	Low	Close
2022............	2,103,096	$4.00	$1.60	$1.71
2021............	1,969,773	$3.25	$2.03	$2.82
2020............	2,101,368	$2.70	$1.30	$2.11
2019............	1,550,616	$2.37	$1.22	$1.48
2018............	1,148,652	$4.21	$1.31	$1.61

Recent Close: $1.90

Capital Stock Changes - There were no changes to capital stock from 2016 to 2022, inclusive.

Long-Term Debt - At Dec. 31, 2022, outstanding long-term debt totaled $8,961,000 (all current and net of $9,000 of financing costs) and consisted entirely of borrowings under a $75,000,000 revolving credit facility, bearing interest at banker's acceptance rate, Canadian or U.S. prime plus a variable spread, and due Feb. 24, 2023.

Note - In February 2023, the company extended the maturity of its revolving credit facility to Feb. 24, 2024. In June 2023, the company terminated its existing $75,000,000 revolving credit facility due Feb. 24, 2024 and entered into a new $120,000,000 secured revolving credit facility due June 15, 2025, bearing interest at banker's acceptance rate or Canadian prime plus a premium based on company's debt ratio, and a new $20,000,000 secured credit facility due on demand, bearing interest at Canadian or U.S. prime plus a premium based on company's debt ratio.

Wholly Owned Subsidiaries

Communications Qolab Inc., Qué.
• 100% int. in **Mels Dubbing Inc.**, Qué.
Incendo Media Inc., Montréal, Qué.
9311-6127 Québec Inc., Qué.
• 0.1% int. in **Mels Studios and Postproduction G.P.**, Qué.
9383-6641 Québec Inc., Montréal, Qué.
• 1.74% int. in **Mels Studios and Postproduction G.P.**, Qué.
TVA Productions Inc., Qué.
TVA Productions II Inc., Qué.
TVA Publications Inc., Montréal, Qué.

Subsidiaries

98.16% int. in **Mels Studios and Postproduction G.P.**, Qué.

Investments

50% int. in **Publications Senior Inc.**, Montréal, Qué.
45% int. in **Tele Inter-Rives Ltd.**, Rivière-du-Loup, Qué.

Financial Statistics

Periods ended:	12m Dec. 31/22[A]		12m Dec. 31/21[A]
	$000s	%Chg	$000s
Operating revenue	**594,409**	**-5**	**622,834**
Salaries & benefits	147,750		139,395
Other operating expense	427,274		403,156
Operating expense	**575,024**	**+6**	**542,551**
Operating income	**19,385**	**-76**	**80,283**
Deprec., depl. & amort.	29,947		32,107
Finance costs, gross	1,305		2,674
Pre-tax income	**(12,797)**	**n.a.**	**40,832**
Income taxes	(3,113)		11,486
After-tax income (expense)	795		1,148
Net income	**(8,889)**	**n.a.**	**30,494**
Net inc. for equity hldrs	**(8,869)**	**n.a.**	**30,504**
Net inc. for non-cont. int	**(20)**	**n.a.**	**(10)**
Cash & equivalent	nil		5,181
Inventories	5,847		5,738
Accounts receivable	175,174		210,814
Current assets	323,134		334,146
Long-term investments	12,017		12,115
Fixed assets, net	157,784		160,288
Right-of-use assets	7,599		9,084
Intangibles, net	36,367		42,255
Total assets	**676,070**	**+2**	**661,091**
Bank indebtedness	1,107		nil
Accts. pay. & accr. liabs	112,976		137,473
Current liabilities	262,547		258,598
Long-term debt, gross	8,961		11,980
Long-term lease liabilities	6,453		7,857
Shareholders' equity	393,376		379,254
Non-controlling interest	nil		1,210
Cash from oper. activs	**28,054**	**-35**	**42,885**
Cash from fin. activs	(4,683)		(20,269)
Cash from invest. activs	(28,552)		(20,273)
Net cash position	**nil**	**n.a.**	**5,181**
Capital expenditures	(20,236)		(17,149)
Pension fund surplus	56,335		32,660
	$		$
Earnings per share*	(0.21)		0.71
Cash flow per share*	0.65		0.99
	shs		shs
No. of shs. o/s*	43,205,535		43,205,535
Avg. no. of shs. o/s*	43,205,535		43,205,535
	%		%
Net profit margin	(1.50)		4.90
Return on equity	(2.30)		8.83
Return on assets	(1.18)		5.19
No. of employees (FTEs)	1,327		1,317

* Class A & B
[A] Reported in accordance with IFRS

Latest Results

Periods ended:	6m June 30/23[A]		6m June 30/22[A]
	$000s	%Chg	$000s
Operating revenue	274,863	-6	291,966
Net income	(31,380)	n.a.	(16,224)
Net inc. for equity hldrs	(31,380)	n.a.	(16,228)
Net inc. for non-cont. int	nil		4
	$		$
Earnings per share*	(0.73)		(0.38)

* Class A & B
[A] Reported in accordance with IFRS

Historical Summary
(as originally stated)

Fiscal Year	Oper. Rev.	Net Inc. Bef. Disc.	EPS*
	$000s	$000s	$
2022[A]	594,409	(8,889)	(0.21)
2021[A]	622,834	30,494	0.71
2020[A]	508,144	32,341	0.75
2019[A]	569,910	16,682	0.38
2018[A]	551,910	8,148	0.19

* Class A & B
[A] Reported in accordance with IFRS

T.16 TWC Enterprises Limited*

Symbol - TWC **Exchange** - TSX **CUSIP** - 87310A
Head Office - 15675 Dufferin St, King City, ON, L7B 1K5 **Telephone** - (905) 841-3730 **Fax** - (905) 841-1134
Website - www.twcenterprises.ca
Email - atamlin@clublink.ca
Investor Relations - Andrew Tamlin (905) 841-5372
Auditors - Deloitte LLP C.A., Calgary, Alta.
Bankers - HSBC Bank USA, N.A.; HSBC Bank Canada
Transfer Agents - TSX Trust Company
FP500 Revenue Ranking - 666
Employees - 650 at Dec. 31, 2022

Profile - (Can. 1997) Owns, operates and manages member golf clubs, daily fee golf clubs and golf resorts primarily in Ontario, Quebec and Florida.

Operates, develops and manages high-quality member golf clubs, daily fee golf clubs and golf resorts with 45.5 18-hole equivalent championship golf courses and 2 18-hole equivalent academy golf courses at 35 locations in the Ontario, Quebec and Florida. Canadian golf clubs are organized into two clusters: the major metropolitan areas of southern Ontario and Muskoka, extending from Hamilton to Huntsville to Pickering and including the Greater Toronto Area; and Quebec/eastern Ontario, extending from the national capital region to Montreal, Que., including Mont-Tremblant, Que. The company's U.S. golf clubs are in Florida.

Golf club operations operate under the trademark ClubLink One Membership More Golf. Member golf clubs are operated in three categories as follows: Prestige, Platinum and Gold. Hybrid golf clubs are available for daily fee (public) play, reciprocal access by members and provide a home club for members with reciprocal access to the ClubLink system; they are operated in three categories as follows: Hybrid - Prestige, Hybrid - Gold and Hybrid - Silver.

Resort properties include The Lake Joseph Club Resort and Sherwood Inn in Port Carling, and Rocky Crest Resort in Mactier, all in Ontario. These resorts provide corporate groups and leisure guests with access to the company's golf clubs in the Muskoka area.

Also holds 83.33% interest in the Highland Gate project, a development project of a former golf course in Aurora, Ont., that includes 157 single family detached homes and a seven story multi-unit residential building with 114 units.

In May 2023, the company closed Sandpiper Golf Club in Sun City Center, Fla.

Recent Merger and Acquisition Activity

Status: pending **Announced:** May 17, 2022
TWC Enterprises Limited and its partner, consisting of a group of former members/shareholders of Club de Golf Islesmere, agreed to sell Club de Golf Islesmere in Laval, Que., to a Quebec developer for $70,000,000. TWC holds a 45% interest in the property. The transaction was expected to close in 2023.

Predecessor Detail - Name changed from ClubLink Enterprises Limited, May 16, 2014.

Directors - K. Rai Sahi, chr., pres. & CEO, Mississauga, Ont.; Donald W. Turple†, Vancouver, B.C.; Fraser R. Berrill, Toronto, Ont.; Patrick S. (Pat) Brigham, Toronto, Ont.; Paul D. Campbell, Toronto, Ont.; Samuel J. B. (Sam) Pollock, Toronto, Ont.; Angela Sahi, Mississauga, Ont.; Jack D. Winberg, Toronto, Ont.

Other Exec. Officers - Andrew Tamlin, CFO; Eugene N. Hretzay, corp. sec.

† Lead director

Capital Stock

	Authorized (shs.)	Outstanding (shs.)[1]
Preferred	unlimited	nil
Common	unlimited	24,605,087

[1] At June 30, 2023

Normal Course Issuer Bid - The company plans to make normal course purchases of up to 1,224,786 common shares representing 5% of the total outstanding. The bid commenced on Sept. 20, 2022, and expires on Sept. 19, 2023.

Major Shareholder - K. Rai Sahi held 79.45% interest at Mar. 23, 2023.

Price Range - TWC/TSX

Year	Volume	High	Low	Close
2022	459,271	$19.86	$15.42	$17.50
2021	1,203,304	$27.00	$15.75	$17.80
2020	2,690,738	$17.05	$7.96	$15.80
2019	992,975	$15.80	$12.75	$13.00
2018	1,120,561	$14.00	$10.83	$13.00

Recent Close: $17.85

Capital Stock Changes - During 2022, 118,656 common shares were issued under dividend reinvestment plan and 57,300 common shares were repurchased under a Normal Course Issuer Bid.

Dividends

TWC com Ra $0.20 pa Q est. Sept. 15, 2022**
Prev. Rate: $0.08 est. June 15, 2016
** Reinvestment Option

Long-Term Debt - Outstanding at Dec. 31, 2022:

Credit facility due 2023[1]	$7,913,000
Revolving credit facility 2024	18,804,000
Credit facility due 2025[2]	32,273,000
Mortgages due to 2029[3]	23,086,000
Promissory note	2,265,000
Less: Deferred fin. costs	190,000
	84,151,000
Less: Current portion	17,433,000
	66,718,000

[1] Consists of $7,900,000 servicing facility bearing interest at bankers' acceptance rates with stamping fees at 2.5% or 7.45%, and $13,000 servicing facility bearing interest at prime rate plus 1%.
[2] Consists of $31,500,000 servicing facility bearing interest at bankers' acceptance rates with stamping fees at 2.5% or 7.45%, and $773,000 servicing facility bearing interest at prime rate plus 1%.
[3] Bear interest at rates ranging from 6.194% to 8.345%.

Wholly Owned Subsidiaries

Clublink Inc., Ont.
• 100% int. in **ClubLink Corporation ULC**, Alta.
3432807 Canada Inc., Canada.
• 100% int. in **ClubLink US LLC**, Del.

Investments

23.9% int. in **Automotive Properties Real Estate Investment Trust**, Toronto, Ont. (see separate coverage)

Financial Statistics

Periods ended:	12m Dec. 31/22[A]		12m Dec. 31/21[A]
	$000s	%Chg	$000s
Operating revenue	**190,806**	**+7**	**178,417**
Cost of sales	35,080		42,881
Other operating expense	102,856		78,720
Operating expense	**137,936**	**+13**	**121,601**
Operating income	**52,870**	**-7**	**56,816**
Deprec., depl. & amort.	17,856		19,440
Finance income	8,578		6,266
Finance costs, gross	7,772		7,470
Investment income	457		1,270
Pre-tax income	**27,822**	**-75**	**110,935**
Income taxes	9,156		21,288
Net income	**18,666**	**-79**	**89,647**
Net inc. for equity hldrs	**18,761**	**-79**	**89,942**
Net inc. for non-cont. int	**(95)**	**n.a.**	**(295)**
Cash & equivalent	44,149		91,395
Inventories	105,447		89,478
Accounts receivable	13,015		5,143
Current assets	297,981		302,344
Long-term investments	442		1,532
Fixed assets, net	400,569		398,482
Right-of-use assets	2,102		6,262
Intangibles, net	11,589		12,931
Total assets	**727,343**	**-3**	**746,806**
Accts. pay. & accr. liabs	25,378		23,903
Current liabilities	82,278		113,036
Long-term debt, gross	84,151		112,561
Long-term debt, net	66,718		73,379
Long-term lease liabilities	1,323		2,520
Shareholders' equity	515,461		494,705
Non-controlling interest	8,588		8,683
Cash from oper. activs	**12,028**	**-82**	**67,730**
Cash from fin. activs	(40,936)		(33,897)
Cash from invest. activs	(22,139)		629
Net cash position	**44,149**	**-52**	**91,395**
Capital expenditures	(13,100)		(23,266)
Capital disposals	483		41,258
	$		$
Earnings per share*	0.76		3.64
Cash flow per share*	0.49		2.75
Cash divd. per share*	0.14		0.08
	shs		shs
No. of shs. o/s*	24,609,280		24,547,924
Avg. no. of shs. o/s*	24,535,000		24,645,000
	%		%
Net profit margin	9.78		50.25
Return on equity	3.71		19.79
Return on assets	3.24		13.88
Foreign sales percent	12		11
No. of employees (FTEs)	650		500

* Common
[A] Reported in accordance with IFRS

Latest Results

Periods ended:	6m June 30/23[A]		6m June 30/22[A]
	$000s	%Chg	$000s
Operating revenue	93,276	+1	92,688
Net income	63	-97	2,501
Net inc. for equity hldrs	21	-99	2,598
Net inc. for non-cont. int	42		(97)
	$		$
Earnings per share*	0.00		0.10

* Common
[A] Reported in accordance with IFRS

Historical Summary
(as originally stated)

Fiscal Year	Oper. Rev.	Net Inc. Bef. Disc.	EPS*
	$000s	$000s	$
2022[A]	190,806	18,666	0.76
2021[A]	178,417	89,647	3.64
2020[A]	131,801	971	0.04
2019[A]	168,787	4,904	0.18
2018[A]	172,638	9,206	0.34

* Common
[A] Reported in accordance with IFRS

T.17 Taiga Building Products Ltd.

Symbol - TBL **Exchange** - TSX **CUSIP** - 87402A
Head Office - 800-4710 Kingsway, Burnaby, BC, V5H 4M2 **Telephone** - (604) 438-1471 **Toll-free** - (800) 663-1470 **Fax** - (604) 439-4242
Website - www.taigabuilding.com
Email - mschneidereit@taigabuilding.com
Investor Relations - Mark Schneidereit-Hsu (800) 663-1470
Auditors - Dale Matheson Carr-Hilton LaBonte LLP C.A., Vancouver, B.C.
Lawyers - Dentons Canada LLP, Vancouver, B.C.
Transfer Agents - Computershare Trust Company of Canada Inc., Vancouver, B.C.
FP500 Revenue Ranking - 206
Employees - 576 at Dec. 31, 2022
Profile - (B.C. 2005) Distributes dimension lumber; panel products including plywood, particle board and oriented strand board (OSB); and allied and treated products such as roofing materials, mouldings, composite decking, polyethylene sheeting, batt and foam insulation, flooring, engineered wood and treated wood.

Building products are distributed through 15 distribution centres in Canada, two in California and one in Washington. The company also distributes through the use of third party reload centres. A majority of the company's revenue is generated from sales in Canada.

In addition, the company operates four wood preservation plants in Langley, B.C., Edmonton, Alta., Monetville, Ont., and Washougal, Wash., that produce pressure-treated wood products.

Primary customers in Canada are "big-box" and other building products retailers, building supply yards and industrial manufacturers, and include national retail chains such as **Lowe's Companies Inc.** and **Home Hardware Stores Limited**; regional retail chains; and members of buying groups such as Sexton, Tim-BR Mart, Castle Building Centres and Independent Lumber Dealers of Canada. Products sold by the California and Washington distribution centres are sold primarily to building supply yards.

Directors - Ian Tong, chr., Singapore; Trent Balog, Calgary, Alta.; Brian Flagel, B.C.; Garson Lee, Vancouver, B.C.; Grant Sali, Vancouver, B.C.; Jim Teh, Singapore, Singapore; Dr. Kooi Ong Tong, Kuala Lumpur, Malaysia

Other Exec. Officers - Russell (Russ) Permann, pres. & CEO; Michael Sivucha, COO; Mark Schneidereit-Hsu, v-p, fin. & admin., CFO & corp. sec.

Capital Stock

	Authorized (shs.)	Outstanding (shs.)[1]
Class A Preferred	unlimited	nil
Class B Preferred	unlimited	nil
Class A Common	unlimited	nil
Common	unlimited	108,139,691

[1] At Mar. 31, 2023

Major Shareholder - Avarga Limited held 71.46% interest at Mar. 29, 2023.

Price Range - TBL/TSX

Year	Volume	High	Low	Close
2022	3,401,806	$3.07	$2.10	$3.00
2021	12,754,951	$3.45	$2.10	$2.62
2020	6,435,084	$2.35	$0.51	$2.30
2019	5,228,609	$1.18	$0.89	$1.15
2018	4,691,183	$1.74	$1.07	$1.16

Recent Close: $2.86

Capital Stock Changes - During 2022, 37,642 common shares were repurchased under a Normal Course Issuer Bid.

Dividends

TBL com N.S.R.
$0.2764◆ .... Mar. 19/21
Paid in 2023: n.a. 2022: n.a. 2021: $0.2764◆
◆ Special

Wholly Owned Subsidiaries

624858 B.C. Ltd., B.C.
- 1% int. in **Taiga Building Products General Partnership**, B.C.

Taiga Building Products (Singapore) Private Limited, Singapore.
Taiga Investment Company Ltd., B.C.
- 1% int. in **Taiga Distribution U.S.A. Limited Partnership**, Nev.

Subsidiaries

99% int. in **Taiga Building Products General Partnership**, B.C.
78.4% int. in **Taiga Building Products USA Ltd.**, Wash.
- 100% int. in **Exterior Wood, Inc.**, Wash.
  - 100% int. in **B & G Trucking, Inc.**, Wash.
- 100% int. in **Taiga Building Products, LLC**, Del.
  - 100% int. in **Taiga Holdings, Inc.**, Del.
    - 100% int. in **Taiga Building Products, Inc.**, Nev.
- 100% int. in **Taiga Building Products (Sanger) LLC**, Del.

99% int. in **Taiga Distribution U.S.A. Limited Partnership**, Nev.
- 21.6% int. in **Taiga Building Products USA Ltd.**, Wash.

Financial Statistics

Periods ended:	12m Dec. 31/22[A]		12m Dec. 31/21[A]
	$000s	%Chg	$000s
Operating revenue	**2,192,705**	**-1**	**2,219,674**
Cost of sales	1,886,579		1,892,380
General & admin expense	163,463		165,851
Operating expense	**2,050,042**	**0**	**2,058,231**
Operating income	**142,663**	**-12**	**161,443**
Deprec., depl. & amort	11,469		11,125
Finance costs, gross	7,322		8,394
Write-downs/write-offs	(3,502)		(15,977)
Pre-tax income	**120,508**	**-4**	**125,662**
Income taxes	31,880		32,976
Net income	**88,628**	**-4**	**92,686**
Cash & equivalent	94,494		69,673
Inventories	226,350		217,698
Accounts receivable	123,098		139,193
Current assets	463,953		430,589
Fixed assets, net	122,144		121,271
Intangibles, net	23,589		23,178
Total assets	**617,832**	**+6**	**583,004**
Accts. pay. & accr. liabs	147,989		155,877
Current liabilities	153,397		205,958
Long-term debt, gross	nil		19,280
Long-term debt, net	nil		6,780
Long-term lease liabilities	92,034		94,132
Shareholders' equity	363,248		267,055
Cash from oper. activs	**53,811**	**-55**	**118,618**
Cash from fin. activs	(26,404)		(46,029)
Cash from invest. activs	(3,972)		(3,160)
Net cash position	**94,494**	**+36**	**69,673**
Capital expenditures	(4,095)		(3,199)
Capital disposals	123		39
	$		$
Earnings per share*	0.82		0.85
Cash flow per share*	0.50		1.09
Extra divd. - cash*	nil		0.28
	shs		shs
No. of shs. o/s*	108,171,321		108,208,963
Avg. no. of shs. o/s*	108,197,000		108,458,000
	%		%
Net profit margin	4.04		4.18
Return on equity	28.12		39.27
Return on assets	15.66		18.71
Foreign sales percent	18		18
No. of employees (FTEs)	576		576

* Common
[A] Reported in accordance with IFRS

Latest Results

Periods ended:	3m Mar. 31/23[A]		3m Mar. 31/22[◻A]
	$000s	%Chg	$000s
Operating revenue	408,492	-33	612,704
Net income	13,516	-66	39,500
	$		$
Earnings per share*	0.12		0.37

* Common
◻ Restated
[A] Reported in accordance with IFRS

Historical Summary
(as originally stated)

Fiscal Year	Oper. Rev.	Net Inc. Bef. Disc.	EPS*
	$000s	$000s	$
2022[A]	2,192,705	88,628	0.82
2021[A]	2,219,674	92,686	0.85
2020[A]	1,589,123	70,826	0.64
2019[A]	1,299,122	25,905	0.23
2018[A]	1,450,985	20,267	0.17

* Common
[A] Reported in accordance with IFRS

T.18 Taiga Motors Corporation

Symbol - TAIG **Exchange** - TSX **CUSIP** - 87402F
Head Office - 2695 ave Dollard, Montréal, QC, H8N 2J8 **Telephone** - (514) 369-7617
Website - taigamotors.ca
Email - shahroz.hussain@taigamotors.ca
Investor Relations - Shahroz Hussain (416) 333-8374
Auditors - KPMG LLP C.A., Montréal, Qué.
Transfer Agents - Odyssey Trust Company, Toronto, Ont.
Employees - 269 at Dec. 31, 2022
Profile - (B.C. 2019) Develops, manufactures and distributes electric recreational powersports vehicles, primarily snowmobiles and personal watercrafts (PWC), in North America and Europe.

Snowmobile models consist of Nomad Utility snowmobile, which is used for sport-utility applications; Ekko Mountain snowmobile, which is used for deep snow and mountain riding; and Atlas Crossover snowmobile, which is used for tail/crossover riding. PWC models consist of Orca Sport, the entry-level model electric PWC; Orca Performance, an advanced middle-level model electric PWC; Orca Carbon, the premium high-level model electric PWC. The Ekko Mountain and the Atlas Crossover snowmobile models, and Orca Sport and the Orca Performance PWC models are under development.

Also sells a range of clothing and apparel in certain territories in several styles adapted to its various product lines, and intends to sell add-on accessories, consumables and replacement parts. A program to develop side-by-sides was also in the plan but was halted to focus on the ramping up of snowmobile and PWC production capacity. In addition, may generate ancillary revenues in the future from data analytics, Software-as-a-service platform or from carbon credit monetization. Moreover, an electric vehicle charging network is being developed with an intention to install DC fast charging stations in strategic locations throughout North America.

Powersports vehicles are manufactured at a location in Montreal, Que., that has two assembly facilities with a research and development facility centre, and are being developed. The combined facilities would have an annual projected production capacity of up to 8,000 vehicles following its completion. A proposed mass-production assembly facility in Shawinigan, Que., is anticipated to increase the total annual production capacity of the company to at least 62,000 units and 3 gigawatt-hours in battery pack and module production. The company is re-evaluating expansion timelines.

Predecessor Detail - Name changed from Canaccord Genuity Growth II Corp., Apr. 23, 2021, pursuant to the Qualifying Acquisition of Taiga Motors Inc. (TMI), and concurrent amalgamation of TMI and wholly owned 9434-3399 Québec inc.; basis 1 new for 5 old shs.

Directors - Samuel Bruneau, co-founder & CEO, Montréal, Qué.; Timothy (Tim) Tokarsky, chr., Westmount, Qué.; Anne Darche, Montréal, Qué.; Michael Fizzell, Toronto, Ont.; Andrew Lapham, Toronto, Ont.; Martin Picard, Westmount, Qué.; Francis C. (Frank) Séguin, Vaughan, Ont.

Other Exec. Officers - Paul Archard, co-founder & chief vehicle devel. officer; Gabriel Bernatchez, co-founder & chief technical officer; Eric Bussières, CFO; Jacques Demont, chief comml. officer; Doug Braswell, v-p, electrification opers.; Mike Jelinek, v-p, global supply chain; Anne Plamondon, gen. counsel & corp. sec.

Capital Stock

	Authorized (shs.)	Outstanding (shs.)[1]
Common	unlimited	31,825,716

[1] At May 1, 2023

Major Shareholder - Northern Private Capital Ltd. held 11.33% interest, Gabriel Bernatchez held 10.52% interest and Samuel Bruneau held 10.52% interest at May 1, 2023.

Price Range - TAIG/TSX

Year	Volume	High	Low	Close
2022	8,756,282	$7.15	$2.21	$2.40
2021	10,181,276	$15.14	$5.58	$6.23

CGGZ.UN/TSX (D)

Year	Volume	High	Low	Close
2021	19,311,738	$4.24	$2.85	$3.18
2020	246,400	$3.30	$2.71	$3.15
2019	1,472,952	$3.70	$2.85	$2.99

Recent Close: $1.43

Capital Stock Changes - During 2022, common shares were issued as follows: 179,330 on exercise of warrants and 148,907 on exercise of options.

Wholly Owned Subsidiaries

CGGZ Finance Corp., Canada. Inactive.
Taiga Motors America Inc., Del.
Taiga Motors Inc., Montréal, Qué.

Financial Statistics

Periods ended:	12m Dec. 31/22[A]		12m Dec. 31/21[A1]
	$000s	%Chg	$000s
Operating revenue	**3,212**	**n.a.**	**nil**
Cost of sales	29,152		nil
Research & devel. expense	9,386		5,895
General & admin expense	18,783		15,851
Operating expense	**57,320**	**+164**	**21,746**
Operating income	**(54,108)**	**n.a.**	**(21,746)**
Deprec., depl. & amort.	4,534		1,019
Finance income	575		361
Finance costs, gross	736		24,769
Write-downs/write-offs	(779)		(753)
Pre-tax income	**(59,516)**	**n.a.**	**(100,141)**
Net income	**(59,516)**	**n.a.**	**(100,141)**
Cash & equivalent	22,838		86,724
Inventories	20,756		20,042
Current assets	53,267		116,740
Fixed assets, net	14,720		8,909
Right-of-use assets	10,075		11,258
Intangibles, net	13,746		7,983
Total assets	**94,315**	**-35**	**144,899**
Accts. pay. & accr. liabs.	11,654		8,536
Current liabilities	16,123		11,435
Long-term debt, gross	2,271		381
Long-term debt, net	2,190		311
Long-term lease liabilities	9,753		10,604
Shareholders' equity	66,249		122,549
Cash from oper. activs	**(46,901)**	**n.a.**	**(43,120)**
Cash from fin. activs	2,666		136,875
Cash from invest. activs	(19,651)		(14,852)
Net cash position	**22,838**	**-74**	**86,724**
Capital expenditures	(12,062)		(8,259)
	$		$
Earnings per share*	(1.88)		(5.72)
Cash flow per share*	(1.48)		(2.46)
	shs		shs
No. of shs. o/s*	31,825,712		31,497,475
Avg. no. of shs. o/s*	31,613,801		17,496,297
	%		%
Net profit margin	n.m.		n.a.
Return on equity	(63.05)		n.m.
Return on assets	(49.14)		(95.83)
Foreign sales percent	25		n.a.
No. of employees (FTEs)	269		187

* Common
[A] Reported in accordance with IFRS
[1] Results reflect the Apr. 21, 2021, reverse takeover acquisition of Taiga Motors Inc.

Latest Results

Periods ended:	3m Mar. 31/23[A]		3m Mar. 31/22[A]
	$000s	%Chg	$000s
Operating revenue	1,729	n.m.	141
Net income	(14,299)	n.a.	(9,123)
	$		$
Earnings per share*	(0.41)		(0.29)

* Common
[A] Reported in accordance with IFRS

Historical Summary
(as originally stated)

Fiscal Year	Oper. Rev.	Net Inc. Bef. Disc.	EPS*
	$000s	$000s	$
2022[A]	3,212	(59,516)	(1.88)
2021[A]	nil	(100,141)	(5.72)
2020[A1,2]	nil	(107,364)	n.a.
2020[A]	nil	(5,118)	n.a.

* Common
[A] Reported in accordance with IFRS
[1] 7 months ended Dec. 31, 2020.
[2] Results pertain to Taiga Motors Inc.

T.19 Tantalus Systems Holding Inc.

Symbol - GRID **Exchange** - TSX **CUSIP** - 87601F
Head Office - 200-3555 Gilmore Way, Burnaby, BC, V5G 0B3 **Telephone** - (604) 299-0458 **Fax** - (604) 451-4111
Website - www.tantalus.com
Email - deborah@adcap.ca
Investor Relations - Deborah Honig (604) 299-0432
Auditors - KPMG LLP C.A., Vancouver, B.C.
Lawyers - Osler, Hoskin & Harcourt LLP, Vancouver, B.C.
Transfer Agents - Computershare Trust Company of Canada Inc., Vancouver, B.C.
Employees - 121 at Mar. 31, 2023
Profile - (B.C. 2018) Provides smart grid technology solutions that enhance the safety, security, reliability and efficiency of public power and electric cooperative utilities across North America.

The company empowers its utility customers to access granular data from both legacy meters and cutting-edge two-way intelligent devices to improve customer service, facilitate consumer engagement, realize cost savings and streamline system operations.

Operations are organized into two segments: Connected Devices and Infrastructure; and Utility Applications and Services.

Connected Devices and Infrastructure - This segment carries out the sale of proprietary edge-computing modules that are integrated into multiple devices deployed across a utility's distribution grid including metres, sensors, street lighting fixtures and distribution automation equipment. Also includes the sale of proprietary multi-relay load control switches and a suite of communications infrastructure devices that are deployed to deliver an industrial network-of things/ Internet-of-Things (IoT) smart grid including base stations, repeaters and collectors.

Utility Applications and Services - This segment carries out the sale of proprietary mission-critical software applications, artificial intelligence-enabled data analytics and a suite of professional services to support utilities.

Has offices in Burnaby and Vancouver, B.C.; Kanata, Ont.; San Jose, Calif.; Norwalk, Conn.; and Raleigh, N.C.

Predecessor Detail - Name changed from RiseTech Capital Corp., Jan. 29, 2021, pursuant to the Qualifying Transaction reverse takeover acquisition of (old) Tantalus Systems Holding Inc., and concurrent amalgamation of (old) Tantalus with wholly owned 12384205 Canada Inc. (and continued as 12384205 Canada Inc.); basis 1 new for 16.4 old shs.

Directors - Laura M. Formusa, chr., Toronto, Ont.; Peter Londa, pres. & CEO, Norwalk, Conn.; Dr. Francis J. Harvey, Los Gatos, Calif.; Thomas (Tom) Liston, Toronto, Ont.; John A. McEwen, Naramata, B.C.; Greg Williams, Tenn.

Other Exec. Officers - Gerard (Gerry) Kaiser, COO; George W. Reznik, CFO; Douglass Campbell, chief solution officer; Michael Julian, chief revenue officer; Hugo Hodge, exec. v-p & gen. mgr., Caribbean basin; P. Randy Aeberhardt, v-p, strategic initiatives; Tom Allen, v-p, product devel.; Harold Hankel, v-p, mfg.; Param Pawar, v-p, fin.; John Ziehl, v-p, cust. opers.; Michael Grandis, gen. counsel & corp. sec.

Capital Stock

	Authorized (shs.)	Outstanding (shs.)[1]
Common	unlimited	44,595,942

[1] At May 9, 2023

Major Shareholder - Redpoint Omega L.P. & Redpoint Omega Associates, LLC collectively held 16.8% interest at May 1, 2023.

Price Range - GRID/TSX

Year	Volume	High	Low	Close
2022	2,112,144	$1.90	$0.69	$1.01
2021	2,298,765	$3.50	$1.75	$1.85
2020	7,195	$2.46	$0.82	$1.48
2019	12,210	$2.46	$0.41	$0.66
2018	1,219	$3.28	$1.64	$1.64

Consolidation: 1-for-16.4 cons. in Feb. 2021
Recent Close: $0.83

Capital Stock Changes - On Feb. 1, 2022, 869,565 common shares were issued pursuant to the acquisition of DLC Systems, Inc. (dba Congruitive). Also during 2022, common shares were issued as follows: 74,074 on vesting of restricted share units and 18,074 on exercise of options.

Wholly Owned Subsidiaries

Energate Inc., Canada.
TSH Canada Inc., Burnaby, B.C. formerly 12384205 Canada Inc.
- 100% int. in **DLC Systems, Inc.**, San Jose, Calif.
- 100% int. in **Tantalus Systems Corp.**, B.C.
- 100% int. in **Tantalus Systems Inc.**, United States.

Financial Statistics

Periods ended:	12m Dec. 31/22[A]		12m Dec. 31/21[A1]
	US$000s	%Chg	US$000s
Operating revenue	**39,603**	**+23**	**32,172**
Cost of sales	20,707		17,820
Research & devel. expense	7,571		5,430
General & admin expense	15,116		13,619
Operating expense	**43,394**	**+18**	**36,868**
Operating income	**(3,791)**	**n.a.**	**(4,696)**
Deprec., depl. & amort.	1,899		1,546
Finance costs, gross	1,070		628
Pre-tax income	**(6,077)**	**n.a.**	**(6,979)**
Income taxes	(882)		41
Net income	**(5,195)**	**n.a.**	**(7,020)**
Cash & equivalent	5,851		14,204
Inventories	5,691		5,687
Accounts receivable	9,042		5,344
Current assets	22,794		26,428
Fixed assets, net	802		1,020
Right-of-use assets	3,335		3,418
Intangibles, net	10,428		160
Total assets	**37,360**	**+20**	**31,026**
Bank indebtedness	8,100		8,100
Accts. pay. & accr. liabs.	12,360		8,975
Current liabilities	27,038		20,953
Long-term debt, gross	2,263		nil
Long-term debt, net	1,163		nil
Long-term lease liabilities	2,618		3,282
Shareholders' equity	3,579		6,791
Cash from oper. activs	**(3,399)**	**n.a.**	**(4,014)**
Cash from fin. activs	1,074		13,748
Cash from invest. activs	(5,862)		(188)
Net cash position	**5,851**	**-59**	**14,204**
Capital expenditures	(177)		(148)
	US$		US$
Earnings per share*	(0.12)		(0.17)
Cash flow per share*	(0.08)		(0.10)
	shs		shs
No. of shs. o/s*	44,595,942		43,634,229
Avg. no. of shs. o/s*	44,498,418		40,309,249
	%		%
Net profit margin	(13.12)		(21.82)
Return on equity	(100.19)		n.m.
Return on assets	(12.52)		(23.42)
Foreign sales percent	99		99

* Common
[A] Reported in accordance with IFRS
[1] Results prior to Jan. 29, 2021, pertain to and reflect the Qualifying Transaction reverse takeover acquisition of (old) Tantalus Systems Holdings Inc. (renamed TSH Canada Inc.).

Latest Results

Periods ended:	3m Mar. 31/23[A]		3m Mar. 31/22[A]
	US$000s	%Chg	US$000s
Operating revenue	10,413	+12	9,291
Net income	(1,637)	n.a.	(1,789)
	US$		US$
Earnings per share*	(0.04)		(0.04)

* Common
[A] Reported in accordance with IFRS

Historical Summary
(as originally stated)

Fiscal Year	Oper. Rev.	Net Inc. Bef. Disc.	EPS*
	US$000s	US$000s	US$
2022[A]	39,603	(5,195)	(0.12)
2021[A]	32,172	(7,020)	(0.17)
2020[A]	33,049	1,485	0.66
2019[A]	41,588	(606)	(0.33)
2018[A]	40,413	(1,469)	n.a.

* Common
[A] Reported in accordance with IFRS
Note: Adjusted throughout for 1-for-16.4 cons. in Feb. 2021

T.20 Target Capital Inc.

Symbol - TCI.H **Exchange** - TSX-VEN (S) **CUSIP** - 876129
Head Office - Bankers Hall West, 4300-888 3 St SW, Calgary, AB, T2P 5C5 **Telephone** - (403) 351-1779
Email - target@5qir.com
Investor Relations - Theo Zunich (403) 351-1779
Auditors - MNP LLP C.A., Calgary, Alta.
Transfer Agents - Computershare Trust Company, Inc.
Profile - (Alta. 1993) Invests in privately held and early-stage publicly traded companies.

The company manages a diversified portfolio of private company investments as well as continued sourcing and evaluation of strategic alternative investments.

In April 2022, the company terminated the proposed reverse takeover acquisition with a private technology company.

Common delisted from CSE, Apr. 16, 2021.

Directors - Theo Zunich, interim pres. & interim CEO, Victoria, B.C.; Ron S. Hozjan, Calgary, Alta.; Nicholas (Nick) Kuzyk, Calgary, Alta.

Other Exec. Officers - Robert Dion, interim CFO; William C. (Bill) Macdonald, exec. v-p, corp. devel.; Jason Kujath, gen. counsel; Sanjib (Sony) Gill, corp. sec.

Capital Stock

	Authorized (shs.)	Outstanding (shs.)[1]
Common	unlimited	106,715,629

[1] At Dec. 23, 2022

Major Shareholder - Widely held at Dec. 23, 2022.

Price Range - TCI.H/TSX-VEN (S)

Year	Volume	High	Low	Close
2020	16,424,935	$0.03	$0.01	$0.02
2019	39,524,260	$0.08	$0.01	$0.03
2018	128,585,894	$0.60	$0.04	$0.04

Capital Stock Changes - There were no changes to capital stock from fiscal 2020 to fiscal 2022, inclusive.

Subsidiaries

95% int. in **Industrial Avenue Development Corporation**, Alta. Inactive.

Financial Statistics

Periods ended:	12m Mar. 31/22[A]		12m Mar. 31/21[A]
	$000s	%Chg	$000s
Total revenue	**23**	**-78**	**103**
General & admin. expense	310		240
Other operating expense	nil		7
Operating expense	**310**	**+26**	**247**
Operating income	**(287)**	**n.a.**	**(144)**
Deprec. & amort.	nil		5
Finance costs, gross	5		nil
Pre-tax income	**(292)**	**n.a.**	**(1,526)**
Net income	**(292)**	**n.a.**	**(1,526)**
Cash & equivalent	26		7
Accounts receivable	nil		34
Current assets	26		151
Long-term investments	nil		5
Total assets	**27**	**-83**	**156**
Current liabilities	304		184
Shareholders' equity	(320)		(27)
Cash from oper. activs.	**(155)**	**n.a.**	**136**
Cash from fin. activs.	60		nil
Cash from invest. activs.	114		(383)
Net cash position	**26**	**+271**	**7**
	$		$
Earnings per share*	(0.00)		(0.01)
Cash flow per share*	(0.00)		0.00
	shs		shs
No. of shs. o/s*	106,715,629		106,715,629
Avg. no. of shs. o/s*	106,715,629		106,715,629
	%		%
Net profit margin	n.m.		n.m.
Return on equity	n.m.		n.m.
Return on assets	(313.66)		(166.59)

* Common

[A] Reported in accordance with IFRS

Latest Results

Periods ended:	6m Sept. 30/22[A]		6m Sept. 30/21[A]
	$000s	%Chg	$000s
Total revenue	249	n.a.	nil
Net income	131	n.a.	(122)
	$		$
Earnings per share*	0.00		(0.00)

* Common

[A] Reported in accordance with IFRS

Historical Summary
(as originally stated)

Fiscal Year	Total Rev. $000s	Net Inc. Bef. Disc. $000s	EPS* $
2022[A]	23	(292)	(0.00)
2021[A]	103	(1,526)	(0.01)
2020[A]	727	(1,760)	(0.02)
2019[A]	593	(931)	(0.01)
2018[A]	704	(3,301)	(0.11)

* Common

[A] Reported in accordance with IFRS

T.21 Targeted Microwave Solutions Inc.

Symbol - TMS.H **Exchange** - TSX-VEN **CUSIP** - 876141

Head Office - 2300-1066 Hastings St W, Vancouver, BC, V6E 3X2 **Telephone** - (778) 995-5833 **Fax** - (604) 601-8436

Email - g.sangha@claredoncapital.com

Investor Relations - Gurminder Sangha (604) 375-6005

Auditors - Dale Matheson Carr-Hilton LaBonte LLP C.A.

Transfer Agents - Computershare Trust Company of Canada Inc., Vancouver, B.C.

Profile - (B.C. 2015) Developing microwave-based application technologies to dry, decontaminate, physically upgrade and fully eliminate or reduce environment harming emissions.

Core technology is a proprietary microwave delivery and process control system designed to achieve uniform moisture reduction across a wide range of industrial aggregates with challenging bulk densities, particle sizes and flow characteristics. The process generates heat within the input material, as opposed to heating the environment around the target material, allowing significantly cooler ambient temperatures during processing, which helps mitigate combustion risk and prevent the unwanted release of volatile gases that generate polluting greenhouse emissions.

The company's Generation 3.0 or WAVEdri® microwave reactors is designed to occupy a small footprint and integrate easily into a variety of manufacturing operations and can deliver up to 2.5 MW of concentrated 0.915 GHz microwave power to a variety of target feedstocks, such as industrial minerals, low-rank coal and wood chips, on a continuous feed basis.

The company plans to explore opportunities outside microwave drying for potential sources of revenue and funding partners.

Directors - Gurminder (Gurm) Sangha, CEO, Vancouver, B.C.; Jurgen A. Wolf, CFO, Vancouver, B.C.; Lyle McLennan, B.C.; Jim Taylor

Other Exec. Officers - Jan Kindler, v-p, bus. devel. & COO

Capital Stock

	Authorized (shs.)	Outstanding (shs.)[1]
Common	unlimited	128,024,439

[1] At May 25, 2023

Price Range - TMS.H/TSX-VEN

Year	Volume	High	Low	Close
2022	3,282,906	$0.06	$0.01	$0.01
2021	4,758,439	$0.07	$0.03	$0.03
2020	2,482,972	$0.06	$0.01	$0.04
2019	4,112,864	$0.04	$0.01	$0.01
2018	18,993,446	$0.06	$0.02	$0.04

Recent Close: $0.01

Capital Stock Changes - There were no changes to capital stock during 2021 or 2022.

Wholly Owned Subsidiaries

TMS-MD, Inc., United States.

Targeted Microwave Solutions USA Inc., Va.

Subsidiaries

51% int. in **Targeted Microwave Solutions Hong Kong Limited**, Hong Kong, People's Republic of China.

Financial Statistics

Periods ended:	12m Dec. 31/22[A]		12m Dec. 31/21[A]
	US$000s	%Chg	US$000s
General & admin expense	42		41
Operating expense	**42**	**+2**	**41**
Operating income	**(41)**	**n.a.**	**(41)**
Pre-tax income	**(33)**	**n.a.**	**(43)**
Net income	**(33)**	**n.a.**	**(43)**
Current assets	4		3
Total assets	**4**	**+33**	**3**
Bank indebtedness	150		150
Accts. pay. & accr. liabs.	238		204
Current liabilities	388		354
Shareholders' equity	(343)		(310)
Non-controlling interest	(42)		(42)
Cash from oper. activs.	**nil**	**n.a.**	**(2)**
	US$		US$
Earnings per share*	(0.00)		(0.00)
	shs		shs
No. of shs. o/s*	128,024,439		128,024,439
Avg. no. of shs. o/s*	128,024,439		128,024,439
	%		%
Net profit margin	n.a.		n.a.
Return on equity	n.m.		n.m.
Return on assets	(942.86)		n.m.

* Common

[A] Reported in accordance with IFRS

Latest Results

Periods ended:	3m Mar. 31/23[A]		3m Mar. 31/22[A]
	US$000s	%Chg	US$000s
Net income	(9)	n.a.	(12)
	US$		US$
Earnings per share*	(0.00)		(0.00)

* Common

[A] Reported in accordance with IFRS

Historical Summary
(as originally stated)

Fiscal Year	Oper. Rev. US$000s	Net Inc. Bef. Disc. US$000s	EPS* US$
2022[A]	nil	(33)	(0.00)
2021[A]	nil	(43)	(0.00)
2020[A]	nil	(49)	(0.00)
2019[A]	nil	(184)	(0.00)
2018[A]	nil	(405)	(0.01)

* Common

[A] Reported in accordance with IFRS

T.22 Telecure Technologies Inc.

Symbol - TELE **Exchange** - CSE (S) **CUSIP** - 87931L

Head Office - 1930-1177 Hastings St W, Vancouver, BC, V6E 3T4 **Telephone** - (604) 398-3432

Website - telecure.com

Email - invest@telecure.com

Investor Relations - Eli Dusenbury (604) 398-3432

Auditors - Charlton & Company C.A., Vancouver, B.C.

Lawyers - Cassels Brock & Blackwell LLP, Vancouver, B.C.

Transfer Agents - Odyssey Trust Company, Vancouver, B.C.

Profile - (B.C. 2018) Provides telemedicine and telehealth services for patients and doctors.

Offers software-as-a-service based health technology solutions, through a subscription-based model, to 250 medical practices, medical providers and nursing homes, serving more than 100,000 users across six countries: the U.S. (in 11 states), Peru, Brazil, Saudi Arabia, Venezuela and the Philippines. Solutions are offered through the CallingDr™ and VisitingDr™ software platforms and the FindingDr™ online appointment booking service, which has more than 2,500 medical providers listed. Clients are also offered complete customization and enhancement of certain features, including the use of a white-label app, which allows clients to place their own branding on the applications.

The company's goal is to digitalize the provision of healthcare services to patients such that patients have access to all points of their care from their smartphone, tablet or computer, thereby increasing accessibility, convenience and affordability of healthcare for patients. In conjunction, the company aims to increase productivity, efficiency and revenue for healthcare providers by enabling them to efficiently capture billable time, reduce the cost associated with no-shows and increase access to patient base and practice reach.

Common suspended from CSE, July 11, 2022.

Directors - Joshua Rosenberg, chr., interim CEO & COO, Leander, Tex.; Faizaan Lalani, Vancouver, B.C.; Prabhjot (Paul) More, Vancouver, B.C.; Amandeep (Aman) Parmar, Vancouver, B.C.; Harwinder Parmar, Vancouver, B.C.

Other Exec. Officers - Eli Dusenbury, CFO

Capital Stock

	Authorized (shs.)	Outstanding (shs.)[1]
Common	unlimited	84,320,299
Class B Non-Vtg.	unlimited	nil

[1] At Aug. 24, 2023

Major Shareholder - Widely held at Feb. 23, 2022.

Price Range - TELE/CSE (S)

Year	Volume	High	Low	Close
2022	2,607,150	$0.33	$0.04	$0.09
2021	20,508,345	$0.51	$0.25	$0.33

Wholly Owned Subsidiaries

MyApps Corp., Altamonte Springs, Fla.

- 100% int. in **Care by CallingDr LLC**, Fla.

11189182 Canada Corp., Canada.

Investments

CloudMD Software & Services Inc., Vancouver, B.C. (see separate coverage)

T.23 Telesat Corporation

Symbol - TSAT **Exchange** - TSX **CUSIP** - 879512

Head Office - 2100-160 Elgin St, Ottawa, ON, K2P 2P7 **Telephone** - (613) 748-0123

Website - www.telesat.com

Email - cdifrancesco@telesat.com

Investor Relations - Christopher S. DiFrancesco (613) 748-8797

Auditors - Deloitte LLP C.A., Toronto, Ont.

Lawyers - Wachtell, Lipton, Rosen & Katz, New York, N.Y.; Stikeman Elliott LLP, Toronto, Ont.

Transfer Agents - Computershare Trust Company, N.A., Canton, Ohio; Computershare Trust Company of Canada Inc., Vancouver, B.C.

FP500 Revenue Ranking - 388

Employees - 455 at Dec. 31, 2022

Profile - (B.C. 2020) Owns and operates a global fleet of satellites along with an integrated teleport infrastructure.

In-orbit satellite fleet consists of 15 GEO (geostationary) satellites, a LEO (low Earth orbit) satellite as well as the Canadian payload on the ViaSat-1 satellite, a jointly owned satellite with **Viasat Inc.** GEO satellites operate in a fixed orbital location about 22,300 miles (35,700 km) above the equator, while LEO satellites travel around the Earth at altitudes between 200 and 870 miles (325 to 1,400 km). The company is developing its Telesat Lightspeed, a constellation of LEO satellites and integrated terrestrial infrastructure with the aim of providing fibre-like global broadband Internet connectivity. Ground station network consists of two satellite control centres in Ottawa, Ont., and Rio de Janeiro,

Brazil, as well as Earth stations in Allan Park, Ont., Victoria, B.C., Fort MacMurray and Calgary, Alta., Hague and Saskatoon, Sask., Winnipeg, Man., Montreal, Que., Iqaluit, Nunavut, St. John's, Nfld., Mount Jackson and Middleton, Va., and Belo Horizonte, Brazil.

Through the combination of its space and ground assets, provides communications solutions to more than 400 customers worldwide, including DTH (direct-to-home) service providers, ISPs (Internet service providers), network service integrators, telecommunications carriers, corporations and government agencies. Solutions include providing video and data services using satellite transponder capacity, providing ground-based transmit and receive services, selling equipment, managing satellite networks for third parties and providing consulting services in the field of satellite communications. Services are provided through three business categories: **Broadcast**, including DTH television, video distribution and contribution, and occasional use services; **Enterprise**, including telecommunication carrier and integrator, government, consumer broadband, resource, maritime and aeronautical, retail and satellite operator services; and **Consulting and Other**, including consulting services related to space and Earth segments, government studies, satellite control services, and research and development.

At Mar. 31, 2023, contract backlog was $1.7 billion, excluding backlog associated with Telesat Lightspeed program.

Directors - Dr. Mark H. Rachesky, chr., New York, N.Y.; Daniel S. (Dan) Goldberg, pres. & CEO, Ottawa, Ont.; Michael T. Boychuk, Baie-d'Urfé, Qué.; Jason A. Caloras, Brooklyn, N.Y.; Dr. A. Jane Craighead, Ont.; Richard Fadden, Ottawa, Ont.; Henry (Hank) Intven, Victoria, B.C.; David Morin, Montréal, Qué.; Guthrie J. Stewart, Westmount, Qué.; Michael B. Targoff, Jupiter, Fla.

Other Exec. Officers - Andrew Browne, CFO; Glenn Katz, chief comml. officer; David N. (Dave) Wendling, chief technical officer; Michèle Beck, sr. v-p, Cdn. sales; Michael C. Schwartz, sr. v-p, corp. & bus. devel.; Christopher S. (Chris) DiFrancesco, v-p, gen. counsel & corp. sec.; John Flaherty, v-p, bus. planning & mktg.; France Teasdale, v-p, people; Philip Harlow, pres., Telesat govt. solutions

Capital Stock

	Authorized (shs.)	Outstanding (shs.)[1]
Cl.A Preferred	unlimited	nil
Cl.A Com.	unlimited	946,118
Cl.B Var. Vtg.	unlimited	12,332,921
Cl.C	unlimited	112,841[2]
Cl.A Special Vtg.	unlimited	1
Cl.B Special Vtg.	unlimited	1
Cl.C Special Vtg.	unlimited	1
Golden	unlimited	1
Cl.A LP Units	unlimited	12,500[3]
Cl.B LP Units	unlimited	18,309,342[4]
Cl.C LP Units	unlimited	18,098,362[5]

[1] At May 2, 2023
[2] All held by Public Sector Pension Investment Board.
[3] Units of Telesat Partnership LP.
[4] Units of Telesat Partnership LP.
[5] Units of Telesat Partnership LP.

Class A Preferred - Non-voting.

Class A Common - Owned by Canadians. One vote per share.

Class B Variable Voting - Owned by non-Canadians. One vote per share provided that any voting power of a single shareholder cannot be more than one-third of the total voting power attached to the shares of the company and LP units of Telesat Partnership LP (via the special voting shares). In such case, any voting power of that shareholder in excess of one-third of the total voting power (less one vote) will be attributed to the golden share and voted by a trustee.

Class C - Consists of class C fully voting (one vote per share) and limited voting (non-voting for directors) shares.

Class A, B & C Special Voting - Held by a trustee, entitling the trustee to a number of votes equal to the number of class A common, class B variable voting and class C shares into which the class A, B and C LP units of Telesat Partnership LP are exchangeable.

Golden Share - Voting power will vary to ensure that the aggregate number of votes cast by Canadians, with respect to a particular matter, will equal a simple majority of all votes cast in respect of such matter, resulting in the dilution of the voting power of non-Canadian shareholders. Entitled to a number of votes equal to the sum of: a number of votes such that the votes cast by the holders of class A common shares and class A LP units, class C shares and class C LP units, and the golden share represent a simple majority of votes cast; and the number of votes transferred from the class B variable voting shares and class B LP units, if applicable.

Class A, B & C LP Units - Exchangeable for class A common, class B variable voting or class C shares on a 1-for-1 basis, or, subject to the company's right as the general partner of Telesat Partnership LP, for cash. Classified as non-controlling interest.

Major Shareholder - Public Sector Pension Investment Board held 36.6% interest and MHR Fund Management LLC held 36.2% interest at May 2, 2023.

Price Range - TSAT/TSX

Year	Volume	High	Low	Close
2022	498,912	$38.54	$8.39	$9.91
2021	66,398	$55.00	$33.00	$35.96

Recent Close: $25.46

Capital Stock Changes - During 2022, class A common or class B variable voting shares were issued as follows: 574,226 on exchange of a like number of class B LP units of Telesat Partnership LP and 210,978 on vesting of restricted share units.

Investments

27% int. in **Telesat Partnership LP**, Ont. Represents general partnership interest.
- 100% int. in **Loral Space & Communications Inc.**, New York, N.Y.
  - 100% int. in **Loral Holdings Corporation**, Del.
    - 20% int. in **Telesat Can ULC**, B.C.
- 100% int. in **Telesat CanHold Corporation**, B.C.
  - 80% int. in **Telesat Can ULC**, B.C.
    - 62.6% int. in **Telesat Canada**, Ottawa, Ont.
  - 37.4% int. in **Telesat Canada**, Ottawa, Ont.
    - 100% int. in **Telesat (IOM) Holdings Limited**, Isle of Man.
      - 100% int. in **Telesat International Limited**, United Kingdom.
    - 100% int. in **Telesat LEO Holdings Inc.**, Canada.
      - 100% int. in **Telesat LEO Inc.**, Canada.
      - 8.5% int. in **Telesat Technology Corporation**, Canada.
    - 100% int. in **Telesat Spectrum General Partnership**, Ont.
      - 87.1% int. in **Telesat Technology Corporation**, Canada.
        - 100% int. in **Telesat Spectrum Holdings Corporation**, Canada.
          - 100% int. in **Telesat Spectrum Corporation**, Canada.
    - 4.4% int. in **Telesat Technology Corporation**, Canada.

Note: The preceding list includes only the major related companies in which interests are held.

Financial Statistics

Periods ended:	12m Dec. 31/22[A]		12m Dec. 31/21[oA]
	$000s	%Chg	$000s
Operating revenue	**759,169**	**0**	**758,212**
Cost of sales	54,004		30,215
Salaries & benefits	84,726		82,389
General & admin expense	52,831		50,622
Stock-based compensation	67,428		73,723
Operating expense	**258,989**	**+9**	**236,949**
Operating income	**500,180**	**-4**	**521,263**
Deprec., depl. & amort.	203,734		219,755
Finance income	23,476		3,418
Finance costs, gross	221,756		187,994
Pre-tax income	**(30,188)**	**n.a.**	**233,402**
Income taxes	49,929		78,377
Net income	**(80,117)**	**n.a.**	**155,025**
Net inc. for equity hldrs	**(23,396)**	**n.a.**	**85,190**
Net inc. for non-cont. int	**(56,721)**	**n.a.**	**69,835**
Cash & equivalent	1,677,792		1,449,593
Inventories	2,023		16,982
Accounts receivable	41,248		122,698
Current assets	1,788,288		1,617,435
Fixed assets, net	1,364,084		1,429,688
Intangibles, net	3,203,481		3,209,262
Total assets	**6,479,593**	**+2**	**6,362,451**
Accts. pay. & accr. liabs	43,555		54,628
Current liabilities	171,396		181,955
Long-term debt, gross	3,850,081		3,792,597
Long-term debt, net	3,850,081		3,792,597
Long-term lease liabilities	31,986		33,729
Shareholders' equity	480,365		415,674
Non-controlling interest	1,355,337		1,280,619
Cash from oper. activs	**228,848**	**-22**	**293,497**
Cash from fin. activs	(104,865)		605,240
Cash from invest. activs	74		(269,968)
Net cash position	**1,677,792**	**+16**	**1,449,593**
Capital expenditures	(32,701)		(31,725)
Pension fund surplus	36,195		12,178
	$		$
Earnings per share*	(1.90)		1.89
Cash flow per share*	18.59		6.50
	shs		shs
No. of shs. o/s*	12,805,291		12,020,087
Avg. no. of shs. o/s*	12,311,264		45,168,650
	%		%
Net profit margin	(10.55)		20.45
Return on equity	(5.22)		9.75
Return on assets	7.92		4.69
Foreign sales percent	56		56
No. of employees (FTEs)	455		471

* Com. & Variable Vtg.
[o] Restated
[A] Reported in accordance with IFRS

Latest Results

Periods ended:	3m Mar. 31/23[A]		3m Mar. 31/22[A]
	$000s	%Chg	$000s
Operating revenue	183,422	-1	185,769
Net income	28,633	-53	60,630
Net inc. for equity hldrs	8,065	-42	13,983
Net inc. for non-cont. int	20,568		46,647
	$		$
Earnings per share*	0.62		1.16

* Com. & Variable Vtg.
[A] Reported in accordance with IFRS

Historical Summary
(as originally stated)

Fiscal Year	Oper. Rev.	Net Inc. Bef. Disc.	EPS*
	$000s	$000s	$
2022[A]	759,169	(80,117)	(1.90)
2021[A]	758,212	157,762	2.29
2020[A1]	820,468	245,578	n.a.
2019[A1]	910,893	187,198	n.a.
2018[A1]	902,932	(90,936)	n.a.

* Com. & Variable Vtg.
[A] Reported in accordance with IFRS
[1] Results pertain to Telesat Canada (predecessor company).

T.24 Telescope Innovations Corp.

Symbol - TELI **Exchange** - CSE **CUSIP** - 87953P
Head Office - 2200-885 Georgia St W, Vancouver, BC, V6C 2E8 **Telephone** - (778) 331-8505 **Fax** - (778) 508-9923
Website - telescopeinnovations.com
Email - jason@telescopeinn.com
Investor Relations - Prof. Jason Hein (604) 822-2211
Auditors - Manning Elliott LLP C.A., Vancouver, B.C.
Transfer Agents - Odyssey Trust Company, Vancouver, B.C.

Profile - (B.C. 2019) Researches and develops manufacturing processes and tools for the pharmaceutical and chemical industry.

The company's proprietary manufacturing processes utilize automated technologies and tools for the production of synthetic psychedelic compounds, with a focus on psilocybin and mental health medicines. These processes can be used for the chemical synthesis of other tryptamine-based compounds, including dimethyltryptamine (DMT), harmaline, miprocin, ibogaine, melatonin, lysergic acid diethylamide, serotonin and bufotenine. The company's flagship product, Direct Inject Liquid Chromatography (DILC™), is a hardware and software ecosystem that enables direct sampling and analysis of chemical reactions, enabling unattended sample capture, quenching, dilution and analysis using a variety of chromatography data system (CDS) platforms.

Predecessor Detail - Name changed from Culmina Ventures Corp., May 19, 2021, pursuant to the reverse takeover acquisition of ClearMynd Technology Solutions Corp.

Directors - Prof. Jason Hein, CEO, B.C.; Henry Dubina, United States; Robert Mintak, Vancouver, B.C.; Ali Pejman, B.C.; Dr. J. Andrew (Andy) Robinson, B.C.

Other Exec. Officers - Dr. Jeffrey Sherman, COO; Robert (Rob) Chisholm, CFO & corp. sec.; Shad Grunert, v-p, innovation; Paloma Prieto, v-p, opers.; Dr. Lars Yunker, v-p, automation & integration

Capital Stock

	Authorized (shs.)	Outstanding (shs.)[1]
Common	unlimited	53,665,569

[1] At May 23, 2023

Major Shareholder - Widely held at May 23, 2023.

Price Range - TELI/CSE

Year	Volume	High	Low	Close
2022	1,898,493	$0.85	$0.22	$0.25
2021	319,094	$1.18	$0.32	$0.85

Recent Close: $0.26

Capital Stock Changes - In November 2022, private placement of 4,879,499 units (1 common share & ½ warrant) at 30¢ per unit was completed, with warrants exercisable at 75¢ per share for two years.

In January 2022, 1,000,000 common shares were issued pursuant to the acquisition of technological developments under the agreement with the University of British Columbia.

Wholly Owned Subsidiaries

ClearMynd Technology Solutions Corp., North Vancouver, B.C.
1280225 B.C. Ltd., B.C.

Financial Statistics

Periods ended:	12m Aug. 31/22[A]		12m Aug. 31/21[A1]
	$000s	%Chg	$000s
Operating revenue	**595**	**n.a.**	**nil**
Research & devel. expense	60		130
General & admin expense	3,274		3,843
Stock-based compensation	2,742		51
Operating expense	**6,076**	**+51**	**4,024**
Operating income	**(5,481)**	**n.a.**	**(4,024)**
Deprec., depl. & amort.	276		nil
Pre-tax income	**(5,747)**	**n.a.**	**(4,025)**
Net income	**(5,747)**	**n.a.**	**(4,025)**
Cash & equivalent	719		3,924
Accounts receivable	504		64
Current assets	1,497		3,474
Fixed assets, net	1,527		600
Total assets	**3,024**	**-26**	**4,073**
Accts. pay. & accr. liabs	480		247
Current liabilities	1,351		247
Shareholders' equity	1,673		3,826
Cash from oper. activs	**(1,371)**	**n.a.**	**(941)**
Cash from fin. activs	nil		4,786
Cash from invest. activs	(1,204)		(600)
Net cash position	**719**	**-78**	**3,294**
Capital expenditures	(1,204)		(600)
	$		$
Earnings per share*	(0.12)		(0.16)
Cash flow per share*	(0.03)		(0.04)
	shs		shs
No. of shs. o/s*	48,786,070		47,786,070
Avg. no. of shs. o/s*	48,424,426		25,886,843
	%		%
Net profit margin	(965.88)		n.a.
Return on equity	(209.02)		(209.96)
Return on assets	(161.96)		(195.29)

* Common
[A] Reported in accordance with IFRS
[1] Results reflect the May 31, 2021, reverse takeover acquisition of ClearMynd Technology Solutions Corp.

Latest Results

Periods ended:	6m Feb. 28/23[A]		6m Feb. 28/22[A]
	$000s	%Chg	$000s
Operating revenue	1,327	n.a.	nil
Net income	(259)	n.a.	(4,011)
	$		$
Earnings per share*	(0.01)		(0.08)

* Common
[A] Reported in accordance with IFRS

Historical Summary
(as originally stated)

Fiscal Year	Oper. Rev.	Net Inc. Bef. Disc.	EPS*
	$000s	$000s	$
2022[A]	595	(5,747)	(0.12)
2021[A]	nil	(4,025)	(0.16)
2020[A1]	nil	(253)	n.a.

* Common
[A] Reported in accordance with IFRS
[1] 13 months ended Aug. 31, 2020.

T.25 Telo Genomics Corp.

Symbol - TELO **Exchange** - TSX-VEN **CUSIP** - 87975M
Head Office - MaRS Centre, South Tower, 200-101 College St, Toronto, ON, M5G 1L7 **Telephone** - (416) 673-8485
Website - www.telodx.com
Email - info@telodx.com
Investor Relations - Dr. Sherif Louis (416) 673-8487
Auditors - Crowe MacKay LLP C.A., Vancouver, B.C.
Lawyers - Blake, Cassels & Graydon LLP, Vancouver, B.C.
Transfer Agents - Computershare Trust Company of Canada Inc., Vancouver, B.C.
Employees - 6 at June 30, 2022
Profile - (Can. 2011) Developing a telomere-based analysis platform, with diagnostic and prognostic applications for cancer and other diseases such as multiple myeloma, Hodgkin's lymphoma, leukemia, myelodysplastic syndromes/acute myeloid leukemia and Alzheimer's disease.

The company's proprietary software platform and diagnostic and prognostic tests are based on the three-dimensional analysis of a patient's individual telomere (the protective caps at the end of chromosomes) organization primarily through a liquid biopsy. The TeloView™ software platform can measure the stage of disease, rate of progression of disease and potential response to treatment for pathologists, clinicians, academic researchers and drug developers. The company's lead application, TELO-MM®, is a prognostic genomics-based test that utilizes TeloView™ to determine the disease stages of multiple myeloma and to provide important actionable information to healthcare professionals.

Predecessor Detail - Name changed from 3D Signatures Inc., Apr. 8, 2019.
Directors - Dr. Sabine Mai, co-founder, Winnipeg, Man.; Guido Baechler, chr., Calif.; Hugh A. D. Rogers, v-p, fin., Vancouver, B.C.; Dr. Ron McGlennen; W. John Meekison, Scottsdale, Ariz.
Other Exec. Officers - Kris Weinberg, CEO; Dr. Sherif Louis, pres. & chief tech. officer; Christopher Ross, CFO

Capital Stock

	Authorized (shs.)	Outstanding (shs.)[1]
Common	unlimited	59,424,433

[1] At Nov. 16, 2022
Major Shareholder - Widely held at Oct. 24, 2022.

Price Range - TELO/TSX-VEN

Year	Volume	High	Low	Close
2022	7,178,192	$0.55	$0.26	$0.36
2021	22,830,579	$1.44	$0.27	$0.41
2020	8,331,945	$0.30	$0.10	$0.27
2019	1,499,054	$0.30	$0.10	$0.18
2018	2,786,574	$2.23	$0.13	$0.18

Consolidation: 1-for-5 cons. in Nov. 2019
Recent Close: $0.27
Capital Stock Changes - In July 2021, private placement of 390,000 units (1 common share & ½ warrant) at 50¢ per unit was completed. Also during fiscal 2022, 3,491,540 common shares were issued on exercise of warrants.

Wholly Owned Subsidiaries

Telo Genomics Holdings Corp., Vancouver, B.C.

Financial Statistics

Periods ended:	12m June 30/22[A]		12m June 30/21[A]
	$000s	%Chg	$000s
Research & devel. expense	1,067		542
General & admin expense	987		653
Operating expense	**2,053**	**+72**	**1,195**
Operating income	**(2,053)**	**n.a.**	**(1,195)**
Deprec., depl. & amort.	57		62
Pre-tax income	**(2,110)**	**n.a.**	**(1,070)**
Net income	**(2,110)**	**n.a.**	**(1,070)**
Cash & equivalent	2,693		3,637
Accounts receivable	38		97
Current assets	2,787		3,761
Fixed assets, net	30		62
Intangibles, net	16		16
Total assets	**2,833**	**-26**	**3,839**
Accts. pay. & accr. liabs	190		114
Current liabilities	190		114
Long-term debt, gross	40		40
Long-term debt, net	40		40
Shareholders' equity	2,603		3,686
Cash from oper. activs	**(1,795)**	**n.a.**	**(1,105)**
Cash from fin. activs	877		3,829
Cash from invest. activs	(25)		(9)
Net cash position	**2,693**	**-26**	**3,637**
Capital expenditures	(25)		(9)
	$		$
Earnings per share*	(0.04)		(0.02)
Cash flow per share*	(0.03)		(0.02)
	shs		shs
No. of shs. o/s*	59,424,433		55,542,893
Avg. no. of shs. o/s*	58,661,088		46,888,865
	%		%
Net profit margin	n.a.		n.a.
Return on equity	(67.10)		(47.97)
Return on assets	(63.25)		(42.73)
No. of employees (FTEs)	6		n.a.

* Common
[A] Reported in accordance with IFRS

Latest Results

Periods ended:	3m Sept. 30/22[A]		3m Sept. 30/21[A]
	$000s	%Chg	$000s
Net income	(616)	n.a.	(479)
	$		$
Earnings per share*	(0.01)		(0.01)

* Common
[A] Reported in accordance with IFRS

Historical Summary
(as originally stated)

Fiscal Year	Oper. Rev.	Net Inc. Bef. Disc.	EPS*
	$000s	$000s	$
2022[A]	nil	(2,110)	(0.04)
2021[A]	nil	(1,070)	(0.02)
2020[A]	nil	(1,242)	(0.04)
2019[A]	nil	(1,074)	(0.08)
2018[A]	nil	(4,695)	(0.40)

* Common
[A] Reported in accordance with IFRS
Note: Adjusted throughout for 1-for-5 cons. in Nov. 2019

T.26 Tempus Capital Inc.

Symbol - TEMP **Exchange** - CSE **CUSIP** - 88024G
Head Office - 200-3310 Service Rd S, Burlington, ON, L7N 3M6 **Telephone** - (905) 681-1925 **Fax** - (905) 681-3648
Email - bcrawford@brantcapital.ca
Investor Relations - Brian L. Crawford (905) 681-1925
Auditors - McGovern Hurley LLP C.A., Toronto, Ont.
Transfer Agents - TSX Trust Company, Toronto, Ont.
Profile - (Ont. 2011) Acquires, develops and owns income producing properties in Canada with a focus on strip mall shopping centres, storefront retail, and mixed residential and commercial properties.

Owns four real estate properties in southwestern Ontario, consisting of a 32,929-sq.-ft. commercial plaza in Strathroy and three mixed commercial/residential buildings in London totaling 22,191 sq. ft.

In addition, holds 18% interest in **2773830 Ontario Inc.** (dba Fritz's Cannabis Company), which processes, packages and distributes handcrafted tetrahydrocannabinol (THC) and cannabidiol (CBD)-infused cannabis edibles.

During the first quarter of 2022, the company sold a 2% interest it held in **2773830 Ontario Inc.** (dba Fritz's Cannabis Company) for $20,000 cash. As a result, the company's interest in Fritz's Cannabis Company decreased from 20% to 18%.

Directors - Russell Tanz, pres. & CEO, Toronto, Ont.; Brian L. Crawford, CFO & corp. sec., Burlington, Ont.; Thomas S. (Tom) Kofman, Thornhill, Ont.; Brian Roberts, Toronto, Ont.; Bernie Tanz, Toronto, Ont.

Capital Stock

	Authorized (shs.)	Outstanding (shs.)[1]
Common	unlimited	30,478,993

[1] At May 30, 2022
Major Shareholder - Mark M. Tanz held 45.7% interest, Russell Tanz held 19.6% interest and 2023920 Ontario Incorporated held 13.1% interest at June 7, 2021.

Price Range - TEMP/CSE

Year	Volume	High	Low	Close
2022	266,061	$0.36	$0.13	$0.20
2021	1,044,396	$0.23	$0.14	$0.20
2020	1,927,203	$0.17	$0.05	$0.17
2019	2,603,367	$0.32	$0.01	$0.08

Recent Close: $0.15

Dividends

TEMP com N.S.R.
$0.05**i** Aug. 15/23
i Initial Payment

Wholly Owned Subsidiaries

Tempus Capital LLC, United States. Inactive.
2335501 Ontario Inc., Ont.
2443578 Ontario Ltd., Ont.
2590197 Ontario Inc., Ont.
2821679 Ontario Inc., Ont.

Investments

18% int. in **2773830 Ontario Inc.**, Ont.

Financial Statistics

Periods ended:	12m Dec. 31/21^A		12m Dec. 31/20^A
	$000s	%Chg	$000s
Total revenue	**1,099**	**+18**	**929**
Rental operating expense	371		335
General & admin. expense	259		225
Stock-based compensation	172		nil
Operating expense	**431**	**-23**	**560**
Operating income	**668**	**+81**	**369**
Investment income	(51)		nil
Finance costs, gross	464		397
Pre-tax income	**856**	**+41**	**606**
Income taxes	167		64
Net income	**689**	**+27**	**542**
Cash & equivalent	8		40
Accounts receivable	51		22
Current assets	143		185
Long-term investments	64		nil
Income-producing props	14,976		12,656
Property interests, net	14,976		12,656
Total assets	**15,183**	**+18**	**12,845**
Accts. pay. & accr. liabs	321		184
Current liabilities	1,841		341
Long-term debt, gross	8,662		7,630
Long-term debt, net	7,264		7,473
Shareholders' equity	5,598		4,686
Cash from oper. activs	**210**	**+775**	**24**
Cash from fin. activs	1,154		(115)
Cash from invest. activs	(1,396)		(30)
Net cash position	**8**	**-80**	**40**
Increase in property	(1,281)		(30)
	$		$
Earnings per share*	0.02		0.02
Cash flow per share*	0.01		0.00
	shs		shs
No. of shs. o/s*	30,478,993		29,878,993
Avg. no. of shs. o/s*	30,340,911		29,878,993
	%		%
Net profit margin	62.69		58.34
Return on equity	13.40		12.28
Return on assets	7.58		7.12

* Common
^A Reported in accordance with IFRS

Latest Results

Periods ended:	3m Mar. 31/22^A		3m Mar. 31/21^A
	$000s	%Chg	$000s
Total revenue	285	+21	235
Net income	24	n.a.	(16)
	$		$
Earnings per share*	0.00		(0.00)

* Common
^A Reported in accordance with IFRS

Historical Summary
(as originally stated)

Fiscal Year	Total Rev.	Net Inc. Bef. Disc.	EPS*
	$000s	$000s	$
2021^A	1,099	689	0.02
2020^A	929	542	0.02
2019^A	977	106	0.00
2018^A	1,002	26	0.00
2017^A1	867	195	0.01

* Common
^A Reported in accordance with IFRS
[1] As shown in the prospectus dated Jan. 14, 2019.

T.27 Tenet Fintech Group Inc.

Symbol - PKK **Exchange** - CSE **CUSIP** - 88035N
Head Office - 705-119 Spadina Ave, Toronto, ON, M5V 2L1 **Telephone** - (416) 428-9954
Website - www.tenetfintech.com
Email - cboyd@tenetfintech.com
Investor Relations - Christina Boyd (416) 428-9954
Auditors - Raymond Chabot Grant Thornton LLP C.A., Montréal, Qué.
Lawyers - Dentons Canada LLP
Transfer Agents - TSX Trust Company, Toronto, Ont.
FP500 Revenue Ranking - 758
Employees - 148 at June 16, 2022
Profile - (Can. 2011; orig. Alta., 2008) Operates as a fintech company in the People's Republic of China where it provides products and services for the commercial lending sector.
Operates through two segments: Fintech Platform and Financial Services.

Fintech Platform

Wholly owned **Asia Synergy Data Solutions Ltd.** (ASDS) operates Cubeler Business Hub (formerly labelled Lending Hub), a centralized commercial lending platform which automates the process of finding, qualifying and extending loans between lenders and borrowers. The platform collects and analyses data of borrowers, primarily entrepreneurs and small and medium-sized businesses, from the businesses' accounting software and other sources and matches the data with the credit criteria of lenders.
Subsidiary **Asia Synergy Supply Chain Ltd.** (ASSC) and wholly owned **Asia Synergy Technologies Ltd.** (AST) provide supply chain services such as credit analysis and various financial and logistics services specifically for supply chain participants, and the Gold River platform, a platform linked to the Business Hub for the procurement and distribution of products.

Financial Services

Operations include wholly owned **Asia Synergy Credit Solutions Ltd.** (ASCS), which provides turnkey credit outsourcing services to banks and other financial institutions; and subsidiary **Asia Synergy Financial Capital Ltd.** (ASFC), which provides commercial loans to small and medium-sized businesses and entrepreneurs.
Predecessor Detail - Name changed from Peak Fintech Group Inc., Nov. 1, 2021.
Directors - Johnson Joseph, pres. & CEO, Montréal, Qué.; Liang (Golden) Qiu, CEO, Tenent China, Montréal, Qué.; Jean Leblond, Qué.; Mayco Quiroz, Montréal, Qué.
Other Exec. Officers - Raji Wahidy, COO; Jean Landreville, CFO; Wendy Kennish, chief legal officer & corp. sec.; Dr. Luis Rocha, chief analytics officer; Claude Theroux, chief tech. officer

Capital Stock

	Authorized (shs.)	Outstanding (shs.)[1]
Preferred	unlimited	nil
Common	unlimited	99,544,183

[1] At Mar. 30, 2023
Major Shareholder - Widely held at May 31, 2022.

Price Range - PKK/CSE

Year	Volume	High	Low	Close
2022	63,974,366	$7.49	$0.67	$0.83
2021	93,006,187	$14.50	$3.20	$7.15
2020	50,603,700	$4.08	$0.34	$3.28
2019	10,352,630	$1.30	$0.40	$0.80
2018	14,099,995	$1.30	$0.40	$0.50

Consolidation: 1-for-2 cons. in July 2021; 1-for-10 cons. in July 2020
Recent Close: $0.27

Wholly Owned Subsidiaries

Asia Synergy Limited, Hong Kong, People's Republic of China.
- 100% int. in **Asia Synergy Holdings Ltd.**, Shanghai, Shanghai, People's Republic of China.
  - 100% int. in **Asia Synergy Data Solutions Ltd.**, People's Republic of China.
    - 100% int. in **Asia Synergy Credit Solutions Ltd.**, Wuxi, Jiangsu, People's Republic of China.
    - 51% int. in **Asia Synergy Supply Chain Ltd.**, People's Republic of China.
    - 100% int. in **Huike Internet Technology Co., Ltd.**
    - 51% int. in **Kailifeng New Energy Technology Co., Ltd.**
    - 51% int. in **Wechain Technology Service Co., Ltd.**
    - 100% int. in **Xinxiang Technologies Ltd.**, People's Republic of China.
  - 100% int. in **Asia Synergy Technologies Ltd.**, Shanghai, Shanghai, People's Republic of China.
    - 100% int. in **Asia Synergy Supply Chain Technologies Ltd.**, Wuxi, Jiangsu, People's Republic of China.
    - 100% int. in **Jiangsu Steel Chain Technology Co., Ltd.**
    - 51% int. in **Shanghai Xinhuizhi Supply Chain Management Co., Ltd.**
    - 100% int. in **Zhejiang Xinjiupin Clean Tech - Oil & Gas Management Co.**, People's Republic of China.
- 100% int. in **Wuxi Aorong Ltd.**, Wuxi, Jiangsu, People's Republic of China.
  - 51% int. in **Asia Synergy Financial Capital Ltd.**, Wuxi, Jiangsu, People's Republic of China.

Cubeler Inc., Montréal, Qué.
- 100% int. in **Tenoris 3 Inc.**

Investments

Rongbang Technology Ltd., People's Republic of China.

Financial Statistics

Periods ended:	12m Dec. 31/22^‡A		12m Dec. 31/21^A
	$000s	%Chg	$000s
Operating revenue	**109,879**	**+6**	**103,633**
Salaries & benefits	...		4,898
General & admin expense	...		6,859
Other operating expense	...		89,836
Operating expense	**...**	**n.a.**	**101,593**
Operating income	**...**	**n.a.**	**2,040**
Deprec., depl. & amort	...		2,644
Finance income	...		53
Finance costs, gross	...		262
Pre-tax income	**...**	**n.a.**	**(50,174)**
Income taxes	...		(1,612)
Net income	**(53,013)**	**n.a.**	**(48,562)**
Net inc. for equity hldrs	**(53,092)**	**n.a.**	**(49,757)**
Net inc. for non-cont. int	**79**	**-93**	**1,195**
Cash & equivalent	...		18,797
Accounts receivable	...		(17,875)
Current assets	...		94,402
Fixed assets, net	...		181
Right-of-use assets	...		1,881
Intangibles, net	...		95,368
Total assets	**141,267**	**-28**	**195,293**
Accts. pay. & accr. liabs	...		5,224
Current liabilities	...		20,327
Long-term debt, gross	374		313
Long-term debt, net	nil		313
Long-term lease liabilities	...		1,315
Shareholders' equity	102,346		151,270
Non-controlling interest	...		14,320
Cash from oper. activs	**...**	**n.a.**	**(40,889)**
Cash from fin. activs	...		69,480
Cash from invest. activs	...		(17,389)
Net cash position	**...**	**n.a.**	**18,797**
Capital expenditures	...		(54)
Capital disposals	...		6
	$		$
Earnings per share*	(0.54)		(0.66)
Cash flow per share*	...		(0.54)
	shs		shs
No. of shs. o/s*	...		97,167,183
Avg. no. of shs. o/s*	...		75,700,826
	%		%
Net profit margin	(48.25)		(46.86)
Return on equity	(41.87)		(57.82)
Return on assets	n.m.		(37.65)
Foreign sales percent	100		100

* Common
‡ Preliminary
^A Reported in accordance with IFRS

Historical Summary
(as originally stated)

Fiscal Year	Oper. Rev.	Net Inc. Bef. Disc.	EPS*
	$000s	$000s	$
2022^‡A	109,879	(53,013)	(0.54)
2021^A	103,633	(48,562)	(0.66)
2020^A	42,698	(5,514)	(0.16)
2019^A	11,709	(1,830)	(0.08)
2018^A	1,682	(3,609)	(0.12)

* Common
‡ Preliminary
^A Reported in accordance with IFRS
Note: Adjusted throughout for 1-for-2 cons. in July 2021; 1-for-10 cons. in July 2020

T.28 TeraGo Inc.

Symbol - TGO **Exchange** - TSX **CUSIP** - 88079F
Head Office - 800-55 Commerce Valley Dr W, Thornhill, ON, L3T 7V9 **Telephone** - (905) 707-5381 **Toll-free** - (866) 837-2461 **Fax** - (905) 707-6212
Website - www.terago.ca
Email - philip.jones@terago.ca
Investor Relations - Philip Jones (877) 982-3688
Auditors - KPMG LLP C.A., Toronto, Ont.
Transfer Agents - Computershare Trust Company of Canada Inc., Toronto, Ont.
Employees - 100 at Dec. 31, 2022
Profile - (Can. 2000) Provides wireless connectivity and private 5G wireless networking services to businesses operating across Canada.
Services include Internet services, which is provided through its carrier-grade Multi-Protocol Label Switching enabled wireline and fixed wireless, Internet Protocol (IP) communications network in Canada using licensed and license-exempt spectrum and fibre-optic wireline infrastructure that supports commercially available equipment with upload and download speeds from 5 Mbps to 1 Gbps; Data services, which allows businesses to connect their multiple sites within a city or across the company's geographic footprint through a Private Virtual Local Area Network (VLAN) with speeds up to 1 Gbps; and 5G fixed

wireless, which delivers higher speeds and lower latency using improved through-put speeds of 1.5 Gbps.

Directors - Kenneth (Ken) Campbell, chr., Ottawa, Ont.; Daniel Vucinic, CEO, Ont.; Pietro Cordova, Rome, Italy; Fred Hrenchuk, Alta.; Tina Pidgeon, Haddonfield, N.J.; Martin (Marty) Pinnes, Ont.; Jim Watson, Ottawa, Ont.

Other Exec. Officers - Matthew Gerber, pres.; Philip Jones, CFO; Osman Mohamednur, v-p, eng. & opers.; Shaunik Katyal, gen. counsel & corp. sec.

Capital Stock

	Authorized (shs.)	Outstanding (shs.)[1]
Class A Non-vtg.	unlimited	nil
Class B	2	nil
Common	unlimited	19,753,282

[1] At May 10, 2023

Class A Non-voting - Rank pari passu with common shares on the winding-up, liquidation or dissolution of the company. Non-voting.

Class B - Entitled to nominate and elect one director for each share held. Redeemable by company at $1.00 per share. Not entitled to receive any assets on the winding-up, liquidation or dissolution of the company. Non-voting.

Common - One vote per share.

Major Shareholder - Cymbria Corporation held 18.32% interest at May 5, 2023.

Price Range - TGO/TSX

Year	Volume	High	Low	Close
2022	5,399,108	$6.50	$1.95	$2.90
2021	3,116,451	$7.45	$4.50	$5.50
2020	3,115,379	$9.18	$4.00	$6.40
2019	6,862,159	$13.06	$7.05	$8.88
2018	15,297,402	$11.49	$4.30	$10.68

Recent Close: $2.03

Capital Stock Changes - During 2022, 68,000 common shares were issued for director's fee.

Wholly Owned Subsidiaries

TeraGo Networks Inc., Thornhill, Ont.
- 100% int. in **TeraGo Networks (US) Inc.**, Del.

Financial Statistics

Periods ended:	12m Dec. 31/22[A]		12m Dec. 31/21[A]
	$000s	%Chg	$000s
Operating revenue	**27,215**	**-37**	**43,303**
Cost of sales	7,437		11,141
Salaries & benefits	12,217		14,401
Stock-based compensation	688		164
Other operating expense	6,187		6,110
Operating expense	**26,529**	**-17**	**31,816**
Operating income	**686**	**-94**	**11,487**
Deprec., depl. & amort.	10,085		14,554
Finance income	123		44
Finance costs, gross	2,089		3,896
Write-downs/write-offs	(423)		(2,125)
Pre-tax income	**(11,571)**	**n.a.**	**(15,172)**
Net income	**(11,571)**	**n.a.**	**(15,172)**
Cash & equivalent	7,378		5,481
Accounts receivable	2,252		1,586
Current assets	10,938		47,569
Fixed assets, net	32,815		33,990
Intangibles, net	11,140		11,152
Total assets	**55,383**	**-41**	**93,230**
Accts. pay. & accr. liabs.	4,711		3,832
Current liabilities	9,861		24,170
Long-term debt, gross	6,157		19,791
Long-term debt, net	6,157		17,541
Long-term lease liabilities	9,318		10,492
Shareholders' equity	29,599		40,262
Cash from oper. activs.	**1,253**	**-87**	**9,322**
Cash from fin. activs.	(19,339)		(1,946)
Cash from invest. activs.	18,825		(7,753)
Net cash position	**6,220**	**+13**	**5,481**
Capital expenditures	(6,212)		(7,380)
	$		$
Earnings per share*	(0.61)		(0.81)
Cash flow per share*	0.07		0.50
	shs		shs
No. of shs. o/s*	19,735,000		19,667,000
Avg. no. of shs. o/s*	19,098,000		18,769,000
	%		%
Net profit margin	(42.52)		(35.04)
Return on equity	(33.13)		(37.40)
Return on assets	(12.76)		(11.48)
No. of employees (FTEs)	100		140

* Com & Cl.A
[A] Reported in accordance with IFRS

Latest Results

Periods ended:	3m Mar. 31/23[A]		3m Mar. 31/22[A]
	$000s	%Chg	$000s
Operating revenue	6,498	-17	7,789
Net income	(2,549)	n.a.	(3,140)
	$		$
Earnings per share*	(0.13)		(0.16)

* Com & Cl.A
[A] Reported in accordance with IFRS

Historical Summary
(as originally stated)

Fiscal Year	Oper. Rev.	Net Inc. Bef. Disc.	EPS*
	$000s	$000s	$
2022[A]	27,215	(11,571)	(0.61)
2021[A]	43,303	(15,172)	(0.81)
2020[A]	45,448	(8,259)	(0.49)
2019[A]	48,437	(6,994)	(0.43)
2018[A]	54,295	(4,820)	(0.32)

* Com & Cl.A
[A] Reported in accordance with IFRS

T.29 Terra Firma Capital Corporation

Symbol - TII **Exchange** - TSX-VEN **CUSIP** - 881002
Head Office - 200-22 St. Clair Ave E, Toronto, ON, M4T 2S3
Telephone - (416) 792-4700 **Fax** - (416) 792-4711
Website - www.tfcc.ca
Email - sochoa@tfcc.ca
Investor Relations - Shelley Ochoa (416) 792-4707
Auditors - KPMG LLP C.A., Toronto, Ont.
Lawyers - Blake, Cassels & Graydon LLP, Toronto, Ont.
Transfer Agents - Computershare Trust Company of Canada Inc., Toronto, Ont.
Employees - 12 at Dec. 31, 2022

Profile - (Ont. 2007) Arranges, creates and manages real estate financings secured by investment properties and real estate developments undertaken by real estate developers and owners throughout Canada and the United States.

Financings provided by the company are in the form of loans and mortgages, such as land and lot inventory loans, term mortgages for acquiring or refinancing income-producing properties, and mezzanine and subordinated debt to fund construction; land bank financing, whereby the company acquires land for residential development from a third party and provides builders with the exclusive right to use and develop the land, and simultaneously grants builders an option to purchase smaller parcels of the initial tract from the company over time at a specified price until it has purchased the entire initial tract; and equity financing through partnerships with developers for the development of real properties or equity investments in an entity that carries on the business of real estate development.

Investment portfolio at Mar. 31, 2023:

Type	Fair Value
First mtges.	US$37,497,355
Unregistered loans	1,996,154
Land banking	58,100,600
Equity invests.	12,187,730
Other invests.	1,514,231
	111,296,070

In July 2023, the company provided an update on its ongoing strategic alternatives review. It has considered several conditional non-binding offers and entered into discussions with potential purchasers for the entire company. However, while the company continues to explore a potential sale of the entire company, no concrete transaction on terms acceptable to the company materialized thus far. The company's board of directors has made the strategic decision to pursue liquidation of its remaining assets with the objective of returning capital to its shareholders.

During 2022, the company disposed its partnership interest in **Terra Firma (Valermo) Corporation**.

Directors - Y. Dov Meyer, exec. chr., Toronto, Ont.; Philip Reichmann†, Toronto, Ont.; Dr. Christopher (Chris) Bart, Hamilton, Ont.; Tristan Kingcott, B.C.; Mike Kirchmair, Ont.

Other Exec. Officers - Glenn Watchorn, pres. & CEO; Seth Greenspan, man. dir.; Carolyn Montgomery, man. dir.; Jeremy Scheetz, man. dir.; Shelley Ochoa, CFO & corp. sec.; Scott Sadleir, v-p

† Lead director

Capital Stock

	Authorized (shs.)	Outstanding (shs.)[1]
Common	unlimited	5,584,134

[1] At May 29, 2023

Major Shareholder - ICM Limited held 20.14% interest and Pathfinder Asset Management Limitied held 15.88% interest at May 18, 2023.

Price Range - TII/TSX-VEN

Year	Volume	High	Low	Close
2022	115,598	$6.50	$4.00	$5.35
2021	910,835	$7.35	$5.20	$6.01
2020	1,184,989	$6.10	$3.90	$5.65
2019	906,299	$6.50	$4.25	$5.60
2018	1,445,183	$7.10	$4.50	$4.60

Consolidation: 1-for-10 cons. in Sept. 2019
Recent Close: $6.91

Capital Stock Changes - During 2022, 16,666 common shares were issued on exercise of options.

Dividends

TII com Ra $0.24 pa Q est. Jan. 14, 2022
Prev. Rate: $0.20 est. Oct. 5, 2019

Wholly Owned Subsidiaries

TFCC Allen Farm LLC, Tex.
TFCC Arroyo LLC, Ariz.
TFCC Cambridge Angier LLC, N.C.
TFCC Coburn LLC, Tex.
TFCC Coyote LLC, United States.
TFCC Delray Inc., United States.
TFCC Dunn's Crossing LLC, Fla.
TFCC Ellington LLC, United States.
TFCC International Ltd., Ont.
TFCC Jacksonville LLC, Fla.
TFCC Kempston Place LLC, United States.
TFCC LanQueen Ltd., Ont.
TFCC San Pablo LLC, United States.
TFCC Saul's Ranch LLC, United States.
TFCC Scotland Heights LLC, United States.
TFCC Stafford LLC, United States.
TFCC Sterling 5A LLC, Colo.
TFCC Sterling LLC, Colo.
TFCC Trailmark LLC, Fla.
TFCC USA II Corporation, Del.
TFCC USA III Corporation, United States.
TFCC USA III Holdings Corporation, Ont.
TFCC USA IV Corporation, Del.
TFCC USA LLC, Del.
TFCC Wilson Trace LLC, United States.
TFCC Windrose LLC, United Arab Emirates.
Terra Firma (Crowdfund) Corporation, Canada.
Terra Firma MA Ltd., Ont.
Terra Firma Queen Developments Inc., Ont.
Terra Firma Senior Debt Fund Corporation, Canada.

Financial Statistics

Periods ended:	12m Dec. 31/22[A]		12m Dec. 31/21[A]
	US$000s	%Chg	US$000s
Total revenue	**15,103**	**-7**	**16,241**
General & admin. expense	3,916		4,014
Stock-based compensation	(97)		127
Other operating expense	60		58
Operating expense	**3,879**	**-8**	**4,199**
Operating income	**11,224**	**-7**	**12,042**
Deprec. & amort.	156		214
Finance costs, gross	9,532		8,589
Pre-tax income	**2,750**	**-39**	**4,472**
Income taxes	1,229		1,131
Net income	**1,521**	**-54**	**3,341**
Cash & equivalent	16,636		18,107
Accounts receivable	764		737
Investments	127,199		115,098
Right-of-use assets	597		852
Total assets	**151,397**	**+9**	**139,306**
Accts. pay. & accr. liabs.	9,221		7,794
Debt	96,727		86,289
Lease liabilities	633		881
Shareholders' equity	44,145		43,579
Cash from oper. activs.	**(630)**	**n.a.**	**2,349**
Cash from fin. activs.	8,246		2,237
Cash from invest. activs.	(9,088)		9,740
Net cash position	**16,636**	**-8**	**18,107**
	US$		US$
Earnings per share*	0.27		0.60
Cash flow per share*	(0.11)		0.42
Cash divd. per share*	$0.24		$0.21
	shs		shs
No. of shs. o/s*	5,584,134		5,567,468
Avg. no. of shs. o/s*	5,575,710		5,565,323
	%		%
Net profit margin	10.07		20.57
Return on equity	3.47		7.89
Return on assets	4.67		7.17
No. of employees (FTEs)	12		11

* Common
[A] Reported in accordance with IFRS

Latest Results

Periods ended:	3m Mar. 31/23[A]		3m Mar. 31/22[A]
	US$000s	%Chg	US$000s
Total revenue	3,861	+1	3,830
Net income	580	0	578
	US$		US$
Earnings per share*	0.10		0.10

* Common
[A] Reported in accordance with IFRS

Historical Summary
(as originally stated)

Fiscal Year	Total Rev.	Net Inc. Bef. Disc.	EPS*
	US$000s	US$000s	US$
2022^A	15,103	1,521	0.27
2021^A	16,241	3,341	0.60
2020^A	15,462	2,169	0.39
2019^A	16,656	3,078	0.54
	$000s	$000s	$
2018^A	17,460	2,771	0.50

* Common
^A Reported in accordance with IFRS
Note: Adjusted throughout for 1-for-10 cons. in Sept. 2019

T.30 Terranueva Corporation

Symbol - TEQ **Exchange** - CSE **CUSIP** - 88105H
Head Office - 803 boul de l'Ange-Gardien, L'Assomption, QC, J5W 1T3 **Telephone** - (450) 681-7744 **Fax** - (450) 681-8400
Website - www.terranueva.ca
Email - info@terranueva.ca
Investor Relations - Dominique St-Louis (450) 591-1011
Auditors - PricewaterhouseCoopers LLP C.A., Montréal, Qué.
Transfer Agents - Computershare Trust Company of Canada Inc., Montréal, Qué.
Profile - (Can. 2007) Developing cannabis operations in Quebec.
Holds licences for cultivation, processing and sale of cannabis issued by Health Canada for the distribution to provincially and territorially authorized retailers and licence holders for recreational and medical purposes. Also implements modular production approach at its certification and research and development unit (CRDU) facility located in L'Assomption, Que.
Common reinstated on CSE, May 16, 2023.
Common suspended from CSE, Feb. 7, 2023.
Predecessor Detail - Name changed from AXE Exploration Inc., Nov. 23, 2018, pursuant to reverse takeover acquisition of Terranueva Pharma Corporation; basis 1 new for 16 old shs.
Directors - Peter A. Polatos, chr. & CEO, Montréal, Qué.; Sylvain Aird, corp. sec., Montréal, Qué.; Sylvain Tremblay
Other Exec. Officers - Dominique St-Louis, v-p, fin. & CFO

Capital Stock

	Authorized (shs.)	Outstanding (shs.)[1]
Common	unlimited	45,969,961

[1] At June 30, 2022

Major Shareholder - Jean-Luc Landry held 26.92% interest, Fiducie Castillo held 16.24% interest and GMTN Inc. held 10.48% interest at Mar. 14, 2022.

Price Range - TEQ/CSE

Year	Volume	High	Low	Close
2022	1,621,843	$0.10	$0.03	$0.03
2021	2,988,085	$0.18	$0.04	$0.09
2020	3,558,324	$0.42	$0.05	$0.10
2019	8,752,485	$1.75	$0.20	$0.40
2018	7,830,306	$2.64	$0.38	$0.64

Recent Close: $0.01

Wholly Owned Subsidiaries
Terranueva Pharma Corporation, L'Assomption, Qué.

Financial Statistics

Periods ended:	12m Sept. 30/21^A		12m Sept. 30/20^A
	$000s	%Chg	$000s
Cost of goods sold	912		722
Salaries & benefits	107		229
General & admin expense	653		471
Stock-based compensation	(39)		236
Operating expense	**1,633**	**-2**	**1,658**
Operating income	**(1,633)**	**n.a.**	**(1,658)**
Deprec., depl. & amort	66		63
Finance costs, gross	515		404
Pre-tax income	**(2,212)**	**n.a.**	**(2,125)**
Income taxes	(22)		nil
Net income	**(2,191)**	**n.a.**	**(2,125)**
Cash & equivalent	118		299
Inventories	566		458
Accounts receivable	99		73
Current assets	875		965
Fixed assets, net	1,428		1,719
Right-of-use assets	2,772		2,838
Total assets	**5,074**	**-8**	**5,522**
Bank indebtedness	963		942
Accts. pay. & accr. liabs	1,298		1,062
Current liabilities	5,230		2,472
Long-term debt, gross	1,216		761
Long-term debt, net	1,183		332
Long-term lease liabilities	nil		2,936
Shareholders' equity	(1,339)		(219)
Cash from oper. activs	**(1,581)**	**n.a.**	**(1,381)**
Cash from fin. activs	1,408		1,217
Cash from invest. activs	(23)		(96)
Net cash position	**118**	**-62**	**314**
Capital expenditures	(23)		(27)
	$		$
Earnings per share*	(0.06)		(0.06)
Cash flow per share*	(0.04)		(0.04)
	shs		shs
No. of shs. o/s*	45,969,961		32,844,961
Avg. no. of shs. o/s*	39,425,440		32,844,961
	%		%
Net profit margin	n.a.		n.a.
Return on equity	n.m.		n.m.
Return on assets	(31.73)		n.a.

* Common
^A Reported in accordance with IFRS

Latest Results

Periods ended:	9m June 30/22^A		9m June 30/21^A
	$000s	%Chg	$000s
Net income	(2,032)	n.a.	(1,397)
	$		$
Earnings per share*	(0.04)		(0.04)

* Common
^A Reported in accordance with IFRS

Historical Summary
(as originally stated)

Fiscal Year	Oper. Rev.	Net Inc. Bef. Disc.	EPS*
	$000s	$000s	$
2021^A	nil	(2,191)	(0.06)
2020^A	nil	(2,125)	(0.06)
2019^A1	nil	(5,494)	(0.17)
2018^A2	nil	(812)	(0.22)
2017^A	nil	(850)	(0.24)

* Common
^A Reported in accordance with IFRS
[1] Results reflect the Dec. 17, 2018, reverse takeover acquisition of Terranueva Pharma Corporation.
[2] Results for fiscal 2018 and prior periods pertain to AXE Exploration Inc.
Note: Adjusted throughout for 1-for-16 cons. in Nov. 2018

T.31 TerrAscend Corp.

Symbol - TSND **Exchange** - TSX **CUSIP** - 88105E
Head Office - East Tower, 501-77 City Centre Dr, Mississauga, ON, L5B 1M5 **Toll-free** - (855) 837-7295 **Fax** - (844) 576-5223
Website - www.terrascend.com
Email - ir@terrascend.com
Investor Relations - Keith Stauffer (855) 837-7295
Auditors - MNP LLP C.A., Toronto, Ont.
Lawyers - Blake, Cassels & Graydon LLP, Toronto, Ont.
Transfer Agents - Odyssey Trust Company, Toronto, Ont.
FP500 Revenue Ranking - 550
Employees - 972 at Dec. 31, 2022
Profile - (Ont. 2017) Cultivates, processes and sells medical and adult-use cannabis products in the U.S. and Canada.
Cultivation, processing and manufacturing facilities consist of a 150,000-sq.-ft. facility in Waterfall, Pa.; a 140,000-sq.-ft. facility in Boonton, N.J.; a 47,000-sq.-ft. facility in Monitor twp., a 14,000-sq.-ft. facility in Harrison twp., and a 17,500-sq.-ft. facility in Warren, all in Michigan; a 156,000-sq.-ft. facility in Hagerstown, Md.; and a 20,000-sq.-ft. facility in San Francisco, Calif. The company also owns Valhalla Confections, which manufactures cannabis-infused artisan edibles from a facility in Santa Rosa, Calif.; and plans to construct a cultivation and manufacturing facility in Phillipsburg, N.J.
Retail operations consist of 38 dispensaries in Pennsylvania (6), Maryland (4), New Jersey (3), Michigan (19), California (5) and Toronto, Ont., which operate primarily under the proprietary The Apothecarium, Gage and Keystone Canna Remedies names, as well as the licensed Cookies brand.
In connection with the company's listing on the TSX on July 4, 2023, the company completed a reorganization in June 2023 to sever its Canadian cannabis operations and interests from its U.S. cannabis operations and interests. The company's 95% ownership in **Cookies Retail Canada Corp.**, owner and operator of a Cookies-branded dispensary in Toronto, Ont., was transferred to wholly owned **TerrAscend Canada Inc.**, the holder of the company's Canadian cannabis business. Wholly owned **TerrAscend Growth Corp.**, the holder of all the company's U.S. cannabis interests, completed a private placement of class A shares with **TERinvest LLC** for gross proceeds of US$1,000,000, representing a 0.2% ownership. As a result, the company retained a 99.8% interest in TerrAscend Growth through ownership of all exchangeable shares.
In April 2023, the company increased its interest in **Cookies Retail Canada Corp.**, which owns and operates a Cookies-branded dispensary in Toronto, Ont., to 95% for an undisclosed amount.
On Mar. 1, 2023, the company sold substantially all the assets of wholly owned **Arise Bioscience Inc.**, which manufactured and distributed hemp-derived wellness products under the Original Hemp and Funky Farms brands from a facility in Boca Raton, Fla. Terms were not disclosed.
During 2022, the company exited its 22,000-sq.-ft. cultivation and processing facility in Frederick, Md., as well as ceased operations at its 67,300-sq.-ft. manufacturing facility in Mississauga, Ont. Cultivation at the Mississauga facility ceased during the fourth quarter of 2020.
Common listed on TSX, July 4, 2023.
Common delisted from CSE, July 4, 2023.

Recent Merger and Acquisition Activity

Status: completed **Revised:** July 10, 2023
UPDATE: The transaction was completed. PREVIOUS: TerrAscend Corp. agreed to acquire Herbiculture Inc. (dba Herbiculture), a medical dispensary in Burtonsville, Md., for US$8,250,000.

Status: completed **Revised:** June 30, 2023
UPDATE: The transaction was completed. PREVIOUS: TerrAscend Corp. agreed to acquire Hempaid, LLC (dba Blue Ridge Wellness), a medical dispensary in Parkville, Md., for US$6,750,000.

Status: completed **Revised:** June 28, 2023
UPDATE: The transaction was completed. PREVIOUS: TerrAscend Corp. agreed to acquire Derby 1, LLC (dba Peninsula Alternative Health), a medical dispensary in Salisbury, Md., near the Delaware border, for US$22,100,000, including cash, debt assumption and issuance of shares.

Status: completed **Announced:** May 23, 2023
TerrAscend Corp. sold its 67,300-sq.-ft. facility in Mississauga, Ont., for Cdn$19,700,000. The facility was focused on producing recreational cannabis under the Haven Street and Legend brands. Cultivation and manufacturing at the facility ceased during the fourth quarters of 2020 and 2022, respectively.

Status: completed **Revised:** Jan. 27, 2023
UPDATE: The transaction was completed. PREVIOUS: TerrAscend Corp. agreed to acquire Allegany Medical Marijuana Dispensary LLC, a medical dispensary in Cumberland, Md., for US$10,000,000. TerrAscend would also acquire the real estate for US$1,700,000.

Status: completed **Revised:** Aug. 22, 2022
UPDATE: The transaction was completed. PREVIOUS: TerrAscend Corp. agreed to acquire KISA Enterprises MI, LLC and KISA Holdings, LLC (collectively Pinnacle), a dispensary operator in Michigan with five operating locations in Addison, Buchanan, Camden, Edmore and Morenci. Total consideration was US$28,500,000, consisting of US$10,000,000 cash, US$10,000,000 in promissory notes and issuance of US$8,500,000 of common shares.

Status: completed **Revised:** Mar. 10, 2022
UPDATE: The transaction was completed. PREVIOUS: TerrAscend Corp. agreed to acquire Gage Growth Corp. on the basis of 0.3001 TerrAscend common shares for each Gage subordinate voting share held. The transaction was valued at US$545,000,000, representing US$2.11 (Cdn$2.66) per Gage share. As part of the transaction, exchangeable units of Gage (each of which is exchangeable into Gage shares) would be transferred (along with all Gage super voting shares) to TerrAscend in exchange for TerrAscend common shares on the same acquisition basis. Gage cultivates, processes and retails cannabis in Michigan, as well as provides support services to licensed cannabis operators. Upon completion, TerrAscend would have operations in five states and Canada, including seven cultivating and processing facilities and 23 operating dispensaries serving both medical and adult-use cannabis markets in the U.S. and Canada. Nov. 11, 2021 - The shareholders of both companies approved the transaction.

Directors - Jason Wild, exec. chr., New York, N.Y.; Craig A. Collard†, N.C.; Kara E. DioGuardi, Me.; Ira Duarte, N.C.; Ed Schutter, Ga.
Other Exec. Officers - Ziad Ghanem, pres. & CEO; Keith Stauffer, CFO; Jeroen De Beijer, chief people & culture officer; Lynn Gefen, chief legal officer & corp. sec.; David Wheeler, sr. v-p & CIO
† Lead director

Capital Stock

	Authorized (shs.)	Outstanding (shs.)[1]
Preferred	unlimited	
Series A	unlimited	12,350
Series B	unlimited	600
Series C	unlimited	nil
Series D	unlimited	nil
Proportionate Voting	unlimited	nil
Exchangeable	unlimited	63,492,037
Common	unlimited	286,563,369[2]

[1] At Apr. 27, 2023

[2] At July 4, 2023.

Preferred - Issuable in series. **Series A, B, C and D** - Convertible at the holder's option at any time into 1,000 common shares (for non-U.S. investors) for each preferred share and into proportionate voting shares (for U.S. investors) an a 1-for-1 basis. Non-voting.

Proportionate Voting - Convertible at the holder's option into 1,000 common shares for each proportionate voting share at any time. 1,000 votes per share.

Exchangeable - Convertible at the holder's option into common shares on a 1-for-1 basis at any time following the satisfaction of: (i) a triggering event being the earlier of (a) the date that federal laws regarding the cultivation, distribution or possession of marijuana in the U.S. are changed and (b) all securities exchanges upon which the securities of the holder are listed for trading have amended their policies to permit listed issuers to invest in entities that are engaged in the cultivation, distribution or possession of marijuana in U.S. states where it is legal to do so; and (ii) all securities exchanges upon which the securities of the holder are listed for trading have approved the exchange of the exchangeable shares into common shares. Non-voting.

Common - Convertible at the holder's option into 0.001 proportionate voting share for each common share at any time. One vote per share.

Major Shareholder - Jason Wild held 32.27% interest at May 10, 2023.

Price Range - TER/CSE (D)

Year	Volume	High	Low	Close
2022	42,754,903	$8.00	$1.35	$1.55
2021	56,143,636	$20.50	$6.09	$7.77
2020	31,125,986	$13.94	$1.74	$12.70
2019	14,384,141	$9.18	$2.28	$2.84
2018	34,361,360	$13.50	$2.25	$5.82

Recent Close: $2.18

Capital Stock Changes - In June 2023, private placement of 6,580,677 units (1 common share & ½ warrant) at US$1.50 per unit was completed, with warrants exercisable at US$1.95 per share for two years.

In March 2022, 51,349,978 common shares and 13,504,500 exchangeable shares were issued pursuant to the acquisition of Gage Growth Corp. In December 2022, 24,601,467 exchangeable shares were issued on conversion of Cdn$125,500,000 of debt. Also during 2022, common shares were issued as follows: 9,186,134 on exercise of warrants, 5,462,874 for business acquisitions, 1,145,819 on conversion of 1,100 series A preferred shares, 10 series B preferred shares and 36 series C preferred shares, 778,245 on exercise of options, 669,478 on vesting of restricted share units and 101,203 for debt settlement.

Wholly Owned Subsidiaries

TerrAscend Canada Inc., Canada.
- 95% int. in **Cookies Retail Canada Corp.**, Ont.

Subsidiaries

99.8% int. in **TerrAscend Growth Corp.**, Ont.
- 100% int. in **Gage Innovations Corp.**, Toronto, Ont.
  - 100% int. in **RI SPE LLC**, United States.
  - 100% int. in **Rivers Innovation, Inc.**, United States.
  - 100% int. in **Rivers Innovations US South LLC**, United States.
- 100% int. in **Spartan Partners Corporation**, Mich.
  - 51.3% int. in **Spartan Partners Holdings, LLC**, Mich.
    - 100% int. in **Mayde US LLC**, Mich.
    - 100% int. in **Spartan Partners Licensing LLC**, Mich.
    - 100% int. in **Spartan Partners Properties LLC**, Mich.
    - 100% int. in **Spartan Partners Services LLC**, Mich.
- 100% int. in **TerrAscend USA Inc.**, United States.
  - 100% int. in **WDB Holding CA, Inc.**, United States.
    - 49.9% int. in **ABI SF, LLC**, Calif.
    - 100% int. in **BTHHM Berkeley, LLC**, Calif.
    - 49.9% int. in **Deep Thought, LLC**, Calif.
    - 49.9% int. in **Howard Street Partners, LLC**, Calif.
    - 49.9% int. in **RHMT, LLC**, Calif.
    - 100% int. in **V Products, LLC**, Calif.
  - 100% int. in **WDB Holding MD, Inc.**, Md.
    - 100% int. in **Allegany Medical Marijuana Dispensary LLC**, Cumberland, Md.
    - 100% int. in **Derby 1, LLC**, Md.
    - 100% int. in **HMS Hagerstown, LLC**, Del.
    - 100% int. in **HMS Health, LLC**, Frederick, Md.
    - 100% int. in **Hempaid, LLC**, Md.
    - 100% int. in **Herbiculture Inc.**, Md.
  - 100% int. in **WDB Holding MI, Inc.**, Mich.
    - 100% int. in **KISA Enterprises MI, LLC**, Mich.
  - 100% int. in **WDB Holding NV, Inc.**, United States.
  - 100% int. in **WDB Holding PA, Inc.**, United States.
    - 100% int. in **IHC Management LLC**, Del.
      - 100% int. in **HMS Processing, LLC**, Frederick, Md.
    - 100% int. in **IHC Real Estate GP, LLC**, Pa.
    - 100% int. in **Ilera Dispensing LLC**, Pa.
    - 100% int. in **Ilera Dispensing 3 LLC**, Pa.
    - 100% int. in **Ilera Dispensing 2 LLC**, Pa.
    - 100% int. in **Ilera Healthcare LLC**, Pa.
      - 50% int. in **IHC Real Estate LP**, Pa.
    - 100% int. in **Ilera InvestCo I LLC**, Pa.
      - 100% int. in **Guadco, LLC**, Pa.
      - 100% int. in **KCR Holdings LLC**, Pa.
    - 100% int. in **Ilera Security LLC**, Pa.
    - 100% int. in **235 Main Street Mercersburg LLC**, Pa.
  - 100% int. in **WDB Management CA LLC**, United States.
  - 100% int. in **Well and Good Inc.**, United States.
    - 87.5% int. in **TerrAscend NJ LLC**, N.J.

Note: The preceding list includes only the major related companies in which interests are held.

Financial Statistics

Periods ended:	12m Dec. 31/22[A]		12m Dec. 31/21[oA]
	US$000s	%Chg	US$000s
Operating revenue	**247,829**	**+28**	**194,210**
Cost of sales	133,359		74,452
Salaries & benefits	44,814		30,256
General & admin expense	58,612		29,909
Stock-based compensation	12,162		14,942
Operating expense	**248,947**	**+66**	**149,559**
Operating income	**(1,118)**	**n.a.**	**44,651**
Deprec., depl. & amort.	22,624		12,789
Finance costs, net	35,893		27,849
Write-downs/write-offs	(312,173)[1]		(8,952)
Pre-tax income	**(310,185)**	**n.a.**	**44,530**
Income taxes	(10,783)		28,877
Net inc bef disc ops, eqhldrs	(303,959)		12,629
Net inc bef disc ops, NCI	4,557		3,024
Net inc. bef. disc. opers	**(299,402)**	**n.a.**	**15,653**
Disc. opers., equity hldrs	(25,949)		(9,518)
Income from disc. opers	(25,949)		(9,518)
Net income	**(325,351)**	**n.a.**	**6,135**
Net inc. for equity hldrs	**(329,908)**	**n.a.**	**3,111**
Net inc. for non-cont. int.	**4,557**	**+51**	**3,024**
Cash & equivalent	29,753		79,642
Inventories	46,335		36,093
Accounts receivable	22,443		12,495
Current assets	121,993		172,489
Fixed assets, net	215,812		112,053
Right-of-use assets	29,451		29,561
Intangibles, net	330,032		258,751
Total assets	**701,587**	**+21**	**581,935**
Accts. pay. & accr. liabs	44,286		27,923
Current liabilities	137,905		66,187
Long-term debt, gross	201,421		179,691
Long-term debt, net	152,565		171,344
Long-term lease liabilities	31,545		30,573
Shareholders' equity	318,797		223,587
Non-controlling interest	2,374		5,367
Cash from oper. activs	**(26,123)**	**n.a.**	**(31,815)**
Cash from fin. activs	3,719		182,201
Cash from invest. activs	(27,579)		(132,421)
Net cash position	**26,763**	**-66**	**79,642**
Capital expenditures	(39,631)		(39,835)
	US$		US$
Earns. per sh. bef disc opers*	(1.24)		0.07
Earnings per share*	(1.35)		0.02
Cash flow per share*	(0.11)		(0.18)
	shs		shs
No. of shs. o/s*	259,624,531		190,930,800
Avg. no. of shs. o/s*	244,351,028		181,056,654
	%		%
Net profit margin	(120.81)		8.06
Return on equity	(112.08)		11.13
Return on assets	(46.65)		2.93
Foreign sales percent	100		100
No. of employees (FTEs)	972		742

* Common

[o] Restated

[A] Reported in accordance with U.S. GAAP

[1] Includes US$170,357,000 and US$140,727,000 of impairments on goodwill and intangible assets, respectively, of the Michigan reporting unit.

Latest Results

Periods ended:	3m Mar. 31/23[A]		3m Mar. 31/22[oA]
	US$000s	%Chg	US$000s
Operating revenue	69,398	+43	48,585
Net inc. bef. disc. opers	(19,178)	n.a.	(13,750)
Income from disc. opers	(3,591)		(2,256)
Net income	(22,769)	n.a.	(16,006)
Net inc. for equity hldrs	(24,955)	n.a.	(16,357)
Net inc. for non-cont. int.	2,186		351
	US$		US$
Earns. per sh. bef. disc. opers.*	(0.08)		(0.07)
Earnings per share*	(0.09)		(0.08)

* Common

[o] Restated

[A] Reported in accordance with U.S. GAAP

Historical Summary
(as originally stated)

Fiscal Year	Oper. Rev.	Net Inc. Bef. Disc.	EPS*
	US$000s	US$000s	US$
2022[A]	247,829	(299,402)	(1.24)
2021[A]	210,419	6,135	0.02
	$000s	$000s	$
2020[B]	198,318	(154,347)	(1.04)
2019[B]	84,868	(218,952)	(2.17)
2018[B]	6,826	(22,144)	(0.24)

* Common

[A] Reported in accordance with U.S. GAAP

[B] Reported in accordance with IFRS

T.32 TerraVest Industries Inc.

Symbol - TVK **Exchange** - TSX **CUSIP** - 88105G

Head Office - 4901 Bruce Rd, Vegreville, AB, T9C 1C3 **Telephone** - (780) 632-7774 **Fax** - (780) 632-7694 **Exec. Office** - 2704-401 Bay St, Toronto, ON, M5H 2Y4 **Telephone** - (416) 855-1928 **Fax** - (416) 640-1834

Website - www.terravestindustries.com

Email - dhaw@terravestindustries.com

Investor Relations - Dr. Dustin Haw (416) 855-1928

Auditors - Raymond Chabot Grant Thornton LLP C.A., Montréal, Qué.

Lawyers - Bennett Jones LLP, Edmonton, Alta.

Transfer Agents - Odyssey Trust Company, Toronto, Ont.

FP500 Revenue Ranking - 662

Employees - 1,653 at Sept. 30, 2022

Profile - (Alta. 2012) Manufactures residential, commercial and industrial liquid and fuel containment products as well as home heating and ventilation equipment; fabricates energy processing equipment; and provides oil and gas well services.

Operates through three business segments: Fuel Containment; Processing Equipment; and Service.

Fuel Containment

Provides products related to liquid and fuel containment to fuel distributors, transportation companies, and industrial, commercial and residential consumers through wholly owned **Pro-Par Inc.**, **Granby Industries LP**, **Granby Composites Inc.**, **Granby Furnaces Inc.**, **Granby FRP Tanks Inc.**, **Fischer Tanks, LLC**, **Signature Truck Systems, LLC**, **ECR International Inc.** and **Granby Heating Products, LLC**. Products include bulk LPG transport trailers, LPG delivery and service trucks, bulk LPG storage tanks, residential and commercial LPG tanks and dispensers, custom pressure vessels, commercial and residential refined fuel tanks, and furnaces and boilers. Also provides complementary products in the home heating and ventilation market.

Processing Equipment

Provides a wide array of equipment primarily to upstream and midstream energy companies, fertilizer distribution companies, propane distribution companies and liquids transportation companies in western Canada and the U.S. through wholly owned **Argo Sales Limited Partnership**, **TerraVest Industries Limited Partnership**, **NWP Industries LP**, **EnviroVault Limited Partnership**, **Iowa Steel Fabrication, LLC**, **TerraVest Leasing LP**, and **MaXfield LP**, and subsidiary **Segretech Inc.** Products include steel skids, pressure vessels, storage and field erected tanks, polyurethane/steel housings, piping, sand separators and ancillary equipment. Also manufactures measurement equipment, separation tanks and remote monitoring equipment; and equipment for complex natural gas wells, as well as for the storage and handling of dangerous goods such as propane, butane and anhydrous ammonia.

Service

Wholly owned **Diamond Energy Services Limited Partnership** provides well servicing to the oil and gas sector in southwestern and central Saskatchewan. Diamond operates 21 oil and gas well service rigs from facilities in Saskatchewan.

Subsidiary **Green Energy Services Inc.** (dba Fraction Energy Services) provides fluid management services including water transfer, containment, heating, fluid trucking and oilfield rentals.

In July 2022, the company agreed to acquire private Calgary, Alta.-based **Platinum Energy Services Ltd.** for $4,850,000. Platinum manufactures energy and processing equipments.

Recent Merger and Acquisition Activity

Status: completed **Announced:** Mar. 11, 2022

TerraVest Industries Inc. acquired Hattiesburg, Miss.-based Mississippi Tank and Manufacturing Company (MS Tank), which produces and distributes storage and distribution equipment for the propane and compressed gas markets in North America, including transport trailers, bobtail delivery trucks and various bulk storage tanks. Terms of the transaction were not disclosed. TerraVest acquired MS Tank using cash and credit facilities.

Predecessor Detail - Name changed from TerraVest Capital Inc., Feb. 28, 2018.

Directors - Charles Pellerin, exec. chr., Victoriaville, Qué.; Dr. Dustin Haw, pres. & CEO, Toronto, Ont.; Blair A. Cook, St. John's, N.L.; Dale H. Laniuk, Vegreville, Alta.; Michael (Mick) MacBean, Calgary, Alta.; Rocco Rossi, Toronto, Ont.

Other Exec. Officers - Marilyn Boucher, CFO; Mitchell Gilbert, chief invest. officer; Mitchell (Mitch) DeBelser, pres., processing equipment div.; Pierre Fournier, pres. & COO, Gestion Jerico Inc.; Michael (Butch) Gering, pres. & CEO, Diamond Energy Services LP

Capital Stock

	Authorized (shs.)	Outstanding (shs.)[1]
Common	unlimited	17,831,318

[1] At Jan. 6, 2023

Normal Course Issuer Bid - The company plans to make normal course purchases of up to 949,963 common shares representing 10% of the public float. The bid commenced on Mar. 17, 2023, and expires on Mar. 16, 2024.

Major Shareholder - Charles Pellerin held 19.7% interest, Mawer Investment Management Limited held 13.6% interest and Dale H. Laniuk held 11.7% interest at Jan. 6, 2023.

Price Range - TVK/TSX

Year	Volume	High	Low	Close
2022	1,004,012	$28.00	$21.11	$27.59
2021	1,636,118	$30.06	$15.15	$27.48
2020	2,419,695	$17.25	$9.50	$15.98
2019	1,449,546	$13.50	$10.22	$13.00
2018	1,485,641	$11.00	$8.75	$10.16

Recent Close: $36.34

Capital Stock Changes - In November 2021, 361,663 common shares were issued pursuant to the acquisition of an additional 44.4% interest in Green Energy Services Inc. Also during fiscal 2022, 43,100 common shares were repurchased under a Normal Course Issuer Bid.

Dividends

TVK com Ra $0.50 pa Q est. Jan. 10, 2023
Prev. Rate: $0.40 est. Jan. 15, 2014

Wholly Owned Subsidiaries

Argo Sales Limited Partnership, Alta.
Diamond Energy Services Limited Partnership, Alta.
EnviroVault Limited Partnership, Alta.
Gestion Jerico Inc., Qué.
- 100% int. in **ECR International Inc.**, N.Y.
- 100% int. in **Fischer Tanks, LLC**, United States.
- 100% int. in **Granby Composites Inc.**, Canada.
- 100% int. in **Granby FRP Tanks Inc.**, Canada.
- 100% int. in **Granby Heating Products, LLC**, Me.
- 100% int. in **Granby Industries L.P.**, Canada.
    - 100% int. in **Granby Furnaces Inc.**, Qué.
- 100% int. in **Granby Industries Transport USA, LLC**, United States.
- 100% int. in **Propar Inc.**, Qué.
- 100% int. in **Signature Truck Systems, Inc.**, Mich.

Maxfield LP
Mississippi Tank and Manufacturing Company, Hattiesburg, Miss.
MTankCo Supply, LLC, United States.
NWP Industries LP, Alta.
Pro-Par Industries, LLC, United States.
TVK West Inc., Alta.
- 100% int. in **Iowa Steel Fabrication, LLC**, Iowa

TerraVest Industries Limited Partnership, Alta.
TerraVest Leasing LP, Canada.

Subsidiaries

66.8% int. in **Green Energy Services Inc.**, Alta.
76.5% int. in **Segretech Inc.**, Calgary, Alta.

Note: The preceding list includes only the major related companies in which interests are held.

Financial Statistics

Periods ended:	12m Sept. 30/22[A]		12m Sept. 30/21[A]
	$000s	%Chg	$000s
Operating revenue	**195,917**	**-36**	**307,463**
Cost of sales	316,161		149,452
Salaries & benefits	152,754		85,723
General & admin expense	21,478		6,907
Operating expense	**174,232**	**-28**	**242,082**
Operating income	**21,685**	**-67**	**65,381**
Deprec., depl. & amort.	35,289		19,253
Finance costs, gross	9,342		4,505
Investment income	(62)		(78)
Pre-tax income	**58,655**	**+27**	**46,046**
Income taxes	11,885		9,636
Net income	**46,770**	**+28**	**36,410**
Net inc. for equity hldrs	**45,252**	**+24**	**36,618**
Net inc. for non-cont. int	**1,518**	**n.a.**	**(208)**
Cash & equivalent	9,394		8,359
Inventories	191,244		136,854
Accounts receivable	108,678		62,926
Current assets	322,152		217,408
Long-term investments	13,418		10,000
Fixed assets, net	160,671		85,933
Right-of-use assets	29,395		27,806
Intangibles, net	60,764		46,978
Total assets	**614,523**	**+51**	**406,338**
Bank indebtedness	3,692		1,129
Accts. pay. & accr. liabs	83,248		51,360
Current liabilities	136,875		80,274
Long-term debt, gross	239,565		158,695
Long-term debt, net	228,459		154,179
Long-term lease liabilities	27,652		26,148
Shareholders' equity	183,573		132,055
Non-controlling interest	12,344		4
Cash from oper. activs	**29,948**	**+30**	**23,064**
Cash from fin. activs	45,160		9,991
Cash from invest. activs	(73,951)		(52,536)
Net cash position	**9,034**	**+21**	**7,481**
Capital expenditures	(35,562)		(18,405)
Capital disposals	10,656		3,719
	$		$
Earnings per share*	2.53		2.02
Cash flow per share*	1.68		1.27
Cash divd. per share*	0.40		0.40
	shs		shs
No. of shs. o/s*	17,886,018		17,567,455
Avg. no. of shs. o/s*	17,877,941		18,099,965
	%		%
Net profit margin	23.87		11.84
Return on equity	28.67		28.39
Return on assets	10.62		11.01
Foreign sales percent	47		44
No. of employees (FTEs)	1,653		1,257

* Common
[A] Reported in accordance with IFRS

Latest Results

Periods ended:	3m Dec. 31/22[A]		3m Dec. 31/21[A]
	$000s	%Chg	$000s
Operating revenue	177,198	+35	131,364
Net income	13,086	+24	10,578
Net inc. for equity hldrs	11,911	+12	10,674
Net inc. for non-cont. int	1,175		(96)
	$		$
Earnings per share*	0.67		0.60

* Common
[A] Reported in accordance with IFRS

Historical Summary
(as originally stated)

Fiscal Year	Oper. Rev.	Net Inc. Bef. Disc.	EPS*
	$000s	$000s	$
2022[A]	195,917	46,770	2.53
2021[A]	307,463	36,410	2.02
2020[A]	304,253	26,628	1.45
2019[A]	306,286	22,555	1.30
2018[A]	269,927	17,152	0.96

* Common
[A] Reported in accordance with IFRS

T.33 Tetra Bio-Pharma Inc.

Symbol - TBP **Exchange** - TSX (S) **CUSIP** - 88166Y
Head Office - 2316 St. Joseph Blvd, Orleans, ON, K1C 1E8 **Telephone** - (343) 780-2020 **Toll-free** - (833) 977-7575 **Fax** - (343) 689-0716
Website - www.tetrabiopharma.com
Email - investors@tetrabiopharma.com
Investor Relations - Natalie Leroux (833) 977-7575
Auditors - PricewaterhouseCoopers LLP C.A., Oakville, Ont.
Lawyers - Stikeman Elliott LLP, Montréal, Qué.
Transfer Agents - Computershare Trust Company of Canada Inc., Montréal, Qué.

Profile - (Can. 2007) Developing cannabinoid-based drug products to relieve symptoms associated with pain, inflammation and cancer diseases.

Priority drug development programs include QIXLEEF™ (REBORN©) for uncontrolled breakthrough pain and (PLENITUDE©) for advanced uncontrolled cancer pain; CAUMZ™ (REBORN©, synthetic version of QIXLEEF™) for fast pain relief in cancer breakthrough pain; REDUVO™ soft gel capsule, REDUVO™ Adversa® mucoadhesive tablet, and REDUVO™ inhaled THC-based product, for chemotherapy-induced nausea and vomiting (CINV) through formulation of cannabinoid Dronabinol based on **IntelGenx Technologies Corp.**'s AdVersa mucoadhesive delivery technology; HCC-011 for CINV and hepatocellular carcinoma, a form of liver cancer; and PPP-004, a topical cream containing THC and CBD for pain and inflammation.

Other drug development programs are ARDS-003 (Onternabez), an intravenous drug for potential treatment of cytokine release syndrome (CRS) and prevention of Acute Respiratory Distress Syndrome (ARDS) in hospitalized COVID-19 patients; PPP-003 for uveitis and proliferative vitreoretinopathy (PVR); and PPP-003v for eye pain associated with indolent corneal ulcers for domestic dogs, which all remains suspended as of May 31, 2022 due to prioritization of other projects or pending funding/partnership.

Also holds interests in **TALLC Corporation Inc.**, which is developing a portfolio of cannabinoid-based drugs to treat acute and chronic conditions in the eye; and **Targeted Pharmaceutical LLC**, which is developing cannabinoid-based drugs for ductal carcinoma in situ (DCIS) breast cancer and HIV-associated dementia. In addition, wholly owned **ENJOUCA Inc.** commercializes non-registered botanical drug candidate under ENJOUCA™ brand.

Also holds license from **Thorne Health Tech, Inc.** to sell prebiotic dietary supplements in the U.S.

In March 2022, wholly owned **2714140 Ontario Inc.** was sold for nominal consideration.

Common suspended from TSX, Aug. 1, 2023.

Predecessor Detail - Name changed from GrowPros Cannabis Ventures Inc., Sept. 28, 2016.

Directors - Dr. H. B. Brent Norton, chr., Collingwood, Ont.; Dr. Guy Chamberland, CEO & chief regulatory officer, Boucherville, Qué.; Catherine Auld, Toronto, Ont.; John M. Kim, Toronto, Ont.; Dale MacCandish Weil, Baie-d'Urfé, Qué.

Other Exec. Officers - Dr. Melanie Kelly, chief scientific officer; Steeve Néron, chief comml. officer; Dr. Aurelia De Pauw, sr. v-p, clinical programs & medical affairs; Dania Scott, sr. v-p, comml. strategy

Capital Stock

	Authorized (shs.)	Outstanding (shs.)[1]
Common	unlimited	423,362,723

[1] At Oct. 12, 2022

Major Shareholder - Widely held at Apr. 14, 2022.

Price Range - TBP/TSX (S)

Year	Volume	High	Low	Close
2022	153,255,280	$0.14	$0.02	$0.02
2021	434,007,470	$0.53	$0.12	$0.13
2020	212,955,506	$0.69	$0.14	$0.20
2019	171,600,171	$1.19	$0.17	$0.46
2018	191,417,356	$1.75	$0.59	$0.82

Recent Close: $0.03

Capital Stock Changes - In December 2021, bought deal public offering of 13,064,000 units (1 common share & 1 warrant) at $0.163 per unit was completed, with warrants exercisable at $0.195 per share for two years. In May 2022, private placement of 8,236,681 common shares was completed at 6¢ per share.

Wholly Owned Subsidiaries

ENJOUCA Inc.
Panag Pharma Inc., Halifax, N.S.
PhytoPain Pharma Inc., Canada.
Tetra Bio-Pharma Australia Pty Ltd., Australia.
Tetra Bio-Pharma Europe Ltd., Malta.

Investments

Lumiera Health Inc., Montréal, Qué. (see separate coverage)
50% int. in **TALLC Corporation Inc.**, Qué.
20% int. in **Targeted Pharmaceutical LLC**, Worcester, Mass.

Financial Statistics

Periods ended:	12m Nov. 30/21[A]		12m Nov. 30/20[A]
	$000s	%Chg	$000s
Research & devel. expense	11,938		11,655
General & admin expense	11,191		8,207
Stock-based compensation	1,054		566
Operating expense	**28,844**	**+41**	**20,428**
Operating income	**(28,844)**	**n.a.**	**(20,428)**
Deprec., depl. & amort.	112		34
Finance income	105		98
Investment income	(949)		(268)
Write-downs/write-offs	(24,630)		(396)
Pre-tax income	**(52,175)**	**n.a.**	**(21,153)**
Net inc. bef. disc. opers	**(52,175)**	**n.a.**	**(21,153)**
Income from disc. opers	nil		(5,323)
Net income	**(52,175)**	**n.a.**	**(26,476)**
Cash & equivalent	4,886		2,501
Current assets	5,950		3,581
Long-term investments	909		2,129
Fixed assets, net	692		435
Intangibles, net	nil		23,194
Total assets	**7,551**	**-74**	**29,339**
Bank indebtedness	3,112		2,000
Accts. pay. & accr. liabs	4,190		4,750
Current liabilities	7,302		6,750
Shareholders' equity	249		22,589
Cash from oper. activs	**(25,276)**	**n.a.**	**19,636**
Cash from fin. activs	29,781		23,519
Cash from invest. activs	(2,120)		(3,420)
Net cash position	**4,886**	**+95**	**2,501**
Capital expenditures	(336)		(242)
	$		$
Earns. per sh. bef disc opers*	(0.12)		(0.08)
Earnings per share*	(0.12)		(0.10)
Cash flow per share*	(0.06)		0.08
	shs		shs
No. of shs. o/s*	401,667,409		283,826,966
Avg. no. of shs. o/s*	445,699,143		258,146,496
	%		%
Net profit margin	n.a.		n.a.
Return on equity	(456.91)		(89.56)
Return on assets	(282.87)		(73.06)
No. of employees (FTEs)	33		33

* Common
[A] Reported in accordance with IFRS

Latest Results

Periods ended:	9m Aug. 31/22[A]		9m Aug. 31/21[A]
	$000s	%Chg	$000s
Net income	(8,832)	n.a.	(21,989)
	$		$
Earnings per share*	(0.02)		(0.06)

* Common
[A] Reported in accordance with IFRS

Historical Summary
(as originally stated)

Fiscal Year	Oper. Rev.	Net Inc. Bef. Disc.	EPS*
	$000s	$000s	$
2021[A]	nil	(52,175)	(0.12)
2020[A]	nil	(21,153)	(0.08)
2019[A]	nil	(14,246)	(0.07)
2018[A]	112	(7,852)	(0.05)
2017[A]	nil	(6,695)	(0.06)

* Common
[A] Reported in accordance with IFRS

T.34 Theralase Technologies Inc.

Symbol - TLT **Exchange** - TSX-VEN **CUSIP** - 88337V
Head Office - 41 Hollinger Rd, Toronto, ON, M4B 3G4 **Telephone** - (416) 699-5273 **Toll-free** - (866) 843-5273 **Fax** - (416) 699-5250
Website - www.theralase.com
Email - khachey@theralase.com
Investor Relations - Kristina Hachey (416) 699-5273 ext. 224
Auditors - Richter LLP C.A., Toronto, Ont.
Bankers - Royal Bank of Canada, Toronto, Ont.
Lawyers - Cassels Brock & Blackwell LLP
Transfer Agents - TSX Trust Company, Toronto, Ont.
Profile - (Can. 1989) Researches and develops light activated Photo Dynamic Compounds (PDCs) used to destroy cancers, bacteria and viruses; and designs, develops, manufactures and markets non-invasive therapeutic laser systems primarily for the treatment of pain.

Operations are divided into two divisions: Anti-Cancer Therapy (ACT) and Cool Laser Therapy (CLT).

The **Anti-Cancer Therapy** division researches and develops PDCs, associated drug formulations and the laser light systems that activate them for the treatment primarily of cancers. PDCs are drugs that are cytotoxic (cell killing) when exposed to light at specific wavelengths and power levels. The company's lead PDC is the anti-cancer drug TLD-1433 (Ruvidar™), which is under Phase II clinical study for the treatment of non-muscle invasive bladder cancer. The treatment involves administering a therapeutic dosage of TLD-1433 to the patient and then activating the drug with the laser light using the company's TLC-3200 laser system, which is being developed with assistance from the CLT division. Additional targets under study for PDCs include glioblastoma multiforme, non-small cell lung cancer and variety of viruses such as H1N1 influenza, Zika and coronaviruses.

The **Cool Laser Therapy** division designs, develops, manufactures and commercializes super-pulsed laser devices for elimination of pain, reduction in inflammation and acceleration of tissue healing to treat chronic knee pain and, when used off-label, to treat numerous nerve, muscle and joint conditions. Product lines include TLC-1000 and TLC-2000 laser systems which can be used for human and veterinary applications.

Predecessor Detail - Name changed from InterStar Group Inc., Nov. 2, 2004.

Directors - Matthew Perraton, chr., Toronto, Ont.; Roger Dumoulin-White, pres. & CEO, Toronto, Ont.; Kristina Hachey, CFO, Toronto, Ont.; Dr. Arkady Mandel, chief science officer, Toronto, Ont.; Guy Anderson, Toronto, Ont.; Randy Bruder, Brampton, Ont.; Kaouthar Lbiati, Boston, Mass.

Capital Stock

	Authorized (shs.)	Outstanding (shs.)[1]
Common	unlimited	216,502,675

[1] At May 30, 2023

Major Shareholder - Widely held at May 19, 2023.

Price Range - TLT/TSX-VEN

Year	Volume	High	Low	Close
2022	33,823,200	$0.48	$0.23	$0.32
2021	61,136,885	$0.38	$0.17	$0.38
2020	90,078,529	$0.38	$0.12	$0.19
2019	121,107,621	$0.60	$0.20	$0.34
2018	60,860,054	$0.46	$0.19	$0.32

Recent Close: $0.25

Capital Stock Changes - In September 2022, private placement of 10,000,000 units (1 common share & 1 warrant) at 25¢ per unit was completed. Also during 2022, common shares were issued as follows: 1,150,000 on exercise of warrants, 1,000,000 by private placement and 76,800 for financing fees.

Wholly Owned Subsidiaries

Theralase Biotech Inc., Del.
Theralase Inc., Markham, Ont.

Financial Statistics

Periods ended:	12m Dec. 31/22[A]		12m Dec. 31/21[A]
	$000s	%Chg	$000s
Operating revenue	**1,139**	**+46**	**781**
Cost of sales	475		441
Research & devel. expense	4,052		2,755
General & admin expense	1,530		1,850
Operating expense	**6,057**	**+20**	**5,046**
Operating income	**(4,918)**	**n.a.**	**(4,265)**
Deprec., depl. & amort.	313		276
Finance income	31		23
Finance costs, gross	21		5
Pre-tax income	**(5,235)**	**n.a.**	**(4,411)**
Net income	**(5,235)**	**n.a.**	**(4,411)**
Cash & equivalent	1,509		3,692
Inventories	486		566
Accounts receivable	296		283
Current assets	2,501		4,998
Fixed assets, net	661		827
Right-of-use assets	446		39
Total assets	**4,161**	**-30**	**5,945**
Accts. pay. & accr. liabs	595		839
Current liabilities	681		875
Long-term lease liabilities	387		nil
Shareholders' equity	3,093		5,070
Cash from oper. activs	**(5,133)**	**n.a.**	**(4,030)**
Cash from fin. activs	3,020		(57)
Cash from invest. activs	(70)		(101)
Net cash position	**1,509**	**-59**	**3,692**
Capital expenditures	(70)		(101)
	$		$
Earnings per share*	(0.03)		(0.02)
Cash flow per share*	(0.02)		(0.02)
	shs		shs
No. of shs. o/s*	216,502,675		204,275,875
Avg. no. of shs. o/s*	207,924,313		204,275,875
	%		%
Net profit margin	(459.61)		(564.79)
Return on equity	(128.26)		(61.98)
Return on assets	(103.19)		(55.19)
Foreign sales percent	11		11

* Common
[A] Reported in accordance with IFRS

Latest Results

Periods ended:	3m Mar. 31/23[A]		3m Mar. 31/22[A]
	$000s	%Chg	$000s
Operating revenue	207	-2	212
Net income	(1,409)	n.a.	(1,701)
	$		$
Earnings per share*	(0.01)		(0.01)

* Common
[A] Reported in accordance with IFRS

Historical Summary
(as originally stated)

Fiscal Year	Oper. Rev.	Net Inc. Bef. Disc.	EPS*
	$000s	$000s	$
2022[A]	1,139	(5,235)	(0.03)
2021[A]	781	(4,411)	(0.02)
2020[A]	929	(5,599)	(0.03)
2019[A]	964	(7,414)	(0.05)
2018[A]	1,734	(3,357)	(0.03)

* Common
[A] Reported in accordance with IFRS

T.35 Theratechnologies Inc.*

Symbol - TH **Exchange** - TSX **CUSIP** - 88338H
Head Office - 1100-2015 rue Peel, Montréal, QC, H3A 1T8 **Telephone** - (514) 336-7800 **Fax** - (514) 331-9691
Website - www.theratech.com
Email - pdubuc@theratech.com
Investor Relations - Philippe Dubuc (514) 336-7800 ext. 297
Auditors - KPMG LLP C.A., Montréal, Qué.
Transfer Agents - Computershare Trust Company, N.A., Canton, Mass.; Computershare Trust Company of Canada Inc., Montréal, Qué.
FP500 Revenue Ranking - 768
Employees - 144 at Nov. 30, 2022
Profile - (Que. 1993) Develops and commercializes therapeutic products that target unmet medical needs in commercially attractive specialty markets, including HIV, oncology and hepatology.

Owns EGRIFTA® and EGRIFTA SV® (tesamorelin for injection), medications for the reduction of excess abdominal fat in HIV-infected patients with lipodystrophy. Tesamorelin, a synthetic human growth hormone releasing factor (GRF) analogue, was developed in the company's laboratories in 1995. The drugs are commercially available in the United States and Canada.

Also holds rights to Trogarzo® (ibalizumab-uiyk), a humanized monoclonal antibody injection for the treatment of multi-drug resistant HIV-1 infection. The company has the exclusive rights to commercialize the drug in Canada and the U.S. The drug is commercially available in the U.S., Germany, Italy, France, Spain and Israel.

Research and development pipeline includes Phase III clinical trial of tesamorelin for the treatment of non-alcoholic steatohepatitis (NASH) in the general population; and Phase I clinical trial of TH-1902 (sudocetaxel zendusortide), a peptide-drug conjugate, for the treatment of the treatment of sortilin-expressing cancers.

On Apr. 27, 2022, the company announced it would cease its Trogarzo® commercialization operations in Europe and focus its commercialization activities on the North American territory only. The company sent a notice of termination to **TaiMed Biologics Inc.**, and would return the European commercialization rights for Trogarzo® to TaiMed by the end of October 2022.

Directors - Dawn Svoronos, chr., Hudson, Qué.; Paul Lévesque, pres. & CEO, Westmount, Qué.; Joseph P. (Joe) Arena, Norristown, Pa.; Frank A. Holler, Summerland, B.C.; Gérald A. Lacoste, Sainte-Adèle, Qué.; Dale MacCandish Weil, Baie-d'Urfé, Qué.; Andrew T. Molson, Westmount, Qué.; Alain Trudeau, Montréal, Qué.

Other Exec. Officers - Philippe Dubuc, sr. v-p & CFO; Dr. Christian Marsolais, sr. v-p & CMO; Marie-Noël Colussi, v-p, fin.; André Dupras, v-p, HR; Jocelyn Lafond, gen. counsel & corp. sec.; John Leasure, global comml. officer

Capital Stock

	Authorized (shs.)	Outstanding (shs.)[1]
Preferred	unlimited	nil
Common	unlimited	24,201,827

[1] At July 31, 2023

Options - At Nov. 30, 2022, options were outstanding to purchase 4,720,160 common shares at prices ranging from Cdn$0.25 to Cdn$10 per share with a weighted average remaining life of 7.36 years, and 426,571 common shares at prices ranging from US$2.01 to US$3.75 per share with a weighted average remaining life of 9.05 years.

Major Shareholder - Soleus Capital Master Fund, L.P. held 10.7% interest at Feb. 14, 2023.

Price Range - TH/TSX

Year	Volume	High	Low	Close
2022	1,512,546	$16.56	$4.12	$4.80
2021	5,739,675	$22.44	$10.88	$15.28
2020	7,863,828	$17.52	$7.72	$12.76
2019	7,846,844	$38.96	$13.76	$17.04
2018	11,644,454	$59.00	$26.64	$33.28

Consolidation: 1-for-4 cons. in July 2023
Recent Close: $1.38
Capital Stock Changes - On July 31, 2023, common shares were consolidated on a 1-for-4 basis.

During fiscal 2022, common shares were issued as follows: 1,600,000 under an at-the-market equity program and 84,660 on exercise of options.

Long-Term Debt - At Nov. 30, 2022, outstanding long-term debt totaled US$64,789,000 (none current) and consisted of US$26,895,000 of 5.75% convertible unsecured senior notes due June 30, 2023, convertible into common shares at US$14.85 per share; and a US$37,894,000 term loan, bearing interest at SOFR plus 9.5%. Equity component of US$2,132,000 was classified as part of shareholders' equity.

Wholly Owned Subsidiaries

Pharma-G Inc., Qué. Inactive.
Theratechnologies Europe Inc., Qué.
Theratechnologies Europe Limited, Dublin, Ireland.
Theratechnologies Intercontinental Inc., Qué.
Theratechnologies U.S., Inc., Del.

Financial Statistics

Periods ended:	12m Nov. 30/22[A]		12m Nov. 30/21[□A]
	US$000s	%Chg	US$000s
Operating revenue	**80,057**	**+15**	**69,823**
Cost of sales	23,019		17,692
Research & devel. expense	36,939		28,274
General & admin expense	47,536		40,345
Operating expense	**107,494**	**+25**	**86,311**
Operating income	**(27,437)**	**n.a.**	**(16,488)**
Deprec., depl. & amort.	12,471		8,748
Finance income	316		195
Finance costs, gross	7,202		6,621
Pre-tax income	**(46,794)**	**n.a.**	**(31,662)**
Income taxes	443		63
Net income	**(47,237)**	**n.a.**	**(31,725)**
Cash & equivalent	33,070		40,354
Inventories	19,688		29,141
Accounts receivable	12,045		10,487
Current assets	73,370		91,908
Fixed assets, net	1,494		743
Right-of-use assets	1,595		2,111
Intangibles, net	16,801		22,009
Total assets	**93,260**	**-22**	**119,212**
Accts. pay. & accr. liabs	41,065		40,376
Current liabilities	49,490		45,076
Long-term debt, gross	64,789		54,227
Long-term debt, net	64,789		54,227
Long-term lease liabilities	1,446		2,055
Equity portion of conv. debs	2,132		4,457
Shareholders' equity	(22,571)		17,760
Cash from oper. activs	**(14,692)**	**n.a.**	**(17,501)**
Cash from fin. activs	9,656		37,863
Cash from invest. activs	8,682		(12,736)
Net cash position	**23,856**	**+17**	**20,399**
Capital expenditures	(985)		(127)
	US$		US$
Earnings per share*	(2.00)		(1.36)
Cash flow per share*	(0.62)		(0.76)
	shs		shs
No. of shs. o/s*	24,201,575		23,780,410
Avg. no. of shs. o/s*	23,813,337		23,087,550
	%		%
Net profit margin	(59.00)		(45.44)
Return on equity	n.m.		(302.37)
Return on assets	(37.62)		(22.88)
Foreign sales percent	100		100
No. of employees (FTEs)	144		87

* Common
□ Restated
[A] Reported in accordance with IFRS

Latest Results

Periods ended:	6m May 31/23[A]		6m May 31/22[A]
	US$000s	%Chg	US$000s
Operating revenue	37,457	-1	37,825
Net income	(20,456)	n.a.	(31,759)
	US$		US$
Earnings per share*	(0.84)		(1.32)

* Common
[A] Reported in accordance with IFRS

Historical Summary
(as originally stated)

Fiscal Year	Oper. Rev.	Net Inc. Bef. Disc.	EPS*
	US$000s	US$000s	US$
2022[A]	80,057	(47,237)	(2.00)
2021[A]	69,823	(31,725)	(1.36)
2020[A]	66,053	(22,667)	(1.16)
2019[A]	63,216	(12,496)	(0.64)
	$000s	$000s	$
2018[A]	58,553	(6,013)	(0.32)

* Common
[A] Reported in accordance with IFRS
Note: Adjusted throughout for 1-for-4 cons. in July 2023

T.36 Therma Bright Inc.

Symbol - THRM **Exchange** - TSX-VEN **CUSIP** - 883426
Head Office - 132-1173 Dundas St E, Toronto, ON, M4M 3P1 **Toll-free** - (844) 274-6837
Website - www.thermabright.com
Email - rfia@thermabright.com
Investor Relations - Roberto Fia (844) 274-6837
Auditors - HS & Partners LLP C.A., Mississauga, Ont.
Lawyers - K MacInnes Law Group, Vancouver, B.C.
Transfer Agents - Computershare Trust Company of Canada Inc.

Profile - (B.C. 2018; orig. Alta., 2001) Provides products for the medical and healthcare industries including rapid COVID-19 tests, medical devices for pain management, devices to improve circulation and devices for the cosmeceutical industry.

Products include AcuVid™ COVID-19 Rapid Antigen Saliva Test, a saliva-based rapid screening solution for the detection of SARS-CoV-2 as well as other prevalent COVID-19 variants; InterceptCS™, a cold sore prevention system, consisting of an ergonomically designed hand held unit and a disposable treatment activator; Venowave®, a lightweight, compact and battery operated medical compression pump which is worn on the calf and produces a peristaltic action that helps move blood from feet and legs back to the heart; and Benepod™, a hot and cold therapy device used for temporary pain relief of chronic pains such as osteoarthritic joint pain, migraine headaches, neuropathic pain and other chronic musculoskeletal aches and pains, as well as short term painful issues including insect bites and localised aches, without the use of medication. Also distributes white-labeled COVID-19 Rapid Antibody Test under the AcuVid™ brand, a test which uses a pinpricked small amount of blood in detecting antibodies of SARS-CoV-2 in those individuals infected or have previously been infected with the virus but went undiagnosed or were unaware of their infection.

TherOZap™ is being developed as a thermal therapy insect device that reduces the inflammatory response, relieving the symptoms of pain, itch and inflammation associated with insect bites and stings; and a beta pain relief device, which incorporates the company's thermal therapy technology with cannabis formulations to reduce general or arthritic pains such as back, hip, knee, foot, hand and other orthopedic pains. TherOZap™ also proved successful at inhabiting Zika virus during in-vitro tests and has moved ahead with further testing against Dengue.

Holds patents pending and the trademarks for Therozap™ and the trademark InterceptCS™ along with regulatory approvals for its breakthrough thermal therapy technology.

In November 2022, the company entered into a letter of intent with **AI4LYF LLC** for the exclusive licensing rights of Digital Cough Test, a patent-pending digital cough-based diagnosis screening technology which detects multiple respiratory diseases including COVID-19 through a smart phone application. Total consideration would include royalty, common shares of the company and up to 2,000,000 warrants exercisable at 17¢ per share.

Recent Merger and Acquisition Activity

Status: pending **Announced:** Dec. 1, 2022
Therma Bright Inc. agreed to acquire 25% interest in each of Rancho Cordova, Calif.-based InStatin, Inc. and InVixa Inc. from 2740162 Ontario Inc. (dba August Therapeutics) and Ketiko Bio Corp. for issuance of 55,000,000 common shares at a deemed price of $0.136364 per share. Therma Bright would also have an option to acquire up to 50% interest in InStatin and 80% interest in InVixa by advancing the drugs to the end of Phase 1 clinical trials. InStatin develops novel treatments using inhaled statins for the treatment and management of patients with chronic lung conditions including asthma and chronic obstructive pulmonary disease and InVixa develops inhaled statins for the prevention and treatment of lung disease caused by COVID-19 pneumonia and acute respiratory distress syndrome.

Predecessor Detail - Name changed from The Jenex Corporation, Feb. 8, 2018.

Directors - Roberto (Rob) Fia, chr., pres. & CEO, Toronto, Ont.; Joseph (Joe) Heng, Toronto, Ont.; Sung Bum (Spencer) Huh, Toronto, Ont.; A. Timothy (Tim) Peterson, Toronto, Ont.

Other Exec. Officers - Victor J. (Vic) Hugo, CFO

Capital Stock

	Authorized (shs.)	Outstanding (shs.)[1]
Preference	unlimited	nil
Common	unlimited	239,526,033

[1] At Oct. 31, 2022

Major Shareholder - Widely held at May 13, 2022.

Price Range - THRM/TSX-VEN

Year	Volume	High	Low	Close
2022	125,150,386	$0.44	$0.05	$0.06
2021	536,748,818	$1.05	$0.22	$0.41
2020	618,619,525	$0.53	$0.01	$0.22
2019	43,288,052	$0.05	$0.01	$0.02
2018	70,767,181	$0.12	$0.02	$0.03

Recent Close: $0.04

Capital Stock Changes - In February 2022, private placement of 20,000,000 units (1 common share & 1 warrant) at 30¢ per unit was completed. Also during fiscal 2022, 118,750 common shares were issued for debt settlement.

Financial Statistics

Periods ended:	12m July 31/22[A]		12m July 31/21[A]
	$000s	%Chg	$000s
Operating revenue	**63**	**n.m.**	**4**
Research & devel. expense	806		1,371
General & admin expense	3,369		2,594
Stock-based compensation	1,574		4,574
Operating expense	**5,748**	**-33**	**8,540**
Operating income	**(5,685)**	**n.a.**	**(8,536)**
Deprec., depl. & amort.	152		58
Finance costs, gross	1		3
Pre-tax income	**(5,881)**	**n.a.**	**(8,610)**
Net income	**(5,881)**	**n.a.**	**(8,610)**
Cash & equivalent	3,082		1,781
Inventories	173		51
Current assets	3,584		1,954
Fixed assets, net	34		83
Right-of-use assets	73		nil
Intangibles, net	105		206
Total assets	**4,001**	**+78**	**2,242**
Accts. pay. & accr. liabs	1,143		887
Current liabilities	1,163		887
Long-term debt, gross	nil		40
Long-term debt, net	nil		40
Equity portion of conv. debs	272		272
Shareholders' equity	2,747		1,315
Cash from oper. activs	**(3,800)**	**n.a.**	**(2,856)**
Cash from fin. activs	5,306		3,875
Cash from invest. activs	(205)		(300)
Net cash position	**3,082**	**+73**	**1,781**
Capital expenditures	nil		(100)
	$		$
Earnings per share*	(0.03)		(0.04)
Cash flow per share*	(0.02)		(0.01)
	shs		shs
No. of shs. o/s*	239,526,033		219,407,283
Avg. no. of shs. o/s*	228,453,636		199,964,619
	%		%
Net profit margin	n.m.		n.m.
Return on equity	(289.56)		(1,118.91)
Return on assets	(188.37)		(507.79)

* Common
[A] Reported in accordance with IFRS

Latest Results

Periods ended:	3m Oct. 31/22[A]		3m Oct. 31/21[A]
	$000s	%Chg	$000s
Operating revenue	6	n.a.	nil
Net income	(451)	n.a.	(2,712)
	$		$
Earnings per share*	(0.00)		(0.01)

* Common
[A] Reported in accordance with IFRS

Historical Summary
(as originally stated)

Fiscal Year	Oper. Rev.	Net Inc. Bef. Disc.	EPS*
	$000s	$000s	$
2022[A]	63	(5,881)	(0.03)
2021[A]	4	(8,610)	(0.04)
2020[A]	4	(627)	(0.01)
2019[A]	7	(422)	(0.01)
2018[A]	14	(1,236)	(0.01)

* Common
[A] Reported in accordance with IFRS

T.37 Thermal Energy International Inc.

Symbol - TMG **Exchange** - TSX-VEN **CUSIP** - 88346B
Head Office - 850-36 Antares Dr, Ottawa, ON, K2E 7W5 **Telephone** - (613) 723-6776 **Fax** - (613) 723-7286
Website - www.thermalenergy.com
Email - bill.crossland@thermalenergy.com
Investor Relations - William M. Crossland (613) 723-6776 ext. 214
Auditors - KPMG LLP C.A., Ottawa, Ont.
Lawyers - LaBarge Weinstein LLP, Ottawa, Ont.
Transfer Agents - TSX Trust Company, Toronto, Ont.

Profile - (Ont. 1991) Develops, engineers and provides heat recovery systems and condensate return solutions for industrial, commercial and institutional customers worldwide.

Energy solutions portfolio includes: FLU-ACE® direct contact waste heat recovery technology, which recovers up to 90% of the heat wasted from power generation systems, evaporator exhausts, dryer exhausts and other industrial heat sources through the boiler flue gas exhaust, and returned to the process; HEATSPONGE® SIDEKICK and RAINMAKER indirect contact condensing heat recovery solutions for use in steam and hot water applications; GEM™ Condensate Return System, a permanent replacement for mechanical steam traps resulting in reduction of steam costs, faster system warm up and improved steam efficiency; and DRY-REX™ low temperature biomass dryer technology, which uses waste heat to evaporate water from sludge and other biomass to significantly increase the thermal or heat producing value of biomass.

The company is headquartered in Ottawa, Ont., with additional offices in the U.K., Italy, Germany and the U.S.

Order backlog at Sept. 27, 2022, totaled $10,300,000 compared with $11,000,000 at Sept. 21, 2021.

Directors - William B. (Bill) White, chr., Palm Coast, Fla.; William M. (Bill) Crossland, pres. & CEO, Toronto, Ont.; William W. (Will) Ollerhead, Toronto, Ont.; David Spagnolo, Calgary, Alta.; Michael Williams, Waterloo, Ont.

Other Exec. Officers - Robert (Rob) Triebe, COO, The Americas & Asia; Jie (Julia) Zhang, CFO; Ken Harden, v-p, sales, North America; Vince Sands, pres., Boilerroom Equipment Inc.

Capital Stock

	Authorized (shs.)	Outstanding (shs.)[1]
Series 1 Preferred	unlimited	nil
Class A Common	unlimited	164,137,606

[1] At Oct. 20, 2022

Major Shareholder - Widely held at Sept. 23, 2022.

Price Range - TMG/TSX-VEN

Year	Volume	High	Low	Close
2022	15,887,928	$0.16	$0.07	$0.10
2021	104,196,381	$0.28	$0.11	$0.15
2020	67,217,346	$0.15	$0.05	$0.11
2019	19,083,009	$0.09	$0.06	$0.07
2018	26,397,452	$0.10	$0.07	$0.08

Recent Close: $0.11

Capital Stock Changes - During fiscal 2022, 250,000 class A common shares were issued on exercise of options.

Wholly Owned Subsidiaries

Thermal Energy International Corporation, Del.
- 100% int. in **Boilerroom Equipment Inc.**, Pa.

Thermal Energy International (UK) Ltd., Bristol, Gloucs., United Kingdom.
- 67% int. in **GEMchem Ltd.**, United Kingdom.

2003356 Ontario Inc., Ont.

2153639 Ontario Inc., Ont.
- 55% int. in **Thermal Energy International (Guangzou) Ltd.**, Guangzhou, Guangdong, People's Republic of China.

Financial Statistics

Periods ended:	12m May 31/22[A]		12m May 31/21[A]
	$000s	%Chg	$000s
Operating revenue	**15,909**	**+4**	**15,349**
Cost of sales	9,177		8,598
Research & devel. expense	(38)		(86)
General & admin expense	7,269		5,734
Stock-based compensation	218		208
Operating expense	**16,626**	**+15**	**14,454**
Operating income	**(717)**	**n.a.**	**895**
Deprec., depl. & amort.	697		559
Finance costs, gross	336		317
Pre-tax income	**(1,749)**	**n.a.**	**19**
Income taxes	89		(204)
Net income	**(1,838)**	**n.a.**	**223**
Net inc. for equity hldrs	**(1,921)**	**n.a.**	**198**
Net inc. for non-cont. int	**83**	**+232**	**25**
Cash & equivalent	2,632		4,241
Inventories	1,055		959
Accounts receivable	3,134		3,193
Current assets	7,014		8,581
Fixed assets, net	349		408
Right-of-use assets	1,192		1,417
Intangibles, net	1,026		1,028
Total assets	**9,599**	**-17**	**11,547**
Accts. pay. & accr. liabs	664		797
Current liabilities	4,237		4,772
Long-term debt, gross	3,936		3,260
Long-term debt, net	3,140		2,409
Long-term lease liabilities	1,178		1,337
Shareholders' equity	1,076		3,042
Non-controlling interest	(33)		(79)
Cash from oper. activs	**(1,640)**	**n.a.**	**(1,186)**
Cash from fin. activs	358		893
Cash from invest. activs	(352)		(125)
Net cash position	**2,632**	**-38**	**4,241**
Capital expenditures	(70)		(115)
Capital disposals	1		nil
	$		$
Earnings per share*	(0.01)		0.00
Cash flow per share*	(0.01)		(0.01)
	shs		shs
No. of shs. o/s*	164,137,606		163,887,606
Avg. no. of shs. o/s*	164,015,688		160,955,437
	%		%
Net profit margin	(11.55)		1.45
Return on equity	(93.30)		7.70
Return on assets	(14.04)		35.87
Foreign sales percent	93		85

* Cl. A com.

[A] Reported in accordance with IFRS

Latest Results

Periods ended:	3m Aug. 31/22[A]		3m Aug. 31/21[A]
	$000s	%Chg	$000s
Operating revenue	3,122	-20	3,879
Net income	(509)	n.a.	(154)
Net inc. for equity hldrs	(513)	n.a.	(181)
Net inc. for non-cont. int	4		28
	$		$
Earnings per share*	(0.00)		(0.00)

* Cl. A com.

[A] Reported in accordance with IFRS

Historical Summary
(as originally stated)

Fiscal Year	Oper. Rev.	Net Inc. Bef. Disc.	EPS*
	$000s	$000s	$
2022[A]	15,909	(1,838)	(0.01)
2021[A]	15,349	223	0.00
2020[A]	21,416	(1,897)	(0.01)
2019[A]	21,083	(451)	(0.00)
2018[A]	17,408	619	0.00

* Cl. A com.

[A] Reported in accordance with IFRS

T.38 Think Research Corporation

Symbol - THNK **Exchange** - TSX-VEN **CUSIP** - 88410J

Head Office - 4000-199 Bay St, Toronto, ON, M5L 1A9 **Telephone** - (416) 977-1955 **Toll-free** - (877) 302-1861

Website - www.thinkresearch.com

Email - mark.sakamoto@thinkresearch.com

Investor Relations - Mark Sakamoto (416) 388-7119

Auditors - Ernst & Young LLP C.A., Toronto, Ont.

Lawyers - Dentons Canada LLP, Toronto, Ont.

Transfer Agents - TSX Trust Company, Toronto, Ont.

Profile - (Ont. 2018) Develops and markets software-as-a-service (SaaS)-based clinical platforms and services that utilizes evidence-based content and technologies to support the clinical decision making process, standardize care and improve patient outcomes for healthcare providers across all phases of care. Also operates contract research organization.

Operations are organized into three business segments:

Software and Data Solutions - Offers patients to find, navigate and connect to health services, as well as connects clinicians to patients, clinical knowledge libraries, data needed to optimize their practice and workflows. The company's Learning Management System (LMS) delivers evidence-based clinical content, knowledge-sharing and education tools that help clinicians learn, integrate and apply clinical research and practice innovation to the frontline.

Clinical Research - Through wholly owned **BioPharma Services Inc.**, provides research and data analysis derived from Phase I clinical trials, bioequivalence studies and bioanalytical services to pharmaceutical, medical device and biotechnology companies worldwide. BioPharma operates two regulatory inspected clinical locations in St. Louis, Mo., and Toronto, Ont.

Clinical Services - The company's clinics act as a test bed for its software and technology which transforms with digital solutions that optimize clinical outcomes, streamline workflows and optimize billing.

The company serves 320,000 primary care, acute care and long-term care clinicians in more than 14,200 healthcare facilities. In addition, the company offers Pharmapod, a SaaS electronic data capture solution that reports medications errors to improve patient safety and simplify pharmacy reporting for more than 9,000 retail pharmacies.

Predecessor Detail - Name changed from AIM4 Ventures Inc., Dec. 23, 2020, pursuant to the Qualifying Transaction reverse takeover acquisition of TRC Management Holdings Corp.; basis 1 new for 24.7612 old shs.

Directors - Dr. Eric Hoskins, chr., Toronto, Ont.; Sachin Aggarwal, CEO, Toronto, Ont.; Cindy Gray, Calgary, Alta.; Barry J. Reiter, Toronto, Ont.; Abraham (Abe) Schwartz, Toronto, Ont.; Kirstine Stewart, Los Angeles, Calif.; Richard J. Wells, Markham, Ont.

Other Exec. Officers - Patrick Craib, COO; John Hayes, CFO; Joanna Carroll, CAO; Saurabh Mukhi, chief tech. officer; Mark Sakamoto, exec. v-p; Kirsten Lewis, sr. v-p, clinical R&D; Michael G. Stewart, gen. counsel & corp. sec.

Capital Stock

	Authorized (shs.)	Outstanding (shs.)[1]
Common	unlimited	77,900,000

[1] At May 29, 2023

Major Shareholder - Widely held at June 21, 2022.

Price Range - THNK/TSX-VEN

Year	Volume	High	Low	Close
2022	9,701,832	$1.58	$0.30	$0.34
2021	12,625,253	$5.05	$1.13	$1.50
2020	539,039	$5.75	$1.61	$4.66
2019	17,972	$4.21	$2.35	$2.48

Consolidation: 1-for-24.7612 cons. in Dec. 2020

Recent Close: $0.28

Capital Stock Changes - In December 2022, private placement of 6,250,000 common shares was completed at 40¢ per share. Also during 2022, common shares were issued as follows: 7,253,229 and 546,388 pursuant to the 2021 acquisitions of Bio Pharma Services Inc. and MDBriefCase Group Inc., respectively, 2,086,203 on conversion of share-based awards, 74,380 for services and 17,350 on exercise of options.

Wholly Owned Subsidiaries

Bio Pharma Services Inc., Toronto, Ont.
Bio Pharma Services USA Inc., United States.
CancerLink Ontario Inc., Ont.
Clinic 360 Inc., North York, Ont.
MDBriefCase Australia Pty Ltd., Australia.
MDBriefCase Group Inc., Toronto, Ont.
MDBriefCase Middle East Inc., Canada.
MDBriefCase South Africa (Pty) Ltd., South Africa.
Pharmapod Canada Ltd., Canada.
Pharmapod Safety Institute PSO, LLC
Pharmapod US Inc., United States.
Think Research (EU) Corp. Limited
Think Research Technology Holdings Corp.
Think Research (UK) Corp. Limited, United Kingdom.
2448430 Ontario Inc., Ont.
2538393 Ontario Inc., Ont.
2538606 Ontario Inc., Ont.

Investments

49% int. in **11419501 Canada Inc.**, Canada.

Financial Statistics

Periods ended:	12m Dec. 31/22[A]		12m Dec. 31/21[oA]
	$000s	%Chg	$000s
Operating revenue	**78,604**	**+64**	**47,791**
Cost of sales	41,217		24,397
Research & devel. expense	6,780		7,263
General & admin expense	36,045		30,966
Operating expense	**84,042**	**+34**	**62,626**
Operating income	**(5,438)**	**n.a.**	**(14,835)**
Deprec., depl. & amort.	14,404		7,986
Finance costs, gross	3,977		2,054
Pre-tax income	**(27,905)**	**n.a.**	**(30,510)**
Income taxes	(2,162)		(1,461)
Net income	**(25,743)**	**n.a.**	**(29,049)**
Cash & equivalent	3,415		6,324
Accounts receivable	14,299		14,934
Current assets	20,660		25,866
Fixed assets, net	2,011		2,193
Right-of-use assets	9,370		11,616
Intangibles, net	81,410		88,003
Total assets	**122,879**	**-10**	**137,106**
Accts. pay. & accr. liabs	13,247		14,680
Current liabilities	59,945		39,030
Long-term debt, gross	36,136		26,984
Long-term debt, net	10,820		26,984
Long-term lease liabilities	8,832		9,771
Shareholders' equity	34,799		49,913
Cash from oper. activs	**(4,749)**	**n.a.**	**(11,148)**
Cash from fin. activs	6,381		33,979
Cash from invest. activs	(4,542)		(27,382)
Net cash position	**3,415**	**-46**	**6,324**
Capital expenditures	(426)		(637)
	$		$
Earnings per share*	(0.42)		(0.62)
Cash flow per share*	(0.08)		(0.24)
	shs		shs
No. of shs. o/s*	74,686,002		58,458,452
Avg. no. of shs. o/s*	60,866,000		46,745,000
	%		%
Net profit margin	(32.75)		(60.78)
Return on equity	(60.78)		n.m.
Return on assets	(17.05)		(36.29)
Foreign sales percent	21		22

* Common

[o] Restated

[A] Reported in accordance with IFRS

Latest Results

Periods ended:	3m Mar. 31/23[A]		3m Mar. 31/22[A]
	$000s	%Chg	$000s
Operating revenue	21,826	+8	20,204
Net income	(3,594)	n.a.	(6,198)
	$		$
Earnings per share*	(0.05)		(0.11)

* Common

[A] Reported in accordance with IFRS

Historical Summary
(as originally stated)

Fiscal Year	Oper. Rev.	Net Inc. Bef. Disc.	EPS*
	$000s	$000s	$
2022[A]	78,604	(25,743)	(0.42)
2021[A1]	47,791	(29,049)	(0.62)
2020[A2]	19,444	(10,016)	n.a.
2019[A]	17,306	(13,284)	n.a.

* Common

[A] Reported in accordance with IFRS

[1] Results reflect the Dec. 23, 2020, Qualifying Transaction with TRC Management Holdings Corp.

[2] Results for fiscal 2020 and prior year pertain to TRC Management Holdings Corp.

Note: Adjusted throughout for 1-for-24.76125 cons. in Dec. 2020

T.39 Thinkific Labs Inc.

Symbol - THNC **Exchange** - TSX **CUSIP** - 884121
Head Office - 400-369 Terminal Ave, Vancouver, BC, V6A 4C4 **Toll-free** - (888) 832-2409
Website - thinkific.com
Email - ed.ma@thinkific.com
Investor Relations - Ed Ma (888) 832-2409
Auditors - KPMG LLP C.A., Vancouver, B.C.
Lawyers - Blake, Cassels & Graydon LLP, Vancouver, B.C.
Transfer Agents - Computershare Trust Company of Canada Inc., Vancouver, B.C.
Employees - 354 at Dec. 31, 2022
Profile - (B.C. 2012) Offers a cloud-based, multi-tenant platform that enables business-building.

The Thinkific platform provides creators of online courses with the functionality needed to launch, grow and diversify their businesses by creating and selling learning products. Learning products include customized courses, communities, membership sites and other experiences that creators can create, sell and deliver using the platform. Course creators include entrepreneurs, business owners, consultants, authors, speakers, coaches, professionals, trainers and social media influencers, as well as large businesses. Also offers Thinkific App Store, an online marketplace which allows third party developers to distribute and monetize solutions and services developed to run on the Thinkific platform as well as custom applications on top of the Thinkific Platform.

In April 2023, the company launched Branded Mobile, a white labeled custom app development solution for creators' online courses and communities, as well as Thinkific Mobile, a dedicated Thinkific app that makes course content and communities more easily available to students.

In September 2022, the company launched Thinkific Communities, a learning product that allows creators to build and sell collaborative learning communities seamlessly with their courses or as stand alone.

Directors - Greg Smith, co-founder & CEO, Vancouver, B.C.; B. Fraser Hall, chr., B.C.; Steve Krenzer, pres., Los Angeles, Calif.; Melanie Kalemba, Austin, Tex.; Katie May, Austin, Tex.; Brandon Nussey, Waterloo, Ont.

Other Exec. Officers - Matt Payne, co-founder & sr. v-p, innovation; Matthew (Matt) Smith, co-founder, chief strategy officer & acting chief rev. officer; Corinne Hua, CFO; Chris McGuire, chief technical officer

Capital Stock

	Authorized (shs.)	Outstanding (shs.)[1]
Preferred	unlimited	nil
Multiple Vtg.	unlimited	56,963,752
Subordinate Vtg.	unlimited	23,594,655

[1] At May 11, 2023

Preferred - Issuable in series.

Multiple Voting - Entitled to dividends. Convertible, at the holder's option, into subordinate voting shares on a one-for-one basis. Automatically convertible into subordinate voting shares in certain other circumstances. Ten votes per share.

Subordinate Voting - Entitled to dividends. Non-convertible. One vote per share.

Major Shareholder - Greg Smith held 43.78% interest, The Rhino group held 34.96% interest and Matthew (Matt) Smith held 17.29% interest at May 11, 2023.

Price Range - THNC/TSX

Year	Volume	High	Low	Close
2022	21,834,908	$9.27	$1.40	$1.88
2021	9,578,202	$19.47	$8.00	$8.91

Recent Close: $1.90

Capital Stock Changes - During 2022, subordinate voting shares were issued as follows: 2,411,941 on exercise of options and 4,256 on vesting of restricted share units.

Wholly Owned Subsidiaries

Thinkific.com Inc., Del.

Financial Statistics

Periods ended:	12m Dec. 31/22[A]		12m Dec. 31/21[A]
	US$000s	%Chg	US$000s
Operating revenue	**51,476**	**+35**	**38,117**
Cost of sales	11,801		8,242
Research & devel. expense	26,145		17,821
General & admin expense	39,905		31,556
Stock-based compensation	2,786		4,124
Operating expense	**80,636**	**+31**	**61,743**
Operating income	**(29,160)**	**n.a.**	**(23,626)**
Deprec., depl. & amort.	1,196		681
Finance costs, net	(1,428)		(245)
Pre-tax income	**(36,422)**	**n.a.**	**(26,375)**
Net income	**(36,422)**	**n.a.**	**(26,375)**
Cash & equivalent	93,846		126,055
Accounts receivable	2,713		1,392
Current assets	98,679		130,376
Fixed assets, net	1,508		767
Right-of-use assets	2,006		754
Intangibles, net	118		99
Total assets	**102,970**	**-22**	**132,404**
Accts. pay. & accr. liabs	4,927		3,286
Current liabilities	13,610		10,430
Long-term lease liabilities	1,512		360
Shareholders' equity	87,848		121,614
Cash from oper. activs	**(25,853)**	**n.a.**	**(18,255)**
Cash from fin. activs	(241)		138,255
Cash from invest. activs	(1,260)		(655)
Net cash position	**93,846**	**-26**	**126,055**
Capital expenditures	(1,233)		(551)
	US$		US$
Earnings per share*	(0.46)		(0.41)
Cash flow per share*	(0.33)		(0.28)
	shs		shs
No. of shs. o/s*	79,671,172		77,254,975
Avg. no. of shs. o/s*	78,701,528		65,107,020
	%		%
Net profit margin	(70.76)		(69.19)
Return on equity	(34.78)		(41.56)
Return on assets	(30.95)		(36.29)
Foreign sales percent	88		90
No. of employees (FTEs)	354		450

* S.V. & M.V.

[A] Reported in accordance with IFRS

Latest Results

Periods ended:	3m Mar. 31/23[A]		3m Mar. 31/22[A]
	US$000s	%Chg	US$000s
Operating revenue	14,093	+20	11,785
Net income	(7,007)	n.a.	(11,987)
	US$		US$
Earnings per share*	(0.09)		(0.16)

* S.V. & M.V.

[A] Reported in accordance with IFRS

Historical Summary
(as originally stated)

Fiscal Year	Oper. Rev.	Net Inc. Bef. Disc.	EPS*
	US$000s	US$000s	US$
2022[A]	51,476	(36,422)	(0.46)
2021[A]	38,117	(26,375)	(0.41)
2020[A1]	21,070	(1,293)	(0.03)
2019[A1]	9,796	291	0.01
2018[A1]	5,996	236	0.00

* S.V. & M.V.

[A] Reported in accordance with IFRS

[1] As shown in the prospectus dated Apr. 22, 2021. Shares and per share figures adjusted to reflect 4-for-1 split effective Apr. 23, 2021.

T.40 Thiogenesis Therapeutics, Corp.

Symbol - TTI **Exchange** - TSX-VEN **CUSIP** - 88410L
Head Office - 401-4 King St W, Toronto, ON, M5H 1B6 **Telephone** - (647) 846-7766
Email - briggins@thiogenesis.com
Investor Relations - Brook G. Riggins 420-776 659 259
Auditors - MNP LLP C.A., Toronto, Ont.
Transfer Agents - TSX Trust Company, Toronto, Ont.
Profile - (Ont. 2018) Developing and commercializing therapeutics that provide thiols/SH groups, particularly precursors to cysteamine-based drugs, for the treatment of a variety of unmet genetic and central nervous system (CNS) diseases.

The company has synthesized and patented three compounds that are precursors to the compound cysteamine, which has multiple mechanisms of action and has long been considered a promising drug candidate for several indications. Cysteamine is a small amino thiol compound (also known as an sulfhydryl or a compound with a functional SH group) that is endogenously derived at low levels from the degradation of Coenzyme A in humans. Two formulations of synthetic cysteamine have already been approved for the treatment of cystinosis, a rare inherited lysosomal storage disease that mostly affects children. The company's lead compound is TTI-0102, a synthesized compound consisting of cysteamine and pantetheine that has the potential as a therapeutic for a variety of applications including Rett syndrome, Mitochondrial Encephalopathy Lactic Acidosis and Stroke (MELAS), traumatic brain injury, Huntington's disease, cystinosis and COVID-19.

Predecessor Detail - Name changed from Rozdil Capital Corporation, Mar. 22, 2022, pursuant to the Qualifying Transaction reverse takeover acquisition of Thiogenesis Therapeutics, Inc.

Directors - Dr. Christopher M. Starr, chr., Sonoma, Calif.; Dr. Patrice P. Rioux, CEO, San Diego, Calif.; Brook G. Riggins, CFO & corp. sec., Prague, Czech Republic; W. Hogan Mullally, Winnipeg, Man.; Kim R. Tsuchimoto, Petaluma, Calif.

Capital Stock

	Authorized (shs.)	Outstanding (shs.)[1]
Common	unlimited	28,242,675

[1] At Aug. 15, 2022

Major Shareholder - Dr. Patrice P. Rioux held 23.86% interest and Vincent P. Stanton Jr. held 14.16% interest at Aug. 15, 2022.

Price Range - TTI/TSX-VEN

Year	Volume	High	Low	Close
2022	3,543,613	$0.72	$0.38	$0.58
2020	494,500	$0.35	$0.14	$0.22
2019	57,000	$0.16	$0.10	$0.15

Recent Close: $0.70

Capital Stock Changes - In April 2022, 12,771,075 common shares were issue pursuant to the Qualifying Transaction reverse takeover acquisition of Thiogenesis Therapeutics, Inc., 10,000,000 common shares were issued without further consideration on exchange of special warrants sold in July 2021 at $0.35 each and 425,000 common shares were issued on exercise of options. In November 2022, private placement of 10,619,400 common shares was completed at 50¢ per share.

Wholly Owned Subsidiaries

Thiogenesis Therapeutics, Inc., San Diego, Calif.
- 100% int. in **Thiogenesis Australia Pty Ltd.**, Australia.
- 100% int. in **Thiogenesis Therapeutics EURL**, France.

Financial Statistics

Periods ended:	12m Dec. 31/21[A1]		12m Dec. 31/20[A]
	US$000s	%Chg	US$000s
Research & devel. expense	1,069		392
General & admin expense	256		60
Stock-based compensation	5		22
Operating expense	**1,330**	**+181**	**474**
Operating income	**(1,330)**	**n.a.**	**(474)**
Finance costs, gross	2		3
Pre-tax income	**(967)**	**n.a.**	**(476)**
Net income	**(967)**	**n.a.**	**(476)**
Cash & equivalent	49		15
Accounts receivable	10		1
Current assets	182		41
Total assets	**182**	**+344**	**41**
Bank indebtedness	364		251
Accts. pay. & accr. liabs	537		31
Current liabilities	1,020		282
Shareholders' equity	(838)		(240)
Cash from oper. activs	**(614)**	**n.a.**	**(373)**
Cash from fin. activs	651		248
Net cash position	**49**	**+227**	**15**
	US$		US$
Earnings per share*	(0.08)		(0.05)
Cash flow per share*	(0.05)		(0.04)
	shs		shs
No. of shs. o/s	n.a.		n.a.
Avg. no. of shs. o/s*	11,556,164		10,000,000
	%		%
Net profit margin	n.a.		n.a.
Return on equity	n.m.		n.m.
Return on assets	(865.47)		(356.98)

* Common
[A] Reported in accordance with IFRS
[1] Results for 2021 and prior years pertain to Thiogenesis Therapeutics, Inc.

Latest Results

Periods ended:	9m Sept. 30/22[A]		9m Sept. 30/21[A]
	$000s	%Chg	$000s
Net income	(3,479)	n.a.	(881)
	$		$
Earnings per share*	(0.15)		(0.08)

* Common
[A] Reported in accordance with IFRS

Historical Summary
(as originally stated)

Fiscal Year	Oper. Rev. US$000s	Net Inc. Bef. Disc. US$000s	EPS* US$
2021[A]	nil	(967)	(0.08)
2020[A]	nil	(476)	(0.05)
2019[A]	nil	(56)	(0.01)

* Common
[A] Reported in accordance with IFRS

T.41 Thomson Reuters Corporation*

Symbol - TRI **Exchange -** TSX **CUSIP -** 884903
Head Office - 300-333 Bay St, Toronto, ON, M5H 2R2 **Telephone -** (416) 687-7500
Website - www.thomsonreuters.com
Email - gary.bisbee@tr.com
Investor Relations - Gary E. Bisbee (646) 540-3249
Auditors - PricewaterhouseCoopers LLP C.P.A., New York, N.Y.
Lawyers - Torys LLP, Toronto, Ont.
Transfer Agents - Computershare Trust Company, N.A., Canton, Mass.; Computershare Investor Services plc, Bristol, Gloucs. United Kingdom; Computershare Trust Company of Canada Inc., Toronto, Ont.
FP500 Revenue Ranking - 72
Employees - 25,200 at Dec. 31, 2022

Profile - (Ont. 1977) Provides information, software and services to professionals and organizations in the private and public sectors worldwide, and operates Reuters, the world's most global multimedia news provider.

Operations are organized into five segments: Legal Professionals; Corporates; Tax & Accounting Professionals; Reuters News; and Global Print.

Legal Professionals - Provides law firms and governments with research and workflow products, which focus on intuitive legal research using emerging technologies and integrated legal workflow solutions which combine content, tools and analytics.

Corporates - Provides corporate customers of all sizes, including the seven largest global accounting firms, with a full suite of content-driven technology solutions for in-house legal, tax, regulatory, compliance and information technology professionals.

Tax & Accounting Professionals - Provides tax, accounting and audit professionals in accounting firms (other than the seven largest served by the Corporates segment) with research and workflow products focused on intuitive tax offerings and automating tax workflows.

Reuters News - Provides business, financial and global news to the world's media organizations, professionals and news consumers through Reuters News Agency, Reuters.com, Reuters Events and Thomson Reuters products, and to financial market professionals exclusively via products of **London Stock Exchange Group plc**. In 2022, the company delivered about 3,500,000 news stories, 1,000,000 pictures/images and 100,000 video stories, as well as various industry events.

Global Print - Provides information primarily in print format to customers, including legal and tax professionals, government, law schools and corporations.

Key product and service brands include: Westlaw, Westlaw Edge, Westlaw Precision, Sweet & Maxwell, La Ley, Practical Law, Practical Law Connect, Practical Law Dynamic Tool Set, CLEAR, CLEAR Risk Inform, CLEAR ID Confirm, CLEAR Adverse Media Sanctions, PeopleMap, HighQ, HighQ Contract Analysis, Case Center, Fraud Analytics, Fraud Detect, ID Risk Analytics, Case Tracking, Checkpoint, Checkpoint Edge, FindLaw, 3E, 3E Cloud, ProLaw, Legal One, Legal Tracker, Regulatory Intelligence, ONESOURCE, ONESOURCE Global Trade, Confirmation, Dominio, Cloud Audit Suite, CS Professional Suite and Onvio.

On June 23, 2023, a US$2.2 billion return of capital transaction was completed, consisting of a distribution of US$4.67 cash per share and a consolidation of common shares on a 0.963957-for-1 basis. The transaction was funded through proceeds from dispositions of shares of **London Stock Exchange Group plc**.

On Jan. 31, 2023, the company and certain investment funds affiliated with **Blackstone Inc.** sold 21,200,000 shares of **London Stock Exchange Group plc** (LSEG) at US$94.50 per share to **Microsoft Corporation**. The shares were co-owned by the company and Blackstone through their interests in **York Parent Limited**; the company indirectly sold 10,500,000 LSEG shares. On Mar. 8, 2023, the company and Blackstone collectively sold 28,000,000 LSEG shares at £71.50 per share through a placement to institutional investors and an offer to retail investors. Of the shares sold, 13,600,000 were indirectly owned by the company. On May 19, 2023, the company and Blackstone collectively sold 33,000,000 LSEG shares at £80.50 per share through a placement to institutional investors and an offer to retail investors; 15,300,000 shares sold were indirectly owned by the company.

Recent Merger and Acquisition Activity

Status: completed **Revised:** July 31, 2023
UPDATE: The transaction was completed. PREVIOUS: Thomson Reuters Corporation agreed to acquire U.K.-based Imagen Ltd., which provides a media management and distribution platform that helps sports organizations, businesses and media companies manage their digital content libraries. Terms of the transaction were not disclosed. Imagen also owns Screenocean, a platform that provides production companies and others the ability to license video and photo content from around the world.

Status: pending **Announced:** June 27, 2023
Thomson Reuters Corporation agreed to acquire San Francisco, Calif.-based Casetext, Inc., which provides artificial intelligence (AI) and machine learning to build technology for legal professionals, for US$650,000,000. Casetext was developing CoCounsel, an AI legal assistant technology that provides document review, legal research memos, deposition preparation and contract analysis within minutes. The transaction was subject to specified regulatory approvals and customary closing conditions, and was expected to be completed in the second half of 2023.

Status: completed **Revised:** June 1, 2023
UPDATE: The transaction was completed. PREVIOUS: Thomson Reuters Corporation agreed to sell a majority interest in its Elite business, a provider of financial and practice management solutions to law firms, to TPG Inc., valuing the business at US$500,000,000. TPG would establish Elite as an independent legal technology company. On closing, Thomson Reuters would receive US$400,000,000 and would retain a 19.9% interest in the business with board representation. Elite offers a suite of solutions, including 3E, ProLaw, eBillingHub and MatterSphere, for automating and streamlining law firm finance and accounting operations, including billing, invoicing, payments and financial reporting. The transaction was expected to close in the second quarter of 2023, subject to regulatory approvals and other customary closing conditions.

Status: completed **Revised:** Jan. 3, 2023
UPDATE: The transaction was completed. PREVIOUS: Thomson Reuters Corporation agreed to acquire Irvine, Calif.-based SurePrep, LLC, a provider of 1040 tax automation software and services, for US$500,000,000. SurePrep's software and services include 1040SCAN, SPbinder and TaxCaddy which are used by more than 23,000 tax professionals at C.P.A. firms, wealth management firms and others.

Status: completed **Announced:** Aug. 31, 2022
Thomson Reuters Corporation acquired Denmark-based PLX AI ApS, a real-time financial news service provider powered by artificial intelligence (AI). PLX AI delivers breaking financials news and insight that moves stock prices, including surprise earnings, outlook changes, mergers and acquisitions, important orders or management decisions, from 1,500 companies across the U.S. and Europe. PLX AI was integrated into Reuters News. Terms were not disclosed.

Status: completed **Announced:** Apr. 26, 2022
Thomson Reuters Corporation acquired São Paulo, Brazil-based Gestta Technology Ltda., a developer of accounting practice management software which enables customers to automate their workflows, people management, customer service and secure document archiving, among other capabilities. Terms were not disclosed.

Status: completed **Revised:** Apr. 14, 2022
UPDATE: The transaction was completed. PREVIOUS: Thomson Reuters Corporation agreed to acquire Houston, Tex.-based ThoughtTrace, Inc., a provider of a document understanding and contract analysis software platform which uses artificial intelligence (AI) and machine learning to read, organize and manage document workflows for customers in various industries. Terms were not disclosed.

Predecessor Detail - Name changed from The Thomson Corporation, Apr. 17, 2008, following acquisition of Reuters Group PLC to form a dual listed company structure.

Directors - David K. R. Thomson, chr., Toronto, Ont.; David W. Binet, deputy chr., Toronto, Ont.; Steve Hasker, pres. & CEO, Toronto, Ont.; Michael E. Daniels†, Hilton Head Island, S.C.; Kirk E. Arnold, Kennebunk, Me.; Dr. W. Edmund (Ed) Clark, Toronto, Ont.; LaVerne H. Council, Great Falls, Va.; Kirk Koenigsbauer, Seattle, Wash.; Deanna Oppenheimer, Seattle, Wash.; Simon Paris, London, Middx., United Kingdom; Kim M. Rivera, Woodside, Calif.; Barry Salzberg, New York, N.Y.; Peter J. Thomson, Toronto, Ont.; Elizabeth D. (Beth) Wilson, Toronto, Ont.

Other Exec. Officers - Michael (Mike) Eastwood, CFO; Kirsty Roth, chief opers. & tech. officer; Mary Alice Vuicic, chief people officer; David Wong, chief product officer; Paul Bascobert, pres., Reuters News; Elizabeth Beastrom, pres., tax & acctg. professionals; Laura A. Clayton McDonnell, pres., corporates; Paul Fischer, pres., legal professionals; Jennifer Prescott, pres., global print; Steve Rubley, pres., govt. div.

† Lead director

Capital Stock

	Authorized (shs.)	Outstanding (shs.)[1]	Par
Preference	unlimited		n.p.v.
Series II	6,000,000	6,000,000	
Common	unlimited	455,303,939	n.p.v.
Thomson Reuters Founders	1	1	n.a

[1] At Aug. 1, 2023

Preference - Issuable in one or more series. Shares of each series rank on a parity with the preference shares of every other series and are entitled to a preference with respect to dividends and the return of capital over the common shares and any other shares ranking junior to the preference shares. **Series II** - Entitled to cumulative preferential dividends payable quarterly at an annual rate of 70% of the Canadian bank prime rate applied to the stated capital of the shares. Redeemable at Cdn$25 per share plus accrued and unpaid dividends. Non-voting.

Common - One vote per share.

Thomson Reuters Founders - Issued to Thomson Reuters Founders Share Company (TRFSC) which enables it to exercise extraordinary voting power to safeguard the Thomson Reuters Trust Principles, including that of integrity, independence and freedom from bias in the gathering and dissemination of information and news, and to thwart those whose holdings of voting shares of the company threaten the Thomson Reuters Trust Principles. Entitled to vote in circumstances where an acquiring person, other than an approved person or an entity within the company, has become or becomes interested in, or the beneficial owner of, 15% or more of the outstanding voting shares of the company or has obtained or is attempting to obtain control or beneficial ownership of 30% or more of the outstanding voting shares of the company. In general, votes cast by TRFSC, alone or in combination with votes cast by approved persons, will be sufficient to negate the voting power of the acquiring person or to constitute the requisite majority voting power.

Equity-based Awards - At Dec. 31, 2022, awards were outstanding to purchase 4,096,000 common shares at a weighted average exercise price of US$78.06 per share. These awards consisted of 1,908,000 stock options, 1,390,000 time-based restricted share units (TRSUs) and 798,000 performance restricted share units (PRSUs).

Major Shareholder - The Woodbridge Company Limited held 69% interest at Aug. 1, 2023.

Price Range - TRI/TSX

Year	Volume	High	Low	Close
2022	97,177,136	$165.80	$123.69	$160.24
2021	88,037,432	$162.48	$102.82	$156.93
2020	140,286,448	$119.99	$78.75	$108.08
2019	122,763,688	$99.94	$65.27	$96.36
2018	203,351,040	$74.21	$53.35	$68.40

Consolidation: 0.963957-for-1 cons. in June 2023

Recent Close: $172.42

Capital Stock Changes - On June 23, 2023, common shares were consolidated on a 0.963957-for-1 basis pursuant to a return of capital transaction.

During 2022, 1,575,342 common shares were issued on exercise of options and other stock plans, 263,730 common shares were issued under the dividend reinvestment plan and 11,872,826 common shares were repurchased under a Normal Course Issuer Bid.

Dividends

TRI com Ra US$1.96 pa Q est. Sept. 15, 2023**
1-for-1 cons eff. June 23, 2023
Prev. Rate: US$1.96 est. Mar. 16, 2023
Prev. Rate: US$1.78 est. Mar. 15, 2022
Prev. Rate: US$1.62 est. Mar. 17, 2021
Prev. Rate: US$1.52 est. Mar. 18, 2020
TRI.PR.B pfd ser II cum. red. Fltg. Ra pa Q
$0.293631 June 30/23 $0.285658 Mar. 31/23
$0.257159 Jan. 3/23 $0.203345 Oct. 3/22
Paid in 2023: $0.836448 2022: $0.450843 2021: $0.428749

** Reinvestment Option

Long-Term Debt - Outstanding at Dec. 31, 2022:

Commercial paper	US$1,048,000,000
4.3% notes due 2023	599,000,000
3.85% notes due 2024	241,000,000
2.239% notes due 2025	1,030,000,000
3.35% notes due 2026	497,000,000
5.5% debs. due 2035	396,000,000
5.85% debs. due 2040	492,000,000
4.5% notes due 2043	116,000,000
5.65% notes due 2043	342,000,000
	4,761,000,000
Less: Current portion	1,647,000,000
	3,114,000,000

Wholly Owned Subsidiaries

Acritas Limited, United Kingdom.
Bedrijfsbeheer TRA B.V., Netherlands.
Capital Confirmation, Inc., Brentwood, Tenn.
HighQ Solutions Limited, London, Middx., United Kingdom.
LN Holdings Limited, Bermuda.
LiveNote Technologies Limited, United Kingdom.
Netmaster Solutions Ltd., London, Middx., United Kingdom.
Reuters News & Media Inc., Del.
Reuters News & Media Limited, United Kingdom.
TR Finance LLC, Del.
TR Holdings Limited, Bermuda.
TR (2008) Limited, London, Middx., United Kingdom.
TR U.S. Inc., Del.
TTC Holdings Limited, Bermuda.
TTC (1994) Limited, United Kingdom.
Thomson Reuters America Corporation, Del.
Thomson Reuters Brasil Conteúdo e Tecnologia Ltda., Brazil.
Thomson Reuters Canada Limited, Toronto, Ont.
Thomson Reuters Enterprise Centre GmbH, Switzerland.
Thomson Reuters Finance S.A., Luxembourg.
Thomson Reuters Group Limited, London, Middx., United Kingdom.
Thomson Reuters Holdco LLC, Del.
Thomson Reuters Holdings B.V., Netherlands.
Thomson Reuters Holdings Inc., Del.
Thomson Reuters Holdings S.A., Luxembourg.
Thomson Reuters Investment Holdings Limited, United Kingdom.
Thomson Reuters (Legal) Inc., Minn.
Thomson Reuters MX Servicios, S.A. de D.V., Mexico.
Thomson Reuters No. 4 Inc., Del.
Thomson Reuters No. 5 LLC, Del.
Thomson Reuters No. 8 LLC, Del.
Thomson Reuters (Professional) Australia Limited, Australia.
Thomson Reuters (Professional) UK Ltd., United Kingdom.
Thomson Reuters (TRI) Inc., Del.
Thomson Reuters (Tax & Accounting) Inc., Tex.
Thomson Reuters U.S. LLC, Del.
3276838 Nova Scotia Company, N.S.
West Publishing Corporation, Minn.

Investments

32.07% int. in **York Parent Limited**, Cayman Islands.

- **London Stock Exchange Group plc**, London, Middx., United Kingdom. Ownership represents 18% economic interest and 11% voting interest.

Note: The preceding list includes only the major related companies in which interests are held.

Financial Statistics

Periods ended:	12m Dec. 31/22[A]		12m Dec. 31/21[A]
	US$000s	%Chg	US$000s
Operating revenue	**6,627,000**	**+4**	**6,348,000**
Salaries & benefits	2,408,000		2,478,000
Stock-based compensation	85,000		76,000
Other operating expense	1,644,000		1,672,000
Operating expense	**4,280,000**	**-2**	**4,370,000**
Operating income	**2,347,000**	**+19**	**1,978,000**
Deprec., depl. & amort.	724,000		770,000
Finance costs, net	(248,000)		188,000
Pre-tax income	**2,082,000**	**+98**	**1,054,000**
Income taxes	259,000		1,607,000
After-tax income (expense)	(432,000)		6,240,000
Net inc. bef. disc. opers	**1,391,000**	**-76**	**5,687,000**
Income from disc. opers	(53,000)		2,000
Net income	**1,338,000**	**-76**	**5,689,000**
Cash & equivalent	1,069,000		778,000
Inventories	29,000		28,000
Accounts receivable	1,069,000		1,057,000
Current assets	2,811,000		2,453,000
Long-term investments	6,199,000		6,736,000
Fixed assets, net	414,000		502,000
Intangibles, net	10,023,000		10,093,000
Total assets	**21,711,000**	**-2**	**22,149,000**
Accts. pay. & accr. liabs	237,000		227,000
Current liabilities	4,891,000		2,581,000
Long-term debt, gross	4,761,000		3,786,000
Long-term debt, net	3,114,000		3,786,000
Long-term lease liabilities	179,000		197,000
Preferred share equity	110,000		110,000
Shareholders' equity	11,885,000		13,834,000
Cash from oper. activs	**1,915,000**	**+8**	**1,773,000**
Cash from fin. activs	(1,156,000)		(2,273,000)
Cash from invest. activs	(462,000)		(504,000)
Net cash position	**1,069,000**	**+37**	**778,000**
Capital expenditures	(595,000)		(487,000)
Unfunded pension liability	392,000		295,000
Pension fund surplus	n.a.		132,000
	US$		US$
Earns. per sh. bef disc opers*	2.98		11.95
Earnings per share*	2.86		11.96
Cash flow per share*	4.11		3.73
Cash divd. per share*	1.85		1.68
	shs		shs
No. of shs. o/s*	458,900,511		468,572,619
Avg. no. of shs. o/s*	466,444,816		475,658,828
	%		%
Net profit margin	20.99		89.59
Return on equity	10.89		48.19
Return on assets	6.34		28.41
Foreign sales percent	97		97
No. of employees (FTEs)	25,200		24,400

* Common
[A] Reported in accordance with IFRS

Latest Results

Periods ended:	6m June 30/23[A]		6m June 30/22[A]
	US$000s	%Chg	US$000s
Operating revenue	3,385,000	+3	3,288,000
Net inc. bef. disc. opers	1,626,000	+72	947,000
Income from disc. opers	24,000		(55,000)
Net income	1,650,000	+85	892,000
	US$		US$
Earns. per sh. bef. disc. opers.*	3.44		2.01
Earnings per share*	3.49		1.90

* Common
[A] Reported in accordance with IFRS

Historical Summary
(as originally stated)

Fiscal Year	Oper. Rev.	Net Inc. Bef. Disc.	EPS*
	US$000s	US$000s	US$
2022[A]	6,627,000	1,391,000	2.98
2021[A]	6,348,000	5,687,000	11.95
2020[A]	5,984,000	1,149,000	2.40
2019[A]	5,906,000	1,570,000	3.25
2018[A]	5,501,000	180,000	0.28

* Common
[A] Reported in accordance with IFRS

Note: Adjusted throughout for 0.963957-for-1 cons. in June 2023

T.42 Three Sixty Solar Ltd.

Symbol - VSOL **Exchange** - NEO **CUSIP** - 88577D
Head Office - Office 8312, 408-55 Water St, Vancouver, BC, V6B 1A1
Toll-free - (877) 684-1972
Website - threesixtysolar.com
Email - athornberry@threesixtysolar.com
Investor Relations - Austin Thornberry (778) 383-6743

Auditors - Dale Matheson Carr-Hilton LaBonte LLP C.A., Vancouver, B.C.

Transfer Agents - National Securities Administrators Ltd., Vancouver, B.C.

Employees - 2 at Dec. 29, 2022

Profile - (B.C. 2015; orig. Ont., 1994 amalg.) Designed and built the patent pending SVS series commercial solar tower, which provides a range of clean energy solutions for small commercial projects all the way up to large utility scale solar farms.

The solar towers are installed vertically, enabling operators to use up to 90% less land space than conventional solar towers and which can co-locate adjacent to homes, retail, agriculture and industry. The towers range between 40 to 120 ft. in height, and each tower can produce up to 250 KW of energy.

The company would purchase completed member components of the towers from steel fabricators, and outsource local labour for the assembly and installation of the towers, with project management and oversight performed directly by the company.

Recent Merger and Acquisition Activity

Status: completed **Revised:** Aug. 4, 2022
UPDATE: The transaction was completed. (New) Three Sixty's post-consolidated common shares commenced trading on the NEO Exchange effective Aug. 15, 2022. PREVIOUS: Liberty One Lithium Corp. entered into a letter of intent for the reverse takeover acquisition of private Vancouver, B.C.-based Three Sixty Solar Ltd., which was designing and developing vertical solar towers to provide a range of energy solutions for small commercial projects all the way up to large utility scale solar farms. Three Sixty would receive common shares of Liberty One as consideration. Feb. 10, 2022 - A definitive agreement was entered into. The basis of share consideration was one-for-one, which would result in the issuance of 19,413,447 Liberty One post-consolidated common shares (following a 1-for-2 share consolidation). Upon completion, Three Sixty would amalgamate with Liberty One's wholly owned 1345100 B.C. Ltd. to form Three Sixty Solar Operations Ltd., and Liberty One would change its name to Three Sixty Solar Ltd. and voluntarily delist its common shares from the TSX Venture Exchange and apply for a listing on the NEO Exchange. June 28, 2022 - Liberty One's common shares were delisted from the TSX Venture Exchange at the close of market. June 29, 2022 - Liberty One's common shares were accepted for listing on the NEO Exchange but were subject to a trading halt pending completion of the transaction. July 26, 2022 - Liberty One effected the 1-for-2 share consolidation.

Predecessor Detail - Name changed from Liberty One Lithium Corp., Aug. 4, 2022, pursuant to the reverse takeover acquisition of (old) Three Sixty Solar Ltd. and concurrent amalgamation of (old) Three Sixty with wholly owned 1345100 B.C. Ltd. (and continued as Three Sixty Solar Operations Ltd.).; basis 1 new for 2 old shs.

Directors - Brian Roth, CEO, B.C.; Robert L. (Rob) Birmingham, North Vancouver, B.C.; Scott McLeod, B.C.; Manavdeep (Mark) Mukhija, W.A., Australia; Ben Parsons; Peter Sherba, B.C.

Other Exec. Officers - Austin Thornberry, CFO

Capital Stock

	Authorized (shs.)	Outstanding (shs.)[1]
Common	unlimited	40,113,313

[1] At May 15, 2023

Major Shareholder - Peter Sherba held 31.83% interest at Oct. 13, 2022.

Price Range - VSOL/NEO

Year	Volume	High	Low	Close
2022	7,300	$1.08	$0.76	$0.77
2021	861,957	$1.80	$0.66	$0.80
2020	725,600	$1.50	$0.80	$1.10
2019	725,119	$3.50	$0.70	$1.00
2018	1,028,952	$20.60	$1.30	$1.60

Consolidation: 1-for-2 cons. in July 2022; 1-for-10 cons. in Dec. 2020

Recent Close: $0.36

Capital Stock Changes - In June 2023, private placement of 1,715,553 units (1 common share & 1 warrant) at 60¢ per unit was completed, with warrants exercisable at 75¢ per share for two years.

On July 26, 2022, common shares were consolidated on a 1-for-2 basis. On Aug. 4, 2022, 19,413,447 post-consolidated common shares were issued pursuant to the reverse takeover acquisition of (old) Three Sixty Solar Ltd.

Wholly Owned Subsidiaries

Liberty One Utah Inc., Utah
Three Sixty Solar Operations Ltd., Vancouver, B.C.
Victory Exploration Inc., Qué.

Financial Statistics

Periods ended:	12m Sept. 30/22[A1]		12m Sept. 30/21[□A]
	$000s	%Chg	$000s
Salaries & benefits	259		163
Research & devel. expense	75		41
General & admin expense	1,329		109
Stock-based compensation	643		nil
Operating expense	**2,306**	**+637**	**313**
Operating income	**(2,306)**	**n.a.**	**(313)**
Deprec., depl. & amort.	30		nil
Finance income	8		nil
Pre-tax income	**(3,340)**	**n.a.**	**(313)**
Net income	**(3,340)**	**n.a.**	**(313)**
Cash & equivalent	2,709		210
Current assets	3,601		210
Fixed assets, net	29		1
Right-of-use assets	123		nil
Total assets	**3,753**	**n.m.**	**211**
Bank indebtedness	13		nil
Accts. pay. & accr. liabs	570		327
Current liabilities	707		340
Shareholders' equity	3,046		(128)
Cash from oper. activs	**(2,505)**	**n.a.**	**(161)**
Cash from fin. activs	1,992		372
Cash from invest. activs	3,011		nil
Net cash position	**2,709**	**n.m.**	**210**
Capital expenditures	(1)		nil
	$		$
Earnings per share*	(0.20)		(0.04)
Cash flow per share*	(0.15)		(0.02)
	shs		shs
No. of shs. o/s*	24,084,730		n.a.
Avg. no. of shs. o/s*	17,021,188		7,666,667
	%		%
Net profit margin	n.a.		n.a.
Return on equity	(92.41)		n.m.
Return on assets	(80.20)		(9.73)

* Common
[□] Restated
[A] Reported in accordance with IFRS
[1] Results reflect the Aug. 4, 2022, reverse takeover transaction of (old) Three Sixty Solar Ltd.

Latest Results

Periods ended:	6m Mar. 31/23[A]		6m Mar. 31/22[□A]
	$000s	%Chg	$000s
Net income	(5,034)	n.a.	(548)
	$		$
Earnings per share*	(0.18)		(0.04)

* Common
[□] Restated
[A] Reported in accordance with IFRS

Historical Summary
(as originally stated)

Fiscal Year	Oper. Rev. $000s	Net Inc. Bef. Disc. $000s	EPS* $
2022[A]	nil	(3,340)	(0.20)
2021[A1]	nil	(2,554)	(0.58)
2020[A]	nil	(1,450)	(0.38)
2019[A]	nil	(1,503)	(0.40)
2018[A]	nil	(4,328)	(1.20)

* Common
[A] Reported in accordance with IFRS
[1] Results for 2021 and prior years pertain to Liberty One Lithium Corp.
Note: Adjusted throughout for 1-for-2 cons. in July 2022; 1-for-10 cons. in Dec. 2020

T.43 Three Valley Copper Corp.

Symbol - TVC.H **Exchange** - TSX-VEN **CUSIP** - 88576E
Head Office - c/o Peterson McVicar LLP, 902-18 King St E, Toronto, ON, M5C 1C4 **Telephone** - (647) 749-5859
Website - threevalleycopper.com
Email - ir@threevalleycopper.com
Investor Relations - Ian M. MacNeily (416) 943-7107
Auditors - PricewaterhouseCoopers LLP C.A., Toronto, Ont.
Lawyers - Peterson McVicar LLP, Toronto, Ont.
Transfer Agents - TSX Trust Company, Toronto, Ont.
Profile - (Can. 2002; orig. B.C., 1997) No current operations.

Formerly held 95.1% interest in **Minera Tres Valles S.p.A.** (MTV), which owns Minera Tres Valles mining complex, 46,000 hectares, 10 km north of Salamanca, Chile, which includes fully integrated processing operations, Don Gabriel open-pit mine (under care and maintenance) and Papomono underground mine (under development), with measured and indicated resource of 18,304,000 tonnes grading 1.034% copper at Jan. 1, 2018. MTV extracts and processes mineralized material to produce copper cathodes. At Jan. 1, 2018, proven and probable reserves at Don Gabriel Manto deposit were 5,168,000 tonnes grading 0.81% total copper. At July 31, 2018, proven and probable reserves at Papomono Masivo deposit were 3,067,000 tonnes grading 1.51% total copper.

On Feb. 17, 2023, the company announced that 95.1%-owned **Minera Tres Valles S.p.A.** (MTV) received court approval to begin bankruptcy liquidation proceedings. A liquidator was appointed and immediately assumed full responsibility for the operations and management of MTV. MTV had operated at a limited capacity since January 2022 while it continued to harvest copper cathodes from its current inventory.

Periods ended:	12m Dec. 31/21	12m Dec. 31/20
Tonnes mined	631,096	408,125
Copper cathodes, tonnes	4,209	4,883
Copper cathode prod., lbs	9,280,000	10,765,172
Copper cathode sales, lbs	8,900,000	8,653,144
Avg real. copper price, US$/lb	3.7	2.58
Copper cash cost, US$/lb	4.44	2.71

Predecessor Detail - Name changed from SRHI Inc., June 21, 2021.
Directors - Mark Pajak, chr. & CEO, London, Middx., United Kingdom; Lenard F. (Len) Boggio, North Vancouver, B.C.; Joan E. Dunne, Calgary, Alta.; Terrence A. (Terry) Lyons, Vancouver, B.C.
Other Exec. Officers - Ian M. MacNeily, CFO & corp. sec.; Luis Vega, CEO, Minera Tres Valles S.p.A.

Capital Stock

	Authorized (shs.)	Outstanding (shs.)[1]
Class A Common	unlimited	112,463,854

[1] At Nov. 25, 2022
Major Shareholder - Widely held at May 20, 2022.

Price Range - TVC.H/TSX-VEN

Year	Volume	High	Low	Close
2022	133,508,878	$0.24	$0.02	$0.03
2021	78,117,468	$1.02	$0.17	$0.17
2020	7,949,440	$0.78	$0.14	$0.29
2019	7,926,811	$1.77	$0.66	$0.76
2018	5,418,801	$3.40	$0.98	$1.12

Recent Close: $0.02

Wholly Owned Subsidiaries

ADI Mining Ltd., Canada.
Sprott Resource Corp., Toronto, Ont.
- 100% int. in **SRH Chile S.p.A.**, Chile.

Financial Statistics

Periods ended:	12m Dec. 31/21[A]		12m Dec. 31/20[A]
	US$000s	%Chg	US$000s
Operating revenue	**32,915**	**+39**	**23,703**
Cost of sales	43,055		23,663
Salaries & benefits	8,455		7,714
Exploration expense	731		nil
General & admin expense	2,211		2,518
Operating expense	**54,452**	**+61**	**33,895**
Operating income	**(21,537)**	**n.a.**	**(10,192)**
Deprec., depl. & amort.	5,102		4,794
Finance costs, net	9,306		6,461
Investment income	(107)		(1,674)
Write-downs/write-offs	(9,377)		(7,628)
Pre-tax income	**(40,792)**	**n.a.**	**(28,087)**
Net inc bef disc ops, eqhldrs	(37,363)		(19,022)
Net inc bef disc ops, NCI	(3,429)		(9,065)
Net inc. bef. disc. opers	**(40,792)**	**n.a.**	**(28,087)**
Income from disc. opers	nil		(2,241)
Net income	**(40,792)**	**n.a.**	**(30,328)**
Net inc. for equity hldrs	**(37,363)**	**n.a.**	**(20,138)**
Net inc. for non-cont. int	**(3,429)**	**n.a.**	**(10,190)**
Cash & equivalent	15,757		14,106
Inventories	16,739		8,426
Accounts receivable	1,705		1,020
Current assets	36,285		27,199
Fixed assets, net	59,733		60,046
Intangibles, net	1,160		1,427
Explor./devel. properties	930		1,046
Total assets	**107,972**	**-2**	**110,374**
Accts. pay. & accr. liabs	18,207		9,860
Current liabilities	95,398		12,072
Long-term debt, gross	74,469		66,250
Long-term debt, net	218		65,623
Shareholders' equity	7,754		26,669
Non-controlling interest	(1,576)		(2,021)
Cash from oper. activs	**(12,045)**	**n.a.**	**(6,159)**
Cash from fin. activs	24,143		2,943
Cash from invest. activs	(10,072)		432
Net cash position	**13,656**	**+14**	**11,961**
Capital expenditures	(10,232)		(3,347)
	US$		US$
Earns. per sh. bef disc opers*	(0.74)		(0.84)
Earnings per share*	(0.74)		(0.91)
Cash flow per share*	(0.22)		(0.18)
	shs		shs
No. of shs. o/s*	112,452,942		34,083,005
Avg. no. of shs. o/s*	54,905,064		33,498,761
	%		%
Net profit margin	(123.93)		(118.50)
Return on equity	(217.08)		(51.43)
Return on assets	(37.36)		(22.16)

* Cl.A Common
[A] Reported in accordance with IFRS

Latest Results

Periods ended:	9m Sept. 30/22[A]		9m Sept. 30/21[A]
	US$000s	%Chg	US$000s
Operating revenue	24,702	+8	22,873
Net income	(17,247)	n.a.	(9,407)
Net inc. for equity hldrs	(16,299)	n.a.	(7,576)
Net inc. for non-cont. int	(948)		(1,831)
	US$		US$
Earnings per share*	(0.15)		(0.20)

* Cl.A Common
[A] Reported in accordance with IFRS

Historical Summary
(as originally stated)

Fiscal Year	Oper. Rev.	Net Inc. Bef. Disc.	EPS*
	US$000s	US$000s	US$
2021[A]	32,915	(40,792)	(0.74)
2020[A]	23,703	(28,087)	(0.84)
2019[A]	35,688	(45,347)	(1.33)
2018[A]	32,700	(29,716)	(0.88)
	$000s	$000s	$
2017[A1]	(35,620)	(42,172)	(1.40)

* Cl.A Common
[A] Reported in accordance with IFRS
[1] Results reflect the Feb. 9, 2017, reverse takeover acquisition of Sprott Resource Corp.
Note: Adjusted throughout for 1-for-20 cons. in Aug. 2018

T.44 ThreeD Capital Inc.

Symbol - IDK **Exchange** - CSE **CUSIP** - 88581L
Head Office - 401-130 Spadina Ave, Toronto, ON, M5V 2L4 **Telephone** - (416) 941-8900
Website - threedcapital.com

Email - chapman@threedcap.com
Investor Relations - Lynn Chapman (416) 941-8900
Auditors - MNP LLP C.A., Toronto, Ont.
Bankers - Royal Bank of Canada, Toronto, Ont.
Lawyers - Cassels Brock & Blackwell LLP, Toronto, Ont.
Transfer Agents - TSX Trust Company, Toronto, Ont.
Profile - (Can. 2011; orig. B.C., 1987) Invests in private and publicly traded companies in the junior resources and disruptive technologies sectors. Also invests in digital assets.

At Sept. 30, 2022, total fair value of investments was $37,150,535 and included equities in private companies such as **Kattegat Mining Inc.**, **SciCann Therapeutics Inc.**, **Nifty Kids Inc.**, **2462344 Ontario Inc.**, **Wolf Acquisitions 1.0 Corp.**, **KOP Therapeutics Corp.** and **One Bullion Limited**; and in public companies such as **Premium Nickel Resources Ltd.**, **Auxico Resources Canada Inc.**, **Nirvana Life Sciences Inc.** and **infinitii ai inc.**

Predecessor Detail - Name changed from Brownstone Energy Inc., June 23, 2016; basis 1 new for 10 old shs.

Directors - Sheldon Inwentash, founder, chr. & CEO, Toronto, Ont.; Jakson Inwentash, v-p, invests. & sr. analyst, Toronto, Ont.; Gerald M. (Gerry) Feldman, Thornhill, Ont.; Steve M. Gray, Kirkland Lake, Ont.; Wayne V. Isaacs, Oakville, Ont.; Alan Myers, Toronto, Ont.

Other Exec. Officers - Lynn Chapman, CFO & corp. sec.; Matthew (Matt) Davis, contr.

Capital Stock

	Authorized (shs.)	Outstanding (shs.)[1]
Common	unlimited	48,641,160

[1] At Nov. 28, 2022

Major Shareholder - Sheldon Inwentash held 17.03% interest at Mar. 18, 2022.

Price Range - IDK/CSE

Year	Volume	High	Low	Close
2022	10,178,498	$0.97	$0.26	$0.31
2021	37,367,198	$2.36	$0.55	$0.70
2020	64,277,764	$0.79	$0.04	$0.71
2019	11,252,578	$1.20	$0.08	$0.22
2018	34,861,324	$10.20	$0.78	$1.02

Consolidation: 1-for-4 cons. in Apr. 2020; 1-for-3 cons. in May 2019
Recent Close: $0.35

Capital Stock Changes - During fiscal 2022, common shares were issued as follows: 4,178,521 on exercise of warrants and 36,666 on exercise of options; 2,306,327 were repurchased under a Normal Course Issuer Bid.

Wholly Owned Subsidiaries

Blockamoto.io Corp. Inactive.
Brownstone Ventures (Barbados) Inc. Inactive.
2121197 Ontario Ltd. Inactive.

Investments

12.9% int. in **Birchtree Investments Ltd.**, Vancouver, B.C. (see separate coverage)

Financial Statistics

Periods ended:	12m June 30/22[A]		12m June 30/21[DA]
	$000s	%Chg	$000s
Realized invest. gain (loss)	5,882		22,053
Unrealized invest. gain (loss)	(5,767)		17,602
Total revenue	**115**	**-100**	**39,655**
Salaries & benefits	1,124		1,308
General & admin. expense	1,566		2,330
Stock-based compensation	1,305		1,385
Operating expense	**3,996**	**-20**	**5,023**
Operating income	**(3,881)**	**n.a.**	**34,632**
Deprec. & amort.	128		148
Finance costs, gross	86		121
Pre-tax income	**(3,739)**	**n.a.**	**34,655**
Net income	**(3,739)**	**n.a.**	**34,655**
Cash & equivalent	394		205
Accounts receivable	80		102
Investments	50,474		55,128
Fixed assets, net	49		63
Right-of-use assets	151		259
Total assets	**51,484**	**-9**	**56,636**
Accts. pay. & accr. liabs	397		1,406
Lease liabilities	174		294
Shareholders' equity	50,912		53,866
Cash from oper. activs	**1,573**	**n.a.**	**(4,070)**
Cash from fin. activs	(1,378)		4,212
Cash from invest. activs	(5)		(7)
Net cash position	**394**	**+92**	**205**
Capital expenditures	(5)		(7)
	$		$
Earnings per share*	(0.08)		0.92
Cash flow per share*	0.03		(0.11)
Net asset value per share*	1.06		1.16
	shs		shs
No. of shs. o/s*	48,245,412		46,336,552
Avg. no. of shs. o/s*	47,607,079		37,839,654
	%		%
Net profit margin	n.m.		87.39
Return on equity	(7.14)		103.30
Return on assets	(6.76)		97.17

* Common
[D] Restated
[A] Reported in accordance with IFRS

Latest Results

Periods ended:	3m Sept. 30/22[A]		3m Sept. 30/21[A]
	$000s	%Chg	$000s
Total revenue	(10,431)	n.a.	13,395
Net income	(11,031)	n.a.	11,703
	$		$
Earnings per share*	(0.23)		0.26

* Common
[A] Reported in accordance with IFRS

Historical Summary
(as originally stated)

Fiscal Year	Total Rev.	Net Inc. Bef. Disc.	EPS*
	$000s	$000s	$
2022[A]	115	(3,739)	(0.08)
2021[A]	39,655	34,655	0.92
2020[A]	(8,227)	(10,526)	(0.43)
2019[A]	(719)	(3,805)	(0.32)
2018[A]	4,842	915	0.12

* Common
[A] Reported in accordance with IFRS

Note: Adjusted throughout for 1-for-4 cons. in Apr. 2020; 1-for-3 cons. in May 2019

T.45 Thunderbird Entertainment Group Inc.

Symbol - TBRD **Exchange** - TSX-VEN **CUSIP** - 88605U
Head Office - 123 7 Ave W, Vancouver, BC, V5Y 1L8 **Telephone** - (604) 683-3555 **Fax** - (604) 707-0378
Website - www.thunderbird.tv
Email - investors@thunderbird.tv
Investor Relations - Jennifer Twiner McCarron (604) 683-3555 ext. 2
Auditors - PricewaterhouseCoopers LLP C.A., Toronto, Ont.
Lawyers - Cassels Brock & Blackwell LLP, Toronto, Ont.
Transfer Agents - Odyssey Trust Company, Vancouver, B.C.
FP500 Revenue Ranking - 708
Profile - (B.C. 1969) Develops, produces and distributes animated, unscripted/factual, and scripted content for world's leading digital platforms, as well as Canadian and international broadcasters.

Owns a library of television, film and digital media content with a focus on children's productions, scripted comedy and drama and unscripted/factual content. Programs are distributed and broadcasted through conventional linear and digital platforms in more than 200 territories worldwide, with a substantial portion of the programming library licensed directly to Internet over-the-top (OTT) platforms such as Netflix, Hulu, Amazon and iTunes.

Operations are conducted through wholly owned **Atomic Cartoons Inc.**, the kids and family content arm, which operates animation studios in Vancouver, B.C., Ottawa Ont., and Los Angeles, Calif., producing two-dimensional and three-dimensional animation with a focus on children's programming; wholly owned **Great Pacific Media Inc.**, the unscripted content arm, which produces factual, lifestyle, reality, game show and documentary programming; and wholly owned **Thunderbird Productions Inc.**, the scripted content arm, which produces scripted programs across a variety of genres including drama, science fiction and comedy series. The company also has a team dedicated to global distribution and consumer products, which develops and manages the media distribution of proprietary and third party content as well as licenses content for merchandise, music, video games and other consumer product opportunities.

The company is headquartered in Vancouver, B.C., with offices in Toronto and Ottawa Ont., and Los Angeles, Calif.

Predecessor Detail - Name changed from Golden Secret Ventures Ltd., Nov. 2, 2018, pursuant to reverse takeover acquisition of Thunderbird Entertainment Inc.; basis 1 new for 10 old shs.

Directors - Jennifer (Jenn) Twiner McCarron, chr. & CEO, North Vancouver, B.C.; Mark Trachuk†, Toronto, Ont.; Lisa Coulman; Asha Daniere, Toronto, Ont.; Dr. Azim Jamal, Vancouver, B.C.; Jérôme Levy, N.Y.; Linda G. Michaelson, Calif.

Other Exec. Officers - Matthew Berkowitz, pres. & chief creative officer; Sarah T. Nathanson, COO, gen. counsel & corp. sec.; Barb Harwood, CFO; Richard Goldsmith, pres., global distrib. & consumer products

† Lead director

Capital Stock

	Authorized (shs.)	Outstanding (shs.)[1]
Class A Preferred	unlimited	415,000
Common	unlimited	49,633,087

[1] At Jan. 16, 2023

Class A Preferred - Entitled to annual dividends of 7¢ per share. Convertible into common shares on a 1-for-3 basis. Retractable and redeemable at $1.025 per share, and increasing to $1.05 per share in March 2023. Non-voting.

Common - One vote per share.

Major Shareholder - Voss Capital LLC held 13.25% interest and Frank Giustra held 12.74% interest at Jan. 16, 2023.

Price Range - TBRD/TSX-VEN

Year	Volume	High	Low	Close
2022	9,544,191	$4.55	$2.33	$3.67
2021	18,503,882	$5.44	$2.84	$4.38
2020	17,381,960	$3.20	$0.66	$3.20
2019	8,419,594	$2.53	$0.96	$1.45
2018	2,168,495	$5.00	$1.40	$1.51

Recent Close: $2.95

Capital Stock Changes - During fiscal 2022, common shares were issued as follows: 470,250 on exercise of options, 79,665 on conversion of 239,000 class A preferred shares and 40,975 as management compensation.

Wholly Owned Subsidiaries

Thunderbird Entertainment Inc., Vancouver, B.C.
- 100% int. in **Atomic Cartoons Inc.**, Vancouver, B.C.
- 100% int. in **Great Pacific Media Inc.**, Vancouver, B.C.

Note: The preceding list includes only the major related companies in which interests are held.

Financial Statistics

Periods ended:	12m June 30/22[A]		12m June 30/21[A]
	$000s	%Chg	$000s
Operating revenue	**148,998**	**+34**	**111,519**
Cost of sales	92,610		57,461
Salaries & benefits	13,337		11,306
General & admin expense	6,825		4,780
Stock-based compensation	938		1,168
Operating expense	**113,710**	**+52**	**74,715**
Operating income	**35,288**	**-4**	**36,804**
Deprec., depl. & amort.	27,932		27,494
Finance income	138		197
Finance costs, gross	1,861		667
Pre-tax income	**5,876**	**-29**	**8,221**
Income taxes	2,278		2,531
Net inc. bef. disc. opers	**3,598**	**-37**	**5,690**
Income from disc. opers	nil		47
Net income	**3,598**	**-37**	**5,737**
Cash & equivalent	30,178		22,420
Accounts receivable	96,161		59,123
Current assets	134,334		86,846
Fixed assets, net	29,735		25,957
Intangibles, net	49,033		35,281
Total assets	**223,718**	**+40**	**160,144**
Bank indebtedness	57,299		32,845
Accts. pay. & accr. liabs	27,441		8,400
Current liabilities	127,061		69,386
Long-term debt, gross	367		576
Long-term lease liabilities	21,328		20,303
Preferred share equity	52		82
Shareholders' equity	69,823		63,930
Cash from oper. activs	**(5,562)**	**n.a.**	**22,786**
Cash from fin. activs	16,868		(11,340)
Cash from invest. activs	(4,115)		(1,429)
Net cash position	**30,178**	**+35**	**22,420**
Capital expenditures, net	(4,115)		(1,429)
	$		$
Earns. per sh. bef disc opers*	0.07		0.12
Earnings per share*	0.07		0.12
Cash flow per share*	(0.11)		0.47
	shs		shs
No. of shs. o/s*	49,386,237		48,795,347
Avg. no. of shs. o/s*	49,139,142		47,990,916
	%		%
Net profit margin	2.41		5.10
Return on equity	5.39		9.70
Return on assets	2.47		3.90
Foreign sales percent	78		60

* Common
[A] Reported in accordance with IFRS

Latest Results

Periods ended:	3m Sept. 30/22[A]		3m Sept. 30/21[A]
	$000s	%Chg	$000s
Operating revenue	43,746	+25	35,072
Net income	93	-95	1,886
	$		$
Earnings per share*	0.00		0.04

* Common
[A] Reported in accordance with IFRS

Historical Summary
(as originally stated)

Fiscal Year	Oper. Rev.	Net Inc. Bef. Disc.	EPS*
	$000s	$000s	$
2022[A]	148,998	3,598	0.07
2021[A]	111,519	5,690	0.12
2020[A]	81,289	4,131	0.09
2019[A]	61,478	(3,820)	(0.11)
2018[A1]	142,402	3,361	n.a.

* Common
[A] Reported in accordance with IFRS
[1] Results for 12 months period ended June 30, 2018, pertain to Thunderbird Entertainment Inc.
Note: Adjusted throughout for 1-for-10 cons. in Nov. 2018

T.46 Tidewater Midstream and Infrastructure Ltd.

Symbol - TWM **Exchange** - TSX **CUSIP** - 886453
Head Office - 900-222 3 Ave SW, Calgary, AB, T2P 0B4 **Telephone** - (587) 475-0210 **Fax** - (587) 475-0211
Website - www.tidewatermidstream.com
Email - bnewmarch@tidewatermidstream.com
Investor Relations - Brian Newmarch (587) 475-0210
Auditors - Deloitte LLP C.A., Calgary, Alta.
Lawyers - DLA Piper (Canada) LLP, Calgary, Alta.
Transfer Agents - TSX Trust Company, Calgary, Alta.
FP500 Revenue Ranking - 176
Employees - 446 at Dec. 31, 2022
Profile - (Alta. 2015) Owns, develops and operates energy infrastructure, including downstream facilities, natural gas processing facilities, natural gas liquids (NGL) infrastructure, pipelines, railcars, export terminals, storage and various renewable fuel projects, primarily in Alberta and British Columbia.

Operations are concentrated in the Western Canadian Sedimentary Basin (Deep Basin, Montney and Edmonton regions) and central British Columbia and consist of refining operations, renewable fuels, natural gas processing, NGL extraction, gas storage, crude oil and NGL terminalling infrastructure, and marketing.

Downstream - Owns and operates the 12,000-bbl-per-day Prince George light oil refinery in British Columbia which mainly produces low sulphur diesel and gasoline. The facility has storage capacity of over 1,000,000 bbls of refined product and crude oil, with pipeline, rail and truck connectivity in place.

Midstream - Owns and operates natural gas plants, pipelines, fractionation and straddle plants, storage and transportation facilities in western Canada. Primary assets include the Pipestone gas plant, a 110-mmcf-per-day sour gas processing plant located west of Grande Prairie, Alta., with 20,000 bbl per day of NGL processing capability; Brazeau River Complex (BRC), a 225-mmcf-per-day gas processing facility located west of Drayton Valley, Alta., with a 10,000-bbl-per-day fractionation facility; and 95% operated working interest in Ram River gas plant, a 600-mmcf-per-day sour gas processing facility located west of Rocky Mountain House, Alta. Operations also include three ethane extraction plants in the greater Edmonton area; the Valhalla liquids blending facility located north of Grande Prairie; and the Acheson Terminal with blending and rail facilities located west of Edmonton. In addition, holds interests in natural gas storage facilities located at the BRC and the Pipestone area in Alberta, with total storage capacity of more than 200 bcf.

Marketing and Other - Purchases, transports, sells, stores and blends crude oil, refined product, natural gas, NGL and renewable products and services to customers across North America, including integrated oil and gas companies, producers, refineries and retail customers. Marketing to customers are conducted through the company's pipeline and rail systems. Also conducts minor oil and gas production primarily in northwestern Alberta.

Through **Tidewater Renewables Ltd.** (68.85% owned), focuses on the production of low carbon fuels, including renewable diesel, renewable hydrogen and renewable natural gas, as well as carbon capture projects.

Recent Merger and Acquisition Activity

Status: completed **Revised:** Dec. 23, 2022
UPDATE: The transaction was completed. PREVIOUS: Tidewater Midstream and Infrastructure Ltd. agreed to acquire the remaining 50% interest in Tidewater Brazeau Gas Storage Limited Partnership for $10,500,000 if the transaction closes prior to Dec. 31, 2022. Tidewater Midstream has until Jan. 31, 2024, to close the transaction, subject to purchase price escalation clause of 15% per annum commencing Jan. 1, 2023. Tidewater Brazeau owns and operates a natural gas storage facility (Brazeau Nisku A) at the Brazeau River Complex in Alberta.

Directors - Thomas P. Dea, chr., Toronto, Ont.; Robert F. (Rob) Colcleugh, interim CEO, Calgary, Alta.; Douglas S. Fraser†, Calgary, Alta.; Neil C. McCarron, Toronto, Ont.; Margaret A. (Greta) Raymond, Calgary, Alta.; Michael J. Salamon, Toronto, Ont.; Gail L. Yester, Calgary, Alta.

Other Exec. Officers - Terrence Dumont, COO, midstream; Brian Newmarch, CFO; Reed L. McDonnell, chief comml. officer; David A. J. Barva, exec. v-p, shared srvcs., chief legal officer & corp. sec.; Brent Booth, exec. v-p, mktg. & comml. bus. devel.; Jeff T. Ketch, exec. v-p, field opers.; Jarvis A. Williams, pres., downstream
† Lead director

Capital Stock

	Authorized (shs.)	Outstanding (shs.)[1]
Preferred	unlimited	nil
Common	unlimited	424,852,930

[1] At Apr. 17, 2023

Major Shareholder - Birch Hill Equity Partners Management Inc. held 22.68% interest at Apr. 17, 2023.

Price Range - TWM/TSX

Year	Volume	High	Low	Close
2022	116,349,011	$1.72	$0.97	$1.01
2021	90,558,502	$1.58	$0.80	$1.30
2020	115,453,186	$1.18	$0.34	$0.82
2019	121,109,948	$1.55	$0.94	$1.17
2018	90,992,579	$1.60	$1.20	$1.30

Recent Close: $0.98

Capital Stock Changes - In August and September 2022, bought deal public offering of 48,392,000 units (1 common share & ½ warrant), including 6,312,000 units on over-allotment option, and concurrent private placement of 31,770,833 units (1 common share & ½ warrant), including 3,020,833 units on over-allotment option, all at $1.20 per unit were completed. Also during 2022, 2,700,000 common shares were issued under long-term incentive plan.

Dividends

TWM com Ra $0.04 pa Q est. Oct. 31, 2015

Wholly Owned Subsidiaries

Tidewater Brazeau Gas Storage Limited Partnership, Alta.

Subsidiaries

85% int. in **Tidewater Pipestone Infrastructure Limited Partnership**, Alta.
68.83% int. in **Tidewater Renewables Ltd.**, Calgary, Alta. (see separate coverage)

Investments

50% int. in **Rimrock Cattle Company Ltd.**, Alta.
Note: The preceding list includes only the major related companies in which interests are held.

Financial Statistics

Periods ended:	12m Dec. 31/22[A]		12m Dec. 31/21[oA]
	$000s	%Chg	$000s
Operating revenue	**2,875,200**	**+69**	**1,698,400**
General & admin expense	36,900		26,300
Stock-based compensation	13,500		6,700
Other operating expense	2,643,800		1,531,200
Operating expense	**2,696,900**	**+72**	**1,564,200**
Operating income	**178,300**	**+33**	**134,200**
Deprec., depl. & amort.	84,400		81,800
Finance costs, gross	69,900		68,400
Investment income	(11,600)		1,300
Write-downs/write-offs	(55,000)[1]		nil
Pre-tax income	**26,500**	**-72**	**94,200**
Income taxes	7,600		20,300
Net income	**18,900**	**-74**	**73,900**
Net inc. for equity hldrs	**8,500**	**-88**	**71,500**
Net inc. for non-cont. int	**10,400**	**+333**	**2,400**
Cash & equivalent	17,000		15,800
Inventories	87,900		59,400
Accounts receivable	269,900		242,900
Current assets	450,900		362,400
Long-term investments	94,500		61,200
Fixed assets, net	1,570,800		1,376,300
Right-of-use assets	92,800		121,300
Total assets	**2,274,600**	**+15**	**1,970,600**
Accts. pay. & accr. liabs	423,400		265,000
Current liabilities	546,600		524,100
Long-term debt, gross	736,700		684,800
Long-term debt, net	736,700		541,200
Long-term lease liabilities	133,600		158,400
Equity portion of conv. debs	4,900		4,900
Shareholders' equity	703,300		616,600
Non-controlling interest	43,000		26,100
Cash from oper. activs	**242,900**	**+92**	**126,700**
Cash from fin. activs	37,900		(140,600)
Cash from invest. activs	(279,600)		19,800
Net cash position	**17,000**	**+8**	**15,800**
Capital expenditures	(349,300)		(116,800)
Capital disposals	14,700		139,200
	$		$
Earnings per share*	0.02		0.21
Cash flow per share*	0.65		0.37
Cash divd. per share*	0.04		0.05
	shs		shs
No. of shs. o/s*	424,500,000		341,600,000
Avg. no. of shs. o/s*	372,100,000		339,800,000
	%		%
Net profit margin	0.66		4.35
Return on equity	1.29		13.71
Return on assets	3.24		6.65
No. of employees (FTEs)	446		419

* Common
[o] Restated
[A] Reported in accordance with IFRS
[1] Pertains to impairment of non-core assets in the Deep Basin CGU.

Latest Results

Periods ended:	3m Mar. 31/23[A]		3m Mar. 31/22[A]
	$000s	%Chg	$000s
Operating revenue	614,500	-7	658,424
Net income	(31,000)	n.a.	47,024
Net inc. for equity hldrs	(24,800)	n.a.	41,220
Net inc. for non-cont. int	(6,200)		5,804
	$		$
Earnings per share*	(0.06)		0.12

* Common
[A] Reported in accordance with IFRS

Historical Summary
(as originally stated)

Fiscal Year	Oper. Rev.	Net Inc. Bef. Disc.	EPS*
	$000s	$000s	$
2022[A]	2,875,200	18,900	0.02
2021[A]	1,698,361	73,910	0.21
2020[A]	979,406	(35,178)	(0.10)
2019[A]	692,268	(15,500)	(0.04)
2018[A]	324,290	19,340	0.06

* Common
[A] Reported in accordance with IFRS

T.47 Tidewater Renewables Ltd.

Symbol - LCFS **Exchange** - TSX **CUSIP** - 88646L
Head Office - 900-222 3 Ave SW, Calgary, AB, T2P 0B4 **Telephone** - (587) 475-0210 **Fax** - (587) 475-0211
Website - tidewater-renewables.com
Email - rkwan@tidewater-renewables.com
Investor Relations - Raymond Kwan (587) 776-0042
Auditors - Deloitte LLP C.A., Calgary, Alta.
Lawyers - DLA Piper (Canada) LLP, Calgary, Alta.
Transfer Agents - TSX Trust Company, Calgary, Alta.
Employees - 36 at Dec. 31, 2022
Profile - (Alta. 2021) Owns, develops and operates clean fuels projects and related infrastructure, with a focus on the production of low carbon fuels, including renewable diesel, renewable hydrogen and renewable natural gas, as well as carbon capture.

Operations are organized into three business units: renewable diesel; renewable hydrogen; and renewable natural gas (RNG).

Renewable diesel and hydrogen assets are co-located at **Tidewater Midstream and Infrastructure Ltd.** (TMIL)'s light oil refinery in Prince George, B.C., and include a 300-bbl-per-day canola co-processing project, which was placed in service in the fourth quarter of 2021 and has been producing renewable diesel and gasoline from canola oil; a 300-bbl-per-day fluid catalytic cracking (FCC) co-processing project (wood-based biocrude), which was placed in service in the second quarter of 2023; and a 3,000-bbl-per-day stand-alone renewable diesel and renewable hydrogen complex capable of processing various renewable feedstock, which was expected to commence commercial operations in late August 2023.

RNG projects include a gas storage facility at TMIL's Brazeau River Complex in Alberta; a 51% interest (**Rimrock RNG Inc.** 49%) in an anaerobic digestion facility near High River, Alta., which was expected to be commissioned by the end of 2023; and a proposed gasifier utilizing woody biomass that may be constructed at TMIL's Ram River gas plant in Alberta.

The company plans to supply low carbon fuels to investment grade offtakers, existing customers, government entities, Indigenous groups and others in the transportation, utilities, refining, marketing and power industries.

In April 2022, the company entered into a partnership agreement with Alberta-based **Rimrock RNG Inc.** to build and evaluate renewable natural gas (RNG) facilities across North America, with the company and Rimrock holding a 51% and 49% interest, respectively, in the partnership.

In addition, the company committed to invest $30,000,000, payable in four equal quarterly instalments commencing in April 2022, in exchange for a 50% interest in Alberta-based **Rimrock Cattle Company Ltd.**, a cattle feeding operation and cattle marketer in North America, with operations in Alberta, Saskatchewan, Colorado, Texas, New Mexico, Iowa and Nebraska. The investment would secure feedstock supply for both the company's RNG and renewable diesel business units.

Directors - Robert F. (Rob) Colcleugh, chr. & interim CEO, Calgary, Alta.; John Adams, Ottawa, Ont.; Simon Bregazzi, Calgary, Alta.; Margaret A. (Greta) Raymond, Calgary, Alta.

Other Exec. Officers - Raymond (Ray) Kwan, CFO; Krasen V. Chervenkov, exec. v-p, bus. devel. & strategy; Andrea Decore, exec. v-p, strategy & corp. devel.; Scott McLean, exec. v-p, opers.; Bryan Morin, corp. sec. & chief legal officer

Capital Stock

	Authorized (shs.)	Outstanding (shs.)[1]
Preferred	unlimited	nil
Common	unlimited	34,726,000

[1] At Aug. 9, 2023

Major Shareholder - Tidewater Midstream and Infrastructure Ltd. held 68.83% interest at Apr. 17, 2023.

Price Range - LCFS/TSX

Year	Volume	High	Low	Close
2022	2,312,685	$15.34	$9.15	$11.51
2021	3,285,625	$15.48	$13.41	$14.72

Recent Close: $7.89

Capital Stock Changes - During 2022, 7,000 common shares were issued under long-term incentive plan.

Subsidiaries

51% int. in **Rimrock Renewables Limited Partnership**, Alta.

Investments

50% int. in **Rimrock Cattle Company Ltd.**, Alta.

Financial Statistics

Periods ended:	12m Dec. 31/22[A]		33w Dec. 31/21[A]
	$000s	%Chg	$000s
Operating revenue	**76,099**	**n.a.**	**23,055**
General & admin expense	5,834		853
Stock-based compensation	3,217		680
Other operating expense	29,971		7,374
Operating expense	**39,022**	**n.a.**	**8,907**
Operating income	**37,077**	**n.a.**	**14,148**
Deprec., depl. & amort.	19,443		6,707
Finance costs, gross	7,547		1,476
Pre-tax income	**35,908**	**n.a.**	**3,997**
Income taxes	9,966		1,234
Net income	**25,942**	**n.a.**	**2,763**
Cash & equivalent	11,379		1,022
Inventories	24,579		nil
Accounts receivable	3,905		7,023
Current assets	54,328		9,062
Long-term investments	30,321		nil
Fixed assets, net	879,677		699,271
Right-of-use assets	19,066		22,659
Total assets	**993,321**	**+36**	**730,992**
Accts. pay. & accr. liabs	55,299		1,780
Current liabilities	81,611		7,315
Long-term debt, gross	198,364		58,952
Long-term debt, net	198,364		58,952
Long-term lease liabilities	14,873		17,377
Shareholders' equity	543,625		515,596
Non-controlling interest	6,500		nil
Cash from oper. activs	**67,444**	**n.a.**	**8,187**
Cash from fin. activs	137,408		205,981
Cash from invest. activs	(194,495)		(213,146)
Net cash position	**11,379**	**n.m.**	**1,022**
Capital expenditures	(244,576)		(30,974)
	$		$
Earnings per share*	0.75		0.14
Cash flow per share*	1.94		0.41
	shs		shs
No. of shs. o/s*	34,719,000		34,712,000
Avg. no. of shs. o/s*	34,712,000		19,901,000
	%		%
Net profit margin	34.09		...
Return on equity	4.90		...
Return on assets	3.64		...
No. of employees (FTEs)	36		3

* Common
[A] Reported in accordance with IFRS

Latest Results

Periods ended:	6m June 30/23[A]		6m June 30/22[A]
	$000s	%Chg	$000s
Operating revenue	33,059	-11	36,980
Net income	(18,823)	n.a.	21,877
	$		$
Earnings per share*	(0.54)		0.63

* Common
[A] Reported in accordance with IFRS

Historical Summary
(as originally stated)

Fiscal Year	Oper. Rev.	Net Inc. Bef. Disc.	EPS*
	$000s	$000s	$
2022[A]	76,099	25,942	0.75
2021[A1]	23,055	2,763	0.14
2020[A2]	4,165	(12,696)	n.a.
2019[A]	4,457	(7,377)	n.a.

* Common
[A] Reported in accordance with IFRS
[1] 33 weeks ended Dec. 31, 2021.
[2] Results represent carve-out financial statements of renewable diesel & hydrogen assets and renewable natural gas business of Tidewater Midstream and Infrastructure Ltd.

T.48 Tier One Capital Limited Partnership

Symbol - TLP.UN **Exchange** - CSE **CUSIP** - 88650W
Head Office - 503-56 The Esplanade, Toronto, ON, M5E 1A7 **Telephone** - (416) 203-7331 **Fax** - (416) 203-6630
Website - www.tier1capital.ca
Email - jrichardson@tier1capital.ca
Investor Relations - John M. A. Richardson (416) 203-7331 ext. 228
Auditors - RSM Canada LLP C.A., Toronto, Ont.
Lawyers - McMillan LLP, Toronto, Ont.
Transfer Agents - TSX Trust Company, Toronto, Ont.
Investment Advisors - B.E.S.T. Investment Counsel Limited, Toronto, Ont.
Profile - (Ont. 2014) Invests primarily in convertible debt, equity and equity-related securities of rapidly growing Canadian companies in the technology, healthcare, resource and financial services industries.

At Mar. 31, 2023, the investment portfolio had a fair value of $22,182,810 compared with $22,745,578 at Dec. 31, 2022. The portfolio includes investments in media technology, health care and health care information technology, security software and services, energy, and other technology and financial sectors.

T1 General Partner LP is the general partner of the limited partnership.

In October 2022, the limited partnership completed the en bloc acquisition of the portfolio of **VentureLink Innovation Fund Inc.** for $1,596,551. The portfolio includes securities of **MMB Research Inc.**, **Pitchpoint Solutions Inc.**, **WF Fund IV Limited Partnership**, **DCT Strategies Inc.**, **Peraso Technologies Inc.**, **Performance Plants Inc.**, **Upsight Inc.** and **Panorama Software Inc.**

Predecessor Detail - Succeeded The Business, Engineering, Science & Technology Discoveries Fund Inc., July 11, 2014, following acquisition of the assets of the fund by Tier One.

Oper. Subsid./Mgt. Co. Directors - John W. Nyholt, chr., Oakville, Ont.; John M. A. Richardson, CEO, Waterdown, Ont.; Thomas W. R. (Tom) Lunan, CFO, Toronto, Ont.; Robert J. (Bob) Roy, Toronto, Ont.; Steven Watzeck

Oper. Subsid./Mgt. Co. Officers - Alan V. Chettiar, corp. sec.

Capital Stock

	Authorized (shs.)	Outstanding (shs.)[1]
Limited Partnership Unit	unlimited	4,613,561

[1] At Mar. 31, 2023

Normal Course Issuer Bid - The company plans to make normal course purchases of up to 227,364 limited partnership units representing 5% of the public float. The bid commenced on Oct. 6, 2022, and expires on Oct. 5, 2023.

Major Shareholder - John M. A. Richardson held 16.72% interest at Mar. 31, 2023.

Price Range - TLP.UN/CSE

Year	Volume	High	Low	Close
2022	255,440	$4.49	$2.01	$3.75
2021	189,831	$4.00	$3.00	$3.60
2020	157,692	$5.15	$3.00	$3.55
2019	397,764	$5.50	$3.50	$5.00
2018	155,133	$6.00	$4.25	$4.80

Recent Close: $2.61

Capital Stock Changes - During 2022, 186,821 limited partnership units were issued under distribution reinvestment plan and 43,700 limited partnership units were repurchased under a Normal Course Issuer Bid.

Dividends

TLP.UN ltd ptnrshp unit Ra $0.50 pa Q est. July 28, 2017**
** Reinvestment Option

Financial Statistics

Periods ended:	12m Dec. 31/22[A]		12m Dec. 31/21[A]
	$000s	%Chg	$000s
Total revenue	**(1,937)**	**n.a.**	**10,201**
General & admin. expense	555		487
Operating expense	**555**	**+14**	**487**
Operating income	**(2,492)**	**n.a.**	**9,713**
Pre-tax income	**(3,289)**	**n.a.**	**8,960**
Net income	**(3,289)**	**n.a.**	**8,960**
Cash & equivalent	1,080		3,183
Accounts receivable	19		2
Investments	22,746		25,737
Total assets	**23,845**	**-18**	**28,922**
Accts. pay. & accr. liabs	120		124
Shareholders' equity	23,540		28,575
Cash from oper. activs	**(357)**	**n.a.**	**3,568**
Cash from fin. activs	(1,746)		(2,029)
Net cash position	**1,080**	**-66**	**3,183**
	$		$
Earnings per share*	(0.73)		2.05
Cash flow per share*	(0.08)		0.82
Cash divd. per share*	0.50		0.50
	shs		shs
No. of shs. o/s*	4,574,397		4,431,276
Avg. no. of shs. o/s*	4,513,664		4,366,739
	%		%
Net profit margin	n.m.		87.83
Return on equity	(12.62)		35.68
Return on assets	(12.47)		35.16

* LP Unit
[A] Reported in accordance with IFRS

Latest Results

Periods ended:	3m Mar. 31/23[A]		3m Mar. 31/22[A]
	$000s	%Chg	$000s
Total revenue	316	n.a.	(35)
Net income	17	n.a.	(394)
	$		$
Earnings per share*	0.00		(0.09)

* LP Unit
[A] Reported in accordance with IFRS

Historical Summary
(as originally stated)

Fiscal Year	Total Rev.	Net Inc. Bef. Disc.	EPS*
	$000s	$000s	$
2022[A]	(1,937)	(3,289)	(0.73)
2021[A]	10,201	8,960	2.05
2020[A]	1,392	(260)	(0.06)
2019[A]	3,004	1,714	0.42
2018[A]	(5,240)	(7,508)	(1.91)

* LP Unit
[A] Reported in accordance with IFRS

T.49 Tiidal Gaming Group Corp.

Symbol - TIDL **Exchange** - CSE **CUSIP** - 88635T
Head Office - 800-365 Bay St, Toronto, ON, M5H 2V1 **Telephone** - (647) 987-5083
Website - tiidal.gg
Email - tom@tiidal.gg
Investor Relations - Thomas Hearne (416) 560-0528
Auditors - MNP LLP C.A., Mississauga, Ont.
Transfer Agents - Odyssey Trust Company, Toronto, Ont.
Employees - 22 at Mar. 10, 2022
Profile - (Ont. 2006) Seeking new business opportunities.

In November 2022, the company sold the assets of wholly owned **Lazarus Esports Inc.**, which is a professional eSports organization that competes in a variety of areas, to **TGS Esports Inc.**

Recent Merger and Acquisition Activity

Status: completed **Revised:** June 9, 2023
UPDATE: The transaction was completed. The sale of Sportsflare constituted the sale of substantially all of the assets and operating activities of Tiidal. PREVIOUS: Tiidal Gaming Group Corp. agreed to sell wholly owned Tiidal Gaming NZ Limited to Entain Holdings (UK) Limited for $13,250,000 in cash. Apr. 26, 2023 - Tiidal Gaming Group shareholders approved the transaction.

Predecessor Detail - Name changed from GTA Financecorp Inc., Nov. 9, 2021, pursuant to the reverse takeover acquisition of Tiidal Gaming Group Inc. and concurrent amalgamation of Tiidal with wholly owned 2852773 Ontario Inc. (and continued as Tiidal Gaming Holdings Inc.).; basis 1 new for 11.2678 old shs.

Directors - Thomas (Tom) Hearne, CEO, Ont.; Neil Duffy, Toronto, Ont.; Zachary Goldenberg, Toronto, Ont.; David Wang, Las Vegas, Nev.

Other Exec. Officers - Carlo Rigillo, CFO; Maksymilian (Max) Polaczuk, chief tech. officer; Charlie Watson, chief gaming officer; Christopher (Chris) Herrmann, v-p, eng.; Kenny Jang, v-p, product

Capital Stock

	Authorized (shs.)	Outstanding (shs.)[1]
Common	unlimited	87,603,908

[1] At June 9, 2023

Major Shareholder - Pritpal Singh held 11.52% interest and Zachary Goldenberg held 10.85% interest at Mar. 27, 2023.

Price Range - TIDL/CSE

Year	Volume	High	Low	Close
2022	12,128,968	$0.35	$0.07	$0.10
2021	2,704,078	$0.30	$0.16	$0.24
2019	449,164	$0.34	$0.17	$0.17
2018	1,042,577	$0.62	$0.17	$0.17

Consolidation: 1-for-11.2678 cons. in Nov. 2021
Recent Close: $0.10

Capital Stock Changes - In December 2022, private placement of 2,961,907 units (1 common share & 1 warrant) at 10¢ per unit was completed, with warrants exercisable at 15¢ per share for three years.

On Nov. 9, 2021, common shares were consolidated on a 1-for-11.2678 basis and 68,460,125 post-consolidated common shares were issued pursuant to the reverse takeover acquisition of Tiidal Gaming Group Inc. Also during fiscal 2022, post-consolidated common shares were issued as follows: 6,950,601 by private placement, 1,237,373 on exercise of warrants, 191,070 on exercise of options and 112,136 for debt settlement.

Wholly Owned Subsidiaries

GTA GW Mergeco, Inc., Del.
Tiidal Gaming Holdings Inc., Toronto, Ont.
- 100% int. in **Lazarus Esports Inc.**, Ont.
- 100% int. in **Space Esports Inc.**, Del.
- 100% int. in **Tiidal Gaming Canada Inc.**, Ont.
- 100% int. in **Tiidal Gaming US Corp.**, United States.

Financial Statistics

Periods ended:	12m Oct. 31/22[A1]		12m Oct. 31/21[A2]
	$000s	%Chg	$000s
Operating revenue	**358**	**-17**	**429**
Cost of sales	196		241
Salaries & benefits	1,978		307
General & admin expense	1,801		1,010
Stock-based compensation	2,268		505
Operating expense	**6,244**	**+203**	**2,063**
Operating income	**(5,886)**	**n.a.**	**(1,634)**
Deprec., depl. & amort.	262		205
Finance income	1		nil
Finance costs, gross	56		37
Write-downs/write-offs	(17)		nil
Pre-tax income	**(7,419)**	**n.a.**	**(1,950)**
Net income	**(7,419)**	**n.a.**	**(1,950)**
Cash & equivalent	16		23
Accounts receivable	302		87
Current assets	356		3,841
Fixed assets, net	15		15
Right-of-use assets	152		224
Intangibles, net	1,573		2,017
Total assets	**2,096**	**-66**	**6,097**
Bank indebtedness	nil		4,000
Accts. pay. & accr. liabs	985		1,137
Current liabilities	1,032		5,195
Long-term lease liabilities	96		177
Shareholders' equity	933		665
Cash from oper. activs	**(3,936)**	**n.a.**	**(430)**
Cash from fin. activs	3,975		388
Cash from invest. activs	(9)		(46)
Net cash position	**16**	**-30**	**23**
Capital expenditures	(19)		(6)
	$		$
Earnings per share*	(0.10)		(0.03)
Cash flow per share*	(0.05)		(0.01)
	shs		shs
No. of shs. o/s*	80,231,301		n.a.
Avg. no. of shs. o/s*	72,799,126		55,880,687
	%		%
Net profit margin	n.m.		(454.55)
Return on equity	(928.54)		n.m.
Return on assets	(179.74)		(61.34)

* Common
[A] Reported in accordance with IFRS
[1] Results reflect the Nov. 9, 2021, reverse takeover acquisition of Tiidal Gaming Group Inc.
[2] Results pertain to Tiidal Gaming Holdings Inc. (formerly Tiidal Gaming Group Inc.)

Latest Results

Periods ended:	3m Jan. 31/23[A]		3m Jan. 31/22[¤A]
	$000s	%Chg	$000s
Operating revenue	76	+485	13
Net inc. bef. disc. opers	(1,062)	n.a.	(3,732)
Income from disc. opers	(5)		(140)
Net income	(1,067)	n.a.	(3,872)
	$		$
Earns. per sh. bef. disc. opers.*	(0.01)		(0.05)
Earnings per share*	(0.01)		(0.06)

* Common
[¤] Restated
[A] Reported in accordance with IFRS

Historical Summary
(as originally stated)

Fiscal Year	Oper. Rev.	Net Inc. Bef. Disc.	EPS*
	$000s	$000s	$
2022[A]	358	(7,419)	(0.10)
2021[A]	429	(1,950)	(0.03)
2020[A1]	578	(1,481)	(0.03)
2019[A1]	5,197	(4,514)	(0.09)
2018[A2]	nil	(1,004)	(0.23)

* Common
[A] Reported in accordance with IFRS
[1] Results pertain to Tiidal Gaming Group Inc.
[2] Results for fiscal 2018 and prior fiscal years pertain to GTA Resources and Mining Inc.

Note: Adjusted throughout for 1-for-11.2678 cons. in Nov. 2021

T.50 Till Capital Corporation

Symbol - TIL **Exchange** - TSX-VEN **CUSIP** - G8875E
Head Office - 1324 N. Liberty Lake Rd, Unit 258, Liberty Lake, WA, United States, 99019 **Telephone** - (208) 635-5415 **Fax** - (208) 635-5465
Website - tillcap.com
Email - info@tillcap.com
Investor Relations - Brian P. Lupien (208) 635-5415
Auditors - PricewaterhouseCoopers LLP C.A., Vancouver, B.C.
Lawyers - Stikeman Elliott LLP, Vancouver, B.C.
Transfer Agents - Olympia Trust Company
Profile - (B.C. 2019; orig. Bermuda, 2012) Holds interests in private and public resource companies, and owns **Omega Insurance Holdings Inc.**, which is held pending for sale.

Subsidiary **Silver Predator Corp.** has mineral interests in Nevada and Idaho. Wholly owned **Golden Predator U.S. Holding Corp.** holds formerly producing Springer tungsten mine and mill in Pershing cty., Nev. The Springer tungsten mine and mill are classified as held for sale. In addition, as at Sept. 30 2022, wholly owned **Till Management Company** holds 33.3% interest in **IG Far East LLC**, which holds a majority interest in Durmin gold property in Russia; 1% interest in **Osisko Development Corp.** (ODV), which has mineral interests in British Columbia, Quebec, Mexico and Utah; and 7.6% interest in **IG Tintic LLC**, which holds a 2% NSR royalty on a property located in the East Tintic District of Utah owned by ODV.

Wholly owned Omega Insurance Holdings operates through **Omega General Insurance Company**, a fully licensed insurance provider and targets the Canadian run-off and start-up phase, and **Focus Group, Inc.**, a provider of management and consulting services to the insurance industry. The company plans to sell Omega Insurance Holdings and has been classified as discontinued operation since 2019.

In June 2021, the company agreed to sell wholly owned **Omega Insurance Holdings, Inc.** to **Accelerant Holdings** for Cdn$13,126,000. As of December 2022, the transaction is still pending. Omega Insurance operates a fully licensed insurance business and a management and consulting services business.

In December 2022, the company entered into a share purchase agreement with a private company for the sale of wholly owned **Springer Mining Company** for terms not yet determined. Springer Mining holds formerly producing Springer tungsten mine and mill in Nevada.

In October 2022, the company terminated its memorandum of understanding for the potential acquisition of Springer tungsten mine and mill in Nevada by a private company for US$5,000,000.

Common reinstated on TSX-VEN, June 20, 2023.
Common suspended from TSX-VEN, June 6, 2023.

Predecessor Detail - Name changed from Till Capital Ltd., Nov. 22, 2019.

Directors - Brian P. Lupien, CEO, Wash.; Robert Forness, Paget, Bermuda; Scott D. McLeod, Reno, Nev.; Dr. John T. (Terry) Rickard, Colo.; James G. Rickards, N.H.

Other Exec. Officers - Weiying (Mary) Zhu, CFO; Edie Nemri, corp. sec.

Capital Stock

	Authorized (shs.)	Outstanding (shs.)[1]	Par
Preference	1,000,000	nil	
Restricted Voting	11,000,000	3,191,462	US$0.001

[1] At Nov. 2, 2022

Restricted Voting - Restricted voting rights, whereby no single shareholder is able to exercise voting rights for more than 9.9% of the voting rights of the total outstanding. However, if any one shareholder beneficially owns or exercises control over more than 50% of the shares outstanding, the 9.9% restriction will no longer apply.

Normal Course Issuer Bid - The company plans to make normal course purchases of up to 253,600 restricted voting shares representing 10% of the public float. The bid commenced on Sept. 26, 2022, and expires on Sept. 27, 2023.

Major Shareholder - Widely held at Nov. 2, 2022.

Price Range - TIL/TSX-VEN

Year	Volume	High	Low	Close
2022	73,864	$7.00	$4.20	$5.40
2021	151,448	$10.45	$4.55	$5.25
2020	81,761	$4.65	$1.60	$4.06
2019	38,283	$2.54	$1.00	$2.00
2018	223,080	$5.60	$1.74	$2.01

Recent Close: $3.18

Wholly Owned Subsidiaries

Omega Insurance Holdings Inc., Toronto, Ont.
- 100% int. in **Focus Group Inc.**, Toronto, Ont.
- 100% int. in **Omega General Insurance Company**, Canada.

Till Capital U.S. Holding Corp., Nev.
- 100% int. in **Golden Predator U.S. Holding Corp.**, Nev.
  - 100% int. in **Springer Mining Company**, Nev.
- 100% int. in **Till Management Company**, Nev.
  - 33.3% int. in **IG Far East LLC**
  - 7.6% int. in **IG Tintic LLC**

Subsidiaries

51.82% int. in **Silver Predator Corp.**, Hayden Lake, Idaho. (see Survey of Mines)

Financial Statistics

Periods ended:	12m Dec. 31/21[A]		12m Dec. 31/20[A]
	US$000s	%Chg	US$000s
Total revenue	**6,761**	**n.a.**	**(450)**
Salaries & benefits	741		464
General & admin. expense	880		566
Stock-based compensation	384		nil
Other operating expense	(1,383)[1]		nil
Operating expense	**623**	**-40**	**1,030**
Operating income	**6,138**	**n.a.**	**(1,480)**
Deprec. & amort.	3		8
Write-downs/write-offs	nil		(484)
Pre-tax income	**5,985**	**n.a.**	**(2,374)**
Income taxes	1,206		(21)
Net inc. bef. disc. opers	**4,779**	**n.a.**	**(2,353)**
Income from disc. opers	(3)		747
Net income	**4,776**	**n.a.**	**(1,606)**
Net inc. for equity hldrs	**4,805**	**n.a.**	**(1,560)**
Net inc. for non-cont. int	**(29)**	**n.a.**	**(46)**
Cash & equivalent	611		1,794
Accounts receivable	3		8
Investments	12,990		3,004
Explor./devel. properties	299		383
Total assets	**70,894**	**+14**	**62,120**
Bank indebtedness	1,212		nil
Accts. pay. & accr. liabs	68		179
Shareholders' equity	25,166		19,405
Non-controlling interest	156		93
Cash from oper. activs	**(1,116)**	**n.a.**	**1,562**
Cash from fin. activs	1,098		(68)
Cash from invest. activs	(1,392)		(5,491)
Net cash position	**611**	**-66**	**1,794**
Capital expenditures, net	54		(142)
	US$		US$
Earns. per sh. bef disc opers*	1.51		(0.72)
Earnings per share*	1.51		(0.49)
Cash flow per share*	(0.35)		0.49
	shs		shs
No. of shs. o/s*	3,191,462		3,191,462
Avg. no. of shs. o/s*	3,191,462		3,191,461
	%		%
Net profit margin	70.68		n.m.
Return on equity	21.57		(11.54)
Return on assets	7.19		(3.77)

* Restricted vtg.
[A] Reported in accordance with IFRS
[1] Exploration expense recovery.

Latest Results

Periods ended:	9m Sept. 30/22[A]		9m Sept. 30/21[A]
	US$000s	%Chg	US$000s
Total revenue	(2,828)	n.a.	6,901
Net inc. bef. disc. opers	(2,277)	n.a.	5,124
Income from disc. opers	323		757
Net income	(1,954)	n.a.	5,881
Net inc. for equity hldrs	(1,876)	n.a.	5,952
Net inc. for non-cont. int	(78)		(70)
	US$		US$
Earns. per sh. bef. disc. opers.*	(0.69)		1.63
Earnings per share*	(0.59)		1.86

* Restricted vtg.
[A] Reported in accordance with IFRS

Historical Summary
(as originally stated)

Fiscal Year	Total Rev.	Net Inc. Bef. Disc.	EPS*
	US$000s	US$000s	US$
2021[A]	6,761	4,779	1.51
2020[A]	(450)	(2,353)	(0.72)
2019[A]	(220)	(1,056)	(0.30)
2018[A]	(1,346)	(1,621)	(0.50)
2017[B]	(245)	(1,582)	(0.47)

* Restricted vtg.
[A] Reported in accordance with IFRS
[B] Reported in accordance with U.S. GAAP

T.51 Tilray Brands, Inc.*

Symbol - TLRY **Exchange** - TSX **CUSIP** - 88688T
Head Office - 245 Talbot St W, Leamington, ON, N8H 4H3 **Toll-free** - (844) 845-7291
Website - www.tilray.com
Email - raphael.gross@icrinc.com
Investor Relations - Raphael Gross (203) 682-8253
Auditors - PricewaterhouseCoopers LLP C.A., Oakville, Ont.
Transfer Agents - Odyssey Trust Company, Calgary, Alta.; Philadelphia Stock Transfer, Inc., Ardmore, Pa.
FP500 Revenue Ranking - 379
Employees - 1,600 at May 31, 2023

Profile - (Del. 2018) Produces, distributes and sells cannabis products, alcoholic beverages and hemp-based wellness products, with operations in Canada, the United States, Europe, Australia and Latin America.

Operates in four segments: Cannabis; Distribution; Beverage Alcohol; and Wellness.

Cannabis

Cultivates, produces, distributes and sells medical and adult-use cannabis products across Canada and in other legal international jurisdictions, including Europe, Australia and Latin America. In Canada, the company serves the medical market under the Tilray, Aphria, Broken Coast and Symbios brands as well as the licensed Charlotte's Web brand, and the adult-use market under the B!NGO, The Batch, Dubon, Good Supply, Solei, Chowie Wowie, Canaca, RIFF, Broken Coast, HEXO, Redecan, Original Stash and Bake Sale brands, among others. Internationally, the company's medical cannabis products are available in 21 countries on five continents under the brands Tilray, Aphria, Broken Coast (in Australia only) and Navcora (in Germany only) for commercial purposes, compassionate access and clinical research. Key international operations are located in Portugal, Germany, Italy, the U.K., Australia, New Zealand and Argentina with strategic relationships in Denmark, Luxembourg and Poland.

Operates the 1,400,000-sq.-ft. Aphria One and 1,500,000-sq.-ft. Aphria Diamond (51% owned) cultivation and processing facilities in Leamington, Ont.; a 134,000-sq.-ft. processing facility in London, Ont.; the 47,000-sq.-ft. Broken Coast cultivation and processing facility in Duncan, B.C.; an 18,000-sq.-ft. processing facility and laboratory in Brampton, Ont.; a 400,000-sq.-ft. cultivation and processing facility in Fenwick, Ont.; a 98-acre cultivation site in Cayuga, Ont.; a 1,292,000-sq.-ft. cultivation facility in Gatineau, Que.; a 50,000-sq.-ft. cannabidiol (CBD) extraction site in Fort Collins, Colo.; a 3,300,000-sq.-ft. cultivation and processing campus in Cantanhede, Portugal; a 65,000-sq.-ft. cultivation facility in Neümunster, Germany; and a 4,700-sq.-ft. distribution facility in Vado Ligure, Italy.

Distribution

Operations consist of the purchase and resale of pharmaceutical products primarily through wholly owned **CC Pharma GmbH**, which imports and distributes pharmaceuticals for the German market from its 70,000-sq.-ft. facility in Densborn, Germany; and wholly owned **ABP, S.A.**, which holds a 10,000-sq.-ft. facility in Buenos Aires, Argentina.

Beverage Alcohol

Manufactures, distributes and sells bottled, canned and draft premium craft beers under the SweetWater, Green Flash, Alpine and Montauk brands, and bourbon whiskey and craft spirits under the Breckenridge Distillery brand. Operations consist of a 158,000-sq.-ft. brewery and taproom in Atlanta, Ga.; a 4,000-sq.-ft. brewery and taproom in Montauk, N.Y.; a 33,000-sq.-ft. brewery and taproom in Fort Collins, Colo.; a 23,000-sq.-ft. distillery in Breckenridge, Colo.; and a 75,000-sq.-ft. warehouse in Denver, Colo. SweetWater, Green Flash, Alpine and Montauk products are distributed in retail stores, restaurants and bars in the U.S., as well as through limited distribution of SweetWater within Ontario and Quebec. Breckenridge products are available in all 50 U.S. states and in two owned tasting and retail store locations in Colorado, as well as in eight different countries.

Wellness

Manufactures, markets and distributes hemp-based food and CBD wellness products under the Manitoba Harvest, Hemp Yeah!, Just Hemp Foods and Happy Flower. brands. Products are sold through retailers, wholesalers and online in the U.S., Canada and 18 other countries. Operations include hemp processing facilities in Winnipeg (15,000 sq. ft.) and St. Agathe (35,000 sq. ft.), Man.

During fiscal 2023, the company sold wholly owned **ASG Pharma Ltd.**, which operated an 8,700-sq.-ft. processing facility and laboratory in Malta. Terms were not disclosed.

In November 2022, the company entered into an agreement with **Charlotte's Web Holdings, Inc.** to license, manufacture and distribute Charlotte's Web™ full spectrum CBD products in Canada. The company would acquire and extract Charlotte's Web's proprietary hemp biomass, harvested from Canadian-grown hemp cultivars, and manufacture into final product at its production facilities in Canada.

Recent Merger and Acquisition Activity

Status: pending **Announced:** Aug. 18, 2023
Tilray Brands, Inc. agreed to acquire the remaining 57.5% interest in private Etobicoke, Ont.-based Truss Beverage Co., which produces and sells cannabis beverages in Canada including XMG, Mollo, House of Terpenes and Little Victory, from Molson Coors Beverage Company for an undisclosed amount.

Status: pending **Announced:** Aug. 7, 2023
Tilray Brands, Inc. agreed to acquire to eight U.S. craft beer and beverage brands from Anheuser-Busch InBev SA/NV for an undisclosed amount payable in cash. The brands Tilray will be acquiring are Shock Top, Breckenridge Brewery, Blue Point Brewing Company, 10 Barrel Brewing Company, Redhook Brewery, Widmer Brothers Brewing, Square Mile Cider Company, and HiBall Energy. The acquisition includes four production facilities and eight brew pubs. The transaction was expected to close in 2023.

Status: completed **Revised:** June 22, 2023
UPDATE: The transaction was completed. PREVIOUS: Tilray Brands, Inc. agreed to acquire HEXO Corp. on the basis of 0.4352 Tilray common shares for each HEXO common share held, which implies a purchase price of US$1.25 per share. Concurrently, the parties also entered into an agreement which, among other things, provides for a waiver by Tilray of, and the amendment to, certain covenants under the amended and restated senior secured convertible note due 2026 issued by HEXO and held by Tilray to mitigate the risk of covenant breaches by HEXO until the consummation of the transaction and to allow HEXO to use existing cash resources to satisfy its ongoing payment and contractual obligations and operate its business. In consideration for the waivers and amendments, HEXO has agreed to pay, and in certain cases accelerate the payment of, various amounts owing to Tilray under the existing services agreement between HEXO and a subsidiary of Tilray, the amended senior secured note and other commercial agreements between the parties and to pay various waiver, amendment and termination fees, which payments in the aggregate total US$18,500,000, with an initial payment of US$9,200,000 made concurrently with entry into the transaction agreement, a second payment of US$1,000,000 in cash or by way of transfer of real property, to be made no later than May 1, 2023 and a final payment of US$2,200,000 to be made on the business day preceding the closing date of the transaction. June 1, 2023 - The transaction was amended to included the purchase of the newly issued HEXO series 1 preferred shares. HEXO issued 25,000,000 series 1 preferred shares at a price of US$1.00 per share.

Status: completed **Announced:** Nov. 7, 2022
Tilray Brands, Inc. acquired New York, N.Y.-based Montauk Brewing Company, Inc., which brews and distributes craft beers, for US$35,110,000, consisting of US$28,688,000 cash and issuance of 1,708,521 class 2 common shares valued at US$6,422,000. Montauk was distributed across more than 6,400 points of distribution. The acquisition expanded Tilray's U.S. beverage-alcohol segment.

Status: completed **Revised:** Nov. 1, 2022
UPDATE: The transaction was completed. The Stellarton facility would be sold. PREVIOUS: Sundial Growers Inc. entered into a purchase agreement, in the form of a stalking horse bid, to acquire Zenabis Global Inc. and the business and assets of Zenabis' wholly owned subsidiaries. Zenabis has filed a petition for protection under the Companies' Creditors Arrangement Act (CCAA) and Ernst & Young Inc. has been appointed as the Monitor to oversee the CCAA proceedings. The assets covered by the agreement include a 380,000-sq.-ft. indoor cultivation facility in Atholville, N.B., and a non-operational 255,000-sq.-ft. indoor facility in Stellarton, N.S., which was used for processing, manufacturing and packaging. The agreement is subject to the approval by the Québec Superior Court supervising the CCAA proceedings, and to potential alternative bids pursuant to bidding procedures that would follow. Zenabis is wholly owned by HEXO Corp., and the CCAA petition is limited to Zenabis and neither HEXO nor any of its subsidiaries, other than the members of the Zenabis, are petitioners or parties to the CCAA proceedings. Sundial, through a special purpose vehicle, holds $51,900,000 principal amount of senior secured debt of Zenabis.

Status: terminated **Revised:** June 30, 2022
UPDATE: The transaction expired. PREVIOUS: Tilray Brands, Inc. agreed to sell its 5.5-acre property in Nanaimo, B.C., where its 60,000-sq.-ft. EU-GMP certified cultivation and processing facility is situated, for Cdn$18,250,000. Closing was targeted in June 2022. Tilray announced in September 2021 the closure of the Nanaimo operations as part of a consolidation.

Predecessor Detail - Name changed from Tilray, Inc., Jan. 10, 2022.

Directors - Irwin D. Simon, chr., pres. & CEO, New York, N.Y.; Renah A. Persofsky†, v-chr., Toronto, Ont.; Jodi L. H. Butts, Ottawa, Ont.; David F. Clanachan, Ont.; John M. Herhalt, Toronto, Ont.; David Hopkinson, N.Y.; Thomas (Tom) Looney, Ridgefield, Conn.

Other Exec. Officers - Carl A. Merton, CFO; Lloyd Brathwaite, CIO; Denise Faltischek, chief strategy officer & head, intl.; Berrin Noorata, chief corp. affairs officer; Nyree Pinto, chief HR officer; Roger Savell, CAO; Mitchell S. (Mitch) Gendel, gen. counsel & corp. sec.; Ty H. Gilmore, pres., U.S. beer; Blair MacNeil, pres., Tilray Canada; Jared Simon, pres., Manitoba Harvest & Tilray Wellness; Bryan Nolt, CEO, Breckenridge Distillery
† Lead director

Capital Stock

	Authorized (shs.)	Outstanding (shs.)[1]	Par
Preferred	10,000,000	nil	US$0.0001
Common	980,000,000	703,257,224	US$0.0001

[1] At July 24, 2023

Major Shareholder - Double Diamond Holdings Ltd. held 19.8% interest at Feb. 22, 2023.

Price Range - TLRY/TSX

Year	Volume	High	Low	Close
2022	479,310,159	$11.28	$3.44	$3.67
2021	243,934,579	$27.88	$8.89	$8.92

TLRY/NASDAQ

Year	Volume	High	Low	Close
2021	1,202,049,292	US$67.00	US$6.98	US$7.03
2020	466,291,521	US$22.93	US$2.43	US$8.26
2019	110,409,905	US$106.00	US$15.57	US$17.13
2018	148,487,005	US$300.00	US$20.10	US$70.54

Recent Close: $3.18

Capital Stock Changes - In June 2023, 39,705,962 class 2 common shares were issued pursuant to the acquisition of HEXO Corp., including 19,551,282 class 2 common shares to acquire all 25,000,000 HEXO series 1 preferred shares. On July 24, 2023, class 2 common shares were reclassified as common shares.

In July 2022, 33,314,412 class 2 common shares were issued pursuant to the acquisition of HEXO Corp.'s senior secured convertible notes. In November 2022, 1,708,521 class 2 common shares were issued pursuant to the acquisition of Montauk Brewing Company, Inc. In February 2023, 120,000 series A preferred shares were issued for debt settlement. In March 2023, class 1 common shares were eliminated from authorized capital and the 233,333,333 authorized class 1 common shares were re-allocated to class 2 common shares, thereby increasing the authorized class 2 common shares to 980,000,000 from 746,666,667. Also in March 2023, all 120,000 series A preferred shares were automatically converted into class 2 common shares. Also during fiscal 2023, class 2 common shares were issued as follows: 38,500,000 as part of a share lending agreement with an affiliate of Jefferies LLC, 32,481,149 under at-the-market offering, 16,114,406 for debt settlement, 1,854,120 on vesting of restricted share units and 7,960 on exercise of options.

In September 2021, authorized common capital was increased to 980,000,000 shares, consisting of 233,333,333 class 1 common shares and 746,666,667 class 2 common shares, from 733,333,333 shares, consisting of 233,333,333 class 1 common shares and 500,000,000 class 2 common shares. Also in September 2021, 9,817,061 class 2 common shares were issued pursuant to the acquisition of a 68% interest in Superhero Acquisition L.P. In December 2021, 12,540,479 class 2 common shares were issued pursuant to the acquisition of Double Diamond Distillery LLC (dba Breckenridge Distillery). Also during fiscal 2022, class 2 common shares were issued as follows: 51,741,710 under at-the-market offering, 4,489,355 on vesting of restricted share units, 2,959,386 for legal settlement, 2,677,596 for debt settlement, 923,320 pursuant to the acquisition of Cheese Grits, LLC, 719,031 on exercise of options and 366,308 pursuant to the acquisition of Alpine and Green Flash brands.

Long-Term Debt - Outstanding at May 31, 2023:

Credit facility due Nov. 2025[1]	US$45,260,000
Mtges.:	
Cdn. prime+1.5% due Aug. 2026	2,104,000
EURIBOR+1.5% due Oct. 2030	20,863,000
Term loans:	
Cdn. prime+1% due July 2023	10,959,000
EURIBOR+1.79% due Dec. 2023	1,558,000
EURIBOR+2.68% due Dec. 2023	803,000
EURIBOR+2% due Apr. 2025	819,000
EURIBOR+2% due June 2025	903,000
Cdn. prime+1.5% due Aug. 2026	346,000
SOFR+margin due June 2028	65,000,000
Cdn. prime+1.5% due Apr. 2032	13,092,000
4% conv. promiss. note due Sept. 2023[2]	47,834,000
5% conv. notes due Oct. 2023[3]	126,544,000
5.25% conv. notes due June 2024[4]	120,568,000
5.2% conv. notes due June 2027[5]	100,476,000
Less: Unamort. financing fees	738,000
	556,391,000
Less: Current portion	198,458,000
	357,933,000

[1] Bears interest at Canadian prime plus a margin.

[2] Convertible into common shares at a conversion price of US$4.03 per share.

[3] Convertible into 5.9735 common shares per US$1,000 principal amount of notes, which is equivalent to an initial conversion price of US$167.41 per share.

[4] Convertible into 89.31162364 common shares per US$1,000 principal amount of notes, which is equivalent to an initial conversion price of US$11.20 per share.

[5] Convertible into 376.6478 common shares per US$1,000 principal amount of notes, which is equivalent to an initial conversion price of US$2.66 per share.

Note - In June 2023, an additional US$22,500,000 principal amount of 5.2% convertible notes due June 2027 were issued.

Wholly Owned Subsidiaries

Aphria Inc., Leamington, Ont.
- 100% int. in **Aphria Malta Limited**, Malta.
- 100% int. in **Aphria Terra S.R.L.**, Italy.
- 100% int. in **Broken Coast Cannabis Ltd.**, Ladysmith, B.C.
- 100% int. in **Four Twenty Corporation**, United States.
  - 100% int. in **Double Diamond Distillery LLC**, Breckenridge, Colo. dba Breckenridge Distillery.
  - 100% int. in **SW Brewing Company, LLC**, United States.
    - 100% int. in **SweetWater Brewing Company, LLC**, Atlanta, Ga.
      - 100% int. in **SweetWater Colorado Brewing Company, LLC**, United States.
- 100% int. in **LATAM Holdings Inc.**, B.C.
  - 100% int. in **ABP, S.A.**, Argentina.
  - 100% int. in **MMJ Colombia Partners Inc.**, Ont.
    - 90% int. in **Colcanna S.A.S.**, Colombia.
  - 100% int. in **Marigold Acquisitions Inc.**, B.C.
- 100% int. in **Nuuvera Holdings Limited**, Toronto, Ont.
  - 100% int. in **ARA - Avanti Rx Analytics Inc.**, Ont.
  - 100% int. in **Aphria Germany GmbH**, Hamburg, Germany.
    - 100% int. in **Aphria RX GmbH**, Germany.
    - 100% int. in **Aphria Wellbeing GmbH**, Germany.
    - 100% int. in **CC Pharma GmbH**, Germany.
      - 75% int. in **CC Pharma Nordic ApS**, Denmark.
      - 100% int. in **CC Pharma Research and Development GmbH**, Germany.
  - 100% int. in **FL Group S.r.l.**, Italy.
  - 100% int. in **Nuuvera Israel Ltd.**, Tel Aviv, Israel.
  - 100% int. in **Nuuvera Malta Ltd.**, Malta.
    - 100% int. in **QSG Health Ltd.**, Malta.
- 51% int. in **1974568 Ontario Ltd.**, Ont. dba Aphria Diamond.

Dorada Ventures, Ltd., Canada.
Earth's Best Cannabis Company, United States.
FHF Holdings Ltd., Winnipeg, Man.
Fresh Hemp Foods Ltd., Canada. dba Manitoba Harvest.
Goodfields Supply Co. Ltd., United Kingdom.
HEXO Corp., Gatineau, Qué.
- 100% int. in **5048963 Ontario Inc.**, Ont.
  - 100% int. in **5054220 Ontario Inc.**, Ont.
  - 100% int. in **9037136 Canada Inc.**, Ridgeville, Ont.
- 100% int. in **48North Cannabis Corp.**, Toronto, Ont.
  - 100% int. in **48North Amalco Ltd.**, Ont.
    - 100% int. in **DelShen Therapeutics Corp.**, Ont.
- 100% int. in **HEXO Operations Inc.**, Ont.
  - 42.5% int. in **Truss Limited Partnership**, Canada.

High Park Botanicals B.V., Netherlands.
High Park Farms Ltd., Canada.
High Park Gardens Inc., Canada.
High Park Holdings B.V., Netherlands.
High Park Holdings, Ltd., Canada.
High Park Shops Inc., Canada.
Manitoba Harvest Japan KK, Japan.
Manitoba Harvest USA LLC, Del.
Montauk Brewing Company, Inc., New York, N.Y.
NC Clinics Pty Ltd., Australia.
Natura Naturals Holdings Inc., Canada.
Natura Naturals Inc., Leamington, Ont.
1197879 B.C. Ltd., B.C.
Pardal Holdings, Lda., Portugal.
Privateer Evolution, LLC, Del.
Tilray Australia New Zealand Pty Ltd., Australia.
Tilray Canada, Ltd., Canada.
Tilray Deutschland GmbH, Germany.
Tilray France S.A.S., France.
Tilray, Inc., Del.
Tilray Latin America S.p.A., Chile.
Tilray Portugal II, Lda., Portugal.
Tilray Portugal Unipessoal, Lda., Portugal.
Tilray Ventures Ltd., Ireland.
2787643 Ontario Inc., Ont.

Subsidiaries

68% int. in **Superhero Acquisition L.P.**, Del.

Investments

42.5% int. in **Truss Beverage Co.**, Etobicoke, Ont.

Financial Statistics

Periods ended:	12m May 31/23[A]		12m May 31/22[oA]
	US$000s	%Chg	US$000s
Operating revenue	**627,124**	**0**	**628,372**
Cost of goods sold	480,164		511,555
Salaries & benefits	57,228		51,693
Research & devel. expense	682		1,518
General & admin expense	134,161		141,656
Stock-based compensation	39,595		35,994
Operating expense	**711,830**	**-4**	**742,416**
Operating income	**(84,706)**	**n.a.**	**(114,044)**
Deprec., depl. & amort.	93,489		115,191
Finance income	33,025		11,736
Finance costs, gross	46,612		39,680
Write-downs/write-offs	(1,180,330)[1]		(378,241)[2]
Pre-tax income	**(1,450,181)**	**n.a.**	**(440,674)**
Income taxes	(7,181)		(6,542)
Net income	**(1,443,000)**	**n.a.**	**(434,132)**
Net inc. for equity hldrs	**(1,452,656)**	**n.a.**	**(476,801)**
Net inc. for non-cont. int	**9,656**	**-77**	**42,669**
Cash & equivalent	448,529		415,909
Inventories	200,551		245,529
Accounts receivable	86,227		95,279
Current assets	773,029		803,503
Long-term investments	12,371		15,002
Fixed assets, net	429,667		587,499
Right-of-use assets	5,941		12,996
Intangibles, net	2,982,628		3,919,180
Total assets	**4,307,259**	**-21**	**5,449,694**
Bank indebtedness	23,381		18,123
Accts. pay. & accr. liabs	175,748		151,281
Current liabilities	432,979		280,342
Long-term debt, gross	556,391		587,651
Long-term debt, net	357,933		519,828
Long-term lease liabilities	7,936		11,329
Shareholders' equity	3,315,692		4,398,805
Non-controlling interest	14,251		42,561
Cash from oper. activs	**7,906**	**n.a.**	**(177,262)**
Cash from fin. activs	70,158		128,196
Cash from invest. activs	(285,111)		(21,533)
Net cash position	**206,632**	**-50**	**415,909**
Capital expenditures	(20,800)		(34,064)
Capital disposals	4,304		12,205
	US$		US$
Earnings per share*	(2.35)		(0.99)
Cash flow per share*	0.01		(0.37)
	shs		shs
No. of shs. o/s*	656,655,455		532,674,887
Avg. no. of shs. o/s*	617,982,589		481,219,130
	%		%
Net profit margin	(230.10)		(69.09)
Return on equity	(37.66)		(10.77)
Return on assets	(28.63)		(6.89)
No. of employees (FTEs)	1,600		1,800

* Common

[o] Restated

[A] Reported in accordance with U.S. GAAP

[1] Includes impairment of US$603,500,000 on cannabis goodwill, US$15,000,000 on wellness goodwill, US$205,000,000 on cannabis intangible assets, US$104,000,000 on capital assets and US$6,500,000 on other current assets; and write-down of US$246,330,000 on convertible notes receivable from HEXO Corp. and MedMen Enterprises Inc.

[2] Includes impairment of US$182,736,000 on goodwill and US$195,504,000 on intangible assets of the cannabis segment.

Historical Summary
(as originally stated)

Fiscal Year	Oper. Rev.	Net Inc. Bef. Disc.	EPS*
	US$000s	US$000s	US$
2023[A]	627,124	(1,443,000)	(2.35)
2022[A]	628,372	(434,132)	(0.90)
2021[A1]	513,085	(336,014)	(1.25)
2020[A]	210,482	(271,073)	(2.15)
2019[A]	166,979	(321,169)	(3.20)

* Common

[A] Reported in accordance with U.S. GAAP

[1] Results reflect the Apr. 30, 2021, reverse takeover acquisition of Aphria Inc.

T.52 Timbercreek Financial Corp.

Symbol - TF **Exchange** - TSX **CUSIP** - 88709B
Head Office - 25 Price St, Toronto, ON, M4W 1Z1 **Telephone** - (416) 923-9967 **Toll-free** - (844) 304-9967
Website - www.timbercreekfinancial.com
Email - kma@timbercreek.com
Investor Relations - Karynna Ma (416) 923-9967
Auditors - KPMG LLP C.A., Toronto, Ont.
Lawyers - McCarthy Tétrault LLP, Toronto, Ont.
Transfer Agents - TSX Trust Company, Toronto, Ont.

Managers - Timbercreek Capital Inc., Toronto, Ont.
FP500 Revenue Ranking - 707
Profile - (Ont. 2016 amalg.) Provides customized mortgage loans typically involving shorter terms to real estate investors requiring funding during the transitional phase of the investment process and secured by income-producing investment grade real estate assets primarily located in large urban markets across Canada.

Customers are typically real estate investors using short-term loans to bridge a period of one to five years where they require temporary capital for property repairs, redevelopment or purchase of another investment. These short-term loans are typically repaid with lower cost, longer-term debt obtained from traditional Canadian financial institutions once the transitional period is over, restructuring completed or from proceeds generated on the sale of assets.

At Mar. 31, 2023, the company had a mortgage investment portfolio of 107 mortgages valued at about $1.15 billion, with a 92% exposure to first mortgages and 68.5% weighted average loan-to-value.

Timbercreek Capital Inc., the manager of the company, receives per annum a management fee of 0.85% on gross assets plus a servicing fee of 0.1% on any senior tranche of a mortgage syndicated by it to a third party on behalf of the company, where the company retains the corresponding subordinated position. In addition, each investment made, involving syndication to another party of a senior tranche with the company retaining a subordinated component, the manager is entitled to retain, from any lender fee generated in respect of such loan, an arrangement fee of 0.2% of the whole loan amount.

Recent Merger and Acquisition Activity

Status: completed **Announced:** Apr. 28, 2022
Timbercreek Financial Corp., through wholly owned Timbercreek Mortgage Investment Fund, sold a 20.46% interest in 14 residential investment properties totaling 1,079 units located in Saskatoon and Regina, Sask., for $43,967,000.

Predecessor Detail - Formed from Timbercreek Mortgage Investment Corporation in Ontario, June 30, 2016, pursuant to amalgamation with Timbercreek Senior Mortgage Investment Corporation; basis 1 new TF sh. for 1 old TMIC sh. and 1.035 new TF shs. for 1 old TSMIC sh.

Directors - R. Blair Tamblyn, chr. & CEO, Toronto, Ont.; Scott Rowland, chief invest. officer, Ont.; W. Glenn Shyba†, Toronto, Ont.; Amar Bhalla, Toronto, Ont.; Deborah Robinson, Toronto, Ont.; Pamela J. (Pam) Spackman, Toronto, Ont.

Other Exec. Officers - Geoff McTait, man. dir., Cdn. origination & head, global syndication; Patrick Smith, man. dir. & head, global credit, Canada; Tracy Johnston, CFO; Karynna Ma, v-p, IR; John Walsh, v-p & corp. sec.

† Lead director

Capital Stock

	Authorized (shs.)	Outstanding (shs.)[1]
Common	unlimited	83,775,016

[1] At May 15, 2023

Normal Course Issuer Bid - The company plans to make normal course purchases of up to 8,305,467 common shares representing 10% of the public float. The bid commenced on May 26, 2023, and expires on May 25, 2024.

Major Shareholder - Widely held at Mar. 29, 2023.

Price Range - TF/TSX

Year	Volume	High	Low	Close
2022	30,409,692	$9.79	$6.87	$7.11
2021	22,885,882	$9.94	$8.56	$9.61
2020	28,189,107	$10.31	$5.91	$8.65
2019	22,277,182	$10.18	$8.67	$9.93
2018	19,156,655	$9.70	$8.50	$8.75

Recent Close: $7.27

Capital Stock Changes - During 2022, common shares were issued as follows: 1,504,300 pursuant to an equity distribution agreement and 641,944 under dividend reinvestment plan; 360,830 common shares were repurchased for dividend reinvestment plan and 117,500 common shares were repurchased under a Normal Course Issuer Bid.

Dividends

TF com N.V. Var. Ra pa M**

$0.0575	Sept. 15/23	$0.0575	Aug. 15/23
$0.0575	July 14/23	$0.0575	June 15/23

Paid in 2023: $0.5175 2022: $0.69 2021: $0.69

** Reinvestment Option

Wholly Owned Subsidiaries

Timbercreek Mortgage Investment Fund, Toronto, Ont.
- 99.99% int. in **Timbercreek CILO II Holdings Partnership**
- 100% int. in **2292912 Ontario Inc.**, Ont.
  - 0.01% int. in **Timbercreek CILO II Holdings Partnership**

Financial Statistics

Periods ended:	12m Dec. 31/22[A]		12m Dec. 31/21[A]
	$000s	%Chg	$000s
Total revenue	**150,030**	**+41**	**106,281**
General & admin. expense	2,109		1,846
Other operating expense	51,991		37,555
Operating expense	**54,100**	**+37**	**39,401**
Operating income	**95,930**	**+43**	**66,880**
Provision for loan losses	7,482		1,660
Finance costs, gross	32,256		19,539
Pre-tax income	**55,896**	**+35**	**41,307**
Net income	**55,896**	**+35**	**41,307**
Cash & equivalent	2,832		6,344
Investments	1,873,451		1,674,869
Properties	30,245		44,063
Total assets	**1,916,039**	**+11**	**1,732,064**
Accts. pay. & accr. liabs	4,450		5,125
Debt	589,767		587,605
Equity portion of conv. debs	4,450		4,450
Shareholders' equity	698,543		684,583
Cash from oper. activs	**83,171**	**+2**	**81,613**
Cash from fin. activs	(42,453)		(54,176)
Cash from invest. activs	(44,180)		(21,384)
Net cash position	**2,832**	**-55**	**6,344**
Capital expenditures	nil		(575)
Capital disposals	7,510		nil
	$		$
Earnings per share*	0.67		0.51
Cash flow per share*	0.99		1.00
Cash divd. per share*	0.69		0.69
	shs		shs
No. of shs. o/s*	83,887,516		82,219,602
Avg. no. of shs. o/s*	83,622,130		81,324,595
	%		%
Net profit margin	37.26		38.87
Return on equity	8.08		6.03
Return on assets	4.83		3.53

* Common
[A] Reported in accordance with IFRS

Latest Results

Periods ended:	3m Mar. 31/23[A]		3m Mar. 31/22[A]
	$000s	%Chg	$000s
Total revenue	45,873	+57	29,147
Net income	18,104	+41	12,882
	$		$
Earnings per share*	0.22		0.16

* Common
[A] Reported in accordance with IFRS

Historical Summary
(as originally stated)

Fiscal Year	Total Rev.	Net Inc. Bef. Disc.	EPS*
	$000s	$000s	$
2022[A]	150,030	55,896	0.67
2021[A]	106,281	41,307	0.51
2020[A]	108,920	32,002	0.39
2019[A]	127,225	54,740	0.66
2018[A]	126,792	53,068	0.67

* Common
[A] Reported in accordance with IFRS

T.53 Timeless Capital Corp.

Symbol - TLC.P **Exchange** - TSX-VEN **CUSIP** - 887333
Head Office - 1900-520 3 Ave SW, Calgary, AB, T2P 0R3
Email - fgadallah@gadallahmanagement.com
Investor Relations - Fahim Gadallah (604) 340-5101
Auditors - Crowe MacKay LLP C.A., Vancouver, B.C.
Transfer Agents - TSX Trust Company, Toronto, Ont.
Profile - (Alta. 2018) Capital Pool Company.
Common reinstated on TSX-VEN, Dec. 21, 2022.

Recent Merger and Acquisition Activity

Status: pending **Revised:** Apr. 5, 2023
UPDATED: Timeless and RBC entered into a definitive agreement whereby RBC and Renaissance Bioscience Holdings Corp. would amalgamate with a wholly owned subsidiary of Timeless. In connection with the transaction, Timeless plans to change its name to Renaissance Bioscience Corp. A concurrent private placement of units at $0.45 per unit would be completed for gross proceeds of $5,000,000, subject to a minimum of $3,600,000. PREVIOUS: Timeless Capital Corp. entered into a letter of intent for the Qualifying Transaction reverse takeover acquisition of Renaissance BioScience Corp. (RBC). Terms are to be negotiated. Timeless shares would be consolidated on a 1-for-2.14 basis and each RBC share would be exchanged for one post-consolidated Timeless share. RBC plans to raise minimum proceeds of $5,000,000 via a private placement. RBC is a bioengineering company whose platform technologies are used to develop innovative, market-ready, functional microorganisms that provide cost-effective solutions to a broad range of environmental, health and industrial efficiency problems.

Status: terminated **Revised:** Mar. 15, 2022
UPDATE: The transaction was terminated. PREVIOUS: Timeless Capital Corp. entered into a letter of intent for the Qualifying Transaction reverse takeover acquisition of private Ottawa, Ont.-based Brane Inc., which provides digital asset custody services, on a share-for-share basis (following an up to 1-for-5 share consolidation). As part of the transaction, Brane would complete a proposed $5,000,000 private placement. Upon completion, Timeless would change its name to Brane Inc. Jan. 12, 2022 - Closing of the transaction was extended to Mar. 15, 2022.

Directors - Fahim Gadallah, CEO, Vancouver, B.C.; Colin Gayford, CFO & corp. sec., Calgary, Alta.; Blair Jordan, West Vancouver, B.C.; Daniel Lanskey, Temora, N.S.W., Australia; Shane W. Shircliff, Saskatoon, Sask.; Danish Wasim, Calgary, Alta.

Capital Stock

	Authorized (shs.)	Outstanding (shs.)[1]
Preferred	unlimited	nil
Common	unlimited	7,000,000

[1] At Sept. 30, 2022

Major Shareholder - Danish Wasim held 11.42% interest at Mar. 16, 2021.

Capital Stock Changes - In February 2023, private placement of 2,110,000 common shares was completed at 10¢ per share.

Wholly Owned Subsidiaries

1219915 B.C. Ltd., Canada.

T.54 Tinkerine Studios Ltd.

Symbol - TTD **Exchange** - TSX-VEN (S) **CUSIP** - 96349P
Head Office - Unit 213A, 8275 92 St, Delta, BC, V4G 0A4 **Telephone** - (604) 288-8778 **Toll-free** - (844) 846-5377
Website - www.tinkerine.com
Email - eugene@tinkerine.com
Investor Relations - Eugene Suyu (604) 288-8778
Auditors - Dale Matheson Carr-Hilton LaBonte LLP C.A., Vancouver, B.C.
Lawyers - McMillan LLP, Vancouver, B.C.
Transfer Agents - Computershare Trust Company of Canada Inc., Vancouver, B.C.
Profile - (B.C. 2006) Designs, manufactures and distributes 3D printers and software, focusing on STEAM-based (Science, Technology, Engineering, Art, Math) educational content and online training tools, to Canada, the U.S. and Asia Pacific region. Also manufactures and sells medical devices or personal protective equipment (PPE) for healthcare and other front-line essential worker environments.

Manufactures Ditto Pro and Ditto Pro R 3D printers that use fused filament fabrication. These printers are made of metal and are available for purchase directly from the company's website. Also sells filaments for 3D printing, including coloured PLA, carbon fiber, stainless steel and copper.

Through its Tinkerine U portal, integrated with the Tinkerine cloud program, the company offers 3D courses and 3D certification for educators, students and professionals; and through its Production of Things 2.0 (Pot2.0), provides a singular platform for businesses with twenty-first century tools as well as a powerful workflow system, which help compete in a fast-paced world and optimize additive manufacturing. Also provides consulting services in areas of hardware, software and business consulting.

In addition, manufactures and sells class 1 medical devices or personal protective equipment (PPE), including face shields, face masks, replacement parts for face shields, TruSight anti-fog coating for face shields and ear relief for face masks, for healthcare institutions and front-line workers. Products under development include test kit swab and ventilator splitter.

Common suspended from TSX-VEN, May 12, 2023.

Recent Merger and Acquisition Activity

Status: pending **Revised:** Sept. 30, 2022
UPDATE: The agreement was due to expire but was extended to Mar. 30, 2023. PREVIOUS: Tinkerine Studios Ltd. entered into a definitive agreement for the reverse takeover acquisition of Surrey, B.C.-based Electrum Charging Solutions Inc., a electric vehicle charging solutions company, for issuance of 17,000,000 post-consolidated common shares (following a 1-for-60 share consolidation). The transaction would be completed by way of three-cornered amalgamation resulting in Electrum becoming a wholly-owned subsidiary of Tinkerine Studios. A private placement for proceeds of up to $7,500,000 would be completed by Electrum.

Predecessor Detail - Name changed from White Bear Resources Inc., Apr. 14, 2014, following reverse takeover acquisition of Tinkerine Studio Inc.

Directors - Eugene Suyu, co-founder, pres. & CEO, Langley, B.C.; Justin Sy, co-founder & chief tech. officer, Richmond, B.C.; Todd Blatt, v-p, market direction, Baltimore, Md.

Other Exec. Officers - Chris Lee, CFO & corp. sec.

Capital Stock

	Authorized (shs.)	Outstanding (shs.)[1]
Preferred	unlimited	nil
Common	unlimited	49,675,849
Non-vtg. Common	unlimited	nil

[1] At Nov. 23, 2022

Major Shareholder - Widely held at Oct. 21, 2021.

Price Range - TTD/TSX-VEN (S)

Year	Volume	High	Low	Close
2022	573,440	$0.06	$0.04	$0.04
2021	29,292,570	$0.19	$0.04	$0.05
2020	147,680,582	$0.32	$0.01	$0.04
2019	5,411,701	$0.04	$0.01	$0.03
2018	8,085,772	$0.05	$0.02	$0.02

Wholly Owned Subsidiaries

Tinkerine 3D Print Systems Ltd., B.C.

Financial Statistics

Periods ended:	12m Dec. 31/21[A]		12m Dec. 31/20[A]
	$000s	%Chg	$000s
Operating revenue	**470**	**+38**	**341**
Cost of goods sold	185		152
Salaries & benefits	283		199
Research & devel. expense	3		1
General & admin expense	236		303
Stock-based compensation	109		275
Operating expense	**816**	**-12**	**929**
Operating income	**(346)**	**n.a.**	**(588)**
Deprec., depl. & amort.	48		48
Finance costs, gross	125		32
Pre-tax income	**(521)**	**n.a.**	**(537)**
Net income	**(521)**	**n.a.**	**(537)**
Cash & equivalent	14		nil
Inventories	72		113
Accounts receivable	26		70
Current assets	123		198
Fixed assets, net	2		nil
Right-of-use assets	44		92
Total assets	**169**	**-42**	**290**
Bank indebtedness	85		142
Accts. pay. & accr. liabs	639		348
Current liabilities	1,404		559
Long-term debt, gross	630		531
Long-term debt, net	nil		511
Long-term lease liabilities	nil		50
Shareholders' equity	(1,235)		(829)
Cash from oper. activs	**121**	**n.a.**	**(181)**
Cash from fin. activs	(52)		119
Cash from invest. activs	(2)		nil
Net cash position	**14**	**n.a.**	**(52)**
Capital expenditures	(2)		nil
	$		$
Earnings per share*	(0.01)		(0.01)
Cash flow per share*	0.00		(0.00)
	shs		shs
No. of shs. o/s*	49,675,849		49,600,849
Avg. no. of shs. o/s*	49,670,301		49,501,534
	%		%
Net profit margin	(110.85)		(157.48)
Return on equity	n.m.		n.m.
Return on assets	(172.55)		(170.03)
Foreign sales percent	72		14

* Common
[A] Reported in accordance with IFRS

Latest Results

Periods ended:	9m Sept. 30/22[A]		9m Sept. 30/21[A]
	$000s	%Chg	$000s
Operating revenue	374	-12	423
Net income	(123)	n.a.	(294)
	$		$
Earnings per share*	(0.00)		(0.01)

* Common
[A] Reported in accordance with IFRS

Historical Summary
(as originally stated)

Fiscal Year	Oper. Rev.	Net Inc. Bef. Disc.	EPS*
	$000s	$000s	$
2021[A]	470	(521)	(0.01)
2020[A]	341	(537)	(0.01)
2019[A]	434	(384)	(0.01)
2018[A]	552	(394)	(0.01)
2017[A]	805	(360)	(0.01)

* Common
[A] Reported in accordance with IFRS

T.55 The Tinley Beverage Company Inc.

Symbol - TNY **Exchange** - CSE **CUSIP** - 887544
Head Office - 1800-181 Bay St, Toronto, ON, M5J 2T9 **Telephone** - (416) 777-6169 **Fax** - (416) 777-6178
Website - www.drinktinley.com
Email - relations@drinktinley.com
Investor Relations - Theodore Zittell (310) 507-9146
Auditors - Zeifmans LLP C.A., Toronto, Ont.
Lawyers - Fogler, Rubinoff LLP, Toronto, Ont.
Transfer Agents - Odyssey Trust Company, Toronto, Ont.

Profile - (Ont. 2005) Manufactures, packs and distributes non-alcoholic, cannabis-infused or non-cannabis plant terpene-infused beverages in the U.S., primarily in California.

Holds licence to produce and package cannabis-infused products, including topicals, edibles and beverages, at its 20,000-sq.-ft. bottling facility in Long Beach, Calif.

Products are sold under various brands including Tinley's™ Tonics and Tinley's™ '27, which are liquor- and cocktail-inspired non-alcoholic, tetrahydrocannabinol (THC)-infused single-serve versions of mixed drinks and elixers, respectively; and Beckett's™ Tonics and Beckett's™ '27, which are non-alcoholic, non-cannabis plant terpene-infused single-serve versions of mixed drinks and classic liquors, respectively. The Tinley's™ branded cannabis-infused beverages are available in licensed dispensaries and delivery services throughout California The Beckett's™ branded non-cannabis versions are available or eligible for sale in mainstream food, beverage and specialty retailers, as well as online across the U.S. Also manufactures cannabis-infused beverages for contract manufacturing clients and their brands. Wholly owned **Lakewood Libations, Inc.** produces beverages containing cannabis-derived cannabidiol (CBD), cannabigerol (CBG) and cannabinol (CBN) for third party brands.

On Mar. 21, 2023, the company announced that it has paused indefinitely the manufacturing and distribution of Tinley's and Beckett's products for and into Canada, due to market complexity and regulatory constraints. Previously, the company's Beckett's™ branded non-cannabis products were sold in grocery and specialty stores in Canada, primarily in Ontario. The company also announced relocation of all production from its Long Beach facility to a new 45,000-sq.-ft. cannabis manufacturing and distribution facility in Canoga Park, Calif., owned by strategic partner **Blaze Life Holdings, LLC.** (BLH) to save overhead operating expenses. The relocation was expected to be completed by the fourth quarter of 2023 and the Long Beach operations would be decommissioned. In January 2023, the company entered into a management services agreement with BLH.

In April 2022, the company acquired California-based **Lakewood Libations, Inc.** from Richard Gillis, an officer of the company, for a nominal amount. Lakewood conducts commercial cannabis manufacturing and distribution operations at the company's Long Beach, Calif., facility.

Common reinstated on CSE, May 11, 2023.

Common suspended from CSE, May 8, 2023.

Predecessor Detail - Name changed from Quia Resources Inc., Oct. 6, 2015; basis 1 new for 5 old shs.

Directors - Theodore (Ted) Zittell, CEO, Toronto, Ont.; Paul Burgis, Los Angeles, Calif.; David N. Ellison, Toronto, Ont.; Anthony (Tony) Yanow, Los Angeles, Calif.

Other Exec. Officers - Manish Z. Kshatriya, CFO

Capital Stock

	Authorized (shs.)	Outstanding (shs.)[1]
Common	unlimited	150,859,565

[1] At Aug. 25, 2023

Major Shareholder - Widely held at Sept. 12, 2022.

Price Range - TNY/CSE

Year	Volume	High	Low	Close
2022	43,992,069	$0.22	$0.07	$0.07
2021	75,281,442	$0.56	$0.08	$0.18
2020	67,019,745	$0.74	$0.19	$0.44
2019	58,617,613	$0.89	$0.33	$0.39
2018	144,576,779	$1.99	$0.39	$0.57

Recent Close: $0.03

Capital Stock Changes - In February 2022, private placement of 5,530,666 units (1 common share & 1 warrant) at 15¢ per unit was completed. Also during 2022, 1,216,857 common shares were issued for services.

Wholly Owned Subsidiaries

Algonquin Springs Beverage Management LLC, Calif.
Beckett's Tonics California Inc.
Beckett's Tonics Canada Inc.
Bolivar Gold Corp., Toronto, Ont. Inactive.
Colombian Mining Corp. Inactive.
Hemplify, Inc., Santa Monica, Calif.
Kulta Corp. Inactive.
Lakewood Libations, Inc.
QBC Holdings Corp. Inactive.
San Lucas Gold Corp. Inactive.
Tinley's Canada Inc., Canada.

Financial Statistics

Periods ended:	12m Dec. 31/22[A]		12m Dec. 31/21[A]
	$000s	%Chg	$000s
Operating revenue	**1,484**	**+85**	**804**
Cost of goods sold	649		493
Salaries & benefits	1,910		1,648
Research & devel. expense	345		206
General & admin expense	2,296		3,419
Stock-based compensation	550		1,788
Operating expense	**5,750**	**-24**	**7,552**
Operating income	**(4,266)**	**n.a.**	**(6,749)**
Deprec., depl. & amort.	1,723		1,615
Finance income	1		nil
Finance costs, gross	549		163
Pre-tax income	**(6,171)**	**n.a.**	**(8,550)**
Net income	**(6,171)**	**n.a.**	**(8,550)**
Cash & equivalent	184		114
Inventories	418		769
Accounts receivable	209		166
Current assets	977		1,393
Fixed assets, net	5,659		6,128
Right-of-use assets	271		863
Total assets	**7,087**	**-17**	**8,518**
Accts. pay. & accr. liabs	916		670
Current liabilities	2,265		1,616
Long-term debt, gross	3,300		nil
Long-term debt, net	2,603		nil
Long-term lease liabilities	nil		357
Shareholders' equity	2,219		6,545
Cash from oper. activs	**(3,660)**	**n.a.**	**(5,259)**
Cash from fin. activs	4,041		3,977
Cash from invest. activs	(259)		(897)
Net cash position	**184**	**+61**	**114**
Capital expenditures	(397)		(897)
Capital disposals	37		nil
	$		$
Earnings per share*	(0.04)		(0.06)
Cash flow per share*	(0.02)		(0.04)
	shs		shs
No. of shs. o/s*	150,859,565		144,112,042
Avg. no. of shs. o/s*	149,628,515		135,265,326
	%		%
Net profit margin	(415.84)		n.m.
Return on equity	(140.83)		(112.85)
Return on assets	(72.05)		(84.07)

* Common
[A] Reported in accordance with IFRS

Latest Results

Periods ended:	6m June 30/23[A]		6m June 30/22[oA]
	$000s	%Chg	$000s
Operating revenue	1,337	+230	405
Net income	(2,132)	n.a.	(3,402)
	$		$
Earnings per share*	(0.01)		(0.02)

* Common
[o] Restated
[A] Reported in accordance with IFRS

Historical Summary
(as originally stated)

Fiscal Year	Oper. Rev.	Net Inc. Bef. Disc.	EPS*
	$000s	$000s	$
2022[A]	1,484	(6,171)	(0.04)
2021[A]	804	(8,550)	(0.06)
2020[A]	304	(7,690)	(0.07)
2019[A]	85	(7,392)	(0.07)
2018[A]	37	(3,661)	(0.04)

* Common
[A] Reported in accordance with IFRS

T.56 Tiny Ltd.

Symbol - TINY **Exchange** - TSX-VEN **CUSIP** - 88770A
Head Office - 400-1152 Mainland St, Vancouver, BC, V6B 4X2 **Telephone** - (416) 418-3881
Website - www.tiny.com
Email - david@tiny.com
Investor Relations - David Charron (416) 418-3881
Auditors - KPMG LLP C.A., Victoria, B.C.
Lawyers - Fasken Martineau DuMoulin LLP
Transfer Agents - Computershare Trust Company of Canada Inc., Vancouver, B.C.
Employees - 153 at June 16, 2022

Profile - (Can. 2023; orig. B.C., 2019) Invests and acquires technology businesses that develop, sell and support website themes and application as well as provide custom solutions to merchants on e-commerce platforms, primarily Shopify.

The company has three core operating segments: (i) **Beam**, a digital service group with many fortune 500 clients and experience helping some of the world's top companies design, build and ship products and services; (ii) **WeCommerce**, an e-commerce software and services group; and (iii) **Dribbble**, a social network and marketplace for digital designers and creatives. Also has several standalone independent software and Internet businesses and ownership of the general partner in a private equity investment fund.

Beam, and its subsidiary companies including **Metalab Design Ltd.**, help start-ups to Fortune 500 companies design, build and ship premium digital products for both mobile and web.

WeCommerce provides merchants with a suite of e-commerce software tools to start and grow their online stores. Its family of companies and brands includes Pixel Union, Out of the Sandbox, KnoCommerce, Archetype, Yopify, SuppleApps, Rehash, Foursixty and Stamped.

Dribbble is a creative network and community that design professionals use to meet, collaborate, and showcase their work. Dribbble also hosts an online marketplace for graphics, fonts, templates and other digital assets.

Standalone businesses include **Tiny Boards Holdings Ltd.** (WeWorkRemotely remote job boards) and **Meteor Software Holdings Ltd.** (a web application hosting company).

On Jan. 1, 2023, the company and wholly owned **Foursixty Holdings Inc.** (formerly **Foursixty Inc.**) and **Pixel Union Design Ltd.** amalgamated to continue as **WeCommerce Holdings Ltd.**

Recent Merger and Acquisition Activity

Status: completed **Revised:** Apr. 18, 2023
UPDATE: The transaction was completed. PREVIOUS: WeCommerce Holdings Ltd. agreed to the reverse takeover acquisition of technology holding company Tiny Capital Ltd. by way of a three-cornered amalgamation of Tiny Capital with a wholly owned subsidiary of WeCommerce. Tiny Capital founded WeCommerce and remains its largest shareholder. Tiny Capital is owned 98% by Andrew Wilkinson and Chris Sparling. Wilkinson holds a 27% interest in WeCommerce through Tiny Holdings Ltd. and Wilkinson Ventures Ltd. Sparling has an indirect interest in WeCommerce through his 20% interest in Tiny Holdings Ltd. The resulting entity would be renamed Tiny Ltd. A total of 146,400,000 WeCommerce common shares were expected to be issued to Tiny shareholders. WeCommerce shareholders Table Holdings, controlled by Bill Ackman, and Freemark Partners, controlled by Howard Marks, who collectively hold 35.9% of WeCommerce shares, have agreed to support the transaction. The transaction was expected to close in April 2023.

Status: completed **Revised:** Mar. 10, 2022
UPDATE: The transaction was completed for a purchase price of US$1,900,000 (Cdn$2,400,000). Subsequently, Kno was renamed Kno Commerce Inc. PREVIOUS: WeCommerce Holdings Ltd. agreed to acquire Kno Technologies Inc., which provides an e-commerce survey and insights platform that enables merchants to capture and act on zero-party data collected directly from customers. Terms of the transaction were not disclosed. WeCommerce expected to fund the upfront consideration with cash on hand, and the earn-out component, if achieved, with cash and/or common shares.

Predecessor Detail - Name changed from WeCommerce Holdings Ltd., Apr. 17, 2023, pursuant to the reverse takeover acquisition of Tiny Capital Ltd.

Directors - Andrew Wilkinson, chr. & co-CEO, Victoria, B.C.; Chris Sparling, v-chr. & co-CEO, Victoria, B.C.; Carla Matheson, Victoria, B.C.; Timothy A. (Tim) McElvaine, Victoria, B.C.; Shane Parrish, Ottawa, Ont.

Other Exec. Officers - Ampere Chan, pres.; David (Dave) Charron, CFO; Susan Min, gen. counsel & corp. sec.

Capital Stock

	Authorized (shs.)	Outstanding (shs.)[1]
Class A Common	unlimited	177,225,512

[1] At May 10, 2023

Normal Course Issuer Bid - The company plans to make normal course purchases of up to 2,078,140 class A common shares representing 5% of the total outstanding. The bid commenced on Sept. 27, 2022, and expires on Sept. 26, 2023.

Major Shareholder - Andrew Wilkinson held 68.72% interest and Chris Sparling held 10.24% interest at Apr. 18, 2023.

Price Range - TINY/TSX-VEN

Year	Volume	High	Low	Close
2022	7,467,921	$14.15	$1.53	$1.90
2021	11,757,320	$31.99	$8.70	$13.34
2020	4,271,794	$30.00	$2.59	$19.08
2019	960	$6.29	$3.70	$3.70

Consolidation: 1-for-36.9763 cons. in Dec. 2020
Recent Close: $3.75

Capital Stock Changes - In April 2023, 146,429,569 class A common shares were issued on the reverse takeover acquisition of Tiny Capital Ltd., and 11,454,725 class A common shares previously held by Tiny Capital Ltd., and Tiny Holdings Ltd. were cancelled.

During 2022, 1,241,742 class A common shares were issued as contingent consideration and 548,817 class A common shares were issued on exercise of options, restricted share units and deferred share units.

Wholly Owned Subsidiaries

Tiny Capital Ltd., Victoria, B.C.
- 100% int. in **Beam Digital Ltd.**, United Kingdom.
  - 60% int. in **Button Inc.**, Victoria, B.C.
  - 66.5% int. in **8020 Design Ltd.**, Canada.
  - 65% int. in **Frosty Studio Ltd.**, Victoria, B.C.
  - 100% int. in **Metalab Design Ltd.**, Victoria, B.C.
  - 70% int. in **Zero to One Digital Production Studio (Canada) Ltd.**, Canada.
  - 70% int. in **Z1 Digital Product Studio S.L.**, Spain.
- 74.5% int. in **Dribbble Holdings Ltd.**, Calif.
- 100% int. in **Meteor Software Holdings Ltd.**, Victoria, B.C.
- 100% int. in **Tiny Boards Holdings Ltd.**, Victoria, B.C.
- 100% int. in **Tiny Holdings Ltd.**, Canada.

WeCommerce Holdings General Partners Ltd., Canada.

Subsidiaries

99.9% int. in **WeCommerce Holdings LP**, Canada.
- 100% int. in **Archetype Themes Limited Partnership**, B.C.
- 100% int. in **Kno Commerce Inc.**, Denver, Colo. formerly Kno Technologies Inc.
- 100% int. in **Stamped Operations Ltd.**, B.C.
- 100% int. in **Stamped Technologies Pte. Ltd.**, Singapore.
- 100% int. in **WeCommerce General Partner Ltd.**, B.C.
- 100% int. in **WeCommerce Operations Ltd.**, Del. formerly Rehash Ltd.

Financial Statistics

Periods ended:	12m Dec. 31/22[A]		12m Dec. 31/21[A]
	$000s	%Chg	$000s
Operating revenue	**48,472**	**+26**	**38,581**
Salaries & benefits	23,863		14,790
General & admin expense	14,233		13,102
Stock-based compensation	3,383		1,890
Operating expense	**41,479**	**+39**	**29,782**
Operating income	**6,993**	**-21**	**8,799**
Deprec., depl. & amort	12,661		10,088
Finance costs, gross	3,463		3,052
Write-downs/write-offs	(11,812)[1]		nil
Pre-tax income	**(22,838)**	**n.a.**	**(545)**
Income taxes	(199)		298
Net income	**(22,639)**	**n.a.**	**(843)**
Cash & equivalent	10,947		26,122
Accounts receivable	2,117		3,049
Current assets	14,334		31,219
Fixed assets, net	183		210
Intangibles, net	155,916		167,076
Total assets	**171,720**	**-14**	**199,523**
Accts. pay. & accr. liabs	4,403		2,532
Current liabilities	15,850		30,919
Long-term debt, gross	46,935		60,203
Long-term debt, net	42,154		50,017
Shareholders' equity	112,331		108,716
Cash from oper. activs	**10,511**	**+31**	**8,002**
Cash from fin. activs	(18,208)		76,815
Cash from invest. activs	(7,434)		(119,449)
Net cash position	**10,947**	**-58**	**26,122**
Capital expenditures	(117)		(204)
	$		$
Earnings per share*	(0.55)		(0.02)
Cash flow per share*	0.26		0.21
	shs		shs
No. of shs. o/s*	41,614,768		39,824,209
Avg. no. of shs. o/s*	41,180,808		38,029,966
	%		%
Net profit margin	(46.71)		(2.19)
Return on equity	(20.48)		(0.97)
Return on assets	(10.35)		2.73
Foreign sales percent	91		87
No. of employees (FTEs)	...		117

* Cl.A Common
[A] Reported in accordance with IFRS
[1] Goodwill impairment related to Stamped business.

Latest Results

Periods ended:	3m Mar. 31/23[A]		3m Mar. 31/22[A]
	$000s	%Chg	$000s
Operating revenue	13,565	+12	12,094
Net income	(4,316)	n.a.	790
	$		$
Earnings per share*	(0.10)		0.02

* Cl.A Common
[A] Reported in accordance with IFRS

Historical Summary
(as originally stated)

Fiscal Year	Oper. Rev. $000s	Net Inc. Bef. Disc. $000s	EPS* $
2022[A]	48,472	(22,639)	(0.55)
2021[A]	38,581	(843)	(0.02)
2020[A1]	21,281	(4,416)	(0.18)
2019[A2]	15,168	129	0.11
2018[A]	12,451	1,090	0.70

* Cl.A Common
[A] Reported in accordance with IFRS
[1] Results reflect the Dec. 9, 2020, Qualifying Transaction reverse takeover acquisition of (old) WeCommerce Holdings Ltd.
[2] Results prior to Nov. 27, 2019, pertain to Pixel Union Design Ltd., the predecessor company to (old) WeCommerce Holdings Ltd., and to (old) WeCommerce thereafter.
Note: Adjusted throughout for 1-for-36.9763 cons. in Dec. 2020

T.57 Titan Logix Corp.

Symbol - TLA **Exchange** - TSX-VEN **CUSIP** - 88831E
Head Office - 4130-93 St NW, Edmonton, AB, T6E 5P5 **Telephone** - (780) 462-4085 **Toll-free** - (877) 462-4085 **Fax** - (780) 450-8369
Website - www.titanlogix.com
Email - invest@titanlogix.com
Investor Relations - Nicholas Forbes (780) 233-1200
Auditors - Kingston Ross Pasnak LLP C.A., Edmonton, Alta.
Bankers - Royal Bank of Canada, Edmonton, Alta.
Transfer Agents - Computershare Trust Company of Canada Inc., Vancouver, B.C.

Profile - (B.C. 1989 amalg.) Develops, manufactures and markets innovative fluid measurement and management solutions, primarily for the upstream/midstream oil and gas industries as well as for the aviation, waste fluid collection and chemical industries.

Provides data driven solutions for Supply Chain Management (SCM) of goods and service supplied to crude oil, produced water, refined fuel, used oil collection, aircraft refuelling, chemical, and vacuum truck markets. The complete solution consists of the company's ruggedized sensor products interconnected by field hardened gateway devices and other handheld smart devices, to the internet and integrated to enable best-in-class data management and end-to-end Industrial Internet of Things (IIoT) solutions for customers.

System solutions include Mobile Monitoring System, which is used in a wide range of applications and liquids, providing accurate level measurement and control of the volume of fluid in mobile tank while preventing overfill and spill incidents; Stationary Monitoring System, which eliminates costly shutdowns and spills with intelligent tank monitoring; Smart Truck System, which uses IIoT software to maintain a 360-degree view of fleet operations and eliminate inaccuracies and errors in fleet monitoring; and Titan-Lite System, a cost effective solution for non-hazardous liquid management which allows for easy, on-the-go access to the information that matters, including tank levels (volume), alarm notification to the Titan Pulse App, locations for multiple tanks or trucks, and up to 6 compartments on a single tank or trailer.

Hardware products include TD Series Coaxial Probe, which measures accurately in fluid with low dielectric constants (low viscosity liquids) including refined fuels, alcohols and low-viscosity lubricants; TD Series Dual Rod Probe, which is meant for high-viscosity, unprocessed fluids, such as crude oil and waste fluids.; TD Series Hastelloy C-276 Alloy Probe, which is meant for use with harsh, corrosive liquids including hydrochloric acid and similar chemicals; 5332 In-Cab display, which monitors liquids from inside the vehicle and controls internal relays to prevent overfills once it detects an alarm state; Finch II, a weatherproof display for exterior installations which displays volume information, alarms and system error codes; TD 100 Transmitter, which incorporates highly accurate liquid level measurement, alarms and overfill prevention system; T-Lite TD100W, which incorporates Titan-Lite System for quick and easy data check in any place; Rack Control Module, a mobile accessory which prevents overfills and is ideal for loading at locations with common optic or thermistor connections; and SFT 881 flow metering, which accepts and amplifies turbine pulses.

Products are sold primarily in Canada and the U.S. through original equipment manufacturers, dealers, distributors, tank manufacturers and fabricators, and service and engineering companies, and directly to end users.

Predecessor Detail - Name changed from Titan Pacific Resources Ltd., July 2, 2002.

Directors - S. Grant Reeves, chr., Awendaw, S.C.; Helen Cornett, Calgary, Alta.; Victor Lee, Alta.; Robert (Rob) Tasker, Alta.

Other Exec. Officers - Nicholas (Nick) Forbes, CEO; Angela Schultz, CFO

Capital Stock

	Authorized (shs.)	Outstanding (shs.)[1]
Common	unlimited	28,536,132

[1] At Jan. 18, 2023

Major Shareholder - Trust for benefit of the family of late Jerry Zucker held 36.8% interest at Dec. 12, 2022.

Price Range - TLA/TSX-VEN

Year	Volume	High	Low	Close
2022	4,906,933	$0.56	$0.40	$0.54
2021	4,038,550	$0.67	$0.35	$0.44
2020	2,782,567	$0.49	$0.28	$0.41
2019	5,109,697	$0.59	$0.41	$0.43
2018	3,282,230	$0.74	$0.43	$0.47

Recent Close: $0.60

Capital Stock Changes - There were no changes to capital stock from fiscal 2018 to fiscal 2022, inclusive.

Wholly Owned Subsidiaries

Titan Logix USA Corp., United States.

Financial Statistics

Periods ended:	12m Aug. 31/22^A		12m Aug. 31/21^A
	$000s	%Chg	$000s
Operating revenue	**4,329**	**+22**	**3,534**
Cost of sales	1,847		1,604
General & admin expense	2,090		1,684
Other operating expense	347		601
Operating expense	**4,284**	**+10**	**3,889**
Operating income	**45**	**n.a.**	**(355)**
Deprec., depl. & amort.	278		459
Finance income	640		663
Finance costs, gross	16		22
Pre-tax income	**1,126**	**n.a.**	**(212)**
Income taxes	nil		16
Net income	**1,126**	**n.a.**	**(227)**
Cash & equivalent	14,271		9,786
Inventories	1,302		924
Accounts receivable	834		730
Current assets	16,541		11,868
Long-term investments	nil		3,080
Fixed assets, net	194		244
Right-of-use assets	236		366
Intangibles, net	528		716
Total assets	**17,499**	**+8**	**16,274**
Accts. pay. & accr. liabs	537		339
Current liabilities	684		482
Long-term lease liabilities	117		254
Shareholders' equity	16,698		15,538
Cash from oper. activs	**(204)**	**n.a.**	**(426)**
Cash from fin. activs	(146)		(153)
Cash from invest. activs	(169)		982
Net cash position	**9,267**	**-5**	**9,786**
Capital expenditures	(3)		(27)
	$		$
Earnings per share*	0.04		(0.01)
Cash flow per share*	(0.01)		(0.01)
	shs		shs
No. of shs. o/s*	28,536,132		28,536,132
Avg. no. of shs. o/s*	28,536,132		28,536,132
	%		%
Net profit margin	26.01		(6.42)
Return on equity	6.99		(1.45)
Return on assets	6.76		(1.23)
Foreign sales percent	77		71

* Common

^A Reported in accordance with IFRS

Latest Results

Periods ended:	3m Nov. 30/22^A		3m Nov. 30/21^A
	$000s	%Chg	$000s
Operating revenue	1,503	+141	624
Net income	415	n.a.	(163)
	$		$
Earnings per share*	0.01		(0.01)

* Common

^A Reported in accordance with IFRS

Historical Summary
(as originally stated)

Fiscal Year	Oper. Rev.	Net Inc. Bef. Disc.	EPS*
	$000s	$000s	$
2022^A	4,329	1,126	0.04
2021^A	3,534	(227)	(0.01)
2020^A	4,110	(578)	(0.02)
2019^A	5,571	110	0.00
2018^A	4,495	(4)	(0.00)

* Common

^A Reported in accordance with IFRS

T.58 Titan Medical Inc.

Symbol - TMD **Exchange** - TSX **CUSIP** - 88830X

Head Office - 76 Berkeley St, Toronto, ON, M5A 2W7 **Telephone** - (416) 548-7522 **Fax** - (416) 368-1608

Website - www.titanmedicalinc.com

Email - chien.huang@titanmedicalinc.com

Investor Relations - Chien Huang (416) 613-6203

Auditors - BDO Canada LLP C.A., Toronto, Ont.

Lawyers - Borden Ladner Gervais LLP, Toronto, Ont.

Transfer Agents - Computershare Trust Company of Canada Inc., Toronto, Ont.

Employees - 33 at Dec. 31, 2022

Profile - (Ont. 2008 amalg.) Licenses its intellectual property related to the enhancement of robotic assisted surgery (RAS).

Prior to June 2023, the company was developing Enos™, a robotic assisted surgery (RAS) system which includes a surgeon-controlled patient cart with a 3D high-definition vision system and multi-articulating instruments for performing surgical procedures, and a surgeon workstation that provides the surgeon with an ergonomic interface to the patient cart and a 3D high-definition view of the surgical procedure.

The company has licensed certain of its RAS technologies and related intellectual property to **Medtronic plc** and **Intuitive Surgical, Inc.**, while retaining global rights to commercialize the technologies for use with the Enos™ System. At June 2023, the company was reviewing and evaluating further strategic alternatives for the business, including a corporate sale, merger or other business combination, a sale of all or a portion of the company's assets, strategic investment or other significant transaction.

In June 2023, the company entered into an asset purchase and licence agreement with **Medtronic plc** for an upfront payment of US$8,000,000 whereby Medtronic would acquire the company's intellectual property (IP) previously exclusively licensed to Medtronic in June 2020. Medtronic would also be granted non-exclusive license to certain other IP of the company, excluding the acquired rights by Medtronic.

On May 29, 2023, the company transitioned from the development and commercialization of robotic assisted surgery (RAS) technologies to the licensing of its intellectual property. It ceased its research and development operations, and was also exploring opportunities for the sale of its testing and manufacturing equipment.

In May 2023, the company entered into a licence agreement with **Intuitive Surgical, Inc.**, a robotic assisted minimally invasive surgery (MIS) device manufacturer, for an upfront payment of US$7,500,000. Under the agreement, Intuitive was granted a non-exclusive licence to all of the company's intellectual property (IP), with the exception of the IP that is exclusively licensed to another party under a license agreement on June 2020.

Common delisted from NASDAQ, Mar. 10, 2023.

Predecessor Detail - Formed from KAM Capital Corp. in Ontario, July 28, 2008, following Qualifying Transaction reverse takeover amalgamation of wholly owned subsid. Titan Medical Inc. (formerly 2174656 Ontario Limited) with Synergist Medical Inc. to continue as Titan Medical Inc., and subsequent amalgamation of KAM Capital with wholly owned subsid. Titan Medical.

Directors - Paul G. Cataford, chr., interim pres. & CEO, Calgary, Alta.; Anthony J. Giovinazzo, Toronto, Ont.; Cathy R. Steiner, Toronto, Ont.; Cary G. Vance, Salt Lake City, Utah

Other Exec. Officers - Chien Huang, CFO

Capital Stock

	Authorized (shs.)	Outstanding (shs.)[1]
Common	unlimited	112,842,297

[1] At June 9, 2023

Major Shareholder - Widely held at May 16, 2023.

Price Range - TMD/TSX

Year	Volume	High	Low	Close
2022	6,310,040	$1.25	$0.49	$0.90
2021	39,752,124	$4.40	$0.75	$0.82
2020	43,277,369	$2.60	$0.15	$2.17
2019	43,719,768	$6.20	$0.51	$0.65
2018	6,338,667	$14.55	$1.44	$1.69

Recent Close: $0.18

Capital Stock Changes - During 2022, 751,417 common shares were issued under restricted share unit plan.

Wholly Owned Subsidiaries

Titan Medical USA Inc., Chapel Hill, N.C.

Financial Statistics

Periods ended:	12m Dec. 31/22^A		12m Dec. 31/21^A
	US$000s	%Chg	US$000s
Operating revenue	**nil**	**n.a.**	**20,093**
Research & devel. expense	33,007		37,955
General & admin expense	6,821		8,390
Stock-based compensation	4,083		4,036
Operating expense	**43,911**	**-13**	**50,381**
Operating income	**(43,911)**	**n.a.**	**(30,288)**
Deprec., depl. & amort.	860		699
Finance income	4,700		15,781
Finance costs, gross	148		125
Write-downs/write-offs	(2,316)		nil
Pre-tax income	**(42,598)**	**n.a.**	**(14,802)**
Income taxes	(56)		56
Net income	**(42,542)**	**n.a.**	**(14,858)**
Cash & equivalent	3,289		32,306
Accounts receivable	nil		8,280
Current assets	5,036		43,662
Fixed assets, net	nil		464
Right-of-use assets	nil		1,177
Intangibles, net	2,083		1,919
Total assets	**7,119**	**-85**	**47,222**
Accts. pay. & accr. liabs	6,993		5,616
Current liabilities	8,860		10,892
Long-term lease liabilities	1,323		981
Shareholders' equity	(3,164)		35,293
Cash from oper. activs	**(27,578)**	**n.a.**	**(36,617)**
Cash from fin. activs	(419)		44,209
Cash from invest. activs	(1,020)		(755)
Net cash position	**3,289**	**-90**	**32,306**
Capital expenditures	(703)		(370)
	US$		US$
Earnings per share*	(0.38)		(0.14)
Cash flow per share*	(0.25)		(0.34)
	shs		shs
No. of shs. o/s*	111,954,284		111,202,690
Avg. no. of shs. o/s*	111,522,192		108,444,405
	%		%
Net profit margin	n.a.		(73.95)
Return on equity	n.m.		n.m.
Return on assets	(156.03)		(38.24)
No. of employees (FTEs)	33		49

* Common

^A Reported in accordance with IFRS

Latest Results

Periods ended:	3m Mar. 31/23^A		3m Mar. 31/22^A
	US$000s	%Chg	US$000s
Net income	(2,571)	n.a.	(9,221)
	US$		US$
Earnings per share*	(0.02)		(0.08)

* Common

^A Reported in accordance with IFRS

Historical Summary
(as originally stated)

Fiscal Year	Oper. Rev.	Net Inc. Bef. Disc.	EPS*
	US$000s	US$000s	US$
2022^A	nil	(42,542)	(0.38)
2021^A	20,093	(14,858)	(0.14)
2020^A	20,000	(24,185)	(0.36)
2019^A	nil	(41,907)	(1.37)
2018^A	nil	(22,639)	(1.36)

* Common

^A Reported in accordance with IFRS

T.59 Titanium Transportation Group Inc.

Symbol - TTNM **Exchange** - TSX **CUSIP** - 888341

Head Office - 32 Simpson Rd, Bolton, ON, L7E 1G9 **Telephone** - (905) 851-1688 **Toll-free** - (800) 785-4369 **Fax** - (905) 851-1180

Website - www.ttgi.com

Email - ted.daniel@ttgi.com

Investor Relations - Theodor Daniel (905) 266-3011

Auditors - KPMG LLP C.A., Vaughan, Ont.

Transfer Agents - TSX Trust Company, Toronto, Ont.

FP500 Revenue Ranking - 469

Employees - 1,100 at Dec. 31, 2022

Profile - (Can. 1989) Provides freight transportation services including truckload, dedicated and cross-border trucking, freight logistics, and warehousing and distribution to more than 1,000 customers throughout North America.

Operations are organized into three divisions: Truck Transportation (Trucking); Logistics; and Warehousing.

Trucking - Provides long-haul, dedicated and local trucking services through a wide array of trailer types including 53' dry vans, flatbeds, step-decks, heavy axle trailers and other specialty equipment, totaling 800 power units and 3,000 trailers. Full-load transport of general merchandise in North America is provided through company-owned vehicles and independent owner-operators.

Logistics - Operates as a non-asset based broker which provides a variety of ancillary transportation services such as third party logistics and freight forwarding. Truckload and less-than-truckload (LTL) freight are transported all over North America on vans, flatbeds and other specialty equipment. The company's network of carrier partners also offers its customers reliable and varied transportation services including intermodal service across North America, international shipping (ocean and air), specialty services (such as for hazardous and fragile products), and emergency and expedited services.

Warehousing - Provides customers with inventory warehousing and distribution services including order management and fulfillment, shipment consolidation/de-consolidation, cross dock, pick 'n pack (packaging, kitting and sub-assembly) and reverse logistics (refurbished and restock processes). Also offers inventory management capabilities.

The company's head office, and trucking, brokerage and warehouse operations are based in Bolton, Ont, with additional terminals in Belleville, Brantford, Bracebridge, Cornwall, Napanee, North Bay and Windsor, Ont., additional parking/switch yards in Sudbury, Brockville and Trenton, Ont., and freight brokerage offices in Montreal, Que., Charlotte, N.C., Nashville, Tenn., Chicago, Ill., Denver, Colo., Atlanta, Ga., and Fayetteville, Ark.

Predecessor Detail - Name changed from Northeastern Group Inc., Apr. 1, 2015, following reverse takeover acquisition of (old) Titanium Transportation Group Inc.

Directors - Luciano (Lu) Galasso, chr., Toronto, Ont.; Theodor (Ted) Daniel, pres. & CEO, Toronto, Ont.; David Bradley, Ont.; William (Bill) Chyfetz, Toronto, Ont.; Grace M. Palombo, Aurora, Ont.

Other Exec. Officers - Marilyn Daniel, COO; Chun Kit (Alex) Fu, CFO

Capital Stock

	Authorized (shs.)	Outstanding (shs.)[1]
Common	unlimited	45,231,785

[1] At Mar. 14, 2023

Normal Course Issuer Bid - The company plans to make normal course purchases of up to 2,242,765 common shares representing 5% of the total outstanding. The bid commenced on Sept. 13, 2022, and expires on Sept. 12, 2023.

Major Shareholder - Trunkeast Investments Canada Limited held 28.9% interest at Mar. 14, 2023.

Price Range - TTNM/TSX

Year	Volume	High	Low	Close
2022	9,716,662	$3.25	$1.85	$2.42
2021	14,130,033	$4.34	$2.32	$3.05
2020	3,460,238	$2.50	$1.06	$2.50
2019	4,065,453	$1.65	$1.20	$1.50
2018	6,087,766	$2.40	$0.82	$1.28

Recent Close: $2.65

Capital Stock Changes - On Jan. 1, 2022, 400,000 common shares were issued pursuant to the acquisition of Bert and Son's Cartage Limited. Also during 2022, common shares were issued as follows: 565,108 under share purchase plan and 120,000 on exercise of options.

Dividends

TTNM com Ra $0.08 pa Q est. Dec. 15, 2020
Listed Aug 3/22.

Wholly Owned Subsidiaries

Bert and Son's Cartage Limited, Brantford, Ont.
Bracebridge Ecclestone 456 Inc., Ont.
Brantford 31 Ewart Inc.
Flexmor Trailers Rentals Inc., Ont.
Flexmore Financial Services Inc., Ont.
ITS Holdings Inc.
- 100% int. in **Haggarty Real Estate Holdings Inc.**
- 100% int. in **ITS Logistics Inc.**
- 100% int. in **International Truckload Services Inc.**, Belleville, Ont.
- 100% int. in **Jachar Developments Limited**

MLRP Holdings Inc.
Muskoka Transport Limited, Bracebridge, Ont.
Napanee Rd41 824 Inc., Ont.
Napanee Rd41 43AC Inc., Ont.
North Bay Birchs 348 Inc., Ont.
Preferred Delivery Systems Inc.
Sudbury Pioneer 1727 Inc., Ont.
Titanium Logistics Inc., Woodbridge, Ont.
- 100% int. in **Titanium Trucking Services Inc.**, Woodbridge, Ont.

Titanium Transportation U.S.A. Inc., United States.
- 100% int. in **Titanium American Logistics, Inc.**, United States.

Windsor Devon 3315 Inc., Ont.

Financial Statistics

Periods ended:	12m Dec. 31/22[A]		12m Dec. 31/21[¤A]
	$000s	%Chg	$000s
Operating revenue	**496,374**	**+24**	**399,443**
Cost of sales	350,310		295,067
Salaries & benefits	72,308		61,736
Stock-based compensation	733		647
Other operating expense	12,335		10,689
Operating expense	**435,686**	**+18**	**368,139**
Operating income	**60,688**	**+94**	**31,304**
Deprec., depl. & amort	27,525		21,337
Finance income	204		233
Finance costs, gross	4,883		3,045
Pre-tax income	**33,590**	**+337**	**7,689**
Income taxes	8,708		2,654
Net income	**24,882**	**+394**	**5,035**
Cash & equivalent	34,892		18,046
Accounts receivable	71,209		68,132
Current assets	110,921		100,508
Fixed assets, net	131,586		76,224
Right-of-use assets	25,683		44,006
Intangibles, net	9,717		10,233
Total assets	**281,142**	**+20**	**233,666**
Bank indebtedness	11,078		21,805
Accts. pay. & accr. liabs	37,114		37,165
Current liabilities	79,452		96,382
Long-term debt, gross	113,114		68,028
Long-term debt, net	86,829		49,680
Shareholders' equity	98,220		73,714
Cash from oper. activs	**43,471**	**+293**	**11,074**
Cash from fin. activs	19,517		49,549
Cash from invest. activs	(46,142)		(45,666)
Net cash position	**34,892**	**+93**	**18,046**
Capital expenditures	(70,529)		(17,731)
Capital disposals	21,804		4,189
	$		$
Earnings per share*	0.56		0.13
Cash flow per share*	0.99		0.28
Cash divd. per share*	0.08		0.08
	shs		shs
No. of shs. o/s*	45,122,621		44,037,513
Avg. no. of shs. o/s*	44,100,792		39,887,331
	%		%
Net profit margin	5.01		1.26
Return on equity	28.94		8.34
Return on assets	11.07		3.77
Foreign sales percent	45		59
No. of employees (FTEs)	1,100		1,100

* Common
[¤] Restated
[A] Reported in accordance with IFRS

Historical Summary
(as originally stated)

Fiscal Year	Oper. Rev.	Net Inc. Bef. Disc.	EPS*
	$000s	$000s	$
2022[A]	496,374	24,882	0.56
2021[A]	399,443	5,035	0.13
2020[A]	200,742	6,266	0.17
2019[A]	167,029	1,585	0.04
2018[A]	184,818	5,801	0.16

* Common
[A] Reported in accordance with IFRS

T.60 Toggle3D.ai Inc.

Symbol - TGGL **Exchange** - CSE **CUSIP** - 88908E

Head Office - PO Box 64039, RPO Royal Bank Plaza, Toronto, ON, M5J 2T6

Website - toggle3d.com

Email - investor.relations@toggle3d.ai

Investor Relations - Evan Gappelberg (631) 655-6733

Auditors - Saturna Group Chartered Accountants LLP C.A., Vancouver, B.C.

Transfer Agents - Computershare Trust Company of Canada Inc., Vancouver, B.C.

Profile - (Ont. 2023) Provides the Toggle3D.ai CAD-3D design studio software-as-a-service (SaaS) platform.

Toggle3D.ai is an augmented reality (AR) enhanced standalone web application which enables product designers, 3D artists, marketing professionals and e-commerce site owners to create, customize and publish high-quality 3D models and experiences without any technical or 3D design knowledge required.

The company was incorporated on Feb. 14, 2023, as a wholly owned subsidiary of **NexTech AR Solutions Corp.** to facilitate the transfer of the Toggle3D.ai CAD-3D design studio software-as-a-service (SaaS) platform to the company. The transfer was completed in June 2023, and the company was spun out to NexTech shareholders. A total of 20,000,000 common shares were issued by the company, of which 13,000,000 were retained by NexTech, representing a 45.4% interest in the company; 4,000,000 were distributed to NexTech shareholders on a pro rata basis; and 3,000,000 were transferred by NexTech to certain service providers in consideration of past services and other indebtedness.

Common listed on CSE, June 14, 2023.

Directors - Evan Gappelberg, CEO, Fla.; Belinda Tyldesley, corp. sec., B.C.; Nidhi Kumra, Toronto, Ont.; Anthony Pizzonia, Toronto, Ont.

Other Exec. Officers - Andrew Chan, CFO

Capital Stock

	Authorized (shs.)	Outstanding (shs.)[1]
Common	unlimited	28,632,473

[1] At June 14, 2023

Major Shareholder - NexTech AR Solutions Corp. held 45.4% interest at June 14, 2023.

Recent Close: $0.62

Capital Stock Changes - In June 2023, 20,000,000 common shares were issued pursuant to the transfer of the Toggle3D.ai CAD-3D design studio software-as-a-service (SaaS) platform from former parent NexTech AR Solutions Corp. to the company and 8,632,473 units (1 common share & 1 warrant) were issued without further consideration on exchange of subscription receipts sold previously by private placement at 25¢ each, with warrants exercisable at 50¢ per share for three years.

T.61 Tokens.com Corp.

Symbol - COIN **Exchange** - NEO **CUSIP** - 88908C

Head Office - 1 First Canadian Place, 3400-100 King St W, Toronto, ON, M5X 1A4 **Telephone** - (647) 578-7490

Website - tokens.com

Email - contact@tokens.com

Investor Relations - Jennifer Karkula (647) 578-7490

Auditors - Raymond Chabot Grant Thornton LLP C.A., Montréal, Qué.

Transfer Agents - Computershare Trust Company of Canada Inc., Vancouver, B.C.

Employees - 4 at Dec. 29, 2022

Profile - (Ont. 2009; orig. B.C., 1998) Owns digital assets and operates businesses utilizing blockchain technology.

Operations are focused on three operating segments: crypto staking; the metaverse; and play-to-earn (P2E) crypto gaming.

Wholly owned **Token.com Capital Corp.** stakes cryptocurrency tokens, which is conducted through third party validators and results in the ownership of digital assets.

Wholly owned **Metaverse Group Ltd.** is an integrated metaverse advertising and media platform that owns its own digital real estate. Revenue is generated from four services activities: metaverse strategy, architecture, digital land assets rental and partnerships.

Subsidiary **Hulk Labs Corp.** (93.6% owned) makes strategic investments in utility-driven non-fungible tokens (NFTs) and upcoming P2E games. Revenue is generated by acquiring both fungible and non-fungible tokens in the P2E sector and uses those tokens to generate a return from activities including playing the games. Hulk is building a software platform that connects owners of in-game assets.

As at Apr. 17, 2023, the value of tokens owned by the company was US$8,600,000 (Cdn$11,500,000).

In June 2023, the company acquired the remaining 44.8% interest in private Ontario-based **Metaverse Group Ltd.**, an integrated metaverse advertising and media platform that owns its own digital real estate, on the basis of 0.347 Tokens.com common shares for each Metaverse share held, which resulted in the issuance of 20,576,941 common shares.

In January 2023, subsidiary **Metaverse Group Ltd.** acquired CocoNFT, a non-fungible token (NFT) platform for non crypto-native creators which allows users to easily mint NFTs from their Instagram. Terms of the transaction were not disclosed.

The company changed its fiscal year end to September 30 from December 31, effective Sept. 30, 2022.

On July 17, 2022, the company acquired private **2839950 Ontario Inc.**, which is focused on building in-house software tools to power the play-to-earn gaming economy, for issuance of 1,000,000 common shares. Concurrently, the company acquired a 93.6% interest in **Hulk Labs Corp.** in exchange for all the assets acquired from the acquisition of 2839950 Ontario Inc.

Predecessor Detail - Name changed from COIN HODL INC., Apr. 27, 2021, pursuant to the reverse takeover acquisition of Tokens.com Inc. and concurrent amlgamation of Tokens.com Inc. with wholly owned 2821956 Ontario Inc. (and continued as Tokens.com Capital Corp.); basis 1 new for 11.9868 old shs.

Directors - Frederick T. (Fred) Pye, exec. chr., Pointe-Claire, Qué.; Andrew G. Kiguel, CEO, Toronto, Ont.; Lorne M. Sugarman, pres., Toronto, Ont.; Andrew D'Souza, St. James, Barbados; Emma Todd, Toronto, Ont.; Demetrios (Jimmy) Vaiopoulos, Toronto, Ont.

Other Exec. Officers - Eric Abrahams, COO; Martin Bui, CFO; Joshua (Josh) Doner, chief NFT officer; Jonathan Okihiro, chief invest. officer; Ian Fodie, corp. sec.

Capital Stock

	Authorized (shs.)	Outstanding (shs.)[1]
Preference	unlimited	nil
Common	unlimited	119,249,959

[1] At Aug. 3, 2023

Normal Course Issuer Bid - The company plans to make normal course purchases of up to 3,000,000 common shares representing 4.1% of the public float. The bid commenced on Nov. 1, 2022, and expires on Oct. 31, 2023.

Major Shareholder - Andrew G. Kiguel held 16% interest at May 25, 2023.

Price Range - COIN/NEO

Year	Volume	High	Low	Close
2022	8,936,800	$2.85	$0.10	$0.11
2021	11,179,304	$4.80	$0.36	$2.56
2020	287,679	$5.87	$0.96	$4.08
2019	365,929	$2.82	$1.44	$2.40
2018	232,199	$4.80	$1.50	$1.56

Consolidation: 1-for-11.9868 cons. in Apr. 2021
Recent Close: $0.18

Capital Stock Changes - In June 2023, 20,576,941 common shares were issued pursuant to the acquisition of the remaining 44.8% interest in Metaverse Group Ltd.

During the nine-month period ended Sept. 30, 2022, common shares were issued as follows: 1,000,000 pursuant to the acquisition of 2839950 Ontario Inc., 434,780 on exercise of warrants, 18,798 on exercise of options and 11,300 for debt conversion.

Wholly Owned Subsidiaries

Metaverse Group Ltd., Ont.
Tokens.com Capital Corp., Toronto, Ont.

Subsidiaries

93.6% int. in **Hulk Labs Corp.**, Ont.

Financial Statistics

Periods ended:	9m Sept. 30/22[A]		12m Dec. 31/21[ᵒA1]
	US$000s	%Chg	US$000s
Operating revenue	**678**	**n.a.**	**1,081**
Cost of sales	28		35
General & admin expense	2,466		5,301
Stock-based compensation	176		976
Operating expense	**2,670**	**n.a.**	**6,311**
Operating income	**(1,991)**	**n.a.**	**(5,230)**
Finance income	nil		3
Finance costs, gross	55		29
Investment income	(265)		(20)
Write-downs/write-offs	(3,790)		nil
Pre-tax income	**(5,727)**	**n.a.**	**(9,201)**
Income taxes	185		(919)
Net income	**(5,913)**	**n.a.**	**(8,282)**
Net inc. for equity hldrs	**(3,816)**	**n.a.**	**(8,260)**
Net inc. for non-cont. int	**(2,097)**	**n.a.**	**(23)**
Cash & equivalent	5,838		9,742
Accounts receivable	383		418
Current assets	6,311		10,398
Long-term investments	285		nil
Intangibles, net	13,450		33,150
Total assets	**20,046**	**n.a.**	**43,548**
Bank indebtedness	475		nil
Accts. pay. & accr. liabs	1,052		2,162
Current liabilities	1,527		2,162
Shareholders' equity	14,882		22,386
Non-controlling interest	3,211		3,744
Cash from oper. activs	**(5,002)**	**n.a.**	**(26,128)**
Cash from fin. activs	1,759		31,995
Cash from invest. activs	(5)		1,907
Net cash position	**5,838**	**n.a.**	**9,742**
	US$		US$
Earnings per share*	(0.04)		(0.12)
Cash flow per share*	(0.05)		(0.05)
	shs		shs
No. of shs. o/s*	97,926,757		96,461,879
Avg. no. of shs. o/s*	97,043,479		66,649,114
	%		%
Net profit margin	...		(766.14)
Return on equity	...		n.m.
Return on assets	...		n.a.

* Common
ᵒ Restated
[A] Reported in accordance with IFRS
[1] Results reflect the Apr. 28, 2021, reverse takeover acquisition of Tokens.com Inc.

Latest Results

Periods ended:	3m Dec. 31/22[A]		3m Dec. 31/21[ᵒA]
	US$000s	%Chg	US$000s
Operating revenue	152	-53	326
Net income	(1,727)	n.a.	(3,720)
Net inc. for equity hldrs	(1,649)	n.a.	(3,698)
Net inc. for non-cont. int	(78)		(23)
	US$		US$
Earnings per share*	(0.02)		(0.05)

* Common
ᵒ Restated
[A] Reported in accordance with IFRS

Historical Summary
(as originally stated)

Fiscal Year	Oper. Rev.	Net Inc. Bef. Disc.	EPS*
	US$000s	US$000s	US$
2022[A1]	678	(5,913)	(0.04)
2021[A]	1,081	(8,282)	(0.12)
	$000s	$000s	$
2020[A]	nil	2,903	2.40
2019[A]	1,669	(40)	(0.03)
2018[A]	(1,481)	(1,806)	(1.44)

* Common
[A] Reported in accordance with IFRS
[1] 9 months ended Sept. 30, 2022.
Note: Adjusted throughout for 1-for-11.9868 cons. in Apr. 2021

T.62 Tony G Co-Investment Holdings Ltd.

Symbol - TONY **Exchange** - CSE **CUSIP** - 89032Q
Head Office - 210-5800 Ambler Dr, Mississauga, ON, L4W 4J4 **Telephone** - (416) 480-2488
Website - tony.holdings
Email - gk@tony.holdings
Investor Relations - Gediminas Klepackas (416) 480-2488
Auditors - Mao & Ying LLP C.A., Vancouver, B.C.
Transfer Agents - TSX Trust Company, Toronto, Ont.

Profile - (Ont. 1988) Invests primarily in securities of companies in the blockchain technology, cryptocurrency, payment processing services, syndicated credit opportunities, online commerce and online gambling industries.

Investments include 51% interest in **News 3.0 Limited** (dba Cryptonews), a crypto-focused online media outlet that delivers original international news coverage on digital assets, blockchain, cryptocurrencies and related content; and 20% interest in **Sportclothes UAB**, a Lithuanian online retailer of high-end basketball, leisure, football and tennis shoes, clothing and accessories. Major company shareholder and director Antanas (Tony) Guoga holds interests in both companies.

Common reinstated on CSE, July 21, 2023.

Predecessor Detail - Name changed from Braingrid Limited, Aug. 11, 2021, pursuant to change of business to an investment company.

Directors - Antanas (Tony) Guoga, exec. chr., Lithuania; Gediminas Klepackas, CEO & interim CFO, Lithuania; Bruno Macchialii; Andrew Parks, Toronto, Ont.

Capital Stock

	Authorized (shs.)	Outstanding (shs.)[1]
Preferred	unlimited	nil
Common	unlimited	7,133,398

[1] At July 31, 2022

Major Shareholder - Antanas (Tony) Guoga held 47.67% interest, Brian Mehler and Fraser Blanchflower held 15.32% interest and European High Growth Opportunities Securitization Fund held 12.62% interest at Oct. 7, 2021.

Price Range - TONY/CSE

Year	Volume	High	Low	Close
2022	41,515	$1.56	$0.31	$0.31
2021	250,401	$1.55	$0.51	$1.55
2020	76,641	$1.50	$0.21	$0.56
2019	929,443	$22.00	$0.50	$1.00
2018	873	$25.50	$18.00	$19.00

Consolidation: 1-for-100 cons. in Nov. 2020
Recent Close: $0.26

Subsidiaries

51% int. in **News 3.0 Limited**, Bahamas. dba Cryptonews

Investments

20% int. in **Sportclothes UAB**, Lithuania.

Financial Statistics

Periods ended:	12m Jan. 31/22[A]		12m Jan. 31/21[ᵒA]
	$000s	%Chg	$000s
Operating revenue	**2,652**	**n.a.**	**nil**
General & admin expense	544		509
Stock-based compensation	173		30
Operating expense	**718**	**+33**	**539**
Operating income	**1,934**	**n.a.**	**(539)**
Finance income	1		392
Finance costs, gross	1,180		8
Pre-tax income	**(4,691)**	**n.a.**	**(156)**
Net inc. bef. disc. opers	**(4,691)**	**n.a.**	**(156)**
Income from disc. opers	(40)		(82)
Net income	**(4,731)**	**n.a.**	**(237)**
Cash & equivalent	193		24
Accounts receivable	8		78
Current assets	202		133
Right-of-use assets	nil		19
Total assets	**3,211**	**n.m.**	**152**
Bank indebtedness	nil		182
Accts. pay. & accr. liabs	212		692
Current liabilities	3,117		1,200
Long-term debt, gross	nil		36
Long-term debt, net	nil		36
Shareholders' equity	93		(1,085)
Cash from oper. activs	**(881)**	**n.a.**	**(139)**
Cash from fin. activs	1,063		193
Net cash position	**193**	**+704**	**24**
	$		$
Earns. per sh. bef disc opers*	(2.50)		(0.13)
Earnings per share*	(2.52)		(0.20)
Cash flow per share*	(0.47)		(0.12)
	shs		shs
No. of shs. o/s*	7,129,698		1,388,417
Avg. no. of shs. o/s*	1,880,254		1,174,111
	%		%
Net profit margin	(176.89)		n.a.
Return on equity	n.m.		n.m.
Return on assets	(208.80)		(90.52)

* Common
ᵒ Restated
[A] Reported in accordance with IFRS

Latest Results

Periods ended:	6m July 31/22[A]		6m July 31/21[ᵒA]
	$000s	%Chg	$000s
Net inc. bef. disc. opers	404	n.a.	(268)
Income from disc. opers	nil		(41)
Net income	404	n.a.	(309)
	$		$
Earns. per sh. bef. disc. opers.*	0.12		(0.20)
Earnings per share*	0.12		(0.23)

* Common
ᵒ Restated
[A] Reported in accordance with IFRS

Historical Summary
(as originally stated)

Fiscal Year	Oper. Rev.	Net Inc. Bef. Disc.	EPS*
	$000s	$000s	$
2022[A]	2,652	(4,691)	(2.50)
2021[A]	114	(237)	(0.20)
2020[A]	153	(2,321)	(4.00)
2019[A1]	194	(3,471)	(16.00)
2018[A2]	nil	(94)	(8.72)

* Common
[A] Reported in accordance with IFRS
[1] Results reflect the Dec. 28, 2018, reverse takeover acquisition of Braingrid Corporation.
[2] Results for 12 months ended Oct. 31, 2018, and prior years pertain to Match Capital Resources Corporation..
Note: Adjusted throughout for 1-for-100 cons. in Nov. 2020; 1-for-8 cons. in Dec. 2018

T.63 Top Strike Resources Corp.

Symbol - VENI **Exchange** - CSE **CUSIP** - 89054L
Head Office - 310-250 6 Ave SW, Calgary, AB, T2P 3H7 **Telephone** - (403) 992-9676
Website - www.vencanna.com
Email - jason@vencanna.com
Investor Relations - Jason Ewasuik (403) 992-9676
Auditors - MNP LLP C.A., Calgary, Alta.
Bankers - ATB Financial
Lawyers - Stikeman Elliott LLP, Calgary, Alta.
Transfer Agents - Odyssey Trust Company, Calgary, Alta.

Profile - (Alta. 2012; orig. B.C., 1989) Doing business as **Vencanna Ventures Inc.**, invests in early stage cannabis companies operating in the U.S. states and other jurisdictions where cannabis is legal.

The company invests throughout the cannabis value chain including cultivation, processing, product placement and distribution, as well as pursues partnerships for cannabis licence applications.

Holdings include **The Cannavative Group LLC**, a cultivator and processor in Nevada, operating a 40,000-sq.-ft. facility situated on 8.5 acres.

Recent Merger and Acquisition Activity

Status: pending **Revised:** Apr. 25, 2022

UPDATE: A definitive agreement was signed. PREVIOUS: Top Strike Resources Corp. entered into a letter of intent for the reverse takeover acquisition of Reno, Nev.-based The Cannavative Group LLC, which cultivates cannabis indoors, used in its products including the Motivator brand infused pre-roll, for issuance of 360,000,000 common shares at a deemed price of US$0.05 per share. Apr. 20, 2022 - The consideration was reduced to 240,000,000 units (1 common share & ½ warrant), with warrants exercisable at US$0.075 per share for 18 months. In addition, US$4,000,000 of debt owed by Cannavative to Top Strike would be converted into 80,000,000 units (1 common share & 0.4 warrant), with warrants exercisable at US$0.05 per share for nine months or US$0.075 per share for 18 months.

Predecessor Detail - Name changed from Colossal Resources Corp., Dec. 13, 2012.

Directors - Jon Sharun, exec. chr. & interim CFO, West Vancouver, B.C.; David McGorman, CEO, Calgary, Alta.; Matthew (Matt) Christopherson, Vancouver, B.C.; Alan Gertner, Toronto, Ont.; W. Scott McGregor, Calgary, Alta.; J. Smoke Wallin, Calif.

Other Exec. Officers - Jason Ewasuik, v-p, originations; Sanjib (Sony) Gill, corp. sec.

Capital Stock

	Authorized (shs.)	Outstanding (shs.)[1]
Preferred	unlimited	nil
Common	unlimited	181,283,390

[1] At July 31, 2022

Major Shareholder - Jon Sharun held 12.26% interest at Oct. 25, 2021.

Price Range - VENI/CSE

Year	Volume	High	Low	Close
2022	8,329,376	$0.06	$0.02	$0.06
2021	38,762,329	$0.08	$0.03	$0.03
2020	47,200,049	$0.04	$0.01	$0.04
2019	33,883,245	$0.17	$0.01	$0.02
2018	2,606,633	$0.55	$0.06	$0.12

Capital Stock Changes - During fiscal 2022, 128,000 common shares were repurchased under a Normal Course Issuer Bid.

Subsidiaries

60% int. in **Galenas New Jersey LLC**, N.J.

Financial Statistics

Periods ended:	12m Apr. 30/22^A		12m Apr. 30/21^A
	$000s	%Chg	$000s
Unrealized invest. gain (loss)	(355)		(227)
Total revenue	**457**	**n.a.**	**(351)**
Salaries & benefits	559		626
General & admin. expense	387		191
Stock-based compensation	6		69
Operating expense	**952**	**+7**	**886**
Operating income	**(495)**	**n.a.**	**(1,237)**
Deprec. & amort.	1		1
Finance costs, gross	149		114
Pre-tax income	**(646)**	**n.a.**	**(1,351)**
Net income	**(646)**	**n.a.**	**(1,351)**
Cash & equivalent	6,644		724
Accounts receivable	11		7
Current assets	9,745		3,217
Long-term investments	nil		6,785
Fixed assets, net	4		5
Total assets	**9,752**	**-3**	**10,010**
Accts. pay. & accr. liabs	333		174
Current liabilities	333		186
Long-term debt, gross	2,473		2,088
Long-term debt, net	2,473		2,088
Shareholders' equity	7,278		7,922
Cash from oper. activs	**5,924**	**n.a.**	**(3,049)**
Cash from fin. activs	(4)		27
Net cash position	**6,644**	**+818**	**724**
	$		$
Earnings per share*	(0.00)		(0.01)
Cash flow per share*	0.03		(0.02)
	shs		shs
No. of shs. o/s*	181,283,390		181,411,390
Avg. no. of shs. o/s*	181,454,343		181,779,061
	%		%
Net profit margin	(141.36)		n.m.
Return on equity	(8.50)		(15.76)
Return on assets	(5.03)		(12.82)

* Common

^A Reported in accordance with IFRS

Latest Results

Periods ended:	3m July 31/22^A		3m July 31/21^A
	$000s	%Chg	$000s
Total revenue	181	-65	510
Net income	(97)	n.a.	281
	$		$
Earnings per share*	(0.00)		0.00

* Common

^A Reported in accordance with IFRS

Historical Summary
(as originally stated)

Fiscal Year	Total Rev. $000s	Net Inc. Bef. Disc. $000s	EPS* $
2022^A	457	(646)	(0.00)
2021^A	(351)	(1,351)	(0.01)
2020^A	1,653	505	0.00
2019^A	nil	(1,913)	(0.02)
2018^A	nil	(20)	(0.00)

* Common

^A Reported in accordance with IFRS

T.64 Top 10 Split Trust

Symbol - TXT.UN **Exchange** - TSX **CUSIP** - 890520

Head Office - c/o Mulvihill Capital Management Inc., Standard Life Centre, 2600-121 King St W, PO Box 113, Toronto, ON, M5H 3T9 **Telephone** - (416) 681-3966 **Toll-free** - (800) 725-7172 **Fax** - (416) 681-3901

Website - www.mulvihill.com

Email - jgermain@mulvihill.com

Investor Relations - John D. Germain (800) 725-7172

Auditors - Deloitte LLP C.A., Toronto, Ont.

Lawyers - Osler, Hoskin & Harcourt LLP, Toronto, Ont.

Transfer Agents - Computershare Trust Company of Canada Inc., Toronto, Ont.

Trustees - RBC Investor Services Trust, Toronto, Ont.

Investment Managers - Mulvihill Capital Management Inc., Toronto, Ont.

Managers - Mulvihill Capital Management Inc., Toronto, Ont.

Profile - (Ont. 1997) Holds a portfolio of common shares of the six largest Canadian banks and the four largest Canadian life insurance companies in order to provide preferred securityholders with quarterly distributions on a fixed, cumulative and preferential basis and capital unitholders with leveraged exposure to the performance of the portfolio holdings including increases or decreases in value and dividends paid.

The trust will generally invest not less than 5% and not more than 15% of its assets in a single issuer.

The trust has a scheduled termination date of Mar. 31, 2026, which will be automatically extended for a further five years and thereafter for additional successive periods of five years. Upon termination, all outstanding preferred shares and class A shares will be redeemed.

The manager receives a management fee and an investment management fee at annual rates equal to 0.1% and 1.0%, respectively, of the net asset value of the fund, calculated and payable monthly in arrears.

Top 10 holdings at Mar. 31, 2023 (as a percentage of net asset value):

Holding	Percentage
iA Financial Corporation Inc.	11.7%
Great-West Lifeco Inc.	11.7%
National Bank of Canada	11.1%
Manulife Financial Corporation	10.9%
Sun Life Financial Inc.	10.2%
Royal Bank of Canada	9.5%
Canadian Imperial Bank of Commerce	8.3%
Bank of Montreal	8.2%
The Toronto-Dominion Bank	8.1%
The Bank of Nova Scotia	7.5%

Oper. Subsid./Mgt. Co. Directors - John P. Mulvihill, chr., CEO & corp. sec., Toronto, Ont.; John P. Mulvihill Jr., pres., Toronto, Ont.; John D. Germain, sr. v-p & CFO, Toronto, Ont.

Oper. Subsid./Mgt. Co. Officers - Jeff Dobson, v-p & portfolio mgr.; Peggy Shiu, v-p & chief compliance officer; Jack Way, v-p & portfolio mgr.

Capital Stock

	Authorized (shs.)	Outstanding (shs.)[1]
Preferred Security	unlimited	559,794[2]
Capital Unit	unlimited	559,794

[1] At Dec. 31, 2022

[2] Classified as debt.

Preferred Security - Entitled to fixed quarterly cash interest payments targeted to be 6.25% per annum of the original issue price of $12.50 per security. Retractable in December of each year, together with a capital unit, at a price equal to the net asset value (NAV) per combined unit (1 capital unit and 1 preferred security). Retractable in any other month, together with a capital unit, at a price equal to 95% of the lesser of: (i) the NAV per combined unit less 50¢; and (ii) the sum of: (a) the weighted average price per capital unit on TSX for the 10 trading days prior the retraction date; and (b) the weighted average price per security on TSX for the 10 trading days prior the retraction date. Payment of interest on preferred securities rank in priority to any distributions on the capital units. Non-voting.

Capital Unit - Entitled to quarterly cash distributions targeted to be 7.5% per annum of the NAV per capital unit. Retractable in December of each year, without a preferred security, at a price equal to the NAV per combined unit less the cost to purchase a preferred security in the market. Retractable in any other month, without a preferred security, at a price equal to 95% of the lesser of: (i) the NAV per combined unit less the cost to purchase a preferred security in the market and 50¢; and (ii) the weighted average price per capital unit on TSX for the 10 trading days prior the retraction date. A holder who surrenders a capital unit together with a preferred security will receive an amount based on the same terms described above. Distributions on capital units rank subordinate to any payment of interest on preferred securities. One vote per capital unit.

Major Shareholder - Widely held at Mar. 27, 2023.

Price Range - TXT.UN/TSX

Year	Volume	High	Low	Close
2022	170,722	$4.96	$2.08	$2.53
2021	239,153	$4.00	$1.60	$3.58
2020	411,913	$4.09	$0.95	$1.51
2019	219,735	$3.96	$2.35	$3.63
2018	161,590	$4.70	$2.57	$2.57

Recent Close: $2.20

Capital Stock Changes - During 2022, 20,100 capital units and 20,100 preferred securities were retracted.

Dividends

TXT.UN cap unit Var. Ra pa Q[1]

$0.02681	June 30/23	$0.04819	Mar. 31/23
$0.03656	Dec. 30/22	$0.02963	Sept. 29/22

Paid in 2023: $0.075 2022: $0.21713 2021: $0.2715

TXT.PR.A pfd 6.25% red. ret. Ra $0.78125 pa Q est. Dec. 30, 2005[2]

[1] Quarterly divd normally payable in June/20 has been omitted.

[2] Distributions are interest income.

Financial Statistics

Periods ended:	12m Dec. 31/22^A		12m Dec. 31/21^A
	$000s	%Chg	$000s
Realized invest. gain (loss)	650		2,302
Unrealized invest. gain (loss)	(1,868)		957
Total revenue	**(807)**	**n.a.**	**3,717**
General & admin. expense	347		396
Operating expense	**347**	**-12**	**396**
Operating income	**(1,154)**	**n.a.**	**3,321**
Finance costs, gross	453		555
Pre-tax income	**(1,607)**	**n.a.**	**2,766**
Net income	**(1,607)**	**n.a.**	**2,766**
Cash & equivalent	116		422
Accounts receivable	19		29
Investments	7,756		8,980
Total assets	**8,131**	**-21**	**10,308**
Accts. pay. & accr. liabs	73		79
Debt	6,997		7,249
Shareholders' equity	781		2,542
Cash from oper. activs	**712**	**-91**	**7,733**
Cash from fin. activs	(1,018)		(7,446)
Net cash position	**116**	**-73**	**422**
	$		$
Earnings per share*	(2.77)		3.81
Cash flow per share*	1.23		10.67
Net asset value per share*	1.40		4.38
Cash divd. per share*	0.22		0.27
	shs		shs
No. of shs. o/s*	559,794		579,894
Avg. no. of shs. o/s*	579,839		725,079
	%		%
Net profit margin	n.m.		74.41
Return on equity	(96.72)		138.51
Return on assets	(12.52)		26.86

* Capital unit

^A Reported in accordance with IFRS

Note: Net income reflects increase/decrease in net assets from operations.

Historical Summary
(as originally stated)

Fiscal Year	Total Rev. $000s	Net Inc. Bef. Disc. $000s	EPS* $
2022^A	(807)	(1,607)	(2.77)
2021^A	3,717	2,766	3.81
2020^A	(1,117)	(2,310)	(2.24)
2019^A	3,635	2,302	2.07
2018^A	(1,877)	(3,201)	(2.88)

* Capital unit

^A Reported in accordance with IFRS

T.65 Topicus.com Inc.

Symbol - TOI **Exchange** - TSX-VEN **CUSIP** - 89072T

Head Office - 1200-20 Adelaide St E, Toronto, ON, M5C 2T5 **Telephone** - (416) 861-9677 **Fax** - (416) 861-2287

Website - www.topicus.com

Email - jbaksh@csisoftware.com

Investor Relations - Jamal Baksh (416) 861-9677
Auditors - KPMG LLP C.A., Toronto, Ont.
Transfer Agents - Computershare Trust Company of Canada Inc., Toronto, Ont.
FP500 Subsidiary Revenue Ranking - 60
Profile - (Ont. 2020) Acquires, manages and builds vertical market software (VMS) businesses, primarily in Europe.

Operates through Topicus and Total Specific Solutions groups which develops, installs and customizes software, as well as provides related professional services and support for public and private clients in more than 20 diverse markets primarily in Europe. Vertical markets served include accountancy, agriculture, associations, automotive, central government, construction, education, facility management, finance, geoscience, healthcare, hospitality, legal, library and archives, local government, manufacturing, maritime, mobility, publishing, real estate and retail.

During the first quarter of 2023, the company agreed to acquire certain businesses for €24,796,000 cash on closing plus total estimated deferred payments of €1,100,000. The business acquisitions operate in the financial services vertical.

In March 2023, the company agreed to acquire private Amsterdam, Netherlands-based **Five Degrees Holding B.V.** for an undisclosed amount. Five Degrees is a cloud-native core banking technology provider to more than 40 banks across western Europe, the United States and Canada.

During 2022, the company completed a number of acquisitions for total cash consideration of €153,828,000 plus cash holdbacks of €20,649,000 and contingent consideration with an estimated fair value of €8,663,000. Most of the businesses acquired during the period were acquisitions of shares of software businesses similar to existing businesses operated by the company.

On July 1, 2022, the company acquired 60% interest in private Scotland-based **Subsurface** and its two interactive software solution for the oil and gas vertical from **Lloyd's Register**. The remaining 40% interest was acquired by **Constellation Software Inc.**'s Vela Software Group.

Recent Merger and Acquisition Activity

Status: completed **Revised:** May 16, 2022
UPDATE: Topicus acquired a 72.68% interest in Sygnity for zl197,000,000. PREVIOUS: Topicus.com Inc. announced its intention to submit a public tender offer to acquire Warsaw, Poland-based Sygnity S.A. at a price of zl12 per ordinary share. Sygnity develops and deploys integrated IT systems and infrastructure to public and private organizations, with a focus on banking, finance and insurance, energy, utilities, industry, local and central administration. Its activities include software production, implementation and maintenance, infrastructure and application integration and IT consulting. The transaction was expected to close by June 30, 2022. Apr. 11, 2022 - The public tender offer was submitted.

Directors - Robin Van Poelje, chr. & CEO, Netherlands; John E. Billowits, Toronto, Ont.; Jane Holden, Toronto, Ont.; J. Alex F. Macdonald, Toronto, Ont.; Donna Parr, Toronto, Ont.
Other Exec. Officers - Jamal Baksh, CFO; Daan Dijkhuizen, CEO, Topicus operating grp.; Han Knooren, CEO, Total Specific Solutions Public operating grp.; Ramon Zanders, CEO, Total Specific Solutions Blue operating grp.

Capital Stock

	Authorized (shs.)	Outstanding (shs.)[1]
Preferred	unlimited	nil
Subordinate Vtg.	unlimited	81,889,763
Super Vtg.	1	1[2]

[1] At Mar. 27, 2023
[2] Held by Constellation Software Inc.

Subordinate Voting - Entitled to dividends. Non-convertible. One vote per share.
Super Voting - Entitled to dividends. Convertible, at any time by Constellation Software Inc., into one subordinate voting share. Entitled to that number of votes that equals 50.1% of the aggregate number of votes attached to all of the outstanding super voting shares and subordinate voting shares at such time.
Preferred (old) - Non-voting. Redeemed on Feb. 1, 2022, at €19.06 per share.
Major Shareholder - Constellation Software Inc. held 74.12% interest at Mar. 27, 2023.

Price Range - TOI/TSX-VEN

Year	Volume	High	Low	Close
2022	11,811,364	$118.00	$61.47	$71.09
2021	17,051,169	$143.00	$57.00	$116.10

Recent Close: $104.80
Capital Stock Changes - On Feb. 1, 2022, all 39,412,385 preferred shares were converted into a like number of subordinate voting shares. Also during 2022, 1,965,000 subordinate voting shares were issued on conversion of a like number of Topicus.com Coöperatief U.A. ordinary units.

Subsidiaries

63.07% int. in **Topicus.com Coöperatief U.A.**, Netherlands.
Note: The preceding list includes only the major related companies in which interests are held.

Financial Statistics

Periods ended:	12m Dec. 31/22[A]		12m Dec. 31/21[A]
	€000s	%Chg	€000s
Operating revenue	**916,681**	**+23**	**742,541**
Salaries & benefits	508,721		398,171
General & admin expense	159,533		120,804
Operating expense	**668,254**	**+29**	**518,976**
Operating income	**248,427**	**+11**	**223,565**
Deprec., depl. & amort.	134,944		109,663
Finance costs, net	9,069		10,748
Write-downs/write-offs	nil		(1,600)
Pre-tax income	**104,418**	**n.a.**	**(2,200,632)**
Income taxes	16,808		21,600
Net income	**87,610**	**n.a.**	**(2,222,233)**
Net inc. for equity hldrs	**52,928**	**n.a.**	**(1,884,042)**
Net inc. for non-cont. int.	**34,682**	**n.a.**	**(338,191)**
Cash & equivalent	136,772		75,333
Inventories	1,419		570
Accounts receivable	95,790		70,725
Current assets	309,795		200,989
Long-term investments	2,130		998
Fixed assets, net	19,579		15,326
Right-of-use assets	54,412		54,382
Intangibles, net	874,000		744,136
Total assets	**1,294,794**	**+26**	**1,028,319**
Bank indebtedness	30,867		29,116
Accts. pay. & accr. liabs	174,824		135,993
Current liabilities	570,141		398,794
Long-term debt, gross	242,555		209,216
Long-term debt, net	41,280		96,113
Long-term lease liabilities	36,634		38,955
Preferred share equity	nil		2,047,473
Shareholders' equity	266,099		(705,604)
Non-controlling interest	201,685		1,061,236
Cash from oper. activs	**203,008**	**+15**	**176,423**
Cash from fin. activs	(8,155)		56,694
Cash from invest. activs	(133,407)		(213,425)
Net cash position	**136,772**	**+82**	**75,326**
Capital expenditures	(7,303)		(5,385)
	€		€
Earnings per share*	0.66		(30.16)
Cash flow per share*	2.52		2.79
	shs		shs
No. of shs. o/s*	81,889,764		40,512,379
Avg. no. of shs. o/s*	80,488,504		63,318,650
	%		%
Net profit margin	9.56		(299.27)
Return on equity	n.m.		n.m.
Return on assets	7.54		(266.22)
Foreign sales percent	100		100

* Subord. Vtg.
[A] Reported in accordance with IFRS

Historical Summary
(as originally stated)

Fiscal Year	Oper. Rev.	Net Inc. Bef. Disc.	EPS*
	€000s	€000s	€
2022[A]	916,681	87,610	0.66
2021[A]	742,541	(2,222,233)	(30.16)
2020[A1]	493,986	63,684	1.08

* Subord. Vtg.
[A] Reported in accordance with IFRS
[1] Results pertain to Topicus.com Coöperatief U.A. (formerly Constellation Software Netherlands Holding Coöperatief U.A.). Shares adjusted to reflect Constellation Software Inc.'s spin-out of Total Specific Solutions operating group (TSS) and Topicus.com B.V.

T.66 Torchlight Innovations Inc.

Symbol - TLX.P **Exchange** - TSX-VEN **CUSIP** - 89103M
Head Office - Five Bentall Centre, 2300-550 Burrard St, Vancouver, BC, V6C 2B5 **Telephone** - (604) 999-4456
Email - fayyaz@zabinacapital.com
Investor Relations - Fayyaz Alimohamed (604) 999-4456
Auditors - Davidson & Company LLP C.A., Vancouver, B.C.
Lawyers - Gowling WLG (Canada) LLP, Vancouver, B.C.
Transfer Agents - Odyssey Trust Company, Vancouver, B.C.
Profile - (B.C. 2021) Capital Pool Company.
Directors - Fayyaz Alimohamed, CEO, CFO & corp. sec., North Vancouver, B.C.; Robert A. (Bob) Archer, Okanagan Falls, B.C.; Frederic W. R. (Fred) Leigh, Toronto, Ont.

Capital Stock

	Authorized (shs.)	Outstanding (shs.)[1]
Common	unlimited	5,500,000

[1] At May 24, 2023

Major Shareholder - Fayyaz Alimohamed held 18.18% interest and Frederic W. R. (Fred) Leigh held 18.18% interest at Feb. 14, 2023.

Price Range - TLX.P/TSX-VEN

Year	Volume	High	Low	Close
2022	1,070,230	$0.21	$0.15	$0.16

Recent Close: $0.15
Capital Stock Changes - On Aug. 8, 2022, an initial public offering of 3,000,000 common shares was completed at 10¢ per share.

T.67 Tornado Global Hydrovacs Ltd.

Symbol - TGH **Exchange** - TSX-VEN **CUSIP** - 89108T
Head Office - 510-7015 McLeod Trail SE, Calgary, AB, T2H 2K6 **Telephone** - (403) 742-6121 **Toll-free** - (877) 340-8141
Website - www.tornadotrucks.com
Email - bnewton@tghl.ca
Investor Relations - Brett Newton (403) 204-6333
Auditors - Ernst & Young LLP C.A., Calgary, Alta.
Transfer Agents - TSX Trust Company
Profile - (Alta. 2016) Designs, fabricates, manufactures and sells hydrovac trucks for excavation service providers to the oil and gas industry and the municipal market in North America.

Hydrovac trucks use high pressure water and vacuum to safely penetrate and cut soil to expose critical infrastructure for repair and installation without damage. This equipment is used in the oil and gas production industry, the pipeline industry and by municipalities to safely expose underground utilities for repair.

Products include F2 Urban, with debris capacity of 7 cubic yard volume and water capacity of 800 U.S. gallons; F3 City, with debris capacity of 10 cubic yard volume and water capacity of 1,250 U.S. gallons; F4 Rural, with debris capacity of 12 cubic yard volume and water capacity of 1,550 U.S. gallons; and F5 Remote, with debris capacity of 12 cubic yard volume and water capacity of 1,950 U.S. gallons.

Manufacturing operations are conducted at its own facility in Red Deer, with a sales office located in Calgary, Alta.

In July 2022, the company entered into a product supply and development agreement for the co-development and supply of customized hydrovac trucks (supply contract) with Ditch Witch, a division of **The Toro Company**. The supply contract contains a commitment for the delivery of a number of hydrovac trucks to Ditch Witch which was estimated to generate minimum gross revenue for the company of US$43,850,000 during the four year term.

Directors - K. Guy Nelson, chr., Toronto, Ont.; George C. Tai, corp. sec., Calgary, Alta.; James (Jie) Chui, Vancouver, B.C.; Robert G. (Bob) Marshall, Toronto, Ont.; Chuyu (Daniel) Wu, Shanghai, Shanghai, People's Republic of China
Other Exec. Officers - Brett Newton, pres. & CEO; Alastair J. (Al) Robertson, CFO; Derek Li, v-p, fin. & contr.

Capital Stock

	Authorized (shs.)	Outstanding (shs.)[1]
Class A Common	unlimited	135,871,119

[1] At May 24, 2023

Major Shareholder - James (Jie) Chui held 39.64% interest at Oct. 27, 2022.

Price Range - TGH/TSX-VEN

Year	Volume	High	Low	Close
2022	3,740,821	$0.75	$0.35	$0.45
2021	6,021,228	$0.57	$0.18	$0.55
2020	10,847,437	$0.21	$0.09	$0.19
2019	6,553,131	$0.23	$0.14	$0.19
2018	6,027,373	$0.16	$0.08	$0.15

Recent Close: $0.52
Capital Stock Changes - During 2022, class A common shares were issued as follows: 6,000,000 on exercise of options and 3,075,000 on exercise of warrants.

Wholly Owned Subsidiaries

Tornado Global Hydrovac (North America) Inc., Canada.
Tornado Hydrovacs Asia Pacific Holdings Ltd., People's Republic of China.
- 100% int. in **Tornado Global Hydrovacs (Shanghai) Ltd.**, Shanghai, People's Republic of China.

Financial Statistics

Periods ended:	12m Dec. 31/22[A]		12m Dec. 31/21[A]
	$000s	%Chg	$000s
Operating revenue	**59,516**	**+81**	**32,876**
Cost of sales	46,088		25,312
Salaries & benefits	6,467		5,572
General & admin expense	2,262		2,074
Stock-based compensation	464		489
Operating expense	**55,281**	**+65**	**33,447**
Operating income	**4,235**	**n.a.**	**(571)**
Deprec., depl. & amort.	1,313		1,575
Finance costs, gross	468		363
Write-downs/write-offs	nil		(953)
Pre-tax income	**2,442**	**n.a.**	**(3,517)**
Income taxes	(13)		(302)
Net income	**2,455**	**n.a.**	**(3,215)**
Cash & equivalent	3,419		834
Inventories	18,535		8,307
Accounts receivable	7,416		2,977
Current assets	30,472		13,255
Fixed assets, net	8,214		9,850
Intangibles, net	1,751		2,210
Total assets	**40,505**	**+60**	**25,315**
Accts. pay. & accr. liabs	14,422		7,142
Current liabilities	19,908		7,969
Long-term debt, gross	9,830		4,732
Long-term debt, net	4,471		4,594
Long-term lease liabilities	90		604
Shareholders' equity	16,036		12,130
Cash from oper. activs	**(3,528)**	**n.a.**	**2,418**
Cash from fin. activs	5,049		(2,654)
Cash from invest. activs	997		(1,061)
Net cash position	**3,419**	**+310**	**834**
Capital expenditures	(517)		(1,118)
Capital disposals	1,715		542
	$		$
Earnings per share*	0.02		(0.03)
Cash flow per share*	(0.03)		0.02
	shs		shs
No. of shs. o/s*	135,871,119		126,796,119
Avg. no. of shs. o/s*	130,231,040		126,775,297
	%		%
Net profit margin	4.12		(9.78)
Return on equity	17.43		(23.85)
Return on assets	8.89		(10.89)
Foreign sales percent	47		35

* Cl.A. Common

[A] Reported in accordance with IFRS

Latest Results

Periods ended:	3m Mar. 31/23[A]		3m Mar. 31/22[A]
	$000s	%Chg	$000s
Operating revenue	21,095	+112	9,952
Net income	785	+66	474
	$		$
Earnings per share*	0.01		0.00

* Cl.A. Common

[A] Reported in accordance with IFRS

Historical Summary
(as originally stated)

Fiscal Year	Oper. Rev.	Net Inc. Bef. Disc.	EPS*
	$000s	$000s	$
2022[A]	59,516	2,455	0.02
2021[A]	32,876	(3,215)	(0.03)
2020[A]	31,038	(667)	(0.01)
2019[A]	60,426	(1,634)	(0.01)
2018[A]	38,908	(1,323)	(0.01)

* Cl.A. Common

[A] Reported in accordance with IFRS

T.68 Toromont Industries Ltd.*

Symbol - TIH **Exchange** - TSX **CUSIP** - 891102
Head Office - 3131 Hwy 7 W, PO Box 5511, Concord, ON, L4K 1B7
Telephone - (416) 667-5511 **Fax** - (416) 667-5555
Website - www.toromont.com
Email - lkorbak@toromont.com
Investor Relations - Lynn M. Korbak (416) 667-5511
Auditors - Ernst & Young LLP C.A., Toronto, Ont.
Transfer Agents - TSX Trust Company, Montréal, Qué.
FP500 Revenue Ranking - 135
Employees - 6,800 at Dec. 31, 2022

Profile - (Can. 1961) Distributes, sells, rents and services a broad range of construction, industrial, compact construction and material handling primarily in Canada; and designs, engineers, installs and supplies industrial and recreational refrigeration systems in Canada and the U.S.

Equipment Group

Toromont CAT is one of the world's largest Caterpillar dealerships with a network of 46 locations in Ontario, Quebec, Manitoba, Newfoundland and Labrador, Nova Scotia, New Brunswick, Prince Edward Island and Nunavut. The company is also the MaK marine engines dealer from the Great Lakes to the eastern seaboard of the U.S., from Maine to Virginia. The dealerships sell a broad range of Caterpillar products, including earthmoving and construction equipment, paving machines, mining equipment, industrial and marine applications, lift trucks and power generation. In addition to the sales and service of equipment, operations include the distribution of replacement parts for Caterpillar products and other equipment lines, and the re-manufacture and repair of engines and engine components. Dealerships also represent products from other manufacturers in equipment lines not served by Caterpillar such as Masaba, Metso and Weiler. Headquarters are located in Concord, Ont.

Battlefield Equipment Rentals - The CAT Rental Store is a single-source supplier of rental equipment, Caterpillar Compact Equipment, new and used equipment sales, specialty tools, building products, safety supplies and safety training programs for construction contractors, trades people, plant maintenance contractors and homeowners. Battlefield Equipment sells brand name products and is the authorized distributor for such brands as Caterpillar, Spectra Precision/Trimble, Wacker Neuson, Stihl, Honda, SkyJack, Genie, Husqvarna, Atlas Copco, Bosch, Gorman-Rupp and many others. Battlefield Equipment has a network of 68 branches and shared locations across Manitoba, Ontario, Quebec, New Brunswick, Prince Edward Island, Nova Scotia, and Newfoundland and Labrador, including its head office facility in Stoney Creek, Ont. Battlefield Equipment also operates Jobsite Industrial Rentals Services, which provides equipment for the plant maintenance, factory and industrial industries, focusing on the electrical, mechanical, welding, millwrighting and rigging trades. Jobsite Industrial Rentals Services operates out of 12 locations in Ontario, New Brunswick, Nova Scotia, Alberta and British Columbia.

Toromont Material Handling is a dealer of material handling equipment from 14 branches and locations in Manitoba, Ontario and Quebec, providing products from a number of large lift truck and battery manufacturers including Mitsubishi, Logisnext, Kalmar, AUSA and Hoppecke targeted to a range of industries including paper product manufacturers, ports and terminals, automotive parts and components manufacturers, beverage makers, and home and hardware retailers.

Wholly owned **SITECH Mid-Canada Ltd.** sells and services Trimble GPS machine control and guidance systems and laser survey equipment, and provides professional services to the earthmoving and mining segments. Sitech operates from locations in London and Burlington, Ont.; Trois-Rivières, Que.; Dartmouth, N.S.; and Winnipeg, Man.

Wholly owned **Toromont Energy Ltd.** develops distributed generation and combined heat and power projects. Core business includes the design, construction, operation and maintenance of high efficiency power plants using Caterpillar's power generation technologies. Toromont Energy operates plants throughout Ontario, including plants in Sudbury (2) and Waterloo, that supply energy to healthcare, agricultural, mining and manufacturing sectors.

CIMCO

Wholly owned **CIMCO Refrigeration Inc.** designs, engineers, installs and services industrial and recreational compression equipment across Canada and the United States. Industrial refrigeration applications include the food, dairy, cold storage and beverage segments. Recreational refrigeration applications include artificial ice surfaces used for various sporting activities and other unusual ice surfaces.

Recent Merger and Acquisition Activity

Status: completed **Announced:** May 1, 2023
Toromont Industries Ltd. sold wholly owned AgWest Ltd. to Mechan International, which is part of Zweegers Equipment Group, for $41,600,000 in cash, subject to post-closing adjustments. AgWest is an agricultural equipment dealer with five locations throughout Manitoba offering farm equipment such as combines and tractors from multiple brands including CLAAS, Fendt, Challenger, RoGator, Massey Ferguson and Schulte.

Predecessor Detail - Name changed from Toromont Industrial Holdings Ltd., Apr. 10, 1974.

Directors - Richard G. Roy, chr., Verchères, Qué.; Scott J. Medhurst, pres. & CEO, Toronto, Ont.; Jeffrey S. Chisholm†, King City, Ont.; Peter J. Blake, Vancouver, B.C.; Benjamin D. (Ben) Cherniavsky, Vancouver, B.C.; Cathryn E. (Cathy) Cranston, Toronto, Ont.; Sharon L. Hodgson, Toronto, Ont.; Frederick J. (Fred) Mifflin, Toronto, Ont.; Katherine A. Rethy, Huntsville, Ont.

Other Exec. Officers - Joel Couture, COO, Toromont Cat; Michael S. H. (Mike) McMillan, exec. v-p & CFO; Jennifer J. Cochrane, v-p, fin.; Michael P. (Mike) Cuddy, v-p & CIO; Lynn M. Korbak, gen. counsel & corp. sec.; Colin Goheen, pres., Battlefield Equipment Rentals Inc.; Miles Gregg, pres., Toromont Cat Construction; William J. Harvey, pres., Toromont Cat Mining; David A. (Dave) Malinauskas, pres., CIMCO Refrigeration

† Lead director

Capital Stock

	Authorized (shs.)	Outstanding (shs.)[1]
Preferred	unlimited	nil
Common	unlimited	82,184,027

[1] At July 26, 2023

Options - At Dec. 31, 2022, options were outstanding to purchase 1,967,892 common shares at a weighted average exercise price of $73.21 per share with a weighted average remaining life of 6.6 years.

Normal Course Issuer Bid - The company plans to make normal course purchases of up to 8,193,292 common shares representing 10% of the public float. The bid commenced on Sept. 19, 2022, and expires on Sept. 18, 2023.

Major Shareholder - Widely held at Feb. 28, 2023.

Price Range - TIH/TSX

Year	Volume	High	Low	Close
2022	32,834,562	$124.25	$93.25	$97.71
2021	33,662,130	$115.23	$84.61	$114.36
2020	52,910,302	$94.86	$52.36	$89.20
2019	31,396,435	$71.15	$52.71	$70.59
2018	33,098,091	$68.11	$46.24	$54.26

Recent Close: $110.36

Capital Stock Changes - During 2022, 347,291 common shares were issued on exercise of options and 473,100 common shares were repurchased under a Normal Course Issuer Bid.

Dividends

TIH com Ra $1.72 pa Q est. Apr. 4, 2023
Prev. Rate: $1.56 est. Apr. 4, 2022
Prev. Rate: $1.40 est. July 5, 2021
Prev. Rate: $1.24 est. Apr. 2, 2020

Long-Term Debt - Outstanding at Dec. 31, 2022:

3.71% sr. debs. due 2025	$150,000,000
3.84% sr. debs. due 2027	500,000,000
Less: Debt issuance costs	2,940,000
	647,060,000
Less: Current portion	nil
	647,060,000

Wholly Owned Subsidiaries

CIMCO Refrigeration Inc., Mobile, Ala.
SITECH Eastern Canada Ltd., Concord, Ont.
Toromont Energy Ltd., Concord, Ont.

Note: The preceding list includes only the major related companies in which interests are held.

Financial Statistics

Periods ended:	12m Dec. 31/22[A]		12m Dec. 31/21[A]
	$000s	%Chg	$000s
Operating revenue	**4,230,736**	**+9**	**3,886,537**
Cost of goods sold	2,952,340		2,776,209
General & admin expense	491,417		476,031
Operating expense	**3,443,757**	**+6**	**3,252,240**
Operating income	**786,979**	**+24**	**634,297**
Deprec., depl. & amort.	162,810		158,360
Finance income	22,232		9,027
Finance costs, gross	27,338		28,161
Pre-tax income	**619,063**	**+36**	**456,803**
Income taxes	164,865		124,093
Net income	**454,198**	**+37**	**332,710**
Cash & equivalent	927,780		916,830
Inventories	1,025,759		720,421
Accounts receivable	579,682		451,944
Current assets	2,569,195		2,108,441
Fixed assets, net	1,086,913		976,346
Right-of-use assets	22,910		18,752
Intangibles, net	472,565		475,043
Total assets	**4,182,125**	**+17**	**3,583,796**
Accts. pay. & accr. liabs	651,259		536,679
Current liabilities	1,056,739		813,702
Long-term debt, gross	647,060		646,337
Long-term debt, net	647,060		646,337
Long-term lease liabilities	16,160		11,780
Shareholders' equity	2,325,359		1,953,329
Cash from oper. activs	**216,953**	**-60**	**542,724**
Cash from fin. activs	(162,159)		(148,143)
Cash from invest. activs	(44,333)		(68,869)
Net cash position	**927,780**	**+1**	**916,830**
Capital expenditures	(69,334)		(71,203)
Capital disposals	25,168		2,467
Unfunded pension liability	n.a.		62,237
Pension fund surplus	11,095		n.a.
	$		$
Earnings per share*	5.52		4.03
Cash flow per share*	2.63		6.57
Cash divd. per share*	1.56		1.36
	shs		shs
No. of shs. o/s*	82,318,159		82,443,968
Avg. no. of shs. o/s*	82,339,480		82,547,961
	%		%
Net profit margin	10.74		8.56
Return on equity	21.23		18.22
Return on assets	12.21		10.19
Foreign sales percent	3		2
No. of employees (FTEs)	6,800		6,400

* Common

[A] Reported in accordance with IFRS

Latest Results

Periods ended:	6m June 30/23[A]		6m June 30/22[oA]
	$000s	%Chg	$000s
Operating revenue	2,221,319	+17	1,903,312
Net inc. bef. disc. opers	229,436	+34	171,278
Income from disc. opers	5,605		(65)
Net income	235,041	+37	171,213
	$		$
Earns. per sh. bef. disc. opers.*	2.79		2.08
Earnings per share*	2.86		2.08

* Common
[o] Restated
[A] Reported in accordance with IFRS

Historical Summary
(as originally stated)

Fiscal Year	Oper. Rev.	Net Inc. Bef. Disc.	EPS*
	$000s	$000s	$
2022[A]	4,230,736	454,198	5.52
2021[A]	3,886,537	332,710	4.03
2020[A]	3,478,897	254,915	3.10
2019[A]	3,678,705	286,800	3.52
2018[A]	3,504,236	251,984	3.10

* Common
[A] Reported in accordance with IFRS

T.69 Toronto Cleantech Capital Inc.

Symbol - YAY.P **Exchange** - TSX-VEN **CUSIP** - 89113K
Head Office - Waterfront Centre, 1200-200 Burrard St, Vancouver, BC, V7X 1T2 **Telephone** - (416) 828-2077
Email - sbrolla@rogers.com
Investor Relations - James J. Sbrolla (416) 828-2077
Auditors - MNP LLP C.A., Calgary, Alta.
Transfer Agents - TSX Trust Company, Calgary, Alta.
Profile - (B.C. 2021) Capital Pool Company.
Directors - James J. Sbrolla, pres. & CEO, Toronto, Ont.; Eric Beutel, CFO, Toronto, Ont.; Lyle Clarke, Whitby, Ont.; Benjamin (Benj) Gallander, Toronto, Ont.; Mark Korol, Toronto, Ont.; Enzo Macri, Woodbridge, Ont.; John Nicholson, Mississauga, Ont.; Andrew White, Toronto, Ont.; William B. (Bill) White, Palm Coast, Fla.
Other Exec. Officers - Dimitris Stubos, corp. sec.

Capital Stock

	Authorized (shs.)	Outstanding (shs.)[1]
Common	unlimited	11,500,000

[1] At Sept. 27, 2022

Major Shareholder - James J. Sbrolla held 34.78% interest at June 30, 2021.

Price Range - YAY.P/TSX-VEN

Year	Volume	High	Low	Close
2022	143,710	$0.28	$0.19	$0.25
2021	386,298	$0.38	$0.16	$0.25

Recent Close: $0.23

T.70 The Toronto-Dominion Bank*

Symbol - TD **Exchange** - TSX **CUSIP** - 891160
Head Office - PO Box 1 Toronto-Dominion Centre, Toronto, ON, M5K 1A2 **Telephone** - (416) 307-6018 **Toll-free** - (866) 567-8888 **Fax** - (416) 308-1943
Website - www.td.com
Email - brooke.hales@td.com
Investor Relations - Brooke Hales (416) 307-8647
Auditors - Ernst & Young LLP C.A., Toronto, Ont.
Lawyers - McCarthy Tétrault LLP
Transfer Agents - Computershare Trust Company, N.A., Providence, R.I.; TSX Trust Company, Montréal, Qué.
FP500 Revenue Ranking - 5
Employees - 94,945 at Oct. 31, 2022
Profile - (Can. 1955 amalg.) A Schedule I Canadian chartered bank providing a full range of retail and commercial banking, wealth and insurance, and wholesale banking products and services to more than 27,000,000 customers around the world.

Canadian Personal and Commercial Banking - Provides personal and business banking products and services to about 15,000,000 customers across Canada. Personal banking provides a full range of financial products and services to retail customers under the TD Canada Trust brand through 1,060 branches, 3,401 automated teller machines (ATMs), mobile specialized salesforce, and telephone, mobile and Internet banking. Products consist of personal deposits, which include chequing, savings and investment products; real estate secured lending; consumer lending, which includes various unsecured financing products; and credit cards and payment products, including debit cards, digital money movement, payment plans and proprietary, co-branded and affinity credit cards. Business banking provides financing, investment, cash management, international trade services and day-to-day banking solutions to small, medium and large businesses, including automobile financing offered through TD Auto Finance Canada. Business banking also offers merchant solutions which include point-of-sale technology and payment solutions for businesses.

U.S. Retail - Provides personal and business banking and wealth management products and services to over 9,900,000 customers in the U.S. under the TD Bank, America's Most Convenient Bank® brand. Operations are located throughout the Northeast, Mid-Atlantic, Metro D.C., the Carolinas and Florida. Personal banking provides a full range of financial products and services through a network of 1,160 stores, 2,693 ATMs, and telephone, mobile and Internet banking. Personal banking solutions include personal deposits, consumer lending, credit cards services and automobile financing (TD Auto Finance U.S.). Business banking provides financing, investment, cash management, international trade and day-to-day banking products and services to U.S. businesses and governments across a wide range of industries. The wealth management business provides wealth products and services to retail and institutional clients, including wealth management advice, financial planning, estate and trust services, insurance and annuity products, and asset management. Asset management solutions are provided through wholly owned **Epoch Investment Partners, Inc.**, the U.S. arm of the bank's TD Asset Management (TDAM) investment business. Operations also include interest in **The Charles Schwab Corporation**, a Westlake, Tex.-based provider of wealth management, securities brokerage, banking, asset management, custody and financial advisory services to individual investors and independent investment advisors.

Wealth Management and Insurance - Serves about 6,000,000 customers across the wealth management and insurance businesses in Canada. The wealth management business offers direct investing through TD Direct Investing online brokerage platform, investment advice, financial planning and asset management to retail and institutional investors. The TDAM business operates in Canada through wholly owned **TD Asset Management Inc.**, which provides investment solutions to corporations, pension funds, endowments, foundations and individual investors. TDAM manages assets on behalf of investors and offers various investment products including mutual funds, managed portfolios and corporate class funds. Under the TD Insurance brand, the bank offers automobile, home, life, health, travel, motorcycle and recreational vehicle, and credit protection insurance products through direct to consumer distribution channels, such as telephone and online, and to members of affinity groups.

Wholesale Banking - Through TD Securities and its division TD Cowen, the bank provides capital markets and corporate and investment banking services to corporate, government and institutional clients through more than 6,500 professionals in 40 cities across North America, Europe and Asia-Pacific. Products and services include sales, trading and research, debt and equity underwriting, client securitization, prime services, trade execution services, corporate lending and syndication, advisory services, trade finance, cash management and investment portfolios.

On Aug. 1, 2022, the bank sold 28,400,000 non-voting common shares of **The Charles Schwab Corporation** for US$1.9 billion. As a result, the bank's interest in Charles Schwab decreased to 12% from 13.4%. The proceeds would be used to fund the proposed acquisition of **Cowen Inc.**

Recent Merger and Acquisition Activity

Status: terminated **Revised:** May 4, 2023
UPDATE: The transaction was terminated as TD was unable to obtain a timetable for regulatory approvals. TD would pay a US$200,000,000 break fee to First Horizon, in addition to a US$25,000,000 fee reimbursement. PREVIOUS: The Toronto-Dominion Bank (TD) agreed to acquire Memphis, Tenn.-based First Horizon Corporation for US$25 cash per share, in a transaction valued at US$13.4 billion. First Horizon has US$89 billion in assets and operates 412 branches and serves over 1,100,000 consumer, business and commercial customers across 12 southeastern U.S. states. On closing, TD's U.S. operations would be a top six U.S. bank with US$614 billion in assets and a network of 1,560 branches serving 10,700,000 customers across 22 states. TD expects to achieve US$610,000,000 in pre-tax cost synergies through a combination of technology and systems consolidation, and other operational efficiencies and incur transaction and integration costs of US$1.3 billion primarily in the first two years following closing. If the transaction does not close prior to Nov. 27, 2022, First Horizon shareholders would receive, at closing, an additional US$0.65 per share on an annualized basis for the period from Nov. 27, 2022, through the day immediately prior to the closing. The transaction was expected to close in the first quarter of TD's 2023 fiscal year. Feb. 9, 2023 - TD and First Horizon announced they had mutually agreed to extend the outside date to May 27, 2023.

Status: completed **Revised:** Mar. 1, 2023
UPDATE: The transaction was completed. PREVIOUS: The Toronto-Dominion Bank (TD) agreed to acquire Cowen Inc., a New York, N.Y.-based investment bank and financial services company listed on the NASDAQ, for US$1.3 billion, representing US$39 cash per Cowen share. TD would finance the transaction with proceeds from the completed sale of non-voting shares of The Charles Schwab Corporation. Cowen provides investment banking, research, sales and trading, prime brokerage, outsourced trading and commission management services. Completion of the transaction would add 1,700 employees from Cowen to TD, where parts of the combined business would operate as TD Cowen, a division of TD Securities. The transaction was expected to be completed in the first quarter of 2023 and was subject to regulatory approvals in Canada and the U.S., as well as a vote by Cowen shareholders. TD would be required to pay a termination fee of US$42,250,000 if the transaction was terminated because of a recommendation change or another superior proposal. Feb. 24, 2023 - all regulatory approvals required were received.

Directors - Brian M. Levitt, chr., Kingston, Ont.; Bharat B. Masrani, grp. pres. & CEO, Toronto, Ont.; Cherie L. Brant, Ont.; Amy W. Brinkley, Charlotte, N.C.; Brian C. Ferguson, Calgary, Alta.; Colleen A. Goggins, Princeton, N.J.; David E. Kepler, Sanford, Mich.; Alan N. MacGibbon, Toronto, Ont.; Karen E. Maidment, Cambridge, Ont.; Claude Mongeau, Montréal, Qué.; S. Jane Rowe, Toronto, Ont.; Nancy G. Tower, Calgary, Alta.; Dr. Ajay K. Virmani, Oakville, Ont.; Mary A. Winston, Charlotte, N.C.

Other Exec. Officers - Riaz Ahmed, grp. head, wholesale banking; Ajai K. Bambawale, grp. head & chief risk officer; Raymond (Chong Ho) Chun, grp. head, wealth & insce.; Barbara Hooper, grp. head, Cdn. bus. banking; Michael G. Rhodes, grp. head, Cdn. personal banking; Leovigildo (Leo) Salom Jr., grp. head, U.S. retail & pres. & CEO, TD Bank, N.A.; Kelvin (Vi Luan) Tran, grp. head & CFO; Gregory M. (Greg) Keeley, sr. exec. v-p, platforms & tech.; Kenneth W. (Kenn) Lalonde, sr. exec. v-p & chief HR officer; Christine Morris, sr. exec. v-p, transformation, enablement & cust. experience; Jane Langford, exec. v-p & gen. counsel; Anita O'Dell, sr. v-p & chief auditor; Gwen Hughes, assoc. v-p & corp. sec.

Capital Stock

	Authorized (shs.)	Outstanding (shs.)[1]
Class A First Preferred	unlimited	
Series 1		20,000,000
Series 3		20,000,000
Series 5		20,000,000
Series 7		14,000,000
Series 9		8,000,000
Series 16		14,000,000
Series 18		14,000,000
Series 20		16,000,000
Series 22		14,000,000
Series 24		18,000,000
Series 27		850,000
Series 28		800,000
Limited Recourse Capital Notes	n.a.	
Series 1		1,750,000
Series 2		1,500,000
Series 3		1,750,000
Common	unlimited	1,827,456,863

[1] At July 31, 2023

Class A First Preferred - Issuable in series at the discretion of the directors. The class A first preferred shares rank in priority to the common shares with respect to the payment of dividends and the distribution of assets in the event of liquidation, dissolution or winding-up of the bank. Pursuant to the Bank Act, approval of the holders of class A first preferred shares is required for creation or issuance of any class of shares ranking prior to or on a parity with the class A first preferred shares. Non-voting except to the extent provided in any series or by the Bank Act.

Series 1 - Entitled to non-cumulative preferential annual dividends of $0.9155 per share payable quarterly to Oct. 31, 2024, and thereafter at a rate reset every five years equal to the five-year Government of Canada bond yield plus 2.24%. Redeemable on Oct. 31, 2024, and on October 31 every five years thereafter at $25 per share plus declared and unpaid dividends. Convertible at the holder's option, on Oct. 31, 2024, and on October 31 every five years thereafter, into floating rate preferred, series 2 shares on a share-for-share basis, subject to certain conditions. The series 2 shares would pay a quarterly dividend equal to the 90-day Canadian Treasury bill rate plus 2.24%. Convertible into common shares upon occurrence of certain trigger events related to financial viability. The contingent conversion formula is 1.0 multiplied by $25 plus declared and unpaid dividends divided by the greater of (i) a floor price of $5.00; and (ii) current market price of the common shares.

Series 3 - Entitled to non-cumulative preferential annual dividends of $0.92025 per share payable quarterly to July 31, 2024, and thereafter at a rate reset every five years equal to the five-year Government of Canada bond yield plus 2.27%. Redeemable on July 31, 2024, and on July 31 every five years thereafter at $25 per share plus declared and unpaid dividends. Convertible at the holder's option, on July 31, 2024, and on July 31 every five years thereafter, into floating rate preferred, series 4 shares on a share-for-share basis, subject to certain conditions. The series 4 shares would pay a quarterly dividend equal to the 90-day Canadian Treasury bill rate plus 2.27%. Convertible into common shares upon occurrence of certain trigger events related to financial viability. The contingent conversion formula is 1.0 multiplied by $25 plus declared and unpaid dividends divided by the greater of (i) a floor price of $5.00; and (ii) current market price of the common shares.

Series 5 - Entitled to non-cumulative preferential annual dividends of $0.969 per share payable quarterly to Jan. 31, 2025, and thereafter at a rate reset every five years equal to the five-year Government of Canada bond yield plus 2.25%. Redeemable on Jan. 31, 2025, and on January 31 every five years thereafter at $25 per share plus declared and unpaid dividends. Convertible at the holder's option, on Jan. 31, 2025, and on January 31 every five years thereafter, into floating rate preferred, series 6 shares on a share-for-share basis, subject to certain conditions. The series 6 shares would pay a quarterly dividend equal to the 90-day Canadian Treasury bill rate plus 2.25%. Convertible into common shares upon occurrence of certain trigger events related to financial viability. The contingent conversion formula is 1.0 multiplied by $25 plus declared and unpaid dividends divided by the greater of (i) a floor price of $5.00; and (ii) current market price of the common shares.

Series 7 - Entitled to non-cumulative preferential annual dividends of $0.80025 per share payable quarterly to July 31, 2025, and thereafter at a rate reset every five years equal to the five-year Government of Canada bond yield plus 2.79%. Redeemable on July 31, 2025, and on July 31 every five years thereafter at $25 per share plus declared and unpaid dividends. Convertible at the holder's option, on July 31, 2025, and on July 31 every five years thereafter, into floating rate preferred, series 8 shares on a share-for-share basis, subject to certain conditions. The series 8 shares would pay a quarterly dividend equal to the 90-day

Canadian Treasury bill rate plus 2.79%. Convertible into common shares upon occurrence of certain trigger events related to financial viability. The contingent conversion formula is 1.0 multiplied by $25 plus declared and unpaid dividends divided by the greater of (i) a floor price of $5.00; and (ii) current market price of the common shares.

Series 9 - Entitled to non-cumulative preferential annual dividends of $0.8105 per share payable quarterly to Oct. 31, 2025, and thereafter at a rate reset every five years equal to the five-year Government of Canada bond yield plus 2.87%. Redeemable on Oct. 31, 2025, and on October 31 every five years thereafter at $25 per share plus declared and unpaid dividends. Convertible at the holder's option, on Oct. 31, 2025, and on October 31 every five years thereafter, into floating rate preferred, series 10 shares on a share-for-share basis, subject to certain conditions. The series 10 shares would pay a quarterly dividend equal to the 90-day Canadian Treasury bill rate plus 2.87%. Convertible into common shares upon occurrence of certain trigger events related to financial viability. The contingent conversion formula is 1.0 multiplied by $25 plus declared and unpaid dividends divided by the greater of (i) a floor price of $5.00; and (ii) current market price of the common shares.

Series 16 - Entitled to non-cumulative preferential annual dividends of $1.57525 per share payable quarterly to Oct. 31, 2027, and thereafter at a rate reset every five years equal to the five-year Government of Canada bond yield plus 3.01%. Redeemable on Oct. 31, 2027, and on October 31 every five years thereafter at $25 per share plus declared and unpaid dividends. Convertible at the holder's option, on Oct. 31, 2027, and on October 31 every five years thereafter, into floating rate preferred, series 17 shares on a share-for-share basis, subject to certain conditions. The series 17 shares would pay a quarterly dividend equal to the 90-day Canadian Treasury bill rate plus 3.01%. Convertible into common shares upon occurrence of certain trigger events related to financial viability. The contingent conversion formula is 1.0 multiplied by $25 plus declared and unpaid dividends divided by the greater of (i) a floor price of $5.00; and (ii) current market price of the common shares.

Series 18 - Entitled to non-cumulative preferential annual dividends of $1.4367 per share payable quarterly to Apr. 30, 2028, and thereafter at a rate reset every five years equal to the five-year Government of Canada bond yield plus 2.7%. Redeemable on Apr. 30, 2028, and on April 30 every five years thereafter at $25 per share plus declared and unpaid dividends. Convertible at the holder's option, on Apr. 30, 2028, and on April 30 every five years thereafter, into floating rate preferred, series 19 shares on a share-for-share basis, subject to certain conditions. The series 19 shares would pay a quarterly dividend equal to the 90-day Canadian Treasury bill rate plus 2.7%. Convertible into common shares upon occurrence of certain trigger events related to financial viability. The contingent conversion formula is 1.0 multiplied by $25 plus declared and unpaid dividends divided by the greater of (i) a floor price of $5.00; and (ii) current market price of the common shares.

Series 20 - Entitled to non-cumulative preferential annual dividends of $1.1875 per share payable quarterly to Oct. 31, 2023, and thereafter at a rate reset every five years equal to the five-year Government of Canada bond yield plus 2.59%. Redeemable on Oct. 31, 2023, and on October 31 every five years thereafter at $25 per share plus declared and unpaid dividends. Convertible at the holder's option, on Oct. 31, 2023, and on October 31 every five years thereafter, into floating rate preferred, series 21 shares on a share-for-share basis, subject to certain conditions. The series 21 shares would pay a quarterly dividend equal to the 90-day Canadian Treasury bill rate plus 2.59%. Convertible into common shares upon occurrence of certain trigger events related to financial viability. The contingent conversion formula is 1.0 multiplied by $25 plus declared and unpaid dividends divided by the greater of (i) a floor price of $5.00; and (ii) current market price of the common shares.

Series 22 - Entitled to non-cumulative preferential annual dividends of $1.30 per share payable quarterly to Apr. 30, 2024, and thereafter at a rate reset every five years equal to the five-year Government of Canada bond yield plus 3.27%. Redeemable on Apr. 30, 2024, and on April 30 every five years thereafter at $25 per share plus declared and unpaid dividends. Convertible at the holder's option, on Apr. 30, 2024, and on April 30 every five years thereafter, into floating rate preferred, series 23 shares on a share-for-share basis, subject to certain conditions. The series 23 shares would pay a quarterly dividend equal to the 90-day Canadian Treasury bill rate plus 3.27%. Convertible into common shares upon occurrence of certain trigger events related to financial viability. The contingent conversion formula is 1.0 multiplied by $25 plus declared and unpaid dividends divided by the greater of (i) a floor price of $5.00; and (ii) current market price of the common shares.

Series 24 - Entitled to non-cumulative preferential annual dividends of $1.275 per share payable quarterly to July 31, 2024, and thereafter at a rate reset every five years equal to the five-year Government of Canada bond yield plus 3.56%. Redeemable on July 31, 2024, and on July 31 every five years thereafter at $25 per share plus declared and unpaid dividends. Convertible at the holder's option, on July 31, 2024, and on July 31 every five years thereafter, into floating rate preferred, series 25 shares on a share-for-share basis, subject to certain conditions. The series 25 shares would pay a quarterly dividend equal to the 90-day Canadian Treasury bill rate plus 3.56%. Convertible into common shares upon occurrence of certain trigger events related to financial viability. The contingent conversion formula is 1.0 multiplied by $25 plus declared and unpaid dividends divided by the greater of (i) a floor price of $5.00; and (ii) current market price of the common shares.

Series 27 - Entitled to non-cumulative preferential annual dividends of $57.50 per share payable semi-annually to Oct. 31, 2027, and thereafter at a rate reset every five years equal to the five-year Government of Canada bond yield plus 3.317%. Redeemable on Oct. 31, 2027, and on October 31 every five years thereafter at $1,000 per share plus declared and unpaid dividends. Convertible into common shares upon occurrence of certain trigger events related to financial viability. The contingent conversion formula is 1.0 multiplied by $1,000 plus declared and unpaid dividends divided by the greater of (i) a floor price of $5.00; and (ii) current market price of the common shares.

Series 28 - Entitled to non-cumulative preferential annual dividends of $72.32 per share payable semi-annually to Oct. 31, 2027, and thereafter at a rate reset every five years equal to the five-year Government of Canada bond yield plus 4.2%. Redeemable on Oct. 31, 2027, and on October 31 every five years thereafter at $1,000 per share plus declared and unpaid dividends. Convertible into common shares upon occurrence of certain trigger events related to financial viability. The contingent conversion formula is 1.0 multiplied by $1,000 plus declared and unpaid dividends divided by the greater of (i) a floor price of $5.00; and (ii) current market price of the common shares.

Limited Recourse Capital Notes (LRCN) - Notes with recourse limited to assets held in a trust consolidated by the bank. **Series 1** - Bear interest at 3.6% per annum until Oct. 31, 2026, and thereafter at an annual rate reset every five years equal to the five-year Government of Canada bond yield plus 2.747% until maturity on Oct. 31, 2081. Trust assets consist of non-cumulative five-year reset class A first preferred series 26 shares. **Series 2** - Bear interest at 7.283% per annum until Oct. 31, 2027, and thereafter at an annual rate reset every five years equal to the five-year Government of Canada bond yield plus 4.1% until maturity on Oct. 31, 2082. Trust assets consist of non-cumulative five-year reset class A first preferred series 29 shares. **Series 3** - Bear interest at 8.125% per annum until Oct. 31, 2027, and thereafter at an annual rate reset every five years equal to the five-year U.S. Treasury yield plus 4.075% until maturity on Oct. 31, 2082. Trust assets consist of non-cumulative five-year reset class A first preferred series 30 shares.

Common - One vote per share.

Options - At Oct. 31, 2022, options were outstanding to purchase 12,800,000 common shares at prices ranging from $40.54 to $95.33 per share and expiring on various dates to Dec. 12, 2031.

Class A First Preferred Series 14 (old) - Were entitled to non-cumulative preferential annual dividends of $1.2125 per share payable quarterly to Oct. 31, 2021. Redeemed on Oct. 31, 2021, at $25 per share.

Normal Course Issuer Bid - The company plans to make normal course purchases of up to 30,000,000 common shares representing 1.6% of the total outstanding. The bid commenced on June 26, 2023, and expires on June 25, 2024.

Major Shareholder - Widely held at May 25, 2023.

Price Range - TD/TSX

Year	Volume	High	Low	Close
2022	1,366,462,397	$109.08	$77.27	$87.67
2021	1,354,645,166	$98.21	$71.65	$96.98
2020	1,439,865,893	$76.10	$49.01	$71.92
2019	852,124,044	$77.96	$67.12	$72.83
2018	816,070,862	$80.05	$65.56	$67.86

Recent Close: $80.37

Capital Stock Changes - In April 2022, offering of 850,000 class A first preferred series 27 shares was completed at $1,000 per share. In July 2022, offering of 800,000 class A first preferred series 28 shares was completed at $1,000 per share. In September 2022, 1,500,000 class A first preferred series 29 shares were issued in conjunction with issuance of $1,500,000,000 of limited recourse capital notes, series 2 priced at $1,000 per note. In October 2022, 1,750,000 class A first preferred series 30 shares were issued in conjunction with issuance of US$1,750,000,000 of limited recourse capital notes, series 3 priced at US$1,000 per note. Also during fiscal 2022, common shares were issued as follows: 17,000,000 under dividend reinvestment plan and 1,800,000 on exercise of options; 21,000,000 common shares were repurchased under a Normal Course Issuer Bid. In addition, 900,000 common shares were released from treasury.

Dividends

TD com Ra $3.84 pa Q est. Jan. 31, 2023**
Prev. Rate: $3.56 est. Jan. 31, 2022
Prev. Rate: $3.16 est. Apr. 30, 2020
TD.PF.A pfd 1st A ser 1 red. exch. Adj. Ra $0.9155 pa Q est. Jan. 31, 2020
TD.PF.B pfd 1st A ser 3 red. exch. Adj. Ra $0.92025 pa Q est. Oct. 31, 2019
TD.PF.C pfd 1st A ser 5 red. exch. Adj. Ra $0.969 pa Q est. Apr. 30, 2020
TD.PF.D pfd 1st A ser 7 red. exch. Adj. Ra $0.80025 pa Q est. Oct. 31, 2020
TD.PF.E pfd 1st A ser 9 red. exch. Adj. Ra $0.8105 pa Q est. Jan. 31, 2021
TD.PF.I pfd 1st A ser 16 red. exch. Adj. Ra $1.57525 pa Q est. Jan. 31, 2023
TD.PF.J pfd 1st A ser 18 red. exch. Adj. Ra $1.43675 pa Q est. July 31, 2023
TD.PF.K pfd 1st A ser 20 red. exch. Adj. Ra $1.1875 pa Q est. Jan. 31, 2019
TD.PF.L pfd 1st A ser 22 red. exch. Adj. Ra $1.30 pa Q est. Apr. 30, 2019
TD.PF.M pfd 1st A ser 24 red. exch. Adj. Ra $1.275 pa Q est. Oct. 31, 2019
pfd 1st A ser 12 red. exch. Adj. Ra $1.375 pa Q est. Apr. 30, 2016[1]
$0.34375**f**............ Apr. 30/21
pfd 1st A ser 14 red. exch. Adj. Ra $1.2125 pa Q est. Oct. 31, 2016[2]
$0.303125**f**........... Oct. 31/21

[1] Redeemed April 30, 2021 at $25 per sh.

[2] Redeemed Oct. 31, 2021 at $25 per sh.

** Reinvestment Option **f** Final Payment

Long-Term Debt - Outstanding at Oct. 31, 2022:

Subord. notes & debs.:	
9.15% due May 2025	$200,000,000
3.589% due Sept. 2028[1]	1,750,000,000
3.224% due July 2029[2]	1,505,000,000
3.105% due Apr. 2030[3]	3,001,000,000
4.859% due Mar. 2031[4]	1,247,000,000
3.625% due Sept. 2031[5]	1,940,000,000
3.06% due Jan. 2032[6]	1,647,000,000
	11,290,000,000

[1] After Sept. 14, 2023, bears interest at the 90-day bankers' acceptance rate plus 1.06%.

[2] After July 25, 2024, bears interest at the 90-day bankers' acceptance rate plus 1.25%.

[3] After Apr. 22, 2025, bears interest at the 90-day bankers' acceptance rate plus 2.16%.

[4] After Mar. 4, 2026, bears interest at the 90-day bankers' acceptance rate plus 3.49%.

[5] After Sept. 15, 2026, bears interest at the five-year mid-swap rate plus 2.205%.

[6] After Jan. 26, 2027, bears interest at the 90-day bankers' acceptance rate plus 1.33%.

Wholly Owned Subsidiaries

Cowen Inc., New York, N.Y.

Meloche Monnex Inc., Montréal, Qué. Book value of shares owned by the bank at Oct. 31, 2022, totaled $2,370,000,000.

- 100% int. in **Security National Insurance Company**, Montréal, Qué.
  - 100% int. in **Primmum Insurance Company**, Montréal, Qué.
  - 100% int. in **TD Direct Insurance Inc.**, Toronto, Ont.
  - 100% int. in **TD General Insurance Company**, Montréal, Qué.
  - 100% int. in **TD Home and Auto Insurance Company**, Toronto, Ont.

TD Auto Finance (Canada) Inc., Toronto, Ont. Book value of shares owned by the bank at Oct. 31, 2022, totaled $3,721,000,000.

TD Group U.S. Holdings LLC, Wilmington, Del. Book value of shares owned by the bank at Oct. 31, 2022, totaled $71,879,000,000.

- 100% int. in **TD Bank US Holding Company**, Cherry Hill, N.J.
  - 100% int. in **Epoch Investment Partners, Inc.**, New York, N.Y.
  - 100% int. in **TD Bank, N.A.**, Cherry Hill, N.J.
    - 100% int. in **TD Equipment Finance, Inc.**, Cherry Hill, N.J.
    - 100% int. in **TD Private Client Wealth LLC**, New York, N.Y.
    - 100% int. in **TD Wealth Management Services Inc.**, Mount Laurel, N.J.
  - 100% int. in **TD Bank USA, N.A.**, Cherry Hill, N.J.
- 100% int. in **Toronto-Dominion Holdings (U.S.A.), Inc.**, New York, N.Y.
  - 100% int. in **TD Prime Services LLC**, New York, N.Y.
  - 100% int. in **TD Securities Automated Trading LLC**, Chicago, Ill.
  - 100% int. in **TD Securities (USA) LLC**, New York, N.Y.
  - 100% int. in **Toronto Dominion Capital (U.S.A.), Inc.**, New York, N.Y.
  - 100% int. in **Toronto Dominion Investments, Inc.**, New York, N.Y.
  - 100% int. in **Toronto Dominion (New York) LLC**, New York, N.Y.
  - 100% int. in **Toronto Dominion (Texas), LLC**, New York, N.Y.

TD Investment Services Inc., Toronto, Ont. Book value of shares owned by the bank at Oct. 31, 2022, totaled $38,000,000.

TD Ireland Unlimited Company, Dublin, Ireland. Book value of shares owned by the bank at Oct. 31, 2022, totaled $2,057,000,000.

- 100% int. in **TD Global Finance Unlimited Company**, Dublin, Ireland.

TD Life Insurance Company, Toronto, Ont. Book value of shares owned by the bank at Oct. 31, 2022, totaled $115,000,000.

TD Mortgage Corporation, Toronto, Ont. Book value of shares owned by the bank at Oct. 31, 2022, totaled $11,737,000,000.

- 100% int. in **The Canada Trust Company**, Toronto, Ont.
- 100% int. in **TD Pacific Mortgage Corporation**, Toronto, Ont.

TD Securities Inc., Toronto, Ont. Book value of shares owned by the bank at Oct. 31, 2022, totaled $2,713,000,000.

TD Securities (Japan) Co. Ltd., Tokyo, Japan. Book value of shares owned by the bank at Oct. 31, 2022, totaled $11,000,000.
TD Vermillion Holdings Limited, Toronto, Ont. Book value of shares owned by the bank at Oct. 31, 2022, totaled $28,723,000,000.
- 100% int. in **TD Financial International Ltd.**, Hamilton, Bermuda.
  - 100% int. in **TD Reinsurance (Barbados) Inc.**, St. James, Barbados.

TD Wealth Holdings Canada Limited, Toronto, Ont. Book value of shares owned by the bank at Oct. 31, 2022, totaled $5,963,000,000.
- 100% int. in **TD Asset Management Inc.**, Toronto, Ont.
  - 100% int. in **GMI Servicing Inc.**, Winnipeg, Man.
  - 100% int. in **TD Waterhouse Private Investment Counsel Inc.**, Toronto, Ont.
- 100% int. in **TD Waterhouse Canada Inc.**, Toronto, Ont.

Toronto Dominion Australia Limited, Sydney, N.S.W., Australia. Book value of shares owned by the bank at Oct. 31, 2022, totaled $94,000,000.
Toronto Dominion Investments B.V., London, Middx., United Kingdom. Book value of shares owned by the bank at Oct. 31, 2022, totaled $1,174,000,000.
- 100% int. in **TD Bank Europe Limited**, London, Middx., United Kingdom.

Toronto Dominion (South East Asia) Limited, Singapore, Singapore. Book value of shares owned by the bank at Oct. 31, 2022, totaled $1,225,000,000.

Investments

12.1% int. in **The Charles Schwab Corporation**, Westlake, Tex.
Note: The preceding list includes only the major related companies in which interests are held.

Financial Statistics

Periods ended:	12m Oct. 31/22A		12m Oct. 31/21A
	$000s	%Chg	$000s
Interest income	**41,032,000**	**+39**	**29,581,000**
Interest expense	13,679,000		5,450,000
Net interest income	**27,353,000**	**+13**	**24,131,000**
Provision for loan losses	1,067,000		(224,000)
Other income	21,679,000		18,562,000
Salaries & pension benefits	13,394,000		12,378,000
Non-interest expense	27,541,000		25,783,000
Pre-tax income	**20,424,000**	**+19**	**17,134,000**
Income taxes	3,986,000		3,621,000
Net income	**17,429,000**	**+22**	**14,298,000**
Cash & equivalent	145,850,000		165,893,000
Securities	572,160,000		509,549,000
Net non-performing loans	1,746,000		1,782,000
Total loans	991,210,000		889,906,000
Fixed assets, net	9,400,000		9,181,000
Total assets	**1,917,528,000**	**+11**	**1,728,672,000**
Deposits	1,229,970,000		1,125,125,000
Other liabilities	564,885,000		492,499,000
Subordinated debt	11,290,000		11,230,000
Preferred share equity	11,246,000		5,690,000
Shareholders' equity	111,383,000		99,818,000
Cash from oper. activs	**38,949,000**	**-22**	**50,129,000**
Cash from fin. activs	(4,819,000)		(5,036,000)
Cash from invest. activs	(31,895,000)		(45,268,000)
Pension fund surplus	1,718,000		554,000
	$		$
Earnings per share*	9.48		7.73
Cash flow per share*	21.51		27.58
Cash divd. per share*	3.56		3.16
	shs		shs
No. of shs. o/s*	1,820,700,000		1,822,000,000
Avg. no. of shs. o/s*	1,810,500,000		1,817,700,000
	%		%
Basel III Common Equity Tier 1	16.20		15.20
Basel III Tier 1	18.30		16.50
Basel III Total	20.70		19.10
Net profit margin	35.55		33.49
Return on equity	17.68		15.27
Return on assets	0.96		0.83
Foreign sales percent	40		38
No. of employees (FTEs)	94,945		89,464

* Common
A Reported in accordance with IFRS

Latest Results

Periods ended:	9m July 31/23A		9m July 31/22A
	$000s	%Chg	$000s
Net interest income	22,450,000	+14	19,723,000
Net income	7,896,000	-27	10,758,000
	$		$
Earnings per share*	4.12		5.86

* Common
A Reported in accordance with IFRS

Historical Summary
(as originally stated)

Fiscal Year	Int. Inc. $000s	Net Inc. Bef. Disc. $000s	EPS* $
2022A	41,032,000	17,429,000	9.48
2021A	29,581,000	14,298,000	7.73
2020A	35,647,000	11,895,000	6.43
2019A	41,999,000	11,686,000	6.26
2018A	36,422,000	11,334,000	6.02

* Common
A Reported in accordance with IFRS

T.71 Torrent Capital Ltd.

Symbol - TORR **Exchange** - TSX-VEN **CUSIP** - 89141P
Head Office - 2001-1969 Upper Water St, Halifax, NS, B3J 3R7 **Telephone** - (902) 442-7187 **Fax** - (902) 491-4281
Website - www.torrentcapital.ca
Email - rrandall@numusfinancial.com
Investor Relations - Robert Randall (902) 442-7187
Auditors - MNP LLP C.A., Toronto, Ont.
Bankers - Royal Bank of Canada, Halifax, N.S.
Lawyers - Fogler, Rubinoff LLP, Toronto, Ont.
Transfer Agents - Computershare Trust Company of Canada Inc., Toronto, Ont.
Profile - (Ont. 1932) Invests in securities of private and public companies.

Investments include **WildBrain Ltd.**, which develops, produces, distributes and licenses children, youth and family content for television, film and online platforms in Canada and international markets; **kneat.com, inc.**, which offers its Kneat Gx software platform for electronic validation lifecycle management designed for pharmaceutical, biotechnology and medical device manufacturers; **The Game Day**, which offers digital sports media platform that includes original content and social distribution network for betting and fantasy fans; **Electrovaya Inc.**, develops and manufactures portable Lithium-ion batteries and battery management systems for warehousing, automotive, vehicles, medical and mobile devices; and **AnalytixInsight Inc.**, provides financial research and content for information providers, investors, media and finance portals in Canada.

Other investments include six public clean technology companies, nine public resource companies and a 50% interest (**Port of Argentia Inc.** 50%) in **Argentia Capital Inc.**, which focuses on the construction of port infrastructure, the provision of services and equity ownership in businesses that support aquaculture, renewable energy, and the oil and gas sectors, as well as other port developments. As at Mar. 31, 2023, the company's total investment fair value was $19,482,067.

Predecessor Detail - Name changed from Metallum Resources Inc., Feb. 6, 2017; basis 1 new for 3 old shs.

Directors - Wade K. Dawe, CEO, Halifax, N.S.; Carl B. Hansen, Mississauga, Ont.; James (Jim) Megann, Fall River, N.S.; Wayne Miles, N.B.; Carl Sheppard, St. John's, N.L.

Other Exec. Officers - Robert (Rob) Randall, CFO; Scott Gardner, chief invest. officer

Capital Stock

	Authorized (shs.)	Outstanding (shs.)[1]
Common	unlimited	25,004,167

[1] At May 23, 2023

Major Shareholder - Wade K. Dawe held 28.3% interest and Glynn David Fisher held 17.2% interest at May 23, 2023.

Price Range - TORR/TSX-VEN

Year	Volume	High	Low	Close
2022	1,540,308	$1.17	$0.60	$0.66
2021	3,038,690	$1.25	$0.78	$1.15
2020	7,966,946	$1.10	$0.25	$0.92
2019	2,546,677	$0.45	$0.28	$0.43
2018	5,549,817	$0.50	$0.21	$0.40

Recent Close: $0.67

Capital Stock Changes - During 2022, common shares were issued as follows: 575,000 on exercise of options and 197,500 on vesting of restricted share units.

Financial Statistics

Periods ended:	12m Dec. 31/22A		12m Dec. 31/21A
	$000s	%Chg	$000s
Realized invest. gain (loss)	322		3,475
Unrealized invest. gain (loss)	(6,649)		(299)
Total revenue	**(6,388)**	**n.a.**	**3,176**
General & admin. expense	939		1,270
Stock-based compensation	244		267
Operating expense	**1,183**	**-23**	**1,537**
Operating income	**(7,571)**	**n.a.**	**1,639**
Pre-tax income	**(7,570)**	**n.a.**	**1,628**
Income taxes	(1,160)		30
Net income	**(6,410)**	**n.a.**	**1,598**
Cash & equivalent	264		459
Accounts receivable	35		50
Long-term investments	21,601		28,689
Total assets	**22,378**	**-24**	**29,479**
Accts. pay. & accr. liabs	249		497
Current liabilities	249		497
Shareholders' equity	21,369		27,362
Cash from oper. activs	**(218)**	**n.a.**	**(2,024)**
Cash from fin. activs	23		nil
Net cash position	**264**	**-42**	**459**
	$		$
Earnings per share*	(0.26)		0.07
Cash flow per share*	(0.01)		(0.08)
	shs		shs
No. of shs. o/s*	25,004,167		24,231,667
Avg. no. of shs. o/s*	24,672,222		24,100,348
	%		%
Net profit margin	n.m.		50.31
Return on equity	(26.31)		6.05
Return on assets	(24.72)		5.53

* Common
A Reported in accordance with IFRS

Latest Results

Periods ended:	3m Mar. 31/23A		3m Mar. 31/22A
	$000s	%Chg	$000s
Total revenue	(1,868)	n.a.	(2,813)
Net income	(1,791)	n.a.	(2,686)
	$		$
Earnings per share*	(0.07)		(0.11)

* Common
A Reported in accordance with IFRS

Historical Summary
(as originally stated)

Fiscal Year	Total Rev. $000s	Net Inc. Bef. Disc. $000s	EPS* $
2022A	(6,388)	(6,410)	(0.26)
2021A	3,176	1,598	0.07
2020A	14,557	10,945	0.46
2019A	4,677	3,849	0.16
2018A	3,735	2,702	0.11

* Common
A Reported in accordance with IFRS

T.72 Total Energy Services Inc.

Symbol - TOT **Exchange** - TSX **CUSIP** - 89154B
Head Office - 1000-734 7 Ave SW, Calgary, AB, T2P 3P8 **Telephone** - (403) 216-3939 **Toll-free** - (877) 818-6825 **Fax** - (403) 234-8731
Website - www.totalenergy.ca
Email - investorrelations@totalenergy.ca
Investor Relations - Yuliya Gorbach (877) 818-6825
Auditors - MNP LLP C.A., Calgary, Alta.
Bankers - ATB Financial; The Bank of Nova Scotia; The Toronto-Dominion Bank; HSBC Bank Canada, Calgary, Alta.
Lawyers - Bennett Jones LLP, Calgary, Alta.
Transfer Agents - Computershare Trust Company of Canada Inc., Calgary, Alta.
FP500 Revenue Ranking - 387
Employees - 2,031 at Dec. 31, 2022
Profile - (Alta. 2009; orig. B.C., 1990 amalg.) Provides contract drilling services, rental and transportation of equipment used in energy and other industrial operations, fabrication, sale, rental and servicing of gas compression and processing equipment, and well servicing to energy and other resource industries in Canada, the U.S. and Australia.

Operations are carried out through four segments: Contract Drilling Services; Rentals and Transportation Services; Compression and Process Services; and Well Servicing.

Contract Drilling Services - Operations are carried out through wholly owned **Savanna Drilling Corp.** in Canada, wholly owned **Savanna Drilling, LLC** in the U.S. and wholly owned **Savanna Energy Services Pty Ltd.** (SESPL) in Australia. At Dec. 31, 2022, the division had a fleet of 94 drilling rigs in Canada (76), the U.S. (13) and Australia (5).

Rentals and Transportation Services - Through Total Oilfield Rentals division, the company provides drilling, completion and production rental equipment and oilfield transportation services from 12 locations in western Canada and three locations in the U.S. At Dec. 31, 2022, the segment had 9,440 pieces of major rental equipment (excluding access matting) and a fleet of 71 heavy trucks.

Compression and Process Services - This segment consists of gas compression services operated by wholly owned **Bidell Gas Compression Ltd.** in Canada and **Bidell Gas Compression Inc.** in the U.S., and process and production services operated by wholly owned **Opsco Process Corp.** (formerly **Spectrum Process Systems Inc.**). Bidell designs, fabricates, sells, leases and services natural gas compression equipments to customers operating in western Canada and internationally. Operations are based out of 160,000 sq. ft. of fabrication facilities in Calgary, Alta., a 100,000-sq.-ft. facility in Weirton, W.Va., and a network of 13 parts and service branch locations in Canada and the U.S. At Dec. 31, 2022, Bidell had 53,300 horsepower of compression in its rental fleet. Opsco designs, engineers and fabricates custom made production and processing equipment for the oil and gas industry from 65,000 sq. ft. of fabrication facilities in Calgary, Alta.

Well Servicing - Operations are carried out through wholly owned **Savanna Well Servicing Inc.** in Canada, wholly owned **Savanna Well Servicing Corp.** in the U.S. and wholly owned SESPL in Australia. This segment provides completion, well workover, well maintenance and abandonment services in Canada, the U.S. and Australia. At Dec. 31, 2022, the division had a fleet of 79 service rigs operating in Canada (56), the U.S. (11) and Australia (12).

Predecessor Detail - Name changed from Biomerge Industries Ltd., May 27, 2009, pursuant to plan of arrangement to convert Total Energy Services Trust (TEST) to a corp. resulting in TEST becoming a wholly owned subsid. of Total Energy Services Inc. (TESI); basis 1 TESI sh. for 1 TEST trust unit, $0.00282 plus 0.000237 TESI shs. for 1 Biomerge vtg. sh. and $0.00389 for 1 Biomerge non-vtg. sh.

Directors - George K. Chow, chr., Calgary, Alta.; Daniel K. Halyk, pres. & CEO, Calgary, Alta.; Glenn O. J. Dagenais, Calgary, Alta.; Jessica Kirstine, Calgary, Alta.; Gregory K. (Greg) Melchin, Calgary, Alta.; Kenneth B. (Ken) Mullen, Calgary, Alta.

Other Exec. Officers - Jeremy Busch-Howell, v-p, legal, gen. counsel & corp. sec.; Yuliya Gorbach, v-p, fin. & CFO; William J. G. (Bill) Kosich, v-p, drilling srvcs.; Bradley J. (Brad) Macson, v-p, opers.; Ashley Ting, contr.

Capital Stock

	Authorized (shs.)	Outstanding (shs.)[1]
Preferred	unlimited	nil
Common	unlimited	40,525,000

[1] At Apr. 3, 2022

Normal Course Issuer Bid - The company plans to make normal course purchases of up to 2,095,015 common shares representing 5% of the total outstanding. The bid commenced on Oct. 19, 2022, and expires on Oct. 18, 2023.

Major Shareholder - EdgePoint Investment Group Inc. held 18.1% interest, Fidelity Investments Inc. held 12.2% interest, Foyston, Gordon & Payne Inc. held 11% interest and Invesco Canada Ltd. held 10.6% interest at Apr. 3, 2023.

Price Range - TOT/TSX

Year	Volume	High	Low	Close
2022	17,578,198	$9.53	$5.94	$8.61
2021	12,059,584	$6.16	$3.09	$6.03
2020	17,908,649	$6.52	$1.40	$3.28
2019	8,494,418	$11.00	$5.30	$6.42
2018	7,425,343	$15.00	$8.83	$9.77

Recent Close: $8.73

Capital Stock Changes - During 2022, 166,000 common shares were issued on exercise of options, 1,644,000 common shares were repurchased under a Normal Course Issuer Bid and 22,000 common shares were redeemed pursuant to acquisition of sunset clause.

Dividends

TOT com N.S.R. [1]

$0.08	July 17/23	$0.08	Apr. 17/23
$0.06	Jan. 16/23	$0.06	Oct. 17/22

Paid in 2023: $0.22 2022: $0.12 2021: n.a.

[1] Quarterly divd normally payable in Apr/20 has been omitted.

Wholly Owned Subsidiaries

Bidell Gas Compression Ltd., Alta.
Opsco Process Corp., Alta.
Savanna Drilling Corp., Alta.
Savanna Energy Services Pty Ltd., Australia.
- 100% int. in **TES Energy Services Pty Ltd.**, Australia.

Savanna Well Servicing Inc., Alta.
TES Investments Ltd., Alta.
TES Services Inc., Nev.
- 100% int. in **Bidell Gas Compression Inc.**, Wyo.
- 100% int. in **Savanna Drilling LLC**, Nev.
- 100% int. in **Savanna Well Servicing Corp.**, Del.
- 100% int. in **TES Land Inc.**, Wyo.
- 100% int. in **Total Oilfield Rentals Inc.**, Wyo.

Total Oilfield Rentals Ltd., Alta.

Note: The preceding list includes only the major related companies in which interests are held.

Financial Statistics

Periods ended:	12m Dec. 31/22[A]		12m Dec. 31/21[A]
	$000s	%Chg	$000s
Operating revenue	**759,813**	**+76**	**431,576**
Cost of sales	589,809		323,092
General & admin expense	39,671		28,234
Stock-based compensation	1,142		804
Operating expense	**630,622**	**+79**	**352,130**
Operating income	**129,191**	**+63**	**79,446**
Deprec., depl. & amort.	78,813		83,065
Finance costs, gross	7,374		6,837
Pre-tax income	**45,133**	**n.a.**	**(3,887)**
Income taxes	7,134		(3,459)
Net income	**37,999**	**n.a.**	**(428)**
Net inc. for equity hldrs	**38,008**	**n.a.**	**(360)**
Net inc. for non-cont. int	**(9)**	**n.a.**	**(68)**
Cash & equivalent	34,061		33,365
Inventories	91,614		89,921
Accounts receivable	154,581		90,543
Current assets	299,977		225,732
Fixed assets, net	567,515		575,913
Right-of-use assets	nil		361
Intangibles, net	4,053		4,053
Total assets	**878,615**	**+8**	**813,522**
Accts. pay. & accr. liabs	114,274		65,513
Current liabilities	187,823		88,428
Long-term debt, gross	119,988		190,517
Long-term debt, net	117,997		187,906
Long-term lease liabilities	9,631		8,101
Shareholders' equity	521,471		492,876
Non-controlling interest	552		561
Cash from oper. activs	**143,401**	**+60**	**89,575**
Cash from fin. activs	(100,443)		(64,953)
Cash from invest. activs	(42,262)		(14,253)
Net cash position	**34,061**	**+2**	**33,365**
Capital expenditures	(56,735)		(28,983)
Capital disposals	6,292		10,507
	$		$
Earnings per share*	0.90		(0.01)
Cash flow per share*	3.40		2.02
Cash divd. per share*	0.18		nil
	shs		shs
No. of shs. o/s*	41,500,000		43,000,000
Avg. no. of shs. o/s*	42,216,000		44,384,000
	%		%
Net profit margin	5.00		(0.10)
Return on equity	7.49		(0.07)
Return on assets	5.23		0.04
Foreign sales percent	51		44
No. of employees (FTEs)	2,031		1,751

* Common
[A] Reported in accordance with IFRS

Historical Summary
(as originally stated)

Fiscal Year	Oper. Rev.	Net Inc. Bef. Disc.	EPS*
	$000s	$000s	$
2022[A]	759,813	37,999	0.90
2021[A]	431,576	(428)	(0.01)
2020[A]	365,750	(30,455)	(0.68)
2019[A]	757,398	10,091	0.23
2018[A]	851,809	24,215	0.53

* Common
[A] Reported in accordance with IFRS

T.73 Total Telcom Inc.

Symbol - TTZ **Exchange** - TSX-VEN **CUSIP** - 89151N
Head Office - 540-1632 Dickson Ave, Kelowna, BC, V1Y 7T2 **Telephone** - (250) 860-3762 **Toll-free** - (877) 860-3762 **Fax** - (250) 860-3763
Website - www.totaltelcom.com
Email - neil.magrath@romcomm.com
Investor Relations - Neil J. Magrath (250) 860-3762 ext. 202
Auditors - Fernandez Young LLP C.A., Vancouver, B.C.
Transfer Agents - TSX Trust Company, Calgary, Alta.

Profile - (Alta. 1987) Develops and provides remote asset monitoring and tracking products and services.

Through wholly owned **ROM Communications Inc.**, develops and markets wireless communications for commercial, industrial and consumer applications enabling the control, tracking, monitoring, data retrieval and management of fixed and mobile assets remotely via the Internet. ROM is an authorized airtime reseller and hardware developer for satellite, cellular and wireless Internet protocol networks.

Products and services are based on the web-to-wireless technology and proprietary second-generation hardware and software platforms marketed as TextAnywhere, ROM Controllers, ROMTraX, MotoTraX, TraX, DataTrax, WaterTrax, SiteTrax, CamTrax and AlarmTrax. The modules consist of wireless modems that utilize microcomputers integrated with sensors, GPS engines and various inputs and outputs and are interfaced by users through the Internet.

Predecessor Detail - Name changed from D.C. Corrosion Corporation, June 10, 1999.

Directors - Neil J. Magrath, CEO, Kelowna, B.C.; Scott Allen, CFO, Sherwood Park, Alta.; David H. Hammermeister, Sask.; Wayne Jamieson, Alta.

Other Exec. Officers - Prof. Lawrence R. (Larry) Cunningham, corp. sec.

Capital Stock

	Authorized (shs.)	Outstanding (shs.)[1]
Common	unlimited	25,990,014

[1] At Nov. 17, 2022

Major Shareholder - Widely held at Aug. 31, 2022.

Price Range - TTZ/TSX-VEN

Year	Volume	High	Low	Close
2022	2,758,283	$0.17	$0.08	$0.16
2021	1,169,764	$0.19	$0.12	$0.13
2020	3,367,502	$0.17	$0.07	$0.12
2019	2,265,596	$0.18	$0.07	$0.12
2018	3,106,450	$0.36	$0.12	$0.17

Recent Close: $0.50

Capital Stock Changes - During fiscal 2022, 675,000 common shares were issued on exercise of options.

Wholly Owned Subsidiaries

ROM Communications Inc., Edmonton, Alta.

Financial Statistics

Periods ended:	12m June 30/22[A]		12m June 30/21[oA]
	$000s	%Chg	$000s
Operating revenue	**1,655**	**-5**	**1,737**
Cost of sales	710		781
Salaries & benefits	249		156
General & admin expense	146		151
Stock-based compensation	45		40
Operating expense	**1,150**	**+2**	**1,128**
Operating income	**505**	**-17**	**609**
Deprec., depl. & amort.	228		221
Finance income	6		6
Finance costs, gross	12		15
Write-downs/write-offs	nil		257
Pre-tax income	**347**	**+313**	**84**
Income taxes	54		(524)
Net income	**293**	**-52**	**608**
Cash & equivalent	1,950		1,792
Inventories	270		150
Accounts receivable	194		167
Current assets	2,426		2,115
Fixed assets, net	208		302
Total assets	**4,327**	**+10**	**3,916**
Accts. pay. & accr. liabs	198		132
Current liabilities	325		269
Long-term debt, gross	40		40
Long-term debt, net	40		40
Long-term lease liabilities	12		178
Shareholders' equity	3,834		3,429
Cash from oper. activs	**476**	**-37**	**755**
Cash from fin. activs	(12)		(9)
Cash from invest. activs	(349)		(390)
Net cash position	**1,345**	**+13**	**1,189**
Capital expenditures	(8)		(1)
Capital disposals	7		3
	$		$
Earnings per share*	0.01		0.02
Cash flow per share*	0.02		0.03
	shs		shs
No. of shs. o/s*	25,315,014		25,315,014
Avg. no. of shs. o/s*	25,708,764		25,056,681
	%		%
Net profit margin	17.70		35.00
Return on equity	8.07		19.70
Return on assets	7.35		19.98
Foreign sales percent	67		71

* Common
[o] Restated
[A] Reported in accordance with IFRS

Latest Results

Periods ended:	3m Sept. 30/22[A]		3m Sept. 30/21[A]
	$000s	%Chg	$000s
Operating revenue	412	+29	320
Net income	123	+98	62
	$		$
Earnings per share*	0.00		0.00

* Common
[A] Reported in accordance with IFRS

Historical Summary
(as originally stated)

Fiscal Year	Oper. Rev.	Net Inc. Bef. Disc.	EPS*
	$000s	$000s	$
2022[A]	1,655	293	0.01
2021[A]	1,737	608	0.02
2020[A]	1,507	321	0.01
2019[A]	1,438	302	0.01
2018[A]	1,781	476	0.02

* Common
[A] Reported in accordance with IFRS

T.74 Totally Hip Technologies Inc.

Symbol - THP **Exchange** - TSX-VEN **CUSIP** - 89152W
Head Office - 702-889 Pender St W, Vancouver, BC, V6C 3B2 **Telephone** - (604) 683-3288
Email - totallyhip2@gmail.com
Investor Relations - James Boyce (604) 683-3288
Auditors - Saturna Group Chartered Accountants LLP C.A., Vancouver, B.C.
Lawyers - Anthony J. Beruschi, Vancouver, B.C.
Transfer Agents - Computershare Trust Company of Canada Inc.
Profile - (B.C. 1999; orig. Alta., 1995) Seeking new business opportunities.
Predecessor Detail - Name changed from Totally Hip Inc., Dec. 23, 2003; basis 1 new for 4 old shs.
Directors - John S. Brydle, pres. & CEO, Coquitlam, B.C.; James Boyce, CFO, North Vancouver, B.C.; Frank J. Garofalo, Mass.; Vincent Teo, B.C.
Other Exec. Officers - Gwen Wegner, corp. sec.

Capital Stock

	Authorized (shs.)	Outstanding (shs.)[1]
Preferred	100,000,000	nil
Common	unlimited	122,590,730

[1] At May 30, 2023

Major Shareholder - Widely held at Mar. 23, 2023.

Price Range - THP/TSX-VEN

Year	Volume	High	Low	Close
2022	106,075	$0.28	$0.10	$0.16
2021	38,417	$0.15	$0.09	$0.12
2020	117,150	$0.17	$0.07	$0.12
2019	253,230	$0.25	$0.10	$0.10
2018	1,207,132	$0.70	$0.11	$0.14

Recent Close: $0.16
Capital Stock Changes - There were no changes to capital stock during fiscal 2022.

Wholly Owned Subsidiaries

Totally Hip Services Inc. Inactive.
Totally Hip Software (B.C.) Inc. Inactive.

Financial Statistics

Periods ended:	12m Sept. 30/22[A]		12m Sept. 30/21[A]
	$000s	%Chg	$000s
Salaries & benefits	nil		13
General & admin expense	111		77
Stock-based compensation	nil		379
Operating expense	**111**	**-76**	**469**
Operating income	**(111)**	**n.a.**	**(469)**
Finance costs, gross	13		8
Pre-tax income	**(228)**	**n.a.**	**(476)**
Net income	**(228)**	**n.a.**	**(476)**
Cash & equivalent	719		991
Accounts receivable	11		8
Current assets	738		1,007
Fixed assets, net	nil		1
Total assets	**738**	**-27**	**1,007**
Bank indebtedness	30		30
Accts. pay. & accr. liabs	1,003		1,044
Current liabilities	1,033		1,074
Shareholders' equity	(295)		(67)
Cash from oper. activs	**(168)**	**n.a.**	**(348)**
Cash from fin. activs	nil		(9)
Net cash position	**719**	**-27**	**991**
	$		$
Earnings per share*	(0.00)		(0.00)
Cash flow per share*	(0.00)		(0.00)
	shs		shs
No. of shs. o/s*	122,590,730		122,590,730
Avg. no. of shs. o/s*	122,590,730		122,604,657
	%		%
Net profit margin	n.a.		n.a.
Return on equity	n.m.		n.m.
Return on assets	(24.64)		(39.48)

* Common
[A] Reported in accordance with IFRS

Latest Results

Periods ended:	6m Mar. 31/23[A]		6m Mar. 31/22[A]
	$000s	%Chg	$000s
Net income	(78)	n.a.	(64)
	$		$
Earnings per share*	(0.00)		(0.00)

* Common
[A] Reported in accordance with IFRS

Historical Summary
(as originally stated)

Fiscal Year	Oper. Rev.	Net Inc. Bef. Disc.	EPS*
	$000s	$000s	$
2022[A]	nil	(228)	(0.00)
2021[A]	nil	(476)	(0.00)
2020[A]	nil	(71)	(0.00)
2019[A]	nil	(179)	(0.00)
2018[A]	nil	(3,305)	(0.03)

* Common
[A] Reported in accordance with IFRS

T.75 Tower One Wireless Corp.

Symbol - TO **Exchange** - CSE (S) **CUSIP** - 89186Q
Head Office - 600-535 Howe St, Vancouver, BC, V6C 2Z4 **Telephone** - (604) 559-8051 **Fax** - (604) 727-1295
Website - www.toweronewireless.com
Email - nick@toweronewireless.com
Investor Relations - Robert Horsley (604) 559-8051
Auditors - Smythe LLP C.A.
Transfer Agents - Computershare Trust Company of Canada Inc., Vancouver, B.C.
Profile - (B.C. 2005) Builds, owns and operates multi-tenant wireless telecommunications infrastructure in Latin America.
Leases space on its towers to mobile network operators and is focused on the build to suit tower industry whereby a long-term lease is secured with a tenant prior to building a tower. Operates in Colombia, Mexico and Ecuador with a combined population of approximately 190,000,000 people. The company has a total of 282 completed wireless towers throughout Colombia, Mexico and Ecuador with 42 collocations, and additional 163 towers in Colombia, 13 towers in Mexico and 50 towers in Ecuador that are under construction. At June 30, 2022, the company has a total of 12 signed master lease agreements with major mobile network operators and has a backlog of more than 400 sites awarded for build-to-suit (BTS) tower construction in Colombia, Mexico and Ecuador.
In the U.S., subsidiary **Tower Construction and Technical Services, LLC** focuses on the 5G rollout of the mobile network operators primarily in Oklahoma and Texas and has completed more than 100 sites for original equipment manufacturers and mobile network operators.
Common suspended from CSE, July 10, 2023.
Predecessor Detail - Name changed from Pacific Therapeutics Ltd., Jan. 12, 2017, following reverse takeover acquisition of Tower Three S.A.S.
Directors - Alejandro (Alex) Ochoa, pres., CEO, interim CFO & corp. sec., Miami, Fla.; Robert (Nick) Horsley, Vancouver, B.C.; Gabriel Tejada Arenas, Colombia; Fabio A. Vasquez, Fla.
Other Exec. Officers - Luis Parra, COO; Abbey Abdiye, chief acctg. officer

Capital Stock

	Authorized (shs.)	Outstanding (shs.)[1]
Class B Preferred		
Series 1	1,500,000	nil
Series 2	1,000,000	nil
Class A Common	unlimited	119,258,849

[1] At Oct. 14, 2022

Major Shareholder - Globo Inmobiliario S.A.S. held 13.65% interest, Alejandro (Alex) Ochoa held 10.06% interest and Fabio A. Vasquez held 10.06% interest at Oct. 14, 2022.

Price Range - TO/CSE (S)

Year	Volume	High	Low	Close
2022	6,623,415	$0.09	$0.05	$0.06
2021	11,503,486	$0.17	$0.05	$0.07
2020	8,905,978	$0.08	$0.03	$0.05
2019	10,713,535	$0.11	$0.03	$0.04
2018	44,931,577	$0.27	$0.07	$0.09

Recent Close: $0.06

Wholly Owned Subsidiaries

Tower One Wireless Colombia S.A.S., Bogota, Colombia.
• 100% int. in **Innervision S.A.S.**, Colombia.
Tower Three S.A., Buenos Aires, Argentina.
Tower Two S.A.S., Argentina.

Subsidiaries

91.25% int. in **Evolution Technology S.A.**, Argentina.
90% int. in **Tower One Wireless Mexico, S.A. de C.V.**, Mexico.
90% int. in **Towerthree Wireless del Ecuador S.A.**, Ecuador.

Investments

50% int. in **Tower Construction and Technical Services, LLC**, United States.

Financial Statistics

Periods ended:	12m Dec. 31/21[A]		12m Dec. 31/20[°A]
	$000s	%Chg	$000s
Operating revenue	**10,688**	**+17**	**9,126**
Cost of sales	6,266		4,951
General & admin expense	3,988		4,495
Stock-based compensation	130		nil
Operating expense	**10,384**	**+10**	**9,446**
Operating income	**304**	**n.a.**	**(320)**
Deprec., depl. & amort.	1,436		1,260
Finance costs, gross	2,127		1,206
Write-downs/write-offs	(1,528)		(480)
Pre-tax income	**(4,509)**	**n.a.**	**(3,488)**
Income taxes	85		187
Net income	**(4,594)**	**n.a.**	**(3,674)**
Net inc. for equity hldrs	**(4,185)**	**n.a.**	**(2,365)**
Net inc. for non-cont. int	**(409)**	**n.a.**	**(1,310)**
Cash & equivalent	1,059		123
Accounts receivable	4,819		1,167
Current assets	7,554		1,691
Fixed assets, net	8,885		6,175
Right-of-use assets	2,537		1,885
Intangibles, net	nil		1,358
Total assets	**21,887**	**+97**	**11,109**
Bank indebtedness	4,083		1,537
Accts. pay. & accr. liabs	10,040		4,368
Current liabilities	24,304		20,816
Long-term debt, gross	6,418		2,048
Long-term debt, net	10,113		144
Long-term lease liabilities	2,139		1,593
Shareholders' equity	(11,972)		(6,911)
Non-controlling interest	(2,826)		(4,532)
Cash from oper. activs	**(5,417)**	**n.a.**	**398**
Cash from fin. activs	8,373		1,049
Cash from invest. activs	(2,074)		(1,379)
Net cash position	**1,059**	**+761**	**123**
Capital expenditures	(5,834)		(2,657)
	$		$
Earnings per share*	(0.04)		(0.03)
Cash flow per share*	(0.06)		0.00
	shs		shs
No. of shs. o/s*	100,473,582		94,103,732
Avg. no. of shs. o/s*	97,423,247		93,867,588
	%		%
Net profit margin	(42.98)		(40.26)
Return on equity	n.m.		n.m.
Return on assets	(14.71)		(17.73)
Foreign sales percent	100		100
No. of employees (FTEs)	68		33

* Cl.A Common
° Restated
[A] Reported in accordance with IFRS

Latest Results

Periods ended:	6m June 30/22[A]		6m June 30/21[A]
	$000s	%Chg	$000s
Operating revenue	6,665	+291	1,703
Net income	(4,166)	n.a.	(2,079)
Net inc. for equity hldrs	(3,936)	n.a.	(1,553)
Net inc. for non-cont. int	(230)		(526)
	$		$
Earnings per share*	(0.04)		(0.02)

* Cl.A Common
[A] Reported in accordance with IFRS

Historical Summary
(as originally stated)

Fiscal Year	Oper. Rev.	Net Inc. Bef. Disc.	EPS*
	$000s	$000s	$
2021[A]	10,688	(4,594)	(0.04)
2020[A]	9,126	(3,674)	(0.03)
2019[A]	5,414	(8,147)	(0.08)
2018[A]	1,557	(8,688)	(0.10)
2017[A1]	200	(9,864)	(0.16)

* Cl.A Common
[A] Reported in accordance with IFRS
[1] Results reflect the Jan. 12, 2017, reverse takeover acquisition of Tower Three S.A.S.

T.76 TrackX Holdings Inc.

Symbol - TKX **Exchange** - TSX-VEN (S) **CUSIP** - 89237Y
Head Office - 7800 E Union Ave, Suite 430, Denver, CO, United States, 80237 **Telephone** - (303) 325-7300
Website - www.trackx.com
Email - gmcconnell@trackx.com
Investor Relations - Gene E. McConnell (720) 505-3050
Auditors - SingerLewak LLP C.P.A., Denver, Colo.
Lawyers - McMillan LLP, Vancouver, B.C.

Transfer Agents - Computershare Trust Company of Canada Inc., Vancouver, B.C.

Profile - (B.C. 2016; orig. Can., 2004) Provides software-as-a-service based enterprise tracing, tracking and collaboration solutions utilizing multiple sensor and automatic identification technologies including radio-frequency identification, Internet of Things and sensor technologies.

The company's Keychain™ platform delivers a system-wide, real-time inventory tracking and optimization solutions. Features and functions of the Keychain™ platform include: TrackX Control Tower, a web and mobile based business intelligence platform which is used to drive efficiency and overall performance; TrackX Verify, which provides proof of supply chain related activity and transactions by recording immutable digital transactions and events in a secure blockchain-based registry; TrackX ESG, which automates performance analytics and reporting capabilities used to monitor, measure and prove progress against ESG and other sustainability standards; and TrackX Mobile, which provides a suite of features in a mobile environment which provides efficient and easy means of extending data entry, visibility and reporting of supply chain events to mobile and android-based consumer phones and tablets.

Customers range across a number of industries including food, beverage, brewery, automotive, retail, financial services, technology and government.

Common suspended from TSX-VEN, Apr. 6, 2023.

Recent Merger and Acquisition Activity

Status: pending **Announced:** Dec. 7, 2022

SpotLite360 IOT Solutions, Inc. entered into a letter of intent to acquire TrackX Holdings Inc. Terms of a definitive agreement were to be finalized. SpotLite360 already holds a software licence to TrackX's supply chain technology platform for use within the healthcare, pharmaceutical and agriculture industries.

Predecessor Detail - Name changed from Cougar Minerals Corp., May 25, 2016, following reverse takeover acquisition of TrackX, Inc.; basis 1 new for 2 old shs.

Directors - Tim Harvie, chr., pres. & CEO, Castle Rock, Colo.; Kirk Ball; Darren P. Devine, West Vancouver, B.C.; Blair Garrou, Houston, Tex.

Other Exec. Officers - Chris Brumett, COO; Gene E. McConnell, interim CFO & corp. sec.; Michael Himmelfarb, chief mktg. officer; Bryan J. Boutté, v-p, opers.; Marc S. Spezialy, contr.

Capital Stock

	Authorized (shs.)	Outstanding (shs.)[1]
Common	unlimited	137,099,835

[1] At Jan. 28, 2022

Major Shareholder - Widely held at June 18, 2021.

Price Range - TKX/TSX-VEN (S)

Year	Volume	High	Low	Close
2022	39,665,402	$0.05	$0.01	$0.01
2021	172,269,735	$0.17	$0.04	$0.05
2020	20,158,758	$0.08	$0.02	$0.05
2019	22,829,512	$0.41	$0.03	$0.04
2018	41,685,711	$0.48	$0.18	$0.35

Recent Close: $0.01

Wholly Owned Subsidiaries

TrackX, Inc., Lone Tree, Colo.

Financial Statistics

Periods ended:	12m Sept. 30/21[A]		12m Sept. 30/20[A]
	$000s	%Chg	$000s
Operating revenue	**3,493**	**-12**	**3,955**
Cost of sales	1,562		1,727
General & admin expense	2,357		2,764
Stock-based compensation	44		(2)
Operating expense	**2,401**	**-47**	**4,489**
Operating income	**1,092**	**n.a.**	**(534)**
Deprec., depl. & amort.	305		1,614
Finance costs, gross	398		527
Pre-tax income	**(759)**	**n.a.**	**185**
Net income	**(759)**	**n.a.**	**185**
Cash & equivalent	61		18
Inventories	nil		165
Accounts receivable	300		209
Current assets	1,263		699
Fixed assets, net	6		19
Right-of-use assets	272		133
Intangibles, net	53		128
Total assets	**1,638**	**+60**	**1,023**
Accts. pay. & accr. liabs	589		793
Current liabilities	2,770		3,391
Long-term debt, gross	1,542		2,656
Long-term debt, net	nil		610
Long-term lease liabilities	254		19
Shareholders' equity	(1,386)		(2,997)
Cash from oper. activs	**(1,184)**	**n.a.**	**273**
Cash from fin. activs	1,630		91
Cash from invest. activs	(214)		(432)
Net cash position	**61**	**+239**	**18**
Capital expenditures	(2)		(7)
	$		$
Earnings per share*	(0.01)		0.01
Cash flow per share*	(0.01)		0.00
	shs		shs
No. of shs. o/s*	134,899,835		88,964,349
Avg. no. of shs. o/s*	110,182,557		82,550,833
	%		%
Net profit margin	(21.73)		4.68
Return on equity	n.m.		n.m.
Return on assets	(27.13)		39.93

* Common

[A] Reported in accordance with IFRS

Historical Summary
(as originally stated)

Fiscal Year	Oper. Rev. $000s	Net Inc. Bef. Disc. $000s	EPS* $
2021[A]	3,493	(759)	(0.01)
2020[A]	3,955	185	0.01
2019[A]	6,288	(3,919)	(0.05)
2018[A]	5,668	(3,452)	(0.04)
2017[A]	5,170	(3,974)	(0.07)

* Common

[A] Reported in accordance with IFRS

T.77 Trail Blazer Capital Corp.

Symbol - TBLZ.P **Exchange** - TSX-VEN **CUSIP** - 892767

Head Office - 918-1030 Georgia St W, Vancouver, BC, V6E 2Y3 **Telephone** - (604) 628-2669

Email - gmarosits@gmail.com

Investor Relations - Grace Marosits (604) 628-2669

Auditors - Dale Matheson Carr-Hilton LaBonte LLP C.A., Vancouver, B.C.

Transfer Agents - Odyssey Trust Company, Vancouver, B.C.

Profile - (B.C. 2021) Capital Pool Company.

Directors - Thomas O'Neill, pres., CEO & corp. sec., Vancouver, B.C.; Grace Marosits, CFO, West Vancouver, B.C.; Warwick Smith, Richmond, B.C.; David Stier, Toronto, Ont.; Marlis Yassin, North Vancouver, B.C.

Capital Stock

	Authorized (shs.)	Outstanding (shs.)[1]
Common	unlimited	15,000,000

[1] At July 26, 2023

Major Shareholder - Widely held at May 30, 2022.

Price Range - TBLZ.P/TSX-VEN

Year	Volume	High	Low	Close
2022	170,500	$0.25	$0.13	$0.14

Recent Close: $0.12

Capital Stock Changes - There were no changes to capital stock during fiscal 2023.

On Nov. 12, 2021, an initial public offering of 5,000,000 common shares was completed at 10¢ per share. Also during fiscal 2022, 500,000 common shares were issued as finder's fee.

T.78 Trail Blazing Ventures Ltd.

Symbol - BLAZ.P **Exchange** - TSX-VEN **CUSIP** - 892766

Head Office - Dome Tower, 800-333 7 Ave SW, Calgary, AB, T2P 2Z1 **Telephone** - (587) 434-5554 **Toll-free** - (800) 503-1875

Website - trailblazingventures.com

Email - darren.bondar@trailblazingventures.com

Investor Relations - Darren Bondar (587) 434-5554

Auditors - Geib & Company Professional Corporation C.A., Calgary, Alta.

Transfer Agents - Odyssey Trust Company, Calgary, Alta.

Profile - (Alta. 2021) Capital Pool Company.

Recent Merger and Acquisition Activity

Status: terminated **Revised:** Nov. 1, 2022

UPDATE: The transaction was terminated. PREVIOUS: Trail Blazing Ventures Ltd. entered into a letter of intent for the Qualifying Transaction reverse takeover acquisition of private Victoria, B.C.-based Ecologyst Outfitters Inc., which produces and sells apparel and accessories made from 100% natural biodegradable materials, on a share-for-share basis, which would result in the issuance of 80,513,934 Trail Blazing post-consolidated common shares (following a 1-for-2 share consolidation).

Directors - Darren Bondar, CEO & CFO, Calgary, Alta.; Craig Steinberg, Calgary, Alta.; L. Russell Wilson, Calgary, Alta.

Other Exec. Officers - Robert R. Verbuck, v-p, legal; Michael Ginevsky, corp. sec.

Capital Stock

	Authorized (shs.)	Outstanding (shs.)[1]
Preferred	unlimited	nil
Common	unlimited	40,000,000

[1] At Jan. 20, 2023

Major Shareholder - Darren Bondar held 16.3% interest at Jan. 20, 2023.

Price Range - BLAZ.P/TSX-VEN

Year	Volume	High	Low	Close
2022	1,860,254	$0.21	$0.08	$0.12

Recent Close: $0.10

Capital Stock Changes - On Jan. 21, 2022, an initial public offering of 20,000,000 common shares was completed at 10¢ per share.

T.79 TransAlta Corporation*

Symbol - TA **Exchange** - TSX **CUSIP** - 89346D

Head Office - 110 12 Ave SW, PO Box 1900 Stn M, Calgary, AB, T2P 2M1 **Telephone** - (403) 267-7110 **Toll-free** - (800) 387-3598 **Fax** - (403) 267-2590

Website - www.transalta.com

Email - investor_relations@transalta.com

Investor Relations - Scott T. Jeffers (800) 387-3598

Auditors - Ernst & Young LLP C.A., Calgary, Alta.

Lawyers - Latham & Watkins LLP, New York, N.Y.; McCarthy Tétrault LLP, Calgary, Alta.

Transfer Agents - Computershare Shareowner Services LLC, Jersey City, N.J.; Computershare Trust Company of Canada Inc., Calgary, Alta.

FP500 Revenue Ranking - 171

Employees - 1,222 at Dec. 31, 2022

Profile - (Can. 1992 amalg.) Produces non-regulated independent power in Canada, the U.S. and Australia. Interests include construction, operation and maintenance of power generation facilities and the management of production sales, natural gas purchases and transmission capacity.

Operations are organized into two segments: Generation and Energy Marketing. Both segments are supported by a corporate group that provides financial, legal, administrative and investing functions.

Generation

This segment includes Hydro, Wind and Solar, Gas and Energy Transition businesses, and is responsible for constructing, operating and maintaining power generation facilities in Canada, the U.S. and Australia. Revenues are derived from the sale of electricity, steam and ancillary services.

The Hydro business holds a net ownership interest of 922 MW of electrical generating capacity, located in Alberta, British Columbia and Ontario.

The Wind and Solar business holds a net ownership interest of 1,878 MW of electrical generating capacity and includes facilities in Alberta, Ontario, New Brunswick, Quebec, Washington, Wyoming, Massachusetts, New Hampshire, Pennsylvania, North Carolina and Minnesota.

The Gas business holds a net ownership interest of 2,775 MW of electrical generating capacity and includes facilities in Alberta, Ontario, Michigan and Western Australia. The business also includes a 270-km Fortescue River Gas pipeline in Western Australia. The gas business includes the previously disclosed North American and Australian Gas businesses.

The Energy Transition business holds a net ownership interest of 671 MW of electrical generating capacity consisting of the Centralia thermal plant and Skookumchuck hydro facility in Washington.

Energy Marketing

This segment manages the transmission needs of the Generation segment by utilizing contracts of various durations for the forward sales of electricity and for the purchase of natural gas and transmission capacity. Revenue and earnings are derived from the wholesale trading of electricity and other energy-related commodities and derivatives.

In April 2022, the company retired its 406-MW Sundance Unit 4 natural gas facility in Alberta.

On Apr. 5, 2022, the company entered into a power purchase agreement with **Meta Platforms, Inc.** (dba Meta) for the offtake of 200 MW from its proposed 200-MW Horizon Hill wind power project, to be located in Logan cty., Okla., for an undisclosed amount. Under the agreement, the company would construct the Horizon Hill project in the fourth quarter of 2022, with a target commercial operation in the second half of 2023. The company would construct, own and operate the facility with a total capital estimated at US$290,000,000 to US$310,000,000.

Recent Merger and Acquisition Activity

Status: pending **Announced:** July 11, 2023
TransAlta Corporation agreed to acquire the remaining 39.9% interest in TransAlta Renewables Inc. for 1.0337 TransAlta Corporation common shares or $13 cash for each TransAlta Renewables share held. The maximum number of common shares that may be issued was 46,441,779 and the maximum aggregate amount of cash was $800,000,000, representing a total consideration of $1,384,051,812. TransAlta Renewables' board of directors unanimously recommended that shareholders vote in favour of the transaction, and TransAlta Corporation's board of directors approved the transaction.

Status: completed **Revised:** Apr. 24, 2023
UPDATE: The transaction was completed. PREVIOUS: TransAlta Corporation agreed to acquire a 50% interest in the Tent Mountain Renewable Energy Complex, an early stage 320-MW pumped hydro energy storage development project in southwestern Alberta, from Montem Resources Limited. TransAlta and Montem would form a partnership and jointly manage the project, with TransAlta acting as project developer. TransAlta would pay Montem $8,000,000 upon closing of the transaction with additional payments of up to $17,000,000 contingent on the achievement of specific development and commercial milestones. The project would be developed over the next four years, with construction targeted to start as early as 2026 with a commercial operation date between 2028 and 2030. The transaction was expected to close in March 2023.

Directors - John P. Dielwart, chr., Calgary, Alta.; John H. Kousinioris, pres. & CEO, Calgary, Alta.; The Hon. Ronalee H. (Rona) Ambrose, Calgary, Alta.; Alan J. Fohrer, Calif.; Laura W. Folse, Tex.; Harry A. Goldgut, Thornhill, Ont.; Candace J. MacGibbon, Toronto, Ont.; Thomas M. O'Flynn, N.J.; Bryan D. Pinney, Calgary, Alta.; James (Jim) Reid, Calgary, Alta.; Manjit K. Sharma, Toronto, Ont.; Sandy R. Sharman, Burlington, Ont.; Sarah A. Slusser, Washington, D.C.

Other Exec. Officers - Jane N. Fedoretz, exec. v-p, people, talent & transformation; Christopher D. Fralick, exec. v-p, generation; Kerry O'Reilly Wilks, exec. v-p, legal, comml. & external affairs; Todd J. Stack, exec. v-p, fin. & CFO; Blain van Melle, exec. v-p, Alta. bus.; Aron J. Willis, exec. v-p, growth; Shasta R. Kadonaga, sr. v-p, shared srvcs.; Brent V. Ward, sr. v-p, M&A, strategy & treas.; Michelle Cameron, v-p & contr.; Scott T. Jeffers, v-p, legal & corp. sec.

Capital Stock

	Authorized (shs.)	Outstanding (shs.)[1]
First Preferred	unlimited	nil
Series A		9,629,913
Series B		2,370,087
Series C		9,955,701
Series D		1,044,299
Series E		9,000,000
Series G		6,600,000
Common	unlimited	263,400,000

[1] At Aug. 3, 2023

First Preferred - Issuable in series and non-voting.

Series A - Entitled to fixed cumulative preferential annual dividends of $0.71925 per share payable quarterly to Mar. 31, 2026, and thereafter at a rate reset every five years equal to the five-year Government of Canada bond yield plus 2.03%. Redeemable on Mar. 31, 2026, and on March 31 every five years thereafter at $25 per share plus declared and unpaid dividends. Convertible at the holder's option on Mar. 31, 2026, and on March 31 every five years thereafter, into floating rate first preferred series B shares on a share-for-share basis, subject to certain conditions.

Series B - Entitled cumulative preferential annual dividends payable quarterly equal to the 90-day Government of Canada Treasury bill rate plus 2.03%. Redeemable on Mar. 31, 2026, and on March 31 every five years thereafter at $25 per share, or at $25.50 per share in the case of redemptions on any date after Mar. 31, 2026, that is not a series B conversion date. Convertible at the holder's option, on Mar. 31, 2026, and on March 31 every five years thereafter, into first preferred series A shares on a share-for-share basis, subject to certain conditions.

Series C - Entitled to fixed cumulative preferential annual dividends of $1.4635 per share payable quarterly to June 30, 2027, and thereafter at a rate reset every five years equal to the five-year Government of Canada bond yield plus 3.1%. Redeemable on June 30, 2027, and on June 30 every five years thereafter at $25 per share plus declared and unpaid dividends. Convertible at the holder's option on June 30, 2027, and on June 30 every five years thereafter, into floating rate first preferred series D shares on a share-for-share basis, subject to certain conditions. The series D shares would pay a quarterly dividend equal to the 90-day Canadian Treasury bill rate plus 3.1%.

Series D - Entitled cumulative preferential annual dividends payable quarterly equal to the 90-day Government of Canada Treasury bill rate plus 3.1%. Redeemable on June 30, 2027, and on June 30 every five years thereafter at $25 per share, or at $25.50 per share in the case of redemptions on any date after June 30, 2027, that is not a series B conversion date. Convertible at the holder's option, on June 30, 2027, and on June 30 every five years thereafter, into first preferred series D shares on a share-for-share basis, subject to certain conditions.

Series E - Entitled to fixed cumulative preferential annual dividends of $1.7235 per share payable quarterly to Sept. 30, 2027, and thereafter at a rate reset every five years equal to the five-year Government of Canada bond yield plus 3.65%. Redeemable on Sept. 30, 2027, and on September 30 every five years thereafter at $25 per share plus declared and unpaid dividends. Convertible at the holder's option on Sept. 30, 2027, and on September 30 every five years thereafter, into floating rate first preferred series F shares on a share-for-share basis, subject to certain conditions. The series F shares would pay a quarterly dividend equal to the 90-day Canadian Treasury bill rate plus 3.65%.

Series G - Entitled to fixed cumulative preferential annual dividends of $1.247 per share payable quarterly to Sept. 30, 2024, and thereafter at a rate reset every five years equal to the five-year Government of Canada bond yield plus 3.8%. Redeemable on Sept. 30, 2024, and on September 30 every five years thereafter at $25 per share plus declared and unpaid dividends. Convertible at the holder's option on Sept. 30, 2024, and on September 30 every five years thereafter, into floating rate first preferred series H shares on a share-for-share basis, subject to certain conditions. The series H shares would pay a quarterly dividend equal to the 90-day Canadian Treasury bill rate plus 3.8%.

Common - One vote per share.

Options - At Dec. 31, 2022, options were outstanding to purchase 3,000,000 common shares at prices ranging between $5 and $12 per share with a weighted average remaining contractual life of 3.89 years.

Normal Course Issuer Bid - The company plans to make normal course purchases of up to 14,000,000 common shares representing 7.3% of the public float. The bid commenced on May 31, 2023, and expires on May 30, 2024.

Major Shareholder - Brookfield Corporation held 13.26% interest and RBC Global Asset Management Inc. held 12.1% interest at Mar. 17, 2023.

Price Range - TA/TSX

Year	Volume	High	Low	Close
2022	194,777,526	$15.28	$10.52	$12.11
2021	145,338,723	$14.61	$9.57	$14.05
2020	196,635,641	$11.23	$5.32	$9.67
2019	150,301,301	$10.14	$5.50	$9.28
2018	143,293,111	$7.90	$5.44	$5.59

Recent Close: $13.17

Capital Stock Changes - On June 30, 2022, 1,044,299 first preferred series C shares were converted into a like number of first preferred series D shares. Also during 2022, common shares were issued as follows: 900,000 as share-based compensation and 500,000 on exercise of options; 4,300,000 common shares were repurchased under a Normal Course Issuer Bid.

Dividends

TA com Ra $0.22 pa Q est. Jan. 1, 2023**
Prev. Rate: $0.20 est. Jan. 1, 2022
Prev. Rate: $0.18 est. Apr. 1, 2021
Prev. Rate: $0.17 est. Apr. 1, 2020

TA.PR.D pfd 1st ser A cum. red. exch. Adj. Ra $0.71925 pa Q est. June 30, 2021

TA.PR.F pfd 1st ser C cum. red. exch. Adj. Ra $1.4635 pa Q est. Sept. 30, 2022

TA.PR.H pfd 1st ser E cum. red. exch. Adj. Ra $1.7235 pa Q est. Dec. 31, 2022

TA.PR.J pfd 1st ser G cum. red. exch. Adj. Ra $1.247 pa Q est. Dec. 31, 2019

TA.PR.E pfd 1st ser B cum. red. exch. Fltg. Ra pa Q

$0.41545	Sept. 30/23	$0.411	June 30/23
$0.37991	Mar. 31/23	$0.337	Dec. 31/22

Paid in 2023: $1.20636 2022: $0.85613 2021: $0.53743

TA.PR.G pfd 1st ser D cum. red. exch. Fltg. Ra pa Q
Listed Jun 30/22.

$0.48287	Sept. 30/23	$0.47769	June 30/23
$0.45578	Mar. 31/23	$0.40442	Dec. 31/22

Paid in 2023: $1.41634 2022: $0.69283**i** 2021: n.a.

** Reinvestment Option **i** Initial Payment

Long-Term Debt - Outstanding at Dec. 31, 2022:

5.9% commercial loan due 2023	$1,000,000
Credit facilities[1]	428,000,000
Debentures[2]	251,000,000
Non-recourse debt[3]	1,781,000,000
Senior notes[4]	934,000,000
Exchangeable securities[5]	739,000,000
Tax equity financing[6]	123,000,000
Finance lease obligs	135,000,000
	4,392,000,000
Less: Current portion	178,000,000
	4,214,000,000

[1] Consists of $396,000,000 term loan facility bearing interest at 6.5% and due 2024; and $32,000,000 credit facility with an effective interest rate of 4.7% (as at Dec. 31, 2022), due 2026.

[2] Bear interest at fixed rates ranging from 6.9% to 7.3%, and due from 2029 to 2030.

[3] Consists of bonds and debentures bearing interest at rates ranging from 3% to 8.9%, and due from 2023 to 2042.

[4] US$700,000,000. Bear interest at rates ranging from 6.5% to 7.8%, and due from 2029 to 2040. A total of US$370,000,000 of the senior notes has been designated as a hedge of the company's net investment of U.S. self-sustaining foreign operations.

[5] Consists of $400,000,000 exchangeable preferred shares series I and $339,000,000 exchangeable debentures due May 2039, and bears interest at 7%. Exchangeable into an equity ownership interest in the company's Alberta Hydro assets.

[6] Consists of tax equity financing for Big Level & Antrim, Lakeswind and North Carolina wind & solar projects bearing interest at rates ranging from 6.6% to 10.5%, and due from 2024 to 2029.

Minimum long-term debt and finance lease obligations repayments were reported as follows:

2023	$163,000,000
2024	531,000,000
2025	146,000,000
2026	180,000,000
2027	158,000,000
Thereafter	2,520,000,000

Wholly Owned Subsidiaries

TransAlta Cogeneration Ltd., Calgary, Alta.
- 0.01% int. in **TransAlta Cogeneration, L.P.**, Ont.

TransAlta Energy Marketing Corp., Canada.
TransAlta Generation Ltd., Canada.
- 0.01% int. in **TransAlta Generation Partnership**, Canada.

TransAlta Investments Ltd., Canada.
- 99.99% int. in **Keephills 3 Limited Partnership**, Alta.

TransAlta Power Ltd.
- 52.26% int. in **TransAlta Holdings ULC**, N.S.

Subsidiaries

57.13% int. in **TEC Limited Partnership**, Alta.
- 100% int. in **TransAlta Energy (Australia), Pty Ltd.**, Australia.
  - 100% int. in **TEC Hedland Pty. Ltd.**, Australia.
  - 100% int. in **TEC Outback Pty. Ltd.**, Australia.
    - 100% int. in **TEC Desert Pty. Ltd.**, Australia.
      - 85% int. in **Southern Cross Energy Partnership**, Perth, W.A., Australia.
      - 100% int. in **TEC Desert No. 2 Pty. Ltd.**, Australia.
        - 15% int. in **Southern Cross Energy Partnership**, Perth, W.A., Australia.
- 100% int. in **TEC Pipe Pty Ltd.**, Australia.

99.99% int. in **TransAlta Generation Partnership**, Canada.
- 65.72% int. in **TA Energy Inc.**, Canada.
- 50% int. in **TransAlta Cogeneration, L.P.**, Ont.
- 22.73% int. in **TransAlta Renewables Inc.**, Calgary, Alta. (see separate coverage)

Investments

0.01% int. in **Keephills 3 Limited Partnership**, Alta.
34.28% int. in **TA Energy Inc.**, Canada.
47.74% int. in **TransAlta Holdings ULC**, N.S.
- 100% int. in **TransAlta Holdings U.S. Inc.**, United States.
  - 100% int. in **Barracuda Wind LLC**, Del.
  - 100% int. in **Bobcat Equity Holdings, LLC**, Del.
  - 100% int. in **TA US Solar Power Holdings LLC**, Del.
  - 100% int. in **TransAlta USA Inc.**, Del.
    - 100% int. in **TECWA Power, Inc.**, Wash.
      - 100% int. in **TransAlta Centralia Generation LLC**, Wash.
  - 100% int. in **TransAlta Wyoming Wind LLC**, United States.

37.38% int. in **TransAlta Renewables Inc.**, Calgary, Alta. (see separate coverage)

Note: The preceding list includes only the major related companies in which interests are held.

Financial Statistics

Periods ended:	12m Dec. 31/22[A]		12m Dec. 31/21[A]
	$000s	%Chg	$000s
Operating revenue	**2,976,000**	**+9**	**2,721,000**
Cost of sales	258,000		277,000
Salaries & benefits	268,000		270,000
Other operating expense	1,369,000		1,038,000
Operating expense	**1,895,000**	**+20**	**1,585,000**
Operating income	**1,081,000**	**-5**	**1,136,000**
Deprec., depl. & amort.	599,000		719,000
Finance income	43,000		36,000
Finance costs, gross	286,000		256,000
Investment income	9,000		9,000
Write-downs/write-offs	(9,000)		(648,000)
Pre-tax income	**353,000**	**n.a.**	**(380,000)**
Income taxes	192,000		45,000
Net income	**161,000**	**n.a.**	**(425,000)**
Net inc. for equity hldrs	**50,000**	**n.a.**	**(537,000)**
Net inc. for non-cont. int.	**111,000**	**-1**	**112,000**
Cash & equivalent	1,134,000		947,000
Inventories	157,000		167,000
Accounts receivable	1,165,000		499,000
Current assets	3,714,000		2,197,000
Long-term investments	129,000		105,000
Fixed assets, net	5,556,000		5,320,000
Right-of-use assets	126,000		95,000
Intangibles, net	716,000		719,000
Total assets	**10,741,000**	**+16**	**9,226,000**
Bank indebtedness	16,000		nil
Accts. pay. & accr. liabs	1,346,000		689,000
Current liabilities	2,888,000		1,931,000
Long-term debt, gross	4,392,000		4,002,000
Long-term debt, net	4,214,000		3,158,000
Preferred share equity	942,000		942,000
Shareholders' equity	1,110,000		1,582,000
Non-controlling interest	879,000		1,011,000
Cash from oper. activs	**877,000**	**-12**	**1,001,000**
Cash from fin. activs	45,000		(282,000)
Cash from invest. activs	(741,000)		(472,000)
Net cash position	**1,134,000**	**+20**	**947,000**
Capital expenditures	(918,000)		(480,000)
Capital disposals	66,000		39,000
Unfunded pension liability	141,000		217,000
	$		$
Earnings per share*	0.01		(2.13)
Cash flow per share*	3.24		3.69
Cash divd. per share*	0.21		0.19
	shs		shs
No. of shs. o/s*	268,100,000		271,000,000
Avg. no. of shs. o/s*	271,000,000		271,000,000
	%		%
Net profit margin	5.41		(15.62)
Return on equity	0.99		(56.20)
Return on assets	2.92		(1.46)
Foreign sales percent	36		32
No. of employees (FTEs)	1,222		1,282

* Common
[A] Reported in accordance with IFRS

Latest Results

Periods ended:	6m June 30/23[A]		6m June 30/22[A]
	$000s	%Chg	$000s
Operating revenue	1,714,000	+44	1,193,000
Net income	431,000	+193	147,000
Net inc. for equity hldrs	368,000	+217	116,000
Net inc. for non-cont. int	63,000		31,000
	$		$
Earnings per share*	1.34		0.39

* Common
[A] Reported in accordance with IFRS

Historical Summary
(as originally stated)

Fiscal Year	Oper. Rev.	Net Inc. Bef. Disc.	EPS*
	$000s	$000s	$
2022[A]	2,976,000	161,000	0.01
2021[A]	2,721,000	(425,000)	(2.13)
2020[A]	2,101,000	(253,000)	(1.22)
2019[A]	2,347,000	176,000	0.18
2018[A]	2,249,000	(90,000)	(0.86)

* Common
[A] Reported in accordance with IFRS

T.80 TransAlta Renewables Inc.*

Symbol - RNW **Exchange** - TSX **CUSIP** - 893463
Head Office - 110 12 Ave SW, PO Box 1900 Stn M, Calgary, AB, T2P 2M1 **Telephone** - (403) 267-7110 **Fax** - (403) 267-7405
Website - www.transaltarenewables.com
Email - investor_relations@transalta.com
Investor Relations - Investor Relations (800) 387-3598
Auditors - Ernst & Young LLP C.A., Calgary, Alta.
Lawyers - McCarthy Tétrault LLP, Calgary, Alta.
Transfer Agents - Computershare Trust Company of Canada Inc., Calgary, Alta.
FP500 Subsidiary Revenue Ranking - 85
Profile - (Can. 2013) Owns, operates and manages renewable power businesses with a focus on wind, hydroelectric, gas and battery storage facilities in Alberta, Ontario, Quebec, New Brunswick and British Columbia. Also holds economic interests in wind, solar and cogeneration facilities in the U.S. and gas-fired power generation facilities and a gas pipeline in Western Australia.

Owns 1,359 MW of net wind generation capacity in 21 wind farms and a battery storage facility in Alberta (13), Ontario (4), Quebec (2) and New Brunswick (3); 109 MW of net hydroelectric generation capacity in 11 hydroelectric facilities in British Columbia (4), Alberta (4) and Ontario (3); and a 499-MW combined-cycle gas cogeneration facility in Sarnia, Ont.

Province	Wind[1,2]	Hydro[1]	Gas[1]
Alberta	636	21	n.a.
Ontario	418	11	499
Quebec	166	n.a.	n.a.
New Brunswick	139	n.a.	n.a.
British Columbia	n.a.	77	n.a.
	1,359	109	499

[1] Net capacity ownership interest (MW).
[2] Includes WindCharger battery storage facility in Pincher Creek, Alta., which has a nameplate capacity of 10 MW and total storage capacity of 20 MWh.

Also holds economic interests based on the cash flows of major shareholder **TransAlta Corporation**'s 140-MW wind farm in Wyoming; 50-MW Lakeswind wind farm in Minnesota; 49% interest in 137-MW Skookumchuck wind farm in Washington; 90-MW Big Level wind farm in Pennsylvania; 29-MW Antrim wind farm in New Hampshire; 21 MW of solar projects in Massachusetts; 122 MW of solar projects in North Carolina; 29-MW Ada cogeneration facility in Michigan; and Western Australian assets consisting of 450 MW of net power generation capacity from six operating gas-fired assets and the 270-km Fortescue River gas pipeline.

In addition, holds economic interest in Northern Goldfields solar project under construction in Western Australia, which includes 27-MW Mount Keith solar farm, 11-MW Leinster solar farm and 10-MW Leinster battery energy, with construction activities started in the first quarter of 2022 and completion expected in the second half of 2023.

On May 3, 2022, the company exercised its option to acquire an economic interest in the expansion of the Mt. Keith 132kV transmission system in Western Australia, to support the Northern Goldfields-based operations of **Billiton Nickel West Pty Ltd.** Total construction capital was estimated between A$50,000,000 and A$53,000,000. Terms were not disclosed.

Recent Merger and Acquisition Activity

Status: pending **Announced:** July 11, 2023
TransAlta Corporation agreed to acquire the remaining 39.9% interest in TransAlta Renewables Inc. for 1.0337 TransAlta Corporation common shares or $13 cash for each TransAlta Renewables share held. The maximum number of common shares that may be issued was 46,441,779 and the maximum aggregate amount of cash was $800,000,000, representing a total consideration of $1,384,051,812. TransAlta Renewables' board of directors unanimously recommended that shareholders vote in favour of the transaction, and TransAlta Corporation's board of directors approved the transaction.

Status: completed **Announced:** Dec. 2, 2022
TransAlta Renewables Inc. sold its 1-MW run-of-river Appleton and 2-MW run-of-river Galetta hydroelectric facilities located in Ontario for an undisclosed amount.

Directors - David W. Drinkwater, chr., B.C.; Todd J. Stack, pres. & acting CEO, Alta.; Brett M. Gellner, Calgary, Alta.; Allen R. Hagerman, Millarville, Alta.; Georganne M. Hodges, Tex.; Michael J. (Mike) Novelli, N.H.; Kerry O'Reilly Wilks, Alta.; Susan M. Ward, Tex.

Oper. Subsid./Mgt. Co. Officers - Brent V. Ward, CFO; Aron J. Willis, exec. v-p, growth; Michelle Cameron, v-p & contr.; Scott T. Jeffers, v-p & corp. sec.; Gary Woods, v-p, gas & renewables

Capital Stock

	Authorized (shs.)	Outstanding (shs.)[1]
Preferred	unlimited	nil
Common	unlimited	266,900,000
Class B	unlimited	nil

[1] At Aug. 2, 2023

Major Shareholder - TransAlta Corporation held 60.1% interest at July 11, 2023.

Price Range - RNW/TSX

Year	Volume	High	Low	Close
2022	118,346,236	$19.45	$10.63	$11.25
2021	126,077,934	$24.47	$18.15	$18.75
2020	134,807,694	$22.63	$10.82	$21.76
2019	78,980,147	$15.79	$10.28	$15.52
2018	74,290,343	$13.50	$9.76	$10.37

Recent Close: $13.22

Capital Stock Changes - There were no changes to capital stock during 2021 or 2022.

Dividends

RNW com Ra $0.93996 pa M est. Sept. 29, 2017

Long-Term Debt - Outstanding at Dec. 31, 2022:

Credit facility[1]	$32,000,000
2.95% Pingston bond due 2023	45,000,000
3.83% Melancthon-Wolfe bond due 2028	202,000,000
3.96% New Richmond bond due 2032	112,000,000
4.45% Kent Hills Wind bond due 2033	206,000,000
3.41% Windrise Green bond due 2041	170,000,000
Lease obligations	23,000,000
	790,000,000
Less: Current portion	109,000,000
	681,000,000

[1] Bearing interest at Canadian prime, banker's acceptances, SOFR or U.S. base rate, due June 2026.

Minimum long-term debt repayments were reported as follows:

2023	$108,000,000
2024	66,000,000
2025	69,000,000
2026	100,000,000
2027	69,000,000
Thereafter	364,000,000

Wholly Owned Subsidiaries

Canadian Hydro Developers, Inc., Calgary, Alta.
- 100% int. in **MW Intermediary Inc.**, Canada.
  - 0.01% int. in **MW Intermediary L.P.**, Ont.
- 99.99% int. in **MW Intermediary L.P.**, Ont.
  - 82.99% int. in **Kent Hills Wind Inc.**, Canada.
    - 0.01% int. in **Kent Hills Wind LP**, Calgary, Alta.
  - 82.99% int. in **Kent Hills Wind LP**, Calgary, Alta.
  - 100% int. in **Melancthon Wolfe Wind Inc.**, Canada.
    - 0.01% int. in **Melancthon Wolfe Wind LP**
  - 99.99% int. in **Melancthon Wolfe Wind LP**
  - 100% int. in **New Richmond Wind Inc.**, Canada.
    - 0.01% int. in **New Richmond Wind L.P.**, Calgary, Alta.
  - 99.99% int. in **New Richmond Wind L.P.**, Calgary, Alta.
- 50% int. in **Pingston Power Inc.**, B.C.
- 100% int. in **TA Kent Breeze Inc.**, Canada.
  - 0.01% int. in **TA Kent Breeze L.P.**, Alta.
- 99.99% int. in **TA Kent Breeze L.P.**, Alta.
- 100% int. in **Windrise Wind Energy Inc.**, Canada.
  - 0.01% int. in **Windrise Wind LP**, Alta.
- 99.99% int. in **Windrise Wind LP**, Alta.

TransAlta (LN) Inc., Canada.
- 0.01% int. in **TransAlta (LN) L.P.**, Alta.

TransAlta (RC) Inc., Canada.
- 0.01% int. in **TransAlta (RC) L.P.**, Alta.

TransAlta (SC) Inc., Canada.
- 0.01% int. in **TransAlta (SC) L.P.**, Alta.

Subsidiaries

99.99% int. in **TransAlta (LN) L.P.**, Alta.
99.99% int. in **TransAlta (RC) L.P.**, Alta.
99.99% int. in **TransAlta (SC) L.P.**, Alta.
- 100% int. in **Sarnia Cogeneration Inc.**, Canada.

Financial Statistics

Periods ended:	12m Dec. 31/22[A]		12m Dec. 31/21[A]
	$000s	%Chg	$000s
Operating revenue	**560,000**	**+19**	**470,000**
Other operating expense	302,000		226,000
Operating expense	**302,000**	**+34**	**226,000**
Operating income	**258,000**	**+6**	**244,000**
Deprec., depl. & amort.	141,000		150,000
Finance income	47,000		115,000
Finance costs, gross	50,000		42,000
Write-downs/write-offs	(31,000)		(17,000)
Pre-tax income	**91,000**	**-39**	**150,000**
Income taxes	17,000		11,000
Net income	**74,000**	**-47**	**139,000**
Net inc. for equity hldrs	**74,000**	**-47**	**140,000**
Net inc. for non-cont. int	**nil**	**n.a.**	**(1,000)**
Cash & equivalent	89,000		244,000
Inventories	9,000		8,000
Accounts receivable	135,000		120,000
Current assets	240,000		430,000
Long-term investments	1,037,000		1,270,000
Fixed assets, net	1,766,000		1,897,000
Right-of-use assets	26,000		26,000
Intangibles, net	81,000		92,000
Total assets	**3,229,000**	**-14**	**3,749,000**
Bank indebtedness	nil		167,000
Accts. pay. & accr. liabs	128,000		82,000
Current liabilities	306,000		593,000
Long-term debt, gross	790,000		814,000
Long-term debt, net	681,000		550,000
Shareholders' equity	1,756,000		2,074,000
Non-controlling interest	49,000		49,000
Cash from oper. activs	**257,000**	**-24**	**336,000**
Cash from fin. activs	(446,000)		(149,000)
Cash from invest. activs	34,000		(525,000)
Net cash position	**89,000**	**-64**	**244,000**
Capital expenditures	(118,000)		(81,000)
Capital disposals	6,000		nil
	$		$
Earnings per share*	0.28		0.52
Cash flow per share*	0.96		1.26
Cash divd. per share*	0.94		0.94
	shs		shs
No. of shs. o/s*	266,900,000		266,900,000
Avg. no. of shs. o/s*	266,900,000		266,900,000
	%		%
Net profit margin	13.21		29.57
Return on equity	3.86		6.47
Return on assets	3.29		4.81

* Common

[A] Reported in accordance with IFRS

Latest Results

Periods ended:	6m June 30/23[A]		6m June 30/22[A]
	$000s	%Chg	$000s
Operating revenue	218,000	-23	282,000
Net income	58,000	+5	55,000
Net inc. for equity hldrs	58,000	+7	54,000
Net inc. for non-cont. int	nil		1,000
	$		$
Earnings per share*	0.22		0.20

* Common

[A] Reported in accordance with IFRS

Historical Summary
(as originally stated)

Fiscal Year	Oper. Rev.	Net Inc. Bef. Disc.	EPS*
	$000s	$000s	$
2022[A]	560,000	74,000	0.28
2021[A]	470,000	139,000	0.52
2020[A]	431,000	97,000	0.35
2019[A]	438,000	183,000	0.68
2018[A]	446,000	241,000	0.92

* Common

[A] Reported in accordance with IFRS

T.81 Transat A.T. Inc.*

Symbol - TRZ **Exchange** - TSX **CUSIP** - 89351T
Head Office - Place du Parc, 600-300 rue Léo-Pariseau, Montréal, QC, H2X 4C2 **Telephone** - (514) 987-1660 **Toll-free** - (866) 322-6649 **Fax** - (514) 987-8035
Website - www.transat.com
Email - patrick.bui@transat.com
Investor Relations - Patrick Bui (514) 987-1660 ext. 4567
Auditors - Ernst & Young LLP C.A., Montréal, Qué.
Transfer Agents - TSX Trust Company, Montréal, Qué.
FP500 Revenue Ranking - 250
Employees - 3,900 at Oct. 31, 2022

Profile - (Can. 1987) Develops, markets and distributes holiday travel products and services to some 60 destinations in more than 25 countries in the Americas and Europe. Operations consist of a Canadian leisure airline, tour operators and a network of travel agencies.

Air transportation operations are carried out through wholly owned **Air Transat A.T. Inc.**, which offers international flights to sun destinations (Caribbean, Mexico, Central and South America) and Europe, as well as transborder flights to the U.S. and domestic flights within Canada. At Oct. 31, 2022, Air Transat's fleet consisted of 24 long-haul aircraft, including 12 Airbus A330s (11 A330-200s and one A330-300) and 12 Airbus A321LRs; and eight medium-haul aircraft, including seven Airbus A321ceos and one Boeing 737-800 (non-operational). During fiscal 2022, Air Transat served 3,216,599 passengers compared with 235,000 passengers in fiscal 2021.

Outgoing tour operators purchase the various components of a trip locally or abroad (airline seats, lodgings, excursions and car rentals among others) and sell them separately or in packages to consumers in their local markets through various distribution channels. Wholly owned **Transat Tours Canada Inc.**, operating under the Transat brand, offers Canadian vacationers with travel vacation packages and aircraft seats to sun, European and U.S. destinations. Transat Tours also offers seats to and from various Canadian cities for its domestic market. All Transat Tours offerings are sold online and through travel agency networks across Canada. Wholly owned **The Airline Seat Company Limited**, operating under the Canadian Affair brand, is the U.K.'s largest single destination tour operator to Canada, offering packaged tours and flights-only products (both Air Transat and third-party airline flights) to Canada for consumers in the U.K. and Ireland through travel agencies and directly to consumers via call centre and online. Wholly owned **Air Consultants France S.A.S.** sells Air Transat's airline tickets for flights from France, Belgium, the Netherlands and Switzerland.

Incoming tour operators purchase tourism services in their own countries and package them into products that are marketed abroad by partners, primarily tour operators or travel agencies. Some incoming tour operators also complement the role of the outgoing tour operators by providing a range of optional services at the destination, such as passenger transfers, excursions, tours or sports activities. Incoming tours to Mexico, the Dominican Republic, Jamaica and Barbados are offered by wholly owned **Trafictours de Mexico S.A. de C.V.**, **Turissimo Caribe Excursiones Dominican Republic C. por A.** and **Caribbean Transportation Inc.**

Products are distributed through 258 travel agencies in Canada, of which 31 are wholly owned, 125 are franchised and 102 are affiliated under the Club Voyages, Marlin Travel/Voyages Marlin, Transat Travel/Voyages Transat, Voyages en Liberté and TravelPlus banners or affiliation programs.

Also holds 50% interest in Marival Armony (formerly Rancho Banderas), a luxury resort in Punta de Mita, Mexico.

Recent Merger and Acquisition Activity

Status: pending **Announced:** July 10, 2023
Transat A.T. Inc. agreed to sell a piece of land in Puerto Morelos, Mexico, to resort company Marena Intracorp B.V. Inc. (dba Finest Resorts) for US$38,000,000. Transat had bought the land in 2018 as part of the development of a hotel subsidiary, which it discontinued in 2021. The sale was part of Transat's plan to focus on its airline business, with the proceeds of the sale to be immediately used to repay debt. The transaction was expected to be completed during Transat's fourth quarter.

Predecessor Detail - Name changed from Groupe Transat A.T. Inc., Aug. 3, 1993.

Directors - Susan Kudzman, chr., Montréal, Qué.; Annick Guérard, pres. & CEO, Montréal, Qué.; Geneviève Brouillette, Montréal, Qué.; Lucie Chabot, Montréal, Qué.; Valérie Chort, Toronto, Ont.; Robert Coallier, Montréal, Qué.; Daniel Desjardins, Montréal, Qué.; Stéphane Lefebvre, Montréal, Qué.; Bruno Matheu, Paris, France; Ian Rae, Montréal, Qué.; Julie Tremblay, Montréal, Qué.

Other Exec. Officers - Patrick Bui, CFO; Michèle Barre, chief revenue officer; Bernard Bussières, chief legal & govt. rel. officer & corp. sec.; Julie Lamontagne, chief people, sustainability & commun. officer; Marc-Philippe Lumpé, chief airline opers. officer; Bruno Leclaire, v-p & chief info. & digital officer; Joseph Adamo, pres., Transat Distribution Canada Inc.

Capital Stock

	Authorized (shs.)	Outstanding (shs.)[1]
Preferred	unlimited	nil
Class A Variable Vtg.	unlimited	1,610,780
Class B Vtg.	unlimited	36,665,278

[1] At Apr. 30, 2023

Class A Variable Voting - Owned or controlled by non-Canadians. One vote per share, unless (i) a single non-Canadian holder or non-Canadians authorized to provide an air service holds more than 25% of the total number of class A shares outstanding; or (ii) the total number of votes that would be cast by or on behalf of a single non-Canadian or non-Canadians authorized to provide an air service would exceed 49% of the total number of votes that would be cast at any meeting. If either of the thresholds is exceeded, the vote attached to each class A share will decrease proportionately and automatically such that (i) the class A shares held by such single non-Canadian or non-Canadians authorized to provide an air service do not carry more than 25% of the aggregate votes attached to all issued and outstanding voting shares, and (ii) the total number of votes cast by or on behalf of all non-Canadians as a class do not exceed 49% of the total number of votes that may be cast at such meeting. Converted into one class B voting share automatically without any further action on the part of the company or the holder, if (i) the class A share is or becomes owned or controlled by a Canadian, or (ii) the provisions under the Canada Transportation Act relating to foreign ownership restrictions are repealed and not replaced with other similar provisions. Maximum ownership level for any single non-Canadian or any one or more non-Canadian authorized to provide an air service is 25%.

Class B Voting - Owned or controlled by Canadians. Converted into one class A variable voting share automatically without any further action on the part of the company or the holder, if the class B share is or becomes owned or controlled by a non-Canadian. One vote per share.

Options - At Oct. 31, 2022, options were outstanding to purchase 480,847 class A or B shares at prices ranging from $4.18 to $10.94 per share with a weighted average remaining life of 4.3 years.

Major Shareholder - Fonds de solidarité des travailleurs du Québec (F.T.Q.) held 11.43% interest and Letko, Brosseau & Associates Inc. held 10.54% interest at Jan. 27, 2023.

Price Range - TRZ/TSX

Year	Volume	High	Low	Close
2022	26,480,350	$5.41	$2.50	$2.94
2021	69,276,476	$7.90	$3.74	$4.03
2020	54,035,544	$16.35	$3.56	$5.49
2019	42,288,144	$17.00	$4.50	$15.94
2018	14,817,178	$11.45	$5.39	$5.95

Recent Close: $4.27

Capital Stock Changes - During fiscal 2022, class B voting shares were issued as follows: 265,646 in exchange for a like number of class A variable voting shares and 265,054 under employee share purchase plan.

Long-Term Debt - Outstanding at Oct. 31, 2022:

Revolving credit facility[1]	$49,644,000
Subordinated credit facility[2]	70,024,000
LEEFF credit facilities[3]	361,972,000
Credit facility related to travel credits[4]	182,520,000
	664,160,000
Less: Current portion	nil
	664,160,000

[1] Bears interest at bankers' acceptance rate or U.S. Secured Overnight Financing Rate (SOFR) plus 4.5% or prime plus 3.5%. Due Apr. 29, 2024.

[2] Bears interest at bankers' acceptance rate plus 6% or prime plus 5%; an additional compounding premium of 3.75% will be added to interest until Oct. 29, 2023. Due Apr. 29, 2024.

[3] Borrowings under the Large Employer Emergency Financing Facility (LEEFF), consisting of a non-revolving and secured credit facility, bearing interest at bankers' acceptance rate plus 4.5% or prime plus 3.5% and due Apr. 29, 2024; and a non-revolving and unsecured credit facility, bearing interest at a rate of 5% until Dec. 31, 2023, increasing to 8% until Dec. 31, 2024, and increasing by 2% per annum thereafter, and due Apr. 29, 2026.

[4] Borrowings for the sole purpose of making refunds to travellers who were scheduled to depart on or after Feb. 1, 2020, and to whom a travel credit was issued as a result of COVID-19. Bears interest at a rate of 1.22%. Due Apr. 29, 2028.

Wholly Owned Subsidiaries

Air Transat A.T. Inc., Canada.
- 100% int. in **Air Consultants France S.A.S.**, France.

The Airline Seat Company Limited, United Kingdom. dba Canadian Affair.
CTI Logistics Inc., Barbados.
Caribbean Transportation Inc., Barbados.
Laminama S.A. de C.V., Mexico.
- 100% int. in **Promociones Residencial Morelos S.A. de C.V.**, Mexico.

11061987 Florida Inc., United States.
Promotora Turistica Regional, S.A. de C.V., Mexico.
Propiedades Profesionales Dominicanas Carhel S.R.L., Dominican Republic.
Servicios y Transportes Punta Cana S.R.L, Dominican Republic.
Sun Excursions Caribbean Inc., Barbados.
TTDR Travel Company S.A.S., Dominican Republic.
Trafictours Canada Inc., Canada.
- 100% int. in **Trafictours de Mexico S.A. de C.V.**, Mexico.
- 100% int. in **Turissimo Caribe Excursiones Dominican Republic C. por A.**, Dominican Republic.
- 100% int. in **Turissimo Jamaica Ltd.**, Jamaica.

Transat Distribution Canada Inc., Montréal, Qué. dba Club Voyages, Voyages en Liberté, Voyages Marlin, Marlin Travel, Voyages Transat, Transat Travel and TravelPlus.
Transat Holidays USA Inc., United States.
Transat Tours Canada Inc., Montréal, Qué. dba Voyages Transat and Transat Travel.

Investments

50% int. in **Desarrollo Transimar S.A. de C.V.**, Mexico.

Note: The preceding list includes only the major related companies in which interests are held.

Financial Statistics

Periods ended:	12m Oct. 31/22[A]		12m Oct. 31/21[oA]
	$000s	%Chg	$000s
Operating revenue	**1,642,038**	**n.m.**	**124,818**
Cost of sales	355,250		31,958
Salaries & benefits	288,889		122,770
Other operating expense	1,143,783		179,271
Operating expense	**1,787,922**	**+435**	**333,999**
Operating income	**(145,884)**	**n.a.**	**(209,181)**
Deprec., depl. & amort.	153,429		159,765
Finance income	12,982		4,441
Finance costs, gross	105,314		77,024
Investment income	(2,477)		(4,704)
Write-downs/write-offs	(783)		(33,450)
Pre-tax income	**(449,473)**	**n.a.**	**(389,415)**
Income taxes	(4,149)		23
Net income	**(445,324)**	**n.a.**	**(389,438)**
Net inc. for equity hldrs	**(445,324)**	**n.a.**	**(389,559)**
Net inc. for non-cont. int	**nil**	**n.a.**	**121**
Cash & equivalent	322,535		433,195
Inventories	26,725		10,514
Accounts receivable	265,050		108,857
Current assets	1,031,890		719,864
Long-term investments	8,820		9,476
Fixed assets, net	1,000,151		974,229
Intangibles, net	13,261		16,849
Total assets	**2,271,131**	**+20**	**1,897,658**
Accts. pay. & accr. liabs	289,897		141,790
Current liabilities	1,053,633		630,546
Long-term debt, gross	664,160		463,180
Long-term debt, net	664,160		463,180
Long-term lease liabilities	950,743		784,801
Shareholders' equity	(750,180)		(315,110)
Cash from oper. activs	**(177,854)**	**n.a.**	**(518,444)**
Cash from fin. activs	99,689		522,071
Cash from invest. activs	(33,783)		4,542
Net cash position	**322,535**	**-26**	**433,195**
Capital expenditures	(32,531)		(5,599)
Capital disposals	nil		422
Unfunded pension liability	20,773		27,120
	$		$
Earnings per share*	(11.77)		(10.32)
Cash flow per share*	(4.70)		(13.73)
	shs		shs
No. of shs. o/s*	38,012,144		37,747,090
Avg. no. of shs. o/s*	37,838,000		37,747,090
	%		%
Net profit margin	(27.12)		(312.00)
Return on equity	n.m.		n.m.
Return on assets	(16.36)		(15.96)
No. of employees (FTEs)	3,900		2,100

* Class A & B
[o] Restated
[A] Reported in accordance with IFRS

Latest Results

Periods ended:	6m Apr. 30/23[A]		6m Apr. 30/22[A]
	$000s	%Chg	$000s
Operating revenue	1,537,568	+174	560,595
Net income	(85,790)	n.a.	(212,621)
	$		$
Earnings per share*	(2.25)		(5.63)

* Class A & B
[A] Reported in accordance with IFRS

Historical Summary
(as originally stated)

Fiscal Year	Oper. Rev.	Net Inc. Bef. Disc.	EPS*
	$000s	$000s	$
2022[A]	1,642,038	(445,324)	(11.77)
2021[A]	124,818	(389,438)	(10.32)
2020[A]	1,302,069	(496,765)	(13.15)
2019[A]	2,937,130	(30,544)	(0.88)
2018[A]	2,992,582	2,416	(0.03)

* Class A & B
[A] Reported in accordance with IFRS

T.82 Transcanna Holdings Inc.

Symbol - TCAN **Exchange** - CSE (S) **CUSIP** - 89356V
Head Office - 2489 Bellevue Ave, West Vancouver, BC, V7V 1E1
Telephone - (604) 207-5548
Website - www.transcanna.com
Email - info@transcanna.com
Investor Relations - James R. Blink (604) 200-8853
Auditors - BF Borgers CPA PC C.P.A., Lakewood, Colo.
Lawyers - Armstrong Simpson, Vancouver, B.C.
Transfer Agents - Odyssey Trust Company, Vancouver, B.C.

Profile - (B.C. 2017) Cultivates, processes and distributes cannabis products and provides cannabis-related services in California.

Operates two facilities in Modesto, Calif., consisting of Jerusalem Court, a 12,000-sq.-ft. indoor cultivation and distribution facility; and Daly, a 196,000-sq.-ft. cultivation, processing and distribution facility, of which 22,500-sq.-ft. of indoor cultivation, 8,000-sq.-ft. of processing space, 6,000-sq.-ft. of packaging area and 11,000-sq.-ft. of storage space are operational. Expansion of Daly is ongoing, which includes construction of four additional 4,700-sq.-ft. cultivation rooms, three curing rooms and vegetative rooms. Completion was expected in the first half of 2023. Products produced include flower, pre-rolls and concentrates which are sold across California under the Lyfted Farms brand.

Also provides white-labelling, co-branding, processing, packaging, cold storage, distribution and crop management services to third party growers and customers throughout California.

Common suspended from CSE, Apr. 6, 2023.

Directors - James R. (Bob) Blink, pres. & CEO, Calif.; Joshua (Josh) Baker, Calif.; Travis Heilman

Other Exec. Officers - Peter Gregovich, CFO

Capital Stock

	Authorized (shs.)	Outstanding (shs.)[1]
Common	unlimited	112,674,180

[1] At Oct. 31, 2022

Major Shareholder - Widely held at Sept. 1, 2021.

Price Range - TCAN/CSE (S)

Year	Volume	High	Low	Close
2022	29,965,828	$0.52	$0.01	$0.02
2021	16,672,516	$1.70	$0.42	$0.48
2020	24,736,294	$2.01	$0.44	$0.77
2019	37,254,407	$7.79	$0.38	$1.18

Recent Close: $0.01

Capital Stock Changes - In April 2022, private placement of 10,000,000 units (1 common share & 1 warrant) at 10¢ per unit was completed, with warrants exercisable at 15¢ per share for two years.

Wholly Owned Subsidiaries

Dalvi, LCC, Calif.
GF Group, Inc., Calif.
Lyfted Farms, Inc., Modesto, Calif.
TransCanna Management, Inc., Calif.
• 100% int. in **TCM Distribution Inc.**, Calif.
Tres Ojos Naturals, LLC, Santa Cruz, Calif.

Financial Statistics

Periods ended:	12m Nov. 30/21[A]		12m Nov. 30/20[A]
	$000s	%Chg	$000s
Operating revenue	**3,999**	**-43**	**6,957**
Cost of goods sold	4,849		6,763
Salaries & benefits	1,882		3,283
General & admin expense	4,529		5,291
Stock-based compensation	1,995		1,456
Operating expense	**13,255**	**-21**	**16,793**
Operating income	**(9,256)**	**n.a.**	**(9,836)**
Deprec., depl. & amort.	1,038		502
Finance costs, gross	2,026		1,762
Write-downs/write-offs	(67)		(5,008)
Pre-tax income	**(13,093)**	**n.a.**	**(17,440)**
Income taxes	nil		(310)
Net income	**(13,093)**	**n.a.**	**(17,130)**
Cash & equivalent	241		1,244
Inventories	377		537
Accounts receivable	365		127
Current assets	1,255		2,507
Fixed assets, net	23,667		22,258
Right-of-use assets	723		973
Intangibles, net	nil		733
Total assets	**25,645**	**-3**	**26,471**
Accts. pay. & accr. liabs	3,093		3,260
Current liabilities	19,436		4,316
Long-term debt, gross	17,943		12,579
Long-term debt, net	2,364		12,000
Long-term lease liabilities	586		816
Shareholders' equity	3,259		9,338
Cash from oper. activs	**(6,060)**	**n.a.**	**(5,807)**
Cash from fin. activs	7,412		4,474
Cash from invest. activs	(2,088)		(656)
Net cash position	**241**	**-81**	**1,244**
Capital expenditures	(2,088)		(830)
	$		$
Earnings per share*	(0.23)		(0.39)
Cash flow per share*	(0.11)		(0.13)
	shs		shs
No. of shs. o/s*	53,404,602		47,867,080
Avg. no. of shs. o/s*	56,357,016		43,763,994
	%		%
Net profit margin	(327.41)		(246.23)
Return on equity	(207.87)		(131.95)
Return on assets	(42.47)		(51.99)
Foreign sales percent	100		100

* Common
[A] Reported in accordance with IFRS

Latest Results

Periods ended:	9m Aug. 31/22[A]		9m Aug. 31/21[oA]
	$000s	%Chg	$000s
Operating revenue	2,190	-5	2,301
Net income	(6,916)	n.a.	(6,528)
	$		$
Earnings per share*	(0.09)		(0.12)

* Common
[o] Restated
[A] Reported in accordance with IFRS

Historical Summary
(as originally stated)

Fiscal Year	Oper. Rev.	Net Inc. Bef. Disc.	EPS*
	$000s	$000s	$
2021[A]	3,999	(13,093)	(0.23)
2020[A]	6,957	(17,130)	(0.39)
2019[A]	240	(25,781)	(0.92)
2018[A]	nil	(2,161)	(0.21)

* Common
[A] Reported in accordance with IFRS

T.83 Transcontinental Inc.*

Symbol - TCL.A **Exchange** - TSX **CUSIP** - 893578
Head Office - 3240-1 Place Ville Marie, Montréal, QC, H3B 0G1
Telephone - (514) 954-4000 **Fax** - (514) 954-4016
Website - tctranscontinental.com
Email - yan.lapointe@tc.tc
Investor Relations - Yan Lapointe (514) 954-3574
Auditors - KPMG LLP C.A., Montréal, Qué.
Bankers - The Toronto-Dominion Bank, Montréal, Qué.; BofA Securities, Inc.; Desjardins Bank, N.A.; National Bank of Canada, Montréal, Qué.; The Bank of Nova Scotia, Montréal, Qué.; Canadian Imperial Bank of Commerce, Montréal, Qué.
Lawyers - Stikeman Elliott LLP, Montréal, Qué.
Transfer Agents - TSX Trust Company, Montréal, Qué.
FP500 Revenue Ranking - 173
Employees - 8,303 at Oct. 30, 2022

Profile - (Can. 1978) Provides flexible plastic packaging solutions primarily in North America, and printing and educational book publishing services primarily in Canada.

Operations are organized into three sectors: Packaging, Printing and Media.

The **Packaging** sector (operating as TC Transcontinental Packaging) manufactures flexible packaging solutions in Canada, the U.S., Mexico, Guatemala, Colombia, Ecuador, the U.K. and New Zealand. Operations include one premedia studio and 28 production plants specializing in extrusion, printing, lamination, converting and recycling. Flexible plastic products offered include rollstock, forming and non-forming films, shrink films and bags, banana tree bags, greenhouse and mulch films, die cut lids, labels, bags and pouches, and advanced coatings. The sector serves a wide variety of markets including dairy, coffee, meat and poultry, pet food, agriculture, beverage, home and personal care, industrial, consumer and medical products. Also provides premedia services including production art, creative and design, photography, brand guideline adaptation and brand extensions, colour management, print quality management, proofing, product innovation, prepress and plate making.

The **Printing** sector (operating as TC Transcontinental Printing) offers a complete line of specialized solutions for the production of printed material, including retail flyers, in-store marketing products, newspapers, magazines, 4-colour books, personalized and mass marketing products, and premedia and door-to-door distribution services. Operations include a network of 13 production plants. The division is divided into five segments: **Retail and Newspaper**, which prints retail flyers and over 175 newspapers, including 13 paid dailies, such as the Toronto Star, The Waterloo Region Record, The Peterborough Examiner, Hamilton Spectator, The Globe and Mail, The Gazette, Calgary Herald, Calgary Sun, The Vancouver Sun and National Post, from four plants in four Canadian provinces; **Magazine and Books**, which consists of three plants in Quebec and Ontario that print more than 300 magazines as well as colour books, catalogues and directories; **Marketing Products**, which includes the creation of digital content and visuals, direct mail and direct marketing solutions, specialty packaging printing, printing and assembly of promotional signs and displays, in-store marketing solutions and full store design-build services as well as printing of corporate materials such as banners, annual reports and identity brochures offered across five plants in Ontario, Quebec and Alberta; **Premedia**, which offers promotional content creation for print and digital and multichannel platforms including strategic creative and design, page production, copywriting and editing, language services, in-studio and external photography and video production; and **Distribution**, which offers door-to-door distribution services through Publisac in Quebec and Targeo, a Canada-wide distribution brokerage service.

The **Media** sector (operating as TC Media) consists of print and digital publication of educational books and specialized publications for construction industry. Activities are divided into two groups: **TC Media Books**, which offers creation, development, adaptation, translation, publication, marketing, sale and distribution of French-language educational resources, including textbooks, teachers' guide, activity books, digital products and other related materials, as well as supplemental materials, general interest books and specialized publications; and **Groupe Constructo**, which specializes in the publication of value-added information for the construction industry in Quebec. TC Media Books holds rights to 20,000 educational book titles used primarily in educational institutions offering French-language courses in Quebec and the rest of Canada, and 950 book titles in French and English for supplemental educational materials (Les Éditions Caractère), general interest books (Les Éditions Transcontinental) and specialized medical books (Edisem). TC Media Books also has the distribution rights in Canada to 70,000 titles of third-party publishers, mainly French. Groupe Constructo publications include Journal Constructo, Les leaders de la construction and Voir Vert. Groupe Constructo also jointly operates with **CGI Inc.** the SEAO, the official website of the Government of Quebec for tenders, allowing suppliers to bid on all government contracts.

Recent Merger and Acquisition Activity

Status: completed **Announced:** June 22, 2022
Transcontinental Inc. acquired Armenia, Colombia-based Banaplast S.A.S., a flexible packaging manufacturer, for $18,400,000. Banaplast is active in the protection of crops in the banana (banana tree bags) and plantain agro-industrial sector and other fruit plantations.

Status: completed **Announced:** June 13, 2022
Transcontinental Inc. acquired Montreal, Que.-based educational publisher Editions du renoveau pédagogique inc. from Pearson plc for $57,200,000, subject to adjustments.

Status: completed **Announced:** Mar. 15, 2022
Transcontinental Inc. acquired Montreal, Que.-based Scolab Inc., which develops digital educational products including Netmath and Buzzmath, for $12,500,000, subject to adjustments.

Predecessor Detail - Name changed from G.T.C. Transcontinental Group Ltd., Apr. 1, 2003; basis 2 new for 1 old sh.

Directors - Rémi Marcoux, founder, Montréal, Qué.; Isabelle Marcoux, exec. chr., Montréal, Qué.; Jacynthe Côté†, Candiac, Qué.; Nelson Gentiletti, Kirkland, Qué.; Yves Leduc, Westmount, Qué.; Nathalie Marcoux, Mount Royal, Qué.; Pierre Marcoux, Mount Royal, Qué.; Anna Martini, Montréal, Qué.; Mario Plourde, Kingsey Falls, Qué.; Jean Raymond, Montréal, Qué.; Annie Thabet, Ile-des-Soeurs, Qué.

Other Exec. Officers - Thomas G. L. Morin, pres. & CEO; Magali Depras, chief strategy & corp. social responsibility officer; Christine Desaulniers, chief legal officer & corp. sec.; Benoît Guilbault, CIO; Eric Morisset, chief corp. devel. officer; Lynda B. Newcomb, chief HR officer; Donald LeCavalier, exec. v-p & CFO; Isabelle Côté, v-p & contr.; Frédérique Deniger, v-p, internal audit; François Taschereau, v-p, corp. commun. & public affairs; Mathieu Hébert, treas.

† Lead director

Capital Stock

	Authorized (shs.)	Outstanding (shs.)[1]
Preferred	unlimited	nil
Class A Subord. Vtg.	unlimited	72,965,844
Class B	unlimited	13,658,326

[1] At May 31, 2023

Preferred - Issuable in series and non-voting.

Class A Subordinate Voting - Convertible into class B shares on a share-for-share basis in the event a takeover bid is made to the majority group. One vote per share.

Class B - Convertible into class A subordinate voting shares on a share-for-share basis at any time. Twenty votes per share.

Normal Course Issuer Bid - The company plans to make normal course purchases of up to 191,343 class B shares representing 1.4% of the total outstanding. The bid commenced on Oct. 3, 2022, and expires on Oct. 2, 2023.

The company plans to make normal course purchases of up to 1,000,000 class A subordinate voting shares representing 1.4% of the total outstanding. The bid commenced on Oct. 3, 2022, and expires on Oct. 2, 2023.

Major Shareholder - Rémi Marcoux held 71.62% interest at Jan. 10, 2023.

Price Range - TCL.A/TSX

Year	Volume	High	Low	Close
2022	49,354,648	$21.62	$14.44	$15.28
2021	49,898,802	$26.45	$18.25	$20.31
2020	69,022,647	$22.93	$9.50	$20.51
2019	67,932,946	$22.25	$12.56	$15.87
2018	69,889,568	$32.89	$18.02	$19.30

Recent Close: $12.75

Capital Stock Changes - During fiscal 2022, 400,800 class A subordinate voting shares were repurchased under a Normal Course Issuer Bid.

Dividends

TCL.B cl B M.V. Ra $0.90 pa Q est. Apr. 7, 2020
Prev. Rate: $0.88 est. Apr. 10, 2019
TCL.A cl A S.V. Ra $0.90 pa Q est. Apr. 7, 2020
Prev. Rate: $0.88 est. Apr. 10, 2019

Long-Term Debt - Outstanding at Oct. 31, 2022:

Credit facilities[1]	$132,700,000
2.667% sr. notes due 2025	190,900,000
2.28% sr. notes due 2026	250,000,000
Term loans due to 2028	314,100,000
4.84% unified debenture due 2028	100,000,000
Other loans due to 2031	6,500,000
Less: Unamort. def. fin. exp.	4,200,000
	990,000,000
Less: Current portion	10,700,000
	979,300,000

[1] Borrowings under a US$25,000,000 credit facility, bearing interest at SOFR plus 1.05% and due March 2023; and a Cdn$400,000,000 (or the U.S. dollar equivalent) credit facility, bearing interest at bankers' acceptance rate or SOFR plus 1.675% or Canadian/U.S. prime rate plus 0.675% and due February 2027.

Wholly Owned Subsidiaries

Transcontinental Media Inc., Qué.
- 100% int. in **Transcontinental Interactive Inc.**, Ont.
  - 91.41% int. in **Transcontinental Media G.P.**, Qué.
- 8.59% int. in **Transcontinental Media G.P.**, Qué.

Transcontinental Printing 2007 Inc., Saint-Laurent, Qué.
- 50% int. in **Transcontinental Packaging Whitby ULC**, N.S.
- 99.7% int. in **Transcontinental Printing Corporation**, Del.
  - 100% int. in **Transcontinental Acquisition LLC**, Del.
    - 100% int. in **CPG Finance, Inc.**, Spartanburg, S.C.
      - 100% int. in **Transcontinental Holding Corp.**, Del.
        - 100% int. in **McNeel International Corp.**, Del.
          - 100% int. in **PIC Guatemala Holdings Corp.**, Del.
            - 99.97% int. in **Olefinas, S.A.**, Guatemala.
        - 0.03% int. in **Olefinas, S.A.**, Guatemala.
        - 100% int. in **Transcontinental NA Holding Corp.**, Del.
          - 100% int. in **Transcontinental Michigan Inc.**, Mich.
        - 100% int. in **Transcontinental US LLC**, Del.
          - 100% int. in **Transcontinental AC US LLC**, Del.
          - 100% int. in **Transcontinental Ontario Inc.**, Calif.
          - 100% int. in **Transcontinental TVL LLC**, Del.
    - 100% int. in **TC Transcontinental Packaging Inc.**, Del.
      - 100% int. in **Transcontinental Ultra Flex Inc.**, N.Y.
    - 100% int. in **Transcontinental Multifilm Inc.**, Ill.
    - 100% int. in **Transcontinental Robbie Inc.**, Del.
- 100% int. in **Transcontinental Printing Inc.**, Canada.
  - 0.01% int. in **Transcontinental Printing Corporation**, Del.
  - 85.1% int. in **Transcontinental Printing 2005 G.P.**, Qué.
- 14.9% int. in **Transcontinental Printing 2005 G.P.**, Qué.

Note: The preceding list includes only the major related companies in which interests are held.

Financial Statistics

Periods ended:	52w Oct. 30/22[A]		53w Oct. 31/21[oA]
	$000s	%Chg	$000s
Operating revenue	**2,956,100**	**+12**	**2,643,400**
Cost of goods sold	2,029,700		1,734,600
Other operating expense	479,700		444,000
Operating expense	**2,509,400**	**+15**	**2,178,600**
Operating income	**446,700**	**-4**	**464,800**
Deprec., depl. & amort.	231,900		217,600
Finance costs, gross	40,000		42,300
Write-downs/write-offs	nil		(700)
Pre-tax income	**177,300**	**-7**	**191,500**
Income taxes	36,500		61,000
Net income	**140,800**	**+8**	**130,500**
Net inc. for equity hldrs	**141,200**	**+8**	**130,600**
Net inc. for non-cont. int.	**(400)**	**n.a.**	**(100)**
Cash & equivalent	45,700		231,100
Inventories	479,300		357,000
Accounts receivable	575,700		496,100
Current assets	1,134,700		1,125,500
Fixed assets, net	756,000		689,700
Right-of-use assets	140,800		140,800
Intangibles, net	1,701,300		1,599,600
Total assets	**3,801,000**	**+5**	**3,612,900**
Accts. pay. & accr. liabs	477,800		435,000
Current liabilities	547,000		700,300
Long-term debt, gross	990,000		965,500
Long-term debt, net	979,300		778,200
Long-term lease liabilities	135,000		137,300
Shareholders' equity	1,877,200		1,759,100
Non-controlling interest	4,800		5,200
Cash from oper. activs	**220,800**	**-30**	**315,300**
Cash from fin. activs	(150,900)		(150,100)
Cash from invest. activs	(257,400)		(181,000)
Net cash position	**45,700**	**-80**	**231,100**
Capital expenditures	(117,100)		(115,000)
Capital disposals	9,800		1,000
Unfunded pension liability	46,700		28,800
	$		$
Earnings per share*	1.63		1.50
Cash flow per share*	2.54		3.62
Cash divd. per share*	0.90		0.90
	shs		shs
No. of shs. o/s*	86,624,170		87,024,970
Avg. no. of shs. o/s*	86,800,000		87,000,000
	%		%
Net profit margin	4.76		4.94
Return on equity	7.77		7.48
Return on assets	4.66		4.42
Foreign sales percent	51		49
No. of employees (FTEs)	8,303		7,904

* Class A & B
[o] Restated
[A] Reported in accordance with IFRS

Latest Results

Periods ended:	6m Apr. 30/23[A]		6m May 1/22[A]
	$000s	%Chg	$000s
Operating revenue	1,454,200	+3	1,406,100
Net income	23,400	-50	46,600
Net inc. for equity hldrs	23,200	-50	46,700
Net inc. for non-cont. int.	200		(100)
	$		$
Earnings per share*	0.27		0.54

* Class A & B
[A] Reported in accordance with IFRS

Historical Summary
(as originally stated)

Fiscal Year	Oper. Rev.	Net Inc. Bef. Disc.	EPS*
	$000s	$000s	$
2022[A]	2,956,100	140,800	1.63
2021[A1]	2,643,400	130,500	1.50
2020[A]	2,574,000	131,800	1.51
2019[A]	3,038,800	166,100	1.90
2018[A]	2,623,500	213,400	2.59

* Class A & B
[A] Reported in accordance with IFRS
[1] 53 weeks ended Oct. 31, 2021.

T.84 Transition Opportunities Corp.

Symbol - TOP.P **Exchange** - TSX-VEN **CUSIP** - 89370J
Head Office - 1900-520 3 Ave SW, Calgary, AB, T2P 0R3 **Telephone** - (403) 801-5015
Email - pantazop.home@gmail.com
Investor Relations - John R. Pantazopoulos (403) 801-5015
Auditors - MNP LLP C.A., Calgary, Alta.
Transfer Agents - Odyssey Trust Company, Calgary, Alta.
Profile - (Alta. 2021) Capital Pool Company.

Directors - John R. Pantazopoulos, CEO & CFO, Calgary, Alta.; Xiaodi Jin, corp. sec., Calgary, Alta.; Jeff Davidson, Calgary, Alta.; Kevin Staveley, Calgary, Alta.

Capital Stock

	Authorized (shs.)	Outstanding (shs.)[1]
Common	unlimited	10,000,000

[1] At Oct. 27, 2022

Major Shareholder - Jeff Davidson held 10% interest, Xiaodi Jin held 10% interest, James Olesko held 10% interest, John R. Pantazopoulos held 10% interest and Kevin Staveley held 10% interest at Feb. 25, 2022.

Price Range - TOP.P/TSX-VEN

Year	Volume	High	Low	Close
2022	111,767	$0.15	$0.08	$0.08

Recent Close: $0.10

Capital Stock Changes - On Apr. 20, 2022, an initial public offering of 5,000,000 common shares was completed at 10¢ per share. Also during fiscal 2022, 5,000,000 common shares were issued by private placement.

T.85 Treatment.com International Inc.

Symbol - TRUE **Exchange** - CSE **CUSIP** - 89465L
Head Office - 700-838 Hastings St W, Vancouver, BC, V6C 0A6 **Telephone** - (604) 559-3511 **Fax** - (604) 559-3501
Website - www.treatment.com
Email - dong.shim@treatment.com
Investor Relations - Dong H. Shim (604) 559-3511 ext. 150
Auditors - A Chan & Company LLP C.A., Burnaby, B.C.
Transfer Agents - National Securities Administrators Ltd., Vancouver, B.C.

Profile - (Can. 2018) Develops artificial intelligence (AI)-driven solutions to manage healthcare concerns for consumers and healthcare providers.

Solutions include a mobile application which serves as a symptom assessment tool based on a user's personalized health profile; a full package solution for medical clinics which assists in the administrative workflow by collecting patient symptom data collection and writing a report of symptoms, risk factors and possible diagnoses; a clinical advisor solution which provides healthcare providers access to peer-reviewed information and suggested diagnoses; and medical education solutions for training student doctors.

The company's solutions are powered by its proprietary AI platform and Global Library of Medicine™ (GLM), a collaborative medical database where medical providers can contribute and exchange up-to-date healthcare information. GLM contains detailed knowledge of complex disease presentations, physical signs, pathology, anatomy, laboratory and x-ray findings, as well as detailed descriptions of where diseases are most likely to occur, how they are transmitted, and who is at the greatest risk.

Directors - John Fraser, co-founder, Minneapolis, Minn.; Dr. Kevin Peterson, chr., interim CEO & CMO, St. Paul, Minn.; Christopher P. (Chris) Cherry, Vancouver, B.C.; Sean Clifford, Vancouver, B.C.; Andrew (Drew) Zimmerman, B.C.

Other Exec. Officers - Dong H. (Don) Shim, CFO

Capital Stock

	Authorized (shs.)	Outstanding (shs.)[1]
Series A Preferred	unlimited	10,000
Series B Preferred	unlimited	nil
Common	unlimited	6,630,115

[1] At July 14, 2023

Series A & B Preferred - Non-voting. Convertible into common shares by company.

Common - One vote per share.

Major Shareholder - John Fraser held 15.47% interest and Dr. Kevin Peterson held 12.7% interest at Mar. 28, 2023.

Price Range - TRUE/CSE

Year	Volume	High	Low	Close
2022............	469,898	$8.60	$0.40	$0.50
2021............	747,204	$63.00	$8.10	$8.20

Consolidation: 1-for-10 cons. in July 2023

Recent Close: $0.17

Capital Stock Changes - On July 14, 2023, preferred shares and common shares were consolidated on a 1-for-10 basis.

Wholly Owned Subsidiaries

Treatment.com Inc., Minneapolis, Minn.

Financial Statistics

Periods ended:	12m Dec. 31/21[A]		12m Dec. 31/20[A]
	$000s	%Chg	$000s
Salaries & benefits..........................	656		327
Research & devel. expense..............	2,186		1,296
General & admin expense................	4,064		821
Stock-based compensation.............	6,991		465
Operating expense.........................	**13,897**	**+378**	**2,908**
Operating income..........................	**(13,897)**	**n.a.**	**(2,908)**
Pre-tax income..............................	**(13,864)**	**n.a.**	**(2,908)**
Net income....................................	**(13,864)**	**n.a.**	**(2,908)**
Cash & equivalent............................	917		312
Accounts receivable........................	1		1
Current assets.................................	943		313
Total assets....................................	**943**	**+201**	**313**
Accts. pay. & accr. liabs..................	833		576
Current liabilities.............................	833		576
Shareholders' equity........................	110		(263)
Cash from oper. activs..................	**(6,290)**	**n.a.**	**(2,012)**
Cash from fin. activs........................	6,942		1,856
Net cash position...........................	**917**	**+194**	**312**
	$		$
Earnings per share*.........................	(2.10)		(0.50)
Cash flow per share*.......................	(0.97)		(0.35)
	shs		shs
No. of shs. o/s*................................	6,614,599		5,971,918
Avg. no. of shs. o/s*.........................	6,484,789		5,715,650
	%		%
Net profit margin..............................	n.a.		n.a.
Return on equity...............................	n.m.		n.m.
Return on assets..............................	n.m.		(702.42)

* Common

[A] Reported in accordance with IFRS

Latest Results

Periods ended:	3m Mar. 31/22[A]		3m Mar. 31/21[A]
	$000s	%Chg	$000s
Net income.......................................	(1,952)	n.a.	(1,076)
	$		$
Earnings per share*.........................	(0.30)		(0.20)

* Common

[A] Reported in accordance with IFRS

Historical Summary
(as originally stated)

Fiscal Year	Oper. Rev.	Net Inc. Bef. Disc.	EPS*
	$000s	$000s	$
2021[A]....................	nil	(13,864)	(2.10)
2020[A]....................	nil	(2,908)	(0.50)
2019[A]....................	nil	(3,004)	(0.90)
2018[A]....................	nil	(70)	(0.03)

* Common

[A] Reported in accordance with IFRS

Note: Adjusted throughout for 1-for-10 cons. in July 2023

T.86 Tree Island Steel Ltd.

Symbol - TSL **Exchange** - TSX **CUSIP** - 89467Q

Head Office - 3933 Boundary Rd, Richmond, BC, V6V 1T8 **Telephone** - (604) 524-3744 **Toll-free** - (800) 663-0955 **Fax** - (604) 524-2362

Website - www.treeisland.com

Email - amahdavi@treeisland.com

Investor Relations - Ali Mahdavi (866) 430-6247

Auditors - KPMG LLP C.A., Vancouver, B.C.

Lawyers - Stikeman Elliott LLP, Vancouver, B.C.

Transfer Agents - Computershare Trust Company of Canada Inc., Toronto, Ont.

FP500 Revenue Ranking - 545

Employees - 450 at Dec. 31, 2022

Profile - (Can. 2012) Manufactures and supplies steel wire and fabricated wire products for the industrial, commercial construction, residential construction and agricultural markets in Canada, the U.S. and internationally.

Product lines include bright and galvanized carbon steel wire, collated and bulk nails, welded wire mesh, stucco reinforcing products, fencing products and other fabricated wire products, which are marketed under the brand names Tree Island®, Halsteel®, TrueSpec®, K-Lath®, TI Wire®, ToughStrand® and ToughPanel™.

A majority of the products are sold to distributors, including wholesale distributors of building products, baling wire and fencing products.

Operating facilities include a 400,000-sq.-ft. facility in Richmond, B.C.; a 70,000-sq.-ft. facility in Calgary, Alta.; and a 200,000-sq.-ft. facility in San Bernardino, Calif.

During fiscal 2022, the company ceased operations in its 134,000-sq.-ft. facility in Etiwanda, Calif. and would relocate higher-performing equipment to other locations. In addition, the company would lay off production staff, as well as certain supervisory, sales and management staff.

Predecessor Detail - Succeeded Tree Island Wire Income Fund, Oct. 3, 2012, pursuant to plan of arrangement whereby Tree Island Steel Ltd. was formed to facilitate the conversion of the fund into a corporation and the fund was subsequently dissolved.

Directors - Amar S. Doman, exec. chr., West Vancouver, B.C.; Peter M. Bull, B.C.; Joe Downes, Fla.; Sam Fleiser, Toronto, Ont.; Theodore A. (Ted) Leja, Blaine, Wash.; Harry Rosenfeld, West Vancouver, B.C.

Other Exec. Officers - Nancy Davies, interim pres., COO & CFO

Capital Stock

	Authorized (shs.)	Outstanding (shs.)[1]
Common	unlimited	28,221,526

[1] At Mar. 16, 2023

Normal Course Issuer Bid - The company plans to make normal course purchases of up to 1,410,000 common shares representing 5% of the total outstanding. The bid commenced on Nov. 9, 2022, and expires on Nov. 8, 2023.

Major Shareholder - Amar S. Doman held 34.7% interest and Peter M. Bull held 23% interest at Mar. 16, 2023.

Price Range - TSL/TSX

Year	Volume	High	Low	Close
2022............	3,924,379	$7.23	$3.15	$3.34
2021............	4,971,867	$5.41	$2.18	$5.16
2020............	3,262,759	$2.85	$1.11	$2.68
2019............	3,183,784	$2.60	$1.51	$2.16
2018............	2,972,170	$3.66	$1.94	$2.13

Recent Close: $3.10

Capital Stock Changes - During 2022, 147,299 common shares were repurchased under a Normal Course Issuer Bid.

Dividends

TSL com Var. Ra pa Q

$0.02◆................	July 14/23	$0.03...............	July 14/23
$0.02◆................	Apr. 14/23	$0.03...............	Apr. 14/23
$0.02◆................	Jan. 16/23	$0.03...............	Jan. 16/23

Paid in 2023: $0.09 + $0.06◆ 2022: $0.12 + $1.29◆ 2021: $0.11 + $0.05◆

◆ Special

Wholly Owned Subsidiaries

Tree Island Industries Ltd., Richmond, B.C.
- 100% int. in **Tree Island Wire (USA) Holdings Inc.**, Del.
  - 100% int. in **Tree Island Wire (USA) Inc.**, Del.

Financial Statistics

Periods ended:	12m Dec. 31/22[A]		12m Dec. 31/21[A]
	$000s	%Chg	$000s
Operating revenue........................	**338,434**	**+12**	**301,848**
Cost of sales.....................................	267,604		227,378
General & admin expense................	14,851		16,367
Operating expense........................	**282,455**	**+16**	**243,745**
Operating income.........................	**55,979**	**-4**	**58,103**
Deprec., depl. & amort.....................	5,497		5,843
Finance costs, gross.........................	2,274		2,532
Write-downs/write-offs.....................	(1,363)[1]		nil
Pre-tax income..............................	**44,211**	**-61**	**113,478**
Income taxes....................................	11,105		25,507
Net income....................................	**33,106**	**-62**	**87,971**
Cash & equivalent............................	14,976		33,251
Inventories.......................................	57,531		77,512
Accounts receivable........................	30,445		38,054
Current assets..................................	10,317		155,602
Fixed assets, net..............................	46,296		49,042
Right-of-use assets..........................	19,401		19,886
Total assets...................................	**176,326**	**-22**	**225,806**
Accts. pay. & accr. liabs..................	16,943		27,278
Current liabilities..............................	20,673		54,278
Long-term debt, gross.......................	nil		13,182
Long-term debt, net..........................	nil		10,363
Long-term lease liabilities.................	23,616		24,289
Shareholders' equity........................	128,096		132,621
Cash from oper. activs...................	**43,375**	**+265**	**11,873**
Cash from fin. activs.........................	(60,252)		(36,986)
Cash from invest. activs....................	(1,456)		57,113
Net cash position...........................	**14,976**	**-55**	**33,251**
Capital expenditures.........................	(1,456)		(12,131)
Capital disposals..............................	nil		69,244
	$		$
Earnings per share*.........................	1.17		3.09
Cash flow per share*........................	1.53		0.42
Cash divd. per share*.......................	0.12		0.12
Extra divd. - cash*............................	1.26		0.10
Total divd. per share*...................	**1.38**		**0.22**
	shs		shs
No. of shs. o/s*................................	28,286,889		28,434,188
Avg. no. of shs. o/s*.........................	28,396,993		28,453,485
	%		%
Net profit margin..............................	9.78		29.14
Return on equity...............................	25.40		95.78
Return on assets..............................	17.31		48.31
Foreign sales percent.......................	67		70
No. of employees (FTEs)..................	450		480

* Common

[A] Reported in accordance with IFRS

[1] Pertains to machinery and equipment impairment in Etiwanda facility.

Historical Summary
(as originally stated)

Fiscal Year	Oper. Rev.	Net Inc. Bef. Disc.	EPS*
	$000s	$000s	$
2022[A]....................	338,434	33,106	1.17
2021[A]....................	301,848	87,971	3.09
2020[A]....................	215,894	5,131	0.18
2019[A]....................	200,405	(5,190)	(0.18)
2018[A]....................	235,306	2,593	0.09

* Common

[A] Reported in accordance with IFRS

T.87 Trees Corporation

Symbol - TREE **Exchange** - NEO **CUSIP** - 89469R

Head Office - 1800-181 Bay St, Toronto, ON, M5J 2T9 **Telephone** - (365) 601-3032

Website - treescorp.ca

Email - jeffh@treescorp.ca

Investor Relations - Jeffrey W. Holmgren (365) 601-3032

Auditors - Zeifmans LLP C.A., Toronto, Ont.

Transfer Agents - Odyssey Trust Company, Calgary, Alta.

Employees - 62 at Mar. 31, 2022

Profile - (Can. 2021 amalg.; orig. B.C., 2021) Owns and operates (at Nov. 28, 2022) 13 retail cannabis stores in Ontario (8) and British Columbia (5).

Also holds a portfolio of cannabis digital platforms including cannabisMD.com and askCMD.com. Products include dried and fresh cannabis flower, cannabis extract, edible cannabis, topicals and cannabis plants and seeds.

In July 2022, the company acquired **2707461 Ontario Ltd.**, which owns and operates a licensed retail cannabis in Burlington, Ont., for $548,000.

During the second quarter of 2022, the company terminated its agreement to acquire **Barnard Cann Ltd.**, which owns and operates four licensed retail cannabis in Ontario for $780,000.

On Mar. 15, 2022, the company acquired private **Miraculo Inc.**, which holds a portfolio of cannabis digital platforms including cannabisMD.com and askCMD.com, for issuance of 13,639,917 units (1 common share

& ½ warrant). Upon completion, Miraculo amalgamated with wholly owned **1000101203 Ontario Inc.**

Recent Merger and Acquisition Activity

Status: pending **Revised:** Sept. 2, 2022
UPDATE: Trees Corporation (new) received its provincial license to operate in British Columbia, which would now complete the acquisition of 101 for the other assets of Cannabis Trees. PREVIOUS: Trees Corporation agreed to acquire private 1015712 B.C. Ltd. (dba Trees Cannabis), which owns and operates five cannabis retail stores in British Columbia, for issuance of 89,000,000 common shares. Dec. 22, 2021 - 1287406 B.C. Ltd. completed the reverse takeover acquisition of and amalgamation with Trees Corporation to form (new) Trees Corporation, which would now complete the acquisition of Trees Cannabis. The purchase price would be the issuance of $11,877,302 of (new) Trees common shares. Mar. 24, 2022 - Trees Corporation (new) and Trees Cannabis amended the transaction whereby Trees Corporation (new) firstly acquired 11391461 Canada Ltd., a wholly owned of 101 that holds all of the registered trademarks of Trees Cannabis including logos. 11391461 also holds license to operate the retail cannabis stores of 101, until the closing of the acquisition of 101 for the other assets of Cannabis Trees. Terms include issuance of 5,933,333 Trees Corporation common shares at $0.045 per share.

Predecessor Detail - Formed from 1287406 B.C. Ltd. in Canada, Dec. 22, 2021, pursuant to the reverse takeover acquisition of and amalgamation with (old) Trees Corporation (deemed acquiror).

Directors - Herbert Fraser Clarke, chr., St. John's, N.L.; Robert W. C. Becher, interim CEO, Caledon, Ont.; Jeffrey W. (Jeff) Holmgren, pres. & CFO, Calgary, Alta.; G. Scott Paterson, Toronto, Ont.; James Ward, Toronto, Ont.

Other Exec. Officers - Melanie Cole, corp. sec.

Capital Stock

	Authorized (shs.)	Outstanding (shs.)[1]
Common	unlimited	159,340,492

[1] At Nov. 14, 2022

Major Shareholder - Widely held at Mar. 31, 2022.

Price Range - TREE/NEO

Year	Volume	High	Low	Close
2022............	898,000	$0.20	$0.01	$0.01

Recent Close: $0.01

Capital Stock Changes - On Mar. 15, 2022, 13,639,917 units (1 common share & ½ warrant) were issued pursuant to the acquisition of Miraculo Inc., with warrants exercisable at 11¢ per share until Dec. 31, 2024. In March 2022, 5,933,333 common shares were issued pursuant to the acquisition of 11391461 Canada Ltd. In May 2022, private placement of 34,166,665 units (1 common share & ½ warrant) at 3¢ per unit was completed, with warrants exercisable at 5¢ per share for two years.

Wholly Owned Subsidiaries

Miraculo Inc.
11391461 Canada Ltd., Canada.
Ontario Cannabis Holdings Corp., Ont.
- 100% int. in **OCH Ontario Consulting Corp.**, Ont.
  - 100% int. in **2707461 Ontario Ltd.**, Ont.
- 100% int. in **11819496 Canada Inc.**, Ont.

Financial Statistics

Periods ended:	12m Dec. 31/21[A1]		12m Dec. 31/20[oA]
	$000s	%Chg	$000s
Operating revenue........................	**4,404**	**+281**	**1,157**
Cost of goods sold..........................	2,995		701
Salaries & benefits..........................	1,421		143
General & admin expense................	1,932		2,002
Stock-based compensation............	927		1,513
Other operating expense.................	514		72
Operating expense........................	**7,789**	**+76**	**4,431**
Operating income.........................	**(3,385)**	**n.a.**	**(3,274)**
Deprec., depl. & amort....................	1,054		575
Finance income...............................	149		27
Finance costs, gross.......................	1,604		249
Write-downs/write-offs....................	(776)		(1,396)
Pre-tax income..............................	**(13,372)**	**n.a.**	**(6,110)**
Net income.....................................	**(13,372)**	**n.a.**	**(6,110)**
Cash & equivalent...........................	1,317		202
Inventories..	192		57
Accounts receivable.........................	162		6
Current assets..................................	2,084		316
Fixed assets, net...............................	3,234		1,061
Right-of-use assets..........................	5,940		3,822
Intangibles, net................................	5,963		21
Total assets.....................................	**20,522**	**+264**	**5,643**
Accts. pay. & accr. liabs..................	1,863		1,557
Current liabilities............................	2,850		3,022
Long-term debt, gross.....................	3,918		3,017
Long-term debt, net.........................	3,810		2,036
Shareholders' equity........................	8,291		(2,792)
Cash from oper. activs..................	**(2,724)**	**n.a.**	**(1,184)**
Cash from fin. activs........................	2,059		1,414
Cash from invest. activs..................	1,779		(325)
Net cash position...........................	**1,317**	**+552**	**202**
Capital expenditures........................	(1,010)		(1,031)
	$		$
Earnings per share*.........................	(1.43)		(0.55)
Cash flow per share*.......................	(0.29)		(0.11)
	shs		shs
No. of shs. o/s*...............................	82,733,911		n.a.
Avg. no. of shs. o/s*........................	9,379,423		11,028,489
	%		%
Net profit margin.............................	(303.63)		(528.09)
Return on equity..............................	n.m.		n.m.
Return on assets..............................	(107.27)		(207.07)
No. of employees (FTEs).................	52		n.a.

* Common
[o] Restated
[A] Reported in accordance with IFRS
[1] Results reflect the Dec. 22, 2021, reverse takeover acquisition of and amalgamation with (old) Trees Corporation.

Latest Results

Periods ended:	9m Sept. 30/22[A]		9m Sept. 30/21[A]
	$000s	%Chg	$000s
Operating revenue..........................	6,457	+129	2,816
Net income..	(3,608)	n.a.	(11,633)
	$		$
Earnings per share*.........................	(0.03)		(1.48)

* Common
[A] Reported in accordance with IFRS

Historical Summary
(as originally stated)

Fiscal Year	Oper. Rev.	Net Inc. Bef. Disc.	EPS*
	$000s	$000s	$
2021[A]..................	4,404	(13,372)	(1.43)
2020[A1].................	nil	(949)	(0.05)
2019[A1].................	nil	(250)	(0.01)

* Common
[A] Reported in accordance with IFRS
[1] Results pertain to (old) Trees Corporation.

T.88 Trench Metals Corp.

Symbol - TMC **Exchange** - TSX-VEN **CUSIP** - 89485U
Head Office - 250-750 Pender St W, Vancouver, BC, V6C 2T7
Telephone - (604) 558-4300
Website - www.trenchmetals.com
Email - simonchengnow+tsi@gmail.com
Investor Relations - Yee Sing Cheng (403) 389-6939
Auditors - Manning Elliott LLP C.A., Vancouver, B.C.
Transfer Agents - Odyssey Trust Company, Vancouver, B.C.

Profile - (B.C. 2019; orig. Alta., 2012) Holds option to acquire Higginson Lake uranium prospect, 5,900 hectares, 52 km northeast of Stony Rapids, Sask.

During fiscal 2022, option to acquire Gorilla Lake uranium prospect in Saskatchewan was terminated and related costs written off.

Predecessor Detail - Name changed from Trench Solutions Inc., Nov. 3, 2020, pursuant to change of business acquistion of uranium property option.; basis 3 new for 1 old sh.

Directors - Yee Sing (Simon) Cheng, CEO, Calgary, Alta.; Scott C. Davis, CFO & corp. sec., Vancouver, B.C.; Mark L. P. Ferguson, Calgary, Alta.

Capital Stock

	Authorized (shs.)	Outstanding (shs.)[1]
Cl.B Preferred	unlimited	nil
Cl.A Common	unlimited	48,937,735

[1] At June 20, 2023

Major Shareholder - Widely held at June 14, 2022.

Price Range - TMC/TSX-VEN

Year	Volume	High	Low	Close
2022............	8,139,904	$0.93	$0.31	$0.31
2021............	25,350,549	$1.11	$0.11	$0.81
2020............	31,300,239	$0.22	$0.04	$0.15
2019............	7,176,933	$0.13	$0.04	$0.05
2018............	5,488,222	$1.03	$0.10	$0.10

Split: 3-for-1 split in Nov. 2020; 1-for-10 cons. in June 2019
Recent Close: $0.27

Capital Stock Changes - During fiscal 2022, 8,587,000 class A common shares were issued on exercise of warrants.

Financial Statistics

Periods ended:	12m Oct. 31/22[A]		12m Oct. 31/21[A]
	$000s	%Chg	$000s
General & admin expense................	180		665
Operating expense........................	**180**	**-73**	**665**
Operating income.........................	**(180)**	**n.a.**	**(665)**
Write-downs/write-offs....................	(115)		nil
Pre-tax income..............................	**(295)**	**n.a.**	**(665)**
Net income.....................................	**(295)**	**n.a.**	**(665)**
Cash & equivalent...........................	584		244
Current assets..................................	590		303
Explor./devel. properties.................	235		155
Total assets.....................................	**825**	**+80**	**459**
Accts. pay. & accr. liabs..................	71		12
Current liabilities............................	72		12
Shareholders' equity........................	753		447
Cash from oper. activs..................	**(115)**	**n.a.**	**(719)**
Cash from fin. activs........................	601		300
Cash from invest. activs..................	(146)		(145)
Net cash position...........................	**584**	**+139**	**244**
Capital expenditures........................	(146)		(145)
	$		$
Earnings per share*.........................	(0.01)		(0.02)
Cash flow per share*.......................	(0.00)		(0.02)
	shs		shs
No. of shs. o/s*...............................	48,937,735		40,350,735
Avg. no. of shs. o/s*........................	42,257,899		36,407,108
	%		%
Net profit margin.............................	n.a.		n.a.
Return on equity..............................	(49.17)		(105.64)
Return on assets..............................	(45.95)		(103.74)

* Cl.A Common
[A] Reported in accordance with IFRS

Historical Summary
(as originally stated)

Fiscal Year	Oper. Rev.	Net Inc. Bef. Disc.	EPS*
	$000s	$000s	$
2022[A]..................	nil	(295)	(0.01)
2021[A]..................	nil	(665)	(0.02)
2020[A]..................	nil	(118)	(0.00)
	US$000s	US$000s	US$
2019[A]..................	nil	(248)	(0.02)
2018[A]..................	2,494	(428)	(0.03)

* Cl.A Common
[A] Reported in accordance with IFRS

Note: Adjusted throughout for 3-for-1 split in Nov. 2020; 1-for-10 cons. in June 2019

T.89 Trenchant Capital Corp.

Symbol - TCC **Exchange** - CSE **CUSIP** - 89485R
Head Office - 2380-1055 Hastings St W, Vancouver, BC, V6E 2E9
Telephone - (604) 307-4274
Website - www.trenchantcapital.net
Email - eric@trenchantcapital.net
Investor Relations - Eric Boehnke (604) 307-4274
Auditors - Dale Matheson Carr-Hilton LaBonte LLP C.A., Vancouver, B.C.
Lawyers - Clark Wilson LLP, Vancouver, B.C.
Transfer Agents - Computershare Trust Company of Canada Inc., Vancouver, B.C.

Profile - (B.C. 2009) Provides special situation debt financing to established companies.

Has a strategic alliance with independent Canadian investment and advisory firm **Hillcore Group Ltd.** for the rights of first negotiation to provide special situation debt financing to Hillcore's pipeline of current and future private equity investments. The financings would include secondary, subordinated, mezzanine or non-traditional debt, asset backed securities and back-leveraged/holdco debt.

At June 30, 2022, the company had loaned $12,183,000 to **ABO Healthcare Limited Partnership**, consisting of 10% loans maturing Jan. 27, 2023.

The ABO loans were funded with 8% convertible debentures due Jan. 27, 2023, and are secured by ABO's 88.73% equity interest in **Omni Health Investments Inc.**, which owns, operates and manages 18 long-term care homes across Ontario.

Predecessor Detail - Name changed from Echelon Petroleum Corp., May 9, 2016.

Directors - Eric Boehnke, CEO, Vancouver, B.C.; Jennie Choboter, CFO & corp. sec., Mission, B.C.; Darren P. Devine, West Vancouver, B.C.; Thomas B. (Tom) English, Toronto, Ont.

Capital Stock

	Authorized (shs.)	Outstanding (shs.)[1]
Series A Preferred	unlimited	nil
Common	unlimited	34,211,286

[1] At Aug. 29, 2022

Major Shareholder - Thomas B. (Tom) English held 18.2% interest and Eric Boehnke held 14.56% interest at Aug. 18, 2022.

Price Range - TCC/CSE

Year	Volume	High	Low	Close
2022	5,100,924	$0.26	$0.03	$0.04
2021	1,616,899	$0.62	$0.07	$0.27
2020	1,089,079	$0.10	$0.03	$0.10
2019	79,357	$0.50	$0.09	$0.09
2018	344,607	$0.83	$0.20	$0.25

Recent Close: $0.06

Capital Stock Changes - There were no changes to capital stock during fiscal 2022.

Wholly Owned Subsidiaries

1141864 B.C. Ltd., B.C.
Trenchant Energy Holdings Inc., Canada.
0960128 B.C. Ltd., B.C. Inactive.

Investments

4% int. in **ASEP Medical Holdings Inc.**, Victoria, B.C. (see separate coverage)

Financial Statistics

Periods ended:	12m Mar. 31/22[A]		12m Mar. 31/21[o][A]
	$000s	%Chg	$000s
Total revenue	**2,304**	**+2**	**2,268**
General & admin. expense	1,040		715
Stock-based compensation	nil		33
Operating expense	**1,040**	**+39**	**748**
Operating income	**1,264**	**-17**	**1,520**
Deprec. & amort.	55		63
Finance costs, gross	1,935		1,888
Write-downs/write-offs	nil		(14)
Pre-tax income	**457**	**n.a.**	**(563)**
Net income	**457**	**n.a.**	**(563)**
Cash & equivalent	883		1,800
Accounts receivable	nil		2
Current assets	22,587		10,856
Long-term investments	1,025		nil
Fixed assets, net	296		42
Total assets	**23,908**	**+4**	**23,081**
Accts. pay. & accr. liabs	1,085		1,012
Current liabilities	20,967		8,822
Long-term debt, gross	19,832		19,779
Long-term debt, net	nil		11,990
Long-term lease liabilities	215		nil
Shareholders' equity	2,726		2,270
Cash from oper. activs	**(457)**	**n.a.**	**107**
Cash from fin. activs	(48)		1,629
Cash from invest. activs	(411)		nil
Net cash position	**883**	**-51**	**1,800**
	$		$
Earnings per share*	0.01		(0.03)
Cash flow per share*	(0.01)		0.01
	shs		shs
No. of shs. o/s*	34,211,286		34,211,286
Avg. no. of shs. o/s*	34,211,286		17,305,769
	%		%
Net profit margin	19.84		(24.82)
Return on equity	18.29		(49.06)
Return on assets	10.18		5.78

* Common
[o] Restated
[A] Reported in accordance with IFRS

Latest Results

Periods ended:	3m June 30/22[A]		3m June 30/21[A]
	$000s	%Chg	$000s
Total revenue	313	-45	572
Net income	(686)	n.a.	(86)
	$		$
Earnings per share*	(0.02)		(0.00)

* Common
[A] Reported in accordance with IFRS

Historical Summary
(as originally stated)

Fiscal Year	Total Rev.	Net Inc. Bef. Disc.	EPS*
	$000s	$000s	$
2022[A]	2,304	457	0.01
2021[A]	2,268	(563)	(0.03)
2020[A]	2,277	(107)	(0.01)
2019[A]	1,888	(47)	(0.00)
2018[A]	863	(349)	(0.03)

* Common
[A] Reported in accordance with IFRS

T.90 Treviso Capital Corp.

Symbol - TRV.P **Exchange** - TSX-VEN **CUSIP** - 89532N
Head Office - 900-885 Georgia St W, Vancouver, BC, V6C 3H1 **Telephone** - (778) 835-2798
Email - davidemelillo@gmail.com
Investor Relations - David Melillo (778) 835-2798
Auditors - Davidson & Company LLP C.A., Vancouver, B.C.
Lawyers - Mauro Palumbo Law Corporation, Vancouver, B.C.
Transfer Agents - Computershare Trust Company of Canada Inc., Vancouver, B.C.
Profile - (B.C. 2021) Capital Pool Company.

Directors - David Melillo, pres., CEO & corp. sec., Kelowna, B.C.; Alexander B. (Alex) Helmel, CFO, Vancouver, B.C.; R. Timothy (Tim) Henneberry, Mill Bay, B.C.; Mauro Palumbo, Vancouver, B.C.

Capital Stock

	Authorized (shs.)	Outstanding (shs.)[1]
Common	unlimited	9,000,000

[1] At May 26, 2023

Major Shareholder - Widely held at Sept. 7, 2022.

Price Range - TRV.P/TSX-VEN

Year	Volume	High	Low	Close
2022	289,074	$0.10	$0.03	$0.04

Recent Close: $0.03

Capital Stock Changes - There were no changes to capital stock during 2022.

T.91 Tribe Property Technologies Inc.

Symbol - TRBE **Exchange** - TSX-VEN **CUSIP** - 89602T
Head Office - 419-1155 Pender St W, Vancouver, BC, V6E 2P4 **Telephone** - (604) 343-2601
Website - tribetech.com
Email - jim.defer@tribetech.com
Investor Relations - James P. Defer (604) 343-2601
Auditors - Dale Matheson Carr-Hilton LaBonte LLP C.A., Vancouver, B.C.
Transfer Agents - TSX Trust Company, Vancouver, B.C.

Profile - (Ont. 2017) Provides property management service for developers, condominium and residential communities, owners and residents through Tribe Home and Pendo.

Offers three software products: condo-living software for strata councils and residents (Tribe Home) which offers secure and easy communication tools with easy-to-find records, on-demand access to shared community documents, amenity booking and a help desk ticketing system; deficiency management software for real estate developers (Tribe Home) which provides management tools necessary to track deficiencies, digitize building data and owners' manuals and facilitate the handover to owners and property managers upon building completion; and rental management software for landlords (Pendo) which streamlines the rental process, allowing users to take advantage of listing websites, online rental applications, tenant vetting and onboarding, digital lease agreements, cashflow management, online rent collection and financial reporting.

Predecessor Detail - Name changed from Cherry Street Capital Inc., Mar. 15, 2021, pursuant to the reverse takeover acquisition of (old) Tribe Property Technologies Inc. and concurrent amalgamation of (old) Tribe with wholly owned 1283534 B.C. Ltd. (and continued as Tribe Property Holdings Inc.).; basis 1 new for 8.4488 old shs.

Directors - Joseph Nakhla, CEO, Port Moody, B.C.; Raymond Choy, Vancouver, B.C.; Charmaine Crooks, Vancouver, B.C.; Andrew G. Kiguel, Toronto, Ont.; Sanjiv Samant, Toronto, Ont.; Michael J. (Mike) Willis, Seattle, Wash.

Other Exec. Officers - Drew Keddy, COO; James P. (Jim) Defer, CFO; Dan Feeny, chief tech. officer; Maureen McMahon, exec. v-p, HR; Fiona Therrien, exec. v-p, mgt. srvcs.; Scott Ullrich, exec. v-p, rental mgt.; Ken Axenty, v-p, fin. srvcs.; Allen Kwok, v-p, eng.; Jenn Laidlaw Kear, v-p, mktg. & commun.; Lawrence Liu, v-p, sales & partnership; Shobana Williams, v-p, IR; John Tims, corp. sec.

Capital Stock

	Authorized (shs.)	Outstanding (shs.)[1]
Preferred	unlimited	nil
Common	unlimited	21,207,516

[1] At May 23, 2023

Major Shareholder - The Aquilini Group held 21.2% interest, Talal Yassin held 14.8% interest, Round 13 Growth II, L.P. held 12.5% interest and Joseph Nakhla held 10.1% interest at May 23, 2023.

Price Range - TRBE/TSX-VEN

Year	Volume	High	Low	Close
2022	722,089	$4.24	$1.35	$1.45
2021	1,392,567	$5.75	$3.10	$4.05
2020	3,905	$3.38	$1.69	$3.38
2019	3,077	$3.38	$3.38	$3.38
2018	1,893	$4.22	$3.38	$3.38

Consolidation: 1-for-8.4488 cons. in Mar. 2021
Recent Close: $0.86

Capital Stock Changes - In January 2022, private placement of 5,250,000 common shares was completed at $4.00 per share.

Wholly Owned Subsidiaries

Tribe Property Holdings Inc., Vancouver, B.C.
- 100% int. in **Gateway Property Management Corp.**, Vancouver, B.C.
  - 100% int. in **Gateway West Management Corp.**, Calgary, Alta.
- 100% int. in **RDC Property Services Ltd.**, Toronto, Ont.
- 100% int. in **Tribe Management Inc.**, Vancouver, B.C.

T.92 Trican Well Service Ltd.*

Symbol - TCW **Exchange** - TSX **CUSIP** - 895945
Head Office - 2900-645 7 Ave SW, Calgary, AB, T2P 4G8 **Telephone** - (403) 266-0202 **Toll-free** - (877) 587-4226 **Fax** - (403) 237-7716
Website - www.tricanwellservice.com
Email - conwuekwe@trican.ca
Investor Relations - Dr. Chika B. Onwuekwe (877) 787-4226
Auditors - KPMG LLP C.A., Calgary, Alta.
Bankers - The Bank of Nova Scotia, Calgary, Alta.
Lawyers - Blake, Cassels & Graydon LLP, Calgary, Alta.
Transfer Agents - Olympia Trust Company, Calgary, Alta.
FP500 Revenue Ranking - 366
Employees - 1,124 at Dec. 31, 2022

Profile - (Alta. 1979) Provides specialized products, equipment, services and technology for use in the drilling, completion, stimulation and re-working of oil and gas wells in western Canada.

Provides services in the Western Canadian Sedimentary Basin including hydraulic fracturing; cementing; coiled tubing; nitrogen services; acidizing; and chemical sales. Operating bases are located in Brooks, Drayton Valley, Grande Prairie, Hinton, Lloydminster, Nisku, Red Deer and Whitecourt, all in Alberta; Fort St. John, B.C.; and Estevan, Sask.

Operating Statistics

Year ended Dec. 31	2022	2021
Number of jobs completed	7,625	7,291
Revenue per job ($)	113,612	77,147
Total proppant pumped[1]	1,335,000	1,364,000

[1] Tonnes.

Predecessor Detail - Name changed from Trican Oilwell Service Co. Ltd., June 11, 1997.

Directors - Thomas M. (Tom) Alford, chr., Calgary, Alta.; Bradley P. D. (Brad) Fedora, pres. & CEO, Calgary, Alta.; Trudy M. Curran, Calgary, Alta.; Michael J. (Mick) McNulty, Calgary, Alta.; Stuart G. O'Connor, Calgary, Alta.; Deborah S. (Debbie) Stein, Calgary, Alta.

Other Exec. Officers - Todd G. Thue, COO; Scott Matson, CFO; Bill Anderson, v-p, quality, health, safety & envir.; Trevor Funk, v-p, well srvcs.; Brian Lane, v-p, sales & mktg.; Daniel Lopushinsky, v-p, planning & analysis; Dr. Chika B. Onwuekwe, v-p, legal, gen. counsel & corp. sec.; Jim Rukin, v-p, fracturing

Capital Stock

	Authorized (shs.)	Outstanding (shs.)[1]
Preferred	unlimited	nil
Common	unlimited	210,594,812

[1] At Aug. 1, 2023

Options - At Dec. 31, 2022, options were outstanding to purchase 9,912,897 common shares at a weighted average price of $1.79 per share with a weighted average remaining life of 3.89 years.

Normal Course Issuer Bid - The company plans to make normal course purchases of up to 23,083,554 common shares representing 10% of the public float. The bid commenced on Oct. 5, 2022, and expires on Oct. 4, 2023.

Major Shareholder - Canoe Financial LP held 14% interest at Mar. 31, 2023.

Price Range - TCW/TSX

Year	Volume	High	Low	Close
2022	275,923,065	$4.90	$2.66	$3.66
2021	304,047,842	$3.68	$1.55	$2.77
2020	170,964,648	$1.69	$0.42	$1.68
2019	274,342,327	$1.73	$0.81	$1.14
2018	737,052,764	$4.42	$0.96	$1.19

Recent Close: $4.65

Capital Stock Changes - During 2022, 2,511,918 common shares were issued on exercise of options and 19,700,033 common shares were repurchased under a Normal Course Issuer Bid.

Dividends

TCW com Var. Ra pa Q[1]

$0.04	Sept. 30/23	$0.04	June 30/23
$0.04	Mar. 31/23		

Paid in 2023: $0.12 2022: n.a. 2021: n.a.

[1] Semiannual divd normally payable in July/15 has been omitted.

Long-Term Debt - At Dec. 31, 2022, outstanding long-term debt totaled $29,817,000 (none current) and consisted entirely of borrowings under a $125,000,000 revolving credit facility, bearing interest at Canadian prime rate, U.S. prime rate, banker's acceptance rate or SOFR plus 1% to 3.5% due Dec. 5, 2024.

Wholly Owned Subsidiaries

Canyon Services Group Inc., Calgary, Alta.

Note: The preceding list includes only the major related companies in which interests are held.

Financial Statistics

Periods ended:	12m Dec. 31/22[A]		12m Dec. 31/21[A]
	$000s	%Chg	$000s
Operating revenue	**866,295**	**+54**	**562,479**
Cost of sales	639,190		434,885
General & admin expense	39,777		28,238
Operating expense	**678,967**	**+47**	**463,123**
Operating income	**187,328**	**+89**	**99,356**
Deprec., depl. & amort.	80,224		87,809
Finance costs, gross	2,570		1,974
Write-downs/write-offs	(71)		50
Pre-tax income	**107,882**	**+801**	**11,978**
Income taxes	28,667		(80)
Net inc. bef. disc. opers	**79,215**	**+557**	**12,058**
Income from disc. opers	nil		5,162
Net income	**79,215**	**+360**	**17,220**
Cash & equivalent	58,114		29,510
Inventories	24,687		19,041
Accounts receivable	175,441		127,793
Current assets	263,264		181,339
Fixed assets, net	396,033		376,337
Right-of-use assets	8,781		6,662
Intangibles, net	3,043		13,501
Total assets	**671,121**	**+16**	**577,839**
Accts. pay. & accr. liabs	90,906		75,167
Current liabilities	93,899		77,581
Long-term debt, gross	29,817		nil
Long-term debt, net	29,817		nil
Long-term lease liabilities	9,581		7,906
Shareholders' equity	504,670		489,400
Cash from oper. activs	**152,232**	**+105**	**74,096**
Cash from fin. activs	(37,830)		(27,841)
Cash from invest. activs	(85,798)		(39,352)
Net cash position	**58,114**	**+97**	**29,510**
Capital expenditures	(103,620)		(53,883)
Capital disposals	20,025		10,160
	$		$
Earns. per sh. bef disc opers*	0.33		0.05
Earnings per share*	0.33		0.07
Cash flow per share*	0.63		0.29
	shs		shs
No. of shs. o/s*	229,776,553		246,964,668
Avg. no. of shs. o/s*	241,410,321		253,153,795
	%		%
Net profit margin	9.14		2.14
Return on equity	15.94		2.46
Return on assets	12.99		2.46
No. of employees (FTEs)	1,124		1,032

* Common
[A] Reported in accordance with IFRS

Latest Results

Periods ended:	6m June 30/23[A]		6m June 30/22[A]
	$000s	%Chg	$000s
Operating revenue	465,267	+25	371,547
Net income	55,873	+277	14,804
	$		$
Earnings per share*	0.25		0.06

* Common
[A] Reported in accordance with IFRS

Historical Summary
(as originally stated)

Fiscal Year	Oper. Rev.	Net Inc. Bef. Disc.	EPS*
	$000s	$000s	$
2022[A]	866,295	79,215	0.33
2021[A]	562,479	12,058	0.05
2020[A]	397,019	(233,317)	(0.88)
2019[A]	636,071	(71,435)	(0.25)
2018[A]	900,592	(233,637)	(0.73)

* Common
[A] Reported in accordance with IFRS

T.93 Tricon Residential Inc.*

Symbol - TCN **Exchange** - TSX **CUSIP** - 89612W
Head Office - 801-7 St. Thomas St, Toronto, ON, M5S 2B7 **Telephone** - (416) 925-7228 **Fax** - (416) 925-5022
Website - www.triconresidential.com
Email - wnowak@triconcapital.com
Investor Relations - Wojtek K. Nowak (416) 925-2409
Auditors - PricewaterhouseCoopers LLP C.A., Toronto, Ont.
Lawyers - Goodmans LLP, Toronto, Ont.
Transfer Agents - TSX Trust Company, Toronto, Ont.
FP500 Revenue Ranking - 323
Employees - 1,010 at Dec. 31, 2022

Profile - (Ont. 1997) Owns and operates single-family rental homes primarily in the United States Sun Belt region. Also invests in adjacent residential businesses including multi-family rental apartments and residential development assets.

Single-family Rental - Owns and operates a portfolio of single-family rental homes primarily in the U.S. sunbelt, with 36,104 homes in 21 markets across 10 states with average monthly rent of US$1,737 and weighted average occupancy of 94.9% at Mar. 31, 2023.

Multi-family Rental - The company operates and holds a 15% interest in one 500-unit class A rental property, The Selby, located in Toronto, Ont., with average monthly rent of Cdn$2,717 and average occupancy of 97.4% at Mar. 31, 2023.

Residential Development - Develops new residential real estate properties including class A multi-unit rental apartments in Canada; single-family rental communities in the U.S.; and land development and home building projects primarily in the U.S. The company had eight projects totaling 4,280 units under construction or in pre-construction in downtown Toronto, Ont., at Mar. 31, 2023. The company's portfolio also includes an existing commercial property, The Shops of Summerhill, adjacent to one of its multi-family development properties. In the U.S., the company's legacy business involves providing equity or equity-type financing to experienced local or regional developers and builders of for-sale housing. These investments are typically made through investment vehicles that hold an interest in land development and home building projects, including master-planned communities (MPC). The company also serves as the developer of certain of its MPCs through its Houston, Tex.-based subsidiary, **The Johnson Companies L.P.**

Private Funds and Advisory - Earns fees from managing third-party capital co-invested in its real estate assets. Activities of this business include providing asset management, whereby the company manages capital on behalf of institutional investors in exchange for management fees, and may earn performance fees provided targeted investment returns are achieved; property management, whereby the company provides resident-facing services from head office in Orange cty., Calif., including marketing, leasing, and repairs and maintenance delivered through a dedicated call center and local field offices; and development management services, whereby the company earns development management fees from its rental development projects in Toronto, Ont., as well as contractual development fees and sales commissions from the development and sale of single-family lots, residential land parcels, and commercial land within the MPCs managed by Johnson. The company manages US$8.1 billion of third-party capital across its business segments.

Revenue from private funds and advisory services:

At Dec. 31	2022	2021
	US$000s	US$000s
Asset mgt. fees	12,431	12,719
Performance fees	110,330	8,909
Development fees	26,826	24,418
Property mgt. fees	10,501	4,647

In June 2022, the company entered into a joint venture with Arizona State Retirement System (ASRS) to invest in master planned communities and the development of single-family "built-to rent" and for-sale housing projects in U.S. Sun Belt markets. ASRS would commit US$400,000,000 with the company committing US$100,000,000. The company previously announced its first joint venture with ASRS in August 2019 and has similar investment strategy with ASRS committing US$400,000,000 and the company with US$50,000,000. In its role as an asset manager, the company would be entitled to receive customary asset management fees, and potentially performance fees for managing third party capital.

In April 2022, the company sold 66.67% of its 20% interest in Queen & Ontario project, a two-tower, 725-unit rental development located in Toronto's Downtown East neighbourhood, to its joint venture partner Canada Pension Plan Investment Board (CPPIB) for an undisclosed amount. The total development cost was expected to be Cdn$600,000,000, including Cdn$192,000,000 of equity capital contributed from the joint venture, of which the company's share is Cdn$58,000,000. Construction commenced in the second quarter of 2022 with completion expected in 2025.

Recent Merger and Acquisition Activity

Status: completed **Revised:** Oct. 18, 2022
UPDATE: The transaction was completed. PREVIOUS: Tricon Residential Inc. agreed to sell its 20% interest in a portfolio of 23 Sun Belt multi-family apartment buildings for gross proceeds of US$315,000,000, including performance fees earned for managing the third-party joint venture through which the portfolio is held. Tricon sold an 80% interest in the portfolio in May 2021. The transaction was expected to close on or about Oct. 18, 2022.

Status: completed **Announced:** Sept. 1, 2022
Tricon Residential Inc. sold its 100% interest in Bryson MPC Holdings LLC to THP JV-2E LLC for US$11,041,000 cash and US$2,760,000 in-kind contribution. Bryson develops a 530-acre master-planned community project in Austin, Tex.

Predecessor Detail - Name changed from Tricon Capital Group Inc., July 7, 2020.

Directors - David Berman, exec. chr., Toronto, Ont.; Gary Berman, pres. & CEO, Toronto, Ont.; Peter D. Sacks†, Toronto, Ont.; Frank Cohen, New York, N.Y.; Camille J. Douglas, New York, N.Y.; Renee L. Glover, Atlanta, Ga.; Ira Gluskin, Toronto, Ont.; J. Michael (Mike) Knowlton, Toronto, Ont.; Siân M. Matthews, Calgary, Alta.; Geoffrey (Geoff) Matus, Toronto, Ont.

Other Exec. Officers - Andrew (Andy) Carmody, sr. man. dir, invests. & head, sustainability; Julie Burdick, man. dir., invests.; Evelyne Dubé, man. dir., private funds; Andrew Joyner, man. dir., invests.; David Mark, man. dir., fin.; Wojtek K. Nowak, man. dir., capital markets; Bill Richards, man. dir., asset mgt. & acqs.; Rick Timmins, man. dir., invests.; Gina McMullan, chief acctg. officer; Alan O'Brien, chief resident experience officer; Douglas P. Quesnel, chief transformation officer; Reshma Block, head, innovation & tech.; John English, head, devel., Canada; Jude Fitzgerald, head, mktg. & commun.; Ali Merali, head, strategic initiatives; Kevin Baldridge, exec. v-p & COO; Jonathan (Jon) Ellenzweig, exec. v-p & chief invest. officer; Wissam Francis, exec. v-p & CFO; Sherrie Suski, exec. v-p & chief people officer; David Veneziano, exec. v-p, chief legal officer & corp. sec.; Sandra Pereira, sr. v-p & head, tax srvcs.; Thomas Walsh, gen. counsel, property opers.

† Lead director

Capital Stock

	Authorized (shs.)	Outstanding (shs.)[1]
Common	unlimited	272,759,578
Exch. Preferred Unit	unlimited	34,744,118[2]

[1] At May 2, 2023
[2] Issued by subsidiary Tricon PIPE LLC

Common - One vote per share.

Exchangeable Preferred Units - Issued by subsidiary Tricon PIPE LLC. Entitled to an annual cash dividend equal to 5.75% of the liquidation preference of the preferred units and payable quarterly to Sept. 3, 2027, with a prescribed annual increase of 1% per year thereafter, up to a maximum rate of 9.75% per year. Mature on Sept. 3, 2032. Exchangeable into common shares at an initial exchange price of US$8.50 per share, which may be adjusted from time-to-time.

Options - At Dec. 31, 2022, options were outstanding to purchase 3,443,770 common shares at a weighted average exercise price of Cdn$10.61 per share expiring from Nov. 14, 2023, to Dec. 15, 2029; and 395,953 common shares at a weighted average exercise price of US$8.54 per share expiring from Dec. 15, 2028, to Dec. 15, 2029.

Normal Course Issuer Bid - The company plans to make normal course purchases of up to 2,500,000 common shares representing 0.9% of the public float. The bid commenced on Oct. 18, 2022, and expires on Oct. 17, 2023.

Major Shareholder - Widely held at May 2, 2023.

Price Range - TCN/TSX

Year	Volume	High	Low	Close
2022	183,775,086	$21.58	$9.83	$10.44
2021	151,930,830	$19.40	$11.00	$19.36
2020	113,756,234	$12.11	$5.45	$11.43
2019	94,620,356	$11.73	$9.51	$10.63
2018	61,732,505	$11.88	$9.33	$9.69

Recent Close: $11.30

Capital Stock Changes - During 2022, common shares were issued as follows: 554,832 on exchange of 4,675 exchangeable preferred units, 483,007 on exercise of deferred share units, 323,048 under dividend reinvestment plan and 8,334 on exercise of options. In addition, 677,666 common shares were repurchased under a Normal Course Issuer Bid and 26,909 common shares were repurchased and reserved for restricted share awards.

Dividends

TCN com Ra US$0.232 pa Q est. Jan. 17, 2022**[1]
Prev. Rate: $0.28 est. Apr. 15, 2018
[1] Divds. paid in Cdn$ prior to January 2022.
** Reinvestment Option

Long-Term Debt - Outstanding at Dec. 31, 2022:

Corporate debt	US$12,717,000
Single-family rental (SFR) props. debt:	
SFR wholly owned props.	1,294,538,000
SFR JV-1 props.	1,568,101,000
SFR JV-2 props.	2,265,066,000
SFR JV-HD props.	616,720,000
Cdn. devel. props. debt	21,095,000
Less: Transaction costs & discounts	50,053,000
	5,728,184,000
Less: Current portion	757,135,000
	4,971,049,000

Wholly Owned Subsidiaries

Tricon Capital GP Inc., Ont.
Tricon Holdings Canada Inc., Ont.
- 100% int. in **Tricon US Topco LLC**, Del.
  - 100% int. in **Tricon Holdings USA LLC**, Del.
    - 100% int. in **THP JV-1E LLC**, Del.
    - 100% int. in **THP JV-2E LLC**, Del.
    - 100% int. in **Tricon JDC LLC**, Del.
      - 50.1% int. in **The Johnson Companies L.P.**, Houston, Tex.
    - 100% int. in **Tricon USA Inc.**, Del.

Tricon Housing Partners US Co-Investment Inc., Del.
Tricon Lifestyle Rentals Investment L.P., Ont.
Tricon US Rental Canco Inc., Del.
- 100% int. in **Tricon US Rental Topco LLC**, Del.
  - 100% int. in **SFR JV-HD Investor LLC**, Del.

- 100% int. in **SFR JV-2 Investor LLC**, Del.
- 100% int. in **Tricon US Rental REIT LLC**, Del.
  - 100% int. in **SFR JV-1 Investor LLC**, Del.
  - 100% int. in **Tricon Single-Family Rental REIT LLC**, Del.
    - 100% int. in **Tricon American Homes LLC**, Del.

Note: The preceding list includes only the major related companies in which interests are held.

Financial Statistics

Periods ended:	12m Dec. 31/22^A		12m Dec. 31/21^oA
	US$000s	%Chg	US$000s
Total revenue	**846,204**	**+56**	**543,575**
Rental operating expense	209,089		149,940
Salaries & benefits	55,040		43,630
General & admin. expense	58,991		41,420
Other operating expense	80,070		88,593
Operating expense	**403,190**	**+25**	**323,583**
Operating income	**443,014**	**+101**	**219,992**
Deprec. & amort.	15,608		12,129
Finance costs, gross	213,932		147,680
Pre-tax income	**934,594**	**+47**	**635,067**
Income taxes	155,220		175,710
Net inc bef disc ops, eqhldrs	773,835		455,085
Net inc bef disc ops, NCI	5,539		4,272
Net inc. bef. disc. opers	**779,374**	**+70**	**459,357**
Disc. opers., equity hldrs	35,106		(9,830)
Income from disc. opers	35,106		(9,830)
Net income	**814,480**	**+81**	**449,527**
Net inc. for equity hldrs	**808,941**	**+82**	**445,255**
Net inc. for non-cont. int	**5,539**	**+30**	**4,272**
Cash & equivalent	204,303		176,894
Accounts receivable	20,846		38,811
Current assets	266,807		251,422
Long-term investments	265,676		441,113
Fixed assets	96,852		84,749
Income-producing props	11,445,659		7,978,396
Properties under devel	136,413		133,250
Property interests, net	11,678,924		8,196,395
Intangibles, net	36,819		39,050
Total assets	**12,450,946**	**+36**	**9,148,617**
Accts. pay. & accr. liabs	87,155		74,012
Current liabilities	991,133		430,365
Long-term debt, gross	5,728,184		3,917,433
Long-term debt, net	4,971,049		3,662,628
Long-term lease liabilities	30,035		28,958
Shareholders' equity	3,790,249		3,053,794
Non-controlling interest	6,776		7,275
Cash from oper. activs	**270,269**	**+127**	**118,917**
Cash from fin. activs	2,178,004		1,611,199
Cash from invest. activs	(2,420,581)		(1,608,380)
Net cash position	**204,303**	**+15**	**176,894**
Capital expenditures	(35,983)		(32,875)
Increase in property	(2,688,645)		(2,031,807)
Decrease in property	80,369		34,528
	US$		US$
Earns. per sh. bef disc opers*	2.82		2.07
Earnings per share*	2.95		2.03
Cash flow per share*	0.98		0.54
Funds from opers. per sh.*	$0.76		$0.57
Adj. funds from opers. per sh.*	$0.64		$0.45
Cash divd. per share*	$0.23		$0.27
Total divd. per share*	**$0.23**		**$0.27**
	shs		shs
No. of shs. o/s*	272,840,692		272,176,046
Avg. no. of shs. o/s*	274,483,264		219,834,130
	%		%
Net profit margin	92.10		84.51
Return on equity	22.61		19.01
Return on assets	8.87		6.94
No. of employees (FTEs)	1,010		968

* Common
^o Restated
^A Reported in accordance with IFRS

Latest Results

Periods ended:	3m Mar. 31/23^A		3m Mar. 31/22^oA
	US$000s	%Chg	US$000s
Total revenue	212,993	+34	158,698
Net inc. bef. disc. opers	29,401	-80	150,124
Income from disc. opers	nil		13,333
Net income	29,401	-82	163,457
Net inc. for equity hldrs	26,959	-83	162,347
Net inc. for non-cont. int	2,442		1,110
	US$		US$
Earns. per sh. bef. disc. opers.*	0.10		0.54
Earnings per share*	0.10		0.59

* Common
^o Restated
^A Reported in accordance with IFRS

Historical Summary
(as originally stated)

Fiscal Year	Total Rev.	Net Inc. Bef. Disc.	EPS*
	US$000s	US$000s	US$
2022^A	846,204	779,374	2.82
2021^A	612,481	517,089	2.34
2020^A	465,416	116,413	0.58
2019^A	246,714	114,135	0.65
2018^A	276,134	193,228	1.40

* Common
^A Reported in accordance with IFRS

T.94 Trillium Acquisition Corp.

Symbol - TCK.P **Exchange** - TSX-VEN **CUSIP** - 89624T
Head Office - 231 Wedgewood Dr, Oakville, ON, L6J 4R6 **Telephone** - (416) 505-0429
Email - kellyhanczyk@yahoo.ca
Investor Relations - Kelly C. Hanczyk (416) 906-2379
Auditors - Richter LLP C.A., Montréal, Qué.
Transfer Agents - TSX Trust Company, Toronto, Ont.
Profile - (Ont. 2019) Capital Pool Company.

Recent Merger and Acquisition Activity

Status: terminated **Revised:** Mar. 24, 2022
UPDATE: The transaction was terminated. PREVIOUS: Trillium Acquisition Corp. agreed to acquire from 104 Nanaimo Holdings Ltd. a multi-family development site and existing shopping centre property in Nanaimo, B.C., covering 64 acres, and rights that include Sports Mall contracts and seven exclusive Canadian trademark rights. Total aggregate consideration was $320,000,000, whereby the conditional allocation would be $120,000,000 for the land and buildings, $100,000,000 for the Sports Mall contracts and $100,000,000 for the trademark rights. The transaction would constitute Trillium's Qualifying Transaction.

Directors - Kelly C. Hanczyk, interim pres., interim CEO & interim CFO, Oakville, Ont.; Deborah Bell, Toronto, Ont.; David Davies, Vancouver, B.C.; Theodore (Ted) Manziaris, Toronto, Ont.

Capital Stock

	Authorized (shs.)	Outstanding (shs.)[1]
Common	unlimited	17,227,400

[1] At July 10, 2023

Major Shareholder - Theodore (Ted) Manziaris held 16.3% interest at July 10, 2023.

Price Range - TCK.P/TSX-VEN

Year	Volume	High	Low	Close
2022	595,502	$0.06	$0.02	$0.02
2020	317,400	$0.15	$0.07	$0.11

Recent Close: $0.03
Capital Stock Changes - There were no changes to capital stock during 2022.

T.95 Trilogy International Partners Inc.

Symbol - TRL.H **Exchange** - TSX-VEN **CUSIP** - 89621T
Head Office - 155 108 Ave NE, Suite 400, Bellevue, WA, United States, 98004 **Telephone** - (425) 458-5900 **Fax** - (425) 458-5999
Website - www.trilogy-international.com
Email - scott.morris@trilogy-international.com
Investor Relations - Scott Morris (425) 458-5900
Auditors - Grant Thornton LLP C.P.A., Seattle, Wash.
Lawyers - Stikeman Elliott LLP, Toronto, Ont.
Transfer Agents - TSX Trust Company, Toronto, Ont.
FP500 Revenue Ranking - 556
Employees - 7 at Mar. 30, 2023
Profile - (B.C. 2017; orig. Ont., 2015) No operations.

Formerly operated wireless and broadband telecommunications subsidiaries in Bolivia and New Zealand.

On July 6, 2023, the company declared a Cdn$0.31 per share return of capital distribution payable July 28, 2023, to shareholders of record on July 19, 2023. The total amount of the distribution is equal to Cdn$27,5000,000.

On June 27, 2022, the company paid Cdn$1.69 per share return of capital distribution to shareholders of record on Jun. 17, 2022. This initial and primary distribution of net cash proceeds follows the sale of the company's interest in **Two Degrees Group Limited** on May 19, 2022.

On May 14, 2022, the company completed the transfer of its 71.5% interest in **Empresa de Telecomunicaciones NuevaTel (PCS de Bolivia) S.A.**, a provider of wireless, long distance, public telephony and wireless broadband communication services under the Viva brand, to **Balesia Technologies, Inc.** for a nominal purchase price. Balesia is a member of the **Balesia Group of Companies**, which collectively develop, own and operate wireless networks, Internet of Things edge and multi-edge computing technologies and supporting infrastructure across Latin America.

On Apr. 6, 2022, the company surrendered its 20% interest in **Salamanca Solutions International LLC** (SSI) to **Salamanca Holding Company** (SHC). SSI owns billing and customer relations management intellectual property, and associated software support and development services that it has licensed to NuevaTel. Following the company's surrender of interest in SSI and in connection with the anticipated sale of **Empresa de Telecomunicaciones NuevaTel (PCS de Bolivia) S.A.** to **Balesia Technologies, Inc.**, Balesia acquired SHC.

Common delisted from TSX, Dec. 28, 2022.
Common listed on TSX-VEN, Dec. 28, 2022.

Recent Merger and Acquisition Activity

Status: completed **Revised:** May 19, 2022
UPDATE: The transaction was completed. PREVIOUS: Trilogy International Partners Inc. (TIP), together with its minority partner Tesbrit BV, agreed to sell Two Degrees Mobile Limited (2degrees) to Voyage Digital (NZ) Limited for NZ$1.315 billion. 2degrees is 73.17%-owned by TIP and 26.83%-owned by Tesbrit. 2degrees offers wireless voice and data communications services, and provides fixed voice and broadband communications services to business and residential customers in New Zealand. Voyage is a joint venture between Macquarie Asset Management and Aware Super that owns Vocus Group Limited (VGL), an international telecommunications company in Australia. TIP had discussions with Macquarie and Aware Super regarding a potential merger of 2degrees and Orcon Group Limited, a wholly owned subsidiary of VGL in October 2021. The potential 2degrees and Orcon merger would create an integrated fixed-mobile business of scale, providing better service to customers in New Zealand's mobile and fixed telecommunication markets. Mar. 15, 2022 - TIP shareholders and New Zealand's Commerce Commission have approved the transaction. Apr. 28, 2022 - The New Zealand Overseas Investment Office has approved the merger of 2degrees with Orcon. This is the final government approval required to complete the sale of 2degrees, which is expected to close during the second quarter of 2022.

Predecessor Detail - Name changed from Alignvest Acquisition Corporation, Feb. 7, 2017, pursuant to the Qualifying Acquisition of Trilogy International Partners LLC.

Directors - John W. Stanton, chr., Wash.; Bradley J. (Brad) Horwitz, pres., CEO & CFO, Wash.; Mark Kroloff, Alaska

Other Exec. Officers - Scott Morris, sr. v-p, gen. counsel & corp. sec.

Capital Stock

	Authorized (shs.)	Outstanding (shs.)[1]
Common	unlimited	88,627,593

[1] At Aug. 10, 2023

Major Shareholder - John W. Stanton and Theresa E. Gillespie together held 19.08% interest and Anson Funds Management L.P. held 10.67% interest at May 8, 2023.

Price Range - TRL.H/TSX-VEN

Year	Volume	High	Low	Close
2022	14,645,634	$2.39	$0.12	$0.22
2021	8,468,737	$2.77	$1.28	$2.38
2020	9,716,697	$2.10	$0.83	$1.43
2019	7,837,849	$3.45	$1.58	$2.05
2018	10,540,187	$6.33	$1.22	$1.64

Recent Close: $0.04

Capital Stock Changes - During 2022, common shares were issued as follows: 3,351,693 on vesting of restricted share units and 489,752 for change in non-controlling interests and others; 1,675,336 common shares were cancelled.

Dividends

TRL.H com N.S.R.
Listed Dec 28/22.
$0.31◆r............... July 28/23 $1.69◆r.......... June 27/22
Paid in 2023: $0.31◆r 2022: $1.69◆r 2021: n.a.

◆ Special **r** Return of Capital

Wholly Owned Subsidiaries

Trilogy International Partners Intermediate Holdings Inc., Del.
- 100% int. in **Trilogy International Partners LLC**, Bellevue, Wash.
  - 100% int. in **Trilogy International Latin America I LLC**, Del.
    - 96.5% int. in **Trilogy International Latin Territories LLC**, Del.
  - 100% int. in **Trilogy International Latin America II LLC**, Del.
    - 96.5% int. in **Trilogy International Latin America III LLC**, Del.
  - 3.5% int. in **Trilogy International Latin America III LLC**, Del.
  - 3.5% int. in **Trilogy International Latin Territories LLC**, Del.
  - 100% int. in **Trilogy International South Pacific Holdings LLC**, Del.
    - 100% int. in **Trilogy International South Pacific LLC**, Del.
      - 100% int. in **Trilogy International New Zealand LLC**, Del.

Financial Statistics

Periods ended:	12m Dec. 31/22[A]		12m Dec. 31/21[A]
	US$000s	%Chg	US$000s
Operating revenue	**238,517**	**-64**	**653,564**
Cost of sales	120,202		338,521
General & admin expense	89,517		209,314
Stock-based compensation	3,572		3,407
Operating expense	**213,291**	**-61**	**551,242**
Operating income	**25,226**	**-75**	**102,322**
Deprec., depl. & amort.	18,418		107,241
Finance costs, gross	22,887		53,713
Write-downs/write-offs	(2,759)		(122,507)
Pre-tax income	**448,507**	**n.a.**	**(183,830)**
Income taxes	11,468		10,542
Net income	**437,039**	**n.a.**	**(194,372)**
Net inc. for equity hldrs	**433,461**	**n.a.**	**(144,689)**
Net inc. for non-cont. int.	**3,578**	**n.a.**	**(49,683)**
Cash & equivalent	25,067		53,486
Inventories	nil		10,918
Accounts receivable	nil		61,073
Current assets	40,628		200,839
Fixed assets, net	12		307,085
Right-of-use assets	nil		120,414
Intangibles, net	nil		71,066
Total assets	**40,640**	**-95**	**803,867**
Accts. pay. & accr. liabs	49		27,171
Current liabilities	7,184		225,623
Long-term debt, gross	nil		663,274
Long-term debt, net	nil		631,685
Long-term lease liabilities	nil		168,437
Shareholders' equity	33,456		(280,889)
Non-controlling interest	nil		34,855
Cash from oper. activs	**(8,590)**	**n.a.**	**48,702**
Cash from fin. activs	(537,262)		(494)
Cash from invest. activs	519,094		(93,806)
Net cash position	**25,067**	**-54**	**55,010**
Capital expenditures	(32,429)		(92,838)
	US$		US$
Earnings per share*	4.93		(2.15)
Cash flow per share*	(0.10)		0.72
Cash divd. per share*	$1.69		$nil
Extra divd. - cash*	$1.69		$nil
Total divd. per share*	**$3.38**		**$nil**
	shs		shs
No. of shs. o/s*	88,627,593		86,461,484
Avg. no. of shs. o/s*	87,844,230		67,412,546
	%		%
Net profit margin	183.23		(29.74)
Return on equity	n.m.		n.m.
Return on assets	108.78		(15.35)
Foreign sales percent	100		100
No. of employees (FTEs)	9		1,630

* Common
[A] Reported in accordance with U.S. GAAP

Historical Summary
(as originally stated)

Fiscal Year	Oper. Rev. US$000s	Net Inc. Bef. Disc. US$000s	EPS* US$
2022[A]	238,517	437,039	4.93
2021[A]	653,564	(194,372)	(2.15)
2020[A]	610,299	(79,687)	(0.83)
2019[A]	693,927	24,022	0.05
2018[A]	798,175	(31,730)	(0.38)

* Common
[A] Reported in accordance with U.S. GAAP

T.96 TripSitter Clinic Ltd.

Symbol - KETA **Exchange** - CSE **CUSIP** - 89680B
Head Office - 700-77 King St W, Toronto, ON, M5K 1G8 **Telephone** - (416) 480-2488
Website - www.tripsitter.clinic
Email - dr.huber@tripsitter.clinic
Investor Relations - Dr. John Huber (416) 480-2488
Auditors - MNP LLP C.A., Toronto, Ont.
Lawyers - McMillan LLP, Toronto, Ont.
Transfer Agents - Olympia Transfer Services Inc., Toronto, Ont.
Profile - (B.C. 2021) Operates a consultative virtual clinic and telehealth software-as-a-service (SaaS) platform through its web app (TripSitter.Clinic) and mobile app (TripSitter) that connect prospective patients to a licensed physician in the U.S. who can evaluate for a prescribed treatment program of low dose, oral ketamine medication.

The ketamine medication is used to treat patients with medical conditions such as depression, anxiety, post traumatic stress disorder (PTSD), bipolar disorder and obsessive compulsive disorder (OCD). Eligible patients enter into either a three-month or six-month subscription plan, which includes consultation with a physician, oral ketamine prescription medication and treatment sessions with a licensed medical practitioner. The company is not a primary care physician (PCP), and a diagnosis from a prospective patient's PCP is required to be submitted to their chosen TripSitter physician, along with other health information. The company's services are available in 23 states in the U.S.

The company generates revenue from the sale of monthly subscription plans.

On Jan. 31, 2023, the company acquired **Insight Systems, PBC** (dba Reconscious Medical), a psychedelic psychotherapy company, for issuance of 1,000,000 units (1 common share & 1 warrant). Reconscious engages in both in-clinic and online virtual care with safety, monitoring and support provided through a proprietary technology platform, with a primary focus on combining psychedelic treatment with psychotherapy in both high and low doses of ketamine.

Predecessor Detail - Name changed from 1284684 B.C. Ltd., Oct. 28, 2021, pursuant to the reverse takeover acquisition of TripSitter Clinic Corp. and concurrent amalgamation of TripSitter with wholly owned 2821573 Ontario Inc.

Directors - Dr. Mark Braunstein, chr.; Dr. John Huber, CEO & corp. sec., Tex.; Richard F. Dolan, Ont.; Matthew Morgan, Fla.

Other Exec. Officers - Muhammad Aziz, interim CFO; Dr. Daniel Hanono, CMO

Capital Stock

	Authorized (shs.)	Outstanding (shs.)[1]
Common	unlimited	30,290,868

[1] At July 31, 2022

Major Shareholder - Cabazon Capital Corp. held 18.62% interest, PF Capital Partners LLC held 18.62% interest and Jason Draizin held 18.62% interest at June 14, 2022.

Price Range - KETA/CSE

Year	Volume	High	Low	Close
2022	4,933,316	$0.58	$0.02	$0.03
2021	745,566	$1.35	$0.21	$0.32

Recent Close: $0.02

Capital Stock Changes - On Jan. 31, 2023, 1,000,000 units (1 common share & 1 warrant) were issued pursuant to the acquisition of Insight Systems, PBC (dba Reconscious Medical), with half the warrants exercisable at US$0.20 per share and the other half exercisable at US$0.50 per share, all until Feb. 28, 2026.

Wholly Owned Subsidiaries

Insights Systems, PBC, United States.
TripSitter Clinic Corp., Toronto, Ont.
- 100% int. in **TripSitter Corp.**, Carson City, Nev.

Financial Statistics

Periods ended:	12m Jan. 31/22[A1]
	$000s
Operating revenue	**87**
Salaries & benefits	232
General & admin expense	1,792
Stock-based compensation	338
Operating expense	**2,362**
Operating income	**(2,275)**
Pre-tax income	**(10,220)**
Net income	**(10,220)**
Cash & equivalent	1,298
Accounts receivable	59
Current assets	1,457
Total assets	**1,457**
Accts. pay. & accr. liabs	191
Current liabilities	198
Shareholders' equity	1,260
Cash from oper. activs	**(1,759)**
Cash from fin. activs	16
Cash from invest. activs	2,297
Net cash position	**1,298**
	$
Earnings per share*	(0.41)
Cash flow per share*	(0.07)
	shs
No. of shs. o/s*	30,290,868
Avg. no. of shs. o/s*	25,107,250
	%
Net profit margin	n.m.
Return on equity	n.m.
Return on assets	n.a.
Foreign sales percent	100

* Common
[A] Reported in accordance with IFRS
[1] Results reflect the Nov. 4, 2021, reverse takeover acquisition of TripSitter Clinic Corp.

Latest Results

Periods ended:	6m July 31/22[A]		6m July 31/21[A]
	$000s	%Chg	$000s
Operating revenue	348	n.m.	3
Net income	(1,255)	n.a.	(692)
	$		$
Earnings per share*	(0.04)		(0.03)

* Common
[A] Reported in accordance with IFRS

T.97 Trisura Group Ltd.

Symbol - TSU **Exchange** - TSX **CUSIP** - 89679A
Head Office - Bay Adelaide Centre, 1610-333 Bay St, Toronto, ON, M5H 2R2 **Telephone** - (416) 214-2555 **Fax** - (416) 214-9597
Website - www.trisura.com/group
Email - bryan.sinclair@trisura.com
Investor Relations - Bryan Sinclair (416) 607-2135
Auditors - Deloitte LLP C.A., Toronto, Ont.
Transfer Agents - TSX Trust Company, Toronto, Ont.
FP500 Revenue Ranking - 454
Employees - 311 at Dec. 31, 2022
Profile - (Ont. 2017) Provides specialty insurance including surety, risk solutions, corporate insurance, fronting and reinsurance products.

Wholly owned **Trisura Guarantee Insurance Company**, a Canadian specialty property and casualty insurance company, operates three business lines: Surety; Risk Solutions; and Corporate Insurance.

Surety business consists of: (i) contract surety bonds, such as performance, labour and material payment bonds for the construction industry; (ii) commercial surety bonds, such as licence and permit, tax and excise, and fiduciary bonds that are issued on behalf of commercial enterprises and professionals to governments, regulatory bodies or courts to guarantee compliance with legal or fiduciary obligations; (iii) developer surety bonds, mainly to secure real estate developers' legislated deposit and warranty obligations on residential projects; and (iv) home warranty insurance for residential homes.

Risk Solutions business includes specialty insurance contracts, primarily warranty programs, that are structured to meet specific requirements of program administrators, managing general agencies, captive insurance companies, affinity groups and reinsurers. Risk Solutions uses four different insurance structures, sometimes in combination, to address clients' insurance requirements: surety structure, fronting structure, retrospectively rated policy structure and risk transfer structure.

Corporate Insurance business includes four primary products: (i) directors' and officers' insurance; (ii) professional liability insurance; (iii) technology and cyber liability insurance; (iv) commercial package insurance; and (v) fidelity insurance.

Trisura Guarantee is headquartered in Toronto, Ont., and has offices in Vancouver, B.C.; Calgary, Alta.; Montreal, Que.; Halifax, N.S.; and Ottawa, Ont. Its distribution network has more than 170 contracted insurance brokerage firms operating across Canada.

Wholly owned **Trisura Specialty Insurance Company** operates in the U.S. as a hybrid fronting carrier with a fee-based business model. It is licensed as a domestic excess and surplus lines insurer in Oklahoma, operating as a non-admitted surplus lines insurer in all U.S. states and as an admitted carrier in 49 states. Trisura Specialty has commenced application for admitted licences in the remaining states.

During 2022, the company determined that its Trisura International segment, which comprised the company's international reinsurance operations, no longer met the quantitative threshold for reportable segment disclosure purposes and has been reclassified to corporate and other. The segment, through wholly owned **Trisura International Insurance Ltd.**, had provided reinsurance and insurance products in a diversified range of property and casualty, and health classes to the specialty insurance marketplace.

In September 2022, the company acquired the surety business of **The Sovereign General Insurance Company** in Canada. Terms were not disclosed.

Directors - Dr. George E. Myhal, chr., Toronto, Ont.; David J. Clare, pres. & CEO, Toronto, Ont.; Paul Gallagher, Toronto, Ont.; Barton Hedges, Stuart, Fla.; Anik Lanthier, Lachine, Qué.; Janice M. Madon, Oakville, Ont.; Gregory (Greg) Morrison, Hamilton, Bermuda; Robert Taylor, Oakville, Ont.

Other Exec. Officers - David Scotland, CFO; Jimmy (James) Doyle, chief risk officer & pres. & CEO, Trisura International Insurance Ltd.; Michael Beasley, pres. & CEO, Trisura Specialty Insurance Company

Capital Stock

	Authorized (shs.)	Outstanding (shs.)[1]
Preference	unlimited	nil
Non-vtg.	unlimited	nil
Common	unlimited	45,959,035

[1] At Mar. 31, 2023

Non-voting - Convertible into common shares on a one-for-one basis in certain circumstances.

Common - One vote per share.

Major Shareholder - Widely held at Mar. 31, 2023.

Price Range - TSU/TSX

Year	Volume	High	Low	Close
2022	30,020,933	$48.60	$29.12	$45.29
2021	47,178,492	$49.43	$20.46	$47.69
2020	24,803,144	$24.19	$8.50	$22.27
2019	10,170,768	$10.96	$6.50	$10.07
2018	7,750,252	$7.07	$6.00	$6.53

Split: 4-for-1 split in July 2021
Recent Close: $31.55

Capital Stock Changes - In August 2023, bought deal public offering of 1,620,000 common shares was completed at $32.90 per share, including 1,000,000 common shares on exercise of over-allotment option.

In July 2022, bought deal public offering of 4,512,000 common shares was completed at $33.25 per share, including 442,000 common shares on exercise of over-allotment option. Also during 2022, 145,141 common shares were issued on exercise of options and 38,811 common shares were repurchased under a restricted share units plan.

Wholly Owned Subsidiaries

Trisura Guarantee Insurance Company, Toronto, Ont.
- 100% int. in **Trisura Warranty Services Inc.**, Canada.

Trisura Insurance Company, Okla.
- 100% int. in **Bricktown Specialty Insurance Company**, Okla.
- 100% int. in **Trisura Specialty Insurance Company**, Okla.

Trisura International Insurance Ltd., Barbados.
- 100% int. in **Trisura International Reinsurance Company Ltd.**, Barbados.

Financial Statistics

Periods ended:	12m Dec. 31/22[A]		12m Dec. 31/21[A]
	$000s	%Chg	$000s
Net premiums earned	418,621		277,909
Net investment income	25,162		7,605
Total revenue	**526,102**	**+50**	**349,877**
Policy benefits & claims	127,192		82,330
Commissions	177,542		107,757
Other operating expense	77,167		73,781
Operating expense	**254,709**	**+40**	**181,538**
Operating income	**144,201**	**+68**	**86,009**
Deprec. & amort.	3,623		3,928
Finance costs, gross	2,644		1,639
Pre-tax income	**35,433**	**-56**	**80,443**
Income taxes	10,782		17,884
Net income	**24,651**	**-61**	**62,559**
Cash & equivalent	406,368		341,319
Accounts receivable	433,165		285,395
Securities investments	1,478,195		897,011
Total investments	765,375		641,140
Total assets	**4,283,370**	**+43**	**3,000,354**
Accts. pay. & accr. liabs.	36,219		33,649
Claims provisions	1,478,195		897,011
Debt	75,000		75,000
Long-term lease liabilities	11,741		9,678
Shareholders' equity	483,294		358,789
Cash from oper. activs.	**150,930**	**-51**	**306,849**
Cash from fin. activs.	141,591		45,153
Cash from invest. activs.	(241,993)		(148,648)
Net cash position	**406,368**	**+19**	**341,319**
Capital expenditures	(877)		(3,264)
	$		$
Earnings per share*	0.57		1.52
Cash flow per share*	3.48		7.46
	shs		shs
No. of shs. o/s*	45,783,528		41,165,198
Avg. no. of shs. o/s*	43,416,000		41,156,000
	%		%
Net profit margin	4.69		17.88
Return on equity	5.85		19.29
Return on assets	0.73		2.71
No. of employees (FTEs)	311		248

* Common
[A] Reported in accordance with IFRS

Historical Summary
(as originally stated)

Fiscal Year	Total Rev.	Net Inc. Bef. Disc.	EPS*
	$000s	$000s	$
2022[A]	526,102	24,651	0.57
2021[A]	349,877	62,559	1.52
2020[A]	226,632	32,442	0.83
2019[A]	145,602	5,094	0.17
2018[A]	103,990	8,638	0.32

* Common
[A] Reported in accordance with IFRS
Note: Adjusted throughout for 4-for-1 split in July 2021

T.98 True North Commercial Real Estate Investment Trust

Symbol - TNT.UN **Exchange** - TSX **CUSIP** - 89784Y
Head Office - Centre Tower, 1400-3280 Bloor St W, Toronto, ON, M8X 2X3 **Telephone** - (416) 234-8444
Website - www.truenorthreit.com
Email - tsherren@starlightinvest.com
Investor Relations - Tracy C. Sherren (416) 234-8444
Auditors - BDO Canada LLP C.A., Toronto, Ont.
Lawyers - Miller Thomson LLP, Toronto, Ont.
Transfer Agents - TSX Trust Company, Toronto, Ont.
Managers - Starlight Group Property Holdings Inc., Toronto, Ont.
FP500 Revenue Ranking - 716

Profile - (Ont. 2012) Acquires and owns office properties in urban and select strategic secondary markets in Canada which focuses on long-term leases with government and credit-rated tenants.

At Mar. 31, 2023, the trust owned 46 office properties totaling 4,950,300 sq. ft.

Region	Props.	Sq. ft.[1]
British Columbia	5	279,400
Alberta	5	606,300
Ontario	26	3,160,900
New Brunswick	8	475,100
Nova Scotia	2	428,600
	46	4,950,300

[1] Gross leasable area.

Recent Merger and Acquisition Activity

Status: completed **Revised:** Mar. 10, 2023
UPDATE: The transaction was completed. PREVIOUS: True North Commercial Real Estate Investment Trust agreed to sell Carlingview property, a 26,800-sq.-ft. single-tenant office building located at 400 Carlingview Drive in Toronto, Ont., for $7,250,000.

Status: pending **Announced:** Jan. 13, 2023
True North Commercial Real Estate Investment Trust agreed to sell Laurier property, an 11-storey office building located at 360 Laurier Avenue West in Ottawa, Ont., for $17,500,000. Closing of the transaction was expected on or about June 15, 2023.

Status: completed **Revised:** Aug. 22, 2022
UPDATE: The transaction was completed. PREVIOUS: True North Commercial Real Estate Investment Trust agreed to acquire an 11-storey, 174,000-sq.-ft. office property in Ottawa, Ont., for $40,500,000, which would be satisfied by a combination of first mortgage financing and the REIT's secured credit facility. The property was Federal government tenanted.

Status: pending **Announced:** Apr. 11, 2022
True North Commercial Real Estate Investment Trust agreed to sell a 52,300-sq.-ft. office property located at 32071 South Fraser in Abbotsford, B.C., for $24,000,000. The transaction was expected to be completed on or about June 30, 2023.

Predecessor Detail - Succeeded Tanq Capital Corporation, Dec. 19, 2012, pursuant to plan of arrangement whereby True North Commercial Real Estate Investment Trust was formed to facilitate the conversion of the corporation into a trust; basis 1 new for 8 old shs.

Trustees - Daniel Drimmer, chr. & CEO, Toronto, Ont.; Martin Liddell, CFO, Toronto, Ont.; Alon S. Ossip‡, Toronto, Ont.; Lindsay Brand, Toronto, Ont.; Lora Gernon, Toronto, Ont.; Sandy I. Poklar, Toronto, Ont.; Tracy C. Sherren, Hammonds Plains, N.S.
‡ Lead trustee

Capital Stock

	Authorized (shs.)	Outstanding (shs.)[1]
Trust Unit	unlimited	92,103,964
Special Voting Unit	unlimited	2,526,414
Class B LP Unit	unlimited	2,526,414[2 3]

[1] At May 9, 2023
[2] Classified as debt.
[3] Issued by True North Commercial Limited Partnership.

Trust Unit - One vote per trust unit.

Special Voting Unit - Issued to holders of class B limited partnership units of wholly owned True North Commercial Limited Partnership. Each special voting unit entitles the holder to a number of votes at unitholder meetings equal to the number of trust units into which the class B limited partnership units are exchangeable.

Class B Limited Partnership Unit - Entitled to distributions equal to those provided to trust units. Directly exchangeable into trust units on a 1-for-1 basis at any time by holder. Puttable instruments classified as financial liabilities under IFRS.

Normal Course Issuer Bid - The company plans to make normal course purchases of up to 8,239,557 trust units representing 10% of the public float. The bid commenced on Apr. 18, 2023, and expires on Apr. 17, 2024.

Major Shareholder - Widely held at May 6, 2022.

Price Range - TNT.UN/TSX

Year	Volume	High	Low	Close
2022	55,250,534	$7.48	$5.48	$5.79
2021	41,883,294	$7.68	$6.18	$7.41
2020	66,841,039	$8.17	$3.83	$6.31
2019	38,358,565	$7.47	$5.56	$7.29
2018	32,248,097	$7.00	$5.30	$5.66

Recent Close: $2.47

Capital Stock Changes - During 2022, trust units were issued as follows: 1,450,800 under an at-the-market equity program, 1,030,273 under dividend reinvestment plan, 496,435 on conversion of a like number of class B LP units, 61,986 on exercise of options and 55,314 on redemption of incentive units.

Dividends

TNT.UN unit Ra $0.297 pa M est. Apr. 17, 2023**
Prev. Rate: $0.297 est. Feb. 15, 2013
** Reinvestment Option

Wholly Owned Subsidiaries

True North Commercial General Partner Corp., Ont.
True North Commercial Limited Partnership, Toronto, Ont.

Financial Statistics

Periods ended:	12m Dec. 31/22[A]		12m Dec. 31/21[A]
	$000s	%Chg	$000s
Total revenue	**143,575**	**+4**	**138,523**
Rental operating expense	36,882		35,940
General & admin. expense	5,389		6,458
Stock-based compensation	665		448
Property taxes	20,209		19,956
Operating expense	**63,145**	**+1**	**62,802**
Operating income	**80,430**	**+6**	**75,721**
Finance costs, gross	32,007		30,549
Pre-tax income	**16,532**	**-68**	**51,004**
Net income	**16,532**	**-68**	**51,004**
Cash & equivalent	9,501		5,476
Accounts receivable	7,264		3,625
Current assets	106,291		12,042
Income-producing props.	1,340,583		1,403,579
Property interests, net	1,340,583		1,403,579
Total assets	**1,450,315**	**+2**	**1,421,177**
Accts. pay. & accr. liabs.	36,974		21,206
Current liabilities	230,156		177,209
Long-term debt, gross	861,317		842,802
Long-term debt, net	698,021		703,575
Shareholders' equity	522,138		540,069
Cash from oper. activs.	**103,271**	**+34**	**77,312**
Cash from fin. activs.	(26,446)		(64,678)
Cash from invest. activs.	(72,800)		(31,738)
Net cash position	**9,501**	**+74**	**5,476**
Capital expenditures	(31,653)		(20,967)
Capital disposals	nil		11,589
Increase in property	(41,147)		(22,360)
	$		$
Earnings per share*	n.a.		n.a.
Cash flow per share*	1.12		0.87
Funds from opers. per sh.*	0.61		0.59
Adj. funds from opers. per sh.*	0.60		0.57
Cash divd. per share*	0.59		0.59
Total divd. per share*	**0.59**		**0.59**
	shs		shs
No. of shs. o/s*	91,813,073		88,718,265
	%		%
Net profit margin	11.51		36.82
Return on equity	3.11		9.58
Return on assets	3.38		5.77

* Trust Unit
[A] Reported in accordance with IFRS

Latest Results

Periods ended:	3m Mar. 31/23[A]		3m Mar. 31/22[A]
	$000s	%Chg	$000s
Total revenue	33,858	-7	36,327
Net income	6,995	-53	14,909
	$		$
Earnings per share*	n.a.		n.a.

[A] Reported in accordance with IFRS

Historical Summary
(as originally stated)

Fiscal Year	Total Rev.	Net Inc. Bef. Disc.	EPS*
	$000s	$000s	$
2022[A]	143,575	16,532	n.a.
2021[A]	138,523	51,004	n.a.
2020[A]	139,431	39,752	n.a.
2019[A]	106,457	24,178	n.a.
2018[A]	87,068	49,620	n.a.

* Trust Unit
[A] Reported in accordance with IFRS

T.99 Trulieve Cannabis Corp.

Symbol - TRUL **Exchange** - CSE **CUSIP** - 89788C
Head Office - 6749 Ben Bostic Rd, Quincy, FL, United States, 32351 **Telephone** - (850) 508-0261
Website - www.trulieve.com
Email - eric.powers@trulieve.com
Investor Relations - Eric Powers (850) 665-3303
Auditors - Marcum LLP C.P.A., West Palm Beach, Fla.
Transfer Agents - Odyssey Trust Company, Vancouver, B.C.
FP500 Revenue Ranking - 255
Employees - 5,900 at Mar. 31, 2023

Profile - (B.C. 2018; orig. Ont., 1940) Cultivates, processes, distributes and retails medical and adult-use cannabis products in the U.S., with leading market positions in Florida, Arizona and Pennsylvania.

Holds licences to operate in three regional hubs: southeast hub, consisting of Florida and Georgia; northeast hub, consisting of Pennsylvania, Maryland, Massachusetts, Connecticut, West Virginia and Ohio; and southwest hub, consisting of Arizona, California and Colorado. At Mar. 31, 2023, owned, operated or managed 18 outdoor, indoor and greenhouse cultivation facilities and processing facilities totaling 3,100,000 sq. ft. in Florida (6) and Georgia; 500,000 sq. ft. in

Pennsylvania (3), West Virginia, Maryland and Massachusetts; and 400,000 sq. ft. in Arizona (4) and Colorado.

Branded retail products that the company cultivates, manufactures and distributes in its regional hubs include premium tier brands Avenue, Cultivar Collection and Muse, mid-tier brands Modern Flower, Alchemy, Momenta and Sweet Talk, and value tier brands Co2lors, Loveli and Roll One. The company also has agreements to sell partner branded products in select markets. Brand partnerships include arrangements with Bellamy Brothers, Bhang, Binske, Black Tuna, Blue River, Connected, DeLisioso, Khalifa Kush, Love's Oven, Miami Mango, Moxie, SLANG, and Sunshine Cannabis. Retail operations at July 1, 2023, consisted of 184 dispensaries located in Florida (125), Arizona (21), Pennsylvania (20), West Virginia (10), Maryland (3), California, Connecticut and Georgia (3).

In June 2023, the company announced the wind down of operations in Massachusetts. All three dispensaries in Northampton, Framingham and Worcester were closed on June 30, and cultivation and manufacturing operations in Holyoke were expected to cease by the end of 2023.

In December 2022, the company acquired **Formula 420 Cannabis LLC**, holder of an adult-use licence in Arizona, for US$5,500,000 in promissory note.

In July 2022, the company discontinued operations in Nevada, which served the wholesale medical and adult-use markets and included a cultivation and manufacturing facility.

In April 2022, the company acquired **Greenhouse Wellness WV Dispensaries, LLC**, holder of a non-operational dispensary permit for a location in Martinsburg, W.Va., for US$300,000.

Predecessor Detail - Name changed from Schyan Exploration Inc., Sept. 21, 2018, following reverse takeover acquisition of Trulieve, Inc.

Directors - Kim Rivers, chr. & CEO, Tallahassee, Fla.; Peter T. Healy†, Hillsborough, Calif.; Giannella Alvarez, Austin, Tex.; Thad Beshears, Monticello, Fla.; Richard May, Quincy, Fla.; Thomas Millner, Monticello, Ga.; Jane Morreau, Louisville, Ky.; Susan Thronson, La Quinta, Calif.

Other Exec. Officers - Steven (Steve) White, pres.; Gina Collins, chief mktg. officer; Nilyum Jhala, chief tech. officer; Kyle Landrum, chief prod. officer; Timothy (Tim) Morey, chief sales officer; Jason Pernell, CIO; Eric Powers, chief legal officer & corp. sec.; Ryan Blust, v-p, fin. & interim CFO; Joy Malivuk, v-p & chief acctg. officer; Nicole Stanton, v-p & gen. counsel

† Lead director

Capital Stock

	Authorized (shs.)	Outstanding (shs.)[1]
Subordinate Vtg.	unlimited	159,761,126
Multiple Vtg.	unlimited	262,264
Super Vtg.	unlimited	nil

[1] At May 3, 2023

Subordinate Voting - One vote per share.

Multiple Voting - Each convertible into 100 subordinate voting shares. Participate equally with subordinate voting shares, assuming conversion of all multiple voting shares into subordinate voting shares. 100 votes per share.

Super Voting - Each convertible into 100 subordinate voting shares, or into multiple voting shares on a 1-for-1 basis. 200 votes per share.

Major Shareholder - Widely held at Apr. 17, 2023.

Price Range - TRUL/CSE

Year	Volume	High	Low	Close
2022	58,261,435	$34.55	$8.72	$10.26
2021	50,607,490	$67.45	$29.57	$32.91
2020	51,646,594	$42.30	$8.10	$40.20
2019	70,672,578	$21.65	$9.91	$15.37
2018	26,779,090	$23.85	$9.10	$11.00

Recent Close: $4.78

Capital Stock Changes - During 2022, subordinate voting shares were issued as follows: 3,626,295 as earnout payments, 1,428,262 on exercise of warrants, 236,756 on release of escrow shares, 179,857 under share compensation plans and 59,971 on exercise of options; 47,801 subordinate voting shares were cancelled as tax withholding related to net share settlements of equity awards. In addition, 256,906.13 multiple voting shares were converted into 25,690,613 subordinate voting shares.

Wholly Owned Subsidiaries

Trulieve Inc., Fla.

- 100% int. in **Harvest Health & Recreation Inc.**, Tempe, Ariz.

Note: The preceding list includes only the major related companies in which interests are held.

Financial Statistics

Periods ended:	12m Dec. 31/22[A]		12m Dec. 31/21[◻A]
	US$000s	%Chg	US$000s
Operating revenue	**1,239,812**	**+32**	**937,981**
Cost of goods sold	505,279		346,096
General & admin expense	454,667		315,655
Operating expense	**959,946**	**+45**	**661,751**
Operating income	**279,866**	**+1**	**276,230**
Deprec., depl. & amort.	171,912		71,302
Finance costs, net	79,771		34,787
Write-downs/write-offs	(3,800)		(3,571)
Pre-tax income	**(43,345)**	**n.a.**	**166,087**
Income taxes	161,820		146,703
Net inc bef disc ops, eqhldrs	(198,502)		19,971
Net inc bef disc ops, NCI	(6,663)		(587)
Net inc. bef. disc. opers	**(205,165)**	**n.a.**	**19,384**
Disc. opers., equity hldrs	(47,562)		(1,939)
Income from disc. opers	(47,562)		(1,939)
Net income	**(252,727)**	**n.a.**	**17,445**
Net inc. for equity hldrs	**(246,064)**	**n.a.**	**18,032**
Net inc. for non-cont. int	**(6,663)**	**n.a.**	**(587)**
Cash & equivalent	212,266		230,085
Inventories	297,815		209,943
Accounts receivable	9,443		8,601
Current assets	592,952		524,932
Fixed assets, net	796,947		779,413
Right-of-use assets	177,610		178,487
Intangibles, net	1,804,141		1,846,598
Total assets	**3,399,048**	**0**	**3,411,384**
Accts. pay. & accr. liabs	83,212		93,801
Current liabilities	209,703		169,448
Long-term debt, gross	831,914		655,626
Long-term debt, net	818,272		644,583
Long-term lease liabilities	178,226		172,814
Shareholders' equity	1,931,160		2,145,821
Non-controlling interest	(3,456)		1,552
Cash from oper. activs	**23,096**	**+79**	**12,898**
Cash from fin. activs	177,796		289,232
Cash from invest. activs	(215,057)		(215,184)
Net cash position	**218,873**	**-6**	**233,098**
Capital expenditures	(177,996)		(296,881)
Capital disposals	739		38
	US$		US$
Earns. per sh. bef disc opers*	(1.06)		0.14
Earnings per share*	(1.31)		0.13
Cash flow per share*	0.12		0.09
	shs		shs
No. of shs. o/s*	185,987,512		180,504,172
Avg. no. of shs. o/s*	187,995,317		139,366,940
	%		%
Net profit margin	(16.55)		2.07
Return on equity	(9.74)		1.54
Return on assets	(6.03)		0.92
Foreign sales percent	100		100
No. of employees (FTEs)	7,600		9,000

* Subord. vtg.
◻ Restated
[A] Reported in accordance with U.S. GAAP

Latest Results

Periods ended:	3m Mar. 31/23[A]		3m Mar. 31/22[◻A]
	US$000s	%Chg	US$000s
Operating revenue	289,089	-9	317,747
Net inc. bef. disc. opers	(65,679)	n.a.	(30,123)
Income from disc. opers	48		(2,359)
Net income	(65,631)	n.a.	(32,482)
Net inc. for equity hldrs	(64,124)	n.a.	(31,975)
Net inc. for non-cont. int	(1,507)		(507)
	US$		US$
Earns. per sh. bef. disc. opers.*	(0.34)		(0.16)
Earnings per share*	(0.34)		(0.17)

* Subord. vtg.
◻ Restated
[A] Reported in accordance with U.S. GAAP

Historical Summary
(as originally stated)

Fiscal Year	Oper. Rev.	Net Inc. Bef. Disc.	EPS*
	US$000s	US$000s	US$
2022[A]	1,239,812	(205,165)	(1.06)
2021[A]	938,385	17,445	0.13
2020[A]	521,533	62,999	0.55
2019[B]	252,819	178,033	1.62
2018[B1]	102,817	42,968	0.42

* Subord. vtg.
[A] Reported in accordance with U.S. GAAP
[B] Reported in accordance with IFRS
[1] Results reflect the Sept. 21, 2018, reverse takeover acquisition of Truelieve, Inc.

T.100 TrustBIX Inc.

Symbol - TBIX **Exchange -** TSX-VEN **CUSIP -** 89835T

Head Office - 200-10607 82 St, Edmonton, AB, T6A 3N2 **Telephone** - (780) 456-2207 **Toll-free -** (866) 456-2207 **Fax -** (800) 475-4603

Website - www.trustbix.com

Email - hlau@trustbix.com

Investor Relations - Hubert Lau (780) 456-2207

Auditors - Kenway Mack Slusarchuk Stewart LLP C.A., Calgary, Alta.

Transfer Agents - Computershare Trust Company of Canada Inc.

Profile - (Alta. 2013) Developing Business InfoXchange (BIX), a cattle and food traceability system; provides solutions for the livestock industry including livestock auction market software, livestock feedlot management software and an electronic system for grading and pricing pork carcasses; and offers solutions to track, protect and identify the movement of high-value moveable equipment in agriculture and other industries.

BIX is a web-based data exchange platform that can be used by cattle producers to collect and deliver information on traceability and chain of custody to prove to customers and retailers that they adhere to the highest standards for food safety, animal care and environmental stewardship. The company creates strategic sourcing for transactional opportunities within a supply chain or value chain where the company creates increased value or volume of agricultural products to upstream suppliers, often ranchers, farmers and producers. The first strategic sourcing was established with The Canadian Beef Sustainability Acceleration, where the company continues to collaborate with industry leaders to provide funding to participants that produce cattle, throughout the entire supply chain. The company is also pursuing to strategically source and supply premium beef products to customers globally.

The company's ViewTrak portfolio of products include Auction MasterPro and MarketMaster livestock auction market software solutions to help build and operate auction activities; Feedlot Solutions, livestock feedlot management software for feedlots in Canada, U.S., Mexico and the People's Republic of China; and Electronic Pork Graders for grading and pricing pork carcasses evaluating carcasses for fat thickness, lean meat thickness, meat percentage and carcass class.

The company's Insight technology offers an edge-to-enterprise supply chain solution that brings asset situational awareness to dealers, equipment fleets, and civil construction managers. The platform allows for the tracking, protection, and identification of movement of assets using self-powered and self-reporting cellular tags and cloud-based suite of tools.

Also holds license from **Green MetricsTechnologies Ltd.** to resell Green MetricsBuildSense® suite of energy management solutions, which include Build Aware for facilitating the collection of energy usage data to benchmark an operation's baseline energy usage against peers; Build Sight for capturing on-premise electrical and mechanical systems for further analysis of load and consumption patterns; and Build Sense for energy management solution based on the insights generated from Build Aware and Build Sight, combined with an ongoing Software-as-a-Service monitoring solution.

Recent Merger and Acquisition Activity

Status: completed **Revised:** Mar. 7, 2022

UPDATE: The transaction was completed. TrustBIX issued an initial 10,000,000 common shares, with up to an additional 20,000,000 common shares to be issued over the following 12 months upon Insight attaining certain net revenue thresholds. PREVIOUS: TrustBIX Inc. signed a letter of intent to acquire a private Canadian company that provides a tracking solutions platform to track, protect and identify the movement of high-value moveable equipment used in the agriculture industry. Mar. 1, 2022 - A definitive agreement was entered into. The target was identified as private Grande Prairie, Alta.-based Insight Global Technology Inc. Consideration would be the issuance of up to 30,000,000 common shares at a deemed price of 18¢ per share.

Predecessor Detail - Name changed from Reco Northern Alberta Inc., Apr. 15, 2019, pursuant to reverse takeover acquisition of ViewTrak Technologies Inc.

Directors - Edward K. (Ted) Power, v-chr. & corp. sec., Edmonton, Alta.; Hubert Lau, pres. & CEO, Edmonton, Alta.; Lap Shing (Andrew) Kao, Hong Kong, People's Republic of China; Nathaniel (Nathan) Mison, Edmonton, Alta.; Frank Yang, Montréal, Qué.

Other Exec. Officers - William Harper, CFO; Deborah Wilson, sr. v-p, channel sales & industry rel.; Dr. Mike Kennedy, v-p, tech. devel.

Capital Stock

	Authorized (shs.)	Outstanding (shs.)[1]
Preferrred	unlimited	nil
Common	unlimited	94,430,474

[1] At Mar. 13, 2023

Major Shareholder - Widely held at Mar. 13, 2023.

Price Range - TBIX/TSX-VEN

Year	Volume	High	Low	Close
2022	12,747,980	$0.25	$0.03	$0.04
2021	19,825,937	$1.05	$0.13	$0.17
2020	550,275	$0.61	$0.02	$0.23
2019	35,300	$0.68	$0.50	$0.60

Recent Close: $0.02

Capital Stock Changes - In February 2023, private placement of 7,142,857 common shares was completed at $0.035 per share. An additional 7,142,857 common shares were to be issued.

In December 2021, private placement of 4,406,250 common shares was completed at 16¢ per share. In February and March 2022, private placement of 6,324,334 units (1 common share & 1 warrant) at 18¢ per unit was completed. Also during fiscal 2022, common shares were issued as follows: 30,000,000 pursuant to the acquisition of Insight Global Technology Inc. and 533,334 on exercise of options.

Wholly Owned Subsidiaries

Insight Global Technology Inc., Grande Prairie, Alta.
ViewTrak Technologies Inc., Edmonton, Alta.

Financial Statistics

Periods ended:	12m Sept. 30/22[A]		12m Sept. 30/21[A]
	$000s	%Chg	$000s
Operating revenue	**1,675**	**-23**	**2,169**
Salaries & benefits	2,288		1,742
Research & devel. expense	339		220
General & admin expense	2,629		2,188
Operating expense	**5,255**	**+27**	**4,150**
Operating income	**(3,580)**	**n.a.**	**(1,981)**
Deprec., depl. & amort.	378		88
Finance income	1		8
Finance costs, gross	129		134
Write-downs/write-offs	nil		(4)
Pre-tax income	**(4,067)**	**n.a.**	**(2,239)**
Net income	**(4,067)**	**n.a.**	**(2,239)**
Cash & equivalent	127		450
Inventories	75		58
Accounts receivable	70		254
Current assets	358		810
Long-term investments	180		334
Fixed assets, net	32		41
Right-of-use assets	32		41
Intangibles, net	1,476		10
Total assets	**2,079**	**+68**	**1,236**
Accts. pay. & accr. liabs.	655		450
Current liabilities	1,426		830
Long-term debt, gross	613		614
Long-term debt, net	613		614
Long-term lease liabilities	26		4
Shareholders' equity	13		(212)
Cash from oper. activs.	**(2,576)**	**n.a.**	**(2,141)**
Cash from fin. activs.	2,075		1,891
Cash from invest. activs.	178		(14)
Net cash position	**127**	**-72**	**450**
Capital expenditures	(3)		(14)
	$		$
Earnings per share*	(0.08)		(0.06)
Cash flow per share*	(0.05)		(0.06)
	shs		shs
No. of shs. o/s*	79,649,831		38,385,913
Avg. no. of shs. o/s*	50,705,085		34,984,110
	%		%
Net profit margin	(242.81)		(103.23)
Return on equity	n.m.		n.m.
Return on assets	(237.59)		(154.89)
Foreign sales percent	47		36

* Common
[A] Reported in accordance with IFRS

Historical Summary
(as originally stated)

Fiscal Year	Oper. Rev.	Net Inc. Bef. Disc.	EPS*
	$000s	$000s	$
2022[A]	1,675	(4,067)	(0.08)
2021[A]	2,169	(2,239)	(0.06)
2020[A]	1,627	(2,335)	(0.09)
2019[A1]	1,641	(3,393)	(0.18)
2018[A]	1,526	(1,245)	n.a.

* Common
[A] Reported in accordance with IFRS
[1] Results prior to Apr. 25, 2019, pertain to and reflect the reverse takeover acquisition of ViewTrak Technologies Inc.

T.101 TruTrace Technologies Inc.

Symbol - TTT **Exchange** - CSE **CUSIP** - 898447
Head Office - 61 Regal Rd, Toronto, ON, M6H 2J6 **Toll-free** - (888) 775-4888 **Fax** - (888) 241-5996
Website - www.trutrace.co
Email - robert@trutrace.co
Investor Relations - Robert Galarza (888) 775-4888
Auditors - Dale Matheson Carr-Hilton LaBonte LLP C.A., Vancouver, B.C.
Transfer Agents - Computershare Trust Company of Canada Inc., Vancouver, B.C.

Profile - (B.C. 2011) Offers a blockchain traceability software platform which gives clients in the food, cosmetics, pharmaceuticals and cannabis industry the ability to store, manage, share and access quality assurance and testing details, Certificates of Authenticity (CoA) and other product information as well as motion and movement intelligence on inventory from batches and lots of serialized items.

Has developed TruTrace Enterprise™, a cloud-based platform specifically designed to power the traceability of testing standards within the nutraceutical, food and pharmaceutical space with a focus on the authentication of source materials or ingredients used in formulation. Features include real-time collaboration module, inventory management system, risk mitigation, recall prevention and management, expanded digital documentation system, updated and enhanced product scan page, expanded application programming interface capabilities, and blockchain and Internet of Things integration capabilities.

Also offers StrainSecure™ is a fully-integrated blockchain platform which registers and tracks intellectual property and mandatory testing data for the cannabis industry, allowing breeders and growers to protect and release their genetics, strain varieties, and validated testing results into the public domain. The platform tracks the quality of products throughout the supply chain, including within the legal cannabis industry from genome to sale. StrainSecure™ records are proprietary, immutable and cryptographically secure, thereby establishing, in a single source, an accurate, validated, and permanent account for cannabis strains from ownership to market.

Predecessor Detail - Name changed from Blockstrain Technology Corp., Apr. 24, 2019.

Directors - Allan O'Dette, chr., Ont.; Robert Galarza, CEO, Vancouver, B.C.; Cesare Fazari, Toronto, Ont.

Other Exec. Officers - Robert Lelovic, CFO; Dr. James LaValle, chief medical mgr.; Thomas (Tommy) Stephenson, chief tech. officer; Swapan Kakumanu, corp. sec.

Capital Stock

	Authorized (shs.)	Outstanding (shs.)[1]
Common	unlimited	152,693,781

[1] At Sept. 28, 2022

Major Shareholder - Thomas (Tommy) Stephenson held 12.9% interest at Aug. 22, 2022.

Price Range - TTT/CSE

Year	Volume	High	Low	Close
2022	19,326,346	$0.05	$0.01	$0.01
2021	64,733,498	$0.23	$0.04	$0.05
2020	39,500,305	$0.13	$0.03	$0.05
2019	78,394,226	$0.50	$0.06	$0.08
2018	66,427,486	$1.20	$0.11	$0.13

Recent Close: $0.01

Capital Stock Changes - There were no changes to capital stock during fiscal 2022.

Wholly Owned Subsidiaries

TruTrace Technologies Group Inc., Vancouver, B.C.
TruTrace Technologies (USA), Inc., Del.

Financial Statistics

Periods ended:	12m Apr. 30/22[A]		12m Apr. 30/21[A]
	$000s	%Chg	$000s
Operating revenue	**118**	**-28**	**163**
Salaries & benefits	555		501
Research & devel. expense	161		371
General & admin expense	464		570
Stock-based compensation	308		189
Operating expense	**1,488**	**-9**	**1,631**
Operating income	**(1,370)**	**n.a.**	**(1,468)**
Deprec., depl. & amort.	79		68
Finance costs, gross	14		45
Write-downs/write-offs	(882)		nil
Pre-tax income	**(2,335)**	**n.a.**	**(1,621)**
Net income	**(2,335)**	**n.a.**	**(1,621)**
Cash & equivalent	4		1,014
Current assets	109		1,100
Fixed assets, net	9		12
Intangibles, net	nil		317
Total assets	**117**	**-92**	**1,429**
Accts. pay. & accr. liabs.	1,952		1,801
Current liabilities	2,592		1,801
Long-term debt, gross	685		121
Long-term debt, net	45		121
Shareholders' equity	(2,520)		(493)
Cash from oper. activs.	**(921)**	**n.a.**	**(826)**
Cash from fin. activs.	552		1,827
Cash from invest. activs.	(640)		nil
Net cash position	**4**	**-100**	**1,014**
	$		$
Earnings per share*	(0.02)		(0.01)
Cash flow per share*	(0.01)		(0.01)
	shs		shs
No. of shs. o/s*	152,693,781		152,693,781
Avg. no. of shs. o/s*	152,693,781		114,500,815
	%		%
Net profit margin	n.m.		(994.48)
Return on equity	n.m.		n.m.
Return on assets	(300.26)		(207.50)

* Common
[A] Reported in accordance with IFRS

Latest Results

Periods ended:	3m July 31/22[A]		3m July 31/21[A]
	$000s	%Chg	$000s
Operating revenue	4	-83	23
Net income	(259)	n.a.	(282)
	$		$
Earnings per share*	(0.00)		(0.00)

* Common
[A] Reported in accordance with IFRS

Historical Summary
(as originally stated)

Fiscal Year	Oper. Rev.	Net Inc. Bef. Disc.	EPS*
	$000s	$000s	$
2022[A]	118	(2,335)	(0.02)
2021[A]	163	(1,621)	(0.01)
2020[A]	403	(4,639)	(0.06)
2019[A1]	10	(14,773)	(0.19)
2018[A2]	nil	(528)	n.a.

* Common
[A] Reported in accordance with IFRS
[1] Results prior to May 17, 2018, pertain to and reflect the Qualifying Transaction reverse takeover acquisition of (old) BlockStrain Technology Corp.
[2] 23 weeks ended Apr. 30, 2018.

T.102 Tucows Inc.

Symbol - TC **Exchange** - TSX **CUSIP** - 898697
Head Office - 96 Mowat Ave, Toronto, ON, M6K 3M1 **Telephone** - (416) 535-0123 **Toll-free** - (800) 371-6992 **Fax** - (416) 531-5584
Website - www.tucows.com
Email - mwebb@tucows.com
Investor Relations - Monica Webb (416) 535-0123 ext. 1238
Auditors - KPMG LLP C.A., Toronto, Ont.
Transfer Agents - Computershare Investor Services, LLC; TSX Trust Company, Toronto, Ont.
FP500 Revenue Ranking - 507
Employees - 1,020 at Dec. 31, 2022

Profile - (Pa. 1992) Provides network access, domain names and other Internet services.

Operations are organized into three segments: Ting; Wavelo; and Tucows Domains.

The **Ting** segment provides fixed high-speed Internet access services in select towns throughout the U.S. As at Dec. 31, 2022, Ting Internet had access to 116,000 owned and partner infrastructure serviceable addresses and 35,000 active accounts under its management compared to having access to 91,000 owned and partner infrastructure serviceable addresses and 26,000 active accounts under its management as at Dec. 31, 2021.

The **Wavelo** segment includes full-service platforms and professional services that provide solutions delivering a wide range of functions, such as subscription and billing management, network orchestration and provisioning and individual developer tools, to communication service providers. The segment also provides billing solutions to Internet service providers under the Platypus brand.

The **Tucows Domains** segment include wholesale and retail domain name registration services and value-added services. OpenSRS®, eNom®, EPAG® and Ascio®, the wholesale services group, manages 24,000,000 domain names under the Tucows®, eNom®, EPAG® and Ascio® ICANN registrar accreditation and for other registrars under their own accreditations. Value-added services include hosted email, which provides email delivery and webmail access to millions of mailboxes, Internet security services, Internet hosting, WHOIS privacy, publishing tools and reseller billing services. The Hover® and eNom® websites, the retail services group, offers domain name registration and email services to individuals and small businesses, as well as Personal Names Service, which is based on more than 36,000 surname domains and allows more than 66% of Americans to acquire an email address based on their last names. Retail services also includes the sale of the rights to the company's portfolio of surname domains used in connection with Realnames email service, as well as the exact hosting service, that provides Linux hosting services for individual and small business websites.

Directors - Allen Karp†, chr., emeritus, Toronto, Ont.; Robin Chase, chr., Cambridge, Mass.; Elliot Noss, pres. & CEO, Toronto, Ont.; Brad Burnham, New York, N.Y.; Marlene Carl; Erez Gissin, Ramat HaSharon, Israel; Jeffrey Schwartz, Toronto, Ont.

Other Exec. Officers - Davinder (Dave) Singh, CFO; Bret Fausett, chief legal officer & gen. counsel; Michael Goldstein, chief revenue officer, Ting; Hanno Liem, chief tech. officer; Justin Reilly, pres., Wavelo; David Woroch, CEO, Tucows Domain Srvcs.
† Lead director

Capital Stock

	Authorized (shs.)	Outstanding (shs.)[1]
Preferred	1,250,000	nil
Common	250,000,000	10,829,711

[1] At Mar. 13, 2023

Major Shareholder - Investmentaktiengesellschaft für langfristige Investoren TGV held 16.66% interest at Apr. 5, 2023.

Price Range - TC/TSX

Year	Volume	High	Low	Close
2022	4,718,602	$106.00	$38.23	$46.03
2021	963,680	$120.21	$89.60	$106.21
2020	697,606	$103.47	$59.12	$94.47
2019	711,395	$120.79	$60.15	$81.83
2018	559,878	$88.99	$62.85	$81.97

Recent Close: $31.04

Capital Stock Changes - During 2022, common shares were issued as follows: 40,459 on exercise options and 32,287 as stock-based compensation; 3,053 common shares were cancelled.

Wholly Owned Subsidiaries

Tucows (Delaware) Inc., Del.
- 100% int. in **Ting Fiber Inc.**, Del.
  - 100% int. in **Cedar Holdings Group, Incorporated**, Durango, Colo.
    - 100% int. in **Zippytech Inc.**, Colo.
    - 100% int. in **Zippytech of New Mexico Inc.**, N.M.
  - 100% int. in **Simply Bits, LLC**, Ariz.
  - 100% int. in **Ting Telecom California LLC**, Del.
  - 100% int. in **Ting Virginia, LLC**, Va.
    - 100% int. in **Blue Ridge Websoft, LLC**, Va.
    - 100% int. in **Fiber Roads, LLC**, Va.
    - 100% int. in **Navigator Network Services, LLC**, Va.
  - 100% int. in **Tucows (Emerald), LLC**, Del.
    - 100% int. in **eNom, LLC**, Del.
      - 100% int. in **eNom Canada Corp.**, N.S.
      - 100% int. in **Secure Business Services, Inc.**, Nev.
      - 100% int. in **Whois Privacy Protection Services, Inc**, Nev.
- 100% int. in **Ting Inc.**, Del.
- 100% int. in **Tucows Corp.**, Miss.
- 100% int. in **Tucows Domains Services, Inc.**, Del.
- 100% int. in **Tucows Fiber, Inc.**, Del.
  - 100% int. in **Ting Fiber, LLC**, Del.
- 100% int. in **Tucows.com Co.**, N.S.
  - 100% int. in **Ascio Technologies Corp.**, N.S.
  - 100% int. in **Contact Privacy Inc.**, Ont.
  - 100% int. in **Tucows (Australia) Pty Limited**, Vic., Australia.
  - 100% int. in **Tucows (Germany) Inc.**, Bonn, Germany.
    - 100% int. in **EPAG Domainservices GmbH**, N.S.
  - 100% int. in **Tucows (UK) Limited**, United Kingdom.
  - 100% int. in **Tucows Domains Inc.**, Ont.
- 100% int. in **Wavelo, Inc.**, Del.

Financial Statistics

Periods ended:	12m Dec. 31/22[A]		12m Dec. 31/21[A]
	US$000s	%Chg	US$000s
Operating revenue	**321,142**	**+6**	**304,337**
Cost of sales	196,268		193,039
General & admin expense	78,638		58,604
Stock-based compensation	7,599		4,592
Other operating expense	30,165		27,724
Operating expense	**312,670**	**+10**	**283,959**
Operating income	**8,472**	**-58**	**20,378**
Deprec., depl. & amort.	39,581		27,993
Finance costs, net	14,456		4,617
Write-downs/write-offs	(92)		(201)
Pre-tax income	**(27,788)**	**n.a.**	**7,270**
Income taxes	(217)		3,906
Net income	**(27,571)**	**n.a.**	**3,364**
Cash & equivalent	23,496		9,105
Inventories	7,284		3,277
Accounts receivable	18,404		14,579
Current assets	16,920		147,004
Long-term investments	2,012		2,012
Fixed assets, net	281,495		172,662
Right-of-use assets	20,489		17,515
Intangibles, net	170,200		180,819
Total assets	**664,747**	**+23**	**539,596**
Accts. pay. & accr. liabs	39,824		25,256
Current liabilities	188,189		173,683
Long-term debt, gross	238,930		190,748
Long-term debt, net	238,930		190,748
Long-term lease liabilities	12,438		11,853
Shareholders' equity	96,657		115,092
Cash from oper. activs	**19,876**	**-33**	**29,637**
Cash from fin. activs	132,007		73,135
Cash from invest. activs	(137,492)		(101,978)
Net cash position	**23,496**	**+158**	**9,105**
Capital expenditures	(136,710)		(73,175)
Capital disposals	nil		510
	US$		US$
Earnings per share*	(2.56)		0.32
Cash flow per share*	1.85		2.78
	shs		shs
No. of shs. o/s*	10,817,110		10,747,417
Avg. no. of shs. o/s*	10,769,280		10,662,337
	%		%
Net profit margin	(8.59)		1.11
Return on equity	(26.04)		3.06
Return on assets	(4.58)		0.68
No. of employees (FTEs)	1,020		1,000

* Common

[A] Reported in accordance with U.S. GAAP

Historical Summary
(as originally stated)

Fiscal Year	Oper. Rev. US$000s	Net Inc. Bef. Disc. US$000s	EPS* US$
2022[A]	321,142	(27,571)	(2.56)
2021[A]	304,337	3,364	0.32
2020[A]	311,202	5,775	0.55
2019[A]	337,145	15,398	1.45
2018[A]	346,013	17,135	1.62

* Common

[A] Reported in accordance with U.S. GAAP

T.103 Turnium Technology Group Inc.

Symbol - TTGI **Exchange** - TSX-VEN **CUSIP** - 90043C
Head Office - 1127 15 St W, North Vancouver, BC, V7P 1M7
Telephone - (778) 945-1075 **Toll-free** - (888) 818-3361
Website - www.ttgi.io
Email - johan@ttgi.io
Investor Relations - Johan Arnet (778) 945-1075
Auditors - Manning Elliott LLP C.A., Vancouver, B.C.
Transfer Agents - Computershare Trust Company of Canada Inc., Vancouver, B.C.

Profile - (B.C. 2017) Develops and commercializes a software-defined wide area networking (SD-WAN) platform, used to build communication networks that connect a business' multiple branches or locations to each other as well as to multiple cloud-hosted applications, data and storage.

The company's SD-WAN product can be hosted, managed, branded and sold by customers and a managed SD-WAN service that customers can buy and resell or use themselves. SD-WAN makes it easy to deploy and manage secure private networks using a combination of Internet, wireless, 4G/LTE, 5G and fibre connections and obtain features comparable to the dedicated networks and connections offered by traditional telecommunications providers.

Provides two products, Turnium Wholesale SD-WAN, a wholesale white-label software platform sold to channel partners that want to own, run, manage, and brand their own SD-WAN solution; and Turnium Managed SD-WAN, a turnkey managed SD-WAN service that is re-sold by channel partners who want to add a Turnium-branded offer to their sales portfolio without the expense or complication of running the platform themselves.

The company hosts and delivers its managed service from its own data centres in Vancouver, B.C., Calgary, Alta., Toronto, Ont., New York, N.Y., and Los Angeles, Calif.

Earns revenue from a combination of upfront site licence fees, set-up fees, support and maintenance fees and monthly per-site licence fees. Through wholly owned **Tenacious Networks Inc.**, resells computer hardware and licensing from brands such as Lenovo and Fortinet and provides professional services.

Recent Merger and Acquisition Activity

Status: completed **Revised:** June 20, 2022

UPDATE: The transaction was completed. TTGI amalgamated with a wholly owned subsidiary of RMR to continue as TTGI OpCo Inc., and RMR changed its name to Turnium Technology Group Inc. PREVIOUS: RMR Science Technologies Inc. entered into a letter of intent for the Qualifying Transaction reverse takeover acquisition of Turnium Technology Group, Inc. (TTGI) on the basis of five RMR common shares for each TTGI share held. TTGI plans to raise up to $1,500,000 through a bridge financing of up to 3,125,000 units at $0.48 per unit and raise up to $10,000,000 via a subscription receipt financing of up to $17,857,143 subscription receipts at $0.56 per receipt. TTGI delivers its software-defined wide area networking (SD-WAN) solution as a managed cloud-native service and as a licensed OEM white label software platform. Dec. 21, 2021 -The parties entered into a definitive amalgamation agreement whereby 1333633 B.C. Ltd., a wholly owned subsidiary of RMR, and TTGI would amalgamate to form TTGI OpCo Inc. RMR would complete the acquisition on a share-for-share basis (following a 1-for-5 share consolidation). Feb. 17, 2022 - Conditional TSX Venture Exchange approval was received.

Predecessor Detail - Name changed from RMR Science Technologies Inc., June 16, 2022, pursuant to the Qualifying Transaction reverse takeover acquisition of Turnium Technology Group, Inc. (old TTGI). and concurrent amalgamation of old TTGI and wholly owned 1333633 B.C. Ltd., to continue as TTGI OpCo Inc.; basis 1 new for 5 old shs.

Directors - Ralph Garcea, chr., Caledon, Ont.; Derek W. Spratt, CEO & interim CFO, Vancouver, B.C.; Johan Arnet, North Vancouver, B.C.; Evelyn Bailey, Port Carling, Ont.; Erin Campbell, Alta.; Peter Green, West Vancouver, B.C.; James S. (Jim) Lovie, Toronto, Ont.; Peter C. Smyrniotis, Vancouver, B.C.

Other Exec. Officers - Geoff Hultin, chief comml. officer; Logan Campbell, exec. v-p, global sales; Josh Hicks, v-p, R&D; Tak Tsan (Simon) Tso, contr.; Aaron Patton, pres., Tenacious Networks Inc.

Capital Stock

	Authorized (shs.)	Outstanding (shs.)[1]
Class B Preferred	unlimited	nil
Class A Common	unlimited	68,865,009

[1] At Mar. 6, 2023

Major Shareholder - Murray Duncan held 12.82% interest, Vassilios (Bill) Mitoulas held 11.52% interest and Ralph Garcea held 10.93% interest at Nov. 19, 2021.

Price Range - TTGI/TSX-VEN

Year	Volume	High	Low	Close
2022	2,001,536	$0.60	$0.07	$0.12
2021	15,600	$0.70	$0.40	$0.50
2018	281,429	$2.50	$1.00	$1.95

Consolidation: 1-for-5 cons. in June 2022

Recent Close: $0.09

Capital Stock Changes - In October 2021, private placement of 2,500,000 class A common shares was completed at 8¢ per share. In June 2022, class A common shares were consolidated on a 1-for-5 basis and 66,492,926 post-consolidated class A common shares were issued pursuant to the Qualifying Transaction reverse takeover acquisition of Turnium Technology Group, Inc. (old TTGI).

Wholly Owned Subsidiaries

TTGI OpCo Inc.
- 100% int. in **Tenacious Networks Inc.**, Vancouver, B.C.

Financial Statistics

Periods ended:	12m Sept. 30/21[A1]		12m Sept. 30/20[A]
	$000s	%Chg	$000s
Operating revenue	**3,950**	**+40**	**2,828**
Cost of goods sold	724		233
Research & devel. expense	810		544
General & admin expense	3,746		3,584
Stock-based compensation	2,317		nil
Operating expense	**7,597**	**+74**	**4,361**
Operating income	**(3,647)**	**n.a.**	**(1,533)**
Deprec., depl. & amort.	51		34
Finance costs, gross	396		293
Write-downs/write-offs	(1,718)		(12)
Pre-tax income	**(5,705)**	**n.a.**	**(1,477)**
Income taxes	(80)		nil
Net income	**(5,624)**	**n.a.**	**(1,477)**
Cash & equivalent	432		437
Accounts receivable	518		335
Current assets	987		779
Fixed assets, net	55		24
Right-of-use assets	nil		45
Intangibles, net	1,451		nil
Total assets	**2,493**	**+194**	**849**
Accts. pay. & accr. liabs.	982		885
Current liabilities	2,509		3,779
Shareholders' equity	(2,977)		(3,015)
Cash from oper. activs.	**(965)**	**n.a.**	**355**
Cash from fin. activs.	920		(85)
Cash from invest. activs.	40		(13)
Net cash position	**432**	**-1**	**437**
Capital expenditures	(38)		(13)
	$		$
Earnings per share*	(0.55)		(0.15)
	shs		shs
No. of shs. o/s	n.a.		n.a.
	%		%
Net profit margin	(142.38)		(52.23)
Return on equity	n.m.		n.m.
Return on assets	(313.20)		n.a.

* Cl.A Common

[A] Reported in accordance with IFRS

[1] Results prior to June 20, 2022, pertain to and reflect the reverse takeover acquisition of Turnium Technology Group, Inc.

Note: Adjusted throughout for 1-for-5 cons. in June 2022

T.104 Two Hands Corporation

Symbol - TWOH **Exchange** - CSE **CUSIP** - 90187E

Head Office - 1035 Queensway E, Mississauga, ON, L4Y 4C1

Telephone - (416) 357-0399

Website - twohandsgroup.com

Email - nadav@twohandsapp.com

Investor Relations - Nadav Elituv (416) 357-0399

Auditors - Sadler, Gibb & Associates, LLC C.P.A., Draper, Utah

Transfer Agents - Transhare Corporation, Englewood, Colo.

Profile - (Del. 2009) Operates gocart.city grocery delivery application for southern Ontario; Grocery Originals, a physical grocery store in Mississauga, Ont.; and Cuore Food Services, a food import and distribution business.

Products offered on gocart.city include produce, meats, pantry items, bakery and pastry goods, gluten free goods and organic items.

Cuore Food Services focuses on bulk delivery of Italian themed oils, pastas and sauces to dry packed goods, exclusive wines, coffees and desserts to food services businesses including retail chains, hotels and restaurants.

Predecessor Detail - Name changed from Innovative Product Opportunities Inc., July 26, 2016.

Directors - Nadav Elituv, pres., CEO, corp. sec. & treas., Toronto, Ont.; Yan Namer, Toronto, Ont.; Bradley Southam, Cambridge, Ont.; Ryan Wilson, Toronto, Ont.

Other Exec. Officers - Steven Gryfe, CFO

Capital Stock

	Authorized (shs.)	Outstanding (shs.)[1]	Par
Preferred	1,000,000		US$0.001
Series A	200,000	25,000	US$0.01
Series B	100,000	17,000	US$0.01
Series C	150,000	90,000	n.p.v.
Series D	200,000	nil	US$0.001
Common	12,000,000,000	123,415,558	n.p.v.

[1] At Aug. 5, 2022

Series A Preferred - Each convertible into 1,000 common shares. Non-voting.

Series B Preferred - Each convertible, at the holder's option after a one-year holding period, into 1,000 common shares. Non-voting.

Series C Preferred - 10,000 of the series C preferred shares are each convertible, at the holder's option after a six-month holding period, into 400 common shares at a conversion price of US$0.25 per share. 80,000 of the series C preferred shares are each convertible, at the holder's option after a six-month holding period, into 100 common shares at a conversion price of US$0.25 per share. Non-voting.

Series D Preferred - Each convertible, at the holder's option after a six-month holding period, into 100 common shares. Non-voting.

Common - One vote per share.

Major Shareholder - Nadav Elituv held 72.99% interest at Aug. 5, 2022.

Price Range - TWOH/CSE

Year	Volume	High	Low	Close
2022	5,179,103	$0.65	$0.01	$0.01

Recent Close: $0.01

Capital Stock Changes - On Apr. 27, 2022, 90,000,000 common shares were issued to president & CEO Nadav Elituv pursuant to an employment agreement. On Apr. 28, 2022, 4,000 series B preferred shares were converted into 4,000,000 common shares. On May 4, 2022, all 40,000 series D preferred shares were converted into 4,000,000 common shares. On July 26, 2022, 175,000 series A preferred shares were returned to treasury and cancelled.

Wholly Owned Subsidiaries

Two Hands Canada Corporation, Thornhill, Ont.

Financial Statistics

Periods ended:	12m Dec. 31/21[A1]		12m Dec. 31/20[A1]
	US$000s	%Chg	US$000s
Operating revenue	**930**	**+485**	**159**
Cost of goods sold	833		138
Salaries & benefits	401		1,972
General & admin expense	1,800		630
Stock-based compensation	1,043		2,922
Operating expense	**4,077**	**-28**	**5,663**
Operating income	**(3,147)**	**n.a.**	**(5,504)**
Deprec., depl. & amort.	2		1
Finance costs, gross	357		239
Write-downs/write-offs	(21)		nil
Pre-tax income	**(16,336)**	**n.a.**	**(7,666)**
Net income	**(16,336)**	**n.a.**	**(7,666)**
Cash & equivalent	533		22
Inventories	155		nil
Accounts receivable	163		41
Current assets	1,609		964
Fixed assets, net	7		3
Right-of-use assets	34		nil
Total assets	**1,649**	**+71**	**967**
Bank indebtedness	6		91
Accts. pay. & accr. liabs.	498		163
Current liabilities	553		608
Long-term debt, gross	728		1,122
Long-term debt, net	728		1,047
Shareholders' equity	(3,736)		(2,784)
Cash from oper. activs.	**(556)**	**n.a.**	**(314)**
Cash from fin. activs.	1,070		338
Cash from invest. activs.	(5)		(2)
Net cash position	**533**	**n.m.**	**22**
Capital expenditures	(5)		(2)
	US$		US$
Earnings per share*	(5.79)		(37.13)
Cash flow per share*	(0.20)		(1.52)
	shs		shs
No. of shs. o/s*	6,000,000		695,576
Avg. no. of shs. o/s*	2,820,094		206,467
	%		%
Net profit margin	n.m.		n.m.
Return on equity	n.m.		n.m.
Return on assets	n.m.		n.a.

* Common

[A] Reported in accordance with U.S. GAAP

[1] As shown in the prospectus dated Apr. 21, 2022. Shares and per share figures adjusted to reflect 1-for-1000 consolidation effective Apr. 27, 2022.

Latest Results

Periods ended:	3m Mar. 31/22[A]		3m Mar. 31/21[A]
	US$000s	%Chg	US$000s
Operating revenue	199	+5	189
Net income	(1,355)	n.a.	(2,891)
	US$		US$
Earnings per share*	(0.20)		(2.99)

* Common

[A] Reported in accordance with U.S. GAAP

U

U.1 UGE International Ltd.

Symbol - UGE **Exchange** - TSX-VEN **CUSIP** - 903510
Head Office - 700-56 Temperance St, Toronto, ON, M5H 3V5 **Telephone** - (416) 789-4655
Website - www.ugei.com
Email - nick.blitterswyk@ugei.com
Investor Relations - Nicolas Blitterswyk (917) 720-5685
Auditors - KPMG LLP C.A., Toronto, Ont.
Lawyers - CP LLP, Toronto, Ont.
Transfer Agents - TSX Trust Company, Toronto, Ont.
Employees - 70 at Dec. 31, 2022

Profile - (Ont. 2011) Develops, builds, owns, operates and finances solar and energy storage projects within the U.S. and the Philippines. Also provides engineering and consulting services globally.

Provides commercial and community solar energy solutions through leasing a building owner's roof space, carports or vacant land, paying annual lease payment to the owner and selling energy to the grid through community solar programs; or the company utilizing the roof space and the client buying the energy through Power Purchase Agreement at a fixed price throughout the contract lifetime.

The company has more than 500 MW of solar project experience since its founding in 2010. At Mar. 31, 2023, the company's total order backlog across the U.S. and the Philippines includes 87 projects with expected average annual revenue of US$22,153,981.

In October 2022, the company acquired a 3.5-MW ground-mounted community solar project in Polk cty., Ore., for an undisclosed amount. Commercial operation for the project is expected in the first quarter of 2024.

Predecessor Detail - Name changed from Way Ventures Inc., July 24, 2014, following Qualifying Transaction reverse takeover acquisition of UGE Holdings Limited; basis 1 new for 5 old shs.

Directors - Nicolas (Nick) Blitterswyk, founder & CEO, New York, N.Y.; Christopher Asimakis, Toronto, Ont.; Stephen (Steve) Blum, N.Y.; Yun (Wendy) Liu, Zurich, Switzerland; Scot Melland; Xiangrong Xie, Beijing, Beijing, People's Republic of China; Jian Yang, Toronto, Ont.

Other Exec. Officers - Brandon McNeil, COO; Stephanie M. Bird, CFO; Tyler Adkins, chief revenue officer; Andrew Hines, chief comml. officer

Capital Stock

	Authorized (shs.)	Outstanding (shs.)[1]
Common	unlimited	32,921,770

[1] At May 24, 2023

Major Shareholder - Junfei Liu held 15.2% interest and Xiangrong Xie held 11.2% interest at May 15, 2023.

Price Range - UGE/TSX-VEN

Year	Volume	High	Low	Close
2022	7,443,884	$1.89	$0.72	$1.40
2021	18,047,752	$3.24	$1.15	$1.69
2020	17,279,594	$2.39	$0.13	$1.98
2019	3,426,944	$0.78	$0.13	$0.13
2018	4,539,536	$1.68	$0.36	$0.44

Consolidation: 1-for-4 cons. in Dec. 2019
Recent Close: $1.30
Capital Stock Changes - During 2022, 655,667 common shares were issued on exercise of options.

Wholly Owned Subsidiaries

UGE Canada RE Ltd., Canada.
UGE Capital LLC
UGE Consulting Services Co. Ltd., Canada.
UGE Dev LLC
UGE EPC LLC
UGE Philippines, Inc., Philippines.
UGE Project HoldCo Ltd., Toronto, Ont.
UGE U.S.A. Inc., N.Y.

Financial Statistics

Periods ended:	12m Dec. 31/22[A]		12m Dec. 31/21[A]
	US$000s	%Chg	US$000s
Operating revenue	**3,831**	**+42**	**2,700**
Cost of sales	2,434		1,829
Salaries & benefits	4,363		3,015
General & admin expense	2,374		1,805
Stock-based compensation	425		652
Operating expense	**9,869**	**+35**	**7,300**
Operating income	**(6,038)**	**n.a.**	**(4,600)**
Deprec., depl. & amort.	128		65
Finance income	49		42
Finance costs, gross	1,146		351
Write-downs/write-offs	(37)		151
Pre-tax income	**(7,448)**	**n.a.**	**(4,325)**
Income taxes	nil		(163)
Net income	**(7,448)**	**n.a.**	**(4,162)**
Cash & equivalent	2,091		1,252
Accounts receivable	1,333		1,116
Current assets	3,875		2,652
Fixed assets, net	5,851		2,658
Right-of-use assets	21,122		12,182
Total assets	**37,784**	**+95**	**19,339**
Accts. pay. & accr. liabs	2,820		2,196
Current liabilities	5,746		3,021
Long-term debt, gross	19,056		5,394
Long-term debt, net	16,808		5,144
Long-term lease liabilities	...		12,150
Shareholders' equity	(7,769)		(1,339)
Cash from oper. activs	**(6,542)**	**n.a.**	**(5,439)**
Cash from fin. activs	13,199		7,730
Cash from invest. activs	(5,694)		(2,074)
Net cash position	**2,091**	**+67**	**1,252**
Capital expenditures	(5,784)		(1,932)
	US$		US$
Earnings per share*	(0.23)		(0.13)
Cash flow per share*	(0.20)		(0.18)
	shs		shs
No. of shs. o/s*	32,895,075		32,239,408
Avg. no. of shs. o/s*	32,536,132		31,015,003
	%		%
Net profit margin	(194.41)		(154.15)
Return on equity	n.m.		n.m.
Return on assets	(22.06)		(29.96)
Foreign sales percent	99		98
No. of employees (FTEs)	70		49

* Common
[A] Reported in accordance with IFRS

Latest Results

Periods ended:	3m Mar. 31/23[A]		3m Mar. 31/22[A]
	US$000s	%Chg	US$000s
Operating revenue	522	+43	364
Net income	(2,827)	n.a.	(1,561)
	US$		US$
Earnings per share*	(0.09)		(0.05)

* Common
[A] Reported in accordance with IFRS

Historical Summary
(as originally stated)

Fiscal Year	Oper. Rev. US$000s	Net Inc. Bef. Disc. US$000s	EPS* US$
2022[A]	3,831	(7,448)	(0.23)
2021[A]	2,700	(4,162)	(0.13)
2020[A]	1,440	(992)	(0.04)
2019[A]	5,062	(2,508)	(0.13)
2018[A]	17,192	(6,143)	(0.52)

* Common
[A] Reported in accordance with IFRS
Note: Adjusted throughout for 1-for-4 cons. in Dec. 2019

U.2 US Financial 15 Split Corp.

Symbol - FTU **Exchange** - TSX **CUSIP** - 90341H
Head Office - c/o Quadravest Capital Management Inc., 2510-200 Front St W, PO Box 51, Toronto, ON, M5V 3K2 **Telephone** - (416) 304-4440 **Toll-free** - (877) 478-2372
Website - www.quadravest.com
Email - info@quadravest.com
Investor Relations - Shari Payne (877) 478-2372
Auditors - PricewaterhouseCoopers LLP C.A., Toronto, Ont.
Lawyers - Blake, Cassels & Graydon LLP, Toronto, Ont.
Transfer Agents - Computershare Trust Company of Canada Inc., Toronto, Ont.
Investment Managers - Quadravest Capital Management Inc., Toronto, Ont.
Managers - Quadravest Capital Management Inc., Toronto, Ont.

Profile - (Ont. 2004) Invests in a diversified portfolio primarily consisting of 15 U.S. financial services companies.

The investment portfolio includes the following 15 U.S. financial services companies: **American Express Company, Bank of America Corp., Bank of New York Mellon Corp., Citigroup Inc., CME Group Inc., Fifth Third Bancorp, Goldman Sachs Group Inc., JPMorgan Chase & Co., Morgan Stanley, PNC Financial Services Group Inc., Regions Financial Corp., State Street Corp., Truist Financial Corporation** (formerly **SunTrust Banks Inc.**), **U.S. Bancorp.** and **Wells Fargo & Co.** Shares held within the portfolio are expected to range between 4% and 8% in weight but may vary from time to time. The portfolio may hold up to 20% of its net asset value in equity securities of other issuers.

To supplement the dividends received on the investment portfolio and to reduce risk, the company will from time to time write covered call options in respect of all or part of the common shares in the portfolio.

The company will terminate on Dec. 1, 2024, or earlier at the discretion of the manager if the class A or 2012 preferred shares are delisted by the TSX or if the net asset value of the company declines to less than $5,000,000. At such time, all outstanding class A and 2012 preferred shares will be redeemed. The termination date may be extended beyond Dec. 1, 2024, for a further six years and thereafter for additional successive periods of six years as determined by the board of directors.

The investment manager receives a management fee at an annual rate equal to 0.65% of the net asset value of the company calculated and payable monthly in arrears. In addition, the manager receives an administration fee at an annual rate equal to 0.1% of the net asset value of the company calculated and payable monthly in arrears, as well a service fee payable to dealers on the class A shares at a rate of 0.5% per annum.

Top 10 holdings at May 31, 2023 (as a percentage of net assets):

Holdings	Percentage
Morgan Stanley	10.9%
Goldman Sachs Group Inc.	9.9%
State Street Corp.	7.8%
JPMorgan Chase & Co.	7.4%
Bank of America Corp.	7.3%
PNC Financial Services Group Inc.	6.2%
Fifth Third Bancorp	5.6%
Citigroup Inc.	5.5%
Regions Financial Corp.	4.4%
American Express Company	4.3%

Directors - S. Wayne Finch, chr., pres. & CEO, Caledon, Ont.; Laura L. Johnson, corp. sec., Oakville, Ont.; Peter F. Cruickshank, Oakville, Ont.; Michael W. Sharp, Toronto, Ont.; John D. Steep, Stratford, Ont.

Other Exec. Officers - Silvia Gomes, CFO

Capital Stock

	Authorized (shs.)	Outstanding (shs.)[1]
Class B	1,000	1,000[2]
2012 Preferred	unlimited	1,900,817[2]
Class A	unlimited	1,900,817

[1] At May 31, 2023
[2] Classified as debt.

Class B - Not entitled to dividends. Retractable at $1.00 per share and are entitled to liquidation value of $1.00 per share. Rank prior to 2012 preferred shares and class A shares with respect to the repayment of capital on the dissolution, liquidation or winding-up of the company. One vote per share.

2012 Preferred - Entitled to receive fixed cumulative preferential monthly dividends equal to 10% per annum of the net asset value (NAV) per unit calculated as at the end of the preceding month, up to a monthly maximum dividend of $0.08333 per share. Retractable at any time at a price per share equal to the lesser of: (i) $10; and (ii) 98% of the NAV per unit (1 2012 preferred share and 1 class A share), less the cost to the company of purchasing a class A share in the market for cancellation. Shareholders who concurrently retract one unit in February of each year are entitled to receive an amount equal to the NAV per unit less any expenses (to a maximum of 1% of the NAV per unit) related to liquidating the portfolio to pay such redemption. The company will redeem all outstanding preferred shares at $10 per share upon termination of the company on or about Dec. 1, 2024. Rank in priority to class A with respect to the payment of dividends and in priority to class A shares but subordinate to class B shares with respect to the repayment of capital on the dissolution, liquidation or winding-up of the company. Non-voting except in certain circumstances.

Class A - The company will endeavour to pay monthly dividends as determined by the directors in their discretion. No monthly dividends will be paid as long as any dividends on the 2012 preferred share are in arrears. Retractable by holder at any time at a price per share equal to 98% of the NAV per unit less the cost to the company of purchasing one preferred share in the market for cancellation. Shareholders who concurrently retract one unit in February of each year are entitled to receive an amount equal to the NAV per unit less any expenses (to a maximum of 1% of the NAV per unit) related to liquidating the portfolio to pay such redemption. The company will endeavour to redeem all outstanding class A shares at $15 per share upon termination of the company on or about Dec. 1, 2024. Class A shareholders are also entitled to receive the balance, if any, of the value of the investment portfolio remaining after returning the original issue price to 2012 preferred and class A shareholders. Rank subsequent to preferred and class B shares with respect to payment of dividends and the repayment of capital on the dissolution, liquidation or winding-up of the company. Non-voting except in certain circumstances.

Major Shareholder - US Financial 15 Split Corp. Holding Trust held 100% interest at Feb. 23, 2023.

Price Range - FTU/TSX

Year	Volume	High	Low	Close
2022	475,545	$0.75	$0.28	$0.36
2021	1,347,565	$0.90	$0.27	$0.51
2020	622,026	$0.51	$0.16	$0.29
2019	600,648	$0.70	$0.13	$0.43
2018	801,644	$1.42	$0.46	$0.46

Recent Close: $0.21

Capital Stock Changes - There were no changes to capital stock from fiscal 2020 to fiscal 2022, inclusive.

Dividends

FTU.PR.B 2012 pfd cum. ret. Var. Ra pa M

$0.05008	Sept. 8/23	$0.0475	Aug. 10/23
$0.04667	July 10/23	$0.05008	June 9/23

Paid in 2023: $0.47575 2022: $0.71457 2021: $0.76964

Financial Statistics

Periods ended:	12m Nov. 30/22[A]		12m Nov. 30/21[A]
	$000s	%Chg	$000s
Realized invest. gain (loss)	1,332		665
Unrealized invest. gain (loss)	(1,968)		3,730
Total revenue	**(215)**	**n.a.**	**4,759**
General & admin. expense	205		213
Other operating expense	186		121
Operating expense	**392**	**+17**	**334**
Operating income	**(607)**	**n.a.**	**4,425**
Finance costs, gross	1,359		1,464
Net income	**nil**	**n.a.**	**nil**
Cash & equivalent	1,425		234
Accounts receivable	19		14
Investments	12,240		15,396
Total assets	**13,683**	**-13**	**15,644**
Accts. pay. & accr. liabs	33		35
Debt	13,496		15,463
Cash from oper. activs	**2,530**	**+87**	**1,350**
Cash from fin. activs	(1,386)		(1,422)
Net cash position	**1,425**	**+509**	**234**
	$		$
Earnings per share*	nil		nil
Cash flow per share*	1.33		0.71
	shs		shs
No. of shs. o/s*	1,901,817		1,901,817
Avg. no. of shs. o/s*	1,901,817		1,901,817
	%		%
Net profit margin	n.a.		n.a.
Return on equity	n.m.		n.m.
Return on assets	n.m.		n.m.

* Class A

[A] Reported in accordance with IFRS

Note: Net income reflects increase/decrease in net assets from operations.

Latest Results

Periods ended:	6m May 31/23[A]		6m May 31/22[A]
	$000s	%Chg	$000s
Total revenue	(2,077)	n.a.	1,352
Net income	nil	n.a.	nil
	$		$
Earnings per share*	nil		nil

[A] Reported in accordance with IFRS

Historical Summary
(as originally stated)

Fiscal Year	Total Rev.	Net Inc. Bef. Disc.	EPS*
	$000s	$000s	$
2022[A]	(215)	nil	nil
2021[A]	4,759	nil	nil
2020[A]	(2,005)	nil	nil
2019[A]	1,265	nil	nil
2018[A]	743	nil	nil

* Class A

[A] Reported in accordance with IFRS

Note: Adjusted throughout for 0.6780904-for-1 cons. in Dec. 2018

U.3 Ucore Rare Metals Inc.

Symbol - UCU **Exchange** - TSX-VEN **CUSIP** - 90348V
Head Office - 106-210 Water Front Dr, Bedford, NS, B4A 0H3 **Telephone** - (902) 482-5214 **Fax** - (902) 492-0197
Website - www.ucore.com
Email - mark@ucore.com
Investor Relations - Mark MacDonald (902) 482-5214
Auditors - KPMG LLP C.A., Halifax, N.S.
Lawyers - Stewart McKelvey LLP, Halifax, N.S.
Transfer Agents - Computershare Trust Company of Canada Inc., Toronto, Ont.

Profile - (Alta. 2005) Holds uranium and rare earth interest in Alaska. Also develops technology for the separation and purification of rare earth elements and critical metals in Canada and the United States.

Holds option to acquire Bokan Mountain/Dotson Ridge uranium-rare earth project, 3,800 hectares, 60 km southwest of Ketchikan. A preliminary economic assessment completed in January 2013 proposed an underground mine with an average annual production of 540,000 tonnes over an 11-year mine life. Initial capital costs were estimated at US$221,300,000. At May 2015, indicated resource was 4,787,900 tonnes grading 0.602% total rare earth oxide.

Through wholly owned **Innovations Metals Corp.** (IMC), offers RapidSX™ platform, an accelerated solvent-extraction based technology for the separation and purification of rare earth elements, lithium, nickel, cobalt and other critical metals. A pilot facility utilizing RapidSX™ is being developed in Kingston, Ont., with commissioning targeted to commence in the third quarter of 2023.

In October 2022, the company entered into a letter of intent with **Louisiana Economic Development** with regards to an investment agreement for the development of a strategic metals complex (SMC) in Louisiana. The application includes a commitment to invest a minimum of US$75,000,000 by December 2027 on the facility, and in return, the company negotiated state grants, payroll rebates and tax incentives, among other items. The SMC was expected to initially produce 2,000 tonnes of rare earth oxide per annum, increasing in stages to 5,000 and then 7,500 of rare earth oxide per annum. The company has selected an 80,800-sq.-ft. brownfield facility in Alexandria, La. at Apr. 6, 2023.

In April 2022, the company entered into a memorandum of understanding with Germany-based **thyssenkrupp Materials Services** to supply the company with 1,000 tons of mixed rare earth carbonate (MREC) annually over a 10-year period. The MREC would be used for the development and processing of a 2,000-tonnes-per-annum strategic metals complex facility in Alaska.

Predecessor Detail - Name changed from Ucore Uranium Inc., June 29, 2010.

Directors - Patrick (Pat) Ryan, chr. & CEO, N.S.; Amira Abouali, Ont.; Geoff Clarke, Ont.; Dr. Jaroslav Dostal, Halifax, N.S.; Randy Johnson, Alaska; Steven Meister, N.W.T.

Other Exec. Officers - Geoff Atkins, v-p, bus. devel.; Mark MacDonald, v-p, IR; Peter Manuel, v-p, CFO & corp. sec.; Mike Schrider, v-p, opers. & eng. & COO; Tyler Dilney, contr.

Capital Stock

	Authorized (shs.)	Outstanding (shs.)[1]
First Preferred	unlimited	nil
Second Preferred	unlimited	nil
Common	unlimited	60,962,425

[1] At July 28, 2023

Major Shareholder - Randy Johnson held 12.25% interest and Concept Capital Management Ltd. held 10.05% interest at May 11, 2023.

Price Range - UCU/TSX-VEN

Year	Volume	High	Low	Close
2022	6,563,207	$1.25	$0.53	$0.68
2021	15,298,156	$2.97	$0.71	$0.73
2020	7,929,571	$2.25	$0.70	$1.18
2019	6,364,163	$3.35	$0.85	$2.25
2018	2,391,262	$2.60	$1.10	$1.15

Consolidation: 1-for-10 cons. in Dec. 2020
Recent Close: $0.80

Capital Stock Changes - In July 2023, brokered private placement of 4,822,500 units (1 common share & ½ warrant) at $1.00 per unit was completed, with warrants exercisable at $1.25 per share for three years.

In December 2022, private placement of 7,055,795 units (1 common share & 1 warrant) at 65¢ per unit was completed.

Wholly Owned Subsidiaries

Alaska SMC, LLC, Alaska
Innovation Metals Corp., B.C.
- 100% int. in **American Innovation Metals, LLC**, Del.
- 100% int. in **IMC REE Holdings Corp.**, Del.

Landmark Minerals Inc., Vancouver, B.C.
- 100% int. in **5621 N.W.T. Ltd.**, N.W.T.
  - 49.95% int. in **Landmark Alaska LP**, Alaska
  - 50% int. in **Mineral Solutions LLC**, Alaska
  - 50% int. in **Rare Earth One LLC**, Alaska
    - 0.1% int. in **Landmark Alaska LP**, Alaska
- 100% int. in **Landmark Minerals US Inc.**

Ucore Rare Metals (US) Inc, Alaska
Ucore Resources LP Inc., N.S.
- 49.95% int. in **Landmark Alaska LP**, Alaska
- 50% int. in **Mineral Solutions LLC**, Alaska
- 50% int. in **Rare Earth One LLC**, Alaska

Financial Statistics

Periods ended:	12m Dec. 31/22[A]		12m Dec. 31/21[A]
	$000s	%Chg	$000s
Salaries & benefits	1,524		2,389
Research & devel. expense	1,055		1,395
General & admin expense	1,425		1,424
Stock-based compensation	747		396
Operating expense	**4,751**	**-15**	**5,603**
Operating income	**(4,751)**	**n.a.**	**(5,603)**
Deprec., depl. & amort.	96		115
Finance income	3		9
Finance costs, gross	534		469
Pre-tax income	**(5,469)**	**n.a.**	**(5,511)**
Net income	**(5,469)**	**n.a.**	**(5,511)**
Cash & equivalent	2,263		3,332
Accounts receivable	434		293
Current assets	2,933		3,858
Fixed assets, net	2,402		73
Right-of-use assets	74		163
Intangibles, net	8,089		8,089
Explor./devel. properties	39,674		37,205
Total assets	**53,241**	**+8**	**49,444**
Accts. pay. & accr. liabs	1,490		903
Current liabilities	2,834		994
Long-term debt, gross	3,441		2,335
Long-term debt, net	2,185		2,335
Long-term lease liabilities	nil		87
Shareholders' equity	48,222		46,028
Cash from oper. activs	**(4,465)**	**n.a.**	**(5,427)**
Cash from fin. activs	5,817		6,551
Cash from invest. activs	(2,427)		1,198
Net cash position	**2,262**	**-32**	**3,331**
Capital expenditures	(2,427)		(359)
	$		$
Earnings per share*	(0.11)		(0.11)
Cash flow per share*	(0.09)		(0.11)
	shs		shs
No. of shs. o/s*	56,139,925		49,084,130
Avg. no. of shs. o/s*	49,258,109		48,223,037
	%		%
Net profit margin	n.a.		n.a.
Return on equity	(11.61)		(12.61)
Return on assets	(9.61)		(10.49)

* Common

[A] Reported in accordance with IFRS

Latest Results

Periods ended:	3m Mar. 31/23[A]		3m Mar. 31/22[A]
	$000s	%Chg	$000s
Net income	(1,640)	n.a.	(1,294)
	$		$
Earnings per share*	(0.03)		(0.03)

* Common

[A] Reported in accordance with IFRS

Historical Summary
(as originally stated)

Fiscal Year	Oper. Rev.	Net Inc. Bef. Disc.	EPS*
	$000s	$000s	$
2022[A]	nil	(5,469)	(0.11)
2021[A]	nil	(5,511)	(0.11)
2020[A]	nil	(5,526)	(0.14)
2019[A]	nil	(10,810)	(0.40)
2018[A]	nil	(4,766)	(0.20)

* Common

[A] Reported in accordance with IFRS

Note: Adjusted throughout for 1-for-10 cons. in Dec. 2020

U.4 Ultra Brands Ltd.

Symbol - ULTA **Exchange** - CSE **CUSIP** - 90387A
Head Office - 400-837 Hastings St W, Vancouver, BC, V6C 3N6 **Telephone** - (604) 235-0010 **Toll-free** - (888) 346-5153 **Fax** - (778) 372-1790
Email - jw@feelfoodsco.com
Investor Relations - Joel T. Warawa (888) 346-5153
Auditors - Sam S. Mah Inc. C.A., Burnaby, B.C.
Transfer Agents - Computershare Trust Company of Canada Inc., Vancouver, B.C.

Profile - (B.C. 2014 amalg.; orig. B.C., 2001) Develops and produces plant-based and keto-friendly foods and operates Plenty Full, an Asian-inspired meal kits service serving Vancouver, Burnaby and Richmond, B.C.

Wholly owned **Be Good Plant Based Foods Ltd.** is developing plant-based chicken, pork and beef products including chicken tenders, nuggets, pork cutlets and burgers, as well as investing in the research and development of keto-friendly plant based candy products.

Wholly owned **Plenty-Full Food Services Corp.** sells meal kits online through its website, www.plenty-full.com, and delivered to customers in Richmond, Vancouver and Burnaby, B.C.

In December 2022, wholly owned **Black Sheep Vegan Cheeze Company Corp.** ceased operations.

Predecessor Detail - Name changed from Feel Foods Ltd., May 17, 2022; basis 1 new for 10 old shs.

Directors - David C. Greenway, CEO, Vancouver, B.C.; Yuying Liang, CFO, Vancouver, B.C.; David Bentil; Bryce A. Clark, Vancouver, B.C.

Capital Stock

	Authorized (shs.)	Outstanding (shs.)[1]
Common	unlimited	18,487,896

[1] At May 30, 2023

Major Shareholder - Widely held at May 1, 2023.

Price Range - ULTA/CSE

Year	Volume	High	Low	Close
2022	11,384,852	$1.05	$0.03	$0.06
2021	2,254,978	$4.70	$0.80	$1.05
2020	39,132	$2.40	$0.20	$1.40
2019	32,084	$3.40	$0.20	$0.60
2018	82,458	$6.80	$1.20	$1.40

Consolidation: 1-for-10 cons. in May 2022; 1-for-4 cons. in Mar. 2021

Recent Close: $0.04

Capital Stock Changes - On May 17, 2022, common shares were consolidated on a 1-for-10 basis. In October 2022, private placement of 10,000,000 units (1 post-consolidated common share & 1 warrant) at 5¢ per unit was completed. Also during 2022, 1,320,000 post-consolidated common shares were issued under restricted share unit plan.

Wholly Owned Subsidiaries

Be Good Plant Based Foods Ltd.

Black Sheep Vegan Cheeze Company Corp., B.C.

Plenty-Full Food Services Corp., Vancouver, B.C.

Financial Statistics

Periods ended:	12m Dec. 31/22[A]		12m Dec. 31/21[oA]
	$000s	%Chg	$000s
Operating revenue	**39**	**-38**	**63**
Cost of sales	9		42
General & admin expense	1,436		3,063
Stock-based compensation	nil		973
Operating expense	**1,445**	**-65**	**4,078**
Operating income	**(1,406)**	**n.a.**	**(4,015)**
Deprec., depl. & amort.	78		33
Finance income	nil		19
Finance costs, gross	37		43
Write-downs/write-offs	(150)		nil
Pre-tax income	**(1,550)**	**n.a.**	**(12,451)**
Net income	**(1,550)**	**n.a.**	**(12,451)**
Cash & equivalent	196		289
Current assets	399		566
Fixed assets, net	117		258
Total assets	**530**	**-38**	**848**
Bank indebtedness	200		nil
Accts. pay. & accr. liabs	259		94
Current liabilities	570		185
Long-term debt, gross	40		103
Long-term debt, net	40		96
Long-term lease liabilities	34		111
Shareholders' equity	(114)		456
Cash from oper. activs	**(668)**	**n.a.**	**(2,345)**
Cash from fin. activs	574		2,904
Cash from invest. activs	nil		(291)
Net cash position	**196**	**-32**	**289**
Capital expenditures	nil		(1,034)
	$		$
Earnings per share*	(0.16)		(20.00)
Cash flow per share*	(0.07)		(3.77)
	shs		shs
No. of shs. o/s*	18,487,896		716,790
Avg. no. of shs. o/s*	9,930,424		621,436
	%		%
Net profit margin	n.m.		n.m.
Return on equity	n.m.		(1,753.66)
Return on assets	(219.59)		(901.42)

* Common
[o] Restated
[A] Reported in accordance with IFRS

Latest Results

Periods ended:	3m Mar. 31/23[A]		3m Mar. 31/22[oA]
	$000s	%Chg	$000s
Operating revenue	nil	n.a.	18
Net income	(147)	n.a.	(838)
	$		$
Earnings per share*	(0.01)		(1.17)

* Common
[o] Restated
[A] Reported in accordance with IFRS

Historical Summary
(as originally stated)

Fiscal Year	Oper. Rev.	Net Inc. Bef. Disc.	EPS*
	$000s	$000s	$
2022[A]	39	(1,550)	(0.16)
2021[A]	63	(12,451)	(2.00)
2020[A]	73	(395)	(0.20)
2019[A]	97	(779)	(1.20)
2018[A]	114	(518)	(0.80)

* Common
[A] Reported in accordance with IFRS

Note: Adjusted throughout for 1-for-10 cons. in May 2022; 1-for-4 cons. in Mar. 2021

U.5 UniDoc Health Corp.

Symbol - UDOC **Exchange** - CSE **CUSIP** - 90468F

Head Office - 220-333 Terminal Ave, Vancouver, BC, V6A 4C1 **Telephone** - (778) 383-6731

Website - unidoctor.com

Email - nina@acmfirm.ca

Investor Relations - Nina Yii (778) 383-6731

Auditors - Dale Matheson Carr-Hilton LaBonte LLP C.A., Vancouver, B.C.

Lawyers - Morton Law, LLP, Vancouver, B.C.

Transfer Agents - Odyssey Trust Company, Vancouver, B.C.

Profile - (B.C. 2021) Designing and developing the Virtual Care model, a telehealth solution integrating a range of physical products (kiosks), web-based services and analytical tools, as well as providing access to a network of healthcare providers, pharmacies and hospitals.

Virtual Care will include virtual/telehealth units providing patients with the ability to have a live virtual visit with a doctor or other health professional.

Solutions include Smart Hospital, a physical telehealth kiosk with integrated diagnostic tools that provide service providers real-time access to the patients' clinical data and vital signs measurements such as body temperature, blood pressure and heart rate, as well as glycaemic and pulse oximetry profiles, and electrocardiogram testing; and Smart Companion, a web-based application that would deliver healthcare services, both at home and via mobile devices, including a service centre, devices for remote or local measurements, training services for medical staff, management services and video consultation services. Smart Hospital and Smart Companion have both been developed and will be provided by **Dedalus Group**.

Virtual Care is also planned to be deployed in the future in locations such as grocery stores, long-term care facilities, post-secondary education campuses and corporate offices.

Directors - Franco Staino, chr., Rome, Italy; Antonio Baldassarre, pres. & CEO, Ont.; Matthew (Matt) Chatterton, Langley, B.C.; Sina S. Pirooz, B.C.; Austin Thornberry, B.C.

Other Exec. Officers - Nina Yii, CFO & corp. sec.; Dr. Sazzad Hossain, chief scientific officer

Capital Stock

	Authorized (shs.)	Outstanding (shs.)[1]
Common	unlimited	10,933,350

[1] At Nov. 30, 2022

Major Shareholder - Antonio Baldassarre held 17.84% interest at June 22, 2022.

Price Range - UDOC/CSE

Year	Volume	High	Low	Close
2022	684,331	$1.50	$0.75	$0.75
2021	387,823	$1.51	$1.25	$1.30

Recent Close: $0.80

Capital Stock Changes - In October 2021, 2,752,100 units (1 common share & ½ warrant) were issued without further consideration on exchange of special warrants sold previously by private placement at $1.25 each. Also during fiscal 2022, 981,250 common shares were issued on exercise of warrants.

Wholly Owned Subsidiaries

Unicheck Holdings Corp., B.C.

Financial Statistics

Periods ended:	12m Mar. 31/22[A]
	$000s
Salaries & benefits	13
Research & devel. expense	353
General & admin expense	2,248
Stock-based compensation	373
Operating expense	**2,988**
Operating income	**(2,988)**
Deprec., depl. & amort.	15
Pre-tax income	**(3,005)**
Net income	**(3,005)**
Cash & equivalent	854
Current assets	1,003
Fixed assets, net	83
Right-of-use assets	89
Total assets	**1,178**
Accts. pay. & accr. liabs	642
Current liabilities	667
Long-term lease liabilities	55
Shareholders' equity	456
Cash from oper. activs	**(2,386)**
Cash from fin. activs	3,010
Cash from invest. activs	(51)
Net cash position	**854**
Capital expenditures	(51)
	$
Earnings per share*	(0.35)
Cash flow per share*	(0.28)
	shs
No. of shs. o/s*	10,933,350
Avg. no. of shs. o/s*	8,519,196
	%
Net profit margin	n.a.
Return on equity	n.m.
Return on assets	n.a.

* Common
[A] Reported in accordance with IFRS

Latest Results

Periods ended:	6m Sept. 30/22[A]		7m Oct. 31/21[A]
	$000s	%Chg	$000s
Net income	(699)	n.a.	(1,305)
	$		$
Earnings per share*	(0.06)		(0.21)

* Common
[A] Reported in accordance with IFRS

U.6 Uniserve Communications Corp.

Symbol - USS **Exchange** - TSX-VEN **CUSIP** - 909172

Head Office - 209-333 Terminal Ave, Vancouver, BC, V6A 4C1 **Telephone** - (604) 395-3900 **Toll-free** - (844) 395-3900

Website - www.uniserve.com

Email - kelly.walker@uniserveteam.com

Investor Relations - Kelly Walker (604) 395-3961

Auditors - Dale Matheson Carr-Hilton LaBonte LLP C.A., Vancouver, B.C.

Transfer Agents - Computershare Trust Company of Canada Inc., Vancouver, B.C.

Profile - (B.C. 2003 amalg.) Provides voice, data and media services, and information technology solutions.

Has more than 13,000 active residential, business and enterprise customers providing more than 45,000 active services in Vancouver, B.C., Calgary, Alta., and Kitchener-Waterloo, Ont. Products are offered across three verticals: residential; small business; and enterprise. For residential customers, products include latest technologies in telecommunications and high-speed Internet services. For small business, the company offers Office-in-a-Box solution which includes hardware for computers and laptops, phones, all networking equipment and productivity software for start-ups, professionals, creative industries and retail outlets. For enterprise customers, the company offers comprehensive managed services focused on security, business continuity, communications, disaster recovery, cloud and application hosting, along with its own T2 data edge centre in Vancouver, B.C. (with backup/disaster recovery, and failover in Calgary, Alta.).

In July 2022, the company terminated the letter of intent to acquire a private Vancouver, B.C.-based cloud solutions company, which provides hosted applications and virtual desktops, as well as secure managed physical terminals to customers, for $3,750,000.

Predecessor Detail - Formed from Technovision Systems, Inc. in British Columbia, Nov. 20, 2003, on amalgamation with PCNet International Inc. with Technovision the deemed acquiror; basis 0.7296 new for 1 PCNet sh. and 1 new for 1 Technovision sh.

Directors - Walter Schultz, chr., Vancouver, B.C.; Kelly Walker, pres. & interim CEO, Vancouver, B.C.; Earnest C. Beaudin, B.C.; Kwin Grauer; Arif Merali, Burnaby, B.C.; Stuart Omsen, B.C.

Other Exec. Officers - Andrej (Andy) Prpic, CFO

Capital Stock

	Authorized (shs.)	Outstanding (shs.)[1]
Series A Preferred	unlimited	2,300[2]
Common	unlimited	80,523,971

[1] At Jan. 27, 2023
[2] Classified as debt.

Series A Preferred - Entitled to 8% cumulative dividends, redeemable at $10 per share, and convertible into common shares at $1.25 per share. During fiscal 2011, the company failed to make the monthly dividend payment. As a result, the series A preferred shares become immediately retractable at $10 per share. At May 31, 2022, dividends in arrears totaled $21,927.

Major Shareholder - Michael C. Scholz held 43.3% interest and Owen Marley held 16.66% interest at Oct. 6, 2021.

Price Range - US$/TSX-VEN

Year	Volume	High	Low	Close
2022	4,110,899	$0.19	$0.04	$0.04
2021	4,818,992	$0.24	$0.05	$0.17
2020	3,381,604	$0.11	$0.04	$0.06
2019	2,771,900	$0.32	$0.07	$0.12
2018	3,244,527	$2.21	$0.18	$0.19

Consolidation: 1-for-3.5 cons. in Feb. 2019

Recent Close: $0.05

Capital Stock Changes - During fiscal 2022, common shares were issued as follows: 12,244,666 on exercise of warrants and 7,000,000 by private placement. In addition, 600 series A preferred shares were redeemed.

Financial Statistics

Periods ended:	12m May 31/22[A]		12m May 31/21[A]
	$000s	%Chg	$000s
Operating revenue	**7,703**	**-4**	**8,064**
Cost of sales	3,721		4,117
Salaries & benefits	2,378		2,377
General & admin expense	763		704
Operating expense	**6,862**	**-5**	**7,197**
Operating income	**841**	**-3**	**867**
Deprec., depl. & amort.	393		506
Finance income	14		9
Finance costs, gross	126		236
Pre-tax income	**393**	**+181**	**140**
Net income	**393**	**+181**	**140**
Cash & equivalent	1,957		412
Inventories	18		49
Accounts receivable	519		2,531
Current assets	2,683		3,141
Fixed assets, net	224		463
Intangibles, net	72		128
Total assets	**3,138**	**-19**	**3,863**
Accts. pay. & accr. liabs.	1,409		3,478
Current liabilities	2,104		5,914
Long-term debt, gross	737		1,907
Long-term debt, net	192		nil
Long-term lease liabilities	nil		60
Shareholders' equity	833		(2,114)
Cash from oper. activs.	**410**	**+87**	**219**
Cash from fin. activs.	1,255		(380)
Cash from invest. activs.	(119)		(102)
Net cash position	**1,957**	**+375**	**412**
Capital expenditures	(122)		(102)
Capital disposals	3		nil
	$		$
Earnings per share*	0.01		0.00
Cash flow per share*	0.01		0.00
	shs		shs
No. of shs. o/s*	80,523,971		61,279,305
Avg. no. of shs. o/s*	71,058,193		61,205,332
	%		%
Net profit margin	5.10		1.74
Return on equity	n.m.		n.m.
Return on assets	14.83		10.00

* Common
[A] Reported in accordance with IFRS

Historical Summary
(as originally stated)

Fiscal Year	Oper. Rev.	Net Inc. Bef. Disc.	EPS*
	$000s	$000s	$
2022[A]	7,703	393	0.01
2021[A]	8,064	140	0.00
2020[A]	12,359	(3,496)	(0.07)
2019[A]	12,251	(3,009)	(0.14)
2018[A]	8,816	(4,017)	(0.28)

* Common
[A] Reported in accordance with IFRS

Note: Adjusted throughout for 1-for-3.5 cons. in Feb. 2019

U.7 Unisync Corp.

Symbol - UNI **Exchange** - TSX **CUSIP** - 90922H
Head Office - 1328-885 Georgia St W, Vancouver, BC, V6C 3E8
Telephone - (778) 370-1725 **Fax** - (604) 909-0299
Website - www.unisyncgroup.com
Email - dgood@unisyncgroup.com
Investor Relations - Douglas F. Good (778) 370-1725
Auditors - MNP LLP C.A., Vancouver, B.C.
Transfer Agents - Computershare Trust Company of Canada Inc., Vancouver, B.C.
FP500 Revenue Ranking - 776
Employees - 379 at Sept. 30, 2022

Profile - (B.C. 2005 amalg.) Designs and manufactures uniforms, work and dress wear, image apparel and harsh weather outerwear primarily for the Canadian government agencies and corporate sectors, and provides a web-based B2B and B2C ordering, distribution and program management system.

Wholly owned **Unisync Group Limited** designs, manufactures and distributes custom and corporate uniforms, work and dress wear and image apparel, and provides related solutions including a web-based B2B and B2C ordering, distribution and program management system. Operations are located in Mississauga, Guelph and Carleton Place, Ont.; Vancouver, B.C.; Saint-Laurent, Que.; and Henderson, Nev. Customers include North American companies in a variety of industries, including Air Canada, Alaska Airlines, Purolator, Canadian Coast Guard, Shoppers Drug Mart, Sobeys, Tim Hortons, WestJet and Allegiant Airlines. Also has Tactical Gear Experts division, which sells outdoor, tactical and lifestyle products through an e-commerce website.

Subsidiary **Peerless Garments Limited Partnership** produces and distributes highly technical protective garments designed to provide water-resistance, windproofing and warmth. Peerless also produces tactical garments made of fire-resistant, anti-static, chemical warfare protective materials and specialized fabrics. Customers include a broad spectrum of federal, provincial and municipal government departments and agencies. Manufacturing is conducted from an 85,000-sq.-ft. owned and operated facility in Winnipeg, Man. Peerless also outsources a portion of its production to subcontractors in Greater Toronto Area of Ontario.

Products are being sold under the Hammill™, York™, Unisync™ and Perfect-Fit brands.

In December 2022, the company sold its N.J.-based hospitality business, which operated under the trade name Red the Uniform Tailor, for $1,405,082 cash on closing and $541,760 promissory note payable in four equal consecutive semi-annual payments commencing six months following the closing.

Predecessor Detail - Name changed from ComWest Enterprise Corp., Aug. 1, 2014.

Directors - Tim Gu, chr., Ont.; C. Scott M. Shepherd, v-chr., Vancouver, B.C.; Douglas F. Good, pres. & CEO, New Westminster, B.C.; Bruce W. Aunger, Maple Ridge, B.C.; Darryl R. Eddy, Vancouver, B.C.; Joel R. McLean, West Vancouver, B.C.; C. Michael O'Brian, Vancouver, B.C.

Other Exec. Officers - Richard Smith, CFO; Abdo (Albert) El Tassi, pres. & CEO, Peerless Garments L.P.; Michael Smith, pres., Unisync Group Limited

Capital Stock

	Authorized (shs.)	Outstanding (shs.)[1]	Par
Class A Preferred	unlimited	nil	$1.00
Common	unlimited	19,012,228	n.p.v.

[1] At Feb. 10, 2023

Major Shareholder - McLean Capital Corporation held 10.8% interest at Feb. 1, 2023.

Price Range - UNI/TSX

Year	Volume	High	Low	Close
2022	1,002,518	$3.29	$1.98	$2.26
2021	3,879,559	$3.58	$2.26	$3.30
2020	1,749,699	$3.65	$1.36	$2.55
2019	1,785,319	$4.07	$3.00	$3.46
2018	853,151	$4.50	$2.90	$3.95

Recent Close: $1.50

Capital Stock Changes - During fiscal 2022, 25,000 common shares were issued on exercise of options.

Wholly Owned Subsidiaries

Peerless Garments GP Inc., Ont.
Utility Garments Inc., Saint-Laurent, Qué.
York Uniforms Holdings Limited, Mississauga, Ont.
- 82% int. in **Unisync Group Limited**, Mississauga, Ont.
  - 90% int. in **Peerless Garments Limited Partnership**, Winnipeg, Man.
  - 100% int. in **Unisync, Inc.**, Del.
    - 100% int. in **Unisync (Nevada) LLC**, Nev.

Investments

18% int. in **Unisync Group Limited**, Mississauga, Ont.

Financial Statistics

Periods ended:	12m Sept. 30/22[A]		12m Sept. 30/21[A]
	$000s	%Chg	$000s
Operating revenue	**96,307**	**+12**	**86,285**
Cost of sales	49,820		48,088
Salaries & benefits	21,539		18,787
General & admin expense	20,029		16,275
Stock-based compensation	408		425
Operating expense	**91,796**	**+10**	**83,574**
Operating income	**4,511**	**+66**	**2,711**
Deprec., depl. & amort.	4,024		3,810
Finance costs, gross	1,733		2,183
Pre-tax income	**(1,246)**	**n.a.**	**(3,282)**
Income taxes	102		(705)
Net income	**(1,348)**	**n.a.**	**(2,577)**
Net inc. for equity hldrs.	**(1,545)**	**n.a.**	**(2,830)**
Net inc. for non-cont. int.	**196**	**-23**	**253**
Cash & equivalent	97		275
Inventories	56,199		36,208
Accounts receivable	13,273		11,726
Current assets	72,118		52,405
Fixed assets, net	8,395		8,887
Right-of-use assets	7,993		9,405
Intangibles, net	13,703		15,060
Total assets	**104,364**	**+19**	**88,020**
Bank indebtedness	25,756		19,020
Accts. pay. & accr. liabs.	12,581		5,009
Current liabilities	58,028		37,714
Long-term debt, gross	9,608		9,847
Long-term debt, net	9,327		9,602
Long-term lease liabilities	8,712		9,912
Shareholders' equity	28,363		29,374
Non-controlling interest	(66)		(82)
Cash from oper. activs.	**(3,082)**	**n.a.**	**9,168**
Cash from fin. activs.	3,523		(7,533)
Cash from invest. activs.	(682)		(1,503)
Net cash position	**97**	**-65**	**275**
Capital expenditures	(239)		(533)
	$		$
Earnings per share*	(0.08)		(0.15)
Cash flow per share*	(0.16)		0.48
	shs		shs
No. of shs. o/s*	19,012,228		18,987,228
Avg. no. of shs. o/s*	19,010,516		18,931,886
	%		%
Net profit margin	(1.40)		(2.99)
Return on equity	(5.35)		(9.34)
Return on assets	0.55		(0.99)
Foreign sales percent	24		15
No. of employees (FTEs)	379		320

* Common
[A] Reported in accordance with IFRS

Latest Results

Periods ended:	3m Dec. 31/22[A]		3m Dec. 31/21[A]
	$000s	%Chg	$000s
Operating revenue	28,872	+32	21,835
Net income	512	n.a.	(101)
Net inc. for equity hldrs.	508	n.a.	(172)
Net inc. for non-cont. int.	4		71
	$		$
Earnings per share*	0.03		(0.01)

* Common
[A] Reported in accordance with IFRS

Historical Summary
(as originally stated)

Fiscal Year	Oper. Rev.	Net Inc. Bef. Disc.	EPS*
	$000s	$000s	$
2022[A]	96,307	(1,348)	(0.08)
2021[A]	86,285	(2,577)	(0.15)
2020[A]	93,103	(1,005)	(0.07)
2019[A]	77,993	(4,005)	(0.23)
2018[A]	76,836	7,238	0.53

* Common
[A] Reported in accordance with IFRS

U.8 United Corporations Limited*

Symbol - UNC **Exchange** - TSX **CUSIP** - 910144
Head Office - 1000-165 University Ave, Toronto, ON, M5H 3B8
Telephone - (416) 947-2578 **Toll-free** - (800) 564-6253 **Fax** - (416) 362-2592
Website - www.ucorp.ca
Email - glosnekf@e-lfinancial.com
Investor Relations - Frank J. Glosnek (416) 947-2578
Auditors - PricewaterhouseCoopers LLP C.A., Toronto, Ont.
Bankers - The Bank of Nova Scotia, Toronto, Ont.
Transfer Agents - Computershare Trust Company of Canada Inc., Toronto, Ont.

Investment Managers - Neuberger Berman Canada ULC, Toronto, Ont.; Comgest Asset Management International Limited, Dublin, Ireland; Causeway Capital Management LLC, Los Angeles, Calif.; Harding Loevner LP, Bridgewater, N.J.

Profile - (Can. 1933) Invests primarily in a global portfolio of equity securities. Investment portfolio includes companies in a wide range of businesses including financial services, oil and gas, precious metals mining, real estate, consumer and industrial goods manufacturing, transportation and communications.

The company is a closed-end investment company with a portfolio of global investments. Majority of the investment portfolio is managed by four external investment managers: **Comgest Asset Management International Limited**, **Harding Loevner LP**, **Causeway Capital Management LLC** and **Neuberger Berman Canada ULC**. The investment managers have been given global investment mandates and are allowed to hedge the foreign currency exposure of any non-Canadian investment. At June 30, 2023, Comgest managed 27%, Harding managed 25%, Causeway managed 24% and Neuberger managed 21% of the investment portfolio. The company's management is responsible for investment decisions regarding its investment in **Algoma Central Corporation**.

Investment allocation by region at June 30, 2023:

Region	Percentage
United States	48.0%
Europe, excl. U.K.	25.4%
Emerging markets	10.4%
United Kingdom	6.5%
Japan	5.8%
Canada	3.5%
Australia	0.4%

In March 2022, **Neuberger Berman Canada ULC** was appointed as portfolio manager for a portion of assets previously managed by **Comgest Asset Management International Limited** and **Harding Loevner LP**. As a result, Comgest, Harding, **Causeway Capital Management LLC** and Neuberger would manage 28%, 28%, 20% and 20% of the company's assets, respectively.

Directors - Duncan N. R. Jackman, chr., pres. & CEO, Toronto, Ont.; Christopher A. Alexander, Ajax, Ont.; David J. Dawson, Ont.; Dr. Trinity O. Jackman, Toronto, Ont.; Fahad Khan, Toronto, Ont.; Kim Shannon, Toronto, Ont.; David R. Wingfield, Ont.

Other Exec. Officers - Scott F. Ewert, v-p; Richard B. Carty, corp. sec.; Frank J. Glosnek, treas.

Capital Stock

	Authorized (shs.)	Outstanding (shs.)[1]
First Preferred	52,237	52,237
Second Preferred	200,000	
1959 Series		80,290
1963 Series		119,710
Third Preferred	15,000,000	nil
Common	unlimited	11,595,748

[1] At June 30, 2023

First Preferred - Each entitled to a cumulative annual dividend rate of $1.50 per share. Redeemable on 60 days' notice at $30 per share plus accrued and unpaid dividends. One vote per share.

Second Preferred - Issuable in series with rights, preferences and priorities subject and subordinate to those attached to first preferred shares. Non-voting, unless the company defaults on dividend payments for one year, when entitled to one vote per share. **1959 Series** - Each entitled to $1.50 cumulative annual dividend. Redeemable on 30 days' notice at $30 per share plus accrued and unpaid dividends. **1963 Series** - Each entitled to $1.50 cumulative annual dividend. Redeemable on 30 days' notice at $31.50 per share plus accrued and unpaid dividends.

Third Preferred - Issuable in series.

Common - Dividends are distributed as regular cash dividends and extra cash dividends from net income and capital gains dividends from net gains realized from the sale of investments. One vote per share.

Normal Course Issuer Bid - The company plans to make normal course purchases of up to 580,102 common shares representing 5% of the total outstanding. The bid commenced on Mar. 9, 2023, and expires on Mar. 8, 2024.

Major Shareholder - E-L Financial Corporation Limited held 54.7% interest and United-Connected Holdings Corp. held 23.5% interest at May 1, 2023.

Price Range - UNC/TSX

Year	Volume	High	Low	Close
2022	307,116	$112.50	$85.00	$99.25
2021	224,207	$114.00	$102.30	$113.15
2020	316,925	$106.59	$74.80	$105.75
2019	292,831	$99.40	$88.50	$98.35
2018	191,289	$106.49	$88.16	$88.68

Recent Close: $104.21

Capital Stock Changes - In September 2022, 454,545 common shares were repurchased under a Substantial Issuer Bid. Also during fiscal 2023, 23,600 common shares were repurchased under a Normal Course Issuer Bid.

During fiscal 2022, 17,300 common shares were repurchased under a Normal Course Issuer Bid.

Dividends

UNC com Ra $1.20 pa Q est. Aug. 15, 2023
Prev. Rate: $1.00 est. June 30, 2023
Prev. Rate: $1.20 est. Aug. 13, 2021
Prev. Rate: $1.20 est. Aug. 15, 2019
$4.50◆............ July 15/22 $1.11◆............ June 30/21
Paid in 2023: $1.45 2022: $1.20 + $4.50◆ 2021: $1.20 + $1.11◆
UNC.PR.A pfd 1st cum. red. Ra $1.50 pa Q
UNC.PR.B pfd 2nd ser 59 $1.50 cum. red. Ra $1.50 pa Q
UNC.PR.C pfd 2nd ser 63 $1.50 cum. red. Ra $1.50 pa Q
◆ Special

Long-Term Debt - At Mar. 31, 2023, the company had no debt.

Wholly Owned Subsidiaries

UNC Holdings No. 3 Limited, Ont.

Financial Statistics

Periods ended:	12m Mar. 31/23[A]		12m Mar. 31/22[A]
	$000s	%Chg	$000s
Realized invest. gain (loss)	(74,220)		82,044
Unrealized invest. gain (loss)	70,053		(112,357)
Total revenue	**31,343**	**n.a.**	**(7,978)**
General & admin. expense	11,878		15,455
Other operating expense	413		392
Operating expense	**12,291**	**-22**	**15,847**
Operating income	**19,052**	**n.a.**	**(23,825)**
Finance costs, gross	956		nil
Pre-tax income	**18,096**	**n.a.**	**(23,825)**
Income taxes	4,225		(733)
Net income	**13,871**	**n.a.**	**(23,092)**
Cash & equivalent	66,438		68,404
Accounts receivable	9,136		11,604
Investments	1,861,226		1,965,258
Total assets	**1,951,850**	**-5**	**2,051,470**
Accts. pay. & accr. liabs.	9,434		11,297
Preferred share equity	6,119		6,119
Shareholders' equity	1,911,779		2,018,799
Cash from oper. activs.	**119,068**	**n.a.**	**(713)**
Cash from fin. activs.	(121,034)		(30,154)
Net cash position	**66,438**	**-3**	**68,404**
	$		$
Earnings per share*	1.14		(1.94)
Cash flow per share*	10.07		(0.06)
Net asset value per share*	164.13		166.49
Cash divd. per share*	1.20		1.20
Extra divd. - cash*	4.50		1.11
Total divd. per share*	**5.70**		**2.31**
	shs		shs
No. of shs. o/s*	11,600,648		12,078,793
Avg. no. of shs. o/s*	11,828,202		12,092,086
	%		%
Net profit margin	44.26		n.m.
Return on equity	0.69		(1.15)
Return on assets	0.73		(1.10)

* Common
[A] Reported in accordance with IFRS

Latest Results

Periods ended:	3m June 30/23[A]		3m June 30/22[A]
	$000s	%Chg	$000s
Total revenue	91,389	n.a.	(272,276)
Net income	75,355	n.a.	(240,378)
	$		$
Earnings per share*	6.49		(19.92)

* Common
[A] Reported in accordance with IFRS

Historical Summary
(as originally stated)

Fiscal Year	Total Rev. $000s	Net Inc. Bef. Disc. $000s	EPS* $
2023[A]	31,343	13,871	1.14
2022[A]	(7,978)	(23,092)	(1.94)
2021[A]	500,522	422,620	34.88
2020[A]	(82,494)	(86,750)	(7.15)
2019[A]	165,206	129,238	10.57

* Common
[A] Reported in accordance with IFRS

U.9 Universal Ibogaine Inc.

Symbol - IBO **Exchange** - TSX-VEN **CUSIP** - 91360F
Head Office - Devon Tower, 1470-400 3 Ave SW, Calgary, AB, T2P 4H2 **Toll-free** - (855) 426-4246
Website - universalibogaine.com
Email - dugan.selkirk@universalibogaine.com
Investor Relations - Dugan Selkirk (855) 426-4246
Auditors - Deloitte LLP C.A., Calgary, Alta.
Lawyers - DLA Piper (Canada) LLP, Calgary, Alta.
Transfer Agents - Odyssey Trust Company, Calgary, Alta.

Profile - (Alta. 2017) Owns and operates the Kelburn Clinic, an addiction treatment facility near Winnipeg, Man. Also researches the use of ibogaine in addiction treatment.

The Kelburn Clinic operates as a traditional addiction treatment centre, with plans to incorporate treatment modalities including ketamine, psilocybin and MDMA assisted psychotherapies.

Also develops medicines for addiction with the medicalization of ibogaine, a naturally-derived plant molecule. In addition, the company plans to expand the treatment centre to include traditional drug detox and to construct an ibogaine detox facility.

In July 2022, the company announced the sale of its 20-acre underdeveloped land in Belize. As a result, the company recorded a $1,242,612 impairment during fiscal 2022.

On Apr. 6, 2022, common shares were listed in the Frankfurt Stock Exchange under the stock symbol JC4.

Predecessor Detail - Name changed from P Squared Renewables Inc., Sept. 15, 2021, pursuant to the Qualifying Transaction reverse takeover acquisition of (old) Universal Ibogaine Inc. and concurrent amalgamation of (old) Universal Ibogaine with wholly owned 1266855 B.C. Ltd. (and continued as Clear Sky Recovery Solutions Inc.).

Directors - Chief Ian Campbell, chr., Vancouver, B.C.; Nicholas (Nick) Karos, CEO, Los Angeles, Calif.; Dr. Alberto Solá, pres., Cancún, Q. Roo., Mexico; Anthony DeCristofaro, Toronto, Ont.; Robert Turner, Ont.

Other Exec. Officers - Gregory J. (Greg) Leavens, CFO & corp. sec.; Dr. Ian Rabb, chief clinics officer

Capital Stock

	Authorized (shs.)	Outstanding (shs.)[1]
Preferred	unlimited	nil
Common	unlimited	191,143,599

[1] At Dec. 22, 2022

Major Shareholder - Widely held at Sept. 12, 2022.

Price Range - IBO/TSX-VEN

Year	Volume	High	Low	Close
2022	51,609,994	$0.20	$0.02	$0.02
2021	11,599,077	$0.25	$0.11	$0.13
2019	643,451	$0.21	$0.10	$0.16
2018	617,460	$0.19	$0.13	$0.17

Recent Close: $0.02

Capital Stock Changes - On Aug. 31, 2021, 154,081,749 common shares were issued pursuant to the Qualifying Transaction reverse takeover acquisition of (old) Universal Ibogaine Inc. and 24,000,000 units (1 common share & 1 warrant) were issued without further consideration on exchange of subscription receipts sold previously by private placement at 25¢ each. Also during fiscal 2022, 176,000 common shares were issued on exercise of options.

Wholly Owned Subsidiaries

Clear Sky Recovery Solutions Inc., Vancouver, B.C.
- 100% int. in **Iboquest Wellness Centres Inc.**, B.C.
- 100% int. in **6887016 Manitoba Ltd.**, Man.
- 100% int. in **Universal Ibogaine Belize Ltd.**, Belize.

Financial Statistics

Periods ended:	12m July 31/22[A1]		12m July 31/21[A]
	$000s	%Chg	$000s
Operating revenue	**1,071**	**n.a.**	**nil**
Salaries & benefits	n.a.		226
Research & devel. expense	409		63
General & admin expense	3,664		3,506
Stock-based compensation	906		nil
Operating expense	**4,979**	**+31**	**3,795**
Operating income	**(3,908)**	**n.a.**	**(3,795)**
Deprec., depl. & amort.	266		70
Finance costs, net	196		(17)
Write-downs/write-offs	(2,707)		nil
Pre-tax income	**(10,496)**	**n.a.**	**(3,867)**
Net income	**(10,496)**	**n.a.**	**(3,867)**
Cash & equivalent	726		142
Current assets	1,017		902
Fixed assets, net	5,301		3,047
Total assets	**6,318**	**+58**	**3,992**
Bank indebtedness	nil		350
Accts. pay. & accr. liabs.	637		638
Current liabilities	2,195		988
Long-term debt, gross	1,738		60
Long-term debt, net	180		60
Shareholders' equity	3,943		2,944
Cash from oper. activs.	**(3,708)**	**n.a.**	**(3,250)**
Cash from fin. activs.	7,006		3,382
Cash from invest. activs.	(2,089)		(43)
Net cash position	**726**	**+411**	**142**
Capital expenditures	(97)		nil
Capital disposals	12		nil
	$		$
Earnings per share*	(0.06)		(0.03)
Cash flow per share*	(0.02)		(0.03)
	shs		shs
No. of shs. o/s*	190,743,599		n.a.
Avg. no. of shs. o/s*	185,636,855		125,189,597
	%		%
Net profit margin	(980.02)		n.a.
Return on equity	(304.81)		n.m.
Return on assets	(203.61)		(170.17)

* Common
[A] Reported in accordance with IFRS
[1] Results prior to Aug. 31, 2021, pertain to and reflect the Qualifying Transaction reverse takeover acquisition of (old) Universal Ibogaine Inc.

Latest Results

Periods ended:	3m Oct. 31/22[A]		3m Oct. 31/21[αA]
	$000s	%Chg	$000s
Operating revenue	nil	n.a.	137
Net income	(842)	n.a.	(4,365)
	$		$
Earnings per share*	(0.00)		(0.03)

* Common
[α] Restated
[A] Reported in accordance with IFRS

Historical Summary
(as originally stated)

Fiscal Year	Oper. Rev.	Net Inc. Bef. Disc.	EPS*
	$000s	$000s	$
2022[A]	1,071	(10,496)	(0.06)
2021[A]	nil	(3,867)	(0.03)
2020[A]	nil	(5,571)	(0.16)
2019[A]	nil	(2,459)	(0.13)

* Common
[A] Reported in accordance with IFRS

U.10 Universal PropTech Inc.

Symbol - UPI.H **Exchange** - TSX-VEN **CUSIP** - 91380M
Head Office - 2905-77 King St W, Toronto, ON, M5K 1H1 **Telephone** - (905) 850-8686
Website - www.universalproptech.com
Email - jberman@universalproptech.com
Investor Relations - Jeffrey Berman (416) 654-7070
Auditors - MNP LLP C.A., Toronto, Ont.
Lawyers - Wildeboer Dellelce LLP, Toronto, Ont.
Transfer Agents - TSX Trust Company, Toronto, Ont.
Profile - (Can. 2008) Seeking new business opportunities.

Formerly through wholly owned **VCI CONTROLS Inc.** supplied building technologies and services that improve comfort, safety, energy efficiency and occupant productivity. Services included digital controls, HVAC mechanical services, real-time performance monitoring and energy efficiency solutions.

In March 2023, the company sold wholly owned **VCI CONTROLS Inc.**, which supplies building technologies and services that improve comfort, safety, energy efficiency and occupant productivity, for total consideration of $4,800,000 consisting of $3,820,000 in cash on closing with a holdback of $980,000 being subject to release over the 12-month period following closing upon meeting certain milestones.

Predecessor Detail - Name changed from Sustainco Inc., Nov. 25, 2020.

Directors - Jeffrey (Jeff) Berman, pres. & CEO; Brian Illion, Toronto, Ont.; Al Quong, Toronto, Ont.

Other Exec. Officers - Amy Stephenson, CFO

Capital Stock

	Authorized (shs.)	Outstanding (shs.)[1]
Common	unlimited	49,217,408

[1] At July 10, 2023

Major Shareholder - Widely held at Dec. 19, 2022.

Price Range - UPI.H/TSX-VEN

Year	Volume	High	Low	Close
2022	11,971,848	$0.16	$0.04	$0.06
2021	65,433,674	$0.75	$0.12	$0.14
2020	5,204,338	$0.40	$0.02	$0.30
2019	1,420,724	$0.24	$0.08	$0.08
2018	527,935	$0.32	$0.12	$0.14

Recent Close: $0.03

Capital Stock Changes - During fiscal 2022, common shares were issued as follows: 907,431 on exercise of warrants and 271,462 for services.

Financial Statistics

Periods ended:	12m Aug. 31/22[A]		12m Aug. 31/21[A]
	$000s	%Chg	$000s
Operating revenue	**7,943**	**-10**	**8,818**
Cost of sales	5,576		6,007
Salaries & benefits	1,526		1,512
General & admin expense	1,134		1,933
Stock-based compensation	104		805
Operating expense	**8,340**	**-19**	**10,257**
Operating income	**(397)**	**n.a.**	**(1,439)**
Deprec., depl. & amort.	248		250
Finance costs, gross	51		127
Write-downs/write-offs	(71)		(7)
Pre-tax income	**(671)**	**n.a.**	**(879)**
Income taxes	(52)		212
Net income	**(619)**	**n.a.**	**(1,090)**
Cash & equivalent	1,032		992
Inventories	149		178
Accounts receivable	2,845		3,288
Current assets	4,137		4,564
Fixed assets, net	366		563
Total assets	**5,504**	**-10**	**6,127**
Accts. pay. & accr. liabs	1,482		1,541
Current liabilities	2,173		2,248
Long-term lease liabilities	153		280
Shareholders' equity	3,168		3,571
Cash from oper. activs	**180**	**n.a.**	**(75)**
Cash from fin. activs	(181)		1,219
Cash from invest. activs	40		(957)
Net cash position	**1,032**	**+4**	**992**
Capital expenditures	(24)		(39)
Capital disposals	65		83
	$		$
Earnings per share*	(0.01)		(0.03)
Cash flow per share*	0.00		(0.00)
	shs		shs
No. of shs. o/s*	49,217,408		48,038,515
Avg. no. of shs. o/s*	49,057,631		34,434,122
	%		%
Net profit margin	(7.79)		(12.36)
Return on equity	(18.37)		(44.99)
Return on assets	(9.83)		(18.56)

* Common
[A] Reported in accordance with IFRS

Historical Summary
(as originally stated)

Fiscal Year	Oper. Rev.	Net Inc. Bef. Disc.	EPS*
	$000s	$000s	$
2022[A]	7,943	(619)	(0.01)
2021[A]	8,818	(1,090)	(0.03)
2020[A]	9,940	(1,215)	(0.08)
2019[A]	15,931	5	0.00
2018[A]	13,687	(124)	(0.01)

* Common
[A] Reported in accordance with IFRS

U.11 UpSnap Inc.

Symbol - UP **Exchange** - CSE **CUSIP** - 916742
Head Office - 200-100 Consilium Pl, Toronto, ON, M1H 3E3 **Telephone** - (416) 619-3900 **Toll-free** - (888) 468-0803 **Fax** - (416) 291-5377
Website - www.upsnap.com
Email - kappleby@upsnap.com
Investor Relations - Kyle Appleby (416) 619-3903
Auditors - SRCO Professional Corporation C.A., Richmond Hill, Ont.
Lawyers - McMillan LLP, Vancouver, B.C.
Transfer Agents - Computershare Trust Company of Canada Inc., Calgary, Alta.
Profile - (Alta. 2004 amalg.) Provides mobile and intent-based advertising services to large brands and small businesses.

Services are offered to national brands and small businesses on a campaign and subscription basis, respectively. Advertising solutions for small businesses are unique, with products including video ads, social media ads and digitally retargeted direct mail ads that have traditionally only been affordable to large businesses. For brands, advertising solutions is based on establishing long-term relationships with advertisers either directly or indirectly through advertising agencies, resellers and other media companies.

The company's Intentional Direct Mail (IDM) service allows advertisers to amplify their digital marketing by sending customized direct mail postcards to potential customers that engage with the advertiser's website or mobile ads.

Also provides software and services that allow customers to perform voice and data searches on proprietary business directories.

Predecessor Detail - Name changed from VoodooVox Inc., July 25, 2014.

Directors - Bruce Howard, chr. & CEO, The Woodlands, Tex.; Heather Burrer, COO, v-p & gen. counsel, The Woodlands, Tex.; Kristina Finch, Ont.; J. Daniel (Dan) Hilton, Ottawa, Ont.; Tom Ross, Ind.

Other Exec. Officers - Kyle Appleby, CFO

Capital Stock

	Authorized (shs.)	Outstanding (shs.)[1]
Preferred	unlimited	nil
Common	unlimited	267,640,941

[1] At May 25, 2023

Major Shareholder - User Friendly Media, LLC held 49.9% interest at Oct. 26, 2021.

Price Range - UP/CSE

Year	Volume	High	Low	Close
2022	11,351,130	$0.01	$0.01	$0.01
2021	147,168,569	$0.06	$0.01	$0.01
2020	46,110,030	$0.03	$0.01	$0.01
2019	2,260,223	$0.01	$0.01	$0.01
2018	39,550,630	$0.06	$0.01	$0.01

Recent Close: $0.01

Wholly Owned Subsidiaries

BTS Logic Europe ApS, Aarhus, Denmark.
Call Genie Europe B.V., Netherlands.
Call Genie (Ontario) Inc., Ont.
UpSnap USA, Inc.
UpSnap USA Holdings, Inc.
VoodooVox Limited, United Kingdom.

Financial Statistics

Periods ended:	12m Dec. 31/21[A]		12m Dec. 31/20[A]
	$000s	%Chg	$000s
Operating revenue	**1,127**	**-29**	**1,594**
Salaries & benefits	82		159
General & admin expense	924		1,164
Stock-based compensation	35		2
Other operating expense	419		585
Operating expense	**1,460**	**-24**	**1,910**
Operating income	**(333)**	**n.a.**	**(316)**
Deprec., depl. & amort.	10		69
Finance costs, gross	108		136
Write-downs/write-offs	nil		(183)
Pre-tax income	**(366)**	**n.a.**	**(523)**
Income taxes	169		nil
Net income	**(535)**	**n.a.**	**(523)**
Cash & equivalent	212		157
Accounts receivable	188		334
Current assets	414		497
Intangibles, net	22		32
Total assets	**436**	**-18**	**529**
Accts. pay. & accr. liabs	1,753		1,627
Current liabilities	3,214		2,815
Long-term debt, gross	800		800
Shareholders' equity	(3,021)		(2,520)
Cash from oper. activs	**33**	**n.a.**	**(41)**
Cash from fin. activs	20		40
Net cash position	**212**	**+35**	**157**
	$		$
Earnings per share*	(0.00)		(0.00)
Cash flow per share*	0.00		(0.00)
	shs		shs
No. of shs. o/s*	267,640,941		267,640,941
Avg. no. of shs. o/s*	267,640,941		267,640,941
	%		%
Net profit margin	(47.47)		(32.81)
Return on equity	n.m.		n.m.
Return on assets	(78.16)		(66.10)

* Common
[A] Reported in accordance with IFRS

Latest Results

Periods ended:	3m Mar. 31/22[A]		3m Mar. 31/21[A]
	$000s	%Chg	$000s
Operating revenue	225	-26	306
Net income	(137)	n.a.	(38)
	$		$
Earnings per share*	(0.00)		(0.00)

* Common
[A] Reported in accordance with IFRS

Historical Summary
(as originally stated)

Fiscal Year	Oper. Rev.	Net Inc. Bef. Disc.	EPS*
	$000s	$000s	$
2021[A]	1,127	(535)	(0.00)
2020[A]	1,594	(523)	(0.00)
2019[A]	1,716	(702)	(0.00)
2018[A]	2,680	(675)	(0.00)
2017[A]	4,082	(167)	(0.00)

* Common
[A] Reported in accordance with IFRS

U.12 Upstart Investments Inc.

Symbol - UPT.P **Exchange** - TSX-VEN **CUSIP** - 91681C
Head Office - 2700-100 rue Sherbrooke O, Montréal, QC, H3A 3G4 **Telephone** - (514) 375-5172
Email - maxime.lemieux@mcmillan.ca
Investor Relations - Maxime Lemieux (514) 375-5172
Auditors - MNP LLP C.A., Montréal, Qué.
Lawyers - McMillan LLP
Transfer Agents - Computershare Trust Company of Canada Inc., Toronto, Ont.
Profile - (Can. 2022) Capital Pool Company.
Common listed on TSX-VEN, June 29, 2023.
Directors - Mena Beshay, CEO, Richmond, B.C.; Franklin Gattinger, CFO, Qué.; Maxime Lemieux, corp. sec., Montréal, Qué.; Linda Dagenbach, Qué.; Anthony Jenkins, Qué.; Ashik Karim, B.C.

Capital Stock

	Authorized (shs.)	Outstanding (shs.)[1]
Common	unlimited	5,411,000

[1] At June 29, 2023

Major Shareholder - Widely held at June 29, 2023.
Recent Close: $0.12
Capital Stock Changes - On June 29, 2023, an initial public offering of 2,611,000 common shares was completed at 10¢ per share.

U.13 Urbana Corporation

Symbol - URB.A **Exchange** - TSX **CUSIP** - 91707P
Head Office - 1702-150 King St W, PO Box 47, Toronto, ON, M5H 1J9 **Telephone** - (416) 595-9106 **Toll-free** - (800) 256-2441 **Fax** - (416) 862-2498
Website - www.urbanacorp.com
Email - enaumovski@urbanacorp.com
Investor Relations - Elizabeth Naumovski (800) 256-2441
Auditors - Deloitte LLP C.A., Toronto, Ont.
Transfer Agents - TSX Trust Company, Montréal, Qué.
Investment Managers - Caldwell Investment Management Ltd., Toronto, Ont.
Employees - 2 at Mar. 23, 2022
Profile - (Ont. 1947) Invests in private and public companies throughout the world.
Top 10 holdings at Mar. 31, 2023 (as a percentage of portfolio):

Holdings	Percentage
CNSX Markets Inc.[1]	21.8%
Morgan Stanley	8.0%
Whitecap Resources Inc.	7.1%
Cboe Global Markets, Inc.	5.4%
Highview Financial Holdings Inc.[1]	5.2%
Tamarack Valley Energy Ltd.	4.3%
Miami International Holdings Inc.[1]	4.1%
Intercontinental Exchange Group Inc.	3.8%
KKR & Co. Inc.	3.8%
Bank of America Corp.	3.7%

[1] Private investments.

Also holds 44 mining claims, 1,154 hectares, Urban twp., Que.
In October 2022, the company acquired an additional 176,798 Class E preferred shares of **Integrated Grain Processors Co-operative Inc.**, increasing its ownership interest to 17.6%.
Predecessor Detail - Name changed from Urban Resources Limited, June 14, 1985; basis 1 new for 5 old shs.
Directors - Thomas S. Caldwell, pres. & CEO, Toronto, Ont.; George D. Elliott†, Toronto, Ont.; Bethann (Beth) Colle, Toronto, Ont.; Michael B. C. Gundy, Toronto, Ont.; Charles A. V. Pennock, Toronto, Ont.
Other Exec. Officers - Sylvia V. Stinson, CFO; Harry K. Liu, gen. counsel & corp. sec.
† Lead director

Capital Stock

	Authorized (shs.)	Outstanding (shs.)[1]
Preferred	unlimited	nil
Class A	unlimited	31,395,100
Common	unlimited	10,000,000

[1] At May 10, 2023

Preferred - Rank prior to class A and common shares with respect to payment of dividends and distribution of assets in the event of the liquidation, dissolution or wind-up of the company. Non-voting.
Class A - Non-voting.
Common - One vote per share.
Normal Course Issuer Bid - The company plans to make normal course purchases of up to 3,139,548 class A sharres representing 10% of the public float. The bid commenced on Sept. 7, 2022, and expires on Sept. 6, 2023.
Major Shareholder - Thomas S. Caldwell held 47.9% interest at Apr. 21, 2023.

Price Range - URB.A/TSX

Year	Volume	High	Low	Close
2022	5,242,634	$4.21	$3.20	$3.88
2021	5,891,796	$3.69	$2.65	$3.56
2020	11,231,859	$2.84	$1.40	$2.77
2019	4,295,592	$2.90	$2.17	$2.75
2018	4,772,572	$3.50	$2.00	$2.21

Recent Close: $4.09
Capital Stock Changes - During 2022, 1,604,900 class A shares were repurchased under a Normal Course Issuer Bid.

Dividends

URB com N.V. Ra $0.11 pa A est. Jan. 31, 2023
Prev. Rate: $0.10 est. Jan. 31, 2022
Prev. Rate: $0.09 est. Jan. 29, 2021
Prev. Rate: $0.08 est. Jan. 31, 2020
URB.A cl A Ra $0.11 pa A est. Jan. 31, 2023
Prev. Rate: $0.10 est. Jan. 31, 2022
Prev. Rate: $0.09 est. Jan. 29, 2021
Prev. Rate: $0.08 est. Jan. 31, 2020

Wholly Owned Subsidiaries

Urbana International Inc., Del.
- 37.31% int. in **Blue Ocean Technologies, LLC**, New York, N.Y.

Subsidiaries

73.42% int. in **Highview Financial Holdings Inc.**, Oakville, Ont.
65.51% int. in **Radar Capital Inc.**, Toronto, Ont.

Investments

49.99% int. in **CNSX Markets Inc.**, Toronto, Ont.
6.19% int. in **Caldwell Canadian Value Momentum Fund**
20% int. in **Caldwell Financial Ltd.**
11.39% int. in **Caldwell Growth Opportunities Fund**, Canada.

Financial Statistics

Periods ended:	12m Dec. 31/22[A]		12m Dec. 31/21[A]
	$000s	%Chg	$000s
Realized invest. gain (loss)	8,718		10,015
Unrealized invest. gain (loss)	19,224		61,758
Total revenue	**32,521**	**-58**	**77,378**
General & admin. expense	9,762		8,666
Operating expense	**9,762**	**+13**	**8,666**
Operating income	**22,759**	**-67**	**68,712**
Finance costs, gross	1,280		719
Pre-tax income	**21,479**	**-68**	**67,993**
Income taxes	2,562		7,999
Net income	**18,917**	**-68**	**59,994**
Cash & equivalent	269		387
Accounts receivable	2,701		533
Investments	364,156		347,179
Total assets	**367,126**	**+5**	**348,099**
Accts. pay. & accr. liabs	1,150		929
Debt	32,000		23,700
Shareholders' equity	309,602		301,140
Cash from oper. activs	**2,036**	**-70**	**6,778**
Cash from fin. activs	2,155		(7,124)
Net cash position	**269**	**-30**	**387**
	$		$
Earnings per share*	0.45		1.37
Cash flow per share*	0.05		0.15
Net asset value per share*	7.48		7.00
Cash divd. per share*	0.10		0.09
	shs		shs
No. of shs. o/s*	42,050,100		43,000,000
Avg. no. of shs. o/s*	42,050,100		43,854,399
	%		%
Net profit margin	58.17		77.53
Return on equity	6.19		21.80
Return on assets	5.61		19.05

* Cl.A & com.
[A] Reported in accordance with IFRS

Latest Results

Periods ended:	3m Mar. 31/23[A]		3m Mar. 31/22[A]
	$000s	%Chg	$000s
Total revenue	8,634	-77	37,965
Net income	5,230	-83	30,960
	$		$
Earnings per share*	0.13		0.72

* Cl.A & com.
[A] Reported in accordance with IFRS

Historical Summary
(as originally stated)

Fiscal Year	Total Rev.	Net Inc. Bef. Disc.	EPS*
	$000s	$000s	$
2022[A]	32,521	18,917	0.45
2021[A]	77,378	59,994	1.37
2020[A]	22,240	13,084	0.27
2019[A]	63,037	50,745	1.02
2018[A]	(38,265)	(38,856)	(0.78)

* Cl.A & com.
[A] Reported in accordance with IFRS

U.14 Urbanfund Corp.

Symbol - UFC **Exchange** - TSX-VEN **CUSIP** - 916910
Head Office - 35 Lesmill Rd, Toronto, ON, M3B 2T3 **Telephone** - (416) 703-1877 **Fax** - (416) 504-9216
Website - www.urbanfund.ca
Email - mcohen@urbanfund.ca
Investor Relations - Mitchell S. Cohen (416) 703-1877 ext. 2025
Auditors - RSM Canada LLP C.A., Toronto, Ont.
Lawyers - Wildeboer Dellelce LLP, Toronto, Ont.
Transfer Agents - Computershare Trust Company of Canada Inc., Toronto, Ont.
Profile - (Ont. 2003; orig. Alta., 1997) Identifies, evaluates and invests in real estate and real estate related projects, with a focus on residential and commercial properties.
Properties consist of an 84-suite townhouse complex in Toronto, Ont.; a 72,796-sq.-ft. shopping centre in Belleville, Ont.; a 16,000-sq.-ft. shopping centre in London, Ont.; an 86.7% interest in a 133-suite multi-residential property in Kitchener, Ont.; a 40% interest in a 100,073-sq.-ft. industrial complex in Etobicoke, Ont.; a 20% interest in a 1,609-unit multi-residential portfolio in Dartmouth, N.S.; a 10% interest in a 1,678-unit multi-family residential portfolio in Quebec City, Montreal and Levis, Que.; and a 10% interest in a 28,084-sq.-ft. commercial centre in Quebec City, Que.
Also holds a 10% interest in a limited partnership which owns a 33.3% interest in One Bloor East, a high-rise condominium and commercial tower at Yonge and Bloor streets in Toronto, Ont.; and a total of $1,870,000 investment in a limited partnership which owns 50% interest in an industrial complex located on 1040 Martin Grove Road in Toronto, Ont.
In November 2022, the company, together with **Takol Real Estate Inc.** and **2074-84 Steeles Avenue East Inc.**, sold 27 units within the industrial complex located on 2074, 2080 and 2084 Steeles Avenue East, Brampton, Ont., for $3,375,000 (representing the company's 25% interest).

Recent Merger and Acquisition Activity

Status: completed **Announced:** Dec. 31, 2022
Urbanfund Corp., and joint venture partners, Takol Real Estate Inc. and 2074-84 Steeles Avenue East Inc., sold all remaining 36 units in commercial properties located on 2074, 2080 and 2084 Steeles Avenue East, Brampton, Ont. for $7,250,000. Urbanfund held a 25% interest in the joint venture.
Directors - Ronald S. Kimel, chr., Toronto, Ont.; Mitchell S. Cohen, pres., CEO & corp. sec., North York, Ont.; Robert A. Barber, Ont.; Steven G. Isenberg, Toronto, Ont.; Thomas S. (Tom) Kofman, Thornhill, Ont.
Other Exec. Officers - Cathy Leung, CFO

Capital Stock

	Authorized (shs.)	Outstanding (shs.)[1]
First Preferred	unlimited	
Series A	20,000,000	7,425,000
Second Preferred	unlimited	nil
Common	unlimited	52,339,637

[1] At May 25, 2023

First Preferred Series A - Convertible at holder's option into common shares on a 1-for-1 basis for no additional consideration unless the aggregate number of common shares held by directors and officers of the company and parties related to such individuals would exceed 80% of outstanding common shares.
Common - One vote per share.
Major Shareholder - Ronald S. Kimel held 49.83% interest and Louis Reznick held 26.65% interest at May 11, 2023.

Price Range - UFC/TSX-VEN

Year	Volume	High	Low	Close
2022	620,345	$1.24	$0.81	$0.81
2021	1,553,263	$1.55	$0.70	$1.20
2020	1,045,327	$0.80	$0.46	$0.74
2019	312,261	$0.87	$0.50	$0.80
2018	817,104	$0.93	$0.59	$0.77

Recent Close: $0.97
Capital Stock Changes - During 2022, 826,326 common shares were issued under dividend reinvestment plan.

Dividends

UFC com Ra $0.05 pa Q est. July 15, 2021**
Prev. Rate: $0.03 est. July 15, 2019
** Reinvestment Option

Subsidiaries

86.67% int. in **Weber Investments Limited Partnership**

Investments

20% int. in **Bellbrook Residential Inc.**, N.S.
20% int. in **Highfield Park Residential Inc.**, N.S.
40% int. in **Takol 67-69 Westmore Inc.**
20% int. in **West Mic Mac Properties Inc.**, N.S.

Financial Statistics

Periods ended:	12m Dec. 31/22[A]		12m Dec. 31/21[A]
	$000s	%Chg	$000s
Total revenue	**23,806**	**+269**	**6,451**
Rental operating expense	3,757		3,024
Cost of real estate sales	10,150		nil
General & admin. expense	577		624
Operating expense	**14,484**	**+297**	**3,647**
Operating income	**9,322**	**+232**	**2,804**
Investment income	1,013		5,630
Finance income	102		28
Finance costs, gross	2,434		1,707
Pre-tax income	**9,693**	**-22**	**12,386**
Income taxes	2,108		1,709
Net income	**7,585**	**-29**	**10,677**
Net inc. for equity hldrs	**7,343**	**-29**	**10,305**
Net inc. for non-cont. int	**241**	**-35**	**372**
Cash & equivalent	12,993		10,367
Accounts receivable	784		370
Long-term investments	21,596		20,983
Income-producing props	104,437		101,537
Residential inventory	10,520		9,288
Property interests, net	114,957		110,825
Total assets	**150,775**	**+4**	**144,473**
Accts. pay. & accr. liabs	1,612		1,868
Long-term debt, gross	65,073		65,777
Preferred share equity	1,114		1,114
Shareholders' equity	71,668		66,474
Non-controlling interest	1,480		1,239
Cash from oper. activs	**8,049**	**n.a.**	**(2,242)**
Cash from fin. activs	(3,020)		10,328
Cash from invest. activs	(2,404)		(4,249)
Net cash position	**12,993**	**+25**	**10,367**
Increase in property	(2,804)		(4,749)
	$		$
Earnings per share*	0.14		0.20
Cash flow per share*	0.16		(0.04)
Funds from opers. per sh.*	0.13		0.06
Cash divd. per share*	0.05		0.05
Total divd. per share*	**0.05**		**0.05**
	shs		shs
No. of shs. o/s*	51,814,741		50,988,415
Avg. no. of shs. o/s*	51,444,726		50,438,531
	%		%
Net profit margin	31.86		165.51
Return on equity	10.81		16.95
Return on assets	6.43		9.05

* Common
[A] Reported in accordance with IFRS

Latest Results

Periods ended:	3m Mar. 31/23[A]		3m Mar. 31/22[A]
	$000s	%Chg	$000s
Total revenue	2,070	+5	1,980
Net income	1,265	+47	863
Net inc. for equity hldrs	1,219	+44	847
Net inc. for non-cont. int	46		16
	$		$
Earnings per share*	0.02		0.02

* Common
[A] Reported in accordance with IFRS

Historical Summary
(as originally stated)

Fiscal Year	Total Rev.	Net Inc. Bef. Disc.	EPS*
	$000s	$000s	$
2022[A]	23,806	7,585	0.14
2021[A]	6,451	10,677	0.20
2020[A]	10,159	8,003	0.17
2019[A]	5,173	6,506	0.14
2018[A]	10,459	4,689	0.11

* Common
[A] Reported in accordance with IFRS

U.15 Urbanimmersive Inc.

Symbol - UI **Exchange** - TSX-VEN **CUSIP** - 91725D
Head Office - 306-3135 boul Moise-Vincent, Longueuil, QC, J3Z 0G7 **Telephone** - (514) 394-7820 **Toll-free** - (877) 360-2883 **Fax** - (514) 394-7821
Website - www.urbanimmersive.com
Email - ghislainlemire@urbanimmersive.com
Investor Relations - Ghislain Lemire (514) 394-7820 ext. 202
Auditors - Raymond Chabot Grant Thornton LLP C.A., Montréal, Qué.
Transfer Agents - TSX Trust Company
Profile - (Can. 2011) Develops and markets software-as-a-service (SaaS) solutions for visual content providers serving the real estate residential, commercial, construction and local business markets; resells dimensional (3D) photographic equipments; and provides photography services to professional photographers.

Operations are carried out through three segments: Software; Photographic Equipment; and Services.

The **Software** segment offers SaaS marketing platform to professional photographers and other immersive visual content providers. The company's core technology is a 3D emulator powered by a visual content recognition post-production algorithm that delivers online and offline alternatives to traditional 3D engines for the creation of immersive digital environments. Products include Immersive 3D Tour, which emulates real 3D environments using spherical images; UiMeet3D, a 3D and video conference technology which enables people to walk through a place and visually interact with other visitors from the convenience of their phones and PCs; UiTags, which integrates information about the premises, room measurements, items for sale and video marketing; Floor Plan, which can edit and add elements for the residential, commercial and/or industrial properties or buildings generated by the company's 3D tours and immersive 3D emulator; and 3D Pocket Website™, which are downloadable single property websites in which backgrounds are replaced by immersive experiences.

The **Photographic Equipment** segment offers resale service of 3D cameras and 360 lenses. This segment also provides custom cases for the protection and transportation of photographic equipment to customers worldwide.

The **Services** segment offers real estate photography, floor plans, measurement and management services.

Recent Merger and Acquisition Activity

Status: completed **Revised:** Oct. 21, 2022
UPDATE: The transaction was completed. PREVIOUS: Urbanimmersive Inc. agreed to acquire real estate photography agency Homevisit, LLC from CoreLogic Solutions, LLC for purchase price of Cdn$9,000,000 payable by issuance of 9,287,707 common shares at a deemed price of $0.25 per share and issuance of a five-year 7.5% secured promissory note for the adjusted balance of the purchase price amounting to $6,678,073. The shares issued represent a 19.9% equity interest. CoreLogic Solutions is owned by CoreLogic, Inc. Chantilly, Va.-based Homevisit provides marketing-focused real estate solutions, including property listing photography, videography, 3D tours, drone imagery, printing services and other related services

Predecessor Detail - Name changed from Urbanimmersive Technologies Inc., Oct. 1, 2015, following amalgamation with wholly owned Urbanimmersive Inc.

Directors - Ghislain Lemire, co-founder, pres. & CEO, Sainte-Julie, Qué.; Jean-François Grou, chr., Montréal, Qué.; Simon Bédard, CFO, Qué.; Judith Brosseau, Laval, Qué.; Glenn Felson, Kinnelon, N.J.; Lynn McDonald, Verdun, Qué.

Other Exec. Officers - Martin Thibault, co-founder & chief mktg. officer; Alexandre Henry-Lebel, chief tech. officer

Capital Stock

	Authorized (shs.)	Outstanding (shs.)[1]
Common	unlimited	62,003,100

[1] At June 30, 2023

Major Shareholder - Widely held at Feb. 22, 2023.

Price Range - UI/TSX-VEN

Year	Volume	High	Low	Close
2022	7,794,243	$0.83	$0.20	$0.22
2021	18,749,313	$1.28	$0.48	$0.79
2020	8,803,207	$0.75	$0.18	$0.75
2019	4,780,768	$0.50	$0.23	$0.30
2018	16,386,272	$1.35	$0.33	$0.45

Consolidation: 1-for-5 cons. in Sept. 2021
Recent Close: $0.07
Capital Stock Changes - In October 2022, 9,287,707 common shares were issued pursuant to the acquisition of HomeVisit, LLC.

During fiscal 2022, common shares were issued as follows: 3,157,115 pursuant to the acquisition of Imoto LLC, 1,518,997 pursuant to the acquisition of Agento Marketing, 690,528 as bonus shares, 585,829 pursuant to the acquisition of Virtual Access Tours LP, 365,292 pursuant to the acquisition of intangible assets, 202,560 on exercise of warrants, 134,894 by private placement, 103,093 pursuant to the acquisition of Immophoto Inc. and 100,000 on exercise of options.

Wholly Owned Subsidiaries

Agence Immophoto Inc.
EGP Technovirtuel Inc., Qué.
8239991 Canada Inc., Canada. dba Immersolution
- 2% int. in **Immersolution Mexico S. de R.L. de C.V.**

Graphique ID Solutions Inc., Qué.
Homevisit, LLC, Chantilly, Va.
10366358 Canada Inc., Gatineau, Qué. dba Agento Marketing
Urbanimmersive USA Corp., United States.
- 100% int. in **Imoto LLC**
- 100% int. in **Stilio LLC**
- 100% int. in **Virtual Access Tours L.P.**

Subsidiaries

98% int. in **Immersolution Mexico S. de R.L. de C.V.**

Financial Statistics

Periods ended:	12m Sept. 30/22[A]		12m Sept. 30/21[A]
	$000s	%Chg	$000s
Operating revenue	**8,337**	**+105**	**4,069**
Cost of goods sold	90		788
General & admin expense	5,054		2,561
Operating expense	**5,144**	**+54**	**3,349**
Operating income	**3,193**	**+343**	**720**
Deprec., depl. & amort	1,266		730
Finance income	nil		3
Finance costs, gross	285		763
Write-downs/write-offs	(232)		(1)
Pre-tax income	**(1,674)**	**n.a.**	**(3,961)**
Income taxes	(83)		(252)
Net income	**(1,590)**	**n.a.**	**(3,709)**
Cash & equivalent	675		1,678
Inventories	32		118
Accounts receivable	309		291
Current assets	1,063		2,163
Fixed assets, net	1,114		1,103
Right-of-use assets	151		nil
Intangibles, net	16,586		9,366
Total assets	**18,914**	**+50**	**12,632**
Accts. pay. & accr. liabs	905		557
Current liabilities	4,695		1,029
Long-term debt, gross	3,682		1,855
Long-term debt, net	70		1,538
Shareholders' equity	12,838		9,416
Cash from oper. activs	**(96)**	**n.a.**	**(26)**
Cash from fin. activs	1,846		2,995
Cash from invest. activs	(2,735)		(2,176)
Net cash position	**675**	**-60**	**1,678**
Capital expenditures	(231)		(360)
Capital disposals	89		nil
	$		$
Earnings per share*	(0.04)		(0.15)
Cash flow per share*	(0.00)		(0.00)
	shs		shs
No. of shs. o/s*	37,318,990		30,460,692
Avg. no. of shs. o/s*	35,459,109		25,224,784
	%		%
Net profit margin	(19.07)		(91.15)
Return on equity	(14.29)		(63.28)
Return on assets	(8.36)		(27.75)
Foreign sales percent	65		60
No. of employees (FTEs)	n.a.		100

* Common
[A] Reported in accordance with IFRS

Historical Summary
(as originally stated)

Fiscal Year	Oper. Rev.	Net Inc. Bef. Disc.	EPS*
	$000s	$000s	$
2022[A]	8,337	(1,590)	(0.04)
2021[A]	4,069	(3,709)	(0.15)
2020[A]	4,594	(413)	(0.05)
2019[A]	4,454	1,942	0.15
2018[A]	2,246	(2,766)	(0.20)

* Common
[A] Reported in accordance with IFRS
Note: Adjusted throughout for 1-for-5 cons. in Sept. 2021

V

V.1 VBI Vaccines Inc.

Symbol - VBIV **Exchange** - NASDAQ **CUSIP** - 91822J
Head Office - 160 Second St, Floor 3, Cambridge, MA, United States, 02142 **Telephone** - (617) 830-3031
Website - www.vbivaccines.com
Email - nbeattie@vbivaccines.com
Investor Relations - Nell Beattie (617) 830-3031 ext. 124
Auditors - EisnerAmper LLP C.P.A., Iselin, N.J.
Transfer Agents - Computershare Trust Company of Canada Inc.
Profile - (B.C. 1965) Develops vaccine candidates that mimic the natural presentation of viruses through a proprietary enveloped virus-like particles (eVLP) platform technology, with a focus on hepatitis B.

The company is pursuing the prevention and treatment of significant infectious diseases including hepatitis B, COVID-19 and coronaviruses, and cytomegalovirus (CMV), as well as aggressive cancers including glioblastoma (GBM).

Product pipeline consists of vaccine and immunotherapeutic candidates developed by VLP technologies to target two distinct, but often related, disease areas: the infectious disease and oncology. Approved vaccine includes PreHevbrio (Hepatitis B Vaccine - Recombinant) for use in the U.S. for the prevention of infection caused by all known subtypes of hepatitis B virus in adults 18 years of age and older, in Israel (under brand name Sci-B-Vac®) for active immunization against hepatitis B virus, and in the European Union (under brand name PreHevbri®) for active immunization against infection caused by all known subtypes of the hepatitis B virus in adults. Vaccine candidates are organized into prophylactic candidates and therapeutic candidates.

Prophylactic candidates include Sci-B-Vac®, a third generation hepatitis B vaccine for adults, children and newborns that contains all three viral surface antigens of the hepatitis B virus; VBI-1501 for treatment of CMV, an infection that can lead to serious complications in babies and people with weak immune systems; VBI-2900, a coronavirus vaccine program utilizing eVLP technology which consists of (i) VBI-2901, a trivalent pan-coronavirus vaccine candidate expressing the SARS-CoV-2 (COVID-19), SARS-CoV (SARS) and MERS-CoV (MERS) spike proteins, (ii) VBI-2902, a monovalent vaccine candidate expressing the SARS-CoV-2 (COVID-19) spike protein, and (iii) VBI-2905, a monovalent vaccine candidate expressing the pre-fusion form of the spike protein from the SARS-COV-2 Beta variant strain; and VBI-2501, a bivalent eVLP vaccine candidate consisting of a modified E glycoprotein (found on the surface of the Zika virus) and NS1 glycoprotein (secreted during Zika viral replication).

Therapeutic candidates include VBI-2601 (BRII-179), a recombinant, protein-based immunotherapeutic treatment of chronic hepatitis B, in the People's Republic of China, Hong Kong, Taiwan and Macau; and VBI-1901 for treatment of recurring GBM, a form of brain cancer. The company has partnered with **Brii Biosciences Limited** to develop VBI-2601 (BRII-179).

The company is headquartered in Cambridge, Mass., with research operations in Ottawa, Ont., and research and manufacturing facilities in Rehovot, Israel.

Predecessor Detail - Name changed from SciVac Therapeutics Inc., May 6, 2016, pursuant to the to acquisition of (old) VBI Vaccines Inc.
Directors - Dr. Steven Gillis, chr., Mercer Island, Wash.; Jeffrey R. (Jeff) Baxter, pres. & CEO, Pa.; Nell Beattie, CFO & head, corp. devel., Boston, Mass.; Linda Bain, Mass.; Damian Braga, N.J.; Joanne Cordeiro, Mass.; Dr. Michel De Wilde, N.J.; Dr. Vaughn B. Himes; Dr. Blaine H. McKee, Mass.
Other Exec. Officers - Dr. David E. Anderson, chief scientific officer; Dr. Francisco Diaz-Mitoma, CMO; John Dillman, chief comml. officer; Adam Buckley, sr. v-p, bus. devel.; Misha Nossov, sr. v-p, market access & comml.

Capital Stock

	Authorized (shs.)	Outstanding (shs.)[1]
Common	unlimited	8,608,583

[1] At Apr. 12, 2023

Major Shareholder - Perceptive Advisors LLC held 20.26% interest at Apr. 25, 2022.

Price Range - VBIV/NASDAQ

Year	Volume	High	Low	Close
2022	4,618,363	US$74.10	US$10.80	US$11.73
2021	8,546,764	US$144.90	US$63.00	US$70.20
2020	14,359,963	US$207.60	US$20.70	US$82.50
2019	3,630,616	US$66.00	US$13.98	US$41.40
2018	625,836	US$138.00	US$36.00	US$48.00

VBV/TSX (D)

Year	Volume	High	Low	Close
2018	7,031	$175.80	$131.10	$144.60

Consolidation: 1-for-30 cons. in Apr. 2023
Capital Stock Changes - On Apr. 12, 2023, common shares were consolidated on a 1-for-30 basis.

Wholly Owned Subsidiaries

SciVac Hong Kong Limited, Hong Kong, People's Republic of China.
SciVac Ltd., Rehovot, Israel.
VBI Vaccines B.V., Netherlands.
VBI Vaccines (Delaware) Inc., Del. formerly (old) VBI Vaccines Inc.
- 100% int. in **Variation Biotechnologies (US), Inc.**, Del.
  - 100% int. in **Variation Biotechnologies, Inc.**, Ottawa, Ont.

Financial Statistics

Periods ended:	12m Dec. 31/21[A]		12m Dec. 31/20[A]
	US$000s	%Chg	US$000s
Operating revenue	**631**	**-41**	**1,061**
Cost of sales	10,770		9,168
Research & devel. expense	19,558		14,859
General & admin expense	36,500		18,999
Operating expense	**66,828**	**+55**	**43,026**
Operating income	**(66,197)**	**n.a.**	**(41,965)**
Deprec., depl. & amort.	1,835		1,652
Finance income	372		613
Finance costs, gross	5,104		3,321
Pre-tax income	**(69,753)**	**n.a.**	**(46,230)**
Net income	**(69,753)**	**n.a.**	**(46,230)**
Cash & equivalent	121,694		119,101
Inventories	2,576		2,152
Accounts receivable	nil		77
Current assets	130,284		132,041
Fixed assets, net	11,037		10,721
Right-of-use assets	3,344		1,554
Intangibles, net	64,352		64,417
Total assets	**210,276**	**0**	**209,372**
Accts. pay. & accr. liabs	31,221		16,149
Current liabilities	32,586		17,348
Long-term debt, gross	28,441		16,329
Long-term debt, net	28,441		16,329
Long-term lease liabilities	2,516		619
Shareholders' equity	143,882		171,705
Cash from oper. activs	**(39,908)**	**n.a.**	**(47,050)**
Cash from fin. activs	44,923		122,392
Cash from invest. activs	23,156		(26,000)
Net cash position	**121,694**	**+30**	**93,825**
Capital expenditures	(1,995)		(1,000)
	US$		US$
Earnings per share*	(8.10)		(6.30)
Cash flow per share*	(4.70)		(6.47)
	shs		shs
No. of shs. o/s*	8,608,342		8,234,634
Avg. no. of shs. o/s*	8,498,240		7,275,633
	%		%
Net profit margin	n.m.		n.m.
Return on equity	(44.21)		(35.57)
Return on assets	(30.81)		(25.88)
Foreign sales percent	100		100
No. of employees (FTEs)	149		127

* Common
[A] Reported in accordance with U.S. GAAP

Latest Results

Periods ended:	3m Mar. 31/22[A]		3m Mar. 31/21[A]
	US$000s	%Chg	US$000s
Operating revenue	126	-58	301
Net income	(21,254)	n.a.	(17,647)
	US$		US$
Earnings per share*	(2.40)		(2.10)

* Common
[A] Reported in accordance with U.S. GAAP

Historical Summary
(as originally stated)

Fiscal Year	Oper. Rev.	Net Inc. Bef. Disc.	EPS*
	US$000s	US$000s	US$
2021[A]	631	(69,753)	(8.10)
2020[A]	1,061	(46,230)	(6.30)
2019[A]	2,221	(54,813)	(13.80)
2018[A]	3,355	(63,600)	(29.10)
2017[A]	865	(38,995)	(26.40)

* Common
[A] Reported in accordance with U.S. GAAP
Note: Adjusted throughout for 1-for-30 cons. in Apr. 2023

V.2 VIP Entertainment Technologies Inc.

Symbol - VIP **Exchange** - TSX-VEN **CUSIP** - 92763B
Head Office - 3200-500 4 Ave SW, Calgary, AB, T2P 2V6 **Telephone** - (587) 436-5635
Website - vipentertaingroup.com
Email - bobl@vipentertaingroup.com
Investor Relations - Robert P. Lunde (604) 763-1034
Auditors - MNP LLP C.A., Calgary, Alta.
Transfer Agents - Computershare Trust Company of Canada Inc., Vancouver, B.C.
Profile - (B.C. 2019) Operates the VipBets.com gaming platform offering online sports betting, casino games and poker to bettors and players.

Recent Merger and Acquisition Activity

Status: completed **Revised:** July 6, 2022
UPDATE: The transaction was completed. ANC issued a total of 74,538,309 common shares at a deemed price of 21¢ per share. PREVIOUS: ANC Capital Ventures Inc. entered into a term sheet for the Qualifying Transaction reverse takeover acquisition of private Calgary, Alta.-based VIP Entertainment Group Inc. on the basis of 1.16739 ANC common shares for each VIP share held, which would result in the issuance of 63,300,000 ANC common shares. VIP operates the VipBets.com gaming platform offering online sports betting, casino games and poker to bettors and players. Upon completion, ANC would change its name to VIP Entertainment Technologies Inc. Apr. 21, 2022 - A definitive agreement was entered into.

Predecessor Detail - Name changed from ANC Capital Ventures Inc., July 6, 2022, pursuant to the Qualifying Transaction reverse takeover acquisition of VIP Entertainment Group Inc.
Directors - Robert P. (Bob) Lunde, CEO, Vancouver, B.C.; Scott Seguin, interim CFO, Calgary, Alta.; David M. (Dave) Antony, Calgary, Alta.; Joel Donais, Calgary, Alta.
Other Exec. Officers - Trevor P. Wong-Chor, corp. sec.

Capital Stock

	Authorized (shs.)	Outstanding (shs.)[1]
Common	unlimited	18,044,862

[1] At Mar. 1, 2023

Major Shareholder - Randy Jennings held 16.68% interest and Theresa Jennings held 16.68% interest at July 14, 2022.

Price Range - VIP/TSX-VEN

Year	Volume	High	Low	Close
2022	2,493,054	$1.25	$0.20	$0.35
2020	20,200	$0.50	$0.40	$0.40

Consolidation: 1-for-5 cons. in Mar. 2023
Recent Close: $0.08
Capital Stock Changes - On Mar. 1, 2023, common shares were consolidated on a 1-for-5 basis.

On July 6, 2022, 74,538,309 common shares were issued pursuant to the Qualifying Transaction reverse takeover acquisition of VIP Entertainment Group Inc.

During fiscal 2022, 350,000 common shares were issued on exercise of options.

Wholly Owned Subsidiaries

VIP Entertainment Group Inc., Calgary, Alta.
- 100% int. in **VIP Entertainment N.V.**, Willemstad, Curacao.
  - 100% int. in **Coal Harbour Developments Limited**, Nicosia, Cyprus.
  - 100% int. in **Westchester Holdings Inc.**, Belize City, Belize.

Financial Statistics

Periods ended:	12m Dec. 31/21[A1]		12m Dec. 31/20[A]
	$000s	%Chg	$000s
Operating revenue	**540**	**-32**	**796**
General & admin expense	1,767		888
Operating expense	**1,767**	**+99**	**888**
Operating income	**(1,227)**	**n.a.**	**(92)**
Finance costs, gross	55		2
Write-downs/write-offs	nil		(66)
Pre-tax income	**(701)**	**n.a.**	**(28)**
Net income	**(702)**	**n.a.**	**(28)**
Cash & equivalent	42		39
Current assets	62		39
Total assets	**62**	**-70**	**204**
Bank indebtedness	267		nil
Accts. pay. & accr. liabs	307		444
Current liabilities	603		586
Long-term debt, gross	nil		210
Long-term debt, net	nil		154
Shareholders' equity	(540)		(536)
Cash from oper. activs	**(559)**	**n.a.**	**(25)**
Cash from fin. activs	563		(10)
Net cash position	**42**	**+8**	**39**
	$		$
Earnings per share*	(0.07)		(0.00)
Cash flow per share*	(0.05)		(0.00)
	shs		shs
No. of shs. o/s	n.a.		n.a.
Avg. no. of shs. o/s*	10,416,826		10,550,020
	%		%
Net profit margin	(129.81)		(3.52)
Return on equity	n.m.		n.m.
Return on assets	(485.71)		n.a.

* Common

[A] Reported in accordance with IFRS

[1] Results prior to July 6, 2022, pertain to and reflect the Qualifying Transaction reverse takeover acquisition of VIP Entertainment Group Inc.

Latest Results

Periods ended:	3m Mar. 31/22[A]		3m Mar. 31/21[A]
	$000s	%Chg	$000s
Operating revenue	107	-45	196
Net income	(81)	n.a.	(143)
	$		$
Earnings per share*	(0.01)		(0.01)

* Common

[A] Reported in accordance with IFRS

Note: Adjusted throughout for 1-for-5 cons. in Mar. 2023

V.3 VIQ Solutions Inc.

Symbol - VQS **Exchange** - TSX **CUSIP** - 91825V
Head Office - 700-5915 Airport Rd, Mississauga, ON, L4V 1T1 **Telephone** - (905) 948-8266 **Toll-free** - (800) 263-9947
Website - www.viqsolutions.com
Email - lhaggard@viqsolutions.com
Investor Relations - Laura Haggard (905) 948-8266
Auditors - Ernst & Young LLP C.A., Toronto, Ont.
Lawyers - McMillan LLP, Toronto, Ont.
Transfer Agents - TSX Trust Company, Toronto, Ont.
Employees - 483 at Dec. 31, 2022

Profile - (Alta. 2004) Develops and provides secure technology and service platform for digital evidence capture, retrieval and content management used by security-focused and regulated public and private sectors.

Operates worldwide with a network of partners including security integrators, audio-video specialists, and hardware and data storage suppliers.

Solutions include CapturePro™, which allows users to securely speed the capture, creation and management of large volumes of official court records, police interrogations or insurance investigations; MobileMic Pro™, a mobile smartphone app which allow users to capture and manage incident reports, recorded statements, case notes and other vital information; NetScribe™, a web-based transcription workflow management platform which provides secure access to single and multi-channel audio recordings; aiAssist™, a multi-tenant workflow and analysis platform which combines advanced technologies, including artificial intelligence, machine learning, and natural language processing, with human intelligence to create documentation from live, multi-channel audio and audio/video; FirstDraft™, which enables clients to convert audio files to text to provide access to interviews, testimonies, recorded calls and dictations; Lexel, which organizes case documents, review recorded testimonies and generate real-time transcript to ensure litigation preparedness, organizational data transparency and streamlined access to critical information of law firms and courts; AccessPoint™, which provides court personnel and legal professionals around the world with instant access to court recordings through a secure, cloud-based portal; and Carbon, a cloud-based media content and text workflow platform which was developed to address broadcast production needs, including administrative controls for organizations with complex workflows and a need for a high level of security.

Also provides recording and transcription services directly to a variety of clients including medical, courtrooms, legislative assemblies, hearing rooms, inquiries and quasi-judicial clients in Canada, the U.K., the U.S. and Australia.

Directors - Larry D. Taylor, exec. chr., Toronto, Ont.; Sebastien Paré, CEO, Ont.; Susan Sumner, pres. & COO, Fla.; Christine Fellowes, Singapore; Harvey Gordon, Ont.; Yixin (Shing) Pan, Calif.; Joseph D. (Joe) Quarin, Toronto, Ont.; Brad Wells, Ont.

Other Exec. Officers - Alexie Edwards, CFO; Laura Haggard, chief mktg. officer; Vahram Sukyas, chief tech. officer; Tony Incardona, sr. v-p, global sales & bus. devel.; Tim Johnson, sr. v-p, intl.

Capital Stock

	Authorized (shs.)	Outstanding (shs.)[1]
Common	unlimited	34,718,139

[1] At May 19, 2023

Major Shareholder - Brad Wells held 12.08% interest at May 19, 2023.

Price Range - VQS/TSX

Year	Volume	High	Low	Close
2022	11,758,269	$2.96	$0.30	$0.36
2021	14,400,860	$9.79	$2.46	$2.99
2020	5,427,512	$6.50	$1.71	$5.85
2019	1,874,742	$3.20	$1.80	$2.18
2018	1,588,574	$5.80	$2.10	$2.80

Consolidation: 1-for-20 cons. in Dec. 2019

Recent Close: $0.34

Capital Stock Changes - In July 2022, private placement of 3,551,852 units (1 common share & 1 warrant) at $1.35 per unit was completed. Also during 2022, common shares were issued as follows: 1,078,901 for financing fees and for 137,227 under restricted share unit plan.

Wholly Owned Subsidiaries

Dataworxs Systems Limited, Mississauga, Ont.
- 100% int. in **Dataworxs Systems Australia Pty Ltd.**, Australia.

VIQ Australia Pty Limited, Australia.
- 100% int. in **VIQ Australia Services Pty Ltd.**, N.S.W., Australia.
- 100% int. in **VIQ Pty Ltd.**, N.S.W., Australia.
- 100% int. in **VIQ Solutions Australia Pty Ltd**, Australia.
- 100% int. in **VIQ Solutions Pty Limited**, Perth, W.A., Australia.

VIQ Services (UK) Limited, United Kingdom.
- 1% int. in **Transcription Agency LLP**, United Kingdom.

VIQ Solutions, Inc., Del.
- 100% int. in **VIQ Services Inc.**
  - 100% int. in **HomeTech, Inc.**, Seattle, Wash.
  - 100% int. in **Net Transcripts, Inc.**, Phoenix, Ariz.
  - 100% int. in **Transcription Express Inc.**, Gilbert, Ariz.
  - 100% int. in **VIQ Media Transcription Inc.**, Del.
  - 100% int. in **wordZXpressed, Inc.**, Atlanta, Ga.

VIQ Solutions (U.K.) Limited, United Kingdom.
- 99% int. in **Transcription Agency LLP**, United Kingdom.

Financial Statistics

Periods ended:	12m Dec. 31/22[A]		12m Dec. 31/21[A]
	US$000s	%Chg	US$000s
Operating revenue	**45,844**	**+48**	**31,047**
Cost of sales	23,918		16,124
Research & devel. expense	734		1,092
General & admin expense	24,426		18,836
Stock-based compensation	2,779		8,495
Operating expense	**51,858**	**+16**	**44,547**
Operating income	**(6,014)**	**n.a.**	**(13,500)**
Deprec., depl. & amort	6,088		4,642
Finance income	2		23
Finance costs, gross	2,284		2,298
Write-downs/write-offs	(115)		(284)
Pre-tax income	**(9,316)**	**n.a.**	**(18,735)**
Income taxes	(610)		944
Net income	**(8,706)**	**n.a.**	**(19,679)**
Cash & equivalent	1,658		10,584
Inventories	38		50
Accounts receivable	5,306		5,594
Current assets	9,156		18,282
Fixed assets, net	1,432		461
Right-of-use assets	1,059		1,134
Intangibles, net	22,779		27,045
Total assets	**35,545**	**-25**	**47,692**
Accts. pay. & accr. liabs	5,938		5,381
Current liabilities	17,173		10,293
Long-term debt, gross	8,654		13,109
Long-term debt, net	20		11,999
Long-term lease liabilities	719		901
Shareholders' equity	15,643		22,090
Cash from oper. activs	**(2,336)**	**n.a.**	**(8,238)**
Cash from fin. activs	(4,014)		(14,441)
Cash from invest. activs	(2,374)		16,522
Net cash position	**1,658**	**-84**	**10,584**
Capital expenditures	(1,202)		(79)
	US$		US$
Earnings per share*	(0.28)		(0.74)
Cash flow per share*	(0.07)		(0.31)
	shs		shs
No. of shs. o/s*	34,649,697		29,881,717
Avg. no. of shs. o/s*	31,648,001		26,448,594
	%		%
Net profit margin	(18.99)		(63.38)
Return on equity	(46.15)		(93.99)
Return on assets	(15.79)		(38.19)
Foreign sales percent	100		99
No. of employees (FTEs)	483		539

* Common

[A] Reported in accordance with IFRS

Latest Results

Periods ended:	3m Mar. 31/23[A]		3m Mar. 31/22[A]
	US$000s	%Chg	US$000s
Operating revenue	10,053	-13	11,525
Net income	(3,460)	n.a.	(2,010)
	US$		US$
Earnings per share*	(0.10)		(0.07)

* Common

[A] Reported in accordance with IFRS

Historical Summary
(as originally stated)

Fiscal Year	Oper. Rev.	Net Inc. Bef. Disc.	EPS*
	US$000s	US$000s	US$
2022[A]	45,844	(8,706)	(0.28)
2021[A]	31,047	(19,679)	(0.74)
2020[A]	31,750	(11,145)	(0.62)
2019[A]	25,096	(4,524)	(0.49)
2018[A]	11,463	(6,067)	(0.80)

* Common

[A] Reported in accordance with IFRS

Note: Adjusted throughout for 1-for-20 cons. in Dec. 2019

V.4 VM Hotel Acquisition Corp.

Symbol - VMH.U **Exchange** - TSX **CUSIP** - 91835A
Head Office - Brookfield Place, 2420-161 Bay St, Toronto, ON, M5J 2S1 **Telephone** - (416) 910-9889
Website - vm-hotel.com
Email - imcauley@vcmgam.com
Investor Relations - Ian McAuley (416) 910-9889
Auditors - KPMG LLP C.A., Toronto, Ont.
Lawyers - Goodmans LLP, Toronto, Ont.
Transfer Agents - TSX Trust Company, Toronto, Ont.

Profile - (B.C. 2020) A Special Purpose Acquisition Corporation formed for the purpose of effecting an acquisition of one or more businesses or assets by way of a merger, share exchange, asset acquisition, share purchase, reorganization or any other similar business combination involving the company.

The company initial had 18 months from Mar. 1, 2021, to complete a Qualifying Acquisition or 21 months if it has executed a definitive agreement for a Qualifying Acquisition within 18 months from Mar. 1, 2021. The date by which to complete Qualifying Acquisition was extended to Sept. 30, 2023. The company plans to execute a Qualifying Acquisition which will aggregate a portfolio of hotel and resort properties and/or related assets and/or businesses. However, the company's search for a Qualifying Acquisition is not limited to a particular industry or geographic region.

In August 2023, the company proposed a further extension of the date by which it has to complete Qualifying Acquisition from Sept. 30, 2023 to Feb. 29, 2024.

In March 2023, the company further extended the date by which it has to complete Qualifying Acquisition from Mar. 31, 2023, to Sept. 30, 2023.

In November 2022, the company extended the date by which it has to complete Qualifying Acquisition from Nov. 30, 2022, to Mar. 31, 2023.

In July 2022, the company executed a non-binding letter of intent in connection with a potential Qualifying Acquisition. The company plans to disclose additional details regarding the acquisition following the execution of a definitive agreement, if applicable. Accordingly, the permitted timeline to complete a Qualifying Acquisition was automatically extended to Nov. 30, 2022.

Recent Merger and Acquisition Activity

Status: pending **Revised:** Apr. 6, 2023

UPDATE: The outside date for the closing of the transaction has passed. An amending agreement was entered to allow for the renegotiation of the terms of the transaction, to reduce the consideration and for Pyure to seek alternative financing agreement with third parties that are not listed on a recognized stock exchange. PREVIOUS: VM Hotel Acquisition Corp. agreed to the Qualifying Acquisition of Boynton Beach, Fla.-based The Pyure Company Inc., which designs and manufactures air and surface purifiers, for issuance of 25,000,000 common shares at a deemed price of US$10 per share. Pyure offered active purification using a proprietary technology that replicates the way sunlight sanitizes the atmosphere by generating hydroxyls and diffusing natural molecules that clean all air and surfaces in the indoor space. Pyure has also developed a cloud-based indoor air quality management platform that delivers indoor air quality as a service. The transaction was expected to be completed during the fourth quarter of 2022.

Status: terminated **Revised:** May 30, 2022

UPDATE: VM decided not to proceed with the acquisition of the remaining assets consisting of Hyatt Regency and the Renaissance hotels in Cleveland, Ohio. PREVIOUS: VM Hotel Acquisition Corp. agreed to the Qualifying Acquisition of five premier hotels, consisting of a total of 2,079 rooms, in Boston, Mass., Cleveland (2), Ohio, Montreal, Que., and Panama City Beach, Fla., for US$411,200,000. The purchase price would be funded through a combination of a US$260,000,000 mortgage financing and US$20,000,000 raised through the issuance of VM shares to a vendor, with the remaining portion funded through cash on hand and a proposed private placement. VM would have a 100% interest in each of the hotels except a 491-room hotel in Cleveland, which VM would have a 90% interest. Upon completion, VM could become a publicly traded real estate operating company. The Qualifying Acquisition was expected to be completed in the first quarter of 2022. Feb. 23, 2022 - VM decided not to proceed with the acquisition of the Battery Wharf and Sheraton Centre hotels in Boston, Mass., and Montreal, Que., respectively. VM was continuing to pursue the acquisition of the three remaining hotels. The acquisition value of just the three hotels was unknown. Mar. 14, 2022 - The agreement to acquire Sheraton Golf & Spa hotel in Panama City Beach, Fla., was terminated.

Directors - Tom A. Vukota, exec. chr. & corp. sec., Nassau, Bahamas; Ian McAuley, pres. & CEO, Toronto, Ont.; Dr. John Andrew, Kingston, Ont.; Tracy C. Sherren, Hammonds Plains, N.S.; Charles Suddaby, Toronto, Ont.

Other Exec. Officers - Tom Wenner, CFO

Capital Stock

	Authorized (shs.)	Outstanding (shs.)[1]
Cl.A Restricted Vtg.	unlimited	46,642
Class B	unlimited	2,937,500

[1] At Aug. 10, 2023

Class A Restricted Voting - Automatically convertible into common shares upon closing of Qualifying Acquisition on a 1-for-1 basis. Not permitted to redeem more than 15% of class A restricted voting shares outstanding. Automatically redeemable if no Qualifying Acquisition is completed. One vote per share on all matters requiring shareholder approval including a proposed Qualifying Acquisition but not on the election and/or removal of directors and auditors.

Class B - Non-redeemable. Automatically convertible into proportionate voting shares upon closing of Qualifying Acquisition on the basis of 1 proportionate voting share for 100 class B shares. One vote per share.

Common - Not issuable prior to closing of Qualifying Acquisition. One vote per share.

Proportionate Voting - Not issuable prior to closing of Qualifying Acquisition. Would be convertible, at the holder's option, into common shares on the basis of 100 common shares for 1 proportionate share. 100 votes per share.

Major Shareholder - VM HA Sponsor Corp. held 53.55% interest and VM HA Sponsor LP held 44.48% interest at Mar. 24, 2023.

Price Range - VMH.U/TSX

Year	Volume	High	Low	Close
2022	169,698	US$10.09	US$9.01	US$9.85
2021	168,415	US$10.00	US$7.24	US$9.65

VMH.V/TSX (D)

Year	Volume	High	Low	Close
2021	119,720	US$9.95	US$9.30	US$9.65

Recent Close: US$9.40

Capital Stock Changes - In March 2023, 1,608,700 class A restricted voting shares were redeemed following the extension of the date by which it has to complete Qualifying Acquisition.

In November 2022, 8,344,658 class A restricted voting shares were redeemed following the extension of the date by which it has to complete Qualifying Acquisition.

V.5 VOTI Detection Inc.

Symbol - VOTI.H **Exchange** - TSX-VEN (S) **CUSIP** - 91833M

Head Office - 790 rue Begin, Saint-Laurent, QC, H4M 2N5 **Telephone** - (514) 752-1566

Website - www.votidetection.com

Email - dan.menard@votidetection.com

Investor Relations - Daniel P. Ménard (514) 782-1566

Auditors -

Transfer Agents - TSX Trust Company, Toronto, Ont.

Profile - (B.C. 2017) Develops X-ray security systems based on proprietary 3D Perspective™ technology.

The company's market includes air cargo, critical infrastructures, events, justice, loss prevention, maritime, precious metals, and transportation and borders.

The company's technology includes 3D Perspective™, which eliminates blind spots for enhanced threat detection and heightened security; BioSans™, which is responsible for generating the 3D Perspective™ images by merging multiple shots into one, with a focus on clarity and quality to provide the highest standard of threat detection and simplify use for the operator; BioSans™ MATRIX, which offers additional applications and differentiated solutions to extend the functionality and value of the customer's current and future equipment; and VotiINSIGHTS™ is a web-based platform for the centralized and remote management of VOTI Detections XR3D scanners.

Software modules include VotiALERT™, which is an application developed to provide easy-to-use automated threat assessment management and material classification recognition; VotiRAM™ (Risk Assessment Management), which has fully customizable detection parameters in addition to five security risk assessment levels and automatically changes system parameters at all levels, adjusting the scanning speed and detection sensitivity; VotiPMD™ (Precious Metal Detector), which offers auto detection solution (platinum, gold, silver and other metals) for miners, jewellers, electronics suppliers, retailers and manufacturers to guard against theft; and VotiTIP™ (Threat Image Projection), a management tool that uses extensive image libraries of false threats to occasionally project onto real scans.

On Oct. 12, 2022, the company filed a Notice of Intention under the Bankruptcy and Insolvency Act (BIA). **PricewaterhouseCoopers Inc.** was appointed proposal trustee.

Common suspended from TSX-VEN, Mar. 7, 2023.

Predecessor Detail - Name changed from Steamsand Capital Corp., Nov. 13, 2018, following Qualifying Transaction reverse takeover acquisition of VOTI Inc. and concurrent amalgamation of VOTI Inc. with wholly owned 10971260 Canada Inc.; basis 1 new for 18 old shs.

Directors - Philip Murray, chr., Ottawa, Ont.; Rory Olson, pres. & CEO, Montréal, Qué.; Marc-André Aubé, Mont-Royal, Qué.; Neil Hindle, Qué.

Other Exec. Officers - Daniel P. Ménard, COO & interim CFO; Kevin McGarr, exec. v-p, corp. affairs; Campbell J. Stuart, corp. sec.

Capital Stock

	Authorized (shs.)	Outstanding (shs.)[1]
Common	unlimited	62,781,238

[1] At July 31, 2022

Major Shareholder - Widely held at Mar. 25, 2022.

Price Range - VOTI.H/TSX-VEN (S)

Year	Volume	High	Low	Close
2022	10,843,477	$0.42	$0.02	$0.02
2021	4,925,301	$1.00	$0.25	$0.39
2020	2,216,682	$1.93	$0.28	$0.35
2019	1,085,327	$3.14	$1.39	$1.75
2018	65,759	$3.78	$2.01	$2.20

Recent Close: $0.02

Capital Stock Changes - In March 2022, private placement of 15,717,434 units (1 common share & ½ warrant) at 15¢ per unit was completed, with warrants exercisable at 20¢ per share for two years.

Wholly Owned Subsidiaries

VOTI Inc., Saint-Laurent, Qué.
- 100% int. in **VOTI Detection Asia Sdn. Bhd.**, Malaysia.
- 100% int. in **VOTI International Inc.**, Canada.
  - 100% int. in **VOTI Security Scanning International**, Dubai, United Arab Emirates.
- 100% int. in **VOTI USA, Inc.**, Del.

Financial Statistics

Periods ended:	12m Oct. 31/21[A]		12m Oct. 31/20[A]
	$000s	%Chg	$000s
Operating revenue	**23,695**	**+25**	**19,014**
Cost of sales	15,677		13,317
Research & devel. expense	1,929		1,179
General & admin expense	7,983		8,758
Stock-based compensation	566		1,251
Operating expense	**26,095**	**+6**	**24,505**
Operating income	**(2,400)**	**n.a.**	**(5,491)**
Deprec., depl. & amort.	1,486		954
Finance costs, gross	3,150		2,175
Write-downs/write-offs	nil		(454)
Pre-tax income	**(6,065)**	**n.a.**	**(6,735)**
Net income	**(6,065)**	**n.a.**	**(6,735)**
Cash & equivalent	2,236		2,172
Inventories	9,353		9,579
Accounts receivable	2,616		1,929
Current assets	14,890		14,810
Fixed assets, net	760		1,037
Right-of-use assets	660		1,014
Intangibles, net	4,758		4,653
Total assets	**21,067**	**-2**	**21,514**
Bank indebtedness	nil		421
Accts. pay. & accr. liabs	5,661		3,664
Current liabilities	8,402		6,333
Long-term debt, gross	4,500		6,205
Long-term debt, net	3,272		5,268
Shareholders' equity	4,800		6,168
Cash from oper. activs	**(171)**	**n.a.**	**(1,515)**
Cash from fin. activs	2,385		3,967
Cash from invest. activs	(1,259)		(2,239)
Net cash position	**2,187**	**+5**	**2,089**
Capital expenditures	(113)		(215)
	$		$
Earnings per share*	(0.17)		(0.25)
Cash flow per share*	(0.00)		(0.06)
	shs		shs
No. of shs. o/s*	46,783,134		26,998,103
Avg. no. of shs. o/s*	36,649,702		26,805,584
	%		%
Net profit margin	(25.60)		(35.42)
Return on equity	(110.59)		(76.33)
Return on assets	(13.69)		(20.42)
Foreign sales percent	97		96

* Common
[A] Reported in accordance with IFRS

Latest Results

Periods ended:	9m July 31/22[A]		9m July 31/21[A]
	$000s	%Chg	$000s
Operating revenue	13,680	-23	17,805
Net income	(3,373)	n.a.	(5,024)
	$		$
Earnings per share*	(0.06)		(0.15)

* Common
[A] Reported in accordance with IFRS

Historical Summary
(as originally stated)

Fiscal Year	Oper. Rev.	Net Inc. Bef. Disc.	EPS*
	$000s	$000s	$
2021[A]	23,695	(6,065)	(0.17)
2020[A]	19,014	(6,735)	(0.25)
2019[A1]	28,427	(4,295)	(0.18)
2018[A]	23,007	(3,688)	n.a.
2017[A]	18,463	(2,464)	n.a.

* Common
[A] Reported in accordance with IFRS
[1] Results prior to Nov. 13, 2018, pertain to and reflect the Qualifying Transaction reverse takeover acquisition of VOTI Inc.

Note: Adjusted throughout for 1-for-18 cons. in Nov. 2018

V.6 VSBLTY Groupe Technologies Corp.

Symbol - VSBY **Exchange** - CSE **CUSIP** - 91834N

Head Office - 206-595 Howe St, Vancouver, BC, V6C 2T5 **Telephone** - (604) 484-7855

Website - www.vsblty.net

Email - lrosanio@vsblty.net

Investor Relations - Linda Rosanio (609) 472-0877

Auditors - Dale Matheson Carr-Hilton LaBonte LLP C.A., Vancouver, B.C.

Transfer Agents - Odyssey Trust Company, Vancouver, B.C.

Employees - 19 at July 6, 2023

Profile - (B.C. 2018) Operates as a software company commercializing various technologies relating to digital display platforms by combining interactive touch-screens and data-capture cameras, with cloud- and edge-based facial analytics.

The company employs its pro-active digital display software-as-a-service (SaaS)-based model for its subscription-based customers. This actively involves the consumer at the point of its purchase decision through its interactive touch-screen display, while capturing key performance indicators including data regarding total brand impressions, engagements and interactions, unique and returning viewers, gender, age of viewers, options, dwell time and emotional engagement.

The company has three primary software modules: VisionCaptor™, an integrated software suite that enables the customer to utilize digital assets (photos, video, multimedia content) to provide a customer experience for a digital display; DataCaptor™, a software module that leverages camera and sensor technology along with artificial intelligence (machine learning and machine vision) to provide real time analytics and audience measurement; and Vector™, a software module that interfaces with a comprehensive database to detect persons of interest within the camera's field of view primarily used for facial recognition and object recognition.

These modules give the company a differentiated suite of software services that allow venues, retailers, or digital out-of-home network providers to deploy sophisticated digital content solutions, coupled with in-depth measurement and analytics as well as a security solution.

Directors - Luiz Felipe Costa Romero de Barros, exec. chr., Ariz.; James (Jay) Hutton, pres. & CEO, Langley, B.C.; Thomas D. Hays III, CFO, Pa.; Alnesh P. Mohan, Vancouver, B.C.; David Roth, Middx., United Kingdom; Amin Shahidi, R.I.

Other Exec. Officers - Tim Huckaby, co-founder; Fred Potok, co-founder & chief sales officer; Linda Rosanio, co-founder & chief strategy officer; Jan Talamo, co-founder & chief creative officer; Gary A. Gibson, chief tech. officer; Sheryl Dhillon, corp. sec.

Capital Stock

	Authorized (shs.)	Outstanding (shs.)[1]
Common	unlimited	246,627,408

[1] At July 6, 2023

Major Shareholder - Widely held at Sept. 12, 2022.

Price Range - VSBY/CSE

Year	Volume	High	Low	Close
2022	103,587,541	$1.21	$0.14	$0.18
2021	208,344,524	$1.99	$0.44	$1.16
2020	122,785,425	$0.72	$0.10	$0.68
2019	30,255,804	$0.75	$0.16	$0.32

Recent Close: $0.07

Capital Stock Changes - In July 2023, private placement of 76,877,000 units (1 common share & 1 warrant) at Cdn$0.05 per unit was completed, with warrants exercisable at Cdn$0.075 per share for four years.

In July 2022, public offering of 19,166,705 units (1 common share & 1 warrant) at Cdn$0.30 per unit was completed, including 2,500,005 units on exercise of over-allotment option. From July to November 2022, private placement of 12,938,394 units (1 common share & 1 warrant) at Cdn$0.30 per unit was completed. Also during 2022, common shares were issued as follows: 11,874,718 on exercise of warrants, 2,158,862 for debt settlement, 970,000 on exercise of options, 383,333 for financing fees, 144,534 for services and 41,750 on vesting of restricted share units; 125,000 common shares were returned to treasury.

Wholly Owned Subsidiaries

VSBLTY, Inc., Philadelphia, Pa.

VSBLTY Mexico, S. de R.L. de C.V., Mexico.

Note: The preceding list includes only the major related companies in which interests are held.

Financial Statistics

Periods ended:	12m Dec. 31/22[A]		12m Dec. 31/21[A]
	US$000s	%Chg	US$000s
Operating revenue	**1,523**	**-5**	**1,600**
Cost of sales	2,647		1,430
Salaries & benefits	2,580		1,430
Research & devel. expense	1,589		1,185
General & admin expense	3,986		5,324
Stock-based compensation	1,286		6,239
Operating expense	**12,088**	**-23**	**15,607**
Operating income	**(10,565)**	**n.a.**	**(14,007)**
Deprec., depl. & amort.	129		76
Finance income	31		9
Finance costs, gross	91		438
Investment income	nil		(26)
Write-downs/write-offs	(1,922)		(866)
Pre-tax income	**(12,375)**	**n.a.**	**(16,237)**
Net income	**(12,375)**	**n.a.**	**(16,237)**
Cash & equivalent	1,064		4,933
Inventories	45		177
Accounts receivable	1,465		1,316
Current assets	3,123		6,756
Long-term investments	1,000		1,000
Fixed assets, net	86		70
Right-of-use assets	173		129
Total assets	**4,468**	**-44**	**7,965**
Accts. pay. & accr. liabs.	1,406		2,383
Current liabilities	1,681		3,233
Long-term debt, gross	93		700
Long-term debt, net	93		700
Long-term lease liabilities	169		100
Shareholders' equity	2,618		4,632
Cash from oper. activs.	**(10,583)**	**n.a.**	**(9,278)**
Cash from fin. activs.	(8,266)		13,988
Cash from invest. activs.	(1,445)		(1,695)
Net cash position	**1,064**	**-78**	**4,933**
Capital expenditures	(61)		(64)
	US$		US$
Earnings per share*	(0.06)		(0.09)
Cash flow per share*	(0.05)		(0.05)
	shs		shs
No. of shs. o/s*	246,090,544		198,537,248
Avg. no. of shs. o/s*	220,717,233		173,582,321
	%		%
Net profit margin	(812.54)		n.m.
Return on equity	(341.38)		n.m.
Return on assets	(197.60)		(299.42)
No. of employees (FTEs)	23		18

* Common
[A] Reported in accordance with IFRS

Latest Results

Periods ended:	3m Mar. 31/23[A]		3m Mar. 31/22[A]
	US$000s	%Chg	US$000s
Operating revenue	77	-94	1,242
Net income	(3,070)	n.a.	(3,651)
	US$		US$
Earnings per share*	(0.01)		(0.02)

* Common
[A] Reported in accordance with IFRS

Historical Summary
(as originally stated)

Fiscal Year	Oper. Rev. US$000s	Net Inc. Bef. Disc. US$000s	EPS* US$
2022[A]	1,523	(12,375)	(0.06)
2021[A]	1,600	(16,237)	(0.09)
2020[A]	607	(6,532)	(0.08)
2019[A1]	106	(7,367)	(0.10)
2018[A2]	79	(2,449)	(0.48)

* Common
[A] Reported in accordance with IFRS
[1] Results reflect the Feb. 15, 2019, reverse takeover acquisition of VSBLTY, Inc.
[2] Results for 2018 and prior years pertain to VSBLTY, Inc.

V.7 Valdor Technology International Inc.

Symbol - VTI **Exchange** - CSE **CUSIP** - 919067
Head Office - 810-789 Pender St W, Vancouver, BC, V6C 1H2
Telephone - (604) 687-2038
Website - www.valdortech.com
Email - info@valdortech.com
Investor Relations - Lucas Stemshorn-Russell (604) 687-2038
Auditors - WDM Chartered Accountants C.A., Vancouver, B.C.
Lawyers - O'Neill & Company, Vancouver, B.C.
Transfer Agents - Endeavor Trust Corporation, Vancouver, B.C.

Profile - (B.C. 1984) Designs, manufactures and markets custom passive fibre optic components in the U.S. using its proprietary patented Impact Mount™ technology.

The patented Impact Mount™ technology is all-mechanical with no epoxy or index matching gel. Field installable termination kits and connectors employing the technology are used in harsh environment applications and allow for quick repair in the field. Other products include LAN patch panels, coupler splitter module, enclosures, laser pigtails, attenuators, multiplexers and singlemode cable assemblies.

Products are manufactured and assembled in Hayward, Calif., primarily for three California-based customers: **Kaiser Optical Systems, Inc.**; **Ceres Technologies, Inc.**; and Gulf Photonics, a division of **Gulf Fiberoptics, Inc.**

Recent Merger and Acquisition Activity

Status: terminated **Revised:** Aug. 26, 2022

UPDATE: The transaction was terminated. PREVIOUS: Valdor Technology International Inc. agreed to acquire Layer 2 Ventures Ltd., which offers solutions leveraging cryptographic technology, like Roll Ups and Zero Knowledge Proofs, to process transactions in bulk beside or above the main chain resulting in a 100x performance increase for just a fraction of the gas fees, for issuance of 16,666,667 common shares at a deemed price of Cdn$0.30 per share.

Predecessor Detail - Name changed from Valdor Fiber Optics Inc., July 21, 2008; basis 1 new for 6.5 old shs.

Directors - Lucas Stemshorn-Russell, pres. & CEO, Victoria, B.C.; Francis Rowe, CFO & corp. sec., Victoria, B.C.; Dorian Banks, Vancouver, B.C.; Steven Inglefield, Victoria, B.C.

Capital Stock

	Authorized (shs.)	Outstanding (shs.)[1]
Preferred	50,000,000	nil
Common	unlimited	65,922,033

[1] At May 1, 2023

Major Shareholder - Widely held at June 29, 2022.

Price Range - VTI/CSE

Year	Volume	High	Low	Close
2022	752,264	$0.25	$0.05	$0.05
2021	2,725,079	$0.48	$0.07	$0.31
2020	1,297,138	$0.11	$0.03	$0.08
2019	992,373	$0.20	$0.05	$0.05
2018	4,686,699	$1.70	$0.10	$0.20

Consolidation: 1-for-20 cons. in Jan. 2019

Recent Close: $0.05

Subsidiaries

94% int. in **Fiberlight Optics, Inc.**, Del. Inactive.
94% int. in **Valdor Fiber Optics, Inc.**, Del.

Financial Statistics

Periods ended:	12m Dec. 31/21[A]		12m Dec. 31/20[A]
	US$000s	%Chg	US$000s
Operating revenue	**263**	**+16**	**227**
Cost of sales	1		6
Salaries & benefits	227		190
General & admin expense	262		99
Stock-based compensation	1,589		nil
Operating expense	**2,079**	**+605**	**295**
Operating income	**(1,816)**	**n.a.**	**(68)**
Pre-tax income	**(1,715)**	**n.a.**	**(61)**
Net inc bef disc ops, eqhldrs	(1,717)		(65)
Net inc bef disc ops, NCI	2		4
Net income	**(1,715)**	**n.a.**	**(61)**
Net inc. for equity hldrs	**(1,717)**	**n.a.**	**(65)**
Net inc. for non-cont. int.	**2**	**-50**	**4**
Cash & equivalent	697		23
Accounts receivable	18		20
Current assets	716		44
Total assets	**716**	**n.m.**	**44**
Bank indebtedness	nil		157
Accts. pay. & accr. liabs.	35		429
Current liabilities	74		1,643
Long-term debt, gross	35		285
Equity portion of conv. debs.	45		45
Shareholders' equity	1,277		(962)
Non-controlling interest	(635)		(637)
Cash from oper. activs.	**(544)**	**n.a.**	**(116)**
Cash from fin. activs.	1,201		132
Net cash position	**697**	**n.m.**	**23**
	US$		US$
Earnings per share*	(0.03)		(0.01)
Cash flow per share*	(0.01)		(0.02)
	shs		shs
No. of shs. o/s*	65,922,033		5,812,033
Avg. no. of shs. o/s*	59,496,307		5,812,033
	%		%
Net profit margin	(652.09)		(26.87)
Return on equity	n.m.		n.m.
Return on assets	(451.32)		(122.00)
Foreign sales percent	100		100

* Common
[A] Reported in accordance with IFRS

Latest Results

Periods ended:	6m June 30/22[A]		6m June 30/21[A]
	US$000s	%Chg	US$000s
Operating revenue	92	-31	133
Net income	(171)	n.a.	(37)
Net inc. for equity hldrs	(171)	n.a.	(36)
Net inc. for non-cont. int	nil		(1)
	US$		US$
Earnings per share*	(0.00)		(0.00)

* Common
[A] Reported in accordance with IFRS

Historical Summary
(as originally stated)

Fiscal Year	Oper. Rev.	Net Inc. Bef. Disc.	EPS*
	US$000s	US$000s	US$
2021[A]	263	(1,715)	(0.03)
2020[A]	227	(61)	(0.01)
2019[A]	199	629	0.11
2018[A]	131	(237)	(0.04)
2017[A]	180	(280)	(0.05)

* Common
[A] Reported in accordance with IFRS
Note: Adjusted throughout for 1-for-20 cons. in Jan. 2019

V.8 Valencia Capital Inc.

Symbol - VAL.P **Exchange** - TSX-VEN **CUSIP** - 91912W
Head Office - 1510-789 Pender St W, Vancouver, BC, V6C 1H2 **Telephone** - (604) 808-4031
Investor Relations - John D. MacPhail (778) 688-7411
Auditors - Saturna Group Chartered Accountants LLP C.A., Vancouver, B.C.
Lawyers - Buttonwood Law Corporation, Vancouver, B.C.
Transfer Agents - Computershare Trust Company of Canada Inc., Vancouver, B.C.
Profile - (B.C. 2019) Capital Pool Company.

On Mar. 6, 2023, the company entered into a letter of intent for the Qualifying Transaction reverse takeover acquisition of **VPP Energy Corp.**, which would complete the acquisition of **Helios Extraction Limited LLC** prior to the company acquiring VPP. Terms and structure of the transaction were to be determined.

Directors - John D. MacPhail, pres. & CEO, North Vancouver, B.C.; Brock Daem, Vancouver, B.C.; Edward J. (Ed) Duda, Burnaby, B.C.; Graham Heal, Vancouver, B.C.

Other Exec. Officers - Robert Wilson, COO; Adam Garvin, CFO & corp. sec.; John A. MacPhail, chief tech. officer; Kim D. M. Oishi, chief mktg. officer

Capital Stock

	Authorized (shs.)	Outstanding (shs.)[1]
Common	unlimited	11,383,900

[1] At Nov. 28, 2022

Major Shareholder - Widely held at Sept. 24, 2021.

Price Range - VAL.P/TSX-VEN

Year	Volume	High	Low	Close
2022	365,000	$0.10	$0.05	$0.06
2021	440,000	$0.10	$0.07	$0.07
2020	126,960	$0.15	$0.11	$0.11

Recent Close: $0.08

Capital Stock Changes - There were no changes to capital stock during fiscal 2022.

V.9 Valeo Pharma Inc.

Symbol - VPH **Exchange** - TSX **CUSIP** - 91915B
Head Office - 16667 boul Hymus, Kirkland, QC, H9H 4R9 **Telephone** - (514) 693-8832 **Toll-free** - (855) 694-0151 **Fax** - (514) 694-0865
Website - www.valeopharma.com
Email - luc.mainville@valeopharma.com
Investor Relations - Luc Mainville (514) 693-8854
Auditors - PricewaterhouseCoopers LLP C.A., Québec, Qué.
Transfer Agents - Computershare Trust Company of Canada Inc., Montréal, Qué.
Employees - 115 at Jan. 27, 2023
Profile - (Can. 2003) Sources, acquires or in-licenses branded and generic pharmaceutical products for sale in Canada.

Acquires exclusive Canadian rights to regulatory approved or late-stage development products, either through acquisitions, long-term in-licensing or distribution agreements with pharmaceutical companies that do not have a presence in Canada, and provides all the services required to register, reimburse and commercialize these pharmaceutical products in Canada. Preferences are for products that are already approved in other territories such as the U.S., Europe, or Asia, and also for innovative products addressing major unmet medical needs.

Operations are divided into the Respiratory, Ophthalmology and Specialty Products business units, plus the Hospital generic division.

The **Respiratory** business unit focuses on the respiratory therapeutic area with an immediate focus on the commercialization of the company's licensed asthma drugs including Enerzair Breezhaler® and Atectura Breezhaler®, which are licensed from **Novartis Pharmaceuticals Canada Inc.**; and Allerject®, a portable epinephrine injector for emergency treatment of serious allergic reactions, which is licensed from **Kaléo Inc.**

The **Ophthalmology** business unit focuses on ophthalmic therapies including XIIDRA®, a prescription eye-drop treatment for dry eye disease; and SIMBRINZA®, an ophthalmic eye-drop treatment for open-angle glaucoma and ocular hypertension, which are licensed from Novartis Pharmaceuticals Canada Inc.

The **Specialty Products** business unit focuses on thrombosis, neurology, oncology and other specialty products. Commercial stage products include Redesca™, licensed from **Shenzhen Techdow Pharmaceuticals Co., Ltd.**, which is an injectable anticoagulant drug used primarily to treat and prevent deep vein thrombosis and pulmonary embolism; Sabizabulin, licensed from **Veru, Inc.**, which is an oral dual antiviral and antiflammatory agent for adults suffering from COVID-19; Onstryv® (Safinamide), licensed from **Zambon S.p.A.**, which is used to treat idiopathic Parkinson's disease as add-on for patients taking a stable dose of levodopa alone or in combination with other Parkinson drugs, to help with "off" episodes; M-Eslon, licensed from **Ethypharm Inc.**, which is an extended release morphine sulphate used for pain management; Yondelis® (trabectedin), licensed from **PharmaMar S.A.**, which is an anti-tumour chemotherapy medication for the treatment of advanced soft-tissue sarcoma and ovarian cancer; Hesperco™, co-developed by the company with **Ingenew Pharma Inc.**, which is a bioflavonoid antioxidant used for immune system support; and Ametop™ Gel 4% (Tetracaine hydrochloride gel), licensed from **Alliance Pharma plc**, which is an anaesthesia of the skin prior to venepuncture or venous cannulation.

The **Hospital Generic** division focuses on pain management, including narcotics, anti-infectives and critical care. Commercial stage products include Benztropine, licensed from an Asia-Pacific generic manufacturer, which is an anticholinergic agent used for treatment of Parkinson's disease; Ethacrynate Sodium, developed by the company, which is a loop diuretic used to treat high blood pressure and the swelling caused by diseases such as congestive heart failure, liver failure and kidney failure; and Amikacin, licensed from a European generic manufacturer, which is an injectable antibiotic.

Also holds rights to Synacthen, licensed from **Atnahs Pharma UK Limited**, which is a specialty neurology therapeutic with 17 approved indications. Sales have been halted since 2019 due to global supply shortage.

In September 2022, the company entered into a commercial and services agreement with **Veru Inc.** for sabizabulin, a dual antiviral and anti-inflammatory agent treatment for COVID-19.

In August 2022, the company entered into a commercial and supply agreement with **Novartis Pharmaceuticals Canada Inc.** for the Canadian rights to two ophthalmic therapies, XIIDRA® and SIMBRINZA® and would be responsible for medical and commercial activities for both drugs for an initial seven-year period. In addition, the company entered into a licence, supply and commercial agreement with **Kaléo Inc.** for the Canadian rights to Allerject®, an autoinjector for the treatment of allergic reactions and would be responsible for its medical and commercial activities for an initial 10-year period.

Directors - Richard J. (Dick) MacKay, chr., Montréal, Qué.; Steven (Steve) Saviuk, v-chr. & CEO, Beaconsfield, Qué.; Maureen C. Brennan, Montréal, Qué.; Tamara Close; Frédéric Fasano, Mount Royal, Qué.; Vincent P. Hogue, Beaconsfield, Qué.; Didier Leconte; Michel C. Trudeau, Montréal, Qué.

Other Exec. Officers - Nelly Komari, sr. v-p, scientific & medical affairs; Luc Mainville, sr. v-p & CFO; Kyle Steiger, sr. v-p & chief comml. officer; Guy-Paul Allard, v-p, legal affairs & corp. sec.; Michelle Brien, v-p, HR & talent mgt.; Helen Saviuk, v-p, opers.; Jeff Skinner, v-p, bus. devel.; Nathalie Therrien, v-p, quality assurance & regulatory affairs

Capital Stock

	Authorized (shs.)	Outstanding (shs.)[1]
Class A	unlimited	82,265,348

[1] At Jan. 30, 2023

Major Shareholder - Manitex Capital Inc. held 29% interest and Richard J. (Dick) MacKay held 14.6% interest at Jan. 30, 2023.

Price Range - VPH/TSX

Year	Volume	High	Low	Close
2022	11,352,054	$0.74	$0.45	$0.57
2021	40,046,971	$1.53	$0.57	$0.74
2020	24,420,014	$1.86	$0.25	$1.22
2019	3,482,950	$0.98	$0.24	$0.45

Recent Close: $0.27

Capital Stock Changes - During fiscal 2022, common shares were issued as follows: 2,603,419 on conversion of debentures, 485,000 on exercise of warrants, 256,250 on exercise of options and 45,505 as compensation.

Wholly Owned Subsidiaries

VPI Pharmaceuticals Inc., Canada.
Valeo Pharma Corp., United States. Inactive.

Financial Statistics

Periods ended:	12m Oct. 31/22[A]		12m Oct. 31/21[□A]
	$000s	%Chg	$000s
Operating revenue	**27,745**	**+105**	**13,557**
Cost of goods sold	20,577		9,250
Salaries & benefits	13,776		7,999
General & admin expense	8,508		6,323
Stock-based compensation	941		996
Other operating expense	1,676		874
Operating expense	**45,478**	**+79**	**25,442**
Operating income	**(17,733)**	**n.a.**	**(11,885)**
Deprec., depl. & amort	1,418		743
Finance income	173		1
Finance costs, gross	7,763		1,277
Write-downs/write-offs	(1,223)		(247)
Pre-tax income	**(26,920)**	**n.a.**	**(14,233)**
Income taxes	(1,174)		nil
Net income	**(25,746)**	**n.a.**	**(14,233)**
Cash & equivalent	22,501		2,043
Inventories	9,980		7,675
Accounts receivable	5,428		1,798
Current assets	40,529		12,350
Fixed assets, net	1,373		1,174
Right-of-use assets	881		967
Intangibles, net	15,482		6,539
Total assets	**58,265**	**+177**	**21,030**
Accts. pay. & accr. liabs	11,064		9,955
Current liabilities	15,339		15,334
Long-term debt, gross	60,276		6,459
Long-term debt, net	59,533		1,605
Long-term lease liabilities	1,114		1,165
Equity portion of conv. debs	3,114		300
Shareholders' equity	(17,848)		2,053
Cash from oper. activs	**(28,503)**	**n.a.**	**(12,315)**
Cash from fin. activs	54,991		15,104
Cash from invest. activs	(6,891)		(3,465)
Net cash position	**22,501**	**n.m.**	**2,043**
Capital expenditures	(359)		(902)
Unfunded pension liability	127		291
	$		$
Earnings per share*	(0.32)		(0.20)
Cash flow per share*	(0.35)		(0.18)
	shs		shs
No. of shs. o/s*	82,190,348		78,800,174
Avg. no. of shs. o/s*	80,858,528		69,930,380
	%		%
Net profit margin	(92.80)		(104.99)
Return on equity	n.m.		(555.76)
Return on assets	(46.21)		(80.99)

* Cl.A
[□] Restated
[A] Reported in accordance with IFRS

Historical Summary
(as originally stated)

Fiscal Year	Oper. Rev.	Net Inc. Bef. Disc.	EPS*
	$000s	$000s	$
2022[A]	27,745	(25,746)	(0.32)
2021[A]	13,557	(14,233)	(0.20)
2020[A]	7,470	(4,761)	(0.08)
2019[A]	6,577	(3,615)	(0.07)
2018[A]	4,382	(2,437)	(0.07)

* Cl.A
[A] Reported in accordance with IFRS

V.10 Vanadiumcorp Resource Inc.

Symbol - VRB **Exchange** - TSX-VEN **CUSIP** - 921428
Head Office - 400-1505 2 Ave W, Vancouver, BC, V6H 3Y4 **Telephone** - (604) 385-4481 **Fax** - (604) 385-4486
Website - www.vanadiumcorp.com
Email - stephen@wildflower.ca
Investor Relations - Stephen W. Pearce (604) 970-3278
Auditors - Crowe MacKay LLP C.A., Vancouver, B.C.
Lawyers - Taylor Veinotte Sullivan, Vancouver, B.C.; Gordon J. Fretwell Law Corporation, Vancouver, B.C.
Transfer Agents - Computershare Trust Company of Canada Inc., Vancouver, B.C.
Profile - (B.C. 1980) Has mineral interests in Quebec. Also developing a hydrometallurgical process technology for the recovery of vanadium and other metals.

Holds Lac Doré vanadium-iron-titanium project, 5,287 hectares, 27 km east-southeast of Chibougamau, with measured and indicated resource of 214,930,000 tonnes grading 0.4% vanadium pentoxide, 27.1% iron, 7.1% titanium dioxide and 24.6% magnetite at October 2020; and Iron-T vanadium-titanium-iron prospect, 4,218 hectares, 18 km east of Matagami.

Owns the patented Vanadiumcorp-Electrochem Process Technology (VEPT) which allows for the sustainable recovery of vanadium, with iron, titanium and silica as coproducts, from various vanadium-bearing sources including mineral concentrates and industrial waste. Recovered vanadium may be used for the preparation of vanadium electrolyte utilized in vanadium redox flow batteries or for preparing various vanadium chemicals.

Predecessor Detail - Name changed from PacificOre Mining Corp., Nov. 22, 2013.

Directors - Ian A. Mallory, exec. chr., Calgary, Alta.; Paul J. McGuigan, interim CEO, Vancouver, B.C.; Dr. Giles Champagne, chief tech. officer, Germany; Gilles Dupuis, Verchères, Qué.; Stephen W. Pearce, Vancouver, B.C.

Other Exec. Officers - James Ross, interim CFO

Capital Stock

	Authorized (shs.)	Outstanding (shs.)[1]
Common	unlimited	49,746,943

[1] At Nov. 21, 2022

Major Shareholder - Roger Shook and Samuel Chen held 11.3% interest at Nov. 25, 2021.

Price Range - VRB/TSX-VEN

Year	Volume	High	Low	Close
2022	9,334,037	$0.55	$0.06	$0.10
2021	3,521,471	$1.30	$0.50	$0.50
2020	4,344,706	$1.20	$0.25	$1.20
2019	2,718,574	$1.00	$0.40	$0.50
2018	2,870,969	$1.60	$0.70	$0.85

Consolidation: 1-for-10 cons. in Apr. 2022

Recent Close: $0.09

Capital Stock Changes - In September and November 2022, private placement of 5,293,333 flow-through units (1 common share & 1 warrant) at 12¢ per unit and 12,528,500 units (1 common share & 1 warrant) at 10¢ per unit was completed, with warrants exercisable at 18¢ per share for two years.

On Apr. 18, 2022, common shares were consolidated on a 1-for-10 basis.

Wholly Owned Subsidiaries

Power Vanadium Corporation, Canada.
Prestige Mining Corporation, Canada.
Pro Minerals Ltd., Canada.
Prosperity Minerals Corporation, Canada.
Vanadiumcorp GmbH, Germany.

Financial Statistics

Periods ended:	12m Oct. 31/21[A]		12m Oct. 31/20[A]
	$000s	%Chg	$000s
Salaries & benefits	399		342
Research & devel. expense	104		250
General & admin expense	1,115		797
Stock-based compensation	578		nil
Operating expense	**2,196**	**+58**	**1,389**
Operating income	**(2,196)**	**n.a.**	**(1,389)**
Deprec., depl. & amort.	59		63
Finance costs, gross	13		6
Pre-tax income	**(2,184)**	**n.a.**	**(672)**
Net income	**(2,184)**	**n.a.**	**(672)**
Cash & equivalent	52		463
Accounts receivable	49		147
Current assets	135		653
Fixed assets, net	22		30
Right-of-use assets	nil		63
Intangibles, net	350		nil
Explor./devel. properties	5,844		5,637
Total assets	**6,351**	**-1**	**6,383**
Bank indebtedness	87		nil
Accts. pay. & accr. liabs	657		481
Current liabilities	745		542
Long-term debt, gross	81		nil
Long-term debt, net	81		nil
Long-term lease liabilities	nil		5
Shareholders' equity	5,525		5,836
Cash from oper. activs	**(1,233)**	**n.a.**	**(1,209)**
Cash from fin. activs	1,411		2,199
Cash from invest. activs	(588)		(1,345)
Net cash position	**29**	**-93**	**440**
Capital expenditures	(238)		(1,345)
	$		$
Earnings per share*	(0.07)		(0.02)
Cash flow per share*	(0.04)		(0.04)
	shs		shs
No. of shs. o/s*	31,925,112		29,925,112
Avg. no. of shs. o/s*	31,655,350		29,038,848
	%		%
Net profit margin	n.a.		n.a.
Return on equity	(38.45)		(12.92)
Return on assets	(34.10)		(10.89)

* Common
[A] Reported in accordance with IFRS

Historical Summary
(as originally stated)

Fiscal Year	Oper. Rev.	Net Inc. Bef. Disc.	EPS*
	$000s	$000s	$
2021[A]	nil	(2,184)	(0.07)
2020[A]	nil	(672)	(0.02)
2019[A]	nil	(1,489)	(0.10)
2018[A]	nil	(2,256)	(0.10)
2017[A]	nil	(755)	(0.04)

* Common
[A] Reported in accordance with IFRS

Note: Adjusted throughout for 1-for-10 cons. in Apr. 2022

V.11 Vaxil Bio Ltd.

Symbol - VXL **Exchange** - TSX-VEN **CUSIP** - 92243L

Head Office - First Canadian Place, 3400-100 King St W, Toronto, ON, M5X 1A4 **Telephone** - (647) 558-5564 **Fax** - (647) 351-6200

Website - vaxil-bio.com

Email - gadi@vaxil-bio.com

Investor Relations - Gadi P. Levin (647) 558-5564

Auditors - Zeifmans LLP C.A., Toronto, Ont.

Transfer Agents - Computershare Trust Company of Canada Inc.

Profile - (B.C. 2009) Developing therapeutic vaccines and antibodies for the treatment of cancer and infectious diseases.

Products are derived from the company's proprietary technology called VaxHit™, which can identify, isolate and produce specific antigen-based immunotherapy products by using the signal peptide domains in selected targets as core antigens. Lead immunotherapy product is ImMucin™, a vaccine to treat multiple myeloma, a type of blood cancer, which has completed Phase I/II clinical trial and has received Orphan Drug Status from the U.S. FDA and European Medicines Agency. Other candidates under development include MTBuVax™, a vaccine for tuberculosis, and CorVax™, a vaccine for coronavirus (COVID-19), which are both under pre-clinical studies. Development of CorVax™ was put on temporary hold as a result of current COVID-19 vaccine market conditions. Also plans to develop its MUC1 signal peptide as an adjunct therapy or combination therapy to synergistically improve the standard of care for solid tumours with high risk of metastasis.

Predecessor Detail - Name changed from Emerge Resources Corp., Feb. 29, 2016, following reverse takeover acquisition of (old) Vaxil Bio Ltd.; basis 1 new for 2 old shs.

Directors - Gadi P. Levin, chr. & CEO, Israel; Daniel N. Bloch, Ont.; Dr. Ari S. Kellen, Teaneck, N.J.; Dr. Shawn Langer, Teaneck, N.J.

Other Exec. Officers - Alan Rootenberg, CFO

Capital Stock

	Authorized (shs.)	Outstanding (shs.)[1]
Common	unlimited	136,978,973

[1] At Aug. 25, 2022

Major Shareholder - Widely held at Dec. 31, 2021.

Price Range - VXL/TSX-VEN

Year	Volume	High	Low	Close
2022	24,030,195	$0.11	$0.01	$0.02
2021	228,673,511	$0.77	$0.06	$0.08
2020	380,653,980	$0.34	$0.03	$0.30
2019	8,650,408	$0.07	$0.03	$0.04
2018	25,546,843	$0.24	$0.03	$0.03

Recent Close: $0.02

Wholly Owned Subsidiaries

Vaxil Bio Ltd., Ness Ziona, Israel.
- 100% int. in **Vaxil Biotherapeutics Ltd.**, Israel.

Financial Statistics

Periods ended:	12m Dec. 31/21[A]		12m Dec. 31/20[oA]
	$000s	%Chg	$000s
Salaries & benefits	63		155
Research & devel. expense	470		411
General & admin expense	358		574
Stock-based compensation	70		150
Operating expense	**961**	**-26**	**1,290**
Operating income	**(961)**	**n.a.**	**(1,290)**
Deprec., depl. & amort.	25		57
Finance costs, gross	nil		11
Pre-tax income	**(986)**	**n.a.**	**(1,358)**
Net income	**(986)**	**n.a.**	**(1,358)**
Cash & equivalent	2,241		1,510
Accounts receivable	35		33
Current assets	2,283		1,634
Fixed assets, net	2		21
Right-of-use assets	nil		6
Total assets	**2,285**	**+38**	**1,661**
Accts. pay. & accr. liabs	585		588
Current liabilities	585		857
Shareholders' equity	1,700		804
Cash from oper. activs	**(1,084)**	**n.a.**	**(1,267)**
Cash from fin. activs	1,808		2,557
Net cash position	**2,241**	**+66**	**1,346**
	$		$
Earnings per share*	(0.01)		(0.01)
Cash flow per share*	(0.01)		(0.01)
	shs		shs
No. of shs. o/s*	136,978,973		118,808,973
Avg. no. of shs. o/s*	136,102,115		101,736,967
	%		%
Net profit margin	n.a.		n.a.
Return on equity	(78.75)		n.m.
Return on assets	(49.97)		(144.37)

* Common
[o] Restated
[A] Reported in accordance with IFRS

Latest Results

Periods ended:	6m June 30/22[A]		6m June 30/21[A]
	$000s	%Chg	$000s
Net income	(272)	n.a.	(467)
	$		$
Earnings per share*	(0.00)		(0.00)

* Common
[A] Reported in accordance with IFRS

Historical Summary
(as originally stated)

Fiscal Year	Oper. Rev.	Net Inc. Bef. Disc.	EPS*
	$000s	$000s	$
2021[A]	nil	(986)	(0.01)
2020[A]	nil	(1,358)	(0.01)
2019[A]	nil	(1,154)	(0.01)
2018[A]	nil	(1,047)	(0.01)
2017[A]	nil	(1,798)	(0.04)

* Common
[A] Reported in accordance with IFRS

V.12 Vecima Networks Inc.

Symbol - VCM **Exchange** - TSX **CUSIP** - 92241Y

Head Office - 771 Vanalman Ave, Victoria, BC, V8Z 3B8 **Telephone** - (250) 881-1982 **Fax** - (250) 881-1974

Website - www.vecima.com

Email - invest@vecima.com

Investor Relations - Investor Relations (250) 881-1982

Auditors - Grant Thornton LLP C.A., Toronto, Ont.

Bankers - Canadian Imperial Bank of Commerce, Saskatoon, Sask.

Transfer Agents - Computershare Trust Company of Canada Inc., Toronto, Ont.

FP500 Revenue Ranking - 671

Employees - 592 at June 30, 2022

Profile - (Can. 2003; orig. Sask., 1988) Designs and manufactures hardware and software solutions in the areas of video and broadband access, content delivery and storage, and telematics.

The **Video and Broadband Solutions** segment provides products which process data from the cable network and deliver Internet connectivity to homes over cable and fibre as well as adapt video services to formats suitable for televisions in commercial properties. Products include Entra, a portfolio of products and platforms that support network migration to a distributed access architecture (DAA); and Terrace, a suite of solutions that enable distribution of analog and digital video to multi-dwelling units and the hospitality industry (hotels, motels and resorts).

The **Content Delivery and Storage** segment includes solutions and software, under the MediaScale brand, that focus on ingesting, producing, storing, delivering and streaming video content for live linear, video on demand (VOD), network digital video recorder (nDVR) and time-shifted services over the Internet.

The **Telematics** segment provides fleet management software to manage mobile and fixed assets across North America under the Contigo and Nero Global Tracking brands.

The company is headquartered in Victoria, B.C., and has facilities in Saskatoon, Sask.; Burnaby, B.C.; Raleigh, N.C.; San Jose, Calif.; Duluth, Ga.; Tokyo, Japan; Qingdao and Shanghai, People's Republic of China; and Amsterdam, Netherlands.

Predecessor Detail - Name changed from VCom Inc., Nov. 29, 2006.

Directors - Dr. Surinder G. Kumar, founder & chr., Victoria, B.C.; Sumit Kumar, pres. & CEO, Victoria, B.C.; Scott B. Edmonds†, Vancouver, B.C.; James A. Blackley, N.Y.; Roderick W. (Rick) Brace, Collingwood, Ont.; Danial Faizullabhoy, Palo Alto, Calif.

Other Exec. Officers - Clay McCreery, COO; Dale R. Booth, CFO; Collin Howlett, chief tech. officer; Richard (Dean) Rockwell, exec. v-p; Paul Boucher, sr. v-p, sales; Brian C. Brown, sr. v-p, cust. opers. & tech.; Laird M. Froese, sr. v-p, R&D, video broadband solutions; Dan Gledhill, sr. v-p, global sales; Kyle Goodwin, sr. v-p & gen. mgr., content delivery & storage bus. unit; David Hobb, sr. v-p, opers.; Ryan Nicometo, sr. v-p & gen. mgr., video & broadband solutions bus. unit; Bernadette Dunn, v-p, mktg.; Lee Ann Fogwell, v-p, R&D, video broadcast solutions; Bill Lee, v-p, global professional srvcs.; Lindsay Y. Ryerson, v-p & gen. mgr., telematics div.; Barry F. Smith, v-p, cust. success; Gerry Vreeswijk, v-p, HR; Heather Asher, gen. counsel & corp. sec.; Osamu (Sammy) Nakamura, pres., Vecima Japan

† Lead director

Capital Stock

	Authorized (shs.)	Outstanding (shs.)[1]
Preferred	unlimited	nil
Common	unlimited	24,301,594

[1] At May 9, 2023

Major Shareholder - Dr. Surinder Kumar & Sumit Kumar held 59.88% interest and Polar Asset Management Partners Inc. held 12.18% interest at Nov. 7, 2022.

Price Range - VCM/TSX

Year	Volume	High	Low	Close
2022	880,647	$20.50	$14.30	$19.39
2021	743,968	$17.45	$12.99	$14.31
2020	1,865,271	$14.90	$7.51	$14.80
2019	1,429,319	$10.45	$8.24	$10.35
2018	1,324,951	$9.80	$8.12	$8.15

Recent Close: $17.11

Capital Stock Changes - In December 2022, private placement of 957,880 common shares was completed at $17.75 per share.

During fiscal 2022, common shares were issued as follows: 187,487 under performance share unit plan and 55,626 on exercise of options; 63,478 common shares were withheld for taxes.

Dividends

VCM com Ra $0.22 pa Q est. Oct. 30, 2015

Wholly Owned Subsidiaries

6105971 Canada Inc., Canada.
Vecima Networks (USA) Inc., United States.
Vecima Solutions Corporation, Japan.
Vecima Technology B.V., Netherlands.
Vecima Technology (Canada) Inc., Canada.
Vecima Technology GmbH, Germany.
Vecima Technology Inc., United States.
Vecima Technology (Qingdao) Co., Ltd., People's Republic of China.
Vecima Technology (Shanghai) Co., Ltd., People's Republic of China.
Vecima Technology (UK) Ltd., United Kingdom.

Financial Statistics

Periods ended:	12m June 30/22[A]		12m June 30/21[A]
	$000s	%Chg	$000s
Operating revenue	**186,814**	**+50**	**124,177**
Cost of sales	96,362		66,995
Research & devel. expense	24,002		16,823
General & admin expense	37,282		26,866
Stock-based compensation	881		1,420
Operating expense	**158,527**	**+41**	**112,104**
Operating income	**28,287**	**+134**	**12,073**
Deprec., depl. & amort.	17,849		14,755
Finance costs, net	272		(69)
Write-downs/write-offs	(712)		nil
Pre-tax income	**11,047**	**n.a.**	**(4,074)**
Income taxes	2,358		(1,889)
Net inc. bef. disc. opers	**8,689**	**n.a.**	**(2,185)**
Income from disc. opers	nil		1,854
Net income	**8,689**	**n.a.**	**(331)**
Cash & equivalent	12,902		28,909
Inventories	49,608		15,578
Accounts receivable	49,655		28,784
Current assets	121,495		77,698
Fixed assets, net	16,483		13,854
Right-of-use assets	2,626		3,660
Intangibles, net	90,730		86,766
Total assets	**262,608**	**+22**	**214,732**
Accts. pay. & accr. liabs	48,172		22,259
Current liabilities	62,924		32,906
Long-term debt, gross	16,897		5,724
Long-term debt, net	15,115		4,107
Shareholders' equity	179,732		174,920
Cash from oper. activs	**3,333**	**-83**	**20,047**
Cash from fin. activs	4,987		(4,606)
Cash from invest. activs	(23,273)		(4,995)
Net cash position	**12,902**	**-55**	**28,909**
Capital expenditures	(5,690)		(2,156)
Capital disposals	4		394
	$		$
Earns. per sh. bef disc opers*	0.38		(0.10)
Earnings per share*	0.38		(0.02)
Cash flow per share*	0.14		0.88
Cash divd. per share*	0.22		0.22
	shs		shs
No. of shs. o/s*	23,101,002		22,921,367
Avg. no. of shs. o/s*	23,079,181		22,748,826
	%		%
Net profit margin	4.65		(1.76)
Return on equity	4.90		(1.23)
Return on assets	3.64		(1.03)
Foreign sales percent	89		89
No. of employees (FTEs)	592		481

* Common
[A] Reported in accordance with IFRS

Latest Results

Periods ended:	9m Mar. 31/23[A]		9m Mar. 31/22[A]
	$000s	%Chg	$000s
Operating revenue	227,915	+80	126,854
Net income	22,102	+325	5,205
	$		$
Earnings per share*	0.94		0.23

* Common
[A] Reported in accordance with IFRS

Historical Summary
(as originally stated)

Fiscal Year	Oper. Rev.	Net Inc. Bef. Disc.	EPS*
	$000s	$000s	$
2022[A]	186,814	8,689	0.38
2021[A]	124,177	(2,185)	(0.10)
2020[A]	96,416	1,806	0.08
2019[A]	85,032	(3,459)	(0.15)
2018[A]	78,104	3,783	0.17

* Common
[A] Reported in accordance with IFRS

V.13 Vegano Foods Inc.

Symbol - VAGN **Exchange** - CSE **CUSIP** - 92255G
Head Office - 415-1040 Georgia St W, Vancouver, BC, V6E 4H1 **Telephone** - (778) 888-9822
Website - veganofoods.com
Email - conor@veganofoods.com
Investor Relations - Conor Power (604) 259-0028
Transfer Agents - Endeavor Trust Corporation, Vancouver, B.C.
Profile - (B.C. 2020) Provides and delivers plant-based meal kits, ready-made meals and vegan grocery items in British Columbia.

Offers a selection of plant-based meal kits on a subscription base through its custom-built online platform www.veganofoods.com, which are delivered to the customers on a weekly basis. The meal kits are able to accommodate the following dietary preferences: vegan, vegetarian, and gluten-free. The meal kits are available for delivery to Metro Vancouver, Vancouver Island, Squamish, Whistler and Pemberton, B.C. Also offers prepared meals that can be ordered through third-party delivery platforms such as SkiptheDishes and DoorDash and Vegano Marketplace, a direct-to-consumer online grocery store featuring a large selection of vegan grocery items.

In April 2022, the company agreed to acquire private **Smpl Oats Ltd.**, which produces dairy-free, gluten free, nut free and plant-based oat milk, on the basis of 0.8936 common shares of the company for each Smpl share held, which would result in the issuance of 28,571,428 common shares at a deemed price of $0.105 per share.

Directors - Conor Power, founder, North Vancouver, B.C.; Ricky Goraya, interim CEO; Jean Laven

Other Exec. Officers - Kaylee Astle, COO; Muhammad M. Memon, CFO

Capital Stock

	Authorized (shs.)	Outstanding (shs.)[1]
Common	unlimited	8,702,445

[1] At Feb. 28, 2023

Major Shareholder - Lorne W. Segal held 12.72% interest at Feb. 15, 2022.

Price Range - VAGN/CSE

Year	Volume	High	Low	Close
2022	2,991,996	$2.60	$0.02	$0.03

Recent Close: $0.07

Capital Stock Changes - On Oct. 25, 2022, common shares were consolidated on a 1-for-10 basis.

Latest Results

Periods ended:	9m Sept. 30/21[A]
	$000s
Operating revenue	228
Net income	(2,462)
	$
Earnings per share*	(0.50)

* Common
[A] Reported in accordance with IFRS

V.14 Veji Holdings Ltd.

Symbol - VEJI **Exchange** - CSE (S) **CUSIP** - 92261K
Head Office - 106-460 Doyle Ave, Kelowna, BC, V1Y 0C2 **Toll-free** - (800) 473-5548
Website - vejiholdings.com
Email - ir@vejiholdings.com
Investor Relations - Kory Zelickson (800) 473-5548
Auditors - Paul J. Rozek Professional Corporation C.A., Calgary, Alta.
Lawyers - Bennett Jones LLP, Vancouver, B.C.
Transfer Agents - Odyssey Trust Company, Vancouver, B.C.
Profile - (B.C. 2019) Operates online marketplace ShopVejii.com and business-to-business focused online marketplace VEDGEco.com which offer more than 2,000 plant-based and sustainable living products throughout the U.S. and Canada.

Products offered include grocery, protein and sports nutrition, personal and home care, vitamins and supplements, wines, pet supplies, and baby and kids supplies. Select products are offered under Veji Express, allowing the company to kit, bundle and pack a wide range of popular products together and guaranteeing customers those products be shipped within two business days across the U.S.

Inventory for the highest velocity products is purchased directly from distributors and held in stock at third party logistics partners' fulfillment centres. Orders are also collected from customers and directed to distribution partners to fulfill on the company's behalf. In addition, brands are offered the ability to apply to list their products directly on ShopVejii.com and access to direct-to-customer distribution through the Veji fulfilment services program.

On Jan. 30, 2023, the company received approval from the Supreme Court of British Columbia for its Division I proposal to the Bankruptcy and Insolvency Act (Canada) in which the company would issue common shares to settle its outstanding creditor liability. **G. Moroso & Associates Inc.** was assigned as trustee. On Apr. 27, 2023, the company issued 25,726,146 common shares to settle $4,000,000 of debt.

On Mar. 16, 2023, the company entered into a letter of intent to acquire certain bakery-related assets from **Keto Caveman Café Ltd.** Terms of the transaction were not disclosed.

In November 2022, the company announced plans to wind down the remainder of its U.S. operations, including wholly owned subsidiaries **Veg Essentials LLC** and **VEDGEco USA Inc.**, due to a lack of funds to continue commercial operations.

In October 2022, the company sold its domain, VeganEssentials.com, and certain associated intellectual property and assets to **PlantX Life Inc.** for $893,000, consisting of $143,000 cash and issuance of 1,071,428 PlantX common shares at a deemed price of 70¢ per share.

On May 2, 2022, the company entered into a letter of intent to acquire United Kingdom-based **Frozenly Limited Inc.**, which operates a direct-to-customer online logistics marketplace and platform for plant-based products, for a purchase price of £2,000,000 consisting of the issuance of £1,000,000 in common shares plus earnout consideration of up to a maximum of £1,000,000 payable in common shares upon meeting certain milestones.

Common suspended from CSE, May 9, 2023.

Predecessor Detail - Name changed from Vejii Holdings Ltd., Aug. 26, 2022.

Directors - Kory Zelickson, CEO, Kelowna, B.C.; Dharamvir (Darren) Gill, pres., COO & corp. sec., Kelowna, B.C.; Kenneth Jones, Mississauga, Ont.; Richard Kelly, Richmond, Va.

Other Exec. Officers - Rick Mah, CFO

Capital Stock

	Authorized (shs.)	Outstanding (shs.)[1]
Preferred	unlimited	nil
Common	unlimited	54,310,772

[1] At Apr. 27, 2023

Major Shareholder - Kory Zelickson held 34.95% interest at Apr. 27, 2023.

Price Range - VEJI/CSE (S)

Year	Volume	High	Low	Close
2022	6,765,876	$0.96	$0.01	$0.01
2021	1,631,072	$1.56	$0.38	$0.80

Consolidation: 1-for-4 cons. in Mar. 2022

Recent Close: $0.01

Capital Stock Changes - On Apr. 27, 2023, 25,726,146 common shares were issued for settlement of $4,000,000 of debt.

On Mar. 25, 2022, common shares were consolidated on a 1-for-4 basis.

Wholly Owned Subsidiaries

VEDGEco USA Inc., Hawaii
Veg Essentials LLC, United States.
Vejii Holdings Ltd., United Kingdom.
Vejii Inc., Del.

Investments

PlantX Life Inc., West Vancouver, B.C. (see Survey of Mines)

Financial Statistics

Periods ended:	12m Dec. 31/21[A]		12m Dec. 31/20[◻A]
	$000s	%Chg	$000s
Operating revenue	**1,722**	**n.m.**	**25**
Cost of goods sold	1,200		43
General & admin expense	9,214		412
Stock-based compensation	316		nil
Operating expense	**10,730**	**n.m.**	**455**
Operating income	**(9,008)**	**n.a.**	**(430)**
Deprec., depl. & amort.	60		2
Finance costs, gross	30		2
Pre-tax income	**(12,252)**	**n.a.**	**(433)**
Net income	**(12,252)**	**n.a.**	**(433)**
Cash & equivalent	283		97
Inventories	746		15
Accounts receivable	188		20
Current assets	1,527		152
Fixed assets, net	76		6
Right-of-use assets	170		nil
Intangibles, net	6,792		56
Total assets	**8,565**	**n.m.**	**214**
Bank indebtedness	1,740		nil
Accts. pay. & accr. liabs	2,447		82
Current liabilities	4,293		327
Long-term lease liabilities	145		nil
Shareholders' equity	2,283		(113)
Cash from oper. activs	**(6,825)**	**n.a.**	**(383)**
Cash from fin. activs	7,429		544
Cash from invest. activs	(554)		(64)
Net cash position	**143**	**+47**	**97**
Capital expenditures	(11)		(6)
	$		$
Earnings per share*	(0.60)		(0.16)
Cash flow per share*	(1.36)		(0.16)
	shs		shs
No. of shs. o/s*	28,584,608		7,500,030
Avg. no. of shs. o/s*	20,025,048		2,418,063
	%		%
Net profit margin	(711.50)		n.m.
Return on equity	n.m.		n.m.
Return on assets	(278.44)		n.a.

* Common
◻ Restated
[A] Reported in accordance with IFRS

Latest Results

Periods ended:	6m June 30/22[A]		6m June 30/21[A]
	$000s	%Chg	$000s
Operating revenue	2,771	+397	557
Net income	(4,353)	n.a.	(4,851)
	$		$
Earnings per share*	(0.15)		(0.28)

* Common
[A] Reported in accordance with IFRS

Note: Adjusted throughout for 1-for-4 cons. in Mar. 2022

V.15 Velan Inc.*

Symbol - VLN **Exchange** - TSX **CUSIP** - 922932
Head Office - 7007 ch de la Côte-de-Liesse, Montréal, QC, H4T 1G2
Telephone - (514) 748-7743 **Fax** - (514) 748-8635
Website - www.velan.com
Email - rishi.sharma@velan.com
Investor Relations - Rishi Sharma (438) 817-4430
Auditors - PricewaterhouseCoopers LLP C.A., Montréal, Qué.
Lawyers - Davies Ward Phillips & Vineberg LLP, Montréal, Qué.
Transfer Agents - TSX Trust Company, Montréal, Qué.
FP500 Revenue Ranking - 461
Employees - 1,647 at Feb. 28, 2023

Profile - (Can. 1952) Designs, manufactures and markets on a worldwide basis a broad range of industrial steel valves for use in many industry applications including power generation, oil and gas, refining and petrochemicals, chemicals, pulp and paper, liquid natural gas and cryogenics, mining, shipbuilding, water and wastewater.

Product lines are grouped into categories consisting of gate, globe, check and quarter-turn valves which are available in sizes varying from ¼" to 72", with pressure ratings from vacuum to more than 10,000 psi, temperature ratings from -458 to more than 1,500 degrees Fahrenheit, and in many material and design options. Other products include bimetallic steam traps, trap stations and manifolds; engineering solutions; Adareg™ control valves; and cable drive actuators. Products are sold directly and through an international network of distributors and agents which are supported by regional sales managers.

The company has 12 manufacturing plants located in Canada (2), South Korea (2), France (2), the U.S., Italy, Portugal, Taiwan, the People's Republic of China and India. In addition, the company has two stocking distribution centres in the U.S. and Germany and more than 50 authorized service/modification shops globally.

Recent Merger and Acquisition Activity

Status: pending **Revised:** May 16, 2023

UPDATE: Court approval was received. PREVIOUS: Flowserve Corporation agreed to acquire Velan Inc. for Cdn$13 in cash per multiple voting and subordinate voting share for a transaction value of US$245,000,000 (Cdn$329,000,000), including the assumption of US$36,300,000 (Cdn$48,900,000) of debt. Flowserve is a provider of flow control products and services for global infrastructure markets. The Velan family, Velan's controlling shareholder with a 92% voting interest, has agreed to vote all of their shares in favour of the transaction. May 5, 2023 - Velan shareholders approved the transaction, which was expected to close in the third quarter of 2023.

Directors - James A. Mannebach, chr., Reno, Nev.; Robert Velan, v-chr. & exec. v-p, intl. opers., Montréal, Qué.; Bruno Carbonaro, pres. & CEO, Montréal, Qué.; Suzanne Blanchet, La Prairie, Qué.; Dahra Granovsky, Toronto, Ont.; Edward H. Kernaghan, Toronto, Ont.; Ivan C. Velan, Montréal, Qué.; Peter O. Velan, Montréal, Qué.; Thomas C. (Tom) Velan, Montréal, Qué.

Other Exec. Officers - Shane Velan, CIO; Sabine Bruckert, exec. v-p, HR, gen. counsel & corp. sec.; Bryan Holt, exec. v-p & gen. mgr., MRO; Laurent Pefferkorn, exec. v-p & gen. mgr., project SBU; Rishi Sharma, exec. v-p, fin. & CFO; Duc T. (Duke) Tran, exec. v-p & gen. mgr., severe srvc.; Paul Dion, sr. v-p, sales, process industries; Victor Apostolescu, v-p, quality assurance; Joe Calabrese, v-p, technical sales, multi-turn products; Hélène Houde, v-p, strategic supply chain & central planning; Yves Lauzé, v-p, eng.; Emanuel Nataf, v-p, corp. fin.; Pierre Sabbagh, v-p, strategic initiatives & PMO; Raffi Sossoyan, v-p, corp. treasury; Daniel Velan, v-p, mktg.

Capital Stock

	Authorized (shs.)	Outstanding (shs.)[1]
Preferred	unlimited	nil
Multiple Voting	unlimited	15,566,567
Subordinate Voting	unlimited	6,019,068

[1] At July 6, 2023

Preferred - Issuable in series.

Multiple Voting - Convertible into subordinate voting shares on a share-for-share basis. Five votes per share.

Subordinate Voting - One vote per share.

Major Shareholder - Velan family held 92.82% interest at July 6, 2023.

Price Range - VLN/TSX

Year	Volume	High	Low	Close
2022	1,246,298	$10.70	$4.76	$5.34
2021	2,036,602	$11.25	$6.90	$8.20
2020	1,265,607	$8.85	$3.51	$7.00
2019	2,028,289	$12.50	$6.50	$8.37
2018	956,358	$20.49	$7.85	$8.86

Recent Close: $10.42

Capital Stock Changes - There were no changes to capital stock from fiscal 2021 to fiscal 2023, inclusive.

Dividends

VLN com S.V. omitted [1]
$0.03 June 30/23 $0.03 June 30/22
Paid in 2023: $0.03 2022: $0.03 2021: n.a.

[1] Quarterly divd normally payable in September/22 has been omitted.

Long-Term Debt - Outstanding at Feb. 28, 2023:

Canadian subsidiary:	
3.8% loan due 2041	US$15,181,000
French subsidiaries:	
0.25% to 2.95% loans due to 2028	3,366,000
Italian subsidiary:	
EURIBOR+3% loan due 2024	487,000
EURIBOR+0.67% to 1.25% loans due to 2027	4,427,000
Other	6,435,000
	29,896,000
Less: Current portion	8,177,000
	21,719,000

Wholly Owned Subsidiaries

Velan Luxembourg S.A.R.L., Luxembourg.
- 42.4% int. in **Velan GmbH**, Willich-Münchheide, Germany.
- 100% int. in **Velan Italy S.r.l.**, Italy.
  - 100% int. in **Velan ABV S.r.l.**, Italy.
    - 60% int. in **Velan Gulf Manufacturing Co. Ltd.**, Dammam, Saudi Arabia.
- 67.5% int. in **Velan Valves India Private Limited**, India.

Velan Valve Corp., Del.
- 100% int. in **Velan Ltd.**, Ansan, South Korea.
- 12% int. in **Velan Valvulas Industriais, Lda.**, Lisbon, Portugal.

Velan Valves Limited, United Kingdom.
- 75% int. in **Ségault S.A.**, Mennecy, France.
- 52.1% int. in **Velan GmbH**, Willich-Münchheide, Germany.
- 100% int. in **Velan S.A.S.**, Lyon, France.

Subsidiaries

85% int. in **Velan-China Holdings Inc.**, Montréal, Qué.
- 100% int. in **Velan Valve (Suzhou) Co., Ltd**, Suzhou, Jiangsu, People's Republic of China.

90% int. in **Velan Valvac Manufacturing Co. Ltd.**, Taichung, Republic of China.
88% int. in **Velan Valvulas Industriais, Lda.**, Lisbon, Portugal.

Investments

5.5% int. in **Velan GmbH**, Willich-Münchheide, Germany.
32.5% int. in **Velan Valves India Private Limited**, India.

Financial Statistics

Periods ended:	12m Feb. 28/23[A]		12m Feb. 28/22[A]
	US$000s	%Chg	US$000s
Operating revenue	**370,429**	**-10**	**411,242**
Cost of sales	183,345		195,606
Salaries & benefits	114,294		122,602
General & admin expense	104,888		58,061
Operating expense	**402,527**	**+7**	**376,269**
Operating income	**(32,098)**	**n.a.**	**34,973**
Deprec., depl. & amort.	10,743		11,648
Finance income	467		392
Finance costs, gross	2,019		2,792
Pre-tax income	**(47,414)**	**n.a.**	**36,176**
Income taxes	8,045		46,431
Net income	**(55,459)**	**n.a.**	**(10,255)**
Net inc. for equity hldrs	**(55,453)**	**n.a.**	**(21,141)**
Net inc. for non-cont. int	**(6)**	**n.a.**	**10,886**
Cash & equivalent	50,550		62,741
Inventories	202,649		223,198
Accounts receivable	121,053		115,834
Current assets	388,113		412,158
Fixed assets, net	68,205		73,906
Intangibles, net	16,153		16,693
Total assets	**477,857**	**-6**	**508,428**
Bank indebtedness	260		550
Accts. pay. & accr. liabs	79,408		80,503
Current liabilities	136,960		154,678
Long-term debt, gross	29,896		31,038
Long-term debt, net	21,719		22,927
Long-term lease liabilities	9,458		11,073
Shareholders' equity	199,889		264,824
Non-controlling interest	946		686
Cash from oper. activs	**522**	**-97**	**17,868**
Cash from fin. activs	(2,620)		(23,519)
Cash from invest. activs	1,759		(26)
Net cash position	**50,253**	**-6**	**53,465**
Capital expenditures	(4,370)		(6,144)
Capital disposals	185		30,183
	US$		US$
Earnings per share*	(2.57)		(0.98)
Cash flow per share*	0.02		0.83
Cash divd. per share*	$0.03		$nil
	shs		shs
No. of shs. o/s*	21,585,635		21,585,635
Avg. no. of shs. o/s*	21,585,635		21,585,635
	%		%
Net profit margin	(14.97)		(2.49)
Return on equity	(23.87)		(7.52)
Return on assets	(10.77)		(2.03)
Foreign sales percent	93		95
No. of employees (FTEs)	1,647		1,658

* M.V. & S.V.
[A] Reported in accordance with IFRS

Latest Results

Periods ended:	3m May 31/23[A]		3m May 31/22[A]
	US$000s	%Chg	US$000s
Operating revenue	67,659	-10	75,005
Net income	(8,290)	n.a.	(7,343)
Net inc. for equity hldrs	(8,284)	n.a.	(7,352)
Net inc. for non-cont. int	(6)		9
	US$		US$
Earnings per share*	(0.38)		(0.34)

* M.V. & S.V.
[A] Reported in accordance with IFRS

Historical Summary
(as originally stated)

Fiscal Year	Oper. Rev. US$000s	Net Inc. Bef. Disc. US$000s	EPS* US$
2023[A]	370,429	(55,459)	(2.57)
2022[A]	411,242	(10,255)	(0.98)
2021[A]	302,063	2,197	0.13
2020[A]	371,625	(16,601)	(0.76)
2019[A]	366,865	(5,394)	(0.23)

* M.V. & S.V.
[A] Reported in accordance with IFRS

V.16 VentriPoint Diagnostics Ltd.

Symbol - VPT **Exchange** - TSX-VEN **CUSIP** - 92281P
Head Office - 101-18 Hook Ave, Toronto, ON, M6P 1T4 **Telephone** - (416) 848-4156
Website - www.ventripoint.com
Email - gadams@ventripoint.com
Investor Relations - Dr. George Adams (519) 803-6937
Auditors - MNP LLP C.A., Mississauga, Ont.
Lawyers - Boyle & Co. LLP, Toronto, Ont.
Transfer Agents - Computershare Trust Company of Canada Inc., Toronto, Ont.
Profile - (Can. 2007; orig. Alta., 2005) Develops and commercializes diagnostic tools to monitor patients with heart disease.
The VentriPoint Medical System™ (VMS), a technology licensed from the University of Washington, generates accurate heart volumetric measurements and a 3D model in a rapid and inexpensive manner. The system produces critical heart information by processing standard information received from existing medical imaging equipment with its patented and proprietary methods incorporating Knowledge Based Reconstruction (KBR) algorithms and proprietary cardiac databases. The KBR method is a form of artificial intelligence which allows for the creation of a 3D model of the all the chambers of the heart, right and left ventricles, and right and left atria using images generated from existing 2D and 3D imaging equipment. The technology is applicable to all major heart diseases.
VMS' hardware and software for 2D and 3D echocardiograms have U.S. FDA marketing clearance, Health Canada licence and European CE Mark for all patients where volumetric information for any of the four chambers of the heart is warranted or desired.
Manufacturing facility is located in Toronto, Ont.
Predecessor Detail - Name changed from Luca Capital Inc., Sept. 26, 2007.
Directors - Dr. George Adams, exec. chr., Guelph, Ont.; Randy AuCoin, Cavan, Ont.; Fiona Fitzgerald, Qué.; Robert L. (Bob) Hodgkinson, Vancouver, B.C.; Hugh MacNaught, North Vancouver, B.C.
Other Exec. Officers - Dr. Alvira Macanovic, pres. & CEO; Victor J. (Vic) Hugo, CFO; Peter Weichler, corp. sec.

Capital Stock

	Authorized (shs.)	Outstanding (shs.)[1]
Preferred	unlimited	nil
Common	unlimited	156,823,905

[1] At Mar. 31, 2023
Major Shareholder - Widely held at July 11, 2022.

Price Range - VPT/TSX-VEN

Year	Volume	High	Low	Close
2022	42,050,330	$0.41	$0.21	$0.27
2021	392,766,280	$0.67	$0.08	$0.35
2020	83,694,979	$0.16	$0.07	$0.09
2019	42,863,035	$0.27	$0.07	$0.08
2018	63,054,434	$0.51	$0.13	$0.16

Recent Close: $0.27
Capital Stock Changes - During 2022, common shares were issued as follows: 1,005,000 on exercise of options and 260,000 on exercise of warrants.

Wholly Owned Subsidiaries

VentriPoint, Inc., Seattle, Wash.

Financial Statistics

Periods ended:	12m Dec. 31/22[A]		12m Dec. 31/21[A]
	$000s	%Chg	$000s
Operating revenue	**68**	**n.a.**	**nil**
Cost of sales	10		nil
Research & devel. expense	990		423
General & admin expense	3,130		2,339
Stock-based compensation	798		898
Other operating expense	nil		6
Operating expense	**4,928**	**+34**	**3,667**
Operating income	**(4,860)**	**n.a.**	**(3,667)**
Deprec., depl. & amort	51		49
Finance costs, net	10		(32)
Pre-tax income	**(4,873)**	**n.a.**	**(3,881)**
Net income	**(4,873)**	**n.a.**	**(3,881)**
Cash & equivalent	5,186		9,269
Accounts receivable	374		197
Current assets	5,663		9,502
Fixed assets, net	7		16
Right-of-use assets	306		26
Total assets	**5,977**	**-37**	**9,545**
Accts. pay. & accr. liabs	964		1,051
Current liabilities	1,056		1,085
Long-term debt, gross	143		125
Long-term debt, net	93		125
Long-term lease liabilities	274		nil
Shareholders' equity	4,554		8,334
Cash from oper. activs	**(4,137)**	**n.a.**	**(3,147)**
Cash from fin. activs	88		11,890
Cash from invest. activs	nil		(4)
Net cash position	**5,186**	**-44**	**9,269**
Capital expenditures	nil		(4)
	$		$
Earnings per share*	(0.03)		(0.03)
Cash flow per share*	(0.03)		(0.02)
	shs		shs
No. of shs. o/s*	156,823,905		155,558,905
Avg. no. of shs. o/s*	155,994,206		136,097,000
	%		%
Net profit margin	n.m.		n.a.
Return on equity	(75.62)		n.m.
Return on assets	(62.79)		(75.02)

* Common
[A] Reported in accordance with IFRS

Latest Results

Periods ended:	3m Mar. 31/23[A]		3m Mar. 31/22[A]
	$000s	%Chg	$000s
Operating revenue	4	-84	25
Net income	(1,345)	n.a.	(1,009)
	$		$
Earnings per share*	(0.01)		(0.01)

* Common
[A] Reported in accordance with IFRS

Historical Summary
(as originally stated)

Fiscal Year	Oper. Rev. $000s	Net Inc. Bef. Disc. $000s	EPS* $
2022[A]	68	(4,873)	(0.03)
2021[A]	nil	(3,881)	(0.03)
2020[A]	36	(1,851)	(0.02)
2019[A]	81	(3,323)	(0.05)
2018[A]	60	(2,084)	(0.04)

* Common
[A] Reported in accordance with IFRS

V.17 Venzee Technologies Inc.

Symbol - VENZ **Exchange** - TSX-VEN **CUSIP** - 92337G
Head Office - 170-422 Richards St, Vancouver, BC, V6B 2Z4 **Toll-free** - (888) 359-8110
Website - www.venzee.com
Email - darren@venzee.com
Investor Relations - Darren Battersby (866) 684-6730
Auditors - Davidson & Company LLP C.A., Vancouver, B.C.
Transfer Agents - Computershare Trust Company of Canada Inc., Vancouver, B.C.
Profile - (B.C. 1996) Provides a cloud-based software-as-a-service (SaaS) content exchange platform which allows suppliers and manufacturers from multiple industries to share real-time product information and inventory updates with retailers.
The company's core product Mesh Connector™ allows brands to automate the distribution of product data to an unlimited number of retail channels which eliminates the retailer's inefficiencies of collecting product data from suppliers. The technology uses automation, machine learning and artificial intelligence to automatically sense, map and send unlimited consumer-facing product attributes to any retail sales channels globally.
Consumer brands pay a monthly recurring fee for each retail destination they choose. Services are paid by consumer brands directly or through a product information management service or a content management service that has a contract-based partner or teaming agreement with the company.
Predecessor Detail - Name changed from Gold Finder Explorations Ltd., Dec. 21, 2017, following reverse takeover acquisition of and amalgamation of Venzee Inc. with a wholly owned subsid.; basis 1 new for 2 old shs.
Directors - Peter Montross, chr. & COO, Ore.; John Sexton Abrams, pres. & CEO, Chicago, Ill.; Marc Bertrand, Hudson, Qué.; Sean Copeland, Delta, B.C.; Thomas J. (Tom) Linden, Chicago, Ill.; John Sviokla, Ill.
Other Exec. Officers - Darren Battersby, CFO & corp. sec.; Marco Sylvestre, v-p, product devel.

Capital Stock

	Authorized (shs.)	Outstanding (shs.)[1]
Common	unlimited	243,041,509

[1] At May 30, 2022
Major Shareholder - Widely held at May 7, 2021.

Price Range - VENZ/TSX-VEN

Year	Volume	High	Low	Close
2022	60,861,600	$0.14	$0.01	$0.01
2021	113,866,390	$0.23	$0.06	$0.14
2020	143,953,267	$0.17	$0.02	$0.08
2019	72,929,191	$0.12	$0.02	$0.04
2018	34,577,586	$1.85	$0.06	$0.12

Recent Close: $0.01
Capital Stock Changes - In May and June 2022, private placement of 8,485,000 units (1 common share & 2 warrant) at 5¢ per unit was completed, with warrants exercisable at 10¢ per share for three years.

Wholly Owned Subsidiaries

Venzee Inc., Wilmington, Del.
Venzee Technologies Canada Inc., Canada.

Financial Statistics

Periods ended:	12m Dec. 31/21[A]		12m Dec. 31/20[A]
	US$000s	%Chg	US$000s
Operating revenue	**68**	**+94**	**35**
Cost of sales	25		44
Research & devel. expense	586		349
General & admin expense	2,347		1,373
Stock-based compensation	801		n.a.
Operating expense	**3,759**	**+165**	**1,417**
Operating income	**(3,691)**	**n.a.**	**(1,382)**
Deprec., depl. & amort	6		17
Finance costs, gross	nil		5
Pre-tax income	**(3,606)**	**n.a.**	**(1,763)**
Net income	**(3,606)**	**n.a.**	**(1,763)**
Cash & equivalent	534		1,325
Accounts receivable	25		12
Current assets	605		1,410
Fixed assets, net	nil		6
Total assets	**605**	**-57**	**1,415**
Bank indebtedness	47		47
Accts. pay. & accr. liabs	175		95
Current liabilities	222		142
Shareholders' equity	384		1,274
Cash from oper. activs	**(2,797)**	**n.a.**	**(1,763)**
Cash from fin. activs	1,980		3,007
Net cash position	**534**	**-60**	**1,325**
	US$		US$
Earnings per share*	(0.02)		(0.01)
Cash flow per share*	(0.01)		(0.01)
	shs		shs
No. of shs. o/s*	231,857,842		208,185,115
Avg. no. of shs. o/s*	222,916,158		157,624,592
	%		%
Net profit margin	n.m.		n.m.
Return on equity	(434.98)		n.m.
Return on assets	(357.03)		(221.83)
Foreign sales percent	100		100

* Common
[A] Reported in accordance with IFRS

Latest Results

Periods ended:	3m Mar. 31/22[A]		3m Mar. 31/21[A]
	US$000s	%Chg	US$000s
Operating revenue	10	+11	9
Net income	(1,009)	n.a.	(657)
	US$		US$
Earnings per share*	(0.00)		(0.00)

* Common
[A] Reported in accordance with IFRS

Historical Summary
(as originally stated)

Fiscal Year	Oper. Rev.	Net Inc. Bef. Disc.	EPS*
	US$000s	US$000s	US$
2021[A]	68	(3,606)	(0.02)
2020[A]	35	(1,763)	(0.01)
2019[A]	164	(3,311)	(0.03)
2018[A]	197	(5,220)	(0.08)
2017[A1]	159	(4,596)	(0.26)

* Common
[A] Reported in accordance with IFRS
[1] Results reflect the Dec. 21, 2017 reverse takeover acquisition of Venzee Inc.
Note: Adjusted throughout for 1-for-2 cons. in Jan. 2018

V.18 Verano Holdings Corp.

Symbol - VRNO **Exchange** - CSE **CUSIP** - 92338D
Head Office - 415 North Dearborn St, 4th Flr, Chicago, IL, United States, 60654 **Telephone** - (312) 265-0730
Website - www.verano.com
Email - julianna.paterra@verano.com
Investor Relations - Julianna Paterra (312) 265-0730
Auditors - Macias Gini & O'Connell LLP C.P.A., San Jose, Calif.
Transfer Agents - Odyssey Trust Company, Vancouver, B.C.
FP500 Revenue Ranking - 314
Employees - 3,780 at Mar. 28, 2023
Profile - (B.C. 2021; orig. Alta., 2014) Cultivates, manufactures, distributes and retails cannabis products in the United States.

The company has active operations in 13 U.S. states (Arizona, Arkansas, Connecticut, Florida, Illinois, Maryland, Massachusetts, Michigan, Nevada, New Jersey, Ohio, Pennsylvania and West Virginia). At Aug. 4, 2023, operations consisted of 14 cultivation and manufacturing facilities with more than 1,000,000 sq. ft. of cultivation space, and 132 retail dispensaries under the Zen Leaf™ and MUV™ banners serving both the medical and adult-use markets. Products include flower, concentrates for dabbing and vaporizing, edibles and topicals which are sold under a portfolio of consumer brands including Verano™, MUV™, Savvy™, BITS™, Encore™ and Avexia™.

On Sept. 7, 2022, the company acquired **WSCC, Inc.** (dba Sierra Well) for US$6,085,000 cash and issuance of 1,536,685 class A subordinate voting shares. Sierra Well has two dispensaries in Reno and Carson City and a 10,000-sq.-ft. cultivation and production facility in Reno, all in Nevada.

On Mar. 11, 2022, the company acquired **420 Capital Management, LLC** (dba GreenGate), operator of two cannabis dispensaries in Lombard and Rogers Park, Ill., for US$21,260,741, consisting of US$7,447,871 cash and issuance of 1,403,067 class A subordinate voting shares.

On Mar. 1, 2022, the company completed the sale of 50% interest in **ILDISP, LLC**, which has dispensary assets in Effingham and Charleston, Ill., for US$22,393,000, subject to certain adjustments.

Recent Merger and Acquisition Activity

Status: terminated **Revised:** Oct. 14, 2022
UPDATE: Verano has provided notice to terminate the transaction. Goodness believes that Verano has no legal basis to terminate the agreement. Verano's repudiation of agreement was acknowledged by Goodness, and the transaction would not proceed. Goodness plans to immediately commence legal proceedings against Verano to seek damages. PREVIOUS: Verano Holdings Corp. entered into a definitive agreement to acquire Goodness Growth Holdings Inc. in an all-share transaction valued at about US$413,000,000. Each Goodness subordinate voting share will be exchanged for 0.22652 Verano class A subordinate voting share and each Goodness multiple voting share and super voting share will be exchanged for 22.652 Verano class A subordinate voting shares. Goodness' active operations include 18 dispensaries; five cultivation and processing facilities; a research and development facility; and the Vireo Spectrum, 1937, LiteBud, Kings & Queens, Hi-Color and Amplifi product brands. The acquisition was intended to add the New York, Minnesota and New Mexico markets to Verano's operations. The transaction was subject to the approvals of Goodness shareholders, the Supreme Court of B.C. and U.S. regulatory bodies. Goodness shareholders holding 36.7% voting interest have agreed to vote in favor of the transaction. A termination fee of US$14,875,000 would be payable by either company under certain circumstances.

Predecessor Detail - Name changed from Majesta Minerals Inc., Feb. 11, 2021, pursuant to reverse takeover acquisition of Verano Holdings, LLC.

Directors - George P. Archos, chr. & CEO, Fla.; John A. Tipton, pres., southern region, Bradenton, Fla.; Lawrence R. Hirsh, Fla.; Charles F. Mueller; Cristina Nuñez, Miami, Fla.

Other Exec. Officers - Darren H. Weiss, pres.; Trip McDermott, COO; Brent Summerer, CFO; Laura Kalesnik, chief legal officer, gen. counsel & corp. sec.; Aaron Miles, chief invest. officer; David Spreckman, chief mktg. officer; Destiny Thompson, chief people officer

Capital Stock

	Authorized (shs.)	Outstanding (shs.)[1]
Cl.A Subordinate Vtg.	unlimited	343,367,514
Cl.B Proportionate Vtg.	unlimited	nil

[1] At Aug. 4, 2023

Class A Subordinate Voting - One vote per share.
Class B Proportionate Voting - Each is convertible into 100 class A subordinate voting shares, subject to restrictions. 100 votes per share.
Major Shareholder - George P. Archos held 16.8% interest at Apr. 27, 2023.

Price Range - VRNO/CSE

Year	Volume	High	Low	Close
2022	82,804,899	$17.45	$3.53	$4.30
2021	60,228,145	$33.00	$12.30	$15.99

Recent Close: $3.55

Capital Stock Changes - On Feb. 14, 2023, 449 class B proportionate voting shares were converted into 44,997 class A subordinate voting shares. On Mar. 24, 2023, all 133,373 class B proportionate voting shares were converted into 13,337,286 class A subordinate voting shares.

During 2022, class A subordinate voting shares were issued as follows: 7,039,977 for acquisitions, 5,310,540 as contingent consideration and 3,320,195 on exercise of restricted share units and options. In addition, 177,212 class B proportionate voting shares were converted into 17,721,188 class A subordinate voting shares.

Wholly Owned Subsidiaries

Verano Holdings USA Corp., Del.
- 100% int. in **A&T SPV II LLC**, Tex.
  - 0.45% int. in **Verano Holdings, LLC**, Chicago, Ill.
- 100% int. in **Nuuvn Holdings, LLC**, Del.
  - 1.69% int. in **Verano Holdings, LLC**, Chicago, Ill.
- 100% int. in **SGI 1 LLC**, Del.
  - 3.01% int. in **Verano Holdings, LLC**, Chicago, Ill.
- 83.43% int. in **Verano Holdings, LLC**, Chicago, Ill.
  - 100% int. in **AGG Wellness, LLC**, Md.
  - 100% int. in **AGOZ Redevelopment, LP**, Pa.
  - 100% int. in **AZGM 3, LLC**, Ariz.
  - 100% int. in **Agri-Kind, LLC**, Pa.
  - 100% int. in **Agronomed Biologics Holdings Inc.**, Pa.
  - 100% int. in **Agronomed Biologics LLC**, Pa.
  - 100% int. in **Agronomed Holdings, Inc.**, Pa.
  - 15% int. in **Agronomed IP LLC**, Pa.
  - 100% int. in **Albion MM, LLC**, Ill.
  - 100% int. in **Ataraxia, LLC**, Ill.
  - 100% int. in **Branchburg Rte. 22, LLC**, N.J.
  - 100% int. in **CTPharma Real Estate Inc.**, Conn.
  - 10% int. in **CTPharma Research Solutions, LLC**, Del.
  - 100% int. in **Caring Nature, LLC**, Conn.
  - 100% int. in **Cave Creek RE, LLC**, Ariz.
  - 100% int. in **ChiVegas Real Estate, LLC**, Nev.
  - 100% int. in **Connecticut Pharmaceutical Solutions, LLC**, Conn.
  - 100% int. in **Cultivation Real Estate Holdings, LLC**, Del.
  - 100% int. in **Custom Strains, LLC**, Ill.
  - 62.5% int. in **DGV Group, LLC**, Del.
  - 100% int. in **Elevele LLC**, Ill.
  - 100% int. in **FGM Processing, LLC**, Md.
  - 100% int. in **Fort Consulting, LLC**, Ariz.
  - 100% int. in **Four Daughters Compassionate Care, Inc.**, Mass.
  - 100% int. in **420 Capital Management, LLC**, Ill.
  - 100% int. in **Freestate Wellness, LLC**, Md.
  - 100% int. in **Glass City Alternatives, LLC**, Ohio
  - 100% int. in **Green RX, LLC**, Ohio
  - 100% int. in **The Healing Center LLC**, Pa.
  - 100% int. in **Healthway Services of Illinois, LLC**, Ill.
  - 100% int. in **The Herbal Care Center, Inc.**, Ill.
  - 100% int. in **Local Dispensaries, LLC**, Pa.
  - 100% int. in **Lone Mountain Partners, LLC**, Nev.
  - 100% int. in **MD MM Logistics, LLC**, Md.
  - 100% int. in **Mad River Remedies, LLC**, Ohio
  - 100% int. in **The Medicine Room, LLC**, Ariz.
  - 100% int. in **Mikran, LLC**, Md.
  - 100% int. in **Mother Grows Best, LLC**, Ohio
  - 100% int. in **Mother Know's Best, LLC**, Ohio
  - 100% int. in **NSE Pennsylvania LLC**, Pa.
  - 100% int. in **NV MM Logistics, LLC**, Nev.
  - 100% int. in **NatureX, LLC**, Nev.
  - 100% int. in **NuTrae, LLC**, Fla.
  - 100% int. in **OH MM Logistics, LLC**, Ohio
  - 100% int. in **Ohio Natural Treatment Solutions, LLC**, Del.
  - 100% int. in **Patient Alternative Relief Center, LLC**, Ariz.
  - 100% int. in **Perpetual Healthcare Inc.**, Ariz.
  - 100% int. in **Plants of Ruskin, LLC**, Fla.
  - 100% int. in **Prospect Heights RE, LLC**, Ill.
  - 100% int. in **RVC 360, LLC**, Del.
  - 100% int. in **RedMed, LLC**, Del.
  - 100% int. in **Retail and Office Real Estate Holdings, LLC**, Del.
  - 100% int. in **TerraVida Holistic Centers LLC**, Pa.
  - 100% int. in **VZL Staffing Services, LLC**, Ill.
  - 100% int. in **Vehicle and Logistics Holdings, LLC**, Del.
  - 100% int. in **Vending Logistics, LLC**, Ariz.
  - 100% int. in **Verano Alabama Holdings, LLC**, Del.
  - 49% int. in **Verano Alabama, LLC**, Ala.
  - 100% int. in **Verano Arizona, LLC**, Del.
  - 100% int. in **Verano Connecticut, LLC**, Del.
  - 100% int. in **Verano El Dorado, LLC**, Ark.
  - 100% int. in **Verano Florida, LLC**, Del.
  - 100% int. in **Verano Four Daughters Holdings, LLC**, Del.
  - 100% int. in **Verano IP, LLC**, Del.
  - 100% int. in **Verano Illinois, LLC**, Ill.
  - 100% int. in **Verano Michigan, LLC**, Del.
  - 100% int. in **Verano NJ Holdings, LLC**, Del.
  - 100% int. in **Verano NJ LLC**, N.J.
  - 100% int. in **Verano Nevada, LLC**, Nev.
  - 100% int. in **Verano Ohio, LLC**, Ohio
  - 100% int. in **Verano Pennsylvania, LLC**, Del.
  - 100% int. in **Verano Virginia, LLC**, Del.
  - 100% int. in **WSCC, Inc.**, Nev.
  - 100% int. in **WSCC Property LLC**, Nev.
  - 100% int. in **West Capital, LLC**, Ill.
  - 100% int. in **Willow Brook Wellness, LLC**, Conn.
  - 100% int. in **Zen Leaf Retail, LLC**, Md.
  - 100% int. in **Zen Leaf Technologies, LLC**, Del.
- 100% int. in **ZNN Holdings, LLC**, Del.
  - 1.64% int. in **Verano Holdings, LLC**, Chicago, Ill.
- 100% int. in **ZenNorth, LLC**, Del.
  - 9.78% int. in **Verano Holdings, LLC**, Chicago, Ill.

Note: The preceding list includes only the major related companies in which interests are held.

Financial Statistics

Periods ended:	12m Dec. 31/22[A]		12m Dec. 31/21[◻A1]
	US$000s	%Chg	US$000s
Operating revenue	**879,412**	**+19**	**737,850**
Cost of goods sold	424,576		386,436
General & admin expense	246,956		195,080
Operating expense	**671,532**	**+15**	**581,516**
Operating income	**207,880**	**+33**	**156,334**
Deprec., depl. & amort.	141,387		96,244
Finance costs, net	57,418		24,270
Investment income	1,558		4,623
Write-downs/write-offs	(229,182)[2]		nil
Pre-tax income	**(163,403)**	**n.a.**	**48,990**
Income taxes	105,470		103,988
Net income	**(268,873)**	**n.a.**	**(54,998)**
Net inc. for equity hldrs	**(269,164)**	**n.a.**	**(57,507)**
Net inc. for non-cont. int.	**291**	**-88**	**2,509**
Cash & equivalent	84,851		99,118
Inventories	164,532		140,703
Accounts receivable	16,580		17,410
Current assets	318,275		277,044
Long-term investments	6,977		7,491
Fixed assets, net	525,905		452,232
Right-of-use assets	82,278		61,346
Intangibles, net	1,449,854		1,748,043
Total assets	**2,396,055**	**-6**	**2,548,655**
Accts. pay. & accr. liabs	82,263		87,321
Current liabilities	386,645		470,516
Long-term debt, gross	413,004		289,925
Long-term debt, net	388,540		276,154
Long-term lease liabilities	76,853		56,812
Shareholders' equity	1,341,550		1,480,530
Non-controlling interest	nil		1,276
Cash from oper. activs	**94,347**	**-48**	**182,872**
Cash from fin. activs	99,245		355,676
Cash from invest. activs	(207,851)		(455,832)
Net cash position	**84,851**	**-14**	**99,118**
Capital expenditures	(119,174)		(141,265)
Capital disposals	6,249		1,894
	US$		US$
Earnings per share*	(0.81)		(0.20)
Cash flow per share*	0.28		0.63
	shs		shs
No. of shs. o/s*	339,983,374		324,312,662
Avg. no. of shs. o/s*	331,409,315		290,443,432
	%		%
Net profit margin	(30.57)		(7.45)
Return on equity	(19.08)		(6.68)
Return on assets	(10.88)		(3.66)
Foreign sales percent	100		100

* Cl.A. S.V.
◻ Restated
[A] Reported in accordance with U.S. GAAP
[1] Results reflect the Feb. 11, 2021, reverse takeover acquisition of Verano Holdings, LLC.
[2] Includes full impairment associated with Arizona cultivation (wholesale) licence of US$116,151,000; and goodwill impairment totaling US$113,031,000 associated with Arizona retail and cultivation (wholesale) units and Pennsylvania retail and cultivation (wholesale) units.

Latest Results

Periods ended:	6m June 30/23[A]		6m June 30/22[A]
	US$000s	%Chg	US$000s
Operating revenue	461,175	+8	425,897
Net income	(22,298)	n.a.	(9,770)
Net inc. for equity hldrs	(22,298)	n.a.	(10,061)
Net inc. for non-cont. int.	nil		291
	US$		US$
Earnings per share*	(0.07)		(0.03)

* Cl.A. S.V.
[A] Reported in accordance with U.S. GAAP

Historical Summary
(as originally stated)

Fiscal Year	Oper. Rev.	Net Inc. Bef. Disc.	EPS*
	US$000s	US$000s	US$
2022[A]	879,412	(268,873)	(0.81)
2021[A]	737,850	(54,998)	(0.20)
2020[B1]	228,530	126,640	n.a.
2019[B]	65,968	(18,194)	n.a.
2018[B]	31,095	3,709	n.a.

* Cl.A. S.V.
[A] Reported in accordance with U.S. GAAP
[B] Reported in accordance with IFRS
[1] Results for 2020 and prior years pertain to Verano Holdings, LLC and subsidiaries.

V.19 Verisante Technology, Inc.

Symbol - VER.H **Exchange** - TSX-VEN **CUSIP** - 92346G
Head Office - 170-422 Richards St, Vancouver, BC, V6B 2Z4 **Telephone** - (604) 605-0507 **Fax** - (604) 605-0508
Website - www.verisante.com
Email - tbraun@verisante.com
Investor Relations - Thomas A. Braun (877) 605-0507
Auditors - Fernandez Young LLP C.A., Vancouver, B.C.
Transfer Agents - Olympia Trust Company, Toronto, Ont.
Profile - (B.C. 2009; orig. Ont., 2006) Seeking new business opportunities.
Prior to 2018, the company was developing non-invasive cancer detection technologies.
Predecessor Detail - Name changed from T-Ray Science Inc., Jan. 18, 2011.
Directors - Thomas A. Braun, pres. & CEO, Vancouver, B.C.; Emmeline Braun, CFO & corp. sec., B.C.; Dr. Jake J. Thiessen, Unionville, Ont.; Vincent Trinh

Capital Stock

	Authorized (shs.)	Outstanding (shs.)[1]
Class A Preferred	unlimited	nil
Class B Preferred	unlimited	nil
Common	unlimited	32,738,004

[1] At Mar. 31, 2023
Major Shareholder - Widely held at Sept. 1, 2018.

Price Range - VER.H/TSX-VEN

Year	Volume	High	Low	Close
2022	679,400	$0.20	$0.01	$0.02
2018	1,668,857	$0.60	$0.15	$0.20

Consolidation: 1-for-10 cons. in June 2022
Recent Close: $0.02
Capital Stock Changes - In June 2022, common shares were consolidated on a 1-for-10 basis and 1,535,418 post-consolidated common shares were issued for settlement of $767,710 of debt. In July 2022, private placement of 9,858,000 post-consolidated common shares was completed at 1¢ per share. In November 2022, 11,483,000 post-consolidated common shares were issued for debt settlement.

Financial Statistics

Periods ended:	12m Dec. 31/21[A]		12m Dec. 31/20[A]
	$000s	%Chg	$000s
General & admin expense	192		159
Operating expense	**192**	**+21**	**159**
Operating income	**(192)**	**n.a.**	**(159)**
Pre-tax income	**(192)**	**n.a.**	**(44)**
Net income	**(192)**	**n.a.**	**(44)**
Cash & equivalent	137		nil
Current assets	146		12
Total assets	**146**	**n.m.**	**12**
Accts. pay. & accr. liabs	125		117
Current liabilities	140		172
Shareholders' equity	(1,560)		(1,367)
Cash from oper. activs	**(41)**	**n.a.**	**(46)**
Cash from fin. activs	178		46
Net cash position	**137**	**n.a.**	**nil**
	$		$
Earnings per share*	(0.02)		(0.00)
Cash flow per share*	(0.00)		(0.00)
	shs		shs
No. of shs. o/s*	9,861,589		9,861,589
Avg. no. of shs. o/s*	9,861,589		9,861,589
	%		%
Net profit margin	n.a.		n.a.
Return on equity	n.m.		n.m.
Return on assets	(243.04)		(366.67)

* Common
[A] Reported in accordance with IFRS

Latest Results

Periods ended:	3m Mar. 31/22[A]		3m Mar. 31/21[A]
	$000s	%Chg	$000s
Net income	(58)	n.a.	(33)
	$		$
Earnings per share*	(0.01)		(0.00)

* Common
[A] Reported in accordance with IFRS

Historical Summary
(as originally stated)

Fiscal Year	Oper. Rev.	Net Inc. Bef. Disc.	EPS*
	$000s	$000s	$
2021[A]	nil	(192)	(0.02)
2020[A]	nil	(44)	(0.00)
2019[A]	nil	(50)	(0.01)
2018[A]	nil	431	0.04
2017[A]	nil	(2,280)	(0.24)

* Common
[A] Reported in accordance with IFRS
Note: Adjusted throughout for 1-for-10 cons. in June 2022

V.20 VersaBank

Symbol - VBNK **Exchange** - TSX **CUSIP** - 92512J
Head Office - 2002-140 Fullarton St, London, ON, N6A 5P2 **Telephone** - (519) 645-1919 **Toll-free** - (866) 979-1919 **Fax** - (519) 645-2060
Website - www.versabank.com
Email - brenth@versabank.com
Investor Relations - Brent T. Hodge (800) 244-1509
Auditors - Ernst & Young LLP C.A., London, Ont.
Bankers - Royal Bank of Canada, Saskatoon, Sask.
Lawyers - Stikeman Elliott LLP, Toronto, Ont.
Transfer Agents - Odyssey Trust Company
FP500 Revenue Ranking - 731
Employees - 110 at Oct. 31, 2022
Profile - (Can. 2017 amalg.; orig. Can., 2002) Operates as a Schedule I Canadian chartered bank providing commercial and consumer lending and deposit solutions to select niche markets across Canada through digital banking. Also provides a comprehensive suite of cyber security solutions to financial institutions, multi-national corporations and government entities worldwide.
Digital Banking - Operations consist of **Point-of-Sale Financing**, which includes financing provided to the bank's network of origination partners, who offer point-of-sale loans and leases to consumers and commercial clients in various markets throughout Canada and the U.S.; and **Commercial Lending**, which includes commercial and residential construction mortgages, commercial term mortgages, commercial insured mortgages, land mortgages, condominium financing loans, and public sector loans and leases which are originated through a network of mortgage brokers and syndication partners as well as directly through the bank.
Deposit solutions consist of guaranteed investment certificates (GICs), tax free savings accounts, registered retirement savings plan accounts, daily interest savings accounts and chequing accounts which are sourced through a network of deposits brokers and insolvency professionals.
DRTC- Wholly owned **DRT Cyber Inc.** offers cyber security protocols, banking and financial technology development, software and supporting systems to mitigate cyber security risks that businesses, governments and other organizations face in the normal course of their operations. Solutions include VersaVault, a digital bank vault for securing cryptocurrency, blockchain-based assets and digital documents; and Digital Boundary Group, a division of DRT that provides a suite of information technology (IT) security assurance services, including external network, web and mobile application penetration testing, physical social engineering engagements, supervisory control and data acquisition (SCADA) system assessments as well as various aspects of training.

Recent Merger and Acquisition Activity

Status: pending **Announced:** June 14, 2022
VersaBank agreed to acquire Minnesota-based Stearns Bank Holdingford, N.A., which operates as a national bank focused on small business lending, from Stearns Financial Services Inc. for US$13,500,000. The transaction would add US$60,000,000 in total assets to VersaBank. Upon completion, Stearns would be renamed VersaBank USA National Association.
Predecessor Detail - Name changed from Pacific & Western Bank of Canada, May 13, 2016.
Directors - The Hon. Thomas A. (Tom) Hockin, chr., Rancho Mirage, Calif.; David R. Taylor, pres. & CEO, Ilderton, Ont.; Gabrielle Bochynek, Stratford, Ont.; Robbert-Jan Brabander, Richmond Hill, Ont.; David A. Bratton, London, Ont.; Peter M. Irwin, Toronto, Ont.; Richard H. L. Jankura, London, Ont.; Arthur R. (Art) Linton, Kitchener, Ont.; Susan T. McGovern, Aurora, Ont.; Paul G. Oliver, Markham, Ont.
Other Exec. Officers - R. Shawn Clarke, CFO; Tammie L. Ashton, chief risk officer; Garry W. G. Clement, chief AML officer; Jim Gardiner, chief risk officer, real estate; Joanne Johnston, chief internal auditor; Wooi Koay, CIO; Nick Kristo, chief credit officer; Jonathan F. P. Taylor, chief HR officer; Dr. Tel G. Matrundola, exec. v-p; John W. Asma, sr. v-p, deposit srvcs. & treas.; Michael R. Dixon, sr. v-p, point-of-sale financing; Brent T. Hodge, sr. v-p, chief compliance officer, gen. counsel & corp. sec.; Scott A. Mizzen, sr. v-p, comml. lending; Rick Smyth, sr. v-p, real estate lending; Saad Inam, v-p, credit; Nancy McCutcheon, v-p, trustee integrated banking bus. devel.; Andrien (Andy) Min, v-p, fin. & corp. acctg.; Deborah Savage, v-p, invest. risk control; David Thoms, v-p, structured fin.; Barbara Todres, v-p, deposit srvcs.; Gurpreet Sahota, pres., DRT Cyber Inc.

Capital Stock

	Authorized (shs.)	Outstanding (shs.)[1]	Par
Preferred	unlimited		
Series 1	unlimited	1,461,460	$10
Series 2	unlimited	nil	
Common	unlimited	27,228,182	n.p.v.

[1] At Dec. 6, 2022
Preferred - Issuable in series and non-voting. **Series 1** - Entitled to non-cumulative annual dividends of $0.6772 per share payable quarterly to Oct. 31, 2024, and thereafter at a rate reset every five years equal to the five-year Government of Canada yield plus 5.43%. Redeemable on Oct. 31, 2024, and on October 31 every five years thereafter at $10 per share plus declared and unpaid dividends. Convertible at the holder's option on Oct. 31, 2024, and on October 31 every five years thereafter, into floating rate preferred series 2 shares on a share-for-share basis, subject to certain conditions. The series 2 shares would pay a quarterly dividend equal to the 90-day Canadian Treasury bill rate plus 5.43%. Convertible into common shares upon occurrence of certain trigger events related to financial viability. The contingent conversion formula is 1.0 multiplied by $10 plus declared and unpaid dividends divided by the greater of (i) a floor price of $0.75; and (ii) current market price of the common shares.
Common - One vote per share.
Major Shareholder - GBH Inc. held 29.88% interest at Dec. 7, 2022.

Price Range - VBNK/TSX

Year	Volume	High	Low	Close
2022	1,429,901	$15.65	$8.75	$10.11
2021	4,154,261	$17.64	$8.91	$15.06
2020	2,328,153	$9.12	$4.41	$8.88
2019	2,782,272	$7.87	$6.50	$7.55
2018	5,011,234	$8.36	$6.10	$7.20

Recent Close: $11.09
Capital Stock Changes - During fiscal 2022, 195,300 common shares were repurchased under a Normal Course Issuer Bid.

Dividends

VBNK com Ra $0.10 pa Q est. Jan. 31, 2020
Prev. Rate: $0.08 est. July 31, 2019
VBNK.PR.A pfd ser 1 red. exch. Adj. Ra $0.6772 pa Q est. Jan. 31, 2020
pfd ser 3 red. exch. Adj. Ra $0.70 pa Q est. July 31, 2015[1]
[1] Redeemed April 30, 2021 at $10 per sh.

Wholly Owned Subsidiaries

DRT Cyber Inc., Washington, D.C.
- 100% int. in **Digital Boundary Group Canada Inc.**, London, Ont. dba Digital Boundary Group
- 100% int. in **Digital Boundary Group Inc.**

VersaHoldings US Corp., United States.
- 100% int. in **VersaFinance US Corp.**, United States.

VersaJet Inc., Canada.

Financial Statistics

Periods ended:	12m Oct. 31/22[A]		12m Oct. 31/21[A]
	$000s	%Chg	$000s
Interest income	**126,817**	**+42**	**89,488**
Interest expense	50,151		29,331
Net interest income	**76,666**	**+27**	**60,157**
Provision for loan losses	451		(438)
Other income	5,726		5,200
Salaries & pension benefits	26,796		20,243
Non-interest expense	49,393		35,006
Pre-tax income	**32,548**	**+6**	**30,789**
Income taxes	9,890		8,409
Net income	**22,658**	**+1**	**22,380**
Cash & equivalent	88,581		271,523
Securities	142,517		953
Total loans	2,992,678		2,103,050
Fixed assets, net	6,868		7,075
Total assets	**3,265,998**	**+35**	**2,415,086**
Deposits	2,657,540		1,853,204
Other liabilities	152,832		134,504
Subordinated debt	104,951		95,272
Preferred share equity	13,647		13,647
Shareholders' equity	350,675		332,106
Cash from oper. activs	**(32,654)**	**n.a.**	**(108,305)**
Cash from fin. activs	(6,301)		131,403
Cash from invest. activs	(141,612)		(8,440)
	$		$
Earnings per share*	0.79		0.96
Cash flow per share*	(1.19)		(4.98)
Cash divd. per share*	0.10		0.10
	shs		shs
No. of shs. o/s*	27,245,782		27,441,082
Avg. no. of shs. o/s*	27,425,479		21,752,930
	%		%
Basel III Common Equity Tier 1	12.00		15.18
Basel III Tier 1	12.50		15.86
Basel III Total	16.52		20.80
Net profit margin	27.50		34.24
Return on equity	6.91		7.64
Return on assets	0.80		1.03
No. of employees (FTEs)	110		145

* Common
[A] Reported in accordance with IFRS

Historical Summary
(as originally stated)

Fiscal Year	Int. Inc. $000s	Net Inc. Bef. Disc. $000s	EPS* $
2022[A]	126,817	22,658	0.79
2021[A]	89,488	22,380	0.96
2020[A]	86,094	19,405	0.82
2019[A]	88,305	20,196	0.85
2018[A]	80,914	18,074	0.75

* Common
[A] Reported in accordance with IFRS

V.21 Verses AI Inc.

Symbol - VERS **Exchange** - NEO **CUSIP** - 92539Q
Head Office - 205-810 Quayside Dr, New Westminster, BC, V3M 6B9 **Telephone** - (323) 868-0514
Website - www.verses.io
Email - kevin.w@verses.io
Investor Relations - Kevin Wilson (323) 868-0514
Auditors - Smythe LLP C.A.
Transfer Agents - Endeavor Trust Corporation, Vancouver, B.C.
Employees - 37 at Mar. 31, 2023
Profile - (B.C. 2020) Operates as a cognitive computing company specializing in next generation Artificial Intelligence (AI) software. Has developed KOSM™, network operating system for distributed intelligence along with software powered by KOSM.

Technologies include KOSM™, a network operating system for managing any resource on a unified network of hardware and software systems which is similar to an operating system like Windows or iOS that manages the resources such as input, output, storage, compute and bandwidth on a single device; WAYFINDER™, a spatial web application, powered by KOSM™, that includes a combination of a handheld app and web-based portal that work together to optimize and automate task-based operations in warehouse and fulfillment operations; and GIA, an AI-powered personal assistant for everyone that was under development.

During fiscal 2023, wholly owned **Verses Holdings Inc.** was dissolved.
Predecessor Detail - Name changed from Verses Technologies Inc., Mar. 31, 2023.
Directors - Jay Samit, chr., Calif.; Gabriel René, CEO, Calif.; Dan Mapes, pres., Calif.; Jonathan De Vos, London, Middx., United Kingdom; G. Scott Paterson, Toronto, Ont.
Other Exec. Officers - Kevin Wilson, CFO & corp. sec.; Dr. Karl Friston, chief scientist; Capm Petersen, chief innovation officer; Philippe Sayegh, chief adoption officer; Steven Swanson, chief admin. officer; Michael Wadden, chief comml. officer; Hari Thiruvengada, v-p, product, enterprise; James Hendrickson, pres. & gen. mgr., Verses enterprise

Capital Stock

	Authorized (shs.)	Outstanding (shs.)[1]
Cl.A Subordinate Vtg.	unlimited	66,061,538
Cl. B Proportionate Vtg.	unlimited	10,000,000

[1] At June 29, 2023

Class A Subordinate Voting - Convertible, at the holder's option, into class B proportionate voting shares on the basis of 1 class B proportionate voting share for 6.25 class A subordinate voting shares. One vote per share.
Class B Proportionate Voting - Convertible, at the holder's option, into class A subordinate voting shares on the basis of 6.25 class A subordinate voting shares for 1 class B proportionate voting share. 6.25 votes per share.
Major Shareholder - Dan Mapes held 24.33% interest and Gabriel René held 24.33% interest at June 29, 2023.

Price Range - VERS/NEO

Year	Volume	High	Low	Close
2022	737,800	$1.06	$0.40	$0.62

Recent Close: $1.45
Capital Stock Changes - In July 2023, private placement of 4,878,048 units (1 class A subordinate voting share & ½ warrant) at US$2.05 per unit was completed, with warrants exercisable at US$2.55 per share for three years.

In August 2022, private placement of 14,907,030 units (1 class A subordinate voting share & ½ warrant) at Cdn$1.00 per unit was completed. Also during fiscal 2023, class A subordinate voting share were issued as follows: 291,325 as finders' fees, 220,000 on exercise of options and 5,070 on exercise of warrants.

On July 20, 2021, 14,434,603 common shares were issued pursuant to the reverse takeover acquisition of Verses Labs Inc. (subsequently renamed Verses Technologies USA, Inc.). Concurrently, the common shares were reclassified as class A subordinate voting shares and a new class of class B proportionate voting shares was created. In February and March 2022, 21,003,077 units (1 class A subordinate voting share & ½ warrant) were issued without further consideration on exchange of special warrants sold previously by private placement at Cdn$0.80 each.

Wholly Owned Subsidiaries

Verses Operations Canada Inc., B.C.
Verses Technologies USA, Inc., Los Angeles, Calif.
- 100% int. in **Verses Global B.V.**, Netherlands.
- 100% int. in **Verses Health Inc.**, Wyo.
- 100% int. in **Verses, Inc.**, Wyo.
- 100% int. in **Verses Logistics Inc.**, Wyo.
- 100% int. in **Verses Realities Inc.**, Wyo.

Financial Statistics

Periods ended:	12m Mar. 31/23[A]		12m Mar. 31/22[A1]
	US$000s	%Chg	US$000s
Operating revenue	**1,605**	**-42**	**2,774**
Cost of sales	1,136		2,384
Salaries & benefits	2,954		1,043
Research & devel. expense	5,882		nil
General & admin expense	8,173		3,741
Stock-based compensation	2,706		nil
Operating expense	**20,850**	**+191**	**7,168**
Operating income	**(19,245)**	**n.a.**	**(4,394)**
Finance costs, gross	132		161
Pre-tax income	**(19,453)**	**n.a.**	**(8,880)**
Income taxes	6		2
Net income	**(19,458)**	**n.a.**	**(8,881)**
Cash & equivalent	4,397		6,370
Accounts receivable	35		329
Current assets	8,297		8,576
Fixed assets, net	235		232
Right-of-use assets	109		220
Total assets	**8,641**	**-4**	**9,028**
Accts. pay. & accr. liabs	1,249		620
Current liabilities	7,656		2,062
Long-term debt, gross	5,049		146
Long-term debt, net	143		146
Long-term lease liabilities	nil		105
Shareholders' equity	841		6,716
Cash from oper. activs	**(17,388)**	**n.a.**	**(6,358)**
Cash from fin. activs	15,872		11,141
Cash from invest. activs	(148)		1,043
Net cash position	**4,397**	**-32**	**6,464**
Capital expenditures	(148)		(252)
	US$		US$
Earnings per share*	(0.18)		(0.11)
Earnings per share**	(1.10)		(0.71)
Cash flow per share***	(0.29)		(0.25)
	shs		shs
No. of shs. o/s***	65,805,937		50,382,512
Avg. no. of shs. o/s***	59,836,021		25,422,225
	%		%
Net profit margin	n.m.		(320.15)
Return on equity	(514.97)		n.m.
Return on assets	(218.76)		(175.50)
Foreign sales percent	100		100
No. of employees (FTEs)	37		32

* Cl.A Subord. Vtg.
** Cl.B Prop. Vtg.
*** Cl.A Subord. Vtg. & Cl.B Prop. Vtg.
[A] Reported in accordance with IFRS
[1] Results prior to July 20, 2021, pertain to and reflect the reverse takeover acquisition of Verses Labs Inc. (subsequently renamed Verses Technologies USA, Inc.).

Historical Summary
(as originally stated)

Fiscal Year	Oper. Rev. US$000s	Net Inc. Bef. Disc. US$000s	EPS* US$
2023[A]	1,605	(19,458)	(0.18)
2022[A]	2,774	(8,881)	(0.11)
2021[A]	97	(2,528)	(0.25)
2020[A]	125	(1,826)	(0.18)

* Cl.A Subord. Vtg.
[A] Reported in accordance with IFRS

V.22 Versus Systems Inc.

Symbol - VS **Exchange** - NASDAQ **CUSIP** - 92535P
Head Office - 1558 Hastings St W, Vancouver, BC, V6G 3J4 **Telephone** - (604) 639-4457 **Fax** - (604) 639-4458
Website - www.versussystems.com
Email - pierce@versussystems.com
Investor Relations - Matthew Pierce (310) 925-6373
Auditors - RJI Ramirez Jimenez International CPAs C.P.A., Irvine, Calif.
Lawyers - Borden Ladner Gervais LLP, Vancouver, B.C.
Transfer Agents - Computershare Trust Company of Canada Inc., Vancouver, B.C.
Profile - (B.C. 2007; orig. Ont., 1988 amalg.) Provides live event production, games, shows and applications for sports teams, leagues, venues, entertainment companies and other content creators to make engaging, rewarding experiences for fans.

Provides customized live event production which includes partnering with multiple professional sports franchises to drive in-stadium audience engagement by creating pump-up videos, player pieces and other live or programmed content. Also develops XEO Engagement platform which is a business-to-business software that allows video game publishers and developers to offer prize-based matches of their games to their players. XEO games and interactions include Bingo, Turbo Trivia, Filter Fan Cam, QB Toss and Predictive Game Play.

On Mar. 1, 2022, the company acquired an additional 15.1% in subsidiary **Versus LLC** for issuance of 171,608 common shares. As a result, the company owned 81.9% interest in Versus LLC.

Predecessor Detail - Name changed from Opal Energy Corp., June 14, 2016, following acquisition of Versus LLC.

Directors - Matthew Pierce, founder & CEO, Los Angeles, Calif.; Keyvan Peymani, exec. chr., Los Angeles, Calif.; Michelle Gahagan, Vancouver, B.C.; Jennifer Prince, Calif.; Shannon Pruitt; Brian J. Tingle, Vancouver, B.C.; Paul Vlasic, Detroit, Mich.

Other Exec. Officers - Craig Finster, pres. & CFO; Amanda Armour, chief people officer; Alex Peachey, chief tech. officer; Kelsey Chin, corp. sec.

Capital Stock

	Authorized (shs.)	Outstanding (shs.)[1]
Class A	unlimited	
Series 1		5,057
Common	unlimited	1,659,961

[1] At Nov. 9, 2022

Class A - Issuable in series. **Series 1** - Convertible into 6.67 common shares for each series 1 share held. Non-voting.

Common - One vote per share.

Major Shareholder - Outblaze Limited held 19.9% interest at Oct. 7, 2022.

Price Range - VS/NASDAQ

Year	Volume	High	Low	Close
2022............	5,559,580	US$37.50	US$0.38	US$0.49
2021............	174,754	US$176.10	US$27.30	US$31.50

MMM/TSX (D)

Year	Volume	High	Low	Close
2021............	133,280	$238.50	$131.10	$189.75
2020............	371,138	$296.25	$42.00	$239.25
2019............	203,766	$118.80	$40.80	$46.80
2018............	85,246	$110.40	$43.20	$57.60

Consolidation: 1-for-15 cons. in Nov. 2022

Capital Stock Changes - In February 2022, public offering of 4,375,000 units (1 common share & 1 warrant) at US$1.60 per unit was completed, with warrants exercisable at US$1.92 per share; an additional 590,625 units were issued on exercise of over-allotment option in March 2022. In July 2022, public offering of 4,145,000 common shares was completed at US$0.52 per share.

On Nov. 9, 2022, common shares were consolidated on a 1-for-15 basis.

Wholly Owned Subsidiaries

Xcite Interactive, Inc., Greeley, Colo.

Subsidiaries

81.9% int. in **Versus Systems (Holdco) Inc.**, Nev. 100% voting control.

- 100% int. in **Versus LLC**, Los Angeles, Calif.
- 100% int. in **Versus Systems UK, Ltd.**, United Kingdom.

Financial Statistics

Periods ended:	12m Dec. 31/21[A]		12m Dec. 31/20[◻A]
	US$000s	%Chg	US$000s
Operating revenue........................	**769**	**-45**	**1,390**
Salaries & benefits........................	5,202		2,565
General & admin expense................	5,317		2,228
Stock-based compensation............	2,146		1,049
Operating expense........................	**12,665**	**+117**	**5,842**
Operating income........................	**(11,896)**	**n.a.**	**(4,452)**
Deprec., depl. & amort....................	2,345		1,531
Finance costs, gross........................	379		511
Pre-tax income........................	**(17,848)**	**n.a.**	**(6,911)**
Net income........................	**(17,848)**	**n.a.**	**(6,911)**
Net inc. for equity hldrs................	**(14,399)**	**n.a.**	**(5,776)**
Net inc. for non-cont. int..............	**(3,449)**	**n.a.**	**(1,135)**
Cash & equivalent........................	1,678		2,283
Accounts receivable........................	124		465
Current assets........................	2,355		3,164
Fixed assets, net........................	327		482
Intangibles, net........................	15,753		2,140
Total assets........................	**18,544**	**+238**	**5,491**
Accts. pay. & accr. liabs..................	832		1,460
Current liabilities........................	3,373		3,960
Long-term debt, gross....................	2,786		4,529
Long-term debt, net........................	679		2,238
Long-term lease liabilities...............	129		432
Shareholders' equity........................	22,624		4,055
Non-controlling interest..................	(8,622)		(5,194)
Cash from oper. activs.................	**(12,893)**	**n.a.**	**(4,237)**
Cash from fin. activs........................	14,800		7,389
Cash from invest. activs..................	(2,512)		(945)
Net cash position........................	**1,678**	**-27**	**2,283**
Capital expenditures........................	(74)		nil
	US$		US$
Earnings per share*........................	(15.15)		(8.85)
Cash flow per share*........................	(13.53)		(6.54)
	shs		shs
No. of shs. o/s*........................	1,036,950		715,572
Avg. no. of shs. o/s*........................	952,828		648,313
	%		%
Net profit margin........................	n.m.		(497.19)
Return on equity........................	(103.90)		(222.89)
Return on assets........................	(142.96)		(155.59)
Foreign sales percent....................	n.a.		100

* Common
◻ Restated
[A] Reported in accordance with IFRS

Latest Results

Periods ended:	6m June 30/22[A]		6m June 30/21[A]
	US$000s	%Chg	US$000s
Operating revenue........................	574	+708	71
Net income........................	(6,582)	n.a.	(13,768)
Net inc. for equity hldrs..................	(5,323)	n.a.	(12,307)
Net inc. for non-cont. int.................	(1,259)		(1,462)
	US$		US$
Earnings per share*........................	(4.20)		(14.10)

* Common
[A] Reported in accordance with IFRS

Historical Summary
(as originally stated)

Fiscal Year	Oper. Rev.	Net Inc. Bef. Disc.	EPS*
	US$000s	US$000s	US$
2021[A]..................	769	(17,848)	(15.15)
	$000s	$000s	$
2020[A]..................	1,865	(9,271)	(12.60)
2019[A]..................	665	(9,628)	(14.40)
2018[A]..................	2	(9,373)	(12.96)
2017[A]..................	nil	(6,982)	(14.40)

* Common
[A] Reported in accordance with IFRS

Note: Adjusted throughout for 1-for-15 cons. in Nov. 2022; 1-for-16 cons. in Dec. 2020

V.23 Vertex Resource Group Ltd.

Symbol - VTX **Exchange** - TSX-VEN **CUSIP** - 92536G
Head Office - 161-2055 Premier Way, Sherwood Park, AB, T8H 0G2
Telephone - (780) 464-3295 **Fax** - (780) 464-3731
Website - www.vertex.ca
Email - sbielopotocky@vertex.ca
Investor Relations - Sherry Bielopotocky (780) 464-3295
Auditors - KPMG LLP C.A., Edmonton, Alta.
Bankers - HSBC Bank Canada, Calgary, Alta.
Lawyers - MLT Aikins LLP, Edmonton, Alta.; Stikeman Elliott LLP, Calgary, Alta.
Transfer Agents - TSX Trust Company, Calgary, Alta.
FP500 Revenue Ranking - 599

Employees - 1,050 at Dec. 31, 2022

Profile - (Alta. 2017 amalg.; orig. Alta., 2014) Provides environmental, consulting and engineering services to clients in the energy, mining, utilities, private development, public infrastructure, construction, telecommunications, forestry, agriculture and government sectors across Canada and select locations in the United States.

Operations are organized into two business segments: Environmental Services and Environmental Consulting.

The **Environmental Services** segment provides various services related to transportation, removal, storage, disposal of materials and maintenance of facilities in an environmentally safe manner. Services include fluid management and logistics, waste recycling, industrial cleaning and maintenance, hydro-excavating and site services. This segment operates and maintains a fleet of specialized equipment with 337 power units and 415 trailers with access to an additional 72 power units and 10 trailers under contract with owner operators, 1,462 pieces of equipment in its rental fleet and a fleet light trucks and equipment.

The **Environmental Consulting** segment provides various services to clients in order to meet internal environmental standards, environmental legislation and related environmental compliance requirements. Services include advisory services related to new capital expenditure and asset development, environmental consulting and monitoring on existing assets, emission management solutions, sub surface engineering, facility engineering, asset retirement and reclamation services.

Recent Merger and Acquisition Activity

Status: completed **Announced:** Sept. 30, 2022
Vertex Resource Group Ltd. acquired private Rocky View County, Alta.-based Young EnergyServe Inc., which provides robotic tank cleaning services, turkey turnaround solutions and various other industrial services throughout Canada, for $13,800,000, consisting of $6,800,000 cash, issuance of a $4,000,000 promissory note and issuance of 5,450,000 common shares at a deemed price of 55¢ per share.

Status: completed **Revised:** Apr. 25, 2022
UPDATE: The transaction was completed. Cordy amalgamated with Vertex Energy Services Ltd., a wholly owned subsidiary of Vertex Resource Group. Cordy will be delisted from TSX on or about Apr. 28, 2022. PREVIOUS: Vertex Resource Group Ltd. agreed to acquire Cordy Oilfield Services Inc. on the basis of 0.081818 Vertex common shares for each Cordy share held, which would result in the issuance of 18,913,253 Vertex common shares. Cordy provides environmental and heavy construction services to the energy, municipal and construction industries in western Canada.

Predecessor Detail - Formed from Vier Capital Corp. in Alberta, Oct. 16, 2017, following Qualifying Transaction reverse takeover of (old) Vertex Resource Group Ltd. and amalgamation of (old) Vertex with the company and a wholly owned subsid.; basis 1 new for 10 old shs.

Directors - Brian F. Butlin, chr., Edmonton, Alta.; Terry A. Stephenson, pres. & CEO, Sherwood Park, Alta.; Trent Baker, Calgary, Alta.; Terry D. Freeman, Edmonton, Alta.; Stuart King, Calgary, Alta.; Stuart G. O'Connor, Calgary, Alta.

Other Exec. Officers - Sherry Bielopotocky, CFO & corp. sec.; Paul Blenkhorn, v-p, cons. srvcs.; Christopher W. (Chris) Challis, v-p, logistics

Capital Stock

	Authorized (shs.)	Outstanding (shs.)[1]
Preferred	unlimited	nil
Common	unlimited	115,620,890

[1] At Aug. 9, 2023

Normal Course Issuer Bid - The company plans to make normal course purchases of up to 5,781,045 common shares representing 5% of the total outstanding. The bid commenced on Aug. 30, 2023, and expires on Aug. 29, 2024.

Major Shareholder - 32 Degrees Capital Advisor Ltd. held 14.72% interest, Terry A. Stephenson held 13.4% interest and Jason Clemett held 12.53% interest at Mar. 24, 2023.

Price Range - VTX/TSX-VEN

Year	Volume	High	Low	Close
2022............	6,901,766	$0.61	$0.28	$0.38
2021............	3,409,648	$0.62	$0.24	$0.44
2020............	3,205,866	$0.40	$0.14	$0.25
2019............	1,825,720	$0.46	$0.24	$0.37
2018............	2,946,515	$0.80	$0.31	$0.31

Recent Close: $0.37

Capital Stock Changes - On Apr. 25, 2022, 18,913,253 common shares were issued pursuant to acquisition of Cordy Oilfield Services Inc. On Sept. 30, 2022, 5,454,545 common shares were issued pursuant to acquisition of Young EnergyServe Inc.

Wholly Owned Subsidiaries

Dominion Leasing Inc., Alta.
Vertex Professional Services Ltd., Alta.
Vertex Resource Services Inc., Nev.
Vertex Resource Services Ltd., Alta.

Investments

Acden-Vertex Partnership Limited, Alta.

Note: The preceding list includes only the major related companies in which interests are held.

Financial Statistics

Periods ended:	12m Dec. 31/22[A]		12m Dec. 31/21[oA]
	$000s	%Chg	$000s
Operating revenue	**257,161**	**+39**	**185,049**
Cost of goods sold	166,127		117,150
General & admin expense	20,066		16,052
Stock-based compensation	200		nil
Operating expense	**186,193**	**+40**	**133,202**
Operating income	**70,968**	**+37**	**51,847**
Deprec., depl. & amort.	20,376		19,621
Finance costs, gross	8,875		6,057
Pre-tax income	**2,734**	**+390**	**558**
Income taxes	692		(1,100)
Net income	**2,042**	**+23**	**1,658**
Cash & equivalent	2,591		nil
Inventories	4,399		4,237
Accounts receivable	71,366		55,197
Current assets	82,073		63,442
Fixed assets, net	82,463		72,790
Right-of-use assets	40,983		21,789
Intangibles, net	40,160		26,978
Total assets	**254,424**	**+36**	**186,570**
Bank indebtedness	nil		400
Accts. pay. & accr. liabs	40,386		28,373
Current liabilities	74,176		58,530
Long-term debt, gross	89,233		79,518
Long-term debt, net	70,725		61,085
Long-term lease liabilities	24,896		13,262
Shareholders' equity	64,736		49,696
Cash from oper. activs	**21,441**	**+65**	**12,958**
Cash from fin. activs	(6,028)		(1,419)
Cash from invest. activs	(12,838)		(11,535)
Net cash position	**2,591**	**n.a.**	**nil**
Capital expenditures	(13,766)		(9,054)
Capital disposals	3,633		2,831
	$		$
Earnings per share*	0.02		0.02
Cash flow per share*	0.20		0.14
	shs		shs
No. of shs. o/s*	115,620,890		91,253,115
Avg. no. of shs. o/s*	105,663,931		91,253,115
	%		%
Net profit margin	0.79		0.90
Return on equity	3.57		3.39
Return on assets	3.93		11.64
No. of employees (FTEs)	1,050		800

* Common
[o] Restated
[A] Reported in accordance with IFRS

Historical Summary
(as originally stated)

Fiscal Year	Oper. Rev.	Net Inc. Bef. Disc.	EPS*
	$000s	$000s	$
2022[A]	257,161	2,042	0.02
2021[A]	159,438	1,658	0.02
2020[A]	136,125	(5,698)	(0.06)
2019[A]	168,070	(11,314)	(0.12)
2018[A]	150,385	2,291	0.03

* Common
[A] Reported in accordance with IFRS

V.24 Vertical Peak Holdings Inc.

Symbol - MJMJ **Exchange** - CSE **CUSIP** - 92539W
Head Office - 2905-77 King St W, PO Box 121, Toronto, ON, M5K 1H1 **Toll-free** - (888) 262-4645 **Fax** - (888) 262-4724
Email - mwilletts@nutritionalhigh.com
Investor Relations - Michael Willetts (888) 262-4645
Auditors - BF Borgers CPA PC C.P.A., Lakewood, Colo.
Transfer Agents - TSX Trust Company
Profile - (B.C. 2023; orig. Can., 2004) Has cannabis manufacturing, retail and cultivation operations in California and owns and operates oil extraction and edibles manufacturing facilities in Colorado and Oregon.
In California, cultivates, manufactures and retails a full line of cannabis products through a 15,000-sq.-ft. vertically-integrated indoor cultivation, extraction and manufacturing facility in El Cajon, and two dispensaries in Escondido and El Cajon. Products include extracts, vapes, tinctures, topicals, capsules and flower under the Outco and Thrive brands.
In Oregon, operates a 5,000-sq.-ft. manufacturing facility in La Pine for the production of cannabis-infused products under the Red Octopus brand.
In Colorado, operates a manufacturing and processing facility in Pueblo, producing vape and edible products under the FLI brand.
On May 18, 2023, the company announced that the spin-out of affiliate **Neural Therapeutics Inc.** (45.6% owned) will become effective May 23, 2023, whereby the company will distribute a portion of its common shares held in Neural to shareholders of the company (of record as of May 19, 2023) on the basis of 0.013884682 Neural common shares for each subordinate voting and multiple voting share held. A total of 4,716,667 Neural common shares will be distributed, representing a 12% interest. Neural, which is focused on developing products and conducting research with psychoactive cacti plants, will apply to list its common shares on a Canadian stock exchange.
On June 30, 2022, the company's agreement to sell its dispensary in Escondido Calif., for US$1,600,000 was terminated.
In March 2022, the company cancelled its management contract for the outdoor cannabis cultivation operation and nursery in Mendocino cty., Calif., and discontinued operations at the property.
Predecessor Detail - Name changed from High Fusion Inc., May 8, 2023.
Directors - Adam K. Szweras, chr. & corp. sec., Toronto, Ont.; William (Bill) Gillespie, CEO, Calif.; Billy A. Morrison, chief tech. officer, Calif.; Austin Birch, Calif.; John Durfy, Oakville, Ont.; Ross Mitgang, Ont.; Rachel Wright, Calif.
Other Exec. Officers - Michael (Mike) Willetts, CFO

Capital Stock

	Authorized (shs.)	Outstanding (shs.)[1]
Multiple Vtg.	unlimited	14,294,891
Subordinate Vtg.	unlimited	179,166,481

[1] At Mar. 20, 2023

MultipleVoting - Convertible into subordinate voting shares on a 10-for-1 basis. 10 votes per share.
Subordinate Voting - One vote per share.
Major Shareholder - Widely held at Mar. 20, 2023.

Price Range - MJMJ/CSE

Year	Volume	High	Low	Close
2022	30,614,122	$0.10	$0.01	$0.01
2021	48,960,942	$1.20	$0.05	$0.05
2020	16,551,919	$1.00	$0.10	$0.20
2019	8,693,089	$7.10	$0.60	$0.80
2018	21,364,542	$18.80	$2.60	$5.30

Consolidation: 1-for-20 cons. in Sept. 2021
Recent Close: $0.01
Capital Stock Changes - On Sept. 2, 2021, common shares were consolidated on a 1-for-20 basis. In November 2021, common shares were reclassified as subordinate voting shares, a new class of multiple voting shares was created and 3,623,243 multiple voting shares were issued without further consideration on exchange of 72,464,861 special warrants issued on Aug. 31, 2021, pursuant to the acquisition of the business of OutCo Labs Inc.

Dividends

MJMJ sub vtg N.S.R.
Listed Dec 16/21.
stk.[1] May 23/23
Paid in 2023: stk. 2022: n.a. 2021: n.a.

[1] Stk. divd. of 0.0138847 Neural Therapeutics Inc com. shs. for ea. 1 sh. held.

Wholly Owned Subsidiaries

Eastgate Property Holding LLC, United States.
NH Bellingham Property Holdings LLC, Bellingham, Wash.
NH Nevada LLC, Nev.
NH Operations LLC, Colo.
NH (Oregon) Properties LLC, Ore.
NH Processing (Nevada) Inc., Nev.
NH Properties Inc., United States.
NH Properties (Nevada) LLC, Nev.
NHC Edibles LLC, Colo.
NHC IP Holdings Corp., Ont.
NHII Holdings Ltd., Ont.
Nutritional High (Colorado) Inc., Colo.
Nutritional High LLC, Calif.
Nutritional High (Oregon) LLC, Ore.
Nutritional IP Holdings LLC, United States.
Nutritional Traditions Inc., United States.
Palo Verde LLC, Colo.
Pasa Verde, LLC, Calif.

Subsidiaries

51% int. in **Eglington Medicinal Advisory Ltd.**, Toronto, Ont.

Investments

45.6% int. in **Neural Therapeutics Inc.**, Ont. Formerly Psychedelic Science Corp.
- 100% int. in **Kruzo LLC**, Ont.

Financial Statistics

Periods ended:	12m July 31/21[A]		12m July 31/20[oA]
	$000s	%Chg	$000s
Operating revenue	**96**	**+773**	**11**
Cost of goods sold	76		14
Salaries & benefits	2,193		2,310
General & admin expense	1,458		1,942
Stock-based compensation	948		1,293
Other operating expense	5		152
Operating expense	**4,680**	**-18**	**5,711**
Operating income	**(4,584)**	**n.a.**	**(5,700)**
Deprec., depl. & amort.	484		1,347
Finance income	218		201
Finance costs, gross	1,277		4,035
Write-downs/write-offs	(5,722)		(1,483)
Pre-tax income	**(11,553)**	**n.a.**	**(10,699)**
Income taxes	68		66
Net inc. bef. disc. opers	**(11,621)**	**n.a.**	**(10,765)**
Income from disc. opers	9,771		(11,324)
Net income	**(1,850)**	**n.a.**	**(22,089)**
Cash & equivalent	1,226		290
Inventories	202		301
Accounts receivable	78		367
Current assets	1,714		3,101
Fixed assets, net	2,690		3,580
Intangibles, net	2,876		nil
Total assets	**7,279**	**+9**	**6,682**
Bank indebtedness	nil		200
Accts. pay. & accr. liabs	4,695		13,421
Current liabilities	6,817		23,665
Long-term debt, gross	6,625		10,701
Long-term debt, net	6,625		4,421
Long-term lease liabilities	nil		468
Equity portion of conv. debs	773		773
Shareholders' equity	(6,148)		(21,885)
Non-controlling interest	(15)		(15)
Cash from oper. activs	**(1,444)**	**n.a.**	**(2,016)**
Cash from fin. activs	(31)		590
Cash from invest. activs	1,262		35
Net cash position	**21**	**-91**	**244**
Capital expenditures	(62)		(240)
	$		$
Earns. per sh. bef disc opers*	(0.26)		(0.65)
Earnings per share*	(0.04)		(1.34)
Cash flow per share*	(0.03)		(0.12)
	shs		shs
No. of shs. o/s*	51,345,746		20,862,321
Avg. no. of shs. o/s*	45,201,322		16,477,169
	%		%
Net profit margin	n.m.		n.m.
Return on equity	n.m.		n.m.
Return on assets	(148.08)		(51.26)
Foreign sales percent	100		100

* S.V. & M.V.
[o] Restated
[A] Reported in accordance with IFRS

Latest Results

Periods ended:	9m Apr. 30/22[A]		9m Apr. 30/21[oA]
	$000s	%Chg	$000s
Operating revenue	4,668	n.m.	51
Net inc. bef. disc. opers	(8,304)	n.a.	(21,048)
Income from disc. opers	19		9,771
Net income	(8,285)	n.a.	(11,277)
Net inc. for equity hldrs	(8,642)	n.a.	(11,277)
Net inc. for non-cont. int	357		nil
	$		$
Earns. per sh. bef. disc. opers.*	(0.12)		(0.54)
Earnings per share*	(0.12)		(0.29)

* S.V. & M.V.
[o] Restated
[A] Reported in accordance with IFRS

Historical Summary
(as originally stated)

Fiscal Year	Oper. Rev.	Net Inc. Bef. Disc.	EPS*
	$000s	$000s	$
2021[A]	96	(11,621)	(0.26)
2020[A]	12,338	(22,089)	(1.34)
2019[A]	23,608	(27,696)	(1.78)
2018[A]	5,815	(9,706)	(0.72)
2017[A]	nil	(5,006)	(0.45)

* S.V. & M.V.
[A] Reported in accordance with IFRS
Note: Adjusted throughout for 1-for-20 cons. in Sept. 2021

V.25 VerticalScope Holdings Inc.

Symbol - FORA **Exchange** - TSX **CUSIP** - 92537Y
Head Office - 600-111 Peter St, Toronto, ON, M5V 2H1 **Telephone** - (416) 341-7166
Website - www.verticalscope.com
Email - ir@verticalscope.com
Investor Relations - Chris Goodridge (416) 341-7174
Auditors - KPMG LLP C.A., Vaughan, Ont.
Lawyers - Norton Rose Fulbright Canada LLP, Toronto, Ont.
Transfer Agents - TSX Trust Company, Toronto, Ont.
FP500 Revenue Ranking - 766
Employees - 212 at Mar. 31, 2023
Profile - (Ont. 2012) Operates Fora, a cloud-based digital community platform for online enthusiast communities in high-consumer spending categories.

The platform, which is intended to and enables people with similar interests to connect, serves more than 100,000,000 monthly active users and 60,000,000 registered community members across 1,264 online communities (as of Dec. 31, 2022).

Revenue is derived from digital advertising, consisting of direct advertising campaigns, custom content solutions and programmatic advertising; and e-commerce, consisting of commissions, referral payments and subscriptions. During 2022, more than 540 direct advertisers were served in the U.S. and Canada. Commissions are generated from more than 100 partners and networks on the company's communities.

The company is headquartered in Toronto, Ont., and has additional offices in Bingham Farms, Mich.; Mountain View, Calif.; Jerusalem, Israel; Estonia; and Camana Bay, Cayman Islands.

During 2022, the company acquired 14 online community sites for total consideration of US$4,410,641.

Directors - Rob Laidlaw, founder, chr. & CEO, Grand Cayman, Cayman Islands; Wayne Bigby†, Ont.; Philip J. Evershed, Toronto, Ont.; Cory Janssen, Edmonton, Alta.; Michael Washinushi, Toronto, Ont.

Other Exec. Officers - Chris Goodridge, pres. & COO; Vincenzo Bellissimo, CFO; Paul Lee, chief product officer; Joe Pishgar, chief community officer; Brandon Seibel, chief tech. officer; Diane Yu, chief legal officer & corp. sec.

† Lead director

Capital Stock

	Authorized (shs.)	Outstanding (shs.)[1]
Preferred	unlimited	nil
Multiple Vtg.	unlimited	2,957,265
Subordinate Vtg.	unlimited	18,407,481[2]

[1] At May 10, 2023
[2] At Aug. 2, 2023.

Preferred - Issuable in series. Entitled to dividends. Non-voting.
Multiple Voting - Entitled to dividends. Convertible at any time, at the holder's option, into subordinate voting shares on a one-for-one basis. Automatically convertible into subordinate voting shares on a one-for-one basis at such time that permitted holders no longer as a group beneficially own, directly or indirectly and in the aggregate, at least 7.5% of the issued and outstanding subordinate and multiple voting shares (on a non-diluted basis). Ten votes per share.
Subordinate Voting - Entitled to dividends. Non-convertible. One vote per share.
Normal Course Issuer Bid - The company plans to make normal course purchases of up to 920,374 subordinate voting shares representing 5% of the total outstanding. The bid commenced on Aug. 16, 2023, and expires on Aug. 15, 2024.
Major Shareholder - Rob Laidlaw held 61.9% interest at Apr. 12, 2023.

Price Range - FORA/TSX

Year	Volume	High	Low	Close
2022	2,484,492	$30.63	$4.01	$6.53
2021	3,844,020	$34.00	$21.67	$30.52

Recent Close: $5.75
Capital Stock Changes - During 2022, subordinate voting shares were issued as follows: 31,626 under restricted and deferred share unit plan and 12,700 on exercise of options; 100,200 subordinate voting shares were repurchased under a Normal Course Issuer Bid.

Wholly Owned Subsidiaries

RateMDs Inc., United States.
Second Media Corp., Canada.
Second Media Inc., San Francisco, Calif.
Threadloom, Inc., Mountain View, Calif.
VerticalScope Inc., Toronto, Ont.
- 100% int. in **Versatile Solutions Holdings Inc.**, Cayman Islands.
  - 100% int. in **Versatile Solutions Inc.**, Cayman Islands.
- 100% int. in **VerticalScope Estonia OÜ**, Estonia.
- 100% int. in **VerticalScope USA Inc.**, Del.
  - 100% int. in **Fomopop, Inc.**, San Francisco, Calif.
  - 100% int. in **Hometalk, Inc.**, New York, N.Y.
    - 100% int. in **Hometalk IL Development Ltd.**, Israel.
  - 100% int. in **Outside Hub Holdings, Inc.**, Del.
    - 100% int. in **Outdoor Hub, LLC**, Mich.

VerticalScope U.S. LLC, United States.
Web Site Acquisitions Inc., Cayman Islands.
Note: The preceding list includes only the major related companies in which interests are held.

Financial Statistics

Periods ended:	12m Dec. 31/22[A]		12m Dec. 31/21[A]
	US$000s	%Chg	US$000s
Operating revenue	**80,488**	**+22**	**65,762**
Salaries & benefits	35,818		26,918
General & admin expense	7,743		10,428
Stock-based compensation	9,809		6,132
Other operating expense	8,816		7,177
Operating expense	**62,186**	**+23**	**50,656**
Operating income	**18,302**	**+21**	**15,106**
Deprec., depl. & amort.	38,659		20,636
Finance income	64		44
Finance costs, gross	3,158		6,118
Write-downs/write-offs	(1,000)		(250)
Pre-tax income	**(27,105)**	**n.a.**	**(14,094)**
Income taxes	(2,333)		(1,830)
Net income	**(24,772)**	**n.a.**	**(12,264)**
Cash & equivalent	8,767		20,494
Accounts receivable	15,713		15,222
Current assets	26,293		37,922
Long-term investments	nil		1,000
Fixed assets, net	1,066		987
Right-of-use assets	1,745		2,629
Intangibles, net	123,215		152,243
Total assets	**177,556**	**-18**	**217,030**
Accts. pay. & accr. liabs.	8,335		9,949
Current liabilities	29,010		24,321
Long-term debt, gross	58,093		79,123
Long-term debt, net	54,884		75,972
Long-term lease liabilities	2,518		3,735
Shareholders' equity	81,496		96,243
Cash from oper. activs.	**20,636**	**+5**	**19,603**
Cash from fin. activs.	(22,474)		84,405
Cash from invest. activs.	(9,658)		(87,756)
Net cash position	**8,767**	**-57**	**20,494**
Capital disposals	57		20
	US$		US$
Earnings per share*	(1.16)		(0.59)
Cash flow per share*	0.97		0.95
	shs		shs
No. of shs. o/s*	21,225,269		21,281,143
Avg. no. of shs. o/s*	21,302,709		20,666,536
	%		%
Net profit margin	(30.78)		(18.65)
Return on equity	(27.87)		n.m.
Return on assets	(11.09)		(4.56)
Foreign sales percent	91		89

* S.V. & M.V.
[A] Reported in accordance with IFRS

Latest Results

Periods ended:	3m Mar. 31/23[A]		3m Mar. 31/22[A]
	US$000s	%Chg	US$000s
Operating revenue	12,872	-36	20,048
Net income	(4,498)	n.a.	(11,871)
	US$		US$
Earnings per share*	(0.21)		(0.56)

* S.V. & M.V.
[A] Reported in accordance with IFRS

Historical Summary
(as originally stated)

Fiscal Year	Oper. Rev.	Net Inc. Bef. Disc.	EPS*
	US$000s	US$000s	US$
2022[A]	80,488	(24,772)	(1.16)
2021[A]	65,762	(12,264)	(0.59)
2020[A1]	56,923	(1,506)	(0.11)
2019[A1]	58,455	(1,733)	(0.12)
2018[A1]	68,348	(14,099)	(1.01)

* S.V. & M.V.
[A] Reported in accordance with IFRS
[1] As shown in the prospectus dated June 14, 2021.

V.26 Veteran Capital Corp.

Symbol - VCC.P **Exchange** - TSX-VEN **CUSIP** - 925501
Head Office - 1422-510 5 St SW, Calgary, AB, T2P 3S2 **Telephone** - (587) 894-0852
Email - don@ricellp.com
Investor Relations - Don Nguyen (587) 894-0852
Auditors - MNP LLP C.A., Calgary, Alta.
Lawyers - Dentons Canada LLP, Calgary, Alta.
Transfer Agents - Olympia Transfer Services Inc., Calgary, Alta.
Profile - (Alta. 2021) Capital Pool Company.
Directors - H. Tyler Rice, pres. & CEO, Nelson, B.C.; Don Nguyen, CFO, Alta.; Grant MacKenzie, corp. sec., Calgary, Alta.; Louis Castro, London, Middx., United Kingdom; Aaron Matlock, Alta.

Capital Stock

	Authorized (shs.)	Outstanding (shs.)[1]
Common	unlimited	4,450,000

[1] At Mar. 31, 2023

Major Shareholder - Grant MacKenzie held 13.48% interest, Aaron Matlock held 13.48% interest and H. Tyler Rice held 13.48% interest at May 27, 2021.

Price Range - VCC.P/TSX-VEN

Year	Volume	High	Low	Close
2022	58,500	$0.18	$0.07	$0.11
2021	56,000	$0.16	$0.14	$0.14

Recent Close: $0.08
Capital Stock Changes - There were no changes to capital stock during 2022.

V.27 Vext Science, Inc.

Symbol - VEXT **Exchange** - CSE **CUSIP** - 925540
Head Office - 2250-1055 Hastings St W, Vancouver, BC, V6E 2E9 **Toll-free** - (844) 211-3725 **Fax** - (778) 329-9361
Website - www.vextscience.com
Email - investors@vextscience.com
Investor Relations - Eric Offenberger (844) 211-3725
Auditors - BF Borgers CPA PC C.P.A., Lakewood, Colo.
Transfer Agents - Odyssey Trust Company, Vancouver, B.C.
Profile - (B.C. 2015) Has cannabis cultivation and retail operations in Arizona and Ohio. Also offers management and advisory services relating to the cultivation, extraction, manufacturing, retail dispensary and wholesale distribution of cannabis products to licensed cannabis and hemp operators in the U.S.

Wholly owned **Herbal Wellness Center Inc.** and **Organica Patient Group, LLC** operate two cannabis dispensaries in Arizona. The dispensaries are supplied by the company's 13,000-sq.-ft. cultivation facility in Phoenix, Ariz., and 11,000-sq.-ft. cultivation facility, with 10-acres of outdoor cultivation area, in Prescott Valley, Ariz. An up to 34,000-sq.-ft. cultivation facility is under construction in Eloy, Ariz., with completion of the first phase, totaling 17,000 sq. ft., which was expected to begin planting in the second quarter of 2023, with a first harvest in the third quarter of 2023.

The company also operates a cannabis dispensary in Jackson, Ohio and initiates operations by rebranding the dispensary to Herbal Wellness Center Ohio (formerly Buckeye Botanicals).

Services are provided to licensed third parties by entering into management agreements, service agreements, and joint ventures/joint operations enabling them to conduct their businesses. Services provided include employee leasing services, the use of a physical plant for cultivation and extraction of cannabis and derivative products, agricultural technology and research services, and related consulting and administrative services. Also provides real property and equipment for lease and enhanced ancillary services.

Services are provided to the following parties: subsidiary **Vapen Kentucky, LLC** (50% owned), which manufactures cannabidiol (CBD) products in Kentucky for distribution worldwide; subsidiary **Vapen-Oklahoma, LLC** (25% owned), which produces and sells tetrahydrocannabinol (THC) products in Oklahoma; **Happy Travels, LLC** (50% voting rights), which operates a cannabis manufacturing, extraction and kitchen facility in San Diego, Calif.; **Las Vegas Wellness and Compassion, LLC**, which produces and sells THC products in Nevada; and subsidiary **Appalachian Pharms Processing, LLC** (37.5% owned), which manufactures cannabis products in Ohio. These parties produce and distribute under contract the company's Vapen brand of THC products and Vapen CBD, Pure Touch and Herbal Wellness brands of hemp-based products.

The company's expansion plans are to continue to invest in the Arizona operations, build out the Ohio cultivation facility and look for accretive opportunities.

Recent Merger and Acquisition Activity

Status: completed **Announced:** Dec. 15, 2022
UPDATE: The transaction was completed for a total consideration of $6,740,000. Concurrently, Buckeye Botanicals would be renamed and operate as Herbal Wellness Center Ohio. PREVIOUS: Vext Science, Inc., through wholly owned Jackson Pharm, LLC, agreed to acquire Buckeye Botanicals, LLC, which operates a cannabis dispensary in Jackson, Ohio, for $6,900,000.

Status: pending **Announced:** Dec. 15, 2022
Vext Science, Inc., through wholly owned Vapen Ohio, LLC, agreed to acquire Appalachian Pharm Processing, LLC, which operates a cannabis manufacturing facility in Jackson, Ohio, together with its subsidiaries and affiliated companies for a total consideration of US$12,500,000, consisting of US$2,000,000 in staged payments on or before Jan. 6, 2023, US$3,000,000 in unsecured promissory notes, US$6,000,000 in unsecured promissory notes on the earlier of the closing of the transaction or on Jan. 1, 2023, and issuance of 8,999,989 common shares. Jan. 1, 2023 - Vext has issued an 8% unsecured promissory notes valued at $9,008,626 to the vendors of Appalachian Pharm Processing, LLC, Appalachian Pharm Products, LLC and APP1803, LLC pursuant to the agreement.

Predecessor Detail - Name changed from Vapen MJ Ventures Corporation, Nov. 12, 2019.
Directors - Thai (Jason) Nguyen, founder & exec. chr., Ariz.; Eric Offenberger, pres., CEO & COO, Ariz.; David Johns, United States; Mark W. Opzoomer; Dr. Jonathan Shelton, Ariz.
Other Exec. Officers - Trevor Smith, CFO; Nalee Pham, corp. sec.

Capital Stock

	Authorized (shs.)	Outstanding (shs.)[1]
Multiple Voting	unlimited	672,747
Subordinate Voting	unlimited	82,485,279

[1] At May 25, 2023

Multiple Voting - Rank equally with subordinate voting shares as to dividends and upon liquidation. Each is convertible, at the holder's option, into 100 subordinate voting shares. 100 votes per share.

Subordinate Voting - One vote per share.

Major Shareholder - Thai (Jason) Nguyen held 36.67% interest and Sopica Special Opportunities Fund Limited held 15.87% interest at Nov. 10, 2022.

Price Range - VEXT/CSE

Year	Volume	High	Low	Close
2022	14,925,701	$0.75	$0.19	$0.24
2021	46,549,934	$1.65	$0.58	$0.64
2020	16,984,440	$1.10	$0.36	$0.99
2019	7,204,044	$2.10	$0.49	$0.70

Recent Close: $0.21

Capital Stock Changes - During 2022, subordinate voting shares were issued as follows: 8,999,989 pursuant to the acquisition of Appalachian Pharm Processing, LLC, 1,541,403 under restricted share unit plan, 586,200 on conversion of multiple voting shares, 369,500 on exercise of warrants and 300,000 to a shareholder as share replacement.

Wholly Owned Subsidiaries

Herbal Wellness Center, Inc., Ariz.
Herbal Wellness Center Ohio, LLC, Ohio
Jackson Pharm, LLC, Ohio
New Gen Holdings Inc., Wyo.
- 100% int. in **Firebrand, LLC**, Ariz.
- 50% int. in **Happy Travels, LLC**, Calif. 50% voting rights.
- 100% int. in **Hydroponics Solutions, LLC**, Phoenix, Ariz.
  - 100% int. in **Pure Touch Botanicals, LLC**, Ariz.
  - 100% int. in **Vapen CBD, LLC**, Ariz.
  - 100% int. in **Vapen, LLC**, Phoenix, Ariz.
    - 37.5% int. in **Appalachian Pharms Processing, LLC**, Ohio
    - 50% int. in **Vapen Kentucky, LLC**, Ky.
    - 25% int. in **Vapen-Oklahoma, LLC**, Okla.
- 100% int. in **New Gen Admin Services, LLC**, Phoenix, Ariz.
- 100% int. in **New Gen Agricultural Services, LLC**, Phoenix, Ariz.
- 100% int. in **New Gen Eloy, LLC**, Eloy, Ariz.
- 100% int. in **New Gen Ohio, LLC**, Ohio
- 100% int. in **New Gen Phoenix (PHX), LLC**, Phoenix, Ariz.
- 100% int. in **New Gen Prescott (PV), LLC**, Prescott, Ariz.
- 100% int. in **New Gen Real Estate Services, LLC**, Phoenix, Ariz.
- 100% int. in **RDF Management, LLC**, Ariz.
- 100% int. in **Step 1 Consulting, LLC**, Phoenix, Ariz.

Organica Patient Group Inc., Ariz.

Financial Statistics

Periods ended:	12m Dec. 31/22[A]		12m Dec. 31/21[A]
	US$000s	%Chg	US$000s
Operating revenue	**35,411**	**-5**	**37,244**
Cost of sales	12,042		8,970
Salaries & benefits	n.a.		10,678
Research & devel. expense	n.a.		150
General & admin expense	8,334		3,997
Stock-based compensation	1,452		950
Operating expense	**21,829**	**-12**	**24,745**
Operating income	**13,581**	**+9**	**12,499**
Deprec., depl. & amort.	6,434		3,289
Finance income	112		739
Finance costs, gross	2,053		2,233
Investment income	(466)		(540)
Pre-tax income	**6,698**	**-2**	**6,820**
Income taxes	(4,221)		1,833
Net income	**10,919**	**+119**	**4,986**
Cash & equivalent	5,934		6,467
Inventories	12,574		215
Accounts receivable	3,296		21,891
Current assets	52,682		31,162
Long-term investments	1,759		1,723
Fixed assets, net	35,651		28,817
Right-of-use assets	797		229
Intangibles, net	28,300		7,172
Total assets	**120,517**	**+44**	**83,704**
Accts. pay. & accr. liabs.	7,019		3,091
Current liabilities	12,975		9,736
Long-term debt, gross	37,259		14,061
Long-term debt, net	31,459		7,432
Long-term lease liabilities	737		251
Shareholders' equity	71,919		59,394
Cash from oper. activs.	**5,923**	**-49**	**11,681**
Cash from fin. activs.	(23,857)		20,138
Cash from invest. activs.	(30,313)		(27,098)
Net cash position	**5,934**	**-8**	**6,467**
Capital expenditures	(8,860)		(18,784)
	US$		US$
Earnings per share*	0.08		0.04
Cash flow per share*	0.04		0.09
	shs		shs
No. of shs. o/s*	148,963,226		137,752,334
Avg. no. of shs. o/s*	138,853,529		136,712,624
	%		%
Net profit margin	30.84		13.39
Return on equity	16.63		10.42
Return on assets	13.97		9.51
Foreign sales percent	100		100

* Suborg. Vtg.
[A] Reported in accordance with IFRS

Latest Results

Periods ended:	3m Mar. 31/23[A]		3m Mar. 31/22[A]
	US$000s	%Chg	US$000s
Operating revenue	9,111	-16	10,791
Net income	73	-98	3,458
	US$		US$
Earnings per share*	0.00		0.03

* Suborg. Vtg.
[A] Reported in accordance with IFRS

Historical Summary
(as originally stated)

Fiscal Year	Oper. Rev. US$000s	Net Inc. Bef. Disc. US$000s	EPS* US$
2022[A]	35,411	10,919	0.08
2021[A]	37,244	4,986	0.04
2020[A]	25,194	2,125	0.02
2019[A]	22,323	2,793	0.04
2018[A1]	18,476	3,749	0.06

* Suborg. Vtg.
[A] Reported in accordance with IFRS
[1] As shown in the prospectus dated Apr. 30, 2019.

V.28 Vibe Growth Corporation

Symbol - VIBE **Exchange** - CSE **CUSIP** - 92556L
Head Office - 250-997 Seymour St, Vancouver, BC, V6B 3M1 **Toll-free** - (833) 420-8423
Website - www.vibebycalifornia.com
Email - michalh@vibebycalifornia.com
Investor Relations - Michal J. Holub (833) 420-8423
Auditors - Davidson & Company LLP C.A., Vancouver, B.C.
Transfer Agents - Odyssey Trust Company, Vancouver, B.C.

Profile - (B.C. 2020; orig. Ont., 2011) Cultivates, manufactures and sells cannabis products in the U.S., primarily in California.

Retail

Operates seven adult-use cannabis dispensaries in Sacramento, Stockton, Redding, Palm Springs, Ukiah and Salinas, Calif., and Portland, Ore., under the Vibe by California brand. Also owns Hype Cannabis Co. marijuana product line, which are sold in the company's retail locations, select third-party dispensaries and its e-commerce platform; and Vibe CBD Spray product line, a proprietary full-spectrum, nano-emulsified cannabidiol oral spray sold in its e-commerce platform.

Cultivation

Operates two cannabis cultivation facilities totaling 20,400 sq. ft. in Sacramento and Crescent City, Calif. Also developing a 70,000-sq.-ft. greenhouse cannabis cultivation facility in Monterey cty., Calif.

Manufacturing and Distribution

Operates a manufacturing and distribution facility of cannabis products in Santa Rosa, Calif.

Predecessor Detail - Name changed from Vibe Bioscience Ltd., Oct. 15, 2020.

Directors - Mark Waldron, CEO, Calgary, Alta.; Joseph L. (Joe) Starr, COO, Calgary, Alta.; Gordon D. (Gord) Anderson, Calgary, Alta.; Aaron Johnson, Salinas, Calif.; James D. (Jim) Walker, High River, Alta.

Other Exec. Officers - Michal J. Holub, CFO; Calvin Yee, v-p, asset devel.

Capital Stock

	Authorized (shs.)	Outstanding (shs.)[1]
Common	unlimited	112,143,071

[1] At Aug. 22, 2022

Normal Course Issuer Bid - The company plans to make normal course purchases of up to 5,607,150 common shares representing 5% of the total outstanding. The bid commenced on Dec. 9, 2022, and expires on Dec. 8, 2023.

Major Shareholder - Joseph L. (Joe) Starr held 19.09% interest and Mark Waldron held 19.03% interest at May 26, 2021.

Price Range - VIBE/CSE

Year	Volume	High	Low	Close
2022	7,488,319	$0.44	$0.10	$0.12
2021	29,257,000	$1.45	$0.32	$0.38
2020	7,886,310	$0.72	$0.01	$0.60
2019	3,725,769	$0.98	$0.06	$0.08
2018	134,772	$1.08	$0.42	$0.60

Consolidation: 1-for-12 cons. in Apr. 2019
Recent Close: $0.08

Wholly Owned Subsidiaries

Desert Organic Solutions Inc., Calif.
Hype Bioscience Corporation, Alta.
Hype Holdings, LLC, Calif.
Lyt Cannabis Co., Calif.
Vibe by California Inc., Nev.
- 100% int. in **Alpine Alternative Naturopathic Inc.**, Sacramento, Calif.
- 100% int. in **EVR Managers, LLC**, Redding, Calif.
- 100% int. in **NGEV, Inc.**, Crescent City, Calif.
- 100% int. in **Port City Alternative of Stockton Inc.**, Stockton, Calif.
- 100% int. in **Portland Asset Holding Corporation**, Ore.
- 100% int. in **Vibe Cultivation LLC**, Calif.
- 100% int. in **Vibe Investments, LLC**, Nev.

Vibe CBD, LLC, Calif.
Vibe Distribution Corporation, Calif.
Vibe Salinas, LLC, Calif.
Vibe Ukiah, LLC, Calif.

Financial Statistics

Periods ended:	12m Dec. 31/21^A	%Chg	12m Dec. 31/20^A
	US$000s	%Chg	US$000s
Operating revenue	**29,288**	**+21**	**24,241**
Cost of goods sold	20,866		15,700
General & admin expense	6,917		5,593
Stock-based compensation	808		134
Operating expense	**28,591**	**+33**	**21,427**
Operating income	**697**	**-75**	**2,814**
Deprec., depl. & amort.	1,196		792
Finance costs, gross	203		147
Write-downs/write-offs	(1,596)		nil
Pre-tax income	**(2,510)**	**n.a.**	**2,421**
Income taxes	1,789		1,692
Net income	**(4,299)**	**n.a.**	**729**
Cash & equivalent	9,098		2,413
Inventories	3,026		3,162
Accounts receivable	135		21
Current assets	12,892		6,209
Fixed assets, net	11,828		4,668
Right-of-use assets	1,297		924
Intangibles, net	6,879		6,541
Total assets	**32,896**	**+79**	**18,342**
Accts. pay. & accr. liabs.	2,915		2,854
Current liabilities	8,539		5,345
Long-term debt, gross	1,441		1,618
Long-term debt, net	1,250		1,427
Long-term lease liabilities	946		643
Shareholders' equity	21,394		10,110
Cash from oper. activs.	**849**	**+17**	**724**
Cash from fin. activs.	14,335		(324)
Cash from invest. activs.	(8,431)		362
Net cash position	**9,098**	**+277**	**2,413**
Capital expenditures	(7,476)		(531)
	US$		US$
Earnings per share*	(0.04)		0.01
Cash flow per share*	0.01		0.01
	shs		shs
No. of shs. o/s*	112,143,071		82,613,028
Avg. no. of shs. o/s*	99,093,174		79,193,961
	%		%
Net profit margin	(14.68)		3.01
Return on equity	(27.29)		n.m.
Return on assets	(15.42)		n.a.
Foreign sales percent	100		100

* Common
^A Reported in accordance with IFRS

Latest Results

Periods ended:	6m June 30/22^A	%Chg	6m June 30/21^A
	US$000s	%Chg	US$000s
Operating revenue	11,399	-26	15,334
Net income	(1,645)	n.a.	(33)
	US$		US$
Earnings per share*	(0.01)		(0.00)

* Common
^A Reported in accordance with IFRS

Historical Summary
(as originally stated)

Fiscal Year	Oper. Rev.	Net Inc. Bef. Disc.	EPS*
	US$000s	US$000s	US$
2021^A	29,288	(4,299)	(0.04)
2020^A	24,241	729	0.01
2019^A1	12,600	(8,618)	(0.11)
	$000s	$000s	$
2018^A2	nil	(2,017)	(0.96)
2017^A	nil	(255)	(0.12)

* Common
^A Reported in accordance with IFRS
[1] Results reflect the Mar. 25, 2019, reverse takeover acquisition of Vibe Bioscience Corporation.
[2] Results for fiscal 2018 and prior fiscal years pertain to Altitude Resources Inc.
Note: Adjusted throughout for 1-for-12 cons. in Apr. 2019

V.29 Vice Health and Wellness Inc.

Symbol - VICE **Exchange** - CSE **CUSIP** - 92561G
Head Office - 734-1055 Dunsmuir St, Vancouver, BC, V7X 1B1 **Telephone** - (236) 317-2812 **Toll-free** - (888) 556-9656
Website - shopgummies.com
Email - robert@shopgummies.com
Investor Relations - Robert Payment (888) 556-9656
Auditors - Davidson & Company LLP C.A., Vancouver, B.C.
Transfer Agents - Odyssey Trust Company, Calgary, Alta.
Profile - (B.C. 2020; orig. Alta., 2018 amalg.) Formulates, manufactures and sells better-for-you, low sugar plant-based gummy and other wellness products to consumers and retailers in Canada and the U.S.

Markets and distributes a line of branded gummies such as proprietary Watermelon Sharks and Peachy Bees. Expansion plans include incorporating vitamins, adaptogens and other nutraceutical ingredients into planned gummy products.

Effective May 26, 2022, the company completed a change of business from a producer of branded cannabis products to a producer of plant-based gummy products. In conjunction, the company changed its name to **The Gummy Project Inc.**

Predecessor Detail - Name changed from The Gummy Project Inc., June 19, 2023.

Directors - Maciej (Magic) Lis, interim pres. & interim CEO, Toronto, Ont.; Robert (Robby) Payment, CFO & corp. sec., Vancouver, B.C.; Michael Hopkinson, Vancouver, B.C.

Other Exec. Officers - Anthony Gindin, chief mktg. officer

Capital Stock

	Authorized (shs.)	Outstanding (shs.)[1]
Preferred	unlimited	nil
Common	unlimited	34,325,993

[1] At May 15, 2023

Major Shareholder - Widely held at May 26, 2022.

Price Range - VICE/CSE

Year	Volume	High	Low	Close
2022	6,484,912	$0.35	$0.03	$0.04
2021	3,039,565	$2.50	$0.30	$0.30
2020	3,145,848	$5.00	$0.40	$0.54
2019	3,700,662	$45.00	$1.88	$2.50
2018	378,497	$77.50	$10.00	$10.63

Consolidation: 1-for-10 cons. in Nov. 2022; 4-for-1 split in Apr. 2021; 1-for-5 cons. in Oct. 2020; 1-for-10 cons. in Jan. 2020

Recent Close: $0.07

Capital Stock Changes - On Nov. 4, 2022, common shares were consolidated on a 1-for-10 basis. In May 2023, private placement of 22,075,884 units (1 post-consolidated common share & 1 warrant) at US$0.018 per unit was completed, with warrants exercisable at US$0.05 per share for two years.

In October 2021, private placement of 15,430,000 units (1 common share & 1 warrant) at Cdn$0.04 per unit was completed. In March 2022, private placement of 13,000,000 units (1 common share & 1 warrant) at Cdn$0.025 per unit was completed. In May 2022, private placement of 8,915,000 units (1 common share & 1 warrant) at Cdn$0.03 per unit was completed. Also during fiscal 2022, 3,590,480 common shares were issued for services.

Wholly Owned Subsidiaries

Elevation Growers Ltd., Canada. Inactive.
The Gummy Project Holdings Inc., Calif.
- 100% int. in **The Gummy Project LLC**, Calif. Inactive.
- 100% int. in **The Gummy Project WA LLC**, Wash. Inactive.

Subsidiaries

70% int. in **Northern Lights Organics Inc.**, Canada. Inactive.

Financial Statistics

Periods ended:	12m Sept. 30/22^A	%Chg	12m Sept. 30/21^A
	US$000s	%Chg	US$000s
Operating revenue	**48**	**+2**	**47**
Cost of goods sold	55		44
General & admin expense	1,506		1,226
Stock-based compensation	13		501
Operating expense	**1,574**	**-11**	**1,772**
Operating income	**(1,526)**	**n.a.**	**(1,724)**
Deprec., depl. & amort.	19		25
Finance costs, net	4		6
Investment income	(121)		18
Write-downs/write-offs	(13)		(246)
Pre-tax income	**(1,683)**	**n.a.**	**(1,983)**
Net income	**(1,683)**	**n.a.**	**(1,983)**
Cash & equivalent	31		717
Inventories	119		nil
Accounts receivable	10		nil
Current assets	238		727
Long-term investments	6		128
Right-of-use assets	14		33
Total assets	**259**	**-71**	**888**
Accts. pay. & accr. liabs.	107		30
Current liabilities	116		41
Long-term lease liabilities	nil		26
Shareholders' equity	247		926
Non-controlling interest	(105)		(105)
Cash from oper. activs.	**(1,565)**	**n.a.**	**(1,260)**
Cash from fin. activs.	892		1,194
Cash from invest. activs.	nil		151
Net cash position	**31**	**-96**	**717**
Capital expenditures	nil		(71)
	US$		US$
Earnings per share*	(0.16)		(0.30)
Cash flow per share*	(0.14)		(0.19)
	shs		shs
No. of shs. o/s*	12,250,109		8,156,609
Avg. no. of shs. o/s*	10,919,603		6,675,433
	%		%
Net profit margin	n.m.		n.m.
Return on equity	(286.96)		(188.50)
Return on assets	(293.46)		(195.56)
Foreign sales percent	n.a.		100

* Common
^A Reported in accordance with IFRS

Latest Results

Periods ended:	6m Mar. 31/23^A	%Chg	6m Mar. 31/22^A
	US$000s	%Chg	US$000s
Net income	(304)	n.a.	(892)
	US$		US$
Earnings per share*	(0.03)		(0.09)

* Common
^A Reported in accordance with IFRS

Historical Summary
(as originally stated)

Fiscal Year	Oper. Rev.	Net Inc. Bef. Disc.	EPS*
	US$000s	US$000s	US$
2022^A	48	(1,683)	(0.16)
2021^A	47	(1,983)	(0.30)
2020^A	133	(2,770)	(0.77)
2019^A1	7	(43,587)	(15.42)
	$000s	$000s	$
2018^A2	nil	875	3.02

* Common
^A Reported in accordance with IFRS
[1] Results reflect the Oct. 10, 2018, merger between Open Source Health Inc. and Weekend Unlimited Inc.
[2] Results for fiscal 2018 and prior fiscal years pertain to Open Source Health Inc.
Note: Adjusted throughout for 1-for-10 cons. in Nov. 2022; 4-for-1 split in Apr. 2021; 1-for-5 cons. in Oct. 2020; 1-for-10 cons. in Jan. 2020; 1-for-2 cons. in Oct. 2018

V.30 Vicinity Motor Corp.

Symbol - VMC **Exchange** - TSX-VEN **CUSIP** - 925654
Head Office - 3168 262 St, Aldergrove, BC, V4W 2Z6 **Telephone** - (604) 607-4000 **Fax** - (604) 607-4004
Website - vicinitymotorcorp.com
Email - jlagourgue@vicinitymotor.com
Investor Relations - John LaGourgue (604) 288-8043
Auditors - PricewaterhouseCoopers LLP C.A., Vancouver, B.C.
Lawyers - Cassels Brock & Blackwell LLP, Vancouver, B.C.
Transfer Agents - Computershare Trust Company of Canada Inc., Vancouver, B.C.
Employees - 60 at Mar. 30, 2023

Profile - (B.C. 2012) Designs, manufactures and distributes mid-size transit buses and medium duty trucks powered by electric, compressed natural gas (CNG), gas and clean-diesel for public and commercial enterprises in Canada and the U.S.

Models consist of Vicinity™ Classic, a purpose-built low-floor bus available in 26 ft. and 28 ft. models with CNG and clean-diesel engines; Vicinity Lightning™, a fully electric zero emission and low-floor bus for transit, airports, community shuttles, para-transit, university shuttles, corporate and other unique applications with 19.5 ft. tires and hydraulic disc brakes; and VMC 1200 Electric Truck, a class 3 commercial electric vehicle (EV) powered by 150 kWh Li-on batter technology which features a 12,000 gross vehicle weight rating medium-duty with 6,000 lbs. load capacity and range up to 15,000 miles on single charge.

Assembly operations are set to commence at the newly constructed 100,000 sq.-ft. U.S. manufacturing campus in Ferndale, Wash., in the first half of 2023. The facility would be used for the manufacturing of both buses and EV trucks for sale in North America.

At Dec. 31, 2022, total firm orders for the year 2023 production were 8 Vicinity™ Classic buses, 10 Vicinity Lightning™ EV buses and chassis and 1,000 VMC 1200 EV trucks. During the twelve-months ended Dec. 31, 2022, 38 Vicinity™ buses, 11 Vicinity trucks and four Optimal shuttles were delivered compared with 131 buses delivered during the year earlier period.

During 2022, the company terminated its 10-year sales and marketing agreement with **Optimal Electric Vehicles, LLC** to distribute and sell the Optimal S1 and E1 electric chassis vehicles in exchange for a licence fee of US$20,000,000.

Predecessor Detail - Name changed from Grande West Transportation Group Inc., Mar. 29, 2021; basis 1 new for 3 old shs.

Directors - Joseph (Joe) Miller, chr., Surrey, B.C.; William R. Trainer, pres. & CEO, Langley, B.C.; John LaGourgue, v-p, sales & corp. devel., Surrey, B.C.; Andrew Imanse, Orange County, Calif.; Christopher Strong, Fort Worth, Tex.; James D. A. White, Toronto, Ont.

Other Exec. Officers - Danial (Dan) Buckle, CFO; Dennis Gore, v-p, eng.; Marion McGrath, corp. sec.

Capital Stock

	Authorized (shs.)	Outstanding (shs.)[1]
Common	unlimited	45,667,706

[1] At May 15, 2023

Major Shareholder - Widely held at Mar. 30, 2023.

Price Range - VMC/TSX-VEN

Year	Volume	High	Low	Close
2022	17,057,085	$5.45	$1.07	$1.30
2021	30,622,781	$13.77	$3.88	$4.45
2020	17,121,168	$6.42	$0.69	$4.71
2019	9,042,292	$2.76	$1.20	$1.41
2018	16,167,200	$7.11	$1.77	$2.13

Consolidation: 1-for-3 cons. in Mar. 2021

Recent Close: $1.40

Capital Stock Changes - During 2022, common shares were issued as follows: 5,118,554 under an at-the-market program, 4,444,445 by direct offering, 166,000 on vesting of restricted share units and 66,661 on exercise of options.

Wholly Owned Subsidiaries

Vicinity Motor (Bus) Corp., B.C.
Vicinity Motor (Bus) U.S.A. Corp., Del. Inactive.
- 100% int. in **Vicinity Motor Property LLC**, Del.

Financial Statistics

Periods ended:	12m Dec. 31/22[A]		12m Dec. 31/21[A]
	US$000s	%Chg	US$000s
Operating revenue	**18,475**	**-56**	**41,708**
Cost of goods sold	17,641		37,104
General & admin expense	9,526		7,812
Stock-based compensation	1,380		1,353
Operating expense	**28,547**	**-38**	**46,269**
Operating income	**(10,072)**	**n.a.**	**(4,561)**
Deprec., depl. & amort	2,966		1,241
Finance costs, gross	2,258		716
Pre-tax income	**(17,746)**	**n.a.**	**(6,859)**
Income taxes	202		464
Net income	**(17,948)**	**n.a.**	**(7,323)**
Cash & equivalent	1,622		4,402
Inventories	10,068		9,416
Accounts receivable	2,655		2,810
Current assets	18,146		20,806
Fixed assets, net	22,613		10,834
Intangibles, net	14,273		22,353
Total assets	**55,032**	**+2**	**53,993**
Bank indebtedness	6,587		7,143
Accts. pay. & accr. liabs	4,942		2,915
Current liabilities	16,573		19,401
Long-term lease liabilities	1,465		19
Shareholders' equity	36,832		34,245
Cash from oper. activs	**(9,082)**	**n.a.**	**3,594**
Cash from fin. activs	17,368		22,945
Cash from invest. activs	(10,698)		(23,120)
Net cash position	**1,622**	**-63**	**4,402**
Capital expenditures	(11,109)		(6,537)
Capital disposals	252		729
	US$		US$
Earnings per share*	(0.45)		(0.24)
Cash flow per share*	(0.23)		0.12
	shs		shs
No. of shs. o/s*	44,742,039		34,946,379
Avg. no. of shs. o/s*	39,650,426		30,827,688
	%		%
Net profit margin	(97.15)		(17.56)
Return on equity	(50.50)		(27.92)
Return on assets	(28.74)		(14.24)
Foreign sales percent	27		68

* Common
[A] Reported in accordance with IFRS

Latest Results

Periods ended:	3m Mar. 31/23[A]		3m Mar. 31/22[A]
	US$000s	%Chg	US$000s
Operating revenue	2,649	-17	3,183
Net income	(2,436)	n.a.	(2,887)
	US$		US$
Earnings per share*	(0.05)		(0.08)

* Common
[A] Reported in accordance with IFRS

Historical Summary
(as originally stated)

Fiscal Year	Oper. Rev.	Net Inc. Bef. Disc.	EPS*
	US$000s	US$000s	US$
2022[A]	18,475	(17,948)	(0.45)
2021[A]	41,708	(7,323)	(0.24)
	$000s	$000s	$
2020[A]	26,069	(4,402)	(0.17)
2019[A]	24,648	(4,985)	(0.21)
2018[A]	70,077	949	0.03

* Common
[A] Reported in accordance with IFRS

Note: Adjusted throughout for 1-for-3 cons. in Mar. 2021

V.31 Victory Opportunities 1 Corp.

Symbol - VOC.P **Exchange** - TSX-VEN **CUSIP** - 92648B
Head Office - 228-1122 Mainland St, Vancouver, BC, V6B 5L1
Email - michael@yeungholdings.com
Investor Relations - Michael Yeung (403) 813-3288
Auditors - Crowe MacKay LLP C.A., Vancouver, B.C.
Transfer Agents - Computershare Trust Company of Canada Inc., Vancouver, B.C.

Profile - (B.C. 2022) Capital Pool Company.

Common listed on TSX-VEN, Dec. 22, 2022.

Directors - Michael Yeung, CEO & corp. sec., Calgary, Alta.; Andrew Ryu, Thornhill, Ont.; Jeffrey J. (Jeff) Stevens, Scarborough, Ont.

Other Exec. Officers - Paul Haber, CFO

Capital Stock

	Authorized (shs.)	Outstanding (shs.)[1]
Common	unlimited	6,388,000

[1] At Dec. 22, 2022

Major Shareholder - Widely held at Dec. 22, 2022.

Recent Close: $0.10

Capital Stock Changes - On Dec. 22, 2022, an initial public offering of 3,018,000 common shares was completed at 10¢ per share.

V.32 Victory Square Technologies Inc.

Symbol - VST **Exchange** - CSE **CUSIP** - 92650P
Head Office - 800-1500 Georgia W, Vancouver, BC, V6G 2Z6 **Telephone** - (604) 283-9166
Website - www.victorysquare.com
Email - sheri@victorysquare.com
Investor Relations - Sheri Rempel (604) 283-9166
Auditors - MNP LLP C.A.
Transfer Agents - Computershare Trust Company of Canada Inc.

Profile - (B.C. 2015) Creates, acquires and invests in startup emerging technology companies that use artificial intelligence (AI), digital health, gaming, cryptocurrencies, augmented reality (AR), virtual reality (VR), mixed reality (MR), cybersecurity, cloud computing and plant-based sciences to disrupt diverse sectors such as fintech, insurance, health, immersive experiences and gaming.

Operating subsidiaries include wholly owned **VS Digital Health Inc.**, which offers connected healthcare solutions including round the clock access to healthcare professionals, prescription delivery services and other related services and products; **Draft Label Technologies Inc.**, which offers custom software development services to various of industries including member-based businesses in exchange for royalty payments; **PDL USA Inc.**, which operates online platforms for fee entry fantasy sports competitions in the U.S.; **Victory Entertainment Inc.**, which develops, finances and produces film, television and digital media products; **IV Hydreight Inc.**, which provides a custom built, proprietary telemedicine service that allows users to book confidential health and wellness and/or medical services at their home, hotel, office or wherever they need discreet assistance; **XR Immersive Tech Inc.** (formerly **Fantasy 360 Technologies Inc.**) (58.75% owned), which designs, builds and installs immersive escape room attractions; **Synthesis VR Inc.**, which operates as a location-based virtual reality (VR) content store; **VS Blockchain Assembly Inc.**, which operates as a software development company; and **BlockX Capital Corp.**, which invests in blockchain and emerging technology companies.

In addition, investments as at Aug. 29, 2022, included interests in **Victory Square Health Inc.**; **Cassia Research Inc.**; **Cloud Benefit Solutions Inc.**; **MLVX Technologies Inc.**; **FansUnite Entertainment Inc.**; **Flo Digital Inc.**; **Grow Academy Technologies Inc.**; **Howyl Ventures Inc.**; **Turnium Technology Group Inc.**; **Next Decentrum Technologies Inc.**; **PayVida Solutions Inc.**; **Silota Research and Development Inc.**; **Shop and Shout Ltd.**; **Cloud Nine Web3 Technologies Inc.**; **Stardust Solar Technologies Inc.**; and **Franchise Global Health Inc.** (formerly **Mercury Acquisitions Corp.**); and **GameOn Entertainment Technologies Inc.**

Recent Merger and Acquisition Activity

Status: completed **Revised:** Nov. 28, 2022

UPDATE: The transaction was completed. PREVIOUS: Perihelion Capital Ltd. entered into a letter of intent for the Qualifying Transaction reverse takeover acquisition of Las Vegas, Nev.-based IV Hydreight Inc., a wholly owned subsidiary of Victory Square Technologies Inc. (VST). IV Hydreight provided a mobile application for booking at-home appointments with medical service providers across the U.S. Upon completion, Perihelion would consolidate its common shares on a 1-for-6.46805 basis. July 12, 2022 - A definitive agreement was entered into. As part of the transaction, Perihelion's wholly owned 1203500 B.C. Ltd. would amalgamate with VST's newly incorporated wholly owned 1362795 B.C. Ltd.; VST would transfer IV Hydreight to 1362795 B.C. Ltd. immediately prior to completion of the transaction for issuance of 27,896,825 common shares of 1362795 B.C. Ltd. Upon completion, Perihelion would issue a total of 28,511,479 post-consolidated common shares at a deemed price of 63¢ per share to indirectly acquire IV Hydreight through the acquisition of 1362795 B.C. Ltd. (representing the 27,896,825 shares issued to VST along with the 614,654 shares it had outstanding). Nov. 25, 2022 - Perihelion changed its name to Hydreight Technologies Inc. and completed the share consolidation. VST also completed the transfer of IV Hydreight to 1362795 B.C. Ltd.

Predecessor Detail - Name changed from Fantasy 6 Sports Inc., June 9, 2017.

Directors - Shafin D. Tejani, pres. & CEO, Vancouver, B.C.; Howard A. Blank, Vancouver, B.C.; Thomas P. Mayenknecht, B.C.; Peter C. Smyrniotis, Vancouver, B.C.

Other Exec. Officers - Vahid Shababi, COO; Sheri Rempel, CFO & corp. sec.

Capital Stock

	Authorized (shs.)	Outstanding (shs.)[1]
Common	unlimited	97,930,700

[1] At Aug. 29, 2022

Major Shareholder - Shafin D. Tejani held 13.26% interest at Oct. 29, 2021.

Price Range - VST/CSE

Year	Volume	High	Low	Close
2022	32,634,696	$0.35	$0.10	$0.11
2021	112,207,702	$1.27	$0.32	$0.33
2020	186,728,915	$1.10	$0.05	$0.55
2019	9,289,641	$0.55	$0.06	$0.08
2018	16,927,779	$3.50	$0.38	$0.46

Recent Close: $0.16

Dividends

VST com
stk.[1]◆.................. Dec. 30/21
Paid in 2023: n.a. 2022: n.a. 2021: stk.◆

[1] Stk. divd. of 45.838991 Fantasy 360 Tchnlgys Inc com. shs. for ea. 1000 shs. held.
◆ Special

Wholly Owned Subsidiaries

BlockX Capital Corp., Canada.
Draft Label Technologies Inc., Canada.
- 100% int. in **PDL USA Inc.**, Del.

VS Blockchain Assembly Inc., Canada.
VS Digital Health Inc., Canada.
Victory Entertainment Inc.

Subsidiaries

73.72% int. in **Hydreight Technologies Inc.**, Vancouver, B.C. (see separate coverage)
58.75% int. in **XR Immersive Tech Inc.**, Vancouver, B.C. (see separate coverage)

Note: The preceding list includes only the major related companies in which interests are held.

Financial Statistics

Periods ended:	12m Dec. 31/21[A]		12m Dec. 31/20[oA]
	$000s	%Chg	$000s
Operating revenue	**1,494**	**0**	**1,487**
Cost of goods sold	584		952
Salaries & benefits	1,756		501
Research & devel. expense	2,308		nil
General & admin expense	5,566		2,327
Stock-based compensation	2,794		nil
Operating expense	**13,008**	**+244**	**3,780**
Operating income	**(11,514)**	**n.a.**	**(2,292)**
Deprec., depl. & amort.	2,595		169
Finance income	785		168
Finance costs, gross	330		24
Investment income	(17)		18
Write-downs/write-offs	(801)		(540)
Pre-tax income	**(13,421)**	**n.a.**	**21,082**
Income taxes	(99)		nil
Net inc. bef. disc. opers	**(13,322)**	**n.a.**	**21,082**
Income from disc. opers	(2,424)		(1,349)
Net income	**(15,746)**	**n.a.**	**19,733**
Net inc. for equity hldrs	**(13,854)**	**n.a.**	**19,915**
Net inc. for non-cont. int.	**(1,892)**	**n.a.**	**(182)**
Cash & equivalent	4,376		4,565
Inventories	144		nil
Accounts receivable	411		193
Current assets	5,442		6,956
Long-term investments	23,945		28,876
Fixed assets, net	284		6
Right-of-use assets	621		nil
Intangibles, net	6,828		4,374
Total assets	**37,331**	**-12**	**42,652**
Bank indebtedness	2,560		295
Accts. pay. & accr. liabs	1,112		1,015
Current liabilities	5,351		3,717
Long-term debt, gross	122		1,675
Long-term debt, net	122		132
Long-term lease liabilities	463		nil
Equity portion of conv. debs	90		200
Shareholders' equity	27,383		32,944
Non-controlling interest	3,776		5,760
Cash from oper. activs	**(8,570)**	**n.a.**	**(3,258)**
Cash from fin. activs	11,900		6,974
Cash from invest. activs	(3,506)		707
Net cash position	**4,376**	**-4**	**4,552**
Capital expenditures	(286)		(2)
Capital disposals	nil		16
	$		$
Earnings per share*	(0.15)		0.27
Cash flow per share*	(0.09)		(0.04)
	shs		shs
No. of shs. o/s*	97,930,700		76,491,818
Avg. no. of shs. o/s*	94,240,905		74,928,905
	%		%
Net profit margin	(891.70)		n.m.
Return on equity	(37.89)		103.04
Return on assets	(32.49)		75.56

* Common
[o] Restated
[A] Reported in accordance with IFRS

Latest Results

Periods ended:	6m June 30/22[A]		6m June 30/21[oA]
	$000s	%Chg	$000s
Operating revenue	2,232	+443	411
Net inc. bef. disc. opers	(10,320)	n.a.	(2,422)
Income from disc. opers	nil		(2,424)
Net income	(10,320)	n.a.	(4,845)
Net inc. for equity hldrs	(8,892)	n.a.	(3,861)
Net inc. for non-cont. int	(1,428)		(984)
	$		$
Earns. per sh. bef. disc. opers.*	(0.09)		(0.02)
Earnings per share*	(0.09)		(0.04)

* Common
[o] Restated
[A] Reported in accordance with IFRS

Historical Summary
(as originally stated)

Fiscal Year	Oper. Rev.	Net Inc. Bef. Disc.	EPS*
	$000s	$000s	$
2021[A]	1,494	(13,322)	(0.15)
2020[A]	1,490	20,101	0.30
2019[A]	3,532	(8,918)	(0.10)
2018[A]	4,488	(12,620)	(0.18)
2017[A]	741	(2,738)	(0.05)

* Common
[A] Reported in accordance with IFRS

V.33 Viemed Healthcare, Inc.

Symbol - VMD **Exchange** - TSX **CUSIP** - 92663R
Head Office - 625 E. Kaliste Saloom Rd, Lafayette, LA, United States, 70508 **Telephone** - (337) 504-3802 **Toll-free** - (866) 852-8343 **Fax** - (337) 500-1972
Website - www.viemed.com
Email - tzehnder@viemed.com
Investor Relations - W. Todd Zehnder (337) 504-3802
Auditors - Ernst & Young LLP C.A.
Transfer Agents - Computershare Trust Company of Canada Inc., Vancouver, B.C.
FP500 Revenue Ranking - 677
Employees - 743 at Dec. 31, 2022

Profile - (B.C. 2016) Provides home medical equipment and home therapy to patients affected by specific respiratory diseases, and in-home sleep testing services for sleep apnea sufferers.

Provides home medical equipment through the following service programs: respiratory disease management, which includes invasive and non-invasive ventilation, percussion vests, other therapies and related equipment and supplies to patients suffering from Chronic Obstructive Pulmonary Disease (COPD); neuromuscular care, which is the provision of respiratory therapy treatments to neuromuscular patients which could lessen the effort required to breathe; oxygen therapy, which provides patients with extra oxygen to manage chronic health problems; and sleep apnea treatment, which provides solutions and equipment including PAP (positive airway pressure), AutoPAP (an automatic continuous positive airway pressure) and BiPAP (bi-level positive airway pressure) machines.

Also offers in-home sleep testing services, which is an alternative to the traditional sleep lab testing environment, as well as healthcare staffing and recruitment services to third party healthcare facilities.

The company's service coverage area consists of all 50 U.S. states.

Recent Merger and Acquisition Activity

Status: pending **Announced:** Apr. 18, 2023
Viemed Healthcare, Inc. agreed to acquire Tennessee-based Home Medical Products, Inc. (HMP) for US$31,750,000, which is adjusted for net working capital and other customary closing adjustments. HMP provides respiratory focused home medical equipment and services, and manages various medical equipment offices in Tennessee, Alabama and Mississippi. Services offered includes home visits and remote monitoring by licensed respiratory therapists and clinical staff, provision of a professional fitter for back, neck, knee and wrist braces, and wound care services.

Directors - Randy Dobbs, chr., Greenville, S.C.; Casey Hoyt, CEO, Lafayette, La.; W. Todd Zehnder, COO, Lafayette, La.; Dr. William Frazier, CMO, Jackson, Miss.; Bruce Greenstein, Seattle, Wash.; Sabrina Heltz, Baton Rouge, La.; Nitin Kaushal, Richmond Hill, Ont.; Timothy Smokoff, Wash.

Other Exec. Officers - Michael (Mike) Moore, pres.; Trae Fitzgerald, CFO; Rob Birkhead, chief mktg. officer; John Collier, chief tech. officer; Michael Freeman, chief bus. devel. officer; Richard Kovacik, chief devel. officer; Ronnie Miller, chief revenue officer; Claudio Munoz, CIO; Brett Stoute, chief compliance officer; Ryan Sullivan, exec. v-p; Jeremy Trahan, exec. v-p, acqs. & strategic transactions & chief legal officer; Jerome Cambre, v-p, sales; Andrew Hill, v-p, sleep & respiratory srvcs.; Max Hoyt, v-p, govt. rel.; Chris Weeks, v-p, HR; Patrick Eagan, gen. counsel & corp. sec.

Capital Stock

	Authorized (shs.)	Outstanding (shs.)[1]
Common	unlimited	38,283,003

[1] At Apr. 19, 2023

Major Shareholder - Thrivent Financial for Lutherans held 10.8% interest at Apr. 19, 2023.

Price Range - VMD/TSX

Year	Volume	High	Low	Close
2022	9,036,253	$10.49	$4.53	$10.27
2021	25,069,248	$13.69	$6.36	$6.60
2020	61,598,982	$16.19	$3.36	$9.95
2019	29,055,339	$11.49	$4.98	$8.13
2018	46,276,028	$8.75	$1.80	$5.23

Recent Close: $10.54

Capital Stock Changes - During 2022, common shares were issued as follows: 148,404 on vesting of restricted share units and 82,822 on exercise of options; 1,821,875 common shares were cancelled.

Wholly Owned Subsidiaries

Viemed, Inc.
- 100% int. in **Home Sleep Delivered, LLC**, Lafayette, La.
- 100% int. in **Sleep Management, LLC**, Lafayette, La.
- 100% int. in **Viemed Clinical Services, LLC**, La.
- 100% int. in **Viemed Healthcare Staffing, LLC**, La.

Investments

DMEscripts, LLC
49% int. in **Solvet Services, LLC**, La.
VeruStat, Inc., Del.

Financial Statistics

Periods ended:	12m Dec. 31/22[A]		12m Dec. 31/21[A]
	US$000s	%Chg	US$000s
Operating revenue	**138,832**	**+19**	**117,062**
Cost of sales	39,533		33,191
Research & devel. expense	2,696		2,110
General & admin expense	68,161		54,893
Stock-based compensation	5,202		5,150
Operating expense	**115,592**	**+21**	**95,344**
Operating income	**23,240**	**+7**	**21,718**
Deprec., depl. & amort.	15,631		11,312
Finance costs, net	197		318
Investment income	935		1,241
Pre-tax income	**8,990**	**-28**	**12,503**
Income taxes	2,768		3,377
Net income	**6,222**	**-32**	**9,126**
Cash & equivalent	16,914		28,408
Inventories	3,574		2,457
Accounts receivable	15,379		12,823
Current assets	39,742		47,310
Fixed assets, net	68,437		62,846
Total assets	**117,043**	**-1**	**117,962**
Accts. pay. & accr. liabs	2,650		3,239
Current liabilities	18,861		17,811
Long-term debt, gross	nil		5,786
Long-term debt, net	nil		4,306
Long-term lease liabilities	199		268
Shareholders' equity	97,094		94,820
Cash from oper. activs	**27,748**	**+23**	**22,494**
Cash from fin. activs	(15,266)		(5,321)
Cash from invest. activs	(23,976)		(19,746)
Net cash position	**16,914**	**-40**	**28,408**
Capital expenditures	(22,898)		(19,743)
Capital disposals	1,063		596
	US$		US$
Earnings per share*	0.16		0.23
Cash flow per share*	0.72		0.57
	shs		shs
No. of shs. o/s*	38,049,739		39,640,388
Avg. no. of shs. o/s*	38,655,403		39,491,117
	%		%
Net profit margin	4.48		7.80
Return on equity	6.48		10.34
Return on assets	5.30		7.92
Foreign sales percent	100		100
No. of employees (FTEs)	743		627

* Common
[A] Reported in accordance with U.S. GAAP

Historical Summary
(as originally stated)

Fiscal Year	Oper. Rev.	Net Inc. Bef. Disc.	EPS*
	US$000s	US$000s	US$
2022[A]	138,832	6,222	0.16
2021[A]	117,062	9,126	0.23
2020[A]	131,309	31,530	0.81
2019[A]	80,256	8,525	0.23
2018[B]	65,271	10,177	0.27

* Common
[A] Reported in accordance with U.S. GAAP
[B] Reported in accordance with IFRS

V.34 Village Farms International, Inc.

Symbol - VFF **Exchange** - NASDAQ **CUSIP** - 92707Y
Head Office - 4700 80 St, Delta, BC, V4K 3N3 **Telephone** - (604) 940-6012 **Fax** - (604) 940-6312 **Exec. Office** - 90 Colonial Center Pkwy, Lake Mary, FL, United States, 32746 **Telephone** - (407) 936-1190 **Fax** - (407) 936-1187
Website - www.villagefarms.com

Email - sruffini@villagefarms.com
Investor Relations - Stephen C. Ruffini (407) 936-1190 ext. 340
Auditors - PricewaterhouseCoopers LLP C.A., Vancouver, B.C.
Lawyers - Torys LLP, Toronto, Ont.
Transfer Agents - Computershare Trust Company of Canada Inc., Vancouver, B.C.
FP500 Revenue Ranking - 518
Employees - 1,800 at Dec. 31, 2022
Profile - (Can. 2003) Grows, markets and distributes vegetable from greenhouse facilities in North America; cultivates, processes, distributes and sells cannabis products and cannabinoid-based health and wellness products in Canada, the U.S. and other international markets; and developing a renewable natural gas facility in British Columbia.

Operations are conducted through five segments: Produce; Canadian Cannabis; U.S. Cannabis; International Cannabis; and Clean Energy.

Produce - Owns and operates a produce greenhouse facility in Delta, B.C., and four greenhouse facilities in Marfa (2), Fort Davis and Monahans, Tex., totaling 8,073,340 sq. ft. and a growing area of 190 acres, where tomatoes, bell peppers and cucumbers are produced. The company also markets and distributes produce from third party greenhouse growers in British Columbia, Ontario and Mexico which operate over 300 acres of growing area. Products are sold primarily under the Village Farms Fresh brand to retail supermarket chains and dedicated fresh food distribution companies in Canada and the U.S.

Canadian Cannabis - Wholly owned **Pure Sunfarms Corp.** cultivates, markets and distributes cannabis products for retail and wholesale channels across 10 Canadian provinces and territories as well as for export markets. Pure Sunfarms operates two 1,100,000-sq.-ft. greenhouse facilities in Delta, B.C. In addition, owns a 70% interest in **ROSE LifeScience Inc.**, which acts as the exclusive, direct-to-retail sales, marketing and distribution partner for well-known Canadian cannabis brands and Quebec-based micro and craft growers to commercialize their products in Quebec. ROSE operates a 55,000-sq.-ft. indoor facility in Huntingdon, Que., where it also cultivates and processes own brands, Tam Tams, DLYS, Pure Laine, Elekt and Promenade.

U.S. Cannabis - Wholly owned **Balanced Health Botanicals, LLC** develops, distributes and sells cannabidiol (CBD) and other cannabinoid-based health and wellness products primarily in the U.S. Products are distributed through brick-and-mortar retailers, its e-commerce platform, CBDistillery, third party e-commerce websites and wholesalers. Balanced Health operates an 8,000-sq.-ft. manufacturing and fulfillment facility in Denver, Colo. Also has a 65% interest in **Village Fields Hemp USA, LLC** for the outdoor cultivation of hemp and CBD extraction in several U.S. states.

International Cannabis - Owns an 85% interest in **Leli Holland B.V.**, which has been granted a cultivation licence in the Netherlands under the Closed Cannabis Supply Chain Experiment program, an experiment to determine whether and how controlled cannabis can be legally supplied to coffee shops and what the effects of this would be. The experiment was expected to begin by mid-2023 and scheduled to operate for a minimum of four years. Leli plans to construct two indoor production facilities.

Clean Energy - Owns a 7-MW co-generation facility, located adjacent to the greenhouse operations in Delta, B.C., which uses landfill gas from the City of Vancouver's landfill to generate electricity for B.C. Hydro and thermal heat for the company's produce greenhouse facility. The company has partnered with Atlanta, Ga.-based **Mas Energy, LLC** to transition the operations into a facility which converts landfill gas to renewable natural gas (RNG). CO_2 generated from the RNG production would be used in the company's vegetable and cannabis greenhouse facilities in Delta. The facility was shut down on Apr. 30, 2022, in preparation for the transition to RNG operations. Construction began during the second quarter of 2022, with operational start up expected in mid-2023.

Recent Merger and Acquisition Activity

Status: completed **Announced:** July 19, 2022
Village Farms International, Inc. acquired an 85% interest in Netherlands-based Leli Holland B.V., one of the applicants selected to receive a licence to cultivate and distribute cannabis to coffee shops under the Dutch Closed Cannabis Supply Chain Experiment program, for €4,250,000 (US$4,568,000).

Directors - John R. McLernon, chr., Vancouver, B.C.; Michael A. DeGiglio, pres. & CEO, Fla.; Stephen C. Ruffini, exec. v-p & CFO, Fla.; John P. Henry, Fla.; David Holewinski, Fla.; Kathy Mahoney, Minn.; Christopher C. (Kip) Woodward, Vancouver, B.C.

Other Exec. Officers - Eric Janke, exec. v-p, sales & mktg.; Ann Gillin Lefever, exec. v-p, corp. affairs; Michael Minerva, sr. v-p, grower rel. supply devel.; Bret T. Wiley, sr. v-p, sales & sales opers.; Lofton Barnes, v-p, corp. HR; Dr. Michael Bledsoe, v-p, food safety & regulatory affairs; Jonathan Bos, v-p, asset devel.; Dirk de Jong, v-p & regl. facility mgr., Canada; Derin Gemmel, v-p, HR admin. & compliance, U.S.A; Andrew Gigante, v-p, finl. planning & analysis; Bill Lowe, v-p, IT; Paul Selina, v-p, applied research & devel.; Patti Smith, v-p & contr.; Arie Van Der Giessen, v-p & regl. facility mgr., U.S.A.; Orville Bovenschen, pres., Pure Sunfarms Corp.; Davide Zaffino, pres. & CEO, ROSE LifeScience Inc.; Phil Jennings IV, CEO, Village Fields Hemp USA, LLC; Chase Terwilliger, CEO, Balanced Health Botanicals, LLC

Capital Stock

	Authorized (shs.)	Outstanding (shs.)[1]
Preferred	unlimited	nil
Special	unlimited	nil
Common	unlimited	110,238,929

[1] At May 1, 2023

Major Shareholder - Widely held at May 1, 2023.

Price Range - VFF/NASDAQ

Year	Volume	High	Low	Close
2022	35,853,992	US$7.21	US$1.22	US$1.34
2021	70,800,375	US$20.31	US$5.62	US$6.42

VFF/TSX (D)

Year	Volume	High	Low	Close
2021	135,310,527	$25.78	$7.25	$8.12
2020	195,864,560	$16.38	$3.01	$12.89
2019	278,794,826	$24.25	$4.21	$8.07
2018	112,046,214	$9.80	$3.98	$4.42

Wholly Owned Subsidiaries

Pure Sunfarms Corp., Delta, B.C.
VF Clean Energy, Inc., Delta, B.C.
Village Farms Canada GP Inc., Delta, B.C.

- 100% int. in **Village Farms Canada Limited Partnership**, Delta, B.C.
  - 100% int. in **VF Operations Canada Inc.**, Delta, B.C.
    - 100% int. in **VF U.S. Holdings Inc.**, Wilmington, Del.
      - 100% int. in **Agro Power Development, Inc.**, Eatontown, N.J.
        - 100% int. in **Village Farms of Delaware, LLC**, Wilmington, Del.
          - 1% int. in **Village Farms, LP**, Wilmington, Del.
      - 100% int. in **Balanced Health Botanicals, LLC**, Englewood, Colo.
      - 99% int. in **Village Farms, LP**, Wilmington, Del.
        - 65% int. in **Village Fields Hemp USA, LLC**, United States.

Subsidiaries

85% int. in **Leli Holland B.V.**, Netherlands.
70% int. in **ROSE LifeScience Inc.**, Huntingdon, Qué.

Investments

Altum International Pty Ltd., Australia.

Financial Statistics

Periods ended:	12m Dec. 31/22[A]		12m Dec. 31/21[A]
	US$000s	%Chg	US$000s
Operating revenue	**293,572**	**+10**	**268,020**
Cost of sales	266,075		222,841
General & admin expense	55,224		33,675
Stock-based compensation	3,987		7,533
Operating expense	**325,286**	**+23**	**264,049**
Operating income	**(31,714)**	**n.a.**	**3,971**
Deprec., depl. & amort.	13,054		12,709
Finance income	207		126
Finance costs, gross	3,244		2,835
Write-downs/write-offs	(43,891)[1]		nil
Pre-tax income	**(94,066)**	**n.a.**	**(12,343)**
Income taxes	4,681		(3,526)
After-tax income (expense)	(2,668)		(308)
Net income	**(101,415)**	**n.a.**	**(9,125)**
Net inc. for equity hldrs	**(101,146)**	**n.a.**	**(9,079)**
Net inc. for non-cont. int	**(269)**	**n.a.**	**(46)**
Cash & equivalent	16,676		53,417
Inventories	70,582		68,677
Accounts receivable	27,867		34,976
Current assets	132,984		174,959
Long-term investments	2,109		2,109
Fixed assets, net	207,701		215,704
Right-of-use assets	9,132		7,609
Intangibles, net	103,382		143,927
Total assets	**465,285**	**-18**	**566,911**
Bank indebtedness	7,529		7,760
Accts. pay. & accr. liabs	51,612		42,762
Current liabilities	72,215		64,313
Long-term debt, gross	53,467		61,835
Long-term debt, net	43,821		50,419
Long-term lease liabilities	7,785		6,711
Shareholders' equity	303,063		408,405
Non-controlling interest	16,931		16,433
Cash from oper. activs	**(19,889)**	**n.a.**	**(39,567)**
Cash from fin. activs	4,496		135,883
Cash from invest. activs	(20,899)		(63,470)
Net cash position	**21,676**	**-63**	**58,667**
Capital expenditures	(14,292)		(21,656)
	US$		US$
Earnings per share*	(1.13)		(0.11)
Cash flow per share*	(0.22)		(0.48)
	shs		shs
No. of shs. o/s*	91,788,929		88,233,929
Avg. no. of shs. o/s*	89,127,000		82,161,000
	%		%
Net profit margin	(34.55)		(3.40)
Return on equity	(28.43)		(2.96)
Return on assets	(18.99)		(1.54)
Foreign sales percent	51		48
No. of employees (FTEs)	1,800		1,800

* Common
[A] Reported in accordance with U.S. GAAP
[1] Includes impairment of US$38,669,000 and US$4,630,000 on goodwill and brand intangible, respectively, of U.S. cannabis operations.

Historical Summary
(as originally stated)

Fiscal Year	Oper. Rev.	Net Inc. Bef. Disc.	EPS*
	US$000s	US$000s	US$
2022[A]	293,572	(101,415)	(1.13)
2021[A]	268,020	(9,125)	(0.11)
2020[A]	170,086	11,608	0.20
2019[A]	144,568	2,325	0.05
2018[B]	150,000	(5,145)	(0.11)

* Common
[A] Reported in accordance with U.S. GAAP
[B] Reported in accordance with IFRS

V.35 Vinergy Capital Inc.

Symbol - VIN **Exchange** - CSE **CUSIP** - 92744H
Head Office - 1000-409 Granville St, Vancouver, BC, V6C 1T2 **Telephone** - (604) 602-0001 **Toll-free** - (800) 674-9731 **Fax** - (604) 608-5448
Website - www.vinergycapital.com
Email - gb@harmonycs.ca
Investor Relations - Geoffrey Balderson (604) 602-0001
Auditors - Saturna Group Chartered Accountants LLP C.A., Vancouver, B.C.
Transfer Agents - Computershare Trust Company of Canada Inc., Vancouver, B.C.
Profile - (B.C. 2011; orig. Alta., 2001) Invests in equity, debt or other securities of both public and private companies involved in Bitcoin mining, Bitcoin derivatives, digital currencies, digital currency marketplaces and exchanges, and blockchain.
Predecessor Detail - Name changed from Vinergy Cannabis Capital Inc., Mar. 10, 2021.
Directors - Alnoor Nathoo, chr. & interim CEO, Calgary, Alta.; Christopher P. (Chris) Cherry, Vancouver, B.C.; Kenneth R. (Ken) Ralfs, Victoria, B.C.
Other Exec. Officers - Geoffrey (Geoff) Balderson, CFO

Capital Stock

	Authorized (shs.)	Outstanding (shs.)[1]
Preferred	unlimited	nil
Common	unlimited	20,984,665

[1] At May 19, 2023

Major Shareholder - Widely held at Nov. 8, 2021.

Price Range - VIN/CSE

Year	Volume	High	Low	Close
2022	5,541,864	$0.30	$0.08	$0.08
2021	19,132,102	$1.45	$0.25	$0.28
2020	5,150,782	$0.40	$0.05	$0.28
2019	1,147,020	$1.00	$0.05	$0.05

Consolidation: 1-for-5 cons. in May 2023
Recent Close: $0.21
Capital Stock Changes - On May 19, 2023, common shares were consolidated on a 1-for-5 basis. In June 2023, private placement of 17,000,000 units (1 post-consolidated common share & 1 warrant) at 5¢ per unit was completed, with warrants exercisable at 6¢ per share for one year, and 2,500,000 post-consolidated common shares were issued for debt settlement.

Financial Statistics

Periods ended:	12m Feb. 28/22[A]		12m Feb. 28/21[A]
	$000s	%Chg	$000s
Realized invest. gain (loss)	398		nil
Unrealized invest. gain (loss)	(81)		nil
Total revenue	**317**	**n.a.**	**nil**
General & admin. expense	828		71
Stock-based compensation	643		376
Operating expense	**1,471**	**+229**	**447**
Operating income	**(1,154)**	**n.a.**	**(447)**
Finance costs, gross	51		78
Pre-tax income	**(1,205)**	**n.a.**	**(719)**
Net income	**(1,205)**	**n.a.**	**(719)**
Cash & equivalent	1,296		128
Accounts receivable	nil		21
Current assets	1,316		299
Long-term investments	780		nil
Total assets	**2,096**	**+601**	**299**
Accts. pay. & accr. liabs	1,120		1,140
Current liabilities	1,355		1,621
Long-term debt, gross	235		481
Equity portion of conv. debs	176		176
Shareholders' equity	741		(1,321)
Cash from oper. activs	**(898)**	**n.a.**	**(180)**
Cash from fin. activs	2,378		377
Cash from invest. activs	(313)		(150)
Net cash position	**1,296**	**+912**	**128**
	$		$
Earnings per share*	(0.05)		(0.05)
Cash flow per share*	(0.04)		(0.01)
	shs		shs
No. of shs. o/s*	21,051,332		15,823,199
Avg. no. of shs. o/s*	20,336,451		12,531,144
	%		%
Net profit margin	(380.13)		n.a.
Return on equity	n.m.		n.m.
Return on assets	(96.37)		(321.30)

* Common
[A] Reported in accordance with IFRS

Latest Results

Periods ended:	3m May 31/22[A]		3m May 31/21[A]
	$000s	%Chg	$000s
Total revenue	(85)	n.a.	50
Net income	(188)	n.a.	(246)
	$		$
Earnings per share*	(0.01)		(0.01)

* Common
[A] Reported in accordance with IFRS

Historical Summary
(as originally stated)

Fiscal Year	Total Rev.	Net Inc. Bef. Disc.	EPS*
	$000s	$000s	$
2022[A]	317	(1,205)	(0.05)
2021[A]	nil	(719)	(0.05)
2020[A]	nil	(2,726)	(0.25)
2019[A]	nil	(1,240)	(0.15)
2018[A]	nil	(272)	(0.05)

* Common
[A] Reported in accordance with IFRS
Note: Adjusted throughout for 1-for-5 cons. in May 2023

V.36 Vision Marine Technologies Inc.

Symbol - VMAR **Exchange** - NASDAQ **CUSIP** - 636992
Head Office - 730 boul du Curé-Boivin, Boisbriand, QC, J7G 2A7 **Telephone** - (450) 951-7009 **Toll-free** - (800) 871-4274
Website - visionmarinetechnologies.com
Email - bn@v-mti.com
Investor Relations - Bruce Nurse (800) 871-4274
Auditors - Ernst & Young LLP C.A., Montréal, Qué.
Lawyers - Dentons US LLP, New York, N.Y.
Transfer Agents - VStock Transfer. LLC, Woodmere, N.Y.
Profile - (Que. 2012) Designs, develops and manufactures outboard power train systems and electric boats featuring lithium-ion batteries. Also operates an electric boat rental business in California.

The company has developed E-Motion, the world's first 180 HP (horsepower) electric propulsion engine. It is a fully electric outboard motor that combines an advanced battery pack, inverter and high efficiency motor. Has yet to commercialize its electric powertrains but has received non-binding letters of intent from original equipment manufacturers for over 1,000 powertrains through the year ended Aug. 31, 2024. The projected sales price for its first electric outboard powertrain system is $100,000.

Manufactures four models of electric recreational powerboats (Bruce 22, Volt 180, Fantail 217 and Quietude 156). Models range in price from $22,995 up to $325,000. Powerboats are sold to retail customers and operators of rental fleets of powerboats. During fiscal 2021, the company sold 49 electric powerboats compared with 47 during the prior fiscal year. The company has manufacturing facilities in Boisbriand, Que., capable of producing up to 300 electric powertrains and 150 boats per year.

Also operates an electric boat rental business in Newport, Calif., with a fleet of 20 electric powerboats, in order to build brand awareness.

Directors - Patrick Bobby, co-founder, Qué.; Alexandre (Alex) Mongeon, co-founder & CEO, Qué.; Carter Murray, chr.; Steve P. Barrenechea, Calif.; Renaud Cloutier, Qué.; Luisa Ingargiola, Tampa, Fla.; Mario Saucier, Montréal, Qué.

Other Exec. Officers - Xavier Montagne, COO & chief tech. officer; Kulwant Sandher, CFO

Capital Stock

	Authorized (shs.)	Outstanding (shs.)[1]
Common	unlimited	9,545,256

[1] At Apr. 12, 2023

Major Shareholder - Alexandre (Alex) Mongeon held 30.1% interest, Patrick Bobby held 26.7% interest and Robert Ghetti held 12.8% interest at Dec. 21, 2021.

Price Range - VMAR/NASDAQ

Year	Volume	High	Low	Close
2022	1,901,283	US$8.74	US$3.35	US$4.61
2021	5,336,066	US$17.46	US$4.55	US$4.84
2020	5,136,628	US$17.89	US$11.00	US$13.45

Wholly Owned Subsidiaries

7858078 Canada Inc., Canada.
- 100% int. in **Electric Boat Rental Ltd.**, Newport Beach, Calif.

Financial Statistics

Periods ended:	12m Aug. 31/21[A]		12m Aug. 31/20[A]
	$000s	%Chg	$000s
Operating revenue	**3,514**	**+45**	**2,417**
Cost of sales	1,677		1,670
Salaries & benefits	1,755		315
Research & devel. expense	1,490		nil
General & admin expense	3,887		1,106
Stock-based compensation	7,121		1,312
Operating expense	**15,930**	**+262**	**4,403**
Operating income	**(12,416)**	**n.a.**	**(1,986)**
Deprec., depl. & amort	417		170
Finance costs, gross	123		107
Pre-tax income	**(15,008)**	**n.a.**	**(2,254)**
Income taxes	106		21
Net income	**(15,114)**	**n.a.**	**(2,276)**
Cash & equivalent	18,148		1,297
Inventories	1,976		492
Accounts receivable	320		79
Current assets	21,321		2,441
Fixed assets, net	1,415		538
Right-of-use assets	2,905		653
Intangibles, net	1,226		nil
Total assets	**38,801**	**+968**	**3,632**
Bank indebtedness	nil		170
Accts. pay. & accr. liabs	848		640
Current liabilities	2,695		1,907
Long-term debt, gross	64		412
Long-term debt, net	54		354
Long-term lease liabilities	2,405		552
Shareholders' equity	33,525		792
Cash from oper. activs	**(8,251)**	**n.a.**	**(435)**
Cash from fin. activs	34,571		1,732
Cash from invest. activs	(468)		(38)
Net cash position	**18,148**	**n.m.**	**1,297**
Capital expenditures	(544)		(78)
Capital disposals	34		nil
	$		$
Earnings per share*	(2.04)		(0.56)
Cash flow per share*	(1.11)		(0.10)
	shs		shs
No. of shs. o/s*	8,324,861		4,585,001
Avg. no. of shs. o/s*	7,412,899		4,179,017
	%		%
Net profit margin	(430.11)		(94.17)
Return on equity	(88.08)		n.m.
Return on assets	(70.65)		(78.17)
Foreign sales percent	84		66

* Common
[A] Reported in accordance with IFRS

Latest Results

Periods ended:	3m Nov. 30/21[A]
	$000s
Operating revenue	1,207
Net income	(3,428)
	$
Earnings per share*	(0.41)

* Common
[A] Reported in accordance with IFRS

Historical Summary
(as originally stated)

Fiscal Year	Oper. Rev.	Net Inc. Bef. Disc.	EPS*
	$000s	$000s	$
2021[A]	3,514	(15,114)	(2.04)
2020[A]	2,417	(2,276)	(0.56)
2019[A1]	2,869	233	0.06
2018[A1]	1,272	(186)	(0.05)

* Common
[A] Reported in accordance with IFRS
[1] All share and per share inforrmation adjusted to reflect a 1-for-3.7 share consolidation on Sept. 3, 2020, and 23,084.86-for-1 share exchange on Jan. 22, 2020.

V.37 Visionary Education Technology Holdings Group Inc.

Symbol - VEDU **Exchange** - NASDAQ **CUSIP** - 92838F
Head Office - Unit 1003, 105 Moatfield Dr, Toronto, ON, M3B 0A2 **Telephone** - (905) 739-0593 **Fax** - (905) 739-0950
Website - visiongroupca.com
Email - vedu@visiongroupca.com
Investor Relations - Katy Liu (905) 739-0593
Auditors - MNP LLP C.A., Vancouver, B.C.
Transfer Agents - Issuer Direct Corporation, Salt Lake City, Utah
Profile - (Can. 2013) Offers private online and in-person educational programs and services in Canada, providing access to secondary school, college, undergraduate and graduate, and vocational education to Canadian and international students through technological innovation developed to provide customized teaching methods.

The company's businesses are organized into three clusters: Degree-oriented Education, Vocational Education and Education Services.

Degree-oriented Education - Programs offered include the Ontario Secondary School Diploma (OSSD) (grades 9-12) program, career-oriented two-year college and four-year university programs, and master's programs. OSSD programs are offered through Visionary Academy (formerly Lowell Academy), Toronto Art School and Toronto ESchool. College and university programs are offered through Conbridge College of Business and Technology, which offers specialized programs, professional examination preparation, and professional development training courses; and MTM College (formerly Max the Mutt College of Animation, Art & Design), which offers college diploma programs in animation, concept art, and illustration and storytelling for sequential arts. Master's degree level programs are offered in collaboration with Niagara University Ontario for which the company is the exclusive student recruiting agent in Canada, China, India and certain other southeast Asian countries.

Vocational Education - Consists of programs implemented on aspects of skilled trades license training, skilled trades career training, and high demand job training. The primary vocational program currently offered is Personal Service Worker (PSW) training, in partnership with Cambrian College.

Education Services - Consists of support services offered to students at the company's schools including study visa and immigration visa services, student housing, career guidance, internship support, job placement, and funding services.

The company's schools are housed in company-owned and leased facilities in the Toronto, Ont., area. Additional facilities include a technology innovation park, a virtual visual production studio centre, a wellness industrial training centre and a smart logistic practice centre.

On July 26, 2022, the company transferred wholly owned subsidiaries **Visionary Study Abroad and Immigration Services Inc., Farvision Human Resource Service Company Inc.** and **The Princeton Career Education Group Inc.** for a nominal amount to their prior owner, Mr. Xiaofeng Wang. Mr. Wang had transferred these companies to the company in 2021 and then worked for the company until his departure in May 2022.

Recent Merger and Acquisition Activity

Status: pending **Announced:** July 31, 2023
Visionary Education Technology Holdings Group Inc. received offers for and agreed to sell two office buildings at 200 and 260 Town Center, Markham, Ont., to two unrelated parties for Cdn$25,300,000 cash. The transaction is estimated to close by Aug. 31, 2023.

Status: completed **Announced:** June 22, 2023
Visionary Education Technology Holdings Group Inc. sold an office building at 41 Metropolitan Road E, Toronto, Ont., to an unrelated party for Cdn$18,000,000 cash.

Status: completed **Announced:** Sept. 23, 2022
Visionary Education Technology Holdings Group Inc. completed the acquisition of two office buildings totaling 433,000 sq. ft. of space at 95-105 Moatfield Drive, Toronto, Ont., for US$69,700,000 (Cdn$94,400,000).

Directors - Fan Zhou, chr., CEO & founder; Dr. Simon Tang, v-chr.; William Chai; The Hon. Peter M. Milliken; Michael Viotto, Canada

Other Exec. Officers - Katy Liu, CFO; John Patrick Hughes, chief tech. dir.; Jin Luo, chief engineer; Harry Lee, v-p & China chief representative; Richard Ng, v-p; Charlotte Ge, education pres.

Capital Stock

	Authorized (shs.)	Outstanding (shs.)[1]	Par
Preference	unlimited	nil	n.p.v.
Common	unlimited	48,729,667	n.p.v.

[1] At Aug. 11, 2023

Major Shareholder - Fan Zhou held 46.7% interest at Aug. 11, 2023.

Price Range - VEDU/NASDAQ

Year	Volume	High	Low	Close
2022............	23,424,589	US$28.00	US$0.37	US$0.39

Capital Stock Changes - In June 2023, 4,546,233 common shares were issued to certain employees for services and 1,326,537 common shares were issued on conversion of a US$400,000 note plus accumulated interest of US$38,809.

On May 17, 2022, an initial public offering of 4,250,000 common shares was completed at US$4.00 per share.

Wholly Owned Subsidiaries

Farvision Career Education Group Inc., Toronto, Ont.
- 80% int. in **Maple Toronto Art Academy Inc.**, Toronto, Ont.
- 70% int. in **Max the Mutt Animation Inc.**, Toronto, Ont.
- 70% int. in **9651837 Canada Inc.**, Canada. dba Lowell Academy.
- 70% int. in **Princeton Career Education Group Inc.**, Toronto, Ont.
- 80% int. in **7621531 Canada Inc.**, Canada. dba Conbridge College of Business and Technology.
- 70% int. in **Toronto eSchool Inc.**, Toronto, Ont.

NeoCanaan Investment Corp., Richmond Hill, Ont.
- 100% int. in **Canada Animation Industry Group Inc.**, Richmond Hill, Ont.
- 100% int. in **Farvision Development Group Inc.**, Scarborough, Ont.

Visionary Education Services and Management Inc., Richmond Hill, Ont.

Financial Statistics

Periods ended:	12m Mar. 31/23[A]		12m Mar. 31/22[A]
	US$000s	%Chg	US$000s
Operating revenue	**8,433**	**+61**	**5,248**
Cost of sales	4,669		2,637
Salaries & benefits	1,137		793
General & admin expense	835		293
Operating expense	**6,641**	**+65**	**4,016**
Operating income	**1,792**	**+45**	**1,232**
Deprec., depl. & amort.	1,361		495
Finance costs, gross	3,433		906
Write-downs/write-offs	nil		(379)
Pre-tax income	**(4,434)**	**n.a.**	**256**
Income taxes	(862)		313
Net income	**(3,572)**	**n.a.**	**(56)**
Net inc. for equity hldrs	**(3,475)**	**n.a.**	**10**
Net inc. for non-cont. int.	**(98)**	**n.a.**	**(66)**
Cash & equivalent	703		798
Accounts receivable	89		2
Current assets	22,345		1,543
Fixed assets, net	69,569		23,240
Right-of-use assets	691		958
Intangibles, net	1,918		2,112
Total assets	**96,202**	**+166**	**36,227**
Accts. pay. & accr. liabs	2,847		1,744
Current liabilities	80,457		13,282
Long-term debt, gross	48,909		18,821
Long-term debt, net	nil		18,278
Long-term lease liabilities	494		747
Shareholders' equity	12,670		3,439
Non-controlling interest	49		236
Cash from oper. activs	**336**	**-95**	**6,362**
Cash from fin. activs	63,872		17,535
Cash from invest. activs	(63,413)		(24,284)
Net cash position	**1,292**	**+60**	**810**
Capital expenditures	(62,702)		nil
	US$		US$
Earnings per share*	(0.09)		0.00
Cash flow per share*	0.01		0.18
	shs		shs
No. of shs. o/s*	39,250,000		35,000,000
Avg. no. of shs. o/s*	38,689,560		35,000,000
	%		%
Net profit margin	(42.36)		(1.07)
Return on equity	(43.13)		0.29
Return on assets	(1.22)		(1.03)

* Common

[A] Reported in accordance with U.S. GAAP

Historical Summary
(as originally stated)

Fiscal Year	Oper. Rev. US$000s	Net Inc. Bef. Disc. US$000s	EPS* US$
2023[A]	8,433	(3,572)	(0.09)
2022[A]	5,248	(56)	0.00
2021[A]	7,725	2,914	0.08
2020[A]	933	242	0.01

* Common

[A] Reported in accordance with U.S. GAAP

V.38 Visionstate Corp.

Symbol - VIS **Exchange** - TSX-VEN **CUSIP** - 92836B
Head Office - 8634 53 Ave, Edmonton, AB, T6E 5G2 **Telephone** - (780) 425-9460 **Toll-free** - (855) 425-9460 **Fax** - (780) 425-9463
Website - www.visionstate.com
Email - jputters@visionstate.com
Investor Relations - John A. Putters (780) 425-9460
Auditors - Kenway Mack Slusarchuk Stewart LLP C.A., Calgary, Alta.
Transfer Agents - Computershare Trust Company of Canada Inc., Calgary, Alta.

Profile - (Alta. 2000) Offers smart touchscreen devices for the facilities management of private and public spaces in North America, and develops applications for the Internet-of-Things (IoT) market.

The company's main product, WANDA (Washroom Attendant Notification Digital Aid), is a tablet-sized smart device that replaces paper-based tracking of cleaning, maintenance and supply utilization in both public and private facilities, such as hospitals, airports, office buildings, recreational centres, casinos, shopping centres and convention centres. Also offers the Wanda QuickTouch IoT button, a device connected to an LTE-M network which allows staff to send an alert to management of an issue in a specific area or restroom, as well as the time the alert was issued; and Wanda Mobile, which allows cleaning staff to track cleaning and maintenance activities throughout any facility including outside of restrooms using a mobile application. The product has an analytics dashboard that collects information on important issues related to restroom management such as public alerts, cleaning times, resources used, and maintenance and cleaning activities performed.

The company's Virtual Customer Care interface (ViCCi™) is an interactive directory designed to assist facility users and displays stores, sales, jobs, promotions and other important information about a facility. Also invests in artificial intelligence (AI) applications through its ViCCi 2.0 product, which integrates conversational AI with customer service in brick and mortar locations.

Predecessor Detail - Name changed from CSM Systems Corp., Sept. 16, 2014.

Directors - John A. Putters, pres. & CEO, Sherwood Park, Alta.; Belinda Davidson, v-p, mktg. & bus. strategy, Alta.; James (Jim) Duke, v-p, corp. devel., Okotoks, Alta.; Ned Dimitrov, Toronto, Ont.; Kevin Gilbank, Calgary, Alta.; Dr. Angel Valov

Other Exec. Officers - Randa Kachkar, CFO & corp. sec.; Erik Johnson, chief tech. officer; Shannon Moore, pres., Visionstate IoT Inc.

Capital Stock

	Authorized (shs.)	Outstanding (shs.)[1]
Preferred	unlimited	nil
Common	unlimited	146,126,335

[1] At May 30, 2023

Major Shareholder - Widely held at Dec. 23, 2022.

Price Range - VIS/TSX-VEN

Year	Volume	High	Low	Close
2022............	11,855,965	$0.05	$0.02	$0.02
2021............	77,385,838	$0.14	$0.03	$0.05
2020............	44,800,244	$0.12	$0.02	$0.04
2019............	6,590,686	$0.14	$0.02	$0.04
2018............	24,708,860	$0.52	$0.08	$0.10

Consolidation: 1-for-4 cons. in Aug. 2019

Recent Close: $0.02

Capital Stock Changes - In December 2022, private placement of 10,045,000 units (1 common share & 1 warrant) at 2¢ per unit was completed, with warrants exercisable at 5¢ per share for two years.

During fiscal 2022, 4,350,400 common shares were issued on exercise of warrants.

Wholly Owned Subsidiaries

NEXT Vision Inc.
Visionstate IoT Inc., Edmonton, Alta. Formerly CSM Systems Inc.
Visionstate U.S. Corp., United States.

Investments

40% int. in **Exceed Solar Inc.**, Edmonton, Alta.
Freedom Cannabis Inc., Acheson, Alta.

Financial Statistics

Periods ended:	12m Sept. 30/22[A]		12m Sept. 30/21[◻A]
	$000s	%Chg	$000s
Operating revenue	**411**	**-24**	**541**
Cost of sales	46		12
Salaries & benefits	324		249
General & admin expense	598		522
Operating expense	**968**	**+24**	**783**
Operating income	**(557)**	**n.a.**	**(242)**
Deprec., depl. & amort.	15		13
Finance income	43		29
Finance costs, gross	20		37
Pre-tax income	**(613)**	**n.a.**	**(1,032)**
Income taxes	8		7
Net income	**(621)**	**n.a.**	**(1,039)**
Cash & equivalent	20		636
Inventories	nil		19
Accounts receivable	34		35
Current assets	64		913
Long-term investments	559		559
Right-of-use assets	72		7
Total assets	**977**	**-34**	**1,485**
Accts. pay. & accr. liabs	373		473
Current liabilities	603		780
Long-term debt, gross	100		100
Long-term debt, net	54		50
Long-term lease liabilities	63		nil
Shareholders' equity	257		655
Cash from oper. activs	**(766)**	**n.a.**	**(537)**
Cash from fin. activs	260		2,470
Cash from invest. activs	(110)		(1,293)
Net cash position	**20**	**-97**	**636**
	$		$
Earnings per share*	(0.01)		(0.01)
Cash flow per share*	(0.01)		(0.01)
	shs		shs
No. of shs. o/s*	110,306,335		105,955,935
Avg. no. of shs. o/s*	108,642,957		82,273,142
	%		%
Net profit margin	(151.09)		(192.05)
Return on equity	(136.18)		n.m.
Return on assets	(48.80)		(112.87)

* Common

◻ Restated

[A] Reported in accordance with IFRS

Historical Summary
(as originally stated)

Fiscal Year	Oper. Rev. $000s	Net Inc. Bef. Disc. $000s	EPS* $
2022[A]	411	(621)	(0.01)
2021[A]	541	(1,039)	(0.01)
2020[A]	130	(723)	(0.02)
2019[A]	114	(953)	(0.03)
2018[A]	200	(762)	(0.04)

* Common

[A] Reported in accordance with IFRS

Note: Adjusted throughout for 1-for-4 cons. in Aug. 2019

V.39 Vitalhub Corp.

Symbol - VHI **Exchange** - TSX **CUSIP** - 92847V
Head Office - 1001-480 University Ave, Toronto, ON, M5G 1V2 **Telephone** - (416) 699-0123 **Toll-free** - (855) 699-0123
Website - www.vitalhub.com
Email - dan.matlow@vitalhub.com
Investor Relations - Daniel Matlow (855) 699-0123
Auditors - MNP LLP C.A., Mississauga, Ont.
Lawyers - CP LLP, Toronto, Ont.
Transfer Agents - TSX Trust Company

Profile - (Ont. 2015) Provides software solutions in the categories of Electric Health Record (EHR), case management, care coordination and optimization and patient flow, engagement and operational visibility solutions to health and human service providers including hospitals, regional health authorities, mental health, long-term care, home health, community and social services.

Products include TREAT, a web-based EHR and care coordination platform with e-prescribing for single and multi-organization providers supporting inpatient, outpatient, community, residential and supportive housing services; B Care, an inpatient and community EHR with electronic medication administration record; Pirouette, a case management solution for smaller agencies such as community and social service organizations; Clarity, a web-based interface and data entry solution for resident assessments and reportings for complex continuing and long-term care settings; Intouch with Health, a patient flow solutions which enables healthcare organizations to manage all aspects of hospital patient journeys; Transforming Systems, a portfolio of real-time patient dashboards which offers simple visualization of large amounts of complex data that span multiple sites, sectors and providers; Shrewd, a platform of data ingestion tools that collate and store data, ready for use by Shrewd modules; S12 solutions, an application and website platform which helps mental health professionals efficiently complete Mental Health Act 1983 process; Jayex, a hospital outpatient flow management system that is hosted on premise; Alamac, a specialist consultancy which helps health and social care systems restore patient flow by providing tools, analytics and delivery expertise; Beautiful Information, which offers real-time information at individual patient level to the U.K.'s National Health Service health and social care sector as well as organizations and industries that sit on the periphery of health such as population health management specialties, residential care home providers, cancer alliance organizations, and health science and academia networks; Hicom, which develops software that automates healthcare and business processes worldwide including mission-critical healthcare centred processes; Community Data Solutions, which offers an online case management system and products which support critical workflows in the community services and not-for-profit organizations; MyPathway, a digital health platform which deals with patient interactions during treatment for long term conditions as well as for individuals visiting acute facilities for shorter term elective or outpatient services; and Coyote, which specializes in tailored software that streamline the workflows of health and social organizations including CaseWORKS, an enterprise-class case management software, as well as formWORKS, ScanWORKS and ShareWORKS, which forms automation, records scanning and document sharing, respectively.

On Jan. 23, 2023, the company acquired private Ontario-based **Coyote Software Corporation**, which offers tailored software solutions that streamline the workflows of health and social service organizations, for $2,373,528, consisting of $2,265,528 cash and issuance of 38,163 common shares at a deemed price of $2.83 per share.

On Jan. 1, 2023, wholly owned **Oculys Health Informatics Inc.** was amalgamated into the company. In addition, wholly owned **Intouch with Health Ltd.**, **Transforming Systems Limited**, **Alamac Limited**, **Beautiful Information Limited** and **The OakGroup (UK) Limited** were amalgamated and continued under **Vitalhub UK Limited**.

In November 2022, the company acquired certain assets of **Advanced Digital Innovation (UK) Limited** for £250,000. The acquisition includes MyPathway, a digital health platform, which is used for patient interactions during treatment for both long term and short term elective conditions as well as outpatient services.

Recent Merger and Acquisition Activity

Status: completed **Announced:** Oct. 11, 2022

Vitalhub Corp. acquired Adelaide, South Australia-based QWAD Community Technologies Pty Ltd. (dba Community Data Solutions) for A$8,197,155. Community Data Solutions (CDS) offers online case management system and supporting products which support critical clinical workflows in the community services sector including counselling, case work, anti-poverty programs, aged care and disability services. CDS generated approximately A$4,000,000 of which A$2,800,000 was identified to be recurring in nature for the trailing 12-month period ended Sept. 30, 2022.

Status: completed **Announced:** Apr. 25, 2022

Vitalhub Corp. acquired England and Wales-based Hicom Technology Limited for £8,700,000 (Cdn$14,113,966) consisting of £7,825,000 cash and issuance of 475,104 common shares at a fair value of L875,000. Hicom develops software which automates healthcare and business processes across a diverse client base of over 200.

Predecessor Detail - Name changed from Quinsam Opportunities I Inc., Nov. 28, 2016, following Qualifying Transaction reverse takeover acquisition of and vertical amalgamation with (old) Vitalhub Corp.

Directors - Chris Schnarr, chr., Mississauga, Ont.; Daniel (Dan) Matlow, pres. & CEO, Thornhill, Ont.; Roger Dent, Toronto, Ont.; Stephen (Steve) Garrington, Sydney, N.S.W., Australia; Anthony P. (Tony) Shen, Toronto, Ont.; Francis N. Shen, Toronto, Ont.; Barry A. Tissenbaum, Toronto, Ont.

Other Exec. Officers - Andre Vandenberk, chief innovation officer; Vijit Coomara, exec. v-p, product devel.; Brian Goffenberg, exec. v-p & CFO; Robert Lazar, exec. v-p, professional srvcs. & support; Patrick Mazza, exec. v-p, performance & opers.; Niels Tofting, exec. v-p, bus. devel. & mktg.

Capital Stock

	Authorized (shs.)	Outstanding (shs.)[1]
Preferred	unlimited	nil
Common	unlimited	43,629,912

[1] At May 12, 2023

Major Shareholder - Shen Capital Corporation held 15.28% interest and Burgundy Asset Management Ltd. held 15.22% interest at May 12, 2023.

Price Range - VHI/TSX

Year	Volume	High	Low	Close
2022	6,532,841	$3.45	$2.19	$2.65
2021	10,978,636	$3.77	$2.63	$3.30
2020	13,411,629	$3.42	$1.20	$2.85
2019	7,111,313	$2.60	$1.40	$1.75
2018	14,490,882	$3.40	$0.95	$1.45

Consolidation: 1-for-10 cons. in Jan. 2020

Recent Close: $2.80

Capital Stock Changes - On Jan. 23, 2023, 38,163 common shares were issued pursuant to the acquisition of Coyote Software Corporation.

In April 2022, bought deal public offering of 5,645,200 common shares was completed at $3.10 per share, including 846,780 common shares on exercise of over-allotment option. Also during 2022, common shares were issued as follows: 495,500 on exercise of options, 475,104 pursuant to the acquisition of Hicom Technology Limited, 90,266 pursuant to the acquisition of Beautiful Information Limited and 45,750 on exercise of warrants; 45,750 common shares were repurchased under a Normal Course Issuer Bid.

Wholly Owned Subsidiaries

B Sharp Technologies Inc., Ont.
- 100% int. in **VitalHub (PVT) Ltd.**, Sri Lanka.

Coyote Software Corporation, Ont.

H.I. Next Inc., Ont.
- 100% int. in **H.I. Next LLC**, Md.

Hicom Technology Limited, United Kingdom.

MyPathway Solutions Limited, United Kingdom.

QWAD Community Technologies Pty Ltd., Adelaide, S.A., Australia. dba Community Data Solutions

Roxy Software Inc., Ont.

S12 Solutions Ltd., United Kingdom.

Vitalhub Australia Pty Ltd., Vic., Australia.

Financial Statistics

Periods ended:	12m Dec. 31/22[A]		12m Dec. 31/21[oA]
	$000s	%Chg	$000s
Operating revenue	**39,971**	**+62**	**24,665**
Cost of sales	7,032		5,237
Research & devel. expense	10,431		6,046
General & admin expense	12,832		8,694
Stock-based compensation	1,140		1,717
Operating expense	**31,435**	**+45**	**21,694**
Operating income	**8,536**	**+187**	**2,971**
Deprec., depl. & amort.	3,873		2,676
Finance costs, net	70		53
Pre-tax income	**1,307**	**n.a.**	**(1,614)**
Income taxes	92		333
Net income	**1,215**	**n.a.**	**(1,947)**
Cash & equivalent	17,452		16,390
Inventories	704		200
Accounts receivable	11,411		5,561
Current assets	30,567		22,624
Fixed assets, net	663		534
Right-of-use assets	766		707
Intangibles, net	74,190		48,907
Total assets	**106,187**	**+48**	**71,772**
Accts. pay. & accr. liabs	6,022		4,064
Current liabilities	23,818		14,734
Long-term debt, gross	nil		29
Long-term lease liabilities	510		522
Shareholders' equity	75,398		54,825
Cash from oper. activs	**6,122**	**n.m.**	**402**
Cash from fin. activs	16,403		(10,476)
Cash from invest. activs	(21,844)		3,167
Net cash position	**17,452**	**+6**	**16,390**
Capital expenditures	(267)		(221)
	$		$
Earnings per share*	0.03		(0.05)
Cash flow per share*	0.15		0.01
	shs		shs
No. of shs. o/s*	43,599,648		36,939,428
Avg. no. of shs. o/s*	41,493,038		36,396,337
	%		%
Net profit margin	3.04		(7.89)
Return on equity	1.87		(3.70)
Return on assets	1.37		(2.87)
Foreign sales percent	505		236

* Common
[o] Restated
[A] Reported in accordance with IFRS

Latest Results

Periods ended:	3m Mar. 31/23[A]		3m Mar. 31/22[A]
	$000s	%Chg	$000s
Operating revenue	12,595	+34	9,423
Net income	162	-89	1,438
	$		$
Earnings per share*	0.01		0.04

* Common
[A] Reported in accordance with IFRS

Historical Summary
(as originally stated)

Fiscal Year	Oper. Rev.	Net Inc. Bef. Disc.	EPS*
	$000s	$000s	$
2022[A]	39,971	1,215	0.03
2021[A]	24,665	(1,947)	(0.05)
2020[A]	13,794	(2,166)	(0.08)
2019[A]	10,228	(626)	(0.04)
2018[A]	9,114	(862)	(0.07)

* Common
[A] Reported in accordance with IFRS

Note: Adjusted throughout for 1-for-10 cons. in Jan. 2020

V.40 Vitality Products Inc.

Symbol - VPI **Exchange** - TSX-VEN **CUSIP** - 92847D

Head Office - 304-837 Hastings St W, Vancouver, BC, V6C 3N6 **Telephone** - (604) 591-1322 **Toll-free** - (888) 855-7776 **Fax** - (604) 662-8524

Website - www.vitality.ca

Email - dgrant@vitality.ca

Investor Relations - W. Douglas Grant (604) 683-6611

Auditors - HLB Cinnamon, Jang, Willoughby & Company C.A., Burnaby, B.C.

Bankers - Bank of Montreal, Vancouver, B.C.

Lawyers - McMillan LLP, Vancouver, B.C.

Transfer Agents - TSX Trust Company, Vancouver, B.C.

Profile - (B.C. 1984) Manufactures, markets and distributes natural health products, including vitamins, minerals and nutritional supplements under the VITALITY® brand.

Markets and licenses its 13 natural health products in Canada and the U.S., through more than 600 retail stores across Canada, and online through www.findmyvitality.com, vitality.ca, well.ca, amazon.ca and amazon.com. Products include Power Iron + Organic Spirulina, Daily Iron + Organic Spirulina, Time Release Super Multi+, Time Release B Complex + C 600 mg, Digest+, Trace Minerals + Organic Chlorella, Magnesium + Chamomile Capsules, Magnesium + Chamomile Powder for Kids, Magnesium + Chamomile Powder for Adults, Relax+, Marine Collagen + Cranberry, Marine Collagen + Biotin and Marine Collagen + Rose.

The company maintains a distribution facility in Vancouver, B.C., and an investment property, which is an undeveloped parcel of land in Whatcom cty., Wash.

Predecessor Detail - Name changed from Startec Marketing Corporation, Feb. 9, 1993; basis 1 new for 5 old shs.

Directors - Cheryl A. Grant, pres. & CEO, Vancouver, B.C.; W. Douglas Grant, v-p, CFO & corp. sec., Vancouver, B.C.; Audra J. Davies, Gabriola, B.C.; Richard V. (Rick) Gannon, Oliver, B.C.; Stuart E. Pennington, Blaine, Wash.; Joanne F. Q. Yan, Vancouver, B.C.

Capital Stock

	Authorized (shs.)	Outstanding (shs.)[1]	Par
Cl.A Pfce.	unlimited		$10
Series 1	27,100	2,500[2]	
Series 2	4,675	nil	
Series 3	39,500	26,920[2]	
Series 4	22,775	nil	
Series 5	32,927	nil	
Series 6	46,000	nil	
Cl.B Pfce.	unlimited	nil	$50
Common	unlimited	41,411,285	n.p.v.

[1] At Sept. 29, 2022
[2] Classified as debt.

Class A Series 1 & 3 Preferred - Entitled to 6% cumulative dividends. Redeemable at $10 per share plus accrued dividends. Non-voting and non-participating. At Sept. 29, 2022, cumulative undeclared dividends totaled $378,701.

Common - One vote per share.

Major Shareholder - The estate of William N. Grant held 27.77% interest at June 9, 2022.

Price Range - VPI/TSX-VEN

Year	Volume	High	Low	Close
2022	2,966,540	$0.12	$0.03	$0.05
2021	6,972,026	$0.40	$0.08	$0.11
2020	4,488,636	$0.21	$0.05	$0.14
2019	1,842,751	$0.24	$0.09	$0.16
2018	5,658,265	$0.29	$0.08	$0.24

Recent Close: $0.04

Financial Statistics

Periods ended:	12m Jan. 31/22[A]		12m Jan. 31/21[□A]
	$000s	%Chg	$000s
Operating revenue	**860**	**+4**	**828**
Cost of sales	228		200
Salaries & benefits	589		342
General & admin expense	550		414
Stock-based compensation	79		24
Operating expense	**1,446**	**+47**	**981**
Operating income	**(586)**	**n.a.**	**(153)**
Deprec., depl. & amort.	8		6
Finance income	3		2
Finance costs, gross	24		22
Pre-tax income	**(617)**	**n.a.**	**(180)**
Net income	**(617)**	**n.a.**	**(180)**
Cash & equivalent	1,003		638
Inventories	188		226
Accounts receivable	197		181
Current assets	1,426		1,055
Long-term investments	239		239
Fixed assets, net	18		13
Total assets	**1,682**	**+28**	**1,317**
Accts. pay. & accr. liabs.	225		177
Current liabilities	2,242		2,301
Long-term lease liabilities	nil		4
Shareholders' equity	(560)		(987)
Cash from oper. activs	**(582)**	**n.a.**	**(277)**
Cash from fin. activs	959		572
Cash from invest. activs	(363)		(353)
Net cash position	**51**	**+38**	**37**
Capital expenditures	(13)		(3)
	$		$
Earnings per share*	(0.02)		(0.01)
Cash flow per share*	(0.01)		(0.01)
	shs		shs
No. of shs. o/s*	41,411,285		35,411,285
Avg. no. of shs. o/s*	40,194,847		33,290,452
	%		%
Net profit margin	(71.74)		(21.74)
Return on equity	n.m.		n.m.
Return on assets	(39.55)		(14.10)
Foreign sales percent	6		11

* Common
[□] Restated
[A] Reported in accordance with IFRS

Latest Results

Periods ended:	6m July 31/22[A]		6m July 31/21[□A]
	$000s	%Chg	$000s
Operating revenue	436	+5	414
Net income	(338)	n.a.	(358)
	$		$
Earnings per share*	(0.01)		(0.01)

* Common
[□] Restated
[A] Reported in accordance with IFRS

Historical Summary
(as originally stated)

Fiscal Year	Oper. Rev.	Net Inc. Bef. Disc.	EPS*
	$000s	$000s	$
2022[A]	860	(617)	(0.02)
2021[A]	803	(180)	(0.01)
2020[A]	618	(63)	(0.00)
2019[A]	528	(355)	(0.01)
2018[A]	429	(27)	(0.00)

* Common
[A] Reported in accordance with IFRS

V.41 Vitreous Glass Inc.

Symbol - VCI **Exchange** - TSX-VEN **CUSIP** - 92852B
Head Office - 212 East Lake Blvd NE, Airdrie, AB, T4B 2B5 **Telephone** - (403) 948-7811 **Fax** - (403) 948-7962
Website - www.vitreousglass.ca
Email - admin@vitreousglass.ca
Investor Relations - Darcy Forbes (403) 948-7811
Auditors - MNP LLP C.A., Calgary, Alta.
Lawyers - Moodys Tax Law LLP, Calgary, Alta.
Transfer Agents - Computershare Trust Company of Canada Inc., Toronto, Ont.
Profile - (Alta. 1992 amalg.) Cleans, crushes and sells waste glass to the fibreglass manufacturing industry in Alberta.
Operates a waste glass processing plant in Airdrie, Alta., which gathers post-consumer waste glass from Alberta and elsewhere, crushes it, removes contaminants and sells the final product to three manufacturers of fibreglass building insulation for use as a raw material.
Predecessor Detail - Name changed from Vitreous Capital Inc., Feb. 15, 2007.
Directors - David G. Birkby, chr., Calgary, Alta.; J. Patrick (Pat) Cashion, pres. & CEO, Calgary, Alta.; Timothy H. Rendell, CFO, Victoria, B.C.; Meredith Cashion, Calgary, Alta.; Joanne A. Hruska, Calgary, Alta.
Other Exec. Officers - Darcy Forbes, v-p & COO; Mary Ann Hickey, corp. sec.

Capital Stock

	Authorized (shs.)	Outstanding (shs.)[1]
Preferred	unlimited	nil
Common	unlimited	6,283,667

[1] At Jan. 27, 2023

Major Shareholder - J. Patrick (Pat) Cashion held 23.6% interest and Meredith Cashion held 13.4% interest at Jan. 27, 2023.

Price Range - VCI/TSX-VEN

Year	Volume	High	Low	Close
2022	711,395	$5.35	$3.61	$4.20
2021	1,773,294	$6.50	$4.00	$4.58
2020	921,794	$4.20	$2.32	$3.97
2019	754,187	$4.10	$3.43	$3.62
2018	477,525	$4.14	$3.26	$3.56

Recent Close: $5.45

Capital Stock Changes - There were no changes to capital stock from fiscal 2017 to fiscal 2022, inclusive.

Dividends

VCI com N.S.R.

$0.06◆	Aug. 15/23	$0.11◆	May 15/23
$0.19◆	Feb. 15/23	$0.06◆	Nov. 15/22

Paid in 2023: $0.36◆ 2022: $0.31◆ 2021: $0.46◆

◆ Special

Financial Statistics

Periods ended:	12m Sept. 30/22[A]		12m Sept. 30/21[A]
	$000s	%Chg	$000s
Operating revenue	**9,623**	**-21**	**12,119**
Cost of sales	4,228		4,757
Salaries & benefits	1,162		1,250
General & admin expense	1,184		1,623
Stock-based compensation	52		nil
Operating expense	**6,626**	**-13**	**7,630**
Operating income	**2,997**	**-33**	**4,489**
Deprec., depl. & amort.	148		125
Pre-tax income	**2,849**	**-35**	**4,364**
Income taxes	677		990
Net income	**2,172**	**-36**	**3,374**
Cash & equivalent	1,744		2,453
Inventories	1,019		521
Accounts receivable	470		448
Current assets	3,381		3,465
Fixed assets, net	2,034		1,584
Right-of-use assets	79		96
Total assets	**5,494**	**+7**	**5,145**
Accts. pay. & accr. liabs.	823		715
Current liabilities	842		734
Long-term lease liabilities	81		100
Shareholders' equity	4,258		4,159
Cash from oper. activs	**1,969**	**-56**	**4,518**
Cash from fin. activs	(2,098)		(3,480)
Cash from invest. activs	(580)		(109)
Net cash position	**1,744**	**-29**	**2,453**
Capital expenditures	(580)		(109)
	$		$
Earnings per share*	0.35		0.54
Cash flow per share*	0.31		0.72
Extra divd. - cash*	0.33		0.55
	shs		shs
No. of shs. o/s*	6,283,667		6,283,667
Avg. no. of shs. o/s*	6,283,667		6,283,667
	%		%
Net profit margin	22.57		27.84
Return on equity	51.61		80.33
Return on assets	40.83		63.36

* Common
[A] Reported in accordance with IFRS

Latest Results

Periods ended:	3m Dec. 31/22[A]		3m Dec. 31/21[A]
	$000s	%Chg	$000s
Operating revenue	2,913	+31	2,218
Net income	731	+39	526
	$		$
Earnings per share*	0.11		0.08

* Common
[A] Reported in accordance with IFRS

Historical Summary
(as originally stated)

Fiscal Year	Oper. Rev.	Net Inc. Bef. Disc.	EPS*
	$000s	$000s	$
2022[A]	9,623	2,172	0.35
2021[A]	12,119	3,374	0.54
2020[A]	9,362	2,316	0.37
2019[A]	8,505	1,769	0.28
2018[A]	8,628	2,120	0.34

* Common
[A] Reported in accordance with IFRS

V.42 Voice Mobility International, Inc.

Symbol - VMY.H **Exchange** - TSX-VEN **CUSIP** - 928622
Head Office - 1600-609 Granville St, Vancouver, BC, V7Y 1C3 **Telephone** - (778) 298-7116 **Fax** - (866) 824-8938
Email - j.hutton@shaw.ca
Investor Relations - James Hutton (778) 298-7116
Auditors - Dale Matheson Carr-Hilton LaBonte LLP C.A., Vancouver, B.C.
Lawyers - Clark Wilson LLP, Vancouver, B.C.; Fasken Martineau DuMoulin LLP, Vancouver, B.C.
Transfer Agents - Computershare Trust Company of Canada Inc., Vancouver, B.C.
Profile - (Nev. 1997) Provides unified communications services to small and medium-size business professionals throughout North America.
Through its Tagline Communications division, the company offers services including 1-800 numbers, voice recognition, fax to email, auto attendant, web-based telephony and conferencing functionality, either individually or as a service bundle.
Directors - James (Jay) Hutton, chr., CEO & acting CFO, Langley, B.C.; Aron Buchman, Vancouver, B.C.; Theresa Carbonneau; Sean O'Mahony, B.C.; Glen Scharf
Other Exec. Officers - Mike Seeley, v-p, global sales

Capital Stock

	Authorized (shs.)	Outstanding (shs.)[1]	Par
Preferred	21,000,000		US$0.001
Series A		1	
Series B		nil	
Series C		19,250,280[2]	
Common	100,000,000	5,242,874	US$0.001

[1] At May 26, 2022
[2] Classified as debt.

Preferred Series A - Issued in trust, providing the mechanism for holders of exchangeable shares of wholly owned Voice Mobility Canada Limited to have voting rights in the company.
Preferred Series C - Convertible into common shares on the basis of 25 preferred shares for one common share. Retractable at Cdn$0.35 per share. Redeemable at any time upon 30 days' notice at Cdn$0.35 per share. Non-voting.
Common - One vote per share.
Major Shareholder - 652420 B.C. Ltd. held 14.42% interest at July 27, 2021.

Price Range - VMY.H/TSX-VEN

Year	Volume	High	Low	Close
2022	34,705	$0.07	$0.01	$0.01
2021	55,700	$0.13	$0.07	$0.07
2020	129,281	$0.08	$0.02	$0.07
2019	155,360	$0.05	$0.02	$0.02
2018	270,108	$0.08	$0.03	$0.04

Recent Close: $0.01

Wholly Owned Subsidiaries

VM Sub Limited, Canada. Inactive.
Voice Mobility Canada Limited, Canada. Inactive.
Voice Mobility Inc., B.C.

Financial Statistics

Periods ended:	12m Dec. 31/21[A]		12m Dec. 31/20[A]
	$000s	%Chg	$000s
Operating revenue	**55**	**-24**	**72**
Cost of sales	23		38
General & admin expense	125		130
Operating expense	**148**	**-12**	**168**
Operating income	**(93)**	**n.a.**	**(96)**
Finance costs, gross	658		571
Pre-tax income	**(756)**	**n.a.**	**(672)**
Net income	**(756)**	**n.a.**	**(672)**
Cash & equivalent	35		48
Accounts receivable	19		24
Current assets	54		422
Total assets	**54**	**-87**	**422**
Bank indebtedness	3,208		3,171
Accts. pay. & accr. liabs	1,032		1,302
Current liabilities	14,368		14,067
Long-term debt, gross	9,872		9,338
Equity portion of conv. debs	4,572		4,572
Shareholders' equity	(14,314)		(13,645)
Cash from oper. activs	**(14)**	**n.a.**	**(31)**
Cash from fin. activs	nil		64
Net cash position	**35**	**-27**	**48**
	$		$
Earnings per share*	(0.17)		(0.17)
Cash flow per share*	(0.00)		(0.01)
	shs		shs
No. of shs. o/s*	5,242,874		3,997,717
Avg. no. of shs. o/s*	4,530,367		3,997,717
	%		%
Net profit margin	n.m.		(933.33)
Return on equity	n.m.		n.m.
Return on assets	(41.18)		(43.82)

* Common
[A] Reported in accordance with IFRS

Latest Results

Periods ended:	3m Mar. 31/22[A]		3m Mar. 31/21[A]
	$000s	%Chg	$000s
Operating revenue	12	-20	15
Net income	(194)	n.a.	(174)
	$		$
Earnings per share*	(0.04)		(0.04)

* Common
[A] Reported in accordance with IFRS

Historical Summary
(as originally stated)

Fiscal Year	Oper. Rev.	Net Inc. Bef. Disc.	EPS*
	$000s	$000s	$
2021[A]	55	(756)	(0.17)
2020[A]	72	(672)	(0.17)
2019[A]	81	196	0.05
2018[A]	96	(1,189)	(0.30)
2017[A]	107	(1,193)	(0.30)

* Common
[A] Reported in accordance with IFRS

V.43 Volatus Aerospace Corp.

Symbol - VOL **Exchange** - TSX-VEN **CUSIP** - 92865G
Head Office - Lake Simcoe Regional Airport, 60 Airport Rd, Oro-Medonte, ON, L0L 2E0 **Telephone** - (905) 676-0092 **Toll-free** - (877) 753-8462 **Fax** - (905) 676-0192
Website - www.volatusaerospace.com
Email - luc.masse@volatusaerospace.com
Investor Relations - Luc Massé (905) 676-0092
Auditors - MS Partners LLP C.A., Toronto, Ont.
Lawyers - Wildeboer Dellelce LLP, Toronto, Ont.
Transfer Agents - TSX Trust Company, Toronto, Ont.
Profile - (Ont. 2021 amalg.) Distributes and sells unmanned aerial (drone) products and services for both civilian and military applications. Also provides full-service flight management and aircraft charter sales, operating a wide range of corporate aircraft.

The company offers unmanned aerial vehicle (UAV) system sales and training, aerial inspection and imaging services, data processing and management, system design engineering, research and development, manufacturing, maintenance and repair. Services are provided to a variety of industries including energy, construction, agricultural, wildlife and forestry, infrastructure and videography and media. It has a physical presence in British Columbia, Alberta, Manitoba, Ontario, Quebec, Prince Edward Island, New York, Pennsylvania, New Jersey, Lima and Emsworth. In addition, designs, manufactures and sells unmanned all-terrain vehicles and has a network of more than 1,200 Transport Canada-qualified UAV pilots available to the company to support service delivery in every province and territory of Canada.

Through Volatus Aviation (Partner Jet) business, provides full-service aircraft management, private aircraft charter sales and flight support services capable of operating a wide range of corporate aircraft. The majority of Volatus Aviation's revenue is generated from aircraft management contracts, which cover the piloting and operation of corporate jets owned by independent corporations, with the balance from charter activities and aircraft maintenance contracts.

In April 2023, the company acquired N.J.-based **Sky Scape Industries, LLC.**, an airborne intelligence data services provider, for issuance 969,737 common shares at a closing price of 38¢ per share and an earn-out issuance of US$310,000 of common shares after the one-year anniversary of acquisition.

In January 2023, the company acquired Syracuse, N.Y.-based **Empire Drone Company LLC**, an unmanned aerial systems distributor and integrator, for US$300,000 cash, issuance of 721,538 common shares at a deemed price of 65¢ per share and issuance of up to 721,538 common shares at a deemed price of 65¢ per share, subject to certain revenue milestones after the one-year anniversary of acquisition.

In November 2022, the company entered into a joint venture agreement with **EOLO Holdings S.A.** to establish Panama-based **Volatus Aerospace LATAM S.A.** (Volatus LATAM). The company owns 75% interest in Volatus LATAM while EOLO holds the remaining 25%. Volatus LATAM develops, markets, and distributes all of the company's products in Central and South America.

In November 2022, the company acquired 51% interest in Emsworth, U.K.-based **iRed Ltd.**, a drone service and training company, for £100,000 and 51% interest in Alberta-based **Synergy Aviation Ltd.**, a oil and gas pipeline inspection and surveillance company, for $2,290,000 and option to acquire the remaining 49% in 2024 upon Synergy meeting certain operational and financial metrics for a maximum issuance of $2,205,000 of common shares.

In April 2022, the company acquired Ontario-based **Canadian Air National Inc,**, a commercial air carrier performing right of way patrol for utility companies, for a total consideration of $90,000.

On Mar. 2, 2022, common shares were listed on the OTCQB market under the stock symbol VLTTF.

Predecessor Detail - Formed from Partner Jet Corp. in Ontario, Dec. 22, 2021, pursuant to reverse takeover acquisition of and amalgamation with (old) Volatus Aerospace Corp.; basis 1 new for 2.95454 old shs.

Directors - Ian A. McDougall, chr., Caledon, Ont.; Glen Lynch, pres. & CEO, Dollard-des-Ormeaux, Qué.; Samuel W. Ingram, Toronto, Ont.; Lt.-Gen. (ret.) Andrew Leslie, Ottawa, Ont.; Gordon Silverman, Fla.

Other Exec. Officers - Abhinav Singhvi, CFO; Luc Massé, exec. v-p & corp. sec.; Robert Walker, v-p, bus. devel. & COO

Capital Stock

	Authorized (shs.)	Outstanding (shs.)[1]
Preferred	unlimited	206,188
Common	unlimited	114,664,617

[1] At May 23, 2023

Preferred - Non-convertible. Non-voting.
Common - One vote per share.
Major Shareholder - Ian A. McDougall held 34.03% interest and Glen Lynch held 33.54% interest at May 23, 2023.

Price Range - VOL/TSX-VEN

Year	Volume	High	Low	Close
2022	8,257,661	$0.89	$0.27	$0.28
2021	75,493	$1.18	$0.59	$1.18
2020	145,301	$1.11	$0.24	$0.65
2019	49,776	$0.83	$0.34	$0.65
2018	237,679	$1.15	$0.64	$0.64

Consolidation: 1-for-2.95454 cons. in Jan. 2022
Recent Close: $0.21
Capital Stock Changes - On Feb. 28, 2022, 349,399 common shares were issued pursuant to the acquisition of MVT Geo-Solutions Inc. In October 2022, bought deal public offering of 11,171,812 units (1 common share & 1 warrant) and concurrent private placement of 569,222 units (1 common share & 1 warrant) all at 36¢ per unit were completed Also during 2022, 16,924 common shares were issued on exercise of options and 351,688 preferred shares were returned.

Wholly Owned Subsidiaries

Canadian Air National Inc., Canada.
Empire Drone Company LLC, N.Y.
MVT Geo-Solutions Inc., Qué.
Partner Jet Inc., Canada.
RPV Aviation Inc., Canada.
Sky Scape Industries, LLC, N.J.
Volatus Aerospace UK Ltd., United Kingdom.

Subsidiaries

51% int. in **iRed Ltd.**, United Kingdom.
51% int. in **Synergy Aviation Ltd.**, Alta.
51% int. in **Synergy Flight Training Inc.**, Canada.
75% int. in **Volatus Aerospace LATAM S.A.**, Panama.
90% int. in **Volatus Aerospace USA Corp.**, United States.
- 100% int. in **ConnexiCore LLC**, Pa.

70% int. in **Volatus Flight Systems Inc.**, Oro Station, Ont.
66% int. in **Volatus Unmanned Services Inc.**, Oro Station, Ont.
- 100% int. in **Canadian UAV Solutions Inc.**, Summerside, P.E.I.
- 100% int. in **M3 Drone Training Zone Inc.**, Winnipeg, Man.
- 100% int. in **M3 Drone Services Inc.**, Winnipeg, Man.
- 100% int. in **OmniView Tech Corp.**, Mississauga, Ont.
- 100% int. in **SkyGate Videography Inc.**, Summerside, P.E.I.
- 100% int. in **UAViation Aerial Solutions Limited**, Coquitlam, B.C.

Investments

49% int. in **Indigenous Aerospace Corp.**, Ohsweken, Ont.

Financial Statistics

Periods ended:	12m Dec. 31/22[A]		12m Dec. 31/21[A1]
	$000s	%Chg	$000s
Operating revenue	**29,771**	**+200**	**9,914**
Cost of goods sold	17,211		6,299
Cost of sales	4,215		1,086
Research & devel. expense	541		nil
General & admin expense	11,887		3,713
Stock-based compensation	1,245		459
Operating expense	**35,099**	**+204**	**11,557**
Operating income	**(5,328)**	**n.a.**	**(1,643)**
Deprec., depl. & amort	1,385		401
Finance costs, gross	526		439
Write-downs/write-offs	nil		(1,399)
Pre-tax income	**(6,974)**	**n.a.**	**(3,679)**
Net income	**(6,974)**	**n.a.**	**(3,679)**
Net inc. for equity hldrs	**(6,626)**	**n.a.**	**(2,781)**
Net inc. for non-cont. int	**(349)**	**n.a.**	**(898)**
Cash & equivalent	3,685		8,807
Inventories	3,762		687
Accounts receivable	4,330		698
Current assets	13,780		10,993
Fixed assets, net	9,330		4,051
Right-of-use assets	995		1,230
Intangibles, net	9,505		6,395
Total assets	**33,610**	**+48**	**22,669**
Bank indebtedness	373		158
Accts. pay. & accr. liabs	3,397		2,459
Current liabilities	6,165		3,621
Long-term debt, gross	12,060		2,912
Long-term debt, net	10,064		2,710
Long-term lease liabilities	826		1,078
Preferred share equity	353		704
Shareholders' equity	13,131		14,971
Non-controlling interest	1,067		289
Cash from oper. activs	**(7,112)**	**n.a.**	**(1,573)**
Cash from fin. activs	2,365		11,757
Cash from invest. activs	(374)		(1,567)
Net cash position	**3,685**	**-58**	**8,807**
Capital expenditures	nil		(254)
Capital disposals	642		nil
	$		$
Earnings per share*	(0.06)		(0.10)
Cash flow per share*	(0.07)		(0.05)
	shs		shs
No. of shs. o/s*	113,943,079		34,467,539
Avg. no. of shs. o/s*	104,932,598		28,582,360
	%		%
Net profit margin	(23.43)		(37.11)
Return on equity	n.m.		(37.54)
Return on assets	n.a.		(24.03)
No. of employees (FTEs)	n.a.		52

* Common
[A] Reported in accordance with IFRS
[1] Results reflect the Dec. 22, 2021, reverse takeover acquisition of (old) Volatus Aerospace Corp.

Latest Results

Periods ended:	3m Mar. 31/23[A]		3m Mar. 31/22[A]
	$000s	%Chg	$000s
Operating revenue	7,412	+54	4,808
Net income	(3,003)	n.a.	(1,774)
Net inc. for equity hldrs	(2,612)	n.a.	(1,855)
Net inc. for non-cont. int	(391)		81
	$		$
Earnings per share*	(0.02)		(0.02)

* Common
[A] Reported in accordance with IFRS

Historical Summary
(as originally stated)

Fiscal Year	Oper. Rev.	Net Inc. Bef. Disc.	EPS*
	$000s	$000s	$
2022[A]	29,771	(6,974)	(0.06)
2021[A]	9,914	(3,679)	(0.10)
2021[A1]	5,068	(1,486)	(0.48)
2020[A]	6,730	(702)	(0.23)
2019[A]	8,910	(66)	(0.02)

* Common
[A] Reported in accordance with IFRS
[1] Results for fiscal 2021 and prior periods pertain to Partner Jet Corp.
Note: Adjusted throughout for 1-for-2.95454 cons. in Jan. 2022

V.44 Volt Carbon Technologies Inc.

Symbol - VCT **Exchange** - TSX-VEN **CUSIP** - 92873M
Head Office - 117-70 Country Hills Landing NW, Calgary, AB, T3K 2L2 **Telephone** - (403) 444-6888 **Fax** - (403) 226-8149
Website - voltcarbontech.com

Email - info@voltcarbontech.com
Investor Relations - V-Bond Lee (647) 546-7049
Auditors - Kenway Mack Slusarchuk Stewart LLP C.A., Calgary, Alta.
Lawyers - MLT Aikins LLP, Calgary, Alta.
Transfer Agents - Computershare Trust Company of Canada Inc., Calgary, Alta.
Profile - (Alta. 2004 amalg.) Developing an air classification system and a solid state battery technology. Also has mineral interests in British Columbia and Quebec.

Owns patent-pending proprietary technologies under development including an air classifier, which separates graphite from ores by means of aerodynamics to produce high purity graphite concentrates; and a solid state electrolyte battery technology. R&D activities for the air classifier and solid electrolyte battery are conducted at leased facilities in Scarborough and Guelph, Ont., respectively.

In addition, holds 25% interest (**Red Bird Resources Ltd.** 75%) in Red Bird molybdenum-copper-rhenium property, 444 hectares, 105 km north of Bella Coola, B.C.; formerly producing Mount Copeland molybdenum property, 730 hectares, 32 km northwest of Revelstoke, B.C.; and Lochaber graphite prospect, 541 hectares, southwestern Quebec.

Predecessor Detail - Name changed from Saint Jean Carbon Inc., Feb. 16, 2022.
Directors - V-Bond Lee, chr., pres. & CEO, Ont.; Dr. Zhongwei Chen, Ont.; Robert Martin, W.A., Australia; Glen Nursey, B.C.
Other Exec. Officers - Carmelo (Carm) Marrelli, CFO

Capital Stock

	Authorized (shs.)	Outstanding (shs.)[1]
First Preferred	unlimited	nil
Second Preferred	unlimited	nil
Common	unlimited	166,220,902

[1] At Nov. 18, 2022

Major Shareholder - Dr. Zhongwei Chen held 10.04% interest at Oct. 17, 2022.

Price Range - VCT/TSX-VEN

Year	Volume	High	Low	Close
2022	14,709,869	$0.17	$0.06	$0.08
2021	59,478,701	$0.24	$0.05	$0.16
2020	20,263,036	$0.06	$0.02	$0.05
2019	17,862,899	$0.04	$0.02	$0.04
2018	24,180,574	$0.24	$0.02	$0.03

Recent Close: $0.08

Capital Stock Changes - In November 2022, private placement of 9,999,999 common shares was completed at 7¢ per share.

From January to March 2022, private placement of 20,000,000 units (1 common share & ½ warrant) at $0.125 per unit was completed, with warrants exercisable at 25¢ per share for two years.

Wholly Owned Subsidiaries

Solid Ultrabattery Inc., Ont.

Financial Statistics

Periods ended:	12m Oct. 31/21[A]		12m Oct. 31/20[◘A]
	$000s	%Chg	$000s
Research & devel. expense	68		nil
General & admin expense	978		672
Stock-based compensation	1,086		nil
Operating expense	**2,132**	**+217**	**672**
Operating income	**(2,132)**	**n.a.**	**(672)**
Deprec., depl. & amort.	126		163
Finance costs, gross	168		11
Write-downs/write-offs	nil		(3,068)[1]
Pre-tax income	**(2,074)**	**n.a.**	**(4,061)**
Net income	**(2,074)**	**n.a.**	**(4,061)**
Cash & equivalent	142		29
Accounts receivable	46		18
Current assets	364		68
Fixed assets, net	438		376
Right-of-use assets	1,113		44
Intangibles, net	1,373		nil
Explor./devel. properties	855		840
Total assets	**4,185**	**+205**	**1,370**
Bank indebtedness	444		140
Accts. pay. & accr. liabs	957		1,544
Current liabilities	1,625		1,854
Long-term lease liabilities	1,040		23
Shareholders' equity	1,520		(508)
Cash from oper. activs	**(1,637)**	**n.a.**	**(200)**
Cash from fin. activs	1,949		222
Cash from invest. activs	(199)		(1)
Net cash position	**142**	**+390**	**29**
Capital expenditures	(164)		nil
Capital disposals	1		nil
	$		$
Earnings per share*	(0.02)		(0.05)
Cash flow per share*	(0.02)		(0.00)
	shs		shs
No. of shs. o/s*	129,393,782		83,797,532
Avg. no. of shs. o/s*	105,309,909		76,389,294
	%		%
Net profit margin	n.a.		n.a.
Return on equity	n.m.		n.m.
Return on assets	(68.62)		(137.57)

* Common
◘ Restated
[A] Reported in accordance with IFRS
[1] Pertains to impairment of mineral properties.

Latest Results

Periods ended:	9m July 31/22[A]		9m July 31/21[◘A]
	$000s	%Chg	$000s
Net income	(2,128)	n.a.	(1,206)
	$		$
Earnings per share*	(0.02)		(0.01)

* Common
◘ Restated
[A] Reported in accordance with IFRS

Historical Summary
(as originally stated)

Fiscal Year	Oper. Rev.	Net Inc. Bef. Disc.	EPS*
	$000s	$000s	$
2021[A]	nil	(2,074)	(0.02)
2020[A]	17	(4,061)	(0.05)
2019[A]	115	(832)	(0.01)
2018[A]	409	(2,188)	(0.03)
2017[A]	nil	(1,720)	(0.03)

* Common
[A] Reported in accordance with IFRS
Note: Adjusted throughout for 1-for-4 cons. in June 2018

V.45 Voxtur Analytics Corp.

Symbol - VXTR **Exchange** - TSX-VEN **CUSIP** - 929082
Head Office - 1105-175 Bloor St E, Toronto, ON, M4W 3R8 **Toll-free** - (866) 963-2015
Website - www.voxtur.com
Email - jordan@voxtur.com
Investor Relations - Jordan Ross (416) 708-9764
Auditors - MNP LLP C.A., Mississauga, Ont.
Lawyers - Stikeman Elliott LLP, Toronto, Ont.
Transfer Agents - TSX Trust Company, Toronto, Ont.
FP500 Revenue Ranking - 778
Profile - (Ont. 2008 amalg.) Provides automated workflows and targeted data analytics to simplify property valuation, tax solutions, and settlement services for investors, lenders, government agencies and mortgage servicers in the U.S. and Canada.

The company primarily offers software and data licences, technology-managed services and settlement services.

In software and data licences, the company provides digital platforms for real-time mortgage asset portfolio analysis, automated appraisal processes, client data commercialization, property assessment accuracy analysis and customizable property review software for assessors and agencies, all supported by proprietary algorithms and a comprehensive suite of add-ons. Through its technology-managed services, offers various real estate valuation services including appraisals, broker price opinions, property tax solutions, outsourcing services and non-legal default services. Also offers settlement service including full-service title, escrow and closing services.

In July 2022, the company acquired **Municipal Tax Equity Consultants Inc.** and **MTE Paralegal Professional Corporation** (collectively MTE) for $4,400,000 consisting of $3,100,000 cash and issuance of 1,313,130 common shares valued at 99¢ per share. MTE provides municipalities with taxation finance software and technology-enabled services to ensure its clients maximize property tax revenue and mitigate future liabilities, optimize operations from emerging opportunities, and develop property tax policy frameworks.

Common reinstated on TSX-VEN, Aug. 1, 2023.

Common suspended from TSX-VEN, July 19, 2023.

Recent Merger and Acquisition Activity

Status: completed **Revised:** Sept. 21, 2022

UPDATE: The transaction was completed. PREVIOUS: Voxtur Analytics Corp. agreed to acquire private U.S.-based Blue Water Financial Technologies Holding Company, LLC for US$101,000,000, consisting of US$30,000,000 cash and issuance of 170,000,000 common shares to be issued in instalments. Of the consideration shares, 101,207,269 common shares would be issued in equal instalments each quarter for the next 16 quarters, and 68,792,731 common shares were to be issued in satisfaction of Blue Water's existing long-term incentive plan and issued in three equal annual instalments. Blue Water offers a digital mortgage asset platform which provides asset valuation, mortgage servicing rights (MSR) distribution, MSR hedging and digital solutions to MSR investors and mortgage lenders.

Predecessor Detail - Name changed from iLOOKABOUT Corp., Feb. 3, 2021, pursuant to the acquisition of Voxtur Technologies, Inc. and Bright Line Title, LLC (dba Brightline), as well as certain technology and non-legal assets of James E. Albertelli, P.A. and certain of its affiliates.

Directors - Nicholas Smith, chr., Minneapolis, Minn.; Gary Yeoman, interim CEO, Toronto, Ont.; Michael D. Harris†, East York, Ont.; James B. Kelsey, Ont.; Grant Moon, Colo.; Christy Soukhamneut, Ga.; Ray Williams, Ont.

Other Exec. Officers - Robin Dyson, interim CFO; Ali Ayub, chief tech. officer; Matt Harrick, chief revenue officer; Stacy Mestayer, chief legal officer & corp. sec.; Jordan Ross, chief invest. officer; Mike Power, v-p, bus. devel.; Mark Sheppard, v-p, opers., iLOOKABOUT Inc.

† Lead director

Capital Stock

	Authorized (shs.)	Outstanding (shs.)[1]
Preference	unlimited	
Series 2		4,081,632[2]
Common	unlimited	618,232,297
Non-Vtg.	unlimited	nil

[1] At June 30, 2023
[2] All held by BMO Capital Partners.

Preference - Issuable in series.

Series 2 - Entitled to fixed and cumulative dividends at a rate of 12% per annum. Convertible, at BMO Capital Partners' (BMOCP) option, into one common share. BMOCP may, at any time with the first five years of issuance, give notice of its election to convert all outstanding preferred shares into common shares. On the third anniversary, any outstanding preferred shares will automatically convert into common shares if the volume weighted average price of the common shares on such date, calculated based on the 20 trading days prior to such date, is at a premium of 10% of more than the conversion price of 98¢. After the third anniversary, the company may at any time elect to redeem all of the outstanding shares for a redemption price equal to the issue price (98¢) plus accrued and unpaid dividends. One vote per share.

Common - One vote per share.

Major Shareholder - James E. (Jim) Albertelli held 18.5% interest at May 11, 2023.

Price Range - VXTR/TSX-VEN

Year	Volume	High	Low	Close
2022	141,372,295	$1.70	$0.21	$0.26
2021	191,372,045	$1.43	$0.43	$1.19
2020	26,583,086	$0.47	$0.11	$0.45
2019	35,985,071	$0.31	$0.13	$0.21
2018	34,266,672	$0.28	$0.12	$0.14

Recent Close: $0.15

Capital Stock Changes - From June to August 2023, private placement of 52,215,262 units (1 common share & 1 warrant) at 20¢ per unit was completed, with warrants exercisable at 20¢ per share for five years.

In May 2022, private placement of 12,260,000 common shares was completed at $1.02 per share. In July 2022, 808,080 common shares were issued pursuant to the acquisition of Municipal Tax Equity Consultants Inc. In October 2022, private placement of 4,081,632 series 2 preference shares was completed at 98¢ per share and 29,256,365 common shares were issued pursuant to the acquisition of Blue Water Financial Technologies Holding Company, LLC. Also during 2022, common shares were issued as follows: 13,572,553 on exercise of warrants, 5,387,423 on vesting of deferred share units, 2,758,000 on vesting of restricted share units, 499,001 on conversion of debentures, 135,865 on exercise of options and 8,655 for loans.

Wholly Owned Subsidiaries

Appraisers Now Ltd., Red Deer, Alta.
Clarocity Inc.
- 100% int. in **iLOOKABOUT (US) Inc.**, Del.
- 100% int. in **Valuation Vision, Inc.**, Carlsbad, Calif.
- 100% int. in **Voxtur Valuation, LLC**, Kansas City, Mo.

iLOOKABOUT Inc., Ont.
Municipal Tax Equity Consultants Inc., Canada.
Voxtur Analytics US Corp., United States.
- 100% int. in **Appraisers Now US LLC**, United States.
- 100% int. in **Blue Water Financial Technologies Holding Company, LLC**, United States.
  - 100% int. in **Blue Water Financial Technologies, LLC**, Del.
  - 100% int. in **Blue Water Financial Technologies Services, LLC**, Minn.
- 100% int. in **RealWealth Technologies LLC**
- 100% int. in **Voxtur Data Services, Inc.**, Calif.
- 100% int. in **Voxtur Services LLC**, United States.
- 100% int. in **Voxtur Settlement Services, LLC**, Fla.
- 100% int. in **Voxtur Technologies U.S., Inc.**, Del.

Voxtur Appraisal Services, LLC, Tex.

Financial Statistics

Periods ended:	12m Dec. 31/22^A		12m Dec. 31/21^oA
	$000s	%Chg	$000s
Operating revenue	**150,878**	**+57**	**95,992**
Cost of sales	61,167		45,056
Salaries & benefits	68,039		33,172
General & admin expense	29,616		19,518
Stock-based compensation	9,734		12,478
Other operating expense	13,563		6,902
Operating expense	**182,119**	**+55**	**117,126**
Operating income	**(31,241)**	**n.a.**	**(21,134)**
Deprec., depl. & amort.	16,611		11,513
Finance income	114		44
Finance costs, gross	3,539		2,291
Write-downs/write-offs	(185,442)		nil
Pre-tax income	**(230,511)**	**n.a.**	**(33,908)**
Income taxes	(17,759)		(1,818)
Net income	**(212,752)**	**n.a.**	**(32,090)**
Cash & equivalent	5,908		18,683
Accounts receivable	9,220		13,965
Current assets	31,464		45,489
Long-term investments	3,979		3,882
Fixed assets, net	532		508
Right-of-use assets	1,718		1,268
Intangibles, net	129,596		216,174
Total assets	**168,343**	**-37**	**268,507**
Accts. pay. & accr. liabs.	13,767		12,213
Current liabilities	32,099		24,176
Long-term debt, gross	60,779		26,197
Long-term debt, net	50,199		19,697
Long-term lease liabilities	1,444		678
Shareholders' equity	74,797		200,594
Cash from oper. activs.	**(22,350)**	**n.a.**	**(18,379)**
Cash from fin. activs.	51,738		74,190
Cash from invest. activs.	(42,262)		(43,118)
Net cash position	**5,908**	**-68**	**18,683**
Capital expenditures	(184)		(197)
	$		$
Earnings per share*	(0.39)		(0.08)
Cash flow per share*	(0.04)		(0.04)
	shs		shs
No. of shs. o/s*	582,797,094		517,091,697
Avg. no. of shs. o/s*	549,525,576		424,524,225
	%		%
Net profit margin	(141.01)		(33.43)
Return on equity	(153.28)		(29.38)
Return on assets	(93.46)		(19.45)
Foreign sales percent	95		91

* Common
^o Restated
^A Reported in accordance with IFRS

Latest Results

Periods ended:	6m June 30/23^A		6m June 30/22^oA
	$000s	%Chg	$000s
Operating revenue	58,619	-26	78,901
Net income	(28,262)	n.a.	(18,266)
	$		$
Earnings per share*	(0.05)		(0.03)

* Common
^o Restated
^A Reported in accordance with IFRS

Historical Summary
(as originally stated)

Fiscal Year	Oper. Rev. $000s	Net Inc. Bef. Disc. $000s	EPS* $
2022^A	150,878	(212,752)	(0.39)
2021^A	95,992	(32,090)	(0.08)
2020^A	20,511	(6,166)	(0.05)
2019^A	14,934	(1,883)	(0.02)
2018^A	9,212	(370)	(0.00)

* Common
^A Reported in accordance with IFRS

V.46 Voyageur Pharmaceuticals Ltd.

Symbol - VM **Exchange** - TSX-VEN **CUSIP** - 92918C
Head Office - 4103B Centre St NW, Calgary, AB, T2E 2Y6 **Telephone** - (403) 818-6086
Website - www.voyageurpharmaceuticals.ca
Email - brent@vpharma.ca
Investor Relations - Brent Willis (403) 818-6086
Auditors - MNP LLP C.A., Calgary, Alta.
Bankers - The Toronto-Dominion Bank, Calgary, Alta.
Lawyers - Dentons Canada LLP, Calgary, Alta.
Transfer Agents - TSX Trust Company, Calgary, Alta.
Profile - (Alta. 2008) Develops and manufactures barium, iodine and carbon (fullerene) active pharmaceutical ingredients (API) and imaging contrast agents for the medical imaging market. Also has mineral interests in British Columbia and Utah.

The company is developing 12 barium products including HDXba, MultiXba, MultiXthin, MutiXS, SmoothX, BarXnectar, BarXthin, BarXhoney, Barpudding, LumenX, VisionX and TagX for sale into the radiology pharmaceutical market. SmoothX, HDXba, MultiXba, MultiXthin and MultiXS have been approved by Health Canada. A pharmaceutical manufacturing and research and development facility in Alberta was targeted to be constructed in 2023. Upon completion of the facility, the processing of barite from the company's Frances Creek barite property to produce pharmaceutical barium contrast media products would commence.

In British Columbia, holds Frances Creek barite property, 839 hectares, 28 km northwest of Radium Hot Springs. A preliminary economic assessment completed in January 2022 proposed an open-pit mine which would produce 10,000 to 15,000 tonnes barite per year over a 10-year mine life for pharmaceutical products and the industrial market for high purity barite. Initial capital costs were estimated at $36,400,000. At January 2022, indicated resource was 214,800 tonnes grading 35.2% barite. Also holds Jubilee Mountain barite-polymetallic prospect, 1,212 hectares, 50 km north-northwest of Radium Hot Springs; and Pedley Mountain barite prospect, 174 hectares, 60 km southeast of Radium Hot Springs.

In Utah, holds 90% interest (**Anson Resources Limited** 10%) in Paradox Basin (ULI) iodine-lithium prospect, 720 hectares, with Anson holding option to earn an additional 60% interest, requiring exploration expenditures of US$2,996,000 and completion of a technical report; and Falcon copper-zinc prospect.

Predecessor Detail - Name changed from Voyageur Minerals Ltd., Dec. 13, 2019.

Directors - Brent Willis, pres. & CEO, Calgary, Alta.; Bradley C. Willis, v-p, explor. & COO, Calgary, Alta.; Eugene (Gene) Fritzel, Pouce Coupe, B.C.; Agustin Gago, New York, N.Y.; Ralph Hesje, Calgary, Alta.; Eric S. Pommer, Calif.; Ronald L. (Ron) Sifton, Alta.

Other Exec. Officers - Albert (Al) Deslauriers, interim CFO

Capital Stock

	Authorized (shs.)	Outstanding (shs.)[1]
Preferred	unlimited	nil
Common	unlimited	132,702,406

[1] At May 24, 2023

Major Shareholder - Widely held at May 24, 2023.

Price Range - VM/TSX-VEN

Year	Volume	High	Low	Close
2022	25,748,490	$0.20	$0.06	$0.09
2021	34,938,352	$0.35	$0.07	$0.09
2020	21,140,096	$0.12	$0.04	$0.07
2019	7,095,962	$0.12	$0.05	$0.08
2018	4,262,910	$0.12	$0.05	$0.07

Recent Close: $0.05

Capital Stock Changes - In December 2022 and January 2023, private placement of 17,142,133 units (1 common share & 1 warrant) at 7¢ per unit was completed, with warrants exercisable at 12¢ per share for two years.

In June 2022, private placement of 11,570,000 units (1 common share & 1 warrant) at 10¢ per unit was completed. Also during 2022, common shares were issued as follows: 848,183 for debt settlement, 796,594 under deferred share unit plan, 300,000 on exercise of warrants and 100,000 on exercise of options.

Wholly Owned Subsidiaries

Voyageur Industrial Minerals Ltd., Calgary, Alta.
Voyageur Minerals Inc., United States.

Financial Statistics

Periods ended:	12m Nov. 30/22^A		12m Nov. 30/21^A
	$000s	%Chg	$000s
Salaries & benefits	412		319
General & admin expense	1,186		992
Stock-based compensation	152		738
Operating expense	**1,749**	**-15**	**2,049**
Operating income	**(1,749)**	**n.a.**	**(2,049)**
Deprec., depl. & amort.	3		2
Pre-tax income	**(1,754)**	**n.a.**	**(2,051)**
Net income	**(1,754)**	**n.a.**	**(2,051)**
Cash & equivalent	32		813
Inventories	10		10
Accounts receivable	24		42
Current assets	157		887
Fixed assets, net	8		30
Explor./devel. properties	1,916		1,636
Total assets	**2,095**	**-18**	**2,567**
Accts. pay. & accr. liabs.	591		585
Current liabilities	591		621
Long-term debt, gross	26		26
Long-term debt, net	26		26
Shareholders' equity	1,465		1,906
Cash from oper. activs.	**(1,719)**	**n.a.**	**(1,654)**
Cash from fin. activs.	1,211		2,896
Cash from invest. activs.	(274)		(432)
Net cash position	**32**	**-96**	**813**
Capital expenditures	(283)		(432)
	$		$
Earnings per share*	(0.02)		(0.02)
Cash flow per share*	(0.02)		(0.02)
	shs		shs
No. of shs. o/s*	115,434,951		101,820,174
Avg. no. of shs. o/s*	107,826,018		94,677,887
	%		%
Net profit margin	n.a.		n.a.
Return on equity	(104.06)		(185.44)
Return on assets	(75.25)		(106.77)

* Common
^A Reported in accordance with IFRS

Latest Results

Periods ended:	3m Feb. 28/23^A		3m Feb. 28/22^A
	$000s	%Chg	$000s
Net income	(374)	n.a.	(247)
	$		$
Earnings per share*	(0.00)		(0.00)

* Common
^A Reported in accordance with IFRS

Historical Summary
(as originally stated)

Fiscal Year	Oper. Rev. $000s	Net Inc. Bef. Disc. $000s	EPS* $
2022^A	nil	(1,754)	(0.02)
2021^A	nil	(2,051)	(0.02)
2020^A	nil	(1,139)	(0.02)
2019^A	nil	(552)	(0.01)
2018^A	nil	(556)	(0.01)

* Common
^A Reported in accordance with IFRS

W

W.1 WELL Health Technologies Corp.

Symbol - WELL **Exchange** - TSX **CUSIP** - 94947L
Head Office - 550-375 Water St, Vancouver, BC, V6B 5C6 **Telephone** - (604) 628-7266 **Fax** - (604) 980-9223
Website - www.well.company
Email - hamed@well.company
Investor Relations - Hamed Shahbazi (604) 628-7266
Auditors - PricewaterhouseCoopers LLP C.A., Vancouver, B.C.
Transfer Agents - Computershare Trust Company of Canada Inc., Vancouver, B.C.
FP500 Revenue Ranking - 443
Employees - 1,710 at Dec. 31, 2022
Profile - (B.C. 2010) Owns and operates an end-to-end healthcare system in Canada, including a network of outpatient medical clinics, and an omni-channel clinical business in the U.S. Also offers a comprehensive practitioner enablement platform, which consists of technologies and services for medical clinics and healthcare practitioners, including electronic medical records (EMR), telehealth platforms, practice management, billing, revenue cycle management (RCM), digital health applications and data protection solutions.

Canadian Patient Services

Owns and operates a network of 148 outpatient medical clinics in British Columbia (WELL Health, Spring Medical, SleepWorks, DERM Lab, Easy Allied and False Creek Wellness), Alberta (INLIV and MCI The Doctor's Office), Ontario (MyHealth, ExecHealth and Uptown Health) and Quebec (ExcelleMD). Clinics provide primary care, allied health, specialized care, executive healthcare and diagnostic healthcare services.

US Patient Services

Offers omni-channel patient services delivered through brick-and-mortar clinics and telehealth platforms as well as digital services. Businesses include CRH Anesthesia, which provides anaesthesiology services primarily for gastrointestinal (GI) procedures in 142 ambulatory surgical centres and GI clinics across 23 states; CRH O'Regan System, a single-use, disposable hemorrhoid banding device for the non-surgical treatment of all grades of hemorrhoids and includes treatment protocols, training, operational and marketing expertise, distributed directly to GI practices as a complete, turnkey package; Circle Medical, a full cycle primary care provider offering virtual and in-person care; Wisp, an online provider of women's health and e-prescription services; and Radar Healthcare Providers, which provides temporary and permanent staffing services focused on anaesthesia providers across 29 states.

Software-as-a-Service (SaaS) and Technology Services

Include electronic medical records (EMR), telehealth services, digital health applications (apps) and services, billing and revenue cycle management (RCM) solutions and cybersecurity solutions.

EMR - Provides EMR software and services to customers across Canada, the U.S., the U.K., Australia and New Zealand. Products include OSCAR Pro, Profile, InSync, Maestro, Cerebrum and Juno EMR.

Telehealth - Provides telehealth and virtual care services across Canada through the platforms Tia Health, VirtualClinic+, Cardiology Now, MyDoctor Now and Focus Mental Wellness.

Digital Health Apps and Services - Includes apps.health, an app marketplace connecting healthcare professionals with new and pioneering apps which integrate with a clinic's EMR software, featuring 54 digital health apps provided by 38 app publishers; and OceanMD, a provider of a suite of software tools that connect patients, providers and healthcare systems such as online booking, patient messaging, digital forms, check-in kiosks, eReferral and eConsult.

Billing and RCM Solutions - Provides billing and back-office services in North America through DoctorCare, Doctor Services, Trillium, ClinicAid and Premium Choice Billing.

Cybersecurity - Provides various cybersecurity protection and data privacy solutions to the company's business units as well as to customers in various industries, including healthcare clients, under the Cycura, Source 44, Secure Solutions Now and Seekintoo names.

In addition, wholly owned **WELL Health Ventures Inc.** invests in the digital health industry globally, with an emphasis on investments that digitize and modernize healthcare in Canada.

In August 2023, the company acquired Calgary, Alta.-based **Seekintoo Ltd.**, a provider of cybersecurity services, for an undisclosed amount.

On July 27, 2023, the company announced that it has rebranded wholly owned **CRH Medical Corporation** as WELL Health USA and launched WELL Health USA as a multidisciplinary healthcare business spanning primary and specialized care with online and offline operations at scale. WELL Health USA integrates U.S. based companies and brands including CRH Anesthesia, CRH O'Regan System, Radar Healthcare Providers, Circle Medical and Wisp.

On July 19, 2023, **MCI Onehealth Technologies Inc.** agreed to sell 11 of its 14 primary care medical clinics in southern Ontario to the company for a purchase price of $1,500,000. The sale was expected to close on or around Oct. 1, 2023. The acquisition brings more than 130 physicians to the company, adding to over 3,000 providers in the company's patient services business units across North America. These clinics are expected to generate annual revenue of more than $21,000,000. MCI plans to focus on AI-powered healthcare technology and clinical research. MCI would complete a 10% convertible debenture financing of between $7,500,000 and $10,000,000, with the company participating for a minimum of $2,500,000. The companies would also enter into a strategic alliance agreement designed to offer the company's clinics and providers technology from MCI. The company would also be granted an option to acquire up to 30,800,000 class A subordinate voting shares and class B multiple voting shares of MCI over time, representing a total voting interest of 81.5%. The exercise of the option is conditional on the achievement by MCI of a number of performance milestones.

On June 1, 2023, the company acquired **MCI Medical Clinics (Alberta) Inc.**, owner and operator of five multidisciplinary primary care clinics in Calgary, Alta., from **MCI Onehealth Technologies Inc.** for $2,000,000.

On May 1, 2023, the company acquired Burlington, Ont.-based **Trillium Medical Billing Agency Inc.**, a provider of full-service medical claim submissions to physicians throughout Ontario, for $2,000,000.

On Jan. 1, 2023, the company completed the following amalgamations of its wholly owned subsidiaries: **Cloud Practice Inc.** into **WELL EMR Group Inc.**; **1330945 B.C. Ltd.**, **HealthVue Ventures Ltd.** and **South Surrey Medical Clinic Inc.** into **WELL Health Clinic Network Inc.**; **2716381 Ontario Inc.** into **MyHealth Caledon Inc.**; and **1507318 Ontario Inc.**, **MyHealth MRI CT Inc.**, **Sleep Disorders Centre Inc.** and **MyHealth Lindsay Inc.** into **MyHealth Partners Inc.**

In December 2022, the company acquired an additional 31% interest in **Focus Mental Wellness Inc.** (formerly **HASU Behavioural Health Inc.**), a virtual online therapy clinic in Canada that provides online video, phone and text therapy for individuals and their families struggling with mental health issues, for $151,000. As a result, the company's interest increased to 51% from 20%.

In November 2022, the company acquired **1330945 B.C. Ltd.**, which holds **PTS Pacific Telemedicine Services Ltd.** (dba False Creek Wellness), a medical centre in Vancouver, B.C., which provides executive health assessments, heart health assessments and medical imaging services. Terms were not disclosed.

On Aug. 1, 2022, the company acquired the assets of Calgary, Alta.-based **INLIV Inc.** from **Coril Holdings Ltd.**, a family enterprise with holdings in various businesses, for $1,609,195 on closing and a holdback of $240,375 payable in cash, common shares or a combination thereof at the company's discretion. INLIV provides consumer preventative health, corporate and executive health, primary care, cosmetics, fitness and integrated health services in the Greater Calgary region through a facility in Calgary and online.

On July 17, 2022, the company announced the formation of wholly owned **WELL Health Clinics Canada Inc.** to consolidate its Canadian outpatient clinics into an integrated hybrid business consisting of brick and mortar and virtual service. The business unit includes the company's primary care, allied health and MyHealth specialized care businesses.

Recent Merger and Acquisition Activity

Status: completed **Announced:** July 13, 2023
WELL Health Technologies Corp. acquired Atlanta, Ga.-based CarePlus Medical Corporation for US$35,000,000, funded from cash on hand and credit facilities. CarePlus has three primary businesses: Radar Healthcare Providers, Inc., which provides staffing and locum tenens services focused on anaesthesia providers in 29 U.S. states; Anaesthesia division, which provides clinical anaesthesia services across nine U.S. states; and Premier Choice Billing, LLC, which provides billing, revenue cycle management (RCM) and collection services.

Status: completed **Announced:** July 1, 2023
WELL Health Technologies Corp. acquired San Antonio, Tex.-based Lone Star Anesthesia Associates, PLLC, which provides anaesthesia services for endoscopic procedures, for US$12,500,000 paid via a combination of cash, common shares and deferred consideration.

Status: completed **Announced:** Apr. 1, 2023
WELL Health Technologies Corp. sold its 51% interest in Western Ohio Sedation Associations, LLC, a gastroenterology anaesthesia practice in Dayton, Ohio, for US$8,172,000.

Status: completed **Announced:** Mar. 1, 2023
WELL Health Technologies Corp. acquired a 51% interest in Tampa, Fla.-based Affiliated Tampa Anesthesia Associates, LLC, which provides anaesthesia services for endoscopic procedures, for US$4,535,000.

Status: completed **Revised:** Nov. 2, 2022
UPDATE: The transaction was completed. PREVIOUS: CloudMD Software & Services Inc. agreed to sell its British Columbia-based primary care clinics and Cloud Practice, its cloud-based electronic medical records (EMR) and practice management software, to WELL Health Technologies for $5,750,000. CloudMD's brick-and-mortar primary care clinics are HealthVue (Richmond [2], B.C.) and South Surrey Medical (Surrey, B.C.). Cloud Practice includes Juno EMR and ClinicAid. CloudMD would retain ownership of its online patient portal, MyHealthAccess, and the right (under a licence granted by WELL at closing of the transaction) to use Juno EMR. CloudMD plans to focus on its core businesses, Enterprise Health Solutions and Digital Health Solutions. The transaction was expected to close in the fourth quarter of 2022.

Status: completed **Announced:** Sept. 26, 2022
WELL Health Technologies Corp. acquired Phoenix, Ariz.-based Grand Canyon Anesthesia, LLC, a group consisting of over 100 anaesthesia providers supporting the delivery of anesthesia for more than 50,000 surgical cases annually, for a net purchase price of US$6,500,000 after adjusting for working capital.

Status: completed **Announced:** Sept. 1, 2022
WELL Health Technologies Corp. sold its 55% interest in West Florida Anesthesia Associates, LLC, a gastroenterology anaesthesia practice, to United Digestive for US$12,400,000.

Status: completed **Announced:** Mar. 7, 2022
WELL Health Technologies Corp. acquired Fairfield, Conn.-based Greater Connecticut Anesthesia Associates, LLC, a gastroenterology anaesthesia services provider in Connecticut, for US$12,500,000.

Predecessor Detail - Name changed from Wellness Lifestyles Inc., July 6, 2018.

Directors - Hamed Shahbazi, chr. & CEO, Vancouver, B.C.; Kenneth A. (Ken) Cawkell, New Westminster, B.C.; John M. Kim, Toronto, Ont.; Sybil E. Jen Lau, Singapore, Singapore; Thomas (Tom) Liston, Toronto, Ont.; Tara McCarville, B.C.

Other Exec. Officers - Amir Javidan, COO; Eva Fong, CFO; Dr. Michael Frankel, CMO; Arjun Kumar, CIO; Iain Paterson, chief info. security officer; Shane Sabatino, chief people officer; Chris Ericksen, sr. v-p, strategic partnerships & mktg.; Brian Levinkind, sr. v-p, corp. devel.; James (Jay) Kreger, CEO, WELL Health USA

Capital Stock

	Authorized (shs.)	Outstanding (shs.)[1]
Common	unlimited	238,212,389

[1] At Aug. 9, 2023

Normal Course Issuer Bid - The company plans to make normal course purchases of up to 5,884,589 common shares representing 2.5% of the total outstanding. The bid commenced on June 5, 2023, and expires on June 4, 2024.

Major Shareholder - Widely held at May 3, 2023.

Price Range - WELL/TSX

Year	Volume	High	Low	Close
2022	215,858,116	$5.64	$2.56	$2.84
2021	257,804,619	$9.84	$4.64	$4.91
2020	217,523,419	$8.70	$1.20	$8.05
2019	77,741,274	$1.87	$0.39	$1.56
2018	33,709,657	$0.75	$0.25	$0.45

Recent Close: $4.33

Capital Stock Changes - In May 2022, bought deal public offering of 9,327,765 common shares was completed at $3.70 per share, including 1,216,665 common shares on exercise of over-allotment option. Also during 2022, common shares were issued as follows: 3,430,767 for deferred acquisition costs and time-based earnouts, 3,133,252 on settlement of restricted and performance share units, 3,132,286 on exercise of options, 2,320,897 for debt settlement and 604,861 for acquisitions; 50,000 common shares were repurchased under a Normal Course Issuer Bid.

Wholly Owned Subsidiaries

CRH Medical Corporation, Vancouver, B.C. dba WELL Health USA.
- 100% int. in **CarePlus Medical Corporation**, Atlanta, Ga.
- 70% int. in **Circle Medical Technologies, Inc.**, San Francisco, Calif.
  - 100% int. in **Circle Medical Technologies (Canada) Inc.**, Qué.
- 53% int. in **WISP, Inc.**, San Francisco, Calif.

Cycura Data Protection Corp., Ont.
DoctorCare Inc., Toronto, Ont.
- 51% int. in **Doctors Services Group Limited**, Toronto, Ont.

Insig Corporation, Toronto, Ont.
Intrahealth Systems Limited, Vancouver, B.C.
Source 44 Consulting Incorporated, Markham, Ont.
WELL Digital Health Apps Inc., Canada.
WELL EMR Group Inc., B.C.
WELL Health Clinics Canada Inc., Canada.
- 100% int. in **WELL Health Clinic Network Inc.**, B.C.
  - 51% int. in **Easy Allied Health Corporation**, B.C.
  - 100% int. in **ExcelleMD Inc.**, Montréal, Qué.
  - 100% int. in **MCI Medical Clinics (Alberta) Inc.**, Alta.
  - 100% int. in **MyHealth Partners Inc.**, Toronto, Ont.
  - 51% int. in **SleepWorks Medical Inc.**, B.C.
  - 51% int. in **Spring Medical Centre Ltd.**, B.C.

WELL Health Ventures Inc., B.C.

Note: The preceding list includes only the major related companies in which interests are held.

Financial Statistics

Periods ended:	12m Dec. 31/22[A]		12m Dec. 31/21[□A]
	$000s	%Chg	$000s
Operating revenue	**569,136**	**+88**	**302,324**
Cost of sales	265,845		148,629
Salaries & benefits	100,352		52,178
General & admin expense	99,271		50,332
Stock-based compensation	24,483		21,012
Operating expense	**489,951**	**+80**	**272,151**
Operating income	**79,185**	**+162**	**30,173**
Deprec., depl. & amort.	55,203		38,710
Finance income	649		555
Finance costs, gross	25,291		9,009
Investment income	(396)		(209)
Pre-tax income	**17,525**	**n.a.**	**(25,485)**
Income taxes	(1,150)		5,802
Net income	**18,675**	**n.a.**	**(31,287)**
Net inc. for equity hldrs	**1,369**	**n.a.**	**(44,179)**
Net inc. for non-cont. int.	**17,306**	**+34**	**12,892**
Cash & equivalent	48,908		61,919
Inventories	1,370		793
Accounts receivable	78,914		66,020
Current assets	150,877		142,336
Long-term investments	10,005		10,845
Fixed assets, net	82,535		83,056
Intangibles, net	1,070,557		1,048,228
Total assets	**1,319,031**	**+2**	**1,287,319**
Accts. pay. & accr. liabs	50,728		38,713
Current liabilities	136,503		137,340
Long-term debt, gross	297,153		340,748
Long-term debt, net	263,000		290,599
Long-term lease liabilities	52,156		53,971
Equity portion of conv. debs	25,042		25,042
Shareholders' equity	732,344		617,845
Non-controlling interest	82,907		89,911
Cash from oper. activs	**76,546**	**+244**	**22,268**
Cash from fin. activs	(52,847)		452,530
Cash from invest. activs	(37,926)		(499,778)
Net cash position	**48,908**	**-21**	**61,919**
Capital expenditures	(6,404)		(2,682)
	$		$
Earnings per share*	0.01		(0.23)
Cash flow per share*	0.35		0.12
	shs		shs
No. of shs. o/s*	231,047,290		209,147,462
Avg. no. of shs. o/s*	220,691,471		190,900,309
	%		%
Net profit margin	3.28		(10.35)
Return on equity	0.20		(10.58)
Return on assets	3.53		(2.61)
No. of employees (FTEs)	1,710		1,507

* Common
□ Restated
[A] Reported in accordance with IFRS

Latest Results

Periods ended:	6m June 30/23[A]		6m June 30/22[□A]
	$000s	%Chg	$000s
Operating revenue	340,347	+28	266,834
Net income	(12,643)	n.a.	(4,020)
Net inc. for equity hldrs	(20,125)	n.a.	(14,840)
Net inc. for non-cont. int	7,482		10,820
	$		$
Earnings per share*	(0.09)		(0.07)

* Common
□ Restated
[A] Reported in accordance with IFRS

Historical Summary
(as originally stated)

Fiscal Year	Oper. Rev.	Net Inc. Bef. Disc.	EPS*
	$000s	$000s	$
2022[A]	569,136	18,675	0.01
2021[A]	302,324	(30,895)	(0.23)
2020[A]	50,240	(3,211)	(0.03)
2019[A]	32,811	(7,794)	(0.08)
2018[A1]	10,560	(2,595)	(0.04)

* Common
[A] Reported in accordance with IFRS
[1] 14 months ended Dec. 31, 2018.

W.2 WPD Pharmaceuticals Inc.

Symbol - WBIO **Exchange** - CSE (S) **CUSIP** - 92941F
Head Office - 1080-789 Pender St W, Vancouver, BC, V6C 1H2 **Telephone** - (604) 428-7050 **Fax** - (604) 428-7052
Website - www.wpdpharmaceuticals.com
Email - investors@wpdpharmaceuticals.com
Investor Relations - Mariusz Olejniczak (604) 428-7050
Auditors - Dale Matheson Carr-Hilton LaBonte LLP C.A., Vancouver, B.C.
Lawyers - Max Pinsky Personal Law Corporation, Vancouver, B.C.
Transfer Agents - Computershare Trust Company of Canada Inc., Toronto, Ont.
Profile - (B.C. 2006) Researches and develops medicinal products involving biological compounds and small molecules, with a focus on oncology and infectious diseases.

The company has nine novel drug candidates, of which four are in the clinical development stage and five are in the pre-clinical development and discovery stages. Products under clinical development stage include Berubicin, an anthracycline for the treatment of glioblastoma multiforme (GBM); Annamycin, an anthracycline for the treatment of acute myeloid leukemia (AML); WP1066, an immune/transcription modulator for the treatment of glioblastoma and melanoma brain metastases; and WP1220, an inhibitor of phosphor (p)-STAT3 for suppressing cutaneous T-cell lymphoma (CTCL). Products under pre-clinical development and discovery stages include WPD101, a biological compound that uses recombinant proteins conjugated with bacterial toxins that targets GBM-specific receptors; WPD102, a targeted therapy against IL-13RA2 by recombinant IL-13 conjugated to a cytotoxic load for the treatment of uveal melanoma in humans; WPD103, a radiopharmaceutical for the diagnosis and treatment of GBM, melanoma and other cancers; WP1732, a water-soluble p-STAT3 inhibitor for the treatment of pancreatic cancer; and WP1122, an antiviral agent against SARS-CoV-2 infection that uses acetylated 2-deoxy-D-glucose (2-DG) to block the glycolysis process and prevent virus replication.

The company has 100 m^2 of laboratory and office space in Warsaw and Wroclaw, Poland, and has access to shared laboratories at the University of Warsaw Biological and Chemical Research Centre and Wroclaw Technology Park.

Common suspended from CSE, July 11, 2022.

Predecessor Detail - Name changed from Westcot Ventures Corp., Jan. 14, 2020, pursuant to reverse takeover acquisition of Poland-based WPD Pharmaceuticals Sp.zo.o.

Directors - Romuald Harwas; Peter Novak, Mich.; Teresa L. Rzepczyk, Kelowna, B.C.

Other Exec. Officers - Mariusz Olejniczak, CEO; Beata Pajak, chief scientific officer; Marek Sipowicz, CMO

Capital Stock

	Authorized (shs.)	Outstanding (shs.)[1]
Common	unlimited	113,438,244

[1] At July 12, 2023

Major Shareholder - Waldemar Priebe held 27.9% interest and Kevan Casey held 10.65% interest at Aug. 6, 2021.

Price Range - WET.H/TSX-VEN (D)

Year	Volume	High	Low	Close
2022	446,213	$0.11	$0.04	$0.05
2021	10,784,259	$0.44	$0.03	$0.04
2020	39,666,765	$1.95	$0.21	$0.30
2019	455,414	$0.70	$0.40	$0.62
2018	635,862	$0.55	$0.23	$0.35

Wholly Owned Subsidiaries

WPD Pharmaceuticals Sp.zo.o, Poland.

W.3 WSM Ventures Corp.

Symbol - WSM.X **Exchange** - CSE **CUSIP** - 92941W
Head Office - 2200-885 Georgia St W, Vancouver, BC, V6C 3E8 **Telephone** - (604) 638-8063
Email - david@springhouseinvestments.com
Investor Relations - David Ebert (604) 685-6747
Auditors - Manning Elliott LLP C.A., Vancouver, B.C.
Lawyers - Blake, Cassels & Graydon LLP, Vancouver, B.C.
Transfer Agents - Computershare Trust Company of Canada Inc., Vancouver, B.C.
Profile - (B.C. 1985 amalg.) Seeking new business opportunities.
Predecessor Detail - Name changed from Avalon Blockchain Inc., Apr. 15, 2020.
Directors - Aleem Nathwani, interim CEO, Vancouver, B.C.; Anthony Alvaro, v-p, bus. devel., B.C.; Darren P. Devine, West Vancouver, B.C.
Other Exec. Officers - David Ebert, CFO

Capital Stock

	Authorized (shs.)	Outstanding (shs.)[1]
Common	unlimited	67,328,936

[1] At May 27, 2022

Major Shareholder - Widely held at Apr. 7, 2021.

Price Range - WSM.X/CSE

Year	Volume	High	Low	Close
2022	850,750	$0.01	$0.01	$0.01
2021	57,846	$0.13	$0.01	$0.01
2020	94,761	$0.01	$0.01	$0.01

Recent Close: $0.01

Wholly Owned Subsidiaries

1158716 B.C. Ltd., B.C.

Financial Statistics

Periods ended:	12m Dec. 31/21[A]		12m Dec. 31/20[A]
	$000s	%Chg	$000s
General & admin expense	101		107
Operating expense	**101**	**-6**	**107**
Operating income	**(101)**	**n.a.**	**(107)**
Pre-tax income	**(101)**	**n.a.**	**(107)**
Net income	**(101)**	**n.a.**	**(107)**
Cash & equivalent	135		245
Current assets	135		245
Total assets	**135**	**-45**	**245**
Accts. pay. & accr. liabs	18		27
Current liabilities	18		27
Shareholders' equity	117		218
Cash from oper. activs	**(110)**	**n.a.**	**(94)**
Net cash position	**135**	**-45**	**245**
	$		$
Earnings per share*	(0.00)		(0.00)
Cash flow per share*	(0.00)		(0.00)
	shs		shs
No. of shs. o/s*	67,328,936		67,328,936
Avg. no. of shs. o/s*	67,328,936		67,328,936
	%		%
Net profit margin	n.a.		n.a.
Return on equity	(60.30)		(39.41)
Return on assets	(53.16)		(36.64)

* Common
[A] Reported in accordance with IFRS

Latest Results

Periods ended:	3m Mar. 31/22[A]		3m Mar. 31/21[A]
	$000s	%Chg	$000s
Net income	(27)	n.a.	(28)
	$		$
Earnings per share*	(0.00)		(0.00)

* Common
[A] Reported in accordance with IFRS

Historical Summary
(as originally stated)

Fiscal Year	Oper. Rev.	Net Inc. Bef. Disc.	EPS*
	$000s	$000s	$
2021[A]	nil	(101)	(0.00)
2020[A]	nil	(107)	(0.00)
2019[A]	nil	(88)	(0.00)
2018[A1]	nil	(2,117)	(0.02)
2017[A2]	nil	(1,665)	(0.15)

* Common
[A] Reported in accordance with IFRS
[1] Results reflect the Mar. 29, 2018, reverse takeover acquisition of 1158716 B.C. Ltd.
[2] Results for 2017 and prior years pertain to World Mahjong Limited.

W.4 WSP Global Inc.*

Symbol - WSP **Exchange** - TSX **CUSIP** - 92938W
Head Office - 1100-1600 boul René-Lévesque O, Montréal, QC, H3H 1P9 **Telephone** - (514) 340-0046
Website - www.wsp.com
Email - alain.michaud@wsp.com
Investor Relations - Alain Michaud (438) 843-7317
Auditors - PricewaterhouseCoopers LLP C.A., Montréal, Qué.
Lawyers - Stikeman Elliott LLP, Montréal, Qué.
Transfer Agents - TSX Trust Company, Montréal, Qué.
FP500 Revenue Ranking - 51
Employees - 66,000 at Dec. 31, 2022
Profile - (Can. 2014) Provides engineering and design services to clients in the transportation and infrastructure, earth and environment, property and buildings, power and energy and industry sectors, as well as offering strategic advisory services.

Operations are carried out through five market segments: Transportation and Infrastructure; Earth and Environment; Property and Buildings; Power and Energy; and Industry.

The **Transportation and Infrastructure** segment helps create mid and long-term transport and infrastructure strategies and provides guidance and support throughout the life cycle of a wide range of projects and assets. The company advises, plans, designs and manages projects for rail transit, aviation, highways, bridges, tunnels, water, maritime and urban infrastructure. Clients include the public and private sector.

The **Earth and Environment** segment works with and advises governments and private-sector clients on key aspects of earth sciences and environmental sustainability. The company advises on matters ranging from clean air, water and land, to biodiversity, green energy solutions, climate change and Environmental, Social and Governance (ESG) issues. Services include due diligence, permit approvals, regulatory compliance, waste/hazardous materials management, geotechnical and mining engineering, environmental/social impact assessments, feasibility and land remediation studies.

The **Property and Buildings** segment provides technical and advisory services ranging from decarbonisation strategies and digital building design to structural and mechanical, electrical, and plumbing (MEP) engineering, which enables clients to maximize the outcome of their projects in sectors from high-rise to healthcare, stadia to stations and commercial to cultural.

The **Power and Energy** segment offers energy sector clients support from pre-feasibility and community engagement to design, operation and maintenance and decommissioning of a project including large-scale power plants, clean energy investments including renewables, smaller on-site power generation and efficiency programs, or energy transmission, storage and distribution.

The **Industry** segment offers a range of manufacturing and engineering services within multiple disciplines that span all stages of a project to clients in almost every industrial sector including food and beverages, pharmaceutical and biotechnology, aerospace, automotive, technology and chemicals.

In addition, the company offers planning and advisory services, management services and technology and sustainability services; and holds 50.5% interest (**Altus Group Limited** 49.5%) in **GeoVerra Inc.**, a Canadian geomatics business providing land surveying, forestry and geospatial solutions to clients in diverse industries with offices across western Canada and Ontario.

In August 2023, the company sold wholly owned **Louis Berger Services, Inc.** (LBS) to **Versar Inc.**, a global engineering, environmental and security services company, for an undisclosed amount. LBS provides operations and maintenance services for complex infrastructure assets at mission-essential defence and civilian facilities worldwide.

In May 2023, the company acquired **LGT Inc.**, a 150-employee building engineering firm based in Quebec, providing advisory services in the areas of mechanical engineering, electricity, sustainable development, structural and civil engineering. Terms were not disclosed.

In October 2022, the company acquired **Odeh Engineers, Inc.**, a 40-person structural engineering firm with offices in Providence, R.I. and Boston, Mass., offering services such as designing complex structures including buildings, bridges and other infrastructure projects; structural and seismic analysis; construction support; and forensic engineering. Terms were not disclosed.

In August 2022, the company acquired **Greencap Holdings Ltd.**, a 250-employee risk management and compliance consulting firm based in Australia, providing advisory services related to health, safety and environmental management. Terms were not disclosed.

In June 2022, the company acquired **BOD Arquitectura e Ingeniería**, a 45-employee architecture and engineering firm based in Madrid, Spain. Terms were not disclosed.

Recent Merger and Acquisition Activity

Status: completed **Revised:** June 5, 2023
UPDATE: The transaction was completed. PREVIOUS: WSP Global Inc. agreed to acquire Australia-based Calibre Professionals Services One Pty Ltd., which provides engineering services focused on rail, infrastructure, rehabilitation and renewable projects, for A$275,000,000 (Cdn$250,000,000).

Status: completed **Revised:** Jan. 31, 2023
UPDATE: The transaction was completed. PREVIOUS: WSP Global Inc. agreed to acquire Enstruct Group Pty Ltd., a 75-employee structural engineering firm with offices in Sydney, Melbourne, and Brisbane, Australia. Terms were not disclosed. The transaction was expected to close in the first quarter of 2023.

Status: completed **Revised:** Jan. 31, 2023
UPDATE: The transaction was completed. PREVIOUS: WSP Global Inc. agreed to acquire Switzerland-based BG Bonnard & Gardel Holding S.A., which provides consulting, engineering and project management services in the infrastructure, building, water, environment and energy sectors. Terms of the transaction were not disclosed. BG's workforce included 480 professionals in Switzerland and 210 in France. BG also had operations in Portugal and Italy. The transaction was expected to be completed in the first quarter of 2023.

Status: terminated **Revised:** Oct. 11, 2022
UPDATE: The transaction was terminated as WSP announced it would not revise its offer. PREVIOUS: WSP Global Inc. agreed to acquire Abingdon, U.K.-based RPS Group plc, which provides specialist services to government and private sector clients with a focus on front-end consulting, for £2.06 cash per share, representing an enterprise value of £625,000,000 (Cdn$975,000,000). WSP would finance the transaction with funds from a new credit facility and proceeds from a bought deal public offering and concurrent private placement. RPS works across six sectors: property; energy; transport; water; resources; and defence and government services. Services span twelve clusters, consisting of: project and program management; design and development; water services; environment; advisory and management consulting; exploration and development; planning and approvals; health, safety and risk; oceans and coastal; laboratories; training; and communication and creative services. The board of directors of RPS unanimously recommended that shareholders vote in favour of the transaction, which was expected to be completed in the fourth quarter of 2022. Sept. 26, 2022 - RPS entered into agreement to be acquired by Tetra Tech, Inc. and RPS's directors have withdrawn their recommendation of WSP's proposed acquisition of RPS.

Status: completed **Revised:** Sept. 23, 2022
UPDATE: The transaction was completed. PREVIOUS: WSP Global Inc. agreed to acquire Capita Real Estate and Infrastructure Ltd. and GL Hearn Ltd., both U.K.-based companies, for a total of £60,000,000. Capita provides specialist advisory, design, engineering, environmental and project management services for land, building and infrastructure owners; and GL Hearn provides cross-sector advisory services to developers, investors and occupiers across business rates and valuation, planning and development, and lease advisory.

Status: completed **Revised:** Sept. 21, 2022
UPDATE: The transaction was completed for US$1.801 billion. PREVIOUS: WSP Global Inc. agreed to acquire the Environment and Infrastructure business of U.K.-based John Wood Group plc for US$1.81 billion (Cdn$2.31 billion), including the present value of US$200,000,000 derived from a transaction related tax benefit, which would be financed with a new US$1.81 billion (Cdn$2.31 billion) fully committed term credit facility. The acquisition would add 20,000 experts to WSP's Earth and Environment consultancy, and would significantly increase WSP's presence in Organisation for Economic Co-operation and Development (OECD) countries such as the U.S., Canada and the U.K. The transaction was expected to be completed in the fourth quarter of 2022.

Predecessor Detail - Succeeded GENIVAR Inc., Jan. 1, 2014, pursuant to plan of arrangement whereby wholly owned WSP Global Inc. was formed to acquire GENIVAR Inc. (renamed WSP Canada Inc.).

Directors - Christopher Cole, chr., Surrey, United Kingdom; Pierre Shoiry, v-chr., Mount Royal, Qué.; Alexandre L'Heureux, pres. & CEO, Saint-Lambert, Qué.; Louis-Philippe Carrière, Lorraine, Qué.; Birgit W. Nørgaard, Denmark; Suzanne Rancourt, Verdun, Qué.; Paul Raymond, Qué.; Linda Smith-Galipeau, Wis.; Macky Tall, Indialantic, Fla.

Other Exec. Officers - Ian Blair, man. dir., New Zealand; Alain Michaud, CFO; Philippe Fortier, chief legal officer & corp. sec.; Juliana Fox, chief ethics & compliance officer; Chadi Habib, chief tech. officer & head, bus. solutions; Gino Poulin, CIO; Megan Van Pelt, chief HR officer; Sandy Vassiadis, chief comml. officer; Marc Rivard, sr. v-p, operational performance; Lewis P. (Lou) Cornell, pres. & CEO, U.S.A.; Marie-Claude Dumas, pres. & CEO, Canada; Guy Templeton, pres. & CEO, Asia Pacific; Ivy Kong, CEO, Asia; Dean McGrail, CEO, Middle East; Dr. Peter Myers, CEO, Latin America & Caribbean; Mark W. Naysmith, CEO, U.K., Europe, Middle East & Africa; Anna-Lena Öberg-Högsta, CEO, Nordics; Eric van den Broek, CEO, Central Europe

Capital Stock

	Authorized (shs.)	Outstanding (shs.)[1]
Preferred	unlimited	nil
Common	unlimited	124,624,209

[1] At Aug. 7, 2023

Options - At Dec. 31, 2022, options were outstanding to purchase 706,602 common shares at prices ranging from $41.69 to $180.65 per share.

Major Shareholder - Caisse de dépôt et placement du Québec held 18.13% interest and Canada Pension Plan Investment Board held 14.67% interest at Mar. 30, 2023.

Price Range - WSP/TSX

Year	Volume	High	Low	Close
2022	44,213,380	$183.47	$130.65	$157.09
2021	34,893,407	$187.94	$109.69	$183.63
2020	55,442,511	$127.54	$59.83	$120.59
2019	38,545,781	$90.83	$56.09	$88.67
2018	60,481,856	$75.42	$56.38	$58.67

Recent Close: $186.53

Capital Stock Changes - In August 2022, bought deal public offering of 3,031,400 common shares, including 395,400 common shares on exercise of over-allotment option, and concurrent private placement of 3,032,550 common shares all at $151.75 per share were completed. Also during 2022, common shares were issued as follows: 584,457 under a dividend reinvestment plan and 22,295 on exercise of options.

Dividends

WSP com Ra $1.50 pa Q est. Aug. 15, 2008

Long-Term Debt - Outstanding at Dec. 31, 2022:

Credit facilities[1]	$2,401,300,000
2.408% sr. notes due 2028	500,000,000
Bank overdraft	4,600,000
Other long-term debt	48,600,000
	2,954,500,000
Less: Current portion	173,400,000
	2,781,100,000

[1] Consist of borrowings under a US$500,000,000 revolving credit facility due April 2025 and a US$1 billion revolving credit facility due April 2027, bearing interest at Canadian prime, U.S.-based rate, bankers' acceptance rate and term SOFR plus an applicable margin of up to 2.25%; and US$750,000,000 of term loans due to April 2025.

Wholly Owned Subsidiaries

BG Bonnard & Gardel Holding S.A., Switzerland.
Berger Group Holdings, Inc., Morristown, N.J.
- 100% int. in **Louis Berger (Canada) Limited**, N.S.

Calibre Professionals Services One Pty Ltd., Australia.
Capita Real Estate and Infrastructure Ltd., United Kingdom.
Enterra Holdings Ltd., Mississauga, Ont.
- 100% int. in **Golder Associates Ltd.**, Ont.
- 100% int. in **Golder Associates Pty Ltd.**, Australia.
- 100% int. in **Golder Associates USA Inc.**, Ga.

GL Hearn Ltd., United Kingdom.
WSP (Asia) Limited, Hong Kong, Hong Kong, People's Republic of China.
WSP Australia Holdings Pty Ltd., Australia.
WSP Australia Pty Ltd., Australia.
WSP Canada Inc., Canada.
WSP International, LLC, Del.
WSP Michigan Inc., Mich.
WSP Middle East Ltd., Jersey.
WSP New Zealand Limited, New Zealand.
WSP Norge AS, Norway.
WSP Sverige AB, Sweden.
WSP UK Limited, United Kingdom.
WSP USA Buildings Inc., N.Y.
WSP USA Environment and Infrastructure Inc., Nev.
WSP USA Inc., N.Y.
WSP USA Services Inc., Del.
WSP USA Solutions Inc., N.Y.

Subsidiaries

50.5% int. in **GeoVerra Inc.**, Edmonton, Alta. 50% voting interest

Note: The preceding list includes only the major related companies in which interests are held.

Financial Statistics

Periods ended:	12m Dec. 31/22[A]		12m Dec. 31/21[A]
	$000s	%Chg	$000s
Operating revenue	**11,932,900**	**+16**	**10,279,100**
Salaries & benefits	6,679,900		5,851,200
Other operating expense	3,769,700		3,155,300
Operating expense	**10,449,600**	**+16**	**9,006,500**
Operating income	**1,483,300**	**+17**	**1,272,600**
Deprec., depl. & amort.	576,500		518,500
Finance income	(16,300)		16,400
Finance costs, gross	145,300		95,900
Investment income	24,000		19,500
Write-downs/write-offs	(21,600)		nil
Pre-tax income	**587,500**	**-9**	**645,100**
Income taxes	152,800		171,000
Net income	**434,700**	**-8**	**474,100**
Net inc. for equity hldrs	**431,800**	**-9**	**473,600**
Net inc. for non-cont. int.	**2,900**	**+480**	**500**
Cash & equivalent	603,000		1,063,000
Accounts receivable	2,625,800		1,916,800
Current assets	5,034,200		4,340,800
Long-term investments	120,200		118,000
Fixed assets, net	398,900		363,600
Right-of-use assets	978,900		861,500
Intangibles, net	7,894,800		5,312,200
Total assets	**14,841,700**	**+32**	**11,250,400**
Accts. pay. & accr. liabs	2,703,100		2,207,000
Current liabilities	4,615,200		3,791,500
Long-term debt, gross	2,954,500		1,776,700
Long-term debt, net	2,781,100		1,479,300
Long-term lease liabilities	856,800		766,100
Shareholders' equity	6,006,000		4,664,500
Non-controlling interest	3,100		700
Cash from oper. activs	**814,800**	**-23**	**1,060,100**
Cash from fin. activs	1,420,700		790,200
Cash from invest. activs	(2,682,700)		(1,344,900)
Net cash position	**491,000**	**-47**	**926,300**
Capital expenditures	(130,900)		(100,700)
Capital disposals	2,000		10,400
	$		$
Earnings per share*	3.59		4.07
Cash flow per share*	6.77		9.10
Cash divd. per share*	1.50		1.50
	shs		shs
No. of shs. o/s*	124,453,717		117,783,015
Avg. no. of shs. o/s*	120,400,365		116,479,695
	%		%
Net profit margin	3.64		4.61
Return on equity	8.09		10.83
Return on assets	4.16		5.42
Foreign sales percent	82		84
No. of employees (FTEs)	66,000		55,000

* Common
[A] Reported in accordance with IFRS

Latest Results

Periods ended:	6m July 1/23[A]		6m July 2/22[A]
	$000s	%Chg	$000s
Operating revenue	7,115,500	+30	5,476,000
Net income	264,600	+43	185,200
Net inc. for equity hldrs	263,200	+43	184,300
Net inc. for non-cont. int	1,400		900
	$		$
Earnings per share*	2.11		1.56

* Common
[A] Reported in accordance with IFRS

Historical Summary
(as originally stated)

Fiscal Year	Oper. Rev. $000s	Net Inc. Bef. Disc. $000s	EPS* $
2022[A]	11,932,900	434,700	3.59
2021[A]	10,279,100	474,100	4.07
2020[A]	8,803,900	277,400	2.51
2019[A]	8,916,100	285,700	2.72
2018[A]	7,908,100	248,800	2.38

* Common
[A] Reported in accordance with IFRS

W.5 Wajax Corporation*

Symbol - WJX **Exchange** - TSX **CUSIP** - 930783
Head Office - 2250 Argentia Rd, Mississauga, ON, L5N 6A5 **Telephone** - (905) 813-8310 **Toll-free** - (888) 504-9941 **Fax** - (905) 812-7203
Website - www.wajax.com
Email - sauld@wajax.com
Investor Relations - Stuart H. Auld (905) 212-3300
Auditors - KPMG LLP C.A., Toronto, Ont.
Lawyers - Norton Rose Fulbright Canada LLP, Toronto, Ont.
Transfer Agents - Computershare Trust Company of Canada Inc., Montréal, Qué.
FP500 Revenue Ranking - 224
Employees - 3,000 at Dec. 31, 2022
Profile - (Can. 2010) Distributes and sells manufacturing infrastructure equipments, power train and power generation products, and industrial components, as well as provides related services, through a network of branch locations in Canada.

Offers equipment sales, industrial parts, product support and equipment rental to the construction, forestry, mining, industrial/commercial, oil sands, transportation, metal processing, government and utilities, and oil and gas sectors. Products offered include construction equipment; material handling equipment; storage equipment; industrial products; power generation solutions; crane and utility equipment; forestry equipment; mining and oil sands equipment; marine power generation equipment, on-highway power; and off highway power.

Also offers engineered repair of equipment such as shop and field services, commissioning, design, repairs and rebuilds, reliability and installation services.

As at Dec. 31, 2022, operated 117 branches across 11 Canadian provinces and territories.

In December 2022, wholly owned **Integrated Distribution Systems Limited Partnership**, **Wajax Industrial Components Limited Partnership** and **Wajax GP Holdco Inc.** ceased to operations to simplify the company's operating structure. All assets, agreements and liabilities have been assigned to wholly owned **Wajax Limited** .

Recent Merger and Acquisition Activity

Status: completed **Announced:** July 4, 2023
Wajax Corporation, through wholly Tundra Process Solutions Ltd., acquired Polyphase Engineered Controls (1977) Ltd., which specializes in producing custom electrical and instrumentation equipment for the oil and gas, utilities, mining, forestry and agricultural sectors. Terms were not disclosed.

Status: completed **Announced:** June 30, 2022
Wajax Corporation, through wholly Tundra Process Solutions Ltd., acquired the valve business of Powell Canada Inc. for $5,360,000. Powell specializes in valve sales, service and support with facilities in Edmonton, Fort McMurray and Lloydminster, Alta.

Predecessor Detail - Succeeded Wajax Income Fund, Jan. 1, 2011, pursuant to plan of arrangement whereby Wajax Corporation was formed to facilitate the conversion of the fund into a corporation and the fund was subsequently dissolved.

Directors - Edward M. (Ed) Barrett, chr., Woodstock, N.B.; Ignacy P. (Iggy) Domagalski, pres. & CEO, Calgary, Alta.; Leslie Abi-Karam, Palm Beach Gardens, Fla.; Thomas M. (Tom) Alford, Calgary, Alta.; Douglas A. Carty, Glen Ellyn, Ill.; Sylvia D. Chrominska, Stratford, Ont.; Dr. A. Jane Craighead, Ont.; David G. Smith, Calgary, Alta.; Elizabeth A. (Beth) Summers, Oakville, Ont.; Alexander S. (Sandy) Taylor, Montréal, Qué.; Susan Uthayakumar, West Palm Beach, Fla.

Other Exec. Officers - Stuart H. Auld, CFO; Mark Edgar, chief people officer; Steven C. (Steve) Deck, sr. v-p, heavy equip. & COO; André Dubé, sr. v-p, ind. parts & engineered repair svcs.; Gregory (Greg) Abtosway, v-p, corp. devel.; Tania Casadinho, v-p & contr.; Cristian Rodriguez, v-p, envir., health, safety & sustainability; Andrew W. H. Tam, gen. counsel & corp. sec.

Capital Stock

	Authorized (shs.)	Outstanding (shs.)[1]
Preferred	unlimited	nil
Common	unlimited	21,489,982

[1] At Aug. 10, 2023

Major Shareholder - Widely held at Mar. 7, 2023.

Price Range - WJX/TSX

Year	Volume	High	Low	Close
2022	12,775,130	$24.57	$17.25	$19.73
2021	17,802,954	$29.67	$16.24	$24.27
2020	23,510,484	$19.60	$4.90	$17.09
2019	11,761,231	$19.95	$13.98	$14.80
2018	7,592,249	$28.17	$15.43	$16.58

Recent Close: $27.65

Capital Stock Changes - During 2022, 71,408 common shares were issued under share-based compensation plan, 23,915 common shares held in trust were released and 33,544 common shares were purchased and held in trust.

Dividends

WJX com Ra $1.32 pa Q est. Apr. 4, 2023
Prev. Rate: $1.00 est. Apr. 20, 2015

Long-Term Debt - Outstanding at Dec. 31, 2022:

Credit facilities[1]	$84,955,000
6% sr. unsec. debs. due 2025	57,000,000
Less: Def. fin. costs	2,591,000
	139,364,000
Less: Current portion	nil
	139,364,000

[1] Consist of $400,000,000 revolving and non-revolving credit facilities which matures in October 2027, and bearing interest at floating rates at margins over Canadian dollar bankers' acceptance yields, U.S. dollar SOFR rates or prime.

Wholly Owned Subsidiaries

Polyphase Engineered Controls (1977) Ltd., Edmonton, Alta.
Tundra Process Solutions Ltd., Calgary, Alta.
Wajax Limited, Mississauga, Ont.
- 100% int. in **Groupe Delom Inc.**, Montréal, Qué.
  - 100% int. in **Delom Services Inc.**, Qué.
  - 100% int. in **Delstar Energie Inc.**, Qué.
  - 100% int. in **Motion Electric Motor Services Inc.**, Ont.
- 100% int. in **NorthPoint Technical Services ULC**, Calgary, Alta.
- 100% int. in **Wajax (U.S.) Limited**, Wash.
  - 100% int. in **Fluid Conditioning Inc.**, Wash.
  - 100% int. in **Pacific North Equipment Company**, Kent, Wash.

Note: The preceding list includes only the major related companies in which interests are held.

Financial Statistics

Periods ended:	12m Dec. 31/22[A]		12m Dec. 31/21[A]
	$000s	%Chg	$000s
Operating revenue	**1,962,822**	**+20**	**1,637,281**
Cost of sales	1,518,841		1,251,814
Other operating expense	264,321		228,634
Operating expense	**1,793,482**	**+20**	**1,489,586**
Operating income	**169,340**	**+15**	**147,695**
Deprec., depl. & amort	55,483		55,394
Finance income	352		229
Finance costs, gross	17,697		19,362
Pre-tax income	**96,512**	**+32**	**73,168**
Income taxes	24,104		19,920
Net income	**72,408**	**+36**	**53,248**
Cash & equivalent	nil		9,988
Inventories	462,164		388,702
Accounts receivable	307,055		223,512
Current assets	860,123		681,364
Fixed assets, net	83,504		85,318
Right-of-use assets	122,720		134,503
Intangibles, net	170,714		171,375
Total assets	**1,249,882**	**+16**	**1,080,847**
Bank indebtedness	5,230		nil
Accts. pay. & accr. liabs	422,704		304,828
Current liabilities	514,078		367,887
Long-term debt, gross	139,364		153,441
Long-term debt, net	139,364		153,441
Long-term lease liabilities	127,099		137,597
Shareholders' equity	449,770		389,913
Cash from oper. activs	**69,132**	**-64**	**190,145**
Cash from fin. activs	(70,004)		(124,198)
Cash from invest. activs	(14,346)		(62,584)
Net cash position	**(5,230)**	**n.a.**	**9,988**
Capital expenditures	(9,224)		(5,939)
Capital disposals	913		17,576
Unfunded pension liability	6,655		8,418
	$		$
Earnings per share*	3.38		2.50
Cash flow per share*	3.23		8.92
Cash divd. per share*	1.00		1.00
	shs		shs
No. of shs. o/s*	21,471,102		21,409,323
Avg. no. of shs. o/s*	21,423,140		21,328,093
	%		%
Net profit margin	3.69		3.25
Return on equity	17.25		14.88
Return on assets	7.35		6.53
No. of employees (FTEs)	3,000		2,800

* Common
[A] Reported in accordance with IFRS

Latest Results

Periods ended:	6m June 30/23[A]		6m June 30/22[A]
	$000s	%Chg	$000s
Operating revenue	1,102,288	+16	950,722
Net income	46,506	+23	37,803
	$		$
Earnings per share*	2.16		1.76

* Common
[A] Reported in accordance with IFRS

Historical Summary
(as originally stated)

Fiscal Year	Oper. Rev.	Net Inc. Bef. Disc.	EPS*
	$000s	$000s	$
2022[A]	1,962,822	72,408	3.38
2021[A]	1,637,281	53,248	2.50
2020[A]	1,422,648	31,653	1.58
2019[A]	1,553,046	39,504	1.98
2018[A]	1,481,597	35,852	1.82

* Common
[A] Reported in accordance with IFRS

W.6 Wall Financial Corporation*

Symbol - WFC **Exchange** - TSX **CUSIP** - 931902
Head Office - 1010 Burrard St, Vancouver, BC, V6Z 2R9 **Telephone** - (604) 893-7131 **Fax** - (604) 893-7179
Website - www.wallfinancialcorporation.com
Email - mlowe@wallcentre.com
Investor Relations - Marion Lowe (604) 893-7255
Auditors - KPMG LLP C.A., Vancouver, B.C.
Transfer Agents - Computershare Trust Company of Canada Inc., Vancouver, B.C.
FP500 Revenue Ranking - 711
Employees - 488 at Jan. 31, 2023
Profile - (B.C. 1969 amalg.) Operates in three segments of the real estate industry, primarily in the Vancouver, B.C., area: ownership and management of revenue-producing residential and commercial properties; ownership and management of hotel properties; and development and sale of residential housing units.

Revenue-Producing Properties

The residential apartment units are leased primarily for a one-year term and all leasing arrangements are governed by the British Columbia Residential Tenancy Act. Rental rates may be increased on tenant turnover or on the anniversary date of each tenant's date of occupancy. The average turnover rate for all of the company's units is about 20% annually. At Apr. 30, 2023, the company owned and managed 1,503 residential and 20 commercial units in 17 properties in the Metro Vancouver Area.

Hotels

Owns and manages the Sheraton Vancouver Wall Centre Hotel in Vancouver, B.C., consisting of two towers with 746 guestrooms and 45,000 sq. ft. of meeting space; and The Westin Wall Centre Vancouver Airport Hotel near the Vancouver International Airport in Richmond, B.C., consisting of 188 guestrooms and 9,900 sq. ft. of meeting space.

Development Properties

At Apr. 30, 2023, two projects were under active development: Eagle Mountain, an 80-acre, single-family subdivision property in Abbotsford, B.C., with approvals in place for 262 single-family lots; and The Trails in North Vancouver, B.C., consisting of 307 townhome and low-rise residential units as well as two strata rental properties to be developed in several phases.

In May 2023, the company acquired a commercial strata unit for $1,275,000.

In March and April 2023, the company acquired two residential strata units in Vancouver, B.C., for $1,379,000.

During fiscal 2023, the company acquired two residential strata units at Wall Centre in Vancouver, B.C., for $1,184,000; and development of The Trails Phase 2B in North Vancouver, B.C. was completed in December 2022.

Recent Merger and Acquisition Activity

Status: completed **Announced:** Apr. 14, 2023
Wall Financial Corporation acquired a 12-unit residential strata property in Vancouver, B.C., for $6,800,000.

Status: completed **Announced:** Jan. 31, 2023
Wall Financial Corporation acquired a 21-unit residential and commercial property at 648-670 East Broadway in Vancouver, B.C., for $21,100,000.

Status: completed **Announced:** Jan. 31, 2023
Wall Financial Corporation acquired a building at 1065 Pacific Street in Vancouver, B.C., for $14,000,000.

Status: completed **Announced:** Mar. 4, 2022
Wall Financial Corporation sold a development property (Cambie and West 43rd Avenue) in Vancouver, B.C., for $76,000,000.

Predecessor Detail - Name changed from Wall & Redekop Corp., Aug. 8, 1988; basis 3 new for 1 old sh.

Directors - Peter W. Ufford, chr., Surrey, B.C.; Bruno Wall, pres., CEO, CFO & treas., Vancouver, B.C.; Sascha A. Voth, v-p, hotel opers. & gen. mgr., North Vancouver, B.C.; Darcee Wise, pres., Peter Wall Mansion & Estates, Langley, B.C.; Oliver J. Borgers, Toronto, Ont.; Michael Redekop, Abbotsford, B.C.

Other Exec. Officers - Grant Myles, v-p, const.; Marion Lowe, contr.

Capital Stock

	Authorized (shs.)	Outstanding (shs.)[1]
Common	54,000,000	32,453,765

[1] At May 8, 2023

Normal Course Issuer Bid - The company plans to make normal course purchases of up to 688,362 common shares representing 10% of the public float. The bid commenced on Mar. 15, 2023, and expires on Mar. 14, 2024.

Major Shareholder - Peter Wall held 54% interest, Bruno Wall held 13% interest and Estate of John Redekop held 10% interest at May 8, 2023.

Price Range - WFC/TSX

Year	Volume	High	Low	Close
2022	131,315	$17.00	$11.00	$13.50
2021	236,651	$21.50	$14.01	$14.12
2020	661,545	$37.95	$15.01	$17.50
2019	266,112	$38.95	$21.21	$33.58
2018	166,429	$29.85	$22.90	$23.99

Recent Close: $19.00

Capital Stock Changes - There were no changes to capital stock during fiscal 2023.

Dividends

WFC com N.S.R.
$3.00 Mar. 3/23
Paid in 2023: $3.00 2022: n.a. 2021: n.a.

Long-Term Debt - Outstanding at Jan. 31, 2023:

Floating rate mtges.[1]	$51,984,416
Fixed rate mtges.[2]	351,806,645
Less: Deferred financing fees	7,684,120
	396,106,941
Less: Current portion	66,634,222
	329,472,719

[1] Bear interest at bankers' acceptance rates plus stamping fees.
[2] Bear interest at fixed rates ranging from 1.48% to 3.77%.

Minimum mortgage repayments were reported as follows:

2024	$66,634,222
2025	7,486,543
2026	36,304,132
2027	49,429,246
2028	5,945,897
Thereafter	237,991,021

Note - In March 2023, principal amount of the credit facility increased from $7,000,000 to $35,000,000, bearing interest at prime plus 0.65% or bankers' acceptance rates plus 2.15%.

Wholly Owned Subsidiaries

Brunswick & 6th Development Ltd.
Cambie and 58th (No. 2) Developments Limited Partnership, Canada.
Cambie and 43rd Developments Limited Partnership
Eagle Mountain Properties Ltd.
588526 British Columbia Ltd.
41st Ave. Development Limited Parternship, Canada.
Hastings Street Developments Limited Partnership, Canada.
1050 Burrard Holdings Ltd.
SWC Hotels LLP
Shannon Condominium Developments Unit Trust
Shannon Estates Utility Ltd., Canada.
W.F.C. Investments Limited Partnership, Canada.
W.F.C. Properties (Broadway) Inc., B.C.
W.F.C. Properties Inc., B.C.
W.F.C. Properties (Pacific) Inc., B.C.
WWC Hotels LLP
Wall Centre Construction Ltd.

Subsidiaries

75% int. in **Wall Centre Central Park Condominiums Limited Partnership**
57% int. in **Wall Trails Rental Development Limited Partnership**, Canada.
75% int. in **Wall University Developments Limited Partnership**, Canada.

Investments

43% int. in **Wall North Vancouver Townhome Development Limited Partnership**, Vancouver, B.C.

Financial Statistics

Periods ended:	12m Jan. 31/23[A]		12m Jan. 31/22[^A]
	$000s	%Chg	$000s
Total revenue	**144,353**	**-40**	**241,048**
General & admin. expense	4,718		3,086
Other operating expense	80,958		181,876
Operating expense	**85,676**	**-54**	**184,962**
Operating income	**58,677**	**+5**	**56,086**
Deprec. & amort.	14,204		15,319
Finance income	374		498
Finance costs, gross	13,289		11,034
Pre-tax income	**61,898**	**+105**	**30,232**
Income taxes	12,622		7,492
Net income	**49,276**	**+117**	**22,741**
Net inc. for equity hldrs	**48,207**	**+230**	**14,615**
Net inc. for non-cont. int.	**1,070**	**-87**	**8,126**
Cash & equivalent	25,413		20,114
Inventories	358		267
Accounts receivable	9,154		9,710
Current assets	75,808		125,617
Long-term investments	nil		137
Fixed assets	242,712		240,575
Income-producing props	642,795		583,783
Properties under devel.	117,175		113,388
Property interests, net	798,331		747,589
Total assets	**874,729**	**0**	**874,063**
Bank indebtedness	143,843		199,456
Accts. pay. & accr. liabs	19,572		21,463
Current liabilities	235,066		348,778
Long-term debt, gross	396,107		380,530
Long-term debt, net	329,473		263,475
Shareholders' equity	235,878		185,080
Non-controlling interest	52,149		62,385
Cash from oper. activs	**44,738**	**-68**	**141,640**
Cash from fin. activs	(44,738)		(89,029)
Cash from invest. activs	5,299		(50,459)
Net cash position	**25,413**	**+26**	**20,114**
Capital expenditures	(2,188)		(1,117)
Capital disposals	64,016		nil
Increase in property	(56,654)		(57,842)
	$		$
Earnings per share*	1.49		0.45
Cash flow per share*	1.38		4.33
	shs		shs
No. of shs. o/s*	32,453,365		32,453,365
Avg. no. of shs. o/s*	32,453,365		32,683,502
	%		%
Net profit margin	34.14		9.43
Return on equity	22.90		7.74
Return on assets	6.85		3.36
No. of employees (FTEs)	488		332

* Common
[^] Restated
[A] Reported in accordance with IFRS

Latest Results

Periods ended:	3m Apr. 30/23[A]		3m Apr. 30/22[A]
	$000s	%Chg	$000s
Total revenue	32,205	-2	32,876
Net income	2,428	-92	30,484
Net inc. for equity hldrs	2,731	-91	29,999
Net inc. for non-cont. int.	(303)		485
	$		$
Earnings per share*	0.08		0.92

* Common
[A] Reported in accordance with IFRS

Historical Summary
(as originally stated)

Fiscal Year	Total Rev.	Net Inc. Bef. Disc.	EPS*
	$000s	$000s	$
2023[A]	144,353	49,276	1.49
2022[A]	241,048	22,741	0.45
2021[A]	191,559	3,572	0.02
2020[A]	474,601	124,263	3.61
2019[A]	452,217	64,049	1.62

* Common
[A] Reported in accordance with IFRS

W.7 Wangton Capital Corp.

Symbol - WT.H **Exchange** - TSX-VEN **CUSIP** - 93390B
Head Office - 145-925 Georgia St W, Vancouver, BC, V6C 3L2 **Telephone** - (778) 989-4999
Email - moedilon@live.com
Investor Relations - Moe Dilon (778) 989-4999
Auditors - Manning Elliott LLP C.A., Vancouver, B.C.
Transfer Agents - Computershare Trust Company of Canada Inc.
Profile - (B.C. 2018; orig. Alta., 2010) Capital Pool Company.

Directors - Moe Dilon, chr., pres. & CEO, B.C.; Tagdeer (Tag) Gill, CFO & corp. sec., Vancouver, B.C.; Cyrus H. Driver, Vancouver, B.C.; The Hon. Jerahmiel S. (Jerry) Grafstein, Toronto, Ont.; Kyle Haddow, Alta.

Capital Stock

	Authorized (shs.)	Outstanding (shs.)[1]
Common	unlimited	24,415,083

[1] At Aug. 29, 2022

Major Shareholder - The Hon. Jerahmiel S. (Jerry) Grafstein held 10.44% interest at June 20, 2022.

Price Range - WT.H/TSX-VEN

Year	Volume	High	Low	Close
2021	1,683,733	$0.09	$0.04	$0.07
2020	1,110,567	$0.09	$0.03	$0.05
2019	727,500	$0.10	$0.06	$0.09
2018	433,633	$0.11	$0.08	$0.09

Capital Stock Changes - In August 2022, a 1-for-16 common share consolidation was proposed.

W.8 Waroona Energy Inc.

Symbol - WHE **Exchange** - TSX-VEN **CUSIP** - 934633
Head Office - Level 20, 140 St Georges Terrace, Perth, WA, Australia, 6000 **Overseas Tel** - 61-8-9200-3428
Website - waroonaenergy.com
Email - contact@waroonaenergy.com
Investor Relations - Anthony J. Wonnacott (604) 737-2303
Auditors - BDO Audit Pty Ltd., Perth, W.A. Australia
Transfer Agents - Computershare Trust Company of Canada Inc., Toronto, Ont.

Profile - (B.C. 2021; orig. B.C., 1993) Developing a solar energy project in Western Australia and has mineral interest in Ontario.

The company is developing a 241-MW solar energy farm, 114 km south of Perth, Australia. The project will be able to sell energy into the spot market and secure offtake via power purchase agreements for renewable electricity.

Holds formerly producing Superior Lake zinc-copper-gold-silver project, 176 km^2, 20 km north of Schreiber, Ont., consisting of Pick Lake deposit and an option to acquire Winston Lake deposit. An updated feasibility study released in November 2021 proposed an underground mining operation with average annual production of 33,401 tonnes zinc concentrate and 1,270 tonnes copper concentrate over a 8.5-year mine life. Initial capital costs were estimated at $145,084,600. At September 2021, proven and probable reserves were 1,960,000 tonnes grading 13.9% zinc, 0.6% copper, 0.2 g/t gold and 26.2 g/t silver.

Recent Merger and Acquisition Activity

Status: completed **Revised:** May 16, 2023

UPDATE: The transaction was completed. PREVIOUS: Metallum Resources Inc. entered into a letter of intent for the reverse takeover acquisition of Waroona Energy Pty Ltd., which is developing a 241-MW solar farm in Western Australia. Metallum plans to complete a concurrent financing for gross proceeds of up to Cdn$9,000,000. A total of 304,500,000 common shares were expected to be issued (excluding the shares to be issued in connection with the concurrent financing) to Waroona shareholders. Dec. 6, 2022 - The companies entered into a definitive agreement. On closing, Metallum was expected to change its name to Waroona Energy Inc. Feb. 9, 2023 - Metallum announced plans to issue up to 150,000,000 subscription receipts at $0.06 per receipt for gross proceeds of $9,000,000.

Predecessor Detail - Name changed from Metallum Resources Inc., May 11, 2023, pursuant to the reverse takeover acquisition of Waroona Energy Pty Ltd.

Directors - Anthony J. (Tony) Wonnacott, chr., Toronto, Ont.; Adam Kiley, pres. & CEO, W.A., Australia; Mark Hanlon, Perth, W.A., Australia; Paul Manias, Ont.

Other Exec. Officers - Sean C. McGrath, CFO; Jan Urata, corp. sec.

Capital Stock

	Authorized (shs.)	Outstanding (shs.)[1]
Common	unlimited	737,979,415

[1] At May 23, 2023

Major Shareholder - Frontier Energy Limited held 17.8% interest at May 23, 2023.

Price Range - WHE/TSX-VEN

Year	Volume	High	Low	Close
2022	21,180,461	$0.11	$0.03	$0.03
2021	7,108,843	$0.20	$0.07	$0.08
2020	2,152,867	$0.35	$0.10	$0.15
2019	1,200,373	$0.50	$0.05	$0.10
2018	1,762,423	$1.20	$0.25	$0.35

Consolidation: 1-for-10 cons. in Apr. 2021

Recent Close: $0.05

Capital Stock Changes - In May 2023, 304,500,000 common shares were issued pursuant to the reverse takeover acquisition of Waroona Energy Pty Ltd., and 150,000,000 common shares were issued without further consideration on exchange of subscription receipts sold previously by private placement at 6¢ each.

In April 2022, private placement of 87,371,674 units (1 common share & 1 warrant) at 6¢ per unit was completed.

Wholly Owned Subsidiaries

Pick Lake Mining Limited, Halifax, N.S.
Waroona Energy Pty Ltd., Australia.
- 100% int. in **SE Waroona Development Pty Ltd.**, Australia.

Note: The preceding list includes only the major related companies in which interests are held.

Financial Statistics

Periods ended:	12m Dec. 31/22[A]		12m Dec. 31/21[A1]
	$000s	%Chg	$000s
Salaries & benefits	249		133
Exploration expense	564		978
General & admin expense	505		349
Stock-based compensation	66		416
Operating expense	**1,384**	**-26**	**1,877**
Operating income	**(1,384)**	**n.a.**	**(1,877)**
Deprec., depl. & amort.	2		1
Finance income	56		1
Finance costs, gross	nil		189
Pre-tax income	**(1,423)**	**n.a.**	**(2,516)**
Income taxes	(30)		(79)
Net income	**(1,393)**	**n.a.**	**(2,437)**
Cash & equivalent	3,460		219
Accounts receivable	nil		2
Current assets	3,519		281
Fixed assets, net	nil		2
Explor./devel. properties	14,431		14,431
Total assets	**17,950**	**+21**	**14,775**
Accts. pay. & accr. liabs.	126		267
Current liabilities	126		593
Shareholders' equity	17,824		14,182
Cash from oper. activs.	**(1,471)**	**n.a.**	**(2,489)**
Cash from fin. activs.	4,673		3,578
Cash from invest. activs.	39		(892)
Net cash position	**3,460**	**n.m.**	**219**
Capital expenditures	nil		(892)
	$		$
Earnings per share*	(0.01)		(0.02)
Cash flow per share*	(0.01)		(0.02)
	shs		shs
No. of shs. o/s*	283,479,415		196,107,741
Avg. no. of shs. o/s*	247,824,063		147,545,051
	%		%
Net profit margin	n.a.		n.a.
Return on equity	(8.70)		n.m.
Return on assets	(8.51)		(29.62)

* Common

[A] Reported in accordance with IFRS

[1] Results reflect the Apr. 1, 2021, reverse takeover acquisition of Pick Lake Mining Limited.

Historical Summary
(as originally stated)

Fiscal Year	Oper. Rev. $000s	Net Inc. Bef. Disc. $000s	EPS* $
2022[A]	nil	(1,393)	(0.01)
2021[A]	nil	(2,437)	(0.02)
2020[A1]	nil	(1,190)	(0.16)
2019[A]	537	(7,373)	(0.80)
2018[A2]	173	(2,634)	(0.50)

* Common

[A] Reported in accordance with IFRS

[1] Results for 2020 and prior years pertain to CROPS Inc.

[2] 13 months ended Dec. 31, 2018.

Note: Adjusted throughout for 1-for-10 cons. in Apr. 2021

W.9 Waste Connections, Inc.*

Symbol - WCN **Exchange** - TSX **CUSIP** - 94106B

Head Office - 600-6220 Hwy 7, Woodbridge, ON, L4H 4G3 **Telephone** - (905) 532-7510

Website - www.wasteconnections.com

Email - maryannew@wasteconnections.com

Investor Relations - Mary Anne Whitney (832) 442-2200

Auditors - Grant Thornton LLP C.P.A., Houston, Tex.

Lawyers - Torys LLP, Toronto, Ont.

Transfer Agents - Computershare Trust Company, Inc., Golden, Colo.; Computershare Trust Company of Canada Inc., Toronto, Ont.

FP500 Revenue Ranking - 65

Employees - 22,109 at Dec. 31, 2022

Profile - (Ont. 2008) Provides non-hazardous solid waste collection, transfer and disposal services, along with resource recovery primarily through recycling and renewable fuels generation, in mostly exclusive and secondary markets across the U.S. and Canada.

Also provides non-hazardous oil and natural gas exploration and production (E&P) waste treatment, recovery and disposal services in several basins across the U.S., as well as offers intermodal services for the rail haul movement of cargo and solid waste containers in the Pacific Northwest.

Operations serve residential, commercial, industrial, and E&P customers in 43 U.S. states and six Canadian provinces.

Operations at Dec. 31, 2022:

Solid waste collection operations	359
Transfer stations	209[1]
Landfills[2]	100[3]
Intermodal facilities	6[4]
Recycling stations	79
E&P liquid waste injections wells	22
E&P waste treatment/oil recovery facilities	18

[1] Includes 52 transfer stations under contracted terms.

[2] Includes active municipal solid waste (MSW), E&P and non-MSWs.

[3] Includes 120 operated landfills under contracted terms.

[4] Includes two intermodal facilities under contracted terms.

During 2022, the company acquired 24 immaterial non-hazardous solid waste collection, transfer, recycling and disposal businesses.

Predecessor Detail - Name changed from Progressive Waste Solutions Ltd., June 1, 2016, pursuant to reverse takeover acquisition of (old) Waste Connections, Inc.; basis 1 new for 2.07684 old shs.

Directors - Michael W. Harlan, chr., Tex.; Ronald J. Mittelstaedt, pres. & CEO, Calif.; Andrea E. Bertone, Houston, Tex.; Edward E. (Ned) Guillet, Sonoma, Calif.; Larry S. Hughes, Vancouver, B.C.; Elise L. Jordan, Tenn.; Susan (Sue) Lee, Vancouver, B.C.; William J. Razzouk, Fla.

Other Exec. Officers - Darrell W. Chambliss, exec. v-p & COO; James M. Little, exec. v-p, eng. & disposal; Patrick J. Shea, exec. v-p, gen. counsel & corp. sec.; Mary Anne Whitney, exec. v-p & CFO; Matthew S. Black, sr. v-p & chief acctg. officer; Robert M. Cloninger, sr. v-p, deputy gen. counsel & asst. sec.; Jason J. Craft, sr. v-p, opers.; David G. Eddie, sr. v-p, performance optimization; Eric O. Hansen, sr. v-p & CIO; Susan R. Netherton, sr. v-p, people, training & devel.; Andrea R. Click, v-p, tax; Keith P. Gordon, v-p, info. sys.; Michelle L. Little, v-p, engagement solutions; Shawn W. Mandel, v-p, safety & risk mgt.; John M. Perkey, v-p & deputy gen. counsel, compliance & govt. affairs; Jason W. Pratt, v-p & contr.; Kurt R. Shaner, v-p, eng. & sustainability; Gregory Thibodeaux, v-p, maint. & fleet mgt.; Colin G. Wittke, v-p, sales

Capital Stock

	Authorized (shs.)	Outstanding (shs.)[1]
Preferred	unlimited	nil
Common	unlimited	257,630,679

[1] At Aug. 2, 2023

Normal Course Issuer Bid - The company plans to make normal course purchases of up to 12,881,534 common shares representing 5% of the total outstanding. The bid commenced on Aug. 10, 2023, and expires on Aug. 9, 2024.

Major Shareholder - The Vanguard Group, Inc. held 10.76% interest at Mar. 24, 2023.

Price Range - WCN/TSX

Year	Volume	High	Low	Close
2022	81,001,992	$196.62	$148.05	$179.48
2021	69,295,315	$176.12	$122.13	$172.40
2020	99,663,592	$143.84	$100.55	$130.52
2019	76,110,808	$128.98	$98.50	$117.95
2018	72,126,552	$107.01	$81.52	$101.33

Recent Close: $187.55

Capital Stock Changes - During 2022, common shares were issued as follows: 318,851 on vesting of restricted share units, 104,253 on exercise of warrants, 57,677 on vesting of performance-based restricted share units, 26,582 under employee share purchase plan, 19,509 on release of restricted share units from deferred compensation plan and 5,203 on sale of common shares held in trust; 3,388,155 common shares were repurchased under a Normal Course Issuer Bid and 210,700 common shares were cancelled.

Dividends

WCN com Ra US$1.02 pa Q est. Dec. 1, 2022
Prev. Rate: US$0.92 est. Nov. 23, 2021
Prev. Rate: US$0.82 est. Nov. 25, 2020

Long-Term Debt - Outstanding at Dec. 31, 2022:

Revolv. credit facility	US$614,705,000
Term loan	1,450,000,000
4.25% sr. notes due 2028	500,000,000
3.5% sr. notes due 2029	500,000,000
2.6% sr. notes due 2030	600,000,000
2.2% sr. notes due 2032	650,000,000
3.2% sr. notes due 2032	500,000,000
4.2% sr. notes due 2033	750,000,000
3.05% sr. notes due 2050	500,000,000
2.95% sr. notes due 2052	850,000,000
Finance lease obligs.[1]	11,464,000
Other notes pay.[2]	37,232,000
Less: Debt disc. & issue costs	66,493,000
	6,896,908,000
Less: Current portion	6,759,000
	6,890,149,000

[1] Bearing interest at 1.89% to 2.16% and due from 2026 to 2027.

[2] Consist of notes payable bearing interest at 2.42% to 10.35%, with due dates ranging from 2024 to 2036.

Principal repayments required in each of the next five years and thereafter were as follows:

2023	US$6,759,000
2024	10,636,000
2025	7,112,000
2026	2,071,152,000
2027	4,862,563,000
Thereafter	6,963,401,000

Wholly Owned Subsidiaries

American Disposal Services, Inc., Manassas, Va.
E.L. Harvey & Sons, Inc., Westborough, Mass.
Groot Industries, Inc., Ill.
R360 Environmental Solutions, LLC, Del.
Waste Connections U.S., Inc., The Woodlands, Tex. formerly Waste Connections, Inc.

Note: The preceding list includes only the major related companies in which interests are held.

Financial Statistics

Periods ended:	12m Dec. 31/22[A]		12m Dec. 31/21[A]
	US$000s	%Chg	US$000s
Operating revenue	**7,211,859**	**+17**	**6,151,361**
Cost of sales	4,336,012		3,654,074
Stock-based compensation	63,485		58,221
Other operating expense	632,982		554,116
Operating expense	**5,032,479**	**+18**	**4,266,411**
Operating income	**2,179,380**	**+16**	**1,884,950**
Deprec., depl. & amort.	918,960		813,009
Finance income	5,950		2,916
Finance costs, gross	202,331		162,796
Pre-tax income	**1,048,963**	**+36**	**770,742**
Income taxes	212,962		152,253
Net income	**836,001**	**+35**	**618,489**
Net inc. for equity hldrs.	**835,662**	**+35**	**618,047**
Net inc. for non-cont. int.	**339**	**-23**	**442**
Cash & equivalent	78,637		147,441
Inventories	55,188		44,257
Accounts receivable	833,862		709,614
Current assets	1,117,645		1,032,777
Fixed assets, net	6,950,915		5,721,949
Right-of-use assets	192,506		160,567
Intangibles, net	8,576,214		7,538,240
Total assets	**17,134,603**	**+17**	**14,699,924**
Bank indebtedness	15,645		16,721
Accts. pay. & accr. liabs.	1,069,975		835,464
Current liabilities	1,512,643		1,232,746
Long-term debt, gross	6,896,908		5,046,520
Long-term debt, net	6,890,149		5,040,500
Long-term lease liabilities	165,462		129,628
Shareholders' equity	7,108,698		6,988,938
Non-controlling interest	4,946		4,607
Cash from oper. activs.	**2,022,492**	**+19**	**1,698,229**
Cash from fin. activs.	1,028,463		(499,496)
Cash from invest. activs.	(3,087,171)		(1,693,482)
Net cash position	**181,364**	**-17**	**219,615**
Capital expenditures	(912,677)		(744,315)
Capital disposals	30,676		42,768
	US$		US$
Earnings per share*	3.25		2.37
Cash flow per share*	7.86		6.50
Cash divd. per share*	0.95		0.85
	shs		shs
No. of shs. o/s*	257,145,716		260,212,496
Avg. no. of shs. o/s*	257,383,578		261,166,723
	%		%
Net profit margin	11.59		10.05
Return on equity	11.86		8.93
Return on assets	6.27		5.22
Foreign sales percent	87		86
No. of employees (FTEs)	22,109		19,998

* Common

[A] Reported in accordance with U.S. GAAP

Latest Results

Periods ended:	6m June 30/23[A]		6m June 30/22[A]
	US$000s	%Chg	US$000s
Operating revenue	3,921,598	+13	3,462,690
Net income	407,006	+1	404,575
Net inc. for equity hldrs.	407,021	+1	404,398
Net inc. for non-cont. int.	(15)		177
	US$		US$
Earnings per share*	1.58		1.57

* Common

[A] Reported in accordance with U.S. GAAP

Historical Summary
(as originally stated)

Fiscal Year	Oper. Rev. US$000s	Net Inc. Bef. Disc. US$000s	EPS* US$
2022[A]	7,211,859	836,001	3.25
2021[A]	6,151,361	618,489	2.37
2020[A]	5,445,990	203,992	0.78
2019[A]	5,388,679	566,681	2.15
2018[A]	4,922,941	547,154	2.07

* Common

[A] Reported in accordance with U.S. GAAP

W.10 Water Ways Technologies Inc.

Symbol - WWT **Exchange** - TSX-VEN **CUSIP** - 941188
Head Office - 3000-77 King St W, PO Box 95 TD Centre, Toronto, ON, M5K 1G8 **Telephone** - (416) 840-3798 **Fax** - (416) 368-5122
Website - www.water-ways-technologies.com
Email - ronnie@waterwt.com
Investor Relations - Ronnie Jaegermann 972-54-420-2054
Auditors - BDO Ziv Haft C.P.A., Tel Aviv, Israel
Transfer Agents - Computershare Trust Company of Canada Inc., Toronto, Ont.
Profile - (Ont. 2007) Designs, supplies, installs and maintains water irrigation systems focused on commercial applications in the micro and precision irrigation segments.

Operations are organized into two business units:

The **Project Services Business Unit** supplies, installs and maintains irrigation systems for application in various agricultural and aqua-cultural operations. Turn-key projects include irrigation systems, water ways, greenhouses, fish farms, silos and other types of agricultural facilities. The company has also developed the DataWays system, a precise irrigation system which collects real-time data from sensors installed in the field that allows analysis of the data and control the system from a mobile device allowing agricultural operators to make data-driven decisions on how and when to irrigate their crops for better functional application with significantly reduced consumption of water. In addition, the company has also developed CANNAWAYS, an Internet-of-Things controlled irrigation and fertilization system for cannabis cultivators and growers which allows higher yields and consistency for cannabis grows while reducing energy, water and fertilization costs. The company has implemented multiple turn-key agricultural and aqua-cultural projects in Canada, Israel, the People's Republic of China, South Africa, Mexico, Peru, Colombia, Ethiopia, Uzbekistan and other countries.

The **Products - Component and Equipment Sales Unit** focuses on purchasing, assembling and exporting technologically advanced irrigation products and systems from Israeli manufacturers. Products include drip laterals, drippers, micro-sprayers, sprinklers water pipes and accessories, manual filtration systems, semi-automatic and automatic filters, self-cleaning screens, disc and media filters, air valves, check valves, agriculture hydraulic controls, unmeasured flow reducers, smart monitoring and control irrigation solutions, single standalone battery-operated controller to multi stations, wireless, web-based irrigation and fertigation systems, and connectors. Also, the company holds the right to sell **Amiad Water Systems Ltd.**'s filtration systems in Canada.

In addition, the company, through 52%-owned **Maravey Corporation S.A.**, plans to obtain a medical cannabis production licence; and through 52%-owned **Zoryan Trade S.A.**, plans to obtain a licence to grow cannabis and extract oil therefrom, both in Uruguay.

In February 2023, the company terminated its agreement to acquire a 51% interest in private Chile-based **Desarrollo de Sistemas Hidraulicos S.A.** (Hidrotop) for US$3,500,000, consisting of US$2,000,000 cash and issuance of 5,686,364 common shares at a deemed price of Cdn$0.33 per share. Both parties agreed to renegotiate a new, reduced acquisition price. Hidrotop is an irrigation and hydraulic engineering company operating in the agricultural and mining industries in Chile and Argentina.

Predecessor Detail - Name changed from Sagittarius Capital Corporation, Mar. 6, 2019, following Qualifying Transaction reverse takeover acquisition of Irri-Al-Tal Ltd.; basis 1 new for 1.49643 old shs.
Directors - Ohad Haber, chr. & CEO, Israel; Yehuda Doron, Tel Aviv, Israel; Ronnie (Ronen) Jaegermann, Tel Aviv, Israel; Nitin Kaushal, Richmond Hill, Ont.; James Lanthier, Toronto, Ont.
Other Exec. Officers - Dor Sneh, CFO; Tomer Bachar, chief tech. officer; Yaron Dichter, v-p, agriculture; Amir Eylon, v-p, opers. & projects

Capital Stock

	Authorized (shs.)	Outstanding (shs.)[1]
Common	unlimited	148,485,345

[1] At Mar. 31, 2023

Major Shareholder - Ohad Haber held 34.5% interest at Nov. 25, 2022.

Price Range - WWT/TSX-VEN

Year	Volume	High	Low	Close
2022	26,441,632	$0.45	$0.14	$0.14
2021	58,578,578	$0.36	$0.05	$0.30
2020	10,512,376	$0.10	$0.04	$0.05
2019	14,381,925	$0.35	$0.06	$0.06

Recent Close: $0.05

Capital Stock Changes - In March 2023, private placement of 2,415,000 units (1 common share & ½ warrant) at Cdn$0.13 per unit was completed, with warrants exercisable at Cdn$0.20 for three years.

During 2022, common shares were issued as follows: 1,492,315 on exercise of warrants, 800,000 on exercise of options and 102,320 for debt settlement.

Wholly Owned Subsidiaries

Heartnut Grove WWT Inc.
Irri-Al-Tal Ltd., Israel.

Subsidiaries

73% int. in **H.D.P. Irrigation Ltd.**, Israel.
• 100% int. in **IRRI-AL TAL (Shanghai) Agriculture Technology Company Ltd.**, People's Republic of China.
52% int. in **Maravey Corporation S.A.**, Uruguay.
52% int. in **Zoryan Trade S.A.**, Uruguay.

Financial Statistics

Periods ended:	12m Dec. 31/22[A]		12m Dec. 31/21[A]
	US$000s	%Chg	US$000s
Operating revenue	**10,809**	**-33**	**16,159**
Cost of sales	8,780		12,901
Salaries & benefits	1,743		1,973
General & admin expense	2,117		1,711
Operating expense	**12,640**	**-24**	**16,585**
Operating income	**(1,831)**	**n.a.**	**(426)**
Deprec., depl. & amort.	262		194
Finance income	27		193
Finance costs, gross	252		414
Pre-tax income	**2,006**	**n.a.**	**(5,308)**
Income taxes	(65)		(5)
Net income	**2,071**	**n.a.**	**(5,303)**
Net inc. for equity hldrs	**2,067**	**n.a.**	**(5,412)**
Net inc. for non-cont. int	**4**	**-96**	**109**
Cash & equivalent	1,064		2,599
Inventories	2,249		1,961
Accounts receivable	2,402		4,393
Current assets	6,890		9,685
Fixed assets, net	414		361
Intangibles, net	1,724		1,875
Total assets	**9,230**	**-24**	**12,085**
Accts. pay. & accr. liabs	2,674		4,336
Current liabilities	4,758		6,078
Long-term debt, gross	2,400		1,374
Long-term debt, net	645		489
Long-term lease liabilities	10		26
Shareholders' equity	1,711		(831)
Cash from oper. activs	**(2,919)**	**n.a.**	**(1,314)**
Cash from fin. activs	1,404		3,625
Cash from invest. activs	(76)		(32)
Net cash position	**1,064**	**-59**	**2,599**
Capital expenditures	(127)		(170)
	US$		US$
Earnings per share*	0.01		(0.05)
Cash flow per share*	(0.02)		(0.01)
	shs		shs
No. of shs. o/s*	145,970,345		143,575,710
Avg. no. of shs. o/s*	145,450,594		117,911,797
	%		%
Net profit margin	19.16		(32.82)
Return on equity	n.m.		n.m.
Return on assets	21.87		(48.85)
Foreign sales percent	57		79

* Common
[A] Reported in accordance with IFRS

Latest Results

Periods ended:	3m Mar. 31/23[A]		3m Mar. 31/22[A]
	US$000s	%Chg	US$000s
Operating revenue	3,040	-17	3,669
Net income	276	-39	449
Net inc. for equity hldrs	264	-41	449
Net inc. for non-cont. int	12		nil
	US$		US$
Earnings per share*	0.00		0.00

* Common
[A] Reported in accordance with IFRS

Historical Summary
(as originally stated)

Fiscal Year	Oper. Rev. US$000s	Net Inc. Bef. Disc. US$000s	EPS* US$
2022[A]	10,809	2,071	0.01
2021[A]	16,159	(5,303)	(0.04)
2020[A]	9,477	(1,166)	(0.01)
2019[A1]	9,628	(2,369)	(0.03)
2018[A2]	12,089	417	n.a.

* Common
[A] Reported in accordance with IFRS
[1] Results reflect the Mar. 6, 2019, Qualifying Transaction reverse takeover acquisition of Irri-Al-Tad Ltd.
[2] Results pertain to Irri-Al-Tal Ltd.
Note: Adjusted throughout for 1-for-1.4964285 cons. in Mar. 2019

W.11 Wavefront Technology Solutions Inc.

Symbol - WEE.H **Exchange** - TSX-VEN (S) **CUSIP** - 94354B
Head Office - 5621 70 St NW, Edmonton, AB, T6B 3P6 **Telephone** - (780) 486-2222 **Fax** - (780) 484-7177
Website - www.onthewavefront.com
Email - investor@onthewavefront.com
Investor Relations - Brett C. Davidson (780) 486-2222
Auditors - Deloitte LLP C.A.
Lawyers - Dentons Canada LLP, Edmonton, Alta.; Bennett Jones LLP, Vancouver, B.C.
Transfer Agents - Computershare Trust Company of Canada Inc., Calgary, Alta.
Profile - (Can. 2003; orig. B.C., 1980) Develops, markets and licenses proprietary dynamic fluid injection technology for performance drilling or milling, oil and gas well stimulation, and improved or enhanced oil recovery.

The Powerwave™ process is an injection technology that improves the flow of fluids (such as oil and gas) in geological materials including sedimentary soils and fractured rock which decreases chemical cost and job execution time.

The Primawave™ process is a method for aiding in-situ (in-ground) environmental groundwater remediation clean-up strategies in contaminated sites.

Common suspended from TSX-VEN, Jan. 6, 2023.

Predecessor Detail - Name changed from Wavefront Energy and Environmental Services Inc., Mar. 27, 2009.
Directors - Brett C. Davidson, pres. & CEO, Cambridge, Ont.; Mark Bernard, Alta.; Dennis R. Minano, Mich.; James (Jimmy) Smith, Colo.

Capital Stock

	Authorized (shs.)	Outstanding (shs.)[1]
Common	unlimited	91,010,165

[1] At Jan. 26, 2022

Major Shareholder - Doug Burger held 16.3% interest at Jan. 20, 2022.

Price Range - WEE.H/TSX-VEN (S)

Year	Volume	High	Low	Close
2022	5,155,309	$0.37	$0.02	$0.02
2021	11,641,297	$0.47	$0.04	$0.38
2020	9,782,981	$0.15	$0.01	$0.05
2019	4,877,630	$0.27	$0.01	$0.08
2018	8,966,599	$0.49	$0.18	$0.22

Recent Close: $0.02

Wholly Owned Subsidiaries

Wavefront Technology Solutions USA Inc., Del.

Financial Statistics

Periods ended:	12m Aug. 31/21[A]		12m Aug. 31/20[A]
	$000s	%Chg	$000s
Operating revenue	**1,606**	**-43**	**2,804**
Cost of sales	75		120
Research & devel. expense	110		211
General & admin expense	2,725		2,685
Operating expense	**2,910**	**-4**	**3,016**
Operating income	**(1,304)**	**n.a.**	**(212)**
Deprec., depl. & amort.	270		371
Finance income	17		24
Finance costs, gross	18		12
Write-downs/write-offs	(119)		(225)
Pre-tax income	**(1,374)**	**n.a.**	**(660)**
Net income	**(1,374)**	**n.a.**	**(660)**
Cash & equivalent	1,202		1,818
Inventories	52		91
Accounts receivable	194		765
Current assets	1,507		2,748
Fixed assets, net	440		485
Right-of-use assets	460		63
Intangibles, net	nil		62
Total assets	**2,420**	**-28**	**3,371**
Accts. pay. & accr. liabs	491		565
Current liabilities	666		709
Shareholders' equity	1,335		2,663
Cash from oper. activs	**(456)**	**n.a.**	**(481)**
Cash from fin. activs	(89)		(149)
Cash from invest. activs	(61)		(151)
Net cash position	**1,202**	**-34**	**1,818**
Capital expenditures	(75)		(84)
Capital disposals	14		nil
	$		$
Earnings per share*	(0.02)		(0.01)
Cash flow per share*	(0.01)		(0.01)
	shs		shs
No. of shs. o/s*	87,572,573		87,572,573
Avg. no. of shs. o/s*	87,572,573		87,572,573
	%		%
Net profit margin	(85.55)		(23.54)
Return on equity	(68.73)		(22.06)
Return on assets	(46.83)		(17.17)
Foreign sales percent	100		100

* Common
[A] Reported in accordance with IFRS

Latest Results

Periods ended:	3m Nov. 30/21^A		3m Nov. 30/20^A
	$000s	%Chg	$000s
Operating revenue	428	-4	446
Net income	(573)	n.a.	(348)
	$		$
Earnings per share*	(0.01)		(0.00)

* Common
A Reported in accordance with IFRS

Historical Summary
(as originally stated)

Fiscal Year	Oper. Rev.	Net Inc. Bef. Disc.	EPS*
	$000s	$000s	$
2021^A	1,606	(1,374)	(0.02)
2020^A	2,804	(660)	(0.01)
2019^A	3,630	(433)	(0.01)
2018^A	3,215	(1,791)	(0.02)
2017^A	2,168	(3,710)	(0.04)

* Common
A Reported in accordance with IFRS

W.12 Waverley Pharma Inc.

Symbol - WAVE **Exchange** - TSX-VEN **CUSIP** - 94357L
Head Office - 4-1250 Waverley St, Winnipeg, MB, R3T 6C6 **Telephone** - (204) 928-7900 **Fax** - (204) 453-1370
Website - www.waverleypharma.com
Email - huddin@waverleypharma.com
Investor Relations - Haaris Uddin (204) 478-5609
Auditors - Ernst & Young LLP C.A., Winnipeg, Man.
Transfer Agents - Computershare Trust Company of Canada Inc., Calgary, Alta.
Profile - (Can. 2017 amalg.) Researches and develops a novel inhibitor for cancer treatment. Also holds licenses to develop and commercialize products for the generic oncology market in the European Union, the U.K. and North America.

The company focuses on the research and development of Poly (ADP-Ribose) Polymerase-1 (PARP-1) inhibitors, which are anti-cancer agents targeting DNA repair enzymes. PARP-1 inhibitors are used as monotherapy to selectively kill cancer cells or in combination with other treatments such as chemotherapy and radiation therapy.

Also holds licenses from **Reliance Life Sciences Private Limited** (RLS) to manufacture and sell capecitabine in the U.K. and Germany, as well as temozolomide and erlotinib in the UK. In addition, holds licenses from RLS to injectable generic chemotherapy drugs under development, pemetrexed (formerly WAV-101) and bortezomib (formerly WAV-102) in the U.S., Canada and the European Union and to sell both drugs in the U.K. Capecitabine is a generic chemotherapy drug for the treatment of breast cancer, gastric cancer and colorectal cancer. Erlotinib is an oral oncology drug for the treatment of non-small cell lung cancer and pancreatic cancer. Temozolomide is a generic chemotherapy drug for the treatment of brain tumours. Pemetrexed is used for the treatment of non-small cell lung cancer and pleural mesothelioma and bortezomib is used for the treatment of multiple myeloma and mantle cell lymphoma. The products are marketed in the European Union and the U.K. through wholly owned **Waverly Pharma Europe Limited**.

In December 2022, wholly owned **Waverly Pharma International Inc.** was wound up.

Predecessor Detail - Formed from Buffalo Capital Inc. in Canada, Oct. 24, 2017, pursuant to Qualifying Transaction amalgamation with (old) Waverley Pharma Inc. (deemed acquiror); basis 1 new com. sh. for 1 Buffalo com. sh. and 400,000 new com. shs. for 1 (old) Waverley com. sh.
Directors - Dr. Albert D. Friesen, chr., Winnipeg, Man.; P. Marcus Enns, Winnipeg, Man.; Hellen Siwanowicz, Toronto, Ont.
Other Exec. Officers - Larry Thiessen, pres. & CEO; Haaris Uddin, CFO

Capital Stock

	Authorized (shs.)	Outstanding (shs.)[1]
Common	unlimited	54,000,000

[1] At May 25, 2023

Major Shareholder - Dr. Albert D. Friesen held 74.61% interest at May 8, 2023.

Price Range - WAVE/TSX-VEN

Year	Volume	High	Low	Close
2022	1,676,942	$0.09	$0.03	$0.03
2021	9,614,703	$0.21	$0.07	$0.08
2020	32,448,110	$0.43	$0.05	$0.13
2019	775,500	$0.24	$0.06	$0.10
2018	673,535	$0.48	$0.15	$0.28

Recent Close: $0.04
Capital Stock Changes - There were no changes to capital stock from 2018 to 2022, inclusive.

Wholly Owned Subsidiaries

Waverley Pharma Europe Limited, Ireland.

Financial Statistics

Periods ended:	12m Dec. 31/22^A		12m Dec. 31/21^A
	$000s	%Chg	$000s
Operating revenue	**1,247**	**-29**	**1,753**
Cost of goods sold	963		1,530
Salaries & benefits	223		245
Research & devel. expense	82		10
General & admin expense	926		710
Operating expense	**1,231**	**-51**	**2,496**
Operating income	**16**	**n.a.**	**(743)**
Deprec., depl. & amort.	212		28
Finance costs, net	17		3
Write-downs/write-offs	nil		(17)
Pre-tax income	**(664)**	**n.a.**	**(797)**
Net income	**(664)**	**n.a.**	**(797)**
Cash & equivalent	134		158
Inventories	62		330
Accounts receivable	193		702
Current assets	633		1,446
Intangibles, net	1,679		1,758
Total assets	**2,687**	**-27**	**3,684**
Bank indebtedness	702		222
Accts. pay. & accr. liabs	737		1,062
Current liabilities	1,596		1,895
Long-term debt, gross	nil		40
Shareholders' equity	1,091		1,789
Cash from oper. activs	**(237)**	**n.a.**	**(799)**
Cash from fin. activs	439		222
Cash from invest. activs	(227)		nil
Net cash position	**134**	**-15**	**158**
	$		$
Earnings per share*	(0.01)		(0.01)
Cash flow per share*	(0.00)		(0.01)
	shs		shs
No. of shs. o/s*	54,000,000		54,000,000
Avg. no. of shs. o/s*	54,000,000		54,000,000
	%		%
Net profit margin	(53.25)		(45.46)
Return on equity	(46.11)		(41.60)
Return on assets	(20.84)		(22.21)
Foreign sales percent	100		100

* Common
A Reported in accordance with IFRS

Latest Results

Periods ended:	3m Mar. 31/23^A		3m Mar. 31/22^A
	$000s	%Chg	$000s
Operating revenue	119	-61	304
Net income	(340)	n.a.	(311)
	$		$
Earnings per share*	(0.01)		(0.01)

* Common
A Reported in accordance with IFRS

Historical Summary
(as originally stated)

Fiscal Year	Oper. Rev.	Net Inc. Bef. Disc.	EPS*
	$000s	$000s	$
2022^A	1,247	(664)	(0.01)
2021^A	1,753	(797)	(0.01)
2020^A	1,375	(706)	(0.01)
2019^A	1,157	(1,215)	(0.02)
2018^A	223	(1,421)	(0.03)

* Common
A Reported in accordance with IFRS

W.13 Way of Will Inc.

Symbol - WAY **Exchange** - CSE (S) **CUSIP** - 94412Y
Head Office - Unit 1-A, 110 Mack Ave, Toronto, ON, M1L 1N3 **Telephone** - (647) 350-2038 **Fax** - (647) 350-3948
Website - wayofwill.com
Email - business@wayofwill.com
Investor Relations - Willie Tsang (647) 350-2038
Auditors - Crowe MacKay LLP C.A., Vancouver, B.C.
Lawyers - McMillan LLP
Transfer Agents - Olympia Trust Company, Vancouver, B.C.
Profile - (Ont. 2016) Manufactures and retails body care, skin care and wellness aromatherapy products that use natural aromatic plant extracts and essential oils to promote healthy outcomes.

Main brand is Way of Will and sub-brands include Nude & Crude and Gu Society. Products include deodorants, body washes and lotions, hand washes, bath soaks and aromatherapy rollers, and are sold both online and in more than 1,000 stores across North America, Europe and Asia.

Common suspended from CSE, Sept. 6, 2022.

Directors - Willie Tsang, founder & CEO, Ont.; Anita Cheng, COO, Ont.; Ravinder (Robert) Kang, CFO, Vancouver, B.C.; Geoffrey (Geoff) Balderson, Vancouver, B.C.; Meetul Patel, B.C.

Capital Stock

	Authorized (shs.)	Outstanding (shs.)[1]
Cl.B Preferred	unlimited	781,821
Common	unlimited	41,923,566

[1] At Jan. 31, 2022

Class B Preferred - Entitled to non-cumulative dividends. Redeemable, at the company's option, at a price equal to the amount paid per share plus any declared and unpaid dividends. Non-voting.
Common - One vote per share.
Major Shareholder - Willie Tsang held 30.66% interest at Jan. 31, 2022.

Price Range - WAY/CSE (S)

Year	Volume	High	Low	Close
2022	1,443,167	$0.25	$0.03	$0.04

Recent Close: $0.04
Capital Stock Changes - In January 2022, 12,600,000 units (1 common share & 1 warrant) were issued without further consideration on exchange of special warrants sold previously by private placement at 10¢ each, with warrants exercisable at 12¢ per share for two years, and 24,147,941 units (1 common share & 1 warrant) were issued at 5¢ per unit on conversion of $1,130,000 principal amount of debentures, with warrants exercisable at $0.075 per share for two years.

Financial Statistics

Periods ended:	12m Apr. 30/21^A		12m Apr. 30/20^A
	$000s	%Chg	$000s
Operating revenue	**3,767**	**+89**	**1,991**
Cost of goods sold	2,051		1,379
Research & devel. expense	nil		1
General & admin expense	1,507		969
Operating expense	**3,559**	**+52**	**2,347**
Operating income	**208**	**n.a.**	**(356)**
Deprec., depl. & amort.	135		124
Finance costs, gross	222		95
Write-downs/write-offs	1		(14)
Pre-tax income	**(203)**	**n.a.**	**(550)**
Net income	**(203)**	**n.a.**	**(550)**
Cash & equivalent	303		200
Inventories	872		454
Accounts receivable	780		54
Current assets	2,134		725
Fixed assets, net	138		76
Right-of-use assets	423		513
Intangibles, net	82		96
Total assets	**2,777**	**+97**	**1,411**
Bank indebtedness	1,949		441
Accts. pay. & accr. liabs	848		299
Current liabilities	2,875		1,358
Long-term lease liabilities	498		571
Equity portion of conv. debs	17		nil
Shareholders' equity	(722)		(558)
Cash from oper. activs	**(800)**	**n.a.**	**(207)**
Cash from fin. activs	994		454
Cash from invest. activs	(92)		(129)
Net cash position	**303**	**+52**	**200**
Capital expenditures	(81)		(9)
	$		$
Earnings per share*	n.a.		n.a.
Cash flow per share*	(0.16)		(0.04)
	shs		shs
No. of shs. o/s*	5,000,000		5,000,000
	%		%
Net profit margin	(5.39)		(27.62)
Return on equity	n.m.		n.m.
Return on assets	0.91		n.a.

* Common
A Reported in accordance with IFRS

Latest Results

Periods ended:	3m July 31/21^A		3m July 31/20^A
	$000s	%Chg	$000s
Operating revenue	799	+73	463
Net income	(667)	n.a.	(98)
	$		$
Earnings per share*	n.a.		n.a.

A Reported in accordance with IFRS

W.14 The Well Told Company Inc.

Symbol - WLCO **Exchange** - TSX-VEN (S) **CUSIP** - 949462
Head Office - 200-99 Yorkville Ave, Toronto, ON, M5R 3K5 **Telephone** - (647) 400-4794 **Toll-free** - (855) 935-5865
Website - www.welltold.ca
Email - info@welltold.com
Investor Relations - Betty Au Yeung (855) 935-5865
Auditors - MNP LLP C.A., Toronto, Ont.
Transfer Agents - Computershare Trust Company of Canada Inc.

Profile - (Ont. 2021; orig. Alta., 1996) Formulates, distributes and sells a variety of supplements, remedies and other functional wellness products.

All ingredients are sourced by the company from suppliers ranging from small boutique to larger commercial outfits on an as needed basis, with products then manufactured by a co-packer in Ontario.

Products include Stress Fighter, Plant-Based Vitamin D, Daily Dose of Turmeric (anti-inflammatory), Sleep, Energy Booster, Antioxidant Booster, Bloating Be Gone™, Skin Nourisher, Age Defier and Beauty Sleep. All products are free of synthetics, fillers and isolates, and are Health Canada approved and U.S. Food and Drug Administration compliant which are available through the company's website, www.welltod.com, and third party e-commerce platforms such as Amazon Canada, Amazon US, League Canada and League US.

Has more than 2,000 active wholesale stores in Canada and the U.S. Active wholesale accounts include CVS Pharmacy, Whole Foods Market, Thrive Market, Rite Aid, the Detox Market, Loblaws, Shoppers Drug Mart, Rexall, smaller independent pharmacies and grocers, spas, salons, gift shops, airports and hotels.

Common suspended from TSX-VEN, May 8, 2023.

Predecessor Detail - Name changed from Agau Resources, Inc., Oct. 14, 2021, pursuant to the reverse takeover acquisition of Well Told Inc. and concurrent amalgamation of Well Told with wholly owned 2835270 Ontario Inc.; basis 1 new for 81.42 old shs.

Directors - Monica Ruffo, pres. & CEO, Toronto, Ont.; Simon Ashbourne, Toronto, Ont.; Sean J. F. Samson, Toronto, Ont.; Linda Sawyer, Larchmont, N.Y.; Dr. Jill Shainhouse, Toronto, Ont.; Harjot Singh, London, Middx., United Kingdom

Other Exec. Officers - Betty Au Yeung, CFO & corp. sec.

Capital Stock

	Authorized (shs.)	Outstanding (shs.)[1]
Common	unlimited	149,679,868

[1] At Nov. 23, 2022

Major Shareholder - Monica Ruffo held 21.86% interest at Aug. 19, 2022.

Price Range - WLCO/TSX-VEN (S)

Year	Volume	High	Low	Close
2022	23,475,933	$0.17	$0.02	$0.02
2021	7,420,897	$0.28	$0.12	$0.14

Recent Close: $0.01

Capital Stock Changes - In September 2022, private placement of 14,125,000 units (1 common share & 1 warrant) at 5¢ per unit was completed, with warrants exercisable at 10¢ per share for two years.

Wholly Owned Subsidiaries

Well Told Inc., Toronto, Ont.

Financial Statistics

Periods ended:	12m Dec. 31/21[A1]		12m Dec. 31/20[A]
	$000s	%Chg	$000s
Operating revenue	**1,158**	**+78**	**651**
Cost of goods sold	668		518
Salaries & benefits	1,072		390
Research & devel. expense	80		29
General & admin expense	2,993		1,276
Stock-based compensation	700		87
Other operating expense	317		11
Operating expense	**5,830**	**+152**	**2,312**
Operating income	**(4,672)**	**n.a.**	**(1,661)**
Deprec., depl. & amort.	46		43
Finance costs, gross	287		206
Pre-tax income	**(10,170)**	**n.a.**	**(2,303)**
Net income	**(10,170)**	**n.a.**	**(2,303)**
Cash & equivalent	597		1,097
Inventories	840		275
Accounts receivable	518		168
Current assets	2,357		1,553
Right-of-use assets	17		54
Intangibles, net	55		33
Total assets	**2,429**	**+48**	**1,640**
Accts. pay. & accr. liabs	2,562		1,086
Current liabilities	2,891		3,669
Long-term debt, gross	276		4,726
Long-term debt, net	112		2,686
Long-term lease liabilities	nil		15
Shareholders' equity	(574)		(4,729)
Cash from oper. activs	**(6,094)**	**n.a.**	**(1,564)**
Cash from fin. activs	5,578		2,667
Cash from invest. activs	16		(14)
Net cash position	**597**	**-46**	**1,097**
Capital expenditures	(30)		(14)
	$		$
Earnings per share*	(0.13)		(0.45)
Cash flow per share*	(0.08)		(0.30)
	shs		shs
No. of shs. o/s*	127,368,372		n.a.
Avg. no. of shs. o/s*	76,692,392		5,126,370
	%		%
Net profit margin	(878.24)		(353.76)
Return on equity	n.m.		n.m.
Return on assets	n.a.		(184.76)

* Common

[A] Reported in accordance with IFRS

[1] Results prior to Oct.14, 2021, pertain to and reflect the reverse takeover acquisition of Well Told Inc.

Latest Results

Periods ended:	9m Sept. 30/22[A]		9m Sept. 30/21[A]
	$000s	%Chg	$000s
Operating revenue	1,201	+52	791
Net income	(1,825)	n.a.	(4,101)
	$		$
Earnings per share*	(0.01)		(0.74)

* Common

[A] Reported in accordance with IFRS

Historical Summary
(as originally stated)

Fiscal Year	Oper. Rev. $000s	Net Inc. Bef. Disc. $000s	EPS* $
2021[A]	1,158	(10,170)	(0.13)
2020[A]	651	(2,303)	(0.45)
2019[†A]	369	(2,330)	(0.46)

* Common

† Unaudited

[A] Reported in accordance with IFRS

Note: Adjusted throughout for 1-for-81.42 cons. in Oct. 2021

W.15 Wellfield Technologies Inc.

Symbol - WFLD **Exchange** - TSX-VEN **CUSIP** - 94950R
Head Office - 100-55 Albert St, Markham, ON, L3P 2T4
Website - investors.wellfield.io
Email - levyc@wellfield.io
Investor Relations - Levy Cohen 972-5-4740-2782
Auditors - Kingston Ross Pasnak LLP C.A., Edmonton, Alta.
Transfer Agents - Odyssey Trust Company, Vancouver, B.C.

Profile - (B.C. 2021) Owns and operates Coinmama, a regulated mobile application for buy and sell of digital currencies such as Bitcoin and Ethereum. Also developing technology infrastructure designed to facilitate decentralized finance (DeFi) by streamlining cross-blockchain trading and making Bitcoin compatible with DeFi.

Owns and operates Coinmama, a full consumer solution for day-to day financial needs covering payments, money transfer, saving, investing and borrowing. Coinmama enables moving funds from bank (directly or with credit card) to the blockchain world, while providing direct access to blockchain-enabled services without the need for cryptocurrency exchanges or centralized custody. Coinmama has more than 3,500,000 registered users globally, each of which has undergone regulatory verification and transacted on the platform.

Also developing permissionless financial services solutions through DeFi technologies internally developed and built on public blockchains, which would include decentralized real-time clearing and settlement infrastructure.

Recent Merger and Acquisition Activity

Status: completed **Revised:** May 27, 2022

UPDATE: The transaction was completed. PREVIOUS: Wellfield Technologies Inc. agreed to acquire Israel-based New Bit Ventures Ltd. (dba Coinmama), which owns and operates a global platform for millions of buyers and sellers of digital currencies using everyday payment methods, for $3,844,500 cash and issuance of 22,988,467 common shares at $1.55 per share.

Predecessor Detail - Name changed from 1290447 B.C. Ltd., Nov. 23, 2021, pursuant to the reverse takeover acquisition of Seamless Logic Software Limited and MoneyClip Inc.

Directors - Marc Lustig, chr., Vancouver, B.C.; Levy Cohen, CEO, Herzliya, Israel; Chanan Steinhart, chief strategy officer, strategy & bus. devel., Fla.; Christie Henderson, Oakville, Ont.; Dr. Neal Sample, Wis.

Other Exec. Officers - Brian Lock, CFO, head, product mktg. & corp. sec.; Yishai Steinhart, v-p, R&D & chief tech. officer

Capital Stock

	Authorized (shs.)	Outstanding (shs.)[1]
Common	unlimited	125,355,789

[1] At Aug. 29, 2022

Major Shareholder - Levy Cohen held 10.8% interest at June 15, 2022.

Price Range - WFLD/TSX-VEN

Year	Volume	High	Low	Close
2022	17,422,939	$2.19	$0.18	$0.18
2021	3,475,877	$2.15	$1.13	$1.90

Recent Close: $0.22

Wholly Owned Subsidiaries

MoneyClip Inc., Markham, Ont.
• 100% int. in **Money Clip Canada Inc.**, Ont.
New Bit Ventures Ltd., Israel.
Seamless Logic Software Limited, Gibraltar.
Wellfield Technology IR Limited, Ireland.

Financial Statistics

Periods ended:	12m Dec. 31/21[A1]		12m Dec. 31/20[oA]
	$000s	%Chg	$000s
Research & devel. expense	1,446		55
General & admin expense	1,655		79
Operating expense	**3,101**	**n.m.**	**134**
Operating income	**(3,101)**	**n.a.**	**(134)**
Deprec., depl. & amort.	156		nil
Pre-tax income	**(5,102)**	**n.a.**	**(134)**
Income taxes	185		nil
Net income	**(5,288)**	**n.a.**	**(134)**
Cash & equivalent	17,650		137
Current assets	19,380		137
Fixed assets, net	82		nil
Intangibles, net	23,992		nil
Total assets	**43,454**	**n.m.**	**137**
Accts. pay. & accr. liabs	1,021		326
Current liabilities	1,466		326
Shareholders' equity	41,782		(1,102)
Cash from oper. activs	**(4,943)**	**n.a.**	**(69)**
Cash from fin. activs	22,097		213
Cash from invest. activs	406		nil
Net cash position	**17,630**	**n.m.**	**137**
Capital expenditures	(2)		nil
	$		$
Earnings per share*	(0.10)		n.a.
Cash flow per share*	(0.09)		n.a.
	shs		shs
No. of shs. o/s*	102,270,376		n.a.
Avg. no. of shs. o/s*	52,996,330		n.a.
	%		%
Net profit margin	n.a.		n.a.
Return on equity	n.m.		n.m.
Return on assets	n.a.		n.a.

* Common

[o] Restated

[A] Reported in accordance with IFRS

[1] Results reflect the Nov. 23, 2021, reverse takeover acquisition of Seamless Logic Software Limited and MoneyClip Inc.

Latest Results

Periods ended:	6m June 30/22[A]		6m June 30/21[A]
	$000s	%Chg	$000s
Operating revenue	5,671	n.a.	nil
Net income	(8,471)	n.a.	(348)
	$		$
Earnings per share*	(0.08)		(0.01)

* Common
[A] Reported in accordance with IFRS

W.16 West Fraser Timber Co. Ltd.*

Symbol - WFG **Exchange** - TSX **CUSIP** - 952845
Head Office - 1500-885 Georgia St W, Vancouver, BC, V6C 3E8 **Telephone** - (604) 895-2700 **Fax** - (604) 681-6061
Website - www.westfraser.com
Email - shareholder@westfraser.com
Investor Relations - Robert B. Winslow (416) 777-4426
Auditors - PricewaterhouseCoopers LLP C.A., Vancouver, B.C.
Lawyers - McMillan LLP, Vancouver, B.C.
Transfer Agents - Computershare Trust Company of Canada Inc., Vancouver, B.C.
FP500 Revenue Ranking - 48
Employees - 11,000 at Dec. 31, 2022

Profile - (B.C. 1966) Produces lumber, oriented strand board (OSB), laminated veneer lumber (LVL), medium density fibreboard (MDF), plywood, particleboard, pulp, newsprint, wood chips, other residuals and renewable energy, with facilities in Canada, the U.S., the U.K. and Europe.

Operations are organized into four segments: Lumber; North America Engineered Wood Products (NA EWP); Pulp & Paper; and Europe Engineered Wood Products (Europe EWP).

Lumber - During 2022, lumber and by-product wood chips were produced from 12 sawmills in Alberta (6) and British Columbia (6) and 22 in the southern United States. Also owns and operates a wood treating facility at its Sundre, Alta., sawmill. Lumber that is produced at Canadian sawmills and sold to North American customers is marketed from a sales office in Quesnel, B.C., while sales to offshore markets are made from an export sales office in Vancouver, B.C. In addition, a customer service centre is maintained in Japan. Lumber produced at the company's U.S. sawmills is marketed by a sales group in Memphis, Tenn.

NA EWP - Operations include 10 multi-opening press OSB mills; three continuous press OSB mills; three plywood mills that primarily produce standard softwood sheathing plywood; two MDF mills; an LVL mill; and a veneer mill that produces veneer for use in the company's Edmonton plywood mill. North American OSB and plywood products are marketed from a sales office in Toronto, Ont., while LVL and MDF products are marketed from a sales office in Quesnel, B.C. NA OSB products are marketed under the following brand names: Durastrand® pointSIX®, Pinnacle® and Stabledge® (premium flooring), TruFlor® pointSIX® and TruFlor® (commodity flooring), Rimboard™, SteadiTred® (industrial), QuakeZone®, Windstorm™, TallWall® and Trubord™ (wall sheathing) and SolarBord™ (radiant barrier sheathing), Trubord™ (roof sheathing), TruDeck® (flat roof sheathing for large industrial/commercial buildings) and StableDeck® (utility trailer floors). Canadian MDF products are marketed under the Ranger™, WestPine™, and EcoGold™ brand names.

Pulp & Paper - This segment includes NBSK pulp produced in Quesnel pulp mill; BCTMP produced primarily at Slave Lake and Quesnel pulp mills; and Unbleached Kraft pulp (UKP) produced in Hinton, Alta., pulp mill. These types of pulp are used by paper manufacturers to produce tissues, printing and writing papers, paperboard and a variety of other paper grades. Newsprint is produced at Whitecourt, Alta., through the joint venture **Alberta Newsprint Company**. The company's share of annual newsprint capacity was 135,000 tonnes at Dec. 31, 2022. Newsprint is sold to various publishers and printers in North America and delivered by rail and truck.

Europe EWP - Operations include EWP mills in Scotland and Belgium, as well as a particleboard mill (including a furniture manufacturing facility) in South Molton, England. OSB, particleboard, MDF and related value-added products are marketed from a sales office in Cowie, Scotland. OSB is sold primarily to customers in the U.K., Germany, BeNeLux, France and Scandinavia while particleboard, MDF and related value-added products are sold primarily to customers in the U.K. Products sold within the U.K. and within continental Europe are shipped by truck and rail while products sold to Scandinavia are shipped by vessel. Products are sold under the SterlingOSB Zero® (OSB), CaberFloor® (particleboard), Conti ® (particleboard) and CaberWood® (MDF) trademarks.

Annual log requirements at the company's Canadian sawmills, plywood facilities and LVL plant totaled 11,500,000 m^3, of which majority is accessible from quota-based tenures, with the balance acquired from third parties holding short or long-term timber harvesting rights. In addition, the company's Canadian OSB operations consume 5,000,000 m^3 of hardwood logs per annum, with majority of log requirements filled within quota-based tenures or wood guarantees with the balance purchased on a competitive market-based system. In the U.S., where SYP lumber and OSB are produced, sawmills consume 20,500,000 tonnes of softwood logs per annum, with majority of log requirements purchased on the open market, with the balance under long-term supply contracts and/or timber deeds. In Europe and the U.K., where OSB, particleboard, MDF and related value-added products are produced, mills consume 2,700,000 m^3 of fibre per annum. Canadian harvesting operations are carried out by independent contractors under the supervision of the company's woodlands staff and reforestation projects are planned and supervised by the company's woodlands staff and are subject to approval by relevant government authorities. In Canada, substantially all requirements for wood chips, shavings and sawdust and hog fuel are supplied from the company's own operations, either directly or indirectly through trades. Fibre requirements of Alberta Newsprint are obtained from local sawmills, including the Blue Ridge sawmill and Slave Lake veneer operation, through chip purchase agreements and log-for-chip trading using logs harvested from Alberta Newsprint's tenures. The Slave Lake deciduous forest management agreement provides most of the fibre requirements of the Slave Lake pulp mill, with the balance being obtained from logs purchased from local suppliers. Majority of the wood chips produced by the company's U.S. sawmill operations are sold to pulp mills at market prices under long-term contracts. The company's European particleboard facilities source recycled fibre from third party suppliers while MDF facilities source wood chips from third party sawmillers in the U.K.

On Jan. 10, 2023, the company announced the indefinite curtailment of its Perry sawmill in Florida, which would reduce lumber production by 100 mmfbm. The decision was made due to high fiber costs and softening lumber markets.

On Aug. 9, 2022, the company announced the permanent curtailment of 170 mmfbm of combined annual production at its Fraser Lake and Williams Lake, B.C., sawmills and 85 msf of plywood production at its Quesnel, B.C., plywood mill. The reduction in capacity was expected to impact 77, 15 and 55 positions at the Fraser Lake, Williams Lake and Quesnel facilities, respectively.

During the first quarter of 2022, the company approved a plan to permanently reduce the capacity at the pulp mill in Hinton, Alta. One of Hinton pulp mill's two production lines would shut and the remaining line would produce unbleached kraft pulp rather than northern bleached softwood kraft pulp.

Periods ended:	12m Dec. 31/22	12m Dec. 31/21
Lumber prod., mfbm	5,652,000	5,857,000
MDF prod., msf	473,000	526,000
Plywood prod., msf	716,000	763,000
LVL prod., mcf	2,439	2,439
BCTMP prod., tonnes	581,000	623,000
NBSK pulp prod., tonnes	359,000	428,000
Newsprint prod., tonnes	106,000	113,000

Recent Merger and Acquisition Activity

Status: pending **Announced:** July 10, 2023
West Fraser Timber Co. Ltd. agreed to sell its unbleached softwood kraft pulp mill in Hinton, Alta., to Mondi plc for US$5,000,000. Mondi planned to invest €400,000,000 to expand the facility, with plans to add a 200,000-tonne-per-year kraft paper machine that was expected to be operational in the second half of 2027. West Fraser would continue to supply fibre to the Hinton mill under a long-term contract. The transaction was subject to regulatory approval and was expected to be completed by the end of 2023.

Directors - Henry H. (Hank) Ketcham, chr., Vancouver, B.C.; Raymond W. (Ray) Ferris, pres. & CEO, Vancouver, B.C.; Doyle N. Beneby Jr., West Palm Beach, Fla.; Eric L. Butler, Neb.; Reid E. Carter, West Vancouver, B.C.; John N. Floren, Oakville, Ont.; Brian G. Kenning, Vancouver, B.C.; Ellis Ketcham Johnson, Greenwich, Conn.; Marian Lawson, Toronto, Ont.; Colleen M. McMorrow, Oakville, Ont.; Janice G. Rennie, Edmonton, Alta.; Gillian D. Winckler, Vancouver, B.C.

Other Exec. Officers - Sean P. McLaren, COO; Kevin J. Burke, sr. v-p, wood products; Keith D. Carter, sr. v-p, western Canada; James W. Gorman, sr. v-p, corp. & govt. rel.; Robin A. Lampard, sr. v-p, fin.; Christopher D. (Chris) McIver, sr. v-p, mktg. & corp. devel.; Alan G. McMeekin, sr. v-p, Europe; Christopher A. (Chris) Virostek, sr. v-p, fin. & CFO; Alan A. Caputo, v-p, HR; Chester R. Fort, v-p, U.S. lumber opers.; D'Arcy R. Henderson, v-p, Cdn. woodlands; James R. Laundry, v-p, Cdn. plywood, MDF & LVL; Adrian A. Plante, v-p, Cdn. lumber; Scott W. Stubbington, v-p, sales, North American wood products; Matthew V. (Matt) Tobin, v-p, sales & mktg.; Charles H. (Chuck) Watkins, v-p, capital & tech.; Shannon D. Webber, v-p & gen. counsel; Tom V. Theodorakis, corp. sec.

Capital Stock

	Authorized (shs.)	Outstanding (shs.)[1]
Preferred	10,000,000	nil
Common	400,000,000	81,274,319
Class B Common	20,000,000	2,281,478

[1] At July 25, 2023

Common & Class B Common - Equal in all respects, except that each class B common share may be exchanged at any time for one common share. One vote per share.

Options - At Dec. 31, 2022, options were outstanding to purchase 841,305 common shares at a weighted average exercise price of Cdn$76.19 per share with a weighted average remaining contractual life of 4.14 years.

Normal Course Issuer Bid - The company plans to make normal course purchases of up to 4,063,696 common shares representing 5% of the total outstanding. The bid commenced on Feb. 27, 2023, and expires on Feb. 26, 2024.

Major Shareholder - James A. (Jim) Pattison held 10.7% interest and Banasino Investments Limited held 10% interest at Feb. 28, 2023.

Price Range - WFG/TSX

Year	Volume	High	Low	Close
2022	109,340,018	$132.91	$89.95	$97.77
2021	182,723,350	$124.74	$73.30	$120.68
2020	111,967,908	$86.50	$21.60	$81.78
2019	93,838,820	$80.13	$43.93	$57.28
2018	114,996,547	$97.99	$60.44	$67.44

Recent Close: $102.24

Capital Stock Changes - During 2022, 11,898,205 common shares were repurchased under a Substantial Issuer Bid and 10,475,115 common shares were repurchased under a Normal Course Issuer Bid.

Dividends

WFG com Ra US$1.20 pa Q est. Oct. 7, 2022[1]
Prev. Rate: US$1.20 est. July 8, 2022
Prev. Rate: US$0.80 est. Jan. 11, 2022
Prev. Rate: $1.00 est. July 6, 2021
Prev. Rate: $0.80 est. Oct. 9, 2018
[1] Divds. paid in Cdn$ prior to Jan. 2022.

Long-Term Debt - Outstanding at Dec. 31, 2022:

Fltg. rate term loan due 2024[1]	US$200,000,000
4.35% sr. notes due 2024	300,000,000
Less: Deferred fin. costs	1,000,000
	499,000,000
Less: Current portion	nil
	499,000,000

[1] Bearing interest at prime, base rate, bankers' acceptances or LIBOR.

Wholly Owned Subsidiaries

Angelina Forest Products, LLC, Tex.
Norbord Inc., Toronto, Ont.
- 100% int. in **Norbord Alabama Inc.**, Ala.
- 100% int. in **Norbord Europe Ltd.**, United Kingdom.
- 100% int. in **Norbord Georgia LLC**, Del.
- 100% int. in **Norbord Minnesota Inc.**, Del.
- 100% int. in **Norbord Mississippi LLC**, Del.
- 100% int. in **Norbord N.V.**, Belgium.
- 100% int. in **Norbord Sales Inc.**, Ont.
- 100% int. in **Norbord South Carolina Inc.**, S.C.
- 100% int. in **Norbord Texas (Jefferson) Inc.**, Del.
- 100% int. in **Norbord Texas (Nacogdoches) Inc.**, Del.
- 100% int. in **West Fraser, Inc.**, Del.
- 100% int. in **West Fraser Wood Products Inc.**, Del.

West Fraser Mills Ltd.
- 100% int. in **Blue Ridge Lumber Inc.**, Blue Ridge, Alta.
- 100% int. in **Manning Forest Products Ltd.**, Manning, Alta.
- 100% int. in **Sundre Forest Products Inc.**, B.C.
- 100% int. in **West Fraser Newsprint Ltd.**, Alta.
  - 50% int. in **Alberta Newsprint Company**, Whitecourt, Alta.

Investments

50% int. in **Cariboo Pulp & Paper Company**, Quesnel, B.C.

Financial Statistics

Periods ended:	12m Dec. 31/22[A]		12m Dec. 31/21[A]
	US$000s	%Chg	US$000s
Operating revenue	**9,701,000**	**-8**	**10,518,000**
Cost of goods sold	5,142,000		4,645,000
General & admin expense	365,000		312,000
Stock-based compensation	5,000		40,000
Other operating expense	981,000		992,000
Operating expense	**6,493,000**	**+8**	**5,989,000**
Operating income	**3,208,000**	**-29**	**4,529,000**
Deprec., depl. & amort.	589,000		584,000
Finance income	27,000		11,000
Finance costs, gross	30,000		56,000
Write-downs/write-offs	(51,000)		nil
Pre-tax income	**2,593,000**	**-33**	**3,898,000**
Income taxes	618,000		951,000
Net income	**1,975,000**	**-33**	**2,947,000**
Cash & equivalent	1,162,000		1,568,000
Inventories	1,032,000		1,061,000
Accounts receivable	350,000		508,000
Current assets	2,749,000		3,217,000
Fixed assets, net	4,333,000		4,468,000
Intangibles, net	2,358,000		2,440,000
Total assets	**9,973,000**	**-4**	**10,433,000**
Accts. pay. & accr. liabs	359,000		411,000
Current liabilities	792,000		1,206,000
Long-term debt, gross	499,000		499,000
Long-term debt, net	499,000		499,000
Long-term lease liabilities	26,000		17,000
Shareholders' equity	7,619,000		7,656,000
Cash from oper. activs	**2,207,000**	**-38**	**3,552,000**
Cash from fin. activs	(2,126,000)		(2,164,000)
Cash from invest. activs	(459,000)		(286,000)
Net cash position	**1,162,000**	**-26**	**1,568,000**
Capital expenditures	(477,000)		(635,000)
Unfunded pension liability	n.a.		118,000
Pension fund surplus	73,000		n.a.
	US$		US$
Earnings per share*	21.06		27.03
Cash flow per share*	23.54		32.58
Cash divd. per share*	1.15		$0.90
	shs		shs
No. of shs. o/s*	83,555,414		105,928,734
Avg. no. of shs. o/s*	93,760,000		109,021,000
	%		%
Net profit margin	20.36		28.02
Return on equity	25.86		57.46
Return on assets	19.58		40.42
Foreign sales percent	84		84
No. of employees (FTEs)	11,000		10,928

* Com. & Cl.B com.

[A] Reported in accordance with IFRS

Latest Results

Periods ended:	6m June 30/23[A]		6m June 30/22[A]
	US$000s	%Chg	US$000s
Operating revenue	3,235,000	-46	5,997,000
Net income	(173,000)	n.a.	1,852,000
	US$		US$
Earnings per share*	(2.07)		18.09

* Com. & Cl.B com.

[A] Reported in accordance with IFRS

Historical Summary
(as originally stated)

Fiscal Year	Oper. Rev.	Net Inc. Bef. Disc.	EPS*
	US$000s	US$000s	US$
2022[A]	9,701,000	1,975,000	21.06
2021[A]	10,518,000	2,947,000	27.03
	$000s	$000s	$
2020[A]	5,850,000	776,000	11.30
2019[A]	4,877,000	(150,000)	(2.18)
2018[A]	6,118,000	810,000	10.88

* Com. & Cl.B com.

[A] Reported in accordance with IFRS

W.17 West Island Brands Inc.

Symbol - WIB **Exchange** - CSE (S) **CUSIP** - 953400
Head Office - 1102-44 Victoria St, Toronto, ON, M5C 1Y2 **Telephone** - (416) 304-9935 **Fax** - (416) 863-1515
Website - www.westislandbrands.com
Email - boris@westislandbrands.com
Investor Relations - Boris I. Ziger (416) 304-9935
Auditors - McGovern Hurley LLP C.A., Toronto, Ont.
Transfer Agents - Capital Transfer Agency Inc., Toronto, Ont.
Profile - (B.C. 2007) Markets and sells cannabis for the medical and recreational markets in Canada.

Cannabis products are marketed through its two brands: OUEST™, which offer high tetrahydrocannabinol (THC) content products; and CITOYEN™, which offer lower THC content products at a lower price. Also offers Matica Ionic Mist, a proprietary odour neutralizing spray for cannabis odours developed with **Yunify Natural Technologies**. Products are sold in Saskatchewan, Manitoba, British Columbia, Ontario, Quebec and the Northwest Territories.

Common suspended from CSE, May 8, 2023.

Predecessor Detail - Name changed from Matica Enterprises Inc., Oct. 20, 2021; basis 1 new for 30 old shs.

Directors - Boris I. Ziger, CEO & interim CFO, Toronto, Ont.; Michael P. Gross; Dr. L. Scott Jobin-Bevans, Santiago, Chile; Ernest J. Royden

Capital Stock

	Authorized (shs.)	Outstanding (shs.)[1]
Common	unlimited	15,109,029

[1] At Nov. 28, 2022

Major Shareholder - Widely held at July 8, 2022.

Price Range - CUZ.H/TSX-VEN (D)

Year	Volume	High	Low	Close
2022	2,120,322	$0.59	$0.09	$0.11
2021	4,282,900	$2.55	$0.31	$0.41
2020	2,858,347	$1.35	$0.60	$0.75
2019	4,451,451	$5.10	$1.05	$1.20
2018	22,886,002	$24.30	$2.10	$2.70

Consolidation: 1-for-30 cons. in Oct. 2021
Recent Close: $0.13

Capital Stock Changes - In January and February 2022, private placement of 2,510,000 units (1 common share & 1 warrant) at 25¢ per unit was completed, with warrants exercisable at 25¢ per share for two years. In March 2022, 1,865,440 common shares were issued for debt settlement.

Wholly Owned Subsidiaries

93802601 Quebec Inc., Qué.
10406619 Canada Inc., Canada.
Ravenline Exploration Ltd., Toronto, Ont.
• 100% int. in **Ravenline USA Ltd.**, Nev.
Trichome Treats Inc., Canada.

Subsidiaries

99.97% int. in **RoyalMax Biotechnology Canada Inc.**, Dorval, Qué.

Financial Statistics

Periods ended:	12m Dec. 31/21[A]		12m Dec. 31/20[□A]
	$000s	%Chg	$000s
Operating revenue	**2,326**	**n.m.**	**121**
Cost of sales	4,853		(309)[1]
General & admin expense	1,609		1,160
Stock-based compensation	724		306
Operating expense	**7,186**	**+521**	**1,157**
Operating income	**(4,860)**	**n.a.**	**(1,036)**
Deprec., depl. & amort.	205		113
Finance income	6		52
Finance costs, gross	76		29
Write-downs/write-offs	nil		(7,097)[2]
Pre-tax income	**(5,144)**	**n.a.**	**(8,514)**
Net income	**(5,144)**	**n.a.**	**(8,514)**
Net inc. for equity hldrs	**(5,143)**	**n.a.**	**(8,404)**
Net inc. for non-cont. int	**(1)**	**n.a.**	**(109)**
Cash & equivalent	236		1,429
Inventories	461		2,573
Accounts receivable	708		113
Current assets	1,762		4,594
Fixed assets, net	3,020		3,303
Right-of-use assets	1,058		1,144
Intangibles, net	190		200
Total assets	**6,141**	**-34**	**9,352**
Bank indebtedness	500		...
Accts. pay. & accr. liabs	1,124		492
Current liabilities	1,716		747
Long-term lease liabilities	1,153		1,207
Shareholders' equity	3,222		7,398
Non-controlling interest	nil		1
Cash from oper. activs	**(1,763)**	**n.a.**	**(1,453)**
Cash from fin. activs	587		(35)
Cash from invest. activs	347		925
Net cash position	**204**	**-80**	**1,032**
	$		$
Earnings per share*	(0.48)		(0.90)
Cash flow per share*	(0.17)		(0.14)
	shs		shs
No. of shs. o/s*	10,712,484		10,514,131
Avg. no. of shs. o/s*	10,679,859		10,616,525
	%		%
Net profit margin	(221.15)		n.m.
Return on equity	(96.85)		(76.11)
Return on assets	(65.42)		(69.77)

* Common

[□] Restated

[A] Reported in accordance with IFRS

[1] Net of unrealized change in fair value of biological assets.

[2] Includes $6,933,477 write-downs of investments in RoyalMax Biotechnologies Inc. and 93802601 Quebec Inc.

Latest Results

Periods ended:	9m Sept. 30/22[A]		9m Sept. 30/21[□A]
	$000s	%Chg	$000s
Operating revenue	3,802	+158	1,471
Net income	(1,353)	n.a.	(2,117)
Net inc. for equity hldrs	(1,353)	n.a.	(2,116)
	$		$
Earnings per share*	(0.09)		(0.20)

* Common

[□] Restated

[A] Reported in accordance with IFRS

Historical Summary
(as originally stated)

Fiscal Year	Oper. Rev.	Net Inc. Bef. Disc.	EPS*
	$000s	$000s	$
2021[A]	2,326	(5,144)	(0.48)
2020[A]	121	(8,514)	(0.90)
2019[A]	nil	(1,976)	(0.30)
2018[A]	nil	(5,261)	(0.60)
2017[A]	nil	(3,903)	(0.60)

* Common

[A] Reported in accordance with IFRS

Note: Adjusted throughout for 1-for-30 cons. in Oct. 2021

W.18 The Westaim Corporation

Symbol - WED **Exchange** - TSX-VEN **CUSIP** - 956909
Head Office - 1700-70 York St, Toronto, ON, M5J 1S9 **Telephone** - (416) 969-3333 **Fax** - (416) 969-3334
Website - www.westaim.com
Email - rkittel@westaim.com
Investor Relations - Robert T. Kittel (416) 969-3337
Auditors - Deloitte LLP C.A., Toronto, Ont.
Lawyers - Baker & McKenzie LLP, Toronto, Ont.
Transfer Agents - Computershare Trust Company of Canada Inc., Calgary, Alta.
Employees - 7 at Dec. 31, 2022
Profile - (Alta. 1996) Invests in companies in the financial services industry.

Investments are **Skyward Specialty Insurance Group, Inc.** and the Arena Group.

Skyward Specialty (26.8% interest) is a specialty insurance provider which underwrites on a non-admitted and admitted basis multiple lines of insurance, including property, casualty, surety and accident and health insurance coverages, in niche markets across the U.S.

The Arena Group manages and structures primarily fundamentals-based, credit and asset-oriented investments, which consist of loans or credit arrangements that are generally secured by assets, through its two businesses: Arena Investors (51%-owned **Arena Investors Group Holdings, LLC**), an investment manager serving institutional clients, insurance companies, investment funds and other pooled investment vehicles; and Arena FINCOs (wholly owned **Westaim Origination Holdings, Inc.** and **Arena Finance Holdings Co., LLC**), specialty finance businesses that source and originate investments mainly for its own account. At June 30, 2023, Arena Investors had committed assets under management (AUM) of US$3.3 billion; and Arena FINCOs had a total investment fair value of US$211,700,000.

On Nov. 30, 2022, the company's interest in **Westaim HIIG Limited Partnership** increased to 98.5% from 62% following the redemption of HIIG units held by non-Canadian limited partners. On July 31, 2023, HIIG was dissolved. HIIG held common shares of **Skyward Specialty Insurance Group, Inc.**, which were distributed to its limited partners, resulting in the company receiving 7,281,780 Skyward common shares.

In July 2023, all 5,000,000 5% subordinate preferred securities maturing on May 26, 2116, held by **Fairfax Financial Holdings Limited** were redeemed at Cdn$10 per share. In connection with the redemption, the company and Fairfax terminated the governance agreement dated June 2, 2017, between the parties; Fairfax surrendered and disposed of, without any further consideration, all of the warrants to purchase common shares of the company held by Fairfax; and the company paid a US$100,000 work fee to Fairfax.

In June 2023, bought deal secondary offering of 3,987,500 common shares of **Skyward Specialty Insurance Group, Inc.** by the company was completed at US$23 per share, including 137,500 common shares on exercise of over-allotment option.

On Jan. 18, 2023, affiliate **Skyward Specialty Insurance Group, Inc.** completed its initial public offering (IPO) of 4,750,000 common shares at US$15 per share. Secondary offering of 5,545,240 Skyward common shares held by certain existing Skyward shareholders was completed at US$15 per share, including 1,342,857 common shares on exercise of over-allotment option. Skyward common shares began trading on the Nasdaq Global Select Market under the symbol SKWD.

On Apr. 1, 2022, **Bernard Partners, LLC** (BP) received a 49% equity ownership in wholly owned **Arena Investors Group Holdings, LLC** following the achievement by BP of certain assets under management (AUM) and cash flow thresholds. As a result, the company's ownership in Arena Investors decreased to 51%. Prior to this, BP and the company were entitled to profit sharing percentage in Arena Investors of 49% and 51%, respectively.

Directors - Ian W. Delaney, exec. chr., Toronto, Ont.; J. Cameron (Cam) MacDonald, pres. & CEO, Ont.; John W. Gildner, Mississauga, Ont.; Lisa Mazzocco, Calif.; Kevin E. Parker, N.Y.; Dr. Bruce V. Walter, Toronto, Ont.

Other Exec. Officers - Robert T. Kittel, COO & corp. sec.; Glenn G. MacNeil, CFO

Capital Stock

	Authorized (shs.)	Outstanding (shs.)[1]
Class A Preferred	unlimited	nil
Class B Preferred	unlimited	nil
Common	unlimited	138,992,118

[1] At June 30, 2023

Normal Course Issuer Bid - The company plans to make normal course purchases of up to 11,005,494 common shares representing 10% of the public float. The bid commenced on Oct. 1, 2022, and expires on Sept. 30, 2023.

Major Shareholder - Widely held at Mar. 31, 2023.

Price Range - WED/TSX-VEN

Year	Volume	High	Low	Close
2022	17,435,305	$2.83	$2.14	$2.63
2021	21,100,146	$2.85	$2.33	$2.50
2020	38,090,124	$2.67	$1.37	$2.49
2019	48,679,902	$2.92	$2.30	$2.65
2018	31,177,546	$3.35	$2.29	$2.58

Recent Close: $3.52

Capital Stock Changes - During 2022, 1,300,000 common shares were repurchased under a Normal Course Issuer Bid.

Dividends

pfd 5% red. Ra $0.50 pa Q est. Apr. 16, 2018[1]
Delisted Jul 18/23.
$0.146575**f**.......... July 17/23
[1] Distributions are interest income.
f Final Payment

Wholly Owned Subsidiaries

Arena Finance Company II Inc., Del.
- 1% int. in **Arena Finance Holdings Co., LLC**, N.Y.

The Westaim Corporation of America, Del.
- 51% int. in **Arena Investors Group Holdings, LLC**, N.Y.
  - 100% int. in **Aedile Advisors Limited**, New Zealand.
  - 100% int. in **Arena Business Solutions, LLC**, United States.
  - 100% int. in **Arena Financial Services, LLC**, Del.
  - 100% int. in **Arena Investment Management (Singapore) Pte. Ltd.**, Singapore.
  - 100% int. in **Arena Investors (HK) Limited**, Hong Kong, People's Republic of China.
  - 100% int. in **Arena Investors, LP**, N.Y.
  - 100% int. in **Arena Investors UK Limited**, United Kingdom.
  - 100% int. in **Arena Management Co., LLC**, N.Y.
- 100% int. in **Westaim Origination Holdings, Inc.**, N.Y.
  - 100% int. in **Arena Origination Co., LLC**, N.Y.

Subsidiaries

99% int. in **Arena Finance Holdings Co., LLC**, N.Y.
- 100% int. in **Arena Finance, LLC**, N.Y.

Investments

26.8% int. in **Skyward Specialty Insurance Group, Inc.**, Houston, Tex.

Financial Statistics

Periods ended:	12m Dec. 31/22[A]		12m Dec. 31/21[A]
	US$000s	%Chg	US$000s
Unrealized invest. gain (loss)	15,972		21,358
Total revenue	**27,437**	**-19**	**33,717**
Salaries & benefits	4,811		4,984
General & admin. expense	2,239		1,736
Stock-based compensation	874		510
Operating expense	**7,924**	**+10**	**7,230**
Operating income	**19,513**	**-26**	**26,487**
Deprec. & amort.	141		145
Finance costs, gross	1,905		1,995
Pre-tax income	**17,604**	**-38**	**28,431**
Income taxes	(357)		221
Net income	**17,961**	**-36**	**28,210**
Cash & equivalent	3,434		6,558
Accounts receivable	291		364
Investments	409,128		394,273
Fixed assets, net	19		34
Right-of-use assets	242		368
Total assets	**413,292**	**+3**	**401,661**
Accts. pay. & accr. liabs	12,679		12,567
Debt	36,939		39,554
Lease liabilities	261		413
Shareholders' equity	363,074		347,677
Cash from oper. activs	**(2,460)**	**n.a.**	**(5,118)**
Cash from fin. activs	(2,564)		(1,055)
Cash from invest. activs	1,900		3,990
Net cash position	**3,434**	**-48**	**6,558**
Capital expenditures	nil		(10)
	US$		US$
Earnings per share*	0.13		0.20
Cash flow per share*	(0.02)		(0.04)
	shs		shs
No. of shs. o/s*	141,386,718		142,686,718
Avg. no. of shs. o/s*	141,901,513		143,079,869
	%		%
Net profit margin	65.46		83.67
Return on equity	5.05		8.44
Return on assets	4.88		7.75
No. of employees (FTEs)	7		7

* Common
[A] Reported in accordance with IFRS

Latest Results

Periods ended:	6m June 30/23[A]		6m June 30/22[A]
	US$000s	%Chg	US$000s
Total revenue	134,701	n.m.	7,399
Net income	125,841	n.m.	1,934
	US$		US$
Earnings per share*	0.89		0.01

* Common
[A] Reported in accordance with IFRS

Historical Summary
(as originally stated)

Fiscal Year	Total Rev.	Net Inc. Bef. Disc.	EPS*
	US$000s	US$000s	US$
2022[A]	27,437	17,961	0.13
2021[A]	33,717	28,210	0.20
2020[A]	(26,025)	(34,400)	(0.24)
2019[A]	19,286	8,524	0.06
2018[A]	21,078	16,793	0.12

* Common
[A] Reported in accordance with IFRS

W.19 WestBond Enterprises Corporation

Symbol - WBE **Exchange** - TSX-VEN **CUSIP** - 95712L
Head Office - 101-7403 Progress Way, Delta, BC, V4G 1E7 **Telephone** - (604) 940-3939 **Toll-free** - (800) 688-8042 **Fax** - (604) 940-9161
Website - www.westbond.ca
Email - gmagistrale@westbond.ca
Investor Relations - Gennaro Magistrale (800) 688-8042
Auditors - PricewaterhouseCoopers LLP C.A., Vancouver, B.C.
Lawyers - DuMoulin Black LLP, Vancouver, B.C.
Transfer Agents - Computershare Trust Company of Canada Inc.

Profile - (B.C. 1989) Manufactures disposable paper products which are sold primarily to major medical and industrial distributors in Canada and the U.S. and to larger end-users on a direct basis.

Product lines include:

Personal hygiene products which include jumbo roll hand towels and bathroom tissues, conventional highsheet-count bathroom tissue and a specialty line of roll towels and bathroom tissue, which are manufactured in one and two ply formats. Products are sold to Canadian and U.S. distributors and janitorial contractors in large order quantities.

Clinical products which are paper products used by clinics, physicians, chiropractors and physiotherapists. Products include examination table paper, sheets, pillowcases, gowns and drapes in roll or sheet format.

Wipe products which include patient wipes and underlays, as well as disinfectant wet-wipes marketed under the brand ViroBan Plus. Products, which are primarily for use in nursing homes, are available in ¼ fold, $^{1}/_{8}$ fold and roll formats, in a variety of widths and perforation length.

Non-Wipe Air Laid products which include bulk air laid parent rolls sold to other paper converters and the company's own line of high quality air laid napkins for use in restaurants. Products are sold through major food service distributors.

Directors - Gennaro Magistrale, pres. & CEO, Delta, B.C.; D. Dan (Danny) Dawson, Vancouver, B.C.; J. Douglas Seppala, Vancouver, B.C.; Peter R. Toigo, B.C.

Other Exec. Officers - Subhashni Prasad, CFO & sec.-treas.

Capital Stock

	Authorized (shs.)	Outstanding (shs.)[1]
Common	unlimited	35,625,800

[1] At June 29, 2023

Major Shareholder - Gennaro Magistrale held 22.8% interest and Mario Grech held 18.1% interest at July 27, 2022.

Price Range - WBE/TSX-VEN

Year	Volume	High	Low	Close
2022	6,035,702	$0.60	$0.21	$0.30
2021	11,105,853	$1.20	$0.45	$0.48
2020	6,420,912	$0.94	$0.17	$0.83
2019	1,031,599	$0.22	$0.12	$0.20
2018	2,007,447	$0.17	$0.09	$0.15

Recent Close: $0.19

Capital Stock Changes - There were no changes to capital stock during fiscal 2022 or fiscal 2023.

Dividends

WBE com N.S.R.
$0.005.................. Dec. 23/22 $0.005.............. Sept. 23/22
$0.005.................. June 21/22 $0.005.............. Mar. 25/22
Paid in 2023: n.a. 2022: $0.02 2021: $0.04

Wholly Owned Subsidiaries

WestBond Industries Inc.

Financial Statistics

Periods ended:	12m Mar. 31/23[A]		12m Mar. 31/22[A]
	$000s	%Chg	$000s
Operating revenue	**11,090**	**-3**	**11,379**
Cost of sales	5,735		6,005
Salaries & benefits	2,162		2,237
General & admin expense	1,062		1,029
Operating expense	**8,959**	**-3**	**9,271**
Operating income	**2,131**	**+1**	**2,108**
Deprec., depl. & amort.	1,150		1,009
Finance costs, gross	143		170
Write-downs/write-offs	(51)		2
Pre-tax income	**836**	**-13**	**959**
Income taxes	262		266
Net income	**575**	**-17**	**693**
Cash & equivalent	73		268
Inventories	1,810		1,923
Accounts receivable	1,082		1,111
Current assets	3,537		3,537
Fixed assets, net	8,193		8,594
Right-of-use assets	1,826		2,103
Total assets	**13,421**	**-6**	**14,263**
Bank indebtedness	12		87
Accts. pay. & accr. liabs.	857		907
Current liabilities	1,753		1,946
Long-term debt, gross	298		1,012
Long-term debt, net	nil		298
Long-term lease liabilities	1,794		2,058
Shareholders' equity	7,831		7,791
Cash from oper. activs	**1,933**	**+87**	**1,036**
Cash from fin. activs	(1,696)		(1,907)
Cash from invest. activs	(432)		(328)
Net cash position	**73**	**-73**	**268**
Capital expenditures	(432)		(328)
	$		$
Earnings per share*	0.02		0.02
Cash flow per share*	0.05		0.03
Cash divd. per share*	0.02		0.03
	shs		shs
No. of shs. o/s*	35,625,800		35,625,800
Avg. no. of shs. o/s*	35,625,800		35,625,800
	%		%
Net profit margin	5.18		6.09
Return on equity	7.36		8.78
Return on assets	4.86		5.47
Foreign sales percent	n.a.		50

* Common
[A] Reported in accordance with IFRS

Historical Summary
(as originally stated)

Fiscal Year	Oper. Rev.	Net Inc. Bef. Disc.	EPS*
	$000s	$000s	$
2023[A]	11,090	575	0.02
2022[A]	11,379	693	0.02
2021[A]	13,980	2,643	0.07
2020[A]	11,668	591	0.02
2019[A]	11,363	421	0.01

* Common
[A] Reported in accordance with IFRS

W.20 Westbridge Renewable Energy Corp.

Symbol - WEB **Exchange** - TSX-VEN **CUSIP** - 81716A
Head Office - 615-800 Pender St W, Vancouver, BC, V6C 2V6 **Telephone** - (604) 687-7767 **Fax** - (604) 688-9895
Website - www.westbridge.energy
Email - sromanin@westbridge.energy
Investor Relations - Stefano Romanin (604) 687-7767
Auditors - Davidson & Company LLP C.A., Vancouver, B.C.
Lawyers - Fogler, Rubinoff LLP, Toronto, Ont.
Transfer Agents - Computershare Trust Company of Canada Inc., Vancouver, B.C.
Profile - (B.C. 1996; orig. Ont., 1956) Develops utility-scale solar photovoltaic (PV) and battery energy storage projects in Canada, the U.S. and the U.K.

Development projects include the Georgetown project in Vulcan cty., Alta., consisting of a 278-MW solar facility and a 100-MW battery energy storage system (BESS); the Sunnynook project (75% owned) in Sunnynook, Alta., consisting of a 332-MW solar plant and a 200-MW BESS; the Dolcy project in Provost, Alta., consisting of a 246-MW solar plant and a 100-MW BESS; Eastervale project in Provost, Alta., consisting of a 274-MW solar plant and a 200-MW BESS; Red Willow project in Stettler County No. 6, Alta., consisting of a 280-MW solar plant and a 100-MW BESS; the 221-MW Accalia Point solar project in Cameron cty., Tex.; and the 53-megavolt-ampere Fiskerton BESS project in Lincoln, U.K.

On June 21, 2022, wholly owned **Portrush Petroleum USA** was dissolved.

Recent Merger and Acquisition Activity

Status: pending **Announced:** June 1, 2023
Westbridge Renewable Energy Corp. agreed to sell five solar photovoltaic (PV) projects with a total capacity of 1,410 MW in Alberta, through the sale of Westbridge's subsidiaries: Georgetown Solar Inc., Sunnynook Solar Energy Inc., Dolcy Solar Inc., Eastervale Solar Inc. and Red Willow Solar Inc. (collectively, SPVs), to Cyprus-based Metka-EGN Ltd., a wholly owned subsidiary of Marousi, Greece-based Mytilineos S.A., for an amount between $217,000,000 to $346,000,000 cash. The purchase price for each SPV is calculated as the product of $167,500 (in respect of the Georgetown) or $165,000 (in respect of the other projects) multiplied by the corresponding project's actually installed maximum solar PV capacity and is subject to standard working capital and indebtedness adjustments, as well as adjustments in the event interconnection costs exceed estimates. The closing of the sale of one project was expected to be in late 2023 and the remainder in 2024. The sale of each SPV is not conditional on the sale of any other SPVs. Accordingly, the transaction is expected to occur in multiple closings as and when the conditions to satisfy the sale of each SPV are satisfied or waived.

Predecessor Detail - Name changed from Westbridge Energy Corporation, Sept. 29, 2022.
Directors - Scott M. Kelly, exec. chr., Toronto, Ont.; Stefano Romanin, CEO, Switzerland; Margaret (Maggie) McKenna, COO, Calgary, Alta.; Marcus Yang, London, Middx., United Kingdom
Other Exec. Officers - Philip Stubbs, CFO; Pandelis Vassilakakis, chief bus. devel. officer; Francesco Paolo Cardi, v-p, devel.

Capital Stock

	Authorized (shs.)	Outstanding (shs.)[1]
Common	unlimited	99,051,085

[1] At July 27, 2023

Major Shareholder - Stefano Romanin held 17.41% interest at Aug. 15, 2022.

Price Range - WEB/TSX-VEN

Year	Volume	High	Low	Close
2022	33,054,713	$0.65	$0.23	$0.60
2021	18,248,683	$0.38	$0.10	$0.33
2020	1,998,898	$0.15	$0.05	$0.10
2019	479,233	$0.24	$0.07	$0.07
2018	604,638	$0.18	$0.07	$0.10

Recent Close: $0.87
Capital Stock Changes - During fiscal 2022, common shares were issued as follows: 16,945,000 on exercise of warrants and 175,000 on exercise of options.

Wholly Owned Subsidiaries

Accalia Point Solar, LLC, Tex.
Dolcy Solar Inc., Alta.
Eastervale Solar Inc., Alta.
Fiskerton BESS Limited, United Kingdom.
Georgetown Solar Inc., Alta.
Red Willow Solar Inc., Alta.
Westbridge Energy UK Limited, United Kingdom.
Westbridge Energy (U.S.) Corp., United States.
Westbridge Renewable Energy Holdco Corp., Alta.

Subsidiaries

75% int. in **Sunnynook Solar Energy Inc.**, Alta.

Financial Statistics

Periods ended:	12m Nov. 30/22[A]		12m Nov. 30/21[A1]
	$000s	%Chg	$000s
General & admin expense	1,381		637
Stock-based compensation	963		470
Operating expense	**2,345**	**+112**	**1,107**
Operating income	**(2,345)**	**n.a.**	**(1,107)**
Deprec., depl. & amort.	47		9
Finance costs, gross	7		15
Pre-tax income	**(2,340)**	**n.a.**	**(3,671)**
Net income	**(2,340)**	**n.a.**	**(3,671)**
Net inc. for equity hldrs	**(2,335)**	**n.a.**	**(3,671)**
Net inc. for non-cont. int.	**(6)**	**n.a.**	**nil**
Cash & equivalent	1,645		3,244
Accounts receivable	1		2
Current assets	1,821		3,293
Fixed assets, net	4,599		1,571
Right-of-use assets	503		24
Total assets	**7,683**	**+57**	**4,888**
Accts. pay. & accr. liabs	654		422
Current liabilities	763		425
Long-term lease liabilities	373		4
Shareholders' equity	6,422		4,359
Non-controlling interest	95		101
Cash from oper. activs	**(1,541)**	**n.a.**	**(426)**
Cash from fin. activs	3,322		733
Cash from invest. activs	(3,380)		2,937
Net cash position	**1,645**	**-49**	**3,244**
Capital expenditures	(2,619)		(1,324)
	$		$
Earnings per share*	(0.03)		(0.10)
Cash flow per share*	(0.02)		(0.01)
	shs		shs
No. of shs. o/s*	96,358,585		79,238,585
Avg. no. of shs. o/s*	83,690,147		35,021,519
	%		%
Net profit margin	n.a.		n.a.
Return on equity	n.m.		(148.92)
Return on assets	n.a.		(131.89)

* Common
[A] Reported in accordance with IFRS
[1] Results reflect the June 17, 2021, reverse takeover acquisition of Georgetown Solar Inc.

Latest Results

Periods ended:	6m May 31/23[A]		6m May 31/22[A]
	$000s	%Chg	$000s
Net income	(1,872)	n.a.	(1,478)
Net inc. for equity hldrs	(1,876)	n.a.	(1,478)
Net inc. for non-cont. int.	5		nil
	$		$
Earnings per share*	(0.02)		(0.02)

* Common
[A] Reported in accordance with IFRS

Historical Summary
(as originally stated)

Fiscal Year	Oper. Rev.	Net Inc. Bef. Disc.	EPS*
	$000s	$000s	$
2022[A]	nil	(2,340)	(0.03)
2021[A]	nil	(3,671)	(0.10)
2020[A1]	nil	624	0.06
2019[A]	nil	(56)	(0.01)
2018[A]	nil	(370)	(0.05)

* Common
[A] Reported in accordance with IFRS
[1] Results for 2020 and prior years pertain to Westbridge Energy Corporation.

W.21 Western Energy Services Corp.

Symbol - WRG **Exchange** - TSX **CUSIP** - 958159
Head Office - 1700-215 9 Ave SW, Calgary, AB, T2P 1K3 **Telephone** - (403) 984-5916 **Fax** - (403) 984-5917
Website - www.wesc.ca
Email - jbowers@wesc.ca
Investor Relations - Jeffrey K. Bowers (403) 984-5916
Auditors - Deloitte LLP C.A., Calgary, Alta.
Bankers - HSBC Bank Canada
Lawyers - Blake, Cassels & Graydon LLP, Calgary, Alta.
Transfer Agents - Computershare Trust Company of Canada Inc., Calgary, Alta.
FP500 Revenue Ranking - 655
Employees - 671 at Dec. 31, 2022
Profile - (Alta. 1996) Provides contract drilling and well servicing in western Canada and the United States, as well as oilfield rental equipment services for the oil and gas industry in western Canada.

Operations are carried out through two segments: Contract Drilling; and Production Services.

Contract Drilling - This segment consists of the Horizon Drilling division, which provides contract drilling services primarily in the Western Canadian Sedimentary Basin (WCSB); and wholly owned **Stoneham Drilling Corporation**, which provides services in the Williston, Permian and Powder River Basins in the United States.

Operating Statistics

Year ended Dec. 31	2022	2021
Canada Contract Drilling:		
No. of rigs	36	49
Drilling rig operating days	3,241	3,124
Drilling rig utilization rate, %	24	18
U.S. Contract Drilling:		
No. of rigs	8	8
Drilling rig operating days	976	387
Drilling rig utilization rate, %	33	13

Production Services - The Eagle Well Servicing division provides well servicing from operation bases in Blackfalds and Grande Prairie, Alta., Lloydminster, Sask. and Virden, Man. Eagle Well owns and operates 65 service rigs which are used for completion, production work-overs, abandonment services and various maintenance activities on producing shallow to deep oil and natural gas wells. The Aero Rental Services division, which operates from facilities in Blackfalds and Grande Prairie, Alta., provides oilfield rental equipment for hydraulic fracturing services, well completions and production work, coil tubing and drilling services to oil and gas exploration and production companies and oilfield service companies.

On Aug. 1, 2022, wholly owned **Western Production Services Corp.** was amalgamated into the company.

On May 18, 2022, the company completed its recapitalization plan which included an agreement with **Alberta Investment Management Corporation** for the conversion of $100,000,000 principal amount of 7.25% term loan facility due January 2023, extension of the remaining principal amount to four years after the completion of the agreement and interest rate increase to 8.5%. On closing, the company completed a $31,500,000 rights offering and $10,000,000 of the proceeds was used to repay the term loan facility. As a result, Alberta Investment's interest in the company increased to 49.7% from 19.18%.

Periods ended:	12m Dec. 31/22	12m Dec. 31/21
No. of drill rigs	44	57
Drill rig operating days	55,625	3,511
Drill rig rev. per oper. day $[1]	29,698	21,931
Drill rig rev. per oper. day US$[2]	25,927	16,615
No. of service rigs	65	63
Service rig operating hrs.	67,077	67,323
Srvc. rig rev. per oper. hr. $	943	735
Service rig util. rate, %	41	29

[1] Represents Canadian operations.
[2] Represents U.S. operations.

Predecessor Detail - Name changed from BBF Resources Inc., July 25, 2005.
Directors - Alex R. N. MacAusland, co-founder, pres. & CEO, Calgary, Alta.; Ronald P. Mathison, chr., Calgary, Alta.; Trent D. Boehm, Calgary, Alta.; Colleen Cebuliak, Edmonton, Alta.; Tomer Cohen, N.S.; Lorne A. Gartner, Calgary, Alta.; John R. Rooney, Calgary, Alta.
Other Exec. Officers - Jeffrey K. Bowers, co-founder, sr. v-p, fin., CFO & corp. sec.; Peter J. Balkwill, v-p, fin.; R. Ross Clancy, v-p, prod. srvcs.; Dan Lundstrom, v-p, health, safety & envir.; J. Aaron MacAusland, v-p, opers., horizontal drilling; April N. Williams, v-p, HR

Capital Stock

	Authorized (shs.)	Outstanding (shs.)[1]
Preferred	unlimited	nil
Common	unlimited	33,841,324

[1] At Apr. 25, 2023

Major Shareholder - Alberta Investment Management Corporation held 49.7% interest, G2S2 Capital Inc. held 15.9% interest and Ronald P. Mathison held 12.3% interest at Mar. 20, 2023.

Price Range - WRG/TSX

Year	Volume	High	Low	Close
2022	3,007,381	$60.00	$2.40	$3.39
2021	37,489	$63.60	$31.20	$34.80
2020	210,332	$58.80	$21.60	$57.60
2019	167,707	$63.60	$19.20	$33.60
2018	323,638	$171.60	$40.80	$54.00

Consolidation: 1-for-120 cons. in Aug. 2022
Recent Close: $3.60
Capital Stock Changes - Pursuant to recapitalization plan completed on May 18, 2022, 16,666,667 post-consolidated common shares were issued on conversion of 7.25% term loan facility. In addition, 16,407,229 post-consolidated common shares were issued at $1.92 per share pursuant to a rights offering. On Aug. 4, 2022, common shares were consolidated on a 1-for-120 basis. Also during 2022, post-consolidated common shares were issued as follows: 2,451 on vesting of restricted share units and 725 on exercise of options.

Wholly Owned Subsidiaries

Stoneham Drilling Corporation, Okla.

Financial Statistics

Periods ended:	12m Dec. 31/22[A]		12m Dec. 31/21[A]
	$000s	%Chg	$000s
Operating revenue	**200,344**	**+52**	**131,678**
Cost of sales	146,560		97,950
General & admin expense	13,863		10,681
Stock-based compensation	1,985		253
Operating expense	**162,408**	**+49**	**108,884**
Operating income	**37,936**	**+66**	**22,794**
Deprec., depl. & amort.	40,096		42,024
Finance income	57		16
Finance costs, gross	14,473		19,680
Pre-tax income	**32,178**	**n.a.**	**(39,269)**
Income taxes	2,858		(3,457)
Net income	**29,320**	**n.a.**	**(35,812)**
Net inc. for equity hldrs	**28,999**	**n.a.**	**(36,134)**
Net inc. for non-cont. int.	**321**	**0**	**322**
Cash & equivalent	8,878		7,478
Inventories	nil		3,595
Accounts receivable	47,213		26,464
Current assets	61,544		40,353
Fixed assets, net	413,840		415,245
Total assets	**475,708**	**+4**	**456,003**
Accts. pay. & accr. liabs	34,459		24,590
Current liabilities	39,621		38,129
Long-term debt, gross	131,689		240,423
Long-term debt, net	126,527		226,884
Shareholders' equity	300,590		184,507
Non-controlling interest	1,940		1,993
Cash from oper. activs	**28,541**	**+72**	**16,631**
Cash from fin. activs	1,811		(22,788)
Cash from invest. activs	(28,952)		(5,687)
Net cash position	**8,878**	**+19**	**7,478**
Capital expenditures	(34,228)		(2,866)
Capital disposals	416		2,212
	$		$
Earnings per share*	1.24		(46.80)
Cash flow per share*	1.21		21.84
	shs		shs
No. of shs. o/s*	33,841,318		764,220
Avg. no. of shs. o/s*	23,581,155		761,439
	%		%
Net profit margin	14.63		(27.20)
Return on equity	11.96		(17.83)
Return on assets	9.12		(3.75)
Foreign sales percent	17		6
No. of employees (FTEs)	671		566

* Common
[A] Reported in accordance with IFRS

Latest Results

Periods ended:	3m Mar. 31/23[A]		3m Mar. 31/22[A]
	$000s	%Chg	$000s
Operating revenue	79,239	+57	50,475
Net income	4,421	n.a.	(3,834)
Net inc. for equity hldrs	4,252	n.a.	(3,993)
Net inc. for non-cont. int.	169		159
	$		$
Earnings per share*	0.13		(5.22)

* Common
[A] Reported in accordance with IFRS

Historical Summary
(as originally stated)

Fiscal Year	Oper. Rev.	Net Inc. Bef. Disc.	EPS*
	$000s	$000s	$
2022[A]	200,344	29,320	1.24
2021[A]	131,678	(35,812)	(46.80)
2020[A]	103,684	(41,301)	(54.00)
2019[A]	196,408	(81,030)	(105.60)
2018[A]	236,410	(41,060)	(54.00)

* Common
[A] Reported in accordance with IFRS
Note: Adjusted throughout for 1-for-120 cons. in Aug. 2022

W.22 Western Forest Products Inc.*

Symbol - WEF **Exchange** - TSX **CUSIP** - 958211
Head Office - Royal Centre, 800-1055 Georgia St W, PO Box 11122, Vancouver, BC, V6E 3P3 **Telephone** - (604) 648-4500 **Fax** - (604) 681-9584
Website - www.westernforest.com
Email - gnontell@westernforest.com
Investor Relations - Glen Nontell (604) 648-4500
Auditors - KPMG LLP C.A., Vancouver, B.C.
Lawyers - DLA Piper (Canada) LLP
Transfer Agents - Computershare Trust Company of Canada Inc., Vancouver, B.C.
FP500 Revenue Ranking - 279
Employees - 2,034 at Dec. 31, 2022

Profile - (Can. 2004) Harvests timber, sawmills logs into lumber, and conducts value-added lumber remanufacturing in the coastal regions of British Columbia and Washington for sale to worldwide markets.

Timber Harvesting

The company's B.C. fibre requirements are primarily met with logs harvested from its timber tenures and private lands, supplemented by logs purchased on the open market, and log trading activities. The company also participates in auctions for the purchase of standing timber through B.C. Timber Sales and sources fibre through timber harvesting joint ventures and limited partnerships with coastal First Nations. Holds tree farm licences, forest licences and timber licences from the Province of British Columbia that provided for an annual allowable cut of 5,914,000 m^3 of logs at Dec. 31, 2022. The long-term species distribution on the company's timber resources at Dec. 31, 2022, was 64% hemlock and balsam, 14% cedar, 12% Douglas fir, 6% yellow cedar and 4% spruce and other minor species.

	2022	2021
Actual Gross Harvest, m^3	3,390,000	3,517,000
Logs purchased, m^3	1,148,000	1,011,000
Logs consumed, m^3	2,576,000	3,089,000
Logs sold, m^3	1,329,000	1,340,000

Logs are sorted according to species, size and grade and directed to sawmills, custom cutting operations and log markets to maximize the return. Most of the company's logging is conducted on government-owned timberlands and some harvesting takes place on private lands external to its tree farm licences.

Manufacturing

Owns six sawmills on Vancouver Island and one in Washington state with a combined annual lumber production capacity of 1,060 mmfbm. The mills process high-quality logs including hemlock and balsam, Douglas fir, yellow cedar and western red cedar into primarily upper grade lumber, lumber with long lengths (over 20 feet) and wide widths (over 10 inches), commodity grades of lumber and residual wood chips sold for pulp production. Lumber is marketed and sold in North America, Japan, the People's Republic of China (PRC) and Europe. Residual wood chips from sawmills are sold under long-term and short term fibre supply agreements, and logs are traded with third parties to secure preferred fibre or for cost benefit.

Also operates a value-added remanufacturing facility, located in Chemainus, B.C., which specializes in value-added processes for all species and provides additional kiln-drying and planer capacity for the primary sawmills. In addition, operates a distribution and processing centre in Arlington, Wash., and a custom cut division which converts logs to lumber on a custom basis to customer specifications. Also has manufacturing facilities in Washougal and Vancouver, Wash., with a combined annual glulam capacity of 35 mmfbm on a two shift basis.

Sawmill production totaled 654,000 m^3 in 2022 and 760,000 m^3 in 2021.

Sales & Marketing

Lumber products are marketed and sold from offices in Vancouver, B.C.; Tokyo, Japan; and Shanghai, PRC. Sales to the United States are made directly to lumber distributors or major manufacturers; sales to Japan are made directly from Vancouver and Washington to Japanese trading houses or through the marketing division in Japan; sales to Europe are made through sales agencies; and sales to the PRC are made through direct sales and local Canadian wholesalers.

In January 2023, the company announced that it would not restart its Alberni Pacific Division (APD) facility's operations in Port Alberni, B.C. The APD sawmill had been curtailed since November 2022 due to market demand and log availability. Also, the company commissioned a third party forest products consulting firm to look at long-term primary manufacturing options for APD considering the factors of rapid change in fibre supply and timber profile, forest policies and global market dynamics. In addition, it was concluded that operating the sawmill is not viable and the investment needed to upgrade the facility would not be economically feasible for the company.

Periods ended:	12m Dec. 31/22	12m Dec. 31/21
Annual allowable cut, m³	5,914,000	5,914,000
Lumber prod., mfbm	654,000	760,000
Log prod., m³	3,110,000	3,090,000
Log purchases, m³	1,093,000	861,000
Log sales, m³	1,329,000	1,340,000

Recent Merger and Acquisition Activity

Status: completed **Revised:** Oct. 31, 2022
UPDATE: HVLP confirmed that it would not complete the second stage acquisition of a further 16% equity interest in Tsawak-qin Forestry Limited Partnership, as well as a 7% equity interest in the Alberni Pacific limited partnership. PREVIOUS: Western Forest Products Inc. (WFP) agreed to sell an incremental 44% equity interest in TFL 44 Limited Partnership (TFL 44 LP), plus a 7% equity interest in a new limited partnership that would own the Alberni Pacific division sawmill, to Huumiis Ventures Limited Partnership (HVLP) for total consideration of $36,200,000. HVLP is a limited partnership owned by Huu-ay-aht First Nations. TFL 44 LP holds certain assets in Port Alberni, B.C., including Tree Farm Licence 44 and associated assets and liabilities. The first stage of the TFL 44 transaction involves the acquisition by HVLP of an additional 28% equity interest in TFL 44 LP, for an interim combined equity interest of 35%. Consideration for the first stage is $22,400,000, of which $2,600,000 would be financed by WFP through vendor take-back with a maturity date of Mar. 31, 2023. The second stage involves the acquisition by HVLP of an additional 16% equity interest in TFL 44 LP for $12,800,000 and was anticipated to close in the first quarter of 2023. WFP may sell to other area First Nations, including HVLP, a further incremental ownership interest of up to 26% in TFL 44 LP, under certain conditions. May 3, 2021 - The first stage was completed. The second stage was anticipated to close in the second quarter of 2023. Nov. 15, 2021 - TFL 44 LP changed its name to Tsawak-qin Forestry Limited Partnership.

Status: completed **Revised:** Aug. 31, 2022
UPDATE: The transaction was completed. PREVIOUS: Western Forest Products Inc. agreed to acquire certain assets of Calvert Company, Inc. located in Washington State for consideration of US$12,000,000, including inventory of US$2,500,000 subject to a customary post-closing inventory adjustment. Calvert manufactures glulam beams in multiple species, including Douglas fir, southern yellow pine and yellow cedar, for industrial, commercial and residential projects. Calvert's operations produced approximately 13 mmfbm of glulam in 2021 on a single shift basis and includes manufacturing facilities in Washougal and Vancouver, Wash., with a combined annual glulam capacity of 35 mmfbm on a two shift basis. The transaction would be financed with cash on hand, and was expected to close in the third quarter of 2022.

Predecessor Detail - Succeeded Doman Industries Limited, July 27, 2004, pursuant to restructuring plan whereby Western Forest Products became the new corporate parent of Doman's operations.

Directors - Daniel L. Nocente, chr., Vancouver, B.C.; J. Steven Hofer, pres. & CEO, Bellingham, Wash.; Laura A. Cillis, Nelson, B.C.; Randy Krotowski, Mass.; Fiona Macfarlane, West Vancouver, B.C.; Noordin S. K. Nanji, Vancouver, B.C.; Peter C. Wijnbergen, Toronto, Ont.; John Williamson, Friday Harbor, Wash.

Other Exec. Officers - Stephen D. A. Williams, exec. v-p & CFO; Bruce L. Alexander, sr. v-p, sales, mktg. & mfg.; Jennifer Foster, sr. v-p, HR & corp. affairs; Jonathan Armstrong, v-p, forest stewardship & fibre supply; Alyce Harper, v-p, legal, gen. counsel & corp. sec.; Donald Holmes, v-p, timberlands; Glen Nontell, v-p, corp. devel.; Dallyn Willis, v-p, fin.

Capital Stock

	Authorized (shs.)	Outstanding (shs.)[1]
Preferred	unlimited	nil
Common	unlimited	316,745,557

[1] At Aug. 3, 2023

Options - At Dec. 31, 2022, options were outstanding to purchase 15,133,457 common shares at prices ranging from $1.05 to $2.74 per share with a weighted average remaining life of 4.8 years.

Normal Course Issuer Bid - The company plans to make normal course purchases of up to 15,837,277 common shares representing 5% of the total outstanding. The bid commenced on Aug. 11, 2023, and expires on Aug. 10, 2024.

Major Shareholder - Letko, Brosseau & Associates Inc. held 15.41% interest at Mar. 20, 2023.

Price Range - WEF/TSX

Year	Volume	High	Low	Close
2022	190,540,257	$2.30	$1.03	$1.16
2021	290,327,451	$2.58	$1.24	$2.11
2020	230,875,989	$1.41	$0.58	$1.28
2019	188,746,840	$2.20	$1.13	$1.22
2018	194,527,952	$2.95	$1.72	$1.89

Recent Close: $0.94

Capital Stock Changes - During 2022, 108,585 common shares were issued on exercise of options and 12,146,409 common shares were repurchased under a Normal Course Issuer Bid.

Dividends

WEF com Var. Ra pa Q[1]

$0.0125	Sept. 15/23	$0.0125	June 16/23
$0.0125	Mar. 17/23	$0.0125	Dec. 16/22

Paid in 2023: $0.0375 2022: $0.0475 2021: $0.04

[1] Quarterly divd normally payable in June/20 has been omitted.

Long-Term Debt - Note - In June 2023, outstanding long-term debt totaled $36,800,000 (none current and net of $300,000 of transaction costs) and consisted of borrowing under a $250,000,000 credit facility, bearing interest at bankers' acceptance rate, Canadian or U.S. prime rate advances, or U.S. base rate advances, and due July 21, 2025.

Wholly Owned Subsidiaries

WFP Holdings US Inc., United States.
- 100% int. in **WFP Engineered Products LLC**, United States.
- 100% int. in **Western Forest Products US LLC**, United States.

WFP Partnerships Ltd., Canada.
Western Forest Products Japan Ltd., Japan.
Western Lumber Sales Limited, Vancouver, B.C.
Western Specialty Lumber Sales US LLC, United States.

Subsidiaries

65% int. in **Tsawak-qin Forestry Limited Partnership**, B.C.

Note: The preceding list includes only the major related companies in which interests are held.

Financial Statistics

Periods ended:	12m Dec. 31/22[A]		12m Dec. 31/21[A]
	$000s	%Chg	$000s
Operating revenue	**1,444,000**	**+2**	**1,417,700**
Cost of goods sold	1,141,600		943,900
General & admin expense	42,200		55,200
Other operating expense	123,300		120,300
Operating expense	**1,307,100**	**+17**	**1,119,400**
Operating income	**136,900**	**-54**	**298,300**
Deprec., depl. & amort.	50,200		50,900
Finance costs, gross	n.a.		1,900
Finance costs, net	(100)		n.a.
Pre-tax income	**84,400**	**-68**	**265,200**
Income taxes	22,600		62,400
Net income	**61,800**	**-70**	**202,800**
Net inc. for equity hldrs	**61,700**	**-69**	**201,400**
Net inc. for non-cont. int.	**100**	**-93**	**1,400**
Cash & equivalent	15,800		130,000
Inventories	224,800		207,200
Accounts receivable	60,000		57,400
Current assets	339,800		411,000
Long-term investments	11,000		12,600
Fixed assets, net	413,800		392,300
Intangibles, net	103,300		100,300
Total assets	**932,800**	**-3**	**959,000**
Accts. pay. & accr. liabs	108,500		112,800
Current liabilities	125,800		194,300
Long-term lease liabilities	16,400		12,800
Shareholders' equity	647,200		612,100
Non-controlling interest	4,500		5,100
Cash from oper. activs	**(10,300)**	**n.a.**	**281,600**
Cash from fin. activs	(44,000)		(193,200)
Cash from invest. activs	(59,900)		38,700
Net cash position	**15,800**	**-88**	**130,000**
Capital expenditures	(60,400)		(31,900)
Capital disposals	2,700		52,000
Unfunded pension liability	2,800		7,800
	$		$
Earnings per share*	0.19		0.56
Cash flow per share*	(0.03)		0.79
Cash divd. per share*	0.05		0.04
	shs		shs
No. of shs. o/s*	316,742,746		328,780,570
Avg. no. of shs. o/s*	322,947,420		358,502,253
	%		%
Net profit margin	4.28		14.30
Return on equity	9.80		36.07
Return on assets	6.53		22.55
Foreign sales percent	60		68
No. of employees (FTEs)	2,034		2,051

* Common
[A] Reported in accordance with IFRS

Latest Results

Periods ended:	6m June 30/23[A]		6m June 30/22[A]
	$000s	%Chg	$000s
Operating revenue	539,800	-32	797,000
Net income	(38,400)	n.a.	76,600
Net inc. for equity hldrs	(38,000)	n.a.	75,900
Net inc. for non-cont. int	(400)		700
	$		$
Earnings per share*	(0.12)		0.23

* Common
[A] Reported in accordance with IFRS

Historical Summary
(as originally stated)

Fiscal Year	Oper. Rev.	Net Inc. Bef. Disc.	EPS*
	$000s	$000s	$
2022[A]	1,444,000	61,800	0.19
2021[A]	1,417,700	202,800	0.56
2020[A]	964,900	33,400	0.09
2019[A]	807,700	(46,700)	(0.12)
2018[A]	1,196,700	69,200	0.18

* Common
[A] Reported in accordance with IFRS

W.23 The Western Investment Company of Canada Limited

Symbol - WI **Exchange** - TSX-VEN **CUSIP** - 95846L
Head Office - 1010 24 St SE, High River, AB, T1V 2A7 **Telephone** - (403) 652-2663 **Fax** - (403) 652-2661
Website - www.winv.ca
Email - scross@winv.ca
Investor Relations - Stacey Cross (403) 703-9882
Auditors - Ernst & Young LLP C.A., Calgary, Alta.
Transfer Agents - Odyssey Trust Company, Calgary, Alta.
Employees - 2 at Apr. 22, 2022

Profile - (Alta. 2015) Invests primarily in western Canadian-based private businesses in the agriculture, distribution and retail, human services, insurance and financial services sectors.

The company targets acquisitions with an enterprise value of between $10,000,000 to $100,000,000 and considers equity ownership interests of between 25% and 100%.

Subsidiary **GlassMasters ARG Autoglass Two Inc.** repairs and replaces windshields, side windows, side mirrors, rear windows and sun roofs through ten retail locations in Calgary (2), Edmonton (2), Airdrie, Red Deer, Lethbridge and Sherwood, Alta., and Saskatoon and Regina, Sask., and mobile repair and installation vehicles. Also imports from the People's Republic of China and wholesales original equipment manufacturer glass and related automotive glass repair and replacement material to GlassMasters and other windshield repair companies in Alberta. Operations include four warehouses in Calgary, Edmonton, Saskatoon and Regina.

Owns 30% interests in three senior care homes in Saskatchewan and 25% interest in **Golden Health Care Management Inc.**, which manages a portfolio of seven retirement homes in Saskatchewan totaling 457 suites.

Subsidiary **Ocean Sales Group Ltd.** is a specialty retailer that imports and sells innovative household products through live demonstrations at leading consumer shows and fairs throughout Canada and the U.S. as well as a wholesale operation to select customers in Canada and the U.S.

Subsidiary **Foothills Creamery Ltd.** produces and distributes butter and ice cream products in western Canada, with distribution facilities in Edmonton, Alta., and Kelowna, B.C.

Subsidiary **Fortress Insurance Company** is a property and casualty insurance company operating in British Columbia, Alberta, Saskatchewan and Manitoba, which writes insurance policies predominantly in property, as well as accident and sickness, boiler and machinery and marine. Also offers third-party automobile liability insurance in Alberta only.

Directors - James F. (Jim) Dinning, chr., Calgary, Alta.; Scott A. Tannas, pres., CEO & corp. sec., High River, Alta.; Dr. Kabir Jivraj, Calgary, Alta.; Jennie Moushos, Maple Ridge, B.C.; Willard H. (Bill) Yuill, Medicine Hat, Alta.

Other Exec. Officers - Shafeen Mawani, COO; Stacey Cross, CFO

Capital Stock

	Authorized (shs.)	Outstanding (shs.)[1]
Preferred	unlimited	nil
Common	unlimited	30,287,756

[1] At Feb. 6, 2023

Normal Course Issuer Bid - The company plans to make normal course purchases of up to 1,500,000 common shares representing 5% of the total outstanding. The bid commenced on Feb. 10, 2023, and expires on Feb. 9, 2024.

Major Shareholder - Widely held at May 26, 2022.

Price Range - WI/TSX-VEN

Year	Volume	High	Low	Close
2022	3,752,332	$0.45	$0.26	$0.37
2021	6,194,912	$0.44	$0.21	$0.36
2020	3,894,469	$0.34	$0.12	$0.23
2019	3,562,564	$0.50	$0.24	$0.33
2018	4,502,378	$0.63	$0.26	$0.39

Recent Close: $0.40

Dividends

WI com Ra $0.005 pa A est. July 29, 2022
$0.005**i** .... July 29/22
i Initial Payment

Subsidiaries

50.4% int. in **Foothills Creamery Ltd.**, Calgary, Alta.
58.2% int. in **GlassMasters ARG Autoglass Two Inc.**, Calgary, Alta.
75% int. in **Ocean Sales Group Ltd.**, Calgary, Alta.

Investments

50% int. in **Fortress Insurance Company**, Alta.
25% int. in **Golden Health Care Management Inc.**, Sask.
30% int. in **The Good Shepherd Villas Inc.**, Prince Albert, Sask.
30% int. in **Hill View Manor Ltd.**, Estevan, Sask.
30% int. in **William Albert House Ltd.**, Emerald Park, Sask.

Financial Statistics

Periods ended:	12m Dec. 31/21[A]		12m Dec. 31/20[oA]
	$000s	%Chg	$000s
Total revenue	**1,375**	**n.a.**	**(2,484)**
General & admin. expense	664		673
Stock-based compensation	64		63
Other operating expense	21		30
Operating expense	**749**	**-2**	**765**
Operating income	**626**	**n.a.**	**(3,250)**
Finance costs, gross	606		556
Pre-tax income	**20**	**n.a.**	**(3,806)**
Net income	**20**	**n.a.**	**(3,806)**
Cash & equivalent	23		366
Investments	18,685		17,783
Total assets	**19,502**	**+3**	**18,989**
Bank indebtedness	1,014		777
Accts. pay. & accr. liabs	145		146
Debt	4,620		4,620
Equity portion of conv. debs	794		794
Shareholders' equity	13,723		13,671
Cash from oper. activs	**(408)**	**n.a.**	**234**
Cash from fin. activs	(99)		457
Cash from invest. activs	164		(475)
Net cash position	**23**	**-94**	**366**
	$		$
Earnings per share*	0.00		(0.13)
Cash flow per share*	(0.01)		0.01
	shs		shs
No. of shs. o/s*	30,338,756		30,460,756
Avg. no. of shs. o/s*	30,398,326		30,523,160
	%		%
Net profit margin	1.45		n.m.
Return on equity	0.14		(23.87)
Return on assets	3.18		(15.64)
No. of employees (FTEs)	2		3

* Common
[o] Restated
[A] Reported in accordance with IFRS

Latest Results

Periods ended:	3m Mar. 31/22[A]		3m Mar. 31/21[A]
	$000s	%Chg	$000s
Total revenue	(408)	n.a.	(168)
Net income	(773)	n.a.	(477)
	$		$
Earnings per share*	(0.03)		(0.02)

* Common
[A] Reported in accordance with IFRS

Historical Summary
(as originally stated)

Fiscal Year	Total Rev.	Net Inc. Bef. Disc.	EPS*
	$000s	$000s	$
2021[A]	1,375	20	0.00
2020[A]	(2,313)	(3,634)	(0.12)
2019[A]	2,359	1,253	0.04
2018[A]	2,174	1,132	0.04
2017[A]	689	(434)	(0.02)

* Common
[A] Reported in accordance with IFRS

W.24 Western Pacific Trust Company

Symbol - WP **Exchange** - TSX-VEN **CUSIP** - 959143
Head Office - 920-789 Pender St W, Vancouver, BC, V6C 1H2 **Telephone** - (604) 683-0455 **Toll-free** - (800) 663-9536 **Fax** - (604) 669-6978
Website - www.westernpacifictrust.com
Email - aalfer@westernpacifictrust.com
Investor Relations - Alison Alfer (604) 683-0455
Auditors - Smythe LLP C.A., Vancouver, B.C.
Bankers - Royal Bank of Canada, Vancouver, B.C.
Lawyers - DuMoulin Black LLP, Vancouver, B.C.
Transfer Agents - Computershare Trust Company of Canada Inc., Vancouver, B.C.

Profile - (B.C. 1964) Provides self-administered investment plans, trust services, client consulting services, private health plans, transfer and collateral agency services.

Provides self-administered investment plans, which permit investors the tax-deferred benefits of a registered plan while maintaining control over their investment choices; trust services that offers strategic counsel, organizational assistance and consults with clients' legal advisors in the establishment and administration of various forms of trusts, an effective vehicle and flexible tool for present and future management of assets; client consulting services that provides a range of accounting, administrative and corporate secretarial services to select clients on a fee-for-service basis; private health care plans through wholly owned **WP Private Health Inc.**, which helps small business owners to save taxes and reduce the after tax costs of health care;

transfer services through wholly owned **WP Private Equity Transfers Inc.**, which offers transfer agency and registrar services to non-reporting, unlisted private organizations; and collateral services through wholly owned **1128668 B.C. Ltd.** and **1211263 B.C. Ltd.** which are maintained solely for the purpose of offering collateral agency services to clients in conduct of its bond business.

Predecessor Detail - Succeeded AME Resource Capital Corp., Sept. 1, 1999, following acquisition of AME Resource Capital (renamed Western Equity Loans Ltd.) by Western Pacific Trust Company; basis 1 new for 4 old shs.

Directors - Dr. Anthony Liscio, chr., Toronto, Ont.; Steve O. Youngman, deputy chr. & corp. sec., B.C.; Alison Alfer, pres. & CEO, Vancouver, B.C.; Bruce H. Bailey, B.C.; G Ben Cutler, B.C.; John C. A. de Wit, B.C.; J. Cowan McKinney, West Vancouver, B.C.

Other Exec. Officers - Sharon Lee, CFO

Capital Stock

	Authorized (shs.)	Outstanding (shs.)[1]
Preferred	100,000,000	nil
Series I		400
Series II		130,550
Common	100,000,000	26,293,558

[1] At Aug. 23, 2023

Preferred Series I - Redeemable, non-retractable, non-cumulative dividends equal to 5% per annum of the aggregate value of $10 per share and a non-cumulative cash payment equal to 1% per annum of the aggregate value of $10 per share payable in respect to waiver of retraction rights. Non-voting.

Preferred Series II - Redeemable, non-retractable, non-cumulative dividends equal to 5% per annum of the aggregate value of $10 per share. Convertible into common shares at 15¢ per common share. Non-voting.

Common - One vote per share.

Major Shareholder - Robert W. (Bob) Macdonald held 15.7% interest, Derek Weston held 14.7% interest and Dr. Anthony Liscio held 11.1% interest at Apr. 26, 2023.

Price Range - WP/TSX-VEN

Year	Volume	High	Low	Close
2022	512,332	$0.48	$0.10	$0.12
2021	485,400	$0.15	$0.09	$0.13
2020	55,000	$0.13	$0.10	$0.10
2019	176,124	$0.27	$0.03	$0.12
2018	395,375	$0.24	$0.09	$0.15

Recent Close: $0.17

Capital Stock Changes - During 2022, 1,275,000 common shares were issued on exercise of options.

Wholly Owned Subsidiaries

1128668 B.C. Ltd., B.C.
1211263 B.C. Ltd., B.C.
WP Private Equity Transfers Inc., B.C.
WP Private Health Inc., B.C.

Financial Statistics

Periods ended:	12m Dec. 31/22^A		12m Dec. 31/21^A
	$000s	%Chg	$000s
Investment income	**1,524**	**+37**	**1,116**
Interest expense	45		22
Net investment income	**1,479**	**+35**	**1,094**
Salaries & pension benefits	542		458
Pre-tax income	**334**	**+215**	**106**
Income taxes	(307)		(740)
Net income	**641**	**-24**	**846**
Cash & equivalent	1,923		1,575
Accounts receivable	88		64
Fixed assets, net	22		18
Total assets	**3,781**	**+45**	**2,611**
Long-term debt	660		526
Preferred share equity	1,273		1,273
Shareholders' equity	2,551		1,868
Cash from oper. activs	**261**	**+46**	**179**
Cash from fin. activs	96		245
Cash from invest. activs	(9)		nil
	$		$
Earnings per share*	0.02		0.03
Cash flow per share*	0.01		0.01
	shs		shs
No. of shs. o/s*	26,293,558		25,018,558
Avg. no. of shs. o/s*	25,826,777		25,018,558
	%		%
Net profit margin	43.34		77.33
Return on equity	61.51		381.42
Return on assets	20.06		40.88

* Common
^A Reported in accordance with IFRS

Latest Results

Periods ended:	6m June 30/23^A		6m June 30/22^A
	$000s	%Chg	$000s
Net invest. income	987	+40	705
Net income	252	+133	108
	$		$
Earnings per share*	0.01		0.00

* Common
^A Reported in accordance with IFRS

Historical Summary
(as originally stated)

Fiscal Year	Invest. Inc. $000s	Net Inc. Bef. Disc. $000s	EPS* $
2022^A	1,524	641	0.02
2021^A	1,116	846	0.03
2020^A	1,060	77	0.00
2019^A	1,087	143	0.00
2018^A	941	32	0.00

* Common
^A Reported in accordance with IFRS

W.25 Western Resources Corp.

Symbol - WRX **Exchange** - TSX **CUSIP** - 95942C

Head Office - 1205-789 Pender St W, Vancouver, BC, V6C 1H2 **Telephone** - (604) 689-9378 **Toll-free** - (866) 689-9378 **Fax** - (604) 620-0775

Website - www.westernresources.com

Email - jerry@westernresources.com

Investor Relations - Jerry Zhang (778) 889-5157

Auditors - MNP LLP C.A., Vancouver, B.C.

Lawyers - Vector Corporate Finance Lawyers, Vancouver, B.C.

Transfer Agents - Computershare Trust Company of Canada Inc., Vancouver, B.C.

Employees - 35 at Sept. 30, 2022

Profile - (B.C. 2017) Has potash interest in Saskatchewan. Also invests in real estate projects in British Columbia.

Holds Milestone potash project, 149,862 acres, 35 km southeast of Regina, Sask. An updated engineering and mine life review released in December 2021 proposed a mine operation with an average annual production of 146,000 tonnes of muriate of potash (MOP) over a 40-year mine life. Initial capital costs were estimated at $149,451,000. At Nov. 30, 2021, proven and probable reserves totaled 116,520,000 tonnes grading 20.91% potassium oxide and 33.1% potassium chloride.

Through wholly owned **Western Garden Properties Corp.**, holds investments in real estate projects in Vancouver, B.C.

In September 2022, **Vantage Chance Limited**, a private investment company based in the British Virgin Islands, exercised its option to convert 157,325,071 common shares of **Western Potash Holdings Corp.** (WPHC) in exchange for 219,726,258 common shares of the company. Previously, the company completed a subscription agreement withVantage for a strategic equity investment of $80,000,000 in **Western Potash Holdings Corp.**, a newly formed company, and received 157,325,071 WPHC common shares. Prior to completion, the company transferred its 100% interest in **Western Potash Corp.** (WPC), which owns the Milestone potash project, to WPHC in exchange for an equivalent number of WPHC common shares, representing 100% interest in WPHC. Upon completion of the subscription agreement, Vantage and the company held 54% and 46% interest in WPHC, respectively. As part of the agreement, Vantage was granted an option to convert all of the 157,325,071 WPHC common shares into 219,726,258 common shares of the company, which would represent 54% interest in the company.

Predecessor Detail - Succeeded Western Potash Corp., Apr. 5, 2017; basis 1 new for 5 old shs.

Directors - Wenye (Bill) Xue, chr., pres. & CEO, Vancouver, B.C.; Xiang (George) Gao, sr. v-p, corp. fin. & CFO, Toronto, Ont.; Guy I. Bentinck, Toronto, Ont.; Mark F. Fracchia, Calgary, Alta.; Andrew C. Hancharyk, Victoria, B.C.; Scott D. Nagel, Minneapolis, Minn.; Justin Xing, Hong Kong, Hong Kong, People's Republic of China

Other Exec. Officers - Jerry Zhang, CAO; Jack Xue, corp. sec.

Capital Stock

	Authorized (shs.)	Outstanding (shs.)[1]
Common	unlimited	408,490,478

[1] At Jan. 25, 2023

Major Shareholder - Justin Xing held 53.79% interest and Wenye (Bill) Xue held 10.88% interest at Jan. 25, 2023.

Price Range - WRX/TSX

Year	Volume	High	Low	Close
2022	11,937,416	$0.48	$0.15	$0.23
2021	10,091,055	$0.37	$0.15	$0.18
2020	10,351,346	$0.31	$0.13	$0.17
2019	38,645,729	$0.55	$0.11	$0.25
2018	4,549,227	$0.45	$0.21	$0.27

Recent Close: $0.24

Capital Stock Changes - In September 2022, 219,726,258 common shares were issued on exercise of conversion option of Vantage Chance Limited. Also during fiscal 2022, 1,590,000 common shares were issued on exercise of options.

Wholly Owned Subsidiaries

Western Garden Properties Corp., B.C.
- 50% int. in **Alabaster (Spires 2) G.P. Ltd.**, B.C.
- 36% int. in **Alabaster (Spires 2) Limited Partnership**, B.C.
- 10.13% int. in **FB 234 Third Avenue Development Limited**, B.C. Voting interest.
- 22.5% int. in **FB 234 Third Development Limited Partnership**, B.C.

Western Potash Corp.
- 72.31% int. in **FB Burrard Development Limited Partnership**, B.C.

Western Potash Holdings Corp., Canada.
0907414 B.C. Ltd., B.C.

Investments

45% int. in **WGP Investment Limited Partnership**

Financial Statistics

Periods ended:	12m Sept. 30/22^A		12m Sept. 30/21^A
	$000s	%Chg	$000s
Salaries & benefits	1,687		659
General & admin expense	1,457		2,065
Stock-based compensation	146		23
Operating expense	**3,290**	**+20**	**2,747**
Operating income	**(3,290)**	**n.a.**	**(2,747)**
Deprec., depl. & amort.	91		143
Finance income	76		84
Finance costs, gross	4,976		3,144
Investment income	(94)		(110)
Pre-tax income	**(328)**	**n.a.**	**(5,596)**
Income taxes	nil		27
Net income	**(328)**	**n.a.**	**(5,623)**
Net inc. for equity hldrs	**(1,231)**	**n.a.**	**(5,623)**
Net inc. for non-cont. int	**903**	**n.a.**	**nil**
Cash & equivalent	30,462		8,091
Accounts receivable	nil		11
Current assets	36,765		9,083
Long-term investments	831		1,402
Fixed assets, net	354		407
Right-of-use assets	nil		34
Intangibles, net	35		nil
Explor./devel. properties	260,023		230,945
Total assets	**305,502**	**+24**	**246,848**
Accts. pay. & accr. liabs	5,453		44,469
Current liabilities	14,377		45,443
Long-term debt, gross	38,763		36,638
Long-term debt, net	29,838		36,638
Shareholders' equity	241,406		160,841
Cash from oper. activs	**(8,331)**	**n.a.**	**(4,257)**
Cash from fin. activs	83,996		(2,259)
Cash from invest. activs	(81,484)		7,824
Net cash position	**2,201**	**-73**	**8,020**
Capital expenditures	(53,237)		(11,161)
	$		$
Earnings per share*	(0.01)		(0.03)
Cash flow per share*	(0.04)		(0.02)
	shs		shs
No. of shs. o/s*	408,490,478		187,174,220
Avg. no. of shs. o/s*	188,778,430		186,236,053
	%		%
Net profit margin	n.a.		n.a.
Return on equity	(0.61)		(3.43)
Return on assets	1.68		(0.96)
No. of employees (FTEs)	35		18

* Common
^A Reported in accordance with IFRS

Latest Results

Periods ended:	3m Dec. 31/22^A		3m Dec. 31/21^A
	$000s	%Chg	$000s
Net income	1,980	n.a.	(2,765)
	$		$
Earnings per share*	0.00		(0.01)

* Common
^A Reported in accordance with IFRS

Historical Summary
(as originally stated)

Fiscal Year	Oper. Rev. $000s	Net Inc. Bef. Disc. $000s	EPS* $
2022^A	nil	(328)	(0.01)
2021^A	nil	(5,623)	(0.03)
2020^A	nil	(1,665)	(0.01)
2019^A	nil	(922)	(0.01)
2018^A	nil	1,952	0.02

* Common
^A Reported in accordance with IFRS

W.26 George Weston Limited*

Symbol - WN **Exchange** - TSX **CUSIP** - 961148
Head Office - 1901-22 St. Clair Ave E, Toronto, ON, M4T 2S7 **Telephone** - (416) 922-2500 **Fax** - (416) 922-4395
Website - www.weston.ca
Email - andrew.bunston@weston.ca
Investor Relations - Andrew Bunston (416) 965-5433
Auditors - PricewaterhouseCoopers LLP C.A.
Transfer Agents - Computershare Trust Company of Canada Inc., Toronto, Ont.
FP500 Revenue Ranking - 8
Employees - 221,285 at Dec. 31, 2022
Profile - (Can. 1928, via letters patent) Operates through two segments: the Loblaw segment, in which 52.6%-owned **Loblaw Companies Limited** provides grocery, pharmacy, health and beauty, apparel, general merchandise, financial services, and wireless mobile products and services across Canada; and the Choice Properties segment, in which 61.7%-owned **Choice Properties Real Estate Investment Trust** owns, manages and develops a portfolio of retail, industrial, and mixed-use, residential and other properties across Canada.

Loblaw

Loblaw Companies Limited (52.6% owned) operates through two segments: the Retail segment, consisting primarily of corporate and franchised retail food and associate-owned drug stores, and includes in-store pharmacies, health care services, other health and beauty products, apparel and other general merchandise; and the Financial Services segment, which provides credit card and everyday banking services, a loyalty program, insurance brokerage services and telecommunication services.

Retail - At Dec. 31, 2022, Loblaw operated 547 corporate stores, 551 franchised stores, 1,346 associate-owned stores and 298 Lifemark healthcare clinics. Loblaw-owned store banners consist of Loblaws (45), Provigo (3), Provigo Le Marché (3), Zehrs (42), Atlantic Superstore (52), Dominion (11), T&T Supermarket (31), Maxi (127), Extra Foods (5), Real Canadian Superstore (120), Cash & Carry (5), Club Entrepôt (4), Presto (6), Real Canadian Wholesale Club (41), Joe Fresh (2), Wellwise by Shoppers (43) Beauty Boutique by Shoppers Drug Mart (1) and The Health Clinic by Shoppers (6). Franchised stores consist of Provigo (55), Provigo Le Marché (10), Valu-Mart (31), Independent (150), City Market (9), Fortinos (23), Extra Foods (2) and No Frills (271). Associate-owned stores consist of Shoppers Drug Mart/Pharmaprix (1,310) and Shoppers Simply Pharmacy/Pharmaprix Simplement Santé (36).

Loblaw also offers control brands, including President's Choice, Life Brand, no name, Farmer's Market, PC Organics, PC Blue Menu, PC Black Label Collection, Everyday Essentials, Life at Home, T&T, Quo Beauty and Joe Fresh, which are available throughout its store and digital networks.

Financial Services - Loblaw's wholly owned **President's Choice Bank** offers financial services to consumers under the President's Choice Financial brand, including the PC MasterCard® and PC Money Account, which enables customers to do their everyday banking and to earn PC Optimum points under Loblaw's PC Optimum loyalty program. Through this loyalty program, Loblaw rewards Canadian consumers for shopping in store or online, including through personalized offers on customers' online accounts. Loblaw also offers guaranteed investment certificates offered through the broker channel and automobile and home insurance through its insurance entities. In addition, Loblaw offers mobile products and services under The Mobile Shop™ brand, as well as prepaid cell phones and giftcards, through its network of grocery stores across Canada.

Choice Properties

Choice Properties Real Estate Investment Trust (61.7% owned) held a portfolio of 574 retail properties, 116 industrial properties, and 12 mixed-use, residential and other properties, totaling 63,900,000 sq. ft. of gross leasable area, at Dec. 31, 2022.

Directors - Galen G. Weston, chr. & CEO, Toronto, Ont.; Gordon M. Nixon†, Toronto, Ont.; M. Marianne Harris, Toronto, Ont.; Nancy H. O. Lockhart, Toronto, Ont.; The Hon. Sarabjit S. (Sabi) Marwah, Toronto, Ont.; Barbara G. Stymiest, Toronto, Ont.; Cornell C. V. Wright, Toronto, Ont.

Other Exec. Officers - Richard Dufresne, pres. & CFO; Khush Dadyburjor, chief strategy officer; Anemona Turcu, chief risk officer; Jeff Gobeil, grp. head, tax; Lina Taglieri, grp. head, contr.; Gordon A. M. Currie, exec. v-p & chief legal officer; Rashid Wasti, exec. v-p & chief talent officer; Andrew Bunston, v-p, gen. counsel & corp. sec.; John Williams, treas. & head, corp. fin.

† Lead director

Capital Stock

	Authorized (shs.)	Outstanding (shs.)[1]
Preferred	unlimited	
Series I	10,000,000	9,400,000
Series III	10,000,000	8,000,000
Series IV	8,000,000	8,000,000
Series V	8,000,000	8,000,000
Common	unlimited	139,080,273

[1] At May 11, 2023

Preferred - Issuable in series and non-voting. **Series I** - Entitled to a fixed cumulative preferred cash dividend of $1.45 per share per annum, payable quarterly. Redeemable at $25 per share together with all accrued and unpaid dividends. **Series III** - Entitled to a fixed cumulative preferred cash dividend of $1.30 per share per annum, payable quarterly. Redeemable at $25 per share together with all accrued and unpaid dividends. **Series IV** - Entitled to a fixed cumulative preferred cash dividend of $1.30 per share per annum, payable quarterly. Redeemable at $25 per share together with all accrued and unpaid dividends. **Series V** - Entitled to a fixed cumulative preferred cash dividend of $1.1875 per share per annum, payable quarterly. Redeemable at $25 per share together with all accrued and unpaid dividends.

Common - One vote per share.

Options - At Dec. 31, 2022, options were outstanding to purchase 1,648,766 common shares at a weighted average exercise price of $106.38 per share with a weighted average remaining life of up to five years.

Normal Course Issuer Bid - The company plans to make normal course purchases of up to 6,954,013 common shares representing 5% of the total outstanding. The bid commenced on May 25, 2023, and expires on May 24, 2024.

Major Shareholder - Galen G. Weston held 56.3% interest at Mar. 13, 2023.

Price Range - WN/TSX

Year	Volume	High	Low	Close
2022	42,889,439	$181.45	$130.81	$167.99
2021	45,762,773	$150.63	$91.95	$146.66
2020	55,388,717	$111.65	$84.01	$95.08
2019	46,314,865	$113.94	$88.08	$103.02
2018	48,271,564	$111.64	$86.72	$90.05

Recent Close: $149.53

Capital Stock Changes - During 2022, 337,615 common shares were issued on exercise of options, 6,389,176 common shares were repurchased under a Normal Course Issuer Bid and 19,359 (net) common shares were purchased and held in trust.

Dividends

WN com Ra $2.852 pa Q est. July 1, 2023**
Prev. Rate: $2.64 est. July 1, 2022
Prev. Rate: $2.40 est. Oct. 1, 2021
Prev. Rate: $2.20 est. Jan. 1, 2021
WN.PR.A pfd ser I cum. red. exch. Ra $1.45 pa Q
WN.PR.C pfd ser III cum. red. exch. Ra $1.30 pa Q
WN.PR.D pfd ser IV cum. red. exch. Ra $1.30 pa Q
WN.PR.E pfd ser V cum. red. exch. Ra $1.1875 pa Q
** Reinvestment Option

Long-Term Debt - Outstanding at Dec. 31, 2022:

4.12% notes due 2024	$200,000,000
7.1% notes due 2032	150,000,000
6.69% notes due 2033	100,000,000
Loblaw Companies Limited debt	7,802,000,000
Choice Properties REIT debt	6,573,000,000
Less: Trans. costs & other	41,000,000
	14,784,000,000
Less: Current portion	1,383,000,000
	13,401,000,000

Minimum long-term debt repayments were reported as follows:

2023	$1,645,000,000
2024	2,257,000,000
2025	1,842,000,000
2026	909,000,000
2027	1,126,000,000
Thereafter	7,046,000,000

Subsidiaries

61.7% int. in **Choice Properties Real Estate Investment Trust**, Toronto, Ont. (see separate coverage)
52.6% int. in **Loblaw Companies Limited**, Brampton, Ont. (see separate coverage)

Note: The preceding list includes only the major related companies in which interests are held.

Financial Statistics

Periods ended:	12m Dec. 31/22[A]		12m Dec. 31/21[oA]
	$000s	%Chg	$000s
Operating revenue	**57,048,000**	**+6**	**53,748,000**
Cost of goods sold	38,528,000		36,435,000
General & admin expense	11,440,000		10,764,000
Stock-based compensation	90,000		78,000
Operating expense	**50,058,000**	**+6**	**47,277,000**
Operating income	**6,990,000**	**+8**	**6,471,000**
Deprec., depl. & amort.	2,407,000		2,419,000
Finance income	71,000		213,000
Finance costs, gross	984,000		1,863,000
Write-downs/write-offs	(30,000)		(25,000)
Pre-tax income	**3,640,000**	**+53**	**2,377,000**
Income taxes	831,000		630,000
Net inc bef disc ops, eqhldrs	1,822,000		753,000
Net inc bef disc ops, NCI	987,000		994,000
Net inc. bef. disc. opers	**2,809,000**	**+61**	**1,747,000**
Disc. opers., equity hldrs	(6,000)		(322,000)
Income from disc. opers	(6,000)		(322,000)
Net income	**2,803,000**	**+97**	**1,425,000**
Net inc. for equity hldrs	**1,816,000**	**+321**	**431,000**
Net inc. for non-cont. int	**987,000**	**-1**	**994,000**
Cash & equivalent	2,816,000		3,863,000
Inventories	5,855,000		5,166,000
Accounts receivable	5,227,000		4,453,000
Current assets	14,653,000		14,222,000
Long-term investments	6,140,000		5,908,000
Fixed assets, net	11,130,000		10,782,000
Right-of-use assets	4,208,000		4,059,000
Intangibles, net	11,380,000		10,909,000
Total assets	**48,958,000**	**+4**	**47,083,000**
Bank indebtedness	708,000		502,000
Accts. pay. & accr. liabs	6,730,000		5,923,000
Current liabilities	10,757,000		9,773,000
Long-term debt, gross	14,784,000		14,010,000
Long-term debt, net	13,401,000		12,490,000
Long-term lease liabilities	4,323,000		4,242,000
Preferred share equity	817,000		817,000
Shareholders' equity	6,841,000		6,959,000
Non-controlling interest	6,339,000		6,178,000
Cash from oper. activs	**4,877,000**	**-5**	**5,119,000**
Cash from fin. activs	(3,011,000)		(4,426,000)
Cash from invest. activs	(2,540,000)		(291,000)
Net cash position	**2,313,000**	**-22**	**2,984,000**
Capital expenditures	(1,474,000)		(1,056,000)
Capital disposals	239,000		334,000
Pension fund surplus	170,000		305,000
	$		$
Earns. per sh. bef disc opers*	12.33		4.73
Earnings per share*	12.29		2.59
Cash flow per share*	33.81		34.15
Cash divd. per share*	2.58		2.30
	shs		shs
No. of shs. o/s*	140,577,477		146,648,397
Avg. no. of shs. o/s*	144,244,034		149,893,834
	%		%
Net profit margin	4.92		3.25
Return on equity	29.23		10.79
Return on assets	7.43		6.55
No. of employees (FTEs)	221,285		215,298

* Common
[o] Restated
[A] Reported in accordance with IFRS

Latest Results

Periods ended:	24w June 17/23[A]		24w June 18/22[A]
	$000s	%Chg	$000s
Operating revenue	27,017,000	+6	25,386,000
Net inc. bef. disc. opers	1,434,000	-4	1,489,000
Income from disc. opers	nil		(6,000)
Net income	1,434,000	-3	1,483,000
Net inc. for equity hldrs	944,000	-7	1,017,000
Net inc. for non-cont. int	490,000		466,000
	$		$
Earns. per sh. bef. disc. opers.*	6.63		6.86
Earnings per share*	6.56		6.82

* Common
[A] Reported in accordance with IFRS

Historical Summary
(as originally stated)

Fiscal Year	Oper. Rev. $000s	Net Inc. Bef. Disc. $000s	EPS* $
2022[A]	57,048,000	2,809,000	12.33
2021[A]	53,748,000	1,747,000	4.73
2020[A]	54,705,000	1,582,000	5.99
2019[A]	50,109,000	823,000	1.29
2018[A]	48,568,000	998,000	4.02

* Common
[A] Reported in accordance with IFRS

W.27 Westport Fuel Systems Inc.*

Symbol - WPRT **Exchange** - TSX **CUSIP** - 960908
Head Office - 1691 75 Ave W, Vancouver, BC, V6P 6P2 **Telephone** - (604) 718-2000 **Fax** - (604) 718-2001
Website - www.wfsinc.com
Email - invest@wfsinc.com
Investor Relations - Ashley Nuell (604) 718-2046
Auditors - KPMG LLP C.A., Vancouver, B.C.
Lawyers - Bennett Jones LLP, Calgary, Alta.
Transfer Agents - Computershare Trust Company, N.A., Golden, Colo.; Computershare Trust Company of Canada Inc., Vancouver, B.C.
FP500 Revenue Ranking - 513
Employees - 1,820 at Dec. 31, 2022
Profile - (Alta. 1995) Engineers, manufactures and supplies advanced alternative fuel delivery components and systems for clean, low-carbon fuels, including natural gas, renewable energy, propane and hydrogen, to the global automotive industry.

Operations are organized into three segments: Original Equipment Manufacturers (OEM); Independent Aftermarket (IAM); and Corporate.

OEM - This segment designs, manufactures and sells alternative fuel systems, components and electronics, including the Westport high pressure direct injection (HPDI) 2.0™, a complete fully-OEM-integrated system that enables heavy-duty trucks to operate on natural gas, and related engineering services, to OEMs and to supplier OEMs. Product offerings utilize a range of alternative fuels including liquefied petroleum gas (LPG), compressed natural gas (CNG), liquefied natural gas (LNG), renewable natural gas (RNG) and hydrogen. Products and services are available for passenger cars, light, medium and heavy-duty truck, cryogenics and hydrogen applications.

IAM - This segment designs, manufactures and sells alternative fuel systems and components that consumers can purchase and have installed onto their vehicles to use LPG or CNG fuels in addition to gasoline. Distribution of such products is realized through a comprehensive distribution network (in more than 70 countries) selling products to the workshops that are responsible for conversion, maintenance and service.

Corporate - This segment is responsible for public company activities, corporate oversight, financing, capital allocation and general administrative duties, including securing the company's intellectual property.

Recent Merger and Acquisition Activity

Status: pending **Announced:** July 19, 2023
Westport Fuel Systems Inc. and Volvo Group signed a non-binding letter of intent to establish a joint venture to accelerate the commercialization and global adoption of Westport's HPDI™ fuel system technology for long-haul and off-road applications. Westport would contribute current HPDI assets and activities including related fixed assets, intellectual property and business into the joint venture. Volvo would acquire a 45% interest in the joint venture for the sum of US$28,000,000 plus up to an additional US$45,000,000 depending on the performance of the joint venture. Completion of the joint venture was conditional on the successful negotiations and execution of a definitive investment agreement, joint venture agreement, supply agreement and development agreement. The joint venture was expected to launch in the first half of 2024.

Predecessor Detail - Name changed from Westport Innovations Inc., June 1, 2016.

Directors - Daniel M. Hancock, chr., Indianapolis, Ind.; Anthony R. (Tony) Guglielmin, interim CEO, Vancouver, B.C.; Michele J. Buchignani, Vancouver, B.C.; Brenda J. Eprile, Toronto, Ont.; Rita Forst, Germany; Philip B. (Phil) Hodge, Calgary, Alta.; Prof. Karl-Viktor Schaller, Munich, Germany; Eileen Wheatman, Petaluma, Calif.

Other Exec. Officers - Hitendra Mishra, man. dir., India; William E. (Bill) Larkin, CFO; Nicola Cosciani, exec. v-p, global opers.; Lance Follett, exec. v-p, corp. devel. & chief legal officer; Fabien G. Redon, exec. v-p, product devel. & chief tech. officer; Tim Smith, exec. v-p & chief of staff; Rohan Athaide, v-p, risk mgt. & assurance & chief compliance officer; Scott Baker, v-p, eng. & gen. mgr., Vancouver opers.; Anders Johansson, v-p, heavy-duty OEM & gen. mgr., Gothenburg opers.; Solomon Samuel, v-p, global HR; Marco Seimandi, v-p, sales & mktg.; Bart van Aerle, v-p, product & bus. strategy

Capital Stock

	Authorized (shs.)	Outstanding (shs.)[1]
Preferred	unlimited	nil
Common	unlimited	17,174,972

[1] At Aug. 8, 2023

Major Shareholder - Kevin G. Douglas held 10.64% interest at Mar. 6, 2023.

Price Range - WPRT/TSX

Year	Volume	High	Low	Close
2022	5,250,115	$31.40	$10.10	$10.40
2021	13,149,427	$164.90	$26.30	$30.10
2020	4,972,617	$80.00	$10.20	$67.70
2019	1,517,463	$44.80	$15.50	$30.70
2018	1,757,460	$54.40	$16.80	$18.10

Consolidation: 1-for-10 cons. in June 2023
Recent Close: $9.57
Capital Stock Changes - On June 6, 2023, common shares were consolidated on a 1-for-10 basis.

During 2022, 503,840 common shares were issued on exercise of performance share units.

Long-Term Debt - Outstanding at Dec. 31, 2022:

Term loan facilities[1]	US$41,934,000
0.55% Bank financing due 2027	512,000
Capital lease obligs.	1,416,000
	43,862,000
Less: Current portion	11,698,000
	32,164,000

[1] Consist of a US$14,683,000 2.01% non-revolving term loan due Sept. 15, 2026, from Export Development Canada (EDC); a US$8,803,000 1.65% Euro denominated term loan due Mar. 31, 2027, a US$2,699,000 1.82% Euro denominated term loan due May 31, 2025, and a US$11,273,000 1.75% Euro denominated term loan due July 31, 2026, all from UniCredit S.p.A.; and a US$5,235,000 1.7% Euro denominated term loan due Aug. 31, 2026, from Deutsche Bank.

Wholly Owned Subsidiaries

Westport Fuel Systems Canada Inc., B.C.
- 100% int. in **Westport Fuel Systems Italia S.r.l.**, Italy.
  - 50% int. in **Minda Westport Technologies Limited**, India.
  - 99.98% int. in **Rohan BRC Gas Equipment Pvt. Ltd.**, India.
  - 100% int. in **Stako Sp.zo.o**, Poland.
  - 100% int. in **TA Gas Technology S.A.**, Argentina.
  - 100% int. in **Westport Fuel Systems Netherlands B.V.**, Netherlands.
- 100% int. in **Westport Fuel Systems Sweden AB**, Sweden.
- 100% int. in **Westport Power Systems (Kunshan) Co. Ltd.**, People's Republic of China.

Note: The preceding list includes only the major related companies in which interests are held.

Financial Statistics

Periods ended:	12m Dec. 31/22[A]		12m Dec. 31/21[A]
	US$000s	%Chg	US$000s
Operating revenue	**305,698**	**-2**	**312,412**
Research & devel. expense	23,161		24,977
General & admin expense	50,245		48,182
Stock-based compensation	2,390		1,911
Other operating expense	261,928		255,524
Operating expense	**337,724**	**+2**	**330,594**
Operating income	**(32,026)**	**n.a.**	**(18,182)**
Deprec., depl. & amort.	11,800		14,035
Finance income	2,285		1,413
Finance costs, gross	3,351		4,937
Investment income	930		33,741
Write-downs/write-offs	nil		(459)
Pre-tax income	**(31,283)**	**n.a.**	**5,527**
Income taxes	1,412		(8,131)
Net income	**(32,695)**	**n.a.**	**13,658**
Cash & equivalent	86,086		124,788
Inventories	81,635		83,128
Accounts receivable	100,822		100,636
Current assets	277,219		338,564
Long-term investments	4,629		3,824
Fixed assets, net	62,641		64,420
Right-of-use assets	23,727		28,830
Intangibles, net	10,775		12,407
Total assets	**407,451**	**-14**	**471,313**
Bank indebtedness	9,102		12,965
Accts. pay. & accr. liabs	90,003		91,114
Current liabilities	135,519		146,447
Long-term debt, gross	43,862		56,402
Long-term debt, net	32,164		45,125
Long-term lease liabilities	20,080		24,362
Shareholders' equity	203,966		236,419
Cash from oper. activs	**(31,578)**	**n.a.**	**(43,793)**
Cash from fin. activs	(22,460)		104,726
Cash from invest. activs	17,647		2,290
Net cash position	**86,184**	**-31**	**124,892**
Capital expenditures	(14,242)		(14,158)
Capital disposals	731		600
	US$		US$
Earnings per share*	(1.90)		0.90
Cash flow per share*	(1.84)		(2.73)
	shs		shs
No. of shs. o/s*	17,130,317		17,079,933
Avg. no. of shs. o/s*	17,122,531		16,023,274
	%		%
Net profit margin	(10.70)		4.37
Return on equity	(14.85)		8.02
Return on assets	(6.64)		6.33
No. of employees (FTEs)	1,820		1,797

* Common
[A] Reported in accordance with U.S. GAAP

Latest Results

Periods ended:	6m June 30/23[A]		6m June 30/22[A]
	US$000s	%Chg	US$000s
Operating revenue	167,262	+7	156,508
Net income	(23,835)	n.a.	(3,869)
	US$		US$
Earnings per share*	(1.39)		(0.23)

* Common
[A] Reported in accordance with U.S. GAAP

Historical Summary
(as originally stated)

Fiscal Year	Oper. Rev. US$000s	Net Inc. Bef. Disc. US$000s	EPS* US$
2022[A]	305,698	(32,695)	(1.90)
2021[A]	312,412	13,658	0.90
2020[A]	252,497	(7,359)	(0.50)
2019[A]	305,338	188	0.01
2018[A]	270,283	(40,770)	(3.10)

* Common
[A] Reported in accordance with U.S. GAAP
Note: Adjusted throughout for 1-for-10 cons. in June 2023

W.28 Westshore Terminals Investment Corporation*

Symbol - WTE **Exchange** - TSX **CUSIP** - 96145A
Head Office - 1800-1067 Cordova St W, Vancouver, BC, V6C 1C7 **Telephone** - (604) 688-6764 **Fax** - (604) 688-2601
Website - www.westshore.com
Email - desmarais@jp-group.com
Investor Relations - Nick Desmarais (604) 488-5214
Auditors - KPMG LLP C.A., Vancouver, B.C.
Transfer Agents - Computershare Trust Company of Canada Inc., Vancouver, B.C.

FP500 Revenue Ranking - 572
Employees - 417 at Dec. 31, 2022
Profile - (B.C. 2010) Operates a bulk coal storage and loading terminal at Roberts Bank, B.C.
The terminal is located on a man-made island, 30 km south of Vancouver, B.C., with a throughput capacity of approximately 33,000,000 tonnes per year. The terminal receives coal on a regular basis from mines in British Columbia and Alberta as well as in the United States. Coal is delivered to the terminal in unit trains operated by **Canadian Pacific Railway Limited**, **Canadian National Railway Company** and **BNSF Railway Company** and is either directly transferred onto a ship or stockpiled for future shiploading. Ultimately, the coal is loaded onto ships destined for about 16 countries worldwide. Services are provided seven days per week and 24 hours per day.

Coal Shipments by Destination

	2022 tonnes	2021 tonnes
Asia	21,375,000	26,350,000
Europe	613 ,000	1,299,000
South America	923 ,000	1,041,000
Other	429,000	165,000
	23,340,000	28,855,000

Predecessor Detail - Succeeded Westshore Terminals Income Fund, Jan. 1, 2011, pursuant to plan of arrangement whereby Westshore Terminals Investment Corporation was formed to facilitate the conversion of the fund into a corporation and the fund was subsequently wound up.
Directors - William W. Stinson, chr., pres. & CEO, Vancouver, B.C.; M. Dallas H. Ross, CFO, Vancouver, B.C.; Nick Desmarais, v-p, corp. devel. & corp. sec., North Vancouver, B.C.; Steve Akazawa, B.C.; Brian A. Canfield, B.C.; Glen D. Clark, Vancouver, B.C.; H. Clark Hollands, Vancouver, B.C.; Dianne L. Watts, Surrey, B.C.
Other Exec. Officers - Glenn Dudar, v-p & gen. mgr.

Capital Stock

	Authorized (shs.)	Outstanding (shs.)[1]
Common	unlimited	62,514,675

[1] At May 5, 2023

Normal Course Issuer Bid - The company plans to make normal course purchases of up to 3,559,056 common shares representing 10% of the public float. The bid commenced on Apr. 13, 2023, and expires on Apr. 12, 2024.
Major Shareholder - James A. (Jim) Pattison held 43.11% interest at May 5, 2023.

Price Range - WTE/TSX

Year	Volume	High	Low	Close
2022	34,433,701	$37.70	$21.59	$22.43
2021	47,967,248	$28.90	$15.21	$26.82
2020	60,927,890	$19.12	$11.88	$15.59
2019	46,877,229	$24.26	$17.64	$18.95
2018	33,862,585	$27.50	$19.95	$20.58

Recent Close: $28.97
Capital Stock Changes - During 2022, 428,376 common shares were repurchased under a Normal Course Issuer Bid.

Dividends

WTE com Ra $1.40 pa Q est. Apr. 15, 2023
Prev. Rate: $1.20 est. Apr. 15, 2022
Prev. Rate: $1.00 est. Oct. 15, 2021
Prev. Rate: $0.80 est. Apr. 15, 2021
Prev. Rate: $0.64 est. Jan. 15, 2016
$1.50◆ Apr. 15/22 $0.50◆ Apr. 15/21
Paid in 2023: $1.00 2022: $1.15 + $1.50◆ 2021: $0.81 + $0.50◆
◆ Special

Long-Term Debt - At Dec. 31, 2022, the company had no long-term debt.

Wholly Owned Subsidiaries

Westshore Terminals Limited Partnership, B.C.
Westshore Terminals Ltd., Delta, B.C.

Financial Statistics

Periods ended:	12m Dec. 31/22[A]		12m Dec. 31/21[A]
	$000s	%Chg	$000s
Operating revenue	**291,960**	**-14**	**340,471**
Cost of sales	147,689		139,735
General & admin expense	12,700		14,983
Operating expense	**160,389**	**+4**	**154,718**
Operating income	**131,571**	**-29**	**185,753**
Deprec., depl. & amort.	30,223		28,419
Finance costs, net	8,673		10,658
Pre-tax income	**91,657**	**-38**	**147,663**
Income taxes	24,819		39,850
Net income	**66,838**	**-38**	**107,813**
Cash & equivalent	156,027		243,491
Inventories	17,625		17,809
Accounts receivable	7,827		14,726
Current assets	195,544		278,390
Fixed assets, net	389,475		364,611
Right-of-use assets	262,165		268,123
Intangibles, net	374,316		365,541
Total assets	**1,258,799**	**-3**	**1,296,852**
Accts. pay. & accr. liabs	45,052		44,567
Current liabilities	78,776		75,330
Long-term lease liabilities	277,740		280,575
Shareholders' equity	712,706		788,471
Cash from oper. activs	**91,202**	**-33**	**136,571**
Cash from fin. activs	(123,738)		(86,399)
Cash from invest. activs	(54,928)		(8,113)
Net cash position	**156,027**	**-36**	**243,491**
Capital expenditures, net	(53,807)		(8,113)
Pension fund surplus	34,604		20,136
	$		$
Earnings per share*	1.06		1.70
Cash flow per share*	1.44		2.16
Cash divd. per share*	1.20		0.90
Extra divd. - cash*	1.50		0.50
Total divd. per share*	**2.70**		**1.40**
	shs		shs
No. of shs. o/s*	62,829,459		63,257,835
Avg. no. of shs. o/s*	63,232,185		63,261,184
	%		%
Net profit margin	22.89		31.67
Return on equity	8.90		14.10
Return on assets	5.23		8.46
No. of employees (FTEs)	417		397

* Common
[A] Reported in accordance with IFRS

Latest Results

Periods ended:	6m June 30/23[A]		6m June 30/22[A]
	$000s	%Chg	$000s
Operating revenue	188,548	+10	170,971
Net income	61,033	+21	50,641
	$		$
Earnings per share*	0.98		0.80

* Common
[A] Reported in accordance with IFRS

Historical Summary
(as originally stated)

Fiscal Year	Oper. Rev. $000s	Net Inc. Bef. Disc. $000s	EPS* $
2022[A]	291,960	66,838	1.06
2021[A]	340,471	107,813	1.70
2020[A]	368,410	126,916	1.96
2019[A]	395,422	139,385	2.09
2018[A]	363,369	124,709	1.80

* Common
[A] Reported in accordance with IFRS

W.29 Whatcom Capital II Corp.

Symbol - WAT.P **Exchange** - TSX-VEN **CUSIP** - 96246G
Head Office - 750-1095 Pender St W, Vancouver, BC, V6E 2M6 **Telephone** - (604) 376-3567
Email - stonerockltd@gmail.com
Investor Relations - Darren Tindale (604) 376-3567
Auditors - SHIM & Associates LLP C.A., Vancouver, B.C.
Lawyers - AFG Law LLP, Vancouver, B.C.
Transfer Agents - Endeavor Trust Corporation, Vancouver, B.C.
Profile - (B.C. 2021) Capital Pool Company.

Recent Merger and Acquisition Activity

Status: terminated **Revised:** June 6, 2023
UPDATE: The transaction was terminated. PREVIOUS: Whatcom Capital II Corp. entered into a letter of intent for the Qualifying Transaction reverse takeover acquisition of Terrazero Technologies Inc., a Metaverse company. A total of 52,947,539 post-consolidated common shares (following a 1-for-3.5 share consolidation) were expected to be issued at a deemed price of $0.70 per share to Terrazero shareholders. Terrazero was expected to complete a private placement financing for gross proceeds of up to $2,000,000. Terrazero has a studio division, which creates immersive Metaverse activations for global brands and companies, a technology division, which creates solutions to bridge the real world with the virtual world, and a data analytics division, which aggregates data from across the Metaverse to help guide Terrazero's and its clients' decision making. BIGG Digital Assets Inc. holds a 29% interest in Terrazero. Feb. 1, 2023 - The companies entered into a definitive agreement whereby Terrazero would amalgamated with a wholly owned subsidiary of Whatcom to continue as TZ technologies Corp. Whatcom would change its name to TerraZero Technologies Inc.
Directors - Darren Tindale, CEO, CFO & corp. sec., North Vancouver, B.C.; Greg Clough, Surrey, B.C.; Ashvani (Ash) Guglani, Vancouver, B.C.; Joerg Schweizer, Munich, Germany; Jeffery M. (Jeff) Tindale, West Vancouver, B.C.

Capital Stock

	Authorized (shs.)	Outstanding (shs.)[1]
Common	unlimited	15,000,000

[1] At July 17, 2023

Major Shareholder - Widely held at Nov. 15, 2022.

Price Range - WAT.P/TSX-VEN

Year	Volume	High	Low	Close
2022	597,500	$0.16	$0.06	$0.07
2021	878,535	$0.29	$0.11	$0.16

Recent Close: $0.08
Capital Stock Changes - There were no changes to capital stock during fiscal 2023.

Wholly Owned Subsidiaries

1396032 B.C. Ltd., Canada.

W.30 Whitewater Acquisition Corp.

Symbol - WWA.P **Exchange** - TSX-VEN **CUSIP** - 96613L
Head Office - c/o Chase Management Ltd., 1305-1090 Georgia St W, Vancouver, BC, V6E 3V7 **Telephone** - (604) 685-9316
Email - ndemare@chasemgt.com
Investor Relations - Nick DeMare (604) 685-9316
Auditors - Davidson & Company LLP C.A., Vancouver, B.C.
Transfer Agents - National Securities Administrators Ltd., Vancouver, B.C.
Profile - (B.C. 2021) Capital Pool Company.
Directors - David A. Henstridge, CEO, CFO & corp. sec., Melbourne, Vic., Australia; Nick DeMare, Vancouver, B.C.; Michael C. Varabioff, Vancouver, B.C.

Capital Stock

	Authorized (shs.)	Outstanding (shs.)[1]
Common	unlimited	8,100,000

[1] At Sept. 16, 2022

Major Shareholder - Nick DeMare held 19.75% interest and David A. Henstridge held 19.75% interest at Oct. 20, 2021.

Price Range - WWA.P/TSX-VEN

Year	Volume	High	Low	Close
2022	110,000	$0.22	$0.15	$0.16
2021	15,019	$0.25	$0.22	$0.22

Recent Close: $0.10
Capital Stock Changes - On Oct. 20, 2021, an initial public offering of 2,500,000 common shares was completed at 10¢ per share.

W.31 Wi2Wi Corporation

Symbol - YTY **Exchange** - TSX-VEN **CUSIP** - 977486
Head Office - 1879 Lundy Ave, Suite 218, San Jose, CA, United States, 95131 **Telephone** - (408) 416-4200
Website - www.wi2wi.com
Email - dawn_l@wi2wi.com
Investor Relations - Dawn Leeder (608) 203-0234
Auditors - Baker Tilly WM LLP C.A., Vancouver, B.C.
Lawyers - Norton Rose Fulbright Canada LLP, Toronto, Ont.
Transfer Agents - Computershare Trust Company of Canada Inc., Toronto, Ont.
Profile - (Can. 2013 amalg.) Develops, manufactures and markets wireless connectivity solutions, precision timing devices, frequency control devices and microwave filters to the global market.
Develops System in Package (SiP) connectivity solutions that are accepted in markets for Internet of Things (IoT), Industrial IoT and portable device embedded applications worldwide. The wireless connectivity modules are based on WiFi, Bluetooth and Near Field Communication (NFC), and satellite navigation systems such as the United States' Global Positioning System (GPS), the People's Republic of China's BeiDou and Russia's Global Navigation Satellite System (GLONASS). Also provides a platform for its frequency control, timing devices and microwave filters which services the avionics, space, industrial, medical and defence markets.
The company's manufacturing plant for its frequency control and precision timing devices and microwave filters is located in Middleton, Wisc., while manufacturing of wireless connectivity products are outsourced. Also has an engineering office in Hyderabad, India, which focuses on the development of wireless connectivity products.
Predecessor Detail - Formed from International Sovereign Energy Corp. in Canada, Jan. 25, 2013, pursuant to reverse takeover acquisition of and amalgamation with (old) Wi2Wi Corporation.
Directors - Gary DuBroc, chr., N.C.; Zachariah J. (Zach) Mathews, pres. & CEO, San Jose, Calif.; Matthew Balazsi, Montréal, Qué.; Francesco (Frank) Ferlaino, Italy; Jason Grelowski, Alta.; Carol Hess, Houston, Tex.

Other Exec. Officers - Dawn Leeder, CFO; Barry Arneson, v-p, eng., frequency control & timing devices

Capital Stock

	Authorized (shs.)	Outstanding (shs.)[1]
Preferred	unlimited	nil
Common	unlimited	152,933,313

[1] At Mar. 31, 2023

Major Shareholder - Widely held at May 19, 2022.

Price Range - YTY/TSX-VEN

Year	Volume	High	Low	Close
2022	45,023,577	$0.05	$0.02	$0.03
2021	50,524,303	$0.10	$0.04	$0.05
2020	14,135,133	$0.09	$0.04	$0.04
2019	4,706,235	$0.12	$0.05	$0.07
2018	9,031,892	$0.18	$0.07	$0.07

Recent Close: $0.03

Capital Stock Changes - There were no changes to capital stock during 2022.

Wholly Owned Subsidiaries

Wi2Wi Inc., Del.
- 100% int. in **Wi2Wi LLC**, Wis.
- 100% int. in **Wi2Wi (India) Pvt. Ltd.**, India.

Investments

Legend Oil & Gas, Ltd., Wash.

Financial Statistics

Periods ended:	12m Dec. 31/22[A]		12m Dec. 31/21[A]
	US$000s	%Chg	US$000s
Operating revenue	**6,857**	**+6**	**6,453**
Cost of sales	5,491		4,558
Salaries & benefits	1,173		1,011
Research & devel. expense	13		6
General & admin expense	659		602
Stock-based compensation	1		21
Operating expense	**7,337**	**+18**	**6,198**
Operating income	**(480)**	**n.a.**	**255**
Deprec., depl. & amort.	794		822
Finance costs, gross	147		176
Pre-tax income	**(1,236)**	**n.a.**	**(204)**
Net income	**(1,236)**	**n.a.**	**(204)**
Cash & equivalent	1,023		1,886
Inventories	2,797		2,756
Accounts receivable	1,242		1,308
Current assets	5,740		6,624
Fixed assets, net	847		1,028
Right-of-use assets	2,416		2,948
Total assets	**9,003**	**-15**	**10,600**
Accts. pay. & accr. liabs	876		713
Current liabilities	1,360		1,240
Long-term debt, gross	60		112
Long-term debt, net	nil		57
Long-term lease liabilities	2,213		2,638
Shareholders' equity	5,280		6,515
Cash from oper. activs	**(305)**	**n.a.**	**504**
Cash from fin. activs	(475)		191
Cash from invest. activs	(81)		(51)
Net cash position	**1,022**	**-46**	**1,883**
Capital expenditures	(81)		(51)
	US$		US$
Earnings per share*	(0.01)		(0.00)
Cash flow per share*	(0.00)		0.00
	shs		shs
No. of shs. o/s*	152,933,313		152,933,313
Avg. no. of shs. o/s*	152,933,313		152,818,394
	%		%
Net profit margin	(18.03)		(3.16)
Return on equity	(20.96)		(3.09)
Return on assets	(11.11)		(0.26)

* Common
[A] Reported in accordance with IFRS

Latest Results

Periods ended:	3m Mar. 31/23[A]		3m Mar. 31/22[A]
	US$000s	%Chg	US$000s
Operating revenue	1,840	+16	1,592
Net income	(233)	n.a.	(371)
	US$		US$
Earnings per share*	(0.00)		(0.00)

* Common
[A] Reported in accordance with IFRS

Historical Summary
(as originally stated)

Fiscal Year	Oper. Rev.	Net Inc. Bef. Disc.	EPS*
	US$000s	US$000s	US$
2022[A]	6,857	(1,236)	(0.01)
2021[A]	6,453	(204)	(0.00)
2020[A]	6,928	(588)	(0.00)
2019[A]	10,369	556	0.00
2018[A]	9,711	143	0.00

* Common
[A] Reported in accordance with IFRS

W.32 WildBrain Ltd.*

Symbol - WILD **Exchange** - TSX **CUSIP** - 96810C

Head Office - 1201-25 York St, Toronto, ON, M5J 2V5 **Telephone** - (416) 363-8034 **Fax** - (416) 363-8919

Website - www.wildbrain.com

Email - james.bishop@wildbrain.com

Investor Relations - James Bishop (902) 423-0260

Auditors - PricewaterhouseCoopers LLP C.A., Halifax, N.S.

Transfer Agents - Computershare Trust Company, N.A., Louisville, Ky.; Computershare Trust Company of Canada Inc., Montréal, Qué.

FP500 Revenue Ranking - 462

Employees - 583 at June 30, 2022

Profile - (Can. 2006; orig. N.S., 2004) Develops, produces and distributes kids and family entertainment content worldwide; owns and operates an ad-supported video-on-demand (AVOD) business; licenses and manages intellectual properties for consumers products and location-based entertainment; and broadcasts television programmes and films through four entertainment channels in Canada.

The company has four business lines: Content Production and Distribution; WildBrain Spark; Consumer Products; and Canadian Television Broadcasting.

Content Production and Distribution - Develops, produces and distributes original animated and live-action content targeted at children and family audiences worldwide. The company's library consists of 13,000 half-hours of primarily animated programming across over 500 proprietary and third-party titles. Animated content is produced at the company's 75,000-sq.-ft. full service animation studio in Vancouver, B.C., and includes Snoopy in Space, The Snoopy Show, Carmen Sandiego, Cloudy with a Chance of Meatballs, Go, Dog. Go!, LEGO Ninjago, The Mr. Peabody & Sherman Show, Bob the Builder, Fireman Sam and The Deep. Live-action comedy and drama series produced include Degrassi, Yo Gabba Gabba!, Malory Towers and Teletubbies. The company's content library is distributed in over 150 countries to more than 500 streaming services, television broadcasters, on-demand services and home entertainment companies. Content is primarily distributed through the company's international sales team in Toronto, Ont.; Paris, France; and Shanghai, People's Republic of China. Production and distribution customers include Apple TV+, Amazon Prime Video, BBC, Warner Media, Disney, Hulu, Netflix, Nickelodeon, ABC, Alibaba, ByteDance, YouTube, Roku, Pluto and Samsung TV Plus.

WildBrain Spark - Owns and operates WildBrain Spark, the company's AVOD business which consists of a network of kids' channels on YouTube and other AVOD platforms featuring owned content and content of third-parties. WildBrain Spark offers channel management, content creation and advertising services for owned and partner brands.

Consumer Products - Licenses rights to merchandisers for fabrication and sale of consumer products, such as toys, games, apparel, publishing, interactive games and applications, live experiences and events, based on proprietary brands, including Peanuts, Strawberry Shortcake, Teletubbies and In the Night Garden, as well as partner brands from Mattel, including Bob the Builder, Fireman Sam, Little People and Polly Pocket. Through WildBrain CPLG, the company's licensing agency business based in London, U.K., represents company-owned brands and third-party lifestyle, entertainment and sports brands worldwide. WildBrain CPLG has offices throughout Europe, Middle East, India, the U.S. and the Asia Pacific region, offering fully-integrated product development, legal and accounting services.

Canadian Television Broadcasting - Operates as WildBrain Television and consists of four children's television channels in Canada, including Family Channel, Family Jr., Télémagino and WildBrain TV (formerly Family CHRGD). In addition to linear television, all four channels have multi-platform applications which allow for their content to be distributed on-demand and via streaming.

In September 2022, the company acquired the rights, title and interest of a children's entertainment property for $1,841,000.

On Apr. 14, 2022, the company acquired the rights, title and interest of a children's entertainment property for $1,000,000.

Recent Merger and Acquisition Activity

Status: completed **Revised:** July 19, 2023

UPDATE: The transaction was completed. PREVIOUS: WildBrain Ltd. agreed to acquire House of Cool Inc., a pre-production studio in the global animation industry, for $15,500,000 consisting of $10,250,000 through issuance of 4,479,406 shares and $5,25,000 in cash. In addition, there is an earnout of up to $6,000,000 based on collection of tax credits earned up to closing. The transaction was expected to close during WildBrain's fiscal 2023 fourth quarter.

Status: completed **Announced:** Mar. 31, 2022

WildBrain Ltd. acquired certain brand representation rights for Peanuts in Asia Pacific under its global licensing agency, WildBrain CPLG. Total consideration was $7,501,000 payable in instalments, plus deferred consideration of $3,749,000 based on certain financial performance conditions.

Predecessor Detail - Name changed from DHX Media Ltd., Dec. 18, 2019.

Directors - Donald A. (Don) Wright, chr., Toronto, Ont.; Josh Scherba, pres. & CEO, Toronto, Ont.; Youssef Ben-Youssef, New York, N.Y.; Karine Courtemanche, Saint-Lambert, Qué.; Deborah A. Drisdell, Montréal, Qué.; Erin J. Elofson, Toronto, Ont.; D. Geoffrey Machum, Halifax, N.S.; Thomas B. McGrath, Los Angeles, Calif.; Rita Middleton, Grimsby, Ont.; Jonathan P. Whitcher, New York, N.Y.

Other Exec. Officers - Deirdre Brennan, COO; Aaron S. Ames, CFO; Stephanie Betts, chief content officer; Tim Erickson, exec. v-p, brand, Peanuts Worldwide LLC; Anne Loi, exec. v-p, M&A & chief comml. officer; Danielle Neath, exec. v-p, fin. & chief acctg. officer; Tara Talbot, exec. v-p, global talent; Maarten Weck, exec. v-p & man. dir., WildBrain Copyright Promotions Licensing Group; James Bishop, gen. counsel & corp. sec.

Capital Stock

	Authorized (shs.)	Outstanding (shs.)[1]
Pref. Variable Vtg.	500,000,000	500,000,000
Common Vtg.	unlimited	25,987,421
Variable Vtg.	unlimited	149,982,437
Non-Vtg.	unlimited	nil

[1] At Mar. 31, 2023

Preferred Variable Voting - Not entitled to dividends. Redeemable at any time at $0.0000001 per share. Number of votes are automatically adjustable so that they, together with shares owned by Canadians, equal 55% of the votes attached to all shares. All held by Josh Scherba.

Common Voting - Held only by Canadians. Convertible into variable voting shares on a 1-for-1 basis if such share becomes owned or controlled by a person who is not a Canadian. One vote per share.

Variable Voting - Held only by non-Canadians and entitled to one vote per share, with the following exceptions: (i) the number of variable voting shares outstanding, as a percentage of the total number of voting shares outstanding, exceeds 33.33%; or (ii) the total number of votes cast by or on behalf of holders of the variable voting shares at a meeting exceeds 33.33% of the total number of votes that may be cast at said meeting. If either of the above noted thresholds is surpassed at any time, the vote attached to each variable voting share will decrease automatically such that: (i) the variable voting shares as a class do not carry more than 33.33% of the total voting rights attached to the aggregate number of issued and outstanding voting shares; and (ii) the variable voting shares as a class do not carry more than 33.33% of the total number of votes that may be cast at said meeting. Convertible into one voting share automatically if the variable voting share becomes owned or controlled by a Canadian, or if the provisions under the Broadcasting Act (Canada) relating to foreign ownership restrictions are repealed and not replaced with other similar provisions.

Options - At June 30, 2022, options were outstanding to purchase 4,308,800 common voting and variable voting shares at prices ranging from $1.50 to $9.49 per share with a weighted average remaining contractual life of 3.42 years.

Major Shareholder - Fine Capital Partners, L.P. held 36.93% interest at Nov. 29, 2022.

Price Range - WILD/TSX

Year	Volume	High	Low	Close
2022	18,432,285	$3.79	$1.84	$3.12
2021	37,879,067	$4.20	$1.67	$3.44
2020	44,245,599	$2.38	$0.71	$1.79
2019	51,246,761	$3.03	$1.40	$1.57
2018	156,138,205	$4.89	$1.09	$2.24

Recent Close: $1.73

Capital Stock Changes - During fiscal 2022, common voting and variable voting shares were issued as follows: 753,430 under restricted share unit plan, 325,000 on exercise of options and 36,087 under employee share purchase plan; 138,190 (net) common voting and variable voting shares held in trust were sold.

Long-Term Debt - Outstanding at June 30, 2022:

Term facility due 2028[1]	$353,387,000
7.5% exch. debs. due 2023[2]	22,662,000
5.875% sr. conv. debs. due 2024[3]	128,090,000
	504,139,000
Less: Current portion	26,335,000
	477,804,000

[1] Bears interest at LIBOR plus 4.25%.
[2] US$18,497,000. Exchangeable into variable voting shares at US$1.0729 per share.
[3] Convertible into common voting or variable voting shares at $7.729 per share.

Wholly Owned Subsidiaries

DHX Global Holdings Ltd., N.S.
- 100% int. in **DHX Media (UK) Limited**, United Kingdom.
  - 100% int. in **DHX Worldwide Limited**, United Kingdom.
    - 100% int. in **The Copyright Promotions Licensing Group Limited**, United Kingdom.
  - 100% int. in **Wild Brain International Limited**, United Kingdom.
    - 100% int. in **Wild Brain Family International Limited**, United Kingdom.
- 100% int. in **DHX SSP Holdings LLC**, Del.
  - 51% int. in **DHX PH Holdings LLC**, Del.
    - 80% int. in **Peanuts Holdings LLC**, Del.
      - 100% int. in **Peanuts Worldwide LLC**, Del.
  - 100% int. in **Shortcake IP Holdings LLC**, Del.
- 100% int. in **Wild Brain Entertainment Inc.**, Los Angeles, Calif.
  - 50% int. in **GabbaCaDabra LLC**, Del.

DHX Media (Halifax) Ltd., N.S.
DHX Media (Toronto) Ltd., Toronto, Ont.

DHX Media (Vancouver) Ltd., Vancouver, B.C.
DHX Television Ltd., Canada.
House of Cool Inc., Toronto, Ont.
Nerd Corps Entertainment Inc., Vancouver, B.C.
WildBrain Holdings LLC, Del.

Note: The preceding list includes only the major related companies in which interests are held.

Financial Statistics

Periods ended:	12m June 30/22[A]		12m June 30/21[oA]
	$000s	%Chg	$000s
Operating revenue	**507,223**	**+12**	**452,534**
General & admin expense	104,129		80,539
Stock-based compensation	7,414		5,075
Other operating expense	291,943		266,259
Operating expense	**403,486**	**+15**	**351,873**
Operating income	**103,737**	**+3**	**100,661**
Deprec., depl. & amort.	34,220		34,024
Finance income	3,041		2,266
Finance costs, gross	33,527		44,405
Write-downs/write-offs	(788)		(7,832)
Pre-tax income	**30,205**	**+52**	**19,811**
Income taxes	(1,557)		(3,298)
Net income	**31,762**	**+37**	**23,109**
Net inc. for equity hldrs	**5,640**	**n.a.**	**(7,077)**
Net inc. for non-cont. int.	**26,122**	**-13**	**30,186**
Cash & equivalent	59,899		78,431
Accounts receivable	249,660		195,240
Current assets	490,540		441,264
Fixed assets, net	39,287		47,229
Intangibles, net	595,712		587,412
Total assets	**1,219,174**	**+8**	**1,127,902**
Bank indebtedness	93,322		65,403
Accts. pay. & accr. liabs	161,849		130,299
Current liabilities	368,912		250,666
Long-term debt, gross	504,139		482,394
Long-term debt, net	477,804		478,862
Long-term lease liabilities	26,056		34,407
Shareholders' equity	79,428		68,588
Non-controlling interest	235,975		234,325
Cash from oper. activs	**33,100**	**-69**	**105,680**
Cash from fin. activs	(46,131)		(79,241)
Cash from invest. activs	(10,839)		(15,165)
Net cash position	**68,734**	**-25**	**92,059**
Capital expenditures	(2,995)		(2,780)
	$		$
Earnings per share*	0.03		(0.04)
Cash flow per share*	0.19		0.62
	shs		shs
No. of shs. o/s*	173,108,668		171,855,961
Avg. no. of shs. o/s*	172,584,000		171,222,000
	%		%
Net profit margin	6.26		5.11
Return on equity	7.62		(9.44)
Return on assets	5.71		6.59
Foreign sales percent	72		68
No. of employees (FTEs)	583		531

* Common & var vtg.
[o] Restated
[A] Reported in accordance with IFRS

Latest Results

Periods ended:	9m Mar. 31/23[A]		9m Mar. 31/22[A]
	$000s	%Chg	$000s
Operating revenue	407,996	+3	395,218
Net income	22,222	-28	31,033
Net inc. for equity hldrs	(1,150)	n.a.	4,500
Net inc. for non-cont. int	23,372		26,533
	$		$
Earnings per share*	(0.01)		0.03

* Common & var vtg.
[A] Reported in accordance with IFRS

Historical Summary
(as originally stated)

Fiscal Year	Oper. Rev.	Net Inc. Bef. Disc.	EPS*
	$000s	$000s	$
2022[A]	507,223	31,762	0.03
2021[A]	452,534	23,109	(0.04)
2020[A]	425,634	(208,791)	(1.51)
2019[A]	439,800	(78,202)	(0.75)
2018[A]	434,416	(6,748)	(0.10)

* Common & var vtg.
[A] Reported in accordance with IFRS

W.33 Wildpack Beverage Inc.

Symbol - CANS **Exchange** - TSX-VEN **CUSIP** - 96812Y
Head Office - 2900-550 Burrard St, Vancouver, BC, V6C 0A3 **Telephone** - (604) 329-6171
Website - www.wildpackbev.com
Email - elijah@wildpackbev.com
Investor Relations - Elijah Clare (604) 329-6171
Auditors - Davidson & Company LLP C.A., Vancouver, B.C.
Lawyers - Fasken Martineau DuMoulin LLP, Vancouver, B.C.
Transfer Agents - Computershare Trust Company of Canada Inc., Toronto, Ont.
Employees - 172 at Dec. 31, 2022

Profile - (B.C. 2017) Provides aluminum can packaging services and private label manufacturing to beverage companies throughout the U.S.

Revenue is primarily earned from can filling and decorating services. Can decorating services include the application of customer label design to blank aluminum cans; and can filling services involve receiving a customer's raw and packaging materials on a consignment basis, mixing them in accordance with formula specifications and packaging them in accordance with their specifications. Also provides brokering services to source and sell aluminum cans and raw ingredients to customers, as well as warehousing services to provide storage to customers for raw materials and/or finished products.

Operates facilities in Baltimore, Md., Grand Rapids, Mich., Las Vegas, Nev., Marietta, Ga., and Sacramento, Calif.

In May 2023, the company has granted an option to convert the loan of its lender **Sandton Credit Solutions Master Fund V, LP** into a 49% interest of newly formed **Thirsty Cat, LLC**, which holds interests in all of the company's U.S. operations, which represent substantially all of the principal business assets of the company. The loan is a non-revolving term credit facility in the principal amount of $25,000,000.

On Jan. 1, 2023, wholly owned **Wildpack Beverage Alberta Inc.** was amalgamated into the company.

Predecessor Detail - Name changed from Ponderous Panda Capital Corp., May 17, 2021, pursuant to the Qualifying Transaction reverse takeover acquisition of Wildpack Beverage Alberta Inc. and concurrent amalgamation of Wildpack with wholly owned 2342700 Alberta Ltd.; basis 1 new for 2.578 old shs.

Directors - Jeffrey R. Mason, chr., Vancouver, B.C.; Mitchell (Mitch) Barnard, CEO, Vancouver, B.C.; Stephen Fader, chief execution officer, Calgary, Alta.; Izhar Basha, Sydney, N.S.W., Australia; Joseph Bubel, Midhurst, Ont.; Sean Clark, Whistler, B.C.; Sara Coyle, Kenilworth, Ill.; Matthew Dwyer, Omaha, Neb.; Rael Nurick, New York, N.Y.

Other Exec. Officers - Ryan Mason, CFO & corp. sec.; Thomas Walker, chief growth officer; David Bower, v-p, sales; Elijah Clare, v-p, IR; Michael Maddox, v-p, opers.; Kim Murray, v-p, packing srvcs.; Tim Murray, v-p, packaging opers.; Dan Wales, v-p, people & culture; Maria Rezvanova, contr.

Capital Stock

	Authorized (shs.)	Outstanding (shs.)[1]
Common	unlimited	112,436,635

[1] At July 25, 2023

Major Shareholder - Stephen Fader held 14.7% interest and Kim Murray held 11.17% interest at Dec. 15, 2022.

Price Range - CANS/TSX-VEN

Year	Volume	High	Low	Close
2022	21,800,169	$0.68	$0.08	$0.08
2021	21,233,600	$1.40	$0.49	$0.54
2020	3,878	$0.39	$0.39	$0.39
2019	3,878	$0.83	$0.83	$0.83

Consolidation: 1-for-2.578 cons. in May 2021
Recent Close: $0.12

Capital Stock Changes - In November 2022, private placement of 8,097,166 common shares was completed at Cdn$0.17 per share. Also during 2022, common shares were issued as follows: 1,271,849 pursuant to the November 2021 acquisition of KT Murray Corporation (dba Land and Sea Packaging) and 958,233 on vesting of restricted share units.

Wholly Owned Subsidiaries

Hungry Hippo Company, United States.
- 100% int. in **Thirsty Cat, LLC**, United States.
  - 100% int. in **Wildpack Holdings US Inc.**, Del.
    - 100% int. in **CraftPac, LLC**, Ga.
    - 100% int. in **KT Murray Corporation**, Grand Rapids, Mich.
    - 100% int. in **Vertical Distilling LLC**, Colo.
    - 100% int. in **Wild Leaf Holdings U.S. LLC**, Del.
    - 100% int. in **Wild Leaf Ventures Group Nevada Inc.**, Nev. Inactive.

Financial Statistics

Periods ended:	12m Dec. 31/22[A]		12m Dec. 31/21[oA]
	US$000s	%Chg	US$000s
Operating revenue	**35,374**	**+25**	**28,281**
Cost of sales	34,919		24,327
Salaries & benefits	7,092		5,152
General & admin expense	6,851		7,526
Stock-based compensation	349		1,090
Other operating expense	128		167
Operating expense	**49,339**	**+29**	**38,262**
Operating income	**(13,965)**	**n.a.**	**(9,981)**
Deprec., depl. & amort.	5,110		3,830
Finance costs, gross	5,885		1,707
Pre-tax income	**(36,645)**	**n.a.**	**(18,066)**
Income taxes	nil		(685)
Net income	**(36,645)**	**n.a.**	**(17,381)**
Cash & equivalent	943		1,450
Inventories	4,852		10,671
Accounts receivable	5,138		3,826
Current assets	12,033		17,949
Fixed assets, net	6,375		5,820
Right-of-use assets	9,503		12,399
Intangibles, net	25,463		36,339
Total assets	**53,703**	**-26**	**73,026**
Bank indebtedness	nil		1,017
Accts. pay. & accr. liabs	16,002		6,882
Current liabilities	27,531		37,717
Long-term debt, gross	33,650		27,434
Long-term debt, net	26,228		391
Long-term lease liabilities	8,168		10,448
Shareholders' equity	(8,224)		24,470
Cash from oper. activs	**(566)**	**n.a.**	**(16,015)**
Cash from fin. activs	713		48,737
Cash from invest. activs	(398)		(31,962)
Net cash position	**943**	**-35**	**1,450**
Capital expenditures	(398)		(3,211)
	US$		US$
Earnings per share*	(0.36)		(0.29)
Cash flow per share*	(0.01)		(0.26)
	shs		shs
No. of shs. o/s*	111,309,169		100,981,921
Avg. no. of shs. o/s*	102,143,314		60,585,175
	%		%
Net profit margin	(103.59)		(61.46)
Return on equity	n.m.		(132.72)
Return on assets	(48.61)		(35.13)
Foreign sales percent	100		100
No. of employees (FTEs)	172		192

* Common
[o] Restated
[A] Reported in accordance with IFRS

Latest Results

Periods ended:	3m Mar. 31/23[A]		3m Mar. 31/22[oA]
	US$000s	%Chg	US$000s
Operating revenue	12,613	+48	8,529
Net income	(5,524)	n.a.	(5,543)
	US$		US$
Earnings per share*	(0.05)		(0.05)

* Common
[o] Restated
[A] Reported in accordance with IFRS

Historical Summary
(as originally stated)

Fiscal Year	Oper. Rev.	Net Inc. Bef. Disc.	EPS*
	US$000s	US$000s	US$
2022[A]	35,374	(36,645)	(0.36)
2021[A1]	28,281	(13,699)	(0.23)
2020[A2]	8,169	(3,467)	(0.27)
	$000s	$000s	$
2020[A]	nil	(1,436)	(0.12)

* Common
[A] Reported in accordance with IFRS
[1] Results prior to May 17, 2021, pertain to and reflect the reverse takeover acquisition of Wildpack Beverage Alberta Inc.
[2] 9 months ended Dec. 31, 2020.

Note: Adjusted throughout for 1-for-2.578 cons. in May 2021

W.34 Willow Biosciences Inc.

Symbol - WLLW **Exchange** - TSX **CUSIP** - 97111B
Head Office - 202-1201 5 St SW, Calgary, AB, T2R 0Y6 **Telephone** - (403) 910-5140
Website - www.willowbio.com
Email - info@willowbio.com
Investor Relations - Travis Doupe (403) 910-5140
Auditors - KPMG LLP C.A., Calgary, Alta.
Lawyers - Stikeman Elliott LLP, Calgary, Alta.

Transfer Agents - Odyssey Trust Company, Calgary, Alta.
Employees - 32 at Dec. 31, 2022
Profile - (Alta. 2019; orig. B.C., 1981) Develops and produces functional ingredients through precision fermentation.

The company's proprietary technology platform, FutureGrown™, allows for the production of compounds from engineered yeast strains through fermentation. The technology can be used to produce cannabinoid and non-cannabinoid functional ingredients with higher purity and consistency for the health and wellness, food and beverage, and personal care sectors. In addition, the company uses BioOxico™, a bio-oxidation technology platform that enables bioconversion-enabled chemical manufacturing which involves the conversion of defined intermediates into ingredients.The platform offers the advantage of eliminating multiple chemical steps and reducing cost and resources. Research and development activities are conducted at a facility in Mountain View, Calif.

The company's first commercialized ingredient is the cannabinoid, cannabigerol (CBG), which is produced by contract manufacturers. The company is also developing ursodeoxycholic acid (UDCA), an active pharmaceutical ingredient (API) used as a medication for the management and treatment of cholestatic liver disease and gallstone conditions; astaxanthin, a red pigment and antioxidant; and an enzyme for use in food preservative.

In August 2022, the company announced the consolidation of research and development operations at its facility in Mountain View, Calif., by closing its Burnaby, B.C., laboratory. Closure and relocation of key personnel were completed in December 2022.

In November 2022, the company entered into an agreement with **Kalsec Inc.**, which produces natural taste and sensory, food protection, colours and hops ingredients for the food and beverage industry, to develop and commercialize a precision fermentation production process for a high volume, natural food preservative.

In May 2022, the company entered into an engagement with **Sandhill One, LLC**, a specialty pharmaceutical company, to optimize an enzyme vital to the development of the large volume of ursodeoxycholic acid (UDCA), an active pharmaceutical ingredient, used in nutraceutical and pharmaceutical products.

Predecessor Detail - Name changed from Makena Resources Inc., Apr. 15, 2019, pursuant to reverse takeover acquisition of BioCan Technologies Inc., and Epimeron Inc.

Directors - Trevor Peters, chr., Calgary, Alta.; Dr. Chris Savile, pres. & CEO, Santa Clara, Calif.; Barbara Munroe†, Calgary, Alta.; Donald F. (Don) Archibald, Calgary, Alta.; Raffi Asadorian, Calif.; Al Foreman, New York, N.Y.; Dr. Fotis Kalantzis, Calgary, Alta.; Dr. Jim Lalonde, San Mateo, Calif.; Dr. Peter Seufer-Wasserthal, Austria

Other Exec. Officers - Travis Doupe, CFO; Dr. Trish Choudhary, sr. v-p, R&D; Sanjib (Sony) Gill, corp. sec.

† Lead director

Capital Stock

	Authorized (shs.)	Outstanding (shs.)[1]
Class A Preferred	unlimited	nil
Common	unlimited	124,220,714

[1] At May 11, 2023

Major Shareholder - Tuatara Capital, L.P. held 21% interest at Apr. 3, 2023.

Price Range - WLLW/TSX

Year	Volume	High	Low	Close
2022	33,016,669	$0.48	$0.11	$0.12
2021	64,564,477	$2.24	$0.39	$0.45
2020	53,243,552	$1.20	$0.30	$1.17
2019	13,063,506	$5.25	$0.51	$0.64
2018	313,966	$5.88	$1.00	$1.13

Consolidation: 1-for-25 cons. in May 2019
Recent Close: $0.08
Capital Stock Changes - During 2022, 174,344 common shares were issued on vesting of restricted share awards.

Wholly Owned Subsidiaries

Epimeron USA, Inc., Del.
Willow Analytics Inc., Calgary, Alta.

Financial Statistics

Periods ended:	12m Dec. 31/22[A]	%Chg	12m Dec. 31/21[A]
	$000s	%Chg	$000s
Operating revenue	**821**	**+517**	**133**
Salaries & benefits	6,871		2,521
Research & devel. expense	3,170		11,511
General & admin expense	5,073		4,380
Stock-based compensation	1,461		1,703
Operating expense	**16,575**	**-18**	**20,115**
Operating income	**(15,754)**	**n.a.**	**(19,982)**
Deprec., depl. & amort.	2,646		3,192
Finance income	300		414
Finance costs, gross	26		27
Write-downs/write-offs	nil		(22)
Pre-tax income	**(14,761)**	**n.a.**	**(6,140)**
Income taxes	53		nil
Net income	**(14,814)**	**n.a.**	**(6,140)**
Cash & equivalent	15,027		30,119
Inventories	277		384
Accounts receivable	282		89
Current assets	16,229		31,271
Fixed assets, net	1,301		2,783
Right-of-use assets	618		867
Total assets	**18,148**	**-48**	**35,016**
Accts. pay. & accr. liabs	1,087		757
Current liabilities	1,719		1,408
Long-term lease liabilities	32		161
Shareholders' equity	16,374		29,682
Cash from oper. activs	**(13,862)**	**n.a.**	**(18,227)**
Cash from fin. activs	(723)		34,126
Cash from invest. activs	(4,553)		(1,674)
Net cash position	**11,007**	**-63**	**30,119**
Capital expenditures	(682)		(1,766)
Capital disposals	123		119
	$		$
Earnings per share*	(0.12)		(0.05)
Cash flow per share*	(0.11)		(0.15)
	shs		shs
No. of shs. o/s*	123,719,667		123,545,323
Avg. no. of shs. o/s*	123,660,080		119,987,680
	%		%
Net profit margin	n.m.		n.m.
Return on equity	(64.33)		n.m.
Return on assets	(55.63)		(21.49)
No. of employees (FTEs)	32		49

* Common
[A] Reported in accordance with IFRS

Latest Results

Periods ended:	3m Mar. 31/23[A]	%Chg	3m Mar. 31/22[A]
	$000s	%Chg	$000s
Operating revenue	274	n.a.	nil
Net income	(4,470)	n.a.	(2,969)
	$		$
Earnings per share*	(0.04)		(0.02)

* Common
[A] Reported in accordance with IFRS

Historical Summary
(as originally stated)

Fiscal Year	Oper. Rev.	Net Inc. Bef. Disc.	EPS*
	$000s	$000s	$
2022[A]	821	(14,814)	(0.12)
2021[A]	133	(6,140)	(0.05)
2020[A]	10	(33,946)	(0.41)
2019[A1]	5	(44,567)	(0.62)
2018[A2]	nil	(1,857)	(2.50)

* Common
[A] Reported in accordance with IFRS
[1] Results reflect the Apr. 12, 2019, reverse takeover acquisition of BioCan Technologies Inc., and Epimeron Inc.
[2] Results for fiscal 2018 and prior fiscal years pertain to Makena Resources Inc.
Note: Adjusted throughout for 1-for-25 cons. in May 2019

W.35 Wilmington Capital Management Inc.

Symbol - WCM.A **Exchange** - TSX **CUSIP** - 971558
Head Office - 1420-205 5 Ave SW, Calgary, AB, T2P 2V7 **Telephone** - (403) 705-8038 **Fax** - (403) 705-8035
Website - www.wilmingtoncapital.ca
Email - pcraddock@wilmingtoncapital.ca
Investor Relations - Patrick Craddock (403) 705-8038
Auditors - PricewaterhouseCoopers LLP C.A., Calgary, Alta.
Transfer Agents - TSX Trust Company, Calgary, Alta.
Employees - 3 at Dec. 31, 2022
Profile - (Ont. 1979 amalg.) Holds investments in the real estate and energy sectors and, in special situations, undervalued assets such as marinas.

Investments consist of **Bow City Self Storage West Limited Partnership** and **Bow City Self Storage East Limited Partnership** (20% interest), which own a 92,000-sq.-ft. self-storage facility under development and an adjacent 32,000-sq.-ft. industrial warehouse in Calgary, Alta.; **Sunchaser RV Resorts Limited Partnership** (16% interest), which owns and operates three recreational vehicle (RV) resorts in Alberta and British Columbia, having 900 RV sites and 70 boat slips on 300 acres of land; **Sunchaser RV Resorts Management Inc.** (16% interest), the manager of Sunchaser RV; **Northbridge Capital Partners Ltd.** (40% interest), which makes private equity investments in the energy sector; **Northbridge Fund 2016 Limited Partnership** (3% interest), a private equity fund administered by Northbridge which invests in private companies in the energy industry; **Northbridge Fund 2021 Limited Partnership** (67% interest), **Northbridge Fund 2022 SP#2 Limited Partnership** (15% interest)and **Northbridge Fund 2022 SP#4 Limited Partnership** (23% interest), all are special purpose funds which invest in specified private oil and gas companies; **Maple Leaf Marinas Holdings Limited Partnership** (17% interest) and **Bay Moorings Marina Holdings Limited Partnership** (18% interest), which own and operate 20 marinas located north of Toronto, Ont., with more than 8,000 boat slips located on 500 acres of waterfront land, including 76 acres of redevelopment and expansion lands; and **Marina Asset Management Inc.** (33% interest), the manager of Maple Leaf and Bay Moorings.

In April 2023, the company invested additional $1,300,000 in **Maple Leaf Marinas Holdings Limited Partnership** and **Bay Moorings Marina Holdings Limited** which represented the company's share to fund Maple Leaf and Bay Moorings' acquisition of a marina in Ontario, having 358 wet and dry rack slips.

In March 2023, the company invested additional $1,100,000 in **Sunchaser RV Resorts Limited Partnership** which represented the company's share to fund Sunchaser's acquisition of a recreational vehicle resort and marina in British Columbia, having approximately 156 full-service recreational vehicle sites and 70 boat slips on 12 lakefront acres of land.

Also during the first quarter of 2023, the company invested additional $2,000,000 in **Northbridge Fund 2022 SP#4 Limited Partnership**, a special purpose fund whose purpose is to invest in a specified private oil and gas company.

In January 2023, the company invested additional $2,600,000 in **Maple Leaf Marinas Holdings Limited Partnership** and **Bay Moorings Marina Holdings Limited** which represented the company's share to fund Maple Leaf and Bay Moorings' acquisition of a marina in Ontario, having 535 boat slips (including dry rack slips) on 29 acres of land.

During 2022, the company invested $1,250,000 and $500,000 in **Northbridge Fund 2022 SP#2 Limited Partnership** and **Northbridge Fund 2022 SP#4 Limited Partnership**, respectively, both are special purpose funds which invest in a specified private oil and gas companies.

Predecessor Detail - Name changed from Unicorp Inc., Mar. 8, 2002, following capital reorganization. Distribution made of 1 $25 preferred hybrid due Dec. 31, 2050, for 4 Unicorp cl. A and/or cl. B shs.

Directors - Ian G. Cockwell, chr., Oakville, Ont.; Joseph F. (Joe) Killi, v-chr., Calgary, Alta.; Christopher J. Killi, man. partner & CEO, Toronto, Ont.; Timothy W. (Tim) Casgrain, Toronto, Ont.; Marc D. Sardachuk, Calgary, Alta.

Other Exec. Officers - Patrick Craddock, v-p, fin., acting CFO & man. partner; Alex Powell, corp. sec.

Capital Stock

	Authorized (shs.)	Outstanding (shs.)[1]
Class I Preference	unlimited	nil
Class II Preference	unlimited	nil
Class III Preference	unlimited	nil
Common	unlimited	nil
Class A	unlimited	11,328,182
Class B	unlimited	997,652

[1] At Mar. 31, 2023

Class A - Rank equally with class B shares in the payment of dividends and on the liquidation, dissolution or winding up of the company. Convertible on a share-for-share basis into class B shares under certain circumstances. Non-voting except, separately as a class, to elect two directors of the company.

Class B - One vote per share and are entitled to elect three directors of the company.

Major Shareholder - Joseph F. (Joe) Killi held 46.2% interest, Ian G. Cockwell held 20.5% interest and Timothy W. (Tim) Casgrain held 10.2% interest at Mar. 28, 2023.

Price Range - WCM.A/TSX

Year	Volume	High	Low	Close
2022	169,379	$4.25	$3.50	$4.25
2021	697,654	$4.10	$3.30	$3.76
2020	1,017,735	$5.00	$3.06	$3.50
2019	91,917	$7.26	$2.75	$4.09
2018	23,624	$3.67	$3.19	$3.50

Recent Close: $3.83
Capital Stock Changes - There were no changes to capital stock during 2021 or 2022.

Subsidiaries

67% int. in **Northbridge Fund 2021 Limited Partnership**

Investments

18% int. in **Bay Moorings Marina Holdings Limited Partnership**, Ont.
20% int. in **Bow City Self Storage East Limited Partnership**, Calgary, Alta.
20% int. in **Bow City Self Storage West Limited Partnership**, Calgary, Alta.
17% int. in **Maple Leaf Marinas Holdings Limited Partnership**, Ont.

33% int. in **Marina Asset Management Inc.**, Alta.
40% int. in **Northbridge Capital Partners Ltd.**, Calgary, Alta.
3% int. in **Northbridge Fund 2016 Limited Partnership**
15% int. in **Northbridge Fund 2022 SP#2 Limited Partnership**
23% int. in **Northbridge Fund 2022 SP#4 Limited Partnership**
16% int. in **Sunchaser RV Resorts Limited Partnership**, Alta.
16% int. in **Sunchaser RV Resorts Management Inc.**, Alta.

Financial Statistics

Periods ended:	12m Dec. 31/22[A]		12m Dec. 31/21[A]
	$000s	%Chg	$000s
Total revenue	**5,637**	**+227**	**1,722**
General & admin. expense	2,013		1,399
Stock-based compensation	328		553
Operating expense	**2,341**	**+20**	**1,952**
Operating income	**3,296**	**n.a.**	**(230)**
Deprec. & amort.	28		124
Finance costs, gross	9		11
Pre-tax income	**3,259**	**n.a.**	**(365)**
Income taxes	463		96
Net income	**2,796**	**n.a.**	**(461)**
Cash & equivalent	26,007		36,924
Accounts receivable	13,083		676
Current assets	39,090		37,600
Long-term investments	31,591		24,243
Total assets	**70,773**	**+11**	**64,021**
Accts. pay. & accr. liabs	790		642
Current liabilities	946		686
Long-term lease liabilities	116		145
Shareholders' equity	68,395		62,616
Cash from oper. activs	**268**	**n.a.**	**(77)**
Cash from fin. activs	(19)		(145)
Cash from invest. activs	1,834		(909)
Net cash position	**4,007**	**+108**	**1,924**
	$		$
Earnings per share*	0.23		(0.04)
Cash flow per share*	0.02		(0.01)
	shs		shs
No. of shs. o/s*	12,325,834		12,325,834
Avg. no. of shs. o/s*	12,326,000		12,326,000
	%		%
Net profit margin	49.60		(26.77)
Return on equity	4.27		(0.74)
Return on assets	4.16		(0.71)
No. of employees (FTEs)	3		4

* Class A & B
[A] Reported in accordance with IFRS

Latest Results

Periods ended:	3m Mar. 31/23[A]		3m Mar. 31/22[A]
	$000s	%Chg	$000s
Total revenue	123	-92	1,570
Net income	(574)	n.a.	866
	$		$
Earnings per share*	(0.05)		0.07

* Class A & B
[A] Reported in accordance with IFRS

Historical Summary
(as originally stated)

Fiscal Year	Total Rev. $000s	Net Inc. Bef. Disc. $000s	EPS* $
2022[A]	5,637	2,796	0.23
2021[A]	1,722	(461)	(0.04)
2020[A]	2,405	657	0.05
2019[A]	41,876	34,145	3.32
2018[A]	1,094	1,427	0.14

* Class A & B
[A] Reported in accordance with IFRS

W.36 Windfall Geotek Inc.

Symbol - WIN **Exchange** - TSX-VEN **CUSIP** - 973242
Head Office - 99-5460 Canotek Rd, Ottawa, ON, K1J 9G9 **Telephone** - (613) 241-2332 **Toll-free** - (855) 946-5145 **Fax** - (613) 421-8406
Website - www.windfallgeotek.com
Email - dinesh@windfallgeotek.com
Investor Relations - Dinesh Kandanchatha (450) 678-8888 ext. 222
Auditors - Davidson & Company LLP C.A., Vancouver, B.C.
Transfer Agents - Computershare Trust Company of Canada Inc., Montréal, Qué.
Profile - (Can. 1996) Has mineral interests in Quebec, Ontario and New Brunswick, and offers data mining consulting services software tool to exploration companies.
In Quebec, holds various properties totaling 1,193 claims including Ashuanipi gold prospect, 115 claims, 30 km west of Schefferville.
In Ontario, holds various properties totaling 5,949 claims including Corallen Lake prospect, 348 claims, 9 km northwest of the Red Lake Main Gold Trend; and Marshall Lake prospect, 20 claims.
In New Brunswick, holds various properties totaling five claims.
Also offers data mining consulting services through a software program that uses the latest artificial intelligence (AI) and pattern recognition algorithms to analyze digital data sets of compiled georeferenced historical exploration data, including geological, geochemical, geophysical and structural data, as well as digital elevation.
Also developing EagleEye™, a drone-based solution for AI-driven aerial surveying and digital exploration in mining.
In March 2023, the company sold the Chapais gold-copper prospect in Quebec to **Quebec Copper & Gold Inc.** for issuance of 500,000 common shares.
During fiscal 2023, the company developed its own software program using the latest artificial intelligence to provide mining exploration targeting services. As a result, the company no longer uses Computer Aided Resources Detection System (CARDS), a software tool which is used to assist exploration companies in identifying mining deposits, and was written down to nil value.
In February 2023, the company sold the West Nine Mile Brook prospect in New Brunswick to **Nine Mile Metals Ltd.** for issuance of 232,143 common shares.
In March 2022, the company sold the Ring of Fire prospect in northern Ontario to **S2 Minerals Inc.** for $300,000.
Predecessor Detail - Name changed from Albert Mining Inc., Oct. 10, 2019.
Directors - Dinesh Kandanchatha, chr. & interim CEO, Brampton, Ont.; Simran Kamboj, pres. & chief tech. officer, Brampton, Ont.; Kulvir Singh Gill, Ont.; Nathan Tribble, Barrie, Ont.
Other Exec. Officers - Scott S. Kelly, CFO

Capital Stock

	Authorized (shs.)	Outstanding (shs.)[1]
Common	unlimited	133,595,628

[1] At July 27, 2023

Major Shareholder - Widely held at Apr. 4, 2022.

Price Range - WIN/TSX-VEN

Year	Volume	High	Low	Close
2022	33,556,008	$0.13	$0.04	$0.04
2021	139,854,118	$0.60	$0.07	$0.11
2020	54,543,341	$0.14	$0.05	$0.08
2019	128,924,875	$0.25	$0.03	$0.08
2018	39,282,230	$0.10	$0.02	$0.03

Recent Close: $0.08
Capital Stock Changes - During fiscal 2023, 900,000 common shares were issued on exercise of warrants.

Wholly Owned Subsidiaries

Ampanihy Ressources S.A.R.L., Madagascar.
Private Ontario Corp., Ont.
SIMACT Alliance Copper Gold Inc., Montréal, Qué.
Tropic Diamonds Inc., Ont.

Investments

BWR Exploration Inc., Toronto, Ont. (see Survey of Mines)
Big Tree Carbon Inc., Toronto, Ont. (see separate coverage)
Blue Thunder Mining Inc., Toronto, Ont. (see Survey of Mines)
Canadian Copper Inc., Toronto, Ont. (see Survey of Mines)
Catalyst Mines Inc., Canada.
Dryden Gold Corp., Canada.
Flow Metals Corp., Vancouver, B.C. (see Survey of Mines)
MacDonald Mines Exploration Ltd., Toronto, Ont. (see Survey of Mines)
Nine Mile Metals Ltd., Vancouver, B.C. (see Survey of Mines)
Pacton Gold Inc., Vancouver, B.C.
Platinex Inc., Toronto, Ont. (see separate coverage)
Playfair Mining Ltd., Vancouver, B.C. (see Survey of Mines)
Power Nickel Inc., Toronto, Ont. (see Survey of Mines)
Puma Exploration Inc., Rimouski, Qué. (see Survey of Mines)
QC Copper & Gold Inc., Toronto, Ont. (see Survey of Mines)
Quebec Precious Metals Corporation, Montréal, Qué. (see Survey of Mines)
S2 Minerals Inc., Toronto, Ont. (see Survey of Mines)

Financial Statistics

Periods ended:	12m Feb. 28/23[A]		12m Feb. 28/22[A]
	$000s	%Chg	$000s
Operating revenue	**658**	**+15**	**571**
Exploration expense	98		1,014
General & admin expense	1,403		3,036
Stock-based compensation	159		1,309
Operating expense	**1,660**	**-69**	**5,359**
Operating income	**(1,002)**	**n.a.**	**(4,788)**
Deprec., depl. & amort.	7		157
Write-downs/write-offs	nil		(10)
Pre-tax income	**(934)**	**n.a.**	**(5,368)**
Net income	**(934)**	**n.a.**	**(5,368)**
Cash & equivalent	2,301		3,137
Accounts receivable	186		26
Current assets	2,515		3,262
Fixed assets, net	12		18
Total assets	**2,527**	**-23**	**3,281**
Accts. pay. & accr. liabs	99		131
Current liabilities	99		141
Long-term debt, gross	nil		10
Shareholders' equity	2,427		3,139
Cash from oper. activs	**(1,082)**	**n.a.**	**(3,687)**
Cash from fin. activs	63		4,218
Cash from invest. activs	429		(174)
Net cash position	**1,283**	**-32**	**1,873**
Capital expenditures	nil		(4)
Capital disposals	320		nil
	$		$
Earnings per share*	(0.01)		(0.04)
Cash flow per share*	(0.01)		(0.03)
	shs		shs
No. of shs. o/s*	133,595,628		132,695,628
Avg. no. of shs. o/s*	133,339,190		123,721,712
	%		%
Net profit margin	(141.95)		(940.11)
Return on equity	(33.56)		(176.14)
Return on assets	(32.16)		(165.70)

* Common
[A] Reported in accordance with IFRS

Latest Results

Periods ended:	3m May 31/23[A]		3m May 31/22[A]
	$000s	%Chg	$000s
Operating revenue	243	+196	82
Net income	(122)	n.a.	(435)
	$		$
Earnings per share*	(0.00)		(0.00)

* Common
[A] Reported in accordance with IFRS

Historical Summary
(as originally stated)

Fiscal Year	Oper. Rev. $000s	Net Inc. Bef. Disc. $000s	EPS* $
2023[A]	658	(934)	(0.01)
2022[A]	571	(5,368)	(0.04)
2021[A]	614	86	0.00
2020[A]	617	(871)	(0.01)
2019[A]	30	(840)	(0.01)

* Common
[A] Reported in accordance with IFRS

W.37 Winpak Ltd.*

Symbol - WPK **Exchange** - TSX **CUSIP** - 97535P
Head Office - 100 Saulteaux Cres, Winnipeg, MB, R3J 3T3 **Telephone** - (204) 889-1015 **Fax** - (204) 888-7806
Website - www.winpak.com
Email - scott.taylor@winpak.com
Investor Relations - Scott M. Taylor (204) 831-2254
Auditors - KPMG LLP C.A., Winnipeg, Man.
Bankers - Bank of America Canada; The Toronto-Dominion Bank
Lawyers - Bond, Schoeneck & King, PLLC, Buffalo, N.Y.; Thompson Dorfman Sweatman LLP, Winnipeg, Man.
Transfer Agents - Computershare Trust Company of Canada Inc., Calgary, Alta.
FP500 Revenue Ranking - 263
Employees - 2,714 at Dec. 25, 2022
Profile - (Can. 1975) Manufactures and distributes high-quality packaging materials and related packaging machines for the protection of perishable foods, beverages and healthcare applications primarily in North America.
Operations are organized into three reportable segments: flexible packaging; rigid packaging and flexible lidding materials; and packaging machinery.
Flexible packaging consists of blown and cast extrusion films, from monolayer to thirteen-layer coextrusions, and laminated films that are suited to modified atmosphere packaging applications, in addition to specialty films such as biaxially oriented nylon and high barrier converter

films including shrink bags, high quality flexographic and rotogravure printed laminations, and vacuum, stand-up and zipper closure pouches. Also manufactures high-quality paper/poly/foil laminated rollstock for various flexible food applications such as dry soup mixes, beverage mixes and powdered coffee flavourings. Pharmaceutical and personal care products include blister foil, pouch stock and film overwrap. For the medical market, products include thermoforming films for device packaging, central supply room wraps and draping films, and both roll-fed and die-cut foil lid stock. Personal care products such as condoms, cosmetics, skin creams, shampoos and shavers are packaged using the company's diverse offering of laminations.

Rigid packaging and flexible lidding materials are manufactured for food, pet food, beverage, dairy, industrial and health care applications. Rigid packaging products include portion control and single-serve containers, such as rigid plastic cups and trays, rigid plastic sheet material, and custom and retort trays. Flexible lidding products include a wide range of standard foil, film and paper material combinations for plastic or metal containers and are available in daisy-chain, die-cut and rollstock formats. Also offers specialized printed packaging solutions including pressure-sensitive pharmaceutical labels, flexible package printing, push-through and blister foil/quick foil, pre-printed thermoformable plastics, inserts, outserts, MedGuides and patient leaflets to the pharmaceutical, healthcare, nutraceutical, cosmetic and personal care markets.

Packaging machinery products include standard and custom vertical form/fill/seal packaging machines used for a variety of pouch applications and horizontal fill/seal packaging machines for preformed plastic cups. The pouch and cup machines are both capable of filling hot, cold, thick and free-flowing liquids in precise volumes. Products packaged with pouch and cup packaging machines include condiments, dips, sauces, salad dressings, cheese, cream cheese, cottage cheese, sour cream, hummus, guacamole, syrup, ketchup, cream, margarine, butter, spreads, yogurt, desserts, ice cream, pudding, applesauce, juice, water, powdered drinks, dry snacks, nuts, cosmetics, beauty/health care products, hand sanitization, and many other liquid, semi-liquid, and dry products. The company also maintains an inventory of replacement parts for packaging machines.

The company has sales representatives located throughout North America and maintains a network of sales agents and distributors throughout North America and in select markets in South America. The majority of products are sold in the U.S., with Canada being the second largest geographical market area, and other markets in Mexico, the Caribbean, certain countries in South America, and in the U.K., with respect to rigid packaging and flexible lidding.

At Dec. 25, 2022, the company had 12 manufacturing facilities in North America, consisting of a 464,000-sq.-ft. integrated plastic film extrusion and conversion facility and a 140,000-sq.-ft. film extrusion facility in Winnipeg, Man.; a 300,000-sq.-ft. film extrusion and conversion facility in Senoia, Ga.; a 68,000-sq.-ft. filling machine manufacturing plant in Rialto, Calif.; a 125,000-sq.-ft. integrated plastic sheet extrusion and conversion facility in Chicago, Ill.; a 615,000-sq.-ft. integrated plastic sheet extrusion and conversion facility in Sauk Village, Ill.; a 154,000-sq.-ft. integrated plastic sheet extrusion and conversion plant in Toronto, Ont.; a 266,000-sq.-ft. integrated lid extrusion and conversion facility at Vaudreuil-Dorion, Que.; a 75,000-sq.-ft. lid die-cutting and conversion plant at Pekin, Ill.; a 55,000-sq.-ft. lid die-cutting and conversion plant in Queretaro, Mexico; and 61,000-sq.-ft. and 21,000-sq.-ft. specialized printing plants in Norwood, N.J.

During fiscal 2022, the company acquired five acres of land and an 88,000-sq.-ft. building for warehouse storage and office space in Winnipeg, Man.

Directors - Antti I. Aarnio-Wihuri, chr., Kaarina, Finland; Martti H. Aarnio-Wihuri, Kaarina, Finland; Rakel J. Aarnio-Wihuri, Kaarina, Finland; Bruce J. Berry, Winnipeg, Man.; Kenneth P. (Ken) Kuchma, Winnipeg, Man.; Dayna Spiring, Winnipeg, Man.; Ilkka T. Suominen, Helsinki, Finland

Other Exec. Officers - Olivier Y. Muggli, pres. & CEO; Mustafa Bilgen, v-p, tech. & innovation; James C. Holland, v-p, pres., Winpak div. & pres., Winpak Films Inc.; Scott M. Taylor, v-p & CFO; Randy W. Zasitko, v-p, supply chain & procurement

Capital Stock

	Authorized (shs.)	Outstanding (shs.)[1]
Common	unlimited	65,000,000

[1] At July 2, 2023

Major Shareholder - Antti I. Aarnio-Wihuri held 52.7% interest at Feb. 28, 2023.

Price Range - WPK/TSX

Year	Volume	High	Low	Close
2022	12,908,801	$48.13	$35.52	$42.06
2021	15,379,204	$45.59	$34.74	$37.17
2020	16,990,532	$52.65	$33.11	$42.82
2019	12,790,869	$49.04	$40.64	$46.98
2018	11,519,636	$50.82	$42.50	$47.75

Recent Close: $39.67

Capital Stock Changes - There were no changes to capital stock from fiscal 2006 to fiscal 2022, inclusive.

Dividends

WPK com Ra $0.12 pa Q est. July 12, 2007
$3.00◆ July 9/21
Paid in 2023: $0.09 2022: $0.12 2021: $0.12 + $3.00◆

◆ Special

Long-Term Debt - At Dec. 25, 2022, the company had no long-term debt.

Wholly Owned Subsidiaries

Winpak Heat Seal Packaging Inc., Vaudreuil-Dorion, Qué.
Winpak Holdings Ltd., Wilmington, Del.
- 100% int. in **Winpak Control Group Inc.**, Del.
- 100% int. in **Winpak Films Inc.**, Senoia, Ga.
- 100% int. in **Winpak Heat Seal Corporation**, Pekin, Ill.
- 100% int. in **Winpak Inc.**, Minneapolis, Minn.
- 100% int. in **Winpak Lane, Inc.**, Calif.
- 100% int. in **Winpak Portion Packaging, Inc.**, Chicago, Ill.

Winpak Portion Packaging Ltd., Etobicoke, Ont.

Subsidiaries

51% int. in **American Biaxis Inc.**, Winnipeg, Man.
99.99% int. in **Grupo Winpak de Mexico, S.A. de C.V.**, Mexico.
- 99.99% int. in **Administracion Winpak de Mexico, S.A. de C.V.**, Mexico.
- 99.99% int. in **Embalajes Winpak de Mexico, S.A. de C.V.**, Mexico.

Investments

0.01% int. in **Administracion Winpak de Mexico, S.A. de C.V.**, Mexico.
0.01% int. in **Embalajes Winpak de Mexico, S.A. de C.V.**, Mexico.

Note: The preceding list includes only the major related companies in which interests are held.

Financial Statistics

Periods ended:	52w Dec. 25/22[A]		52w Dec. 26/21[A]
	US$000s	%Chg	US$000s
Operating revenue	**1,181,133**	**+18**	**1,001,994**
Cost of sales	799,983		680,282
Research & devel. expense	18,249		17,831
General & admin expense	134,161		115,404
Operating expense	**952,393**	**+17**	**813,517**
Operating income	**228,740**	**+21**	**188,477**
Deprec., depl. & amort.	49,386		47,264
Finance income	6,414		913
Finance costs, gross	4,612		1,738
Pre-tax income	**174,086**	**+23**	**141,613**
Income taxes	45,861		35,265
Net income	**128,225**	**+21**	**106,348**
Net inc. for equity hldrs	**128,343**	**+24**	**103,808**
Net inc. for non-cont. int	**(118)**	**n.a.**	**2,540**
Cash & equivalent	398,673		377,461
Inventories	288,118		187,058
Accounts receivable	204,040		177,382
Current assets	900,006		758,428
Fixed assets, net	518,590		515,247
Intangibles, net	33,110		34,472
Total assets	**1,462,489**	**+11**	**1,321,694**
Accts. pay. & accr. liabs	101,061		90,403
Current liabilities	124,724		97,037
Long-term lease liabilities	11,212		12,179
Shareholders' equity	1,202,774		1,079,620
Non-controlling interest	36,001		36,119
Cash from oper. activs	**77,569**	**-20**	**97,055**
Cash from fin. activs	(6,896)		(166,404)
Cash from invest. activs	(49,461)		(48,536)
Net cash position	**398,673**	**+6**	**377,461**
Capital expenditures	(49,125)		(48,291)
Unfunded pension liability	3,819		4,724
	US$		US$
Earnings per share*	1.97		1.60
Cash flow per share*	1.19		1.49
Cash divd. per share*	$0.12		$0.12
Extra divd. - cash*	$nil		$3.00
Total divd. per share*	**$0.12**		**$3.12**
	shs		shs
No. of shs. o/s*	65,000,000		65,000,000
Avg. no. of shs. o/s*	65,000,000		65,000,000
	%		%
Net profit margin	10.86		10.61
Return on equity	11.25		9.38
Return on assets	9.45		8.11
Foreign sales percent	87		87
No. of employees (FTEs)	2,714		2,563

* Common
[A] Reported in accordance with IFRS

Latest Results

Periods ended:	27w July 2/23[A]		26w June 26/22[A]
	US$000s	%Chg	US$000s
Operating revenue	591,980	+1	586,236
Net income	78,753	+16	68,037
Net inc. for equity hldrs	79,293	+17	67,541
Net inc. for non-cont. int	(540)		496
	US$		US$
Earnings per share*	1.22		1.04

* Common
[A] Reported in accordance with IFRS

Historical Summary
(as originally stated)

Fiscal Year	Oper. Rev.	Net Inc. Bef. Disc.	EPS*
	US$000s	US$000s	US$
2022[A]	1,181,133	128,225	1.97
2021[A]	1,001,994	106,348	1.60
2020[A]	852,493	108,915	1.64
2019[A]	873,843	118,064	1.77
2018[A]	889,641	111,577	1.68

* Common
[A] Reported in accordance with IFRS

W.38 Wishpond Technologies Ltd.

Symbol - WISH **Exchange** - TSX-VEN **CUSIP** - 97730P
Head Office - 170-422 Richards St, Vancouver, BC, V6B 2Z4 **Telephone** - (604) 889-4790 **Toll-free** - (800) 921-0167
Website - www.wishpond.com
Email - investor@wishpond.com
Investor Relations - Pardeep S. Sangha (604) 572-6392
Auditors - BDO Canada LLP C.A.
Transfer Agents - Computershare Trust Company of Canada Inc., Vancouver, B.C.
Employees - 300 at Mar. 31, 2023
Profile - (B.C. 2018) Provides digital marketing, promotion, lead generation, sales automation, ad management, referral marketing and sales conversion to small-to-medium size businesses for generating, managing and nurturing leads.

The company's cloud-based Propel IQ platform provides an artificial intelligence (AI) powered website builder for lead generation, marketing automation and analytics, including landing pages, website pop-ups, online forms, cart abandonment tools, call tracking, marketing funnels, sales automation, appointment bookings, payment features, social promotion, email marketing, short messaging service marketing, lead management, native ads management, referral marketing campaigns and digital marketing services.

Also provides subscription-based marketing services which supports the design, launch and maintenance of effective digital marketing campaigns including campaign design and management, online advertising, search engine optimization and landing page design. Serves more than 4,000 customers who are primarily small-to-medium size businesses in various industries. Customers subscribe to the company's software and services through annual or monthly recurring plans.

In May 2023, the company acquired certain assets including the software, brand, website and client relationships of Wilmington, Del.-based **Essential Studio Manager LLC** (ESM) for an undisclosed amount. ESM provides business management software, including invoicing and customer relationship management solutions for small businesses in the services industry.

In January 2023, wholly owned **Wishpond Solutions Ltd.**, **Wishpond Marketing Group Ltd.**, **Invigo Media Ltd.**, **Wishpond Technology Group Ltd.**, **Winback Technologies Inc.**, **Brax Technologies Inc.**, and **Viral Loops Technologies Inc.** were amalgamated and continued as **Wishpond Technology Group Ltd.**

In April 2022, the company acquired substantially all of the business and assets of **Viral Loops Ltd.** for US$1,380,000 and a one year earn-out based on the projected revenue of the business. Viral Loops provides Software-as-a-Service template-based marketing platform which designs, creates and manages marketing campaigns for e-commerce merchants.

Predecessor Detail - Name changed from Antera Ventures I Corp., Dec. 8, 2020, pursuant to Qualifying Transaction reverse takeover acquisition of (old) Wishpond Technologies Ltd.; basis 1 new for 4.64672 old shs.

Directors - Ali Tajskandar, chr. & CEO, North Vancouver, B.C.; Jordan Gutierrez, COO, Vancouver, B.C.; Lloyed Lobo, Sunnyvale, Calif.; Hossein Malek, West Vancouver, B.C.; Olivier Vincent, North Vancouver, B.C.

Other Exec. Officers - David Pais, CFO; Dennis Zelada, chief tech. officer; Kevin Ho, gen. mgr., Brax; Nicholas Steeves, gen. mgr., PersistIQ; Kendra Low, corp. sec.

Capital Stock

	Authorized (shs.)	Outstanding (shs.)[1]
Common	unlimited	53,768,620

[1] At June 12, 2023

Normal Course Issuer Bid - The company plans to make normal course purchases of up to 2,688,431 common shares representing 5% of the total outstanding. The bid commenced on June 30, 2023, and expires on June 29, 2024.

Major Shareholder - Hossein Malek held 21.5% interest and Ali Tajskandar held 15.9% interest at Apr. 12, 2023.

Price Range - WISH/TSX-VEN

Year	Volume	High	Low	Close
2022	4,375,840	$1.39	$0.56	$0.70
2021	14,010,896	$2.50	$1.02	$1.34
2020	4,306,431	$2.79	$0.28	$2.06
2019	28,945	$0.70	$0.28	$0.56

Consolidation: 1-for-4.64672 cons. in Dec. 2020
Recent Close: $0.62

Capital Stock Changes - During 2022 common shares were issued as follows: 1,977,423 pursuant to the acquisition of PersistIQ Inc. and Brax Technologies Inc., 70,110 on exercise of warrants and 44,100 on exercise of options; 152,600 common shares were repurchased under a Normal Course Issue Bid.

Wholly Owned Subsidiaries

PersistIQ Inc., San Mateo, Calif.

Financial Statistics

Periods ended:	12m Dec. 31/22[A]		12m Dec. 31/21[A]
	$000s	%Chg	$000s
Operating revenue	**20,479**	**+39**	**14,761**
Cost of sales	6,922		4,781
Salaries & benefits	4,239		3,039
General & admin expense	8,670		6,885
Stock-based compensation	1,139		2,323
Operating expense	**20,970**	**+23**	**17,028**
Operating income	**(491)**	**n.a.**	**(2,267)**
Deprec., depl. & amort.	1,297		879
Finance income	11		nil
Finance costs, gross	nil		9
Pre-tax income	**(2,338)**	**n.a.**	**(4,794)**
Income taxes	(588)		94
Net income	**(1,750)**	**n.a.**	**(4,888)**
Cash & equivalent	2,965		6,412
Accounts receivable	178		170
Current assets	3,456		7,150
Fixed assets, net	27		30
Intangibles, net	12,648		9,566
Total assets	**16,278**	**-3**	**16,793**
Accts. pay. & accr. liabs	2,275		1,232
Current liabilities	5,666		6,604
Shareholders' equity	10,590		9,672
Cash from oper. activs	**1,032**	**n.a.**	**(1,538)**
Cash from fin. activs	(107)		6,743
Cash from invest. activs	(4,475)		(6,268)
Net cash position	**2,693**	**-57**	**6,242**
Capital expenditures	(6)		(20)
	$		$
Earnings per share*	(0.03)		(0.10)
Cash flow per share*	0.02		(0.03)
	shs		shs
No. of shs. o/s*	53,705,324		51,766,291
Avg. no. of shs. o/s*	52,572,676		51,183,732
	%		%
Net profit margin	(8.55)		(33.11)
Return on equity	(17.27)		(71.20)
Return on assets	(10.58)		(37.70)
Foreign sales percent	86		90
No. of employees (FTEs)	300		235

* Common
[A] Reported in accordance with IFRS

Latest Results

Periods ended:	3m Mar. 31/23[A]		3m Mar. 31/22[A]
	$000s	%Chg	$000s
Operating revenue	5,624	+38	4,078
Net income	(790)	n.a.	(1,133)
	$		$
Earnings per share*	(0.01)		(0.02)

* Common
[A] Reported in accordance with IFRS

Historical Summary
(as originally stated)

Fiscal Year	Oper. Rev.	Net Inc. Bef. Disc.	EPS*
	$000s	$000s	$
2022[A]	20,479	(1,750)	(0.03)
2021[A]	14,761	(4,888)	(0.10)
2020[A1]	7,882	(2,215)	(0.08)
2019[A]	6,050	(428)	(0.23)
2018[A]	4,308	(1,027)	(0.60)

* Common
[A] Reported in accordance with IFRS
[1] Results prior to Dec. 8, 2020, pertain to and reflect the Qualifying Transaction reverse takeover acquisition of (old) Wishpond Technologies Ltd.

Note: Adjusted throughout for 1-for-4.6467206 cons. in Dec. 2020

W.39 Wittering Capital Corp.

Symbol - WITT.P **Exchange** - TSX-VEN **CUSIP** - 97749Q
Head Office - 1710-1050 Pender St W, Vancouver, BC, V6E 3S7 **Telephone** - (604) 609-3355
Email - tobypierce@hotmail.com
Investor Relations - Toby R. Pierce (604) 609-3355
Auditors - De Visser Gray LLP C.A., Vancouver, B.C.
Lawyers - S. Paul Simpson Law Corporation, Vancouver, B.C.
Transfer Agents - Odyssey Trust Company, Vancouver, B.C.
Profile - (B.C. 2021) Capital Pool Company.
Common reinstated on TSX-VEN, Jan. 30, 2023.
Common suspended from TSX-VEN, Jan. 9, 2023.
Directors - Mark Colucci, pres., CEO, CFO & corp. sec., Calgary, Alta.; Dain Currie, George Town, Cayman Islands; Peter Laflamme, Toronto, Ont.; Toby R. Pierce, Vancouver, B.C.

Capital Stock

	Authorized (shs.)	Outstanding (shs.)[1]
Common	unlimited	7,000,000

[1] At Dec. 20, 2021

Major Shareholder - Dain Currie held 11.43% interest and Toby R. Pierce held 11.43% interest at Dec. 20, 2021.

Price Range - WITT.P/TSX-VEN

Year	Volume	High	Low	Close
2022	198,208	$0.40	$0.12	$0.12

Recent Close: $0.05

Capital Stock Changes - On Dec. 20, 2021, an initial public offering of 3,000,000 common shares was completed at 10¢ per share.

W.40 Wolverine Energy and Infrastructure Inc.

Symbol - WEII **Exchange** - TSX-VEN **CUSIP** - 977891
Head Office - 1711 9 St, Nisku, AB, T9E 0R3 **Telephone** - (780) 438-3451
Website - www.wnrgi.com
Email - acowie@wnrgi.com
Investor Relations - Alison Cowie (780) 476-6916
Auditors - Deloitte LLP C.A., Calgary, Alta.
Transfer Agents - Odyssey Trust Company, Calgary, Alta.
Profile - (Alta. 2017) Provides civil infrastructure construction and management services, heavy equipment sales and rentals, oilfield and energy equipment rentals, above ground water management services, a variety of oil and gas services, and transportation and trailer rentals in western Canada and the United States.

Services include: **Oilfield/ Energy Equipment Rentals**, which provides oilfield and energy rental services consisting of 400 barrel insulated tanks, well site accommodations, combination units, boilers and heat exchangers, water heating alternatives, safe work platforms, mobile recycle units and sewage containment solutions; **Heavy Equipment Sales and Rentals**, which sells and provides rentals for equipments including articulated rock trucks, graders, dozers, scrapers, excavators, wheel loaders, fire guards, earth compactors, skid steers, access mats and light towers; **Civil/Infrastructure Construction & Management**, which provides construction and seismic services consisting of water and sewer servicing, site excavation, utilities service and maintenance, horizontal directional drilling, underground gas line installation, polyethylene fusion, snow management solutions, mulching and slashing, and seismic line cutting; **Transportation Services & Trailer Rentals**, which provides hauling service as well as various trucking services for construction, agriculture and residential including the rents for Highboy, Step Decks, Multi Axle, Sliding Axle, Super B's and Trombones; **Water Management**, which includes water transfer, water management and water heating services; **Wide Ranging Oil & Gas Services** (such as **Production Testing** and **Sand Management**), which includes surface and/or downhole pressure and temperature data reporting, production testing reporting, well test analysis, as well as a fleet of testing vessels for short-term or long-term rentals.

Directors - Jesse Douglas, exec. chr., Nisku, Alta.; Christopher G. (Chris) Hoose, Edmonton, Alta.; Dirk Le Poole, Edmonton, Alta.; Darrell R. Peterson, Calgary, Alta.
Other Exec. Officers - Shannon Ostapovich, pres.; Richard (Rick) Quigley, COO; Alison Cowie, CFO; John P. Smith, gen. counsel, corp. sec. & dir., capital allocation

Capital Stock

	Authorized (shs.)	Outstanding (shs.)[1]
Common	unlimited	110,345,823

[1] At Dec. 31, 2022

Major Shareholder - Jesse Douglas held 45.71% interest at Nov. 1, 2022.

Price Range - WEII/TSX-VEN

Year	Volume	High	Low	Close
2022	8,769,185	$0.45	$0.05	$0.07
2021	5,231,029	$1.15	$0.17	$0.20
2020	3,462,562	$0.80	$0.20	$0.50
2019	3,922,139	$1.25	$0.60	$0.76

Recent Close: $0.07

Capital Stock Changes - In December 2021, 4,347,826 common shares were issued pursuant to the acquisition of Western Canadian Mulching Ltd. and certain assets of Seisline Resource Services Ltd.

Wholly Owned Subsidiaries

HD Northern Equipment Sales and Rentals Inc., Alta.
PetroMaroc Corporation, Nisku, Alta.
- 100% int. in **Longreach Oil and Gas (Canada) Limited**, Canada.
- 100% int. in **Longreach Oil and Gas Ventures Limited**, Jersey.

Western Canadian Mulching Ltd., Alta.
Wolverine Construction Inc., Alta.
Wolverine Equipment Inc., Alta.
- 100% int. in **Bearing Transport Ltd.**, Alta.
- 100% int. in **Flo-Back Equipment Rentals and Sales Ltd.**, Edmonton, Alta.
- 100% int. in **HD Energy Rentals Ltd.**, Grande Prairie, Alta.
- 100% int. in **Liberty Energy Services Ltd.**, Edson, Alta.
- 100% int. in **WTI Rentals Limited**, Edmonton, Alta.

Investments

25.4% int. in **Green Impact Partners Inc.**, Calgary, Alta. (see separate coverage)

Financial Statistics

Periods ended:	12m Mar. 31/22[A]		12m Mar. 31/21[¤A]
	$000s	%Chg	$000s
Operating revenue	**66,200**	**-43**	**116,828**
Cost of sales	33,694		88,956
Salaries & benefits	22,287		21,073
General & admin expense	9,878		6,425
Operating expense	**65,859**	**-43**	**116,454**
Operating income	**341**	**-9**	**374**
Deprec., depl. & amort.	24,469		26,485
Finance costs, gross	9,425		8,778
Investment income	(6,085)		(1,266)
Pre-tax income	**(4,863)**	**n.a.**	**(27,418)**
Income taxes	(682)		(4,549)
Net income	**(4,181)**	**n.a.**	**(22,869)**
Cash & equivalent	3,863		2,830
Inventories	2,254		5,582
Accounts receivable	27,451		24,724
Current assets	33,898		38,642
Long-term investments	51,567		7,350
Fixed assets, net	76,550		169,648
Intangibles, net	2,173		10,417
Total assets	**174,663**	**-24**	**229,668**
Bank indebtedness	9,171		12,915
Accts. pay. & accr. liabs	16,260		17,222
Current liabilities	55,225		72,463
Long-term debt, gross	98,617		120,342
Long-term debt, net	68,823		78,016
Shareholders' equity	41,436		58,694
Cash from oper. activs	**(1,237)**	**n.a.**	**(5,098)**
Cash from fin. activs	(37,963)		2,875
Cash from invest. activs	40,234		1,171
Net cash position	**3,863**	**+37**	**2,830**
Capital expenditures	(3,693)		(6,977)
Capital disposals	11,334		8,149
	$		$
Earnings per share*	(0.04)		(0.22)
Cash flow per share*	(0.01)		(0.05)
	shs		shs
No. of shs. o/s*	110,345,824		105,997,998
Avg. no. of shs. o/s*	107,248,742		105,997,998
	%		%
Net profit margin	(6.32)		(19.57)
Return on equity	(8.25)		(31.91)
Return on assets	1.93		(6.36)

* Common
[¤] Restated
[A] Reported in accordance with IFRS

Latest Results

Periods ended:	9m Dec. 31/22[A]		9m Dec. 31/21[A]
	$000s	%Chg	$000s
Operating revenue	38,665	-12	44,138
Net income	(27,970)	n.a.	(4,999)
	$		$
Earnings per share*	(0.25)		(0.05)

* Common
[A] Reported in accordance with IFRS

Historical Summary
(as originally stated)

Fiscal Year	Oper. Rev.	Net Inc. Bef. Disc.	EPS*
	$000s	$000s	$
2022[A]	66,200	(4,181)	(0.04)
2021[A]	116,828	(21,602)	(0.20)
2020[A]	237,389	12,592	0.13
2019[A]	58,006	16,902	0.24
2018[A]	39,951	(627)	n.a.

* Common
[A] Reported in accordance with IFRS

W.41 WonderFi Technologies Inc.

Symbol - WNDR **Exchange** - TSX **CUSIP** - 97818W
Head Office - 2200-885 Georgia St W, Vancouver, BC, V6C 3E8 **Telephone** - (778) 843-9637
Website - www.wonder.fi
Email - dean.skurka@wonder.fi
Investor Relations - Dean Skurka (778) 843-9637
Auditors - Raymond Chabot Grant Thornton LLP C.A., Montréal, Qué.
Transfer Agents - Computershare Trust Company of Canada Inc., Vancouver, B.C.
Profile - (B.C. 1990 amalg.) Owns and operates four registered Canadian cryptocurrency asset trading platforms and has other investments in the digital asset ecosystem.

Owns and operates cryptocurrency trading platforms: Coinsquare, Bitbuy, Coinsmart and Coinberry, with a combined user base of over 1,600,000 registered users and a combined assets under custody exceeding $600,000,000. The company's crypto payment processing division, SmartPay, provides an easy way for businesses to send and receive cryptocurrency payments across the globe. Also owns a 43% interest in **Tetra Trust Company**, Canada's first and only trust company licensed to custody digital assets.

Other ventures and investments include wholly owned **Blockchain Foundry Inc.**, a North American blockchain development firm; BetLegend; a Canadian sports betting and gaming platform which is awaiting regulatory approval; UniiFi (formerly known as WonderFi), an aggregator platform which was launched in January 2022, that provides users with a convenient interface for transacting in crypto assets using DeFi (Decentralized Finance) protocols; and wholly owned **WonderFi Interactive Inc.**, which is pursuing play-to-earn gaming opportunities.

Recent Merger and Acquisition Activity

Status: completed **Revised:** July 10, 2023
UPDATE: The transaction was completed. PREVIOUS: WonderFi Technologies Inc. agreed to acquire private Coinsquare Ltd. and public CoinSmart Financial Inc., both Toronto, Ont.-based companies operating cryptocurrency trading platforms, for issuance of 269,727,080 and 119,181,733 common shares, respectively. The combined company would have transacted more than $17 billion since 2017 and have more than $600,000,000 in assets under custody, with a registered user base in excess of 1,650,000 Canadians. Upon completion, WonderFi, Coinsquare and CoinSmart shareholders would hold a 38%, 43% and 19% interest, respectively, in the combined company. Mogo Inc., which held a 34% interest in Coinsquare, would become the largest shareholder of the combined company with a 14% interest.

Status: terminated **Revised:** Feb. 2, 2023
UPDATE: The transaction was terminated. PREVIOUS: CoinSmart Financial Inc. agreed to sell wholly owned Simply Digital Technologies Inc., which operates CoinSmart's cryptocurrency trading platform, to Coinsquare Ltd. for $29,215,555, consisting of $3,000,000 and issuance of 5,222,222 common shares and contingent consideration of up to $20,000,000 and issuance of 1,100,000 common shares upon achieving certain milestones. The sale constitutes the sale of all or substantially all of the operations of CoinSmart. Upon completion, CoinSmart would hold 12% of the shares of Coinsquare and it is anticipated that CoinSmart will change its name to SMRT Financial Inc. The transaction is expected to close in the fourth quarter of 2022. Jan. 17, 2022 - Coinsquare Ltd. has delivered a notice to terminate the transaction. CoinSmart has rejected the notice and considers that Coinsquare remains bound by the agreement and plans to hold Coinsquare to its obligations under the agreement.

Status: completed **Revised:** Nov. 7, 2022
UPDATE: The transaction was completed. PREVIOUS: WonderFi Technologies Inc. agreed to acquire Blockchain Foundry Inc. (BCF) on the basis of 0.2155 WonderFi common shares for each BCF share held, which would result in the issuance of 26,285,794 WonderFi common shares, representing 13.4% of the issued and outstanding WonderFi shares. BCF develops and commercializes blockchain-based business solutions. Nov. 1, 2022 - BCF shareholders approved the transaction.

Status: completed **Revised:** July 4, 2022
UPDATE: The transaction was completed. PREVIOUS: WonderFi Technologies Inc. agreed to acquire private Toronto, Ont.-based Coinberry Limited, which operates Coinberry.com, a cryptocurrency asset trading platform that offers investors a safe and simple way to buy, sell and process payments made with Bitcoin, Ethereum and other cryptocurrencies in Canada, for issuance of 29,107,000 common shares valued at $38,300,000. Coinberry featured 29 of the top cryptocurrency trading pairs, and serviced more than 220,000 users. Coinberry earned $13,000,000 in revenue during 2021 and had more than $100,000,000 of assets under custody as at Dec. 31, 2021.

Status: completed **Revised:** Mar. 25, 2022
UPDATE: The transaction was completed. First Ledge was amalgamated into wholly owned Bitbuy Holdings Inc. PREVIOUS: WonderFi Technologies Inc. agreed to acquire private Toronto, Ont.-based First Ledger Corp., which operates an online trading platform (BitBuy.ca) enabling users to buy and sell digital currencies, for $206,000,000, consisting of $50,000,000 cash and issuance of 70,000,000 common shares. The boards of directors of both companies approved the transaction.

Predecessor Detail - Name changed from Austpro Energy Corporation, Aug. 25, 2021, pursuant to the reverse takeover acquisition of DeFi Ventures Inc. and concurrent amalgmation of DeFi with wholly owned 1302107 B.C. Ltd. (and continued as WonderFi Digital Inc.).; basis 1 new for 8.727 old shs.

Directors - Dean Skurka, pres. & CEO, Toronto, Ont.; Robert Halpern, Toronto, Ont.; Justin Hartzman, Toronto, Ont.; Christopher Marsh, Toronto, Ont.; G. Scott Paterson, Toronto, Ont.; Wendy Rudd, Ont.; Nicholas Thadaney, Toronto, Ont.; Jason Theofilos, Toronto, Ont.; Michael A. Wekerle, Caledon, Ont.

Other Exec. Officers - Gordon Brocklehurst, CFO; Torstein Braaten, chief compliance officer; Adam Garetson, chief legal officer & gen. counsel; Cong Ly, chief tech. officer; Dean Sutton, chief strategy officer; Jeff Fitzgerald, v-p, sales, private wealth & corp. solutions; Sheona Docksteader, corp. sec.; Andrei Poliakov, pres., Coinberry

Capital Stock

	Authorized (shs.)	Outstanding (shs.)[1]
First Preferred	unlimited	nil
Common	unlimited	648,103,634

[1] At July 11, 2023

Major Shareholder - Mogo Inc. held 14% interest at July 10, 2023.

Price Range - WNDR/TSX

Year	Volume	High	Low	Close
2022	60,738,438	$2.80	$0.11	$0.14
2021	5,308,600	$3.01	$1.24	$2.22
2020	11,862	$2.18	$1.35	$2.18
2019	4,375	$2.23	$1.79	$1.83
2018	38,556	$5.24	$0.35	$1.92

Consolidation: 1-for-8.727 cons. in Aug. 2021
Recent Close: $0.16

Capital Stock Changes - In January 2023, private placement of 22,800,000 units (1 common share & 1 warrant) at $0.22 per unit was completed, with warrants exercisable at $0.30 per share for two years. In July 2023, 270,920,353 common shares were issued on acquisition of Coinsquare Ltd., and 117,924,334 common shares were issued on acquisition of CoinSmart Financial Inc. In addition, 15,863,554 common shares were issued to advisors.

In October 2021, private placement of 13,520,001 units (1 common share & ½ warrant) at $1.95 per unit was completed. In February 2022, private placement of 18,750,000 units (1 common share & ½ warrant) at $2.40 per unit was completed. In March 2022, 66,640,584 common shares were issued on acquisition of BitBuy. In July 2022, 25,825,645 common shares were issued on acquisition of Coinberry. In November 2022, 19,740,846 common shares were issued on acquisition of Blockchain Foundry Inc. Also during the 15-month period ended Dec. 31, 2022, common shares were issued as follows: 6,124,168 for services, 4,808,733 to settle contingent liabilities, 1,148,839 as restricted shares, 596,375 on exercise of options, 541,677 on exercise of warrants. In addition, 4,008,300 common shares were repurchased under a Normal Course Issued Bid.

Wholly Owned Subsidiaries

Bitbuy Holdings Inc., Ont.
- 100% int. in **Bitbuy Technologies Inc.**, Toronto, Ont.
  - 100% int. in **Bitbuy Gaming Inc.**, Ont.
  - 100% int. in **Blockchain Markets Inc.**, Ont.
  - 100% int. in **Twenty One Digital Inc.**, Ont.

Blockchain Foundry Inc., Toronto, Ont.
- 100% int. in **Blockchain Foundry 2018 Ltd.**, Canada.

Coinberry Limited, Toronto, Ont.
- 100% int. in **Coinberry USA, LLC**, United States.

CoinSmart Financial Inc., Toronto, Ont.
- 100% int. in **Simply Digital Technologies Inc.**, Toronto, Ont.
  - 100% int. in **S.D.T. OU**, Estonia.
  - 100% int. in **SDT USA Inc.**, United States.
  - 100% int. in **S.D.T. UAB**, Lithuania.

Coinsquare Ltd., Toronto, Ont.
- 100% int. in **Coin Capital Asset Management Ltd.**, Ont.
  - 100% int. in **Coin Capital Investment Management Inc.**, Ont.
- 100% int. in **Coinsquare Canada Ltd.**, Canada.
  - 100% int. in **Bigterminal.com Inc.**, Canada.
  - 100% int. in **Cryptiv Inc.**, Toronto, Ont.
  - 42.63% int. in **Tetra Trust Company**, Calgary, Alta.
- 100% int. in **Coinsquare Capital Markets Ltd.**, Canada.
- 100% int. in **Coinsquare Investments Ltd.**, Canada.

WonderFi Digital Inc., Vancouver, B.C.
WonderFi Entertainment Inc., B.C.
WonderFi Interactive Inc., B.C.

Financial Statistics

Periods ended:	15m Dec. 31/22[A]		8m Sept. 30/21[oA1]
	$000s	%Chg	$000s
Operating revenue	**9,088**	**n.a.**	**nil**
Salaries & benefits	12,871		135
General & admin expense	33,081		3,936
Stock-based compensation	9,919		1,068
Operating expense	**55,871**	**n.a.**	**5,140**
Operating income	**(46,783)**	**n.a.**	**(5,140)**
Deprec., depl. & amort.	5,515		2
Finance income	96		2
Finance costs, gross	28		nil
Write-downs/write-offs	(120,536)[2]		nil
Pre-tax income	**(175,565)**	**n.a.**	**(5,063)**
Income taxes	(3,411)		nil
Net income	**(172,154)**	**n.a.**	**(5,063)**
Cash & equivalent	10,252		20,347
Accounts receivable	2,390		95
Current assets	217,266		21,253
Long-term investments	537		n.a.
Fixed assets, net	432		9
Right-of-use assets	229		nil
Intangibles, net	41,993		4,110
Total assets	**260,457**	**n.a.**	**25,372**
Bank indebtedness	844		nil
Accts. pay. & accr. liabs	10,019		470
Current liabilities	210,314		535
Long-term debt, gross	70		nil
Long-term debt, net	70		nil
Shareholders' equity	45,123		24,837
Cash from oper. activs	**(25,269)**	**n.a.**	**(2,692)**
Cash from fin. activs	51,667		26,061
Cash from invest. activs	(36,493)		(3,053)
Net cash position	**10,252**	**n.a.**	**20,347**
Capital expenditures	(74)		(11)
	$		$
Earnings per share*	(1.20)		(0.15)
Cash flow per share*	(0.18)		(0.08)
	shs		shs
No. of shs. o/s*	214,637,855		60,910,825
Avg. no. of shs. o/s*	144,011,212		34,467,516
	%		%
Net profit margin	...		...
Return on equity	...		...
Return on assets	...		...

* Common
[o] Restated
[A] Reported in accordance with IFRS
[1] Results reflect the Aug. 30, 2021, reverse takeover acquisition of DeFi Ventures Inc. (concurrently renamed WonderFi Digital Inc.).
[2] Includes a $108,023,000 goodwill impairment related to Bitbuy.

Latest Results

Periods ended:	3m Mar. 31/23[A]
	$000s
Operating revenue	2,469
Net income	(7,629)
	$
Earnings per share*	(0.03)

* Common
[A] Reported in accordance with IFRS

Historical Summary
(as originally stated)

Fiscal Year	Oper. Rev.	Net Inc. Bef. Disc.	EPS*
	$000s	$000s	$
2022[A1]	9,088	(172,154)	(1.20)
2021[A2,3]	nil	(5,063)	(0.15)
2021[A4]	nil	(238)	(0.14)
2020[A]	nil	(154)	(0.10)
2019[A]	nil	(393)	(0.35)

* Common
[A] Reported in accordance with IFRS
[1] 15 months ended Dec. 31, 2022.
[2] 8 months ended Sept. 30, 2021.
[3] Results reflect the Aug. 30, 2021, reverse takeover acquisition of DeFi Ventures Inc. (concurrently renamed WonderFi Digital Inc.).
[4] Results for fiscal 2021 and prior fiscal years pertain to Austpro Energy Corporation.
Note: Adjusted throughout for 1-for-8.727 cons. in Aug. 2021

W.42 Woodbridge Ventures II Inc.

Symbol - WOOD.P **Exchange** - TSX-VEN **CUSIP** - 97888Q
Head Office - 7 Graymar Ave, Toronto, ON, M3H 3B5 **Telephone** - (416) 884-0840
Email - raphaeldanon@gmail.com
Investor Relations - Raphael Y. Danon (416) 884-0840

Auditors - MNP LLP C.A., Toronto, Ont.
Transfer Agents - TSX Trust Company, Toronto, Ont.
Profile - (Ont. 2021) Capital Pool Company.

Recent Merger and Acquisition Activity

Status: pending **Announced:** Nov. 17, 2022
Woodbridge Ventures II Inc. entered into a letter of intent for the Qualifying Transaction reverse takeover acquisition of Sparq Naturals, Inc., which manufactures inhalation devices that promote wellness by trading in nicotine and harmful chemicals for lab-tested, health-focused formulations that include vitamins, amino acids, botanicals and natural flavouring. Woodbridge would issue post-consolidated common shares on a to-be-determined basis.

Directors - Raphael Y. Danon, CEO, CFO & corp. sec., Toronto, Ont.; Carey Berdock; Patrick S. (Pat) Brigham, Toronto, Ont.

Capital Stock

	Authorized (shs.)	Outstanding (shs.)[1]
Common	unlimited	7,000,000

[1] At Apr. 27, 2023

Major Shareholder - Raphael Y. Danon held 25.71% interest at Nov. 16, 2021.

Price Range - WOOD.P/TSX-VEN

Year	Volume	High	Low	Close
2022	142,500	$0.15	$0.07	$0.07
2021	2,700	$0.15	$0.15	$0.15

Recent Close: $0.07

Capital Stock Changes - On Nov. 16, 2021, an initial public offering of 5,000,000 common shares was completed at 10¢ per share.

W.43 World Financial Split Corp.

Symbol - WFS **Exchange** - TSX **CUSIP** - 98146P
Head Office - c/o Mulvihill Capital Management Inc., Standard Life Centre, 2600-121 King St W, PO Box 113, Toronto, ON, M5H 3T9 **Telephone** - (416) 681-3966 **Toll-free** - (800) 725-7172 **Fax** - (416) 681-3901
Website - www.strathbridge.com
Email - jgermain@mulvihill.com
Investor Relations - John D. Germain (416) 681-3966
Auditors - Deloitte LLP C.A., Toronto, Ont.
Lawyers - Osler, Hoskin & Harcourt LLP, Toronto, Ont.
Transfer Agents - Computershare Trust Company of Canada Inc., Toronto, Ont.
Trustees - RBC Investor Services Trust, Toronto, Ont.
Investment Managers - Mulvihill Capital Management Inc., Toronto, Ont.
Managers - Mulvihill Capital Management Inc., Toronto, Ont.
Profile - (Ont. 2003) Holds a portfolio of common shares of financial services and real estate companies in order to provide preferred shareholders with quarterly distributions on a fixed, cumulative and preferential basis and class A shareholders with leveraged exposure to the performance of the portfolio holdings including increases or decreases in value and dividends paid.

The investment portfolio consists of common equity securities selected from the ten largest financial services or real estate companies by market capitalization in each of Canada, the U.S. and the rest of the world (the portfolio universe), having a minimum credit rating of A (excluding Canadian issuers) from Standard and Poor's or an equivalent rating agency. In addition, up to 25% of the net asset value may be invested in common equity securities of financial services or real estate companies not included in the portfolio universe provided such companies have a market capitalization of at least US$10 billion and, for non-Canadian issuers, a minimum credit rating of A- from Standard and Poor's or an equivalent rating agency.

The company has a scheduled termination date of June 30, 2025, which will be automatically extended for a further seven years and thereafter for additional successive periods of seven years. Upon termination, all outstanding preferred shares and class A shares will be redeemed.

The manager receives a management fee and an investment management fee at annual rates equal to 0.1% and 1.0%, respectively, of the net asset value of the company, calculated and payable monthly in arrears.

Top 10 holdings at Mar. 31, 2023 (as a percentage of net asset value):

Holding	Percentage
Royal Bank of Canada	5.7%
JPMorgan Chase & Co.	5.7%
Great-West Lifeco Inc.	5.3%
Sun Life Financial Inc.	5.2%
Manulife Financial Corporation	5.1%
National Bank of Canada	5.0%
Cboe Global Markets Inc.	4.9%
The Progressive Corporation	4.9%
The Toronto-Dominion Bank	4.2%
Canadian Imperial Bank of Commerce	3.9%

Directors - John P. Mulvihill, chr., CEO & corp. sec., Toronto, Ont.; John D. Germain, sr. v-p & CFO, Toronto, Ont.; Dr. Robert (Bob) Bell, Toronto, Ont.; Robert G. (Bob) Bertram, Aurora, Ont.; R. Peter Gillin, Toronto, Ont.

Capital Stock

	Authorized (shs.)	Outstanding (shs.)[1]
Preferred	unlimited	912,102[2]
Class A	unlimited	912,102
Class J	unlimited	100[2]

[1] At Dec. 31, 2022
[2] Classified as debt.

Preferred - Entitled to fixed cumulative preferential quarterly cash distributions of $0.13125 per share to yield 5.25% per annum on the original $10 issue price. Retractable in June of each year, together with a class A share, at a price equal to the net asset value (NAV) per unit (1 class A share and 1 preferred share). Retractable in any other month, without a class A share, at a price equal to 96% of the lesser of: (i) the difference between (a) the NAV per unit and (b) the cost to purchase a class A share in the market for cancellation; and (ii) the lesser of (a) the sum of the weighted average price per class A share and the weighted average price per preferred share on TSX for the 10 trading days prior the retraction date less the cost to purchase a class A share in the market for cancellation and (b) $10. All outstanding preferred shares will be redeemed on June 30, 2025, at a price per share equal to the lesser of: (i) the NAV per share; and (ii) $10. Rank in priority to the class A and class J shares with respect to the payment of distributions and the repayment of capital on the dissolution, liquidation or winding-up of the company. Non-voting.

Class A - Entitled to non-cumulative quarterly cash distributions targeted to be 8% per annum of the NAV per share. No distributions will be paid if the distributions payable on the preferred shares are in arrears or, after payment of the distribution, the NAV per unit would be less than $15. In addition, no special distributions will be paid if, after payment of the distribution, the NAV per unit would be less than $23.50 unless the company has to make such distributions to fully recover refundable taxes. Retractable in June of each year, together with a preferred share, at a price equal to the NAV per unit. Retractable in any other month, without a preferred share, at a price equal to 96% of the lesser of: (i) the difference between (a) the NAV per unit and (b) the cost to purchase a preferred share in the market for cancellation; and (ii) the difference between (a) the sum of the weighted average price per class A share and the weighted average price per preferred share on TSX for the 10 trading days prior the retraction date and (b) the cost to purchase a preferred share in the market for cancellation. If the NAV per unit is less than $10, the class A retraction price will be nil. All outstanding class A shares will be redeemed on June 30, 2025, at a price per share equal to the greater of: (i) the NAV per unit minus $10; and (ii) nil. Rank subordinate to the preferred shares but in priority to the class J shares with respect to the payment of distributions and the repayment of capital on the dissolution, liquidation or winding-up of the company. Non-voting.

Class J - Not entitled to receive distributions. Retractable and redeemable at any time at $1.00 per share. Rank subordinate to both preferred and class A shares with respect to distributions on the dissolution, liquidation or winding-up of the company. One vote per share.

Major Shareholder - World Financial Split Trust held 100% interest at Mar. 27, 2023.

Price Range - WFS/TSX

Year	Volume	High	Low	Close
2022	181,052	$3.45	$0.99	$1.84
2021	135,765	$3.15	$1.59	$2.90
2020	317,311	$3.35	$0.75	$1.75
2019	121,590	$3.31	$2.07	$3.08
2018	285,978	$5.30	$2.02	$2.07

Recent Close: $1.20

Capital Stock Changes - During 2022, 15,532 preferred shares and 15,532 class A shares were retracted.

Dividends

WFS.PR.A pfd cum. red. ret. Ra $0.525 pa Q

Financial Statistics

Periods ended:	12m Dec. 31/22[A]		12m Dec. 31/21[A]
	$000s	%Chg	$000s
Realized invest. gain (loss)	(406)		1,926
Unrealized invest. gain (loss)	(1,141)		564
Total revenue	**(1,224)**	**n.a.**	**2,849**
General & admin. expense	408		482
Operating expense	**408**	**-15**	**482**
Operating income	**(1,632)**	**n.a.**	**2,367**
Finance costs, gross	483		509
Pre-tax income	**(2,114)**	**n.a.**	**1,857**
Net income	**(2,114)**	**n.a.**	**1,857**
Cash & equivalent	175		213
Accounts receivable	17		20
Investments	10,091		12,339
Total assets	**10,283**	**-19**	**12,620**
Accts. pay. & accr. liabs	86		88
Debt	9,121		9,276
Shareholders' equity	1,053		3,186
Cash from oper. activs	**618**	**-64**	**1,697**
Cash from fin. activs	(657)		(1,594)
Net cash position	**175**	**-18**	**213**
	$		$
Earnings per share*	(2.30)		1.91
Cash flow per share*	0.67		1.74
Net asset value per share*	1.15		3.43
	shs		shs
No. of shs. o/s*	912,102		927,634
Avg. no. of shs. o/s*	920,423		972,592
	%		%
Net profit margin	n.m.		65.18
Return on equity	(99.74)		78.07
Return on assets	(14.24)		19.42

* Class A
[A] Reported in accordance with IFRS

Note: Net income reflects increase/decrease in net assets from operations.

Historical Summary
(as originally stated)

Fiscal Year	Total Rev.	Net Inc. Bef. Disc.	EPS*
	$000s	$000s	$
2022[A]	(1,224)	(2,114)	(2.30)
2021[A]	2,849	1,857	1.91
2020[A]	(1,321)	(2,296)	(2.14)
2019[A]	1,986	891	0.77
2018[A]	(1,948)	(3,470)	(2.10)

* Class A
[A] Reported in accordance with IFRS

X

X.1 X1 Entertainment Group Inc.

Symbol - XONE **Exchange** - CSE **CUSIP** - 983787
Head Office - 615-800 Pender St W, Vancouver, BC, V6C 2V6 **Telephone** - (604) 229-9445 **Toll-free** - (833) 923-3334
Website - www.x1ent.com
Email - info@x1ent.com
Investor Relations - Adam Giddens (604) 229-9445
Auditors - Smythe LLP C.A., Vancouver, B.C.
Lawyers - McMillan LLP, Vancouver, B.C.
Transfer Agents - Odyssey Trust Company, Vancouver, B.C.
Employees - 12 at May 19, 2022
Profile - (B.C. 2020) Seeking new business opportunities.

On Apr. 6, 2023, the company wound down operations of wholly owned **X1 Talent Corp.** (formerly Tyrus, LLC), a boutique talent management group for digital content creators. X1 Talent continues to have ongoing operations related to the collection of accounts receivable but would no longer be representing talent or engaging in new contracts with brands seeking talent.

On Mar. 17, 2023, the company sold the assets of ShiftRLE, inclusive of Octane.GG, in exchange for the vendors and ongoing service providers forgoing any termination payments in connection with their consulting agreements at a value of US$35,250.

On Mar. 9, 2023, the company ceased operations of wholly owned **Rix.GG Europe Ltd.**, which holds and operates the company's esports franchise. Rix currently has one team competing in League of Legends: Wild Rift. The team would no longer compete in Wild Rift effective March 2023 as a result of Riot Games' recent announcement that it would discontinue support for Wild Rift esports operations outside of Asia. As this team represents the sole team competing within the Rix franchise, the operations supporting the team are being terminated as well.

In November 2022, the company incorporated the assets of Octane.GG into ShiftRLE to create a single website dedicated to Rocket League news, reporting and statistical analysis operating under the name, Shift.

On Oct. 4, 2022, the company acquired the assets of Octane.GG, an online fan statistics platform focused on the video game, Rocket League, for US$35,000 cash, US$17,500 of which was paid on closing, and the remaining US$17,500 was paid during the second quarter of fiscal 2023.

On Aug. 10, 2022, the company acquired the assets of ShiftRLE including websites, social media accounts, goodwill, and intellectual property for US$50,000 cash, issuance of 333,333 common shares and a 7% share of gross revenues in the first three years following closing to a maximum of US$250,000. ShiftRLE is an online news outlet focused on the popular video game Rocket League.

On Aug. 5, 2022, the company acquired **Tyrus, LLC**, an influencer management firm empowering gamers, content creators and influencers, for US$150,000 in cash, issuance of 555,555 common shares at a deemed price of 45¢ per share and a bonus payment of US$100,000, payable if Tyrus reaches US$1,750,000 in its first full year of revenue, which may be settled in cash or common shares at the option of the company.

Predecessor Detail - Name changed from X1 Esports and Entertainment Ltd., Oct. 19, 2022.

Directors - Adam Giddens, CEO, B.C.; Oliver Bales; Latika D. Prasad, Vancouver, B.C.

Other Exec. Officers - Bobby S. Dhaliwal, CFO

Capital Stock

	Authorized (shs.)	Outstanding (shs.)[1]
Common	unlimited	47,577,491

[1] At Apr. 28, 2023

Major Shareholder - Widely held at Mar. 2, 2023.

Price Range - XONE/CSE

Year	Volume	High	Low	Close
2022	9,759,511	$0.48	$0.05	$0.07

Recent Close: $0.01

Capital Stock Changes - On June 30, 2022, an initial public offering of 6,914,820 units (1 common share & 1 warrant) at 45¢ per unit was completed. On Aug. 4, 2022, 555,555 common shares were issued pursuant to the acquisition of Tyrus, LLC. On Aug. 10, 2022, 333,333 common shares were issued pursuant to the acquisition of ShiftRLE. Also during fiscal 2022, 66,667 common shares were issued for financing fees.

Wholly Owned Subsidiaries

Forward Agency Ltd., United Kingdom.
Mechanics Agency Ltd., United Kingdom. Inactive.
Rix.GG Europe Ltd., Malta. Inactive.
X1 Talent Corp., United States. Inactive. Formerly Tyrus, LLC.

Financial Statistics

Periods ended:	12m Aug. 31/22[A]		50w Aug. 31/21[A1]
	$000s	%Chg	$000s
Operating revenue	**391**	**n.m.**	**27**
Salaries & benefits	417		307
General & admin expense	2,694		1,531
Stock-based compensation	317		nil
Operating expense	**3,427**	**+86**	**1,838**
Operating income	**(3,036)**	**n.a.**	**(1,811)**
Pre-tax income	**(3,065)**	**n.a.**	**(2,015)**
Net income	**(3,065)**	**n.a.**	**(2,015)**
Cash & equivalent	1,624		1,910
Accounts receivable	274		19
Current assets	2,416		2,147
Intangibles, net	603		nil
Total assets	**3,023**	**+41**	**2,147**
Bank indebtedness	36		nil
Accts. pay. & accr. liabs	478		143
Current liabilities	708		143
Shareholders' equity	2,252		2,004
Cash from oper. activs	**(2,956)**	**n.a.**	**(1,911)**
Cash from fin. activs	2,814		1,974
Cash from invest. activs	(111)		1,839
Net cash position	**1,624**	**-15**	**1,910**
	$		$
Earnings per share*	(0.08)		(0.15)
Cash flow per share*	(0.07)		(0.15)
	shs		shs
No. of shs. o/s*	47,577,491		38,257,688
Avg. no. of shs. o/s*	40,746,977		13,018,570
	%		%
Net profit margin	(783.89)		n.m.
Return on equity	(144.03)		n.m.
Return on assets	(118.57)		n.a.

* Common
[A] Reported in accordance with IFRS
[1] Results reflect the Apr. 16, 2021, reverse takeover acquisition of Rix.GG Europe LLC (from Sept. 16, 2020, the incorporation date of Rix.GG).

Latest Results

Periods ended:	6m Feb. 28/23[A]		6m Feb. 28/22[A]
	$000s	%Chg	$000s
Operating revenue	308	+51	204
Net income	(3,171)	n.a.	(1,380)
	$		$
Earnings per share*	(0.07)		(0.04)

* Common
[A] Reported in accordance with IFRS

X.2 XBiotech Inc.

Symbol - XBIT **Exchange** - NASDAQ **CUSIP** - 98400H
Head Office - 5217 Winnebago Lane, Austin, TX, United States, 78744 **Telephone** - (512) 386-2900 **Fax** - (512) 386-5505
Website - www.xbiotech.com
Email - wwei@xbiotech.com
Investor Relations - Wenyi Wei (737) 207-4600
Auditors - Ernst & Young LLP C.P.A., Austin, Tex.
Lawyers - Quarles & Brady LLP, Naples, Fla.; Stikeman Elliott LLP, Vancouver, B.C.
Transfer Agents - American Stock Transfer & Trust Company, LLC, New York, N.Y.
Employees - 96 at June 30, 2022
Profile - (B.C. 2005; orig. Can., 2005) Discovers, develops and commercializes therapeutic antibodies based on its True Human™ proprietary technology for treating a variety of diseases.

The company is advancing a pipeline of therapies by harnessing naturally occurring antibodies from patients with immunity to certain diseases. To develop a True Human™ antibody therapy, donors are screened to find an individual that has a specific antibody that matches the desired characteristics needed to obtain the intended medical benefit. White blood cells from such individuals are obtained, the unique gene that produced the antibody is cloned, and the genetic information is used to produce an exact replica of the antibody sequence. Patents relating to the composition of matter and methods of use of the company's True Human™ antibodies are developed internally, and antibodies are manufactured using a proprietary expression system licensed from **Lonza Sales AG.**

Lead products under development include Natrunix™, a new anti-interleukin-1alpha (IL-1a) antibody candidate to be used in all areas of medicine with the exception of dermatology. Has received approval from U.S. Food and Drug Administration for clinical studies using Natrunix to treat pancreatic cancer in combination with ONIVYDE/5-FU (Phase I/II); for colorectal cancer with Trifluridine/Tipiracil (Phase II/III); for reducing brain injury after stroke (Phase I/II); and for rheumatoid arthritis (Phase I/II). Also developing product candidates against C. difficile bacteria, the cause of debilitationg and deadly intestinal infections; S.aureus infections (bacteremia), which has immune evasion mechanism that can allow it to overwhelm defense and establish uncontrolled and lethal infections; and through collaboration with **BioBridge Global**, the company is developing FLUVID™ for treating illness caused by combined infections with influenza and COVID-19 by combining influenza and COVID-19 True Human antibodies.

The company is also using its proprietary manufacturing technology to manufacture bermekimab for **Janssen Biotech Inc.**, a subsidiary **Johnson & Johnson Inc.**, under a one-year supply agreement ending Dec. 31, 2023. The agreement was valued at US$4,700,000.

The company has 63,000-sq.-ft. manufacturing and research facility in Austin, Tex.

Directors - John Simard, founder, chr., pres. & CEO; Dr. Peter Libby; Donald H. MacAdam, Port Dover, Ont.; W. Thorpe McKenzie; Jan-Paul Waldin, Ont.

Other Exec. Officers - Dr. Sushma Shivaswamy, chief scientific officer; Norma I. Gonzalez, v-p, quality; Qian Wu, v-p, quality control

Capital Stock

	Authorized (shs.)	Outstanding (shs.)[1]
Preferred	unlimited	nil
Common	unlimited	30,439,275

[1] At Aug. 9, 2022

Major Shareholder - John Simard held 16.3% interest and Thomas Gut held 12.9% interest at Mar. 15, 2023.

Price Range - XBIT/NASDAQ

Year	Volume	High	Low	Close
2022	7,665,545	US$11.90	US$3.01	US$3.51
2021	8,873,232	US$20.74	US$10.80	US$11.13
2020	32,942,977	US$26.40	US$8.75	US$15.65
2019	16,615,284	US$22.95	US$4.78	US$18.67
2018	7,099,369	US$6.50	US$2.13	US$5.08

Wholly Owned Subsidiaries

XBiotech Germany GmbH, Germany.
XBiotech USA, Inc., Del.

Financial Statistics

Periods ended:	12m Dec. 31/21[A]		12m Dec. 31/20[A]
	US$000s	%Chg	US$000s
Operating revenue	**18,394**	**-58**	**43,997**
Cost of goods sold	5,538		33,062
Salaries & benefits	16,206		6,590
Research & devel. expense	14,013		3,348
General & admin expense	607		4,454
Stock-based compensation	4,464		12,581
Operating expense	**43,476**	**-28**	**60,035**
Operating income	**(25,082)**	**n.a.**	**(16,038)**
Deprec., depl. & amort.	2,648		2,238
Finance income	467		2,456
Pre-tax income	**(25,458)**	**n.a.**	**(12,827)**
Income taxes	(8,044)		(1,606)
Net income	**(17,414)**	**n.a.**	**(11,221)**
Cash & equivalent	236,983		237,366
Accounts receivable	nil		4,113
Current assets	246,870		325,875
Fixed assets, net	28,307		27,336
Total assets	**275,177**	**-22**	**353,744**
Accts. pay. & accr. liabs	3,443		3,842
Current liabilities	3,453		3,984
Shareholders' equity	269,385		348,639
Cash from oper. activs	**69,445**	**n.a.**	**(65,149)**
Cash from fin. activs	(67,008)		(409,724)
Cash from invest. activs	(3,525)		(3,727)
Net cash position	**236,983**	**0**	**237,366**
Capital expenditures	(3,525)		(3,727)
	US$		US$
Earnings per share*	(0.58)		(0.36)
Cash flow per share*	2.31		(2.11)
	shs		shs
No. of shs. o/s*	30,439,275		29,304,396
Avg. no. of shs. o/s*	30,043,380		30,823,458
	%		%
Net profit margin	(94.67)		(25.50)
Return on equity	(5.64)		(2.03)
Return on assets	(5.54)		(1.92)
No. of employees (FTEs)	97		91

* Common
[A] Reported in accordance with U.S. GAAP

Latest Results

Periods ended:	6m June 30/22[A]		6m June 30/21[A]
	US$000s	%Chg	US$000s
Operating revenue	2,030	-78	9,375
Net income	(17,039)	n.a.	(7,686)
	US$		US$
Earnings per share*	(0.56)		(0.26)

* Common
[A] Reported in accordance with U.S. GAAP

Historical Summary
(as originally stated)

Fiscal Year	Oper. Rev. US$000s	Net Inc. Bef. Disc. US$000s	EPS* US$
2021[A]	18,394	(17,414)	(0.58)
2020[A]	43,997	(11,221)	(0.36)
2019[A]	nil	668,629	17.17
2018[A]	nil	(21,138)	(0.59)
2017[A]	nil	(33,150)	(0.95)

* Common
[A] Reported in accordance with U.S. GAAP

X.3 XORTX Therapeutics Inc.

Symbol - XRTX **Exchange** - TSX-VEN **CUSIP** - 98420Q
Head Office - 3710 33 St NW, Calgary, AB, T2L 2M1 **Telephone** - (403) 455-7727
Website - www.xortx.com
Email - adavidoff@xortx.com
Investor Relations - Dr. Allen Davidoff (403) 607-2621
Auditors - Smythe LLP C.A., Vancouver, B.C.
Transfer Agents - TSX Trust Company, Vancouver, B.C.
Profile - (B.C. 2011) Develops therapies to treat progressive kidney disease modulated by aberrant purine and uric acid metabolism in orphan disease indications such as autosomal dominant polycystic kidney disease and type 2 diabetic nephropathy, and acute kidney injury associated with respiratory virus infection.

Advance programs include XRx-008 for the treatment of autosomal dominant polycystic kidney disease (ADPKD); and XRx-101 (a new formulation of Oxypurinol) as treatment for acute kidney injury associated with respiratory virus infection and associated health consequences. XRx-008 is a proprietary formulation of oxypurinol designed to decrease and maintain serum uric acid levels intended to treat certain prevalent conditions including pre-diabetes, insulin resistance and metabolic syndrome, as well as the health consequences of diabetes, including diabetic nephropathy and fatty liver disease, by lowering serum uric acid levels. XRx-101 acts as an anti-viral, uric acid lowering treatment and organ-protective therapy by inhibiting xanthine oxidase expression due to hypoxia, or tissue destruction, thereby preventing increased serum uric acid concentration from reaching saturation levels at which uric acid crystals could trigger acute organ injury.

Other program includes XRx-225, a pre-clinical stage program for the treatment of type 2 diabetic nephropathy.

The company has been granted U.S. and European patents for the use of all uric acid lowering agents to treat insulin resistance or diabetic nephropathy; for metabolic syndrome, diabetes and fatty liver disease; and for unique proprietary formulations of xanthine oxidase inhibitors. In addition, the U.S. FDA has granted oxypurinol an orphan drug designation to treat ADPKD.

Predecessor Detail - Name changed from APAC Resources Inc., Jan. 11, 2018, following reverse takeover acquisition of XORTX Pharma Corp.

Directors - Anthony J. Giovinazzo, chr., Toronto, Ont.; Dr. Allen Davidoff, pres. & CEO, Alta.; William (Bill) Farley, N.Y.; Ian M. Klassen, Vancouver, B.C.; Jacqueline H. R. Le Saux, Toronto, Ont.; Dr. Raymond Pratt, Md.; Paul J. Van Damme, Toronto, Ont.

Other Exec. Officers - James N. (Jim) Fairbairn, CFO; Dr. Stacy Evans, chief bus. officer; Dr. Stephen Haworth, CMO; Brian Mangal, v-p, bus. devel.

Capital Stock

	Authorized (shs.)	Outstanding (shs.)[1]
Common	unlimited	17,989,687

[1] At May 16, 2023

Major Shareholder - Widely held at May 16, 2023.

Price Range - XRTX/TSX-VEN

Year	Volume	High	Low	Close
2022	2,166,484	$3.00	$0.97	$1.12
2021	12,366,710	$9.98	$1.53	$2.50
2020	845,369	$3.17	$1.12	$1.70
2019	342,816	$3.46	$1.23	$1.88
2018	365,218	$5.87	$1.53	$1.53

Consolidation: 1-for-11.74 cons. in Sept. 2021
Recent Close: $0.86
Capital Stock Changes - In October 2022, public offering of 1,400,000 units (1 common share & 1 warrant) at US$1.00 per unit was completed. Also during 2022, 641,000 common shares were issued on exercise of warrants.

Wholly Owned Subsidiaries

XORTX Pharma Corp., Calgary, Alta.

Financial Statistics

Periods ended:	12m Dec. 31/22[A]		12m Dec. 31/21[A]
	$000s	%Chg	$000s
Salaries & benefits	842		286
Research & devel. expense	8,808		853
General & admin expense	3,027		1,993
Stock-based compensation	633		499
Operating expense	**13,310**	**+266**	**3,632**
Operating income	**(13,310)**	**n.a.**	**(3,632)**
Deprec., depl. & amort.	75		18
Finance costs, gross	n.a.		6
Finance costs, net	(138)		n.a.
Pre-tax income	**(9,485)**	**n.a.**	**(1,652)**
Net income	**(9,485)**	**n.a.**	**(1,652)**
Cash & equivalent	14,126		18,851
Accounts receivable	111		52
Current assets	14,750		20,173
Fixed assets, net	22		nil
Right-of-use assets	103		n.a.
Intangibles, net	271		256
Total assets	**16,753**	**-24**	**22,036**
Accts. pay. & accr. liabs	1,961		701
Current liabilities	2,050		701
Long-term lease liabilities	16		n.a.
Shareholders' equity	9,466		16,738
Cash from oper. activs	**(11,968)**	**n.a.**	**(6,063)**
Cash from fin. activs	6,431		24,457
Cash from invest. activs	(60)		(40)
Net cash position	**14,126**	**-25**	**18,851**
Capital expenditures	(26)		nil
	$		$
Earnings per share*	(0.71)		(0.17)
Cash flow per share*	(0.90)		(0.62)
	shs		shs
No. of shs. o/s*	15,030,687		12,989,687
Avg. no. of shs. o/s*	13,319,226		9,847,641
	%		%
Net profit margin	n.a.		n.a.
Return on equity	(72.39)		(18.36)
Return on assets	(48.91)		(13.53)

* Common
[A] Reported in accordance with IFRS

Latest Results

Periods ended:	3m Mar. 31/23[A]		3m Mar. 31/22[DA]
	$000s	%Chg	$000s
Net income	(1,832)	n.a.	(2,704)
	$		$
Earnings per share*	(0.11)		(0.21)

* Common
[D] Restated
[A] Reported in accordance with IFRS

Historical Summary
(as originally stated)

Fiscal Year	Oper. Rev. $000s	Net Inc. Bef. Disc. $000s	EPS* $
2022[A]	nil	(9,485)	(0.71)
2021[A]	nil	(1,652)	(0.17)
2020[A]	nil	(1,285)	(0.23)
2019[A]	nil	(630)	(0.12)
2018[A1]	nil	(3,776)	(0.70)

* Common
[A] Reported in accordance with IFRS
[1] Results reflect the Jan. 10, 2018, reverse takeover acquisition of XORTX Pharma Corp.
Note: Adjusted throughout for 1-for-11.74 cons. in Sept. 2021

X.4 XR Immersive Tech Inc.

Symbol - VRAR **Exchange** - CSE **CUSIP** - 98383L
Head Office - 240-577 Great Northern Way, Vancouver, BC, V5T 1E1 **Telephone** - (604) 834-2968 **Fax** - (604) 428-7052
Website - www.immersivetech.co
Email - srempel@aroconsulting.ca
Investor Relations - Sheri Rempel (604) 428-7050
Auditors - SRCO Professional Corporation C.A., Richmond Hill, Ont.
Transfer Agents - Odyssey Trust Company, Vancouver, B.C.
Profile - (B.C. 2016) Designs, builds and installs immersive escape room attractions, utilizing technologies from the video game development, theme park engineering and virtual reality/augmented reality/mixed reality (VR/AR/MR) industries.

The attractions are developed for customers for a variety of purposes such as brand engagement, product announcement and activation events, edutainment opportunities, revenue generating attractions for family entertainment centres, and corporate training and events.

Flagship product is UNCONTAINED, a standalone plug and play VR attraction built in a 40-foot container, with 5D environmental haptics including motion floor, pneumatic air blasts, temperature augmentation effects, scents and physical object interaction. UNCONTAINED is also capable of mining various cryptocurrencies in off-hours, earning operators additional income while the unit is sitting idle. The company has developed an in-house hyper-immersive game for UNCONTAINED called Deep Signal, which offers a multiplayer sci-fi narrative experience taking players on an interstellar journey into unexplored galaxies through the Pathseeker Titan ship.

Through wholly owned **Synthesis VR Inc.**, the company also provides complete management, game enhancement and licensing software platform for location-based VR (LBVR) entertainment centres. The platform features support for free roam games, multiple experiences, mixed reality, memberships, video recording and streaming. Synthesis nearly has 400 operators using the software to manage their centres and nearly 400 VR games in its marketplace being licensed to these operators.

The company's customers include **Intel Corporation**, **Bayer AG**, **Capital One**, **The Bank of Nova Scotia**, the U.S. Food and Drug Administration and **Allegiant Airlines**.

Predecessor Detail - Name changed from Fantasy 360 Technologies Inc., Feb. 3, 2022.

Directors - A. Shabeer Sinnalebbe, CEO; Sheri Rempel, CFO & corp. sec., Vancouver, B.C.; Shafin Diamond; Kamen Petrov; Alexandros (Alexander) Tzilios, North Vancouver, B.C.

Other Exec. Officers - Adrian Duke, chief design officer

Capital Stock

	Authorized (shs.)	Outstanding (shs.)[1]
Common	unlimited	90,393,641

[1] At Nov. 29, 2022

Major Shareholder - Victory Square Technologies Inc. held 58.75% interest at June 30, 2022.

Price Range - VRAR/CSE

Year	Volume	High	Low	Close
2022	10,729,607	$0.28	$0.03	$0.03
2021	3,474,150	$0.83	$0.24	$0.27

Recent Close: $0.03
Capital Stock Changes - On Feb. 22, 2022, 12,285,714 common shares were issued pursuant to the acquisition of Synthesis VR Inc.

Wholly Owned Subsidiaries

Synthesis VR Inc., Calif.

Investments

AlphaGen Intelligence Corp., Vancouver, B.C. (see separate coverage)

Financial Statistics

Periods ended:	12m Dec. 31/21[A]		12m Dec. 31/20[A1]
	$000s	%Chg	$000s
Operating revenue	**108**	**-93**	**1,441**
Cost of goods sold	96		889
Salaries & benefits	688		242
Research & devel. expense	1,609		...
General & admin expense	1,427		420
Stock-based compensation	1,087		nil
Operating expense	**4,907**	**+641**	**662**
Operating income	**(4,799)**	**n.a.**	**779**
Deprec., depl. & amort.	13		6
Finance costs, gross	65		6
Pre-tax income	**(4,345)**	**n.a.**	**81**
Net income	**(4,345)**	**n.a.**	**81**
Cash & equivalent	2,933		192
Inventories	144		nil
Accounts receivable	17		64
Current assets	3,341		295
Long-term investments	nil		3
Fixed assets, net	33		4
Right-of-use assets	45		n.a.
Total assets	**3,419**	**+305**	**845**
Bank indebtedness	2,560		nil
Accts. pay. & accr. liabs	294		228
Current liabilities	4,052		1,500
Long-term debt, gross	40		34
Long-term debt, net	40		34
Long-term lease liabilities	34		nil
Shareholders' equity	(707)		(689)
Cash from oper. activs	**(3,266)**	**n.a.**	**(225)**
Cash from fin. activs	6,042		395
Cash from invest. activs	(36)		nil
Net cash position	**2,933**	**n.m.**	**192**
Capital expenditures	(36)		nil
	$		$
Earnings per share*	(0.06)		0.00
Cash flow per share*	(0.05)		(0.00)
	shs		shs
No. of shs. o/s*	76,050,803		63,308,820
Avg. no. of shs. o/s*	69,685,094		63,308,820
	%		%
Net profit margin	n.m.		5.62
Return on equity	n.m.		n.m.
Return on assets	(200.75)		15.85

* Common
[A] Reported in accordance with IFRS
[1] Shares and per share figures adjusted to reflect 2.6378675-for-1 split effective Mar. 12, 2021.

Latest Results

Periods ended:	6m June 30/22[A]		6m June 30/21[A]
	$000s	%Chg	$000s
Operating revenue	525	n.m.	41
Net income	(3,467)	n.a.	(1,418)
	$		$
Earnings per share*	(0.04)		(0.02)

* Common
[A] Reported in accordance with IFRS

Historical Summary
(as originally stated)

Fiscal Year	Oper. Rev.	Net Inc. Bef. Disc.	EPS*
	$000s	$000s	$
2021[A]	108	(4,345)	(0.06)
2020[A1]	1,441	81	0.00
2019[A1]	2,029	(588)	(0.01)

* Common
[A] Reported in accordance with IFRS
[1] Shares and per share figures adjusted to reflect 2.6378675-for-1 split effective Mar. 12, 2021.

X.5 XRApplied Technologies Inc.

Symbol - XRA **Exchange** - CSE (S) **CUSIP** - 98422K
Head Office - 908-510 Burrard St, Vancouver, BC, V6C 3A8 **Telephone** - (604) 608-6314 **Toll-free** - (877) 324-7245 **Fax** - (604) 682-1666
Website - xrapplied.com
Email - grw@grwinc.ca
Investor Relations - Geoffrey R. Watson (604) 682-1643
Auditors - Baker Tilly WM LLP C.A., Vancouver, B.C.
Lawyers - Thomas, Rondeau LLP, Vancouver, B.C.
Transfer Agents - Computershare Trust Company of Canada Inc., Vancouver, B.C.
Profile - (B.C. 2008) Provides augmented reality (AR)/virtual reality (VR) e-commerce applications to businesses through a suite of proprietary products and services.
Offers a vertically agnostic proprietary Software Development Kit (SDK) platform for implementation of augmented reality/virtual reality/mixed reality (AR/VR/MR) experiences. SDK can be used in many sectors but the company is initially targeting AR/VR cataloguing for e-commerce, AR/VRgames and the gamification of toys.
Using its SDK platform, the company has developed three separate products to demonstrate the various uses of the SDK platform: (i) a commercial app (the Technology News app); (ii) a retail /commercial consumer product (ARFlooring Made Easy); and (iii) a VR game (Balloon Pop). Also in the process of adapting a fourth product to become a VR game (The Rifters AR Shooting Game).
In the longer term, the majority of revenue was expected to be earned from software-as-a-service (SaaS) and platform-as-a-service (PaaS) contracts, where as the SDK platform would be used to create XR games for third parties in return for development fees and future revenue sharing.
Common suspended from CSE, Dec. 5, 2022.
Predecessor Detail - Name changed from Zadar Ventures Ltd., July 19, 2021, following the acquisition of immersive technology solutions provider XRApplied S.A.S.
Directors - Mark T. Tommasi, chr., North Vancouver, B.C.; Geoffrey R. (Geoff) Watson, CFO & corp. sec., North Vancouver, B.C.; Kostiantyn (Constantine) Makeiev, chief tech. officer, Berlin, Germany; Oleksiy (Aleksey) Andriychenko, Berlin, Germany; Jean Vignon, France
Other Exec. Officers - Lior Ishai, CEO

Capital Stock

	Authorized (shs.)	Outstanding (shs.)[1]
Common	unlimited	68,544,584

[1] At Jan. 28, 2022

Major Shareholder - Oleksiy (Aleksey) Andriychenko held 14.92% interest and Kostiantyn (Constantine) Makeiev held 14.92% interest at July 23, 2021.

Price Range - ZAD/TSX-VEN (D)

Year	Volume	High	Low	Close
2022	3,566,639	$0.29	$0.02	$0.03
2021	3,736,052	$0.45	$0.23	$0.24
2020	3,416,837	$0.35	$0.10	$0.30
2019	1,599,629	$0.25	$0.08	$0.09
2018	2,893,418	$1.25	$0.25	$0.25

Consolidation: 1-for-10 cons. in Apr. 2019
Recent Close: $0.03

Wholly Owned Subsidiaries

XRApplied S.A.S., France.

Investments

Global Resources Investment Trust plc

Financial Statistics

Periods ended:	12m July 31/21[A]		12m July 31/20[□A]
	$000s	%Chg	$000s
General & admin expense	688		334
Operating expense	**688**	**+106**	**334**
Operating income	**(688)**	**n.a.**	**(334)**
Deprec., depl. & amort.	690		42
Finance costs, gross	4		3
Pre-tax income	**(1,357)**	**n.a.**	**(313)**
Net inc. bef. disc. opers	**(1,357)**	**n.a.**	**(313)**
Income from disc. opers	nil		(6)
Net income	**(1,357)**	**n.a.**	**(319)**
Cash & equivalent	814		229
Accounts receivable	206		110
Current assets	1,211		740
Right-of-use assets	210		49
Intangibles, net	11,744		nil
Explor./devel. properties	nil		28
Total assets	**13,165**	**n.m.**	**816**
Bank indebtedness	1		1
Accts. pay. & accr. liabs	316		50
Current liabilities	398		136
Long-term lease liabilities	162		6
Shareholders' equity	12,605		674
Cash from oper. activs	**(672)**	**n.a.**	**(726)**
Cash from fin. activs	1,101		592
Cash from invest. activs	190		(6)
Net cash position	**793**	**+305**	**196**
Capital expenditures	nil		(6)
	$		$
Earnings per share*	(0.05)		(0.02)
Cash flow per share*	(0.02)		(0.04)
	shs		shs
No. of shs. o/s*	67,294,584		23,429,134
Avg. no. of shs. o/s*	28,420,218		19,591,702
	%		%
Net profit margin	n.a.		n.a.
Return on equity	(20.44)		(62.10)
Return on assets	(19.35)		(48.44)

* Common
[□] Restated
[A] Reported in accordance with IFRS

Latest Results

Periods ended:	3m Oct. 31/21[A]		3m Oct. 31/20[A]
	$000s	%Chg	$000s
Net income	(2,412)	n.a.	(78)
	$		$
Earnings per share*	(0.04)		(0.00)

* Common
[A] Reported in accordance with IFRS

Historical Summary
(as originally stated)

Fiscal Year	Oper. Rev.	Net Inc. Bef. Disc.	EPS*
	$000s	$000s	$
2021[A]	nil	(1,357)	(0.05)
2020[A]	nil	(319)	(0.02)
2019[A]	nil	(602)	(0.05)
2018[A]	nil	(1,418)	(0.20)
2017[A]	nil	(829)	(0.10)

* Common
[A] Reported in accordance with IFRS
Note: Adjusted throughout for 1-for-10 cons. in Apr. 2019

X.6 XS Financial Inc.

Symbol - XSF **Exchange** - CSE **CUSIP** - 983861
Head Office - 1901 Avenue of the Stars, Suite 120, Los Angeles, CA, United States, 90067 **Telephone** - (310) 683-2336
Website - www.xsfinancial.com
Email - ir@xsfinancial.com
Investor Relations - Antony Radbod (310) 683-2336
Auditors - Macias Gini & O'Connell LLP C.P.A., San Francisco, Calif.
Transfer Agents - Odyssey Trust Company, Calgary, Alta.
Profile - (B.C. 2009) Provides capital financing solutions to the cannabis and hemp industries in the United States.
Financing provided by the company are used for equipment and other qualified capital expenditures of cannabis and hemp operators, including cultivators, processors, manufacturers and testing laboratories. Solutions include equipment-specific leasing, sale-leasebacks, purchasing solutions and equipment procurement solutions. The company has partnered with more than 250 original equipment manufacturers (OEMs) which provide access to various equipment and financing options.
Predecessor Detail - Name changed from Xtraction Services Holdings Corp., June 26, 2020.
Directors - David Kivitz, pres. & CEO, Los Angeles, Calif.; Antony Radbod, COO, Los Angeles, Calif.; Stephen Christoffersen, Newport Beach, Calif.; Gary Herman, New York, N.Y.; Andrew Mitchell
Other Exec. Officers - Justin Vuong, CFO; Trevor Kross, v-p, procurement

Capital Stock

	Authorized (shs.)	Outstanding (shs.)[1]
Subordinate Voting	unlimited	75,526,443
Proportionate Voting	unlimited	28,358

[1] At Nov. 28, 2022

Subordinate Voting - One vote per share.
Proportionate Voting - Each convertible, at the holder's option, into 1,000 subordinate voting shares. 1,000 votes per share.
Major Shareholder - Archytas Ventures, LLC held 18.5% interest and Greenlane Holdings, Inc. held 10.2% interest at July 12, 2022.

Price Range - XSF/CSE

Year	Volume	High	Low	Close
2022	13,750,740	$0.22	$0.04	$0.07
2021	26,812,042	$0.54	$0.15	$0.21
2020	8,292,750	$0.43	$0.10	$0.24
2019	3,225,494	$0.80	$0.17	$0.28
2018	204,520	$1.57	$0.50	$0.69

Consolidation: 1-for-6.262 cons. in Sept. 2019
Recent Close: $0.02

Wholly Owned Subsidiaries

CA Licensed Lenders LLC, Calif.
CSI Princesa Inc., Ont.
XSF SPC, LLC, Del.
Xtraction Services, Inc., Clermont, Fla.

Investments

Greenlane Holdings, Inc.

Financial Statistics

Periods ended:	12m Dec. 31/21[A]		12m Dec. 31/20[A]
	US$000s	%Chg	US$000s
Operating revenue	**3,159**	**+367**	**676**
Salaries & benefits	1,204		259
General & admin expense	2,178		1,934
Stock-based compensation	688		341
Operating expense	**4,070**	**+61**	**2,534**
Operating income	**(911)**	**n.a.**	**(1,858)**
Deprec., depl. & amort.	17		95
Finance costs, net	2,321		845
Pre-tax income	**(2,985)**	**n.a.**	**(5,053)**
Net income	**(2,985)**	**n.a.**	**(5,053)**
Cash & equivalent	17,205		862
Current assets	26,805		2,396
Fixed assets, net	27		45
Total assets	**52,307**	**+617**	**7,294**
Accts. pay. & accr. liabs	4,387		3,414
Current liabilities	7,482		4,476
Long-term debt, gross	35,621		3,090
Long-term debt, net	34,334		2,284
Equity portion of conv. debs	931		940
Shareholders' equity	9,418		534
Cash from oper. activs	**(29,650)**	**n.a.**	**(3,476)**
Cash from fin. activs	45,420		206
Cash from invest. activs	87		1,347
Net cash position	**17,119**	**n.m.**	**546**
Capital expenditures	nil		(252)
Capital disposals	nil		605
	US$		US$
Earnings per share*	(0.03)		(0.10)
Cash flow per share*	(0.31)		(0.07)
	shs		shs
No. of shs. o/s*	103,884,443		55,444,724
Avg. no. of shs. o/s*	95,509,221		53,145,555
	%		%
Net profit margin	(94.49)		(747.49)
Return on equity	(59.99)		n.m.
Return on assets	(10.02)		n.a.
Foreign sales percent	100		100

* Subord. Vtg.
[A] Reported in accordance with IFRS

Latest Results

Periods ended:	6m June 30/22[A]		6m June 30/21[A]
	US$000s	%Chg	US$000s
Operating revenue	2,946	+201	978
Net income	(5,315)	n.a.	(884)
	US$		US$
Earnings per share*	(0.05)		(0.01)

* Subord. Vtg.
[A] Reported in accordance with IFRS

Historical Summary
(as originally stated)

Fiscal Year	Oper. Rev.	Net Inc. Bef. Disc.	EPS*
	US$000s	US$000s	US$
2021[A]	3,159	(2,985)	(0.03)
2020[A]	676	(5,053)	(0.10)
2019[A1]	2,290	(6,947)	(0.18)
	$000s	$000s	$
2019[A2]	nil	(102)	(0.03)
2018[A]	nil	(110)	(0.06)

* Subord. Vtg.
[A] Reported in accordance with IFRS
[1] Results reflect the Sept. 12, 2019, reverse takeover acquisition of Xtraction Services, Inc.
[2] Results for fiscal 2019 and prior fiscal years pertain to Caracara Silver Inc.
Note: Adjusted throughout for 1-for-6.262 cons. in Sept. 2019

X.7 XTM Inc.

Symbol - PAID **Exchange** - CSE **CUSIP** - 98388T
Head Office - 437-67 Mowat St, Toronto, ON, M6K 3E3 **Telephone** - (416) 260-1641
Website - www.xtminc.com
Email - mschaffer@xtminc.com
Investor Relations - Marilyn Schaffer (416) 400-5629
Auditors - MNP LLP C.A.
Transfer Agents - Computershare Trust Company of Canada Inc., Toronto, Ont.
Profile - (Ont. 2005) Designs, builds and maintains mobile banking and payments platform for disseminating earned wages, gratuities and expense reimbursements to workers in the hospitality, personal care, food delivery space and services staffing industries.

Products include Today™, a mobile and enterprise software platform specifically designed for restaurateurs and personal care services operators and their staff and consisting of free mobile app and a Visa or Mastercard debit card with free banking features; Tipstoday™, a gratuity pooling and tip allocation software platform which allows establishments to set up a tip distribution plan; and QRails AnyDay™, a early wage access platform which enables employees to receive a portion of their earned pay when they need it.

Provides on-demand pay for many large brands including Earls, Maple Leaf Sports & Entertainment, Cactus Club, Marriott Hotels and Live Nation.

In June 2023, the company agreed to acquire **Qrails Inc.**, a prepaid payments issuer-processor and one of the first vertically integrated providers of earned wage access, for total consideration of US$3,500,000, consisting of US$100,000 cash and issuance of 28,333,333 common shares at a deemed value of US$3,400,000.

In May 2022, the company discontinued the bills payment feature in Today™ platform due to negative margin being a free way in which users could deplete the Today™ wallet of its funds while incurring a transactional cost for the company and eliminating the possibility of interchange revenue from point of sale transactions.

Common reinstated on CSE, Aug. 10, 2023.
Common suspended from CSE, July 19, 2023.

Directors - Marilyn Schaffer, founder & CEO, Mississauga, Ont.; Olga Balanovskaya, Oakville, Ont.; Randy Khalaf, St. Louis, Mo.; Keith McKenzie, Ont.
Other Exec. Officers - Paul Dowdall, CFO; Chad Arthur, chief tech. officer; Jessika Cabral, chief compliance officer & dir., HR; Cary Strange, chief revenue officer; Michael Li, sr. v-p, opers.; Keeya Nunes, v-p, mktg.

Capital Stock

	Authorized (shs.)	Outstanding (shs.)[1]
Common	unlimited	171,839,374
Class A Special	unlimited	nil
Class B Special	unlimited	nil
Class C Special	unlimited	nil

[1] At Mar. 31, 2023
Major Shareholder - Widely held at Sept. 9, 2022.

Price Range - PAID/CSE

Year	Volume	High	Low	Close
2022	49,301,615	$0.46	$0.10	$0.12
2021	125,788,393	$0.68	$0.15	$0.38
2020	48,415,382	$0.25	$0.06	$0.17

Recent Close: $0.17
Capital Stock Changes - During 2022, common shares were issued as follows: 1,510,422 on exercise of options, 1,082,417 on exercise of warrants, 999,784 as share-based compensation and 143,034 under restricted share unit plan.

Wholly Owned Subsidiaries
XTM USA Inc., United States.

Financial Statistics

Periods ended:	12m Dec. 31/22[A]	%Chg	12m Dec. 31/21[oA]
	$000s	%Chg	$000s
Operating revenue	**4,734**	**+110**	**2,256**
Cost of sales	3,803		2,195
Salaries & benefits	3,699		2,122
General & admin expense	3,554		2,482
Stock-based compensation	358		531
Operating expense	**11,415**	**+56**	**7,330**
Operating income	**(6,682)**	**n.a.**	**(5,074)**
Deprec., depl. & amort.	191		216
Finance costs, gross	35		159
Pre-tax income	**(7,266)**	**n.a.**	**(5,450)**
Net income	**(7,266)**	**n.a.**	**(5,450)**
Cash & equivalent	2,688		8,383
Accounts receivable	579		869
Current assets	55,572		36,784
Fixed assets, net	216		271
Intangibles, net	998		1,050
Total assets	**56,786**	**+49**	**38,106**
Accts. pay. & accr. liabs.	1,288		830
Current liabilities	54,600		29,409
Long-term lease liabilities	87		90
Shareholders' equity	2,187		8,610
Cash from oper. activs.	**(5,860)**	**n.a.**	**(4,383)**
Cash from fin. activs.	272		12,552
Cash from invest. activs.	(83)		(72)
Net cash position	**2,688**	**-68**	**8,383**
Capital expenditures	(83)		(72)
	$		$
Earnings per share*	(0.04)		(0.04)
Cash flow per share*	(0.03)		(0.03)
	shs		shs
No. of shs. o/s*	171,569,084		167,833,427
Avg. no. of shs. o/s*	170,402,299		141,723,786
	%		%
Net profit margin	(153.49)		(241.58)
Return on equity	(122.85)		(115.31)
Return on assets	(15.42)		(22.78)

* Common
[o] Restated
[A] Reported in accordance with IFRS

Latest Results

Periods ended:	3m Mar. 31/23[A]	%Chg	3m Mar. 31/22[A]
	$000s	%Chg	$000s
Operating revenue	1,428	+79	797
Net income	(1,890)	n.a.	(1,524)
	$		$
Earnings per share*	(0.01)		(0.01)

* Common
[A] Reported in accordance with IFRS

Historical Summary
(as originally stated)

Fiscal Year	Oper. Rev.	Net Inc. Bef. Disc.	EPS*
	$000s	$000s	$
2022[A]	4,734	(7,266)	(0.04)
2021[A]	2,381	(4,756)	(0.03)
2020[A]	853	(3,597)	(0.04)
2019[A]	863	(2,010)	(0.02)
2018[A1]	664	(1,134)	(0.02)

* Common
[A] Reported in accordance with IFRS
[1] As shown in the prospectus dated Feb. 18, 2020.

X.8 Xebra Brands Ltd.

Symbol - XBRA **Exchange** - CSE **CUSIP** - 98402E
Head Office - 1090 Hamilton St, Vancouver, BC, V6B 2R9 **Telephone** - (604) 634-0970 **Fax** - (604) 638-3474
Website - xebrabrands.com
Email - ir@xebrabrands.com
Investor Relations - Rodrigo Gallardo (604) 424-4200
Auditors - Dale Matheson Carr-Hilton LaBonte LLP C.A., Vancouver, B.C.
Lawyers - McMillan LLP, Vancouver, B.C.
Transfer Agents - Computershare Trust Company of Canada Inc., Vancouver, B.C.
Profile - (B.C. 2019) Cultivates, manufactures and distributes cannabidiol (CBD) products ranging from beverages to wellness.

Develops and produces cannabis-infused beverages brands including its retail product Vicious Citrus™, which is a non-carbonated, tetrahydrocannabinol (THC) lemonade beverage available in Canada and under research and development beverages including MADCAP™ (Crazy Good!™; seltzers and sodas); HIGHJACK™ (Enjoy the Trip!™; energy drinks); HOLAHI™ (It's High Time!™; iced teas), Conquer™ (Protect™; sports beverages); and HIGHCASTLE™ (Drink Like a King™; waters).In addition, the company has filed the equivalent of more than 400 trademark applications for the Xebra brands in more than 40 countries.

Wholly owned **Desart MX S.A. de C.V.** holds an injunction grant in cultivating and processing hemp, and manufacturing and distributing low-levels of THC wellness products such as tinctures, oils, topicals, edibles, beverages, concentrates, distillates, emulsions, and biomass in Mexico.

Also has a licensing agreement with **New Age Nano Tech LLC** for the right to develop and use New Age's technology that converts oil-based products into water-soluble oil, with the licence exclusive in Mexico and Colombia, and non-exclusive in Europe and the rest of the Americas, including Canada, but limited to only California in the U.S.

In June 2022, the company announced the sale of its operations including cultivation, harvest and distribution of cannabis seeds and products in Colombia due to saturated licences and in the Netherlands due to high cultivation costs.

Directors - Jay Garnett, CEO, B.C.; Todd Dalotto, chief science officer, Ore.; Jordi Chemonte, Mexico; Keith Dolo, B.C.; Antonio Grimaldo, Mexico
Other Exec. Officers - Rodrigo Gallardo, pres.; Jorge Martínez, COO; Omar Garcia, CFO & corp. sec.; Diego Chiguachi, chief agronomist & breeder

Capital Stock

	Authorized (shs.)	Outstanding (shs.)[1]
Class A Common	unlimited	54,426,312
Class B Common	unlimited	nil

[1] At Aug. 17, 2023
Class A and B Common - One vote per share.
Major Shareholder - Widely held at July 19, 2022.

Price Range - XBRA/CSE

Year	Volume	High	Low	Close
2022	7,182,700	$1.90	$0.13	$0.15
2021	4,403,659	$4.15	$0.40	$1.90

Consolidation: 1-for-5 cons. in Feb. 2023
Recent Close: $0.04
Capital Stock Changes - In March 2023, private placement of 15,086,731 units (1 class A common share & ½ warrant) at 6¢ per unit was completed, with warrants exercisable at 10¢ per share for 18 months.

In April 2022, private placement of 3,000,000 units (1 post-consolidated class A common share & ½ warrant) at 60¢ per unit was completed, with warrants exercisable at $1.25 per share for one year. On Feb. 28, 2023, class A common shares were consolidated on a 1-for-5 basis.

In April 2022, private placement of 15,000,000 units (1 class A common share & ½ warrant) at 12¢ per unit was completed, with warrants exercisable at 25¢ per share for one year. On Feb. 28, 2023, class A common shares were consolidated on a 1-for-5 basis.

Wholly Owned Subsidiaries
Bleuflor Logistics Ltd., B.C.
- 100% int. in **Bleuflor Logistica S.A.S.**, Colombia.

Medicannabis S.A.S., Colombia.
- 100% int. in **Desart MX S.A. de C.V.**, Mexico.
- 100% int. in **Elements Bioscience S.A.P.I. de C.V.**, Mexico.
- 100% int. in **Sativa Group Biosciences S.A.P.I. de C.V.**, Mexico.

Xebra Brands Mexico S.A. de C.V., Mexico.

Subsidiaries
75% int. in **Xebra Brands Europe B.V.**, Netherlands.

Financial Statistics

Periods ended:	12m Feb. 28/22[A]		12m Feb. 28/21[A]
	$000s	%Chg	$000s
General & admin expense	2,504		1,280
Stock-based compensation	557		nil
Operating expense	**3,061**	**+139**	**1,280**
Operating income	**(3,061)**	**n.a.**	**(1,280)**
Deprec., depl. & amort.	603		550
Finance income	1		nil
Finance costs, gross	11		8
Write-downs/write-offs	2,537		nil
Pre-tax income	**(6,261)**	**n.a.**	**(1,881)**
Net income	**(6,261)**	**n.a.**	**(1,881)**
Net inc. for equity hldrs	**(6,143)**	**n.a.**	**(1,860)**
Net inc. for non-cont. int.	**(118)**	**n.a.**	**(21)**
Cash & equivalent	647		93
Current assets	1,151		334
Fixed assets, net	330		213
Intangibles, net	1,310		2,970
Total assets	**2,902**	**-19**	**3,597**
Accts. pay. & accr. liabs	429		552
Current liabilities	429		552
Long-term lease liabilities	29		67
Shareholders' equity	2,582		3,002
Non-controlling interest	(137)		(24)
Cash from oper. activs	**(2,707)**	**n.a.**	**(911)**
Cash from fin. activs	4,034		202
Cash from invest. activs	(770)		(145)
Net cash position	**647**	**+596**	**93**
Capital expenditures	(687)		(83)
	$		$
Earnings per share*	(0.25)		(0.10)
Cash flow per share*	(0.11)		(0.04)
	shs		shs
No. of shs. o/s*	36,241,394		20,714,675
Avg. no. of shs. o/s*	24,308,060		20,428,727
	%		%
Net profit margin	n.a.		n.a.
Return on equity	(220.02)		(49.36)
Return on assets	(192.34)		(42.86)

* CL.A & B Common
[A] Reported in accordance with IFRS

Latest Results

Periods ended:	6m Aug. 31/22[A]		6m Aug. 31/21[A]
	$000s	%Chg	$000s
Operating revenue	54	n.a.	nil
Net income	(2,046)	n.a.	(724)
Net inc. for equity hldrs	(1,948)	n.a.	(719)
Net inc. for non-cont. int	(98)		(4)
	$		$
Earnings per share*	(0.05)		(0.05)

* CL.A & B Common
[A] Reported in accordance with IFRS

Historical Summary
(as originally stated)

Fiscal Year	Oper. Rev.	Net Inc. Bef. Disc.	EPS*
	$000s	$000s	$
2022[A]	nil	(6,261)	(0.25)
2021[A]	nil	(1,881)	(0.10)
2020[A]	nil	(2,791)	(0.20)

* CL.A & B Common
[A] Reported in accordance with IFRS
Note: Adjusted throughout for 1-for-5 cons. in Feb. 2023

X.9 Xenon Pharmaceuticals Inc.

Symbol - XENE **Exchange** - NASDAQ **CUSIP** - 98420N
Head Office - 200-3650 Gilmore Way, Burnaby, BC, V5G 4W8 **Telephone** - (604) 484-3300 **Fax** - (604) 484-3450
Website - www.xenon-pharma.com
Email - imortimer@xenon-pharma.com
Investor Relations - Ian C. Mortimer (604) 484-3300
Auditors - KPMG LLP C.A., Vancouver, B.C.
Lawyers - Wilson Sonsini Goodrich & Rosati Professional Corporation, Palo Alto, Calif.; McCarthy Tétrault LLP, Vancouver, B.C.
Transfer Agents - American Stock Transfer & Trust Company, LLC, New York, N.Y.; TSX Trust Company, Vancouver, B.C.
Employees - 203 at Dec. 31, 2022
Profile - (Can. 2000; orig. B.C., 1996) Discovers and develops differentiated therapeutics for neurological disorders, with a focus on epilepsy.

Product candidates include XEN1101, for the treatment of adult focal epilepsy and primary generalized tonic clonic seizures (Phase III clinical trial), and major depressive disorder (MDD) and anhedonia (Phase II clinical trial); and XEN496 (Phase III clinical trial), a paediatric formulation of ezogabine for the treatment of KCNQ2 developmental and epileptic encephalopathy (KCNQ2-DEE) for infants and children. The U.S. FDA has granted Fast Track designation for XEN496 for the treatment of seizures associated with KCNQ2-DEE, and Orphan Drug Designation for the treatment of KCNQ2-DEE.

Also has partnership with **Neurocrine Biosciences, Inc.** for the development of NBI-921352 (formerly XEN901, Phase II clinical trial), which is being developed to treat paediatric patients with SCN8A developmental and epileptic encephalopathy (SCN8A-DEE), and adult patients with focal onset seizures.

In November 2022, the company together with its partner, **Pacira BioSciences, Inc.**, made the strategic decision to no longer pursue the clinical development of PCRX301 (formerly FX301), a product candidate for the treatment of post-operative pain.

Directors - Dr. Simon N. Pimstone, co-founder & exec. chr., Vancouver, B.C.; Ian C. Mortimer, pres. & CEO, Burnaby, B.C.; Dawn Svoronos†, Hudson, Qué.; Dr. Mohammad Azab, San Francisco, Calif.; Dr. Gillian M. Cannon, N.Y.; Steven Gannon, Montréal, Qué.; Dr. Elizabeth (Betsy) Garofalo, Ann Arbor, Mich.; Justin Gover, Calif.; Patrick Machado, Sydney, N.S.W., Australia; Dr. Gary Patou, Los Altos Hills, Calif.

Other Exec. Officers - Sherry Aulin, CFO; Andrea DiFabio, chief legal officer & corp. sec.; Dr. Christopher Kenney, CMO; Dr. Christopher E. (Chris) Von Seggern, chief comml. officer; Dr. James R. Empfield, exec. v-p, drug discovery; Dr. Robin P. Sherrington, exec. v-p, strategy & innovation; Sheila M. Grant, sr. v-p, R&D opers.; Shelley McCloskey, sr. v-p, HR
† Lead director

Capital Stock

	Authorized (shs.)	Outstanding (shs.)[1]
Preferred	unlimited	
Series 1	unlimited	nil
Common	unlimited	63,562,303

[1] At May 5, 2023

Common - One vote per share.
Series 1 Preferred (old) - All preferred shares were converted into common shares on a one-for-one basis in March 2022. Previously held by BVF Partners L.P. One vote per share.
Major Shareholder - Widely held at Apr. 4, 2023.

Price Range - XENE/NASDAQ

Year	Volume	High	Low	Close
2022	31,455,343	US$41.31	US$24.60	US$39.43
2021	33,176,055	US$36.42	US$13.23	US$31.24
2020	12,634,098	US$18.38	US$7.00	US$15.38
2019	5,355,586	US$14.90	US$6.20	US$13.11
2018	7,472,033	US$15.90	US$2.70	US$6.31

Capital Stock Changes - In March 2022, all 1,016,000 series 1 preferred shares were converted into a like number of common shares. In June 2022, public offering of 9,098,362 common shares was completed at US$30.50 per share, including 1,229,508 common shares on exercise of over-allotment option. Also during 2022, common shares were issued as follows: 579,601 on exercise of options and 258,986 on exercise of warrants.

Wholly Owned Subsidiaries
Xenon Pharmaceuticals U.S.A. Inc., Del.

Financial Statistics

Periods ended:	12m Dec. 31/22[A]		12m Dec. 31/21[A]
	US$000s	%Chg	US$000s
Operating revenue	**9,434**[1]	**-49**	**18,437**
Research & devel. expense	98,001		71,729
General & admin expense	18,576		14,778
Stock-based compensation	20,376		10,017
Operating expense	**136,953**	**+42**	**96,524**
Operating income	**(127,519)**	**n.a.**	**(78,087)**
Deprec., depl. & amort.	1,624		906
Finance costs, net	(5,779)		253
Pre-tax income	**(125,255)**	**n.a.**	**(78,888)**
Income taxes	118		(6)
Net income	**(125,373)**	**n.a.**	**(78,882)**
Cash & equivalent	592,087		551,774
Accounts receivable	986		2,765
Current assets	600,298		559,020
Long-term investments	128,682		nil
Fixed assets, net	6,500		4,466
Right-of-use assets	10,406		8,056
Total assets	**754,146**	**+32**	**572,007**
Accts. pay. & accr. liabs	22,214		13,717
Current liabilities	22,702		14,322
Long-term lease liabilities	9,947		7,652
Preferred share equity	nil		7,732
Shareholders' equity	721,497		550,033
Cash from oper. activs	**(98,430)**	**n.a.**	**(69,502)**
Cash from fin. activs	278,471		447,543
Cash from invest. activs	(296,003)		(246,770)
Net cash position	**57,242**	**-67**	**175,688**
Capital expenditures	(2,894)		(2,050)
	US$		US$
Earnings per share*	(2.06)		(1.77)
Cash flow per share*	(1.63)		(1.59)
	shs		shs
No. of shs. o/s*	62,587,701		51,634,752
Avg. no. of shs. o/s*	60,542,142		43,627,452
	%		%
Net profit margin	n.m.		(427.85)
Return on equity	(19.77)		(21.84)
Return on assets	(18.91)		(20.73)
No. of employees (FTEs)	203		149

* Common
[A] Reported in accordance with U.S. GAAP
[1] Represents collaboration revenue from Neurocrine Biosciences, Inc. and Pacira BioSciences, Inc.

Latest Results

Periods ended:	3m Mar. 31/23[A]		3m Mar. 31/22[A]
	US$000s	%Chg	US$000s
Operating revenue	nil	n.a.	8,766
Net income	(41,727)	n.a.	(19,670)
	US$		US$
Earnings per share*	(0.63)		(0.35)

* Common
[A] Reported in accordance with U.S. GAAP

Historical Summary
(as originally stated)

Fiscal Year	Oper. Rev.	Net Inc. Bef. Disc.	EPS*
	US$000s	US$000s	US$
2022[A]	9,434	(125,373)	(2.06)
2021[A]	18,437	(78,882)	(1.77)
2020[A]	32,166	(28,837)	(0.81)
2019[A]	6,829	(41,595)	(1.54)
2018[A]	nil	(34,497)	(1.63)

* Common
[A] Reported in accordance with U.S. GAAP

X.10 Xigem Technologies Corporation

Symbol - XIGM **Exchange** - CSE **CUSIP** - 98422W
Head Office - 67-70 Great Gulf Dr, Vaughan, ON, L4K 0K7 **Telephone** - (647) 250-9824
Website - www.xigemtechnologies.com
Email - investors@xigemtechnologies.com
Investor Relations - Brian Kalish (647) 250-9824 ext. 4
Auditors - SRCO Professional Corporation C.A., Richmond Hill, Ont.
Transfer Agents - Capital Transfer Agency Inc., Toronto, Ont.
Profile - (Can. 2017) Provides software-as-a-service (SaaS) technology platforms that are capable of improving the capacity, productivity and overall remote operations for businesses, consumers and other organizations.

iAgent, which is premised on U.S. patented and Canadian patent pending technology, is a mobile, geo-targeted customer acquisition, conversion and retention application which matches sales and services with consumers, treatment seekers and students across a broad range of sectors, in real time.

F00i is commercialized, SaaS, cloud-based and peer-to-peer mobile payment application.

In November 2022, entered into a letter of intent to acquire substantially all of the assets of **EAFdigital Inc.** for issuance of common shares to be determined upon completion of due diligence and signing of a definitive agreement. EAFdigital provides fintech solutions including agency marketing, information architecture and mining, content creation and design, and lead generation organized to capture, convert and close purchases of automobiles. The transaction was expected to close in January 2023.

In May 2022, the company's management is of the view that the vendor of **2747524 Ontario Inc.** (dba Cylix Data Group) has breached certain key provisions in relation to its asset purchase agreement with the company making it highly improbable for the company to recognize sole control of the Cylix asset and the books and records associated with it, resulting in the company's inability to formally control the Cylix asset. The company is pursuing resolution with the vendor of the Cylix asset.

Predecessor Detail - Name changed from 10557536 Canada Corp., Mar. 4, 2021, pursuant to the reverse takeover acquisition of (old) Xigem Technologies Corporation and concurrent amalgamation of (old) Xigem with wholly owned 2792189 Ontario Inc. (and continued as Xigem Technology Solutions Inc.).

Directors - Brian Kalish, CEO & corp. sec., Toronto, Ont.; Conor S. Bill, Toronto, Ont.; Stephen Coates, Toronto, Ont.; Ezio D'Onofrio, Toronto, Ont.; Dr. Scott Wilson, Toronto, Ont.

Other Exec. Officers - Igor Kostioutchenko, CFO; Anthony Cozzi, chief tech. officer

Capital Stock

	Authorized (shs.)	Outstanding (shs.)[1]
Preferred	unlimited	nil
Common	unlimited	15,316,847

[1] At Nov. 24, 2022

Major Shareholder - Widely held at Mar. 9, 2022.

Price Range - XIGM/CSE

Year	Volume	High	Low	Close
2022	1,475,385	$2.20	$0.01	$0.14
2021	1,836,174	$9.50	$0.70	$0.90

Consolidation: 1-for-10 cons. in July 2022

Recent Close: $0.03

Capital Stock Changes - On Jan. 24, 2022, 6,470,000 units (1 post-consolidated common share & 1/7 warrant) were issued $1.40 per unit pursuant to the acquisition of substantially all of the assets and operations of 2747524 Ontario Inc. (dba Cylix Data Group), with warrants exercisable at $6.00 per share for two years.On July 21, 2022, commons shares were consolidated on a 1-for-10 basis.

Wholly Owned Subsidiaries

2747524 Ontario Inc., Ont.
Xigem Technology Solutions Inc., Toronto, Ont.

Note: The preceding list includes only the major related companies in which interests are held.

Financial Statistics

Periods ended:	12m Dec. 31/21[A1]		29w Dec. 31/20[A2]
	$000s	%Chg	$000s
General & admin expense	2,074		154
Stock-based compensation	1,313		25
Operating expense	**3,387**	**n.a.**	**179**
Operating income	**(3,387)**	**n.a.**	**(179)**
Deprec., depl. & amort.	223		25
Finance costs, gross	6		nil
Pre-tax income	**(5,980)**	**n.a.**	**(204)**
Income taxes	5		2
Net income	**(5,985)**	**n.a.**	**(206)**
Cash & equivalent	684		2,166
Current assets	1,072		2,374
Fixed assets, net	419		nil
Intangibles, net	1,318		607
Total assets	**2,809**	**-6**	**2,981**
Accts. pay. & accr. liabs	507		176
Current liabilities	543		176
Long-term lease liabilities	128		nil
Shareholders' equity	2,131		2,803
Cash from oper. activs	**(1,689)**	**n.a.**	**14**
Cash from fin. activs	830		2,159
Cash from invest. activs	(622)		(7)
Net cash position	**684**	**-68**	**2,166**
Capital expenditures	(313)		nil
	$		$
Earnings per share*	(0.75)		(0.01)
Cash flow per share*	(0.21)		nil
	shs		shs
No. of shs. o/s*	8,517,765		n.a.
Avg. no. of shs. o/s*	7,935,938		31,023,226
	%		%
Net profit margin	n.a.		...
Return on equity	(242.60)		...
Return on assets	(206.53)		...

* Common
[A] Reported in accordance with IFRS
[1] Results prior to Mar. 4, 2021, pertain to and reflect the reverse takeover acquisition of (old) Xigem Technologies Corporation.
[2] Represents period from (old) Xigem Technologies Corporation's June 15, 2020, incorporation date.

Latest Results

Periods ended:	9m Sept. 30/22[A]		9m Sept. 30/21[A]
	$000s	%Chg	$000s
Net income	(11,807)	n.a.	(4,224)
	$		$
Earnings per share*	(0.79)		(0.67)

* Common
[A] Reported in accordance with IFRS

Note: Adjusted throughout for 1-for-10 cons. in July 2022

X.11 Xtract One Technologies Inc.

Symbol - XTRA **Exchange** - TSX **CUSIP** - 98422Q
Head Office - 400-257 Adelaide St W, Toronto, ON, M5H 1X9
Telephone - (888) 782-1832 **Toll-free** - (888) 728-1332
Website - xtractone.com
Email - investors@xtractone.com
Investor Relations - Investor Relations (888) 728-1332
Auditors - Davidson & Company LLP C.A., Vancouver, B.C.
Lawyers - Miller Thomson LLP, Vancouver, B.C.
Transfer Agents - TSX Trust Company, Vancouver, B.C.
Employees - 69 at July 31, 2022

Profile - (B.C. 2010) Develops and commercializes an integrated, layered and artificial intelligence (AI)-powered threat detection platform designed to detect and combat active threats for arenas, stadiums, ticket venues and attractions, casinos, workplaces and schools.

The platform offers AI-powered patron screening security solutions and features SafeGateway, which automatically scans entrants for concealed weapons such as guns, knives and improvised explosive device components more efficiently and accurately than conventional security measures like metal detectors; SmartGateway, which unobtrusively scans patrons for guns, knives and other prohibited items as they enter the facility using AI-powered sensors to detect threats without invading the sense of privacy and comfort of the patrons and is ideal for stadiums and other ticketed venues that need to get thousands of people quickly, safely and in alignment with security standard requirements; and Xtract One Insights, a software which analyzes massive amount of venue data in real-time, automatically detects incidents and alerts the appropriate personnel for immediate action and uses AI to integrate multiple data sources including Xtract One Gateways, security cameras and access control systems into a single view of the venue.

Predecessor Detail - Name changed from Patriot One Technologies Inc., Nov. 28, 2022.

Directors - Peter van der Gracht, chr., B.C.; Peter J. Evans, CEO, Fla.; John Gillies, B.C.; William (Bill) Maginas, Ont.; Lea M. Ray, Toronto, Ont.

Other Exec. Officers - Karen Hersh, CFO & corp. sec.; Joshua (Josh) Douglas, sr. v-p, product & eng.; Christopher Feusner, v-p, sales

Capital Stock

	Authorized (shs.)	Outstanding (shs.)[1]
Common	unlimited	163,181,722

[1] At Oct. 31, 2022

Major Shareholder - Widely held at Sept. 30, 2022.

Price Range - XTRA/TSX

Year	Volume	High	Low	Close
2022	36,718,716	$0.92	$0.31	$0.50
2021	46,266,975	$0.75	$0.36	$0.37
2020	87,385,202	$1.61	$0.39	$0.57
2019	125,094,192	$2.86	$1.12	$1.29
2018	230,281,696	$3.01	$1.11	$1.67

Recent Close: $0.74

Capital Stock Changes - In March 2022, public offering of 11,471,850 units (1 common share & 1 warrant) at 60¢ per unit was completed. Also during fiscal 2022, 978,750 common shares were issued on exercise of options.

Wholly Owned Subsidiaries

EhEye Inc., Saint John, N.B.
Patriot One (UK) Limited, United Kingdom.
Xtract One Detection Ltd., Vancouver, B.C.
Xtract One (US) Technologies Inc., United States.
• 49% int. in **Sotech Secure, LLC**, Del.
Xtract Technologies Inc., Vancouver, B.C.

Financial Statistics

Periods ended:	12m July 31/22[A]		12m July 31/21[A]
	$000s	%Chg	$000s
Operating revenue	**3,619**	**+234**	**1,082**
Salaries & benefits	5,284		4,362
Research & devel. expense	4,464		2,757
General & admin expense	4,291		3,622
Stock-based compensation	1,064		1,180
Other operating expense	772		28
Operating expense	**15,874**	**+33**	**11,949**
Operating income	**(12,255)**	**n.a.**	**(10,867)**
Deprec., depl. & amort.	1,571		1,813
Finance income	31		25
Finance costs, gross	67		99
Write-downs/write-offs	(26,085)		nil
Pre-tax income	**(39,717)**	**n.a.**	**(16,732)**
Income taxes	nil		(170)
Net income	**(39,717)**	**n.a.**	**(16,562)**
Cash & equivalent	6,277		9,652
Inventories	1,106		1,458
Accounts receivable	1,725		2,940
Current assets	9,947		14,724
Long-term investments	394		219
Fixed assets, net	1,478		1,505
Right-of-use assets	590		913
Intangibles, net	5,650		32,038
Total assets	**18,058**	**-63**	**49,398**
Accts. pay. & accr. liabs	2,639		1,266
Current liabilities	3,156		1,883
Long-term lease liabilities	357		677
Shareholders' equity	14,545		46,838
Cash from oper. activs	**(9,271)**	**n.a.**	**(11,695)**
Cash from fin. activs	5,992		(515)
Cash from invest. activs	(96)		(545)
Net cash position	**6,277**	**-35**	**9,652**
Capital expenditures	(96)		(492)
	$		$
Earnings per share*	(0.25)		(0.11)
Cash flow per share*	(0.06)		(0.08)
	shs		shs
No. of shs. o/s*	163,179,222		150,728,622
Avg. no. of shs. o/s*	155,744,354		150,728,622
	%		%
Net profit margin	n.m.		n.m.
Return on equity	(129.41)		(30.37)
Return on assets	(117.56)		(28.53)
No. of employees (FTEs)	69		68

* Common
[A] Reported in accordance with IFRS

Latest Results

Periods ended:	3m Oct. 31/22[A]		3m Oct. 31/21[A]
	$000s	%Chg	$000s
Operating revenue	647	-9	709
Net income	(4,918)	n.a.	(1,088)
	$		$
Earnings per share*	(0.03)		(0.01)

* Common
[A] Reported in accordance with IFRS

Historical Summary
(as originally stated)

Fiscal Year	Oper. Rev.	Net Inc. Bef. Disc.	EPS*
	$000s	$000s	$
2022^A	3,619	(39,717)	(0.25)
2021^A	1,082	(16,562)	(0.11)
2020^A	2,071	(25,126)	(0.17)
2019^A	nil	(17,432)	(0.13)
2018^A	nil	(11,986)	(0.13)

* Common
[A] Reported in accordance with IFRS

X.12 Xybion Digital Inc.

Symbol - XYBN **Exchange** - TSX-VEN **CUSIP** - 98423T
Head Office - 105 College Rd E, Princeton, NJ, United States, 08540 **Telephone** - (609) 512-5790 **Toll-free** - (844) 291-4430 **Fax** - (609) 482-3823
Website - xybion.com
Email - pbanerjee@xybion.com
Investor Relations - Dr. Pradip K. Banerjee (609) 512-5790 ext. 122
Auditors - Marcum LLP C.P.A.
Transfer Agents - TSX Trust Company, Vancouver, B.C.
Profile - (B.C. 2020) Provides software solutions for automating and streamlining complex business processes.
The solutions offer cloud-based unified end-to-end sub-platforms as a software-as-a-service (SaaS) under its Xybion digital acceleration platform for core business processes like research and development, testing laboratory operations, workplace and employee health, and safety management with embedded compliance, quality, risk and Enterprise Content management systems. Solutions offered include:: Pristima® XD, a pre-clinical R&D execution system; Labwise® XD, an all-in-one digital lab management system; CQRM XD, a compliance and quality risk management with real time data integrity monitoring platform; Emidence® XD, a workplace health, safety and worker's compensation platform; and ECM-XD, a content management system.
Also provides consulting services for project management, computer system validation and software development and testing.
Serves more than 160 customers in 25 countries. Customers include major global corporations in pharmaceutical, biotechnology, contract research, diagnostic and testing laboratories, health systems and government agencies.
Predecessor Detail - Name changed from Gravitas One Capital Corp., Nov. 12, 2021, pursuant to the reverse takeover acquisition of Xybion Corporation and concurrent amalgamation of Xybion with wholly owned Gravitas US Corp.; basis 1 new for 10.65 old shs.
Directors - Dr. Pradip K. Banerjee, chr. & CEO, N.J.; Peter Bailey†, N.J.; John McCoach, Vancouver, B.C.
Other Exec. Officers - Kamal Biswas, pres. & COO; Steven L. Porfano, CFO & corp. sec.
† Lead director

Capital Stock

	Authorized (shs.)	Outstanding (shs.)[1]
Cl.A Subord. Vtg.	unlimited	1,513,245
Cl.B Proportionate Vtg.	unlimited	60,532
Cl.C Proportionate Non-Vtg.	unlimited	4,479

[1] At Nov. 16, 2022
Class A Subordinate Voting - One vote per share.
Class B Proportionate Voting - Each convertible into 100 class A subordinate voting shares. 100 votes per share. All held by Dr. Pradip K. Banerjee.
Class C Proportionate Non-Voting - Each convertible into 10,000 class A subordinate voting shares or 100 Class B proportionate voting shares. All held by Dr. Pradip K. Banerjee.
Major Shareholder - Dr. Pradip K. Banerjee held 79.92% interest at Nov. 8, 2022.

Price Range - XYBN/TSX-VEN

Year	Volume	High	Low	Close
2022	534,290	$3.50	$1.10	$2.00
2021	296,022	$5.27	$1.75	$2.55

Recent Close: $0.49
Capital Stock Changes - On Nov. 15, 2021, common shares were consolidated on a 1-for-10.65 basis and reclassified as class A subordinate voting shares, 60,532 class B proportionate voting shares (newly created) and 4,479 class C proportionate non-voting shares (newly created) were issued pursuant to the Qualifying Transaction reverse takeover acquisition of Xybion Corporation, and 696,404 class A subordinate voting shares were issued without further consideration on exchange of subscription receipts sold previously by Xybion Corporation at $3.20 each.

Wholly Owned Subsidiaries

Xybion Corporation, Princeton, N.J.
- 100% int. in **Services Informatique Xybion**, Québec, Qué.
- 100% int. in **Xybion India Private Ltd.**, India.
- 100% int. in **Xybion Medical Systems Corporation**, N.J.
- 100% int. in **Xybion Technology Solutions, Inc.**, Del.

Financial Statistics

Periods ended:	12m Mar. 31/22^A1		12m Mar. 31/21^A
	US$000s	%Chg	US$000s
Operating revenue	**16,767**	**+17**	**14,316**
Cost of sales	5,617		4,911
Salaries & benefits	4,842		4,598
Research & devel. expense	1,290		1,180
General & admin expense	2,100		967
Stock-based compensation	33		29
Other operating expense	445		285
Operating expense	**14,327**	**+20**	**11,970**
Operating income	**2,440**	**+4**	**2,346**
Deprec., depl. & amort.	461		459
Finance costs, gross	18		13
Write-downs/write-offs	(183)		(95)
Pre-tax income	**(562)**	**n.a.**	**2,791**
Income taxes	419		513
Net income	**(981)**	**n.a.**	**2,278**
Cash & equivalent	8,146		6,460
Accounts receivable	4,333		4,787
Current assets	13,973		11,973
Right-of-use assets	624		954
Intangibles, net	2,315		2,314
Total assets	**17,477**	**+8**	**16,143**
Accts. pay. & accr. liabs	690		807
Current liabilities	7,710		7,459
Long-term lease liabilities	442		668
Shareholders' equity	9,325		8,016
Cash from oper. activs	**1,148**	**-55**	**2,548**
Cash from fin. activs	(69)		2
Cash from invest. activs	710		(237)
Net cash position	**8,146**	**+26**	**6,460**
Capital expenditures	(72)		(237)
	US$		US$
Earnings per share*	(1.56)		n.a.
Cash flow per share*	1.83		0.02
Cash divd. per share*	0.00		0.05
	shs		shs
No. of shs. o/s*	1,578,317		n.a.
Avg. no. of shs. o/s*	628,873		n.a.
	%		%
Net profit margin	(5.85)		15.91
Return on equity	(11.31)		31.59
Return on assets	(5.65)		15.77

* Cl.A Subord. Vtg.
[A] Reported in accordance with IFRS
[1] Results prior to Nov. 15, 2021, pertain to and reflect the Qualfiying Transaction reverse takeover acquisition of Xybion Corporation.

Latest Results

Periods ended:	6m Sept. 30/22^A		6m Sept. 30/21^A
	US$000s	%Chg	US$000s
Operating revenue	7,636	-6	8,166
Net income	(2,052)	n.a.	606
	US$		US$
Earnings per share*	(1.30)		n.a.

* Cl.A Subord. Vtg.
[A] Reported in accordance with IFRS

Historical Summary
(as originally stated)

Fiscal Year	Oper. Rev.	Net Inc. Bef. Disc.	EPS*
	US$000s	US$000s	US$
2022^A	16,767	(981)	(1.56)
2021^A	14,316	2,278	n.a.
2020^A	15,144	1,386	n.a.
2019^A	13,643	1,501	n.a.

* Cl.A Subord. Vtg.
[A] Reported in accordance with IFRS
Note: Adjusted throughout for 1-for-10.65 cons. in Nov. 2021

Y

Y.1 YANGAROO Inc.

Symbol - YOO **Exchange** - TSX-VEN **CUSIP** - 984747
Head Office - 203-360 Dufferin St, Toronto, ON, M6K 3G1 **Telephone** - (416) 534-0607 **Toll-free** - (855) 534-0607 **Fax** - (416) 534-9427
Website - www.yangaroo.com
Email - grant.schuetrumpf@yangaroo.com
Investor Relations - Grant Schuetrumpf (416) 534-0607 ext. 162
Auditors - Baker Tilly WM LLP C.A., Toronto, Ont.
Lawyers - ECS Law Professional Corporation, Toronto, Ont.; Gowling WLG (Canada) LLP, Toronto, Ont.
Transfer Agents - Computershare Trust Company of Canada Inc., Toronto, Ont.
Profile - (Ont. 1999) Provides a secure business-to-business (B2B) cloud-based media content distribution solution, the Digital Media Distribution System (DMDS), for the advertising, music and awards industry. Also provides media asset distribution and content management services.

The DMDS platform is a cloud-based technology that provides customers with a fully integrated workflow and broadcaster connected managed network for digital content delivery and related data management across the advertising, music and entertainment award show markets.

In addition, wholly owned **Digital Media Solutions Inc.** provides media asset distribution and content management services to marketers, advertisers, media agencies, broadcasters, publishers and film makers. Services include advertising distribution and other post-production services.

The company has offices in Toronto Ont.; New York, N.Y.; Los Angeles, Calif.; and New Jersey.

The company changed its reporting currency to the U.S. dollar from the Canada dollar, effective Jan. 1, 2022.

Predecessor Detail - Name changed from Musicrypt Inc., July 18, 2007.

Directors - Anthony G. (Tony) Miller, chr., Toronto, Ont.; Grant Schuetrumpf, pres. & CEO, New York, N.Y.; Philip (Phil) Benson, Toronto, Ont.; Horace Shepard (Shep) Boone, Cos Cob, Conn.

Other Exec. Officers - Jeff Wagner, CFO; Richard Klosa, chief tech. officer; Adam Hunt, exec. v-p, music

Capital Stock

	Authorized (shs.)	Outstanding (shs.)[1]
Common	unlimited	62,437,140

[1] At May 25, 2023

Major Shareholder - Ingalls & Snyder, LLC held 24.89% interest and Horace Shepard (Shep) Boone held 16.21% interest at May 19, 2023.

Price Range - YOO/TSX-VEN

Year	Volume	High	Low	Close
2022	5,181,575	$0.17	$0.03	$0.05
2021	5,094,662	$0.28	$0.13	$0.14
2020	8,966,426	$0.22	$0.09	$0.15
2019	6,886,626	$0.21	$0.09	$0.13
2018	12,082,728	$0.39	$0.12	$0.13

Recent Close: $0.05

Capital Stock Changes - During 2022, common shares were issued as follows: 1,160,000 under restricted share unit plan and 580,000 on exercise of options.

Wholly Owned Subsidiaries

Digital Media Services Inc., New York, N.Y.

Financial Statistics

Periods ended:	12m Dec. 31/22[A]		12m Dec. 31/21[oA]
	US$000s	%Chg	US$000s
Operating revenue	**7,735**	**0**	**7,727**
Salaries & benefits	5,260		5,426
Research & devel. expense	640		614
General & admin expense	1,224		844
Operating expense	**7,124**	**+3**	**6,884**
Operating income	**611**	**-28**	**843**
Deprec., depl. & amort.	811		535
Finance income	31		nil
Finance costs, gross	270		156
Write-downs/write-offs	(123)		36
Pre-tax income	**1,584**	**n.a.**	**(47)**
Income taxes	14		7
Net income	**1,570**	**n.a.**	**(54)**
Cash & equivalent	297		768
Accounts receivable	1,567		1,737
Current assets	2,412		3,024
Fixed assets, net	685		682
Intangibles, net	5,503		5,249
Total assets	**9,138**	**+2**	**8,955**
Bank indebtedness	845		nil
Accts. pay. & accr. liabs	879		851
Current liabilities	2,194		2,112
Long-term debt, gross	2,147		2,424
Long-term debt, net	2,038		2,004
Long-term lease liabilities	275		255
Shareholders' equity	4,631		2,967
Cash from oper. activs	**57**	**-95**	**1,101**
Cash from fin. activs	501		2,169
Cash from invest. activs	(776)		(4,107)
Net cash position	**297**	**-61**	**768**
Capital expenditures	(105)		(141)
	US$		US$
Earnings per share*	0.03		(0.00)
Cash flow per share*	0.00		0.02
	shs		shs
No. of shs. o/s*	62,437,140		60,697,140
Avg. no. of shs. o/s*	62,174,961		60,512,836
	%		%
Net profit margin	20.30		(0.70)
Return on equity	40.75		(1.89)
Return on assets	20.17		1.98
Foreign sales percent	90		89

* Common
[o] Restated
[A] Reported in accordance with IFRS

Latest Results

Periods ended:	3m Mar. 31/23[A]		3m Mar. 31/22[A]
	US$000s	%Chg	US$000s
Operating revenue	1,845	-7	1,989
Net income	(365)	n.a.	(598)
	US$		US$
Earnings per share*	(0.01)		(0.01)

* Common
[A] Reported in accordance with IFRS

Historical Summary
(as originally stated)

Fiscal Year	Oper. Rev.	Net Inc. Bef. Disc.	EPS*
	US$000s	US$000s	US$
2022[A]	7,735	1,570	0.03
	$000s	$000s	$
2021[A]	9,696	(59)	(0.00)
2020[A]	7,948	910	0.02
2019[A]	7,432	(151)	(0.00)
2018[A]	7,488	513	0.01

* Common
[A] Reported in accordance with IFRS

Y.2 Yellow Pages Limited*

Symbol - Y **Exchange** - TSX **CUSIP** - 985572
Head Office - 8300-1751 rue Richardson, Montréal, QC, H3K 1G6 **Telephone** - (514) 934-2611 **Toll-free** - (800) 361-6010 **Fax** - (514) 934-2918
Website - www.corporate.yp.ca/en
Email - franco.sciannamblo@yp.ca
Investor Relations - Franco Sciannamblo (800) 268-5637
Auditors - Deloitte LLP C.A., Montréal, Qué.
Transfer Agents - TSX Trust Company, Montréal, Qué.
FP500 Revenue Ranking - 593
Employees - 600 at Dec. 31, 2022
Profile - (B.C. 2020; orig. Can., 2014 amalg.) Provides digital media and marketing solutions, and offers tools to local businesses, national brands and consumers allowing them to interact and transact.

Offers small- and medium-sized enterprises (SMEs) digital and traditional marketing solutions including online and mobile placement on Yellow Pages digital media properties, content syndication, search engine solutions, website fulfilment, social media campaign management, digital display advertising, video production, e-commerce solutions and print advertising. At June 30, 2023, the company served 86,500 SMEs, through a national sales force of 300 media consultants. Digital and print media properties include YP™, an online and mobile application platform which allows users to discover and transact through comprehensive merchant profiles, relevant editorial content, reviews and booking functionalities; Canada411 (C411), an online and mobile destination for personal and local business information; and 411.ca, a digital directory service which helps users find other people and local businesses.

The company is the official directory publisher for **Bell Canada**, **TELUS Communications Inc.**, **Bell Aliant Inc.**, **Bell MTS Inc.** and for a number of other incumbent telephone companies in Canada. During 2022, the company published more than 330 different telephone directories.

Predecessor Detail - Formed from Yellow Media Limited in Canada, Dec. 31, 2014, on amalgamation with wholly owned Yellow Pages Limited.

Directors - Susan Kudzman, chr., Montréal, Qué.; David A. Eckert, pres. & CEO, Mass.; Craig I. Forman, Calif.; Rob Hall, Cheshire, United Kingdom; Paul W. Russo, Tel Aviv, Israel

Other Exec. Officers - John R. Ireland, sr. v-p, org. effectiveness; Sherilyn King, sr. v-p, sales, mktg. & cust. srvc.; Franco Sciannamblo, sr. v-p & CFO

Capital Stock

	Authorized (shs.)	Outstanding (shs.)[1]
Common	unlimited	18,658,347

[1] At Aug. 8, 2023

Major Shareholder - GoldenTree Asset Management, LP held 31.36% interest, Empyrean Capital Partners, LP held 23.66% interest and Canso Investment Counsel Ltd. held 23.29% interest at Mar. 24, 2023.

Price Range - Y/TSX

Year	Volume	High	Low	Close
2022	1,615,512	$14.65	$12.43	$13.62
2021	1,207,612	$15.20	$11.47	$13.66
2020	2,609,600	$13.25	$6.00	$12.53
2019	2,833,099	$9.63	$5.43	$9.06
2018	13,014,547	$10.73	$5.30	$6.09

Recent Close: $12.30

Capital Stock Changes - In October 2022, 7,949,125 common shares were repurchased and cancelled. Also during 2022, common shares were issued as follows: 18,873 on exercise of options and 48 on exercise of warrants; 871,135 common shares were repurchased under a Normal Course Issuer Bid.

Dividends

Y com Ra $0.80 pa Q est. June 15, 2023
Prev. Rate: $0.60 est. June 30, 2021
Prev. Rate: $0.44 est. June 15, 2020

Long-Term Debt - At Dec. 31, 2022, the company had no long-term debt.

Wholly Owned Subsidiaries

YPG (USA) Holdings, Inc., United States.
Yellow Pages Digital & Media Solutions Limited, Montréal, Qué.
Yellow Pages Digital & Media Solutions, LLC, United States.

Financial Statistics

Periods ended:	12m Dec. 31/22[A]		12m Dec. 31/21[A]
	$000s	%Chg	$000s
Operating revenue	**268,278**	**-7**	**287,646**
Salaries & benefits	74,780		82,200
Other operating expense	94,508		95,896
Operating expense	**169,288**	**-5**	**178,096**
Operating income	**98,990**	**-10**	**109,550**
Deprec., depl. & amort.	15,397		19,635
Finance income	1,819		1,877
Finance costs, gross	3,627		11,220
Write-downs/write-offs	(2,422)		(7,550)
Pre-tax income	**76,132**	**+27**	**59,914**
Income taxes	2,700		(10,721)
Net income	**73,432**	**+4**	**70,635**
Cash & equivalent	43,907		123,559
Accounts receivable	38,415		42,267
Current assets	89,506		173,393
Fixed assets, net	4,169		5,249
Right-of-use assets	7,085		9,752
Intangibles, net	49,662		58,747
Total assets	**207,298**	**-32**	**305,229**
Accts. pay. & accr. liabs.	33,623		34,931
Current liabilities	56,014		65,888
Long-term lease liabilities	43,733		46,939
Shareholders' equity	65,781		116,131
Cash from oper. activs.	**49,500**	**-53**	**104,579**
Cash from fin. activs.	(125,486)		(130,031)
Cash from invest. activs.	(3,666)		(4,481)
Net cash position	**43,907**	**-64**	**123,559**
Capital expenditures	(93)		(117)
Unfunded pension liability	18,818		45,684
	$		$
Earnings per share*	3.10		2.68
Cash flow per share*	2.09		3.97
Cash divd. per share*	0.60		0.56
	shs		shs
No. of shs. o/s*	18,658,347		27,459,686
Avg. no. of shs. o/s*	23,669,723		26,337,343
	%		%
Net profit margin	27.37		24.56
Return on equity	80.73		97.14
Return on assets	30.02		24.92
No. of employees (FTEs)	600		700

* Common
[A] Reported in accordance with IFRS

Latest Results

Periods ended:	6m June 30/23[A]		6m June 30/22[A]
	$000s	%Chg	$000s
Operating revenue	125,451	-9	137,373
Net income	25,119	-8	27,308
	$		$
Earnings per share*	1.41		1.06

* Common
[A] Reported in accordance with IFRS

Historical Summary
(as originally stated)

Fiscal Year	Oper. Rev.	Net Inc. Bef. Disc.	EPS*
	$000s	$000s	$
2022[A]	268,278	73,432	3.10
2021[A]	287,646	70,635	2.68
2020[A]	333,538	60,298	2.27
2019[A]	403,213	94,669	3.57
2018[A]	577,195	82,809	3.13

* Common
[A] Reported in accordance with IFRS

Y.3 Yerbaé Brands Corp.

Symbol - YERB.U **Exchange** - TSX-VEN **CUSIP** - 98582P
Head Office - 18801 N Thompson Peak Pkwy, Suite 380, Scottsdale, AZ, United States, 85255 **Telephone** - (480) 471-8391
Website - yerbae.com
Email - investors@yerbae.com
Investor Relations - Todd Gibson (480) 471-8391
Auditors - MNP LLP C.A., Toronto, Ont.
Transfer Agents - Odyssey Trust Company
Employees - 20 at Nov. 13, 2022
Profile - (B.C. 2000) Manufactures, markets and distributes sugar-free, naturally caffeinated, plant-based energy drinks in the United States under the Yerbaé brand.

The company offers two primary beverage lines with a total of fifteen flavours. Its two primary product lines are the 12 oz. Energy Seltzer Water and 16 oz. Energy Drink. Each beverage contains Yerba Mate, a South American herb and a natural source of caffeine. Yerbaé beverages are sold online, direct to consumer and through a network of more than 10,000 U.S. retail location, including convenience stores, natural product stores and grocery chains. The company uses a contract manufacturer for production.

Common listed on TSX-VEN, Feb. 13, 2023.
Common delisted from TSX-VEN, Feb. 10, 2023.

Recent Merger and Acquisition Activity

Status: completed **Revised:** Feb. 9, 2023
UPDATE: The transaction was competed. PREVIOUS: Kona Bay Technologies Inc. agreed to the reverse takeover acquisition of Scottsdale, Ariz.-based Yerbaé Brands Co. on a share-for-share basis (following a 1-for-5.8 share consolidation) which would result in the issuance of an estimated 32,544,609 Kona post-consolidated common shares at a deemed price of US$1.23 per share. Yerbaé manufactures and markets plant-based energy drinks and seltzers. The transaction would be completed by the merger of Kona Bay Technologies (Delaware) Inc., a newly incorporated wholly owned subsidiary of Kona, with and into Yerbaé. A wholly owned British Columbia subsidiary of Kona intends to complete a private placement of subscription receipts at US$1.23 per receipt for proceeds of a minimum of US$5,000,000. Oct. 31, 2022 - TSX Venture Exchange conditional approval was received. Dec. 21, 2022 - Kona shareholders approved the transaction

Predecessor Detail - Name changed from Kona Bay Technologies Inc., pursuant to the reverse takeover acquisition of Yerbaé Brands Co.
Directors - Todd Gibson, CEO, Ariz.; Karrie Gibson, COO, Ariz.; Andy Dratt, Ill.; Carl Sweat, Ga.; Rose Zanic, Vancouver, B.C.
Other Exec. Officers - Nick Cranny, interim CFO; Seth Smith, v-p, sales; Renata Kubicek, corp. sec.

Capital Stock

	Authorized (shs.)	Outstanding (shs.)[1]
Preferred	100,000,000	nil
Common	unlimited	54,493,953

[1] At Feb. 13, 2023

Major Shareholder - Karrie Gibson held 15.56% interest and Todd Gibson held 15.56% interest at Feb. 9, 2023.

Price Range - KBY.H/TSX-VEN (D)

Year	Volume	High	Low	Close
2022	614,022	$1.45	$0.23	$1.45
2021	168,996	$1.39	$0.35	$0.58
2020	25,281	$0.58	$0.15	$0.58
2018	17,120	$0.87	$0.26	$0.38

Consolidation: 1-for-5.8 cons. in Feb. 2023
Recent Close: US$2.09
Capital Stock Changes - In February 2023, common shares were consolidated on a 1-for-5.8 basis and 49,524,861 post-consolidated common shares were issued pursuant to reverse takeover acquisition of Yerbaé Brands Co.

During fiscal 2022, 1,925,000 common shares were issued on exercise of warrants.

Wholly Owned Subsidiaries

Yerbaé Brands Co., Scottsdale, Ariz.
- 100% int. in **Yerbaé, LLC**, Scottsdale, Ariz.

Financial Statistics

Periods ended:	12m Sept. 30/22[A1]		12m Sept. 30/21[A]
	$000s	%Chg	$000s
General & admin expense	315		221
Operating expense	**315**	**+43**	**221**
Operating income	**(315)**	**n.a.**	**(221)**
Finance costs, gross	nil		2
Pre-tax income	**(316)**	**n.a.**	**(90)**
Net inc. bef. disc. opers	**(316)**	**n.a.**	**(90)**
Income from disc. opers	nil		18
Net income	**(316)**	**n.a.**	**(72)**
Cash & equivalent	28		115
Current assets	47		117
Total assets	**47**	**-60**	**117**
Accts. pay. & accr. liabs.	162		26
Current liabilities	171		26
Shareholders' equity	(124)		91
Cash from oper. activs.	**(196)**	**n.a.**	**(739)**
Cash from fin. activs.	109		654
Cash from invest. activs.	nil		194
Net cash position	**28**	**-76**	**115**
	$		$
Earns. per sh. bef disc opers*	(0.06)		(0.02)
Earnings per share*	(0.06)		(0.02)
Cash flow per share*	(0.04)		(0.19)
	shs		shs
No. of shs. o/s*	4,969,075		4,637,178
Avg. no. of shs. o/s*	4,697,192		3,687,721
	%		%
Net profit margin	n.a.		n.a.
Return on equity	n.m.		n.m.
Return on assets	(385.37)		(75.86)

* Common
[A] Reported in accordance with IFRS
[1] Results for fiscal 2022 and prior periods pertain to Kona Bay Technologies Inc.

Latest Results

Periods ended:	3m Dec. 31/22[A]		3m Dec. 31/21[A]
	$000s	%Chg	$000s
Net income	(153)	n.a.	(29)
	$		$
Earnings per share*	(0.06)		(0.01)

* Common
[A] Reported in accordance with IFRS

Historical Summary
(as originally stated)

Fiscal Year	Oper. Rev.	Net Inc. Bef. Disc.	EPS*
	$000s	$000s	$
2022[A]	nil	(316)	(0.06)
2021[A]	nil	(90)	(0.02)
2020[A]	114	(219)	(0.17)
2019[A]	100	(177)	(0.17)
2018[A]	155	(166)	(0.17)

* Common
[A] Reported in accordance with IFRS

Y.4 Ynvisible Interactive Inc.

Symbol - YNV **Exchange** - TSX-VEN **CUSIP** - 985844
Head Office - 830-1100 Melville St, PO Box 43, Vancouver, BC, V6E 4A6 **Telephone** - (778) 683-4324 **Toll-free** - (866) 637-5138
Website - www.ynvisible.com
Email - ir@ynvisible.com
Investor Relations - Darren C. Urquhart (604) 638-4324
Auditors - Baker Tilly WM LLP C.A., Vancouver, B.C.
Lawyers - McMillan LLP, Vancouver, B.C.
Transfer Agents - Computershare Trust Company of Canada Inc., Vancouver, B.C.
Profile - (B.C. 1983) Develops, manufactures and commercializes electrochromic displays (ECDs), which are printable on flexible materials such as plastic or paper, to be integrated into smart labels, smart indicators, smart products and Internet of Things (IoT) applications.

Develops and integrates know-how, design skill, development acumen, scale manufacturing capability and intellectual property in ECDs, materials, inks, display systems and complementing electronic components.

Provides interactive printed graphics solutions, which is a mix of standard and customized ultra-low power, mass deployable, & easy-to-use electronic displays and indicators, for everyday smart objects, IoT devices, and ambient intelligence (intelligent surfaces). Printed displays can be easily scaled up in production and integrated into finished, scalable product solutions like packaging labels, smart cards, and at-home electronic devices.

Other products and services include contracted research, prototyping, development, pilot production, production, and contract manufacturing services based on printed electronics, pilot and volume production of electrochromic displays, and tailored display solutions. Also offers a mix of services, materials and technology to brand owners developing smart objects and IoT products.

Predecessor Detail - Name changed from Network Exploration Ltd., Jan. 12, 2018, pursuant to reverse takeover acquisition of a 94.19% interest in YD Ynvisible S.A.
Directors - Ramin Heydarpour, chr. & CEO, Beverly Hills, Calif.; Jani-Mikael Kuusisto, v-chr., Tampere, Finland; Dr. Inês Henriques, COO, Lisbon, Portugal; Alexander B. (Alex) Helmel, Vancouver, B.C.; Alexander (Alex) Langer, North Vancouver, B.C.; Benjamin D. Leboe, B.C.
Other Exec. Officers - Darren C. Urquhart, CFO; Dr. Carlos Pinheiro, chief tech. officer; Keith Morton, v-p, sales & mktg.

Capital Stock

	Authorized (shs.)	Outstanding (shs.)[1]
Class A Common	unlimited	124,671,915
Class B Common	unlimited	nil

[1] At May 30, 2023

Class A Common - One vote per share.
Class B Common - Convertible on a share-for-share basis into class A common shares. Non-voting.
Major Shareholder - Widely held at Oct. 27, 2022.

Price Range - YNV/TSX-VEN

Year	Volume	High	Low	Close
2022	7,816,872	$0.37	$0.06	$0.08
2021	49,524,812	$2.05	$0.23	$0.27
2020	35,316,160	$0.93	$0.08	$0.70
2019	18,807,347	$0.54	$0.18	$0.25
2018	9,461,564	$0.48	$0.23	$0.24

Recent Close: $0.11
Capital Stock Changes - In April 2022, 5,000 class A common shares were issued in exchange for a like number of common shares of YD Ynvisible S.A.

Wholly Owned Subsidiaries

YD Ynvisible S.A., Portugal.
- 100% int. in **Ynvisible GmbH**, Freiburg im Breisgau, Germany.

Ynvisible Production AB, Sweden.

Financial Statistics

Periods ended:	12m Dec. 31/22[A]		12m Dec. 31/21[A]
	$000s	%Chg	$000s
Operating revenue	**686**	**-50**	**1,378**
Cost of sales	285		1,012
Salaries & benefits	2,877		3,011
General & admin expense	2,185		2,536
Stock-based compensation	716		1,167
Operating expense	**6,063**	**-22**	**7,725**
Operating income	**(5,377)**	**n.a.**	**(6,347)**
Deprec., depl. & amort.	605		570
Finance costs, gross	11		15
Write-downs/write-offs	nil		(39)
Pre-tax income	**(5,105)**	**n.a.**	**(5,885)**
Income taxes	4		1
Net income	**(5,109)**	**n.a.**	**(5,886)**
Cash & equivalent	11,844		16,107
Inventories	61		74
Accounts receivable	769		1,068
Current assets	12,792		17,439
Fixed assets, net	1,659		1,976
Right-of-use assets	307		372
Intangibles, net	316		387
Total assets	**15,080**	**-25**	**20,179**
Accts. pay. & accr. liabs	946		1,100
Current liabilities	1,464		2,003
Long-term lease liabilities	9		73
Shareholders' equity	13,607		18,104
Cash from oper. activs	**(3,903)**	**n.a.**	**(4,607)**
Cash from fin. activs	(271)		19,344
Cash from invest. activs	(67)		(275)
Net cash position	**11,844**	**-26**	**16,107**
Capital expenditures	(62)		(171)
	$		$
Earnings per share*	(0.04)		(0.05)
Cash flow per share*	(0.03)		(0.04)
	shs		shs
No. of shs. o/s*	124,671,915		124,666,915
Avg. no. of shs. o/s*	124,670,312		116,087,901
	%		%
Net profit margin	(744.75)		(427.14)
Return on equity	(32.22)		(54.31)
Return on assets	(28.92)		(44.79)

* Cl. A & B com.

[A] Reported in accordance with IFRS

Latest Results

Periods ended:	3m Mar. 31/23[A]		3m Mar. 31/22[A]
	$000s	%Chg	$000s
Operating revenue	265	+43	185
Net income	(1,193)	n.a.	(1,276)
	$		$
Earnings per share*	(0.01)		(0.01)

* Cl. A & B com.

[A] Reported in accordance with IFRS

Historical Summary
(as originally stated)

Fiscal Year	Oper. Rev.	Net Inc. Bef. Disc.	EPS*
	$000s	$000s	$
2022[A]	686	(5,109)	(0.04)
2021[A]	1,378	(5,886)	(0.05)
2020[A]	388	(3,795)	(0.05)
2019[A]	313	(3,467)	(0.05)
2018[A1]	nil	(5,419)	(0.11)

* Cl. A & B com.

[A] Reported in accordance with IFRS

[1] Results reflect the Jan. 19, 2018 reverse takeover acquisition of 94.19% of YD Ynvisible, S.A.

Y.5 Yongsheng Capital Inc.

Symbol - YSC.H **Exchange** - TSX-VEN (S) **CUSIP** - 98606Q
Head Office - 700-595 Burrard St, Vancouver, BC, V7X 1S8
Email - hildasung@gmail.com
Investor Relations - Hilda Sung 86-75-525-839-921
Auditors - A Chan & Company LLP C.A., Burnaby, B.C.
Lawyers - Clark Wilson LLP, Vancouver, B.C.
Transfer Agents - Computershare Trust Company of Canada Inc., Toronto, Ont.

Profile - (B.C. 2011) Capital Pool Company.

Common suspended from TSX-VEN, Apr. 8, 2020.

Directors - Hilda Sung, pres., CEO & interim CFO, Hong Kong, People's Republic of China; Shuen Chuen (Joseph) Chan, Richmond Hill, Ont.

Capital Stock

	Authorized (shs.)	Outstanding (shs.)[1]
Common	unlimited	5,150,000

[1] At Aug. 2, 2022

Price Range - YSC.H/TSX-VEN (S)

Year	Volume	High	Low	Close
2020	10,000	$0.03	$0.03	$0.03
2019	42,166	$0.06	$0.05	$0.05
2018	196,666	$0.07	$0.04	$0.05

Y.6 Yooma Wellness Inc.

Symbol - YOOM **Exchange** - CSE (S) **CUSIP** - 98615V
Head Office - 900-135 Yorkville Ave, Toronto, ON, M5R 0C7 **Telephone** - (416) 419-7046
Website - yooma.ca
Email - jgreenberg@yooma.ca
Investor Relations - Jordan Greenberg (416) 419-7046
Auditors - BF Borgers CPA PC C.P.A., Lakewood, Colo.
Transfer Agents - Odyssey Trust Company, Toronto, Ont.

Profile - (Ont. 2021 amalg.) Manufactures, markets, distributes and sells wellness products, including hemp seed oil and hemp-derived and cannabinoid ingredients.

Products include tea, infusion, cannabidiol (CBD) oils, protein, chocolate bars, cookies, vegetable mince, bites, granolas, spreads, and hemp seeds, oil and flour under the hello Joya brand; CBD beauty, cosmetic and personal care products under the Blossom brand; essential amino acids, functional sprays, superfood blends, pre and probiotics, and plant proteins under the MYO Plant Nutrition brand; granolas, and CBD infusions and oils under the What The Hemp brand; disposable vapes, oils, drops, sprays, active CBD range, support CBD range, balms, infused cosmetics, gummies and e-liquids under the Vitality CBD brand. Other brands include Branfine, Ems, mondiale, Sakai Premium and Vertex. Products are sold through sales channels and e-commerce networks primarily in the U.K. and France.

In February 2023, the company reached a settlement with the vendors of **Vertex Co., Ltd.** (acquired by the company on Oct. 1, 2021) which will discharge US$12,000,000 in debts and other obligations of the company, consisting of US$2,500,000 paid on closing, and deferred payments of US$6,500,000 due Apr. 30, 2023, and US$3,000,000 due Apr. 30, 2023. As a result, the company exited from the Japanese market.

During the period ended Sept. 30, 2022, operations of wholly owned **Socati Corp.**, which manufactures cannabidiol (CBD) ingredients, and wholly owned **Big Swig Inc.**, which operates a sparkling water business, were suspended; and wholly owned **N8 Essentials, LLC**, which manufactures and sells wellness products, ceased all operations as part of the company's re-evaluation of operations in the U.S. In addition, Socati's real estate asset in Montana was sold for US$2,500,000; and all assets of N8 were sold to a third party for US$200,000.

Common suspended from CSE, May 8, 2023.

Predecessor Detail - Formed from Globalive Technology Inc. in Ontario, Feb. 10, 2021, pursuant to the reverse takeover acquisition of and amalgamation with Yooma Corp.

Directors - Lorne K. Abony, chr., Austin, Tex.; Jordan Greenberg, pres., CEO & corp. sec., Toronto, Ont.; Antonio Costanzo, London, Middx., United Kingdom; Simon Dryan; Anthony (Tony) Lacavera, Toronto, Ont.

Other Exec. Officers - Joshua Lebovic, interim CFO

Capital Stock

	Authorized (shs.)	Outstanding (shs.)[1]
Common	unlimited	100,859,744

[1] At Nov. 28, 2022

Major Shareholder - Widely held at Oct. 11, 2021.

Price Range - LIVE/TSX-VEN (D)

Year	Volume	High	Low	Close
2022	4,504,418	$0.24	$0.01	$0.02
2021	6,253,826	$1.75	$0.16	$0.16
2020	202,196	$2.60	$0.60	$1.10
2019	1,015,250	$5.50	$0.80	$1.80
2018	965,574	$30.40	$3.00	$3.70

Consolidation: 1-for-20 cons. in June 2020
Recent Close: $0.01

Wholly Owned Subsidiaries

Big Swig, Inc., United States.
Entertainment District Asia Ltd., British Virgin Islands.
N8 Essentials LLC, United States.
Socati Corp., Austin, Tex.
Vertex Co., Ltd., Tokyo, Japan.
Yooma Europe Limited, United Kingdom.
- 100% int. in **Green Leaf Company S.A.S.**, France.
- 100% int. in **Vitality CBD Limited**, United Kingdom.

Yooma Japan KK, Japan.

Financial Statistics

Periods ended:	12m Dec. 31/21[A1]		12m Dec. 31/20[¤A]
	US$000s	%Chg	US$000s
Operating revenue	**10,185**	**n.m.**	**43**
Cost of sales	7,812		86
Salaries & benefits	3,320		704
Research & devel. expense	9		nil
General & admin expense	9,877		1,474
Stock-based compensation	428		nil
Operating expense	**21,445**	**+847**	**2,264**
Operating income	**(11,260)**	**n.a.**	**(2,221)**
Deprec., depl. & amort.	912		17
Write-downs/write-offs	(22,504)		nil
Pre-tax income	**(33,332)**	**n.a.**	**(2,274)**
Income taxes	(215)		nil
Net income	**(33,117)**	**n.a.**	**(2,274)**
Cash & equivalent	1,233		2,482
Inventories	2,458		117
Accounts receivable	3,059		85
Current assets	8,341		2,701
Fixed assets, net	3,043		nil
Intangibles, net	25,029		1,366
Total assets	**36,589**	**+800**	**4,067**
Accts. pay. & accr. liabs	4,471		816
Current liabilities	7,097		873
Long-term debt, gross	10,886		nil
Long-term debt, net	10,886		nil
Long-term lease liabilities	1,107		n.a.
Shareholders' equity	15,297		3,194
Cash from oper. activs	**(10,968)**	**n.a.**	**(1,673)**
Cash from fin. activs	9,288		2,345
Cash from invest. activs	482		320
Net cash position	**1,233**	**-50**	**2,482**
	US$		US$
Earnings per share*	(0.43)		(0.08)
Cash flow per share*	(0.14)		(0.00)
	shs		shs
No. of shs. o/s*	100,859,744		n.a.
Avg. no. of shs. o/s*	77,554,161		26,822,087
	%		%
Net profit margin	(325.15)		n.m.
Return on equity	(217.00)		(21.69)
Return on assets	(126.40)		(20.76)

* Common

[¤] Restated

[A] Reported in accordance with IFRS

[1] Results reflect the Feb. 10, 2021 reverse takeover acquisition of Yooma Corp.

Latest Results

Periods ended:	9m Sept. 30/22[A]		9m Sept. 30/21[A]
	US$000s	%Chg	US$000s
Operating revenue	8,914	+82	4,910
Net income	(4,450)	n.a.	(8,203)
	US$		US$
Earnings per share*	(0.04)		(0.14)

* Common

[A] Reported in accordance with IFRS

Historical Summary
(as originally stated)

Fiscal Year	Oper. Rev.	Net Inc. Bef. Disc.	EPS*
	US$000s	US$000s	US$
2021[A]	10,185	(33,117)	(0.43)
	$000s	$000s	$
2020[A1]	nil	(6,146)	(0.88)
2019[A]	nil	(14,094)	(2.02)
2018[A2,3]	674	(23,698)	(3.90)

* Common

[A] Reported in accordance with IFRS

[1] Results for 2020 and 2019 pertain to Globalive Technology Inc.

[2] 10 months ended Dec. 31, 2018.

[3] Results reflect the June 8, 2018, reverse takeover acquisition of Globalive Technology Partners Inc.

Note: Adjusted throughout for 1-for-20 cons. in June 2020

Y.7 Yorkton Equity Group Inc.

Symbol - YEG **Exchange** - TSX-VEN **CUSIP** - 98721W
Head Office - Manulife Place, 3165-10180 101 St NW, Edmonton, AB, T5J 3S4 **Telephone** - (780) 409-8228 **Toll-free** - (886) 409-8228
Fax - (780) 409-9228
Website - yorktonequitygroup.com
Email - ben.lui@yorktongroup.com
Investor Relations - Ben Lui (780) 409-8228 ext. 222
Auditors - Kenway Mack Slusarchuk Stewart LLP C.A., Calgary, Alta.
Transfer Agents - Computershare Trust Company of Canada Inc., Calgary, Alta.

Profile - (Alta. 2016) Owns and acquires residential and commercial real estate properties in Alberta and British Columbia.

At Mar. 31, 2023, portfolio consisted of nine residential properties in Kelowna, Langford, Penticton, and Fort St. John (4), B.C., and Edmonton, Alta., totaling 393 units; and a two-storey commercial property known as Pacific Rim Mall in Edmonton, Alta., which features tenants including large banquet restaurant and HSBC bank branch.

Recent Merger and Acquisition Activity

Status: completed **Revised:** Feb. 28, 2023

UPDATE: The transaction was completed. PREVIOUS: Yorkton Equity Group Inc. agreed to acquire a 188-unit multi-family apartment complex in Edmonton, Alta., for $41,736,000, which was funded with cash on hand and an insured mortgage. The complex, known as The Dwell, consisted of two luxury condominium grade buildings situated on 3.31 acres of land.

Status: completed **Revised:** Apr. 11, 2022

UPDATE: The transaction was completed for $6,480,000. PREVIOUS: Yorkton Equity Group Inc. agreed to acquire a 50-unit townhouse portfolio in Fort St. John, B.C., consisting of two adjacent townhouse complexes situated on a 3.28-acre parcel of land. Terms of the transaction would be disclosed following completion.

Predecessor Detail - Name changed from Trusted Brand 2016 Inc., Nov. 20, 2020, pursuant to Qualifying Transaction reverse takeover acquisition of 1421526 Alberta Ltd.

Directors - Bill Smith, chr., Edmonton, Alta.; Ben Lui, pres. & CEO, Edmonton, Alta.; Jason Theiss, Edmonton, Alta.; Mark Wilbert, Edmonton, Alta.

Other Exec. Officers - William Harper, CFO & corp. sec.; R. (Reg) Liyanage, exec. v-p

Capital Stock

	Authorized (shs.)	Outstanding (shs.)[1]
Preferred	unlimited	nil
Common	unlimited	112,657,427

[1] At May 29, 2023

Normal Course Issuer Bid - The company plans to make normal course purchases of up to 5,633,871 common shares representing 5% of the total outstanding. The bid commenced on Jan. 27, 2023, and expires on Jan. 26, 2024.

Major Shareholder - Ben Lui held 73.23% interest at May 8, 2023.

Price Range - YEG/TSX-VEN

Year	Volume	High	Low	Close
2022	2,387,801	$0.20	$0.12	$0.15
2021	4,071,461	$0.45	$0.17	$0.18
2020	973,955	$0.25	$0.15	$0.25

Recent Close: $0.15

Capital Stock Changes - During 2022, 101,605 common shares were issued on exercise of options.

Wholly Owned Subsidiaries

Canterbury YXJ Properties Ltd., Fort St. John, B.C.
- 100% int. in **Canterbury YXJ Holdings Ltd.**, Fort St. John, B.C.

Larson Nickel Properties Ltd., B.C.
- 100% int. in **Larson Nickel Holdings Ltd.**, B.C.

Midtown YXJ Properties Ltd., Fort St. John, B.C.
- 100% int. in **Midtown YXJ Holdings Ltd.**, Fort St. John, B.C.

1205946 Alberta Ltd., Edmonton, Alta.
1305271 B.C. Ltd., B.C.
1421526 Alberta Ltd., Edmonton, Alta.
1999988 Alberta Ltd., Alta.
Pacific Central Properties Ltd., B.C.
- 100% int. in **Pacific Central Holdings Ltd.**, B.C.

Windsor Shamrock YXJ Properties Ltd., B.C.
- 100% int. in **Shamrock YXJ Holdings Ltd.**, B.C.
- 100% int. in **Windsor YXJ Holdings Ltd.**, Fort St. John, B.C.

Winton Terrace Properties Ltd., Penticton, B.C.
- 100% int. in **Winton Terrace Holdings Ltd.**, Penticton, B.C.

Investments

25% int. in **Yorkton 108 Limited Partnership**, B.C.

Financial Statistics

Periods ended:	12m Dec. 31/22[A]		12m Dec. 31/21[oA]
	$000s	%Chg	$000s
Total revenue	**3,422**	**+129**	**1,492**
Rental operating expense	1,577		931
Operating expense	**2,320**	**+22**	**1,899**
Operating income	**1,102**	**n.a.**	**(407)**
Deprec. & amort.	3		2
Non-operating overhead	724		946
Finance costs, gross	1,576		479
Write-downs/write-offs	(125)		(116)
Pre-tax income	**69**	**n.a.**	**(1,219)**
Income taxes	231		37
Net income	**(162)**	**n.a.**	**(1,257)**
Cash & equivalent	2,951		2,330
Accounts receivable	291		30
Current assets	3,725		3,057
Long-term investments	40		40
Fixed assets	14		12
Income-producing props	6,360		6,400
Properties for future devel	7,000		6,620
Property interests, net	54,630		42,500
Total assets	**58,611**	**+28**	**45,862**
Accts. pay. & accr. liabs	436		483
Current liabilities	4,492		14,044
Long-term debt, gross	35,383		21,571
Long-term debt, net	31,760		10,242
Equity portion of conv. debs	408		nil
Shareholders' equity	20,941		20,511
Cash from oper. activs	**781**	**n.a.**	**(976)**
Cash from fin. activs	11,225		20,084
Cash from invest. activs	(11,235)		(17,929)
Net cash position	**2,951**	**+35**	**2,180**
Capital expenditures	(5)		nil
Increase in property	11,478		20,431
	$		$
Earnings per share*	(0.00)		(0.01)
Cash flow per share*	0.01		(0.01)
	shs		shs
No. of shs. o/s*	112,677,427		112,575,822
Avg. no. of shs. o/s*	112,635,393		97,338,049
	%		%
Net profit margin	(4.73)		(84.25)
Return on equity	(0.78)		(8.01)
Return on assets	(7.39)		(2.51)

* Common
[o] Restated
[A] Reported in accordance with IFRS

Latest Results

Periods ended:	3m Mar. 31/23[A]		3m Mar. 31/22[A]
	$000s	%Chg	$000s
Total revenue	11,280	n.m.	722
Net income	1	n.a.	(219)
	$		$
Earnings per share*	nil		(0.00)

* Common
[A] Reported in accordance with IFRS

Historical Summary
(as originally stated)

Fiscal Year	Total Rev.	Net Inc. Bef. Disc.	EPS*
	$000s	$000s	$
2022[A]	3,422	(162)	(0.00)
2021[A]	1,492	(1,257)	(0.01)
2020[A1]	925	(422)	(0.01)
2019[A]	1,033	208	n.a.
2018[A]	1,007	176	n.a.

* Common
[A] Reported in accordance with IFRS
[1] Results prior to Nov. 18, 2020, pertain to and reflect the reverse takeover acquisition of 1421526 Alberta Ltd.

Y.8 YourWay Cannabis Brands Inc.

Symbol - YOUR **Exchange** - CSE (S) **CUSIP** - 987812
Head Office - 2200-885 Georgia St W, Vancouver, BC, V6C 3E8
Telephone - (604) 961-0296
Website - www.yourwaycannabis.com
Email - glen@yourwaycannabis.com
Investor Relations - Glen Shear (437) 218-1445
Auditors - Semple, Marchal & Cooper, LLP C.P.A., Phoenix, Ariz.
Transfer Agents - Olympia Trust Company, Vancouver, B.C.

Profile - (B.C. 2019) Manufactures and distributes cannabis products in California and Arizona. Also developing non-psychoactive mushroom-based natural health products.

Operates a 37,061-sq.-ft. facility in Hollister, Calif., where 2,061 sq. ft. is used, and an 11,000-sq.-ft. facility in Phoenix, Ariz., to process and manufacture cannabis products. The company plans to build-out the remaining portion of the Hollister facility to allow for additional processing, manufacturing and packaging projects, including its nanoemulsified cannabis concentrate, NanoPure, to be used in sublingual sprays, beverages, edibles and capsules. Also holds a 30-acre property in Cottonwood, Ariz., where it plans to develop in phases over 700,000 sq. ft. of canopy for cultivation and a 28,500-sq.-ft. processing and manufacturing facility. Offers products for the medicinal and recreational markets, including distillates, concentrates, pre-packaged flower, pre-roll, hash-infused pre-roll, bubble hash, tinctures, vape products and pet tinctures. Proprietary brands include Venom Extracts in Arizona and HashBone, Purity Petibles and Hollister Cannabis Co. in California. In addition, offers white labeling manufacturing for other brands, including Tommy Chong's, Tactical Relief, Easyriders and Heavy Grass. The company's products are sold in about 400 dispensaries across Arizona and California and through its direct-to-consumer delivery platform, Dreamy Delivery, in select areas in California.

Operations also include wholly owned **AlphaMind Brands Inc.**, which is developing legal mushroom-based natural health products.

Common suspended from CSE, May 10, 2022.

Recent Merger and Acquisition Activity

Status: pending **Announced:** Apr. 20, 2022

YourWay Cannabis Brands Inc. agreed to acquire Ionic Brands Corp. on the basis of 0.0525 YourWay common share for each Ionic Brands held, including all Ionic Brands' Shares issuable on conversion of Ionic Brands' issued and outstanding preferred shares.

Predecessor Detail - Name changed from Hollister Biosciences Inc., Dec. 13, 2021.

Directors - Jakob Ripshtein, exec. chr. & acting CEO, Toronto, Ont.; Jacob (Jake) Cohen, Ariz.; Lily Dash, Barbados; Kevin Harrington, Fla.; Brett Mecum, Ariz.

Other Exec. Officers - Sandra Ceccacci, CFO; Christopher (Chris) Lund, chief comml. officer; Damian Solomon, exec. v-p, cultivation; Jill Karpe, sr. v-p, fin. & admin.

Capital Stock

	Authorized (shs.)	Outstanding (shs.)[1]
Common	unlimited	197,191,152
Proportionate	unlimited	75,564

[1] At June 29, 2022

Common - One vote per share.

Proportionate - Each convertible, at the holder's option, into 1,000 common shares. 1,000 votes per share.

Major Shareholder - Jacob (Jake) Cohen held 17.9% interest, Ischgl Management LLC held 11.6% interest and Carl Saling held 10.6% interest at June 29, 2022.

Price Range - YOUR/CSE (S)

Year	Volume	High	Low	Close
2022	12,797,690	$0.19	$0.09	$0.09
2021	90,949,990	$0.53	$0.15	$0.17
2020	192,759,096	$0.36	$0.04	$0.26
2019	8,232,756	$0.22	$0.09	$0.16

Wholly Owned Subsidiaries

AlphaMind Brands Inc., Canada.
Labtronix, Inc., Ariz. dba Venom Extracts
Rebel Hemp Company, United States.
Weldon Manor LLC, San Diego, Calif. dba Hollister Cannabis
- 100% int. in **Hollister Holistics 1**, Hollister, Calif. dba Hollister Cannabis Co.
- 100% int. in **Hollister Holistics 2**, San Diego, Calif.

Y.9 Yubba Capital Corp.

Symbol - YUB.P **Exchange** - TSX-VEN **CUSIP** - 988365
Head Office - 207-2131 Lawrence Ave E, Toronto, ON, M1R 5G4
Telephone - (647) 241-7202
Email - yubbacapital@gmail.com
Investor Relations - Jason Smart (647) 241-7202
Auditors - MNP LLP C.A., Mississauga, Ont.
Transfer Agents - TSX Trust Company, Toronto, Ont.
Profile - (Ont. 2021) Capital Pool Company.

Recent Merger and Acquisition Activity

Status: pending **Announced:** Dec. 2, 2022

Yubba Capital Corp. entered into a letter of intent for the Qualifying Transaction reverse takeover acquisition of Impact Housing Corporation, (IHC), a Panamanian based real estate developer. Each share of IHC would be exchanged for one common share of Yubba. The structure of the transaction was to be determined. IHC plans to complete a private placement offering of a minimum US$6,000,000 of subscription receipts. IHC provides affordable housing supported by a long standing subsidized government program with multiple product offerings. It builds and develops affordable and subsidized houses and in the Republic of Panama to support the middle class market.

Directors - Jason Smart, CEO, CFO & corp. sec., Toronto, Ont.; Brian Morales, Toronto, Ont.; Edward (Ted) Yew, Toronto, Ont.

Capital Stock

	Authorized (shs.)	Outstanding (shs.)[1]
Common	unlimited	5,220,000

[1] At May 30, 2022

Major Shareholder - Jason Smart held 40.23% interest at Oct. 21, 2021.

Price Range - YUB.P/TSX-VEN

Year	Volume	High	Low	Close
2022	65,000	$0.08	$0.05	$0.05
2021	120,000	$0.16	$0.12	$0.16

Recent Close: $0.05

Y.10 The Yumy Candy Company Inc.

Symbol - TYUM **Exchange** - CSE **CUSIP** - 98873A
Head Office - 2500-700 Georgia St W, Vancouver, BC, V7Y 1B3 **Telephone** - (604) 449-2026
Website - yumybear.com
Email - investors@yumybear.com
Investor Relations - Investor Relations (604) 449-2026
Auditors - Dale Matheson Carr-Hilton LaBonte LLP C.A., Vancouver, B.C.
Transfer Agents - Endeavor Trust Corporation, Vancouver, B.C.
Profile - (B.C. 1997) Develops, manufactures and distributes a line of better-for-you, plant-based, low-sugar gummy bears to wholesalers, retailers and consumers in Canada.

The gummy bears are free of gelatin, soy, gluten, nuts, dairy, eggs, sugar alcohols, artificial sweeteners and genetically modified organisms. Products such as proprietary Yumy Bear™ are manufactured through an overseas partnership, and are distributed to wholesalers and retail trade partners in Canada, as well as directly to consumers online. Most of the company's sales have been from the metropolitan areas of British Columbia. The company is working on expanding its products in the United States through large grocery chains, as well as its confectionary product line beyond gummy products to become an all-encompassing confectionery company. The expanded product line will include lollipops, chews and hard candy logs.

Predecessor Detail - Name changed from Yumy Bear Goods Inc., Dec. 30, 2021.

Directors - Cassidy McCord, CEO, Vancouver, B.C.; Yinshun (Sue) He, CFO, B.C.; Quinn Field-Dyte, Vancouver, B.C.; Pegah Manavikherad

Capital Stock

	Authorized (shs.)	Outstanding (shs.)[1]
Common	unlimited	29,208,132

[1] At May 1, 2023

Major Shareholder - Widely held at May 1, 2023.

Price Range - TYUM/CSE

Year	Volume	High	Low	Close
2022	4,188,800	$2.70	$0.31	$0.50
2021	3,455,457	$5.75	$0.36	$2.70

Consolidation: 1-for-3 cons. in July 2021
Recent Close: $0.28
Capital Stock Changes - During fiscal 2023, 1,720,000 common shares were issued on exercise of warrants.

Wholly Owned Subsidiaries

1295304 B.C. Ltd., Vancouver, B.C.
Yumy Bear Goods (US) Inc., United States.

Financial Statistics

Periods ended:	12m Jan. 31/23[A]		12m Jan. 31/22[A1]
	$000s	%Chg	$000s
Operating revenue	**775**	**+113**	**364**
Cost of sales	522		429
Research & devel. expense	412		413
General & admin expense	1,304		2,717
Operating expense	**2,238**	**-37**	**3,559**
Operating income	**(1,463)**	**n.a.**	**(3,195)**
Deprec., depl. & amort.	nil		6
Finance costs, gross	7		10
Pre-tax income	**(1,471)**	**n.a.**	**(11,253)**
Net income	**(1,471)**	**n.a.**	**(11,253)**
Cash & equivalent	101		639
Inventories	105		320
Accounts receivable	137		85
Current assets	382		1,152
Total assets	**382**	**-67**	**1,152**
Bank indebtedness	216		nil
Accts. pay. & accr. liabs	1,583		1,185
Current liabilities	1,800		1,185
Shareholders' equity	(1,418)		(33)
Cash from oper. activs	**(837)**	**n.a.**	**(3,536)**
Cash from fin. activs	299		747
Cash from invest. activs	nil		937
Net cash position	**101**	**-84**	**639**
	$		$
Earnings per share*	(0.05)		(0.45)
Cash flow per share*	(0.03)		(0.14)
	shs		shs
No. of shs. o/s*	29,208,132		27,488,132
Avg. no. of shs. o/s*	27,789,721		25,227,110
	%		%
Net profit margin	(189.81)		n.m.
Return on equity	n.m.		n.m.
Return on assets	n.a.		(615.21)

* Common
[A] Reported in accordance with IFRS
[1] Results reflect the June 30, 2021, reverse takeover acquisition of (old) Yumy Bear Goods Inc.

Latest Results

Periods ended:	3m Apr. 30/23[A]		3m Apr. 30/22[A]
	$000s	%Chg	$000s
Operating revenue	74	-62	197
Net income	(432)	n.a.	(353)
	$		$
Earnings per share*	(0.01)		(0.01)

* Common
[A] Reported in accordance with IFRS

Historical Summary
(as originally stated)

Fiscal Year	Oper. Rev.	Net Inc. Bef. Disc.	EPS*
	$000s	$000s	$
2023[A]	775	(1,471)	(0.05)
2022[A]	364	(11,253)	(0.45)
2020[A1]	nil	(161)	(0.15)
2019[A]	nil	(193)	(0.18)

* Common
[A] Reported in accordance with IFRS
[1] Results for fiscal 2020 and prior fiscal years pertain to Fire River Gold Corp.
Note: Adjusted throughout for 1-for-3 cons. in July 2021

Z

Z.1 ZTEST Electronics Inc.

Symbol - ZTE **Exchange** - CSE **CUSIP** - 989930
Head Office - 523 McNicoll Ave, North York, ON, M2H 2C9 **Telephone** - (416) 297-5155 **Fax** - (416) 297-5156
Website - www.ztest.com
Email - stevesmith15@shaw.ca
Investor Relations - Stephen Smith (416) 297-5155
Auditors - Wasserman Ramsay C.A., Markham, Ont.
Transfer Agents - TSX Trust Company, Toronto, Ont.
Profile - (Ont. 1996 amalg.) Designs, develops and assembles printed circuit boards and other electronic equipment.

Wholly owned **Permatech Electronics Corporation** provides materials management, printed circuit board assembly, testing and design services to customers including the medical, power, computer, telecommunication, wireless, industrial and consumer electronics markets. Operations are located at a 20,000-sq.-ft. facility in North York, Ont.

Affiliate **Conversance Inc.** (25.29% owned) develops and markets proprietary artificial intelligence (AI) supported distributed ledger technologies.

Predecessor Detail - Formed from Panthco Resources Inc. in Ontario, July 1, 1996, on amalgamation with ZTEST Electronics Inc., constituting a reverse takeover by ZTEST; basis 1 new for 1 ZTEST sh. and 1 new com. and 1 new cl. A special for 8 old shs.

Directors - Stephen (Steve) Smith, chr., pres. & CEO, White Rock, B.C.; Don Beaton, Burlington, Ont.; K. Michael Guerreiro, Cambridge, Ont.; Derrick Strickland, Vancouver, B.C.; Dean Tyliakos, St. Albert, Alta.

Other Exec. Officers - Michael D. (Mike) Kindy, v-p, fin. & CFO; William R. (Bill) Johnstone, corp. sec.

Capital Stock

	Authorized (shs.)	Outstanding (shs.)[1]
Common	unlimited	26,687,196

[1] At May 30, 2023

Common shares - One vote per share.
Preferred shares series 2 (old) - Were redeemable, non-voting, with no dividend rights and subject to conversion into common shares on completion of financing by Conversance Inc. Redeemed on June 30, 2022, for $1.
Major Shareholder - Widely held at Aug. 15, 2022.

Price Range - ZTE/CSE

Year	Volume	High	Low	Close
2022	2,424,408	$0.34	$0.02	$0.03
2021	3,896,751	$0.45	$0.18	$0.27
2020	3,158,769	$0.39	$0.10	$0.37
2019	1,531,795	$0.44	$0.08	$0.20
2018	4,389,093	$1.06	$0.10	$0.41

Recent Close: $0.12
Capital Stock Changes - During fiscal 2022, common shares were issued as follows: 2,260,000 on exercise of warrants and 200,000 on exercise of options; 1,250,000 convertible preferred shares series 2 were redeemed.

Wholly Owned Subsidiaries

Permatech Electronics Corporation
Twenty49 Ltd. Inactive.

Subsidiaries

66.7% int. in **Northern Cross Minerals Inc.** Inactive.

Investments

25.29% int. in **Conversance Inc.**, Waterloo, Ont.
- 28% int. in **3955 Trading Inc.**, Canada. dba Cannamerx.

Financial Statistics

Periods ended:	12m June 30/22[A]		12m June 30/21[A]
	$000s	%Chg	$000s
Operating revenue	**4,415**	**+10**	**4,009**
Cost of sales	3,209		2,740
General & admin expense	1,181		1,056
Operating expense	**4,390**	**+16**	**3,796**
Operating income	**25**	**-88**	**213**
Deprec., depl. & amort.	249		162
Finance costs, gross	38		11
Pre-tax income	**(267)**	**n.a.**	**46**
Net income	**(267)**	**n.a.**	**46**
Cash & equivalent	268		557
Inventories	857		488
Accounts receivable	783		655
Current assets	1,920		1,718
Fixed assets, net	505		581
Right-of-use assets	657		822
Total assets	**3,082**	**-1**	**3,121**
Accts. pay. & accr. liabs	1,250		960
Current liabilities	1,470		1,168
Long-term debt, gross	305		364
Long-term debt, net	244		305
Long-term lease liabilities	485		644
Shareholders' equity	883		1,004
Cash from oper. activs	**(195)**	**n.a.**	**356**
Cash from fin. activs	(86)		394
Cash from invest. activs	(8)		(413)
Net cash position	**268**	**-52**	**557**
Capital expenditures	(8)		(413)
	$		$
Earnings per share*	(0.01)		0.00
Cash flow per share*	(0.01)		0.01
	shs		shs
No. of shs. o/s*	26,687,196		24,227,196
Avg. no. of shs. o/s*	25,780,073		24,227,196
	%		%
Net profit margin	(6.05)		1.15
Return on equity	(28.30)		5.20
Return on assets	(7.38)		2.31

* Common
[A] Reported in accordance with IFRS

Latest Results

Periods ended:	3m Sept. 30/22[A]		3m Sept. 30/21[A]
	$000s	%Chg	$000s
Operating revenue	1,169	+86	630
Net income	(87)	n.a.	(170)
	$		$
Earnings per share*	(0.00)		(0.01)

* Common
[A] Reported in accordance with IFRS

Historical Summary
(as originally stated)

Fiscal Year	Oper. Rev.	Net Inc. Bef. Disc.	EPS*
	$000s	$000s	$
2022[A]	4,415	(267)	(0.01)
2021[A]	4,009	46	0.00
2020[A]	3,889	(819)	(0.04)
2019[A]	4,399	(344)	(0.02)
2018[A]	3,686	(884)	(0.05)

* Common
[A] Reported in accordance with IFRS

Z.2 ZYUS Life Sciences Corporation

Symbol - ZYUS **Exchange** - TSX-VEN **CUSIP** - 989960
Head Office - 204-407 Downey Rd, Saskatoon, SK, S7N 4L8 **Telephone** - (306) 242-2357 **Toll-free** - (888) 651-9987
Website - zyus.com
Email - michelle.gursky@zyus.com
Investor Relations - Michelle Gursky (888) 651-9987
Auditors - KPMG LLP C.A.
Transfer Agents - TSX Trust Company
Profile - (Ont. 1944) Focuses on development and commercialization of cannabinoid-based drug product candidates.

The company's first drug product candidate for pain management in patients suffering from chronic pain is Trichomylin softgel capsules, for which it has completed a Phase I clinical trial. Has a production facility Saskatoon, Sask.

During the second quarter of 2022, the company sold for $1.00 its remaining gas interests, nominal interests in a mature gas field which had ceased operation. The company paid $12,000 in estimated abandonment and reclamation costs in exchange for indemnification with respect to all potential remediation costs.

Recent Merger and Acquisition Activity

Status: completed **Revised:** June 12, 2023
UPDATE: The transaction was completed. PREVIOUS: Phoenix Canada Oil Company Limited entered into a letter of intent for the reverse takeover acquisition of Saskatoon, Sask.-based ZYUS Life Sciences Inc., which is researching and developing cannabinoid products for pain management. ZYUS shareholders would receive common shares of Phoenix at an exchange ratio to be determined. A subscription receipt financing for gross proceeds of up to $25,000,000 would be completed by ZYUS. On closing, ZYUS would change its name to ZYUS Life Sciences Corporation. July 7, 2022 - Phoenix paid $1,700,000 to ZYUS in exchange for $1,700,000 in 12% promissory notes which become automatically convertible into common shares of ZYUS at a price equal to 85% of the deemed price of such shares in the proposed business combination plus 680,000 warrants exercisable at $2.50 per share until Jan. 7, 2025. Nov. 16, 2022 - A definitive agreement was signed. June 6, 2023 - Conditional TSX Venture Exchange approval was received

Predecessor Detail - Name changed from Phoenix Canada Oil Company Limited, June 9, 2023, pursuant to the reverse takeover acquisition of ZYUS Life Sciences Inc.

Directors - Richard Hoyt, chr., Mo.; Brent H. Zettl, pres., CEO & corp. sec., Saskatoon, Sask.; Wayne R. Brownlee, Saskatoon, Sask.; John L. Knowles, Winnipeg, Man.; Dr. Charlotte Moore Hepburn, Toronto, Ont.; Garnette Weber, Sask.

Other Exec. Officers - John M. Hyshka, CFO; Keith Carpenter, chief strategy & invest. officer; Dr. Lionel Marks De Chabris, CMO

Capital Stock

	Authorized (shs.)	Outstanding (shs.)[1]
Common	unlimited	69,847,381

[1] At June 19, 2023

Major Shareholder - Brent H. Zettl held 49% interest at June 19, 2023.

Price Range - ZYUS/TSX-VEN

Year	Volume	High	Low	Close
2022	25,154	$1.50	$0.60	$0.85
2021	74,871	$1.75	$1.16	$1.16
2020	104,558	$1.80	$1.10	$1.80
2019	67,350	$1.40	$1.16	$1.20
2018	375,842	$1.60	$1.30	$1.45

Recent Close: $1.07
Capital Stock Changes - In June 2023, 64,533,278 common shares issued pursuant to the reverse takeover acquisition of ZYUS Life Sciences Inc. (old ZYUS), including 17,070,085 shares on conversion of over $31,100,000 of (old) ZYUS convertible debt and 8,862,758 shares without further consideration on exchange of (old) ZYUS subscription receipts sold previously for proceeds of $20,130,131.

Wholly Owned Subsidiaries

ZYUS Life Sciences Inc., Saskatoon, Sask.
- 100% int. in **ZYUS Life Sciences Australia Pty Ltd.**, Australia.
- 100% int. in **ZYUS Life Sciences Europe S.A.R.L.**, Luxembourg.
  - 100% int. in **ZYUS Life Sciences Germany GmbH**, Germany.
  - 100% int. in **ZYUS Sociedade Unipessoal Lda.**, Portugal.
- 100% int. in **ZYUS Life Sciences US Ltd.**, United States.
- 100% int. in **ZYUS S.H. Bio Manufacturing Pty Ltd.**, Australia.

Financial Statistics

Periods ended:	12m Dec. 31/22[A1]		12m Dec. 31/21[A]
	$000s	%Chg	$000s
General & admin expense	463		201
Other operating expense	(1)		28
Operating expense	**463**	**+102**	**229**
Operating income	**(463)**	**n.a.**	**(229)**
Investment income	289		103
Pre-tax income	**(362)**	**n.a.**	**351**
Net income	**(362)**	**n.a.**	**351**
Cash & equivalent	6,948		8,593
Accounts receivable	170		44
Current assets	7,118		8,636
Total assets	**8,818**	**+2**	**8,636**
Accts. pay. & accr. liabs	202		96
Current liabilities	202		96
Shareholders' equity	8,615		8,540
Cash from oper. activs	**(193)**	**n.a.**	**(333)**
Cash from fin. activs	437		nil
Cash from invest. activs	(1,700)		(579)
Net cash position	**4,839**	**-23**	**6,295**
	$		$
Earnings per share*	(0.07)		0.07
Cash flow per share*	(0.04)		(0.07)
	shs		shs
No. of shs. o/s*	5,314,103		5,029,194
Avg. no. of shs. o/s*	5,067,360		5,029,194
	%		%
Net profit margin	n.a.		n.a.
Return on equity	(4.22)		4.20
Return on assets	(4.15)		4.09

* Common
[A] Reported in accordance with IFRS
[1] Results for 2022 and prior periods pretain to Phoenix Canada Oil Company Limited.

Latest Results

Periods ended:	3m Mar. 31/23[A]		3m Mar. 31/22[A]
	$000s	%Chg	$000s
Net income	1	-99	104
	$		$
Earnings per share*	0.00		0.02

* Common
[A] Reported in accordance with IFRS

Historical Summary
(as originally stated)

Fiscal Year	Oper. Rev.	Net Inc. Bef. Disc.	EPS*
	$000s	$000s	$
2022[A]	nil	(362)	(0.07)
2021[A]	nil	351	0.07
2020[A]	nil	(728)	(0.14)
2019[A]	nil	274	0.05
2018[A]	1	(664)	(0.13)

* Common
[A] Reported in accordance with IFRS

Z.3 Zedcor Inc.

Symbol - ZDC **Exchange** - TSX-VEN **CUSIP** - 98923V
Head Office - 300-151 Canada Olympic Rd SW, Calgary, AB, T3B 6B7 **Telephone** - (403) 930-5430 **Fax** - (403) 460-6216
Website - zedcorsecurity.ca
Email - aladha@zedcor.ca
Investor Relations - Amin Ladha (403) 930-5434
Auditors - MNP LLP C.A., Calgary, Alta.
Bankers - ATB Financial, Calgary, Alta.
Lawyers - Borden Ladner Gervais LLP, Calgary, Alta.
Transfer Agents - Computershare Trust Company of Canada Inc., Calgary, Alta.
Employees - 76 at Dec. 31, 2022
Profile - (Alta. 2011) Provides technology-based security and surveillance services throughout Canada.

Wholly owned **Zedcor Security Solutions Corp.** provides remote surveillance, live monitoring and security personnel to customers involved in pipeline construction, civil and municipal construction, oil and gas exploration, retail industries and emergency response through its fleet of light towers equipped with high resolution security cameras and equipment monitored by a central command centre. At Dec. 31, 2022, the fleet of light towers include 254 Solar Hybrid MobileyeZ towers, 231 Electric MobileyeZ towers and 21 Diesel MobileyeZ towers.

During the first quarter of 2023, the company added to its fleet 18 Electric MobileyeZ towers and 21 Solar Hybrid MobileyeZ towers.

During 2022, the company added to its fleet 178 Electric MobileyeZ towers and 64 Solar Hybrid MobileyeZ towers.

Predecessor Detail - Name changed from Zedcor Energy Inc., Sept. 21, 2020.

Directors - Wade Felesky, chr., Calgary, Alta.; Brian McGill, Alta.; Dean Shillington, B.C.; Dean S. Swanberg, Grande Prairie, Alta.

Other Exec. Officers - Todd Ziniuk, pres. & CEO; Amin Ladha, CFO; James Leganchuk, chief revenue officer; Tony Ciarla, exec. v-p; Jan M. Campbell, corp. sec.

Capital Stock

	Authorized (shs.)	Outstanding (shs.)[1]
Preferred	unlimited	nil
Common	unlimited	72,908,925

[1] At Apr. 12, 2023

Common - One vote per share.
Preferred (old) - Were entitled to a cumulative cash dividend of 10% of the stated value (70¢). Redeemed on Apr. 7, 2022, at 70¢ per share. Non-voting.
Major Shareholder - Dean S. Swanberg held 32.64% interest at Apr. 12, 2023.

Price Range - ZDC/TSX-VEN

Year	Volume	High	Low	Close
2022	3,533,471	$0.60	$0.31	$0.60
2021	4,711,481	$0.45	$0.15	$0.41
2020	4,246,108	$0.18	$0.02	$0.17
2019	6,026,122	$0.17	$0.05	$0.07
2018	5,371,237	$0.34	$0.08	$0.11

Recent Close: $0.64
Capital Stock Changes - In March and April 2022, private placement of 5,233,930 units (1 common share & ½ warrant) at 50¢ per unit was completed. In addition, 4,400,000 common shares were issued in exchange for a like number of preferred shares. Also during 2022, common shares were issued as follows: 2,883,386 for the cumulative dividend payable on the conversion of preferred shares and 75,000 on exercise of options.

Wholly Owned Subsidiaries

Zedcor Industrial Services Corp., Alta.
Zedcor Security Solutions Corp., Alta.
Zedcor Security Solutions (USA) Corp., United States.

Financial Statistics

Periods ended:	12m Dec. 31/22[A]		12m Dec. 31/21[A]
	$000s	%Chg	$000s
Operating revenue	**22,099**	**+63**	**13,550**
Cost of sales	9,164		5,892
Salaries & benefits	4,426		2,538
General & admin expense	930		757
Stock-based compensation	129		135
Operating expense	**14,649**	**+57**	**9,322**
Operating income	**7,450**	**+76**	**4,228**
Deprec., depl. & amort.	3,350		2,274
Finance costs, gross	1,063		3,164
Write-downs/write-offs	(10)		nil
Pre-tax income	**3,993**	**n.a.**	**(1,580)**
Income taxes	(2,005)		nil
Net inc. bef. disc. opers	**5,998**	**n.a.**	**(1,580)**
Income from disc. opers	nil		(2,321)
Net income	**5,998**	**n.a.**	**(3,901)**
Cash & equivalent	571		108
Inventories	1,315		383
Accounts receivable	4,699		3,143
Current assets	7,542		4,442
Fixed assets, net	17,563		11,073
Right-of-use assets	2,939		1,290
Total assets	**32,578**	**+65**	**19,796**
Accts. pay. & accr. liabs	3,409		2,380
Current liabilities	7,379		5,962
Long-term debt, gross	13,729		11,063
Long-term debt, net	11,531		8,832
Long-term lease liabilities	5,179		4,604
Preferred share equity	nil		2,864
Shareholders' equity	8,489		398
Cash from oper. activs	**6,190**	**+36**	**4,543**
Cash from fin. activs	2,880		(11,771)
Cash from invest. activs	(8,607)		6,575
Net cash position	**571**	**+429**	**108**
Capital expenditures	(8,988)		(5,760)
Capital disposals	225		167
	$		$
Earns. per sh. bef disc opers*	0.09		(0.03)
Earnings per share*	0.09		(0.07)
Cash flow per share*	0.09		0.08
	shs		shs
No. of shs. o/s*	70,892,259		58,299,943
Avg. no. of shs. o/s*	67,639,086		57,885,234
	%		%
Net profit margin	27.14		(11.66)
Return on equity	199.17		n.m.
Return on assets	29.00		6.06
No. of employees (FTEs)	76		62

* Common
[A] Reported in accordance with IFRS

Latest Results

Periods ended:	3m Mar. 31/23[A]		3m Mar. 31/22[A]
	$000s	%Chg	$000s
Operating revenue	6,443	+39	4,631
Net income	752	+76	428
	$		$
Earnings per share*	0.01		0.01

* Common
[A] Reported in accordance with IFRS

Historical Summary
(as originally stated)

Fiscal Year	Oper. Rev.	Net Inc. Bef. Disc.	EPS*
	$000s	$000s	$
2022[A]	22,099	5,998	0.09
2021[A]	13,550	(1,580)	(0.03)
2020[A]	13,762	(4,678)	(0.08)
2019[A]	16,962	(8,035)	(0.15)
2018[A]	17,452	(20,160)	(0.39)

* Common
[A] Reported in accordance with IFRS

Z.4 Zenith Capital Corporation

Symbol - ZENI.P **Exchange** - TSX-VEN **CUSIP** - 98936P
Head Office - 400-725 Granville St, Vancouver, BC, V7Y 1G5 **Telephone** - (604) 836-6667
Email - zenithcapital@shaw.ca
Investor Relations - Charalambos Katevatis (604) 836-6667
Auditors - Manning Elliott LLP C.A., Vancouver, B.C.
Transfer Agents - Odyssey Trust Company, Vancouver, B.C.
Profile - (B.C. 2019) Capital Pool Company.

Recent Merger and Acquisition Activity

Status: pending **Announced:** Mar. 9, 2023
Zenith Capital Corporation entered into a letter of intent for the Qualifying Transaction reverse takeover acquisition of Mongolia-based Grand Samsara Consulting LLC, which holds the Tsagaan Zalaa silica prospect in Mongolia, and British Columbia-based CBGB Ventures Corp., which has no assets other than a nominal amount of cash. The basis of the share consideration would be subsequently disclosed. Concurrent or prior to completion, CBGB was expected to complete a private placement of a minimum of $1,500,000.

Status: terminated **Revised:** Jan. 23, 2023
UPDATE: The transaction was terminated. PREVIOUS: Zenith Capital Corporation entered into a letter of intent for the Qualifying Transaction reverse takeover acquisition of Israel-based Venda Robotix Ltd. for issuance of 88,314,700 Zenith common shares plus issuance of additional 25,000,000 Zenith common shares upon achieving certain performance milestones. Upon closing, Zenith and Venda shareholders would hold 30% and 70% interest, respectively. Venda develops a robotic platform for preparing and delivering natural, good-for-you food. Feb. 28, 2022 - Pursuant to an amended letter of intent, Zenith would acquire Venda by way of a three-cornered amalgamation. Consideration includes issuance of 83,499,989 Zenith common shares plus issuance of additional 25,400,000 Zenith common shares upon achieving certain performance milestones. In connection, Zenith would change its name to Venda Robotix Holdings Inc. and would continue into Ontario. An entity (finco) would be incorporated to complete a brokered private placement of up to 13,636,364 subscription receipts at 22¢ per receipt and a non-brokered private placement of subscription receipts on the same terms as the brokered private placement. Concurrently, Zenith would also complete a private placement of subscription receipts. Each finco and Zenith subscription receipt would entitle the holder to 1 Zenith unit (1 common share & 1 warrant), without payment of additional consideration or further action, upon closing of the transaction. May 31, 2022 - The closing date of the transaction was extended to July 31, 2022. June 30, 2022 - The closing date of the transaction was extended to Sept. 30, 2022. Aug. 30, 2022 - The closing date of the transaction was extended to Oct. 31, 2022. Oct. 26, 2022 - The closing date of the transaction was extended to Jan. 31, 2023.

Directors - Charalambos (Harry) Katevatis, pres., CEO, CFO & corp. sec., West Vancouver, B.C.; Vivian A. Katsuris, Vancouver, B.C.; Theofilos (Theo) Sanidas, North Vancouver, B.C.

Capital Stock

	Authorized (shs.)	Outstanding (shs.)[1]
Common	unlimited	7,390,421

[1] At Mar. 28, 2023

Major Shareholder - Charalambos (Harry) Katevatis held 24.54% interest and Theofilos (Theo) Sanidas held 20.41% interest at Oct. 25, 2022.

Price Range - ZENI.P/TSX-VEN

Year	Volume	High	Low	Close
2021	126,414	$0.31	$0.12	$0.14
2020	384,570	$0.33	$0.12	$0.33

Recent Close: $0.11
Capital Stock Changes - In February 2023, private placement of 2,500,000 common shares was completed at 8¢ per share.
During fiscal 2022, 90,420 common shares were issued on exercise of warrants.

Z.5 Zentek Ltd.

Symbol - ZEN **Exchange** - TSX-VEN **CUSIP** - 98942X
Head Office - 24 Corporate Crt, Guelph, ON, N1G 5G5 **Telephone** - (705) 618-0900 **Toll-free** - (844) 730-9822
Website - www.zentek.com
Email - gfenton@zentek.com
Investor Relations - Greg Fenton (705) 618-0900
Auditors - BDO Canada LLP C.A., Vancouver, B.C.
Lawyers - Irwin Lowy LLP, Toronto, Ont.
Transfer Agents - TSX Trust Company, Toronto, Ont.
Employees - 25 at June 29, 2023
Profile - (Ont. 2008) Has developed and is commercializing ZENGuard™, an antimicrobial coating for use on surgical masks, other personal protective equipment (PPE) and heating, ventilation, and air conditioning (HVAC) filters. Also developing certain rapid detection technologies and other nanomaterials-based technologies.

ZENGuard™ is a patent-pending graphene oxide/silver coating that effectively inactivates over 99% of the SARS-CoV-2 virus and has the potential to be used in similar compounds as products against infectious diseases. The company also holds exclusive worldwide rights to commercialize a SARS-CoV-2 rapid detection technology developed by McMaster University. A provisional patent was also filed on the use of ZENGuard™ as an anti-inflammatory agent for dermatological conditions.

In addition, the company is developing a stable graphene-based fuel additive to improve combustion, increase burn rate, reduce greenhouse gas emissions and to improve fuel economy of diesel fuels; a carbon-based, nanotechnology-enhanced coating (Icephobic coating) designed to prevent or reduce ice accretion for aviation and wind energy applications; a fire-retardant additive which could potentially create a fire-resistant plastic that could be used in electrical vehicles; a battery technology that would improve automotive battery components including anode, cathode, electrolyte and separator; and ZenArmor™, a corrosion protection technology based on functionalized graphene oxide, for potential use in naval and marine infrastructure, bridges, buildings and pipelines industries.

The company is also working with various research institutions to develop processes to synthesize graphene, graphene oxide and graphene quantum dots along with new applications for graphene. Potential markets for graphene include composites such as concrete, rubber, plastic polymers and ceramics; sensors; water purification and filtration; coatings and solid-state lubricants; silicon-graphene; and graphene aerogel anode material for next generation batteries along with aerospace and military applications.

The company purchases graphene oxide from third parties used to produce ZenGUARD™ coating at its 25,680-sq.-ft. production facility in Guelph, Ont. Also plans to construct a manufacturing plant to produce its own graphene oxide.

Wholly owned **Albany Graphite Corp.** holds Albany graphite property, 9,816 hectares, 86 km northwest of Hearst, Ont. A preliminary economic assessment released in June 2015 contemplated an average annual production of 30,000 tonnes graphite over a 22-year mine life. Initial capital costs were estimated at US$411,465,000. At April 2023, indicated resource was 22,900,000 tonnes grading 4.07% graphitic carbon.

On May 5, 2023, the company completed the transfer of its Albany graphite property in Ontario into newly formed wholly owned **Albany Graphite Corp.** in exchange for 59,999,900 Albany common shares. The company plans to list the common shares of Albany on a Canadian stock exchange.

On Mar. 22, 2022, common shares were listed on the Nasdaq Capital Market under the symbol ZTEK.

Predecessor Detail - Name changed from ZEN Graphene Solutions Ltd., Nov. 1, 2021.

Directors - Dr. Francis Dubé, exec. chr. & COO, Welland, Ont.; Greg Fenton, CEO, St. James, Barbados; Brian Bosse, Toronto, Ont.; Lisa Sim, B.C.; Ilse Treurnicht, Ont.; Eric Wallman, Winnipeg, Man.

Other Exec. Officers - Wendy Ford, CFO; Dr. Colin van der Kuur, chief scientific officer; Ryan Shacklock, sr. v-p, strategy, bus. devel. & IR; Nick Hansford, v-p, strategy & product devel.; Peter C. Wood, v-p, devel.

Capital Stock

	Authorized (shs.)	Outstanding (shs.)[1]
Common	unlimited	99,586,981

[1] At June 29, 2023

Normal Course Issuer Bid - The company plans to make normal course purchases of up to 4,979,349 common shares representing 5% of the total outstanding. The bid commenced on June 1, 2023, and expires on May 31, 2024.

Major Shareholder - Widely held at Aug. 25, 2022.

Price Range - ZEN/TSX-VEN

Year	Volume	High	Low	Close
2022	23,751,992	$5.19	$1.72	$2.02
2021	57,586,977	$7.50	$1.71	$4.98
2020	48,313,808	$3.77	$0.26	$3.58
2019	14,469,945	$0.63	$0.28	$0.36
2018	10,088,599	$0.84	$0.34	$0.45

Recent Close: $1.93

Capital Stock Changes - During fiscal 2023, 285,924 common shares were issued on exercise of options.

In January 2022, bought deal public offering of 4,424,050 common shares and concurrent private placement of 1,924,812 common shares, all at $5.85 per share, were completed. Also during fiscal 2022, common shares were issued as follows: 4,256,064 on exercise of warrants, 1,735,199 by private placement, 673,333 on exercise of options, 19,157 for debt settlement and 15,592 as share issuance cost.

Wholly Owned Subsidiaries

Albany Graphite Corp., B.C.
1000114904 Ontario Inc. Inactive.
Zentek USA Inc., United States. Inactive.

Financial Statistics

Periods ended:	12m Mar. 31/23[A]		12m Mar. 31/22[oA]
	$000s	%Chg	$000s
Operating revenue	**73**	**-79**	**340**
Salaries & benefits	3,598		1,437
Research & devel. expense	1,646		1,542
General & admin expense	5,923		4,590
Stock-based compensation	3,203		4,727
Operating expense	**14,370**	**+17**	**12,295**
Operating income	**(14,297)**	**n.a.**	**(11,955)**
Deprec., depl. & amort.	540		615
Finance income	510		21
Finance costs, gross	121		64
Write-downs/write-offs	(134)		(19,672)[1]
Pre-tax income	**(14,414)**	**n.a.**	**(31,694)**
Net income	**(14,414)**	**n.a.**	**(31,694)**
Cash & equivalent	10,357		26,675
Inventories	2,849		666
Accounts receivable	569		656
Current assets	17,953		31,959
Fixed assets, net	8,336		6,025
Explor./devel. properties	7,000		7,000
Total assets	**33,289**	**-26**	**44,985**
Accts. pay. & accr. liabs	1,292		1,205
Current liabilities	2,420		2,035
Long-term debt, gross	998		1,949
Long-term debt, net	nil		998
Long-term lease liabilities	485		133
Shareholders' equity	30,384		41,549
Cash from oper. activs	**(12,957)**	**n.a.**	**(7,989)**
Cash from fin. activs	(1,054)		38,825
Cash from invest. activs	(2,307)		(7,253)
Net cash position	**10,357**	**-61**	**26,675**
Capital expenditures	(2,273)		(4,303)
	$		$
Earnings per share*	(0.14)		(0.34)
Cash flow per share*	(0.13)		(0.09)
	shs		shs
No. of shs. o/s*	99,533,982		99,248,058
Avg. no. of shs. o/s*	99,436,264		92,091,983
	%		%
Net profit margin	n.m.		n.m.
Return on equity	(44.40)		(91.85)
Return on assets	(40.11)		(84.08)

* Common
[o] Restated
[A] Reported in accordance with IFRS
[1] Pertains to the impairment of Albany graphite property in Ontario.

Historical Summary
(as originally stated)

Fiscal Year	Oper. Rev.	Net Inc. Bef. Disc.	EPS*
	$000s	$000s	$
2023[A]	73	(14,414)	(0.14)
2022[A]	340	(12,022)	(0.13)
2021[A]	nil	(3,869)	(0.05)
2020[A]	nil	(1,541)	(0.02)
2019[A]	nil	(2,428)	(0.04)

* Common
[A] Reported in accordance with IFRS

Z.6 01 Communique Laboratory Inc.

Symbol - ONE **Exchange** - TSX-VEN **CUSIP** - 67088Q
Head Office - 700-789 Don Mills Rd, Toronto, ON, M3C 1T5 **Telephone** - (905) 795-2888 **Fax** - (905) 795-0101
Website - www.01com.com
Email - brian.stringer@01com.com
Investor Relations - Brian Stringer (800) 668-2185
Auditors - McGovern Hurley LLP C.A., Toronto, Ont.
Lawyers - Fogler, Rubinoff LLP, Toronto, Ont.
Transfer Agents - TSX Trust Company, Toronto, Ont.
Profile - (Ont. 1992) Developing post-quantum cybersecurity technologies and provides remote access software solutions for the North American and Japanese markets.

Developing Post-Quantum Cryptography (PQ-Crypto) and Post-Quantum Blockchain (PQBC) technologies which are aimed to secure data, communications and blockchain networks against cyber attacks especially from Quantum Computers, which has exponentially faster computing power than conventional computers and has the potential capacity to breach existing blockchain networks.

The PQ-Crypto and PQBC technologies based solution is IronCAP™, a patent-pending cryptography system designed to operate on conventional computer systems. Products based on IronCAP™ include IronCAP™ API, which was released in August 2019 and allows third party developers to build highly secure post-quantum systems for blockchain, 5G/IoT, data storage, remote access/VPN, encryption, digital signing and others; and IronCAP X™, which was released on Apr. 23, 2020, and is a cybersecurity product for email/file encryption.

Also continues to offer remote access solutions to individuals, small businesses and workgroups within a larger corporation. These remote access products and services include:

I'm InTouch™ - A platform that provides users with the ability to access and/or remotely control their desktop PC from anywhere, anytime using any device connected to the Internet. Affiliated products under this platform includes I'm InTouch Go, which is a mobile app that allows for remote access to an employee's computer without the use of an Internet browser; I'm InTouch GoMail, which is a mobile mailbox that does not store any messages on employee's device for enhanced security but simply mobilizes the employee's Microsoft Outlook account; and I'm InTouch server edition, which allows employees to remotely access their office computers via the organization's own I'm InTouch servers instead of the servers hosted by the company. DoMobile, a remote access service in Japan based on I'm InTouch remote access service, is being marketed by **Hitachi Business Solution Create Ltd.**

I'm OnCall™ - A secure online help desk software which allows organizations to offer remote support over the Internet to their customers. The software also provides a live-chat support to their customers and allows for up to 10 simultaneous chat sessions per agent.

I'm InTouch Meeting™ - An online meeting, web conferencing and phone conferencing tool that has several features including real-time screen sharing, whiteboard (annotation) to allow moderator and attendees to annotate on moderator's screen, file transfer, remote printing, and administrative or statistics tools for moderators to manage meetings, review historical sessions, manage users and customize invitation email.

Directors - William A. Train, chr., Oakville, Ont.; Andrew Cheung, pres. & CEO, Toronto, Ont.; Gary F. Kissack, Toronto, Ont.; Tyson Macaulay, Ont.

Other Exec. Officers - Brian Stringer, CFO; Sergey Strakhov, chief tech. officer; Gigi Loo, contr. & corp. sec.

Capital Stock

	Authorized (shs.)	Outstanding (shs.)[1]
Preference	unlimited	
Series A	50,000	nil
Common	unlimited	96,364,554

[1] At June 14, 2023

Major Shareholder - Andrew Cheung held 11.5% interest at Mar. 15, 2023.

Price Range - ONE/TSX-VEN

Year	Volume	High	Low	Close
2022	8,967,361	$0.36	$0.09	$0.12
2021	15,031,596	$0.42	$0.20	$0.22
2020	21,063,142	$0.51	$0.08	$0.40
2019	10,587,323	$0.19	$0.06	$0.12
2018	22,505,939	$0.12	$0.02	$0.07

Recent Close: $0.10

Capital Stock Changes - During fiscal 2022, common shares were issued as follows: 562,500 by private placement, 541,666 on exercise of warrants and 246,667 on exercise of options.

Wholly Owned Subsidiaries

01 Communique (GP) Inc., Ont.
01 Communique Laboratory Hong Kong Limited

Financial Statistics

Periods ended:	12m Oct. 31/22[A]		12m Oct. 31/21[A]
	$000s	%Chg	$000s
Operating revenue	**1,027**	**+16**	**885**
Research & devel. expense	816		614
General & admin expense	646		585
Stock-based compensation	160		203
Operating expense	**1,622**	**+16**	**1,403**
Operating income	**(595)**	**n.a.**	**(518)**
Deprec., depl. & amort.	51		53
Finance income	4		1
Finance costs, gross	5		4
Pre-tax income	**(586)**	**n.a.**	**(570)**
Income taxes	76		86
Net income	**(662)**	**n.a.**	**(657)**
Cash & equivalent	637		995
Accounts receivable	316		206
Current assets	1,018		1,232
Fixed assets, net	91		126
Total assets	**1,110**	**-18**	**1,358**
Accts. pay. & accr. liabs	273		182
Current liabilities	325		231
Long-term debt, gross	40		40
Long-term debt, net	40		40
Long-term lease liabilities	21		67
Shareholders' equity	725		1,019
Cash from oper. activs	**(498)**	**n.a.**	**(400)**
Cash from fin. activs	158		381
Cash from invest. activs	168		52
Net cash position	**487**	**-51**	**995**
Capital expenditures	(17)		(8)
	$		$
Earnings per share*	(0.01)		(0.01)
Cash flow per share*	(0.01)		(0.00)
	shs		shs
No. of shs. o/s*	95,802,054		94,451,221
Avg. no. of shs. o/s*	94,850,618		92,788,400
	%		%
Net profit margin	(64.46)		(74.24)
Return on equity	(75.92)		(61.78)
Return on assets	(53.19)		(49.35)
Foreign sales percent	99		99

* Common
[A] Reported in accordance with IFRS

Historical Summary
(as originally stated)

Fiscal Year	Oper. Rev. $000s	Net Inc. Bef. Disc. $000s	EPS* $
2022[A]	1,027	(662)	(0.01)
2021[A]	885	(657)	(0.01)
2020[A]	522	(657)	(0.01)
2019[A]	283	(314)	(0.00)
2018[A]	203	(388)	(0.01)

* Common
[A] Reported in accordance with IFRS

Z.7 ZeU Technologies, Inc.

Symbol - ZEU **Exchange** - CSE **CUSIP** - 98955W
Head Office - 2700-1000 rue Sherbrooke O, Montréal, QC, H3A 3G4 **Telephone** - (514) 996-6342
Website - zeuniverse.com
Email - neha_tally@dumasbancorp.com
Investor Relations - Neha Tally (514) 996-6342
Auditors - Kingston Ross Pasnak LLP C.A., Edmonton, Alta.
Transfer Agents - Computershare Trust Company of Canada Inc., Montréal, Qué.
Profile - (Can. 2018) Developing Peer-to-Peer and blockchain-based technologies which provide transparency, security, scalability and big data management for applications and financial transactions of clients in the payment, gaming, data and healthcare sector.

Flagship application is the Mula platform, comprised of MulaMail, Mula Office, MulaMicrofinance, MulaMarketplace, MulaWallet, MulaKeep and MulaMessage, which uses the company's patented technology to anonymize and protect user's local data and online information from unwanted access.

Projects being developed with partners include ZeU Gaming, which charges a network/platform fee for the operation of the infrastructure enabling users to gamble in a peer-to-peer environment; ZeUPay, which provides custodial and legacy banking support for the Mula platform as well as the company's other Decentralize Finance and gaming initiatives; and a virtual identity and user management which manages user authentication, data sharing, wallet custody, and identity validations without the use of third-party infrastructure such as banks or government databases.

Also developing technologies including a system for augmenting database applications; a biocrypt digital wallet; a block-chain based secure email system; a global multi- payment and e-money services platform; a blockchain random number generator for lottery and online gaming; a derivative data marketplace platform; a system to complete cross-chain transactions; a transactional decentralized communication protocol infrastructure; a system for distributed data real time back-up and recovery; a system for converting database applications into blockchain applications; a symmetric asynchronous generative encryption (SAGE); a method and system for safe custody of private data using blockchain; and a permission-based multi-level scheme document for decentralized storage.

The company announced plans to spin-out wholly owned **ZeUPay Inc.** to its shareholders on a pro-rata basis and is subject to approval by qualified shareholders. The spin-out will mitigate issues related the company owning conflicting types of financial platforms and required licenses involved.

Predecessor Detail - Name changed from ZeU Crypto Networks Inc., Oct. 15, 2020.

Directors - François (Frank) Dumas, pres. & CEO, Montréal, Qué.; Patricia Popert-Fortier, COO, Montréal, Qué.; Mark A. Billings, CFO, Montréal, Qué.; Neha Tally, corp. sec., Montréal, Qué.; Jasseem Allybokus, Bucharest, Romania; Lord Timothy E. Razzall, London, Middx., United Kingdom

Other Exec. Officers - Jean-Philippe Beaudet, chief tech. officer

Capital Stock

	Authorized (shs.)	Outstanding (shs.)[1]
Common	unlimited	37,177,948

[1] At Nov. 28, 2022

Major Shareholder - St-Georges Eco-Mining Corp. held 27.3% interest at Mar. 31, 2022.

Price Range - ZEU/CSE

Year	Volume	High	Low	Close
2022	4,425,741	$0.46	$0.03	$0.06
2021	7,940,615	$1.08	$0.30	$0.55
2020	8,587,766	$1.11	$0.10	$0.45
2019	370	$2.50	$2.00	$2.50

Recent Close: $0.02

Capital Stock Changes - In December 2021, private placement of 1,975,000 units (1 common share & 1 warrant) at 40¢ per share was completed. Also during the 15-month period ended Mar. 31, 2022, common shares were issued as follows: 2,500,000 by private placement, 2,500,000 pursuant to the acquisition of Prego International Group AS, 1,935,555 on exercise of warrants, 1,817,391 for debt settlement, 650,000 on exercise of options and 276,030 on conversion of debentures.

Wholly Owned Subsidiaries

ZeU Gaming Inc., Canada.
ZeUPay Inc, Canada.
- 100% int. in **ZeUPay AS**, Norway.

Financial Statistics

Periods ended:	15m Mar. 31/22[A]		12m Dec. 31/20[A]
	$000s	%Chg	$000s
Operating revenue	**nil**	**n.a.**	**355**
Salaries & benefits	198		nil
Research & devel. expense	863		588
General & admin expense	1,624		664
Stock-based compensation	728		527
Operating expense	**3,413**	**n.a.**	**1,780**
Operating income	**(3,413)**	**n.a.**	**(1,425)**
Finance costs, gross	2,435		397
Write-downs/write-offs	(13,321)[1]		nil
Pre-tax income	**(14,274)**	**n.a.**	**(9,504)**
Net income	**(14,274)**	**n.a.**	**(9,504)**
Cash & equivalent	24		2
Current assets	585		17
Total assets	**585**	**n.a.**	**17**
Accts. pay. & accr. liabs	2,046		1,367
Current liabilities	6,457		5,183
Long-term debt, gross	10,615		8,070
Long-term debt, net	6,224		4,253
Shareholders' equity	(12,096)		(9,420)
Cash from oper. activs	**(2,245)**	**n.a.**	**(61)**
Cash from fin. activs	2,291		nil
Cash from invest. activs	(24)		nil
Net cash position	**24**	**n.a.**	**2**
	$		$
Earnings per share*	(0.41)		(0.39)
Cash flow per share*	(0.06)		(0.00)
	shs		shs
No. of shs. o/s*	37,177,948		25,523,972
Avg. no. of shs. o/s*	34,631,932		24,513,955
	%		%
Net profit margin	...		n.m.
Return on equity	...		n.m.
Return on assets	...		(81.19)

* Common
[A] Reported in accordance with IFRS
[1] Consisting of impairment of goodwill.

Latest Results

Periods ended:	6m Sept. 30/22[A]		6m Sept. 30/21[oA]
	$000s	%Chg	$000s
Net income	(1,561)	n.a.	(3,041)
	$		$
Earnings per share*	(0.04)		(0.09)

* Common
[o] Restated
[A] Reported in accordance with IFRS

Historical Summary
(as originally stated)

Fiscal Year	Oper. Rev. $000s	Net Inc. Bef. Disc. $000s	EPS* $
2022[A1]	nil	(14,274)	(0.41)
2020[A]	355	(9,504)	(0.39)
2019[A]	nil	(4,947)	(0.25)
2018[A]	nil	(4,412)	(0.22)

* Common
[A] Reported in accordance with IFRS
[1] 15 months ended Mar. 31, 2022.

Z.8 Zidane Capital Corp.

Symbol - ZZE.H **Exchange** - TSX-VEN **CUSIP** - 98953U
Head Office - 845 8 St, West Vancouver, BC, V7T 1S1 **Telephone** - (604) 417-6375 **Fax** - (604) 628-9875
Email - casper.bych@gmail.com
Investor Relations - Casper K. Bych (604) 417-6375
Auditors - De Visser Gray LLP C.A., Vancouver, B.C.
Transfer Agents - TSX Trust Company, Vancouver, B.C.
Profile - (B.C. 2010) Capital Pool Company.

Recent Merger and Acquisition Activity

Status: terminated **Revised:** May 30, 2022
UPDATE: The transaction was terminated. PREVIOUS: Zidane Capital Corp. entered into a letter of intent for the Qualifying Transaction reverse takeover acquisition of British Virgin Islands-based Millennial Technologies Limited. Terms of the transaction would be disclosed upon entering into a definitive agreement. Millennial was pursuing the acquisition of Trans Energo Invest LLC, which has secured the right to construct a 100-MW crypto mining operation in the Maimak Free Economic Zone of the Kyrgyzstan Republic.

Directors - Casper K. Bych, pres., CEO, CFO & corp. sec., Vancouver, B.C.; Raymond Fortier, Prince George, B.C.; David J. Salmon, North Vancouver, B.C.

Capital Stock

	Authorized (shs.)	Outstanding (shs.)[1]
Common	unlimited	5,225,276

[1] At May 30, 2023

Major Shareholder - Casper K. Bych held 11.96% interest at Nov. 25, 2022.

Price Range - ZZE.H/TSX-VEN

Year	Volume	High	Low	Close
2022	56,500	$0.05	$0.03	$0.03
2021	47,750	$0.14	$0.05	$0.08
2020	35,220	$0.20	$0.04	$0.11
2019	12,750	$0.06	$0.04	$0.06

Recent Close: $0.04

Capital Stock Changes - There were no changes to capital stock during fiscal 2022 or fiscal 2023.

Z.9 Zimtu Capital Corp.

Symbol - ZC **Exchange** - TSX-VEN **CUSIP** - 989589
Head Office - 1450-789 Pender St W, Vancouver, BC, V6C 1H2 **Telephone** - (604) 681-1568 **Toll-free** - (877) 377-6222 **Fax** - (604) 681-8240
Website - www.zimtu.com
Email - info@zimtu.com
Investor Relations - Jody Bellefleur (877) 377-6222
Auditors - WDM Chartered Accountants C.A., Vancouver, B.C.
Bankers - Bank of Montreal
Lawyers - Clark Wilson LLP, Vancouver, B.C.
Transfer Agents - Odyssey Trust Company, Vancouver, B.C.
Profile - (B.C. 2006) Invests in and provides management and administrative services to various mineral exploration companies, and holds interests in mineral prospects across Canada.

At May 31, 2022, the company's equity investment portfolio had a market value of $18,810,997. Core holdings include **Commerce Resources Corp.**, **Aduro Clean Energy Technologies Inc.** (formerly **Dimension Five Technologies Inc.**), **Zinc8 Energy Solutions Inc.**, **Saville Resources Inc.**, **Core Assets Corp.**, **Swmbrd Sports Inc.** and **Eagle Bay Resources Corp.**

The company offers corporate development and marketing services to companies through its ZimtuADVANTAGE program, a program designed to provide opportunities, guidance, cost savings and assistance to companies covering multiple aspects of being a public company.

Additionally, the company evaluates and acquires prospective resource properties to make available for sale, option or joint venture. The company has interests in several mineral property claims throughout Canada.

In July 2022, the company agreed to sell four claims which comprise the Wicheeda extension property in northeast British Columbia to **Eagle Bay Resources Corp.** for issuance of 800,000 Eagle Bay common shares valued at $60,000. Wicheeda extension was acquired by the company on Dec. 13, 2021, for $20,000 cash, issuance of 200,000 common shares and commitment to transfer 200,000 Eagle Bay common shares to the vendor.

Predecessor Detail - Name changed from Flow Energy Ltd., July 31, 2008, following Qualifying Transaction reverse takeover acquisition of 755032 B.C. Ltd.

Directors - Sean Charland, pres. & CEO, Whistler, B.C.; Kevin J. Bottomley, Vancouver, B.C.; J. Christopher (Chris) Grove, North Vancouver, B.C.; Robert P. Leckie, Toronto, Ont.

Other Exec. Officers - Jody Bellefleur, CFO & corp. sec.

Capital Stock

	Authorized (shs.)	Outstanding (shs.)[1]
Common	unlimited	63,413,303

[1] At July 24, 2023

Major Shareholder - Widely held at June 5, 2023.

Price Range - ZC/TSX-VEN

Year	Volume	High	Low	Close
2022	12,680,368	$0.30	$0.07	$0.09
2021	4,835,643	$0.30	$0.14	$0.23
2020	2,959,188	$0.28	$0.08	$0.20
2019	3,446,095	$0.35	$0.09	$0.13
2018	2,814,452	$0.40	$0.20	$0.22

Recent Close: $0.06

Capital Stock Changes - In March 2023, private placement of up to 18,750,000 units (1 common share & 1 warrant) at 8¢ per unit was arranged, with warrants exercisable at 10¢ per share for three years.

In February 2022, private placement of 9,892,500 units (1 common share & 1 warrant) at 20¢ per unit was completed.

Investments

3% int. in **Aduro Clean Technologies Inc.**, Sarnia, Ont. (see separate coverage)
Alpha Lithium Corporation, Vancouver, B.C. (see Survey of Mines)
Arctic Star Exploration Corp., Vancouver, B.C. (see Survey of Mines)
Commerce Resources Corp., Vancouver, B.C. (see Survey of Mines)
10.06% int. in **Core Assets Corp.**, Vancouver, B.C. (see Survey of Mines)
39.9% int. in **Eagle Bay Resources Corp.**, Vancouver, B.C. (see Survey of Mines)
Lion Rock Resources Inc., Vancouver, B.C. (see Survey of Mines)
Maple Gold Mines Ltd., Vancouver, B.C. (see Survey of Mines)
Ophir Gold Corp., Vancouver, B.C. (see Survey of Mines)
Pegasus Resources Inc., Vancouver, B.C. (see Survey of Mines)
SWMBRD Sports Inc., Vancouver, B.C. (see separate coverage)
Saville Resources Inc., Vancouver, B.C. (see Survey of Mines)
Sceptre Ventures Inc., Vancouver, B.C. (see separate coverage)
Zinc8 Energy Solutions Inc., Vancouver, B.C. (see separate coverage)

Financial Statistics

Periods ended:	12m Nov. 30/21[A]		12m Nov. 30/20[A]
	$000s	%Chg	$000s
Realized invest. gain (loss)	n.a.		1,092
Unrealized invest. gain (loss)	n.a.		3,500
Total revenue	**12,338**	**+110**	**5,876**
Salaries & benefits	1,180		1,265
General & admin. expense	512		550
Stock-based compensation	244		nil
Operating expense	**1,937**	**+7**	**1,815**
Operating income	**10,401**	**+156**	**4,061**
Deprec. & amort.	145		144
Finance costs, gross	8		5
Write-downs/write-offs	46		(156)
Pre-tax income	**10,292**	**+178**	**3,700**
Income taxes	55		nil
Net income	**10,237**	**+177**	**3,700**
Cash & equivalent	17,799		8,978
Accounts receivable	920		777
Current assets	19,263		10,294
Long-term investments	1,538		266
Explor./devel. properties	13		16
Total assets	**20,814**	**+97**	**10,577**
Bank indebtedness	nil		19
Accts. pay. & accr. liabs	129		470
Current liabilities	412		901
Long-term debt, gross	211		22
Long-term debt, net	211		22
Shareholders' equity	20,136		9,654
Cash from oper. activs	**(531)**	**n.a.**	**(360)**
Cash from fin. activs	(130)		(106)
Cash from invest. activs	695		649
Net cash position	**254**	**+16**	**219**
Capital expenditures	(29)		(38)
Capital disposals	89		23
	$		$
Earnings per share*	0.64		0.23
Cash flow per share*	(0.03)		(0.02)
	shs		shs
No. of shs. o/s*	16,106,483		16,106,483
Avg. no. of shs. o/s*	16,106,483		16,106,483
	%		%
Net profit margin	82.97		62.97
Return on equity	68.73		47.41
Return on assets	65.27		43.83

* Common
[A] Reported in accordance with IFRS

Latest Results

Periods ended:	6m May 31/22[A]		6m May 31/21[A]
	$000s	%Chg	$000s
Total revenue	1,126	-89	10,094
Net income	(174)	n.a.	9,482
	$		$
Earnings per share*	(0.01)		0.59

* Common
[A] Reported in accordance with IFRS

Historical Summary
(as originally stated)

Fiscal Year	Total Rev.	Net Inc. Bef. Disc.	EPS*
	$000s	$000s	$
2021[A]	12,338	10,237	0.64
2020[A]	5,876	3,700	0.23
2019[A]	(70)	(2,743)	(0.17)
2018[A]	(2,696)	(5,623)	(0.37)
2017[A]	8,449	5,280	0.34

* Common
[A] Reported in accordance with IFRS

Z.10 Zinc8 Energy Solutions Inc.

Symbol - ZAIR **Exchange** - CSE **CUSIP** - 98959U

Head Office - Unit 1, 8765 Ash St, Vancouver, BC, V6P 6T3 **Telephone** - (604) 558-1406

Website - www.zinc8energy.com

Email - ron@zinc8energy.com

Investor Relations - Ronald J. MacDonald (604) 366-5918

Auditors - D & H Group LLP C.A., Vancouver, B.C.

Transfer Agents - Computershare Trust Company of Canada Inc., Vancouver, B.C.

Profile - (B.C. 2011) Develops zinc-air flow batteries which provides peak shaving, bill management, peak demand reduction, backup power and demand response, energy arbitrage, and distribution and transmission deferral, for utilities, microgrid, commercial and industrial markets.

The company's zinc-air technology consists of three major components: the fuel tank where zinc particles and a potassium hydroxide (KOH) electrolyte are stored; the cell stack where the fuel is converted to electrical power; and the regenerator unit where the electrical power is converted back to fuel. In operation, electrical energy from a source is used to convert zinc oxide to zinc metal in the regenerator unit. The zinc "fuel" thus created is stored in the fuel tank until required. When stored energy is to be released, the zinc fuel is pumped into the cell stack where it reacts with atmospheric oxygen to produce electricity. The technology is designed to deliver power ranging from 20KW to 1MW and energy in the range of 160KWh to 8MWh.

The company has commenced development of a scaled-up 20-KW/160-KWh system for use in utility-scale battery storage.

Predecessor Detail - Name changed from MGX Renewables Inc., Mar. 20, 2020.

Directors - Ronald J. (Ron) MacDonald, exec. chr., pres. & CEO, Ont.; Gurcharn S. (Charn) Deol, Richmond, B.C.; David I. (Dave) Hodge, Vancouver, B.C.; Bernard Pinsky, B.C.

Other Exec. Officers - Sorin Spinu, CFO; Dr. Simon Fan, chief tech. officer & v-p, product mgt.; Mark Baggio, v-p, bus. devel.; Serge Drobatschewsky, v-p, opers.; John McLeod, v-p, eng.

Capital Stock

	Authorized (shs.)	Outstanding (shs.)[1]
Common	unlimited	162,577,317

[1] At Oct. 28, 2022

Major Shareholder - Widely held at Oct. 28, 2022.

Price Range - ZAIR/CSE

Year	Volume	High	Low	Close
2022	75,782,196	$0.38	$0.14	$0.18
2021	76,114,913	$0.90	$0.20	$0.27
2020	90,595,806	$0.62	$0.11	$0.57
2019	25,176,353	$0.53	$0.08	$0.13

Recent Close: $0.06

Wholly Owned Subsidiaries

Zinc8 Energy Solutions (USA) Inc., N.Y. Inactive.

Financial Statistics

Periods ended:	12m Dec. 31/21[A]		12m Dec. 31/20[A]
	$000s	%Chg	$000s
Salaries & benefits	340		204
Research & devel. expense	4,855		2,718
General & admin expense	2,112		2,217
Stock-based compensation	4,211		978
Operating expense	**11,518**	**+88**	**6,117**
Operating income	**(11,518)**	**n.a.**	**(6,117)**
Deprec., depl. & amort.	466		104
Finance income	300		3,736
Finance costs, gross	n.a.		164
Finance costs, net	(17)		n.a.
Write-downs/write-offs	(4,950)		nil
Pre-tax income	**(16,272)**	**n.a.**	**(2,044)**
Net income	**(16,272)**	**n.a.**	**(2,044)**
Cash & equivalent	10,203		1,577
Accounts receivable	72		46
Current assets	10,950		1,721
Fixed assets, net	1,940		511
Intangibles, net	nil		4,950
Total assets	**12,890**	**+79**	**7,182**
Bank indebtedness	nil		60
Accts. pay. & accr. liabs	751		1,254
Current liabilities	1,040		1,392
Long-term lease liabilities	61		61
Shareholders' equity	11,064		5,728
Cash from oper. activs	**(7,600)**	**n.a.**	**(3,733)**
Cash from fin. activs	16,983		5,501
Cash from invest. activs	(756)		(278)
Net cash position	**10,203**	**+547**	**1,577**
Capital expenditures	(666)		(278)
	$		$
Earnings per share*	(0.11)		(0.03)
Cash flow per share*	(0.05)		(0.05)
	shs		shs
No. of shs. o/s*	152,218,629		105,222,567
Avg. no. of shs. o/s*	145,217,965		80,418,849
	%		%
Net profit margin	n.a.		n.a.
Return on equity	(193.81)		n.m.
Return on assets	(162.14)		(29.43)

* Common
[A] Reported in accordance with IFRS

Latest Results

Periods ended:	6m June 30/22[A]		6m June 30/21[A]
	$000s	%Chg	$000s
Net income	(5,316)	n.a.	(6,965)
	$		$
Earnings per share*	(0.03)		(0.05)

* Common
[A] Reported in accordance with IFRS

Historical Summary
(as originally stated)

Fiscal Year	Oper. Rev.	Net Inc. Bef. Disc.	EPS*
	$000s	$000s	$
2021[A]	nil	(16,272)	(0.11)
2020[A]	nil	(2,044)	(0.03)
2019[A]	nil	(5,147)	(0.14)
2018[A]	nil	(2,596)	(0.09)
2017[A]	nil	(8,040)	(0.27)

* Common
[A] Reported in accordance with IFRS

Z.11 Zoglo's Food Corp.

Symbol - ZOG **Exchange** - CSE **CUSIP** - 98979D
Head Office - 75 Addiscott Crt, Markham, ON, L6G 1A6 **Telephone** - (647) 478-9585
Website - zoglos.com
Email - hari@varshneycapital.com
Investor Relations - Hari B. Varshney (647) 478-9585
Auditors - SRCO Professional Corporation C.A., Richmond Hill, Ont.
Lawyers - McMillan LLP, Vancouver, B.C.
Transfer Agents - Olympia Trust Company, Vancouver, B.C.
Profile - (B.C. 2020) Seeking new business opportunities.

Previously designed, developed, produced, distributed and sold plant-based appetizers, veggies and meat substitutes. Operations were suspended on June 5, 2023.

Effective May 15, 2023, the company announced to move its distribution network to **Altra Foods**, a full-service food distributor with complete inventory and multi-temperature storage facilities in Montreal and Toronto. Altra Foods has a national reach from Atlantic Provinces to British Columbia, supporting Canadian grocery stores and specialty food distribution networks.

In December 2022, the company amended the agreement with Israel-based **Naknik Nahariya Kasher Soglowek Ltd.** (NNKS) relating to its acquisition of all NNKS's assets, patents, intellectual property (IP), licensing rights and manufacturing rights relating to a line of heat and serve kosher plant-based food products, which granted the company the right to sell these products in North America. Consideration previously consisted of $2,000,000 cash and issuance of $3,000,000 note payable. Terms of the amended agreement include: (i) the parties would waive the company's existing debt balance of $2,500,000; (ii) the company would pay 3% royalties to NNKS from any product sold under the Zoglo's brand in perpetuity to NNKS; (iii) the company would have the right to use the IP, as long as royalties are paid; and (iv) the ownership of the IP would remain with NNKS.

Recent Merger and Acquisition Activity

Status: terminated **Revised:** May 26, 2023
UPDATE: The transaction was terminated. PREVIOUS: Odd Burger Corporation signed a letter of intent to acquire Zoglo's Food Corp., which designs, develops, produces, distributes and sells plant-based appetizers, veggies and meat substitutes. Odd Burger would issue common shares whereby Zoglo's shareholders would hold 25% of the Odd Burger shares issued and outstanding upon completion of the transaction.

Predecessor Detail - Name changed from Zoglo's Incredible Food Corp., Feb. 28, 2023.
Directors - Hari B. Varshney, CEO & CFO, Vancouver, B.C.

Capital Stock

	Authorized (shs.)	Outstanding (shs.)[1]
Common	unlimited	106,191,360

[1] At May 30, 2023

Major Shareholder - Henry Ender held 44.29% interest at May 4, 2022.

Price Range - ZOG/CSE

Year	Volume	High	Low	Close
2022	14,557,631	$0.23	$0.02	$0.02
2021	19,142,188	$0.80	$0.16	$0.21

Recent Close: $0.01

Wholly Owned Subsidiaries

Zoglo's Incredible Food Inc., Richmond Hill, Ont.

Financial Statistics

Periods ended:	12m Dec. 31/21[A1]		25w Dec. 31/20[A]
	$000s	%Chg	$000s
Operating revenue	**796**	**n.a.**	**nil**
Cost of goods sold	945		nil
Salaries & benefits	301		nil
General & admin expense	2,265		10
Stock-based compensation	2,377		nil
Operating expense	**5,887**	**n.a.**	**10**
Operating income	**(5,091)**	**n.a.**	**(10)**
Deprec., depl. & amort.	230		nil
Finance income	5		nil
Finance costs, gross	162		nil
Pre-tax income	**(7,974)**	**n.a.**	**(10)**
Net income	**(7,974)**	**n.a.**	**(10)**
Cash & equivalent	2,503		840
Inventories	2,280		86
Accounts receivable	194		nil
Current assets	5,468		936
Fixed assets, net	91		nil
Intangibles, net	4,148		nil
Total assets	**9,707**	**+937**	**936**
Accts. pay. & accr. liabs	1,422		96
Current liabilities	3,376		96
Long-term debt, gross	2,528		nil
Long-term debt, net	1,805		nil
Shareholders' equity	4,525		840
Cash from oper. activs	**(2,844)**	**n.a.**	**(10)**
Cash from fin. activs	6,610		850
Cash from invest. activs	(2,103)		nil
Net cash position	**2,503**	**+198**	**840**
Capital expenditures	(103)		nil
	$		$
Earnings per share*	(0.09)		(0.00)
Cash flow per share*	(0.03)		(0.00)
	shs		shs
No. of shs. o/s*	104,187,100		n.a.
Avg. no. of shs. o/s*	84,747,275		59,000,000
	%		%
Net profit margin	n.m.		...
Return on equity	(297.26)		...
Return on assets	(146.80)		...

* Common
[A] Reported in accordance with IFRS
[1] Results prior to Mar. 23, 2021, pertain to and reflect the reverse takeover acquisition of (old) Zoglo's Incredible Food Corp.

Latest Results

Periods ended:	9m Sept. 30/22[A]		9m Sept. 30/21[A]
	$000s	%Chg	$000s
Operating revenue	1,984	+9	1,826
Net income	(2,370)	n.a.	(5,774)
	$		$
Earnings per share*	(0.02)		(0.07)

* Common
[A] Reported in accordance with IFRS

Z.12 Zomedica Corp.

Symbol - ZOM **Exchange** - NYSE MKT **CUSIP** - 98980M
Head Office - 100 Phoenix Dr, Suite 125, Ann Arbor, MI, United States, 48108 **Telephone** - (734) 369-2555 **Fax** - (734) 436-8680
Website - www.zomedica.com
Email - pdonato@zomedica.com
Investor Relations - Peter L. Donato (734) 780-4453
Auditors - Grant Thornton LLP C.A.
Lawyers - Fasken Martineau DuMoulin LLP
Transfer Agents - TSX Trust Company, Toronto, Ont.
Employees - 85 at Dec. 31, 2022
Profile - (Alta. 2013) Researches, develops and commercializes diagnostic and therapeutic medical devices for companion animals (canine, feline and equine).

Product lines under commercialization includes TRUFORMA™, a biosensor platform for the detection of adrenal and thyroid disorders in cats and dogs; VetGuardian™, a vital signs remote monitoring system that enable contact-free monitoring of a pet's temperature, pulse, respiration and other vital signs with real-time notifications if vital signs fall outside a customizable range; PulseVet®, which provides electro-hydraulic shock wave technology treatment for musculoskeletal issues in horses and small animals; and Assisi Loop®, a line of devices designed to treat pain and inflammation, as well as separation anxiety in small animals through delivery of targeted pulsed electromagnetic field focused energy (tPEMF).

Platforms under development include TRUVIEW™ (formerly MicroView®) digital microscopy, which utilizes a liquid lens imaging technology and has an automated slide preparation feature; and TRUSOUND™, a line of digital ultrasound products that comes with remote training and coaching.

Corporate headquarters, and research and development laboratory are in an 18,966-sq.-ft. property in Ann Arbor, Mich. Also has a 61,500-sq.-ft. global manufacturing and distribution centre in Roswell, Ga.

In May 2023, the company exercised its option to acquire Elyria, Ohio-based **Structured Monitoring Products, Inc.** (SMP) for an undisclosed amount. The acquisition was rooted in a convertible note investment by the company in SMP. The company paid a deposit of US$250,000 to SMP and expects finalization of a definitive agreement. SMP has developed a vital signs remote monitoring platform, VetGuardian, which provides veterinarians the ability to monitor stressed or aggressive animal patients without wires or wearables. The company has been distributing the VetGuardian system since January 2023.

On Jan. 18, 2023, the company restructured its prior development and commercialization agreement with **Qorvo Biotechnologies, LLC** for TRUFORMA™ wherein the company would take control of aspects of the product line previously provided by Qorvo including development of new assays and manufacturing of instruments and assay cartridges. The company would provide up-front licensing and certain milestone payments, and an option payment if the company exercises its option to extend exclusive rights for TRUFORMA™ in the veterinary health market in perpetuity. A related agreement provides the company with the right to acquire Bulk Acoustic Wave sensors from Qorvo for inclusion in the TRUFORMA™ products. TRUFORMA™ is a biosensor platform for the detection of adrenal and thyroid disorders in cats and dogs.

On Jan. 13, 2023, the company was granted non-exclusive rights to distribute VetGuardian remote animal vital sign and surveillance monitoring device from **Structured Monitoring Products, Inc.** (SMP) following the company's exercise of its right to commercialize the product pursuant to a note purchase agreement with SMP. Under the agreement, the company would acquire the products from SMP for resale and would share service fees with SMP. The agreement has a term of two years with automatic renewals of 12 months unless either party provides written notice of intent not to renew.

Recent Merger and Acquisition Activity

Status: completed **Announced:** July 18, 2022
Zomedica Corp. acquired substantially all of the assets of private Pinehurst, N.C.-based Assisi Animal Health LLC for US$23,000,000 payable in cash and equity. Assisi Animal Health Assisi Loop® has developed a line of veterinary devices designed to treat pain and inflammation, as well as separation anxiety in small animals through delivery of targeted pulsed electromagnetic field focused energy (tPEMF).

Status: completed **Revised:** July 6, 2022
UPDATE: The transaction was completed. PREVIOUS: Zomedica Corp. agreed to acquire substantially all of the assets of private Marietta, Ga.-based Revo Squared, LLC for US$7,800,000 payable in cash and equity. Revo Squared develops MicroView®, a digital cytology imaging system for animals that utilizes liquid lens imaging technology, and has a feature that enables automatic smearing and staining of hematology and cytology slides inside a microscope, eliminating human error in slide preparation.

Predecessor Detail - Name changed from Zomedica Pharmaceuticals Corp., Oct. 5, 2020.
Directors - Jeffrey (Jeff) Rowe, chr., Flushing, Mich.; Larry Heaton, pres. & CEO; Robert A. Cohen, Eden Prairie, Minn.; Christopher R. (Chris) MacLeod, Oakville, Ont.; Dr. Pamela Nichols; Dr. Johnny D. Powers, Scottsdale, Ariz.; Sean Whelan; Rodney J. Williams, Rancho Cucamonga, Calif.
Other Exec. Officers - Peter L. Donato, CFO; Tony Blair, exec. v-p, opers.; Greg Blair, v-p, bus. devel. & strategic planning; William Campbell, v-p, imaging sys.; Kristin Domanski, v-p, HR; Adrian Lock, v-p & gen. mgr.; Evan St. Peter, v-p, tech. innovation; Nicole Westfall, v-p, mktg.; Ashley Wood, v-p, R&D; Karen DeHaan-Fullert, gen. counsel & corp. sec.

Capital Stock

	Authorized (shs.)	Outstanding (shs.)[1]
Preferred	20	nil
Common	unlimited	979,949,668

[1] At May 11, 2023

Major Shareholder - Widely held at Apr. 24, 2023.

Price Range - ZOM/NYSE MKT

Year	Volume	High	Low	Close
2022	255,158,638	US$0.50	US$0.15	US$0.16
2021	700,155,199	US$2.91	US$0.25	US$0.31
2020	431,874,301	US$0.50	US$0.06	US$0.23

ZOM/TSX-VEN (D)

Year	Volume	High	Low	Close
2020	17,150	$0.45	$0.29	$0.29
2019	526,202	$1.70	$0.29	$0.44
2018	765,118	$3.73	$1.87	$2.00

Capital Stock Changes - During 2022, 50,000 common shares were issued on exercise of warrants.

Wholly Owned Subsidiaries

Zomedica Inc., Ann Arbor, Mich.
- 100% int. in **HMT High Medical Technologies (Japan) Co. Ltd.**, Japan.
- 100% int. in **PVT NeoPulse Acquisition GmbH**
  - 100% int. in **NeoPulse, GmbH**, Germany.

Financial Statistics

Periods ended:	12m Dec. 31/22[A]		12m Dec. 31/21[oA]
	US$000s	%Chg	US$000s
Operating revenue	**18,930**	**+358**	**4,133**
Cost of sales	5,278		1,079
Research & devel. expense	2,578		1,673
General & admin expense	21,064		14,523
Stock-based compensation	7,891		7,092
Operating expense	**36,811**	**+51**	**24,367**
Operating income	**(17,881)**	**n.a.**	**(20,234)**
Deprec., depl. & amort.	4,042		1,140
Finance income	2,701		357
Finance costs, gross	1		6
Pre-tax income	**(19,381)**	**n.a.**	**(20,716)**
Income taxes	(2,366)		(2,333)
Net income	**(17,015)**	**n.a.**	**(18,383)**
Cash & equivalent	115,092		194,952
Inventories	2,746		2,848
Accounts receivable	1,864		765
Current assets	123,501		200,408
Fixed assets, net	7,501		1,550
Right-of-use assets	1,665		1,320
Intangibles, net	105,778		76,464
Total assets	**279,610**	**0**	**280,399**
Accts. pay. & accr. liabs.	6,698		3,225
Current liabilities	7,811		4,340
Long-term lease liabilities	1,097		964
Shareholders' equity	267,392		270,885
Cash from oper. activs.	**(11,670)**	**n.a.**	**(14,275)**
Cash from fin. activs.	8		219,159
Cash from invest. activs.	(155,880)		(71,925)
Net cash position	**27,399**	**-86**	**194,952**
Capital expenditures	(2,551)		(147)
	US$		US$
Earnings per share*	(0.02)		(0.05)
Cash flow per share*	(0.01)		(0.01)
	shs		shs
No. of shs. o/s*	979,949,668		979,899,668
Avg. no. of shs. o/s*	979,924,052		956,533,761
	%		%
Net profit margin	(89.88)		(444.79)
Return on equity	(6.32)		(11.86)
Return on assets	(6.08)		(10.61)
No. of employees (FTEs)	85		47

* Common
[o] Restated
[A] Reported in accordance with U.S. GAAP

Latest Results

Periods ended:	3m Mar. 31/23[A]		3m Mar. 31/22[A]
	US$000s	%Chg	US$000s
Operating revenue	5,482	+46	3,751
Net income	(6,385)	n.a.	(3,937)
	US$		US$
Earnings per share*	(0.01)		(0.00)

* Common
[A] Reported in accordance with U.S. GAAP

Historical Summary
(as originally stated)

Fiscal Year	Oper. Rev.	Net Inc. Bef. Disc.	EPS*
	US$000s	US$000s	US$
2022[A]	18,930	(17,015)	(0.02)
2021[A]	4,133	(18,383)	(0.05)
2020[A]	nil	(16,912)	(0.05)
2019[A]	nil	(19,784)	(0.19)
2018[A]	nil	(16,648)	(0.18)

* Common
[A] Reported in accordance with U.S. GAAP

Z.13 Zonetail Inc.

Symbol - ZONE **Exchange** - TSX-VEN **CUSIP** - 98979N
Head Office - 1460-70 University Ave, Toronto, ON, M5J 2M4
Telephone - (416) 583-3773 **Toll-free** - (855) 668-7690
Website - www.zonetail.com
Email - mark@zonetail.com
Investor Relations - Mark Holmes (416) 583-3373 ext. 228
Auditors - MNP LLP C.A., Toronto, Ont.
Transfer Agents - TSX Trust Company, Toronto, Ont.

Profile - (Ont. 2014) Develops mobile platforms for high-rise residential condominiums and apartments, as well as hotels designed to connect residents or guests to the amenities and services of their building through the residents' or guests' mobile device.

Mobile applications (app) include Zonetail, Zonetail Home and Shiftsuite. Zonetail app, which was built in association with Asian American Hotel Owners Association, helps travellers find hotels, connects them to amenities and services of the hotel, as well as the businesses in the surrounding neighbourhood. Zonetail Home app, which was integrated with Yardi Systems, creates and tracks maintenance requests and allows residents to get community updates and push messaging for information on building maintenance and security. Shiftsuite app, built in partnership with **Shift Next Level Innovations Inc.**, allows residents to have direct access to all of a property's services, view status certificates, create and track maintenance requests, as well as get community updates and push messaging on building maintenance and security. The company also has an integration and strategic partnership agreement with MRI Software that would enable MRI clients to efficiently leverage the company's residential mobile platform to connect people with products, amenities and services in the community. Partnership with Yardi, Shift and MRI Software together account for an estimated 50,000,000 households across North America.

Predecessor Detail - Name changed from Revelstoke Equity Inc., Nov. 8, 2018, pursuant to Qualifying Transaction reverse takeover acquisition of (old) Zonetail Inc. by way amalgamation of (old) Zonetail with a wholly owned subsidiary of Revelstoke Equity Inc. which was then vertically amalgamated into the company.

Directors - Mark Holmes, co-founder, pres. & CEO, Toronto, Ont.; Paul Scott, chr., Calif.; J. Errol Farr, CFO & corp. sec., Bradford, Ont.; Geoffrey Gelb, Calif.; W. David Oliver, Toronto, Ont.; William M. (Chip) Rogers, Atlanta, Ga.

Other Exec. Officers - Grant Rickhoff, chief tech. officer; Brian Davies, exec. v-p, sales & strategic partnerships; James Jenkins, exec. v-p, U.S. markets; Ken Singh, v-p, bus. devel. & opers.

Capital Stock

	Authorized (shs.)	Outstanding (shs.)[1]
Common	unlimited	193,838,134

[1] At Aug. 26, 2022

Major Shareholder - Paul Scott held 12.33% interest at Dec. 16, 2021.

Price Range - ZONE/TSX-VEN

Year	Volume	High	Low	Close
2022	35,095,603	$0.06	$0.03	$0.03
2021	129,954,367	$0.17	$0.04	$0.05
2020	64,139,710	$0.11	$0.01	$0.08
2019	23,553,135	$0.10	$0.01	$0.02
2018	1,597,138	$0.18	$0.05	$0.05

Recent Close: $0.02

Capital Stock Changes - In October 2022, private placement of 12,794,750 units (1 common share & ½ warrant) at 4¢ per unit was completed, with warrants exercisable at 6¢ per share for three years.

Wholly Owned Subsidiaries

9827200 Canada Limited, Ont.
Zonetail Inc., Toronto, Ont.
Zonetail US Inc., Wyo.

Financial Statistics

Periods ended:	12m Dec. 31/21[A]		12m Dec. 31/20[A]
	$000s	%Chg	$000s
Operating revenue	**41**	**+2**	**40**
Salaries & benefits	607		540
Research & devel. expense	382		148
General & admin expense	780		432
Stock-based compensation	99		134
Operating expense	**1,868**	**+49**	**1,255**
Operating income	**(1,827)**	**n.a.**	**(1,215)**
Deprec., depl. & amort.	10		45
Finance costs, gross	100		119
Pre-tax income	**(1,934)**	**n.a.**	**(1,220)**
Net income	**(1,934)**	**n.a.**	**(1,220)**
Cash & equivalent	1,088		149
Accounts receivable	119		72
Current assets	1,251		237
Fixed assets, net	nil		7
Total assets	**1,251**	**+413**	**244**
Bank indebtedness	325		325
Accts. pay. & accr. liabs.	225		371
Current liabilities	797		1,130
Long-term debt, gross	223		416
Shareholders' equity	454		(886)
Cash from oper. activs.	**(1,983)**	**n.a.**	**(1,042)**
Cash from fin. activs.	2,921		1,180
Net cash position	**1,088**	**+630**	**149**
	$		$
Earnings per share*	(0.01)		(0.01)
Cash flow per share*	(0.01)		(0.01)
	shs		shs
No. of shs. o/s*	193,838,134		131,215,760
Avg. no. of shs. o/s*	171,464,021		99,324,913
	%		%
Net profit margin	n.m.		n.m.
Return on equity	n.m.		n.m.
Return on assets	(245.35)		(537.07)

* Common
[A] Reported in accordance with IFRS

Latest Results

Periods ended:	6m June 30/22[A]		6m June 30/21[A]
	$000s	%Chg	$000s
Operating revenue	10	-78	45
Net income	(1,071)	n.a.	(874)
	$		$
Earnings per share*	(0.01)		(0.01)

* Common
[A] Reported in accordance with IFRS

Historical Summary
(as originally stated)

Fiscal Year	Oper. Rev.	Net Inc. Bef. Disc.	EPS*
	$000s	$000s	$
2021[A]	41	(1,934)	(0.01)
2020[A]	40	(1,220)	(0.01)
2019[A]	78	(1,880)	(0.03)
2018[A1]	41	(2,915)	(0.07)
2017[A2]	44	(728)	n.a.

* Common
[A] Reported in accordance with IFRS
[1] Results reflect the Nov. 8, 2018, reverse takeover acquisition of (old) Zonetail Inc.
[2] Results pertain to (old) Zonetail Inc.

Z.14 ZoomAway Technologies Inc.

Symbol - ZMA **Exchange** - TSX-VEN **CUSIP** - 98980C
Head Office - 2600 Mill St, Suite 400, Reno, NV, United States, 89502
Toll-free - (888) 586-1475
Website - zoomaway.com
Email - sean@zoomaway.com
Investor Relations - Sean M. Schaeffer (888) 586-1475
Auditors - MNP LLP C.A., Toronto, Ont.
Transfer Agents - Computershare Trust Company of Canada Inc., Vancouver, B.C.

Profile - (B.C. 2010; orig. B.C., 1987) Provides technology and marketing platforms for the hospitality and travel industries including hotels, golf courses, ski resorts and other lodging and activity providers, as well as other markets including the financial technology sector.

Flagship product is ZoomedOUT©, a digital based hospitality game. The game is location-based and allows users to "conquer" certain buildings or establishments through completion of certain requirements and quests. The game is initially designed for Las Vegas, Nev.

Also provides white label booking interfaces embedded on the client's website that performs booking actions such as bundling hotel rooms with activities and other real-time reservation services; customized group and event registration portal branded for the client's group or event; and customized golf registration portal for leisure and corporate golf outings, meetings and conferences.

Other products include LoanCache, which allows consumers to easily find, compare reviews and apply for a wide range of loan types; The ZoomAway Events technology, which provides registration management and group travel services, including hotel rooms, meal, conference and conventions, events/ticketing and transportation; and the Tripsee platform, a communication technology which combines travel, concierge and registration management. Tripsee's Retail Travel Website enables retail users to plan and book vacations via www.tripsee.travel while its Concierge Platform (www.tripsee.travel/concierge) provides virtual concierge functionality for a diverse portfolio of hotels and resorts around the world.

In April 2022, the company entered into a letter of intent to acquire a privately held specialty retailer with locations throughout Ontario. Concurrently, the company would spin off its current business to wholly owned **Zoom Tech Inc.** including all intellectual property and related rights to its retail and hospitality technology platforms. The acquisition would constitute a change of business.

Predecessor Detail - Name changed from ZoomAway Travel Inc., Apr. 15, 2021; basis 1 new for 9 old shs.

Directors - Sean M. Schaeffer, pres. & CEO, Reno, Nev.; Steven D. (Steve) Rosenthal, acting CFO, Reno, Nev.; Jayahari (Jay) Balasubramaniam, Toronto, Ont.; Jeremy Green; Alexey (Alex) Kanayev, Toronto, Ont.; Umeshan (Mason) Shanmugadasan, Toronto, Ont.

Other Exec. Officers - Sandra E. Buschau, corp. sec.

Capital Stock

	Authorized (shs.)	Outstanding (shs.)[1]
Common	unlimited	16,331,038

[1] At June 30, 2022

Major Shareholder - AIP Convertible Private Debt Fund LP held 46.34% interest at Nov. 8, 2021.

Price Range - ZMA/TSX-VEN

Year	Volume	High	Low	Close
2022	214,826	$0.25	$0.16	$0.20
2021	4,288,648	$0.54	$0.16	$0.20
2020	8,029,731	$0.95	$0.14	$0.41
2019	18,947,140	$1.31	$0.09	$0.81
2018	9,368,811	$1.22	$0.09	$0.18

Consolidation: 1-for-9 cons. in Apr. 2021

Wholly Owned Subsidiaries

Zoom Tech Inc.
ZoomAway, Inc., Reno, Nev.

Financial Statistics

Periods ended:	12m Dec. 31/21[A]		12m Dec. 31/20[◻A]
	US$000s	%Chg	US$000s
Operating revenue	**82**	**n.a.**	**(3)**
Salaries & benefits	148		165
General & admin expense	556		785
Stock-based compensation	nil		213
Operating expense	**704**	**-39**	**1,162**
Operating income	**(622)**	**n.a.**	**(1,165)**
Deprec., depl. & amort.	nil		3
Finance costs, net	1,314		553
Pre-tax income	**(1,927)**	**n.a.**	**(1,697)**
Net income	**(1,927)**	**n.a.**	**(1,697)**
Cash & equivalent	715		2
Accounts receivable	nil		4
Current assets	767		2,151
Total assets	**767**	**-64**	**2,156**
Accts. pay. & accr. liabs	265		482
Current liabilities	5,277		2,430
Long-term debt, gross	4,425		4,244
Long-term debt, net	nil		3,004
Shareholders' equity	(4,511)		(3,278)
Cash from oper. activs	**(1,157)**	**n.a.**	**(916)**
Cash from fin. activs	(293)		2,678
Net cash position	**715**	**-67**	**2,147**
	US$		US$
Earnings per share*	(0.12)		(0.21)
Cash flow per share*	(0.07)		(0.12)
	shs		shs
No. of shs. o/s*	16,412,538		9,738,186
Avg. no. of shs. o/s*	15,912,858		8,107,340
	%		%
Net profit margin	n.m.		n.m.
Return on equity	n.m.		n.m.
Return on assets	n.a.		n.a.
Foreign sales percent	100		100

* Common
◻ Restated
A Reported in accordance with IFRS

Latest Results

Periods ended:	6m June 30/22[A]		6m June 30/21[A]
	US$000s	%Chg	US$000s
Operating revenue	123	+262	34
Net income	(1,101)	n.a.	(803)
	US$		US$
Earnings per share*	(0.06)		(0.06)

* Common
A Reported in accordance with IFRS

Historical Summary
(as originally stated)

Fiscal Year	Oper. Rev.	Net Inc. Bef. Disc.	EPS*
	US$000s	US$000s	US$
2021[A]	82	(1,927)	(0.12)
2020[A]	(3)	(1,697)	(0.21)
2019[A]	57	(653)	(0.09)
2018[A]	151	(504)	(0.09)
2017[A]	348	(1,560)	(0.36)

* Common
A Reported in accordance with IFRS
Note: Adjusted throughout for 1-for-9 cons. in Apr. 2021

Z.15 Zoomd Technologies Ltd.

Symbol - ZOMD **Exchange** - TSX-VEN **CUSIP** - 98981L
Head Office - 2500-700 Georgia St W, Vancouver, BC, V7Y 1B3
Website - www.zoomd.com
Email - ir@zoomd.com
Investor Relations - Amit Bohensky 972-72-220-0555
Auditors - Brightman Almagor Zohar & Co. C.P.A., Tel Aviv, Israel
Lawyers - Goodmans LLP, Vancouver, B.C.
Transfer Agents - TSX Trust Company, Vancouver, B.C.
Profile - (Alta. 2013) Offers an internal site search engine to publishers for increased monetization, and better management of online advertising focusing on user acquisition for media agencies and advertisers, through a single proprietary patented platform.

The company has unified publisher-focused search and advertiser-focused mobile user acquisition under one platform. The company offers publishers a fully customized software-as-a-service (SaaS)-based search engine tool for free, using a revenue-share model with the publisher (as a partner) for their websites that helps increase engagement and monetization of their site content. It offers advertisers a platform for mobile app user acquisition, integrating more than 600 media channels, consolidating all data and streaming it into a centralized dashboard, giving the advertiser the ability to view, analyse and optimize their campaign on hundreds of channels in a single platform, thereby saving the advertiser resources and maximizing their advertising budget.

In March 2022, wholly owned **Zoomd Ltd.** acquired U.S.-based **Albert Technologies Ltd.** for $125,000 cash and issuance of $375,000 common shares on closing, and an additional payment of $125,000 cash and issuance of $375,000 common shares upon achievement of certain performance-based metrics. Albert Technologies offers an artificial intelligence marketing platform for advertisers which primarily uses the Google and Facebook platforms.

Predecessor Detail - Name changed from DataMiners Capital Corp., Aug. 28, 2019, pursuant to Qualifying Transaction reverse takeover acquisition of Zoomd Ltd.; basis 1 new for 2.5 old shs.

Directors - Amit Bohensky, chr., Israel; Amnon Argaman, Israel; Darryl S. Cardey, Vancouver, B.C.; Ofer Eitan, Israel; Avigur Zmora, Israel

Other Exec. Officers - Ido Almany, CEO; Yair Yaskerovitch, COO; Tsvika Adler, CFO & corp. sec.; Omir Argaman, chief growth officer; Niv Sharoni, chief tech. officer; Deborah Cohen, v-p, cust. success; Nir Levy, v-p, R&D

Capital Stock

	Authorized (shs.)	Outstanding (shs.)[1]
Preferred	unlimited	nil
Common	unlimited	98,055,837

1 At May 30, 2023

Major Shareholder - Widely held at Nov. 2, 2022.

Price Range - ZOMD/TSX-VEN

Year	Volume	High	Low	Close
2022	14,375,419	$0.60	$0.15	$0.18
2021	19,543,280	$1.50	$0.23	$0.49
2020	6,828,855	$0.69	$0.15	$0.25
2019	653,622	$1.30	$0.60	$0.70
2018	47,640	$2.50	$0.53	$0.53

Consolidation: 1-for-2.5 cons. in Sept. 2019
Recent Close: $0.06
Capital Stock Changes - During 2022, common shares were issued as follows: 1,315,582 pursuant to the acquisition of Albert Technologies Ltd. and 339,715 on exercise of options.

Wholly Owned Subsidiaries

Performance Revenue Ltd., Israel.
Zoomd Ltd., Herzliya, Israel.
- 100% int. in **Moblin Asia Pte. Ltd.**, Singapore.

Financial Statistics

Periods ended:	12m Dec. 31/22[A]		12m Dec. 31/21[A]
	US$000s	%Chg	US$000s
Operating revenue	**53,023**	**+1**	**52,585**
Cost of sales	36,415		36,294
Salaries & benefits	9,931		6,757
Research & devel. expense	2,451		1,626
General & admin expense	3,351		2,992
Stock-based compensation	277		110
Operating expense	**52,425**	**+10**	**47,779**
Operating income	**598**	**-88**	**4,806**
Deprec., depl. & amort.	2,712		1,802
Finance income	108		6
Finance costs, gross	560		512
Pre-tax income	**(2,566)**	**n.a.**	**2,498**
Income taxes	287		nil
Net income	**(2,853)**	**n.a.**	**2,498**
Cash & equivalent	3,776		5,238
Accounts receivable	5,818		8,478
Current assets	10,390		14,133
Fixed assets, net	316		80
Right-of-use assets	2,874		734
Intangibles, net	11,154		11,332
Total assets	**24,954**	**-6**	**26,575**
Bank indebtedness	2,001		2,003
Accts. pay. & accr. liabs	3,422		9,014
Current liabilities	9,076		11,017
Long-term lease liabilities	2,271		96
Shareholders' equity	13,087		14,991
Cash from oper. activs	**1,843**	**-52**	**3,825**
Cash from fin. activs	(642)		1,319
Cash from invest. activs	(2,663)		(2,477)
Net cash position	**3,776**	**-28**	**5,238**
Capital expenditures	(296)		(31)
	US$		US$
Earnings per share*	(0.03)		0.02
Cash flow per share*	0.02		0.04
	shs		shs
No. of shs. o/s*	97,250,914		95,595,617
Avg. no. of shs. o/s*	102,583,043		100,988,841
	%		%
Net profit margin	(5.38)		4.75
Return on equity	(20.32)		18.28
Return on assets	(8.66)		13.08

* Common
A Reported in accordance with IFRS

Latest Results

Periods ended:	3m Mar. 31/23[A]		3m Mar. 31/22[A]
	US$000s	%Chg	US$000s
Operating revenue	8,649	-47	16,250
Net income	(3,578)	n.a.	821
	US$		US$
Earnings per share*	(0.03)		0.01

* Common
A Reported in accordance with IFRS

Historical Summary
(as originally stated)

Fiscal Year	Oper. Rev.	Net Inc. Bef. Disc.	EPS*
	US$000s	US$000s	US$
2022[A]	53,023	(2,853)	(0.03)
2021[A]	52,585	2,498	0.02
2020[A]	25,423	(5,705)	(0.06)
2019[A1]	27,052	(6,296)	(0.07)
2018[A]	28,649	(2,338)	n.a.

* Common
A Reported in accordance with IFRS
1 Results prior to Aug. 28, 2019, pertain to and reflect the Qualifying Transaction reverse takeover acquisiton of Zoomd Ltd.
Note: Adjusted throughout for 1-for-2.5 cons. in Sept. 2019

Z.16 ZoomerMedia Limited

Symbol - ZUM **Exchange** - TSX-VEN **CUSIP** - 98978C
Head Office - 70 Jefferson Ave, Toronto, ON, M6K 1Y4 **Telephone** - (416) 607-7735 **Fax** - (416) 363-8747
Website - www.zoomermedia.ca
Email - leanne@zoomer.ca
Investor Relations - Leanne H. Wright (416) 886-6873
Auditors - BDO Canada LLP C.A., Markham, Ont.
Lawyers - CP LLP, Toronto, Ont.
Transfer Agents - Computershare Trust Company of Canada Inc., Toronto, Ont.
Profile - (Can. 2008 amalg.) Serves its diversified demographic through television, radio, magazine, Internet, conferences, trade shows and digital platforms for local news and platforms.

Television properties include: VisionTV, a multi-cultural, multi-faith, family friendly specialty television service; ONE TV, which offers fitness, healthy living and entertainment programs; JoyTV in Vancouver, Victoria and Surrey, B.C., as well as the Fraser Valley; FaithTV, a television service from Winnipeg, Man., devoted to broadcasting Christian, multi-faith, and local content; and TVL Channel 5, a linear channel guide available to Rogers households in Ontario and New Brunswick.

Radio properties include: CFMZ-FM Toronto (The New Classical 96.3FM), CFMX-FM Cobourg (The New Classical 103.1FM) and CFMO-FM Collingwood (The New Classical 102.9FM), which are commercial classical music radio stations serving the Greater Toronto Area (GTA), eastern Ontario and Collingwood, respectively; CFZM-AM 740 Toronto; and CFZM-FM 96.7 FM Toronto (Zoomer Radio, Toronto's "Timeless Hits" Station).

Magazines/print properties include: ZOOMER magazine, a paid circulation mature magazine published six times a year; On The Bay Magazine, a quarterly regional lifestyle magazine for 20 towns and villages of the Southern Georgian Bay, Ont.; and Tonic Magazine, a regional health and wellness magazine published every two months and distributed in Toronto.

Online/digital properties include: www.EverythingZoomer.com, is the lifestyle site for the 45-plus age group, with features ranging from food and entertainment, style and fashion, arts and entertainment, sex and relating, health, finance, travel and spirit; www.blogto.com, Canada's unrivalled local publisher across digital and social media platforms which caters to the interest of the Greater Toronto Region, bringing in 8,000,000 monthly active users, and more than 360,000,000 page views annually; www.dailyhive.com, a digital source for local news, culture, and what's happening in Western Canada, with more than 9,000,000 million monthly active users, nearly 300,000,000 annual page views, and 3,100,000 followers across Instagram, TikTok, Facebook, Twitter, and Linkedin. Other websites include CARP.ca, VisionTV.ca, ONEtv.ca, Zoomerradio.ca/am740.ca and ClassicalFM.ca. Royalty revenue is derived through the provision of exclusive marketing and membership services to CARP (Canadian Association of Retired Persons), Canada's largest national senior and retiree advocacy group.

In addition, the company has a trade show and conference divisions that conduct the ZoomerShows, an annual lifestyle expos in Toronto, Ont. and Vancouver, B.C.; and ideaCity, an annual Canadian conference also known as Canada's Premiere Meeting of the Minds, which presents the "Smartest People with The Biggest Ideas".

Recent Merger and Acquisition Activity

Status: completed **Announced:** Sept. 12, 2022
ZoomerMedia Limited acquired Buzz Connected Media Inc., owner and publisher of Daily Hive, a digital source for local news, culture, and what's happening in western Canada, for a purchase price of $16,400,000 consisting of $6,000,000 in cash, a $5,000,000 promissory note, $3,000,000 of ZoomerMedia preference shares at $0.15 per share and assumption of $2,400,000 of debt.

Predecessor Detail - Formed from Fifty-Plus.Net International Inc. in Canada, July 1, 2008, on amalgamation with wholly owned subsidiaries Fifty-Plus.Net Inc. and ZoomerMedia Limited (previously Kemur Publishing Co. Ltd.).

Directors - Moses Znaimer, chr., pres. & CEO, Ont.; Diane M. Francis, Ont.; Wayne Ingram, Ont.; Julia J. Johnston, Ont.; Dr. David R. Morgenthau, Ont.; Peter Palframan, Thornhill, Ont.; Chandran Ratnaswami, Toronto, Ont.

Other Exec. Officers - Omri Tintpulver, COO & chief digital officer; Terence Chan, CFO; Dan K. Hamilton, chief revenue officer & gen. mgr., radio div.; Beverley Shenken, chief content officer & gen. mgr., television div.; Leanne H. Wright, sr. v-p, commun.; Richard Lumsden, v-p, creative srvcs.

Capital Stock

	Authorized (shs.)	Outstanding (shs.)[1]
Class A Preference	unlimited	
Series 1		131,974,099
Series 2		255,905,030
Common	unlimited	273,646,964

[1] At Apr. 26, 2023

Class A Preference Series 1 & 2 - Entitled to dividends. Convertible into common shares on a 1-for-1 basis. Non-voting.

Common - One vote per share.

Major Shareholder - Moses Znaimer held 62.83% interest and Fairfax Financial Holdings Limited held 16.09% interest at Jan. 13, 2023.

Price Range - ZUM/TSX-VEN

Year	Volume	High	Low	Close
2022	12,923,847	$0.14	$0.04	$0.05
2021	10,499,156	$0.15	$0.07	$0.10
2020	15,163,016	$0.09	$0.04	$0.08
2019	101,388,882	$0.29	$0.02	$0.04
2018	11,164,813	$0.07	$0.02	$0.03

Recent Close: $0.04

Capital Stock Changes - During fiscal 2022, 483,667 common shares were issued on exercise of options.

Dividends

ZUM com N.S.R.

$0.003 ... Jan. 9/23 $0.003 ... Dec. 31/21
$0.0025**i** ... Sept. 2/21
Paid in 2023: $0.003 2022: n.a. 2021: $0.0055**i**

i Initial Payment

Wholly Owned Subsidiaries

Buzz Connected Media Inc., Vancouver, B.C.
Freshdaily Inc., Toronto, Ont.
JTM Amalco Inc.
JTM Healing Gardens Inc.
JTM Hit Parade Inc., Canada.
JTM Hit Parade 3 Inc., Canada.
JTM Unholy Inc., Canada.
On The Bay Magazine Inc.
2585882 Ontario Inc., Ont.

Investments

Canopy Growth Corporation, Smiths Falls, Ont. (see separate coverage)
Heritage Cannabis Holdings Corporation

Financial Statistics

Periods ended:	12m Aug. 31/22[A]		12m Aug. 31/21[A]
	$000s	%Chg	$000s
Operating revenue	**54,243**	**+11**	**48,861**
Cost of sales	16,726		13,559
Salaries & benefits	22,083		20,573
Stock-based compensation	341		384
Operating expense	**39,149**	**+13**	**34,516**
Operating income	**15,094**	**+5**	**14,345**
Deprec., depl. & amort.	9,614		8,502
Finance income	130		119
Finance costs, gross	1,399		1,296
Pre-tax income	**4,778**	**-2**	**4,870**
Income taxes	1,296		1,136
Net income	**3,481**	**-7**	**3,734**
Net inc. for equity hldrs	**3,245**	**-8**	**3,529**
Net inc. for non-cont. int.	**236**	**+15**	**205**
Cash & equivalent	20,856		33,322
Accounts receivable	9,024		7,876
Current assets	33,248		43,824
Fixed assets, net	3,649		3,663
Right-of-use assets	20,013		21,473
Intangibles, net	32,750		15,907
Total assets	**92,453**	**+4**	**88,623**
Accts. pay. & accr. liabs.	4,789		6,797
Current liabilities	11,470		14,889
Long-term debt, gross	5,000		nil
Long-term debt, net	5,000		nil
Long-term lease liabilities	21,126		22,061
Shareholders' equity	54,550		52,924
Non-controlling interest	(1,787)		(2,023)
Cash from oper. activs.	**3,635**	**-56**	**8,225**
Cash from fin. activs.	(5,870)		(1,722)
Cash from invest. activs.	(3,374)		(7,498)
Net cash position	**11,067**	**-34**	**16,675**
Capital expenditures	(805)		(1,113)
	$		$
Earnings per share*	0.01		0.01
Cash flow per share*	0.01		0.01
Cash divd. per share*	0.00		0.00
	shs		shs
No. of shs. o/s*	273,646,964		273,163,297
Avg. no. of shs. o/s*	661,376,561		655,202,108
	%		%
Net profit margin	6.42		7.64
Return on equity	6.04		6.84
Return on assets	4.97		5.44

* Common
[A] Reported in accordance with IFRS

Latest Results

Periods ended:	6m Feb. 28/23[A]		6m Feb. 28/22[A]
	$000s	%Chg	$000s
Operating revenue	32,470	+21	26,764
Net income	382	-89	3,588
Net inc. for equity hldrs	372	-89	3,480
Net inc. for non-cont. int.	10		108
	$		$
Earnings per share*	0.00		0.01

* Common
[A] Reported in accordance with IFRS

Historical Summary
(as originally stated)

Fiscal Year	Oper. Rev.	Net Inc. Bef. Disc.	EPS*
	$000s	$000s	$
2022[A]	54,243	3,481	0.01
2021[A]	48,861	3,734	0.01
2020[A]	50,686	4,591	0.01
2019[A]	52,691	1,559	0.00
2018[A]	50,666	52	0.00

* Common
[A] Reported in accordance with IFRS

At Last Report

The following is a list of "valid and subsisting" companies, for which limited information is available.

A

Name	Incorp. Date	Date of Last Report	Remarks
A.A.A. Stamp Coin Bullion Inc.	B.C. 1987	July 1998	Delisted VSE Jan. 30, 1998
ACEnetx Inc.	Ont. 2000, amalg.	Nov. 2002	Delisted TSX-VEN Nov. 14, 2002
A.E. Ventures Ltd.	Alta. 1993	June 2001	Delisted TSX-VEN June 5, 2002
AJA Ventures Inc.	B.C. 2020; orig. Alta. 1998	July 2012	Delisted TSX-VEN Apr. 19, 2021
AML International Inc.	Ont. 1981	Mar. 1988	Delisted CDN Jan. 3, 1995
ANB Canada Inc.	Ont. 2007	Sept. 2016	Delisted TSX-VEN Sept. 29, 2016
ARV Corp.	Alta. 1996	Nov. 1999	Delisted CDNX May 15, 2001
Abattis Bioceuticals Corp.	B.C. 1997	Feb. 2021	Delisted CSE Feb. 16, 2021
AbitibiBowater Canada Inc.	Can. 1998	May 2009	Delisted TSX May 19, 2009
Acadian Energy Inc.	Ont. 2007	Apr. 2015	Delisted TSX-VEN Apr. 13, 2015
Acer Capital Corp.	Alta. 1993	Oct. 2000	Delisted CDNX May 31, 2001
Ad Com Marketing Inc.	B.C. 1979	Nov. 1988	Delisted VSE Jan. 10, 1990
Adaptive Technologies (Canada) Inc.	B.C. 1983	Aug. 1986	Delisted VSE July 6, 1988
Admiral Inc.	Ont. 1992	Mar. 2002	Delisted TSX-VEN June 20, 2003
Advanced Strategic Solutions Inc.	Alta. 1997	May 2001	Delisted CDNX Feb. 1, 2002
Afitex Financial Services Inc.	Ont. 1981	Feb. 1999	Delisted CDN Oct. 13, 2000
Agrios Global Holdings Ltd.	B.C. 2017	Feb. 2021	Delisted CSE Feb. 4, 2021
Aiviv Ventures Inc.	B.C. 1995	Dec. 2001	Delisted TSX-VEN May 13, 2002
Aladin International Inc.	Ont. 1975	Sept. 1990	Delisted ASE Sept. 5, 1990
Alava Ventures Inc.	Alta. 1987	May 2002	Delisted ASE Sept. 18, 1995
Albarton Technologies Inc.	Alta. 1987	Mar. 1991	Delisted ASE Mar. 18, 1991
Alcina Development Corporation	B.C. 1962	June 1985	Delisted VSE Apr. 7, 1986
Aldea Solutions Inc.	Can. 2006	Jan. 2008	Delisted TSX-VEN Jan. 25, 2008
Alliance Growers Corp.	B.C. 2014	May 2023	Delisted CSE May 9, 2023
Alpha Group Industries Inc.	Ont. 1994; orig. Can. 1989	July 2009	Delisted TSX-VEN July 15, 2009
Alpha Peak Capital Inc.	B.C. 2015, amalg.	Apr. 2021	Delisted TSX-VEN Apr. 20, 2021
Alternate Health Corp.	B.C. 2014	July 2022	Delisted CSE July 29, 2022
Aludra Inc.	Ont. 1997	June 2003	Delisted TSX-VEN June 20, 2003
American Lightwave Corp.	B.C. 1980	Nov. 1988	Delisted VSE Jan. 10, 1990
American Wireless Corp.	Alta. 1996	May 2002	Delisted TSX-VEN May 14, 2002
Analytical Software, Inc.	B.C. 1998	Dec. 2000	Delisted TSX-VEN May 31, 2002
Groupe André Perry Incorporated	Que. 1974	Dec. 1990	Delisted ME Jan. 25, 1991
Annidis Corporation	Ont. 2010	Nov. 2019	Delisted TSX-VEN Dec. 14, 2020
Ansar Financial and Development Corporation	Ont. 2008	Mar. 2022	Delisted CSE Mar. 29, 2022
Applause Corporation	Alta. 1994	June 2003	Delisted TSX-VEN June 20, 2003
Ardent Ventures Inc.	Alta. 1994	Feb. 1999	Delisted ASE July 29, 1998
Asean Holdings Inc.	B.C. 1984	May 1999	Delisted CDNX Mar. 1, 2000
Aspen Venture Capital Corporation	Alta. 1993	Apr. 1999	Delisted ASE Apr. 18, 1996
Asset Management Software Systems Corp.	Ont. 1992	July 2002	Delisted TSX-VEN June 20, 2003
Atlantic Systems Group Inc.	N.B. 1988	June 2003	Delisted TSX-VEN June 20, 2003
Aurelian Developers Ltd.	Ont. 1979	June 2007	Delisted TSX-VEN June 20, 2003
Austin Investment Corporation Ltd.	B.C. 1957	Aug. 1979	Delisted VSE Oct. 1, 1981
Avanté Technologies Inc.	Alta. 1996	Apr. 2002	Delisted TSX-VEN June 20, 2003
Avisa Diagnostics Inc.	Ont. 1984	July 2023	Delisted CSE July 14, 2023
Axiom International Development Corporation	B.C. 1984	Apr. 1991	Delisted VSE Mar. 4, 1992
Axiotron Corp.	Ont. 2005	Dec. 2011	Delisted TSX-VEN Dec. 19, 2011
Axis.Port Inc.	Alta. 1996	Nov. 2001	Delisted TSX-VEN June 5, 2002
Aztech Innovations Inc.	Can. 2010	July 2011	Delisted TSX-VEN July 21, 2011

B

Name	Incorp. Date	Date of Last Report	Remarks
BLOK Technologies Inc.	B.C. 2013	Oct. 2020	Delisted CSE Oct. 22, 2020
Babylon Technologies Inc.	Alta. 1999	Dec. 2004	Delisted TSX-VEN Dec. 15, 2004
Bald Eagle Golf Corp.	Man. 2000	Nov. 2002	Delisted TSX-VEN Nov. 17, 2004
Bassett Media Group Corp.	Ont. 2007	Dec. 2011	Delisted TSX-VEN Dec. 19, 2011
Battery & Wireless Solutions Inc.	Alta. 1993	Oct. 2007	Delisted TSX-VEN Oct. 2, 2007
Battery Technologies Inc.	Ont. 1988, amalg.	May 2003	Delisted TSX May 27, 2004
Bauska Manufacturing (B.C.) Ltd.	B.C. 1985	Dec. 1987	Delisted VSE July 7, 1989
Beckett Technologies Corp.	Ont. 1994; orig. Alta. 1983	Aug. 1997	Delisted ASE May 4, 1998
Betacom Corporation	Ont. 1922	Feb. 2003	Delisted TSX-VEN Apr. 20, 2004
betterU Education Corp.	Can. 2017; orig. B.C. 2007	Aug. 2023	Suspended TSX-VEN Sept. 21, 2020
Bio-Feed Industries Limited	B.C. 1983	Mar. 1992	Delisted VSE Mar. 4, 1991
Bio-Med Laboratories Inc.	Can. 1995	Sept. 2005	Delisted CDN Oct. 13, 2000
BioExx Specialty Proteins Ltd.	Ont. 2006	Nov. 2013	Delisted TSX Nov. 7, 2013
Biolix Corporation	Can. 1998	Dec. 2005	Delisted TSX-VEN June 25, 2007
Biologix International Ltd.	B.C. 1966	Mar. 1993	Delisted VSE May 2, 1991
Biophage Pharma Inc.	Can. 2001; orig. Alta. 2000	June 2010	Delisted TSX-VEN June 9, 2010
Biosign Technologies Inc.	Ont. 2006, amalg.	May 2016	Delisted TSX-VEN Aug. 18, 2016
Bloom Health Partners Inc.	B.C. 2011	May 2023	Delisted CSE May 9, 2023
Blue Hill Capital Corp.	Alta. 1988	May 1998	Delisted ASE Oct. 31, 1996
Blue Zen Memorial Parks Inc.	Can. 1994	May 2016	Delisted CSE May 31, 2016
BluePoint Data, Inc.	Yuk. 1993; orig. B.C. 1987	July 2012	Delisted TSX-VEN July 23, 2012
Bold Stroke Ventures Inc.	B.C. 2011	Nov. 2019	Delisted TSX-VEN May 25, 2021
Boost Capital Corp.	Ont. 2011	Aug. 2017	Delisted TSX-VEN Aug. 18, 2017
Border Chemical Company Limited	Man. 1959	June 2007	Delisted CDN Oct. 13, 2000
Borkin Industries Corp.	B.C. 1983	June 1987	Delisted VSE Mar. 2, 1988
Boswell International Technologies Ltd.	B.C. 1982	Jan. 1997	Delisted VSE June 12, 1996
Brandevor Enterprises Ltd.	B.C. 1985	Oct. 1997	Delisted TSE Apr. 1, 1999
Brighter Minds Media Inc.	Ont. 2004	July 2009	Delisted TSX-VEN July 14, 2009
Browning Communications Canada Inc.	Ont. 1983	Dec. 1989	Delisted ASE Aug. 21, 1990

C

Name	Incorp. Date	Date of Last Report	Remarks
C & E Furniture Industries Inc.	B.C. 1976	May 1994	Delisted VSE May 4, 1994
CANCRETE Environmental Solutions Inc.	Alta. 1995	Apr. 1999	Delisted ASE Nov. 23, 1999
CD ROM Network Corp.	Ont. 1987	Mar. 2003	Delisted CDN Oct. 13, 2000
CDNet Canada Inc.	Ont. 1986	Oct. 2001	Delisted TSX-VEN June 5, 2002
CIM International Group Inc.	Ont. 2010	July 2022	Delisted CSE July 28, 2022
CLN Ventures Inc.	Ont. 1986	June 2003	Delisted TSX-VEN June 20, 2003
CMAC Computer Systems Ltd.	B.C. 1982	Jan. 1988	Delisted VSE Oct. 25, 1988
CME Capital Inc.	Ont. 1939	Oct. 1995	Delisted CDN May 31, 1996

Name	Incorp. Date	Date of Last Report	Remarks
CNI Computer Networks International Ltd.	B.C. 1985	Dec. 1987	Delisted VSE June 20, 1988
CO2 Solutions Inc.	Que. 1997	Oct. 2021	Delisted TSX-VEN Dec. 7, 2021
CPI Crown Properties International Corporation	Alta. 1997	July 2009	Delisted TSX-VEN July 14, 2009
Ca-Network Inc.	Ont. 1967	Oct. 2002	Delisted CDN Oct. 13, 2000
Caara Ventures Inc.	B.C. 1983	Feb. 1987	Delisted VSE May 2, 1988
Cachet Communications Inc.	Alta. 1994	Sept. 1998	Delisted ASE Nov. 22, 1999
Caddev Industries Inc.	B.C. 1986	Oct. 1990	Delisted VSE Nov. 16, 1990
Calcap Investments Ltd.	Alta. 1987	Feb. 1994	Delisted ASE Feb. 7, 1994
Caldera Technologies Corporation	Yuk. 1994; orig. B.C. 1988	Mar. 1997	Delisted VSE Mar. 15, 1996
Calibre Technologies Corporation	B.C. 1986	Jan. 1997	Delisted VSE Dec. 10, 1996
Callitas Health Inc.	Alta. 2014; orig. Ont. 2003	Dec. 2021	Delisted CSE Dec. 9, 2021
Calyx Ventures Inc.	B.C. 2008	Nov. 2022	Suspended TSX-VEN July 22, 2020
Cam-Turf Corporation	Ont. 1983	June 1988	Delisted ASE Mar. 14, 1989
Camarico Investment Group Ltd.	B.C. 1996	July 2023	Delisted CSE July 24, 2023
Can-Med Technology Inc.	Ont. 1982	Nov. 1995	Delisted ASE Oct. 12, 1995
Canada Renewable Bioenergy Corp.	Alta. 2007	Aug. 2016	Delisted CSE Aug. 15, 2016
Canadian Food Products Limited	Ont. 1928	June 1981	Delisted CDN Aug. 31, 1992
Canadian Roxana Resources Limited	B.C. 1985	May 1995	Delisted VSE May 18, 1995
Canadiana Genetics Inc.	Alta. 1990, amalg.	May 1996	Delisted ASE Feb. 28, 1995
Cancorp Technologies Inc.	Alta. 1988	Jan. 1997	Delisted ASE July 15, 1992
Canex Resources Corporation	B.C. 1984	Jan. 1991	Delisted VSE May 4, 1994
CannAmerica Brands Corp.	B.C. 2017	Jan. 2023	Delisted CSE Jan. 27, 2023
CannTrust Holdings Inc.	Ont. 2015	May 2020	Delisted TSX May 7, 2020
Capha Pharmaceuticals Inc.	B.C. 2004; orig. Alta. 1998	Apr. 2016	Delisted CSE Apr. 6, 2016
Capital Pro-Egaux inc.	Que. 2003	Dec. 2018	Delisted TSX-VEN Dec. 17, 2018
Caprice-Greystoke Enterprises Ltd.	B.C. 1986	Sept. 1996	Delisted VSE Sept. 30, 1996
Carbiz Inc.	Ont. 1998	June 2007	Delisted TSX-VEN Oct. 4, 2006
Carlyle Entertainment Ltd.	B.C. 2013	May 2019	Delisted CSE May 27, 2019
Carthew Bay Technologies Inc.	Ont. 1987; orig. Alta. 1981	Oct. 2000	Delisted CDN Oct. 13, 2000
Cascadia Technologies Ltd.	B.C. 1987	Jan. 1998	Delisted VSE Mar. 2, 1998
The Cash Store Australia Holdings Inc.	Ont. 2009, amalg.	Sept. 2015	Delisted TSX-VEN Oct. 1, 2015
The Cash Store Financial Services Inc.	Ont. 2002, amalg.	May 2014	Delisted TSX May 26, 2014
Ced-Or Corporation	Que. 1980	June 2007	Delisted TSX-VEN June 23, 2006
Le Château Inc.	Can. 1969	July 2021	Delisted TSX-VEN July 5, 2021
Chelsea Mercantile Bancorp Ltd.	Alta. 1993	Dec. 1998	Delisted CDNX Mar. 16, 2001
ChitrChatr Communications Inc.	B.C. 2013	Mar. 2017	Delisted CSE Mar. 7, 2017
Cinequity Corporation	Ont. 1981	May 1983	Delisted CDN Aug. 31, 1992
Claremont Industries Inc.	Ont. 1974	Dec. 1988	Delisted CDN Jan. 3, 1995
Cleanfield Alternative Energy Inc.	Ont. 2009; orig. B.C. 2004	Mar. 2015	Delisted TSX-VEN Mar. 12, 2015
CleanSoils Limited	Ont. 1992	Dec. 1997	Delisted CDN Jan. 14, 2000
Clement Systems Inc.	Alta. 1997	Apr. 2001	Delisted TSX-VEN Dec. 22, 2006
Coffee Tea or Me Cafe Inc.	Ont. 1995	Nov. 2001	Delisted CDN Oct. 13, 2000
Colours International Inc.	Ont. 1983	July 1988	Delisted CDN Jan. 3, 1995
Concord Capital Corp.	Ont. 1979, amalg.	Sept. 1991	Delisted TSE Sept. 21, 1992
ConPak Seafoods Inc.	Can. 1987; orig. B.C. 1978	Jan. 1998	Delisted TSE Apr. 1, 1999
Consolidated Indescor Corp.	B.C. 1981	Oct. 1989	Delisted VSE Mar. 1, 1989
Consolidated Niche Peripherals Inc.	B.C. 1986	Sept. 1998	Delisted CDNX Apr. 18, 2001
Consolidated Trout Lake Mines Ltd.	B.C. 1985	Jan. 1992	Delisted VSE May 4, 1993
Contach Industries Inc.	Ont. 1980	Nov. 1988	Delisted CDN Jan. 3, 1995
Contact Image Corporation	Alta. 2003	Oct. 2007	Delisted TSX-VEN June 25, 2007
Control Networks Corporation	B.C. 1986	June 1987	Delisted VSE May 2, 1988
Cosmoz.com Inc.	B.C. 1979	Feb. 1999	Delisted CDN Jan. 26, 1999
Cotinga Pharmaceuticals Inc.	Ont. 2006, amalg.	Oct. 2021	Delisted TSX-VEN Oct. 8, 2021
Crimson Bioenergy Ltd.	B.C. 2009	Aug. 2020	Delisted TSX-VEN Oct. 8, 2021
Crossland Industries Corporation	B.C. 1980	Feb. 1988	Delisted VSE Mar. 2, 1989
Crownbridge Industries Inc.	Ont. 1963	July 1992	Delisted ASE July 17, 1992
Crownia Holdings Ltd.	B.C. 2012	Mar. 2023	Delisted TSX-VEN Mar. 16, 2023
Cumulus Ventures Ltd.	B.C. 1985	Aug. 2000	Delisted TSE Dec. 12, 1994
Cybersurf Corp.	Alta. 1995	June 2010	Delisted TSX-VEN June 9, 2010

D

Name	Incorp. Date	Date of Last Report	Remarks
DMI Technology Inc.	Alta. 1993	Sept. 2002	Delisted ASE May 2, 1997
DRT Resources Ltd.	B.C. 1978	May 1995	Delisted VSE Mar. 5, 1996
DVO Industries Ltd.	B.C. 1972, amalg.	Apr. 1995	Delisted VSE Jan. 6, 1994
Darkhorse Technologies Ltd.	Que. 1971; orig. Ont. 1958	Apr. 1997	Delisted VSE Mar. 1, 1999
Data Trax Systems Ltd.	Alta. 1991	Jan. 1999	Delisted ASE Jan. 15, 1999
Davis Distributing Limited	Ont. 1953	Sept. 1997	Delisted CDN Jan. 14, 2000
DecorStone Industries Inc.	B.C. 1981	May 1989	Delisted VSE Mar. 2, 1990
Desen Computer Industries Inc.	B.C. 1982	Mar. 1988	Delisted VSE Mar. 2, 1988
Devon Industries Inc.	B.C. 1979	Sept. 1985	Delisted VSE Apr. 7, 1986
Dilmont Inc.	Que. 1955	June 1988	No recent report
Dimensional Media Inc.	Ont. 1987	May 2002	Delisted CDN Oct. 13, 2000
Dimples Group Inc.	B.C. 1984	July 1994	Delisted VSE Mar. 6, 1995
Dino International Inc.	Ont. 1985	Jan. 1994	Delisted CDN Jan. 3, 1995
Dion Entertainment Corp.	Can. 1987	Dec. 2002	Delisted TSX Jan. 15, 2004
Discover Wellness Solutions Inc.	Alta. 2018	Apr. 2023	Delisted CSE Apr. 3, 2023
Discovery Technologies Corp.	B.C. 1983	Mar. 1996	Delisted VSE Mar. 5, 1996
Diversified Investment Strategies Inc.	Alta. 1987	May 2000	Delisted CDNX May 31, 2001
Dominco Industries Corp.	B.C. 1986	Nov. 1990	Delisted VSE Mar. 4, 1991
Dover Enterprises Ltd.	Alta. 1987	Aug. 1995	Delisted ASE Nov. 2, 1992
Dragon Legend Entertainment (Canada) Inc.	B.C. 1990	Apr. 2018	Delisted CSE Apr. 9, 2018
Duck Book Communications Limited	B.C. 1982	June 1986	Delisted VSE Nov. 7, 1988
Dynastar Inc.	Alta. 1979	June 2010	Delisted TSX-VEN June 9, 2010

E

Name	Incorp. Date	Date of Last Report	Remarks
E Automotive Inc.	Can. 2017	May 2023	Delisted TSX May 25, 2023
E-International Fund Management Inc.	B.C. 1982	June 1985	Delisted VSE Nov. 21, 1986
e-Manufacturing Networks Inc.	Alta. 1996	Dec. 2002	Delisted TSX-VEN June 20, 2003
E-Ventures Inc.	Ont. 1986; orig. Ont. 1951	Oct. 2000	Delisted CDN Oct. 13, 2000
ENTREC Corporation	Alta. 2009	June 2020	Delisted TSX June 25, 2020
EXO U Inc.	Can. 2013, amalg.	Dec. 2018	Delisted TSX-VEN Dec. 17, 2018
Earthwhile Developments Inc.	Alta. 1994, amalg.	Jan. 1997	Delisted ASE Jan. 28, 1997
Easy Technologies Inc.	B.C. 2009	May 2019	Delisted CSE May 27, 2019
Eco Technologies International Inc.	Ont. 1991, amalg.	July 2001	Delisted TSE July 6, 2001
Ecology Pure Air International, Inc.	B.C. 1987	Apr. 1998	Delisted VSE Mar. 5, 1996
Eden Empire Inc.	B.C. 2020, amalg.	June 2023	Delisted CSE June 7, 2023
El Dorado Systems (Canada) Inc.	B.C. 1980	June 1987	Delisted VSE Oct. 3, 1988
Electric-Spin Ltd.	Ont. 2004	Oct. 2012	Delisted TSX-VEN Oct. 12, 2012
EleTel Inc.	Que. 1996	June 2003	Delisted TSX-VEN Dec. 22, 2006

Name	Incorp. Date	Date of Last Report	Remarks
Ellipsiz Communications Ltd.	Ont. 1996, amalg.	Oct. 2021	Delisted TSX-VEN Oct. 8, 2021
Emfax International Ltd.	Ont. 1974	May 2000	Delisted CDN Nov. 25, 1994
Empire Alliance Properties Inc.	Ont. 1986	June 2001	Delisted CDN Oct. 13, 2000
Empower Technologies Corporation	B.C. 2003	Dec. 2018	Delisted TSX-VEN Dec. 17, 2018
Enercan Group Inc.	Ont. 1984; orig. Alta. 1982	May 1989	Delisted ASE May 26, 1989
Energold Drilling Corp.	B.C. 1973	Mar. 2021	Delisted TSX-VEN Mar. 22, 2021
Energy Conversion Technologies Inc.	Ont. 1999	Oct. 2000	Delisted CDN Oct. 13, 2000
Enssolutions Group Inc.	Can. 2007	Aug. 2020	Delisted TSX-VEN May 25, 2021
Entec Systems Inc.	Alta. 1987	Oct. 1991	Delisted ASE Oct. 11, 1991
Entertainment Royalties Inc.	Alta. 2000	Aug. 2002	Delisted TSX-VEN Nov. 19, 2003
Environmental Reclamation Inc.	Ont. 1994, amalg.	Feb. 2002	Delisted TSE Feb. 13, 2002
EnviroPower Industries Inc.	Alta. 1987	June 1997	Delisted ASE June 15, 1998
Epicure Food Products, Inc.	B.C. 1987	June 1991	Delisted VSE Mar. 4, 1992
Equitec Products Corp.	Alta. 1987	Oct. 1989	Delisted ASE July 29, 1991
Etrion Corporation	B.C. 2009; orig. Ont. 1993	Sept. 2021	Delisted TSX Sept. 20, 2021
Euro-American Financial Services Ltd.	B.C. 1981	Nov. 1985	Delisted VSE Apr. 7, 1986
Euro-Net Investments Ltd.	Ont. 1986	June 2007	Delisted TSX-VEN June 25, 2004
Even Technologies Inc.	Can. 1996; orig. Ont. 1928	July 2009	Delisted TSX-VEN July 14, 2009
Eviana Health Corporation	B.C. 2011	May 2023	Delisted CSE May 9, 2023
Exclamation Investments Corporation	Can. 2007	Nov. 2019	Delisted TSX-VEN Oct. 13, 2020

F

Name	Incorp. Date	Date of Last Report	Remarks
FSFC Developments Inc.	Alta. 1996	July 2002	Delisted TSX-VEN July 10, 2002
FSPI Technologies Corp.	Alta. 1996	Aug. 1999	Delisted CDNX May 31, 2000
Falcon Group Ltd.	Ont. 1987	July 1996	Delisted CDN Jan. 3, 1995
FaxMate.Com Inc.	Alta. 1996	June 2003	Delisted TSX-VEN June 20, 2003
Filter Queen Ltd.	Ont. 1984	July 1986	No recent report
Fiore Cannabis Ltd.	B.C. 2007	May 2023	Delisted CSE May 17, 2023
Fire & Flower Holdings Corp.	Can. 2019; orig. Ont. 2017	July 2023	Delisted TSX July 17, 2023
First Choice Products Inc.	Alta. 2008, amalg.	July 2016	Delisted CSE July 4, 2016
First Global Data Limited	Ont. 2011	Dec. 2020	Delisted TSX-VEN Dec. 17, 2020
First Global Investments Inc.	B.C. 1989	Apr. 2008	Delisted VSE Mar. 4, 1991
First Interactive Inc.	Ont. 1997; orig. Can. 1928	Apr. 1999	Delisted CDN Apr. 14, 2000
First United Capital Corp.	Ont. 1960	Mar. 1985	No recent report
Fiscal Investments Limited	Ont. 1954	June 2000	Delisted CDN Oct. 13, 2000
Flemdon Limited	Ont. 1974	Mar. 1986	Delisted CDN Aug. 31, 1992
The Flowr Corporation	Ont. 2018; orig. Alta. 2016	Mar. 2023	Delisted TSX-VEN Mar. 7, 2023
The Follgard Group Inc.	Alta. 1994	Sept. 1998	Delisted ASE Oct. 15, 1999
FootSource Inc.	Alta. 1992	Dec. 2003	Delisted TSX-VEN Dec. 13, 2006
Foremost Income Fund	Alta. 2005	Dec. 2010	Delisted TSX Dec. 16, 2010
Forest Hill Capital Corporation	Ont. 1986	Nov. 1998	Delisted CDN Oct. 13, 2000
FormerXBC Inc.	Can. 2009, amalg.	Nov. 2022	Delisted TSX Nov. 15, 2022
Fortress Global Enterprises Inc.	B.C. 2006	Jan. 2020	Delisted TSX Jan. 20, 2020
Freshlocal Solutions Inc.	B.C. 2018	July 2022	Delisted TSX July 4, 2022
Friendly Fuels Group Inc.	Alta. 1993	June 1997	Delisted ASE Sept. 23, 1999
The Fulcrum Investment Company Limited	Can. 1966	July 1986	Delisted CDN Oct. 13, 2000
Fusion Technologies Limited	N.B. 1956	May 1989	Inactive
Future Farm Technologies Inc.	B.C. 1984	July 2022	Delisted CSE July 28, 2022
Fytokem Products Inc.	Sask. 1994	July 2009	Delisted TSX-VEN July 14, 2009

G

Name	Incorp. Date	Date of Last Report	Remarks
GDI Global Data Inc.	Ont. 1989	Feb. 2005	Delisted TSX-VEN June 30, 2005
G.I.E. Environment Technologies Ltd.	Alta. 1997	Dec. 2011	Delisted TSX-VEN Dec. 19, 2011
The Gambol Group Incorporated	Alta. 1994	May 1998	Delisted CDNX May 31, 2000
Gametek Systems Inc.	B.C. 1981	July 1988	Delisted VSE Mar. 1, 1989
General Cybernetics Corporation	B.C. 1982	Oct. 1989	Delisted VSE Oct. 6, 1989
General Leaseholds Limited	Ont. 1964	Apr. 1995	Delisted TSE Nov. 7, 1997
Genoil Inc.	Can. 1996, amalg.	May 2014	Delisted TSX-VEN May 27, 2014
GetSwift Technologies Limited	B.C. 2020	Mar. 2023	Delisted NEO Mar. 7, 2023
Glentronic International Inc.	B.C. 1986	Jan. 1987	Delisted VSE Mar. 2, 1990
Global Biotech Inc.	Ont. 1986	Jan. 1998	Delisted CDN Jan. 3, 1995
Global Gaming Technologies Corp.	B.C. 2010	Apr. 2020	Delisted CSE Apr. 9, 2020
Global Gardens Group Inc.	B.C. 2014	Apr. 2020	Delisted TSX-VEN Apr. 2, 2020
Global Key Investment Limited	B.C. 2007	Mar. 2016	Delisted TSX-VEN Mar. 24, 2016
Global Teleworks Corp.	Man. 1988	Jan. 1995	Delisted VSE Mar. 3, 1997
GlobeeCom International Inc.	Can. 2001	July 2009	Delisted TSX-VEN July 14, 2009
Golden Fortune Investments Limited	Alta. 1994	June 2003	Delisted TSX-VEN Apr. 20, 2004
Golden Moor Inc.	Ont. 1987	July 2014	Delisted CSE May 1, 2014
Golden Seven Industries Inc.	B.C. 1971	Nov. 1988	Delisted VSE Mar. 2, 1990
Goran Capital Inc.	Can. 1985	Mar. 2005	Delisted TSX Mar. 4, 2005
GoverMedia Plus Canada Corp.	B.C. 2017	Apr. 2020	Delisted CSE Apr. 27, 2020
Great Lakes Graphite Inc.	Ont. 2004	Dec. 2021	Delisted TSX-VEN Dec. 7, 2021
Great Weighs! Industries Inc.	B.C. 1983	Nov. 1987	Delisted VSE Jan. 9, 1989
Grecian Specialty Foods Inc.	Alta. 1993	Dec. 1996	Delisted ASE Dec. 31, 1997
Green Environmental Technologies Inc.	Ont. 1994	Oct. 2007	Delisted TSX-VEN Oct. 12, 2007
Greenlight Communications Inc.	Ont. 1975	Nov. 1999	Delisted CDN Oct. 13, 2000
Guard Inc.	Ont. 1994	May 2002	Delisted TSX-VEN Dec. 23, 2005

H

Name	Incorp. Date	Date of Last Report	Remarks
H-Source Holdings Ltd.	B.C. 2014	Aug. 2023	Suspended TSX-VEN Aug. 5, 2021
HPY Industries Ltd.	B.C. 1983	June 1992	Delisted VSE Jan. 31, 1991
Haemacure Corporation	Can. 1991	Feb. 2010	Delisted TSX Feb. 8, 2010
Halo Gaming Corporation	B.C. 1965	Aug. 1999	Delisted CDNX May 31, 2001
Hardwood Properties Ltd.	Alta. 1997	June 2004	Delisted TSX-VEN June 25, 2004
Harken Technologies Inc.	B.C. 1980	Jan. 1988	Delisted VSE Feb. 2, 1989
Health and Environment Technologies Inc.	Ont. 1989, amalg.	May 1988	Delisted CDN Jan. 3, 1995
HeartLink Canada (1999) Inc.	Can. 1999	June 2007	Delisted TSX-VEN Feb. 1, 2007
HempNova Lifetech Corporation	B.C. 1989, amalg.	May 2019	Delisted TSX-VEN May 2, 2019
Hillestad Pharmaceuticals Inc.	Can. 2006; orig. B.C. 1983	July 2009	Delisted TSX-VEN July 14, 2009
Hirose Group Ltd.	Man. 1989	Mar. 1990	Delisted ASE Aug. 20, 1992
Hollinger Inc.	Can. 1985, amalg.	Aug. 2008	Delisted TSX Aug. 25, 2008
Home Products Inc.	B.C. 1985; orig. Ont. 1966	Sept. 1997	Delisted CDN Jan. 14, 2000
HomeXpress Limited	Alta. 1999	Dec. 2001	Delisted TSX-VEN June 5, 2002
Horton Technologies Ltd.	B.C. 1986	Dec. 1987	Delisted VSE July 7, 1989
Hotline to HR Inc.	Ont. 2011	July 2013	Delisted CNSX July 3, 2013
How to Web TV Inc.	Alta. 1996	June 2007	Delisted TSX-VEN June 23, 2006
Huaxing Machinery Corp.	B.C. 2008	Nov. 2019	Delisted TSX-VEN Mar. 15, 2023
Humantics (B.C.) Ltd.	B.C. 1987	Mar. 1989	Delisted VSE May 14, 1992
Hunter Financial Group Ltd.	Alta. 1998, amalg.	Feb. 1999	Delisted CDNX Oct. 23, 2001

Name	Incorp. Date	Date of Last Report	Remarks
Hyatt Financial Corporation Ltd.	Alta. 1980	Apr. 2003	Delisted TSX-VEN June 20, 2003
HydraLogic Systems Inc.	Ont. 2004, amalg.	July 2016	Delisted TSX-VEN July 8, 2016
HydroMet Environmental Recovery Ltd.	Alta. 1986	Dec. 2003	Delisted TSX-VEN June 30, 2005
Hyduke Energy Services Inc.	Alta. 1995	Oct. 2020	Delisted TSX-VEN Oct. 14, 2020
Hytec Flow Systems, Inc.	B.C. 1965	Mar. 1999	Delisted CDNX Mar. 22, 2001

I

IATRA Life Sciences Corporation	Ont. 1994	Apr. 2008	Delisted TSX-VEN Apr. 7, 2008
ICCI Integrated Credit and Commerce Inc.	B.C. 1986	Oct. 1996	Delisted VSE Dec. 10, 1996
IDYIA Innovations Inc.	Man. 2000	June 2007	Delisted TSX-VEN June 23, 2006
I.E.S. Technologies Corp.	B.C. 1987	June 1991	Delisted VSE Mar. 4, 1992
IMC Integrated Marketing Communications Inc.	Ont. 1986; orig. Ont. 1937	Apr. 1992	Delisted ASE June 12, 1990
IMV Inc.	Can. 2007	June 2023	Suspended TSX May 1, 2023
INDVR Brands Inc.	B.C. 2007	Feb. 2023	Delisted CSE Feb. 6, 2023
INSCAPE Corporation	Ont. 1989, amalg.	Feb. 2023	Delisted TSX Feb. 22, 2023
I.S.L. Industries Ltd.	B.C. 1979	Apr. 1985	Delisted VSE Apr. 1, 1985
Image Data International Corporation	Ont. 1993; orig. B.C. 1988	Mar. 1996	Delisted VSE Mar. 5, 1996
Image West Entertainment Corporation	B.C. 1970	Dec. 1987	Delisted VSE Feb. 2, 1989
ImaSight Corp.	Ont. 2000	July 2009	Delisted TSX-VEN July 14, 2009
Imex Systems Inc.	Ont. 1985	May 2021	Delisted TSX-VEN May 26, 2021
Impatica Inc.	Ont. 1998	June 2007	Delisted CDN Oct. 13, 2000
Impertex Inc.	Que. 1957	Nov. 1989	Delisted ME Jan. 16, 1991
Infocorp Computer Solutions Ltd.	Man. 1983	Aug. 2005	Delisted TSX Aug. 4, 2005
Innovative Environmental Services Ltd.	Alta. 1988	Aug. 1995	Delisted ASE Aug. 4, 1995
Innovium Media Properties Corp.	Can. 1992, amalg.	Oct. 2012	Delisted TSX-VEN Oct. 12, 2012
Insurcom Financial Corporation	Alta. 1993	July 2001	Delisted CDNX May 31, 2001
Intellectual Capital Group Ltd.	Ont. 1962	Mar. 2015	Delisted TSX-VEN Mar. 12, 2015
Intelligent Web Technologies Inc.	Ont. 2000, amalg.	June 2003	Delisted TSX-VEN June 20, 2003
Inter Cable Communications Inc.	B.C. 1980	Apr. 1994	Delisted TSE July 26, 1991
Inter Canadian Development Corp.	B.C. 1980	Sept. 1995	Delisted VSE Mar. 3, 1997
Interactive Capital Partners Corporation	Ont. 2008	Jan. 2014	Delisted TSX-VEN Jan. 31, 2014
Intercable ICH Inc.	Can. 2002	Dec. 2011	Delisted TSX-VEN Dec. 19, 2011
Intercept America Corp.	Ont. 1982	Nov. 1988	Delisted CDN Jan. 3, 1995
Intercept Energy Services Inc.	Alta. 1995	Aug. 2020	Delisted TSX-VEN May 26, 2021
Interchem (N.A.) Industries Inc.	B.C. 1984	Mar. 1996	Delisted VSE Mar. 5, 1996
Interex Minerals Ltd.	Alta. 1986	June 2005	Delisted TSX-VEN June 30, 2005
International Accord Inc.	Ont. 1982	Apr. 1997	Delisted ASE Aug. 27, 1997
International Display Corporation	B.C. 1973	Dec. 1987	Delisted VSE Jan. 10, 1990
International Fitness Unlimited Centres Inc.	Ont. 1983, amalg.	Oct. 1986	Delisted ASE Feb. 2, 1989
International Frecom Communications Inc.	B.C. 1986	Feb. 1993	Delisted VSE Mar. 5, 1993
International Health and Beauty Inc.	B.C. 1989	Oct. 1999	Delisted CDNX Aug. 3, 2001
International Hi-Tech Industries Inc.	Can. 1996; orig. B.C. 1987	June 2007	Delisted TSX-VEN Apr. 18, 2007
International Mitek Computer Inc.	B.C. 1981	Apr. 1991	Delisted VSE May 14, 1992
International PLC Autopark Inc.	B.C. 1985	May 1991	Delisted VSE Apr. 20, 1992
International Pharmadyne Ltd.	B.C. 1966	Oct. 1992	Delisted VSE Mar. 5, 1993
International Phasor Telecom Ltd.	B.C. 1982, amalg.	Jan. 1999	Delisted VSE July 10, 1990
International Texcan Technology Corp.	B.C. 1983	May 1990	Delisted VSE Mar. 7, 1990
International Transtech Inc.	B.C. 1987	June 2003	Delisted TSX-VEN June 20, 2003
Internet Shopping Catalog Inc.	Ont. 2001, amalg.	Mar. 2002	Delisted CDN Oct. 13, 2000
Interprovincial Venture Capital Corporation	Ont. 1996, amalg.	July 2001	Delisted CDN Oct. 13, 2000
Isodiol International Inc.	B.C. 2014	Dec. 2021	Delisted CSE Dec. 7, 2021
iTV Games, Inc.	Alta. 1996	Sept. 2002	Delisted TSX-VEN June 5, 2002
Izone International Ltd.	B.C. 1969	Mar. 1996	Delisted VSE Mar. 3, 1997

J

JPY Holdings Ltd.	Can. 2007; orig. B.C. 1985	Mar. 2005	Delisted TSX-VEN Mar. 30, 2005
James E. Wagner Cultivation Corporation	Ont. 2017	July 2022	Delisted TSX-VEN July 20, 2022
Jardin Financial Group Inc.	Alta. 1987	Oct. 1996	Delisted ASE Oct. 4, 1996
Jefjen Capital Corporation	B.C. 1985	July 1992	Delisted VSE Mar. 5, 1993
Jentan Resources Ltd.	Alta. 1987	July 1997	Delisted ASE Apr. 17, 1997
Jeotex Inc.	Can. 2014	May 2021	Delisted TSX-VEN May 26, 2021
Jetcom Inc.	Ont. 1968	Oct. 2013	Delisted CNSX Oct. 16, 2013
Job Industries Ltd.	B.C. 1987	Nov. 1999	Delisted CDNX May 31, 2000

K

KT Capital Corporation	Alta. 1981	June 2007	Delisted ASE May 11, 1993
Kane Investment Corp.	Alta. 1986	June 2005	Delisted TSX-VEN June 2, 2005
Kasten Energy Inc.	Alta. 2007; orig. Ont. 1996, amalg.	Jan. 2008	Delisted TSX July 4, 2006
Kazz Industries Inc.	Alta. 1996	Jan. 2002	Delisted TSX-VEN June 20, 2003
Kendall Venture Funding Ltd.	Alta. 1993	June 2007	Delisted ASE May 8, 1996
Kingly Enterprises Inc.	Ont. 1988	June 2007	Delisted CDN Oct. 13, 2000
KnightHawk Inc.	Can. 1998; orig. B.C. 1993	Dec. 2022	Suspended TSX-VEN Mar. 9, 2021
Knightscove Media Corp.	Ont. 2004	Oct. 2013	Delisted TSX-VEN Oct. 3, 2013
Knowledge House Inc.	N.S. 1984	July 2002	Delisted TSX-VEN June 20, 2003
Koba Capital Corporation	B.C. 1980	Feb. 1989	Delisted VSE Feb. 2, 1989

L

LYRtech inc.	Que. 2000	Oct. 2012	Delisted TSX-VEN Oct. 12, 2012
Lambus Enterprises Inc.	Alta. 1995	Feb. 2003	Delisted TSX-VEN Sept. 30, 2004
Landmark Global Financial Corporation	Ont. 1992, amalg.	Oct. 2014	Delisted TSX-VEN Oct. 21, 2014
Larken Capital Corporation	Alta. 1987	July 1992	Delisted ASE May 29, 1992
Laser Publishing Inc.	B.C. 1986	Dec. 1987	Delisted VSE July 7, 1989
Lattice Biologics Ltd.	B.C. 1985	Aug. 2023	Suspended TSX-VEN June 7, 2021
Lehman Trikes, Inc.	Alta. 1993	Oct. 2013	Delisted TSX-VEN Oct. 3, 2013
Lessonware Ltd.	Yuk. 1991	July 1993	Delisted VSE Mar. 4, 1994
Life Investors International Limited	Ont. 1973	July 1973	CTO issued Mar. 1, 1974
Liquid Media Group Ltd.	B.C. 1986	Aug. 2023	Delisted NASDAQ Aug. 23, 2023
Loh's Sinfully Good Ice Cream & Cookies Inc.	Ont. 1981	Jan. 1988	Delisted VSE Mar. 2, 1990
LottoGopher Holdings Inc.	B.C. 2016	Apr. 2020	Delisted CSE Apr. 21, 2020

M

MAACKK Capital Corp.	Alta. 2013; orig. B.C. 2009	Mar. 2018	Delisted TSX-VEN Mar. 29, 2018
M. C. Beverages, Ltd.	B.C. 1984	Jan. 1989	Delisted VSE Mar. 1, 1989
MDC Financial Inc.	B.C. 1983	Apr. 1995	Delisted VSE May 11, 1990
MGX Minerals Inc.	B.C. 2012	Aug. 2023	Delisted CSE Aug. 1, 2023
MPL Communications Inc.	Alta. 1988	Mar. 2010	Delisted TSX-VEN July 12, 2010
MTW Solutions Online Inc.	Ont. 1996	Sept. 2001	Delisted TSX-VEN June 5, 2002

Name	Incorp. Date	Date of Last Report	Remarks
Maclos Capital Inc.	Can. 2003	July 2009	Delisted TSX July 6, 2009
Madenta Inc.	Alta. 1988	Aug. 1999	Delisted CDNX May 31, 2000
The Madison Companies Limited	Alta. 1997	June 2003	Delisted TSX-VEN June 20, 2003
Madonna Educational Group of Canada Ltd.	B.C. 1982, amalg.	June 1989	Delisted VSE July 14, 1989
Maghemite Inc.	B.C. 1981	Mar. 1991	Delisted VSE Mar. 4, 1992
MagIndustries Corp.	Can. 2006; orig. Ont. 1997, amalg.	Aug. 2015	Delisted TSX Aug. 20, 2015
Magnum Resources Ltd.	Alta. 1951	Aug. 1994	Delisted ASE Aug. 8, 1994
Magor Corporation	Can. 2009	Mar. 2019	Delisted TSX-VEN Mar. 19, 2019
MailBoxCity Corporation	Alta. 1998	Nov. 2002	Delisted TSX-VEN Nov. 14, 2002
Majesty Resources Limited	B.C. 1980	Mar. 1993	Delisted VSE Mar. 4, 1991
Mandate National Mortgage Corporation	Can. 1989, amalg.	June 2007	Delisted CDNX Dec. 23, 1999
Marlborough Productions Ltd.	B.C. 1983	Oct. 1988	Delisted VSE Nov. 16, 1990
Maxcard Systems International Inc.	B.C. 1980	May 1995	Delisted VSE Mar. 6, 1995
Mecachrome International Inc.	Can. 2003	Jan. 2009	Delisted TSX Jan. 26, 2009
Medical Intelligence Technologies Inc.	Can. 2004	July 2010	Delisted TSX-VEN July 12, 2010
Medilase Industries Inc.	B.C. 1987	Mar. 1994	Delisted VSE May 4, 1994
Medipure Holdings Inc.	B.C. 2014	Aug. 2016	Delisted CSE Aug. 17, 2016
Meditrust Healthcare Inc.	Ont. 1992	Dec. 1996	No recent report
Megalode Corporation	Ont. 1983	May 1995	Delisted CDN Jan. 3, 1995
Mercator Transport Group Corporation	Can. 2004	July 2016	Delisted TSX-VEN July 8, 2016
Merch Performance Inc.	Alta. 1990	Sept. 2003	Delisted TSX-VEN June 16, 2004
Merged Enterprises Inc.	Ont. 1943	May 1998	Delisted CDN Aug. 31, 1992
Metaverse Capital Corp.	B.C. 2017	Apr. 2020	Delisted CSE Apr. 9, 2020
Metaville Labs Inc.	B.C. 2006	Mar. 2018	Delisted TSX-VEN Mar. 29, 2018
mHealth Capital Corp.	Alta. 2010	Nov. 2013	Delisted TSX-VEN Nov. 6, 2013
Micro Mining Technologies Ltd.	Alta. 1996	Nov. 2002	Delisted TSX-VEN June 20, 2003
Microbe Corporation	Ont. 1982	Mar. 1992	Delisted CDN Jan. 3, 1995
Microkey Communication Systems, Inc.	B.C. 1964	June 1998	Delisted CDNX May 31, 2001
MicroPlanet Technology Corp.	Alta. 2004	May 2017	Delisted TSX-VEN May 11, 2017
Milton Group Ltd.	Ont. 1936	Aug. 1977	Delisted TSE Nov. 14, 1978
Minerva Venture Technologies Ltd.	Can. 2000	July 2009	Delisted TSX-VEN July 14, 2009
Minpro International Ltd.	Ont. 1998, amalg.	Nov. 2001	Delisted CDN Oct. 13, 2000
Mintron Enterprises Ltd.	Ont. 1980	Feb. 1992	Delisted ASE Feb. 28, 1992
Mr. Tube Steak Canada, Ltd.	Alta. 1995	May 1999	Delisted ASE Dec. 2, 1998
Mode Products Inc.	B.C. 1977	May 1992	Delisted VSE Mar. 5, 1993
Montco Ltd.	Que. 1956	June 1988	Delisted ME June 10, 1988
Monte Cristo Capital Inc.	Alta. 1997	June 2002	Delisted TSX-VEN June 13, 2002
Multi-Step Industries Inc.	B.C. 1984	Nov. 1988	Delisted VSE Jan. 10, 1990
Myriad Concepts, Ltd.	B.C. 1983	Dec. 1987	Delisted VSE July 7, 1989
N			
NTV Oil Services Industries Inc.	B.C. 1985	Dec. 1987	Delisted VSE July 7, 1989
NX Phase Capital Inc.	Can. 2000	July 2010	Delisted TSX-VEN July 12, 2010
National Healthcare Manufacturing Corporation	Man. 1993	Feb. 2000	Delisted NASDAQ Dec. 22, 1999
National Nova Marketing Inc.	B.C. 1980	May 1995	Delisted VSE Oct. 19, 1994
National Scientific Products Corp.	B.C. 1980	Mar. 1987	Delisted VSE Mar. 2, 1990
National Steel Corp. of Canada	unknown	June 1988	No recent report
National Training Rinks Corp.	Alta. 1996	June 2003	Delisted TSX-VEN June 20, 2003
NatQuote Financial Incorporated	Ont. 1982	Aug. 1997	Delisted CDN Jan. 3, 1995
Nelma Information Inc.	Ont. 1984, amalg.	May 1987	No recent report
Network One Holdings Corp.	B.C. 1983	Mar. 2004	Delisted CDN Oct. 13, 2000
Nevada Bob's Golf Inc.	Alta. 1996	Mar. 2002	Delisted TSX Mar. 7, 2003
Nevasco Corporation	Ont. 1974	May 1991	Delisted CDN Jan. 3, 1995
New Spirit Research & Development Corp.	B.C. 1987	Apr. 1988	Delisted VSE Mar. 4, 1991
NewKidCo International Inc.	N.B. 1998; orig. B.C. 1982	Dec. 2002	Delisted TSX Nov. 5, 2004
Newline Development Corporation	B.C. 1975	June 1989	Delisted VSE Oct. 6, 1989
Newlook Industries Corp.	Ont. 2009; orig. B.C. 1999	Sept. 2013	Delisted CNSX Sept. 30, 2013
Nexia Health Technologies Inc.	Ont. 2005, amalg.	Dec. 2022	Suspended TSX-VEN July 10, 2020
Nobilis Health Corp.	B.C. 2007	Sept. 2019	Delisted NYSE MKT Sept. 11, 2019
Nortel Networks Corporation	Can. 2000	June 2009	Delisted TSX June 29, 2009
North Bud Farms Inc.	Can. 2016	May 2023	Delisted CSE May 9, 2023
Northern Sphere Mining Corp.	Can. 2011, amalg.	Jan. 2020	Delisted CSE Jan. 23, 2020
Northland Helicopters Ltd.	B.C. 1965	May 1986	No recent report
Northside Minerals International Inc.	Alta. 1987	Mar. 1999	Delisted CDNX May 31, 2000
Northwest Shroom Industries Ltd.	B.C. 1986	July 1988	Delisted VSE Mar. 2, 1990
Norwich Ventures Ltd.	B.C. 1986	Aug. 1991	Delisted ASE Feb. 8, 1993
Norzan Enterprises Ltd.	B.C. 1985	Nov. 2019	Suspended TSX-VEN Aug. 6, 2015
Novelion Therapeutics Inc.	B.C. 1981	Oct. 2019	Delisted NASDAQ Oct. 9, 2019
O			
O.E.X. Electromagnetic Inc.	B.C. 1978	Jan. 1989	Delisted VSE Mar. 1, 1989
OceanLake Commerce Inc.	Ont. 2003; orig. B.C. 1984	July 2009	Delisted TSX-VEN July 14, 2009
Odesia Group Inc.	Can. 2005	Mar. 2018	Delisted TSX-VEN Mar. 29, 2018
Odin Industries Ltd.	B.C. 1979	Jan. 2002	Delisted TSX-VEN Mar. 26, 2003
Odyssey Industries Incorporated	Ont. 1980	Aug. 1992	Delisted CDN Aug. 31, 1992
Old PSG Wind-down Ltd.	B.C. 2010	Dec. 2016	Delisted TSX Dec. 9, 2016
Oliver Iron & Steel Corp. Ltd.	Que. 1957	June 1981	No recent report
Omnex International Inc.	unknown	June 1988	No recent report
OneRoof Energy Group, Inc.	Ont. 2010	Nov. 2019	Delisted TSX-VEN Apr. 2, 2020
Online Direct Inc.	Can. 1999, amalg.	Nov. 2001	Delisted TSX-VEN June 5, 2002
Orbus Pharma Inc.	Alta. 2002, amalg.	Jan. 2012	Delisted TSX-VEN Jan. 26, 2012
Orchid Ventures, Inc.	B.C. 2011	May 2023	Delisted CSE May 8, 2023
Otter Dorchester Insurance Co. Ltd.	unknown	Dec. 1987	No recent report
OutdoorPartner Media Corporation	Ont. 2004	Apr. 2014	Delisted TSX-VEN Apr. 17, 2014
Outlook Resources Inc.	Ont. 1984	Apr. 2012	Delisted TSX-VEN Apr. 20, 2012
P			
PBB Venture Corporation	Yuk. 1997; orig. B.C. 1984	Jan. 1999	Delisted CDNX May 31, 2000
PC Chips Corporation	Ont. 1993	Aug. 2002	Delisted CDN Oct. 13, 2000
PCL Industries Limited	Ont. 1969	Mar. 1993	Delisted TSE Mar. 5, 1993
PDC Biological Health Group Corporation	B.C. 2013, amalg.; orig. Ont. 2011	Oct. 2016	Delisted CSE Oct. 3, 2016
PESA Corporation	Ont. 2005, amalg.	Dec. 2010	Delisted TSX-VEN Dec. 29, 2010
PPC Capital Corp.	Alta. 1986	May 2002	Delisted CDNX May 31, 2000
P.S.M. Technologies Inc.	B.C. 1982	Oct. 1989	Delisted VSE Mar. 4, 1991
Pacific Orient Capital Inc.	Ont. 2009	May 2015	Delisted TSX-VEN May 14, 2015
Pacific Vista Industries Inc.	Yuk. 1993; orig. B.C. 1988	Aug. 1999	Delisted VSE Mar. 15, 1999
Palcan Power Systems Inc.	Yuk. 1998; orig. B.C. 1987	Sept. 2009	Delisted TSX-VEN May 9, 2011
Pallet Pallet Inc.	Ont. 1994, amalg.	June 2000	Delisted CDN Oct. 13, 2000
Pan Pacific Strategies Corp.	Ont. 1987	Jan. 1998	Delisted CDN Oct. 13, 2000

Name	Incorp. Date	Date of Last Report	Remarks
Pan Smak Pizza Inc.	B.C. 1983	Nov. 1998	Delisted CDNX Mar. 22, 2001
Paradise Capital Inc.	Alta. 1995	Jan. 2002	Delisted CDNX Jan. 23, 2002
Parallax Development Corporation	B.C. 1986	May 1995	Delisted VSE Mar. 6, 1995
Paron Resources Inc.	B.C. 1982	June 2007	Delisted CDNX Mar. 19, 2001
Parton Capital Inc.	Alta. 1987	Oct. 2002	Delisted TSX-VEN June 20, 2003
Patchgear.com Inc.	Alta. 1996	June 2001	Delisted TSX-VEN June 5, 2002
PathTechnics Ltd.	Ont. 1979	Mar. 1989	Delisted VSE Nov. 16, 1990
Paul Martin Inc.	Que. 1985	Mar. 1990	Delisted ME Jan. 16, 1991
Pay Linx Financial Corporation	Alta. 2004	July 2009	Delisted TSX-VEN July 14, 2009
Pega Capital Corporation	Ont. 1980	Aug. 1995	Delisted TSE Sept. 26, 1997
Perennial Energy Inc.	B.C. 1950	Mar. 1995	Delisted VSE Mar. 7, 1995
Performance Optician Software Corporation	Alta. 2000, amalg.	June 2005	Delisted TSX-VEN June 21, 2005
Periscope Investments Limited	Alta. 1993	Nov. 2001	Delisted ASE Sept. 26, 1995
Peritronics Medical, Ltd.	B.C. 1981	May 1998	Delisted VSE Mar. 1, 1999
Pharmaglobe Inc.	Ont. 1959	Nov. 2003	Delisted CDN Dec. 31, 1997
The Phoenician Fund Corporation I	Ont. 2006	Sept. 2015	Delisted TSX-VEN Oct. 10, 2013
Phoenix Capital Income Trust	Ont. 2005	Nov. 2007	Delisted TSX-VEN June 25, 2007
Pineridge Capital Group Inc.	B.C. 1987	Sept. 1993	Delisted VSE Mar. 6, 1995
Pivotal Therapeutics Inc.	Can. 2011	Oct. 2017	Delisted CSE Oct. 24, 2017
Plant-Based Investment Corp	Can. 2017	June 2023	Delisted CSE June 9, 2023
Plantable Health Inc.	B.C. 2021	Aug. 2023	Delisted NEO Aug. 9, 2023
Plasticycle Inc.	Alta. 1992	July 1996	Delisted ASE July 23, 1996
Pleasant Realty & Financial Corp.	Ont. 1959	Jan. 1995	Delisted CDN Jan. 3, 1995
Plus International Corporation	Alta. 1988	June 2003	Delisted TSX-VEN June 25, 2004
Plus Products Inc.	B.C. 2018	Sept. 2021	Delisted CSE Sept. 21, 2021
Polyphalt Inc.	Ont. 1992	Dec. 2003	Delisted TSX-VEN June 16, 2004
Ponder Oils Ltd.	Alta. 1951	Aug. 1983	Delisted CDN Jan. 3, 1995
Ponderosa Ventures Inc.	B.C. 1981	Dec. 1987	Delisted VSE July 7, 1989
Portex Minerals Inc.	Ont. 2006	Sept. 2016	Delisted CSE Sept. 12, 2016
Postec Systems Inc.	Alta. 1992	May 2002	Delisted CDNX Oct. 22, 2001
Posters Plus Marketing Corp.	Ont. 1983	Jan. 1987	Delisted CDN Jan. 3, 1995
Pounce Technologies Inc.	Alta. 2014; orig. Can. 2007	Oct. 2021	Delisted TSX-VEN Oct. 19, 2021
Power Tech Corporation Inc.	Que. 2005, amalg.	Dec. 2011	Delisted TSX-VEN Dec. 19, 2011
PowerNova Technologies Corporation	B.C. 1986	Feb. 2005	Delisted TSX-VEN June 20, 2003
Precision Assessment Technology Corporation	Alta. 1987	May 2008	Delisted TSX May 22, 2008
Prefco Enterprises Inc.	B.C. 1999	Mar. 2004	Delisted TSX-VEN June 16, 2004
Preferred Dental Technologies Inc.	B.C. 2010	Feb. 2021	Delisted CSE Feb. 22, 2021
Primaria Capital (Canada) Ltd.	B.C. 2011	Mar. 2016	Delisted CSE Mar. 1, 2016
PrimeWest Mortgage Investment Corporation	Sask. 2005	Nov. 2019	Delisted CSE Nov. 12, 2019
Primo Nutraceuitcals Inc.	B.C. 2014	Mar. 2021	Delisted CSE Mar. 16, 2021
Le Print Express International Inc.	Ont. 1993, amalg.	May 1999	Delisted CDN Oct. 13, 2000
Prize Puzzle Inc.	Ont. 1982	Aug. 1984	Delisted ASE July 31, 1985
Pro-Tech Venture Corp.	B.C. 1982	Oct. 2000	Delisted CDNX Dec. 28, 2001
Pro-Trans Ventures Inc.	Alta. 2007	Feb. 2016	Delisted TSX-VEN Feb. 25, 2016
Process Capital Corp.	Alta. 1996	July 2012	Delisted TSX-VEN July 23, 2012
Profab Energy Services Ltd.	Alta. 1997	Jan. 2001	Delisted TSX-VEN Apr. 15, 2003
Proflex Limited	Ont. 1980; orig. Can. 1967	Dec. 1987	Delisted VSE Nov. 7, 1988
Promethean Technologies Inc.	B.C. 1983	Apr. 1988	Delisted VSE Mar. 2, 1990
Prosys Tech Corporation	Can. 2004	Jan. 2014	Delisted TSX-VEN Jan. 31, 2014
Protection Technology Inc.	B.C. 1987	Apr. 1995	Delisted VSE Mar. 5, 1996
Proteo Technology Corporation	Can. - unspecified	Aug. 1992	Delisted CDN Aug. 31, 1992
Proteus Environmental Inc.	Alta. 1993	May 2001	Delisted CDNX May 31, 2001
Provident Ventures Corporation	Alta. 1988	May 1998	Delisted ASE July 30, 1999
PsiNaptic Inc.	Alta. 1999	Oct. 2010	Delisted TSX-VEN Oct. 28, 2010
Punters Graphics Inc.	Can. - unspecified	July 1987	Delisted CDN Jan. 3, 1995
Pure Energy Visions Corporation	Ont. 1996	Mar. 2015	Delisted TSX-VEN Mar. 19, 2015
Pure Lean Incorporated	Alta. 1999	Nov. 2003	Delisted TSX-VEN June 21, 2005
Purichlor Technology Ltd.	B.C. 1984	Dec. 1987	Delisted VSE July 7, 1989
Python Corporation	Ont. 1966	June 1988	Delisted CDN Jan. 3, 1995

Q

Name	Incorp. Date	Date of Last Report	Remarks
Q-Entertainment Inc.	N.B. 1995	Nov. 1997	Delisted CDN Feb. 23, 1999
QSolar Limited	Alta. 1999	July 2015	Delisted CSE July 2, 2015
QSound Labs, Inc.	Alta. 1990; orig. B.C. 1968	May 2009	Delisted NASDAQ Apr. 3, 2009
QZZ Inc.	Ont. 1946	Mar. 1987	Delisted CDN Jan. 3, 1995
Quantitative Alpha Trading Inc.	Ont. 2011; orig. B.C. 1987	May 2013	Delisted CNSX May 29, 2013
Quillo Technologies Inc.	B.C. 1983	Sept. 1995	Delisted VSE Mar. 5, 1996

R

Name	Incorp. Date	Date of Last Report	Remarks
RDX Technologies Corporation	Alta. 2006; orig. B.C. 2003	July 2016	Delisted TSX-VEN July 8, 2016
REALM Group Inc.	Alta. 1994	May 2002	Delisted TSX-VEN June 5, 2002
RHN-Recreational Enterprises Ltd.	Alta. 1997	Mar. 2005	Delisted TSX-VEN June 20, 2003
RPV Industries (Canada) Inc.	Alta. 1987	Mar. 1994	Delisted ASE Mar. 3, 1994
RTICA Corporation	Ont. 2001; orig. Alta. 1997	May 2007	Delisted TSX-VEN Dec. 22, 2006
RYM Capital Corp.	Ont. 2004	Oct. 2007	Delisted TSX-VEN Oct. 29, 2007
Radical Advanced Technologies Corp.	B.C. 1989	July 1997	Delisted VSE Mar. 2, 1998
Radiko Holdings Corp.	Alta. 2011	Aug. 2021	Delisted CSE Aug. 16, 2021
Ramm Venture Corporation	B.C. 1968	Mar. 2001	Delisted VSE May 21, 1997
RangeStar Telecommunications Ltd.	B.C. 1987	Mar. 1999	Delisted VSE Mar. 24, 1999
Ravenquest BioMed Inc.	B.C. 2004; orig. B.C. 1987	May 2021	Delisted CSE May 14, 2021
Real Time Measurements Inc.	Alta. 1995	Nov. 2019	Delisted TSX-VEN Oct. 8, 2020
RealCap Holdings Limited	Ont. 1962	June 2007	Delisted CDN Oct. 13, 2000
Red Hill Marketing Group Ltd.	B.C. 1981	Nov. 1988	Delisted VSE Mar. 2, 1990
Redlaw Industries Inc.	Ont. 1978; orig. Ont. 1961	June 2000	Delisted CDN Oct. 13, 2000
Reefco Manufacturing Corporation	B.C. 1989	Nov. 1994	Delisted VSE Mar. 6, 1995
Registered Plan Private Investments Inc.	B.C. 2016	May 2020	Delisted CSE May 5, 2020
David S. Reid Limited	Ont. 1997	Mar. 2002	Delisted TSX-VEN June 20, 2003
Remworks Inc.	Ont. 1984	May 2002	Delisted CDNX May 31, 2001
Renfield Enterprises Inc.	Yuk. 1998; orig. Alta. 1989	June 2000	Delisted CDNX May 31, 2001
Reocito Capital Inc.	Can. 2007	June 2009	Delisted TSX-VEN June 22, 2009
Rhand Industries Inc.	Alta. 1986	Apr. 1995	Delisted ASE Apr. 11, 1995
Richwest Holdings Inc.	Ont. 1989; orig. Alta. 1988	Dec. 1999	Delisted CDN Oct. 13, 2000
RoaDor Industries Ltd.	Ont. 2002; orig. Alta. 1998	July 2010	Delisted TSX-VEN July 12, 2010
Robix Environmental Technologies, Inc.	Alta. 2011	July 2019	Delisted CSE July 3, 2019
Robop.tek (Canada) Inc.	B.C. 1983	Dec. 1987	Delisted VSE Mar. 2, 1989
Rockford Technology Corporation	Alta. 1985	June 2007	Delisted ASE Dec. 18, 1995
Rockvale Resources Limited	Alta. 1997	Feb. 2003	Delisted TSX-VEN June 20, 2003
Rodin Communications Corporation	Ont. 2000; orig. Can. 1994	Sept. 2001	Delisted TSE Apr. 16, 2001
Rothwell Corporation	Ont. 1963	Mar. 1996	Delisted CDN May 31, 1996

Name	Incorp. Date	Date of Last Report	Remarks
Rutel Networks Corporation	Can. 1998	Oct. 2008	Delisted TSX-VEN Oct. 28, 2008

S

Name	Incorp. Date	Date of Last Report	Remarks
S-VISION Corporation	Que. 1995	June 1998	Delisted ME May 22, 1998
SAMsports.com Inc.	Alta. 1997	June 2002	Delisted TSX-VEN June 5, 2002
S.C.O. Medallion Healthy Homes Ltd.	B.C. 1999	July 2007	Delisted CNQ July 24, 2007
SEL Exchange Inc.	Ont. 2010	Aug. 2016	Delisted TSX-VEN Aug. 18, 2016
SFP International Ltd.	Ont. 1982	Jan. 1993	Delisted ASE May 13, 1993
SKG Interactive Inc.	Can. 1999; orig. B.C. 1985	Apr. 2002	Delisted TSE Mar. 8, 2002
SPVC Capital Corporation	Sask. 2007	July 2010	Delisted TSX-VEN July 9, 2010
S.T.I. Industries Inc.	Ont. 1978	May 1997	Delisted CDN Jan. 3, 1995
SURE Print and Copy Centres, Inc.	Alta. 1996	June 2003	Delisted TSX-VEN June 20, 2003
SVL Holdings Inc.	Ont. 1954	June 2007	Delisted CDN Oct. 13, 2000
Sabra-Dent Dental Supplies Ltd.	Ont. 1983	May 1987	No recent report
Sackport Ventures Inc.	Alta. 2004	Sept. 2007	Delisted TSX-VEN Sept. 21, 2007
Saltbae Capital Corp.	B.C. 1986	Aug. 2023	Suspended CSE Nov. 4, 2019
Samia Ventures Inc.	B.C. 1980	June 1995	Delisted VSE Mar. 2, 1998
Saratoga Capital Corp.	Ont. 1937	Dec. 2003	Delisted CDN Oct. 13, 2000
Score Athletic Products Inc.	B.C. 1983	June 1993	Delisted VSE Mar. 3, 1997
Seaway Multi-Corp Limited	Ont. 1963	Feb. 1987	Delisted TSE May 19, 1988
Seaway Trust Company	Ont. 1978	July 1985	Delisted CDN Aug. 31, 1992
Second Chance Corp.	Alta. 1996	Sept. 2002	Delisted TSX-VEN June 20, 2003
Secured Communication Canada 95 Inc.	B.C. 1983	Dec. 1997	Delisted VSE July 7, 1998
Segami Images Incorporated	B.C. 1970	May 2002	Delisted TSX-VEN June 5, 2002
Selco International Properties, Inc.	B.C. 1965	Oct. 1991	Dissolution in progress June 1, 1998
Senco Sensors Inc.	B.C. 1988	June 2003	Delisted TSX-VEN June 20, 2003
Sensat Technologies Ltd.	B.C. 1980	May 2001	Delisted VSE May 23, 1991
Sense Technologies Inc.	B.C. 2007; orig. B.C. 1988	June 2007	Delisted NASDAQ Apr. 25, 2002
Sensorstat Systems, Inc.	B.C. 1983	Sept. 1986	Delisted ASE Feb. 26, 1988
Sentry U.S. Growth and Income Fund	Ont. 2005	June 2009	Delisted TSX June 17, 2009
Service Plastics & Chemicals Corp.	Que. 1951	July 1985	No recent report
Service Track Enterprises Inc.	Alta. 1996	June 1998	Delisted ASE Mar. 12, 1999
Setanta Ventures Inc.	B.C. 1987	June 2001	Delisted CDNX Nov. 5, 2001
Severide Environmental Industries Inc.	B.C. 1984	Oct. 1995	Delisted VSE Mar. 2, 1998
Shayna International Industries Ltd.	B.C. 1984	Sept. 1987	Delisted VSE Nov. 16, 1990
Shelter Products Inc.	Alta. 1994	Nov. 1996	Delisted ASE June 11, 1997
Sherbrook SBK Sport Corp.	Can. 2010; orig. B.C. 2006	July 2012	Delisted TSX-VEN July 23, 2012
Shift Networks Inc.	Alta. 2002, amalg.	June 2008	Delisted TSX-VEN June 30, 2008
Sightus Inc.	Can. 2003; orig. Alta. 1985	June 2008	Delisted TSX-VEN June 30, 2008
Siltronics Ltd.	Ont. 1974	Apr. 2003	Delisted TSE Nov. 11, 1987
SilverBirch Inc.	Ont. 2004	July 2009	Delisted TSX-VEN July 14, 2009
Simmonds Capital Limited	B.C. 1980	Dec. 2001	Delisted TSX Mar. 7, 2003
Simplex Solutions Inc.	Ont. 1997, amalg.	Apr. 2008	Delisted CNQ Apr. 9, 2008
SineTec Holdings Corporation	Alta. 1997	June 2003	Delisted TSX-VEN June 20, 2003
Skylon All Asset Trust	Ont. 2004	Dec. 2014	Delisted TSX Dec. 24, 2014
Smartor Products Inc.	Alta. 1995	Nov. 1999	Delisted CDNX Mar. 19, 2002
Snow Leopard Resources Inc.	Alta. 1990	June 2004	Delisted TSX June 25, 2004
So-Luminaire Systems Corp.	B.C. 1977	Dec. 1987	Delisted VSE Feb. 2, 1989
Sofame Technologies Inc.	Can. 1994	Mar. 2017	Delisted TSX-VEN Mar. 31, 2017
Software Control Systems International Inc.	Alta. 1993	May 2002	Delisted CDNX May 31, 2001
Softwex Technologies Inc.	Alta. 1996	Oct. 2001	Delisted CDNX Apr. 10, 2001
Solar Pharmaceutical Ltd.	B.C. 1980	Nov. 2000	Delisted CDNX May 3, 2001
Solucorp Industries Ltd.	B.C. 1987	Jan. 2000	Delisted VSE Aug. 6, 1996
SolutionInc Technologies Limited	N.S. 2004; orig. B.C. 1980	Nov. 2019	Suspended TSX-VEN Aug. 9, 2011
Solutrea Corp.	Alta. 2004	July 2009	Delisted TSX-VEN July 14, 2009
SonnenEnergy Corp.	Ont. 2006	July 2011	Delisted TSX-VEN July 21, 2011
Sonomax Technologies Inc.	Can. 2010	Oct. 2014	Delisted CSE Oct. 10, 2014
Sophiris Bio Inc.	B.C. 2003, amalg.	July 2020	Delisted NASDAQ Mar. 12, 2020
Sorata Developments Inc.	B.C. 1985	Feb. 1996	Delisted VSE Nov. 15, 1995
Southwest Technologies Inc.	B.C. 1983	May 1988	Delisted VSE May 21, 1991
Spartec International Corporation	Ont. 1972	June 1998	Delisted CDN Jan. 14, 2000
Speakeasy Cannabis Club Ltd.	B.C. 2018; orig. Ont. 2010	Dec. 2022	Delisted CSE Dec. 12, 2022
Specialty Foods Group Income Fund	Ont. 2002	Mar. 2010	Delisted TSX-VEN Mar. 1, 2010
Spectrum Digital Holdings Inc.	B.C. 2013; orig. B.C. 1988	Mar. 2016	Delisted TSX-VEN Mar. 28, 2016
Spinlogic Technologies Inc.	Can. 2004	June 2008	Delisted TSX-VEN June 30, 2008
Spinnaker Development Corporation	Ont. 1990; orig. Can. 1982	Sept. 1996	Delisted TSE Sept. 2, 1994
Sport Specific International Inc.	Alta. 1988	Nov. 1996	Delisted ASE June 11, 1997
Stamford International Inc.	Ont. 1987; orig. Can. 1973	Oct. 2000	Delisted CDN Oct. 13, 2000
Star Properties Inc.	B.C. 1983	Jan. 1999	Delisted VSE Mar. 1, 1999
Starfire Industries Limited	B.C. 1979	Dec. 1986	Delisted VSE Oct. 9, 1987
Staront Technologies Inc.	Ont. 1998	May 2005	Delisted TSX-VEN Aug. 5, 2008
StartMonday Technology Corp.	B.C. 2016	Jan. 2020	Delisted CSE Jan. 13, 2020
Steadfast Ventures Inc.	B.C. 1983	Feb. 1999	Delisted CDNX May 31, 2000
Steed Ventures Corporation	B.C. 1972	June 1986	Delisted VSE July 7, 1989
Sterling Leaf Income Trust	Alta. 2003	June 2007	Delisted TSX-VEN June 23, 2006
Stockguard Corporation	Ont. 1984	July 1998	Delisted CDN Jan. 14, 2000
Stone Mark Capital Inc.	Yuk. 1993; orig. B.C. 1980	Feb. 1993	Delisted VSE Mar. 4, 1994
Stonebridge Inc.	Ont. 1988	Apr. 1991	Delisted TSE Apr. 29, 1991
Stoneset Equity Development Corp.	Alta. 2006	Nov. 2011	Delisted CNSX Nov. 9, 2011
Stornaway Capital Development Corp.	B.C. 1980	Aug. 1990	Delisted VSE May 2, 1991
Straight Forward Marketing Corporation	Ont. 2000	June 2007	Delisted CNQ Nov. 7, 2006
Stratas Corporation Ltd.	Ont. 1982, amalg.	Jan. 1990	Delisted CDN Jan. 3, 1995
Strategic Data Ltd.	Alta. 1994	Dec. 2001	Delisted TSX-VEN Feb. 10, 2003
Strathearn House Group Limited	Ont. 1965	Feb. 1992	Delisted TSE Mar. 5, 1993
Studebaker's Resource Development Ltd.	B.C. 1981	Dec. 1987	Delisted ASE Feb. 21, 1989
Sumabus Inc.	Que. 1982	June 1987	Delisted ME Feb. 4, 1988
Sun Free Enterprises Ltd.	B.C. 1987	July 1998	Delisted VSE Mar. 3, 1997
Sungold International Holdings Corp.	Can. 2003; orig. B.C. 1986	June 2007	Delisted VSE Dec. 11, 1997
Sunrise International Inc.	Alta. 1986	Mar. 2008	Delisted TSX-VEN Mar. 11, 2008
Sweet Natural Trading Co. Limited	Ont. 2008	Sept. 2020	Delisted TSX-VEN Sept. 22, 2020
Synapse Software Inc.	B.C. 1992	May 1996	Delisted ASE May 7, 1996
Synaptec, A Knowledge Engineering Corporation	B.C. 1983	Dec. 1988	Delisted VSE Jan. 10, 1990
Synergex Corporation	Ont. 2005, amalg.	Feb. 2011	Delisted TSX Feb. 25, 2011

T

Name	Incorp. Date	Date of Last Report	Remarks
TCR Environmental Corp.	Ont. 1991	May 2001	Delisted CDNX May 31, 2001
TER Thermal Retrieval Systems Ltd.	Alta. 1996	Jan. 2003	Delisted TSX-VEN Oct. 7, 2004
TG Residential Value Properties Ltd.	B.C. 2011	Sept. 2015	Delisted TSX-VEN Oct. 1, 2015
T.I. Travel International Inc.	B.C. 1979	June 1989	Delisted VSE Mar. 2, 1990

Name	Incorp. Date	Date of Last Report	Remarks
TMI Technology Inc.	Alta. 1987	Sept. 2002	Delisted TSX-VEN Sept. 25, 2002
TWX Group Holding Limited	B.C. 2020; orig. Ont. 1995	Apr. 2021	Delisted CSE Apr. 8, 2021
Tactex Controls Inc.	Alta. 2000, amalg.	Apr. 2009	Delisted TSX-VEN Apr. 22, 2009
Tagalder (2000) Inc.	Ont. 1996, amalg.	Jan. 2003	Delisted CDNX Jan. 17, 2001
Tahiti Resort Hotels Ltd.	B.C. 1986	Dec. 1987	Delisted VSE Mar. 2, 1989
Tajac Capital Inc.	Alta. 2006	Oct. 2009	Delisted TSX-VEN Oct. 30, 2009
Talisman Enterprises Inc.	Ont. 1978	May 2002	Delisted NASDAQ May 24, 2001
Tallagium Corporation	Alta. 1998	Aug. 2007	Delisted TSX-VEN Aug. 2, 2007
Talware Networx Inc.	Alta. 1998	July 2009	Delisted TSX-VEN July 14, 2009
Tampico Capital Corporation	B.C. 1972	July 1993	Delisted VSE Mar. 6, 1995
Tap Capital Corp.	Ont. 1987	Mar. 1994	Delisted TSE Mar. 4, 1994
Teal Valley Health Inc.	B.C. 2016; orig. Can. 1994	June 2007	Delisted TSX Sept. 22, 2004
Techniscope Development Corp.	B.C. 1984	Mar. 1996	Delisted VSE Mar. 5, 1993
Tek-Net International (Canada) Ltd.	B.C. 1985	Dec. 1986	Delisted VSE Sept. 1, 1988
Telekom Advanced Systems Corporation	Que. 1996	Mar. 2000	Delisted ME Mar. 10, 2000
Telephony Communications International Incorporated	Ont. 1980	Aug. 1990	Delisted ASE May 23, 1991
Telepost Communications Inc.	B.C. 1986	Jan. 2002	Delisted TSX-VEN Apr. 20, 2004
Telescan Industries Inc.	Ont. 1980	May 1988	Delisted CDN Jan. 3, 1995
Tellza Inc.	Ont. 1984	Mar. 2019	Delisted TSX Mar. 4, 2019
Terrabiogen Technologies Inc.	B.C. 1993	June 2012	Delisted TSX-VEN June 12, 2012
Terrawest Industries Inc.	B.C. 1986	July 1997	Delisted CDNX May 31, 2000
Tevana Traders Corp.	Ont. 1989	Dec. 1995	Delisted VSE Mar. 1, 1999
Theme Restaurants Incorporated	Ont. 1945	May 1987	Delisted CDN Jan. 3, 1995
Thermal Control Technologies Corp.	Alta. 1997, amalg.; orig. Alta. 1988	May 2002	Delisted CDNX May 31, 2000
Thoughtful Brands Inc.	B.C. 2010	July 2022	Delisted CSE July 18, 2022
3 Sixty Risk Solutions Ltd.	B.C. 2006	Apr. 2022	Delisted CSE July 15, 2021
Titan Trading Analytics Inc.	Alta. 2005; orig. B.C. 1993	Oct. 2015	Delisted TSX-VEN Oct. 1, 2015
Tokyo Trading Ltd.	B.C. 1988	Apr. 1995	Delisted VSE Mar. 3, 1997
Tomahawk Corporation	Alta. 1986	Mar. 1999	Delisted CDNX May 31, 2001
Toptent inc.	Can. 2007	May 2011	Delisted TSX-VEN May 9, 2011
Torrent Capital Corp.	Alta. 1996	Dec. 1998	Delisted ASE Sept. 23, 1999
Total Image Capital Corp.	Alta. 1997	June 2001	Delisted TSX-VEN Oct. 1, 2002
Toxin Alert Inc.	Ont. 1998	July 2011	Delisted TSX-VEN Oct. 10, 2013
TraceAbility Solutions Inc.	Alta. 1998, amalg.	June 2002	Delisted TSX-VEN June 5, 2002
Tracker Software International Inc.	Yuk. 1996; orig. B.C. 1993	Feb. 1997	Delisted VSE Mar. 1, 1999
Transmedica Enterprises Inc.	B.C. 1983	June 1988	Delisted VSE Oct. 6, 1989
Transnational Cannabis Ltd.	B.C. 2006	Dec. 2019	Delisted CSE Dec. 23, 2019
Transtide Industries Ltd.	Man. 1946	Feb. 1993	Delisted NEO Feb. 12, 1993
Trellis Technology Corporation	B.C. 1983	June 1999	Delisted VSE Feb. 12, 1996
Trend Vision Technologies, Inc.	B.C. 1984	June 1994	Delisted VSE Mar. 7, 1995
Trez Capital Mortgage Investment Corporation	Can. 2012	Aug. 2019	Delisted TSX Aug. 1, 2019
Tribute Resources Inc.	Alta. 1997	May 2021	Delisted TSX-VEN May 26, 2021
Trirak Industries Corporation	Sask. 1986	Apr. 1988	Delisted ASE Feb. 5, 1990
TriTec Power Systems Ltd.	Ont. 1994	May 2002	Delisted TSX-VEN May 21, 2002
Triton Industries Inc.	Que. 1965	Dec. 1993	Delisted ME Dec. 31, 1993
Tropika International Limited	Ont. 1975	June 2003	Delisted TSX-VEN June 20, 2003
Tru-Wall Group Limited	Ont. 1956	Sept. 1997	Delisted TSE Sept. 19, 1997
Turbo Power Systems Inc.	Yuk. 2004; orig. Alta. 1987	July 2012	Delisted TSX July 4, 2012
2980304 Canada Inc.	Can. 1993	Jan. 2009	Delisted TSX-VEN Jan. 13, 2009

U

Name	Incorp. Date	Date of Last Report	Remarks
U.F.X. Enterprises Inc.	Alta. 1996	Apr. 2003	Delisted TSX-VEN Apr. 23, 2003
U.T. Technologies Limited	B.C. 1986	May 1989	Delisted VSE Jan. 10, 1990
The Unicorn Corp.	Can.	June 1991	Delisted ASE Mar. 26, 1992
Uniglobe.com Inc.	Can. 1995	June 2004	Delisted TSX-VEN June 16, 2004
Unilink Tele.com Inc.	B.C. 1999	June 2004	Delisted TSX-VEN June 25, 2004
Unisphere Satellite Corp.	Ont. 1928	Nov. 1989	Delisted CDN Jan. 3, 1995
United Industrial Services Ltd.	Alta. 1987	May 2000	Delisted TSX-VEN June 5, 2002
United International Industries Ltd.	Alta. 1962	July 1973	No recent report
United Liberty Financial Corporation	B.C. 1983	Sept. 1989	Delisted VSE Oct. 6, 1989
Upland Global Corporation	Alta. 1993	June 2007	Delisted TSX-VEN June 23, 2006
UrtheCast Corp.	Ont. 2014, amalg.; orig. Ont. 2004	Oct. 2020	Delisted TSX Oct. 19, 2020

V

Name	Incorp. Date	Date of Last Report	Remarks
V-Tech Diagnostics (Canada) Inc.	B.C. 1986	Oct. 1994	Delisted VSE Oct. 31, 1994
V.R.D. Entertainment Ltd.	Ont. 1987	Nov. 1998	Delisted CDN May 31, 1996
VSC Technology Inc.	B.C. 1981	Apr. 1996	Delisted VSE May 4, 1994
VSM MedTech Ltd.	Alta. 1995	June 2007	Delisted TSX Oct. 18, 2006
Société d'entraide économique de Val-d'Or	Que. 1982	Dec. 1988	Delisted ME Feb. 3, 1989
Valmec Capital Inc.	Que. 1995	May 1999	Delisted ASE Aug. 20, 1998
Valucap Investments Inc.	Ont. 2008; orig. B.C. 1981	Nov. 2019	Delisted TSX-VEN Sept. 11, 2020
Venga Aerospace Systems Inc.	Ont. 1979, amalg.	May 2015	Delisted TSX-VEN May 14, 2015
Ventura Cannabis and Wellness Corp.	B.C. 2013	Nov. 2020	Delisted CSE Nov. 2, 2020
Vert Infrastructure Ltd.	B.C. 2011	May 2021	Delisted CSE May 13, 2021
Vertex Properties Inc.	Alta. 1993	May 2002	Delisted CDNX Aug. 22, 2001
Vestronix Corporation	Ont. 1988; orig. U.K. 1986	Sept. 1990	Delisted CDN Jan. 3, 1995
Viridis Holdings Corp.	B.C. 1998	Aug. 2023	Suspended TSX-VEN May 9, 2022
Vision Incorporated	Alta. 1986	Oct. 1994	Delisted ASE May 14, 1998
Vision SCMS Inc.	Alta. 1998	Aug. 2003	Delisted TSX-VEN June 24, 2004
Visionwall Incorporated	Alta. 1992	Mar. 2008	Delisted TSX-VEN Mar. 1, 2010
Visiphor Corporation	Can. 2005; orig. B.C. 1998	July 2009	Delisted TSX-VEN July 15, 2009
Vital Retirement Living Inc.	Alta. 1998	Oct. 2004	Delisted TSX-VEN Oct. 7, 2004
The Vivant Group Inc.	Alta. 1988	Dec. 1999	Delisted CDNX May 31, 2000
Vivione Biosciences Inc.	Alta. 2011	Aug. 2020	Suspended TSX-VEN Apr. 25, 2017
Vogue Investments (1987) Ltd.	Alta. 1987	Jan. 1989	Delisted ASE Sept. 24, 1990
Voyager Digital Ltd.	B.C. 1990	Aug. 2022	Delisted TSX Aug. 18, 2022

W

Name	Incorp. Date	Date of Last Report	Remarks
WASTECORP. International Investments Inc.	Can. 1990	June 2007	Delisted TSX-VEN June 23, 2006
Wagon Train Estates Ltd.	B.C. 1968	Nov. 1985	No recent report
Waitsfield Capital Inc.	Que. 1973	June 2007	Delisted CDN Apr. 14, 2000
Warwick Universal Ltd.	Que. 1972	June 1978	Delisted CDN Aug. 31, 1992
Wavve Telecommunications, Inc.	Yuk. 1996; orig. B.C. 1995, amalg.	Aug. 2001	Delisted TSX-VEN June 5, 2002
Wayland Group Corp.	Ont. 1998; orig. Alta. 1996	Oct. 2020	Delisted CSE Oct. 13, 2020
Wellbeing Digital Sciences Inc.	B.C. 2017	Aug. 2023	Delisted NEO Aug. 9, 2023
West Bay Capital Corp.	Alta. 1993	Sept. 1995	Delisted ASE Dec. 23, 1996
Westwater Industries Ltd.	B.C. 1980	Mar. 1993	Delisted TSE Mar. 5, 1993
WildCard Technologies Inc.	Ont. 1996, amalg.	Feb. 1997	Delisted ASE Sept. 22, 1997
Wildflower Brands Inc.	B.C. 1983	July 2022	Delisted CSE July 28, 2022

Name	Incorp. Date	Date of Last Report	Remarks
The Winchester Group Inc.	Ont. 1987	June 1998	Delisted CDN Oct. 13, 2000
Windsor Raceway Inc.	Ont. 1962	May 1989	No recent report
Winfield Resources Limited	B.C. 1987	Oct. 2010	Delisted TSX-VEN Oct. 28, 2010
Winzen Properties Inc.	B.C. 1986, amalg.	July 2013	Delisted TSX-VEN July 29, 2013
World Environmental Inc.	Alta. 1987	Mar. 1996	Delisted ASE Mar. 25, 1996
World Enzymes Ltd.	B.C. 1979	Dec. 1987	Delisted VSE July 7, 1989
World Famous Pizza Company Ltd.	B.C. 2007	Mar. 2015	Delisted TSX-VEN Mar. 19, 2015
World Marketing Corporation	B.C. 1980	Oct. 1998	Delisted VSE May 4, 1994
World Outfitters Corporation Safari Nordik	Can. 1988	July 2011	Delisted TSX-VEN July 21, 2011
World Sales & Merchandising Inc.	Ont. 1986	Feb. 2002	Delisted TSX-VEN June 20, 2003
World Videophone Teleconferencing Technologies Ltd.	B.C. 1963	Mar. 1990	Delisted VSE Mar. 23, 1990
World Wise Technologies Inc.	Ont. 1998; orig. B.C. 1987	June 2003	Delisted TSX-VEN June 20, 2003
Worldtec Sciences Incorporated	Ont. 1990	Dec. 1995	Delisted CDN Dec. 31, 1997
Worldwide Monitoring Corporation	B.C. 1987; orig. Del. 1985	Dec. 1987	Delisted VSE Jan. 10, 1990
X			
XS Technologies Inc.	Alta. 1996	Mar. 2003	Delisted TSX-VEN June 20, 2003
Xcel Consolidated Ltd.	Alta. 1999	July 2010	Delisted TSX-VEN July 12, 2010
Xgen Ventures Inc.	Ont. 1974	Dec. 2011	Delisted TSX-VEN Dec. 19, 2011
Xianburg Data Systems Canada Corporation	Alta. 2008	Sept. 2012	Delisted TSX-VEN Sept. 17, 2012
xRM Global Inc.	Ont. 2008	Aug. 2011	Delisted TSX-VEN Aug. 2, 2011
Y			
YDx Innovation Corp.	B.C. 2007	Aug. 2023	Suspended TSX-VEN May 7, 2021
Yaletown Capital Corp.	Alta. 2007	Mar. 2015	Delisted TSX-VEN Mar. 19, 2015
Z			
Zecotek Photonics Inc.	B.C. 1983	Dec. 2022	Delisted TSX-VEN Jan. 30, 2023
0187279 B.C. Ltd.	B.C. 1979	June 2007	Delisted CDNX Dec. 15, 1999
Zlin Aerospace Inc.	Ont. 1987; orig. Ont. 1982	June 2002	Delisted TSX-VEN Sept. 30, 2004
ZoomMed Inc.	Can. 2005	Aug. 2020	Suspended TSX-VEN Oct. 5, 2018
Zupintra Corporation, Inc.	Ont. 1984	June 2007	Delisted CDN Oct. 13, 2000
Zytec Systems Inc.	B.C. 1983	June 1993	Delisted TSE June 11, 1993

Companies by Global Industry Classification Standard

The Global Industry Classification Standard (GICS) was developed by Standard & Poor's and Morgan Stanley Capital International, two leading providers of global indices, and was launched in 1999. GICS was developed in response to the global financial community's need for one complete, consistent set of global sector and industry definitions.

Standard & Poor's and the Toronto Stock Exchange introduced GICS to Canada in 2002 with the revision of the benchmark equity index, the S&P/TSX Composite Index, which was launched on May 1, 2002. GICS has rapidly gained worldwide acceptance and its use in the S&P/TSX Composite is meant to allow investors to accurately compare the performance of Canadian indices with those around the world.

GICS classifications consist of 11 economic sectors aggregated from 25 industry groups, 74 industries and 163 sub-industries. All Economic Sectors, have a 2-digit identification code, all Industry Groups have a 4-digit identification code, all Industries have a 6-digit identification code and all Sub-Industries have an 8-digit identification code.

The Financial Post DataGroup uses both GICS and SIC (Standard Industrial Classifiation) codes, and either standard can be used when conducting a search using our FP Corporate Survey online product. Classification of the universe of companies in the Survey of Industrials is produced and verified by our analysts, except for companies in the S&P/TSX Composite Index which have been classified by Standard & Poor's. All companies have been assigned one or more 4-digit SIC codes and, except for those deemed non-classifiable such as shell or Capital Pool Companies (SIC code is 9999), all companies have been assigned an 8-digit GICS code.

Companies are shown below by GICS Sub-Industry, arranged alphabetically.

50201010 Advertising

EQ Inc.
Mobio Technologies Inc.

20101010 Aerospace & Defense

Aether Global Innovations Corp.
Bombardier Inc.
CAE Inc.
Draganfly Inc.
Drone Delivery Canada Corp.
Héroux-Devtek Inc.
KWESST Micro Systems Inc.
Kraken Robotics Inc.
MDA Ltd.
Magellan Aerospace Corporation
Maritime Launch Services Inc.
Omni-Lite Industries Canada Inc.
RDARS Inc.
Star Navigation Systems Group Ltd.
Volatus Aerospace Corp.

20106015 Agricultural & Farm Machinery

Ag Growth International Inc.
Buhler Industries Inc.
Clean Seed Capital Group Ltd.
CubicFarm Systems Corp.
Sprout AI Inc.

30202010 Agricultural Products & Services

DLC Holdings Corp.
Digicann Ventures Inc.
Global Food and Ingredients Ltd.
Green Rise Foods Inc.
Greenrise Global Brands Inc.
Greenway Greenhouse Cannabis Corporation
Imperial Ginseng Products Ltd.
Pontus Protein Ltd.
SunOpta Inc.
Sweet Earth Holdings Corporation
Terranueva Corporation
Vext Science, Inc.
Village Farms International, Inc.

20301010 Air Freight & Logistics

Cargojet Inc.
PUDO Inc.
ParcelPal Logistics Inc.

50101010 Alternative Carriers

Telesat Corporation

25504010 Apparel Retail

Aritzia Inc.
lululemon athletica inc.
Peekaboo Beans Inc.
RYU Apparel Inc.
Reitmans (Canada) Limited
Roots Corporation

25203010 Apparel, Accessories & Luxury Goods

Canada Goose Holdings Inc.
Gildan Activewear Inc.
iFabric Corp.
Mene Inc.
Unisync Corp.

45103010 Application Software

ARHT Media Inc.
ATW Tech Inc.
Acceleware Ltd.
Ackroo Inc.
Adcore Inc.
AdRabbit Limited
AirIQ Inc.
Aisix Solutions Inc.
Alphinat inc.
Anonymous Intelligence Company Inc.
Arway Corporation
BYND Cannasoft Enterprises Inc.
BlueRush Inc.
BnSellit Technology Inc.
Boardwalktech Software Corp.
Carbeeza Inc.
CardioComm Solutions, Inc.
Ceridian HCM Holding Inc.
Certive Solutions Inc.
CoinAnalyst Corp.
Computer Modelling Group Ltd.
Constellation Software Inc.
Contagious Gaming Inc.
Copperleaf Technologies Inc.
Coveo Solutions Inc.
Cryptoblox Technologies Inc.
CyberCatch Holdings, Inc.
D2L Inc.
DGTL Holdings Inc.
DXStorm.com Inc.
Datable Technology Corporation
DeepSpatial Inc.
The Descartes Systems Group Inc.
Destiny Media Technologies Inc.
Direct Communication Solutions, Inc.
Docebo Inc.
Dye & Durham Limited
Edge Total Intelligence Inc.
Energy Plug Technologies Corp.
Enghouse Systems Limited
EonX Technologies Inc.
FLYHT Aerospace Solutions Ltd.
Fandifi Technology Corp.
Farmers Edge Inc.
Geekco Technologies Corporation
Generative AI Solutions Corp.
Givex Corp.
Global Compliance Applications Corp.
HS GovTech Solutions Inc.
Hank Payments Corp.
Hello Pal International Inc.
Hero Innovation Group Inc.
Hunter Technology Corp.
Identillect Technologies Corp.
infinitii ai inc.
InsuraGuest Technologies Inc.
Intellabridge Technology Corporation
Interfield Global Software Inc.
Intouch Insight Ltd.
iSign Media Solutions Inc.
Jasper Commerce Inc.
Katipult Technology Corp.
Kidoz Inc.
Kinaxis Inc.
kneat.com, inc.
Lightspeed Commerce Inc.
Liquid Avatar Technologies Inc.
Lumine Group Inc.
Lynx Global Digital Finance Corporation
Martello Technologies Group Inc.
mCloud Technologies Corp.
MediaValet Inc.
Mijem Newcomm Tech Inc.
MiMedia Holdings Inc.
Mobi724 Global Solutions Inc.
Mogo Inc.

Moovly Media Inc.
NamSys Inc.
NetCents Technology Inc.
NexTech AR Solutions Corp.
NowVertical Group Inc.
Nubeva Technologies Ltd.
OOOOO Entertainment Commerce Limited
Oculus VisionTech Inc.
OneSoft Solutions Inc.
Open Text Corporation
Parvis Invest Inc.
Perk Labs Inc.
Pioneer Media Holdings Inc.
Playgon Games Inc.
Pluribus Technologies Corp.
Plurilock Security Inc.
PowerBand Solutions Inc.
ProntoForms Corporation
ProStar Holdings Inc.
Pushfor Tech Inc.
Q4 Inc.
Quorum Information Technologies Inc.
RESAAS Services Inc.
RIWI Corp.
Radial Research Corp.
Railtown AI Technologies Inc.
Reklaim Ltd.
RenoWorks Software Inc.
RevoluGROUP Canada Inc.
Route1 Inc.
Scope Carbon Corp.
Snipp Interactive Inc.
Solvbl Solutions Inc.
Sparx Technology Inc.
Spetz Inc.
SponsorsOne Inc.
SpotLite360 IOT Solutions, Inc.
Steer Technologies Inc.
SuperBuzz Inc.
Swarmio Media Holdings Inc.
Sylogist Ltd.
TECSYS Inc.
Tenet Fintech Group Inc.
Thinkific Labs Inc.
Tiny Ltd.
Toggle3D.ai Inc.
Topicus.com Inc.
TrackX Holdings Inc.
TrustBIX Inc.
UpSnap Inc.
VIQ Solutions Inc.
Verses AI Inc.
VerticalScope Holdings Inc.
Victory Square Technologies Inc.
Visionstate Corp.
Wishpond Technologies Ltd.
XRApplied Technologies Inc.
Xigem Technologies Corporation
Xtract One Technologies Inc.
Xybion Digital Inc.
01 Communique Laboratory Inc.
Zonetail Inc.
Zoomd Technologies Ltd.

40203010 Asset Management & Custody Banks

AGF Management Limited
AI Artificial Intelligence Ventures Inc.
Aberdeen International Inc.
abrdn Asia-Pacific Income Fund VCC
Aimia Inc.
Alaris Equity Partners Income Trust
Australian REIT Income Fund
Axcap Ventures Inc.
Axiom Capital Advisors Inc.
Axion Ventures Inc.
B.E.S.T. Venture Opportunities Fund Inc.
BIP Investment Corporation
Belgravia Hartford Capital Inc.
Big Banc Split Corp.
Big Pharma Split Corp.
Birchtree Investments Ltd.
The Bitcoin Fund
Blackhawk Growth Corp.
BlockchainK2 Corp.
Bloom Select Income Fund
Blue Ribbon Income Fund
Brompton Lifeco Split Corp.
Brompton Oil Split Corp.
Brompton Split Banc Corp.
Brookfield Asset Management Ltd.
Brookfield Corporation
Brookfield Global Infrastructure Securities Income Fund
Brookfield Investments Corporation
CI Financial Corp.
CULT Food Science Corp.
Canadian Banc Corp.
Canadian General Investments, Limited
Canadian High Income Equity Fund
Canadian Investment Grade Preferred Share Fund
Canadian Life Companies Split Corp.
Canadian Nexus Team Ventures Corp.
Canoe EIT Income Fund
Canso Credit Income Fund
Canso Select Opportunities Corporation
Capitan Investment Ltd.
Carbon Streaming Corporation
Chemistree Technology Inc.
Ciscom Corp.
Citadel Income Fund
Clairvest Group Inc.
Clarke Inc.
Cliffside Capital Ltd.
Coloured Ties Capital Inc.
Consolidated Firstfund Capital Corp.
Copland Road Capital Corporation
CoTec Holdings Corp.
Cymbria Corporation
Cypher Metaverse Inc.
Cypherpunk Holdings Inc.
DevvStream Holdings Inc.
Dividend 15 Split Corp.
Dividend 15 Split Corp. II
Dividend Growth Split Corp.
Dividend Select 15 Corp.
Dundee Corporation
E Split Corp.
Eat & Beyond Global Holdings Inc.
Eat Well Investment Group Inc.
Economic Investment Trust Limited
Elixxer Ltd.
Elysee Development Corp.
Enlighta Inc.
Esstra Industries Inc.
Ether Capital Corporation
The Ether Fund
Faircourt Gold Income Corp.
Faircourt Split Trust
Fiera Capital Corporation
Financial 15 Split Corp.
FinCanna Capital Corp.
First Growth Funds Limited
Flow Capital Corp.
49 North Resources Inc.
GCC Global Capital Corporation
GOAT Industries Ltd.
Global Dividend Growth Split Corp.
Grand Peak Capital Corp.
GreenBank Capital Inc.
Guardian Capital Group Limited
Healthcare Special Opportunities Fund
IC Capitalight Corp.
IGM Financial Inc.
Immutable Holdings Inc.
Income Financial Trust
International Clean Power Dividend Fund
JFT Strategies Fund
Lanebury Growth Capital Ltd.
Life & Banc Split Corp.
Lions Bay Capital Inc.
Lorne Park Capital Partners Inc.
M Split Corp.
MINT Income Fund
Magnetic North Acquisition Corp.
Manitex Capital Inc.
Maple Peak Investments Inc.
Marret High Yield Strategies Fund
Marret Multi-Strategy Income Fund
Middlefield Global Real Asset Fund
Minco Capital Corp.
Montfort Capital Corp.
Mount Logan Capital Inc.
New Commerce Split Fund
North American Financial 15 Split Corp.
Northfield Capital Corporation
Olive Resource Capital Inc.
Olympia Financial Group Inc.
Onex Corporation
Origin Therapeutics Holdings Inc.
PIMCO Global Income Opportunities Fund
PIMCO Multi-Sector Income Fund
PIMCO Tactical Income Fund
PIMCO Tactical Income Opportunities Fund
Palisades Goldcorp Ltd.
Partners Value Investments LP
Partners Value Split Corp.
Pender Growth Fund Inc.
Picton Mahoney Tactical Income Fund
Pinetree Capital Ltd.
Planet Ventures Inc.
Plank Ventures Ltd.
Polaris Northstar Capital Corp.
Premium Income Corporation
Prime Dividend Corp.
Prophecy DeFi Inc.
Prospect Park Capital Corp.
Queen's Road Capital Investment Ltd.
Quinsam Capital Corporation
RF Capital Group Inc.
Ravensource Fund
Real Estate Split Corp.
Reservoir Capital Corp.
Ridgewood Canadian Investment Grade Bond Fund
Right Season Investments Corp.
S Split Corp.
SOL Global Investments Corp.
Senvest Capital Inc.
Sixty Six Capital Inc.
Sonor Investments Limited
Spackman Equities Group Inc.
Sprott Inc.
Sprott Physical Gold and Silver Trust
Sprott Physical Gold Trust
Sprott Physical Platinum and Palladium Trust
Sprott Physical Silver Trust
Stack Capital Group Inc.
Stock Trend Capital Inc.
Strategem Capital Corporation
Sustainable Innovation & Health Dividend Fund
Sustainable Power & Infrastructure Split Corp.
Sustainable Real Estate Dividend Fund
Symphony Floating Rate Senior Loan Fund
TDb Split Corp.
Target Capital Inc.
Terra Firma Capital Corporation
ThreeD Capital Inc.
Tier One Capital Limited Partnership

Till Capital Corporation
Tony G Co-Investment Holdings Ltd.
Top Strike Resources Corp.
Top 10 Split Trust
Torrent Capital Ltd.
US Financial 15 Split Corp.
United Corporations Limited
Urbana Corporation
Vinergy Capital Inc.
The Westaim Corporation
The Western Investment Company of Canada Limited
Western Pacific Trust Company
Wilmington Capital Management Inc.
World Financial Split Corp.
Zimtu Capital Corp.

25102010 Automobile Manufacturers

Electrameccanica Vehicles Corp.
First Hydrogen Corp.

25101010 Automotive Parts & Equipment

ABC Technologies Holdings Inc.
Aether Catalyst Solutions, Inc.
Linamar Corporation
Magna International Inc.
Martinrea International Inc.
Spectra Products Inc.
TUGA Innovations, Inc.

25504050 Automotive Retail

AutoCanada Inc.
EV Technology Group Ltd.

35201010 Biotechnology

AEterna Zentaris Inc.
ASEP Medical Holdings Inc.
Aptose Biosciences Inc.
Arch Biopartners Inc.
Asia Green Biotechnology Corp.
Aurinia Pharmaceuticals Inc.
BetterLife Pharma Inc.
biOasis Technologies Inc.
Biocure Technology Inc.
BioMark Diagnostics Inc.
BioNxt Solutions Inc.
BioVaxys Technology Corp.
BriaCell Therapeutics Corp.
Ceapro Inc.
ChitogenX Inc.
Defence Therapeutics Inc.
DiaMedica Therapeutics Inc.
ESSA Pharma Inc.
Edesa Biotech, Inc.
Fennec Pharmaceuticals Inc.
Fusion Pharmaceuticals Inc.
GLG Life Tech Corporation
Gemina Laboratories Ltd.
GeneTether Therapeutics Inc.
Global Hemp Group Inc.
IBEX Technologies Inc.
ImmunoPrecise Antibodies Ltd.
IntelGenx Technologies Corp.
Kane Biotech Inc.
Liminal BioSciences Inc.
MedMira Inc.
Microbix Biosystems Inc.
NanoSphere Health Sciences Inc.
NeutriSci International Inc.
Oncolytics Biotech Inc.
ProMIS Neurosciences Inc.
Psyched Wellness Ltd.
Quest PharmaTech Inc.
Radient Technologies Inc.
Rakovina Therapeutics Inc.
Rapid Dose Therapeutics Corp.
Sirona Biochem Corp.
Solarvest BioEnergy Inc.
Sona Nanotech Inc.
Spectral Medical Inc.
StageZero Life Sciences Ltd.
Telo Genomics Corp.
Theratechnologies Inc.
VBI Vaccines Inc.
Vaxil Bio Ltd.
WPD Pharmaceuticals Inc.
Waverley Pharma Inc.
Willow Biosciences Inc.

30201010 Brewers

Big Rock Brewery Inc.
Molson Coors Canada Inc.

50201020 Broadcasting

Asian Television Network International Limited
Corus Entertainment Inc.
TVA Group Inc.
ZoomerMedia Limited

25503030 Broadline Retail

Canadian Tire Corporation, Limited
Dollarama Inc.
PesoRama Inc.

20102010 Building Products

ADF Group Inc.
AgriFORCE Growing Systems Ltd.
Cymat Technologies Ltd.
DIRTT Environmental Solutions Ltd.
Imaflex Inc.
Masonite International Corporation
Minaean SP Construction Corp.

50201030 Cable & Satellite

COGECO Inc.
Cogeco Communications Inc.
QYOU Media Inc.
Quebecor Inc.
Stingray Group Inc.

20304030 Cargo Ground Transportation

Andlauer Healthcare Group Inc.
Desert Mountain Energy Corp.
Mullen Group Ltd.
TFI International Inc.
Titanium Transportation Group Inc.

25301010 Casinos & Gaming

Bragg Gaming Group Inc.
FansUnite Entertainment Inc.
Gamehost Inc.
I3 Interactive Inc.
Kings Entertainment Group Inc.
NorthStar Gaming Holdings Inc.
React Gaming Group Inc.
Real Luck Group Ltd.
Rivalry Corp.
VIP Entertainment Technologies Inc.

10102050 Coal & Consumable Fuels

Cameco Corporation

40201050 Commercial & Residential Mortgage Finance

Atrium Mortgage Investment Corporation
Builders Capital Mortgage Corp.
Dominion Lending Centres Inc.
Findev Inc.
Firm Capital Mortgage Investment Corporation
First National Financial Corporation
Home Capital Group Inc.
MCAN Mortgage Corporation
Sagen MI Canada Inc.
Standard Mercantile Acquisition Corp.
Timbercreek Financial Corp.

20201010 Commercial Printing

DATA Communications Management Corp.
Pollard Banknote Limited

15101010 Commodity Chemicals

CO2 Gro Inc.
Char Technologies Ltd.
Chemtrade Logistics Income Fund
Earth Alive Clean Technologies Inc.
EcoSynthetix Inc.
FendX Technologies Inc.
Methanex Corporation
Neo Performance Materials Inc.
Organic Potash Corporation

45201020 Communications Equipment

Baylin Technologies Inc.
BeWhere Holdings, Inc.
Blackline Safety Corp.
C-COM Satellite Systems Inc.
Critical Infrastructure Technologies Ltd.
Edgewater Wireless Systems Inc.
Enablence Technologies Inc.
Evertz Technologies Limited
Gatekeeper Systems Inc.
Haivision Systems Inc.
INEO Tech Corp.
Jemtec Inc.
Liberty Defense Holdings, Ltd.
Lite Access Technologies Inc.
Novra Technologies Inc.
Nuran Wireless Inc.
Sangoma Technologies Corporation
Siyata Mobile Inc.
Total Telcom Inc.
Vecima Networks Inc.
Wi2Wi Corporation

25504020 Computer & Electronics Retail

Advent-AWI Holdings Inc.

20103010 Construction & Engineering

Aecon Group Inc.
BYT Holdings Ltd.
Badger Infrastructure Solutions Ltd.
Bird Construction Inc.
Brookfield Business Corporation
Delta CleanTech Inc.
Plaintree Systems Inc.
Reco International Group Inc.
SNC-Lavalin Group Inc.
Spark Power Group Inc.
Three Sixty Solar Ltd.
Tower One Wireless Corp.
WSP Global Inc.

20106010 Construction Machinery & Heavy Transportation Equipment

GreenPower Motor Company Inc.
Kelso Technologies Inc.
The Limestone Boat Company Limited
The Lion Electric Company
NFI Group Inc.
Tornado Global Hydrovacs Ltd.
Vicinity Motor Corp.
Vision Marine Technologies Inc.
Westport Fuel Systems Inc.

15102010 Construction Materials

Athabasca Minerals Inc.
Cematrix Corporation
Northstar Clean Technologies Inc.
Source Energy Services Ltd.

25201010 Consumer Electronics

BEACN Wizardry & Magic Inc.
D-BOX Technologies Inc.

40202010 Consumer Finance
Axis Auto Finance Inc.
goeasy Ltd.
Marble Financial Inc.
Nicholas Financial, Inc.
Propel Holdings Inc.
Solution Financial Inc.

15104025 Copper
Battery Mineral Resources Corp.

20202030 Data Processing & Outsourced Services
Abaxx Technologies Inc.
BTQ Technologies Corp.
Banxa Holdings Inc.
Bitfarms Ltd.
Blockchain Venture Capital Inc.
Blockmint Technologies Inc.
Bluesky Digital Assets Corp.
Cathedra Bitcoin Inc.
CryptoStar Corp.
DMG Blockchain Solutions Inc.
DataMetrex AI Limited
DeepMarkit Corp.
DeFi Technologies Inc.
Digihost Technology Inc.
Graph Blockchain Inc.
Green Block Mining Corp.
HIVE Digital Technologies Ltd.
Hut 8 Mining Corp.
iMining Technologies Inc.
Information Services Corporation
LQWD Technologies Corp.
Liquid Meta Capital Holdings Ltd.
Looking Glass Labs Ltd.
Luxxfolio Holdings Inc.
MCX Technologies Corporation
MetaWorks Platforms, Inc.
MineHub Technologies Inc.
Mobilum Technologies Inc.
NFT Technologies Inc.
Neptune Digital Assets Corp.
Nuvei Corporation
P2Earn Inc.
Pivotree Inc.
Quisitive Technology Solutions, Inc.
SATO Technologies Corp.
Skychain Technologies Inc.
Spirit Blockchain Capital Inc.
TELUS International (Cda) Inc.
Tokens.com Corp.
TruTrace Technologies Inc.
Venzee Technologies Inc.
Voxtur Analytics Corp.
Wellfield Technologies Inc.
ZeU Technologies, Inc.

30201020 Distillers & Vintners
Andrew Peller Limited
Corby Spirit and Wine Limited
Diamond Estates Wines & Spirits Inc.
Forbidden Spirits Distilling Corp.
Hill Incorporated
SBD Capital Corp.

25501010 Distributors
ADENTRA Inc.
Doman Building Materials Group Ltd.
Goodfellow Inc.
Harrys Manufacturing Inc.
Humble & Fume Inc.
Jewett-Cameron Trading Company Ltd.
Lifeist Wellness Inc.
Taiga Building Products Ltd.

40101010 Diversified Banks
Bank of Montreal
The Bank of Nova Scotia
Canadian Imperial Bank of Commerce
HSBC Bank Canada
Laurentian Bank of Canada
National Bank of Canada
Royal Bank of Canada
The Toronto-Dominion Bank
VersaBank

15101020 Diversified Chemicals
Aluula Composites Inc.
FRX Innovations Inc.
ReGen III Corp.

15104020 Diversified Metals & Mining
AmmPower Corp.
Arctic Fox Lithium Corp.
BacTech Environmental Corporation
Bonanza Mining Corporation
Currie Rose Resources Inc.
5N Plus Inc.
Foraco International S.A.
Generation Gold Corp.
Geodrill Limited
Green River Gold Corp.
Hispania Resources Inc.
IBC Advanced Alloys Corp.
International Zeolite Corp.
Kintavar Exploration Inc.
Lomiko Metals Inc.
Major Drilling Group International Inc.
Manganese X Energy Corp.
Mason Graphite Inc.
Norsemont Mining Inc.
Platinex Inc.
Radius Gold Inc.
RecycLiCo Battery Materials Inc.
Royalties Inc.
Sherritt International Corporation
Silver Bullet Mines Corp.
Southern Arc Minerals Inc.
Sparton Resources Inc.
Spearmint Resources Inc.
St-Georges Eco-Mining Corp.
Stria Lithium Inc.
Three Valley Copper Corp.
Trench Metals Corp.
Ucore Rare Metals Inc.
Vanadiumcorp Resource Inc.
Volt Carbon Technologies Inc.
Windfall Geotek Inc.

60201010 Diversified Real Estate Activities
DREAM Unlimited Corp.

60101010 Diversified REITs
Artis Real Estate Investment Trust
BTB Real Estate Investment Trust
H&R Real Estate Investment Trust
Melcor Real Estate Investment Trust
Morguard Real Estate Investment Trust
PRO Real Estate Investment Trust

20201070 Diversified Support Services
Affinor Growers Inc.
Bee Vectoring Technologies International Inc.
Black Diamond Group Limited
Boyd Group Services Inc.
Ceres Global Ag Corp.
Dexterra Group Inc.
Everyday People Financial Corp.
FTI Foodtech International Inc.
GDI Integrated Facility Services Inc.
K-Bro Linen Inc.
Mission Ready Solutions Inc.
RB Global, Inc.
RediShred Capital Corp.
Starrex International Ltd.
Wildpack Beverage Inc.

30101010 Drug Retail
CareRx Corporation
Goodness Growth Holdings Inc.
ManifestSeven Holdings Corporation
Mednow Inc.
Neighbourly Pharmacy Inc.
Quizam Media Corporation
StateHouse Holdings Inc
Vibe Growth Corporation

25302010 Education Services
China Education Resources Inc.
Everybody Loves Languages Corp.
Global Education Communities Corp.
Visionary Education Technology Holdings Group Inc.

55101010 Electric Utilities
Altius Renewable Royalties Corp.
Caribbean Utilities Company, Ltd.
Emera Incorporated
Fortis Inc.
Hydro One Limited
New Brunswick Power Corporation
Nova Scotia Power Incorporated
Ontario Power Generation Inc.
Saskatchewan Power Corporation

20104010 Electrical Components & Equipment
Ballard Power Systems Inc.
Braille Energy Systems Inc.
Cleantech Power Corp.
dynaCERT Inc.
Eguana Technologies Inc.
Electrovaya Inc.
Exro Technologies Inc.
Fuelpositive Corporation
GBLT Corp.
Hammond Manufacturing Company Limited
Hillcrest Energy Technologies Ltd.
Hypercharge Networks Corp.
Li-Metal Corp.
Loop Energy Inc.
NEO Battery Materials Ltd.
Nano One Materials Corp.
Novanta Inc.
Pioneering Technology Corp.
PowerTap Hydrogen Capital Corp.
SPARQ Systems Inc.
Zinc8 Energy Solutions Inc.

45203015 Electronic Components
American Aires Inc.
Danavation Technologies Corp.
Firan Technology Group Corporation
PR Technology Inc.
Valdor Technology International Inc.
Ynvisible Interactive Inc.
ZTEST Electronics Inc.

45203010 Electronic Equipment & Instruments
AI/ML Innovations Inc.
ATI AirTest Technologies Inc.
Aurora Solar Technologies Inc.
Cannabix Technologies Inc.
Clear Blue Technologies International Inc.
Eddy Smart Home Solutions Ltd.
Frequency Exchange Corp.
Kontrol Technologies Corp.
Legend Power Systems Inc.
Midwest Energy Emissions Corp.

Nanalysis Scientific Corp.
NexOptic Technology Corp.
Ocumetics Technology Corp.
Quarterhill Inc.
SQI Diagnostics Inc.
Smartcool Systems Inc.
Tantalus Systems Holding Inc.
Titan Logix Corp.

45203020 Electronic Manufacturing Services

Celestica Inc.

20201050 Environmental & Facilities Services

Anaergia Inc.
BQE Water Inc.
BluMetric Environmental Inc.
Canadian Oil Recovery & Remediation Enterprises Ltd.
Cielo Waste Solutions Corp.
Current Water Technologies Inc.
Earthworks Industries Inc.
Ecolomondo Corporation
Environmental Waste International Inc.
Full Circle Lithium Corp.
GFL Environmental Inc.
PlasCred Circular Innovations Inc.
Questor Technology Inc.
Sharc International Systems Inc.
Sparta Capital Ltd.
Vertex Resource Group Ltd.
Waste Connections, Inc.

15101030 Fertilizers & Agricultural Chemicals

Argo Living Soils Corp.
EarthRenew Inc.
Itafos Inc.
MustGrow Biologics Corp.
Nutrien Ltd.
Progressive Planet Solutions Inc.
Western Resources Corp.

40203040 Financial Exchanges & Data

BIGG Digital Assets Inc.
Cascadia Blockchain Group Corp.
Fineqia International Inc.
The INX Digital Company, Inc.
TMX Group Limited
WonderFi Technologies Inc.

30101020 Food Distributors

Astron Connect Inc.
Colabor Group Inc.
Organto Foods Inc.
Sweet Poison Spirits Inc.

30101030 Food Retail

Alimentation Couche-Tard Inc.
DAVIDsTEA INC.
Empire Company Limited
Loblaw Companies Limited
Lords & Company Worldwide Holdings Inc.
METRO Inc.
The North West Company Inc.
ORAGIN Foods Inc.
Two Hands Corporation
Vegano Foods Inc.
Veji Holdings Ltd.
George Weston Limited

25203020 Footwear

Grounded People Apparel Inc.

15105010 Forest Products

Acadian Timber Corp.
Atlas Engineered Products Ltd.
Big Tree Carbon Inc.
Canfor Corporation
Conifex Timber Inc.
GreenFirst Forest Products Inc.
Interfor Corporation
Klimat X Developments Inc.
Stella-Jones Inc.
West Fraser Timber Co. Ltd.
Western Forest Products Inc.

55102010 Gas Utilities

AltaGas Ltd.
CF Energy Corp.
Superior Plus Corp.

15104030 Gold

Cerrado Gold Inc.
Goldcliff Resource Corporation

35102010 Health Care Distributors

Medexus Pharmaceuticals Inc.
Quipt Home Medical Corp.
Relevium Technologies Inc.
Therma Bright Inc.

35101010 Health Care Equipment

Aquarius Surgical Technologies Inc.
Aurora Spine Corporation
Avricore Health Inc.
CVR Medical Corp.
Cloud DX Inc.
Covalon Technologies Ltd.
DiagnaMed Holdings Corp.
Hamilton Thorne Ltd.
Hapbee Technologies, Inc.
Imagin Medical Inc.
Imaging Dynamics Company Ltd.
Izotropic Corporation
MedX Health Corp.
MyndTec Inc.
NuGen Medical Devices Inc.
Opsens Inc.
Perimeter Medical Imaging AI, Inc.
Predictmedix AI Inc.
Profound Medical Corp.
RYAH Group, Inc.
Salona Global Medical Device Corporation
Savaria Corporation
Theralase Technologies Inc.
Titan Medical Inc.
VOTI Detection Inc.
VentriPoint Diagnostics Ltd.
Zomedica Corp.

35102020 Health Care Facilities

Chartwell Retirement Residences
Element Lifestyle Retirement Inc.
Extendicare Inc.
Greenbrook TMS Inc.
Medical Facilities Corporation
Sienna Senior Living Inc.

60105010 Health Care REITs

NorthWest Healthcare Properties Real Estate Investment Trust
Pine Trail Real Estate Investment Trust

35102015 Health Care Services

ARCpoint Inc.
Akumin Inc.
Braxia Scientific Corp.
CareSpan Health, Inc.
dentalcorp Holdings Ltd.
Empower Clinics Inc.
Field Trip Health & Wellness Ltd.
Global Health Clinics Ltd.
Jack Nathan Medical Corp.
Justera Health Ltd.
Leveljump Healthcare Corp.
Levitee Labs Inc.
MCI Onehealth Technologies Inc.
Moss Genomics Inc.
NeuPath Health Inc.
Nova Leap Health Corp.
Optimind Pharma Corp.
Pathway Health Corp.
Revitalist Lifestyle and Wellness Ltd.
Skylight Health Group Inc.
TripSitter Clinic Ltd.
Universal Ibogaine Inc.
WELL Health Technologies Corp.

35101020 Health Care Supplies

Bausch + Lomb Corporation
WestBond Enterprises Corporation
Zentek Ltd.

35103010 Health Care Technology

Binovi Technologies Corp.
Carebook Technologies Inc.
CloudMD Software & Services Inc.
Cognetivity Neurosciences Ltd.
Comprehensive Healthcare Systems Inc.
Diagnos Inc.
Dialogue Health Technologies Inc.
Empatho Holdings Inc.
EvokAI Creative Labs Inc.
Highmark Interactive Inc.
Hydreight Technologies Inc.
InMed Pharmaceuticals Inc.
KDA Group Inc.
Kovo Healthtech Corporation
LifeSpeak Inc.
Medivolve Inc.
nDatalyze Corp.
NetraMark Holdings Inc.
PanGenomic Health Inc.
Reliq Health Technologies Inc.
Sernova Corp.
Telecure Technologies Inc.
Think Research Corporation
Treatment.com International Inc.
UniDoc Health Corp.
Vitalhub Corp.

20104020 Heavy Electrical Equipment

Hammond Power Solutions Inc.

25201020 Home Furnishings

Dorel Industries Inc.

25504030 Home Improvement Retail

BuildDirect.com Technologies Inc.

25504060 Homefurnishing Retail

BMTC Group Inc.
Leon's Furniture Limited
Sleep Country Canada Holdings Inc.

60103010 Hotel & Resort REITs

American Hotel Income Properties REIT LP
NexPoint Hospitality Trust
R&R Real Estate Investment Trust

25301020 Hotels, Resorts & Cruise Lines

Civeo Corporation
Spacefy Inc.
Transat A.T. Inc.
ZoomAway Technologies Inc.

25201040 Household Appliances

Brüush Oral Care Inc.

30301010 Household Products

Ambari Brands Inc.
BIOSENTA Inc.
CleanGo Innovations Inc.
International Parkside Products Inc.

MAV Beauty Brands Inc.
Mary Agrotechnologies Inc.
NAVCO Pharmaceuticals Inc.
Pure to Pure Beauty Inc.
SureNano Science Ltd.
Way of Will Inc.

25201050 Housewares & Specialties

TILT Holdings Inc.
Vitreous Glass Inc.

20202010 Human Resource & Employment Services

The Caldwell Partners International Inc.
Hire Technologies Inc.
Premier Health of America Inc.

55105010 Independent Power Producers & Energy Traders

Capital Power Corporation
Maxim Power Corp.
TransAlta Corporation

20105010 Industrial Conglomerates

Brookfield Business Partners L.P.
Decisive Dividend Corporation

15101040 Industrial Gases

Charbone Hydrogen Corporation

20106020 Industrial Machinery & Supplies & Components

ATS Corporation
Aduro Clean Technologies Inc.
Appulse Corporation
Atmofizer Technologies Inc.
Biorem Inc.
California Nanotechnologies Corp.
Composite Alliance Group Inc.
EnWave Corporation
Exco Technologies Limited
Forward Water Technologies Corp.
Greenlane Renewables Inc.
H2O Innovation Inc.
HPQ Silicon Inc.
Inventronics Limited
Next Hydrogen Solutions Inc.
Pool Safe Inc.
PyroGenesis Canada Inc.
Reko International Group Inc.
Targeted Microwave Solutions Inc.
TerraVest Industries Inc.
Thermal Energy International Inc.
Velan Inc.

60102510 Industrial REITs

AIP Realty Trust
Dream Industrial Real Estate Investment Trust
Granite Real Estate Investment Trust
Nova Net Lease REIT

60101020 Industrial REITs - discontinued 03/17/2023

Nexus Industrial REIT

10102010 Integrated Oil & Gas

Imperial Oil Limited
Suncor Energy Inc.

50101020 Integrated Telecommunication Services

Adamant Holdings Inc.
Adya Inc.
BCE Inc.
TELUS Corporation
TeraGo Inc.
Uniserve Communications Corp.

50202020 Interactive Home Entertainment

AlphaGen Intelligence Corp.
Backstageplay Inc.
East Side Games Group Inc.
ePlay Digital Inc.
GameOn Entertainment Technologies Inc.
GameSquare Holdings, Inc.
Good Gamer Entertainment Inc.
KuuHubb Inc.
Playground Ventures Inc.
PopReach Corporation
Royal Wins Corporation
TGS Esports Inc.

50203010 Interactive Media & Services

ApartmentLove Inc.
Champion Gaming Group Inc.
Darelle Online Solutions Inc.
EarthLabs Inc.
Enthusiast Gaming Holdings Inc.
Gamelancer Media Corp.
illumin Holdings Inc.
Legible Inc.
Personas Social Incorporated
Playmaker Capital Inc.
Sabio Holdings Inc.

45102030 Internet Services & Infrastructure

AMPD Ventures Inc.
BBTV Holdings Inc.
Fobi AI Inc.
ICEsoft Technologies Canada Corp.
ImagineAR Inc.
Ivrnet Inc.
mdf commerce inc.
NameSilo Technologies Corp.
Optiva Inc.
ShiftCarbon Inc.
Shopify Inc.
Sphere 3D Corporation
Tucows Inc.
Turnium Technology Group Inc.
VSBLTY Groupe Technologies Corp.

40203020 Investment Banking & Brokerage

Base Carbon Inc.
Canaccord Genuity Group Inc.
DelphX Capital Markets Inc.
FRNT Financial Inc.
Galaxy Digital Holdings Ltd.
Hampton Financial Corporation
Mackenzie Master Limited Partnership
Ostrom Climate Solutions Inc.
Raffles Financial Group Limited

45102010 IT Consulting & Other Services

Alithya Group inc.
AnalytixInsight Inc.
CGI Inc.
Calian Group Ltd.
Converge Technology Solutions Corp.
Cybeats Technologies Corp.
genifi inc.
IGEN Networks Corp.
Memex Inc.
NTG Clarity Networks Inc.
Nerds On Site Inc.
Predictiv AI Inc.
Scryb Inc.
Softchoice Corporation
Sparc AI Inc.
Urbanimmersive Inc.
Voice Mobility International, Inc.
YANGAROO Inc.

25301030 Leisure Facilities

Canlan Ice Sports Corp.
Pathfinder Ventures Inc.
TWC Enterprises Limited
XR Immersive Tech Inc.

25202010 Leisure Products

BRP Inc.
Jackpot Digital Inc.
SWMBRD Sports Inc.
Spin Master Corp.
TUT Fitness Group Inc.
Taiga Motors Corporation

40301020 Life & Health Insurance

E-L Financial Corporation Limited
Great-West Lifeco Inc.
iA Financial Corporation Inc.
Manulife Financial Corporation
Power Corporation of Canada
Power Financial Corporation
Sagicor Financial Company Ltd.
Sun Life Financial Inc.

35203010 Life Sciences Tools & Services

AbCellera Biologics Inc.
Principal Technologies Inc.
RepliCel Life Sciences Inc.

35102030 Managed Health Care

NexgenRx Inc.

20305030 Marine Ports & Services

Logistec Corporation
Westshore Terminals Investment Corporation

20303010 Marine Transportation

Algoma Central Corporation

15103010 Metal, Glass & Plastic Containers

CCL Industries Inc.
good natured Products Inc.
Pearl River Holdings Limited
Richards Packaging Income Fund
Transcontinental Inc.
Winpak Ltd.

50202010 Movies & Entertainment

Amcomri Entertainment Inc.
Boat Rocker Media Inc.
Cineplex Inc.
ESE Entertainment Inc.
IMAX Corporation
Lions Gate Entertainment Corp.
Network Media Group Inc.
OverActive Media Corp.
Thunderbird Entertainment Group Inc.
Versus Systems Inc.
WildBrain Ltd.

60106010 Multi-Family Residential REITs

BSR Real Estate Investment Trust
Boardwalk Real Estate Investment Trust
Canadian Apartment Properties Real Estate Investment Trust
Dream Residential Real Estate Investment Trust
European Residential Real Estate Investment Trust
InterRent Real Estate Investment Trust
Killam Apartment Real Estate Investment Trust
Lanesborough Real Estate Investment Trust
Marwest Apartment Real Estate Investment Trust
Minto Apartment Real Estate Investment Trust
Morguard North American Residential Real Estate Investment Trust
Northview Residential REIT
Sun Residential Real Estate Investment Trust

40201030 Multi-Sector Holdings

Fairfax India Holdings Corporation
Helios Fairfax Partners Corporation

Highwood Asset Management Ltd.
Premier Diversified Holdings Inc.

55103010 Multi-Utilities

ATCO Ltd.
Algonquin Power & Utilities Corp.
Brookfield Infrastructure Partners L.P.
CU Inc.
Canadian Utilities Limited

99999999 Non-classifiable

A-Labs Capital II Corp.
A-Labs Capital IV Corp.
A-Labs Capital V Corp.
A2ZCryptocap Inc.
AADirection Capital Corp.
AAJ Capital 3 Corp.
AD4 Capital Corp.
AF2 Capital Corp.
AIM5 Ventures Inc.
AIM6 Ventures Inc.
ALDD Ventures Corp.
AMG Acquisition Corp.
AZN Capital Corp.
Aardvark 2 Capital Corp.
Adagio Capital Inc.
Advanced Proteome Therapeutics Corporation
Agrinam Acquisition Corporation
Albatros Acquisition Corporation Inc.
Alset Capital Inc.
Altina Capital Corp.
Amego Capital Corp.
American Biofuels Inc.
Anacott Acquisition Corporation
Aneesh Capital Corp.
Ankh II Capital Inc.
Ankh Capital Inc.
Anquiro Ventures Ltd.
Antera Ventures II Corp.
Apolo IV Acquisition Corp.
Argo Opportunity Corp.
Arkadia Capital Corp.
Aster Acquisition Corp.
Atlas One Capital Corporation
Atoro Capital Corp.
Audrey Capital Corporation
Auka Capital Corp.
Aurum Lake Mining Corporation
Auston Capital Corp.
Axe2 Acquisitions Inc.
Badger Capital Corp.
Baltic I Acquisition Corp.
Baymount Incorporated
Beretta Ventures Ltd.
Better Plant Sciences Inc.
Beyond Medical Technologies Inc.
Bigstack Opportunities I Inc.
Biome Grow Inc.
Bird River Resources Inc.
BitRush Corp.
Bold Capital Enterprises Ltd.
Bow Lake Capital Corp.
Brachium2 Capital Corp.
Butte Energy Inc.
Buzz Capital Inc.
Buzz Capital 2 Inc.
CNJ Capital Investments Inc.
Can-Gow Capital Inc.
Canaccord Genuity G Ventures Corp.
Cann-Is Capital Corp.
Canna 8 Investment Trust
Caplink Ventures Inc.
CarbonTech Capital Corp.
Carcetti Capital Corp.
Castlebar Capital Corp.
Castlecap Capital Inc.
Cavalry Capital Corp.
Celestial Acquisition Corp.
Chicane Capital I Corp.
China Keli Electric Company Ltd.
Cinaport Acquisition Corp. III
Clover Leaf Capital Corp.
Compass Venture Inc.
Constellation Capital Corp.
Cranstown Capital Corp.
Crossover Acquisitions Inc.
Cuspis Capital II Ltd.
Cuspis Capital III Ltd.
DGL Investments No.1 Inc.
DXI Capital Corp.
Dash Capital Corp.
Daura Capital Corp.
Deal Pro Capital Corporation
Departure Bay Capital Corp.
Dominus Acquisitions Corp.
Draxos Capital Corp.
Drummond Ventures Corp.
ECC Ventures 4 Corp.
ECC Ventures 5 Corp.
ECC Ventures 6 Corp.
EVP Capital Inc.
EXMceuticals Inc.
Eastower Wireless Inc.
Endurance Capital Corp.
Eureka Capital Corp.
eXeBlock Technology Corporation
Exelerate Capital Corp.
FG Acquisition Corp.
Faction Investment Group Corp.
Fairplay Ventures Inc.
Farstarcap Investment Corp.
Fibre-Crown Manufacturing Inc.
Fife Capital Corp.
First and Goal Capital Corp.
First Responder Technologies Inc.
First Tidal Acquisition Corp.
5D Acquisition Corp.
Florence One Capital Inc.
FluroTech Ltd.
Fountainhall Capital Corp.
Four Arrows Capital Corp.
Fraser Mackenzie Accelerator Corp.
GABY Inc.
GHP Noetic Science-Psychedelic Pharma Inc.
GOLO Mobile Inc.
G2M Cap Corp.
Galaxy Ventures Inc.
Gencan Capital Inc.
Genesis AI Corp.
Genesis Acquisition Corp.
Gentor Resources Inc.
Global Investments Capital Corp.
Global UAV Technologies Ltd.
GlobalBlock Digital Asset Trading Limited
Glorious Creation Limited
Golden Star Capital Ventures Inc.
Goodbridge Capital Corp.
Good2Go4 Corp.
Gourmet Ocean Products Inc.
Green Panda Capital Corp.
Grosvenor CPC I Inc.
Gstaad Capital Corp.
H2 Ventures 1 Inc.
Hakken Capital Corp.
Hansco Capital Corp.
Harmony Acquisitions Corp.
Haviland Enviro Corp.
Haw Capital 2 Corp.
Health Logic Interactive Inc.
High Mountain 2 Capital Corporation
Hopefield Ventures Two Inc.
Hoshi Resource Corp.
Hydaway Ventures Corp.
ICWHY Capital Ventures Inc.
IDG Holdings Inc.
Icarus Capital Corp.
Ikigai Capital Corp.
Impact Acquisitions Corp.
Inceptus Capital Ltd.
Intertidal Capital Corp.
Iocaste Ventures Inc.
J4 Ventures Inc.
JM Capital II Corp.
JVR Ventures Inc.
Jabbo Capital Corp.
Jade Power Trust
Jesmond Capital Ltd.
KMT-Hansa Corp.
Kalma Capital Corp.
Kalon Acquisition Corp.
Kelly Ventures Ltd.
Keon Capital Inc.
Kua Investments Inc.
Kure Technologies, Inc.
LDB Capital Corp.
Left Field Capital Corp.
Lendified Holdings Inc.
LexaGene Holdings Inc.
Lincoln Ventures Ltd.
Little Fish Acquisition I Corp.
Logica Ventures Corp.
M3 Capital Corp.
MDK Acquisition Inc.
MX Gold Corp.
Mandala Capital Inc.
Mandeville Ventures Inc.
Many Bright Ideas Technologies Inc.
Mapath Capital Corp.
Mayfair Acquisition Corporation
Meed Growth Corp.
Mega View Digital Entertainment Corp.
Meraki Acquisition One, Inc.
Michichi Capital Corp.
Midasco Capital Corp.
Mind Cure Health Inc.
Miza III Ventures Inc.
Mojave Brands Inc.
Monaghan Capital Fund Ltd.
Monarch West Ventures Inc.
Moon River Capital Ltd.
Must Capital Inc.
NL2 Capital Inc.
Nabati Foods Global Inc.
Navigator Acquisition Corp.
New Frontier Ventures Inc.
New Media Capital 2.0 Inc.
Noble Iron Inc.
Nurcapital Corporation Ltd.
ONEnergy Inc.
Ocean Shore Capital Corp.
Odessa Capital Ltd.
Opensesame Acquisition Corp.
Ord Mountain Resources Corp.
Orion Nutraceuticals Inc.
Osisko Green Acquisition Limited
PC 1 Corp.
POCML 7 Inc.
Pacific GeoInfo Corp.
Panorama Capital Corp.
Pardus Ventures Inc.
Peak Discovery Capital Ltd.
Penbar Capital Ltd.
Pender Street Capital Corp.
Pentagon I Capital Corp.
Planet X Capital Corp.
Planet X II Capital Corp.
Prestwick Capital Corporation Limited
Proton Capital Corp.
Quinto Resources Inc.

Raging Rhino Capital Corp.
Railtown Capital Corp.
Red Rock Capital Corp.
Reem Capital Corp.
Riverwalk Acquisition Corp.
Rockport Capital Corp.
Ronin Ventures Corp.
Roshni Capital Inc.
Rumbu Holdings Ltd.
Rupert's Crossing Capital Inc.
SIQ Mountain Industries Inc.
St. Davids Capital Inc.
Samurai Capital Corp.
Sanibel Ventures Corp.
Savanna Capital Corp.
Sayward Capital Corp.
Scaling Capital 1 Corp.
Sceptre Ventures Inc.
Schwabo Capital Corporation
Searchlight Innovations Inc.
Seven Oaks Capital Corp.
ShellRon Capital Ltd.
Shine Box Capital Corp.
Shooting Star Acquisition Corp.
Sleeping Giant Capital Corp.
Smartset Services Inc.
Smithe Resources Corp.
Solid Impact Investments Corp.
Space Kingdom Digital Capital Corp.
Spectre Capital Corp.
Spitfyre Capital Inc.
Steep Hill Inc.
Sunniva Inc.
Sunshine Agri-Tech Inc.
TUP Capital Inc.
Tiidal Gaming Group Corp.
Timeless Capital Corp.
Torchlight Innovations Inc.
Toronto Cleantech Capital Inc.
Totally Hip Technologies Inc.
Trail Blazer Capital Corp.
Trail Blazing Ventures Ltd.
Transition Opportunities Corp.
Treviso Capital Corp.
Trillium Acquisition Corp.
Trilogy International Partners Inc.
Universal PropTech Inc.
Upstart Investments Inc.
VM Hotel Acquisition Corp.
Valencia Capital Inc.
Verisante Technology, Inc.
Veteran Capital Corp.
Victory Opportunities 1 Corp.
WSM Ventures Corp.
Wangton Capital Corp.
Whatcom Capital II Corp.
Whitewater Acquisition Corp.
Wittering Capital Corp.
Woodbridge Ventures II Inc.
X1 Entertainment Group Inc.
Yongsheng Capital Inc.
Yubba Capital Corp.
Zenith Capital Corporation
Zidane Capital Corp.
Zoglo's Food Corp.

60104010 Office REITs

Allied Properties Real Estate Investment Trust
Dream Office Real Estate Investment Trust
Inovalis Real Estate Investment Trust
True North Commercial Real Estate Investment Trust

60101040 Office REITs - discontinued 03/17/2023

Slate Office Real Estate Investment Trust

10101010 Oil & Gas Drilling

AKITA Drilling Ltd.
Cathedral Energy Services Ltd.
Ensign Energy Services Inc.
PHX Energy Services Corp.
Precision Drilling Corporation
Total Energy Services Inc.

10101020 Oil & Gas Equipment & Services

CES Energy Solutions Corp.
CWC Energy Services Corp.
Calfrac Well Services Ltd.
Cleantek Industries Inc.
Divergent Energy Services Corp.
Enerflex Ltd.
Essential Energy Services Ltd.
FLINT Corp.
High Arctic Energy Services Inc.
McCoy Global Inc.
NXT Energy Solutions Inc.
North American Construction Group Ltd.
Pason Systems Inc.
Pulse Seismic Inc.
STEP Energy Services Ltd.
Secure Energy Services Inc.
Shawcor Ltd.
Stampede Drilling Inc.
Trican Well Service Ltd.
Wavefront Technology Solutions Inc.
Western Energy Services Corp.
Wolverine Energy and Infrastructure Inc.

10102020 Oil & Gas Exploration & Production

EF EnergyFunders Ventures, Inc.
Frontera Energy Corporation
G2 Energy Corp.
Jericho Energy Ventures Inc.
Kiwetinohk Energy Corp.
MEG Energy Corp.
Matachewan Consolidated Mines, Limited
Metalore Resources Limited
Razor Energy Corp.

10102030 Oil & Gas Refining & Marketing

Parkland Corporation
Tidewater Renewables Ltd.

10102040 Oil & Gas Storage & Transportation

Brookfield Infrastructure Corporation
Enbridge Inc.
Gibson Energy Inc.
Keyera Corp.
Pembina Pipeline Corporation
TC Energy Corporation
Tidewater Midstream and Infrastructure Ltd.

60108010 Other Specialized REITs

Automotive Properties Real Estate Investment Trust

25504040 Other Specialty Retail

Birks Group Inc.
CLS Holdings USA, Inc.
CanaFarma Hemp Products Corp.
Captor Capital Corp.
Choom Holdings Inc.
CordovaCann Corp.
Delota Corp.
Delta 9 Cannabis Inc.
Emerge Commerce Ltd.
Friday's Dog Holdings Inc.
Happy Belly Food Group Inc.
Herbal Dispatch Inc.
High Tide Inc.
Indigo Books & Music Inc.
Jushi Holdings Inc.
Kiaro Holdings Corp.
Kits Eyecare Ltd.
LXRandCo, Inc.
MedMen Enterprises Inc.
Nova Cannabis Inc.
1CM Inc.
PeakBirch Commerce Inc.
Pet Valu Holdings Ltd.
Rocky Mountain Liquor Inc.
SNDL Inc.
Shiny Health & Wellness Corp.
Simply Better Brands Corp.
Trees Corporation

30202030 Packaged Foods & Meats

Adaptogenics Health Corp.
Aretto Wellness Inc.
Bettermoo(d) Food Corporation
Beyond Oil Ltd.
BioNeutra Global Corporation
Blender Bites Limited
Boosh Plant-Based Brands Inc.
Burcon NutraScience Corporation
Cannibble Foodtech Ltd.
Canyon Creek Food Company Ltd.
EastWest Bioscience Inc.
Element Nutritional Sciences Inc.
Else Nutrition Holdings Inc.
The Good Flour Corp.
The Good Shroom Co Inc.
GreenSpace Brands Inc.
High Liner Foods Incorporated
Inter-Rock Minerals Inc.
Just Kitchen Holdings Corp.
Komo Plant Based Foods Inc.
Lassonde Industries Inc.
Maple Leaf Foods Inc.
Modern Plant Based Foods Inc.
Naturally Splendid Enterprises Ltd.
Nepra Foods Inc.
Odd Burger Corporation
Pangea Natural Foods Inc.
Planet Based Foods Global Inc.
Plant Veda Foods Ltd.
Plantify Foods, Inc.
The Planting Hope Company Inc.
Pond Technologies Holdings Inc.
Premium Brands Holdings Corporation
Rogers Sugar Inc.
Saputo Inc.
Sensible Meats Inc.
Swiss Water Decaffeinated Coffee Inc.
Ultra Brands Ltd.
Vice Health and Wellness Inc.
The Yumy Candy Company Inc.

15103020 Paper & Plastic Packaging Products & Materials

Cascades Inc.

15105020 Paper Products

Canfor Pulp Products Inc.
KP Tissue Inc.
Nexe Innovations Inc.
Supremex Inc.

20302010 Passenger Airlines

Air Canada
Canada Jetlines Operations Ltd.
Chorus Aviation Inc.
Exchange Income Corporation
Global Crossing Airlines Group Inc.

30302010 Personal Care Products

Irwin Naturals Inc.
Jamieson Wellness Inc.
SLANG Worldwide Inc.

Vitality Products Inc.

35202010 Pharmaceuticals

AREV Life Sciences Global Corp.
Acasti Pharma Inc.
Acreage Holdings, Inc.
Adastra Holdings Ltd.
Aequus Pharmaceuticals Inc.
Aion Therapeutic Inc.
Akanda Corp.
Albert Labs International Corp.
Aleafia Health Inc.
Algernon Pharmaceuticals Inc.
Alpha Cognition Inc.
Antibe Therapeutics Inc.
Appili Therapeutics Inc.
Arbutus Biopharma Corporation
Ascend Wellness Holdings, Inc.
Atlas Global Brands Inc.
Aurora Cannabis Inc.
Australis Capital Inc.
Auxly Cannabis Group Inc.
Avant Brands Inc.
Avicanna Inc.
Avivagen Inc.
Awakn Life Sciences Corp.
Ayr Wellness Inc.
Ayurcann Holdings Corp.
The BC Bud Corporation
BC Craft Supply Co. Ltd.
BZAM Ltd.
Bausch Health Companies Inc.
Bhang Inc.
BioHarvest Sciences Inc.
Biomind Labs Inc.
BioSyent Inc.
Blueberries Medical Corp.
Body and Mind Inc.
Bright Minds Biosciences Inc.
C21 Investments Inc.
CBD Global Sciences Inc.
CRAFT 1861 Global Holdings Inc.
CanadaBis Capital Inc.
Cannara Biotech Inc.
Canntab Therapeutics Limited
Canopy Growth Corporation
Cansortium Inc.
Cardiol Therapeutics Inc.
Chalice Brands Ltd.
Charlotte's Web Holdings, Inc.
Christina Lake Cannabis Corp.
Cipher Pharmaceuticals Inc.
City View Green Holdings Inc.
Clearmind Medicine Inc.
Clever Leaves Holdings Inc.
Columbia Care Inc.
Core One Labs Inc.
Craftport Cannabis Corp.
Crescita Therapeutics Inc.
Cresco Labs Inc.
Cronos Group Inc.
Curaleaf Holdings, Inc.
Cybin Inc.
DRI Healthcare Trust
Decibel Cannabis Company Inc.
Delivra Health Brands Inc.
Devonian Health Group Inc.
Doseology Sciences Inc.
Eastwood Bio-Medical Canada Inc.
Emergence Global Enterprises Inc.
Entourage Health Corp.
Eupraxia Pharmaceuticals Inc.
Eve & Co Incorporated
FSD Pharma Inc.
Filament Health Corp.
Flora Growth Corp.
Flower One Holdings Inc.
4Front Ventures Corp.
Gaia Grow Corp.
Genix Pharmaceuticals Corporation
Glass House Brands Inc.
Glow LifeTech Corp.
Gnomestar Craft Inc.
Gold Flora Corporation
Green Thumb Industries Inc.
Grey Wolf Animal Health Corp.
Grown Rogue International Inc.
HAVN Life Sciences Inc.
HLS Therapeutics Inc.
HTC Purenergy Inc.
Halo Collective Inc.
The Hash Corporation
Helix BioPharma Corp.
Hemostemix Inc.
Hempsana Holdings Ltd.
Heritage Cannabis Holdings Corp.
IM Cannabis Corp.
iAnthus Capital Holdings, Inc.
Indigenous Bloom Hemp Corp.
Indiva Limited
InnoCan Pharma Corporation
IntelliPharmaCeutics International Inc.
Ionic Brands Corp.
Isracann Biosciences Inc.
Jolt Health Inc.
Juva Life Inc.
Khiron Life Sciences Corp.
Knight Therapeutics Inc.
LSL Pharma Group Inc.
LeanLife Health Inc.
Leef Brands Inc.
Lobe Sciences Ltd.
Lotus Ventures Inc.
Lowell Farms Inc.
Lumiera Health Inc.
MPX International Corporation
MTL Cannabis Corp.
MYND Life Sciences Inc.
Maple Leaf Green World Inc.
MariMed Inc.
Marvel Biosciences Corp.
Maven Brands Inc.
Medcolcanna Organics Inc.
Medicenna Therapeutics Corp.
Medicine Man Technologies, Inc.
Medicure Inc.
MediPharm Labs Corp.
Milestone Pharmaceuticals Inc.
Mind Medicine (MindMed) Inc.
MindBio Therapeutics Corp.
Mindset Pharma Inc.
Mountain Valley MD Holdings Inc.
Mydecine Innovations Group Inc.
Nass Valley Gateway Ltd.
Neptune Wellness Solutions Inc.
NervGen Pharma Corp.
Nextleaf Solutions Ltd.
Nirvana Life Sciences Inc.
Nova Mentis Life Science Corp.
NurExone Biologic Inc.
1933 Industries Inc.
Optima Medical Innovations Corp.
Optimi Health Corp.
OrganiGram Holdings Inc.
Ovation Science Inc.
PharmaCielo Ltd.
Pharmadrug Inc.
Pharmala Biotech Holdings Inc.
PharmaTher Holdings Ltd.
Planet 13 Holdings Inc.
PlantFuel Life Inc.
Poko Innovations Inc.
PreveCeutical Medical Inc.
PsyBio Therapeutics Corp.
Psyence Group Inc.
Pure Extracts Technologies Corp.
RIV Capital Inc.
Ramm Pharma Corp.
Red Light Holland Corp.
Red White & Bloom Brands Inc.
Repare Therapeutics Inc.
Resverlogix Corp.
Revive Therapeutics Ltd.
Rubicon Organics Inc.
Satellos Bioscience Inc.
Silo Wellness Inc.
Small Pharma Inc.
Sproutly Canada, Inc.
Stem Holdings, Inc.
THC BioMed Intl Ltd.
TRYP Therapeutics Inc.
Telescope Innovations Corp.
TerrAscend Corp.
Tetra Bio-Pharma Inc.
Thiogenesis Therapeutics, Corp.
Tilray Brands, Inc.
Transcanna Holdings Inc.
Trulieve Cannabis Corp.
Valeo Pharma Inc.
Verano Holdings Corp.
Vertical Peak Holdings Inc.
Voyageur Pharmaceuticals Ltd.
The Well Told Company Inc.
West Island Brands Inc.
XBiotech Inc.
XORTX Therapeutics Inc.
Xenon Pharmaceuticals Inc.
Yooma Wellness Inc.
YourWay Cannabis Brands Inc.
ZYUS Life Sciences Corporation

15104040 Precious Metals & Minerals

Lucara Diamond Corp.

40301040 Property & Casualty Insurance

Co-operators General Insurance Company
Definity Financial Corporation
Fairfax Financial Holdings Limited
Intact Financial Corporation
Trisura Group Ltd.

50201040 Publishing

Armada Data Corporation
FP Newspapers Inc.
Glacier Media Inc.
Postmedia Network Canada Corp.
Yellow Pages Limited

20304010 Rail Transportation

Canadian National Railway Company
Canadian Pacific Kansas City Limited

60201030 Real Estate Development

Captiva Verde Wellness Corp.
Genesis Land Development Corp.
Greenbank Ventures Inc.
Greenbriar Capital Corp.
Melcor Developments Ltd.
Realia Properties Inc.

60201020 Real Estate Operating Companies

The Becker Milk Company Limited
Brookfield Office Properties Inc.
Brookfield Property Preferred L.P.
Brookfield Property Split Corp.
Coho Collective Kitchens Inc.
Comet Industries Ltd.
Dream Impact Trust
Emergia Inc.
Gulf & Pacific Equities Corp.
Halmont Properties Corporation

Imperial Equities Inc.
Invesque Inc.
Kadestone Capital Corp.
Madison Pacific Properties Inc.
Mainstreet Equity Corp.
Mongolia Growth Group Ltd.
Morguard Corporation
NexLiving Communities Inc.
NextGen Food Robotics Corp.
Parkit Enterprise Inc.
Regent Pacific Properties Inc.
Starlight U.S. Multi-Family (No. 2) Core Plus Fund
Starlight U.S. Residential Fund
StorageVault Canada Inc.
Tempus Capital Inc.
Tricon Residential Inc.
Urbanfund Corp.
Wall Financial Corporation
Yorkton Equity Group Inc.

60201040 Real Estate Services

Altus Group Limited
Bridgemarq Real Estate Services Inc.
Colliers International Group Inc.
FirstService Corporation
The Real Brokerage Inc.
Real Matters Inc.
Tribe Property Technologies Inc.

40101015 Regional Banks

Canadian Western Bank

40301050 Reinsurance

Brookfield Reinsurance Ltd.

55105020 Renewable Electricity

Alaska Hydro Corporation
Boralex Inc.
British Columbia Hydro and Power Authority
Brookfield Renewable Corporation
Brookfield Renewable Partners L.P.
Brookfield Renewable Power Preferred Equity Inc.
Capstone Infrastructure Corporation
EverGen Infrastructure Corp.
Hydro-Québec
Innergex Renewable Energy Inc.
The Manitoba Hydro-Electric Board
Nalcor Energy
Northland Power Inc.
Oceanic Wind Energy Inc.
Polaris Renewable Energy Inc.
RE Royalties Ltd.
ReVolve Renewable Power Corp.
Solar Alliance Energy Inc.
SolarBank Corporation
Synex Renewable Energy Corporation
TransAlta Renewables Inc.
UGE International Ltd.
Waroona Energy Inc.
Westbridge Renewable Energy Corp.

20202020 Research & Consulting Services

Berkley Renewables Inc.
Britannia Life Sciences Inc.
Deveron Corp.
EGF Theramed Health Corp.
Green Scientific Labs Holdings Inc.
Innovotech Inc.
Intermap Technologies Corporation
Lexston Life Sciences Corp.
Metamaterial Exchangeco Inc.
New Leaf Ventures Inc.
Numinus Wellness Inc.
Quantum eMotion Corp.
Sixth Wave Innovations Inc.
Stantec Inc.
Thomson Reuters Corporation

25301040 Restaurants

A&W Revenue Royalties Income Fund
Aegis Brands Inc.
Boston Pizza Royalties Income Fund
General Assembly Holdings Limited
The Keg Royalties Income Fund
MTY Food Group Inc.
Pizza Pizza Royalty Corp.
Restaurant Brands International Inc.
Restaurant Brands International Limited Partnership
SIR Royalty Income Fund
SPoT Coffee (Canada) Ltd.

60107010 Retail REITs

CT Real Estate Investment Trust
Canadian Net Real Estate Investment Trust
Choice Properties Real Estate Investment Trust
Crombie Real Estate Investment Trust
Firm Capital Property Trust
First Capital Real Estate Investment Trust
Plaza Retail REIT
Primaris Real Estate Investment Trust
RioCan Real Estate Investment Trust
Slate Grocery REIT
SmartCentres Real Estate Investment Trust

20201080 Security & Alarm Services

Avante Corp.
SSC Security Services Corp.
Zedcor Inc.

45301020 Semiconductors

Canadian Solar Inc.
Inspire Semiconductor Holdings Inc.
Micromem Technologies Inc.
POET Technologies Inc.
Spectra7 Microsystems Inc.

15104045 Silver

Andean Precious Metals Corp.

60106020 Single-Family Residential REITs

Flagship Communities Real Estate Investment Trust

30201030 Soft Drinks & Non-alcoholic Beverages

BevCanna Enterprises Inc.
CENTR Brands Corp.
Flow Beverage Corp.
The Fresh Factory B.C. Ltd.
GURU Organic Energy Corp.
Jones Soda Co.
Koios Beverage Corp.
Molecule Holdings Inc.
Primo Water Corporation
The Tinley Beverage Company Inc.
Xebra Brands Ltd.
Yerbaé Brands Corp.

25302020 Specialized Consumer Services

Goodfood Market Corp.
MiniLuxe Holding Corp.
Newtopia Inc.
NextPoint Financial Inc.
Park Lawn Corporation

40201040 Specialized Finance

Accord Financial Corp.
Armada Mercantile Ltd.
Automotive Finco Corp.
Chesswood Group Limited
Crown Capital Partners Inc.
ECN Capital Corp.
Element Fleet Management Corp.
Fountain Asset Corp.
IOU Financial Inc.
Richco Investors Inc.
Trenchant Capital Corp.
XS Financial Inc.

15101050 Specialty Chemicals

Black Swan Graphene Inc.
G6 Materials Corp.
Graphene Manufacturing Group Ltd.
HydroGraph Clean Power Inc.
NanoXplore Inc.
Oceansix Future Paths Ltd.
Strong Global Entertainment, Inc.

15104050 Steel

Algoma Steel Group Inc.
Century Global Commodities Corporation
Stelco Holdings Inc.
Tree Island Steel Ltd.

45103020 Systems Software

BlackBerry Limited
LeoNovus Inc.
Sekur Private Data Ltd.

45202030 Technology Hardware, Storage & Peripherals

A2Z Smart Technologies Corp.
POSaBIT Systems Corporation
Tinkerine Studios Ltd.

25203030 Textiles

Fab-Form Industries Ltd.

40102010 Thrifts & Mortgage Finance - discontinued 03/17/2023

EQB Inc.

25101020 Tires & Rubber

AirBoss of America Corp.

30203010 Tobacco

The Hempshire Group, Inc.

20107010 Trading Companies & Distributors

Bri-Chem Corp.
Diversified Royalty Corp.
Enterprise Group, Inc.
Finning International Inc.
Nevis Brands Inc.
Richelieu Hardware Ltd.
Russel Metals Inc.
Toromont Industries Ltd.
Viemed Healthcare, Inc.
Wajax Corporation

40201060 Transaction & Payment Processing Services

Advantex Marketing International Inc.
Bitcoin Well Inc.
Blockmate Ventures Inc.
Clip Money Inc.
Currency Exchange International, Corp.
Fintech Select Ltd.
GoldMoney Inc.
The Mint Corporation
Payfare Inc.
SQID Technologies Limited
XTM Inc.

55104010 Water Utilities

Green Impact Partners Inc.
Prime Drink Group Corp.
Water Ways Technologies Inc.

50102010 Wireless Telecommunication Services

GINSMS Inc.
Rift Valley Resources Corp.

General Index

In response to customer requests, we have added page numbers to the index in addition to the alpha-numeric designation (e.g., A.1, A.2, A.3). Each principal company and its subsidiaries carry the same alpha-numeric designation, along with the page number on which the company's principal coverage is found.

For example, if Canadian Utilities Limited is a principal company with the alpha-numeric designation C.46, with coverage beginning on page 254. All subsidiaries of Canadian Utilities Limited are indexed to C.46 as well on page 254. In addition, Canadian Utilities Limited is also referenced under coverage A.29 on page 53, since it is a subsidiary of ATCO Ltd. and the index shows this information as well.

The designation ALR refers to AT LAST REPORT, a list of companies from which information is solicited but for which limited information is available and companies which are delisted or in receivership. An alphabetical listing of these companies is found in a separate section of this book, beginning on page 1167.

A

B

C

D

E

F

G

H

I

J

K

L

M

N

O

P

Q

R

S

T

U

V

W

X

Y

Z

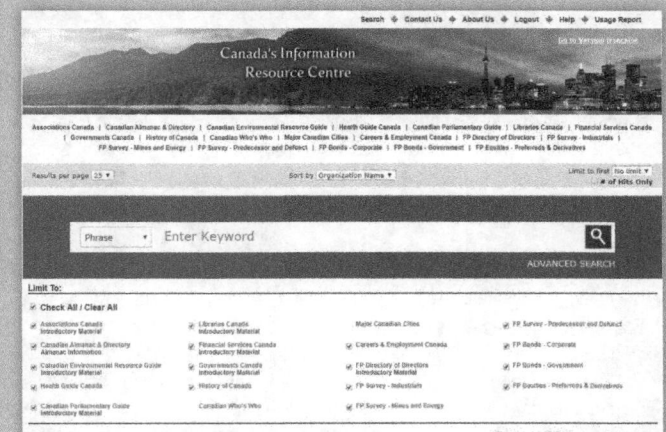

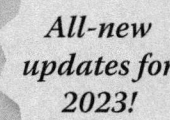

CENTRE DE DOCUMENTATION DU CANADA (CDC)

Consultez en tout temps toutes ces excellentes ressources en ligne grâce au Centre de documentation du Canada (CDC) à http://circ.greyhouse.ca

Le Centre de documentation du Canada (CDC) regroupe sous une seule ressource en ligne conviviale tout le contenu des ouvrages de référence primés de Grey House Canada. Répertoriant plus de **100 000 entreprises canadiennes, et plus de 140 600 personnes-ressources**, faits et chiffres, il s'agit de la ressource la plus complète en matière de bases de données spécialisées au Canada! Grâce à l'ajout de sept bases de données, le Canada Info Desk Complete est plus avantageux que jamais alors qu'il coûte 50 % que l'abonnement aux ouvrages individuels. Accédez aux 20 bases de données dès maintenant – le Canadian Info Desk Complete vous offre un ensemble complet!

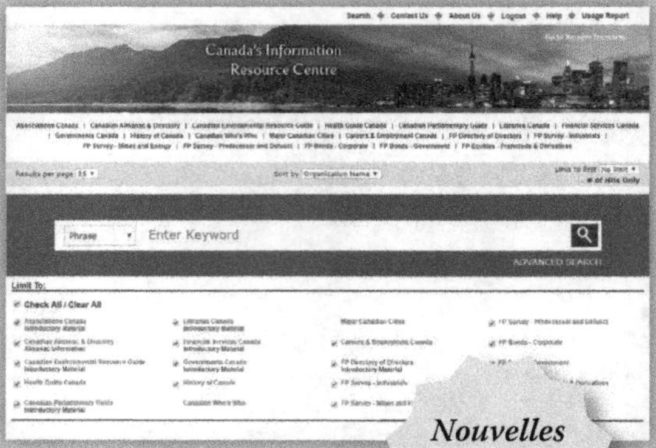

Nouvelles mises à jour pour 2023!

PRINCIPAUX AVANTAGES DU CDC

- Recherche transversale efficace dans le contenu des bases de données
- Sauvegarde des résultats de recherche pour consultation future
- Lien direct aux sites Web et aux adresses électroniques
- Grâce à l'affichage lisible de vos résultats, il est dorénavant plus facile de compiler les résultats ou d'ajouter des critères à vos recherches

CONCEPTION PERSONNALISÉE DE VOS LISTES DE PERSONNES-RESSOURCES!

Le CDC vous permet de définir et d'extraire vos propres listes, et ce, en quelques secondes.
Découvrez des clients potentiels, effectuez des recherches par mot-clé, trouvez les participants à une conférence à venir : l'information dont vous avez besoin, au bout de vos doigts.

CHOISISSEZ ENTRE RECHERCHES MOT-CLÉ ET AVANCÉE!

Grâce au CDC, vous pouvez choisir entre une recherche Mot-clé ou Avancée pour localiser l'information avec précision. Vous avez la possibilité d'effectuer des recherches en texte simple ou booléennes puissantes – les recherches sont conçues à l'intention des chercheurs débutants et avancés.

LES PROFILS DU CDC COMPRENNENT :

- Numéros de téléphone, adresses électroniques, numéros de télécopieur et adresses complètes pour toutes les succursales d'un organisme
- Comptes de médias sociaux, comme Twitter et Facebook
- Personnes-ressources clés en fonction des appellations d'emploi
- Budgets, frais d'adhésion, tailles du personnel et plus!

Effectuez des recherches dans le CDC à l'aide de champs uniques ou communs, personnalisés selon vos besoins!

SEULS LES RÉPERTOIRES DE GREY HOUSE VOUS OFFRENT UN CONTENU PARTICULIER QUE VOUS NE TROUVEREZ NULLE PART AILLEURS!

- **Le répertoire des associations du Canada :** sources de financement, activités, publications, congrès, membres, prix, profil de membre
- **Guide parlementaire canadien :** carrières privées et politiques des membres élus, liste complète des comtés et des représentants
- **Services financiers :** type de propriétaire, nombre d'employés, année de la fondation, immobilisations, revenus, symbole au téléscripteur
- **Bibliothèques Canada :** personnel, collections particulières, services, année de la fondation, symbole de bibliothèque national, système régional
- **Gouvernements du Canada :** population municipale
- **Canadian Who's Who :** ville d'origine, publication, formation (diplômes et alma mater), carrière/emploi et employeur
- **Principales villes canadiennes :** données démographiques, ethnicité, immigration, langue, éducation, logement, revenu, main-d'œuvre et transport
- **Guide canadien de la santé :** maladies chroniques et mentales, ressources generales, annexes et statistiques
- **Cannabis au Canada :** type d'entreprise, activité à l'étranger, type de propriété, sources de revenus
- **Guide des ressources environnementales canadiennes :** périmètre organisationnel, budget, nombre d'employés, activités, réglementations, domaines de spécialité environnementale
- **Carrières et emplois Canada :** associations professionnelles, sites Web d'emplois, employeurs, recruteurs, bourses, et emplois d'été
- **Répertoire des administrateurs :** prénom, nom de famille, poste de cadre et d'administrateur, parcours scolaire et professionnel et adresse électronique des cadres supérieurs canadiens; liste des sociétés les plus importantes au Canada et l'information complète des compagnies
- **FPbonds :** information sur les obligations en format PDF, avec tableaux à trier
- **FPsurvey :** profils détaillés de sociétés cotées en bourse et changements organisationnels antérieurs

Le nouveau CDC facilite la recherche au sein de toutes nos ressources au Canada et procure plus rapidement des résultats plus poussés – des associations au gouvernement en passant par les principales entreprises et les zoos, sans oublier tout un éventail d'organisations! Que vous ayez besoin d'information très détaillée au sujet de votre personne-ressource ou d'une simple adresse électronique, vous pouvez personnaliser votre requête afin qu'elle réponde à vos besoins. Contactez-nous sans tarder pour obtenir un **essai gratuit** ou visitez http://circ.greyhouse.ca

GREY HOUSE PUBLISHING CANADA

Pour obtenir plus d'information, veuillez contacter Grey House Publishing Canada

par tél. : 1 866 433-4739 ou 416 644-6479 par téléc. : 416 644-1904 | info@greyhouse.ca | www.greyhouse.ca

Répertoire et almanach canadien

La ressource de référence au sujet des données et des faits relatifs au Canada

Le *Répertoire et almanach canadien* constitue le guide canadien le plus rigoureux depuis 176 ans. Publié annuellement depuis 1847, il est toujours grandement utilisé dans le monde des affaires, les bureaux gouvernementaux, par les spécialistes de l'information, les chercheurs, les éditeurs ou quiconque est à la recherche d'information actuelle et accessible sur tous les sujets imaginables à propos des gens qui vivent et travaillent au Canada.

À la fois répertoire et guide, le *Répertoire et almanach canadien* dresse le tableau le plus complet du Canada, des caractéristiques physiques jusqu'aux revues économique et commerciale, en passant par les loisirs et les activités récréatives. Il combine des documents textuels, des représentations graphiques, des photographies en couleurs et des listes de répertoires accompagnées de profils détaillés. Autant d'information pointue et organisée de manière à ce qu'elle soit facile à obtenir. Le *Répertoire et almanach canadien* foisonne de renseignements généraux. Il présente des statistiques nationales sur la population, l'emploi, l'IPC, l'importation et l'exportation ainsi que des images des prix nationaux, des symboles canadiens, des drapeaux, des emblèmes et des leaders parlementaires canadiens.

Si vous cherchez des personnes-ressources essentielles un peu partout au Canada, peu importe qu'il s'agisse de projets d'affaires ou d'une question factuelle anecdotique, le Répertoire et almanach canadien vous fournira les pistes dont vous ignoriez l'existence – rapidement et facilement!

TOUTE L'INFORMATION DONT VOUS AUREZ BESOIN, ORGANISÉE EN 17 CATÉGORIES DISTINCTES POUR UNE CONSULTATION FACILE!

Almanach—un aperçu informatif du Canada, notamment l'histoire, la géographie, l'économie et les statistiques essentielles.

Arts et culture—comprends 9 sujets, des galeries aux zoos.

Associations—des milliers d'organisations classées selon plus de 120 sujets différents, de l'actuariat au jeunesse.

Radiodiffusion—les principales sociétés de radiodiffusion au Canada, les stations radiophoniques et de télévision ainsi que les entreprises de câblodistribution et les diffuseurs thématiques.

Commerce et finance—comptabilité, services bancaires, assurances, principales entreprises et bourses canadiennes.

Éducation—organisé par province et comprend les arrondissements scolaires, les organismes gouvernementaux, les écoles spécialisées et indépendantes, les universités et les établissements techniques.

Gouvernement—s'étend sur trois sections et comprend un guide de référence, des listes fédérales et provinciales, les comtés et arrondissements municipaux ainsi que les cours canadiennes.

Santé—organismes gouvernementaux, hôpitaux, centres de santé communautaires, établissements de soins pour personnes retraitées et de soins de santé mentale.

Sociétés d'avocats—toutes les principales sociétés d'avocats, suivies des sociétés plus petites, classées par province et en ordre alphabétique.

Bibliothèques—la bibliothèque et les archives principales du Canada ainsi que les bibliothèques des ministères, suivis des listes provinciales et des systèmes régionaux.

Édition—livres, magazines et journaux classés par province, y compris leur fréquence et les données relatives à leur diffusion.

Religion—information générale au sujet des groupes religieux et des associations religieuses de 37 dénominations.

Sports—associations de 110 sports distincts; comprend des listes de ligues et d'équipes.

Transport—des listes complètes des principaux modes de transport.

Services publics—associations, organismes gouvernementaux et entreprises de services publics provinciales.

FORMAT PAPIER OU EN LIGNE— ACCÈS RAPIDE À TOUS LES RENSEIGNEMENTS DONT VOUS AVEZ BESOIN!

Offert sous couverture rigide ou en format électronique grâce au web, le *Répertoire et almanach canadien* offre invariablement un accès instantané aux représentants du gouvernement et aux faits qui font l'objet de vos recherches.

La version imprimée du Répertoire et almanach canadien est vérifiée et mise à jour annuellement. La version en ligne est mise à jour mensuellement. Cette version vous permet de circonscrire la recherche grâce aux champs de l'index comme le nom ou le type d'organisme, le sujet, l'emplacement, le nom ou le titre de la personne-ressource et le code postal.

Les abonnés au service en ligne peuvent générer instantanément leurs propres listes de contacts et les exporter en format feuille de calcul pour une utilisation approfondie – une solution de rechange géniale aux services dispendieux d'un commissionnaire en publipostage.

GREY HOUSE PUBLISHING CANADA

Pour obtenir plus d'information, veuillez contacter Grey House Publishing Canada

par tél. : 1 866 433-4739 ou 416 644-6479 par téléc. : 416 644-1904 | info@greyhouse.ca | www.greyhouse.ca

Canadian Who's Who

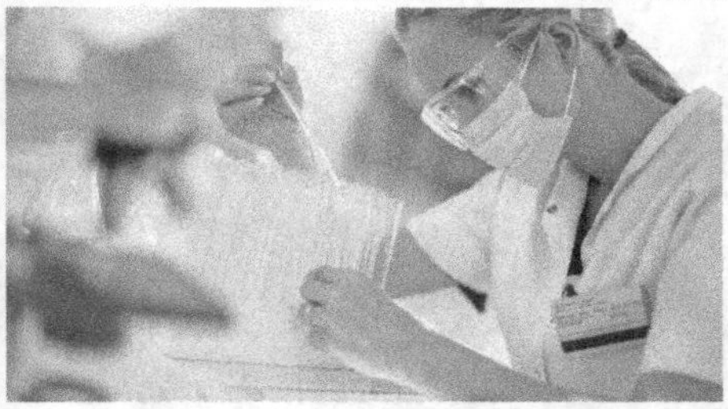

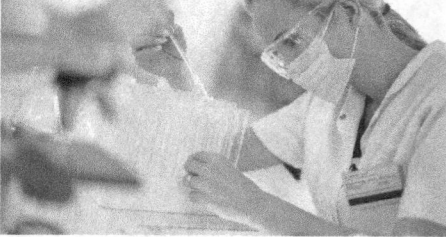

Directory of Directors

Your Best Source for Hard-to-Find Business Information

Since 1931, the *Financial Post Directory of Directors* has been recognizing leading Canadian companies and their execs. Today, this title is one of the most comprehensive resources for hard-to-find Canadian business information, allowing readers to access roughly 16,800 executive contacts from Canada's top 1,400 corporations. This prestigious title offers a definitive list of directorships and offices held by noteworthy Canadian business people. It also provides details on leading Canadian companies—publicly traded and privately-owned, including company name, contact information and the names of their executive officers and directors.

ACCESS THE COMPANIES & DIRECTORS YOU NEED IN NO TIME!

The updated 2023 edition of the *Directory of Directors* is jam-packed with information, including:

- ALL-NEW **front matter**: An infographic drawn from data in the book, a report on how companies can help women overcome barriers to networking, reports on diversity disclosure practices and executive compensation in Canada, and rankings from the FP500.
- **Personal listings**: First name, last name, gender, birth date, degrees, schools attended, executive positions and directorships, previous positions held, main business address and more.
- **Company listings**: Boards of directors and executive officers, head office address, phone and fax numbers, toll-free number, web and email addresses.

Powerful indexes enabling researchers to target just the information they need include:

- An **industrial classification index**: List of key Canadian companies, sorted by industry type according to the Global Industry Classification Standard (GICS®).
- A **geographic location index** grouping all companies in the Company Listings section according to the city and province/state of the head office; and
- An **alphabetical list of abbreviations** providing definitions of common abbreviations used for terms, titles, organizations, honours/fellowships and degrees throughout the Directory.

AVAILABLE ONLINE!

The Directory is also available online, through Canada's Information Resource Centre. Readers can access this title's in-depth and vital networking content in the format that best suits their needs—in print, by subscription or online.

Create your own contact lists! Online subscribers can instantly generate their own contact lists and export information into spreadsheets for further use. A great alternative to high cost list broker services!

GREY HOUSE PUBLISHING CANADA

For more information please contact Grey House Publishing Canada

Tel.: (866)-433-4739 or (416) 644-6479 Fax: (416) 644-1904 | info@greyhouse.ca | www.greyhouse.ca

Répertoire des administrateurs

Votre source par excellence de renseignements professionnels difficiles à trouver

Depuis 1931, le Financial Post Directory of Directors (Répertoire des administrateurs du Financial Post) reconnaît les sociétés canadiennes importantes et leur haute direction. De nos jours, cet ouvrage compte parmi certaines des ressources les plus exhaustives lorsqu'il est question des renseignements d'affaires canadiens difficiles à trouver. Il permet aux lecteurs d'accéder à environ 16 800 coordonnées d'administrateurs provenant des 1 400 sociétés les plus importantes au Canada. Ce document prestigieux comprend une liste définitive des postes d'administrateurs et des fonctions que ces gens d'affaires canadiens remarquables occupent. Il offre également des détails sur des sociétés canadiennes importantes – privées ou négociées sur le marché – y compris le nom de l'entreprise, ses coordonnées et le nombre des membres de sa haute direction et de ses administrateurs.

UN ACCÈS RAPIDE ET FACILE À TOUS LES ENTREPRISES ET DIRECTEURS DONT VOUS AVEZ BESOIN!

La version mise à jour de 2023 du Répertoire des administrateurs du Financial Post est remplie d'information, notamment:

- **NOUVELLE section de textes préliminaires** –une infographie inspirée des données de l'ouvrage; un rapport sur la manière dont les entreprises peuvent aider les femmes à surmonter les obstacles au réseautage; rapports sur les pratiques de divulgation de la diversité et la rémunération des dirigeants au Canada; le classement le plus récent au FP500.
- **Données personnelles** – prénom, nom de famille, sexe, date de naissance, diplômes, écoles fréquentées, poste de cadre et d'administrateur, postes occupés préalablement, adresse professionnelle principale et plus encore.
- **Listes de sociétés** – conseils d'administration et cadres supérieurs, adresse du siège social, numéros de téléphone et de télécopieur, numéro sans frais, adresse électronique et site Web.

Des index puissants permettent aux utilisateurs de cibler l'information dont ils ont besoin, notamment:

- **Index de classement industriel** - énumère les sociétés classées par type d'industrie général selon le Global Industry Classification Standard (GICS^MD).
- l'**Index des emplacements géographiques** qui comprend toutes les sociétés de la section Liste des sociétés en fonction de la ville et de la province/de l'état où se trouve le siège social;
- une **liste des abréviations en ordre alphabétique** définit les abréviations courantes pour la terminologie, les titres, les organisations, les distinctions/fellowships et les diplômes mentionnés dans le Répertoire.

OFFERT EN FORMAT ÉLECTRONIQUE!

Le Répertoire est également accessible en ligne par l'entremise du Centre de documentation du Canada. Les lecteurs peuvent accéder au contenu approfondi et essentiel au réseautage de cet ouvrage dans le format qui leur convient le mieux - version imprimée, en ligne ou par abonnement.

Créez vos propres listes! Les abonnés au service en ligne peuvent générer instantanément leurs propres listes de contacts et les exporter en format feuille de calcul pour une utilisation approfondie – une solution de rechange géniale aux services dispendieux d'un commissionnaire en publipostage.

GREY HOUSE PUBLISHING CANADA

Pour obtenir plus d'information, veuillez contacter Grey House Publishing Canada

par tél. : 1 866 433-4739 ou 416 644-6479 par téléc. : 416 644-1904 | info@greyhouse.ca | www.greyhouse.ca

Guide parlementaire canadien

Votre principale source d'information en matière de résultats d'élections fédérales!

Publié annuellement depuis avant la Confédération, le *Guide parlementaire canadien* est une source fondamentale de notices biographiques des membres élus et nommés aux gouvernements fédéral et provinciaux. Il y est question, notamment, d'établissements gouvernementaux comme la résidence du gouverneur général, le Conseil privé et la législature canadienne. Ce recueil exhaustif présente les résultats historiques et actuels accompagnés de données statistiques, provinciales et politiques.

LE GUIDE PARLEMENTAIRE CANADIEN EST DIVISÉ EN CINQ CATÉGORIES EXHAUSTIVES:

La monarchie—des renseignements biographiques sur Sa Majesté le Roi Charles III, la famille royale et le gouverneur général.

Le gouvernement fédéral—un chapitre distinct pour chacun des sujets suivants: Conseil privé, sénat, Chambre des communes (y compris une brève description de l'institution, son historique sous forme de textes et de graphiques et une liste des membres actuels) suivi de notes biographiques sans pareil.*

Les élections fédérales

1867–2019

- Les renseignements sont présentés en ordre alphabétique par province puis par circonscription.
- Les notes de chaque circonscription comprennent : La date d'établissement, la date d'abolition, l'ancienne circonscription, les circonscriptions ultérieures, etc. puis l'année d'élection ainsi que le nom et le parti des candidats élus.
- Viennent ensuite des renseignements sur l'élection partielle.

2021

- Les renseignements de l'élection 2021 sont organisés de la même manière, mais comprennent également de l'information sur tous les candidats qui se sont présentés dans chaque circonscription, leur appartenance politique et le nombre de voix récoltées.

Gouvernements provinciaux et territoriaux—Chaque chapitre portant sur le gouvernement provincial comprend :

- des renseignements statistiques
- une description de l'Assemblée législative
- des notes biographiques sur le lieutenant-gouverneur ou le commissaire
- une liste des ministres actuels
- les dates de périodes législatives depuis la Confédération
- une liste des membres et des circonscriptions
- des notes biographiques*
- les résultats d'élections générales et partielles, y compris les dernières élections provinciales et territoriales.

Cours : fédérale—chaque chapitre comprend : une description de la cour (suprême, fédérale, cour d'appel fédérale, cour d'appel de la cour martiale et cour de l'impôt), son histoire, une liste des juges qui y siègent ainsi que des notes biographiques.*

* Les notes biographiques respectent un format concis, bien qu'approfondi :

Renseignements personnels—lieu de naissance, formation, renseignements familiaux

Carrière politique—cheminement politique et service public

Carrière privée—antécédents professionnels, membre d'organisations, antécédents militaires

OFFERT EN FORMAT PAPIER ET DÉSORMAIS ÉLECTRONIQUE!

Offert sous couverture rigide ou en format électronique grâce au web, le *Guide parlementaire canadien* donne invariablement un accès instantané aux représentants du gouvernement et aux faits qui font l'objet de vos recherches. Servez-vous de la version en ligne afin de circonscrire vos recherches grâce aux champs spéciaux de l'index comme l'institution, la province et le nom.

Créez vos propres listes! Les abonnés au service en ligne peuvent générer instantanément leurs propres listes de contacts et les exporter en format feuille de calcul pour une utilisation approfondie – une solution de rechange géniale aux services dispendieux d'un commissionnaire en publipostage!

GREY HOUSE PUBLISHING CANADA

Pour obtenir plus d'information, veuillez contacter Grey House Publishing Canada

par tél. : 1 866 433-4739 ou 416 644-6479 par téléc. : 416 644-1904 | info@greyhouse.ca | www.greyhouse.ca

Bibliothèques Canada

Accédez aux renseignements complets et détaillés au sujet des bibliothèques canadiennes

Bibliothèques Canada combine les renseignements les plus à jour provenant du secteur des bibliothèques de partout au Canada, y compris les bibliothèques et leurs succursales, les bibliothèques éducatives, les systèmes régionaux, les centres de ressources, les archives, les périodiques pertinents, les écoles de bibliothéconomie et leurs programmes, les organismes provinciaux et gouvernementaux ainsi que les associations.

Principal répertoire des bibliothèques depuis plus de 35 ans, *Bibliothèques Canada* vous donne accès à près de 10 000 noms et adresses de personnes-ressources pour ces établissements. Il comprend également des détails précieux comme le symbole d'identification de bibliothèque, le nombre de membres du personnel, les systèmes d'exploitation, le type de bibliothèque et le budget attribué aux acquisitions, les heures d'ouverture – autant d'information minutieusement indexée et facile à trouver.

Offert en version imprimée et en ligne, *Bibliothèques Canada* offre des renseignements de qualité, facile d'accès, qui ont été vérifiés et organisés afin de les obtenir facilement. Cinq index conviviaux vous aident dans la navigation du numéro imprimé tandis que la version en ligne vous permet de saisir plusieurs champs d'index pour vous aider à découvrir l'information voulue.

ACCÈS INSTANTANÉ AUX RENSEIGNEMENTS DU DOMAINE DES BIBLIOTHÈQUES CANADIENNES

Conçu pour les éditeurs, les groupes de revendication, les fournisseurs de matériel informatique, les fournisseurs de services Internet et autres groupes qui offrent produits et services aux bibliothèques; les associations qui ont besoin de conserver une liste à jour des ressources bibliothécaires au Canada; les services de recherche, les organismes étudiants et gouvernementaux qui ont besoin d'information au sujet des types de services et de programmes offerts par divers établissements de recherche, *Bibliothèques Canada* vous aide à trouver l'information nécessaire – rapidement et simplement.

LA VERSION EN LIGNE COMPREND DES OPTIONS DE RECHERCHE POUSSÉES...

À partir de l'interface du Centre de documentation du Canada de Grey House Publishing Canada, vous pouvez choisir entre la recherche poussée et rapide pour cibler votre information. Vous pouvez effectuer des recherches par texte simple, conçues à la fois pour les chercheurs débutants et chevronnés, ainsi que des recherches booléennes puissantes. Vous pouvez également restreindre votre recherche à l'aide des champs d'index, comme le nom ou le type d'établissement, le siège social, l'emplacement, l'indicatif régional, le nom de la personne-ressource ou son titre et le code postal. Enregistrez vos recherches pour vous en servir plus tard ou utilisez la fonction de marquage pour afficher, imprimer, envoyer par courriel ou exporter les dossiers sélectionnés.

Les abonnés au service en ligne peuvent générer instantanément leurs propres listes de contacts et les exporter en format feuille de calcul pour une utilisation approfondie – une solution de rechange géniale aux services dispendieux d'un commissionnaire en publipostage.

BIBLIOTHÈQUES CANADA VOUS DONNE TOUS LES RENSEIGNEMENTS ESSENTIELS RELATIFS À CHAQUE ÉTABLISSEMENT :

Leurs nom et adresse, les coordonnées de la personne-ressource, les membres clés du personnel, le nombre de membres du personnel

L'information relative aux collections, le type de bibliothèque, le budget attribué aux acquisitions, le domaine, les collections particulières

Les services aux utilisateurs, le nombre de succursales, les heures d'ouverture, les renseignements relatifs au PEB, les services de photocopie et de microforme, la recherche rémunérée, l'accès à Internet

L'information relative aux systèmes, des détails sur l'accès électronique, les systèmes d'exploitation et ceux en ligne, Internet et le logiciel de messagerie électronique, la connectivité à Internet, l'accès aux ressources électroniques

L'information supplémentaire, y compris les associations, les publications et les systèmes régionaux

Alors que près de 60 % des données sont modifiées annuellement, il est plus important que jamais de posséder la plus récente version de *Bibliothèques Canada*.

GREY HOUSE PUBLISHING CANADA

Pour obtenir plus d'information, veuillez contacter Grey House Publishing Canada

par tél. : 1 866 433-4739 ou 416 644-6479 par téléc. : 416 644-1904 | info@greyhouse.ca | www.greyhouse.ca

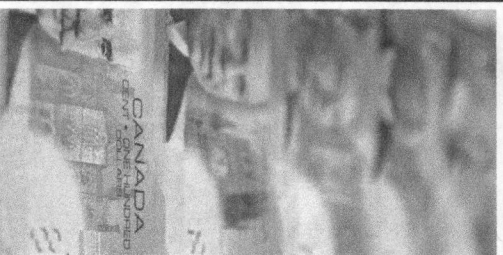

Services financiers au Canada

Une couverture sans pareille de l'industrie des services financiers canadiens

Grâce à plus de 30 000 organisations et renseignements commerciaux rares, *Services financiers du Canada* est la source la plus à jour de noms et de coordonnées de professionnels, de membres de la haute direction, de gestionnaires de portefeuille, de conseillers financiers, de fonctionnaires et de représentants élus de l'industrie.

Services financiers du Canada intègre les plus récentes modifications à l'industrie afin de vous offrir les détails les plus à jour au sujet de chaque entreprise, notamment le nom, le titre, l'organisation, les numéros de téléphone et de télécopieur, le courriel et l'adresse du site Web. Servez-vous de la base de données en ligne et raffinez votre recherche selon le symbole, le revenu, l'année de création, les immobilisations, le type de propriété ou le nombre d'employés.

DES INDEX PUISSANTS VOUS AIDENT À TROUVER LES RENSEIGNEMENTS FINANCIERS ESSENTIELS DONT VOUS AVEZ BESOIN.

C'est avec l'utilisateur en tête que Services financiers au Canada a été conçu; il contient des listes catégorisées et quatre index faciles d'utilisation :

Alphabétique—les organisations financières apparaissent en ordre alphabétique, selon le nom de l'entreprise.

Géographique—les institutions financières sont détaillées par ville.

Nom de directeur—tous les agents, directeurs et cadres supérieurs sont classés en ordre alphabétique, selon leur nom de famille.

Classe d'assurance—toutes les entreprises selon leur type d'assurance.

Passez moins de temps à préparer des listes, à faire des recherches ou à chercher des contacts et des courriels. Que vous soyez intéressé à contacter un avocat en droit des affaires au sujet de projets conjoints internationaux et nationaux, que vous ayez besoin de générer une liste des banques étrangères au Canada ou que vous souhaitiez communiquer avec la Bourse de Toronto, *Services financiers au Canada* vous permet de trouver toutes les données dont vous avez besoin.

OFFERT EN FORMAT PAPIER OU EN LIGNE – UN ACCÈS RAPIDE ET FACILE À TOUS LES RENSEIGNEMENTS DONT VOUS AVEZ BESOIN!

Offert sous couverture rigide ou en format électronique grâce au Web, Services financiers du Canada donne invariablement un accès instantané aux personnes et aux faits dont vous avez besoin. Si la version imprimée est vérifiée et mise à jour annuellement, des changements continus sont apportés mensuellement à la base de données en ligne. Servez-vous de la version en ligne afin de circonscrire vos recherches grâce à des champs spéciaux de l'index comme le nom de l'organisation ou son type, le sujet, l'emplacement, le nom de la personne-ressource ou son titre et le code postal.

Créez vos propres listes! Les abonnés au service en ligne peuvent générer instantanément leurs propres listes de contacts et les exporter en format feuille de calcul pour une utilisation approfondie – une solution de rechange géniale aux services dispendieux d'un commissionnaire en publipostage.

ACCÉDEZ AUX LISTES ACTUELLES...

Banques et institutions de dépôt
- Banques nationales et d'épargne
- Banques étrangères et leurs succursales
- Bureaux des représentants de banques étrangères
- Sociétés de fiducie
- Coopératives d'épargne et de crédit

Établissements financiers
- Entreprises de notation des obligations
- Agences de placement
- Compagnies de carte de crédit
- Sociétés de financement et de prêt
- Syndics de faillite

Sociétés de gestion de placements, y compris les valeurs et marchandises
- Entreprises de planification financière et de gestion des investissements
- Maisons de courtage de valeurs Courtiers en épargne collective
- Entreprises de gestion de la pension/de trésorerie
- Bourses
- Sociétés de portefeuille

Compagnies d'assurance, fédérales et provinciales
- Compagnies de réassurance
- Sociétés fraternelles
- Sociétés de secours mutuel
- Échanges selon la formule de réciprocité

Comptabilité et droit
- Comptables
- Cabinets d'actuaires-conseils
- Cabinets d'avocats (spécialisés en finance)

Principales entreprises canadiennes
- Principaux contacts financiers pour les sociétés de capitaux publiques, privées et de la Couronne

Les associations et Technologie et services financiers

Accès à plus de contenu en ligne: Gouvernement et Publications
- Personnes-ressources aux paliers fédéral, provinciaux et territoriaux
- Principales publications qui desservent l'industrie des services financiers

GREY HOUSE PUBLISHING CANADA

Pour obtenir plus d'information, veuillez contacter Grey House Publishing Canada

par tél. : 1 866 433-4739 ou 416 644-6479 par téléc. : 416 644-1904 | info@greyhouse.ca | www.greyhouse.ca

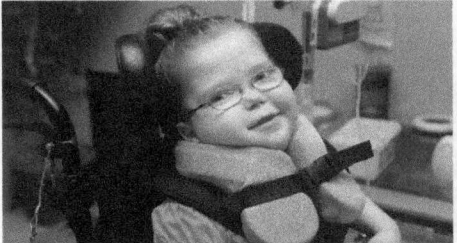

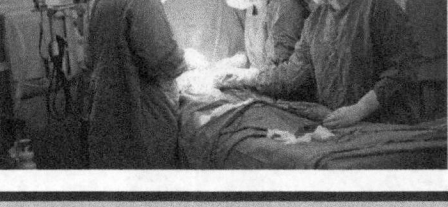

Guide canadien de la santé

Un manuel informatif au sujet des services en santé au Canada

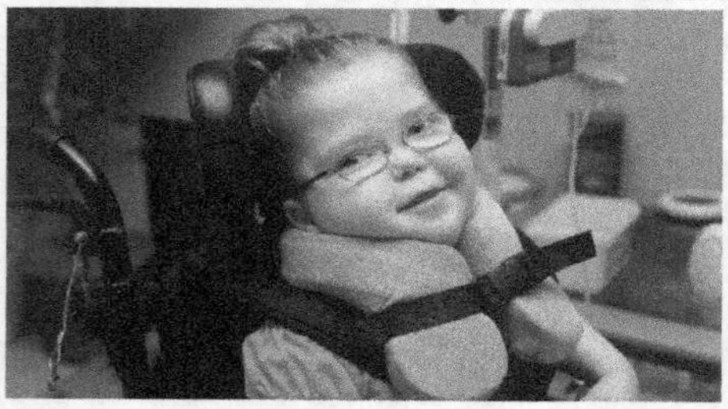

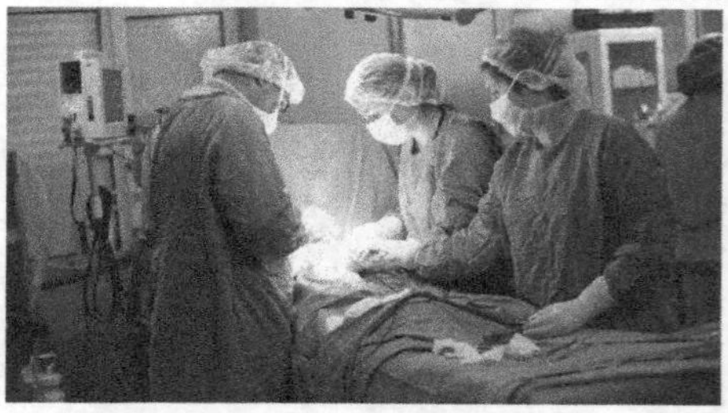

Le *Guide canadien de la santé : un manuel informatif au sujet des maladies chroniques et mentales de même que des services en santé au Canada* donne un aperçu exhaustif de 107 maladies chroniques et mentales, de la maladie d'Addison à celle de Wilson. Chaque chapitre comprend une description médicale facile à comprendre, une vaste gamme de services de soutien particuliers à l'état et des ressources documentaires qui portent sur diverses questions relatives aux personnes qui sont aux prises avec une maladie chronique ou mentale et à ceux qui soutiennent la communauté liée à cette maladie.

Le *Guide canadien de la santé* contient des milliers de moyens pour composer avec divers aspects d'une maladie chronique ou d'un problème de santé mentale. Il comprend des associations, des organismes gouvernementaux, des bibliothèques et des centres de documentation, des services d'éducation, des hôpitaux et des publications. En plus des chapitres qui portent sur des états chroniques ou mentaux, un chapitre traite de l'industrie de la santé en général; d'autres abordent les fondations qui réalisent des rêves, les groupes de soutien axés sur le décès et le deuil, la médecine homéopathique, les questions autochtones et les sports pour les personnes handicapées. Les sections incluent

- Matériel didactique
- Section I : Les maladies chroniques ou mentales
- Section II : Les ressources génériques
- Section III : Les annexes
- Section IV : Les statistiques

Chaque entrée comprend une description, une adresse (y compris le site Web, le courriel et les liens des médias sociaux, lorsque possible), les noms et titres des directeurs de même que plusieurs détails particuliers à ce type d'organisme.

Les membres du personnel des hôpitaux et des centres médicaux peuvent trouver, au même titre que parents et familles, le soutien dont ils ont besoin dans le cadre de leur travail ou de leurs études. Le *Guide canadien de la santé* est rempli de ressources capitales pour les personnes qui souffrent d'une maladie chronique alors qu'elles passent du diagnostic au retour à la maison, de la maison au travail et du travail à la vie au sein de la communauté.

OFFERT EN FORMAT PAPIER OU EN LIGNE – UN ACCÈS RAPIDE ET FACILE À TOUS LES RENSEIGNEMENTS DONT VOUS AVEZ BESOIN!

Offert sous couverture souple ou en format électronique grâce au web, le *Guide canadien de la santé* donne invariablement un accès instantané aux personnes et aux faits dont vous avez besoin. Si la version imprimée est vérifiée et mise à jour annuellement, des changements continus sont apportés mensuellement à la base de données en ligne. Servez-vous de la version en ligne afin de circonscrire vos recherches grâce à des champs spéciaux de l'index comme le nom de l'organisation ou son type, le sujet, l'emplacement, le nom de la personne-ressource ou son titre et le code postal.

LE GUIDE CANADIEN DE LA SANTÉ VOUS AIDERA À TROUVER CE DONT VOUS AVEZ BESOIN GRÂCE À CES OUTILS DE REPÉRAGE PRÉCIEUX!

Répertoire nominatif—une list alphabétique offrant un moyen rapide et facile d'accéder à toute liste de cette edition.

Onglets—les sections principals possèdent un onglet pour une consultation facile. Les notes en tête de chaque page vous aident à trouver les données voulues.

Créez vos propres listes! Les abonnés au service en ligne peuvent générer instantanément leurs propres listes de contacts et les exporter en format feuille de calcul pour une utilisation approfondie – une solution de rechange géniale aux services dispendieux d'un commissionnaire en publipostage.

GREY HOUSE PUBLISHING CANADA

Pour obtenir plus d'information, veuillez contacter Grey House Publishing Canada

par tél. : 1 866 433-4739 ou 416 644-6479 par téléc. : 416 644-1904 | info@greyhouse.ca | www.greyhouse.ca

Cannabis au Canada

Cannabis du Canada est une ressource unique qui porte sur tous les aspects de cette industrie en pleine expansion. Il comprend des entrées exhaustives ainsi qu'une vaste gamme de rapports et de statistiques : vous y trouverez tout ce qu'il y a à savoir sur ce marché désormais légal, y compris des renseignements à portée internationale.

La première édition inclut le document l'État de l'industrie du cannabis 2019 sur l'histoire de la marijuana, les réglementations en vigueur ainsi que des rapports éclairants et des annonces de salons commerciaux et de congrès à venir.

Les lecteurs découvriront également le tout nouveau guide de l'acheteur de l'industrie du cannabis qui couvre un vaste éventail de sujets : des producteurs autorisés aux sociétés de conseil en passant par les sociétés de sécurité et plus encore. Toutes les entrées comprennent des champs spécialisés qui vont bien plus loin que le nom et l'adresse : elles regorgent de contacts essentiels et actuels.

PARMI LES RESSOURCES SUPPLÉMENTAIRES, MENTIONNONS :

- Associations de l'industrie
- Sociétés financières et de capital de risque
- Cabinets d'avocats
- Agences gouvernementales
- Établissements de soins de santé et de traitement
- Publications

Des annexes avec des statistiques détaillées et plusieurs index vous aident à parcourir cet ouvrage exhaustif.

UN EXAMEN PLUS APPROFONDI DU CONTENU :

L'état de l'industrie du cannabis en 2019—Une section détaillée volumineuse : de l'histoire du cannabis à la réglementation actuelle. S'y trouvent également des rapports objectifs portant sur tous les aspects de l'industrie, des entrées relatives aux salons professionnels ainsi qu'aux conférences, au Canada et à l'étranger.

Guide de l'acheteur—Industrie du cannabis : entrées commerciales exhaustives sur tous les aspects essentiels de l'industrie. Il constitue votre source d'information par excellence de personnes-ressources essentielles à l'expansion de votre entreprise et de votre réseau ou à la recherche de réponses.

Associations—Des associations professionnelles aux organismes de santé, y compris les organismes internationaux essentiels à l'industrie.

Finances et capital-risque—Toute l'information dont vous avez besoin au sujet de l'assurance, des services banquiers et du secteur des placements.

Cabinets d'avocats—Découvrez les cabinets d'avocats qui offrent des services reliés aux enjeux du cannabis, jusqu'aux domaines de spécialité d'avocats précis!

Gouvernement—Les agences et ministères fédéraux et provinciaux qui réglementent et surveillent l'industrie du cannabis au Canada. Cette source vous offre les meilleurs contacts à l'échelle du gouvernement.

Enseignement—Collèges, universités et écoles spécialisées qui offrent des cours ayant trait au cannabis ou qui comptent le faire.

Santé—L'emplacement d'établissements de santé spécialisés, notamment en santé mentale et en programmes de traitement des dépendances, partout au pays.

Publications—Listes de magazines, canadiens et étrangers, imprimés et en ligne, que peuvent consulter les participants du secteur du cannabis.

OFFERT EN LIGNE!

Le *Guide canadien du cannabis* sera également offert en ligne dans le Centre de documentation du Canada (CIRC). Un seul clic vous donne accès à des milliers d'entreprises et de personnes-ressources! Effectuez une recherche par nom ou par type d'organisation, par sujet, par emplacement, par code postal, par personne-ressource ou par titre. Exportez les résultats pour créer des listes d'envoi grâce à cette base de données en ligne conviviale, un outil essentiel tant pour les chercheurs, étudiants, professionnels du marketing que pour les experts de l'industrie.

GREY HOUSE PUBLISHING CANADA

Pour obtenir plus d'information, veuillez contacter Grey House Publishing Canada

par tél. : 1 866 433-4739 ou 416 644-6479 par téléc. : 416 644-1904 | info@greyhouse.ca | www.greyhouse.ca